The Almanac of American Politics

2018

Members of Congress and Governors:
their Profiles and Election Results,
their States and Districts

Richard E. Cohen
James A. Barnes

Introductions by
Charlie Cook
Michael Barone

Senior Authors
Louis Jacobson
Louis Peck

Columbia Books & Information Services
National Journal

Printed in the United States of America

ISBN-13: 978-1-938939-58-7 (cloth)

ISBN-13: 978-1-938939-56-3 (paper)

ISBN-13: 978-1-938939-59-4 (e-book)

THE ALMANAC OF AMERICAN POLITICS 2018

Chief Author	Richard E. Cohen
Co-author	James A. Barnes
Managing Editor	Emma Griffin
Editorial Director	Duncan Bell
Senior Contributing Authors	Charlie Cook, Michael Barone (Founding Author)
Senior Authors	Louis Jacobson, Louis Peck
Senior Editor	John Bicknell
Senate Editor	Jennifer Duffy
Data Editor	Dr. Emil Pitkin
Director of Research/Writer	Charles Aull
Writers	Cam Joseph, David Wasserman; Emily Aubert, Kelly Coyle, Nicholas Katers (Ballotpedia)
Researchers	Jackie Beran, Jessica Dravecky (researcher-writers); Lauren Arnold, Anna Wendland
Election Results	Dave Leip's Atlas of U.S. Presidential Elections (uselectionatlas.org)
District Maps	Polidata

Columbia Books & Information Services
President: Joel Poznansky

About the Authors

Richard E. Cohen has four decades of experience covering Capitol Hill, chiefly for *National Journal*. He was co-author of the Almanac from 2001 to 2010, and has been chief author since 2015. He has authored other books about Congress, including a biography of former House Ways and Means Committee chairman Dan Rostenkowski. He won the Everett Dirksen award for distinguished reporting on Congress, and is an adjunct professor at George Mason University.

James A. Barnes has covered every presidential election and national party convention since 1984. He is a consultant to CNN where he projects the outcomes of presidential, congressional and gubernatorial races for its election and primary night coverage. He was the chief political correspondent for *National Journal* and founder of the *National Journal* Insiders Poll. He was a contributor to *The State of American Politics.*

Louis Jacobson is the senior correspondent for PolitiFact. Since 2002, he has handicapped political races, including state legislatures, governors and state attorneys general, Congress and the electoral college, currently for *Governing*. He has served as deputy editor of *Roll Call* and as founding editor of its legislative wire service, *CongressNow*. Earlier, he spent more than a decade as a reporter for *National Journal.*

Louis Peck is the politics editor for *Bethesda* magazine. Since 1978, he has been a Washington-based journalist who writes and edits coverage of Congress and national politics. For nearly two decades, he was editor-in-chief of *National Journal's Congress Daily*. Earlier, he was editor of *Campaigns and Elections* magazine and a national political correspondent for the Washington bureau of Gannett newspapers.

Acknowledgements

The authors owe a debt of gratitude to several people and organizations that have contributed to the 2018 edition of *The Almanac of American Politics* and sustained it for decades. Most notably, Michael Barone co-founded and authored the original 1972 *Almanac,* and since then his insights have been the heart and soul of this essential work on American politics and government. John Fox Sullivan, the former president and publisher of *National Journal,* and David Bradley, the owner of *National Journal's* parent company, Atlantic Media, nurtured the *Almanac* for many years. Ballotpedia, led by its president Leslie Graves and editor in chief Geoff Pallay, have provided essential research and editorial support for the 2018 *Almanac,* without which this edition would not have been possible. Charlie Cook and his staff at the Cook Political Report made significant contributions to this latest edition. The Brookings Institution graciously allowed usage of key figures from their report "Vital Statistics on Congress". Dave Leip provided election and other data. Clark Benson, at Polidata, contributed updated congressional district maps. Beth Hahn, historical editor at the Senate Historical Office, gave vital research assistance. We also are grateful to Brittany Carter, Matthew Barnes, Jamie Herring, Adem Gokturk, and the staff of Columbia Books and Information Services for their efforts in getting this book to press.

TABLE OF CONTENTS

★ GUIDE TO USAGE ★

The following guide explains the information sources used by The Almanac of American Politics. Major sources of information include the U.S. Census Bureau, Ballotpedia, the Center for Responsive Politics, The Cook Political Report and the Almanac's writers and researchers. The 2018 Almanac offers significant updates from the previous edition of the book, published in 2015. Figures released by the Census Bureau may vary slightly from those used by the Almanac due to different methods of data aggregation or tabulation. Percentages used in the book may not add up to 100% because of rounding.

Biography

This section lists the date each governor, senator, and representative was elected or appointed, the date and place of birth, academic degrees earned, religion, marital status, and, if applicable, spouse's name and number of children. Also provided is a brief outline of the subject's past elected offices, professional career and military service, and office addresses, telephone numbers, and websites. Committee and subcommittee assignments are current as of June 2017. (Note: On many committees, the chairman and ranking minority member are ex officio members of subcommittees. Leaders in the House typically do not serve on committees.)

Group Ratings

The congressional ratings by 10 interest groups provide insight into a legislator's general ideology and the degree to which he or she reflects the group's point of view. Some organizations provided just one rating for 2015 and 2016, the two sessions of the 114th Congress.

ADA: Americans for Democratic Action

Liberal: Since ADA's founding in 1947, the Annual Voting Records have served as the standard measure of political liberalism. Rating is calculated by combining 20 key votes on a wide range of social and economic issues, both domestic and international. Only 2015 ratings were available at the time of publication.

ACLU: American Civil Liberties Union

Pro-individual liberties: ACLU seeks to protect individuals from what it views as legal, executive, and congressional infringements on civil liberties. The ACLU compiles a combined score for each two-year Congress. (C = Combined)

AFL-CIO: American Federation of Labor Congress of Industrial Organizations

Liberal labor: The AFL-CIO is a federation of 56 unions representing some 12.5 million members that advocates for social and economic justice and improved working conditions through collective bargaining. Its analysis is based on roll call votes in 2015. Its 2016 analysis was not available at press time.

LCV: League of Conservation Voters

Environmental: Formed in 1970, LCV is the arm of the environmental movement that works to elect pro-environmental protection candidates to Congress. LCV ratings are based on key votes on energy, environment, and natural resources legislation in 2015 and 2016

ITI: Information Technology Industry Council

High-tech industry: ITI represents the leading U.S. providers of information technology products and services. It compiles a combined score for each two-year Congress. (C = Combined)

COC: U.S. Chamber of Commerce

Pro-business: Founded in 1912, COC represents local, regional, and state chambers of commerce in addition to trade and professional organizations. It promotes free market policies and ranks members of Congress for key business votes.

HAFA: Heritage Action for America

Conservative: HAFA advocates for conservative policies, many of which are developed by its sister organization, the Heritage Foundation. Key votes in this rating encompass a broad range of conservative issues. It compiles a combined score for each two-year Congress. (C = Combined)

ACU: American Conservative Union

Conservative: Since 1971, ACU ratings have provided a means of gauging the conservatism of members of Congress on foreign policy, social, and budget issues. Its scores are annual.

CFG: Club for Growth

Pro-tax limitation: CFG supports limited government, lower taxes, and policies it deems favorable to economic growth. CFG's annual ratings are based on key votes on taxes, trade, and the economy.

FRC: Family Research Council

Social conservative: The FRC promotes traditional marriage and family and advocates for policies that uphold Judeo-Christian values. Its annual ratings are based on votes on abortion and family issues. It compiles a combined score for each two-year Congress. (C = Combined)

Almanac Vote Ratings

Emil Pitkin, CEO of GovPredict, has computed the Almanac congressional vote ratings for 2015. Almanac editors have selected a list of key congressional roll call votes and classified them as economic, social, or foreign policy-related. Within each issue area, a principal component analysis (PCA) is applied to the votes. PCA is a general statistical procedure that reduces a complex data set with many dimensions into its most descriptive constituent parts, called principle components. This blind statistical procedure found that the most salient, one-number summary of how a legislator voted across dozens of votes corresponds to the liberalism or conservatism of each Member of Congress. That one number is known as the score of the first principal component.

The Members of Congress have been ranked according to their score, and their scores are normalized to fit in the 0 to 100 range, both for the "conservative score" and for their "liberal score." The liberal score is simply 100 minus the conservative score, and vice versa. The composite score is an average of a member's three issue-based scores.

There was not an analysis of 2016 roll call votes because there was an insufficient number of meaningful votes in both the House and Senate. Only Members of Congress who participate in at least half of the votes in an issue area receive ratings. Members who miss more than half the votes are not scored (shown as *). Absences are not scored, while abstentions are scored as a 0.5, with an aye vote scored as a 1 and a nay vote as an 0.

Key Votes

The key votes section presents the positions of Senators and House members on important issues. The following key votes, selected by the Almanac staff, took place during the 114th Congress (2015-2016). There are 12 votes in the Senate and 12 votes in the House, which are split among economic, foreign policy, and social issues. A member who was absent or declined to vote receives NV for "not voting." The letter P signifies a vote of "present." No listings are provided for members who were not in office at the time. Roll-call data were obtained from the clerk of the House and Secretary of the Senate.

Senate Votes

- *Keystone pipeline:* (Senate Vote 49, S. 1) Permit TransCanada to start work immediately on the Keystone XL pipeline. Jan. 29, 2015. Passed 62-36. (R: 53-0; D: 9-34; I: 0-2)
- *Trade deals:* (Senate Vote 193, H.R. 1314) Grant Trade Promotion Authority for the President to negotiate international trade agreements and for Congress to vote without amendments, plus extend Trade Adjustment Assistance. May 21, 2015. Passed 62-37. (R: 48-5; D: 14-30; I: 0-2)
- *Export-Import Bank:* (Senate Vote 206, H.R. 1735) Table proposal to extend the authority of the Export-Import Bank. June 10, 2015. Passed 31-65. (R: 30-22; D: 0-42; I: 1-1)
- *Debt ceiling increase:*(Senate Vote 290, H.R. 1314) Increase discretionary spending caps and suspend the debt limit. Oct. 30, 2015. Passed 64-35. (R: 18-35; D: 44-0; I: 2-0)
- *Homeland Security $$$:* (Senate Vote 62, H.R. 240) Appropriate Fiscal 2015 funds for the Homeland Security Department. Feb. 27, 2015. Passed 68-31. (R: 23-31; D: 43-0; I: 2-0)
- *National Security data:* (Senate Vote 201, H.R. 2048) Prohibit the National Security Agency from bulk collection and storage of telephone meta-data and limit the collection of other bulk data. June 2, 2015. Passed 67-32. (R: 23-30; D: 43-1; I: 1-1)

- *Iran nuclear deal:* (Senate Vote 264, H Res 61) Invoke cloture on proposal to disapprove the nuclear agreement reached with Iran by the United States and five other nations. Sept. 10, 2015. Defeated 58-42. (Failed to get the required 60 votes) (R: 54-0; D: 4-40; I: 0-2)
- *Puerto Rico debt:* (Senate Vote 116, S 2328) Establish a financial oversight board for Puerto Rico to assist in restructuring of the island's debts. June 29, 2016. Passed 68-30. (R: 36-18; D: 31-11; I: 1-1)
- *Loretta Lynch A.G.:* (Senate Vote 165) Confirm Loretta Lynch as Attorney General. April 23, 2015. Approved 56-43. (R: 10-43; D: 44-0; I: 2-0)
- *Sanctuary cities:* (Senate Vote 280, S. 2146) Invoke cloture on proposal to withhold funds from "sanctuary cities" and other localities that fail to enforce immigration laws. Oct. 20, 2015. Defeated 54-45. (Failed to get the required 60 votes) (R: 52-1; D: 2-42; I: 0-2)
- *Gun sales checks:* (Senate Vote 321, H.R. 3762) Expand federal background checks of gun sales on the Internet or at gun shows. Dec. 3, 2015. Defeated 48-50. (R: 4-50; D: 44-0; I: 2-0)
- *Planned Parenthood:* (Senate Vote 329, H.R. 3762) Revise provisions of the Affordable Care Act, including a one-year funding ban for Planned Parenthood. Dec. 3, 2015. Passed 52-47. (R: 52-2; D: 0-44; I: 0-1)

House Votes

- *Keystone pipeline:* (House Vote 75, S. 1) Permit TransCanada to start work immediately on the Keystone XL pipeline. Feb. 11, 2015 Passed 270-152. (R: 241-1; D: 29-151)
- *Trade Deals:* (House Vote 362, H.R. 1314) Grant Trade Promotion Authority for the President to negotiate international trade agreements, and for Congress to vote without amendments. June 12, 2015. Passed: 219-211. (R: 191-54; D: 28-157)
- *Export-Import Bank:*(House Vote 569, HRes 450) Force House debate on reauthorization of the Export-Import Bank. Oct. 26, 2015. Passed: 246-177. (R: 62-177; D: 184-0)
- *Debt ceiling increase:*(House Vote 579, H.R. 1314) Increase discretionary spending caps and suspend the debt limit. Oct. 28, 2015. Passed: 266-167. (R: 79-167; D: 187-0)
- *Homeland Security $$$:*(House Vote 109, H.R. 240) Agree to the Senate amendment on Fiscal 2015 appropriations for the Homeland Security Department. March 3, 2015. Passed 257-167. (R: 75-167; D: 182-0)
- *Troops in Iraq:*(House Vote 370, HCon Res 370) Direct President Obama to remove most U.S. Armed Forces that were deployed to Iraq and Syria on or after August 7, 2014. June 17, 2015. Defeated: 139-288. (R: 19-222; D: 120-66)
- *Trade Adjustment Aid:*(House Vote 388, H.R. 1295) Revise tariff and trade laws, including Trade Adjustment Assistance for workers. June 25, 2015. Passed: 286-138. (R: 111-132; D: 175-6)
- *Puerto Rico debt:*(House Vote 278, H.R. 5278) Establish a financial oversight board for Puerto Rico to assist in restructuring of the island's debts. June 9, 2016. Passed: 297-127. (R: 139-103; D: 158-24)
- *Offenses by aliens:*(House Vote 31, H.R. 240) Require that the Department of Homeland Security enforce strict civil enforcement standards against any alien convicted of various offenses. Jan. 14, 2015. Passed 278-149. (R: 243-1; D: 35-148)
- *Medical marijuana:*(House Vote 283, H.R. 2578) Prohibit funds that seek to supersede State law that have legalized the use of medical marijuana. June 3, 2015. Passed 242-186. (R: 67-176; D: 175-10)
- *Armor-piercing bullets:*(House Vote 289, H.R. 2578) Limit funds to restrict the use of armor-piercing ammunition. June 3, 2015. Passed 250-171. (R: 238-2; D: 12-169)
- *Sanctuary cities:*(House Vote 294, H.R. 2578) Prohibits law enforcement assistance funding that violates restriction on the establishment of sanctuary cities. June 3, 2015. Passed: 227-198. (R: 227-14; D: 0-184)

NOTE: Freshman members of the House, because they took office in January 2017, do not have key votes, vote scores from the interest groups, or ratings from the Almanac for the 114th Congress (2015-2016). Freshman senators have vote scores if they served in the House. Freshmen who won in a special election to fill a vacancy may have some key votes and vote scores from some interest groups.

Election Results

The most recent election results are listed for senators and governors. For House members, the results are from the 2016 primary and general elections, as well as any runoffs in 2016 or special elections held since November 2016. Candidates in primaries receiving less than 5% (before rounding) of the total vote and candidates in general elections receiving less than 2% (before rounding) of the total were excluded. Election results were supplied by Ballotpedia and Secretary of State websites. Prior Winning percentages: The incumbent's winning percentages in earlier elections.

Campaign Finance

Campaign finance data in the Almanac was sourced from the Federal Elections Commission (FEC) website. The FEC makes bulk campaign finance data available in several reports, however principally two were used for the purposes of the Almanac: Operating Expenditures and Independent Expenditures. The Operating Expenditures file was referenced to gather all spending activity for each candidate's principal campaign committee during the relevant election cycle; the Independent Expenditures file was referenced to gather all spending from outside groups attempting to influence an election result.

In the "Election Results" section of each Senator and Member profile, campaign finance data can be found in the 3 columns aligned to the right of each candidate election result. "Cand. Spent" provides the spending total for the principal campaign committee of the candidate during the election cycle in question. "Ind. Exp. Support" and "Ind. Exp. Oppose" both relate to the Intendent Expenditures file, which reports any spending from outside groups to impact an election outcome. The FEC requires that these filers indicate the relevant candidate, as well as whether they "support" or "oppose" the election of that candidate. "Outside groups" may include Super PACs, social welfare 501(c)(4) organizations, trade associations, unions, political parties, corporations, individuals or other groups. However, the monies may not account for all outside money spent in a race, as some outside spending is subject to different federal campaign finance disclosure rules.

The FEC Operating Expenses file for the 2015-2016 cycle was downloaded in April of 2017; the Independent Expenditures file for the 2015-2016 cycle was downloaded in May of 2017. These were mapped to the Candidate Master and Committee Master files, downloaded in April of 2017. Campaign finance data for 2017 special elections (CA-34, GA-6, KS-4, MT-AL, and SC-5) was downloaded from the FEC website on June 21st, 2017.

Demographics

Population: Figures are from the 2015 American Community Survey (ACS) one-year estimates reported by the U.S. Census Bureau.

Born in state: Percent of entire population of the district that was born in the state in which that district is located.

Race and ethnicity: Figures are from the 2015 ACS reported by the Census Bureau. As defined by the Census Bureau, race reflects individual respondents' perception of their racial identity. Latino origin is defined as an ethnicity. The Census Bureau initially reports data for whites, blacks, and other racial groups that include both Latinos and non-Latinos, but traditionally will follow this initial report with figures that breaks racial and ethnic data into results that are more useful for political analysis. As a result, the 2016 version of the Almanac uses the following definitions:

- *White* refers to people who describe their race as white and who say they are not of Latino ancestry or descent.
- *Black* refers to people who describe their race as black or African-American and who say they are not of Latino ancestry or descent.
- *Latino* refers to people who say they are of Latino or Hispanic ancestry, regardless of how they answer questions about their racial identity.
- *Asian* refers to people who describe their race as Asian and who say they are not of Latino ancestry or descent.
- *Two races* refer to people who choose more than one racial category (white, black, Asian,American Indian or Pacific Islander) to describe themselves. This does not include people who describe themselves as Latino.
- *Other* is comprised of the following groups: American Indian, Pacific Islander and those who report "Other".

- *American Indian* refers to people who describe their race as American Indian or Alaska Native and who say they are not of Latino ancestry or descent.
- *Pacific Islander* refers to people who describe their race as black or Native Hawaiian or "other Pacific Islander" and who say they are not of Latino ancestry or descent.

Education: H.S. grad or less refers to people who did not attend college. Some college refers to people who attended college but did not receive a diploma, or who received an associate's degree but not a bachelor's degree. College degree, 4 yr. refers to people who received a bachelor's degree but did not receive a graduate or professional degree after attending college. Post-grad study refers to people who received a graduate or professional degree. All groups are a percentage of people 25 years and older.

Veteran: This category includes both men and women in the civilian population who served in the U.S. military.

Active duty: This category refers to men and women currently employed in the U.S. armed forces.

Median income: This figure represents the median income (not the average income) for all households in the congressional district (or state) for 2015. The numbers in parentheses immediately below indicates where the district ranks among all 435 districts, with the richest district indicated by (1 of 435) and the poorest by (435 of 435).

Income: Each category represents the number of households in each district (or state) with a reported income that fell within that bracket in 2015. Poverty rate: This figure indicates the poverty rate computed by the Census Bureau for 2015 for each district using the definition outlined in the Office of Management and Budget's (OMB) Statistical Policy Directive 14.

Work: The Census Bureau asks all respondents over the age of 16 who are employed in the civilian workforce about their occupation and assigns each respondent to one of five occupation codes defined by the federal government.

- *White collar* refers to civilian workers assigned to the category titled "Management, Business, Science and Arts occupations."
- *Blue collar* refers to workers assigned to two categories: "Natural Resources, Construction and Maintenance occupations" and "Production, Transportation and Material Moving occupations."
- *Sales and service* refers to workers assigned to the final two categories: "Service occupations" and "Sales and Office occupations."
- *Govt. workers* refers to the percentage of respondents over the age of 16 who are employed in the civilian government workforce.

Language: This is percentage of households in the nation speaking a certain language as a percentage of people 5 years and older. The abbreviation other European refers to other Indo-European languages.

Place of Birth: The Census asks people if they are native or foreign born, and if they currently reside in the state in which they were born or if they were born in a different state.

Foreign-born Citizenship Status: This category shows the percentage of foreign-born residents in the U.S. who are citizens.

Region of Foreign Born: This category shows the regions of the world where foreign-bornresidents were born.

Abbreviations

ACLU	American Civil Liberties Union
ACU	American Conservative Union
ADA	Americans for Democratic Action
AFDC	Aid to Families with Dependent Children
AFL-CIO	American Federation of Labor and Congress of Industrial Organizations
AID	Agency for International Development
ANWR	Arctic National Wildlife Refuge
BL	Better Life Party
C	Conservative Party (NY
CAFE	Corporate Average Fuel Economy
CAFTA	Central America Free Trade Agreement
CFG	Club for Growth
CHMN	Chairman
CHOB	Cannon House Office Building
CIA	Central Intelligence Agency
CNP	Constitution Party
COC	United States Chamber of Commerce
COLA	Cost of Living Adjustment
D	Democratic Party
DCCC	Democratic Congressional Campaign Committee
DCS	District of Columbia Statehood
DFL	Democratic-Farmer-Labor Party (MN)
DLC	Democratic Leadership Council
DNC	Democratic National Committee
DSCC	Democratic Senatorial Campaign Committee
DSOB	Dirksen Senate Office Building
EMILY	EMILY's List (Early Money is Like Yeast)
ERISA	Employee Retirement Income Security Act
FEC	Federal Election Commission
FERC	Federal Energy Regulatory Commission
FRC	Family Research Council
GOP	Republican Party (Grand Old Party)
G	Green Party
H	Capitol Building Room (House side)
HAFA	Heritage Action for America
HSOB	Hart Senate Office Building
I	Independent
IAP	Independent American Party (NV)
IC	Independent Conservative
ID	Independent Democrat
IG	Independent Green
Ind	Independence Party
ITI	Information Technology Industry Council
IVP	Independent Voters Party
LCV	League of Conservation Voters
LHOB	Longworth House Office Building
Lib	Libertarian Party
Mod	Moderate Party
NAFTA	North American Free Trade Agreement
NARAL	NARAL Pro-Choice America
NL	Natural Law Party
NP	Non-Partisan
NPA	No Party Affiliation
NRSC	National Republican Senatorial Committee
NSA	National Security Agency
NTU	National Taxpayers Union
PF	Peace and Freedom Party
PNP	New Progressive Party (PR) (Spanish: Partido Nuevo Progresista)
POP	Populist Party
PPD	Popular Democratic Party (PR) (Spanish: Partido Popular Democrático)
PRG	Progressive Party
R	Republican Party
Ref	Reform Party
RHOB	Rayburn House Office Building
RMM	Ranking Minority Member
RNC	Republican National Committee
RSOB	Russell Senate Office Building
RTL	Right-to-Life Party
S	Capitol Building Room (Senate side)
SOC	Socialist Party
SW	Socialist Workers Party
UAW	United Auto Workers
UMJ	United States Marijuana Party
WF	Working Families

Throwing Out the Political Rulebook, An Overview

By Charlie Cook

If 2016 was the year when the political rulebook was thrown out, whether it will apply in 2017 and 2018 is a good question. In 2016, the normally predictable Republican Party ignored its historic tendency to nominate whoever's turn it was to be the party's standard-bearer and did something completely different. Donald Trump, the first GOP nominee not to be an established political personal, the first in modern history to run against the party establishment as well as becoming the first president in American history to have never served in government at any level, elected or appointed, civilian or military, it all defied history.

Conversely, Democrats, who have historically been more likely than Republicans to opt for someone new, fresh and very different, did the opposite. By nominating Hillary Clinton, the person next in line having been passed over in 2008 for Barack Obama, Democrats ignored polls showing her with incredibly high negative ratings and arguably unelectable against anyone whose negatives were lower than Donald Trump's.

Unquestionably Trump's victory was the biggest upset in presidential election history, one that will be studied and argued about for decades. There was very little, if anything, that was normal about Donald Trump's candidacy, his campaign, his general election victory, his presidential transition period and now about his presidency. Forty out of our 45 presidents came into the office by either winning the most popular votes, or moving up from the vice presidency on the death or resignation of a predecessor. While Trump won the most votes in 30 states, winning the Electoral College 306 to 232, he lost the popular vote by 2.1 percentage points, or more than 2.8 million votes (technically the Electoral College vote was 304 to 227, two electors who "should" have voted for Trump voted for someone else, bringing the Republican total down to 304, five electors who were supposed to vote for Clinton cast their ballots for someone else, bringing her down to 227). Trump joined John Quincy Adams, Rutherford B. Hayes, Benjamin Harrison and George W. Bush as presidents who lost the popular vote, but won in the Electoral College, or in Adams case, losing the popular vote to Andrew Jackson who also won a plurality but not a majority in the Electoral College. Adams prevailed in the vote by the House of Representatives, becoming president. Trump's deficit in both numbers of popular votes and percentage point difference was greater than the other four.

Normally after winning election to the presidency, the incoming chief executive benefits some from a halo effect, at least some of the negative baggage from the campaign is usually left behind, his favorability ratings rising from before the election. Typically, Americans become hopeful that the new president will work out, whether they supported him or not, and at least for a time, give him the benefit of the doubt. But Trump's post-election/pre-inaugural favorable ratings hardly went up, in the January 4-8 Gallup Poll, 40 percent of Americans had a favorable opinion of him, 55 percent and unfavorable view. By comparison, 78 percent had a favorable opinion of Barack Obama, 18 percent an unfavorable opinion in the period preceding his taking office. For George W. Bush, even after his contested election, 62 percent had a favorable view, 36 percent unfavorable, while for Bill Clinton, 66 percent viewed him favorably, 26 percent unfavorably.

Every new presidency experiences something of a problematic shakedown cruise with a new chief executive, a new White House staff and Cabinet adjusting to their new jobs, but President Trump missed out on the champagne celebration christening, too. The Gallup Poll for Trump's first week in office put his job approval rating at 45 percent, 1.1 percentage points below his share of the popular vote (disapproval was 47 percent). That honeymoon period usually extends for some time. George H.W. Bush went 1,336 days into his administration before his disapproval rating in the Gallup Poll ever hit 50 percent. For his son, George W. Bush it took 1,205 days, Barack Obama went 936 days before his disapproval hit 50 percent, for Ronald Reagan it was 727 days and Bill Clinton got there after 573 days. But for Donald Trump it took just eight days.

By early spring, Trump's approval ratings had dropped below those of any newly elected president, at least as far back as polling exists, though quite a few subsequently dropped this low or lower. A legitimate question of to what extent this was a reflection of an era of increasing hyper-partisanship and how much was unique to Trump and his presidency was impossible to know. The old rule of thumb was that a favorability or job approval rating above 50 percent was good and below was bad, but that may no longer be as applicable. To the extent that Trump's favorable and approval ratings are below his 46.1 percent share of the popular vote, it suggests that at least some of this is specific to Trump. Worth noting is that Bill Clinton's Gallup approval rating dropped as low as 37 percent in early June 1993, his first year in office, he bounced back to get re-elected in 1996, something that should hearten Republicans worried about Trump's approval ratings in early 2017.

For a Republican president who was certainly not the choice of his party's establishment, was hardly a traditional candidate and had quite a few detractors in the GOP all the way to the Republican National Convention, he did consolidate his party, garnering 90 percent of the vote of self-identified Republicans in the network exit polls and at least for his first few months in office drew 84 to 88 percent approval ratings among self-identified Republicans each week in the Gallup tracking, with almost identical disapproval ratings among self-described Democrats. Among independents, his approval ratings were typically in the mid-to-high 30s after an initial week at 41 percent. The partisan lines that we have seen in recent years were clearly in place.

One of the norms for presidents is mid-term election losses, not quite as inevitable as death and taxes, but close. In 36 out of the 39 (92 percent) midterm elections held since the beginning of the Civil War, the party holding the White House lost ground in the House of Representatives, averaging losses of 33 seats, while in 20 out of the 25 midterms since the direct election of senators went into effect in 1914, the White House lost Senate seats as well, averaging a net loss of four seats.

Many political scientists subscribe to the "surge and decline" theory, that when a presidential candidate is elected or re-elected, down-ballot candidates of that same party tend to benefit from the coattails of their presidential candidate as well as the voter turnout and circumstances that enabled the top of the ticket to succeed. It follows that going into the subsequent midterm election, that party is numerically over-exposed. In many cases, candidates who would not have won without the presidential victors' coattails at the top of the ticket were unable to survive the next midterm election when they were more on their own and the circumstances are very different from when they were elected or re-elected the previous election. Midterm elections are often dominated by unhappy voters. Voters of the party that is out of power tend to be angry, more passionate and energized, turning out in proportionally higher numbers than the more complacent voters of the president's party. Given that midterm elections have significantly lower participation rates than presidential elections, a party benefiting from disproportionately high turnout will benefit.

Though midterm elections generally go bad for the party in the White House, exceptions do occur. In 1934, two years after Republican Herbert Hoover lost re-election to Franklin Roosevelt, voters were not yet finished punishing Hoover's GOP and lashed Republicans again to the tune of net losses of 10 Senate and nine House seats. Republicans under President George W. Bush actually gained one Senate and eight House seats in 2002, his first-term midterm election - aided by the election being just 14 months after the 9/11 attacks and Bush's 63 percent approval rating, having topped out at a sky-high 86 percent immediately after the attacks. But by the time of Bush's second midterm election, the Iraq War had turned radioactive and in a more normal midterm pattern, Bush's GOP lost six Senate and 30 House seats in that 2006 election. For Clinton it was the other way around, the normal midterm pattern manifested itself in 1994, his first-term midterm election, when Democrats lost eight Senate and 54 House seats in 1994. But in Clinton's second midterm election, in a backlash against Republicans impeaching him in the House though he was acquitted in the Senate, Democrats broke even in the Senate and gained five seats in the House.

Overall, since the beginning of the Civil War, there is an important distinction between first-term and second-term midterm elections. In first-term, midterm elections, the party in the White House has averaged a net loss of just one Senate seat since direct elections began, and 26 House seats. It was the second-term, midterm elections when losses were often catastrophic, averaging nine Senate and 35 House seats.

So will those normal patterns hold and how will President Trump and his Republican Party fare in 2018? One concern for Republicans was whether they could suffer the same turnout problem that plagued Democrats in the 2010 and 2014 midterm elections. While Barack Obama was able to draw a strong vote that benefited down-ballot Democrats in 2008, many of those Obama voters did not return for the 2010 midterm when his name was not on the ballot, resulting in substantial Democratic losses. Those voters returned in 2012 for his successful re-election, again benefiting down-ballot Democrats, but didn't for the 2014 midterms, again resulting in Democratic losses. Obama supporters were uniquely his, and did not convey in midterm elections to other Democratic candidates. As Democratic pollster Fred Yang put it, "they don't call them Obama voters for nothing." Now Republicans have the same worry about Trump voters -- will they return in 2018 for Joe and Jane generic Republican candidates, who don't look or sound like Donald Trump. To the extent that Trump has problems with his own party members in Congress, this could become even more of a challenge. Maybe we shouldn't call them Trump voters for no reason.

Both the political environment and other circumstances are very important. Incumbents generally make their decisions whether to run for re-election during that odd-numbered, off-election year. If the political environment seems favorable a year out, an incumbent is often more likely to run for re-election than if the public mood looks ominous. Over the last 20 elections, 94 percent of House incumbents and 83 percent of Senate incumbents who have sought re-election won, so normally (there are exceptions), the more of a party's incumbents running for re-election the better it is for that party. Similarly when the political environment looks favorable for the Loyal Opposition during that year preceding an election, that party often is able to recruit better challengers and open seat candidates than if the prospects look more foreboding. While a couple of states have congressional filing deadlines as early as December 2017 and a few have deadlines in early summer, most occur between January and May, so the political environment up until then is important.

After the first few months of the Trump administration, things looked very concerning for Republicans, though obviously that can change. It would be reasonable to assume that the environment this year would be somewhat encouraging for Democratic candidates and incumbents and less so for Republicans. But again, that can change.

In terms of circumstances beyond the political climate, numerical exposure for parties is an important factor. In the House there are several exposure elements that are important. A party that enjoys large seat gains in a presidential election year is more exposed in the next midterm election than one that picked up very few or even lost seats in that presidential year. With Republicans having lost six House seats in 2016, they enter 2018 with relatively small exposure levels. Few freshmen or other incumbents are sitting in seats previously held by the other party and thus usually more vulnerable. So this would argue that Republicans might be somewhat less vulnerable to House losses.

Another key factor has to do with the drawing of congressional district boundaries and distribution of voters. For many years, Democrats dominated the governorships and state legislatures that in most states draw congressional district (and state legislative) boundaries and, not surprisingly, they drew maps that tended to benefit their party. But in the 2010 midterm elections, Republicans enjoyed major gains in both governorships and state legislative seats (more state races are in the midterm than presidential election cycles) and as a result, were able to draw congressional and state legislative boundaries that benefited GOP candidates enormously. Modern computer technology and data bases have made partisan mapmakers even more effective in drawing boundaries for maximum benefit than in previous decades, exacerbating that problem for the party out of power in each state. This too would argue for lower Republican losses in the House.

Beyond this gerrymandering practice is one that is less sinister but also important -- population distribution. Democratic voters tend to be heavily concentrated in urban areas and college towns while Republican voters are more spread out in suburban and rural areas and smaller towns. Once a party wins a congressional (or state legislative) race by one vote, every additional vote is effectively wasted. As a result, Republican voters are more efficiently allocated than Democratic voters, giving the GOP an additional advantage.

Another factor to be considered is that while presidential elections usually have bigger, broader and more diverse electorates than midterms, when the electorate is older, whiter, more conservative and more Republican, in 2016 this difference was less than in most other presidential years. Thus a midterm electorate is often more generous to Republicans than presidential-year electorates. This does not mean that the GOP is immune to bad midterm elections. The GOP suffered large losses in 2006 and substantial

House losses in 1982 as well as large Senate losses in 1986 under President Reagan. This is yet another factor that would argue against larger House losses.

These factors are all potentially important in reducing House losses but they do not make Republicans immune to the laws of political physics. When a party controls the White House, the Senate and the House going into an election with their own voters either complacent or disenchanted, and the other party's voter are agitated and highly motivated, bad things can happen to the party in power. Similarly if Trump voters stay home in the 2018 midterm elections just as 2008 Obama voters stayed home in 2010, that can result in an unfavorable outcome for Republicans. While the late former Democratic Speaker of the House Tip O'Neill famously said, "all politics is local," my variation on that is that "all politics is local, except when it isn't." From time to time there are "wave" elections in which the are larger forces at work with the result of one party having a strong political tail wind while the other party has to contend with a headwind. It occasionally happens in presidential election years like 1980, but it is more commonly seen in midterm elections like 1946, 1958, 1966, 1974, 1994 and 2010, when it is not unusual for weak candidates to beat strong candidates and poor campaigns beat good campaigns. The factors suggested above might well reduce the severity of a wave election but might not eliminate it. A wave election that in past decades might result in House losses for a party of between 40 and 65, as each of the six midterms mentioned earlier, might end up with losses of just 20 to 30.

As of spring 2017, Democrats needed a net gain of 24 seats to take control of the House, slightly less than the average number of first-term, midterm election losses for the party holding the White House. If President Trump's job approval ratings remained in the 30s or lower, one could consider the GOP majority in the House in considerable danger.

The Senate is a very different situation. Keeping in mind that Senate terms are six years, the results of elections six and 12 years earlier become highly relevant, determining the relative exposure of each party. Democrats scored a net gain of six Senate seats in 2006, President George W. Bush's second-term, midterm election, picking up two additional seats in 2012, the next time this class of Senate seats were up. As a result, Democrats have 25 Senate seats up in 2018, to just nine for Republicans. Exacerbating this overall disproportionate exposure for Senate Democrats is that five Democratic incumbents were up in states where Mitt Romney won by nine or more points and Trump won by 19 or more points: Joe Donnelly of Indiana, Heidi Heitkamp of North Dakota, Joe Manchin of West Virginia, Claire McCaskill of Missouri and Jon Tester of Montana. Five more Democratic incumbents were up in other states that Trump won: Tammy Baldwin of Wisconsin , Sherrod Brown of Ohio, Bob Casey of Pennsylvania , Bill Nelson of Florida and Debbie Stabenow of Michigan. Note that many of these Democratic Senate incumbents are in northern rust belt states with disproportionate shares of working class white voters, a group that Democrats have had problems with of late. Conversely, there is only one Republican up in a state that Hillary Clinton won, Dean Heller of Nevada. Only two Republicans are up in states that Trump won by single digits, Jeff Flake of Arizona and Ted Cruz of Texas.

Clearly, Senate Democrats are vastly more exposed to losses in 2018 than Republicans, limiting the downside risk potential for Republicans if the political environment is unfavorable or circumstances turn against them.

So are the midterm rules re-written in the era of Donald Trump? At least in the Senate they might be. But in the House, the potential for losses clearly exist, perhaps enough to endanger their majority. The potential for House losses of three dozen or more as has often occurred to the president's party in midterm elections seems less likely in 2018.

It's a pretty good bet that there will be few normal weeks or even days during the Trump presidency, at least anytime soon. This most unconventional of candidates has become the least conventional president in history and many of the normal rules won't apply.

Sources for various data:

http://www.gallup.com/poll/201977/trump-pre-inauguration-favorables-remain-historically-low.aspx

http://www.gallup.com/poll/203198/presidential-approval-ratings-donald-trump.aspx

http://www.gallup.com/interactives/185273/presidential-job-approval-center.aspx

Two Nations

By Richard Cohen

As the 2016 election dramatically revealed, the United States has split into two political nations. In both the Republican and Democratic wings, the majority party holds at least two-thirds of the presidential Electoral Votes, the seats in Congress, and the governorships. That leaves the balance of power with roughly 20 percent of the states and voters—from Ohio to Wisconsin, and Colorado to Arizona—where partisan control is up for grabs and the nation's political control is determined. For the foreseeable future, significant shifts in the overwhelming numbers on each side seem unlikely.

These dynamics were shown in the past eight years when Washington shifted from Democratic control of the White House and Congress to Republican control of both branches. Elections during that interval revealed that the balance point is so narrow that either party can reign supreme—for the short term, at least. Following the 2008 election, Democrats proclaimed that Barack Obama—the first Democrat since 1964 to win the presidency with a majority of the popular vote and more than 300 electoral votes—had ushered in their political dominance. By June 2009, they had a filibuster-proof 60 Senate seats and a seemingly solid 256-seat House majority.

Starting a few months later, their dominance steadily declined in a succession of steps that hit a painful bottom for them in November 2016. They lost their Senate lock in January 2010, when Republican Scott Brown stunningly won the seat of the late Edward Kennedy of Massachusetts. The following November, House Democrats suffered a cataclysmic 63-seat loss, which Republicans then reinforced during the subsequent redistricting in several key states. In 2014, it was the Senate's turn, as Democrats suffered a wipe-out with the loss of nine seats and their majority. Finally, Donald Trump won the presidency, when he unexpectedly took Wisconsin, Michigan and Pennsylvania, where Republicans had been shut out since 1988.

Following their 2016 disaster, a Democratic takeover of the House or Senate in 2018 initially seemed unlikely. Those prospects in Congress as well as the White House seemed more likely to improve in 2020. As always, there are caveats and uncertainties. In the early months of the Trump presidency, the durability of the Republican coalition seemed as uncertain as the Democrats' dominance eight years earlier.

Regardless of the outcome of upcoming elections, the political math revealed the challenges facing each party. The United States has evolved to two distinct political coalitions: A Republican hammer-lock in the South and the nation's heartland, which provides 219 electoral votes in 24 states— all of which are contiguous except for Alaska; A Democratic coalition based on the Atlantic and Pacific coasts, where they hold a solid grip on 203 electoral votes in 16 states; and 116 electoral votes in 10 states in the Great Lakes region and Southwest that are up for grabs.

As the following tables and maps reveal, the split between the two parties has become so clear-cut and overwhelming that the numbers are easy to present and describe. This introductory overview provides an essential primer to the profiles of the nation's top elected officials, plus the states and House districts that they serve, as the 2018 Almanac of American Politics describes in detail. This political evolution dates back a half-century. In those days, Democrats—mostly conservatives--remained dominant in the South, and Republicans could succeed in most other states, with both strong liberals and strong conservatives.

Now that the two parties have lined up on opposite ends of the ideological spectrum, this new status quo likely will remain in place until one party or the other successfully moves into the opposition's domain. How soon that might happen is among the many challenges facing the Trump presidency and its Democratic opposition. Even with the seemingly entrenched party coalitions of recent years, events have shown that breath-taking change can arrive quickly and unexpectedly.

The following tables describe the components of the two separate party coalitions and the swing groups. The data are vital to understanding political control in the United States, and potential avenues for change. Included below are the presidential results of 2012 and 2016, plus control of governor, Senate and House offices in 10 regions across the nation following the November 2016 election. In each case, the Republican total is followed by the Democratic total. The numbers are based on the actual results of the November 2016 election, prior to subsequent House vacancies and special elections. They ignore the vicissitudes of the casting of Electoral College votes. (The grouping of some states--such as Virginia and Florida—might stir disagreement. But, as the numbers reveal, recent election results have created obvious patterns.)

Republican Coalition (24 States)							
		Presidential		Governors	Senate	House
Region	States	2012	2016	November 2016		
South Atlantic	FL, GA, NC, SC	40-29	69-0	3-1	7-1	42-19
Mid South	AR, KY, TN, WV	30-0	30-0	3-1	7-1	19-3
Deep South	AL, LA, MS, OK, TX	68-0	68-0	4-1	10-0	44-14
Plains	IA, KS, MO, NE, ND, SD	27-6	33-0	6-0	10-2	18-3
Mountain	AK, ID, MT, UT, WY	19-0	19-0	3-1 (1 Indep.)	9-1	9-0
	Sub-Total	**184-35**	**219-0**	**19-4 (1 Indep.)**	**43-5**	**132-39**

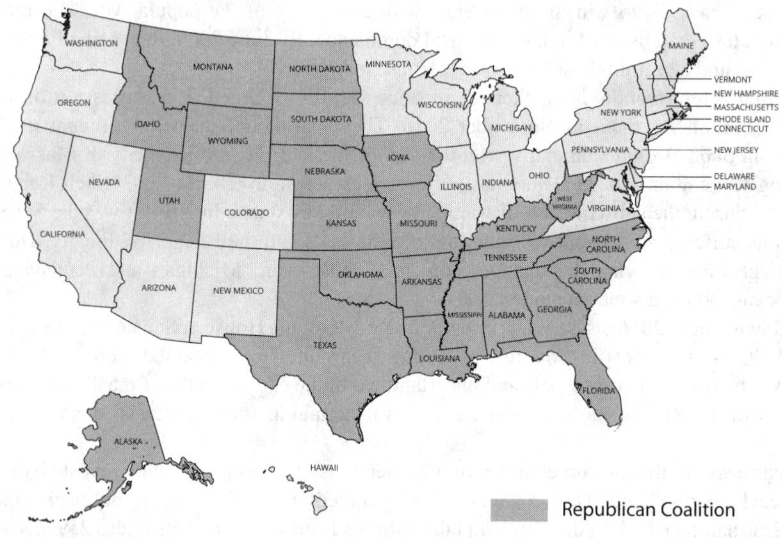

Democratic Coalition (16 States)						
		Presidential		Governors	Senate	House
Region	States	2012	2016	November 2016		
New England	CT, ME, MA, NH, RI, VT	0-33	1-32	4-2	1-11*	1-20
Mid-Atlantic	DE, MD, NJ, NY, PA, VA	0-92	20-72	2-4	1-11	35-42
Far West	CA, HI, OR, WA	0-78	0-78	0-4	0-8	19-51
	Sub-Total	**0-203**	**21-182**	**6-10**	**2-30**	**55-113**

* Two Senators elected as Independents are grouped as Democrats, with whom they caucus.

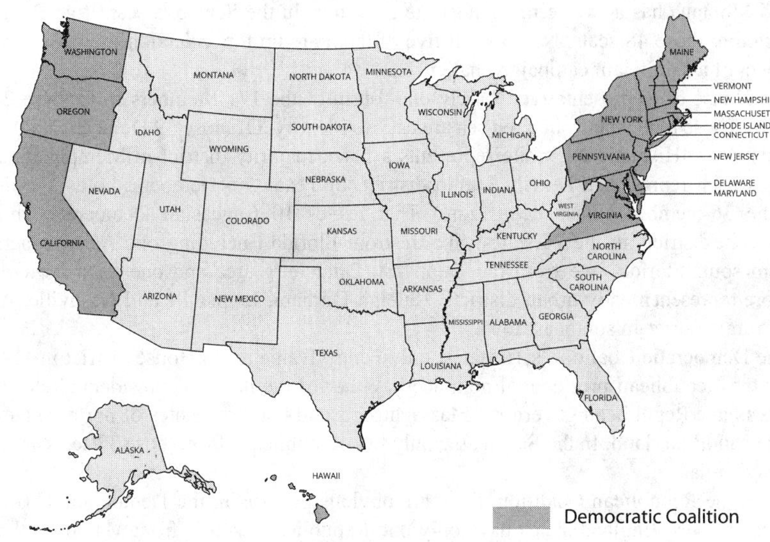

Up for Grabs (10 States)						
		Presidential		Governors	Senate	House
Region	States	2012	2016	November 2016		
Great Lakes	IL, IN, MI, MN, OH, WI	11-74	55-30	5-1	3-9	43-30
Southwest	AZ, CO, NV, NM	11-20	11-20	3-1	4-4	11-12
	Sub-Total	**22-94**	**66-50**	**8-2**	**7-13**	**54-42**

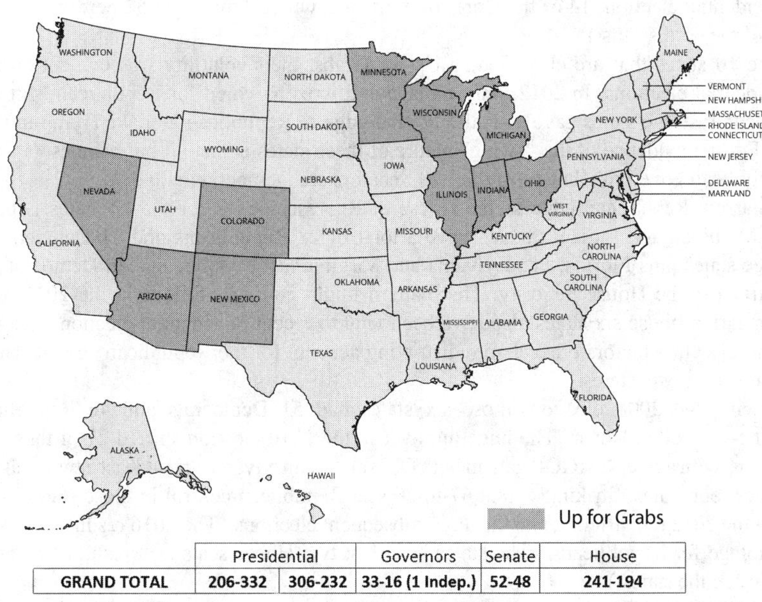

	Presidential		Governors	Senate	House
GRAND TOTAL	**206-332**	**306-232**	**33-16 (1 Indep.)**	**52-48**	**241-194**

More detailed review of the data demonstrates the dramatic sweep of these partisan splits. Of the Republican Coalition's 24 states, only Florida and Iowa in 2012 voted for the Democratic presidential nominee in either of the past two presidential elections. Only four of those states have a Democratic governor: Louisiana, North Carolina and West Virginia each elected a new Chief Executive in 2015 or 2016, and Montana has a two-term Democratic governor. In the Senate, a scant five Democrats have been elected to those 48 seats. Notably, all five of them are up for reelection in 2018, and each faced the prospect of a significant campaign challenge.

In the House of Representatives, barely one-fourth of the 171 Members from those 24 states are Democrats. Those blue islands in a red sea are easy to identify. Of those 39 Democrats, 20 are African-Americans, 5 are Hispanics, 1 white represents a black-majority district in Memphis and 3 Anglos from Texas each represent a heavily Latino district.(In Texas, no Democrat holds a white-majority seat in the 36-member House delegation.) That leaves 10 Caucasian Democrats who represent majority-white districts in the 24 states: Six are from Florida (including one Asian-American), with three from south Florida, two from the Tampa-St. Petersburg area and one from the Orlando area. Three more represent mostly urban districts: Raleigh-Durham, Louisville and Nashville. And one has a mostly rural district in southeast Iowa.

Of the Democratic Coalition's 16 states, only Pennsylvania and a House district in Maine in 2016 voted for the Republican presidential nominee in either of the past two presidential elections. Six of these states have Republican governors: Massachusetts and the three states of northern New England, New Jersey and Maryland. In the Senate, the only two Republicans from those 32 seats are from Maine and Pennsylvania.

As with the Republican Coalition, there are obvious patterns in the Democratic Coalition. In the House, the six New England states have only one Republican, who is from Maine. In the Far West, California's 53-seat House delegation has 14 Republicans; two of them serve districts that are on the Pacific coast; only 2 of the other 12 represent outlying parts of the 16 districts in at least part of Los Angeles County, and none serve in any of the 10 districts in the San Francisco Bay Area. Of the four GOP Members from Washington and one from Oregon, only the Representative from suburban Seattle is from either state's dominant metropolitan area.

There is a vital anomaly for the six states in the Democratic Coalition's Mid-Atlantic region. Nearly half of the 77 House Members from those six states are Republicans. They include 13 from Pennsylvania, 9 from New York, 7 from Virginia, 5 from New Jersey and 1 from Maryland. Some of those from Pennsylvania and Virginia have benefited from partisan redistricting. But 22 of those 35 Republicans serve suburban districts where Donald Trump won less than 55 percent of the vote in the 2016 presidential election; 14 of them are from districts where Trump got 52 percent or less. (He won all but 5 of the 35 districts.)

Of the 10 states that are classified as Up for Grabs, their volatility was evident during the past two presidential elections. In 2012, only Indiana and Arizona voted for Republican Mitt Romney. In 2016, by contrast, the states gave a small but vital edge to Republican Donald Trump in the Electoral College. Further evidence of the "swing" nature of these states is that all but Minnesota and Colorado have Republican governors, but 13 of their 20 Senators are Democrats.

The narrow Republican edge in the House of Representatives for the 10 states is based chiefly in Ohio, Michigan and Indiana, which have a total of 28 Republicans and 11 Democrats. In effect, those three states plus Florida, Pennsylvania and Virginia (36 Republicans, 20 Democrats) determine which party has the House majority. That pattern might continue following the 2022 redistricting. As shown earlier, those six states also have been vital to recent presidential election outcomes. These results reinforce that factors other than redistricting account for the Republican strength in the House delegation of those six states.

Following the 2008 election, those six states had 51 Democrats and 46 Republicans in the Democratic-controlled House. The huge turnover in the 2010 election shifted 21 of those seats to the Republicans, with a five-seat GOP gain in both Ohio and Pennsylvania and at least a two-seat gain in each of the other four states. Strikingly, that 67-to-30 seat Republican control in those states barely shifted following the 2012 redistricting and the three subsequent elections. The 2016 results yielded a 64-to-31 seat advantage for Republicans. (The states have lost two House seats as a result of reapportionment shifts between the states.)

Only a handful of House districts in those six states have been competitive since 2012, even though many of them have been competitive in presidential elections. Two House seats in those six states have shifted party control since 2012: In Florida and Virginia, the Democrats gained one seat in each state, which resulted largely from their unusual court-drawn mid-decade redistricting in 2016.No other House seats have changed party control in the four other states since 2010. One other point is worth noting for those six states: Of those 31 Democratic-held House seats, each is in a large metropolitan area—either in a dominant city or close-in suburbs. Republicans control all of the exurban and rural districts in the six states.

The 10 states that we classify as Up for Grabs have provided much of the battleground for recent presidential elections. Similar patterns have also applied in congressional results. In Senate elections in 2016, Republican victories in competitive contests in Ohio, Indiana, Wisconsin and Arizona were instrumental in the party's retaining control. For 2018, the fate of Democratic incumbents in Ohio, Michigan, Indiana, Wisconsin and Minnesota, plus the Republican Senators in Nevada and Arizona, will be crucial to the outcome of Senate elections.

In the House, many Democrats expect that their best opportunity to regain control will come in 2022 following the decennial Census. Their prospects will be substantially influenced by whether they can replace five Republican governors in the Midwest battleground--each of those six states except for Minnesota. Not coincidentally, Republicans since 2010 have controlled the state House and Senate in four of those five states: Ohio, Michigan, Indiana and Wisconsin. Prior to 2010, Democrats had control of the House in each of those four states, plus the Senate in Wisconsin.

It's important to emphasize that the huge switch in party fortunes in those six states during Obama's first mid-term election came prior to the subsequent redistricting in 2011-12. That most recent redrawing of political boundaries reinforced the partisan trends in the House that began in 2010 and have continued since then.

As for the Senate, Republicans have an obvious benefit, given that each state gets two Senators regardless of its size. Their coalition is based in 24 states, while the Democratic Coalition is in only 16 states. Given that Democrats are at risk in 2018 of losing their five Senators in the 24 GOP states (while Republicans have only two Senators in the 16 states of the Democratic Coalition), that increases the imperative for them to hold firm with their 13 (of 20) Senate seats in the "Up for Grabs" Great Lakes and Southwest states.(For the purpose of this review, the "Independent" Senators from Maine and Vermont are listed with Democrats, with whom each receives committee assignments and is included in the party caucus.)

A similar point applies in the House to many of the 55 Republican-held seats in the 16 states of the Democratic Coalition. Democrats' opportunities to increase their seats in New York, New Jersey and California—in addition to Florida, Pennsylvania and Virginia—are essential to control of the House.

In politics, of course, change is constant and nothing remains the same forever. A half-century ago, Democrats controlled the South and Republicans were dominant in New England. Just as Republicans benefited in 2016 when Donald Trump climbed over the "Blue Wall" in what had been viewed as Democratic strongholds, Democrats in Congress need to find the keys to open the locks in states and districts that have slipped from their control in shifts between the Two Nations.

★ The President and Vice President ★

By Michael Barone

President

Donald J. Trump (R)

Elected 2016, term expires Jan. 2021, 1st term; b. June. 14, 1946, New York, NY; University of Pennsylvania Wharton School of Business (PA), B.A.; Presbyterian; married (Melania Trump); 5 children (4 from previous marriages), 8 grand-children.

Professional Career: Real estate developer & Owner, The Trump Organization, 1971-2016; Television Producer, "The Apprentice", 2004-2015.

On a cold, sunny day, November 21, 1964, a crowd of 5,000 attended the ceremony opening the Verrazano Narrows Bridge between Brooklyn and Staten Island, then the longest suspension bridge in the world and still the longest in the United States. At the front of the dais were Governor Nelson Rockefeller, Mayor Robert Wagner and Francis Cardinal Spellman. Not far away was an 18-year-old Fordham freshman from Queens named Donald Trump. Robert Moses, head of the Triborough Bridge and Tunnel Authority, opened the ceremony by paying tribute to the architect of this and many other bridges, the 85-year-old Swiss-American Othmar H. Ammann—but neglected to mention his name.

Donald Trump noticed—and remembered. Years later he told a New York Times reporter, "I realized then and there that if you let people treat you how they want, you'll be made a fool. I realized then and there something I would never forget: I don't want to be made anybody's sucker." The things he would build would have his name prominently displayed.

What was the teenage Trump doing in a crowd of politically connected celebrities? The answer is that Donald Trump's entire life and career have been marinated in politics. His father Fred Trump made millions building apartments in Brooklyn and Queens. In assembling land and qualifying for public subsidies, it didn't hurt that he was a key supporter of Brooklyn machine Democrats and a close friend and ally of Abraham Beame, city controller in 1964 and mayor from 1973 to 1977, and Hugh Carey, governor from 1974 to 1982. Most college freshmen would not ask their fathers to get them included in a crowd of politicians at a bridge dedication. But Donald Trump obviously understood the importance of political connections in his father's business—and in the vastly expanded business he may already have been dreaming about launching.

And launch it he did, less than ten years after the bridge dedication, and in as much defiance of conventional wisdom as his widely mocked decision to run for president some four decades later. He took over running the family real estate business in 1971, a year after graduating from the University of Pennsylvania's Wharton School, and soon decided to plunge into Manhattan real estate. New York City was in the process of losing nearly 1 million inhabitants in the 1970s, and the city government was headed toward bankruptcy by 1975; New York seemed caught in a spiral of decline, and Manhattan real estate values plunged. Trump negotiated with the bankrupt Penn Central Railroad and in 1976 took over the Commodore Hotel, next door to Grand Central Station, and turned it into the Grand Hyatt, complete with a 40-year tax abatement. In 1978 he launched what became the Trump Tower, on Fifth Avenue and 56th Street. In 1984, after New Jersey legalized casino gambling in Atlantic City, Trump opened his first of several casino hotels there.

All these enterprises involved extensive negotiations and interactions with various levels of government and were accompanied by extensive publicity generated by Trump as well as critical journalists like the Village Voice's Wayne Barrett. Trump saw to it that, unlike Othmar Ammann, his name would not go unmentioned. His propensity for controversial utterances, his movie-star good looks, his gaudy lifestyle and his 1987 number one bestselling book The Art of the Deal made him a national celebrity. His reliance on political connections and favorable treatment by government provided upward leverage in the 1980s but downward leverage in the 1990s: after casino gambling was legalized in other East Coast states, his Atlantic City properties were thrown into bankruptcy, and in the early 1990s he only avoided personal bankruptcy by restructuring relations with creditors. He provided his own version of this passage of his life in his 1997 book, The Art of the Comeback.

Through his entire business career, as he went into one enterprise after another, Trump took care to generate maximum publicity: no one was going to forget his name. It was prominently displayed on Trump Tower, on his 44-story tower on Columbus Circle and his 72-story apartment tower across from the United Nations, on his 40 Wall Street building, once the highest in the world. His enterprises included an airline (the Trump Shuttle between New York and Washington), golf courses in the United States and foreign countries, a U.S. Football League team, boxing matches, the Tour de Trump bicycle race, the Miss Universe beauty pageant, a modeling agency, Trump University, a hotel in Washington's Old Post Office Tower on Pennsylvania Avenue and, from 2003 to 2015, the NBC television show The Apprentice. A major, perhaps majority, share of the value of the Trump Organization, it has been estimated, is the Trump brand.

Many of Trump's businesses, starting with Manhattan real estate, have depended on political decisions; not surprisingly, in heavily Democratic New York City, he started off identifying himself, like his father, as a Democrat. But that identification has always been malleable (he registered as a Republican in 1987) and he has contributed to candidates of both parties. He also voiced politically heterodox opinions early on. In the 1980s he ran newspaper ads arguing that "America should stop paying to defend countries that can afford to defend themselves" and in the 1990s he questioned the wisdom of free trade agreements—positions that became familiar in the 2016 campaign cycle. He undoubtedly noticed the success of another celebrity billionaire, Ross Perot, in rising to lead the polls in the 1992 presidential race, before his inexplicable and temporary withdrawal, and in 1999 he explored the possibility of running for president himself as a candidate of the Reform party Perot had founded. As a registered Democrat, he opposed the Iraq war policy of George W. Bush, though not as early as he later claimed. But in 2008 he endorsed the candidacy of John McCain. In 2011 he spoke at the conservative CPAC conference in February but in May announced he would not seek the Republican nomination—while saying he would be elected if he did. That same month he was ridiculed by Barack Obama at the White House Correspondents Association dinner for his charges that Obama was not born in the United States.

On June 16, 2015 Donald Trump descended on the escalator at the Trump Tower and announced his candidacy for president and his slogan "Make America Great Again." Press accounts focused on his provocative statements that "when Mexico sends its people, they're not sending their best. . . . They're sending people that have lots of problems. . . . They're bringing drugs. They're bringing crime. They're rapists. And some, I assume, are good people." In response to widespread criticism, Trump refused to back down and asserted that he would not be bound by "political correctness." This clearly struck a chord with many Republican voters. By mid-July Trump had passed the erstwhile leader in primary polls, Jeb ("low energy") Bush and but for a few weeks in the fall maintained a poll lead up through the Republican National Convention. His presence surely accounted for the enormous viewership, three times the previous record, of the early Republican candidate debates, and the record turnout, more than 30 million, in Republican primaries and caucuses. He attracted giant crowds at rallies across the country.

Trump's positions on immigration and trade were different from those of all of his 16 rivals for the Republican nomination, just as they were different from those of every Republican presidential nominee for the preceding four decades. They were not necessarily the majority view among the Republican and he profited from the rivalry of other candidates, who tended to attack each other in the hopes of appealing to Trump voters when, it was assumed, his candidacy would fall by the wayside. But it didn't. Trump narrowly lost the first contest, the Iowa caucuses, to Ted Cruz, but won with pluralities in the first two primaries in New Hampshire (35%) and South Carolina (32%) and won a solid 46% in the Nevada caucus. In the March 1 primaries, Trump won the 255 of 595 delegates at stake; his largest percentages were in Alabama and Massachusetts, while Ted ("Lyin' Ted") Cruz won his home state of Texas and next-door Oklahoma, and Marco ("Little Marco") Rubio won the Minnesota caucuses. Results in contests between March 5 and 12 were mixed, with Trump carrying five states, Cruz four, Rubio Puerto Rico and the District of Columbia. On March 15 Trump did much better, besting Rubio by a 46%-27% margin in his home state of Florida and thereby winning all its delegates, beating Cruz narrowly in Missouri and North Carolina and by a wider margin in Illinois, while John Kasich won his home state of Ohio (outside of which he won a total of only seven counties, four in Vermont, two in Michigan and Trump's own Manhattan).

In retrospect, this was the critical moment putting Trump on the cusp of winning the 1,237 delegates needed for the nomination. But the struggle continued: Trump won Arizona solidly, while majority-Mormon Utah voted 70% for Cruz; Trump was third, with 14%. On April 5, Cruz beat Trump 48%-35% in Wisconsin. On April 19, Trump won a smashing 59% in his home state of New York; Cruz finished third, with 15%. This was the first contest in which Trump won an absolute majority of the vote, and he followed it up a week later with majority wins in five other Northeastern states. The final contested primary was in Indiana May 3, where Governor Mike Pence endorsed Cruz but had positive words for Trump. Trump won 53%-37% over Cruz, a reversal of the Wisconsin result in a larger Midwestern state. Cruz immediately dropped out and Kasich "suspended" his campaign.

The contours of support were different in 2016 from those in the 2008 and 2012 Republican primaries. Those elections boiled down to contests between establishment candidates—John McCain and Mitt Romney—and candidates associated with religious conservatives—Mike Huckabee and Rick Santorum. McCain and Romney prevailed by carrying suburban and higher income areas; Huckabee and Santorum carried rural and lower income areas. In contrast, Trump ran about as strong in suburbs as in rural areas, and about as well among religious conservatives as among more secular voters. One constant was that Trump ran strongest among non-college graduates, and weaker among college graduates, who tended to favor Marco Rubio and John Kasich. One clear divide came along lines of social capital or social connectedness, as defined by scholars Charles Murray and Robert Putnam. Groups with a high degree of social connectedness and involvement in voluntary associations proved resistant to the Trump appeal; these included most notably Mormons and also Dutch-, German- and Scandinavian-Americans in states like Iowa, Michigan, Minnesota and Wisconsin. Trump's strongest groups were those with low social capital, most notably Scots-Irish along the Appalachian chain from western Pennsylvania southwest to Arkansas and Louisiana and also Italian- and Irish-Americans from the Northeast (including those who moved to Florida).

Meanwhile Democrats were also having a primary contest in which a candidate out of line with previous nominees—a protest candidate—was running much better than expected, the self-described socialist Bernie Sanders. He ran just slightly behind Hillary Clinton in the Iowa caucuses (and may have won more votes, given the Democrats' weighted state-convention-delegate-equivalent counting system) and won a solid victory in New Hampshire, next door to his home state of Vermont. Overall Sanders won primaries or caucuses in 22 states and came within 2% of winning in five more (Illinois, Iowa, Kentucky, Massachusetts, Missouri). At no point did it seem likely that Sanders would actually win a majority of delegates: after New Hampshire, Clinton won narrowly in the Nevada caucuses, but won by a smashing 73%-26% margin in the South Carolina primary. She replicated that victory in every other Southern state except Oklahoma and West Virginia and beat Sanders in the 14 Southern states combined by nearly a 2-1 margin, 63%-34%. In the rest of the country, however, the race was closer: Clinton prevailed over Sanders by just 53%-46%. Demographically, Clinton carried black and Hispanic voters by wide margins and ran just about even with Sanders among white Democratic voters. Outside the South, Sanders typically won by wide margins among young voters, including young women; Clinton won solidly among older voters. As in the Republican contests, so among Democrats the voting patterns differed from the last contested primaries, in 2008. Then Barack Obama carried black voters over Clinton by wide margins; this time she was winning them by similar margins, while she carried Hispanics by wide margins in both years. But Clinton was not able to replicate her 2008 wide margins among downscale whites; to the contrary, she lost them to Sanders in most states, while carrying high-income areas (perhaps because Sanders spoke favorably of 77% top income tax rates).

The novel alignments in the parties' primaries turned out to be an indicator in the changes—marginal but significant changes—in the voting patterns that have become so familiar in general elections over the past two decades. Voters continued to be divided more along cultural than along economic lines, with the demographic variable most closely correlated with voting behavior continuing to be religion, or degree of religiosity within each sectarian group. The percentages of the national popular vote won by each of the two parties' nominees were within the historically narrow range that they have been starting in the 1990s. Despite predictions that his calls for restricting immigration and building a wall on the southern border would antagonize Hispanics, exit polls indicated that Donald Trump received about the same percentage from them as Mitt Romney did in 2012; actually his numbers among Hispanics, and among blacks and Asians, were slightly better than Romney's. Among whites, there was a significant difference depending on levels of education. Exit polls showed Romney carrying white college graduates 56%-42% and Trump carrying them by only 49%-45%. But among non-college- graduate whites, Romney's substantial 61%-36% margin was eclipsed by Trump's huuuge 67%-28% margin. This group, considerably larger than the combined number of Hispanics and Asians, gave the Republican a percentage margin comparable to Hillary Clinton's percentage margins among those two non-white groups. Trump showed the same strength as he had in the primaries among groups with low degrees of social connectedness, Scots-Irish along the Appalachian chain and Italian-Americans in the Northeast and Florida. And he showed the same weakness as he had there in the affluent suburbs, not only in the North, where Democrats have been carrying these areas since the 1990s, but in the South as well.

In effect, the author of The Art of the Deal made a deal, a trade. He would give up college whites that had previously gone Republican in states like California, Arizona, Colorado, Texas and Georgia. In all but Colorado he ran behind previous Republicans. Net electoral vote loss, as compared to the 2008 and 2012 Republican nominees: zero. All those states voted as they had voted before. In return, as part of the deal, he would gain votes among non-college whites who had previously voted Democratic, in states including Florida, Pennsylvania, Ohio, Michigan, Wisconsin, Iowa and the 2nd congressional district of Maine, all of which voted Democratic in 2008 and 2012. Net electoral vote gain: 100. To be sure, he won 46 of those electoral votes, without which he would not have been elected, in Pennsylvania, Michigan and Wisconsin, by margins of less than 1 percent. There was relatively little difference in voting in metropolitan areas of more than 1 million population in the Midwest and Pennsylvania: Barack Obama carried them by a 15% margin in 2012, 57%-42%, and Hillary Clinton carried them by a 14% margin in 2016, 54%-40%. But a majority of votes in this region are cast outside these major metropolitan areas, and in these "outstate" areas there was a major shift. In 2012 Mitt Romney carried those areas 53%-46%, a 7% margin. In 2016 Donald Trump carried them 57%-37%, a 20% margin. These outstate areas had been evenly split between the candidates in 2008, and in 2004 George W. Bush had carried them over John Kerry by a 55%-43% margin. Donald Trump ran 2% better there than Bush, and Clinton ran 6% behind Kerry.

All of which raises the question: Was Donald Trump's victory the result of brilliant and original insight, or was it just blind dumb luck? Surely it was a mixture of both, in proportions that people will be arguing about for decades to come.

His victory is all the more remarkable because, once the nominations were clinched, Hillary Clinton seemed to be leading by all conventional measures. She had and spent far more money; she had a more successful and less fraught national convention; she was supported heartily by the incumbent president, whose job approval hovered (just) above 50 percent during the campaign period; she performed better, according to polls, in all three presidential debates, especially the first. She led in almost every national poll and in most target state polls throughout the summer and fall. The dominant memes in political commentary pointed to a Democratic victory.

Many analysts noted that Democrats had carried states with 242 electoral votes in all of the preceding six presidential elections: a "blue wall" that made it almost impossible for a Republican nominee to get to 270. But it turned out that it was possible to punch holes in the blue wall, which Included Pennsylvania, Michigan and Wisconsin, which one might have predicted if one looked back and saw how narrowly the Democrats carried those states in some recent elections. Other analysts argued that an increasingly non-white ascendant America required Republicans to win an historically almost unprecedented (with the exception of 1984) percentage of white voters in order to win. And indeed that was reflected in the national popular vote, which Hillary Clinton won 48%-46%.

But the states with what turned out to be the decisive 100 electoral votes have (with the exception of Florida) relatively few Hispanic and Asian voters and either flat or declining percentages of black voters—and lots of non-college whites. The widespread assumption among pundits was that non-college whites who voted for Barack Obama would vote for Hillary Clinton as well, and polling evidence to the contrary was scanty since their responses are not usually broken out in statewide polls. But there was evidence the unexpected was happening, notably the polls in Iowa and Ohio, which showed Clinton trailing, as she did in November there and in the parts of Florida, Pennsylvania, Michigan and Wisconsin outside million-plus metropolitan areas. There were a few analysts who raised the possibility that this might happen: the blogger Steve Sailer back in 2002, political scientist Sean Trende of realclearpolitics.com in a series of articles in 2013, analyst Nate Cohn in a perceptive piece in the New York Times's Upshot blog in June 2016. Nate Silver, proprietor of fivethirtyeight.com, noted that Clinton's polling leads in critical states were shakier, with more voters undecided between two highly unpopular major party nominees, than did the analysts who gave her a 99% chance of winning. Going into election day, Silver pegged Trump chances at 29% and, as he pointed out, something with a 29% probability happens just about one out of three times.

On November 8, some time between nine and ten o'clock Eastern time, it became clear, to the suddenly downcast Clinton crowd under the glass ceiling of the Javits Center and to the suddenly jubilant Trump crowd several blocks away at the New York Hilton, that the 2016 presidential election was one of those in which something with a one-in-three chance was happening. America and the world live with the consequences.

Vice President

Mike Pence (R)

Elected 2016, term expires Jan. 2021, 1st term; b. June. 7, 1959, Columbus, IN; Hanover College, B.A., 1981, Indiana University School of Law, J.D. 1986; Disciples of Christ; married (Karen Batten); 3 children.

Elected Office: U.S House, 2001-2003 (IN 2nd District), 2003-2013 (IN 6th District); IN Governor, 2013-2017.

Professional Career: Practicing attorney; President, Indiana Policy Review Foundation 1991-1994; Network Indiana talk show host, 1994-2000.

The 42nd, 43rd and 44th presidents of the United States each ran for the House of Representatives and lost: Bill Clinton in 1974, George W. Bush in 1978 and Barack Obama in 2000. Mike Pence, the 48th vice president of the United States, ran for the House of Representatives and lost twice, in 1988 and 1990, and later won six successive elections to the House starting in 2000. Pence grew up in Columbus, Indiana, a small courthouse town distinguished by numerous examples of tasteful modern architecture. The Pence family members were Roman Catholics and Democrats, admirers of John F. Kennedy and Martin Luther King, Jr., who was assassinated when Mike Pence was eight years old. Pence's grandparents were Irish immigrants and his father owned several gas stations. Pence graduated from Hanover College, Indiana's first private college near the banks of the Ohio River and down the road from the old river town of Madison. At college Pence became an evangelical Christian. After graduation, he worked as an admissions officer at Hanover and then went to Indiana University Law School in Indianapolis, graduating in 1986 and practicing law.

In 1988, at 31, Pence ran for Congress against 14-year Democratic incumbent Philip Sharpin the 2nd district, southeast and east of Indianapolis. It included the industrial town of Muncie, the "Middletown" described in the books of that name by sociologists Robert and Helen Lynd in the 1930s; Richmond, founded by Quakers and home of Earlham College; Columbus and southeastern suburbs of Indianapolis. Sharp, first elected in the Watergate year of 1974, had become a Commerce Committee subcommittee chairman and had a genial manner which appealed to many non-liberal Hoosier voters. In 1988, as George H.W. Bush and Dan Quayle carried the district by nearly a 2-1 margin over Michael Dukakis and Dan Quayle, Pence held Sharp to a 53%-47% margin, his closest re-election race in what turned out to be 20 years in the House. In 1990 Pence ran again, and this time lost by a wider 59%-41% margin.

For a while Pence adjured elective office, and entered into two professions then opening up for conservatives—think tanks and talk radio. In 1991-93 he ran the pro-free enterprise Indiana Policy Review Foundation, and in 1993-99 he conducted a morning talk program on an Indianapolis and 17 other stations in the state. In these years he wrote an essay, "Confessions of a Negative Campaigner," regretting some of his tactics in House campaigns, and described his radio program as "Rush Limbaugh on decaf." He missed the years of the Gingrich revolution in Congress, one of the leaders of which was David McIntosh, who won the 2nd district seat after Sharp retired in 1994. When McIntosh ran unsuccessfully for governor in 2000, Pence ran for Congress again. He ran first in a six-candidate primary, with 44% of the vote; running third was Luke Messer, since 2012 congressmen from the renumbered (after 2000) 6th district. Pence won the general election with 51%, to 39% for Democrat Robert Rock and 9% for independent conservative Bill Frazier, who had run four times against Sharp. In subsequent House races, as Indiana like the rest of the nation increasingly voted straight-party tickets, he was re-elected by between 64% and 67% of the vote.

Pence has repeatedly described himself as "a Christian, a conservative and a Republican, in that order," and proceeded in the House to vote accordingly. He opposed the McCain-Feingold campaign-finance law and became a plaintiff, along with Senator Mitch McConnell, in a court case challenging its constitutionality. In 2001 he was one of 34 Republicans to vote against the education bill, christened "No Child Left Behind," supported by George W. Bush, Edward Kennedy and House committee chairman John Boehner. In 2003 he was just one of 19 Republicans to oppose the Medicare prescription drug bill supported by Bush and for which the House Republican leadership kept the roll call open for three hours in a successful effort to squeeze out the needed votes. It did not come from Mike Pence.

In 2005 Pence became chairman of the conservative Republican Study Committee, a group sometimes critical of the House leadership. After House Republicans lost their majority in the 2006 election, Pence challenged Boehner for the position of minority leader; he lost 168-27. After the 2008 election, when House Republicans lost more seats, Pence was selected chairman of the Republican Conference, a leadership position, with Boehner's support.

In May 2011 launched a campaign for governor, to replace the highly successful Republican Mitch Daniels, who was term-limited. He promised to "build an even better Indiana on the solid foundation that Governor Daniels has poured," in part by cutting individual and corporate tax rates and eliminating the estate tax. He also emphasized education, particularly his support of school choice. His only announced opponent for the Republican nomination was ruled off the ballot when he was found to be 14 short of the petition signatures required. In the general election he faced former state House Speaker John Gregg, who attacked him for his opposition to Planned Parenthood and for an essay in a book his former think tank produced calling for repeal of the Americans with Disabilities Act. Pence focused on jobs and education, and called for "family impact statements" from state officials assessing how regulations promoted or discouraged marriage.

Pence had an immense financial advantage, but may have been hurt by his refusal to run negative advertisements and by the fallout from Republican Senate candidate Richard Mourdock's statement that pregnancy resulting from rape is "something that God intended to happen." Pence won by just 49%-47%, the closest margin in a gubernatorial race since 1960. Gregg carried industrial Northern Indiana and rural counties around his home base in southwest Indiana. Pence lost Indianapolis's Marion County, but won big in suburban counties and carried the Indianapolis metropolitan area.

As governor, Pence pushed a 10% personal income tax cut, reduced by half by the legislature. He signed a "right to try" bill allowing terminal patients to use drugs not yet approved by the Food and Drug Administration and a bill requiring inmates to serve at least three-quarters of their sentences. He authorized a temporary exception to the state's anti-needle exchange program in response to an outbreak of HIV in southern Indiana. On Pence's watch, Indiana became the first state to drop out of the Common Core education program. He worked to expand vocational training in a state that continues to have the largest share of manufacturing jobs of any in the nation. He obtained HHS approval for his Healthy Indiana Plan 2.0, an expansion and revision of a Daniels policy. It expanded Medicaid for the poor and also required participants to contribute to a Health Savings Account, penalizing non-payers by suspending coverage for six months. Pence aroused controversy over a proposal for a state-run news outlet which he dropped under criticism. He stirred more controversy by backing a religious freedom law which critics said would enable businesses to discriminate against gay and lesbian customers. Business leaders were especially critical, and after days of outcry Pence and Republican legislative leaders agreed to a legislative fix that banned discrimination based on sexual orientation and gender identity. Pence successfully backed increased funding of charter schools and restrictions on abortion providers.

Pence was one of many Republican officeholders who were considered a potential presidential candidate in 2016—and one of the considerably smaller number who did not run. In June 2015, the same month when Donald Trump announced his candidacy, Pence announced he would run for a second term as governor in 2016. But he found his way into the spotlight in the presidential campaign nonetheless. The April primaries had mixed results: Ted Cruz beat Donald Trump decisively in Wisconsin, while Trump won in New York and "Acela corridor" states from Rhode Island to Maryland. Indiana voted May 3: would a Midwestern state with an economy similar to Wisconsin's vote for Cruz or would it vote for the candidate who had won absolute majorities in Eastern states? On April 29 Pence endorsed Cruz, but he also praised Trump and said, "I'm not against anybody." He noted that Trump has "given voice to the frustration of millions of working Americans with the lack of progress in Washington, D.C.," and pledged to support the winner of the Republican nomination. Indiana proved to be the opposite of Wisconsin: Trump beat Cruz 53%-37%, with 8% for John Kasich of next-door Ohio. Trump carried 87 of the state's 92 counties, and Cruz and Kasich withdrew from the race.

In that same primary, Pence was re-nominated as the Republican candidate for governor, but it was also clear that he was under serious consideration by Trump for the vice-presidential nomination. He had experience both in Congress and as governor, and was one of the few prominent Republicans who had not said disparaging things about the presumptive presidential nominee. On July 15, three days before the opening of the Republican National Convention, Trump announced that Pence was his choice for vice president, noting that Pence's non-endorsement was the most positive he had received. Pence was duly nominated and resigned the governorship nomination; he was replaced at a Republican state convention by Lieutenant Governor Eric Holcomb, who won in November. On October 4, he debated Democratic vice-presidential nomination in Farmville Virginia and, despite Kaine's hectoring tone and numerous interruptions, put in what most observers considered a winning performance. Many observers, relying on a strained interpretation of the polling evidence, supposed that Pence's political career was over. Instead, as the returns were counted on the evening of November 8, it was apparent that he was elected vice president of the United States. No Hoosier has ever been president, but Pence is the sixth to serve as vice-president, after Republican Schuyler Colfax (1869-73); Democrat Thomas A. Hendricks, a fellow graduate of Hanover College (1885); Republican Charles W. Fairbanks (1905-09); Democrat Thomas R. Marshall (1913-21); and Republican Dan Quayle (1989-93).

The United States of America

Population	
Total	316,515,021
% change since 2010	4.0%
Land area (sq. miles)	3,797,000
Pop/ sq mi	83.4

Race and Ethnicity	
White	62.3%
Black	12.3%
Latino	17.1%
Mexican	10.9%
Puerto Rican	1.6%
Cuban	0.6%
Other Hispanic or Latino	3.9%
Asian	5.1%
Pacific Islander	0.2%
American Indian and Alaska Native	0.7%
Two or more races	2.2%
Other	0.2%

Language	
English only	79.0%
Spanish	13.0%
Other European	3.7%
Asian	3.4%

Work	
White Collar	36.7%
Sales and Service	42.2%
Blue Collar	21.1%
Government	14.3%

Place of Birth	
Native	86.8%
Born in US	85.4%
State of residence	58.7%
Different state	26.7%
Puerto Rico, U.S Islands or abroad to american parent	1.5%
Foreign Born	13.2%

Foreign-born Citizenship Status	
Naturalized U.S citizen	46.6%
Not a U.S citizen	53.4%

Region of Foreign Born	
Europe	11.5%
Asia	29.7%
Africa	4.4%
Oceania	0.6%
Latin America	51.8%
Northern America	2.0%

Education	
H.S grad or less	41.1%
Some college	29.2%
College Degree, 4 yr	18.5%
Post grad	11.2%

Military	
Veteran	8.3%
Active Duty	0.4%

Age Groups	
Under 18	23.3%
18-34	23.3%
35-64	39.1%
Over 64	14.1%

18 years and over	
Male	48.6%
Female	51.4%

65 years and over	
Male	43.8%
Female	56.2%

Income	
Median Income	$53,889
Under $50,000	46.6%
$50,000-$99,999	29.9%
$100,000-$199,999	18.2%
$200,000 or more	5.3%
Poverty Rate	15.5%

Health Insurance	
With health insurance coverage	87.0%

Public Assistance	
Cash public assistance income	2.8%
Food stamp/SNAP benefits	13.2%

2016 Presidential Vote		
Hillary Clinton (D)	65,853,652	(48%)
Donald Trump (R)	62,985,134	(46%)
Gary Johnson (L)	4,489,235	(3%)

2012 Presidential Vote		
Barack Obama (D)	65,915,795	(51%)
Mitt Romney (R)	60,933,504	(47%)

★ ALABAMA ★

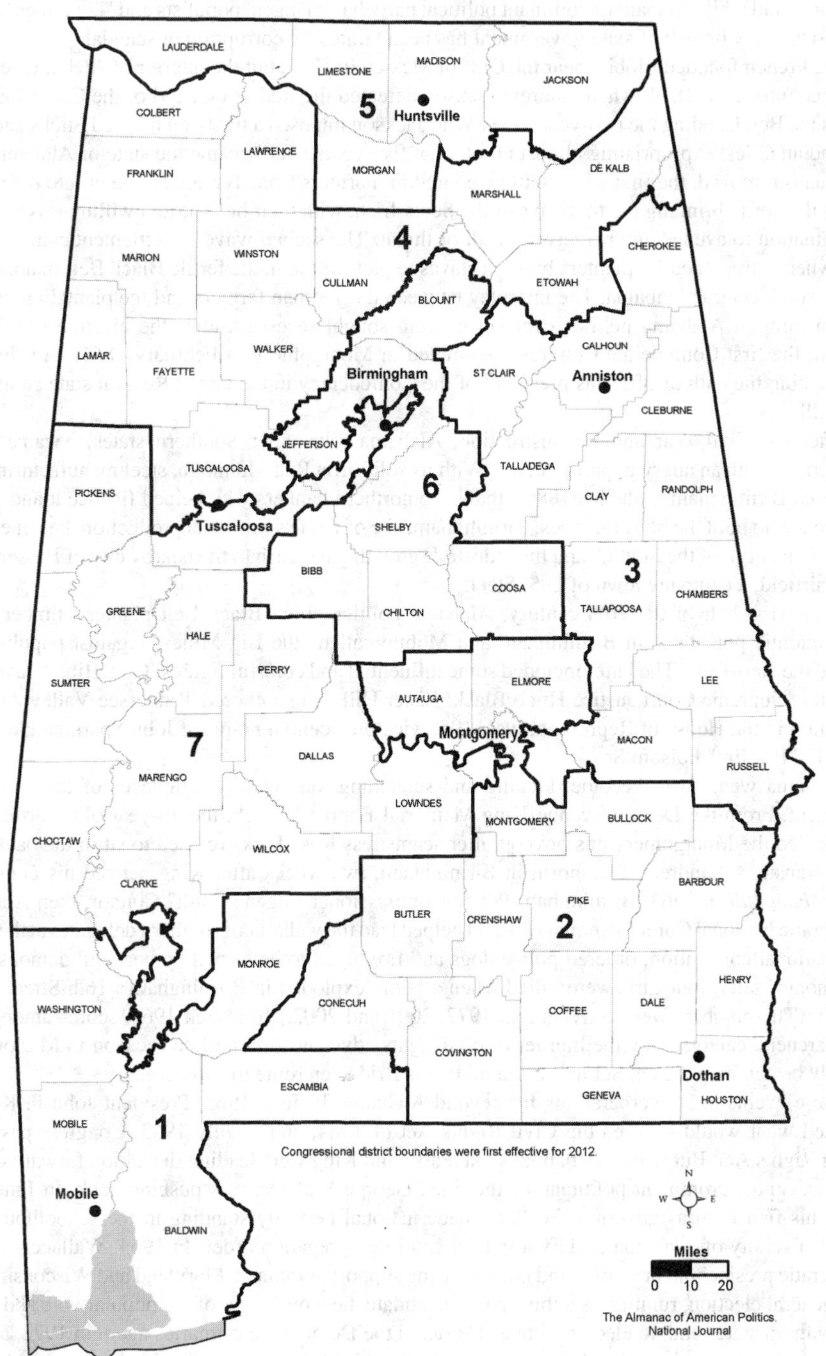

Congressional district boundaries were first effective for 2012.

The past hangs over Alabama like its tall yellow pines: Refrains from decades-old civil rights struggles recur in the debate on gay marriage, and the state's manufacturing base has once again been built with the help of outsiders. The state continues to struggle with poverty and low rates of education, and while Alabama's dominant political party has changed, populists and "big mules" remain. Only now, every branch of state government has been tainted by corruption or scandal.

The French founded Mobile near the Gulf of Mexico in 1702, but the interior of Alabama remained Indian country until 1814, when Andrew Jackson defeated the Red Stick band of the Creek Indians at Horseshoe Bend, ending the two-year Creek War. Jackson imposed a treaty on the Red Sticks and on his own Indian allies, expropriating almost all of what five years later became the state of Alabama. With the Indians removed, the first white settlers poured in. Farmers from Tennessee swept into the red clay hills in the north, bringing the folkways of the Scots-Irish, with their hot-spirited willingness and fierce determination to avenge any perceived insult or threat. The second wave of settlement came a decade later, when entrepreneurial planters brought slaves to pick cotton in the fertile Black Belt (named for its soil) in south central Alabama. The interplay between the yeoman farmers and the plantation grandees has run through Alabama politics ever since. Both sought secession after the election of Abraham Lincoln; the first Confederate Congress assembled in Montgomery in February 1861, with Jefferson Davis taking the oath of office as president of the Confederacy in the Greek Revival state capitol atop Goat Hill.

After the Civil War and Reconstruction, Alabama, like other Southern states, became solidly Democratic, with an angry populist accent. With its solid-iron Red Mountain, steel manufacturing grew up around Birmingham in the late1880s, thanks to northern bankers who helped finance it and Yankee engineers who built the blast furnaces. Birmingham, site of Dixie's first steel production, became known as the "Pittsburgh of the South," and the industry's growth gave birth to the nearby city of Bessemer and later Fairfield, a company town of U.S. Steel.

In the first half of the 20th century, Alabama politics pitted Black Belt planters, timber barons and economic potentates in Birmingham and Mobile called "the Big Mules," against populists who favored the New Deal. The latter included some influential and colorful figures: Gov. Bibb Graves; Sen. and future Supreme Court Justice Hugo Black; Lister Hill, who authored Tennessee Valley Authority legislation in the House of Representatives; 1952 vice presidential nominee John Sparkman; and Gov. James E. "Big Jim" Folsom Sr.

Alabama went on to become, kicking and screaming, one of the birthplaces of the civil rights movement. From the Dexter Avenue King Memorial Baptist Church, the 26-year-old Martin Luther King Jr. led the Montgomery bus boycott after seamstress Rosa Parks refused to sit in the back of the public transit. A hundred miles north in Birmingham, two weeks after King penned his *Letter from Birmingham Jail* in 1963, Birmingham Police Commissioner Eugene "Bull" Connor, then Alabama's Democratic National Committeeman who had helped lead the walkout of southern delegates at the party's 1948 national convention, ordered police dogs and fire hoses to be turned on peaceful demonstrators. Four months later, four girls were killed when a bomb exploded in Birmingham's 16th Street Baptist Church. (The bombers were convicted in 1977, 2001 and 2002.) In March 1965, scores among some 600 marchers, catalyzed by the murder of civil rights advocate Jimmie Lee Jackson in Marion, were severely beaten by police at Selma's Edmund Pettus Bridge en route to Montgomery.

These events had reverberations far beyond Alabama. In June 1963, President John F. Kennedy endorsed what would become the Civil Rights Act of 1964, and in July 1965, Congress passed the Voting Rights Act. But while Alabamians like Parks and King were leading the nation forward on race, Alabama's most prominent politician of the time, George Wallace, was pushing back. In June 1963, during his first term as governor, Wallace made national news by standing in the schoolhouse door at the University of Alabama to defy a federal court desegregation order. In 1964, Wallace ran in the Democratic presidential primaries and got surprising support in Indiana, Maryland and Wisconsin. In the 1968 general election, running as a third-party candidate, he won 13.5% of the popular vote and carried five southern states and 46 electoral votes. He ran in the Democratic primaries again in 1972, and was shot and partially paralyzed while campaigning in Laurel, Maryland. He remained a formidable figure nationally until Jimmy Carter beat him in the 1976 Florida Democratic primary. He dominated Alabama politics, winning the governorship in 1962, running his wife to succeed him in 1966 (she died midterm), regaining the governorship in 1970 and 1974, then running and winning one last time in 1982. He spent his final years apologizing for his earlier acts and met with Vivian Malone Jones, one of the students he tried to block from attending the University of Alabama, professing, "The South has changed, and for the better." He died in 1998.

Today, civil rights tourism is a major business. Not far from the state capitol, Montgomery boasts sculptor-architect Maya Lin's circular Civil Rights Memorial, Troy University's Rosa Parks Museum, and the Dexter Parsonage. The Selma to Montgomery National Historic Trail runs along U.S. Highway 80, and the Alabama Civil Rights Museum Trail includes the Tuskegee Airmen National Historic Site and the 16th Street Baptist Church.

Economically, Alabama lost ground during the Wallace years. While Atlanta was peacefully desegregating and beginning decades of white-collar growth, Birmingham was violently resisting the civil rights movement, only to see its blue-collar base in the steel industry shrink and its most talented residents of all races flee to calmer climes. Agriculture remains a significant industry, including the third-highest percentage of timber acreage in the country, behind Oregon and Georgia; timber covers 69 percent of the state. But where the state has gained ground is in manufacturing.

Automobiles became a major part of Alabama's economy, and as with the steel industry a century before, outsiders helped fuel the rebirth. Mercedes opened its first American assembly line in 1997 near Tuscaloosa, while Honda has a major plant in Lincoln and Hyundai has one in Montgomery. These operations spawned dozens of auto supplier and subcontractor firms. Honda alone employs more than 4,500 workers and indirectly supports more than nine times that number throughout the state, according to the University of Alabama's Center for Business and Economic Research.

Aerospace has been another key to Alabama's economy, due heavily to the presence of the Marshall Space Flight Center in Huntsville. Boeing has a workforce of 2,750 developing NASA's Space Launch System, and Raytheon opened a missile integration facility in 2012. In conventional aviation, Airbus selected Mobile as the location of its first U.S. assembly plant for A320 aircraft; in 2016, within three years of breaking ground, the first airplane, destined for JetBlue, rolled off the assembly lines. Lesser-known companies have flocked to the area as well. Pennsylvania-based Carpenter Technologies built a premium metals plant near Huntsville to provide alloy steel products for aerospace engines and medical devices.

The gains in manufacturing facilities have been driven by weaker unionization than in the north, although Alabama does rank first among the former Confederate states with 10.2 percent of workers holding union cards in 2014. (Most members are public employees, including teachers in the politically potent Alabama Education Association.) Economic health has been strongest around Huntsville, the Mobile suburbs and the resort communities of Baldwin County. But prosperity has largely eluded rural Alabama, where joblessness and grinding poverty persist. Overall, Alabama's unemployment rate in November 2016 was 5.9 percent, the fifth-worst of any state. The state also has the fifth-lowest median income and the sixth-lowest rate of bachelor's degrees in the nation. The trade publication Education Week ranked Alabama's K-12 education system 47th in the nation, and no less than the governor, Robert Bentley, said in 2016, "Our education system in this state sucks."

In the 30-plus years since George Wallace's name last appeared on an Alabama ballot, the state has become solidly Republican, first in national politics and then in state politics. For a while, many of the talented state politicians were Democrats who, along with their allies - the AEA, major black political associations, and trial lawyers - could defeat less experienced Republicans with regularity. But even these canny Democratic survivors were overcome. Gov. Don Siegelman was defeated for a second term in 2002 and convicted on corruption charges in 2006; Lt. Gov. Jim Folsom Jr. - a former governor in the 1990s - got swamped by the 2010 Republican wave; a year later, legendary AEA political chief Paul Hubbert stepped down at the age of 76; and in 2012, Alabama's last Democratic statewide elected official, Lucy Baxley, 74, saw her political career end when she lost her reelection bid for Public Service Commission president to Twinkle Cavanaugh.

At the same time, the local Democratic machinery atrophied and the party's longstanding control of the state legislature also disappeared in 2010, when midterm voters propelled Republicans to almost a two-to-one advantage in the state Senate and a 27-seat upper hand in the state House - the first GOP majorities in Montgomery since Reconstruction. Two of the prime movers in that victory, state Rep. Mike Hubbard, the Republican state party chairman, and state Sen. Del Marsh, president pro tem of that chamber, led a disciplined and relentless campaign. Just like national GOP strategists who learned long ago that the path to congressional majorities ran through conservative districts and states in the South that had reflexively elected centrist Democrats, Hubbard, in particular, aggressively backed candidates in seats that had previously been conceded to conservative Democratic legislators and were ripe for Republican takeover.

But in surprisingly short order, power proved corrupting. By 2016, the leaders of each of the three branches of state government – all Republicans – were mired in troubles of one kind or another. Hubbard was sentenced to four years in prison, plus eight years of probation and a $210,000 fine, after being convicted on 12 felony ethics charges, revolving around the use of his office to make $1.1 million for his businesses. In the judicial branch, Roy Moore -- the chief justice of the Alabama Supreme Court who had in 2003 defied a federal judge's order to remove a 5,280-pound granite monument to the Ten Commandments that he had installed in his Montgomery courthouse, leading to his ouster – was once again removed from his position, this time for defying federal court orders on same-sex marriage. But the most spectacular implosion was the governor. Bentley was secretly recorded having a cringe-worthy extramarital affair with a top adviser; the episode led to an impeachment inquiry and an investigation by the state attorney general's office.

Taken together, these scandals turned Alabama into a national poster child for dysfunctional government and prompted soul-searching among local thinkers. "The saddest thing is, this state has so much potential," wrote Kyle Whitmire, a political commentator for the Alabama Media Group. "In person -- one-on-one -- our people are decent and selfless. We make great music. We cook good food. We tell funny jokes. We love our children and would sacrifice everything for their futures. … [But] rather than holding our elected officials to higher standards, we lower our expectations." Josh Moon, a Montgomery Advertiser columnist, despaired that the traditional refrain that "the voters deserve better" was wrong. "The people of this state do not deserve better," Moon wrote. "The people of this state are getting exactly what they deserve, because the people of this state have, time and again, ignored reasonable, smart candidates, both Republican and Democratic."

Population		**Race and Ethnicity**		**Income**	
Total	4,830,620	White	66.3%	Median Income	$43,623 (47 out of 50)
Land area	50,645	Black	26.3%		
Pop/ sq mi	95.4	Latino	4.0%	Under $50,000	55.4%
Born in state	70.0%	Asian	1.2%	$50,000-$99,999	28.2%
		Two races	1.5%	$100,000-$199,999	13.8%
Age Groups		Other	0.6%	$200,000 or more	2.7%
Under 18	23.0%			Poverty Rate	18.8%
18-34	20.1%	**Education**			
35-64	39.4%	H.S grad or less	46.8%	**Health Insurance**	
Over 64	14.9%	Some college	29.8%	With health insurance coverage	87.3%
		College Degree, 4 yr	14.8%		
Work		Post grad	8.7%		
White Collar	33.3%			**Public Assistance**	
Sales and Service	40.9%	**Military**		Cash public assistance income	1.8%
Blue Collar	25.8%	Veteran	9.8%		
Government	16.3%	Active Duty	0.3%	Food stamp/SNAP benefits	16.1%

Voter Turnout			
2015 Total Citizens 18+	3,620,994	2016 Pres Turnout as % CVAP	59%
2016 Pres Votes	2,123,372	2012 Pres Turnout as % CVAP	59%

Legislature	
Senate:	8D, 26R
House:	37D, 66R, 1I, 1V

Presidential Politics

2016 Democratic Primary		
Hillary Clinton (D)	311,141	(78%)
Bernie Sanders (D)	76,878	(19%)
2016 Republican Primary		
Donald Trump (R)	373,721	(43%)
Ted Cruz (R)	181,479	(21%)
Marco Rubio (R)	160,606	(19%)
Ben Carson (R)	88,094	(10%)

2016 Presidential Vote		
Donald Trump (R)	1,318,255	(62%)
Hillary Clinton (D)	729,547	(34%)
Gary Johnson (L)	44,467	(2%)
2012 Presidential Vote		
Mitt Romney (R)	1,255,925	(61%)
Barack Obama (D)	795,696	(38%)

Alabama normally doesn't play much of a role in presidential politics. It's been a reliably Republican state in the presidential race since 1980. Jimmy Carter, a son of the South, in 1976 was the last Democratic nominee to carry Alabama, winning 60 of its 67 counties. But in 2015, a huge August rally at Ladd-Peebles Stadium outside of Mobile for Donald Trump's nascent bid for the 2016 GOP presidential nomination, attracted some 30,000 boisterous supporters and signaled the candidate's unique appeal to many Republican voters who had become alienated from the party establishment. The event also drew Alabama's leading populist, then GOP Sen. Jeff Sessions, who praised Trump's stance on halting illegal immigration. Six months later, Sessions formally endorsed Trump's candidacy - the first senator to do so - and the New York real estate developer handily captured the state's March 1 GOP presidential primary with 43 percent over Texas Sen. Ted Cruz, the runner-up with 21 percent. Trump's victory in Alabama and elsewhere in the South that day was a major blow to the Cruz campaign, which had been counting on a strong showing in the region to bolster his candidacy. President Trump repaid Sessions by nominating him for Attorney General. The Democrats' primary between former Secretary of State Hillary Clinton and Vermont Sen. Bernie Sanders was even more lopsided. Clinton trounced Sanders 78%-19%, largely with her support from African Americans, who made up a majority of the state's Democratic primary voters. According to the television network exit poll, Clinton swept African Americans by roughly 15-to-1 over Sanders, who campaigned lightly in the state. In 2008, Clinton lost the Alabama primary to then Illinois Sen. Barack Obama, 56%-42%. Turnout in the Democratic primary was down from 2008, while Republicans saw record turnout in their presidential primary.

The general election was a foregone conclusion: Trump bested Clinton 62%-34%. Trump carried 54 of the state's 67 counties. Clinton won 12 counties in the state's Black Belt, named for the rich dark soil that was once worked by cotton plantation slaves and sharecroppers. The region has a high share of African-American voters. Clinton also captured Jefferson County (Birmingham), marking the third consecutive time that a Democratic presidential nominee had carried the state's largest vote-producing county. But the share of the statewide vote for Jefferson was less than 14 percent in 2016, down from 19 percent in 1980. That decline reflects the growth of Birmingham's Republican suburbs and exurbs in Shelby and St. Clair counties, where Trump swamped Clinton. Trump, like other GOP candidates, dominated fast-growing counties like Limestone, suburban Huntsville; and Baldwin, a recreational haven on the Gulf Coast that includes suburbs of Mobile. Republican Gov. Robert Bentley, who had endorsed Ohio Gov. John Kasich in the GOP primary, said he would not vote for Trump or Clinton in the general election.

Congressional Districts

115th Congress Lineup	6R 1D	114th Congress Lineup	6R 1D

Alabama's shift to its predominantly Republican delegation came more slowly than in other southern states. As recently as 2010, it was split between four Republicans and three Democrats. But that year's election eliminated the final white Democrats (in the Montgomery and Huntsville-area districts), and the subsequent redistricting further entrenched the Democrats' hold on the African-American 7th District by adding most of Montgomery's black precincts to its Birmingham-area black population. The prospect of a competitive partisan congressional election in the state is remote, at least until the next redistricting. Even then, it will be unlikely.

Another way in which Alabama has contrasted with most of the South has been its shrinking number of House districts. As recently as 1960, it had nine seats. Current Census Bureau population forecasts project that it will drop to six seats after the 2020 reapportionment. That loss almost surely would be a Republican seat. With the likelihood of continued GOP districts based in the urban centers of Mobile, Montgomery, Birmingham and Huntsville, that likely would result in elimination of one of the mostly rural districts in the central part of Alabama, which have been held by veteran Reps. Mike Rogers and Robert Aderholt. Aderholt is next in line to chair the House Appropriations Committee. His eager self-promotion to win the appointment of Gov. Robert Bentley to fill the Senate seat of Attorney General Jeff Sessions revealed that Aderholt is not committed to the House. He might have other Senate opportunities before 2022.

Governor

Kay Ivey (R)

Assumed office in 2017, term expires 2019, 1st term; b. Oct. 15, 1944, Camden, AL; Auburn U 1967; Baptist; Single.

Elected Office: AL House, 1980-1982; AL Treasurer, 2002-2010; AL Lt. Governor, 2011-2017.

Professional Career: High School teacher; Assistant Vice President, Merchants National Bank/Regions Bank, 1970-1979; Consultant, American Bankers Association, 1979; Reading Clerk, Assistant Director, Alabama Development Office, 1982-1985; Director of Government Affairs,Alabama Commission on Higher Education, 1985-1998.

Office: 600 Dexter Avenue, Montgomery, 36130; 334-242-7100; Fax: 334-353-0004; Website: alabama.gov.

Republican Kay Ivey became governor of Alabama in April 2017, ending a long, soap-opera-like scandal involving fellow Republican Robert Bentley, who resigned under the threat of impeachment. Ivey took office at age 72, becoming only the second woman to serve as Alabama's governor, after Lurleen Burns Wallace, the wife of former Gov. George Wallace, who served until her death in 1968.

Ivey was raised on a family cattle farm in Camden, served as lieutenant governor at Alabama Girls State while in high school, and earned a degree from Auburn University in 1967. While a student, she helped the Wallace campaign organize on campus. She received additional education at Duke University's Governor's Center for Public Policy, the Alabama Banking School and the University of Colorado School of Banking. She worked as a high school teacher, as assistant vice president of Merchants National Bank/Regions Bank, as a reading clerk in the state House, as assistant director of the Alabama Development Office, and as director of government affairs for the Alabama Commission on Higher Education. In 1982, she ran as a Democrat (as most Alabamians did at the time) for her first statewide office – state auditor – but lost.

Two decades later, Ivey began a more successful phase of her electoral career, as a Republican, a label that was becoming advantageous in the state. She was elected state treasurer in 2002 and 2006, then, after a brief flirtation with a gubernatorial bid in 2010, ran for lieutenant governor. Ivey's biggest albatross was her past leadership of the state's Prepaid Affordable College Tuition program, which closed in 2008 due to financial pressures. "Only market conditions caused this, not staff or the board. It's due solely to the economic conditions of the country," Ivey said. Still, she was able to narrowly defeat Democratic incumbent Jim Folsom Jr. to win the lieutenant governorship, and she was reelected in 2014 before being elevated to governor on Bentley's resignation.

Bentley's ethical problems were separate from -- but occurred at roughly the same time as -- serious troubles within the leadership of the other two branches of Alabama government. House Speaker Mike Hubbard, the architect of the Republicans' legislative majority, was sentenced to four years in prison after being convicted on 12 felony ethics counts, while state Supreme Court justice Roy Moore's refusal to follow orders from the federal bench led to his removal as chief justice (for the second time). Bentley's troubles, though, became the biggest embarrassment, revealing the sexual peccadilloes of a seemingly mild-mannered politician who had gotten himself elected governor twice.

In March 2016, Bentley fired Spencer Collier, the former head of the Alabama Law Enforcement Agency and an old friend. Collier proceeded to go public with the allegation that Bentley had been having an affair with a top adviser, Rebekah Caldwell Mason. Mason was married, and Bentley had been until a sudden divorce after 50 years of marriage. In a secretly recorded tape, AL.com reported, the governor was heard engaging in sexually tinged banter, including "improper comments about her breasts and behind." Both denied having a "physical affair," but that did nothing to quell the scandal. For more than a year, it severely damaged Bentley's credibility and his ability to govern. As the House began impeachment proceedings after months of delays in April 2017, Bentley reached a deal with prosecutors and pled guilty to misdemeanor campaign-finance charges stemming from the relationship with Mason. At her swearing-in, Ivey said, "Today is a dark day in Alabama but also one of opportunity. Together we steady the ship of state and improve the image of the state. These are my two priorities as governor."

Indeed, much of Ivey's early tenure in office was devoted to cleaning up Bentley's mess. One of her most notable moves was to accelerate the date of the election to fill one of the state's two Senate seats. The seat had become vacant with the elevation of Jeff Sessions to attorney general under President Donald Trump. Bentley had appointed state Attorney General Luther Strange to the seat. But the two men had a history – Strange had urged the legislature to hold off on impeachment for months as his own office investigated the case. Seemingly seeking to move past reminders of the episode, Ivey set an August 2017 primary, a September runoff and a December general election – instead of waiting until November 2018.

Ivey was expected to run for a term of her own in 2018, though with the GOP's dominance in the state there was no guarantee that she would be renominated without a primary challenge. The Democrats, for their part, have been decimated in Alabama and seemed unlikely to be a factor in the gubernatorial race.

Senior Senator

Richard Shelby (R)

Elected 1986, term expires 2022, 6th term; b. May 06, 1934, Birmingham; University of Alabama, B.A.; University of Alabama School of Law, LL.B.; Presbyterian; Married (Annette Nevin Shelby); 2 children; 2 grandchildren.

Elected Office: AL Senate, 1970-1978; U.S. House, 1979-1987.

Professional Career: Practicing attorney, 1963-1978; City prosecutor, Tuscaloosa, 1963-1971; U.S magistrate, 1966-1970; Spec. Assistant to Alabama Attorney General, 1969-1971.

DC Office: 304 RSOB 20510, 202-224-5744, Fax: 202-224-3416, shelby.senate.gov.

State Offices: Birmingham, 205-731-1384; Huntsville, 256-772-0460; Mobile, 251-694-4164; Montgomery, 334-223-7303; Tuscaloosa, 205-759-5047.

Committees: *Appropriations*: Commerce, Justice, Science & Related Agencies (Chmn), Department of Defense, Department of Homeland Security, DOL, HHS & Education & Related Agencies, Energy & Water Development, Transportation, HUD & Related Agencies. *Banking, Housing & Urban Affairs*: Financial Institutions & Consumer Protection, Housing, Transportation & Community Development, Securities, Insurance & Investment. *Environment & Public Works*: Clean Air & Nuclear Safety, Fisheries, Water, and Wildlife, Transportation & Infrastructure. *Rules & Administration (Chmn)*.

Group Ratings

	ADA	ACLU	AFL-CIO	LCV	ITI	COC	HAFA	ACU	CFG	FRC
2016	-	11%	-	0%	40%	83%	82%	83%	79%	100%
2015	0%	C	43%	4%	C	50%	C	96%	92%	100%

Almanac Ratings 2015

	Economy	Social	Foreign	Composite
Liberal	17%	0%	0%	6%
Conservative	83%	100%	100%	94%

Key Votes of the 114th Congress

1. Keystone pipeline	Y	5. National Security Data	N	9. Gun Sales Checks	N
2. Export-Import Bank	Y	6. Iran Nuclear Deal	Y	10. Sanctuary Cities	Y
3. Debt Ceiling Increase	N	7. Puerto Rico Debt	N	11. Planned Parenthood	Y
4. Homeland Security $$	N	8. Loretta Lynch A.G	N	12. Trade deals	N

Election Results

Election	Name (Party)	Vote (%)	Cand. Spent	Ind. Exp. Support	Ind. Exp. Oppose
2016 General	Richard Shelby (R)	1,335,104 (64%)	$11,473,078	$479,359	
	Ron Crumpton (D)	748,709 (36%)	$22,060		
2016 Primary	Richard Shelby (R)	505,586 (65%)			
	Jonathan McConnell (R)	214,770 (28%)			
	John Martin (R)	23,558 (3%)			

Prior winning percentages: 2004 (68%), 1998 (63%), 1992 (65%), 1986 (50%); House: 1984 (97%), 1982 (97%), 1980 (73%), 1978 (94%)

As a former chairman of both the Banking, Housing and Urban Affairs Committee and the Intelligence Committee, Alabama senior Sen. Richard Shelby, a Republican, has tangled with the nation's spy chiefs and has battled against bank bailouts, while also resisting stiffer regulation of the nation's financial industry. Shelby has been a vocal critic of the so-called Dodd-Frank law cracking down on banks and tightening consumer protections in the wake of the 2008 financial crisis. But, due to Senate Republican Conference rules on term limits for committee chairs, Shelby was forced to relinquish the Banking Committee gavel at the end of 2016. His departure came as the incoming administration of President Donald Trump was vowing to take aim at the Dodd-Frank law, counted among the signature legislative achievements of President Barack Obama. While shuttled to a lower profile post chairing the Senate Rules and Administration Committee during the 115th Congress, term limits law could work to Shelby's favor in the foreseeable future: If the GOP retains Senate control in the 2018 election, it would enable him to take over the chairmanship of the powerful Appropriations Committee, where Shelby has been a member for more than two decades.

If there is an issue responsible for Shelby's political longevity in the Heart of Dixie -- where he has been elected to the Senate twice as a Democrat and four times as a Republican -- it has been the ability to steer federal funds to his home state from his Appropriations Committee perch. A total of a half-dozen buildings that bear Shelby's name can be found on the campuses of the University of Alabama as well as at Auburn University and the University of South Alabama. In the 2016 Republican primary, facing his first significant political challenge since being elected to the Senate in 1986, Shelby repeatedly emphasized the benefits of his seniority. It enabled him to turn back an upstart opponent hoping to ride a wave of anti-incumbent voters energized by outsider presidential candidates such as Trump and Sen. Ted Cruz of Texas. *The Washington Post* recounted a stop in the Anniston area during the campaign, where Shelby brought the crowd to its feet by declaring: "If things go right, maybe I'll chair the Appropriations Committee. And I'll tell you: Calhoun County would know it! And Alabama would know it. I'm about one step from that!" (The current Appropriations chair, Republican Sen. Thad Cochran of Mississippi, is in his final two years in the committee post under the GOP's term limit rules.)

On the surface, Shelby is much in the mold of Southern politicians of another era -- quick to backslap and recount political war stories during downtime on the Senate floor. But when it comes to legislation, he is a notoriously tough negotiator, known for keeping his cards close to his chest and preserving his options for as long as possible. Now 82, Shelby has honed his skills in a career in elected office that goes back nearly a half-century. He grew up the son of a steelworker in Birmingham, and, after earning both an undergraduate and law degree at the University of Alabama, he remained in Tuscaloosa and practiced law with future Democratic Rep. Walter Flowers -- who, as a member of the House Judiciary Committee, was part of an informal group of conservative Democrats and Republicans that played a key role in the 1974 impeachment of President Richard Nixon. Shelby was elected to the state Senate in

1970 as a Democrat, and, when Flowers unsuccessfully sought to move up to the U.S. Senate in 1978, Shelby ran for his House seat. The critical contest was the Democratic runoff against Chris McNair, an African-American state legislator whose daughter was one of the four young girls killed in the 1963 Birmingham church bombing. Although the district had the highest percentage of black residents at the time, Shelby won 59%-41%.

In the House, Shelby had a conservative voting record, opposing the Voting Rights Act extension and the Martin Luther King Jr. holiday. He was part of a significant bloc of conservative Democrats primarily from the South, known at the time as the Boll Weevils, who were often allied with House Republicans. Shelby ran for the Senate in 1986 and won a five-way Democratic primary with 51 percent after then-Alabama Secretary of State (and later governor) Don Siegelman withdrew. In the general election, he took on Republican Sen. Jeremiah Denton, a retired admiral and former Vietnam prisoner of war who had been swept into office by President Ronald Reagan's landslide victory six years earlier. Shelby slammed Denton for voting to cut Social Security and for owning two Mercedes-Benz cars, and won a slim majority in the general election, coming out on top by 7,000 votes. As one of a half dozen or so conservative Southern Democrats in the Senate in the mid-1980s, Shelby at first attracted little notice, and was comfortably re-elected in 1992 by a nearly 2-1 margin, as Democrat Bill Clinton won the presidency (but ran nearly 25 points behind Shelby in Alabama).

Soon after Clinton took office, Shelby broke ranks with the new administration. At a meeting with Vice President Al Gore -- who had been a Senate colleague of Shelby's from the neighboring state of Tennessee -- Shelby turned to the assembled Alabama television cameras and criticized the Clinton program as "high on taxes, low on spending cuts." The administration retaliated, announcing that a multimillion-dollar space facility would be built not in Alabama but in Texas (although it eventually was built in Alabama). The more he defied Clinton, the better Shelby's favorable ratings were at home.

The day after Republicans regained control of the Senate in 1994, Shelby announced he was switching parties, increasing the GOP majority to 53-47. Republicans happily allowed him to keep his seniority on the Banking Committee and gave him seats on Appropriations and its Defense Subcommittee. In an interview with CNN several years later, Shelby attributed his switch to the leftward shift of the Democratic party as the factor that drove him away, and rejected the idea that he made the move to gain power. "What I did didn't cause a political earthquake here," he said. "I just crossed the aisle and voted just like I've always been voting, and feel very comfortable there."

The switch, however, quickly paid dividends for Shelby's clout, as he assumed the first of three Senate committee chairmanships he has held -- the Intelligence panel -- in 1997. One of his first acts was to scuttle the nomination of Clinton's national security adviser, Anthony Lake, to be director of the director of the Central Intelligence Agency. By the time of the Sept. 11 attacks, the Senate was back in Democratic hands, but Shelby, as the ranking Republican on the Intelligence Committee, was an important player in the ensuing weeks and months. He had adopted an adversarial posture toward the intelligence agencies during the Clinton and Bush presidencies, and soon after the terrorist attacks, Shelby stopped just short of calling for the resignation of CIA Director George Tenet. When Tenet announced his resignation in mid-2004, Shelby declared, "What was a surprise was that he held onto the job as long as he did." Notwithstanding such differences, Shelby was mostly supportive of the Bush administration's conduct of the war on terrorism. Three months after Sept. 11, he was one of 10 senators to sign a letter calling for a plan "to eliminate the threat from Iraq." He was out front in calling for the creation of a director of national intelligence after the intelligence community, in his view, was unable to share information. That position was later adopted in the intelligence bill approved by Congress in 2004.

Control of the Senate went back to the Republicans following the 2002 election, opening the way for Shelby, over the next decade and a half, to exert substantial influence over the nation's financial and housing industries during a time for crisis for both. He chaired the Banking Committee from 2003 to 2007, and then, with the Democrats back in the Senate majority, was the ranking Republican until the beginning of 2013. Two years later, when the Senate majority flipped again following the 2014 election, Shelby was back for his third and final term as Banking chairman.

While noted for his opposition of the 2010 Dodd-Frank law -- Shelby believes it has overreached in setting rules for regional and smaller community banks -- he has exhibited a populist streak when it comes to Wall Street and the county's largest financial institutions. As far back as 1999, Shelby was the only Senate Republican to vote against a financial services deregulation bill that repealed the so-called Glass-Steagall Act, a Depression Era law that barred banks from expanding into investment-related businesses. Recently, there have been calls from members of both parties, including such disparate figures as Trump and Democratic Sen. Bernie Sanders of Vermont, to reinstate Glass-Steagall to forestall a repeat of the 2008 financial crisis.

During that crisis, Shelby opposed the $700 billion rescue of the financial markets, although President Bush was pushing the Troubled Asset Relief Program -- TARP -- legislation and signed it into law in the fall of 2008. Not long afterward, Shelby protested the massive government loan for the Big Three domestic automakers, which he called "dinosaurs." He threatened to filibuster; the bill did not pass the Senate, but Obama proceeded administratively with a successful auto industry bailout. When Shelby was accused of defending foreign automakers with plants in Alabama, he cited a vote years earlier against a Chrysler bailout before the foreign automaker's plant had been built. Amid his objections to the creation of TARP to assist failing banks, Shelby drew praise from the program's special inspector general, Neil Barofsky. In a 2012 book criticizing Congress and the Treasury Department for its handling of the issue, Barofsky singled out Shelby for being more interested in substance than were many of his colleagues. Of one briefing with the senator, he wrote, "I probably covered more in fifteen minutes of rapid-fire questions and answers than in most hour-long meetings with other members of Congress."

Five years before the financial crisis, during his first year as Banking chairman, Shelby presciently quizzed Federal Reserve Chairman Alan Greenspan about the increasing number of home loans to borrowers with weak credit histories, a trend that led to the home mortgage market collapse. In 2008, the Democratic chairman of the Banking Committee, Sen. Christopher Dodd of Connecticut, pushed a compromise housing bill that would allow bankruptcy judges to restructure mortgages and another proposal to refinance mortgages for millions of homeowners at risk of defaulting. While consumer groups pushed for both, they could not get by Shelby.

As efforts to reform the nation's financial regulatory system geared up in 2009, Shelby and Dodd agreed, at least in theory, on the creation of a consumer financial protection division or agency. But a persistent sticking point surfaced over its structure. While Dodd and Obama wanted the consumer protection agency to be housed within the Federal Reserve and given more independence, Shelby called for making it a division of the Federal Deposit Insurance Corp. His substitute plan failed on the Senate floor, 61-38, and when the final Dodd-Frank bill was passed in May 2010, Shelby voted against it. Shelby remained at the forefront of GOP efforts to delay the Obama administration's implementation of the bureau in 2011, demanding changes before he would consider approving a director to lead it. These objections eventually prompted Obama to circumvent the Senate in January 2012 and make a recess appointment of former Ohio Attorney General Richard Cordray as director. Shelby's stance toward to the bureau has not softened. "Because of the bureau's structure and the means by which it is financed, it remains one of least accountable agencies in the federal government," he charged during an April 2016 hearing, a reference to the fact that the bureau gets its funding from the Federal Reserve -- a provision inserted by Democratic supporters to prevent congressional Republicans from blocking funding for it.

One of the more controversial episodes of Shelby's tenure in the leadership of the Banking panel came in 2010, when he blocked the nomination of MIT economics professor Peter Diamond to the board of the Federal Reserve. Shelby's insistence that Diamond lacked experience and knowledge in monetary economics were derided by national media outlets after Diamond won the Nobel Prize in economics in October of that year. Diamond withdrew his nomination in 2011. Responding to Diamond's withdrawal, Shelby urged Obama to nominate a candidate "capable of garnering bipartisan support in the Senate," adding, "It would be my hope that the president will not seek to pack the Fed with those who will use the institution to finance his profligate spending and agenda."

The term limits rule forced Shelby to step aside after three terms as ranking minority member on Banking, and he became ranking member on Appropriations beginning in 2013. But Cochran, re-elected in November 2014, reclaimed the Appropriations chairmanship he had held earlier, sending Shelby back to the Banking panel as chairman. Back in the majority, Shelby sought to move a Dodd-Frank overhaul. "Although Dodd-Frank was touted by its Democrat advocates as 'Wall Street reform,' the law has put in place a structure where Main Street banks and other financial companies that had nothing to do with the crisis are being treated as if they caused it," he said in an op-ed piece for Alabama media. But Shelby's bill, after clearing the Banking panel in June 2015, went no further, with Sen. Sherrod Brown of Ohio, the committee's ranking Democrat, joining other Democrats in expressing concerns about Shelby's handling of the issue. Brown, in late 2016, voiced barely concealed pleasure that Shelby would be departing due to term limits, to be replaced by Republican Sen. Mike Crapo of Idaho. According to *The Hill*, Brown told a D.C. think tank that he was optimistic about bipartisan Dodd-Frank reform in the 115th Congress, pointedly noting that he and Crapo "have a working relationship."

Shelby appeared to enjoy a warmer relationship with Maryland's crusty then-senior senator, Democrat Barbara Mikulski, who chaired the Appropriations Committee during Shelby's stint as ranking member. In 2014, Mikulski agreed to boost spending for the Space Launch System, an important project at the Marshall Space Flight Center in Huntsville. Critics have derided SLS as a "rocket to nowhere," asserting that its technology is outmoded and much costlier than using private alternatives to propel heavy payloads into space. But Shelby and Mikulski, with her own home-state interest at the Goddard Space Flight Center, worked collaboratively to fund NASA programs. Said the liberal Mikulski of Shelby at a hearing that year, "He's a true partner."

While boasting on his Senate Web site that he has biennially introduced a balanced budget constitutional amendment since being elected to the Senate, Shelby makes no apologies for amount of federal dollars he seeks to direct to his home state. When it comes to earmarking, the special provisions tucked into spending bills by individual lawmakers, Shelby has "made a kind of art form out of it," former Alabama GOP Rep. Jack Edwards -- himself a long-time member of the House Appropriations Committee -- told the Mobile *Press-Register*. In early 2010, in a gambit to break loose funding for a couple of Alabama-based defense projects, Shelby put a hold for several days on 70 executive branch nominations before the Senate; it enraged the Obama White House, with a spokesman decrying Shelby's ploy as "the poster child for how this town needs to change the way it works." A decade earlier, a GOP crusader against earmarks, Arizona Sen. John McCain, took aim at a $3.5 million Shelby earmark to refurbish a statue of Vulcan, the Roman god of fire that sits atop Birmingham's Red Mountain.

Shelby was critical of the Senate's earmark ban adopted in November 2010, saying it would put a significant crimp in his long-term goal of securing $1 billion for science, engineering, and research projects at the state's colleges. Such efforts are one reason that he went for three decades, both as a Democrat and a Republican, easily winning re-election. Another is the massive campaign treasury that, until the 2016 primary, scared off competitive challengers. Much of that war chest was stocked by individuals and political action committees representing a variety of interests over which the Banking Committee has jurisdiction -- but lawyers and law firms have been the biggest single source of campaign contributions during Shelby's career, according to the Center for Responsive Politics. Despite his party switch, Shelby has remained friendly with trial lawyers, who usually support Democrats in Alabama. (It may help to explain why Shelby voted against a controversial 2004 measure to protect gun manufacturers from liability for the actions of users of their products. It put Shelby, who describes himself as a "stalwart support of Second Amendment rights," on the same side as gun control advocates.)

By the end of 2014, Shelby had amassed a campaign treasury of $18 million. He took hits that fall in the media -- notably the *Wall Street Journal* -- for directing a mere fraction of that, a little over $17,000 to the NRSC at a time that his party was seeking to recapture the Senate. But Shelby objected, on principle, to Senators financing the NRSC and other campaigns, despite the committee's generous assistance to him. After easily dispensing of a primary opponent in 2010 by a more than 5-1 margin, Shelby faced a significant threat in 2016 from former Marine Capt. Jonathan McConnell, owner of a maritime security company. McConnell said Shelby was "too old" and how been in Washington for "too long", while taking aim at Shelby's role as an appropriator. "People are sick of his big spending ways," McConnell told the *Post*, adding: "People are frustrated with the status quo, and that's why you've seen Trump's success. I don't think they're going to cancel out their vote by voting for Richard Shelby."

Shelby's nervousness was apparent. "My primary is Tuesday!" Shelby snapped at a *New York Times* reporter when asked about presidential nominations stalled at the Banking Committee. "We can talk about this later." But, five days before the primary, the Tea Party Patriots Citizens Fund endorsed Shelby, citing his 2008 opposition to the TARP legislation. That PAC joined groups ranging from the National Rifle Association to the National Right to Life Committee that had earlier endorsed the incumbent. And Shelby outspent McConnell by 15-1, pumping $11.8 million into his primary campaign against just over $780,000 for McConnell. Seeking to avoid a runoff, Shelby scored 65 percent to 28 percent for McConnell, with the remainder spread among three other candidates. In November, Shelby won a sixth term by 64%-36%, mirroring his margins in four previous re-election campaigns. He returned to Capitol Hill to assume his third chairmanship at Senate Rules, with the big prize -- the Appropriations gavel -- not far in the distance.

Junior Senator

Luther Strange (R)

Appointed 2017, term expires 2020, 1st term; b. Mar 01, 1953, Sylacauga; Tulane University (LA), J.D.; Episcopalian; Married (Melissa Strange); 2 children; 1 grandchild.

Elected Office: AL Attorney General, 2011-2017.

Professional Career: Practicing attorney & Founder, Strange LLC.

DC Office: 326 RSOB 20510, 202-224-4124, Fax: 202-224-3149, strange.senate.gov.

State Offices: Birmingham, 205-731-1500; Dothan, 334-792-4924; Huntsville, 256-553-0979; Mobile, 251-414-3083; Montgomery, 334-230-0698.

Committees: *Agriculture, Nutrition & Forestry*: Conservation, Forestry & Natural Resources, Nutrition, Agricultural Research & Specialty Crops (Chmn), Rural Development & Energy. *Armed Services*: Readiness & Management Support, Seapower. *Budget*. *Energy & Natural Resources*: Energy, Public Lands, Forests & Mining, Water & Power.

When Republican Luther Strange, Alabama's junior senator, was appointed on Feb. 9, 2017 to fill the vacancy that arose when his predecessor, Republican Jeff Sessions, was named as attorney general in the Trump Administration, he immediately established a record of sorts. At 6'9", the former Tulane University basketball player known in Alabama political circles as "Big Luther" became the tallest person ever to serve in the Senate, eclipsing 6'7" former Wyoming Sen. Alan Simpson, who had retired two decades earlier. But, even before he was sworn in, questions surrounding the circumstances of Strange's appointment by state's embattled governor, Robert Bentley, hovered over the new senator's towering frame.

As Alabama's attorney general for the previous six years, Strange in late 2016 had asked the state House of Representatives to delay impeachment hearings against Bentley -- engulfed in a sex scandal -- due to "related work" by the attorney general's office. His appointment by Bentley to the Senate vacancy just a few months later, while welcomed by a number of leading Republicans, prompted several within the Alabama GOP to suggest the appearance of political payback. Strange, in fact, managed to raise $300,000 for a federal campaign in December 2016, the only prospective Senate candidate who bothered to raise money. And, notwithstanding Strange's background as a one-time Eagle Scout who made fighting corruption a high priority as attorney general, the controversy surrounding his appointment could persist as Strange runs in a 2017 special election to fill the remaining three years of Sessions' term. "It's grimly problematic that the attorney general who blocked the impeachment investigation and who has not gone forward with the Bentley criminal investigation is rewarded with the U.S. Senate appointment," State Auditor Jim Zeigler, a frequent critic of Bentley's, told *The New York Times*. Asserted Zeigler, who voiced interest in running and sued Bentley over the delayed timing of the special election, "There will be a challenger to Luther Strange in the special Senate election, and this will be an issue." Still, there was a widespread sentiment that Strange's incumbency and fundraising ability would establish him as a clear favorite in a GOP primary in what has become one of the nation' most reliably red states.

The outspokenly conservative Sessions, elected to a fourth term in 2014 without opposition, embraced Donald Trump's candidacy early in the campaign for the Republican presidential nomination; he was later on the short list for Trump's vice presidential running mate. As the Senate's leading foe of loosening the nation's immigration laws and a frequent critic of international trade deals, he often echoed the nativism of such old style Southern populists as the late Alabama Gov. James "Big Jim" Folsom -- while connecting to the modern-day version of populism embodied by Trump. In a 2013 attack on a bipartisan immigration bill, Sessions, the son of a country store owner who was raised in rural Alabama, thundered: "I know who I work for, and that is the hard-working people of Alabama and the United States. A small group of CEOs don't get to set immigration policy for the country, no matter how much money they have."

Strange's background stands in marked contrast to that of Sessions: While a solid conservative who joined in lawsuits brought by other Republican attorneys general against the Obama Administration over both labor and environmental regulations, he is a creature of both the Republican establishment and corporate America. "Luther is not a stranger in Washington," Bentley wisecracked in announcing the appointment. Specifically, he is no stranger to Washington's K Street lobbying corridor: Strange ran the D.C.-based lobbying office of an Alabama-based energy holding company for nearly a decade before returning home to become a partner in one of Alabama's leading corporate law firms.

Strange, who turned 64 less than a month after his Senate appointment, has never been shy about desire to climb the political ladder. In December 2016, after Sessions' appointment to the Trump Cabinet was announced, Strange declared he would run in the special election whether or not he was appointed to fill the expected vacancy. "The voters will make the ultimate decision about who will represent them, and I look forward to making my case to the people of Alabama in the months to come as to why they can trust me to keep protecting and fighting for our conservative values," he said in a statement. Strange was raised in Homewood, a comfortable suburb of Birmingham, Alabama's largest city. As an undergraduate, he attended Tulane University in New Orleans on a basketball scholarship. He went on to earn his law degree from Tulane in 1979. Strange went from law school to work for Birmingham-based Sonat, which had grown from a natural gas utility into a Fortune 500 oil and gas exploration and production company. He was named to run the company's Washington office in 1985, and remained in that position until 1994.

Returning to Birmingham to go into private law practice, he became a partner in 1998 of what was then Bradley, Arant, Rose & White; currently Bradley, Arant, Boult Cummings LLP, the firm today employs more than 500 attorneys in nine offices throughout the South and in Washington, D.C. Strange left in 2008 to start his own firm focusing on economic development matters. By that time, he had made his first run for elected office: a 2006 bid for Alabama lieutenant governor. He found himself up against a couple of candidates with storied political names. In the Republican primary runoff, Strange defeated George C. Wallace Jr., son of the late governor, by a 55%-45% margin. But he narrowly lost the general election to Democrat James Folsom Jr., son of the legendary "Big Jim" Folsom and himself a former governor and lieutenant governor. Four years later, Strange challenged the incumbent Republican attorney general, Troy King, and ousted him by a 60%-40% margin. Strange won the general election by a similar margin, and was handily re-elected in 2014.

As attorney general, Strange won praise for a settlement he negotiated with BP for damage done to Alabama's Gulf of Mexico coastline by the 2010 Deepwater Horizon oil spill, which resulted in about $1 billion being paid to the state. He also continued an effort by former Gov. Bob Riley, who left office at the end of 2010, to crack down on gambling in Alabama. In April 2012, Strange was behind formation of the Special Prosecutions Alliance, a collaboration among several state agencies dedicated to combating public corruption. He vowed that officials who violated the public trust could expect to be held to account "regardless of their political affiliation or position." The following year, his office began an ethics investigation into Alabama House Speaker Mike Hubbard, who had helped to lead the Republican takeover of the state Legislature in 2010. Strange recused himself from the Hubbard investigation, citing donations Hubbard had made to Strange's campaign for attorney general, and a special prosecutor was appointed. Hubbard was convicted of 12 felony ethics charges in mid-2016, leading to his removal from office. In spite of Strange's recusal, Hubbard accused Strange of using the investigation to knock him out of the 2018 gubernatorial race.

By the time that Hubbard was convicted, the ethics-related controversy involving Gov. Bentley had moved to center stage. In the summer of 2015, Bentley's wife of 50 years had filed for divorce. In March 2016, the governor ousted the head of the Alabama Law Enforcement Agency, saying that an investigation had turned up evidence of misused funds. Days after the ouster, the former agency chief alleged that Bentley was having an affair with his political adviser, Rebekah Caldwell Mason, and charged that Bentley had misused state money in carrying on the affair. Following closely was a leaked phone recording in which Bentley is heard making sexually suggestive comments to Mason. While apologizing for the language, the governor denied a physical affair with the aide and refused to resign, leading to demands for his impeachment. In November 2016, less than a week before Trump was elected -- opening the way for Sessions to be appointed to the Cabinet member and for a Senate vacancy to occur -- Strange made his request in writing to a state House committee to hold off on impeachment hearings so that his office could complete "necessary related work."

Appointed just hours after Sessions was narrowly confirmed as attorney general after a bruising Senate battle in which all but one Democrat voted against him, Strange refused to confirm or deny that his office was conducting a probe of Bentley. He also declined to elaborate on his earlier request for a delay in the impeachment hearings, saying that his letter "speaks for itself." Before naming Strange, Bentley was reported to have narrowed the list of possible appointees to a half-dozen names, including veteran Rep. Robert Aderholt, first elected to the House in 1996.

Bentley's plan for the special election in November 2018 was overturned by his successor as governor, Kay Ivey, who accelerated the schedule by a year, with the primaries in August 2017. The chief GOP challengers to Strange included Rep. Mo Brooks and former state Supreme Court Chief Justice Roy Moore.

FIRST DISTRICT

Bradley Byrne (R)

Elected 2013, 3rd term; b. Feb 16, 1955, Mobile; University of Alabama School of Law, LL.D.; University Military School (AL); Duke University (NC), B.A.; Episcopalian; Married (Rebecca Dukes); 4 children; 1 grandchild.

Elected Office: AL Senate, 2002-2007.

Professional Career: Practicing attorney, 1980-1994, 2010-2013; AL State Board of Ed., 1994-2002; Chancellor of AL Department of Postsecondary Ed., 2007-2009.

DC Office: 119 CHOB 20515, 202-225-4931, Fax: 202-225-0562, byrne.house.gov.

State Offices: Mobile, 251-690-2811; Summerdale, 251-989-2664.

Committees: *Armed Services*: Seapower & Projection Forces, Strategic Forces. *Education & the Workforce*: Higher Education & Workforce Development, Workforce Protections (Chmn). *Rules*: Legislative & Budget Process, Rules & Organization of the House.

Group Ratings

	ADA	ACLU	AFL-CIO	LCV	ITI	COC	HAFA	ACU	CFG	FRC
2016	-	5%	-	0%	100%	100%	71%	92%	77%	100%
2015	0%	C	17%	0%	C	78%	C	96%	77%	100%

Almanac Ratings 2015

	Economy	Social	Foreign	Composite
Liberal	4%	0%	7%	4%
Conservative	96%	100%	93%	96%

Key Votes of the 114th Congress

1. Keystone Pipeline	Y	5. Puerto Rico Debt	Y	9. Offenses by Aliens	Y
2. Trade Deals	Y	6. Medical Marijuana	N	10. Troops in Iraq	NV
3. Export-Import Bank	N	7. Sanctuary Cities	Y	11. Homeland Security $$	N
4. Debt Ceiling Increase	N	8. Armor-piercing Bullets	Y	12. Trade Adjustment aid	N

Election Results

Election	Name (Party)	Vote (%)	Cand. Spent	Ind. Exp. Support	Ind. Exp. Oppose
2016 General	Bradley Byrne (R)	208,083 (96%)	$1,021,574	$250,000	
2016 Primary	Bradley Byrne (R)	70,883 (60%)			
	Dean Young (R)	47,021 (40%)			

Prior winning percentages: 2014 (68%)

Republican Bradley Byrne won a special election in December 2013 to replace Jo Bonner, who resigned to become vice chancellor at the University of Alabama. Like his predecessor, Byrne showed skills as a back-room operator who cooperated with party leaders and was not eager for publicity.

Byrne was born and raised in Mobile, where he practiced law for 14 years. He began his political career in 1994, successfully seeking a seat on the Alabama State Board of Education. He ran as a Democrat but left to join the Republican Party in 1997. "I learned there was no place for a conservative in the Alabama Democratic Party," Byrne told a reporter in 2013. After serving a second term on the state's Board of Education, he was elected to two terms in the state Senate. He stepped aside in 2007 when he was appointed chancellor of the Alabama Community College System, where he drew high marks for cleaning up a corrupt system.

Byrne didn't stay away from electoral politics for long, resigning in 2009 to launch a campaign for governor in 2010. With much of the state's Republican establishment and business community behind him, Byrne was the early frontrunner. He finished first in a tight four-way June Republican primary with 28 percent of the vote, but lost the runoff to state Rep. Robert Bentley, 56%-44%. Byrne returned to practicing law in Mobile, but didn't hide his itch to seek elected office again. In May 2013, Byrne got the opening he needed when Bonner, coincidentally, took a high-ranking state education post.

Once again, Byrne entered the race as the favorite with strong support from the business community and Mobile-area establishment. In a nine-candidate Republican field, he finished first with 35 percent of the primary vote. His opponent in the Republican run-off was businessman Dean Young, an outspoken social conservative, who got 23 percent. Little separated Byrne and Young in terms of policy, but the differences in their respective campaign styles were stark. Young stirred up controversy on the trail. He called for President Barack Obama's impeachment, said he would not support House Speaker John Boehner, and objected to "homosexuals pretending like they're married." Byrne, meanwhile, kept his focus on attacking Obama and a dysfunctional Congress, while touting his own record as a public official. The U.S. Chamber of Commerce spent more than $185,000 on direct mail and digital ads to boost Byrne in the week before the run-off vote. In an unexpectedly narrow outcome, the far better-funded Byrne won the November 2013 runoff, 52.5%-47.5%. A month later, he handily won the general election with 71 percent against real-estate agent Burton LeFlore, grandson of Alabama civil-rights leader John LeFlore.

In the House, Byrne won committee assignments consistent with his local and personal interests: Armed Services, and Education and the Workforce. With his insider credentials, he later got a seat on the Rules Committee, which traditionally functions as an arm of the leadership. He teamed with other Republicans on reforms in elementary and secondary education that would restore local control and empower parents and teachers. In February 2015, the House passed his bill to repeal - not for the first time - the Affordable Care Act. The measure also called for House committees to prepare alternatives.

Following an intensive push by Mobile business interests, Byrne praised outgoing Defense Secretary Chuck Hagel's decision to resume procurement of an updated version of the Navy's Littoral Combat Ships, relatively small vessels that are built at the Austral Shipyard in Mobile. During 2016 debate on the annual defense spending bill, Byrne successfully led opposition to a plan by the Obama administration to reduce the number of ships. But a December 2016 report by the Government Accountability Office raised new questions about the costs of the program.

Byrne responded to constituent concerns by helping to create and becoming a co-chair of the bipartisan Congressional Coastal Communities Caucus. The group was organized to help address often controversial policy issues, including weather-related disasters, marine habitats, erosion, and tourism. When the Obama administration in January 2015 released recommendations for off-shore oil and gas leasing, Byrne applauded the decision to open some areas off the Atlantic Coast, and advocated additional sites for exploration.

In a 2016 rematch with Young in the Republican primary, Byrne had a more comfortable - but not secure - victory, 60%-40%. The 1st Congressional District has had a tradition in the past half-century of electing Republicans who become hard-working and politically secure. Byrne could fit that mold.

Following the resignation of Sen. Jeff Sessions to become Attorney General, Byrne joined other Alabama Republicans who voiced interest in the seat. He failed to secure Gov. Bentley's appointment as temporary successor and showed no immediate interest for the seat in 2018. Byrne may have damaged his prospects when he initially said that Donald Trump should step aside as Republican presidential nominee following the release in early October 2016 of a 2005 tape in which Trump made lewd comments about women. A week later, Byrne reiterated his support for Trump and noted that the alternative was Hillary Clinton. Because Byrne had no challenger in the November election, he suffered no immediate political fallout.

Southwest Alabama: Mobile Bay

Population		Race and Ethnicity		Income	
Total	695,961	White	65.4%	Median Income	$44,309 (348 out of 435)
Land area	6,067	Black	27.7%		
Pop/ sq mi	114.7	Latino	3.0%		
Born in state	68.5%	Asian	1.4%	Under $50,000	54.9%
		Two races	1.5%	$50,000-$99,999	29.0%
Age Groups		Other	1.0%	$100,000-$199,999	13.3%
Under 18	23.6%			$200,000 or more	2.6%
18-34	21.7%	**Education**		Poverty Rate	18.3%
35-64	39.2%	H.S grad or less	47.1%		
Over 64	15.5%	Some college	30.2%	**Health Insurance**	
Work		College Degree, 4 yr	15.2%	With health insurance coverage	85.5%
		Post grad	7.6%		
White Collar	31.8%				
Sales and Service	49.5%	**Military**		**Public Assistance**	
Blue Collar	24.4%	Veteran	10.5%	Cash public assistance income	1.9%
Government	13.8%	Active Duty	0.2%		
				Food stamp/SNAP benefits	16.0%

Voter Turnout			
2015 Total Citizens 18+	521,401	2016 House Turnout as % CVAP	41%
2016 House turnout	215,893	2014 House Turnout as % CVAP	29%

2012 Presidential Vote		
Mitt Romney	184,743	(62%)
Barack Obama	11,712	(37%)

2016 Presidential Vote		
Donald Trump	192,633	(63%)
Hillary Clinton	103,363	(34%)
Gary Johnson	6,153	(2%)

Cook Partisan Voting Index: R+15

Mobile, the port where the Tombigbee and Alabama rivers flow into the Gulf of Mexico, was a strategic point on the American frontier. Spanish after the Revolutionary War, it was wrested away by threats of war from Secretary of State John Quincy Adams. During the Civil War, it was one of the major Confederate ports. In 1864, Admiral David Farragut, while steaming into the harbor lashed to his mast, cried, "Damn the torpedoes! Full speed ahead." Today, Mobile is full of graceful signs of its exotic past. Behind the docks and rail lines are downtown buildings and old houses with Spanish motifs, French accents, or tropical Art Deco lines. Further inland are neighborhoods with spacious houses, often with double porches, overhung by huge live oaks graced with Spanish moss. Mobile is a Gulf Coast version of Charleston or a smaller, more comfortable New Orleans, with a taste for shellfish and spicy food and an even older Mardi Gras, which the locals have been celebrating since 1703. As befits a frontier city with a martial past, Mobile is bristling with arms: One of the city's proudest possessions is the battleship *USS Alabama,* moored at the head of Mobile Bay, with its guns aimed out toward the Gulf.

Mobile's economy was based originally on docks and shipyards, factories and terminals, but with a determination to impose touches of beauty on its hot, flat landscape. The capital improvements include Mobile's State Docks, which serve Alabama's booming Mercedes, Honda, and Hyundai auto factories. Mobile's $300 million container terminal opened in 2008 and immediately more than doubled annual shipments with an alternative shipping route to Midwest markets. Three recent developments have attracted more business to the port: expansion of the Panama Canal; the opening of a new assembly line by European aircraft manufacturer Airbus for its A320 airline (which delivered its first aircraft in December 2016); and the return of Carnival Cruise Lines, which provided a boost for local tourism. In 2014, the nearby Daphne-Fairhope-Foley area in Baldwin County ranked among the top 10 fast-growing metro areas in the nation with a population less than 200,000, according to *Site Selection* magazine.

In August 2005, Hurricane Katrina struck Mobile and its beaches with Category 4 intensity. On Dauphin Island, the 14-mile spit of land south of Mobile Bay, 300 homes were swept away, and a one-mile gash created a new island. Elsewhere in Mobile and Baldwin counties, Katrina caused major damage to pecan, peanut and cotton crops. Disaster struck the area again in 2010. After the explosion of BP's Deepwater Horizon offshore drilling rig, oil washed up on beaches and into Mobile Bay, prompting concerns that neighboring Louisiana was receiving more cleanup attention. In 2016, the Mobile Bay National Estuary Program updated its comprehensive plan to finance restoration of the Bay.

Mobile is the focus of Alabama's 1st Congressional District, which extends north along the usually lazy Tombigbee and Alabama rivers, with their old forts and mansions. Monroeville is the home of Harper Lee, whose classic *To Kill a Mockingbird* and her best-selling 2015 novel *Go Set a Watchman*, are set here. Her childhood playmate was noted author Truman Capote. She died in February 2016 following controversy over the origins of her recent book. There are also surviving backcountry settlements of blacks and Cajans (who may or may not be descended from Louisiana Cajuns) and Creek Indians. Once cotton fields, this is now timberland, a major contributor to Alabama's economy. East of Mobile Bay, along the shores of the Gulf of Mexico, are condominium communities in Baldwin County. The area hosts the annual National Shrimp Festival, and its glorious Gulf beaches are among the South's best.

For years, this southern seaboard of the Confederacy has been among the most hawkish parts of America, and today it is solidly Republican in national elections. Donald Trump made early appearances here during his 2016 campaign, and was well-received. In 2005, in elections held after Katrina, Mobile elected its first African-American mayor, Sam Jones, a liberal Democrat who served with Sen. John McCain during the Vietnam War. After he was reelected in 2009 running unopposed, Jones lost in 2013 to Republican businessman Sandy Stimpson.

SECOND DISTRICT

Martha Roby (R)

Elected 2010, 4th term; b. Jul 26, 1976, Montgomery; New York University; b.M.; Samford University Cumberland School of Law (AL) Cumberland School of Law, J.D.; Presbyterian; Married (Riley Roby); 2 children.

Elected Office: Montgomery City Council, 2003-2010.

Professional Career: Practicing attorney, 2002-2004.

DC Office: 442 CHOB 20515, 202-225-2901, Fax: 202-225-8913, roby.house.gov.

State Offices: Andalusia, 334-428-1129; Dothan, 334-794-9680; Montgomery, 334-262-7718.

Committees: *Appropriations*: Commerce, Justice, Science & Related Agencies, Defense, Labor, Health & Human Services, Education & Related Agencies. *Judiciary*: Crime, Terrorism, Homeland Security & Investigations.

Group Ratings

	ADA	ACLU	AFL-CIO	LCV	ITI	COC	HAFA	ACU	CFG	FRC
2016	-	5%	-	3%	100%	93%	59%	71%	62%	92%
2015	0%	C	21%	3%	C	80%	C	75%	64%	100%

Almanac Ratings 2015

	Economy	Social	Foreign	Composite
Liberal	1%	0%	0%	1%
Conservative	99%	100%	100%	99%

Key Votes of the 114th Congress

1. Keystone Pipeline	Y	5. Puerto Rico Debt	Y	9. Offenses by Aliens	Y
2. Trade Deals	Y	6. Medical Marijuana	N	10. Troops in Iraq	N
3. Export-Import Bank	N	7. Sanctuary Cities	Y	11. Homeland Security $$	N
4. Debt Ceiling Increase	N	8. Armor-piercing Bullets	Y	12. Trade Adjustment aid	N

Election Results

Election	Name (Party)	Vote (%)		Cand. Spent	Ind. Exp. Support	Ind. Exp. Oppose
2016 General	Martha Roby (R)	134,886	(49%)	$1,563,892	$282,230	
	Nathan Mathis (D)	112,089	(41%)			
2016 Primary	Martha Roby (R)	78,001	(67%)			
	Becky Gerritson (R)	32,510	(28%)			
	Robert Rogers (R)	6,850	(6%)			

Prior winning percentages: 2014 (67%), 2012 (64%), 2010 (51%)

Alabama 2nd District Republican Martha Roby has won notice as an articulate and more visible conservative in a party trying to reach out to women voters. She has advanced in the House, with prime committee assignments and as a leadership ally. She is young enough to chart her course to increased influence in the House or potentially a Senate seat, although she has drawn flak from the tea party wing for being insufficiently committed to its agenda. Her political problems at home deepened when her disavowal of Donald Trump caused an unexpected drop in her voter support in 2016.

Roby is the daughter of Joel Dubina, a senior judge on the U.S. Court of Appeals for the 11th Circuit. She grew up in Montgomery and received a bachelor's degree in music from New York University in 1998. After earning a law degree from Samford University in Birmingham, she returned to her hometown to practice law. In 2003, she was elected to the Montgomery City Council. In that role, she led efforts to adopt an ordinance barring city businesses from hiring undocumented workers.

Immigration emerged as a major issue in her 2010 House challenge to freshman Democratic Rep. Bobby Bright. A former mayor of Montgomery, Bright criticized Roby for moving too slowly on her undocumented workers initiative. Roby and the Republicans kept Bright on the partisan defensive. He announced that he would not vote again to elect California liberal Nancy Pelosi as speaker of the House. In one campaign ad, Bright boasted of having voted with then-House Minority Leader John Boehner of Ohio 80 percent of the time. He also played up his endorsements from the National Rifle Association and the National Right to Life PAC. He sometimes campaigned in a "Fire Congress" T-shirt. The Democratic Congressional Campaign Committee spent about $1 million for Bright, but that was not enough to save him. Roby pulled out a close win, 51%-49%.

On the Armed Services Committee during her first term, she advocated for the Maxwell-Gunter Air Force Base and the Army post at Fort Rucker in her district. After a bipartisan deal was reached between Republican leaders and President Barack Obama to raise the debt ceiling, Roby said she voted against passage because she feared it might lead to severe defense cuts. "This bill goes much too far," she said in a statement, arguing that it could result in "devastating and unjustified cuts to our national security." *Politico* named her the most underrated member of the freshman class, saying, "If she's able to win reelection, she could be a leader of her party." Recognizing her appeal to younger voters, Mitt Romney's presidential campaign brought Roby to North Carolina for a September 2012 rally. But a few conservative activists weren't satisfied with some of her votes. Erick Erickson of the influential *RedState.com* charged, "She has carried water for the leadership" and "betrayed her conservative constituents."

After the 2012 election, Roby made a bid to join the House Republican leadership as GOP conference vice chair. She lost to the slightly more senior Lynn Jenkins of Kansas, but she got an impressive consolation prize in 2013 with a seat on the Appropriations Committee. She displayed her conservative credentials by joining the Select Committee on Benghazi, where she criticized the State Department's failure to upgrade security at its Libyan facility. She remained a hawk on defense, joining with Democratic Rep. Tulsi Gabbard of Hawaii to warn of the "devastating" effect if automatic military spending cuts took effect in 2016. Also that year, she backed the proposed shift of about 18 F-35s to the 187th Fighter Wing at Montgomery's Dannelly Field Air Guard Station. Roby was outspoken in her criticism of mismanagement by the Veterans Affairs Department, and led the call for top officials to resign. She told Labor Secretary Thomas Perez that he should apologize for criticizing the safety record of the Hyundai plant in Montgomery. Two days later, the Labor Department clarified that Perez was referring to Hyundai suppliers.

Cooperating with Democratic Rep. Terri Sewell as co-sponsor of the March 2015 commemoration of the 50th anniversary of the Selma to Montgomery civil rights march, Roby organized significant participation by other House Republicans, plus former President George W. Bush. She passed legislation giving the Congressional Gold Medal to the 1965 marchers.

The redistricting shifts in 2012 seemed to ensure that Roby was secure for another decade. In her next two campaigns, she sailed to reelection with 64 percent and 67 percent of the vote. Those strong showings, plus her firm base in the state's southeast corner and her consensus-building style, reinforced speculation that she would seek a Senate seat when it became available.

But her progress encountered a speed bump when Roby said a month before the 2016 election that Trump's language was "unacceptable" for a presidential candidate and that she would not vote for him, following the release of a 2005 video in which he made crude sexual comments about women. She did not back down, even when other congressional Republicans later toned down their criticism of Trump. Her remarks sparked a furor at home. The Pike County Republican Women withdrew an invitation for Roby to speak. Trump supporters protested when she spoke to a Republican women's group in Houston County. "I cannot look my children in the eye [Margaret, age 11, and George, age 7] and justify a vote for a man who promotes and boasts about sexually assaulting women," Roby responded. That led to a write-in campaign for Becky Gerritson, a local Tea Party leader whom Roby had defeated, 66%-28%, in the March primary. In the official results, Roby led Democrat Nathan Morris, 49%-41%, with Gerritson getting 29,609 write-ins. Following the election, Roby stood by her criticism but said that she was "eager" to work with Trump and his administration. Local critics raised the possibility of a primary challenge in 2018. The ultimate political impact may depend on whether voters fault Roby for her criticism, credit her for backbone or simply dismiss the incident.

Southeast Alabama: Montgomery, Dothan

Population		**Race and Ethnicity**		**Income**	
Total	684,660	White	62.7%	Median Income	$42,645 (364 out of 435)
Land area	10,142	Black	30.4%		
Pop/ sq mi	67.5	Latino	3.5%		
Born in state	69.2%	Asian	1.1%	Under $50,000	56.8%
		Two races	1.7%	$50,000-$99,999	28.4%
Age Groups		Other	0.6%	$100,000-$199,999	12.8%
Under 18	23.3%			$200,000 or more	2.1%
18-34	22.9%	**Education**		Poverty Rate	19.5%
35-64	38.7%	H.S grad or less	48.8%		
Over 64	15.1%	Some college	29.7%	**Health Insurance**	
		College Degree, 4 yr	13.5%	With health insurance coverage	87.5%
Work		Post grad	8.0%		
White Collar	31.4%				
Sales and Service	48.6%	**Military**		**Public Assistance**	
Blue Collar	26.8%	Veteran	12.1%	Cash public assistance income	1.6%
Government	19.7%	Active Duty	1.2%		
				Food stamp/SNAP benefits	16.8%

Voter Turnout			
2015 Total Citizens 18+	513,877	2016 House Turnout as % CVAP	54%
2016 House turnout	276,584	2014 House Turnout as % CVAP	32%

2012 Presidential Vote		
Mitt Romney	182,146	(63%)
Barack Obama	105,636	(36%)

2016 Presidential Vote		
Donald Trump	185,504	(64%)
Hillary Clinton	94,300	(33%)

Cook Partisan Voting Index: R+16

Thick green countryside blankets southern Alabama. Even in Montgomery, the stone and brick buildings of the downtown district do not mask the contours of the hills or hide the lush foliage. One can look downhill from the restored Greek Revival capitol toward Dexter Avenue King Memorial Baptist Church, where the young Martin Luther King Jr. was pastor in the 1950s, or out past the impressive Carolyn Blount Theatre, host of the Alabama Shakespeare Festival, toward new subdivisions and shopping malls, and easily imagine when this land was covered with cotton fields and pine trees and a young Wilson Pickett, the legendary soul singer, was still performing in Baptist church choirs in Prattville. The atmosphere is especially rural in southeast Alabama's Wiregrass region, named for the stiff native grass. There is the fishing town of Eufaula, along the Chattahoochee River; the Army's

Fort Rucker, the home of Army aviation flight training; Maxwell-Gunter Air Force Base, which is the largest employer in the Montgomery area; and Enterprise, site of the Boll Weevil Monument that commemorates the insect that destroyed two-thirds of the cotton crop in 1915 and then spread throughout the South.

Timber is an important resource here, and peanuts have replaced cotton as the main crop in the area surrounding Dothan, which calls itself the "peanut capital of the world," though more fame has accrued to the peanut farm of former President Jimmy Carter across the state line in Plains, Georgia. Each fall, Dothan holds the National Peanut Festival, the largest of its kind, to celebrate peanut growers and the harvest season. A statue of peanut innovator George Washington Carver can be found here. Dothan also is the home of the expanded Wayne Farms chicken processing plant, which processes 1.3 million chickens weekly.

The area's industrial diversification has been led by the automobile industry. Hyundai, the world's fifth largest automaker, built its first U.S. assembly plant in southwest Montgomery County, with about 3,100 local jobs and more than 400 robots to meet annual production capacity of 395,000 cars. The company calls the facility one of the most advanced in the North American auto industry, producing Sonata and Elantra sedans.

The 2nd Congressional District of Alabama covers 14 counties in the southeast corner of the state. It includes a thin link in the heart of Montgomery, but shares the surrounding metropolitan area with the 3rd and 7th districts to the east and west. The more heavily black precincts in west Montgomery, as well as mostly African-American Lowndes County, have become part of the sprawling majority-minority 7th. The remaining Montgomery County precincts in the 2nd district vote heavily Republican, as do suburban Elmore and Autauga counties and Houston County in the Wiregrass region; each gave Donald Trump more than 70 percent of the vote in the 2016 election. These areas outvote the district's "Black Belt" counties, including Bullock, with a large black majority and the only Democratic county in the district, and Barbour on the Georgia border, which was George Wallace's home base. Like all of Alabama except for the 7th, this district is solidly Republican.

THIRD DISTRICT

Mike Rogers (R)

Elected 2002, 8th term; b. Jul 16, 1958, Hammond, IN; Birmingham School of Law (AL), J.D.; Jacksonville State University (AL), M.P.A.; Jacksonville State University (AL), B.A.; Baptist; Married (Beth Rogers); 3 children.

Elected Office: Calhoun County Commission, 1986-1990; AL House, 1994-2002; Min. Leader, 1998-2000.

Professional Career: Practicing attorney, 1991-2002.

DC Office: 2184 RHOB 20515, 202-225-3261, Fax: 202-226-8485, mikerogers.house.gov.

State Offices: Anniston, 256-236-5655; Opelika, 334-745-6221.

Committees: *Agriculture*: Commodity Exchanges, Energy & Credit, General Farm Commodities & Risk Management. *Armed Services*: Readiness, Strategic Forces (Chmn). *Homeland Security*: Border & Maritime Security, Transportation & Protective Security.

Group Ratings

	ADA	ACLU	AFL-CIO	LCV	ITI	COC	HAFA	ACU	CFG	FRC
2016	-	11%	-	3%	100%	93%	64%	76%	60%	92%
2015	0%	C	21%	0%	C	85%	C	75%	59%	92%

Almanac Ratings 2015

	Economy	Social	Foreign	Composite
Liberal	9%	15%	4%	9%
Conservative	91%	85%	96%	91%

Key Votes of the 114th Congress

1. Keystone Pipeline	Y	5. Puerto Rico Debt	N	9. Offenses by Aliens	Y
2. Trade Deals	Y	6. Medical Marijuana	Y	10. Troops in Iraq	N
3. Export-Import Bank	Y	7. Sanctuary Cities	Y	11. Homeland Security $$	N
4. Debt Ceiling Increase	Y	8. Armor-piercing Bullets	Y	12. Trade Adjustment aid	Y

Election Results

Election	Name (Party)	Vote (%)		Cand. Spent	Ind. Exp. Support	Ind. Exp. Oppose
2016 General	Mike Rogers (R)	192,164	(67%)	$894,659	$32,230	
	Jesse Smith (D)	94,549	(33%)	$7,350		
2016 Primary	Mike Rogers (R)	76,781	(76%)			
	Larry DiChiara (R)	24,291	(24%)			

Prior winning percentages: 2014 (66%), 2012 (64%), 2010 (59%), 2008 (53%), 2006 (59%), 2004 (61%), 2002 (50%)

Republican Mike Rogers of Alabama, elected in 2002, is well-placed on three House committee that deal with national security and agriculture issues. In the southern tradition, he has gained seniority and may be close to getting the brass ring as a House committee chairman.

Rogers is a fifth-generation resident of Calhoun County, the son of a textile worker and a fireman. At the age of 28 in 1986, he was the first Republican elected to the county commission. In 1994, he won a seat in the Alabama House, and in his second term, he became minority leader. After Republican Bob Riley gave up the 3rd District seat to run for governor, Rogers easily won the GOP nomination to succeed him. In the general election, he had stiff competition from Democrat Joe Turnham Jr., who served three years as state party chairman and challenged Riley unsuccessfully in 1998. Turnham and Rogers tried to "out-bubba" each other, with Turnham calling for a congressional auto racing caucus and demanding that Rogers prove he had hunting and fishing licenses. Rogers touted his working-class values and support from the National Rifle Association. He also emphasized his opposition to abortion rights and support for a constitutional amendment permitting prayer in public schools. Though both national parties targeted the race, Turnham did not risk bringing in national Democrats to campaign for him in the socially conservative district, while Rogers got frequent visits from national Republican leaders. The contrast in national party support was evident in Rogers's big fundraising advantage. Rogers won, but only 50%-48%.

On the Armed Services Committee, Rogers is chairman of the Strategic Forces Subcommittee. He seeks to protect Anniston Army Depot as well as Maxwell-Gunter Air Force Base and Fort Benning just across the state line in Georgia. He is a leading Republican hawk on defense issues. At a hearing of his subcommittee, he said that the growing nuclear threat to the United States, especially from Russia, should force increased attention to missile defense. After Sen. Dianne Feinstein of California said in 2014 that current spending for nuclear weapons is "unsustainable," Rogers wrote a letter to *The Washington Post* that her comment shows a disregard for reality. "Nuclear weapons are not undermining other national security priorities-they are undergirding them." President Donald Trump later picked up on that theme. Rogers also has advocated space defense technology as a vital feature of American military strength. "Our adversaries know that we cannot fight and win a war without using space," he told a December 2016 panel at the Reagan presidential library.

Rogers has sought to enhance Alabama's role in domestic protection against terrorism. His district includes the Federal Emergency Management Agency's Center for Domestic Preparedness. He has been highly critical of the Transportation Security Administration, saying that the aviation security agency must become "smarter, leaner and tougher." After the 2012 election, he competed to fill a vacancy as chairman of the House Homeland Security Committee. He lost narrowly to Rep. Mike McCaul of Texas, who was supported by Speaker John Boehner. When McCaul was briefly under consideration for a position in Trump's Cabinet, Rogers voiced interest in McCaul's post. The House's limit of three terms for committee chairmen likely will give Rogers another opportunity after the 2018 election.

Rogers has been outspoken in describing security threats facing the nation and potential responses. With the Islamic State, he said during a meeting in his district, "Let's go over there and kill them and get out. … We cannot ignore this problem. We can't put our head in the sand because all of us are tired of war. We're tired of Iraq, we're tired of Afghanistan, we're tired of all of these little nuts around the world … but the fact is, the threats [ISIL] has are going to hit us."

Rogers has shown populist leanings on economic issues. He bucked the Bush administration and won local praise by opposing the free trade agreement with Morocco on the grounds that it would reduce local textile and apparel jobs. In 2009, he proposed allowing new car buyers a tax deduction of up to $7,500. Following the 2016 election, he stirred discussion among House Republicans to revive the practice of legislative earmarks for members of Congress to direct federal spending to their constituents. "This proposal would allow the conservative, Republican-controlled House to reassert its constitutional authority over the Obama administration and the spending decisions it is currently making," Rogers said. But House Speaker Paul Ryan objected and shut down that internal debate. Still, Rogers mostly has been a reliable Republican vote since the GOP regained the majority, including the showdown June 2015 vote to give trade promotion authority to the president. That has reinforced his electoral confidence in what had been a "yellow dog" Democratic bastion. His *Almanac* vote ratings in 2015 placed toward the center of House Republicans.

In this ancestrally Democratic district with a 27 percent African-American population, Rogers has worked hard to entrench himself and raise money to discourage Democratic opposition. In 2008, he faced a serious contest with Josh Segall, a 29-year-old Montgomery bankruptcy lawyer who stuck with Democratic doctrine on most issues except gay rights and gun control, spent more than $1 million, and had the support of the Democratic Congressional Campaign Committee. He attacked Rogers for backing the $700 billion government rescue of the financial markets, and also accused him of harming the local textile industry with his support of the Central America Free Trade Agreement. Rogers attacked Segall for his "Hollywood and New York" campaign contributions and his liberal views that "don't reflect east Alabama's conservative values." Segall won Montgomery County 62%-38% and three nearby counties, but Rogers prevailed 53%-47% overall. He has made himself a fixture ever since.

In September 2015, Rogers endorsed Jeb Bush for president. Once Trump became the Republican nominee, Rogers was a stalwart supporter.

Eastern Alabama: Auburn, Anniston

Population		**Race and Ethnicity**		**Income**	
Total	697,296	White	68.6%	Median Income	$41,695 (377 out of 435)
Land area	7,544	Black	25.1%		
Pop/ sq mi	92.4	Latino	2.9%		
Born in state	65.8%	Asian	1.4%	Under $50,000	57.3%
		Two races	1.5%	$50,000-$99,999	28.3%
Age Groups		Other	0.4%	$100,000-$199,999	12.4%
Under 18	22.5%			$200,000 or more	2.0%
18-34	24.2%	**Education**		Poverty Rate	20.4%
35-64	38.8%	H.S grad or less	49.3%		
Over 64	14.5%	Some college	29.9%	**Health Insurance**	
		College Degree, 4 yr	12.5%	With health insurance coverage	88.2%
Work		Post grad	8.3%		
White Collar	32.0%				
Sales and Service	48.0%	**Military**		**Public Assistance**	
Blue Collar	28.5%	Veteran	10.2%	Cash public assistance income	1.7%
Government	18.0%	Active Duty	0.6%		
				Food stamp/SNAP benefits	16.9%

Voter Turnout			
2015 Total Citizens 18+	528,588	2016 House Turnout as % CVAP	54%
2016 House turnout	287,104	2014 House Turnout as % CVAP	30%

2012 Presidential Vote		
Mitt Romney	174,620	(62%)
Barack Obama	103,089	(37%)

2016 Presidential Vote		
Donald Trump	188,476	(65%)
Hillary Clinton	93,301	(32%)
Gary Johnson	5,766	(2%)

Cook Partisan Voting Index: R+16

The 3rd Congressional District of Alabama is centered geographically and philosophically in Lineville. The small town's progress from Ku Klux Klan country to an integrated community where crowds regularly cheer mixed black and white high school teams and people of all races work together echoes that of America's most integrated institution, the military. Lineville produced more men and women per capita for Operation Desert Storm than any other community in the nation. When the United States invaded Iraq in 2003, Alabama was the nation's top contributor of National Guard personnel. The local military presence is unmistakable: Calhoun County is home to the Anniston Army Depot. Horseshoe Bend is where Andrew Jackson won a climactic battle against the Upper Creek Indians. Fort Mitchell, a 19th-century frontier military outpost, is the site of a national military cemetery sometimes referred to as the "Arlington of the South." Phenix City, across the Chattahoochee River from Georgia's Fort Benning, served as a "sin city" in the 1940s and 1950s, with virtually every imaginable vice for pleasure-seeking soldiers, a place so sleazy that Gen. George Patton threatened to level it with his tanks. Today, the huge military installation plays a more constructive role in the local economy.

There are other places of distinction in the district: Tuskegee is the home of Booker T. Washington's Tuskegee Institute (now Tuskegee University), the training ground for the Tuskegee Airmen, the first black pilots trained to fly for the U.S. military. Auburn is the home of Auburn University and its renowned sports teams and veterinary school. Talladega is the site of the Alabama Institute for the Deaf and Blind, and is perhaps America's most user-friendly city for people with disabilities. NASCAR fans know it as the home of a famed speedway and for the International Motorsports Hall of Fame - the Cooperstown of auto racing.

This looks and feels like rural country, though few people here make a living off their farms. Rather, they work at Tyson Foods or Walmart or in dozens of small and medium-sized factories. An economy once dependent on cotton mills is today more diverse, and interstates have brought in new businesses. A huge Honda assembly plant in Talladega County employs 4,500, perhaps the largest concentration of manufacturing employees in the state. With the growth of auto manufacturing has come an increase in related businesses; Gerhardi, a German parts supplier announced in July 2016 a $38 million facility in Montgomery.

Politically, this was long one of the heartlands of the conservative wing of the Democratic Party, the home of white Democrats who are patriotic supporters of the military and cautious supporters of some domestic programs. There is also a large population of African-American descendants of slaves from plantations. But the area has become safely Republican. Tuskegee's Macon County is the only Democratic County in the district. St. Clair County, close to Birmingham and solidly Republican, grew by 29 percent from 2000 to 2010, almost four times faster than the growth rate of the state.

Democrats have remained competitive in some state elections. In the old incarnation of the district, George W. Bush won 52 percent here in 2000, and 58 percent in 2004. Barack Obama increased black turnout in 2008, but John McCain still won with 56 percent. Redistricting changes boosted Republicans, and Democrats have had a more difficult time competing here. Donald Trump won the district with 65 percent of the vote.

FOURTH DISTRICT

Robert Aderholt (R)

Elected 1996, 11th term; b. Jul 22, 1965, Haleyville; Birmingham-Southern College (AL), B.A.; Samford University Cumberland Law School (AL), J.D.; Methodist; Married (Caroline McDonald Aderholt); 2 children.

Professional Career: Haleyville Municipal Judge, 1992-1995; Assistant legal advisor, Gov. Fob James, 1995-1996.

DC Office: 235 CHOB 20515, 202-225-4876, Fax: 202-225-5587, aderholt.house.gov.

State Offices: Cullman, 256-734-6043; Gadsden, 256-546-0201; Jasper, 205-221-2310; Tuscumbia, 256-381-3450.

Committees: *Appropriations*: Agriculture, Rural Development, FDA & Related Agencies (Chmn), Commerce, Justice, Science & Related Agencies, Defense. *Joint Security & Cooperation in Europe*.

Group Ratings

	ADA	ACLU	AFL-CIO	LCV	ITI	COC	HAFA	ACU	CFG	FRC
2016	-	5%	-	3%	83%	93%	62%	71%	61%	100%
2015	5%	C	21%	3%	C	85%	C	71%	60%	100%

Almanac Ratings 2015

	Economy	Social	Foreign	Composite
Liberal	14%	5%	8%	9%
Conservative	86%	95%	92%	91%

Key Votes of the 114th Congress

1. Keystone Pipeline	Y	5. Puerto Rico Debt	N	9. Offenses by Aliens	Y
2. Trade Deals	N	6. Medical Marijuana	N	10. Troops in Iraq	N
3. Export-Import Bank	Y	7. Sanctuary Cities	Y	11. Homeland Security $$	N
4. Debt Ceiling Increase	N	8. Armor-piercing Bullets	Y	12. Trade Adjustment aid	Y

Election Results

Election	Name (Party)	Vote	(%)	Cand. Spent	Ind. Exp. Support	Ind. Exp. Oppose
2016 General	Robert Aderholt (R)	235,925	(99%)	$1,210,279		
2016 Primary	Robert Aderholt (R)	102,348	(81%)			
	Phil Norris (R)	23,343	(19%)			

Prior winning percentages: 2014 (99%), 2012 (74%), 2010 (100%), 2008 (75%), 2006 (70%), 2004 (75%), 2002 (87%), 2000 (61%), 1998 (56%), 1996 (50%)

Robert Aderholt, a Republican first elected in 1996, is a mild-mannered conservative and a senior member of the Appropriations Committee who is next in line to chair the panel. He considers obtaining federal money for the state to be an essential part of his job, and he often takes a constituent-based approach. But he also offers his own imprint on spending, such as stringent rules for program beneficiaries.

Aderholt is from Winston County, the one ancestrally Republican county in north Alabama; it opposed secession in the Civil War and declared itself the Free State of Winston. His father was a circuit judge for more than 30 years; his wife's father was a state senator and state commissioner of Agriculture and Industry. In 1992, Aderholt was appointed Haleyville municipal judge. Three years later, he became a top aide to Republican Gov. Fob James. With that pedigree, he decided to run for Congress when 30-year veteran Rep. Tom Bevill, a Democrat and a pork-barrel spending appropriator, retired. As the Republican nominee, he faced state Sen. Bob Wilson Jr., who called himself a Democrat "in the Tom Bevill tradition." In this culturally conservative district, Aderholt emphasized social issues, opposing abortion rights, gun control, same-sex marriage, and prohibitions against school prayer. "We want to go to Washington to deliver a message, and that is, don't mess with our traditional family values," he said. He also attacked Wilson for his support from labor unions and trial lawyers. This was a nationally targeted race, seriously contested, and Aderholt won 50%-48%. Two year following the Republican capture of the House for the first time in 40 years, the outcome was a landmark in the Republican takeover of rural southern districts.

Aderholt's voting record is generally conservative, and he was among the first House Republicans to join the Tea Party Caucus in July 2010. But he often sides with labor and economic populists on trade issues, mainly because of local imperatives. His Almanac vote ratings in 2015 were toward the center of the House GOP. He has supported quotas on steel imports and sponsored a bill assessing additional antidumping duties on foreign steel. He voted against normalizing trade relations with China and opposed free-trade agreements with Chile, Morocco and Singapore. In June 2015, he was one of 50 Republicans to vote against the measure giving fast-track authority to negotiate trade deals to President Barack Obama and his successors. In 2005, however, Aderholt was a crucial vote for the Central America Free Trade Agreement after he got a last-minute letter from President George W. Bush delaying the phase-out of tariffs on socks. In another populist leaning, he was the only House member from Alabama in 2008 to vote against the $700 billion rescue of the financial markets. He cited public "discontent" with the plan and the need for a more market-based approach.

Recognizing Aderholt's electoral vulnerability when he took office, Republican leaders put him on the Appropriations Committee, where he has secured more highway and water projects money than most of his GOP colleagues. In the old-style southern tradition, he has worked his way up the ranks by learning how deals are made and trading favors. After Republicans assumed House control in 2011, he became chairman of the Homeland Security Subcommittee. When a tornado hit his district hard that year, he increased spending on disaster relief while offsetting the cost with other cuts to the Homeland Security and Energy department budgets.

On behalf of Alabama's aerospace industry, Aderholt has worked with delegation members to have a new NASA heavy-lift rocket designed to carry astronauts into deep space built at Huntsville's Marshall Space Flight Center.

In 2013, Aderholt became chairman of the Agriculture Appropriations Subcommittee, an area of interest for many of his constituents. His panel faces the limitation that about $120 billion under its control is for "mandatory" programs - chiefly food stamps - and therefore subject to limited appropriations tinkering. He lists his priorities as "cutting edge" agricultural research, vibrant rural communities, nutrition for the most vulnerable, competitive markets in the global economy and the safest food and drug supply in the world. He also is mindful of agri-business needs. He scored a legislative coup when the 2014 omnibus spending bill adopted his modified plan to limit federal standards advocated by first lady Michelle Obama that would require more whole grains in school foods. Aderholt later mocked her use of the school lunch program to reduce obesity. "The purpose of the school lunch program is to make sure that hungry kids can eat," he said. When a federal advisory panel urged consideration of the environmental impact of nutrition plans, Aderholt criticized "politically motivated" steps such as taxes on certain foods that he said were at odds with sound science. In 2016, he filed a bill that would allow states to require drug testing for recipients of food stamps.

At Appropriations, he retained his interest in social issues. In 2012, he added an amendment to the department's spending bill specifying that none of the funds provided to Immigration and Customs Enforcement (ICE) could be used to pay for an abortion, except under certain circumstances. In response to President Barack Obama's executive actions on immigration, he prepared House Republican legislation in 2015 to nullify presidential action and toughen enforcement against undocumented immigrants, especially the surge of unaccompanied children who have crossed the southern border. The previous year, the House approved his plan to make it more difficult for other countries to deport unaccompanied children. The American people were looking to Republicans for leadership on the issue, he said. When Alabama Chief Justice Roy Moore called for a new law to prevent federal judges from interfering with public displays of the Ten Commandments, Aderholt filed a bill toward that goal. "The acknowledgment of God is not a legitimate subject of review by the federal courts," Aderholt said.

Aderholt faced serious challenges in his first two reelections, but has won easily since. With his relative youth, he is positioned as the next Republican to chair the Appropriations Committee behind Rep. Rodney Frelinghuysen of New Jersey. The chief obstacle standing in his way might be that Alabama's prospective loss of a House seat after the 2020 census could place at risk his rural district, with its lack of a population center. When President-Elect Donald Trump tapped Alabama Sen. Jeff Sessions for attorney general, Aderholt said that he would like to be appointed as his successor. "I would be someone who could hit the ground running," he told the Yellowhammer News. For the heir apparent as Appropriations Committee chairman to seek a switch to the Senate would have been viewed in decades past as blasphemy by House insiders. Although he didn't get the appointment, Aderholt, with his relatively young age, could have other opportunities for the Senate.

North-Central Alabama: Gadsden

Population		**Race and Ethnicity**		**Income**	
Total	682,859	White	84.1%	Median Income	$39,147 (402 out of 435)
Land area	8,889	Black	6.8%		
Pop/ sq mi	76.8	Latino	6.1%		
Born in state	75.1%	Asian	0.6%	Under $50,000	60.3%
		Two races	1.7%	$50,000-$99,999	27.7%
Age Groups		Other	0.7%	$100,000-$199,999	10.2%
Under 18	23.0%			$200,000 or more	1.8%
18-34	20.3%	**Education**		Poverty Rate	19.2%
35-64	40.0%	H.S grad or less	54.4%		
Over 64	16.8%	Some college	29.8%	**Health Insurance**	
Work		College Degree, 4 yr	9.7%	With health insurance coverage	86.4%
White Collar	28.4%	Post grad	6.2%		
Sales and Service	44.1%	**Military**		**Public Assistance**	
Blue Collar	33.7%	Veteran	8.8%	Cash public assistance income	1.4%
Government	14.9%	Active Duty	0.1%		
				Food stamp/SNAP benefits	16.7%

Voter Turnout			
2015 Total Citizens 18+	508,870	2016 House Turnout as % CVAP	47%
2016 House turnout	239,444	2014 House Turnout as % CVAP	27%

2012 Presidential Vote		
Mitt Romney	205,589	(75%)
Barack Obama	65,852	(24%)

2016 Presidential Vote		
Donald Trump	233,662	(80%)
Hillary Clinton	50,722	(17%)

Cook Partisan Voting Index: R+30

The Appalachian Mountains' corduroy ridges, dividing the Atlantic coast from the interior, make up America's coal-and-steel industrial spine, from the black coal country of western Pennsylvania to the red hill country of northern Alabama. Here rose America's two premier steel cities, Pittsburgh and Birmingham. Around both, and for many miles in between, is countryside settled by feisty Scots-Irish farmers in the years between the Revolution and the Civil War. In valley land accessible to railroads, great steel factories were built in the 80 years after the Civil War, along with smaller factories that produced socks, tires, glass and chemicals, and butchered chickens. Northern Alabama was solidly Democratic through the 1950s. It was populist on economics, conservative on cultural issues. Since then, the region has become firmly Republican, even though it has benefited from massive federal public works programs. The movement is most pronounced in counties close to Birmingham and along the interstates.

Alabama's 4th Congressional District is a collection of small towns - Cullman, Jasper, Russellville, Fort Payne and Albertville. The last is the home of a military helicopter plant and other aerospace facilities. Sandwiched between Huntsville to the north and Birmingham to the south, the 4th District crosses the state and the Appalachian ridges, from the Georgia line to Mississippi. Decades of coal mining scarred 150 square miles of landscape, about one-fourth of which has been reclaimed, with pockets of jobs. Gritty Gadsden (pop. 36,500) is the biggest city, with a Goodyear tire plant built in 1929 - with about 1,650 workers and daily production exceeding 20,000 tires. Plant managers in 2014 introduced a new tire for the Ford F-150 aluminum body truck. In 2016, the company spent $30 million to expand the aging facility and its operations. The plant's most famous employee was activist Lilly Ledbetter, who, after discovering that her salary was much lower than men in similar positions, waged a nine-year battle on behalf of equal pay for women. Her case became a *cause celebre* for Democrats, and President Barack Obama in 2009 signed into law the Lilly Ledbetter Fair Pay Act extending the statute of limitations on equal-pay discrimination lawsuits. In Jasper, Japanese-based Yoruzu Automotive built a $100 million plant to manufacture stamped parts.

This area was hard hit by deadly tornadoes that struck Alabama on April 27, 2011. Of the 253 people who died statewide, 122 lived in northwest Alabama. The Category EF-5 twister, the strongest there is, cleared a three-quarter-mile wide path 25 miles long, killing more than 70 people. The small town of Hackleburg in Marion County was already struggling with nearly 13 percent unemployment when the storm destroyed a Wrangler jeans distribution center. Two years later, Hackleburg and Wrangler celebrated the opening of a new 369,000 square-foot plant, with a conveyer system capable of handling 27 million pairs of jeans annually along two miles of belts. The $31 million facility is the largest employer in town, with about 200 workers.

The 4th is Alabama's premier Scots-Irish district, with the lowest African-American population percentage of the state's seven congressional districts. Though family income is low and poverty above national averages, high marriage rates provide some social stability. There are few vestiges of its Democratic heritage. Mitt Romney's 75 percent made this district his 7th-best performance in the nation in 2012 and his best in Alabama. In 2016, the 80 percent for Donald Trump was his highest in the nation. Census Bureau mid-decade population estimates project that Alabama will lose a seat in the reapportionment following the 2020 Census. The 4th district could be at risk because it's the only one in Alabama without an urban population center.

FIFTH DISTRICT

Mo Brooks (R)

Elected 2010, 4th term; b. Apr 29, 1954, Charleston, SC; Duke University (NC), B.A.; University of Alabama School of Law, J.D.; Christian Church; Married (Martha Brooks); 4 children; 3 grandchildren.

Elected Office: AL House, 1983-1992; Madison County Commissioner, 1996-2010.

Professional Career: Tuscaloosa County prosecutor, 1978-1980; Clerk, Circuit Ct. Judge John Snodgrass, 1980-1982; Madison County district Attorney, 1991-1993; AL special Assistant Attorney General, 1995-2002; practicing Attorney, 1993-2010.

DC Office: 2400 RHOB 20515, 202-225-4801, brooks.house.gov.

State Offices: Decatur, 256-355-9400; Florence, 256-718-5155; Huntsville, 256-551-0190.

Committees: *Armed Services*: Strategic Forces, Tactical Air & Land Forces. *Foreign Affairs*: Asia & the Pacific, Western Hemisphere. *Science, Space & Technology*: Energy, Environment, Space.

Group Ratings

	ADA	ACLU	AFL-CIO	LCV	ITI	COC	HAFA	ACU	CFG	FRC
2016	-	11%	-	3%	67%	86%	94%	92%	87%	92%
2015	5%	C	13%	9%	C	65%	C	96%	92%	92%

Almanac Ratings 2015

	Economy	Social	Foreign	Composite
Liberal	12%	15%	1%	9%
Conservative	88%	85%	99%	91%

Key Votes of the 114th Congress

1. Keystone Pipeline	Y	5. Puerto Rico Debt	N	9. Offenses by Aliens	Y
2. Trade Deals	N	6. Medical Marijuana	Y	10. Troops in Iraq	N
3. Export-Import Bank	N	7. Sanctuary Cities	Y	11. Homeland Security $$	N
4. Debt Ceiling Increase	N	8. Armor-piercing Bullets	Y	12. Trade Adjustment aid	N

Election Results

Election	Name (Party)	Vote (%)		Cand. Spent	Ind. Exp. Support	Ind. Exp. Oppose
2016 General	Mo Brooks (R)	205,647	(67%)	$113,530		
	Will Boyd (D)	102,234	(33%)	$51,646		
2016 Primary	Mo Brooks (R)		(100%)			

Prior winning percentages: 2014 (74%), 2012 (65%), 2010 (58%)

Mo Brooks, the 5th District congressman, in 2010 became the first Republican to be elected to the seat since 1868. A member of the maverick Freedom Caucus, he has a boisterous style that has not prevented him from enjoying some legislative successes.

Brooks was born in Charleston, South Carolina. His father was raised "dirt poor" in Chattanooga, Tennesseee, and later worked as an electrical engineer. His mother grew up without electricity or indoor plumbing, and later taught high school economics and government in Huntsville. "Out of that poverty, my parents learned that you'd better work, and work hard," Brooks said. He studied economics and political science at Duke University and got his law degree from the University of Alabama. In 1982, he was elected as one of 11 Republicans in the state House, where the Alabama Taxpayers' Defense Fund gave him its No. 1 ranking for opposing tax increases. He served two years as district attorney, lost reelection, and in 1996 was elected to the Madison County Commission.

Brooks won his House seat in two hard-fought battles. In the Republican primary, he defeated first-term Rep. Parker Griffith,who had been elected as a Democrat but switched parties in December 2009. Brooks campaigned on the theme that the district "deserves a congressman who acts honorably." He defeated Parker, 51%-33%. In the general election, he was opposed by Steve Raby, the longtime chief of staff to former Sen. Howell Heflin of Alabama. The Democrat shunned his party label in most of his ads, focusing almost exclusively on local issues. Brooks took on hot-button issues, declaring that he favored repealing President Barack Obama's health care legislation and deporting all illegal immigrants. He said the country was veering dangerously toward socialism and that the trend must be reversed. Brooks won, 58%-42%.

He made a quick impression. Within four months, he charged in a House speech that the United States is at "risk of insolvency and bankruptcy because the socialist members of this body choose to spend money that we do not have." Several months later, at a forum back home, Brooks said he supported any measure "short of shooting them" to force illegal immigrants back to their home countries. Latino lawmakers and groups condemned his remarks.

When he circulated a letter in 2011 urging House GOP leaders to hold a vote on a Senate-passed Chinese currency manipulation measure, the conservative anti-tax group Club for Growth assailed Brooks for "standing with Senate liberals like [Democratic Sens.] Sherrod Brown and Chuck Schumer." Brooks was unapologetic. "Americans cannot stand idly by and watch Communist China undermine our economy via unfair trade practices," he said.

Brooks landed in an even bigger controversy in 2014. Asked by conservative radio host Laura Ingraham about a statement that the Republican Party was alienating non-white voters, Brooks responded: "This is a part of the war on whites that's being launched by the Democratic Party. And the way in which they're launching this war is by claiming that whites hate everybody else. It's a part of the strategy that Barack Obama implemented in 2008, continued in 2012, where he divides us all on race, on sex, greed, envy, class warfare, all those kinds of things." Ingraham responded that the characterization was "a little out there," and numerous Democrats blasted Brooks for playing the race card. But he was unapologetic.

His committee assignments have matched up well with his district. On Science, Space and Technology, he has been vice-chair of the Space Subcommittee. Brooks has been part of a bipartisan coalition that has sought to reshape space policy with a stepping-stone approach to exploration. That plan featured access by American astronauts on American rockets to an international space station, and envisioned long-term plans for deep-space destinations such as Mars. On the Armed Services Committee, he said that the United States should spend what it takes to fight terrorism. If the Europeans "choose to be halfhearted about it, if our interests are at stake and the security of the American people is at stake, then I think we gotta be there," he said.Following House passage in May 2016 of the defense spending bill, he claimed credit for provisions that support Redstone Arsenal programs for military capability in space and small satellite technology development.

After John Boehner stepped down as House Speaker in September 2015, Brooks joined other Freedom Caucus members in backing Rep. Daniel Webster of Florida for the post. When Rep. Paul Ryan won the support of the Republican Conference, Brooks agreed to support him after Ryan pledged that the House would not consider immigration reform legislation while Obama was president, and subsequently only if a majority of House Republicans supported such a proposal.

In what had been an entrenched Democratic district less than a decade ago, Brooks has secured his House seat. In the 2012 primary, he again dispatched Griffith in the Republican primary, with 71 percent of the vote. He has won each general election without serious competition. He endorsed Ted Cruz and kept his distance from Donald Trump during the presidential campaign. In February 2016, Brooks used terms such as "serial adultery," "notorious flip-flopper" and "gutter mouth" to describe Trump and said that he would never endorse him. After Trump won the Republican nomination, Brooks said that he was supporting the entire Republican ticket without mentioning Trump by name.

In May 2017, Brooks joined the campaign to fill the remainder three years of the term of former Sen. Jeff Sessions, who resigned in February to become Attorney General for President Donald Trump. That pitted Brooks against Sen. Luther Strange, who was appointed to the seat by the since-resigned Gov. Robert Bentley. With a Super PAC linked to Senate Majority Leader Mitch McConnell spending millions of dollars on behalf of Strange, Brooks positioned himself as a political outsider and "grass roots conservative" who would stand with Trump, though the President and other leading conservatives initially were neutral in the contest. With his strong opposition to illegal immigration, he reasserted his support from tea party groups.

North Alabama: Huntsville, Decatur

Population		**Race and Ethnicity**		**Income**	
Total	700,501	White	73.4%	Median Income	$50,392 (251 out of 435)
Land area	3,677	Black	17.1%	Under $50,000	49.5%
Pop/ sq mi	190.5	Latino	4.9%	$50,000-$99,999	28.7%
Born in state	61.3%	Asian	1.6%	$100,000-$199,999	17.9%
		Two races	2.3%	$200,000 or more	3.7%
		Other	0.8%	Poverty Rate	15.1%
Age Groups		**Education**		**Health Insurance**	
Under 18	22.6%	H.S grad or less	41.0%	With health insurance coverage	87.4%
18-34	22.3%	Some college	29.2%		
35-64	40.5%	College Degree, 4 yr	18.8%		
Over 64	14.6%	Post grad	10.9%		
Work		**Military**		**Public Assistance**	
White Collar	37.7%	Veteran	10.8%	Cash public assistance income	1.6%
Sales and Service	53.5%	Active Duty	0.2%	Food stamp/SNAP benefits	13.0%
Blue Collar	23.1%				
Government	17.4%				

Voter Turnout			
2015 Total Citizens 18+	525,764	2016 House Turnout as % CVAP	59%
2016 House turnout	308,326	2014 House Turnout as % CVAP	29%

2012 Presidential Vote		
Mitt Romney	189,838	(64%)
Barack Obama	103,601	(35%)

2016 Presidential Vote		
Donald Trump	200,570	(64%)
Hillary Clinton	97,159	(31%)
Gary Johnson	10,223	(3%)

Cook Partisan Voting Index: R+18

After the Soviets put up Sputnik in 1957, the Redstone Arsenal in Huntsville became the nation's foremost missile development center. Then a sleepy town huddled around a well-preserved, early-19th-century settlement, Huntsville grew to become the center of Alabama's northern tier. Residents are fond of referring to their hometown as "Rocket City." The first of the large U.S. ballistic missiles were developed here. On the grounds of Redstone, NASA built its Marshall Space Flight Center in the 1960s, and the Huntsville-Decatur area soon achieved high-tech critical mass. With leadership from Wernher von Braun and other German engineers, Redstone and Marshall built Explorer 1, the first American orbiting satellite; the Mercury-Redstone vehicle that boosted astronaut Alan Shepard into suborbital flight; and the Saturn V rocket that sent men to the moon. In the 1970s, Marshall produced Skylab and developed the space shuttle's main engines and solid-rocket boosters. The Boeing research center here, in a consortium with Lockheed Martin, produces the Delta IV heavy rocket booster at its factory in Decatur, about 20 miles west of Huntsville.

With the retirement of the space shuttle, NASA expected that Marshall would have a major role in preparing the next generation of space vehicles, including the Ares I rocket and the Constellation project aimed at returning humans to the moon. But the Obama administration, wary of large-scale space exploration programs funded entirely by the government, scuttled the Constellation program and officials estimated that the area lost 1,500 contractor jobs. Still, the Arsenal has more than 35,000 employees.

Huntsville has diversified its high-tech economy in recent years, and has been able to weather the Arsenal setbacks. Space-related jobs have evolved with a broader defense focus. In 2005, the Pentagon base-closing commission moved 1,800 jobs in the Missile Defense Agency from northern Virginia to Redstone. More than two dozen aerospace companies subsequently moved or expanded to Huntsville to remain close to the agency. A Verizon Wireless call center now employs 1,300 people in the city, mostly for customer service. Other companies that have expanded their operations include Boeing, Toyota and Remington. Over several decades, city leaders carefully cultivated the Cummings Research Park, which claims that it is the second-largest research park in the nation and home to more than 300 companies and 29,000 employees specializing in technology-based manufacturing, biotechnology and pharmaceuticals. In addition to the usual tax incentives and grants, the city took the novel approach of offering to train or retrain high-tech manufacturing employees at city facilities for free. In 2016, the area was among the national leaders in new construction. Demographers project that Huntsville, which has long been the fourth largest city in Alabama, could become the largest within a decade.

Huntsville gained a new kind of identity in early 2015 when a federal judge ruled that same-sex marriages were legal in Alabama. Unexpectedly, the city became a destination wedding spot for gays in the South. Like high-tech centers in places like Cambridge, Massachusetts, Austin, Texas, and California's Silicon Valley, Huntsville has attracted many educated and motivated people who also are socially liberal, though they haven't made much change in the area's conservative politics.

The 5th Congressional District of Alabama takes in most of the space counties. For decades, most voters here were staunch New Deal Democrats, liberal on economics and not much interested in race issues. Sen. John Sparkman was the party's vice presidential nominee in 1952. But professional and technical people in the space business tended to be conservative, and this made much of northern Alabama marginal-to-Republican country in the 1990s. The district has voted Republican for president since 1980, but did not elect a Republican to Congress until 2010. Parker Griffith was elected as a Democrat in 2008, and switched to the GOP a year later.

Of the five counties in the district, Huntsville-based Madison County has about 60 percent of the voters. With its more corporate lifestyle, Donald Trump got a relatively small 55 percent of the vote. In the district's other four counties, his vote share ranged between 71 and 84 percent.

SIXTH DISTRICT

Gary Palmer (R)

Elected 2014, 2nd term; b. May 14, 1954, Hackleburg; University of Alabama, B.S.; Northwest Alabama Junior College, Att.; Presbyterian; Married (Ann Cushing); 3 children.

Professional Career: Engineer, 1977-1989; Founder/President, AL Policy Institute (formerly AL Family Alliance), 1989-2013; Founding board member, State Policy Network, 1992-1998.

DC Office: 330 CHOB 20515, 202-225-4921, Fax: 202-225-2082, palmer.house.gov.

State Offices: Birmingham, 205-968-1290; Clanton, 205-280-6846; Oneonta, 205-274-2136.

Committees: *Budget*. *Oversight & Government Reform*: Intergovernmental Affairs (Chmn), Interior, Energy & Environment. *Science, Space & Technology*: Environment, Oversight.

Group Ratings

	ADA	ACLU	AFL-CIO	LCV	ITI	COC	HAFA	ACU	CFG	FRC
2016	-	5%	-	0%	83%	86%	95%	100%	94%	100%
2015	5%	C	4%	6%	C	60%	C	100%	97%	100%

Almanac Ratings 2015

	Economy	Social	Foreign	Composite
Liberal	8%	0%	0%	3%
Conservative	93%	100%	100%	98%

Key Votes of the 114th Congress

1. Keystone Pipeline	Y	5. Puerto Rico Debt	N	9. Offenses by Aliens	Y
2. Trade Deals	N	6. Medical Marijuana	N	10. Troops in Iraq	N
3. Export-Import Bank	N	7. Sanctuary Cities	Y	11. Homeland Security $$	N
4. Debt Ceiling Increase	N	8. Armor-piercing Bullets	Y	12. Trade Adjustment aid	N

Election Results

Election	Name (Party)	Vote (%)	Cand. Spent	Ind. Exp. Support	Ind. Exp. Oppose
2016 General	Gary Palmer (R)	245,313 (75%)	$584,805		
	David Putman (D)	83,709 (25%)	$72,786		
2016 Primary	Gary Palmer (R)	(100%)			

Prior winning percentages: 2014 (76%)

Republican Gary Palmer was elected to Congress in 2014 as a political outsider in one of the nation's strongest Republican districts. On his opening day, he allied with conservative and free-spirited Republicans, and showed his independent credentials by voting against a new term for House Speaker John Boehner. But he later joined GOP leaders in efforts to earn his party stripes.

Palmer grew up on a small farm in Hackleburg, Alabama. He was the first in his family to go to college, where he studied engineering. He started his career in the private sector before cofounding the Alabama Policy Institute (API) in 1989. As president of the think tank with ties to the right-leaning American Legislative Exchange Council, Palmer engaged for years in state-level policy issues, including tax and regulatory affairs. In 2012, API joined a coalition that successfully campaigned against a public referendum on a measure to transfer money from the Alabama Trust Fund - which collects royalties from offshore gas exploration - into the state's cash-strapped General Fund, which covers many social services. Palmer and other conservatives argued that a "no" vote on the transfer would force the state government to downsize and allocate its spending more efficiently. Palmer also recommended a proposal to congressional Republicans that any debt-ceiling deal should contain language allowing oil and gas exploitation on federal lands as a way to pay down the national debt.

Following the retirement of Rep. Spencer Bachus, a former chairman of the House Financial Services Committee and ally of Speaker Boehner, there was a wide-open contest to succeed him. The path to victory focused on the party primary, which began with a seven-candidate field. Palmer came in second in the initial June vote, trailing GOP state Rep. Paul DeMarco, 33%-19%. DeMarco led the field in each of the district's six counties. In the run-off, the Club for Growth weighed in for Palmer after deeming DeMarco pro-tax. Palmer got the Club's endorsement, along with $250,000 for ads that helped him go on the offensive. He also won the backing of prominent national Republicans such as Indiana Gov. Mike Pence and former presidential candidate Rick Santorum. Palmer won the July runoff handily, 64%-36%. In this district, he didn't need to break a sweat to claim his general election victory over Democrat Mark Lester, with 76 percent of the vote.

Even before taking office, Palmer joined forces with several incoming GOP members who said they would not back Boehner for a third term as Speaker. In a debate before the runoff, Palmer told the audience: "I cannot in good conscience support John Boehner because I think he lost his legitimacy to lead" after bringing to the House floor bills that most Republican members opposed. Palmer later said he regretted making that pledge because it jeopardized his ability to land good committee assignments. But he said that he had told Boehner before the election that he would need to keep his word to his constituents

- unlike some other freshmen who reneged on their campaign promises. As he later recounted his conversation with the Speaker, "not only would I lose their confidence, but I would lose his. I think he respected that." Instead, Palmer voted for then-Alabama Sen. Jeff Sessions; under the Constitution, the Speaker does not need to be a member of the House.

As he predicted, Palmer fell short on influential committee posts. In a delegation where each of the other five Republicans serves on either the Appropriations or Armed Services Committee, Palmer was assigned to Science, Space and Technology (potentially useful for Alabama), plus the Budget and Oversight and Government Reform panels. He was outspoken throughout his first term. In March 2015, he opposed the bipartisan agreement to fund the Homeland Security Department. Instead, he urged another three days of debate to drive a tougher compromise on the measure, which already had consumed two months. When he claimed on a Birmingham radio program that temperature data used to measure global climate change have been falsified and manipulated, a review by *Factcheck.org* cited studies by the National Oceanic and Atmospheric Administration and other meteorological organizations to conclude that Palmer was wrong.

Summarizing his first term, Palmer told a local reporter that he had become "one of the top policy thinkers in our [Republican] conference." He cited his participation with a handful of Budget Committee members who crafted a compromise on the annual budget resolution with Majority Leader Kevin McCarthy. He also cited his contribution to Speaker Paul Ryan's "Better Way" policy agenda, which included eliminating the Environmental Protection Agency's authority to regulate greenhouse gasses. Still, Palmer received no new committee assignment in 2017.

In this district, Palmer's chief reelection concern is a Republican challenge from a more "establishment" candidate. In 2016, his political start-up showed his success in seeking a balance. He got a free pass in the primary and won 74 percent against Democratic David Putnam, a former manager at Alabama Power. Palmer raised $1.2 million, which was 10 times Putnam's receipts. In the presidential campaign, Palmer condemned as "offensive and inappropriate" the lewd remarks that Donald Trump made on a 2005 video recording. But he subsequently added that supporting Trump over Hillary Clinton "is not a difficult choice."

Central Alabama: Birmingham Suburbs, Shelby County

Population		**Race and Ethnicity**		**Income**	
Total	692,738	White	77.2%	Median Income	$59,659
Land area	4,171	Black	14.5%		(145 out of
Pop/ sq mi	166.1	Latino	5.0%		435)
Born in state	70.5%	Asian	1.8%	Under $50,000	42.2%
		Two races	1.1%	$50,000-$99,999	32.2%
Age Groups		Other	0.4%	$100,000-$199,999	20.3%
Under 18	23.6%			$200,000 or more	5.3%
18-34	21.3%	**Education**		Poverty Rate	11.0%
35-64	40.8%	H.S grad or less	36.5%		
Over 64	14.3%	Some college	29.0%	**Health Insurance**	
		College Degree, 4 yr	21.4%	With health insurance coverage	90.5%
Work		Post grad	13.2%		
White Collar	41.4%				
Sales and Service	55.2%	**Military**		**Public Assistance**	
Blue Collar	19.5%	Veteran	8.7%	Cash public assistance income	1.4%
Government	13.8%	Active Duty	0.1%		
				Food stamp/SNAP benefits	8.5%

Voter Turnout			
2015 Total Citizens 18+	510,018	2016 House Turnout as % CVAP	65%
2016 House turnout	329,306	2014 House Turnout as % CVAP	35%

2012 Presidential Vote		
Mitt Romney	233,803	(74%)
Barack Obama	77,235	(25%)

2016 Presidential Vote		
Donald Trump	233,494	(70%)
Hillary Clinton	86,117	(26%)
Gary Johnson	8,709	(3%)

Cook Partisan Voting Index: R+26

Birmingham, once one of America's booming industrial cities, was better known in the middle of the 20th century as a center of white resistance to the civil rights movement. Its prospects in the 21st century have been more hopeful. This is a new city by Southern standards. Before the Civil War, there was nothing here but a few creeks running below Red Mountain. But Red Mountain is almost pure iron ore. With the additional mining of coal, Birmingham - the self-styled Magic City - had by 1890 the South's largest steel mills. In the early 20th century, as the statue of Vulcan, the Roman god of fire and metalworking, looked out over the smokestack-filled valley, Birmingham seemed prosperous and the most progressive city in the South. But the worldwide overcapacity of steel and technological obsolescence at home sent the American steel industry into long-term decline starting in the 1950s.

Meanwhile, Birmingham's political leaders plotted to avoid desegregation. The city's violent reaction to the civil rights movement made a vivid impression on the rest of the country. Police Commissioner (and Democratic National Committeeman at the time) Bull Connor set dogs and fire hoses against peaceful demonstrators, and Ku Klux Klansmen bombed the 16th Street Baptist Church, killing four young girls in 1963. Those images haunted Birmingham for a generation. As the more civic-minded Atlanta became the new heart of the South, Birmingham suffered from uninspired business leadership. An example remains its mid-sized airport terminal, which is dwarfed by Atlanta's world-class Hartsfield-Jackson Airport.

In recent years, Birmingham has worked to improve race relations and develop a new economic base. Health care is a major industry. The city has some of the largest and most advanced medical care centers in the South, and is renowned for its sports medicine facilities and specialists who tend to the ailments of famous athletes. Banking is also important. While Atlanta's banks foundered and were acquired by outsiders, Birmingham became the largest Southern banking center outside Charlotte, North Carolina. But city leaders have worried that the viability of the downtown area and white movement to newer suburbs have caused an uptick in racial polarization.

The city's population has declined by 100,000 since 1960 and was 73 percent African American in 2010. Whites have been moving out of Birmingham's Jefferson County southeast to Shelby County, which grew 44 percent in the 1990s, 36 percent in the next decade and 7 percent from 2010 to 2015 - the fastest growth in the state. (The migration to Shelby has not been entirely white flight. Its African-American population has increased as well, though the county is about 84 percent white.) Jefferson County, once more Republican than most of Alabama, votes Democratic in close statewide elections, while Shelby County is overwhelmingly Republican. Metropolitan planners projected an 85 percent population increase for Shelby County from 2005 to 2035, but only a 2 percent increase for Jefferson, where physical expansion is limited by the hills.

Shelby County played a vital role in a recent civil rights debate, to the dismay of many local and national activists, when it argued that it no longer engaged in racially discriminatory practices in elections and challenged the constitutionality of the federal rule that most southern states are required to report ballot changes under the Voting Rights Act. In a landmark 2013 ruling that overturned a central provision of that law, the U.S. Supreme Court agreed with Shelby County that it was no longer required to get Justice Department approval of each voting change - which, in this case, removed a black-majority district in the small town of Calera. On behalf of the 5-4 majority, Chief Justice John Roberts ruled that the formula for determining which jurisdictions are covered by the law was unconstitutional and that the "preclearance" requirement was no longer required. "Things have changed dramatically" for the better in the South, he wrote. Critics of Congress blamed lawmakers for the bipartisan failure to update the law - both before and after the ruling.

The 6th Congressional District of Alabama, which once included all of Birmingham and most of Jefferson County, is now the suburban Birmingham-area district and strongly Republican. It includes Shelby County and parts of Jefferson County, such as prosperous Mountain Brook with upscale shopping malls, and stretches southwest toward Tuscaloosa and south along Interstate 65 halfway to Montgomery. Jefferson retains a slight majority of the district vote and Shelby has 30 percent. The remaining population is in four outlying counties. This has been one of the most Republican districts in the nation. Under its previous borders, it voted 74 percent for George W. Bush in 2000 - his second-best district outside Texas. The new district lines also gave 74 percent to Mitt Romney in 2012, his ninth-best district in the nation. In 2016, the vote for Donald Trump fell to 71 percent.

SEVENTH DISTRICT

Terri Sewell (D)

Elected 2010, 4th term; b. Jan 01, 1965, Huntsville; Princeton University (NJ), B.A.; Oxford University (England), M.A.; Harvard University Law School (MA), J.D.; Protestant; Divorced.

Professional Career: Clerk, U.S. District Court judge, 1993-1994; practicing Attorney, 1994-2010.

DC Office: 2201 RHOB 20515, 202-225-2665, Fax: 202-226-9567, sewell.house.gov.

State Offices: Birmingham, 205-254-1960; Montgomery, 334-262-1919; Selma, 334-877-4414; Tuscaloosa, 205-752-5380.

Committees: *Permanent Select on Intelligence*. *Ways & Means*: Health, Human Resources.

Group Ratings

	ADA	ACLU	AFL-CIO	LCV	ITI	COC	HAFA	ACU	CFG	FRC
2016	-	76%	-	82%	75%	73%	11%	4%	6%	8%
2015	65%	C	82%	71%	C	65%	C	5%	0%	17%

Almanac Ratings 2015

	Economy	Social	Foreign	Composite
Liberal	73%	85%	76%	78%
Conservative	27%	15%	24%	22%

Key Votes of the 114th Congress

1. Keystone Pipeline	Y	5. Puerto Rico Debt	Y	9. Offenses by Aliens	N
2. Trade Deals	Y	6. Medical Marijuana	N	10. Troops in Iraq	N
3. Export-Import Bank	Y	7. Sanctuary Cities	N	11. Homeland Security $$	Y
4. Debt Ceiling Increase	Y	8. Armor-piercing Bullets	N	12. Trade Adjustment aid	Y

Election Results

Election	Name (Party)	Vote (%)		Cand. Spent	Ind. Exp. Support	Ind. Exp. Oppose
2016 General	Terri Sewell (D)	229,330	(98%)	$669,282		
2016 Primary	Terri Sewell (D)		(100%)			

Prior winning percentages: 2014 (98%), 2012 (76%), 2010 (73%)

Soon after Democrat Terri Sewell, the congresswoman from the 7th District, was elected in 2010, *The Washington Post* lauded her as "the breakout star" of the Congressional Black Caucus. A personable consensus builder, Sewell has shown policy interests that go beyond the usual focus on civil rights and an ideology that doesn't always fit liberal pigeonholes.

Sewell was born in Huntsville and raised in Selma, a hotbed of activity for the civil rights movement. She grew up near the famed Edmund Pettus Bridge, the site of the "Bloody Sunday" clash between protest marchers and state troopers. Sewell's family offered shelter for wayward travelers making the famed march from Selma to Montgomery in 1965. Hailing from such a place, "you appreciate the significance of your elders' fight for voting rights and civil rights," said Sewell, who was two months old during the march. Her mother, Nancy Sewell, was the first African-American woman elected to the Selma City Council. Her father was the high school basketball coach at Selma High School, where Sewell was the first black valedictorian. "Well, when you can get no dates because your daddy is a coach, all you can really do is study, right?" she joked.

Sewell earned her undergraduate degree from Princeton University. During that time, she took part in a Big Sister program and drew inspiration from the mentor assigned to her, Michelle Robinson, later first lady Michelle Obama. While Sewell was writing her senior thesis at Princeton, she met former Democratic Rep. Shirley Chisholm of New York, the first African-American woman elected to Congress and later a candidate for president, who was retired by then and teaching at Mount Holyoke College. "I don't know if anybody could ever follow in Shirley Chisholm's footsteps, but I can tell you that I was inspired by her whole life story," Sewell said.

Sewell later studied politics at Oxford University on a scholarship, earning a master's degree. A theater buff, she dabbled in drama while at Oxford, directing and starring in the play *For Colored Girls Who Have Considered Suicide When the Rainbow is Enuf* by Ntozake Shange. Later, while earning her law degree from Harvard, Sewell was a classmate of future President Barack Obama. At Harvard, she took a year off to turn her master's thesis into a book called *Black Tribunes: Race and Representation in British Politics*.

After graduating, Sewell clerked for a U.S. District Court judge in Birmingham, then in 1994 moved to New York City to work as a lawyer on Wall Street. Returning home to Alabama to help care for her ailing father after he suffered several strokes, she was a bond lawyer and a partner in a Birmingham law firm.

When Democratic Rep. Artur Davis decided to leave the House after four terms to run for governor, Sewell jumped into the primary contest against eight other candidates. They included prominent local figures Earl Hilliard Jr., son of former Rep. Earl Hilliard, and Jefferson County Commissioner Shelia Smoot. Sewell had lower name recognition than Hilliard or Smoot, but she made up for it by outraising the other candidates with both a local and national fundraising network. She finished first in the Democratic primary with 37 percent of the vote. Smoot snagged second place with 29 percent, setting up a runoff. Smoot got the endorsement of House Majority Whip James Clyburn, but Sewell outspent Smoot by nearly $1 million. In a relatively congenial runoff, Sewell won, 55%-45%. She has not faced a competitive contest since.

In the House, Sewell has been more of a centrist than most of her Black Caucus colleagues. She serves as vice-chair of the New Democrat Coalition - moderate House Democrats who work on job promotion and innovation, often with business groups. Her Almanac vote ratings in 2015 ranked her among the more conservative House Democrats. She hit it off with her classmate from Alabama, Republican Martha Roby. As first-term members of the Agriculture Committee, they worked together on a bill to reduce some of the most fertile acreage eligible for the federal Conservation Reserve Program in response to farmers who said that too much cropland was being lost to the program. In 2016, they jointly advocated moving F-35 fighter planes to Montgomery's Dannelly Field Air Guard Station. On the Science, Space, and Technology Committee, Sewell joined Alabama Republicans in looking out for the state's NASA installations. She broke with Obama in supporting construction of the Keystone XL pipeline. But she also showed her loyalty to her party. When Davis switched parties and spoke at the 2012 Republican National Convention, Sewell blasted him for being "out of touch" and "never connected to the best interests of this district."

With increased seniority, Sewell gained assignments to influential House committees. In 2014, she joined the bipartisan support of legislation to preserve access to financing for manufactured housing, especially for low-income rural Americans. In 2015, Sewell became the ranking Democrat on the Intelligence subcommittee with oversight of Pentagon agencies. In 2017, she joined Ways and Means, where she said that she brought a unique voice as an African-American woman with the perspective of underserved communities in the industrial and rural South.

On other issues, she worked with a bipartisan group to file the Voting Rights Amendment Act of 2015, which was designed to restore a key section of the law that the Supreme Court had overturned in 2013. "I am pleased that both Democrats and Republicans recognize the need to strengthen federal voter protections," she said, while voicing regret that the limited proposal would not restore full Justice Department review of election-law changes in Alabama. At her urging, Obama designated parts of downtown Birmingham as a national historic monument, which made some of the sites eligible for renovation and tourist promotion.

Sewell gained national prominence and an emotional personal moment during the 50th anniversary commemoration in Selma of the march to Montgomery, which she and Roby helped to organize. Two years later, she took a more adversarial stance when she warned Alabama Republican Sen. Jeff Sessions that she would hold him accountable as attorney general "for protecting the precious civil and human rights of all Americans."

Central Alabama: Birmingham, Tuscaloosa, Parts of Montgomery

Population		**Race and Ethnicity**		**Income**	
Total	676,605	White	32.3%	Median Income	$32,245 (431 out of 435)
Land area	10,156	Black	63.1%		
Pop/ sq mi	66.6	Latino	2.7%		
Born in state	80.2%	Asian	0.7%	Under $50,000	67.0%
		Two races	0.9%	$50,000-$99,999	22.7%
Age Groups		Other	0.3%	$100,000-$199,999	8.9%
Under 18	22.6%			$200,000 or more	1.3%
18-34	26.9%	**Education**		Poverty Rate	28.8%
35-64	37.0%	H.S grad or less	50.9%		
Over 64	13.5%	Some college	30.4%	**Health Insurance**	
		College Degree, 4 yr	12.0%	With health insurance coverage	85.4%
Work		Post grad	6.6%		
White Collar	28.3%				
Sales and Service	50.2%	**Military**		**Public Assistance**	
Blue Collar	26.4%	Veteran	7.5%	Cash public assistance income	3.3%
Government	16.8%	Active Duty	0.1%		
				Food stamp/SNAP benefits	25.1%

Voter Turnout			
2015 Total Citizens 18+	512,476	2016 House Turnout as % CVAP	45%
2016 House turnout	233,028	2014 House Turnout as % CVAP	27%

2012 Presidential Vote		
Barack Obama	228,468	(73%)
Mitt Romney	85,106	(27%)

2016 Presidential Vote		
Hillary Clinton	204,585	(69%)
Donald Trump	83,916	(28%)

Cook Partisan Voting Index: D+20

Alabama has learned to celebrate its black heritage, building striking memorials to the civil rights movement in Montgomery and Birmingham, acknowledging its history as ground zero of white resistance to the empowerment of blacks in the 1950s and 1960s. Blacks first came here as slaves. The last slave ship to the United States, the *Clotilde*, docked in Mobile in 1859, where its cargo was then set free. Blacks were part of the great migration into the cotton lands after the Jacksonians swept the Indians out of the Southeast and sent them on their Trail of Tears to what is now Oklahoma. Today, Alabama's rural African Americans are still clustered in the Black Belt of fertile dark soil across the center of the state. In Selma, founded by Alabama's one vice president, William Rufus King, Sheriff Jim Clark's troops beat up peaceful marchers on the Edmund Pettus Bridge in demonstrations that led to the march on Montgomery and the 1965 Voting Rights Act. All 11 of Alabama's majority-black counties are in the rich farm country of the Black Belt, but most Alabama blacks now live in urban areas - one-quarter of them in metropolitan Birmingham.

After decades of urban decline, Birmingham has undergone a renaissance in recent years. The city pulled itself out of the spiral of abandoned neighborhoods, soaring joblessness and crime through the savvy use of public-private partnerships and other incentives. Numerous vacant and boarded up buildings have been supplanted by lofts and cafes for young professionals and empty-nesters, slowing the migration to the suburbs. The industrial flats of downtown Birmingham are reemerging as a population center. Crime zones like the Metropolitan Gardens public housing project were leveled and replaced with mixed-income apartments. 2015 brought new hotels and an entertainment district downtown. In 2016, planners unveiled specifics to expand Legacy Stadium in nearby Uptown. But change has come too slowly to stem the exodus from the city. Birmingham's population declined 12.6 percent from 2000 to 2010, though it remained steady from 2010 to 2015.

The 7th Congressional District of Alabama, which was created in 1992, is a majority African-American district that sprawls from Birmingham and Tuscaloosa to the western black precincts of Montgomery and nearly to Mobile County. Republican redistricting in 2011 made the 2nd and 3rd districts whiter and safer for the GOP, and further solidified the 7th for the Democrats. Some Democratic legislators protested these moves because they made it harder for the party to compete in the rest of the state.

The Alabama River flows on the district's eastern edge, while the Tombigbee River straddles the western border. The area is filled with old plantations and a thriving catfish industry. The district takes in part of Tuscaloosa, home of the University of Alabama, and nearby Vance, site of a Mercedes factory. In 2015, company officials announced a $1.3 billion expansion at the Vance plant that will raise employment to 3,500 and increase production by 60 percent to 300,000 cars annually. The Mercedes growth has been accompanied by two large parts manufacturers nearby. In Montgomery, the huge Hyundai assembly plant has spurred worker-training programs in local high schools and colleges. Even with some recent economic progress, this remains one of the poorest districts in the nation. Growth in Birmingham continues to be outpaced by other southern metro areas.

The district is 64 percent African American and solidly Democratic - the only district in Alabama where Democrats have an expectation of victory. In his two campaigns, Barack Obama, who spoke in Selma in March 2015 to commemorate the 50th anniversary of the bloody march to Montgomery, swept each Black Belt county by a large margin. Overall, he won this district with 72% in 2008 and 73% in 2012. In her losing campaign in 2016, Hillary Clinton won the Black Belt counties and 69% of the district vote.

★ ALASKA ★

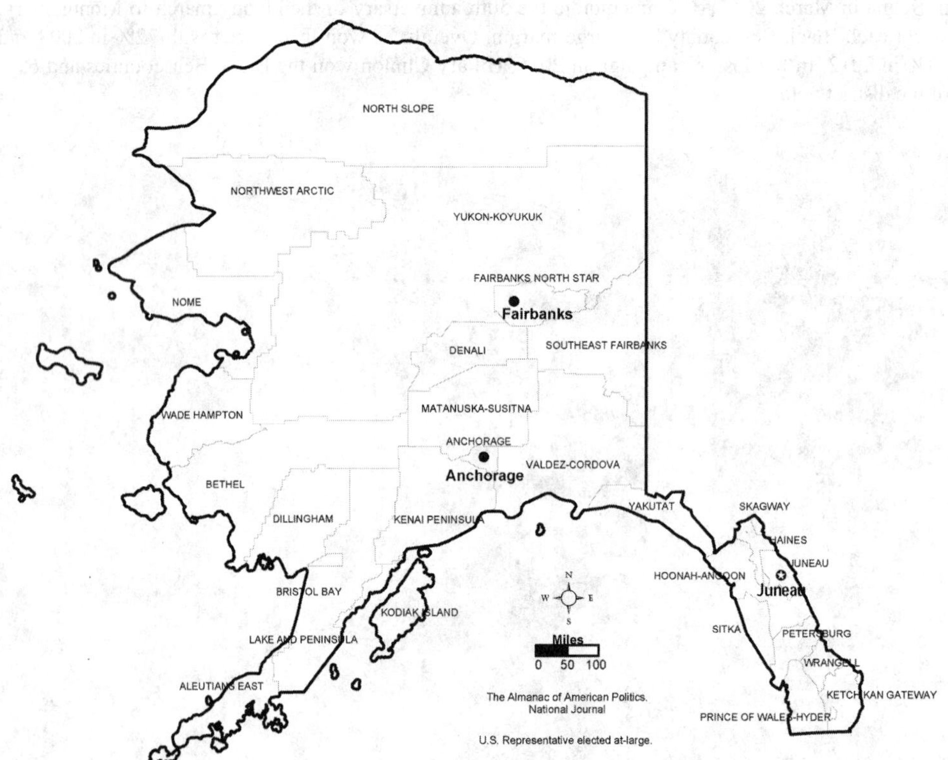
NORTH SLOPE
NORTHWEST ARCTIC
YUKON-KOYUKUK
FAIRBANKS NORTH STAR
Fairbanks
NOME
DENALI
SOUTHEAST FAIRBANKS
MATANUSKA-SUSITNA
WADE HAMPTON
ANCHORAGE
Anchorage
VALDEZ-CORDOVA
BETHEL
DILLINGHAM
KENAI PENINSULA
YAKUTAT
SKAGWAY
HAINES
JUNEAU
Juneau
HOONAH-ANGOON
BRISTOL BAY
KODIAK ISLAND
SITKA
PETERSBURG
LAKE AND PENINSULA
Miles
0 50 100
WRANGELL
ALEUTIANS EAST
KETCHIKAN GATEWAY
PRINCE OF WALES-HYDER
N
W
E
S
The Almanac of American Politics.
National Journal
U.S. Representative elected at-large.

Alaska -- far removed from the Lower 48, what Alaskans sometimes refer to as "Outside" -- maintains an individualistic culture that has responded with creativity to its unique conditions. But while it is dependent on Washington for federal largesse, the relationship between Washington and Alaska is often fraught. Alaska at once depends on subsidies and special treatment and is resentful of what it considers Washington's heavy-handed intervention.

The father of Alaska was Secretary of State William Seward, who took advantage of an opportunity in 1867 to create an American Pacific empire by purchasing the region from Russia for $7.2 million. The Alaska territory owes much of its early growth to federal decisions. While the state burst into national consciousness with the Klondike Gold Rush of 1897, its largest city, Anchorage, had its beginnings in 1914 as the chief worksite for the federal government's Alaska Railroad, completed in 1923. Its famous sled dog race, the Iditarod, started in 1973 on a trail originally cleared and graded by the Army after Congress established the Alaska Road Commission in 1905. The race honors the 1925 emergency 20-team relay that delivered medicine from Nenana across nearly 700 miles to icebound Nome in 127 hours, saving hundreds of lives from a diphtheria outbreak, a feat that generated headlines in the lower 48. Alaska became strategic territory in World War II, when the Aleutian Islands of Attu and Kiska were invaded by a small force of Japanese, the only part of the United States occupied by a foreign enemy since the War of 1812. Alaska, with only 72,000 people when the war began, was connected to the states by the Army's Alcan Highway, completed in 1942; by 1943, there were 152,000 troops in the territory. Alaska is the only state abutting Russia, across the Bering Strait and over the North Pole-you actually can see Russia from part of Alaska-and the state maintains a strategic geographic position. The military is a major presence at Joint Base Elmendorf-Richardson near Anchorage and at Fort Wainwright and Eielson Air Force Base near Fairbanks, with interceptors for the national missile defense system not far to the south at Fort Greely. The state also has the highest per capita rate of military veterans in the nation.

The third least-populated state and the least densely populated state, Alaska's 741,000 people amount to less than one-quarter of 1 percent of the nation's population, yet Alaska's land area is equal to one-fifth of the Lower 48. If superimposed on the continental United States, Alaska would stretch from Florida to California. The westernmost Aleutians are closer to Tokyo than to Juneau and farther west than Wellington, New Zealand. Many Alaskans have no access to state roads and are reachable only by boat, airplane, dog sleds and snowmachines. About two-thirds of the population resides in Anchorage and the nearby Kenai Peninsula and Matanuska-Susitna ("Mat-Su") Valley. This plus the Fairbanks area, accounting for about one-eighth of the population, are the fastest-growing parts of Alaska. The Panhandle, with about one-tenth of the population, is the old Alaska, its towns settled by Russians built up against steep mountains on inlets from the Pacific. This includes the state capital of Juneau, which is inaccessible by road or highway-you have to ferry or fly in. The rest of the population lives in the Bush and the Aleutians, scattered in small towns, Native settlements and the wilderness. (Only in Alaska does the term "Bush Democrat" not refer to a cross-party supporter of the presidential dynasty.)

Alaska became a state in January 1959. While this technically ended federal dominance,Washington remains the largest landowner in Alaska, with roughly 60 percent of the state's total area under the supervision of more than a dozen federal agencies, including national parks, wildlife refuges, national forests, military bases and the North Slope National Petroleum Reserve. A 2014 Pew Charitable Trusts study found that Alaska ranked third in the nation in terms of per capita total federal spending in the states, trailing only Maryland and Virginia, home to legions of federal employees. In federal grants alone, Alaska ranked number one. Alaskans continue to seek federal subsidies for intrastate air service, loan guarantees for the fishing industry and funding for the Alaska Railroad. The state's special needs, its longtime Sen. Ted Stevens used to argue, justify its special treatment. Sometimes the state and the federal government agree –in 2015, President Obama acted to rename Mt. McKinley, the nation's highest peak, "Denali," its ancestral name. The move, which countered longstanding efforts by the Ohio congressional delegation to honor one of the state's presidents, was popular in Alaska. But such agreement is not always the case.

Alaska's forbidding terrain is responsible for some of its economic assets. In 1959, Alaska's economy depended on fishing, oil production in Cook Inlet around Anchorage and the military-all federally regulated or controlled-and they continue to be important. It has more aircraft per capita than any other state, supporting a sizable general aviation sector. Private contractors provide much of the Post Office's service to the Bush. Alaska's fisheries accounted for more than half of the nation's seafood harvest in 2012, according to a report by the National Marine Fisheries Service. Tourism, the No. 2 private employer, has been on the rise, with cruise ships prowling the intra-coastal inlets amid glaciers and grizzlies, docking in Anchorage for side trips to Denali National Park and Preserve. Alaska has major mines producing gold, copper, coal and zinc. Twelve corporations created by the Alaska Native Claims Settlement Act have proved to be successful, not only in providing dividend income, elderly benefits and scholarships and employment opportunities for Natives, but also in helping them preserve Native traditions and adapt to Alaska's market economy at their own pace. The corporate model allows more continuity in office for the Alaska Native corporations' managers-although some have made bad decisions and been thrown out. This cumulative voting method, by which a minority can get a seat on the board, has produced management that is sensitive to all opinions. Huge windfalls are avoided because all corporations share 70 percent of profits from mineral sales. In 2010, the Native corporations had gross revenues of more than $8 billion and employed some 16,000 Alaskans. But not all is rosy. Native villages in the Bush have little in the way of a private-sector economy, and alcoholism, domestic violence and suicide rates remain high. Just 57 percent of Alaska Natives graduated from high school on time in 2013, more than 20 points below the rate for white students, while a mere 7 percent of Native Alaskan fourth-graders were rated proficient in reading by the 2013 National Assessment of Educational Progress.

But something else has transformed Alaska-something not fully envisioned by those who successfully obtained statehood in 1959. Within a decade, Alaska's economy and public life were reshaped by the discovery of North Slope oil. It began suddenly, almost accidentally, as Arco chief executive Robert Anderson, after seven dry wells on Prudhoe Bay, decided to use a nearby drilling rig to make another try-and as a natural gas flare shot 30 feet in the air discovered the 12-billion barrel North Slope oil field. This was the greatest single oil strike in U.S. history and the beginning of much of today's Alaska.

Finding oil in Prudhoe Bay was somewhat akin to finding it on the moon. It was not clear in 1968 who owned the oil or how it could be taken out. The Statehood Act of 1959 gave the state the right to choose its own public lands, but only after settling Native land claims. Because the Arctic Ocean ice broke up in late July in those days, and for only six weeks, the only feasible way to get the oil out was a pipeline. But environmentalists opposed that option for fear it would destroy the delicate permafrost and interfere with caribou migrations. Development-minded Alaskans got a pipeline bill through Congress in 1973, but the pipeline had to be built on stilts and wasn't opened until 1977. Then in 1980, after astute lobbying by environmentalists, Congress passed- over the objections of Alaska's two senators and Rep. Don Young-the Alaska National Interest Lands Conservation Act (ANILCA), which set aside 159 million acres as national parks, national monuments or wilderness: one-third of the state was protected (or barred) from development. Much, if not all, of this turned out to be for the best. The pipeline came on line just as oil prices were approaching a peak, thus generating maximum revenues to the state, which gets most of the royalties. At the same time, the environment was protected far better than it would have been without the safeguards. With fluctuations, the Western Arctic herd of caribou grew from 75,000 in 1976 to 235,000 in 2013, and Native Alaskans got more autonomy than the non-Native majority of Alaskans would have given them. With oil providing some 85 percent of its revenue, the state government abolished its income tax in 1980-it doesn't have a state sales tax either-and created a low-tax regime. Wisely, Alaska did not squander its windfall. In 1976, Republican Gov. Jay Hammond persuaded the legislature to establish a Permanent Fund for most of the oil revenues. Each year, it presents every resident with a dividend based on a five-year rolling average of the Permanent Fund's financial performance, which is now largely generated by stock, bond and real estate investments, not oil revenue. The dividend was more than $2,000 in 2015, only the second time it exceeded that threshold since distributions to Alaskans began in 1982.

Over the years, Alaskans' efforts to develop energy resources outside of the North Slope have been frustrated, causing no end of friction. Its congressional delegation, despite its relative seniority, was unable to overcome the opposition of environmental groups to oil drilling in the Arctic National Wildlife Refuge (ANWR) east of Prudhoe Bay. ANWR was estimated to have 9 to 16 billion barrels, and horizontal drilling techniques meant that the drilling footprint could be reduced to the size of Washington's Dulles Airport. Congress was on the verge of approving ANWR drilling in 1989 when the *Exxon Valdez* ran aground in Prince William Sound near the pipeline terminus at Valdez. The ensuing uproar over environmental damage stalled the drilling proposal, and Democrats managed to block its approval in subsequent Congresses. Then, in January 2015, Obama proposed the largest-ever wilderness designation in ANWR, which would place its potentially oil-rich coastal plain and millions of additional acres off-limits to future oil and gas development. The month prior to his announcement on ANWR, the president had ordered an indefinite ban on oil and gas drilling in Alaska's Bristol Bay. While Obama did approve an application by Royal Dutch Shell to drill for oil and gas in the Chukchi Sea based on a lease signed during the presidency of George W. Bush, his administration – concerned about climate change, which was predicted to cause erosion and melting through large swaths of Alaska – continued to erect barriers. In December 2016, Obama ordered 125 million acres of the Arctic Ocean, holding perhaps 27 billion barrels of oil, closed to future extraction permanently, though it was unclear whether President Donald Trump or another future president could reverse the decision. While it would likely take decades for the oil to begin flowing even if it had been approved, the state's politicians blasted the decision, as they have previous decisions to bar resource development. "To lock it up against any further exploration or development activity is akin to saying that the voices of activists who live in Lower 48 cities have a greater stake than those to whom the Arctic is our front yard and our backyard," said Bill Walker, the state's independent governor.

A more immediate threat to the state's petro-fueled hayride, however, is the global petroleum price slump. North Slope oil production had already been falling for decades, peaking in 1988 at almost 2 million barrels a day and settling in 2014 at less than 500,000 barrels a day. Initially, the decline was cushioned by a steady rise in global demand and the price for oil. Then the wellhead price for Alaskan crude began a long slide, prompting a drop in the state's flow of oil royalties. At the same time, receipts from the corporate, production and property taxes that the state levies on oil companies also tumbled. By late 2016, statewide unemployment was 6.8 percent, more than 2 percentage points higher than the national average. "It's safe to say that by all measures, we are in a recession," said state economist Caroline Schultz in 2016 – just as many Americans felt they were finally crawling out of the shadow of the Great Recession. The fiscal hit from the oil slump led the state to project that it could run out of savings by 2019, threatening the dividend that residents had come to depend on.

Alaska's congressional delegation has been notable for longevity. GOP Rep. Don Young won his seat in a 1973 special election and, despite occasional turbulence, has been reelected ever since. Meanwhile, despite the fact that the state is about one-third non-white, the intense focus on the oil sector has helped make Alaska pretty solidly Republican; it did not elect a Democrat to the Senate between 1974 and 2008, when Nick Begich was elected for just one term. Initially, the state appeared not to be enamored of Donald Trump; he placed second in the Republican primary behind Ted Cruz, and for a while, the state seemed surprisingly close in general-election polling. On Election Day, however, Trump won the state by a margin similar to what previous Republicans have achieved. Punctuating the state's maverick streak, however, a coalition of 17 Democrats, two independents and three Republicans forged a majority in the state House after the 2016 elections, seemingly aligned with Walker, who himself had been elected in 2014 as a Republican-turned-Independent with a Democratic running mate. That said, don't count on a widespread Democratic resurgence. "The Democrats who think Alaska is tending blueward or at least purple have mistaken the tattooed waiter at their favorite bistro for the voter of tomorrow," wrote Michael Carey, an Alaska Dispatch News columnist. "Alaska may be going artisanal, but it is not going Democratic."

Population		Race and Ethnicity		Income	
Total	733,375	White	62.4%	Median Income	$72,515 (2 out of 50)
Land area	570,641	Black	3.2%		
Pop/ sq mi	1.3	Latino	6.5%	Under $50,000	33.5%
Born in state	41.1%	Asian	5.8%	$50,000-$99,999	33.2%
		Two races	7.4%	$100,000-$199,999	27.2%
Age Groups		Other	14.7%	$200,000 or more	6.1%
Under 18	25.7%			Poverty Rate	10.2%
18-34	23.9%	**Education**			
35-64	38.8%	H.S grad or less	35.7%	**Health Insurance**	
Over 64	9.0%	Some college	36.3%	With health insurance coverage	81.8%
		College Degree, 4 yr	17.9%		
Work		Post grad	10.1%	**Public Assistance**	
White Collar	36.2%				
Sales and Service	40.2%	**Military**		Cash public assistance income	6.3%
Blue Collar	23.6%	Veteran	13.1%		
Government	25.1%	Active Duty	3.0%	Food stamp/SNAP benefits	10.5%

Voter Turnout			
2015 Total Citizens 18+	523,946	2016 Pres Turnout as % CVAP	61%
2016 Pres Votes	318,608	2012 Pres Turnout as % CVAP	61%

Legislature	
Senate:	6D, 14R
House:	17D, 21R, 2I

Presidential Politics

2016 Democratic Caucus		
Bernie Sanders (D)	8,447	(80%)
Hillary Clinton (D)	2,146	(20%)
2016 Republican Caucus		
Ted Cruz (R)	8,369	(36%)
Donald Trump (R)	7,740	(34%)
Marco Rubio (R)	3,488	(15%)
Ben Carson (R)	2,492	(11%)

2016 Presidential Vote		
Donald Trump (R)	163,387	(51%)
Hillary Clinton (D)	116,454	(37%)
Gary Johnson (L)	18,725	(6%)
2012 Presidential Vote		
Mitt Romney (R)	164,676	(55%)
Barack Obama (D)	122,640	(41%)
Gary Johnson (L)	7,392	(2%)

Cook Partisan Voting Index: R+9

While some pre-election polling suggested Hillary Clinton might have a shot at carrying the Last Frontier, Donald Trump handily won the state 51%-37%. That 14-percentage point advantage was almost identical to Mitt Romney's margin over Barack Obama four years earlier. Notwithstanding the flow of federal resources to the state, Alaska's voters have a healthy suspicion of Washington, particularly when it comes to the federal government's oversight of Alaska's natural resources. Many Alaskans chafed at Obama administration environmental orders limiting oil and gas extraction in the state. Trump's comfortable victory came despite the public declarations of the state's two GOP senators that they wouldn't vote for him in November, after a 2005 tape surfaced in which Trump made lewd comments about women to then *Access Hollywood* host Billy Bush.

Both parties hold caucuses to allocate their national convention delegates, which didn't work to the advantage of either Trump or Clinton. With just over 23,000 participants, Texas Sen. Ted Cruz edged out Trump in the GOP caucuses, 36%-34%. Vermont Sen. Bernie Sanders overwhelmed Clinton 80%-20%, among 10,593 Democratic caucus attendees. Alaska gave Sanders his second-largest margin of victory over Clinton in the Democratic nominating contest, eclipsed only by his showing in his home state.

Alaska has traditionally been hospitable to third-party candidates: in 1992 Ross Perot won 28 percent here, his second-best showing in the country; and in 2000, Ralph Nader captured 10 percent of the vote, his best showing. But in 2016, Alaskans seemed less enthralled by third-party options. Libertarian nominee Gary Johnson won less than 6 percent, and Green Party standard-bearer Jill Stein managed less than 2 percent.

When Alaska and Hawaii were admitted to the union in 1959, it was expected that Alaska would vote Democratic and Hawaii Republican. It has turned out to be the other way around. Alaska has voted for the GOP nominee in every presidential election except for 1964, the LBJ landslide year. Rural areas in the northern and western regions of the state, including hundreds of tiny settlements of Native Alaskans are the most Democratic, while Republicans are strongest in the "Mat-Su" territory (short for the borough of Matanuska-Susitna), containing the northern suburbs of Anchorage. Roughly 40 percent of the state's population lives in Anchorage, its largest city, which tends to vote Republican; Democrats have some bastions there, as well.

Neither Trump nor Clinton made a 2015-16 campaign stop in Alaska. The state is remembered for the visit Richard Nixon paid in 1960, two days before Election Day, in order to fulfill his pledge to campaign in all 50 states. The distant stop on the presidential trail consumed precious time on Nixon's closing days' schedule that might have been better spent stumping in Texas or Illinois, states with far more electoral votes that Nixon lost by a whisker.

Congressional Districts

115th Congress Lineup	1R	114th Congress Lineup	1R

Governor

Bill Walker (I)

Elected 2014, term expires 2018, 1st term; b. Apr. 16, 1951, Fairbanks, AK; Lewis and Clark College, B.S. 1973; U. of Puget Sound, J.D. 1983; Christian; Married (Donna); 4 children.

Elected Office: Valdez City Council, 1977-1979; Valdez Mayor, 1979.

Professional Career: Commercial fisherman, 1969; Construction worker, 1970-1974; Owner, Bill Walker Construction Company, 1975-1980; Practicing attorney, 1983-1995; Owner/Attorney, Walker and Levesque LLC/Walker Richards LLC Law Firm, 1995-present.

Office: 120 4th Street, Juneau, 99801; Website: gov.alaska.gov.

Election Results

Election	Name (Party)	Vote (%)
2014 General	Bill Walker (I)	134,658 (48%)
	Sean Parnell (R)	128,435 (46%)
	Carolyn "Care" Clift (L)	8,985 (3%)
	J.R. Myers (C)	6,987 (3%)

Bill Walker won the governor's seat in November 2014 as an independent, defeating Republican incumbent Sean Parnell in a campaign that was unconventional, even by Alaska's eccentric political standards. And Walker, a former Republican serving with a Democratic lieutenant governor, continued to display a feisty independence.

Walker was born in Fairbanks, the youngest of four children, and raised in Delta Junction and Valdez. His father, a World War II veteran, was working in home construction when the 1964 earthquake struck, destroying the family's home and much of the town of Valdez. At 12, Walker helped provide for the family by working as a janitor at the local post office. He worked his way through Lewis and Clark College in Portland, Oregon, as a carpenter and laborer on the Trans-Alaska Pipeline and joined the family construction trade after graduating from college with a B.S. in business administration. He won a seat on the Valdez City Council in 1977 and two years later, at the age of 27, was elected the city's youngest-ever mayor. After one term he went to law school and, after graduating in 1983, joined an old-line Anchorage firm. He founded his own firm, Walker Richards, in 1995, with a primary focus on oil and gas and municipal law. He represented several local communities and served as general counsel to the Alaska Gasline Port Authority. Walker ran for governor in 2010, but lost to incumbent Sean Parnell in the GOP primary. In the 2014 cycle, he began running against Parnell for the Republican nod, then dropped out of the primary to run as an independent and head directly to the general election.

Although his popularity was ebbing in 2014, Parnell looked like a reasonable bet to win a three-way race with Walker and Democrat Byron Mallott, the former mayor of Juneau and a native Alaskan. But the contest was upended in September when Mallott dropped his bid for governor and agreed to become Walker's running mate on a "unity ticket," something the independent had been urging in order to have a better chance at dislodging Parnell. (An unusually high 53 percent of the Alaska electorate is registered as nonpartisan or undeclared.) This was not the first time Mallott had backed an independent - in 2010 he strayed from the party line and signed on to co-chair Lisa Murkowski's independent Senate bid. The Alaska Democratic state central committee, eager to oust Parnell, endorsed Mallott's switch and an Anchorage judge subsequently upheld his pairing with Walker. The fusion ticket did not agree on everything - Walker was pro-life and Mallott was pro-choice-but the two vowed to work together on the major issues confronting the state.

Parnell was weakened with the release of a federal report in September about a sexual-assault scandal in the Alaska National Guard. Walker also opposed Parnell on his decision to sign legislation in 2013 that significantly lowered the oil-production taxes that had been raised by GOP Gov. Sarah Palin, whom Parnell had served with as lieutenant governor. Walker, echoing Palin's populism, declared he would not bow to oil companies' interests to gain votes. The independent also supported expanding Medicaid coverage in Alaska, which Parnell opposed. And when a U.S. District Court struck down the state's ban on same-sex marriage in October, Walker criticized Parnell for pledging to appeal the ruling. Walker said he did not agree with same-sex marriage but would "uphold the laws of the land," and warned that spending state resources on an appeal was unwise. The race was already one of the most exotic contests of 2014 when in the waning days of the campaign, tea party heroine Palin endorsed Walker and accused Parnell, her ex-running mate, of "caving" to Big Oil. The Walker-Mallott ticket won by about 6,200 votes out of 285,000 cast, making it one of the closest elections in state history.

Of Walker's first seven major selections to head state agencies, only one, Craig Richards, Walker's former law partner and his pick for attorney general, was a registered Republican. His choices to run the departments of health and social services, environmental conservation, labor, natural resources, revenue, and public safety were not enrolled in either of the two major parties. Not long after he took office, Walker booted three energy careerists off the Alaska Gasline Development Corporation, the public entity that is working with major oil companies to build a pipeline to transport natural gas from the North Slope to the Kenai Peninsula for export overseas. Walker's management of the corporation rankled Republican House Speaker Mike Chenault, who had personally backed one of the booted commissioners, a veteran Texas-based pipeline construction consultant. The early jousting between Walker and Chenault, seemed to foreshadow a rocky relationship between the two leaders. It didn't help matters that Chenault's chief of staff had been Parnell's campaign manager.

In March, Chenault introduced legislation that blocked Walker from using the Development Corporation to come up with alternatives to the Alaska LNG Project Pipeline. Walker seemed to take Chenault's move as an affront to his authority. At press conference he brandished a copy of the bill and asked, in an annoyed tone, "Are you kidding me?" A month later, he carried out his promise to veto the measure. In May, the Republican-run House Finance Committee effectively tabled Walker's Medicaid expansion proposal. A few days later, Walker returned the favor and vetoed most elements of a budget passed by Republican lawmakers, claiming it was woefully underfunded, a result of the collapse in oil revenues coming into the state coffers.

During the second year of his governorship, a worsening oil and gas slump sent the economy reeling, which in turn walloped the state budget to the tune of a $4 billion deficit. It was feared that the state could run out of savings by 2019 – meaning an end to the state permanent fund dividend program that shares oil proceeds with residents. Walker and the Republican-led legislature were on a collision course for a government shutdown by July 2016; the legislature rejected his $700 million proposal for new sales and income taxes. But the two sides reached a compromise in May 2016, averting a shutdown. Walker also prevailed in the battle over Medicaid expansion, with the program beginning in September 2015 and helping nearly 18,000 Alaskans secure coverage (and setting up a future budget debate when federal subsidies are reduced and the state share of the costs increase). After Walker prevailed in court to keep the program alive, a House-Senate committee that had been appealing the decision moved to end its lawsuit, effectively enshrining the program.

A recall effort promoted by former U.S. Senate candidate Joe Miller has not gathered much steam, and Walker's surgery to treat prostate cancer appeared to be successful. Then, soon after the 2016 election, he got good news when Democrats and breakaway Republicans formed a new leadership coalition in the state House that broadly shares Walker's fiscal approach. As Walker runs for a second term in 2018, he can expect support from Democrats but a challenge from Republicans, whether it's from Parnell or someone else on the GOP's deep Alaska bench.

Senior Senator

Lisa Murkowski (R)

Appointed Dec. 2002, term expires 2022, 3rd full term; b. May 22, 1957, Ketchikan; Willamette University (OR), Att., 1977; Georgetown University (DC), B.A., 1980; Willamette University College of Law (OR), J.D., 1985, Roman Catholic; Married (Verne Martell); 2 children.

Elected Office: AK House, 1998-2002.

Professional Career: Anchorage Dist. Court Clerk's Office, Attorney, 1987-1989; Practicing attorney, 1989-1998.

DC Office: 522 HSOB 20510, 202-224-6665, Fax: 202-224-5301, murkowski.senate.gov.

State Offices: Anchorage, 907-271-3735; Fairbanks, 907-456-0233; Juneau, 907-586-7277; Kenai, 907-283-5808; Ketchikan, 907-225-6880; Wasilla, 907-376-7665.

Committees: *Appropriations*: Commerce, Justice, Science & Related Agencies, Department of Defense, Department of Homeland Security, Department of the Interior, Environment & Related Agencies (Chmn), Energy & Water Development, Military Construction & Veteran Affairs & Related Agencies. *Energy & Natural Resources (Chmn)*: Energy, National Parks, Public Lands, Forests & Mining, Water & Power. *Health, Education, Labor & Pensions*: Children & Families, Primary Health & Retirement Security. *Indian Affairs*.

Group Ratings

	ADA	ACLU	AFL-CIO	LCV	ITI	COC	HAFA	ACU	CFG	FRC
2016	-	64%	-	29%	100%	88%	35%	54%	50%	100%
2015	25%	C	42%	4%	C	93%	C	48%	49%	50%

Almanac Ratings 2015

	Economy	Social	Foreign	Composite
Liberal	55%	15%	31%	33%
Conservative	45%	86%	69%	67%

Key Votes of the 114th Congress

1. Keystone pipeline	Y	5. National Security Data	Y	9. Gun Sales Checks	N
2. Export-Import Bank	N	6. Iran Nuclear Deal	Y	10. Sanctuary Cities	Y
3. Debt Ceiling Increase	Y	7. Puerto Rico Debt	Y	11. Planned Parenthood	Y
4. Homeland Security $$	Y	8. Loretta Lynch A.G	N	12. Trade deals	Y

Election Results

Election	Name (Party)	Vote (%)		Cand. Spent	Ind. Exp. Support	Ind. Exp. Oppose
2016 General	Lisa Murkowski (R)	138,149	(44%)	$5,905,748	$147,178	
	Joe Miller (L)	90,825	(29%)	$727,527		
	Margaret Stock (I)	41,194	(13%)	$708,297		
	Ray Metcalfe (D)	36,200	(12%)	$12,355		
2016 Primary	Lisa Murkowski (R)	39,545	(72%)			
	Bob Lochner (R)	8,480	(15%)			
	Paul Kendall (R)	4,272	(8%)			
	Thomas Lamb (R)	2,996	(5%)			

Prior winning percentages: 2010 (39%), 2004 (49%)

Since the seating of the first Congress nearly 230 years ago, there have been no less than 45 instances of sons following their fathers into Senate service. To date, there has been only one woman in this category: Republican Lisa Murkowski, now Alaska's senior senator, who was appointed in 2002 by her father, then-Gov. Frank Murkowski, to fill the Senate vacancy created when he resigned to become governor. Father and daughter have occupied not only the same Senate seat, but the same committee chairmanship: Energy and Natural Resources, whose legislative jurisdiction is crucial to their vast, sparsely populated home state, where more than 60 percent of the land area is owned by the federal government, and 90 percent of the state's revenues are derived from the oil industry. Lisa Murkowski assumed the chairmanship of Energy and Natural Resources in 2015, after the Republicans regained control of the chamber following eight years in the minority; Frank Murkowski claimed the chairman's gavel 20 years earlier, in 1995, and held it for more than six years.

But, philosophically, Lisa Murkowski is often not her father's daughter. If Frank Murkowski, now 84 and retired, was largely a traditional conservative, his offspring has been more of a Republican moderate with a decided libertarian streak: She supports abortion rights, while her father was an abortion opponent, and she has been at odds with GOP conservatives on issues ranging from gay rights to climate change. Such independence has at times created political problems for her back home. Lisa Murkowski, in three statewide election general election campaigns, has never won more than 49 percent. In fact, she is the only Senator to ever have done so. Re-election to her second term, in 2010, proved particularly arduous. Ousted by a tea party conservative in the Republican primary, she won the general election as a write-in candidate. She became only the second senator ever to win via write-in, matching an electoral feat that the late Strom Thurmond had accomplished in South Carolina more than a half-century earlier.

The candidate who upset Murkowski in the 2010 primary, attorney Joe Miller, contended that, "compromise is destroying the nation." In contrast, Murkowski has established a reputation for a willingness to reach across the aisle throughout her Senate tenure; during her first year as Energy and Natural Resources chairman, she crafted a bipartisan energy bill that cleared the Senate with 85 votes. Murkowski does hew to a hardline in terms of what she sees as the economic prerogatives of her home state, fiercely resisting efforts by the federal government to restrict Alaska's ability to access its energy resources. But if the state's long-time senior senator, the late Republican Ted Stevens, was known for berating colleagues on the Senate floor while wearing a tie emblazoned with the Incredible Hulk, the personable Murkowski is known more forher calm albeit steely resolve. "Channeling my inner #Hulk while meeting with the press," she once posted on her Instagram account, according to a 2015 profile of her in *High Country News*.

Murkowski, the first Alaskan-born U.S. senator,was born in Ketchikan, at the southern end of Alaska's Panhandle, in 1957, two years before Alaska achieved statehood. The family moved up the Panhandle in the early 1960s to Wrangell, then known as the timber capital of Alaska, where Frank Murkowski -- a native of Seattle, Washington -- managed a bank. A decade later, the Murkowskis moved 900 miles further north, to Fairbanks, then reaping the economic benefits of construction of the Trans-Alaska Pipeline, which opened in 1977.

Lisa Murkowski graduated from Georgetown University in 1980, the year her father was first elected to the Senate, and went on toearn a law degree from the Willamette University College of Law in Salem, Oregon, in 1985. She settled in Anchorage, serving as an Anchorage District Court attorney before going into private law practice. But in 1998, Murkowski -- said to have been bitten by the political bug when she was just 13, during her father's unsuccessful 1970 race for Alaska's at-large U.S. House seat -- launched her own political career. Motivated to run in part by concern about declines in two mainstays of the Alaskan economy, oil and timber, she was elected to the state House from a district that includes north Anchorage.

The independent streak that Murkowski has displayed throughout her political career was evident during her state legislative tenure. When Alaska faced a $1.1 billion budget shortfall in 2002, she was a leader in the bipartisan Fiscal Policy Caucus that pushed for a tax hike, including raising the alcohol tax from 3 cents to 10 cents a drink. It put her at odds with her father, then running for governor on a pledge of no new taxes. Her bill was enacted, making Alaska the state with the highest alcohol tax in the country. Some conservatives derisively referred to her and her allies as "RIMs"-Republican Invertebrate Moderates. Facing a conservative challenger in the 2002 primary, Murkowski was renominated by a margin of just 57 votes. Nonetheless, after the general election, she was chosen as the state House majority leader.

She was not in that leadership position for long. Alaskans elected her father to the governorship by a wide margin, though he had two years left in his Senate term. (Republican state legislators saw to it that he-not outgoing Democratic Gov. Tony Knowles-appointed a successor. Earlier in 2002, they passed, over Knowles' veto, a law barring a governor from appointing a successor until five days after the vacancy occurred.) Frank Murkowski compiled a long list of possible successors, saying he looking for someone whose views on Alaska issues were in sync with his, had legislative experience, and was young enough to serve many years. Among the candidates: then-state Sen. Ben Stevens, Ted Stevens' son, and a rising political star named Sarah Palin, the former mayor of Wasilla. In an interview more than a decade afterward, Frank Murkowski recalledputting the candidates' names on a spreadsheet to compare qualifications. At first, he wasn't particularly serious about his daughter as a potential appointee -- but, as he studied the spreadsheet, she began moving up the list.

It was the first time in U.S. history that a governor had appointed his or her child to the Senate. "Lisa, who's your daddy?" read the derisive bumper stickers at the time. Even though most Republicans and many Democrats praised her abilities, others said her selection was all about nepotism. In response, Murkowski sought to highlight her political differences with the man who had appointed her. "We have always maintained very separate identities, at least for the time I have been in the legislature," she said. "I haven't called him for counseling, and typically he doesn't offer."

Still, Murkowski knew that, as she completed her father's term, critics would be watching to see if she was up to the job. In learning the ropes, Murkowski got significant help from Ted Stevens, whose senior position on the Appropriations Committee made him one of Capitol Hill's most influential lawmakers.Murkowski pushed through a bill, with Stevens' help, that included federal loan guarantees for a 3,500-mile pipeline that would bring natural gas from the North Slope to the lower 48 states-a major venture for Alaska. Stevens, in his characteristic blunt manner, praised Murkowski's work, declaring that she "is a hell of a lot better senator than her Dad ever was." (She later returned that loyalty in 2009 by asking President George W. Bush to pardon Stevens, who lost a 2008 re-election bid after he was convicted for concealing $250,000 in gifts from an oil executive. Bush declined, but Stevens' conviction eventually was tossed out because of prosecutorial misconduct.)

Nonetheless, as Murkowski entered the 2004 campaign, she was vulnerable. She turned back a challenge from the right, 58%-37%, in the primary, but in the general election, faced a tough challenge against Knowles. A Vietnam veteran and Yale classmate and friend of President George W. Bush, Knowles had twice been elected the city's mayor and twice won gubernatorial races. The nepotism issue loomed over the campaign. Fifty thousand voters signed a ballot measure to ban governors from appointing new senators, and it later passed with 56 percent of the vote. Stevens campaigned for Murkowski, stressing that she, at age 47, would have a chance of amassing more seniority than would 61-year-old Knowles. This strongly red state voted to give Bush a second term by a 25-point margin, helping Murkowski to eke out victory, 49%-46%, over the president's old college friend.

Murkowski's victory made her the first woman ever to be elected to Congress from Alaska. And it was Frank Murkowski rather than his daughter who ended up paying the political price for the nepotism controversy. Seeking a second term as governor in 2006, he finished third in a three-way primary, as Sarah Palin toppled him and went on to win the general election. Residual public anger over Murkowski's appointment of his daughter played a role in his electoral demise, although purchase of a state jet for his personal use and a pipeline deal criticized for its concessions to major oil companies contributed as well.

Two years later, Ted Stevens' re-election defeat -- eight days after his 2008 conviction on corruption charges for concealing gifts -- led to Lisa Murkowski assuming a much larger role in the Senate on Alaska-centric issues. With Stevens gone, she secured a seat on the Appropriations Committee, a critical post for a state so dependent on federal spending. (When the Republicans regained control of the Senate in 2014, Murkowski would find herself chairing not only the Energy and Natural Resources Committee but also the Appropriations Subcommittee on Interior, Environment and Related Agencies, giving her leverage over federal departments and agencies that wield broad jurisdiction within her home state.)

Republican leaders helped her in other ways during her first full term. She joined the GOP leadership as a counsel to then-Minority Leader Mitch McConnell, and when there was a reshuffling in the leadership structure in 2009, Murkowski become vice chair of the Senate Republican Conference. At the same time, Murkowski continued to demonstrate her independent streak. She joined just three other Republican senators to seek more civil liberties protections in the USA Patriot Act after President Bush asked Congress to reauthorize it. And, after President Barack Obama took office in 2009, Murkowski was one of just five Senate Republicans to help pass into law the so-called Matthew Shepard Act, expanding the federal hate crimes statute to cover a victim's sexual orientation or gender identity.

Murkowski's work on state issues, as well as frequent trips home to showcase her growing influence,was not enough to stave off Miller's vigorous primary challenge in 2010. A graduate of West Point and Yale Law School, the self-described "constitutional conservative" charged that Murkowski was a Washington insider who had abandoned Republican values by supporting abortion rights and higher taxes. His candidacy was backed by former Gov. Palin, two years after her 2008 stint as the Republican vice-presidential nominee. Palin's followers in the tea party movement flocked to Miller, who was also boosted by an anti-abortion referendum on the ballot that brought thousands of voters to the polls. Miller narrowly prevailed, 51%-49%.

Murkowski conceded, and, for a time, appeared ready to move back to Alaska with her husband, Verne Martell, and their two sons. But after repeated urgings from friends and supporters, she announced seven weeks before the general election that she would pursue a long shot write-in effort. Invoking the slogan "Let's Make History," she waged a spirited campaign, pointing to the considerable seniority that federallydependent Alaska would forsake if she lost. Her GOP colleagues in the Senate, prohibited by party rules from endorsing her as an independent, lined up behind Miller because, they said, Republican voters had spoken in the primary. But many were not enthusiastic, and Miller's campaign suffered from numerous missteps. A number of former staffers to Ted Stevens, who had died in a plane crash just weeks earlier, pitched into the Murkowski write-in effort. With the support of some Democrats seeking to block Miller from the Senate, Murkowski won a three-way contest with 39 percent to 35 percent for Miller; the Democratic candidate, Scott McAdams, was a distant third with 23 percent.

After the successful write-in campaign, there was some question about whether Murkowski would steer a moderate course and continue to show her independent bent -- or seek out issues to appease her conservative critics. In March 2011, *The New York Times* ran a story highlighting Murkowski's support for a bill to cut $2 billion from Head Start, a preschool program for impoverished children that she had supported in the past. Murkowski defended her vote,saying, "I did not get caught up in the individual cuts….My vote was a marker for moving towards a greater degree in a reduction in spending." However, two months later, in May 2011, she was one of only five Republican senators to vote against a House-passed budget bill by then- House Budget Committee Chairman Paul Ryan of Wisconsin that included a sweeping plan to restructure Medicare. For the most part, Murkowski's difficult victory appeared to accelerate her march to the political middle. *Almanac* vote ratings for 2015 showed her to be the second least conservative member of the 54-member Republican Conference on economic issues, the seventh least conservative on social issues.

In the 2010 lame-duck session that followed her re-election to a second full term, she was among just seven Republican senators to support the repeal of the military's "don't ask, don't tell policy" and in 2013, became the third GOP senator to publicly express support for gay marriage. Two years later, Murkowski was the lead Republican on a bill designed to restore several provisions of the Voting Rights Act ruled unconstitutional by the U.S. Supreme Court. Politically, her stance reflected the strong support that Alaska Natives had given her in the 2010 write-in effort. "The question of whether Alaska Natives have fair access to the voting booth has been litigated multiple times over the past several years. Impediments to voting in many of our rural communities because of distance and language need to be addressed, and my hope is that this legislation will resolve these issues," Murkowski declared.

During the Obama Administration's second term, Murkowski was supportive on several fronts. In March 2015, she was one of only seven GOP senators not to sign an open letter intended to undermine the Obama's efforts to reach a nuclear deal with Iran. Earlier, Murkowski was the only Republican not to back a GOP filibuster against a couple of Obama's appellate court nominees, arguing that judicial nominees should receive up-or-down votes. She initially was among a handful of Republicans to support holding hearings on Obama's 2016 nomination of Merrick Garland to the fill the Supreme Court vacancy created by the death of Antonin Scalia, although she later retreated from that position as Senate Republican leaders held firm to not allowing Obama to fill the slot during his last year in office. "Senator Murkowski respects the decision of the chair and members of the Judiciary Committee not to hold hearings on the nominee," Murkowski's spokeswoman told the *Times*.

One source of repeated confrontation with the Obama Administration was the state delegation's long-standing goal of opening up the Alaska National Wildlife Refuge to oil and gas exploration-a popular idea in the state, but one that has been rebuffed repeatedly in Washington. While the area houses a wide array of wildlife, it also is thought to hold large oil and gas reserves. Murkowski was incensed when Obama in 2015 said that he would ask Congress to designate 12 million of ANWR's 19 million acres as wilderness. She blasted the move as "a stunning attack on our sovereignty."Murkowski was perhaps equally enraged when Obama, a month before leaving office, invoked a 1953 law to bar new oil leases in most of the U.S. Arctic offshore waters by executive fiat. "The only thing more shocking than this reckless, short-sighted last-minute gift to the extreme environmental agenda is that President Obama had the nerve to claim he is doing Alaska a favor," Murkowski declared.

Such rhetoric has tended to mask the collaborative manner in which Murkowski has operated within the Energy and Natural Resources Committee as chairman, and, prior to that, in three terms as ranking minority member (2009-2015). Just prior to chairing the panel, Murkowski helped negotiate a sweeping compromise on public land use that was attached to must-pass defense legislation and signed by Obama at the end of 2014. It created 250,000 acres of Western wilderness and 140 miles of wild and scenic rivers, while also opening 110,000 acres to logging and mining. One provision that furthered Murkowski's long-time objectives transferred 70,000 acres of the Tongass National Forest to an Alaska Native corporation for logging.

In early 2015, Murkowski and the Energy and Natural Resources Committee ranking member, Maria Cantwell of Washington, went to work on comprehensive energy legislation. Environmental advocates, while complaining it did nothing to address climate change, liked its provisions for energy research and modernizing the electric grid. Congressional Democrats praised its inclusion of a permanent reauthorization of the Land and Water Conservation Fund for public land acquisition, while Republicans liked provisions to expedite the processing for liquefied natural gas terminals. But, after clearing the Senate in the spring of 2016 on an overwhelmingly bipartisan vote, it ran into a far more partisan House counterpart bill in conference committee. The legislation died in the lame duck session at the end of the year, as an irritated Murkowski told the *Alaska Journal of Commerce* that Ryan, by now the House Speaker, had opted to adjourn for a holiday gathering in New York rather than round up votes for the finalconference report on the bill. "The Speaker said 'We've run out of time' because they wanted to get on the party train," she gibed.

Murkowski entered the 2016 election in an unfamiliar position -- heavily favored to win a third full term. But, while far from a repeat of 2010, it was short of a cakewalk. Former Anchorage Mayor Dan Sullivan (no relation to Murkowski's junior colleague, GOP Sen. Dan Sullivan, who had ousted Democrat Mark Begich in 2014) filed to take on Murkowski, but then dropped his bid. Murkowski, taking no chances this time, started earlier and spent more money, winning the primary with 72 percent. She also benefitted from a split in the Democratic ranks: Democratic nominee Ray Metcalfe was a long-time critic of Begich, who returned the favor by endorsing independent candidate Margaret Stock, an attorney and former MacArthur Foundation "genius grant" awardee. Joe Miller, who opted not to challenge Murkowski in the primary, ran on the Libertarian Party line in the general election, and several officers of the state Republican Party organization resigned their posts to back him. Miller garnered 29 percent, second to Murkowski's victorious 44 percent showing.

During the campaign, Murkowski kept her distance from Republican presidential nominee Donald Trump. She never endorsed him, and, after the videotape surfaced of Trump making lewd comments about women, Murkowski called on him to step aside, saying he had "forfeited the right to be our party's nominee." After the November election, Murkowski was conciliatory; Trump's aggressive stance on energy exploration could help further her goal of increased oil and gas drilling at home. "When they want to work with us to do good things for Alaska, we'll be working together," Murkowski told *Alaska Public Media* about Trump."And if there are things that we need to block because they're bad for Alaska, we're going to do that." She continued, "So yes, I can absolutely [work] with anyone."

Junior Senator

Dan Sullivan (R)

Elected 2014, term expires 2020, 1st term; b. Nov 13, 1964, Fairview Park, OH; Harvard University, Bach. Deg.; Georgetown University Law Center (DC), J.D.; Georgetown University Law Center (DC), M.S.; Roman Catholic; Married (Julie Fate); 3 children.

Military Career: U.S Marine Corps, 1993-1997, U.S. Marine Corps Reserves, 1997-present (Afghanistan).

Professional Career: Law clerk, U.S Court of Appeals for the Ninth Circuit, 1997-1998; Law clerk, AK Supreme Court, 1998-1999; Assistant Secretary of State for Economic, Energy, and Business Affairs, U.S Department of State, 2006-2009; AK Attorney General, 2009-2010; Commissioner, AK Department of Natural Resources, 2010-2013.

DC Office: 702 HSOB 20510, 202-224-3004, Fax: 202-224-6501, sullivan.senate.gov.

State Offices: Anchorage, 907-271-5915; Fairbanks, 907-456-0261; Juneau, 907-586-7277; Kenai, 907-283-4000; Ketchikan, 907-225-6880; Wasilla, 907-357-9956.

Committees: *Armed Services*: Airland, Seapower, Strategic Forces. *Commerce, Science & Transportation*: Aviation Operations, Safety & Security, Communications, Technology, Innovation &

the Internet, Oceans, Atmosphere, Fisheries & Coast Guard (Chmn), Space, Science & Competitiveness. *Environment & Public Works*: Fisheries, Water, and Wildlife, Superfund, Waste Management, & Regulatory Oversight, Transportation & Infrastructure. *Veterans' Affairs*.

Group Ratings

	ADA	ACLU	AFL-CIO	LCV	ITI	COC	HAFA	ACU	CFG	FRC
2016	-	52%	-	24%	50%	86%	58%	80%	73%	100%
2015	5%	C	14%	0%	C	86%	C	88%	79%	91%

Almanac Ratings 2015

	Economy	Social	Foreign	Composite
Liberal	21%	0%	25%	15%
Conservative	79%	100%	75%	85%

Key Votes of the 114th Congress

1. Keystone pipeline	Y	5. National Security Data	Y	9. Gun Sales Checks	N
2. Export-Import Bank	Y	6. Iran Nuclear Deal	Y	10. Sanctuary Cities	Y
3. Debt Ceiling Increase	N	7. Puerto Rico Debt	Y	11. Planned Parenthood	Y
4. Homeland Security $$	N	8. Loretta Lynch A.G	N	12. Trade deals	Y

Election Results

Election	Name (Party)	Vote (%)	Cand. Spent	Ind. Exp. Support	Ind. Exp. Oppose
2014 General	Dan Sullivan (R)	135,445 (48%)	$7,797,250	$4,548,858	$15,791,064
	Mark Begich (D)	129,431 (46%)	$11,082,246	$7,103,335	$13,709,045
	Mark Fish (L)	10,512 (4%)			
	Ted Gianoutsos (I)	5,636 (2%)			
2014 Primary	Dan Sullivan (R)	44,740 (40%)			
	Joe Miller (R)	35,904 (32%)			
	Mead Treadwell (R)	27,807 (25%)			

Until his election in 2014, Republican Dan Sullivan, Alaska's junior senator, was sometimes referred to in his home state as the "other" Dan Sullivan -- so as not to confuse him with former Anchorage Mayor Dan Sullivan, an Alaska native. Foes of the future senator sometimes derided him as "Ohio Dan," an allusion to his upbringing in a Cleveland suburb and a continuing debate over precisely how long he had resided in Alaska. But as a Marine officer with a long resume of state and federal jobs, Sullivan overcame two high-profile opponents in the 2014 GOP Senate primary. And, in a very bad year for Democrats, Sullivan proved too formidable for Democratic incumbent Mark Begich, another former Anchorage mayor who is the second generation of a prominent Alaska political family; Sullivan triumphed by a narrow margin after a bruising campaign.

Once on Capitol Hill, Sullivan landed a seat on the Armed Services Committee and quickly served notice that he would bring his hawkish views to the debate over defense issues. During an Armed Services hearing in March 2015, Sullivan accused President Barack Obama of holding an "almost delusional view of the world environment" after the President suggested in his State of the Union address that the shadow of crisis had passed on various threats, from ISIS's advance to Russia's aggression and Iran's nuclear program. The same month, Sullivan was among 47 Republican signers of a controversial letter to the leaders of Iran, spearheaded by fellow freshman Sen. Tom Cotton of Arkansas, that sought to stymie an Iran nuclear deal by suggesting that an agreement could be revoked once Obama left office. Sullivan's in-state senior colleague, Lisa Murkowski, was among a handful of Republicans who declined to sign the letter.

Meanwhile, Sullivan -- who has spent two decades as a reservist after four years of active duty in the Marines -- repeatedly took aim at what he saw as the Obama White House's downplaying of the battle against ISIS. In May 2016, when a Navy SEAL was killed by ISIS forces while advising Kurdish forces in Iraq, a White House spokesman told reporters that the SEAL had not been on a combat mission. "The White House continues to diminish the service and sacrifice of our troops serving in Iraq, Syria, Afghanistan and elsewhere by peddling the fiction that they are not engaged in combat," snapped Sullivan, who has been called up for three tours of active duty as Marine reservist, most recently a six-week stint in Afghanistan in 2013. Sullivan is currently the only senator serving in the military reserves.

(Two other senators, Republicans Joni Ernst of Iowa and Lindsey Graham of South Carolina, resigned from the reserves in 2015.) But while Sullivan remains in the Marine Corps Forces Reserve with the rank of lieutenant colonel, he was forced to give up command of a California-based reserve unit shortly after he became a senator. At issue is the so-called Ineligibility Clause of Section I, Article 6 of the Constitution, prohibiting members of Congress from holding office in the executive branch. While his military experience was regarded as a significant political asset in his campaign for Senate, Sullivan contended it had given him a legislative edge as well. "Having first-hand experience, being able to talk about just how incredible Alaska is for military training, I think, gives me a lot of credibility as a senator to make the case to not only my fellow senators but to senior administration officials," he told *Alaska Public Media*.

His comments came as Sullivan sought to apply pressure on Army officials to slow or halt the transfer of troops from Joint Base Elmendorf-Richardson north of Anchorage. "They [Russia] have positioned four brigade size combat teams and built 11 new airfield in the Arctic. What are we doing? Squat," he complained in an interview with the *Alaska Journal of Commerce* at the end of 2015. Sullivan's other committee assignments have enabled him to look out for Alaskan interests as well: He chairs subcommittees of both the Commerce Committee and Environment and Public Works Committee that have jurisdiction over fisheries. About 60 percent of the seafood caught in the United States comes from Alaskan waters.Sullivan grew up in Fairview Park, Ohio, as a member of a family prominent in the Cleveland area. His paternal grandfather started a business just after World War II that today has grown into to RPM International, which employs more than 10,000 employees in the manufacture of commercial and residential paints, coatings and sealants. Sullivan's father later ran and grew the firm; one of his brothers is the current CEO and another is a vice president. Sullivan chose a different course. He graduated from Harvard University with a bachelor's degree in economics and earned a joint law and foreign service degree from Georgetown University. It was while Sullivan was attending Georgetown that he stumbled onto the path that would take him to Alaska: He met Julie Fate, a staffer for then-Sen. Ted Stevens, and later a reporter for the *Los Angeles Times*. They were married in Fairbanks in 1994, where Fate -- now Julie Fate Sullivan -- was part of a prominent Alaska Native family. Her mother was the first woman co-chair of the Alaska Federation of Natives, while her father served in the state legislature.

Upon his graduation from law school in 1993, Sullivan enlisted in the Marines, was commissioned a second lieutenant and began a four-year active tour of duty. He then moved to Alaska, where he clerked for a federal appeals court judge in Fairbanks before heading to Anchorage to clerk for the chief justice of the Alaska Supreme Court. He then spent a couple of years in the Anchorage office of the Seattle-based Perkins Coie law firm. But, he left Alaska after five years, a move that would come back to haunt him politically in his run for office. He and his family moved away in 2002 for good reason, Sullivan told the *Alaska Dispatch News* during the Senate campaign: "9/11 happened and that changed everything." He spent more than two years on a fellowship at the White House of President George W. Bush, working for the National Security Council under then-National Security Adviser Condoleeza Rice, as well as the National Economic Council. At the end of 2004, he started a 16-month active duty deployment in the Marines; in mid-2006, with Rice by now secretary of state, Sullivan became assistant secretary of state for economic, energy and business affairs.

Out of a job at the end of the Bush administration in early 2009, Sullivan returned to Alaska to stay that June, when Gov. Sarah Palin appointed him state attorney general a month before resigning the governorship. Palin's successor, Republican Sean Parnell, named Sullivan to head the state's Department of Natural Resources 18 months later. Sullivan resigned that post in September 2013, shortly before announcing his candidacy for Senate. His primary opponents included Parnell's lieutenant governor, Mead Treadwell, and Fairbanks attorney Joe Miller, a tea party favorite who had defeated Murkowski in the 2010 primary before she went on to win as a write-in candidate in the general election. Treadwell sought to depict Sullivan as a carpetbagger -- "I've got a jar of mayonnaise in my refrigerator that's been there longer than Dan Sullivan's been in Alaska," Treadwell gibed to *Politico* -- while Palin endorsed Miller. But the prospect of the GOP retaking Senate control prompted national conservative interest groups to pull out the stops, and they decided to throw their efforts behind Sullivan. The Club for Growth, which backs fiscal conservatives, endorsed Sullivan, as did the U.S. Chamber of Commerce: They were clearly betting he had the best shot to defeat Begich. Sullivan won the primary with 40 percent, with Miller at 32 percent and Treadwell at 25 percent.

Begich had toppled Stevens in 2008 after a 40-year tenure, winning by a mere 4,000 votes following Stevens' conviction on corruption charges just days before the election. (The charges, involving concealment of $250,000 in work done on Stevens' Alaska residence, were eventually dismissed.) As a Democrat from a deep-red state, Begich focused intensely on parochial issues and worked to show his independence from Obama as well as most of his fellow congressional Democrats. He was one of only four Senate Democrats to vote against a bill ending tax breaks for oil companies and also opposed a ban on so-called earmark spending -- a device that had been used with regularity by Stevens to steer federal appropriations to his huge, sparsely populated state.

Begich's campaign also apparently saw Sullivan as their toughest opponent: Democrats began sounding the carpetbagger theme during the primary, and continued to use it right up until the general election. Sullivan committed an early gaffe when he criticized Begich in an ad filmed atop an Anchorage convention center, saying Alaskans wanted someone who delivered real results; construction of the center was considered a significant achievement for Begich when he was mayor. But, otherwise, Sullivan ran a carefully managed campaign whose overriding goal was to tie Begich to Obama, who was deeply unpopular in Alaska. Ultimately, the bitter battle consumed $61 million, making it the most expensive race in Alaska history. Despite Begich's skills as a campaigner, Republicans had a superior ground game -- and this red state simply was not going to return Begich during a national Republican wave that swept the GOP into Senate control and solidified the party's hold on the House. Sullivan eked out a 48%-46% victory, with about 6,000 votes separating them; Begich declined to throw in the towel until all votes across the nation's largest state were tallied, calling Sullivan two weeks after Election Day to congratulate him.

In a controversial move, Begich sought to appear nonpartisan during the campaign by running an ad that featured the image of his Republican Senate colleague, Murkowski, and touted their close relationship. Murkowski told Begich to stop using her image, and made clear that she supported Sullivan. Nonetheless, during their time representing Alaska together, the political daylight between the more conservative Sullivan and Murkowski on both policy and political matters had been evident. On the political front, Sullivan, unlike Murkowski, endorsed Donald Trump after he emerged as the Republican presidential nominee. Both senators did condemn Trump's behavior and call for him to step aside as the nominee after the release of the "Access Hollywood" video containing lewd comments about women. But Sullivan went a step further than his senior colleague and urged that Trump be replaced by now-Vice President Mike Pence, a leading social conservative. During the 2014 campaign, Sullivan had staked out positions at odds with Murkowski on abortion and same-sex marriage, saying that he opposed both.

For a time, there was at least a possibility that the 2016 campaign could result in two Alaska senators named Dan Sullivan. The former Anchorage mayor by that name (no relation to the current senator) filed to mount a right-wing challenge to Murkowski in the Republican primary just before the deadline. But the former mayor dropped out after barely two weeks.

REPRESENTATIVE-AT-LARGE

Don Young (R)

Elected 1973, 23th term; b. Jun 09, 1933, Meridian, CA; California State University, Chico, B.A.; Yuba Junior College (CA), A.A.; Episcopalian; Married (Anne Garland Walton); 2 children; 14 grandchildren; 1 great-grandchild.

Military Career: U.S Army, 1955-1957.

Elected Office: Fort Yukon City Council, 1960-1964; Fort Yukon Mayor, 1964-1968; AK House, 1966-1970; AK Senate, 1970-1973.

Professional Career: School teacher, Fort Yukon, 1960-1968; Riverboat captain, 1968-1972.

DC Office: 2314 RHOB 20515, 202-225-5765, Fax: 202-225-0425, donyoung.house.gov.

State Offices: Anchorage, 907-271-5978; Fairbanks, 907-456-0210.

Committees: *Natural Resources*: Federal Lands, Indian, Insular & Alaska Native Affairs. *Transportation & Infrastructure*: Aviation, Coast Guard & Maritime Transportation, Highways & Transit.

Group Ratings

	ADA	ACLU	AFL-CIO	LCV	ITI	COC	HAFA	ACU	CFG	FRC
2016	-	5%	-	3%	100%	100%	46%	71%	53%	92%
2015	5%	C	48%	6%	C	89%	C	50%	44%	73%

Almanac Ratings 2015

	Economy	Social	Foreign	Composite
Liberal	25%	20%	6%	17%
Conservative	75%	80%	94%	83%

Key Votes of the 114th Congress

1. Keystone Pipeline	Y	5. Puerto Rico Debt	Y	9. Offenses by Aliens	Y
2. Trade Deals	N	6. Medical Marijuana	Y	10. Troops in Iraq	N
3. Export-Import Bank	Y	7. Sanctuary Cities	Y	11. Homeland Security $$	N
4. Debt Ceiling Increase	N	8. Armor-piercing Bullets	Y	12. Trade Adjustment aid	N

Election Results

Election	Name (Party)	Vote (%)		Cand. Spent	Ind. Exp. Support	Ind. Exp. Oppose
2016 General	Don Young (R)	155,088	(50%)	$1,308,196	$21,285	
	Steve Lindbeck (D)	111,019	(36%)	$1,021,866	$1,318	
	Jim C. McDermott (L)	31,770	(10%)			
	Bernie Souphanavong (I)	9,093	(3%)			
2016 Primary	Don Young (R)	34,540	(72%)			
	Stephen Wright (R)	8,946	(19%)			
	Gerald Heikes (R)	2,511	(5%)			

Prior winning percentages: 2014 (51%), 2012 (64%), 2010 (69%), 2008 (50%), 2006 (57%), 2004 (71%), 2002 (75%), 2000 (70%), 1998 (63%), 1996 (59%), 1994 (57%), 1992 (47%), 1990 (52%), 1988 (63%), 1986 (57%), 1984 (55%), 1982 (71%), 1980 (74%), 1978 (55%), 1976 (71%), 1974 (54%), 1972 (56%)

Don Young has been Alaska's congressman-at-large since 1973. He is the most-senior Republican in the House and number-two behind Democrat John Conyers of Michigan. He has served longer than any House Republican other than former Speaker Joe Cannon, who retired in 1923 after 46 years. Young's long political career was nearly destroyed by an influence-peddling scandal in 2008, when he narrowly survived reelection. He remains a forceful figure in Washington. But after having served six years each as chairman of two House committees that are vital to his home state, he has lost much of his internal clout.

Young grew up on his family's farm in the Sacramento Valley of California, served in the Army, and graduated from college. He had a thirst for adventure and the rugged outdoors: He remembers that *The Call of the Wild* by Jack London was a favorite book growing up. He moved to Alaska in 1959, the year that the vast, untamed U.S. territory became a state. Young worked in construction, fishing, trapping, and gold prospecting. He taught elementary school to indigenous Alaskan children in Fort Yukon, population 700. After spring thaws, he worked as a tugboat captain on the Yukon. He is a licensed mariner, which, in his words, is definitely not a typical profession of "one of these smooth, namby-pamby politicians." Young was elected mayor of Fort Yukon in 1964, to the state House in 1966, and to the state Senate in 1970. He ran for Congress in 1972. His opponent, incumbent Democrat Nick Begich, was killed in a plane crash in October and reelected posthumously. Young won the March 1973 special election to succeed him. Young is not a free-market conservative and has voted with liberals on some cultural issues, but he is a consistent, fierce advocate for Alaska's interests. He is temperamental and salty-tongued. To critics who once proposed shifting money for Alaska bridges to Hurricane Katrina recovery efforts, he said, "They can kiss my ear."

Soon after taking his seat in the House, Young voted for building the Alaska oil pipeline. He often found that his aggressive pursuit of economic development for his state conflicted with the environmental lobby and its interest in preserving wildlife. On what was then the Interior Committee, he called his critics a "self-centered bunch, the waffle-stomping, Harvard-graduating, intellectual idiots."

When Republicans have controlled the House, Young occupied power positions that allowed him to work around his adversaries. On both committees, he proved capable of forging bipartisan consensus. He chaired the Resources Committee from 1995 to 2001 and the Transportation and Infrastructure Committee from 2001 to 2007. In each case, his tenure was limited by the House GOP term-limits rule for committee chairmen. He steered to House passage bills allowing oil drilling in the Arctic National Wildlife Refuge in 1995, 2001, and 2006, only to see them defeated or bottled up in the Senate. On the Resources Committee, his attempts to roll back environmental rulings, such as the one that barred logging in the Tongass National Forest, were frustrated in the 1990s by Democratic President Bill Clinton or by adverse votes cast by moderate Republicans. In 2000, he got Congress to pass the Conservation and Reinvestment Act to dedicate royalties from offshore oil and gas wells to state purchases of land.

On the Transportation and Infrastructure Committee, he led arguably the most bipartisan panel in the House because its chairmen traditionally have larded their bills to make sure every cooperating committee member received plenty of highway or mass transit projects for his or her district. In 2003, Young proposed a surface transportation bill with $375 billion in spending, financed with a gas tax increase. But the Bush administration and the House Republican leadership were stoutly opposed to any such hike. In 2005, he tried again and got the House to pass a $284 billion bill in March. But there was mounting criticism of the bill's earmarks - special projects for certain lawmakers - particularly of two bridges in Alaska. One was from Anchorage to the largely uninhabited land across the Knik Arm; the other was from the town of Ketchikan (pop. 14,000) to the island of Gravina (pop. 50), whose airport could be reached by local ferry. They were derisively dubbed the "bridges to nowhere." In July, both chambers passed by near-unanimous votes a $286 billion bill with more than 6,300 earmarks. They included $230 million for the Knik Arm bridge and $220 million for the Ketchikan-Gravina bridge. The bill contained about $941 million for Young's Alaska, more than any other state except California, Illinois and New York.

That likely would have been the end of the earmark controversy, except that Hurricane Katrina struck the Gulf Coast in August. Suddenly, there were demands that money be shifted from Alaska's "bridges to nowhere" to New Orleans and other parts of the devastated region. "That is the dumbest thing I ever heard," Young said. But criticism of earmarks and the bridges continued. Conservative Republicans as well as Democrats chimed in, and profligate spending, symbolized by the two spans, emerged as an issue in the 2006 election. It was among the factors that helped wipe out the Republican majorities that year.

For an incumbent with his lengthy seniority, Young has had a bumpy history with Alaska voters and has frequently drawn serious challengers. In recent years, his acerbic personality has been accompanied by ethical problems. In April 2007, a former Young aide pleaded guilty to accepting cash from disgraced lobbyist Jack Abramoff in exchange for inside government information. Records showed 120 contacts between Young and his staff with Abramoff and his clients. The next month, Rick Smith, an associate of Young's and a former lobbyist with the oil services firm VECO, a major Young contributor since 1989, pleaded guilty to bribing Alaska state legislators. *The New York Times* published a story about a Young staffer altering the 2005 transportation bill to add $10 million for an interstate interchange in Florida that would help real estate developer Daniel Aronoff, who had raised $40,000 for the lawmaker. Young dismissed the allegations, telling the *Anchorage Daily News* that it was just "a recycled story." Plus, he said, Florida Gulf Coast University supported the Coconut Road interchange. In April 2008, House Speaker Nancy Pelosi ordered an ethics investigation, and the Justice Department conducted its own review. Following lengthy inquiries, no charges were lodged against Young.

That year, Republican Lt. Gov. Sean Parnell announced he would challenge Young in the primary. Parnell was endorsed by GOP Gov. Sarah Palin. Polls in summer 2008 showed Young trailing, but he professed to be unfazed, saying he was used to tough reelections. During a debate with Parnell, he said: "I've been accused of being arrogant, being a bully, and sometimes I'll plead to being both of those. Most of the time and every time I've done that is because I'm fighting for this state." Parnell spent $572,000, with strong support from the anti-tax Club for Growth. "We're tired of being the nation's symbol of excess and greed," Parnell said in an August debate. Young beat Parnell by just 304 votes.

His battle was far from over. Former Alaska House Minority Leader Ethan Berkowitz, a Democrat, ran against him in the general election. Berkowitz was well funded, with $1.6 million, while Young's resources were depleted by legal fees and by the primary contest. The Democratic Congressional Campaign Committee spent $1.4 million on ads charging that Young was the subject of multiple investigations. Berkowitz framed the choice as one of style, contrasting his consensus-building approach to Young's tendency to "bully and intimidate." He said he would seek earmarks if communities and citizens asked for them, but not for lobbyists. Young responded during a debate, tongue in cheek, that he is "one of the nicest, kindest persons in the world." He added, "But when you mess with the state, you're messing with me." Young defeated Berkowitz 50%-45%.

Young returned to Washington, but he remained under a political cloud. He lost the ranking minority member position on Resources, the committee on which he had served for 36 years. Young issued a press release saying he would regain the post when "my name is cleared." For one reason or another, that has not happened. Ethics problems lingered for Young. In 2014, the House Ethics Committee rebuked him for "improperly accepting nearly $60,000 in hunting trips, rides on private planes and other gifts and failing to report them on his financial disclosure forms." The gifts dated back to 2001. Young repaid the donors of the gifts, plus his campaign account. "I've been under a cloud all my life," Young told reporters in Juneau. "It's sort of like living in Juneau. It rains on you all the time. You don't even notice it."

He has remained an active legislator. He got a provision attached to the 2012 Interior appropriations bill that forbids the National Park Service from regulating waters in Alaska's Yukon-Charley Rivers National Preserve. He also introduced a sweeping bill - with long odds of passage and designed to make a political point - that would require the Obama administration to review and justify every regulation implemented in the past 20 years. After Interior Secretary Sally Jewell rejected what Young viewed as a potentially life-saving road through an Alaska refuge, he wagged his finger at her and told her at a 2014 committee hearing, "I think your decision stunk."

Young has remained as feisty and vocal as ever. In a 2013 radio interview in Alaska, he referred to Latino immigrants as "wetbacks." Other Republicans who were keen on making political inroads with Hispanic voters swiftly condemned him, and Young apologized for what he acknowledged was an "insensitive" term. During a 2015 hearing with Jewell, during which he objected to placing gray wolves on the endangered species list, Young said that wolves could be put to good use in many areas. "You wouldn't have a homeless problem anymore," he said. In 2016, he showed his libertarian bent when he filed with Democratic Rep. Steve Cohen of Tennessee a bill that would end prosecution for possession of medical marijuana in states where it has been legalized. In the *Almanac* vote ratings for 2015, his ranking on social issues placed him near the center of the House.

Young was reelected in 2016, 50%-36%, against Democrat Steve Lindbeck, a former public broadcasting executive. Each raised $1.1 million. Libertarian Jim McDermott got 10 percent. A new ethics issue arose in the campaign after Young disclosed in August that he had written the House Clerk in May that he had accidentally failed to disclose for 25 years his interest in a family farm in California, for which he received $250,000 when it was sold in 2015. Lindbeck's campaign cited the incident as cause to "fire" Young.

Young has no plans to retire. "The only time I'll retire is when people want to retire me," he told the *Daily News* after the 2014 election. "The people decide I can't serve them anymore, they'll get rid of me. It's that simple." His real enthusiasm is no longer legislation, he added, but "helping people that have problems."

★ ARIZONA ★

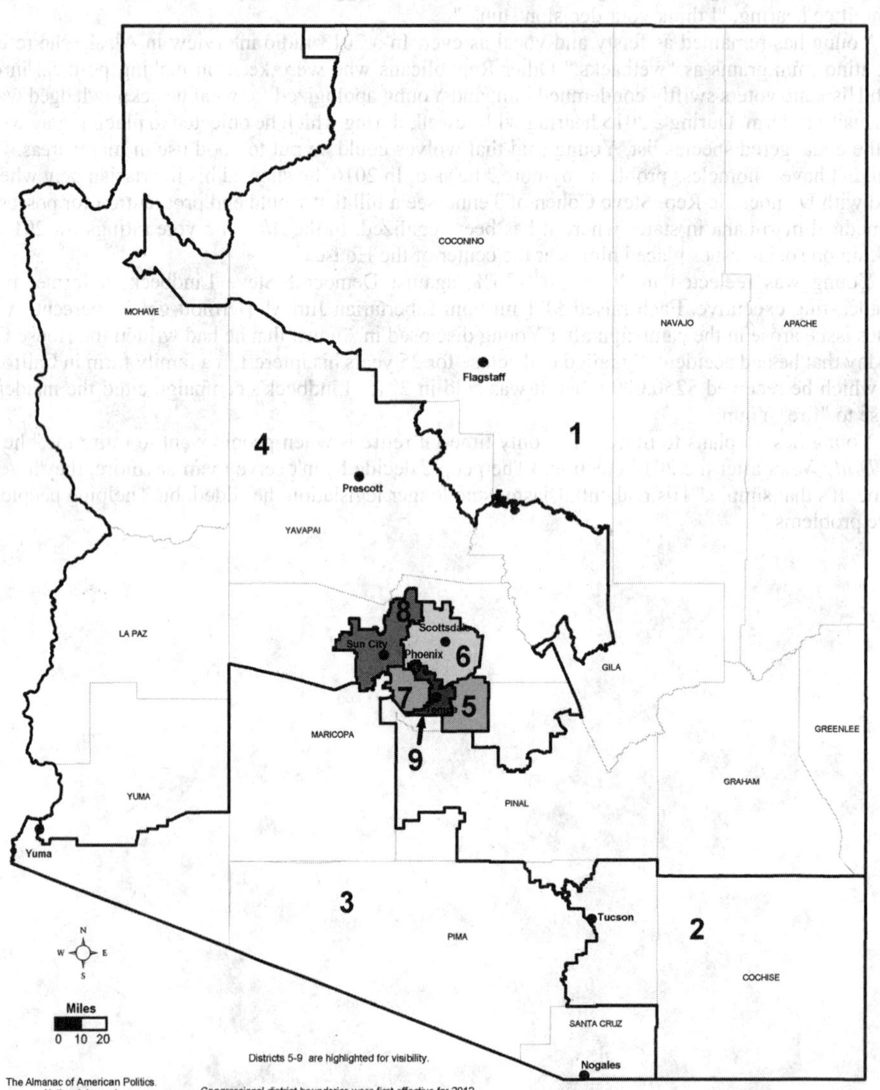
COCONINO
MOHAVE
NAVAJO
APACHE
Flagstaff
4
1
Prescott
YAVAPAI
8
Scottsdale
Sun City
Phoenix
6
LA PAZ
GILA
7
5
Tempe
MARICOPA
9
GREENLEE
YUMA
GRAHAM
PINAL
Yuma
3
Tucson
2
PIMA
COCHISE
SANTA CRUZ
Nogales
N
W
E
S
Miles
0 10 20
Districts 5-9 are highlighted for visibility.
The Almanac of American Politics.
National Journal
Congressional district boundaries were first effective for 2012.

Arizona is at the crossroads of some of America's most urgent demographic and political trends – the migration from colder states to the sunbelt, the role of immigration, and the increase in Hispanic influence on American politics. But it remains to be seen whether the Democrats' incremental gains during the 2016 election in Arizona portend a shift in the state from reliably red to something more like purple.

Growing and changing more rapidly in recent decades than most states, Arizona is also home to America's oldest continuous community, the Hopi Indians, who have lived as shepherds on the plateaus east of the Grand Canyon for more than 900 years. They have spurned Christianity since 1680, when they killed the local Franciscan priests and burned their churches. Their land disputes with the more numerous Navajo have dragged on for centuries. Efforts by the federal government to get the two tribes to share lands came to naught, and it has cost more than $500 million to relocate primarily the Navajo to new homes. Separately, the Obama administration agreed in 2014 to a record $544 million tribal settlement with the Navajo Nation over claims that its reservation had been mismanaged by the government for decades.

Other than the Native American population, the rugged desert, mountains and forested lands of Arizona were sparsely populated when the United States obtained them as part of the treaty that ended the Mexican War in 1848 (and another chunk a few years later to provide land for a southern route for a transcontinental railroad). Arizona was made a separate territory in 1863 after some locals tried to join the Confederacy. Nearly half a century later, in 1912, it became the 48th state.

Back then few imagined that Arizona would transcend its frontier roots. For decades it relied on the five Cs, memorialized in the state seal. The first C was copper: The dome of the state Capitol is encased in copper, and one of the state's leading public figures was Lewis Douglas, scion of a prominent Arizona mining family, a congressman, Franklin D. Roosevelt's first budget director, and Harry Truman's ambassador to Britain. The second C was cattle: As late as the mid-1960s a dozen or so cattle barons ran the state legislature. The third C was cotton: The signature achievement of Carl Hayden, a Democratic senator from 1927 to 1969, was the Central Arizona Project, a massive irrigation program that brought cotton farms to the flatlands around Phoenix. The water also helped with the fourth C: citrus. The fifth C was climate: Dry, clear air drew visitors seeking its therapeutic benefits, as well as tourists, but the scorching summer heat deterred permanent transplants for many years.

Then came air conditioning. In the years after World War II, Arizona became less dependent on federal largesse, except for its military bases and defense contracts. Businessmen, lawyers, developers and water companies, notably the Salt River Project, built Arizona and fostered an environment that welcomed new technological ideas. Their political champion was Barry Goldwater, a Phoenix City Council member, senator and the 1964 GOP presidential nominee who was the nation's most recognizable conservative for much of the 1950s and 1960s (and someone who today would be considered a libertarian -- a strain of Republicanism with especially strong roots in the West). Goldwater helped to make Arizona solidly Republican, the only state to vote Republican for president in every election from 1952 to 1992.

For years, Arizona's growth was based more on high-tech and low taxes than the influx of retirees. Phoenix began attracting technology industries when Motorola built a research center for military electronics there in 1948. Other major employers, Honeywell, Raytheon, Intel, Avnet and General Dynamics, followed. Defense industries are important here, especially the manufacture of unmanned aircraft. The state counts two Air Force bases and a Marine air station, plus the huge Barry M. Goldwater Range, where many of America's pilots have trained. Private companies have invested as well: In 2015, Apple Inc. announced it was building a $2 billion center in Mesa that was envisioned as the seed for a new tech hub; the center was planned for a 1.3 million-square-foot former solar-panel manufacturing plant and would provide cloud storage for data and music. The technology sector has also given a boost to renewable-energy jobs in the state. Over three square miles of the desert near Gila Bend, the Solana solar plant is able to make electricity without direct sunlight and to generate power at night. The state can use the juice: 25 percent of the energy consumed in Arizona homes is for air conditioning, about four times the national average. Arizona's Renewable Energy Standard requires 15 percent of the state's electricity consumption to come from renewables by 2025. In 2014, 2.8 percent of its electricity generation came from solar. This is one of the ways in which the state is coming to grips with the expectation of a changing climate, which could include a mix of rising temperatures, smaller snowpacks, reduced Colorado River flow and more frequent wildfires. Since 1984, more than 2 percent of Arizona has burned per decade.

Arizona has been one of the nation's boom states and its population nearly doubled from 3.7 million in 1990 to 6.9 million in 2016, driven by the relocation of retirees from the Midwest and elsewhere. Second to Nevada, it grew faster than any other state from 2000 to 2010. That kind of growth led developers to buy out the cotton farms, and the Valley of the Sun around Phoenix lost nearly half its farmland between 1975 and 2000. But Arizona's boom took a major blow with the Great Recession and the collapse of the housing market. Prior to that, construction and real estate accounted for about a third of the state's economy. When Arizona became a leader in home foreclosures, those industries stalled. Unemployment peaked at 11.1 percent in late 2009. Seven years later, it had fallen to 5 percent, slightly above the national average. Slowly, the housing market came back; Realtor.com projected Phoenix and Tucson as the first- and ninth-hottest markets for 2017. University of Arizona projections foresee growth rates above the national average in the coming years, but slower than the pace of growth during the 30 years prior to the Great Recession.

In the boom years and after the bust, Arizona was a focal point of illegal immigration. With strong border enforcement in Texas and a border fence near San Diego, the hilly Arizona desert in Cochise and Santa Cruz counties became a major entry point for illegal immigrants. Anger at the flood of contributed to the passage of ballot propositions denying welfare benefits to them and requiring government employees to report illegal residents. Other ballot measures, supported by some 40 percent of Hispanic voters, declared English Arizona's official language and barred in-state tuition for illegal residents at state colleges. The crisis deepened when illegal immigrants murdered a local rancher and kidnappings involving illegal immigrants became common. In 2010, the legislature passed Senate Bill 1070 authorizing law enforcement officials to check the immigration status of people stopped for other reasons. After hesitating, Republican Gov. Jan Brewer signed the bill. Up for election that year, she had been running poorly in GOP primary polls and trailed Democratic Attorney General Terry Goddard in general election trial heats. But after approving the controversial legislation, her poll numbers soared and she bested Goddard by double digits in the fall. President Barack Obama denounced the law, saying it encouraged racial profiling, and Hispanic organizations called for a boycott of the state, which led to cancellation of some conventions and lower hotel bookings. The Justice Department brought a lawsuit to stop enforcement and won at the trial and appellate levels. But in June 2012, the Supreme Court upheld the main provision requiring law enforcement officers to check immigration status of people stopped for other reasons.

Gradually, the crisis atmosphere in the state ebbed. In 2011, the heavily Republican state Senate, heeding the opposition of the Arizona business lobby, rejected several new measures that would have cracked down further on illegal immigration. (Similarly, the state Chamber of Commerce & Industry came out against Senate Bill 1062, a religious-freedom bill some saw as anti-gay. Gov. Brewer vetoed it in 2014.) Brewer's executive order denying driver's licenses for qualified immigrant youth under the Deferred Action for Childhood Arrivals, or "DACA" program, was upended in 2014 when the Supreme Court upheld a lower court ruling that overturned her order. Also that year, a federal judge ruled that Arizona authorities could no longer enforce the state's 2005 immigrant smuggling law, signed into law by Democratic Gov. Janet Napolitano, which local officials, including Maricopa County Sheriff Joe Arpaio, had embraced.

The state was a source of other headaches for the Obama administration. The Justice Department's Operation Fast and Furious, the misbegotten gun-trafficking investigation by the Bureau of Alcohol, Tobacco, Firearms and Explosives, began in Arizona in 2009 and led to the killing of border Patrolman Brian Terry in 2010. In the wake of the fiasco, the acting director and the deputy director of the ATF resigned their posts. Meanwhile, the Phoenix VA Health Care System was the epicenter of the 2014 Veterans Health Administration scandal. And just days before the 2016 election, Arizona stood out as the state with the highest projected increase in premiums under the Affordable Care Act – 116 percent. That may have been enough to nudge some late deciders toward Donald Trump, enabling him to win the state despite an energized Latino vote.

Indeed, Latino voters have been the big story in Arizona in recent election cycles. For some time, Arizona has seemed on the verge of becoming less Republican and more competitive, fueled by demographic changes and an increase in independent voters. But it has never quite gotten there.

Democrats posted a few notable victories: Bill Clinton carried the state 47%-44% in 1996, and Janet Napolitano was elected governor in both 2002 and 2006. Democrats have hoped that the increasing Hispanic population - currently 37 percent - would tip the state their way in presidential contests; a 2015 study projected that by 2023, the state will have a majority-minority population, though it won't be until 2038 that minorities are expected to constitute a majority of Arizona's eligible voters. Still, John Kerry and Barack Obama lost by almost identical margins. The immigration issue seems to have made Latinos more Democratic and whites more Republican. In 2004 and 2008, George W. Bush and John McCain – both of whom were in favor of immigration reform -- both captured more than 40 percent of the Hispanic vote. But Mitt Romney lost Latinos 74%-25% and carried whites, 66%-32%, running ahead of the 59 percent white vote for Bush and McCain.

These trends came to a head in 2016, with Trump's aggressive rhetoric on illegal immigration. Cementing the issue's place at center stage was the presence of Arpaio on the ballot, seeking a seventh term. Hillary Clinton made a few high-profile visits to the state, though it was never entirely clear whether the campaign considered Arizona a state seriously in play, a possible hedge against losses elsewhere, or a feint to distract Trump. Ultimately, Trump, with slightly higher support from Latinos than Romney, won the state, though by 3.5 percentage points – about one-third of Romney's margin over Obama in 2012. In populous Maricopa County, Clinton came within about 40,000 votes of defeating Trump. Meanwhile, in a race that sometimes seemed to take precedence over the presidential contest, Maricopa voters ousted Arpaio by a double-digit margin. (Statewide, voters also enacted a $12 minimum wage by a surprisingly large 17-point margin, though they dealt a narrow, and rare, loss to marijuana legalization.) Despite Democratic gains, Arizona is still a state with a Republican governor and legislature, as well as two GOP senators. It remains to be seen whether the Democrats can make a lasting breakthrough – especially without Trump and Arpaio on the ballot.

Population		**Race and Ethnicity**		**Income**	
Total	6,641,928	White	56.5%	Median Income	$50,255 (30 out of 50)
Land area	113,594	Black	4.0%		
Pop/ sq mi	58.5	Latino	30.3%	Under $50,000	49.7%
Born in state	38.7%	Asian	2.9%	$50,000-$99,999	30.3%
		Two races	2.0%	$100,000-$199,999	16.1%
Age Groups		Other	4.3%	$200,000 or more	3.8%
Under 18	24.3%			Poverty Rate	18.2%
18-34	20.5%	**Education**			
35-64	37.0%	H.S grad or less	38.3%	**Health Insurance**	
Over 64	15.4%	Some college	34.2%	With health insurance coverage	85.0%
		College Degree, 4 yr	17.3%		
Work		Post grad	10.2%		
White Collar	35.1%			**Public Assistance**	
Sales and Service	46.1%	**Military**		Cash public assistance income	2.3%
Blue Collar	18.9%	Veteran	10.1%		
Government	14.6%	Active Duty	0.3%	Food stamp/SNAP benefits	13.5%

Voter Turnout			
2015 Total Citizens 18+	4,526,594	2016 Pres Turnout as % CVAP	57%
2016 Pres Votes	2,573,165	2012 Pres Turnout as % CVAP	55%

Legislature	
Senate:	12D, 18R
House:	24D, 36R

Presidential Politics

2016 Democratic Primary		
Hillary Clinton (D)	262,459	(56%)
Bernie Sanders (D)	192,962	(41%)
2016 Republican Primary		
Donald Trump (R)	286,743	(46%)
Ted Cruz (R)	172,294	(28%)
Marco Rubio (R)	72,304	(12%)
John Kasich (R)	65,965	(11%)

2016 Presidential Vote		
Donald Trump (R)	1,252,401	(48%)
Hillary Clinton (D)	1,161,167	(45%)
Gary Johnson (L)	106,327	(4%)
2012 Presidential Vote		
Mitt Romney (R)	1,233,654	(54%)
Barack Obama (D)	1,025,232	(45%)

As the demographics of the Arizona electorate become more diverse, the state is becoming more of a presidential battleground state. While Donald Trump kept the state in the Republican column, his 49%-45% victory over Hillary Clinton was a much slimmer margin than GOP nominees had garnered in recent White House contests.

The reason Clinton was able to make Arizona a competitive race is that she lost the state's dominant Maricopa County by roughly three percentage points while Obama lost it by nine points in both 2008 and 2012. Maricopa, which contains metro Phoenix with its fast-growing suburbs and exurbs such as Surprise, Buckeye, Goodyear and Gilbert, and large cities such as Glendale, Mesa and Scottsdale, cast some 60 percent of the state's votes in 2016. The county overall tilts Republican, but Tempe, home to Arizona State University, provides Democratic votes. Pima County, dominated by Tucson, the state's second largest city, is a Democratic stronghold, but only about one-sixth of the state's ballots were are cast there in 2016. The remainder of Arizona's largely rural territory had been home to conservative ranchers and others who were known as "Pinto" or "Goldwater" Democrats. But today it is strong GOP turf, except for Apache County with its tribal reservations; Coconino County, with Flagstaff and Northern Arizona University; and Santa Cruz County where four of five residents are Hispanic. This largely rural portion of the state (Mohave County now includes Las Vegas exurbs) delivered heavily for Trump, backing him 56%-39%, better than Mitt Romney did in 2012 or home state Sen. John McCain performed in 2008. In order to prevail, a Democratic presidential candidate needs to battle a Republican at least close to a draw in Maricopa, score a big turnout in Pima, and hold down the losses in the rest of the state. That was essentially the formula Bill Clinton followed in 1996, when he became the first Democrat to carry Arizona since Harry Truman in 1948.

Immigration roiled the state's politics in the previous decade, but it was a less critical issue in 2016 general election. By a margin of more than 4-1, the television network exit poll found that voters in the presidential election favored allowing illegal immigrants working in the United States to apply for "legal status," as opposed to deporting them. One of Trump's early Arizona backers was Maricopa County Sheriff Joe Arpaio who advocated an immigration crackdown. But the controversial Arpaio was defeated in his bid for a seventh election. In the Republican primary in late March, Arpaio's support along with the backing of former GOP governor Jan Brewer, helped Trump romp over his rivals with 46 percent of the vote, followed by Texas Sen. Ted Cruz who captured 28 percent. In a winner-take-all contest, Trump took all of the state's GOP convention delegates. Clinton likewise won the Democratic primary handily, defeating Sanders 56%-41%. She did well in high Hispanic counties and won all nine of the state's congressional districts; Sanders was most competitive in the 4th and 9th Districts, containing Phoenix suburbs and exurbs.

The primary was marred by long voting lines in Maricopa, because officials there reduced the number of polling places from 200 in the 2012 primary to 60. Lawsuits by Democrats and voting rights advocates against state and county officials over the primary delays helped prompt moves to ease long waits at polling places in November. However, there were still challenges in tallying Arizona's votes. The day after the election, more than 627,000 votes, mostly provisional and late-arriving early ballots, remained uncounted, including 470,000 in Maricopa.

Congressional Districts

115th Congress Lineup	5R 4D	114th Congress Lineup	5R 4D

Arizona has become a competitive battleground for House seats. Its nine-member delegation includes four solidly Republican districts, two solidly Democratic districts (with large Hispanic majorities), and three districts that could remain "toss-up" for the remainder of the decade. Those three districts - now represented by two Democrats and one Republican - are based in the sprawling rural eastern part of the state, Tempe and Tucson.

That map has been drawn by a five-member Independent Redistricting Commission, which was created by a statewide referendum in 2000. Its members include two Democrats, two Republicans and an independent picked by the other four. The commission's map resulted in a delegation of six Republican and two Democrats after the 2002 election, but it shifted to five Democrats and three Republicans in 2008. The GOP wave of 2010 restored Republicans to a 5-3 majority. When Arizona gained a seat from the 2010 census, replicating its pattern of increasing its delegation by at least one seat following each decennial count since 1960, Democrats unexpectedly emerged from a state dominated by a Republican governor and legislature with the map of their dreams and five of the state's nine House seats.

The Democrats' good fortune resulted when the commission's Republicans agreed to select as the panel's chair Colleen Coyle Mathis, a Tucson health care administrator who described herself as a "post-partisan" ex-Republican. She quickly sided with the commission's Democrats on the need to draw more competitive districts. The result was a plan that sought to protect the two heavily Hispanic districts in the Phoenix area plus the Democratic-leaning 2nd district in Tucson. The commission also drew two others that Democrats could win: a new 9th District anchored by the university bastion of Tempe, and an altered northern Arizona 1st District linking the feuding Hopi and Navajo tribes, who had agreed to consolidate their votes after years of being split into different districts.

The map infuriated Republicans: Not only did it maximize Democratic opportunities, it forced Republicans David Schweikert and Ben Quayle to run against each other even though the state was gaining a seat. GOP Gov. Jan Brewer chose to void the map and accused Mathis of "gross misconduct." The state Senate removed her from the commission on a 21-6 vote, with several Democrats abstaining in protest. The *Arizona Republic* slammed Brewer for running "roughshod over the public."

Less than three weeks after Mathis' removal, the Arizona Supreme Court rebuked Brewer and reinstated Mathis. The commission voted to re-pass the map. Republicans' worst fears were confirmed when Schweikert and Quayle were forced to duel in an ugly primary and Democrats picked up both the 1st and 9th districts in November. In 2014, Democrats retained those two districts but narrowly lost the 2nd district. Democrats retained the 1st in 2016 after Republicans ran a flawed campaign.

The Republican-controlled legislature, meanwhile, challenged the map in federal court. Its lawyers contended that the 2000 referendum violated the Constitution by removing its authority over the congressional district map. A three-judge federal court ruled against the legislature in 2014, with two of the judges dismissing the complaint on the grounds that the Arizona constitution reserved the initiative power to its people, and that the federal Constitution permits "legislative" power to be exercised through a referendum. The U.S. Supreme Court, in a 5-4 decision, ruled that Arizona voters had the authority to create a redistricting commission. Its ruling could encourage citizen referenda in other states, though both political parties likely will remain reluctant to relinquish their control.

If Republicans retain control of the governor and Legislature in 2018, they could seek other steps to limit the authority of the commission. With the Census Bureau's projection that Arizona will gain a tenth seat after the 2020 census, that opening likely will be in the Phoenix area and could be politically competitive. The three current swing seats likely will be in play during the next redistricting.

Governor

Doug Ducey (R)

Elected 2014, term expires 2019, 1st term; b. Apr. 9, 1964, Toledo, OH; Arizona State U., B.S. 1986; Catholic; Married (Angela); 3 children.

Elected Office: AZ Treasurer, 2010-2014.

Professional Career: Beer Distributorship Marketing Coordinator, Hensley & Co., 1982-1986; Sales and Marketing Executive, Proctor & Gamble, 1986-1993; CEO and Chairman, Cold Stone Creamery, 1996-2007; Chairman, iMemories, 2008-2012.

Office: 1700 W. Washington St., Phoenix, 85007; 602-542-4331; Fax: 602-542-7601; Website: azgovernor.gov.

Election Results

Election	Name (Party)	Vote (%)
2014 General	Doug Ducey (R)	805,062 (53%)
	Fred DuVal (D)	626,921 (42%)
	Barry J. Hess (L)	57,337 (4%)
2014 Primary	Doug Ducey (R)	200,607 (37%)
	Scott Smith (R)	119,107 (22%)
	Christine Jones (R)	89,922 (17%)
	Ken Bennett (R)	62,010 (12%)
	Andrew Thomas (R)	43,822 (8%)

Republican Doug Ducey is the self-professed "conservative ice cream guy" who won the governorship in 2014, succeeding GOP incumbent, Jan Brewer, whose tenure had a habit of attracting controversy. As governor, Ducey has largely conformed to that description, especially when it comes to state spending and taxes, but he has also avoided confrontation on some issues.

Ducey grew up in Toledo Ohio, and graduated from St. John's Jesuit High School in 1982. He drove west in his Datsun B210, leaving his recession-ravaged state to attend Arizona State University and seek his fortune in the Sunbelt. He found it in a Tempe ice cream store. After graduating with a degree in finance in 1986, and a brief stint in marketing at Procter & Gamble, Ducey joined up with the founder of Cold Stone Creamery and helped turn it into a global brand with more than 1,400 stores. He eventually became CEO. In 2007, at the age of 43, Ducey helped engineer a merger with another Arizona franchising heavyweight, Kahala Corp. He got rich in the process, but that corporate marriage didn't work out, an experience Ducey described to *Bloomberg Business* as "incredibly frustrating and disappointing, but equally liberating all at once." Ducey took some time off, refocused, and became the lead investor and chairman of the board of iMemories, a friend's technology startup in Scottsdale, which helps people digitize their home movies and share them online. "As an entrepreneur, you're constantly navigating your way through a proverbial hallway of new opportunities," said Ducey. "Identifying and capitalizing on the right open door defines your success."

A new opportunity knocked in 2010, when Ducey made his first foray into elective politics and sought the state treasurer's post, vowing to bring his business background to state government to help promote jobs and economic growth. That's not a core function of the state treasurer's office, and at the time many viewed his bid for the treasurer's job as a warm-up for a Senate or gubernatorial run. Nevertheless, with his connections to the Phoenix business elite, Ducey significantly outraised and outspent his more credentialed GOP opponents, including a conservative favorite, and he handily won the primary and prevailed in the fall. While he was Treasurer, Ducey raised his political profile by leading a successful fight to defeat a 2012 ballot initiative that would have made a temporary one-cent sales tax increase permanent. In 2014, in the spirited Republican contest to replace Brewer, Ducey played up his business know-how again, but this time he had plenty of backing from prominent conservatives, including Sen. Ted Cruz of Texas, former Alaska Gov. Sarah Palin, and Maricopa County Sheriff Joe Arpaio, an immigration hardliner who had supported one of Ducey's GOP primary rivals four years prior. Brewer backed former Mesa Mayor Scott Smith in the primary, and another opponent, Christine Jones, the former legal counsel of GoDaddy, the Scottsdale Internet domain company, spent $5.4 million of her own money on the race and was aided by another $2 million independent effort funded by the company's founder. Ducey's stewardship of Cold Stone Creamery was criticized for a high default rate on Small Business Administration loans used to finance franchises, but he easily won the nomination.

In the general election, Ducey faced former Board of Regents member Fred DuVal, a centrist Democrat, former Clinton White House staffer and long-time adviser to former Arizona Democratic Gov. Bruce Babbitt. Ducey campaigned as the champion of business, favoring cuts in state regulations and dramatic reductions in business and personal income taxes. With looming state deficits, DuVal called Ducey's tax plans unrealistic and stressed more state funding for education to improve the Arizona workforce as a way to attract and expand business. Ducey campaigned against Common Core education standards, favored limiting the definition of marriage to that between a man and a woman, and opposed benefits to domestic partners of gay state employees, but added that he would always comply with the law. The campaign had its low points, including minor infractions in both candidates' driving records that came under scrutiny. Republicans painted DuVal as a career lobbyist with sinister clients, while liberals touted stories linking some of Ducey's Italian-American relatives in Ohio to organized crime. Ducey pumped about $5 million of his own money into the campaign which, along with allied groups, resulted in more than $10 million being spent on his behalf in the election, compared withabout $3 million spent by DuVal and his outside backers. Ducey won by nearly 12 percentage points while his party swept every statewide office, and Arizonans extended a more than three-decade long streak of not electing a governor who was a native of the state (The last native elected governor was Bruce Babbitt in 1982.)

In office, and confronting a yawning state deficit, Ducey pushed through an austere budget that cut nearly $100 million in funding to higher education, borrowed more than $100 million from the state's rainy day fund and clawed back some $220 million in unspent agency funds. Ducey had proposed raising the state vehicle registration fee, but GOP lawmakers in Phoenix balked and rejected the governor's argument that a fee increase was not a tax hike. The state legislature did adopt a one-year lifetime cap on Temporary Assistance to Needy Families, making the state's support program for low-income families with children among the most tightfisted in the nation. (In 2016, after the fiscal picture had stabilized, Ducey and Republicans dismissed critics' efforts to once again ease the limit.) Doctors and hospitals were also slated for a 5 percent cut in state Medicaid reimbursements. Even though Arizona's aid to public school students still ranks near the bottom of the states, Ducey backed off a plan to prune non-classroom K-12 education spending and negotiated a deal with legislators giving schools more flexibility in this regard. Later in 2015, under pressure from a lawsuit challenging school funding short of what had been mandated by a voter-approved ballot measure, Ducey signed a legislative package to devote $3.5 billion toward K-12 education over a decade. Schools would get about 70 percent of what a lawsuit would have secured, if the suit had been successful.

To the chagrin of his more conservative backers, Ducey steered clear of some controversial topics. He rejected their demands for scrapping Common Core standards and instead asked the Arizona Board of Education to review, modify and possibly replace some of the K-12 learning benchmarks. When Ducey learned that the Arizona Department of Child Safety had stopped granting joint foster care licenses and adoptions for same-sex couples while the U.S. Supreme Court was weighing the issue of same-sex marriage-the U.S. Court of Appeals for the 9th Circuit had overturned Arizona's ban in 2014-the governor quickly stepped in and ordered the state agency to allow all legally married couples in Arizona to serve as foster parents and adopt.

In 2016, Ducey once again melded conservative positions with more moderate ones. He demanded that the federal government stop sending Syrian refugees to the state; Arizona had become the third most-common destination, behind Michigan and California. And he signed legislation that would allow the state to withhold funding from local jurisdictions that pursue policies at odds with the state. Given Arizona's unified Republican government at the state level and the predominance of Democratic governance in many of the state's big cities, this law held the potential for sinking liberal policies on the minimum wage, sick leave, gun restrictions and other issues. At the same time, Ducey sought to smooth the rough edges of Donald Trump's call to renegotiate NAFTA – a policy that would be an economic dagger at the state's heart. After Trump's election, Ducey visited Mexico, noting that it is "our No. 1 trading partner, times four, for the state of Arizona. We've built that relationship."

Indeed, Ducey's relationship with Trump ran hot and cold in 2016, particularly compared with his predecessor, Brewer, who was all in for Trump early on. In March, Ducey didn't explicitly endorse Trump but pledged to support the GOP nominee, whoever it turned out to be, saying, "I don't want to see another four or eight years of the policies of Barack Obama." At the Republican National Convention in Cleveland, Ducey led the state's delegation and said, "I'm proud to be here." But it took until Aug. 31 for Ducey to appear in person alongside Trump, when he spoke at a rally in Phoenix touting Trump's promises to nominate conservative judges and toughen border security. Then, when the tape of Trump's sexually explicit comments to Billy Bush became public in early October, Ducey called the remarks "insulting and terribly demeaning to women" and said he disavowed them "100 percent." Even so, just days before the election, Ducey addressed a Trump rally in Mesa. Speaking after Trump's victory, Ducey said he looked forward to the repeal and replacement of Obamacare and improved border security – two of Trump's key positions.

Ducey had a productive legislative session in 2017. Highlights included expansion of the state's Empowerment Scholarship Account program to allow any student to use taxpayer dollars to pay private school tuition or for other educational expenses; tougher penalties for assaulting a police officer, even if the officer is off duty; and a $9.8 billion budget, featuring two percent pay hikes for school teachers and a modest income-tax cut for residents. A bill to punish organizers of public protests that turn violent failed to win passage.

Senior Senator

John McCain (R)

Elected 1986, term expires 2022, 6th term; b. Aug 29, 1936, Canal Zone, Panama; National War College (DC), Att.; U.S. Naval Academy (MD), B.S.; Baptist; Married (Cindy Hensley McCain); 7 children (3 from previous marriage); 5 grandchildren.

Military Career: U.S Navy, 1958-1980 (Vietnam, POW).

Elected Office: U.S. House, 1982-1986.

Professional Career: Director, Navy Senate Liaison Office, 1977-1981.

DC Office: 218 RSOB 20510, 202-224-2235, Fax: 202-228-2862, mccain.senate.gov.

State Offices: Phoenix, 602-952-2410; Tucson, 520-670-6334.

Committees: *Armed Services (Chmn)*: Airland, Cybersecurity, Emerging Threats & Capabilities, Personnel, Readiness & Management Support, Seapower, Strategic Forces. *Homeland Security & Government Affairs*: Investigations, Regulatory Affairs & Federal Management. *Indian Affairs*. *Intelligence*.

Group Ratings

	ADA	ACLU	AFL-CIO	LCV	ITI	COC	HAFA	ACU	CFG	FRC
2016	-	11%	-	12%	60%	88%	49%	88%	78%	0%
2015	10%	C	15%	4%	C	86%	C	67%	70%	100%

Almanac Ratings 2015

	Economy	Social	Foreign	Composite
Liberal	30%	10%	22%	21%
Conservative	70%	90%	78%	79%

Key Votes of the 114th Congress

1. Keystone pipeline	Y	5. National Security Data	N	9. Gun Sales Checks	Y
2. Export-Import Bank	N	6. Iran Nuclear Deal	Y	10. Sanctuary Cities	Y
3. Debt Ceiling Increase	Y	7. Puerto Rico Debt	Y	11. Planned Parenthood	Y
4. Homeland Security $$	Y	8. Loretta Lynch A.G	N	12. Trade deals	Y

Election Results

Election	Name (Party)	Vote (%)		Cand. Spent	Ind. Exp. Support	Ind. Exp. Oppose
2016 General	John McCain (R)	1,359,267	(54%)	$10,958,109	$2,833,528	$203,385
	Ann Kirkpatrick (D)	1,031,245	(41%)	$8,793,944	$42,974	$1,303,929
2016 Primary	John McCain (R)	302,532	(51%)			
	Kelli Ward (R)	235,988	(40%)			
	Alex Meluskey (R)	31,159	(5%)			

Prior winning percentages: 2010 (59%), 2004 (77%), 1998 (69%), 1992 (56%), 1986 (60%); House: 1984 (78%), 1982 (66%)

He is now an octogenarian, and it has been nearly a decade since his ambitions to occupy the White House were permanently foreclosed. But Republican John McCain, Arizona's senior senator, remains a political icon, outspokenly independent and an influential force in Washington and the nation at large. For years, he was among the Democrats' favorite Republican legislators, unafraid to work cross the aisle on issues such as campaign finance and immigration reform. After losing to Barack Obama in the 2008 presidential race, however, McCain rebranded himself as the GOP's chief critic of Obama's national security policies, using his high-profile status to advocate a hawkish approach in the Middle East and elsewhere. But, since Donald Trump's surprise White House victory, McCain has eclipsed even leading Democrats as Trump's most prominent critic on Capitol Hill -- taking on the new president on a variety of issues dealing with the United States' role in the world community, notably the U.S. relationship with Russia.

Notwithstanding his maverick image, McCain, for the most part, has been -- and remains -- a conservative in terms of his voting record. But that record has as many quirks as the man himself. He supported funding of embryonic stem cell research, in opposition to most other Republicans. On the environmental front, he has at various times co-authored bills to increase fuel efficiency standards for car and lights trucks and to reduce global warming-related carbon dioxide emissions. Before 2013 Supreme Court decision to legalize same-sex marriage, McCain opposed a constitutional amendment to ban such marriages as "antithetical in every way to the core philosophy of Republicans" to respect states' rights to govern themselves. He is a pragmatic legislator who has shown little patience for ideological litmus tests imposed by many conservatives. "You've got to be 110 percent, otherwise you're out," he lamented to a home-state audience during his 2016 re-election campaign, while asserting, "We've got to be a big-tent party." Such a view has forced McCain, notwithstanding his national renown, to walk a political tightrope in his home state in recent years: He had serious primary challenges from the right during his last two reelection bids.

McCain entered the national consciousness well before entering politics: As a 31-year old bomber pilot, he was shot down during the Vietnam War, and spent the next five and a half years suffering through often brutal treatment as a prisoner-of-war. Born John Sidney McCain III in the Canal Zone, he was the namesake of a father and grandfather who both graduated from the Naval Academy and who both achieved the rank of admiral. McCain also attended Annapolis, albeit he was something short of the model midshipman: He graduated fifth from the bottom of his class academically, and was high in demerits. But he volunteered for service in Vietnam, and flew ground-attack aircraft from carriers at sea. In October 1967, on his 23rd bombing mission, his A-4E Skyhawk was shot down by a missile, and McCain ejected from the plane, breaking both of his arms and a leg in a fall into a lake near Hanoi. After pulling him from the water, his North Vietnamese "rescuers" crushed one of his shoulders with a rifle butt, bayoneted him, and then refused him medical treatment during his stay at a prison dubbed the Hanoi Hilton by U.S. soldiers.

Besides being subjected to repeated torture by Communist captors, he spent two years in solitary confinement.(That period is recounted in detail in Robert Timberg's *The Nightingale's Song* and in McCain's own 1999 memoir, *Faith of My Fathers*.) Less than a year after he was shot down, McCain's father was named head of the U.S. Pacific Command. When the younger McCain was offered release because of his father's rank, he refused to be let out ahead of those who had been imprisoned longer. As a former victim of torture, McCain later reacted strongly against the "waterboarding" used on suspected terrorists in the wake of the 9/11 attacks. Responding to Trump's support of reviving such tactics during the 2016 campaign, McCain bluntly told an international security forum. "If they started waterboarding, I swear to you a whole bunch of us would have them in court in a New York minute, and there's no judge in America that wouldn't say they're in violation of the law." It was a reference to an amendment McCain successfully attached to a 2005 defense spending bill over the initial objections of President George W. Bush.

McCain returned to the United States in March 1973 with other POWs. Despite intensive physical therapy, he was left with permanent injuries, including restricted movement of his arms. As a senator, McCain, in the 1990s, served on a commission headed by Massachusetts Democratic Sen. John Kerry, another Vietnam veteran, which sought a full accounting of POWs and MIAs from the Vietnam War, and worked with Kerry to end the trade embargo on Vietnam and to establish diplomatic relations. But first, on top of the many medals and commendations he received upon his homecoming,McCain's heroism was rewarded with an assignment in 1977 as the Navy's liaison to the Senate: The experience launched his career in politics. On the personal front, McCain's first marriage failed, and, in 1980, he was remarried to Cindy Lou Hensley, daughter of a wealthy Phoenix beer distributor. Two years later, he ran for an open House seat in Arizona. Attacked as an outsider, he responded, "The longest place I ever lived in was Hanoi." He won a four-way primary with 32 percent, and had no trouble in a Republican-dominated district that fall.

For all of the attention he now commands, McCain kept a low profile during his early years in Congress. Though a strong supporter of the Reagan administration, McCain, as a newlyelected House member, did demonstrate his independence by opposing the president's dispatch of troops to Lebanon in 1982, arguing they were too few to be effective and too vulnerable to attack. He was vindicated when a truck bomb blasted Marine barracks and killed 241 U.S. servicemen-a stunning loss that led Reagan to withdraw troops. In 1986, McCainmoved to the Senate, easily defeating a former Democratic state legislator by a 3-2 margin to succeed retiring Republican Barry Goldwater. McCain eventually built a reputation as someone who refused to engage in business as usual: Early on,such behavior nearly ended his political career. In the late1980s, McCain was one of the Keating Five senators investigated for allegedly pressuring regulators on behalf of Charles Keating's savings and loan enterprise. Ultimately, McCain received a slap on the wrist for exercising poor judgment, but there was no finding of improper conduct. Vindicated by his reelection in 1992, he reinvented himself as a reformer.

When Republicans won control of Congress in 1994, McCain sought out Democrat Russ Feingold of Wisconsin,who was pushing legislation to clamp down on campaign finance abuses. Over the next several years, the McCain-Feingold bills went through several transformations. Key features included prohibitions on so-called soft money-unlimited, largely unregulated contributions to political parties -- and restrictions on advertising by independent expenditure groupsclose to an election. The changes were fiercely opposed as an infringement on free speech and a threat to the Republican Party by future Senate GOP Leader Mitch McConnell of Kentucky, who used threats of filibusters to prevent the bill from coming to a vote. In response, McCain threatened to tie up the Senate in early 2001 unless then-Majority Leader Trent Lott of Mississippi set aside time for debate on the issue. After two weeks of McCain and Feingold fending off poison-pill amendments, the legislation passed in early April 2001 on a 59-41 vote. The House passed its version in February 2002, and McCain-Feingold became law.

After a series of mixed rulings on the new law, the Supreme Court in January 2010 struck down a key reform when it ruled in *Citizens United vs. Federal Election Commission* that curbs on political spending by corporations were an unconstitutional infringement on free speech. "I think there will be scandals associated with the worst decision of the United States Supreme Court in the 21st century," McCain declared afterward. But he refused to join Democrats in supporting the DISCLOSE Act aimed at mitigating the effects of *CitizensUnited*, calling it "closer to a clever attempt at political gamesmanship than actual reform."Another of his reform crusades was a war on earmarks, the practice of slipping high-dollar projects into bills to benefit a particular congressional district or state. Each year, McCain highlighted the pork-barrel spending he found in appropriations bills -- to the irritation of his colleagues in both parties, who were accustomed to using earmarks to curry favor with voters. But McCain's lonely campaign was eventually joined by House conservatives, and both chambers in 2011 adopted an earmark ban.

His biggest act of ideological heresy came on immigration. "The truth is, border enforcement alone does not work," McCain declared, as most conservatives were pursuing tougher enforcement strategies. In 2005, McCain joined with a leading liberal, Massachusetts Democratic Sen. Edward Kennedy, on a bill that gave illegal immigrants a path to legal status. "Some Americans believe we must find all these millions, round them up, and send them back to the countries they came from. I don't know how you do that. And I don't know why you would want to," McCain said. But a comprehensive immigration bill failed in 2006 and again in 2007. In 2010, McCain retreated from his earlier out-front support for a path to citizenship as he battled a competitive challenge to his renomination to a fifth term. But two years later, when immigration resurfaced as a front-burner issue after the 2012 elections, McCainveered back to the center and joined a bipartisan group, the so-called "Gang of Eight," that crafted a proposal.

That exercise required working closely with another leading liberal, New York Sen. Charles Schumer, one of the few other senators whose ubiquitous media presence rivals that of McCain's. The once frosty relationship between McCain and Schumer -- who ascended to Senate Democratic leader at the outset of the 115th Congress in 2017 -- had thawed after 2012 talks involving Senate rules on filibusters of presidential nominations. "He said, 'You know? You're a much different person than I thought you were,'" Schumer, in a *New Yorker* interview, later recalled McCain saying to him. A comprehensive bill that combined a path to citizenship for illegal immigrants with tough border-security measures passed the Senate in 2013 on a bipartisan vote, but the Republican-controlled House refused to take it up. When a frustrated Obama issued an executive order on immigration in November 2014, he received no support from McCain -- who complained it was "a cynical action that means that the president isn't that interested in comprehensive reform. He's only interested in placating his base."

Even before Obama and Trump, McCain was an equal opportunity critic of the White House, regardless of the party in control. While supporting President Bill Clinton's use of air strikes against Serbia in 1999, he knocked the Clinton administration for ruling out ground troops and for not using "all necessary force" against the Serbs.McCain strongly supported George W. Bush in the war on terrorism after 9/11, as well as when Bush decided to invade Iraq in 2003. But McCain pushed for a larger army and more troops to get the job done, leading to frequent clashes with Defense Secretary Donald Rumsfeld. At one point, McCain declared that the Bush administration's handling of the war "will go down as one of the worst" mistakes in U.S. military history.

Clearly, the Bush-McCain relationship bore scars from their 2000 battle for the GOP presidential nomination. McCain skipped the delegate caucuses in corn-dependent Iowa (McCain had long denounced ethanol subsidies as pork barrel spending) and instead concentrated on the New Hampshire primary. Traveling around in his "Straight Talk Express" bus, McCain attracted increasingly large and enthusiastic crowds as he told his personal story in self-deprecating terms.McCain did not have much support from his Senate colleagues, and *The Arizona Republic* wrote editorials warning of his "volcanic" temper. But, on Feb. 1, he beat Bush in New Hampshire -- where independents can vote in the Republican primary -- by a nearly 20-point margin. However, the "Straight Talk Express" stalled in South Carolina, where the GOP establishment and Christian conservatives had lined up with Bush. McCain's emphasis on campaign finance regulation and his criticism of Bush's proposed tax cuts for giving too much to the rich helped with independents, but sounded like enemy talk to Republicans. On Feb. 18, Bush won South Carolina, which turned out to be a decisive victory. On "Super Tuesday" in March, McCain won four New England states, but lost in New York, Ohio, and California. He suspended his campaign shortly afterward, grudgingly endorsing Bush two months later.

Four years later, as Bush headed into his 2004 reelection campaign, McCain was a popular national figure, with high positive ratings among Republicans and very low negatives among Democrats. Always enchanted with him, the news media-which McCain would laughingly refer to as his base-provided lavish coverage. (Years later, when Trump excoriated the media as "the enemy of the American people", McCain defended the media's role. "The first thing that dictators do is shut down the press," he gibed on NBC's *Meet The Press* in early 2017.) As his fellow Vietnam veteran Kerry clinched the Democratic nomination in March 2004, there even was talk he might ask McCain to be his vice presidential nominee on a fusion ticket. After some days of speculation, McCain firmly rejected the idea. "I am a pro-life, deficit-hawk, free-trade Republican," he declared. Subsequently, the Bush and McCain camps made peace, butwhen the independent expenditure "Swift Boat Veterans for Truth" ads appeared attacking Kerry, McCain called them "dishonorable" and said they should be pulled.

As the 2008 GOP presidential contest neared, McCain voiced more frequently and fervently his long-standing opposition to abortion rights. Even so, many conservatives were not enthusiastic about McCain. Their skepticism doomed his early strategy, which was to campaign as the next-in-line Republican for the presidential nomination. By late June 2007, the McCain campaign was broke, and its top managers were fired. Backed into a corner, McCain adopted the strategy on which some of the best consultants rely: Campaign on what you believe. His backup strategy: Wait for the other candidates' strategies to fail.They both worked.

After a trip to Iraq, McCain said in July 2007 that he was convinced the controversial troop surge strategy was working. In September, he launched his "No Surrender" tour, and, in primary debates, he was quick to jab at any rival who expressed skepticism about the surge. As in 2000, McCainwrote offIowa and focused on New Hampshire -- where, in January 2008, he defeated Mitt Romney, whohad been governor in neighboring Massachusetts. Next up was Michigan, where Romney had grown up:He promised to bring back jobs to the state's important automobile industry, while McCain, in his "straight talk" manner, bluntly said that many jobs would never return. Romney prevailed there, but attention quickly turned to South Carolina, where McCain had lost decisively to Bush in 2000. This time, McCain scored a narrow victory, and, on Super Tuesday, Feb. 5, he effectively sewed up the nomination.

But McCain faced difficult general election dynamics -- including Bush's low job rating and the continuing unpopularity of the Iraq war, doubts about the course of the economy, and enthusiasm among young, Hispanic and black voters for Obama. Given these factors, it's perhaps surprising that McCain made a contest of it at all.When McCain chose Alaska Gov. Sarah Palin as the second woman ever to appear on a major party national ticket, she initially sparked great enthusiasm among the Republican base, and, for about two weeks, McCain-Palin actually led Obama and his running mate, Sen. Joe Biden of Delaware, by narrow margins. But it became apparent that Palin was unprepared for the rigors of a national campaign, and her rambling interviews and verbal gaffes provided fodder for *Saturday Night Live* and late-night comics. She also was mercurial in temperament, clashing with McCain's aides and eventually overshadowing the senator's own campaign.

On Sept. 15, 2008, Lehman Brothers, a global financial services firm, went into bankruptcy, precipitating a far-reaching crisis. The same day, McCain said, "The fundamentals of our economy are strong." But four days later, Treasury Secretary Henry Paulson and Federal Reserve Chairman Ben Bernanke called for a $700 billion rescue of the financial markets. Obama's campaign scoffed at McCain's "strong" comment, surged in the polls, and never relinquished the lead after that. On Sept. 24, McCain announced he was suspending his campaign, and returning to the Capitol to work on the financial industry bill. When the House initially rejected the financial rescue on Sept. 29, McCain was blamed for not bringing along a sufficient number of House Republicans. He struggled to find traction on what had become the key issue of the campaign. When asked in a debate about the economy, McCain fell back on his determination to stop spending on earmarks-hardly a comprehensive economic agenda. McCain also touted his Senate experience, telling CBS' *60 Minutes,* "I was chairman of the

Commerce Committee, which oversights all of the commercial aspects of America's economy." In fact, the committee -- which McCain chaired for six years beginning in the late 1990s -- does not have jurisdiction over the financial services industry; several observers of the panel described McCain's time at the helm as lacking in major accomplishment.

On Election Day, Obama won 53%-46%, the best Democratic percentage since 1964. For McCain, it triggered a difficult period in which he displayed that volcanic temper that had erupted from time to time throughout his career. "It took me three years of feeling sorry for myself," McCain told to a group of reporters in 2012. Flashes of resentment persist, such as when McCain -- in early 2017 -- was asked about the prospect of an alliance with the Democrats in light of his sharp criticism of Trump. "These are the same Democrats that shredded me in 2008," he told *New York Magazine*. "I get along with the Democrats, but please, I'm not their hero…We will work with them, but have no doubt, their agenda is not our agenda." After his 2008 defeat, he resumed playing the prominent role that had characterized much of his Senate career, although he took a more conservative tack thanin earlier years. Despite past support of legislation to reduce carbon emissions, he called the Democrats' so-called "cap-and-trade bill" early in Obama's first term "bad economic policy that would cost businesses billions of dollars and allow for little to no transition into a low carbon system."He also spoke out strongly against repeal of the ban on openly gay military personnel.

McCain's positive image with the public had been built on his tendency toward political independence. But that imageacquired chinks in 2010 when, for the first time, he faced a serious primary challenge -- from ex-Rep. J.D. Hayworth, a conservative radio talk show host. McCain backed away from some of his earlier stances, telling *Newsweek* in April 2010, "I never considered myself a maverick."One of his most telling changes of heart was on immigration.He said that voters had spoken and that the border must be protected first, before any comprehensive bill would be passed. Most Republican primary voters in Arizona strongly opposed legalization of undocumented aliens, viewing it as a form of amnesty, and McCain no doubt was angling to eliminate an easy line of attack for Hayworth. In March 2009, McCain had snapped to a Hispanic group, "You people made your choice during the election," a reference to exit polls showing he lost Latinos to Obama by more than 2-1.

With his long Senate career on the line, McCain campaigned nonstop and beat Hayworth in the August primary 56%-32%. He went on to score an equally comfortable general election victory against Democratic nominee Rodney Glassman, the former vice mayor of Tucson, in a year in which Democratic Senate candidates were struggling nationwide. The Republican gains in the 2010 elections appeared to whet McCain's inclinations toward partisanship, leaving his onetime Democratic allies disappointed. "I just hope he goes back to his roots," then-Senate Majority Whip Dick Durbin of Illinois told *The New York Times* in July 2012. But from his perch as ranking Republican on the Armed Services Committee -- a post he held from 2007 to 2013 -- McCain's attacks on Obama escalated, as he blasted the administration's "feckless foreign policy that abandons American leadership." And, as the war in Iraq wound down, he gave the credit not to Obama, but to his predecessor, notwithstanding his many criticisms of Bush's handling of it. "Though most Democrats still cannot bear to admit it, the war in Iraq is ending successfully because the surge worked," he told *The Wall Street Journal*.

When Obama won reelection in 2012 and considered nominating United Nations Ambassador Susan Rice as secretary of state, McCain and his close ally, Sen. Lindsey Graham of South Carolina emerged as Rice's most full-throated critics. McCain called her "unqualified," citing her erroneous public statements about the September 2012 terrorist attack on the U.S. embassy in Libya. It prompted an angry Obama to retort, "If Senator McCain and Senator Graham and others want to go after somebody, they should go after me." The senators, however, won the battle when Rice withdrew her name, though she later became Obama's national security adviser. The two senators next took aim at Obama's nomination of their former Senate colleague, Nebraska's Chuck Hagel, to become defense secretary. Hagel was another Vietnam War veteran who had been close to McCain -- he was among the first supporters of McCain's 2000 presidential bid -- before political and policy differences drove them apart. McCain and Graham questioned Hagel's loyalty to Israel and willingness to intervene militarily overseas, but were unable to stop Hagel from being confirmed.

With Republicans regaining the Senate majority in the 2014 election, McCain assumed the chairmanship of Armed Services. At a hearing soon after he took over, he flashed his legendary temper at a group of Code Pink anti-war protesters who shouted for the arrest of Henry Kissinger while the Vietnam era secretary of state testified. "Get out of here, you lowlife scum!" he barkedin an exchange that went viral. As chairman, McCain said he hoped to shape a legacy as someone who played "a significant role in defeating the forces of radical Islam that want to destroy America." He had caused a stir in 2013 when he ventured into Syria to meet with opposition leaders whom he hoped could topple Bashar al-Assad. (He made a similar visit four years later, in February 2017, to meet with Kurdish fighters.)

McCain did applaud the Obama Administration for providing arms to Syrian rebels, but said it was not enough. "It is delusional for them to think that what they're doing is succeeding," McCain charged, as he called for more of a military presence to combat Islamic State forces (ISIS) operating in Iraq and Syria. Later that year, he blasted the Obama Administration's Iran nuclear agreement as a deal with "the patron of the Assad regime."

In 2015, McCain made clear that he planned to run for a sixth term the following year, when he would turn 80. His sharp criticisms of the Obama Administration did little to assuage hardline conservatives at home: In January 2014, the Maricopa County (Phoenix) Republican Party voted overwhelmingly to censure him, and the state GOP followed suit a couple of weeks later. A couple of members of the state's House delegation, Reps. Matt Salmon and David Schweikert, kept the door open but ultimately opted not to launch a primary challenge.Instead, the less-experienced former state Sen. Kelli Ward ran, and McCain caught a break when a number of national conservative groups -- believing Ward had limited prospects for toppling McCain -- opted to put their resources elsewhere. In the August 2016 primary, McCain bested Ward by a 51%-40% margin, boosted by a pro-McCain independent expenditure "super PAC" that poured close to $2.7 million into the primary. Given his role as a long-time advocate of campaign reform, McCain acknowledged the irony, telling *Politico*: "You've got to play the game by the rules, but I don't think there's any doubt that there will be future scandals. We've gone through a cycle ever since Teddy Roosevelt of corruption, reform, a period of time, corruption, reform."

One wealthy Trump backer, hedge fund manager Robert Mercer, donated $200,000 to another super PAC that spent about $600,000 on ads on behalf of Ward slamming McCain on immigration. The McCain-Trump relationship had gotten off to an acrimonious start a year earlier, when Trump had launched his presidential campaign with an anti-immigrant blast. It prompted McCain to criticize the New York businessman for characterizing Mexicans as "rapists." Trump shot back by belittling McCain's "war hero" status. "I like people that weren't captured," Trump sneered. The volatile McCain remained surprisingly restrained in the ensuing months, notwithstanding a couple of additional swipes at Trump over the latter's use of racially tinged rhetoric. "I'm running my own campaign, and I just don't really want to keep talking about Trump," McCain insisted as he focused on winning renomination. His stance was widely attributed to a need to attract Trump supporters in the August primary.

"If Donald Trump is at the top of the ticket, here in Arizona, with over 30 percent of the vote being the Hispanic vote, no doubt that this may be the race of my life," McCain had acknowledged to supporters at a fundraiser a couple of months prior to Trump's nomination. A day after winning the primary, McCain appeared to write off Trump's chances in November, as he prepared to face three-term Democratic Rep. Ann Kirkpatrick."My opponent...is a good person," McCain declared in a video. "But if Hillary Clinton is elected president, Arizona will need a senator who will act as a check - not a rubber stamp - for the White House." His statement came as polls showed Clinton with a shot at becoming only the second Democratic presidential candidate to win Arizona in the past 70 years.

Kirkpatrick focused her campaign on tying McCain to Trump, while suggesting he was no longer the outspoken independent of the past."The fact that he continues to support Donald Trump in spite of the fact that Trump insulted him, in spite of the fact that Trump insulted a Gold Star family, shows that he's changed," Kirkpatrick told *Politico*. She wasalluding to Trump's criticism of Khizr Khan, father of an Army captain killed during the Iraq war, after Khan addressed the 2016 Democratic National Convention. "There was a day that he would have stood up for that family, would have stood up for himself," said Kirkpatrick, who acknowledged having voted for McCain several times in previous elections. McCain renounced his endorsement of Trump about a month before the November election, following release of a decade-old videotape in which Trump made lewd comments about women. He said he would not vote for Trump, and suggested he might write in his good friend, Graham, who was briefly a candidate for the 2016 presidential nomination. (McCain later declined to say for whom he voted.) On Election Day, Trump took Arizona by 49%-45% margin, as McCain scored a comfortable 54%-41% victory over Kirkpatrick. CNN exit polls showed him attracting 90 percent of Republicans along with peeling off 16 percent of Democrats, while besting Kirkpatrick by 50%-41% among independents.

Returning to Capitol Hill, McCain again sought to go silent on the surprise winner of the White House. "I'm not talking about President-elect Trump. Now look, tell all your friends, OK?" he barked at reporters. But, given his deep-seated differences with the incoming president, the verbal floodgates opened after Trump was sworn in. McCain called Trump's efforts to restrict travel from several predominantly Muslim countries a "self-inflicted wound" that would hamper efforts to recruit Muslim allies in battle against terrorism. He blasted Trump's decision to abandon the Trans Pacific Partnership, the 12-nation trade deal negotiated by the Obama Administration -- saying Trump's move "creates an opening for China." McCain even engaged in a bit of trans-Pacific diplomacy himself: After reports surfaced of Trump confronting the Australian prime minister in their initial phone conversation, McCain called Australia's ambassador to the United States and issued a statement expressing "unwavering support for the U.S.-Australian alliance."

McCain's criticism of a raid in Yemen a little more than a week into the Trump presidency -- in which a Navy SEAL and two dozen Yemeni citizens were killed -- sparked one of Trump's pungent Twitter messages. "Sen. McCain should not be talking about the success or failure of a mission to the media. Only emboldens the enemy! He's been losing so long he doesn't know how to win anymore," Trump asserted. But it was the subject of relations with Russia that most clearly highlighted the differences between McCain's world view and that of the new president.

McCain denounced Russia's "interfering" in the presidential election via cyberspace, telling *New York Magazine*: "The severity of this issue, the gravity of it, is so consequential because if you succeed in corrupting an election, then you've destroyed the foundation of democracy…I view it more seriously than Orlando, or San Bernardino. As tragic as that was, the far-reaching consequences of an election hack are certainly far in excess of a single terrorist attack." He characterized Russian President Vladimir Putin as a "former KGB agent who has plunged his country into tyranny," and took sharp issue with a Trump comment that appeared to put Putin's actions on a moral plain similar to that of the United States. "That moral equivalency is a contradiction of everything the United States has ever stood for in the 20th and 21st centuries," McCain said during a "Meet the Press" appearance. He issued a joint statement with his sometime Democratic ally, Schumer, pressing for a special committee to look into Russian efforts to influence the election -- putting him on a collision course with his own party leader, McConnell. At the same time, as the Democrats sought to derail several controversial Trump appointees, McCain voted for all but one -- Office of Management and Budget Director Mick Mulvaney, whom he considered insufficiently supportive of military spending.

On Election Night 2016, McCain suggested that "I think this might be the last" campaign for him, telling the crowd in an emotional moment, "I'll say good night and thank you, one last time, for making me the luckiest guy I know." But, in an interview several days later with the *Arizona Republic,* he said he wouldn't rule out a running again in 2022 -- saying he wouldn't make a decision on a seventh term for about three years. "I feel great," he said, pointedly adding, "My mother will be 105 in February."

Junior Senator

Jeff Flake (R)

Elected 2012, term expires 2018, 1st term; b. Dec 31, 1962, Snowflake; Brigham Young University (UT), M.A.; Brigham Young University (UT), B.A.; Mormon; Married (Ms. Kathleen Slattery); 5 children.

Elected Office: U.S. House, 2000-2012.

Professional Career: Owner, public affairs firm, 1987; Executive Director, Foundation for Democracy (Namibia), 1989-1990; Executive Director, Goldwater Inst., 1992-1999.

DC Office: 413 RSOB 20510, 202-224-4521, Fax: 202-228-0515, flake.senate.gov.

State Offices: Phoenix, 602-840-1891; Tucson, 520-575-8633.

Committees: *Aging*. *Energy & Natural Resources*: Energy, Public Lands, Forests & Mining, Water & Power (Chmn). *Foreign Relations*: Africa & Global Health Policy (Chmn), Internat'l Dev Instit & Internat'l Econ, Energy & Environ Policy, West Hem Crime Civ Sec Dem Rights & Women's Issues. *Judiciary*: Border Security & Immigration, Oversight, Agency Action, Federal Rights & Federal Courts, Privacy, Technology & the Law (Chmn).

Group Ratings

	ADA	ACLU	AFL-CIO	LCV	ITI	COC	HAFA	ACU	CFG	FRC
2016	-	35%	-	6%	80%	63%	67%	79%	8400%	0%
2015	5%	C	8%	0%	C	77%	C	79%	93%	91%

Almanac Ratings 2015

	Economy	Social	Foreign	Composite
Liberal	15%	9%	40%	22%
Conservative	85%	91%	60%	78%

Key Votes of the 114th Congress

1. Keystone pipeline	Y	5. National Security Data	Y	9. Gun Sales Checks	N
2. Export-Import Bank	Y	6. Iran Nuclear Deal	Y	10. Sanctuary Cities	Y
3. Debt Ceiling Increase	N	7. Puerto Rico Debt	Y	11. Planned Parenthood	Y
4. Homeland Security $$	Y	8. Loretta Lynch A.G	Y	12. Trade deals	Y

Election Results

Election	Name (Party)	Vote (%)	Cand. Spent	Ind. Exp. Support	Ind. Exp. Oppose
2012 General	Jeff Flake (R)	1,104,457 (49%)	$9,557,420	$4,606,334	$8,514,069
	Richard Carmona (D)	1,036,542 (46%)	$6,373,544	$1,138,072	$8,035,923
2012 Primary	Jeff Flake (R)	357,360 (69%)			
	Wil Cardon (R)	110,150 (21%)			
	Clair Van Steenwyk (R)	29,159 (6%)			

Prior winning percentages: House: 2010 (66%), 2008 (62%), 2006 (75%), 2004 (79%), 2002 (66%),2000 (54%)

Republican Jeff Flake, Arizona's junior senator, occupies the Senate seat held by the late Barry Goldwater for the 12 years leading up to Goldwater's 1964 presidential campaign -- which he lost by a landslide, albeit while triggering a long-term transformation of the national political landscape. But if Goldwater is often referred to as the father of modern-day conservativism, he adhered to a brand with a more libertarian bent than many of today's conservatives. And Flake -- executive director of the Phoenix-based Goldwater Institute for seven years prior to his first run for Congress in 2000 -- fits into Goldwater's philosophical mold to a significant degree.

After six terms in the House, Flake won election to the Senate in 2012, where he has shared representation of Arizona with fellow Republican John McCain. If the two have differed on some significant issues, Flake and McCain have in common an independent streak that, for both, has occasionally alienated GOP colleagues on Capitol Hill --while creating political headaches back in the Grand Canyon State. McCain has faced competitive primary challenges in his last two re-election races, and a similar situation confronts Flake as he prepares to seek a second Senate term in 2018. Among the nine Republican senators up for another term in the coming election, Flake appears to be the one most vulnerable to a primary challenge, in part because of his rocky relationship with President Donald Trump. While numerous congressional Republicans, including McCain, have been critical of Trump's tone and policies, few have been as publicly vocal as Flake -- who also confronted Trump during a closed meeting on Capitol Hill in July 2016, telling the then-Republican presidential candidate to cease his rhetorical attacks on Mexicans. Trump returned the favor a couple of months later in tweets that derided Flake as "very weak and ineffective."

A fifth-generation Arizonan, Flake is a Mormon who was born and raised on a ranch in Snowflake, a town named after his great-great-grandfather. The fifth of 11 children, he graduated with a degree in international studies from Brigham Young University and did missionary work in South Africa and Zimbabwe. In 1989, he moved to Namibia to become executive director of the Foundation for Democracy, which monitored democratic progress in that country. After Namibia gained independence in 1990, Flake returned to Arizona to lead the Goldwater Institute, where he was out front in the fight for Arizona's charter school law. When Rep. Matt Salmon -- elected in 1994 as Republicans won a House majority for the first time four decades -- kept his pledge to serve only three terms in the House, he anointed Flake to succeed him. Flake triumphed in a hard-fought primary, in which he ran as the most conservative candidate against four opponents, and went on to easily win the general election.

Flake promised to "continue to rock the boat" as Salmon had, as a principled conservative who bucked the Republican leadership. Flake became the House's leading opponent of earmarking -- a practice that McCain was frequently lambasting on the Senate side of the Capitol at the same time -- and regularly tried to amend legislation to ban such special-interest funding provisions from being added to spending bills. His willingness to take on special projects in the districts of fellow Republicans and Democrats made him a darling of conservative groups such as the Club for Growth, which favors limiting federal government spending. After Republicans regained control of the House in 2010 after four years of a Democratic majority, Flake won a spot on the Appropriations Committee, whose members strongly favored earmarks. (While earmarking has now been curtailed in both the House and Senate, Flake continues to produce regular reports detailing examples of what he regards as government waste.)

Flake did not hesitate to demonstrate an independent streak on other fronts during his House tenure. During the George W. Bush Administration, Flake voted against the new Republican president's 2001 No Child Left Behind education overhaul and the 2003 law extending Medicare benefits for prescription drugs. In 2010, he was one of only three Republicans to oppose a bill overhauling how the Defense Department buys goods and services through an expansion of the Pentagon's acquisition authority. At the same time, Flake's libertarian beliefs on occasion led him to support Democratic-sponsored measures that many Republicans abhorred. He supported a 2007 bill to prohibit workplace discrimination against gays, although he said in 2010 that he wouldn't support a revised version because of its expansion to include transgender rights. An avid backer of free trade, he also joined Democrats in calling for an end to the 1962 trade embargo with Cuba -- which many staunchly anti-Communist Republicans have refused to support lifting, despite President Barack Obama's move to re-establish diplomatic relations with the island nation in 2015.

When Republican Sen. Jon Kyl decided against seeking a fourth term in 2012, Flake joined the race. He faced a primary challenge from real estate investor Wil Cardon, and the two men waged an acrimonious campaign. Cardon inveighed against "career politicians" and ran an ad using Flake's own words to highlight a broken pledge not to serve more than three House terms. "What can I say? I lied," Flake joked in an interview with Reason TV. Flake won easily, 69%-21%, with the rest split between two other candidates -- although Cardon outspent him 2-to-1. But the late August primary meant that he had less time to focus on the fall campaign against Democrat Richard Carmona, a former U.S. surgeon general. In a traditionally Republican state that has become more competitive in recent presidential elections, Carmona stressed doing more to assist veterans and took the middle ground on many issues, including immigration and health care.

Flake, meanwhile, emphasized his fiscal conservatism. His campaign ran one of the most explosive ads of the 2012 election cycle in which Cristina Beato, Carmona's former boss at the Health and Human Services Department, alleged that he twice angrily banged on her door and yelled at her in the middle of the night after workplace disputes. Carmona's campaign denied the charges and released its own spot featuring Cecilia Rosales, a University of Arizona professor, who called her former colleague "respectful and supportive of his coworkers." Carmona closed the gap in polls but could not overcome Arizona's Republican tilt. Flake won the endorsement of *The Arizona Republic*, which declared, "With the exception of Rep. Paul Ryan, perhaps no candidate for federal office in this election cycle is more committed to forcing sanity back into the nation's finances." Flake narrowly prevailed, 49%-46%, as Republican presidential nominee Mitt Romney was besting Obama by 54%-45% in the state.

Having been outspoken for many years in advocating an end to travel and trade restrictions with Cuba, it was little surprise that the Obama Administration asked Flake, in December 2014, to be the only Republican in a secret delegation that flew to Cuba. In a prisoner swap, the group brought Alan P. Gross, a jailed U.S. government contractor, back to the United States as a prelude to Obama's move to normalize diplomatic relations. (Flake made another trip to Cuba in March 2016, accompanying the president as Obama visited the island for the first time.) Even as most other Republicans lambasted the Cuban government as tyrannical and repressive and opposed Obama's action, Flake has consistently viewed issues involving the two countries in terms of freedom, including the freedom to travel.

In the spring of 2015, Flake also parted company with most of his Senate Republican colleagues in supporting the Obama's nomination of Loretta Lynch to be attorney general. He voted for her as a member of the Judiciary Committee and, again, when her nomination came to the Senate floor. Similarly, Flake was one of only seven Republicans who in early 2015 declined to sign a controversial letter to Iran's leaders. The letter warned that an agreement with Obama regarding nuclear facilities without congressional approval was nothing more than an executive agreement that could be short-lived, since it could be undone by a future president or Congress. However, while regarded as one of the few Republicans who might back the Iran deal, Flake came out against it several months later, contending that the benefits of limiting Iran's ability to produce a nuclear bomb were outweighed by "severe limitations" on Congress and future administrations "in responding to Iran's non-nuclear behavior in the region."

Each of those stances-favoring the opening of diplomatic relations with Cuba, backing the Lynch nomination and declining to sign the letter to the Iranian leaders-put Flake at odds with McCain. But the two senators have worked on other issues, including in 2013, when, as members of the so-called bipartisan "Gang of Eight," they helped to craft a comprehensive immigration bill that cleared the Senate but was blocked in the Republican-controlled House. And, as representatives of a border state that abuts Mexico, the two joined together in early 2017 to defend the North American Free Trade Agreement as Trump was vowing to renegotiate it. "Improvements can be made, but it would be very difficult to renegotiate NAFTA in a way that benefits the U.S. and penalizes Mexico," Flake told the *Arizona Republic* in a swipe at Trump. During the campaign, Flake dismissed Trump's calls for building a wall along the Mexican border as a "joke."

In the closing weeks of the 2016 campaign, Flake and McCain both called for Trump to step aside as the Republican nominee following release of the decade-old video showing Trump making lewd comments about women. But while McCain had previously said he would support Trump as the party's nominee, Flake never offered his endorsement, in large part because of Trump's anti-immigrant rhetoric toward both Mexicans and Muslims. Flake suggested several times prior to Election Day that Trump's controversial statements had put Arizona -- with a Hispanic-American population of more than 30 percent, according to the latest census figures -- in play for Democratic presidential nominee Hillary Clinton. (Trump ended up winning the state by a 49%-45% margin.)

And, in his confrontation with Trump during the July 2016 meeting with Republican senators, Flake brought up Trump's comments about McCain early in the campaign -- in which Trump had belittled McCain's status as a prisoner of war in Vietnam, saying that he likes people who don't get captured. "I'm the other senator from Arizona -- the one who didn't get captured -- and I want to talk to you about statements like that," Flake was reported by *The Washington Post* as telling Trump during a tense exchange between the two men. Notwithstanding his testy relationship with Trump, Flake has a close friendship with Trump's running mate, Vice President Mike Pence: Flake and Pence served in the House together for 12 years, and both headed conservative think tanks before being elected to office. Flake is also good friends with the other 2016 vice-presidential nominee: Democratic Sen. Tim Kaine of Virginia. He and Kaine sit on the Foreign Relations Committee, where -- in the face of resistance from the Obama Administration -- they pushed for a new authorization for the use of military force, in order to more clearly define the fight against terrorist groups such as ISIS.

Following a loss to McCain in the August 2016 primary, former state Sen. Kelli Ward quickly announced she would take on Flake in 2018. A bigger potential threat to the incumbent may be state Treasurer Jeff DeWit, a strong Trump supporter who headed Trump's Arizona campaign before becoming chief operating officer of his national campaign. If DeWit opts against a run, Arizona GOP Chairman Robert Graham, an outspoken Trump supporter, is a possibility. A mid-November 2016 poll of likely Arizona Republican primary voters showed Trump with an 82 percent favorability rating as compared to just 30 percent for Flake; DeWit led Flake by 9 points in a head-to-head matchup, though the poll results may have been affected by the post-election timing. "For those of us who opposed [Trump's] candidacy, you can expect your numbers to be down pretty far," Flake observed during a press conference shortly after the poll was released, while adding, "But that's why you run campaigns ... I'm glad I took the position that I did, and we'll go forward."

FIRST DISTRICT

Tom O'Halleran (D)

Elected 2016, 1st term; b. Jan 24, 1946, Chicago, IL; Lewis University, 1966; DePaul University, Att., 1993; Catholic; Married (Pat O'Halleran); 3 children; 3 grandchildren.

Elected Office: AZ House, 2001-2007; AZ Senate, 2007-2009.

Professional Career: Police officer, 1966-1979; Bond trader/business owner.

DC Office: 126 CHOB 20515, 202-225-3361, Fax: 202-225-3462, ohalleran.house.gov.

State Offices: Casa Grande, 520-316-0839; Flagstaff, 928-286-5338; Tucson, 928-304-0131.

Committees: *Agriculture*: Commodity Exchanges, Energy & Credit, Conservation & Forestry, General Farm Commodities & Risk Management. *Armed Services*: Oversight & Investigations, Tactical Air & Land Forces.

Election Results

Election	Name (Party)	Vote (%)		Cand. Spent	Ind. Exp. Support	Ind. Exp. Oppose
2016 General	Tom O'Halleran (D)	142,219	(51%)	$1,563,186	$27,461	
	Paul Babeu (R)	121,745	(43%)	$1,250,945	$71,495	$3,484,797
	Ray Parrish (G)	16,746	(6%)		$3,400	
2016 Primary	Tom O'Halleran (D)	26,289	(59%)			
	Miguel Olivas (D)	18,119	(41%)			

Democrat Tom O'Halleran, a former Republican state legislator who switched parties to run for the House, was elected in 2014 to an open seat in Arizona. In this competitive district, he benefited from an ethically flawed opponent whom national Republicans refused to support. O'Halleran, age 70 when he entered Congress, will need to strengthen his political support at home and cannot assume that his opposition will again self-destruct in 2018.

He was born in Chicago. His father grew up on a dairy farm that his family lost during the Depression, and he worked in a steel foundry and later was a janitor. His mother was a secretary. He joined the Chicago police department in 1966, serving as an officer and later a sergeant in a special operations unit. He received numerous department awards. In 1979, O'Halleran became a government bond trader and served two terms on the Chicago Board of Trade's executive board of directors, including as an officer of its finance, floor operations and planning committees.

He retired and moved with his family to Arizona, where he became involved in local politics. He initially was an advocate for Yavapai County in the state legislature, where he focused on preservation of natural resources. He was elected as a Republican to the state House in 2000, where he served three terms and was chairman of the Natural Resources and Agriculture Committee. In 2006, he was elected to the state Senate, where he chaired the Higher Education Committee, but was defeated in 2008. Citing Republicans' inability to legislate on issues such as education, child welfare and water problems, he changed his registration in 2014 to Independent and ran again for the Senate. He lost to Republican Sylvia Allen, 51%-49%.

When Democratic Rep. Ann Kirkpatrick challenged Sen. John McCain, O'Halleran ran for the open seat. He continued to reside in Yavapai County, which is a small slice of the district. In the Democratic primary, he defeated Miguel Olivas 59%-41%. Republicans nominated Paul Babeu, who got 31 percent of the vote in a six-candidate field. Babeu was well-known as the Sheriff of Pinal County, where he has been a hard-liner and outspoken on illegal immigration. He made an initial run for the House in 2012 against Rep. Paul Gosar in the 4th Congressional District, but became embroiled in controversy when a former boyfriend (and illegal immigrant) accused him of threatening deportation to keep their friendship quiet. Babeu came out as gay but denied the allegations, and withdrew from the contest before the Republican primary.

In the 2016 general election, Babeu emphasized immigration issues. "I'm for enforcing the law, securing the border and protecting America. I don't feel our nation is more secure or more safe than it was eight years ago," he said, according to a report by Arizona Public Media. O'Halleran called for improved security at the border, with the best technology and experts.

The campaign was overwhelmed by new charges against Babeu, stemming from reports of alleged abuses while he was headmaster of a private Massachusetts school for troubled children, which subsequently was shut down; a state investigation concluded that the school's disciplinary practices were abusive and inhumane. With Babeu's mountain of personal baggage, Republican spokesmen tried to dismiss the various charges as old news but the National Republican Congressional Committee decided to steer clear of the contest and spent no money in this competitive district. Two of his sisters advised voters not to support Babeu. National Democratic groups and their allies spent $3 million, chiefly on ads attacking Babeu's personal history. O'Halleran out-spent Babeu, $1.6 million to $1.3 million.

O'Halleran won, 51%-43%. He led by a 2-to-1 margin in Apache and Coconino counties, and narrowly in Navajo County. Babeu had small leads in Pinal and Pima counties. In the House, O'Halleran got a seat on the Agriculture Committee.

Northeast/Central Arizona: Southern Phoenix, Navajo Nation, Flagstaff

Population		**Race and Ethnicity**		**Income**	
Total	727,454	White	50.0%	Median Income	$47,531 (291 out of 435)
Land area	55,040	Black	2.2%	Under $50,000	52.0%
Pop/ sq mi	13.2	Latino	21.3%	$50,000-$99,999	30.8%
Born in state	51.8%	Asian	1.6%	$100,000-$199,999	14.5%
Age Groups		Two races	1.9%	$200,000 or more	2.7%
Under 18	24.8%	Other	1.8%	Poverty Rate	21.9%
18-34	23.0%	**Education**		**Health Insurance**	
35-64	36.5%	H.S grad or less	41.7%	With health insurance coverage	84.4%
Over 64	15.7%	Some college	34.8%	**Public Assistance**	
Work		College Degree, 4 yr	14.3%	Cash public assistance income	3.0%
White Collar	33.1%	Post grad	9.2%	Food stamp/SNAP benefits	16.1%
Sales and Service	45.1%	**Military**			
Blue Collar	21.7%	Veteran	10.1%		
Government	23.7%	Active Duty	0.1%		

Voter Turnout			
2015 Total Citizens 18+	521,711	2016 House Turnout as % CVAP	54%
2016 House turnout	280,710	2014 House Turnout as % CVAP	36%

2012 Presidential Vote		
Mitt Romney	131,115	(50%)
Barack Obama	124,550	(48%)

2016 Presidential Vote		
Donald Trump	135,928	(47%)
Hillary Clinton	132,874	(46%)
Gary Johnson	11,732	(4%)

Cook Partisan Voting Index: R+2

Beyond Phoenix, Arizona is a vast state of stunning beauty: the awe-inspiring Grand Canyon, the subtle pastel hues of the Painted Desert, the sheer cliff walls of Canyon de Chelly, the still waters of Lake Powell, the mountainous pine forests around Flagstaff, and the rust-and-rose red rocks of Sedona. It also has man-made landmarks. The celebrated U.S. 66, now mostly superseded by Interstate 40, traverses the district, and it's dotted with old copper mining towns like Globe.

All of these places are in the 1st Congressional District in northeastern Arizona, an area larger than Pennsylvania and the tenth largest district in the nation. The district has wide variations in economic strength and commercial development. It encompasses Flagstaff, a university town and growing retirement mecca that has lured snowbirds with its climate and well-priced housing. The boom in home construction made the city vulnerable to the housing bust of the late 2000s and created both winners and losers. From 2006 to 2012, the median home value in Flagstaff was slashed from $400,000 to $225,000. By the summer of 2016, the median value had returned to $354,000.

There have been ample signs of economic recovery in the district. Investors have been buying up land to develop shopping centers and housing in fast-growing Pinal County. In Casa Grande, a town between Phoenix and Tucson, Phoenix Mart was scheduled for a delayed opening in 2018 as a 1.6-million square foot commercial complex that styles itself as "North America's most complete global product marketplace," designed to connect manufacturers, distributors, wholesalers and retailers. In 2016, other developers in Casa Grande announced separate plans to build a $700 million plant to manufacture luxury electric vehicles and a huge new motorsports center with two roads of 2.8 miles each. In Flagstaff, Northern Arizona University continued its rapid growth. The city has been designated an International Dark Sky City, which permits lighting to be controlled.

The 1st is also home to the nation's largest Indian population. A full 23 percent of its residents identify themselves as Native Americans, who slightly outnumber Hispanics in the district. Redistricting after the 2010 census united the Navajo and Hopi reservations in the same congressional district for the first time in the state's history. The two tribes, historic enemies, concluded they could wield more political clout together than apart. Other tribes with a presence here are the Fort Apache, San Carlos, Havasupai, Hualapai, Kaibab, Gila River, and Zuni.

By far the largest is the Navajo Nation. Most of the Navajo are in Apache County, with the rest in Navajo and Coconino counties and others on parts of the reservation that extend into corners of New Mexico and Utah. There are about 286,000 Navajo in the three states, of whom an estimated 73 percent speak the language, and many still practice the traditional Navajo lifestyle. They have a history of fiercely contested tribal elections and considerable social problems. Unemployment recently has been close to 50 percent. A large number of dwellings are without telephone service, and 21 percent of homes lack complete plumbing systems. Alcoholism and drug abuse are rampant, violent crime is a problem, and there is little economic development. Following a failed decades-long $500 million effort to encourage the Navajo and Hopi to share land, the federal government has begun to remove members of each tribe from the property of the other. The relocation is scheduled for completion in 2018.

The 1st District was drawn to be competitive politically. With its diversity and huge size, it is one of the most difficult in the nation to manage. Although Democrats have held a 10-point voter registration advantage, the district has leaned slightly Republican in recent presidential elections. Donald Trump won by 1 percent, a slightly smaller margin than John McCain and Mitt Romney had when they won the district. Apache County, with its Navajo majority, is heavily Democratic. Coconino County has moved in that direction. Pinal County, which has the most voters, leans Republican, as does the sliver of Pima County included in the 1st. A Republican needs a strong performance in those exurban areas south of Phoenix to neutralize the Democratic vote to the north and east in the district.

SECOND DISTRICT

Martha McSally (R)

Elected 2014, 2nd term; b. Mar 22, 1966, Warwick, RI; United States Air Force Academy, B.S.; Harvard University John F. Kennedy School of Government (MA), M.PP; National Air War College, Mast. Deg.; Single.

Military Career: U.S. Air Force, 1988-2010 (Iraq, Afghanistan).

Professional Career: Legislative fellow, 1999-2000; National Security Studies professor, George C. Marshall Ctr, 2011-2012.

DC Office: 510 CHOB 20515, 202-225-2542, Fax: 202-225-0378, mcsally.house.gov.

State Offices: Sierra Vista, 520-459-3115; Tucson, 520-881-3588.

Committees: *Armed Services*: Military Personnel, Readiness, Tactical Air & Land Forces. *Homeland Security*: Border & Maritime Security (Chmn), Emergency Preparedness, Response & Communications.

Group Ratings

	ADA	ACLU	AFL-CIO	LCV	ITI	COC	HAFA	ACU	CFG	FRC
2016	-	23%	-	3%	100%	100%	43%	76%	64%	58%
2015	5%	C	17%	3%	C	100%	C	58%	53%	83%

Almanac Ratings 2015

	Economy	Social	Foreign	Composite
Liberal	15%	28%	10%	18%
Conservative	85%	72%	90%	82%

Key Votes of the 114th Congress

1. Keystone Pipeline	Y	5. Puerto Rico Debt	Y	9. Offenses by Aliens	Y
2. Trade Deals	Y	6. Medical Marijuana	N	10. Troops in Iraq	N
3. Export-Import Bank	N	7. Sanctuary Cities	N	11. Homeland Security $$	Y
4. Debt Ceiling Increase	Y	8. Armor-piercing Bullets	Y	12. Trade Adjustment aid	Y

Election Results

Election	Name (Party)	Vote (%)	Cand. Spent	Ind. Exp. Support	Ind. Exp. Oppose
2016 General	Martha MCSally (R)....................	179,806 (57%)	$7,548,870	$45,086	$30,000
	Matt Heinz (D)..........................	135,873 (43%)	$1,551,530		$632,678
2016 Primary	Martha McSally (R).................................	(100%)			

Prior winning percentages: 2014 (50%)

Republican Martha McSally, elected in 2014, made history by being the first woman to fly and command an Air Force squadron in combat. Two years after a narrow loss to Democratic Rep. Ron Barber, she campaigned on her extensive military background to win a rematch that wasn't officially decided for more than six weeks. In the House, she quickly became a player on security issues, which are apt for McSally and for her district.

A Rhode Island native, McSally came to Tucson in the early 1990s when she was assigned to Davis-Monthan Air Force Base. She had graduated from the Air Force Academy in 1988 with a biology degree. Two years later, she received a master's in public policy from Harvard University. In 1999, McSally was selected for a Washington, D.C.-based fellowship program, where she served as a national security adviser to Sen. Jon Kyl of Arizona.

McSally retired as a colonel in the Air Force with more than 2,600 flight hours, including 325 combat hours. She served multiple tours in the Middle East and supervised the execution of an air campaign based in Saudi Arabia for Operation Iraqi Freedom. She led a combat deployment to Afghanistan for Operation Enduring Freedom, and taught senior military officials. In 2007, McSally received her second master's degree from the Air Force Air War College.

She drew national attention after she filed - and won - a 2001 lawsuit against the Defense Department (*McSally v. Rumsfeld*) to overturn a policy that required U.S. servicewomen based in Saudi Arabia to wear a body-covering Muslim *abaya* and headscarf. Her initiative also resulted in subsequent legislation. In an interview on CBS's *60 Minutes*, she criticized other forms of discrimination in the conservative Saudi culture. "I can fly a single-seat aircraft in enemy territory, but [in Saudi Arabia] I can't drive a vehicle," she said.

Barber, a former aide to Rep. Gabrielle Giffords who was grievously injured alongside the former congresswoman in a 2011 mass shooting in Tucson, won a 2012 special election to fill her vacated seat. McSally finished second among five candidates in the Republican primary for the special election, but handily won the 2012 primary for the two-year term. Barber's race against McSally drew controversy: The Democratic-backed House Majority PAC changed an ad that showed McSally in a kitchen cooking "a recipe for disaster" after she called it sexist. Meanwhile, McSally was criticized for saying, "I resemble Gabby Giffords more than the man who worked for her." Barber prevailed with a 2,454-vote margin.

In their rematch, Barber and McSally sparred over stricter gun-control laws, with McSally criticizing an ad by Giffords' Americans for Responsible Solutions political committee that said the Republican "opposes making it harder for stalkers to get a gun." McSally, who revealed that she was a victim of stalking, called the ad "horrendous." Giffords' group spent more than $2 million on behalf of Barber in one of the most expensive House races of the year. McSally raised about $4.8 million compared with $4 million for Barber. Spending by outside groups exceeded $10 million, and was roughly equal for each side.

Election night didn't end the skirmishing between the candidates. Just over a week after the election, McSally held a lead of fewer than 200 votes and declared victory. But the narrow margin triggered a mandatory recount under Arizona law. Barber sought several ways to get additional provisional and early ballots counted, but failed each time. On December 17, Maricopa County Superior Court Judge Katherine Cooper ruled McSally the winner by 161 votes. *National Journal* wrote that McSally's military background shaped her politically "not only because it cultivated toughness, but because it made her an expert in refusing to take no for an answer."

In the House, McSally won her coveted seat on the Armed Services Committee even before she was declared the election winner. She vowed to be a strong voice for both the military and for Raytheon's missile programs in Tucson. In 2015, she praised the Pentagon's decision to lift its ban on women soldiers taking on combat roles as "long overdue." In contrast to the other four House Republicans in the Arizona delegation, she voted with party leaders in March 2015 to support full-year funding of the Homeland Security Department. During 2016 debate on the annual defense spending bill, she took credit for full funding for aircraft at Davis-Monthan, including the A-10 Warthog, which she flew in combat in Iraq and later trained other pilots to fly. On the Homeland Security Committee, she chaired the Border and

Maritime Security Subcommittee. In 2015, she won approval of amendments to strengthen preparedness against cyber-attacks.

In contrast to the recent history of close contests in this district, McSally handily won reelection, 57%-43%, against Matt Heinz, an emergency-room physician and former state representative who is a gay man. For the first time, she led comfortably in Pima County. McSally took no chances, with campaign spending of an impressive $8.3 million; Heinz spent $1.6 million. A month before the election, she condemned as "disgusting" and "unacceptable" Trump's lewd comments about women in a 2005 video. She never endorsed him during the campaign.

Southeast Arizona: Tucson Metro

Population		**Race and Ethnicity**		**Income**	
Total	719,851	White	62.5%	Median Income	$47,507 (292 out of 435)
Land area	7,838	Black	3.8%		
Pop/ sq mi	91.8	Latino	27.2%		
Born in state	36.1%	Asian	2.8%	Under $50,000	52.2%
		Two races	2.5%	$50,000-$99,999	29.6%
Age Groups		Other	3.1%	$100,000-$199,999	14.9%
Under 18	20.7%			$200,000 or more	3.4%
18-34	23.0%	**Education**		Poverty Rate	16.3%
35-64	37.2%	H.S grad or less	31.2%		
Over 64	19.1%	Some college	36.5%	**Health Insurance**	
		College Degree, 4 yr	18.8%	With health insurance coverage	88.6%
Work		Post grad	13.6%		
White Collar	38.1%				
Sales and Service	46.3%	**Military**		**Public Assistance**	
Blue Collar	15.6%	Veteran	13.9%	Cash public assistance income	2.7%
Government	19.7%	Active Duty	1.5%		
				Food stamp/SNAP benefits	13.0%

Voter Turnout			
2015 Total Citizens 18+	535,224	2016 House Turnout as % CVAP	59%
2016 House turnout	315,679	2014 House Turnout as % CVAP	41%

2012 Presidential Vote		
Mitt Romney	149,651	(50%)
Barack Obama	144,966	(48%)

2016 Presidential Vote		
Hillary Clinton	156,676	(49%)
Donald Trump	141,196	(44%)
Gary Johnson	12,989	(4%)

Cook Partisan Voting Index: R+1

Arizona's first frontier was just south of today's Tucson, where Franciscan friars built Mission San Xavier del Bac in the 18th century. To the east, the late-19th century mining towns of Tombstone and Bisbee sprang up on mountainsides, where miners dug up gold, silver, and much of America's copper. In those wild and wicked mining days, the Earp brothers waged their famous gunfight against a gang of outlaws at the O.K. Corral in Tombstone. A 1957 movie starring Burt Lancaster and Kirk Douglas told that tale and helped put the city on the tourism map. Cochise County, where Tombstone and Bisbee are located, was the most populous county when Arizona became the 48th state in 1912. Here the white man finally quashed the rebellion of the land-starved American Indian, when the Apache leader Geronimo surrendered in 1886.

In recent years, Cochise County became an active frontier again. After the Border Patrol reduced illegal crossings in California and Texas, Mexicans trying to enter the United States illegally began coming to Agua Prieta, just across the border from the town of Douglas. There they fanned out, crossed the border and used the area's numerous roads, mountain trails and ranch lands to get to Tucson and Phoenix. The Tucson sector became the Border Patrol's most active in both apprehensions and illegal drug seizures. Stepped-up border enforcement and a reduced flow of illegal immigrants have significantly decreased these metrics: down to 123,000 arrests in 2010, which was the lowest total in the Tucson sector since 1993, and to 63,000 in 2015. But the bodies of many who didn't make it are still found in the mountains and in the desert. Border Patrol agent Brian Terry was killed in December 2010 as he patrolled in nearby Santa Cruz County. His death attracted widespread attention after two weapons from the shooting were traced to the Bureau of Alcohol, Tobacco, Firearms and Explosives' failed "Fast and Furious" gun-trafficking operation. Drug trafficking remains active. Local law enforcement officials worry that legalization of marijuana in Western states will increase business for illegal cartels, including more powerful drugs.

One immigrant destination is Tucson, Arizona's second metropolis. It is much smaller and politically less conservative than Phoenix. Tucson is a high-tech city and home to the University of Arizona. Defense giant Raytheon Co. has a huge missile plant at Tucson International Airport, which is in the 3rd District. In November 2016, Raytheon announced an increase of nearly 2,000 employees at its local headquarters. Planners projected a continuing upturn in jobs. It is also a tourist destination, with famed resorts. The Davis-Monthan Air Force base near downtown Tucson is home to F-16 fighter jets and drone pilot training, and contributes $1 billion a year to the area economy. Tucson does not share the wealth of Phoenix. In February 2015, the Census Bureau reported that Tucson was the nation's fifth-poorest city, with one in four residents in poverty.

The 2nd Congressional District includes most of Tucson, except the Latino-dominated west and south sides. It also includes the eastern half of surrounding Pima County. Also here are southeastern Arizona high desert real estate, including all of mountainous Cochise County, the small, border-crossing town of Douglas, and the city of Sierra Vista near Fort Huachuca, the site of the Army Military Intelligence Center, where military interrogators are trained. About 85 percent of the district is in Pima. Politically, it is very closely divided, voting for Arizona GOP favorite son John McCain by less than a percentage point in 2008 and for Republican Mitt Romney by just two points in 2012. Donald Trump lost much of the swing vote in 2016, and Hillary Clinton won the district by five points. This remains among the most competitive districts in the nation, a place where political centrism can be rewarded.

THIRD DISTRICT

Raul Grijalva (D)

Elected 2002, 8th term; b. Feb 19, 1948, Tucson; University of Arizona (AZ), B.A.; Roman Catholic; Married (Ramona Grijalva); 3 children.

Elected Office: Tucson Unified School District Governing Board, 1974-1986; Pima County Board of Supervisors, 1988-2002.

Professional Career: Assistant dean of Hispanic Affairs, University of AZ., 1987.

DC Office: 1511 LHOB 20515, 202-225-2435, Fax: 202-225-1541, grijalva.house.gov.

State Offices: Avondale, 623-536-3388; Somerton, 928-343-7933; Tucson, 520-622-6788.

Committees: *Education & the Workforce*: Early Childhood, Elementary & Secondary Education, Workforce Protections. *Natural Resources (RMM)*: Energy & Mineral Resources, Federal Lands, Indian, Insular & Alaska Native Affairs, Oversight & Investigations, Water, Power & Oceans.

Group Ratings

	ADA	ACLU	AFL-CIO	LCV	ITI	COC	HAFA	ACU	CFG	FRC
2016	-	94%	-	95%	33%	50%	21%	0%	4%	0%
2015	100%	C	96%	97%	C	32%	C	4%	4%	0%

Almanac Ratings 2015

	Economy	Social	Foreign	Composite
Liberal	95%	100%	96%	97%
Conservative	5%	0%	4%	3%

Key Votes of the 114th Congress

1. Keystone Pipeline	N	5. Puerto Rico Debt	Y	9. Offenses by Aliens	N
2. Trade Deals	N	6. Medical Marijuana	Y	10. Troops in Iraq	Y
3. Export-Import Bank	Y	7. Sanctuary Cities	N	11. Homeland Security $$	Y
4. Debt Ceiling Increase	Y	8. Armor-piercing Bullets	N	12. Trade Adjustment aid	N

Election Results

Election	Name (Party)	Vote (%)	Cand. Spent	Ind. Exp. Support	Ind. Exp. Oppose
2016 General	Raul Grijalva (D)........................	148,973 (99%)	$585,984		
2016 Primary	Raul Grijalva (D).....................................	(100%)			

Prior winning percentages: 2014 (56%), 2012 (58%), 2010 (50%), 2008 (63%), 2006 (61%), 2004 (62%), 2002 (59%)

RaÚl Grijalva, a Democrat first elected in 2002, is one of the House's most liberal members. He took over in 2015 as ranking Democrat on the Natural Resources Committee, which he has used as a platform for his outspoken progressive views that often feature a border perspective. He also was an early and vocal supporter of Bernie Sanders for president in 2016.

Grijalva was born and grew up in Tucson, the son of a *bracero*, or guest worker, who emigrated from Mexico in 1945. He graduated from the University of Arizona and has deep roots in the immigrant community on the city's southwest side. He was director of El Pueblo Neighborhood Center and assistant dean for Hispanic student affairs at the university. In 1974, he was elected to the Tucson school board and served 12 years. In 1988, he was elected a Pima County supervisor and served 14 years. As supervisor, he backed an effort to extend medical and dental benefits to same-sex domestic partners of county employees and focused on affordable health care, family and children services, and economic growth. Developers and builders helped elect him to office, but his support for planned growth and impact fees later alienated them. He won election to the House in a new seat created by redistricting. His chief opponent was state Sen. Elaine Richardson, who was endorsed by EMILY's List, which spent more than $500,000 on ads. Mocking his opponent's national funding, Grijalva created "Adelita's List," an allusion to the independent women who fought in the Mexican Revolution. He won the primary, 41%-21% and swept the general election in the heavily Democratic district.

In the House, his rhetoric often matches the fervor of his voting record. In 2008, Grijalva was elected co-chair of what was then the 75-member Progressive Caucus. In that position, he initially insisted that any health care overhaul include a government-run insurance option to compete with private insurers, but he later backed away from that demand. He also espoused a "war tax" that year to finance military operations in Afghanistan, an effort he considered immoral. In December 2014, he spoke out against the bipartisan omnibus spending bill and said Democrats need to do a better job of defining where they stand.

Much of his effort has been focused on immigration policy. He has co-sponsored bills to raise the number of low-skill visas from 5,000 to 400,000 and to allow legalization for some illegal immigrants, provided they pay a $500 civil fine. After Arizona state lawmakers passed a controversial immigration bill in 2010 expanding law enforcement's powers to detain suspected immigrants, Grijalva took the unusual step of urging a boycott of his state, calling on sympathetic organizations to refrain from using Arizona as a convention site. He abandoned the boycott idea after a federal judge halted implementation of most of the immigration law. In 2014, he encouraged the efforts of Republican Mario Diaz-Balart of Florida to find common ground on a bipartisan plan to approve immigration changes that he viewed as "low-hanging fruit." When a federal judge in Texas in February 2015 ordered a stop to Obama's executive order aimed at protecting some illegal immigrants, Grijalva said: "This injunction is not the result of sound legal action - it is the result of a lawsuit shopped around by attorneys general and governors intent on undermining the president's efforts."

His initial focus on environmental and energy issues was popular at home. He worked to stop uranium mining in the Kaibab National Forest and on federal lands near the Grand Canyon, and he was behind efforts to create a Sonoran Desert conservation system, which would protect 3.3 million acres and 56 miles of trails. Grijalva sponsored legislation creating a Public Lands Service Corps to train federal land managers as well as to protect parts of Pima and Santa Cruz counties from future mining claims, and he has stuck up for the San Carlos Apache Tribe in battling copper-mining operations around its lands. Combining his interests in the environment and immigration, he has implored Homeland Security Department officials to take into account protecting native plants and species when building fences and other security checkpoints at the border.

At the Natural Resources Committee, Grijalva in 2015 wrote to seven universities requesting detailed records when documents were released that suggested fossil-fuel companies were underwriting the research of climate-change skeptics. As the panel's senior Democrat, he worked with party leaders in opposing Republican efforts to require approval of the Keystone XL pipeline. And he sought opportunities to view environmental issues from the viewpoint of Hispanics and other minority groups. In December 2016, when the Obama administration halted construction of the Dakota Access pipeline in North Dakota, he hailed the action as a "big win for tribal rights, for environmental quality and for every American who has stood in solidarity with the water protectors."

Despite the strongly Democratic leaning of his district, Grijalva has faced reelection challenges. In 2010, Republican Ruth McClung, a 28-year-old physicist, voiced the slogan "Boycott Grijalva, not Arizona." She got help from tea party groups, along with a televised endorsement from Republican Sen. John McCain, and pulled nearly even in polls. But national Democrats raced to his assistance with ads, and he eked out a 50%-44% victory. When the *Arizona Republic* reported in 2014 that Grijalva had missed 13 percent of the previous year's congressional votes, giving him one of the worst attendance records in Congress, he shrugged it off. "I had perfect attendance in the fifth grade," he told the newspaper. "That didn't make me the smartest kid in the class." In a 2014 rematch with conservative activist Gabriela Saucedo Mercer, he won with 56 percent. In Pima County, which cast nearly half of the total vote, Grijalva led 61%-39%. But he trailed narrowly in Maricopa County and barely led in Yuma. Saucedo Mercer spent only $103,000. Although he won both the primary and general in 2016 without opposition, he might remain vulnerable to a well-financed challenger.

In October 2015, Grijalva was the first member of Congress to endorse the Sanders presidential campaign. "The positions he has taken and the values he holds are ones I share. ... I couldn't sit on the sidelines and wait for the tea leaves to be read better," Grijalva told *The New York Times*. When supporters of Hillary Clinton called Sanders anti-immigrant, Grijalva responded, "Latino voters were thinking for themselves and not being herded into any particular direction." He was a key ally of Sanders during the debate on the Democratic platform, when the two sides sought to reconcile their differences. After the 2016 election, Grijalva was an early supporter of Rep. Keith Ellison to chair the Democratic National Committee. The two have worked together closely in the Progressive Caucus.

Southwest Arizona: Tucson West, Western Phoenix Exurbs, Yuma

Population		**Race and Ethnicity**		**Income**	
Total	732,596	White	27.7%	Median Income	$41,293 (387 out of 435)
Age Groups		Black	4.3%		
Under 18	28.3%	Latino	61.5%		
18-34	27.7%	Pop/ sq mi	46.7	Under $50,000	58.6%
Land area	15,689	Asian	1.7%	$50,000-$99,999	29.5%
35-64	34.0%	Two races	1.2%	$100,000-$199,999	10.5%
Over 64	10.1%	Other	1.9%	$200,000 or more	1.3%
		Education		Poverty Rate	24.5%
Work		H.S grad or less	52.7%	**Health Insurance**	
White Collar	25.4%	Some college	31.7%	With health insurance coverage	80.5%
Sales and Service	48.4%	College Degree, 4 yr	10.1%		
Blue Collar	26.0%	Post grad	5.5%		
Government	18.1%	Born in state	47.3%	**Public Assistance**	
				Cash public assistance income	3.2%
		Military			
		Veteran	7.5%	Food stamp/SNAP benefits	22.6%
		Active Duty	0.3%		

Voter Turnout			
2015 Total Citizens 18+	439,591	2016 House Turnout as % CVAP	38%
2016 House turnout	169,135	2014 House Turnout as % CVAP	24%

2012 Presidential Vote		
Barack Obama	108,902	(61%)
Mitt Romney	65,482	(37%)

2016 Presidential Vote		
Hillary Clinton	130,466	(62%)
Donald Trump	67,952	(32%)
Gary Johnson	7,197	(3%)

Cook Partisan Voting Index: D+13

Southern Arizona, although technically part of Mexico for hundreds of years, was never a home to Latin American civilization the way northern New Mexico has been. Here the hot desert land was inhabited mainly by Native American tribes such as the Apache and Cocopah. They kept their culture and language alive in the region until they were uprooted by English-speaking whites who came in on cavalry horses and in miners' wagons and railroad cars in the late 19th century. In 1854, the Gadsden Purchase - $10 million to Mexico for 30,000 square miles of desert - cleared the way for a southern transcontinental railroad. Today's Hispanic Arizonans are mostly descendants of later emigrants from Mexico, some of whom came over the border in the sleepier days before World War II, when *la frontera* was scarcely patrolled. Many more came in the 1980s to partake in the dazzling economic growth in the region. That immigration pattern slowed considerably in recent years, with the collapse of the real estate market in Arizona and stronger enforcement along the Mexican border.

The 3rd Congressional District is one of the state's two Hispanic-majority districts, with a population that is 60 percent Hispanic and 21 percent foreign-born. One of the two overwhelmingly Democratic districts in the state, it shares a 293-mile border with Mexico. The district is a collection of four distant communities connected by many square miles of uninhabited Sonoran desert.

One is the suburb of Avondale west of downtown Phoenix, home to Phoenix International Raceway. Avondale is also the site of the Palo Verde Nuclear Generating Station, the nation's largest nuclear power plant and the only one not located by a large body of water. The second community is the heavily Latino and mostly low-income west and south sides of Tucson, where the University of Arizona, the largest employer in southern Arizona, is located. The third is the Mexican border town of Nogales, which is 95 percent Hispanic and located near many maquiladora plants. It is one of the busiest cargo terminals along the Mexican border, but it also has long been an entry point for the drug trade and the scene of many illegal border crossings in recent years. The twin smuggling tides - drugs and people - have inflicted damage on the fragile desert ecosystem. The federal government has responded with money-laundering restrictions that have adversely affected some banks' dealings with produce companies. The fourth is Yuma, located on the California border at a Colorado River crossing in an irrigated agricultural valley that is often the hottest place in the nation. The lower Colorado is the second-largest producer of the nation's lettuce. In winter, the Yuma area produces 90 percent of the nation's leafy green vegetables, with an estimated 30,000 Mexican workers crossing the border daily. The area also is a magnet for RV campers.

Out in the desert you find the Organ Pipe Cactus National Monument, the Sonoran Desert National Monument, the Tohono O'odham Indian Reservation, and the Barry M. Goldwater Air Force Range, the largest aerial gunnery range after Nevada's Nellis Air Force Range. However, 95 percent of it is not used for target practice in order to protect the habitat of the endangered Sonoran pronghorn antelope. Near Nogales, other unique forms of wildlife are found in the Tumacacori Highlands, including endangered species such as the jaguar, peregrine falcon, Chiricahua leopard frog and the Mexican spotted owl. With its brutal desert heat, the Baboquivari trail that runs north to the Tohono O'odham Nation has been the deadliest immigrant crossing in the nation. In November 2016, the Border Patrol reported a sharp increase in the number of Central American families and unaccompanied minors entering the country illegally in the Yuma area - chiefly from Honduras, El Salvador and Guatemala.

In 2016, Hillary Clinton defeated Donald Trump, 62%-33%. That margin was a few points higher than Barack Obama's local performance in 2012.

FOURTH DISTRICT

Paul Gosar (R)

Elected 2010, 4th term; b. Nov 27, 1958, Rock Springs, WY; Creighton University, B.S.; Creighton Boyne School of Dentistry (NE), D.D.S.; Roman Catholic; Married (Maude Gosar); 3 children.

Professional Career: Owner, dental practice.

DC Office: 2057 RHOB 20515, 202-225-2315, Fax: 202-226-9739, gosar.house.gov.

State Offices: Gold Canyon, 480-882-2697; Kingman, 928-445-1683; Prescott, 928-445-1683.

Committees: *Natural Resources*: Energy & Mineral Resources (Chmn), Water, Power & Oceans. *Oversight & Government Reform*: Interior, Energy & Environment, National Security.

Group Ratings

	ADA	ACLU	AFL-CIO	LCV	ITI	COC	HAFA	ACU	CFG	FRC
2016	-	17%	-	0%	60%	100%	93%	100%	100%	100%
2015	10%	C	5%	3%	C	50%	C	96%	94%	100%

Almanac Ratings 2015

	Economy	Social	Foreign	Composite
Liberal	15%	0%	12%	9%
Conservative	85%	100%	88%	91%

Key Votes of the 114th Congress

1. Keystone Pipeline	Y	5. Puerto Rico Debt	N	9. Offenses by Aliens	Y
2. Trade Deals	N	6. Medical Marijuana	N	10. Troops in Iraq	N
3. Export-Import Bank	N	7. Sanctuary Cities	Y	11. Homeland Security $$	N
4. Debt Ceiling Increase	N	8. Armor-piercing Bullets	Y	12. Trade Adjustment aid	N

Election Results

Election	Name (Party)	Vote (%)		Cand. Spent	Ind. Exp. Support	Ind. Exp. Oppose
2016 General	Paul Gosar (R)	203,487	(72%)	$683,893	$64,339	$277,028
	Mikel Weisser (D)	81,296	(29%)	$28,897		
2016 Primary	Paul Gosar (R)	51,349	(71%)			
	Ray Strauss (R)	21,122	(29%)			

Prior winning percentages: 2014 (70%), 2012 (67%), 2010 (50%)

Republican Paul Gosar, first elected in 2010, survived two competitive elections. He then settled into the Republican-friendly 4th District and signed on with other party renegades in the House, all of which seemed natural for this self-styled outsider. Unexpectedly, Gosar faced a well-financed challenger in the 2016 primary. He easily survived. But his experience likely caught the attention of other House GOP rebels who have gone their own way in the Capitol.

Gosar grew up in Pinedale, Wyoming, a town of fewer than 2,000 residents near the headwaters of the Green River. Gosar's father, a geologist with Belco Petroleum and Union Pacific, was often away working on rigs, and an uncle, who was a dentist, stepped in as a role model during those absences. Gosar went on to study dentistry at Creighton University with the expectation that he would return to Wyoming to enter practice with his uncle. His father, however, advised him to seek a more vibrant locale. "My dad took me aside and said, 'I don't think the right time is here. I think the minerals, the oil, and gas are going to crash,'" Gosar recalled. After receiving his D.D.S. in 1985, Gosar landed in Flagstaff. Appealing to a local banker for financing to launch his practice in 1985, Gosar says he emphasized his frugality, vowing to eat nothing but peanut-butter-and-jelly sandwiches until his business was established.

When he decided to challenge freshman 1st District Democratic Rep. Ann Kirkpatrick in the 2010 election, Gosar was motivated by his contempt for the health care overhaul that the Democratic Congress enacted. In his campaign, Gosar sharply criticized her votes for President Barack Obama's agenda. He also took a hard line on immigration, touting his endorsement from Maricopa County Sheriff Joe Arpaio, who aggressively pursued illegal immigrants in Arizona. Kirkpatrick refused to distance herself from the administration. Her ads highlighted her support for Obama's initiatives and cast Gosar as an irresponsible millionaire who was late paying business and property taxes 12 times. Going into the closing weeks of the contest, Kirkpatrick had $870,000 to spend, compared with Gosar's $49,000. But he received help from the American Dental Association and other medical groups that opposed the health care law. He also got help from tea party activists. The national GOP wave in high-growth areas like this district helped to seal his 50%-44% victory.

In Washington, Gosar immediately made clear his contempt for Washington's typical ways. He told a reporter that the formal swearing-in ceremony on the House floor felt awkward, and that Congress should have held a barbecue with legislators serving people. On the Oversight and Government Reform Committee in 2011, he became one of the first House members to call on Attorney General Eric Holder to resign because of the failed "Operation Fast and Furious," a program that facilitated the sale of thousands of weapons to Mexican drug cartels. In an interview with *The Daily Caller*, he accused Holder and other government officials of possibly being "accessories to murder" for their roles. Gosar continued to lead attacks on Holder, which resulted in the House vote in 2012 to cite the attorney general for contempt of Congress.

On the Natural Resources Committee, Gosar enacted a law aimed at eliminating red tape on a dam project spanning the Coconino and Tonto national forests. In 2014, Congress approved as part of its annual defense spending bill his proposal to swap 2,400 acres of Tonto forest land - which includes the San Carlos Apache reservation - to make way for a new $4 billion copper mine. In exchange, the Resolution Copper Co. gave up land scattered across the state. Sen. John McCain of Arizona strongly backed the proposal, which removed restrictions that were imposed in 1955. Gosar spoke out against the Obama administration's management of national forests and grasslands, saying that constituents were left "vulnerable to catastrophic wildfires."

Concerned over his reelection prospects and faced with new redistricting lines that bolstered Democrats, Gosar in January 2012 announced he would move out of his Flagstaff home and run in the more Republican-leaning 4th District. (Kirkpatrick won back the 1st District seat until her unsuccessful campaign against McCain.) Pinal County Sheriff Paul Babeu, a hard-liner on illegal immigration, initially was considered the front-runner in the primary, but his campaign's momentum halted when a former boyfriend (and illegal immigrant) accused him of threatening deportation to keep their relationship quiet. Babeu came out as gay but denied the allegations, and he was reelected as sheriff. (In what has become a game of musical chairs, Babeu ran in 2016 for the open seat in the 1st District, where he was defeated after being abandoned by national Republicans.)

That left Gosar with two challengers in the August 2012 GOP primary: state Sen. Ron Gould of Lake Havasu City and radio station owner Rick Murphy of Bullhead City. Gould, one of the Arizona legislature's most conservative members, attacked Gosar for being the only House Republican from Arizona to support the 2011 deal to raise the nation's debt limit. The anti-tax group Club for Growth contributed heavily to Gould's campaign, but the American Dental Association's political action committee again countered with help for a fellow dentist. Gosar won with 51 percent to Gould's 32 percent and Murphy's 17 percent. Gosar won easily in November against a largely unknown Democrat. In 2014, he breezed to reelection without a GOP primary.

On the opening day of Congress in January 2015, Gosar was one of 25 House Republicans who opposed giving John Boehner another term as Speaker. Instead, he voted for Rep. Daniel Webster of Florida. "Our leadership in D.C. should be bold and determined," Gosar said in a statement. "We do not need more status quo." He became an active participant in the House GOP's Freedom Caucus, which prepared conservative strategy and policy alternatives. In September, Boehner announced his resignation as Speaker under pressure from that faction. Coincidentally, Boehner's move came a day after Pope Francis spoke to a joint session of Congress, which the Roman Catholic Gosar boycotted because of the Pope's advocacy of fighting climate change. "When the Pope chooses to act and talk like a leftist politician, then he can expect to be treated like one," Gosar wrote. A month later, Gosar was one of nine House Republicans who voted against Paul Ryan as the new Speaker.

But Gosar's independence had riled some of his constituents. When Ray Strauss, a local pastor, challenged him in the 2016 primary, the contest gained added attention when Washington-based business groups spent $300,000 to run ads critical of Gosar, which were sponsored by The Right Way Super PAC. That group's biggest contributor was the Western Growers Association, an agri-business group that advocates immigration reform, in part to provide foreign workers to aid farmers. "Mr. Gosar chose to denigrate our members and dismiss their legitimate concerns. We find that unacceptable," Western Growers executive vice president Dave Puglia told *National Review*. Gosar won the primary, 71%-29%, and he defeated a token Democratic challenger in November.

In December 2016, Gosar was elected chairman of the Congressional Western Caucus. The group has sought to protect the interests of western and rural communities, including their opposition to the growth of public lands.

Western Arizona: Eastern Phoenix Exurbs, Prescott, Lake Havasu City

Population		**Race and Ethnicity**		**Income**	
Total	730,220	White	75.0%	Median Income	$44,345 (346 out of 435)
Land area	33,199	Black	1.7%		
Pop/ sq mi	22.0	Latino	18.5%		
Born in state	27.5%	Asian	1.1%	Under $50,000	55.8%
		Two races	1.8%	$50,000-$99,999	30.9%
Age Groups		Other	1.4%	$100,000-$199,999	11.4%
Under 18	20.7%			$200,000 or more	1.8%
18-34	17.7%	**Education**		Poverty Rate	16.4%
35-64	37.0%	H.S grad or less	43.8%		
Over 64	24.6%	Some college	37.8%	**Health Insurance**	
		College Degree, 4 yr	11.7%	With health insurance coverage	86.8%
Work		Post grad	6.5%		
White Collar	29.8%				
Sales and Service	48.4%	**Military**		**Public Assistance**	
Blue Collar	21.9%	Veteran	14.9%	Cash public assistance income	2.0%
Government	16.6%	Active Duty	0.5%		
				Food stamp/SNAP benefits	13.2%

Voter Turnout			
2015 Total Citizens 18+	543,540	2016 House Turnout as % CVAP	52%
2016 House turnout	284,783	2014 House Turnout as % CVAP	32%

2012 Presidential Vote		
Mitt Romney	173,394	(67%)
Barack Obama	80,035	(31%)

2016 Presidential Vote		
Donald Trump	202,043	(67%)
Hillary Clinton	82,192	(27%)
Gary Johnson	10,965	(4%)

Cook Partisan Voting Index: R+21

Beyond the cities of Phoenix and Tucson, much of Arizona looks as it did a century ago. Some places maintain a timeless Western look, like Wickenburg, the oldest Arizona town north of Tucson. Others preserve antiquated ways of life, such as the polygamist community of Colorado City, just south of Utah. In some cases, nature and settlement juxtapose jarringly: The real London Bridge has been transplanted to Lake Havasu City, a retirement community on the Colorado River and a popular spring break destination for college students.

Approximately the size of Massachusetts, the expansive 4th Congressional District stretches from the Hoover Dam and Lake Mead in the northwest corner of the state down all the way to the outskirts of Yuma and nearly to the border of Mexico, and it spans east to Prescott and beyond to the Phoenix exurbs in Pinal County. The district covers La Paz County, most of Mohave and Yavapai counties, and parts of Yuma, Gila, and Pinal counties, along with a tiny slice of Maricopa. Its population center is in fast-growing Prescott, the place where Barry Goldwater announced his presidential campaign in 1964. Once a gold mining camp, Prescott has been home since 1888 to America's oldest annual rodeo and it retains the charming markers of an older city. Its Yavapai County Courthouse Plaza has been called one of America's Great Public Spaces by the American Planning Association, which described it as "a majestic, man-made urban forest in the heart of a historic commercial district." In November 2016, Arizona's employment report showed that Prescott had the strongest job growth in the state. Yavapai County has a bit more than one-third of the district's voters.

The district's economy is fueled by tourism, with visitors coming to explore Western folklore. Jerome, a mining town built improbably on hillside stilts, has been reborn as an artist colony. Bullhead City is home to the annual River Regatta, where participants take an eight-mile float down the Colorado. The district also is a retirement haven and a mecca for second homes. Prescott and Lake Havasu City are among the most popular retirement destinations in the country. According to the Census Bureau, Lake Havasu City has become the "remarriage capital" of the nation; in this self-styled "party town," 42 percent of women and 41 percent of men have married at least twice. The number of retirees, along with upwardly striving and family-oriented young transplants, infuse the area with a cultural and political conservatism, placing it among the top 10 percent Republican districts nationwide. The rapid growth in this area, which is across the state line from the California desert, has increased demands for additional water supply. Donald Trump won 66 percent of the vote in 2016, by far his strongest district in Arizona.

FIFTH DISTRICT

Andy Biggs (R)

Elected 2016, 1st term; b. Nov 07, 1958, Tucson; Brigham Young University (UT), B.A., 1982; University of Arizona James E. Rogers College of Law (AZ), J.D., 1984; Arizona State University, M.A., 1999; Mormon; Married (Cindy Biggs); 6 children.

Elected Office: AZ house, 2003-2011; AZ Senate, 2011-2016, Majority Leader, 2011-2012, Senate President, 2013-2016.

Professional Career: Practicing attorney.

DC Office: 1626 LHOB 20515, 202-225-2635, biggs.house.gov.

State Offices: Mesa, 480-699-8239.

Committees: *Judiciary*: Courts, Intellectual Property & Internet, Immigration & Border Security. *Science, Space & Technology*: Environment (Chmn), Space.

Election Results

Election	Name (Party)	Vote (%)	Cand. Spent	Ind. Exp. Support	Ind. Exp. Oppose
2016 General	Andy Biggs (R)	205,184 (64%)	$795,973	$230,286	
	Talia Fuentes (D)	114,940 (36%)	$15,115		
2016 Primary	Christine Jones (R)	20,195 (30%)			
	Andy Biggs (R)	19,319 (29%)			
	Don Stapley (R)	14,477 (22%)			
	Justin Olson (R)	13,315 (20%)			

Andy Biggs was elected to the House to fill a seat vacated by fellow Republican Matt Salmon, who had returned to the House in 2010 after having earlier served a separate six years. After a lengthy recount, Biggs won the GOP primary by 27 votes in the closest contest that determined a House election in 2016. He has been a strong conservative, with lengthy experience in state government.

Biggs got his undergraduate degree in Asian studies from Brigham Young University, his master's degree in political science from Arizona State University and a law degree from the University of Arizona. After practicing law in Phoenix and then Gilbert, he was elected in 2002 to the state House, where he served eight years. He moved to the Senate in 2010, and became majority leader and then president of the Senate. He was a hard-liner on illegal immigration, and a conservative icon. Americans for Prosperity's Arizona Chapter named him a "Champion of the Taxpayer;" the Goldwater Institute tapped him as a "Friend of Liberty;" and the American Conservative Union gave him its "Conservative Excellence Award." In 1993, he won $10 million in the Publishers Clearing House sweepstakes.

After Salmon announced his retirement, Biggs was the initial frontrunner among four Republican candidates in the primary. He had an exceedingly tight battle with Christine Jones, a former legal counsel with GoDaddy, an Internet domain company; in 2014, Jones had finished third in the five-candidate Republican primary for governor. Jones contributed $1.9 million to her own campaign. Biggs, who was endorsed by Salmon, spent nearly $1 million on the campaign and received another $560,000 in support from the Club for Growth. The other candidates were state Rep. Justin Olson and former Maricopa

County Supervisor Don Stapley. Biggs and Olson were the most conservative candidates in the contest, while Jones ran as an outsider who emphasized her business record. Stapley identified with the GOP establishment and advocated controls on federal spending.

Jones was the leader in the vote count on the evening of the Aug. 30 primary, and she delivered a victory speech. The tight result led to an automatic recount by Maricopa County election officials and a court review. The recount showed that as many as 728 voters had gone to the wrong voting precinct and then cast a provisional ballot. When Superior Court Judge Joshua Rogers announced the official result, he conceded that many voters had been "disenfranchised." In a bitter statement during that court hearing, Jones said, "I do want to say this for the record. This has been a very eye-opening experience."

The official results of the primary showed that Biggs defeated Jones, 25,244 to 25,217. Each received 29.5 percent of the vote, while Stapley had 20.7 percent and Olson had 20.3 percent. In the pro forma general election, Biggs defeated Democrat Talia Fuentes, 64%-36%. She was a 31-year-old single mother who had supported Bernie Sanders for president.

Biggs got seats on the Judiciary Committee and Science, Space and Technology, where he chaired the Environment Subcommittee. When House Republicans in May 2017 passed their American Health Care Act, he was among the few conservatives who voted against it. He called the proposal "an ill-considered, ill-defined, and an almost certainly ill-fated three-stage plan to completely repeal Obamacare at an unspecified later date."

Eastern Phoenix Suburbs: Eastern Mesa, Gilbert

Population		**Race and Ethnicity**		**Income**	
Total	761,257	White	71.7%	Median Income	$66,620 (81 out of 435)
Land area	293	Black	2.8%		
Pop/ sq mi	2594.0	Latino	17.5%	Under $50,000	37.0%
Born in state	36.2%	Asian	4.6%	$50,000-$99,999	32.8%
		Two races	2.1%	$100,000-$199,999	24.8%
Age Groups		Other	4.9%	$200,000 or more	5.4%
Under 18	27.0%			Poverty Rate	9.5%
18-34	19.6%	**Education**			
35-64	37.9%	H.S grad or less	29.1%	**Health Insurance**	
Over 64	15.5%	Some college	36.4%	With health insurance coverage	90.2%
Work		College Degree, 4 yr	22.4%		
		Post grad	12.0%		
White Collar	41.9%			**Public Assistance**	
Sales and Service	43.0%	**Military**		Cash public assistance income	1.6%
Blue Collar	15.2%	Veteran	10.2%		
Government	11.9%	Active Duty	0.1%	Food stamp/SNAP benefits	7.0%

Voter Turnout			
2015 Total Citizens 18+	520,176	2016 House Turnout as % CVAP	62%
2016 House turnout	320,124	2014 House Turnout as % CVAP	35%

2012 Presidential Vote		
Mitt Romney	187,304	(64%)
Barack Obama	101,511	(35%)

2016 Presidential Vote		
Donald Trump	191,432	(56%)
Hillary Clinton	121,280	(36%)
Gary Johnson	15,845	(5%)

Cook Partisan Voting Index: R+15

The city of Phoenix is exceedingly young. Conservative trailblazer Barry Goldwater, born in 1909, grew up knowing people who remembered when the Valley of the Sun - or the Valley, as most people say - was virtually empty, with a few parched settlements set above a dry riverbed. As late as 1950, only 107,000 people lived in Phoenix and 332,000 in all of Maricopa County. But the air conditioner and military technology transformed Phoenix into today's high-rise studded metropolis, with 1.6 million city dwellers and 4.2 million people in Maricopa County, as of 2015. From 2000 to 2010, Maricopa's population grew by 26 percent. The growth slowed to 9 percent from 2010 to 2015, following the collapse of the local housing market and the state's crackdowns on illegal immigration. Still, most parts of the nation would welcome such an increase. Gilbert's population doubled to 208,543 from 2000 to 2010, with an additional 9 percent increase in the next five years. In April 2016, a national real estate website listed Gilbert as the leading boomtown in the nation. Phoenix is not, as some people think, a giant retirement village, nor is it overrun by crooked land salesmen and fast-buck artists, though the area has attracted its share of each.

Maricopa's second-largest city is Mesa, south of the Salt River and east of Phoenix. It was founded by Mormons in 1878 on one square mile and was laid out Salt Lake City-style on broad streets with large lots. A gleaming white Mormon temple was built in 1927, one of the few in the United States then. In 1950, Mesa had 17,000 people, and more than half of its residents earned their living from farming, primarily citrus and cotton. In 2015, it had 472,000 people, more than Miami or Minneapolis. A former Air Force base is now the Phoenix-Mesa Gateway Airport, with stalled plans for it to become a major center for passengers and freight. In 2016, Allegiant Air was the only carrier providing commercial service. Valley Metro, the regional transit authority broke ground in October 2016 for a 2-mile light-rail extension from Mesa to Gilbert, which was scheduled to open in 2018.

The 5th Congressional District of Arizona is made up of Phoenix's East Valley suburbs: Mesa, Chandler, Gilbert, and Queen Creek. Nicknamed the Silicon Desert, Chandler has become one of the fastest-growing high-tech centers in the country, with companies drawn to relatively cheap real estate and semiconductor chip maker Intel's longstanding presence. But not every project has a happy ending. In April 2016, Intel, the largest employer in the region, abandoned its newly built neighboring facility known as Fab 42, which had been expected to manufacture additional chips. Those plans suffered when sales of Intel's desktop and notebook computers failed to keep pace with tablet personal computers. In late 2016, Apple began to hire workers for its new $2 billion data center in Mesa, which was planned as the control center for its four other U.S.-based data operations.

The 5th includes some high-income precincts, but the district's cultural tone is resolutely middle class. Donald Trump won 56 percent of the vote here in 2016, compared with Mitt Romney's 64 percent in 2012.

SIXTH DISTRICT

David Schweikert (R)

Elected 2010, 4th term; b. Mar 03, 1962, Los Angeles, CA; Arizona State University, B.A.; Scottsdale Community College (AZ), A.A.; Arizona State University, M.B.A.; Roman Catholic; Married (Joyce Schweikert); 1 child.

Elected Office: AZ House, 1989-1994; Treasurer, Maricopa County, 2004-2006.

Professional Career: Member, AZ State Board of Equalization, 1995-2003; Owner, Sheridan Equities & Sheridan Equities Holdings.

DC Office: 2059 RHOB 20515, 202-225-2190, Fax: 202-225-0096, schweikert.house.gov.

State Offices: Scottsdale, 480-946-2411.

Committees: *Joint Economic*. *Ways & Means*: Oversight, Social Security.

Group Ratings

	ADA	ACLU	AFL-CIO	LCV	ITI	COC	HAFA	ACU	CFG	FRC
2016	-	17%	-	0%	83%	100%	85%	96%	95%	92%
2015	5%	C	4%	0%	C	58%	C	100%	99%	83%

Almanac Ratings 2015

	Economy	Social	Foreign	Composite
Liberal	6%	15%	1%	7%
Conservative	94%	85%	99%	93%

Key Votes of the 114th Congress

1. Keystone Pipeline	Y	5. Puerto Rico Debt	Y	9. Offenses by Aliens	Y
2. Trade Deals	Y	6. Medical Marijuana	Y	10. Troops in Iraq	N
3. Export-Import Bank	N	7. Sanctuary Cities	Y	11. Homeland Security $$	N
4. Debt Ceiling Increase	N	8. Armor-piercing Bullets	Y	12. Trade Adjustment aid	N

Election Results

Election	Name (Party)	Vote	(%)	Cand. Spent	Ind. Exp. Support	Ind. Exp. Oppose
2016 General	David Schweikert (R)	201,578	(62%)	$353,046		
	W. John Williamson (D)	122,866	(38%)	$6,624		
2016 Primary	David Schweikert (R)	52,956	(80%)			
	Russ Wittenberg (R)	13,121	(20%)			

Prior winning percentages: 2014 (65%), 2012 (61%), 2010 (52%)

Republican David Schweikert was elected in 2010 by defeating a two-term House Democrat and succeeded two years later by defeating a fellow freshman Republican in a nasty redistricting-created primary. Then he was stripped of his prime House committee assignment because he flaunted his independence of the GOP leadership. Despite that brass-knuckle background, Schweikert is a wonkish fiscal conservative who settled into his work with reduced controversy. Eventually, he was rehabilitated with a seat on the Ways and Means Committee, where he showed signs of being a team player.

Schweikert was born in a Catholic home for unwed mothers in downtown Los Angeles; he was adopted and raised by a family in Arizona. Growing up in Scottsdale, he credits his early affinity for politics to former President Ronald Reagan. "We had a president [Jimmy Carter], who would go on television wearing a sweater and demanding that we adjust our thermostats because we were living in a world of shortages," Schweikert recalled. Along came Reagan, who galvanized a "wave of young people," he said. As an undergraduate at Arizona State University, where he later got an M.B.A., Schweikert focused on finance and real estate. "I have spent almost all my life within a 20-mile radius," he said. He acquired a real estate license at age 18, worked full-time while taking classes at night and graduated in six years.

He ventured into the political arena at 26, when he lost a bid for the Arizona House. Two years later, he won an open seat in the Scottsdale area, and at the end of his freshman term, he became majority whip at age 30. He worked to pass legislation that laid the foundation for tax cuts, tort reform and charter schools, as well as a bill shortening the legislative session from 170 to 98 days. He next was elected as Maricopa County treasurer. In that role, he managed a $4 billion budget, created a program to help low-income seniors pay their property taxes and corrected thousands of deed errors.

In 2008, Schweikert challenged Democratic Rep. Harry Mitchell, who had taken a GOP seat two years earlier. Schweikert lost by 9 percentage points in an inhospitable year for Republicans. Two years later, their rematch told the larger tale of the 2010 election. It featured an incumbent under fire for supporting the Obama administration agenda and a conservative challenger touting his outsider credentials. Schweikert made Mitchell's vote for President Barack Obama's $787 billion economic stimulus bill a central theme, and his campaign signs called Mitchell a "lap dog" for liberal House Speaker Nancy Pelosi. Mitchell countered that he had been among the Democrats most likely to buck his party. The incumbent raised about twice as much money. But Schweikert won convincingly, 53%-42%.

In the House, Schweikert became known for his studiousness. In May 2011, he told *The Washington Post* that he spent five hours a day as a member of the Financial Services Committee learning about government-sponsored mortgage giants Fannie Mae and Freddie Mac. In the summer of 2011, he strongly opposed raising the federal debt ceiling. He accused Treasury Secretary Tim Geithner of having "his hair on fire. ... It's absolutely silly. We have plenty of cash flow to pay debt." In January 2012, he introduced a bill proposing a constitutional amendment that would force Congress to get approval from a majority of the states before increasing the debt limit in the future. But he ultimately voted for a final compromise that was enacted.

After the 2010 census, the state's independent redistricting commission lumped Schweikert in a district with Rep. Ben Quayle, the son of former Vice President Dan Quayle. The younger Quayle represented two-thirds of the new district. House Republican leaders and outgoing Arizona Sen. Jon Kyl lined up to support Quayle, whom they considered the more loyal Republican. Schweikert ran as a self-styled reformer up against the GOP establishment, which he said his opponent embodied. He cast Quayle as immature, reviving allegations from 2010 that his opponent had made offensive comments on a racy nightlife website, DirtyScottsdale.com. Quayle at first denied any connection with the site, but later in their campaign acknowledged that he had written for it.

Quayle labeled Schweikert "Dishonest Dave" and accused him of being the source of a *Politico* story alleging that Quayle was one of the GOP congressmen who took a late-night swim in the Sea of Galilee during a 2011 trip to Israel. (Quayle said he took a brief swim and brought home some of the water to baptize his daughter.) The acrimony peaked when Schweikert's campaign sent out a mailer claiming that Quayle "goes both ways" on conservative issues. Quayle and his supporters, including Sen. John McCain, angrily accused Schweikert of sexual innuendo, a charge that the congressman denied. Schweikert prevailed, 51%-49%. The general-election race was a formality in this safe Republican district. Since 2012, he has won reelection without breaking a sweat.

In 2013, House Republican leaders took the rare step of booting Schweikert off Financial Services. His aides claimed that it resulted from his proclivity to challenge the leadership, although the bitterness of his race with Quayle may have been a factor. He also left the Republican whip team. Still, Schweikert did not make a complete break. He was not among the 10 House Republicans who voted against John Boehner for Speaker. He moved to the Science, Space and Technology Committee and quietly reestablished his party credentials. He voted for the annual budget resolution, even though other conservatives left the reservation. After the 2014 election, he regained his seat on Financial Services, though his earlier seniority was not restored. Then, Schweikert again voted for Boehner for Speaker - despite continued objections to his leadership. The appropriate time to challenge his Speakership would have been in the private meetings of the Republican Conference, not in a public vote where his opponent was Nancy Pelosi, he told reporters. Following the 2016 election, Speaker Paul Ryan closed the book on his earlier transgressions by awarding Schweikert a seat on the blue-ribbon Ways and Means Committee. He worked with other Republicans to pass their American Health Care Act in May 2017.

Conservative activists urged him to oppose McCain in the 2016 Republican primary, but he did not show strong interest in what likely would have been an uphill contest. He supported Ted Cruz for president. Following the election, he called for a more pragmatic approach by House conservatives. Instead of blocking legislation, as he and others had occasionally done in the past, he said that they should work with President Donald Trump and the Republican-controlled Congress. "If you have someone who's not necessarily an ideologue, be the first one to show up with the details worked out and all of a sudden your idea becomes the base of the discussion," he told *Buzzfeed*.

Northeastern Phoenix Suburbs: Scottsdale

Population		Race and Ethnicity		Income	
Total	739,321	White	73.3%	Median Income	$62,482 (115 out of 435)
Land area	625	Black	2.6%		
Pop/ sq mi	1182.8	Latino	15.9%		
Born in state	30.6%	Asian	4.5%	Under $50,000	40.4%
		Two races	2.1%	$50,000-$99,999	29.9%
Age Groups		Other	4.7%	$100,000-$199,999	20.9%
Under 18	21.0%			$200,000 or more	8.9%
18-34	21.1%	**Education**		Poverty Rate	12.5%
35-64	41.6%	H.S grad or less	27.1%		
Over 64	16.3%	Some college	31.4%	**Health Insurance**	
		College Degree, 4 yr	25.7%	With health insurance coverage	87.8%
Work		Post grad	15.7%		
White Collar	43.6%				
Sales and Service	44.5%	**Military**		**Public Assistance**	
Blue Collar	11.9%	Veteran	8.6%	Cash public assistance income	1.6%
Government	9.5%	Active Duty	0.0%		
				Food stamp/SNAP benefits	7.9%

Voter Turnout			
2015 Total Citizens 18+	535,194	2016 House Turnout as % CVAP	61%
2016 House turnout	324,444	2014 House Turnout as % CVAP	37%

2012 Presidential Vote		
Mitt Romney	186,537	(60%)
Barack Obama	121,661	(39%)

2016 Presidential Vote		
Donald Trump	177,332	(52%)
Hillary Clinton	143,571	(42%)
Gary Johnson	13,891	(4%)

Cook Partisan Voting Index: R+9

In May 1998, conservative trailblazer Barry Goldwater died at his home in the Phoenix suburb of Paradise Valley. He could remember when Arizona was the "baby state," with fewer people than any state except Delaware, Wyoming and Nevada. When he returned from military service in World War II, Paradise Valley was still undeveloped, and Phoenix - founded after the Civil War as a hay market for cavalry horses at Fort McDowell - was not much more than a tiny outpost of American civilization, a metropolitan area of fewer than 300,000 in the sizzling desert. By 2015, there were 4.2 million people in Maricopa County. And the city had been transformed from a frontier outpost to a diversified high-tech center, an example of how creativity and ingenuity can build a sophisticated city even in the most unwelcoming environs.

Like Los Angeles and San Francisco, Phoenix is dotted with mountains that rise grandly from the valley and are preserved as undeveloped parkland. Some, such as Shaw Butte, contain archaeological evidence that Indians used them as a base for sophisticated astronomical observations. From the landmark Camelback Mountain, 1,800 feet above Phoenix and Paradise Valley, one can appreciate with comparable awe what the land was originally like and how impressively Phoenix has grown.

Over the mountains, east of the affluent part of Phoenix and north of Tempe and the Salt River Indian Reservation, is Scottsdale, a city that grew in population from 130,000 in 1990 to 237,000 in 2015. Scottsdale is home to Frank Lloyd Wright's Taliesin West, the architect's onetime winter home and studio, which was beyond the reach of electricity and telephone lines when built in the McDowell Mountain foothills in the 1940s. Today, the city boasts luxury shopping malls, resorts, the renowned WestWorld equestrian center and the most expensive real estate market in Arizona. Local politicians argue over whether Scottsdale should keep marketing itself as a Western town or emphasize its new live-work downtown. The advocates of growth appear to be winning. In October 2016, Arizona State University and the Mayo Clinic announced they were building a $200 million Health Solutions Innovation Center. The next month, the San Francisco-based McKesson Corp., a health care services firm, unveiled plans for a new facility in Scottsdale that could house 2,200 workers. The city also touts its importance in the Cactus League of warm-weather cities that host spring training camps for Major League Baseball, and its reputation as one of the most retiree-friendly cities in the country. Twenty percent of its residents are 65 and older, the largest percentage among cities with 100,000 or more people. Only 4 percent are younger than five years old.

The 6th Congressional District of Arizona includes the northern part of Phoenix, most of Scottsdale, plus Paradise Valley, Cave Creek and Carefree, so named in 1955 by developers who hoped to lure snowbird retirees. As with four other Arizona districts, the 6th is contained entirely in Maricopa County. But it has the most college graduates and is the only one that borders each of the other four. This is an affluent and comfortably Republican district. Donald Trump won 52 percent of the vote in 2016, a notable dip from the 60 percent that Mitt Romney took in 2012. That outcome was comparable to Trump's relatively weak showing in other upscale locales.

SEVENTH DISTRICT

Ruben Gallego (D)

Elected 2014, 2nd term; b. Nov 20, 1979, Chicago, IL; Harvard University, B.A.; Catholic; Divorced.

Military Career: U.S. Marine Corps, 2002-2006 (Iraq).

Elected Office: AZ House, 2010-2014.

Professional Career: Public affairs consultant 2007-2008; Delegate, DNC 2008; Vice chair, AZ Democratic Party, 2009.

DC Office: 1218 LHOB 20515, 202-225-4065, rubengallego.house.gov.

State Offices: Phoenix, 602-256-0551.

Committees: *Armed Services*: Military Personnel, Tactical Air & Land Forces. *Natural Resources*: Federal Lands, Indian, Insular & Alaska Native Affairs, Oversight & Investigations.

Group Ratings

	ADA	ACLU	AFL-CIO	LCV	ITI	COC	HAFA	ACU	CFG	FRC
2016	-	100%	-	97%	67%	57%	14%	0%	4%	0%
2015	95%	C	100%	97%	C	37%	C	8%	2%	0%

Almanac Ratings 2015

	Economy	Social	Foreign	Composite
Liberal	94%	100%	99%	97%
Conservative	6%	0%	1%	3%

Key Votes of the 114th Congress

1. Keystone Pipeline	N	5. Puerto Rico Debt	Y	9. Offenses by Aliens	N
2. Trade Deals	N	6. Medical Marijuana	Y	10. Troops in Iraq	Y
3. Export-Import Bank	Y	7. Sanctuary Cities	N	11. Homeland Security $$	Y
4. Debt Ceiling Increase	Y	8. Armor-piercing Bullets	N	12. Trade Adjustment aid	Y

Election Results

Election	Name (Party)	Vote (%)	Cand. Spent	Ind. Exp. Support	Ind. Exp. Oppose
2016 General	Ruben Gallego (D)	119,465 (75%)	$506,351		
	Eve Nunez (R)	39,286 (25%)	$30,997		
2016 Primary	Ruben Gallego (D)	(100%)			

Prior winning percentages: 2014 (75%)

Democrat Ruben Gallego, a first-generation American with an impressive bio, was easily elected in 2014. With his experience in the military and local politics plus his engaging persona, he quickly gained notice in the House and showed a willingness to rock the boat among House Democrats - sometimes working with other newcomers.

Gallego's life story is made for a political candidate, including a hardscrabble upbringing, a Harvard degree, and military service in Iraq. Born in Chicago to Hispanic immigrant parents, Gallego and his family struggled after his father left home, something Gallego has said helps him relate to the low-income people in his district. He got his undergraduate degree in international relations. While attending Harvard, he enlisted in the Marine Corps. He served in Iraq as an assistant machine gunner and fought in more than 10 combat operations in urban areas; his best friend died in combat. That experience, including his anger over the quality of the troops' equipment, led him to get involved in politics and to help veterans.

Gallego was elected to the Arizona Senate in 2010, rising to assistant minority leader in 2012. When 12-term Democratic Rep. Ed Pastor retired, Gallego left the legislature to run. In this ultra-blue district, where the Democratic nominee was considered a shoo-in, the true contest came in the August primary. His chief competitor was Mary Rose Wilcox, who is Hispanic and had high name recognition as a

Maricopa County supervisor. She was endorsed by Pastor, but may have suffered because she was 30 years older than Gallego.

Gallego appealed to Latino voters, noting his opposition to the Arizona law requiring police officers in some circumstances to determine the immigration status of arrested or detained persons. He founded Citizens for Professional Law Enforcement, which sought to recall Maricopa County Sheriff Joe Arpaio. The controversial sheriff had been criticized for alleged racial profiling and for investigating President Barack Obama's birth certificate. A Wilcox supporter challenged Gallego's nominating petitions for not using his legal name. The suit was withdrawn when Gallego explained he had changed his name in 2008 from Ruben Marinelarena (his father's name) to Ruben Marinelarena Gallego to honor the mother who raised him. He combined a social media presence with aggressive door-to-door campaigning, and out-raised Wilcox by about $300,000.

In the five-candidate field, Gallego won with 48.4 percent to 35.9 percent for Wilcox. In November, he won without Republican opposition. His success, he said, is "living proof that the American Dream still exists." He said that he hoped to serve his career in the House. "I'll be trying to work my way fast into leadership," he told a local reporter. "As a congressman, you can do more for your state the more seniority you have, the better committees you get."

With seats on the Armed Services and Natural Resources committees, he got off to a good start. He opposed additional U.S. military action in Iraq, which he described as "a horrible sequel to a horrible movie." He cited the many men and women who died because of the decisions of officials in Washington and at the Pentagon, and said that additional steps to assist Iraq should not come at the risk of losing more American lives. The United States "should support our allies in the region, but limit the scope of our involvement on the ground," he said in response to Obama's request to authorize the use of force against the Islamic State. Gallego joined a new congressional caucus of lawmakers who had served in the military since 2001. At home, he opposed Republican lawsuits that challenged Obama's authority to assist undocumented immigrants. Instead, he said, they penalize communities that "work legally here, pay their taxes, raise their families and become part of the social fabric of America." At Gallego's request, the Federal Aviation Administration agreed to review flight paths at Sky Harbor Airport to limit the noise over local neighborhoods.

Gallego was an early supporter of Hillary Clinton in 2016, saying that she was "our best-known, most experienced, most electable candidate." Following the election, he was among the first congressional Democrats to oppose the required waiver for recently retired Marine General James Mattis to serve as secretary of Defense. "As a veteran, I believe strongly in the principle of civilian leadership of the military," he said. He urged the House to oppose the infrastructure plan of President Donald Trump. "We must not lift a finger to help him scam our country," he said. "We must, instead, put every effort into stopping him."

Gallego was an outspoken critic of Minority Leader Nancy Pelosi, following House Democrats' poor performance in the 2016 election and was an early supporter of Rep. Tim Ryan of Ohio in his bid to replace Pelosi as party leader. The 63 votes cast for Ryan in the Democratic Caucus were "a message directly to leadership to be more responsive and actually make the Democratic caucus more democratic," Gallego said. Grijalva, the other Phoenix-area Hispanic member of the House, voted for Pelosi. With Reps. Seth Moulton of Massachusetts and Kathleen Rice of New York, Gallego won Caucus approval to require election of additional Democratic leadership positions, rather than appointment by the Democratic leader. Post-election discussion about the future of the Caucus, he said, "were difficult and contentious, but also necessary and inspiring."

In December 2016, Gallego's wife Kate, the vice mayor of Phoenix, wrote on Facebook that her "marriage is ending" and she was preparing for a divorce.

Central and Western Phoenix

Population		**Race and Ethnicity**		**Income**	
Total	744,743	White	20.2%	Median Income	$34,186 (426 out of 435)
Land area	205	Black	9.2%	Under $50,000	66.3%
Pop/ sq mi	3630.8	Latino	64.6%	$50,000-$99,999	24.1%
Born in state	47.1%	Asian	2.2%	$100,000-$199,999	8.3%
		Two races	1.3%	$200,000 or more	1.3%
		Other	2.5%	Poverty Rate	34.6%
Age Groups		**Education**		**Health Insurance**	
Under 18	31.4%	H.S grad or less	60.6%	With health insurance coverage	73.0%
18-34	28.0%	Some college	25.7%		
35-64	33.8%	College Degree, 4 yr	9.2%		
Over 64	6.8%	Post grad	4.6%		
Work		**Military**		**Public Assistance**	
White Collar	21.1%	Veteran	5.0%	Cash public assistance income	3.2%
Sales and Service	48.8%	Active Duty	0.0%	Food stamp/SNAP benefits	28.3%
Blue Collar	30.1%				
Government	10.4%				

Voter Turnout			
2015 Total Citizens 18+	371,197	2016 House Turnout as % CVAP	43%
2016 House turnout	158,811	2014 House Turnout as % CVAP	19%

2012 Presidential Vote		
Barack Obama	101,028	(72%)
Mitt Romney	37,353	(27%)

2016 Presidential Vote		
Hillary Clinton	117,958	(71%)
Donald Trump	37,232	(22%)
Gary Johnson	6,228	(4%)

Cook Partisan Voting Index: D+23

Phoenix is a relatively new American metropolis. It has grown to a big city just in the past two generations. Yet it is also an ancient city, or, built on top of one. The Arizona Canal, several miles north of downtown Phoenix, runs along the route of a canal built about 600 years ago by the Hohokam aboriginal people. They distributed irrigated water diverted from the Salt River in its wet moments to farmers in what today is called the Valley of the Sun, and they made sophisticated astronomical observations from the mountains that jut up from the desert. This society disappeared for reasons unknown less than half a century before the Spaniards arrived in North America. So, today's Phoenix is the second civilization to prosper in this desert region. Half a century ago, Phoenix spread six miles north, west and east of the downtown and only a few miles south. Downtown was its only office district and its main shopping area, and people blew fans over boxes of ice to cool off. Today, the view from downtown Phoenix's office towers stretches toward other office towers many miles to the north, northeast and northwest.

The city opened its first light-rail transit line in 2008, connecting residents of the Tempe and Mesa suburbs to downtown Phoenix on a 20-mile route. Annual ridership increased from 5 million in 2009 to 14 million in 2015. Separate three-mile extensions at each end, which were delayed when the state's economy collapsed, are under construction. In 2015, the city council approved a 35-year, $32 billion transportation plan for 40 more miles of light rail across the area, plus additional bus service, with financing from a sales tax hike. Work has begun on the $1.9 billion, 22-mile Loop 202 highway extension between downtown Phoenix and Chandler, which will connect Interstate 10 on each end. The controversial project shares financing from the sales tax.

The 7th Congressional District of Arizona is centered in downtown Phoenix and is based entirely in Maricopa County. It covers the capitol, in a rundown neighborhood a couple of miles to the west, and Sky Harbor International Airport, situated in an industrial corridor several miles east. It includes most of southern Phoenix, and its boundaries follow approximately the southern and western city limits. It stretches south into Guadalupe and northwest into parts of Glendale. Geographically, the district covers most of the land between South Mountain and Camelback Mountain. The district is 63 percent Hispanic, and its median income is among the lowest in the nation. Most of the immigrants have been Mexican, but there has been an influx of Guatemalans.

The area was hit hard by the economic downturn in the late-2000s. The median home price in metropolitan Phoenix fell from $245,000 in September 2006 to $115,000 in September 2011. By 2015, about half of that dip had been recovered. 2016 brought several positive developments. In December, a national real estate website forecast that the area in 2017 would have the largest home sales increase in the nation. Developers planned several downtown commercial and residential developments in the hundreds of millions of dollars. In August, Grand Canyon University in West Phoenix announced plans to expand its campus to 400 acres, with 5,000 employees. Total enrollment was 67,000, including part-time and on-line students. One downside: In late 2016, Sky Harbor airport reported decreased passenger traffic, due to double-digit percentage cuts by its largest tenant, American Airlines.

In 2014, the local veterans' hospital became the unfortunate symbol of the nationwide failure of the Veterans Affairs Department's health system: delayed or inadequate care, fabricated records and flawed management. During a 2015 visit to the hospital, President Barack Obama said that the care was "outstanding," but that there was a need to restore "trust and confidence" in the VA and that he was creating another committee to review how veterans' needs could be met. During campaign visits to Arizona, Donald Trump criticized the Phoenix hospital and promised improvements for veterans. "Nobody has been treated worse and there is no more corrupt group in terms of government than what's happening with the VA in Arizona. You're the poster child for everybody. And we're going to fix it, and we're going to take care of our vets, our greatest people," he told a June 2016 rally in Phoenix.

Politically, this is the most Democratic district in the state. Hillary Clinton got 71 percent of the vote, the same as Obama in 2012.

EIGHTH DISTRICT

Trent Franks (R)

Elected 2002, 8th term; b. Jun 19, 1957, Uravan, CO; Center for Constitutional Studies (UT), Att.; Ottawa University (KS), Att.; Baptist; Married (Josephine Franks); 2 children (twins).

Elected Office: AZ House, 1984-1986.

Professional Career: Director, AZ Gov.'s Office for Children, 1987-1988; Executive Director, AZ Family Research Inst., 1989-1993; Writer-commentator, AZ radio station KTKP; Co-owner, Franks Brothers Independent Drilling; President-CEO, Liberty Petroleum Corporation.

DC Office: 2435 RHOB 20515, 202-225-4576, Fax: 202-225-6328, franks.house.gov.

State Offices: Glendale, 623-776-7911.

Committees: *Armed Services*: Emerging Threats & Capabilities, Strategic Forces. *Joint Congressional-Executive Commission on China*. *Judiciary*: Constitution & Civil Justice, Courts, Intellectual Property & Internet.

Group Ratings

	ADA	ACLU	AFL-CIO	LCV	ITI	COC	HAFA	ACU	CFG	FRC
2016	-	5%	-	3%	100%	86%	90%	96%	90%	100%
2015	0%	C	4%	3%	C	65%	C	100%	95%	100%

Almanac Ratings 2015

	Economy	Social	Foreign	Composite
Liberal	1%	0%	0%	0%
Conservative	99%	100%	100%	100%

Key Votes of the 114th Congress

1. Keystone Pipeline	Y	5. Puerto Rico Debt	N	9. Offenses by Aliens	Y
2. Trade Deals	Y	6. Medical Marijuana	N	10. Troops in Iraq	N
3. Export-Import Bank	N	7. Sanctuary Cities	Y	11. Homeland Security $$	N
4. Debt Ceiling Increase	N	8. Armor-piercing Bullets	Y	12. Trade Adjustment aid	N

Election Results

Election	Name (Party)	Vote (%)	Cand. Spent	Ind. Exp. Support	Ind. Exp. Oppose
2016 General	Trent Franks (R)	204,942 (69%)	$244,061		
	Mark Salazar (G)	93,954 (32%)			
2016 Primary	Trent Franks (R)	49,763 (71%)			
	Clair Van Steenwyk (R)	20,724 (29%)			

Prior winning percentages: 2014 (76%), 2012 (63%), 2010 (65%), 2008 (59%), 2006 (59%), 2004 (59%), 2002 (60%)

Trent Franks, a Republican first elected in 2002, is best known for his fervent opposition to abortion rights. As chairman of a House Judiciary subcommittee that handles such issues, he has unsuccessfully pushed a measure that would criminalize some abortions. But some Republican leaders and rank-and-file members object to his agenda as bad politics. Franks also has been an active conservative at the Armed Services Committee.

Franks grew up in Colorado, attended college briefly, and started his own oil-and-gas exploration business. His political career began when he won a single term in the Arizona House in 1984. There, he was known for wearing a tie tack in the shape of the feet of a fetus, as a constant reminder of his anti-abortion views. In 1987, he was director of the Governor's Office for Children under Evan Mecham, a conservative Republican who was later impeached. In 1989, Franks became executive director of the Arizona Family Research Institute, an organization associated with James Dobson's Focus on the Family, and he was a consultant to conservative Pat Buchanan's presidential campaign. Franks designed the state's 1997 scholarship tax credit legislation, a much litigated measure that ultimately was upheld by the U.S. Supreme Court. The plan provides tax credits for donations to nonprofit organizations to help families pay for private education.

Franks first ran for a House seat in 1994 but lost to John Shadegg in the Republican primary, 43%-30%. In 2002, Republican Rep. Bob Stump announced he was retiring and endorsed Lisa Atkins, his chief of staff. Franks was not thought to be in the top tier of candidates, but his base of Christian conservatives and abortion opponents, plus his spending of $300,000 of his own money, made him a contender. He called for overturning the Supreme Court's *Roe v. Wade* decision legalizing abortion and for constitutional protection for fetuses. He endorsed a flat tax to replace the federal income tax, supported individual investment accounts in Social Security, and called for tougher enforcement of immigration laws. His base of activists made the difference. He finished first with 28 percent of the vote, only 797 votes ahead of Atkins. He has not faced a serious reelection threat since.

In the House, Franks has accumulated a conservative voting record while emerging as a fierce rhetorical firebrand. He was among the first House Republicans to join the Tea Party Caucus in 2010. Despite the House Republican majority's desire to focus on economic rather than social issues, he used his post as chairman of the Judiciary Subcommittee on Constitution and Civil Justice to seek votes on abortion-related bills. In 2012, the leadership brought to the floor his measure to criminalize abortions based on the fetus' sex or gender, on the heels of a similar Arizona law. It needed two-thirds to pass under the House rule for handling that bill, but it fell 30 votes short on the 246-168 roll call.

In 2013, the House passed his Pain Capable Unborn Child Protection Act, which was designed to prevent an abortion after five months of pregnancy; the Senate took no action. In 2015, a similar bill stirred objections from House Republican women, including newly elected members, and GOP leaders pulled the bill from debate. Franks said he was disappointed, and that party leaders had assured him that he would have another opportunity. The House passed the bill in May with minor tweaks, 242-184. On another social issue, he joined leading conservatives participating in a 2015 documentary that contended gay rights threaten Christianity.

Franks was a long-time critic of a provision in the Voting Rights Act empowering the Justice Department to approve or challenge changes to voting laws in some states, including Arizona. He said it was "ludicrous" that his state had to get preclearance before new congressional redistricting maps could take effect. The Supreme Court agreed in a 2014 ruling on a challenge that had been brought by Shelby County, Ala.

On the Armed Services Committee, Franks has strongly supported missile defense, plus protections against electromagnetic pulse (EMP) attacks. Such attacks involve a powerful shock wave that can disrupt magnetic fields and potentially damage electric systems. In 2014, the House approved a bill that would strengthen protection for the nation's electric grid.

His strong rhetoric has caused him occasional problems. In 2010, Franks angered African Americans when he declared that their population has been decimated more by abortions than by slavery. Discussing President Barack Obama's reelection prospects, he said in March 2011, "He is a left-wing ideologue of the first magnitude, and if we don't understand that now, then I'm afraid that somehow he may get back in in two years, and I don't know that the country can survive that."

In the 2016 presidential campaign, Franks initially supported three other Republican candidates before he endorsed Donald Trump, who had wrapped up the nomination. "Jesus is not on the ballot. We always need to choose between two flawed people," he told an Arizona radio station. "Here's the bottom line. As a conservative, I may not be able to trust Donald Trump to do the right thing," Franks said. "But I can trust Hillary Clinton to do the wrong thing every time." During the fall campaign, he joined Trump's pro-life advisory council.

On a personal note, he has encouraged public awareness of facial deformity similar to the one he has battled. Franks has had multiple surgeries to correct a cleft palate.

Western Phoenix Suburbs: Glendale, Peoria

Population		Race and Ethnicity		Income	
Total	744,439	White	70.5%	Median Income	$59,256 (149 out of 435)
Land area	540	Black	4.2%		
Pop/ sq mi	1379.5	Latino	19.0%		
Born in state	34.3%	Asian	3.2%	Under $50,000	41.3%
		Two races	2.3%	$50,000-$99,999	35.1%
Age Groups		Other	3.4%	$100,000-$199,999	20.0%
Under 18	23.5%			$200,000 or more	3.5%
18-34	19.3%	**Education**		Poverty Rate	9.7%
35-64	37.3%	H.S grad or less	33.5%		
Over 64	19.9%	Some college	38.4%	**Health Insurance**	
		College Degree, 4 yr	18.2%	With health insurance coverage	90.2%
Work		Post grad	9.8%		
White Collar	37.1%				
Sales and Service	46.1%	**Military**		**Public Assistance**	
Blue Collar	16.8%	Veteran	12.7%	Cash public assistance income	1.7%
Government	13.5%	Active Duty	0.4%		
				Food stamp/SNAP benefits	7.4%

Voter Turnout			
2015 Total Citizens 18+	541,977	2016 House Turnout as % CVAP	55%
2016 House turnout	298,971	2014 House Turnout as % CVAP	32%

2012 Presidential Vote		
Mitt Romney	179,555	(62%)
Barack Obama	107,335	(37%)

2016 Presidential Vote		
Donald Trump	190,163	(57%)
Hillary Clinton	120,992	(36%)
Gary Johnson	12,712	(4%)

Cook Partisan Voting Index: R+13

In 1938, when most of Phoenix's West Valley was barren, desert landscape, Flora Mae Statler paid 35 cents an acre to acquire land on the site of what became the city of Surprise. Statler chose the name, she later recalled, because she'd "be surprised if this town ever amounted to much." But the city got the last laugh on Statler: Over the past half-century, it has become one of the fastest-growing cities in Maricopa County. From 2000 to 2010, its population nearly quadrupled.

Once a haven for retirees looking for warmer climates, Surprise and Phoenix's surrounding western suburbs have been booming, although the collapse of the housing market slowed the tempo. Astride

Grand Avenue, the only diagonal street in the rigorous grid of metro Phoenix, is the suburb of Glendale, not so long ago just a crossroads but now home to 240,000 people. The city is the home of the Phoenix Coyotes hockey stadium and the University of Phoenix Stadium, which has a retractable roof and capacity of more than 78,000. The stadium has hosted the 2015 Super Bowl, the 2016 NCAA football championships and the April 2017 NCAA "Final Four" basketball tournament; each is a financial boon for the host city. Nearby Westgate City Center is one of several edge cities in Phoenix's Valley of the Sun. Tucked between Surprise and Glendale are Peoria, as middle-American as its namesake in Illinois, and Sun City, a huge retirement community started in the 1950s. Peoria has spent close to $100 million to revive its older community as an historic area. The planned community of Anthem, 30 miles north of downtown and established in 1998, has about 22,000 residents.

All of these cities are part of the 8th Congressional District of Arizona, which covers Phoenix's West Valley. Because this has been an area of rapid growth, it was particularly hard hit by the housing bust and subsequent economic downturn in the mid-2000s. After a slow recovery, real estate values have been on the rise, with home values in Surprise increasing 70 percent from 2011 to 2016, though those prices remain below pre-recession levels. In 2015, Goodyear and Buckeye to the west of Glendale were among the 15 fastest-growing cities in the nation. A new casino opened in Glendale in December 2015, despite strong opposition from state and local officials over the use of the property. A few miles beyond Glendale is Luke Air Force Base, which has the largest fighter training wing in the Air Force and the only active duty F-16 training base in the United States. In May 2015, Luke began functioning as the chief operational training base for pilots of the F-35A Lightning II fighter jets, many of which have been purchased by other nations.

This is conservative territory. It grew more compact in the 2012 redistricting, shedding counties along the Colorado River. Donald Trump won this district, 57%-36%, compared with Mitt Romney's 62%-37% lead in the 2012 presidential election.

NINTH DISTRICT

Kyrsten Sinema (D)

Elected 2012, 3rd term; b. Jul 12, 1976, Tucson; Arizona State University Law School, J.D.; Arizona State University, M.A.; Harvard University Kennedy School of Government (MA); Brigham Young University (UT), Bach. Deg.; Arizona State University, Ph.D.; Harvard University Kennedy School of Government, 2010; None; Single.

Elected Office: AZ House, 2004-2010; AZ Senate, 2010-2012.

Professional Career: Social worker, 1995-2002; Practicing lawyer, 2005-present; Instructor, Center for Progressive Leadership, 2006-present.

DC Office: 1725 LHOB 20515, 202-225-9888, Fax: 202-225-9731, sinema.house.gov.

State Offices: Phoenix, 602-956-2285.

Committees: *Financial Services*: Capital Markets, Securities & Investment, Terrorism & Illicit Finance.

Group Ratings

	ADA	ACLU	AFL-CIO	LCV	ITI	COC	HAFA	ACU	CFG	FRC
2016	-	64%	-	87%	83%	79%	21%	8%	4%	0%
2015	35%	C	73%	60%	C	79%	C	21%	9%	17%

Almanac Ratings 2015

	Economy	Social	Foreign	Composite
Liberal	54%	80%	26%	53%
Conservative	46%	20%	74%	47%

Key Votes of the 114th Congress

1. Keystone Pipeline	N	5. Puerto Rico Debt	Y	9. Offenses by Aliens	Y
2. Trade Deals	N	6. Medical Marijuana	Y	10. Troops in Iraq	N
3. Export-Import Bank	Y	7. Sanctuary Cities	N	11. Homeland Security $$	Y
4. Debt Ceiling Increase	Y	8. Armor-piercing Bullets	N	12. Trade Adjustment aid	Y

Election Results

Election	Name (Party)	Vote (%)		Cand. Spent	Ind. Exp. Support	Ind. Exp. Oppose
2016 General	Kyrsten Sinema (D)	169,055	(61%)	$2,382,716	$44,076	
	Dave Giles (R)	108,350	(39%)	$180,495		
2016 Primary	Kyrsten Sinema (D)		(100%)			

Prior winning percentages: 2014 (55%), 2012 (49%)

Democrat Kyrsten Sinema, elected to the newly created 9th District in 2012, overcame deep poverty to achieve academic success. In addition to being the first openly bisexual member of Congress, she established her mark in the House with outspoken and sometimes iconoclastic views - among Democrats, and sometimes across the aisle.

Sinema grew up in Tucson. Her parents divorced, and her mother remarried a teacher. When her stepfather lost his job, the family took shelter for two years in an abandoned gas station without running water or electricity. They eventually moved into a home, but remained poor. At 16, Sinema graduated as her high school's valedictorian and went on to earn a bachelor's degree in social work from Brigham Young University, followed by a master's degree in social work, a law degree, and a doctorate in justice studies from Arizona State University - all while working full-time. After graduating from BYU at 18, she became a social worker in a central Phoenix school district. Before her election to Congress, she worked as a lawyer, an adjunct professor at Arizona State, and an instructor at the Center for Progressive Leadership, a Washington-based institute that trains activists in progressive policies. Sinema is a fitness addict: She has run more than 10 marathons, including Boston, and is the first member of Congress to complete a triathlon. She also has taught spin classes to colleagues in the House Gym. Another first for Sinema, according to *U.S. News & World Report*: She is a rare Member of Congress to describe her religion as "none."

Sinema, who says she faced adversity by using Helen Keller as a role model, was motivated to enter politics to assist people with backgrounds similar to hers. "I'm a Democrat today … because they taught me the best of both ideas: help each other when you're struggling, but work very hard on your own," she told *National Journal*. After losing her first bid for the Arizona House as an independent in 2002, she ran as a Democrat and won in 2004. She served there until 2010, when she was elected to the state Senate. As a liberal advocate in the legislature, she promoted gay rights issues and sponsored several bills aimed at reining in the tough tactics of Maricopa County Sheriff Joe Arpaio on illegal immigration. She also worked with Republicans to pass legislation on human trafficking and other issues.

Running for the new 9th District seat, she voiced frustration with the partisan divide in Congress. She won the Democratic primary with 41 percent of the vote; state Sen. David Schapira got 30 percent and former Arizona Democratic Party Chairman Andrei Cherny, a former speechwriter for President Bill Clinton, got 29 percent. Her general election opponent was Vernon Parker, a former Paradise Valley mayor who served in both Bush administrations. They fiercely competed for the independent vote, with each painting the other as extreme in attack ads. Sinema echoed President Barack Obama's call to develop an economy "that rewards those who work hard and play by the rules,. She supported closing corporate tax loopholes and protecting payroll tax cuts for working families. Parker followed the national GOP playbook in vowing to repeal the health care law and rein in runaway spending. Sinema won, 49%-45%.

In the House, Sinema worked on housing and consumer issues on the Financial Services Committee. The panel approved several of her proposals, including a 2016 measure to help law enforcement officials track down financial criminals who target seniors. Her actions have been unpredictable. She joined organizations of moderate Democrats, occasionally criticized Obama and has worked across the aisle with House Republicans. She co-founded the United Solutions Caucus, a bipartisan House group seeking consensus policies. "I'm just doing my thing," she told *Roll Call* in February 2015. "I know my thing's a little bit different than other people, but I don't think there's anything wrong with that at all. And, you know what? I don't mind if some people like it or don't like it. That's OK."

Minority Whip Steny Hoyer named Sinema a chief deputy whip, and said she brought "dynamism and fresh ideas that will surely enhance the work of the whip operation." In the *Almanac* vote ratings for 2015, she ranked among the most conservative Democrats in each of the three issue categories. She objected to the prospective Asian-Pacific trade pact on the grounds that LGBT people can be caned and imprisoned for up to 20 years under Malaysian law. Based on her teaching experience, she has worked on legislation to provide additional protections to the victims of sexual violence on campus. With her leadership role, she has shown notable independence from Minority Leader Nancy Pelosi. In January 2015, she was one of four House Democrats to vote for someone other than Pelosi for Speaker. Following the 2016 election, she was one of 63 Democrats who voted for Rep. Tim Ryan of Ohio as party leader; it was time for "clear-eyed change, not a time to rubber-stamp the failed strategy of the past," Sinema said.

At home, Sinema has settled in politically. In her 2014 contest that had been expected to be tight, she defeated Wendy Rogers, 55%-42%. Sinema spent $3.5 million to $1.4 million for Rogers, who doubted the constitutionality of Social Security. Sinema benefited from another $700,000 of party spending on her behalf. In 2016, she defeated political newcomer David Giles, 61%-39%. Earlier, she decided not to challenge Sen. John McCain, but kept the door open for a future Senate bid and created a leadership PAC that would be a useful fundraising vehicle. In a May 2017 Phoenix radio interview, she said that she was "running for reelection," though she subsequently kept the door open for a challenge to Sen. Jeff Flake in 2018. If she runs statewide, she would draw national support from the LGBT community.

Central and Eastern Phoenix Suburbs: Tempe, Western Mesa

Population		**Race and Ethnicity**		**Income**	
Total	742,047	White	57.4%	Median Income	$50,832 (242 out of 435)
Land area	165	Black	5.0%	Under $50,000	49.1%
Pop/ sq mi	4503.0	Latino	27.5%	$50,000-$99,999	29.5%
Born in state	37.5%	Asian	4.6%	$100,000-$199,999	16.9%
		Two races	2.6%	$200,000 or more	4.5%
		Other	5.1%	Poverty Rate	18.8%
Age Groups		**Education**		**Health Insurance**	
Under 18	21.5%	H.S grad or less	31.3%	With health insurance coverage	83.2%
18-34	30.7%	Some college	32.8%		
35-64	37.3%	College Degree, 4 yr	22.5%		
Over 64	10.4%	Post grad	13.5%		
Work		**Military**		**Public Assistance**	
White Collar	39.5%	Veteran	7.4%	Cash public assistance income	2.3%
Sales and Service	45.7%	Active Duty	0.0%	Food stamp/SNAP benefits	11.2%
Blue Collar	14.8%				
Government	12.0%				

Voter Turnout			
2015 Total Citizens 18+	517,984	2016 House Turnout as % CVAP	54%
2016 House turnout	277,507	2014 House Turnout as % CVAP	32%

2012 Presidential Vote		
Barack Obama	135,244	(51%)
Mitt Romney	123,263	(47%)

2016 Presidential Vote		
Hillary Clinton	155,158	(54%)
Donald Trump	109,123	(38%)
Gary Johnson	14,768	(5%)

Cook Partisan Voting Index: D+4

As metropolitan Phoenix has expanded in the Valley of the Sun over the past half century, it has absorbed the crossroads towns that were once separate and distinct. One such town is Tempe, east of downtown Phoenix. It was founded in 1871 as Hayden's Ferry by the father of future Democratic Sen. Carl Hayden, who held that office from 1927 to 1969, and it was renamed in 1879 for an ancient Greek vale. The old town centered on Arizona State University, and both the town and the university have expanded greatly over the decades. The campus, which sits astride a rise with a fine view of much of metropolitan Phoenix, has an undergraduate enrollment of 42,000 students. The research park on the campus has 51 business tenants with 6,000 employees. The Mayo Clinic has formed a partnership with the university to develop the Mayo Medical School, with the first class of students scheduled to enter in summer 2017. Located near the Mayo Hospital campus in North Scottsdale, the medical school plans to emphasize innovative, patient-centered care. It will be accompanied by a new biosciences center.

Tempe is relatively affluent, with 176,000 people in 2015, up from 142,000 in 1990, which is slower growth than other Phoenix suburbs. The city has nine stations along the original 20-mile light rail system from the city. Its Mill Avenue district across from the ASU campus is a pedestrian-friendly downtown featuring red brick sidewalks and turn-of-the-century buildings. The day before college football's Fiesta Bowl in Glendale, Tempe hosts a parade and block party. In November 2016, the National Hockey League's Arizona Coyotes announced plans to move from Glendale to a new arena in Tempe. In 2016, the Fort-Worth based American Airlines closed the Tempe headquarters building of US Airways, following their corporate merger.

The 9th Congressional District of Arizona includes Tempe and parts of Scottsdale, Mesa, Chandler and Phoenix. It was drawn to be the only politically competitive district in the Phoenix area, but its demographic characteristics are favorable for Democrats. The district contains high shares of college graduates and high-income households, drawn to Democrats on cultural issues. Hillary Clinton won the district in 2016, 54%-38%, a boost for Democrats over the 51%-47% local win by President Barack Obama in 2012. Outside of Arizona's two majority-minority districts, the 9th contains the largest concentration of Hispanics, at 29 percent.

★ ARKANSAS ★

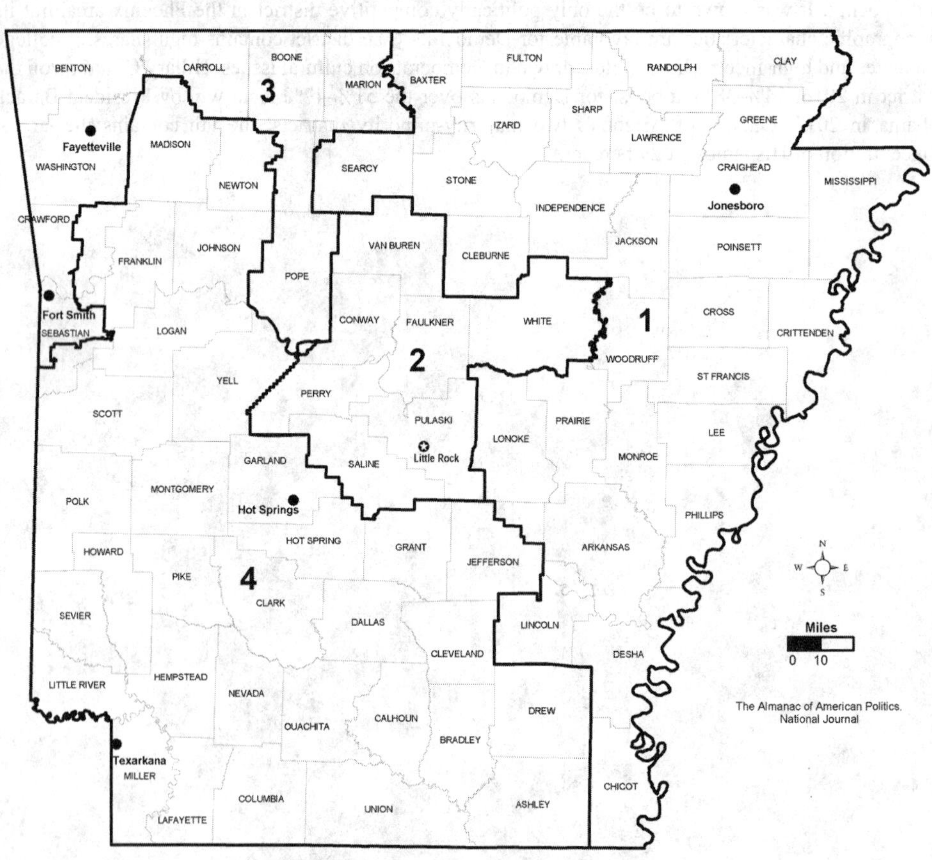

Congressional district boundaries were first effective for 2012.

Even before this state's former first lady lost the 2016 presidential election, Arkansas had already turned decisively away from the Democrats. Just eight years earlier, in 2008, the state's governor, both senators and three of its four House members were Democrats. Today, the GOP asserts unified control of the governorship, both chambers of the state legislature and every House and Senate seat. And in a state that's whiter, poorer, older, more rural and with lower rates of college education than the national average – five key demographic factors in determining partisan leanings today – there's little chance that Democrats will be returning to influence in Arkansas any time soon, despite the reality that its greatest politician, very much alive to see the transition, was Democrat Bill Clinton.

Like Clinton, Arkansas began life without many advantages. It consists of the land left over when Louisiana and Missouri were carved out of the Louisiana Purchase and what is now Oklahoma was fenced off as Indian Territory. In area, it is the second-smallest state between the Mississippi River and the Pacific Ocean. In population, it is the smallest Southern state except for West Virginia (though it is now neck and neck with Mississippi). Arkansas was not blessed with great natural resources, unless you count bauxite, once the main source of aluminum, or flame-retarding bromine. Historically, it was home to no major industry. Its first two senators could not agree on how to pronounce the state's name, but since 1881, it's been illegal to call it *ar-KAN-sas*. Settled by poor farmers with large families, few slaves, and little cash, Arkansas has had no major city like Atlanta, Dallas or even Memphis. Arkansas was settled more by Scots-Irish dirt farmers than by grand plantation owners. It fought for the Confederacy, except for a few Union men in the northwest, and followed other Southern states in establishing government-enforced racial segregation. It is the birthplace of Pentecostal denominations like the Church of God in Christ, which had roots in late 1800s Little Rock, and the Assemblies of God, founded in Hot Springs in 1914 and now headquartered in Springfield, Missouri.

When Clinton returned to the state from Yale Law School in 1973, the dominant figure in Arkansas, as far as most Americans were concerned, was Orval Faubus, governor from 1954 to 1966. Faubus was famous for blocking desegregation of Little Rock's Central High School in 1957, until President Dwight Eisenhower sent in federal troops to enforce the court order. And Arkansas was one of five states to vote for segregationist George Wallace for president in 1968. But Arkansas was changing, culturally and economically, in ways that made Clinton's career possible. Faubus had been succeeded by governors who repudiated his legacy: Republican Winthrop Rockefeller in 1966 and Democrat Dale Bumpers in 1970. Their politics made Clinton, then 28, a plausible candidate in the Republican-dominated third Congressional District in 1974. He narrowly lost to the incumbent Republican but probably came to the notice of leading entrepreneurs in the northwest corner of Arkansas, none of whom had quite yet achieved national fame: Sam Walton, whose first Wal-mart had opened only a dozen years before; Don Tyson of chicken-producing Tyson Food; and J. B. Hunt and his trucking firm. In less than two decades, Walton was America's richest man, and Clinton was elected president.

Arkansas still ranks low on many national indexes - its median household income is the nation's third-lowest, and nearly one-in-five residents (and 28 percent of children) live in poverty - but it has achieved above-average population growth over the past two decades. Educational achievement is hit-and-miss - higher-than-average high-school graduation rates but lower-than-average rates of college degrees. The state's prison population grew by 26 percent from 2004 to 2013 -- the nation's third fastest growth rate and more than three times the state's overall population growth. Arkansas lost some 30,000 manufacturing jobs between 2007 and 2012. There has been a natural gas boom in the Fayetteville area, and Arkansas continues to lead the nation in rice production while ranking No. 2 in chickens, No. 3 in cotton and No. 4 in timber. State government finances have been in good shape thanks to budget reforms instituted after the state defaulted on bonds in the 1930s (its bank balance in January 1933 was supposedly $4.80). Little Rock has become a vibrant regional center, with exurban growth spreading out past the Pulaski County line, and it has been attracting tourists thanks to the William J. Clinton Presidential Center, the nation's largest presidential library. Northwest Arkansas has been booming even more, including Bentonville (where Wal-mart's headquarters are housed and where Sam Walton's daughter, Alice Walton, in 2011 opened the Crystal Bridges museum, with a magnificent collection of American art) and the University of Arkansas, along with the research and technology firms its presence has midwifed. By November 2016, the unemployment rate was down to an impressive 3.8 percent. Left behind, however, are the aging, shrinking rural regions of the state; in 33 rural counties, more than one of every three children is living in poverty

Politically, Arkansas was long solidly Democratic, with Republican pockets in the mountains of the northwest. For years, it produced Democratic politicians who accumulated great seniority and power in Washington: longtime House Ways and Means Chairman Wilbur Mills; Sens. John McClellan and J. William Fulbright, who represented the state for a total of 65 years from the 1940s to the 1970s; and Sens. Dale Bumpers and David Pryor, who served for 42 years from the 1970s to the 1990s. Republicans won some gubernatorial races - Winthrop Rockefeller in the 1960s, Frank White in 1980 (when he beat Clinton), and future presidential candidate Mike Huckabee in 1998 and 2002 - and John Paul Hammerschmidt amassed influence in the House, serving from 1967 to 1993. Still, as late as the 1990s, Arkansas remained one of the most Democratic states in the South in presidential and congressional elections.

Not so anymore; as throughout the Scots-Irish belt of America, which runs from western Pennsylvania southwest along the Appalachian chain and west to Texas, President Barack Obama was unpopular. Hillary Clinton, who decided to run for the Senate in New York rather than returning to Arkansas after her husband vacated the White House, won the state's 2016 presidential primary by a 2-1 margin over Bernie Sanders, but she was trounced by Donald Trump in the general, 61%-34%. Down ballot, the GOP has been relentlessly ascendant. In 2010, the GOP claimed the offices of lieutenant governor, secretary of state and land commissioner, even as Democratic Gov. Mike Beebe was reelected. The same year, Democratic Sen. Blanche Lincoln was defeated 58%-37% by Republican Rep. John Boozman, while two of the state's three Democratic congressmen retired rather than run for reelection, to be replaced by Republicans. The third retired in 2012 and was succeeded by Republican Tom Cotton. Then, in 2014, Mark Pryor, a second-generation Democratic senator and the only Democrat left in the Arkansas delegation - lost big to Cotton, 57%-40%. Credible Democratic candidates for House seats lost, including respected former FEMA head James Lee Witt, who was swamped by double digits.

Meanwhile, the state legislature, heavily Democratic since Reconstruction, is now securely Republican, with more farmers serving than lawyers. The GOP steered the legislature to the right, voting to cut $140 million in taxes by fiscal 2016 and passing a raft of socially conservative legislation, including a measure declaring that life begins at conception and a ban on most abortions after 12 weeks. There is a residual strain of populism in Arkansas - even during the 2014 Republican wave, voters approved a three-phase minimum-wage hike -- and voters, against the wishes of GOP Gov. Asa Hutchinson, approved a medical marijuana initiative in 2016. But unlike other Southern states such as North Carolina and Virginia that have turned purple due to an influx of liberal-leaning outsiders, Arkansas has seen its fastest growth in the historically Republican northwest and in the GOP-leaning Little Rock exurbs. In Arkansas, Clintonism is the past, not the future.

Population		**Race and Ethnicity**		**Income**	
Total	2,958,208	White	73.6%	Median Income	$41,371 (49 out of 50)
Land area	52,035	Black	15.4%		
Pop/ sq mi	56.8	Latino	6.9%	Under $50,000	58.2%
Born in state	61.4%	Asian	1.4%	$50,000-$99,999	27.7%
		Two races	1.9%	$100,000-$199,999	11.8%
Age Groups		Other	0.9%	$200,000 or more	2.4%
Under 18	23.9%			Poverty Rate	19.3%
18-34	20.0%	**Education**			
35-64	38.0%	H.S grad or less	50.2%	**Health Insurance**	
Over 64	15.3%	Some college	28.8%	With health insurance coverage	85.8%
		College Degree, 4 yr	13.6%		
Work		Post grad	7.5%		
White Collar	32.0%			**Public Assistance**	
Sales and Service	41.0%	**Military**		Cash public assistance income	2.4%
Blue Collar	27.1%	Veteran	9.8%		
Government	16.4%	Active Duty	0.2%	Food stamp/SNAP benefits	14.8%

Voter Turnout			
2015 Total Citizens 18+	2,164,083	2016 Pres Turnout as % CVAP	52%
2016 Pres Votes	1,130,635	2012 Pres Turnout as % CVAP	51%

Legislature	
Senate:	11D, 24R
House:	24D, 76R

Presidential Politics

2016 Democratic Primary		
Hillary Clinton (D)	146,057	(66%)
Bernie Sanders (D)	66,236	(30%)
2016 Republican Primary		
Donald Trump (R)	134,744	(33%)
Ted Cruz (R)	125,340	(31%)
Marco Rubio (R)	101,910	(25%)
Ben Carson (R)	23,521	(6%)

2016 Presidential Vote		
Donald Trump (R)	684,872	(61%)
Hillary Clinton (D)	380,494	(34%)
Gary Johnson (L)	29,829	(3%)
2012 Presidential Vote		
Mitt Romney (R)	647,744	(61%)
Barack Obama (D)	394,409	(37%)

Like most Southern states, Arkansas voted more Democratic than the nation as a whole in presidential elections from Reconstruction to 1960. Since then, it has done so only when Jimmy Carter and Bill Clinton were atop the Democratic ticket. In the past five elections, it has voted 51 and 54 percent for George W. Bush, 59 percent for John McCain, and 61 percent for Mitt Romney and Donald Trump. Between the presidential elections of 2000 and 2016, only in West Virginia has the Democratic percentage declined more precipitously than it has in Arkansas. In 1996, Bill Clinton carried all but nine of the state's 75 counties. In 2016, his wife, Hillary Clinton won just eight. The Democratic base in presidential contests is Pulaski County, home to Little Rock, the state's largest city and capital. More than a third of the county's residents are African American. Jefferson County (Pine Bluff) also leans Democratic. Northwest Arkansas, the Ozark Mountain region, is historically Republican and home to the corporate headquarters of Wal-Mart in Bentonville. Relatively fast growing suburban counties of Falkner and Saline around Little Rock are also GOP strengths.

The 2016 GOP presidential primary was a competitive affair in which Trump edged out Texas Sen. Ted Cruz, 33%-31%. Florida Sen. Marco Rubio won 25 percent. Trump's strength in the primary was in the rural eastern counties of the state along the Mississippi River and in the rural southwestern corner of the state. He also narrowly beat Cruz in Northwest Arkansas. Cruz prevailed in the counties around Little Rock, including Falkner and Saline; Rubio won Pulaski, where Trump finished third. In the Democratic primary, Clinton, the former first lady of the state, prevailed easily over Vermont Sen. Bernie Sanders, 66%-30%. She won 73 counties, losing only tiny Carroll and Newton counties in the northwest. But familiarity did not help Clinton in the general election in which she captured only 34% of the vote, trailing the 37% Obama scored in 2012.

Congressional Districts

115th Congress Lineup	4R	**114th Congress Lineup**	4R

The rapid Republican takeover of Arkansas since 2010, when it was the last remaining Southern state where Democrats still held the governorship and both houses of the legislature, has also extended to the congressional delegation. When Republicans that year flipped Democrats' usual 3-to-1 seat majority by picking up the open 1st and 2nd districts, national Democratic strategists applied pressure on their Arkansas counterparts to radically revamp the state's map by creating a solidly Democratic black-influenced district linking Little Rock with the state's Delta region.

But what party strategists in Washington wanted fell on deaf ears in Little Rock, where Democrats' first order of business was protecting sole surviving Blue Dog Democrat Mike Ross in the southern 4th District. In 2011, Gov. Mike Beebe signed off on a map that barely changed the 1st and 2nd districts but pushed the slow-growing 4th District north to take a big bite of rural Republican counties out of the 3rd District. Three months later, Ross announced his retirement, and Democrats lost the 4th District in a landslide, embarrassingly locking them out of the state's House delegation for the first time since Reconstruction.

Since then, Democrats have not come close to winning any seat despite strong bids in 2014 for open seats in the 2nd and 4th districts With Republicans likely to retain control in Little Rock for the next redistricting, litigation appears to be the only option for Democrats to gain a district with black influence.

Governor

Asa Hutchinson (R)

Elected 2014, term expires 2019, 1st term; b. Dec. 3, 1950, Bentonville, AR; Bob Jones U., B.S. 1972; U of AR (Fayetteville), J.D. 1975; Christian; Married (Susan); 4 children.

Elected Office: Chairman, AR Republican Committee, 1990-95; U.S. House, 1996-2001.

Professional Career: Bentonville City Attorney, 1997-1978; U.S. Attorney, 1982-1985; Director, DEA, 2001-2003; Under Secretary for Border & Transportation Security, Department Homeland Security, 2003-2005.

Office: State Capitol, Room 250, Little Rock, 72201; 501-682-2345; Fax: 501-682-1382; Website: governor.arkansas.gov.

Election Results

Election	Name (Party)	Vote (%)
2014 General	Asa Hutchinson (R)	470,429 (55%)
	Mike Ross (D)	352,115 (42%)
2014 Primary	Asa Hutchinson (R)	130,752 (73%)
	Curtis Coleman (R)	48,473 (27%)

Republican Asa Hutchinson was elected governor in 2014, succeeding Democrat Mike Beebe. After three unsuccessful tries for statewide office, Hutchinson prevailed over fellow former Rep. Mike Ross. He has governed as a conservative in this increasingly Republican state, but with heterodox views on such issues as the federal Medicaid expansion and trade with Cuba.

Hutchinson grew up on a farm with his brother Tim, who later became a senator. Their parents also operated a Christian radio station and school. After graduating from Bob Jones University, Asa Hutchinson attended the University of Arkansas law school at the same time Bill Clinton started teaching there. He became U.S. attorney in western Arkansas and prosecuted Clinton's half-brother, Roger, for cocaine possession. He lost a longshot 1986 bid for the Senate against Democrat Dale Bumpers, then ran for attorney general in 1990 and lost again. He spent the next five years as the state GOP chairman.

Hutchinson easily won election to the House in 1996 to succeed his brother, who moved to the Senate. He combined a conservative voting record with a pleasant demeanor to become an important player in a short time. In 1998, he served as one of the House's impeachment managers against Clinton. When George W. Bush became president, he tapped Hutchinson to head the Drug Enforcement Administration, then as undersecretary for transportation and border security in the new Homeland Security Department. Hutchinson returned to Arkansas to run for governor in 2006, but lost.

After the 2012 mass shooting in Newtown Connecticut-when National Rifle Association executive vice president Wayne LaPierre decisively rejected national pressure to moderate the group's stance against gun control-LaPierre offered his solution, which was to ensure the presence of guns in schools as a defensive measure. LaPierre tapped Hutchinson to head a "multifaceted" education and training program "available to every school in America free of charge."

With Beebe term-limited, Hutchinson prepared for a race in 2014. He ended up facing Ross, who in 12 years in the House had been a Blue Dog with the kind of moderate voting record that would have seemed appropriate for the Republican-trending state, including a vote against the Affordable Care Act. Hutchinson took less ideological stands during the campaign than he had in the past: He backed a November ballot measure to increase the state minimum wage and to provide additional funding for early-childhood education, two proposals that Democrats nationally have favored. He also aired an ad targeting women that featured his school-age granddaughter, who helped him advocate a plan to put computer-science classes in every high school and to help women compete for high-tech jobs. Backed by $6.2 million from the Republican Governors Association aimed at tying Ross to President Barack Obama and other national Democrats, Hutchison prevailed, 55%-42%.

Once in office-and leading the state's first unified Republican government since Reconstruction-Hutchinson succeeded in getting much of his agenda enacted, including a middle-class tax cut, scaled back from $100 million to $80 million.

In his first two years, a pair of legislative battles stood out. One was the latest chapter in the fight over the state's "private option"-Beebe's creative way of getting a red state to accept Medicaid expansion under the Affordable Care Act, by applying federal funds for Medicaid-eligible residents toward securing them private health coverage. It was approved narrowly in 2013 and reauthorized even more narrowly in 2014. Facing fierce conservative opposition in the legislature, Hutchinson took something of a middle course, keeping the program in place through the end of 2016 as a task force drew up recommendations for a possible new direction after that. In April 2016, he went so far as to use a line-item veto against a Republican provision to keep the state's Medicaid expansion alive. Ultimately, the expansion held, signing up some 300,000 residents.

The other conflict Hutchinson had to grapple with was a religious freedom measure that blew up shortly after a similar bill in Indiana drew fire for potentially enabling businesses to refuse to serve gays and lesbians. As in Indiana, disapproval from the business community was critical in forestalling the measure; in Arkansas, the key opposition came from Walmart, and Hutchinson's son Seth attracted notice for signing a petition urging a veto. Hutchinson rejected the first version he received from lawmakers, ordering up changes to the most controversial provisions. The legislature complied, and Hutchinson signed the revised measure. "I think it's sending the right signal, the way this has been resolved, to the world and the country that Arkansas understands the diversity of our culture and workforce but also the importance of balancing that with our sincerely held religious convictions," Hutchinson said. All in all, the controversy proved to be much less messy, and with more limited economic fallout, than in Indiana.

Hutchinson has taken a hard line on some issues – he opposed the settlement of Syrian refugees in Arkansas, and he criticized an Obama administration effort to pressure public schools to allow transgender students to use bathrooms and locker rooms for their chosen gender, calling it "offensive, intrusive and totally lacking in common sense." In other areas, however, Hutchinson has followed a moderate approach, much as he did with the 2010 health care overhaul and the religious freedom bill. He signed a measure to "implement wide-ranging reforms to the criminal justice system in order to address prison overcrowding" and to "promote seamless reentry into society." He sought $3 million to start implementation of medical marijuana, even though he had opposed the ballot measure that approved it. He backed agricultural sales to Cuba, even visiting the island nation after the Obama administration's reopening of ties. And he advocated an end to the state's simultaneous observance of Martin Luther King Jr. Day and Robert E. Lee Day, saying that it's important that King's day "be distinguished and separate and focused on that civil rights struggle and what he personally did in that effort."

As he prepared his 2018 reelection bid, Hutchinson sought a $50.5 million tax cut as well as legislation to tie higher-education funding to student performance. With Arkansas now tilting heavily Republican, he is considered an easy bet for reelection.

Hutchison had several legislative successes during the 2017 session. He won enactment of new voter ID requirements to replace an earlier plan that had been struck down by the state Supreme Court; revision of Medicaid to impose additional work requirements for some beneficiaries; and separation of the Martin Luther King Jr. and Robert E. Lee holidays. In April 2017, he gained extensive national and international attention for the execution by lethal-injection drugs of four death-row inmates in eight days; four other scheduled executions were delayed by legal challenges.

Senior Senator

John Boozman (R)

Elected 2010, term expires 2022, 2nd term; b. Dec 10, 1950; Shreveport, LA; Southern College of Optometry (TN), O.D.; University of Arkansas; Baptist; Married (Cathy Marley Boozman); 3 children; 2 grandchildren.

Elected Office: Rogers School Board, 1994-2001; U.S. House, 2001-2011.

Professional Career: Optometrist, Boozman-Hof Regional Eye Clinic, 1977-2001.

DC Office: 141 HSOB 20510, 202-224-4843, Fax: 202-228-1371, boozman.senate.gov.

State Offices: El Dorado, 870-863-4641; Fort Smith, 479-573-0189; Jonesboro, 870-268-6925; Little Rock, 501-372-7153; Lowell, 479-725-0400; Mountain Home, 870-424-0129; Stuttgart, 870-672-6941.

Committees: *Agriculture, Nutrition & Forestry*: Commodities, Risk Management & Trade (Chmn), Conservation, Forestry & Natural Resources, Nutrition, Agricultural Research & Specialty Crops, Rural Development & Energy. *Appropriations*: Commerce, Justice, Science & Related Agencies, Department of Homeland Security (Chmn), Financial Services & General Government, Military Construction & Veteran Affairs & Related Agencies, State, Foreign Operations & Related Programs, Transportation, HUD & Related Agencies. *Budget*. *Environment & Public Works*: Clean Air & Nuclear Safety, Fisheries, Water, and Wildlife (Chmn), Transportation & Infrastructure. *Joint Security & Cooperation in Europe*. *Veterans' Affairs*.

Group Ratings

	ADA	ACLU	AFL-CIO	LCV	ITI	COC	HAFA	ACU	CFG	FRC
2016	-	11%	-	6%	80%	88%	64%	77%	82%	100%
2015	0%	C	14%	0%	C	79%	C	96%	79%	100%

Almanac Ratings 2015

	Economy	Social	Foreign	Composite
Liberal	7%	0%	9%	5%
Conservative	93%	100%	91%	95%

Key Votes of the 114th Congress

1. Keystone pipeline	Y	5. National Security Data	Y	9. Gun Sales Checks	N
2. Export-Import Bank	Y	6. Iran Nuclear Deal	Y	10. Sanctuary Cities	Y
3. Debt Ceiling Increase	N	7. Puerto Rico Debt	N	11. Planned Parenthood	Y
4. Homeland Security $$	N	8. Loretta Lynch A.G	N	12. Trade deals	Y

Election Results

Election	Name (Party)	Vote (%)		Cand. Spent	Ind. Exp. Support	Ind. Exp. Oppose
2016 General	John Boozman (R)	661,984	(60%)	$4,097,463	$164,806	
	Conner Eldridge (D)	400,602	(36%)	$2,227,706		$29,991
	Frank Gilbert (L)	43,866	(4%)			
2016 Primary	John Boozman (R)	298,039	(77%)			
	Curtis Coleman (R)	91,795	(24%)			

Prior winning percentages: 2010 (57%), House: 2008(79%), 2006 (62%), 2004 (59%), 2002 (99%), 2001 special (56%)

Republican John Boozman, Arkansas' senior senator, was the only Republican in the state's congressional delegation when he won a special election to the House in 2001. Less than a decade later, in 2010, he became only the second Republican to represent Arkansas in the Senate since Reconstruction, ousting Democratic incumbent Blanche Lincoln by a wide margin. Today, Boozman -- as the longest-serving member of a six-person, all-Republican state delegation on Capitol Hill -- reflects Arkansas' dramatic political shift since the turn of the century, when it was the last remaining Democratic stronghold in the Deep South. An amiable conservative, he generally hews to the party line in the Senate -- though he occasionally works across the aisle, as he also did from time to time during his five terms in the House. He had little trouble winning re-election to a second Senate term in 2016, notwithstanding the Democrats' touting of their nominee as a leading prospect for an upset.

Boozman was born in Shreveport Louisiana and grew up in Fort Smith, the second-largest city in Arkansas. He credits his upbringing-his father was an Air Force master sergeant -- for his appreciation of difficult issues that military families face. His current committee assignments include the Senate Veterans Affairs panel, where he has pushed for several measures -- often with Democratic co-authors -- to provide assistance for veterans. Boozman attended the University of Arkansas, where he played offensive guard on the football team. He left after completing his pre-optometry requirements and went on to graduate from the Southern College of Optometry in 1977. He opened a clinic in Rogers with his older brother, Fay Boozman, an ophthalmologist. As a sidelight, John Boozman raised Polled Hereford cattle that were competitive in the show ring.

The father of three children, Boozman had his first experience in public office as a member of the Rogers Board of Education, a seat he won in 1994. Four years later, Fay Boozman -- by then a member of the state Senate -- unsuccessfully ran against Lincoln for an open U.S. Senate seat, as John Boozman got a taste of statewide politics working in his brother's campaign. Fay Boozman went on to serve for six years as director of the state health department under Gov. Mike Huckabee until Boozman's 2005 death in an accident on his farm. John Boozman in 2001 sought the 3rd District seat vacated by Republican Rep. Asa Hutchinson to head the Drug Enforcement Administration, and had Huckabee's support in the special election. Boozman was the only Republican in the contest to back President George W. Bush's push for limited federal funding of stem cell research. After emerging from a first-round of the primary followed by a 57%-43% runoff victory, Boozman won the general election by a 56%-42% margin in the general election. Boozman benefitted from a strong GOP get-out-the-vote operation in what was at the time the only district in the state with a history of electing Republicans.

When Boozman traveled to Capitol Hill to claim his seat, it marked his first trip to Washington.

Boozman showed independence from the George W. Bush White House by voting to end the trade embargo with Cuba -- a stance that reflected a longstanding desire by Arkansas agricultural interests to export two of the state's leading agricultural products, rice and chickens to Cuba -- and by backing a measure to allow the importation of prescription drugs from Canada. But he exhibited his more conservative side in opposing Bush's immigration proposal, calling it amnesty for illegal aliens. A devout evangelical Christian (he co-chaired the annual National Prayer Breakfast in Washington in early 2017), Boozman sponsored measures to display the Ten Commandments in the House and Senate chambers, and sought to weaken restrictions on churches' political activities. Boozman created a dust-up in 2005 by sponsoring and then withdrawing a bill to increase the maximum workday for truckers to 16 hours. It was a move sought by Arkansas-based Wal-mart, but that was lambasted by critics as a "sweatshop on wheels" that would have jeopardized safety.

Boozman never garnered less than 59 percent of the vote in winning re-election to four House terms; in two of those races, the Democrats did not field a candidate against him. In 2010, Boozman entered the Senate race against Lincoln, who was seeking a third term. The political dynamics in the state had changed markedly since his initial election to the House; GOP presidential nominee John McCain had trounced Democratic nominee Barack Obama in 2008. But Boozman had some potential vulnerabilities in an eight-candidate primary contest: He had backed Bush's controversial 2008 legislation to bail out the nation's financial institutions in the midst of the Great Recession -- an issue that tea party supporters used against some Republican incumbents in primaries in 2010. But the endorsement of former vice presidential nominee Sarah Palin helped to inoculate Boozman. As the best-known candidate and having represented a district that was home to the largest concentration of the state's GOP voters, Boozman captured 53 percent of the primary vote, avoiding a runoff.

Meanwhile, Lincoln's re-election bid was hampered by a spirited primary challenge from the left by Democratic Lt. Gov. Bill Halter, who not only made her drain her campaign war chest but also forced her into a runoff. She narrowly won, but the battle left her weakened. Like other Republican Senate candidates in 2010, Boozman sought to exploit the state's disenchantment with Obama by seeking to tie Lincoln to the White House. He blasted her as out of step with the conservative values of the state, while citing his endorsements from the National Rifle Association and Arkansas Right to Life. He criticized Lincoln's vote for the $787 billion economic stimulus in Obama's first year, and especially targeted her support of the Affordable Care Act. Lincoln tried to distance herself from Obama and to stress the importance to the state of her position as chair of the Agriculture Committee. Republican Senate Leader Mitch McConnell gave Boozman a boost by promising him a seat on that panel if he won. Echoing an attack line used against Boozman in his first congressional campaign, Lincoln criticized him for supporting Social Security "privatization." Boozman countered that Lincoln was taking a card out of the old Democratic playbook by trying to scare seniors.

The Senate race was no contest: Boozman swept to a big win as part of the national GOP tide as well as Arkansas' increasing shift to the Republican column. Boozman moved across the Capitol to assume his promised slot on the Senate Agriculture Committee, and saw his clout enhanced a couple of years later when he was named to an opening on the Appropriations Committee.

In the Senate, Boozman has continued to compile a consistently conservative record. A staunch abortion opponent, he introduced a measure to require parental notification at least four days before their minor daughter could have an abortion. In 2015, with Republicans back in control of the Senate, Boozman became chair of the Appropriations Subcommittee on Financial Services and General Government, and teamed with fellow Republicans in the continuing attacks on the Consumer Financial Protection Bureau -- created as part of the 2010 so-called Dodd-Frank law. Boozman joined several Republicans in withdrawing support for legislation aimed at cracking down on the theft of Internet content after critics -- including websites such as Google and Wikipedia and their users -- contended it would give the Justice Department the power to force Internet service providers to block access to sites accused of stealing intellectual property. On the environmental front, Boozman opposed the Environmental Protection Agency for what he saw as an attack on coal, especially the agency's proposed rules to reduce carbon emissions at power plants-a move he said would drive up costs in Arkansas.

On farm policy, Boozman's stances have appeared to reflect state and regional interests more than ideology. In 2012, he joined 34 colleagues in voting against the Senate version of the farm bill reauthorization; the opponents included many fellow Southerners who felt it did too little for farmers in their region, particularly rice and peanut growers. A year later, Boozman switched and voted for another version of the farm bill that had been revised to the liking of Southern agricultural interests; conservative groups such as FreedomWorks lobbied strongly against that measure. Boozman has praised Obama's move to normalize relations with Cuba, splitting from hardline conservatives -- including his in-state junior Senate colleague, Republican Tom Cotton -- but aligning himself with many other Arkansas Republicans. "Arkansas is uniquely positioned…to export goods to Cuba. Cuba imports about 80 percent of its food, making it an attractive export market for farmers in Arkansas," Boozman declared in late 2015. The following year, he joined with Sen. Jon Tester of Montana, a centrist Democrat, to attach an amendment to an Appropriations Committee measure to lift a ban on private banks and companies offering credit for export of agricultural commodities to Cuba.

Boozman had emergency heart surgery in April 2014 after discovery of an aortic aneurysm, but returned to Capitol Hill a couple of months later. In 2016, at 65, he ran for a second term. His Democratic opponent, Conner Eldridge, was a quarter of a century younger, and had served as U.S. attorney for the Western District of Arkansas from 2010-2015 after earlier working as a congressional aide and bank executive. Boozman criticized Eldridge, an Obama appointee, as someone who would enable "a third term of Barack Obama." Eldridge distanced himself from Obama on issues such as the Second Amendment, while citing his record prosecuting child abusers and pornographers as U.S. attorney. He promised to press for tougher penalties on child pornographers and greater access to high-speed Internet service in rural Arkansas as well as campaign finance reform -- while pumping nearly $600,000 in personal contributions and loans into his candidacy.

Eldridge was clearly banking on the anti-incumbent mood evident in the 2016 election. "I am convinced that while they did vote against a two-term Democratic incumbent senator last time, those voters are fed up," Eldridge said in an interview with *Roll Call*, alluding to the 2014 defeat of Arkansas Sen. Mark Pryor. "And many of them are going to vote against a 14-year Republican incumbent senator because they're ready for new leadership." But on Election Day, Boozman came out on top by 60%-36%. Like other down-ballot candidates, Boozman had to deal with controversy from the top of the ticket. After release of the decade-old video with then-Republican presidential candidate Donald Trump's lewd comments about women, Boozman characterized the comments as evidence that the presidential race was a "race to the bottom of humanity," declaring, "As a husband, father of three daughters, and grandfather of two precious little girls, if I ever heard anyone speak this way about them, they would be shopping for a new set of teeth." But Boozman never withdrew his support of Trump. And, during a debate a week after the video surfaced, he said he supported Trump because the next president would likely nominate several Supreme Court justices over the next four years.

Junior Senator

Tom Cotton (R)

Elected 2014, term expires 2020, 1st term; b. May 13, 1977, Dardanelle; Harvard University, A.B.; Harvard University Law School (MA), J.D.; Claremont Graduate University, Att.; Methodist; Married (Anna Cotton); 2 children.

Military Career: U.S. Army, 2004-2009 (Iraq).

Elected Office: U.S. House, 2012-2014.

Professional Career: Clerk, U.S Court of Appeals, 2002-2003; Practicing attorney, 2003-2004; Management consultant, McKinsey & Co., 2010-2011.

DC Office: 124 RSOB 20510, 202-224-2353, Fax: 202-228-0908, cotton.senate.gov.

State Offices: El Dorado, 870-864-8582; Jonesboro, 870-933-6223; Little Rock, 501-223-9081; Springdale, 479-751-0879.

Committees: *Armed Services*: Airland (Chmn), Seapower, Strategic Forces. *Banking, Housing & Urban Affairs*: Economic Policy (Chmn), Financial Institutions & Consumer Protection, National Security & International Trade & Finance. *Intelligence*. *Joint Congressional-Executive Commission on China*.

Group Ratings

	ADA	ACLU	AFL-CIO	LCV	ITI	COC	HAFA	ACU	CFG	FRC
2016	-	5%	-	0%	60%	86%	77%	92%	82%	100%
2015	0%	C	7%	0%	C	64%	C	96%	91%	91%

Almanac Ratings 2015

	Economy	Social	Foreign	Composite
Liberal	2%	0%	0%	1%
Conservative	98%	100%	100%	99%

Key Votes of the 114th Congress

1. Keystone pipeline	Y	5. National Security Data	N	9. Gun Sales Checks	N
2. Export-Import Bank	Y	6. Iran Nuclear Deal	Y	10. Sanctuary Cities	Y
3. Debt Ceiling Increase	N	7. Puerto Rico Debt	N	11. Planned Parenthood	Y
4. Homeland Security $$	N	8. Loretta Lynch A.G	N	12. Trade deals	Y

Election Results

Election	Name (Party)	Vote	(%)	Cand. Spent	Ind. Exp. Support	Ind. Exp. Oppose
2014 General	Tom Cotton (R)	478,819	(57%)	$13,948,938	$8,004,645	$15,802,295
	Mark Pryor (D)	334,174	(40%)	$14,578,504	$987,646	$15,005,636
	Nathan LaFrance (L)	17,210	(2%)			
	Mark Swaney (G)	16,797	(2%)			
2014 Primary	Tom Cotton (R)	Unopposed				

Prior winning percentages: House: 2012 (60%)

Republicans won back control of the Senate in 2014 thanks to a pickup of nine seats, the lion's share of them in states that have been increasingly dominated by the GOP in recent elections. The result was a freshman class that was avowedly conservative -- but perhaps no member more outspokenly so than Republican Tom Cotton, Arkansas' junior senator. It took Cotton -- then and now the Senate's youngest member -- only a couple of months into his term to demonstrate his unapologetically bold approach, as he authored and rounded up signatures for a controversial letter to Iran's leaders.

Intended to head off what Cotton saw as the White House negotiating a bad nuclear deal with Iran, the letter warned Iran's leaders that striking an agreement with President Barack Obama without congressional approval was nothing more than an executive agreement that could be short-lived -- since it could be undone by a future president. While Cotton convinced 46 of his Senate Republican colleagues -- all but seven members of the GOP majority -- to join him in signing the letter, it infuriated White House officials as an inappropriate interference in the conduct of foreign policy. Democratic Sen. Chris Murphy of Connecticut, a member of the Foreign Relations Committee, called the letter"unprecedented" and said it was "undermining the authority of the president." Shot back Cotton on CNN, "The only thing unprecedented is an American president negotiating a nuclear deal with the world's leading state sponsor of terrorism without submitting it to Congress." The Senate overwhelmingly approved the plan for congressional review of an agreement, although Obama ultimately rounded up enough supporters to block a super-majority needed to disapprove the deal.

A Harvard-educated military veteran of the wars in Iraq and Afghanistan, Cotton's political ascent has been little short of meteoric: He ousted Democratic Sen. Mark Pryor, the bearer of a well-known name in Arkansas politics, after serving just one term in the House. And, prior to President Trump's surprise 2016 victory, there was buzz about Cotton as a potential presidential contender in 2020. Hardly a natural politician, Cotton -- notwithstanding his often blunt rhetoric and occasional wry humor -- is more the cerebral, introverted, principled conservative than a back-slapper who enjoys mixing it up on the campaign trail. Still, his tough-minded views caught the attention of national groups when he sought an open House seat in 2012, earning endorsements from the anti-tax Club for Growth and the National Republican Congressional Committee as well as Sen. John McCain of Arizona, who shares Cotton's hawkish beliefs.

A sixth-generation Arkansan, Cotton grew up on his family's cattle farm in Dardanelle. Even at a young age, his serious, studious demeanor made an impression, as did his growing interest in conservative thought and teachings. Friends remember him as a contrarian and a deep admirer of Winston Churchill. He studied government as an undergraduate at Harvard, and went on to earn a degree from Harvard Law School in 2002. Cotton clerked for a federal appeals court judge and later went to work at two law firms.He enlisted in the Army in 2004 in the wake of the 9/11 attacks, and turned down an opportunity to join the Judge Advocate General Corps, preferring to serve in combat.

Cotton was deployed to Baghdad in May 2006 as a platoon leader in the 101st Airborne Division, leading daily patrols through the city. His ferocity came through after his deployment when he wrote a letter in to *The New York Times* in response to a story the newspaper broke about the George W. Bush administration's program to trace financial transactions of people suspected of ties to terrorist organizations. "You may think you have done a public service," he wrote, "but you have gravely endangered the lives of my soldiers and all other soldiers and innocent Iraqis here." He went on: "Next time I hear that familiar explosion-or next time I feel it-I will wonder whether we could have stopped that bomb had you not instructed terrorists how to evade our financial surveillance. By the time we return home, maybe you will be in your rightful place: not at the Pulitzer announcements, but behind bars."

Though the *Times* chose not to publish the letter, Cotton had copied PowerLine, a conservative blog, which did publish it. His tough words made a big impression on some leading conservatives. William Kristol, the editor of *The Weekly Standard*, befriended Cotton and became his champion. In 2007, Cotton joined the Old Guard at Arlington National Cemetery, the regiment that guards the Tomb of the Unknowns. The following year, he went to Afghanistan as an operations officer for a provincial construction team. After completing his military service, Cotton considered launching a campaign against Democratic Sen. Blanche Lincoln in 2010, but instead postponed pursuit of political office and joined McKinsey & Co., a high-powered management consulting firm.

When conservative Democratic Rep. Mike Ross announced in June 2011 that he would not seek reelection, Cotton decided it was the right time to take the plunge into politics. He won the GOP primary with 58 percent of the vote over Beth Anne Rankin, a former aide to Republican Gov. Mike Huckabee. He then trounced Democratic state Rep. Gene Jeffress in the 2012 general election with 60 percent of the vote, becoming only the second Republican ever elected in the traditionally Democratic 4th District.

In the House, Cotton quickly compiled a strongly conservative record and began to exhibit an uncompromising streak. He opposed an initial version of the 2014 farm bill, which he scorned as a "food-stamp bill." He later backed a version that didn't contain food-stamp programs. He opposed disaster relief for those who took a hit from Hurricane Sandy along the Atlantic coast. After the 2013 Boston Marathon bombing, he blasted the Obama Administration for "failing in its mission to stop terrorism before it reaches its targets in the United States." But Cotton didn't spare his party's own anti-interventionist wing and, just months later, he joined with another military veteran, Rep. Mike Pompeo of Kansas -- who later became the CIA director -- to author an op-ed in *The Washington Post* urging fellow Republicans to support Obama's call for military intervention in Syria.

In the Senate, Mark Pryor held the same seat that his father, one-time Gov. David Pryor, had occupied for three terms ; Mark Pryor first won the seat in 2002, and Republicans hadn't even bothered to field a candidate against him in 2008. But Arkansas' increasingly rightward shift, combined with Obama's deep unpopularity there, provided an opening for the GOP. Cotton, with his military background and strong conservative credentials, was quickly seen as the party's best prospect to unseat Pryor. Though Republicans couldn't depict Pryor, one of the most conservative Democrats in the chamber, as a liberal Obama ally, they did hammer him for backing the Affordable Care Act. Pryor also had supported the administration's $787 billion economic stimulus bill. But he was one of a small number of Democrats who opposed additional background checks on gun purchases. He also parted company with the administration by backing the Keystone XL pipeline and, in 2012, he was the only Democrat to oppose the so-called "Buffett rule" requiring millionaires to pay an effective 30 percent minimum tax rate.

The Democratic strategy was to paint Cotton as an extremist, driven by ideological convictions that put him at odds with most Arkansans. They highlighted his vote against lower student loan interest rates-the only member of the state's delegation to oppose it-as well as his opposition to the farm bill. Cotton countered that hometown banks should finance student loans rather than allowing the federal government to have a monopoly.And he again took aim at the food-stamp component of the farm bill, saying he opposed a food stamp program "that isn't reformed, that doesn't have job training and work requirements [and] that doesn't have drug testing requirements, so we can get people who are addicted the help they need. Or make sure that long-term addicts or recidivists are not abusing taxpayer dollars."

The debate became particularly nasty after Cotton raised the 2014 *Hobby Lobby* case -- in which the Supreme Court ruled that certain businesses did not have to pay for the Affordable Care Act's contraception mandate if it conflicted with their religious beliefs -- to take a swipe at Pryor. "It's another example of how Obamacare infringes on the liberties of all Arkansans. Barack Obama and Mark Pryor think that faith is something that only happens at 11:00 on Sunday mornings," declared Cotton. Responded Pryor, "He and I may disagree on issues, but for him to question my faith is out of bounds."But the Democratic tactic of depicting Cotton as too far to the right did not make a dent in Arkansas' decade-long trend toward backing GOP candidates. While a number of polls showed an extremely tight race up until just weeks before the election, Cotton ended up winning easily, 57%-40%.His victory marked a milestone for the state, as the first time since Reconstruction that Republicans held every seat in its congressional delegation.

Even before his Iran letter garnered him national attention in 2015, Cotton made an impression -- as a newly minted member of the Senate Armed Services Committee -- in grilling an Obama Defense Department official about Guantanamo. Obama had promised to close that facility, used to detain foreigners suspected of terrorism, during his 2008 campaign.But Cotton asserted, "The only problem with Guantanamo Bay is that there are too many empty cells."

Cotton voiced a similar attitude with regard to domestic prisons. While a number of his fellow conservatives united with liberals to vote a criminal justice reform bill out of the Judiciary Committee in 2015, Cotton emerged as the Senate's most vocal critic of the legislation -- putting him at odds with the committee chairman, Republican Sen. Charles Grassley of Iowa. "If anything, we have an under-incarceration problem," Cotton declared. While supporters of the measure argued that prisons are currently overcrowded with those incarcerated for non-violent offenses, Cotton contended the proposed reforms could lead to release of those convicted of violent crimes. "Some members of Congress would reduce mandatory minimum sentences for drug traffickers and other violent felons, while giving liberal judges more discretion in sentencing again," he said in a May 2016 speech to the conservative Hudson Institute. "These policies are not merely wrong. They are dangerous. They threaten a return to the worst days of the 1990s, when law-abiding citizens lived in fear of their lives."

At times, Cotton's sharp tongue has made even some members of his own party uncomfortable, according to a report in *Politico* -- such as when he called the leadership of then-Senate Minority Leader Harry Reid of Nevada "cancerous" in a 2016 floor speech. He also publicly characterized Reid as "incoherent." Sen. Lindsey Graham of South Carolina, another outspoken Republican conservative, said of Cotton: "He's feisty. I've been feisty. But you've got to balance being feisty and being effective." Added Graham, "I think he can do both." Cotton's uncompromising attitude has been in evidence even when home-state economic interests are involved. When Obama acted to restore diplomatic relations with Cuba in 2015 after more than a half-century, most of Arkansas' all-Republican congressional delegation -- along with the state's GOP governor -- welcomed the move, seeing the prospect of a new export market for the state's abundant rice crop. Cotton was the lone holdout in the delegation, joining other hardline Republican conservatives on Capitol Hill. He termed the normalization of relations with Cuba a "grave mistake," while vowing, "Rest assured, I will work to maintain and increase sanctions on the regime, block the confirmation of a new ambassador, demand the extradition of U.S. fugitives from justice, and hold the Castro regime accountable."

A Trump tweet praising Cotton in the run-up to the 2016 Republican National Convention fueled speculation that the Arkansan was on a short list of possible nominees for vice president. He was an in-demand speaker at the July gathering in Cleveland, including appearances before the delegations from Iowa, New Hampshire and South Carolina -- states that would be the first to select delegates in advance of the 2020 convention. When Trump's candidacy hit the rocks in the fall following the release of the "Access Hollywood" video in which he made lewd comments about women, Cotton joined many other Republicans in putting distance between himself and the party's nominee. "He needs to throw himself on the mercy of the American people," Cotton said of Trump. "If he doesn't. . . then he should step aside and allow the Republican Party to replace him with an elder statesman who will." But, several days later, after what was generally regarded as a strong performance by Trump in his second debate with Democratic nominee Hillary Clinton, Cotton walked back those comments. He said that Trump had apologized and could "change his ways," and reaffirmed his endorsement of the Republican nominee.

Both comments on Trump were made as Cotton was in the midst of a four-day tour of Iowa, site of the first-in-the-nation delegate caucuses, which included speeches at two fundraising dinners. The trip, a month before Election Day, fueled further speculation about Cotton's presidential ambitions -- perhaps as early as 2020 if Trump was unsuccessful. Starting with the presidential transition,Cotton was an informal adviser to Trump on national security matters. Cotton has time to wait: He entered middle age, having reached 40 in May 2017.

FIRST DISTRICT

Rick Crawford (R)

Elected 2010, 4th term; b. Jan 22, 1966, Homestead Air Force Base, FL; Arkansas State University, Jonesboro, B.A.; Southwest Missouri State University, Att.; Baptist; Married (Stacy Crawford); 2 children.

Military Career: U.S. Army, 1985-1989 (Pakistan).

Professional Career: News anchor; Agri-reporter; Marketing Manager, John Deere; Owner, AgWatch Network.

DC Office: 2422 RHOB 20515, 202-225-4076, Fax: 202-225-5602, crawford.house.gov.

State Offices: Cabot, 501-843-3043; Jonesboro, 870-203-0540; Mountain Home, 870-424-2075.

Committees: *Agriculture*: General Farm Commodities & Risk Management (Chmn), Nutrition. *Permanent Select on Intelligence*. *Transportation & Infrastructure*: Economic Dev't, Public Buildings & Emergency Management, Highways & Transit, Water Resources & Environment.

Group Ratings

	ADA	ACLU	AFL-CIO	LCV	ITI	COC	HAFA	ACU	CFG	FRC
2016	-	5%	-	3%	100%	100%	68%	86%	63%	100%
2015	0%	C	17%	3%	C	75%	C	88%	74%	100%

Almanac Ratings 2015

	Economy	Social	Foreign	Composite
Liberal	7%	0%	0%	2%
Conservative	93%	100%	100%	98%

Key Votes of the 114th Congress

1. Keystone Pipeline	Y	5. Puerto Rico Debt	N	9. Offenses by Aliens	Y
2. Trade Deals	Y	6. Medical Marijuana	N	10. Troops in Iraq	N
3. Export-Import Bank	NV	7. Sanctuary Cities	Y	11. Homeland Security $$	N
4. Debt Ceiling Increase	N	8. Armor-piercing Bullets	Y	12. Trade Adjustment aid	N

Election Results

Election	Name (Party)	Vote (%)	Cand. Spent	Ind. Exp. Support	Ind. Exp. Oppose
2016 General	Rick Crawford (R)	183,866 (76%)	$471,710		
	Mark West (L)	57,181 (24%)			
2016 Primary	Rick Crawford (R)	(100%)			

Prior winning percentages: 2014 (63%), 2012 (56%), 2010 (52%)

First District Rep. Rick Crawford, who in 2010 became the first Republican since Reconstruction to win this eastern Arkansas district, has settled in and delivers federal payments and projects back home. Like the many Democrats who served this and similar rural Southern districts in decades past, he is usually a loyalist who quietly produces farm and other legislation for party leaders. A former news anchor and owner of an agricultural broadcasting business, he keeps an eye out for the region's cotton and rice farmers. As with other areas in Arkansas, his district has become safely Republican.

Crawford was born in Florida on the former Homestead Air Force Base, where his father, a munitions expert, was stationed. Growing up in a military family meant a lot of "bouncing around," says Crawford, who attended a dozen schools as a child. After graduating from high school in Hudson, New Hampshire, he enlisted in the Army, where he trained as a bomb-disposal technician, disabling suspected live explosive devices. Crawford became a sergeant, did a tour of duty in Pakistan, and later served on U.S. Secret Service details for Presidents Ronald Reagan and George H.W. Bush.

When his military service ended, he enrolled at Arkansas State University in Jonesboro to study agribusiness and economics. He competed on the college rodeo circuit until injuries forced him to quit. In 1994, he declared personal bankruptcy, but eventually found full-time employment - and discovered he had some skills - in rodeo announcing. He worked some 100 shows a year before finishing his degree. Working the rodeo-broadcasting gigs helped Crawford land a news-anchor job in Jonesboro after graduation. His experience in agricultural broadcasting led to his own business called the AgWatch Network, a farm-news outlet that broadcast on dozens of radio stations in the mid-South, as well as on television stations in Little Rock and Jonesboro.

When Crawford decided to challenge seven-term Democratic Rep. Marion Berry for the 1st District seat, national Republicans were at first cool to the idea, hoping to recruit a more seasoned candidate. Crawford gained traction after Berry announced he wouldn't run, which made the district ripe for a GOP takeover. Crawford coasted to an easy primary victory over 26-year-old congressional aide Princella Smith, and he launched a general election campaign with the theme that Democrats had lost touch with the region's rural and small-town conservative voters. Democrat Chad Causey, Berry's former chief of staff, made an issue of Crawford's personal bankruptcy, attacking the Republican for failing to release his financial records. Crawford sought to portray Causey as a Washington insider beholden to national Democrats. The national parties jumped in with independent expenditures for ads. Former President Bill Clinton returned to his home state to help raise money for Causey, to no avail. Crawford won, 52%-44%.

In the House, Crawford sits on the Agriculture Committee, where he focuses on ways to protect farmers from what he considers overly burdensome regulations. He is chairman of the General Farm Commodities and Risk Management Subcommittee, which has jurisdiction over major commercial crops plus farm credit and crop insurance. That positioned him well to protect his district's interests on farm legislation. He conducted oversight of the Agriculture Department's implementation of the 2014 farm bill, including crop insurance improvements that he helped enact. He took the lead among a bipartisan group of House members from Delta districts who opposed a move by the Obama administration to reverse a provision in the new law that shifted inspection of catfish imports from the Agriculture Department to the Food and Drug Administration. He filed a bill to promote farm exports to Cuba. On the Transportation and Infrastructure Committee, Crawford added a provision to the 2015 highway bill that permitted farm vehicles to use a three-mile stretch of the redesignated Interstate 555 near Jonesboro.

His inclination to seek bipartisan consensus occasionally has caused problems for Crawford, including charges of flip-flopping. When he supported a 5 percent surtax on incomes exceeding $1 million to break a budget stalemate in 2012 - but only if Congress first passed a balanced-budget constitutional amendment - Crawford told *The New York Times* that "many conservatives (are) calling for my head. … But this does not deter me, because the alternative is economic calamity." He has urged a more flexible approach on illegal immigration, arguing that immigrants are an important economic force.

Democrats in 2012 thought they might have a shot at unseating Crawford, claiming that redistricting had weakened him politically. But the national party's favored candidate, state Rep. Clark Hall, lost the primary to a little-known prosecutor. Crawford won his first reelection with 56 percent of the vote. In

2016, Democrats failed to run a candidate against him. Libertarian Party challenger Mark West opposed abortion and said the government should not be issuing marriage licenses. Crawford did not break a sweat. With a Republican-controlled Legislature to protect the GOP congressional delegation from redistricting mischief, Crawford appears to have become entrenched in what a decade ago was a "Yellow Dog" Democratic district.

Eastern Arkansas: The Delta, Jonesboro

Population		**Race and Ethnicity**		**Income**	
Total	726,282	White	76.5%	Median Income	$36,928 (417 out of 435)
Land area	19,318	Black	18.0%		
Pop/ sq mi	37.6	Latino	3.1%		
Born in state	66.0%	Asian	0.5%	Under $50,000	62.9%
		Two races	1.4%	$50,000-$99,999	26.5%
Age Groups		Other	0.4%	$100,000-$199,999	9.2%
Under 18	23.6%			$200,000 or more	1.5%
18-34	21.1%	**Education**		Poverty Rate	21.4%
35-64	38.5%	H.S grad or less	56.3%		
Over 64	16.8%	Some college	28.3%	**Health Insurance**	
		College Degree, 4 yr	10.2%	With health insurance coverage	85.6%
Work		Post grad	5.1%		
White Collar	28.8%				
Sales and Service	40.3%	**Military**		**Public Assistance**	
Blue Collar	30.8%	Veteran	10.2%	Cash public assistance income	2.4%
Government	16.8%	Active Duty	0.2%		
				Food stamp/SNAP benefits	18.7%

Voter Turnout			
2015 Total Citizens 18+	547,005	2016 House Turnout as % CVAP	44%
2016 House turnout	241,047	2014 House Turnout as % CVAP	36%

2012 Presidential Vote		
Mitt Romney	154,551	(61%)
Barack Obama	92,085	(36%)

2016 Presidential Vote		
Donald Trump	169,438	(65%)
Hillary Clinton	78,688	(30%)
Gary Johnson	5,489	(2%)

Cook Partisan Voting Index: R+17

The Mississippi Delta, the flat, mucky, river-crossed lowland on both sides of the great river, was some of the country's first industrial farmland. This land was uncultivated in most of the 19th century, when plows were still pulled by mules and muddy flatlands were impassable. Then, big landowners used machines to drain the marshlands and persuaded poor blacks to move here to tend fields of cotton, rice and, later, soybeans. The results were bountiful agriculture and impoverished people. Around 1940, the Delta began to slowly change: The first minimum-wage and war-industry jobs up North drew young people out of the region, and the introduction of the mechanical cotton picker idled many farm workers.

But this land - stretching flat as far as the eye can see, along ribbons of asphalt that shimmer in the heat - remains poor by national standards. The people are undereducated and the area has substantial pockets of unemployment. Local rice farmers are among the biggest recipients of federal farm subsidies. In Stuttgart, Riceland Foods is a farmer-owned agricultural marketing cooperative and the world's largest miller and marketer of rice. With more than 6,000 farmer-members and $1.3 billion in annual revenues, it is a major exporter. The local rice fields also attract ducks, helping put Arkansas on the map as the most productive state for mallard hunters. In the small town of Gillett, a political highlight is the annual Coon Supper. Governors Bill Clinton and Mike Huckabee, among others, frequently mingled with guests who added enough barbecue sauce to ease the dining.

The local economy is increasingly supported by manufacturing. In the Jonesboro area, which has become a rail-car manufacturing center, the Southwest Steel Processing Company in Newport announced plans to develop a new forging line. Several big auto parts plants operate in Marion, across the Mississippi River from Memphis. Big River Steel built a $1.1 billion flat-rolled flex mill facility in Blytheville, with plans to hire 450 workers.

The 1st Congressional District of Arkansas includes almost all of the state's Delta lands and stretches west to the cool, green Ozarks. The largest city in the district is Jonesboro, whose cheap labor and flat land have made it a hub for food-processing companies like Nestle and Frito-Lay. Jonesboro native John Grisham makes a number of references to the city in his book *A Painted House.* The district's natural beauty draws outdoorsmen to the sleepy Ozark town of Mountain Home.

For decades, the Delta was the most Democratic part of Arkansas. Some of the hill counties are ancestrally Republican. Craigshead County (Jonesboro) and Lonoke County, which is part of the Little Rock metro area, are the largest in the district and both have become heavily Republican. The district is among the lowest 5 percent in the nation in median income. Even though six rural and sparsely populated counties along the Mississippi River voted for Hillary Clinton, the vote elsewhere in the district resulted in 65 percent support overall for Donald Trump - barely replacing the long-time Republican and more business-friendly 3rd District as the state's biggest backer of Trump.

SECOND DISTRICT

French Hill (R)

Elected 2014, 2nd term; b. Dec 05, 1956, Little Rock; Vanderbilt University (TN), B.S.; Roman Catholic; Married (Martha Hill); 2 children.

Professional Career: Staff, U.S. Senate Committee on Banking, Housing & Urban Affairs, 1982-1984; Deputy Assistant, U.S. Treasury, 1989-1991; Special Assistant, Economic Policy Council, 1991-1993; Sr. advisor, Gov. Huckabee, 2008; Banker, Businessman.

DC Office: 1229 LHOB 20515, 202-225-2506, Fax: 202-225-5903, hill.house.gov.

State Offices: Conway, 501-358-3481; Little Rock, 501-324-5941.

Committees: *Financial Services*: Capital Markets, Securities & Investment, Monetary Policy & Trade, Terrorism & Illicit Finance.

Group Ratings

	ADA	ACLU	AFL-CIO	LCV	ITI	COC	HAFA	ACU	CFG	FRC
2016	-	5%	-	5%	100%	100%	66%	88%	72%	100%
2015	0%	C	13%	3%	C	80%	C	88%	71%	100%

Almanac Ratings 2015

	Economy	Social	Foreign	Composite
Liberal	3%	0%	0%	1%
Conservative	97%	100%	100%	99%

Key Votes of the 114th Congress

1. Keystone Pipeline	Y	5. Puerto Rico Debt	Y	9. Offenses by Aliens	Y
2. Trade Deals	Y	6. Medical Marijuana	N	10. Troops in Iraq	N
3. Export-Import Bank	N	7. Sanctuary Cities	Y	11. Homeland Security $$	N
4. Debt Ceiling Increase	N	8. Armor-piercing Bullets	Y	12. Trade Adjustment aid	N

Election Results

Election	Name (Party)	Vote (%)		Cand. Spent	Ind. Exp. Support	Ind. Exp. Oppose
2016 General	French Hill (R)	176,472	(58%)	$1,608,638		$75,828
	Dianne Curry (D)	111,347	(37%)	$22,370		
	Chris Hayes (L)	14,342	(5%)			
2016 Primary	French Hill (R)	86,365	(85%)			
	Brock Olree (R)	15,788	(16%)			

Prior winning percentages: 2014 (52%)

French Hill, elected in 2014, won easy reelection following his initial competitive campaign in this Republican-leaning district. In the House, he has been a mostly reliable Republican and has focused chiefly on his work at the Financial Service Committee, where he has brought his extensive private-sector experience in banking. With Republicans seeking major cutbacks in banking controls enacted by Democrats, Hill was positioned to serve as a leading advocate.

A ninth-generation Arkansan, Hill's career as an investment banker linked his business and policy interests. The son and grandson of commercial and investment bankers, he earned a bachelor's degree in economics from Vanderbilt University. He worked as a banking officer and senior financial analyst for Interfirst Bank in Dallas until 1982, when he moved to Washington as a legislative aide for Republican Sen. John Tower of Texas, who was a senior member of the Banking Committee. When Tower retired two years later, Hill became director of the Dallas-based Mason Best Co. After returning to Washington in 1989 as a deputy assistant Treasury secretary, he became a senior policy adviser for President George H.W. Bush and the Economic Policy Council. Hill returned to investment banking as chairman of First Commerce Trust and First Commercial Investments. In 1999, he joined with other investors to form Delta Trust & Bank in Little Rock, serving as its chairman.

In 2008, Hill served as senior adviser for former Arkansas Gov. Mike Huckabee's run for the White House. The following year, GOP strategists urged Hill to challenge Democratic Rep. Vic Snyder. When Snyder chose not to run, Hill instead contributed to Republican Tim Griffin's successful campaign.

Hill sought the open House seat when Griffin ran successfully for lieutenant governor. Against two credible opponents in the primary, he campaigned on a platform of fiscal conservatism that he highlighted in ads promoting "old Blue," a dusty 1998 Volvo. He took some heat for failing to mention his other cars, including a BMW and Mercedes-Benz. He easily won the primary with 55 percent of the vote, and took each of the seven counties. In the general election, Hill advocated approval of the Keystone pipeline, the delay of which had adversely affected the Little Rock pipe-manufacturing firm Welspun. He pushed for a reduction in the corporate income tax while opposing efforts to hike the minimum wage - a stance he modified when voters approved a referendum to put the issue on the ballot.

National Democrats were enthusiastic about former North Little Rock Mayor Patrick Henry Hays. The Democratic Congressional Campaign Committee poured more than $1 million into the race and former President Bill Clinton campaigned for Hays. Democrats slammed Hill for contributing to former state Treasurer Martha Shoffner, who "directed $700 million in taxpayer dollars to Hill's bank." Shoffner had been convicted in March 2014 on bribery and corruption charges. Hill had a heavy fundraising advantage, particularly with contributions from the securities and investment industry. Hill won with 52 percent of the vote, slightly underperforming the district's recent vote history. Hays won 54 percent of the vote in Pulaski County, which cast 54 percent of the district vote. But that wasn't nearly enough to overcome Hill's big leads in the outlying counties, including 65 percent in Saline and 60 percent in Faulkner, the next two largest counties.

With his assignment to the Financial Services Committee, where he has obvious expertise, Hill sought changes in the 2010 Dodd-Frank banking law and worked to enhance the accountability of federal agencies that handle banking issues. In March 2016, the committee reported his bill to weaken the Dodd-Frank risk-retention requirements for commercial real estate loans. Hill warned that the rules could impair economic development and job creation. The House did not consider the legislation. On a local issue, Hill criticized the Veterans Affairs Department for wasting money by failing to use solar panels that had been installed in 2013 at the VA hospital in Little Rock, as reported by a local television station.

In 2016, Hill was the only House Republican from Arkansas to face a Democratic challenger. But Dianne Curry, who had served two terms as president of the Little Rock School Board, raised only $33,000, while Hill reported $2 million in contributions. The contest received little local or national attention. Hill won 58 percent of the vote - safe, but not overwhelming. Unless Democrats reverse their declining influence in Arkansas, Hill should be secure.

Central Arkansas: Little Rock, Pulaski

Population		**Race and Ethnicity**		**Income**	
Total	750,711	White	69.3%	Median Income	$47,206 (300 out of 435)
Land area	4,978	Black	22.0%		
Pop/ sq mi	150.8	Latino	5.0%		
Born in state	66.7%	Asian	1.5%	Under $50,000	52.3%
		Two races	1.9%	$50,000-$99,999	29.4%
Age Groups		Other	0.4%	$100,000-$199,999	15.1%
Under 18	23.7%			$200,000 or more	3.1%
18-34	24.3%	**Education**		Poverty Rate	16.3%
35-64	38.1%	H.S grad or less	42.1%		
Over 64	13.9%	Some college	29.8%	**Health Insurance**	
		College Degree, 4 yr	17.8%	With health insurance coverage	87.0%
Work		Post grad	10.2%		
White Collar	36.7%				
Sales and Service	42.5%	**Military**		**Public Assistance**	
Blue Collar	20.8%	Veteran	10.1%	Cash public assistance income	2.3%
Government	19.1%	Active Duty	0.5%		
				Food stamp/SNAP benefits	12.5%

Voter Turnout			
2015 Total Citizens 18+	555,464	2016 House Turnout as % CVAP	54%
2016 House turnout	302,464	2014 House Turnout as % CVAP	43%

2012 Presidential Vote		
Mitt Romney	160,140	(55%)
Barack Obama	125,527	(43%)

2016 Presidential Vote		
Donald Trump	160,782	(52%)
Hillary Clinton	127,883	(42%)
Gary Johnson	8,630	(3%)

Cook Partisan Voting Index: R+7

Little Rock has been the capital of Arkansas and also its largest city for more than a century. It is at the geographic center of an otherwise rural state, and it is home to the presidential library of Bill Clinton, the former Arkansas governor. The city was harshly criticized for its role at the dawn of the civil rights movement. In September 1957, Democratic Gov. Orval Faubus sent in the National Guard to block a desegregation order at Central High School. President Dwight D. Eisenhower sent in U.S. troops and federalized the National Guard to enforce the order, and Little Rock became a synonym for bigotry around the world. Forty years later, the Little Rock Nine who integrated the high school returned for an anniversary commemoration with Clinton. "It was Little Rock that made racial equality a driving obsession in my life," he said.

Today, Little Rock is still the political center of Arkansas, setting the tone of the public life of its state as do only a few other state capitals - Boston, Providence, Atlanta, Denver and Honolulu. On the banks of the Arkansas River is the Clinton Presidential Center and Park, opened in 2004 with his personal imprint. It has promoted local economic revitalization, with architecture evocative of a "bridge to the 21st century." But the political influence of the Clintons in the city that they once dominated has faded. Other than biographical details that she voiced at the Democratic convention that year, Hillary Clinton largely ignored her former home during her 2016 presidential campaign.

The 2nd Congressional District of Arkansas includes Little Rock and North Little Rock, a kind of industrial suburb across the Arkansas River and known informally for years as Dog Town. The district also takes in Saline (named for its early salt works) and Faulkner (named for fiddle player Sanford C. Faulkner, the original Arkansas Traveler) counties, which have grown rapidly as people move farther out on the freeways. With its large shipping facilities, Little Rock is a robust market for trade.

Welspun Corp., a Bombay India-based producer of large-diameter steel pipes, chiefly for oil and gas companies, manufactured at its Little Rock plant more than 700 miles of the 36-inch-diameter steel pipe for the Keystone XL Pipeline project prior to the November 2015 announcement by President Barack Obama that rejected TransCanada's proposal. Another 350 miles of pipe remained idle awaiting possible revival of the project. In 2016, Welspun announced a $47 million contract to manufacture pipe for the 440-mile Diamond Pipeline, a controversial project to ship crude oil from Cushing, Oklahoma, to Memphis, Tennessee. In a notable reversal of textile manufacturing activity, the Chinese-based sport apparel manufacturer Suzhou Tianyuan Garments Company announced in 2016 that it planned to invest more $20 million in a plant that would bring 400 jobs to the Little Rock area.

This is the least conservative of the state's four districts, though it has a GOP lean. Pulaski County (Little Rock) is entirely in the 2nd District and includes a bit more than half of the district voters. It performs comfortably Democratic in competitive elections. The outlying areas, led by Faulkner and Saline, have become heavily Republican and they outweigh the Pulaski vote. In the 2016 presidential election, Donald Trump won 52 percent of the district vote - a dip from the 55 percent for Republican Mitt Romney in 2012. In a pattern similar to the 2014 contests for governor and senator, Hillary Clinton won 56 percent of the vote in Pulaski, but Trump's lead in Sabine and Faulkner more than made up for that margin. This is the seat once held by House Ways and Means Chairman Wilbur Mills, a legendary Democrat who reigned at the committee for 17 years and retired in 1976.

THIRD DISTRICT

Steve Womack (R)

Elected 2010, 4th term; b. Feb 18, 1957, Russellville, AZ; Arkansas Tech University, Bach. Deg., 1979; Southern Baptist; Married (Terri Williams Womack); 3 children; 2 grandchildren.

Military Career: AR Army National Guard, 1979-2009.

Elected Office: Rogers Mayor, 1998-2010.

Professional Career: Stn. Manager, KURM Radio, 1979-1990; Rogers Cty. Council, 1983-1984, 1997-1998; Executive officer, Army ROTC, University of AR, 1990-1996; Financial consultant, Merrill Lynch, 1996.

DC Office: 2412 RHOB 20515, 202-225-4301, Fax: 202-225-5713, womack.house.gov.

State Offices: Fort Smith, 479-424-1146; Harrison, 870-741-6900; Rogers, 479-464-0446.

Committees: *Appropriations*: Defense, Labor, Health & Human Services, Education & Related Agencies, Military Construction, Veterans Affairs & Related Agencies. *Budget*.

Group Ratings

	ADA	ACLU	AFL-CIO	LCV	ITI	COC	HAFA	ACU	CFG	FRC
2016	-	5%	-	3%	100%	100%	55%	80%	71%	100%
2015	0%	C	21%	3%	C	95%	C	58%	49%	92%

Almanac Ratings 2015

	Economy	Social	Foreign	Composite
Liberal	10%	0%	0%	3%
Conservative	90%	100%	100%	97%

Key Votes of the 114th Congress

1. Keystone Pipeline	Y	5. Puerto Rico Debt	Y	9. Offenses by Aliens	Y
2. Trade Deals	Y	6. Medical Marijuana	N	10. Troops in Iraq	N
3. Export-Import Bank	N	7. Sanctuary Cities	Y	11. Homeland Security $$	N
4. Debt Ceiling Increase	Y	8. Armor-piercing Bullets	N	12. Trade Adjustment aid	N

Election Results

Election	Name (Party)	Vote (%)	Cand. Spent	Ind. Exp. Support	Ind. Exp. Oppose
2016 General	Steve Womack (R)	217,192 (77%)	$480,698		
	Steve Isaacson (L)	63,715 (23%)			
2016 Primary	Steve Womack (R)	(100%)			

Prior winning percentages: 2014 (79%), 2012 (76%), 2010 (72%)

Republican Steve Womack, first elected in 2010, has become an active Republican lawmaker with a knack for cutting deals and working across the aisle. With his growing seniority on the Appropriations Committee and his leadership alliances, he is well-positioned for a subcommittee chairmanship.

Womack was born in Russellville, Arkansas, and spent a good portion of his childhood in Moberly, Missouri. His father, a local radio broadcaster, introduced him to popular political figures in the region, including former Sens. Tom Eagleton and Stuart Symington and Gov. Warren Hearnes, all Missouri Democrats. "If I 'Dr. Phil' myself about what got me involved in public service, it's that I always admired political leaders," Womack said. After high school, Womack earned his bachelor's degree at Arkansas Tech University. He and his father subsequently established KURM Radio, which focused on community news, the weather, the county fair, and high school football and Little League baseball games. Womack covered local politics for the station. "I always would second-guess things, and say, 'could I do that better?'" he recalled.

In 1990, as a member of the Army National Guard, Womack served as executive officer of the Army ROTC program at the University of Arkansas. In 2002, he led a peacekeeping task force of 500 troops in the Sinai Desert in Egypt - a mission established by the peace accord between Israel and Egypt. Womack was elected mayor of Rogers in 1998 and worked to turn the city into a shopping destination, including the issuance of bonds to develop infrastructure to attract business. He also had a reputation for tough enforcement of immigration laws. Local Hispanic leaders were incensed when Womack maintained that a majority of crimes in the city were committed by illegal immigrants, which they said was untrue. In 2007, Womack directed city officials to cooperate with raids by federal immigration agents on a Northwest Arkansas Mexican restaurant chain. After Hispanic motorists filed a lawsuit charging racial profiling by Rogers and its police department, a settlement was reached without an award of damages or an admission of guilt; Womack formed a committee to build better relations with the immigrant community.

When then-Rep. John Boozman ran for the Senate, Womack stepped into a crowded field of Republicans interested in the seat. His chief opponent was Cecile Bledsoe, a state senator endorsed by former Alaska Gov. Sarah Palin and Asa Hutchinson, now the Arkansas governor. Bledsoe tried to portray herself as the true conservative in the race, promising to repeal President Barack Obama's health care overhaul. Womack touted his record of job creation and attacked Bledsoe for her votes to increase taxes when she was in the legislature. Womack eked out a victory, 52%-48%. In this solidly Republican district, he defeated Democrat David Whitaker, a former assistant city attorney in Fayetteville, 72%-28%.

In the House, Womack established himself as firmly conservative. To win a coveted slot on the Appropriations Committee as a freshman, he told Chairman Harold Rogers of Kentucky that being a mayor had taught him how to say "no." But he has been eager to say "yes" to local interests in their dealings with the federal government. With Democratic Rep. Jackie Speier of California and others, he filed a bill to allow states to require Amazon and other out-of-state retailers to collect sales tax when they sell products over the Internet, something that benefitted brick-and-mortar retailers such as Arkansas' Walmart, which already collect state sales taxes online. He joined with Rep. Jim Costa, another California Democrat, to create the Chicken Caucus; the poultry industry maintains more than 2,000 chicken houses in Benton County.

In January 2013, Womack was the only Arkansas Republican who supported the budget and tax deal to avoid across-the-board tax hikes. Speaker John Boehner invited him to join a 2014 delegation to Afghanistan, a sign that he was a favorite of GOP leaders. He has shown insider skills on the Appropriations Committee, where he sits on three prime subcommittees.

Womack, who earlier endorsed Sen. Marco Rubio of Florida for the presidential nomination, displayed his moderate credentials prior to the 2016 Republican national convention when he advised Donald Trump to select Ohio Gov. John Kasich as his running mate. "I think that would be the very best possible outcome for [Trump's] sake and for the sake of our party in terms of some sustainability," he said in a local newspaper interview. At the convention, his parliamentary skill led Republican officials to select him to preside during what they feared might be a contentious debate over the convention rules.

Back home, Womack has achieved the impressive combination of avoiding a Republican primary and a Democratic challenger in all three of his reelections. In 2016, he got 77 percent of the vote against Libertarian Party challenger Steve Isaacson, who had failed to qualify to run in the Republican primary. Although his centrism could prompt a challenge from a conservative Republican, the strong corporate influence in this district would offer Womack some protection.

Northwest Arkansas: Fayetteville, Fort Smith

Population		Race and Ethnicity		Income	
Total	761,175	White	76.4%	Median Income	$45,185 (338 out of 435)
Land area	5,401	Black	2.7%		
Pop/ sq mi	140.9	Latino	13.5%		
Born in state	48.9%	Asian	2.7%	Under $50,000	54.9%
		Two races	2.6%	$50,000-$99,999	28.3%
Age Groups		Other	2.0%	$100,000-$199,999	13.4%
Under 18	25.2%			$200,000 or more	3.5%
18-34	24.7%	**Education**		Poverty Rate	17.9%
35-64	36.8%	H.S grad or less	46.9%		
Over 64	13.3%	Some college	28.0%	**Health Insurance**	
		College Degree, 4 yr	16.0%	With health insurance coverage	85.5%
Work		Post grad	9.1%		
White Collar	33.2%				
Sales and Service	40.8%	**Military**		**Public Assistance**	
Blue Collar	26.0%	Veteran	8.9%	Cash public assistance income	2.1%
Government	11.6%	Active Duty	0.1%		
				Food stamp/SNAP benefits	11.5%

Voter Turnout			
2015 Total Citizens 18+	523,147	2016 House Turnout as % CVAP	54%
2016 House turnout	280,907	2014 House Turnout as % CVAP	37%

2012 Presidential Vote		
Mitt Romney	168,703	(66%)
Barack Obama	81,413	(32%)

2016 Presidential Vote		
Donald Trump	180,921	(62%)
Hillary Clinton	89,081	(31%)
Gary Johnson	10,587	(4%)

Cook Partisan Voting Index: R+19

The northwest corner of Arkansas has become one of America's boom areas, with major corporate headquarters and dozens of small factories, tourist attractions, and retirement developments in the Ozarks. Anchoring the local economy are three major employers: Walmart Stores, Tyson Foods, and J.B. Hunt Transport Services. The area has a rapidly growing population of Hispanics working at these companies in Springdale and Rogers. About 10,000 "climate refugees" from the Marshall Islands in the South Pacific moved here to escape the long-term risk of high tides.

This is also home to the handsome University of Arkansas in Fayetteville, where young lawyers Bill Clinton and Hillary Rodham settled. "One day I was driving her to the airport to fly back to Chicago when we passed this little brick house that had a for sale sign on it. And she said, boy, that's a pretty house. It had 1,100 square feet, an attic, fan and no air conditioner in hot Arkansas, and a screened-in porch," Bill Clinton recounted during his speech to the Democratic national convention in 2016. "We were married in that little house on October the 11th, 1975. I married my best friend."

The friendly atmosphere, the prevalence of religious faith, and the natural backdrop of rounded green mountains and wide valleys in northwest Arkansas have contributed to the economic creativity. There have also been touches of genius. Sam Walton, who opened his first Walmart on the town square of Bentonville (it's now a small museum), had the inspiration to build a retail chain in tradition-minded small towns and rural areas using sophisticated computerized management. It made him the richest man in America before he died in 1992, though he still drove a pickup truck and kept the corporate headquarters in a deliberately unglitzy building in Bentonville. The corporate headquarters are by far the largest employer in this corner of the state - with about 18,000 employees before 450 were laid off in 2015. Don Tyson built Tyson Foods into the world's leading chicken producer and processor. In April 2016, the company announced plans to build a second processing facility across the street from its headquarters outside Springdale.

Other firms have flocked in, especially to do business with Walmart, the world's largest food retailer. The region's unemployment is low, but local leaders have moved to diversify into professional services and tourism. Fort Smith was dealt a blow in 2012 when Whirlpool closed its refrigerator production plant and shed 1,000 jobs. But that area has also strengthened, with increases in tech jobs and expanded commercial use of local waterways. In Fayetteville, which *U.S. News and World Report* in March 2016 ranked as the third best place to live in the United States, voters in September 2015 approved an ordinance to ban discrimination based on gender identity or sexual orientation.

The 3rd Congressional District covers Northwest Arkansas, including Bentonville, Fayetteville and Springdale, plus Fort Smith on the Oklahoma line. Politically, this area has been consistently the most Republican part of Arkansas since the Civil War. John Paul Hammerschmidt was elected to the House in 1966 as one of the first Republican congressmen from the South, and the district has not elected a Democrat since. He beat 28-year-old Bill Clinton in the Democratic year of 1974, ending Clinton's first bid for public office with a loss (although he got an impressive 48 percent of the vote). Lately, Christian conservatives have entered politics, and new migrants and millionaires have voted heavily for the GOP. In 2016, Donald Trump won 62 percent, in contrast to the 66 percent support for Mitt Romney in the 2012 presidential election. That dropped it to the third-most Republican district in Arkansas behind the two lower-income rural districts. As with other campus towns across the nation, Trump fared relatively poorly in Washington County (Fayetteville), the largest county in the district, with 51 percent.

FOURTH DISTRICT

Bruce Westerman (R)

Elected 2014, 2nd term; b. Nov 18, 1967, Hot Springs; University of Arkansas, B.S., 1990; Yale University (CT), M.S., 2001; Southern Baptist; Married (Sharon French); 4 children.

Elected Office: AR House, 2010-2014, Minority Leader, 2012-2013, Majority Leader, 2013-2014.

Professional Career: Fountain Lake School Board, 2006-2010, President, 2009-2010; Engineer, forester, Mid-South Engineering; Deacon, Walnut Valley Baptist Church.

DC Office: 130 CHOB 20515, 202-225-3772, Fax: 202-225-1314, westerman.house.gov.

State Offices: El Dorado, 870-864-8946; Hot Springs, 501-609-9796; Ozark, 479-667-0075; Pine Bluff, 870-536-8178.

Committees: *Budget*. *Natural Resources*: Energy & Mineral Resources, Federal Lands. *Transportation & Infrastructure*: Aviation, Highways & Transit, Railroads, Pipelines & Hazardous Materials.

Group Ratings

	ADA	ACLU	AFL-CIO	LCV	ITI	COC	HAFA	ACU	CFG	FRC
2016	-	5%	-	0%	100%	100%	74%	96%	78%	100%
2015	0%	C	13%	3%	C	75%	C	88%	79%	100%

Almanac Ratings 2015

	Economy	Social	Foreign	Composite
Liberal	0%	0%	0%	0%
Conservative	100%	100%	100%	100%

Key Votes of the 114th Congress

1. Keystone Pipeline	Y	5. Puerto Rico Debt	Y	9. Offenses by Aliens	Y
2. Trade Deals	Y	6. Medical Marijuana	N	10. Troops in Iraq	N
3. Export-Import Bank	N	7. Sanctuary Cities	Y	11. Homeland Security $$	N
4. Debt Ceiling Increase	N	8. Armor-piercing Bullets	Y	12. Trade Adjustment aid	N

Election Results

Election	Name (Party)	Vote (%)	Cand. Spent	Ind. Exp. Support	Ind. Exp. Oppose
2016 General	Bruce Westerman (R)	182,885 (75%)	$396,466		
	Kerry Hicks (L)	61,274 (25%)			
2016 Primary	Bruce Westerman (R)	(100%)			

Prior winning percentages: 2014 (54%)

Republican Bruce Westerman, with strong social conservative credentials, was elected in 2014 to the district that had been the home until 2012 of the most recent House Democrat from Arkansas. With his defeat of James Lee Witt, who was the Federal Emergency Management Agency director in the Clinton administration, the former president's legacy in the area continued to diminish. Westerman was reelected without Democratic opposition.

Born in Hot Springs, Westerman earned his B.S. in biological and agricultural engineering at the University of Arkansas, where he played for the Razorbacks football team. He completed his master's in forestry at Yale. He worked as a plant engineer for Riceland Foods and as an engineer and forester for Mid-South Engineering. Westerman was elected to the Arkansas House in 2010. When the GOP two years later took control of both chambers of the state Legislature for the first time since Reconstruction, Westerman became House majority leader. He had a solid record as a conservative, voting to override a gubernatorial veto of a voter ID law and to approve a bill banning abortions after 20 weeks. He supported legislation expanding gun rights; setting dress codes in public schools; and requiring that tests for driver's licenses be offered only in English. He also was a fiscal conservative, as an architect of the "SIMPLE Plan" to reduce taxes and cut government regulation, a GOP agenda that has helped entrench a Republican majority, Westerman said. He opposed the so-called Private Option, Arkansas's expansion of Medicaid under the Affordable Care Act.

The 4th District, with its strong Old South flavor, had elected just two Republicans since Reconstruction - now-Sen. Tom Cotton and Jay Dickey, a four-term congressman who lost in 2000 to Mike Ross after Dickey voted to impeach home-towner Bill Clinton, who remained popular in the district. In the 2014 primary, Westerman defeated energy businessman Tommy Moll 54%-46%. Westerman ran stronger in the southern part of the district, while Moll swept most of the northern counties. Westerman's 4,345-vote margin in Garland County accounted for his victory. Both candidates resided in Hot Springs. In the general election, Witt ran a vigorous and old-style campaign. He was one of the few prominent Democratic candidates in recent years who opposed gay marriage and abortion and supported gun rights. Despite a campaign visit from Clinton and outspending his opponent by $250,000, Witt could not overcome the GOP tide in the district. Westerman won easily, 54%-43%.

In the House, he served on the Budget Committee and applauded the panel's fiscal 2016 budget plan, which sought to balance the budget in 10 years with no tax increases. He filed legislation to give state governments more flexibility to set work requirements for Medicaid beneficiaries and he called for reducing Medicaid spending to add funding for the highway trust fund. On the Natural Resources Committee, Westerman used his academic background in forestry and took an interest in the 2.5 million acres of timber on the public lands in his district. He sponsored the Resilient Federal Forests Act, which set management policies on federally owned timber and would impose legal hurdles on litigants who seek to limit forestry plans. The House in 2015 passed the bill, 262-167, with 19 Democrats in favor. The Senate failed to act on a companion measure that had been approved by its Agriculture, Nutrition and Forestry Committee. He joined the House Republican Whip team.

In 2016, Westerman won 75 percent against Libertarian Kerry Hickey, who endorsed large cuts in defense spending.

Western Arkansas: Hot Springs, Pine Bluff

Population		**Race and Ethnicity**		**Income**	
Total	720,040	White	72.1%	Median Income	$37,037 (416 out of 435)
Land area	22,338	Black	19.5%		
Pop/ sq mi	32.2	Latino	5.6%		
Born in state	64.6%	Asian	0.6%	Under $50,000	62.7%
		Two races	1.5%	$50,000-$99,999	26.4%
Age Groups		Other	0.6%	$100,000-$199,999	9.4%
Under 18	23.2%			$200,000 or more	1.6%
18-34	20.5%	**Education**		Poverty Rate	21.7%
35-64	38.9%	H.S grad or less	55.2%		
Over 64	17.4%	Some college	28.9%	**Health Insurance**	
		College Degree, 4 yr	10.5%	With health insurance coverage	85.3%
Work		Post grad	5.4%		
White Collar	27.9%				
Sales and Service	40.1%	**Military**		**Public Assistance**	
Blue Collar	32.0%	Veteran	10.2%	Cash public assistance income	2.9%
Government	18.3%	Active Duty	0.0%		
				Food stamp/SNAP benefits	16.7%

Voter Turnout			
2015 Total Citizens 18+	538,467	2016 House Turnout as % CVAP	45%
2016 House turnout	244,159	2014 House Turnout as % CVAP	38%

2012 Presidential Vote		
Mitt Romney	164,350	(62%)
Barack Obama	95,384	(36%)

2016 Presidential Vote		
Donald Trump	173,731	(64%)
Hillary Clinton	84,842	(31%)

Cook Partisan Voting Index: R+17

West from the Delta flatlands along the Mississippi River, where the water-soaked fields produce America's largest rice crop, are small cities like Pine Bluff and El Dorado and the Ouachita Mountains. Southern Arkansas might well be called the northwest corner of the Deep South. It includes the state's largest African-American population, a reminder that parts of southern Arkansas near the Delta were once plantation country. There is also oil production, and the broiler-chicken industry looms large in these parts. The accent is clearly Arkansan: El Dorado, Nevada and Lafayette are all pronounced with long a's and accents on the penultimate syllable, and Ouachita, with a bow to the original French rendition of the Indian name, is *WASH-i-taw*.

The 4th Congressional District occupies much of the southern half of Arkansas, stretching from the eastern part of the state all the way west to Texarkana. Not far from the Texas border is the little railroad-crossing, county-seat town of Hope, where former President Bill Clinton and his first White House chief of staff, Mack McLarty, were classmates in Miss Mary's kindergarten room and where former Gov. Mike Huckabee grew up a decade later. Hot Springs is the spa resort and gambling haven where Clinton's stepfather sold Buicks, his mother bet on the horses, and he excelled in high school. Established in 1832, Hot Springs National Park is the oldest federal reserve in the country, predating Yellowstone by 40 years (though Hot Springs was not declared a national park until 1921).

To the east is Pine Bluff, where a century and a half ago Union soldiers withstood a Confederate attack on the fortified courthouse square. Despite the presence of poultry giant Tyson Foods, the region has taken hits to its economy lately. More than 1,000 workers were idled with the closing in 2014 of the Pine Bluff Chemical Agent Disposal Facility, which held the second largest stockpile before the United States joined an international effort to eradicate chemical weapons. Pine Bluff got a boost in November 2016 when Highland Pellets opened a wood pellet facility that planned to produce 600,000 metric tons annually, which will permit power plants to lower their carbon footprint. In Camden, Lockheed Martin relocated its production of the Tactical Missile System.

The 4th includes territory in the Ozark National Forest to the northwest, including Madison, Johnson and Franklin counties. The district leans substantially Republican. Jefferson County (Pine Bluff), just south of Little Rock and 55 percent African-American, was its only county that voted for Hillary Clinton in 2016.

★ CALIFORNIA ★

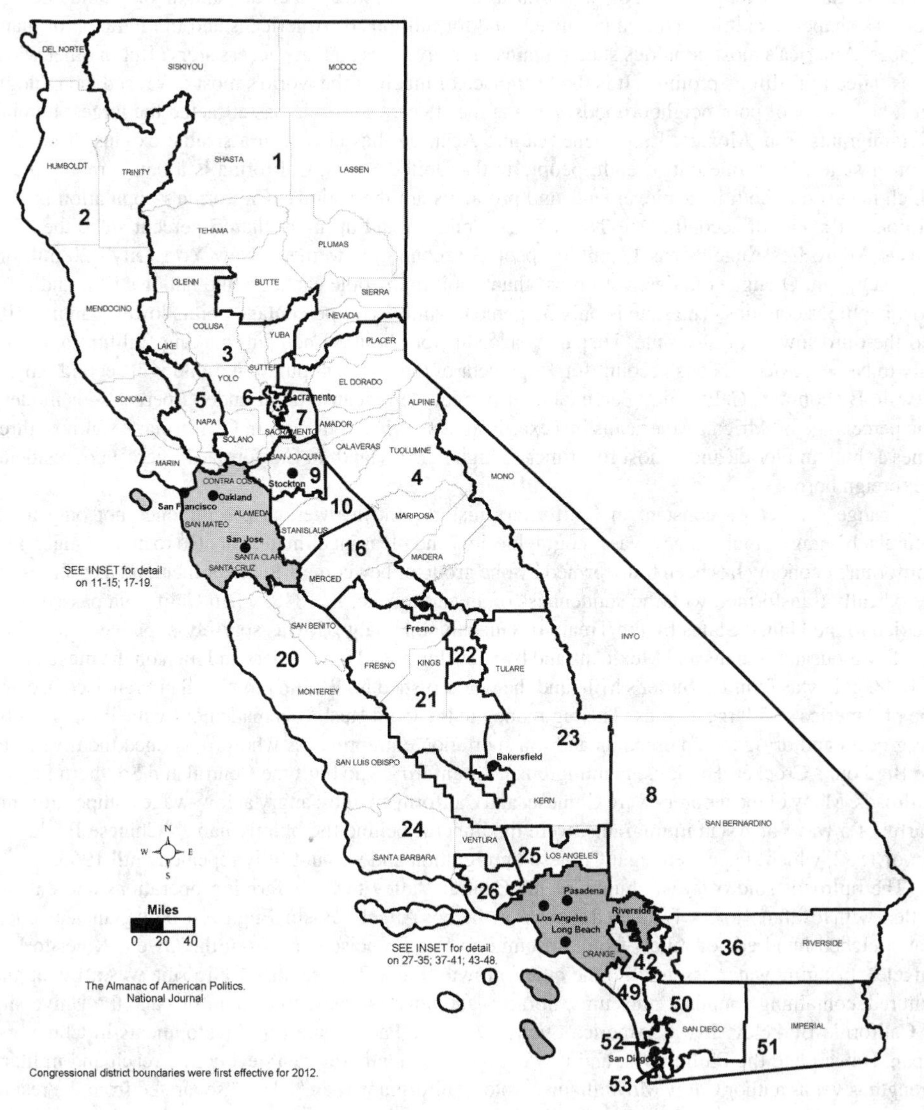
DEL NORTE
SISKIYOU
MODOC
SHASTA
1
LASSEN
HUMBOLDT
TRINITY
2
TEHAMA
PLUMAS
GLENN
BUTTE
SIERRA
MENDOCINO
NEVADA
COLUSA
YUBA
PLACER
LAKE
3
SUTTER
YOLO
6
Sacramento
EL DORADO
SONOMA
5
7
ALPINE
NAPA
SACRAMENTO
AMADOR
SOLANO
CALAVERAS
TUOLUMNE
MARIN
SAN JOAQUIN
9
Stockton
4
MONO
CONTRA COSTA
Oakland
San Francisco
10
ALAMEDA
MARIPOSA
SAN MATEO
STANISLAUS
San Jose
16
SANTA CLARA
MADERA
SANTA CRUZ
SEE INSET for detail on 11-15; 17-19.
MERCED
SAN BENITO
Fresno
INYO
20
22
FRESNO
KINGS
TULARE
MONTEREY
21
23
SAN LUIS OBISPO
Bakersfield
KERN
8
SAN BERNARDINO
24
N
W
E
S
VENTURA
25
LOS ANGELES
SANTA BARBARA
26
Pasadena
Miles
0 20 40
Los Angeles
Riverside
Long Beach
36
RIVERSIDE
SEE INSET for detail on 27-35; 37-41; 43-48.
ORANGE
42
The Almanac of American Politics.
National Journal
49
50
SAN DIEGO
IMPERIAL
52
51
San Diego
Congressional district boundaries were first effective for 2012.
53

Both sides of America's political divide have taken the opportunity to emphasize how different California is from the rest of the country. After the 2016 presidential election, supporters of Donald Trump complained that were it not for Hillary Clinton's margin of victory in California, Trump would have won the popular vote. For their part, California's Democratic politicians have taken a leading role in opposing Trump's vision for America; some Californians are even flirting with seceding from the union, though "Calexit" faces constitutional obstacles that make it highly improbable. Despite such antagonism, California and the United States need each other, even if it no longer seems like it.

Americans have long thought of California as the Golden State -- a distant and dreamy land initially, then as a shaper of culture and as a promised land for millions of Americans and immigrants for many decades. America's most populous state remains in many ways a great success story. But in other ways, it has failed to fulfill its promise. It is the birthplace of much of the world's most advanced technology, yet it has plenty of poor neighborhoods. Among the states, California has attracted the largest number of immigrants from Mexico, Latin America and Asia, but has also seen a sizable exodus of citizens to other states. With one out of eight people in the United States, California is a demographic giant, which means that both its achievements and problems are the nation's. California's population is 39.3 million, far ahead of second-place Texas at 27.9 million and up more than 5 percent since the 2010 census. Metro Los Angeles has 13 million people, second only to metro New York City's 20 million. San Diego and Orange counties, with more than 3 million people each, are the nation's fifth and sixth most populous counties. The state is only 38 percent white – two percentage points lower than in 2010, and the third lowest of any state. Hispanics account for about 39 percent, making California second only to New Mexico. Asians account for 15 percent of the state's population, ranking it second only to Hawaii. By contrast, California's percentage of African Americans – a bit under 7 percent – is modest. The percentage of African Americans in Texas is almost twice as high as in California; it's almost three times as high in Florida and almost five times as high in Maryland. In California, 27 percent of residents are foreign born.

Change has been a constant in California's history, and it owes its preeminence not only to its natural advantages, including its vast geographic area and pleasant climate, but also to human ingenuity. California's economy has been transformed by one group of newcomers after another, and its politics are periodically transformed with the suddenness of an earthquake. In 1848, when California passed from Mexico to the United States by the Treaty of Guadalupe Hidalgo, it was sparsely populated, inhabited by a few thousand Indians and Mexicans and by a few hundred U.S. soldiers and men on the make. Then in 1848, gold was found at Sutter's Mill, and the world rushed in. Within months, San Francisco became one of America's 25 largest cities. The big money in the Gold Rush was made not by the miners but by the grocers and dry-goods merchants and transportation entrepreneurs who provisioned them, such as the Big Four - Crocker, Hopkins, Huntington and Stanford - who built the Central and Southern Pacific Railroads. Many of the laborers were Chinese, and California whites, angry at low-wage competition and fearful of a wave of Asian immigrants, were the impetus behind the bluntly named Chinese Exclusion Act of 1882, which suspended legal Chinese immigration and was not fully repealed until 1965.

The railroads sold off vast chunks of the Central Valley to large farming operations and enticed settlers with low fares to newly created suburbs in the Los Angeles Basin. Engineers built giant aqueducts that stretched hundreds of miles, from Yosemite to San Francisco and from the Owens River to Los Angeles, bringing water essential to the cities' growth. Early 20th century California was affluent and cultured, containing abundant museums, libraries and universities such as Stanford and the University of California-Berkeley. It was America's window on the Pacific, alert to developments in China and Japan, Hawaii and the Philippines, and it was eager to extend America's economic reach and military strength -- yet as author Carey McWilliams wrote, California was an "island" separated from the rest of the country. That began to change in World War II, when it became one of the great defense industry states, building ships and airplanes by the thousands. Millions of Americans came and millions stayed. The population rose from 7 million in 1940 to 17 million in 1963, when California passed New York as the nation's most populous state.

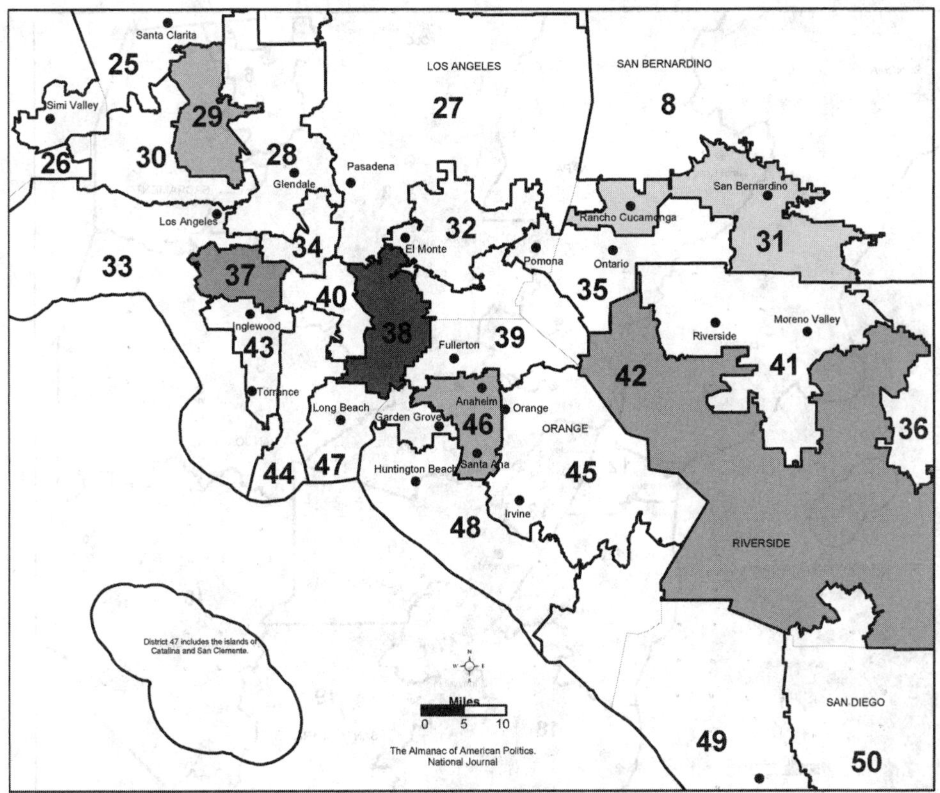

Congressional district boundaries were first effective for 2012.

Districts 29, 31, 37, 38, 42, and 46 are highlighted for visibility.

The heads of the big units of government and business planned California's future - leaders such as President Franklin D. Roosevelt and industrial mogul Henry J. Kaiser, who constructed vast shipyards and steel and aluminum factories. Republican Gov. Earl Warren husbanded tax monies after the war to build schools and the freeways that did as much as Detroit's auto factories – if not more -- to cement the automobile's place in American culture. Educators Robert Sproul and Clark Kerr transformed the University of California into what Kerr called "the multiversity," and Democratic Gov. Pat Brown added to the vast system of canals and aqueducts that brought water from the wet north to the dry south. But the real engine of growth was the little people who took advantage of this infrastructure and built a humming economy. When California's defense plants closed down after World War II, government and civic leaders imagined that hundreds of thousands would head back east. But in those days before universal air conditioning and thermal winter clothing, people had experienced a climate in which it was comfortable to be outdoors all year. They wanted to stay, and so, as urbanologist Jane Jacobs pointed out, they created one-eighth of all the new jobs in the nation in the late 1940s in metro Los Angeles. This growth, multiplied thousands of times over, helped make California a mega-state. Meanwhile, Los Angeles County became what New York City was 100 years before: the great entry point in the United States, with some of the largest concentrations of Mexicans, Iranians, Samoans, Filipinos, Salvadorans, Armenians, Guatemalans, Koreans and Thais outside their native lands. The farmlands of Imperial County are 83 percent Hispanic. San Francisco County is 35 percent Asian and Santa Clara County in Silicon Valley is 36 percent Asian.

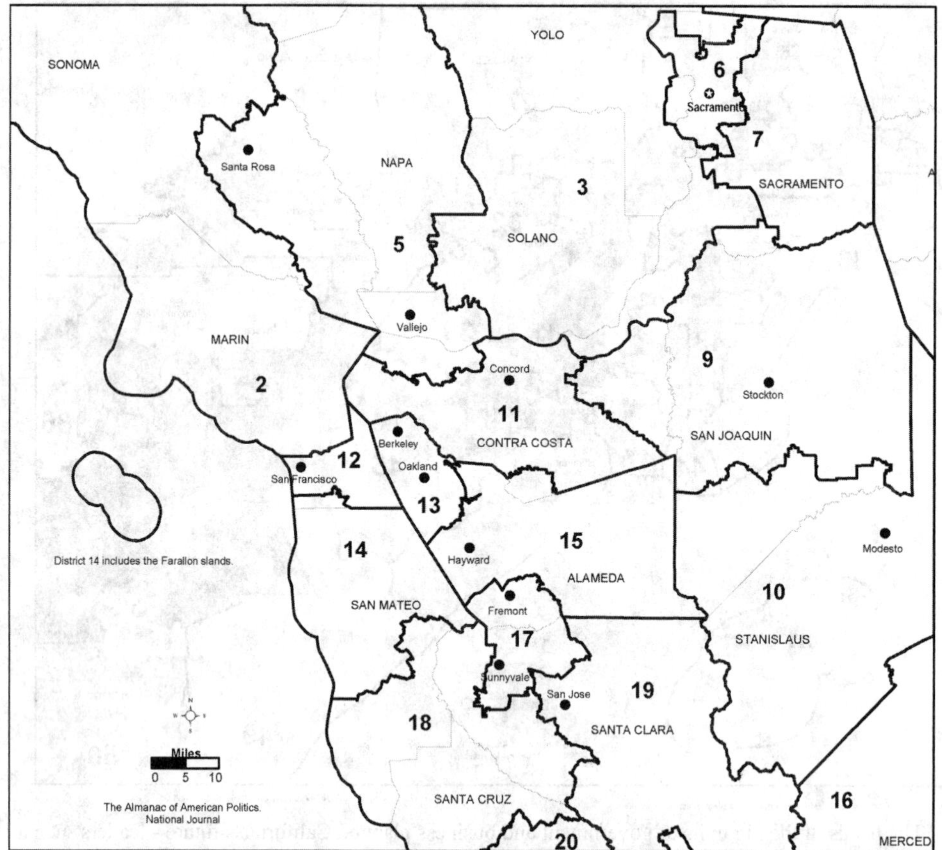

Congressional district boundaries were first effective for 2012.

The demographic changes transformed California politically. Before the war, it was a Republican state with progressive leanings. Most of the struggles for political power took place within the Republican Party. The in-rush of the GI generation, with its allegiance to the New Deal, and the building of auto and steel factories with unionized workforces, transformed California into a two-party state. These new migrants were middle- and working-class -- family men and women enjoying a life in suburbs in the lovely California climate. Warren's progressive Republicans remained dominant through the mid-1950s, but with Brown's election as governor in 1958, a group of talented liberal Democrats took over. Things turned sour in the mid-1960s, when student rebellions at Berkeley and the Watts riots upset the New Deal order. Californians responded by calling in a disillusioned New Dealer espousing the conformist cultural conservatism of the GI generation -- Ronald Reagan. Then, in 1974, California elected Pat Brown's son Jerry as governor and for a time was entranced by his fresh vision of baby boomer liberalism. California's laid-back lifestyle became a magnet for highly educated boomers, lawyers, scientists, techies and show-biz types. But it took time for them to become the dominant force in state politics. California voted Republican in every presidential election from 1968 to 1988, and Brown's administration was not wholly successful on policy, partly because he always seemed to have one eye on the presidency. In 1978, voters froze property taxes by passing Proposition 13 and ousted three of his state Supreme Court justices in 1986, after Brown had left office. Republicans followed Brown in the governorship: George Deukmejian, elected in 1982 and 1986, and Pete Wilson, elected in 1990 and 1994.

As Reagan was occupying the White House, California's defense industry boomed, and Silicon Valley began to flower south of San Francisco. Immigration continued in vast numbers, with newcomers living in the stucco bungalows and garden apartments that white, blue-collar workers left behind in neighborhoods like those south and east of downtown Los Angeles. Large swaths of the San Fernando Valley and Santa Ana in Orange County became predominantly Latino. Public policy was increasingly set by the Democratic legislature, led from 1980 to 1995 by Assembly Speaker Willie Brown. In the 1990s, disaster struck in several forms. Defense industry cutbacks hit the Los Angeles area hard, corporate mergers and relocations caused additional upheaval, and television screens were filled with seemingly apocalyptic news - floods, wildfires, earthquakes, riots and sensational trials. The state government responded competently to the natural disasters, but less well to those that were man-made. Lou Cannon's *Official Negligence*, the definitive story of the Rodney King case, is a story of public-sector incompetence as dismaying as that spotlighted for the nation in the O.J. Simpson murder trial.

Since the recession of the early 1990s, California has seen an outflow of people -- mostly white and middle-class-to-affluent – that to a large degree has offset the flow of people from other countries. In the meantime, from the late 1990s to the housing bust of 2007, federal policies encouraging mortgages for borrowers of more modest means produced a housing and construction boom in the Inland Empire - the sprawling San Bernardino and Riverside Counties east of Los Angeles - and in the Central Valley. Latinos moved out from central Los Angeles County and bought new houses with little or no down payment and hopes of windfall profits from what everyone assumed would be endlessly rising house prices. But the market crashed in 2007, and the Inland Empire and Central Valley had some of the nation's highest foreclosure rates. For the next five years, California also had one of the nation's highest unemployment rates, exceeded only by much smaller states such as Nevada or Rhode Island. Between 2010 and 2016, the state's population grew by 5.4 percent – but that represented a slowdown from the heady years of the 20th century. Part of the reason: the state's birthrate, which in 2015-2016 sank to its lowest level since the Great Depression. International migration, especially from Mexico, also declined. For the first time, the 2010 reapportionment did not add any seats to California's House delegation, and it's not on pace to add any in 2020, either.

In the decades after World War II, California was a key target in presidential elections. In Reagan's time, it went Republican in presidential elections while usually tilting Democratic in congressional and state contests. But starting in the early 1990s, it has become one of the bedrock Democratic states. The shift occurred slowly: While Bill Clinton carried California 46%-33% in 1992 and proceeded to lavish attention on the state, Republican Gov. Pete Wilson won reelection in 1994 by a 14-point margin while supporting Proposition 187, which barred state aid to illegal immigrants. But ever since, California's increasing Latino voter share has given Democrats enormous margins.

Two other voting blocs have helped make California solidly Democratic. One group consists of affluent, highly educated whites living in lush corners of the big metropolitan areas, many with ties to the state's two resilient economic and cultural behemoths - Silicon Valley and Hollywood. They tend to be liberal on cultural issues such as abortion rights and same-sex marriage, more moderate on fiscal issues, and hostile to the religious conservatives who hold sway within the national Republican Party. These voters have been similarly repelled by the increasingly conservative edge of the state's vestigial GOP. In the Reagan years, affluent neighborhoods, except for the heavily Jewish west side of Los Angeles, usually cast large Republican majorities; since then, they have voted increasingly Democratic. This has helped Democrats maintain large majorities in California's House delegation and in both houses of the state legislature since 1996. The second group now bolstering Democratic fortunes is Asian Americans. In 1992, they favored George H.W. Bush over Clinton, but by the 2016 election, they backed Hillary Clinton over Trump, 70%-17%. Asian voters have become an important factor in the lopsided margins by which Democrats carry the San Francisco Bay Area and Los Angeles County.

California's two governors from 1998 to 2010 -- Democrat Gray Davis and Republican Arnold Schwarzenegger -- tried to exert some discipline over the state's finances, with limited success. The power of the public employee unions has continued upward pressure on government spending, especially when California's progressive tax structure brings in gushers of revenue in prosperous years. When revenues plummet, as they did after the tech boom ended in 2000 or when the housing market crashed in 2007, the pressure is then to increase taxes. Davis was unable to hold spending down and was blamed for electricity blackouts. He was recalled, 55%-45%, and on the replacement ballot, Schwarzenegger finished first with 49 percent. In office, the ex-bodybuilder/actor sought a conservative shift via ballot measures, but voters rebuffed him, and his job rating flagged. He turned things around by backing liberal measures like carbon emissions reduction legislation and bonds for a high-speed rail line, and it was enough to easily win him reelection in 2006.

California's economy was slowing even before the housing market crashed in 2007. But the Great Recession made things far worse. One-third of California homeowners owed more on their mortgages than their houses were worth; the proportion hit 60 percent in parts of the Inland Empire. Corporate executive complained that high taxes, stringent regulations, complex land-use controls and high litigation risks hampered the economic recovery. Public employee unions' success in negotiating large pension benefits led to some municipal bankruptcies, such as Vallejo in 2008 and Stockton and San Bernardino in 2012. Seemingly adrift, California voters turned to a familiar face - Jerry Brown. In 2010, he defeated former eBay chief executive Meg Whitman for the governorship, 54%-41%, despite her spending $141.5 million of her own money. Once mocked as the flaky "Governor Moonbeam," Brown gained ground-level experience as a two-term mayor of troubled Oakland and matured into a moderate technocrat who knew the inside game; crucially, he was at last undistracted by presidential ambitions. Task No. 1 was fixing the state's fiscal outlook; Brown made great strides, ultimately squeezing out an annual surplus that, while modest, would have been unthinkable a few years earlier. While the nation's overall economic comeback helped, Brown also played a role by successfully urging passage of a 2012 ballot measure that temporarily hiked sales taxes and income taxes on higher-earners.

By the middle of the decade, California had the sixth-largest economy on the planet – bigger than France and Brazil. To be sure, poverty persisted – one of every five Californians is at or below the poverty line when adjusted for the cost of living. And the main reason for the high cost of living is the high cost of housing. The real estate firm PropertyShark.com determined that 70 of the priciest 100 zip codes for housing are in California, including No. 2, Atherton in Silicon Valley. California needs about 3.5 million new homes - three times its current pace of construction -- to keep up with population growth and keep housing costs down, according to McKinsey Global Institute. In its coastal environs, California has an increasingly two-tiered society, with not much of a middle class in between; San Francisco ranks as the second-most unequal metro area in the nation and saw the fastest growth in inequality in recent years, according to the Brookings Institution.

Once upon a time, people used to analyze California politics by distinguishing between Northern California and Southern California. Northern California - the Central Valley and the North Coast as well as the San Francisco Bay Area - tended to vote Democratic. Southern California - Los Angeles County as well as the smaller suburban and desert counties - tended to vote for Republicans. Today, the geographic divisions run the other way. The dichotomy is now between coastal California - all the counties that touch the ocean or San Francisco Bay - and interior California. Politically, coastal California votes Democratic and furthers liberal policies; California was ahead of the curve on same-sex marriage (and on electoral reform, including voter-backed experiments in non-partisan redistricting and top-two-finisher primaries), and in 2016 it made marijuana legal. In California's interior, the income gap is not nearly as wide, and the cost of living is lower, but private-sector job creation was not stellar before 2007 and has been dismal since. If interior California were a separate state, it would be competitive in presidential elections and would have 19 electoral votes. But coastal California, more than twice as populous as interior California, is dominant politically. For the most part, since Prop 187, the state is out of reach for Republicans. Even in the 2014 wave year for Republicans, California's GOP candidates for statewide office secured between 41 and 47 percent of the vote, and the Democrats who coasted to victory included not just Brown but several younger politicians with bigger ambitions - Attorney General Kamala Harris, who succeeded Barbara Boxer in the Senate in 2016, and Lt. Gov. Gavin Newsom, who is poised to run for governor in 2018.

In the 2016 election, California voted for Clinton by 30 points, up from Barack Obama's 23-point margin in 2012. Clinton's raw vote total was 11 percent higher than Obama's in 2012, while Trump's total fell by 7 percent from Mitt Romney's. Four counties switched from red to blue – Riverside, Fresno, Nevada and, most strikingly, Orange, which hadn't voted for a Democrat since Franklin Roosevelt in 1936 but which swung 15 points in the Democratic direction in 2016. Eight other counties stayed blue but increased the Democratic victory margin by double digits between 2012 and 2016. In San Diego, Democrats expanded their winning presidential margin by 11 percentage points; double-digit increases, or close, also came in San Mateo, Marin, Ventura, Santa Barbara, Santa Clara, Contra Costa and Napa counties. In each of the seven biggest counties in the state, Clinton improved on Obama's 2012 raw vote totals, by between 36,000 (San Bernardino) and 247,000 votes (Los Angeles). Trump's raw vote mostly fell in these seven counties, rising modestly only in Riverside and San Bernardino, two counties experiencing weak recoveries. Meanwhile, Brown – backed by a Democratic super majority in both chambers of the legislature, making it one of the nation's few remaining Democratic "trifectas" – spoke out strongly against the newly elected president's policies, articulating support for policies to address climate change and protect illegal immigrants. Such positions should prove popular in a state that voted overwhelmingly against Trump, unless and until he finds a way to leverage federal power to punish the state.

Population		**Race and Ethnicity**		**Income**	
Total	38,421,464	White	38.7%	Median Income	$61,818 (9 out of 50)
Land area	155,779	Black	5.6%	Under $50,000	41.3%
Pop/ sq mi	246.6	Latino	38.4%	$50,000-$99,999	28.8%
Born in state	54.7%	Asian	13.5%	$100,000-$199,999	22.0%
Age Groups		Two races	2.8%	$200,000 or more	7.9%
Under 18	23.9%	Other	1.0%	Poverty Rate	16.3%
18-34	22.2%	**Education**		**Health Insurance**	
35-64	38.7%	H.S grad or less	38.9%	With health insurance coverage	85.3%
Over 64	12.5%	Some college	29.6%	**Public Assistance**	
Work		College Degree, 4 yr	19.8%	Cash public assistance income	3.9%
White Collar	37.3%	Post grad	11.6%	Food stamp/SNAP benefits	9.2%
Sales and Service	42.5%	**Military**			
Blue Collar	20.2%	Veteran	6.1%		
Government	13.8%	Active Duty	0.4%		

Voter Turnout			
2015 Total Citizens 18+	24,280,349	2016 Pres Turnout as % CVAP	58%
2016 Pres Votes	14,181,595	2012 Pres Turnout as % CVAP	57%

Legislature	
Senate:	27D, 13R
House:	55D, 25R

Presidential Politics

2016 Democratic Primary		
Hillary Clinton (D)	2,745,302	(53%)
Bernie Sanders (D)	2,381,722	(46%)
2016 Republican Primary		
Donald Trump (R)	1,665,135	(75%)
John Kasich (R)	252,544	(11%)
Ted Cruz (R)	211,576	(9%)

2016 Presidential Vote		
Hillary Clinton (D)	8,753,792	(62%)
Donald Trump (R)	4,483,814	(32%)
Gary Johnson (L)	478,500	(3%)
Jill Stein (G)	278,658	(2%)
2012 Presidential Vote		
Barack Obama (D)	7,854,285	(60%)
Mitt Romney (R)	4,839,958	(37%)

California has 55 electoral votes. Since 1972, it has had substantially more than any other state. That fact gave Republicans a near lock on the presidency in the 1970s and 1980s. Then, from 1992 to 2016, Democrats swept the state, giving them a structural advantage in the Electoral College. The state's vote for Democratic presidential candidates has grown from 46 percent in 1992 to 62 percent in 2016. Democrats are winning where the voters are: In the 10 counties that cast the most ballots in the 2016 presidential race, Hillary Clinton captured all 10, including, for the first time since 1936, Orange County, the one-time home of GOP conservatism in California. Clinton received a higher percentage of votes than any presidential candidate since FDR won 67 percent in California in 1936. Clinton won the vote in seven congressional districts represented by Republicans; Donald Trump, who captured only 32 percent of the vote, won no district represented by a Democrat.

For years, California's June primary was a kingmaker. In 1964, the state was the center of national attention when Nelson Rockefeller lost here to Barry Goldwater in the GOP contest. California returned to the limelight in 1968; Robert Kennedy prevailed over Eugene McCarthy in the Democratic contest, but was assassinated by Palestinian Sirhan Sirhan on primary night. Four years later, George McGovern edged out Hubert Humphrey in the Democratic primary. The state's delegation was the focus of a pivotal credentials fight at the Democratic National Convention where McGovern prevailed, assuring him the 1972 nomination. But the state lost its marquee status in four of the next five election cycles when both parties' nominations were essentially clinched long before California voted. For the 1996 campaign, California moved its presidential primary from the first week in June to March 26, which was still too late to make a difference. So in 2000 and 2004, California held its primary in the first week of March, and it became one of several states that clinched nominations for George W. Bush in 2000 and for John Kerry in 2004. In 2008, California joined 14 other states holding primaries on Feb. 5, Super Tuesday (eight other states conducted a caucus). Still, the Golden State primary never achieved the status it once held. In order to save public funds, the legislature switched California's presidential primary back to its traditional date in early June, when state and congressional primaries are held.

As the Democratic primary approached the finish line in 2016, both Clinton and Vermont Sen. Bernie Sanders campaigned vigorously in the state. Sanders had camped out in the state and held dozens of events and rallies, hoping that an upset victory might give him enough momentum to keep contesting the Democratic race to the convention in Philadelphia. Clinton, leaving nothing to chance, devoted the final five days before the primary campaigning in the state and dispatched her husband and other surrogates to dozens of events. While Sanders promoted his liberal agenda, Clinton argued that she would be the strongest candidate to take on Trump in the general election. But the primary was a bit anti-climactic: The day before voters went to the polls, the Associated Press and CNN reported that Clinton had wrapped up enough Democratic convention delegates, including super delegates, to claim the nomination. Nonetheless, more than 5 million turned out to give Clinton a 53%-46% victory. She carried all of the major metropolitan areas. Sanders won most of the state's counties above Sacramento. Because Trump wrapped up the Republican nomination in May, California had little importance for Republicans. But eager to remain in the limelight, Trump held rallies around the state and won 75 percent of the primary vote.

Congressional Districts

115th Congress Lineup	14R 39D	**114th Congress Lineup**	14R 39D

California has a rich tradition of partisan gerrymandering and incumbent protection: Republicans drew the lines to their advantage in the 1940s and 1950s, Democrats in the 1960s, 1970s, and 1980s. Democratic Rep. Phillip Burton, the former godfather of the process, used to defend the drawing of safe seats by deviously arguing it was inhumane to make congressmen catch red-eye flights to Washington every week. In 2001, consultant Michael Berman, the brother of then-Rep. Howard Berman, charged every incumbent Democrat $20,000 to draw a map that granted Democrats 33 and Republicans 20 safe seats.

In 2012, for the first time since it was admitted to the Union in 1850, California did not gain House seats following the decennial census. But thanks to 2010 voter approval, by 61%-39%, of a ballot proposition spearheaded by GOP Gov. Arnold Schwarzenegger, the state became a large laboratory for redistricting reform. The Democratic-dominated legislature was forced to cede power to a 14-member Citizens Redistricting Commission barred from taking into account any partisan data or where incumbents live. Chosen by a byzantine application and lottery selection process, the commission included a chiropractor, a bookstore owner, and a businessman who just happened to be director of the U.S. Census Bureau under Presidents Richard Nixon and Gerald Ford.

After months of tedious meetings and mountains of public testimony, the commission in August 2011 adopted a new map that radically -- and more logically -- rearranged the state's 53 seats. Under the 2001 map, mangled lines had produced a delegation so safe that just one House seat changed partisan hands one time in 10 years' worth of elections. Moreover, clever incumbent protection had delayed advancements in Latino representation; in 2010, Latinos were 38 percent of California's population, but held just nine of the state's 53 seats. The new map threw 27 incumbents into 13 districts and created 14 seats with no resident incument. It also created three new or altered districts with functional majorities of Latino citizens: one in the fast-growing Central Valley, another in the San Fernando Valley, and a third anchored by San Diego.

Both parties worked frantically to adapt to the new order, pushing to avoid intra-party battles by awkwardly shoehorning affected members into nearby districts. Largely locked out of the process, some members had done their homework in advance by hiring consultants to drum up "grass-roots" community input before the commission, with some success: One incumbent, Republican Gary Miller, moved to (and won one term in) an entirely new district. Still, seven members - three Democrats and four Republicans - decided 2012 would be an ideal year to retire.

The end result was the most upheaval and loss of seniority California's delegation had ever seen. Not only did the new commission scramble the map, the state's new top-two jungle primary law meant candidates of the same party advanced to the November election in eight districts. In addition to retirees in 2012, 40-year Democratic veterans George Miller and Henry Waxman retired in 2014, and several senior members lost reelection, such as veteran Democrats Berman and Pete Stark and Republican Dan Lungren. What incumbents viewed as seniority, many voters saw as entrenchment, and reformers got the burst of competition and new blood they wanted.

Ironically, this "nonpartisan" map has turned out to be much more beneficial for Democrats than the one the Democratic legislature passed in 2001. In 2014, spurred by House Majority Leader Kevin McCarthy of Bakersfield, Republicans waged a half-dozen competitive challenges. But, stunningly, every Democrat survived - a few by narrow margins. With the defeat of Republican Gary Miller, the Democrats increased their control of the delegation to 39-14. California has 12 percent of all House seats, but 20 percent of the Democratic Caucus, 19 percent of the House's women Members, and 39 percent of Hispanic members (including those of Portuguese ancestry). Despite a few more close contests in 2016, including the defeat of veteran Democratic Rep. Mike Honda by another Democrat in the 17th District, another cycle passed with no changes in party control.

Following the poor performance of Donald Trump in several Republican-held districts in 2016, California Democrats believed they could find ways to squeeze out a few more Republicans. Even with the current prospect of no change to the size of the delegation for 2022, some tweaks of district lines here and there could easily place several Republicans in jeopardy, especially in the Central Valley and on the periphery of Los Angeles County. At least a couple of Democratic incumbents will need to be watchful. Latinos will be pushing for more seats.

Governor

Jerry Brown (D)

Elected 2010, term expires 2019, 4th term; b. Apr. 7, 1938, San Francisco, CA; U. of CA Berkeley, B.A. 1961; Yale U., J.D. 1964; Catholic; Married (Anne Gust).

Elected Office: Los Angeles Community College Board of Trustees, 1969-1971; CA Secretary of State, 1970-1974; CA Governor, 1974-1982; Chairman, CA Democratic Party, 1989-1991; Oakland Mayor, 1998-2006; CA Attorney General, 2006-10.

Professional Career: Law clerk, CA Supreme Court; Practicing attorney, Tuttle & Taylor; Practicing attorney, Fulbright & Jaworski; Radio host, KPFA Berkeley, 1995-1998.

Office: State Capitol Building, Suite 1173, Sacramento, 95814; 916-445-2841; Fax: 916-558-3160; Website: gov.ca.gov.

Election Results

Election	Name (Party)	Vote (%)
2014 General	Jerry Brown (D)	4,388,368 (60%)
	Neel Kashkari (R)	2,929,213 (40%)
2014 Primary	Jerry Brown (D)	2,354,769 (54%)
	Neel Kashkari (R)	839,767 (19%)
	Tim Donnelly (R)	643,236 (15%)

Prior winning percentage: 2010 (54%), 1978 (56%), 1974 (50%)

No other high-ranking political figure in the United States has a longer electoral career than Jerry Brown, a creative, intellectual and independent-minded Democrat who was elected governor of California in 2010 and won an unprecedented fourth term in 2014. He first won statewide office as California's secretary of state in 1970, went on to serve two terms as governor, then was defeated in a bid for senator in 1982. He's also been the mayor of Oakland and a three-time presidential candidate.

Edmund G. Brown Jr. grew up in San Francisco, in the upper-middle-class and then heavily Catholic neighborhood of St. Francis Wood, the grandson of a cigar-store owner and a policeman, and the son of lawyer Edmund G. Brown, universally known as Pat. In 1943, when Jerry was five, Pat Brown ran for district attorney of the city and county of San Francisco and won. He went on to serve two terms as state attorney general, and, beginning in 1959, two terms as governor of California. At a time when many California Republicans joined with Democrats in favoring activist government, Pat Brown embarked on a vast program of public spending - a water system transferring northern California water to the Central Valley and Los Angeles, a public university and state college system promising higher education for all who qualified, and a freeway program to connect the sprawling metropolitan areas that were growing rapidly in the interstices between mountain ranges and the Pacific Ocean. Voters heartily endorsed this record when they reelected Pat Brown 52%-47% in 1962 over Richard Nixon, the future president.

At first, Pat Brown's son was put off by politics. A year after graduating from St. Ignatius High School in 1955, Jerry Brown entered the Sacred Heart Novitiate, where he set out to become a priest. But after several years, he felt unfulfilled by a religious life and left the Jesuit seminary. He entered the University of California, Berkeley, where he earned a degree in classics in 1961. This was before the tumultuous Berkeley rebellion of 1964, but Brown was a rebel against his father in some ways. He opposed capital punishment and championed the cause of Caryl Chessman, who was sentenced to death for rape and other crimes. His father, who also opposed capital punishment, delayed the execution for a time but finally allowed it to go forward in 1960. After college, Brown went to Yale Law School, where he graduated in 1964 in the same class with future Sen. Gary Hart of Colorado.

After law school, Brown clerked for a state Supreme Court justice and then traveled in Latin America. When he returned to California, he settled not in his native San Francisco, but in Los Angeles. He worked for a large law firm, and in 1969, three years after his father was defeated by Republican Ronald Reagan 58%-42%, Brown ran for the board of trustees of Los Angeles Community College and, aided by name recognition, finished first among 124 candidates. In 1970, he ran statewide for secretary of state and won easily, even as Reagan was winning a second term. The victory put Brown in position to run for governor in 1974, when it was presumed Reagan would retire (many assumed from political life forever) at the age of 63. In the Democratic primary, Brown had serious competition from San Francisco Mayor Joseph Alioto, state Assembly Speaker Bob Moretti and Rep. Jerome Waldie. He won with 38 percent of the vote doubling second-place finisher Alioto. It was a very favorable year for Democrats, but California then was not nearly as Democratic as it is now, and in the general election, Brown faced Controller Houston Flournoy, a moderate Republican. Brown won by only 50%-47%.

At age 36, Brown was governor of California. He turned out to be a different kind of Democrat than his father. Brown refused to stay in the governor's mansion and instead hung out in a sparely furnished apartment. He parked the governor's limousine and drove around in a Plymouth. He largely stopped highway construction and tried to encourage mass transportation. He created a Wellness Commission and an Office of Appropriate Technology. Brown also legalized the practice of acupuncture. He opposed the death penalty, but his veto of a capital punishment bill was overridden by the legislature. If he was liberal on cultural issues, Brown was relatively conservative on economic issues. He was tight-fisted on spending, but he also gave bargaining rights to public employee unions.

Brown's eccentricity and unusual policy positions made him a regular target for late-night comics. Still, in 1976, at age 38, he ran for president. In the primaries, he won his first victory in May in Maryland, 48%-37%, over frontrunner Jimmy Carter of Georgia, with the help of San Francisco housewife and Democratic activist Nancy Pelosi, who later became Speaker of the House. One week later, he won in Nevada and ran a fairly close third to Frank Church of Idaho and Carter in dovish Oregon. Brown won 59 percent of the vote in the California primary, making him second in the national popular vote to Carter. But he was unable to keep pace with Carter in subsequent contests, and he finished third at the 1976 Democratic convention with about 300 delegates.

His political career continued. In 1978, Brown won a second term as governor, defeating GOP state Attorney General Evelle Younger 56%-37%. That year, a taxpayers' revolt led to passage of Proposition 13 to freeze property taxes in a period of rapidly rising housing prices. Like most Democrats, Brown opposed it, but when it passed, he came around and became a big booster, cutting state spending in order to funnel revenue to localities. His second term is considered less successful than his first. In 1981 he came under harsh attack by the state's important farm sector for refusing to order use of the pesticide malathion when California crops were hit by an infestation of medflies. But Brown was also ahead of his time. He appointed openly gay judges to the state courts, and he embraced satellite technology for emergency communications systems before it was common. His novel and sometimes far-fetched ideas inspired Chicago columnist Mike Royko to dub him "Governor Moonbeam," a nickname that, unfortunately for Brown, stuck. He ran for president again in 1980 and finished far behind Carter and Massachusetts Sen. Edward Kennedy everywhere, even in California. In 1982, Brown ran for the Senate seat being vacated by Republican S. I. Hayakawa. He was far better known than his Republican opponent, San Diego Mayor Pete Wilson. But Wilson out-debated him and won 52%-45%. Brown carried Los Angeles County and the San Francisco Bay area narrowly, but lost in all but one county in the rest of the state.

In the mid-1980s, as Reagan was basking in public approval in the White House, Brown traveled to China, Japan, Russia and India, where he worked with Mother Teresa's humanitarian projects. He practiced law in Los Angeles, and in 1989, embarked on a two-year stint as California Democratic chairman. In 1992, he ran for president a third time, refusing contributions over $100 and inviting listeners to call his 800 number to send him money. He finished a poor fifth in New Hampshire but beat Bill Clinton and Paul Tsongas in the Colorado and Connecticut primaries and in the caucuses in Maine, Vermont and Nevada. He aroused Clinton's ire by suggesting that there might be something improper about Hillary Clinton's work at the Rose Law Firm in Little Rock. By the time California voted in June, Clinton was the sure nominee, but he beat Brown there by only 47%-40%.

During most of the Clinton administration, Brown was out of favor at the White House. In time, he moved to Oakland, and in 1998, ran for mayor of that troubled city. In an 11-candidate primary, he was elected with 59 percent of the vote. To a much greater extent than his tenure as governor, he took a hands-on approach to being mayor. He won passage of a proposal creating a strong mayoral form of government, ordered innovative policing that sharply reduced crime, stimulated significant development in the bedraggled downtown and established both the Oakland School for the Arts and the Oakland Military Institute as an alternative high school option. He won a second term as mayor in 2002 with 64 percent of the vote.

In 2006, Brown, finishing his second term as Oakland mayor, ran for attorney general and defeated state Sen. Chuck Poochigian 56%-38%. As attorney general, Brown in 2009 asked the Supreme Court to stay a three-judge federal court decision requiring the state to release 40,000 inmates from California prisons. He sued the city of San Bernardino for a zoning plan that encouraged sprawl. After voters in 2008 passed Proposition 8 overturning the state Supreme Court decision authorizing same-sex marriage, Brown initially promised to defend it in court but reversed himself in December, making the novel argument that the people could not revoke rights discovered by the courts to be "inalienable."

His most recent turn as governor came about after actor-turned-politician Arnold Schwarzenegger was term-limited and California was hobbled by legislative dysfunction and mired in financial straits. The Republicans had a fierce primary between two Silicon Valley magnates, former eBay chief Meg Whitman and state Insurance Commissioner Steve Poizner. Spending some $60 million, Whitman won the primary 64%-27%. In the general election, Whitman spent $160 million, $141.5 million of it her own money. Whitman faced problems on immigration policy, as California Republicans have since 1996, and from seeming to mimic Schwarzenegger's agenda. Despite a national Republican tide, Brown beat Whitman, 54%-41%. In 2010, Brown won 63 percent of the vote in Los Angeles County and 67 percent in the San Francisco Bay area, way up from 53 percent in both places in 1974. He was modestly down elsewhere compared with 1974.

In his first weeks in office, Brown called for reductions in welfare programs, health care for the poor, community colleges, and a $1 billion cut from the budgets for the University of California and California State University systems. He followed with a state hiring freeze in February 2011, then incensed mayors when he called for shutting down the state's nearly 400 municipal redevelopment agencies to save $1.7 billion. Brown ordered half of the state's employees to turn in their cell phones and directed all state departments to turn in non-essential vehicles and to halt all new auto purchases.

At the same time, Brown made several moves that went against the grain of other, less progressive states. He signed into law in April 2011 the nation's most aggressive clean-energy standard, which required the state's utilities to get one-third of their electricity from renewable sources, such as geothermal, wind and solar, by 2020. Another bill he signed made California the first state to require that school textbooks and history lessons include the contributions of gay, lesbian, bisexual, and transgender Americans. Later that year, he signed a host of bills aimed at greater acceptance of illegal immigrants, including one to allow thousands of undocumented students to apply for financial aid at state colleges and universities. And he enacted the nation's most far-reaching new gun laws by banning most residents from openly carrying unloaded handguns in public places and requiring that all rifles be registered. At the same time, though, he refused to sign a bill that would have required young skiers to wear helmets, decrying without a hint of self-awareness the "continuing and seemingly inexorable transfer of authority from parents to the state."

To show his commitment to personal frugality, Brown rented a loft apartment blocks from the Capitol and flew coach class - always taking the senior citizens' discount - without the security entourage that had surrounded Schwarzenegger. He further reinforced his unconventional image in June 2011 when he vetoed a state budget that was seen as laden with gimmicks. Unable to negotiate tax hikes with state Republicans, he eventually signed a budget that cut spending by $26.6 billion. At the end of the year, he announced nearly $1 billion in new budget cuts, slashing spending on higher education and eliminating funding for free school-bus service. The public approved of Brown's frugality; polls showed he was popular at a time when most politicians were not.

But Brown also had grander visions. "At this stage, as I see many of my friends dying - I went to the funeral of my best friend a couple of weeks ago - I want to get (expletive) done." He unveiled a plan to build a $14 billion pair of tunnels - to be paid for by farmers and other water users - to move water from the north to the south to address the region's chronic water shortages. Environmentalists and Northern California lawmakers howled with outrage at the tunnel project, but Brown was unfazed. He also signed an $8 billion bill to kick off high-speed rail construction. Meanwhile, he pushed for voters to approve Proposition 30, an income tax hike on those earning at least $250,000, combined with a sales-tax increase. Thanks in large part to Brown's political skills, it ended up passing, 55%-45%. A jubilant Brown got more good news on Election Night 2012: Democrats gained a supermajority in both houses of the legislature, giving them the two-thirds majority needed to pass legislation to increase taxes. Brown announced plans to increase education spending and balance the state's budget.

In the 2014 election - the first gubernatorial race to use the new top-two primary system - Brown's opponent in the general was Neel Kashkari, the U.S. Treasury Department official under President George W. Bush who spearheaded the Troubled Assets Relief Program, better known as the Wall Street bailout. Kashkari was more moderate on social issues and immigration than most state or national Republican officeholders, and he had enough money to compete. He actually ended up outspending Brown, $7.1 million to $5.9 million. But few voters gave him much thought (Brown assented to only one debate, aired alongside the U.S. Open tennis tournament and the NFL season opener), and Kashkari's week-long sojourn to Fresno, when he slept behind a dumpster while posing as a homeless job-seeker, only made the onetime Gov. Moonbeam seem sober by comparison. Most of Brown's reelection efforts consisted of pushing two ballot measures - a $7.5 billion water bond and an effort to stabilize the state's budgetary rainy-day fund. Both measures passed - and, in what was almost an afterthought, Brown defeated Kashkari, 60%-40%, to win an unprecedented fourth term (something the state constitution no longer allows).

While Brown continued to show flashes of quirkiness - at his 2014 State of the State address, Brown offered playing cards featuring his (now deceased) Welsh corgi, Sutter, and after winning reelection, he tweeted archly that he "didn't get here by being pusillanimous" - his fiscal achievements were hard to dismiss. Brown's combination of spending cuts and tax increases, bolstered by the nation's slow but steady economic recovery, helped turn the $26.6 billion deficit he inherited into billions of dollars of surplus by 2015. With the fiscal situation greatly improved, Brown moved aggressively on other fronts, including his three-decade quest for high-speed rail, which could cost as much as $68 billion; climate change, capped by an April 2015 proposal to cut carbon emissions to 40 percent below 1990 levels by 2030; and efforts to ease the state's historic drought, for which he imposed mandatory 25 percent cuts in water use and an effort to turn 50 million square feet of lawns into "drought-tolerant landscape." He also faced down a growing movement in some corners of California to avoid vaccinations by signing a bill in June 2015 that eliminated personal and religious beliefs as permitted justifications for opting out of childhood immunizations. A few months later, after grappling with the issue, the onetime Jesuit novitiate signed an assisted suicide bill, making California the fourth state to enact such a law. In a break with his past, Brown moved into the newly renovated governor's mansion, last occupied by Reagan.

In early 2016, Brown continued to urge fiscal restraint, emphasizing the ability to "pay for the commitments we already have" rather than dreaming up new ones, and pushed to shore up the state's rainy-day fund. This concern for the fiscal future became somewhat prophetic by early 2017, when the state was looking at the possibility of its first deficit in five years. Brown's cautious approach reflected the "popular, dominant side of Gov. Jerry Brown's emerging legacy - the adult in the state Capitol, the political tutor, the check on runaway spending," wrote the *Los Angeles Times'* George Skelton. Brown followed moderate impulses on other issues. On guns, he signed laws in July 2016 that tightened rules for certain classes of semi-automatic weapons and ammunition, but he vetoed several other gun-related bills, including limits on the number of gun purchases residents could make and an expansion of the definition of "firearm." (Not that his choosiness cut it with the National Rifle Association; a spokeswoman said the new laws made "California the most anti-gun state in America.") Brown also vetoed a family leave bill, opposed stronger oversight of charter schools, and nixed several tax cuts, including one to exempt diapers and tampons from the sales tax, citing the likelihood of revenue losses. Other measures he signed were more pleasing to progressives. After initial misgivings, Brown signed a minimum wage hike -- to $15 by 2022 -- and sped up targets for cutting greenhouse gas emissions. Brown's approach seemed fine to most voters, who rewarded him with approval ratings in the mid-to-high 50s.

After Donald Trump's victory in 2016, Brown, emboldened by his state's overwhelming rejection of the Republican nominee, became an irritant to the new president. "It's hard for me to keep my thoughts just on California," Brown said during his 2017 state of the state address. "We've seen the bald assertion of 'alternative facts,' whatever those are. We've heard the blatant attacks on science. Familiar signposts of our democracy - truth, civility, working together - have been obscured or even swept aside." In the address, he touted California as a "beacon of hope to the rest of the world," and in a speech to scientists in San Francisco -- in which he attacked Trump's climate-change skepticism -- Brown promised, "If Trump turns off the satellites, California will launch its own damn satellites." As Brown was turning the twilight of his governorship into an alternative to Trumpism, the rest of the California political community began strategizing about possible successors. Given the contemporary realities of California politics, that almost certainly means a Democrat; in contrast to other states with weakened Democratic farm teams, the party's bench in California is deep. The top tier of candidates included Lt. Gov. Gavin Newsom, state Treasurer John Chiang and former Los Angeles Mayor Antonio Villaraigosa, with the possibility that others could enter the race as well, including former hedge fund executive and liberal donor Tom Steyer.

In June 2017, Brown took additional steps to position himself as the anti-Trump when he signed in Beijing a non-binding agreement to lower greenhouse gas emissions and then met with Chinese president Xi Jinping.

Senior Senator

Dianne Feinstein (D)

Elected 1992, term expires 2018, 5th term; b. Jun 22, 1933, San Francisco; Stanford University (CA), Bach. Deg.; Jewish; Married (Richard C. Blum); 1 child; 3 stepchildren.

Elected Office: San Francisco Board of Supervisors, 1970-1978, President, 1970-1971, 1974-1975, 1978; San Francisco Mayor, 1978-1988.

Professional Career: CA Women's Parole Board, 1960-1966; Director, Bank of CA, 1988-1989.

DC Office: 331 HSOB 20510, 202-224-3841, Fax: 202-228-3954, feinstein.senate.gov.

State Offices: Fresno, 559-485-7430; Los Angeles, 310-914-7300; San Diego, 619-231-9712; San Francisco, 415-393-0707.

Committees: *Appropriations*: Agriculture, Rural Development, FDA & Related Agencies, Commerce, Justice, Science & Related Agencies, Department of Defense, Department of the Interior, Environment & Related Agencies, Energy & Water Development (RMM), Transportation, HUD & Related Agencies. *Intelligence*. *Judiciary (RMM)*: Border Security & Immigration. *Rules & Administration*.

Group Ratings

	ADA	ACLU	AFL-CIO	LCV	ITI	COC	HAFA	ACU	CFG	FRC
2016	-	70%	-	94%	100%	63%	2%	8%	900%	0%
2015	75%	C	54%	88%	C	57%	C	0%	6%	0%

Almanac Ratings 2015

	Economy	Social	Foreign	Composite
Liberal	79%	100%	73%	84%
Conservative	21%	0%	27%	16%

Key Votes of the 114th Congress

1. Keystone pipeline	N	5. National Security Data	Y	9. Gun Sales Checks	Y
2. Export-Import Bank	N	6. Iran Nuclear Deal	N	10. Sanctuary Cities	N
3. Debt Ceiling Increase	Y	7. Puerto Rico Debt	Y	11. Planned Parenthood	N
4. Homeland Security $$	Y	8. Loretta Lynch A.G	Y	12. Trade deals	Y

Election Results

Election	Name (Party)	Vote (%)		Cand. Spent	Ind. Exp. Support	Ind. Exp. Oppose
2012 General	Dianne Feinstein (D)	7,864,624	(63%)	$12,152,230	$78,552	
	Elizabeth Emken (R)	4,713,887	(37%)	$910,209	$17,851	
2012 Primary	Dianne Feinstein (D)	2,392,822	(49%)			
	Elizabeth Emken (R)	613,613	(13%)			
	Dan Hughes (R)	323,840	(7%)			

Prior winning percentages: 2006 (59%), 2000 (56%), 1994 (47%), 1992 special (54%)

In early 2017, Dianne Feinstein, California's senior senator, became the top Democrat on the Judiciary Committee -- the first woman to occupy the chairmanship or ranking member's slot on that panel. It was but the latest in a series of firsts in a political career that began nearly a half-century ago: Feinstein also was the first woman ever to be seated on Senate Judiciary, following her arrival in the chamber after a 1992 special election. The latter election itself was precedent-setting. Barbara Boxer, who went on to serve four terms as Feinstein's California colleague, was chosen the same year -- marking the first time in history that a state had elected two female senators. The two campaigned together that year, with Feinstein at one point declaring: "Just as Cagney had Lacey and Thelma had Louise, Dianne has Barbara and Barbara has Dianne."

Notwithstanding the allusion to "Thelma and Louise" -- the 1991 celluloid feminist classic in which two friends turn into outlaws during a road trip -- Feinstein has crafted a reputation as a law-and-order liberal throughout her career. She became San Francisco's first woman mayor after her predecessor was assassinated by a deranged former public official, and her support of capital punishment puts her at odds with many fellow Democrats. But Feinstein also has been perhaps the Senate's most persistent advocate of gun control legislation. On the national security front, she has been a staunch defender of government surveillance programs and federal intelligence gathering agencies, a stance that has subjected her to blowback from civil libertarians and digital privacy advocates. But she sharply criticized the harsh interrogation techniques used on terrorism suspects in the wake of 9/11. And she fought a lengthy, often nasty battle with the Central Intelligence Agency and the Obama White House to secure release of a 2014 report that questioned whether such practices had improved national security.

Feinstein grew up in San Francisco in lush Presidio Heights. Her father was a prominent physician who was Jewish, while her mother belonged to the Russian Orthodox faith. Feinstein attended San Francisco's Convent of the Sacred Heart before officially converting to Judaism at age 20. She had hoped to follow in her father's professional footsteps, but, in her first semester at Stanford University, she got a D in genetics and decided she did not have the aptitude for medicine. But she did love a class she took on American political thought, and an uncle active in local Democratic politics is said to have fueled her interest in moving in that direction. Feinstein graduated with a degree in criminology and then, while on an internship, wrote a paper about post-conviction phases of the justice system that she thought contained valuable ideas for the state of California. She sent her paper to Gov. Edmund (Pat) Brown: Feinstein's father was Brown's personal physician. Despite her youth-she was just 27-the governor appointed her to the California Women's Board of Terms and Parole.

In 1969, she won her first election, to the San Francisco County Board of Supervisors, eventually rising to serve as its president. However, she was defeated in bids for mayor in 1971 and 1975. Feinstein, who describes herself as a pragmatist, began to question her future amid San Francisco's polarized politics. "I was convinced I was not electable," she recalled years later.

One day in late November 1978, Feinstein -- who had lost her second husband, neurosurgeon Bertram Feinstein, to cancer just months earlier -- was talking to reporters, openly contemplating leaving politics. Hours later, as president of the Board of Supervisors, she became the city's acting mayor, after Mayor George Moscone and Harvey Milk -- a fellow supervisor -- were shot and killed by former Supervisor Dan White. Feinstein was the first to discover Milk's body, and had to announce to the world what had happened.

In the subsequent weeks, she displayed a steadiness and a sense of command that calmed the city, and went on to be elected to full terms in 1979 and 1983 -- even as she angered the city's large gay community by vetoing a 1982 bill that would have extended to gay couples the health insurance benefits enjoyed by the spouses of city employees. (As senator, Feinstein has been an outspoken proponent of gay rights, introducing legislation to repeal the Defense of Marriage Act two years prior to the 2013 Supreme Court ruling recognizing same sex marriage -- and later pushing a bill to repeal portions of DOMA not covered by the high court decision.) As a supervisor, Feinstein for a time carried a .38-caliber pistol after being the target of two failed bomb attacks. But, in the wake of the circumstances of her ascension to the mayor's office, she launched a citywide campaign urging residents to turn in their guns.

In 1984, Democratic presidential candidate Walter Mondale seriously considered Feinstein as a running mate. But he passed over her for Geraldine Ferraro in part due to qualms about the business dealings of Feinstein's third husband, Richard Blum, whom she married in 1980. Feinstein presided gracefully that year over the Democratic National Convention in San Francisco, while, ironically, Ferraro confronted questions about her husband's business dealings. Blum's extensive holdings have helped make Feinstein the eighth wealthiest member of Congress, according to a recent *Roll Call* compilation; they also have yielded periodic political headaches for her, in the form of conflict-of-interest allegations. (Feinstein's first marriage, to attorney Jack Berman, produced a daughter, Katherine, who in 2012 stepped down as presiding judge of the San Francisco Superior Court after 12 years on the bench.)

Ineligible for a third term, Feinstein left the mayor's office in 1987 and ran for governor in 1990, buoyed by a $3 million loan that she and her husband made to the effort. She won the Democratic primary by 52%-41% over state Attorney General John Van de Kamp, then lost 49%-46% to Republican Pete Wilson in the general election. During that campaign, Feinstein -- who had been strongly anti-death penalty as a young member of the Board of Terms and Parole -- said she had changed her mind, in the belief that capital punishment was a deterrent for certain types of crimes. When Wilson appointed little-known state Sen. John Seymour to replace him in the Senate, Feinstein quickly announced for the 1992 special election to fill the remainder of the term. She defeated then-state Controller Gray Davis by 58%-33% in a heated primary that permanently soured her relationship with Davis, who went on to be elected governor in 1998. Seymour struggled throughout the campaign, flip-flopping to support abortion rights and seeing attacks on illegal immigration and Feinstein's fundraising fall flat. Feinstein won, 54%-38%.

As a junior senator, Feinstein's tough-on-crime background led her to sponsor a ban on the manufacture and sale of assault weapons in 1994, which President Bill Clinton signed into law. "The [Senate] leadership basically said, "If you want to do this, terrific, you're on your own'," long-time Feinstein staffer Michael Schiffer told the *New Yorker* two decades later. "She went out, senator to senator, buttonholed people, found out what was necessary to cobble together enough votes." When Idaho Republican Sen. Larry Craig argued that her definition of assault weapons was not rigorous enough and challenged her knowledge of firearms, she stopped the argument in its tracks by reminding the Senate of the horrific tragedy earlier in her political career. "I know something about what firearms can do," Feinstein said. She pressed unsuccessfully for reauthorization of the assault weapons ban in 2004, when Congress was under Republican control.

As the Democratic Party's support for gun control waned -- some put a portion of the blame for the party's loss of the House and Senate in 1994 on the assault weapons ban -- Feinstein had a harder time convincing her colleagues to consider new gun restrictions. After a gunman at a Colorado movie theatre killed 12 people and injured 58 others in July 2012, she lamented that "there is no outrage out there" to spur a crackdown on guns. The public mood changed just a few months later, with the December 2012 mass shooting of 26 small children and teachers at an elementary school in Newtown, Connecticut. Feinstein immediately became the point person in the Democratic-controlled Senate for legislation even tougher than the 1994 law; it sought to ban assault weapons and high-capacity magazines.

Democratic leaders subsequently abandoned pushing for the new ban to focus on measures they hoped could draw more bipartisan support, such as expanding criminal background checks for gun purchases. After those proposals failed as well, Feinstein blamed the National Rifle Association for making colleagues afraid to vote on gun control legislation. "A fear has set in that if they vote for the bill they won't be re-elected. It's that plain, it's that simple," she told a San Francisco audience in April 2013. Three years later, after the Orlando Florida nightclub shooting in which 49 were killed by a lone gunman, Feinstein tried again -- sponsoring a measure to deny the sale of firearms to those in the federal government's terrorist screening database. With the Senate back in GOP control, the proposal was defeated on a largely party-line vote, with just two Republicans backing it.

Feinstein has had a moderate to liberal voting record throughout her career on Capitol Hill; 2015 Almanac ratings pegged her as the 37th most liberal member of the Senate. During the Bush Administration, she supported the 2001 tax cuts and the Iraq war resolution in 2002 -- although she said later that she had been misled into voting for the war by an exaggeration of the threat, and regretted her vote. She supported the GOP-sponsored Medicare prescription drug bill in 2003, as well. In 2006, she was the only Democrat on the Judiciary panel to support a constitutional amendment barring desecration of the American flag.

Feinstein was less bipartisan in the battle over some of Bush's judicial nominees. After an interview with Supreme Court nominee John Roberts in July 2005, she called him "very impressive" but opposed his confirmation out of concern that he might overturn the *Roe v. Wade* decision legalizing abortion. She also opposed confirmation of appeals court judge Samuel Alito in early 2006. Bush nominated Alito after his initial choice of White House counsel Harriet Miers ran into trouble, prompting Feinstein to declare, "I don't believe they would have attacked a man the way she was attacked." A decade later, as the Judiciary Committee's top Democrat, Feinstein also highlighted her concerns about *Roe v. Wade* when President Donald Trump's Supreme Court nomination of appeals court judge Neil Gorsuch came before the panel in March 2017. She defended the 1973 decision as "settled law," while noting Trump's campaign promise to appoint judges whom he considered "pro-life." Although Gorsuch had not ruled directly on abortion, "his writings do raise questions," Feinstein added.

In an interview with the *San Francisco Chronicle* prior to the Gorsuch hearings, she excoriated as "appalling" the failure of Senate Republicans to grant appeals court judge Merrick Garland, Obama's nominee for the vacancy, a hearing or vote. "The humiliation that he went through," declared Feinstein. "Asking people just to meet with him and getting turned down… Bringing volumes, literally box after box after box of records, putting it all together, walking these halls day and night, and getting the back of the Republican hand. Many of us haven't recovered from that."

Feinstein became chairman of the Senate Intelligence Committee in 2009 and held the gavel until 2015, when the Republican retook Senate control. She then spent another two years as the panel's ranking Democrat. As a committee member during the Bush Administration, she charted an independent course. In 2007, she supported immunity for telecommunications companies that had allowed the government to listen in on telephone calls from suspected terrorists abroad to persons in the United States, even though many Democrats opposed immunity. Feinstein also disagreed with other Democrats who claimed the USA Patriot Act, the Bush administration's centerpiece anti-terrorism law, had led to violations of civil liberties -- a statement cited by Bush in pressing for renewal of the act.

Later, Feinstein was the Obama Administration's most prominent Democratic defender when former National Security Agency contractor Edward Snowden leaked details of the NSA's domestic surveillance efforts in 2013. She accused Snowden of "treason" and, while taking the agency to task for being unable to prevent him from accessing so much highly classified material, defended the NSA's far-reaching covert collection of Americans' telephone call records. The situation caused her approval ratings among Californians to plummet. Feinstein shrugged it off, telling the *Los Angeles Times*, "Numbers go down, numbers go up. I don't think people understand" the NSA's work. But in spring 2015, as debate raged over reauthorizing the Patriot Act, she did back ending the NSA's bulk collection of phone records -- putting her in league with Democrats and libertarian-leaning Republicans. She again took a hard line after the San Bernardino shooting rampage in late 2015, as the Justice Department sought access to an iPhone used by one of the shooters. She pushed a draft bill to give law enforcement a "back door" to encrypted communications, putting her at odds with technology firms and civil libertarians.

As chairman of the Senate Rules Committee, Feinstein headed the Joint Congressional Committee on Inaugural Services in 2009 -- giving her the role of overseeing Obama's swearing-in. Both posts were firsts for a female legislator, as was Feinstein's assumption of the Intelligence Committee chairmanship immediately after the inauguration. "My view is that it's time for a new start. I want to see the Senate Intelligence Committee with much closer oversight and a much closer relationship with the intelligence community," she declared. But it was a bumpy start, as Clinton White House Chief of Staff Leon Panetta -- a former member of the California congressional delegation -- was named the new CIA director without advance notice to Feinstein. She reacted by saying she thought the president should have appointed "an intelligence professional" before the White House moved to smooth things over. But it was not with Panetta, but rather with John Brennan -- who took over the CIA at the beginning of Obama's second term -- that Feinstein would really bang heads.

Brennan, previously the White House counterterrorism adviser under Obama, had been named deputy executive director of the CIA under Bush in early 2001 -- just months before 9/11. Feinstein repeatedly questioned both the rationale and effectiveness behind the use of waterboarding and other so-called "enhanced interrogation techniques" on terrorism suspects following 9/11. She attached amendments to the 2007 and 2008 intelligence authorization bills to require all government interrogations to be conducted under the rules of the Army Field Manual. In January 2009, she called for closing the detention camp for terrorism suspects at Guantanamo Bay, Cuba, calling it a "failed experiment." Upon taking over the committee, Feinstein won nearly unanimous approval for an investigation into the CIA's program of harsh interrogation tactics.

In late 2012, it yielded a 6,700 page report. With the aim of making a 500-page "executive summary" public, the committee forwarded it to the White House for review. To Feinstein's displeasure, the White House turned the document over to the target of the probe -- the CIA -- for review. What followed were protracted negotiations with the Obama administration over the report's release. Although Obama, early in his presidency, had signed an executive order barring future use of the Bush-era interrogation techniques, the Obama White House appeared sympathetic to the CIA's reluctance to allow a detailed airing of that period. Feinstein and other Intelligence panel Democrats felt the administration was redacting far too much information, with Feinstein complaining about the White House dragging its feet on the matter.

The tensions spilled out into public view in the spring of 2014, when media reports appeared in which the CIA accused Senate staffers working on the investigation of hacking into the agency's computers. In March 2014, Feinstein, in a Senate floor speech, angrily responded that it was the CIA that had secretly removed classified documents from the committee staff's computers in the middle of the investigation. "I have asked for an apology and a recognition that this CIA search of computers used by its oversight committee was inappropriate. I have received neither," she said. The agency conducted an investigation and apologized four months later; Feinstein stopped short of joining several of her committee colleagues in seeking Brennan's resignation.

In late 2014, the Intelligence Committee finally released the so-called "torture report" slamming the "deeply flawed" Bush-era approach to harsh interrogation methods used by the CIA on detainees. Some Republicans ripped the report, which the CIA also derided, but Feinstein was defiant. "America is big enough to admit when it's wrong and confident enough to learn from its mistakes," she told CNN. "History will judge us by our commitment to a just society governed by law and the willingness to face an ugly truth and say: 'Never again.'" Vermont Sen. Patrick Leahy, whom Feinstein later succeeded as the Judiciary panel's top Democrat, told *Roll Call* that the report "never would have gotten released if [Feinstein] hadn't worked so hard." Added, Leahy, "She was under enormous pressure to allow a cover-up. She didn't."

The end of 2016 marked the close of a 24-year political partnership between the often reserved, consensus-seeking Feinstein -- whom her predecessor as Intelligence chairman, former West Virginia Sen. Jay Rockefeller, described to the New Yorker as "so West Coast, calm, cool, stately" -- and the voluble, more ideological Boxer. But California's first two female senators were said to have forged a close professional relationship, and were widely credited with complementing each other to the state's benefit The partnership did end on a bumpy note, when at the end of 2016, Boxer -- ranking member of the Environmental and Public Works Committee -- sought to move a massive bill dealing with a topic of supreme importance to California: water. Feinstein, as ranking member of the Senate Appropriations Energy and Water Subcommittee, successfully attached a rider to allow water in a river delta where fish stocks are depleted to be diverted to agriculture. An enraged Boxer, believing Feinstein's move violated the Endangered Species Act, felt compelled to speak against her own legislation. Boxer termed the episode "heartbreaking," while Feinstein told the *Los Angeles Times* that it was "very difficult for me."

Feinstein has had only one serious challenge since she was elected to the Senate. Running for her first full term in the Republican year of 1994, she faced Rep. Michael Huffington, who spent $30 million of his own money. (He was then married to Arianna Huffington, who founded the liberal *Huffington Post* news website.) Days before the election, it was revealed that Feinstein, despite earlier denials, had employed a woman whose work permit had expired. She won narrowly, 47%–45%, carrying Los Angeles County and the San Francisco Bay Area to offset Huffington's margins elsewhere. In 2000, moderate GOP Rep. Tom Campbell, a Stanford Law professor, challenged her. Feinstein far outspent him, $10.3 million to $4.4 million, and won 56%-37%, carrying all major regions of the state. In her 2006 and 2012 reelection contests, she defeated little known opponents by margins of 59%-35% and 63%-37%, respectively.

Feinstein is currently the Senate's oldest member: Her Republican counterpart on the Judiciary panel, Chairman Charles Grassley of Iowa, is three months her junior. She delayed a decision on whether she will seek a fifth full term in 2018, when she turns 85, in a state that is now reliably blue. Feinstein had a pacemaker implanted in January 2017, but was back at work on Capitol Hill within a day at confirmation hearings for Trump administration nominees. "I did not see a senator [during the confirmation hearings] that was anywhere close to retiring, pacemaker or not," Democratic strategist Michael Trujillo told the

Los Angeles Times. "This senator still has a lot more legacy policy moves that she wants to get through and ... I think she's going to feel this great sense of patriotic duty to be there and to be a check on Donald Trump."

Junior Senator

Kamala Harris (D)

Elected 2016, term expires 2022, 1st term; b. Oct 24, 1964, Oakland; Howard University (DC), Bach. Deg.; University of California Hastings College of Law, J.D.; Baptist; Married (Douglas Emhoff).

Elected Office: District Attorney, San Francisco, 2004-2011; CA Attorney General, 2011-2016

DC Office: 112 HSOB 20510, 202-224-3553, Fax: 202-224-2200, harris.senate.gov.

State Offices: Fresno, 559-497-5109; Los Angeles, 213-894-5000; Sacramento, 916-448-2787; San Diego, 619-239-3884; San Francisco, 415-355-9041.

Committees: *Budget*. *Environment & Public Works*: Superfund, Waste Management, & Regulatory Oversight (RMM), Transportation & Infrastructure. *Homeland Security & Government Affairs*: Federal Spending Oversight & Emergency Management, Regulatory Affairs & Federal Management. *Intelligence*.

Election Results

Election	Name (Party)	Vote (%)		Cand. Spent	Ind. Exp. Support	Ind. Exp. Oppose
2016 General	Kamala Harris (D)	7,542,757	(62%)	$14,718,666	$1,512,017	$3,000
	Loretta Sanchez (D)	4,701,419	(38%)	$2,951,762	$104,488	
2016 Primary	Kamala Harris (D)	2,051,048	(40%)			
	Loretta Sanchez (D)	943,002	(19%)			
	Duf Sundheim (R)	406,964	(8%)			

In 2004, not long she was first elected as San Francisco's district attorney, Kamala Harris raised money for a young Democratic state senator embarking on a campaign for the Senate half a continent away, in Illinois. Even before Barack Obama had captured that seat, there was speculation about him as a future presidential contender. More than a decade later, as Obama entered the final weeks of his presidency, a similar buzz surrounded Harris as she was sworn in at the beginning of 2017 as California's junior senator. The intensity of the talk was such that Harris -- who, like the immediate past president, is the offspring of a multiracial marriage -- was already being referred to in some party circles as the "female Obama" two years before her arrival on Capitol Hill.

Whatever the future may hold for the former California attorney general, her election to the Senate was precedent-setting on several fronts. She is the first African-American to represent the Golden State, as well as the first woman of color to be elected senator from California. Nationwide, she is only the second African-American woman ever to serve in the Senate. And the election of Harris -- born just months after passage of the Civil Rights Act of 1964 -- marks the first time three African-Americans have served simultaneously as senators. Such milestones aside, Harris -- who, like Obama, came of age in the post-civil rights era -- has been ambivalent about making racial issues central to her political persona. "I don't feel compelled to sing long ballads about my experiences with injustice," she told the *Los Angeles Times* in a 2015 interview.

But such experiences were part of Harris' upbringing, even in the left-leaning northern California of the 1960s and 1970s. Her parents -- her father was Jamaican, her mother an emigrant from India -- met as graduate students at the University of California Berkeley. (In yet another first, Harris' election made her the first senator of Indian-American descent.) Even liberal Berkeley took its time implementing the dictates of the 1954 Supreme Court ruling in *Brown vs. Board of Topeka;* in the early 1970s, Harris' elementary school class became only the second to integrate Berkeley schools by use of busing. Her parents divorced when she was five, and Harris and her younger sister -- Maya Harris, now a civil rights attorney who was a senior policy adviser to Hillary Clinton's 2016 presidential bid -- visited their father, a Stanford University economics professor, on weekends. "The neighbors' kids were not allowed to play with us because we were black," Kamala Harris recounted during the *Times* interview. "In Palo Alto. The home of Google."

Harris spent her high-school years in Montreal, where her mother worked as a breast cancer researcher affiliated with McGill University. Harris earned her undergraduate degree at Howard University in Washington, D.C., the nation's oldest historically black college; she interned in the Capitol Hill office of California Democratic Sen. Alan Cranston, who occupied the seat she now holds. Harris returned to the San Francisco area to get her law degree at the University of California's Hastings College of Law. She took a job in the Alameda County (Oakland) district attorney's office, prosecuting crimes ranging from homicide and robbery to child sexual assault cases. In 1998, she transferred to the San Francisco district attorney's office, before moving to the city attorney's office as head of its division on families and children.

Harris' 2016 election to the Senate was a glide compared to her early outings in the electoral arena. In 2003, she challenged her onetime boss, San Francisco District Attorney Terence Hallinan. Under Hallinan, the office had come under criticism for low conviction rates and an antiquated administrative operation. Fighting for his political life, Hallinan sought to link Harris to Willie Brown, a colorful and often controversial figure who was then completing his final term as San Francisco's mayor. Harris had dated Brown in the 1990s while he was speaker of the California Assembly, and he had appointed her to a couple of state boards that added nearly $100,000 in annual compensation to her district attorney's office salary. Citing the patronage jobs, Hallinan attacked Harris as part of "the old Willie Brown machine." (Harris and Brown had stopped dating shortly after he became mayor in 1996; in 2014, Harris married Douglas Emhoff, West Coast managing director of Venable LLP, a Baltimore-based law firm.)

In November 2003, Hallinan ran slightly ahead of Harris, 36%-34%, with the rest going to a third candidate. It set up a runoff a month later, which Harris won, 56%-44%. Harris faced a political firestorm early in her first term, when, three days after the murder of a San Francisco police officer, Isaac Espinoza, she announced she would not seek the death penalty in the case. At the time, Democratic Sen. Dianne Feinstein, now Harris' in-state colleague, called for the death penalty and suggested she would not have backed Harris for district attorney if she had known Harris was opposed to capital punishment. Democratic Sen. Barbara Boxer, Harris' immediate predecessor on Capitol Hill, called on San Francisco's U.S. attorney to prosecute the killer under federal death penalty laws. Harris later conceded she had been "politically naive" to rule out the death penalty so soon after Espinoza's killing, but argued the subsequent second-degree murder conviction and sentence of life without parole in the case had justified her action. In 2016, Feinstein and Boxer endorsed Harris for Senate, albeit their move came months after Gov. Jerry Brown and much of the rest of the California Democratic establishment had done so.

Harris won praise for being among the first district attorneys in the nation to emphasize alternatives to incarceration for drug-related offenses, and she ran unopposed for a second term in 2007. But she faced another controversy during her initial race in 2010 for state attorney general. The theft of cocaine by a technician in San Francisco's police crime lab had forced Harris to drop drug charges in nearly 1,300 cases, and a local judge accused her office of hiding damaging information about the technician. Harris denied the charge, but her Republican opponent, Los Angeles District Attorney Steve Cooley, sought to use it against her -- while also highlighting the Espinoza controversy. For her part, Harris criticized Cooley for saying he would go to court to defend Proposition 8, a ban on same-sex marriage narrowly approved by California voters in 2008. Final returns gave Harris victory by a razor-thin margin, 46.1%-45.3%, making her the state's first female attorney general.

Harris' ties to Obama, whom she counts as a personal friend, grew closer throughout her tenure as district attorney and, later, state attorney general. She co-chaired Obama's California campaign during the race for the 2008 Democratic presidential nomination, and the president helped to put her into the national spotlight with a prime-time speaking role at the 2012 Democratic National Convention in North Carolina. Obama caused a stir at a 2013 San Francisco area fundraiser when he declared of Harris: "She's brilliant and she's dedicated, she's tough. She also happens to be, by far, the best-looking attorney general in the country." The president later called Harris to apologize. A year later, Harris was mentioned as a possible replacement for Attorney General Eric Holder; then in the midst of a campaign for re-election, which she won by a 15-point margin, Harris disavowed interest in moving to the Obama Administration. When Obama endorsed Harris' Senate candidacy in July 2016, her opponent, Democratic Rep. Loretta Sanchez, drew political blowback after she grumbled that Obama had backed Harris because they were both black.

Harris and Sanchez found themselves facing off in the 2016 general election thanks to California's adoption in a ballot initiative six years earlier of the so-called "blanket" primary system, in which the two top vote-getters in the first round primary advance to a runoff, regardless of party. Harris had quickly jumped into the Senate race after Boxer announced her retirement in January 2015, and soon emerged as the frontrunner when two other leading Democrats -- Lt. Gov. Gavin Newsom and former Los Angeles Mayor Antonio Villaraigosa -- chose not to run, opting instead to wait until the governorship came open in 2018. Sanchez, hoping for a path to victory in a state that is nearly 40 percent Latino, entered the contest four months after Harris. Harris won the endorsement of the California Democratic Party in February 2016, garnering 78 percent of the delegates to the party's state convention. In the June 2016 first-round primary, she won 40 percent of the vote in a 34-candidate field, with Sanchez a distant second at 19 percent. The leading GOP contender, George "Duf" Sundheim, a former chairman of the struggling California Republican Party, was third with 8 percent.

Although Sanchez entered the general election against Harris clearly lagging in both the polls and in fundraising, the matchup had several intriguing aspects. While featuring two women who were members of minority groups, it also marked the first high-profile contest between two candidates of the same party since the adoption of the state's blanket primary -- as well as being California's first open seat Senate race in nearly 25 years. The candidates presented a contrast in style: Harris was on occasion criticized for an overabundance of caution, as compared to the shoot-from-the-hip reputation Sanchez had accumulated during her 20-year career in Congress. Amid the tumult of the presidential race, the Senate contest -- in which neither camp had the funds to underwrite saturation advertising blitzes in a huge state with expensive media market -- struggled to attract voter interest, with reporters often utilizing adjectives such as "sleepy" to describe it.

As fellow Democrats, there was limited ideological daylight between the two women. However, as the campaign entered its closing weeks, Sanchez did adjust her pitch to attract Republicans and independents. She collected endorsements from GOP officeholders, and went on a conservative radio talk show to tout her record against "Islamic extremists." She tried to peel away some Democratic support by pointing to $6,000 in donations made by Republican presidential nominee Donald Trump to Harris' attorney general re-election campaign in 2011 and 2013. (Harris gave the money to charity following disparaging remarks Trump made about Mexicans in 2015.) When Sanchez sought to tie these donations to Harris' failure to open an investigation of Trump University following a 2010 federal class action lawsuit against the latter, Harris pointed to a $1.1 billion judgment her office had won against another large for-profit institution, Corinthian Colleges. Seeking to emphasize her accomplishments as attorney general; she also cited her role in brokering a $25-billion nationwide settlement with several large mortgage institutions for improper foreclosure practices during the housing market crash.

Sanchez's last-ditch efforts failed to translate into much additional support; Harris won overwhelmingly, 62%-38%, and even outpolled Sanchez among Latino voters. In the Senate, Harris was assigned to the Environment and Public Works Committee -- which Boxer chaired while the Democrats were in the majority -- along with the Homeland Security and Governmental Affairs, Budget and Intelligence panels.

Harris outlined a progressive agenda in line with that of her predecessor, even if her style is more measured than the outspokenly liberal Boxer. As with past freshman senators arriving on Capitol Hill with an element of celebrity, those close to Harris sought to downplay any interests outside representation of her home state. "Kamala Harris has always carried enormous expectations on her back, but her sole focus is on representing California in the U.S. Senate," her political strategist, Sean Clegg, told *Politico*. But the buzz continued about whether Harris might be the one to finally crack the glass ceiling following Clinton's 2016 defeat. "The dirty little secret is that the Democrats currently don't have much of a bench," Democratic consultant Garry South said, adding, "Barack Obama had only been in the Senate two years when he announced he was running for president - stranger things have happened."

FIRST DISTRICT

Doug LaMalfa (R)

Elected 2012, 3rd term; b. Jul 02, 1960, Oroville; California Polytechnic State University, San Luis Obispo, B.S.; Butte College (CA), A.A.; Evangelical; Married (Jill LaMalfa); 4 children.

Elected Office: CA Assembly, 2002-2008; CA Senate, 2010-2012.

Professional Career: Manager family rice farm.

DC Office: 322 CHOB 20515, 202-225-3076, Fax: 202-226-0852, lamalfa.house.gov.

State Offices: Auburn, 530-878-5035; Oroville, 530-534-7100; Redding, 530-223-5898.

Committees: *Agriculture*: Commodity Exchanges, Energy & Credit, Conservation & Forestry. *Natural Resources*: Indian, Insular & Alaska Native Affairs (Chmn), Water, Power & Oceans. *Transportation & Infrastructure*: Aviation, Highways & Transit, Water Resources & Environment.

Group Ratings

	ADA	ACLU	AFL-CIO	LCV	ITI	COC	HAFA	ACU	CFG	FRC
2016	-	11%	-	3%	100%	100%	68%	92%	78%	100%
2015	0%	C	13%	0%	C	79%	C	100%	84%	92%

Almanac Ratings 2015

	Economy	Social	Foreign	Composite
Liberal	7%	0%	0%	2%
Conservative	93%	100%	100%	98%

Key Votes of the 114th Congress

1. Keystone Pipeline	Y	5. Puerto Rico Debt	Y	9. Offenses by Aliens	Y
2. Trade Deals	Y	6. Medical Marijuana	N	10. Troops in Iraq	N
3. Export-Import Bank	N	7. Sanctuary Cities	Y	11. Homeland Security $$	N
4. Debt Ceiling Increase	N	8. Armor-piercing Bullets	Y	12. Trade Adjustment aid	N

Election Results

Election	Name (Party)	Vote (%)		Cand. Spent	Ind. Exp. Support	Ind. Exp. Oppose
2016 General	Doug LaMalfa (R)	185,448	(59%)	$731,643	$94,682	
	Jim Reed (D)	128,588	(41%)	$131,530		
2016 Primary	Doug LaMalfa (R)	59,037	(40%)			
	Jim Reed (D)	42,543	(29%)			
	Joe Montes (R)	25,203	(17%)			
	David Peterson (D)	9,167	(6%)			

Prior winning percentages: 2014 (61%), 2012 (57%)

Republican Doug LaMalfa was elected in 2012 in this isolated district, with the endorsement of his predecessor Wally Herger, and has caused few ripples in Congress. His committee work has focused on local issues. In 2017, he took over as chairman of the Indian, Insular and Alaskan Native Subcommittee at Natural Resources.

LaMalfa hails from what he calls "the real California," a wide swath of rural country north of Sacramento. A fourth-generation rice farmer from Richvale in Butte County, he was born in Oroville and attended area schools. He later graduated with degrees in agriculture and business from California Polytechnic State University in San Luis Obispo. LaMalfa and his wife, Jill, operate in Richvale the farm his great-grandfather started in 1931.

He served on various agricultural commissions before winning election in 2002 to the state Assembly, where he spent six years. In 2010, he was elected to the Senate, earning the most votes of any candidate for the legislature that year. LaMalfa made his name in Sacramento by promoting agricultural interests and fighting new government spending and regulation. He sought unsuccessfully to freeze funding for the state's voter-approved high-speed rail project, citing its cost overruns. He opposed a state-level Dream Act proposal giving financial aid to children of illegal immigrants. LaMalfa started "There Ought Not to Be a Law" contests, where citizens across California were invited to submit ideas for removing burdensome laws, with LaMalfa sponsoring the winning proposal.

Herger endorsed LaMalfa immediately after announcing his retirement, inviting criticism from those in Republican circles who objected to his "kingmaker" politics. The LaMalfa campaign became embroiled in controversy when it was discovered that a staffer had set up an anonymous website attacking LaMalfa's chief Republican rival, former state Sen. Sam Aanestad. The site, which criticized Aanestad's record in the Senate and questioned whether he was truly a dentist, was taken down. In the primary, LaMalfa came in first under California's all-party system, getting 38 percent of the vote. The second-highest vote getter was Democrat Jim Reed, an estate and tax attorney, with 25 percent. Annestad finished third with 14 percent. LaMalfa amassed five times more money than Reed, with the largest sums coming from agricultural interests. He ran on a platform that heavily criticized excessive government spending, prompting critics to highlight the total $4.7 million in federal agricultural subsidies he received for his family's rice farm. LaMalfa claimed the federal help was necessary for a small farm to comply with onerous federal regulations; rice farmers have long received sizable support. His 57%-43% win was less than stellar, but in line with the recent presidential vote in the district. He won all 11 counties, but had only 51 percent in Butte - which had the largest turnout.

In the House, LaMalfa worked with neighboring Democratic Rep. John Garamendi on a bill to create a large new reservoir in Glenn and Colusa counties to serve northern California, mostly with state funding. LaMalfa said that private interests were ready to support the Sites Reservoir. It would be twice as large as Folsom Lake, which has served much of the region. He worked on a Republican bill to assure that metropolitan water districts would receive all available water from the reservoir, but the measure has been opposed by Democrats. In 2016, he criticized the lack of open procedures when the Interior Department collaborated with California and Oregon to remove four dams on the Klamath River. He has called for shifting $3 billion from the state's high-speed rail project to pay for new water storage. An aide to LaMalfa said that she favored a local movement for Siskiyou County to secede from the state; LaMalfa encouraged the supporters but did not explicitly back their movement.

In 2014, LaMalfa was reelected 61%-39% over Heidi Hall, a conservation expert with the state's Department of Water Resources, who promised to "break through the bitter partisanship" in Washington. She spent $233,000 - not enough to be competitive in this sprawling district. LaMalfa increased his support in Butte County to 56 percent. In 2016, he had a rematch of his 2012 contest with Reed, and slightly increased his overall margin to 59%-41%. His vote share in Butte fell back to 51 percent.

Northeast: Redding, Chico

Population		**Race and Ethnicity**		**Income**	
Total	704,448	White	77.9%	Median Income	$45,741 (330 out of 435)
Land area	28,089	Black	1.3%		
Pop/ sq mi	25.1	Latino	12.9%		
Born in state	69.1%	Asian	2.6%	Under $50,000	28.6%
		Two races	3.5%	$50,000-$99,999	14.7%
Age Groups		Other	1.8%	$100,000-$199,999	2.9%
Under 18	20.3%			$200,000 or more	18.5%
18-34	22.0%	**Education**		Poverty Rate	18.5%
35-64	38.8%	H.S grad or less	36.1%		
Over 64	18.9%	Some college	40.8%	**Health Insurance**	
		College Degree, 4 yr	15.2%	With health insurance coverage	87.0%
Work		Post grad	7.8%		
White Collar	33.6%				
Sales and Service	46.1%	**Military**		**Public Assistance**	
Blue Collar	20.2%	Veteran	11.1%	Cash public assistance income	3.9%
Government	19.0%	Active Duty	0.1%		
				Food stamp/SNAP benefits	10.2%

Voter Turnout			
2015 Total Citizens 18+	540,736	2016 House Turnout as % CVAP	58%
2016 House turnout	314,036	2014 House Turnout as % CVAP	40%

2012 Presidential Vote		
Mitt Romney	171,902	(56%)
Barack Obama	122,379	(40%)

2016 Presidential Vote		
Donald Trump	176,358	(56%)
Hillary Clinton	114,727	(36%)
Gary Johnson	14,110	(4%)
Jill Stein	7,501	(2%)

Cook Partisan Voting Index: R+11

Rising 14,000 feet over low foothills and the Central Valley, visible for 100 miles, is the snow-capped volcanic cone of Mount Shasta, one of a string of (supposedly) burnt-out volcanoes up and down the Pacific Coast. This is the far northern tier of California, where truck traffic on Interstate 5 is the only reminder of the choked metropolitan areas where most of the state's people live. This is lumber country mostly, where the mountains that rise on all sides - the Coast Range to the west, the Sierra Nevada to the east, the scattered mountains sealing off the Central Valley north of Redding - are thick with trees. It's rugged, flannel-shirt, two-lane-road country that was left behind economically when Los Angeles and San Francisco boomed after World War II. Since the 1980s, this northern end of California has been attracting people, mostly young families who come here to raise their children in a small-town environment, plus retirees looking for a calm atmosphere and low cost of living.

The 1st Congressional District of California is mountainous and mostly rural. It is the largest district in the state, with two major population areas. One is Redding, south of Mount Shasta, where increased high-altitude snowfall from Pacific Ocean moisture has allowed the Whitney Glacier to defy global warming trends by growing in the past century, the only glacier to do so. The second is farther south, at the edge of the Sierra foothills, around the Butte County communities of Paradise and Chico, home to a state university campus and Sierra Nevada Pale Ale, where the brewery is powered by a solar installation. Butte produces about 60 percent of the nation's almonds and 10 percent of the walnuts - a nearly $500 million business. The district takes in thinly populated mountain counties like Modoc, site of a World War II detention facility for Japanese Americans. In June 2016, the National Park Service proposed turning what remained of the facility into a national historic site. Local interests sought to retain local control under the proposal. In the closing days of his administration, President Barack Obama created local controversy when he issued an executive order that expanded the Cascade-Siskiyou National Monument along the Oregon border. In 2014, the severe statewide drought fueled devastating fires in the mountains, which led to the evacuation of Weed and other neighboring towns. The January 2017 rain and snow resulted in the first release of water from the spillway of the Shasta Dam in six years. The bad news came from the Oroville Dam, the tallest in the nation, which developed a hole that forced a shutdown of the spillway into Lake Oroville. By spring, state officials had resumed limited releases at the reservoir and began work on $275 million in repairs. They had not fully described the problem or the long-term prospects for the dam.

The 1st District covers the northeast corner of California, sharing borders with Oregon to the north and Nevada to the east. Politically, it has a Democratic heritage but is culturally conservative and often angry at intrusions by urban environmentalists. Until 1980, the area elected rough-and-ready Democrats who pulled strings in Sacramento and Washington to build roads and dams. Since then, it has elected abstemious Republicans who have solidly conservative voting records and tend to local needs. The mountain areas have a stronger Republican lean. Chico, with its state university, is more centrist. Its 55 percent of the vote for Donald Trump in 2016 made this his second-best district in the state, behind the Bakersfield-based 23rd District.

SECOND DISTRICT

Jared Huffman (D)

Elected 2012, 3rd term; b. Feb 18, 1964, Independence, MO; University of California, Santa Barbara, B.A., 1986; Boston College Law School (MA), J.S.D., 1990; Protestant; Married (Susan Huffman); 2 children.

Elected Office: Board member, Marin Municipal Water District, 1994- 2006; CA Assembly, 2006-2012.

Professional Career: Attorney, McCutchen, Doyle, Brown & Enersen, 1990-1992; Managing partner, Boyd, Huffman & Williams, 1992-1996; Managing partner, The Legal Solutions Group, 1996-2001; Sr. Attorney, Natural Resources Defense Cncl., 2001-2006.

DC Office: 1406 LHOB 20515, 202-225-5161, Fax: 202-225-5163, huffman.house.gov.

State Offices: Eureka, 707-407-3585; Fort Bragg, 707-962-0933; Petaluma, 707-981-8967; San Rafael, 415-258-9657; Ukiah, 707-671-7449.

Committees: *Natural Resources*: Energy & Mineral Resources, Oversight & Investigations, Water, Power & Oceans (RMM). *Transportation & Infrastructure*: Coast Guard & Maritime Transportation, Highways & Transit, Water Resources & Environment.

Group Ratings

	ADA	ACLU	AFL-CIO	LCV	ITI	COC	HAFA	ACU	CFG	FRC
2016	-	100%	-	100%	67%	36%	12%	4%	4%	0%
2015	95%	C	100%	100%	C	40%	C	4%	0%	0%

Almanac Ratings 2015

	Economy	Social	Foreign	Composite
Liberal	98%	100%	93%	97%
Conservative	2%	0%	7%	3%

Key Votes of the 114th Congress

1. Keystone Pipeline	N	5. Puerto Rico Debt	Y	9. Offenses by Aliens	N
2. Trade Deals	N	6. Medical Marijuana	Y	10. Troops in Iraq	Y
3. Export-Import Bank	Y	7. Sanctuary Cities	N	11. Homeland Security $$	Y
4. Debt Ceiling Increase	Y	8. Armor-piercing Bullets	N	12. Trade Adjustment aid	Y

Election Results

Election	Name (Party)	Vote (%)		Cand. Spent	Ind. Exp. Support	Ind. Exp. Oppose
2016 General	Jared Huffman (D)	254,194	(77%)	$561,092		
	Dale Mensing (R)	76,572	(23%)	$2,311		
2016 Primary	Jared Huffman (D)	104,520	(69%)			
	Dale Mensing (R)	24,690	(16%)			
	Erin Schrode (D)	12,333	(8%)			
	Matthew Wookey (I)	10,307	(7%)			

Prior winning percentages: 2014 (75%), 2012 (71%)

Democrat Jared Huffman, first elected in 2012, has joined activist lawmakers in the California delegation and beyond. With his deep interest and expertise on resource issues, he has taken a committee leadership position and has had policy impact in the Republican-controlled House, with both partisan and bipartisan initiatives.

Huffman was born in former President Harry Truman's hometown of Independence, Missouri. He attended the University of California, Santa Barbara, on a volleyball scholarship, later becoming a three-time NCAA All-American. Three years later, Huffman earned his law degree and went to work on antitrust litigation at a San Francisco-based firm before opening his own practice. His interest in student athletics led to his involvement in a variety of Title IX cases, including a landmark case in which California State University agreed to guarantee gender equity in its men's and women's athletic programs.

In 1994, Huffman ran for and won a position on the board of the Marin Municipal Water District, which led to a job as a senior attorney on water and fisheries issues with the Natural Resources Defense Council. In 2006, he defeated a 14-year Marin County supervisor in the primary and was elected to the state Assembly, with a focus on environmental policy. During his three terms, he helped block efforts by Republican Gov. Arnold Schwarzenegger to construct a $356 million death row complex at San Quentin.

When he ran for the House in 2012, Huffman had the support of his district's retiring Rep. Lynn Woolsey and Rep. Mike Thompson of the neighboring district, both Democrats, and a celebrity endorsement from Mickey Hart, former drummer for the Grateful Dead. In California's jungle primary, eight Democrats split the progressive vote. Huffman finished first with 37 percent, and the splintered Democratic voting narrowly eliminated Norman Solomon, an antiwar activist and media critic who would have been Huffman's toughest opponent in the general election. Instead, the second spot went to Republican Daniel Roberts. In the solidly Democratic district, Huffman won 71%-29%.

He quickly showed his activist stripes on the Natural Resources panel, with an initial focus on his district's diverse interests - including fishing and forestry. The House approved his bill to add Mendocino public lands to the California Coastal National Monument, and he worked with Republican Jamie Herrera Beutler of Washington on their bill to sustain Pacific coast fishing communities by reducing interest rates for groundfish fishing boats. Huffman spoke out regularly on climate change and raised options that might appeal to Republicans, such as energy efficiency and weather resiliency. With Democratic Rep. Jackie Speier, he filed disaster-relief legislation on behalf of California fishery workers and businesses.

As ranking Democrat on the influential Water, Power and Oceans Subcommittee, which handles local projects that are vital to many lawmakers, Huffman has sought to use the post to tackle "the complex natural resource issues that we face in a constructive, problem-solving manner." In January 2017, he was tapped for the new position of vice-ranking member on Natural Resources, which the Democratic Caucus had created to give added responsibilities to a junior member at each House committee. He pledged to use the position to combat "President Trump's radical agenda to expand dirty energy and undermine public health safeguards."

On the Transportation and Infrastructure panel, Huffman filed a bill to replace the 18.4 cents-per-gallon federal tax on gasoline with a carbon tax, which might average about 50 cents per gallon and be designed to finance highway and transit improvements. Despite their aversion to tax hikes, some Republicans have been open to changes in fuel taxes. He has been active on issues outside his committee work. In January 2016, after making contacts with Iranian officials, he played a role in the release from prison of *Washington Post* reporter Jason Rezaian, a Marin County native. In May 2016, the House passed on a 265-159 vote his amendment to prohibit the Confederate battle flag from being flown at cemeteries run by the Veterans Affairs Department. The House had earlier passed by voice vote a similar amendment on another appropriations bill, but that led to a revolt by some Republicans and GOP leaders pulled that bill. During the transition to President Donald Trump, Huffman pointedly filed a bill to clarify that a president-elect cannot conduct U.S. foreign policy.

Huffman's hobby is winemaking, and his collection features his own "Homemade Hooch" wine. On the pop culture front, he held his own in a broadcast interview with Stephen Colbert, who enjoys mocking Congress. He has won reelection with minimal major-party opposition.

Coastal North: Marin, Sonoma

Population		**Race and Ethnicity**		**Income**	
Total	712,526	White	71.7%	Median Income	$62,964
Land area	12,952	Black	1.5%		(111 out of 435)
Pop/ sq mi	55.0	Latino	17.2%		
Born in state	59.2%	Asian	3.7%	Under $50,000	27.2%
		Two races	3.5%	$50,000-$99,999	21.3%
Age Groups		Other	2.5%	$100,000-$199,999	10.6%
Under 18	20.4%			$200,000 or more	13.3%
18-34	19.5%	**Education**		Poverty Rate	13.3%
35-64	42.6%	H.S grad or less	29.0%		
Over 64	17.5%	Some college	31.7%	**Health Insurance**	
		College Degree, 4 yr	23.8%	With health insurance coverage	88.8%
Work		Post grad	15.5%		
White Collar	41.9%				
Sales and Service	42.0%	**Military**		**Public Assistance**	
Blue Collar	16.1%	Veteran	8.2%	Cash public assistance income	2.6%
Government	15.2%	Active Duty	0.2%		
				Food stamp/SNAP benefits	6.8%

Voter Turnout			
2015 Total Citizens 18+	517,691	2016 House Turnout as % CVAP	64%
2016 House turnout	330,766	2014 House Turnout as % CVAP	42%

2012 Presidential Vote		
Barack Obama	230,212	(69%)
Mitt Romney	89,908	(27%)

2016 Presidential Vote		
Hillary Clinton	238,157	(68%)
Donald Trump	80,545	(23%)
Gary Johnson	12,239	(4%)
Jill Stein	12,778	(4%)

Cook Partisan Voting Index: D+22

The North Coast of California is unlike any other place in America. It is the only part of the lower 48 states first settled by Russians, who built Fort Ross in 1812. They sold it in 1841 to a Swiss pioneer named John Augustus Sutter; a Sutter employee's discovery of gold near Sacramento seven years later started the Gold Rush. It is the only part of the world with large numbers of redwood trees, shooting up hundreds of feet in the drizzly air. It is wet country, and for years it was one of America's prime lumbering areas. Coastal Eureka and smaller lumber towns are filled with filigreed Victorian houses and old mills, but also art galleries, hiking trails, pubs and waterfront hotels.

Humboldt County is known for its quality marijuana fields, and the local economy relies heavily on the product, as depicted in the eponymous 2008 movie. With about 35,000 pot growers along the North Coast, the saturation of marijuana growers led to increased production and a drop in prices. Environmental groups gave grown concerned about the impact pot growers are having on the region's salmon streams. Their farms consume enormous amounts of water while also spilling pesticides, fertilizers and other products into the Eel and Klamath Rivers, which historically have produced large salmon harvests. The problem was compounded by California's extended drought, plus the proliferation of marijuana fields and influx of young people from around the world who can get good pay and are eager to join in the harvest - typically from September to November. The November 2016 approval of the statewide referendum for recreational use of marijuana added to the market and the environmental concerns. Some experts believe that the weed industry in northern California eventually might rival the size of wine production. By contrast, the local seafood industry has suffered in recent years, due in part to warmer and more acidic ocean waters. The harvest decreased by $109 million - 40 percent - from 2014 to 2015. The price of Chinook salmon and Dungeness crab soared, as a result.

Encouraged by local Democrats, President Barack Obama set aside some of these land and ocean areas. In 2015, the National Oceanic and Atmospheric Administration more than doubled the size of two large marine sanctuaries off the coast of Marin and Sonoma counties. That left NOAA with control of 350 miles off the California coast and the many species that thrive there. Obama in January 2017 designated three sites in Humboldt County as part of the California Coastal National Monument. One problem for Humboldt: Since 2011, it has annually had the largest earthquake in the nation. That hasn't stopped the inflow. Eureka, the county seat of Humboldt, in October 2016 was 15th in a list of the nation's hottest real estate markets, according to realtor.com.

The 2nd Congressional District of California runs from the Oregon border in the northwest corner of the state down through Marin County to San Francisco Bay. It includes all of the coastal counties of Del Norte, Humboldt, Mendocino and Marin, which are connected by Highway 101, and inland Trinity County. The North Coast lumbering area, from Mendocino north, was once filled with rough-hewn working men, and was historically Democratic. Now the focus is on sustainable forestry and the area remains heavily Democratic, but with more socially liberal views. The district takes in nearly half of Sonoma County, including Healdsburg, the Alexander Valley and Simi Winery, one of the oldest boutique wineries in the state. About 40 percent of the voters are in upscale Marin, which identifies more with the Bay Area than with the North Coast.

Hillary Clinton won Marin County in 2016 with a huge 79 percent of the vote. She took the district, 68%-23%, lower than her performance in several other Bay Area districts.

THIRD DISTRICT

John Garamendi (D)

Elected 2009, 5th term; b. Jan 24, 1945, Camp Blanding, FL; University of California, Berkeley, B.A., 1966; Harvard Business School (MA), M.B.A., 1970; Christian Church; Married (Patricia Wilkinson Garamendi); 6 children; 10 grandchildren.

Elected Office: CA Assembly, 1974-1976; CA Senate, 1976-1990; CA state ins. commissioner, 1991-1994, 2002-2006; CA Lt. Governor, 2007-2009.

Professional Career: U.S. Peace Corps, Ethiopia, 1966-1968; Deputy Secretary, U.S. Department of Interior, 1995-1998.

DC Office: 2438 RHOB 20515, 202-225-1880, Fax: 202-225-5914, garamendi.house.gov.

State Offices: Davis, 530-753-5301; Fairfield, 707-438-1822; Yuba City, 530-329-8865.

Committees: *Armed Services*: Seapower & Projection Forces, Strategic Forces. *Transportation & Infrastructure*: Coast Guard & Maritime Transportation (RMM), Railroads, Pipelines & Hazardous Materials, Water Resources & Environment.

Group Ratings

	ADA	ACLU	AFL-CIO	LCV	ITI	COC	HAFA	ACU	CFG	FRC
2016	-	82%	-	87%	67%	71%	13%	0%	10%	0%
2015	75%	C	100%	91%	C	56%	C	4%	0%	8%

Almanac Ratings 2015

	Economy	Social	Foreign	Composite
Liberal	82%	84%	85%	84%
Conservative	18%	16%	16%	16%

Key Votes of the 114th Congress

1. Keystone Pipeline	N	5. Puerto Rico Debt	Y	9. Offenses by Aliens	NV
2. Trade Deals	N	6. Medical Marijuana	Y	10. Troops in Iraq	Y
3. Export-Import Bank	Y	7. Sanctuary Cities	N	11. Homeland Security $$	NV
4. Debt Ceiling Increase	Y	8. Armor-piercing Bullets	N	12. Trade Adjustment aid	Y

Election Results

Election	Name (Party)	Vote (%)		Cand. Spent	Ind. Exp. Support	Ind. Exp. Oppose
2016 General	John Garamendi (D)	152,519	(59%)	$790,283		
	Eugene Cleek (R)	104,456	(41%)	$374,700		
2016 Primary	John Garamendi (D)	73,000	(63%)			
	Eugene Cleek (R)	27,634	(24%)			
	Ryan Detert (R)	14,447	(13%)			

Prior winning percentages: 2014 (53%), 2012 (54%), 2010 (59%), 2009 special (53%)

John Garamendi is one of the House's most politically seasoned Democrats, with a public service career spanning more than 40 years. An active legislator, he was jolted when redistricting in 2011 moved him from a relatively secure seat to one where he might need to battle every two years to win reelection.

Garamendi was raised on his family's cattle ranch in Calaveras County. At the University of California, Berkeley, he was an All-American offensive lineman in football and a competitive wrestler. After graduating, he joined the Peace Corps in Ethiopia, where his wife, Patti, also was a volunteer. The experience launched his career in public service. After returning to California, he won his first campaign in 1974 to the state Assembly. In 1976, he was elected to the state Senate, where he eventually became majority leader. During his career, he did two stints as the state's insurance commissioner and also was President Bill Clinton's deputy secretary of the Interior. He failed twice in bids to become governor of California. In the 2006 Democratic primary for lieutenant governor, Garamendi narrowly defeated Jackie Speier. He went on to beat Republican Tom McClintock in the general election. Speier and McClintock now hold House seats from northern California. Garamendi was planning to seek an open seat for governor in 2010 when Ellen Tauscher resigned from the House in June 2009 to become President Barack Obama's undersecretary of State for arms control and international security.

In the jockeying before the all-party primary in September, state Sen. Mark DeSaulnier was an early favorite among Democrats and gained endorsements from Tauscher and Rep. George Miller, who held an adjoining district. DeSaulnier was better known locally, but Garamendi had higher name identification from his statewide campaigns, and he also was endorsed by Clinton and former Vice President Al Gore. In the September primary, Garamendi prevailed among Democrats, winning 26 percent to DeSaulnier's 18 percent. DeSaulnier, too, later was elected to the House. Because no candidate received the requisite 50 percent of the vote, Garamendi faced a runoff election against Republican attorney David Harmer. Harmer, though competitive financially, faced an uphill battle in a suburban San Francisco district that tilted Democratic. Garamendi embraced Obama's agenda while Harmer opposed the president and his bailouts of the financial and auto industries. Garamendi won 53%-43%.

In the House, Garamendi has been an ardent environmentalist. He was among the strongest critics of offshore oil drilling in the wake of the BP oil spill in the Gulf of Mexico, pressing for his proposal to bar new federal drilling leases off the coasts of California, Oregon and Washington. He has been outspoken in opposing Democratic Gov. Jerry Brown's ambitious plan to build two tunnels to pipe Sierra Nevada snowmelt to San Joaquin Valley farms and Southern California cities. He called the proposal "a boondoggle" for the benefit of wealthy farmers in the Southland and said that it "wouldn't create a drop of new water for the state and would serve only to reignite the California water wars." In early 2017, Brown was pushing for final state and federal approval.

On Transportation and Infrastructure, as the ranking minority member of the Coast Guard and Maritime Transportation Subcommittee, Garamendi has sought to enhance farm and manufacturing exports. In December 2016, he introduced a bill that would strengthen the maritime industry by requiring that up to 30 percent of strategic energy exports be shipped on U.S.-flagged vessels. He has pressed to increase penalties for physical or verbal attacks on airport security officials who are performing their job. He helped to win enactment in a broader water-resources bill of a measure to restore parts of the Lake Tahoe area. His *Almanac* vote ratings in 2015 placed him toward the center of the House in each of the three issue areas.

California's independent redistricting commission put Garamendi's residence in the newly redrawn 3rd District, where 77 percent of voters were new to him, making him ripe for a GOP challenge in 2012. He was flipped from a mostly suburban Bay Area district to a more exurban and rural district, which shifted his focus to the water needs of drought-stricken farms. In the June primary, he got 51 percent of the vote, setting up a general election with Republican Kim Vann, a Colusa County supervisor. Vann sought to broaden her appeal by refusing to sign the Republicans' no-tax pledge and by embracing popular provisions in Obama's health care legislation. She ran a strong campaign and the U.S. Chamber of Commerce spent $600,000 on her behalf. But Garamendi won with 54 percent, precisely the district's vote for Obama.

In 2014, Garamendi faced another competitive reelection and was targeted by the National Republican Congressional Committee. Garamendi won the June "all-party" primary against Assemblyman Dan Logue with 53.5 percent of the vote. In the general election, Logue opposed a minimum-wage hike and comprehensive immigration reform. Garamendi supported those two goals, plus high-speed rail for California. Both opposed Obama's handling of the war against the Islamic State. Garamendi had a fundraising advantage: $1.3 million to $800,000. The outcome was similar to the primary: Garamendi got 52.7 percent of the total vote. After Sen. Barbara Boxer announced her retirement in 2015, Garamendi said he was considering a run for her seat. But he sparked little interest. In 2016, he had an easy reelection, 59%-41%, against Republican Eugene Cleek, a physician. Even with additional state offices up for grabs in 2018, when he will be 73, Garamendi seems likely to end his career in the House.

North Central: Western Sacramento Suburbs, Solano

Population		Race and Ethnicity		Income	
Total	716,206	White	48.9%	Median Income	$56,306 (170 out of 435)
Land area	6,184	Black	5.8%		
Pop/ sq mi	115.8	Latino	28.7%		
Born in state	60.7%	Asian	10.8%	Under $50,000	30.5%
		Two races	4.3%	$50,000-$99,999	20.2%
Age Groups		Other	1.5%	$100,000-$199,999	4.7%
Under 18	24.2%			$200,000 or more	17.2%
18-34	26.2%	**Education**		Poverty Rate	17.2%
35-64	37.0%	H.S grad or less	40.5%		
Over 64	12.6%	Some college	35.5%	**Health Insurance**	
Work		College Degree, 4 yr	14.8%	With health insurance coverage	88.0%
		Post grad	9.2%		
White Collar	33.5%				
Sales and Service	42.8%	**Military**		**Public Assistance**	
Blue Collar	23.8%	Veteran	9.6%	Cash public assistance income	4.1%
Government	22.5%	Active Duty	1.2%		
				Food stamp/SNAP benefits	10.2%

Voter Turnout			
2015 Total Citizens 18+	478,008	2016 House Turnout as % CVAP	54%
2016 House turnout	256,966	2014 House Turnout as % CVAP	32%

2012 Presidential Vote		
Barack Obama	131,237	(54%)
Mitt Romney	104,145	(43%)

2016 Presidential Vote		
Hillary Clinton	138,882	(52%)
Donald Trump	105,860	(40%)
Gary Johnson	11,300	(4%)

Cook Partisan Voting Index: D+5

In California's Central Valley, north and west of Sacramento, are the farm counties of Colusa, Sutter and Yuba. Marysville, the county seat of Yuba County, sits on the east bank of the Feather River. This heavily agricultural region includes locally cultivated rice hybrids from Colusa County, the leading rice-producing county in the nation. Sutter County is the nation's largest producer of prunes and the third-largest producer of walnuts. Yuba City is the headquarters for Sunsweet Growers, which operates a large dried fruit processing facility there.

The local farm economy has suffered in recent years, however, and Colusa County has lost thousands of farm jobs with scant recovery. In November 2016, its unemployment rate of 15.5 percent was second-highest in the state, behind Imperial County. In adjacent Sutter and Yolo counties, farm-based employment dropped from 7,100 in 1997 to 4,600 in 2013. Despite its high poverty rate, new residential development in Yolo made it the fastest-growing county in the state in 2016. Passage of a state water bond in November 2016 was another step toward construction of the giant Sites Reservoir in Colusa.

That county also is the home of a large family ranch where Gov. Jerry Brown plans to retire after he is term-limited in 2018.

Solano County, which is about midway between the Bay Area and Sacramento, has been thriving economically as an exurban commuter locale and styles itself as "a place of opportunity." The Yuba City area has one of the largest Sikh populations in the United States. In 2014, a Sikh woman was elected to the city council - likely one of the first Sikh political victories in the nation. Davis is home to a branch of the University of California, with an activist faculty and student body. The campus generated $8.1 billion in economic activity and supported 72,000 jobs in 2013-14, according to a university report. In January 2017, protests of Donald Trump forced the cancellation of a speech by conservative activist Milo Yiannopoulos.

The 3rd Congressional District of California includes Republican-leaning areas like Colusa, Sutter and Yuba counties, along with a large portion of more Democratic Lake County closer to the wine country. Solano County, which includes about 40 percent of the district, is comfortably Democratic. To the west are Fairfield and Vacaville, in the outskirts of the Bay Area. Fairfield is home to Travis Air Force Base, which has more than 10,000 personnel and is home to the military's airlift and aerial refueling, including the new KC-46A tanker. Politically, the 3rd District became more competitive after the 2012 redistricting. In 2016, Hillary Clinton led in the district, 52%-40%.

FOURTH DISTRICT

Tom McClintock (R)

Elected 2008, 5th term; b. Jul 10, 1956, Bronxville, NY; University of California, Santa Barbara, B.S.; Baptist; Married (Lori McClintock); 2 children.

Elected Office: CA Assembly, 1982-1992, 1996-2000; CA Senate, 2000-2008.

Professional Career: Newspaper columnist, journalist, public policy analyst.

DC Office: 2312 RHOB 20515, 202-225-2511, Fax: 202-225-5444, mcclintock.house.gov.

State Offices: Roseville, 916-786-5560.

Committees: *Budget. Natural Resources*: Federal Lands (Chmn), Water, Power & Oceans.

Group Ratings

	ADA	ACLU	AFL-CIO	LCV	ITI	COC	HAFA	ACU	CFG	FRC
2016	-	23%	-	0%	83%	93%	84%	100%	93%	92%
2015	5%	C	0%	0%	C	58%	C	100%	97%	82%

Almanac Ratings 2015

	Economy	Social	Foreign	Composite
Liberal	5%	20%	1%	8%
Conservative	95%	80%	99%	92%

Key Votes of the 114th Congress

1. Keystone Pipeline	Y	5. Puerto Rico Debt	N	9. Offenses by Aliens	Y
2. Trade Deals	Y	6. Medical Marijuana	Y	10. Troops in Iraq	N
3. Export-Import Bank	N	7. Sanctuary Cities	Y	11. Homeland Security $$	N
4. Debt Ceiling Increase	N	8. Armor-piercing Bullets	Y	12. Trade Adjustment aid	N

Election Results

Election	Name (Party)	Vote (%)	Cand. Spent	Ind. Exp. Support	Ind. Exp. Oppose
2016 General	Tom McClintock (R)	220,133 (63%)	$835,347		
	Bob Derlet (D)	130,845 (37%)	$88,337		
2016 Primary	Tom McClintock (R)	97,204 (61%)			
	Bob Derlet (D)	44,582 (28%)			
	Sean White (D)	17,109 (11%)			

Prior winning percentages: 2014 (60%), 2012 (61%), 2010 (61%), 2008 (50%)

Republican Tom McClintock, who was first elected in 2008, is one of the California delegation's most conservative members, actively espousing his limited-government views in floor speeches, television interviews and op-ed columns. In contrast to tea party and other junior House Republicans, he has spent most of his career in public office and he often deliberately pursues a separate course from the self-styled outsiders.

McClintock spent his early childhood in White Plains, New York. After graduating from the University of California, Los Angeles, he worked briefly as a political columnist and a state Senate aide before winning a seat in the California Assembly at age 26. From his earliest days in the legislature, McClintock was perhaps its most vocal, if not the most effective, budget hawk, railing against tax increases and high spending under Democratic and Republican administrations alike. Supporters saw an eloquent champion of conservative ideas, a policy wonk with a penchant for quoting Abraham Lincoln.

McClintock tested the limits of his statewide appeal in an increasingly liberal California through a relentless effort to win higher office. He ran for state controller in 1994 and again in 2002, narrowly losing each time. In 2006, he was unsuccessful as his party's nominee for lieutenant governor, even as Republican Gov. Arnold Schwarzenegger sailed to reelection. No race elevated McClintock's profile in the state as much as his quixotic campaign for governor in the 2003 recall election. As star-struck Republicans lined up behind former actor Schwarzenegger, McClintock forged ahead, presenting himself as the true Republican. He finished with 13 percent.

Opportunity struck again for McClintock in 2008. After nine-term Republican Rep. John Doolittle announced he would step down from the 4th District seat amid a federal probe of disgraced Republican lobbyist Jack Abramoff, McClintock ran in an intense, three-month primary campaign against former Rep. Doug Ose, a Republican moderate who held the neighboring district seat from 1999 to 2005. Ose, who also lived outside the district, attacked McClintock as a career politician and carpetbagger who had represented the Thousand Oaks area in southern California during more than two decades in the Legislature. McClintock ran ads branding Ose as a liberal who had voted to raise taxes and had earmarked millions of dollars for federal projects in his district. McClintock won the primary 54%-39%.

In the general election, McClintock faced Democrat Charlie Brown, a retired Air Force officer who came within 10,000 votes of beating Doolittle in 2006. Brown, who raised his family in Roseville, renewed criticism of McClintock as an opportunist who didn't live in the district. McClintock asserted that Brown supported gay marriage but not the troops in Iraq. McClintock's expected easy victory actually took weeks to unfold. He won by precisely 1,800 votes, 50.2%-49.8%, and took six of the nine counties.

McClintock has been a faithful conservative vote, though an occasionally nettlesome one to House GOP leaders seeking to limit internal dissent. He promised to eschew spending earmarks for his district, and called for the earmarking process to be abolished instead of simply reformed. McClintock has consistently filed amendments to slash funding, even after Republicans took control of the House. He joined Democratic Rep. Jared Huffman of California in winning House passage of an amendment to strike a special-interest provision that required U.S. military bases in Europe to burn anthracite coal from Pennsylvania; the earmark had survived for more than four decades.

In January 2013, he was an outspoken foe of spending without offsets on disaster relief for individuals and local governments in New Jersey and New York that had been devastated by Hurricane Sandy three months earlier. Most Republicans agreed with him and Speaker John Boehner was forced to rely on Democrats to pass the bill. In a clash with fellow conservatives in September 2015, a few days before Boehner resigned, McClintock resigned from the House Freedom Caucus because, he wrote, its tactics of bucking the GOP "thwarted vital conservative policy objectives and unwittingly become Nancy Pelosi's tactical ally."

On the Natural Resources Committee, McClintock chaired the Water and Power Subcommittee for four years. He complained that about half of the state's water supply is consumed to meet various environmental regulations, a particular problem during the state's frequent droughts. In 2015, he became chairman of the Federal Lands Subcommittee, which has jurisdiction over many large national forests and parks that are in or near McClintock's district. The House passed his bill to speed emergency timber salvage as a tool to reduce fire hazards in the parks. In a review of his first year as Lands chairman, a liberal former reporter wrote in *The Sacramento Bee* that McClintock had enormous potential to address the many problems with the parks, but that he "chooses to waste this potential" by attacking federal bureaucrats and opening the door to more concessionaires at the parks, while preparing little legislation.

After the redistricting changes in 2011, neighboring Rep. Dan Lungren considered a challenge to McClintock, but he ran and lost in the 7th District. McClintock has not faced a serious contest from Democrats in this district. He faced an unusual election challenge in 2014, when his chief opponent was a moderate Republican who criticized McClintock as too conservative for his district. Art Moore, a West Point graduate who had spent more than two years deployed overseas and then worked on intelligence issues as a consultant, voiced the conventional outsider's pitch against gridlock and dysfunction in Washington and added that competition was good for the GOP. McClintock dismissed Moore as a Democratic front. He outspent the challenger, $1.75 million to about $200,000. Even with the endorsement of the *Sacramento Bee*, Moore underperformed. In the all-party primary, he trailed McClintock 56%-23% and barely made it to the general election ahead of a third-party contender. In November, Moore got little more than the standard opposition vote as he held McClintock to 60 percent, nearly the same vote share as in his two previous election wins.

In 2016, no Republican challenged McClintock and he breezed to reelection with his best-yet 63 percent of the vote.

East Central: Northern Sacramento Suburbs, Madera

Population		**Race and Ethnicity**		**Income**	
Total	712,747	White	77.0%	Median Income	$66,547 (82 out of 435)
Land area	12,836	Black	1.2%		
Pop/ sq mi	55.5	Latino	12.8%	Under $50,000	30.3%
Born in state	65.2%	Asian	4.6%	$50,000-$99,999	24.7%
		Two races	3.2%	$100,000-$199,999	7.0%
Age Groups		Other	1.1%	$200,000 or more	10.4%
Under 18	21.4%			Poverty Rate	10.4%
18-34	17.9%	**Education**			
35-64	42.2%	H.S grad or less	29.2%	**Health Insurance**	
Over 64	18.4%	Some college	39.1%	With health insurance coverage	90.7%
		College Degree, 4 yr	21.1%		
Work		Post grad	10.6%		
White Collar	39.9%			**Public Assistance**	
Sales and Service	44.4%	**Military**		Cash public assistance income	2.7%
Blue Collar	15.8%	Veteran	10.9%		
Government	17.5%	Active Duty	0.2%	Food stamp/SNAP benefits	6.2%

Voter Turnout			
2015 Total Citizens 18+	533,389	2016 House Turnout as % CVAP	66%
2016 House turnout	350,978	2014 House Turnout as % CVAP	40%

2012 Presidential Vote		
Mitt Romney	195,388	(58%)
Barack Obama	133,473	(40%)

2016 Presidential Vote		
Donald Trump	190,924	(53%)
Hillary Clinton	138,790	(39%)
Gary Johnson	17,650	(5%)

Cook Partisan Voting Index: R+10

California sprang into existence with the Gold Rush of 1849. Statehood and the creation of the first 27 counties followed in 1850. The new state's first boom area was the Mother Lode Country in the foothills of the Sierra Nevada above Sacramento. Mining camps the size of Eastern cities grew up almost overnight in vacant valleys locked amid steep hills, with thousands of would-be millionaires gathered to find gold. Most of those who actually got rich did so by providing goods and services that catered to miners' needs. In Placerville, John Studebaker had a buggy shop, Philip Armour ran a butcher shop, and Mark Hopkins had a dry goods store. The biggest mine in California was in Grass Valley in 1857 and was worked for half a century. But long before that, most of the Mother Lode Country emptied out, leaving ghost towns and villages with hundreds of deserted houses, an antique vacation country left behind in time.

When local residents celebrated the sesquicentennial, the area had been resurrected as a booming exurban and tourist mecca. Thousands of Californians - many of them families from smog-filled, middle-class suburbs of the Los Angeles Basin and the San Francisco Bay Area - went looking for a more pleasant, small-town, orderly environment and found it along fast-flowing creeks where the '49ers camped. Placer County, which includes Sacramento suburbs and part of the Mother Lode Country, grew 50 percent from 2000 to 2015, among the most rapid in California. It also ranks among its wealthiest counties. Near Lake Tahoe, the development of ski resorts has promoted growth in Truckee. *USA Today* described the region this way: "The American River near Coloma becomes a virtual freeway of whooping rafters on summer weekends. The Mother Lode also offers modern-day prospectors an intriguing pastiche of bed-and-breakfast inns, musty antique stores and such blink-and-you'll-miss-'em outposts as Volcano, Fiddletown, and Rough and Ready."

The 4th Congressional District of California takes in the Mother Lode counties of Mariposa and Tuolumne and a large share of Yosemite National Park. Placer County is the largest in the district. Many residents are concentrated in Sacramento suburbs like Roseville, which has grown 60 percent since 2000. In 2017, a builders' website ranked Roseville fourth nationally in its appeal to millennials. Developers plan more than 14,000 homes in Placers' Vineyards, a 5,230-acre planned community just west of Roseville, which will also include commercial centers, business parks and schools.

A swath of the district also has a large elderly population. In Amador, Calaveras, and Tuolumne counties, senior citizens make up 25 percent of the population, twice the state average. Calaveras County is perhaps best known as the setting for Mark Twain's famous short story about a jumping frog. This has been the most solidly Republican district in northern California. Calaveras gained a different kind of attention in February 2015 when the American Civil Liberties Union filed a lawsuit against the county after its Board of Supervisors approved a resolution that invited young women to "test and see for themselves the many blessings that can come from living the teachings of Christ." The following month, the board voted unanimously to repeal the resolution.

The 4th was Mitt Romney's third-best district in California, when he won 58%-40%. Donald Trump slipped a bit when he took the district, 53%-39%.

FIFTH DISTRICT

Mike Thompson (D)

Elected 1998, 10th term; b. Jan 24, 1951, St. Helena; California State University, Chico, M.A.; California State University, Chico, B.A.; Roman Catholic; Married (Janet Thompson); 2 children; 3 grandchildren.

Military Career: U.S. Army 1969-1972 (Vietnam).

Elected Office: CA Senate, 1990-1998.

Professional Career: Supervisor, Beringer Winery; CA Assembly fellow, 1982-1983; Chief of Staff, CA Assemblyman Lou Papan, 1984-1987; Chief of Staff, CA Assemblywoman Jackie Speier, 1987-1990; Owner, vineyard.

DC Office: 231 CHOB 20515, 202-225-3311, Fax: 202-225-4335, mikethompson.house.gov.

State Offices: Napa, 707-226-9898; Santa Rosa, 707-542-7182; Vallejo, 707-645-1888.

Committees: *Ways & Means*: Health, Tax Policy.

Group Ratings

	ADA	ACLU	AFL-CIO	LCV	ITI	COC	HAFA	ACU	CFG	FRC
2016	-	82%	-	100%	67%	57%	7%	0%	0%	0%
2015	85%	C	100%	91%	C	47%	C	0%	0%	0%

Almanac Ratings 2015

	Economy	Social	Foreign	Composite
Liberal	93%	93%	89%	92%
Conservative	7%	7%	11%	8%

Key Votes of the 114th Congress

1. Keystone Pipeline	N	5. Puerto Rico Debt	Y	9. Offenses by Aliens	N
2. Trade Deals	NV	6. Medical Marijuana	Y	10. Troops in Iraq	Y
3. Export-Import Bank	Y	7. Sanctuary Cities	N	11. Homeland Security $$	Y
4. Debt Ceiling Increase	Y	8. Armor-piercing Bullets	N	12. Trade Adjustment aid	Y

Election Results

Election	Name (Party)	Vote (%)	Cand. Spent	Ind. Exp. Support	Ind. Exp. Oppose
2016 General	Mike Thompson (D)	224,526 (77%)	$1,389,143		
	Carlos Satntamaria (R)	67,565 (23%)	$2,700		
2016 Primary	Mike Thompson (D)	88,322 (67%)			
	Carlos Santamaria (R)	25,453 (19%)			
	Nils Palsson (D)	15,399 (12%)			

Prior winning percentages: 2014 (76%), 2012 (75%), 2010 (63%), 2008 (68%), 2006 (66%), 2004 (67%), 2002 (64%), 2000 (65%), 1998 (62%)

Democrat Mike Thompson, first elected in 1998, has a moderate voting record that has been among the least liberal of coastal Californians. He is a trusted ally of Minority Leader Nancy Pelosi, a major fundraiser for his party and a member of the powerful Ways and Means Committee, where he watches out for the interests of the wine industry.

Thompson grew up in the Napa Valley town of St. Helena, dropped out of high school, served in the Army in Vietnam, and earned a Purple Heart. Later, he got a bachelor's and master's degree from what is now California State University, Chico. He owned a vineyard and worked as a maintenance supervisor for Beringer, a big winery in the valley. From 1984 to 1990, he was chief of staff to two Assembly members from the Bay Area. In 1990, he was elected to the state Senate, where he chaired the Budget Committee. In 1998, he ran for the House seat of Republican Frank Riggs, who planned to challenge Democratic Sen. Barbara Boxer that year. Thompson faced weak opposition and had support from almost every interest group that matters in the district: unions, medical providers, vintners, oil and timber interests, environmental advocates, law enforcement groups and fishermen. His issue stands - opposition to oil drilling off the California coast, support of abortion rights and the death penalty - were broadly popular. He won the primary 78%-22% and the general election 62%-33%.

In the House, Thompson has joined both the centrist New Democrats and the Blue Dog Coalition. He agrees with Republicans on the need to abolish the estate tax, which he said unfairly burdens family farms. He co-founded the Congressional Wine Caucus, and wineries such as Gallo and Sutter Home have been among his largest campaign contributors. His leadership political action committee, the Victory in November Election PAC (VINE PAC), has raised at least $260,000 each election cycle since 2006.

For several years, Thompson and the caucus have battled lawmakers allied with beer and alcohol wholesalers over a bill giving states new power to restrict sales over the internet. When a bipartisan group of lawmakers in 2011 introduced a bill to ensure state governments can continue to regulate alcohol under the 21st Amendment, Thompson warned the bill would allow states to pass laws effectively banning direct shipping of spirits. "The federal government has no business picking winners and losers in the wine, beer and distilled spirits industry," he said. In April 2016, he introduced with Ways and Means Republican Rep. Dave Reichert of Washington a bill to reduce the excise tax on sparkling wine to the rate charged for still wine. On another local farm issue, he filed with neighboring Democratic Rep. Jared Huffman a bill to strengthen criminal penalties for illegal marijuana farms.

On Ways and Means, he enacted a tax break for landowners who place their land under conservation easements, a way to preserve farmland. In 2007, he sponsored the Airline Passenger Bill of Rights, which requires airlines to provide basic necessities, like food, water and well-ventilated facilities when flights are delayed for long periods. Although it stalled in Congress, the Obama administration issued a rule modeled after the legislation in 2010, and it eventually was included in a 2012 bill to reauthorize the Federal Aviation Administration. In June 2016, the House passed his Small Business Health Care Relief Act to provide protections for tax benefits under health reimbursement arrangements, despite conflicts with the Affordable Care Act. The measure became part of the 21st Century Cures Act, which was enacted later that year.

He remains a reliable lieutenant for Pelosi. Following the deadly school massacre in Newtown, Connecticut, in December 2012, she named Thompson, a hunter and former chair of the Congressional Sportsmen's Caucus, to head a House Democratic task force to develop a response on gun issues. He has continued to sponsor an updated version of that proposal, which would close the internet and gun-show loopholes in existing rules and expand background checks to all gun sales. He emphasized that his legislation protected hunters and gun owners. Although the National Rifle Association has given him a D grade for his legislative record, its political action committee has not contributed to his opponents. Earlier, Pelosi tapped him to coordinate redistricting efforts for Democrats following the 2010 census.

In 2016, Thompson was reelected, 77%-23%, his highest share ever, against Republican Carlos Santamaria, a businessman from Napa County. Whenever Pelosi leaves the House, that could also signal his exit. It's unlikely that he would have nearly as close a relationship with the next Democratic leader.

Wine Country: Sonoma, Napa

Population		Race and Ethnicity		Income	
Total	720,557	White	51.1%	Median Income	$64,524 (99 out of 435)
Land area	1,731	Black	6.2%		
Pop/ sq mi	416.3	Latino	27.2%	Under $50,000	31.6%
Born in state	59.7%	Asian	10.6%	$50,000-$99,999	23.1%
		Two races	3.8%	$100,000-$199,999	6.6%
Age Groups		Other	1.1%	$200,000 or more	12.7%
Under 18	21.4%			Poverty Rate	12.7%
18-34	22.8%	**Education**			
35-64	40.6%	H.S grad or less	34.8%	**Health Insurance**	
Over 64	15.2%	Some college	35.1%	With health insurance coverage	88.0%
		College Degree, 4 yr	20.4%		
Work		Post grad	9.7%		
White Collar	34.9%			**Public Assistance**	
Sales and Service	44.3%	**Military**		Cash public assistance income	2.8%
Blue Collar	20.9%	Veteran	7.8%		
Government	14.5%	Active Duty	0.1%	Food stamp/SNAP benefits	7.9%

Voter Turnout			
2015 Total Citizens 18+	495,649	2016 House Turnout as % CVAP	59%
2016 House turnout	292,091	2014 House Turnout as % CVAP	34%

2012 Presidential Vote		
Barack Obama	199,924	(70%)
Mitt Romney	78,703	(27%)

2016 Presidential Vote		
Hillary Clinton	210,950	(68%)
Donald Trump	74,088	(24%)
Gary Johnson	11,171	(4%)
Jill Stein	7,681	(3%)

Cook Partisan Voting Index: D+21

In sunny valleys sealed off from the Coast Range, some of the nation's premium wine grapes are grown on ridges. Three decades ago, there were only 20 wineries in Napa Valley. Today, there are several hundred, with more just west of the ridges in Sonoma County. Wineries were a favorite investment for Silicon Valley millionaires until the recession caused production cutbacks and thousands of layoffs in 2008. But the vineyards continue to attract millions of visitors every year. The tourism industry in Sonoma County has had double-digit annual increases, with more marketing of the region to foreign tourists. In Napa, the emphasis has turned from the vineyards to bottling and tourism; in 2014, more than two-thirds of the grapes used for wine were from outside the county. Olive trees are also grown here. Some of California's earliest literary haunts were in the region's beautiful, lush valleys. Robert Louis Stevenson took his honeymoon near Calistoga in Napa, and Jack London owned a giant house in Sonoma that mysteriously burned down in 1913. Santa Rosa, wine country's largest city, is increasingly upscale, and laborers have become hard-pressed to find housing. All is not mellow in wine country. Solano and

Napa counties have persistently high rates of binge drinking and smoking, and Napa has had the highest obesity rate of the nine Bay Area counties, according to the UCLA Center for Health Policy Research.

Vallejo is named for a Mexican general and early member of the California Senate. From 1853 to 1996, the city was the site of the giant Mare Island Naval Shipyard, where 41,000 people worked during World War II. When the shipyard closed, Vallejo filed for bankruptcy in 2008, a dire turn of events also blamed on the huge public employee salaries and pensions the city was paying - 292 of 411 city workers earned more than $100,000 a year. Although it emerged from bankruptcy, the city retained huge pension costs. The Kaiser Permanente Medical Center in Vallejo had nearly 4,000 workers. Faraday Future, an electric car company, has plans for Vallejo as its manufacturing and delivery center. Some of the shipyard's huge dry docks remain in operation for ship repair. Despite high crime and underperforming schools, Vallejo has become a popular housing alternative to the prohibitively expensive San Francisco.

The 5th Congressional District includes all of Napa County and parts of Contra Costa, Lake, Solano and Sonoma counties. Sonoma is the population center, with about 40 percent of the district. In 2011, the state's redistricting commission aimed to unite much of California's wine-growing region. All of these areas are heavily Democratic, and the district is unlikely to be competitive any time soon. Hillary Clinton in 2016 took the district, 68%-24%. In his two presidential victories, Barack Obama got 70 percent of the vote.

SIXTH DISTRICT

Doris Matsui (D)

Elected 2005, 7th term; b. Sep 25, 1944, Poston, AZ; University of California, Berkeley, B.A., 1966; Methodist; Widow; 1 child; 2 grandchildren.

Professional Career: Transition team, President-elect Bill Clinton, 1992-1993; Deputy Assistant to the President, deputy Director of public liaison, White House, 1993-1998; Lobbyist, 1998-2005.

DC Office: 2311 RHOB 20515, 202-225-7163, Fax: 202-225-0566, matsui.house.gov.

State Offices: Sacramento, 916-498-5600.

Committees: *Energy & Commerce*: Communications & Technology, Digital Commerce & Consumer Protection, Environment, Health.

Group Ratings

	ADA	ACLU	AFL-CIO	LCV	ITI	COC	HAFA	ACU	CFG	FRC
2016	-	100%	-	97%	67%	69%	10%	0%	4%	0%
2015	100%	C	100%	97%	C	40%	C	0%	0%	0%

Almanac Ratings 2015

	Economy	Social	Foreign	Composite
Liberal	98%	100%	93%	97%
Conservative	2%	0%	7%	3%

Key Votes of the 114th Congress

1. Keystone Pipeline	N	5. Puerto Rico Debt	Y	9. Offenses by Aliens	N
2. Trade Deals	N	6. Medical Marijuana	Y	10. Troops in Iraq	Y
3. Export-Import Bank	Y	7. Sanctuary Cities	N	11. Homeland Security $$	Y
4. Debt Ceiling Increase	Y	8. Armor-piercing Bullets	N	12. Trade Adjustment aid	Y

Election Results

Election	Name (Party)	Vote (%)		Cand. Spent	Ind. Exp. Support	Ind. Exp. Oppose
2016 General	Doris Matsui (D)	177,565	(75%)	$830,896		
	Bob Evans (R)	57,848	(25%)	$2,805		
2016 Primary	Doris Matsui (D)	61,518	(71%)			
	Robert Evans (R)	16,166	(19%)			
	Jrmar Jefferson (D)	4,393	(5%)			

Prior winning percentages: 2014 (73%), 2012 (75%), 2010 (72%), 2008 (74%), 2006 (71%), 2005 special (68%)

Democrat Doris Matsui won a special election in 2005 to replace her late husband, Robert Matsui, a long-time member of the Ways and Means Committee. She lacks his flair in attracting attention, but may have matched him as a legislator with a choice seat on the Energy and Commerce panel, where she has had an impact on health and communications policy.

Matsui, who was born in a Japanese internment camp in Arizona, was a well-known political figure during her husband's career in Congress. She grew up in Dinuba in Fresno County and graduated from the University of California, Berkeley. In Sacramento, she chaired the board of the local public television station and participated in many civic organizations. After working on Bill Clinton's presidential campaign, she joined his transition team and then served as deputy director of public liaison, where she worked on economic and budget issues. When she left the White House in 1998, she became a senior adviser at a Washington law firm.

Robert Matsui died of complications from a rare blood disorder in January 2005, after serving 13 terms. A few days after his memorial services, Doris Matsui announced that she would run in the special election. With urging from House Minority Leader Nancy Pelosi, other prominent Sacramento Democrats decided not to run. None of Matsui's 10 opponents in the nonpartisan contest had significant political experience or name recognition. She emphasized her support for local water projects and her opposition to President George W. Bush's proposal for personal retirement accounts in Social Security. She also opposed the war in Iraq. Her investment in a partnership with a longtime friend who was a Sacramento land developer sparked a brief flurry of criticism, but she emphasized that her husband had nothing to do with the deal while he was in office and that there was no conflict of interest. Some called the contest a "coronation," but the lack of competition surely reflected the respect the Matsuis had won over the years. She won the all-party primary with 68 percent of the vote to 9 percent for the runner-up. Since then, she has not faced a competitive major-party challenger for reelection.

With her seat on Energy and Commerce, she has taken the initiative on telecommunications and consumer issues. In January 2015, she filed a bill that would ban companies from charging more for faster internet access. The following month, she praised the decision by the Federal Communications Commission to approve a comparable approach with its "net neutrality" rules. She has filed legislation to remove roadblocks to health care technology. In December 2016, Congress enacted legislation that she filed with Republican Rep. Mike Burgess of Texas: the Expanding Capacity for Health Outcomes (ECHO) Act, which was designed to use technology to provide expertise in community health centers and among other providers in underserved areas.

When Congress in 2014 reauthorized the Coast Guard, it included a provision by Matsui to update crime data on passenger cruise ships, with more accessible information on their web sites. That strengthened a comparable law that she enacted in 2010. She joined Republican Rep. Randy Hultgren of Illinois in 2012 in lobbying conference committee members on the transportation reauthorization bill to strip out a provision, sought by Pennsylvania Democratic Sen. Bob Casey, that lowered the diesel/electric standard for new high-speed rail locomotives from 125 mph to 110 mph. They said the provision would make such trains less energy-efficient, and it was removed. In response to recent derailments, she urged federal regulators in 2015 to implement stronger safety rules for trains carrying oil. In 2015-16 Matsui co-chaired, with Republican Rep. Kristi Noem of South Dakota, the Congressional Caucus on Women's Issues, where she helped to enact the Human Trafficking Prevention, Intervention, and Recovery Act of 2015.

Matsui sometimes invokes her family's experience in internment camps to warn of potential civil liberties abuses in the war on terrorism. When President Barack Obama in 2013 issued an executive order aimed at improving cybersecurity, she praised the decision to consider the implications for privacy. Following the November 2016 election of Donald Trump, she criticized his call for restrictions on immigration from Muslim-majority countries. "Casting a shadow on everyone, not just individuals doing these bad things, is not the American way," she told *The Sacramento Bee*. "We are a nation of immigrants inviting people from all over the world. And that is our greatness, that's why we have so much culture, art, innovation and creativity."

Sacramento

Population		Race and Ethnicity		Income	
Total	725,594	White	37.8%	Median Income	$47,433 (295 out of 435)
Land area	175	Black	12.1%		
Pop/ sq mi	4145.3	Latino	27.8%		
Born in state	59.5%	Asian	15.3%	Under $50,000	29.1%
		Two races	4.9%	$50,000-$99,999	16.0%
Age Groups		Other	2.1%	$100,000-$199,999	2.9%
Under 18	24.9%			$200,000 or more	22.9%
18-34	27.5%	**Education**		Poverty Rate	22.9%
35-64	36.3%	H.S grad or less	39.7%		
Over 64	11.3%	Some college	34.0%	**Health Insurance**	
		College Degree, 4 yr	17.2%	With health insurance coverage	85.9%
Work		Post grad	9.0%		
White Collar	34.8%				
Sales and Service	47.4%	**Military**		**Public Assistance**	
Blue Collar	17.8%	Veteran	6.9%	Cash public assistance income	6.9%
Government	22.0%	Active Duty	0.1%		
				Food stamp/SNAP benefits	15.7%

Voter Turnout			
2015 Total Citizens 18+	471,099	2016 House Turnout as % CVAP	50%
2016 House turnout	235,413	2014 House Turnout as % CVAP	28%

2012 Presidential Vote		
Barack Obama	156,141	(69%)
Mitt Romney	63,862	(28%)

2016 Presidential Vote		
Hillary Clinton	168,687	(68%)
Donald Trump	59,549	(24%)
Gary Johnson	9,354	(4%)
Jill Stein	4,975	(2%)

Cook Partisan Voting Index: D+21

Sacramento, capital of the nation's most populous state and with its 43-mile light-rail system, is no longer just a small city with a lot of civil servants and a vegetable-packing economy. It is a vibrant metropolis that has struggled recently along with the rest of the Golden State. Sacramento started as a port on the sluggish waters of the Sacramento and American rivers. It was the destination of many overland migrants, the site of Sutter's Fort, where workers for John Augustus Sutter found the gold that set off the Gold Rush of 1848, and the western terminus of the Pony Express in 1860. This was the natural choice at the time to be California's capital, halfway between San Francisco Bay and the Mother Lode Country in the foothills of the Sierras, and in the middle of California's vast valley. It has the corporate home of the world's largest almond processing plant, and agriculture continues to be important in Sacratomato, or Sacto, as some locals call it. Former NBA star Kevin Johnson, its first African-American mayor and later the president of the U.S. Conference of Mayors, served eight years before stepping down in 2016. He was replaced by Darrell Steinberg, former president of the state Senate. Efforts to strengthen the authority of the mayor and weaken the city manager, who has been the executive officer, have been defeated. Even with the recent drought, the confluence of the two rivers has made the area a major flood hazard and more than $2 billion has been spent on levees and other steps to reduce risk.

In the old days, government was not a big business. Just a few lobbyists hung out in saloons on K or J streets, the governor's mansion was a musty antique, and the summers' 100-plus degree days emptied out what there was of the city. Air conditioning long ago replaced awnings, and freeways and shopping malls have followed the city's growth east and north toward the Sierra foothills. Platoons of lobbyists, lawyers and consultants set up permanent shop, and new hotels have been built to serve them. Today, more than 1,750 registered lobbyists prowl the halls of the capitol, transforming the once working-class bastion. In 2015, its 2.7 million people - an increase from about 800,000 in 1980 -- were about the same as metro Portland or San Antonio. The middle class in the area dropped below 50 percent, according to a 2014 study by the Pew Research Center, with increases in both the poor and the rich.

Most of the growth has been outside the city. Technology firms have moved east from Silicon Valley into the metro area, with Intel and Hewlett-Packard maintaining large campuses. Bay Area refugees have welcomed less expensive living standards. The growth has continued in recent years, but was temporarily slowed by housing shortages and the recession. The future of the city's NBA franchise, the Kings, had been in jeopardy, with threats that it might move to Seattle. But a deal was reached for new ownership and a new high-tech sports arena that opened in October 2016, with solar panels on its roof.

The 6th Congressional District of California consists of the city of Sacramento, West Sacramento in Yolo County and parts of Sacramento County. The majority-minority district contains affluent neighborhoods and scattered low-income Latino and black neighborhoods, plus new condominiums north of the American River and middle-class subdivisions south of downtown. Its ethnically diverse communities include, among others, Hmong refugees from Laos, Vietnamese, Russians and Ukrainians. In contrast to the 7th District, which is a politically mixed area, this is the solidly Democratic part of greater Sacramento.

SEVENTH DISTRICT

Ami Bera (D)

Elected 2012, 3rd term; b. Mar 02, 1965, Los Angeles; University of California, Irvine, B.S.; University of California, Irvine, M.D.; Unitarian; Married (Janine Bera); 1 child.

Professional Career: Professor, University of CA Davis, 2004-2012, Association dean, 2004-2008; Chief med. officer, Sacramento County Department of Health & Human Services, 1999-2004; Med. Director, Mercy Healthcare Sacramento, 1998-1999; MedClinic Med. Group, physician, 1999, Assistant med. Director, 1997-1998, chief of internal med. Department, 1996-1997.

DC Office: 1431 LHOB 20515, 202-225-5716, Fax: 202-226-1298, bera.house.gov.

State Offices: Sacramento, 916-635-0505.

Committees: *Foreign Affairs*: Africa, Global Health, Global Human Rights & Internat'l Orgs, Asia & the Pacific. *Science, Space & Technology*: Research & Technology, Space (RMM).

Group Ratings

	ADA	ACLU	AFL-CIO	LCV	ITI	COC	HAFA	ACU	CFG	FRC
2016	-	76%	-	97%	100%	64%	9%	4%	4%	0%
2015	55%	C	79%	86%	C	65%	C	8%	0%	0%

Almanac Ratings 2015

	Economy	Social	Foreign	Composite
Liberal	57%	87%	50%	65%
Conservative	43%	13%	50%	35%

Key Votes of the 114th Congress

1. Keystone Pipeline	N	5. Puerto Rico Debt	Y	9. Offenses by Aliens	Y
2. Trade Deals	Y	6. Medical Marijuana	Y	10. Troops in Iraq	N
3. Export-Import Bank	Y	7. Sanctuary Cities	N	11. Homeland Security $$	Y
4. Debt Ceiling Increase	Y	8. Armor-piercing Bullets	N	12. Trade Adjustment aid	Y

Election Results

Election	Name (Party)	Vote (%)	Cand. Spent	Ind. Exp. Support	Ind. Exp. Oppose
2016 General	Ami Bera (D)	152,133 (51%)	$3,824,308	$689,719	$4,690,863
	Scott Jones (R)	145,168 (49%)	$1,344,931	$1,362,250	$4,196,393
2016 Primary	Ami Bera (D)	93,506 (54%)			
	Scott Jones (R)	79,640 (46%)			

Prior winning percentages: 2014 (50%), 2012 (52%)

Democrat Ami Bera has had four consecutive tight elections, losing the first and winning the next three against a current and former House Republican member plus the local sheriff. Despite some votes in the House to separate himself from the Democratic mainstream, he seems likely to remain in the Republican Party's crosshairs.

Bera was born in Hollywood, the son of parents who emigrated from India to the United States in the 1950s to attend college. His mother studied education and became a public elementary school teacher; his father paid for his engineering degree by ushering at Los Angeles Dodgers baseball games. The younger Bera said he grew up believing that he lived in a land of opportunity where "if you worked hard and played by the rules, you could reach your full potential." Bera excelled in science and math, and went to the University of California, Irvine, to study biology and then earn his medical degree. As a second-year medical student, he met his future wife, Janine, then an undergraduate and now also a physician.

After several years practicing internal medicine, Bera became the medical director of care management for Mercy Healthcare Sacramento. There, he discovered the inefficiency within the health care sector and set about identifying and implementing "simple solutions" to reduce waste. In one project, his unit reviewed 911 calls that weren't actually emergencies and found that most originated from a small group of widows and widowers. By reaching out to that group, the unit dramatically reduced unnecessary calls. He became the county's chief medical officer and realized that the county was unprepared to meet the demands of its uninsured population, which became a top priority for Bera. He said that the Affordable Care Act "is not the direction I would have gone," but believes that the law offers a solid starting point to bring down spiraling medical costs.

In 2010, Bera challenged eight-term Republican Rep. Dan Lungren, who had a close election in 2008. Bera showed impressive strength as a fundraiser, drawing on donations from Indian Americans across the country. He accused Lungren of being out of touch with district voters, while the incumbent portrayed him as a rubber stamp for then-House Speaker Nancy Pelosi's liberal agenda. A late-breaking wave of nearly $700,000 in ads from GOP strategist Karl Rove's American Crossroads organization helped seal Lungren's win. Bera began almost immediately to make a second run. In 2012, he challenged Lungren in the post-redistricting 7th District, which was three percentage points more Democratic than Lungren's old district. Bera benefited from a *Sacramento Bee* endorsement that said "Bera has matured, and Lungren has failed to meet local expectations." He won, 52%-48%.

Bera has been one of the California delegation's most moderate and politically attuned members. In 2014, he was one of four California Democrats from competitive districts who voted against funding for the California high-speed rail project. And he backed an unsuccessful version of the farm bill that cut $20 billion from the federal food stamp program, an amount that many of his fellow Democrats abhorred. He described the vote as a signal of his willingness to compromise. With Republican Rep. Phil Roe of Tennessee, another physician, he filed a bill to fund disposal of old or unused prescription drugs, which the House overwhelmingly approved.

Bera was one of 28 House Democrats who voted in June 2015 for presidential authority to make international trade deals, which caused heartburn for many Democrats. Angry leaders of organized labor targeted Bera and said they would not back him for reelection, to which he responded that he would not succumb to "bullying" tactics or "special-interest" groups. Bera sought opportunities to collaborate with House Republicans. In 2017, he became co-chairman with Republican Rep. Tom Reed of New York of the new bipartisan Problem Solver Caucus, which he described as "a great way to get members from both sides of the aisle to focus on areas where we agree and can make progress." In the *Almanac* vote ratings for 2015, Bera was among the least liberal Democrats in each of the three issue groups.

On the Foreign Affairs Committee, Bera worked to improve ties between India and Afghanistan and spent a week in his parents' home region to encourage students there to attend California colleges. As one of four congressional Democrats who accompanied President Barack Obama to India, he praised the civilian nuclear agreement that was reached with Prime Minister Narenda Modi. Bera regularly spoke out against the Obama administration's contemplation of military action against Syria, preferring to let diplomacy work. He extended his opposition when he was one of 47 House Democrats who voted against aid for resettlement of Syrian refugees. Despite that independence, Bera became vice-ranking member of the Foreign Affairs panel in 2017. He responded, "I'm energized to continue advancing the role America plays in ensuring stability and security in an increasingly complex global landscape."

Bera remained a top GOP campaign target. In 2014, he faced former Rep. Doug Ose, who served six years before abiding by his term-limits pledge to retire in 2004. This became the most expensive House campaign in the 2014 cycle. National Republican groups poured more than $6 million into the general election on Ose's behalf, while Democrats spent more than $5 million for Bera. Ose spent $5.1 million from his own campaign treasury, compared with $4.3 million for Bera. The Democrat released an ad showing him with patients and touting his decision to forego his salary during the 2013 government shutdown. In a contest that took several days to resolve, he eked out a win over Ose, 50.4%-49.6%.

The 2016 contest was nearly as close. Unions remained unhappy with Bera's support for Obama's Trans-Pacific Partnership trade deal, but they failed to find a primary challenger. Local Democrats gave him a belated endorsement after he was the only Democrat on the ballot. Minority Leader Nancy Pelosi called him "a valued member of the Congress [with] a great base of support at the grassroots level." Republicans cleared the field for Sacramento County Sheriff Scott Jones, who was attacked by Democrats over decade-old allegations that he sexually harassed a young woman who was a deputy sheriff, which he denied. Bera faced his own ethical problems after his 83-year-old father in May 2016 pleaded guilty to election fraud in the financing of his son's first two campaigns for the House and was sentenced to a year in prison. Bera said that his father made "a grave mistake" and prosecutors said they had no evidence that he knew of his father's actions, but Jones and other Republicans challenged those assertions. The campaign was nearly as expensive as Bera's contest in 2014. Bera out-raised Jones, $4.3 million to $1.3 million, but Republicans had the advantage in party support, roughly $5 million to $4 million. Jones conceded 10 days following Election Day, after late-counted votes gave Bera a 51.2%-48.8% win.

Eastern Sacramento Suburbs

Population		**Race and Ethnicity**		**Income**	
Total	729,192	White	55.1%	Median Income	$65,159 (93 out of 435)
Land area	549	Black	7.1%		
Pop/ sq mi	1329.1	Latino	16.7%	Under $50,000	31.7%
Born in state	60.5%	Asian	14.7%	$50,000-$99,999	24.2%
Age Groups		Two races	4.8%	$100,000-$199,999	5.8%
Under 18	24.3%	Other	1.6%	$200,000 or more	13.5%
18-34	22.1%	**Education**		Poverty Rate	13.5%
35-64	40.2%	H.S grad or less	31.0%	**Health Insurance**	
Over 64	13.4%	Some college	36.8%	With health insurance coverage	89.9%
Work		College Degree, 4 yr	21.4%		
White Collar	41.2%	Post grad	10.7%	**Public Assistance**	
Sales and Service	43.5%	**Military**		Cash public assistance income	4.5%
Blue Collar	15.3%	Veteran	9.1%		
Government	22.0%	Active Duty	0.1%	Food stamp/SNAP benefits	9.0%

Voter Turnout			
2015 Total Citizens 18+	506,320	2016 House Turnout as % CVAP	59%
2016 House turnout	297,301	2014 House Turnout as % CVAP	37%

2012 Presidential Vote		
Barack Obama	145,147	(51%)
Mitt Romney	133,888	(47%)

2016 Presidential Vote		
Hillary Clinton	159,066	(52%)
Donald Trump	124,249	(40%)
Gary Johnson	14,747	(5%)

Cook Partisan Voting Index: D+3

Until recently, Sacramento was chiefly the metropolis of a fertile valley that produced a marvelous variety of crops: rice, plums, almonds, olives, asparagus, pears, hops, beans, celery, onions and potatoes, plus caviar-yielding sturgeon in pools of filtered water. The farmlands remain, and the capital city flourishes as a center of government. Until the recession struck in 2007, greater Sacramento was one of the fastest-growing metro areas in the country. Almost all of the growth was away from the floodplain of the Sacramento River, in the higher land east of the city that eventually turns into hills rising toward the Sierra Nevada. Home sales plunged and foreclosures soared in 2007, which led to service cutbacks in Sacramento County. The county's housing market rebounded, with a 10 percent increase in both sales and prices in 2014; two years later, the sales increase was only 2 percent but prices climbed by 11 percent. In Rancho Cordova, which won an All-America City award in 2010, local leaders created a New Urbanist development plan to replace aging strip malls with a traditional downtown. Voters there in November 2014 approved a half-percentage point increase in the sales tax to improve services and infrastructure. After some hesitation, city officials decided to spend the money to finance projects in its community enhancement fund.

The 7th Congressional District of California includes suburban Sacramento and much of Sacramento County outside the neighboring and mostly urban 6th District. All of its residents are in Sacramento County, in suburbs like Arden-Arcade and Carmichael. There is also the old town of Folsom, where the Intel campus has downsized from 6,300 to about 5,800 employees in 2016. With $146,000 average pay for engineers, the prosperous company town has moved beyond the image singer Johnny Cash created in his song, "Folsom Prison Blues." A WalletHub survey in 2016 found that Folsom was the best place in California to raise a family. Intel calls the research lab its "nerve center," where engineers develop its core intellectual property. The company's chips once dominated the market, but the decline in the share of personal computers and laptops in the world led Intel to shift some of its production to semiconductors. The city of Sacramento historically has been Democratic. But Sacramento County, with its rapid growth, was marginal in the early 2000s. In the 2004 presidential race, Democrat John Kerry won the county over George W. Bush by just 1,118 votes. By 2016, the Democratic advantage had grown to 59%-35% for Hillary Clinton. With the more conservative parts of the county in the 7th, Clinton took the District, 52%-40%.

EIGHTH DISTRICT

Paul Cook (R)

Elected 2012, 3rd term; b. Mar 03, 1943, Meriden, CT; Southern Connecticut State University, B.S., 1966; California State University, San Bernardino, M.P.A., 1996; University of California, Riverside, M.A., 2000; Roman Catholic; Married (Jeannie Cook); 2 children.

Military Career: U.S. Marine Corps, Colonel, 1966-1992 (Vietnam).

Elected Office: CA Assembly, 2006-2012; Yucca Valley Town Council, Yucca Valley Mayor, 1998-2006.

Professional Career: Professor, U of CA Riverside, 2002-2012; Assistant Professional, Copper Mountain College, 1998-2002; Executive Director, Yucca Valley Chamber of Commerce, 1993-1994.

DC Office: 1222 LHOB 20515, 202-225-5861, Fax: 202-225-6498, cook.house.gov.

State Offices: Apple Valley, 760-247-1815; Yucaipa, 909-797-4900.

Committees: *Armed Services*: Seapower & Projection Forces, Tactical Air & Land Forces. *Foreign Affairs*: Middle East & North Africa, Terrorism, Nonproliferation & Trade. *Natural Resources*: Energy & Mineral Resources, Indian, Insular & Alaska Native Affairs.

Group Ratings

	ADA	ACLU	AFL-CIO	LCV	ITI	COC	HAFA	ACU	CFG	FRC
2016	-	5%	-	3%	100%	100%	51%	72%	59%	100%
2015	5%	C	42%	3%	C	90%	C	71%	54%	91%

Almanac Ratings 2015

	Economy	Social	Foreign	Composite
Liberal	18%	0%	0%	6%
Conservative	83%	100%	100%	94%

Key Votes of the 114th Congress

1. Keystone Pipeline	Y	5. Puerto Rico Debt	N	9. Offenses by Aliens	Y
2. Trade Deals	N	6. Medical Marijuana	N	10. Troops in Iraq	N
3. Export-Import Bank	N	7. Sanctuary Cities	Y	11. Homeland Security $$	N
4. Debt Ceiling Increase	Y	8. Armor-piercing Bullets	Y	12. Trade Adjustment aid	N

Election Results

Election	Name (Party)	Vote (%)	Cand. Spent	Ind. Exp. Support	Ind. Exp. Oppose
2016 General	Paul Cook (R)	136,972 (62%)	$887,732	$329,242	
	Rita Ramirez (D)	83,035 (38%)	$30,417	$22,642	
2016 Primary	Paul Cook (R)	38,740 (43%)			
	Rita Ramirez (D)	19,124 (21%)			
	Tim Donnelly (R)	18,039 (20%)			
	John Pinkerton (D)	8,522 (10%)			
	Roger LaPlante (D)	4,925 (6%)			

Prior winning percentages: 2014 (68%), 2012 (57%)

Republican Paul Cook, a 26-year Marine Corps veteran and Vietnam-era war hero, won this seat in 2012 at the age of 69. He became a diligent and policy-focused lawmaker, and one of the least publicity-minded among GOP newcomers. His military and community backgrounds make him a throwback to an era when many Republicans styled themselves as representative of Main Street and were reliable supporters of party leaders.

Cook grew up and attended school in Meriden, Connecticut. He studied education at Southern Connecticut State University and joined the Marines after graduating. His first assignment sent him to Vietnam, where he served as an infantry officer and platoon commander. During the war, he received the Bronze Star and two Purple Heart citations. He returned to the United States in 1968, eventually earning a promotion to captain while training infantry in North Carolina. He rose through the ranks and, as a colonel, became the area commander for the Marine base at Camp Pendleton in California.

After he retired from the military in 1992, Cook moved to Yucca Valley and was executive director of the local Chamber of Commerce before heading back to school to earn degrees in public administration and political science. He taught political science and history at several California universities before earning tenure at Copper Mountain College, which has a close relationship with the local Marine base. Cook told *National Journal*, "When I retired from active duty, I still felt that I owed something to my community. That's why I pursued education. ... I still miss the classroom and recall those days fondly."

Cook won a seat on the Yucca Valley Town Council and ultimately served as the town's mayor. In 2006, Cook ran for the state Assembly and won the seat against better-known candidates. As chairman of the Assembly's Veterans Affairs Committee (while serving in the minority party), he worked on issues related to retirement homes, child custody, higher education and other services for veterans. He also worked to protect children from sexual predators, a legislative accomplishment of which he said he is particularly proud.

In his race for Congress, Cook enjoyed the support of a host of California Republicans, including former Gov. Pete Wilson. He was endorsed by the U.S. Chamber of Commerce and California Taxpayers Association. In a crowded field of 13 candidates, Cook trailed a newcomer tea party candidate, Gregg Imus, in the primary by just 237 votes; he was 240 votes ahead of third-place finisher Phil Liberatore, who also was a Republican. Cook picked up momentum in the general-election campaign, outraising Imus more than 5-to-1. He ran on promises not to raise taxes and to fight for veterans and military families, while distancing himself from Democrats. "Military and veterans seem to be a low priority with [the Obama] administration, but I won't let Washington replicate the past, where they forgot about veterans returning from Vietnam," he said. Under California's top-two, all-party primary system, Cook defeated his fellow Republican, 57%-43%.

With his natural base on the Armed Services Committee, he has focused on national security and has mostly been a Pentagon loyalist. Cook filed a bill to permit continued pay checks to Pentagon employees furloughed during a government shutdown. In 2014, he wrote in a column in the *San Bernardino Sun* that the Obama administration had "faltered in our commitment to Iraq," and he called for military action against the Islamic State in Iraq and Syria by arming proxy groups, but not with U.S. troops. On the Resources Committee, he won House passage in 2016 of his bill to establish the Alabama Hill National Scenic Area on the eastern slope of the Sierra Nevada in Inyo County. Though he has not served on the Veterans Affairs Committee, Cook also won House passage that year of his HIRE Vets bill, which provides incentives for the private-sector hiring of military vets. A separate veterans bill was enacted that included his provision to authorize independent analysis of the effectiveness of the Labor Department's veterans training programs. In the *Almanac* vote ratings for 2015, Cook was firmly conservative on social and foreign issues, but a centrist on the economy.

He organized the Semper Fi leadership PAC, which raised nearly $80,000 during each of his cycles in the House. Cook has twice breezed to reelection against weakly funded Democrats. In the 2016 primary, Cook got 42 percent of the vote. Tea party candidate Tim Donnelly got 21 percent, only 1,439 votes behind Democrat Rita Ramirez in California's "top two" runoff system. Cook appears to be entrenched in his seat, at least until the next redistricting.

High Desert: San Bernardino County

Population		**Race and Ethnicity**		**Income**	
Total	712,224	White	47.6%	Median Income	$46,927 (308 out of 435)
Land area	32,867	Black	7.6%		
Pop/ sq mi	21.7	Latino	38.3%		
Born in state	64.7%	Asian	2.8%	Under $50,000	30.2%
		Two races	2.3%	$50,000-$99,999	15.1%
Age Groups		Other	1.4%	$100,000-$199,999	2.3%
Under 18	27.7%			$200,000 or more	21.8%
18-34	23.5%	**Education**		Poverty Rate	21.8%
35-64	36.4%	H.S grad or less	46.6%		
Over 64	12.4%	Some college	37.6%	**Health Insurance**	
		College Degree, 4 yr	9.6%	With health insurance coverage	85.7%
Work		Post grad	6.1%		
White Collar	28.3%				
Sales and Service	45.5%	**Military**		**Public Assistance**	
Blue Collar	26.2%	Veteran	9.8%	Cash public assistance income	6.5%
Government	21.0%	Active Duty	2.0%		
				Food stamp/SNAP benefits	16.9%

Voter Turnout			
2015 Total Citizens 18+	469,449	2016 House Turnout as % CVAP	47%
2016 House turnout	220,007	2014 House Turnout as % CVAP	24%

2012 Presidential Vote		
Mitt Romney	118,278	(56%)
Barack Obama	88,579	(42%)

2016 Presidential Vote		
Donald Trump	127,471	(54%)
Hillary Clinton	92,238	(39%)
Gary Johnson	8,210	(4%)

Cook Partisan Voting Index: R+9

The eastern High Desert of California runs along the Nevada border, with a huge swath of land uninhabited for dozens of miles. In the west are the towns of Apple Valley and Victorville, a high-growth area that was once home to cowboy stars Roy Rogers and Dale Evans. Other San Bernardino County cities and towns dot the landscape: the heavily Hispanic city of Adelanto; Hesperia, a wayside on the Mormon Trail; and Needles, where the fictional Joad family stops soon after entering California in *The Grapes of Wrath*. To the north, off Interstate 15 heading to Las Vegas, are Barstow and the military training center at Fort Irwin. A fork splits Interstates 15 and 40, and both highways straddle the outskirts of the Mojave National Preserve before moving into Nevada. The Inland Empire struggled to climb out of the recession and the high unemployment rate, which peaked at 14.8 percent in mid-2010. Finally, the rate in San Bernardino County dropped to 5 percent in December 2016, which was below the state rate and nearly as low as the national average. A plan for renewable energy projects in the desert has generated opposition from several counties, including San Bernardino, which has been partly based on the impact on private lands. Proponents welcome the broad vision for land use in the plan, which would cover 22 million acres. San Bernardino has the most land of any county in the nation, but more than 80 percent of it is publicly owned.

The 8th Congressional District of California covers Mono and Inyo counties, as well as the rural parts of San Bernardino County; more than 90 percent of the population is in San Bernardino. The 8th does not include the city of San Bernardino, which accounts for only 10 percent of the county's 2.1 million population. The remainder of the county is part of four other districts to the south and west, three of which are majority-minority seats held by Democrats. Its geography is vast. It sweeps in the sleepy Mojave Desert and mountains, Death Valley (where the International Dark-Sky Association laments the visibility of lights from Las Vegas), and Owens Valley, the source of Los Angeles' water supply and the site of the California "Water Wars" that became the inspiration for the movie *Chinatown;* the conflict finally was resolved in 2014 when the county agreed on a new method to suppress the dust from the dry bed of Owens Lake. In 2016, Death Valley National Park had more than 1.3 million visitors, its most ever. The district includes Mammoth Lakes and the Mammoth ski resort area in the Inyo National Forest, where more than 40 feet of snow fell during the winter of 2016-17. Despite pockets of Democratic support - the scant population in Mono County voted for Hillary Clinton in the 2016 presidential race - this is strong Republican territory. Donald Trump won the district, 54%-39%, virtually the same partisan outcome as in the previous two presidential elections.

NINTH DISTRICT

Jerry McNerney (D)

Elected 2006, 6th term; b. Jun 18, 1951, Albuquerque, NM; U.S. Military Academy (NY), Att.; University of New Mexico, B.S.; University of New Mexico, M.S.; University of New Mexico, Ph.D.; St. Joseph's Military Academy (KS); Roman Catholic; Married (Mary McNerney); 3 children.

Professional Career: National security contractor, Sandia National Labs., 1979-1985; Engineer, U.S. Windpower Kenetech, 1985-1994; Energy consultant, 1994-1999; CEO, start-up wind turbine manufacturer, 2000-2006.

DC Office: 2265 RHOB 20515, 202-225-1947, Fax: 202-225-4060, mcnerney.house.gov.

State Offices: Antioch, 925-754-0716; Stockton, 209-476-8552.

Committees: *Energy & Commerce*: Communications & Technology, Energy, Environment. *Science, Space & Technology*: Energy, Oversight.

Group Ratings

	ADA	ACLU	AFL-CIO	LCV	ITI	COC	HAFA	ACU	CFG	FRC
2016	-	100%	-	100%	67%	50%	12%	4%	0%	0%
2015	90%	C	100%	100%	C	55%	C	0%	0%	0%

Almanac Ratings 2015

	Economy	Social	Foreign	Composite
Liberal	88%	100%	86%	91%
Conservative	12%	0%	14%	9%

Key Votes of the 114th Congress

1. Keystone Pipeline	N	5. Puerto Rico Debt	Y	9. Offenses by Aliens	N
2. Trade Deals	N	6. Medical Marijuana	Y	10. Troops in Iraq	Y
3. Export-Import Bank	Y	7. Sanctuary Cities	N	11. Homeland Security $$	Y
4. Debt Ceiling Increase	Y	8. Armor-piercing Bullets	N	12. Trade Adjustment aid	Y

Election Results

Election	Name (Party)	Vote (%)		Cand. Spent	Ind. Exp. Support	Ind. Exp. Oppose
2016 General	Jerry McNerney (D)	133,163	(57%)	$1,135,566		
	Tony Amador (R)	98,992	(43%)	$57,110		
2016 Primary	Jerry McNerney (D)	45,571	(55%)			
	Antonio Amador (R)	18,017	(22%)			
	Kathryn Nance (R)	15,785	(19%)			

Prior winning percentages: 2014 (52%), 2012 (56%), 2010 (48%), 2008 (55%), 2006 (53%)

Democrat Jerry McNerney has been one of the most politically vulnerable members of his party: In six elections since 2007, he has never won more than 57 percent of the vote. Though he is more moderate than most California Democrats, he has usually been a party loyalist and behind-the-scenes operator, and an ally of Minority Leader Nancy Pelosi.

McNerney's father was a union organizer in the 1930s and later worked for the U.S. Geological Survey in Albuquerque, where Jerry McNerney was born. Along with his twin brother, he was sent to a military boarding school in Hays, Kansas, and later won an appointment to the U.S. Military Academy. He left West Point after two years in the late 1960s because he opposed the war in Vietnam. He transferred to the University of New Mexico, where he earned his bachelor's degree and a doctorate in differential geometry. He spent several years as a contractor for Sandia National Laboratories, working on national security programs. In 1985, he moved to the private sector with U.S. Windpower and later was chief executive of a wind turbine firm. McNerney, who named his daughter Windy, claimed that his work contributed to keeping 8.3 million tons of carbon dioxide out of the atmosphere.

In 2006, McNerney was an unlikely winner against Republican Rep. Richard Pombo, a local rancher in an area that was dubbed "Pombo Country." As chairman of the House Resources Committee, Pombo was leader of the property-rights movement backed by ranchers and farmers. In the primary, the Democratic Congressional Campaign Committee endorsed Steve Filson, an airline pilot and political neophyte who turned out to be a disappointment. McNerney, endorsed by the state party and by local organized labor, soundly defeated Filson, 53%-28%. In the general election, Pombo outspent McNerney by nearly 2-to-1. McNerney turned the election into a referendum on Pombo, who was hated by national environmental groups, which called him an "eco-thug" and "Wildlife Enemy No. 1." Bolstered by a strong anti-Republican tide, McNerney won 53%-47%.

In the House, McNerney established a moderate voting record. He joined a majority of Republicans in 2011 in voting to extend several anti-terrorism provisions of the 2001 Patriot Act. He was vocal in publicly calling for President Barack Obama to take more action on housing foreclosures, and he introduced a measure in 2012 aimed at expediting short sales, which occur when lenders agree to allow a homeowner to sell property for less than what is owed on the mortgage. With Republican Rep. Walter Jones of North Carolina, McNerney launched the Congressional Campaign Finance Reform Caucus.

On the influential Energy and Commerce Committee, he won a provision regulating carbon emissions as part of a measure to encourage electric vehicle usage. In response to the economic peril in Stockton, he filed in September 2014 a bill to aid homeowners who may be facing foreclosure. He has used his seat on the Veterans Affairs Committee to assist ex-servicemembers, including a House-passed bill in October 2016 to expand broadband access for veterans. His House-passed bill to encourage disabled veterans to become small business owners was enacted in December 2016 as part of a broader package of veterans' measures. The *Almanac* vote ratings in 2015 ranked him as a party centrist on economic and foreign issues.

His history of tight reelection races has been beneficial, McNerney has said. "I have to be more moderate," he told *The Modesto Bee* in May 2012. "If I alienate Republicans, I can't win. If I alienate Democrats, I can't win." He has kept a low profile on Capitol Hill.

Republicans came after McNerney in 2010. They fielded a credible challenger in David Harmer, son of John Harmer, who was Ronald Reagan's lieutenant governor. The younger Harmer was a high-profile education activist and author, as well as a financial executive at JPMorgan Chase. Harmer promised to shun earmarks, calling them "the gateway drug of federal spending." Democratic interest groups attacked Harmer for a 2000 op-ed column calling for the abolition of public education. The race was close and ballot-counting continued for days after the election, until McNerney prevailed with 48 percent of the vote.

In 2012, McNerney's opponent was Ricky Gill, an ambitious 25-year-old Indian American hailed as a rising GOP star. Gill graduated a semester early from law school in order to run for Congress. He raised nearly $3 million, and the National Republican Congressional Committee spent another $2.5 million on his behalf. As a Lodi native, Gill had ties to the area, while redistricting forced McNerney to move. Gill described himself as a "different kind of Republican," holding moderate stances on immigration and education. McNerney called Gill a novice who was propped up by his wealthy parents' business ties; local newspapers echoed concerns about Gill's lack of real-world experience and endorsed McNerney. He also benefitted from Obama's strong showing in California to win, 56%-44%.

The 2014 election shaped up as an easier contest. Republican challenger Tony Amador was a former police officer and U.S. Marshal who had become a perennial political loser; he spent only $62,000 and had no national party assistance. But McNerney led by only 2,150 votes in San Joaquin, which cast two-thirds of the vote. He got a boost in the vote from Contra Costa to win the district with 52.4 percent. Kathryn Nance, president of the local police union in Stockton, failed to pursue a possible challenge in 2016. Amador ran again and spent a similar amount of money; with the higher presidential-election turnout, McNerney won, 57%-43%.

Central Valley: Stockton, San Joaquin

Population		**Race and Ethnicity**		**Income**	
Total	730,863	White	35.3%	Median Income	$55,958 (173 out of 435)
Land area	1,245	Black	8.3%	Under $50,000	29.3%
Pop/ sq mi	586.9	Latino	38.1%	$50,000-$99,999	21.5%
Born in state	63.6%	Asian	13.8%	$100,000-$199,999	4.1%
		Two races	3.6%	$200,000 or more	18.4%
Age Groups		Other	0.9%	Poverty Rate	18.4%
Under 18	27.8%				
18-34	23.5%	**Education**		**Health Insurance**	
35-64	37.0%	H.S grad or less	45.6%	With health insurance coverage	86.4%
Over 64	11.8%	Some college	34.9%		
		College Degree, 4 yr	13.6%	**Public Assistance**	
Work		Post grad	6.0%	Cash public assistance income	5.8%
White Collar	29.2%			Food stamp/SNAP benefits	13.3%
Sales and Service	43.4%	**Military**			
Blue Collar	27.3%	Veteran	6.5%		
Government	15.5%	Active Duty	0.1%		

Voter Turnout			
2015 Total Citizens 18+	448,129	2016 House Turnout as % CVAP	52%
2016 House turnout	232,155	2014 House Turnout as % CVAP	28%

2012 Presidential Vote		
Barack Obama	127,418	(58%)
Mitt Romney	88,403	(40%)

2016 Presidential Vote		
Hillary Clinton	134,719	(56%)
Donald Trump	90,484	(38%)
Gary Johnson	8,518	(4%)

Cook Partisan Voting Index: D+8

California is often defined by its cosmopolitan cities, its gorgeous Pacific coastline and its world-class vineyards. But beyond Beverly Hills and Nob Hill, there is another California that likes to get its hands dirty. This is an old part of the state, settled in the 1840s. When the Gold Rush fortune seekers departed, the land was left to a determined population of farmers. Crisscrossed with railroads and canals, the Central Valley became one of the world's greatest agricultural regions. The San Joaquin River channel was deepened to 37 feet, and Stockton today is the Central Valley's port. (The city is named after Robert Stockton, the second U.S. military governor of California, who captured Santa Barbara and Los Angeles from Mexico and proclaimed California U.S. territory.) The rich land attracted immigrants from all over: Mexicans came up Route 99 and joined Germans from the Dakotas flocking to the town of Lodi. Italian and Yugoslavian immigrants brought their Old World crops. Yankees and Okies brought their distinct churches and beliefs. Recently, Southeast Asian refugees have crowded into the old streets of Stockton. The region endures the usual plagues of a farm economy, such as the difficulty attracting migrant workers at harvest time, and some that are unique to California, such as chronic concerns about the water supply. The heavy rains during the 2017 winter overwhelmed local reservoirs and came after three years in which the federal government had denied water to Central Valley Project farmers and some were forced to shut down production. With large use of chemicals and pesticides, air pollution in the San Joaquin Valley has been ranked as the worst in the nation, with high levels of cancer and asthma.

In recent decades, the Central Valley has also become a suburban zone. Because of the high cost of living in the San Francisco Bay Area, racial minorities have been pushed to outlying suburbs and workers with modest incomes bought lower-priced houses around Tracy and Stockton and commute to work on Interstate 580, past the windmills of Altamont. The population in San Joaquin County in 2015 was 41 percent Hispanic, 16 percent Asian and 8 percent black. Stockton has become a poster child for urban dysfunction. *Forbes* magazine named it the most miserable city in America in 2011. At the time, city officials tried to tackle mounting debt, slashing spending by $90 million and cutting police and fire department budgets. Their efforts fell short. In June 2012, facing close to $1 billion in long-term debt, Stockton became the biggest city in American history to declare bankruptcy; the following year, the record went to Detroit. In October 2014, a bankruptcy judge approved the city's plan, with higher taxes and slashed payments to bondholders, but little impact on public pensions. Stockton exited bankruptcy in February 2015. San Joaquin County's jobless rate remained at 8 percent in 2016, and CNBC ranked it as the worst city in the United States in which to start a business. In November, voters elected as mayor Michael Tubbs, a 26-year-old African American and Stanford University graduate.

The 9th Congressional District contains most of San Joaquin County, plus an eastern slice of Contra Costa County and a southern nip of Sacramento County. It contains all of Stockton, plus Lodi, a town with a sizable Muslim community and a thriving downtown. About one-third of the county is in the 10th District, to the south. The district takes in Brentwood in Contra Costa County, the fastest-growing city in the Bay Area in the 2000s. Brentwood nearly doubled in population from 2000 to 2006, slowed considerably after the housing bust, then grew another 11 percent from 2010 to 2015.

The creation of this district generated controversy. The state's nonpartisan redistricting commission was designed to preclude interference from elected and party officials. But an investigation by the online watchdog *ProPublica* found that Democratic Rep. Jerry McNerney hired a mapping consultant who set up a Facebook page called "OneSanJoaquin" to push for a San Joaquin-based district, which eventually came to pass. The district became more Democratic, but it is not overwhelmingly Democratic and could be competitive in the future, especially with continued economic woes. Hillary Clinton got 56 percent of the vote in 2016, which was two percentage points less than Barack Obama received in 2012 and a point lower than his 2008 vote.

TENTH DISTRICT

Jeff Denham (R)

Elected 2010, 4th term; b. Jul 29, 1967, Hawthorne; California Polytechnic State University, San Luis Obispo, B.A.; Victor Valley Junior College (CA), A.A.; Presbyterian; Married (Sonia Denham); 2 children.

Military Career: U.S. Air Force, 1984-1988; Air Force Reserves, 1988-2000 (Persian Gulf).

Elected Office: CA Senate, 2002-2010.

Professional Career: Project Manager, Fresh Express, 1992-1998; Almond rancher; Owner, Denham Plastics.

DC Office: 1730 LHOB 20515, 202-225-4540, Fax: 202-225-3402, denham.house.gov.

State Offices: Modesto, 209-579-5458.

Committees: *Agriculture*: Biotechnology, Horticulture & Research, Conservation & Forestry. *Natural Resources*: Indian, Insular & Alaska Native Affairs, Water, Power & Oceans. *Transportation & Infrastructure*: Aviation, Highways & Transit, Railroads, Pipelines & Hazardous Materials (Chmn).

Group Ratings

	ADA	ACLU	AFL-CIO	LCV	ITI	COC	HAFA	ACU	CFG	FRC
2016	-	5%	-	3%	100%	100%	34%	58%	59%	75%
2015	0%	C	33%	6%	C	100%	C	42%	42%	92%

Almanac Ratings 2015

	Economy	Social	Foreign	Composite
Liberal	10%	31%	18%	20%
Conservative	90%	69%	82%	80%

Key Votes of the 114th Congress

1. Keystone Pipeline	Y	5. Puerto Rico Debt	Y	9. Offenses by Aliens	Y
2. Trade Deals	Y	6. Medical Marijuana	N	10. Troops in Iraq	N
3. Export-Import Bank	N	7. Sanctuary Cities	N	11. Homeland Security $$	Y
4. Debt Ceiling Increase	Y	8. Armor-piercing Bullets	Y	12. Trade Adjustment aid	Y

Election Results

Election	Name (Party)	Vote (%)	Cand. Spent	Ind. Exp. Support	Ind. Exp. Oppose
2016 General	Jeff Denham (R)	124,671 (52%)	$4,172,963	$342,186	$1,725,793
	Michael Eggman (D)	116,470 (48%)	$1,569,729	$4,538,155	$3,368,419
2016 Primary	Jeff Denham (R)	35,008 (47%)			
	Michael Eggman (D)	21,179 (28%)			
	Michael Barkley (D)	18,576 (15%)			
	Robert Hodges (R)	13,130 (10%)			

Prior winning percentages: 2014 (56%), 2012 (53%), 2010 (65%)

Jeff Denham, a Republican elected in 2010, is a vocal conservative whose views on local economics and politics occasionally move on a separate track from his party, notably on agriculture and immigration. His background as an Air Force veteran and farmer has given him hands-on experience with many issues. His election campaigns have become a national battleground.

Denham was born near Los Angeles and lived in Indiana for five years, but he spent most of his childhood in the Northern California town of Pescadero. His parents divorced when he was in high school, and Denham spent much of his time at his grandparents' home. At age 17, Denham enlisted in the Air Force. He was a crew chief, preparing and maintaining aircraft such as F-4 fighter jets and C-5 transport planes. After transitioning to the Reserve for more than a dozen years, Denham attended community college and then transferred to Cal Poly, San Luis Obispo, where he was active in College Republicans and received a bachelor's degree in political science. During the Persian Gulf War, he worked on an air base in Saudi Arabia. He also maintained aircraft in the peacekeeping mission in Somalia in 1992. Back home after his service, Denham became manager of a packaged salad company, and in 1998, he founded his own business, Denham Plastics, an agricultural container supply firm. In 2004, he bought a ranch in Merced County, where he grows almonds.

Denham first ran for public office in 2000, losing a bid for the California Assembly. Two years later, he ran for the state Senate and eked out a victory in a district where Democrats held a 12-point registration advantage. His roommate for several years in Sacramento was Kevin McCarthy, now the House majority leader. In 2007, Democrats needed Republican support to approve a budget. Because of the makeup of Denham's district, Democratic leaders hoped that he would agree to a compromise that included spending cuts and tax increases. After he refused, Democratic Senate Leader Don Perata organized a recall campaign against him. In June 2008, a resounding 75 percent of district voters chose not to recall Denham.

When the House seat opened in 2010, Denham did not have a clear path. Former Rep. Richard Pombo, who had been ousted in a neighboring district in 2006, and former Fresno Mayor Jim Patterson also ran in the primary. They criticized Denham for flying on a corporate jet with Republican strategist Karl Rove, a possible violation of federal election law, and for his ties to an Indian tribe that sponsored ads attacking his opponents. With strong fundraising and the support of the popular retiring Rep. George Radanovich, Denham won the primary with 36 percent; Patterson got 31 percent and Pombo placed third with 21 percent. Denham took the general election, 65%-35%.

In the House, Denham got off to a shaky start when he ignored new Republican Speaker John Boehner's admonition to keep GOP inaugural celebrations austere, throwing a $2,500-a-person fundraiser featuring country singer LeAnn Rimes. In recognition of his state legislative experience, he got the chairmanship of the Subcommittee on Economic Development, Public Buildings and Emergency Management at the Transportation and Infrastructure Committee. In 2012, the House agreed to his plan to create a commission to study whether federal offices were being used efficiently. He fought, unsuccessfully, to block plans to build a new $400 million courthouse in Los Angeles that was a priority for other California lawmakers, and he criticized the Securities and Exchange Commission for leasing 900,000 square feet of space, which he said was unneeded and cost the taxpayers $556 million.

Denham in 2013 became chairman of the Railroads, Pipelines and Hazardous Materials Subcommittee, where he pursued numerous agriculture-related issues. He strongly opposed California's high-speed rail project, which Gov. Jerry Brown has pursued despite political and regional divisions in California. Following the January 2015 groundbreaking in Fresno, Denham complained, "California voters were promised jobs, ridership numbers, speeds and costs that look nothing like the current proposal. … It's hard to celebrate breaking ground on what is likely to become abandoned pieces of track that never connect to a usable segment." Two months later, the House passed his rail bill with provisions to modernize the business operations of Amtrak, which Denham said would prevent "another disaster like California high-speed rail from wasting taxpayer dollars," including a requirement for state matching funds and deadlines for new projects. The bill won unanimous Democratic support, but only a slight majority of Republicans. With the nation's "unprecedented energy renaissance," he said, the nation's freight rails and pipelines have not kept pace with the increased demand. He enacted three bills from his committee work in 2016: Two dealt with federal property management, and the other with pipeline safety. In January 2017, after a confidential federal analysis of the California project showed that the state had not purchased parcels along half of its 118-mile rail route in the Central Valley, Denham called for a federal audit.

Denham has pushed for compromise on immigration legislation. On the defense spending bill in 2014, he sought to add his "Enlist Act" to provide legal status to undocumented immigrants who serve in the military. Republican leaders blocked a vote on his plan, but the Defense Department four months later moved forward with a scaled-down version of his plan for a limited number of immigrants with language or medical skills. Denham praised the "step forward." In January 2017, he revived his proposal for legal status for immigrants who served in the military and seized on a positive comment from Donald Trump during his campaign.

In 2012, Denham faced Democrat Jose Hernandez, a former astronaut, in the general election. Hernandez criticized him for using taxpayers' money to stay in hotels near the district. Denham accused Hernandez of carpetbagging because he had lived in Houston during the years he worked at NASA. The race tightened, but Denham pulled off a 53%-47% win. He had another competitive race in 2014 against beekeeper Michael Eggman, who spent $1.3 million. Denham spent $1.8 million, and benefited from a favorable Republican year. He won 56%-44%. When Eggman returned for a rematch in 2016, national Democrats spent $3.9 million for him, while Denham benefited from $3.3 million in GOP spending. Denham, who originally backed Jeb Bush for president, kept his distance from Trump and his hostility toward immigrants, but did not disavow him. *The Modesto Bee* for the first time failed to endorse Denham, citing his support for "dangerous demagogue" Trump as "a disqualifier." In his campaign, Eggman chiefly sought to link Denham to Trump. Denham won by his closest margin, 51.7%-48.3%, with narrow leads in both Stanislaus and San Joaquin counties.

Central Valley: Modesto, Stanislaus

Population		**Race and Ethnicity**		**Income**	
Total	723,880	White	44.5%	Median Income	$54,111 (197 out of 435)
Land area	1,819	Black	3.0%	Under $50,000	31.5%
Pop/ sq mi	398.0	Latino	41.7%	$50,000-$99,999	19.0%
Born in state	65.0%	Asian	6.5%	$100,000-$199,999	3.4%
		Two races	3.0%	$200,000 or more	17.6%
Age Groups		Other	1.2%	Poverty Rate	17.6%
Under 18	27.7%	**Education**		**Health Insurance**	
18-34	23.6%	H.S grad or less	49.6%	With health insurance coverage	86.9%
35-64	37.3%	Some college	33.1%	**Public Assistance**	
Over 64	11.3%	College Degree, 4 yr	11.9%	Cash public assistance income	5.4%
Work		Post grad	5.4%	Food stamp/SNAP benefits	14.2%
White Collar	27.4%	**Military**			
Sales and Service	42.6%	Veteran	6.5%		
Blue Collar	30.0%	Active Duty	0.1%		
Government	14.0%				

Voter Turnout			
2015 Total Citizens 18+	447,597	2016 House Turnout as % CVAP	54%
2016 House turnout	241,141	2014 House Turnout as % CVAP	28%

2012 Presidential Vote		
Barack Obama	108,923	(51%)
Mitt Romney	101,160	(47%)

2016 Presidential Vote		
Hillary Clinton	116,335	(48%)
Donald Trump	109,145	(45%)
Gary Johnson	9,370	(4%)

Cook Partisan Voting Index: EVEN

The Central Valley of California is a miraculous landscape, an outdoor factory stretching as far as the eye can see. Nature created the vast flatlands, rimmed by mountains rising in the distant haze. In the 20th century, people disciplined the land with a remorseless mile-square grid of roads, the California Aqueduct, and dozens of arrow-straight canals. Pipes fitted with valves and gauges pump water, fertilizer and pesticides to the fields in measured quantities with industrial precision. The crops grow in carefully spaced rows. The rich soil and the irrigated water were too precious to waste on decorative fountains or flower gardens. Throughout history, farming here has been a business, not a way of life. In the 19th century, the U.S. government did not give the land to 160-acre homesteaders but rather sold it to large enterprises in thousands-of-acres parcels. Among the most famous local capitalists were the Gallo brothers, Ernest and Julio, who started a winery in Modesto in 1933 with virtually no money. It now covers more than 16,000 acres of vineyards, with 60 brands that produce more than 80 million cases of wine each year.

In recent years, the Central Valley became one of California's boom areas, not just for crops, but also for people. Middle-income workers in the San Francisco Bay Area drive east at the end of the day on Interstate 580, past surreal windmills whirling on the bare hills of Altamont Pass, to modestly priced homes in Modesto, the town immortalized (when it was much smaller) in the 1973 film *American Graffiti.* Warehouses and factories have sprung up on land that for all its farming value is cheaper than industrial land in the Bay Area. But there have been costs: Traffic is a problem, air-pollution levels on bad days can be among the worst in the nation, and the pace of life has become more hectic. The over-pumping of groundwater has caused the Valley to sink a half-inch each month, the *Los Angeles Times* reported. Escalated by the drought prior to 2017, the result was "cracking irrigation canals, buckling roads and permanently depleting storage space in the vast aquifer that underlies California's heartland." The aquifer extends 400 miles below the Valley. In 2015, 20,000 of nearly 770,000 farmland acres were left fallow. After record farming revenues in Stanislaus County of $4.4 billion in 2014, the drought in

2015 was a factor in reducing that to $3.9 billion, with almonds the leading crop. Milk and walnuts were other profitable products.

The 10th Congressional District of California includes all of Stanislaus County and part of San Joaquin County, including Tracy, Ripon and the almond center of Manteca. Nearly three-fourths of the voters are in Stanislaus. It takes in Modesto, Oakdale and Riverbank. The political tradition here had been Democratic. In the 1960s, Democrats in Washington and Democratic Gov. Pat Brown built the irrigation canals and authorized the water subsidies. This area produced two House Democratic whips, John McFall in the mid-1970s and Tony Coelho in the 1980s. But the Central Valley, with the highest proportion of families and children in California, grew to be more culturally conservative than other parts of the state. In recent decades, it has trended Republican, and even the Latinos here are less solidly Democratic than those in Los Angeles. Still, with a 43 percent Hispanic population, this has become one of the few political "swing" areas in California. In the 2016 presidential election, Stanislaus County favored Hillary Clinton over Donald Trump, 47.4%-46.7%; President Barack Obama in 2012 won reelection, 51%-47%. In each of the past three presidential elections, Democrats have won the district by about three percentage points.

ELEVENTH DISTRICT

Mark DeSaulnier (D)

Elected 2014, 2nd term; b. Mar 31, 1952, Lowell, MA; College of the Holy Cross (MA), B.A., 1974; Harvard University John F. Kennedy School of Government (MA), 2002; Roman Catholic; Divorced; 2 children.

Elected Office: Concord City Council, 1991-1994; Concord Mayor, 1993; Contra Costa County Board Supervisors, 1994-2006, chair, 1994; CA Assembly 2006-2008; CA Senate, 2008-2014.

Professional Career: Deputy probation officer; Warehouse worker; Hotel service; Restauranteur; Business owner; Fellow, JFK School of Gov't, Harvard University, 2003.

DC Office: 115 CHOB 20515, 202-225-2095, Fax: 202-225-5609, desaulnier.house.gov.

State Offices: Richmond, 510-620-1000; Walnut Creek, 925-933-2660.

Committees: *Education & the Workforce*: Higher Education & Workforce Development, Workforce Protections. *Oversight & Government Reform*: Intergovernmental Affairs, National Security. *Transportation & Infrastructure*: Highways & Transit, Railroads, Pipelines & Hazardous Materials.

Group Ratings

	ADA	ACLU	AFL-CIO	LCV	ITI	COC	HAFA	ACU	CFG	FRC
2016	-	88%	-	100%	67%	50%	12%	0%	0%	0%
2015	100%	C	100%	97%	C	45%	C	4%	0%	0%

Almanac Ratings 2015

	Economy	Social	Foreign	Composite
Liberal	97%	100%	99%	99%
Conservative	3%	0%	1%	1%

Key Votes of the 114th Congress

1. Keystone Pipeline	N	5. Puerto Rico Debt	Y	9. Offenses by Aliens	N
2. Trade Deals	N	6. Medical Marijuana	Y	10. Troops in Iraq	Y
3. Export-Import Bank	Y	7. Sanctuary Cities	N	11. Homeland Security $$	Y
4. Debt Ceiling Increase	Y	8. Armor-piercing Bullets	N	12. Trade Adjustment aid	Y

Election Results

Election	Name (Party)	Vote (%)	Cand. Spent	Ind. Exp. Support	Ind. Exp. Oppose
2016 General	Mark DeSaulnier (D)	214,868 (72%)	$307,331		
	Roger Petersen (R)	83,341 (28%)	$7,047		
2016 Primary	Mark DeSaulnier (D)	133,317 (75%)			
	Roger Peterson (R)	43,654 (25%)			

Prior winning percentages: 2014 (67%)

Democrat Mark DeSaulnier, elected to a solidly blue district in 2014, has shown his legislative experience and expertise. With particular interest in education and transportation policy, he was unusually productive for a freshman in the minority party.

DeSaulnier is a veteran of California politics with blue-collar bona fides. He had been a trucker, probation officer, and hotel worker before entering the restaurant business, eventually owning several Bay Area dining locales. A keen interest in local politics inspired him to run for Concord City Council in 1991, and he became mayor in 1993. In those early years, he was a Republican. Gov. Pete Wilson appointed him to the influential state Air Resources Board in 1997. As he saw the GOP move to the right, DeSaulnier switched parties and became a Democrat. He was elected to the state Assembly in 2006 and the state Senate in 2008. He chaired the Transportation Committee in each chamber. DeSaulnier had not always marched with his party in Sacramento. He opposed proposals to revive California's troubled high-speed rail project, and he pledged to work with business groups to amend his corporate tax bill so it had a better chance of passage.

In January 2014, when 40-year veteran George Miller, an influential liberal leader and close ally of Minority Leader Nancy Pelosi, announced his retirement, DeSaulnier got his opening. He had lost a special election five years earlier to a better-known candidate, John Garamendi. This time, DeSaulnier made sure he was well positioned. Armed with the biggest war chest and a slew of endorsements, DeSaulnier quickly became the front-runner. He used his day job in the state Senate to advance liberal priorities. That included a bill to adjust the state corporate tax rate according to the wage disparity in each firm – a measure that resonated with Democrats but fell short of the required two-thirds majority to pass. He proposed another bill to set up a pilot project to reform the state's gasoline tax so that motorists pay based on mileage rather than by the gallon. That measure passed. DeSaulnier easily won election to the open seat. He took 59 percent of the vote in the first round of voting, well ahead of 28 percent for Republican Tue Phan-Quang. In the general election, he took 67 percent of the vote. This was a relatively low-cost contest, with DeSaulnier spending $540,000.

In the House, DeSaulnier continued his predecessor Miller's long-time tenure on the Education and the Workforce Committee. He filed legislation to make the income from student Pell Grants tax-exempt for low-income recipients. The first bill he introduced would expand the John Muir National Historic Site with 44 additional acres of donated land in Martinez. Muir, a conservationist, was the father of the national parks. The House passed the bill in May 2016. In response to incidents in which law-enforcement agents had their firearms stolen from their cars, DeSaulnier proposed a bill that would require federal agents to store their guns in a locked box while they are in a car.

He took several steps to call attention to the case of the Port Chicago 50, a group of African Americans who were found guilty of mutiny in 1944 when they refused to return to work following a huge munitions explosion during the loading of a ship at the Naval Magazine in Concord, which killed 320 persons. The House-passed defense spending bill in May 2016 included his amendment to require that the Navy investigate their treatment at the time to determine if there was racial bias. President Bill Clinton in 1999 pardoned Freddie Meeks, the last surviving member of the Port Chicago 50. In 2015, outgoing Navy Secretary Ray Mabus said that he favored a posthumous pardon for the group.

Prior to his reelection in 2016, which he won easily, DeSaulnier announced he had had months of chemotherapy treatment for a form of leukemia, which was a blood cancer that is not curable but is manageable. In a follow-up from his experience in Sacramento, DeSaulnier got a seat in 2017 on the Transportation and Infrastructure Committee. "I understand that our transportation is failing the Bay Area, and that we need radical and immediate change," he said, in taking the assignment.

Outer East Bay: Concord, Richmond

Population		**Race and Ethnicity**		**Income**	
Total	732,078	White	47.4%	Median Income	$75,633 (49 out of 435)
Land area	494	Black	8.4%		
Pop/ sq mi	1483.1	Latino	26.1%	Under $50,000	28.0%
Born in state	53.8%	Asian	13.1%	$50,000-$99,999	25.4%
		Two races	3.9%	$100,000-$199,999	13.0%
Age Groups		Other	1.1%	$200,000 or more	12.2%
Under 18	22.8%			Poverty Rate	12.2%
18-34	21.4%	**Education**			
35-64	41.0%	H.S grad or less	30.0%	**Health Insurance**	
Over 64	14.8%	Some college	28.2%	With health insurance coverage	89.2%
		College Degree, 4 yr	25.9%		
Work		Post grad	15.9%		
White Collar	43.6%			**Public Assistance**	
Sales and Service	40.7%	**Military**		Cash public assistance income	2.9%
Blue Collar	15.7%	Veteran	6.3%		
Government	12.6%	Active Duty	0.1%	Food stamp/SNAP benefits	6.7%

Voter Turnout			
2015 Total Citizens 18+	480,164	2016 House Turnout as % CVAP	62%
2016 House turnout	298,209	2014 House Turnout as % CVAP	36%

2012 Presidential Vote		
Barack Obama	203,699	(68%)
Mitt Romney	90,226	(30%)

2016 Presidential Vote		
Hillary Clinton	223,559	(71%)
Donald Trump	70,869	(23%)
Gary Johnson	10,993	(4%)

Cook Partisan Voting Index: D+21

The journey inward from the Pacific Ocean to the vast flatness of California's Central Valley passes through a wondrous variety of terrain. The traveler starts at the Golden Gate Bridge, with the lush green Presidio on one side and the bluffs of mountains in Marin County on the other. The journey continues through the San Francisco Bay, through the narrow Carquinez Strait to Suisun Bay, with its sloughs and marshes and ships ready for scrap, and finally past the mountains, to the flat, fertile expanse of California's great interior. This is not a journey most tourists make, but it was a familiar route to the first Americans in California, and it passes by much of the industrial base of the Bay Area. On the east side of Suisun Bay is Richmond, developed almost instantaneously during World War II when Henry J. Kaiser built a shipyard in its deep-water port and 91,000 people from all over the country were put to work building ships for the Pacific theater. What became known as Rosie the Riveter Memorial Park is now a national park. The recession landed a severe blow here - median household earnings plummeted by more than $3,000 in two years. The state Employment Development Department issued a report in 2015 that the East Bay had experienced a robust jobs recovery.

In recent years, Richmond citizens have harbored doubts about safety at a Chevron refinery plant, the scene of frequent fires and explosions. After an August 2012 fire at the plant, some residents blasted Chevron for causing high asthma rates and pollution, while business leaders defended the company as a jobs creator. The federal Chemical Safety Board issued a report in February 2015 that Chevron was responsible for the disaster because it failed to respond when experts warned of defects at the plant. In the 2014 election, Chevron fueled a backlash when it endorsed four candidates for the Richmond city council, and spent more than $3 million on their behalf. Sen. Bernie Sanders of Vermont campaigned locally against the Chevron candidates. All of them lost. A local political science professor said the result showed that "ordinary people can defeat huge corporate power." Activist writer Steve Early described the saga in a book published in January 2017, *Refinery Town: Big Oil, Big Money, and the Remaking of an American City,* which also reported on the council's subsequent approval of rent-control measures in response to a surge of new homeowners and tenants. In November 2016, Contra Costa voters defeated a referendum for a sales tax increase to pay for new transportation projects.

The 11th District of California is entirely in Contra Costa County, including all of Richmond and Concord, which is the largest city in the county. About 30 percent of the county's voters are in three adjoining districts. Interstate 680 running north-south provides a spine for businesses and shopping centers up and down the San Ramon Valley, from burgeoning Concord to Walnut Creek. The district also takes in the "Lamorinda" area of Lafayette, Moraga and Orinda. Officials in Concord lobbied the Pentagon to close the mostly unused Concord Naval Weapons Station so they could use the land for business and residential development. After California State University in 2014 dropped plans to build a new campus at the site, the city council updated development plans that envisioned more than 12,000 housing units and 6 million square feet of commercial space; about 70 percent was expected to be used as parkland and open space. The district is solidly Democratic, but less culturally liberal than San Francisco. The Democratic presidential vote increased from 68 percent in 2012 to 71 percent in 2016.

TWELFTH DISTRICT

Nancy Pelosi (D)

Elected 1987, 16th term; b. Mar 26, 1940, Baltimore, MD; Trinity College (DC), A.B., 1962; Roman Catholic; Married (Paul F. Pelosi); 5 children; 9 grandchildren.

Professional Career: CA Dem. Party, Northern Chairman, 1977- 81, St. Chairman, 1981-1983; DSCC finance Chairman, 1985-1986; PR Executive, Ogilvy & Mather, 1986-1987.

DC Office: 233 CHOB 20515, 202-225-4965, Fax: 202-225-8259, pelosi.house.gov.

State Offices: San Francisco, 415-556-4862.

Group Ratings

	ADA	ACLU	AFL-CIO	LCV	ITI	COC	HAFA	ACU	CFG	FRC
2016	-	100%	-	100%	67%	42%	14%	0%	0%	0%
2015	95%	C	100%	100%	C	45%	C	0%	0%	0%

Almanac Ratings 2015

	Economy	Social	Foreign	Composite
Liberal	98%	90%	99%	95%
Conservative	2%	11%	1%	5%

Key Votes of the 114th Congress

1. Keystone Pipeline	N	5. Puerto Rico Debt	Y	9. Offenses by Aliens	N
2. Trade Deals	N	6. Medical Marijuana	Y	10. Troops in Iraq	Y
3. Export-Import Bank	Y	7. Sanctuary Cities	NV	11. Homeland Security $$	Y
4. Debt Ceiling Increase	Y	8. Armor-piercing Bullets	NV	12. Trade Adjustment aid	Y

Election Results

Election	Name (Party)	Vote (%)		Cand. Spent	Ind. Exp. Support	Ind. Exp. Oppose
2016 General	Nancy Pelosi (D)	274,035	(81%)	$1,164,034	$1,963	$19,718
2016 Primary	Nancy Pelosi (D)	119,941	(78%)			
	Bob Miller (R)	12,287	(8%)			
	Preston Picus (I)	10,936	(7%)			
	Barry Hermanson (G)	10,171	(7%)			

Prior winning percentages: 2014 (83%), 2012 (85%), 2010 (80%), 2008 (72%), 2006 (80%), 2004 (83%), 2002 (80%), 2000 (84%), 1998 (86%), 1996 (84%), 1994 (82%), 1992 (83%), 1990 (77%), 1988 (76%)

Nancy Pelosi, Speaker of the House from 2007 to 2011 and minority leader since Democrats lost control of the chamber, is one of the most polarizing figures in politics. Detested by Republicans for her proudly liberal views and assertive style, she has been beloved in her party for her legislative accomplishments as well as her fundraising and politicking, which continued unabated in her mid-70s. Pelosi was the first woman to achieve the speakership, and those four years were among the most productive for the House in the past century. Since then, she and her depleted caucus have struggled, though GOP splits have given her opportunities to shape legislation.

Elected to Congress in June 1987, she has the energy and shrewdness of one who has handled the most delicate of political chores, and the charm and unflappability of one who is the mother of five and grandmother of nine. As minority leader, Pelosi's public image has receded since 2010, when Republicans ran thousands of ads vilifying her in their successful campaign to gain control of the House. GOP strategists and candidates still warn that a return of Democratic control under Pelosi would be tantamount to the Apocalypse.

Democrats' dismal showings in the 2010 and 2014 midterm elections fueled speculation and some internal demands that it was time for her to step aside. But she has proven far too skilled at hauling in campaign funds; she collected more than $128 million, a personal record, during the 2016 cycle. "I'm the one that brung everyone to the party by winning the House in the first place," she told *The Washington Post*. "I could have walked away, but we built something and then we want to take it to the next step" - winning back control of the House. Recent elections have made that goal seem unattainable, at least until redistricting for the 2022 election, when she will be 82.

Since 2014, Pelosi has bowed to the demands for new, younger faces in leadership. She appointed Rep. Ben Ray Luján of New Mexico, a Latino, to head the Democratic Congressional Campaign Committee. Later, she installed Eric Swalwell, a Bay Area upstart, as co-chair of the powerful Steering and Policy Committee along with longtime ally Rosa DeLauro of Connecticut. But her diminished influence was reflected in her inability to get her close friend and fellow Californian Anna Eshoo the ranking member post on the Energy and Commerce Committee. New Jersey's Frank Pallone, working with Minority Whip Steny Hoyer and other allies, beat out Eshoo for the job on a secret ballot. News reports revealed growing frustration among younger rank-and-file members with what they saw as the entrenchment of longtime, and aging, figures in leadership and top committee slots. Most of them were Pelosi allies. The 63 votes for 43-year-old Rep. Tim Ryan of Ohio in November 2016 when he challenged Pelosi for leader were a manifestation of economic populism and the desire for change, though she remained secure with a majority of the Democratic Caucus. She responded that "our values" continued to unify Democrats but made limited tinkering, including the creation of a new "vice ranking member" slot for a junior Democrat at each House committee.

Her lingering legislative influence has been both positive and negative. In March 2015, Pelosi worked with Speaker John Boehner in an impressive joint show of strength to win overwhelming House passage of a "doc fix" bill that solved long-standing problems with Medicare and other health care programs. Then, she had a showdown with Obama in June 2015 when she joined with rank-and-file Democrats who mostly opposed the expedited congressional procedures on the prospective Trans-Pacific Partnership agreement that the president and his aides were negotiating with Asian allies and had become a centerpiece of his second-term agenda. Backers of the deal had worked to get support from Pelosi and other Democrats, at least on the "trade adjustment" worker assistance, which was an auxiliary part of the trade deal and had long been a signature part of the Democratic agenda. In effect, Pelosi abandoned the lame-duck president for the Democrats' steadfast allies in organized labor, even though Obama made a last-minute personal plea for support at a closed-door meeting of the caucus. The resulting disarray among Democrats was a stark reminder of the limitations that Pelosi faced since she lost her gavel in 2010.

Earlier, Pelosi began the 112th Congress in January 2011 with 19 Democrats voting against her - the most defections that any party leader had suffered since 1913. Most of those votes were cast by the diminishing corps of moderate "Blue Dog" Democrats. As Republicans voted repeatedly to repeal the health care law that had been her signature achievement, she stood stubbornly against their criticisms.

Despite her furious fundraising, Pelosi and her lieutenants have been unsuccessful in crafting a path to the majority that would circumvent the twin Democratic demons of redistricting and demographic shifts in many large metropolitan areas. In many parts of the nation, from Pennsylvania and Ohio to Florida and Texas, where Democrats once dominated the House delegations, her cultural liberalism and the relentless attacks of Republicans kept her from making credible appearances in public events on behalf of Democratic candidates or House members with whom she worked regularly at the Capitol. An early sign of that erosion of support came when her close ally, Rep. John Murtha of Pennsylvania, died in early 2010 and Pelosi's role was limited chiefly to fundraising assistance. In the southwest corner of Pennsylvania, the four House Democrats in 2002 shrunk to one a decade later. That pattern was repeated across the nation. Talk has occasionally circulated about whether she would continue as Democratic leader, and her daughter, Alexandra, in 2011 told a blogger that her mother was "done" with Washington and "wants to have a life," if her donors "didn't want her to stay so badly." Then, perhaps unwilling to hand the reins to Minority Whip Steny Hoyer of Maryland, Pelosi said that she would seek another term as party leader. The unpopularity of President Donald Trump and the Republican agenda sparked new enthusiasm among Democratic activists about their prospects for big House gains in 2018.

Pelosi grew up on Albemarle Street in Baltimore's Little Italy, just east of downtown. Her father, Thomas D'Alesandro Jr., served in the House from 1939 to 1947 and was mayor of Baltimore for 12 years after that. Her mother, Annunciata D'Alesandro, was an indefatigable political organizer, and her brother, Thomas, was mayor from 1967 to 1971. Pelosi says of her parents, "What I got from them was about economic fairness. That was the difference between Democrats and Republicans all those years ago." She graduated from Trinity University in Washington, D.C., where she met her husband Paul. After marrying, they moved to his hometown of San Francisco. There he became a successful real estate investor, and she raised their children and got into local Democratic politics. The couple eventually became extremely wealthy, with a home in San Francisco, a vineyard in the Napa Valley, a townhome in the Sierras, and a condominium in Washington. Their diversified investments have placed Pelosi among the five wealthiest House members, though she generally does not flaunt it in public. For her 75th birthday, she told reporters that she wanted a pool table.

In the 1970s, Pelosi struck rough-hewn Rep. John Burton of California as just another stylish hostess in a city that had many of them. But she soon got Burton's attention and that of his older brother, Rep. Phillip Burton, the de facto liberal leader of the House, who lost his race for majority leader to Texas Democrat Jim Wright by one vote in 1976. That year, Pelosi returned east to run the Maryland campaign of presidential candidate Jerry Brown, then and later governor of California. She was able to relate both to "Governor Moonbeam," as Brown was dubbed, and to the practical-minded politicians she had met through her parents. In 1977, she became chairwoman of the Northern California Democratic Party, and four years later, she became chairwoman of the California Democratic Party. The positions required a considerable amount of diplomacy, including dealing with fractious regional antagonisms. But Pelosi managed to remain on good terms with various warring Democrats and help the party hold majorities in the legislature.

Then in 1982, John Burton declined to run for reelection in a new Marin- and San Francisco-based district. Some Democrats sounded out Pelosi, whose Presidio Heights home was in the district, but she declined to run, and the seat went to Marin-based Democrat Barbara Boxer. Instead, Pelosi worked with Mayor Dianne Feinstein to land the 1984 Democratic National Convention for San Francisco. In 1985, she ran for Democratic National Chairman but lost to Paul Kirk. Before long, though, she had another opportunity. Phil Burton's widow, Sala Burton, was elected to succeed her husband after his death in 1983, but her health failed too. In 1987, as she was dying of cancer, she told her friends whom she wanted to succeed her: Nancy Pelosi.

This time, she ran, moving her residence from Presidio Heights to a Pacific Heights rental apartment. Her chief opponent in the Democratic primary was San Francisco Supervisor Harry Britt, who had succeeded Harvey Milk after he was assassinated. San Francisco's gay community at that time was not as mainstream as it is now, but Britt, who was gay, had a good record in office and Pelosi had to work hard to beat him, 35%-31%.

In her early days in Congress, Pelosi focused on important issues of local sensitivity. One was the Presidio. Burton had enacted a provision that transferred the Presidio from the military to the Interior Department. The problem was that it was so expensive to maintain, it threatened to exceed the National Park Service's budget. Through several Congresses, Pelosi worked to get bipartisan support for a funding source, and in 1997 created the Presidio Trust.

Another sensitive issue was human rights, especially in China. After the Tiananmen Square massacre in 1989, Pelosi sponsored an amendment to give Chinese students the right to remain in the United States, but President George H. W. Bush vetoed it. In 1991, she became lead sponsor of the bill to make China's most-favored-nation status conditional on human rights reforms. The House overrode Bush's veto, but it was upheld in the Senate. After that, Pelosi led the annual fight against normalizing trade relations with China. She did all this at some political risk. Pelosi's position was by no means universally popular with Asian Americans in her district; many thought the United States should trade and negotiate quietly with China. One of her chief adversaries was her San Francisco neighbor, Feinstein; for many years, they lived in houses just a few blocks apart in Presidio Heights. Pelosi courted support from people on the opposite end of the ideological spectrum, especially religious conservatives in the Republican caucus who also wanted to remain vigilant on China's human rights record.

Pelosi rose to the position of senior Democrat on the Intelligence Committee. Following the September 11 attacks, she joined in the committee's conclusion that, while the intelligence community did not have specific evidence in advance, it did have information that was relevant to the attacks.

Her move into the leadership was persistent, shrewd and well-organized. In 1997, as a member of the Ethics Committee, she doggedly pursued charges against Republican Speaker Newt Gingrich and worked with Minority Whip David Bonior in using scorched-earth tactics against him. In 1999, she launched a campaign for majority whip, anticipating that Democrats would win a majority in 2000. Her opponent was Hoyer. They were old acquaintances, having served as interns for Sen. Daniel Brewster of Maryland in the 1960s, but not confreres: there were considerable stylistic and ideological differences.

But in 2000, Republicans held onto their majority, and the race for majority whip was moot. Not for long, though. Michigan's Republican legislature, in drawing new congressional districts, put Bonior in a district that he could not win, and he decided to run for governor. He resigned as minority whip, and Pelosi was off and running against Hoyer. Some supporters played up her potential to become a celebrity - "a glamorous grandmother who knocks people off their feet," as then-Rep. Neil Abercrombie of Hawaii put it. With nearly unanimous support from the 32 California Democrats and from most women members, Pelosi started off with a strong base. In October 2001, she won by a convincing 118-95.

As whip, Pelosi moved quickly to assert herself, sometimes independently from then-Minority Leader Dick Gephardt of Missouri. Her biggest conflict came in the fall of 2002, when she actively encouraged opponents of the resolution authorizing the use of force in Iraq, which Gephardt had enthusiastically endorsed. Pelosi contended that supporters had not made the case for using force and that she had seen no evidence that Iraq "poses an imminent threat to our nation." To the surprise of many, her efforts helped win 126 Democratic votes against the resolution, while 81 backed Gephardt's position. In retrospect, the split signaled a transition in the caucus. Once the disappointing 2002 election results were in and Gephardt said that he was stepping down, Pelosi had all but locked up the support of a majority of the caucus. Rep. Martin Frost of Texas announced his candidacy with warnings that the selection of Pelosi might create a "permanent minority party." He withdrew from the contest a day later, conceding that he could not win, though he claimed substantial private support. Harold Ford of Tennessee made a belated, quixotic bid designed to appeal to a combination of blacks and New Democrats, but Pelosi won 177-29.

As the Democratic leader in the House, she brought a burst of energy - and favorable press coverage - to a party that badly needed both. She showed hands-on management in selecting members for committee vacancies and in developing a Democratic message criticizing the agenda of President George W. Bush. As Republicans pressed their agenda, Pelosi declared that Democrats would take "a party position" in opposition to the Republican Medicare prescription-drug bill. But 16 Democrats voted for the final deal in November 2003, providing the critical margin for passage. She was largely silent about the renegades, many of whom were responding to local pressures favoring the bill.

Pelosi traveled the country in 2004 raising money and boosting local candidates. If she became Speaker, Pelosi pledged, she would reform the House to give a greater voice to all members and to assure fairness. The three-seat loss in the November election that year turned out to be yet another disappointment for House Democrats, although Pelosi noted correctly that they won a net gain apart from the effects of the 2003 Texas redistricting. Bush's declining job approval ratings and the rising prospects of Democrats in the 2006 election helped Pelosi maintain party discipline.

For months, House Democrats worked to come up with a platform for 2006 and emerged with a "Six for '06" program, including an increase in the minimum wage and approval of the remaining recommendations of the 9/11 Commission. Pelosi campaigned tirelessly across the country and was rewarded when Democrats gained 31 seats, enough for a Democratic majority, on Election Day.

As she assumed the office that put her second in line for the presidency, Pelosi said in January 2007, "This is an historic moment, for Congress, and for the women of this country. It is a moment for which we have waited more than 200 years. For our daughters and granddaughters, today we have broken the marble ceiling. To our daughters and granddaughters, the sky is the limit." Much of her leadership team was already in place. Although she had vigorously supported Murtha for majority leader, Hoyer had the support of most of the conservative Blue Dog Democrats, most freshmen and senior incoming committee chairmen. Hoyer won the No. 2 spot, 149-86. The third-ranking spot, majority whip, went to the well-liked James Clyburn of South Carolina, an African American who brought racial diversity to the new lineup. Influential Illinois Rep. Rahm Emanuel had wanted to be whip, but Pelosi persuaded him to take the fourth-ranking job, that of caucus chairman, with new responsibilities.

Beneath the velvet glove, Pelosi continued to operate with an iron fist. One of her key issues was reducing carbon dioxide emissions to curb global warming. So she announced the creation of a Select Committee on Energy Independence and Global Warming, to be headed by Energy and Commerce member Edward Markey of Massachusetts. Energy and Commerce Chairman John Dingell of Michigan protested that he was being sidelined, but Pelosi had her way.

She had some early and impressive legislative successes, but also some disappointments, especially when Democratic leaders in the closely divided Senate failed to rally the 60 votes needed to pass bills from the House. Her greatest frustration was being unable to end military involvement in Iraq. Pelosi conceded that she had underestimated Republicans' willingness to stick with Bush on the war, a position at odds with statements she said they had made to her privately and also at odds with the public mood in some Republican districts.

On domestic policy, Pelosi and her Democratic leadership ran a tight ship and were largely successful, at least in the House. The Democrats' bill to expand the State Children's Health Insurance Program was passed by both chambers, but Bush vetoed it. When gasoline hit $4 a gallon and public opinion began to favor more offshore oil drilling, Pelosi refused to allow a roll call vote. "I'm trying to save the planet," she said. But Democrats too were coming under pressure to act on gas prices, and Pelosi agreed to allow a vote on a bill that gave states a role in offshore drilling decisions.

Then, crisis struck, as the financial industry teetered on the verge of collapse, with the potential to send the United States into a second Great Depression. Treasury Secretary Henry Paulson and Federal Reserve Chairman Ben Bernanke confronted the House in September 2008 with a request for $700 billion to bail out big, failing financial firms. Pelosi, with Financial Services Committee Chairman Barney Frank of Massachusetts, decided to grant the request. But a few days later, it became clear that many Democrats were unwilling to vote for it. Pelosi announced she would bring Democrats along if 100 Republicans supported it as well. When the bill came to a vote on Sept. 29, it was defeated, and Republicans blamed Pelosi for speaking harshly about Bush administration economic policies. The Senate changed some of the terms of the bill, and it passed on Oct. 1. The House took up the Senate version and, with some vote switches prompted by Pelosi, passed it two days later.

In the November 2008 election, Democrats gained 21 House seats, and Pelosi entered 2009 as the leader of 257 Democrats - the biggest majority a Speaker had enjoyed since Democrat Thomas Foley of Washington in 1993-94. Pelosi made it plain to the new Obama administration that she expected it to work through her and not make side deals with Democratic factions, much less Republicans. She presided over a record of legislative accomplishments that many consider the most impressive since the Great Society Congress of 1965-66.

The first order of business was Obama's massive economic stimulus bill. Pelosi largely delegated the specifics to Appropriations Chairman David Obey of Wisconsin. The $819 billion measure was passed without a single Republican vote. The size of the stimulus was reduced in the Senate, and Pelosi negotiated hard to get the price tag to $787 billion. That amount was enacted in mid-February, less than a month after Obama's inauguration.

On Iraq, Pelosi said she was unhappy with Obama's decision to leave 50,000 troops there and also with the Justice Department's decision not to prosecute Bush administration officials for approving enhanced interrogation techniques. She was embarrassed in May 2009 when the Central Intelligence Agency released documents indicating that she had been present at a September 2002 briefing where water boarding was discussed. In a tense press conference, she said, "In that or any other briefing, we were not and, I repeat, were not told that water boarding or any of these other enhanced interrogation techniques were used" - only that they were legal. Republicans' call for an inquiry was rejected on partisan lines.

As in the previous Congress, Pelosi pushed hard for legislation restricting carbon emissions, her signature issue. She quietly supported California Rep. Henry Waxman's successful campaign to replace Dingell as chairman of Energy and Commerce, with prime jurisdiction over the issue. And she worked closely with Waxman and Markey on the contents of the bill, including Waxman's concessions to win over conservative Democrats. She even met with 11 Republican moderates to get their support. In late June, the bill passed, 219-212, with eight Republicans voting yes. But the Senate did not act.

The other major initiative for Pelosi was Obama's health care overhaul. But finding agreement on complex and far-reaching changes to the medical insurance system, including a controversial proposal to let people opt into a federally sponsored plan, delayed the bill in committee for many weeks. As Pelosi had feared, opposition to the bill gained momentum at town hall meetings across the country during the August recess, including many in Democratic districts. Lawmakers were more skittish about the legislation when they returned. Pelosi agreed to changes in the controversial public option but refused to give in to pressure from conservative Democrats to drop it from the bill. And, in the 11th hour and to the dismay of abortion-rights supporters, she agreed to accept Michigan Rep. Bart Stupak's amendment barring coverage for abortions. A 1,990-page draft was unveiled on Oct. 29 and the bill was passed 220-215 on Nov. 7, with 39 Democrats voting no and 1 Republican voting yes.

The public option proved to be an even tougher sell in the Senate, which ultimately voted on Christmas Eve for a health care overhaul minus the government insurance provision. Then on Jan. 19, 2010, Republican Scott Brown won the special Senate election in Massachusetts for the seat vacated by the death of Ted Kennedy. In his campaign, Brown had promised to be the 41st vote against the health care bill, denying Democrats the 60 votes they needed to stop a filibuster. The obstacles were great. But Pelosi characteristically braced for the fight. "We're in the majority," she told Obama. "We'll never have a better majority in your presidency in numbers than we've got right now. We can make this work."

Public opinion polls in early 2010 showed the public to be increasingly wary of the changes to the health care system. Pelosi agreed to drop a House-passed surtax on high-income earners, which was replaced by an excise tax on high-end insurance plans. She also got Stupak and other anti-abortion lawmakers to agree to changes to their provision that they had previously deemed unacceptable. On the day of the vote, March 21, Pelosi marched with fellow Democrats from their offices to the Capitol, while an angry crowd, held back by Capitol police, chanted "Kill the bill." Pelosi's attitude toward the anti-Obama health care forces was clear in a statement in January of that year: "We will go through the gate. If the gate is closed, we will go over the fence. If the fence is too high, we will pole vault in. If that doesn't work, we will parachute in. But we are going to get health care reform passed for the American people." The final roll call was 219-212, without a single Republican vote. The Senate acquiesced to the House changes and Obama signed the bill.

Its passage was the defining moment of Pelosi's speakership and showcased her skills at putting together complex legislation and rounding up reluctant votes, amid volatile public opinion. Polls around the country showed a disturbing number of Democratic incumbents trailing their Republican challengers. In September, she hoped to send Democrats home to campaign on a high note by having them vote to extend the Bush-era income tax cuts except for upper income-earners of $200,000 or more. But when it became clear the votes weren't there, she moved to adjourn a week earlier than scheduled. It was acknowledgement that her ability to control a majority, after four years of doing so time and again, was in the hands of a restless electorate in November.

That fall, Pelosi campaigned for Democrats across the country, but she was more a liability than an asset in conservative-leaning districts where Democratic incumbents were bombarded with GOP-orchestrated ads labeling them as "Pelosi-Reid Democrats." Democrats lost 63 seats, the most the party had lost since the 1938 election, and Republicans took majority control in January.

In 2011, it was widely expected that Pelosi would relinquish her hold on her leadership position. But after two days of prayer and conversations, Pelosi announced she wanted to run for minority leader again. She could not stop North Carolina's conservative Heath Shuler from launching a quixotic challenge. Pelosi prevailed in the caucus vote 150-43. When asked to explain why she won, she said, "Because I'm an effective leader, because we got the job done on health care and Wall Street reform and consumer protection, the list goes on. Because they know that I'm the person that can attract the resources, both intellectual and otherwise, to take us to victory because I have done it before." After two more elections, House Democrats in January 2015 held 188 seats, their smallest total since 1928. In the 2016 election, Democrats surprisingly regained only six seats. The bigger shock of Hillary Clinton losing to Donald Trump left House Democrats with an even weaker legislative hand.

Back home, Pelosi has been overwhelmingly reelected. In 2008, antiwar protester Cindy Sheehan ran against her as an independent. Pelosi refused to debate or acknowledge Sheehan, who wound up getting 16 percent of the vote, more than the Republican nominee's 10 percent. Pelosi got 72 percent.

San Francisco

Population		Race and Ethnicity		Income	
Total	731,379	White	43.5%	Median Income	$81,189 (32 out of 435)
Land area	39	Black	5.4%		
Pop/ sq mi	18767.7	Latino	14.9%	Under $50,000	22.8%
Born in state	38.2%	Asian	31.6%	$50,000-$99,999	26.0%
		Two races	3.6%	$100,000-$199,999	16.7%
Age Groups		Other	1.1%	$200,000 or more	13.3%
Under 18	13.0%			Poverty Rate	13.3%
18-34	30.9%	**Education**			
35-64	42.1%	H.S grad or less	24.7%	**Health Insurance**	
Over 64	14.0%	Some college	20.0%	With health insurance coverage	91.6%
		College Degree, 4 yr	33.4%		
Work		Post grad	22.0%		
White Collar	55.1%			**Public Assistance**	
Sales and Service	36.5%	**Military**		Cash public assistance income	2.8%
Blue Collar	8.4%	Veteran	3.6%		
Government	10.8%	Active Duty	0.0%	Food stamp/SNAP benefits	5.3%

Voter Turnout			
2015 Total Citizens 18+	541,740	2016 House Turnout as % CVAP	63%
2016 House turnout	338,845	2014 House Turnout as % CVAP	35%

2012 Presidential Vote		
Barack Obama	269,461	(84%)
Mitt Romney	40,003	(13%)

2016 Presidential Vote		
Hillary Clinton	309,221	(86%)
Donald Trump	31,158	(9%)
Jill Stein	8,881	(3%)
Gary Johnson	7,949	(2%)

Cook Partisan Voting Index: D+37

On Feb. 20, 1915, a crowd of 150,000 gathered on the grounds of the Panama-Pacific International Exposition to see the Spanish-Italian baroque-style structure built on reclaimed land in what was to become San Francisco's Marina district. The Exposition ostensibly celebrated the completion of the Panama Canal, but it was clearly intended to show off San Francisco's recovery from the 1906 earthquake. It also spotlighted the city as the central focus of America's efforts to open an economic door to the eastern part of the world, especially in light of the acquisition of Hawaii and the Philippines and of its interest in an open-door policy with China and trade with Japan. The Exposition established the physical style of San Francisco, encouraging the use of Mediterranean color, accent and detail that characterizes many of the post-Victorian houses and commercial structures in The City, as the *San Francisco Examiner* called it for years. It set the tone for the picturesque Marina district, and for Fisherman's Wharf and Ghirardelli Square. On a sunny day, San Francisco can look almost tropical, with brown mountains baking in the sun and light shining off the pastel stucco buildings. When the clouds scud in from the Pacific, it can look sinister, full of dark corners where a private detective's partner might encounter unexpected temptations. The buildings can be majestic, like the monumental Beaux-Arts City Hall. The tawdry hotels of the Tenderloin District have become a gritty neighborhood with its own charms. The hills can be a grueling hike.

San Francisco grew from nothing to a major city in the single year of 1850, an instant product of the California Gold Rush. Within just a few years, culture was flourishing in the city, and San Francisco developed a parochial pride in the great writers who worked there - Jack London, Ambrose Bierce, Frank Norris - and in giving birth to the Arts and Crafts movement. Later, San Francisco newspaper scribe Herb Caen coined the term "beatnik" to describe the youthful penchant for freedom in the 1950s and wrote definitively about the hippies who thronged Haight-Ashbury in 1967. In the 1970s, the city was among the first to embrace the gay rights movement, in The Castro district. Gays lately have been moving to the suburbs and straights have been moving into the city. Perhaps surprisingly, a 2014 Gallup survey found that the overall metro area had the largest LGBT share of the population in the nation, at 6.2 percent, but the city itself was only 3.6 percent. Over the years, the city's booming economy - based initially on food processing, but now on finance, high-tech, and clothing (Levi Strauss, the Gap) - attracted talented newcomers, though its population is increasingly polarized between high-income and low-income. The dot-com crash in 2000 took a brutal toll, but the city rallied in mid-decade, as new high-rise office buildings and condominiums sprang up on the waterfront and south of Market. In a growing entertainment district in Mission Bay, the NBA's Warriors planned to open their new arena in 2019; in *The Mercury News*, a critic from their home in Oakland lamented the "elite takeover" by "the Silicon Valley crowd."

The housing bust in 2008 did not hit as hard here as in California's Central Valley subdivisions, where many modest-income Bay Area residents had been fleeing. The income inequality ratio in San Francisco is especially high chiefly because the wealthy are really wealthy. Thanks to the flood of high-tech workers pouring in, many of whom commute daily to Silicon Valley on luxurious corporate buses ("Google buses"), the city's housing costs are so high that low-income persons have become virtually precluded from living in most parts of the city. In October 2016, the median home-sale price was $1.2 million. This hyper-gentrification has led to economic stratification and has produced growing protests of activists and low-income groups that target the tech industry and developers. San Francisco has the lowest percentage of children, 13 percent, of any major city, raising questions about its post-modern future. Although it is proudly tolerant, San Francisco is one of California's whitest cities, with only about half as many black residents as it had in 1970. The population on the west side is substantially Asian, but Asian communities are increasingly migrating to other parts of the Bay Area. Demographers projected that the gentrified city could regain its white-majority status.

Politically, San Francisco was a progressive Republican town, like the two men who led the way into the Exposition: Mayor "Sunny Jim" Rolph and California Gov. Hiram Johnson. The sour-tempered Johnson made his name as a reformer, throwing out crooked city politicians. His administration gave California primary and recall elections, referenda and strong civil-service laws. Rolph, mayor from 1911 to 1930 and then governor, built the civic center, parks, schools, streetcars, and the Hetch Hetchy aqueduct - the antique infrastructure of San Francisco today. Sympathetic to the conservation movement, willing to deal with organized labor in a union town that had America's only general strike in 1934, and tolerant of California's diversity, these progressive Republicans were the recognizable ancestors of the generally liberal San Franciscans of today.

More recently, the city has elected staunch liberal politicians, notably Mayor George Moscone and the first openly gay supervisor, Harvey Milk. Both were shot to death in 1978 by Dan White, a former city supervisor, who was found guilty of the lesser crime of voluntary manslaughter. Over the next decade, the city's cultural liberalism was tempered by Democratic Mayor Dianne Feinstein, who vetoed a domestic partnership ordinance and opposed commercial rent control. In 1995, Willie Brown, ousted after 15 years as speaker of the state Assembly, returned home and was elected mayor. Brown's political flair was always in evidence, but high taxes and an increasing homeless population drove out blue-collar families and immigrants.

As his successor, San Francisco installed Gavin Newsom, who in 2004 started issuing marriage licenses to same-sex couples, although California voters had outlawed same-sex marriage. The state Supreme Court ordered him to stop and voided the marriages. In 2008, Newsom was vindicated when the same court declared the ban on same-sex marriage unconstitutional. But his victory statement - "this door's wide open, it's going to happen, whether you like it or not" - was featured in ads for proponents of Proposition 8, which by a 52%-48% vote reversed the court's decision. The U.S. Supreme Court nullified that referendum in its seminal ruling in June 2013, when it ruled that supporters of the ballot measure had no standing to defend the referendum in court. In 2010, Newsom was elected California's lieutenant governor. The Board of Supervisors appointed City Administrator Ed Lee as interim mayor. Lee, the first Asian American to serve in that office, subsequently won two four-year terms.

The 12th Congressional District of California takes in most of the city and county of San Francisco, except that the southwest corner is in the 14th District. It includes all of San Francisco's high-rise downtown area, the crowded and bustling Chinatown, Telegraph Hill, Nob Hill and Russian Hill, North Beach, Pacific Heights, and the Marina District (which does not have a very big marina). In the valleys are the Fillmore and Western Addition areas. The 12th also has Noe Valley; the Castro, still mainly gay; Haight-Ashbury, once the bedraggled center of hippie culture and now another gentrifying San

Francisco neighborhood; and Potrero Hill, with its restored houses overlooking downtown. The Asian population of the district has grown to 33 percent, African Americans have dropped to 5 percent and Hispanics are 15 percent. James Fang, the overwhelmingly Democratic city's only elected Republican office-holder, was defeated in 2014 after serving as a Bay Area Rapid Transit director for 24 years. Hillary Clinton won 86 percent of the vote in 2016, placing the 12th among the top ten most Democratic districts in the nation.

THIRTEENTH DISTRICT

Barbara Lee (D)

Elected 1998, 10th term; b. Jul 16, 1946, El Paso, TX; Mills College (CA), B.A., 1973; University of California, Berkeley, M.S.W., 1975; Baptist; Divorced; 2 children; 5 grandchildren.

Elected Office: CA Assembly, 1991-1997; CA Senate, 1997-1998.

Professional Career: Chief of Staff, U.S. Rep. Ron Dellums, 1975-1987.

DC Office: 2267 RHOB 20515, 202-225-2661, Fax: 202-225-9817, lee.house.gov.

State Offices: Oakland, 510-763-0370.

Committees: *Appropriations*: Labor, Health & Human Services, Education & Related Agencies, Military Construction, Veterans Affairs & Related Agencies, State, Foreign Operations & Related Programs. *Budget*.

Group Ratings

	ADA	ACLU	AFL-CIO	LCV	ITI	COC	HAFA	ACU	CFG	FRC
2016	-	100%	-	100%	33%	46%	16%	4%	4%	0%
2015	95%	C	100%	91%	C	42%	C	4%	0%	0%

Almanac Ratings 2015

	Economy	Social	Foreign	Composite
Liberal	86%	100%	100%	95%
Conservative	15%	0%	0%	5%

Key Votes of the 114th Congress

1. Keystone Pipeline	NV	5. Puerto Rico Debt	Y	9. Offenses by Aliens	N
2. Trade Deals	N	6. Medical Marijuana	Y	10. Troops in Iraq	Y
3. Export-Import Bank	Y	7. Sanctuary Cities	N	11. Homeland Security $$	Y
4. Debt Ceiling Increase	Y	8. Armor-piercing Bullets	N	12. Trade Adjustment aid	Y

Election Results

Election	Name (Party)	Vote (%)		Cand. Spent	Ind. Exp. Support	Ind. Exp. Oppose
2016 General	Barbara Lee (D)	293,117	(91%)	$1,080,545		
	Sue Caro (R)	29,754	(9%)	$3,736		
2016 Primary	Barbara Lee (D)	192,227	(92%)			
	Sue Caro (R)	16,818	(8%)			

Prior winning percentages: 2014 (89%), 2012 (87%), 2010 (84%), 2008 (86%), 2006 (86%), 2004 (85%), 2002 (81%), 2000 (85%), 1998 (83%)

Democrat Barbara Lee, who won an April 1998 special election, is one of Congress' most liberal members, which has diminished her influence in a GOP-controlled House. From her prize seat on the Appropriations Committee, she seeks to help the poor while condemning U.S. military involvement overseas. Some of her proposals gained a receptive ear from the Obama administration, notably the opening of diplomatic relations with Cuba. She suffered a setback to fellow Californian Linda Sanchez in a bid for a leadership post.

Lee spent her childhood in Texas and says her political thinking was shaped by her early exposure to race discrimination. While in labor with her, Lee's mother was at first denied treatment at an El Paso hospital. Lee attended a segregated school in that city until her parents sent their children to a Catholic school. In 1960, the family moved to Southern California, where Lee was the first black cheerleader in her high school, a distinction she won after enlisting the help of the local chapter of the NAACP. In 2008, Lee authored a memoir, *Renegade for Peace and Justice*, in which she discussed her experiences as a single welfare mother raising two children while attending college and her early days of social advocacy. "In order to go the policy front, I had to do the personal," she said. Lee graduated from Mills College in Oakland and got a degree in social work at the University of California, Berkeley. She started a community mental health center in Berkeley and then worked as a staffer for 12 years for Rep. Ron Dellums, who chaired the House Armed Services Committee. She was elected to the California Assembly in 1990 and to the Senate in 1996. After Dellums announced he was resigning, he endorsed Lee as his successor, and she won the special election with 67 percent of the vote. She has not faced a serious primary or general election challenge.

Lee agitates for a reduction in the nation's weapons stockpiles and sharp cuts in Pentagon spending. She was a founder of the Out of Iraq Caucus, a group of the most vocal antiwar House members. In 2008, the House passed, 399-24, her bill to prevent permanent U.S. military bases in Iraq or U.S. control of Iraqi oil. In 2009, as a long-time advocate of ending the trade embargo, she led a delegation of Democrats to Cuba to discuss trade and other issues with its Communist-run government, and two years later helped to get charter passenger flights to the island nation from Oakland's airport. In January 2015, after President Barack Obama announced his plan to restore diplomatic relations with Cuba, the *San Francisco Chronicle* reported that she had a "gentlewoman's agreement" with Obama that she would become the ambassador to Havana. Lee denied the report and full-scale diplomatic relations were not restored, but she enthusiastically backed his efforts to lift the embargo and reach out to Cuba. She visited Cuba more than two dozen times and met senior officials to facilitate relatively minor agricultural and tourist dealings and to encourage more trust. When Fidel Castro died in November 2016, she extended her "deepest condolences" - a view that was not universally shared in Congress.

Lee's consistent opposition to military action occasionally has made her a lonely voice. As most Democrats voted to authorize the Clinton administration to bomb Serbia in 1999, Lee was the only House member to oppose a resolution supporting U.S. troops. In September 2001, she was the only member of Congress to vote against the resolution authorizing the use of force in response to the terrorist attacks. "If we rush to launch a counterattack, we run too great a risk that women, children and other noncombatants will be caught in the crossfire," she said. Her vote brought a torrent of national attention, though her concern turned out to be valid. Lee received threats of violence, and the Capitol police provided her with 24-hour protection. But she had supportive rallies in her district. Years later, she defended her vote on the basis that the resolution had yielded "perpetual war." During the debate in October 2002 to authorize the use of force in Iraq, Lee offered an alternative calling for diplomatic action, which was defeated 355-72. In May 2016, the House rejected, 285-138, her amendment to remove any authority for the president to use military force against the Islamic State.

In 2007, House Speaker Nancy Pelosi gave Lee a seat on the Appropriations Committee. She was one of 14 Democrats to vote against the Iraq war funding bill on the House floor. "My conscience is that we can't put up more money to fund this war," Lee said. As the co-chair of the Progressive Caucus, she laid out an agenda with three priorities: economic justice and security, protection of civil rights and liberties, and promotion of global peace. As Republican criticism mounted over earmarked spending, Lee remained a staunch defender of the practice. "I'll tell them to come to my community and see what we can accomplish with whatever federal dollars we can get," she said in 2009.

After the 2008 election, Lee became chairwoman of the Congressional Black Caucus, which she calls "the conscience of the Congress." She and other caucus members lamented Obama's failure to pay more attention to minorities. Unlike many other Black Caucus members who backed Hillary Clinton in 2008, Lee was his early supporter, in large part because of Obama's opposition to the Iraq war. In 2016, she did not take sides between Clinton and Sen. Bernie Sanders, which surprised some of her pro-Sanders progressive allies.

Pursuing her long-standing ambition for a leadership post, Lee ran for vice chair of the House Democratic Caucus following the 2016 election. Running against Rep. Linda Sanchez from Los Angeles, Lee was respected by many Caucus members. But multiple factors posed obstacles: The party leadership already included Pelosi from the Bay Area and Rep. James Clyburn of South Carolina from the Black Caucus. Sanchez, at 47, was a generation younger and better connected to various Democratic factions. Sanchez won, 98-96. Pelosi subsequently named Lee vice-chair of the Democratic Steering and Policy

Committee. A few days before the inauguration of President Donald Trump, Lee said, "I will be organizing and preparing for resistance."

East Bay: Oakland, Berkeley

Population		**Race and Ethnicity**		**Income**	
Total	733,401	White	34.4%	Median Income	$61,663 (127 out of 435)
Land area	97	Black	17.8%		
Pop/ sq mi	7577.2	Latino	21.5%		
Born in state	49.0%	Asian	20.6%	Under $50,000	26.7%
		Two races	4.5%	$50,000-$99,999	21.8%
Age Groups		Other	1.2%	$100,000-$199,999	9.7%
Under 18	19.4%			$200,000 or more	17.5%
18-34	28.0%	**Education**		Poverty Rate	17.5%
35-64	40.0%	H.S grad or less	30.2%		
Over 64	12.6%	Some college	24.2%	**Health Insurance**	
		College Degree, 4 yr	25.0%	With health insurance coverage	88.5%
Work		Post grad	20.7%		
White Collar	47.9%				
Sales and Service	37.9%	**Military**		**Public Assistance**	
Blue Collar	14.3%	Veteran	4.7%	Cash public assistance income	4.2%
Government	16.6%	Active Duty	0.2%		
				Food stamp/SNAP benefits	8.7%

Voter Turnout			
2015 Total Citizens 18+	498,750	2016 House Turnout as % CVAP	65%
2016 House turnout	322,871	2014 House Turnout as % CVAP	39%

2012 Presidential Vote		
Barack Obama	268,093	(88%)
Mitt Romney	27,474	(9%)

2016 Presidential Vote		
Hillary Clinton	291,926	(87%)
Donald Trump	22,743	(7%)
Jill Stein	12,039	(4%)

Cook Partisan Voting Index: D+40

On the East Bay opposite San Francisco, Oakland and Berkeley stand today on one of the lushest sites in America, overlooking the San Francisco-Oakland Bay Bridge and the Golden Gate Bridge and basking in the sunshine that is more common here than across the bay. Both cities host great institutions. In different ways they became museum pieces, antiques from a moment in the 1960s when both, especially Berkeley, gained identities that became hard to shake. But Oakland, in particular, has become transformed by the wealth that has made San Francisco accessible chiefly to the top income classes.

Berkeley was founded as a university town, named after the 18th-century Irish philosopher Bishop George Berkeley for his proclamation, "Westward the course of empire takes its way." Famous for years as the home of first-rate scholarship at the University of California, Berkeley became famous politically in 1964 as ground zero of student rebellion when an administrator's refusal to let students set up a table to sign up volunteers for Democrat Lyndon Johnson's presidential campaign led to months of riots, student strikes and classroom confrontations. In 1969, students led protests at "People's Park," a lot owned by the university, and Republican Gov. Ronald Reagan sent in the National Guard to protect state property, an episode in which both sides relished the confrontation. Berkeley gave birth to a street culture that still exists. Its denizens made common cause with the quasi-political Black Panthers from nearby Oakland and smoked marijuana with the Hell's Angels motorcycle gang. With its view of the bay, the campus is beautiful, and old buildings like the shingled Claremont Hotel are grand, although construction of new offices and apartment buildings have created a more modern look in the past couple decades.

Oakland has a different history, centered on commerce. (Gertrude Stein was wrong: There is a there there.) It became the western terminus of the transcontinental railroad in 1870 and was connected by ferry to San Francisco. It has always had heavy industry, and its port today is the fifth-busiest in the country. The docks attracted young roustabouts like the writer Jack London, after whom a downtown square is named. Civic affairs were run by the local elite like the Knowland family, who owned the *Oakland Tribune*. With the Bay Area's largest black community, Oakland spawned the Black Panthers, a militant organization that came to define late 1960s radicalism. "The Black Panthers were mostly young activists whose personal lives and oftentimes limited professional opportunities were defined by Oakland's increasingly impoverished landscape," wrote Peniel Joseph in his history of the Black Power movement, *Waiting 'Til the Midnight Hour.* African-American leaders began to dominate city government in the 1970s and the *Tribune* came under black ownership in the 1980s.

In 1994, Jerry Brown arrived. Governor of California 20 years earlier and an unsuccessful presidential candidate several times over, he ran an unorthodox campaign for mayor and won. Brown irritated local factions by firing department heads and ignoring long-standing alliances, but he seemed to take seriously his mission of propelling Oakland to prominence. With his tough talk on crime and advocacy of big development projects that drove up rents, he sounded like a conservative. Crime rates dropped, and the local economy thrived, partly with the growth of middle-income refugees from the exorbitant housing costs of San Francisco. Many longtime residents, especially African Americans, complained about rising costs, and they moved to the outskirts. The city's black population fell from 47 percent in 1980 to 28 percent in 2010.

After Brown's departure, community leaders in 2007 created a public-private initiative called the Oakland Partnership, with the goal of attracting 10,000 jobs over five years. Although poverty has remained prevalent, the Oakland real estate market rebounded, partly because it had become undervalued in the booming Bay Area. Population, after falling by 10,000 from 2000 to 2010, increased by 30,000 in the next five years. In the gentrifying city, Hispanics increased to 25 percent and Asians to 17 percent. The "housing frenzy" was shifting eastward across the bay, Bloomberg News reported in August 2016. "Despite persistently high crime rates and political turmoil, Oakland is attracting residents for its relative affordability, vibrant cultural scene, diverse population and urban environment within commuting distance to San Francisco." Residential prices increased 16 percent in the previous year, and the median home sale price soared 178 percent from 2011 to 2016, according to real estate data. Commercial office rents rose 43 percent in two years. The Oakland Airport, even though its passenger load was less than one-fourth of San Francisco's airport, had sits own growth spurt, with new routes and plans to complete a $200 million renovation of its main terminal.

Problems remained, including a massive strike that shut down businesses and Oakland's bustling port in 2011. Racial tensions were buttressed by a 2014 police report that 62 percent of local police stops were made on blacks. The local sports scene was in turmoil. After winning the NBA championship in 2015 at Oracle Arena in Oakland, the Golden State Warriors broke ground in January 2017 on an extravagant arena in San Francisco's Mission Bay. The NFL's Raiders, following the failure of lengthy discussions for a new stadium in Oakland, made tentative plans to move to a lush publicly financed stadium in Las Vegas. The December 2016 Ghost Ship fire that killed 36 persons at a warehouse in an entertainment district was horrific, though it put a spotlight on the bustling arts scene in Oakland.

The 13th Congressional District of California consists of Oakland and Berkeley; the suburb of San Leandro, originally settled by Portuguese immigrants; and the island city of Alameda. It's the most Democratic district in California and one of the most liberal in the nation. The 7 percent of the vote in 2016 for Donald Trump in the 13th was lower than all but two districts in New York City.

FOURTEENTH DISTRICT

Jackie Speier (D)

Elected 2008, 5th term; b. May 14, 1950, San Francisco; University of California Davis, B.A., 1972; University of California Hastings College of Law, J.D., 1976; Roman Catholic; Married (Barry Dennis); 2 children.

Elected Office: San Mateo County Board of Supervisors, 1980-1986; CA Assembly, 1986-1998; CA Senate, 1998-2006.

Professional Career: Staff aide, Rep. Leo Ryan, 1973-1978; Director, gov. affairs, Community Gatepath, 1996-1998; Director, gov. affairs, Electronic Arts, 1996-1998; Attorney, 2007-2008.

DC Office: 2465 RHOB 20515, 202-225-3531, Fax: 202-226-4183, speier.house.gov.

State Offices: San Mateo, 650-342-0300.

Committees: *Armed Services*: Emerging Threats & Capabilities, Military Personnel (RMM). *Permanent Select on Intelligence*.

Group Ratings

	ADA	ACLU	AFL-CIO	LCV	ITI	COC	HAFA	ACU	CFG	FRC
2016	-	94%	-	100%	60%	50%	11%	4%	4%	0%
2015	75%	C	100%	91%	C	50%	C	5%	0%	0%

Almanac Ratings 2015

	Economy	Social	Foreign	Composite
Liberal	85%	88%	96%	90%
Conservative	15%	12%	4%	10%

Key Votes of the 114th Congress

1. Keystone Pipeline	N	5. Puerto Rico Debt	N	9. Offenses by Aliens	Y
2. Trade Deals	NV	6. Medical Marijuana	Y	10. Troops in Iraq	Y
3. Export-Import Bank	Y	7. Sanctuary Cities	N	11. Homeland Security $$	NV
4. Debt Ceiling Increase	Y	8. Armor-piercing Bullets	N	12. Trade Adjustment aid	Y

Election Results

Election	Name (Party)	Vote (%)		Cand. Spent	Ind. Exp. Support	Ind. Exp. Oppose
2016 General	Jackie Speier (D)	231,630	(81%)	$406,672	$1,963	
	Angel Cardenas (R)	54,817	(19%)	$3,578		
2016 Primary	Jackie Speier (D)	144,719	(99%)			

Prior winning percentages: 2014 (77%), 2012 (79%), 2010 (76%), 2008 (75%)

Democrat Jackie Speier, who won a special election in April 2008, brought with her a unique experience as a young House aide and a continuing interest in national security. A committed liberal, she has focused on consumer-protection issues as well as on exposing rapes and sexual assaults within the military and in society as a whole. She has become an outspoken advocate for gender equity.

Born in San Francisco's Sunset district, Speier graduated from the University of California, Davis, and got her law degree at UC Hastings College of the Law. While an undergraduate, she interned in Sacramento for Democratic Assemblyman Leo Ryan and later joined his staff after he was elected to Congress. In November 1978, Speier accompanied third-term Rep. Ryan to Jonestown, Guyana, to investigate claims that some of Ryan's constituents, who were members of a church called the Peoples Temple, were being held against their will by the Rev. Jim Jones of San Francisco. Some defectors from the church joined Ryan's entourage for the journey home, but the group made it only as far as the airport. Four assassins sent by Jones opened fire on the defenseless group. Ryan and four others, including two journalists, were killed. Speier was shot five times and left for dead on the airstrip, where she waited 15 hours before the Guyana police rescued her. In the meantime, Jones, back at his jungle camp, set in motion events that shocked the world. He forced his cult followers to commit "revolutionary suicide" by drinking poison-laced punch, which resulted in the deaths of more than 900 followers, some of them babies and children.

Once back in California, Speier underwent 10 surgeries, including skin grafts. Despite her injuries, she ran in the special election to succeed Ryan, gaining only 15 percent of the total vote and finishing third among Democrats in the primary. She then went local to build her political career, starting on the San Mateo County Board of Supervisors and serving 18 years in the state Legislature. Her pinnacle achievement was legislation protecting consumers' privacy from invasive practices by banks and insurance companies. In 2006, she unsuccessfully sought the nomination for lieutenant governor. A year later she joined three other women in co-authoring a book, *This Is Not the Life I Ordered: 50 Ways to Keep Your Head Above Water When Life Keeps Dragging You Down.*

When Democratic Rep. Tom Lantos, chairman of the House Foreign Affairs Committee and the only Holocaust survivor to serve in Congress, announced his retirement in January 2008, he endorsed Speier as his successor. He died in February of complications from cancer of the esophagus. Speier immediately became the front-runner. She won the all-party election with 75 percent of the vote against four little-known opponents.

Immediately after she took her oath of office, she caused a ruckus when she launched a sharp partisan attack on President George W. Bush's handling of the war in Iraq. "History will not judge us kindly if we sacrifice four generations of Americans because of the folly of one," she declared. Her remarks triggered a volley of boos among Republican members on the floor and prompted Republican Rep. Darrell Issa of California to walk out of the chamber, claiming she had violated House rules of decorum. Speier responded that she had been "forthright." Later, in March 2010, Speier joined 59 other Democrats in voting for a resolution requiring the withdrawal of troops from Afghanistan. Since then, as a member of the Armed Services Committee, she regularly has appeared on the House floor to speak about military men and women who have been raped or sexually assaulted, and she has taken a lead role in improving delivery of benefits to Bay Area veterans. She also would give women in the military access to free birth control and counseling. In 2017, she became ranking Democrat on the committee's military personnel panel. In addition to continuing her earlier work on sexual violence and harassment plus whistleblower protection, she said that she would work "to ensure that our government demonstrates the same level of commitment to our military personnel that they demonstrate by putting their lives on the line to defend our country."

Speier has expanded her focus on sexual assault to academia, where she has shined the spotlight on sexual harassers, especially in science and engineering. "Left in their wake is a trail of broken, damaged careers and lives," she wrote. "Survivors (often graduate students and post-docs) lose years of research, their funding, their confidence, and even sometimes their careers." In September 2016, she filed a bill to require universities to operate under greater transparency with respect to substantiated cases of sex discrimination. Following reports of an increase in sexual assaults on college campuses, she was part of a bipartisan House group in 2014 that said one response should be to include the data for each school in the annual college rankings of *U.S. News & World Report*. "The issue has not been taken seriously enough," she said, although the studies have been widely criticized. Also that year, she called on NFL Commissioner Roger Goodell to resign because of his handling of domestic-violence cases involving several of the league's players.

In February 2011, during a House debate over funding for abortion providers, Speier emotionally discussed her own experience with abortion. She said that she had to terminate a pregnancy in the second trimester because of a serious medical complication, and she suggested that ardent anti-abortion rights Republican Rep. Chris Smith of New Jersey was mischaracterizing the procedure she had. "For you to stand on this floor and to suggest, as you have, that somehow this is a procedure that is either welcomed or done cavalierly or done without any thought is preposterous," Speier said. In 2016, she said that she wants to repeal the "pink tax," which she described as the higher prices that women pay for comparable goods and services.

Earlier in her career, Speier focused on more traditional consumer and fairness issues. She drew attention in 2010 when she spent five days living on a food-stamp budget of $4.50 a day to call attention to rising poverty. During debate on a major financial services regulatory bill in 2009, Speier passed in the House an amendment requiring big banks to have at least $1 in capital for every $15 in assets. In the final bill, lawmakers watered down the requirement, giving federal regulators the option of enforcing the limit only if a firm posed a "grave threat" to financial stability.

After the massive 2010 pipeline explosion in her district killed eight people, Speier introduced a pipeline safety bill. The measure, enacted in January 2012, doubled the maximum fine for safety violations to $2 million, authorized more pipeline inspectors, and required automatic shut-off valves on new or replaced pipelines.

Speier considered running for state attorney general in 2010 but opted to stay in the House. She has not faced a serious reelection challenge.

San Francisco Peninsula: San Mateo

Population		**Race and Ethnicity**		**Income**	
Total	736,622	White	35.2%	Median Income	$89,241 (19 out of 435)
Land area	260	Black	3.1%		
Pop/ sq mi	2838.6	Latino	24.4%	Under $50,000	27.4%
Born in state	47.0%	Asian	32.0%	$50,000-$99,999	29.1%
Age Groups		Two races	3.5%	$100,000-$199,999	16.0%
Under 18	20.5%	Other	1.8%	$200,000 or more	8.6%
18-34	22.8%	**Education**		Poverty Rate	8.6%
35-64	42.4%	H.S grad or less	29.6%	**Health Insurance**	
Over 64	14.4%	Some college	27.1%	With health insurance coverage	91.1%
Work		College Degree, 4 yr	27.1%		
White Collar	43.1%	Post grad	16.1%	**Public Assistance**	
Sales and Service	42.8%	**Military**		Cash public assistance income	1.7%
Blue Collar	14.1%	Veteran	4.6%		
Government	12.5%	Active Duty	0.0%	Food stamp/SNAP benefits	3.7%

Voter Turnout			
2015 Total Citizens 18+	480,880	2016 House Turnout as % CVAP	60%
2016 House turnout	286,447	2014 House Turnout as % CVAP	31%

2012 Presidential Vote		
Barack Obama	200,343	(74%)
Mitt Romney	63,589	(24%)

2016 Presidential Vote		
Hillary Clinton	229,008	(76%)
Donald Trump	54,229	(18%)
Gary Johnson	8,126	(3%)

Cook Partisan Voting Index: D+27

The city of San Francisco sits at the tip of the San Francisco Peninsula on the California coast. This is geologically interesting country. The San Andreas Fault runs just east of the Coast Range, underneath the reservoirs that store San Francisco's water supply. To the west are green mountains running down to the ocean. To the east is a zone of flat land between mountain and San Francisco Bay, an unbroken chain of suburbs and urban settlement, with light industry and salt flats along the bay front. Daly City and Pacifica on the ocean are a kind of extension of San Francisco's old working-class districts, with boxy houses on streets looking out on the ocean or the freeway. Today, these neighborhoods are home to many of the Bay Area's Asian immigrants. Pacific Islanders are prominent, too. A large concentration of Samoans is in Daly City, and San Bruno is home to a sizable Tongan community. A strip of Highway 1 that winds along the coastal cliffs south of Pacifica has passed through an area known as "Devil's Slide" for the mudslides that often follow heavy storms. A tunnel now bypasses Devil's Slide.

On the Bay side is South San Francisco, where Herb Boyer and Bob Swanson sketched on a napkin their plans for the first biotechnology company, Genentech. They bought space in an old warehouse on the waterfront near a Bethlehem Steel plant. In 2009, Genentech was purchased by the Swiss pharmaceutical firm Roche and had a market capitalization exceeding $100 billion. The area is one large biotech campus overlooking the Bay, with lawns, parkways and earth-toned office complexes, the center of the industry. *YouTube*, started in 2005, is headquartered in San Bruno. Oracle, a computer software company, is based in a cluster of gleaming glass buildings in Redwood City. The exorbitant cost of real estate has imposed a premium on large employers. In November 2014, Google bought more than a million square feet of office space in Redwood City, most of which was leased at the time. On the site of the former Bay Meadows racetrack near San Mateo, an 83-acre master-planned community is being developed. Stanford University in 2016 began construction of a $568 million project that is scheduled to house 2,400 employees on 35 acres in Redwood City, a few miles up El Camino Real from Leland Stanford's original "farm," as many refer to the campus.

Between the Bayshore Freeway and Interstate 280 are middle class suburbs that grew up to be cities with office complexes - Millbrae, Burlingame, San Mateo and San Carlos. Bolstered by many large and creative local companies, the area weathered the recession better than most. In December 2016, the county's unemployment rate was 2.7 percent, the lowest in the state. The average monthly rent in 2016 for a two-bedroom apartment was $3,018. In the county, agricultural production dropped $20 million in 2015, chiefly in floral and nursery crops, due to such factors as the paucity of migrant labor, the high cost of land and the drought. Otherwise, the local economy remained booming. The county council voted to raise the minimum wage to $15 hourly, and voters approved a half-cent increase in the sales tax, which resulted in a combined sales tax of 9 percent in San Mateo. The area has been the source of incredible athletic talent: Junipero Serra, an all-boys Catholic high school in San Mateo, enrolled both New England Patriots quarterback Tom Brady and former San Francisco Giants slugger Barry Bonds.

On Sept. 9, 2010, a ruptured gas line in San Bruno caused a massive explosion that killed eight people and destroyed 38 homes. Federal investigators found cracks in welds that held sections of the pipe together, and it was revealed that pipeline owner Pacific Gas and Electric Co. had cut corners in its safety inspections. California regulators have imposed $1.6 billion in penalties, its largest ever. PG&E responded that it was "deeply sorry" and that the penalty was appropriate.

The 14th Congressional District of California consists of these northern peninsula suburbs plus the southwest corner of San Francisco, which has less than 20 percent of the district population. It takes in about 80 percent of affluent San Mateo County. The 14th is 34 percent Asian and 24 percent Hispanic. The economic orientation here was historically toward San Francisco, then later toward Silicon Valley. But now the district has its own burgeoning biotech industry, and income levels are among the highest in California. Politically, the 14th District is overwhelmingly Democratic. The 76 percent of the vote for Hillary Clinton in 2016 was slightly more than Barack Obama received in his two elections.

FIFTEENTH DISTRICT

Eric Swalwell (D)

Elected 2012, 3rd term; b. Nov 16, 1980, Sac City, IA; University of Maryland - College Park, B.A., 2003; University of Maryland School of Law, J.D., 2006; Christian - Non-Denominational; Married (Brittany Ann Watts).

Elected Office: Dublin City Council, 2010-2012.

Professional Career: Deputy District Attorney, Alameda County, 2006-2012.

DC Office: 129 CHOB 20515, 202-225-5065, Fax: 202-226-3805, swalwell.house.gov.

State Offices: Castro Valley, 510-370-3322.

Committees: House Democratic Steering and Policy Committee Co-Chair. *Judiciary*: Courts, Intellectual Property & Internet, Regulatory Reform, Commercial & Antitrust Law. *Permanent Select on Intelligence*.

Group Ratings

	ADA	ACLU	AFL-CIO	LCV	ITI	COC	HAFA	ACU	CFG	FRC
2016	-	82%	-	97%	67%	57%	12%	0%	11%	0%
2015	85%	C	100%	97%	C	55%	C	0%	0%	0%

Almanac Ratings 2015

	Economy	Social	Foreign	Composite
Liberal	85%	100%	93%	93%
Conservative	15%	0%	7%	7%

Key Votes of the 114th Congress

1. Keystone Pipeline	N	5. Puerto Rico Debt	Y	9. Offenses by Aliens	N
2. Trade Deals	N	6. Medical Marijuana	Y	10. Troops in Iraq	Y
3. Export-Import Bank	Y	7. Sanctuary Cities	N	11. Homeland Security $$	Y
4. Debt Ceiling Increase	Y	8. Armor-piercing Bullets	N	12. Trade Adjustment aid	Y

Election Results

Election	Name (Party)	Vote (%)		Cand. Spent	Ind. Exp. Support	Ind. Exp. Oppose
2016 General	Eric Swalwell (D).........................	198,578	(74%)	$1,032,031		
	Danny Turner (R).........................	70,619	(26%)	$369		
2016 Primary	Eric Swlawell (D).........................	110,803	(77%)			
	Danny Turner (R).........................	34	(24%)			

Prior winning percentages: 2014 (70%), 2012 (52%)

Democrat Eric Swalwell, whose defeat of 40-year Democratic Rep. Pete Stark in 2012 alarmed some Democrats who prefer the comfort of seniority, moved quickly to mend fences with Minority Leader Nancy Pelosi and her team. With his youth and focus on tech and intelligence issues, Swalwell has brought fresh thinking into the mostly retirement-age Democratic delegation in the Bay Area and to the House more broadly.

Born in Sac City, Iowa, Swalwell grew up in Dublin California. He attended the University of Maryland, where he was bitten by the political bug and graduated with a bachelor's in government and politics and then a law degree. He got his start in politics as an unpaid intern on Capitol Hill, working for then-Rep. Ellen Tauscher, a moderate Bay Area Democrat. To make ends meet, he worked two summer jobs around the Capitol, at the local gym and a restaurant, where he kept an eye out for members of Congress. "In the morning I would serve them gym towels," he said. "In the evening, I would serve them dinner." After graduation, Swalwell moved back to California and got a job as a prosecutor in the Alameda County district attorney's office, where he rose to the post of deputy district attorney. "I put a lot of bad guys away," he told voters on the campaign trail. In 2010, he ran successfully for city council in Dublin, an outer suburb of San Francisco.

Other prominent California Democrats had been patiently waiting for Stark to retire, including former Obama administration official Ro Khanna, who raised more than $1 million for a congressional bid. But as the 2012 election approached, Khanna and others opted to let Stark serve another term unchallenged. Swalwell jumped the line. Much of the Democratic establishment backed Stark. Swalwell got support from a smattering of local officials, including Tauscher, his former boss. Swalwell began the campaign by pointedly competing in running races across the district, a series his campaign dubbed the "race for change." The contrast between the 80-year-old incumbent and the 31-year-old challenger was hard to miss. Beyond his hustle, Swalwell's campaign was largely fueled by Stark's own missteps.

During a debate, Stark made multiple mistakes for which he had to apologize. He wrongly accused Swalwell of taking bribes. He wrongly accused a local newspaper columnist of donating to his opponent. He threatened the family and livelihood of a local politician who endorsed Swalwell, but claimed he was provoked. After the slip-ups, the notoriously mercurial Stark was largely cloistered out of sight, instead relying on hard-hitting mailers, the rare scripted appearance, and high name recognition after his decades of service. Swalwell reached out to Republicans and independents dissatisfied with Stark's long liberal tenure. He didn't promise to vote all that differently from Stark-he describes himself as a solid Democrat, though he believes "every human problem does not need a legislative solution"-but said that he would at least listen intently as their congressman. His 52%-48% victory in the November run-off was an ironic way for Stark to exit: Four decades earlier, Stark had made much the same argument in unseating the previous octogenarian congressman.

In the House, Swalwell took action on what he called a series of "small steps." He enacted his Philippines Charitable Giving Assistance Act, which permitted tax deductions for contributions to recovery in the Philippines following a typhoon that devastated the islands in 2013. He attributed his success to bipartisan outreach. "The reason that the Bay Area, especially Silicon Valley, has led the way in innovation is that it's a collaborative environment," he told the *San Francisco Chronicle*, in reviewing his first term. Swalwell joined the Intelligence Committee and has served as the ranking Democrat on its CIA Subcommittee, which oversees the agency's policy, activities and budget. The House-passed intelligence authorization bill in 2016 included his proposal to keep Congress informed about foreign fighters traveling to terrorist safe havens. In 2017, he joined the Judiciary Committee, where he filed with veteran Republican Rep. Jim Sensenbrenner of Wisconsin the Rapid DNA bill, which encourages technology for quick analysis of DNA.

Swalwell kept busy with non-legislative work. He joined with other junior House Democrats to create the Future Forum-chiefly to engage with millennials, especially on campuses. With his social-media skills, he became the Snapchat king of Congress. Pelosi gave him a political assignment to oversee Democratic outreach to young voters. She also appointed Swalwell to an insider post as co-chair of Democratic Steering and Policy Committee.

In 2014, Swalwell began his campaign with warnings from Stark and his allies that they planned to get even. His chief challenger was Democratic state Senate Majority Leader Ellen Corbett. She attacked Swalwell's inexperience and lack of Democratic credentials. Turning the tables, the incumbent claimed support from the party establishment. Swalwell benefited from a huge fundraising advantage. Despite Stark's earlier promise to give her a big boost, Corbett raised only $225,000 to Swalwell's $2 million for the cycle. Surprisingly, Corbett failed to survive the all-party primary. Swalwell got 49 percent of the total vote, and Corbett ran 430 votes behind Republican candidate Hugh Bussell. The general election became an after-thought, with Swalwell winning, 70%-30%. In 2016, his challenger had scant campaign presence.

Swalwell appeared to have made all of the right moves, and was settling in for a potentially long tenure.

Southern East Bay: Hayward, Fremont

Population		**Race and Ethnicity**		**Income**	
Total	741,528	White	34.7%	Median Income	$92,311 (14 out of 435)
Land area	599	Black	6.0%	Under $50,000	27.0%
Pop/ sq mi	1237.0	Latino	23.2%	$50,000-$99,999	32.3%
Born in state	51.2%	Asian	30.4%	$100,000-$199,999	14.3%
		Two races	4.1%	$200,000 or more	8.2%
Age Groups		Other	1.6%	Poverty Rate	8.2%
Under 18	24.5%				
18-34	21.8%	**Education**		**Health Insurance**	
35-64	42.2%	H.S grad or less	31.5%	With health insurance coverage	91.4%
Over 64	11.5%	Some college	27.5%		
		College Degree, 4 yr	26.1%		
Work		Post grad	14.9%	**Public Assistance**	
White Collar	45.3%			Cash public assistance income	3.1%
Sales and Service	38.0%	**Military**		Food stamp/SNAP benefits	5.8%
Blue Collar	16.6%	Veteran	5.1%		
Government	11.8%	Active Duty	0.1%		

Voter Turnout			
2015 Total Citizens 18+	460,000	2016 House Turnout as % CVAP	59%
2016 House turnout	269,197	2014 House Turnout as % CVAP	31%

2012 Presidential Vote		
Barack Obama	177,243	(68%)
Mitt Romney	77,748	(30%)

2016 Presidential Vote		
Hillary Clinton	198,964	(69%)
Donald Trump	68,808	(24%)
Gary Johnson	10,604	(4%)

Cook Partisan Voting Index: D+20

The East Bay is the workaday, unglamorous side of the San Francisco Bay Area - a narrow strip of land between the Bay and the surprisingly high mountains that rise just to the east. The shoreline is not picturesque, with its closed-down Navy bases and its docks, airports and salt evaporators. The Bay Bridge cuts an inspiring figure, though it has required constant patching. A new span was opened in September 2013, but complaints continued about its safety. The San Mateo Bridge to the south is at best utilitarian. In World War II, when the shipyards of Richmond were buzzing, the East Bay south of Oakland was still largely uninhabited farm fields. After the war, the area filled up, south along old Route 17: Hayward, with its California State University campus and seafood industry; Union City, with its rail yards; and Newark, with dozens of industrial plants ranging from salt processing to computer network servers. Hit hard by the dot-com bust at the turn of the century, the East Bay revived with biotech, construction and health care, only to be set back like the rest of California during the recession.

The national labs are a vital presence here. At the Lawrence Livermore National Laboratory, the federal government conducts nuclear-warhead and energy research. Also in Livermore is a part of the Albuquerque-based Sandia National Labs, which offers scientific and technological expertise on the nation's most challenging security issues. The labs respectively have 6,300 and more than 1,000 employees in Livermore. Since the 1980s, anti-nuclear protestors have gathered at Livermore to commemorate historical events and denounce nuclear weapons.

Underneath the East Bay is the Hayward Fault, not as famous as the San Andreas, but a branch of it that is just as dangerous. An earthquake there in 1868 registered about 7.0 on the Richter scale. Another rupture is overdue, and 7 million people in the region might be shaken significantly, with damage likely to exceed $100 billion.

The 15th Congressional District of California is made up of East Bay towns in southern Alameda County and part of Castro Valley. It includes a small slice of Contra Costa County near San Ramon. The majority-minority district is racially and ethnically mixed: 34 percent Asian, 22 percent Hispanic, and 6 percent black. It includes Hayward, with its significant Asian and Hispanic populations, and Union City, which has become more than 50 percent Asian. In Pleasanton, an Asian shopping center - the Pacific Pearl - was scheduled to open in 2017. Politically, this is a safe Democratic district. In 2016, Hillary Clinton got 69 percent of the vote, which was smaller than her vote in seven other Bay Area districts.

SIXTEENTH DISTRICT

Jim Costa (D)

Elected 2004, 7th term; b. Apr 13, 1952, Fresno; California State University, Fresno, B.S., 1974; Roman Catholic; Single.

Elected Office: CA Assembly, 1978-1994; CA Senate, 1994-2002.

Professional Career: Consultant, 2002-2004.

DC Office: 2081 RHOB 20515, 202-225-3341, Fax: 202-225-9308, costa.house.gov.

State Offices: Fresno, 559-495-1620; Merced, 209-384-1620.

Committees: *Agriculture*: Biotechnology, Horticulture & Research, Livestock & Foreign Agriculture (RMM). *Natural Resources*: Energy & Mineral Resources, Water, Power & Oceans.

Group Ratings

	ADA	ACLU	AFL-CIO	LCV	ITI	COC	HAFA	ACU	CFG	FRC
2016	-	76%	-	55%	83%	86%	17%	4%	17%	8%
2015	45%	C	75%	43%	C	89%	C	4%	15%	8%

Almanac Ratings 2015

	Economy	Social	Foreign	Composite
Liberal	48%	100%	50%	66%
Conservative	52%	0%	50%	34%

Key Votes of the 114th Congress

1. Keystone Pipeline	Y	5. Puerto Rico Debt	Y	9. Offenses by Aliens	N
2. Trade Deals	Y	6. Medical Marijuana	Y	10. Troops in Iraq	N
3. Export-Import Bank	Y	7. Sanctuary Cities	N	11. Homeland Security $$	Y
4. Debt Ceiling Increase	Y	8. Armor-piercing Bullets	N	12. Trade Adjustment aid	Y

Election Results

Election	Name (Party)	Vote (%)		Cand. Spent	Ind. Exp. Support	Ind. Exp. Oppose
2016 General	Jim Costa (D)	97,473	(58%)	$1,625,897	$31,627	
	Johnny Tacherra (R)	70,483	(42%)	$509,829		
2016 Primary	Jim Costa (D)	33,956	(54%)			
	Johnny Tacherra (R)	21,200	(34%)			
	David Rogers (R)	7,574	(12%)			

Prior winning percentages: 2014 (51%), 2012 (57%), 2010 52%), 2008 (74%), 2006 (0%), 2004 (53%)

Democrat Jim Costa, elected in 2004, is a third-generation farmer who concentrates on the agricultural issues that affect his district's rural residents, often trying to find a middle ground between production and resource protection. For now, he is the only remaining Democrat from the Central Valley who fits the traditional mold of voting conservative on many economic and social policies but taking his party's side on most big issues. He has survived competitive reelection challenges.

Born in Fresno, he was raised on his family's dairy farm. He is the grandson of Portuguese immigrants who settled in the San Joaquin Valley near the turn of the 20th century. In 1978, Costa was elected to the state Assembly, where he was known as a moderate Democrat. In 2002, after he was forced to retire at age 50 because of term limits, Costa founded a consulting firm. Two years later, when Democratic Rep. Cal Dooley retired after 14 years, Costa entered the race with solid name recognition. His former state Senate district covered the entire congressional district. In the March primary, he faced a bruising challenge from Lisa Quigley, Dooley's chief of staff. Quigley grew up in the Central Valley, but she hadn't lived in the district in nearly two decades. Costa questioned her residency and her agricultural credentials. Quigley was endorsed by Dooley and national abortion rights groups and she painted Costa as a special-interest lobbyist. In the campaign's final days, Quigley ran ads mentioning Costa's 1986 arrest for soliciting a prostitute and a 1994 incident in which police found drug paraphernalia in his home. Costa shrugged off the attacks and won the primary by an unexpectedly large 73%-27%.

In the general election, Costa began as a clear favorite in the Democratic-leaning district. But the Republican nominee, state Sen. Roy Ashburn, ran a formidable campaign. He criticized Costa for supporting tax policies that he said hurt low-income families. The National Republican Congressional Committee ran $1.5 million in ads saying, "Jim Costa - he's gonna cost ya." But Costa's lengthy legislative record didn't readily lend itself to the "liberal" label. In a relatively low turnout event, Costa won 53%-47%.

Costa sits on the Agriculture and Natural Resources committees, both important to his district. He is the ranking Democrat on the re-named Livestock and Foreign Agriculture Committee. In 2016, he helped to enact the sweeping water resources bill, with vital provisions that steered more water to the San Joaquin Delta. Costa called it a positive step "to create more reliable water supplies for the valley and all Californians." Among the provisions he cited were flood planning for Merced County, steps to stretch the water supply of the San Joaquin River and expedited review of proposed water transfers.

Local water supply has been a continuing preoccupation for Costa. With then-Rep. Dennis Cardoza, a fellow Blue Dog from the valley, he was among the final undecided votes in 2010 on President Barack Obama's health care overhaul. Republicans charged that they were given extra public water allocations for their region, though both denied there was any connection. Costa was one of 10 Democrats to vote for California GOP Rep. Devin Nunes' House-passed bill in 2012 to change California's system of water laws to benefit San Joaquin Valley farmers. Costa supported lifting the ban on oil drilling 50 to 100 miles off the nation's coast, but he sought to maintain the federal ban on drilling within 25 miles of shore. Costa has bucked his party on fiscal issues that bring out his conservative impulses. He was one of 22 House Democrats to support a failed proposal in 2012 to adopt the Simpson-Bowles commission's budget, which imposed politically painful spending reductions to balance the budget.

Costa did not face a significant reelection challenge until 2010. That year, Republican rancher Andy Vidak sought to blame Costa for the area's weak economy, running billboards depicting him as the pitchfork-holding "American Gothic" farmer with Speaker Nancy Pelosi at his side. Vidak surged in the polls, and in the closing weeks the race became a toss-up. Costa put in a month of heavy retail politicking, and he got last-minute help from the Democratic Congressional Campaign Committee. The Obama administration announced a few days before the election that California would get $715 million for high-speed rail, contingent on money being spent quickly on a San Joaquin Valley segment. In a recount that dragged on for three weeks, Costa won 52%-48%.

The 2012 redistricting gave Costa what seemed to be the favorable 16th District, though three-fourths of it was new political territory for him. Initially, national Republicans focused their attention elsewhere. The 2014 election became a big surprise. In the first round of voting in June, Fresno County dairyman Johnny Tacherra easily led three other Republican candidates and moved into the general election with Costa. Before he decided to make the challenge, Tacherra met with Costa in his Washington office and pleaded for more water assistance for local farmers. But he felt rebuffed when the meeting ended. "I'm going to run for Congress against this guy because he does not represent us, he's not going to help us," Tacherra later recounted to *National Review*.

Running with no national-party assistance and one modestly paid campaign aide, Tacherra worked the grass roots to show his connection to the drought-stricken district, and he painted the incumbent as out of touch. Costa outspent the challenger by nearly 5-to-1. He was so confident that he made contributions to endangered Democrats elsewhere during the closing weeks of the campaign. When the votes were tallied on election night, and for the following week, Tacherra shockingly held a narrow lead. He flew to Washington to join the bipartisan freshman orientation. But Costa prevailed just before Thanksgiving. He won by 1,334 votes on the strength of taking 64 percent of the Fresno County vote. Tacherra handily won Madera and Merced counties. Following that scare, Costa sided with Republicans on multiple House votes, including support of the Keystone XL pipeline and new restrictions on Obama's regulatory authority.

Costa was better prepared when Tacherra returned for a rematch in 2016. Donald Trump, a Republican handicap in this Latino-majority district, gave Democrats an opportunity to increase turnout. The 168,000 voters were nearly twice the turnout in the 2014 mid-term, and more than 20,000 more than in the 2012 presidential election. In contrast to 2014 when Costa left more than $600,000 in his campaign account, this time he spent all of the $1.7 million that he raised. With only $526,000 raised and the National Republican Congressional Committee more focused on support for two vulnerable GOP incumbents in the Central Valley, Tacherra had less opportunity to make his case. Costa won 58%-42%. Virtually all of his 27,000-vote margin came from Fresno.

As has been the case throughout Costa's career, he managed to find a way.

Central Valley: Merced, Part of Fresno

Population		**Race and Ethnicity**		**Income**	
Total	717,984	White	23.5%	Median Income	$37,291 (412 out of 435)
Land area	2,840	Black	5.6%	Under $50,000	26.0%
Pop/ sq mi	252.9	Latino	59.2%	$50,000-$99,999	10.3%
Born in state	64.3%	Asian	9.1%	$100,000-$199,999	1.7%
		Two races	1.8%	$200,000 or more	31.4%
		Other	0.9%	Poverty Rate	31.4%
Age Groups		**Education**		**Health Insurance**	
Under 18	31.0%	H.S grad or less	59.1%	With health insurance coverage	81.9%
18-34	26.6%	Some college	29.1%		
35-64	32.9%	College Degree, 4 yr	8.2%		
Over 64	9.6%	Post grad	3.5%		
Work		**Military**		**Public Assistance**	
White Collar	21.4%	Veteran	5.3%	Cash public assistance income	10.4%
Sales and Service	41.8%	Active Duty	0.0%	Food stamp/SNAP benefits	25.4%
Blue Collar	36.7%				
Government	15.7%				

Voter Turnout			
2015 Total Citizens 18+	384,570	2016 House Turnout as % CVAP	44%
2016 House turnout	167,956	2014 House Turnout as % CVAP	24%

2012 Presidential Vote		
Barack Obama	88,973	(59%)
Mitt Romney	59,808	(39%)

2016 Presidential Vote		
Hillary Clinton	98,504	(57%)
Donald Trump	61,813	(36%)
Gary Johnson	5,546	(3%)

Cook Partisan Voting Index: D+9

Under orders from the Spanish governor of California to explore what lay beyond the coastal mountains, army officer Gabriel Moraga became one of the first Europeans to behold the Central Valley, a fertile expanse teaming with wildlife-heron, antelope, elk, and grizzly bears. He brought his soldiers through the Pacheco Pass, which would become the main route for exporting the natural riches of the Valley to the port cities springing up along the coast. During his travels in the early 1800s, Moraga bestowed Spanish names on the places and rivers he encountered. So the region he was inspired to call "Blessed Sacrament" became Sacramento. After one long and dusty day, he stumbled on a much-welcomed river, which he called Merced, or, "River of Our Lady of Mercy." Like much of the rest of the valley, Merced grew to be a hub of agriculture. Located north of Fresno, its economy was long hitched to agribusiness. Harvest time attracted thousands of itinerant farmworkers from Mexico and elsewhere, and later, the region's affordable housing inspired new waves of migration. With the 2010 census, Latinos became a majority in surrounding Merced County. The empowered community approved a referendum in 2014 switching local elections from at-large to district voting.

The 16th District of California encompasses all of Merced County and takes in parts of Madera and Fresno counties. These parts of the San Joaquin Valley are 60 percent Hispanic, and include much of the city of Fresno and its lower-income neighborhoods. The neighboring 22nd District includes more populous and suburban parts of Fresno County, and much of the county's farmland is in the 21st. A bit more than a third of the population of the 16th is in Merced, where the per capita income is lower than in Fresno city and county. Unemployment here in recent years has been among the nation's highest, and Merced County's jobless rate hit 20 percent in early 2012. Its 10.8 per cent unemployment rate in December 2016 was the county's lowest in a decade. The University of California, Merced, the 10th university in the vast UC system, opened in 2005 and has 7,300 students, with plans for continued rapid growth. Highway 99 connects most of the key cities and towns in the district, with their shared agricultural and water interests: Livingston, Atwater, Merced, Chowchilla, Madera, and down to Fresno. After the drought had become a new job crippler, with major cutbacks in water supply forcing many farmers to reduce their expenses or abandon their fields, the increased water supply created a sudden turnaround. Following the deluge of rain and snow in the 2017 winter, the San Luis reservoir that serves the San Joaquin Valley rose more than 110 feet.

With its heavy concentration of Latinos and other immigrant groups, which respond to Voting Rights Act imperatives for fair Hispanic representation, Hillary Clinton won the 16th with 57% in 2016, after Barack Obama took 58% and 59% in his two campaigns. Voter registration and turnout have been relatively low.

SEVENTEENTH DISTRICT

Ro Khanna (D)

Elected 2016, 1st term; b. Sep 13, 1976, Philadelphia, PA; University of Chicago (IL), B.A., 1998; Yale Law School (CT), J.D., 2001; Hinduism; Married (Ritu Ahuja).

Professional Career: Law Professor; Author; Deputy Assistant Secretary, United States Department of Commerce.

DC Office: 513 CHOB 20515, 202-225-2631, Fax: 202-225-2699; Website: khanna.house.gov.

State Offices: Santa Clara, 408-436-2720.

Committees: *Armed Services*: Readiness, Strategic Forces. *Budget*.

Election Results

Election	Name (Party)	Vote (%)		Cand. Spent	Ind. Exp. Support	Ind. Exp. Oppose
2016 General	Ro Khanna (D)	142,268	(61%)	$3,646,452	$177,090	
	Mike Honda (D)	90,924	(39%)	$2,946,103	$80,267	$321,065
2016 Primary	Ro Khanna (D)	33,785	(38%)			
	Mike Honda (D)	33,608	(38%)			
	Peter Kuo (R)	7,793	(9%)			
	Ron Cohen (R)	7,461	(9%)			

Democrat Ro Khanna was elected in 2016 in a rematch of his tight contest two years earlier with veteran Democratic Rep. Mike Honda. Khanna won by an unexpectedly wide margin, partly as a result of self-inflicted wounds by Honda. Although their views were mostly similar, Khanna offered a more conciliatory approach and an outsider style against Honda, who had been in elected office since before Khanna began grade school. Despite their differences in age, the candidates shared an unusual bond. Each was a first-generation Asian American, with immediate ancestors who had been victims of political prosecution.

Khanna was born in Philadelphia. Shortly before, his parents had emigrated from India to seek a better life for their children. His father was an electrical engineer and his mother was a substitute school teacher. Khanna's maternal grandfather had joined the independence movement in India led by Mahatma Gandhi and was imprisoned for several years for promoting human rights. Khanna got his bachelor's in economics from the University of Chicago and his law degree from Yale University. He claimed to have been a volunteer campaigner in Barack Obama's successful bid for the state Senate in 1996.

Khanna worked for a law firm in the Silicon Valley where he specialized in intellectual property issues and wrote the book *Entrepreneurial Nation: Why Manufacturing is Still Key to America's Future.* He taught economics at Stanford and law at Santa Clara University. He has shown interest in three separate Bay Area congressional districts. In his first political campaign, he challenged Democratic Rep. Tom Lantos in the 2004 Democratic primary, with criticism for his support of the war in Iraq; Khanna got 20 percent of the vote. He was a deputy assistant secretary at the Commerce Department during Obama's first term as president. Gov. Jerry Brown appointed Khanna to the California Workforce Investment Board. He set his eyes on the House seat held by Democratic Rep. Pete Stark of California, but Eric Swalwell beat him to the punch by defeating Stark in 2012.

With a strong corps of campaign contributors, many of them Indian Americans, Khanna decided to take on Democratic Rep. Mike Honda in 2014 in an adjacent district. Honda spent 14 months as a youngster with his Japanese family in a World War II internment camp in Colorado, though his father spent the war working for the U.S. Military Intelligence Service. Honda became a school teacher in San Jose and was first elected to the school board in 1980. He served in the California Assembly before he was elected to the House in 2000. With help from House Speaker Nancy Pelosi, he got a seat on the powerful Appropriations Committee and focused on trying to win more funding for education programs.

In their initial contest, Honda led Khanna in the primary 48%-28%. Republican candidates took the remaining votes. Honda was endorsed by major Democratic leaders, including Obama and Pelosi. Khanna had some endorsements from local technology leaders. Khanna styled himself as more tech-friendly and half Honda's age. "There's nothing wrong with Congressman Honda personally," Khanna told *The New Yorker*. "But there is something static about the political system, and I think the valley gets that." Honda supporters dismissed Khanna as a "tech groupie." The November 2014 contest was much closer than the primary, with Honda prevailing 51.8%-48.2%. Khanna outspent Honda $4.4 million to $3.4 million, but learned the difficulty of ousting a generally popular incumbent.

Khanna barely stopped campaigning and expanded his message to talk about broader economic issues, including automation. Honda was hindered by an investigation by the House Ethics Committee for his failure to keep his official House staff separate from his 2014 campaign. Though the case was not formally resolved before the election, it resulted in loss of political support, including the endorsements of Obama and some local tech leaders. Honda's campaign ran a negative ad in which a south Asian actor depicted Khanna taking a call from "Wall Street" on his cell phone. Khanna showed that the political dynamics had changed, when he led the 2016 primary, 39.1%-37.4%. In the general election, Khanna out-raised Honda, $3.7 million to $3 million. Support for Honda collapsed, which Khanna later attributed to "a frustration with Washington." Others cited the growing political clout of the Indian-American community. Khanna won, 61%-39%.

In the House, Khanna got seats on the Armed Services and Budget committees, and became a vice-chairman of the Progressive Caucus. He repeated his campaign advocacy for congressional term limits and a ban on contributions from political action committees.

South Bay: San Jose suburbs, Central San Jose

Population		**Race and Ethnicity**		**Income**	
Total	740,121	White	25.3%	Median Income	$1,02,886 (4 out of 435)
Land area	185	Black	2.5%		
Pop/ sq mi	4003.9	Latino	17.0%	Under $50,000	24.7%
Born in state	39.5%	Asian	51.3%	$50,000-$99,999	34.6%
		Two races	3.0%	$100,000-$199,999	17.5%
Age Groups		Other	0.9%	$200,000 or more	7.5%
Under 18	22.5%			Poverty Rate	7.5%
18-34	24.6%	**Education**			
35-64	41.7%	H.S grad or less	25.0%	**Health Insurance**	
Over 64	11.3%	Some college	21.4%	With health insurance coverage	92.3%
Work		College Degree, 4 yr	28.2%		
		Post grad	25.4%		
White Collar	56.7%			**Public Assistance**	
Sales and Service	30.5%	**Military**		Cash public assistance income	2.5%
Blue Collar	12.8%	Veteran	3.8%		
Government	8.2%	Active Duty	0.0%	Food stamp/SNAP benefits	3.7%

Voter Turnout			
2015 Total Citizens 18+	424,706	2016 House Turnout as % CVAP	55%
2016 House turnout	233,192	2014 House Turnout as % CVAP	31%

2012 Presidential Vote		
Barack Obama	163,862	(72%)
Mitt Romney	58,193	(26%)

2016 Presidential Vote		
Hillary Clinton	184,151	(73%)
Donald Trump	51,079	(20%)
Gary Johnson	8,314	(3%)

Cook Partisan Voting Index: D+25

A few decades ago, the broad valley of Santa Clara County around San Jose was mostly orchards and vineyards. Sheltered by mountains from the chilly ocean fogs, with soil incredibly fertile once it was irrigated, this valley produced peaches, plums, prunes, apricots and grapes and made San Jose the nation's biggest fruit-packing center. Today, subdivisions, shopping centers, and office buildings have replaced the orchards, and the population of the county exceeds 1.9 million. Its steady growth was stunted by the recession, but the recovery has had a strong bounce back: Real estate prices in Santa Clara County have been soaring. In late 2016, the average sales price for a single-family home exceeded $1 million, a 5 percent increase in the past year. The average monthly rental of a one-bedroom apartment was close to $2,200. Nearby Fremont in Alameda County has experienced economic rejuvenation. A shuttered General Motors/Toyota plant was taken over by Tesla Motors, which has been building high-end electric cars there. With assembly line upgrades, the company planned to produce 500,000 cars in 2018. Fremont could become "the Detroit of the 21st century," gushed the newsletter *California Planning & Development Report.* Fremont is also home to the Little Kabul neighborhood, which may be the largest Afghan enclave in the western world. The San Francisco 49ers in 2014 moved to Levi Stadium in the city of Santa Clara, close to the southern tip of San Francisco Bay.

The 17th Congressional District consists of the city of Santa Clara and a northern wedge of Santa Clara County, the sixth biggest county in the state, with large numbers of Chinese, Vietnamese and Mexican immigrants. The district also takes in a part of San Jose, part of Fremont, Newark, Sunnyvale and Cupertino, where Steve Jobs started Apple in a garage in the 1970s and where the company is still based. Apple planned to open its solar-powered "spaceship" headquarters by late-2017, a state-of-the-art building in Cupertino that will house some 13,000 employees on a 176-acre site. The hallways in the round building exceed one mile. Technology firms are an important driver of the district's economy. LinkedIn opened its "net zero energy" campus in Sunnyvale. On the less successful side of the ledger is Solyndra, the Fremont-based solar energy company that received economic stimulus money from the Obama administration and then went bankrupt in 2011. SolarCity, a California-based solar power company, has taken over its complex in Fremont.

Both Cupertino and Milpitas are more than 60 percent Asian, and this growing population has become a political force. The 17th District as a whole is 53 percent (and climbing) Asian American, by far the largest percentage of any district in California. Its median household income of $111,000 was among the top 10 in the nation. Hillary Clinton won this district, 73%-20%.

EIGHTEENTH DISTRICT

Anna Eshoo (D)

Elected 1992, 13th term; b. Dec 13, 1942, New Britain, CT; Canada College (CA), A.A.; University of San Francisco (CA), Att.; Roman Catholic; Divorced; 2 children.

Elected Office: San Mateo County Board of Supervisors, 1983-1992, President, 1986.

Professional Career: San Mateo County Dem. Party, 1980-1992; Speakr pro tempore, CA assembly speaker, 1981-1982.

DC Office: 241 CHOB 20515, 202-225-8104, Fax: 202-225-8890, eshoo.house.gov.

State Offices: Palo Alto, 650-323-2984.

Committees: *Energy & Commerce*: Communications & Technology, Health.

Group Ratings

	ADA	ACLU	AFL-CIO	LCV	ITI	COC	HAFA	ACU	CFG	FRC
2016	-	100%	-	97%	50%	46%	12%	0%	4%	0%
2015	90%	C	100%	100%	C	42%	C	0%	0%	0%

Almanac Ratings 2015

	Economy	Social	Foreign	Composite
Liberal	91%	100%	93%	95%
Conservative	9%	0%	7%	5%

Key Votes of the 114th Congress

1. Keystone Pipeline	N	5. Puerto Rico Debt	Y	9. Offenses by Aliens	N
2. Trade Deals	N	6. Medical Marijuana	Y	10. Troops in Iraq	Y
3. Export-Import Bank	Y	7. Sanctuary Cities	N	11. Homeland Security $$	Y
4. Debt Ceiling Increase	Y	8. Armor-piercing Bullets	N	12. Trade Adjustment aid	Y

Election Results

Election	Name (Party)	Vote (%)		Cand. Spent	Ind. Exp. Support	Ind. Exp. Oppose
2016 General	Anna Eshoo (D)	230,460	(71%)	$1,017,012		
	Richard Fox (R)	93,470	(29%)	$17,950		
2016 Primary	Anna Eshoo (D)	85,242	(68%)			
	Richard Fox (R)	31,385	(25%)			
	Bob Harlow (D)	8,920	(7%)			

Prior winning percentages: 2014 (68%), 2012 (71%), 2010 (69%), 2008 (70%), 2006 (71%), 2004 (70%), 2002 (68%), 2000 (70%), 1998 (69%), 1996 (65%), 1994 (61%), 1992 (57%)

Democrat Anna Eshoo, first elected in 1992, has much in common with her close friend Nancy Pelosi: They are nearly the same age, Roman Catholic, wealthy East Coast transplants and prodigious fundraisers for their party. Eshoo has had impressive accomplishments on a range of issues on the powerful Energy and Commerce Committee. Following the 2014 election, they shared an unexpected setback among House Democrats when Eshoo sought the top Democratic slot on the committee, but lost to Frank Pallone of New Jersey.

Born in Connecticut, Eshoo is the only member of Congress of Assyrian descent. Her father, a jeweler and an FDR Democrat, sparked her interest in politics at a young age by taking her to political rallies. As a youngster, her mother briefly lived in Baghdad. The family moved to California. Eshoo married, had two children, and for a while was a stay-at-home mother working on a degree in English literature. (She later divorced.) She was active in civic groups, chaired the San Mateo County Democratic Party and in 1982 was elected to the San Mateo Board of Supervisors. In 1988, she ran for the House against Republican Rep. Tom Campbell. The two spent a total of $2.5 million, which was big bucks in those days. Campbell won 52%-46%. In 1992, Campbell gave up his seat to run for the Senate, and Eshoo again ran. In the primary, she beat Assemblyman Ted Lempert, who had strong backing from environmentalists but lost ground by making unsubstantiated attacks against Eshoo. She prevailed 40%-36%. In what was still a swing district, she had a tough contest against Republican Tom Huening, the San Mateo supervisor who was backed by David Packard and other Silicon Valley business leaders. Eshoo won by a convincing 57%-39%. She has not had a serious challenge for reelection.

As shown by her *Almanac* vote ratings for 2015, Eshoo's voting record has been mostly liberal, with more-moderate views on issues such as taxes that affect high-income earners in her district. She joined Republicans and high-tech interests in votes on securities litigation and normalizing trade relations with China. But she joined most Democrats in 2015 in opposing trade promotion authority for President Barack Obama, chiefly to conclude the Trans-Pacific Partnership. Eshoo fought telecommunications legislation that would have allowed internet carriers to have a two-tier pricing system, contending that it would put start-up firms at a disadvantage.

As a senior member of the Energy and Commerce Committee, Eshoo in 2011 defeated Illinois' Bobby Rush to take over the senior Democrat post on the panel's Subcommittee on Communications and Technology - a panel with obvious importance to her district. She has been a strong supporter of net neutrality, the concept that broadband providers should be prohibited from blocking certain traffic or setting up tiered pathways for internet content. In 2015, she praised the Federal Communications Commission for adopting net neutrality rules. "This is an epic battle between David and Goliath, and David won this round," Eshoo said. She argued in favor of ensuring that the FCC provides an adequate supply of spectrum that any company can use for free. She was the leading Democratic supporter of the permanent moratorium on internet access taxes paid by consumers, which was enacted in February 2016. Following the election, she voluntarily gave up the subcommittee post. "Senior members like myself must consider the best interest of our party and our need to develop leaders for the future. In other words, it's time to walk my talk," said the 74-year-old Eshoo.

In return, Eshoo got a seat on the Health Subcommittee. She has a lengthy record on health technology issues. In 2009, she prevailed over committee Chairman Henry Waxman in winning passage of a measure allowing makers of "biologic" drugs up to 12 years of protection from competition from the generic drug industry. In 2011, she enacted a bill to reduce the volume of television commercials. Other achievements include bills to increase internet access for schools, to allow the use of electronic signatures in business transactions, and to require insurance companies to pay for reconstructive surgery for cancer patients. The 21st Century Cures Act, which was enacted in December 2016, had a section that she prepared with Republican Rep. Susan Brooks of Indiana that strengthened the nation's biodefense to respond to public health emergencies.

Eshoo has been the closest friend of Pelosi. Confidants since they met at a Democratic event in the Bay Area in the early 1970s. Eshoo officiated at the marriage ceremony of Pelosi's daughter, Christine, in 2008. When the House passed the health care overhaul in 2010, Eshoo lauded her friend's political will in her dealings with Obama and Senate Majority Leader Harry Reid. "I think (Pelosi) is the one who has kept the steel in the president's back - and I think she represents that to Harry Reid, too," Eshoo told *Politico*.

Following the 2014 election, Pelosi sought to return the favor when Eshoo moved to replace Waxman as the ranking Democrat on Energy and Commerce. But that proved to be a step too far. Eshoo was stymied by several factors: Rep. Frank Pallone of New Jersey had more seniority, and he emphasized that point. The secret vote became an opportunity for some Democrats to express unhappiness with Pelosi and their deepening minority status in the House. Plus, Pelosi and her allies stirred resentment with heavy-handed tactics to prevent Iraqi war veteran and double-amputee Rep. Tammy Duckworth from voting by proxy on the Pallone-Eshoo contest during her final weeks of pregnancy.

As other senior Democrats in Washington - including from California - have stepped down, it might not be long before the two Bay Area friends take their final working trip home.

Silicon Valley: Western San Jose, Palo Alto

Population		**Race and Ethnicity**		**Income**	
Total	728,724	White	56.2%	Median Income	$1,07,319 (2 out of 435)
Land area	696	Black	1.8%		
Pop/ sq mi	1046.8	Latino	16.6%	Under $50,000	22.6%
Born in state	48.1%	Asian	20.9%	$50,000-$99,999	28.6%
		Two races	3.8%	$100,000-$199,999	24.8%
Age Groups		Other	0.6%	$200,000 or more	7.2%
Under 18	22.8%			Poverty Rate	7.2%
18-34	20.9%	**Education**			
35-64	42.3%	H.S grad or less	18.4%	**Health Insurance**	
Over 64	14.1%	Some college	22.2%	With health insurance coverage	92.9%
		College Degree, 4 yr	29.6%		
Work		Post grad	29.8%		
White Collar	59.4%			**Public Assistance**	
Sales and Service	31.1%	**Military**		Cash public assistance income	1.5%
Blue Collar	9.5%	Veteran	5.4%		
Government	9.5%	Active Duty	0.1%	Food stamp/SNAP benefits	2.7%

Voter Turnout			
2015 Total Citizens 18+	475,128	2016 House Turnout as % CVAP	68%
2016 House turnout	323,930	2014 House Turnout as % CVAP	41%

2012 Presidential Vote		
Barack Obama	218,082	(68%)
Mitt Romney	92,457	(29%)

2016 Presidential Vote		
Hillary Clinton	246,464	(73%)
Donald Trump	67,842	(20%)
Gary Johnson	13,894	(4%)

Cook Partisan Voting Index: D+23

Silicon Valley is a place and a state of mind, an area that had no distinctive identity four decades ago but that people all over the world today recognize and imitate. In the 1980s and 1990s, Silicon Valley emerged as the center of America's computer industry, a place where creative minds developed products that large corporations never thought would sell. Its beginnings can be traced back to 1939, when William Hewlett and David Packard started their electronics firm in a Palo Alto garage, or perhaps even to 1891, when Stanford University was founded on the estate of a California governor and senator. Not every aspect of the computer business is centered here: Microsoft, routinely disparaged in every Palo Alto espresso shop and bar, is in Redmond, Washington, and the downsized IBM is in Armonk, New York. But the compact Silicon Valley is where most of the giants and much of the creativity of the technology business - as well as many dot-coms - have been based, and where they continue to grow in their pricey surroundings and generate extraordinary wealth.

How did Silicon Valley come to be where it is? One factor is Stanford, the students it attracts and produces, and its tradition of encouraging faculty members to pursue profit-making activity. Another key component is venture capital, widely available from innovation-minded old San Francisco money. A third ingredient is the presence of smart young innovators, attracted to the valley's lifestyle. Elite law and medical school graduates head to the prestigious, high-salary jobs of central cities. But techies are free to live in this pleasant, healthy environment. Sheltered by hills from coastal fogs and rains, Silicon Valley boasts a sunny climate with perceptible but gentle seasons, perfect for year-round outdoor sports. These communities were rustic but never poor, rural but not small-minded, country-like but still easily accessible to urban luxuries. People here were ahead of the rest of the nation in fighting for the environment, in favoring natural over processed foods and in incorporating regular exercise into busy lives. In one of his final official actions, President Barack Obama gave national monument status to a six-mile stretch between Davenport and Santa Cruz along Highway 1 that features rolling hills, redwoods and spectacular ocean views.

The area has been quick to adapt to change. In the 1980s, in the face of threats from Japanese firms, Silicon Valley shifted to microprocessors and personal computers. In the 1990s, when PCs became a low-profit commodity business, Silicon Valley shifted to the internet. Yahoo and Hotmail reportedly were conceived at Buck's restaurant, the networking nexus in Woodside. When the internet bubble burst in 2000, Silicon Valley fell on hard times. By one estimate, the area lost 220,000 jobs, nearly two-thirds of the 350,000 created during the dot-com boom. Stock prices plummeted and real estate prices did too. Billions of dollars in paper wealth disappeared, and technology exports from California fell. In 2010, unemployment in the San Jose-Sunnyvale-Santa Clara region was above 11 percent. The question became whether Silicon Valley still had the ability to adapt. Since then, it has had a strong revival. In 2015, the valley exceeded 1.5 million jobs, higher than in 2000, according to the Silicon Valley Index; its 4.3 percent increase in 2015 was the highest during that 15-year period. Housing prices have roared back and are again among the highest in the nation, and there has been an accompanying surge in apartment construction. Half of the employees in the valley are foreign-born. Innovation and investment opportunities have accelerated. In Menlo Park, Facebook opened its third campus in 2015, with 2,800 employees and CEO Mark Zuckerberg's desk in the middle. Menlo Park voters in 2014 rejected a referendum that would have capped local growth

The 18th Congressional District of California includes large portions of Silicon Valley, along with Palo Alto and Stanford University. It includes a slice of San Jose and a slice of Menlo Park. Further south along El Camino Real are Mountain View and Google, with ambitious expansion plans for its more than 60,000 employees. There are some ultra-wealthy enclaves here: Woodside, with its mansions in the hills, and Los Altos Hills, with its stark contemporary homes overlooking San Francisco Bay. The district takes in small San Jose-area cities such as Campbell, Los Gatos, and the increasingly Asian Saratoga. To the west is a long stretch of hills and wilderness areas, and Route 1 that overlooks the Pacific Ocean. About three-fourths of the population is in Santa Clara County, with the remainder in southern San Mateo and northern Santa Cruz. The district's median household income of $120,000 ranked as the highest in the nation.

The area's political heritage is progressive, with a sort of environmentalist, dovish, culturally liberal but entrepreneurial Republicanism, typified until the 1990s by former Reps. Pete McCloskey and Tom Campbell. But that brand of Republican has become virtually extinct here, as in most of the nation. The Republican vote in the 18th dropped from 29 percent for Mitt Romney in 2012 to 20 percent for Donald Trump in 2016.

NINETEENTH DISTRICT

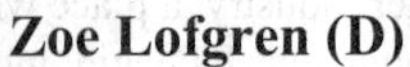

Zoe Lofgren (D)

Elected 1994, 12th term; b. Dec 21, 1947, San Mateo; Stanford University (CA), B.A., 1970; Santa Clara University Law School (CA), J.D., 1975; Lutheran; Married (John Marshall Collins); 2 children.

Elected Office: Santa Clara Board of Supervisors, 1980-1994.

Professional Career: Staff Assistant, U.S. Rep. Don Edwards, 1970-1978; Practicing attorney, 1978-1980; Professor, University of Santa Clara School of Law, 1977-1980.

DC Office: 1401 LHOB 20515, 202-225-3072, Fax: 202-225-3336, zoelofgren.house.gov.

State Offices: San Jose, 408-271-8700.

Committees: *House Administration*. *Judiciary*: Courts, Intellectual Property & Internet, Immigration & Border Security (RMM). *Science, Space & Technology*: Energy, Space.

Group Ratings

	ADA	ACLU	AFL-CIO	LCV	ITI	COC	HAFA	ACU	CFG	FRC
2016	-	94%	-	100%	67%	46%	16%	4%	4%	0%
2015	95%	C	100%	66%	C	35%	C	10%	3%	0%

Almanac Ratings 2015

	Economy	Social	Foreign	Composite
Liberal	85%	100%	93%	93%
Conservative	15%	0%	7%	7%

Key Votes of the 114th Congress

1. Keystone Pipeline	N	5. Puerto Rico Debt	Y	9. Offenses by Aliens	N
2. Trade Deals	N	6. Medical Marijuana	Y	10. Troops in Iraq	Y
3. Export-Import Bank	Y	7. Sanctuary Cities	N	11. Homeland Security $$	Y
4. Debt Ceiling Increase	Y	8. Armor-piercing Bullets	N	12. Trade Adjustment aid	Y

Election Results

Election	Name (Party)	Vote (%)		Cand. Spent	Ind. Exp. Support	Ind. Exp. Oppose
2016 General	Zoe Lofgren (D)	181,802	(74%)	$674,926	$1,772	
	G. Burt Lancaster (R)	64,061	(26%)	$5,500		
2016 Primary	Zoe Lofgren (D)	107,773	(76%)			
	G. Burt Lancaster (R)	33,889	(24%)			

Prior winning percentages: 2014 (67%), 2012 (67%), 2010 (68%), 2008 (71%), 2006 (73%), 2004 (71%), 2002 (67%), 2000 (72%), 1998 (73%), 1996 (66%), 1994 (65%)

The congresswoman from the 19th District is Zoe Lofgren, a Democrat first elected in 1994. She has been an active legislator on multiple issues, and perhaps the savviest defender of high technology's interests in the House. As a senior member of the Judiciary Committee with extensive experience in dealing with constitutional controversies related to presidents, she moved quickly in 2017 to raise concerns about President Donald Trump.

Lofgren grew up in the Bay Area, where her father was a Teamsters truck driver and her mother worked for the Machinists Union. She graduated from Stanford University, then moved to Washington to work for Democratic Rep. Don Edwards while he was a leader on the Judiciary Committee that voted to impeach President Richard Nixon. She stayed on for eight years as an aide to Edwards. She met her husband, a lawyer, one Election Night. Lofgren returned to California to get a law degree, and specialized in immigration law. In 1980, she was elected to the Santa Clara County Board of Supervisors. When Edwards retired, Lofgren ran for his House seat. Her chief Democratic opponent, former San Jose Mayor Tom McEnery, was better known. But Lofgren raised twice as much money, with support from liberal women's organizations and women in the California delegation. She gained considerable recognition after she insisted on listing herself as a county supervisor/mother on the ballot. Election officials refused, and the national press covered the ensuing controversy. Lofgren won the primary 45%-42% and easily took the general election. Lofgren has had no trouble winning reelection every two years.

Lofgren's voting record, while mostly liberal, includes bipartisan free-market positions that often are responsive to local businesses and law enforcement. Working with Republicans, she won expanded allotments of visas for high-tech workers. She pushed for looser controls on encryption exports, securities litigation limitations and relaxation of trade restraints on supercomputers, all big Silicon Valley causes. When the House split 210-210 on a proposal to restrict government access to library records, Lofgren was the only House member to vote "present." She said the amendment went too far in preventing legitimate law enforcement searches. In 2013, she introduced "Aaron's Law," in memory of Aaron Swartz, a young Harvard University professor and internet entrepreneur who committed suicide after challenging book copyright rules and becoming the target of what Lofgren said were "disproportionate charges" by the Justice Department. Her proposal failed to get a House vote. With Republican Rep. Ted Poe of Texas, she filed a bill in 2015 to prevent privacy intrusions by drones and other unmanned aircraft. In July 2016, she and Poe formed a Fourth Amendment Caucus to protect the privacy and security of Americans in the digital age. Three months later, President Barack Obama signed the Survivors' Bill of Rights Act, which provides protections for survivors of sexual assault; Lofgren was an original sponsor with Republican Rep. Mimi Walters of California.

When Democrats won the majority in 2006, Lofgren, a trusted lieutenant of House Speaker Nancy Pelosi, became chairwoman of the Judiciary Subcommittee on Immigration and related issues. She hoped for a major overhaul of immigration policy, but the politically charged issue bogged down. When Republicans regained control of the House, Lofgren was an outspoken supporter of a bill to change the visa system to allow more highly skilled immigrants from China and India to become permanent legal residents. In 2011, the bill passed the House easily, with Lofgren joining Judiciary Chairman Lamar Smith of Texas. On another immigration-related measure, Lofgren was the chief sponsor of a new law to allow overseas military personnel and their spouses more time to file for permanent resident status through marriage.

Lofgren was a leading opponent of the controversial Stop Online Piracy Act, an intellectual property enforcement measure favored by movie studios and the recording industry but opposed by some of her Silicon Valley interests. It would give larger sites the power to kill rogue or upstart websites believed to be engaged in theft or copyright infringement. Lofgren told the tech media site *CNET* that the bill would signal "the end of the internet as we know it." After Google and Wikipedia sponsored an "Internet Black Out" day in January 2012, chairman Smith officially withdrew it.

With Republican Rep. Robert Goodlatte of Virginia, the new Judiciary Committee chairman, she criticized in 2015 the backlog of "green card" visa applications for talented foreign workers. In July 2016, she filed with Democratic Sen. Patrick Leahy of Vermont the Refugee Protection Act of 2016, which reaffirmed the nation's commitment to refugees and strengthened safeguards for those seeking protection from persecution and violence

Lofgren tried to get a foothold in leadership by running for vice chair of the Democratic Caucus in 2003. But Pelosi, who is also from the Bay Area, had just been elected minority leader and the Congressional Black Caucus pressed for one of its members to join the leadership. Lofgren got 53 votes to 95 for the victorious James Clyburn of South Carolina.

In 2009, Lofgren took over as chairman of the House Ethics Committee just as it launched a politically sensitive inquiry of House Ways and Means Chairman Charles Rangel of New York, and as questions were being raised about the connections of other senior Democrats to lobbyists. Lofgren's skills as a former staffer and law professor were tested by the politically combustible cases. She told the House Administration Committee in early 2010 that at least 36 lawmakers - around 8 percent of the House - had been subjected to scrutiny for their dealings with special interests the previous year. Her panel subsequently found that no House members colluded with lobbyists. The Rangel case dragged on for months. Finally, just after the election, he was afforded a trial but walked out in protest after complaining that he hadn't been granted enough time to hire a new attorney. Lofgren and the rest of the panel refused to back down, and a few days later voted 9-1 to censure him - a decision Lofgren called "quite wrenching."

Lofgren joined the dozens of House Democrats who boycotted in January 2017 the inauguration of President Donald Trump. "I acknowledge the fact that he is the incoming president, but I'm not in the mood to celebrate that fact," she told the *Los Angeles Times*. After he released his executive order that temporarily banned refugees and some immigrant groups, she filed a bill to prohibit the use of federal funds to enforce his action. Republicans refused her call for immediate action on the bill.

South Bay: Southern San Jose

Population		**Race and Ethnicity**		**Income**	
Total	738,243	White	25.7%	Median Income	$81,193 (31 out of 435)
Land area	915	Black	2.9%		
Pop/ sq mi	806.5	Latino	41.0%	Under $50,000	27.2%
Born in state	50.8%	Asian	26.7%	$50,000-$99,999	28.4%
		Two races	2.9%	$100,000-$199,999	12.2%
Age Groups		Other	0.8%	$200,000 or more	12.5%
Under 18	24.1%			Poverty Rate	12.5%
18-34	24.8%	**Education**			
35-64	40.0%	H.S grad or less	39.8%	**Health Insurance**	
Over 64	11.1%	Some college	27.8%	With health insurance coverage	88.3%
		College Degree, 4 yr	21.0%		
Work		Post grad	11.4%	**Public Assistance**	
White Collar	37.5%				
Sales and Service	41.7%	**Military**		Cash public assistance income	3.3%
Blue Collar	20.7%	Veteran	4.1%		
Government	10.6%	Active Duty	0.0%	Food stamp/SNAP benefits	8.3%

Voter Turnout			
2015 Total Citizens 18+	450,347	2016 House Turnout as % CVAP	55%
2016 House turnout	245,863	2014 House Turnout as % CVAP	29%

2012 Presidential Vote		
Barack Obama	165,530	(71%)
Mitt Romney	61,643	(27%)

2016 Presidential Vote		
Hillary Clinton	188,304	(72%)
Donald Trump	55,489	(21%)
Gary Johnson	8,620	(3%)

Cook Partisan Voting Index: D+24

With more people than San Francisco, a tradition of high-tech innovation, and a professional sports team, San Jose finally has claims on national attention and respect. Yet San Jose does not register on the national consciousness as it should. At the southern end of San Francisco Bay, it remains in the shadow of the city on the Golden Gate. San Francisco is every tourist's idea of a city: geographically compact, with picturesque housing; old and new immigrant groups; an economy historically based on heavy industry and sea trade; a large city bureaucracy; and a monumental City Hall. San Jose is quite different. It got its start as a farm-market town, with canneries and fruit-packing operations for the produce from the surrounding fertile plains. Farm labor icon Cesar Chavez settled with his family in the East San Jose barrio of Sal Si Puedes ("Get out if you can"). The modest Our Lady of Guadalupe Mission Chapel, where he learned community organizing, was designated by the outgoing Obama administration as a national historic landmark. San Jose sits not on the bay but on the Southern Pacific rail line above the marshes and salt evaporators. Its major transportation arteries are the freeways - U.S. 101, Interstates 280, 680, and 880, California 87 - that encircle its revitalized downtown plus the larger Bay Area.

Starting in the 1950s, San Jose grew in every direction, with developers hopscotching across the farmland and at times putting up subdivisions faster than the few city employees could update the street maps. It now has a popular National Hockey League team, the San Jose Sharks. Its population passed 1 million in 2014, not far below San Francisco and Oakland combined; it is growing faster than the other two, but has more available land. In January 2017, the realtor.com website ranked San Jose as the second hottest market in the nation, behind San Francisco; it has been ranked the most "unaffordable" city in the nation. Economically, San Jose has been sustained by everything from its traditional agriculture to manufacturing to the high-tech businesses that are centered in Silicon Valley towns just to the west and north, and are omnipresent here: an American city, 21st-century style. Santa Clara County not long ago had the highest median household income in the nation. Now, it is merely the highest in California.

For many years, San Jose has been a focal point for immigration issues. It has Northern California's largest Mexican-American community, many of them farmworkers. Recent years have brought a diverse and substantial presence from Latin America and East and South Asia. Half of all Santa Clara County residents speak a language other than English at home, mostly Spanish, Vietnamese or Chinese, 38 percent are foreign born. Among the signs of new growth: In May 2016, the San Jose city council approved a huge development project for its Diridon district, which may have been the largest in downtown's history. County voters approved in November ballot measures with a $950 million bond for affordable housing and a half-cent increase in the sales tax for transportation projects, which likely will extend BART down the East Bay to San Jose.

The 19th Congressional District of California consists of substantial portions of San Jose, including much of the city's downtown area and the neighborhoods of Alum Rock and East Foothills. The district takes in eastern and southern parts of Santa Clara County, including Morgan Hill, a traditional farming town that has branched into technology. Near the southern edge of the district is Gilroy, which is 58 percent Hispanic, the garlic capital of the world and home of the huge annual garlic festival. Politically, the district is solidly Democratic. Along with the 17th and 18th Districts, this is one of three Santa Clara-based districts where Hillary Clinton got at least 72 percent of the vote in 2016.

TWENTIETH DISTRICT

Jimmy Panetta (D)

Elected 2016, 1st term; b. Oct 01, 1969, Washington, DC; Monterey Peninsula College (CA), A.A., 1989; University of California Davis, B.A., 1991; Santa Clara University (CA), J.D., 1996; Catholic; Married (Carrie Panetta); 2 children.

Military Career: U.S Navy Reserve (Afghanistan), 2003-2011.

Elected Office: Monterey County Deputy District Attorney, 2010-2016.

Professional Career: Clerk, United States Department of State, 1992; Alameda County Deputy District Attorney, 1996-2010; Vice Chairman, Monterey Country Central Democratic Committee, 2012-2016.

DC Office: 228 CHOB 20515, 202-225-2861, Fax: 202-225-6791, panetta.house.gov.
State Offices: Salinas, 831-424-2229; Santa Cruz, 831-429-1976.

Committees: *Agriculture*: Biotechnology, Horticulture & Research, Nutrition. *Natural Resources*: Federal Lands, Water, Power & Oceans.

Election Results

Election	Name (Party)	Vote (%)		Cand. Spent	Ind. Exp. Support	Ind. Exp. Oppose
2016 General	Jimmy Panetta (D)	180,980	(71%)	$991,443		
	Casey Lucius (R)	74,811	(29%)	$414,020	$52,913	
2016 Primary	Jimmy Panetta (D)	67,104	(72%)			
	Casey Lucius (R)	18,552	(20%)			

Democrat Jimmy Panetta was easily elected to the House in 2016. Following his father's high-level service in Congress and as a respected top official for Presidents Bill Clinton and Barack Obama, young Panetta had a strong head start with local voters and with national party leaders and contributors. With a pledge of bipartisanship, his initial work in Congress focused on grass-roots issues.

The youngest of three sons of former Defense Secretary and CIA Director Leon Panetta, Jimmy grew up in Carmel Valley. He got his bachelor's degree from the University of California, Davis, and his law degree from Santa Clara University. Growing up, he got up-close insight on Washington through the eyes of his father. Panetta began his legal career as a prosecutor for the Alameda County District Attorney. Later, he was appointed to the California Council on Criminal and Juvenile Justice, which provided guidance to the governor's office on criminal justice programs. In 2003, he was commissioned as an intelligence officer with the U.S. Navy Reserve. Four years later, he took a leave of absence from work and served with a special operations task force deployed to Afghanistan, as an intelligence officer with the Joint Special Operations Command. Before his election to Congress, he was the deputy district attorney in Monterey County.

Panetta worked on veterans' issues as a board member of the Veterans Transition Center, and on missile and chemical weapons nonproliferation issues for the State Department and the Monterey Institute of International Studies. He also managed his family's large walnut farm in the area. His wife, Carrie McIntyre Panetta, was a Superior Court judge in Monterey County. His father, who held this seat for 16 years and chaired the House Budget Committee, chaired the Panetta Institute on Public Policy.

After Democrat Sam Farr -- who held this seat for nearly 24 years after Leon Panetta resigned to join the Clinton White House -- announced his retirement, Jimmy Panetta was the immediate front-runner. Other potential Democratic candidates decided not to challenge him. Prior to his campaign, Monterey County Supervisor Dave Potter, an active Democrat, told the *Mercury News* that Panetta has "the personality, he's got the record, the charisma. This guy's going to be able to break down some partisan walls." His only major-party opponent was Republican Casey Lucius, a city councilwoman in Pacific Grove and a professor of national security at the Naval Postgraduate School. An Ohio native, she was a strong conservative on most national security and economic issues, and relatively liberal views on social issues. Lucius raised $420,000, compared with $1.4 million for Panetta. She offered a credible candidacy. But she probably never had a chance against the iconic family name in this district. Panetta led the "top two" primary, 71%-20%, and took the general election, 71-29%.

In the House, Panetta got seats on the Agriculture and Natural Resources committees, where he was positioned to take care of local issues. As his father's son, he seemed positioned to wield some influence. Given the friendship and similar career paths of their fathers Leon Panetta and Dick Cheney, one potential working partner was freshman Republican Rep. Liz Cheney of Wyoming, who also got a seat on Natural Resources.

Central Coast: Monterey, Southern Santa Cruz

Population		Race and Ethnicity		Income	
Total	725,254	White	37.8%	Median Income	$60,807 (138 out of 435)
Land area	4,874	Black	1.9%		
Pop/ sq mi	148.8	Latino	52.0%		
Born in state	56.5%	Asian	5.2%	Under $50,000	31.0%
		Two races	2.4%	$50,000-$99,999	21.2%
Age Groups		Other	0.7%	$100,000-$199,999	6.4%
Under 18	24.9%			$200,000 or more	16.6%
18-34	26.5%	**Education**		Poverty Rate	16.6%
35-64	36.9%	H.S grad or less	44.9%		
Over 64	11.7%	Some college	28.5%	**Health Insurance**	
		College Degree, 4 yr	16.4%	With health insurance coverage	83.7%
Work		Post grad	10.2%		
White Collar	30.8%				
Sales and Service	41.7%	**Military**		**Public Assistance**	
Blue Collar	27.5%	Veteran	5.7%	Cash public assistance income	2.7%
Government	15.1%	Active Duty	1.1%		
				Food stamp/SNAP benefits	8.1%

Voter Turnout			
2015 Total Citizens 18+	419,858	2016 House Turnout as % CVAP	61%
2016 House turnout	255,791	2014 House Turnout as % CVAP	33%

2012 Presidential Vote		
Barack Obama	168,956	(71%)
Mitt Romney	62,427	(26%)

2016 Presidential Vote		
Hillary Clinton	180,499	(70%)
Donald Trump	59,580	(23%)
Gary Johnson	8,425	(3%)
Jill Stein	6,737	(3%)

Cook Partisan Voting Index: D+23

The California coast around Monterey Bay is for many a working definition of paradise. This kernel of California, site of the first state capital, still makes a fine living off the land and sea, as it has for 150 years. The inspiration for *The Grapes of Wrath* and many other John Steinbeck novels, the fields around Salinas provide much of the nation's lettuce and cauliflower. The area is often referred to as "the salad bowl of the world." Nearby, the farmlands around Castroville supply the country with its artichokes, and the vast greenhouses around Watsonville have been a popular supplier of roses. The fishing fleet and the 18 now-closed canneries of Monterey (the last sardines were canned in 1964) have generated a new industry. Once described by Steinbeck as "a poem, a stink, a grating noise, a quality of light, a tone, a habit, nostalgia, a dream," Cannery Row now is refurbished with upscale shops and hotels. The magnificent Monterey Bay Aquarium is one of California's top tourist destinations, and the National Marine Sanctuary holds more than 400 shipwrecks and ditched aircraft.

The Monterey Bay area calls itself the world's language-learning capital, with the Defense Language Institute, Language Line Services, and Cal State Monterey Bay's School of World Languages and Cultures. This area was also a magnet for the 1960s counterculture. The three-day Monterey Pop Festival in 1967 became the stuff of rock 'n' roll legend. Both The Who and Jimi Hendrix wanted to perform first. The Who won the deciding coin toss, and band members subsequently destroyed much of the stage after their set. Not to be outdone, Hendrix, during his performance, set his guitar on fire. The wealthy now entertain themselves with the annual Monterey Car Week, which sells many classic models.

For many, the main attraction of the Monterey peninsula is the lush 17-Mile Drive along the Pacific Coast Highway, with Pebble Beach's golf courses, the Del Monte Lodge, and Carmel, whose restrictive laws - no house numbers, no door-to-door mail delivery, no stoplights, no wearing of high-heeled shoes without permits - reflect an effort to maintain the atmosphere of nearly a century ago, when it was an artists' colony. Monterey has suffered its own affordability gap. These days, the top-flight buyers include many investors from China, many of whom initially spent time in the area for language training. In August 2016, Apple Computer received federal approval to sell power from its solar farm, part of an $850 million investment that could power 60,000 homes. Monterey County has been spending for its future. In November 2016, voters approved - following two defeats in the past decade - a sales tax increase to finance transportation improvements. In another referendum in Monterey, which is the fourth-largest oil-producing county in California, voters approved a ban on fracking to find more petroleum reserves. Construction was planned to start in 2017 on extension of Salinas Rail service to the Bay Area and Sacramento. In Santa Cruz, officials struggled to prevent erosion along the famed boardwalk.

The 20th Congressional District of California includes the entire coast of Monterey Bay and follows the stunning Big Sur coastline south along the steep slopes, taking in extensive wilderness areas and some of the most beautiful scenery in America. To the north along Monterey Bay, it runs past Watsonville to Santa Cruz. The district extends inland, into sunny valleys sheltered from ocean mists, and covers some of the nation's richest farmland. Most of the farmworkers are Latino, mainly Mexican. The end of the drought in 2017 was a positive local development All of Monterey and San Benito counties are located here, and the district takes in most of Santa Cruz County and a small portion of Santa Clara. About half of the population is in Monterey.

The gap between rich and poor in Monterey County is wide. It has thousands of homes valued at more than $1 million, but 15 percent of households live below the poverty line and 54 percent do not live in an English-speaking home. Forty years ago, this was a solidly Republican area, dominated politically by the landowners in Salinas and the townspeople who sympathized with them, plus retirees in Santa Cruz and on the Monterey peninsula. But an influx of young people, attracted less by the economy than by the atmosphere, moved these counties - like most of the California coast -- nearly as far to the left as much of the Bay Area. In the 2016 presidential, Hillary Clinton got 75 percent of the vote from Santa Cruz and 67 percent from Monterey, which was precisely the same as the 2012 vote for President Barack Obama. This district has climbed steadily to 53 percent Hispanic and is solidly Democratic.

TWENTY-FIRST DISTRICT

David Valadao (R)

Elected 2012, 3rd term; b. Apr 14, 1977, Hanford; College of the Sequoias (CA), Att.; Roman Catholic; Married (Terra Valadao); 3 children.

Elected Office: CA Assembly, 2010-2012.

Professional Career: Partner, Valadao Dairy and Triple V Dairy, 1992-present.

DC Office: 1728 LHOB 20515, 202-225-4695, Fax: 202-225-3196, valadao.house.gov.

State Offices: Bakersfield, 661-864-7736; Hanford, 559-582-5526.

Committees: *Appropriations*: Agriculture, Rural Development, FDA & Related Agencies, Military Construction, Veterans Affairs & Related Agencies, Transportation, HUD & Related Agencies.

Group Ratings

	ADA	ACLU	AFL-CIO	LCV	ITI	COC	HAFA	ACU	CFG	FRC
2016	-	5%	-	5%	100%	100%	33%	48%	55%	92%
2015	0%	C	29%	3%	C	100%	C	42%	40%	92%

Almanac Ratings 2015

	Economy	Social	Foreign	Composite
Liberal	10%	35%	18%	21%
Conservative	90%	65%	82%	79%

Key Votes of the 114th Congress

1. Keystone Pipeline	Y	5. Puerto Rico Debt	Y	9. Offenses by Aliens	Y
2. Trade Deals	Y	6. Medical Marijuana	N	10. Troops in Iraq	N
3. Export-Import Bank	N	7. Sanctuary Cities	N	11. Homeland Security $$	Y
4. Debt Ceiling Increase	Y	8. Armor-piercing Bullets	Y	12. Trade Adjustment aid	Y

Election Results

Election	Name (Party)	Vote (%)		Cand. Spent	Ind. Exp. Support	Ind. Exp. Oppose
2016 General	David Valadao (R)	75,126	(57%)	$2,783,454	$488,229	$37,708
	Emilio Huerta (D)	57,282	(43%)	$642,552	$1,997,748	$593,623
2016 Primary	David Valadao (R)	28,772	(58%)			
	Daniel Parra (D)	10,583	(21%)			
	Emilio Huerta (D)	10,116	(20%)			

Prior winning percentages: 2014 (58%), 2012 (58%)

Republican David Valadao, a dairy farmer of Portuguese descent elected in 2012, has won the 21st District seat against credible Democratic opponents who have consistently under-performed initial expectations. His skill and independence in addressing the area's agricultural and immigration issues have gained admiration from House Republicans for his success in one of the most daunting districts for them to retain. His tolerance clashed with the hard line of Donald Trump.

Valadao's father emigrated to California from Portugal's Azores Islands and started a small dairy farm in Kings County in 1969. Valadao was born in 1977, and his family lived on a farm in Hanford. In 1992, he and his brother became partners in the growing Valadao Dairy. He recalled riding in the car with his parents the day that all three voted for the first time. He was 18 and a registered Republican; his parents, who became naturalized citizens, were Democrats, although they later switched parties. Valadao worked on the family's farm, which also grew grains as dairy feed stock and increased to more than 1,000 acres; he drove the tractor that carried feed for animals, and handled contracts and purchases. He was a part-time student at the College of the Sequoias but did not graduate. The single political science class he took "piqued my interest in politics, but I never considered running for office," he said.

His appetite for politics was whetted when he was elected regional leadership council chairman of Land O'Lakes, a member-owned agricultural cooperative. Valadao began traveling to Sacramento and Washington, where he spoke with elected officials and groups on issues affecting dairy farmers, such as his region's aging water infrastructure. "The more I got involved in dairy and agricultural issues, the more I saw how much of an importance government and policies play in our lives," he said. He became active with the California Milk Advisory Board and the Western States Dairy Trade Association.

In 2010, Valadao was elected to the Assembly. He successfully sponsored legislation that eliminated millions of dollars in state funding to subsidize the production of corn-based ethanol. He also passed a bill that placed restrictions on people with criminal convictions who care for the elderly or disabled.

In the 2012 race for this new House seat, Valadao got an early fundraising advantage and finished first in the all-party primary, with 57 percent of the vote; Democrat John Hernandez came in second with 22 percent. As the head of the Central California Hispanic Chamber of Commerce, Hernandez hoped he could make inroads with Latino voters. But he suffered from not living in the district and as a first-time candidate. The *Bakersfield Californian* endorsed Valadao, saying that the district's constituents "deserve a representative who has been tested politically a little more." In his surprisingly comfortable 58%-42% victory, Valadao led by large margins in Fresno and Kings counties, while Hernandez won narrowly in more urban Kern County.

With help from House GOP leader Kevin McCarthy, who represents a neighboring district, Valadao gained a rare plum for a freshman: a seat on the Appropriations Committee, where he focused on securing funds for his district. He split with most Republicans on immigration legislation by cosponsoring in 2013 the Democrats' sweeping reform plan and speaking positively about the bipartisan bill that passed the Senate that spring. He was one of six House Republicans to vote against an amendment by GOP Rep. Steve King of Iowa that would give immigration authorities wider discretion to deport undocumented immigrants. In discussing these proposals, he incongruously cited the legal immigration experience of his parents. The U.S. Chamber of Commerce gave Valadao its Spirit of Enterprise award for his work on immigration. In 2014, Valadao worked with California Republicans on a bill to reject an Obama administration decision to limit water supplies to home, farms and businesses in the Central Valley. Anyone voting against the bill, which passed on a nearly party-line vote, was stating, "I want to raise the cost of food to everybody in the United States," he said.

In 2014, Democrats recruited and actively promoted Amanda Renteria, a Latina who had been chief of staff to Democratic Sen. Debbie Stabenow of Michigan. In the June primary, she easily defeated Hernandez, but Valadao got 63 percent of the total vote. That diminished some of the enthusiasm for Renteria, plus California Democrats were more focused on protecting their several vulnerable incumbents. Renteria raised an impressive $1.7 million, though much of her money came from outside the district, which reinforced her image as disconnected locally. She fell short of Valadao's $2.7 million. Despite Democrats' expectations of a tighter race, Valadao had another 58%-42% victory, validating his bipartisan legislative approach.

Once again in 2016, Democrats were enthusiastic about their prospects. Their candidate, lawyer and businessman Emilio Huerta, had a magical name as the son of the iconic United Farmworkers co-founder Dolores Huerta. Valadao separated himself from the "divisive rhetoric" of Republican presidential nominee Trump and said he could not support Trump's candidacy. Huerta suffered from a big fundraising disparity, $2.8 million to $767,000, though he got more than $2 million in support from national Democratic groups.

The outcome was similar to Valadao's two previous victories. He won 57%-43%, with big leads in the rural parts of Fresno and Kern counties while trailing in Kings. Valadao helped himself at home with his work on legislation. McCarthy gave him a prominent role on behalf of a bill to increase local water flow and storage. Valadao pushed his bill to forgive the $375 million debt of Westland Water District, which gave the district time to complete its irrigation drainage plan, with new financing. As the *Los Angeles Times* headlined in a pre-election report, "In this California congressional district, water is more important than Donald Trump." Valadao was a rare Republican supporter of legislation to protect from deportation undocumented immigrants who entered the United States as children.

Even with his continuing campaign success, House Republicans continued to worry about his political future. In February 2017, the National Republican Congressional Committee included Valadao among the first 10 incumbents in its "Patriots" program, receiving special attention for reelection.

Central Valley: Southern Fresno Suburbs, Eastern Bakersfield

Population		**Race and Ethnicity**		**Income**	
Total	711,866	White	18.0%	Median Income	$37,950 (410 out of 435)
Land area	6,730	Black	4.0%		
Pop/ sq mi	105.8	Latino	72.9%		
Born in state	61.0%	Asian	3.1%	Under $50,000	26.1%
		Two races	1.4%	$50,000-$99,999	9.8%
Age Groups		Other	0.7%	$100,000-$199,999	1.6%
Under 18	31.7%			$200,000 or more	31.1%
18-34	27.5%	**Education**		Poverty Rate	31.1%
35-64	33.0%	H.S grad or less	67.4%		
Over 64	7.8%	Some college	24.3%	**Health Insurance**	
		College Degree, 4 yr	5.9%	With health insurance coverage	79.0%
Work		Post grad	2.4%		
White Collar	16.5%				
Sales and Service	36.2%	**Military**		**Public Assistance**	
Blue Collar	47.4%	Veteran	4.8%	Cash public assistance income	9.2%
Government	14.7%	Active Duty	0.8%		
				Food stamp/SNAP benefits	23.5%

Voter Turnout			
2015 Total Citizens 18+	340,997	2016 House Turnout as % CVAP	39%
2016 House turnout	132,408	2014 House Turnout as % CVAP	24%

2012 Presidential Vote		
Barack Obama	65,146	(55%)
Mitt Romney	51,917	(44%)

2016 Presidential Vote		
Hillary Clinton	73,773	(55%)
Donald Trump	52,972	(39%)
Gary Johnson	4,029	(3%)

Cook Partisan Voting Index: D+5

By car, California's Central Valley is a monotonous landscape: mile after mile of farmland with mile-square grid roads, intersected by railroads and canals, with an occasional cluster town. The land is hilly and gets more water near the Sierra Nevada mountains, and this is where the larger cities are. On the other side are the Westlands, where the land is flatter and the water scarcer. Its 600,000 acres are the nation's largest irrigation district. Here the land was always developed and sold in big plots; today, it has some of the world's largest farming operations. The land produces abundantly: alfalfa, cantaloupes, cotton, grapes, lima beans, olives, peaches, plums, raisins, sugar beets, tomatoes, walnuts, wheat. The landowners are a hardy and politically independent lot, but they have been happy to receive government help over the years, with money for crop price supports (in the case of cotton), agricultural research, irrigation systems, and, most important, subsidized and plentiful water.

Landowners have fought hard against liberals' efforts to change their way of life, from Democratic Gov. Jerry Brown's encouragement of Cesar Chavez's United Farm Workers in the 1970s to former House Natural Resources Committee Chairman George Miller's 1992 law to draw off more water to the Sacramento delta and charge higher prices for it in the valley. They have been stymied when conservatives in Congress have deadlocked on expansion of guest-worker programs pushed by valley farmers. Landowners also worry that Los Angeles users might outbid them for scarce water. In the Westlands, several hundred thousand acres went fallow during the drought. This region is a major contributor to California's oil production, and Kern County has the most oil wells in the state. Census Bureau data have shown that the population growth in Kings County has been heavily Hispanic, poor and less likely to be married. Workers in the area's growing food-processing industry were often seasonal. In January 2017, Kings County planners moved toward final discussions with developers of a new city, Quay Valley, with a projected 75,000 people on 7,200 acres along Interstate 5. Skeptics questioned how developers would cope with decreased water availability, which already had adversely affected the local economy. The abundant rains during the winter of 2017 filled local reservoirs and were a huge relief for the short term. But the continuing shortfall of groundwater was a warning that the turnaround was not guaranteed.

The 21st Congressional District is very rural, includes large portions of the Westlands Water District, and links communities with similar agricultural and water interests. It takes in all of heavily Hispanic Kings County and parts of Fresno and Kern counties. Fresno and Kern each have about one-third of the district voters and Kings has one-fourth. The remainder are in a small corner of Tulare. The Naval Air Station Lemoore in January 2017 received its first new wing of F-35 fighter jets, as the new home of the Strike Fighter base of the Navy's Pacific Fleet. The town of Delano is Cesar Chavez's old headquarters, and at the southeastern foot of the district is the Latino part of downtown Bakersfield, which is split between the 21st and the 23rd. The district has increased to 75 percent Hispanic, but Hispanic voter registration and turnout typically remain low. The district leans Democratic. Hillary Clinton in 2016 duplicated the 55 percent that Barack Obama won in 2012. But a local Republican can win with the right background and political appeal.

TWENTY-SECOND DISTRICT

Devin Nunes (R)

Elected 2002, 8th term; b. Oct 01, 1973, Tulare County; California State Polytechnic University, B.S.; California State Polytechnic University, M.S.; College of the Sequoias (CA), A.A.; Roman Catholic; Married (Elizabeth Tamariz Nunes); 3 children.

Elected Office: Col. of the Sequoias Governing Board, 1996-2002.

Professional Career: Appt. Director, USDA Rural Development, 2001.

DC Office: 1013 LHOB 20515, 202-225-2523, Fax: 202-225-3404, nunes.house.gov.

State Offices: Clovis, 559-323-5235; Visalia, 559-733-3861.

Committees: *Permanent Select on Intelligence (Chmn). Ways & Means*: Health, Trade.

Group Ratings

	ADA	ACLU	AFL-CIO	LCV	ITI	COC	HAFA	ACU	CFG	FRC
2016	-	5%	-	3%	100%	100%	46%	80%	60%	100%
2015	0%	C	17%	0%	C	100%	C	58%	48%	92%

Almanac Ratings 2015

	Economy	Social	Foreign	Composite
Liberal	10%	12%	11%	11%
Conservative	90%	88%	90%	89%

Key Votes of the 114th Congress

1. Keystone Pipeline	Y	5. Puerto Rico Debt	Y	9. Offenses by Aliens	Y
2. Trade Deals	Y	6. Medical Marijuana	N	10. Troops in Iraq	N
3. Export-Import Bank	N	7. Sanctuary Cities	Y	11. Homeland Security $$	Y
4. Debt Ceiling Increase	Y	8. Armor-piercing Bullets	Y	12. Trade Adjustment aid	Y

Election Results

Election	Name (Party)	Vote (%)		Cand. Spent	Ind. Exp. Support	Ind. Exp. Oppose
2016 General	Devin Nunes (R)	158,755	(68%)	$871,798		
	Louie Campos (D)	76,211	(32%)			
2016 Primary	Devin Nunes (R)	59,410	(65%)			
	Louie Campos (D)	26,297	(29%)			
	Teresita Andres (R)	5,785	(6%)			

Prior winning percentages: 2014 (72%), 2012 (62%), 2010 (100%), 2008 (68%), 2006 (67%), 2004 (73%), 2002 (71%)

Devin Nunes, a Republican first elected in 2002 at age 29, is an influential conservative with ambitions within and beyond the House. He has briefly toyed with running for the Senate and in 2016 he joined the Trump transition discussion of selection of Cabinet members. Speaker John Boehner tapped him to chair the House Intelligence Committee and he has been an ardent ally of new Speaker Paul Ryan and his desire to shrink government and reshape entitlement programs. Nunes works closely with Majority Leader Kevin McCarthy, who represents the adjacent 23rd District. As House Intelligence Committee chairman, his mishandling in early 2017 of the panel's investigation of alleged Russian influence in the 2016 presidential election led to harsh criticism of Nunes and his decision to transfer control of that inquiry to other committee Republicans. .

Nunes is the descendant of Portuguese immigrants from the Azores. His grandfather established the 600-acre-plus dairy farm that his parents ran when he was growing up in Tulare County. He graduated from California Polytechnic State University, San Luis Obispo, with degrees in agriculture, worked on the family farm, and married a local elementary schoolteacher whose family roots are also in Portugal. In 1998, Nunes ran for the House in a neighboring district and finished second in the primary, 52%-48%.

In 2000, he was the Tulare County campaign chairman for Republican Rep. Bill Thomas, who chaired the Ways and Means Committee before he retired. In 2001, with Thomas' help, Nunes was appointed California director of rural development for the U.S. Department of Agriculture.

When California's redistricting plan was unveiled in September 2001, the 21st District was left without an incumbent, and Nunes moved quickly. He was supported by Thomas, whose deep-pocketed campaign contributors in the pharmaceutical and insurance industries agreed to help Nunes. At home, Nunes won the endorsement of the California Farm Bureau, the state's largest farm organization and a powerful voice in Central Valley politics. He faced serious primary challenges from Jim Patterson, Fresno's conservative former mayor, who was backed by the anti-tax group Club for Growth, and California Assembly member Mike Briggs. They had few differences on policy. All three promised to seek new water sources for farmers about to lose the San Joaquin River as a primary source after environmentalists successfully lobbied to restore the river, which for years had been dammed for irrigation. The candidates all called for tax cuts, fewer federal regulations and expanded guest-worker programs for immigrants. Nunes won with 37 percent of the vote to 33 percent for Patterson and 26 percent for Briggs. In November, Nunes won easily, 70%-26%. He has not been seriously challenged since.

Nunes has a mostly conservative voting record. In the *Almanac* vote ratings for 2015, he was near the center of House Republicans. "I draw my inspiration from the Founding Fathers," he told *Time* magazine after being named one of its "40 Under 40" leaders in 2010. "These political heroes brought us a republican form of government that centered on liberty. The struggle to preserve that liberty grows every time our federal government takes power and rights from the people." Nunes can deliver a cutting sound bite, once comparing government spending with the actions of "a broke gambler who desperately keeps doubling down in a vain effort to break even." He said that conservative Republicans who were blamed by many for shutting down part of the government in 2013 because they opposed the Affordable Care Act were "lemmings with suicide vests."

Legislatively, Nunes has dived into his district's most pressing issue: the use of water from the San Joaquin River. He clashed with supporters of alternatives to increase water flow over the Friant Dam so salmon could be returned to the parched lower reaches of the San Joaquin. Nunes contended that the move would seriously deplete the area's water supply for irrigation. Leaders of such projects were like "communist politburo members who collect big checks and do nothing," he said.

When California's drought worsened, Nunes lashed out at the Obama administration for allying with "radical environmentalists" in preventing farmers from getting sufficient water for their crops. He got a bill through the House in 2012 to reshape California's water-rights system to deliver more San Joaquin water for farmers; Democrats condemned the move as a "water grab" and it did not move in the Senate, something Nunes attributed to California's Democratic senators for defending "their environmental wacko friends."

A member of Ways and Means, at the outset of the health care debate in 2009 Nunes joined Ryan in introducing a bill providing tax credits for people to buy insurance and ending the tax exemption for businesses providing workers with the benefit. Their strategy pre-empted other Republicans who preferred to take more time to craft a plan. Nunes introduced his own bill in 2012 to create a voluntary pilot program in which Medicare and Medicaid recipients would be given a debit-style "Medi-choice" card to buy health insurance. He has proposed to overhaul the tax code by replacing business taxes with a new system he said would create more economic growth. Following the 2016 election, he praised Trump's call for a border adjustment tax that would tax imports and invest in the domestic economy, and said that opposition from some business groups was "a little offensive," given that other nations have comparable fees.

Nunes has used his sizable contributions from dairy interests and other agricultural businesses to donate to colleagues' campaigns, thus increasing his growing internal clout. With the retirement of Rep. Sam Johnson of Texas, he is in line to chair Ways and Means in the next few years, assuming that Republicans retain control of the House.

As Intelligence Committee chairman since 2015, Nunes revamped the panel's subcommittees, forming new ones to concentrate on scrutinizing the CIA, as well as the NSA and cybersecurity. He has been an advocate for intelligence agencies and he kept a low profile, though he traveled widely. "My goal is to make sure we are getting our members out to every corner of the world," Nunes told McClatchy Newspapers. "You cannot conduct serious oversight work without getting on the ground and actually talking to the folks that are doing the work."

On the executive committee of Donald Trump's presidential transition team, which advised on the selection of Cabinet members, he was among the first to recommend the selection of James Mattis for Defense Secretary. From the House, he advocated fellow Reps. Mike Pompeo for director of the CIA and Tom Price for Secretary of Health and Human Services. He said that he had no interest of his own in those positions.

Nunes initially voiced reluctance after the 2016 election to investigate ties between Russia and the Trump campaign, but he joined a bipartisan investigation of the claims following the inauguration. With ranking Democratic Rep. Adam Schiff of California, Nunes said in January that the Intelligence Committee would review Russian cyber-activity against the United States and its allies, plus the response of the intelligence community. He voiced concern about the leaking of Trump-related material to the news media.

Oddly, Nunes got into trouble when he apparently received classified information from a friendly source at the White House and then discussed the report with journalists, among others. In April 2017, the House Ethics Committee announced that it would investigate Nunes for possible "unauthorized disclosures." On the same day, he said that he would transfer control of the Intelligence Committee inquiry to other members, though he retained his chairmanship at the time.

Central Valley: Eastern Fresno City and Suburbs

Population		**Race and Ethnicity**		**Income**	
Total	734,495	White	40.6%	Median Income	$52,897 (211 out of 435)
Land area	1,165	Black	2.8%		
Pop/ sq mi	630.4	Latino	46.5%		
Born in state	68.3%	Asian	7.2%	Under $50,000	30.1%
		Two races	2.1%	$50,000-$99,999	18.5%
Age Groups		Other	0.7%	$100,000-$199,999	4.1%
Under 18	28.4%			$200,000 or more	20.8%
18-34	25.1%	**Education**		Poverty Rate	20.8%
35-64	35.0%	H.S grad or less	42.8%		
Over 64	11.5%	Some college	33.7%	**Health Insurance**	
		College Degree, 4 yr	15.6%	With health insurance coverage	86.1%
Work		Post grad	7.9%		
White Collar	32.8%				
Sales and Service	42.3%	**Military**		**Public Assistance**	
Blue Collar	24.9%	Veteran	6.5%	Cash public assistance income	6.7%
Government	18.5%	Active Duty	0.1%		
				Food stamp/SNAP benefits	16.0%

Voter Turnout			
2015 Total Citizens 18+	453,955	2016 House Turnout as % CVAP	52%
2016 House turnout	234,966	2014 House Turnout as % CVAP	29%

2012 Presidential Vote		
Mitt Romney	125,213	(57%)
Barack Obama	92,005	(42%)

2016 Presidential Vote		
Donald Trump	125,089	(52%)
Hillary Clinton	102,292	(42%)
Gary Johnson	8,628	(4%)

Cook Partisan Voting Index: R+8

In California's Central Valley, between the flat Westlands and the Sierras, is Fresno, a city that is both agricultural and industrial, middle American and ethnically diverse. Although it began as a farm-market center, the city has long since grown out to the north, east and west from its downtown, and its economy has expanded to other sectors - construction, transportation and financial services. It is in fact a creation of the Industrial Age and the Central Pacific Railroad. Historian Kevin Starr described the San Joaquin Valley, at the heart of the Central Valley, as "the most productive unnatural environment on Earth." Fresno's city fathers bred the local wine grape, developed the raisin industry and introduced the Smyrna fig. These are among the area's 300-plus crops, which include cotton, lima beans, nectarines, almonds, tomatoes, cantaloupes, plums, peaches and alfalfa. Dairy, however, is now the biggest commodity and Tulare County leads the nation in milk and dairy sales, with more than 600,000 cattle. In 2015, Tulare also was the number-one county in the United States in the total dollar value of farm production; it surpassed Fresno County, which suffered because of the drought. Those two counties, plus nearby Kern, have been exchanging places in recent years for the highest annual farm exports, with more than $6 billion each.

Central Valley agriculture is industrial in its thoroughness and in its ownership by large corporations. The vineyards outside Fresno radiate in mechanical precision, with vines just 10 feet apart and exposed to the relentless summer sun: nothing romantic or quaint about it. Until recently, times were good. The weak dollar boosted farm exports, large citrus groves benefited from losses in hurricane-plagued Florida and nuts found new export markets. Then, the recession and severe drought hit the area hard. After having peaked at 16.7 percent in 2010, unemployment in Fresno County was still at 9.5 percent in December 2016. Jobs in education and health services were up; farming was down. Tulare's 28 percent poverty rate in 2015 was among the highest in the nation; Fresno was at 25 percent.

Construction of the bullet train from San Francisco to Los Angeles began in the Central Valley, where the project has been fiercely opposed by many local officials worried that it could attract too many people to the Fresno area, forcing residents out of single-family homes and into dense, urban communities. As the pace of rail construction increased, Gov. Jerry Brown hailed the prospect of concentrating new home development. "We can't keep paving over agricultural land," he said in February 2015. A confidential report of the federal Department of Transportation revealed that the original cost of $6.4 billion for the 118 miles from Merced to Bakersfield had increased to more than $9.5 billion.

The 22nd District covers a bit more than half of Fresno County and most of Tulare. The city of Fresno is split between the 22nd and the Hispanic majority 16th, which leans Democratic. Route 99, the old Farm-to-Market Corridor, runs through the district and leads to the Hispanic-majority city of Tulare. In the northern part of the district is Clovis, billed as the "gateway to the Sierras." The central area takes in the smaller city of Dinuba and Visalia, which is the district's largest whole city. It is a largely agricultural district that leans strongly Republican. Fresno County is one of the most conservative urban centers in the nation. As was the case throughout California, Donald Trump under-performed in 2016. In Fresno, where Mitt Romney got 51 percent in 2012, Trump got 46 percent. In Tulare, the Republican vote dropped from 58 percent to 53 percent.

TWENTY-THIRD DISTRICT

Kevin McCarthy (R)

Elected 2006, 6th term; b. Jan 26, 1965, Bakersfield; Bakersfield College (CA), 1985; California State University, Bakersfield, B.A., 1989; University of California, Bakersfield, M.B.A., 1994; Baptist; Married (Judy McCarthy); 2 children.

Elected Office: Trustee, Kern Commissioner Col. Board, 2000-2002; CA Assembly, 2002-2007, Minority Leader, 2004-2006.

Professional Career: Owner, Kevin O's Deli, 1986-1987, Mesa Marin Batting Range, 1991-1992; Staff, U.S. Rep. Bill Thomas, 1987-2002.

DC Office: 2421 RHOB 20515, 202-225-2915, Fax: 202-225-2908, kevinmccarthy.house.gov.

State Offices: Bakersfield, 661-327-3611.

Group Ratings

	ADA	ACLU	AFL-CIO	LCV	ITI	COC	HAFA	ACU	CFG	FRC
2016	-	5%	-	3%	100%	100%	52%	88%	69%	100%
2015	0%	C	13%	0%	C	95%	C	79%	68%	92%

Almanac Ratings 2015

	Economy	Social	Foreign	Composite
Liberal	10%	5%	10%	9%
Conservative	90%	95%	90%	91%

Key Votes of the 114th Congress

1. Keystone Pipeline	Y	5. Puerto Rico Debt	Y	9. Offenses by Aliens	Y
2. Trade Deals	Y	6. Medical Marijuana	N	10. Troops in Iraq	N
3. Export-Import Bank	N	7. Sanctuary Cities	Y	11. Homeland Security $$	Y
4. Debt Ceiling Increase	Y	8. Armor-piercing Bullets	Y	12. Trade Adjustment aid	Y

Election Results

Election	Name (Party)	Vote (%)		Cand. Spent	Ind. Exp. Support	Ind. Exp. Oppose
2016 General	Kevin McCarthy (R)	167,116	(69%)	$4,522,370	$130,629	
	Wendy Reed (D)	74,468	(31%)	$30,992		$13,166
2016 Primary	Kevin McCarthy (R)	51,298	(57%)			
	Wendy Reed (D)	24,158	(27%)			
	Ken Mettler (R)	11,493	(13%)			

Prior winning percentages: 2014 (75%), 2012 (73%), 2010 (99%), 2008 (100%), 2006 (71%)

Kevin McCarthy, a gregarious former Capitol Hill staffer elected in 2006, has combined hard work, some luck and the ability to reach across the party as the No. 2 House GOP leader. In June 2014, he moved up to majority leader in the fallout from Virginia Rep. Eric Cantor's stunning primary defeat. But he fell short in October 2015, when John Boehner unexpectedly announced his resignation as House Speaker and McCarthy was the heir apparent. He ran into numerous obstacles, including opposition from conservatives and self-induced errors. When it became clear that he could not get 218 votes in the House, he magnanimously stepped aside for Paul Ryan and remained as majority leader. The two have had a close political friendship.

McCarthy grew up in Bakersfield, where his blue-collar family has lived for generations and often voted Democratic. He moved in the other direction. At 19, he won $5,000 in the state lottery and invested it in a deli, which helped pay for business school at Cal State, Bakersfield. In college, he was elected chairman of the California Young Republicans and later headed the national Young Republicans organization. After he sold the deli, he got a job in the local office of Rep. Bill Thomas, who was on his way to chairing the powerful Ways and Means Committee. McCarthy eventually became Thomas' district director and protégé. In 2000, he was elected to the Kern County Community College Board, and in 2002 he was elected to the Assembly. He was immediately chosen Republican leader (which, because of California's term limits, is a little easier than it looks). McCarthy worked with Republican Gov. Arnold Schwarzenegger on the budget, workers' compensation issues, and redistricting procedures. His Republican colleague from the Central Valley, Rep. Devin Nunes, says McCarthy "lives and breathes politics."

When Thomas announced his retirement in March 2006, just four days before the filing deadline, McCarthy was the obvious candidate to succeed him. He faced token Republican primary opposition. In November, he won 71%-29%. Looking ahead, he raised more than $1 million and traveled the country campaigning for other Republican candidates. That attracted the attention of party leaders, and he quickly rocketed to influence. After the election, he was chosen the freshman representative on the Republican Steering Committee, which makes committee assignments. He chaired the Platform Committee at the 2008 Republican National Convention, winning praise for soliciting a wide spectrum of views and uniting conservatives and moderates.

McCarthy landed a leadership position in 2009 when Minority Whip Cantor appointed him chief deputy whip - an unusual responsibility for a House member in his second term. On the night of President Barack Obama's inauguration, he reportedly implored a gathering of leading GOP lawmakers and activists plotting strategy to be aggressive. "If you act like you're the minority, you're going to stay in the minority," McCarthy said, according to Robert Draper's 2012 book *Do Not Ask What Good We Do: Inside the U.S. House of Representatives*. "We've gotta challenge them on every single bill and challenge them on every single campaign." In a sign of his media savvy, McCarthy cooperated extensively with Draper.

In the next two years, McCarthy wore multiple hats. He was the head of recruiting for the National Republican Congressional Committee, in what turned out to be the highly successful 2010 election for the GOP. He traveled widely looking for candidates, identifying challengers to take on Democrats accustomed to weak opposition. Ultimately, Republicans had candidates in 430 of the 435 congressional districts, the highest number ever. Even after he recruited the candidates, McCarthy kept in constant contact with the top contenders, often with quick cell phone calls while he was heading to meet other prospects. With Cantor and Ryan, he led the party's "Young Guns" program to spotlight and finance Republican challengers. Minority Leader John Boehner assigned McCarthy and Rep. Peter Roskam of Illinois to draw up a document similar to the House Republicans' 1994 Contract with America. They solicited ideas from the public on the internet, and ultimately compiled the "Pledge to America" policy manifesto. Kept deliberately vague to deter Democratic attacks, it did not make as big an impression as the 1994 document. It sought to commit incoming and veteran Republicans to a single set of policies, such as extending the Bush-era tax cuts and repealing Obama's health care overhaul.

McCarthy was rewarded for his impressive efforts after Republicans won control of the House. He was the overwhelming choice for whip, the third-ranking position for the House majority. Rep. Pete Sessions of Texas, another influential Republican, wanted the post, but was persuaded by Boehner to remain for a second term as chairman of the NRCC, clearing the way for McCarthy to run unopposed.

In his new job, McCarthy avoided the tensions with Boehner that Cantor experienced and employed a nice-guy approach in building trust. He mountain-biked with Republican members in the mornings and rounded up others in the evenings for group dinners, drawing them out by asking questions such as, "What's the most embarrassing thing that happened to you at college?" and "What was the first concert you went to?" He encouraged lawmakers to hang around his whip office on the first floor of the Capitol and he got acquainted with their families.

"A conference united around policies creates better legislation than using intimidation," McCarthy told *The New York Times*. But he did not go out of his way to build bridges to senators of either party. "The Senate is like a country club, and the House is like stopping at a truck stop for breakfast," he told reporters at a 2012 gathering. "We are a microcosm of society, and we reflect it first."

McCarthy paid particular attention to the often-rambunctious tea party freshmen elected in 2010. He offered them advice, including telling them to vote their conscience at times even if it meant disagreeing with the leadership. Sometimes the results were disastrous - especially for the whip, whose job is to assure the majority party prevails. When the leadership decided in April 2011 to back a continuing resolution to keep the federal government operating, 59 Republicans defected. And at the height of the "fiscal cliff" negotiations in December 2012, when the two parties struggled against a deadline to reach agreement on spending and tax cuts, Boehner's "Plan B" proposal was pulled from the floor when it became clear that it lacked sufficient Republican votes.

McCarthy's whip operation faced periodic criticism for its failure to unite Republicans. But there was little second-guessing after Cantor stepped down as majority leader following his unexpected 2014 primary defeat. With the support of friendly colleagues and the GOP's establishment wing, McCarthy geared up a campaign within hours to replace his fallen friend. Early on, there were rumblings that he might face stiff competition from two committee chairs from Texas who previously had served in leadership - Jeb Hensarling of Financial Services and Sessions of Rules. But neither pursued the clash, leaving Idaho maverick Raul Labrador as his only opponent. The secret ballot among House Republicans was held barely a week after Cantor's defeat. Labrador never stood a chance against McCarthy's formidable vote-counting operation.

In his new job, McCarthy laid out broad-based objectives that were designed to appeal across the board: a simpler and fairer tax code, energy independence, local control of education, and ending "the stale policies of the past." When it came to specifics, he showed his allegiance to House conservatives. He endorsed closing the U.S. Export-Import Bank when its charter expired. McCarthy had voted in 2012 to renew the charter of the bank, which many conservatives contend engages in crony capitalism. After their big election victories in 2014, he promised to overhaul how the House did its work by giving committee chairmen more autonomy, assuring that GOP leaders work more closely with their Senate counterparts, and finding issues to draw a clear contrast between the parties.

In early 2015, McCarthy helped create a working group of committee chairs to develop a Republican alternative to the Affordable Care Act. But after a month, Republicans were second-guessed for their sporadic success in passing major legislation. They picked what many saw as an unwinnable fight with Obama over immigration policy by trying to use a Department of Homeland Security spending bill to force an end to his executive order. At the last minute, the leadership jettisoned a planned vote on a controversial anti-abortion bill after some Republican women lawmakers complained it was too harsh. With slight modifications, the House passed that bill a few months later.

The continuing Republican infighting that led to Boehner's September 2015 resignation as Speaker helped to stymie the move by McCarthy to take over as his successor. The conservative Freedom Caucus made a series of demands before several of its members would support him for Speaker. When a partisan firestorm erupted after he claimed credit in a broadcast interview with Sean Hannity of Fox News for the hearings on Benghazi, Libya, which resulted in political damage to Hillary Clinton, McCarthy was slow to respond and proved to be unprepared to fill the big shoes. Eventually, McCarthy advised Ryan that he was the best hope for House Republicans. Some conservatives claimed the McCarthy setback as a victory. Still, he became a key lieutenant to Ryan and remained a major campaign fundraiser and advocate.

McCarthy is no close friend of Democrats. But he makes an effort to have at least some relationships. Facing partisan criticism of scant Republican participation at the 50th anniversary celebration of civil rights protests in Selma, Alabama, in March 2015, he made a last-minute decision to join the festivities. With his home-state Democratic Sen. Dianne Feinstein, he vowed to work closely to ease the problems caused by California's crippling drought. They agreed in December 2016 on a California-focused piece of the water-resources bill, including expanded reservoir storage, financing of water recycling in the cities, and desalination projects. Outgoing Democratic Sen. Barbara Boxer blasted their "poison pill," but Obama signed the measure. Even with ample rainfall in the following months, the infrastructure improvements promised long-term drought relief. In January 2017, McCarthy was the lead supporter in the House of the final bill that Obama enacted as president, which codified the Presidential Innovation Fellows program.

At home, McCarthy had no major party opposition in his first three reelection bids. In 2016, he faced Wendy Reed, an administrator of the Antelope Valley Conservancy. His 69 percent of the vote was the smallest in his six election victories. But the contest was barely a nuisance. McCarthy has continued to suffer embarrassing setbacks, often by excruciatingly close margins, in well-funded efforts to elect more Republicans to the House from California, giving Democrats (and Nancy Pelosi) a 39-14 control of the state delegation. GOP problems in California certainly resulted from factors beyond his control. But their miseries are a reminder of McCarthy's limitations at home - in contrast to GOP leaders who could cite their dominance of home-state delegations, for example, in Ohio and Texas.

When Donald Trump became president, McCarthy became a prominent and unabashed ally. During the campaign, they had spoken frequently. He was a go-between in the more difficult relationship between Trump and Ryan. "As majority leader, my role is to keep a team together," he told *The Washington Post*. "I think it's been helpful." The *Post* described their relationship as "light on policy nitty-gritty but heavy on back-slapping, deal-making and personal rapport." During a celebratory lunch the day before his inauguration, Trump called him out, "There's my Kevin."

Central Valley: Central and Western Bakersfield and Suburbs

Population	
Total	723,632
Land area	9,898
Pop/ sq mi	73.1
Born in state	68.0%

Age Groups	
Under 18	27.5%
18-34	24.3%
35-64	36.7%
Over 64	11.6%

Work	
White Collar	32.0%
Sales and Service	41.5%
Blue Collar	26.6%
Government	21.1%

Race and Ethnicity	
White	48.1%
Black	6.1%
Latino	37.5%
Asian	4.9%
Two races	2.4%
Other	0.9%

Education	
H.S grad or less	45.0%
Some college	35.8%
College Degree, 4 yr	12.7%
Post grad	6.6%

Military	
Veteran	8.5%
Active Duty	0.3%

Income	
Median Income	$55,574 (177 out of 435)
Under $50,000	30.7%
$50,000-$99,999	19.7%
$100,000-$199,999	4.0%
$200,000 or more	19.3%
Poverty Rate	19.3%

Health Insurance	
With health insurance coverage	87.2%

Public Assistance	
Cash public assistance income	6.0%
Food stamp/SNAP benefits	13.2%

Voter Turnout			
2015 Total Citizens 18+	472,814	2016 House Turnout as % CVAP	51%
2016 House turnout	241,584	2014 House Turnout as % CVAP	28%

2012 Presidential Vote		
Mitt Romney	139,816	(62%)
Barack Obama	82,119	(36%)

2016 Presidential Vote		
Donald Trump	142,351	(58%)
Hillary Clinton	88,314	(36%)
Gary Johnson	9,850	(4%)

Cook Partisan Voting Index: R+14

Bakersfield, near the southern end of California's Central Valley, has been the focus of great migrations four times: in the gold rush of 1885; in the boomlet that followed the discovery of oil in 1899; in the 1930s flight of Dust Bowl refugees from Oklahoma, Kansas and Texas; and in a flood of newcomers in the past two decades, when Bakersfield and Kern County grew more rapidly than California's biggest metro areas. The migration that made the deepest imprint was in the 1930s. The Okies drove across a thousand miles of brown landscape, then through the Tehachapi Pass, and found this vast green valley, with its irrigated fields and its eucalyptus-shaded towns - the richest farming country in the world. The story is told vividly in novelist John Steinbeck's *The Grapes of Wrath* and in Dan Morgan's *Rising in the West*, which explains how the Okies' descendants prospered in California. As a result, the area around Bakersfield is the one Southern-accented part of California, the home of a thriving country-music scene that included the late singers Merle Haggard and Buck Owens. Haggard first learned his craft as a prisoner at San Quentin, including an appearance by Johnny Cash. When he died in April 2016, he was praised as one of the most influential country-music singers of his generation.

People here are culturally conservative with little empathy for Los Angeles-style liberalism. More recently, Latinos have been coming in large numbers for farm work. The result is that the Central Valley, including Bakersfield, has had both high population growth and high unemployment for a decade. Its 41 percent population increase from 2000 to 2010 placed Bakersfield among the top 10 fastest-growing cities in the nation; by 2015, it had grown by another 7 percent. The flip side was that unemployment at the end of 2016 remained at 9.9 percent.

Reduced oil prices, and the accompanying disincentive for drilling, became another hit to the Kern County economy, which is home to 70 percent of the oil production in California and produces more oil than any other county in the nation. In 2015, the local oil and gas industry laid off more than 2,000 of its 12,000-plus workers. That cut county revenues by $40 million and reduced local property values by about 10 percent. The drought added to the miseries for the farm sector, though the heavy rains in early 2017 significantly improved conditions.

The 23rd Congressional District includes about 80 percent of Kern County, with the remainder of the district in rural Tulare and a northern tip of Los Angeles County. It includes much of downtown Bakersfield, though the city and much of the rich farmland along Interstate 5 spill into the Kings County-based 21st District. The 23rd covers the southern part of the Sierras, including Sequoia National Forest and Lake Isabella. The Cesar Chavez National Monument is part of the National Park in Keene. The southern end of the district encompasses the sprawling Edwards Air Force Base, where Chuck Yeager flew the X-1 and where the Space Shuttle has frequently landed, and the Naval Air Weapons Station China Lake. The district takes in part of Lancaster in Antelope Valley. About 80 percent of its voters are in Kern. The 23rd is 38 percent Hispanic. As in 2012, this was the most Republican district in California in the 2016 presidential election. Donald Trump led Hillary Clinton, 58%-36%, a dip from 62 percent for Mitt Romney. Kern, the most populous county in Trump Country in California, gave him 53 percent of the vote.

TWENTY-FOURTH DISTRICT

Salud Carbajal (D)

Elected 2016, 1st term; b. Nov 18, 1964, Moroleon, Mexico; Fielding University (CA); University of California, Santa Barbara, B.A., 1990; Catholic; Married (Gina Carbajal); 2 children.

Military Career: U.S Marine Corps Reserves.

Elected Office: Staff, County Supervisor Naomi Schwartz, 1993-2004; Member, Santa Barbara County Board of Supervisors, 2004-2016.

DC Office: 212 CHOB 20515, 202-225-3601, Fax: 202-225-5632, carbajal.house.gov.

State Offices: San Luis Obispo, 805-546-8348; Santa Barbara, 805-730-1710.

Committees: *Armed Services*: Readiness, Tactical Air & Land Forces. *Budget*.

Election Results

Election	Name (Party)	Vote (%)		Cand. Spent	Ind. Exp. Support	Ind. Exp. Oppose
2016 General	Salud Carbajal (D)	166,034	(53%)	$3,076,664	$824,112	$1,418,406
	Justin Fareed (R)	144,780	(47%)	$2,269,955	$442,602	$745,962
2016 Primary	Salud Carbajal (D)	47,618	(33%)			
	Justin Fareed (R)	29,902	(21%)			
	Katcho Achadjian (R)	27,545	(19%)			
	Helene Schneider (D)	20,992	(14%)			
	William Ostrander (D)	8,048	(6%)			
	Matt Kokkonen (R)	7,779	(5%)			

Democrat Salud Carbajal was elected in 2016 in a contentious contest for an open seat that Democrats had held for 20 years. The competitive and costly campaign required two additional weeks of vote-counting before the outcome was assured.

Carbajal was born in Mexico, and his family moved to a small mining town in Arizona when he was five. His father worked in a copper mine until it closed. One of eight children, he was the first in his family to graduate from college. He got his bachelor's in Iberian studies from the University of California, Santa Barbara, and a master's in organizational management from Fielding University. Carbajal was a member of the U.S. Marine Corps Reserve for eight years, including two years of active stateside duty during the Gulf War. He had several jobs on the public payroll, including chief of staff to a county supervisor and program director in the Santa Barbara Public Health Department. He served for 12 years on the Santa Barbara County Board of Supervisors, where he worked to improve local schools, protect the environment and advocate sustainable, clean energy sources. Carbajal has participated in several broader public forums, including President Barack Obama's State, Local and Tribal Leaders Task Force on Climate Preparedness and Resilience, and a local government advisory committee of the Environmental Protection Agency.

Carbajal was the favorite of the Democratic establishment when Rep. Lois Capps announced her retirement in April 2015. Her daughter Laura Capps, a former aide to President Bill Clinton, explored a bid but decided not to run. Santa Barbara Mayor Helene Schneider, who spoke positively about Vermont Sen. Bernie Sanders in the presidential campaign, was another Democratic contender. Capps and Democratic Leader Nancy Pelosi were early supporters of Carbajal. "This is not a foregone-conclusion Democratic district," Pelosi told *The Los Angeles Times*. On the Republican side, the chief candidates were Assemblyman Katcho Achadjian and businessman Justin Fareed, whose family owned a sports business; Fareed had run for this seat in 2014 and fell 614 votes short in the primary of making it into the November election. In the "top two" non-partisan primary, Carbajal and Fareed were the front-runners with 31.9 percent and 20.5 percent. Schneider and Achadjian ran competitive challenges, but they fell short with 18.1 percent and 14.9 percent.

In the general election, Fareed, who had served a year in Washington as an aide to Republican Rep. Ed Whitfield of Kentucky, accused Carbajal of being long on "political rhetoric and not actual solutions to the problems we're facing." He said that Carbajal's "puppet masters in Washington" deceived the public in an attempt to turn the campaign into a contest about Donald Trump. Carbajal described himself as a public servant who worked across party lines. In September, he apologized for what he thought was a private remark when he referred to Lompoc, a military town that includes the Vandenberg base, as the "armpit" of Santa Barbara. Carbajal raised $3.1 million to $2.3 million for Fareed. National Republican spent $2 million on behalf of Fareed, while Democrats responded with more than $1.5 million for Carbajal. The contest turned out closer than had been expected. Fareed took San Luis Obispo with 51.5 percent of the vote. But Carbajal won the more populous Santa Barbara with 57 percent, and led overall, 53%-47%. Fareed conceded on Nov. 23 after the late counting made little change in the tally.

Carbajal got seats on the Armed Services and Budget committees. His first bill was to bar oil and gas drilling off of California's Central Coast. During a news conference with other members of the Hispanic Caucus on Trump's inauguration day, Carbajal responded to his anti-Mexican rhetoric, "Mr. Trump, I ask you, am I a threat to our democracy?"

Central Coast: Santa Barbara, San Luis Obispo

Population		**Race and Ethnicity**		**Income**	
Total	722,051	White	55.6%	Median Income	$62,276 (118 out of 435)
Land area	6,883	Black	1.8%	Under $50,000	30.1%
Pop/ sq mi	104.9	Latino	35.3%	$50,000-$99,999	22.2%
Born in state	59.5%	Asian	4.4%	$100,000-$199,999	6.8%
Age Groups		Two races	2.3%	$200,000 or more	15.7%
Under 18	20.9%	Other	0.6%	Poverty Rate	15.7%
18-34	28.4%	**Education**		**Health Insurance**	
35-64	35.8%	H.S grad or less	34.7%	With health insurance coverage	85.7%
Over 64	14.9%	Some college	32.7%	**Public Assistance**	
Work		College Degree, 4 yr	19.9%	Cash public assistance income	2.3%
White Collar	36.1%	Post grad	12.7%	Food stamp/SNAP benefits	6.5%
Sales and Service	43.0%	**Military**			
Blue Collar	20.9%	Veteran	7.7%		
Government	17.5%	Active Duty	0.6%		

Voter Turnout			
2015 Total Citizens 18+	493,986	2016 House Turnout as % CVAP	63%
2016 House turnout	310,814	2014 House Turnout as % CVAP	40%

2012 Presidential Vote		
Barack Obama	158,119	(54%)
Mitt Romney	126,049	(43%)

2016 Presidential Vote		
Hillary Clinton	176,979	(56%)
Donald Trump	113,887	(36%)
Gary Johnson	13,426	(4%)
Jill Stein	6,733	(2%)

Cook Partisan Voting Index: D+7

In a state where stunning coastal landscapes and charming small towns are a dime a dozen, Santa Barbara stands out as someplace special. It is a collection of red tile roofs and leafy live oaks, sheltered by towering mountains just above the sea. The impression is a bit misleading, for Santa Barbara has its problems. Most of its quaint white stucco buildings were put up not as part of 18th-century mission settlement, but after a 1925 earthquake leveled much of the town. Like Disneyland, it is not authentically old, but rather a bigger, more attractive, cleaner version of a historical artifact, one that is maintained not by a company, but by an architectural review board. The city has long been one of the nation's richest retirement communities, one comfortable with its high living costs and determined to preserve its pristine environment and serenity.

Both features came under threat spectacularly in 1969, when an underwater oil well ruptured, coating the beach with oil. Pictures of the oil slick in the channel, and of volunteers trying to wash oil off grounded birds, helped to launch the 1970s environmental movement. Almost all of the wells are closed now, though some old 19th-century wells mysteriously still wash up globs of oil to the beach at nearby Summerland. The oil spill left a long-lasting residue in Santa Barbara's politics. This was once a mostly Republican community, uninterested in redistribution of wealth, but always concerned about the environment and having moderate-to-liberal impulses on cultural issues. Like most of coastal California, it has moved decisively to the left. Despite that, 61 percent of voters opposed in November 2014 a Santa Barbara County referendum to impose a ban on fracking. In one of his final actions as president, Barack Obama added Piedras Blancas, which is not far from San Simeon, to the California Coastal Monument.

Much of the Santa Barbara coastline is occupied by Vandenberg Air Force Base, which was the site in December 1958 of the first U.S. test missile launch and now sends unmanned government and commercial satellites into polar orbit. The largest towns in northern Santa Barbara County, like San Luis Obispo, are pleasant, comfortable places, as untrendy as you can find in coastal California. One problem is that the cost of rental housing in both counties has become unaffordable for many local workers. In

San Luis Obispo, PG&E moved to shut down the Diablo Canyon nuclear power plant starting in 2024, when the permits for its reactors expire.

The 24th Congressional District of California includes all of San Luis Obispo and Santa Barbara counties. Santa Barbara is the larger of the two, and its 45 percent Latino population is twice that of SLO. Santa Maria is the largest city in Santa Barbara County. The 24th also brings in the northwest corner of Ventura County and a small coastal part of the city of San Buenaventura to the south, and encompasses much of the Los Padres National Forest. Politically, the district favors Democrats. Closer to Los Angeles, Santa Barbara leans more heavily Democratic.

TWENTY-FIFTH DISTRICT

Steve Knight (R)

Elected 2014, 2nd term; b. Dec 17, 1966, Edwards Air Force Base; Antelope Valley College (CA), A.A., 2006; Roman Catholic; Married (Lily Knight); 2 children.

Military Career: U.S. Army, 1985-1987; U.S. Army Reserve, 1987-1993.

Elected Office: Palmdale City Council, 2005-2008; CA Assembly, 2008-2012, Assistant Minority Leader, 2010-2012; Vice Mayor, Palmdale; CA Senate 2012-2014.

Professional Career: Police officer, 18 years.

DC Office: 1023 LHOB 20515, 202-225-1956, Fax: 202-226-0683, knight.house.gov.

State Offices: Palmdale, 661-441-0320; Santa Clarita, 661-255-5630; Simi Valley, 805-581-7130.

Committees: *Armed Services*: Seapower & Projection Forces, Tactical Air & Land Forces. *Science, Space & Technology*: Energy, Research & Technology, Space. *Small Business*: Contracting & Workforce (Chmn), Economic Growth, Tax & Capital Access.

Group Ratings

	ADA	ACLU	AFL-CIO	LCV	ITI	COC	HAFA	ACU	CFG	FRC
2016	-	5%	-	0%	100%	100%	61%	100%	84%	92%
2015	0%	C	13%	0%	C	89%	C	71%	56%	92%

Almanac Ratings 2015

	Economy	Social	Foreign	Composite
Liberal	12%	9%	6%	9%
Conservative	88%	91%	94%	91%

Key Votes of the 114th Congress

1. Keystone Pipeline	Y	5. Puerto Rico Debt	N	9. Offenses by Aliens	Y
2. Trade Deals	Y	6. Medical Marijuana	N	10. Troops in Iraq	N
3. Export-Import Bank	Y	7. Sanctuary Cities	Y	11. Homeland Security $$	Y
4. Debt Ceiling Increase	N	8. Armor-piercing Bullets	Y	12. Trade Adjustment aid	N

Election Results

Election	Name (Party)	Vote (%)		Cand. Spent	Ind. Exp. Support	Ind. Exp. Oppose
2016 General	Steve Knight (R)	138,755	(53%)	$1,604,738	$12,707	$4,223,944
	Bryan Caforio (D)	122,406	(47%)	$1,689,852	$775,258	$1,693,305
2016 Primary	Steve Knight (R)	46,568	(49%)			
	Bryan Caforio (D)	27,332	(29%)			
	Lou Vince (D)	14,197	(15%)			
	Jeffrey Moffatt (R)	6,978	(7%)			

Prior winning percentages: 2014 (53%)

Steve Knight beat expectations in 2014 to defeat fellow Republican Tony Strickland, for the open seat of retiring House Armed Services Committee Chairman Buck McKeon. The GOP benefited from

Democrats' divisions in the primary that shut them out of the general-election vote. Democrats contend that demographic shifts make it only a matter of time before they take this seat, which is the sole Republican-held House district that is predominantly in Los Angeles County.

Knight was born into a military family and grew up in Palmdale. He enlisted in the Army after high school. After completing his military service, he joined the Los Angeles Police Department, where he served for 18 years. Citing the inspiration of his father - who had served as mayor, and then in the state Assembly and Senate for 12 years - Knight was elected to the Palmdale City Council. He established a reputation as tough on crime and government spending. In 2008, he was elected to the Assembly, which was followed four years later with election to the state Senate. In those years, he compiled a solidly conservative record, especially on immigration and gun control.

Democrats initially were skeptical that McKeon's retirement gave them a pick-up opportunity. Their failure became a certainty thanks to the state's all-party primary system. With eight candidates in the June primary, Strickland topped the field at 30 percent, Knight had 28 percent, and the top Democrat Lee Rogers got 22 percent. The four GOP candidates on the June ballot got a total of 65 percent of the vote. In the November run-off, Strickland was the early favorite, thanks to a big fundraising advantage and his lead in the primary.

The focus on personality and political base gave their contest elements of an election to the state Legislature, where each had served. Knight attacked Strickland as a carpetbagger from nearby Ventura County, where he lost a House bid in 2012, 53%-47%, in the blue-leaning 26th District. He contended that Strickland moved to the neighboring 25th only because he couldn't win in his own base. Knight played up his local roots and more socially conservative bona fides. He encountered his own troubles, especially after he was one of only three state senators to vote against a bill banning Confederate symbols on state property. He ran his campaign on a shoestring budget while getting outspent 5-to-1. In the end, Strickland was unable to shake the label of opportunist. Knight won 53%-47%, less than a firm grip on his district.

In the House, Knight took a seat on the Armed Services Committee near the bottom of the seniority list that McKeon had climbed over nearly two decades. With an amendment to the annual defense spending bill in 2015, he sought to resolve a long-standing dispute over protective regions for sea otters near the Point Mugu Naval Air Station in Ventura County by permitting Defense Department testing in two specific areas while protecting the sea otters elsewhere. The Small Business Committee approved two bills by Knight, making it easier for companies to form joint ventures and compete for federal contracts, and simplifying the eligibility for small businesses to participate in the Defense Department's mentor-protégé program. Each measure was enacted as part of larger defense spending bills. In 2017, he became chairman of the Contracting and Workforce Subcommittee. Knight received some unwanted attention in April 2015 when he told an immigration protester outside his Simi Valley office, "If you touch me again, I'll drop your ass."

As expected, Knight was a top target in 2016 for Democrats, who viewed him as a bad fit for this district. Their preferred candidate, trial lawyer Bryan Caforio, took second in the primary, 29%-15%, against retired LAPD Lt. Lou Vince, whom Democratic campaign strategists had dismissed as not a viable candidate. Knight and one other Republican took 56 percent of the first-round vote. Caforia was well-financed and argued that Knight was out of touch with his changing constituency, but he suffered from the taint of being a carpetbagger who moved to Santa Clarita shortly before he declared his candidacy.

Democrats attacked Knight for not sufficiently distancing himself from presidential nominee Donald Trump. In October, Knight condemned Trump's "reprehensible behavior" and said that he did not support either major-party candidate; following the election, he said that he had voted for Trump. Each candidate raised about $1.7 million. Democratic groups spent another $3.5 million on behalf of Cafario, which doubled what Republicans spent for their candidate. But Knight prevailed with a relatively comfortable 53%-47%. Whether that was enough to entrench him remained to be seen.

Northern LA Exurbs: Santa Clarita, Palmdale

Population		**Race and Ethnicity**		**Income**	
Total	718,475	White	43.4%	Median Income	$72,342 (64 out of 435)
Land area	1,691	Black	7.7%	Under $50,000	30.5%
Pop/ sq mi	425.0	Latino	37.3%	$50,000-$99,999	26.4%
Born in state	61.6%	Asian	7.9%	$100,000-$199,999	7.9%
		Two races	3.1%	$200,000 or more	14.0%
		Other	0.6%	Poverty Rate	14.0%
Age Groups		**Education**		**Health Insurance**	
Under 18	27.5%	H.S grad or less	37.9%	With health insurance coverage	87.8%
18-34	22.2%	Some college	35.0%		
35-64	40.1%	College Degree, 4 yr	18.1%		
Over 64	10.1%	Post grad	8.8%		
Work		**Military**		**Public Assistance**	
White Collar	38.3%	Veteran	6.4%	Cash public assistance income	3.5%
Sales and Service	42.8%	Active Duty	0.1%	Food stamp/SNAP benefits	7.5%
Blue Collar	18.9%				
Government	14.3%				

Voter Turnout			
2015 Total Citizens 18+	460,444	2016 House Turnout as % CVAP	57%
2016 House turnout	261,161	2014 House Turnout as % CVAP	25%

2012 Presidential Vote		
Mitt Romney	125,258	(50%)
Barack Obama	120,701	(48%)

2016 Presidential Vote		
Hillary Clinton	137,491	(50%)
Donald Trump	119,249	(43%)
Gary Johnson	9,969	(4%)

Cook Partisan Voting Index: EVEN

For decades, as the mild-temperature flatlands of the Los Angeles Basin and San Fernando Valley filled up with people, the rugged mountains and hot desert to the north in Los Angeles County remained mostly empty. But as L.A. and the valley filled up, people began moving north through Newhall pass on Interstate 5 and northeast on Route 14 to the high desert country. Immediately north of the pass is Santa Clarita, the third-largest city in the county with more than 180,000 residents, and the Six Flags Magic Mountain theme park. Northeast on Route 14, past the former gold-mining center of Acton, the mountains stop at the San Andreas Fault and the desert stretches out low and flat. This is Antelope Valley, with huge aerospace plants and military bases around Palmdale and Lancaster, where more than 320,000 people live. Not far from upscale shopping centers, there has been a resurgence of specialty farm crops such as baby carrots, organic onions and parsnips. Access to health care has been a problem in Antelope Valley and the life expectancy of African Americans here has been four years shorter than for blacks in the rest of Los Angeles County.

The Air Force Plant 42 is home to many defense contractors, with projects that include the B-2 Stealth Bomber, the F-117 Stealth Fighter, and the F-35 Joint Strike Fighter. The RQ-170 Sentinel, a next-generation drone reportedly used in stealth CIA operations, has been developed at Lockheed Martin's Skunk Works facility in Palmdale. In October 2015, the Pentagon awarded Northrop Grumman a deal to build as many as 100 of the B-2 Long-Range Strike Bombers, with much of the work expected at Palmdale.

After several years as one of the fast-growing areas in California, with relatively cheap housing and easy mortgages, housing prices collapsed early during the Great Recession and this area had one of the nation's highest foreclosure rates. Following a slow recovery, low prices resulted in some improvement of the housing market. In a welcome diversification, Santa Clarita has become a favorite alternative production site for Hollywood studios 30 miles to the south, though many of these "movie ranches" suffered major damage when a huge fire spread from the mountains in August 2016. Allegations of police brutality in Antelope Valley were filed with the Justice Department in 2015, which two years earlier had found instances of illegal targeting of racial minorities; Palmdale is Hispanic-majority.

The 25th Congressional District of California includes all of the Santa Clarita Valley and the high desert parts of Los Angeles County. The district extends to most of Simi Valley in Ventura County, including the Ronald Reagan Presidential Foundation and Library, which has become one of the most popular tourist attraction north of Los Angeles. Housed there are 55 million pages of presidential documents and a large piece of the Berlin Wall, which Reagan famously urged Soviet leader Mikhail Gorbachev to tear down. About one-fifth of the district is in Ventura. The high desert, not surprisingly, suffered from the statewide drought. At Castaic Lake, water had to be pumped uphill in 2014 to get it to the local treatment plant. Beaches at the lake were closed and boats could no longer be launched from a trailer. The storms in the winter of 2017 resulted in a welcome replenishment of local reservoirs.

Politically, the district had been comfortably Republican. During the past decade, the influx of Latinos, which have grown to 37 percent of the 25th, and the extension of the L.A. psyche to this once-rural area have eliminated the GOP's voter-registration advantage and made this a competitive district. Barack Obama won it by a sliver in 2008 and lost narrowly in 2012. Hillary Clinton won more comfortably in 2016, 50%-43%.

TWENTY-SIXTH DISTRICT

Julia Brownley (D)

Elected 2012, 3rd term; b. Aug 28, 1952, Aiken, SC; George Washington University (DC), B.A.; American University (DC), M.B.A.; Episcopalian; Divorced; 2 children.

Elected Office: CA Assembly, 2006-2012; Santa Monica Malibu School Board, 1994-2006.

Professional Career: Product Manager, Steelcase, 1984-1992; Sales Manager, Pitney Bowes, 1981-1984; Sales Manager, Burroughs Corporation, 1976-1981.

DC Office: 1019 LHOB 20515, 202-225-5811, Fax: 202-225-1100, juliabrownley.house.gov.

State Offices: Oxnard, 805-379-1779; Thousand Oaks, 805-379-1779.

Committees: *Transportation & Infrastructure*: Aviation, Highways & Transit, Water Resources & Environment. *Veterans' Affairs*: Disability Assistance & Memorial Affairs, Health (RMM).

Group Ratings

	ADA	ACLU	AFL-CIO	LCV	ITI	COC	HAFA	ACU	CFG	FRC
2016	-	70%	-	100%	83%	64%	12%	4%	4%	0%
2015	70%	C	100%	100%	C	55%	C	4%	0%	0%

Almanac Ratings 2015

	Economy	Social	Foreign	Composite
Liberal	78%	94%	40%	71%
Conservative	22%	6%	60%	29%

Key Votes of the 114th Congress

1. Keystone Pipeline	N	5. Puerto Rico Debt	Y	9. Offenses by Aliens	Y
2. Trade Deals	N	6. Medical Marijuana	Y	10. Troops in Iraq	N
3. Export-Import Bank	Y	7. Sanctuary Cities	N	11. Homeland Security $$	Y
4. Debt Ceiling Increase	Y	8. Armor-piercing Bullets	N	12. Trade Adjustment aid	Y

Election Results

Election	Name (Party)	Vote (%)		Cand. Spent	Ind. Exp. Support	Ind. Exp. Oppose
2016 General	Julia Brownley (D)	169,248	(60%)	$1,739,600		
	Rafael Dagnesses (R)	111,059	(40%)	$176,221		
2016 Primary	Julia Brownley (D)	108,937	(64%)			
	Rafael dagnesses (R)	61,219	(36%)			

Prior winning percentages: 2014 (51%), 2012 (53%)

Democrat Julia Brownley in 2012 took the Ventura County seat that had long been held by Republicans. With a political base that had been in Santa Monica south of the 26th District, she was slow to establish control of the district or her mark in the House. But she has carved out a niche on veterans' health issues and she breezed to reelection in 2016.

Brownley grew up in Virginia in a Republican household. It wasn't until she went to Washington, D.C.'s, all-girls Mount Vernon College that she began to consider her personal politics. There, shaped by the emerging women's movement and the war in Vietnam, Brownley said she felt at home in the Democratic Party. After college, she pursued a career in marketing, earning a master's degree from American University and then working as a sales manager for several large companies. The career introduced her to her husband (they are now divorced) and brought her to California. Brownley's experiences with her children helped to push her into politics. Her daughter, Hannah, suffered from dyslexia. Working with the school system to improve Hannah's education inspired Brownley to run for the Santa Monica-Malibu school board in 1994. She stayed on the board for 12 years, and served as its president.

Frustrated with what she considered insufficient funding for the school district, Brownley in 2006 won a seat in the state Assembly. There, Brownley chaired the Education Committee, advocating higher spending on the state's schools at every level. She worked on legislation to prevent human trafficking, to improve the foster care system, and to reduce the prevalence of single-use plastic bags. She pushed for a state version of the Disclose Act that would require more disclosure of political donors.

In the contest for the open seat in the 26th District, Democrats had counted on Ventura County Supervisor Steve Bennett, but he dropped out before the filing deadline. Brownley moved up the coast from Santa Monica and prevailed in the primary over Linda Parks, a Republican-turned-independent hoping to steal moderate votes from Brownley. Nearly $1 million in advertising, including a $600,000 television buy from a Democratic super PAC, moved Brownley to the general election against state Sen. Tony Strickland. He led the all-party primary with 44 percent, to 27 percent for Brownley and 18 percent for Parks. In the general election, Strickland attacked Brownley for moving to the district, while emphasizing his own history in the area. The U.S. Chamber of Commerce and other groups contributed to his campaign, leading Brownley to call him a captive of "Washington special interests." The *Los Angeles Times* endorsed her, saying that the "ideologically rigid" Strickland lacked the "real-world pragmatism" of other Southern California Republicans. She won, 52.7%-47.3%, barely short of President Barack Obama's 54 percent in the district. Strickland in 2014 ran - and lost - to a Republican in the adjacent GOP-leaning 25th District.

Brownley had continuing problems in finding a comfort level with her new constituency. Her official House bio listed that she served on a school board for 12 years, for example, but it did not say where. She became active on the Veterans Affairs Committee, where she was ranking Democrat on the Health Subcommittee. In February 2016, the House passed her bill to identify the best mental-health and suicide-prevention program for at-risk women veterans. For 2017, her agenda included several proposals to expand and improve the quality of veterans' care.

She pursued her interest in education issues by calling for increased funding of bilingual programs. As co-chair of the House Dyslexia Caucus with Republican Rep. Lamar Smith of Texas, she won enactment of the Research Excellence and Advancements for Dyslexia (READ) Act to require the National Science Foundation to spend at least $2.5 million annually for dyslexia research. In December 2016, the House passed her bill to name a local post office in honor of the fallen heroes of the west coast Seabees battalion stationed in Ventura.

Brownley faced another competitive campaign in 2014. This time, her opponent was Republican Assemblyman Jeff Gorell, who showcased his moderate voting record in Sacramento. In September 2014, a Democratic official in Washington told *Roll Call* that, "This is a tight race and a difficult seat." Brownley was far better-funded, $3.4 million to $1.3 million, and benefited in the expensive L.A. media market from more than $2 million in national party funding. She won narrowly, 51.3%-48.7%. It took more than a week to declare the winner.

In the next cycle, the Democratic Congressional Campaign Committee included Brownley among the first 14 members of its Frontline program of House Democrats who were expected to be vulnerable in 2016. Perhaps that scared off potential challengers. Republican challenger Rafael Dagnesses, a real estate agent, was little-known politically and raised only $184,000, including $100,000 of self-financing. Brownley won, 60%-40%.

Southern Ventura: Oxnard, Thousand Oaks

Population		**Race and Ethnicity**		**Income**	
Total	717,882	White	44.4%	Median Income	$76,002 (47 out of 435)
Land area	939	Black	1.7%		
Pop/ sq mi	764.4	Latino	44.5%	Under $50,000	30.5%
Born in state	56.3%	Asian	6.7%	$50,000-$99,999	26.9%
Age Groups		Two races	2.2%	$100,000-$199,999	9.8%
Under 18	24.8%	Other	0.5%	$200,000 or more	11.8%
18-34	23.2%	**Education**		Poverty Rate	11.8%
35-64	38.7%	H.S grad or less	36.6%	**Health Insurance**	
Over 64	13.3%	Some college	31.5%	With health insurance coverage	85.7%
Work		College Degree, 4 yr	19.8%		
White Collar	36.2%	Post grad	12.1%	**Public Assistance**	
Sales and Service	41.3%	**Military**		Cash public assistance income	2.6%
Blue Collar	22.5%	Veteran	7.1%		
Government	13.7%	Active Duty	0.6%	Food stamp/SNAP benefits	7.5%

Voter Turnout			
2015 Total Citizens 18+	451,525	2016 House Turnout as % CVAP	62%
2016 House turnout	280,307	2014 House Turnout as % CVAP	38%

2012 Presidential Vote		
Barack Obama	147,753	(54%)
Mitt Romney	119,677	(44%)

2016 Presidential Vote		
Hillary Clinton	169,083	(57%)
Donald Trump	105,259	(36%)
Gary Johnson	11,301	(4%)

Cook Partisan Voting Index: D+7

For many Americans, Simi Valley remains best known as the site of the 1992 trial where four Los Angeles police officers were acquitted for the beating of taxi driver Rodney King, who famously said, "People, I just want to say, can we all get along?" Increasingly overlooked has been that the incident took place during riots in South Los Angeles. The city of Simi Valley is a very different place -- a product of the 1960s, the expansive postwar years when migrants from points across the United States moved west to Los Angeles and then spread beyond city and county limits to fill up the valleys between the mountains. With their work ethic, varied skills, and appreciation of the local environment, they brought a distaste for the crime and civil strife that seemed all too common in Los Angeles during that turbulent decade in U.S. history. In the valleys of Ventura County, northwest of Los Angeles, people built communities in what had been orange and lemon groves. Like California overall, the Ventura County population has trended socially liberal and economically conservative. To the south is upscale Thousand Oaks, one of the safest large cities in the nation and the headquarters of biotechnology giant Amgen Inc. Farther west in Pleasant Valley is Camarillo, which is home to numerous technology firms.

The local economy has a strong export market, including pharmaceuticals, semiconductors and citrus fruit. A downside is that the economic growth and high cost of living have created a shortage of housing for farm workers. The once-robust local farming, especially strawberries, has been reduced - a victim of imports, labor costs and the drought. In the inland valleys still farther west is Ojai, which remains a center for tourism. During the filming of the 1937 Frank Capra movie *Lost Horizon*, an aerial shot of the Ojai Valley was used to represent the mythical earthly paradise of Shangri-La. Also present here is the Santa Clara River Valley, with Fillmore, Piru and Santa Paula. Despite its affluence, the area did not escape the recession and suffered for a short time with its unemployment rate in the double digits.

The 26th Congressional District includes about 80 percent of Ventura County, including its largest city, Oxnard. The district takes in Thousand Oaks and the Santa Clara River Valley. Simi Valley is split with the 25th, despite the objections of many residents who wanted a single district entirely in Ventura County. Instead, the 26th has a thin slice of Los Angeles county, but with only a few thousand voters.

The 26th District leans Democratic, though it is more competitive than any Democratic-held district in L.A. County. Hillary Clinton led Donald Trump, 57%-36%. She took the county overall, 56%-38%.

TWENTY-SEVENTH DISTRICT

Judy Chu (D)

Elected 2009, 5th term; b. Jul 07, 1953, Los Angeles; California School Professional Psychology, Los Angeles, Ph.D.; California School Professional Psychology, Los Angeles, M.A.; University of California, Los Angeles, B.A.; University of California, Santa Barbara, Att.; Married (Michael Eng).

Elected Office: Garvey School Board, 1985-1988; Monterey Park City Council, 1988-2001; Mayor, Monterey Park; CA Assembly, 2001-2006; CA Board Of Equalization, 2006-2009, vice Chairman, 2009.

Professional Career: Professor, Los Angeles City College, Psychology Department, 1981-1988; E. Los Angeles College, Psychology Department, 1988-2001.

DC Office: 2423 RHOB 20515, 202-225-5464, Fax: 202-225-5467, chu.house.gov.

State Offices: Claremont, 909-625-5394; Pasadena, 626-304-0110.

Committees: *Small Business*: Economic Growth, Tax & Capital Access. *Ways & Means*: Health, Human Resources.

Group Ratings

	ADA	ACLU	AFL-CIO	LCV	ITI	COC	HAFA	ACU	CFG	FRC
2016	-	88%	-	97%	50%	54%	12%	0%	4%	0%
2015	100%	C	100%	100%	C	40%	C	0%	0%	0%

Almanac Ratings 2015

	Economy	Social	Foreign	Composite
Liberal	95%	100%	99%	98%
Conservative	5%	0%	1%	2%

Key Votes of the 114th Congress

1. Keystone Pipeline	N	5. Puerto Rico Debt	Y	9. Offenses by Aliens	N
2. Trade Deals	N	6. Medical Marijuana	Y	10. Troops in Iraq	Y
3. Export-Import Bank	Y	7. Sanctuary Cities	N	11. Homeland Security $$	Y
4. Debt Ceiling Increase	Y	8. Armor-piercing Bullets	N	12. Trade Adjustment aid	Y

Election Results

Election	Name (Party)	Vote (%)		Cand. Spent	Ind. Exp. Support	Ind. Exp. Oppose
2016 General	Judy Chu (D)	168,977	(67%)	$465,766		
	Jack Orswell (R)	81,655	(33%)	$185,550		
2016 Primary	Judy Chu (D)	67,318	(66%)			
	Jack Orswell (R)	29,057	(28%)			
	Tim Sweeney (I)	5,850	(6%)			

Prior winning percentages: 2014 (59%), 2012 (64%), 2010 (71%), 2009 special (62%)

Democrat Judy Chu, who won a 2009 special election, became the first Chinese-American woman in the House. She is a strong liberal and has been active in the Congressional Asian Pacific-American Caucus. After Rep. Xavier Becerra resigned in January 2017 to become attorney general of California, Chu got his seat on the Ways and Means Committee.

Chu grew up in Los Angeles as the daughter of an electrical technician who brought his wife from China under the War Brides Act. The family moved to the Bay Area when she was in junior high school. She graduated from the University of California, Los Angeles, got a Ph.D. in psychology, and then taught for 13 years at East Los Angeles Community College. She served on the Garvey School District board for three years and was mayor of Monterey Park for 12 years. In 2000, Chu was elected to the

California Assembly, where she focused on criminal justice and environmental issues. As chairwoman of the Appropriations Committee, she sponsored a tax amnesty program that brought in significant sums for the state. In 2006, she was elected to the state Board of Equalization, where she worked on closing tax loopholes.

After Rep. Hilda Solis was appointed as President Barack Obama's first Secretary of Labor, the contest for the Democratic nomination became a race between Chu and state Sen. Gil Cedillo, the leading Hispanic candidate. Rather than simply an ethnic showdown between an Asian and a Latino, the race was more nuanced. Chu was endorsed by much of the Democratic establishment, including prominent Hispanics such as Los Angeles Mayor Anthony Villaraigosa and members of Solis' family. The Los Angeles County Labor Federation, which was impressed by Chu's support for farm workers, backed her, as did EMILY's List, the national advocacy group for pro-abortion rights Democratic women. A third candidate was also a Hispanic and siphoned off some likely Cedillo voters: political novice Emanuel Pleitez, a 26-year-old financial analyst who had worked on Obama's presidential campaign. Chu raised nearly $1 million, Cedillo more than $700,000, and Pleitez $200,000. Chu won the primary with 32 percent, to 23 percent for Cedillo and 14 percent for Pleitez. Because Judy Chu failed to receive a majority of the total vote, she faced a runoff with Republican Betty Chu, a Monterey Park councilwoman who was Chu's distant cousin by marriage. The Democrat won by nearly 2-to-1, 62%-33%.

Chu joined the Out of Afghanistan Caucus and voted against a 2010 spending bill to fund military operations there. After her nephew, a lance corporal in the Marine Corps stationed in Afghanistan, committed suicide in 2011 after being beaten up by his fellow soldiers, she began introducing anti-military hazing bills. In the fiscal 2017 defense spending bill, the House included her proposal to require the Defense Department to create a national database of hazing incidents and submit an annual report on its efforts to stop hazing. Chu has sought to designate a large slice of the San Gabriel Mountains as a national park.

As chair of the Asian Pacific-American Caucus, Chu campaigned for Asian Americans to support Obama's reelection in 2012. "No other U.S. president in history has had such a deep understanding of the vibrancy of Asia," she wrote in an op-ed piece shortly before the election. She sponsored a House-passed resolution in 2012 to have the United States apologize for the anti-immigrant Chinese Exclusion Act of 1882, explaining that her grandfather was forced to carry a certificate of U.S. residence for about 40 years. "It is for my grandfather, and for all Chinese Americans who were told for six decades by the U.S. government that the land of the free wasn't open to them, that we must pass this resolution," she said. In 2014, she unveiled for the caucus a package of immigration reforms, including deferral of deportations for young undocumented immigrants. Following the 2016 election, she urged Obama to grant pardons to immigrants without legal status to reduce their vulnerability to deportation by President Donald Trump. When Trump took office, she voiced concern that discrimination against Muslims could parallel the Japanese internment camps during World War II.

In the 2014 campaign, Republican Jack Orswell, a small business owner and former FBI agent, challenged Chu and got 40.6 percent of the vote. That was the first time Chu was held below 60 percent, but she does not appear to be in jeopardy. A month after the election, the House Standards of Official Conduct (Ethics) Committee issued Chu a letter of reproval after concluding that she interfered with the panel's investigation of whether her House aides had performed campaign work. "The committee acknowledged that my intention was to ease the staff member's anxiety and that I expressed regret for this one moment of contact," Chu said in a subsequent statement. In a 2016 rematch with Orswell, Chu won with 67 percent.

When Chu got a seat on Ways and Means in February 2017, the committee's ranking Democrat Richard Neal cited her experience with tax issues on the Board of Equalization plus her commitment to tax fairness. She criticized the committee's handling of Republican efforts to repeal and revise the Affordable Care Act. "This plan was rushed to committee, there has not been time for the Congressional Budget Office to release their analysis of how much this will cost or how many Americans will be covered," Chu said.

San Gabriel Foothills: Pasadena, Monterey Park

Population		**Race and Ethnicity**		**Income**	
Total	716,789	White	28.2%	Median Income	$68,755 (77 out of 435)
Land area	700	Black	4.4%		
Pop/ sq mi	1024.1	Latino	27.5%	Under $50,000	28.4%
Born in state	47.2%	Asian	37.1%	$50,000-$99,999	24.3%
Age Groups		Two races	2.2%	$100,000-$199,999	9.8%
Under 18	19.7%	Other	0.7%	$200,000 or more	12.8%
18-34	22.1%	**Education**		Poverty Rate	12.8%
35-64	42.3%	H.S grad or less	33.1%	**Health Insurance**	
Over 64	15.9%	Some college	25.9%	With health insurance coverage	87.0%
Work		College Degree, 4 yr	24.6%		
White Collar	45.4%	Post grad	16.3%	**Public Assistance**	
Sales and Service	41.4%	**Military**		Cash public assistance income	2.3%
Blue Collar	13.2%	Veteran	4.1%		
Government	14.1%	Active Duty	0.0%	Food stamp/SNAP benefits	4.2%

Voter Turnout			
2015 Total Citizens 18+	482,042	2016 House Turnout as % CVAP	52%
2016 House turnout	250,632	2014 House Turnout as % CVAP	26%

2012 Presidential Vote		
Barack Obama	161,528	(63%)
Mitt Romney	90,278	(35%)

2016 Presidential Vote		
Hillary Clinton	174,544	(66%)
Donald Trump	74,984	(28%)
Gary Johnson	7,862	(3%)
Jill Stein	5,717	(2%)

Cook Partisan Voting Index: D+16

In the early part of the 20th century, when Los Angeles was growing rapidly and on its way to becoming one of America's major cities, its richest citizens settled not on the beach (too clammy and cold) or on the west side (too dusty and remote), but in communities they built at the base of the San Gabriel Mountains. Their snow-capped peaks, rising 10,000 feet above the city, are visible most of the year. The place to be was Pasadena, home of the Rose Bowl, Cal Tech and a baroque-domed city hall. Pasadena and South Pasadena have carefully preserved their bungalow neighborhoods, and Pasadena preserved and rebuilt the 80-year-old curving Colorado Boulevard Bridge over Arroyo Seco. With 15 percent of Pasadena living below the poverty level, city officials have sought to develop additional options for affordable housing. Nearby is luxurious San Marino, home of the Huntington Library, one of the world's great museums and scholarly institutions, with more than 150 acres of botanical gardens. Arcadia has the Santa Anita Park racetrack and the Los Angeles County Arboretum & Botanic Garden. Wealthy Chinese have invested in business opportunities in the area.

Parts of this area have significant Asian populations. Chinese and other Asians are 67 percent of the population in Monterey Park, which has been called America's first suburban Chinatown, and 61 percent in Rosemead. The late *New York Times* food maven R.W. Apple Jr. reported that "it is easier to buy bok choy than iceberg" in Monterey Park. Young Asian Americans produced a *YouTube* rap video titled "626" - the area code for much of the San Gabriel Valley - and it went viral. Pasadena is only 11 percent Asian, but its population is 59 percent minority.

The 27th Congressional District includes much of the Pasadena area and other portions of Los Angeles County. It takes in San Marino and the San Gabriel foothills communities of Altadena, Glendora, Sierra Madre and San Antonio Heights, where vicious cycles of drought, fire, rain and mudslides have become familiar. Also in the district are San Gabriel, Temple City and Claremont, dubbed "The City of Trees and PhD's" after its Claremont Colleges -- plus the conservative-leaning Claremont Institute, which has been a source of ideas for advocates of Donald Trump. The 27th has a small indentation of San Bernardino County, near Upland, which leans Republican, but it is less than 10 percent of the district. Proposals to designate a large part of the San Gabriel Mountains as a national monument drew protests, especially from bikers, hunters and other recreational users. The 27th is 38 percent Asian American, the second-highest of any California district, and 28 percent Hispanic. Politically, it is solidly Democratic. Hillary Clinton won the district, 66%-28%, a bigger lead than President Barack Obama had in his two victories but not as strongly Democratic as some other L.A.-area districts.

TWENTY-EIGHTH DISTRICT

Adam Schiff (D)

Elected 2000, 9th term; b. Jun 22, 1960, Framingham, MA; Stanford University (CA), B.A., 1982; Harvard University Law School (MA), J.D., 1985; Jewish; Married (Eve Sanderson Schiff); 2 children.

Elected Office: CA Senate, 1996-2000.

Professional Career: Prosecutor, U.S. Attorney General Office, L.A., 1987- 93; Practicing attorney, 1986-1987, 1995-1996.

DC Office: 2372 RHOB 20515, 202-225-4176, Fax: 202-225-5828, schiff.house.gov.

State Offices: Burbank, 818-450-2900.

Committees: *Permanent Select on Intelligence (RMM).*

Group Ratings

	ADA	ACLU	AFL-CIO	LCV	ITI	COC	HAFA	ACU	CFG	FRC
2016	-	88%	-	100%	67%	54%	15%	0%	10%	0%
2015	85%	C	100%	100%	C	45%	C	0%	0%	0%

Almanac Ratings 2015

	Economy	Social	Foreign	Composite
Liberal	98%	100%	99%	99%
Conservative	2%	0%	1%	1%

Key Votes of the 114th Congress

1. Keystone Pipeline	N	5. Puerto Rico Debt	Y	9. Offenses by Aliens	N
2. Trade Deals	N	6. Medical Marijuana	Y	10. Troops in Iraq	Y
3. Export-Import Bank	Y	7. Sanctuary Cities	N	11. Homeland Security $$	Y
4. Debt Ceiling Increase	Y	8. Armor-piercing Bullets	N	12. Trade Adjustment aid	Y

Election Results

Election	Name (Party)	Vote (%)		Cand. Spent	Ind. Exp. Support	Ind. Exp. Oppose
2016 General	Adam Schiff (D)	210,883	(78%)	$689,027		
	Lenore Solis (R)	59,526	(22%)			
2016 Primary	Adam Schiff (D)	81,806	(71%)			
	Lenore Solis (R)	21,741	(19%)			
	Sal Genovese (D)	12,492	(11%)			

Prior winning percentages: 2014 (77%), 2012 (77%), 2010 (65%), 2008 (69%), 2006 (64%), 2004 (65%), 2002 (63%), 2000 (53%)

Adam Schiff, a Democrat elected in 2000, has been an active and often independent voice on national security and intellectual property issues. He is more of a fiscal moderate than most Southern California Democrats, and repeatedly has called for Congress to provide more active oversight of the executive branch's national security actions. When Donald Trump became president, Schiff became an outspoken critic who demanded answers to allegations of misbehavior, including possible encouragement of Russian interference in the 2016 election. His leadership has increased speculation about his ambitions beyond the House, which Schiff has encouraged.

Schiff's father was a traveling salesman and later owned a lumberyard. Schiff grew up throughout the country, graduating from high school in Northern California. He went on to Stanford University and Harvard Law School. From 1987 to 1993, he worked in the U.S. attorney's office in Los Angeles. He ran for the California Assembly and lost three times. In 1996, he was elected to the state Senate. In his first two years, he enacted dozens of measures, including a bill guaranteeing up-to-date textbooks in classrooms and another reforming the child support system. Schiff also taught political science at Glendale Community College.

Schiff ran for the House in the first election following the 1998 impeachment of President Bill Clinton. He challenged Republican James Rogan, who was a Judiciary Committee leader and a persuasive voice for the case against Clinton, which centered on the president's lying under oath about an affair with a White House intern. Clinton pal and entertainment mogul David Geffen promised to raise millions of dollars to oppose him. The Schiff-Rogan race became a fundraising marathon, and was then the most expensive House race on record. The candidates raised more than $10 million combined, and much more was spent independently by Clinton's supporters as well as his detractors. Rogan branded his opponent as a traditional tax-and-spend liberal, who would "run naked through the Treasury, spending everything he can." Schiff attacked Rogan for calling abortion a holocaust for the African-American community. Schiff won by an unexpectedly large 53%-44% vote, and has been easily reelected since.

In the House, Schiff joined the Blue Dog Coalition of moderate to conservative Democrats and has sometimes worked across party lines. Schiff served as co-chairman of the Congressional International Anti-Piracy Caucus. He joined Republican Lamar Smith of Texas in sponsoring a bill to provide law enforcement and copyright holders with new tools to target websites based offshore that offer pirated music, movies and other counterfeit goods. He was instrumental in bipartisan legislation that made identity theft a crime. Schiff stirred complaints from liberal constituents when he supported the resolution approving the use of force in Iraq in 2002 and for voting for the USA Patriot Act, the anti-terrorism law that gave new powers to law enforcement.

As the years passed, his views became more conventionally liberal. When the Justice Department's failed gun-tracking operation known as "Fast and Furious" became a political controversy in 2011, he called for implementing tougher penalties on straw-purchase gun buyers as an alternative to Republican demands for Attorney General Eric Holder's resignation. After the fatal police shooting of an unarmed black man in Ferguson, Missouri, in 2014, Schiff pushed Holder to help state and local law enforcement agencies acquire body-worn cameras. In the *Almanac* vote ratings for 2015, Schiff ranked consistently among the most liberal members of the House.

His contribution to congressional ethics reform was a bill passed by the House in 2007 preventing lawmakers from placing their spouses on campaign payrolls. The bill was not enacted, but alleged abuses have grown. After the Supreme Court in the 2012 *Citizens United* case overturned a Montana law barring corporate spending in state elections, he worked with Harvard constitutional law scholar Laurence Tribe to introduce a constitutional amendment making it clear that Congress and the states have the authority to impose limitations on independent campaign expenditures.

On foreign policy, Schiff has pressed for recognition of the Armenian genocide as the responsibility of the Ottoman Empire, a move Turkey adamantly opposes. His resolution was approved by the House Foreign Affairs Committee in 2007, but he agreed to postpone further action after a strong response from Turkey. Schiff has been concerned that major national security actions should not be left solely to a president's discretion. He introduced a bill in 2013 to repeal the Authorization for Use of Military Force, which Congress passed after the 2001 attacks. He said it "was never intended to authorize a war without end, and it now poorly defines those who pose a threat to our country." When he offered an amendment based on the measure to the fiscal 2014 defense appropriations bill, it was defeated 185-236 after Republicans said it was dangerous to set a specific timeline for replacing the 2001 resolution. Following the election of Trump in 2016, Schiff voiced new concern that the failure to limit presidential action was "very troubling."

When the Islamic State terrorist group (ISIS) began capturing large swaths of territory in the Middle East in 2014, Schiff sought to call attention to the threat of Americans and Europeans carrying out attacks at home. "As with so much else in the post-9/11 era, the United States and its democratic allies must balance security and freedom as we seek to prevent our citizens from becoming radicalized and turning on us," he wrote in a *Los Angeles Register* op-ed column. Later, when Obama outlined a plan to deal with ISIS, Schiff became heavily involved in unsuccessful efforts to have Congress authorize the president's actions. "It's hard to explain the relative silence of my libertarian colleagues at a time when the president is about to announce a war effort that may take years," Schiff told *The Washington Post*. He also pressed for lawmakers to have a role in the administration's look at surveillance and privacy following revelations of the National Security Agency's domestic snooping. Schiff strongly objected to the Republican push to investigate the terrorist attacks on U.S. facilities in Benghazi, Libya. In May 2014, he told Fox News that a select committee on the matter was "a colossal waste of time" and that his party should boycott it - something that House leaders refused to do. He subsequently became a member of the select committee.

Minority Leader Nancy Pelosi gave Schiff a significant niche on national security issues when she named him ranking Democrat on the House Intelligence Committee in 2015. He brought to the table new proposals on intelligence policy. He has filed legislation to require greater transparency for the U.S. military drone program. He has opposed paying ransoms to free Americans held by rebel groups, such as ISIS. He also advocated major changes in the National Security Agency's phone metadata surveillance program, which would require the government to request phone company records on a case-by-case basis.

Schiff used his Intelligence Committee post to criticize the failure of the Obama administration to sanction Russia for its computer hacking that he said had been designed to influence the 2016 election, and he demanded that Congress investigate. "They didn't just steal data, they weaponized it. They dumped it during an election with the specific intent of influencing the outcomes of that election and sowing discord in the United States," he said. Schiff voiced early warnings of Trump's use of "alternative facts," which he said "undermines his credibility" and is "a crisis waiting to happen." In March 2017, a profile in *New Yorker* wrote that Schiff had become "an unlikely face of Democratic resistance" and that he "has gained a quiet respect among foreign-policy liberals and reporters for his nuanced views on surveillance, war powers, and press freedoms."

Schiff, who has competed in triathlons, in 2014 participated in a week-long 545-mile bike ride down California's coast, on behalf of L.A.'s LGBT Center and the San Francisco AIDS Foundation. After Sen. Barbara Boxer in 2015 said she would not seek reelection, Schiff thought seriously about running for the open seat. After he quietly announced that he would remain in the House, he kept the door open to "other challenges in the future." In 2017, he voiced interest in succeeding Dianne Feinstein whenever she leaves the Senate.

Northern Los Angeles: Westside and Hollywood

Population		**Race and Ethnicity**		**Income**	
Total	716,256	White	54.7%	Median Income	$56,103 (172 out of 435)
Land area	218	Black	2.4%		
Pop/ sq mi	3278.8	Latino	26.2%		
Born in state	37.2%	Asian	13.3%	Under $50,000	26.6%
		Two races	2.6%	$50,000-$99,999	19.4%
Age Groups		Other	0.7%	$100,000-$199,999	8.9%
Under 18	16.2%			$200,000 or more	15.5%
18-34	27.2%	**Education**		Poverty Rate	15.5%
35-64	42.3%	H.S grad or less	30.3%		
Over 64	14.2%	Some college	26.3%	**Health Insurance**	
		College Degree, 4 yr	29.1%	With health insurance coverage	83.0%
Work		Post grad	14.3%		
White Collar	47.4%				
Sales and Service	40.7%	**Military**		**Public Assistance**	
Blue Collar	11.9%	Veteran	3.4%	Cash public assistance income	3.3%
Government	9.4%	Active Duty	0.0%		
				Food stamp/SNAP benefits	5.5%

Voter Turnout			
2015 Total Citizens 18+	488,001	2016 House Turnout as % CVAP	55%
2016 House turnout	270,409	2014 House Turnout as % CVAP	25%

2012 Presidential Vote		
Barack Obama	187,441	(70%)
Mitt Romney	70,757	(27%)

2016 Presidential Vote		
Hillary Clinton	208,645	(72%)
Donald Trump	64,607	(22%)
Jill Stein	7,433	(3%)
Gary Johnson	7,050	(2%)

Cook Partisan Voting Index: D+23

The Westside of Los Angeles is perhaps the most glamorous and flashiest concentration of affluence in the world. It is the heartland of one of America's most productive and creative industries and one of the nation's major exports, show business. The first moviemakers came here looking for a place to shoot silent films where the sunlight was more dependable than in Astoria, Queens, or Englewood, New Jersey. They found it in Hollywood, a suburb just annexed by burgeoning Los Angeles when the first movie studio was built in 1911. In 1923 came the "Hollywood" sign (it said "Hollywoodland" then), overlooking the soon-famous intersection of Hollywood and Vine. By the 1930s, big studio lots were scattered around town, over the mountains in Burbank, or out toward the ocean in Westwood and Culver City. Miraculously, the studio bosses of that era - most of them Jewish immigrants with little ancestral experience of America - created a popular culture that was universally accessible and embodied the American spirit in a way that still rings true.

Beneath the Verdugo Mountains is Burbank, which Dr. David Burbank, a dentist, founded as a large ranch, on what is now a backlot of Warner Brothers. The city has become the "media capital of the world," including the headquarters for Warner Brothers, NBC Studios, ABC Studios and Disney, plus many small entertainment and multimedia companies. Millions of Americans recognized Burbank from having watched *The Tonight Show*, until Jimmy Fallon replaced Jay Leno as host and returned the show to Manhattan. The movie studios have been an integral part of the local economy. Warner Brothers remained the largest employer in Burbank, though it dropped to 5,000 jobs in 2016, following industry downturns. More middle-class is Glendale, north of downtown Los Angeles, site of Forest Lawn Cemetery and DreamWorks Animation. Glendale is a diverse city with a large concentration of Armenians, a politically influential community that has remained hostile to Turkey. In August 2016, a federal judge upheld the decision to erect a bronze statue in a city park to commemorate the Korean "comfort women" who were sex slaves for Japanese soldiers during World War II.

The entertainment industry here has pushed for greater protection of intellectual property and a crackdown on online piracy. The industry-favored Stop Online Piracy Act generated an "Internet Black Out" day of protest on Jan. 18, 2012, from Wikipedia and Google, and the controversy pitted Hollywood movie studios in Southern California against Northern California dot.coms and Silicon Valley. Following 70 percent approval of a referendum in November 2016, a new terminal is planned for 2023 at the Hollywood Burbank Airport, which has dropped the name of legendary comedian Bob Hope; the time that has passed since his death in 2003 has dimmed many memories of the former icon. West Hollywood has a large gay community. It is home to the Sunset Strip, a launching pad for many rock 'n' roll acts, including The Doors, Guns N' Roses and Led Zeppelin, although these days the Strip attracts mostly lesser-known bands and cover acts.

The 28th Congressional District includes parts of the Westside and Los Angeles County, including La Crescenta-Montrose and La CaÑada Flintridge, home of NASA's Jet Propulsion Laboratory. The largest cities are Glendale and Burbank, although part of the latter spills into the 30th District. Celebrity Kim Kardashian in 2012 expressed interest in becoming mayor of Glendale, but apparently has not followed up. This is a solidly Democratic district, with 24 percent Hispanic and 14 percent Asian population. Hillary Clinton got 72 percent of the vote in 2016.

TWENTY-NINTH DISTRICT

Tony Cardenas (D)

Elected 2012, 3rd term; b. Mar 31, 1963, Pacoima; University of California, Santa Barbara, B.S.; Christian Church; Married (Norma Cárdenas); 4 children.

Elected Office: Los Angeles City Council, 2004-2012; CA Assembly, 1996-2002.

Professional Career: Real-estate broker, 1987-1996; Life ins. salesman, 1986-1987; Electrical engineer, Hewlett-Packard, 1986.

DC Office: 1510 LHOB 20515, 202-225-6131, Fax: 202-225-0819, cardenas.house.gov.

State Offices: Panorama City, 818-221-3718.

Committees: *Energy & Commerce*: Digital Commerce & Consumer Protection, Environment, Health.

Group Ratings

	ADA	ACLU	AFL-CIO	LCV	ITI	COC	HAFA	ACU	CFG	FRC
2016	-	94%	-	84%	67%	69%	11%	5%	9%	0%
2015	90%	C	96%	94%	C	58%	C	0%	3%	0%

Key Votes of the 114th Congress

1. Keystone Pipeline	N	5. Puerto Rico Debt	Y	9. Offenses by Aliens	N
2. Trade Deals	N	6. Medical Marijuana	Y	10. Troops in Iraq	Y
3. Export-Import Bank	Y	7. Sanctuary Cities	N	11. Homeland Security $$	Y
4. Debt Ceiling Increase	Y	8. Armor-piercing Bullets	N	12. Trade Adjustment aid	Y

Election Results

Election	Name (Party)	Vote (%)		Cand. Spent	Ind. Exp. Support	Ind. Exp. Oppose
2016 General	Tony Cardenas (D)	128,407	(75%)	$1,583,627		
2016 Primary	Tony Cardenas (D)	42,892	(62%)			
	Richard Alarcon (D)	9,021	(13%)			
	Joseph Shammas (D)	7,671	(11%)			
	Benito Bernal (D)	6,787	(10%)			

Prior winning percentages: 2014 (75%), 2012 (74%)

Democrat Tony Cárdenas, elected in 2012 as the first Latino congressman to represent Los Angeles's San Fernando Valley, has moved into prominent positions in the House and has been a player on issues that affect his district.

As the youngest of 11 children of Mexican immigrant parents, Cárdenas was born and raised in the Valley city of Pacoima. His father was a self-employed gardener who would take young Cárdenas and his brothers to work with him. He earned a bachelor's degree in electrical engineering from the University of California, Santa Barbara. He subsequently went to work for Hewlett-Packard but left just five months later. "There has to be something different for me," he remembered thinking.

He returned home to Pacoima to live with his parents and sold life insurance for a year, then worked selling real estate for five years before opening his own brokerage firm in the San Fernando Valley. During that time, the Valley had become more Latino - but, he observed, political representation did not mirror that change. One day, a friend suggested that he run for political office. He did, and in 1996 became the first Latino to represent the Valley in the state Assembly. Cárdenas became known for his work to reform California's gang prevention and intervention programs. In 2000, the Legislature passed a bill he co-sponsored authorizing $121 million in annual funding for local juvenile justice programs. Cárdenas says he became interested in gang-intervention programs after many of his childhood friends had run-ins with the law, lamenting, "They weren't exactly living a life that we had dreamed of."

In 2003, Cárdenas was elected to the Los Angeles City Council, where he continued to work on gang prevention. He also sought to create opportunities for minority-owned businesses to compete for the city's bond underwriting work. He pushed for policies to fight human trafficking and prevent the mistreatment of animals.

When he decided to run for Congress in a re-drawn district with no incumbent, Cárdenas was a strong favorite and he received 64 percent of the vote in the primary. His closest competitor was "No Party Preference" perennial candidate David Hernandez, an insurance adjuster and Vietnam veteran. Hernandez mocked Cárdenas for touting his Latino roots. A message on Hernandez's Facebook page said, "Tony Cárdenas wants to be the first Latino congressman from the San Fernando Valley. David Hernandez wants to be the congressman who represents and brings prosperity to the area which has suffered under failed leadership." Those attacks barely resonated in the Democratic district, and Cárdenas won 74%-26%.

Cardenas has worn several hats in the House. He co-chaired the Crime Prevention and Youth Development Caucus with Rep. David Reichert of Washington, and the Congressional Student-Athlete Protection Caucus with Rep. Charlie Dent of Pennsylvania, both Republicans. With Republican Rep. Carlos Curbelo of Florida, he created the Connecting the Americas Caucus, to strengthen business opportunities between the United States and Latin American nations. In November 2014, Cardenas became chairman of BOLD PAC, the fundraising arm of the Congressional Hispanic Caucus, which increased its fundraising from $1 million to close to $6 million during the next two years. Following the 2016 election, he won a newly created Democratic leadership position for a member who has served less than three terms. He defeated Rep. Debbie Dingell of Michigan, 91-76.

With a prized seat on the Energy and Commerce Committee, Cardenas became one of the first House members to oppose the proposed merger of Comcast and Time Warner Cable, which he said would harm competition, raise costs and "eliminate good jobs in California." Following regulatory overview, the deal was scuttled. During committee debate on a data security bill in 2015, he worked with Republican Rep. Marsha Blackburn of Tennessee to gain approval of amendments that required the Federal Trade Commission to take a more active role in preventing data breaches and to improve education of consumers.

Cardenas persistently sought votes on comprehensive immigration legislation, and told CNN in 2014 that "the Latino community is frustrated with [President Obama] but pissed off with Republicans," over the delay. Also that year, the annual defense spending bill was enacted with his amendment that directed the Government Accountability Office to review gaps and weaknesses in the Pentagon's cybersecurity, including their impact on businesses.

In 2016, he faced Democrat Richard Alarcon, a former member of the Los Angeles City Council who subsequently had his conviction overturned on charges that he and his wife committed perjury in misstating their home address for a political campaign. Alarcon raised only $70,000 to $1.7 million for Cardenas and was defeated, 75%-25%.

Central San Fernando Valley: Van Nuys

Population		**Race and Ethnicity**		**Income**	
Total	714,303	White	18.3%	Median Income	$47,073 (304 out of 435)
Land area	92	Black	3.7%		
Pop/ sq mi	7761.6	Latino	68.6%		
Born in state	46.1%	Asian	7.7%	Under $50,000	29.6%
		Two races	1.2%	$50,000-$99,999	15.4%
Age Groups		Other	0.5%	$100,000-$199,999	2.4%
Under 18	24.9%			$200,000 or more	22.1%
18-34	28.1%	**Education**		Poverty Rate	22.1%
35-64	37.7%	H.S grad or less	57.4%		
Over 64	9.3%	Some college	23.6%	**Health Insurance**	
		College Degree, 4 yr	14.4%	With health insurance coverage	76.2%
Work		Post grad	4.5%		
White Collar	24.9%				
Sales and Service	47.6%	**Military**		**Public Assistance**	
Blue Collar	27.5%	Veteran	2.9%	Cash public assistance income	5.1%
Government	9.0%	Active Duty	0.0%		
				Food stamp/SNAP benefits	11.8%

Voter Turnout			
2015 Total Citizens 18+	369,549	2016 House Turnout as % CVAP	46%
2016 House turnout	171,824	2014 House Turnout as % CVAP	19%

2012 Presidential Vote		
Barack Obama	129,323	(77%)
Mitt Romney	34,454	(21%)

2016 Presidential Vote		
Hillary Clinton	152,517	(78%)
Donald Trump	32,963	(17%)
Jill Stein	4,863	(3%)
Gary Johnson	4,328	(2%)

Cook Partisan Voting Index: D+29

A hiker looking north from the crest of the Santa Monica Mountains in 1912 would have seen a valley almost totally empty and barren, 20 miles long and 12 miles wide. Separated by the Cahuenga Pass from rapidly growing Los Angeles and Hollywood, the San Fernando Valley was bought up in massive tracts by civic leaders as they were urging city engineer William Mulholland to build a huge 250-mile aqueduct from the Owens Valley to bring water to Los Angeles and persuading the city in 1915 to annex 200 square miles of the Valley. In the years after World War II, this was modern suburbia, filled with *Leave It to Beaver* families. More recently, the San Fernando Valley became postmodern urban. The driver topping the crest saw office towers looming out over slightly hazy air, shopping centers, occasional palm trees, stucco subdivisions and the squat factory and warehouse buildings that once made Los Angeles County a top manufacturing locale.

Many of the big plants have closed and the Valley has changed. The 1950s white families with stay-at-home moms have been replaced by Latino families with parents juggling two jobs and trying to raise children who will have a better chance than they had. Pacoima, at the northern end of the Valley, is mostly Latino. Farther south, in Van Nuys, Canoga Park and Burbank, was the industrial base - the GM plants were mostly shut down in the 1980s, and the last large factory, the Pratt and Whitney Rocketdyne plant, was sold to manufacturer GenCorp in 2012. The big factories have been supplanted by hundreds of small factories and multimedia plants.

The southern rim of the Valley, around the North Hollywood area, remains heavily Jewish and is attracting new families who often send their kids to religious schools. People with money cluster near the foot of the mountains around the Valley; those less well-off settle on the flatlands beyond. The Valley was hit hard when the housing bubble burst in 2007, with prices dropping 50 percent or more in some areas. The business and housing markets have improved, with foreclosures down sharply, but times have remained tough. In 2014, Nestle and Sunkist closed plants. Permits for adult film productions in the Valley plummeted after Los Angeles voters in 2012 approved a referendum requiring actors to wear condoms on-camera, though adult-entertainment entrepreneurs moved to other technologies and products. The Valley has been plagued by increased crime, including gangs, which has accompanied a rise in homelessness. In 2015, the housing market neared a recent low in sales; the median price for a home rose 8 percent to $600,000.

The 29th Congressional District of California consists of the eastern part of the San Fernando Valley in the city of Los Angeles. It includes affluent North Hollywood, as well as Van Nuys, North Hills and Panorama City. The southeast part of the district takes in the NoHo Arts District. Parts of the northern end of the Valley, including economically declining Pacoima and the small city of San Fernando, are in the district. Whiteman Airport and Los Angeles Valley College are also here. The District is 69 percent Hispanic, and solidly Democratic. Hillary Clinton got 78 percent of the vote here in 2016.

THIRTIETH DISTRICT

Brad Sherman (D)

Elected 1996, 11th term; b. Oct 24, 1954, Los Angeles; Orange Coast University (CA), Att.; University of California, Los Angeles, B.A., 1974; Harvard University Law School (MA), J.D., 1979; Jewish; Married (Lisa Kaplan Sherman); 3 children.

Elected Office: CA Board of Equalization, 1990-1995, Chairman, 1991-1995.

Professional Career: Practicing attorney, Accountant, 1980-1990.

DC Office: 2181 RHOB 20515, 202-225-5911, Fax: 202-225-5879, sherman.house.gov.

State Offices: Sherman Oaks, 818-501-9200.

Committees: *Commission Congressional Mailing Standards*. *Financial Services*: Capital Markets, Securities & Investment, Housing & Insurance, Monetary Policy & Trade. *Foreign Affairs*: Asia & the Pacific (RMM), Europe, Eurasia & Emerging Threats.

Group Ratings

	ADA	ACLU	AFL-CIO	LCV	ITI	COC	HAFA	ACU	CFG	FRC
2016	-	94%	-	100%	67%	57%	12%	4%	4%	0%
2015	80%	C	100%	100%	C	45%	C	4%	2%	0%

Almanac Ratings 2015

	Economy	Social	Foreign	Composite
Liberal	91%	100%	78%	90%
Conservative	10%	0%	22%	11%

Key Votes of the 114th Congress

1. Keystone Pipeline	N	5. Puerto Rico Debt	Y	9. Offenses by Aliens	N
2. Trade Deals	N	6. Medical Marijuana	Y	10. Troops in Iraq	N
3. Export-Import Bank	Y	7. Sanctuary Cities	N	11. Homeland Security $$	Y
4. Debt Ceiling Increase	Y	8. Armor-piercing Bullets	N	12. Trade Adjustment aid	Y

Election Results

Election	Name (Party)	Vote (%)		Cand. Spent	Ind. Exp. Support	Ind. Exp. Oppose
2016 General	Brad Sherman (D)	205,279	(73%)	$395,666		
	Mark Reed (R)	77,325	(27%)			
2016 Primary	Brad Sherman (D)	68,719	(61%)			
	Mark Reed (R)	15,793	(14%)			
	Patrea Patrick (D)	9,962	(9%)			
	Raji Rab (D)	6,025	(5%)			

Prior winning percentages: 2014 (66%), 2012 (60%), 2010 (65%), 2008 (69%), 2006 (69%), 2004 (62%), 2002 (62%), 2000 (66%), 1998 (57%), 1996 (49%)

Brad Sherman, a Democrat first elected in 1996, has shown that he is a rough and ready political scrapper - on behalf of Israel and against Wall Street, for example. His reelection brawl in 2012 against more senior Democrat Howard Berman left wounds that were slow to heal, especially with Minority Leader Nancy Pelosi. He remains outspoken, especially on foreign policy, and sometimes cooperates with Republicans.

Sherman grew up in Monterey Park, in the San Gabriel Valley east of Los Angeles. He started working on Democratic campaigns at age 6, stuffing envelopes for Rep. George Brown. He set up his own stamp-wholesaling firm at age 14. He graduated with high honors from the University of California, Los Angeles, worked as an accountant, and then went to Harvard Law School. He came back to the Los Angeles area to practice tax law, and represented the Philippines in its successful effort to seize the assets of deposed President Ferdinand Marcos.

In 1990, Sherman was elected from Los Angeles County to the state Board of Equalization, which is a sort of tax court. He was known as a stickler for detail, a "tax nerd," as one former staffer said, who used the office with a keen scent for political advantage. He irritated cartoonists with a ruling that exempted artwork from the state tax but not illustrations. They took their revenge by setting up a website, the Sherman Gallery, where they vied in caricaturing the balding and bespectacled Sherman.

In 1996, Sherman moved his residence from Santa Monica to Sherman Oaks, where a House seat had opened. Both he and his Republican opponent, businessman Rich Sybert, were self-financers; Sherman spent $578,000 of his own money. And both stressed their moderation. Sherman campaigned against then-House Speaker Newt Gingrich and the Republican Congress, but he also supported the death penalty, called for phasing out racial quotas and preferences, and favored tough measures on illegal immigration. Sybert stressed his independence from Gingrich as well as his support for abortion rights and environmental protection. Sherman won 49%-44%.

In the House, his voting record has been more moderate than those of most other Los Angeles County Democrats, and he has shown occasional independence from party leaders. Sherman has taken an interest in some of the more arcane aspects of government. He sponsored bills for several years to overhaul the presidential succession process and another measure to set up a commission to reduce delays in processing Freedom of Information Act requests.

One of the few certified public accountants in Congress, Sherman serves on the Financial Services Committee, where his experience has been useful in congressional attempts to unravel recent corporate accounting scandals. In 2008, he was an outspoken foe of the bill creating the Troubled Assets Relief Program to bail out the financial services industry, dubbing it "cash for trash." When domestic auto company executives testified in favor of a proposed bailout for that industry, Sherman got them to concede that they had all flown separately to Washington in private airplanes, a revelation that sparked a public backlash. In 2009, he advocated a 70 percent surtax on all compensation exceeding $1 million for executives of financial institutions receiving large federal bailouts. Sherman helped form the new Consumer Financial Protection Bureau as part of the 2010 Dodd-Frank financial overhaul law. But one of the bill's namesakes, Rep. Barney Frank of Massachusetts, accused him of "arrogance" and of overstating his role after Sherman boasted that he had "more to do with Dodd-Frank than anyone except Dodd and Frank."

Sherman faced his first serious opposition when redistricting following the 2010 census redrew the lines in the San Fernando Valley and lumped him together in 2012 with Berman, a 30-year House veteran who had chaired the Foreign Affairs Committee. Berman had the backing of much of the state's Democratic establishment as well as the support of Hollywood elites for his work on anti-piracy legislation; even some prominent Republicans such as Rep. Darrell Issa of California and Sen. John McCain of Arizona came out publicly for him. But Berman was at a serious geographic disadvantage: The new 30th District covered twice as much of Sherman's old turf as Berman's base, which was in the new 29th District.

Both candidates raised plenty of money. The final tab for the race was $16.3 million, making it one of the nation's most expensive for the House. Sherman went on the attack, depicting Berman as a Washington insider who didn't understand constituents' concerns. The normally mild-mannered Berman followed suit, launching a weekly "BS Report" on his opponent and highlighting his inability to get more than a handful of bills into law, while criticizing him for loaning his campaigns money and then charging interest, an allegation that Sherman heatedly denied. The acrimony reached its peak at an October debate when the two loudly bickered over immigration legislation, and Sherman threw his arm around his opponent's shoulders and demanded, "You want to get into this?" A sheriff's deputy and a debate organizer stepped between them to prevent an escalation. Berman sent out a *YouTube* video of the incident accusing Sherman of trying to start a fight, prompting Sherman to apologize. But it was too little, too late for Berman. Sherman won easily, 60%-40%.

Sherman soon paid the price when Pelosi objected to his bid to become the senior Democrat on the Foreign Affairs Committee, where he had been next in line among Democratic members behind Berman; instead, Democrats selected Rep. Eliot Engel of New York. In a further dig, Sherman was denied the ranking Democrat position on the Middle East and North African Subcommittee, and that position went to far more junior Rep. Ted Deutch of Florida. As the top Democrat on the Asia and the Pacific Subcommittee, he strongly opposed President Barack Obama's deal with Iran on nuclear weapons, which he described as "preposterous." Later, he opposed the sales of Boeing aircraft to Iran. As a staunch supporter of Israel, he contended that liberals suffer from "the David and Goliath inversion" regarding the Israel-Palestinian conflict. "Liberals always root for David, never Goliath," and they assume Israel is the aggressor, Sherman said. When many Democrats boycotted the speech of Israeli Prime Minister Benjamin Netanyahu in March 2015, Sherman said he was "honored" to serve on the escort committee that accompanied him into the House chamber. After Democratic Rep. Tulsi Gabbard of Hawaii made a controversial visit to Syrian President Bashar al-Assad, Sherman was among the few in Congress to defend her assertion of legislative prerogatives. "Congress has an equal role in the conduct of American foreign policy," he said.

Since 2012, Sherman has had much easier reelections. In 2016, he got 60 percent of the vote in the primary against six other candidates, including three Democrats. In the general, against Republican small businessman Mark Reed, who did not file a campaign-finance report, Sherman won 73%-27%. His hold on this district appears secure.

Southern and Western San Fernando Valley: The Valley, Reseda

Population		**Race and Ethnicity**		**Income**	
Total	745,240	White	50.8%	Median Income	$70,750 (70 out of 435)
Land area	136	Black	4.3%		
Pop/ sq mi	5482.1	Latino	28.9%	Under $50,000	28.6%
Born in state	45.7%	Asian	12.2%	$50,000-$99,999	24.5%
		Two races	3.2%	$100,000-$199,999	10.6%
Age Groups		Other	0.6%	$200,000 or more	12.3%
Under 18	20.4%			Poverty Rate	12.3%
18-34	24.2%	**Education**			
35-64	41.5%	H.S grad or less	30.2%	**Health Insurance**	
Over 64	14.0%	Some college	28.2%	With health insurance coverage	85.5%
		College Degree, 4 yr	27.3%		
Work		Post grad	14.4%		
White Collar	46.2%			**Public Assistance**	
Sales and Service	40.8%	**Military**		Cash public assistance income	2.3%
Blue Collar	13.0%	Veteran	4.5%		
Government	8.9%	Active Duty	0.0%	Food stamp/SNAP benefits	4.3%

Voter Turnout			
2015 Total Citizens 18+	498,515	2016 House Turnout as % CVAP	57%
2016 House turnout	282,604	2014 House Turnout as % CVAP	27%

2012 Presidential Vote		
Barack Obama	186,301	(65%)
Mitt Romney	91,680	(32%)

2016 Presidential Vote		
Hillary Clinton	209,149	(69%)
Donald Trump	77,701	(26%)
Gary Johnson	8,278	(3%)
Jill Stein	6,244	(2%)

Cook Partisan Voting Index: D+18

In the early 20th century, when the movie business was young, the San Fernando Valley was a vast expanse of empty land that had been annexed to Los Angeles in 1915. Moviemakers, looking for filming sites for a western, drove past the vacant lots of Westwood, up narrow roads through the Santa Monica Mountains, and into the vast Valley, sheltered from ocean breezes and rain-bearing clouds by the mountains. This big bowl of land was transformed, first into 1950s suburbia, and then into a postmodern city of its own, economically vital and diversely ethnic. Even in its suburban years, the San Fernando Valley was not entirely residential. Big factories provided jobs. In those years, this was fast-growing, family-friendly territory. Plenty of upscale territory remains in the uplands of the Valley, in Granada Hills and Tarzana; and the office blocks and mini-malls show unmistakable signs of affluence. But in a not so family-friendly development, the Valley became a hub for the adult-film industry. After Los Angeles County voters approved a measure in 2012 that required actors to wear condoms in sex scenes to control the spread of sexually transmitted disease, some adult-movie producers moved studio operations out of the region. What had been an annual total of about 500 permits for such motion pictures, television and commercial production across Los Angeles declined by 90 percent. Other porn businesses diversified to new forms of technology and paraphernalia, and their headquarters remained in the area. In 2016, a similar statewide adult-movie initiative in California was defeated, 54%-46%.

Parts of the Valley have been unhappy to be linked with the city of Los Angeles, whose City Council has imposed high taxes and irksome regulations. A secession movement arose, and the issue was put on the 2002 ballot. The Valley voted 51%-49% for it, with stronger support in the southern and western sections. But it failed to get the needed majority in all of Los Angeles to pass. Partly in response, the L.A. City Council in 2013 tightened rules on who can participate in such neighborhood elections, eliminating what had been called "Starbucks shareholders." After being hit hard by the recession, the Valley's economy began improving, thanks in part to a massive expansion in California's enterprise zone program. Nevertheless, many thousands of middle-class residents have relocated in recent years to less-costly places. After six years of construction, the widening of Interstate 405, a.k.a. the San Diego Freeway, was completed in 2016 with debatable impact on congestion.

The 30th Congressional District covers the western and southern parts of the San Fernando Valley within Los Angeles. Along its southern border, the 30th includes Tarzana, Encino and Hidden Hills - which in 2015 ranked eighth in its list of America's most expensive ZIP codes, according to *Forbes* Magazine. In the center of the district are industrial Canoga Park, Winnetka and largely Hispanic Reseda. On the northern end are Granada Hills, where the San Fernando Valley's first oil well was drilled in 1916, and O'Melveny Park, one of the largest parks in Los Angeles. Also in the district is California State University, Northridge. Less than 1 percent of the 30th reaches into Ventura County. Although not as Hispanic as the neighboring 29th District, it is solidly Democratic territory. In a district that is 29 percent Hispanic and 13 percent Asian, Hillary Clinton led, 69%-26%.

THIRTY-FIRST DISTRICT

Pete Aguilar (D)

Elected 2014, 2nd term; b. Jun 19, 1979, Fontana; University of Redlands; b.R.E., 2001; Roman Catholic; Married (Alisha Aguilar); 2 children.

Elected Office: Redlands City Council, 2006-2014; Mayor, Redlands, 2010-2014.

Professional Career: Business owner; Interim Director & deputy Director, Inland Empire regional office of the Gov., 2001.

DC Office: 1223 LHOB 20515, 202-225-3201, Fax: 202-226-6962, aguilar.house.gov.

State Offices: San Bernardino, 909-890-4445.

Committees: *Appropriations*: Energy & Water Development & Related Agencies, Transportation, HUD & Related Agencies.

Group Ratings

	ADA	ACLU	AFL-CIO	LCV	ITI	COC	HAFA	ACU	CFG	FRC
2016	-	64%	-	100%	83%	64%	14%	4%	10%	0%
2015	65%	C	86%	94%	C	53%	C	4%	0%	0%

Almanac Ratings 2015

	Economy	Social	Foreign	Composite
Liberal	71%	94%	41%	69%
Conservative	29%	6%	59%	31%

Key Votes of the 114th Congress

1. Keystone Pipeline	N	5. Puerto Rico Debt	Y	9. Offenses by Aliens	Y
2. Trade Deals	N	6. Medical Marijuana	Y	10. Troops in Iraq	N
3. Export-Import Bank	Y	7. Sanctuary Cities	N	11. Homeland Security $$	Y
4. Debt Ceiling Increase	Y	8. Armor-piercing Bullets	N	12. Trade Adjustment aid	Y

Election Results

Election	Name (Party)	Vote (%)		Cand. Spent	Ind. Exp. Support	Ind. Exp. Oppose
2016 General	Pete Aguilar (D)	121,070	(56%)	$1,860,317	$22,438	
	Paul Chabot (R)	94,866	(44%)	$619,261	$27,919	$3,559
2016 Primary	Pete Aguilar (D)	34,721	(43%)			
	Paul Chabot (R)	19,088	(24%)			
	Joe Baca (R)	9,452	(12%)			
	Sean Flynn (R)	8,956	(11%)			
	Kaisar Ahmed (D)	8,007	(10%)			

Prior winning percentages: 2014 (52%)

Democrat Pete Aguilar's 2014 win returned the 31st District seat to the Democrats, who had long held it. The quirks of redistricting and an open primary gave the predominantly Hispanic district to the GOP in 2012, and turbulent local politics remained unpredictable. With his relatively smooth reelection and a seat on the Appropriations Committee, Aguilar seemed to restore stability.

Aguilar was born in Fontana and grew up in San Bernardino. He earned undergraduate degrees in government and business administration at the University of Redlands. One of his first jobs was at the San Bernardino County Courthouse cafeteria, where his blind grandfather was the operator. In 2001, Gov. Gray Davis appointed Aguilar as deputy director of the Inland Empire Regional Office of the Governor. In 2006, Aguilar was appointed to the Redlands City Council, making him the youngest council member in the city's 140-year history. He ran successfully for two more terms and was elected mayor in 2010 by his fellow council members.

In 2012, he ran in this redrawn minority district. Four Democrats divided the vote in the primary. Aguilar was the frontrunner among them with 23 percent of the total vote. But the two Republicans who sought the seat emerged at the top, with 27 and 25 percent. Rep. Gary Miller - who decided to run here for his eighth term, despite not having represented any of the district - won in November over fellow Republican Bob Dutton, 55%-45%.

Miller announced he would not seek reelection in 2014, and Aguilar again sought the seat. History almost repeated itself in June, as four Democrats faced off against three Republicans. GOP candidate Paul Chabot came in first with 27 percent, and Aguilar had 17 percent and hung onto a 209-vote lead over Republican Leslie Gooch. This time, the four Democratic candidates in the primary got 53 percent of the total vote. Aguilar hammered Chabot for what he called his too-conservative views on education, immigration and heath care. National Democratic ads referred to Chabot's support of Arizona's SB 1070, a law that requires police in certain circumstances to determine the immigration status of detainees. Chabot, an Iraq war vet and Naval Reserve intelligence officer, focused on those experiences and how to combat terrorism. Aguilar won with 51 percent to Chabot's 49 percent. Aguilar out-spent Chabot, $2.2 million to $469,000, and was boosted by more than $1.5 million in national party money. Republicans seem to have missed an opportunity by steering clear of this contest, to Chabot's dismay.

Aguilar initially focused on issues relevant to the Inland Empire. He criticized President Barack Obama's executive action on immigration reform as not good enough. "To truly fix our broken immigration system and put our country on a path forward, Congress must pass a bill, much like the one passed by the Senate more than a year ago, that addresses all aspects of this issue," he wrote in a December 2014 op-ed. He filed a bill to provide a tax credit for the job-training expenses of employers. After the terrorist attack in San Bernardino, he heard from other members of Congress who had endured similar searing experiences. They advised him what to expect and how to help San Bernardino recover. In 2017, Aguilar got a seat on the Appropriations Committee, which he said gave him "a louder voice when it comes to standing up for Inland Empire families." He was named an assistant whip in Rep. Steny Hoyer's Democratic Whip organization, and also became the whip for the Hispanic Caucus.

Early in the 2016 campaign cycle, the National Republican Congressional Committee placed Aguilar on its "Donkeys List" of vulnerable incumbents. Chabot, who had written an e-book about his 2014 campaign experience, decided to run again. He cited Aguilar's failure to improve the continuing weak local economy. Chabot referred to his opponent as "Agu-liar" and generated controversy when he issued "terrorist hunting permits" to campaign donors. In the first round of voting in June, Aguilar led Chabot, 43%-23%; another Democrat got 11 percent of the vote. Aguilar again had a big fundraising advantage, $2.9 million to $622,000, and national Republicans spent little money to back up their attacks on Aguilar. The higher presidential-year turnout provided a boost for Aguilar, who this time won 56%-44%.

Southwestern San Bernardino: Rancho Cucamonga

Population		**Race and Ethnicity**		**Income**	
Total	729,036	White	27.9%	Median Income	$53,700 (204 out of 435)
Land area	218	Black	10.3%		
Pop/ sq mi	3340.5	Latino	50.8%		
Born in state	63.5%	Asian	7.6%	Under $50,000	30.4%
		Two races	2.5%	$50,000-$99,999	19.0%
Age Groups		Other	0.8%	$100,000-$199,999	4.1%
Under 18	27.6%			$200,000 or more	20.4%
18-34	27.2%	**Education**		Poverty Rate	20.4%
35-64	35.7%	H.S grad or less	44.9%		
Over 64	9.5%	Some college	32.3%	**Health Insurance**	
		College Degree, 4 yr	14.2%	With health insurance coverage	83.8%
Work		Post grad	8.6%		
White Collar	31.7%				
Sales and Service	44.4%	**Military**		**Public Assistance**	
Blue Collar	23.9%	Veteran	5.6%	Cash public assistance income	5.7%
Government	17.3%	Active Duty	0.1%		
				Food stamp/SNAP benefits	16.0%

Voter Turnout			
2015 Total Citizens 18+	447,834	2016 House Turnout as % CVAP	48%
2016 House turnout	215,936	2014 House Turnout as % CVAP	22%

2012 Presidential Vote		
Barack Obama	118,043	(54%)
Mitt Romney	83,822	(41%)

2016 Presidential Vote		
Hillary Clinton	131,966	(57%)
Donald Trump	83,706	(36%)
Gary Johnson	7,729	(3%)

Cook Partisan Voting Index: D+8

In the 1970s, as the coastal portions of the Los Angeles Basin became fully developed, and in the 1980s, as real estate values skyrocketed, people with modest incomes and young families increasingly moved east, from the high-cost, high-crime coast to the smoggier, hotter valleys inland. There was a lot of empty, low-priced land in what people began calling the Inland Empire, defined usually as San Bernardino and Riverside counties, and even more in the desert to the north and east of the passes through the mountains that rim the Basin. This was a high-growth area, with a population that expanded from 1.6 million in 1980 to 4.2 million in 2010. In the century's first decade, there was a boom in commercial real estate, especially warehouses to store merchandise offloaded at the port of Los Angeles-Long Beach. The uptick in construction attracted many Latinos, both citizens and immigrants. San Bernardino has become the second-largest county in the nation - behind Miami-Dade in Florida - with a population that is majority Latino, an increase in Latino population from 241,000 in 1980 to 1.11 million in 2015. New subdivisions sprang up and subprime mortgages were readily available with little or no money down.

In 2007 the housing bubble burst, and in the ensuing recession, commercial real estate went sour. Millions of square feet of warehouses stood empty. The Inland Empire had one of the nation's highest foreclosure rates and housing values fell by half. Many of the job losses were in the construction industry. Poverty has been a persistent challenge in the Inland Empire. Nowhere were the problems greater than in the city of San Bernardino, which was declared one of the weakest metropolitan areas in the country for job creation. The city was criticized for carrying inflated pension costs and high government salaries, with nearly one in four city employees earning more than $100,000 a year in 2010. Facing a $45.8 million budget shortfall, San Bernardino voted to declare bankruptcy in July 2012.

Since then, financial conditions have improved. In 2014, the city announced plans to repay fully its pension debt. Rancho Cucamonga had improved to the top third of cities nationwide to find a job according to the financial website WalletHub, and economic growth there had shut down most of the orange groves. Amazon opened in March 2016 a second fulfillment center in San Bernardino, with combined employment of 2,500. County development officials announced later in the year that they had created more than 10,000 jobs - more than the earlier total -- at the site of the Norton Air Force Base, which closed in 1994. Amazon was among those employers, who were primarily in logistics. In January 2017, the county achieved a milestone in its economic recovery: Its unemployment rate dropped to 5 percent.

In December 2015, San Bernardino gained unwanted attention as it joined the international list of terrorism sites. A disgruntled five-year county employee, wearing military fatigues and firing a rifle, killed 14 and wounded 22 in a mass shooting at a holiday reception with many of his fellow workers. Police killed him with his wife in a shoot-out a few hours later as they were pursued in a fleeing sports utility vehicle. The Chicago-born shooter and his Pakistani-born wife, both Muslims, made a Facebook statement in support of the Islamic State terrorist organization. The event was described at the time as the deadliest terrorist act on American soil since September 2001, though that mark was overtaken six months later by the attack at a night club in Orlando, Florida. The county later received a $4 million anti-terrorism grant from the Justice Department to reimburse some of its costs and assist the survivors.

The 31st Congressional District is the only district that is entirely within San Bernardino County; four other districts are partly in the county. This includes the cities of Colton, Loma Linda, Redlands and most of downtown San Bernardino. Also here is Rancho Cucamonga. Its population had been soaring, but with only a slight increase to 175,000 since 2005. This city has a local baseball team, the Quakes, who play at the Epicenter. Rialto and Upland are split between this district and the 35th. The 31st was designed to comply with Voting Rights Act rules against racial discrimination. The district is 52 percent Hispanic and politically leans Democratic. Hillary Clinton got 57 percent of the vote, the same as Barack Obama won in each of his campaigns, though the area has been competitive locally.

THIRTY-SECOND DISTRICT

Grace Napolitano (D)

Elected 1998, 10th term; b. Dec 04, 1936, Brownsville, TX; Texas Southmost College, Att.; Cerritos College (CA), Att.; Roman Catholic; Married (Frank Napolitano); 5 children (5 from previous marriage); 14 grandchildren; 2 great-grandchildren.

Elected Office: Norwalk City Council, 1986-1992; Norwalk Mayor, 1990- 92; CA Assembly, 1992-1998.

Professional Career: Employee, Ford Motor Co., 1970-1992.

DC Office: 1610 LHOB 20515, 202-225-5256, Fax: 202-225-0027, napolitano.house.gov.

State Offices: El Monte, 626-350-0150.

Committees: *Natural Resources*: Water, Power & Oceans. *Transportation & Infrastructure*: Aviation, Economic Dev't, Public Buildings & Emergency Management, Highways & Transit, Water Resources & Environment (RMM).

Group Ratings

	ADA	ACLU	AFL-CIO	LCV	ITI	COC	HAFA	ACU	CFG	FRC
2016	-	100%	-	92%	67%	62%	10%	77%	4%	0%
2015	95%	C	100%	94%	C	37%	C	4%	0%	0%

Almanac Ratings 2015

	Economy	Social	Foreign	Composite
Liberal	100%	100%	89%	96%
Conservative	0%	0%	11%	4%

Key Votes of the 114th Congress

1. Keystone Pipeline	N	5. Puerto Rico Debt	Y	9. Offenses by Aliens	N
2. Trade Deals	N	6. Medical Marijuana	Y	10. Troops in Iraq	Y
3. Export-Import Bank	Y	7. Sanctuary Cities	N	11. Homeland Security $$	Y
4. Debt Ceiling Increase	Y	8. Armor-piercing Bullets	N	12. Trade Adjustment aid	NV

Election Results

Election	Name (Party)	Vote (%)		Cand. Spent	Ind. Exp. Support	Ind. Exp. Oppose
2016 General	Grace Napolitano (D)	114,926	(62%)	$816,003		
	Roger Hernandez (D)	71,720	(38%)	$113,569		
2016 Primary	Grace Napolitano (D)	41,423	(52%)			
	Gordon Fisher (R)	19,439	(24%)			
	Roger Hernandez (D)	19,217	(24%)			

Prior winning percentages: 2014 (60%), 2012 (66%), 2010 (74%), 2008 (82%), 2006 (75%), 2004 (100%), 2002 (71%), 2000 (71%), 1998 (68%)

Grace Napolitano, a Democrat first elected in 1998, has concentrated on issues affecting lower-income Hispanics in her Southern California district, including jobs, water scarcity and mental health. Her committee assignments have given her clout on pork-barrel projects, on both land and water. In the Republican-controlled House, she has had some legislative success.

Napolitano grew up in the lower Rio Grande Valley of Texas, married at age 18, and eventually had five children. When she was 23, the family moved to California. She got a job as a secretary at Ford Motor Co. and stayed for 22 years. After her first husband died, she married Frank Napolitano, and in 1980, they started a pizzeria. (*Washingtonian* magazine has praised her egg and tortilla hash, known as *migas*.) She served on the Norwalk City Council from 1986 to 1992 and served one term as mayor, becoming the first Latino to hold the position. In 1992, she was elected to the California Assembly.

Term-limited in 1998, she got the opportunity to run for Congress when 16-year Democratic Rep. Esteban Torres announced three days before the filing deadline that he was retiring. Torres's surprise move was designed to promote the election of Jamie Casso, his son-in-law and chief of staff, who immediately announced his candidacy. Napolitano was not deterred, and got into the race. She criticized Casso for not living in the district, and he criticized a $180,000 loan she made to her campaign at an unusual 18 percent interest rate. Napolitano had the financial backing of liberal women's organizations, including EMILY's List, plus the benefit of higher name recognition. The two candidates had few differences on major issues. Napolitano signed a pledge to serve only three terms. She won the primary by 618 votes, assuring her victory in November in the heavily Democratic district.

Napolitano has been among the most liberal members of the House. In the *Almanac* vote ratings for 2015, she had perfect liberal scores on economic and social issues and was near the center of House Democrats on foreign issues. She is a former chairwoman of the Congressional Hispanic Caucus and has been more consensus-oriented on immigration legislation than some caucus members. She has been a long-time advocate on issues related to the mentally ill, an interest that was sparked by a report that one in three Hispanic girls contemplates suicide. "Mental health is treatable. But [the Latino community has] a stigma attached to it," Napolitano said. During the 2010 health care debate, she said affordable health care was "critical to the future of women who suffer in silence from mental illness." As chair of the Congressional Mental Health Caucus, she has written that most people who commit suicides use guns, and she advocated steps to reduce such incidents.

On the Natural Resources Committee, she was chairwoman of the panel's Water and Power Subcommittee from 2007 until 2011, with a focus on Southern California's acute need for an adequate water supply. She held hearings to examine possible long-term solutions to address water needs, and she called for continued funding of water desalination research in 2012, saying, "Our water supply continues to be strained by population growth and climate change, and the ability to convert saltwater into drinking water is fast becoming a critical source of economic growth and international competition." In 2014, she unveiled her "Water in the 21st Century" bill, which provided $2 billion in loans and grants for water recycling, storm water capture and treatment, ground water management and water infrastructure projects. After the 2014 election, she decided not to seek the vacant post as senior Democrat on the full committee, which instead went to Rep. Raul Grijalva of Arizona.

As a member of the Transportation and Infrastructure Committee, she has been ranking Democrat on the Water Resources and Environment Subcommittee, where she has worked to fix "our nation's crumbling water infrastructure." She has encouraged regulators to find ways to recycle water for irrigation use and groundwater replenishment and to assist local water agencies to find more ways to recapture water for their reservoirs. She worked with Republican Rep. Jeff Denham on behalf of several California-related provisions in the 2015 highway bill that was enacted. During debate on the House-passed surface transportation bill in 2012, she defeated proposed changes that would have weakened safety measures. She won an extension of a program to speed up transportation projects and lower costs by relieving California of the need for a review under the National Environmental Policy Act when a more stringent review already was completed.

In 2003, Napolitano abandoned her earlier pledge to serve only three terms. She has not been seriously challenged for reelection. In 2012, she won with 66 percent of the vote in the redrawn 32nd District, in which more than 80 percent of voters were new to her and her Norwalk residence was in the 38th District. In 2014, she was held to 60 percent by Arturo Alas, a real estate agent who opposed the move by President Barack Obama to create a national monument in the San Gabriel Mountains. Alas was part of what *Reuters* described as a group of "ethnically diverse young libertarians" who have sought to revive the Republican Party in Los Angeles. In 2016, she had an unusual campaign when Democratic Assemblyman Roger Hernandez finished second in the June all-party primary but then faced allegations of domestic violence from his ex-wife. In August, he formally ended his campaign, though his name remained on the ballot and he got 38 percent of the vote against Napolitano.

At an endorsement meeting of Young Democrats in February 2016, Napolitano suffered a small stroke and took a few weeks to recover. "It hasn't slowed my brain. It's slowed my body somewhat," including her ability at age 79 to write, she told *The Los Angeles Times*.

Eastern L.A. Suburbs: Azusa, West Covina

Population		**Race and Ethnicity**		**Income**	
Total	718,864	White	16.8%	Median Income	$59,558 (147 out of 435)
Land area	124	Black	2.5%		
Pop/ sq mi	5786.6	Latino	62.1%		
Born in state	56.2%	Asian	16.7%	Under $50,000	32.8%
		Two races	1.4%	$50,000-$99,999	21.5%
Age Groups		Other	0.4%	$100,000-$199,999	3.6%
Under 18	23.8%			$200,000 or more	14.5%
18-34	25.8%	**Education**		Poverty Rate	14.5%
35-64	38.1%	H.S grad or less	52.4%		
Over 64	12.3%	Some college	27.7%	**Health Insurance**	
		College Degree, 4 yr	14.2%	With health insurance coverage	81.6%
Work		Post grad	5.7%		
White Collar	27.4%				
Sales and Service	46.7%	**Military**		**Public Assistance**	
Blue Collar	25.9%	Veteran	4.2%	Cash public assistance income	3.9%
Government	12.6%	Active Duty	0.1%		
				Food stamp/SNAP benefits	8.7%

Voter Turnout			
2015 Total Citizens 18+	436,821	2016 House Turnout as % CVAP	43%
2016 House turnout	186,646	2014 House Turnout as % CVAP	20%

2012 Presidential Vote		
Barack Obama	133,061	(65%)
Mitt Romney	66,269	(33%)

2016 Presidential Vote		
Hillary Clinton	146,459	(66%)
Donald Trump	60,921	(28%)
Gary Johnson	5,996	(3%)
Jill Stein	4,678	(2%)

Cook Partisan Voting Index: D+17

It was the great route west to California in the first half of the 20th century: Passengers on the Santa Fe Railroad's *Super Chief* or motorists on U.S. 66, after hours and days in barren desert, would descend through Cajon Pass into the Los Angeles Basin, and come upon orange groves and exotic plants thriving beneath the 10,000-foot snow-capped San Gabriel Mountains. The railroad and highway ran through a line of towns built by Midwestern Protestants as independent communities. Foothills communities such as La Verne and San Dimas have horse trails and their own rodeos. Azusa has suffered both forest fires and mudslide threats from the nearby mountains.

The small city of Irwindale continued its long-running legal dispute in which it cited the Huy Fong Foods company as a public nuisance because of the odor from Sriracha hot sauce production. The chili sauce has a devoted following. *Bon Appetit* has named it one of its favorite foods. David Tran, a refugee from Vietnam, built the successful company from its start in a van. Another classic L.A. food note: After a popular In-n-Out burger stand, which had been constructed in 1948, was demolished in Baldwin Park in 2011, public protests prompted the owner to build a 100-square-foot replica, with an antique Coldspot refrigerator, vintage fryers and two-way speakers in the drive-through lane. That building was purely promotional. For food, customers were directed less than a mile near the site of the original stand, in the shadow of Interstate 10.

The 32nd District is 63 percent Hispanic and 17 percent Asian. The western parts of the compact 32nd District - the areas closer to downtown Los Angeles - are heavily Latino: Covina, West Covina and Azusa all are Hispanic-majority cities. In Baldwin Park, which is 80 percent Hispanic and 14 percent Asian, more than 80 percent of its population speaks a language other than English at home. Chinese investors in 2015 gained approval for major investments in El Monte, including a Hilton hotel plus office and retail space. In March 2016, L.A. Metro opened an 11-mile light-rail extension of the Gold Line from Pasadena to Asuza. With approval of a November 2016 referendum to extend a sales tax increase for transit funding, Metro planned further extensions to the Ontario Airport. Outlying areas to the east, such as La Verne and San Dimas, have lower poverty rates and higher household incomes. The I-10 freeway connects the district to downtown Los Angeles. The heavily Hispanic composition of this district makes it safe Democratic territory. The demographic shifts helped to account for an increase in the Democratic margin from 62%-36% for Barack Obama in 2008 to 66%-28% for Hillary Clinton in 2016.

THIRTY-THIRD DISTRICT

Ted Lieu (D)

Elected 2014, 2nd term; b. Mar 29, 1969, Taipei, Taiwan; Stanford University (CA), B.S.; Georgetown University Law Center (DC), J.D.; Stanford University (CA), B.A.; Roman Catholic; Married (Betty Lieu); 2 children.

Military Career: U.S. Air Force JAG, 1995-1999; U.S. Air Force Reserve, 2000-present.

Elected Office: Torrance City Council, 2002-2005; CA Assembly, 2005-2010. CA Senate, 2011-2014.

Professional Career: Clerk, U.S. Court of Appeals, 9th Circuit; Practicing attorney.

DC Office: 236 CHOB 20515, 202-225-3976, Fax: 202-225-4099, lieu.house.gov.

State Offices: Los Angeles, 310-652-3095; Manhattan Beach, 310-321-7664.

Committees: *Foreign Affairs*: Middle East & North Africa. *Joint Congressional-Executive Commission on China*. *Judiciary*: Courts, Intellectual Property & Internet, Crime, Terrorism, Homeland Security & Investigations.

Group Ratings

	ADA	ACLU	AFL-CIO	LCV	ITI	COC	HAFA	ACU	CFG	FRC
2016	-	100%	-	89%	33%	58%	18%	0%	11%	0%
2015	80%	C	96%	91%	C	40%	C	8%	2%	0%

Almanac Ratings 2015

	Economy	Social	Foreign	Composite
Liberal	87%	100%	92%	93%
Conservative	13%	0%	8%	7%

Key Votes of the 114th Congress

1. Keystone Pipeline	N	5. Puerto Rico Debt	NV	9. Offenses by Aliens	N
2. Trade Deals	N	6. Medical Marijuana	Y	10. Troops in Iraq	Y
3. Export-Import Bank	Y	7. Sanctuary Cities	N	11. Homeland Security $$	Y
4. Debt Ceiling Increase	Y	8. Armor-piercing Bullets	N	12. Trade Adjustment aid	Y

Election Results

Election	Name (Party)	Vote (%)		Cand. Spent	Ind. Exp. Support	Ind. Exp. Oppose
2016 General	Ted Lieu (D)	219,397	(66%)	$704,644		
	Kenneth Wright (R)	110,822	(34%)	$49,586		
2016 Primary	Ted Lieu (D)	127,733	(69%)			
	Kenneth Wright (R)	56,976	(31%)			

Prior winning percentages: 2014 (59%)

Democrat Ted Lieu was elected in 2014 in one of the nation's richest and most liberal House districts. He replaced the iconic liberal Henry Waxman, who for 40 years played a major role in legislation ranging from health care to environmental protection and was aggressive at congressional oversight. Lieu displayed his own activism, with both new liberal initiatives and occasional bipartisan action.

A Taiwanese American whose working-class family came to the United States when he was a toddler, he got his bachelor's degree from Stanford and a law degree from Georgetown University. Lieu's early career centered on law and military service. After four years of active duty in the Air Force, including a posting in the JAG Corps, he divided his time between working in the private sector and serving on the Torrance City Council. In 2005, he won a special election to serve in the state Assembly, followed by election to the state Senate in 2010 to represent much of the territory in the 33rd District. He backed a successful bill allowing undocumented immigrants to take the bar exam, and called for a statewide referendum expressing opposition to the *Citizens United* campaign-finance ruling. On affirmative action, he staked out a more centrist position, opposing a bill that would have overturned the affirmative action ban at California state universities. That move drew criticism from black and Latino lawmakers.

When Waxman announced his retirement in 2013, he set off a primary fight that attracted no fewer than 18 candidates. Along with Lieu, the best known were Republican Elan Carr, who served with the Army in Iraq and was a deputy in the L.A. District Attorney's office, former L.A. mayoral candidate Wendy Greuel, and self-help guru Marianne Williamson, an independent. Lieu ran an aggressive campaign that leveraged his deep political ties to the district, his liberal voting record in Sacramento, and a lineup of top Democratic endorsements, including L.A. Mayor Eric Garcetti, as well as the *Los Angeles Daily News*. He underscored the need for more Asian-American representation in Congress. In the June primary, he came in second to Carr, 21%-19%; Greuel was third with 17 percent. That set Lieu up for an easy victory in a party stronghold, and his wealthy voters could help raise money for other Democrats. He won in November, 59%-41%.

In the House, Lieu was president of the Democrats' freshman class. He became the first House Democrat to announce opposition to the request by President Barack Obama to authorize the use of military force against the Islamic State. "I do not believe the administration has made the case that ISIL represents a direct, grave threat to our nation," he said. He joined several other junior House members in launching the bipartisan Post-9/11 Veterans Caucus. Noting that his district has one of the nation's largest populations of homeless veterans, plus a huge VA health care system, he emphasized the need for innovative solutions to the problems of returned service members but he opposed suggestions to privatize veterans' health care services. Lieu enacted a bill in September 2016 to authorize leases for the VA's campus in West Los Angeles that would construct 1,200 units for homeless vets. He secured $35 million for seismic retrofits at the existing facility.

Lieu filed a bill in February 2016 with Republican Rep. Blake Farenthold of Texas to prohibit states from requiring tech companies to build encryption weaknesses into their products. The legislation was prompted by concerns from law-enforcement authorities that criminal suspects might use powerful encryption to prevent investigators from gaining access to smartphones.

In 2017, with seats on the Foreign Affairs and Judiciary Committees, Lieu filed a bill with Sen. Edward Markey of Massachusetts to prevent the president from authorizing a nuclear first strike without a declaration of war by Congress. The legislation had virtually no chance of enactment, but it expressed concerns by Democrats about the mixed signals that Donald Trump had sent during his campaign.

Lieu was challenged for reelection by Kenneth Wright, a pediatric eye surgeon from South Bay and a first-time candidate who described himself as a progressive Republican. Lieu refused to debate and he won, 66%-34%.

Coastal and Central L.A.: Westside, Santa Monica

Population		Race and Ethnicity		Income	
Total	715,480	White	65.9%	Median Income	$96,398 (9 out of 435)
Land area	289	Black	2.8%		
Pop/ sq mi	2479.3	Latino	12.5%	Under $50,000	23.9%
Born in state	46.3%	Asian	14.0%	$50,000-$99,999	28.0%
Age Groups		Two races	4.1%	$100,000-$199,999	20.8%
Under 18	18.5%	Other	0.7%	$200,000 or more	9.1%
18-34	23.6%	**Education**		Poverty Rate	9.1%
35-64	41.8%	H.S grad or less	14.5%	**Health Insurance**	
Over 64	16.0%	Some college	22.9%	With health insurance coverage	92.9%
Work		College Degree, 4 yr	35.7%		
White Collar	61.3%	Post grad	26.8%	**Public Assistance**	
Sales and Service	32.1%	**Military**		Cash public assistance income	1.3%
Blue Collar	6.5%	Veteran	5.2%		
Government	10.3%	Active Duty	0.1%	Food stamp/SNAP benefits	1.7%

Voter Turnout			
2015 Total Citizens 18+	525,289	2016 House Turnout as % CVAP	63%
2016 House turnout	330,219	2014 House Turnout as % CVAP	35%

2012 Presidential Vote		
Barack Obama	210,010	(61%)
Mitt Romney	127,421	(37%)

2016 Presidential Vote		
Hillary Clinton	239,982	(68%)
Donald Trump	93,706	(26%)
Gary Johnson	12,485	(4%)

Cook Partisan Voting Index: D+16

Showbiz still sets the tone for the Westside of Los Angeles. It remains tremendously profitable, and not just for the big conglomerate-owned studios. There are tens of thousands of entrepreneurs, actors, writers and craftsmen who are the best in the world at what they do and who tend to cluster on the Westside because so many others in the entertainment business work there. Not everyone is in show business, of course. The Westside is metro Los Angeles's biggest office center, with horrific traffic during the morning and evening rush hours. Most office workers can't afford to live in the limited and expensive neighborhoods nearby. The city's Purple Line subway is being extended to the Westside, a nine-mile extension from Wilshire/Western. Over the objections of Beverly Hills school district officials, the $5.6 billion project includes a tunnel underneath Beverly Hills High School. Construction broke ground in 2014 and was scheduled to be completed in 2023. In August 2016, a federal judge found that the environmental studies were inadequate and demanded revision. Metro officials said their route and construction timetable would not be affected.

The area has a large and diverse Jewish community. Iranian Jews have poured in since 1979 and make up about one-fifth of the population of Beverly Hills. The old Fairfax district is home to many Russian Jewish immigrants and a number of corner delis, including the historic Canter's Deli that opened in 1931 and remains open 24/7. Beverly Hills and the Westside remain the locus of some of America's most expensive residential real estate, where people buy houses for millions of dollars, tear them down, and build new houses for many more millions. Rodeo Drive is one of the world's premier high-priced shopping areas. These communities experienced significant foreclosures following the housing bubble. Unlike in much of California, the average price for local real estate sales has surpassed the earlier levels, including a return to some stratospheric prices. The L.A. City Council responded in March 2015 with restrictions in 20 neighborhoods on what residents described as "mansionization," the building of mansion-like homes that are unusually large for their lots. In August 2016, the local council voted to close the Santa Monica airport by 2018.

The 33rd Congressional District of California contains the upscale cities of Beverly Hills, Brentwood and parts of Westside Los Angeles, which it shares with the 28th District. In the hills of Bel Air, $100 million homes have become common - and relatively modest. It takes in the campus of the University of California, Los Angeles and the J. Paul Getty Museum. Santa Monica is in the 33rd, as is the whole 21 miles of Malibu on the Pacific Ocean. It dips south to take in Marina del Rey, which offers yacht moorings, and skirts along the ocean past Los Angeles International Airport to El Segundo, Manhattan Beach and Redondo Beach. Its southernmost point is Rancho Palos Verdes, where, on cliffs overlooking the ocean, is famed architect Frank Lloyd Wright's Wayfarers Chapel, also known as "The Glass Church." Nearby is the Trump National Golf Club where hundreds of employees in 2013 settled a class-action suit over working conditions. With a racial composition that is almost three-fourths white, the district is less ethnically diverse than other congressional districts in greater Los Angeles. But it is solid Democratic territory comparable to less-white areas nearby, though with a loftier median household income that placed the district among the wealthiest in the nation. Hillary Clinton in 2016 got 68 percent of the vote, compared with 61 percent for President Barack Obama in 2012. Many typically Republican voters in the 33rd abandoned Donald Trump.

THIRTY-FOURTH DISTRICT

Jimmy Gomez (D)

Elected 2017, 1st term; b. Nov. 25, 1974, Fullerton; University of California, Los Angeles, BA; Harvard University, MPP; married (Mary Hodge).

Elected Office: CA Assembly, 2012- present, Majority Whip, 2012-2015; Democratic National Committee, Member.

Professional Career: Political Director, United Nurses Association of California.

State Offices: Los Angeles, 213-481-1425.

Election Results

Election	Name (Party)	Vote (%)		Cand. Spent	Ind. Exp. Support	Ind. Exp. Oppose
2017 Special	Jimmy Gomez (D)	19,761	(60%)	$734,844	$1,877	
	Robert Lee Ahn (D)	13,108	(40%)	$1,268,675		
2017 Primary	Jimmy Gomez (D)	10,728	(25%)			
	Robert Lee Ahn (D)	9,415	(22%)			
	Maria Cabildo (D)	4,259	(10%)			
	Sara Hernandez (D)	2,358	(6%)			
	Arturo Carmona (D)	2,205	(5%)			
	Wendy Carrillo (D)	2,195	(5%)			

Democrat Jimmy Gomez won the June 2017 special election to replace Rep. Xavier Becerra, who resigned in January after Gov. Jerry Brown selected him as Attorney General of California. Gomez won the run-off against Robert Lee Ahn, 60%-40%, after they were the top two candidates among 24 who ran in the April primary. Ahn, an attorney who worked in his family's real estate business, had been a member of the Los Angeles Planning Commission. He had strong support from the local Korean-American community.

Gomez, an Assemblyman who had represented much of the congressional district while elected to three terms in Sacramento, was supported by much of the local Democratic establishment, including Becerra. He was born and raised in southern California; his parents had immigrated from Mexico in the early 1970s. After graduating from high school, Gomez for several months worked 16 hours daily at a fast-food restaurant and a local superstore. In search of a quality education, he enrolled in a community college and got his bachelor's degree at UCLA and then a master's in public policy from the John F. Kennedy School of Government at Harvard University.

He spent more than a decade working with local and federal officials, including former Rep. Hilda Solis, at the Democratic National Committee and labor unions - most recently as political director of the United Nurses Associations of California. In the Assembly, where he was first elected in 2012, Gomez styled himself as a progressive. He authored an expansion of California's Paid Family Leave program to cover all workers who paid into it, which was enacted.

The vacancy was created when Becerra resigned on Jan. 24 to fill the attorney general vacancy created when Kamala Harris was elected to the Senate. The first Latino to serve in that position, Becerra said that part of his job would be to challenge the policies of President Donald Trump that conflict with or seek to reverse California law on issues ranging from energy and the environment to immigration, marriage equality and health care. "If you want to take on a forward-leading state that is prepared to defend its rights and interests, then come at us," he said. First elected to the House in 1992, he chaired the Democratic Caucus for four years, making him the most prominent Latino in the House. He was a senior member of the Ways and Means Committee.

Becerra's resignation spurred a wide-open contest for his successor. The 24 candidates, who did not include a single Republican, featured several women candidates and supporters of presidential candidate Sen. Bernie Sanders. None of them emerged from the pack. Nine candidates raised more than $100,000. They were led by Ahn, who self-financed $303,000 of the $767,000 that he reported spending through the primary, and Gomez, whose initial $439,000 in spending included $163,000 from political action committees, by far the highest amount for any candidate. In the primary, Gomez got 25 percent of the vote and Ahn had 22 percent. No other candidate got more than 10 percent. Because the election had no partisan impact in the House, it received less national attention than the four other special elections that were held during the spring of 2017.

Downtown/Northeast L.A.

Population		**Race and Ethnicity**		**Income**	
Total	714,351	White	10.0%	Median Income	$35,836 (422 out of 435)
Land area	48	Black	4.0%		
Pop/ sq mi	14988.5	Latino	64.8%		
Born in state	41.5%	Asian	19.4%	Under $50,000	23.2%
		Two races	1.2%	$50,000-$99,999	10.4%
Age Groups		Other	0.5%	$100,000-$199,999	2.6%
Under 18	21.7%			$200,000 or more	28.6%
18-34	29.3%	**Education**		Poverty Rate	28.6%
35-64	38.5%	H.S grad or less	57.0%		
Over 64	10.5%	Some college	20.1%	**Health Insurance**	
		College Degree, 4 yr	16.6%	With health insurance coverage	70.8%
Work		Post grad	6.3%		
White Collar	26.9%				
Sales and Service	47.7%	**Military**		**Public Assistance**	
Blue Collar	25.5%	Veteran	2.1%	Cash public assistance income	5.2%
Government	9.0%	Active Duty	0.0%		
				Food stamp/SNAP benefits	12.2%

Voter Turnout			
2015 Total Citizens 18+	350,317	2016 House Turnout as % CVAP	45%
2016 House turnout	159,156	2014 House Turnout as % CVAP	18%

2012 Presidential Vote		
Barack Obama	127,510	(83%)
Mitt Romney	21,739	(14%)

2016 Presidential Vote		
Hillary Clinton	154,259	(83%)
Donald Trump	19,784	(11%)
Jill Stein	6,129	(3%)

Cook Partisan Voting Index: D+35

Downtown L.A. "is undergoing its largest construction boom in modern times," the *Los Angeles Times* reported in January 2017. With 79 developments of at least 50,000 square feet completed since 2010 or under construction, the area has gained thousands of apartments, new hotels, shop and restaurants. Much of the financing has come from foreign investment. The downtown construction in the 1970s and 1980s, by contrast, were relatively bland corporate office towers. Although driving a few blocks can be a Manhattan-type nightmare, the area has become surprisingly pedestrian-friendly, with attractive plazas like the one around the Los Angeles Public Library.

South of downtown is the garment district, with factories in nondescript buildings, an economically vibrant area that has helped make Los Angeles one of the largest manufacturing cities in America today. In 2014, the manufacturing workforce of 511,000 in the Los Angeles-Long Beach area was the largest in the nation; Chicago and New York City were next in line. Its products include apparel, chemicals, foods, furniture and electronics. In September 2016, the California Labor Commission found labor-law violations by 18 local garment manufacturers and contractors, and warned, "Sweatshop operators threaten garment workers' rights and undermine honest employers in the industry." The number of skilled workers has been declining as the result of many factors, including the recession, automation, offshoring, improved productivity, local costs and paralyzing traffic. The Los Angeles County Economic Development Corporation worried that it has become difficult to find workers with sufficient education and skill sets. Only three *Fortune* 500 companies are based in the city.

Surrounding downtown Los Angeles and largely detached from it are ethnically diverse neighborhoods, many of them built in the mid-20th century. They have changed character with every new immigration flow. To the north is Lincoln Heights, one of the oldest neighborhoods in the city and a heavily Hispanic area centered on the busy shopping street of North Broadway, where residents have been fighting gangs and graffiti with some success. Authorities credit the growing use of community policing. Highland Park and Eagle Rock, which were white middle-class enclaves 30 years ago, are now ethnically mixed and middle-class with large numbers of Latinos and Asians. Eagle Rock is the home of Occidental College, which former President Barack Obama attended his first two years of college. West of downtown is Pico Union, an entry point for new immigrants where Greeks, Mexicans and Central Americans co-mingle. Historic Filipinotown, known locally as Hi-Fi, was settled by Filipinos in the early 1900s and in recent years has become more of a polyglot. Further west is bustling and increasingly hip Koreatown, with boutique hotels plus clubs and restaurants for a busy night life. Beyond the commercial strips in Koreatown, the Asian community has gained a social and political identity as it has moved to the middle class.

These areas, plus Montecito Heights, Dodger Stadium and Elysian Park, are parts of California's 34th Congressional District. The district also takes in Chinatown and Boyle Heights, once an entry neighborhood for Irish and Jewish immigrants and for the past 40 years predominantly Mexican American. In Los Angeles' booming 1980s, these neighborhoods were suddenly thronged with immigrants, with small houses and garden apartments full of large families and many children. Since then, the population surge stopped, and this became a slow-growing district, as the newcomers of the decade before moved out to middle-class neighborhoods and incoming immigrants spread more evenly around the Los Angeles Basin. The district is 64 percent Hispanic and 20 percent Asian. Politically, it is in the top 5 percent of Democratic districts in the nation.

THIRTY-FIFTH DISTRICT

Norma Torres (D)

Elected 2014, 2nd term; b. Apr 04, 1965, Escuintla, Guatemala; National Labor College (MD), Bach. Deg.; Mount San Antonio College (CA), Att.; Rio Hondo College, Att.; Roman Catholic; Married (Louis Torres); 3 children.

Elected Office: Pomona City Council, 2000-2006; Pomona Mayor, 2006-2008; CA Assembly, 2008-2013; CA Senate, 2013-2014.

Professional Career: Emergency dispatcher; Sales rep..

DC Office: 1713 LHOB 20515, 202-225-6161, Fax: 202-225-8671, torres.house.gov.

State Offices: Ontario, 909-481-6474.

Committees: *Foreign Affairs*: Terrorism, Nonproliferation & Trade, Western Hemisphere. *Natural Resources*: Federal Lands, Indian, Insular & Alaska Native Affairs (RMM).

Group Ratings

	ADA	ACLU	AFL-CIO	LCV	ITI	COC	HAFA	ACU	CFG	FRC
2016	-	88%	-	100%	60%	64%	14%	0%	0%	0%
2015	80%	C	100%	91%	C	50%	C	0%	0%	0%

Almanac Ratings 2015

	Economy	Social	Foreign	Composite
Liberal	88%	100%	93%	94%
Conservative	12%	0%	7%	6%

Key Votes of the 114th Congress

1. Keystone Pipeline	N	5. Puerto Rico Debt	N	9. Offenses by Aliens	N
2. Trade Deals	N	6. Medical Marijuana	Y	10. Troops in Iraq	Y
3. Export-Import Bank	Y	7. Sanctuary Cities	N	11. Homeland Security $$	Y
4. Debt Ceiling Increase	Y	8. Armor-piercing Bullets	N	12. Trade Adjustment aid	Y

Election Results

Election	Name (Party)	Vote (%)	Cand. Spent	Ind. Exp. Support	Ind. Exp. Oppose
2016 General	Norma Torres (D)	124,044 (72%)	$318,123		
	Tyler Fischella (R)	47,309 (28%)	$3,748		
2016 Primary	Norma Torres (D)	65,226 (76%)			
	Tyler Fischella (R)	21,089 (24%)			

Prior winning percentages: 2014 (64%)

Democrat Norma Torres, a state lawmaker deeply involved in health care and immigration debates, easily defeated another Democrat to take an open seat in 2014 after the incumbent decided to return home and run for county government. In the House, she has taken an interest in issues affecting her Central American homeland.

Torres was born in Guatemala but entered the United States at age 5, when her parents sent her to live with relatives in Whittier, California, so she would be safe from that country's bloody civil war. Her interest in community safety led to work as a 911 dispatcher in Pomona, where she soon developed a deeper interest in public service. One episode was particularly profound: In 1994, while she was handling other calls, a fellow dispatcher put a frantic Spanish-speaking woman on hold because no one else could speak with her. When Torres finally picked up, she heard a domestic dispute escalate on the other line, resulting in the shooting death of an 11-year-old. Shaken, she led a successful fight to compel the police to hire more bilingual dispatchers. She helped to secure a $350,000 federal grant for improved technology. At age 47, she received her bachelor's degree in labor studies from the National Labor College in Silver Spring, Maryland, where she took online courses.

Torres became involved in broader community issues, especially union organizing and immigrants' rights. She was elected to the Pomona City Council in 2000 and was elected mayor in 2006. The following year, when she returned for the first time to her hometown in Guatemala, she was treated like a celebrity. In 2008, her rise continued as she won a seat in the state Assembly. She chaired the Housing and Community Development Committee, where she helped to secure $2 billion for the "Keep Your Home" program to assist homeowners to avoid foreclosure. She wrote a law that modernized the 911 system by directing cell phone callers to their local police department during an emergency.

Torres's next big opening came in a 2013 special election, after Gloria Negrete McLeod was elected to the House and gave up her state Senate seat. Torres won the Senate seat, and introduced two bills to increase diversity on the state board overseeing health care expansion, following a rollout period that many critics said was inadequate for Latinos. She also championed a law to generate more revenue for programs that train and place doctors in medically underserved communities. To assist immigrants, she coauthored a measure that transferred $3 million to help unaccompanied minors fleeing Central America.

In 2014, Negrete McLeod handed Torres another opportunity, announcing she would not seek reelection to the House and instead ran for a seat on the San Bernardino County Board of Supervisors, which she ultimately lost. In the blanket primary in June, Torres faced three other Democrats and a Republican. Bolstered by a sizable cash advantage, name recognition, and endorsements by major unions and liberal women's groups, she got 67 percent to Democrat Christina Gagnier's 15 percent. Under California's "top two" rules, those two advanced to the general election in November, which was another easy contest for Torres. During the full campaign, she outspent Gagnier $423,000 to $84,000, and won with 63 percent. More than three-fourths of that vote was cast in San Bernardino County.

During her first term, she used her seat on the Homeland Security Committee as an opportunity to oversee ports of entry in her district's Ontario International Airport and the inland port serving the maritime ports of Los Angeles and Long Beach. She told a reporter for the *Inland Valley Daily Bulletin* that she was surprised and dismayed by the pervasive partisanship, including in her committee work. "Homeland Security, you think 'that's life and death,'" she said. "But we're not able to work together on this issue."

She gravitated toward international issues and founded the bipartisan Central America Caucus with more than 30 members to enhance understanding of the region, including immigration issues. In 2017, she got a seat on the Foreign Affairs Committee. Unlike many House Democrats, she decided to attend the inauguration of President Donald Trump. "I am the embodiment of everything Trump has demonized and demeaned," she said in a statement. "I will stand over his shoulder, just as I will during the next four years, to remind him that I and people like me deserve a seat at the table, and we will watch his every move."

Torres was easily reelected with 72 percent of the vote against Republican Tyler Fischella, a little-known business development associate. She hoped for a lengthy tenure in the House.

Inland Empire: Fontana, Ontario

Population		**Race and Ethnicity**		**Income**	
Total	727,007	White	14.7%	Median Income	$54,748 (186 out of 435)
Land area	169	Black	6.3%		
Pop/ sq mi	4304.9	Latino	70.0%		
Born in state	60.3%	Asian	6.5%	Under $50,000	35.3%
		Two races	1.8%	$50,000-$99,999	17.3%
Age Groups		Other	0.7%	$100,000-$199,999	2.1%
Under 18	27.9%			$200,000 or more	18.5%
18-34	27.6%	**Education**		Poverty Rate	18.5%
35-64	36.6%	H.S grad or less	57.3%		
Over 64	7.9%	Some college	28.4%	**Health Insurance**	
		College Degree, 4 yr	10.6%	With health insurance coverage	79.1%
Work		Post grad	3.7%		
White Collar	22.1%				
Sales and Service	44.6%	**Military**		**Public Assistance**	
Blue Collar	33.3%	Veteran	3.8%	Cash public assistance income	5.5%
Government	12.2%	Active Duty	0.0%		
				Food stamp/SNAP benefits	14.4%

Voter Turnout			
2015 Total Citizens 18+	402,167	2016 House Turnout as % CVAP	43%
2016 House turnout	171,353	2014 House Turnout as % CVAP	15%

2012 Presidential Vote		
Barack Obama	108,983	(67%)
Mitt Romney	49,433	(31%)

2016 Presidential Vote		
Hillary Clinton	127,761	(67%)
Donald Trump	50,824	(27%)
Gary Johnson	5,069	(3%)

Cook Partisan Voting Index: D+19

The gateway to the Los Angeles Basin for decades was San Bernardino. This was an agricultural zone until World War II, when Henry J. Kaiser built the West Coast's first major steel mill between the Santa Fe and Southern Pacific rail lines in Fontana, just west of San Bernardino. Today, these lands have largely filled up. The Inland Empire, as it is called, may be where the smog piles up against the mountains, but it also has some of the lowest real estate prices in the Los Angeles Basin and an energetic small business economy. After the large Kaiser steel mill closed in Fontana in 1994, new businesses moved in to supplant it. At this site, future California Gov. Arnold Schwarzenegger had a knock-down, drag-out fight with the enemy metal alloy machine in the 1991 blockbuster *Terminator 2: Judgment Day*.

Business growth has been spurred by huge distribution and warehouse centers that service overseas cargo from the Long Beach port. The recession hit hard in the Inland Empire, with home foreclosures among the highest in the nation and many residents fleeing the region. Partly because of the earlier excess of cheap credit, the foreclosure crisis and scarcity of bank loans remained major local problems long after conditions improved in most of the nation. Jobs returned slowly, with some help from the local California Steel plant that employed about 1,000 workers. Like much of California, after Gov. Jerry Brown imposed statewide water restrictions in 2015, local governments in this area imposed strict conservation measures. Despite these problems, a new entertainment district in downtown Pomona enlivened the nightlife.

The 35th District is mostly in San Bernardino County, taking in heavily Hispanic areas in Fontana and Ontario. Ontario Mills is one of the largest shopping malls in the United States. Also here is part of Chino, a meatpacking area. This district covers Pomona Valley and the city of Pomona in Los Angeles County, though Pomona College is part of the Claremont Colleges a few miles away in the 27th District. The three largest cities - Fontana, Ontario and Pomona - are similar in size and each is about 70 percent Hispanic. This is a safe Democratic district, where Hillary Clinton got 67 percent of the vote in 2016.

THIRTY-SIXTH DISTRICT

Raul Ruiz (D)

Elected 2012, 3rd term; b. Aug 25, 1972, Zacatecas, Mexico; University of California, Los Angeles, B.S., 1994; Harvard University, M.PP, 2001; Harvard University, M.D., 2001; Harvard University, M.PH, 2007; Seventh-Day Adventist; Married (Monica Ruiz); 2 children (twins).

Professional Career: Emergency physician, Eisenhower Med. Center, 2007-2013; Association dean, University of CA Riverside School of Med., 2011-2012.

DC Office: 1319 LHOB 20515, 202-225-5330, Fax: 202-225-1238, ruiz.house.gov.

State Offices: Hemet, 951-765-2304; Palm Desert, 760-424-8888.

Committees: *Energy & Commerce*: Communications & Technology, Environment, Oversight & Investigations.

Group Ratings

	ADA	ACLU	AFL-CIO	LCV	ITI	COC	HAFA	ACU	CFG	FRC
2016	-	76%	-	100%	83%	64%	15%	4%	10%	0%
2015	70%	C	96%	94%	C	61%	C	5%	0%	0%

Almanac Ratings 2015

	Economy	Social	Foreign	Composite
Liberal	79%	90%	41%	70%
Conservative	21%	10%	59%	30%

Key Votes of the 114th Congress

1. Keystone Pipeline	NV	5. Puerto Rico Debt	Y	9. Offenses by Aliens	Y
2. Trade Deals	N	6. Medical Marijuana	Y	10. Troops in Iraq	N
3. Export-Import Bank	Y	7. Sanctuary Cities	N	11. Homeland Security $$	Y
4. Debt Ceiling Increase	Y	8. Armor-piercing Bullets	N	12. Trade Adjustment aid	Y

Election Results

Election	Name (Party)	Vote (%)		Cand. Spent	Ind. Exp. Support	Ind. Exp. Oppose
2016 General	Raul Ruiz (D)	144,348	(62%)	$2,432,814	$124,363	
	Jeff Stone (R)	88,269	(38%)	$320,037		
2016 Primary	Raul Ruiz (D)	48,924	(57%)			
	Jeff Stone (R)	28,809	(33%)			
	Stephan Wolkowicz (R)	8,654	(10%)			

Prior winning percentages: 2014 (54%), 2012 (53%)

Emergency room doctor Raul Ruiz, a Democrat, narrowly defeated a veteran incumbent in 2012, with effective criticism of the Republican's stance on Medicare. Ruiz pursued health care issues and was rewarded with a seat on the influential Energy and Commerce Committee, where he focused on the consequences of repeal of the Affordable Care Act.

The son of farmworkers, Ruiz was born and raised in the Coachella Valley. He dreamed of being a doctor from a very young age. A family friend paid for Ruiz to apply to the University of California, Los Angeles, but he needed money for tuition. Ruiz went door-to-door in his hometown of Coachella with a handmade contract, asking neighbors and local businesses to contribute to his college fund in exchange for his future medical service to the community. He raised almost $2,000. After graduating from UCLA, Ruiz went to Harvard Medical School. As a student, he spent almost a year in Chiapas, Mexico, through a health and social justice organization, Partners in Health. "I came out of there realizing the tremendous nature of poverty and how real policies can actually affect human lives," he later told *The Desert Sun* newspaper. After graduating from Harvard with three degrees, Ruiz returned to the Coachella Valley and served in the emergency room of a nonprofit hospital. He returned to Chiapas in 2008 to work with the government on implementing health policy changes for the region.

Ruiz was Mary Bono Mack's first Hispanic opponent since she won the seat of her late husband, musician Sonny Bono, who died in a skiing accident in 1998. Ruiz had a demographic advantage in a newly redrawn district, where nearly half the voters were Latino. Bono Mack won the first round of the match-up, 58%-42%. Ruiz got more than $1.1 million in support from the Democratic Congressional Campaign Committee. Conservative super PACs supported Bono Mack, painting Ruiz as a minion of House Minority Leader Nancy Pelosi and attacking his support of the Affordable Care Act.

In the final weeks of the race, a local newspaper received an eight-page document from Bono Mack's campaign that outlined a Thanksgiving protest in which Ruiz was arrested and charged with two misdemeanors while attending Harvard. At issue was Ruiz's participation in the National Day of Mourning, which takes place annually at Plymouth Rock to publicize the suffering of Native Americans since the Pilgrims' arrival in 1620. Both charges were dropped in a deal that also discharged claims of police brutality. Bono Mack's campaign cast Ruiz's participation in the event as anti-American and as left-wing extremism, and released a recording of a speech he gave at the protest. Ruiz characterized her efforts as desperate. The pro-Democratic House Majority PAC ran ads accusing Bono Mack and her then-husband, Republican Rep. Connie Mack of Florida, of benefiting from tax exemptions in Florida. Ruiz was endorsed by *The Desert Sun*, which said that Bono Mack had gotten too comfortable in Congress. He won, 53%-47%.

On the Veterans Affairs Committee, the former emergency room doctor took on problems with VA hospitals. He catalogued complaints of poor services, and filed bills designed to reduce the claims backlog and to make it easier for veterans to use video conferencing for hearings before the Board of Veterans' Appeals. He served two years as the senior Democrat on the Natural Resources Subcommittee on Indian, Insular and Native American Affairs, where he explored ways to improve health care and economic growth for Native Americans. He relinquished those assignments when he moved to Energy and Commerce. He warned that Republican plans to replace the Affordable Care Act would adversely and disproportionately affect Latinos.

In 2014, Ruiz was a top target of the National Republican Congressional Committee, which was counting on lower turnout in a midterm election. He benefited from unexpected events that drew extensive local media coverage, including two airplane flights during which he provided emergency service to other passengers. His opponent, Brian Nestande, a Republican Assemblyman and a former top aide to Bono Mack, proved to be a mediocre fundraiser. Ruiz out-spent him $3.1 million to $1.3 million. The NRCC contributed far less money to this contest than to its defense of Bono Mack in 2012. Ruiz won 54%-46%.

Ruiz showed interest in the open seat of retiring Democratic Sen. Barbara Boxer, but deferred to two better-known Democrats. The candidacy of Democratic Rep. Loretta Sanchez limited his opportunity to rally Latino support. In 2016, he was opposed for reelection by Republican state Sen. Jeffrey Stone, who was the former mayor of Temecula. Stone raised $362,000, but the NRCC was more focused on defending its incumbents in California and again spent little money against Ruiz. The outcome was a 62%-38% blowout for Ruiz, who raised $3.2 million and seemed to have taken control of a once-secure Republican seat. Following the election, Ruiz said that he was not interested in appointment to a vacancy on the five-member Board of Supervisors for Riverside County.

Here's a campaign-finance story with a bizarre twist: After actor Sean Penn did an interview for *Rolling Stone* magazine with Mexican drug lord Joaquin (El Chapo) Guzman, who was in hiding, Republicans demanded that Ruiz donate to heroin-treatment clinics the $17,600 in campaign contribution that Penn earlier gave him. "We don't respond to political stunts," said a campaign consultant to Ruiz.

Eastern Riverside County: Indio, Palm Springs

Population		**Race and Ethnicity**		**Income**	
Total	733,025	White	41.7%	Median Income	$45,295 (337 out of 435)
Land area	5,913	Black	4.0%	Under $50,000	27.8%
Pop/ sq mi	124.0	Latino	48.4%	$50,000-$99,999	14.1%
Born in state	54.0%	Asian	3.2%	$100,000-$199,999	3.9%
		Two races	1.8%	$200,000 or more	20.8%
		Other	0.9%	Poverty Rate	20.8%
Age Groups		**Education**		**Health Insurance**	
Under 18	24.5%	H.S grad or less	47.8%	With health insurance coverage	81.9%
18-34	20.7%	Some college	31.9%		
35-64	35.4%	College Degree, 4 yr	12.6%		
Over 64	19.4%	Post grad	7.7%		
Work		**Military**		**Public Assistance**	
White Collar	25.9%	Veteran	9.0%	Cash public assistance income	4.4%
Sales and Service	51.6%	Active Duty	0.1%	Food stamp/SNAP benefits	11.6%
Blue Collar	22.6%				
Government	12.8%				

Voter Turnout			
2015 Total Citizens 18+	458,941	2016 House Turnout as % CVAP	51%
2016 House turnout	232,617	2014 House Turnout as % CVAP	30%

2012 Presidential Vote		
Barack Obama	107,914	(51%)
Mitt Romney	101,156	(48%)

2016 Presidential Vote		
Hillary Clinton	123,795	(52%)
Donald Trump	103,051	(43%)
Gary Johnson	6,172	(3%)

Cook Partisan Voting Index: D+2

From the air a few decades ago, a night flight east from Los Angeles flew over the lights of homes of 10 million people and then into almost perfect darkness. The city then was a vast metropolis surrounded by almost uninhabited territory. Today, the sprinkled pattern of white lights has spread into the Inland Empire around Riverside and San Bernardino and has multiplied outward into the desert. Over the 10,000-foot-high San Jacinto Mountains, desert communities boomed: Palm Springs was once the lone winter resort for the stars but now is popular for its retro architecture and as a destination for gay couples. It is one of a string of communities along Highway 111 and Frank Sinatra and Bob Hope drives. Among rich retirees, the coast's cachet lessened as beach cities filled up with roller-bladers and rent-control crusaders. The clean, dry, roomy desert, where the days are almost always crystal clear and the sky usually cloudless, became more attractive with the prevalence of air-conditioning. Two presidents retired to the desert and its many golf courses here: Dwight Eisenhower wintered in Palm Desert, and Gerald Ford resided for 30 years after his presidency in nearby Rancho Mirage.

The population of 87,500 in the unincorporated areas of the Coachella Valley in 2008 was projected to exceed 300,000 by 2035, chiefly in heavily Latino and fast-growing agricultural cities. The nine cities in the Valley extend from Palm Springs to Coachella. Of its roughly 1 million acres, 700,000 have been designated for conservation, which keeps them mostly pristine. Landholders have the option of getting compensation for their properties at market rates. The area produces roughly 95 percent of the dates consumed in the U.S. The annual music and arts festival in Coachella, which began in 1999, has become one of the leading music festivals in the nation and has drawn the largest revenue. In 2016, it sold out each of its six days of performance during two weekends in April, with daily sales of 99,000. A third weekend for the Stagecoach country music festival attracted 70,000 daily. That brought an estimated

$106 million to the local economy. With its scenic location in the desert and a relatively short drive from Los Angeles, the events draw extensive attention in the entertainment world.

The drought-imposed water restrictions raised concerns in the desert splendor of places like Rancho Mirage, with its cascading waterfalls and significant water usage at many residences. Communities were slow to respond to the state's quotas, though local leaders pointed out that the area sits on a massive aquifer that has been regularly replenished. Tourist growth in the desert has remained strong. In 2015, National Public Radio reported that Palm Springs had evolved to "Mad Men aesthetic," with abundant cocktail parties and vintage fashion. Although the heavy rains during the winter of 2017 were mostly welcomed here, one prominent visitor was inconvenienced: On the day that he left office, former President Barack Obama, with his entourage on the Air Force One plane that he borrowed from his successor Donald Trump, flew west to Palm Springs. But the heavy storms forced them to land 50 miles to the west at March Air Reserve Base in Riverside.

The 36th District covers eastern Riverside County. Interstate 10 runs through the district, taking in Banning and Beaumont on the western side and stretching east to Blythe at the Arizona border. There are huge socio-economic contrasts: Per capita income of $36,000 in Palm Springs is nearly twice that of Indio and three times Coachella. Joshua Tree National Park, with its high-desert sands, is a popular tourist spot here (part of the park spills into the neighboring 8th District). The 36th is the largest and least urban of three congressional districts that are entirely within Riverside. Its Hispanic population has grown to 50 percent. This has been a politically competitive district, though Hillary Clinton's 52%-43% win was three times the margin by which President Barack Obama won each of his two campaigns.

THIRTY-SEVENTH DISTRICT

Karen Bass (D)

Elected 2010, 4th term; b. Oct 03, 1953, Los Angeles; California State University - Dominguez Hills, B.S.; San Diego State University; University of Southern California School of Medicine; Baptist; Divorced; 2 children (1 deceased); 4 stepchildren.

Elected Office: CA Assembly, 2005-2010, speaker, 2008-2010.

Professional Career: Physician's Assistant, Los Angeles County General Hosp.; Instructor, University of S. CA; Executive Director, Community Coalition, 1990-2004.

DC Office: 2241 RHOB 20515, 202-225-7084, Fax: 202-225-2422, bass.house.gov.

State Offices: Los Angeles, 323-965-1422.

Committees: *Foreign Affairs*: Africa, Global Health, Global Human Rights & Internat'l Orgs (RMM). *Judiciary*: Courts, Intellectual Property & Internet, Crime, Terrorism, Homeland Security & Investigations.

Group Ratings

	ADA	ACLU	AFL-CIO	LCV	ITI	COC	HAFA	ACU	CFG	FRC
2016	-	76%	-	95%	33%	54%	13%	0%	1%	0%
2015	95%	C	100%	86%	C	44%	C	0%	0%	9%

Almanac Ratings 2015

	Economy	Social	Foreign	Composite
Liberal	95%	87%	93%	92%
Conservative	5%	14%	7%	8%

Key Votes of the 114th Congress

1. Keystone Pipeline	N	5. Puerto Rico Debt	Y	9. Offenses by Aliens	N
2. Trade Deals	N	6. Medical Marijuana	N	10. Troops in Iraq	Y
3. Export-Import Bank	Y	7. Sanctuary Cities	N	11. Homeland Security $$	NV
4. Debt Ceiling Increase	Y	8. Armor-piercing Bullets	N	12. Trade Adjustment aid	Y

Election Results

Election	Name (Party)	Vote (%)		Cand. Spent	Ind. Exp. Support	Ind. Exp. Oppose
2016 General	Karen Bass (D)	192,490	(81%)	$421,567		
	Chris Wiggins (D)	44,782	(19%)			
2016 Primary	Karen Bass (D)	84,031	(81%)			
	Chris Blake Wiggins (D)	10,288	(10%)			
	Shariff Hasan (R)	9,371	(9%)			

Prior winning percentages: 2014 (84%), 2012 (86%), 2010 (86%)

Karen Bass, elected in 2010, is a former California Assembly speaker and a Democratic up-and-comer who has drawn flattering comparisons to another Californian who once presided as Speaker of the House, Minority Leader Nancy Pelosi. Although she has served only in the minority while in Congress, Bass has shown impressive leadership skills, including on Africa-related legislation and on Democratic Party organization.

Bass was born and raised in Los Angeles. Her father was a letter carrier and her mother was a homemaker. Her father had moved to California from Texas after World War II; her mother was a Los Angeles native who learned to speak Spanish as a child. In middle school, Bass was a student representative on a committee overseeing integration of the school. At age 14, she got involved in Democratic Sen. Robert F. Kennedy's 1968 presidential campaign by signing up her mother as a precinct captain and then doing all the neighborhood canvassing herself. At her high school in West Los Angeles, Bass joined her teachers in protests against the Vietnam War. She attended San Diego State University and stayed active in community organizing. "School wound up being rather secondary for me," she said. Bass served on a committee that investigated accusations of police abuses in Los Angeles.

Bass received a nursing certificate from the University of Southern California and a bachelor's degree from California State University, Dominguez Hills. She was married in 1980 and had a daughter; the couple divorced in 1986. She and her ex-husband cooperated on raising their daughter and four stepchildren. In 2006, her daughter and son-in-law died in a car accident.

In 1990, Bass founded the Community Coalition, a nonprofit that works with African-American and Latino communities in South Los Angeles to combat drug use and gang violence by shutting down liquor stores and motels. The group campaigned against Proposition 187, which sought to deny public services to illegal immigrants, and Proposition 209, which prohibited affirmative action admissions policies in public universities. Bass served as executive director of the organization for 14 years.

Bass won election to the state Assembly in 2004. She sponsored several bills aimed at reforming the state's foster care system and expanding health insurance programs for children. In her first term, she was the majority whip; in her second, she was majority leader; and in her third term, she became the first black female speaker in any state legislature in the United States. Trying to balance California's budget in the midst of a fiscal crisis consumed much of her tenure. She negotiated budget compromises with Gov. Arnold Schwarzenegger that included deep cuts to education and social spending. Bass described her two years as speaker as "painful" and said, "I ran for office because I wanted to create, build, and expand programs, not tear them apart."

When Rep. Diane Watson announced she would retire, she supported Bass as her successor. Other prominent Democrats stayed out of the race, assuming that Bass would easily win on turf she had represented in the Assembly. She won the Democratic primary in 2010 with 85 percent of the vote. In the general election, she got 86 percent against Republican lawyer James Andion.

Bass has taken on leadership assignments. On Foreign Affairs, as the senior Democrat on the Subcommittee on Africa, Global Health, Global Human Rights and International Organizations, her work has included successful efforts to extend the African Growth and Opportunity Act. During the Ebola crisis in 2014, she joined Democratic Reps. Keith Ellison of Minnesota and Barbara Lee of California to urge President Barack Obama to send U.S. troops to care for Ebola patients in west Africa. In 2015, the House passed the bill she introduced with Republican Rep. John Kline of Minnesota, which was designed to connect child victims of trafficking to appropriate services and prevent further exploitation. At home, Bass maintained her advocacy of the poor and disadvantaged. She created the Congressional Caucus on Foster Youth, which she has co-chaired with Republican Rep. Tom Marino of Pennsylvania, and has filed several bills to improve foster care.

Bass has pursued partisan interests. She was made an assistant Democratic whip and became co-chair of the Democratic Congressional Campaign Committee's Women LEAD program, charged with recruiting more female candidates. Colleagues lauded her political skills, and she worked the talk-show circuit to spread the party's message. She has been an active campaign fundraiser, both in Sacramento and in Congress. *Politico* in 2011 named her the freshman Democrat "most likely to succeed" and said she "looks more and more like a (Nancy) Pelosi-in-waiting each day." She has charged that Republican voter identification legislation was aimed at curtailing minorities' voting participation. "One of the darkest shadows of the past century is creeping into this one: one of our most basic rights - the right to vote, a right that we fought for and won - is under attack," she said. In 2015, after an intensive review of House Democratic internal rules, she said that the best way to resolve internal conflicts was to elect more Democrats to the House. "The way to get more opportunities is to get the majority, not to go after each other," she told *The Washington Post*.

In addition to her legislative and political work, Bass drew attention for her avid interest in martial arts. She has brown belts in taekwondo and hapkido, a Korean self-defense technique. She likely won't need those skills to retain this seat.

Western L.A./South L.A., Culver City

Population		**Race and Ethnicity**		**Income**	
Total	719,856	White	24.9%	Median Income	$50,191 (254 out of 435)
Land area	55	Black	23.4%		
Pop/ sq mi	13026.7	Latino	38.1%		
Born in state	47.0%	Asian	10.1%	Under $50,000	26.3%
		Two races	2.7%	$50,000-$99,999	16.8%
Age Groups		Other	0.9%	$100,000-$199,999	7.0%
Under 18	20.2%			$200,000 or more	21.6%
18-34	29.6%	**Education**		Poverty Rate	21.6%
35-64	38.4%	H.S grad or less	37.9%		
Over 64	11.8%	Some college	25.1%	**Health Insurance**	
		College Degree, 4 yr	22.5%	With health insurance coverage	81.0%
Work		Post grad	14.4%		
White Collar	41.1%				
Sales and Service	43.6%	**Military**		**Public Assistance**	
Blue Collar	15.3%	Veteran	3.5%	Cash public assistance income	4.5%
Government	11.2%	Active Duty	0.0%		
				Food stamp/SNAP benefits	9.3%

Voter Turnout			
2015 Total Citizens 18+	446,601	2016 House Turnout as % CVAP	53%
2016 House turnout	237,272	2014 House Turnout as % CVAP	25%

2012 Presidential Vote		
Barack Obama	222,329	(85%)
Mitt Romney	33,307	(13%)

2016 Presidential Vote		
Hillary Clinton	236,621	(85%)
Donald Trump	26,608	(10%)
Jill Stein	6,355	(2%)

Cook Partisan Voting Index: D+37

Since the Los Angeles riots of 1992 and 1965, the city has had to live down its reputation as being inhospitable to African Americans, a problem exacerbated by racial tensions in the city's police department. This was the epicenter of L.A.'s two postwar riots, in the Watts district in 1965 and at the corner of Florence and Normandie in 1992. But by other measures - levels of income and degree of residential integration with non-blacks - blacks in Los Angeles have been doing better than those elsewhere in the United States. According to a 2011 National Urban League report, Los Angeles was the second-best city in the country for black-owned businesses. Job opportunities in Los Angeles - up to and including the office of mayor for 20 years - have been relatively good for blacks. The long-simmering tension between the LAPD and the African-American community has been ameliorated by the region's changing demographics. Former Los Angeles Mayor Antonio Villaraigosa proudly noted that two-thirds of the city's police officers were non-white, though the command staff remained 55 percent white. A less positive side of the story has developed in recent years. Partly due to the high cost of housing, the black population in Los Angeles dropped 12 percent since 2000. Watts has become more than 70 percent

Latino. The city ranked 40th out of 52 cities in the nation in terms of housing and income for blacks, L.A.-based urban-affairs scholar Joel Kotkin wrote.

Baldwin Hills, where on clear days one can see the snow-capped San Gabriel Mountains, is a high-income, African-American neighborhood. Near View Park-Windsor Hills along Slauson Avenue are other comfortable black-majority neighborhoods. Crenshaw, an Art Deco neighborhood built in the 1920s and 1930s, is the birthplace of West Coast hip hop music. In one of the more rundown sections of Crenshaw, former L.A. Lakers basketball star (and current Lakers executive) Magic Johnson built his multiplex theaters. The once desolate Culver City, which features sprawling studios and media businesses, has experienced an urban renaissance and is home to trendy new restaurants and a historically restored Culver Hotel.

These parts of Los Angeles are the heart of the 37th Congressional District, which is bisected by the Santa Monica Freeway. The district encompasses Century City, Ladera Heights, Baldwin Hills and Hyde Park. It includes the University of Southern California, a private university with more than 43,000 students, and the adjacent Los Angeles Memorial Coliseum, which has hosted two Olympics and is where the USC Trojans play football. The former St. Louis Rams returned to L.A. in 2016 and moved into the Coliseum until their gaudy new stadium in Inglewood is completed. Nearby Exposition Park will be the site of a new museum that will house the huge art collection of film-maker George Lucas, who earlier sought to base the museum in the heart of Chicago. The 37th takes in several cultural landmarks, including the California Science Center, the Natural History Museum, and the California African American Museum. The District is about 38 percent Latino and 24 percent black. It is one of the most Democratic districts in the nation. Hillary Clinton got 85 percent of the local vote, which was one point better than President Barack Obama during each of his campaigns.

THIRTY-EIGHTH DISTRICT

Linda Sanchez (D)

Elected 2002, 8th term; b. Jan 28, 1969, Orange; University of California, Los Angeles, J.D.; University of California, Santa Barbara, B.A.; Roman Catholic; Married (James M. Sullivan); 1 child; 3 stepchildren.

Professional Career: Practicing attorney, 1995-1998; Executive Secretary treas. Of Orange County AFL-CIO, 2000-2002.

DC Office: 2329 RHOB 20515, 202-225-6676, Fax: 202-226-1012, lindasanchez.house.gov.

State Offices: Norwalk, 562-860-5050.

Committees: House Democratic Caucus Vice Chairman. *Ways & Means*: Social Security, Tax Policy.

Group Ratings

	ADA	ACLU	AFL-CIO	LCV	ITI	COC	HAFA	ACU	CFG	FRC
2016	-	100%	-	95%	67%	67%	12%	4%	4%	0%
2015	100%	C	95%	100%	C	40%	C	4%	0%	0%

Almanac Ratings 2015

	Economy	Social	Foreign	Composite
Liberal	98%	96%	99%	98%
Conservative	2%	4%	1%	2%

Key Votes of the 114th Congress

1. Keystone Pipeline	N	5. Puerto Rico Debt	Y	9. Offenses by Aliens	N
2. Trade Deals	N	6. Medical Marijuana	Y	10. Troops in Iraq	Y
3. Export-Import Bank	Y	7. Sanctuary Cities	N	11. Homeland Security $$	Y
4. Debt Ceiling Increase	Y	8. Armor-piercing Bullets	N	12. Trade Adjustment aid	Y

Election Results

Election	Name (Party)	Vote (%)		Cand. Spent	Ind. Exp. Support	Ind. Exp. Oppose
2016 General	Linda Sanchez (D)	163,590	(71%)	$1,213,249		
	Ryan Downing (R)	68,524	(30%)			
2016 Primary	Linda Sanchez (D)	64,258	(70%)			
	Ryan Downing (R)	19,452	(21%)			
	Scott Michael Adams (I)	8,129	(9%)			

Prior winning percentages: 2014 (59%), 2012 (68%), 2010 (63%), 2008 (70%), 2006 (66%), 2004 (61%), 2002 (55%)

Linda Sánchez, first elected in 2002, has become the newest member of the Democratic leadership, with promises for a younger and outspoken voice. As a member of the Ways and Means Committee, she has been a defender of the Affordable Care Act. Her sister Loretta Sánchez ran unsuccessfully in 2016 for the Senate after having served for 20 years in the House from an Orange County district.

The sisters are two of the seven children of Mexican immigrant parents Ignacio Sánchez, a machinist, and Maria Macias, a bilingual education aide in an elementary school. Their parents met while trying to organize a union at a tire shop where they worked when they were young. Linda Sánchez earned her bachelor's degree in Spanish literature at the University of California, Berkeley, and her law degree at the University of California, Los Angeles, working her way through school with jobs as a security guard, nanny and teacher's aide. She became a civil rights lawyer and was executive secretary-treasurer of the Orange County Federation of Labor. "She's definitely the more liberal one," Loretta said. She's also considered the funnier one. Sanchez has won kudos from Washington insiders for her routines at the D.C. Improv, a professional comedy club that often features members of Congress.

When the new district lines were unveiled after the 2000 census, Linda Sánchez was one of six Democrats who ran for the seat. Her most important asset was her sister's support. She tapped Loretta's extensive fundraising network, walked precincts with her, and appeared in a television commercial with her. In a Spanish ad, their mother urged voters to send both of her daughters to Capitol Hill. These connections gave Linda Sánchez an advantage over her two chief opponents, who were better known when the race began: Assemblywoman Sally Havice and South Gate Councilman Hector De La Torre. The three candidates differed very little on the issues.

Sánchez's ties to labor helped her build a strong voter-turnout operation. She won the endorsement of then-House Minority Whip Nancy Pelosi of California. Her opponents noted that no Latino members of Congress endorsed Sánchez, and they charged that she was a political opportunist who changed her name and residence to run in the newly created district. She won the primary with 33 percent of the vote; De La Torre received 29 percent and Havice had 19 percent. In November, Republican Tim Escobar, a financial adviser and former Army helicopter pilot, called her an inexperienced liberal extremist. Sánchez won 55%-41%, and she has been reelected easily since.

Sánchez has a strongly liberal voting record. In the *Almanac* vote ratings for 2015, her scores ranked among the most liberal on economic and foreign issues. She has sponsored bills to end the Social Security Administration's policy to deny benefits to same-sex couples and to establish a federal definition of school bullying to protect vulnerable students, including those who have been targeted because of their sexual orientation. She can be quick to use her sharp tongue against political foes. In 2011, bloggers on the right derided her for saying on MSNBC that a potential government shutdown would hurt her financially. "I have to tell you that I live paycheck-to-paycheck, like most Americans," Sánchez said. "I'm still paying off my student loans. I have a 2-year-old son who I have to support, and I have to maintain residences on both coasts."

When Democrats held the majority, Sánchez chaired the Judiciary Subcommittee on Commercial and Administrative Law, where she held hearings to oversee allegations that the George W. Bush administration had initiated politically motivated firings of U.S. attorneys around the country. After senior White House political adviser Karl Rove refused to cooperate, Sánchez initiated a contempt of Congress action. The House dropped its lawsuit against him when Rove capitulated in March 2009. As the top Democrat on the Ethics Committee, she was at the center of several thorny cases. Later, as co-founder of the House Trade Working Group, Sánchez pledged tougher review of proposed international trade deals that she feared would ship jobs overseas. She helped to lead opposition to the Trans-Pacific Partnership agreement.

Following the 2016 election, Sánchez became the first woman of color elected to the Democratic leadership. She cited her background as a working mother in the contest for Caucus vice chair with Rep.

Barbara Lee, also of California, which she won 98-96. "My role in the next four years is to be as vocal an advocate as I can for what my constituents want and need, and I will put myself in Donald Trump's path at every turn to confront him about these issues," Sánchez told *The Los Angeles Times*. "My goal is to be front and center. … I'm going to be the biggest pain in the neck that I can be." She said that Democrats would work with Republicans if they wanted to "fine tune" the Affordable Care Act, but not if "they want to dismantle real progress for working families."

Her husband, James Sullivan, drew attention for possible conflicts of interest as a lobbyist and former chairman of the Connecticut Municipal Electric Energy Cooperative. In January 2017, he told the New London *Day* newspaper that he was under investigation by the FBI. Sánchez got advice from the Ethics Committee before attending related events as his spouse, according to her spokesman.

Eastern L.A. suburbs: Whittier, Norwalk

Population		**Race and Ethnicity**		**Income**	
Total	717,038	White	17.5%	Median Income	$61,842 (122 out of 435)
Land area	101	Black	3.8%		
Pop/ sq mi	7067.2	Latino	61.6%		
Born in state	59.9%	Asian	14.9%	Under $50,000	32.8%
		Two races	1.4%	$50,000-$99,999	22.7%
Age Groups		Other	0.8%	$100,000-$199,999	4.2%
Under 18	23.9%			$200,000 or more	12.6%
18-34	24.7%	**Education**		Poverty Rate	12.6%
35-64	38.4%	H.S grad or less	47.9%		
Over 64	13.0%	Some college	30.6%	**Health Insurance**	
Work		College Degree, 4 yr	14.7%	With health insurance coverage	82.8%
White Collar	30.3%	Post grad	6.8%		
Sales and Service	45.7%	**Military**		**Public Assistance**	
Blue Collar	24.0%	Veteran	4.7%	Cash public assistance income	4.1%
Government	14.7%	Active Duty	0.0%	Food stamp/SNAP benefits	8.0%

Voter Turnout			
2015 Total Citizens 18+	455,186	2016 House Turnout as % CVAP	51%
2016 House turnout	232,114	2014 House Turnout as % CVAP	21%

2012 Presidential Vote		
Barack Obama	149,141	(65%)
Mitt Romney	75,780	(33%)

2016 Presidential Vote		
Hillary Clinton	166,224	(67%)
Donald Trump	68,033	(27%)
Gary Johnson	6,730	(3%)
Jill Stein	5,055	(2%)

Cook Partisan Voting Index: D+17

In the years just after World War II, much of southeast Los Angeles County was farmland - citrus groves and dairy farms. In the next two decades, housing subdivisions were built and new cities incorporated so that what had been a few towns separated by farmland became one continuous swath of suburbia. The towns were different in character. Whittier, founded by Midwestern Quakers, was the hometown of Richard Nixon, a young lawyer who decided to run for Congress in 1946. Lakewood, just north of Long Beach, used to be an area of lima bean fields. Developers built it up so rapidly in the 1950s that *Life* magazine featured it as one of the first mass-produced suburbs. Other towns were late-bloomers. There were still dairy farms in Cerritos in the 1970s, though few remain now.

Most of these communities are known as Gateway Cities in southeast Los Angeles County: Artesia, which Dutch and Portuguese dairy experts developed into a major dairy center for Southern California; Pico Rivera, which is 91 percent Hispanic; and La Mirada, named by Rand McNally Publishing founder Andrew McNally when he purchased 2,300 acres in the area in the late 1800s. After World War II, Montebello became a center of the large community of displaced Armenians. They built a monument to the Armenian genocide martyrs. In the northern part of Montebello, a few miles from downtown Los

Angeles, Southern California Gas Co. has a few dozen wells that produce oil and natural gas; as recently as the 1990s, some leaked onto nearby properties. Officials of the L.A. Metro planned to extend their light-rail Green Line from Norwalk to connect it with the transit station to LAX Airport, which could become a commuter alternative to the crowded freeways.

Montebello is home to blimp-maker Worldwide Aeros Corp. The company's original plan for a new engineering facility to build a 120-mph aircraft to carry cargo loads for the military failed in 2013 when a large section of the ceiling collapsed and damaged the experimental aircraft. Instead, the company dedicated a smaller version of the Goodyear blimp, a commercial airship that was designed for use in advertising, tourism, surveillance or to move cargo. In July 2015, the company unveiled a new model at the Paris Air Show that could travel at 90 miles per hour, with a cost of $40 million. It was uncertain whether the vehicle would be commercially successful.

The 38th Congressional District encompasses Whittier and some of the Gateway Cities in southeast Los Angeles County. It extends from outside of Monterey Park nearly to Long Beach. It includes Norwalk, which is 70 percent Hispanic and the district's largest city, South El Monte, Montebello and a small northern tip of Orange County. The 38th is 62 percent Hispanic and solidly Democratic. Hillary Clinton got 67 percent of the vote in 2016, a significant increase from the 62 percent for Barack Obama in 2008.

THIRTY-NINTH DISTRICT

Ed Royce (R)

Elected 1992, 13th term; b. Oct 12, 1951, Los Angeles; California State University Fullerton, B.A.; Roman Catholic; Married (Marie Therese Porter Royce).

Elected Office: CA Senate, 1983-1992.

Professional Career: Tax Manager, 1979-1982.

DC Office: 2310 RHOB 20515, 202-225-4111, Fax: 202-226-0335, royce.house.gov.

State Offices: Brea, 714-255-0101; Rowland Heights, 626-964-5123.

Committees: *Financial Services*: Financial Institutions & Consumer Credit, Housing & Insurance. *Foreign Affairs (Chmn)*: Africa, Global Health, Global Human Rights & Internat'l Orgs, Asia & the Pacific, Europe, Eurasia & Emerging Threats, Middle East & North Africa, Terrorism, Nonproliferation & Trade, Western Hemisphere.

Group Ratings

	ADA	ACLU	AFL-CIO	LCV	ITI	COC	HAFA	ACU	CFG	FRC
2016	-	5%	-	5%	100%	100%	58%	88%	89%	100%
2015	0%	C	8%	0%	C	95%	C	83%	70%	92%

Almanac Ratings 2015

	Economy	Social	Foreign	Composite
Liberal	10%	14%	10%	12%
Conservative	90%	86%	90%	89%

Key Votes of the 114th Congress

1. Keystone Pipeline	Y	5. Puerto Rico Debt	Y	9. Offenses by Aliens	Y
2. Trade Deals	Y	6. Medical Marijuana	N	10. Troops in Iraq	N
3. Export-Import Bank	N	7. Sanctuary Cities	Y	11. Homeland Security $$	Y
4. Debt Ceiling Increase	Y	8. Armor-piercing Bullets	Y	12. Trade Adjustment aid	Y

Election Results

Election	Name (Party)	Vote (%)		Cand. Spent	Ind. Exp. Support	Ind. Exp. Oppose
2016 General	Ed Royce (R)	150,777	(57%)	$3,435,733		
	Brett Murdock (D)	112,679	(43%)	$74,804		
2016 Primary	Ed Royce (R)	85,035	(61%)			
	Brett Murdock (D)	55,520	(40%)			

Prior winning percentages: 2014 (69%), 2012 (58%), 2010 (67%), 2008 (63%), 2006 (67%), 2004 (68%), 2002 (68%), 2000 (63%), 1998 (63%), 1996 (63%), 1994 (66%), 1992 (57%)

Ed Royce, a Republican first elected in 1992, is a hawkish conservative and fervent supporter of free trade. As chairman of the House Foreign Affairs Committee, he actively asserted those views and sought to influence legislative actions and the policy debate. Often, he was at odds with President Barack Obama. With the political shifts in his district, Royce took a cautious approach with President Donald Trump.

Royce's profile almost precisely spans Orange County's. He grew up in Fullerton and belonged to the conservative Young Americans for Freedom at Cal State Fullerton. He was later the head of Youth for Reagan in California during Reagan's 1976 presidential primary challenge to Gerald Ford. Royce worked several years as a tax and capital projects manager for a cement company. In 1982, a group of conservative state legislators known as the "Cave Men" took him to a Black Angus restaurant - no avocado-and-sprout sandwiches for them - and persuaded him to run for the state Senate. He won at age 31. When the legislature refused to pass Royce's bill allowing crime victims to object to trial delays, giving grand juries more power and ending "jury-shopping," he got the measure on the ballot as an initiative and it passed by a wide margin. He wrote the first law making it a felony to stalk someone. In 1992, Royce ran for an open seat in a district where President George H.W. Bush had won with 66 percent of the vote in 1988. With the blessing of Orange County Republican leaders, he was unopposed in the primary and won the general, 57%-38%. He has been reelected by wide margins since.

In the House, Royce has a conservative voting record, and he has been a faithful fundraiser for Republicans. That helped him to prevail over New Jersey Rep. Chris Smith in taking the helm at Foreign Affairs in 2013. As chairman, he pursued aggressive oversight of President Barack Obama and his administration. He blasted what he called Obama's "unimaginative and moribund" handling of North Korea, and endorsed an alternative approach of cutting off money so that "the regime collapses." In February 2016, Royce enacted a bill that further tightened sanctions on North Korea. He called Iran's quest to attain nuclear weapons "a grave threat that demands constant attention and great pressure on Tehran." In April 2015, Royce voiced deep reservations about the agreement that Secretary of State John Kerry had reached with Iran. "I think when the ayatollah is calling for death to the little Satan, death to Israel, he's also calling for death to America, death to the great Satan," he said in an interview with PBS. When it was revealed that the United States subsequently delivered $1.7 billion to Iran as part of the release of American prisoners in Iran that accompanied completion of the nuclear deal, an angry Royce demanded that Kerry explain the payment of "ransom." Following the 2016 election, he sponsored a bill to extend U.S. sanctions against Iran until 2026. In an unusual procedure, the bill automatically became law after Obama took no action within 10 days.

In 2014, Royce pressed for legislation providing aid to Ukraine while imposing sanctions on Russia. He called for more exports of American natural gas to Europe to compete with Russia in those markets. "Until we do something decisive on energy policy, until we have a strategy and a policy that actually is something that the Russians would really worry about long term, we don't have that hammer," Royce said.

He developed a good working relationship with New York's Eliot Engel, the committee's ranking Democrat. Both are strong supporters of Israel. They have issued numerous joint news releases, and they appeared together in a 2014 CNN interview to call for greater action against the Islamic State. Royce sought to develop closer ties with the Senate Foreign Relations Committee, saying on his blog, "It doesn't make a lot of sense to pass legislation in the House with little Senate support." Despite that logic, senators often respond to different public-relations imperatives, especially on international issues.

During Republican control of the House prior to 2007, Royce chaired the Subcommittee on Africa. Although he had never set foot in Africa, he was widely praised for getting up to speed on the issues. He was instrumental in getting bipartisan support to enact an Africa free trade bill. He was among the sponsors of a bipartisan bill in 2009 requiring Obama to develop a comprehensive plan to end the brutal two-decade war in Uganda.

In 2011, he became chairman of the Terrorism, Nonproliferation, and Trade Subcommittee, where he focused on the spread of radical Islam. He won enactment of a bill establishing Radio Free Afghanistan and another measure to promote nuclear nonproliferation in North Korea. He helped win the release of two journalists from a North Korean prison in 2009. He urged stronger strategic and trade relationships between the United States and India, and condemned discrimination against Hindus in Pakistan, Bangladesh and Bhutan. Royce was a vocal critic of the Obama administration's approach to immigration, calling for tighter enforcement of existing laws rather than enactment of new ones.

On the Financial Services Committee, he worked with Democrats to expand lending authority for credit unions and to put them on an equivalent status with banks, something that put him at odds with most Republicans, who aligned more closely with the banking industry. He enacted a bill in 2014 that expanded federal deposit insurance to include interest on lawyer trust accounts and similar escrow accounts housed within credit unions. During conference committee negotiations on the 2010 financial industry overhaul, he tried without success to persuade conferees to make major changes to government-backed mortgage giants Fannie Mae and Freddie Mac, arguing that reshaping the oft-criticized institutions was crucial to any reform effort. His *Almanac* vote ratings in 2015 ranked him toward the center of House Republicans.

Throughout his House career, Royce has been blessed with a solidly GOP district where, unlike other California Republicans, he has not had to worry about primaries or new voters. In 2016, Democratic challenger Brett Murdock had an impressive bio: a lawyer in private practice, American government instructor at Cal State Fullerton, member of the Brea city council and mayor in 2014. His political record had some downsides: In 2014, he ran fourth in the Brea council contest in which the top three were elected. Murdock was weakly funded against Royce with $79,000 to $4.5 million. But he held Royce to 57%-43%, his lowest share since he was first elected. Royce showed hesitation about Donald Trump during the 2016 campaign. The FiveThirtyEight website listed him with elected Republicans who supported Trump without naming him.

Eyeing the 2016 results after the election, Democrats designated Royce as a GOP incumbent primed for a serious challenge in 2018. They could test whether his political career has come full circle with the political changes in Orange County. Royce backed the travel ban on refugees that Trump issued a week after his inauguration. "Pausing the intake of refugees from terror hot spots is the right call to keep America safe," Royce said, with the caveat that cases of individuals who were traveling with U.S. visas should be resolved quickly.

Northern Orange County: Fullerton, Yorba Linda

Population		**Race and Ethnicity**		**Income**	
Total	722,109	White	32.0%	Median Income	$79,814 (35 out of 435)
Land area	204	Black	2.2%		
Pop/ sq mi	3532.8	Latino	33.6%	Under $50,000	30.4%
Born in state	53.1%	Asian	29.4%	$50,000-$99,999	29.2%
		Two races	2.2%	$100,000-$199,999	9.7%
Age Groups		Other	0.5%	$200,000 or more	10.4%
Under 18	22.5%			Poverty Rate	10.4%
18-34	23.7%	**Education**			
35-64	40.7%	H.S grad or less	30.1%	**Health Insurance**	
Over 64	13.1%	Some college	30.2%	With health insurance coverage	86.6%
		College Degree, 4 yr	26.5%		
Work		Post grad	13.1%		
White Collar	42.4%			**Public Assistance**	
Sales and Service	42.7%	**Military**		Cash public assistance income	2.3%
Blue Collar	14.9%	Veteran	4.9%		
Government	13.3%	Active Duty	0.0%	Food stamp/SNAP benefits	5.0%

Voter Turnout			
2015 Total Citizens 18+	470,646	2016 House Turnout as % CVAP	56%
2016 House turnout	263,456	2014 House Turnout as % CVAP	28%

2012 Presidential Vote		
Mitt Romney	133,742	(51%)
Barack Obama	124,108	(47%)

2016 Presidential Vote		
Hillary Clinton	140,231	(51%)
Donald Trump	116,783	(43%)
Gary Johnson	9,850	(4%)

Cook Partisan Voting Index: EVEN

During the Southern California land boom in the 1880s, Massachusetts grain merchants George and Edward Amerige headed west in search of new business opportunities. They went on a duck hunting trip near Anaheim and eventually opened a real estate business in the city. Through negotiations with railroad agent George Fullerton, the Ameriges eventually purchased 430 acres of land for $68,000 and allowed the railroad the right-of-way - provided, of course, that the railway's route include the new town they were developing. Local residents later voted to name the locale Fullerton, and it developed as a prime source of juicy Valencia oranges.

Today, the city is home to California State University, Fullerton, which enrolls more than 40,000 students and has the largest business school in the state. Following a challenge by the American Civil Liberties Union and an Asian-American civil rights group, voters in November 2016 approved a referendum that replaced the at-large voting system with five districts for the city council in Fullerton, where the population was 34 percent Hispanic and 23 percent Asian. Nearby is affluent Yorba Linda, which has a median household income of $118,000 and is one of the wealthiest cities in the nation. In May 2015, voters defeated recall petitions to remove the mayor and a council member who supported high-density residential development. But two Yorba Linda council members were recalled in November 2016 following voter protests over a scheduled 380 percent increase in water rates over five years, which the council had approved unanimously; a third board member lost reelection, and a fourth did not seek another term.

The 39th Congressional District of California is based in northern Orange County and includes the southeast corner of Los Angeles County and the southwest corner of San Bernardino County. More than two-thirds of the voters are in Orange County. In San Bernardino, it includes part of Chino, which had been the site of a large youth prison. It also has large meatpacking plants, whose smell can carry across the valley on a windy day, and Chino Hills, incorporated in 1991 and full of subdivisions for commuters who battle the heavy traffic on Interstate 5. In Los Angeles County, the 39th includes La Habra Heights and Diamond Bar, which is almost 53 percent Asian. The Orange County section takes in parts of Anaheim. Yorba Linda is the birthplace of President Richard Nixon and the site of his presidential library.

Only 40,000 people lived in Orange County in 1913 when Nixon was born; 3.2 million live there today. The district is 35 percent Hispanic and 31 percent Asian. Politically, the 39th has included some of the few remaining areas of Los Angeles County that elect a Republican. That has been changing. Hillary Clinton led Donald Trump in the district, 51%-43%, and she ran even better in the L.A. County portion. Republican presidential nominees edged Barack Obama with 50 and 51 percent in 2008 and 2012.

FORTIETH DISTRICT

Lucille Roybal-Allard (D)

Elected 1992, 13th term; b. Jun 12, 1941, Boyle Heights; California State University, Los Angeles, B.A.; Catholic; Married (Edward T. Allard III); 2 children; 2 stepchildren; 9 grandchildren.

Elected Office: CA Assembly, 1987-1992.

Professional Career: Community relations; Nonprofit Executive.

DC Office: 2083 RHOB 20515, 202-225-1766, Fax: 202-226-0350, roybal-allard.house.gov.

State Offices: Commerce, 323-721-8790.

Committees: *Appropriations*: Homeland Security (RMM), Labor, Health & Human Services, Education & Related Agencies.

Group Ratings

	ADA	ACLU	AFL-CIO	LCV	ITI	COC	HAFA	ACU	CFG	FRC
2016	-	94%	-	100%	67%	57%	14%	0%	0%	0%
2015	100%	C	100%	100%	C	40%	C	0%	0%	0%

Almanac Ratings 2015

	Economy	Social	Foreign	Composite
Liberal	98%	95%	93%	95%
Conservative	2%	5%	7%	5%

Key Votes of the 114th Congress

1. Keystone Pipeline	N	5. Puerto Rico Debt	Y	9. Offenses by Aliens	N
2. Trade Deals	N	6. Medical Marijuana	Y	10. Troops in Iraq	Y
3. Export-Import Bank	Y	7. Sanctuary Cities	N	11. Homeland Security $$	Y
4. Debt Ceiling Increase	Y	8. Armor-piercing Bullets	N	12. Trade Adjustment aid	Y

Election Results

Election	Name (Party)	Vote (%)	Cand. Spent	Ind. Exp. Support	Ind. Exp. Oppose
2016 General	Lucille Roybal-Allard (D)............	106,554 (71%)	$434,844		
	Roman Gabriel Gonzalez (I)..........	24,743 (19%)			
2016 Primary	Lucille Roybal-Allard (D).............	60,691 (76%)			
	Roman Gabriel Gonzalez (I)..........	18,844 (24%)			

Prior winning percentages: 2014 (61%), 2012 (59%), 2010 (77%), 2008 (77%), 2006 (77%), 2004 (75%), 2002 (74%), 2000 (85%), 1998 (87%), 1996 (82%), 1994 (82%), 1992 (63%)

Lucille Roybal-Allard, first elected in 1992, was the first Mexican-American woman to be elected to Congress. Immigration reform is one of her main priorities, along with social programs serving the poor. As ranking Democrat on the Appropriations Subcommittee on Homeland Security, she was well-positioned to protect funding for that federal agency and work on immigration issues, though she maintained a low-profile approach.

Roybal-Allard grew up in the Los Angeles area, the daughter of longtime Democratic Rep. Edward Roybal, who was the first Latino to serve on the Los Angeles City Council and became a founder of the Congressional Hispanic Caucus. She dreamed of a show business career as a teenager and later worked as a department store clerk and for nonprofit organizations. After raising a family - two of her children are lawyers - she followed her father into politics when she was 45 years old. She was elected to the California Assembly in 1986. Six years later he retired from the House, and she ran for the seat in a district that took in much of the territory he had represented for 30 years. Roybal-Allard won easily with 75 percent of the vote in the primary and 63 percent in the general election.

Roybal-Allard has compiled a solidly liberal voting record and was among the Hispanic lawmakers pushing President Barack Obama to act boldly on immigration reform. One session between lawmakers and Obama domestic policy adviser Cecilia Munoz grew so testy that Roybal-Allard walked out, *The Washington Post* reported in April 2012. She called Obama's reelection a mandate to focus on a comprehensive immigration overhaul, predicting that opponents would revive "the usual scare tactics, misinformation, and misguided thinking. … But the truth is that the facts are on our side, the majority of Americans are on our side and the momentum is on our side."

For the Obama presidency, she was proven incorrect. With the Republican takeover of Congress, and later the presidency, Roybal-Allard's role on immigration became increasingly defensive in seeking to hold the line. When Republicans in March 2015 sought to use the Homeland Security appropriations bill to restrict Obama's executive actions, she became more visible and vocal in what was becoming a fight against increased deportations of those in the country illegally.

She has a long history of advocacy for immigrants of all sorts. Among the immigration-related bills Roybal-Allard has introduced has been the Help Separated Families Act to ensure that children are not taken away from relatives because of a parent's immigration status, including deportation. When Senate Finance Committee Democrats proposed restrictions on illegal immigrants participating in health care programs as part of the 2010 overhaul, she joined a group of Hispanics who succeeded in modifying the provision. She was an early co-sponsor of the DREAM Act, which would provide a path to legal status for college- or military-bound students. During Obama's final weeks in office, she requested that he issue a blanket pardon to the estimated 750,000 Dreamers. The official White House response was, "Only Congress can create legal status for undocumented individuals."

Roybal-Allard has pushed for in-state college tuition rates for illegal immigrants. She has filed legislation aimed at raising labor standards and protections for children of migrant farm workers to the same level as occupations outside of agriculture. When Obama in November 2014 posthumously gave the Presidential Medal of Freedom to her father, she recalled his success in working on bipartisan terms, including with Republican presidents, on behalf of undocumented immigrants.

As a member of the Appropriations Committee, Roybal-Allard championed a new federal courthouse in Los Angeles. In October 2016, the $350 million building officially opened with 24 courtrooms and chambers for 32 judges. "We knew building a new courthouse would be a multi-year project, but we had no idea of the many obstacles we would face and how many years the project would actually take," she said at the ribbon-cutting ceremony. She got a bill signed into law to coordinate federal programs and research on underage drinking, and to fund a media campaign on its dangers. Another success was a new law in 2008 that authorized federal grants for newborn health screening for congenital, genetic and metabolic disorders.

Roybal-Allard isn't as close to Minority Leader Nancy Pelosi and her inner circle as have been other Democratic women from California, which sometimes limits her leverage in the House. In 2006, Roybal-Allard seconded the nomination of Steny Hoyer of Maryland for majority leader, in opposition to Pelosi's preferred candidate, John Murtha of Pennsylvania. Hoyer won the contest, so Roybal-Allard retained a friend in high places.

At home in 2012, under the state's new top-two, all-party primary rules, Roybal-Allard found herself with a Democratic challenger, college instructor David Sanchez. He held her to 59 percent of the vote, her lowest ever. They faced each other again in 2014, when she won, 61%-39%. Sanchez did not report spending any campaign money in either contest. In 2016, her only opponent, Roman Gonzalez, had no party preference or funding. This time, Roybal-Allard won with 71 percent.

Eastern Los Angeles: Bell Gardens, Downey

Population		**Race and Ethnicity**		**Income**	
Total	709,734	White	4.9%	Median Income	$40,385 (397 out of 435)
Land area	58	Black	4.7%		
Pop/ sq mi	12302.5	Latino	87.4%		
Born in state	53.5%	Asian	2.3%	Under $50,000	28.0%
		Two races	0.4%	$50,000-$99,999	10.5%
Age Groups		Other	0.4%	$100,000-$199,999	1.4%
Under 18	30.0%			$200,000 or more	27.8%
18-34	27.2%	**Education**		Poverty Rate	27.8%
35-64	35.2%	H.S grad or less	71.7%		
Over 64	7.6%	Some college	19.4%	**Health Insurance**	
		College Degree, 4 yr	6.7%	With health insurance coverage	72.5%
Work		Post grad	2.2%		
White Collar	15.6%				
Sales and Service	45.7%	**Military**		**Public Assistance**	
Blue Collar	38.7%	Veteran	1.9%	Cash public assistance income	7.3%
Government	8.9%	Active Duty	0.0%		
				Food stamp/SNAP benefits	18.4%

Voter Turnout			
2015 Total Citizens 18+	306,875	2016 House Turnout as % CVAP	49%
2016 House turnout	149,297	2014 House Turnout as % CVAP	16%

2012 Presidential Vote		
Barack Obama	115,637	(82%)
Mitt Romney	23,446	(17%)

2016 Presidential Vote		
Hillary Clinton	135,472	(82%)
Donald Trump	21,077	(13%)
Jill Stein	3,805	(2%)

Cook Partisan Voting Index: D+33

East Los Angeles is a piece of Latin America transplanted to California. Hard-working immigrants from Mexico and also from Central and South America come to find affordable housing, doubling and tripling up with other families in places that are close enough to drive an old car to work in factories and warehouses south and east of downtown Los Angeles. The Gold Line extension of L.A.'s transit agency made their commutes considerably easier by bringing light rail service to the area. This part of Los Angeles includes the 1940s working-class suburb of Huntington Park, with its shopping strip on the wide Pacific Boulevard, plus Bell Gardens, Downey and Maywood, all of which are now predominantly Latino. Each calls itself a "sanctuary city" for illegal immigrants, as do both the city and county of Los Angeles.

This area, which already was struggling to make ends meet and suffering the consequences of other malfeasance, took a brutal hit from the recession. After Maywood laid off all but one of its public workers in 2010 and arranged for its city services to be performed by outsourced contractors, its plan for collaboration with neighboring Bell fell apart because of that city's corruption. Bell residents threw the bums out when they discovered that their city manager was paid an annual salary of $787,000 and their police chief $457,000; both resigned their posts. Both pleaded guilty to corruption charges and were sentenced in 2014, as did several other former city officials. His successors said that taxpayers of the impoverished city continued to pay a "Rizzo tax," named for former city manager Robert Rizzo. Maywood, meanwhile, was struggling in 2016 with $16 million in debt in its square-mile community. Cudahy also has been scandal-plagued; three city officials arrested on bribery charges in 2012 reached a plea deal, amid continuing investigations of corruption. Somewhat more affluent Bellflower, once a prime shopping area, has made a comeback with multiple shopping centers. Downey is home to Raytheon's Public Safety Regional Technology Center, which won a contract to upgrade Los Angeles County's emergency dispatch system. In more cosmic terms, Downey is home to the world's oldest surviving McDonald's hamburgers site; it was started by Dick and Mac McDonald in 1948 and featured golden arches.

These are all communities in the 40th Congressional District of California, radiating south from East Los Angeles and downtown L.A. Bisecting much of the district is the concrete-lined Los Angeles River. Environmentalists have pushed the city for years to clean it up and return it to a more natural condition, with adjacent parkland and bicycle paths, while preserving its flood-control assets. In November 2016, county voters overwhelmingly approved a $1 billion plan for an 11-mile restoration that was designed to dig up the cement and restore the river, and create an urban greenway from Glendale to downtown with additional land the city had purchased. The 40th District also takes in Paramount, where local businessmen Frank and Lawrence Zamboni invented refrigeration technology for the dairy industry and the Zamboni ice-resurfacing machine for skating rinks. With an 88 percent (and climbing) Latino population, and 41 percent foreign-born, this has become the most Hispanic district in California. Its 82 percent vote for Hillary Clinton in 2016 was only her fourth-best district in the L.A. area.

FORTY-FIRST DISTRICT

Mark Takano (D)

Elected 2012, 3rd term; b. Dec 10, 1960, Riverside; Harvard College (MA), B.A.; School of Education, University of California, Riverside, M.F.A.; Methodist; Single.

Elected Office: Board of Trustees, Riverside Commissioner Col. District, 1990-2012, President, 1992, 1997-198, 2005-2006.

Professional Career: Teacher, Rialto Unified School District, 1988-2013; Substitute teacher, Boston, 1984-1985.

DC Office: 1507 LHOB 20515, 202-225-2305, Fax: 202-225-7018, takano.house.gov.

State Offices: Riverside, 951-222-0203.

Committees: *Education & the Workforce*: Higher Education & Workforce Development, Workforce Protections (RMM). *Science, Space & Technology*: Energy. *Veterans' Affairs*: Economic Opportunity, Health.

Group Ratings

	ADA	ACLU	AFL-CIO	LCV	ITI	COC	HAFA	ACU	CFG	FRC
2016	-	100%	-	100%	33%	64%	14%	0%	4%	0%
2015	100%	C	100%	100%	C	35%	C	4%	2%	0%

Almanac Ratings 2015

	Economy	Social	Foreign	Composite
Liberal	99%	100%	100%	99%
Conservative	2%	0%	0%	1%

Key Votes of the 114th Congress

1. Keystone Pipeline	N	5. Puerto Rico Debt	Y	9. Offenses by Aliens	N
2. Trade Deals	N	6. Medical Marijuana	Y	10. Troops in Iraq	Y
3. Export-Import Bank	Y	7. Sanctuary Cities	N	11. Homeland Security $$	Y
4. Debt Ceiling Increase	Y	8. Armor-piercing Bullets	N	12. Trade Adjustment aid	Y

Election Results

Election	Name (Party)	Vote (%)	Cand. Spent	Ind. Exp. Support	Ind. Exp. Oppose
2016 General	Mark Takano (D)	128,164 (65%)	$791,011	$11,788	
	Doug Shepherd (R)	69,159 (35%)	$250,678		
2016 Primary	Mark Takano (D)	36,700 (63%)			
	Doug Shepherd (R)	10,864 (19%)			
	Randy Fox (R)	9,157 (16%)			

Prior winning percentages: 2014 (57%), 2012 (59%)

Political newcomer Mark Takano, a Democrat elected in 2012, brought his experience as an inner-city schoolteacher, and he has shown dexterity on social media in pursuing education issues. He is the first openly gay person of a racial minority - "gaysian," as he jokingly describes himself -- to hold a seat in Congress.

Born and raised in Riverside, Takano grew up in a self-described "typical Japanese-American family" with a strong emphasis on education, self-reliance and public service. In his youth, he played junior football. He was fascinated by politics and remembers watching as a boy the televised Watergate hearings of the House Judiciary Committee, entranced by the opening remarks of Democratic Rep. Barbara Jordan of Texas. He got his bachelor's in government from Harvard University. He was planning to go to law school but decided instead to try teaching, taking a job as a substitute teacher in the Boston area. The diverse region gave him the experience of working in wealthier districts like Brookline and also inner-city schools. He returned to school to get a teaching certificate, and took a job as an English and social studies teacher at the Rialto Unified School District. In 1990, Takano was elected to the Riverside Community College District's Board of Trustees. He became the board's longest-serving member, spending two separate terms as the board's president.

Takano made a bid for an open House seat in 1992 but lost to Republican Ken Calvert in one of the closest elections in California history. Calvert defeated him by a double-digit margin in 1994. He jokingly calls the ensuing time his "wilderness years," when he traveled to foreign countries while continuing to teach. Takano stayed active in his community, with roles on the California Community College Trustees board and the Board of the Chancellor's Asian Pacific Islander Community Advisory Center at the University of California, Riverside.

In 2012, he ran in the redrawn 41st District in California's jungle primary. Republican John Tavaglione, a veteran Riverside County supervisor, came in first with 45 percent of the vote and Takano second, with 37 percent. The district leans Democratic, giving Takano an edge in the general election. Tavaglione had worked with Democrats in Riverside County, and he slightly outperformed Takano in fundraising. Tavaglione took some moderate positions, declining to sign conservative activist Grover Norquist's "no new taxes" pledge. Takano ran as a populist, attacking lobbyists and oil and insurance companies. He stressed job creation, job training and education reform. Neither candidate received much party financing. In the much higher turnout election in November, Takano won 59%-41%. Takano said that he hoped his victory would be a breakthrough for LGBT rights.

Takano cited his teaching experience as integral to his membership on the Education and the Workforce Committee. He worked with other House Democrats to form a Public Education Caucus, which protested the lack of public school experience for Betsy DeVos, whom President Donald Trump chose as his Education Secretary. Takano spent six months as the acting ranking minority member of the Veterans Affairs Committee after Democratic Rep. Corrine Brown of Florida was indicted and forced to step aside in July 2016. In January 2017, he yielded the position to Rep. Tim Walz of Minnesota, who was more senior in the House and had deep experience in the military. Takano became the number-two ranking member on the Veterans panel, and the ranking Democrat on the Workforce Protection Subcommittee at Education and the Workforce. He offered a creative proposal, the Let it Go Act, to require former members of Congress to shut down their campaign account within six years of their departure. The problem with the practice, he said, was "It becomes an extension of your lobbying salary and another tool for leverage on the political process."

As a junior member of the minority party with modest influence, Takano made creative use of social media and his communications skills to score rhetorical points and attempt to influence Washington debates. He used a red pen to grade a letter that House Republicans had privately circulated among themselves about immigration. He gave the letter an "F," scrawled multiple comments in red, advised the GOP members to "See me after work," and posted the results on his Tumblr page. He criticized Sen. Rand Paul of Kentucky for comparing the overreach of President Barack Obama's executive actions on immigration to Franklin D. Roosevelt's internment of Japanese Americans during World War Two. Takano cited his Japanese-American parents, who were among those held prisoners, calling Paul's comment "insulting," and said that the action of Obama, in contrast to FDR, was designed to protect "vulnerable, hardworking immigrants."

In 2014, Takano faced a competitive challenger. Steve Adams, a Republican councilman from Riverside who called himself "apolitical" and said that an increase in the minimum wage would cost jobs. He advocated more spending on infrastructure, and said Obama had "fundamentally changed America, not for the good." Takano outspent Adams more than 5-to-1, and won 57%-43%. Takano faced a routine reelection in 2016 against Doug Shepherd, who self-financed nearly two-thirds of the $252,000 that he raised for his campaign. Takano won with 65 percent of the vote.

Inland Empire: Central and Western Riverside, Moreno Valley

Population		**Race and Ethnicity**		**Income**	
Total	729,223	White	24.5%	Median Income	$54,917 (185 out of 435)
Land area	317	Black	8.9%		
Pop/ sq mi	2303.7	Latino	58.2%		
Born in state	62.1%	Asian	5.4%	Under $50,000	33.8%
		Two races	2.1%	$50,000-$99,999	17.6%
Age Groups		Other	0.8%	$100,000-$199,999	3.1%
Under 18	28.0%			$200,000 or more	20.0%
18-34	28.2%	**Education**		Poverty Rate	20.0%
35-64	35.2%	H.S grad or less	52.5%		
Over 64	8.7%	Some college	30.8%	**Health Insurance**	
		College Degree, 4 yr	10.6%	With health insurance coverage	80.0%
Work		Post grad	6.1%		
White Collar	24.5%				
Sales and Service	45.1%	**Military**		**Public Assistance**	
Blue Collar	30.4%	Veteran	5.7%	Cash public assistance income	5.2%
Government	15.8%	Active Duty	0.1%		
				Food stamp/SNAP benefits	13.6%

Voter Turnout			
2015 Total Citizens 18+	430,958	2016 House Turnout as % CVAP	46%
2016 House turnout	197,323	2014 House Turnout as % CVAP	19%

2012 Presidential Vote		
Barack Obama	114,040	(62%)
Mitt Romney	67,314	(36%)

2016 Presidential Vote		
Hillary Clinton	126,197	(61%)
Donald Trump	68,526	(33%)
Gary Johnson	6,847	(3%)
Jill Stein	4,219	(2%)

Cook Partisan Voting Index: D+12

Riverside was a sleepy town of 34,000 people, a couple hours' drive from Los Angeles, when Richard and Pat Nixon were married there in 1940 at the Mission Inn, built in 1876 and, with its bell towers, fountains and stained glass windows, an inspired setting for a wedding. Riverside was not much larger, with 46,000 people, when Ronald and Nancy Reagan spent their honeymoon at the Mission Inn a dozen years later. Riverside then was a citrus center, a market town amid orange groves, where the local agricultural college developed, among other things, the navel orange. Today the Mission Inn is again doing business, after being shuttered from 1985 to 1992, but Riverside has changed completely. The city has grown to more than 330,000 people. Riverside County has about 2.4 million, nearly a quadrupling of its population since 1980. This has been a boom part of California, where modest-income families found new houses in inexpensive developments and small businesses found steady markets.

The Great Recession halted that progress. Since then, the local economy has begun to turn around. In 2014, Riverside surpassed the borough of Queens in New York and became the tenth largest county in the nation. The University of California opened a new medical school in Riverside. Its accreditation was delayed because of questions about the school's long-term funding, but it enrolled its first students in 2013. A 42-million-square-foot warehouse by World Logistics Center, which would be the largest in the nation and create perhaps 20,000 jobs, reached a settlement in October 2016 on an air-cleanup program. Construction of the giant complex was scheduled to begin on farmland in the eastern Moreno Valley. In 2015, population growth and housing starts accelerated in the county. The Spring Mountain Ranch home development closed on nearly 400 of the planned 1,400 homes in its master plan community, which will be the largest development for Riverside in more than 20 years.

The 41st District includes western parts of Riverside County and all of Riverside city, and the towns of Moreno Valley and Perris. Of the three House districts in the county, this is the most urban. Politically, it leans comfortably Democratic, but less so than in Los Angeles or San Francisco urban districts. In 2016, Hillary Clinton defeated Donald Trump, 61%-33%.

FORTY-SECOND DISTRICT

Ken Calvert (R)

Elected 1992, 13th term; b. Jun 08, 1953, Corona; Chaffey Community College (CA), A.A.; San Diego State University, B.A.; Protestant; Divorced.

Professional Career: Restaurant owner, 1975-1980; Real estate broker, 1980-1992; Chairman, Riverside County Repub. Party, 1984-1988.

DC Office: 2205 RHOB 20515, 202-225-1986, Fax: 202-225-2004, calvert.house.gov.

State Offices: Corona, 951-277-0042.

Committees: *Appropriations*: Defense, Energy & Water Development & Related Agencies, Interior, Environment & Related Agencies (Chmn).

Group Ratings

	ADA	ACLU	AFL-CIO	LCV	ITI	COC	HAFA	ACU	CFG	FRC
2016	-	5%	-	5%	100%	100%	50%	79%	70%	100%
2015	0%	C	22%	3%	C	100%	C	48%	48%	92%

Almanac Ratings 2015

	Economy	Social	Foreign	Composite
Liberal	10%	14%	11%	11%
Conservative	90%	86%	90%	89%

Key Votes of the 114th Congress

1. Keystone Pipeline	Y	5. Puerto Rico Debt	Y	9. Offenses by Aliens	Y
2. Trade Deals	Y	6. Medical Marijuana	N	10. Troops in Iraq	N
3. Export-Import Bank	N	7. Sanctuary Cities	Y	11. Homeland Security $$	Y
4. Debt Ceiling Increase	Y	8. Armor-piercing Bullets	Y	12. Trade Adjustment aid	Y

Election Results

Election	Name (Party)	Vote (%)	Cand. Spent	Ind. Exp. Support	Ind. Exp. Oppose
2016 General	Ken Calvert (R)	149,547 (59%)	$1,131,569		
	Tim Sheridan (D)	104,689 (41%)	$132,461		
2016 Primary	Ken Calvert (R)	41,366 (56%)			
	Tim Sheridan (D)	27,336 (37%)			
	Kerri Condley (I)	5,210 (7%)			

Prior winning percentages: 2014 (66%), 2012 (61%), 2010 (56%), 2008 (51%), 2006 (60%), 2004 (62%), 2002 (64%), 2000 (74%), 1998 (56%), 1996 (55%), 1994 (55%), 1992 (47%)

Ken Calvert, a Republican first elected in 1992, has been relatively centrist and an ally of GOP leadership. He holds a plum spot on the Appropriations Committee, where he is a "cardinal" who chairs a subcommittee whose domain is the center of frequent conflicts with Democrats.

Calvert grew up in Corona. While at San Diego State University, where he majored in economics, he was a congressional intern at the Senate Watergate hearings of 1973. Later, he ran the family restaurant back home and, in 1980, got into the commercial real estate business. In 1982, at age 29, he ran for Congress in a district that included almost all of Riverside County and lost a nine-candidate primary to Al McCandless by 868 votes. In 1992, he ran in a new district and won the GOP primary with 28 percent of the vote. His Democratic opponent was Mark Takano, a middle-school teacher who had the support of teachers' unions and Japanese Americans. Calvert beat Takano by 519 votes (Takano was elected to represent the neighboring 41st District in 2012.) Three decades after Calvert first ran, Riverside County has three entire districts in Congress and a small corner of a fourth.

Soon after he was elected, Calvert ran into trouble at home when the Riverside *Press-Enterprise* reported that he had been stopped by police with a prostitute in his car. Calvert apologized and said that he was upset because his wife had divorced him the month before and his father had recently committed suicide. His opponents in 1994 used the incident against him. Calvert won the primary 51%-49%, with only an 884-vote margin, against business professor Joseph Khoury. Takano, running again in the general election, ran an ad that accused Calvert of "flagrant womanizing." But with the Republican tide that year, Calvert won 55%-38%.

Calvert has compiled a moderate-to-conservative voting record. He broke with most GOP colleagues in 2008 by supporting housing finance legislation, citing his district's high foreclosure rate. He has introduced bills to open more of California's coast to offshore drilling, something many Democrats oppose. He has been a major backer of E-Verify, an online system he helped enact that allows employers to confirm the immigration status of new hires. Critics have faulted the system's accuracy, while farm groups have complained it has hurt their efforts to recruit workers. He called for lie-detector tests for refugees attempting to enter the United States from Syria or Iraq. In January 2017, he reintroduced a bill to cut off funds to local governments that style themselves as "sanctuary cities" and resist federal efforts to deport undocumented immigrants who have been jailed.

In 2007, Calvert snagged a coveted seat on Appropriations, where he aggressively sought spending earmarks for his district. In 2010, taxpayer groups criticized him for more than $33 million in solo provisions, the third-largest amount in the California delegation behind then-Speaker Nancy Pelosi and Appropriations ranking Republican Jerry Lewis. He took over in November 2013 the plum position as chairman of the Subcommittee on Interior and the Environment. He said he was interested in finding ways to strengthen domestic energy production on federal lands. Calvert has emphasized the funds in the bill for wildfire fighting and prevention programs, including activities to reduce dead timber, and funds for domestic energy production. To encourage the building of more infrastructure projects, he has backed legislation to streamline highway construction timelines and eliminate the need for redundant environmental reviews. He has been an enthusiastic supporter of the Keystone XL pipeline.

In 2003, Calvert abandoned his 1992 pledge to serve only 12 years in Congress. He was reelected easily. In recent years, campaign opponents have called into question his ethics. In 2006, the *Los Angeles Times* reported that he and his real estate partner had bought a four-acre tract for $550,000, then sold it less than a year later for $985,000, after Calvert secured an $8 million spending earmark for expansion of a nearby freeway interchange. Calvert denied wrongdoing, noting that it was not illegal for a member of Congress to make personal investments.

In 2008, Calvert had a close contest against Democrat Bill Hedrick, a Corona-Norco school board member who was poorly funded and had no national party help but benefited from Calvert's ethics problems. Calvert won by a little more than 6,000 votes, 51.2%-48.8%. Hedrick returned for a rematch in 2010. This time, he got help from the Democratic Congressional Campaign Committee, which ran ads slamming Calvert for voting against the economic stimulus bill, children's health legislation and other initiatives. But they were two years late. The National Republican Congressional Committee stepped in to help Calvert, and the DCCC eventually turned its focus to more-winnable races in that strongly Republican year. Calvert won 56%-44%, spending more than $1.5 million to Hedrick's $493,000. He has twice been challenged by Tim Sheridan, a lawyer and official of the National Treasury Employees Union. Calvert got 66 percent in 2014 but was held to a 59%-41% win in 2016, when turnout more than doubled from two years earlier.

Inland Empire: Corona, West Riverside

Population		**Race and Ethnicity**		**Income**	
Total	749,374	White	44.7%	Median Income	$72,324 (65 out of 435)
Land area	936	Black	5.2%		
Pop/ sq mi	800.6	Latino	37.2%	Under $50,000	33.1%
Born in state	60.2%	Asian	8.9%	$50,000-$99,999	27.3%
		Two races	3.2%	$100,000-$199,999	5.5%
Age Groups		Other	0.9%	$200,000 or more	10.9%
Under 18	27.4%			Poverty Rate	10.9%
18-34	22.9%	**Education**			
35-64	38.8%	H.S grad or less	39.5%	**Health Insurance**	
Over 64	10.8%	Some college	36.3%	With health insurance coverage	86.7%
		College Degree, 4 yr	15.9%		
Work		Post grad	8.3%		
White Collar	34.7%			**Public Assistance**	
Sales and Service	44.2%	**Military**		Cash public assistance income	2.7%
Blue Collar	21.2%	Veteran	8.1%		
Government	15.7%	Active Duty	0.4%	Food stamp/SNAP benefits	7.6%

Voter Turnout			
2015 Total Citizens 18+	481,354	2016 House Turnout as % CVAP	53%
2016 House turnout	254,236	2014 House Turnout as % CVAP	24%

2012 Presidential Vote		
Mitt Romney	131,438	(57%)
Barack Obama	96,212	(41%)

2016 Presidential Vote		
Donald Trump	143,175	(53%)
Hillary Clinton	111,103	(41%)
Gary Johnson	9,587	(4%)

Cook Partisan Voting Index: R+9

The fastest growth in the Los Angeles metropolitan area over the past 25 years has been in the Inland Empire, at the eastern end of the Los Angeles Basin. Mostly orange groves and dairy farms a few decades ago, this territory is now the site of personal upward mobility and ethnic and cultural diversity. The main ingredient of the growth has been small entrepreneurial businesses, many of them started by people with Asian or Latino immigrant backgrounds. California has never been a land of leisure, as stereotype would have it, but rather a place for hard work, where the fertility of the soil and the productivity of the people have led to prosperity and, more recently, relative tolerance toward newcomers.

Anti-Asian sentiment expressed itself in the Chinese Exclusion Act of 1882 and the Japanese-American internment camps of 1942-45. Despite occasional tensions since World War II, this area otherwise has styled itself as a welcoming destination for immigrants. That mindset may have changed or become more complex with the immigration problems on the southern border. In July 2014, local protestors in Murrietta surrounded and forced back three buses filled with immigration detainees who had been sent to Riverside County from Texas and were approaching a local Border Patrol station. The local mayor said that protesters were worried whether the town could safely house the detainees. Border problems continued in June 2016, when law-enforcement authorities in Corona targeted illegal drugs and firearms trafficking from a Mexican prison gang.

During the Great Recession, the Inland Empire had high foreclosure rates, with significant numbers of people moving out, rather than in, for the first time in decades. One area where the recovery has been strong is Murrieta. It doubled in population from 2000 to 2010, though growth has slowed since then. Its families are mostly young, with a 26 percent Hispanic share that is below the state average.

The 42nd Congressional District is based in Riverside County, which is the largest part of the Inland Empire. It takes in most of the western parts of Riverside to the south of the 41st District, which centers on the city of Riverside and nearby areas. That includes the towns of Corona, Norco, Murrieta, Lake Elsinore and the new city of Menifee. Parts of Temecula are shared with the 50th district. The district is solidly Republican, with 38 percent Hispanic population. Donald Trump led Hillary Clinton, 53%-41%, one of seven districts in California where he had a majority of the vote.

FORTY-THIRD DISTRICT

Maxine Waters (D)

Elected 1990, 14th term; b. Aug 15, 1938, St. Louis, MO; California State University, Los Angeles, B.A., 1970; Christian Church; Married (Amb. Sidney Williams); 2 children; 2 grandchildren.

Elected Office: CA Assembly, 1977-1991.

Professional Career: Head Start teacher, 1966; Deputy, City Councilman David Cunningham, 1973-1976.

DC Office: 2221 RHOB 20515, 202-225-2201, Fax: 202-225-7854, waters.house.gov.

State Offices: Los Angeles, 323-757-8900.

Committees: *Financial Services (RMM)*: Capital Markets, Securities & Investment, Financial Institutions & Consumer Credit, Housing & Insurance, Monetary Policy & Trade, Oversight & Investigations, Terrorism & Illicit Finance.

Group Ratings

	ADA	ACLU	AFL-CIO	LCV	ITI	COC	HAFA	ACU	CFG	FRC
2016	-	94%	-	89%	33%	58%	21%	0%	8%	0%
2015	100%	C	100%	97%	C	32%	C	8%	6%	0%

Almanac Ratings 2015

	Economy	Social	Foreign	Composite
Liberal	91%	100%	100%	97%
Conservative	9%	0%	0%	3%

Key Votes of the 114th Congress

1. Keystone Pipeline	N	5. Puerto Rico Debt	N	9. Offenses by Aliens	N
2. Trade Deals	N	6. Medical Marijuana	Y	10. Troops in Iraq	Y
3. Export-Import Bank	Y	7. Sanctuary Cities	N	11. Homeland Security $$	Y
4. Debt Ceiling Increase	Y	8. Armor-piercing Bullets	N	12. Trade Adjustment aid	Y

Election Results

Election	Name (Party)	Vote (%)		Cand. Spent	Ind. Exp. Support	Ind. Exp. Oppose
2016 General	Maxine Waters (D)	167,017	(76%)	$736,766		
	Omar Navarro (R)	52,499	(24%)	$2,611		
2016 Primary	Maxine Waters (D)	92,909	(76%)			
	Omar Navarro (R)	29,152	(24%)			

Prior winning percentages: 2014 (71%), 2012 (71%), 2010 (79%), 2008 (83%), 2006 (84%), 2004 (81%), 2002 (78%), 2000 (87%), 1998 (89%), 1996 (86%), 1994 (78%), 1992 (483%), 1990 (79%)

Maxine Waters, a Democrat first elected in 1990, for years was known chiefly for her incendiary rhetoric and a protracted ethics controversy involving her husband. That changed in 2013, when she became ranking Democrat on the Financial Services Committee. She has settled into a substantive role, amid occasional clashes with the panel's conservative chairman, Jeb Hensarling of Texas. Prior to his inauguration, she was a harsh critic of President Donald Trump.

Waters grew up in St. Louis, one of 13 children. She has said, "I know all about welfare. I remember the social workers peeking in the refrigerator and under the beds." She moved to California in 1961, worked in a garment factory and raised two children. Waters got a sociology degree at California State University in Los Angeles and became an assistant Head Start teacher after the Watts riot of 1965. She likes to call herself "The Organizer" and has shown the capacity to draw big supportive crowds to her protests over the years. From 1973 to 1976, she worked on the staff of a Los Angeles city councilman. In 1976, she won a seat in the California Assembly, where she helped pass legislation divesting state pension funds from apartheid South Africa, setting up a child abuse prevention training program, and prohibiting police strip searches for nonviolent offenses. When Democratic Rep. Augustus Hawkins retired in 1990 after 28 years in the House, Waters was the obvious choice for the seat and won it easily. Her husband, Sidney Williams, a former professional football player and Mercedes-Benz salesman, became President Bill Clinton's ambassador to the Bahamas.

Having grown up in poverty and under Jim Crow, Waters believes fervently in federal aid for the poor and for racial preferences to help blacks overcome the legacies of slavery, segregation and discrimination. She has favored big reductions in defense spending in favor of domestic spending. She voted against the Gulf War resolution in 1991 and was a staunch opponent a decade later of the Iraq war as well as the subsequent troop buildup in Afghanistan. She has brought an intensity bordering on fury to her work, asserting herself regardless of protocol. Her anger is a political weapon she uses shrewdly to get both publicity and results. "I don't have time to be polite," Waters says.

The 1992 riots in L.A. exemplified her best and worst moments. She flew home immediately and roused the Department of Water and Power to restore service to the riot area, and she later was effective in adding provisions to the post-riot emergency act that were eventually signed into law. But she also suggested rioters were morally justified and claimed ominously, "Los Angeles is under siege. ... The violence could spill over to many other cities in this country."

Waters isn't afraid to step on toes. When House Appropriations Chairman David Obey of Wisconsin sought to ban spending earmarks named after members in 2009, she heatedly confronted him over his refusal to fund her request for the Maxine Waters Employment Preparation Center. Obey eventually prevailed. She pushed for federal loan guarantees to cities for economic and infrastructure development. Waters successfully sponsored an amendment to triple spending to erase the debts of poor nations, mostly in Africa. She has sponsored bills to repeal mandatory minimum sentences for drug crimes, and charges that the war on drugs has created "apartheid" in the United States.

She was an occasional thorn in the side of President Barack Obama, starting with her endorsement of Hillary Clinton over Obama during the 2008 Democratic presidential primaries. She and other Congressional Black Caucus members held up a vote on the financial services overhaul in November 2009 because they said the administration wasn't addressing the needs of segments of the black community. Waters repeatedly discussed the need to "educate" people advising Obama. At an Atlanta jobs fair in 2011, she warned of growing disillusionment within minority communities over the unemployment rate, and she encouraged Obama to fight harder when negotiating with the GOP on budget matters and the economy. "The Congressional Black Caucus loves the president, too. We're supportive of the president, but we're getting tired," she said. "The unemployment is unconscionable. We don't know what the strategy is."

On the Financial Services Committee, she has a long history of working to address housing issues. When former committee Chairman Barney Frank retired in 2012, Waters succeeded him as the ranking member, giving her a larger platform to push her pro-regulatory, pro-consumer agenda. She sponsored measures to overhaul discredited housing finance programs, expand affordable housing programs and aid local governments to rehabilitate foreclosed homes. In 2016, Congress enacted a bill that included her provision to expand the use of rental vouchers for Section 8 housing. She harshly criticized the Federal Reserve Board and big bankers for their financing practices and the tight credit that resulted. She told a panel of banking executives in 2009, "to the captains of the universe sitting here before all of us, all of my political life I have been in disagreement with the banking industry." During a September 2016 committee hearing, she responded to admissions by Wells Fargo of its wrongdoing in creating 2 million fake accounts by urging the break-up of the bank. "It's too big to manage," she said. In January 2017, Waters joined Sen. Sherrod Brown of Ohio in intervening in a federal appeals court case to defend the structure of the Consumer Financial Protection Bureau.

As leader of Financial Services Committee Democrats, *Politico* reported in 2014, Waters skillfully exploited divisions between conservative Republicans and big business. She had become "a sympathetic ally for corporate America" - notably on extension of the Export-Import Bank, which makes loans to businesses involved in trade. Her position has given her the opportunity to work with various interests, she said, "even if you've never worked with them before and even if you're never going to work with them again." In response to industry concerns about unintended consequences, she helped to tweak changes in flood-insurance regulations. Waters remained a regulatory stalwart, as when she filed a bill in 2015 to set limits on the Securities and Exchange Commission before it can grant waivers to those she called "bad actors" who have previously pled guilty to fraudulent activity. She also retained her focus on broader economic conflicts, including income inequality. In 2014, she returned to her home town of St. Louis for the funeral of Michael Brown, whose shooting by police sparked riots in nearby Ferguson. She joined the community in "calling for justice."

In recent years, Waters' personal finances have become the target of watchdogs. In 2005, the liberal-leaning Citizens for Responsibility and Ethics in Washington criticized the fact that members of her family had made more than $1 million in eight years doing business with companies, candidates and causes that she had helped in her official capacity. Her reply: "They do their business and I do mine." In March 2009, news stories raised the issue of whether Waters had urged federal regulators to give favorable treatment to a bank in which she and her husband had a financial interest. Federal regulators told *The New York Times* that Waters in 2008 helped set up a meeting with bankers, including one whose chief executive asked them for $50 million in government bailout funds. Waters defended her actions, saying, "I have been an outspoken advocate for minority communities and businesses in California and nationally for decades."

The House Ethics Committee launched an investigation in 2009 and subsequently charged her with three counts of breaking House rules barring lawmakers from taking actions in their own financial interest. Hoping to seize political advantage, Republicans clamored to have ethics trials of Waters and Charles Rangel of New York held before the November 2010 elections, and accused Ethics Chairwoman Zoe Lofgren of California of stalling. Her trial was postponed when committee leaders cited the discovery of additional evidence. Waters contended that the delay proved that the case against her was weak. "I have been denied basic due process," she said. In September 2012, the committee announced that Waters would not be charged with violating House rules.

Waters is a force to be reckoned with in L.A. politics and she has been reelected without difficulty. The rising Hispanic percentage in her district has been viewed as the biggest threat to her career. Even with more than twice as many Hispanics than blacks, she has had no trouble keeping this seat.

During the formal ceremony to count the electoral votes for the 2016 presidential election, she sought unsuccessfully to get a senator to join her in objecting to the certification of the vote and forcing debate about the victory of Donald Trump. "I don't honor him, I don't respect him and I don't want to be involved with him," she said in explaining her decision not to attend Trump's inauguration.

Southern and Western L.A.: Inglewood, Torrance

Population		**Race and Ethnicity**		**Income**	
Total	718,044	White	14.5%	Median Income	$48,781 (272 out of 435)
Land area	72	Black	22.7%	Under $50,000	28.6%
Pop/ sq mi	9968.7	Latino	46.8%	$50,000-$99,999	16.5%
Born in state	54.2%	Asian	12.4%	$100,000-$199,999	3.9%
Age Groups		Two races	2.8%	$200,000 or more	21.0%
Under 18	24.8%	Other	0.8%	Poverty Rate	21.0%
18-34	26.0%	**Education**		**Health Insurance**	
35-64	38.1%	H.S grad or less	46.3%	With health insurance coverage	80.6%
Over 64	11.0%	Some college	29.4%	**Public Assistance**	
Work		College Degree, 4 yr	16.7%	Cash public assistance income	5.3%
White Collar	29.8%	Post grad	7.5%	Food stamp/SNAP benefits	11.4%
Sales and Service	48.4%	**Military**			
Blue Collar	21.7%	Veteran	4.5%		
Government	12.5%	Active Duty	0.0%		

Voter Turnout			
2015 Total Citizens 18+	422,221	2016 House Turnout as % CVAP	52%
2016 House turnout	219,516	2014 House Turnout as % CVAP	23%

2012 Presidential Vote		
Barack Obama	173,342	(78%)
Mitt Romney	44,485	(20%)

2016 Presidential Vote		
Hillary Clinton	183,434	(78%)
Donald Trump	39,039	(17%)
Gary Johnson	5,546	(2%)
Jill Stein	4,637	(2%)

Cook Partisan Voting Index: D+29

In the years just after World War II, Los Angeles was the fastest-growing metropolitan area in America. LAX, today the world's seventh-busiest airport in the number of passengers, with eight central terminals, was then a small airfield amid open country. The mile-square grids east, north and south of the airport were just filling up with subdivisions. Inglewood, east of the airport around the Hollywood Park racetrack, attracted the young families of people who had moved to Los Angeles during the war - workers in the giant aircraft factories or in the small factories that every day were making California less dependent on goods from back East. In Hawthorne, near what has become the southeast corner of the airport, future celebrities were growing up - Sonny Bono, the Beach Boys and, during her early years, Marilyn Monroe. Gardena, east of Hawthorne, was known for its legal poker clubs and its Japanese-American residents, back from the wartime internment camps. Hawthorne had been home to a big Northrop Grumman plant. Now, Space Exploration Technologies (Space X) is based in Hawthorne and is sending cargo shipments to the International Space Station; NASA, with its limited manned space flight program, is pushing Space X to seek out private contractors.

In this area is South Central or, more recently, South Los Angeles, after the City Council in 2003 officially renamed the community in an effort to rid it of the stigma of gang wars and race riots. In the days of residential segregation, much of this area was the home of Los Angeles' black community, its numbers greatly expanded by migration from the South during and after the war. As the nation's focus on civil rights receded in the 1980s and 1990s, this part of Los Angeles continued to deal with racial tensions. That led to chronic economic problems. An almost bankrupt Inglewood Unified School District was given $55 million as part of an emergency state takeover in 2012, with the school board voting to cut salaries by 15 percent to keep the school district afloat. Inglewood has a brighter future as the planned site for the lavish stadium and shopping complex that will be home for both the former St. Louis Rams and San Diego Chargers of the National Football League.

The 43rd Congressional District covers much of this section of Los Angeles County, including Gardena, and the heavily Hispanic areas of Alondra Park, Hawthorne and Lawndale. It also takes in part of Torrance, which is home to large Korean and Japanese communities and to the North American headquarters of Honda, though Toyota has moved its headquarters from Torrance to Plano, Texas. On the northern end of the district is Inglewood and to the south is West Carson. The district takes in Los Angeles International Airport, though a narrow strip that separates the airport from the Pacific Ocean is in the 33rd District. It is safe Democratic territory. Hillary Clinton got 78 percent of the district vote in 2016, as did President Barack Obama in 2012. The current district lines are 48 percent Hispanic and 23 percent black. But the black community wields more political clout.

FORTY-FOURTH DISTRICT

Nanette Barragan (D)

Elected 2016, 1st term; b. Sep 15, 1976, San Pedro; University of California, Los Angeles, B.A., 2000; University of Southern California, J.D., 2005; Catholic; Single.

Elected Office: Hermosa Beach City Council, 2013-2015; Mayor Pro Tem, Hermosa Beach, 2015.

Professional Career: Practicing attorney.

DC Office: 1320 LHOB 20515, 202-225-8220, barragan.house.gov.

State Offices: Carson, 310-831-1799; San Pedro, 310-831-1799; South Gate, 310-831-1799.

Committees: *Homeland Security*: Border & Maritime Security, Oversight & Management Efficiency. *Natural Resources*: Energy & Mineral Resources, Water, Power & Oceans.

Election Results

Election	Name (Party)	Vote (%)		Cand. Spent	Ind. Exp. Support	Ind. Exp. Oppose
2016 General	Nanette Barragan (D)	93,124	(52%)	$1,873,946	$432,277	$27,411
	Isadore Hall III (D)	85,289	(48%)	$1,910,598	$237,743	$405,583
2016 Primary	Isadore Hall (D)	30,219	(42%)			
	Nanette Barragan (D)	15,737	(22%)			
	Armando Sotomayor (D)	7,040	(10%)			
	Sylvia Ortiz (D)	4,313	(6%)			
	Michael De Mauricio (I)	4,201	(6%)			
	Ronald Siegel (R)	4,030	(6%)			

Democrat Nanette Barragán was elected to an open seat in 2016 in a close contest with an African-American state senator. She benefited from the support of activist Democratic women and the large Hispanic community in the district, plus an impressive professional background.

Barragán was the youngest of 11 children of undocumented immigrants from Mexico. She succeeded with what the *Los Angeles Times* described as "an up-from-the-bootstraps story" from the hard-scrabble streets of Carson to graduate from UCLA and get a law degree from the University of Southern California. At the Clinton White House, she worked on African-American outreach in the Office of Public Liaison. She returned to California as an extern for a California Supreme Court justice and later worked for the Los Angeles Legal Aid Foundation and the U.S. attorney's office. As a lawyer with Latham & Watkins, a top Los Angeles firm, she handled an immigration asylum case on behalf of a mother and child from Guatemala that lasted for three years.

In 2012, Barragán took a leave from her law firm to work on the reelection campaign of President Barack Obama. A year later, she was elected to the Hermosa Beach City Council. She served barely a month as mayor before stepping down to run for Congress. She gained attention for working to impose a ban on oil drilling in Santa Monica Bay, where an oil company had planned to set up rigs.

When Rep. Janice Hahn retired after two full terms to mount a successful bid for a seat on the Los Angeles County Board of Supervisors, the front-runners were Barragán and state Sen. Isadore Hall III, who was endorsed by much of the California Democratic establishment, including Gov. Jerry Brown.

In its editorial, the *Times* wrote that Hall's self-styled "moderate" appeal benefited from large campaign donations from oil companies, casinos, tobacco companies and the alcohol lobby. In the first round of voting, Hall led the 10-candidate field with 40 percent of the vote to 22 percent for Barragán. Each candidate raised about $1.9 million. Barragán got a big boost with nearly $700,000 in support from Women Vote!, a Super PAC created by EMILY'S List, the abortion-rights group. She won in November, 52.2%-47.8%, a margin of 7,835 votes.

In a post-election interview with the *Daily Breeze*, Barragán described her reaction to her victory. "I think the first thing I feel is pride that, once again, I beat the odds. That's been my life story." She got seats on the Homeland Security and Natural Resources committees. She was selected as an assistant whip and as one of three co-presidents of the Democrats' freshman class. She said that she decided to attend the inauguration of President Donald Trump, while wearing a symbolic pink fleece hat, because "I want to show Donald Trump that immigrants have always added immeasurable value to our nation and we will not go away. We are here to stay."

Southern L.A.: San Pedro, Compton

Population		**Race and Ethnicity**		**Income**	
Total	719,482	White	6.7%	Median Income	$46,448 (317 out of 435)
Land area	79	Black	15.4%		
Pop/ sq mi	9066.1	Latino	69.9%		
Born in state	56.7%	Asian	5.5%	Under $50,000	30.1%
Age Groups		Two races	1.5%	$50,000-$99,999	14.9%
Under 18	28.8%	Other	1.0%	$100,000-$199,999	1.9%
18-34	26.9%	**Education**		$200,000 or more	23.6%
35-64	35.3%	H.S grad or less	62.5%	Poverty Rate	23.6%
Over 64	9.0%	Some college	25.9%	**Health Insurance**	
Work		College Degree, 4 yr	8.7%	With health insurance coverage	77.6%
White Collar	19.1%	Post grad	3.0%		
Sales and Service	46.5%	**Military**		**Public Assistance**	
Blue Collar	34.2%	Veteran	3.1%	Cash public assistance income	8.2%
Government	11.6%	Active Duty	0.1%	Food stamp/SNAP benefits	17.3%

Voter Turnout			
2015 Total Citizens 18+	373,212	2016 House Turnout as % CVAP	48%
2016 House turnout	178,413	2014 House Turnout as % CVAP	19%

2012 Presidential Vote		
Barack Obama	155,459	(85%)
Mitt Romney	24,995	(14%)

2016 Presidential Vote		
Hillary Clinton	164,251	(83%)
Donald Trump	24,261	(12%)
Jill Stein	4,213	(2%)

Cook Partisan Voting Index: D+35

Just five days after President Lyndon Johnson signed the landmark Voting Rights Act into law, a police arrest gone wrong led to the explosion of the Watts riots. Six days later, 34 people were dead, more than 1,000 were injured, and Los Angeles had a wound that would take years to heal. Postmodern novelist Thomas Pynchon, in a story about the riots in *The New York Times* magazine, wrote, "The heart of L.A.'s racial sickness is the coexistence of two very different cultures: one white and one black. Watts is country which lies, psychologically, uncounted miles further than most whites seem at present willing to travel." But the area also has a rich cultural heritage. In Compton, the Central Avenue entertainment district during the postwar years was filled with clubs and theaters hosting Ella Fitzgerald, Sarah Vaughan, Duke Ellington and Louis Armstrong.

Still, Compton symbolizes many of the problems still facing South Los Angeles: high crime rates, gang violence, drugs and poverty. The influential late 1980s rap group N.W.A. expressed the frustration of many city residents with the song *Straight Outta Compton*. That led to a full-length hit movie in 2015 with the same title, which told the story of the rappers. In the past 20 years, Latinos have been arriving in increasing numbers, buying homes and opening businesses. The Bloods and Crips street gangs have seen the rise of Hispanic counterparts. Blacks are disproportionately the victims, and they are most of the gang members. Compton struggled with a poor economy and unemployment that topped 22 percent in 2011 and remained at 13 percent in December 2014 before it dropped to 7.4 percent in December 2016. A notable success story: Serena and Venus Williams grew up in Compton before they became world-class tennis champions. Local gangs protected the sisters as their prominence grew.

The once-dominant blacks in Compton have been overtaken by Hispanics, 65 percent to 33 percent. The first Latino member of the city council was elected in 2013. Aja Brown, the black woman and urban planner who was elected mayor at age 31 in 2013, said after her election that she planned to take a Spanish class. Her timing may have been right. After taking office, Brown reached out to the gangs. The Bloods and Crips eventually reached a truce, which contributed to a reduction in crime. At the same time, real estate prices in Compton began to soar, spurred partly by investors speculating on the long-term prospect. In 2015, CNN profiled Brown's success in increasing jobs and renegotiating the city's debt.

The 44th Congressional District includes Carson, Compton, Willowbrook and Rancho Dominguez, plus the overwhelmingly Hispanic South Gate and Lynwood - 95 percent and 87 percent Latino, respectively. The district stretches south to include coastal areas, including San Pedro and some of Long Beach, which are more middle-class in character and adjacent to the massive ports of Los Angles and Long Beach. Similar to other coastal parts of Los Angeles, a 44 percent plurality of San Pedro is white. Overall, the district is 69 percent Hispanic and 15 percent black. Politically, it is solidly Democratic. Hillary Clinton got 83 percent of the vote here in 2016 and Barack Obama won 85 percent in 2012. Until 2012, this area of Los Angeles elected a series of African-Americans to the House - one of three blacks representing the city. But the changing demographics have left barely enough blacks to influence the selection of two African-American members.

FORTY-FIFTH DISTRICT

Mimi Walters (R)

Elected 2014, 2nd term; b. May 14, 1962, Pasadena; University of California, Los Angeles, B.A., 1984; Roman Catholic; Married (David Walters); 4 children.

Elected Office: Laguna Niguel City Council, 1996-2004, Laguna Mayor, 2000; CA Assembly, 2005-2008; CA Senate, 2008-2015.

Professional Career: Sales rep.; Investment Executive, Drexel, Burnham, & Lambert; Kidder Peabody & Co..

DC Office: 215 CHOB 20515, 202-225-5611, Fax: 202-225-9177, walters.house.gov.

State Offices: Irvine, 949-263-8703.

Committees: *Energy & Commerce*: Communications & Technology, Digital Commerce & Consumer Protection, Oversight & Investigations.

Group Ratings

	ADA	ACLU	AFL-CIO	LCV	ITI	COC	HAFA	ACU	CFG	FRC
2016	-	5%	-	5%	100%	100%	52%	76%	75%	92%
2015	0%	C	17%	3%	C	100%	C	75%	53%	92%

Almanac Ratings 2015

	Economy	Social	Foreign	Composite
Liberal	10%	5%	10%	9%
Conservative	90%	95%	90%	91%

Key Votes of the 114th Congress

1. Keystone Pipeline	Y	5. Puerto Rico Debt	Y	9. Offenses by Aliens	Y
2. Trade Deals	Y	6. Medical Marijuana	N	10. Troops in Iraq	N
3. Export-Import Bank	N	7. Sanctuary Cities	Y	11. Homeland Security $$	Y
4. Debt Ceiling Increase	Y	8. Armor-piercing Bullets	Y	12. Trade Adjustment aid	Y

Election Results

Election	Name (Party)	Vote (%)		Cand. Spent	Ind. Exp. Support	Ind. Exp. Oppose
2016 General	Mimi Walters (R)	182,618	(59%)	$1,603,119		
	Ron Varasteh (D)	129,231	(41%)	$41,389		
2016 Primary	Mimi Walters (R)	47,136	(41%)			
	Ron Varasteh (D)	31,042	(27%)			
	Greg Raths (R)	21,721	(19%)			
	Max Gouron (D)	14,279	(13%)			

Prior winning percentages: 2014 (65%)

Republican Mimi Walters, first elected to represent California's heavily Republican 45th District in 2014, touted her long experience in public office. Her pro-business, anti-tax platform resonated in the district and has played well with House GOP leaders. In 2017, she joined the Energy and Commerce Committee and was the deputy chair of the National Republican Congressional Committee.

Walters is the daughter of a Marine Corps captain who later became a major in the Reserve. She worked as a stockbroker and then for seven years as an investment executive before she won her first race to the Laguna Niguel City Council in 1996. She served as Laguna Niguel mayor before being elected to the state Assembly and then to the state Senate. "When I first entered public service I firmly believed, and still do, that our prosperity does not come from government; it comes in spite of it," she said. As a state senator, she joined other Republicans in opposing many of the measures backed by California Gov. Jerry Brown. Those initiatives included a 2012 sales tax hike, the plan to redirect $250 million from the state's cap-and-trade program to high-speed rail and an increase in the minimum wage. On environmental and immigration issues, she staked out a more moderate approach. With her husband, David Walters, she owned a business that staffed California prisons with medical professionals. The California Fair Political Practices Commission dismissed a conflict of interest complaint against her.

When Republican Rep. John Campbell announced his retirement in 2013, Walters took advantage of her support from donors. She entered the June primary with a 2-to-1 fundraising edge over all of her competitors combined. Unlike many other Republicans, her association with the GOP establishment has helped rather than hurt her. At first, her strongest opposition came from fellow Republican Greg Raths, a retired Marine colonel. Walters focused her attacks on him rather than on any Democrat. The tactic paid off. She led Raths 45%-24%, and she was left to face Democrat Drew Leavens, who got 28 percent, in a district where Republicans held a 15-point registration advantage.

After the primary, she used her cash advantage to contribute nearly $130,000 to help Republicans facing a tougher fight in the general election, then used that political capital once elected to Congress. She outspent Leavens 10-to-1, and took 65 percent of the vote in the general.

In the House, her game plan proved successful. The freshman class selected Walters as its representative in the Republican leadership. She said that Congress must become "solution-oriented," especially in creating jobs. On behalf of more than two dozen members of her class, she joined Republican Rep. Tom Emmer of Minnesota in sending a letter to President Barack Obama urging him to seek legislation granting him trade promotion authority. She was among several House Republican women who successfully urged GOP leaders to defer action on a bill restricting abortions, which subsequently was revised. In July 2016, she won enactment of her Survivors' Bill of Rights Act, which focused especially on the victims of sexual assault.

Walters gained attention for her party views. As a "practical conservative," she told *The New York Times*, she wanted to limit taxes and spending but added that "government's job is to sometimes help those people who need help - not to give them money to just give them money, but to give them tools to help bring them out of poverty." After earlier supporting Jeb Bush and then Marco Rubio, she said in May 2016 that she would vote for Donald Trump for president. "The alternative, a Clinton presidency and four more years of [President Barack] Obama's economic and national security policies, is not an outcome I find acceptable," she said.

In her second term, Walters retained her leadership seat as a representative of the 2014 class. With her seat on the Energy and Commerce Committee, she said that she would help to enact real solutions to "reforming our health care system, keeping energy affordable, and growing our economy." She became a co-vice chair of the Congressional Women's Caucus, and said that "women in America still face serious obstacles in the workplace and academia." Her assignment at the NRCC gave her responsibility for its current operations.

In the 2016 campaign, Raths ran again and finished third in the primary with 19 percent. Walters defeated Democrat Ron Varaseth in the general, 59%-41%; Varaseth raised $13,000 and had scant campaign presence. Hillary Clinton's win in the 45th District led the Democratic Congressional Campaign Committee to list Walters as an early reelection target for 2018.

Central Orange: Irvine, Lake Forest

Population		**Race and Ethnicity**		**Income**	
Total	740,844	White	53.2%	Median Income	$92,378 (13 out of 435)
Land area	330	Black	1.7%		
Pop/ sq mi	2242.3	Latino	18.7%	Under $50,000	26.6%
Born in state	49.3%	Asian	22.4%	$50,000-$99,999	32.1%
		Two races	3.3%	$100,000-$199,999	14.8%
Age Groups		Other	0.6%	$200,000 or more	8.9%
Under 18	22.0%			Poverty Rate	8.9%
18-34	23.0%	**Education**			
35-64	41.5%	H.S grad or less	20.0%	**Health Insurance**	
Over 64	13.6%	Some college	27.7%	With health insurance coverage	91.1%
		College Degree, 4 yr	31.9%		
Work		Post grad	20.3%		
White Collar	52.3%			**Public Assistance**	
Sales and Service	38.0%	**Military**		Cash public assistance income	1.7%
Blue Collar	9.8%	Veteran	5.5%		
Government	11.1%	Active Duty	0.1%	Food stamp/SNAP benefits	2.6%

Voter Turnout			
2015 Total Citizens 18+	499,008	2016 House Turnout as % CVAP	62%
2016 House turnout	311,849	2014 House Turnout as % CVAP	32%

2012 Presidential Vote		
Mitt Romney	169,489	(55%)
Barack Obama	133,114	(43%)

2016 Presidential Vote		
Hillary Clinton	162,449	(49%)
Donald Trump	144,713	(44%)
Gary Johnson	13,200	(4%)

Cook Partisan Voting Index: R+3

Orange County is the sixth most populous county in the United States, having grown steadily from 130,000 people in 1940, to nearly 2 million in 1980, to 3.2 million in 2015. It narrowly trails its neighbor San Diego County. It is now a community with the patina of maturity, and in some respects, of an aging community fraying at the edges. In recent years, its economy has been constantly reshaped: Tourism remains key, but there is no single industry responsible for Orange County's prosperity. The region was hit hard by the defense spending cutbacks and recession of the early 1990s, but it bounced back, fueled by start-ups and small entrepreneurial successes. Orange County was again rocked by recession in 2008, when the hyperinflation of the local housing market abruptly burst and home values slid as much as 20 percent. Rapid moves by local governments to cut costs and attract new projects, such as alternative energy jobs, helped the county recover faster than other California counties, though slower than in recent decades.

Always Republican since 1936, Orange County became a symbol of conservatism, first in California and then nationally. This was a solid base for Ronald Reagan in his campaigns for governor and president. In 1988, the district's 317,000-vote plurality for George H.W. Bush was his largest in any county in the nation. Over the years, Orange County has become racially and ethnically more diverse. The all-white Orange County stereotype is now thoroughly out of date, exemplified by the election in

2007 of the county's first Vietnamese-American supervisor. Nearly one-third of the county's residents were born in another country, and 46 percent speak a language other than English at home. Its majority-minority population in 2015 had grown to 34 percent Hispanic and 20 percent Asian, though only 2 percent black. The GOP advantage, which had dwindled in 2012 to 70,000 votes when Republican Mitt Romney beat President Barack Obama, has vanished - and not by a small amount. Hillary Clinton led Donald Trump in Orange County, 51%-43%, a margin of 103,000 votes.

The third-largest city in Orange County is Irvine. Irvine Ranch was purchased by Gold Rush merchant James Irvine from the Sepulveda and Yorba families. As Orange County grew up to the limits of the Irvine Ranch, the Irvine family was sitting on some immensely valuable territory, the last large plot of vacant land in metro Los Angeles. In 1959, the Irvines donated a site for the University of California, Irvine, which has grown to 31,000 students. In the 1970s, they sold the rest to developers. Irvine was born as a planned community, with eight-lane parkways, huge office parks, shopping malls and attractive subdivisions. It attracted high-tech and high-growth businesses, highly educated and affluent people. From 2010 to 2015, its population grew by 21 percent. More than 45 percent are Asian, including large numbers of Koreans and Vietnamese, and the city is home to a Chinese-language library. In March 2015, agents of the Homeland Security Department raided a luxury "maternity hotel" in Irvine, where women from China gave birth to American babies for up to $80,000.

The 45th Congressional District is made up of central and south Orange County. Its population center is Irvine, and it also takes in parts of Anaheim, Orange and Mission Viejo. It is 25 percent Asian and 18 percent Hispanic. This is one of three districts that are based entirely in Orange County, while three others are partly in the county. Its once strongly Republican lean has been shifting. In a district that Romney won 55%-43% in 2012, Clinton led 49%-44%, a drop of one-fifth in the Republican vote.

FORTY-SIXTH DISTRICT

Lou Correa (D)

Elected 2016, 1st term; b. Jan 24, 1958, Los Angeles; California State University Fullerton, B.S.; University of California, Los Angeles, J.D.; University of California, Los Angeles, M.B.A.; Catholic; Married (Esther Reynoso Correa); 4 children.

Elected Office: CA Assembly, 1998-2004; Orange County Board of Supervisors, 2005-2006; CA Senate, 2006-2014.

Professional Career: Investment banker/ real estate broker; California High Speed Rail Authority, 2015-2016.

DC Office: 1039 LHOB 20515, 202-225-2965, correa.house.gov.

State Offices: Santa Ana, 714-621-0102.

Committees: *Homeland Security*: Border & Maritime Security, Oversight & Management Efficiency (RMM). *Veterans' Affairs*: Economic Opportunity, Health.

Election Results

Election	Name (Party)	Vote	(%)	Cand. Spent	Ind. Exp. Support	Ind. Exp. Oppose
2016 General	Lou Correa (D)	115,248	(70%)	$854,029	$713,909	$19,680
	Bao Nguyen (D)	49,345	(30%)	$253,289		
2016 Primary	Lou Correa (D)	24,184	(42%)			
	Bob Peterson (R)	8,446	(15%)			
	Bao Nguyen (D)	7,954	(14%)			
	Joe Dunn (D)	7,414	(13%)			
	Lynn Schott (R)	5,014	(9%)			

Democrat Lou Correa, elected to an open seat in 2016, has a lengthy political bio and a close connection to the Mexican-American immigrant community. His grass-roots political style emphasizes deal-making over ideology.

He was born in East Los Angeles. His grandfather and American-born father returned to Mexico to look for work. When he was a year old, his mother died in an automobile accident in Mexico. After spending five more years in Mexico, he returned with his father plus aunts and uncles to Anaheim, where they struggled in subsistence-living in small apartments. "I had enough to eat, and I had a roof over me when I slept. That's all I really cared about," he told the *Los Angeles Times*. After graduating from Anaheim High School, he got his bachelor's at California State University, Fullerton, and then a law degree and MBA from UCLA. He worked as an attorney, investment banker and real estate broker.

The passage in 1994 of Proposition 187, which targeted illegal immigration, made Correa politically active. He ran for the state Assembly in 1996 and lost by 93 votes. Two years later, he easily defeated the Republican incumbent. After six years in the Assembly, he was elected to the Orange County Board of Supervisors, and the state Senate. In 2014, he narrowly lost a bid to return to the board. Correa styled himself as a political moderate, often to the annoyance of Democratic leaders. "A lot of politicians will wring their hands and put a wet finger in the air to get a feel for what he should do," former Senate Majority Leader Donn Perata told the *Times*. "Lou just intuitively knew." He was consistent in his advocacy of immigrants' rights, and criticized President Barack Obama for his deportations.

When 10-term Democratic Rep. Loretta Sanchez decided to run for the Senate, Correa sought the open seat and was endorsed by Sanchez and many Democratic Party leaders. In the eight-candidate first round of voting, he got 44 percent. Runner-up with 15 percent was Garden Grove mayor Bao Nguyen, who had fled Vietnam as a baby with his parents. Nguyen, a Democrat, appealed to supporters of Sen. Bernie Sanders. Correa, who was an early supporter of Hillary Clinton for president, appealed chiefly to Latinos in this heavily Hispanic district. With a fundraising advantage of $920,000 to $270,000, he had another easy win in the general election, 70%-30%.

In the House, Correa got seats on the Homeland Security and Veterans Affairs committees. Unlike many other House Democrats, he attended the inauguration of President Donald Trump. "I'm going to D.C. to be at the table when decisions are made that affect my constituents. Either we are at the table or we are on the menu," he said in statement.

Northern Orange: Santa Ana, Central and Western Anaheim

Population		**Race and Ethnicity**		**Income**	
Total	721,847	White	18.5%	Median Income	$55,172 (182 out of 435)
Land area	72	Black	1.6%		
Pop/ sq mi	10064.8	Latino	66.2%		
Born in state	49.9%	Asian	12.2%	Under $50,000	33.4%
		Two races	1.1%	$50,000-$99,999	18.6%
Age Groups		Other	0.5%	$100,000-$199,999	3.0%
Under 18	27.0%			$200,000 or more	19.7%
18-34	28.6%	**Education**		Poverty Rate	19.7%
35-64	35.8%	H.S grad or less	58.1%		
Over 64	8.7%	Some college	24.6%	**Health Insurance**	
Work		College Degree, 4 yr	12.7%	With health insurance coverage	76.4%
White Collar	22.2%	Post grad	4.5%		
Sales and Service	49.3%	**Military**		**Public Assistance**	
Blue Collar	28.5%	Veteran	3.2%	Cash public assistance income	3.8%
Government	7.8%	Active Duty	0.0%		
				Food stamp/SNAP benefits	13.6%

Voter Turnout			
2015 Total Citizens 18+	352,031	2016 House Turnout as % CVAP	47%
2016 House turnout	164,593	2014 House Turnout as % CVAP	23%

2012 Presidential Vote		
Barack Obama	95,479	(61%)
Mitt Romney	56,252	(36%)

2016 Presidential Vote		
Hillary Clinton	119,762	(66%)
Donald Trump	50,403	(28%)
Gary Johnson	5,630	(3%)
Jill Stein	3,711	(2%)

Cook Partisan Voting Index: D+15

When Walt Disney began planning Disneyland in the late 1940s, he did not have to drive far from downtown Los Angeles before finding undeveloped land. Dairy farms and orange groves covered most of southeast Los Angeles County and adjacent Orange County, which had only 216,000 people in 1950. As Disneyland opened there in 1955 and became a great success, the area around it - a mass of flatland surrounded by mountains and sea - found itself directly in the path of the most explosively growing metropolitan area in the United States. With 3.2 million people, this has become the nation's sixth-largest county.

Just as Orange County was once transformed by newcomers from Los Angeles County and the Midwest, so it is again being transformed by immigrants, from Mexico and other parts of Latin America, and from Vietnam, Taiwan, Korea and other parts of East Asia. The county seat of Santa Ana is a major arrival point for immigrants from Mexico and is 78 percent Hispanic, of whom nearly half have been counted as non-citizens. Other immigrants have moved farther out, like so many Southern Californians before them, working multiple jobs, commuting on freeways, and living in stucco subdivisions. There are concentrations in various places - Latinos in Santa Ana and much of Anaheim and Vietnamese in Garden Grove, who constitute the largest Vietnamese community in the nation. Many of these new Californians are scattered throughout the county. Overall, the county has the third largest Asian population in the nation, behind Los Angeles and Santa Clara counties. These demographic changes have made for some political wobble. Until the mid-1990s, Asians were split between the parties, and few Latinos were registered to vote. After the 1994 approval of Proposition 187, which sought to deny most social services to illegal immigrants, many more Latinos began voting, mostly Democratic. Following the 2016 election, the Santa Ana city council declared the community a "sanctuary city."

The 46th Congressional District covers central and western areas of Orange County. It takes in parts of Santa Ana, which is the second-largest city in Orange County, and Orange. It includes a significant portion of Anaheim, Orange County's largest city. The district is the Democratic core of the county, with population that is 67 percent Hispanic and 12 percent Asian. The Democratic presidential vote increased from 58 percent in 2008 to 66 percent in 2016. During the Democratic presidential primary, Sen. Bernie Sanders took on Disney - while speaking in Anaheim, no less. "People are asking, is it right that at Disneyland you have a CEO making $46 million while they're paying their workers starvation wages."

FORTY-SEVENTH DISTRICT

Alan Lowenthal (D)

Elected 2012, 3rd term; b. Mar 08, 1941, New York (Manhattan), NY; Hobart College (NY), B.A., 1962; Ohio State University, M.A., 1965; Ohio State University, Ph.D., 1967; Jewish; Married (Deborah Malumed); 2 children; 1 grandchild.

Elected Office: Long Beach City Council, 1992-1998; CA Assembly, 1998-2004; CA Senate, 2004-2012.

Professional Career: Professor, CA. St. University Long Beach, 1969-1998.

DC Office: 125 CHOB 20515, 202-225-7924, Fax: 202-225-7926, lowenthal.house.gov.

State Offices: Long Beach, 562-436-3828.

Committees: *Natural Resources*: Energy & Mineral Resources (RMM), Federal Lands. *Transportation & Infrastructure*: Coast Guard & Maritime Transportation, Highways & Transit, Water Resources & Environment.

Group Ratings

	ADA	ACLU	AFL-CIO	LCV	ITI	COC	HAFA	ACU	CFG	FRC
2016	-	100%	-	100%	33%	50%	12%	0%	4%	0%
2015	95%	C	100%	100%	C	40%	C	0%	0%	0%

Almanac Ratings 2015

	Economy	Social	Foreign	Composite
Liberal	100%	100%	100%	100%
Conservative	0%	0%	0%	0%

Key Votes of the 114th Congress

1. Keystone Pipeline	N	5. Puerto Rico Debt	Y	9. Offenses by Aliens	N
2. Trade Deals	N	6. Medical Marijuana	Y	10. Troops in Iraq	Y
3. Export-Import Bank	Y	7. Sanctuary Cities	N	11. Homeland Security $$	Y
4. Debt Ceiling Increase	Y	8. Armor-piercing Bullets	N	12. Trade Adjustment aid	Y

Election Results

Election	Name (Party)	Vote (%)	Cand. Spent	Ind. Exp. Support	Ind. Exp. Oppose
2016 General	Alan Lowenthal (D)	154,759 (64%)	$299,171		
	Andy Whallon (R)	88,109 (36%)	$68,243		
2016 Primary	Alan Lowenthal (D)	62,967 (66%)			
	Andy Whallon (R)	21,064 (22%)			
	Sanford Kahn (R)	11,506 (12%)			

Prior winning percentages: 2014 (56%), 2012 (57%)

Alan Lowenthal, a Democrat first elected in 2012, is a rare academician seeking to bring pragmatic problem-solving to Washington. With lengthy experience at home and in Sacramento, he has raised thoughtful ideas, though he has been limited as a junior member of the minority party.

Lowenthal was born in New York City, grew up in Queens and went to high school on Long Island. Lowenthal studied psychology at Hobart College, where he got a bachelor's degree, and he continued his studies at Ohio State University, earning a masters and a doctorate. During his doctoral training, he had an internship in San Francisco and decided that he wanted to live in California. Lowenthal took a position at California State University, Long Beach, in 1969 as an assistant professor.

He joined Long Beach Area Citizens Involved, an umbrella group of community organizations trying to influence local government, and eventually became the group's president. He ran for office in 1992, winning a seat on the Long Beach City Council. He was elected to the state Assembly in 1998, and to the state Senate six years later. In the legislature, Lowenthal focused on reducing air pollution at California ports and protecting public health. "I wanted to make sure the community was livable and the port economically viable," he said.

Long Beach Councilman Gary DeLong, Lowenthal's opponent in 2012, ran as a moderate Republican who said he would not be bound by the decisions of the House Republican leadership. Even so, Lowenthal did his best to tie DeLong to the GOP establishment. He seized on a comment DeLong made at a community event in which he said he had not seen scientific evidence that confirms the existence of climate change. DeLong had the edge in spending, $1.4 million to $1.2 million. In this comfortably Democratic district, Lowenthal won 57%-43%.

Lowenthal, who claimed that his work in the Assembly helped to pave the way for the public referendum creating a citizens' redistricting commission in California, used his wider platform in the House to urge an end to political gerrymandering and to the practice of politicians across the nation drawing their own districts. He filed a bill that would create a redistricting panel in each state that would be based on the California model, and conceded that success would be much more difficult to achieve in Congress.

Serving on the House Foreign Affairs Committee, he focused especially on human-rights issues that have concerned his Vietnamese and other Asian constituents. In 2015, Lowenthal took over as senior Democrat on the Natural Resources Subcommittee on Energy and Mineral Resources, where he focused on renewable energy development, especially on public lands. In September 2016, he filed a bipartisan bill to require the online posting of information about energy production on federal lands. With Republican Rep. Steve Chabot of Ohio, he formed and co-chaired the Congressional Cambodia Caucus. Long Beach has the largest community of Cambodians outside that nation. In June 2016, the House passed his resolution condemning the government of Cambodia for its physical attacks and other persecution of the opposition. Lowenthal and Republican Rep. Ted Poe of Texas co-chaired the Ports Caucus.

In the 2014 campaign, Republican Andy Whallon, a former aeronautical engineer, promised more job creation. Whallon spent only $60,000, and Lowenthal's 56%-44% victory was close to his initial election. In 2016, the turnout was twice as large and Lowenthal won a rematch with Whallon, 64%-36%.

Coastal L.A./Inland Orange: Long Beach, Garden Grove

Population		**Race and Ethnicity**		**Income**	
Total	719,582	White	32.0%	Median Income	$58,674 (152 out of 435)
Land area	216	Black	7.1%	Under $50,000	29.6%
Pop/ sq mi	3328.2	Latino	34.8%	$50,000-$99,999	21.4%
Born in state	53.9%	Asian	21.6%	$100,000-$199,999	5.9%
		Two races	3.1%	$200,000 or more	17.6%
Age Groups		Other	1.4%	Poverty Rate	17.6%
Under 18	23.3%	**Education**		**Health Insurance**	
18-34	24.9%	H.S grad or less	38.7%	With health insurance coverage	84.5%
35-64	39.9%	Some college	31.5%	**Public Assistance**	
Over 64	11.9%	College Degree, 4 yr	19.8%	Cash public assistance income	4.0%
Work		Post grad	10.1%	Food stamp/SNAP benefits	9.7%
White Collar	36.1%	**Military**			
Sales and Service	44.3%	Veteran	5.6%		
Blue Collar	19.7%	Active Duty	0.1%		
Government	13.7%				

Voter Turnout			
2015 Total Citizens 18+	460,890	2016 House Turnout as % CVAP	53%
2016 House turnout	242,868	2014 House Turnout as % CVAP	27%

2012 Presidential Vote		
Barack Obama	147,456	(60%)
Mitt Romney	92,010	(38%)

2016 Presidential Vote		
Hillary Clinton	161,743	(62%)
Donald Trump	80,162	(31%)
Gary Johnson	9,260	(4%)
Jill Stein	5,690	(2%)

Cook Partisan Voting Index: D+13

With 474,000 people, Long Beach would be a major metropolis almost anywhere but in Los Angeles County, where it seems just the largest of many suburbs. But it has an identity of its own. Founded as a beach resort in 1888, it soon became a port when Los Angeles civic leaders decided that if their town was to be a world-class city, it must have a world-class harbor. Since nature had not provided one, they built it where the Los Angeles River flows into the ocean at the western edge of Long Beach. By 1909, Los Angeles had annexed the harbor towns of San Pedro and Wilmington on the other side of the river. Over the next decades, the two cities persuaded the federal government to dredge channels and build a breakwater and turning basins. Long Beach was developing other businesses as well. It sprouted oil derricks in the 1920s and briefly became one of the nation's big oil producers. It was the site of major aircraft plants in the 1940s and beyond.

Since then, the Los Angeles-Long Beach port has become the nation's busiest cargo center, with huge steel-gray container ships pulling up to enormous automated loading facilities. The two ports in the complex compete with each other on business terms, but collaborate on many issues. The overall port, with 30,000 employees and 66 gantry cranes, handles the equivalent of 18,600, 20-foot containers daily docked at 10 piers and 80 berths. From there, nearly half the cargo leaves by rail in more than 40 daily trains along the high-speed, 20-mile Alameda Corridor to the large rail yards near downtown Los Angeles. Trucking accounts for a declining share of the $180 billion in annual cargo on 2,000 vessels through the port. These facilities handle 43 percent of goods imported into the nation, and 27 percent of exports. More than 90 percent of the port shipments are to or from East Asia. Economists disagreed about the impact of the failure of Congress to approve the Trans-Pacific Partnership, which President Barack Obama had reached with 11 Asian nations; President Donald Trump officially scuttled the deal.

The *Queen Mary,* converted into a floating hotel, is a big tourist attraction in Long Beach, and there are new high-rises and a huge aquarium along the beach. The city has suffered from downsized manufacturing. In November 2015, Boeing shut down production of its Globemaster III military transports, which had manufactured more than 250 planes and brought thousands of jobs. The Long Beach plant had been the last aircraft-manufacturing facility in California. Virgin Galactic, the commercial space flight company, filled part of the space.

The 47th Congressional District is centered on Long Beach, and takes in Signal Hill, where oil rigs are still pumping. Parts are in Orange County, including Los Alamitos and Cypress, which has a large Asian-American population and is the birthplace of golfing great Tiger Woods. Parts of Garden Grove and Westminster, founded as a Presbyterian temperance colony in 1870, are shared with the 48th District. Politically, it leans strongly Democratic. In 2016, Hillary Clinton led Donald Trump, 62%-31%, a big increase for Democrats over Barack Obama's 58%-39% win over John McCain in 2008.

FORTY-EIGHTH DISTRICT

Dana Rohrabacher (R)

Elected 1988, 15th term; b. Jun 21, 1947, Coronado; Los Angeles Harbor College (CA), Att., 1967; California State University, San Bernardino, B.A., 1969; University of Southern California, M.A., 1975; Baptist; Married (Rhonda Carmony Rohrabacher); 3 children (triplets).

Professional Career: Radio & print journalist, 1970-1980; Assistant press sect. Ronald Reagan, 1976, 1980; Sr. speechwriter, special Assistant to President Reagan, 1981-1988.

DC Office: 2300 RHOB 20515, 202-225-2415, Fax: 202-225-0145, rohrabacher.house.gov.

State Offices: Huntington Beach, 714-960-6483.

Committees: *Foreign Affairs*: Asia & the Pacific, Europe, Eurasia & Emerging Threats (Chmn). *Science, Space & Technology*: Energy, Environment, Space.

Group Ratings

	ADA	ACLU	AFL-CIO	LCV	ITI	COC	HAFA	ACU	CFG	FRC
2016	-	11%	-	0%	67%	92%	86%	96%	99%	92%
2015	10%	C	4%	3%	C	65%	C	100%	91%	73%

Almanac Ratings 2015

	Economy	Social	Foreign	Composite
Liberal	24%	15%	7%	15%
Conservative	76%	85%	93%	85%

Key Votes of the 114th Congress

1. Keystone Pipeline	Y	5. Puerto Rico Debt	N	9. Offenses by Aliens	Y
2. Trade Deals	N	6. Medical Marijuana	Y	10. Troops in Iraq	N
3. Export-Import Bank	N	7. Sanctuary Cities	Y	11. Homeland Security $$	N
4. Debt Ceiling Increase	N	8. Armor-piercing Bullets	Y	12. Trade Adjustment aid	N

Election Results

Election	Name (Party)	Vote (%)		Cand. Spent	Ind. Exp. Support	Ind. Exp. Oppose
2016 General	Dana Rohrabacher (R).................	178,701	(58%)	$597,760		
	Suzanne Savary (D)......................	127,715	(42%)	$99,939		
2016 Primary	Dana Rohrabacher (R).....................	67,218	(57%)			
	Suzanne Savary (D)........................	34,379	(29%)			
	Robert John Banuelos (D).............	17,213	(15%)			

Prior winning percentages: 2014 (64%), 2012 (61%), 2010 (62%), 2008 (53%), 2006 (60%), 2004 (62%), 2002 (62%), 2000 (62%), 1998 (59%), 1996 (61%), 1994 (69%), 1992 (55%), 1990 (59%), 1988 (64%)

A self-described "surfer Republican" who sports an American-flag surfboard on his lapel, Dana Rohrabacher likes to make waves in the House. Since coming to Capitol Hill in 1989, he has provoked people on both the left and right with his hyperbolic rhetoric and non-conformity. But he professes not to care, and says his motto is, "Fighting for freedom and having fun." Long before Donald Trump launched his presidential campaign, Rohrabacher was the chief congressional defender of Russian president Vladimir Putin.

Rohrabacher grew up in Southern California, went to college and experimented with drugs, and once had a folk band called the Goldwaters. By the mid-1970s, he was on a far straighter path as a press aide in Ronald Reagan's 1976 and 1980 presidential campaigns. He wrote editorials for *The Orange County Register* and later was a speechwriter in the Reagan White House. He returned to Southern California in 1988, when the heavily Republican seat opened. Rohrabacher won the primary with 35 percent of the vote and coasted to victory in November. During the campaign, Rhonda Carmony, one of his volunteers and a surfer, entered him in a surfing contest. They later married and, in 2004, became the parents of triplets.

Rohrabacher's voting record can lean toward the center, as shown by the *Almanac* vote ratings for 2015. He supports the legal use of medical marijuana and joined with liberal Rep. Barney Frank of Massachusetts on a bill to decriminalize possession of less than 100 grams. He invited Frank, who is gay, and his partner, a surfer, to visit Huntington Beach. Rohrabacher has doubled down in his support for legalization of marijuana, especially in the District of Columbia. He told his fellow Republicans: "Wake up! . . . The American people are shifting on this issue." In June 2015, the House on a 242-186 vote passed his amendment to prevent federal interference with medical marijuana in states where it is legal. He became the first member of Congress to use marijuana for medical purposes (as a topical rub to treat arthritis pain in his shoulder), *Huffington Post* reported in May 2016.

Rohrabacher is a congressional skeptic of human-caused global warming. Despite the widespread view in the scientific world, Rohrabacher told *Science* magazine in 2012 that "in the global warming debate, we won. ... I think that after 10 years of debate, we can show that there are hundreds if not thousands of scientists who have come over to being skeptics." In his free-spirit ways, Rohrabacher has taken on some unusual causes. He has repeatedly sponsored a bill that would give District of Columbia residents full voting rights in Maryland but would maintain a separate District government.

On the Foreign Affairs Committee, he has taken a special interest in efforts to fight the Taliban in Afghanistan. After the Sept. 11, 2001, attacks, he visited the exiled king of Afghanistan in Rome, encouraged him to return to Kabul, and promised that the United States would oust the Taliban and help rebuild the country. He was a strong critic of former Afghan President Hamid Karzai, accusing him of having a "corrupt little clique." Karzai responded by refusing to let the congressman enter the country with a delegation in 2012. Rohrabacher has been a longtime critic of China's rulers. He strongly opposed normal trade relations with China and has backed export controls to bar advanced technology to non-democratic governments, sometimes referring to the nation as "Red China."

Rohrabacher has had an odd history with Russian leader Putin. In the early 1990s, he claims to have arm-wrestled - and lost to - Putin in a Capitol Hill bar. Rohrabacher has defended Putin's invasion of Ukraine on the basis that post-Communist Russia had become a more open society, and said that Russia could be a valuable ally in defeating the greater threat of "radical Islam." An April 2016 article in *Commentary* magazine was headlined "The Kremlin's Congressman." Following the election, he told a radio talk-show program in Los Angeles that alleged Russian hacking of the Democratic National Committee's computers and release of information during the campaign was "terrific" because it gave voters more information about Hillary Clinton.

For years, Rohrabacher has advocated stronger action against illegal immigration. In 2003, he delayed his support for the Republicans' Medicare prescription drug bill until GOP leaders, in exchange for his vote, gave him a vote on his bill to require hospitals to report potential illegal immigrants to the Homeland Security Department. He has led voter initiatives to remove illegal immigrants from California's welfare and school rolls, and he successfully urged President George W. Bush to commute the sentences of two former Border Patrol agents who shot a Mexican drug dealer. In 2013, he said that if John Boehner brought an immigration bill to the House floor without the support of a majority of House Republicans, he should be removed as Speaker. By the time that Boehner quit as Speaker in 2015, most House Republicans agreed with Rohrabacher on immigration.

As a maverick, Rohrabacher has been frustrated in his pursuit of a committee gavel. In 2006, he lost the top minority post on the full Science and Technology Committee to the more senior Ralph Hall of Texas. Rohrabacher again sought to chair the committee in 2012, but the slot went to Texas' Lamar Smith, who will be term-limited after the 2018 election. Likewise, at the Foreign Affairs Committee, more junior members have jumped over him to become chairman. There have been occasional other cases where senior House members have been denied chairmanships, but they are rare.

Rohrabacher usually has little trouble getting reelected. In 2008, he faced Huntington Beach Mayor Debbie Cook, a Democratic lawyer and environmental activist who claimed he had done little during his time in Congress. With no help from the national party, she raised $482,000. Rohrabacher criticized Cook's opposition to more oil drilling and her support for the rescue of the financial markets. He won by a reduced 53%-43%. In the strongly Republican 2010, he won by a more customary, 62%-38%. In October 2011, *OC Weekly* reported that more than half of his campaign donations over a three-month period went to his wife, who was acting as his campaign manager. Against Suzanne Savary in 2016, a retired professor and management consultant, Rohrabacher was held to a 58%-42% win.

Rohrabacher was an enthusiastic supporter of Trump during the 2016 campaign. When many congressional Republicans, including Speaker Paul Ryan, voiced reservations after the release of the Access Hollywood video with crude comments by Trump, Rohrabacher warned that GOP critics will destroy the Republican Party, not Trump. "The choice is not between Donald Trump and a better candidate. It is a choice between Donald Trump and Hillary Clinton," he wrote in *USA Today*. "The crude sexual references made 11 years ago in a private conversation were appalling, but they're nowhere near as appalling as the record of corruption and abusive sexual behavior by the Clintons when they occupied the White House." He sponsored an inaugural ball for the new president at the Library of Congress. He praised the selection of Secretary of State Rex Tillerson as "a man who knows the players in Russia," but turned down suggestions that he take a senior position with the State Department.

Coastal Orange: Huntington Beach, Costa Mesa

Population		**Race and Ethnicity**		**Income**	
Total	722,403	White	56.1%	Median Income	$81,680 (30 out of 435)
Land area	145	Black	1.0%		
Pop/ sq mi	4966.0	Latino	21.5%	Under $50,000	27.6%
Born in state	51.7%	Asian	17.8%	$50,000-$99,999	27.4%
		Two races	2.8%	$100,000-$199,999	13.7%
Age Groups		Other	0.7%	$200,000 or more	10.7%
Under 18	20.4%			Poverty Rate	10.7%
18-34	22.2%	**Education**			
35-64	42.0%	H.S grad or less	25.9%	**Health Insurance**	
Over 64	15.4%	Some college	30.6%	With health insurance coverage	88.3%
Work		College Degree, 4 yr	27.8%		
		Post grad	15.7%		
White Collar	45.1%			**Public Assistance**	
Sales and Service	41.7%	**Military**		Cash public assistance income	1.7%
Blue Collar	13.2%	Veteran	6.0%		
Government	9.5%	Active Duty	0.1%	Food stamp/SNAP benefits	4.4%

Voter Turnout			
2015 Total Citizens 18+	511,959	2016 House Turnout as % CVAP	60%
2016 House turnout	306,416	2014 House Turnout as % CVAP	34%

2012 Presidential Vote		
Mitt Romney	169,249	(55%)
Barack Obama	133,103	(43%)

2016 Presidential Vote		
Hillary Clinton	152,035	(48%)
Donald Trump	146,595	(46%)
Gary Johnson	13,127	(4%)

Cook Partisan Voting Index: R+4

In the 1950s, when the Beach Boys were at Hawthorne High School in L.A., surfers would drive far down the coast to the vast expanse of Huntington Beach in Orange County to catch a wave. This was empty country then, vegetable fields and orange groves mainly, with nary a freeway or shopping center in sight. Today, the 42-mile shoreline of Orange County is pretty much filled in with pricey coastal resorts and other developments. Huntington Beach, a city of nearly 202,000, is a mixture of family subdivisions and garden apartments and home of the International Surfing Museum. Its eight miles of beach and self-depiction as Surf City make it a tourist draw in the summer. In 2015, city officials were exploring a new use for the ocean: a desalination plant to counter the state's water crisis. But they were struggling with the estimated $2 billion cost. As part of a January 2017 executive order, President Barack Obama designated some rock formations at local beaches as part of the California Coastal National Monument.

To the north is Westminster, the center of a prominent Vietnamese-American community, with miles of shops with Vietnamese names and its own Vietnamese-language daily newspaper. Southeast along San Diego Freeway is Fountain Valley, the central focus of many Asian-owned technology businesses. Near the coast is Costa Mesa, site of South Coast Plaza's luxury stores and a grand performing arts center. Like other California cities, it has experienced a huge influx of Hispanic immigrants, and adapting has been rocky. The Costa Mesa City Council shut down a day-laborer center and declared itself a "rule of law city" - a message to illegal immigrants to stay away. The city is 36 percent Hispanic.

The 48th Congressional District takes in much of coastal Orange County and is anchored by Huntington Beach. It includes the oceanside cities of Laguna Beach, with its art galleries and cute shops, and Newport Beach, one of California's richest cities, which was rated in 2016 by Coldwell Banker as the second-most expensive housing market in the country (behind Saratoga, California), with an average listing of $2.1 million. Newport Beach was the setting for the popular teen drama, *The O.C.* Westminster is split with the neighboring 47th District, but the area known as Little Saigon is in the 48th. With their entrepreneurial spirit, many of the Vietnamese communities compete with each other, for example, in celebrating the Lunar New Year ("Tet"), or in a more contentious battle between a Vietnamese newspaper publisher in Little Saigon and anti-Communist refugees who continued to fight the war that ended in 1975.

Parts of Garden Grove and Santa Ana are also in the district, as are Fountain Valley, Seal Beach and Leisure World, its large gated community for seniors. These coastal areas share many common interests in managing state beaches and coastal estuaries. Politically, this district has leaned firmly Republican. In April 2016, Costa Mesa was the site of Donald Trump's first campaign speech in California. In the district, Mitt Romney led President Barack Obama in 2012, 55%-43%. That changed in 2016, when Hillary Clinton prevailed over Trump, 48%-46%

FORTY-NINTH DISTRICT

Darrell Issa (R)

Elected 2000, 9th term; b. Nov 01, 1953, Cleveland, OH; Kent State University (OH), A.A.; Siena Heights University (MI), B.A.; Christian Church; Married (Kathy Issa); 1 child.

Military Career: U.S. Army, 1970-1972, 1976-1980.

Professional Career: Founder & President, Directed Electronics, 1982-1999.

DC Office: 2269 RHOB 20515, 202-225-3906, Fax: 202-225-3303, issa.house.gov.

State Offices: Dana Point, 949-281-2449; Vista, 760-599-5000.

Committees: *Foreign Affairs*: Middle East & North Africa, Terrorism, Nonproliferation & Trade. *Judiciary*: Courts, Intellectual Property & Internet (Chmn), Regulatory Reform, Commercial & Antitrust Law. *Oversight & Government Reform*: Health Care, Benefits & Administrative Rules, Information Technology.

Group Ratings

	ADA	ACLU	AFL-CIO	LCV	ITI	COC	HAFA	ACU	CFG	FRC
2016	-	11%	-	3%	75%	100%	61%	82%	56%	90%
2015	0%	C	13%	0%	C	85%	C	83%	78%	92%

Almanac Ratings 2015

	Economy	Social	Foreign	Composite
Liberal	10%	4%	12%	8%
Conservative	90%	96%	88%	92%

Key Votes of the 114th Congress

1. Keystone Pipeline	Y	5. Puerto Rico Debt	N	9. Offenses by Aliens	Y
2. Trade Deals	Y	6. Medical Marijuana	N	10. Troops in Iraq	N
3. Export-Import Bank	N	7. Sanctuary Cities	Y	11. Homeland Security $$	N
4. Debt Ceiling Increase	N	8. Armor-piercing Bullets	Y	12. Trade Adjustment aid	Y

Election Results

Election	Name (Party)	Vote (%)	Cand. Spent	Ind. Exp. Support	Ind. Exp. Oppose
2016 General	Darrell Issa (R)	155,888 (50%)	$6,094,953	$5,886	$560,829
	Doug Applegate (D)	154,267 (50%)	$2,032,703	$4,263,366	
2016 Primary	Darrell Issa (R)	56,013 (51%)			
	Douglas Applegate (D)	49,792 (45%)			

Prior winning percentages: 2014 (60%), 2012 (58%), 2010 (63%), 2008 (58%), 2006 (63%), 2004 (63%), 2002 (77%), 2000 (61%)

Darrell Issa is a Republican first elected in 2000. As chairman of the Oversight and Government Reform Committee from 2011 to 2015, he made himself President Barack Obama's chief investigative nemesis. His aggressive, headline-grabbing pursuits of alleged waste, fraud and abuse in the administration made him a hero to conservatives and the scourge of liberals. In his new post as chairman of the subcommittee in charge of patent policy, he has not captured nearly as much attention but he wields more policy influence.

Issa grew up in a working-class section of Cleveland, the son of an X-ray technician. Hampered by dyslexia, Issa found academics difficult, and he dropped out of high school to join the Army. After his service, the military paid for him to finish school, and he graduated from Siena Heights University in Michigan. A brother's run-ins with the law for car theft spurred Issa's idea for his first business venture. He invested all of his savings, some $7,000, in a car-alarm business in Cleveland, eventually taking it over with his wife, Kathy, and relocating the business to Vista, California, north of San Diego. Their Directed Electronics became the nation's largest manufacturer of vehicle security systems, including the popular Viper system, and earned them a fortune. Issa became active in the high-technology lobby, serving as chairman of the Consumer Electronics Association. In 2010, the Center for Responsive Politics ranked Issa as the wealthiest member of Congress, with an estimated average net worth of $448 million. In January 2016, *Roll Call* reported that his estimated net worth had dropped to $255 million, but he remained the wealthiest, with more than twice the net worth of the runner-up, Republican Rep. Michael McCaul of Texas. (The Center estimated Issa's net worth in 2014 as somewhere between $230 million and $643 million.)

In the early 1990s, Issa turned to politics, contributing to Republicans and chairing the 1996 campaign to pass Proposition 209, which banned the use of racial quotas and preferences in California. In 1998, he ran for the Republican nomination to challenge Sen. Barbara Boxer and spent $9.8 million of his own money. He lost the primary 45%-40% to Matt Fong. In November 1999, when Rep. Ron Packard announced his retirement, 10 candidates ran in the Republican primary. This turned into a contest between Issa and state Sen. Bill Morrow. Morrow questioned Issa's business practices, and Issa raised questions about Morrow's honesty. On most issues, the candidates took similar positions. Issa spent $1.5 million of his own money on the primary and beat Morrow 46%-30%. In the fall, the Democratic nominee abandoned his campaign after getting little national party support, and Issa won 61%-28%.

Issa's voting record has had occasional moderate notes, especially on foreign affairs, as was the case with his *Almanac* ratings in 2015. Of Lebanese descent, he has condemned the sponsorship of terrorism by Arab nations while urging the United States to build coalitions with friendly Arab nations. That earned him enemies among pro-Israel groups.

After the 2008 election, House Republican leaders chose Issa over several more senior Republicans as ranking member on Oversight and Government Reform, with broad authority to investigate the federal government. As chairman, during the early days of the Republican Congress in 2011, he called the

Obama administration "one of the most corrupt administrations ever." He later said that he meant it was guilty of overspending and inefficiency. He began his chairmanship by accusing the Department of Homeland Security of letting political appointees interfere with Freedom of Information Act requests, and subsequently made a regular point of describing the administration's refusal to release documents as inconsistent with its stated philosophy of openness. His committee issued a stinging report on the handling of the Deepwater Horizon oil spill disaster in the Gulf of Mexico, accusing Obama and his administration of giving BP too much control over cleanup operations and failing to ensure that affected Gulf Coast residents were paid fairly and quickly for their losses.

The so-called "Fast and Furious" investigation dominated the committee's early agenda. The Bureau of Alcohol, Tobacco, Firearms and Explosives operation, which began in 2009, allowed guns to be shipped illegally into Mexico in an effort to track them to drug cartels. Two of the guns were found a year later at the scene of the killing of a U.S. Border Patrol agent in Arizona. Issa and other committee Republicans repeatedly pressed the administration to discuss who at the Justice Department was aware of the operation, as well as who authorized it. Justice officials, citing executive privilege, said releasing material Issa sought could jeopardize ongoing investigations. The spat became a hot topic for the far right and conspiracy theories flourished, including one floated by Issa at a National Rifle Association convention that the Obama administration deliberately lost the guns to later push for renewal of a ban on so-called assault weapons.

Attorney General Eric Holder landed in Issa's crosshairs. House Republicans voted in 2012 to hold him in contempt of Congress for allegedly withholding information. Seventeen Democrats joined the GOP, immunizing the Republicans from accusations of pure partisanship. Still, the White House accused Issa and the GOP of a witch hunt against Holder. The Justice Department's inspector general issued a 2012 report faulting ATF for misguided strategies and errors in judgment and management, which Issa said proved his point.

He turned his attention to the administration's handling of the Sept. 11, 2012, tragedy at the U.S. mission in Benghazi, Libya, in which four Americans were killed. Issa's office released 166 pages of "sensitive but unclassified" State Department communications related to Libya. But it did not redact identifying information about Libyans working with the United States. Ethics watchdog groups, who earlier had filed complaints against Issa for releasing wiretap information related to Fast and Furious, joined Democrats in expressing outrage. Former Obama White House Chief of Staff Rahm Emanuel called Issa "reckless." Issa responded that, "Anything below 'Secret' (classification) is in fact just a name on a piece of paper." In May 2014, the House voted to create a select committee to investigate the events surrounding the attack in Benghazi, which superseded the work of Issa's committee.

Probably Issa's most highly charged inquiry was his panel's extended review in 2013-14 of the Internal Revenue Service and its allegedly unfair treatment of tea party groups that had applied for tax-exempt status. Issa and his staff documented examples of the IRS treating conservative activists with a double standard compared to their liberal counterparts. When Lois Lerner, the head of the IRS division on tax-exempt organizations, was discovered to have "lost" tens of thousands of files in her office computer, and Lerner then cited her Fifth Amendment right not to testify before the Issa committee because she might incriminate herself, the committee in May 2014 asked the Justice Department to investigate whether she had broken the law. Nearly a year later, the department concluded that there were not sufficient grounds on which to charge her. Lerner earlier was placed on administrative leave at the IRS.

Issa occasionally pursued investigations on a bipartisan basis, notably his review of misbehavior by Secret Service agents while they were supposedly on the job protecting Obama or incidents in which intruders ran loose on the White House grounds. With the Oversight Committee's ranking Democrat, Elijah Cummings of Maryland, Issa wrote that there was a "bipartisan apprehension about a series of dangerous security breaches."

In 2015, Issa became chairman of the Judiciary Subcommittee on Courts, Intellectual Property and Internet. He pursued, in particular, patent reform issues. Drawing on his experience as a patent holder (he holds 37 of them), he had sponsored a bipartisan bill that became law in 2011 giving district court judges hearing patent cases access to clerks trained in patent law. He also has co-sponsored bipartisan legislation to create a review process of already-issued patents and to tighten rules for calculating damages in patent lawsuits. The technology industry had led the charge for patent reform, contending it has been held hostage by "patent trolls" who obtain patents solely for the purpose of launching infringement suits to cash in on multibillion-dollar damage awards. Working with Judiciary Committee Chairman Bob Goodlatte of Virginia, Issa pursued legislation to restrict such practices. They ran into opposition from other conservatives, who feared that the proposal would stifle innovation and entrepreneurship. Issa also supported requiring radio stations to pay royalties to record companies and performers as well as to composers of music.

With ambitions for statewide office, Issa in 2003 spent $1.7 million of his own money to get the signatures needed for a recall election of Democratic Gov. Gray Davis. His hopes of getting unified GOP support as a replacement candidate were dashed when Arnold Schwarzenegger got in the race. Issa tearfully announced that he would not run.

After that, he was reelected easily, until his political fortunes had an abrupt change in 2016. Democratic challenger Doug Applegate, a retired Marine Corps colonel and political neophyte, sought to take advantage of local voters' hostility to Republican presidential nominee Donald Trump. "I knew one thing the Democrats never have tried is to run a Marine," Applegate told *The Washington Post*. "And I know that in the military, if you say anything that's racist or misogynistic, nine out of 10 times you'll be disciplined for it." He said that Issa was "Trump before there was Trump." In the weeks before the election, Applegate ran excerpts from the *Hollywood Access* video with Trump's crude comments about women. Issa helped the Democrats make their case by introducing Trump at an enthusiastic rally in San Diego a few days before the June primary in California.

Issa was slow to respond to the challenge, even when he led the first round of voting by a mere 50. %-45.5%. He was a "high-profile Trump booster in a rapidly changing, well-educated district where Trump is toxic," David Wasserman of the Cook Political Report wrote a month before the election. The Democratic Congressional Campaign Committee and its liberal allies spent $3.6 million, in addition to the $2.1 million that Applegate raised. The deep-pocket Issa raised $2.9 million, but self-financed only $36,000 and had no national party assistance. When Issa finally attacked, he raised Applegate's messy divorce records. Three weeks after the election, Issa was declared the winner, 50.3%-49.7%, a margin of 1,621 votes. Issa led by more than 16,000 votes among the 79,000 that were cast in Orange County, while the San Diego-based Applegate led by 15,000 among the 231,000 votes in his home county. Applegate said he planned a rematch in 2018.

Northwest San Diego: Oceanside, Vista

Population		**Race and Ethnicity**		**Income**	
Total	724,280	White	61.4%	Median Income	$74,916 (54 out of 435)
Land area	553	Black	2.6%		
Pop/ sq mi	1309.5	Latino	25.9%	Under $50,000	27.8%
Born in state	49.5%	Asian	6.6%	$50,000-$99,999	24.9%
		Two races	2.7%	$100,000-$199,999	12.9%
Age Groups		Other	0.9%	$200,000 or more	11.2%
Under 18	23.4%			Poverty Rate	11.2%
18-34	24.1%	**Education**			
35-64	39.2%	H.S grad or less	26.6%	**Health Insurance**	
Over 64	13.2%	Some college	31.6%	With health insurance coverage	88.1%
		College Degree, 4 yr	25.6%		
Work		Post grad	16.1%		
White Collar	43.7%			**Public Assistance**	
Sales and Service	41.9%	**Military**		Cash public assistance income	1.8%
Blue Collar	14.4%	Veteran	9.1%		
Government	11.8%	Active Duty	4.8%	Food stamp/SNAP benefits	3.6%

Voter Turnout			
2015 Total Citizens 18+	495,907	2016 House Turnout as % CVAP	63%
2016 House turnout	310,155	2014 House Turnout as % CVAP	33%

2012 Presidential Vote		
Mitt Romney	153,856	(52%)
Barack Obama	134,447	(46%)

2016 Presidential Vote		
Hillary Clinton	159,081	(50%)
Donald Trump	135,576	(43%)
Gary Johnson	13,636	(4%)

Cook Partisan Voting Index: R+1

The California coast between Los Angeles and San Diego has never entirely filled up with development - and never will as long as the Marine Corps retains custody of Camp Pendleton, the giant training base just south of the Orange-San Diego County line and the Corps' largest expeditionary training facility on the West Coast. The land along the coast and inland in northern San Diego County, usually referred to as North County, was largely empty territory a half-century ago - never fertile enough to produce a large farm community, never endowed with much manufacturing, never actively promoted as a retirement community. But North County has been growing rapidly since then. Today more than 800,000 people live here, and who can blame them? This is one of America's most beautiful and comfortable environments, with ocean and mountain scenery, sunny and warm weather, and low crime. Amid dry but not desert landscape, there are miles of rolling hills, with occasional sagebrush-like bushes. It has attracted thousands of new migrants - many, but by no means all, retirees. New construction and home sales fell off during the Great Recession, but the local economy has been on the upswing.

Southern California Edison announced in 2013 the permanent shutdown of the San Onofre nuclear plant because of the financial costs and regulatory uncertainty of restarting a reactor following discovery of a radiation leak in 2012, plus flaws in the plant's steam generators. The company said that it planned to start the decommissioning in 2018, which it estimated as a 20-year, $4.4 billion project. In return, homeowners in the area expected that their properties would appreciate several billion dollars in value. In Carlsbad, a Boston-based company opened in December 2015 a $1 billion desalination plant, partly in response to the California water crisis. The San Diego County Water Authority, the region's main water manager, had a 30-year agreement to purchase the desalinated water. At least 15 other such plants have been proposed in California.

The 49th Congressional District covers the southernmost coastal area of Orange County, including Laguna Niguel and the heavily Republican San Clemente. Known as the "Spanish Village by the Sea," San Clemente is where Richard Nixon retired to write his memoirs after resigning the presidency. Nixon purchased his 5.5 acre estate in 1969, reportedly for a bit less than $1 million, though the financing was complicated and later controversial. He sold it in 1980. In April 2016, it was reported that the subsequent owner, the retired chief executive of Allergan pharmaceutical company, listed the property for sale at $69 million. The district takes in parts of northern San Diego County and the North County, including Oceanside, Encinitas and Carlsbad, home of the La Costa resort and a big tourist destination. About three-fourths of the voters in the 49th are in San Diego.

Politically, the district has leaned Republican. In 2012, Mitt Romney led President Barack Obama, 52%-46%. Hillary Clinton turned that around in 2016, when she led Donald Trump, 50%-43%.

FIFTIETH DISTRICT

Duncan Hunter (R)

Elected 2008, 5th term; b. Dec 07, 1976, San Diego; Marine Corps Officer Candidate School (VA); San Diego State University, B.A.; Baptist; Married (Margaret Hunter); 3 children.

Military Career: U.S. Marine Corps, 2002-2005 (Iraq); Marine Reserves, 2005-present (Afghanistan).

Professional Career: Business analyst, Cayenta Inc., 2000-2002; Residential developer, 2005-2007.

DC Office: 2429 RHOB 20515, 202-225-5672, Fax: 202-225-0235, hunter.house.gov.

State Offices: El Cajon, 619-448-5201; Temecula, 951-695-5108.

Committees: *Armed Services*: Seapower & Projection Forces, Strategic Forces. *Education & the Workforce*: Early Childhood, Elementary & Secondary Education, Workforce Protections. *Transportation & Infrastructure*: Aviation, Coast Guard & Maritime Transportation (Chmn), Highways & Transit.

Group Ratings

	ADA	ACLU	AFL-CIO	LCV	ITI	COC	HAFA	ACU	CFG	FRC
2016	-	5%	-	0%	83%	100%	69%	88%	63%	92%
2015	5%	C	25%	3%	C	75%	C	92%	71%	83%

Almanac Ratings 2015

	Economy	Social	Foreign	Composite
Liberal	13%	15%	0%	9%
Conservative	87%	85%	100%	91%

Key Votes of the 114th Congress

1. Keystone Pipeline	Y	5. Puerto Rico Debt	Y	9. Offenses by Aliens	Y
2. Trade Deals	N	6. Medical Marijuana	Y	10. Troops in Iraq	N
3. Export-Import Bank	Y	7. Sanctuary Cities	Y	11. Homeland Security $$	N
4. Debt Ceiling Increase	N	8. Armor-piercing Bullets	Y	12. Trade Adjustment aid	N

Election Results

Election	Name (Party)	Vote (%)	Cand. Spent	Ind. Exp. Support	Ind. Exp. Oppose
2016 General	Duncan Hunter (R)	179,937 (64%)	$859,347		
	Patrick Malloy (D)	103,646 (37%)	$22,523		
2016 Primary	Duncan Hunter (R)	55,311 (57%)			
	Patrick Malloy (D)	20,987 (22%)			
	David Secor (D)	10,866 (11%)			
	Scott Meisterlin (R)	6,630 (7%)			

Prior winning percentages: 2014 (71%), 2012 (68%), 2010 (63%), 2008 (56%)

Republican Duncan D. Hunter, elected in 2008, holds the seat that his father, Duncan Hunter, former chairman of the House Armed Services Committee, held for 28 years before him. The younger Hunter is a Marine Corps veteran and just as much of a defense hawk as his father, occasionally going his own way on military issues.

The younger Hunter grew up in El Cajon and got a degree in business administration from San Diego State University, after having started a website design company with a friend during his sophomore year. He worked in the computer industry for several years during the technology boom of the late 1990s. He says that the Sept. 11, 2001, terrorist attacks prompted him to rethink his career plans. The next day, Hunter quit his job and enlisted in the Marine Corps. After completing officer training, Hunter was commissioned as a lieutenant. He was deployed to Iraq in 2003, served in Baghdad after the fall of the city, and in 2004 fought in the battle of Fallujah. In 2006, he was promoted to captain and placed on reserve status.

Though he earlier had shown little interest in following his father into politics, he said his battlefield experiences led him to reconsider public service. Shortly after announcing his candidacy in March 2007 for his retiring father's House seat, Hunter was again called to active duty, this time in Afghanistan. Hunter was prohibited from any campaign activities, including fundraising and planning, and held only one event before leaving. In his absence, the management of his nascent campaign fell to his wife, Margaret Hunter. She took over all appearances and campaign duties in addition to caring for their three young children. When Hunter called home from Afghanistan, it was illegal for him even to inquire how the campaign was going, and he remained largely in the dark until his duty ended in December 2007. He returned home to resume campaigning full-time.

In the June primary, Hunter faced Santee Councilman Brian Jones and San Diego Board of Education President Bob Watkins. Although both were well known locally and campaigned actively, Hunter and his family surrogates effectively ran on the basis of his military credentials. Hunter also benefited from his father's political and congressional connections, raising nearly three times as much as his Republican challengers. Hunter cruised to victory in the June primary with 72 percent of the vote. In the general election, Democrats paid little attention to the contest, and Hunter prevailed, 56%-39%. He has won reelection with more than 60 percent since.

Hunter shares many of his father's political beliefs. On the Armed Services Committee, he cites national security as his top priority. "I can tell you what the guys on the ground, the men and women out there fighting, actually need," Hunter said. "We have a whole lot of brass out there at the Pentagon and in the DOD who haven't left their offices in six or seven years." He has been vocal about the need for more defense spending. In 2012, he said that the Obama administration should consider building fewer littoral combat ships that operate close to the shore, and use the savings to construct more traditional amphibious warships that could be used to support Marine Corps operations. The shortage of amphibious ships is "one of the most glaring gaps in the Navy," he said.

Hunter has been outspoken on military personnel issues. He strongly opposed repealing the "don't ask, don't tell" policy prohibiting openly gay military personnel, telling National Public Radio that the bond between soldiers "is broken if you open up the military to transgenders, to hermaphrodites, to gays and lesbians." He opposed requiring women to register for the military draft with the Selective Service. When he offered such a proposal in April 2016 during the Armed Services Committee debate of the annual defense spending bill, a bare majority of the committee unexpectedly voted in favor, though Hunter opposed his own amendment. After Navy Secretary Ray Mabus said that he supported making women eligible for combat posts in the Marines, Hunter said that such a plan was "a greater threat to the Marine Corps than ISIS."

During a 2013 visit to the Syria-Jordan border, he said that President Barack Obama needed to provide additional support to rebel groups in Syria. But Hunter opposed the aid in 2014 when the House voted on a request from Obama, saying that he had "no confidence we are arming the right people." Hunter pressed the Pentagon to do more to confront the threat posed by the Islamic State. He told Fox News in a 2014 interview that their fighters had crossed the Mexican border into Texas. The Homeland Security Department firmly denied his claim.

Hunter's other interests include tougher immigration laws and finding ways to halt the outflow of jobs overseas. In 2014, he opposed the creation in Escondido of a shelter for children who had crossed the border illegally. In January 2017, he was part of a contentious event on Capitol Hill in which he removed from a public exhibit a painting that depicted police as pigs. Hunter returned the painting to Democratic Rep. William Lacy Clay of Missouri, who had sponsored it. Clay then returned the painting to the site, after which it was removed again.

As chairman of the Transportation and Infrastructure Subcommittee on Coast Guard and Maritime Transportation, Hunter took the lead in the House during the December 2015 enactment of a Coast Guard authorization bill, which included more authority to crack down on smuggling and funding for a polar icebreaker. Hunter's work on this legislation has been useful for the San Diego region, where the Coast Guard has operated since 1937 and now patrols for illegal immigration and drug enforcement.

In February 2016, Hunter was one of the first congressional Republicans to endorse Donald Trump for president, saying that they agreed on many national security and immigration issues. During his campaign, his Democratic opponent, Patrick Malloy, criticized Hunter for being "joined at the hip" with Trump. Malloy cited reports that Hunter had used campaign funds for personal purposes. Hunter largely ignored the charges, and he was reelected 63%-37%. In December 2016, the House Ethics Committee issued a statement that it was investigating the financial allegations.

Inland San Diego: Escondido, El Cajon

Population		**Race and Ethnicity**		**Income**	
Total	730,427	White	57.6%	Median Income	$62,468 (116 out of 435)
Land area	2,787	Black	2.3%		
Pop/ sq mi	262.1	Latino	30.2%		
Born in state	54.8%	Asian	5.3%	Under $50,000	30.7%
		Two races	3.2%	$50,000-$99,999	23.7%
Age Groups		Other	1.4%	$100,000-$199,999	5.2%
Under 18	24.5%			$200,000 or more	13.9%
18-34	23.0%	**Education**		Poverty Rate	13.9%
35-64	39.5%	H.S grad or less	38.1%		
Over 64	13.0%	Some college	35.9%	**Health Insurance**	
Work		College Degree, 4 yr	17.5%	With health insurance coverage	85.3%
White Collar	33.7%	Post grad	8.6%		
Sales and Service	45.6%	**Military**		**Public Assistance**	
Blue Collar	20.6%	Veteran	10.1%	Cash public assistance income	3.2%
Government	13.6%	Active Duty	0.8%		
				Food stamp/SNAP benefits	7.4%

Voter Turnout			
2015 Total Citizens 18+	476,835	2016 House Turnout as % CVAP	59%
2016 House turnout	283,583	2014 House Turnout as % CVAP	33%

2012 Presidential Vote		
Mitt Romney	165,104	(60%)
Barack Obama	102,649	(38%)

2016 Presidential Vote		
Donald Trump	159,822	(54%)
Hillary Clinton	115,864	(39%)
Gary Johnson	12,240	(4%)

Cook Partisan Voting Index: R+11

San Diego began as a port, but today most metropolitan-area residents live out of sight of the sea, in hilltop neighborhoods that look out over distant ridges and freeways or in warm, sunny valleys amid the mountains that become dense and taller as one travels east from the Pacific Ocean. There is a discernible difference in attitudes and values between those who have settled inland and those who live nearer the ocean, part of the split between coastal California and interior California that has been at the heart of the state's political struggles and culture wars. Outside of the city of San Diego, these groups in San Diego County have tended to identify as Republicans. Coastal residents tend to be more affluent, and those who settle inland are more likely to be culturally traditional, supportive of the military and dubious about the ability of government to help society's have-nots. Part of this can be explained by the area's large military presence. A 2016 report estimated that the Pentagon accounts for about $45 billion in annual spending in San Diego County, which is about 20 percent of the local economy. That includes 134,000 civilians and active-duty military and 53 ships home-ported in San Diego, and two aircraft carriers based in Coronado. Many veterans and military retirees have settled in the area.

North of San Diego on Interstate 15 is Escondido, a conservative city that is 49 percent Hispanic. Tensions between the Escondido political leadership and Latino activists have heightened in recent years, as the City Council passed several tough ordinances cracking down on illegal immigration. In response to a lawsuit against the city over its at-large electoral system that activists said was discriminatory against Latinos, the city agreed to divide its council into four districts, one of which had a Hispanic majority. In the November 2016 election, Latina Olga Diaz was elected, though not in the Hispanic-majority district.

The 50th Congressional District of California takes in much of the mountain and desert interior of San Diego County. The district includes a small slice of Riverside County, which is mostly in Temecula. It touches neither the Pacific Ocean nor the border with Mexico, but it comes within a few miles of each. Eastern parts of the district are lightly inhabited. In the mountains is tiny Alpine and in the desert is the town of Borrego Springs, amid the giant Anza-Borrego Desert State Park. El Cajon, which is split with the 51st District, has the nation's second-largest community of Chaldeans, Catholic Arabs from Iraq. That Chaldean community has had conflicts with the church's international leadership over possible excommunication of local priests unless they recognized the authority in Baghdad. In 2015, Pope Francis sided with the San Diego church. Politically, this district is solidly Republican. This was the strongest California district for Donald Trump south of Bakersfield. He led Hillary Clinton, 54%-39%.

FIFTY-FIRST DISTRICT

Juan Vargas (D)

Elected 2012, 3rd term; b. Mar 07, 1961, National City; University of San Diego, B.A.; Fordham University (NY); Harvard University Law School (MA), J.D.; Roman Catholic; Married (Adrienne D'Ascoli); 2 children.

Elected Office: San Diego City Council, 1993-2000; CA Assembly, 2000-2006, Assistant Majority Leader, 2000; CA Senate, 2010-2012.

Professional Career: Practicing attorney, Luce, Forward, Hamilton, & Scripps; Vice President., external affairs, Safeco Ins., 2006-2008; Vice President., corporate legal, Liberty Mutual Group, 2008-2010.

DC Office: 1605 LHOB 20515, 202-225-8045, Fax: 202-225-2772, vargas.house.gov.

State Offices: Chula Vista, 619-422-5963; El Centro, 760-312-9900.

Committees: *Financial Services*: Capital Markets, Securities & Investment, Monetary Policy & Trade, Terrorism & Illicit Finance.

Group Ratings

	ADA	ACLU	AFL-CIO	LCV	ITI	COC	HAFA	ACU	CFG	FRC
2016	-	94%	-	100%	67%	57%	11%	0%	0%	0%
2015	85%	C	100%	97%	C	53%	C	4%	0%	0%

Almanac Ratings 2015

	Economy	Social	Foreign	Composite
Liberal	88%	100%	71%	86%
Conservative	12%	0%	29%	14%

Key Votes of the 114th Congress

1. Keystone Pipeline	N	5. Puerto Rico Debt	N	9. Offenses by Aliens	N
2. Trade Deals	NV	6. Medical Marijuana	Y	10. Troops in Iraq	N
3. Export-Import Bank	Y	7. Sanctuary Cities	N	11. Homeland Security $$	Y
4. Debt Ceiling Increase	Y	8. Armor-piercing Bullets	N	12. Trade Adjustment aid	Y

Election Results

Election	Name (Party)	Vote (%)		Cand. Spent	Ind. Exp. Support	Ind. Exp. Oppose
2016 General	Juan Vargas (D)	145,162	(73%)	$517,416		
	Juan Hidalgo (R)	54,362	(27%)	$63,806	$461	
2016 Primary	Juan Vargas (D)	39,460	(67%)			
	Juan Hidalgo Jr. (R)	9,697	(16%)			
	Juan Mercado-Flores (D)	5,133	(9%)			
	Carlos Sanchez (R)	4,953	(8%)			

Prior winning percentages: 2014 (69%), 2012 (72%)

Democrat Juan Vargas, first elected in 2012, has taken control of the district that he had sought for years. In this border district, he has spent much of his time on immigration. His committee assignment has been on Financial Services, which has few links to local issues but has been an area of personal expertise.

Vargas was born in National City, just south of San Diego. He is the son of *braceros*, who were among the millions of legal Mexican immigrants brought to the U.S. for cheap labor. He grew up on a chicken ranch in an urbanized area. While other kids at school had dogs and cats, Vargas had pet ducks. He considered entering the priesthood but said he was wary of going straight into a seminary. Instead, he graduated from the University of San Diego. After college, Vargas studied with the Jesuits, working with the poor, orphans, and refugees in El Salvador and elsewhere. The Jesuits sent him to Fordham University, where he studied philosophy and earned a master's degree. At Fordham, he met his future wife, Adrienne, a fellow student who worked with him at a soup kitchen in the Bronx. At Harvard, he earned a law degree alongside a student named Barack Obama. Vargas guarded the future president in pickup basketball games and said that Obama was the more talented player.

After law school, Vargas settled in San Diego and briefly worked at a large corporate law firm. He served on the City Council for seven years and then won election to the California Assembly, where he stayed for six years. In 2010, he won election to the state Senate, where he chaired the Banking and Financial Institutions Committee and advocated government support for children and the elderly. He sponsored a bill mandating the reporting of child abuse by athletic coaches in California, a direct response to the Pennsylvania State University sex abuse scandal. Between his stints in the Legislature, he was an executive with two insurance companies.

Vargas ran three unsuccessful campaigns for Congress against Rep. Bob Filner in Democratic primaries. Filner stepped down and was elected mayor of San Diego, but quickly faced allegations of sexual harassment and resigned under pressure. In 2012, political observers expected Vargas and fellow Latino Democrat Denise Moreno Ducheny to advance in California's new jungle primary, in which the top two finishers, regardless of party, compete in the general election. But Vargas lavished attention on the Republican candidate, Michael Crimmins, in order to help him slide into second place. Vargas refused to participate in a debate unless Crimmins was included. Meanwhile, Vargas hammered Ducheny for a previous drunken-driving arrest. Crimmins edged Ducheny 20%-15%, and faced Vargas in the fall election, when his defeat was all but assured in the strongly Democratic district. It was a smart strategy. Vargas won 71%-29%. He has had no trouble with reelection.

Vargas has sought to provide a sympathetic ear to immigrants and refugees, no matter their circumstances. After protesters turned away busloads in Murrieta, he met with them the next day in El Centro in 2014. Carrying a Bible, Vargas prayed with them and told them that they would be treated "fairly and with dignity." He did not promise that they would remain in the United States. In 2016, he filed legislation that would require the military to inform recruits who are not citizens about the citizenship process while they are in training. Even while Donald Trump during his presidential campaign was promising to build a wall along the border with Mexico, Vargas told civic groups in his district that he wanted to build more bridges. With Republican Rep. Duncan Hunter, Vargas filed a bill to provide protection and a "safe haven" for local Chaldean Christians who had been threatened by their religious leaders in Iraq. In February 2017, he proposed an Imperial Valley conservation bill that sought to protect habitats and create new recreational areas for motor bikes on designated routes.

On the Financial Services Committee, Vargas worked with members who shared his interest in insurance issues. With Republican Rep. Bruce Poliquin of Maine, he won House approval in December 2016 of a provision that required the Securities and Exchange Commission to respond to any findings and recommendations from the SEC's annual Government-Business Forum on Small Business Capital Formation. Vargas cosponsored with Republican Rep. Peter Roskam of Illinois a provision that conditioned free-trade agreements with the nations of the European Union on their rejection of the anti-Israel boycott, divestment and sanctions movement. The provision was enacted in 2015 as part of the measure that gave trade promotion authority to Obama.

San Diego to Nevada: Eastern Chula Vista, Imperial

Population		**Race and Ethnicity**		**Income**	
Total	728,256	White	13.5%	Median Income	$41,357 (382 out of 435)
Land area	4,792	Black	6.5%		
Pop/ sq mi	152.0	Latino	69.8%		
Born in state	51.9%	Asian	8.1%	Under $50,000	27.9%
		Two races	1.5%	$50,000-$99,999	12.5%
Age Groups		Other	0.7%	$100,000-$199,999	1.5%
Under 18	27.0%			$200,000 or more	24.2%
18-34	28.0%	**Education**		Poverty Rate	24.2%
35-64	34.5%	H.S grad or less	57.0%		
Over 64	10.4%	Some college	29.6%	**Health Insurance**	
		College Degree, 4 yr	9.8%	With health insurance coverage	78.2%
Work		Post grad	3.6%		
White Collar	20.8%				
Sales and Service	53.6%	**Military**		**Public Assistance**	
Blue Collar	25.5%	Veteran	6.6%	Cash public assistance income	5.7%
Government	17.0%	Active Duty	2.6%		
				Food stamp/SNAP benefits	17.3%

Voter Turnout			
2015 Total Citizens 18+	399,674	2016 House Turnout as % CVAP	50%
2016 House turnout	199,524	2014 House Turnout as % CVAP	21%

2012 Presidential Vote		
Barack Obama	115,610	(69%)
Mitt Romney	48,108	(29%)

2016 Presidential Vote		
Hillary Clinton	147,603	(71%)
Donald Trump	46,825	(23%)
Gary Johnson	5,714	(3%)
Jill Stein	4,065	(2%)

Cook Partisan Voting Index: D+22

Anchoring a corner of the continental United States, San Diego not so long ago was a small Navy town known for its good harbor and splendid weather. It is now a major metropolis of 1.4 million people and the center of a county of 3.3 million. To its occasional discomfort, it is also one of the largest cities directly on an international border, situated between countries with strikingly different economic conditions, political systems and cultural traditions. San Diego sits on the busiest border crossing in the world, and on a daily basis agents for the Border Patrol play a sometimes violent cat-and-mouse game with people trying to cross illegally. The Great Recession slowed traffic considerably. Apprehensions in the San Diego sector, which numbered around 300,000 a year in the 1980s, dropped to 26,000 in 2015. The apprehensions jumped to 32,000 in 2016, when there was only a 2 percent increase nationwide. Border agents said that the enforcement policies of President Donald Trump will result in a further increase as they are permitted to do their job. In 2014, local agents seized 48 percent of the amphetamines and 38 percent of cocaine of the totals that were seized nationwide. Credit was due, in part, to the discovery of two tunnels that connected warehouses on the two sides of the border.

Thousands of legal workers cross the border daily to reach the industrial zone on San Diego's southern edge, in Otay Mesa and San Ysidro and the industrial suburbs of Chula Vista and National City. Many children from Mexico cross daily to attend public and private schools. Latinos pour billions of dollars into the San Diego economy and are scattered in various parts of the city. Oddly, there is not much evidence of Mexican style in San Diego - less than in Los Angeles.

The thinly-populated and agricultural Imperial County to the east has faced enormous economic adversity. Its unemployment rate is routinely the highest in California, earning that distinction again in November 2016 with a 20.3 percent jobless rate. El Centro, a center for lettuce growers, earlier in the year had the highest jobless rate of any city in the nation, with 19.6 percent. The county is 83 percent Hispanic. Its salvation may lie in energy innovation. The first solar energy project in the Imperial Valley opened in 2013. In 2015, San Diego Gas & Electric was five years ahead of schedule in meeting state requirements for the use of solar and wind power. Tesla moved production of its battery-operated cars to Las Vegas, though it struck a more limited economic deal with a large plant to draw lithium - used in electric car batteries - from the Salton Sea. In January 2017, two start-up companies said they planned to develop a geothermal power plant near the Salton Sea, as soon as 2020. Even in the desert, California's water shortage has had consequences. A plan to restore the sea, which was created when the Colorado River overran its dikes in 1905, has suffered because its disappearing wetlands and fish now attract fewer migrating birds. That makes the remaining sea even saltier, and will have consequences, in turn, for human activity. In 2016, the drought placed additional demands on the limited water supply from the Colorado River. Local officials threatened to cut back their participation in statewide sharing.

The 51st Congressional District of California covers California's entire border with Mexico, from the Arizona state line to the southeast corner of the city of San Diego near Balboa Park, the eastern side of San Diego Bay, plus National City and Chula Vista. It includes the Salton Sea basin in the eastern desert and the Tijuana River National Estuarine Research Reserve on the western coast. About one-fourth of the vote is cast in Imperial County, all of which is in the 51st, with the remainder in San Diego County. The district is 71 percent Hispanic. The Democratic share of the presidential vote increased from 66 percent in 2008 to 71 percent in 2016.

FIFTY-SECOND DISTRICT

Scott Peters (D)

Elected 2012, 3rd term; b. Jun 17, 1958, Springfield, OH; Duke University (NC), B.A.; New York University Law School, J.D., 1984; Lutheran; Married (Lynn Gorguze); 2 children.

Elected Office: San Diego City Council, 2000-2008, President, 2006-2008.

Professional Career: Economist, U.S. Environmental Protection Agency, 1980-1981; Deputy Attorney, San Diego City, 1991-1996; Practicing attorney, 1984-1991, 1996-2000; CA Commission on Tax Policy in the New Economy, 2002-2003; CA Coastal Commission, 2002-2005; San Diego Unified Port District Commission, 2009-2012.

DC Office: 1122 LHOB 20515, 202-225-0508, Fax: 202-225-2558, scottpeters.house.gov.

State Offices: San Diego, 858-455-5550.

Committees: *Energy & Commerce*: Energy, Environment, Oversight & Investigations. *Veterans' Affairs*: Oversight & Investigations.

Group Ratings

	ADA	ACLU	AFL-CIO	LCV	ITI	COC	HAFA	ACU	CFG	FRC
2016	-	76%	-	97%	100%	71%	10%	0%	10%	0%
2015	60%	C	83%	89%	C	65%	C	0%	1%	0%

Almanac Ratings 2015

	Economy	Social	Foreign	Composite
Liberal	52%	90%	58%	67%
Conservative	48%	10%	42%	33%

Key Votes of the 114th Congress

1. Keystone Pipeline	N	5. Puerto Rico Debt	Y	9. Offenses by Aliens	Y
2. Trade Deals	Y	6. Medical Marijuana	Y	10. Troops in Iraq	N
3. Export-Import Bank	Y	7. Sanctuary Cities	N	11. Homeland Security $$	Y
4. Debt Ceiling Increase	Y	8. Armor-piercing Bullets	N	12. Trade Adjustment aid	Y

Election Results

Election	Name (Party)	Vote (%)	Cand. Spent	Ind. Exp. Support	Ind. Exp. Oppose
2016 General	Scott Peters (D)	181,253 (57%)	$2,399,175	$258,286	
	Denise Gitsham (R)	139,403 (44%)	$1,373,038		
2016 Primary	Scott Peters (D)	64,811 (59%)			
	Denise Gitsham (R)	17,761 (16%)			
	Jacquie Atkinson (R)	14,785 (13%)			

Prior winning percentages: 2014 (52%), 2012 (51%)

Scott Peters, first elected in 2012 with help from a redrawn congressional district, has survived two costly and tight campaigns against experienced local Republicans. That success has benefited from a centrist voting record and his occasional distancing from the liberal views of most congressional Democrats from California.

Peters is the son of a Lutheran minister who fought against redlining in Detroit in the 1960s, when African Americans and Jews were prevented from buying homes in some neighborhoods. A threat against his family sparked a police chief to suggest his father take them out of town for a week. At age 14, while the family was briefly living in Chicago, Peters had his first taste of politics campaigning for Democrat George McGovern's unsuccessful 1972 presidential race. He studied political science and economics at Duke, taking a low-wage job cleaning pigeon cages for the psychology department to support himself. He went on to graduate from New York University's law school.

His wife, Lynn Gorguze, forged a successful career in private equity, and her work brought them to San Diego in 1988. She is the daughter of a wealthy La Jolla industrialist who was a contributor to Republican presidential candidate Mitt Romney. Peters had a wide-ranging, 16-year career as a lawyer handling environmental regulation, corporate taxes and litigation at various firms; served as a deputy county counsel; and opened a private practice before being elected to the city council in 2000. During two back-to-back terms- the last three years as president - Peters worked on reducing sewage spills, redeveloping neighborhoods to make them more walkable, boosting jobs with support for a downtown ballpark and creating the city's first ethics commission. For 2015, *Roll Call* ranked Peters as the 11th wealthiest member of Congress, with a net worth of $40 million.

In 2012, Peters endured a bruising primary battle against Lori SaldaÑa, a former state Assembly member. She drew support from a left-leaning coalition of environmentalists and other liberal activists, but Peters snagged endorsements from a host of Democratic officials. Despite outspending SaldaÑa by 5-to-1, Peters eked out a victory by just 700 votes.

Running against three-term Republican Rep. Brian Bilbray, Peters found himself on the defensive against GOP attacks that he underfunded public-employee pensions during his tenure on the council, something that had marred his unsuccessful race for city attorney in 2009. He responded by accusing Bilbray of talking as a moderate while voting as a conservative, and he regularly touted his desire not to be bound by ideology. "I'm just not a purist. You set goals and you have to work with everyone to figure out how to get what you can," he said. Peters financed his campaign with more than $1 million from his own wealth and was one of the Democratic Congressional Campaign Committee's top "Red to Blue" candidates for picking up Republican-leaning seats. He outspent the incumbent, $4.3 million to $2.8 million and won 51.2%-48.8%.

His votes in the House, as shown by the *Almanac* vote ratings for 2015, have stamped him as a centrist. He tried to remain a political outsider by creating and publicizing his #FixCongressNow plan of broad changes in how Congress and elections operate, including five-day work weeks. He said Democrats "must move beyond economic fairness and now take the lead on creating an agenda for economic growth." His June 2015 vote to give trade promotion authority to President Barack Obama infuriated the AFL-CIO, which denied him the support of organized labor in the 2016 campaign. In November 2015, he was one of 47 Democrats who voted for tighter screening of refugees from Syria and Iraq. Peters pursued some actions of a congressional insider, including his post as a senior whip with House Minority Whip Steny Hoyer. He lined up in favor of steps to combat climate change, protect seniors on Medicare and promote immigration reform. On the House Armed Services Committee, he encouraged bipartisanship and protection of San Diego's Navy interests.

Even with all of these steps, he faced a difficult reelection in 2014 against Republican Carl DeMaio, a former member of the city council who had been praised for his efforts to improve the shaky finances of the city and narrowly lost a 2012 run for mayor of San Diego. DeMaio, who is openly gay, sought to move beyond traditional Republican support. In the first round of the election, Peters got 42 percent of the vote with DeMaio at 36 percent, and three Republicans divided the remainder. That was a clear sign that Peters was vulnerable. DeMaio styled himself as a "next generation Republican," but Peters ran a tough ad campaign that focused on the challenger's sometimes abrasive style and hardline positions on the city council. DeMaio was put on the defensive by charges of sexual harassment and bribery that were made by a former campaign aide. Peters outspent DeMaio, $4.5 million to $3.4 million, and the two candidates split another $7 million in national party money. In a close count that was not settled until three days after the election, Peters won 51.6%-48.4%. No charges were filed against DeMaio and the accuser later admitted that some of his charges were lies.

In 2016, Peters faced Denise Gitsham, who had worked in Texas for Karl Rove during the 2000 presidential campaign of Gov. George Bush and then joined Bush's White House staff. Gitsham emphasized her small-business values and raised $1.4 million. But Peters raised $3.5 million and won 57%-43%, with some likely benefit from the strong showing of Hillary Clinton in the presidential campaign. Republican Jacquie Atkinson, an openly lesbian Marine Corps combat veteran, finished third with 13 percent in the primary to 16 percent for Gitsham.

Northern San Diego: La Jolla, Mission Bay

Population		**Race and Ethnicity**		**Income**	
Total	731,075	White	59.2%	Median Income	$84,054 (26 out of 435)
Land area	267	Black	2.9%		
Pop/ sq mi	2738.1	Latino	13.9%	Under $50,000	28.4%
Born in state	42.3%	Asian	19.4%	$50,000-$99,999	29.5%
		Two races	3.8%	$100,000-$199,999	12.4%
Age Groups		Other	0.8%	$200,000 or more	9.6%
Under 18	19.7%			Poverty Rate	9.6%
18-34	28.5%	**Education**			
35-64	38.8%	H.S grad or less	17.2%	**Health Insurance**	
Over 64	13.0%	Some college	26.5%	With health insurance coverage	91.7%
		College Degree, 4 yr	32.1%		
Work		Post grad	24.2%		
White Collar	55.7%			**Public Assistance**	
Sales and Service	35.5%	**Military**		Cash public assistance income	1.3%
Blue Collar	8.8%	Veteran	9.7%		
Government	14.6%	Active Duty	3.5%	Food stamp/SNAP benefits	2.5%

Voter Turnout			
2015 Total Citizens 18+	522,003	2016 House Turnout as % CVAP	61%
2016 House turnout	320,656	2014 House Turnout as % CVAP	38%

2012 Presidential Vote		
Barack Obama	163,911	(52%)
Mitt Romney	143,726	(46%)

2016 Presidential Vote		
Hillary Clinton	191,325	(57%)
Donald Trump	117,057	(35%)
Gary Johnson	14,807	(4%)

Cook Partisan Voting Index: D+6

When the United States was dictating the terms of the Treaty of Guadalupe Hidalgo in 1848 after its successful war with Mexico, it made sure the southern boundary of its new California territory was just south of the port of San Diego. This is one of three splendid natural harbors on the Pacific Coast, and in 1914, the Marine Corps established a base on North Island. This was just the first of many military bases in San Diego, with its mild climate, deep harbor, and plentiful land for aircraft maneuvers. Naval Base San Diego has been the major West Coast U.S. Navy base for more than 50 years, the second-largest Navy port behind Norfolk, and home to 134,000 active-duty personnel, with more than one-fourth of the nation's Marines. Separate from the Navy facilities, the port generates more than 43,000 jobs and $5.4 billion in economic activity. Also located here are about 230,000 veterans, and the retired aircraft carrier *Midway*.

The port and Navy base in the sheltered harbor remain the central focus of a rapidly growing metropolis that now stretches far inland and to the north. Downtown features post-modern buildings like the Horton Plaza amid a few well-preserved early-20th-century relics like the Spreckels Theatre. Across the harbor, on the sand spit that guards it against the ocean, is the white frame castle of the Hotel Del Coronado, with its dark wooden interior - the U.S.'s largest wooden structure, opened in 1888 and a favored resort of past American presidents. The San Diego metro area economy has had slow, steady growth. Growth in life sciences, biotech and telecommunications contribute to what San Diego calls its "innovation industry," though local claims that this is the next Silicon Valley have been exaggerated.

The coastal area is not all Navy. To the north, the Pacific waves pound against the beach beneath unique rock formations along the coast. Part of La Jolla is here, including the Scripps Institute of Oceanography. To the south are raffish Mission Beach; Ocean Beach, with its strong rip currents; and Point Loma, overlooking the entrance to the harbor. The weather - a sunny 70 degrees most of the time - lures tourists and new residents. The area's warm climate nourishes prodigious baseball talent. Boston Red Sox great Ted Williams grew up here. In his book *Moneyball*, author Michael Lewis says Rancho Bernardo High School in San Diego came to be known in baseball circles as "The Factory," because it produced so many big league prospects. San Diego is also home to Comic-Con International, a four-day comic book and pop culture event that caps its attendance at 130,000 people annually. The January 2017 move of the National Football League's San Diego Chargers up the freeway to Los Angeles was a blow to civic pride, but an acknowledgment of the smaller local market that objected to the team's demand for a new stadium.

The 52nd Congressional District includes much of the city of San Diego. It is one of two districts that are entirely within San Diego County. It runs along the west coast, taking in most of the city's Navy installations, ports and beaches. Inland and north of San Diego, it includes high-income Poway. It shares La Jolla with the 49th District to its north. The Asian population of the 52nd exceeds the Hispanic community, 19 percent to 16 percent. Its median income is the highest of the five San Diego-based districts. Politically, it has been a competitive congressional battleground, though it leans to Democrats in presidential contests. Hillary Clinton defeated Donald Trump, 57%-35%, a big increase from President Barack Obama's 52%-46% lead over Mitt Romney in 2012.

FIFTY-THIRD DISTRICT

Susan Davis (D)

Elected 2000, 9th term; b. Apr 13, 1944, Cambridge, MA; University of California, Berkeley, B.S., 1965; University of North Carolina, Chapel Hill, M.A., 1968; Jewish; Married (Dr. Steve Davis); 2 children; 3 grandchildren.

Elected Office: San Diego School Board, 1983-1992, President, 1989-1992; CA Assembly, 1994-2000.

Professional Career: Devel. Association, KPBS Radio, 1980-1982.; Executive Director, Aaron Price Fellows, 1990-1994.

DC Office: 1214 LHOB 20515, 202-225-2040, Fax: 202-225-2948; Website: susandavis.house.gov.

State Offices: San Diego, 619-280-5353.

Committees: *Armed Services*: Seapower & Projection Forces, Strategic Forces. *Commission Congressional Mailing Standards (RMM)*. *Education & the Workforce*: Early Childhood, Elementary & Secondary Education, Higher Education & Workforce Development (RMM).

Group Ratings

	ADA	ACLU	AFL-CIO	LCV	ITI	COC	HAFA	ACU	CFG	FRC
2016	-	82%	-	100%	83%	62%	9%	71%	0%	0%
2015	90%	C	96%	97%	C	55%	C	0%	0%	0%

Almanac Ratings 2015

	Economy	Social	Foreign	Composite
Liberal	83%	100%	85%	89%
Conservative	17%	0%	15%	11%

Key Votes of the 114th Congress

1. Keystone Pipeline	N	5. Puerto Rico Debt	Y	9. Offenses by Aliens	N
2. Trade Deals	Y	6. Medical Marijuana	Y	10. Troops in Iraq	N
3. Export-Import Bank	Y	7. Sanctuary Cities	N	11. Homeland Security $$	Y
4. Debt Ceiling Increase	Y	8. Armor-piercing Bullets	N	12. Trade Adjustment aid	Y

Election Results

Election	Name (Party)	Vote (%)		Cand. Spent	Ind. Exp. Support	Ind. Exp. Oppose
2016 General	Susan Davis (D)	198,988	(67%)	$287,074		
	James Veltmeyer (R)	97,968	(33%)	$118,795		
2016 Primary	Susan Davis (D)	67,166	(65%)			
	Jim Ash (R)	16,085	(16%)			
	James Veltmeyer (R)	15,958	(15%)			

Prior winning percentages: 2014 (59%), 2012 (61%), 2010 (62%), 2008 (69%), 2006 (68%), 2004 (66%), 2002 (62%), 2000 (50%)

Susan Davis, a Democrat first elected in 2000, is a low-profile member who avoids the media spotlight in favor of working quietly behind the scenes on issues that range from education and women's health to local and national military matters.

Davis grew up in Richmond, California, the daughter of a pediatrician. She graduated from the University of California, Berkeley, and got a degree in social work at the University of North Carolina. After she married, she and her husband lived for a time in Japan while he served as an Air Force doctor during the Vietnam War. They moved to San Diego, where she was a producer for a local television station while also volunteering in civic groups, including as president of the local League of Women Voters. In 1983, Davis was elected to the San Diego school board. In 1994, she won the first of three terms in the California Assembly, where she chaired the Consumer Protection Committee.

Facing term limits, Davis in 2000 challenged Rep. Brian Bilbray, a Republican who had won three close elections. She portrayed him as too conservative for the district, though he took liberal and moderate positions on abortion rights and environmental protection. Bilbray had voted with conservatives to impeach President Bill Clinton in 1998, and Davis also attacked him for supporting bills that would deny citizenship to U.S.-born children of illegal immigrants. The AFL-CIO ran so much advertising on her behalf that Davis asked the union to stop. Davis won 50%-46%, and has been reelected without a serious challenge. Bilbray returned to Congress in June 2006 when he won a special election in the neighboring district, though he lost his seat a second time in 2012.

Davis' voting record tends to be in the center of House Democrats, though more liberal on social issues, as shown by the *Almanac* vote ratings for 2015. Assigned to the Armed Services and Education and the Workforce committees, her priorities have included higher military pay, increased aid for school districts with a large military presence, increased student loans, and incentives for better teachers. She angered organized labor by voting to give both Presidents George W. Bush and Barack Obama wide authority to negotiate international trade deals. San Diego is a city that has been built on trade. When organized labor rescinded its endorsement of her in 2015, she had a big drop in campaign contributions from unions, but there was no discernible electoral impact. In 2017, she became senior Democrat on the Higher Education Subcommittee, where she said her priorities were increased access to a college degree, equal opportunity in education and the workplace, student safety, and career and technical training – especially for women. She is the number-two Democrat on the Education and the Workforce Committee behind Rep. Bobby Scott of Virginia.

On Armed Services, she has been active on women's health issues, including abortion services for military women. In 2009, as chairman of the Armed Services' Personnel Subcommittee, she helped secure a higher military pay raise than President Barack Obama requested. She supported Obama's troop buildup in Afghanistan, but cautioned that greater civilian support and involvement from U.S. allies were essential. In November 2016, she proposed the Military Hunger Prevention Act to make it easier for needy military families to get food stamps. She found herself in an unusual position that month when she opposed a 2.1 percent military pay hike because of the potential impact on other programs. "I am concerned that by increasing [pay] above the requested amount, we are taking funds away from other critical priorities, including readiness," she said.

Davis has been reelected with ease. She received an unusual amount of attention in 2012 when she filed a lawsuit to try to recover $160,000 in campaign funds that were siphoned by her one-time campaign treasurer, who pleaded guilty to stealing more than $7 million from Davis and other California lawmakers. The conflict was resolved in 2014 with a legal settlement that returned $90,000 to her campaign account. In 2014, against modest Republican opposition, Davis posted weak reelection performances. In the first round, she got 56 percent of the vote against seven other candidates, none of them a Democrat. In November against Larry Wilske, whom she outspent more than 5-to-1, Davis won with 59 percent. She improved her performance in 2016. A Democratic opponent in the all-party primary got only 4 percent of the vote and Davis won in November with 67 percent.

East San Diego, La Mesa

Population		**Race and Ethnicity**		**Income**	
Total	745,567	White	41.1%	Median Income	$63,458 (108 out of 435)
Land area	135	Black	7.7%		
Pop/ sq mi	5505.2	Latino	33.4%		
Born in state	50.2%	Asian	12.9%	Under $50,000	32.9%
		Two races	3.8%	$50,000-$99,999	23.2%
Age Groups		Other	1.0%	$100,000-$199,999	5.0%
Under 18	21.1%			$200,000 or more	13.6%
18-34	29.3%	**Education**		Poverty Rate	13.6%
35-64	37.8%	H.S grad or less	30.4%		
Over 64	11.8%	Some college	34.2%	**Health Insurance**	
		College Degree, 4 yr	23.0%	With health insurance coverage	86.2%
Work		Post grad	12.5%		
White Collar	41.7%				
Sales and Service	43.7%	**Military**		**Public Assistance**	
Blue Collar	14.6%	Veteran	11.0%	Cash public assistance income	2.7%
Government	18.0%	Active Duty	1.7%		
				Food stamp/SNAP benefits	6.7%

Voter Turnout			
2015 Total Citizens 18+	517,582	2016 House Turnout as % CVAP	57%
2016 House turnout	296,956	2014 House Turnout as % CVAP	29%

2012 Presidential Vote		
Barack Obama	174,616	(61%)
Mitt Romney	103,513	(36%)

2016 Presidential Vote		
Hillary Clinton	200,237	(64%)
Donald Trump	91,822	(29%)
Gary Johnson	11,325	(4%)
Jill Stein	6,132	(2%)

Cook Partisan Voting Index: D+14

Often thought of as California's most conservative, straight-arrow city because of its long association with the U.S. Navy and the military, San Diego is now a multi-ethnic metropolis, with a population that is 29 percent Hispanic and 16 percent Asian. In a sense, the city is returning to its roots. Although it was the first European settlement in what is now California, San Diego was a part of newly independent Mexico in the early 1800s, and did not join the United States until after the Mexican-American War. It sits directly across the border from the Tijuana metropolitan area, and roughly 300,000 people a day cross from one city to the other, including 20,000 pedestrians. The drive across the border at the San Ysidro port of entry, the busiest entry point in the Western Hemisphere, often takes as long as two hours. Regular users can move more quickly through the Ready Lane if they have the requisite electronic documents. Expansion in 2014 increased northbound capacity to 46 booths, with additional expansion planned for 2019.

San Diego recently has had a stormy and unconventional political history. In 2012, the city elected 10-term Democratic Rep. Bob Filner as mayor. He was the city's first Democratic leader in 20 years. But he quickly ran into ethical problems and survived only seven months before he resigned under pressure in the face of sexual harassment allegations by at least 18 women. He said he had been the victim of "the hysteria of a lynch mob." He later pleaded guilty to a false imprisonment charge, and served three months of home confinement. In 2014, Republican Kevin Faulconer, a former public relations executive, won a special election to complete Filner's term. He was easily reelected in 2016, with 58 percent of the vote. Of all the Republican mayors in the nation, he has led the largest city. San Diego is projected to continue its rapid growth rate, with a nearly 50 percent increase by 2050. Most of that likely will come from Hispanics.

The 53rd Congressional District is geographically the smallest San Diego-area district, taking in the eastern edge of the city and points inland to include the suburbs of Lemon Grove and Spring Valley. It includes La Mesa and La Presa, which is 50 percent Hispanic, and extends about two miles short of the border with Mexico. Like the neighboring 52nd, this district has an active gay and lesbian presence. In January 2017, *Forbes* magazine reported that San Diego could be the city that is "ground zero" and that its economy would be at risk of "a massive, sudden blow" if President Donald Trump pursued aggressive deportation of illegal immigrants. The district has a number of parks, lakes and open space preserves. The zoo is among the 10 largest in the world. Politically, this is a safe Democratic district. The Republican presidential vote fell from 36 percent in 2012 to 29 percent in 2016.

★ COLORADO ★

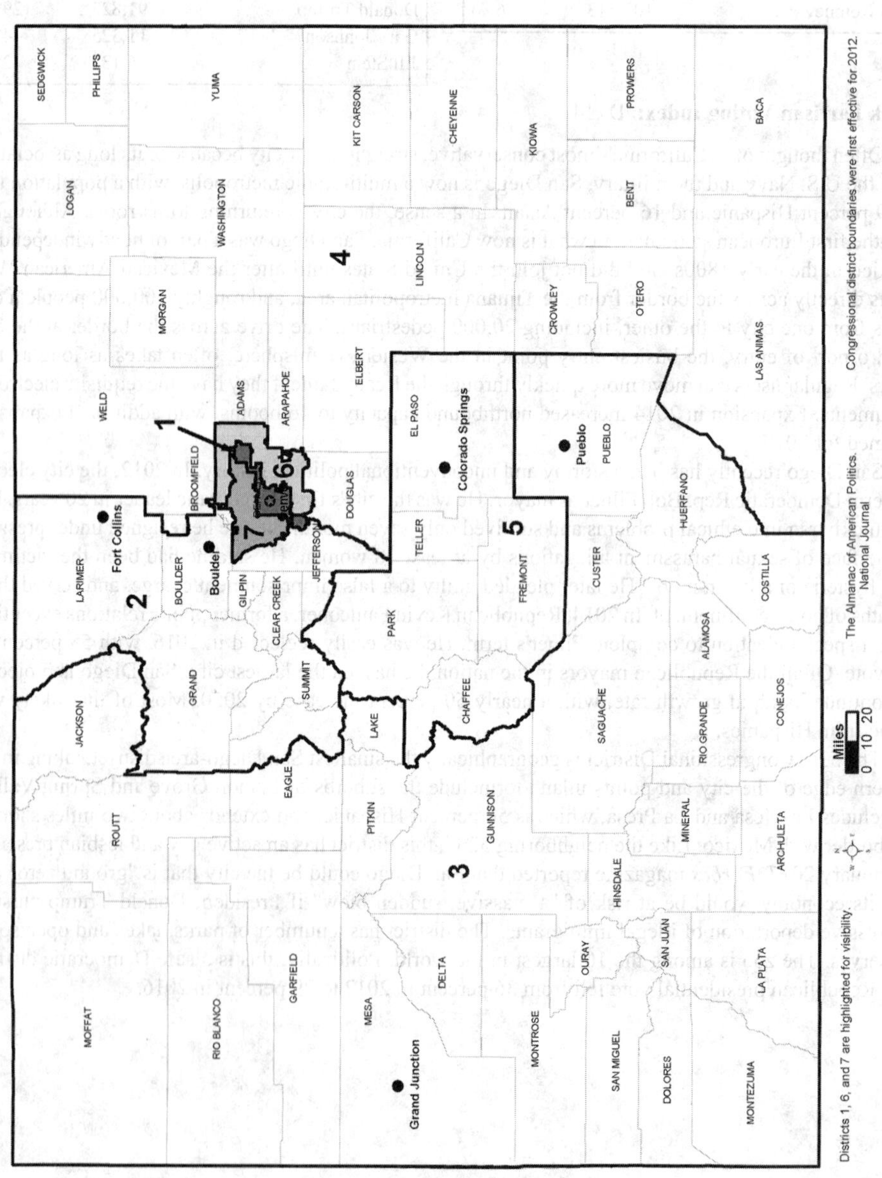
SEDGWICK
PHILLIPS
YUMA
KIT CARSON
CHEYENNE
KIOWA
PROWERS
BACA
LOGAN
WASHINGTON
LINCOLN
4
MORGAN
CROWLEY
OTERO
BENT
LAS ANIMAS
WELD
ADAMS
ARAPAHOE
ELBERT
EL PASO
Colorado Springs
Pueblo
PUEBLO
1
BROOMFIELD
6
7
Fort Collins
Boulder
DOUGLAS
JEFFERSON
TELLER
5
HUERFANO
CUSTER
FREMONT
LARIMER
BOULDER
GILPIN
CLEAR CREEK
PARK
COSTILLA
ALAMOSA
2
GRAND
SUMMIT
CHAFFEE
SAGUACHE
CONEJOS
RIO GRANDE
JACKSON
LAKE
ROUTT
EAGLE
PITKIN
GUNNISON
MINERAL
ARCHULETA
HINSDALE
3
GARFIELD
OURAY
SAN JUAN
DELTA
LA PLATA
MOFFAT
RIO BLANCO
MESA
MONTROSE
SAN MIGUEL
DOLORES
MONTEZUMA
Grand Junction
Miles
0 10 20
Congressional district boundaries were first effective for 2012.
The Almanac of American Politics.
National Journal
Districts 1, 6, and 7 are highlighted for visibility.

Colorado is the kind of state Democrats can point to when they dream of a future where their party is ascendant – fast-growing, well-educated, economically successful, tech-savvy, demographically diverse, and beautifully situated. But in Colorado, it's been a winding and sometimes uncertain path to this Democratic nirvana.

One summer day in 1893, Katherine Lee Bates, an English teacher at Colorado College, made her way by prairie wagon and mule up 14,114-foot Pikes Peak. Inspiration struck as she looked out over the spacious skies from the purple mountain's majesty to the amber waves of grain on the fruited plain, and she wrote the first version of *America the Beautiful*. Set to music, her words have resonated ever since, even though more than 90 percent of Americans up through World War II lived east of the Rockies, which rise above Denver, Boulder and Colorado Springs on the mile-high plateau. With its magnificent and contrasting landscapes, Colorado, the "Centennial State" admitted to the Union in 1876, has long had a hold on the American imagination. And as it has developed over the years, Colorado has been at the leading edge of economic, cultural and political change. For all its scenery, it is demographically an urban state; nearly half of its 5 million people reside in metropolitan Denver and four-fifths within the urban strip paralleling the Front Range. And it is a healthy state, with the nation's lowest rates of obesity and highest rates of physical activity. You burn off more calories when you live around 5,000 feet above sea level – and near alluring mountain scenery -- as most Coloradans do.

Colorado's history has been typified by occasional booms punctuated by long pauses of moderate growth. The first boom came just before the Civil War, when gold and silver were discovered in the Rockies; you can still see the grand opera houses and courthouses built in cities from that era, such as Cripple Creek, Central City, Aspen and Telluride. But mining boom towns tend to go bust, and Denver, on the South Platte River just east of the mountains, soon became the region's leading city, driven by meatpacking, banking and manufacturing, as well as state government and the regional operations of the federal government. Colorado's Capitol building, standing exactly 5,280 feet above sea level, sports a dome of gold leaf, which was refurbished in 2011 and 2012 with a donation of 72 ounces of gold from the same mine in Cripple Creek that supplied the original gold.

To the north and west, the Capitol overlooks Denver's vigorous downtown, with skyscrapers built during the energy boom of the 1970s and the telecom boom of the 1990s. Off toward the usually dry river bed are the retro Coors Field baseball park and the Lower Downtown ("LoDo") neighborhood with its warehouses renovated into restaurants and clubs. Metro Denver stretches in all directions. To the east is the startling architecture of the Denver International Airport on the plains, its canopy simultaneously suggesting the snow-capped Rockies, pioneers' covered wagons and Native American teepees. To the south is the sprawling Denver Tech Center, and all around are fast-growing tracts of subdivisions. Colorado has grown faster than the national average, but it has not experienced the explosive growth experienced by Arizona and Nevada in recent decades – or, importantly, their debilitating housing bubbles. Unemployment has tracked below the national average, peaking at 8.9 percent in the fall of 2010 and falling to 3.2 percent in November 2016, and even lower -- 2.9 percent -- in the Denver-Aurora-Lakewood metropolitan area. Colorado has attracted fewer retirees and low-skill immigrants than those states, and more young adults. Its attainment rates for bachelor's degrees rank among the nation's highest, and the graduates that settle in the state are eager to make a good living in what has generally been a growth economy and a place with natural and manmade amenities. Denver is famous for its parks and bike paths, and Boulder is a national center for bungee jumping, mountain biking, snowshoe running and hot-air ballooning. The public and local officials were angered in August 2015 by an EPA-caused spill of mining waste water at a site near Durango that federal officials had been cleaning up

For Colorado, the 1980s brought a bust, when an energy slump hit the state's relatively undiversified economy. But big and small tech firms boomed in the 1990s, accompanied by other types of high-salary work, including financial services, aerospace and satellites. From 2014 to 2015, Colorado saw the second-fastest rate of population growth in the nation. An affluent electorate was willing to chip in to expand amenities, at least cautiously. A new rail line connecting the airport with downtown, plus efforts to support cultural institutions "required people to vote to raise their taxes," Tom Clark, chief executive of the Metro Denver Economic Development Corporation, told the *New York Times*.

Most strikingly, Coloradans voted to make their state the first jurisdiction in the world to fully license the manufacture, cultivation and sale of marijuana. In its first legal year, 2014, marijuana became a $700 million industry, with hundreds of shops opening for recreational and medicinal sales, mostly in the highest-population areas. (Jurisdictions can choose whether to allow marijuana sales.) Then, in 2016, Colorado marijuana shops rang up more than $1.1 billion in sales. Local jurisdictions have been thrilled with the new revenue; Denver alone took in $29 million in taxes and licensing fees. Unexpected problems emerged - difficulty in regulating "edibles," smaller-than-expected tax revenues due to the persistence of the black market - but with public opinion heading in a pro-marijuana direction, no one expected the clock to be turned back.

Colorado has been reshaped politically by its successive waves of newcomers, who have increased the state's population from 1.7 million in 1960 to more than 5.5 million today. The conservative and boosterish Colorado of the 1960s was transformed in the 1970s by young liberal migrants who swept the state's politics by calling for environmental protections and slow growth. The state's national leaders reflected this trend - Gov. Dick Lamm, Sen. Gary Hart, Rep. Patricia Schroeder, and Rep. Tim Wirth. Then in the 1990s, a new wave of migrants - tech-savvy, family-oriented cultural conservatives looking for an environment in which to prosper - moved Colorado's politics to the right. In that decade, private-school enrollment was up 33 percent and the number of home-schooled children tripled. If the spirit of the 1970s newcomers was embodied by Boulder, with its pedestrian mall, outdoor sports shops, vegetarian restaurants and politically dominant environmentalist liberals, the spirit of the 1990s newcomers was dominated by religious conservatives in Colorado Springs, home of the Air Force Academy, Fort Carson, and Dr. James Dobson's Focus on the Family. In 2014, the *New York Times* pithily contrasted neighboring Weld County, GOP-dominated territory with 20,000 oil and gas wells, and Boulder, 15 miles to the west, "where a Buddhist-inspired university offers classes in yoga and the Tibetan language, and nature activists are working to carve out legal rights for ecosystems and wild species." Today, some of the state's fastest growing areas are on the northern edge of the Front Range -- Loveland and Fort Collins. Less than 20 miles from Wyoming, they are slowly turning bluer, matching the state.

Over the long term, Colorado has maintained a notably even balance politically, albeit with dominance by one party or the other in certain offices and certain time periods. For years, Colorado elections were, to a certain extent, contests between these groups to determine which one prevails. The victories of the liberal Democrats in the 1970s, starting with the 1972 referendum keeping the Winter Olympics out of Denver, were followed by a long period in which Republicans held control of the legislature and the state's congressional delegation. The victories of the conservative Republicans in the 1990s, starting with the 1990 referendum imposing term limits and the 1992 Taxpayers' Bill of Rights requiring referenda to raise taxes, were followed by a resurgence of the Democratic Party, led by liberal entrepreneurs such as Jared Polis, now the 2nd District representative, who was part of a "Gang of Four" that also included QuarkXPress founder Tim Gill, medical device heiress Patricia Stryker and geophysicist and MicroMAX software creator Rutt Bridges. The group nurtured a web of liberal activist organizations and shrewdly framed and targeted issues, ultimately reshaping the political landscape, including taking control of both legislative chambers in 2004. They took advantage of favorable demographic trends. Colorado's Latino population now stands at 21 percent, the seventh-highest percentage of any state. The state also has one of the nation's youngest populations, with many millennials living in university enclaves. Denver and Boulder attract young professionals imbued with progressive values, while the ski resorts - Telluride, Aspen, Vail, Crested Butte, Steamboat Springs - are inhabited by the wealthy and the people who wait on them in boutiques and restaurants, both demographics that lean Democratic.

Voters like these tipped the balance toward Democrats starting around 2008. Republicans -- dominant in 2002, with majorities in both houses of the legislature, both Senate seats, and five of the seven House seats – had largely relinquished control to Democrats by 2008, a year when Democrats held their national party convention in Denver and when a victory in the state helped send Barack Obama off to the White House. In 2010, the partisan split was closer; appointed Sen. Michael Bennet held on against tea party-supported Weld County District Attorney Ken Buck 48%-47%, while Democratic Denver Mayor John Hickenlooper succeeded fellow Democrat Bill Ritter with 51 percent of the vote in a three-way race for governor. But further down the ballot, Republicans won all four statewide races, regained the 3rd and 4th district House seats they'd lost in 2006 and 2008, and secured a majority in the state House. Then, in 2012, Democrats did a little better, as Obama carried the state, 51%-46%, and Democrats won sufficient state House seats to secure unified control of the legislature. But Republicans held onto four of the seven U.S. House seats.

In 2013 and 2014, Democrats were disabused of any sense of invincibility. The newly Democratic-controlled legislature ruffled feathers by enacting several liberal-leaning bills, most notably a gun control measure in the wake of a massacre at a movie theater in suburban Aurora. The measure imposed background checks for private gun sales and a cap on ammunition magazines of 15 rounds. In a low-turnout recall election, two Democratic lawmakers who had voted for the gun bill were ousted in a fight that drew in both the National Rifle Association and gun-control supporters like New York City Mayor Michael Bloomberg. On Election Day 2014, Democratic Sen. Mark Udall, who began the election cycle seeming not especially vulnerable, lost to GOP Rep. Cory Gardner by 2 points after focusing excessively on abortion and other social issues; the GOP took over the state Senate and fell just short in the state House. Hickenlooper - like Gardner, buoyed by his personality - prevailed by 3 points.

In 2016, the candidacy of Donald Trump only increased the polarization between ascendant Colorado and lagging Colorado. Statewide, Hillary Clinton beat Trump by nearly 5 points, similar to Obama's edge over Mitt Romney in 2012. But this time, swingy suburban areas tilted more to Clinton and blue-collar areas moved toward Trump. In Jefferson County, an older Denver suburb that had backed George W. Bush in 2000 and 2004 and Obama in 2008 and 2012, Clinton's 4-point edge over Trump represented an improvement over Obama's 4.4-point margin in 2012. The pro-Clinton tilt was even greater in Arapahoe County, another Denver suburb that includes Aurora. Once Republican, it now has a sizable immigrant population to go along with long-settled communities of working- and middle-class whites. In 2016, Clinton won Arapahoe by nearly 14 points, up from Obama's 10-point margin in 2012 (though GOP Rep. Mike Coffman won the county and was returned to the House). The flip side is represented by Pueblo County, a historically Democratic stronghold but one with blue-collar, religious, gun-friendly voters. In 2016, it shifted decisively in Trump's direction. Obama had won the county by 14 points; Trump won it narrowly, even as Bennet, the Democratic senator, won the county by about 7,000 votes. Meanwhile, Colorado's split results on ballot measures underscored a continuing preference in the state for social liberalism and fiscal moderation: Voters rejected a cigarette tax increase and a proposal to provide universal health care, but they approved a hike in the minimum wage as well as assisted suicide for terminally ill patients. Republicans can still win the state, but these days, unless the Democrats self-destruct, the GOP needs a good candidate and a strong campaign to do it.

Population		**Race and Ethnicity**		**Income**	
Total	5,278,906	White	69.1%	Median Income	$60,629 (13 out of 50)
Land area	103,642	Black	3.9%		
Pop/ sq mi	50.9	Latino	21.1%	Under $50,000	41.5%
Born in state	42.7%	Asian	2.8%	$50,000-$99,999	31.5%
		Two races	2.3%	$100,000-$199,999	21.1%
Age Groups		Other	0.8%	$200,000 or more	5.8%
Under 18	23.5%			Poverty Rate	12.7%
18-34	21.9%	**Education**			
35-64	39.6%	H.S grad or less	31.1%	**Health Insurance**	
Over 64	12.3%	Some college	30.8%	With health insurance coverage	87.7%
		College Degree, 4 yr	24.1%		
Work		Post grad	14.0%		
White Collar	40.4%			**Public Assistance**	
Sales and Service	41.3%	**Military**		Cash public assistance income	2.2%
Blue Collar	18.3%	Veteran	9.8%		
Government	13.9%	Active Duty	0.8%	Food stamp/SNAP benefits	8.7%

Voter Turnout			
2015 Total Citizens 18+	3,750,953	2016 Pres Turnout as % CVAP	74%
2016 Pres Votes	2,780,247	2012 Pres Turnout as % CVAP	74%

Legislature	
Senate:	17D, 18R
House:	37D, 28R

Presidential Politics

2016 Democratic Caucus		
Bernie Sanders (D)	72,846	(59%)
Hillary Clinton (D)	49,789	(40%)

2016 Presidential Vote		
Hillary Clinton (D)	1,338,870	(48%)
Donald Trump (R)	1,202,484	(43%)
Gary Johnson (L)	144,121	(5%)
2012 Presidential Vote		
Barack Obama (D)	1,323,102	(51%)
Mitt Romney (R)	1,185,243	(46%)

Colorado, once a Republican state in presidential elections, has cast its ballots in three consecutive elections for Democrats. Hillary Clinton defeated Donald Trump 48%-43%, on the strength of support from Hispanics and college-educated white voters. Not surprisingly, that kind of backing has made the greater Denver area a Democratic stronghold. In the 2016, nearly half of the state's presidential vote came from Denver, its three major suburban counties -- Adams, Arapahoe and Jefferson -- and the adjacent Boulder County, home to the University of Colorado. (That turnout was down from just over half in 2012.) This area gave Clinton almost three-out-of-five votes cast for president. Nearby Douglas County, which includes some Denver exurbs, remained a Republican bastion and Trump won it handily, along with other more urban counties on the southern Front Range like El Paso (Colorado Springs) and, narrowly, Pueblo. Pueblo is home to blue collar Democrats, some of whom work at the Evraz Rocky Mountain Steel Mill, a Russian-owned foundry. Pueblo is also home to a Grupo Cementos de Chihuahua cement plant, a Mexican company. Voters in this aging manufacturing community behaved like their brethren in the Midwestern Rust Belt and voted for Trump, who became the first GOP presidential nominee to carry Pueblo County since Richard Nixon in 1972. Incumbent Democratic Sen. Michael Bennet, who was up for reelection in 2016, carried the county by nine percentage points. Nearby, the old coal mining counties of Las Animas and Huerfano also switched to Trump after having backed Obama in 2012.

Colorado wasn't always hospitable to Democratic presidential nominees. Between LBJ in 1964 and Obama and Clinton since 2008, the only Democrat to carry Colorado was Bill Clinton in 1992, and it's likely that independent candidate Ross Perot siphoned off enough Republican voters from George H.W. Bush to produce that outcome. But Democrats had Colorado in their sights when they selected Denver as the location for their 2008 national convention. Obama formally accepted the nomination in Mile High Stadium, the only outdoor venue for an acceptance speech since John F. Kennedy addressed Democratic delegates in the Los Angeles Coliseum.

Colorado held an early March presidential primary from 1992 until 2000, which never attracted much national attention. In 2003, to save money, the legislature voted to eliminate the presidential primary and let the parties hold caucuses. The 2016 Republican and Democratic versions were both notable. Hoping to increase the state's leverage at a possible contested convention, Colorado GOP officials opted not to hold a typical presidential preference poll at their local caucuses, with the aim of sending uncommitted delegates to the party confab in Cleveland. But Texas Sen. Ted Cruz skillfully organized the subsequent congressional district conventions and the state convention and packed the delegation with his supporters, prompting Trump to complain that the Colorado GOP caucuses were "rigged" and had denied his supporters a chance to vote for him. Meanwhile, Vermont Sen. Bernie Sanders swamped Clinton in the March 1 Democratic caucuses, 59%-40%. The turnout of more than 122,000 exceeded the roughly 120,000 who participated in the party caucuses eight years earlier when Obama defeated Clinton 67%-32%, and was one of the few contests where Democratic turnout was up from 2008.

Congressional Districts

115th Congress Lineup	4R 3D	114th Congress Lineup	4R 3D

After the 2010 census, the two parties had a lengthy and bitter stalemate in the state legislature that forced the federal courts to intervene. A Denver district judge chose a Democratic plan for the sake of making the Republican-held 6th District south of Denver more "competitive."

The latest map's biggest shift was to remove nearly all of heavily Republican Douglas County from the 6th District and replace it with increasingly Hispanic Aurora to the north, making Republican Mike Coffman's seat seven percentage points less Republican. But the payoff for Democrats has not been immediate. After Coffman escaped with a 48%-46% win when Democrats failed to recruit a strong candidate, he showed increased strength against competitive challengers.

The state appears likely to gain an additional House seat after the 2020 census, which again could be located in competitive suburban or exurban areas outside Denver. With an open seat for governor in 2018 and narrow majorities in the Legislature, which is one of only three in the nation with divided control, national party strategists likely will give much attention to Colorado.

Governor

John Hickenlooper (D)

Elected 2010, term expires 2019, 2nd term; b. Feb. 7, 1952, Narberth, PA; Wesleyan U., B.A. 1974, M.A. 1980; Episcopalian; Separated; 1 child.

Elected Office: Denver Mayor, 2003-2010.

Professional Career: Geologist; Restaurateur, 1980-2003.

Office: 136 State Capitol, Denver, 80203-1792; 303-866-2471; Fax: 303-866-2003; Website: colorado.gov.

Election Results

Election	Name (Party)	Vote (%)
2014 General	John Hickenlooper (D)	1,006,433 (49%)
	Bob Beauprez (R)	938,195 (46%)

Prior winning percentage: 2010 (51%)

Democrat John Hickenlooper, a beer entrepreneur with a penchant for reaching across the aisle, was elected governor of Colorado in 2010. During his first two years in office, his response to two major crises won him plaudits, and *Esquire* magazine named him one of its "Americans of the Year" in 2012. His approval rating subsequently plummeted, and though he found himself in a tough reelection fight, he managed to prevail despite a strong GOP tide in 2014. In 2016, Hickenlooper was in the mix as a potential running mate for Hillary Clinton, but his past efforts to bridge partisan differences proved to be out of step with a highly polarized presidential campaign.

"Hick," as he's known in Colorado newspaper headlines, grew up in the Philadelphia suburbs, raised by a frugal widowed mother. He is a descendant of the Revolutionary War financier Robert Morris. "My great-grandparents were Quakers. And I tried to take that ethic into business. Quaker honesty, Quaker mindfulness, that effort to build community across differences," he told *The Philadelphia Inquirer*. He graduated from Wesleyan University, first studying English and then getting a master's degree in geology. He moved to Colorado in 1981 and took a job in the oil industry. When oil prices fell in the 1980s, he was laid off. On a trip to the San Francisco Bay area, he stopped in at a brewpub, then a rarity. He thought the concept might work in Denver, and in 1988, he opened the state's first brewpub, Wynkoop Brewery, in a warehouse district northwest of downtown Denver. He ended up launching 14 restaurants, which spearheaded development of the Lower Downtown as an entertainment district. Today, "LoDo" is buzzing with activity.

Hickenlooper's business success got his friends talking about him running for mayor of Denver in 2003 to succeed term-limited incumbent Wellington Webb. Hickenlooper and city Auditor Don Mares were the top two finishers in a six-candidate field; their June 2003 runoff was noteworthy for its lack of vitriol. Hickenlooper refused to run negative ads (a policy he has continued, although independent groups have sometimes done so on his behalf) and he campaigned against "the nonsense of government," including parking meter rates. One television ad showed Hickenlooper with a change-maker around his waist, thrusting quarters into meters. He also pledged to cut the city payroll by 4 percent. He beat Mares, 65%-35%.

As mayor, Hickenlooper reached out to suburban officials and to Republican Gov. Bill Owens. In 2004, he got all 32 mayors in metro Denver to support a ballot proposition instituting a 0.4% sales tax to raise $4.7 billion for a light-rail system. He also got voters to approve the largest bond issue in the city's history, a property tax increase and a tax increase for early childhood education. Hickenlooper also took control of the city's troubled public schools and installed his chief of staff, Michael Bennet, now a senator, as superintendent, charging him with finding innovative ways to increase school performance. Hickenlooper's 2005 program to increase energy efficiency and decrease carbon emissions reduced energy use per passenger by 11 percent at Denver International Airport and increased recycling in the city by 69 percent.

In 2007, Hickenlooper won a second term as mayor. When Democrat Bill Ritter was elected governor, the two worked together successfully to bring the 2008 Democratic National Convention to Denver. But they differed on other issues. Ritter favored restrictions on abortion rights, a position that put him at odds with many Democrats, and he favored limits on oil and gas drilling, which the business community opposed. Hickenlooper tended to take the opposite stands. In December 2008, when President Barack Obama named Democratic Sen. Ken Salazar as his Interior secretary, it was widely expected that Ritter would appoint Hickenlooper to fill Salazar's Senate seat. Instead, Ritter appointed schools chief Bennet.

In January 2010, Ritter said he would not seek a second term. Obama called Hickenlooper and asked him to run. A week later, he agreed. While he quickly won Ritter's endorsement, he also criticized Ritter's rulemaking process and said he was "coming from a very different place" on oil and gas issues, saying he wanted to cut red tape, not increase it. (Hickenlooper once went so far as to taste a newly created fracking fluid to demonstrate its safety.) Despite Hickenlooper's popularity in the Denver media market, which covers much of the state, Republicans seemed to have a serious chance to regain the office they lost in 2006. But one by one, their candidates imploded. The narrow GOP primary winner, tea party-aligned businessman Daniel Maes, eventually became so hobbled by revelations about his past that former Rep. Tom Tancredo, who had run a quixotic presidential campaign in 2008 as a hard-core opponent of illegal immigration, announced a bid on a third-party line. Blessed with not one but two flawed opponents, Hickenlooper won with 51 percent, with 36 percent for Tancredo and just 11 percent for the Republican nominee, Maes.

Hickenlooper used the story of his work in converting Colorado Springs' old Cheyenne Hotel into a successful brewpub as a metaphor for how the state could emerge from the recession. He created an economic-development initiative that subsequently came out with a report called "the Colorado Blueprint," which called for creating a business-friendly environment. He submitted a spending plan that made $570 million in cuts on top of those that Ritter had proposed - with spending on elementary education taking the biggest hit - while raising the state's general fund reserve from 2 percent to 4 percent. An improved revenue forecast helped bring down the size of the education cuts, and Hickenlooper won positive marks for his willingness to broker differences between the Democratic-controlled Senate and the Republican-led House. The split between the chambers prevented bills on contentious issues such as gun rights and illegal immigration from reaching his desk. But he was able to get through a measure creating state health care exchanges as part of Obama's new federal health care law. Polls showed him with strong approval ratings among both Republicans and Democrats, and even conservative columnist George Will hailed him as an example for the Democratic Party to follow.

Entering his second year, Hickenlooper called for substantially increasing spending for economic development and announced plans to follow neighboring New Mexico in creating a "spaceport" for commercial rockets. He got into a tussle with Republicans over a property tax break for seniors that cost the state $100 million a year. Hickenlooper said suspending the tax break would help avoid further cuts to schools, while Republicans countered that the state should instead reduce spending on Medicaid. When revenues were forecast to come in an estimated $231 million higher than previously expected, the governor boosted spending on schools. But Hickenlooper was unable to overcome Republican resistance to a bill allowing civil unions for same-sex couples.

To deal with wildfires that ravaged the state, Hickenlooper flew home from a trade mission to Mexico to be on the front lines, listening to rescue workers' requests. He subsequently called for more water storage and conservation to ease the effects of future droughts. His approval rating reached 60 percent, prompting some in Colorado political circles to begin wondering if he would be a future presidential candidate. Despite a foray to New Hampshire, Hickenlooper downplayed such talk, saying he didn't feel like he was the right type of person for the job. In 2012, he amicably separated from his wife of 10 years, author Helen Thorpe; their announcement included the guidance, "Please feel free to include both of us in social gatherings as we will not find it awkward." In 2016, after more than a year of dating, Hickenlooper married Robin Pringle, 37, a vice president of corporate development at a media company.

Ironically, Democratic legislative gains in the 2012 election helped dim Hickenlooper's popularity, as lawmakers from his own party pushed him to the left. Hickenlooper took heat for signing controversial gun control legislation in the wake of the movie theater massacre for which 24-year-old James Holmes in Aurora was convicted in July 2015, but spared the death penalty. Hickenlooper reportedly told an audience of county sheriffs that he regretted signing the measures because of the uproar that they caused, and that he had not spoken to New York City Mayor Michael Bloomberg - a staunch backer of gun control - about the bills, though he acknowledged later that the two had talked. Hickenlooper also took heat for his stances on energy issues, especially his refusal to express an opinion about the Keystone XL pipeline project. "I've avoided taking a position because it's just going to piss off a lot of people in Washington that I don't need to piss off," he told the *Durango Herald*, "and my opinion is not going to change anybody's opinion there." Another unpopular move was his decision to grant what he called a "temporary reprieve" to Nathan Dunlap, a murderer convicted of the shooting deaths of four people at a Chuck E. Cheese in suburban Denver in 1993.

In 2014, former Rep. and 2006 gubernatorial nominee Bob Beauprez, a late Republican entrant against Hickenlooper as the incumbent sought a second term, managed to win the four-way GOP primary with 30 percent. By mid-September, polls showed the race tightening. Despite the Democrats' dismal showing nationally and in Colorado, Hickenlooper pulled off a 49%-46% victory. The win enabled Hickenlooper to continue as chairman of the National Governors Association, a post he had assumed in July 2014.

By 2015, the state had completed the first year of voter-approved legalization of recreational marijuana. Hundreds of shops opened for recreational and medicinal sales, but it also brought public-safety challenges and lower-than-expected tax revenues for the state. Hickenlooper, who had opposed legalization from the beginning, said afterward that "if I could've waved a wand the day after the election, I would've reversed the election and said, 'This was a bad idea.'" Since then, legalization has become popular and Hickenlooper has come around on the issue, acknowledging in national media appearances that the scale of the problems may have been overstated initially. At a Milken Institute Global Conference in Los Angeles in 2016, he said, "If I had that magic wand now, I don't know if I would wave it," he said. "It's beginning to look like it might work." With the success of the marijuana rollout and unemployment below the national average, Hickenlooper saw his popularity rise again after his close electoral call in November 2014. In the spring of 2015, he had a 53%-37% job approval rating., and in the sparse polling for the rest of 2015 and 2016 he was comfortably above water.

In the first two years of his second term, Hickenlooper continued to spar over fiscal policy with Republicans in the legislature, who had taken back the Senate in 2014 while the Democrats retained the House. The governor and Republican lawmakers repeatedly butted heads over the scale of Medicaid spending and whether the state's Taxpayer Bill of Rights (TABOR) refund should remain sacrosanct. But some of the biggest fights were over energy policy. While environmentalists appreciated Hickenlooper's proposal to spend more than $100 million on bike infrastructure, they were unhappy about his continued support for fracking. In fact, there was widespread speculation that his energy views torpedoed his chances to become Clinton's running mate or to be tapped as Interior Secretary had she won. Still, the governor supported Obama's emissions-curbing Clean Power Plan and opposed a lawsuit against it filed by Colorado's attorney general, Cynthia Coffman. After the U.S. Supreme Court kept the Obama administration from implementing the plan until further judicial review was complete, Hickenlooper sought to continue state efforts to prepare for its eventual enactment anyway. This drew fierce opposition from Republican lawmakers, who threatened to defund the work. A subsequent draft executive order by Hickenlooper pleased neither side -- yet another sign that Hickenlooper's attempts at finding common ground were out of tune with the times.

Early candidates to replace the term-limited Hickenlooper included Arapahoe County District Attorney George Brauchler, a Republican, and Democratic Rep. Ed Perlmutter. Jared Polis, another House Democrat, was considering a bid.

Senior Senator

Michael Bennet (D)

Appointed Jan. 2009, term expires 2022, 2nd full term; b. Nov 28, 1964; New Delhi, India; Wesleyan University (CT), B.A., 1987; Yale University Law School (CT), J.D., 1993; Episcopalian; Married (Susan Daggett Bennet); 3 children.

Professional Career: Deputy Attorney General, U.S Department of Justice, 1995-1997; Managing Director, Anschutz Investment Co., 1997-2003; Chief of staff, Denver Mayor John Hickenlooper, 2003-2005; Superintendent, Denver Public School, 2005-2009.

DC Office: 261 RSOB 20510, 202-224-5852, Fax: 202-228-5097, bennet.senate.gov.

State Offices: Alamosa, 719-587-0096; Colorado Springs, 719-328-1100; Denver, 303-455-7600; Durango, 970-259-1710; Fort Collins, 970-224-2200; Grand Junction, 970-241-6631; Pueblo, 719-542-7550.

Committees: *Agriculture, Nutrition & Forestry*: Commodities, Risk Management & Trade, Conservation, Forestry & Natural Resources (RMM), Rural Development & Energy. *Finance*: Energy, Natural Resources & Infrastructure (RMM), Taxation & IRS Oversight. *Health, Education, Labor & Pensions*: Children & Families, Primary Health & Retirement Security.

Group Ratings

	ADA	ACLU	AFL-CIO	LCV	ITI	COC	HAFA	ACU	CFG	FRC
2016	-	88%	-	100%	100%	63%	5%	4%	5%	0%
2015	85%	C	71%	84%	C	64%	C	0%	6%	0%

Almanac Ratings 2015

	Economy	Social	Foreign	Composite
Liberal	70%	100%	80%	83%
Conservative	30%	0%	20%	17%

Key Votes of the 114th Congress

1. Keystone pipeline	Y	5. National Security Data	Y	9. Gun Sales Checks	Y
2. Export-Import Bank	N	6. Iran Nuclear Deal	N	10. Sanctuary Cities	N
3. Debt Ceiling Increase	Y	7. Puerto Rico Debt	Y	11. Planned Parenthood	N
4. Homeland Security $$	Y	8. Loretta Lynch A.G	Y	12. Trade deals	Y

Election Results

Election	Name (Party)	Vote (%)		Cand. Spent	Ind. Exp. Support	Ind. Exp. Oppose
2016 General	Michael Bennet (D)	1,370,710	(50%)	$24,460,995	$1,277,047	$705,306
	Darryl Glenn (R)	1,215,318	(44%)	$4,955,031	$2,987,974	$90,511
	Lily Tang Williams (L)	99,277	(4%)	$6,810		
2016 Primary	Michael Bennet (D)	unopposed				

Prior winning percentages: 2010 (48%)

Colorado's senior senator, Michael Bennet, started the 2016 cycle as the Senate Democrats' most endangered incumbent, with national conservative groups training their sights on him. He finished the cycle as one of the luckiest incumbents of either party: His path to a second full term in a "purple" state was paved by Republican recruiting failures, followed by a GOP primary notable for its embarrassing controversies. But, then again, Bennet has been an improbable senator from the get-go, notwithstanding his upbringing in the Washington establishment. He was a surprise choice for a vacant seat in 2009 -- appointed over several far better known contenders -- and emerged victorious in tough primary and general election battles in his first run for the job in 2010, with a little luck that time around as well. Between campaigns, Bennet has gained a reputation as an affable legislator who is a very quick study. While supportive of most major initiatives of President Barack Obama, who took office the month that

Bennet arrived on Capitol Hill, Bennet -- still boyish-looking at 52 -- has sought to craft a reputation as a centrist ready to reach across party lines to achieve legislative progress.

Bennet's pre-Senate resume is among the more eclectic among members of that chamber. He moved from law and politics to finance, where he became a multimillionaire, and then on to education, where he was superintendent of a large urban school district, before returning to politics in his current role. His lineage is also intriguing: His father's family dates back to the arrival of the Mayflower, while his mother was born in the Jewish ghetto of Warsaw, Poland, immigrating to the United States after being hidden from the Nazis during World War II. Bennet was born in New Delhi, India, in 1964, where his father, Douglas Bennet, was an aide to Ambassador Chester Bowles. Michael Bennet grew up and attended private schools in Washington, D.C.; he was a Senate page in high school. His father, after serving an aide to such leading Democratic senators as Hubert Humphrey, Edmund Muskie and Thomas Eagleton, went on to become a top State Department official in the Carter and Clinton administrations as well as president of National Public Radio. (Michael Bennet's younger brother, James, has become the editorial page editor of *The New York Times*.)

Michael Bennet became the third generation of his family to graduate from Wesleyan University -- his father later served as president of the school -- and then went to work as an aide to Ohio Democratic Gov. Richard Celeste, a family friend. In 1990, Bennet entered Yale Law School, where he went on to be editor-in-chief of the *Yale Law Journal*. He was an associate in Lloyd Cutler's influential law firm in Washington before being named counsel to Deputy Attorney General Jamie Gorelick in the Clinton Administration; he wrote speeches for Attorney General Janet Reno. Bennet's move west came in 1997 when his wife, Susan Daggett, a natural resources lawyer, accepted a job with the Earthjustice Legal Defense Fund in Denver. Bennet went to work for an investment company headed by billionaire Philip Anschutz, a political conservative. While Bennet had never read a balance sheet, Anschutz was impressed by Bennet and hired him -- while ordering Bennet to attend accounting school at night at his own expense.

Eventually, Bennet landed major assignments such as overseeing the consolidation of three theater chains into Regal Entertainment Group, the world's largest movie theater company. After six years with Anschutz, during which he accumulated a personal fortune of $12 million, Bennet returned to the public sector when a fellow Wesleyan alumnus, John Hickenlooper, was elected Denver mayor and asked him to be his chief of staff. Bennet says he gave up millions in stock options to accept "an opportunity that wouldn't come around again." His accomplishments in that post included a plan to balance the city's budget by cutting 10 percent -- without laying off any workers. "I have referred to him as the second mayor, the hidden mayor," Hickenlooper, who later became governor, told *The Denver Post*.

In 2005, the position of Denver Public Schools superintendent came open, and Bennet was among the top candidates-even though he had no experience in education, had attended private schools, and was sending his daughter to a private kindergarten. The board picked him to head a system of 73,000 students, three-quarters of whom were Latino or African-American and two-thirds of whom were from low-income families. He quickly triggered controversy by moving to close a problem-plagued high school in the city's African-American community, and disperse its student to other schools. But he also instituted a plan to boost performance standards in the schools, while creating workshops to teach principals how to lead schools to reform. Proficiency in reading and math rose by six percent during Bennet's four-year tenure, and has continued to rise since, according to the Washington-based Council of Great City Schools.

When Obama was running for president in 2008, Bennet co-hosted a fundraiser for the then-Illinois senator, and was later included in the Democratic candidate's weekly education conference calls. After Obama was elected, Bennet was on the short list to head the U.S. Department of Education, although Obama ultimately chose Chicago schools chief Arne Duncan. But Bennet was not even regarded as a long shot for the Senate after Obama named Sen. Ken Salazar as his Interior secretary. Bennet had limited national political experience that consisted mainly of a 2004 speech he gave to a group of business leaders denouncing the Iraq war and President George W. Bush. The more obvious candidates included outgoing state House Speaker Andrew Romanoff, who had ties to Democratic politicians and activists across the state, and Hickenlooper, Bennet's mentor.

But on Jan. 2, 2009, Democratic Gov. Bill Ritter astonished just about everyone by naming Bennet to fill the remainder of Salazar's term, which had a couple of years to run. Ritter said he was impressed with his record of bringing diverse interests together to solve problems and by his pragmatic approach to turning around troubled public and private enterprises. Republican leaders relished the prospect of taking on a candidate far less formidable electorally than Hickenlooper or Romanoff in 2010. And some Democratic leaders were not happy. In a 2016 profile of Bennet, *The Washington Post* recounted that now-Senate Democratic Leader Charles Schumer of New York called Ritter at the time and sarcastically thanked him for throwing away a Democratic seat on an unknown who could not win re-election.

Once sworn in, Bennet dug into legislating with gusto. On the Health, Education, Labor, and Pensions Committee, he introduced a bill in 2010 to strengthen the Food and Drug Administration's ability to identify and prevent tainted drugs from reaching consumers. In one of the rare examples of bipartisan cooperation that followed the 2010 election, Bennet's proposal ultimately became law in 2012. Drawing on his experience with Denver's schools, he added more than half a dozen proposals as the Obama administration sought to reauthorize the No Child Left Behind education law in 2010, such as tying new teacher licensing to performance and increasing the flexibility of school districts in spending federal money. His colleagues credit Bennet with moving both parties to the middle in that debate, which ultimately led to passage of a new law, the Every Student Succeeds Act, in late 2015. "He bridged the gap with the Republicans," the HELP panel's ranking Democrat, Sen. Patty Murray of Washington state, told the *Post*, terming Bennet "the pragmatic voice of reason."

As he prepared to seek election to the seat in his own right in 2010 -- crisscrossing the state to introduce himself to voters outside of Denver -- Bennet drew a fierce primary challenge from former state House Speaker Romanoff, who portrayed himself as the outsider. Drawing on Bennet's work for Anschutz, Romanoff attacked the incumbent as a tool of Wall Street. He also accused Bennet of failing to support the public insurance option of health care reform, which liberals favored. Bennet insisted that he had supported the public option, which was left out of the Affordable Care Act of 2010 because of opposition from party conservatives. Bennet proved to be a strong fundraiser and heavily outspent Romanoff. While Romanoff surged in the closing days of the primary in a year that was tough for incumbents, Bennet hung on to win, 54%-46%.

In November, Bennet faced another tough contest against Weld County District Attorney Ken Buck, who had won the GOP nomination over the establishment Republican candidate, former Lt. Gov. Jane Norton, with the backing of tea party activists. Buck portrayed Bennet as part of the problem in big-spending Washington, and attacked his votes for Obama's $787 billion economic stimulus bill as well as the health care legislation. But Buck proved to be gaffe-prone. Bennet and the Democrats made an issue of his 2005 decision as district attorney not to prosecute an accused rapist; Buck said at the time that a jury would likely conclude that the victim's complaint was a case of "buyer's remorse." In an appearance on *Meet the Press*, Buck made controversial remarks about homosexuality, saying, "I think that birth has an influence over it, like alcoholism and some other things. But I think that basically, you have a choice."

With $11.5 million in campaign funds, Bennet saturated the airwaves with Buck's missteps and portrayed him as too extreme for Colorado's independent-minded voters; Buck called for dismantling the Department of Education and said he opposed abortion in all circumstances.

Buck raised $5 million of his own, and had help from the GOP-friendly American Crossroads, which invested another $5 million in negative ads against Bennet. But the Republicans arguably had nominated the weaker of their two potential Senate nominees, and Bennet held the upper hand in spite of his votes for major elements of the Obama agenda, which were hurting Democratic incumbents elsewhere. Colorado College political scientist Bob Loevy told *The Denver Post*, "To a very large extent, Bennet made the issue not about the national economy, but about the characteristics of Ken Buck." Bennet won 48%-46%. (Four years later, Buck won a House seat from Colorado's predominantly Republican 4th District.)

Returning to Capitol Hill, where the House had flipped to Republican control and the Senate had a decreased Democratic majority in the wake of the 2010 election, Bennet looked for opportunities to reach across the political aisle. He became part of a bipartisan "Gang of Eight" seeking ways to avoid the "fiscal cliff" looming at the end of 2012. A leader of that group was Bennet's close friend, Sen. Mark Warner of Virginia, a centrist Democrat who shared Bennet's appetite for bipartisanship. However, the "fiscal cliff" solution ultimately adopted by Congress at the end of 2012 was largely the result of negotiations between the Obama White House and Senate Republican leaders, and Bennet was one of only three Senate Democrats to oppose it. He complained it "does not put in place a real process to reduce the debt down the road." In 2013, Bennet was part of another "Gang of Eight" that crafted an immigration reform proposal that passed the Senate. But the House refused to take up the bill.

Shortly after the 2012 election, Senate Majority Leader Harry Reid offered Bennet the chairmanship of the DSCC, but it took Bennet three weeks to agree to take the position. He was reluctant for fear that it would interfere with his efforts to work across the aisle. Bennet finally decided to accept the challenge and, as sweetener to take on the difficult task, he was awarded a coveted seat on the powerful Finance Committee. It turned out to be a disastrous election cycle for Democrats, who lost nine seats as well as control of the Senate. Among the political casualties was Bennet's good friend and Colorado colleague, Sen. Mark Udall, who ran a race similar to Bennet's in 2010, by stressing his opponent's "extreme" positions. In turn, Udall's Republican opponent, now-Sen. Cory Gardner -- upset about DSCC ads aimed at him -- skewered Bennet as "the chief partisan of the United States Senate." Despite the Democrats' dismal showing at the polls, Bennet largely escaped the second-guessing that inevitably follows such failures, as many in the party quietly blamed the White House.

Bennet gave up the DSCC chairmanship in 2015 to prepare for his coming re-election campaign. At the same time, he showed his independence from the Obama White House on a couple of fronts. He joined only 13 other Senate Democrats to back construction of the controversial Keystone XL Pipeline. And while supporting Obama's plan to close down the U.S. prison at Guantanamo Bay, Cuba -- saying that it "is a symbol all over the world for our not living up to our own values" -- Bennet vehemently objected to an administration plan in February 2016 that envisioned a couple of Colorado prisons as possible locations for detainees accused of terrorist acts. "...I believe military detainees should be held in military prisons. Colorado does not have that type of facility," declared Bennet.

On the other hand, Bennet came out forcefully against the 2015 letter signed by 47 Republicans, including his Colorado colleague Gardner, that warned Iran's leaders that reaching a deal on nuclear facilities with Obama without congressional approval could be short-lived -- since it could be undone by a future President or Congress. The letter infuriated the White House and a number of Democratic senators, including Bennet, as an inappropriate interference in the conduct of foreign policy. "This letter is completely counterproductive and I cannot say enough about the seven Republicans who were wise enough not to sign it," Bennet said in a statement.

Nonetheless, Bennet and Gardner developed a bipartisan bromance of sorts. Shortly after his arrival in the Senate, the newly elected Republican senator met with Bennet, and both stressed their desire to work together. It was followed by Gardner inviting Bennet on a tour of Colorado's Eastern Plains, where he grew up, with Bennet then hosting a tour of his former bailiwick, the Denver city school system. The two have found common ground on energy issues -- agreeing not only on building the Keystone XL Pipeline, but also on the need for an "all of the above" approach to energy in which they favor renewable sources while also vowing to protect Colorado's liquid natural gas industry. All told, Bennet and Gardner co-authored more than a dozen pieces of substantive legislation in 2015-2016. Several related to issues specific to Colorado, but also included was an unusual measure to impose strict rules -- including the possibility of arrest -- on the Senate anytime one or more federal agencies were in a shutdown mode. The rationale, the two said, was to force legislators to stay in town to negotiate.

Gardner's upset victory over Udall in 2014, coming after Gardner had jumped into the Senate race just months earlier, emboldened national Republicans -- who targeted Bennet as the one incumbent Democrat that they had a chance of ousting in 2016. However, problems on the GOP side provided Bennet with a continuing series of breaks. First, Republicans failed to attract a top-tier candidate: Their first choice, Rep. Mike Coffman, announced in mid-2015 that he planned to seek re-election to his suburban Denver seat. Then, Coffman's wife, newly elected state Attorney General Cynthia Coffman said no to a Senate race, followed by Arapahoe County District Attorney George Brauchler, who had gained statewide attention as the prosecutor in the 2012 Aurora movie theater shooting in which 12 died.

As five lesser known Republicans crowded into the race for their party's nomination in early 2016, Bennet took advantage of the $7.6 million in his campaign treasury to hit the airwaves touting his legislative accomplishments. On the GOP side, former state Rep. Jon Keyser emerged as the choice of the party establishment, and claimed to have secured significant multi-million dollar funding commitments from around the country. But, barely two months before the June primary, Keyser was removed from the ballot after a number of the signatures on his nominating petition were deemed invalid. He was subsequently reinstated, but had to fight a lawsuit seeking to have him removed again amid a controversy over whether some of the signatures had been forged. He ended up finishing a distant fourth in the primary, with El Paso County Supervisor Darryl Glenn winning with 38 percent of the vote. Glenn, an African-American and Air Force veteran with service in Iraq and Afghanistan, was boosted by endorsements from such conservative luminaries as Sen. Ted Cruz of Texas and former Alaska Gov. Sarah Palin.

But Glenn was at a major financial disadvantage: He had raised a mere $11,000 by the spring of 2016, and he ended up being outspent by Bennet by a 4-1 margin. The Bennet campaign hammered away at a remark Glenn had made during a primary debate -- in which the Republican had declared "it's not about reaching across the aisle" to compromise -- to suggest Glenn was too politically extreme for Colorado. A CBS survey during the summer showed Bennet with an approval rating of 60 percent, and polls three weeks from the general election showed him with a double-digit lead. It ended up being closer in the end, with Bennet on top 50%-44%, his victory largely tracking Democratic presidential candidate Hillary Clinton's 48%-43% win in the state on a county-by-county basis. Exit polls showed Bennet with a large advantage among women voters, with Glenn holding a slight edge among male voters and independents.

Bennet's name appeared on some lists of possible running mates for Clinton, and, as a twice-elected senator from a swing state, he is likely to be the subject of national ticket speculation going forward. But his tendency toward political independence and compromise could prove to be problematic for the Democrats' vocal progressive wing. Labor and environmental groups were critical of Bennet as he became one of the few congressional Democrats to support the 12-nation Pacific trade deal pushed by Obama (and now jettisoned by President Donald Trump).And his speech to the 2016 Colorado Democratic convention was frequently drowned out by boos from supporters of Sen. Bernie Sanders of Vermont, angry that Bennet was sticking with Clinton as a national convention "superdelegate" despite Sanders' win in the state caucuses.

Junior Senator

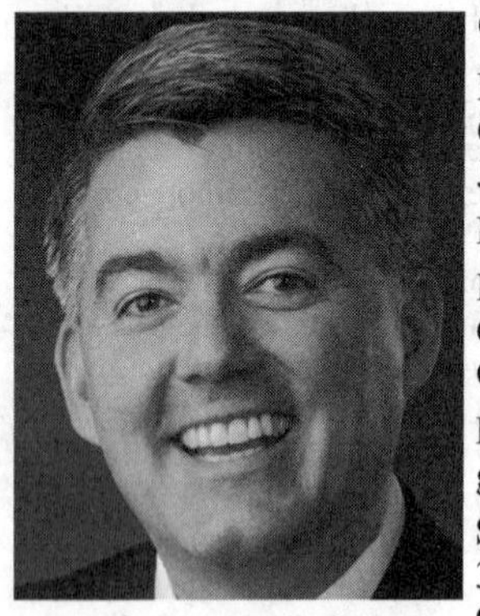

Cory Gardner (R)

Elected 2014, term expires 2020, 1st term; b. Aug 22, 1974, Yuma; Colorado State University, B.A.; University of Colorado School of Law, J.D.; Lutheran; Married (Jamie Gardner); 2 children.

Elected Office: CO House, 2005-2010; U.S. House, 2011-2015.

Professional Career: Communications Director, National Corn Growers Assn., 2001-2002; Staffer, Sen. Wayne Allard, 2002-2005; Owner, Farmers Implement dealership.

DC Office: 354 RSOB 20510, 202-224-5941, Fax: 202-224-6524, gardner.senate.gov.

State Offices: Colorado Springs, 719-632-6706; Denver, 303-391-5777; Durango, 970-415-7416; Fort Collins, 970-484-3502; Grand Junction, 970-245-9553; Greeley, 970-352-5546; Pueblo, 719-543-1324; Yuma, 970-848-3095.

Committees: Senate National Republican Senatorial Committee Chairman. *Budget*. *Commerce, Science & Transportation*: Aviation Operations, Safety & Security, Communications, Technology, Innovation & the Internet, Oceans, Atmosphere, Fisheries & Coast Guard, Space, Science & Competitiveness, Surface Trans., Merchant Marine Infra., Safety & Security. *Energy & Natural Resources*: Energy (Chmn), National Parks, Public Lands, Forests & Mining. *Foreign Relations*: East Asia, the Pacific & International Cybersecurity Policy (Chmn), Internat'l Dev Instit & Internat'l Econ, Energy & Environ Policy, West Hem Crime Civ Sec Dem Rights & Women's Issues. *Joint Security & Cooperation in Europe*.

Group Ratings

	ADA	ACLU	AFL-CIO	LCV	ITI	COC	HAFA	ACU	CFG	FRC
2016	-	58%	-	29%	100%	100%	56%	73%	6100%	100%
2015	5%	C	14%	16%	C	85%	C	79%	75%	100%

Almanac Ratings 2015

	Economy	Social	Foreign	Composite
Liberal	17%	0%	31%	16%
Conservative	83%	100%	69%	84%

Key Votes of the 114th Congress

1. Keystone pipeline	Y	5. National Security Data	Y	9. Gun Sales Checks	N
2. Export-Import Bank	Y	6. Iran Nuclear Deal	Y	10. Sanctuary Cities	Y
3. Debt Ceiling Increase	N	7. Puerto Rico Debt	Y	11. Planned Parenthood	Y
4. Homeland Security $$	Y	8. Loretta Lynch A.G	N	12. Trade deals	Y

Election Results

Election	Name (Party)	Vote (%)	Cand. Spent	Ind. Exp. Support	Ind. Exp. Oppose
2014 General	Cory Gardner (R)	983,891 (48%)	$12,490,384	$9,012,838	$30,646,858
	Mark Udall (D)	944,203 (46%)	$20,463,869	$6,684,190	$23,665,575
	Gaylon Kent (L)	52,876 (3%)			
2014 Primary	Cory Gardner (R)	338,324 (100%)			

Prior winning percentages: House: 2012 (58%), 2010 (52%)

At the outset of the 2014 election cycle, Republican strategists had one-term Democratic Sen. Mark Udall firmly in their sights. But they had a significant problem: finding a top-tier candidate to challenge him. After a long list of contenders -- among them three current members of Congress and one former member, as well as the state's attorney general -- had turned them down, the GOP finally found their candidate in two-term Rep. Cory Gardner. The youthful Republican House member, with an ever-present upbeat disposition, took advantage of plummeting ratings for President Barack Obama to topple Udall and become Colorado's junior senator -- overcoming criticism he was too conservative for a state that has turned a distinct shade of purple in recent years.

Gardner became a protégé of the House Republican leadership following his election to that chamber in 2010, the year the GOP regained control of the House majority. And, in late 2016, after two years in the Senate, he took on the task of chairing the National Republican Senatorial Committee, hoping to boost the Republican majority in 2018 in an election in which half of Senate Democratic incumbents will have to defend their seats. But, while reliably conservative throughout his time on Capitol Hill, Gardner has shown an ability to reach across the aisle -- including the development of a close working relationship with Colorado's senior senator, Democrat Michael Bennet, which has seen the two co-author several pieces of legislation of relevance nationally as well as to their home state.

A fifth-generation Coloradan, Gardner grew up in Yuma, a tiny farming and ranching town 150 miles east of Denver. After graduating from Colorado State University, Gardner returned to Yuma in pursuit of a pastoral lifestyle. But his father urged him to consider a profession less closely tied to the vagaries of Colorado's Eastern Plains. In 2001, Gardner earned a law degree from the University of Colorado and took a job as communications director for the National Corn Growers Association. The following year, he became an aide to Republican Sen. Wayne Allard, whose former seat Gardner now occupies. In the summer of 2005, Gardner was appointed to fill a vacancy in the Colorado House, and a year later he won election to a full term.

Believing one-term Democratic Rep. Betsy Markey to be vulnerable in early 2010 in a district that had previously been held by Republicans since 1973, the state GOP coalesced around Gardner: They saw him as a rising star and emphasized his deep roots in the 4th District's heavily Republican Eastern Plains. Gardner pounded Markey for supporting Obama's spending policies while he skirted the social issues that could have potentially alienated voters in some of the district's suburban areas. His strategy worked, as Markey was on the defensive after having supported Obama's $787 billion economic stimulus bill and his health insurance overhaul. At age 36, Gardner was elected to Congress with 52 percent of the vote.

In the House, Gardner was one of his freshman class's most faithful followers of the GOP leadership. He befriended then-Budget Committee Chairman Paul Ryan of Wisconsin -- now the House speaker -- while often joining Ryan on the vice presidential campaign trail in 2012. Gardner received a choice seat on the influential Energy and Commerce Committee and frequently assisted in House Republican messaging on energy matters. Gardner authored bills to open parts of Alaska to oil drilling and to require the president to promote a policy to lower gas prices by tapping the Strategic Petroleum Reserves. Both passed the House, but went nowhere in a Senate then under Democratic control. But Gardner's moves weren't all partisan, as he formed an Energy Savings Performance Caucus with Rep. Peter Welch, a liberal Vermont Democrat, in 2012.

After easily winning reelection in 2012 with 58 percent of the vote over state Senate President Brandon Shaffer, Gardner initially rejected the idea of running for the Senate two years later. "I've got work to do, I'm not in a hurry to run for another office," he told *The Denver Post* in April 2013. But 10 months later, Gardner changed his mind after a list of other potential candidate -- including fellow Colorado GOP Reps. Mike Coffman, Doug Lamborn, and Scott Tipton -- also said no. "YES!!!" Thank you, Cory! Republicans now have a viable option for winning!" former state Rep. B.J. Nikkel exclaimed on her Facebook page, capturing the sentiments of leading Republicans in Colorado and elsewhere. Gardner's entry into the contest prompted five other candidates who were seeking the GOP Senate nod to drop out -- including 2010 Republican Senate nominee Ken Buck, who opted instead to run for the House seat that Gardner was vacating. Gardner received 73 percent of the vote at the state Republican assembly in April 2014 over two remaining candidates to secure the Senate nomination. An independent poll that month showed Gardner, despite never having run statewide and only entering the race weeks earlier, to be in a dead heat with Udall.

Gardner decided to take on Udall by running as a political outsider, while portraying Udall -- who had spent a decade in the House prior to winning the Senate seat opened up in 2008 by Allard's retirement -- as a rubberstamp for then-Senate Majority Leader Harry Reid of Nevada and a captive of Washington. He also hammered away at Udall's support for Obama's health care law. Udall responded by painting Gardner as extreme on social issues and ran ads attacking him on birth control and abortion. His charges that Gardner held positions that were hostile to women, reinforced by outside groups that spent lavishly, saturated the airwaves throughout the campaign. But he did little to make a positive case for his re-election, and his campaign strategy ultimately backfired. In a major blow to Udall, *The Denver Post,* the state's largest newspaper that typically backs Democrats, endorsed Gardner. "Udall is trying to frighten voters rather than inspire them. His obnoxious one-issue campaign is an insult to those he seeks to convince," the editorial said. Noting that Congress is hardly functional, the newspaper said that it needs "fresh leadership, energy and ideas," while adding: "In every position [Gardner] has held over the years-from the state legislature to U.S. House of Representatives-he has quickly become someone to be reckoned with and whose words carry weight."

Gardner defended himself against Udall's attacks by saying that he had listened to voters and changed his stance on a "personhood" bill that could have resulted in a ban on certain forms of birth control. He went so far as to advocate in an op-ed piece during the campaign that birth control pills be available over the counter." On another major issue in a state that is 20 percent Hispanic-American, Gardner shifted his position on immigration and supported a move to give undocumented immigrants who serve in the armed forces a path to citizenship. He also was one of only a handful of House Republicans to oppose a bill that sought to prevent Obama from granting work permits to immigrants who were brought to the U.S. illegally as children. Such moves appeared to reassure voters that he was not the inflexible ideologue that the Democrats charged he was. On Election Day, Gardner scored a 48%-46% win over Udall.

After taking his Senate seat, Gardner continued to work to undercut charges during the campaign that his policies constituted a "war on women." He followed through on his campaign op-ed and sponsored legislation with other Republican senators to make certain forms of contraception available over the counter. The bill also sought to repeal the Affordable Care Act's restriction on the use of health, medical and flexible savings accounts to pay for prescriptions for other forms of contraception. But the Gardner initiative came under attack from reproductive health groups who charged that it could again force women to pay for birth control out of pocket. Senate Democrats, including Gardner's in-state colleague Bennet, introduced a rival bill. Shot back Gardner: "It's unfortunate they have decided to bring partisanship to an issue that could have brought support on Capitol Hill, but we are pleased they are following our lead."

But Gardner also moved to mend fences with Bennet after a 2014 campaign in which Bennet, as the chairman of the Democratic Senatorial Campaign Committee, aggressively sought to stave off Udall's defeat with tactics that prompted Gardner to criticize Bennet as "the chief partisan of the United States Senate." The two men have found common ground on issues ranging from energy to education reform. Among their efforts is legislation -- on which Gardner joined Oregon's two Democratic senators as well as Bennet -- to legalize banking for recreational marijuana companies; Colorado and Oregon were the first states to legalize recreational marijuana.

]One of Gardner's most significant achievements] was legislation co-sponsored with Democratic Sen. Gary Peters of Michigan. It resolved a three-year battle between House Republican leaders and the scientific community over how the National Science Foundation should operate. While the House had passed a series of proposals along partisan lines, Gardner and Peters -- working together as members of the Commerce, Science and Transportation Committee --crafted a bipartisan measure that scientists saw as much more supportive of the NSF. Legislation signed into law by Obama in late 2016 reflected the Gardner-Peters approach.

Gardner has demonstrated independence on the political as well as policy front. During the 2016 presidential campaign, when the video emerged showing Republican nominee Donald Trump making lewd comments about women, Gardner declared, "I cannot and will not support someone who brags about degrading and assaulting women." He called for Trump to step aside in favor of his running mate, now-Vice President Mike Pence, adding, "If he fails to do so, I will not vote for Hillary Clinton but instead will write-in my vote for Mike Pence." And just days after being elected NRSC chairman, Gardner joined fellow GOP Sens. John McCain of Arizona and Lindsey Graham of South Carolina -- as well as several leading Democrats -- in advocating a select committee on cybersecurity, in part to look into investigate allegations of Russian hacking during the 2016 election. Gardner's position was at odds with that of Senate Majority Leader Mitch McConnell of Kentucky, who was resisting calls for such a special committee in favor of a probe by the Senate's existing committee structure. Earlier in 2016, Gardner joined Virginia Democratic Sen. Mark Warner establishing a bipartisan Senate Cybersecurity Caucus.

Such stances underscore that Gardner is not about to let Democrats pigeonhole him as he looks ahead to re-election in 2020 in a state that has voted Democratic in the last three presidential elections. He knows that Colorado's population growth is driven partly by immigrants from California. And, in 2014, he defeated Udall in a race in which self-identified moderates cast over one-third of the ballots. Given those political dynamics, Gardner is likely to continue to try to thread the needle of reassuring moderates and independents that he is no reflexive ideologue, while also maintaining the support of those on the right.

FIRST DISTRICT

Diana DeGette (D)

Elected 1996, 11th term; b. Jul 29, 1957, Tachikawa, Japan; Colorado College, B.A., 1979; New York University Law School, J.D., 1982; Presbyterian; Married (Lino Lipinsky); 2 children.

Elected Office: CO House, 1992-1996, Assistant Minority Leader, 1994-1995.

Professional Career: Practicing attorney, 1982-1996.

DC Office: 2111 RHOB 20515, 202-225-4431, Fax: 202-225-5657, degette.house.gov.

State Offices: Denver, 303-844-4988.

Committees: *Energy & Commerce*: Environment, Health, Oversight & Investigations (RMM).

Group Ratings

	ADA	ACLU	AFL-CIO	LCV	ITI	COC	HAFA	ACU	CFG	FRC
2016	-	100%	-	100%	50%	46%	12%	0%	0%	0%
2015	95%	C	100%	100%	C	40%	C	0%	0%	0%

Almanac Ratings 2015

	Economy	Social	Foreign	Composite
Liberal	95%	100%	100%	98%
Conservative	6%	0%	0%	2%

Key Votes of the 114th Congress

1. Keystone Pipeline	N	5. Puerto Rico Debt	Y	9. Offenses by Aliens	N
2. Trade Deals	N	6. Medical Marijuana	Y	10. Troops in Iraq	Y
3. Export-Import Bank	Y	7. Sanctuary Cities	N	11. Homeland Security $$	Y
4. Debt Ceiling Increase	Y	8. Armor-piercing Bullets	N	12. Trade Adjustment aid	Y

Election Results

Election	Name (Party)	Vote (%)		Cand. Spent	Ind. Exp. Support	Ind. Exp. Oppose
2016 General	Diana DeGette (D)	257,254	(68%)	$840,210		
	Casper Stockham (R)	105,030	(28%)	$47,493		
	Darrell Dinges (L)	16,752	(4%)			
2016 Primary	Diana DeGette (D)	55,438	(87%)			
	Charles Norris (D)	8,676	(14%)			

Prior winning percentages: 2014 (66%), 2012 (68%), 2010 (67%), 2008 (72%), 2006 (80%), 2004 (74%), 2002 (66%), 2000 (69%), 1998 (67%), 1996 (57%)

Diana DeGette, first elected in 1996, is an energetic liberal and a chief deputy whip who has been among the House Democrats anxiously awaiting the chance to succeed the party's older, entrenched leaders. That blockage at the top has stymied the succession to a younger generation of Democrats. As a senior member of the Energy and Commerce Committee, DeGette was instrumental in the bipartisan enactment in 2016 of the 21st Century Cures Act, which was designed to promote health care innovation with increased research spending.

DeGette is a fourth-generation resident of Denver, though she was born on a military base in Japan. She says that she was inspired at age 13 by the television show *Storefront Lawyers* to "crusade for justice," and decided she would be a public interest lawyer. She attended New York University's law school on a full scholarship, then returned to Denver to practice employment law. In 1992, at age 35, DeGette was elected to the Colorado House. Her signature accomplishment was the Bubble Bill, which was aimed at protecting women at abortion clinics by making it illegal for protesters to come within eight feet of a person entering or leaving a health care facility. The U.S. Supreme Court upheld the constitutionality of the law in a 6-3 decision. In 1995, when Rep. Patricia Schroeder, a pioneer of the feminist left, announced she was retiring, DeGette ran for the seat. Organizationally adept, legislatively creative and politically progressive, she proved a worthy successor to Schroeder, one of the best-known figures in Colorado politics.

In both the minority and the majority, she has achieved legislative successes. On Energy and Commerce she has focused on health care issues. She teamed with Republican Rep. Mike Castle of Delaware to expand federal funding for stem cell research, which employs excess embryos from in vitro fertilization. President George W. Bush opposed more money for such research, and in 2006 vetoed their bill. In 2009, President Barack Obama, using his executive powers, removed most federal restrictions on stem cell research. She wrote a book on the topic called *Sex, Science, and Stem Cells*. She explained that she was inspired to take on the cause after one of her daughters was diagnosed with diabetes at age 4.

On other health issues, she co-sponsored in 2009 the Food Safety Enhancement Act. She secured two key provisions giving the Food and Drug Administration the power to mandate product recalls and authorizing the FDA to establish a food-tracking system. The bill was passed by the House but stalled in the Senate. Mandatory recall authority for the FDA became law in the Food Safety Modernization Act in 2011. During the health care overhaul debate in 2009 and 2010, DeGette played a major role in shaping the final abortion provisions in the legislation. With Republican Energy and Commerce Chairman Fred Upton of Michigan, she launched an initiative in 2015 to reduce the time for getting "breakthrough drugs" into the hands of needy patients. Their goal, she said, was to make the United States "the health care innovation capital of the world," including the approval of experimental pharmaceutical research plus more aggressive federal policy to promote mental health care. Their 21st Century Cures bill was one of the few major bipartisan measures enacted during Obama's final two years as president. DeGette called the legislation "a watershed moment in this country for bio-medical research."

DeGette has been active on other issues affecting Colorado and the West. She introduced a measure to provide health insurance to seasonal firefighters - an idea that Obama also implemented with an executive order. After Colorado and Washington state in 2012 passed laws legalizing marijuana, she filed legislation that bars the federal government from pre-empting such state laws. "My constituents have spoken, and I don't want the federal government denying money to Colorado or taking other punitive steps that would undermine the will of our citizens," she said. On Energy and Commerce, where DeGette is the senior Democrat on the Oversight and Investigations Subcommittee, she has pushed to address climate change, including U.S.-led international funding of renewable energy production.

DeGette has been active in House leadership politics, but has had setbacks. In 2001, she supported Maryland's Steny Hoyer in his unsuccessful bid for Democratic whip against California's Nancy Pelosi, who went on to become House Speaker. When Hoyer got the job as party whip in 2002, DeGette moved into the role of party strategist. When Democrats gained control of the House in 2007, Hoyer became majority leader, and DeGette seriously considered running for whip against South Carolina's James Clyburn. She said she ultimately decided that it would have been disruptive to have another internal struggle. Clyburn made DeGette his chief deputy whip. "If the opportunity arose, I would love to be whip," DeGette said. "I love to whip!"

As a mother of two children, who were 2 and 6 years old when she was elected, DeGette tries to help newer members of Congress with children find a balance between family and public life. She has had limited campaign opposition. In 2002, Ramona Martinez, a 15-year member of the Denver City Council and a Democratic National Committeewoman, criticized her for having lost touch with the district. DeGette returned her family to Denver from the Maryland suburbs in 2001 and won impressively, 73%-27%. DeGette did not face another primary challenge until 2016. Chuck Norris, a geologist and enthusiastic supporter of Bernie Sanders, ran on the "time for a change" theme. Sanders had easily won Colorado's Democratic Caucus against Hillary Clinton, whom DeGette had backed. But DeGette defeated Norris, 86%-14%. In November, she defeated Republican Charles Stockham, 68%-28%, which was consistent with recent results.

Denver Metro

Population		**Race and Ethnicity**		**Income**	
Total	771,214	White	57.2%	Median Income	$55,945 (174 out of 435)
Land area	190	Black	8.2%		
Pop/ sq mi	4067.2	Latino	28.2%		
Born in state	42.2%	Asian	3.3%	Under $50,000	45.0%
Age Groups		Two races	2.3%	$50,000-$99,999	29.2%
Under 18	21.0%	Other	0.8%	$100,000-$199,999	9.2%
18-34	29.4%	**Education**		$200,000 or more	19.1%
35-64	38.6%	H.S grad or less	30.7%	Poverty Rate	16.1%
Over 64	10.9%	Some college	24.7%	**Health Insurance**	
Work		College Degree, 4 yr	27.3%	With health insurance coverage	86.2%
White Collar	44.3%	Post grad	17.2%		
Sales and Service	40.3%	**Military**		**Public Assistance**	
Blue Collar	15.4%	Veteran	6.7%	Cash public assistance income	2.5%
Government	11.3%	Active Duty	0.1%	Food stamp/SNAP benefits	9.9%

Voter Turnout			
2015 Total Citizens 18+	540,651	2016 House Turnout as % CVAP	70%
2016 House turnout	379,036	2014 House Turnout as % CVAP	51%

2012 Presidential Vote		
Barack Obama	254,400	(69%)
Mitt Romney	106,334	(29%)

2016 Presidential Vote		
Hillary Clinton	277,790	(69%)
Donald Trump	93,486	(23%)
Gary Johnson	18,996	(5%)

Cook Partisan Voting Index: D+21

Denver is serious about being the Mile High City: There are three markers on the granite steps of the gold-domed Capitol that proclaim the elevation of 5,280 feet. Denver is situated a few miles from where the High Plains yield to the sharp peaks of the Front Range of the Rockies. With 683,000 people in 2015, the city for a century has been the economic and cultural capital of the Rocky Mountain region. On top of its Old West heritage and early-20th-century elegance, Denver has developed an exuberant postmodern style. The National Western Stock Show held here every year and the LoDo entertainment district along the South Platte River evoke the Old West. The Capitol, the spacious parks, the aspens that line the streets, give the city a lush, burnished air, in contrast to the dry plains and stark peaks.

Amid its downtown grid are the skyscrapers of the 1970s energy boom and the 1990s tech boom, plus Coors Field, where Major League Baseball's Colorado Rockies play, the Elitch Gardens Theme and Water Park, and the Denver Museum of Nature & Science. Barack Obama claimed the Democratic presidential nomination at Mile High Stadium in 2008, with grand expectations. Rather than losing population as many central cities have, Denver has gained people since 1990. In 2015, it moved past Detroit as the nation's 19th-largest city, and it ranked ninth that year among cities with the largest population increase. Most of its neighborhoods have strong housing demand, including the African-American neighborhoods of northeastern Denver, filled with neat 1950s bungalows, and the Hispanic quarter northwest of downtown. But more than three-quarters of the metro area's people now live in the suburbs, and Denver has disproportionate numbers of singles and cultural liberals who value an urban and physically active lifestyle in the gentrified areas south of the Capitol.

The local gay and lesbian population is the ninth largest among the nation's metropolitan areas. In early 2015, a local bakery that had prepared many cakes for gay-themed events generated national attention when it refused to prepare a cake with an anti-gay message. The state's civil rights division ruled that the baker did not discriminate for refusing to include the biblical phrases on the cakes. In November 2016, city voters approved a referendum to allow the social use of marijuana at local facilities that get a permit. Following the election, Denver Mayor Michael Hancock said the city's police officers would not cooperate with enforcement of federal immigration laws.

Denver is the liberal heart of Colorado. The city remains majority Anglo, but has elected Hispanic and black mayors and is now 32 percent Latino. In the early 1970s, Denver liberals were hostile to growth and boosterism. Today's Denver has shown that growth can produce more of the distinctiveness that people here appreciate. There was good reason: Denver has been ranked among the nation's top 10 cities in business climate, livability, libraries and bikeways. The metro economy remained strong in 2016, with 2.7 percent unemployment, the lowest of any metro area in the nation with a population above 1 million.

The 1st Congressional District covers all of Denver and stretches northeast to include Denver International Airport. It includes affluent suburbs, long-settled Englewood and recently settled Cherry Hills Village in Arapahoe County. The district drops southwest to include suburban parts of Jefferson County, where Columbine High School was the location in 1999 of a mass shooting, when two teenage boys killed 13 people. More than 80 percent live in Denver County. In an era when cultural attitudes often are a better clue to voting behavior than economic status, this district, which last elected a Republican in 1970, is the only solid Democratic district in the state.

SECOND DISTRICT

Jared Polis (D)

Elected 2008, 5th term; b. May 12, 1975, Boulder; Princeton University (NJ), B.A.; Jewish; Domestic Partner (Marlon Reis); 2 children.

Elected Office: CO Board of Education, 2001-2007, Chairman 2004, Vice Chairman, 2005-2006.

Professional Career: Entrepreneur, 1996-2008.

DC Office: 1727 LHOB 20515, 202-225-2161, Fax: 202-226-7840, polis.house.gov.

State Offices: Boulder, 303-484-9596; Fort Collins, 970-226-1239; Frisco, 970-409-7301.

Committees: *Education & the Workforce*: Early Childhood, Elementary & Secondary Education (RMM), Higher Education & Workforce Development. *Ethics*. *Rules*: Legislative & Budget Process.

Group Ratings

	ADA	ACLU	AFL-CIO	LCV	ITI	COC	HAFA	ACU	CFG	FRC
2016	-	100%	-	100%	50%	50%	15%	12%	23%	0%
2015	80%	C	92%	91%	C	40%	C	13%	5%	0%

Almanac Ratings 2015

	Economy	Social	Foreign	Composite
Liberal	81%	87%	93%	87%
Conservative	19%	13%	7%	13%

Key Votes of the 114th Congress

1. Keystone Pipeline	N	5. Puerto Rico Debt	Y	9. Offenses by Aliens	Y
2. Trade Deals	Y	6. Medical Marijuana	Y	10. Troops in Iraq	Y
3. Export-Import Bank	Y	7. Sanctuary Cities	N	11. Homeland Security $$	Y
4. Debt Ceiling Increase	Y	8. Armor-piercing Bullets	Y	12. Trade Adjustment aid	Y

Election Results

Election	Name (Party)	Vote (%)		Cand. Spent	Ind. Exp. Support	Ind. Exp. Oppose
2016 General	Jared Polis (D)	260,175	(57%)	$1,186,443		
	Nic Morse (R)	170,001	(37%)	$160,186		
	Richard Longstreth (L)	27,136	(6%)			
2016 Primary	Jared Polis (D)		(100%)			

Prior winning percentages: 2014 (57%), 2012 (56%), 2010 (67%), 2008 (63%)

Jared Polis, a Democrat first elected in 2008, is the first man who was openly gay when he was elected to Congress. The multi-talented multimillionaire entrepreneur has diverse policy interests plus partisan ambitions, and he has been an active fundraiser for his party. In 2015, after Republican Rep. Steve King of Iowa introduced a bill to block federal courts from hearing cases to legalize same-sex marriage, Polis showed his creativity by filing his own bill - apparently satirical - to block the courts from enforcing King's proposal.

Polis was born in Boulder but grew up in San Diego. His mother, a poet, and his father, an artist, were both politically active during the anti-war movement of the late 1960s. Polis and his younger brother and sister frequently accompanied their parents to demonstrations and rallies. Their activism spurred Polis' interest in politics and progressive ideas. He graduated from high school in three years, and got his bachelor's degree in political science at Princeton University. Also fascinated by technology and business, Polis banded together with two friends in their sophomore year to launch American Information Systems, an Internet access provider. Soon afterward, he founded *bluemountainarts.com*, an electronic greeting card site that at its height was the eighth most popular on the Internet. His next venture was *Proflowers.com*, which enables customers to order fresh flowers directly from growers. All three were successful, and Polis sold them for profits of upwards of $300 million. (He has distributed business cards in which he calls himself a "retired florist.")

Financial security allowed Polis to focus on his other passions. "I was always interested in public service. Education is an issue I feel very passionately about, providing an opportunity to all Americans," he said. In 2000, four years out of college, he was elected to the Colorado State Board of Education. He served for six years and as chairman for one year. Polis was most proud of his advancement of school choice through charter schools and his work improving accountability standards for schools. In part with his own money, he founded two innovative charter schools in Colorado, which helped new immigrants assimilate, especially with flexible day or evening programs, and teachers trained to help students learn English. "We really needed a school to cater to their unique needs," Polis said. At the same time, he partnered with three other Colorado multimillionaires - who were dubbed the "Gang of Four" in newspapers - and built a Democratic fundraising operation that raised $3.6 million in 2004.

When the House seat opened in 2008, Polis ran. In the Democratic primary, he faced former state Senate President Joan Fitz-Gerald and conservationist Will Shafroth. Most of the state's Democratic establishment backed Fitz-Gerald, based on her political seasoning. Pouring in his own money, Polis outspent his opponents 4-to-1. He got 42 percent of the vote, followed by Fitz-Gerald with 38 percent and Shafroth with 20 percent. At age 33, he breezed through the general election, 63%-34%. In the entire campaign, he spent $7 million, of which $6 million was his own. Since then, he has not been seriously challenged in a primary or general election. The nonpartisan watchdog Center for Responsive Politics ranked Polis in 2015 as the second-richest member of the House, pegging his net worth at $388 million, based on his financial disclosure reports.

In Washington, Democratic leaders gave Polis a seat on the influential Rules Committee, whose majority-party members control the terms of debate for major bills on the House floor. He has had a medley of interests. In 2009, Polis jumped into the health care debate, fighting a proposal by his own party that would pay for elements of the overhauled system with a tax on the highest-earning Americans. Polis maintained that the tax would hurt small business owners who aren't large enough to organize as corporations. The proposed surtax was dropped from the sweeping overhaul enacted in 2010. He has taken an interest in budget issues. He was one of 22 Democrats in 2012 who voted for a plan that was based on the recommendations of President Barack Obama's Simpson-Bowles deficit-reduction commission. In 2015, he was one of 28 House Democrats who voted to give trade promotion authority to Obama. On gay rights, he was the chief House sponsor of the Employee Non-Discrimination Act. Responding to objections from gay-rights groups in 2014, he narrowed the religious exemption in his proposal. He has called for the Food and Drug Administration to rescind a requirement that gay and bisexual men be celibate for a year before donating blood. With Rep. Earl Blumenauer of Oregon, he filed a bill that would legalize marijuana as a controlled substance and tax it, initially at 10 percent.

At home, he clashed with state Democratic leaders in 2014 when he threatened to force public votes in November on two referenda that would limit hydraulic fracking for oil and gas in Colorado. Many Democrats feared that the move would backfire by increasing the turnout of conservative voters. Polis backed down at the August deadline after Gov. John Hickenlooper agreed to review alternative policy options.

Polis has displayed impressive fundraising skills among House Democrats, collecting from liberal interest groups and investment companies while donating money to politically vulnerable colleagues through his Jared Polis Victory Fund. He suffered a setback following the 2014 election when Minority Leader Nancy Pelosi named Rep. Ben Ray Lujan of New Mexico to chair the Democratic Congressional Campaign Committee. Polis had openly sought the position, though he responded that he was "relieved" that he would not be taking on the partisan post. The outcome has not quelled his enthusiasm. After he announced support for Hillary Clinton for the Democratic presidential nomination, the *Daily Camera* newspaper in Boulder reported that Polis received a written note urging him to "Feel the Bern" when he ordered at a Boulder carry-out. Polis tweeted with a photo of the note, "Even my food takeout is lobbying me for #FeelTheBern." In June 2017, Polis announced that he was joining the wide-open contest for governor in 2018. His agenda included 100 percent renewable energy by 2040; free full-day preschool or kindergarten for children age 3 and older; and encouraging companies to provide stock options to employees.

Northern Front Range: Fort Collins, Boulder

Population		**Race and Ethnicity**		**Income**	
Total	757,740	White	83.3%	Median Income	$69,304 (75 out of 435)
Land area	7,535	Black	0.8%		
Pop/ sq mi	100.6	Latino	10.3%	Under $50,000	36.9%
Born in state	35.8%	Asian	3.0%	$50,000-$99,999	30.5%
		Two races	2.0%	$100,000-$199,999	109.2%
Age Groups		Other	0.6%	$200,000 or more	24.5%
Under 18	20.2%			Poverty Rate	11.9%
18-34	26.8%	**Education**			
35-64	40.6%	H.S grad or less	19.6%	**Health Insurance**	
Over 64	12.4%	Some college	27.6%	With health insurance coverage	90.9%
		College Degree, 4 yr	31.1%		
Work		Post grad	21.6%		
White Collar	47.4%			**Public Assistance**	
Sales and Service	38.2%	**Military**		Cash public assistance income	1.5%
Blue Collar	14.4%	Veteran	7.7%		
Government	15.0%	Active Duty	0.1%	Food stamp/SNAP benefits	4.9%

Voter Turnout			
2015 Total Citizens 18+	576,459	2016 House Turnout as % CVAP	79%
2016 House turnout	457,312	2014 House Turnout as % CVAP	60%

2012 Presidential Vote		
Barack Obama	255,208	(58%)
Mitt Romney	174,028	(40%)

2016 Presidential Vote		
Hillary Clinton	264,966	(56%)
Donald Trump	164,769	(35%)
Gary Johnson	24,820	(5%)

Cook Partisan Voting Index: D+9

Nestled against the Front Range of the Rocky Mountains is Boulder, home of the 30,000-student University of Colorado, once billed by the city as "a combination of Lycra-clad athletes, New Age artists, and thoughtful intellectuals sipping cappuccinos." Boulder is one of the nation's leading centers for bungee jumping, mountain biking, snowshoeing, rock and ice climbing, downhill skiing, land surfing and hot-air ballooning. It has been called the nation's No. 1 town for outdoor sports by *Outdoor* magazine, and in 2016 ranked fifth among mid-sized metropolitan areas with the best quality of life. Marathoners from around the world train in several camps here. It is also the home of Boulder College of Massage Therapy and the Buddhist Naropa University, where Allen Ginsberg helped start a poetry school in 1974.

All have come here because of the setting. The streets of Boulder look up at craggy peaks rising to 14,000 feet from a mile-high plain stretching farther east than the eye can see. It has become a magnet for technology firms dissatisfied with the more congested Silicon Valley. The economics also have been appealing. Unemployment in Boulder has been among the lowest in the nation, hovering at around 3 percent. *Business Insider* in 2015 ranked Boulder fourth best in the nation among city economies. The Fort Collins-Loveland area, which is north of Boulder, continues to grow and in 2015 ranked fourth in Gallup's Well-Being index that measures emotional and physical health in U.S. cities. Fort Collins has faced some challenges. The demographic changes have widened the local income gap. And grass-roots groups were displeased when the state Supreme Court in June 2016 unanimously ruled that the Fort Collins moratorium on hydraulic fracking violated the state's authority to regulate oil and gas.

The 2nd Congressional District is centered in Boulder. Interstate 70 charts a scenically awesome course through the mountains as it takes in Rocky Mountain acreage, and it is often congested with cars loaded with skis and snowboards. The district includes the old coal mining town of Central City, which describes itself as "the richest square mile on earth" and is home to multiple casinos. The lodges and resorts of Vail are farther west on Interstate 70. Once dependent on mining and agriculture, Vail evolved into an international resort city after the 10th Mountain Division ski troops were introduced to the Eagle River Valley in the 1940s. After World War II, a group of Army buddies returned and developed a ski resort.

The district is comfortably Democratic. Boulder County is a partisan hub for Democrats, but the rest of the district is relatively balanced politically. Larimer County, with Fort Collins and Loveland, is the largest county with more than 40 percent of the voters in the district. Boulder has about 30 percent.

THIRD DISTRICT

Scott Tipton (R)

Elected 2010, 4th term; b. Nov 09, 1956, Espanola, NM; Fort Lewis College (CO), B.A.; Anglican; Married (Jean Tipton); 2 children.

Elected Office: CO House, 2009-2011.

Professional Career: Owner, CEO, Mesa Verde Pottery.

DC Office: 218 CHOB 20515, 202-225-4761, Fax: 202-226-9669, tipton.house.gov.

State Offices: Alamosa, 719-587-5105; Durango, 970-259-1490; Grand Junction, 970-241-2499; Pueblo, 719-542-1073; Steamboat Springs, 970-640-9718.

Committees: *Financial Services*: Financial Institutions & Consumer Credit, Oversight & Investigations, Terrorism & Illicit Finance. *Natural Resources*: Energy & Mineral Resources, Federal Lands.

Group Ratings

	ADA	ACLU	AFL-CIO	LCV	ITI	COC	HAFA	ACU	CFG	FRC
2016	-	11%	-	0%	100%	93%	75%	100%	81%	100%
2015	5%	C	4%	3%	C	74%	C	91%	87%	82%

Almanac Ratings 2015

	Economy	Social	Foreign	Composite
Liberal	3%	15%	0%	6%
Conservative	97%	85%	100%	94%

Key Votes of the 114th Congress

1. Keystone Pipeline	Y	5. Puerto Rico Debt	Y	9. Offenses by Aliens	Y
2. Trade Deals	Y	6. Medical Marijuana	Y	10. Troops in Iraq	N
3. Export-Import Bank	N	7. Sanctuary Cities	Y	11. Homeland Security $$	N
4. Debt Ceiling Increase	N	8. Armor-piercing Bullets	Y	12. Trade Adjustment aid	N

Election Results

Election	Name (Party)	Vote (%)		Cand. Spent	Ind. Exp. Support	Ind. Exp. Oppose
2016 General	Scott Tipton (R)	204,220	(55%)	$1,997,600	$38,908	$2,227,842
	Gail Schwartz (D)	150,914	(40%)	$1,400,846	$940,455	$2,643,247
	Gaylon Kent (L)	18,903	(5%)			
2016 Primary	Scott Tipton (R)	43,697	(79%)			
	Alex Beinstein (R)	11,708	(21%)			

Prior winning percentages: 2014 (58%), 2012 (53%), 2010 (50%)

The congressman from the 3rd District is Scott Tipton, a conservative Republican elected in 2010 who has been known to buck his party's leadership and show occasional bipartisanship in dealing with local resource issues. In 2016, he easily survived a well-financed Democratic challenge.

Tipton was born in EspaÑola, New Mexico. His family moved to Cortez, Colorado, three months after he was born. His father was a construction worker for a Denver-based company, but the family's finances were often strained by the medical needs of Tipton's brother, who was diabetic. When Tipton enrolled in Fort Lewis College in Durango, he became the first member of his family to go beyond high school. After getting his degree, Tipton returned to his hometown to establish a production facility for Native American pottery and jewelry, employing childhood friends who belonged to the Ute and Navajo tribes. When his fledgling business was encumbered by onerous and redundant government paperwork, he said that the experience made him a critic of government interference with small businesses.

In 2006, he mounted his first political campaign against Democrat John Salazar, then a freshman in the 3rd District. Salazar won 62%-37% in a Democratic year, but Tipton increased his visibility. Two years later, he won a seat in the Colorado House. As a Republican legislator, Tipton said that he sometimes felt marginalized by the Democratic Party's hegemony in the state capital.

In 2010, Tipton again challenged Salazar. In the GOP primary, retired Army lawyer Bob McConnell was the preferred candidate of tea party activists. Some tea partiers viewed Tipton suspiciously as a member of the Republican establishment, but he refrained from criticizing McConnell and won 54%-46%. In the fall campaign, Tipton portrayed Salazar as too deferential to the Democratic leadership, slamming the incumbent for his votes in favor of President Barack Obama's $787 billion economic stimulus bill and the Affordable Care Act. Salazar also was perceived as having close ties to Obama, who had tapped his younger brother, Ken Salazar, as Interior secretary. For his part, John Salazar deemphasized his party label, calling himself "An Independent Voice for Rural Colorado." The incumbent was well-funded, raising more than $2 million to Tipton's $1.2 million. The district's conservative voters were energized and Tipton prevailed, 50%-46%.

Early in his first term, defying the House Republican leadership, Tipton voted against a major spending bill because he favored steeper cuts. He joined other conservatives in opposing House Speaker John Boehner's deal with the White House to raise the debt limit that year. On the Financial Services Committee, Tipton has filed several proposals to reduce regulations imposed by the 2010 Dodd-Frank banking law.

Tipton has been more centrist on non-fiscal issues. *The Denver Post* pointed out that he favored government funding for a local bicycle trail, a popular position in an environmentally conscious district. He supported funding to preserve groundwater in the San Luis Valley in the southern part of his district. He criticized the slow response and "poor communication" by the Environmental Protection Agency after the blowout at the King Gold Mine deluged the Durango area with wastewater. And he has attacked the excesses of federal regulators, including the EPA. In 2015, he proposed a 30-year plan for American energy that would rely on all sources.

Democrats targeted Tipton in 2012, backing the challenge of state Rep. Sal Pace. The National Republican Congressional Committee derided Pace as one of liberal House Minority Leader "Nancy Pelosi's hand-picked puppets," but he took some conservative positions, such as calling for a balanced budget constitutional amendment. Pace attacked Tipton's vote for Rep. Paul Ryan's Medicare reform plan. "If you dare put an idea on the table, you get demonized," Tipton complained during an August candidates' debate. Tipton slightly outspent Pace, $2.2 million to $1.9 million, and won, 53%-41%.

After his victory margin grew to 58%-36% in an uncompetitive reelection in 2014, Tipton voiced interest in challenging Democratic Sen. Michael Bennet in 2016, with the potential to emulate the 2014 success of then-Rep. Cory Gardner over Sen. Mark Udall in another match-up of a rural Republican and a metro Democrat. But Tipton turned down what would have been an uphill challenge to Bennet.

Instead, he again found himself a reelection target of national Democrats. This time, his opponent was Gail Schwartz, a former state senator from Crested Butte, who attacked Tipton for circulating draft legislation that had been prepared with assistance from an energy company that was a large campaign contributor to him. She called for expansion of the district's tourism and recreation industries, while preserving its public lands. Tipton said that Schwartz's support for higher renewable energy standards had cost the area hundreds of energy-related jobs, especially in the coal industry. Tipton outpaced Schwartz in fundraising, $1.9 million to $1.7 million, but Schwartz received large support from national liberal groups, including $2.9 million from the House Majority PAC. Tipton prevailed by an impressive 55%-40%, with 66 percent in Mesa (Grand Junction) and 53 percent in Pueblo - the two largest counties. Schwartz led in 13 of the 29 counties, especially in the high-mountain resort areas.

With his second double-digit victory against a competitive challenger, Tipton seemed likely to reduce his exposure to another well-financed Democratic candidate.

Western Slope: Grand Junction, Pueblo

Population		**Race and Ethnicity**		**Income**	
Total	723,937	White	71.1%	Median Income	$49,013 (267 out of 435)
Land area	49,732	Black	0.8%		
Pop/ sq mi	14.6	Latino	24.4%		
Born in state	49.0%	Asian	0.7%	Under $50,000	50.8%
		Two races	1.5%	$50,000-$99,999	31.0%
Age Groups		Other	1.5%	$100,000-$199,999	209.2%
Under 18	22.6%			$200,000 or more	15.1%
18-34	21.9%	**Education**		Poverty Rate	15.8%
35-64	40.0%	H.S grad or less	37.5%		
Over 64	15.6%	Some college	32.5%	**Health Insurance**	
		College Degree, 4 yr	19.8%	With health insurance coverage	84.5%
Work		Post grad	10.1%		
White Collar	32.6%				
Sales and Service	43.8%	**Military**		**Public Assistance**	
Blue Collar	23.6%	Veteran	10.4%	Cash public assistance income	3.0%
Government	15.8%	Active Duty	0.1%		
				Food stamp/SNAP benefits	11.9%

Voter Turnout			
2015 Total Citizens 18+	532,819	2016 House Turnout as % CVAP	70%
2016 House turnout	374,037	2014 House Turnout as % CVAP	53%

2012 Presidential Vote		
Mitt Romney	185,459	(52%)
Barack Obama	163,885	(46%)

2016 Presidential Vote		
Donald Trump	195,966	(52%)
Hillary Clinton	151,057	(40%)
Gary Johnson	17,687	(5%)

Cook Partisan Voting Index: R+6

On a clear night from the air, they look like tiny mottled veins, thickest near Denver. These are the lights of the civilization Americans have built on the Western Slope of the Rockies in Colorado. The lights follow the trails of valley roads and mountainside switchbacks. The nodes mark the dozens of little towns built during mining boom years: the Gold Rush of the 1870s, the uranium boom of the 1950s, and the oil-shale boomlet of the 1970s. The Western Slope - everything west of the Front Range, with dozens of peaks over 14,000 feet - has always blocked east-west movement. Except for mining and skiing, few would have followed the Ute Indians and settled here. The miners who tracked gold and silver and lead ores also built Victorian towns with opera houses and gingerbread storefronts in Aspen and Telluride, in valleys and defiles scarcely accessible to the outside world. Now many of these towns have been restored by ski resort operators and joined by dozens of new condominiums and shopping malls. Cries of overdevelopment have followed. More than half of the area's iconic aspen trees have died in recent years from fire or natural causes.

Amid the tourism, resource development continues of gas deposits trapped beneath the Roan Plateau. In 2014, following bipartisan encouragement by the Colorado congressional delegation, the federal government agreed with the state to permit limited drilling in designated areas of the plateau. The energy-rich Western Slope has suffered from the steep nationwide drop in natural gas prices. But long-term prospects strengthened in June 2016 when the U.S. Geological Service increased by 40 times its estimate of natural gas reserves in the area's Piceance Basin, which would be the second largest in the nation behind the Marcellus Shale centered in Pennsylvania. A large share of the western Colorado reserves are on federal lands, where drilling companies expect to use hydraulic fracturing. In September 2016, the Environmental Protection Agency listed the Gold King Mine in Silverton for Superfund cleanup after a blow-out a year earlier contaminated the Animas River with 5.4 million gallons of acid metals daily for several months.

The political map of the Western Slope is as diverse as its history. A ribbon of counties along the Wasatch Range, from Wyoming on the northern border to New Mexico on the southern border, votes mostly Democratic. They include Aspen and the former coal mining centers of Crested Butte and Steamboat Springs, once Republican, today sporting ski lodges. Durango, an old frontier town, has moved in the same direction. Some areas are still heavily Republican and hostile to environmentalists and liberals generally: the rough-handed mining area around Grand Junction, the population center of the district, where piles of tailings still crackle with radioactivity; and the northwest corner of the state, where people remember the oil shale boom with nostalgia. Generally on the Western Slope, the high-income areas, with lots of residents opposed to new oil and gas drilling, are the most Democratic, while more modest-income, working-class towns are the most Republican.

The 3rd Congressional District of Colorado includes most of the Western Slope, and occupies nearly half of Colorado. It extends east of the Front Range to include the industrial city of Pueblo. There, on the banks of the Arkansas River, the Rockefellers built large steel factories before World War I to make barbed wire and rails. In September 2016, the Army began to operate a $4.5 billion plant at the Pueblo Chemical Depot to destroy the largest remaining stockpile of chemical weapons: more than 2,600 tons of a mustard gas agent. The target date for completion was 2020. Pueblo County is the second-largest in the district and has been comfortably Democratic, with a 43 percent Hispanic population. In 2016, Donald Trump won by 390 votes, with his blue-collar and rural appeal. (These inhabitants are Hispanics but not necessarily Mexican-Americans: Spanish-speaking people have been living here, as in northern New Mexico, for 350 years.) The 3rd has the lowest median income and education levels in the state. With the chief exception of the resort counties toward the center of the state, the district has leaned increasingly Republican. After John McCain won the district 50%-49% in 2008, Trump increased the Republican spread to 52%-40%.

FOURTH DISTRICT

Ken Buck (R)

Elected 2014, 2nd term; b. Feb 16, 1959, Ossining, NY; Princeton University (NJ), B.A.; University of Wyoming (WY), J.D.; Wesleyan; Married (Perry Lynn); 2 children (2 from previous marriage).

Elected Office: Weld County, CO, DA 2005-2014.

Professional Career: Practicing attorney, 1987-2002; Staff, U.S. Committee to Investigate Cover Arms Transactions with Iran, 1986-1987.

DC Office: 1130 LHOB 20515, 202-225-4676, buck.house.gov.

State Offices: Castle Rock, 720-639-9165; Greeley, 970-702-2136.

Committees: *Judiciary*: Immigration & Border Security, Regulatory Reform, Commercial & Antitrust Law. *Rules*: Legislative & Budget Process.

Group Ratings

	ADA	ACLU	AFL-CIO	LCV	ITI	COC	HAFA	ACU	CFG	FRC
2016	-	17%	-	0%	83%	79%	100%	100%	100%	91%
2015	10%	C	9%	3%	C	58%	C	100%	97%	80%

Almanac Ratings 2015

	Economy	Social	Foreign	Composite
Liberal	22%	20%	0%	14%
Conservative	78%	80%	100%	86%

Key Votes of the 114th Congress

1. Keystone Pipeline	Y	5. Puerto Rico Debt	N	9. Offenses by Aliens	Y
2. Trade Deals	N	6. Medical Marijuana	Y	10. Troops in Iraq	N
3. Export-Import Bank	N	7. Sanctuary Cities	Y	11. Homeland Security $$	N
4. Debt Ceiling Increase	N	8. Armor-piercing Bullets	Y	12. Trade Adjustment aid	N

Election Results

Election	Name (Party)	Vote (%)		Cand. Spent	Ind. Exp. Support	Ind. Exp. Oppose
2016 General	Ken Buck (R)	248,230	(64%)	$580,948		
	Bob Seay (D)	123,642	(32%)	$62,842		
	Bruce Griffith (L)	18,761	(5%)			
2016 Primary	Ken Buck (R)		(100%)			

Prior winning percentages: 2014 (65%)

Republican Ken Buck achieved a political revival in 2014 in Colorado's red-leaning 4th District race after narrowly losing four years earlier a Senate contest to Democrat Michael Bennet that many expected Buck would win. In the House, he quickly settled in as an outspoken conservative, including as a Freedom Caucus member.

Buck cultivated his political chops early in his career. Fresh out of the University of Wyoming law school, he worked for then-Rep. Dick Cheney on the House's 1986-87 probe into the Iran-Contra scandal and later served as a trial attorney in the Justice Department. He returned to Colorado in the 1990s as chief of the Criminal Division in the U.S. Attorney's Office. In 2005, he successfully ran for Weld County district attorney and was reelected twice. But his political hopes crashed in 2010. In the GOP primary for a Senate seat, he attracted national attention by commenting that he would make a better candidate than his opponent, Lt. Gov. Jane Norton, because he didn't "wear heels." Buck won the primary, 52%-48%. Further damage was done when he compared homosexuality to alcoholism on *Meet the Press*. He lost to Bennet by less than 2 percentage points, prompting many Republicans to view Colorado, along with Delaware and Nevada, as Senate pickup opportunities that the party squandered with weak candidates.

Sporting a more professional image and emphasizing his career in law enforcement, Buck launched another shot at the Senate in 2014 against first-term Democratic Sen. Mark Udall. But when Rep. Cory Gardner threw his hat in the ring, Buck decided to step aside to compete instead for the open 4th District, where the turf is friendly for Republicans. GOP strategists, with their negative memories of Buck, were grateful to get a stronger Senate challenger. The softer-edged Gardner was relieved to avoid a competitive primary. In the June primary for Gardner's House seat, Buck's name recognition and conservative reputation gave him a big edge over three GOP opponents, and he was largely immune from attacks from the right by state Sen. Scott Renfroe. He steered away from making controversial comments, even distancing himself from Washington Republicans who backed the government shutdown in 2013. Instead, he highlighted issues such as energy independence, touting his support for the Keystone XL pipeline. Boosted by endorsements from Gardner and other top Republicans, as well as the local newspaper, *The Greeley Tribune*, Buck topped the primary field with 44 percent, while Renfroe trailed by more than 20 points. In the general election, Buck easily beat Vic Meyers, 65%-29%. In this district, he seems secure.

He got a quick start in the House, with his election as president of the Republican freshman class. He said that he would focus on problem-solving, not partisanship. But he maintained his blunt-spoken style.

Criticizing President Barack Obama for abusing his executive authority, he said, "No more acting like King Barack." Buck was quick to stir his own controversy. Three months after he took office, he brought an AR-15 assault rifle to his office on Capitol Hill. The weapon is illegal in the District of Columbia. Buck said the rifle was not loaded and that he had received approval from the Capitol Police

In June 2015, Buck faced the threat of insurrection from his freshman class after he was one of 34 Republicans who failed to support the party leadership on a procedural vote related to legislation to provide trade promotion authority to Obama. That caught the attention of Speaker John Boehner, whose allies alerted Buck to Boehner's unhappiness. That led to criticism of Buck's leadership of the freshman class. Freshman Republican Carlos Curbelo of Florida told *The Hill* newspaper after he and other freshmen shared their gripes with Buck, "We haven't met enough, we haven't gotten to know each other enough, we're not communicating enough. That's what it boils down to. ... [Buck] listened to everyone, and he acknowledged everyone's concerns."

On the legislative front, the House Ways and Means Committee approved Buck's bill to loosen restrictions on water storage and delivery companies that seek to maintain their nonprofit status. A member of the Judiciary Committee, he filed a bill to make assault on a police officer a federal hate crime.

Buck easily won reelection against Bob Seay, a school teacher who raised $73,000 compared with Buck's $1 million. Buck led in every county except for Boulder, which accounts for only 12 percent of the district's voters.

Eastern Colorado: Weld, Douglas

Population		**Race and Ethnicity**		**Income**	
Total	751,207	White	72.7%	Median Income	$66,030 (87 out of 435)
Land area	38,103	Black	1.3%		
Pop/ sq mi	19.7	Latino	21.7%	Under $50,000	38.3%
Born in state	48.6%	Asian	1.8%	$50,000-$99,999	31.7%
		Two races	1.8%	$100,000-$199,999	309.2%
Age Groups		Other	0.7%	$200,000 or more	23.6%
Under 18	26.2%			Poverty Rate	11.1%
18-34	21.6%	**Education**			
35-64	40.2%	H.S grad or less	34.4%	**Health Insurance**	
Over 64	12.0%	Some college	32.7%	With health insurance coverage	89.3%
		College Degree, 4 yr	22.0%		
Work		Post grad	10.8%		
White Collar	38.7%			**Public Assistance**	
Sales and Service	39.9%	**Military**		Cash public assistance income	1.9%
Blue Collar	21.4%	Veteran	9.1%		
Government	14.1%	Active Duty	0.1%	Food stamp/SNAP benefits	8.3%

Voter Turnout			
2015 Total Citizens 18+	519,538	2016 House Turnout as % CVAP	75%
2016 House turnout	390,549	2014 House Turnout as % CVAP	54%

2012 Presidential Vote		
Mitt Romney	210,019	(59%)
Barack Obama	140,855	(39%)

2016 Presidential Vote		
Donald Trump	230,945	(57%)
Hillary Clinton	137,784	(34%)
Gary Johnson	20,104	(5%)

Cook Partisan Voting Index: R+13

The High Plains of eastern Colorado are dusty brown, gently rolling up toward the Rocky Mountains. The land is fertile, but dry. Rainfall is rare, the rivers are just a trickle most of the year, and in many places, groundwater is scarce. It is fine wheat country when irrigated, and one of the foremost beef cattle regions. But it has been squeezed in recent decades by declining prices for wheat, declining demand for beef and increased prices for water because of the high demand in Denver and along the Front Range. Bitter confrontations have erupted over who gets access to the South Platte River, leading to limitations on pumping from the basin. Local farmers have found that the value of their water rights to metro Denver far exceeds what they could hope to gain by farming. Their neighbors have condemned them for selling out and betraying a way of life. But the free market that once made the High Plains the scene of farm protests has caused some of it to empty out and revert to untamed land, ready again for increasingly numerous buffalo, elk, deer and bighorn sheep.

This area stretches into the Denver suburbs, which have continued their rapid population growth. Until the 1970s, Douglas County was a sparsely populated patch of the High Plains just east of the Front Range and south of Denver. From 2000 to 2010, it grew 62 percent, making it the fastest-growing county in the state. In 2016, the county was the ninth wealthiest in the nation with a median income of $95,324. This is Patio Land, as conservative writer David Brooks has described it: an area with a high-tech economy, highly educated families with relatively conservative cultural values and looking for a safe environment for children, with the serenity - if not the close personal ties - of a small town and the creativity of a metropolis.

The 4th Congressional District covers much of the Eastern Plains and nearly the entire eastern half of the state, sharing borders with New Mexico, Oklahoma, Kansas, Nebraska, and Wyoming. It includes all of Weld County and two-thirds of Douglas. Its large share of the land in Adams and Arapahoe counties is sparsely populated and stops short of the Denver exurbs. A small slice of Boulder County is a Democratic outlier. Douglas County, which has welcomed a surge of telecom and aerospace companies, has a significant Republican voter registration edge. Donald Trump won the county, 56%-37%, a bit tighter than the 62%-36% vote for Mitt Romney in 2012. Conservative activists there have pressed for a more free-enterprise approach to governance, including education; elementary schools compete for students. The southern part of the county retains open space, including cattle range. Weld County, which grew 13 percent from 2010 to 2015, has a lower per capita income than neighboring Boulder and Larimer counties. Weld, whose producers account for about three-fourths of Colorado's jobs in the mining sector, suffered a small job loss in 2015, chiefly because of a downturn in oil and gas production. The economy of Weld County is as dependent on oil and gas as are North Dakota and Oklahoma. The 4th is a solidly Republican district.

The district has pockets of feisty conservatism. In 2014, five small counties in the northeast corner of the state voted for a referendum to "pursue becoming the 51st state." Six other counties, including the larger Weld, defeated the proposal, which likely killed the immediate prospects for the plan. The movement was a cry of disenfranchisement for local officials and voters, which was directed especially at liberal rule in Denver. Citing energy regulation, they said that they were fighting "a war on rural Colorado." Ironically, farmers in eastern Colorado, who have suffered from drought, depend heavily for their water supply on reservoirs and pipelines in the western part of the state, and officials have sought to increase that diversion.

FIFTH DISTRICT

Doug Lamborn (R)

Elected 2006, 6th term; b. May 24, 1954, Leavenworth, KS; University of Kansas School of Journalism, B.S., 1978; University of Kansas School of Law, J.D., 1985; Christian Church; Married (Jeanie Lamborn); 5 children.

Elected Office: CO House, 1995-1999; CO Senate, 1998-2006.

Professional Career: Practicing attorney, 1987-2007.

DC Office: 2402 RHOB 20515, 202-225-4422, Fax: 202-226-2638, lamborn.house.gov.

State Offices: Buena Vista, 719-520-0055; Colorado Springs, 719-520-0055.

Committees: *Armed Services*: Emerging Threats & Capabilities, Strategic Forces. *Natural Resources*: Energy & Mineral Resources, Water, Power & Oceans (Chmn).

Group Ratings

	ADA	ACLU	AFL-CIO	LCV	ITI	COC	HAFA	ACU	CFG	FRC
2016	-	11%	-	0%	100%	100%	89%	91%	78%	100%
2015	0%	C	0%	0%	C	63%	C	96%	95%	100%

Almanac Ratings 2015

	Economy	Social	Foreign	Composite
Liberal	3%	0%	0%	1%
Conservative	98%	100%	100%	99%

Key Votes of the 114th Congress

1. Keystone Pipeline	Y	5. Puerto Rico Debt	N	9. Offenses by Aliens	Y
2. Trade Deals	Y	6. Medical Marijuana	N	10. Troops in Iraq	N
3. Export-Import Bank	N	7. Sanctuary Cities	Y	11. Homeland Security $$	N
4. Debt Ceiling Increase	N	8. Armor-piercing Bullets	Y	12. Trade Adjustment aid	N

Election Results

Election	Name (Party)	Vote (%)	Cand. Spent	Ind. Exp. Support	Ind. Exp. Oppose
2016 General	Doug Lamborn (R)	225,445 (62%)	$302,317		
	Misty Plowright (D)	111,676 (31%)	$10,029		
	Mike McRedmond (L)	24,872 (7%)			
2016 Primary	Doug Lamborn (R)	50,867 (68%)			
	Calandra Vargas (R)	23,889 (32%)			

Prior winning percentages: 2014 (60%), 2012 (65%), 2010 (66%), 2008 (60%), 2006 (60%)

The congressman from the 5th District is Doug Lamborn, a conservative Republican first elected in 2006 and a fierce partisan. Despite the strong Republican lean of his district, he has been slow to shut down competitive challenges from either party. But Democrats have turned their attention elsewhere in Colorado. After the 2016 election, House Republicans defeated his bid to take over as chairman of the Veterans Affairs Committee.

The son of a prison guard, Lamborn was born in Leavenworth, Kansas. He studied journalism and ultimately earned a law degree at the University of Kansas. He said he voted for Jimmy Carter in 1976, but was then drawn to the Republican politics of Ronald Reagan in the 1980s. In 1987, Lamborn moved his family to Colorado Springs, where he practiced business and real estate law and became an avid mountain climber. In 1994, he was elected to the state House, and he was appointed in 1998 to a Senate seat. During 12 years in the legislature, Lamborn compiled a firmly conservative record on social and fiscal issues.

When Republican Joel Hefley retired and created an open seat in 2006, he endorsed Jeff Crank, a former aide. Lamborn won the backing of the anti-tax Club for Growth and the Colorado Christian Coalition. At the May GOP convention, Crank won the delegate vote 46%-40%, but Lamborn had more than the 30% required to secure a place on the primary ballot. Lamborn emphasized his conservative voting record and vowed never to raise taxes. The Christian Coalition sent a mailer suggesting Crank backed the "radical homosexual lobby." In the August primary, Crank won five of the district's six counties and appeared headed to victory. But absentee ballots flipped the results, and Lamborn won by 892 votes, 27%-25%.

In November, Lamborn faced Democrat Jay Fawcett, an Air Force Academy graduate who won a Bronze star during the Persian Gulf War -- a strong selling point in the military-oriented district. In most years, the Democratic nominee would not have drawn a second look; no Democrat had won the seat since it was created in 1972. But this became an unusually competitive general election. Hefley accused Lamborn of running a "sleazy" primary and refused to endorse him. Fawcett purchased a newspaper ad featuring the names and photos of three dozen prominent local Republicans who also declined to endorse their party's nominee. Despite October polls showing a dead heat, voters gave Lamborn a 60%-40% victory.

In the House, Lamborn became one of his party's most conservative members. He was an original member of the Tea Party Caucus. During the 2011 debt and budget talks, he bucked House Speaker John Boehner because he wanted President Barack Obama to agree to deeper cuts. During the 2013 budget debate, Lamborn helped to prepare the budget plan of the conservative Republican Study

Committee, which made further large cuts in domestic programs. Later, he called for cuts in Social Security, Medicare and farm programs to pay for increased defense spending. He voiced concern that military cutbacks would affect personnel and missile programs in the Colorado Springs area. In October 2015, Lamborn described as "outrageous and unacceptable" a Defense Department proposal to move Guantanamo detainees to one of two prisons in his district.

His bid for the Veterans Affairs Committee chairmanship fell short in the leadership-controlled Republican Steering Committee. Lamborn, who was the most senior GOP member of the committee, was defeated by Phil Roe of Tennessee. As chairman of the Natural Resources Subcommittee on Energy and Mineral Resources, Lamborn has supported more development of all forms of energy.

Back home, he has continued to face problems. Lingering resentment over the 2006 primary led to a rematch with Crank in 2008. This time, Lamborn won 44%-30%. In 2014, he barely won the GOP primary, 53%-47%, over Bentley Rayburn, a retired Air Force general who had challenged Lamborn in two earlier primaries. Bradley complained that Lamborn was "out of touch" with local concerns about possible military base closings in the area. Similar criticisms were raised in the general election by Democratic foe Irving Halter, also a retired Air Force general. Halter cited the district's large federal payroll in criticizing the incumbent as the only member of the Colorado delegation to vote for the government shutdown in October 2013. Lamborn kept a low profile during the campaign and refused to debate, contending that his views were well-known and that Halter was trying to hide his. Halter raised $834,000 compared with only $490,000 for Lamborn, an unusual contrast for a veteran incumbent. Neither national party spent money on the contest. Lamborn won 60%-40%, which signaled Lamborn's personal weakness in a Republican year, though it was not enough to encourage Democrats that they can win this seat.

His 2016 campaign suffered a self-imposed wound when he failed to take his opponent seriously. Calandra Vargas, a political neophyte, challenged Lamborn at the Republican convention. In a rousing speech that Vargas called "a statement on behalf of my generation," she "brought some of the crowd to its feet," the Colorado Springs *Gazette* reported. Vargas got 58 percent of the vote - just short of the 60 percent required to prevent a primary challenge. Lamborn got 35 percent of the convention vote, a bit more than the 30 percent required to run in the primary. In the subsequent primary, Lamborn won 68%-32%; Vargas did not raise enough money to file a report with the Federal Election Commission. In November, Lamborn won 62%-31% against Misty Plowright, a trans-gender Democrat who said that her campaign was inspired by Bernie Sanders.

Central Colorado: Colorado Springs

Population		**Race and Ethnicity**		**Income**	
Total	751,270	White	72.3%	Median Income	$56,622 (166 out of 435)
Land area	7,266	Black	5.4%		
Pop/ sq mi	103.4	Latino	15.2%		
Born in state	32.9%	Asian	2.5%	Under $50,000	43.6%
Age Groups		Two races	3.8%	$50,000-$99,999	32.6%
Under 18	24.3%	Other	0.9%	$100,000-$199,999	409.2%
18-34	25.2%	**Education**		$200,000 or more	19.6%
35-64	38.4%	H.S grad or less	29.5%	Poverty Rate	11.8%
Over 64	12.1%	Some college	36.4%	**Health Insurance**	
Work		College Degree, 4 yr	20.9%	With health insurance coverage	88.9%
White Collar	39.6%	Post grad	13.2%		
Sales and Service	43.5%	**Military**		**Public Assistance**	
Blue Collar	16.8%	Veteran	17.9%	Cash public assistance income	2.7%
Government	18.1%	Active Duty	4.8%		
				Food stamp/SNAP benefits	9.9%

Voter Turnout			
2015 Total Citizens 18+	546,548	2016 House Turnout as % CVAP	66%
2016 House turnout	361,993	2014 House Turnout as % CVAP	48%

2012 Presidential Vote		
Mitt Romney	200,558	(59%)
Barack Obama	129,904	(38%)

2016 Presidential Vote		
Donald Trump	212,558	(57%)
Hillary Clinton	123,537	(33%)
Gary Johnson	22,195	(6%)

Cook Partisan Voting Index: R+14

In 1893, Katherine Lee Bates took the cog railway up from Colorado Springs to the top of 14,110-foot Pikes Peak, and looking out at the purple mountain's majesty above amber waves of grain, she wrote the lines of "America the Beautiful." Pikes Peak, espied by Zebulon Pike in 1806, and Colorado Springs, with the Garden of the Gods and the Broadmoor hotel, have been tourist attractions for more than 100 years. In the second half of the 20th century, Colorado Springs, safe in the vastness of North America, also became a great American military fortress. During the Cold War in the 1960s, the Pentagon constructed the North American Aerospace Defense Command more than 1,000 feet below Cheyenne Mountain, a fortified bunker theoretically able to survive a nuclear strike from a Soviet Union missile. The Pentagon, in part because of local traffic congestion, moved NORAD's surveillance operations to nearby Peterson Air Force Base, site of space-based defense research, with the option of a rapid return to secure Cheyenne Mountain in an emergency. Other military installations dominate the landscape as well: the Army installation at Fort Carson, the Air Force Academy, and Schriever Air Force Base, named for Gen. Bernard A. Schriever, a pioneer in the development of ballistic missile programs.

Colorado Springs has built a high-tech, innovative economy. In 2016, it ranked fifth among all cities in the *U.S. News & World Report's* quality-of-life rankings. One downside locally: The area must contend with occasional out-of-control fires that have become the bane of the West. A forest fire broke out here in 2012 that destroyed 346 homes and forced the evacuation of about 35,000 people. The following year, an even larger fire laid waste 509 homes and burned 14,000 acres

Led by the arrival of James Dobson's Focus on the Family in 1994, Colorado Springs has been a center of conservative Christianity, the home of Colorado's young conservatism and the counterpoint to Denver's liberalism. This was the birthplace of Colorado's anti-tax initiatives and of Amendment 2, which in 1992 repealed the city's gay rights ordinances only to be later overturned by the U.S. Supreme Court. It is one of America's most Republican metropolitan areas.

The 5th Congressional District takes in Colorado Springs and all of El Paso County. It also includes all or part of four rural counties: Park, Teller, Fremont and Chaffee. More than 85 percent of the district's voters are in El Paso County. Along with the 4th District, it has been the strongest Republican district in Colorado. Still, its 57 percent for Donald Trump in 2016 had less impact than did the 69 percent vote for Hillary Clinton in the 1st District (Denver), when Clinton won statewide 48%-43%.

SIXTH DISTRICT

Mike Coffman (R)

Elected 2008, 5th term; b. Mar 19, 1955, Fort Leonard Wood, MO; D.G. Vaishnav College (India), Att., 1976; University of Veracruz (Mexico), 1977; University of Colorado - Boulder, B.A., 1979; Harvard University John F. Kennedy School of Government (MA), 1995; Methodist; Married (Cynthia Coffman).

Military Career: U.S Army, 1972-1979; U.S Marine Corps, 1979-1994 (Persian Gulf), 2005-2006 (Iraq).

Elected Office: CO House, 1988-1994; CO Senate, 1994-1998; CO Treasurer, 1999-2007 CO Secretary of State., 2007-2008.

Professional Career: Property Management firm owner, 1983-2000.

DC Office: 2443 RHOB 20515, 202-225-7882, Fax: 202-226-4623, coffman.house.gov.

State Offices: Aurora, 720-748-7514.

Committees: *Armed Services*: Military Personnel (Chmn), Strategic Forces. *Veterans' Affairs*: Disability Assistance & Memorial Affairs.

Group Ratings

	ADA	ACLU	AFL-CIO	LCV	ITI	COC	HAFA	ACU	CFG	FRC
2016	-	17%	-	3%	100%	93%	55%	76%	69%	58%
2015	0%	C	0%	3%	C	85%	C	83%	81%	67%

Almanac Ratings 2015

	Economy	Social	Foreign	Composite
Liberal	6%	27%	22%	18%
Conservative	94%	73%	78%	82%

Key Votes of the 114th Congress

1. Keystone Pipeline	Y	5. Puerto Rico Debt	Y	9. Offenses by Aliens	Y
2. Trade Deals	Y	6. Medical Marijuana	Y	10. Troops in Iraq	N
3. Export-Import Bank	N	7. Sanctuary Cities	Y	11. Homeland Security $$	Y
4. Debt Ceiling Increase	N	8. Armor-piercing Bullets	Y	12. Trade Adjustment aid	Y

Election Results

Election	Name (Party)	Vote (%)	Cand. Spent	Ind. Exp. Support	Ind. Exp. Oppose
2016 General	Mike Coffman (R)	191,973 (51%)	$3,491,869	$980,376	$5,938,083
	Morgan Carroll (D)	160,372 (43%)	$3,100,200	$278,770	$7,756,685
	Norm Olsen (L)	18,778 (5%)			
2016 Primary	Mike Coffman (R)	(100%)			

Prior winning percentages: 2014 (52%), 2012 (48%), 2010 (66%), 2008 (61%)

The congressman from the 6th District is Mike Coffman, first elected as a conservative Republican in 2008. Following major redistricting shifts in 2012 that created a very competitive battleground, including a big increase in Hispanics, Coffman moderated his views and has won three high-profile and costly contests. In the House, he has built on his military service to become an activist on defense and veterans' issues.

The son of an Army doctor, Coffman enlisted in the Army before he finished high school and completed his diploma in the military. He went to the University of Colorado on the G.I. Bill, then officers' school in the Marine Corps. After his active duty service ended, he started several Denver-area property management firms, which he sold in 2000. In 1988, Coffman was elected to the Colorado House. Two years later, he was called back to active duty with the Marines to serve in the first Gulf War. His colleagues draped his desk with a Marine Corps flag and yellow ribbons, and read his letters from the front lines on the House floor. After his service, Coffman returned to public life, first as a state senator and then as Colorado treasurer. Military duty called again in 2005. Coffman resigned as treasurer to deploy for six months in Iraq, where he helped establish local governments in the Western Euphrates River Valley. In 2006, he was elected secretary of state, touting his experience with the Iraqi elections. In that office, he drew criticism for taking several voting machines out of commission because of possible problems and not having replacement machines ready. The August 2008 primary was plagued with errors, and many voters did not receive absentee ballots.

In 2007, after conservative Republican firebrand Tom Tancredo retired from this House seat to wage a long-shot race for president, Coffman announced his candidacy. In the GOP primary, he was challenged by businessman Wil Armstrong, the son of former Republican Sen. Bill Armstrong, and state senators Ted Harvey and Steve Ward. The four were nearly uniformly conservative. All supported the Iraq war and, like Tancredo, were staunch opponents of giving citizenship to illegal immigrants. But Coffman had the highest name recognition, thanks to his statewide offices, and he also outraised his challengers. He won with 40 percent of the vote, to 33 percent for Armstrong. In the general election, he cruised to victory against Democrat Hank Eng with 61 percent of the vote.

Once in Congress, Coffman opposed President Barack Obama's initiatives, telling the conservative publication *Human Events* in 2009 that "they are taking us down the road to a European-style social welfare state." He was appointed to the House Armed Services Committee, and got a bill through the House in March 2010 to extend re-employment protections for National Guard members. With the Republican takeover of the House in 2011, Coffman pushed for several internal reforms. He introduced a bill for a 10 percent salary reduction for members of Congress and sought to end congressional pensions.

In 2013, Coffman became chairman of the Veterans Affairs Subcommittee on Oversight and Investigations. The VA Department had been widely criticized for inefficient and potentially criminal malfeasance in handling the health care problems of veterans, in addition to huge cost overruns at its hospital under construction in Aurora. Coffman aggressively pursued the problem. At a February 2015 hearing with VA Secretary Robert McDonald, Coffman asked when he would clean up the "corruption" and "incompetence" in his agency. The angry McDonald, who had been chief executive of Procter & Gamble, replied, "I've run a large company, sir. What have *you* done?"

Since 2012, Coffman has faced the challenge of representing a district that lost much of its Republican base.

Redistricting more than doubled the Hispanic population of the district, and increased Obama's local vote share by six percentage points. Coffman took intensive Spanish training, and spent time in immigrant neighborhoods. As recently as August 2011, he had introduced legislation to allow communities to use English-only campaign ballots.

His opponent in 2012 was Democrat Joe Miklosi, a state representative in the Denver suburbs. Miklosi highlighted his opponent's anti-abortion rights views and accused him of seeking to dismantle Medicare. Coffman was forced to apologize in May for telling supporters that "in his heart, [President Obama] is not an American." But Coffman fought back hard, criticizing Miklosi for supporting tax hikes and running what newspaper fact-checkers called misleading ads. "It is a different ballgame," Coffman acknowledged to *The New York Times*. "It is clearly a competitive district, and it is a big transition." Though the national Democratic Party targeted Coffman, he outraised Miklosi, \$3.4 million to \$1.7 million and squeezed out a victory, 48%-46%. He was one of 17 House Republicans who were elected that year even though Obama prevailed in their district.

After the election, Coffman softened his stance on immigration, with a bill to allow noncitizens, such as foreign students in the U.S. on visas, to serve in the military. "Like it did for my father and me, the prospect of military service would give these young people something to aspire to," he wrote in an op-ed column. He sponsored multiple bills aimed at helping the military and veterans, including a 2013 bill that became law to pay military officials during a government shutdown.

In 2014, he drew a top-tier challenger in Andrew Romanoff, a former state House speaker who had run for the Senate in 2010. Romanoff touted his bipartisan accomplishments as a state lawmaker while seeking to highlight public unhappiness with Congress and, by extension, with Coffman. "If we elect the same crowd to Congress, nothing is going to change and nothing is going to get done," Romanoff said at one debate. Coffman stressed his foreign-policy credentials and depicted himself as a workhorse. Both candidates and their national parties spent huge sums of money, a total of more than \$17 million. Coffman won in a surprisingly comfortable 52%-43% outcome. He led in all three counties; Arapahoe and Adams were tight, but Douglas gave him 62 percent.

His impressive strength in his swing battleground district led Republican strategists to urge him to run against Sen. Michael Bennet in 2016. Coffman's wife, Cynthia, who was elected state attorney general in November 2014 after having served as deputy attorney general, was also touted as a potential challenger to Bennet. To the relief of House GOP campaign officials, he turned down a Senate challenge. Cynthia Coffman made the same decision two weeks later.

Democrats backed another expensive challenge to Coffman in 2016. This time, they hoped for a favorable climate in the presidential election. The challenger was state Sen. Morgan Carroll, who sought to link Coffman with the locally unpopular Donald Trump. Coffman attacked Carroll's liberal record as a legislator and said that his party's presidential nominee should step aside. "I don't know if I'll cast a vote for president," Coffman told a TV interviewer in mid-October. "I'm not going to vote for Hillary Clinton or Donald Trump. I'm struggling with it like many other Americans." Each candidate spent more than \$3 million, and received about \$5 million in national party assistance. The outcome was familiar. Coffman won, 51%-43%, with a narrow lead in Arapahoe and a nearly 2-to-1 margin in Douglas. Given Trump's weak showing in the district, Coffman's independence was a smart move.

Following the 2016 result, a Democratic political consultant in Colorado offered what seemed like sound advice for his party. "[Coffman] can have that seat as long as he wants it," Eric Sondermann told *The Denver Post*. "I have a hard time seeing Democrats continuing to invest serious resources in this race."

Eastern and Southern Denver Suburbs: Arapahoe County, Aurora

Population		**Race and Ethnicity**		**Income**	
Total	766,265	White	62.5%	Median Income	$69,909 (73 out of 435)
Land area	475	Black	8.8%		
Pop/ sq mi	1614.3	Latino	19.8%	Under $50,000	34.9%
Born in state	40.2%	Asian	5.4%	$50,000-$99,999	32.1%
		Two races	2.8%	$100,000-$199,999	509.2%
Age Groups		Other	0.8%	$200,000 or more	25.5%
Under 18	26.6%			Poverty Rate	10.4%
18-34	22.3%	**Education**			
35-64	40.6%	H.S grad or less	28.3%	**Health Insurance**	
Over 64	10.5%	Some college	30.8%	With health insurance coverage	87.4%
Work		College Degree, 4 yr	26.8%		
White Collar	42.1%	Post grad	14.1%	**Public Assistance**	
Sales and Service	41.5%	**Military**		Cash public assistance income	1.8%
Blue Collar	16.2%	Veteran	8.8%		
Government	11.7%	Active Duty	0.3%	Food stamp/SNAP benefits	7.2%

Voter Turnout			
2015 Total Citizens 18+	503,361	2016 House Turnout as % CVAP	75%
2016 House turnout	376,417	2014 House Turnout as % CVAP	55%

2012 Presidential Vote		
Barack Obama	182,464	(52%)
Mitt Romney	164,398	(47%)

2016 Presidential Vote		
Hillary Clinton	191,099	(50%)
Donald Trump	157,115	(41%)
Gary Johnson	19,727	(5%)

Cook Partisan Voting Index: D+2

Two generations ago, most people in metropolitan Denver lived in the city itself. At the city limits, the tree-shaded sidewalks gave way to the empty High Plains. Today, more than three-quarters of metro Denver residents live outside the city, some in long-settled suburbs, some in large new subdivisions on rolling land with magnificent views of the Rocky Mountains. Littleton, originally a small, long-settled suburb just south of Denver, now extends to vast new tracts. Other areas that surround Denver were once quite rural but have grown into modern suburbs. To the east of the now-closed Stapleton Airport is Aurora, with an increasing number of middle-class African Americans. The area has developed as a hub for alternative energy firms, where new technologies can be studied for their commercial value. Just south of Littleton is fast-growing Douglas County and Highlands Ranch, whose 100,000 residents form one of the largest unincorporated communities in the nation.

Much of the growth in Arapahoe County, which includes many of the suburbs south and east of downtown Denver, has resulted from a large number of immigrants to the area. There are 120 languages spoken in the Aurora public schools. Solidly Republican until a few years ago, the county has become a hard-fought political battleground in one of the most competitive states. Its population has increased 10 percent between 2010 and 2015. Hispanics make up 19 percent of the population, blacks 11 percent. Those increases have led to social tensions in what had been mostly working-class white communities. The economy of the Denver metro area has been strong, but rapid growth has created economic pressures. In 2016, Arapahoe had a 7 percent increase in its price for rental properties.

Aurora, which is the largest city in Arapahoe, has been the site not only of innovation but also of unspeakable tragedy. At a July 2012 midnight showing of the movie *The Dark Knight Rises*, a mentally unstable gunman shot and killed 12 people and injured 58 others, an event that sparked an outpouring of public outrage and sympathy. In July 2015, James Holmes was found guilty of the murders. But the jury deadlocked and failed to impose the death penalty. That pain was compounded because nearby Littleton was the location of Columbine High School, which suffered in 1999 what had been the nation's worst school massacre when two teenagers killed 13 people and themselves. More recently, Aurora suffered another kind of controversy with huge cost overruns at a new VA hospital, whose price exceeded $1.7

billion, more than three times the estimate when ground was broken in 2009. Expected completion date was 2018.

The 6th Congressional District covers Aurora, Littleton and other south Denver suburbs. About 75 percent of the district is in Arapahoe County, with the remainder in small slices of Adams and Douglas counties. Aurora had long been a Republican-leaning city, but it has been trending Democratic in recent years. Barack Obama won this district, with 52 percent and then 54 percent in his presidential runs. Hillary Clinton led Donald Trump, 50%-41% in the district and had a slightly larger lead in the Arapahoe vote.

SEVENTH DISTRICT

Ed Perlmutter (D)

Elected 2006, 6th term; b. May 01, 1953, Denver; University of Colorado - Boulder, B.A., 1975; University of Colorado School of Law, J.D., 1978; Protestant; Married (Deana M. Perlmutter); 3 children.

Elected Office: CO Senate, 1995-2003.

Professional Career: Practicing attorney, 1979-2006.

DC Office: 1410 LHOB 20515, 202-225-2645, Fax: 202-225-5278, perlmutter.house.gov.

State Offices: Lakewood, 303-274-7944.

Committees: *Financial Services*: Terrorism & Illicit Finance (RMM). *Science, Space & Technology*: Oversight, Space.

Group Ratings

	ADA	ACLU	AFL-CIO	LCV	ITI	COC	HAFA	ACU	CFG	FRC
2016	-	94%	-	97%	67%	57%	14%	0%	1%	0%
2015	85%	C	96%	83%	C	53%	C	0%	1%	0%

Almanac Ratings 2015

	Economy	Social	Foreign	Composite
Liberal	76%	91%	83%	83%
Conservative	24%	9%	17%	17%

Key Votes of the 114th Congress

1. Keystone Pipeline	N	5. Puerto Rico Debt	Y	9. Offenses by Aliens	Y
2. Trade Deals	N	6. Medical Marijuana	Y	10. Troops in Iraq	N
3. Export-Import Bank	Y	7. Sanctuary Cities	N	11. Homeland Security $$	Y
4. Debt Ceiling Increase	Y	8. Armor-piercing Bullets	N	12. Trade Adjustment aid	Y

Election Results

Election	Name (Party)	Vote (%)	Cand. Spent	Ind. Exp. Support	Ind. Exp. Oppose
2016 General	Ed Perlmutter (D)	199,758 (55%)	$1,729,994		
	George Athanasopoulos (R)	144,066 (40%)	$49,566		
	Martin Buchanan (L)	18,186 (5%)			
2016 Primary	Ed Perlmutter (D)	(100%)			

Prior winning percentages: 2014 (55%), 2012 (54%), 2010 (53%), 2008 (64%), 2006 (55%)

Ed Perlmutter, first elected in 2006, has been the most centrist member of Colorado's congressional delegation and a self-described "business-oriented Democrat." As a mirror of the county that he chiefly represents, he is not predictably partisan. He usually backs his party on major issues, but regularly has sought out Republicans to work on financial, homeland security and energy matters.

Perlmutter grew up in Jefferson County, walking precincts with his father on Democratic campaigns. His family owned a concrete business. He attended the University of Colorado and earned a law degree in 1978, then went into private practice. In 1994, Perlmutter won election to the state Senate from a northern Jefferson County district that had not elected a Democrat in nearly 30 years. In the legislature, he gained a reputation as a mediator and served two years as Senate president pro tem. As chairman of the renewable energy caucus, he worked on legislation protecting consumer rights and promoting responsible growth.

In 2002, Perlmutter was considered the early front-runner for the new 7th District seat. But he opted not to run, citing the time it would take him from his three daughters. The district elected Republican Bob Beauprez by just 121 votes. When Beauprez ran unsuccessfully for governor in 2006, Democrats immediately touted the 7th as one of their top pickup opportunities. This time, Perlmutter entered the race, with his first campaign ad in favor of federal funding for embryonic stem cell research. His most significant primary opposition came from Peggy Lamm, a former state representative who had been the sister-in-law of former Democratic Gov. Richard Lamm. He won the primary 53%-38%.

In the general election, he faced Republican Rick O'Donnell, a rising star who had been executive director of the Colorado Department of Higher Education. At a time of multiple ethics scandals in Congress, O'Donnell argued that Perlmutter's marriage to a Denver lobbyist for a D.C.-based lobbying firm would lead to conflicts of interest. (They later divorced and he re-married to a school teacher.) With differing views on immigration, Perlmutter supported a guest worker program and O'Donnell opposed it. Each candidate was well-financed. Beauprez's poor showing in the governor's race, and President George W. Bush's unpopularity worked against O'Donnell. Perlmutter won, 55%-42%.

In the House, Perlmutter has been a fairly consistent but not automatic Democratic vote. He split with other Colorado Democrats and immigration groups in 2011 in supporting Secure Communities, a federal program to speed up deportations of illegal immigrants convicted of crimes. On the centrist New Democrat Coalition, he chaired its energy task force. In sync with local interests in energy, he has promoted an all-of-the-above energy policy, including incentives to lenders who create a market for energy-efficient buildings. He got a provision in the House-passed climate change bill in 2009 to benefit environmentally conscious banks, drawing criticism from Republicans when it was revealed that he was an investor in one of them.

Inspired by his daughter's struggles with epilepsy, Perlmutter won passage of a bill creating epilepsy centers for returning combat veterans. He repeatedly pushed the Department of Veterans Affairs to build a long-delayed local hospital, at one point threatening to show up at the site with veterans and shovels if construction didn't start as scheduled. (It did).

On the Financial Services Committee, Perlmutter joined Republicans in adding protections for taxpayers to the $700 billion government rescue of financial markets in 2008. He has filed a bill to permit banks to do business with marijuana retailers in states where they can operate legally. The legislation went nowhere in the Republican-controlled House. In 2015, he stuck with most House Democrats and opposed trade promotion authority for President Barack Obama. In the *Almanac* vote ratings for 2015, his overall centrist scores leaned a bit more conservative on economic issues.

In 2010, Perlmutter decided against running for governor. His reelection in that big Republican year proved considerably tougher than his initial contest. His challenger, Aurora GOP Councilman Ryan Frazier, an African-American Navy veteran, attacked him for contributing to government overspending. Perlmutter accused his opponent's software developer company of outsourcing its consulting services. Frazier got considerable help from national Republicans and outside groups, but he couldn't keep pace financially with Perlmutter, who spent nearly $3 million and won with 53 percent of the vote.

Perlmutter drew another formidable challenger two years later in Joe Coors, a wealthy heir to his family's brewing empire. Coors emphasized his record as a ceramics manufacturing executive. He sought to make an issue of Perlmutter's ex-wife's work as a lobbyist for California solar manufacturer Solyndra, which failed after getting significant federal help. Perlmutter fired back by accusing Coors of outsourcing jobs, which Coors denied. Perlmutter got last-minute help from the Democratic Congressional Campaign Committee and prevailed 53%-41%. Since then, he has not been seriously threatened.

Following the 2016 election, he showed his independence with public support for Rep. Tim Ryan of Ohio in his challenge to Minority Leader Nancy Pelosi. "We need a change," Perlmutter said. In April 2017, Perlmutter announced his candidacy to succeed term-limited Gov. John Hickenlooper in 2018, with a call for Colorado to "keep moving forward." His self-styled independence should play well in an expected wide-open Democratic primary, though the state Democrats' support for Bernie Sanders in the 2016 presidential caucus raises questions about his centrist appeal. Colorado voters haven't chosen a member of Congress for the governor's office since Democratic Senator Edwin Johnson was elected in 1954.

Western and Northern Denver Suburbs: Jefferson County

Population		**Race and Ethnicity**		**Income**	
Total	757,273	White	64.9%	Median Income	$60,874 (137 out of 435)
Land area	342	Black	1.4%		
Pop/ sq mi	2213.5	Latino	28.0%		
Born in state	50.7%	Asian	3.1%	Under $50,000	40.8%
		Two races	1.9%	$50,000-$99,999	34.2%
Age Groups		Other	0.8%	$100,000-$199,999	609.2%
Under 18	23.8%			$200,000 or more	20.7%
18-34	24.7%	**Education**		Poverty Rate	11.6%
35-64	39.3%	H.S grad or less	37.6%		
Over 64	12.2%	Some college	31.4%	**Health Insurance**	
		College Degree, 4 yr	20.3%	With health insurance coverage	86.5%
Work		Post grad	10.7%		
White Collar	36.3%				
Sales and Service	42.4%	**Military**		**Public Assistance**	
Blue Collar	21.3%	Veteran	8.7%	Cash public assistance income	1.9%
Government	12.6%	Active Duty	0.0%		
				Food stamp/SNAP benefits	8.5%

Voter Turnout			
2015 Total Citizens 18+	531,577	2016 House Turnout as % CVAP	68%
2016 House turnout	362,010	2014 House Turnout as % CVAP	51%

2012 Presidential Vote		
Barack Obama	196,386	(56%)
Mitt Romney	144,446	(42%)

2016 Presidential Vote		
Hillary Clinton	192,637	(51%)
Donald Trump	147,645	(39%)
Gary Johnson	20,592	(6%)

Cook Partisan Voting Index: D+6

West of Denver, on broad avenues running toward the mountains, the inner circle of suburbs comprise Jefferson County. Affluent in the south and more marginal near the Denver city limits, its population is nearly as large as Denver. In contrast to the Mile High City, the politics of Jeffco make it one of the nation's most competitive battlegrounds. Its voters backed George W. Bush in 2000 and 2004, then supported Barack Obama in 2008 and 2012. National political campaigns battle-test their message here, and many political reporters have flocked to the county in an attempt to get their fingers on the pulse of the nation. Jefferson is "one of the most important counties in the nation and symbolic in every way of the battle for the soul of the middle class," a local political observer told *Governing*. "As 'Jeffco' goes, so goes the state, and probably, the country."

To the west of the city is the town of Golden, with the old Colorado School of Mines and the Coors brewery. Denver's light-rail line extends 12 miles from downtown to Golden. To the northwest are Arvada and Wheat Ridge, middle-income suburbs with an increasing number of Latinos. Farther north along Interstate 25 are rapidly growing Federal Heights, Northglenn and Thornton. Commerce City, with its large oil refinery, more than doubled its population from 2000 to 2015. One of the civic jewels of the region is strong public education. Of the 50 largest school districts in the nation, Jefferson County was tied for the second-highest graduation rate in 2012. In a November 2015 recall, voters by nearly 2-to-1 ousted three conservative school board members who were accused of attempting to censure classes in U.S. history, with bullying tactics against students and parents. The election drew more than $1 million from local and national donors.

The 7th Congressional District covers the suburbs north and west of Denver, sweeping in Arvada, Lakewood, Thornton and Westminster, which are the district's largest cities. It also takes in the Rocky Mountain Arsenal National Wildlife Refuge, as well as other parks, lakes and recreational spots. Nearly two-thirds of the district is in Jefferson County, with small slices of the county in the 1st and 2nd Congressional Districts. In the 2012 presidential race, President Barack Obama won Jefferson, 51%-46%. Although the county and state were out of sync with the nation in 2016, its voting pattern remained similar, with Hillary Clinton leading Donald Trump, 49%-42%. Still, the county leaned to Republicans in other contests that year. The remainder of the district population is in the western end of Adams County, extending just north of the airport. With Clinton having an overall margin of 51%-39%, the district is a tad more Democratic than is Jeffco.

★ CONNECTICUT ★

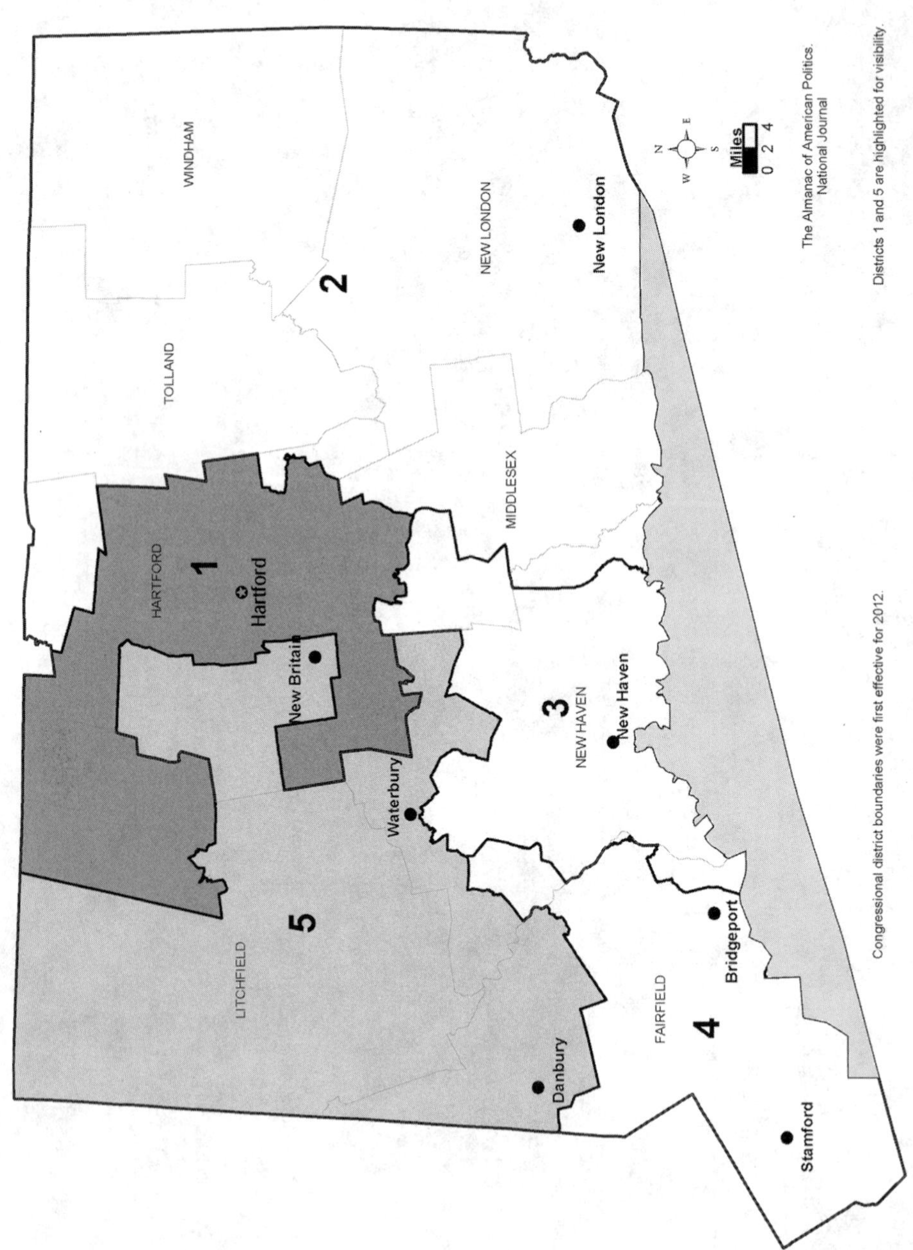

Connecticut is in some respects America's highest achieving state, with one of the highest rates of bachelor's degrees, one of the top median incomes, and great accumulations of wealth - but it is also a state with a yawning gap between the rich and poor, visible in the contrast between hedge fund managers' estates in Greenwich and the slums of Bridgeport not all that far away. The state that is home to Yale University is in the upper tier of states competitive in the global knowledge economy, yet it has grown achingly slowly. By late 2016, the employment level in Connecticut remained below its 2008 peak, and even below its earlier apex in 2000; the state's unemployment rate in late 2016 was no better than the national average, despite its great advantages. Even among its peers in New England, Connecticut's post-Great Recession jobs recovery was the weakest. The state's population has only treaded water in recent years, and economic stagnation has created budgetary pressures that have put Democrats on the defensive.

Connecticut was founded by Puritans who considered Massachusetts too lenient. Connecticut Yankees for years were flintier and more unyielding, more tightfisted and set in their ways than other New Englanders. Yet they were also open to certain reforms. In 1784, Connecticut voted for gradual emancipation of the state's slaves, one of the first societies anywhere to do so. The state now exhibits significant diversity – 9 percent of residents are black, 15 percent Hispanic, and 4 percent are Asian-American, while the city's capital and largest city, Hartford, is 28 percent foreign born, peopled by immigrants from Cape Verde, the Middle East, Asia and the Caribbean. Connecticut's affluence came not from any windfall but from a knack for tinkering and making productive use of savings. George Washington called it the "provision state" for the supplies of food and cannon it provided his Revolutionary War forces. Connecticut made clocks, hats, combs, cigars, silk thread, pins, matches, brass and furniture. It invented and still manufactures Pez candy in the town of Orange, Nivea skin cream in Norwalk, and the Wiffle ball in Shelton. The quintessential Connecticut Yankee, Eli Whitney, was the inventor not only of the cotton gin but also of rifles with interchangeable parts. The state has been a major arms maker ever since Samuel Colt won a War Department contract to manufacture guns for the Mexican-American War; the company's disused, blue-onion-domed factory in Hartford received a National Park Service designation in 2014. (The state's longstanding gun connections caused tension following the 2012 shooting massacre at Sandy Hook Elementary School in Newtown; when Gov. Dan Malloy shepherded a tough anti-gun bill into law, he faced fierce opposition from the gun industry.)

During the Reagan defense buildup of the 1980s, Connecticut produced Air Force jets and Army helicopters and, in the Electric Boat Shipyard in New London, most of the Navy's nuclear submarines, continuing a long seafaring tradition memorialized at Mystic Seaport. These industries, like Connecticut's civilian manufacturers, depend heavily on meticulous work. Through decades of immigration, its workers never lost the Yankee knack: Connecticut ranks high in patents per capita. Over the years, the state has accumulated capital and invested shrewdly, with great skill at assessing risk. It has long been home to several of the nation's great insurance companies -- its laws are unusually friendly to creditors and harsh on debtors – and more recently, hedge funds have sprouted in suburbs like Greenwich on the fringes of New York City.

Today, Pratt & Whitney makes engines for the Airbus A320 and the F-35 Lightning II in Connecticut, and the company's president said it plans to add thousands of jobs over the next decade. United Technologies Corp., which owns Pratt & Whitney, remains the state's largest employer (it sold Sikorsky Aircraft to Lockheed Martin in 2015). But overall aerospace employment in the state has declined somewhat in recent years. Meanwhile, Connecticut's insurance companies have sustained casualty losses from natural disasters, and the state's modestly sized central cities - New Haven, Hartford and Bridgeport - have been plagued by crime and have been bleeding manufacturing jobs and people for years. In 1950, the three cities had 500,000 people in a state of 2 million; in 2010, they had 400,000 in a state of 3.6 million. In "Corrupticut," mayors of Waterbury and Bridgeport were sent to prison, and the mayor of Hartford was convicted on bribery charges in 2010. Republican Gov. John Rowland, elected three times, went to prison in 2005 for corruption. Then, in 2015, he was sentenced to 30 months in another political case altogether. The same year, the Bridgeport mayor who had served time, Joe Ganim, was returned to the mayor's office by voters just five years after leaving prison.

Connecticut's economic growth in the 1990s and 2000s was concentrated in two corners of the state, on opposite sides of the invisible divide that separates Yankee fans and Red Sox fans. (Bristol-based ESPN sits roughly along that line.) In the southeast are the Foxwoods Resort Casino, opened in

1992 and owned by the 900-member Mashantucket Pequot tribe, and its big competitor, Mohegan Sun, owned by the 1,700-member Mohegans. Collectively, the state's casinos employ about 20,000, though these are mostly lower-wage jobs, and the industry has faced struggles. New and expanded casinos in Pennsylvania, New York, Rhode Island and Maine have cut the combined revenues of Foxwoods and the Mohegan Sun from $3.2 billion in 2006 to $1.9 billion in 2014, according to the Northeastern Gaming Research Project.

Meanwhile, even as Greenwich and the rest of southwestern Connecticut have prospered from high finance, the shift from manufacturing to finance was not necessarily a boon for job creation. Bridgewater, a $150 billion hedge fund, employs only about 1,400 (very well-compensated) people. This has created what is by some measures the nation's most unequal state. "Get out of Greenwich, in other words, and you encounter lovely but stagnant suburbs - grist for so many ennui-afflicted short stories - studded with the occasional pocket of urban poverty," Annie Lowrey wrote in New York magazine.

The most prominent economic development stories in recent years have involved companies leaving the state – prompted, pro-business interests argue, by high taxes and heavy regulation. In a bombshell announcement in 2016, General Electric said it would quit its 70-acre, 800-job headquarters in Fairfield, where it had been based since 1974, for greener pastures in Boston. The decision was smoothed by incentives from Massachusetts worth as much as $145 million. But some of Connecticut's own spending on economic incentives has been called into question, such as $22 million for one hedge fund, Bridgewater, and $35 million for another, AQR Capital Management. State comptroller Kevin Lembo was among those who suggested that such aid from the state would be better spent on companies that provide middle-class jobs. One initiative that has gained the support of both environmentalists and business is the "Green Bank," created in 2011 and funded by electric ratepayer fees and corporate cap-and-trade payments. Since its creation, the bank has funded 17,000 solar projects, among other efforts.

For much of the 20th century, Connecticut politics was an ethnic struggle between Yankee Republicans and Catholic Democrats. Slowly, as Catholic birthrates exceeded those of Protestants, Democrats gained ground. Their great leader was John Bailey, state party chairman from 1946 to 1975, a master legislative strategist and ticket-balancer who was one of the first to endorse John F. Kennedy for president. For a long historical moment, the central cities and Catholic suburbs voted Democratic, and the WASP-y suburbs and rural towns voted Republican. But those days are gone. In 2004, 2008 and 2012, white Protestants and Catholics voted Republican; secular whites, blacks and Latinos went heavily Democratic. Cultural issues have played a role. The state whose ban on contraceptives produced the U.S. Supreme Court's *Griswold* decision in 1965, the precursor of *Roe v. Wade*, now solidly supports abortion rights. In 2005, the legislature legalized civil unions for same-sex couples, and in 2008, the state Supreme Court converted all these into same-sex marriages. Connecticut legislators have also voted for in-state college tuition for children of illegal immigrants, for public financing of state legislative races, and for strict carbon emission reductions.

In congressional races, Connecticut has become solidly Democratic. As recently as 2006, Republicans (albeit moderate ones) held a majority in the state's five-member U.S. House delegation. Since 2009, all five seats have been Democratic. Meanwhile, in the Senate, Connecticut was represented by a pair of Democrats for more than two decades -- Christopher Dodd (himself the son of a Democratic senator, Thomas Dodd) and Joe Lieberman, both of whom at one point ran for president. In both 2010 and 2012, Republican Linda McMahon, head of World Wrestling Entertainment, spent lavishly on television ads to try to win an open Senate seat - some $100 million in those two races - but was unable to run far enough ahead of her party to win. In 2010, she lost 55%-43% to Richard Blumenthal, and in 2012 she lost 55%-40% to Rep. Chris Murphy.

Oddly, Connecticut did not have a Democratic governor for two decades. Former liberal Republican Sen. Lowell Weicker, elected on the alphabetically advantaged "A Connecticut Party" line in 1990, pushed through the income tax in 1991 and retired in 1994. Rowland, elected with a plurality in 1994 and majorities in 1998 and 2002, resigned due to scandal; low-key Republican lieutenant governor Jodi Rell succeeded him and then won a full term by a wide margin in 2006. In 2010, Democrat Dannel Malloy, longtime mayor of Stamford, defeated former Ambassador to Ireland Tom Foley by a hair. Malloy and the Democratic legislature pushed through a thoroughgoing liberal program, and the state's resilient partisan leanings enabled him to win reelection in 2014 despite mediocre approval ratings. Amid continued economic stagnation, fiscal challenges and worries about the state's pension burden,

Malloy's approval ratings sunk low enough to endanger the rest of the Democratic ticket in 2016. In that election, Republicans gained enough seats to tie the state Senate and shave the Democratic edge in the state House to just a couple of seats.

But the 2016 election between Donald Trump and Hillary Clinton pushed the state's internal realignment further than ever. Connecticut once again voted Democratic for president – as it has since 1992 – and Clinton's 14-point margin was down, but not dramatically, from Barack Obama's 17-point margin four years earlier. But some affluent, historically Republican towns that felt warmly toward Mitt Romney in 2012 swung heavily toward Clinton, while some working-class, historically Democratic towns felt kinship with Trump's blue-collar appeals and flipped their vote. In affluent Darien, Romney won in 2012 by 31 points, but Clinton beat Trump by 12 points – a 43-point swing. In neighboring New Canaan, the swing toward Clinton was 42 points, and in Greenwich, it was 29 points. In more lightly populated areas, however, Trump did impressively for a Republican. Plainfield, near the border with Rhode Island, went for Obama by 10 points in 2012 but backed Trump by 22; Naugatuck, south of Waterbury, backed Obama narrowly, but Trump by 16. Whether such patterns persist beyond the unusual 2016 election season remains to be seen.

Population		**Race and Ethnicity**		**Income**	
Total	3,593,222	White	69.2%	Median Income	$70,331 (4 out of 50)
Land area	4,842	Black	9.6%	Under $50,000	36.6%
Pop/ sq mi	742.0	Latino	14.7%	$50,000-$99,999	29.0%
Born in state	55.2%	Asian	4.2%	$100,000-$199,999	24.7%
Age Groups		Two races	1.9%	$200,000 or more	9.7%
Under 18	21.8%	Other	0.4%	Poverty Rate	10.5%
18-34	18.8%	**Education**		**Health Insurance**	
35-64	41.3%	H.S grad or less	37.6%	With health insurance coverage	92.1%
Over 64	15.0%	Some college	24.9%	**Public Assistance**	
Work		College Degree, 4 yr	21.0%	Cash public assistance income	3.4%
White Collar	41.7%	Post grad	16.6%	Food stamp/SNAP benefits	12.1%
Sales and Service	41.3%	**Military**			
Blue Collar	17.0%	Veteran	7.1%		
Government	13.2%	Active Duty	0.3%		

Voter Turnout			
2015 Total Citizens 18+	2,574,178	2016 Pres Turnout as % CVAP	64%
2016 Pres Votes	1,644,920	2012 Pres Turnout as % CVAP	62%

Legislature	
Senate:	18D, 18R
House:	78D, 71R, 2V

Presidential Politics

2016 Democratic Primary		
Hillary Clinton (D)	170,045	(52%)
Bernie Sanders (D)	152,379	(46%)
2016 Republican Primary		
Donald Trump (R)	123,523	(58%)
John Kasich (R)	60,522	(28%)
Ted Cruz (R)	24,987	(12%)

2016 Presidential Vote		
Hillary Clinton (D)	897,572	(55%)
Donald Trump (R)	673,215	(41%)
Gary Johnson (L)	48,676	(3%)
2012 Presidential Vote		
Barack Obama (D)	905,083	(58%)
Mitt Romney (R)	634,892	(41%)

Hillary Clinton favored higher taxes on the rich while billionaire Donald Trump winced at that idea. But the Democrat nonetheless defeated Trump 55%-41% in one of the nation's highest-income states, where many corporate executives who work in New York live to avoid relatively high Empire State taxes. What gives? Liberal stands on cultural issues have trumped economic concerns among wealthy Connecticut voters and many of the state's white ethnics still adhere to their Democratic roots of generations past. The wealthy "gold coast" towns of Darien, Greenwich, New Canaan and Westport in Fairfield County, home to hedge fund investors and old WASP money, once a Republican bastion in the state, have been alienated by the influence of Christian evangelicals in the GOP. Nor did Trump's brand of populism play well among these voters: those four towns saw double-digit percentage increases in the vote for Clinton over the Obama vote four years earlier. Trump did manage to prevail in one portion of the state, the more rural western portion of Connecticut north of the New York City suburbs in Fairfield. This is an area of horse farms and old mill towns. Its only significant city is Waterbury, a former manufacturing center, which Clinton easily won, although by a smaller margin than Obama did in 2012.

The GOP primary was held on April 26, and Trump rolled to victory, 58%-28%, over Ohio Gov. John Kasich, who had hoped that the state's more moderate electorate might embrace his brand of pragmatic centrism. But the Connecticut GOP primary was limited to registered Republicans and they delivered all of the state's convention delegates to Trump. The Democratic primary was much more spirited and Vermont Sen. Bernie Sanders was hoping that his demonstrated popularity with New England voters would enable him to bounce back from a stinging defeat in the New York primary a week earlier. After all, Obama had beaten Clinton in the primary eight years earlier, 51%-47%. But Sanders' past support for limiting the liability of gun manufacturers was a handicap in a state that saw 20 children and six adults murdered at the Sandy Hook Elementary School mass shooting in Newtown in 2012. Gov. Dan Malloy, a top Clinton Connecticut surrogate and gun-control advocate made sure to remind his fellow Democrats of Sanders' past liability position. Clinton won the New York City suburbs and the Gold Coast, where Sanders' hostility toward Wall Street was not welcomed. She also captured the state's major cities, including New Haven, which had one of the lowest turnouts in the state. Sanders prevailed in western Connecticut and in the eastern portion of the state, which has a number of rural townships, more conservative communities such as Groton and New London, both of which Sanders carried, and the University of Connecticut at Storrs. It was a hard-fought primary, but Clinton won 52%-46%. Despite the closeness of the contest, all 15 of the superdelegates from Connecticut backed Clinton, a prime example of what the Sanders camp felt was unfair about this class of Democratic convention delegates made up of elected and party officials.

It's easy to forget that from 1972 to 1988, Republican presidential candidates won the Nutmeg State. In 1988, Democratic nominee Michael Dukakis won only one of the state's eight counties, Hartford. In 2016, Clinton won six, losing only Litchfield and Windham. Democrats were not always the liberal party on social issues. The legendary John Bailey, who chaired the Connecticut Democratic Party from 1946 until his death in 1975, was a key early supporter of John F. Kennedy's 1960 presidential bid. Culturally conservative working-class Irish, Italian and Polish Catholics in Hartford, New Britain, New Haven, Bridgeport and New London were the backbone of his Connecticut machine.

Congressional Districts

115th Congress Lineup	5D	**114th Congress Lineup**	5D

Connecticut has a bipartisan redistricting process. Two Republicans and two Democrats from each chamber of the legislature meet to draw the lines. If their map is approved by a two-thirds vote in both chambers, it becomes law. Otherwise, a ninth member is chosen by the other eight, and they try to reach consensus. The customary collaboration didn't work in 2011, when Democrats controlled all five House seats. Republicans wanted to remove the heavily Democratic cities of Bridgeport and New Britain from the 4th and 5th districts respectively, in order to make both seats' boundaries smoother and more competitive. When the commission failed to meet its Supreme Court-extended deadline, the court stepped in and appointed Columbia Law Professor Nathaniel Persily as special redistricting master.

With instructions from the court to make minimal changes, Persily shifted only 28,975 residents between districts. In the subsequent two elections, Democrat Elizabeth Esty narrowly won the 5th District, with a big boost from New Britain. The long-time Republican success in western Connecticut districts has been relegated to the increasingly distant past.

Governor

Dannel Malloy (D)

Elected 2010, term expires 2019, 2nd term; b. Jul. 21, 1955, Stamford, CT; Boston Col., B.A. 1977, J.D. 1980; Catholic; Married (Cathy); 3 children.

Elected Office: Stamford Mayor, 1995-2009.

Professional Career: Assistant District Attorney, Brooklyn, NY, 1980-1984; Partner, Abate & Fox, 1984-1995.

Office: State Capitol, 210 Capitol Ave., Hartford, 06106; 860-566-4840; Fax: 860-524-7395; Website: ct.gov.

Election Results

Election	Name (Party)	Vote (%)
2014 General	Dannel Malloy (D)	554,314 (51%)
	Tom Foley (R)	526,295 (48%)

Prior winning percentage: 2010 (50%)

Democrat Dannel Malloy was elected governor of Connecticut in 2010. Like his better-known counterparts Andrew Cuomo of New York and Chris Christie of New Jersey, he is a former prosecutor; unlike them, he has lacked the celebrity cachet of being a future presidential possibility, and he has had to contend with low approval ratings while trying to champion a generally progressive agenda within a challenging fiscal landscape. While he was able to win reelection narrowly in 2014, he continued to struggle with some of the lowest approval ratings in the nation and saw sizable Republican gains in the legislature in the 2016 elections.

Malloy, the youngest of eight children, grew up in Stamford with a learning disability; he had difficulties with reading and motor coordination and after several years was diagnosed as dyslexic. He graduated from Boston College and its law school, taking the bar exam orally. He was an assistant district attorney in Brooklyn from 1980 to 1984, and in that role, obtained 22 convictions in 23 felony cases. He moved back to Stamford to practice law. In 1995, he beat Republican incumbent Mayor Stanley Esposito and served in that job until 2009. In those years, Malloy recruited big financial houses to set up shop in Stamford, eventually generating about 5,000 new jobs. He sponsored citywide preschool and a Stamford Urban Transitway. The one blight on his record was an accusation of favoritism to campaign contributors and contractors who did work on his house. After a 17-month investigation, prosecutors said there was no evidence of wrongdoing.

Stamford is not Connecticut's biggest city, but it often casts a large number of votes, which was helpful for Malloy when he set his sights on statewide office. In 2006, he ran for governor, won the endorsement of the Democratic state convention by a single vote and then lost the Democratic primary to New Haven Mayor John DeStefano, 51%-49%. DeStefano went on to lose, 63%-35%, to Republican incumbent Jodi Rell, whose low-key approach was a relief to voters disgusted with Republican Gov. John Rowland, who resigned amid corruption-related charges that ultimately sent him to prison. Rell announced in November 2009 that she would not run again. In March 2010, Malloy got into the contest as an underdog in the Democratic primary against investor Ned Lamont, who had beaten Sen. Joe Lieberman in the 2006 Senate primary but then lost to him when Lieberman ran as an independent in the general election. Although Lamont led in initial polls, Malloy won the primary, 57%-43%. In the general, Malloy faced former Ambassador to Ireland Tom Foley. The candidates had sharp issue differences: Malloy opposed the death penalty and favored legalizing same-sex marriage; he also supported a union-backed bill to require companies with more than 50 employees to grant workers paid sick days and he called for requiring 20 percent of Connecticut's electricity to be produced from renewable sources by 2020. Malloy was well ahead in the polls in early fall, but the race tightened in October. Malloy was eventually declared the winner the Friday after the election, 50%-49%.

In early 2011, his first order of business was figuring out ways to address a projected $3.5 billion budget shortfall. He took the politically unpopular step of asking the Democratic-controlled General Assembly for tax increases, saying, "It's what's right for my state. Connecticut would not be Connecticut if we cut $3.5 billion out of the budget." Lawmakers eventually approved a $40.2 billion budget that included $1.5 billion in tax hikes, including an increase in the general sales tax. They refused, however, to grant Malloy's request for a 3-cents-a-gallon gasoline tax increase, citing high gas prices. He also had to battle the state's 45,000 unionized employees, who in June rejected his call for $1.6 billion in concessions to balance the budget. In response, he called for eliminating 6,500 jobs. After two months of negotiations, the unions agreed to a modified version of the deal. On a more positive note, he signed into law his campaign-promised bill to require companies to provide employees with paid sick leave. But his anemic approval rating in a June Quinnipiac University poll, 37 percent, reflected the public's unease over the tax hikes.

To promote economic development in a state that had no net gain in employment in more than two decades, Malloy unveiled a "First Five" plan that called for benefits for the first five companies to expand business in the state. NBC Sports accepted the deal and announced plans in October 2011 to add studio, production and office space in Stamford in exchange for $20 million in tax breaks. He got lawmakers to approve a $626 million package of hiring incentives, job training and infrastructure repair, with most of it intended to help small businesses. He also unveiled an ambitious education reform plan that drew fire from teachers' unions because of a proposal to make it easier for school districts to fire underperforming teachers with tenure. "I believe education reform is the civil rights issue of our time," he said in May 2012 after lawmakers passed his proposal. Malloy also signed a bill the following month to legalize and regulate medical marijuana. But at the end of 2012 the state's finances remained precarious. After projecting a manageable $60 million deficit in November, state officials revised the number upward a month later to $363 million. And they warned that the deficit was expected to grow to $1.1 billion by 2014.

In all, Malloy, in concert with the heavily Democratic legislature, was able to implement one of the nation's most solidly progressive agendas - a $10.10 minimum wage, mandatory paid sick leave, a death penalty repeal, relaxed laws on marijuana, a ban on discrimination based on "gender identity or expression," unabashed support for the Affordable Care Act, a measure allowing undocumented immigrants to secure driver's licenses, and tougher gun control. The conservative *National Review* called him "America's Worst Governor," and Malloy gained a reputation for arrogance and combativeness, without a gift for schmoozing to smooth his rougher edges. The silver lining was a certain steeliness and a cool-under-fire approach amid crises. Malloy gained respect for his handling of natural disasters, and he took a central role after the December 2012 massacre at Sandy Hook Elementary School in Newtown, when a troubled young man opened fire on small children and their teachers, killing 26, including 20 children. When Malloy arrived at the scene, he learned that it fell to him to inform anxious parents that their children had been killed; he decided to do so before awaiting formal identifications of the victims, a task he described afterward with great emotion. Later, he spearheaded the legislative response, pushing through a ban on so-called assault weapons and high-capacity magazines in the face of fierce opposition from the gun industry, some of which has centuries-old ties to his state.

The reverberations from the tax hike and the state's zigzagging economic recovery left Malloy with weak approval ratings as he approached his reelection in 2014. For most of the election cycle, handicappers rated Malloy's rematch with Foley as a toss-up, despite Connecticut's increasingly blue hue in major races. In a brutal election year for Democrats, Malloy did something many other candidates in his party were unwilling to do - invite Barack Obama to campaign for him, which the president did in Bridgeport shortly before Election Day. Ultimately, though, there was enough of an economic recovery - tentative though it may have been - to save him. By a somewhat more comfortable margin than in 2010, Malloy defeated Foley, 51%-48%.

After his reelection victory, Malloy kept the bold moves coming. In 2015, he signed a criminal-justice overhaul known as the Second Chance Society. It reclassified drug-possession crimes without an intent to distribute as misdemeanors and ended mandatory-minimum sentences for drug possession in school zones. It also accelerated the processes for parole and pardons and provided funding for education and employment assistance following release from prison. Meanwhile, Malloy pushed for $100 billion in spending on highways and mass transit over 30 years and greater use of rooftop solar energy. When Indiana passed a law that critics said could allow businesses to discriminate against gays and lesbians - a law later modified under national pressure - Malloy became the first governor to sign an executive order barring state-funded travel to Indiana. In 2016, Malloy received the John F. Kennedy Profile in Courage Award for his stance on accepting Syrian refugees in the state.

One area where Malloy proceeded more cautiously was on gun control. In March 2015, the Sandy Hook Advisory Commission, a panel Malloy established, issued a 277-page report that recommended tighter laws on gun registration, expanded use of trigger locks, serial numbers for shell casings, and the ability of law enforcement to take firearms, ammunition and gun permits from those facing a restraining order. But Malloy threw cold water on the report, saying that "there's just not a big appetite for even talking about guns at the moment in the state of Connecticut." He did, however, win kudos from advocates for victims of domestic violence by signing a bill in May 2016 to ban gun possession by persons subject to a temporary restraining order.

But the state's fiscal picture continued to pose headaches. In 2015 he signed a budget that raised taxes not just on higher-income residents and corporations but also more moderate earners, through changes to the property tax credit, an extension of the sales tax on clothing, and a hike in cigarette taxes. The following year, Malloy and lawmakers had to close a nearly $1 billion budget deficit, though this time they worked to avoid tax increases. The state also continued to face a significant shortfall in what it needed to cover future pension obligations, forcing Malloy to negotiate cuts with public-sector employee unions. The continuing fiscal angst helped drag down Malloy's approval ratings into the 20s and is widely credited with enabling Republicans on Election Day 2016 to pull into a tie in the Senate and come within a few seats in the House. Despite these difficulties back home, Malloy reinforced his stature nationally when he was reelected to a second one-year term as chairman of the Democratic Governors Association. In that post, he would be tasked with helping steer his party's efforts to rebuild their depleted gubernatorial ranks in the crucial 2018 election cycle, the last major gubernatorial cycle in advance of the redistricting process that will shape the party's state-level outlook for another decade. In April 2017, to the relief of many Democrats in Connecticut, he announced that he would not seek reelection, which added to the prospect of a wide-open primary in each party and a competive contest in November.

Senior Senator

Richard Blumenthal (D)

Elected 2010, term expires 2022, 2nd term; b. Feb 13, 1946, Brooklyn, NY; Harvard College (MA), A.B., 1967; Cambridge University (England), Att., 1968; Yale University Law School (CT), J.D., 1973; Jewish; Married (Cynthia Allison Malkin); 4 children.

Military Career: U.S. Marine Corps Reserves, 1970-1976.

Elected Office: CT House, 1984-1987; CT Senate, 1987-1990; CT Attorney General, 1991-2010.

Professional Career: Teacher, Washington D.C. public School, 1968-1969; Staff Assistant, White House Office of Economic Opportunity, 1969-1970; Clerk, Supreme Court Justice Harry Blackmun, 1974-1975; Administrative Assistant, Sen. Abraham Ribicoff, 1975-1976; U.S Attorney CT, 1977-1981; Practing Attorney, 1981-1990.

DC Office: 706 HSOB 20510, 202-224-2823, Fax: 202-224-9673, blumenthal.senate.gov.
State Offices: Bridgeport, 203-330-0598; Hartford, 860-258-6940.

Committees: *Aging*. *Armed Services*: Airland, Cybersecurity, Seapower. *Commerce, Science & Transportation*: Aviation Operations, Safety & Security, Communications, Technology, Innovation & the Internet, Consumer Protection, Product Safety, Ins & Data Security (RMM), Oceans, Atmosphere, Fisheries & Coast Guard, Surface Trans., Merchant Marine Infra., Safety & Security. *Judiciary*: Antitrust, Competition Policy & Consumer Rights, Border Security & Immigration, Constitution (RMM), Oversight, Agency Action, Federal Rights & Federal Courts. *Veterans' Affairs*.

Group Ratings

	ADA	ACLU	AFL-CIO	LCV	ITI	COC	HAFA	ACU	CFG	FRC
2016	-	88%	-	100%	80%	50%	9%	4%	5%	0%
2015	95%	C	100%	100%	C	43%	C	0%	4%	0%

Almanac Ratings 2015

	Economy	Social	Foreign	Composite
Liberal	100%	100%	80%	93%
Conservative	0%	0%	20%	7%

Key Votes of the 114th Congress

1. Keystone pipeline	N	5. National Security Data	Y	9. Gun Sales Checks	Y
2. Export-Import Bank	N	6. Iran Nuclear Deal	N	10. Sanctuary Cities	N
3. Debt Ceiling Increase	Y	7. Puerto Rico Debt	Y	11. Planned Parenthood	N
4. Homeland Security $$	Y	8. Loretta Lynch A.G	Y	12. Trade deals	N

Election Results

Election	Name (Party)	Vote (%)	Cand. Spent	Ind. Exp. Support	Ind. Exp. Oppose
2016 General	Richard Blumenthal (D)............	1,008,714 (63%)	$6,794,120		
	Dan Carter (R)............................	552,621 (35%)	$244,556		
2016 Primary	Richard Blumenthal (D)...........unopposed				

Prior winning percentages: 2010 (54%)

For two decades, Democrat Richard Blumenthal -- Connecticut's senior senator -- was the Nutmeg State's aggressive, media-savvy attorney general, focusing on one consumer protection issue after another and becoming the state's most popular elected official in the process. Blumenthal's *modus operandi* changed little during his first term in the Senate: His focus remained on acting as a consumer advocate in high-profile controversies involving enterprises ranging from auto manufacturers to professional sports leagues. If Blumenthal's frequent jawboning didn't often translate into enacted legislation, he contended that it nonetheless helped prod the targeted industries to do the right thing. It also appears that it reinforced his political standing back home. After being roughed up during his first run for Senate in 2010 by a Republican opponent who made a fortune thanks to professional wrestling, Blumenthal had no trouble winning a second term in 2016 after failing to attract a high-profile challenger. He was re-elected by 28 points, twice the margin by which Democratic presidential nominee Hillary Clinton -- once Blumenthal's classmate at Yale Law School --- carried the state.

Blumenthal was born in the New York City borough of Brooklyn; his father, Martin, had fled Nazi Germany in 1935 and became wealthy by trading commodities in his adopted country. (Based on available disclosure reports for 2014, the Center for Responsive Politics ranked Blumenthal as the third wealthiest member of the Senate, with an estimated fortune of almost $82 million. It is due largely to his wife, Cynthia, whose father, New York real estate magnate Peter Malkin, counts the iconic Empire State Building among his recent holdings.) After graduating from Harvard with a degree in political science, Blumenthal moved on to Yale Law School, where he edited the *Yale Law Journal.* Blumenthal's post-college list of employers reads like a Who's Who of the Washington elite in the 1970s. They included longtime *Washington Post* publisher Katharine Graham, future New York Sen. Daniel Patrick Moynihan when the latter was a top adviser in the Nixon White House, and Supreme Court Justice William Brennan-for whom Blumenthal clerked.

After a two-year stint as a top aide to Sen. Abraham Ribicoff-who then held the seat Blumenthal now occupies-President Jimmy Carter in 1977 appointed the 31-year old Blumenthal as U.S. attorney for Connecticut. Entering private law practice in the early 1980s, Blumenthal-doing volunteer work for the NAACP Legal Defense Fund-gained further visibility by winning a stay of execution for a prisoner on Florida's death row just hours before it was to take place, and later convincing an appeals court to overturn the murder conviction against the prisoner, Joseph Green Brown. Later, Blumenthal said the Brown case changed his view of the death penalty "because it provided such a dramatic illustration of how the system could be fallible and cause the death of an innocent person." But the case came back to haunt Blumenthal after he was elected to the Senate: Brown's wife was found dead in September 2012, and Brown was arrested again and charged with first degree murder.

Elected to the Connecticut Assembly in 1984 and to the state Senate in 1987 before his successful run for attorney general in 1990, Blumenthal used the latter position to pursue lawsuits against health insurers and polluters as well as Big Tobacco and some of the nation's leading banks. Detractors derided him as "Sue 'Em All Blumenthal", but voters elected him to five terms, never with less than 59 percent of the vote. Although seemingly unhesitant to take on a series of powerful corporate targets, Blumenthal earned a reputation for caution when it came to tackling his own political future: He resisted repeated entreaties from fellow Democrats to run for governor, a post occupied by Republicans during much of his tenure as the state's top lawyer. Finally, just as Blumenthal finally seemed ready to take the plunge for higher office-eyeing a 2012 challenge to Democratic-turned-independent Sen. Joe Lieberman -- an unexpected opening occurred. Veteran Democratic Sen. Christopher Dodd, at the height of his power on Capitol Hill but politically embattled at home over allegations that he had accepted political favors, abruptly announced his retirement at the beginning of 2010. Blumenthal switched from seeking re-election to a sixth term to run for Dodd's seat.

At first, Blumenthal's initial Senate race looked to be an electoral stroll in the park, given his popularity in a one-time swing state that had titled heavily blue. But it was also the year that the tea party took flight, and the Republican nominee, Linda McMahon-who, with her husband, Vince McMahon had started World Wrestling Entertainment-harnessed an upswing in GOP voter energy to make it a real contest. The first sign things were not going to be easy for Blumenthal was his apparent exaggeration of his military service. A member of the Marine Corps Reserve from 1970 to 1975, Blumenthal claimed on several occasions to have served in Vietnam, though he never in fact was deployed. The McMahon campaign attacked him for distorting his record, putting a chink in his best asset: his image as a selfless crusader. Blumenthal apologized, but the episode sparked a nasty back-and-forth campaign, with Blumenthal's initial wide lead in the polls tightening considerably. (The controversy resurfaced in early 2017, when President Donald Trump derisively mentioned it in a tweet aimed at Blumenthal after the senator charged that Trump's firing of FBI Director James Comey had created "a looming constitutional crisis that is deadly serious" and "may well produce impeachment proceedings…." In an episode with hints of a contretemps between two powerful New York real estate families, Trump fired back: " 'Richie' devised one of the greatest military frauds in U.S. history….He should be the one investigated for his acts.")

McMahon proved to be a tireless campaigner, and, to appeal to Democrats and independents, she billed herself as a centrist who supported abortion rights and the prerogative of states to decide the same-sex marriage issue. Blumenthal's camp went after McMahon over sexism and use of steroids in professional wrestling, where McMahon had earned a fortune as WWE president. By the end of the campaign, she had spent more than $50 million-almost six times as much as Blumenthal-with most of it coming from her own pocket. Blumenthal took aim at McMahon's spending, declaring that voters deserved "an election, not an auction." The *Hartford Courant* noted that McMahon "had persistent trouble winning over women voters, despite the fact she would have become the first female senator in the state's history. Some women were turned off by some of the racier images of WWE; others didn't like her aggressive advertising strategy." Blumenthal scored a comfortable, if less than overwhelming, 55%-43% win.

Much of Blumenthal's consumer advocacy efforts during his first Senate term were aimed at transportation safety. He called for General Motors to create a compensation fund for victims of defective ignition switches in the company's automobiles; after the company announced it was setting up such a fund in mid-2014, Blumenthal joined Democratic Sen. Edward Markey of Massachusetts in keeping up the pressure on GM. A year later, Blumenthal called on Takata to establish a similar fund for victims of its ruptured air bags. Company officials rejected Blumenthal's request, but later agreed to set up such a fund in early 2017 as part of a $1 billion settlement with the U.S. Justice Department. With an eye toward his constituents, Blumenthal pressured the Federal Railroad Administration to adopt new regulations after a series of accidents on Metro North, the commuter line that thousands of Connecticut residents ride to get to jobs in New York City.

Professional sports leagues were another favorite Blumenthal target. He has credited a bill that he sponsored with Republican Sen. John McCain of Arizona, a fellow member of the Commerce, Science and Transportation Committee, with pushing the Federal Communications Commission to change its rules on the blackout of televised sporting events, And, in late 2014, Blumenthal held a hearing on the incidence of domestic violence among National Football League players, followed by the NFL donating $25 million to a domestic violence hotline. "My friends at the hotline say it was a $25 million hearing," Blumenthal afterward told the *Connecticut Mirror*. And, appearing to address critics -- past and present -- who have accused him of being more interested in attention than results, Blumenthal pointedly added: "One lesson to me is that legislation is only one lever to fight for benefits for the people of Connecticut. I can use my position to shine a light on problems."

Blumenthal's committee assignments include the Armed Services panel; the defense industry is a major employer in eastern Connecticut. In early 2015, Blumenthal became ranking Democrat on the Veterans' Affairs Committee. (One son, Matthew, is an officer in the Marine Corps Reserve and has served in Afghanistan; another son, Michael, entered the Navy midway through Blumenthal's first Senate term.) Blumenthal teamed with the Veterans' Affairs panel chairman, Republican Johnny Isakson of Georgia, to sponsor a 400-page bill to overhaul the troubled Veterans Affairs Department -- including provisions to facilitate the firing of problem employees while protecting whistleblowers, and to expand mental health programs for veterans. A stripped-down version of the bill was adopted during the lame duck session in December 2016. Sen. Jon Tester of Montana, who outranked Blumenthal in seniority, opted to take over his position in advance of a tough 2018 re-election. "The position or the title is less important than the work," shrugged Blumenthal, vowing to "work with even greater determination to improve services for our veterans."

Despite efforts to reach across the aisle, Blumenthal has for the most part been a reliable partisan. A notable exception occurred a month prior to the 2016 election, when he was at the forefront of the successful effort to override President Barack Obama's veto of a bill allowing families of 9/11 victims to sue the Saudi Arabian government in U.S, courts. "I stood up to the president," Blumenthal said afterward. "Trust me, there was a lot of pressure to back down." A year earlier, he came under heavy lobbying pressure from both sides as one of the last Democratic holdouts on taking a position on the Obama Administration's nuclear agreement with Iran. Blumenthal ultimately came out for it; by that time, Obama had obtained enough Senate support to sustain a veto of a resolution disapproving the deal. While Blumenthal's vote was not crucial to allowing the agreement to go forward, Larry Kudlow, a conservative commentator for CNBC who served in the Reagan administration, vowed to challenge Blumenthal if he voted for the Iran deal.

But, after seven months of talking about taking on Blumenthal, Kudlow abruptly announced he would not run -- preferring to keep his CNBC gig and his nationally syndicated Saturday radio show. "I love being a broadcaster. I love it so much I don't want to give it up," declared Kudlow, foreclosing what might have been one of the more visible and colorful matchups of the 2016 election cycle. While early polls showed Kudlow to be a distinct underdog in a state that has not elected a Republican to the Senate in one-third of a century, he was well-positioned to raise the kind of campaign funds needed to make such a race competitive. And before deciding not to run, Kudlow had served notice that he was planning to make an issue not only of Blumenthal's record in the Senate, but his entire public career. "All these anti-business lawsuits never went anywhere," Kudlow told the *Courant*, referring to Blumenthal's tenure as attorney general. "It was death by 1,000 press releases."' Blumenthal, in a pre-emptive strike, sent out mailings calling Kudlow "anti-Main Street" and seeking to tie him to Trump, then a contender for the Republican presidential nomination. "He called the recession 'therapeutic' and workers laid off in 2008 'whiners'," one Blumenthal fundraising letter charged of Kudlow.

Kudlow's withdrawal, three months before the state GOP's nomination convention, left August Wolf -- a little known businessman whose claim to fame was as a shot putter in the 1984 Olympics -- as the Republican frontrunner. But adverse publicity surrounding Wolf -- due to staff turnover in his campaign and a lawsuit that included allegations of sexual harassment -- prompted state Republicans to search for an alternative. A month before the convention, conservative state Rep. Dan Carter entered the race, and was overwhelmingly chosen by delegates to the nomination convention. Wolf failed to collect enough signatures to get on the primary ballot, allowing the GOP to avoid a primary. Carter, a former Air Force pilot, was virtually unknown statewide, and was outspent 20-1 by Blumenthal, who cruised to a 63%-35% victory. When Blumenthal's current term ends in 2022, he will be 76 -- including nearly four decades of holding elected office in Connecticut.

Junior Senator

Chris Murphy (D)

Elected 2012, term expires 2018, 1st term; b. Aug 03, 1973, White Plains, NY; University of Connecticut School of Law, J.D.; Williams College, B.A.; Oxford University Exeter College (England), Att.; Protestant; Married (Catherine Holahan Murphy); 2 children.

Elected Office: CT House, 1999-2003; CT Senate, 2003-2006; U.S. House, 2007-2013.

Professional Career: Southington CT Planning & Zoning Commission, 1997-1999; Practicing attorney, 2002-2006.

DC Office: 136 HSOB 20510, 202-224-4041, Fax: 202-224-9750, murphy.senate.gov.

State Offices: Hartford, 860-549-8463.

Committees: *Appropriations*: DOL, HHS & Education & Related Agencies, Legislative Branch (RMM), Military Construction & Veteran Affairs & Related Agencies, State, Foreign Operations & Related Programs, Transportation, HUD & Related Agencies. *Foreign Relations*: East Asia, the Pacific & International Cybersecurity Policy, Europe & Regional Security Cooperation (RMM), Near East,

South Asia, Central Asia & Counterterrorism. *Health, Education, Labor & Pensions*: Employment & Workplace Safety, Primary Health & Retirement Security.

Group Ratings

	ADA	ACLU	AFL-CIO	LCV	ITI	COC	HAFA	ACU	CFG	FRC
2016	-	88%	-	100%	80%	50%	9%	0%	0%	0%
2015	95%	C	100%	100%	C	43%	C	0%	7%	0%

Almanac Ratings 2015

	Economy	Social	Foreign	Composite
Liberal	98%	100%	80%	93%
Conservative	2%	0%	20%	8%

Key Votes of the 114th Congress

1. Keystone pipeline	N	5. National Security Data	Y	9. Gun Sales Checks	Y
2. Export-Import Bank	N	6. Iran Nuclear Deal	N	10. Sanctuary Cities	N
3. Debt Ceiling Increase	Y	7. Puerto Rico Debt	Y	11. Planned Parenthood	N
4. Homeland Security $$	Y	8. Loretta Lynch A.G	Y	12. Trade deals	N

Election Results

Election	Name (Party)	Vote (%)	Cand. Spent	Ind. Exp. Support	Ind. Exp. Oppose
2012 General	Chris Murphy (D)	792,983 (52%)	$10,436,219	$1,879,868	$85,309
	Linda E. McMahon (R)	604,569 (40%)	$49,496,249	$1,022,818	$7,426,239
2012 Primary	Chris Murphy (D)	94,424 (67%)			
	Susan Bysiewicz (D)	47,109 (33%)			

Prior winning percentages: House: 2010 (54%), 2008 (59%), 2006 (56%)

On the morning of June 15, 2016, Democrat Chris Murphy, Connecticut's junior senator, began a filibuster -- three days after the Orlando nightclub shooting, in which 49 were killed and 53 were injured. Murphy held the Senate floor for nearly 15 hours -- accompanied for much of the time by his in-state colleague, Democratic Sen. Richard Blumenthal, and New Jersey Democratic Sen. Cory Booker -- and, before he yielded, won concessions from the GOP leadership for votes to be scheduled on several gun control measures. But the ultimate result was the same as = what followed other episodes of gun violence in recent years: Proposals to expand background checks to cover gun shows and sales over the Internet and to bar sale of guns to those on terrorist watch lists fell short of the 60-vote supermajority needed for cloture early the following week. Murphy reacted angrily, declaring, "I'm mortified by today's vote but I'm not surprised by it. The NRA has a vise-like grip on this place."

By his own admission, Murphy arrived in the Senate in early 2013 without a driving purpose. That changed dramatically five weeks after Election Day 2012, when a mass shooting at the Sandy Hook Elementary School in Newtown -- located in the House district that Murphy had represented for three terms -- resulted in 26 deaths, most of them children. "There wasn't one issue that was driving me to get up every day and go to work. There is today," Murphy declared in a 2016 interview with *Politico*. He said of the Sandy Hook shooting: "This was something different…in part because my son just graduated from first grade. I'm the same age as all of these parents. I walked out of that tragedy feeling like I had just been handed my mission in public service."

Murphy was also handed a political opportunity: He strove to make the 2016 election a referendum on gun control, while raising money and campaigning for like-minded candidates. His name showed up on a list of potential running mates compiled internally by the Hillary Clinton campaign, and it is currently being tossed around in Democratic presidential speculation for 2020. If many members of the Senate see a presidential contender when they look in the mirror -- as the well-worn wisecrack suggests -- most are coy about it. But Murphy, who was just short of 40 when elected to the Senate, bluntly conceded to the *Washington Post* during a 2016 walk across his home state that he is a "big ball of political ambition." He continued: "Everyone doing this job is fooling themselves if they don't admit that we are attracted to the show business element of it. We are all doing this in part because we enjoy being in front of the cameras."

Raised in the Hartford suburb of Wethersfield-his father for many years was managing partner of a large Hartford law firm-Murphy has been in in the political spotlight virtually his entire adult life. Upon his graduation from Williams College in 1996, he signed on as campaign manager for Democrat Charlotte Koskoff, who came within 1,600 votes of toppling Republican Nancy Johnson in what was then Connecticut's 6th District. Two years later, Murphy ran for office himself, winning a seat in the state House when he was just 25. He also pursued a law degree, which he received in the spring of 2002; later that year, he won election to the state Senate.

In early 2005, Murphy moved into the 5th District, which had been significantly redrawn after Connecticut's loss of a House seat following the 2000 census. Murphy announced plans to challenge her. Besides the war in Iraq, the debate focused on the Medicare prescription drug benefit that Johnson had helped design in 2003 as chairman of the House Ways and Means panel's Health Subcommittee. Murphy contended that the prescription drug program's enrollment deadlines penalized seniors, and spotlighted drug industry contributions to Johnson. Johnson, who had served in Congress for nearly a quarter of a century, counterattacked with ads accusing Murphy of voting to raise taxes 27 times, and outspent Murphy by 2-1. But, as the Democrats rode a national wave to retake the House majority, Murphy won easily, 56%-44%.

In the House, Murphy was a fairly loyal Democrat, although he boasted of his role in Center Aisle Caucus, which he described as "one of the few places in the House where Republicans and Democrats are…getting together to try and talk about the importance of civility." While his district was home to many insurance industry employees, he backed a government-run public option to compete with private insurers during the 2009-2010 debate over the Affordable Care Act. An ardent advocate for "buy American" requirements throughout his congressional career, he introduced bills to require federal contracting officials to accept and solicit information from businesses regarding how many U.S. jobs would be retained or created if their bid was chosen. (Following the swearing-in of President Donald Trump, Murphy expressed hope that the rhetoric of Trump's inaugural address would translate into the new administration's support of Murphy's buy-American plan. "I've said from Election Day that I'm willing to work with President Trump when his policies align with those of my constituents," Murphy told a press conference, not long after announcing opposition to several of Trump's Cabinet appointments.)

When four-term Sen. Joe Lieberman announced he would not seek re-election in 2012, Murphy announced for the seat and faced a primary against former Connecticut Secretary of State Susan Bysiewicz. She ran a controversial TV ad seeking to link Murphy to Wall Street in the wake of the 2008 financial meltdown; it cited more than $700,000 in contributions to Murphy from Wall Street sources over a six-year period. But Bysiewicz found herself on the defensive after having to acknowledge that the ad had overstated Murphy's donations from hedge funds. Murphy triumphed in the primary by 2-1. The general election turned out to be *déjà vu*. Linda McMahon, the former professional wrestling magnate who had lost the 2010 Senate race to Blumenthal, was again the Republican nominee. And, like Blumenthal two years earlier, Murphy struggled in the general election despite being an odds-on favorite at the start of the campaign.

While Blumenthal had stumbled due to inflated claims on his military record, Murphy was tripped up over revelations that he missed mortgage payments and was sued over failure to pay rent. Murphy blamed a busy schedule for the missed payments. As she had in 2010, McMahon tapped into her personal wealth to float her campaign-burning through nearly $50 million. Like two years earlier, she sought to move to the political center-but it prompted questions about her true ideological leanings. Murphy targeted McMahon -- later appointed by Trump to head the Small Business Administration -- on issues affecting seniors, arguing she would pose a threat to Social Security and Medicare. On Election Day, McMahon lost by the same 55%-43% spread by which she had come up short to Blumenthal.

Lieberman had long been one of the Democratic Party's leading hawks: His support for the Iraq war was largely responsible for the party's 2000 vice-presidential nominee losing a bid for renomination to the Senate in 2006. It forced Lieberman to run as an independent to win election to a fourth term. In contrast, Murphy has emerged as one of the Senate's most outspoken doves with regard to U.S. involvement in the Middle East. He found himself at odds with both President Barack Obama and Obama's 2008 Republican opponent, Arizona Sen. John McCain-for whom Lieberman bolted the Democratic Party to support in that year's presidential race.

Murphy, who sits on the Foreign Relations Committee, found accord with McCain on another foreign policy front: the tensions in Ukraine. In December 2013, Murphy traveled to Ukraine, where he and McCain stood in Kiev's Independence Square and addressed thousands of protesters seeking the ouster of Ukraine's Russian-backed president. Murphy's views on Ukrainian independence were influenced, he says, by his Polish-American mother, a retired school teacher. As he was growing up, he recalls her relating the struggles of relatives in the old country living in the shadow of Russian power. He also represents a state with a significant Ukrainian-American community. In early 2015, McCain traveled to Hartford to appear with Murphy at the Ukrainian National Home, a cultural center, where he praised Murphy as "a worthy successor" to Lieberman in his "deep and active" involvement in foreign policy issues.

Murphy's more dovish views with regard to the Middle East appear to date back to his first race for Congress in 2006, when he campaigned as a strong opponent of the war in Iraq. He gained widespread attention in September 2013 when he told Obama-who had called Murphy at home-that he could not support the administration's plan to take military action against Syria. "I can't say that it was a comfortable position to be in, having a public dispute with the president so early in my freshman term," Murphy told the *Connecticut Mirror*. A year later, he came out solidly against the Obama Administration's efforts to train and arm Syrian rebels to fight the Islamic militant force ISIS. Murphy says he became wary of U.S. military involvements because of what he saw as the failures of the wars in Afghanistan as well as Iraq. "I want ISIS defeated in Syria," he said in a floor speech. "But too much can go wrong, for not enough possible gain, for the U.S. to increase our involvement in the Syrian civil war." His stance on Syrian refugees is in sharp contrast to the policies of the Trump Administration: In late 2015, he circulated a letter, signed by 26 other Senate Democrats, calling for increased funding to allow for admission of more refugees. "We can and must do more to address the plight of Syrian refugees," the letter declared.

On domestic policy, *Almanac* vote rankings show Murphy to be among the most liberal senators in the chamber. As a member of the Senate Health, Education, Labor and Pensions Committee, he was an outspoken defender of the Affordable Care Act, Obama's signature legislative achievement and he volunteered to take the lead role among Senate Democrats in seeking to rebut relentless Republican criticism of "Obamacare". His willingness to perform this politically onerous task served him well with Democratic leaders: Murphy was given a coveted seat on the Appropriations Committee in 2015.

In contrast to Blumenthal, Murphy is among the Senate's poorer members: His 2014 financial disclosure form showed student loan debt of as much as $50,000. Murphy and Sen. Brian Schatz in late 2013 teamed up on a bill to provide incentives to college administrators to bring down the cost of higher education. Perhaps Murphy's major legislative achievement to date was a mental health bill, co-authored with Republican Sen. Bill Cassidy of Louisiana, which was signed into law by Obama at the end of 2016. Hailed as the first major piece of mental health legislation in a decade, it was designed to strengthen insurance coverage for mental health treatment while providing grants to increase the number of psychiatrists and psychologists nationwide. A state report following the Sandy Hook shooting found that the gunman, Adam Lanza, had gone untreated for psychiatric as well as physical disorders.

Absent the late emergence of a candidate with high name recognition or deep pockets, Murphy appears unlikely to be seriously challenged for re-election in 2018 in a state with a decidedly Democratic tilt. He will be 45 in November 2018, and, if opportunities to seek higher office do not present themselves, he could be around the Senate long enough to accumulate a lot of seniority-and influence. He boasts he is the first Connecticut senator in almost 30 years to sit on the Appropriations panel, and longevity could make him chairman down the road. "I'm young. I only get a six-year term," Murphy told a reporter for the *Connecticut Post* in 2014, "but I'm planning to be around the Senate long enough to beat the gun lobby." Two years later, with little progress on that front on Capitol Hill, Murphy was nonetheless encouraged by three states passing referenda in 2016 to curb gun ownership. And he said gun control advocates are looking for other states that could be ready to take similar steps, while preparing to fight possible pro-gun initiatives put forth by the Trump Administration. "We will make change one state at a time, and we will hold the line here in Washington," he vowed.

FIRST DISTRICT

John Larson (D)

Elected 1998, 10th term; b. Jul 22, 1948, Hartford; Central Connecticut State University (CT), B.S.; Trinity College (CT); Catholic; Married (Leslie Best Larson); 3 children.

Elected Office: E. Hartford Board of Education, 1977-1979; E. Hartford Town Council, 1979-1983; CT Senate, 1986-1998, President pro-tem, 1990-1998.

Professional Career: H.S. teacher, 1972-1977; Ins. broker, 1977-1998; Sr. fellow, Yale Bush Center, 1995-1998.

DC Office: 1501 LHOB 20515, 202-225-2265, Fax: 202-225-1031, larson.house.gov.

State Offices: Hartford, 860-278-8888.

Committees: *Ways & Means*: Social Security (RMM), Tax Policy.

Group Ratings

	ADA	ACLU	AFL-CIO	LCV	ITI	COC	HAFA	ACU	CFG	FRC
2016	-	82%	-	100%	67%	57%	12%	0%	0%	0%
2015	95%	C	100%	97%	C	42%	C	4%	0%	0%

Almanac Ratings 2015

	Economy	Social	Foreign	Composite
Liberal	93%	97%	84%	91%
Conservative	7%	4%	16%	9%

Key Votes of the 114th Congress

1. Keystone Pipeline	N	5. Puerto Rico Debt	Y	9. Offenses by Aliens	N
2. Trade Deals	N	6. Medical Marijuana	Y	10. Troops in Iraq	Y
3. Export-Import Bank	Y	7. Sanctuary Cities	N	11. Homeland Security $$	Y
4. Debt Ceiling Increase	Y	8. Armor-piercing Bullets	N	12. Trade Adjustment aid	Y

Election Results

Election	Name (Party)	Vote (%)	Cand. Spent	Ind. Exp. Support	Ind. Exp. Oppose
2016 General	John Larson (D)	200,686 (64%)	$1,187,447		
	Matthew Corey (R)	105,674 (34%)	$20,982		
	Mike DeRosa (G)	6,565 (2%)			

Prior winning percentages: 2014 (62%), 2012 (70%), 2010 (60%), 2008 (72%), 2006 (74%), 2004 (73%), 2002 (67%), 2000 (72%), 1998 (58%)

Democrat John Larson, first elected in 1998, has been an influential figure among House Democrats and popular with colleagues. With a break in the seniority logjam atop the tax-writing Ways and Means Committee, he became ranking Democrat on the Social Security Subcommittee. After having been a long-time ally of Democratic Leader Nancy Pelosi, Larson has become a cautious critic in the wake of poor election results by House Democrats. Nearing age 70, he seemed unlikely to win a return to the Democratic leadership.

One of eight children, Larson grew up in the Mayberry Village public-housing project in East Hartford, and is fond of saying that he is a "product of public housing, public education, and public service." His father was a fireman at Pratt & Whitney and also worked as an auto mechanic and butcher. His mother had a job at the state Capitol and served on the town council. Speaking at the 2012 Democratic National Convention, he said that his mother had dementia and required round-the-clock care, paid for in part through her Social Security benefits. "Don't ever tell me or any American that's a handout," he said. "It's the insurance they paid for."

After graduating from Central Connecticut State University, Larson taught high school and coached athletics. He also worked in the hometown industry as an insurance agent. In 1982, Larson was elected to the state Senate. Four years later, he earned a promotion to Senate president. He sponsored one of the nation's first family medical leave laws, a prototype for the federal bill signed into law by President Bill Clinton in 1993.

Larson seemed headed for governor and, in 1994, won the party designation at the state convention. But Comptroller Bill Curry built an organization of unionists and liberal activists and beat him 55%-45% in the primary. When Democratic Rep. Barbara Kennelly decided to run for governor in 1998, Larson ran for her seat. In the primary, he raised impressive sums, built a local organization, campaigned door-to-door and got help from Hartford Mayor Mike Peters. He won 46%-43% over Secretary of State Miles Rapoport. In the general election, he competed against Kevin O'Connor, a 31-year-old Securities and Exchange Commission lawyer. Larson won 58%-41% and has not been seriously challenged since.

Larson's voting record places him near the center of his party. He doesn't hesitate to work with Republicans on legislation, especially at Ways and Means - with Texas' Kevin Brady, now the committee chairman, on a measure to make permanent a research and development tax credit. He showed his bipartisan stripes on a local issue in 2013 when he became co-chairman of the Congressional Joint Strike Fighter Caucus, which backs the F-35, whose engines are made by Pratt & Whitney. In 2014, he won enactment of a provision that designated Hartford's Coltsville as a national historical park, a 260-acre site along the river, which includes 19th century factories.

In 2003, Pelosi tapped Larson as the senior Democrat on the House Administration Committee, the congressional housekeeping panel that handles office space assignments and other perks of interest to colleagues. Among his legislative interests at the committee was campaign finance reform, including a proposal to allow the federal government to match funds raised by a candidate who agrees to accept contributions of $100 or less. He also has proposed a constitutional amendment that would give members of the House four-year terms with elections staggered every two years. Longer terms would make legislators more effective by allowing them to spend less time campaigning, Larson said.

Pelosi brought Larson into her circle of advisers, and his influence grew. In 2006, he won a hotly contested race for Democratic Caucus vice chairman. His competitors were the better-known Jan Schakowsky of Illinois and Joseph Crowley of New York. When Schakowsky finished third on the first ballot and was eliminated, she threw her support to Larson. With Schakowsky's former supporters, Larson prevailed on the second ballot 116-87 over Crowley, who was allied with Maryland's Steny Hoyer, Pelosi's arch-rival in leadership. In 2007, Larson planned to run for caucus chairman, but stepped aside when it became clear that Rahm Emanuel of Illinois had locked up support for the job. When Emanuel quit the House in November 2008 to become chief of staff to President Barack Obama, then-Speaker Pelosi cleared the field for Larson to finally become caucus chairman.

Larson took on a number of leadership assignments, including dealing with party dissidents who complained that Pelosi's Iraq strategy was too accommodating to President George W. Bush and later coordinating the Democrats' strategy on energy policy. Some Democrats privately derided him as Pelosi's cheerleader, but he shrugged off such comments, saying that his "bottom-up, member's member" approach was very different from the imperious style Emanuel was known for, but no less effective. But the caucus chairmanship position had a four-year limit. Because Democrats did not reclaim the majority in 2012, there was no place for Larson to move up. He continued to serve as a mentor to younger members and said he would welcome a return to a position in party leadership.

In June 2016, he gained attention for himself and for House Democrats when he and Rep. John Lewis of Georgia organized an overnight House sit-in to demand legislative action on gun control following the terrorist attack that killed 49 at an Orlando nightclub. With the group making ample use of social media, Larson called the result "a mix of '60s activism with21stcentury millennial technology." With House Speaker Paul Ryan calling the effort "a publicity stunt," Larson's group did not get Republican agreement for House votes. But he won the gratitude of many House Democrats. His voice grew more independent following the election when he joined critics of Pelosi who pushed for a delay in choosing Democratic leaders. The Democratic Caucus needed "a frank discussion about what happened," he said. Coincidentally, at the same time, his close friend Rep. Richard Neal of Massachusetts - who has also shown independence of Pelosi - became the top Democrat at the Ways and Means Committee.

The frustration of many Democrats with House election results left him looking for an opportunity. "I'm not running, but it's unfair to say I'm not interested in running" for a leadership position, he told a local reporter.

North-central Connecticut: Hartford

Population		Race and Ethnicity		Income	
Total	716,277	White	63.0%	Median Income	$66,349 (84 out of 435)
Land area	675	Black	14.2%		
Pop/ sq mi	1060.4	Latino	15.7%	Under $50,000	38.5%
Born in state	58.5%	Asian	4.8%	$50,000-$99,999	30.3%
		Two races	1.9%	$100,000-$199,999	24.2%
Age Groups		Other	0.4%	$200,000 or more	6.9%
Under 18	21.6%			Poverty Rate	11.8%
18-34	21.8%	**Education**			
35-64	40.9%	H.S grad or less	38.4%	**Health Insurance**	
Over 64	15.7%	Some college	25.9%	With health insurance coverage	92.9%
		College Degree, 4 yr	20.3%		
Work		Post grad	15.4%		
White Collar	42.9%			**Public Assistance**	
Sales and Service	40.7%	**Military**		Cash public assistance income	4.6%
Blue Collar	16.5%	Veteran	6.9%		
Government	14.5%	Active Duty	0.1%	Food stamp/SNAP benefits	14.5%

Voter Turnout			
2015 Total Citizens 18+	514,755	2016 House Turnout as % CVAP	61%
2016 House turnout	312,925	2014 House Turnout as % CVAP	42%

2012 Presidential Vote		
Barack Obama	200,910	(63%)
Mitt Romney	112,962	(36%)

2016 Presidential Vote		
Hillary Clinton	195,305	(59%)
Donald Trump	119,395	(36%)
Gary Johnson	9,468	(3%)

Cook Partisan Voting Index: D+12

The Puritans who founded Hartford certainly never expected, or even hoped, that Connecticut's Yankees would turn out to be shrewd businessmen. Yet this is exactly what happened. Mark Twain moved to Hartford in 1871 to become director of an insurance company, and in time became the Connecticut capital's most famous citizen. Some have departed, but Connecticut retains one of the largest concentration of financial and insurance firms in the nation, mostly in the Hartford area. Its merchants wrote fire insurance, using the capital they had accumulated in the Napoleonic Wars to finance their ventures. The native Samuel Colt played a foundational role in developing the state's armaments base; he conceived of the revolving-barrel pistol after watching the wheel of a ship spin while on a year-long voyage at sea. His gun factory, just south of downtown Hartford, became one of the nation's great arms plants. Thanks to the broad Connecticut River, Hartford also became a seaport.

Despite their downsizing, insurance and armaments remain economic mainstays of Hartford, Connecticut's biggest metropolitan area. But many employers have moved out of Hartford itself, hastening the sad decline of this once rich city. Insurance industry employment dropped to 47,000 statewide in 2014 from 50,000 in 2011. Since the 1980s, the central core has been filled with bedraggled, high-crime neighborhoods littered with abandoned buildings. Downtown landmarks, such as the Broadcast House, have been demolished. Where 177,000 people lived in 1950, there were about 125,400 residents in 2014. The population is 39 percent African American and 43 percent Hispanic. But there have been signs of recovery and hopes for a business turnaround. The University of Connecticut plans to open in 2017 a large downtown campus, Hartford Hospital has opened a new Bone and Joint Institute, inter-city train service has expanded, and new housing and retail facilities are under construction. A baseball stadium just north of downtown was nearly completed in 2016, though it ran into financing problems. Luke Bronin, a former Rhodes Scholar who served with the Navy in Afghanistan, has brought a youthful urgency as Mayor. After Donald Trump was elected president, Bronin said that Hartford would remain a "sanctuary city" that would protect illegal immigrants from federal authority.

Across the river is the Pratt & Whitney jet engine plant in East Hartford, cornerstone of Connecticut-based United Technologies. Though its operations have been shrunk by Pentagon spending cutbacks and its local workforce is less than one-fourth its size in 1980, it still builds engines for more than 600 customers around the world. The areas west of Hartford are more affluent and faring much better.

The 1st Congressional District of Connecticut is centered on Hartford. In its present incarnation, it looks like a lobster claw. The top half of the claw passes through Windsor, where Amy Archer-Gilligan's poisoning spree in the late 1910s at the retirement home she oversaw shocked the citizenry and inspired the play *Arsenic and Old Lace,* and the film version that followed. The claw then swings west across the northern border of the state, excluding some affluent suburbs while taking in small towns and part of Torrington. The bottom half of the district swings southwest of Hartford. It includes Bristol, site of the sprawling headquarters of ESPN, the multimedia network that prior to cutbacks in 2017 employed about 4,000 people locally of its nearly 8,000 worldwide. ESPN Plaza includes almost 1.2 million square feet in 17 buildings on 123 acres. Bristol has gained national attention for its municipal fiber optic network that provides Internet access to the city's agencies and in public places.

The Hartford area has long been more Democratic than the rest of Connecticut. The 2016 election produced a twist, when Hillary Clinton dropped below 60 percent and got a slightly larger vote in the upscale 4th District.

SECOND DISTRICT

Joe Courtney (D)

Elected 2006, 6th term; b. Apr 06, 1953, West Hartford; Tufts University (MA), B.A., 1975; University of Connecticut School of Law, J.D., 1978; Roman Catholic; Married (Audrey Courtney); 2 children.

Elected Office: CT House, 1987-1994.

Professional Career: Practicing attorney, 1978-2006; CT coordinator, John Edwards President campaign, 2004.

DC Office: 2348 RHOB 20515, 202-225-2076, Fax: 202-225-4977, courtney.house.gov.

State Offices: Enfield, 860-741-6011; Norwich, 860-886-0139.

Committees: *Armed Services*: Readiness, Seapower & Projection Forces (RMM). *Education & the Workforce*: Health, Employment, Labor & Pensions, Higher Education & Workforce Development.

Group Ratings

	ADA	ACLU	AFL-CIO	LCV	ITI	COC	HAFA	ACU	CFG	FRC
2016	-	88%	-	100%	67%	57%	14%	0%	0%	0%
2015	75%	C	100%	97%	C	45%	C	4%	0%	0%

Almanac Ratings 2015

	Economy	Social	Foreign	Composite
Liberal	91%	100%	71%	87%
Conservative	9%	0%	29%	13%

Key Votes of the 114th Congress

1. Keystone Pipeline	N	5. Puerto Rico Debt	Y	9. Offenses by Aliens	N
2. Trade Deals	N	6. Medical Marijuana	Y	10. Troops in Iraq	N
3. Export-Import Bank	Y	7. Sanctuary Cities	N	11. Homeland Security $$	Y
4. Debt Ceiling Increase	Y	8. Armor-piercing Bullets	N	12. Trade Adjustment aid	Y

Election Results

Election	Name (Party)	Vote (%)	Cand. Spent	Ind. Exp. Support	Ind. Exp. Oppose
2016 General	Joe Courtney (D)	208,818 (63%)	$1,083,870		
	Daria Novak (R)	111,149 (34%)	$48,014		

Prior winning percentages: 2014 (62%), 2012 (68%), 2010 (59%), 2008 (66%), 2006 (50%)

Democrat Joe Courtney, elected in 2006, has tirelessly promoted issues that are important to him, chiefly defense and education. With his position as ranking member of the Armed Services Subcommittee on Seapower and Projection Forces, he has delivered local benefits as a vigilant guardian of General Dynamics' Electric Boat plant and the New London Naval Submarine Base.

Courtney was raised in West Hartford. He studied at Tufts University, graduated from the University of Connecticut law school and went into private practice. In 1986, he won the first of four terms in the state House, where he served as chairman of the public health and human services committees. He ran unsuccessfully for lieutenant governor in 1998, then unsuccessfully in 2002 against Republican Rep. Rob Simmons, who won 54%-46%. Courtney returned for a rematch in 2006. Democrats worked diligently to nationalize the race by exploiting voter anger over the Iraq war and GOP ethics scandals in Congress. Simmons touted his independence from the Bush administration on partial-birth abortion and same-sex marriage votes. He also touted his successful lobbying to keep the submarine base off the 2005 base-closing list. Courtney prevailed in the closest House race of the 2006 election, with a winning margin of 83 votes out of the more than 242,000 cast.

In the House, Courtney's new colleagues gave him a nickname, "Landslide Joe." He got a seat on Armed Services, where he could more effectively lobby for the Navy's shipbuilding program at Groton. He worked with other Connecticut and Rhode Island lawmakers in 2007 to secure an extra $588 million in the defense appropriations bill for submarines, paving the way for the Navy to double its sub production from one to two a year. That led to another nickname from colleagues: "Two Sub Joe." During negotiations on so-called "fiscal cliff" tax and spending legislation in late 2012, he told the *Hartford Courant* that he faithfully studied Electric Boat employment listings like baseball box scores, looking for signs of anxiety because of the threat of massive defense cuts.

Courtney took over as co-chair of the Congressional Shipbuilding Caucus and worked to prevent a one-year cut in submarine production in 2014 while protecting the appropriation for a "stretched" version of a *Virginia*-class sub with cruise-missile tubes, which was designed at the Electric Boat yard. He successfully lobbied the Pentagon to include in its Quadrennial Defense Review the need for a future fleet of as many as 55 submarines, up from the 48 called for in 2006. In the 2014 defense spending bill, he secured as much as $3.5 billion for a "National Sea-Based Deterrence Fund" that would allow the Pentagon to finance a new class of submarines in Groton. In 2015, he touted his new senior position on the Seapower Subcommittee as "not only vital to Connecticut, but to our nation's security today and in the future." He worked closely in 2015 with Republican Rep. Randy Forbes of Virginia, who chaired the subcommittee, to defeat an attempt by members of the House Appropriations Committee to restore annual funding for the new submarines. "We haven't seen this much work [at Electric Boat] since the late '80s and early '90s," Courtney told the *Hartford Courant* in September 2016.

He has generally been a loyal Democrat. Representing a district that includes the University of Connecticut, Courtney has been the leading champion of keeping interest rates low on federally backed college loans. With Sen. Elizabeth Warren of Massachusetts, he filed a bill in 2015 that would save the average student borrower $2,000. During the 2009 health care debate, he led House Democratic opposition to a proposed "Cadillac tax" on high-cost health insurance plans, which he said would harm millions in the middle class. He helped change it to a 3.8 percent tax on non-wage income.

Unlike most Democrats elected in 2006, Courtney has had a much easier time keeping his office than he did in winning it, never receiving less than 60 percent in his next five campaigns.

Eastern Connecticut: New London, Norwich

Population		**Race and Ethnicity**		**Income**	
Total	712,023	White	82.6%	Median Income	$71,458 (69 out of 435)
Land area	1,988	Black	3.6%		
Pop/ sq mi	358.2	Latino	7.7%	Under $50,000	34.7%
Born in state	56.7%	Asian	3.2%	$50,000-$99,999	31.7%
Age Groups		Two races	2.6%	$100,000-$199,999	27.0%
Under 18	20.4%	Other	0.3%	$200,000 or more	6.8%
18-34	22.5%	**Education**		Poverty Rate	8.5%
35-64	41.7%	H.S grad or less	38.2%	**Health Insurance**	
Over 64	15.4%	Some college	28.0%	With health insurance coverage	94.3%
Work		College Degree, 4 yr	18.9%		
White Collar	39.6%	Post grad	14.8%	**Public Assistance**	
Sales and Service	42.1%	**Military**		Cash public assistance income	3.3%
Blue Collar	18.4%	Veteran	9.9%		
Government	16.4%	Active Duty	1.2%	Food stamp/SNAP benefits	10.3%

Voter Turnout			
2015 Total Citizens 18+	546,830	2016 House Turnout as % CVAP	60%
2016 House turnout	330,257	2014 House Turnout as % CVAP	41%

2012 Presidential Vote		
Barack Obama	177,522	(56%)
Mitt Romney	135,212	(43%)

2016 Presidential Vote		
Hillary Clinton	165,799	(49%)
Donald Trump	155,975	(46%)
Gary Johnson	13,080	(4%)

Cook Partisan Voting Index: D+3

When Puritans from Massachusetts and England arrived in eastern Connecticut, the flinty hills were the home of small Indian tribes, whose numbers had been decimated by warfare and even more by disease. Factories quickly developed around mills in little villages on the fast-flowing Quinebaug and Shetucket rivers. Soon, New London and Norwich were among the 13 colonies' leading workshops and ports. The infamous plot of Connecticut native Benedict Arnold to deliver West Point in New York to the British was uncovered during the American Revolution, but his company did succeed in burning New London to the ground in 1781 and sacking Fort Griswold. The region's deep vein of human industriousness sustained it into the 20th century, when new technology took over in shaping the area. Four nuclear power plants were built here, more than in any similarly populated part of the United States. In Groton, the "Submarine Capital of the World" situated across the Thames River from New London, is General Dynamics' Electric Boat company, which built its first submarines in 1915 and later, nuclear submarines.

The 1990s brought a serious downturn in the local economy. The end of the Cold War and accompanying reductions in military spending were painful for the region and the long-term survival for the port has been in doubt. But Congress approved additional spending for submarines and the Navy chose Electric Boat to be the prime contractor for a new class of 12 ballistic-missile submarines, with an ultimate price tag of perhaps $100 billion. That could increase the payroll at Groton from roughly 14,000 to an estimated 18,000 by 2030. The shipyard also helps to build two attack submarines annually. The submarine programs sustain nearly 500 suppliers across Connecticut. A $100 million national Coast Guard museum is scheduled to open in 2020 on the New London waterfront.

The area's economic base has relied heavily on entertainment, specifically gambling. The Foxwoods Resort Casino, built by the 650-member Mashantucket Pequot tribe, is the largest casino in the Western Hemisphere. But its number of employees has dropped from 10,500 to 7,600 in 2014. Uncasville is the site of the Mohegan Sun casino, the second-largest in the Western Hemisphere with a slightly smaller payroll. Competition from nearby states and the slow national economy are stunting the growth of gaming in the area. Foxwoods has struggled to restructure billions of dollars in debt. Concerned about competition from an MGM casino under construction in Springfield, Massachusetts, the two tribes have discussed plans for a new casino across the border in Connecticut to compete with MGM.

The 2nd Congressional District includes most of the eastern half of the state, centering on the small cities of New London and Norwich and including mill towns and the University of Connecticut in Storrs. The northeastern edge of Windham County, long known as "Quiet Corner" for its small towns and dairy farms, has lured away many Rhode Island and Massachusetts residents looking to escape higher taxes and housing prices. The district stretches west to the outskirts of Hartford and to antique-filled small towns like Essex and Old Lyme on Long Island Sound.

For many years, this was a politically marginal district, with close battles between Yankee Republicans and Catholic Democrats. More recently, it had trended comfortably Democratic. But the 49%-46% margin by Hillary Clinton over Donald Trump in 2016 was 10 points less than Barack Obama's 56%-43% local win over Mitt Romney in 2012.

THIRD DISTRICT

Rosa DeLauro (D)

Elected 1990, 14th term; b. Mar 02, 1943, New Haven; Queen Mary College - London School of Economics (England), 1963; Marymount College (NY), B.A., 1964; Columbia University (NY), M.A., 1966; Roman Catholic; Married (Stanley Greenberg); 3 children; 4 grandchildren.

Professional Career: Executive Assistant, New Haven Mayor Frank Logue, 1976-1977; Executive Assistant & develop. admin., City of New Haven, 1977-1979; Chief of Staff, U.S. Sen. Christopher Dodd, 1981-1987; Executive Director, Countdown '87, 1987-1988; Executive Director, EMILY's List, 1989-1990.

DC Office: 2413 RHOB 20515, 202-225-3661, Fax: 202-225-4890, delauro.house.gov.

State Offices: Derby, 203-735-5005; Naugatuck, 203-729-0204; New Haven, 203-562-3718.

Committees: House Democratic Steering and Policy Committee Co-Chair. *Appropriations*: Agriculture, Rural Development, FDA & Related Agencies, Labor, Health & Human Services, Education & Related Agencies (RMM).

Group Ratings

	ADA	ACLU	AFL-CIO	LCV	ITI	COC	HAFA	ACU	CFG	FRC
2016	-	100%	-	97%	50%	57%	17%	4%	0%	0%
2015	95%	C	100%	97%	C	47%	C	4%	5%	0%

Almanac Ratings 2015

	Economy	Social	Foreign	Composite
Liberal	85%	100%	99%	94%
Conservative	15%	0%	1%	6%

Key Votes of the 114th Congress

1. Keystone Pipeline	N	5. Puerto Rico Debt	Y	9. Offenses by Aliens	N
2. Trade Deals	N	6. Medical Marijuana	Y	10. Troops in Iraq	Y
3. Export-Import Bank	Y	7. Sanctuary Cities	N	11. Homeland Security $$	Y
4. Debt Ceiling Increase	Y	8. Armor-piercing Bullets	N	12. Trade Adjustment aid	Y

Election Results

Election	Name (Party)	Vote (%)	Cand. Spent	Ind. Exp. Support	Ind. Exp. Oppose
2016 General	Rosa DeLauro (D)	213,572 (69%)	$641,090		
	Angel Cadena (R)	95,786 (31%)			

Prior winning percentages: 2014 (67%), 2012 (75%), 2010 (64%), 2008 (77%), 2006 (76%), 2004 (72%), 2002 (66%), 2000 (72%), 1998 (71%), 1996 (71%), 1994 (68%), 1992 (57%), 1990 (52%)

Rosa DeLauro, a Democrat first elected in 1990, is an outspoken liberal - "a live wire whose words rush out like sparks," *The New York Times* once wrote - and a prominent party leader on women's health as well as food safety issues. She is a senior House appropriator on domestic funding issues, and a confidant of Minority Leader Nancy Pelosi of California at the Democratic leadership table as co-chair of the Steering and Policy Committee.

DeLauro grew up in New Haven's Wooster Square. Both of her parents were New Haven aldermen. Her mother, Luisa DeLauro, retired from the Board of Aldermen in 1999 after 35 years, the longest tenure in New Haven history. In Wooster Square Park, a granite monument of a table, bench and two chairs honors the family's home as a social services center. Rosa DeLauro's husband, Stanley Greenberg, was Bill Clinton's chief pollster from 1991 to 1994 and worked for Al Gore's presidential campaign in 2000 and John Kerry's in 2004. As Obama's White House chief of staff, Rahm Emanuel, a family friend who lived for a while in the basement of DeLauro's Capitol Hill home, officiated at the wedding of Greenberg's daughter Anna, a partner in their political consulting firm.

DeLauro has been in politics nearly all of her life. She was a development administrator in New Haven in the 1970s, chief of staff to Democratic Sen. Christopher Dodd from 1980 to 1987, then spent a year working to stop U.S. military aid to Nicaraguan contras before she became director of EMILY's List, the women's campaign fundraising group that supports abortion rights. When the 3rd District seat opened in 1990, DeLauro prevailed 52%-48% over anti-tax and anti-abortion Republican state Sen. Tom Scott. She has not faced serious competition since 1992, when she won a rematch against Scott, 66%-34%.

As a close ally of Pelosi, DeLauro is one of the Democratic leadership's most vocal champions in debate. Pelosi in 2011 admiringly described her as "a force of nature." She is an active and ardent supporter of feminist issues. A cancer survivor, she sponsored the law to require that patients and doctors, not insurance companies, decide on 48-hour hospital stays for mastectomies. She also lobbied for insurance coverage of early-detection tests for cervical cancer, and helped to enact "Johanna's Law" to increase awareness of gynecological cancers. In 2009, she introduced a bill to require employers to give workers seven paid sick days annually. Also that year, the House passed her bill, which eventually became law as the Lilly Ledbetter Fair Pay Act, which provided remedies to victims of wage discrimination, reversing a Supreme Court decision that had made it more difficult to ensure that women and men doing the same job are paid comparable wages. Since the Democrats' loss of the House majority in 2010, DeLauro has been less prolific as a legislator.

As a former chair of the Appropriations Subcommittee on Agriculture, Rural Development, Food and Drug Administration, and Related Agencies, DeLauro has taken a keen interest in food safety, which she said should have the same priority as prescription drug and medical device safety. Her subcommittee in 2008 increased by $1.8 billion President George W. Bush's funding request for the FDA. But she said a year later that the agency remained "badly broken," and faulted the Obama administration for not doing enough to address food safety. After the Centers for Disease Control and Prevention released figures in late 2010 showing that food-borne disease remained a public health threat, she introduced a bill to create a single agency to regulate the food supply. At a May 2016 event with Sen. Richard Blumenthal of Connecticut, she said that food companies are "preying on consumers good intentions" by putting artificial ingredients in "natural" products, given the lack of any prohibition; she urged the FDA to define the use of "natural" when it is applied to food. Since 2011, she has been ranking Democrat on the Labor, HHS and Education Subcommittee at Appropriations, where the Republican majority has held the line on spending.

In an unusual and often testy clash with President Barack Obama during his final two years in office, DeLauro was a leader among House Democrats in siding with unions to oppose the proposed Trans-Pacific Partnership trade agreement that the United States was negotiating with 11 nations. Despite the prospect of lower tariffs, her greater concern was that the deal would kill good-paying jobs. It was vital, she said, that "everyone who works hard and plays by the rules has a chance to succeed." Responding to Obama's criticism that she had her facts wrong on the issue, DeLauro said, "We have been framed as 'opposed to trade,' but we're not. ... We are opposed to corporate-driven trade agreements written by lobbyists."

Still, DeLauro strongly embraced Obama's opening to Cuba and accompanied him in March 2016 when he was the first president to visit the island since 1928. DeLauro has cautioned that diplomatic progress with Cuba would be slow. "No one has their head in the sand or is wearing rose-colored glasses," she said.

As co-chair of the Steering and Policy Committee, DeLauro is instrumental in advising on committee assignments for House Democrats. She has "an encyclopedic knowledge of members' committee aspirations," Pelosi said. Often, she uses the position to advance her interests. In December 2014, DeLauro and Pelosi got into an awkward situation when they denied the request of then-Rep. Tammy Duckworth of Illinois to vote by proxy in a Democratic Caucus leadership contest in which both were supporting California Rep. Anna Eshoo, another close ally. Duckworth, a double amputee, was at home in her final weeks of pregnancy and under doctor's orders not to travel. Duckworth was denied her request, but Eshoo fell short on the vote.

DeLauro has run twice for chairwoman of the Democratic Caucus and suffered two painfully close setbacks. In 1998, she lost 108-97 to Martin Frost of Texas; Minority Leader Richard Gephardt then named her an assistant leader in charge of the party's message. In 2002, she lost 104-103 to Robert Menendez of New Jersey after an intense year-long contest. DeLauro has been an active supporter of Pelosi in her leadership races, which helped cement the bond between the two Italian-American liberal women. In 2004, she led the drafting of the Democratic platform when John Kerry was nominated for president. She has remained an influential voice on platform fights and other policy conflicts among Democrats, with her skillful blend of policy and politics.

South Central Connecticut: New Haven

Population		**Race and Ethnicity**		**Income**	
Total	717,105	White	66.6%	Median Income	$62,939 (112 out of 435)
Land area	470	Black	12.8%		
Pop/ sq mi	1524.7	Latino	14.1%		
Born in state	62.3%	Asian	4.2%	Under $50,000	40.4%
Age Groups		Two races	1.8%	$50,000-$99,999	29.1%
Under 18	20.4%	Other	0.5%	$100,000-$199,999	24.1%
18-34	24.3%	**Education**		$200,000 or more	6.5%
35-64	40.0%	H.S grad or less	39.8%	Poverty Rate	11.8%
Over 64	15.2%	Some college	24.7%	**Health Insurance**	
Work		College Degree, 4 yr	19.1%	With health insurance coverage	92.7%
White Collar	40.8%	Post grad	16.4%		
Sales and Service	41.6%	**Military**		**Public Assistance**	
Blue Collar	17.5%	Veteran	6.7%	Cash public assistance income	3.5%
Government	13.1%	Active Duty	0.1%	Food stamp/SNAP benefits	12.8%

Voter Turnout			
2015 Total Citizens 18+	528,512	2016 House Turnout as % CVAP	59%
2016 House turnout	309,379	2014 House Turnout as % CVAP	40%

2012 Presidential Vote		
Barack Obama	191,197	(63%)
Mitt Romney	110,867	(36%)

2016 Presidential Vote		
Hillary Clinton	179,832	(56%)
Donald Trump	129,968	(40%)
Gary Johnson	7,628	(2%)

Cook Partisan Voting Index: D+9

The New Haven Colony was founded in 1637 by a group of Puritan settlers who opted to bypass the Massachusetts Bay Colony after concluding the religious practices near Boston weren't strict enough. Their new colony was successful and grew rapidly. More than 150 years later, a young Yale graduate named Eli Whitney won an order from the young U.S. government to produce 10,000 muskets at $13.40 each. Whitney had invented the cotton gin six years earlier, which had embroiled him in a lengthy patent suit. He was determined to make a quick profit on the musket contract, so he set up a system of interchangeable parts and invented a milling machine and gauges: the birth of standardized American manufacturing. For the next 150 years or so, New Haven mass-produced rifles, clocks, locks, hardware and toys - anything its tinkerers and entrepreneurs could fashion. Today, few factories remain in New Haven. The factory that produced Winchester rifles and guns for 140 years closed in 2006. In recent years, southern Connecticut around New Haven discovered a new source of prosperity in scores of small technology and biomedical firms. Although the area's defense contracts are modest compared with those of the city's heyday, Stratford-based Sikorsky Aircraft envisions 8,000 employees and a doubling of its spending by 2032, chiefly for the King Stallion heavy-lift cargo helicopter for the U.S. Marines.

The city, with significant crime rates and many neighborhoods scarred by abandoned homes, has shrunk in population. In 2015, it had 130,000 people, down from 164,000 in 1950. Yale University, with its Gothic spires and red-brick halls, has always been the visual focus of New Haven and is now its largest employer. With two new residential colleges scheduled to open in August 2017, the university planned a 15 percent increase in undergraduate enrollment. Local revival was sparked by a state development program that turned old retail and office buildings into residences and by $1 billion in investments by biotech firms. Racial minorities and immigrants have had an influential voice in New Haven. In 2015, the Community Foundation for Greater New Haven reported that "immigrants are critical assets and are committed to making New Haven a more welcoming community." In the midst of the occasional urban chaos, the *Record Journal* in Meriden had a reassuring report in March 2015 about local nature: Two bald eagles nested along the Quinnipiac River in Hampden, a sign the local bald eagle population was increasing. The news story quoted a wildlife biologist that the return of the eagles was a sign that pollution of state waterways had decreased. A year later, the bald eagles returned to the river bank, an indication they were planning a family.

The 3rd Congressional District covers the New Haven metropolitan area, and extends to the outskirts of the former industrial cities of Bridgeport, Waterbury and Meriden. The metro area has long since spread beyond the narrow city limits into what were once Yankee villages and countryside. The suburb of Hamden has made it onto the CNNMoney list of the 100 best places to live. Politically, the 3rd was once a marginal district, regularly changing partisan hands in the 1980s. It is now strongly Democratic, though slightly less so than the Hartford-based 1st District. President Barack Obama got 63 percent of the vote in each of his campaigns. But in a notable twist, Hillary Clinton got only 56 percent in 2016, while the Democratic presidential vote in the adjacent 4th District, which is more upscale, rose from 55 percent to 60 percent.

FOURTH DISTRICT

Jim Himes (D)

Elected 2008, 5th term; b. Jul 05, 1966, Lima, Peru; Harvard University, B.A.; Oxford University (England), M.Phil; Presbyterian; Married (Mary Himes); 2 children.

Elected Office: Greenwich Board of Estimate & Taxation, 2006-2007.

Professional Career: Financial analyst & Vice President., Goldman Sachs, 1990-2002; Chairman, Greenwich Housing Authority, 2003-2006; Vice President., Enterprise Community Partners, 2004-2008.

DC Office: 1227 LHOB 20515, 202-225-5541, Fax: 202-225-9629, himes.house.gov.

State Offices: Bridgeport, 866-453-0028; Stamford, 203-353-9400.

Committees: *Financial Services*: Capital Markets, Securities & Investment, Terrorism & Illicit Finance. *Permanent Select on Intelligence*.

Group Ratings

	ADA	ACLU	AFL-CIO	LCV	ITI	COC	HAFA	ACU	CFG	FRC
2016	-	88%	-	97%	83%	57%	14%	4%	4%	0%
2015	80%	C	96%	89%	C	55%	C	8%	3%	0%

Almanac Ratings 2015

	Economy	Social	Foreign	Composite
Liberal	76%	94%	78%	83%
Conservative	24%	6%	22%	17%

Key Votes of the 114th Congress

1. Keystone Pipeline	N	5. Puerto Rico Debt	Y	9. Offenses by Aliens	Y
2. Trade Deals	Y	6. Medical Marijuana	Y	10. Troops in Iraq	Y
3. Export-Import Bank	Y	7. Sanctuary Cities	N	11. Homeland Security $$	Y
4. Debt Ceiling Increase	Y	8. Armor-piercing Bullets	N	12. Trade Adjustment aid	Y

Election Results

Election	Name (Party)	Vote (%)		Cand. Spent	Ind. Exp. Support	Ind. Exp. Oppose
2016 General	Jim Himes (D)	187,811	(60%)	$846,230		
	John Shaban (R)	125,724	(40%)	$157,331		

Prior winning percentages: 2014 (54%), 2012 (60%), 2010 (52%), 2008 (50%)

Jim Himes, a Democrat elected in 2008, is a former investment banker who puts his understanding of Wall Street to use at the Financial Services Committee and in conversations with colleagues. Given the growing hostility of many Democrats to deep-pocket financiers - especially hedge funds, which are based predominantly in his district - his influence in the Democratic Caucus has faced some limitations. But he has found ways to assert himself as a business-friendly Democrat, a dwindling cohort that likely needs to expand for the party to regain House control.

Though he represents one of the wealthiest areas of the country, Himes grew up in different surroundings. Born in Lima Peru, he spent his early years in Peru and Colombia, where his father worked for the Ford Foundation. Around the time of his 10th birthday, after his parents divorced, he came to the United States with his mother and two sisters and settled in Pennington, New Jersey. He speaks fluent Spanish and maintains a deep interest in Latin America. Himes earned his undergraduate degree from Harvard University and was a Rhodes scholar at Oxford. When he returned to the United States, he worked for Goldman Sachs as a financial analyst. On Sept. 11, 2001, he was at his office in Lower Manhattan and did volunteer work with ambulance crews. After 12 years, he left the investment house in 2002 as a vice president. The following year, he joined Enterprise Community Partners, a Columbia Maryland-based nonprofit dedicated to alleviating urban poverty. Beginning in 2004, he managed its offices in the Northeast.

Like many other Wall Street executives, Himes raised a family with his wife Mary in the affluent suburb of Greenwich. He became active in the town Democratic committee, and served as chairman from 2003 to 2007. He was a campaign volunteer in 2006 for Democrat Diane Farrell, who finished about 7,000 votes behind Rep. Christopher Shays, a moderate Republican who had withstood repeated Democratic campaign assaults. The following April, Himes announced his own challenge against Shays. Himes set a torrid fundraising pace, aided in large measure by his Wall Street connections. The Democratic Congressional Campaign Committee made him a top prospect. After easily dispatching a minor challenger in the primary, Himes focused on Shays and the George W. Bush administration and attempted to link the two over the Iraq war. Himes embraced the national Democratic establishment, frequently reminding voters that he was running with presidential nominee Barack Obama. In the past, Shays' moderate record and Capitol Hill seniority helped him weather political storms. But in 2008, the enthusiasm for Obama provided a powerful final push that gave Himes a 51%-48% win. He comfortably took the district's urban centers and managed to stay competitive in the affluent suburbs that tend to break Republican.

Himes has taken a centrist approach in Congress, supporting Obama's major priorities but also asserting his independence on behalf of his district. He riled some Democratic leaders when he joined several other junior lawmakers in 2010 to form a working group to propose large spending cuts in defense, energy, housing, and agriculture. In March 2012, he was one of 22 Democrats who supported a failed amendment to implement the recommendations of the Simpson-Bowles deficit reduction commission.

On the Financial Services Committee, he has engaged on district-related issues. When the committee took up what became the sweeping Dodd-Frank financial overhaul bill, he helped craft a provision regulating the complex financial instruments known as derivatives. Consumer advocates criticized Himes and other centrist Democrats, accusing them of watering down derivatives controls passed by the Senate in an effort to appease Wall Street. Himes argued that the bill took significant steps to crack down on abuses at investment firms.

During the furor in 2009 over bonuses paid to executives at AIG International and other firms receiving federal rescue money, he cosponsored a measure requiring all future compensation to be performance-based; it passed the House but stalled in the Senate. He routinely speaks with colleagues about the industry. "He can explain things like derivatives and credit default swaps in plain English so [members] can have some degree of fluency in this, which is extremely helpful," fellow Connecticut Democrat Joe Courtney told the *Connecticut Post*.

Following the 2014 election, he failed in his bid to be Nancy Pelosi's choice to chair the Democratic Congressional Campaign Committee. She gave the post to Rep. Ben Ray Lujan of New Mexico, who was more junior but represented a much lower income district than Himes, who had been the DCCC's finance chairman. An anti-Wall Street activist praised Pelosi for "rejecting the Wall Street wing of the Democratic Party."

Himes has worked on national-security issues as a member of the Select Intelligence Committee, and filed a bill that states that only Congress has the power to declare and wage war. After the 2016 election, he became chairman of the House's New Democrat Coalition, a self-described "fiscally responsible, moderate bloc of lawmakers." He said that he would defend and support Americans "who get left behind."

He has occasionally voiced his frustration with Congress. In a June 2016 op-ed piece in *The Washington Post*, he wrote that he walked out of the House chamber during a "moment of silence" following the gun massacre that killed 49 in an Orlando night club. "If the House of Representatives had a solitary moral fiber, even a wisp of human empathy…" he wrote, "We'd invite parents and partners and siblings up from Orlando, and ask them to speak, openly, rawly, honestly about their pain. We'd listen. And maybe, just maybe, we'd hear."

Republicans hoped to unseat Himes without Obama on the ballot. In 2010, against state Sen. Dan Debicella, Himes portrayed him as an extremist and won 53%-47%. Debicella tried again in 2014, and the outcome was similar. Himes won 54%-46%. He got 71% in Bridgeport and Norwalk, which cast 21% of the total vote. Debicella won seven of the other nine communities and hill towns, but that upscale vote was not enough to overcome the urban support for Himes.

Southwest Connecticut: Bridgeport, Stamford

Population		**Race and Ethnicity**		**Income**	
Total	732,795	White	62.8%	Median Income	$86,773 (24 out of 435)
Land area	461	Black	11.6%		
Pop/ sq mi	1590.5	Latino	18.4%	Under $50,000	31.3%
Born in state	42.9%	Asian	5.1%	$50,000-$99,999	24.3%
		Two races	1.6%	$100,000-$199,999	23.8%
Age Groups		Other	0.5%	$200,000 or more	20.6%
Under 18	24.5%			Poverty Rate	9.3%
18-34	20.2%	**Education**			
35-64	41.5%	H.S grad or less	31.2%	**Health Insurance**	
Over 64	13.8%	Some college	20.6%	With health insurance coverage	89.2%
Work		College Degree, 4 yr	26.8%		
		Post grad	21.5%		
White Collar	45.5%			**Public Assistance**	
Sales and Service	41.0%	**Military**		Cash public assistance income	2.5%
Blue Collar	13.4%	Veteran	5.0%		
Government	9.5%	Active Duty	0.0%	Food stamp/SNAP benefits	9.4%

Voter Turnout			
2015 Total Citizens 18+	474,290	2016 House Turnout as % CVAP	66%
2016 House turnout	313,540	2014 House Turnout as % CVAP	43%

2012 Presidential Vote		
Barack Obama	170,827	(55%)
Mitt Romney	136,527	(44%)

2016 Presidential Vote		
Hillary Clinton	195,494	(60%)
Donald Trump	119,976	(37%)
Gary Johnson	9,144	(3%)

Cook Partisan Voting Index: D+7

No one in colonial America imagined that southern Connecticut would someday lodge one of the largest concentrations of wealth in the world. The soil was stony, the terrain unaccommodating and the harbors not as convenient as those in New York, Rhode Island and Massachusetts. For 200 years, this was the home of unnoticed Yankee farmers, sailors, and tinkerers. Before starting his famous circus, P.T. Barnum was involved in abolitionist causes and cast a vote for the 13th Amendment while representing Fairfield in the state legislature; he also served a term as Bridgeport's mayor. Around the same time, rich New Yorkers began taking the train north to country houses in Connecticut. In the 20th century, Greenwich and other Yankee villages clustered around commuter railroad stations became the home of New York's elite.

Starting in the 1950s, New York City-based executives, eager to minimize their commutes and avoid New York's income taxes, moved their headquarters to Greenwich and farther into Fairfield County. Greenwich, sometimes referred to as "Wall Street by the Sea" for its proliferation of hedge fund offices and financial firms, is closest to New York and commands the highest commercial rents of all these places. But not all is well in the corporate suites: General Electric, which has been headquartered in Fairfield, in 2016 announced plans to move to Boston - in part, to escape high taxes.

The 4th Congressional District is the wealthiest district in the nation's wealthiest state. The district covers most of the southwest corner of Connecticut along Long Island Sound, from industrial Bridgeport, now the state's largest city, to affluent Greenwich. The district's waterfront towns include bustling and pricey Stamford, woodsy Darien, modest Norwalk, artsy-craftsy Westport, and Fairfield. In low-income Bridgeport, some downtown revitalization ensued when the state-financed Harbor Yard sports complex opened for minor league baseball. This social disparity within Fairfield County has ranked the 4th District as the fourth highest in the nation in income inequality, according to a January 2016 *Bloomberg BusinessWeek* listing. In an attempt to adjust the balance, local developers have sought to encourage more millennials to move into the area. In late 2016, construction began on a roughly $500 million project in Norwalk to replace the swing Walk Bridge, which was built in the 19th century. The Norwalk bridge is one of four movable bridges on the main line to New Haven, all in need of major repair. Additional plans to redevelop downtown and the waterfront in Bridgeport have been making slow progress, local leaders reported in 2016. In Stamford, financial constraints became apparent when a $500 million plan to upgrade and expand the train station was abandoned in October 2016 after state officials said the real estate and construction team failed to meet requirements.

For many years, the heavily affluent suburbs outvoted Bridgeport and elected moderate-to-liberal Republicans such as Clare Boothe Luce, Lowell Weicker and Chris Shays to Congress. But the influence of Christian conservatives in the national GOP repelled Episcopalians and other mainline Protestants, and they have been increasingly voting Democratic. At the same time, the district has been diversifying. It is now only 57 percent non-Hispanic white, the lowest percentage in the state. After President Barack Obama's share of the vote here dropped from 60 percent in 2008 to 55 percent in 2012, support for Hillary Clinton in 2016 climbed back to 60 percent. For now, this socially liberal and economically flush district remains comfortably Democratic - and largely hostile to President Donald Trump.

FIFTH DISTRICT

Elizabeth Esty (D)

Elected 2012, 3rd term; b. Aug 25, 1959, Oak Park, IL; L'Institut d'études politiques, Paris (France); Harvard University, A.B., 1981; Yale University Law School (CT), J.D., 1985; Congregationalist; Married (Dan Esty); 3 children.

Elected Office: Cheshire Town Council, 2005-2008; CT House, 2008-2010.

Professional Career: Clerk, Judge Robert Keeton of MA; Practicing attorney, 1986-1990; Adjunct Professional, American University, 1991-1992; Health care policy analyst, 1990-2002; Sr. research scholar, Yale Law School, 1994-2009.

DC Office: 221 CHOB 20515, 202-225-4476, esty.house.gov.

State Offices: New Britain, 860-223-8412.

Committees: *Science, Space & Technology*: Research & Technology. *Transportation & Infrastructure*: Highways & Transit, Railroads, Pipelines & Hazardous Materials, Water Resources & Environment. *Veterans' Affairs*: Disability Assistance & Memorial Affairs (RMM).

Group Ratings

	ADA	ACLU	AFL-CIO	LCV	ITI	COC	HAFA	ACU	CFG	FRC
2016	-	76%	-	100%	67%	57%	14%	0%	0%	0%
2015	80%	C	100%	100%	C	45%	C	4%	0%	0%

Almanac Ratings 2015

	Economy	Social	Foreign	Composite
Liberal	82%	94%	84%	87%
Conservative	18%	6%	16%	13%

Key Votes of the 114th Congress

1. Keystone Pipeline	N	5. Puerto Rico Debt	Y	9. Offenses by Aliens	Y
2. Trade Deals	N	6. Medical Marijuana	Y	10. Troops in Iraq	Y
3. Export-Import Bank	Y	7. Sanctuary Cities	N	11. Homeland Security $$	Y
4. Debt Ceiling Increase	Y	8. Armor-piercing Bullets	N	12. Trade Adjustment aid	Y

Election Results

Election	Name (Party)	Vote (%)	Cand. Spent	Ind. Exp. Support	Ind. Exp. Oppose
2016 General	Elizabeth Esty (D)	179,252 (58%)	$1,136,787		
	Clay Cope (R)	129,801 (42%)	$92,055	$15,000	

Prior winning percentages: 2014 (53%), 2012 (51%)

Democratic lawyer Elizabeth Esty, first elected in the 5th District in 2012, initially was challenged by two tough campaigns and she was at the epicenter of a national debate on gun control with her representation of a town that suffered great tragedy. Esty is more of a policy wonk and has not sought the spotlight at home. She was prominent in the House Democratic sit-in that protested the Republican stand against gun control. As with most of New England, Republicans have turned their campaign attention elsewhere.

Esty was born in Oak Park, Illinois, but moved around growing up because of her father's work as a construction engineer. She described herself as the latest in "a long line of feisty women" on her mother's side, including her grandmother, who lobbied for civil rights. After graduating from high school in Minnesota, she came east to attend Harvard University, where she met her husband, Dan. After Yale Law School, she was a clerk for U.S. District Judge Robert Keeton of Massachusetts. She moved to Washington to work for the large law firm Sidley Austin, where she wrote legal briefs in several cases that defended abortion rights. After teaching and some policy work on health care, she moved to Connecticut in 1994 when her husband started an environmental law and policy program at Yale.

Her first elected position was on the Cheshire Town Council, where she backed tax relief for senior citizens. In 2008, Esty was elected as a state representative, but her tenure was short-lived. She voted to abolish the death penalty after two convicts killed three people in Cheshire in one of the highest-profile crimes in state history. She lost re-election to a Republican who backed capital punishment.

When Rep. Chris Murphy ran for the Senate in 2012, state House Speaker Chris Donovan was the early Democratic favorite. But a pay-to-play scandal engulfed two of Donovan's top aides. With the help of a $500,000 self-loan to her campaign, Esty brushed past Donovan and businessman Dan Roberti in the primary. She led Donovan, 45%-32%. In the general election against Sen. Andrew Roraback, her economic agenda promised infrastructure improvements, training of future manufacturers and increased access to credit for small businesses. The Democratic Congressional Campaign Committee went on the attack, running ads saying that Roraback would "fit right in" with images of strident conservatives in Congress. Roraback, who supported abortion rights and same-sex marriage, denounced the ads as "outright lies." Esty maintained an edge in fundraising and was endorsed by *The New York Times*, which pointed to her capital punishment vote in the state legislature as "the kind of political fortitude Washington desperately needs." She won, 51%-49%, with a margin of more than 7,000 votes.

Just before Esty took office, she was confronted with a massive tragedy in her district: the December 2012 Sandy Hook school shooting in Newtown in which 26 people were killed, including 20 children.

On the day of the shooting, she rushed to Newtown from a freshman orientation session at Harvard University. "It's refocused my agenda; I know that," she told *The Connecticut Mirror*. President Barack Obama attended a local prayer vigil two days later, and described that day as the worst of his presidency. A day after she took office, Esty was named one of 12 vice chairs of the House Democrats' Gun Violence Prevention Task Force. "The status quo is unacceptable, and action is long overdue," she said, and later added that she was "very encouraged" by Obama's commitment to "real, meaningful change." Among other steps, she cosponsored a bill requiring background checks for all commercial gun sales. But, as often has been the case with firearms legislation, nothing happened in Congress. Esty won praise inside the Democratic Caucus and from advocacy groups for her efforts. She voiced frustration over the stalemate. "We should be ashamed," she said. During the June 2016 House sit-in on guns, she spent time seated on the floor next to civil-rights icon Rep. John Lewis of Georgia. She protested that the House had not voted on a single gun-control measure since she was elected. She repeated her call for universal background checks.

As a junior member of the House minority party, she had few legislative accomplishments. Congress enacted her Collinsville Renewable Energy Production Act, which required the Federal Energy Regulatory Commission to reinstate expired licenses for hydropower dams at two old mills in the town on the Farmington River. "We have the opportunity to reinvent a dormant dam into a dam producing local, clean energy," she told the House. In March 2016, the House overwhelmingly passed her bill to encourage women entrepreneurs in science and math.

Esty showed occasional independence from her party. When she voted in 2013 for a Republican bill to delay for one year the mandate for coverage in the Affordable Care Act, the liberal advocacy group moveon.org launched online petitions asking Esty and other Democrats to explain their vote. She said she was responding to constituent requests for more time. In 2015, Esty was among 33 Democrats who voted to extend certain tax breaks. "Predictability is important, which is why I voted to make these tax incentives permanent and give local business owners the peace of mind they deserve," she explained to the *Connecticut Mirror*.

In 2014, Esty faced another competitive opponent, wealthy Litchfield real-estate businessman Mark Greenberg, who had lost the Republican primary in 2010 and 2012. She broadcast an ad claiming that Greenberg was seeking to end guaranteed Social Security payments, which the *Hartford Courant* determined was false. They disagreed on other issues, including the death penalty, abortion and gun control. Greenberg self-financed more than $1.1 million of his $1.8 million campaign. Esty spent nearly $3 million, and had more than $600,000 in national party aid. She won, 53%-46%, with nearly two-thirds of the combined vote in the urban centers of Meriden, New Britain and Waterbury. In 2016, she outspent Republican challenger Clay Cope, the First Selectman of Sherman, by nearly $2 million to $100,000, and increased her margin to 58%-42%. That was close to Murphy's high-water mark during his three terms representing the district.

Western and Central Connecticut: Waterbury, Danbury, New Britain

Population		**Race and Ethnicity**		**Income**	
Total	715,022	White	71.3%	Median Income	$67,805 (79 out of 435)
Land area	1,248	Black	5.9%		
Pop/ sq mi	572.9	Latino	17.2%	Under $50,000	37.6%
Born in state	55.7%	Asian	3.5%	$50,000-$99,999	29.7%
		Two races	1.6%	$100,000-$199,999	24.4%
Age Groups		Other	0.5%	$200,000 or more	8.5%
Under 18	22.2%			Poverty Rate	11.2%
18-34	20.1%	**Education**			
35-64	42.4%	H.S grad or less	39.9%	**Health Insurance**	
Over 64	15.3%	Some college	25.4%	With health insurance coverage	91.6%
		College Degree, 4 yr	19.7%		
Work		Post grad	15.1%		
White Collar	39.7%			**Public Assistance**	
Sales and Service	41.1%	**Military**		Cash public assistance income	3.3%
Blue Collar	19.3%	Veteran	7.0%		
Government	12.6%	Active Duty	0.0%	Food stamp/SNAP benefits	13.0%

Voter Turnout			
2015 Total Citizens 18+	509,791	2016 House Turnout as % CVAP	61%
2016 House turnout	309,082	2014 House Turnout as % CVAP	41%

2012 Presidential Vote		
Barack Obama	164,627	(54%)
Mitt Romney	139,324	(45%)

2016 Presidential Vote		
Hillary Clinton	161,142	(50%)
Donald Trump	147,901	(46%)
Gary Johnson	9,356	(3%)

Cook Partisan Voting Index: D+2

Over the years, Connecticut's stony soil has become home to some of the most affluent people in the world. This is true in the hills of northwest Connecticut, distant from the interstates and from Connecticut's small urban capital of Hartford. In Litchfield County are exquisite Yankee towns like Washington and Kent, where Connecticut's ship owners once invested their accumulated capital in factories and mills. They now are considered the "anti-Hamptons," a weekend country-home mecca for ultra-rich New Yorkers seeking to avoid the glitz of Southampton and East Hampton. Avon and Simsbury have become comfortable bedroom communities to Hartford.

Not far away are grittier parts, small industrial cities like New Britain, America's ball-bearing capital for years; Meriden, which turned from making ivory combs, clocks and cutlery to producing electrical signaling equipment, biotech filters and nuclear instruments; and Waterbury, once the nation's largest producer of brass. Like many manufacturing centers, these towns have fallen on hard times, though there have been recovery efforts. In September 2016, Meriden opened a new urban park and flood-control plain. Danbury was once the nation's leading producer of hats, and has become a center for clean energy technology. In December 2016, Danbury-based FuelCell Energy - which manufactures and serves technology for clean power plants - laid off 96 of its roughly 600 workers.

East of Danbury is the small town of Newtown, where gunman Adam Lanza shocked the nation and ignited debates - but little action - over gun control, care for the mentally ill and the marketing of violence to the young when he killed 26 people, 20 of them children, at Sandy Hook Elementary School, in December 2012. The old building was demolished out of respect for the victims, and a new school opened in August 2016.

The 5th Congressional District of Connecticut covers much of the northwestern corner of the state, including the northern towns of Fairfield County. It has two arms that reach into the hills of central Connecticut - one to Democratic Meriden and the other to the affluent and Republican-leaning Farmington Valley suburbs of Hartford. It has been a Democratically leaning district. But Republicans have been competitive here. Barack Obama won it by 14 points in 2008, and by a narrower 54%-45% margin in 2012. Hillary Clinton's margin fell further, to 50%-46%. She won the four old industrial cities, but Donald Trump took most of the towns west of Avon and Farmington and from Litchfield to the east.

★ DELAWARE ★

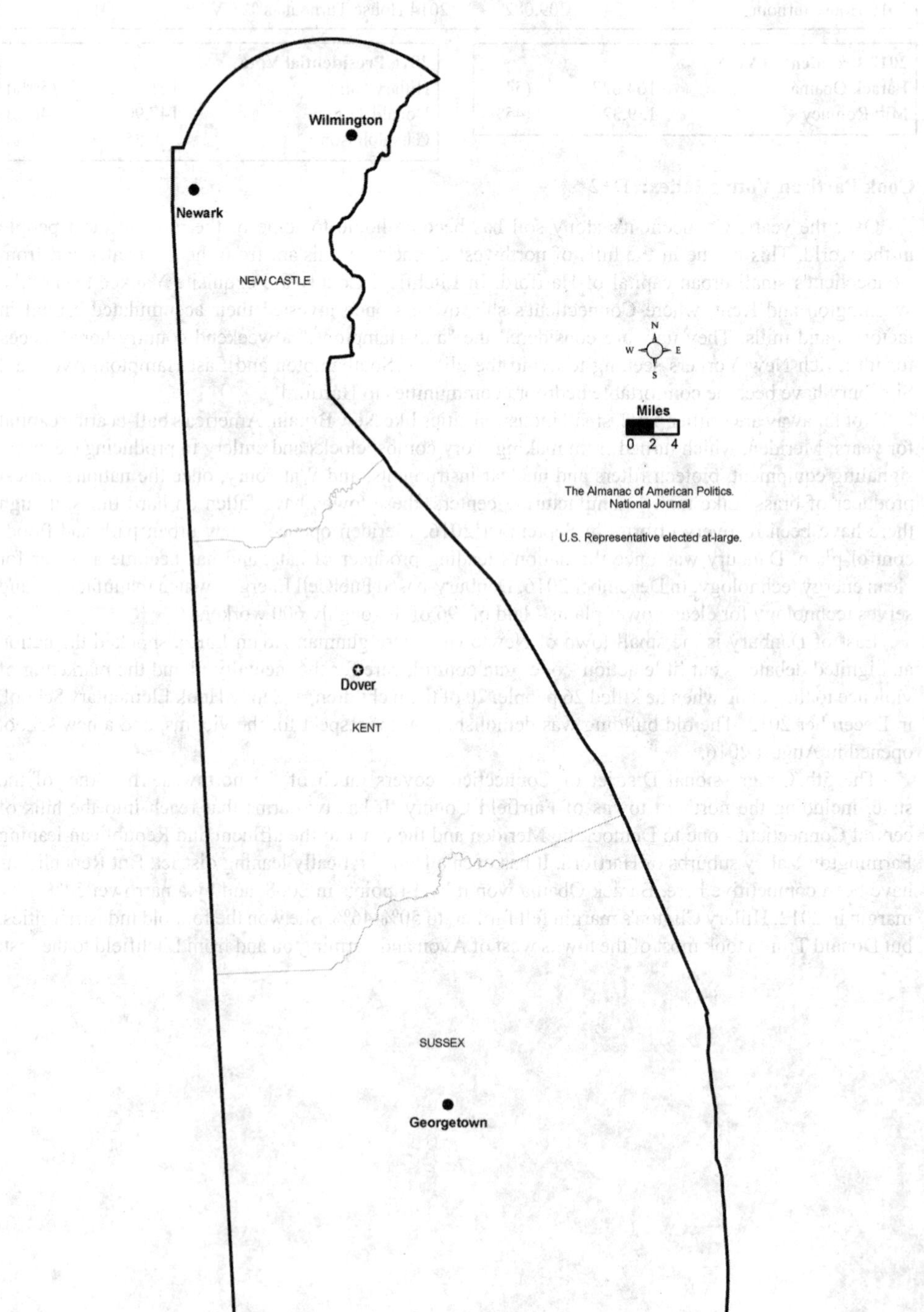
Wilmington
Newark
NEW CASTLE
N
W
E
S
Miles
0 2 4
The Almanac of American Politics.
National Journal
U.S. Representative elected at-large.
Dover
KENT
SUSSEX
Georgetown

On December 7, 1787, 30 Delawareans met at the Golden Fleece Tavern in Dover and voted unanimously to ratify the Constitution. And thus, the second smallest state in area became, as it likes to boast, the First State. This small corner of America has a long history. The mouth of the Delaware River was explored by Henry Hudson, and the Dutch and Swedes built settlements on the west bank in the 1630s. But the three counties of Delaware owe their separate existence to the politics of the proprietors of William Penn's colony to the north and to Delawareans' determination even before July 4, 1776, to declare independence not only from Britain but also from Pennsylvania.

Throughout most of its history, Delaware has been unusually affluent. Its income levels during the early 20th century were the nation's highest, and they remain close to the top today. The many members of the du Pont family maintain beautiful cobblestone mansions in its chateau country, and the charming Brandywine Valley, which spills across the 12-mile semicircular border with Pennsylvania, includes a trove of refined tourist attractions. The Mason-Dixon Line forms Delaware's western border with Maryland, and the state has both Northern and Southern heritages. It was still a slave state when the Civil War broke out, but 92 percent of its blacks were free. Today, its population is 21 percent black, almost twice the national average; in 2016, Lisa Blunt Rochester became the first African American (and first woman) to represent Delaware in Congress. On his train ride to Washington in January 2009, newly elected President Barack Obama, joined by native son Joe Biden, paid tribute to Delaware's Underground Railroad and diplomatically did not mention that Abraham Lincoln, during his 1861 train ride to Washington, decided not to risk a stop in slaveholding Delaware.

The state today has immigrant communities in the Wilmington area, and it has Southern-accented farmers in Kent and Sussex counties, plus Latino migrants working in its chicken plants (chickens outnumber people by 300 to 1 and produce tons of processed chicken dung known as "broiler litter") as well as in its beach-tourism industry (residents of the Washington, D.C., area flock to such Atlantic Ocean resorts as Rehoboth Beach and Bethany Beach during the summer). The state is 10 percent Hispanic, two points higher than neighboring Pennsylvania, and 4 percent Asian. Newark has grown from a country crossroads to a small city as the University of Delaware has expanded. Well-preserved 18th century buildings line the streets of New Castle, the capital from 1704 to 1777; it is the home of the First State National Historical Park, a collection of vintage buildings dedicated by Obama in 2013, making Delaware the last state to secure a National Park Service unit.

For much of the last two centuries, the central focus of Delaware's economy was the business started by Éleuthère Irénée du Pont, the practical-minded son of a dreamy, idealistic French immigrant. He built a gunpowder mill on the banks of Brandywine Creek in 1802-the first enterprise of the du Pont family. Over time it became one of America's great munitions and chemical companies. It switched from gunpowder to dynamite in the 1880s, and the company grew especially rapidly during World War I, generating so much capital that it bought a large share of General Motors stock in 1914 and for 30 years controlled GM, which was for much of that time the nation's largest corporation. DuPont capital also financed what was arguably the world's finest research and development program. In the years on either side of World War II, DuPont prospered by bringing to the consumer and industrial markets new synthetics and plastics such as rayon, nylon, synthetic dyes, cellophane, Lucite, Teflon, and Dacron: "Better Living Through Chemistry." But just before Christmas 2015, DuPont announced that because of its merger with Dow Chemical the company would be shedding 1,700 jobs in the state, or 28 percent of its Delaware workforce, after already having already undergone rounds of belt-tightening in the state. The company decided, however, to keep two of the merged entity's three subsidiary headquarters in Delaware.

Delaware has had an outsized impact on national policy. In the late 19th century, the state passed pioneering laws of incorporation, giving more flexibility and power to managers and owners. Most of the companies in the *Fortune* 500 and on the New York Stock Exchange and Nasdaq are incorporated in Delaware. Their legal births take place in a federal-style building near the Capitol in Dover, which means that much of the nation's corporate law, especially on mergers and acquisitions, is made in Delaware's Chancery Court. And one of their primary residences is 1209 North Orange St. in Wilmington, a "nondescript, two-story office building" just north of the city's "rundown downtown," as *The Guardian* put it. In that unassuming locale, the newspaper reported, 285,000 companies are domiciled – "more than any other known address in the world" – including Apple, American Airlines, Coca-Cola and Walmart, as well as companies started by both Hillary Clinton and Donald Trump. "We have 378 entities registered in the state of Delaware, meaning I pay you a lot of money, folks," Trump said at a campaign rally in Delaware. "I don't feel at all guilty, OK?"

Delaware also helped foster a new industry: credit cards. In 1981, Republican Gov. Pete du Pont pushed through a law abolishing Delaware's usury laws and lowering its bank franchise tax. Inflation was high, and banks were looking for a state with no limit on interest rates to locate their credit card operations. MBNA Corporation moved there from Maryland in 1982, invented the affinity card in 1983, and became the nation's largest credit card issuer; its chief executive officer, Charles Cawley, replaced the du Pont family as Delaware's most visible philanthropist and community leader. Cawley retired in 2003, and Bank of America acquired MBNA in 2005. Two years later, the financial crisis hit the credit card business hard, helping to send Delaware into recession. The troubles in the domestic auto industry reverberated as well. More than 1,000 people lost their jobs when Chrysler closed its plant in Newark in 2008, and Obama administration efforts to locate the Fisker electric car plant there foundered. White-collar sectors have also lost thousands of jobs since 2001 in the wake of corporate consolidation, though JPMorgan Chase said it plans to add 1,800 jobs in the state by 2019. On paper, at least, Delaware continues to have a strong job market; its unemployment rate peaked during the Great Recession at 8.7 percent, which was well under the national average, and by late 2016 was 4.3 percent, still below the much-improved national average. Delaware's population growth has seemingly been unaffected. The state grew by 18 percent in the 1990s, 15 percent from 2000 to 2010, and has risen by 6 percent so far this decade. One reason has been a flow of retirees from Pennsylvania, Maryland and New Jersey; Delaware now has the 11th largest population of seniors of any state.

Delaware's state budget relies heavily on unconventional revenue sources. Repossession of unclaimed property accounts for 15 percent of the state's revenue – a cash stream so alluring that 23 states are going to the Supreme Court to try to claw it back. The state also gets 3 percent of its budget from turnpike tolls ($4 for just 11 miles on heavily trafficked I-95), 22 percent from corporate and franchise taxes and 7 percent from the lottery and slot machines. It allows betting on football parley cards at racetracks, bars and restaurants. "The organizing principle of Delaware government is to subsidize its people at the rest of the country's expense," grumbled journalist Jonathan Chait in *The New Republic*. But this has been popular at home. Exporting taxes has allowed Delaware to be one of the five states with no sales tax, and its property taxes are among the nation's lowest. A bipartisan mix of governors has lowered the income tax several times in recent years.

From the 1950s through the 1980s, the state produced robust two-party politics in which tiny Delaware's vote mirrored that of the nation. But since the 1990s, Delaware has trended Democratic. Delaware has not elected a Republican governor since 1988. Democrat Jack Markell, then state treasurer, effectively clinched the governorship when he defeated Lt. Gov. John Carney in the 2008 Democratic primary, and was easily reelected in 2012. In 2016, Carney, by then serving as the state's sole House member, was elected to succeed him, 58%-39%.

From 1972 to 2000, Delaware had a bipartisan presence in the Senate, with Republican William Roth, first elected in 1970, getting along well with Democrat Biden, first elected in 1972 at age 29 (he turned the constitutional age of 30 before the term started). But Roth, at 79, was defeated in 2000 by former Gov. Tom Carper, who has been reelected twice with ease. After Biden won the vice presidency in 2008, his seat went to Democrat Chris Coons. The state House turned Democratic in 2008, joining the state Senate and the governorship for unified control. During this period, the state pursued generally liberal policies. Delaware's Supreme Court abolished the death penalty, the state approved same-sex marriage and transgender rights, and Markell signed a marijuana decriminalization bill, with full legalization being floated for the 2017 legislative agenda. Biden remained the state's preeminent political figure, even after leaving the vice president's mansion and transitioning into dual professorships at the University of Delaware and the University of Pennsylvania, located in the state he actually represented in the Senate and the one for which he was often called the "third senator." But hope for a new generation of Delaware political leaders named Biden was tragically cut short when his son -- former state attorney general, decorated combat veteran and presumed gubernatorial candidate Beau -- died of brain cancer in 2015.

The 2016 election provided some notes of caution for Democrats. Hillary Clinton won the state, but her margin was 11 points, well short of Barack Obama's 19 in 2012. Donald Trump even won two of the state's three counties, albeit the smallest and most rural -- Kent, which had backed Obama in 2012, and Sussex. In each of Delaware's three counties, Clinton's vote total was steady or slightly down, but Trump consistently pushed above Mitt Romney's 2012 total – up 10,000 in Sussex, 5,000 in Kent and even 4,000 in New Castle, the urban and suburban linchpin of Clinton's win.

Delaware elections are not usually bitter. Thanks to the state's small size, politics remain intimate. Personal campaigning is important, and successful Delaware politicians are almost always nice people; they couldn't get elected otherwise. Historically, "the Delaware Way" prevails -- a habit of party establishments exerting tight control and minimizing ideological and personal conflicts. (This made Carper's decision to challenge the long-tenured Roth in 2000 a bold and atypical move.) There's even a unique custom, dating back to 1792, of "Return Day." On the Thursday after an election, winning and losing candidates go to the Sussex County seat of Georgetown and ride together in carriages to receive the bipartisan cheers of the voters and, literally, bury a hatchet in a box of Lewes Beach sand. Not a bad example for the other 49 states.

Population		**Race and Ethnicity**		**Income**	
Total	926,454	White	63.9%	Median Income	$60,509 (14 out of 50)
Land area	1,949	Black	21.1%		
Pop/ sq mi	475.5	Latino	8.7%	Under $50,000	41.2%
Born in state	45.7%	Asian	3.6%	$50,000-$99,999	32.6%
		Two races	2.2%	$100,000-$199,999	21.0%
Age Groups		Other	0.5%	$200,000 or more	5.1%
Under 18	22.0%			Poverty Rate	12.0%
18-34	20.0%	**Education**			
35-64	39.2%	H.S grad or less	42.8%	**Health Insurance**	
Over 64	15.9%	Some college	27.2%	With health insurance coverage	91.8%
		College Degree, 4 yr	17.8%		
Work		Post grad	12.2%		
White Collar	38.4%			**Public Assistance**	
Sales and Service	42.7%	**Military**		Cash public assistance income	2.5%
Blue Collar	19.0%	Veteran	9.9%		
Government	14.5%	Active Duty	0.4%	Food stamp/SNAP benefits	13.0%

Voter Turnout			
2015 Total Citizens 18+	681,606	2016 Pres Turnout as % CVAP	65%
2016 Pres Votes	443,814	2012 Pres Turnout as % CVAP	64%

Legislature	
Senate:	11D, 10R
House:	25D, 16R

Presidential Politics

2016 Democratic Primary		
Hillary Clinton (D)	55,954	(60%)
Bernie Sanders (D)	36,662	(39%)
2016 Republican Primary		
Donald Trump (R)	42,472	(61%)
John Kasich (R)	14,225	(20%)
Ted Cruz (R)	11,110	(16%)

2016 Presidential Vote		
Hillary Clinton (D)	235,603	(53%)
Donald Trump (R)	185,127	(42%)
Gary Johnson (L)	14,757	(3%)
2012 Presidential Vote		
Barack Obama (D)	242,584	(59%)
Mitt Romney (R)	165,484	(40%)

Cook Partisan Voting Index: D+6

Delaware used to be a presidential bellwether: It mimicked the popular vote winner of every presidential election voted from 1952 to 2000, the longest winning streak of any state. But starting with the disputed election of 2000, this relatively wealthy state also began to vote significantly more Democratic than the national average. While Al Gore won the 2000 popular vote by about half a percentage point nationwide, he carried Delaware by 13 points. But lately, that Democratic margin has dropped from a high of 25 points in 2008 to roughly 11 in 2016 when Hillary Clinton defeated Donald Trump 53%-42%. In a sense, tiny Delaware is two states: New Castle County and its suburbs dominate the state and nearly three out of five ballots in presidential election are cast there. New Castle, like affluent parts of other major metropolitan areas, starting in the middle 1990s, tilted toward the Democrats and away from the Republicans on cultural issues, and it voted 2-to-1 or more for Obama in 2008 and 2012. The state's largest city, Wilmington, has a majority African-American population. In 2016, New Castle voted for Clinton, 62%-33%. Lower Delaware, the other part of the state, is made up of more rural Kent and Sussex counties, the latter of which is also home to the state's popular beach towns. That area votes Republican and this year it backed Trump over Clinton, 55%-40%. Four years earlier it only sided with Mitt Romney 52%-47% over Barack Obama. Most Delaware voters still see plenty of ads, because in the past three elections, all candidates have targeted Pennsylvania, and New Castle and Kent are in the Philadelphia media market. (Sussex is in the Salisbury, Maryland, market.)

In 2016, Delaware held its primary on April 26 along with four other states and was overshadowed by the more pivotal contest in next-door Pennsylvania. Trump defeated Ohio Gov. John Kasich 61%-20%, winning New Castle by 51%-27% and lower Delaware by a whopping 69%-14%. More than 65,000 votes were cast in the GOP primary, more than double the amount in 2012. The Democratic contest was a bit more competitive: Clinton dispatched Vermont Sen. Bernie Sanders 60%-39%, winning each section of the state by roughly the same margin. Democratic turnout was more than 92,000 votes, only 4,000 less than the mark set in 2008 when Obama defeated Clinton 53%-42%, winning by a big margin in both black neighborhoods and affluent suburbs in New Castle County.

Congressional Districts

115th Congress Lineup	1D	**114th Congress Lineup**	1D

Governor

John Carney (D)

Elected 2017, term expires 2021, 1st term; b. May. 20, 1956, Wilmington, DE; Dartmouth College, BA 1978; Univ. Del. MPA 1987; Roman Catholic; Married (Tracey); 2 children.

Elected Office: DE Finance Secretary, 1997-2000; DE Lt. Governor, 2001-2009; US House, 2011-2017.

Office: 150 Martin Luther King Jr. Blvd., 2nd Floor, Dover, 19901; 302-744-4101; Fax: 302-739-2775; Website: delaware.gov.

Election Results

Election	Name (Party)	Vote (%)
2016 General	John Carney (D)	248,404 (58%)
	Colin Bonini (R)	166,852 (39%)
2016 Primary	John Carney (D)	unopposed (0%)

John Carney, a former congressman elected to the governorship in 2016, is, like several of Delaware's recent governors, a centrist devoted to bipartisanship. Carney, the second of nine children born to two teachers, has lived in Wilmington for most of his life. He has been careful to stress his humble upbringing and the fact that he, his wife, and their two children live in a modest row house. Carney has spent nearly his entire adult life in public office, except for brief stints as president and chief operating officer of Transformative Technologies, a Delaware technology firm, and as executive vice president of a wind farm start-up called DelaWind. After earning an English degree at Dartmouth College and a master's from the University of Delaware, Carney served as an aide to Joe Biden, the state's legendary Democratic senator. In the 1990s, he became a top aide to then-Gov. Thomas Carper, also a Delaware senator. Carney was the state secretary of finance under Carper from 1997 to 2000. That year, he won the first of two terms as lieutenant governor. Then in 2008, he lost a high-profile gubernatorial primary against Jack Markell, a former telecommunications executive and self-described "card-carrying capitalist."

Carney began the 2008 race as the favorite of party officials who, hoping to avoid a primary, urged Markell to run for lieutenant governor instead. But Markell was steadfast about wanting the top job. Deprived of his anticipated coronation, Carney lined up support from much of the party establishment, including outgoing Gov. Ruth Ann Minner, state legislators and unions. But Markell campaigned tirelessly across the state and raised more than $4 million, including $725,000 of his own money, a record fundraising haul in a Delaware governor's race. As Minner's popularity flagged after two terms in office, Carney subtly distanced himself from her by campaigning on a theme of change. Still, Markell's victory in the September primary was a stunner. He took 51 percent to Carney's 49 percent, a margin of about 1,700 votes.

Carney regrouped for 2010 and ran for the state's at-large House seat, which was vacated by moderate Republican Michael Castle, who was running (unsuccessfully as it turned out) for the Senate. Carney faced largely self-funding Republican Glen Urquhart, a Rehoboth Beach developer. Carney ran on his support for renewable energy technology and jobs as well as his opposition to oil drilling off the Delaware shoreline. Urquhart also called attention to Carney's attempt to lobby the state for assistance in 2009, when he worked for DelaWind. But liberal-leaning Delawareans were skittish about Urquhart's conservative positions, which included favoring a repeal the Affordable Care Act and abolition of the departments of Energy and Education. Carney declared Urquhart too "radical" and "extreme" to represent the neighborly state, citing his opponent's comparison of liberals to Nazis while claiming that Hitler, not Thomas Jefferson, coined the phrase "separation of church and state." Carney won, 57%-41%, a rare instance of a Democratic takeover of a seat in that GOP-friendly year.

In the House, Carney followed the example of his predecessor Castle, a nine-term centrist Republican. Not long after taking office, Carney was assigned to the Financial Services Committee and struck up a friendship with fellow freshman Jim Renacci, a Republican from Ohio, in whom he saw a common-sense approach to problems. They started a breakfast group that eventually grew to 14 lawmakers. "If our group can sit down, hear each other out, and come up with solutions we all agree on, that says something," Carney said in September 2011. "Can we move the needle nationally? I don't know, but it has to start somewhere." Carney became the first freshman Democrat to pass an amendment in the House when he added a provision to a bill in May 2011 making rail security a priority for U.S. intelligence agencies. Carney joined another Republican, Stephen Fincher of Tennessee, in drafting legislation to make it easier for small and medium-sized companies to undertake an initial public offering and become a public company. Their measure passed the Financial Services Committee on a 54-1 vote in February 2012 and became law two months later after House Republicans included it in their job-creation agenda; in Delaware, corporate franchise and related fees are more than one-third of state revenue. Carney showed a more partisan edge when he joined a June 2016 sit-in on the House floor over expanding gun background checks. In his two reelection campaigns, Carney won easily.

Carney still harbored gubernatorial ambitions, and he would have set them aside, at least temporarily, had Biden's son Beau – a rising star and the odds-on favorite to win the governorship had he run in 2016 -- not died of brain cancer in 2015. After the younger Biden's death, all attention turned to Carney. His prominence in the state and Delaware's weak Republican bench combined to make the 2016 gubernatorial contest arguably the least competitive in the nation that year. After some uncertainty about who the GOP would field as a candidate, state Sen. Colin Bonini jumped in. But Carney's fundraising edge was on the order of 20 to 1 and Markell's two terms hadn't inspired the sort of fatigue that would have given the Republican an opening, especially in a presidential election year when Hillary Clinton was almost certain to win the state. Indeed, a September 2016 University of Delaware poll found Markell with 64 percent approval and 17 percent disapproval. In the end, Carney lost Republican-leaning Sussex County by eight points and narrowly won Kent County, but he crushed Bonini in the most populous county by far, New Castle, by a roughly 2-to-1 margin.

Senior Senator

Tom Carper (D)

Elected 2000, term expires 2018, 3rd term; b. Jan 23, 1947, Beckley, WV; Ohio State University, B.A.; University of Delaware, Newark, M.B.A.; Presbyterian; Married (Martha Ann Stacy Carper); 2 children.

Military Career: U.S. Navy, 1968-1973 (Vietnam); U.S Naval Reserves, 1973-1991.

Elected Office: DE Treasurer, 1976-1983; U.S. House, 1983-1993; DE Governor, 1993-2001.

Professional Career: Industrial devel. specialist, DE Div. of Econ. Devel., 1975-1976; Chmn, National Governors Association, 1998-1999.

DC Office: 513 HSOB 20510, 202-224-2441, Fax: 202-228-2190, carper.senate.gov.

State Offices: Dover, 302-674-3308; Georgetown, 302-856-7690; Wilmington, 302-573-6291.

Committees: *Environment & Public Works (RMM)*: Clean Air & Nuclear Safety, Fisheries, Water, and Wildlife, Superfund, Waste Management, & Regulatory Oversight, Transportation & Infrastructure. *Finance*: Energy, Natural Resources & Infrastructure, Health Care, Taxation & IRS Oversight. *Homeland Security & Government Affairs*: Investigations (RMM), Regulatory Affairs & Federal Management.

Group Ratings

	ADA	ACLU	AFL-CIO	LCV	ITI	COC	HAFA	ACU	CFG	FRC
2016	-	76%	-	94%	100%	63%	7%	13%	12%	0%
2015	75%	C	43%	84%	C	57%	C	0%	18%	0%

Almanac Ratings 2015

	Economy	Social	Foreign	Composite
Liberal	70%	100%	88%	86%
Conservative	30%	0%	12%	14%

Key Votes of the 114th Congress

1. Keystone pipeline	Y	5. National Security Data	Y	9. Gun Sales Checks	Y
2. Export-Import Bank	N	6. Iran Nuclear Deal	N	10. Sanctuary Cities	N
3. Debt Ceiling Increase	Y	7. Puerto Rico Debt	Y	11. Planned Parenthood	N
4. Homeland Security $$	Y	8. Loretta Lynch A.G	Y	12. Trade deals	Y

Election Results

Election	Name (Party)	Vote (%)	Cand. Spent	Ind. Exp. Support	Ind. Exp. Oppose
2012 General	Tom Carper (D)	265,415 (66%)	$5,324,026	$3,075	
	Kevin Wade (R)	115,700 (29%)	$181,600	$10,000	
	Alexander Pires (I)	15,300 (4%)	$413,774		
2012 Primary	Tom Carper (D)	43,587 (88%)			
	Keith Spanarelli (D)	6,028 (12%)			

Prior winning percentages: 2006 (70%), 2000 (56%); Governor: 1996 (70%), 1992 (65%); House: 1990 (66%), 1988 (68%), 1986 (66%), 1984 (59%0, 1982 (52%)

Democrat Thomas Carper is arguably the most successful politician in the history of the First State: He has won 13 consecutive statewide elections, and has never lost a race in four decades in public office. Serving as state treasurer, House member and governor before his election to the Senate in 2000, Carper's reputation as a centrist consensus-builder has made him well-liked on both sides of the aisle on Capitol Hill as well as popular at home. Now Delaware's senior senator, he fits squarely into what the home state establishment refers to as the "Delaware Way": a low-key, pragmatic brand of politics favored in a pocket-sized state that often has the feel of an extended town, in which most of the key players know each other well.

Carper's long-time leading role on the Senate Homeland Security and Governmental Affairs Committee-which he chaired in 2013-2014 -- reinforced his image as a results-oriented legislator focused on issues outside of the political limelight, such as Postal Service reform, that are nonetheless important to the efficiency of government. In 2017, Carper leveraged his seniority to take over as ranking Democrat on the Environment and Public Works Committee, succeeding retiring California Sen. Barbara Boxer. The moderate, consensus-oriented Carper is a pronounced contrast to the avowedly liberal Boxer, and environmentalists -- particularly given Carper's 2015 vote for the Keystone XL pipeline -- were less than overjoyed. But Carper sought to quickly underscore his pro-environment credentials, as he joined in widespread Democratic criticism of President Donald Trump's nomination of Scott Pruitt to head the Environmental Protection Agency. "We cannot roll back the progress we made in the past eight years to protect the environment," Carper tweeted. "Anyone leading EPA who wants to ignore science or lookout for special interests at the expense of public health can expect a fight with me."

Carper grew up in Southside Virginia and attended Ohio State University on a Navy ROTC scholarship. He first came to Delaware as a Navy ensign. After service in Southeast Asia during the Vietnam War, where he was a mission commander piloting submarine-hunting planes, Carper returned to earn his M.B.A. at the University of Delaware. More than four decades later, Carper traveled to Vietnam with President Barack Obama as part of an effort to bring about closer ties with that nation; an earlier trip in 1991, when he led a bipartisan congressional delegation, is credited with having helped to create a path toward normalizing U.S.-Vietnamese relations.

In 1976, at the age of 29, Carper was elected as Delaware's state treasurer. Six years later, leading state Democrats-including Sen. Joe Biden-prodded Carper to leave his politically secure post to challenge Republican incumbent Thomas Evans for the state's at-large House seat. The ensuing race was a relatively rare detour from the Delaware Way; the tabloid *New York Post* labeled it as "the nation's dirtiest campaign" that year. Evans had been politically damaged by an acknowledged "association" with a young female lobbyist named Paula Parkinson, and the state of Carper's marriage was also dragged into the campaign. (Carper has since divorced and remarried.) Carper won with 52 percent, and the civility for which Delaware politics is known ultimately resurfaced: Carper and Evans became friendly, and Evans even contributed to Carper's campaign committee during the 2012 and 2014 election cycles.

After a decade in the House of accumulating a moderate voting record-his strong support of a constitutional amendment requiring a balanced budget set him apart from many fellow Democrats-Carper in 1992 was party to what is still referred to as "The Swap" by Delaware insiders. Carper and Republican Gov. Michael Castle were personal friends who, despite differing partisan affiliations, were considered near-ideological twins. Castle was term-limited and ran for the House, while Carper ran to succeed Castle as governor and won with nearly two-thirds of the vote. As governor, Carper pursued an agenda that was in many ways more conservative than liberal. He continued former Republican Gov. Pete du Pont's policy of cutting taxes, reducing income tax rates by about 10 percent. Delaware's strong economy helped him keep the budget in the black, and he boosted the state's credit rating to a historic high even as state spending rose 40 percent in eight years. He also signed a bill authorizing charter schools.

After easily winning re-election in 1996, Carper-barred from seeking a third term in 2000-faced a possible interruption in a nearly quarter century of unbroken electoral success. Some thought Republican Sen. William Roth would retire after one-third of a century on Capitol Hill, and that Castle would run to succeed him; Carper went so far as to say publicly that, under such a scenario, he would have bowed out of politics, at least temporarily, rather than run against his friend Castle. But Roth decided to seek re-election, Castle shied away from a primary challenge to the incumbent, and Carper ran for the Senate.

In contrast to the Carper vs. Evans confrontation almost two decades earlier, this was a battle of positives. Both candidates had high approval ratings at home and were familiar figures to voters. Roth had a record of achievements that paid direct benefits to residents of this generally affluent state, starting with the Kemp-Roth tax cut of 1981. Later, as chairman of the Senate Finance Committee, he engineered the eponymous Roth IRA as well as reform of the Internal Revenue Service. Roth's main problem was that he was 79 years old. The then 53-year-old Carper was careful not to campaign negatively against Roth, but his slogan, "A Senator for Our Future," spotlighted the generational contrast. While Carper regularly spent 16 hours per day campaigning, Roth stayed in Washington and made only a few appearances in the state. In October, Roth fainted twice on the campaign trail, once in full view of cameras. On Election Day, Carper won by a solid 56%-44% margin.

As was the case during his House tenure, Carper has amassed one of the more middle-of-the-road voting records among Senate Democrats, and is often at the center of efforts to build bipartisan coalitions when important legislation bogs down, as illustrated by the push to pass a health care overhaul at the outset of the Obama Administration. Carper bucked liberals in his party by opposing creation of a government-run insurance plan for those who could not afford private plans. But rather than attack the public option idea, he tried to broker a compromise he and other centrist Democrats could support. The public option was ultimately dropped from the final legislation, but Carper first sought to advance an alternative that would allow states to individually decide whether to offer a public option to compete with private insurers.

In addition to shaping health care policy, Carper has utilized his seat on the influential Finance Committee to strongly back free trade: In early 2015, as many of Congress' left-leaning Democrats were putting distance between themselves and Obama on a free trade agreement with 12 Asian nations, Carper was among those in his party to support not only the deal itself-but also a proposal to grant the president special authority to expedite negotiations of its provisions. In a May 2015 procedural vote on the matter in which Senate Democrats deserted Obama *en masse*, Carper was the sole Democrat to vote with the president. A month later, after White House lobbying and reassurances to several wavering senators, Carper was joined by a dozen fellow Democrats in the final procedural vote that granted Obama special negotiating authority for the agreement -- a deal from which President Donald Trump withdrew the United States shortly after entering the White House.

Carper has been considered a budget hawk. In late 2012, he called for a deficit reduction blueprint similar to one developed earlier by the so-called Simpson-Bowles commission, which had backed proposals to overhaul the tax code and gradually raise the Medicare eligibility age. His affinity for Simpson-Bowles led him to be one of just three Senate Democrats to oppose a final budget deal on New Year's Eve 2013, intended to avert the so-called "fiscal cliff" of tax hikes and spending cuts.

In his portfolio on the Homeland Security and Governmental Affairs Committee, Carper enacted legislation beefing up protections against government payments to ineligible claimants of retiree or disability benefits, and requiring audits to identify billions lost through waste and fraudulent claims, while also shepherding passage of bills designed to beef up government cybersecurity efforts. Carper has been in the forefront of seeking to highlight conflict-of-interest issues posed by Trump's business holdings. When the director of the Office of Government Ethics, responding to a letter from Carper, came under criticism for suggesting that Trump should divest of himself of his holdings, Carper issued a strongly worded defense of the director, Walter Shaub. "We as members of Congress should be focused on how our president-elect has no plan to resolve his massive conflicts of interest before assuming the highest office in our country," Carper declared.

But the issue with the committee's jurisdiction with which Carper has been most identified is the so-far unsuccessful effort to rescue the ailing Postal Service. He worked with a fellow centrist, Republican Susan Collins of Maine, in 2006 to pass the first major revision of Postal Service operations since 1970. (Delaware is a major center for the credit card industry, which accounts for about one-quarter of the Postal Service's mail.) As the Postal Service continued to run large deficits, Carper in 2012 engineered bipartisan Senate passage of legislation that allowed the service to offer buyout and early retirement incentives to 100,000 employees, while reducing six-day delivery to five days after giving officials time to come up with an alternative to save costs. But the bill stalled in the House, leaving Carper so frustrated that he created a Facebook page complaining about the lack of action. In the summer of 2016, a House panel passed Postal Service legislation on a bipartisan basis for the first time, raising hopes that Carper's long-term goal of reforming the troubled enterprise might finally come about.

A former chairman of the Environment and Public Works' subcommittee on clean air, Carper also has focused on legislation to reduce air pollution and halt climate change, while again reaching across the political aisle. With Republican `Lamar Alexander of Tennessee as a partner, he authored legislation almost a decade ago to limit emissions of sulfur dioxide, nitrous oxide, mercury and carbon dioxide; the pair later pushed for another bill to substantially reduce emissions from power plants. Such efforts have made little headway on Capitol Hill, and Carper later was supportive of Obama Administration efforts to accomplish such aims through EPA regulations. He has defended the EPA against Republican criticism, citing a 2012 American Lung Association study showing improvements in 18 of the 25 most pollution-plagued cities as evidence that "we can have a strong economy, clean air, and protect public health all at the same time."

Carper ranks sixth from the bottom among Senate Democrats on the lifetime voting scorecard compiled by the League of Conservation Voters -- the result, in recent years, of his support of free trade pacts opposed by environmental groups, and his backing of the controversial Keystone XL pipeline. In early 2015, he was one of just eight Democrats to join all Senate Republicans in an unsuccessful effort to override Obama's veto of legislation to construct the $8 billion pipeline. Carper said the controversy over the pipeline, designed to run from Canada through the Midwest, had "impeded our ability to work together and make progress even on issues that we're in agreement on," while declaring, "We need to address this issue and we need to move on."

Such comments bespeak a broader frustration on the part of the former governor with the pace of getting things done on Capitol Hill. "My worst day as governor was better than my best day as a United States senator," he is said to have told colleagues. But he is said to be planning to seek a fourth term in 2018, when he turns 71. In a 2016 interview with *Roll Call,* Carper boasted of working out daily, and of not having missed work due to illness in 35 years. In 2012, Carper defeated Republican engineer Kevin Wade while winning 66 percent of the vote, down only slightly from Carper's victory margin six years earlier in a state that has trended increasingly Democratic over the past couple of decades. And his influence and impact within Delaware have perhaps never been greater: At the outset of 2017, the state's new governor and new House member were both onetime Carper aides, as was the chief justice of Delaware's highest court.

Should Carper change his mind and decide that 42 years in elected office is enough, the apparent favorite to succeed him would be former Gov. Jack Markell, a Democrat who left the statehouse in January 2017 due to term limits -- with approval ratings almost as high as Carper's. Despite a few gains in recent years, the Delaware Republican bench remains thin. State Treasurer Ken Simpler, elected for the first time in 2014, is mentioned as a future candidate for higher office.

Junior Senator

Chris Coons (D)

Elected 2010, term expires 2020, 2nd term; b. Sep 09, 1963, Greenwich, CT; Amherst College (MA), B.A.; Yale University Law School (CT), J.D.; Yale University Divinity School (CT), Mast. Deg.; University of Nairobi (Kenya); Tower Hill School (DE); Presbyterian; Married (Annie Lingenfelter); 3 children.

Elected Office: President, New Castle County Council, 2001-2005; New Castle County Executive, 2005-2010.

Professional Career: Practicing attorney, W.L. Gore & Associates, 1996-2004.

DC Office: 127-A RSOB 20510, 202-224-5042, Fax: 202-228-3075, coons.senate.gov.

State Offices: Dover, 302-736-5601; Wilmington, 302-573-6345.

Committees: *Appropriations*: Commerce, Justice, Science & Related Agencies, Energy & Water Development, Financial Services & General Government (RMM), State, Foreign Operations & Related Programs, Transportation, HUD & Related Agencies. *Ethics*. *Foreign Relations*: Africa & Global Health Policy, Internat'l Dev Instit & Internat'l Econ, Energy & Environ Policy, State Dept & USAID Mngmnt, Internat'l Ops & Internat'l Dev. *Judiciary*: Constitution, Crime & Terrorism, Oversight, Agency Action, Federal Rights & Federal Courts (RMM), Privacy, Technology & the Law. *Small Business & Entrepreneurship*.

Group Ratings

	ADA	ACLU	AFL-CIO	LCV	ITI	COC	HAFA	ACU	CFG	FRC
2016	-	94%	-	94%	80%	57%	2%	4%	5%	0%
2015	95%	C	62%	92%	C	54%	C	0%	9%	0%

Almanac Ratings 2015

	Economy	Social	Foreign	Composite
Liberal	83%	100%	92%	92%
Conservative	17%	0%	8%	8%

Key Votes of the 114th Congress

1. Keystone pipeline	N	5. National Security Data	Y	9. Gun Sales Checks	Y
2. Export-Import Bank	N	6. Iran Nuclear Deal	N	10. Sanctuary Cities	N
3. Debt Ceiling Increase	Y	7. Puerto Rico Debt	Y	11. Planned Parenthood	N
4. Homeland Security $$	Y	8. Loretta Lynch A.G	Y	12. Trade deals	Y

Election Results

Election	Name (Party)	Vote (%)		Cand. Spent	Ind. Exp. Support	Ind. Exp. Oppose
2014 General	Chris Coons (D)	130,655	(56%)	$8,958,014	$57,744	
	Kevin Wade (R)	98,823	(42%)	$111,823	$72,702	
2014 Primary	Chris Coons (D)	Unopposed				

Prior winning percentages: 2010 special (57%)

"Chris Coons may turn out to be the luckiest politician in America this year," CNN declared in mid-September of 2010. Indeed, at the outset of that year, Coons was hardly on the radar screen as a potential contender for the seat occupied for nearly four decades by Democrat Joe Biden. It took the biggest upset of the 2010 primary season-the Republican primary season, that is-to transform Coons from distinct underdog to overwhelming favorite to fill out the final four years of Biden's Senate term after the latter became vice president. In style, Delaware's low-key junior senator-easily re-elected to a full term in 2014-is a marked contrast to the voluble Biden; in substance, he has been a bipartisan-oriented, business-friendly Democrat in the mold of Virginia's Mark Warner, Colorado's Michael Bennet, and his home-state senior colleague, Thomas Carper. At times, Coons has shown an interest in taking on a more partisan role and moving up the Senate leadership ladder. But he waved off opportunities to chair the Democratic Senatorial Campaign Committee -- and the seat at the leadership table which accompanies that post -- after both the 2014 and 2016 elections.

Coons' family moved to Delaware during his early childhood; bankruptcy wiped out much of his father's business success, and his parents later divorced. His mother, Sally, a schoolteacher, later remarried: Coons' stepfather, Robert Gore, played a key role in the founding of a highly successful family enterprise, Newark, Del.-based W.L. Gore and Associates. (Holder of the patent for water-resistant Gore-Tex fabric, the firm is among the top 200 privately held companies in the United States.) As a student at Wilmington's elite Tower Hill School, Coons considered himself a Republican and volunteered for Ronald Reagan's 1980 presidential campaign. His conversion to the Democratic Party came while he was a student at Amherst College. Studying in Kenya for a semester in 1984, Coons said that observing his host family changed the way he thought about poverty and free markets. It also led him to write a tongue-in-cheek column for the college newspaper, titled "Chris Coons: The Making of a Bearded Marxist," which would crop up as an issue in his Senate bid a quarter of a century later.

After graduating from Amherst with a dual major in chemistry and political science, Coons did relief work with a church group in South Africa before attending Yale Law School. He also enrolled in Yale's Divinity School, graduating from both programs in 1992 with doctor of jurisprudence and Master of Arts in religion degrees, respectively. He initially worked with low-income students in New York City, but moved back to Delaware in 1996 after getting married-and went to work as an attorney for W.L. Gore, of which his stepfather was then president. Coons' first foray into politics came in 2000, when he was elected president of the New Castle County Council. Four years later, he was elected county executive on an anti-corruption platform; his predecessor had been dogged by corruption allegations. Despite promising in his campaign not to increase taxes, Coons wound up doing so to close a budget gap.

When Biden was elected vice president in 2008-winning re-election to the Senate at the same time-the heavy favorite on the Democratic side for the open seat was his son, state Attorney General Beau Biden. Ted Kaufman, a long-time aide to the elder Biden, received a temporary appointment to the job, while ruling out running himself; it was seen as a move to keep the seat warm for the younger Biden until the 2010 election. But Beau Biden, who died in May 2015, declined to run, busy with his work as state attorney general and perhaps influenced by leading Democrats' appraisal that the race was, at best, an uphill battle against moderate-to-liberal Republican Rep. Michael Castle. Elected statewide 12 times in 30 years, Castle, also a former governor, was seen as a heavy favorite in the general election despite the state's increasingly Democratic tilt. But, in a year in which the tea party emerged as a major force in Republican politics, Castle lost the September GOP primary in a stunning upset to tea party-backed Christine O'Donnell, a consultant and TV commentator who had been defeated by Joe Biden by a 2-1 margin two years earlier.

Coons, seen as a heavy underdog against Castle, immediately catapulted to a double-digit lead over O'Donnell in the polls. Predictions that she would be a weak opponent were fulfilled in spades. O'Donnell was put on the defensive by old TV footage -- most notably a videotape in which she claimed to have dabbled in witchcraft while an occasional guest more than a decade earlier on Bill Maher's nightly talk show, "Politically Incorrect." She was compelled to tape a now-famous campaign ad in which she reassured her supporters, "I am not a witch. I'm nothing you've heard. I am you." The ad accomplished little but to provide fodder for late-night comics. O'Donnell sought to focus on Coons' record of raising taxes as county executive, dubbing him "The Tax Man." Neither that nor Republican efforts to use his "Bearded Marxist" essay as a line of attack gained much traction. "I am a clean-shaven capitalist," Coons retorted. Mostly, Coons kept a low profile while O'Donnell's campaign came apart with one controversy after another. On Election Day, he won in a 57%-40% landslide, with exit polls showing him with a significant crossover vote from Republicans.

Even before winning the race, Coons' status as the electoral bulwark against an upstart tea party candidate won him a special place among national Democrats. "He's my favorite candidate. He's my pet," then-Majority Leader Harry Reid gushed to *The Hill* newspaper following the primary. But Coons also has made a determined effort to work with Republicans. He teamed with a fellow freshman, Florida Republican Marco Rubio, to introduce a jobs bill in 2011. He joined with Texas Republican John Cornyn on a bill to make the illegal streaming of television shows or movies a felony. As a member of the Energy and Natural Resources Committee, Coons worked with Republican James Inhofe of Oklahoma in a 2012 effort to scrutinize the renewable fuels standard, earlier mandated by Congress to increase production of biofuels. (Coons later gave up his seat on the energy panel when a sought-after seat on the Appropriations Committee opened up.)

Following his 2010 election, Coons was given the chairmanship of Foreign Relations' Africa subcommittee in recognition of the time he spent on that continent. He struck up a friendship with the subcommittee's then ranking Republican, Georgia's Johnny Isakson, and they led the Senate's effort in 2012 to formally condemn Joseph Kony and his Lord's Resistance Army for its notorious reign of killings and child abductions across central Africa . In 2017, Coons was named the ranking Democrat on the Senate Ethics Committee -- once again pairing him with Isakson, who had become the Ethics Committee chairman when the Republicans regained control of the Senate following the 2014 election. In between, Coons and Isakson teamed up in 2013 to start the Senate Chicken Caucus, in recognition of the importance of the poultry industry to their home states. And in late 2016, the pair cosponsored legislation to require the nation's most selective colleges to either add low-income students or pay a fee to remain in the federal student aid program; money raised from such fees would then be used to help improve graduation rates at schools that admit a large percentage of low-income students.

Coons, who also serves on the Judiciary Committee, has found himself at odds with some leading congressional Republicans on the perennial issue of curbing patent abuses. A patent reform bill Coons introduced early in 2015-co-sponsored by Senate Minority Whip Dick Durbin of Illinois-was praised by university groups as well as the biotechnology and pharmaceutical industries. However, it was criticized by the consumer electronics sector as doing little to restrain "patent trolls"-firms that purchase patents largely to seek financial settlements for infringement from other firms.

In September 2015, Coons joined most Senate Democrats in endorsing the Iran nuclear agreement, giving President Barack Obama sufficient votes to block a congressional resolution disapproving the deal. A couple of months earlier, Coons was in the minority of his party when he and 12 other Democrats voted to give Obama expedited authority to negotiate the Trans Pacific Partnership, a 12-trade deal later jettisoned by President Donald Trump. As a Foreign Relations Committee member, Coons joined a handful of senators from both parties in advocating that the U.S. effort against the Islamic terrorist group ISIS be debated and specifically authorized by Congress -- a position resisted by the Obama administration. Writing in an op-ed piece for *The Philadelphia Inquirer* at the end of 2015, Coons also advocated a surtax to pay for the war against ISIS, arguing that taxes had been raised to underwrite most wars in the nation's history until the post-9/11 involvement in Iraq and Afghanistan. "When we pay for our wars with a credit card, and when the pain of war is felt only by our troops and their families, it is far too easy for our nation's leaders to send soldiers into harm's way without a national conversation about the merits of our involvement, and far too easy for those conflicts to drag on," he contended.

Defeating his 2014 Republican opponent, Kevin Wade-who unsuccessfully ran against Carper two years earlier-by 13 points in a difficult year for Democrats, Coons emerged with what he described as a rekindled appetite for campaigning. He expressed interest in heading the Senate Democrats' campaign arm, the DSCC, as the party began its quest to regain the Senate majority lost in the 2014 election. While success at the DSCC has often translated into an ascent into the top rungs of the Senate Democratic leadership, Coons ultimately withdrew from consideration. "He...decided it wasn't the right time for him to do it," said a spokesman, citing Coons' three teenage children at home and the travel demands of the DSCC job. (Like Carper and, earlier, Biden, Coons commutes from Wilmington to Washington on most days when Congress is in session.) The Coons spokesman added, "He's also inherently a pretty bipartisan guy and was concerned it would be harder to make real progress on some of his legislative priorities while running the DSCC." Senate Democratic leaders again eyed Coons for the post following the 2016 election, when there was a paucity of takers -- given that the Democrats faced an election cycle in which the party would be defending 25 seats nationwide, as compared to just eight Republican-held seats. Again, Coons pleaded family considerations in passing on the job.

The 2016 campaign took a toll on Coons' normally bipartisan mien: In the fall of 2015, he lambasted Republican presidential contender Donald Trump as "a thin-skinned reality TV star" and "a Cheeto-faced short-fingered vulgarian" during a Democratic rally in southern Delaware. A year later, it fell to the Yale Divinity School graduate to journey to New York and invite Trump -- by then the president-elect -- to the January 2017 National Prayer Breakfast, which Coons was co-chairing. Coons said he avoided partisan issues during his 20-minute meeting at Trump Tower with the president-elect, a fellow Presbyterian, and focused on his own experiences attending weekly prayer breakfasts with other senators; the matter of his campaign remarks did not come up during the session, Coons added. "I said it's tough to throw a punch at someone on the floor of the Senate when you've held hands with them in prayer that morning," Coons told the Wilmington *News Journal* afterward. He also expressed remorse to the newspaper about the insults hurled at Trump a year earlier, saying he regretted "that one incident of my not keeping a measured tone in the campaign."

REPRESENTATIVE-AT-LARGE

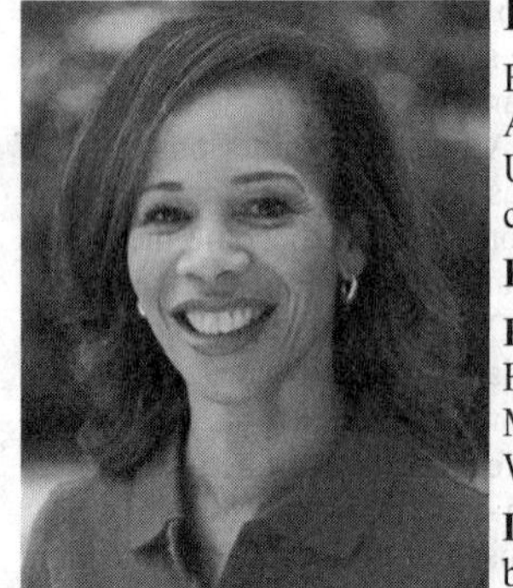

Lisa Rochester (D)

Elected 2016, 1st term; b. Feb 10, 1962, Philadelphia, PA; Padua Academy (DE); Fairleigh Dickinson University, Bach. Deg., 1985; University of Delaware, M.A., 2002; Christian Church; Widow; 2 children.

Elected Office: Delaware Secretary of Labor, 1998-2001.

Professional Career: Deputy Secretary, Delaware Department of Health and Social Services; Personnel Director, Delaware Office of Management and Budget, 2001-2004; Chief Executive, Metropolitan Wilmington Urban League, 2004-2007.

DC Office: 1123 LHOB 20515, 202-225-4165, bluntrochester.house.gov.

State Offices: Wilmington, 302-830-2330.

Committees: *Agriculture*: Biotechnology, Horticulture & Research, General Farm Commodities & Risk Management. *Education & the Workforce*: Health, Employment, Labor & Pensions, Higher Education & Workforce Development.

Election Results

Election	Name (Party)	Vote (%)		Cand. Spent	Ind. Exp. Support	Ind. Exp. Oppose
2016 General	Lisa Rochester (D)	233,554	(56%)	$1,332,932	$190,702	
	Hans Reigle (R)	172,301	(41%)	$211,652		
2016 Primary	Lisa Rochester (D)	27,919	(44%)			
	Bryan Townsend (D)	15,847	(25%)			
	Sean Barney (D)	12,891	(20%)			
	Michael Miller (D)	3,500	(6%)			

Lisa Blunt Rochester was elected in 2016 to the open seat in Delaware. She had extensive experience in local government and public affairs. But this was her first political campaign. She joined the growing number of Congressional Black Caucus members who represent a constituency that is not predominantly African American.

Blunt Rochester was born in Philadelphia and moved with her family to Wilmington, Delaware, when she was a child. She has a political pedigree as a Democrat. Her father was president of the Wilmington City Council. Her sister was an aide to Joe Biden in his Senate office, and state director for the Obama-Biden campaign. Blunt Rochester got her bachelor's in international relations from Fairleigh Dickinson University, and received a master's degree in urban affairs and public policy from the University of Delaware. In 1987, she began her political career as an intern for then-Rep. Tom Carper, and recalls her experience as a case-worker dealing with Social Security benefits, disability insurance claims, IRS disputes and housing needs. She continued with Carper when he was elected governor in

1992. She initially was a policy advisor and eventually served three years as secretary of labor in the governor's cabinet, where she focused on connecting employers to resources and jobseekers.

When Carper was elected to the Senate in 2000, Blunt Rochester joined the cabinet of new Democratic Gov. Ruth Ann Minner, as personnel director. In that job, her responsibilities included an investigation of the Delaware State Police for racial and sexual discrimination. She moved to the private sector as chief executive officer of the Metropolitan Wilmington Urban League, a public policy think tank. There, she met her husband Charles Rochester, an engineer working in China. She moved to Shanghai after they married in 2006, writing a book, *Thrive*, that profiled women who reinvented themselves while living in a foreign country. She decided to write the book after nothing fell into place during her job search in China until she attended a 10-day meditation retreat in Hong Kong that helped her to clarify what she wanted from life. She wrote the book with two co-authors - women from Mexico and Kenya who also had accompanied their husbands to Shanghai. Blunt Rochester moved back to the United States when her husband was transferred to Boston. She returned to Delaware after her husband died suddenly in 2014 after rupturing his Achilles tendon.

When John Carney decided to run for governor, Blunt Rochester was an early front-runner to take his seat in the House. In the competitive six-candidate Democratic primary, she won with 44 percent of the vote. The runners-up were state Sen. Bryan Townsend and Iraq War veteran Sean Barney, who got 25 and 20 percent respectively. Townsend was the only candidate who had held elective office. Barney had been an aide to Carper and outgoing Gov. Jack Markell. Each of the three front-runners raised about $700,000. Blunt Rochester loaned her campaign an additional $400,000 for the primary. Her net worth exceeded $5 million, which she inherited from her late husband.

In the general election against Republican Hans Reigle, Blunt Rochester criticized Donald Trump for supporting "hateful, racist and discriminatory" policies. She said that she favored making Delaware a sanctuary state to prevent the federal government from detaining people who are living illegally in the United States. Reigle, who had been mayor of the small town of Wyoming, called for more steps to prevent illegal immigration. Blunt Rochester won 56%-41%. She took 64 percent in New Castle County, including Wilmington. Reigle won the two smaller counties.

Blunt Rochester is the first woman and person of color to represent Delaware in Congress. She got seats on the Agriculture and Education and Workforce committees. Entering the House at age 54, she could be positioned for an eventual move to the Senate.

★ DISTRICT OF COLUMBIA ★

The capital of the most powerful and affluent nation in history, Washington is a physically beautiful city of great achievements and astonishing contrasts that go back more than 200 years. In 1787, the Constitution's framers, familiar with contemporary London and Paris mobs and remembering how unruly crowds had threatened the Continental Congress in Philadelphia, gave the new federal government control over the 10-mile-square that came to be called the District of Columbia. The Residence Act of 1790 located the District on the Potomac River along the borders of Maryland and Virginia, though in 1848 the portion west of the Potomac was retroceded to Virginia on the grounds that the federal government would never need it.

Over the years, Congress kept control of the District for its own advantage and, at times, out of distrust of the city's large African-American population. In the late 18th century, African Americans made up one-quarter of Washington's residents. Although slavery was legal, the city was something of a refuge for free blacks before the Civil War, and also right after emancipation. Radical Republicans gave the District self-government in 1871, but the experiment ended three years later after Gov. Alexander Shepherd spent the city into bankruptcy. In the 20th century, Washington's growth spurts, starting with the New Deal and World War II, resulted in the development of large, mostly white suburbs in Virginia and Maryland. It was at this time that African Americans became a larger percentage of the city's population, reaching a majority in the 1960 census.

With the civil rights movement, the way that many District residents viewed their lack of voting rights began to change. In 1961, Congress amended the Constitution to give District residents the right to vote for president; in 1968, residents began voting for the school board; in 1971, they received a non-voting delegate in Congress; and in 1973, the District of Columbia Home Rule Act allowed the city to elect a mayor and a city council, though Congress retained control over the District's budget and the ability to review its legislation. For some time, self-government worked no better than it did in the 1870s. The Alexander Shepherd of modern times was the late Marion Barry, who held office for 16 of 20 years between 1978 and 1998. Under Barry, the District struggled. Neighborhoods fell into disarray and violent crime rates increased. Meanwhile, the size of local government soared to 51,000 employees. Barry nonetheless regularly won re-election. In January 1990, District police arrested him at a D.C. hotel for cocaine possession. After a six-month stint in prison, he returned to city government. Barry was elected to the city council in 1992 and won a fourth term as mayor in 1994.

At that time, D.C. was experiencing a dire fiscal crisis, and Congress stepped in. Republican House Speaker Newt Gingrich tasked Rep. Tom Davis, a Republican from northern Virginia, with the job of stabilizing the District's finances. Working closely with D.C.'s elected delegate, Democrat Eleanor Holmes Norton, Davis set up a financial control board whose head, Anthony Williams, hacked away at the payroll and reformed management practices. In 1998, Barry chose not to run for a fifth term. Williams ran and went on to win the Democratic primary and general election. The financial control board immediately relinquished power to the new mayor, and in 2000, a court returned control of most District departments to the city.

Beginning with William's tenure, the District's population started rising, from 572,000 in 2000 to 681,000 in 2016, with a substantial portion of this increase coming from well-educated, unmarried young people: almost 55 percent of the D.C. adult population has at least a bachelor's degree-one of the highest percentages in the country-while it is estimated that 71 percent are unmarried (a decline from 76 percent in 2011). Approximately 35 percent can be categorized as millennials. In the November 2014 municipal elections, voters between the ages of 25 and 34 outnumbered senior citizens for the first time in 40 years. With youth and population growth have come gentrification and an exceptionally high cost of living. Condominiums and rental apartments targeted at singles were built in what had been high-crime areas. A 2015 study found the D.C. rental market was fourth most expensive in the country. The rental market, in turn, has sprouted new bars and restaurants, rental bikes and bike lanes, food trucks and cupcake stores, dog parks and streetcar tracks. The city's black population has dropped since its peak of 71 percent in 1970, as low-income black neighborhoods emptied out and middle-income blacks moved to majority-black suburbs. 2011 marked the first year in almost a half century that African Americans were not the majority in the District. As of July 2015, an estimated 48.3 percent of the city was African American.

The city's white population, on the other hand, grew from 30 percent in 2000 to an estimated 44 percent 15 years later.

Adrian Fenty succeeded Williams in 2007. As mayor, Fenty's biggest initiative was improving the floundering public schools. For years D.C. schools, despite one of the highest per-pupil spending rates in the nation, had low achievement levels and plunging enrollments. In 2007, at Fenty's behest, the city council transferred control of the schools from an independent board of education to the mayor's office. He installed as his superintendent Michelle Rhee, an alumna of the Teach for America Program and founder of the New Teacher Project. Rhee closed nonperforming and underused schools and negotiated a contract with the union that gave teachers the option of earning merit pay and gave her the power to dismiss low-performing teachers. Rhee also encouraged the charter school movement. Charter school enrollments in D.C. rose from 25 percent in 2006 to 46 percent in 2016, one of the highest enrollment rates in the country.

In 2010, Council President Vincent Gray harnessed African-American discontent with gentrification to defeat Fenty for the Democratic nomination. He won the primary 54%-44%, carrying almost every black-majority precinct and losing just about all the others. Gray continued many of the initiatives championed by his immediate predecessors but soon found his administration derailed by a series of scandals and a federal investigation, which set the stage for a grueling primary election in 2014. Gray ended up losing 44%-32% to Muriel Bowser, a second-term councilwoman with close ties to Fenty. Bowser went on to defeat David Catania, a Republican-turned-independent councilman, in a contentious general election 54%-34%.

Often viewed as a cautious politician, Bowser has taken some risks as mayor, especially when it comes to the matter of District autonomy. In February 2015, Bowser defied Congress by allowing to take effect a voter-approved ballot measure that effectively legalized marijuana. House Republicans had previously attached a rider to the 2015 federal budget prohibiting the city from implementing the law. Bowser's administration ignored the rider by arguing that the measure had gone into effect before Congress passed the budget (though her office did refrain from setting up a framework for taxing and regulating marijuana in the city). Bowser threw her support behind the Budget Autonomy Act the city council passed in 2013. The act, which grants D.C. more control over its internal finances, had been tied up in courts since Gray's administration challenged it. After a 2015 legal ruling in favor of the act, congressional Republicans moved to nix it the following year. Bowser has also been a vocal proponent of the D.C. statehood movement. In 2016, she supported placing a referendum on the November ballot that proposed making D.C. the 51st state and establishing a smaller federal district for government buildings and monuments. It received 79 percent of the vote. Hillary Clinton publicly backed statehood ahead of the March 2016 primaries in D.C., and Barack Obama was also a supporter, though he never actively pressed the issue as president. Donald Trump, when asked by *The Washington Post* about his stance on D.C. statehood, said that he had no position but suggested that he could be open to D.C. receiving full voting rights in the House.

The federal government is the city's chief employer, and roughly 15 percent of the federal workforce is based in the metro area. Federal spending and lobbying activity kept the city's economy buoyant throughout the recession. President Donald Trump announced a hiring freeze throughout the federal government, exempting military and national security agencies. The hospitality and tourism industrieshave continued to prosper. More than 19 million Americans visited the capital in 2015, spending $7.1 billion on local transportation, hotels and restaurants.

Politically, the District is liberal. In the 2016 general election, Trumpreceived only 4 percent% of the vote, down from the 7.3 percent that Mitt Romney received in 2012. In D.C.'s Republican caucuses, Trump won less than 14 percent, third behind Gov. John Kasich and Sen. Marco Rubio. Trump's presence in the city is accentuated by a hotel that he owns on Pennsylvania Avenue, about halfway between the Capitol and the White House. The hotel, which opened in September 2016, has been a focal point of concerns about potential conflicts of interest and has given rise to tensions between D.C. business owners and the president. In March 2017, two restaurant owners in the District launched a lawsuit against the hotel, alleging that it violates local laws on unfair competition.

The District's liberalism has often led to run-ins with congressional conservatives. In March 2015, Sen. Ted Cruz sought to overturn two D.C. laws: one aimed at prohibiting discrimination based on religious objections to abortion or birth control, and another that repealed an exemption for religious educational institutions from the city's LGBT anti-discrimination law. The following month, Rubio continued a decades-long battle between the District and gun-rights advocates by introducing a bill that overturned some of the city's restrictive firearms laws. Some Republicans have sympathized with the District's lack of budget autonomy and full voting rights. In February 2017, Rep. Darrell Issa of California voted with Democrats on the House Oversight Committee not to overturn D.C.'s assisted suicide law. Issa, a former chairman of the committee, also supported budget autonomy for the District, once saying, "what the city does with city funds should be primarily city decisions." Conservative firebrand Rep. Louie Gohmert of Texas argued that requiring District residents to pay federal income taxes without full voting rights amounted to "taxation without representation," a phrase that has become the unofficial slogan of the D.C. statehood movement. In 2015, he proposed abolishing federal income taxes for District residents until they receive a full-voting representative in Congress.

Population		**Race and Ethnicity**		**Income**	
Total	647,484	White	35.6%	Median Income	$70,848
Land area	68	Black	48.0%	Under $50,000	38.1%
Pop/ sq mi	9474.5	Latino	10.2%	$50,000-$99,999	24.7%
Born in state	36.8%	Asian	3.6%	$100,000-$199,999	23.7%
		Two races	2.1%	$200,000 or more	13.5%
Age Groups		Other	0.5%	Poverty Rate	18.0%
Under 18	17.2%				
18-34	31.7%	**Education**		**Health Insurance**	
35-64	36.4%	H.S grad or less	28.7%	With health insurance coverage	94.2%
Over 64	11.2%	Some college	16.8%		
		College Degree, 4 yr	23.3%		
Work		Post grad	31.3%	**Public Assistance**	
White Collar	60.9%			Cash public assistance income	3.7%
Sales and Service	32.6%	**Military**			
Blue Collar	6.6%	Veteran	5.4%	Food stamp/SNAP benefits	14.9%
Government	25.4%	Active Duty	0.6%		

Voter Turnout			
2015 Total Citizens 18+	485,116	2016 Pres Turnout as % CVAP	64%
2016 Pres Votes	311,268	2012 Pres Turnout as % CVAP	66%

Presidential Politics

2016 Democratic Primary		
Hillary Clinton (D)	76,704	(78%)
Bernie Sanders (D)	20,361	(21%)
2016 Republican Convention		
Marco Rubio (R)	1,059	(37%)
John Kasich (R)	1,009	(36%)
Donald Trump (R)	391	(14%)
Ted Cruz (R)	351	(12%)

2016 Presidential Vote		
Hillary Clinton (D)	282,830	(91%)
Donald Trump (R)	12,723	(4%)
2012 Presidential Vote		
Barack Obama (D)	267,070	(91%)
Mitt Romney (R)	21,381	(7%)

DELEGATE

Eleanor Holmes Norton (D)

Elected 1990, 14th term; b. Jun 13, 1937, Washington; Antioch College (OH), B.A., 1960; Yale University (CT), M.A., 1963; Yale University Law School (CT), J.D., 1964; Episcopalian; Divorced; 2 children.

Professional Career: Clerk, Judge A. Leon Higginbotham, 1964-1965; Assistant legal Director, ACLU, 1965-1970; Adjunct Assistant Professional, NY University Law School, 1970-1971; Staff, NY mayor, 1971-1974; Chair, NYC Human Rights Comm., 1970-1977; Chair, US Equal Empl. Oppor. Comm., 1977-1981; Sr. fellow, Urban Inst., 1981-1982; Professor, Georgetown University Law Center, 1982-1990.

DC Office: 2136 RHOB 20515, 202-225-8050, Fax: 202-225-3002, norton.house.gov.

State Offices: Washington, 202-408-9041; Washington, 202-678-8900.

Committees: *Oversight & Government Reform*: Government Operations, Health Care, Benefits & Administrative Rules. *Transportation & Infrastructure*: Aviation, Coast Guard & Maritime Transportation, Economic Dev't, Public Buildings & Emergency Management, Highways & Transit (RMM).

Election Results

Election	Name (Party)	Vote (%)		Cand. Spent	Ind. Exp. Support	Ind. Exp. Oppose
2016 General	Eleanor Holmes Norton (D)	265,178	(89%)			
	Martin Moulton (L)	18,713	(6%)			
	Natale Stracuzzi (G)	14,336	(5%)			

Prior winning percentages: 2014 (97%), 2012 (89%), 2010 (89%), 2008 (92%), 2006 (100%), 2004 (91%), 2002 (93%), 2000 (90%), 1998 (90%), 1996 (90%), 1994 (89%), 1992 (85%), 1990 (62%)

Eleanor Holmes Norton is a Democrat who was first elected delegate from the District of Columbia in 1990. The daughter of a District government employee and a school teacher, Norton graduated from Dunbar High School, and went on to get a law degree at Yale. She volunteered for the Student Nonviolent Coordinating Committee and traveled to Mississippi in 1963 to help register African-American voters. On June 11 of that year, she met with civil-rights activist Medgar Evers, who tried to convince her to move to Jackson and work as a civil rights lawyer. Just hours after Evers dropped her off at a bus station, a white supremacist shot and killed him in his driveway. Norton worked for the American Civil Liberties Union and the New York City Commission on Human Rights, and was head of the Equal Employment Opportunity Commission in the Carter administration. Afterward, she taught law at Georgetown University. When the delegate seat came open in 1990, she edged past Council Member Betty Anne Kane, 39%-33%, in the primary. Norton has been re-elected easily since; in 2016, she won 89% of the vote.

Her relationship with congressional Republicans active on District matters has been mixed. She worked closely with former Republican Rep. Tom Davis of Virginia on several issues. In 1995, she collaborated with Davis and Speaker Newt Gingrich to create the fiscal control board that oversaw the District's financial recovery. In 1999, she and Davis also worked together to pass a law providing in-state tuition for District students at colleges and universities in any state. But Norton has clashed with Republicans seeking to impose restrictions on District policies. When Maryland Republican Rep. Andy Harris announced his intentions to challenge a voter-approved ballot measure decriminalizing marijuana in 2014, Norton stated, "D.C. residents can rest assured that when a mandate comes directly from the people, they haven't seen a fight like the fight I'm preparing to make against Rep. Andy Harris and any other member of Congress who attempts to undo our democratic process."

She has clashed with presidents in recent years. Norton was frustrated by President Barack Obama's 2011 budget deal with House Republicans because it kept a school voucher program in the

District's budget. She also disagreed with Obama's opposition to a 2013 House bill to allow the District to tap local revenues for government operations. She has been a vocal opponent of President Donald Trump. In November 2016, she called for him to withdraw his selection of Steve Bannon as chief strategist. She has continued her opposition to school voucher programs under the Trump administration, which supported expanding the program during budget deliberations in 2017.

Norton has been frustrated in one of her top priorities: securing full voting rights for D.C. in the House, even with Democratic majorities in both houses of Congress from 2007 to 2011. "We must never retreat from our full citizenship rights, and we must always seize any part of our rights that we can get," she told *The Washington Post*. Davis came up with the idea of creating two new House seats, one for the District of Columbia and the other for the state entitled to the 436th district under the statutory reapportionment formula, which after the 2000 census happened to be heavily Republican Utah. That gave Republicans an incentive to vote for the bill. In 2007, the House passed her bill 241-177. But in the Senate, it fell three votes short of the 60 necessary to prevent a filibuster. In 2009, with increased Democratic majorities, Norton revived the bill and it was approved by the House Judiciary Committee in February 2009. In March, the Senate passed it, 61-37, but with an amendment sponsored by Republican Sen. John Ensign of Nevada overturning the District's gun control laws. Norton looked for a path to compromise, but then House conservatives added more constraints on the District's ability to regulate guns and Norton threw up her hands. The legislation died soon thereafter. In January 2015, she introduced the New Columbia Admission Act, proposing to carve out a 51st state around the White House, Capitol, Supreme Court and National Mall. Companion legislation was introduced in the Senate, but neither bill advanced. Norton introduced another statehood bill in March 2017.

Norton has had a number of successes on local issues, including the Southeast Federal Center Public-Private Development Act, which promoted development around the Washington Navy Yard, and the decision to place the Coast Guard headquarters on the grounds of the old St. Elizabeth's Hospital. She sponsored a financial transparency act for D.C. judges that Obama signed into law in 2016. In addition, Norton has managed to get senators and the White House to recognize her recommendations for federal trial judges and the U.S. attorney for the District of Columbia, a privilege enjoyed by members of the Senate. In March 2017, she sent a letter to Trump, requesting that he too consult her on nominations for federal judicial and law enforcement positions in the District. Norton's legislative and policy agenda is not solely local. As the ranking Democrat on the Transportation and Infrastructure Highways and Transit Subcommittee, she has advocated increased funding for road and mass transit projects. In every Congress since 1993, she has introduced or co-sponsored a bill to dismantle the U.S. nuclear weapons program.

★ FLORIDA ★

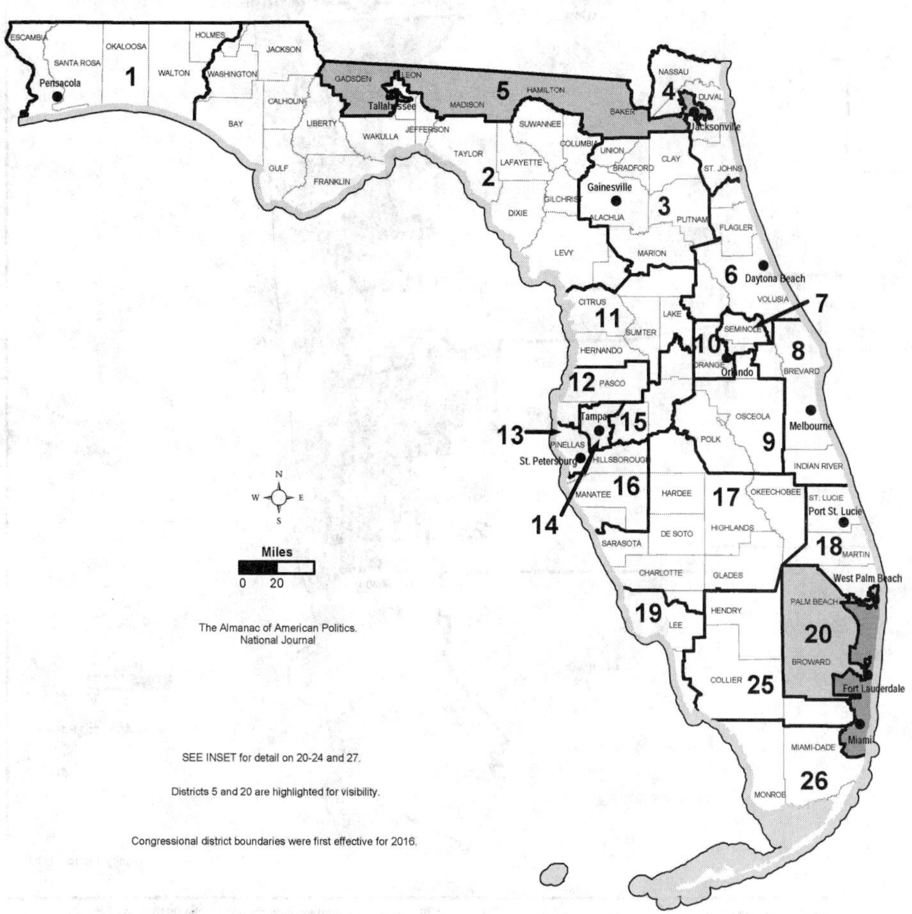

ESCAMBIA
SANTA ROSA
OKALOOSA
WALTON
HOLMES
WASHINGTON
JACKSON
CALHOUN
BAY
GULF
LIBERTY
FRANKLIN
WAKULLA
GADSDEN
LEON
Tallahassee
JEFFERSON
MADISON
HAMILTON
TAYLOR
SUWANNEE
LAFAYETTE
COLUMBIA
BAKER
NASSAU
DUVAL
Jacksonville
UNION
BRADFORD
CLAY
ST. JOHNS
Gainesville
ALACHUA
GILCHRIST
DIXIE
LEVY
PUTNAM
FLAGLER
MARION
Daytona Beach
VOLUSIA
CITRUS
SUMTER
LAKE
SEMINOLE
HERNANDO
ORANGE
Orlando
BREVARD
PASCO
Tampa
PINELLAS
St. Petersburg
HILLSBOROUGH
OSCEOLA
POLK
Melbourne
INDIAN RIVER
MANATEE
HARDEE
OKEECHOBEE
ST. LUCIE
Port St. Lucie
HIGHLANDS
DE SOTO
SARASOTA
MARTIN
CHARLOTTE
GLADES
West Palm Beach
PALM BEACH
LEE
HENDRY
BROWARD
COLLIER
Fort Lauderdale
Miami
MIAMI-DADE
MONROE
Pensacola
1
2
3
4
5
6
7
8
9
10
11
12
13
14
15
16
17
18
19
20
25
26
N
W
E
S
Miles
0 20
The Almanac of American Politics.
National Journal
SEE INSET for detail on 20-24 and 27.
Districts 5 and 20 are highlighted for visibility.
Congressional district boundaries were first effective for 2016.

On election night 2000, television journalist Tim Russert – seeing the close margins in the Sunshine State -- famously told viewers that the contest was coming down to "Florida, Florida, Florida." Ever since that interminable recount was decided by the Supreme Court, Florida has refused to give up its prized position in presidential politics, attracting countless candidate visits and siding with the winner every time, by margins between just one and five percentage points.

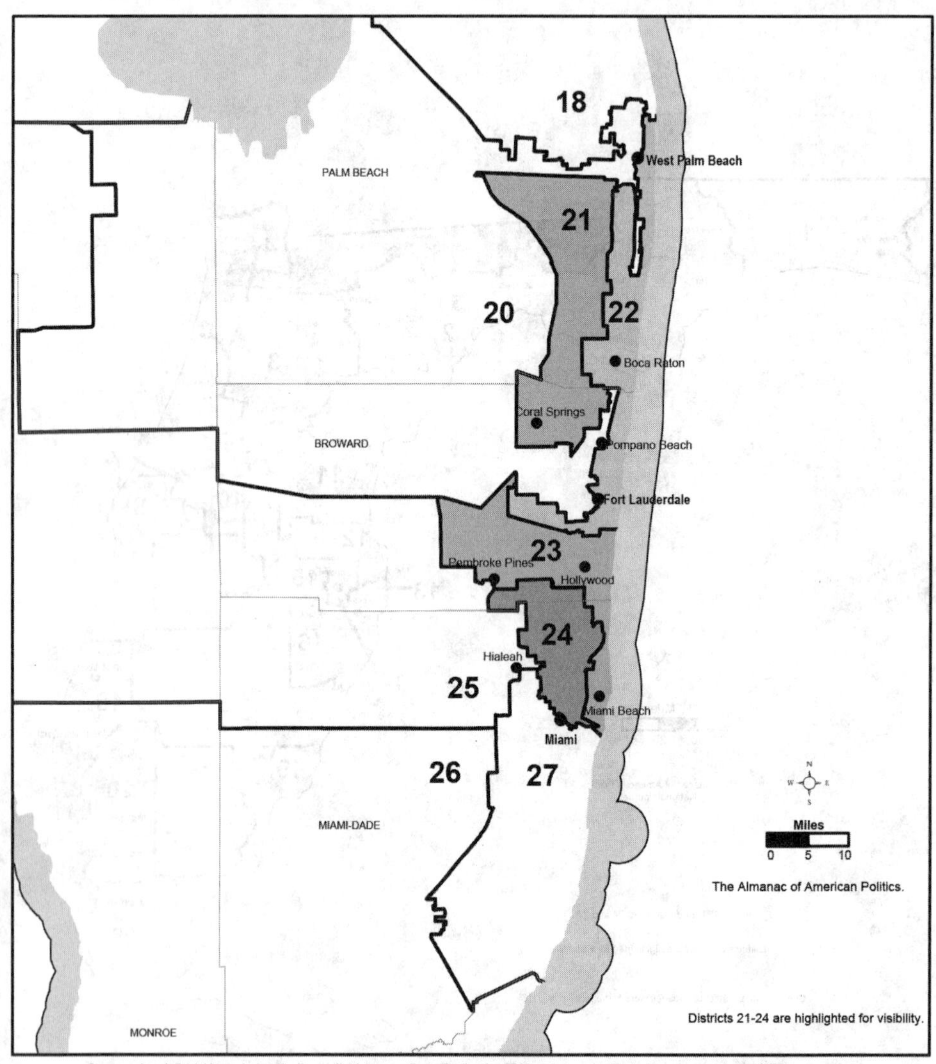

Congressional district boundaries for these districts were first effective for 2012 and were unaffected by changes in the 2015 map..

More than 500 years ago, in March 1513, the Spanish conquistador Juan Ponce de León spied the coast of Florida. For the next 400 years, anyone sailing along Florida's 1,197 miles of coastline and 663 miles of beach would not have seen anything much different from what Ponce de Leon saw. But within the past century the state has been transformed, from a swampy, under-settled, mostly rural state of 1.5 million people (the smallest population in the South), to a metropolitan powerhouse of more than 20 million people that overtook New York as the third most populous state in 2014. The result is a heterogeneous nation-state, historically Southern, demographically Northeastern and Midwestern, and culturally, at least partly, Latin American. It has been economically vibrant for most of the past century, but vulnerable to sudden contractions, as in the mid-1920s when a hurricane abruptly ended the Miami real estate boom and during the Great Recession. But Florida has bounced back before, and it is growing again – a population spike of almost 10 percent since 2010 alone.

Florida is the only Atlantic Coast state that was not part of the colonial United States. In 1819, it was acquired from Spain, through the exertions of John Quincy Adams and Andrew Jackson. Adams thought that in foreign hands Florida could block the Gulf of Mexico and the Mississippi Valley, while Jackson saw it as a haven for runaway slaves and a launching pad for Indians to raid the farmers and planters of what was then the American Southwest. Florida was a minor agricultural state until the early 20th century, when its sunshine economy based on citrus production and tourism took hold. After the Civil War, orange groves sprang up along the St. John's River and outside of Tampa, but the "Great Freeze" of 1894-95 devastated the state's nascent citrus industry. Growers responded by expanding croplands further south and by 1915, citrus output in the state was roughly double its pre-freeze level. Florida's balmy winter climate inspired railroad barons Henry Flagler and Henry Plant to build grand resort hotels and accompanying rail lines (Flagler on the Atlantic coast and Plant on the Gulf) which not only brought vacationers to Florida but also helped transport Florida oranges north to urban markets. Later, auto entrepreneur Carl Fisher promoted tourism to Florida and construction of the Dixie Highway, which in the 1920s helped millions of visitors travel to the state, many of whom decided to stay. Miami, founded in 1896, boomed until the hurricane hit in 1926 (and Fisher, who had become a local real estate magnate, lost his fortune). In the 1930s, New Yorkers started retiring to art deco apartments in Miami Beach.

By the 1960s, retirees from further north were flocking to the state looking for year-round sunshine – driving down I-95 from the northeast and ending up on the Atlantic coast, or down I-75 from the Midwest to reach the Gulf coast. Retirees joined agriculture and tourism as Florida's main economic drivers, but new industries, many related to the space program, also migrated to the state. In the 1980s and 1990s, the percentage of families with children as a share of Florida's population grew rapidly, lured by jobs and opportunities in communities that hadn't existed a generation earlier. The state's tourism sector, no longer dependent solely on beautiful beaches, was transformed as Orlando became the "Theme Park Capital of the World," starting, but hardly ending, with the Disney empire. The cruise business exploded, Port Miami was the global leader for cruise travel while Port Canaveral, about an hour's drive east from Orlando, and Port Everglades, outside of Fort Lauderdale, have huge terminals as well. If normalization with Cuba continues, it could eventually spur even more embarkations from the state's ports.

Florida is also an aviation industry hub. Brazilian manufacturer Embraer assembles executive jets in Melbourne, and it recently added a new maintenance facility to its North American headquarters complex in Fort Lauderdale. Likewise, the European turboprop maker ATR relocated its North American operations to Miami Springs. And aerospace giant Northrop Grumman has invested heavily in its operations in Melbourne, building a new design center there and adding capacity to produce the Air Force's Long Range Strike Bomber. Florida's "Space Coast" is seeing a revival after cutbacks, with entrepreneurial space companies like SpaceX testing the next generation of launch vehicles, although accidents like the September 2016 explosion of a SpaceX Falcon 9 on the Cape Canaveral launch pad have prompted delays. The Florida Panhandle is home to several military installations, including the Pensacola Naval Air Station and Eglin Air Force Base, which helped attract defense contractors, commercial aviation companies and industrial airparks to the region.

With three state universities as lead partners, central Florida is developing a high-tech corridor that runs from Tampa (home of the University of South Florida) through Orlando (the University of Central Florida) to the Space Coast and reaches up to Gainesville (the University of Florida). An example of the rapid development in the corridor is Lake Nona, a 7,000-acre parcel south of Orlando. What a decade ago was a downtrodden golf course and vacant land next to the airport is now a medical multiplex that includes Sanford Burnham, which conducts research in obesity and other diseases, the University of Central Florida's College of Medicine, Nemours Children's Hospital, and the massive new Orlando VA Medical Center. Cisco chose Lake Nona and its pedestrian-friendly residential and commercial developments as the first U.S. community, and only the ninth in the world, to become a networked "Smart+Connected" city.

But like other fast-growing states, Florida's economy has also been built on construction and real estate, which makes it subject to sudden downturns. As real estate values plummeted during the Great Recession, the foreclosure crisis hit few states as hard as Florida. Many banks there compounded the problem by their inability to process the glut of distressed properties though the state's court system, and fraud was not uncommon. Local tax receipts, heavily dependent on property values and the construction industry, slumped. Unemployment rose from 3.5 percent in January 2007 to a peak of 11.2 percent in

January 2010, and more people left Florida than moved there for the first time since post-World War II demobilization. The recession lasted longer in Florida than it did most other states, with the economy not really picking up until 2012. Even then the housing sector remained troubled, and while unemployment had fallen to 4.9 percent by late 2016, that was still higher than the nation as a whole, and median incomes were roughly $8,000 below the national average

One of the state's original economic pillars, the citrus industry, has been crippled by citrus greening disease, which has destroyed about three-quarters of the crop. Much of the rest of the agriculture sector has either remained stagnant or shrunk; agriculture currently accounts for less than 1 percent of the state's workforce. Now, horticulture – including such humble products as sod and outdoor plants -- is on the verge of overtaking the vaunted citrus fruit as the state's biggest agricultural product. "Just since the early 2000s, the value of agriculture as a share of the state economy has been nearly cut in half," the *Tampa Bay Times* reported. No wonder, then, that developers have purchased 1 million acres of farmland over the last decade. One potential growth area related to agriculture: medical marijuana, approved in a ballot measure on its second try in 2016. One market research firm predicted a $1.6 billion industry for the state by 2020.

Retirees continue to come to Florida; 19 percent of the population is 65 or older, the nation's highest percentage. But Florida is also increasingly diverse. Nearly a quarter of the population is Latino, up two percentage points just since the 2010 Census, while the white population has fallen from about 58 percent to just above 55 percent over the same period. More than half of the state's children are minorities, up from a little more than a third in 1980. For refugees from Cuba and Haiti and for immigrants from the Caribbean and Latin America, Florida has been a land of freedom from authoritarian and turbulent lands. Its population has been continually replenished with people from other states, foreign countries and the U.S. territory of Puerto Rico. Today, a little more than one-third of Florida residents are natives. Miami has long been the economic and commercial capital of Latin America: You can fly nonstop from Miami to just about any major city in Latin America, and both English and Spanish are common and Portuguese not unknown. Spurred by a weak economy and a debt crisis, large numbers of Puerto Ricans have been moving to Orlando and Osceola County, as have Venezuelans, Colombians and Dominicans; Mexicans are more prevalent in the state's verdant southwestern farmlands (Hendry, Collier and Hardee Counties). While Cubans still dominate Miami-Dade, they make up less than a third of the state's overall Hispanic population. The I-4 Corridor is mostly family country, although The Villages site in Sumter County is a fast-growing haven for retirees. Further south along the Gulf Coast are a necklace of affluent communities. The Panhandle, the so-called Redneck Riviera around Pensacola and Panama City, is culturally Southern. State government is headquartered in Tallahassee, chosen because it was midway between the population centers of Jacksonville and Pensacola at a time when almost no one lived on the peninsula; Tallahassee and the university town of Gainesville are liberal bastions in a sea of conservatism.

Florida has a fragile civil society, and it can be chaotic and disorderly at times; the state has often ranked in the top 10 in violent crime. Most people do not have deep roots in the state - most communities sprang into existence within living memory - and if Florida gives people more freedom and options than elsewhere, it also gives them more disruption than many anticipated. (Aggregating stories of weird crimes in Florida has become a cottage industry.) Florida has more gun permits than any other state, and it pioneered the right for citizens to carry concealed weapons in 1987. The state's "stand-your-ground" law, which allows Floridians to use deadly force when they believe their lives are threatened, became a focal point in the tragic 2012 shooting death of an unarmed black teenager, Trayvon Martin, in Sanford. Guns came to the fore again with the terrorism-inspired incident at the Pulse nightclub in Orlando in June 2016 – the deadliest mass shooting in modern U.S. history, with 49 killed and 53 injured. Another terror-related mass shooting, also possibly stemming from the gunman's mental problems, came in early 2017 at the Fort Lauderdale-Hollywood International Airport, leaving five dead. But political polarization seemed to make any overhaul of firearms policy unlikely. Meanwhile, the state was forced to grapple with the apparent consequences of climate change, including a projected sea level rise of between one and four feet over the next century. At least the state was lucky to avoid a major hurricane between Wilma in October 2005 and Matthew in November 2016; the latter storm strafed the Atlantic coast, causing an estimated $729 million in damage.

The nation's other three largest states are one-sided politically, with California and New York heavily Democratic and Texas heavily Republican. Florida remains closely divided. In 2008 and 2012, Floridians voted narrowly for Barack Obama, who rallied the liberal Democratic base; then they flipped in the subsequent governor's races, electing and reelecting conservative Republican Rick Scott by even narrower margins. But the trend in state politics has been toward Republicans since the 1990s, when they captured the state House in 1994, the state Senate in 1996, and the governorship in 1998. Republicans in 2015 held all of the major elected statewide offices and had big majorities in the legislature. In 2014, none of the Democratic candidates for attorney general, chief financial officer or commissioner of agriculture could muster more than 42 percent of the vote. Republican state legislators have been helped by term limits and redistricting: Democratic communities of African Americans and Jews are concentrated in a few districts, while Republican voters are more evenly spread around.

In 2016, both Donald Trump and Hillary Clinton devoted major attention to the state – Clinton with a precision ground game and Trump seemingly winging it. But after strong Democratic results in early voting, Trump ended up ahead, winning by 112,000 votes, or just over 1 percent of the 9.5 million cast. (The 2012 margin for Obama had been fewer than 75,000 votes.) Clinton, targeting minority voters, actually did pretty well -- she won Hispanics, 62%-35%, and secured about 267,000 more votes than Obama had in 2012, including six-digit increases in the Democratic bastions of Miami-Dade, Broward (Fort Lauderdale), Palm Beach and Orange counties. But the first female presidential nominee did three points worse among women than Obama had, and Trump benefited from a white surge. Running strong in the I-4 corridor, the Republican nominee got a whopping 454,000 more votes than Mitt Romney had in 2012, flipped such counties as Pinellas (St. Petersburg) and St. Lucie from blue to red, and saw six-digit raw-vote increases in Lee (Fort Myers), Pasco, Volusia (Daytona Beach), Polk, Manatee (Bradenton), Hernando, Sarasota and Charlotte counties. (Traditional bellwether county Hillsborough, which includes Tampa, voted for Clinton – a rare lapse.) The New York Times' Upshot column noted that if not for a historical quirk – the inclusion of the panhandle in Florida rather than in Alabama -- an affiliation that residents had sought for decades – then Clinton might well have become president. Either way, Florida's demographic churn should make it a national political battleground for the foreseeable future.

Population		**Race and Ethnicity**		**Income**	
Total	19,645,772	White	56.1%	Median Income	$47,507 (38 out of 50)
Land area	53,625	Black	15.5%		
Pop/ sq mi	366.4	Latino	23.7%	Under $50,000	52.1%
Born in state	35.8%	Asian	2.5%	$50,000-$99,999	29.3%
		Two races	1.7%	$100,000-$199,999	14.6%
Age Groups		Other	0.5%	$200,000 or more	4.1%
Under 18	20.6%			Poverty Rate	16.5%
18-34	19.2%	**Education**			
35-64	39.3%	H.S grad or less	42.6%	**Health Insurance**	
Over 64	18.5%	Some college	30.1%	With health insurance coverage	82.0%
		College Degree, 4 yr	17.5%		
Work		Post grad	9.8%	**Public Assistance**	
White Collar	34.1%				
Sales and Service	47.9%	**Military**		Cash public assistance income	2.2%
Blue Collar	18.0%	Veteran	9.7%		
Government	12.5%	Active Duty	0.3%	Food stamp/SNAP benefits	14.8%

Voter Turnout			
2015 Total Citizens 18+	13,933,052	2016 Pres Turnout as % CVAP	68%
2016 Pres Votes	9,420,039	2012 Pres Turnout as % CVAP	65%

Legislature	
Senate:	15D, 25R
House:	41D, 79R

Presidential Politics

2016 Democratic Primary		
Hillary Clinton (D)	1,101,414	(64%)
Bernie Sanders (D)	568,839	(33%)
2016 Republican Primary		
Donald Trump (R)	1,079,870	(46%)
Marco Rubio (R)	638,661	(27%)
Ted Cruz (R)	404,891	(17%)
John Kasich (R)	159,976	(7%)

2016 Presidential Vote		
Donald Trump (R)	4,617,886	(49%)
Hillary Clinton (D)	4,504,975	(47%)
Gary Johnson (L)	207,043	(2%)
2012 Presidential Vote		
Barack Obama (D)	4,237,756	(50%)
Mitt Romney (R)	4,163,447	(49%)

Florida may not always decide the outcome of the presidential race, but it is likely to maintain its status as the largest and one of the most competitive battleground states in the country. Florida has 29 electoral votes, the same number as New York; only California and Texas have more. And according to Florida Democratic strategist Steven Schale, one of the state's savviest political observers, since 1992, when the Sunshine State became a true White House battleground, more than 50 million votes have been cast in seven presidential elections and the two parties are separated by a miniscule 0.02 percent: Republican candidates having received a net 12,000 votes more than Democrats. Donald Trump scored a more comfortable margin over Hillary Clinton in 2016, nearly 113,000 votes, defeating her 49%-48%. But the outcome was hardly a foregone conclusion. Just over 69 percent of Florida's voters cast their ballots before Election Day and daily pre-election data from state and local election officials indicated that Clinton was leading in the early vote. Indeed, among all ballots cast before Election Day, Clinton garnered an advantage of roughly 247,000. But among voters who went to their precinct polling stations on Nov. 8, Trump prevailed by some 360,000, tipping the state into his column. How, and where, did Trump succeed? Both Trump and Clinton turned out their respective partisan bases in the state: Republicans in the Panhandle and the northern tier of the state, as well as those in the Fort Myers media market, voted solidly for Trump; voters in Tallahassee (the state capital and home of Florida State University) and Gainesville (the University of Florida) and the Democratic bastion of Miami-Dade and Broward counties went decisively for Clinton. In the third county on the so-called "Gold Coast," Palm Beach, the Democratic vote lagged, but Clinton still prevailed. Comparing the vote in the base regions of the two parties, Clinton came out ahead by about 140,000 votes, a margin slightly higher than Obama's advantage over Mitt Romney in 2012.

In other words, inadequate Democratic turnout in the party's base territory did not cause Clinton's loss. The election was decided in the state's famed I-4 corridor, which stretches from Daytona on the Atlantic Coast, through the burgeoning Orlando area, to the Tampa-St. Petersburg metro on the Gulf Coast. The early vote from the I-4 corridor gave Trump a scant 11,000-vote lead, an advantage that wouldn't suggest he could overcome the lead Clinton had from the "base" counties. But on Election Day, Trump voters surged to the polls and his 11,000-vote lead along I-4 swelled to more than 250,000, securing the state for the GOP standard-bearer. According to a post-election analysis by Schale, Trump's victory in the I-4 corridor was fueled largely by his strength in the suburbs and exurbs of the region. While Clinton outpolled Trump in the more urban portions -- Orange, Osceola and Seminole counties around Orlando, as well as Tampa-St. Petersburg -- by about 200,000 votes, the future president won 15 other counties along I-4 by a whopping 450,000. In just three -- Hernando and Pasco north of Tampa-St. Pete and Volusia (Daytona Beach) -- Romney's margin over Obama was some 24,000 votes in 2012. Trump's advantage over Clinton in these three counties was more than 112,000. That difference alone would have been more than enough to wipe out Obama's statewide victory margin of 74,309 in 2012. Floridians got to know the candidates very well during the campaign. According to an analysis by Kantar Media, both pumped more advertising dollars into Florida than any other state. An ABC News report just prior to the election found that in the last month of the general election campaign, Trump and Clinton spent more days in Florida - Trump, 10; Clinton, 8 -than any other state. And the voters responded: 9.4 million Floridians cast ballots in the presidential election, up from 8.5 million in 2012.

Florida's presidential primary was not crucial in determining a nomination between 1976, when Democrat Jimmy Carter defeated George Wallace and ended Wallace's career in national politics, and 2008, when Arizona Sen. John McCain defeated Romney, a victory that propelled him to success one week later in the more than 20 states that held primaries or caucuses on Super Tuesday. In 2016, the GOP primary saw Trump dispatch one of his chief rivals, Florida Sen. Marco Rubio, from the Republican nominating contest. Rubio's campaign had flagged by the time of the Florida primary on March 15 and he waged a last-ditch effort to win it. But he could not rally his home-state voters and former Florida Gov. Jeb Bush, who had pulled out of the GOP nominating contest earlier, declined Rubio's overtures to his former mentor to endorse him. Trump breezed to a victory over Rubio 46%-27%, and Texas Sen. Ted Cruz finished third. In the end, Rubio won only one of the state's 67 counties, Miami-Dade, with its sizeable Cuban-American electorate. Trump swept the rest of the state and Florida's winner-take-all primary netted him the state's 99 GOP convention delegates, a huge haul that helped him solidify his grip on the Republican nomination. In his concession speech on primary night, Rubio announced he was suspending his campaign and lamented, "America's in the middle of a real political storm, a real tsunami, and we should have seen this coming." Ironically, Rubio had ridden an anti-establishment wave to his upset victory in the 2010 Republican Senate primary. But by the time he sought the presidency, many Florida Republicans saw him as a more establishment figure, having backed bipartisan immigration reform in the Senate, while others viewed him as a typical pol who put his White House ambitions ahead of serving his Florida constituents. The Democratic race was less critical to Clinton. In a primary where roughly half the voters were non-white, Clinton was able to rally African Americans and Hispanics to defeat Vermont Sen. Bernie Sanders 64%-33%. Sanders carried just nine rural counties in the Panhandle and northern rim of the state.

Congressional Districts

115th Congress Lineup	16R 11D	**114th Congress Lineup**	17R 10D

Florida has gained congressional districts after every Census since 1930, when it elected four House members. Its 15-seat gain since 1960 is more than any other state, including Texas, during that half-century. Following the 2010 Census, Florida increased from 25 to 27, leaving it with a delegation the same size as New York's. Republican Gov. Rick Scott's narrow victory and big GOP margins in the legislature after 2010 meant that Republicans controlled the redistricting process. But their growth opportunities were limited by two factors: Republicans' already robust 19-6 edge in the delegation following a banner year, and a new voter-approved law seeking to rein in the kind of gerrymandering that had created one of the strangest patchworks of districts in the country.

In November 2010, while four Florida Democrats lost their seats, voters simultaneously gave Democrats a silver lining by approving a set of ballot propositions backed by the reform group Fair Districts Florida. The Fair Districts amendments require legislators to draw compact districts conforming to county and city boundaries and prohibit them from taking into account partisan data or incumbent residences. Black Democrat Corrine Brown, whose district snaked through the North Florida swamp from Jacksonville to Orlando, as well as Cuban-American Republican Mario Diaz-Balart, whose party's interests were threatened by the new law, unsuccessfully sued in federal court to block the law, claiming it would harm minority voters.

Allies of Democrats and the Fair Districts movement then sued in state court to overturn the Republican-drawn map in 2012, arguing Republicans had secretly used partisan data to preserve their edge. In particular, many Democrats (except Brown) would have liked for her egregiously shaped 5th District to be unpacked and for St. Petersburg's black neighborhoods to be reattached to the 13th District. But Republicans defended their handiwork by noting they had shoved two of their own into the same suburban Orlando seat. In April 2012, the Obama Justice Department granted the Republican map federal preclearance and a state circuit judge refused to block implementation.

Fair Districts proponents continued to press for change. After Leon County Circuit Judge Terry Lewis ruled that the districts of Brown and Republican Daniel Webster failed to meet the Fair Districts standard, the legislature in August 2014 adopted a new map that altered seven of the state's districts and shifted nearly 400,000 voters in central and north Florida; that map took effect after the 2014 election. Lewis approved the map, but the reformers appealed again. In July 2015, the state Supreme Court threw out major pieces of the map, ruling that it was a political gerrymander in violation of the 2010 referendum. The Court gave the Legislature explicit instructions on a new map, and the Legislature complied with those guidelines. It changed virtually every district in the state, effectively ending the career of one incumbent from each party and causing major headaches for a few others.

In the 2016 election, the changes helped Democrats gain two seats in the Orlando area and one in St. Petersburg. But they lost seats in the Tallahassee and Treasure Coast areas. That gave the Democrats a one-seat gain and reduced Republican control of the delegation to 16-11. In addition, Corrine Brown lost her seat in the Democratic primary, the victim of a major shift in her district, plus a federal indictment.

Florida likely will gain two seats following the 2020 reapportionment, according to Census Bureau projections. An easy option might be for the Republicans to take a seat in the north and Democrats a seat in the south, and for each party to entrench some of its incumbents. But the recent history of redistricting suggests that neither party in Florida has been inclined to take the course of least resistance, and that citizens groups will assert their prerogatives. The election of a new governor in 2018 likely will have some impact on the outcome. Regardless, it's a safe bet that the state and federal courts will have additional opportunities for influence.

Governor

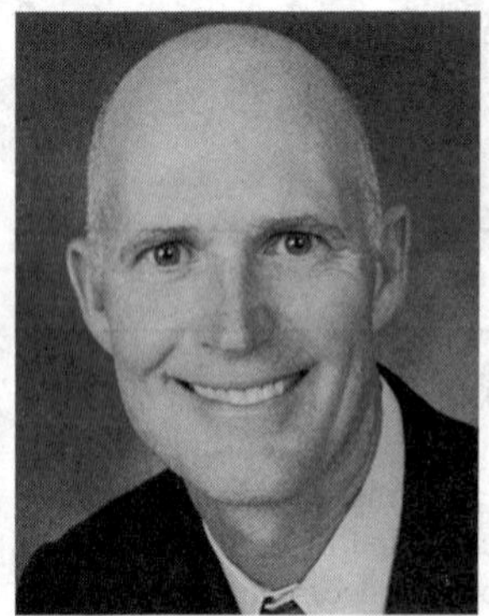

Rick Scott (R)

Elected 2010, term expires 2019, 2nd term; b. Dec. 1, 1952, Bloomington, IL; U. of MO, Kansas City, B.A. 1975, Southern Methodist U., J.D. 1978; Christian; Married (Ann); 2 children.

Military Career: U.S. Navy, 1971-1974.

Professional Career: Co-founder, Chairman & CEO, Columbia/HCA, 1987-1997; Venture Capitalist, 1997-2010; Practicing attorney, Johnson & Swanson, Dallas.

Office: 400 S. Monroe St., Tallahassee, 32399-0001; 850-488-7146; Fax: 850-487-0801; Website: flgov.com.

Election Results

Election	Name (Party)	Vote (%)
2014 General	Rick Scott (R)	2,865,343 (48%)
	Charlie Crist (D)	2,801,198 (47%)
	Adrian Wyllie (L)	223,356 (4%)
2014 Primary	Rick Scott (R)	831,887 (88%)
	Elizabeth Cuevas-Neunder (R)	100,496 (11%)

Prior winning percentage: 2010 (49%)

Republican Rick Scott, a conservative former healthcare CEO, has won two close contests for the governorship of Florida, yet in office, Scott has regularly irritated his own party in Tallahassee -- to say nothing of the Democrats. In 2016, Scott broke early for Donald Trump and helped the GOP nominee carry his electoral-vote-rich state, seemingly brightening his political future as his tenure as governor was nearing an end.

Scott grew up in Kansas City, Missouri, the son of a truck driver and a JCPenney clerk. He enlisted in the Navy after one year of community college. After his military service, Scott enrolled at the University of Missouri-Kansas City and, displaying an early entrepreneurial streak, financed his education by buying two donut shops and hiring his mother to manage them. Undergraduate degree in hand, he went to Southern Methodist University in Texas for a law degree. After college, he went to work for a large firm, where he specialized in health care mergers and acquisitions. In 1987, Scott put together a $6 billion bid to purchase Nashville-based HCA, the hospital company founded by Drs. Thomas Frist and Thomas Frist Jr., father and brother, respectively, of former GOP Sen. Bill Frist of Tennessee. When that offer was rejected, Scott and Texas billionaire Richard Rainwater started their own hospital company called Columbia with $125,000 in savings.

Columbia started off in 1988 with two hospitals in El Paso, and for the next nine years bought up dozens of hospitals, many of them nonprofit operations, and offered ownership shares to doctors who made referrals. Columbia became highly profitable, and in 1994, it made a successful bid for HCA. Scott worked to reduce costs and to require more accountability while opening heart bypass surgery facilities. By 1997, Columbia/HCA was the nation's largest health care company and its seventh largest employer, with 340 hospitals, $20 billion in revenue and 285,000 employees. But the FBI was investigating charges that Columbia/HCA overbilled the Medicare and Medicaid programs, twice raiding the firm's hospitals seeking evidence. Nine days after the second raid, the board of directors ousted Scott, with Thomas Frist Jr. made chief executive officer. In settlements in 2000 and 2002, the firm pleaded guilty to federal fraud charges and paid $1.7 billion in fines. In a deposition in a civil suit in which he was a witness, Scott invoked his Fifth Amendment right against self-incrimination 75 times rather than answer questions – a spectacle that came to haunt his future campaigns. His business associates told *The New York Times* at the time that Scott was a brilliant and incisive businessman who was undone by his fatal flaws, including arrogance and aggressiveness that had permeated the company. Still, Scott was richly rewarded for his work at Columbia/HCA, leaving with $10 million in cash and $300 million in stock and options. In rehabilitating his image later, Scott maintained that he was never charged with wrongdoing. "I learned very hard lessons from what happened, and those lessons have helped me become a better businessman and leader," he said. Scott later bought control of America's Health Network cable channel, and in 2001 co-founded Solantic, which operates walk-in urgent care centers throughout Florida and specializes in patients without insurance. In 2003, he moved to Naples, Florida.

In March 2009, Scott cut a check for $5 million to found Conservatives for Patients' Rights, which ran TV ads featuring Scott criticizing President Barack Obama and congressional Democrats' health care reform bills, particularly the provision creating a government-financed insurance option. The Affordable Care Act passed in March 2010, and the next month, Scott announced that he was running for governor as a Republican to succeed Charlie Crist, who had opted to run for the Senate rather than seek a second term. Scott, who declared a $218 million net worth, immediately spent $4.7 million on ads. The front-runner in the primary was Attorney General Bill McCollum, a former House member and the GOP nominee for the Senate in 2000, who was choice of the state's GOP establishment. But the two rivals assailed each other in a barrage of ads, with Scott ultimately getting the better of McCollum. Scott unveiled a catchy economic plan with seven steps to create 700,000 jobs in seven years, with corporate and property tax cuts, public payroll reductions, and the streamlining of government agencies. Scott spent nearly $50 million and beat McCollum 46%-44%. Soon afterward, he picked as his running mate GOP state Sen. Jennifer Carroll, the first African-American Republican woman elected to the Legislature. The Democratic nominee was Alex Sink, a banker who became the state's elected chief financial officer, who easily won her primary. The Scott-Sink race continued in the same acrimonious vein as the GOP primary, as Democratic ads revived the Columbia/HCA case and Republican ads painted Sink as a "Tallahassee insider" and a supporter of Obama, who was toxic in that year's midterm election. Scott charged her with cheating during a debate and ran ads featuring his mother, wife and adult daughters to soften his image. Scott won, 49%-48%; he carried Latinos 50%-48%, won 62 percent of whites without college degrees, and ran just barely ahead in the I-4 Corridor. Overall, his campaign and political committee spent $85 million on his election, $73 million of which he financed himself. Republicans also expanded their majorities in both houses of the legislature.

In his first year in office, Scott cut the state budget to just over $69 billion, about $1.3 billion smaller than in the previous fiscal year. He also vetoed bills totaling a record $615 million, winning praise from tea party groups for cutting Tallahassee lawmakers' prized earmark measures. Scott took on teachers' unions, and in the summer of 2011 he signed several education bills that expanded the use of school vouchers and increased enrollment at high-performing charter schools. He also rejected $2.4 billion in federal transportation funds for a high-speed train line between Tampa and Orlando. The project had been in the works for years, and legislators from both parties criticized Scott's decision. Scott insisted that Florida taxpayers would ultimately be asked to pick up the tab for some of the construction costs. Scott enraged state Democrats by requiring welfare recipients to take drug tests. The law made national headlines and proved popular with conservatives in other states, but in late October, a U.S. District Court judge halted implementation on constitutional grounds and claimed that, contrary to data provided by the state, the program would not save money. Scott also waded into Florida's knotty Cuba politics when he signed a bill in May 2012 cracking down on companies doing business with Cuba and Syria. He was initially praised by the Cuban exile community, but after he signed the bill, he issued a statement complaining that the law was unenforceable without support from the federal government. Republican state legislators and Cuban exiles complained that Scott had undermined the new policy, and Florida Republican Sen. Marco Rubio publicly disagreed with the statement.

As Scott prepared to run for re-election, he shifted toward the political center. Having made good on most of his 2010 campaign promises, according to PolitiFact Florida's count, Scott shed the tea party image of his first years in office and portrayed himself as a champion of education. In 2014, he signed a record $77 billion budget that increased funding for public schools, universities, child protection services and the environment. He also used a light touch with his veto pen, rejecting only $69 million in the legislators' priority items. After vetoing a bill in 2013 to permit undocumented Florida residents to apply for a temporary drivers' license, he signed legislation providing in-state college tuition to them in 2014, over strong objections from some conservatives in his party. Still, Scott's brash manner, combined with a sluggish economic recovery, kept his poll numbers low, sinking to 31 percent in 2012. The governor's vulnerability inspired former governor Charlie Crist to try for a comeback, this time as a Democrat. Crist rapped Scott for cutting education and restricting abortion, and he vowed to raise the minimum wage; Scott promised to pump money into education, environmental protection, airports and seaport infrastructure and to cut taxes by up to $1 billion while maintaining his overall focus on creating jobs. In a bizarre episode at a mid-October debate, Scott refused to go on stage because a small, portable fan had been placed underneath the Democrat's podium – an amenity perennially requested by Crist, but in a possible violation of the debate rules. After several agonizing minutes of live TV with only one candidate on stage, Scott relented and went to his podium; while the incumbent held his own on the issues, the snit over the fan became predictable chum for late-night comedians.

In the end, Scott edged Crist by a point. Scott contributed more than $12 million of his personal fortune to help pay for a TV ad blitz in the closing days of the campaign that Democrats believe tipped the election his way. Estimates vary, but between his campaign, his political committee and the money he steered to the state GOP, Scott's reelection bid was likely better funded than his previous campaign. Crist was hardly a pauper in the money race. His campaign spent more than $40 million, and California billionaire environmentalist Tom Steyer's NextGen Climate political committee anted up roughly $20 million. Crist won almost a quarter million more votes than Sink had four years earlier, but voting in the Democratic strongholds of Miami-Dade and Broward counties was ten and six percentage points, respectively, below the statewide turnout of registered voters. Higher turnout came in GOP bastions like Collier, St. John's, Manatee and Sumter Counties. Scott carried white voters by a wide margin; Crist overwhelmingly won the votes of African Americans and easily carried Hispanics, who had split their votes four years earlier. Crist even carried Cubans narrowly.

With a projected $1 billion state surplus, Scott appeared well-positioned to increase spending on education and cut taxes. But he experienced some self-inflicted wounds. Scott forced out the widely respected commissioner of the Florida Department of Law Enforcement (FDLE), Gerald Bailey, and he had to backtrack from an initial claim that Bailey had resigned on his own. The revelation embarrassed Florida Cabinet members Attorney General Pam Bondi, state CFO Jeff Atwater and Agriculture Commissioner Adam Putman, all Republicans, who said they would not have rubber-stamped Scott's pick to replace Bailey had they known the true nature of his departure. Bailey accused Scott's office of frequent political meddling in the FDLE's work, including requests to run interference in a federal money-laundering probe of a GOP donor and to implicate falsely an Orange County clerk in an investigation of a prison release scandal. Scott denied Bailey's allegations.

Scott also faced turbulence for his shifting stance on Medicaid expansion. Early in his first term, Scott, a long-time critic of the Affordable Care Act, opposed its Medicaid expansion because the state would eventually have to pick up more of the costs once the feds reduced their subsidy. After his mother died in an ICU unit and Obama had carried Florida for a second time, Scott reversed course and endorsed Medicaid expansion in early 2013, calling it a "compassionate, common-sense step forward." But Scott didn't aggressively push the idea, as the GOP-controlled state legislature remained hostile. Then, in February 2015, the Centers for Medicare and Medicaid Services said it would not renew a Medicaid waiver that had provided more than $1 billion as a "low income pool" for the state to compensate hospitals for treating uninsured and poor patients. That prompted the Republican majority in the state Senate to get behind Medicaid expansion to help state hospitals pay for uninsured care. But after Scott was unable to persuade federal officials to extend the state's Medicaid waiver, he abruptly announced that he couldn't support Medicaid expansion, saying the federal government couldn't be trusted to cover the costs. Scott's Medicaid reversal antagonized Republican senators, who also complained that the governor was AWOL during much of the budget impasse - the worst since the GOP takeover of the statehouse in the mid-1990s - spending too much time on business recruiting trips or minor public events outside of Tallahassee. Republicans in the state House opposed the Senate's Medicaid expansion plans, and when Scott did try to intervene in the budget dispute, he did so in a way lawmakers found counterproductive.

Republican lawmakers were also peeved by Scott's Let's Get to Work political committee, which aired TV spots touting his tax cut proposals as GOP lawmakers in both legislative chambers were trying to scale them back to help resolve their budget differences.

Scott's awkward persona, polarizing policies and an impulse to counterattack collided in a most unexpected location in April 2016 – a Gainesville Starbucks where Cara Jennings, a liberal activist, happened to be working when Scott and his retinue walked in. In an exchange that would quickly go viral, Jennings angrily laid into Scott's policies on Medicaid and funding for Planned Parenthood and called the governor "an embarrassment to our state." Scott claimed (with some legitimacy) to have created 1 million jobs, to which Jennings countered, "A million jobs? Great, who here has a great job?" At that point, Scott left -- without his coffee – but in short order, his PAC fired back at Jennings through a video of its own. It answered Jennings' question about great jobs with this riposte: "Well, almost everybody – except those that are sitting around coffee shops, demanding public assistance, surfing the internet, and cursing at customers who come in." Scott fared better with the legislature later that year, when he signed a budget with relatively little fuss that raised public school student spending by 1 percent and allocated $151 million for Everglades restoration, while reducing the number of line-item vetoes, a move seen as an olive branch to legislators. Scott also said he had fulfilled his promise to cut taxes by $1 billion in his second term, a claim PolitiFact Florida rated Mostly True.

Disasters, both natural and manmade, made their mark on 2016. Florida grappled with the threat of Zika virus; Scott declared a state of emergency, called for more federal assistance, and offered free testing for pregnant women, who were at highest risk. (Less noticed: Five years earlier, Scott and lawmakers had slashed the state's mosquito-control budget.) In June, an ISIS-inspired gunman killed 49 and injured 53 at the Pulse nightclub in Orlando -- the deadliest mass shooting in modern U.S. history. And in October, the state's Atlantic Coast was hit by Hurricane Matthew, ending a decade-long run without a significant hurricane in the state. Scott received good reviews for his response, though he was rebuked in the courts for refusing to extend the state's voter-registration deadline because of the storm. Ultimately, an estimated 100,000 more voters registered for the general election thanks to the court-ordered extension.

The other big story of 2016, of course, was Trump. Prior to the Florida primary, Scott was officially neutral, though he wrote an op-ed favorable to Trump in *USA Today* in January – long before it was clear that Trump would be the nominee. After Trump won the Florida primary in March, Scott endorsed him – and by May, Scott's Trump ties were already so strong that he had to brush off vice presidential rumors. Then, in July, Scott was named national chairman of the pro-Trump Rebuilding America Now Super PAC. After Trump's victory, there was widespread agreement that Scott would have Trump's ear, an improvement after six years of relatively frosty relations with Obama – and an asset for a state with lots riding on federal cooperation, including funding to fight Zika. With strong encouragement from Trump, Scott emerged in the spring of 2017 as the likely challenger in 2018 to Sen. Bill Nelson, the only remaining statewide elected Democrat in Florida. Their expected contest seemed likely to be high-profile and expensive.

Senior Senator

Bill Nelson (D)

Elected 2000, term expires 2018, 3rd term; b. Sep 29, 1942, Miami; University of Virginia Law School, J.D.; Yale University (CT), B.A.; Episcopalian; Married (Grace H. Cavert Nelson); 2 children.

Military Career: U.S. Army Reserves, 1965-1968, 1970-1971; U.S. Army, 1968-1970.

Elected Office: FL House, 1972-1978; U.S. House, 1978-1990; FL Treasurer, Insurance Commissioner & Fire Marshal, 1994-2000.

Professional Career: Practicing attorney, 1970-1979, 1991-1994; Legislative Assistant, FL Governor Reubin Askew, 1971; Crew member, Space Shuttle Columbia, 1986.

DC Office: Hart 520 HSOB 20510, 202-224-5274, Fax: 202-228-2183, billnelson.senate.gov.

State Offices: Coral Gables, 305-536-5999; Fort Lauderdale, 954-693-4851; Fort Myers, 239-334-7760; Jacksonville, 904-346-4500; Orlando, 407-872-7161; Tallahassee, 850-942-8415; Tampa, 813-225-7040; West Palm Beach, 561-514-0189.

Committees: *Aging*. *Armed Services*: Cybersecurity (RMM), Emerging Threats & Capabilities. *Commerce, Science & Transportation (RMM)*: Aviation Operations, Safety & Security, Communications, Technology, Innovation & the Internet, Consumer Protection, Product Safety, Ins & Data Security, Oceans, Atmosphere, Fisheries & Coast Guard, Space, Science & Competitiveness, Surface Trans., Merchant Marine Infra., Safety & Security. *Finance*: Energy, Natural Resources & Infrastructure, International Trade, Customs & Global Competitiveness.

Group Ratings

	ADA	ACLU	AFL-CIO	LCV	ITI	COC	HAFA	ACU	CFG	FRC
2016	-	47%	-	100%	100%	63%	2%	4%	5%	0%
2015	90%	C	57%	84%	C	57%	C	0%	7%	0%

Almanac Ratings 2015

	Economy	Social	Foreign	Composite
Liberal	78%	95%	96%	90%
Conservative	22%	5%	4%	10%

Key Votes of the 114th Congress

1. Keystone pipeline	N	5. National Security Data	Y	9. Gun Sales Checks	Y
2. Export-Import Bank	N	6. Iran Nuclear Deal	N	10. Sanctuary Cities	N
3. Debt Ceiling Increase	Y	7. Puerto Rico Debt	Y	11. Planned Parenthood	N
4. Homeland Security $$	Y	8. Loretta Lynch A.G	Y	12. Trade deals	Y

Election Results

Election	Name (Party)	Vote (%)		Cand. Spent	Ind. Exp. Support	Ind. Exp. Oppose
2012 General	Bill Nelson (D)	4,523,451	(55%)	$17,125,413	$3,790,749	$9,747,183
	Connie Mack (R)	3,458,267	(42%)	$7,508,151	$6,249,161	$3,598,471
2012 Primary	Bill Nelson (D)	690,112	(79%)			
	Glen Burkett (D)	185,629	(21%)			

Prior winning percentages: 2006 (60%); 2000 (51%); House: 1988 (61%); 1986 (73%); 1984 (61%);1982 (71%); 1980 (70%); 1978 (61%)

Bill Nelson, Florida's senior senator, is among a rapidly diminishing breed in the Senate: the Southern Democrat. The aftermath of the 2014 mid-term election left Nelson as the only Democrat representing a state in the Deep South. Like other Southern Democrats of recent decades, Nelson has crafted an image as a centrist, and some aspects of his voting record place him firmly among his party's more moderate members. At the same time, representing a battleground state that twice voted narrowly for President Barack Obama, Nelson was a reliable supporter of the White House during the Obama presidency, while joining most other Democrats in voicing criticism of the early White House tenure of President Donald Trump.

Nelson also has been the only Democrat holding statewide office in purple Florida, and is all but certain to face a fierce battle to hold on to his seat in 2018. It could be a marquee race if term-limited Gov. Rick Scott -- a solid supporter of Trump in a state that swung to him by a small margin -- opts to take on Nelson. While he will turn 76 just weeks before Election Day 2018, Nelson has given every indication that he is running for a fourth term. "Whoever it is, I run my race like there's no tomorrow," Nelson told *The Tampa Bay Times* of the prospect of facing Scott. And, even if Nelson faced relatively weak opponents in winning previous re-election bids in 2006 and 20012, few are underestimating the appeal and durability of a politician whose career in elective office in the Sunshine State dates back to the early 1970s.

While many of his current constituents have emigrated from elsewhere, Nelson's Florida roots go back generations: He likes to recall that his great-grandfather arrived in the Florida from Denmark as a stowaway on a ship. His grandparents moved the family from the state's northern Panhandle to central Florida, and Nelson -- formally named Clarence William Nelson -- grew up in Melbourne. From the family home, he could see rockets take off in the 1950s and 1960s from what is now Cape Kennedy, where he later blasted off in his own mission . His mother was a schoolteacher, and his father was an attorney and real estate investor who died when Nelson was just 14. In high school, Nelson was active in student government, where he was -- and remains -- something of a straight arrow: He doesn't smoke, drink or swear.

He attended the University of Florida for two years, and then transferred to Yale University, where he earned his undergraduate degree before going on to the University of Virginia law school. After a two-year hitch in the Army, he returned to Melbourne where he briefly practiced law and worked on the staff of Democratic Gov. Reubin Askew. In 1972, at age 30, he was elected to the state House of Representatives. In 1978, when Republican Rep. Louis Frey unsuccessfully sought his party's gubernatorial nomination, Nelson ran to succeed Frey in a congressional district that then included the Space Coast's Brevard County and most of Orlando's Orange County. Nelson's religious faith -- he is a nondenominational Christian who was baptized Baptist -- and traditional values, along with his folksy manner, made him popular in an area that was trending Republican. He won the seat 61%-39%;. In five succeeding elections, he never received less than 61 percent of the vote in a district where just 29 percent voted for Democrat Michael Dukakis in the 1988 presidential race.

In the House, he became chairman of the Science Committee's Space Subcommittee, a post of obvious importance to the district. Nelson not only boosted the space program in every possible way, but became the second sitting member of Congress to orbit the Earth in January 1986. (Then-Sen. Jake Garn of Utah had done so a year earlier.) Nelson safely returned aboard the Columbia just 10 days before another shuttle, the Challenger, blew up shortly after liftoff, killing all seven crew members. A visibly distraught Nelson appeared on the House floor that morning to pay tribute to the fallen astronauts. Three decades later, he emphasized the happier memories of that period -- noting that in space he saw no racial or political divides on Earth, just a single unified planet.

In 1989, with the support of leading Florida Democrats, Nelson set out to run against Republican Gov. Bob Martinez. However, some Democrats subsequently became concerned about his prospects and persuaded Lawton Chiles, who had retired from the Senate in 1988 after three terms, to run. Chiles won the September 1990 primary by better than 2-1, and Nelson returned to his 77-acre oceanfront residence in Melbourne, his political career seemingly over. But in 1994, he found an opening when an elected statewide office became vacant. Nelson ran for and won a position whose full title was treasurer, insurance commissioner, and state fire marshal. (The latter duties have since been combined with those of the former comptroller to create the elected position of chief financial officer.) Nelson proceeded to compile an activist record, including prodding European insurers to pay Holocaust era claims -- an issue of painful significance to numerous families in a state with the nation's second highest percentage of Jewish residents.

Nelson's chance to run for higher office came when Republican Sen. Connie Mack decided not to seek re-election in 2000. Mack's retirement left a seat up for grabs in a state that, as that Election Night returns in the Bush-Gore presidential contest would show, was closely divided between the parties. Republicans nominated veteran, Orlando-based Rep. Bill McCollum, one of the House managers of the impeachment of President Bill Clinton. While Washington observers believed it would be a political test of the wisdom of impeachment, the race was in large measure a battle of competing styles. Running his fourth statewide race in 10 years, Nelson's easygoing manner contrasted favorably with McCollum's stiff and sometimes caustic demeanor. With a long conservative record on abortion rights and gun control, McCollum attempted to moderate his positions, but only succeeded in antagonizing his base supporters. Nelson won, 51%-46%; the two candidates spent more $15 million between them, then a Florida record.

Nelson is not particularly well known nationally, even if his name did pop up on a list of possible running mates floated by Hillary Clinton's campaign in mid-2016. But his activity on a variety of fronts relevant to large segments of what is today the nation's third most populous state has raised his profile. He did draw attention in May 2012, when former CIA official Jose Rodriguez said in a book that Nelson, as a member of the Intelligence Committee, had volunteered to be waterboarded to see what the controversial interrogation procedure was like; the agency declined the offer. Meanwhile, some Republicans grouse that he prefers to avoid the tougher issues. "He is a connoisseur of low-hanging fruit," Florida Republican strategist J.M. "Mac" Stipanovich gibed during Nelson's 2012 re-election bid. Nelson responded by citing his work on energy exploration and health care, among other issues.

Nelson has vehemently fought oil drilling anywhere close to the Florida coast throughout his political career. The most recent chapter came in 2016, when he utilized Senate procedures to put a "hold" on an energy bill that included a provision expanding a revenue sharing program for states that allow offshore drilling. In the process, Nelson delayed an aid package attached to the bill designed to alleviate the crisis in Flint Michigan, where dangerous levels of lead had leached into the drinking water. But he nonetheless refused to budge, arguing that the revenue sharing provision could ultimately lead to drilling off the coast of his home state. "For 40 years, I've fought to keep rigs off of the state of Florida and I will not let that happen here to satisfy Sen. Cassidy," asserted Nelson, referring to Louisiana Republican Bill

Cassidy, sponsor of the revenue sharing provision. After a weeks-long standoff, Cassidy withdrew the amendment from the bill, and Nelson dropped his hold on the legislation. The jockeying came a year after Nelson succeeded in getting the Obama administration to ban drilling off Florida's coast through 2022.

Almanac rankings of Senate voting scores in 2015 pegged Nelson as the seventh most conservative Democratic senator on economic issues, while placing him closer to his party's left wing on social issues. A few years earlier, gay-rights groups derided Nelson for his cautiousness after Obama declared his support for same-sex marriage in 2012. "I believe marriage should be left to the states," Nelson said at the time, noting that Florida had voted on the issue in 2008 -- when the electorate there approved a constitutional ban on gay marriage. Nonetheless, Nelson flipped to supporting gay marriage in 2013, part of a groundswell of moderate Democrats who backed it ahead of the Supreme Court decision that overturned parts of the Defense of Marriage Act.

Nelson was a consistent supporter of many of Obama's major second-term initiatives. In 2015, he joined most Senate Democrats in supporting the Iranian nuclear agreement, and sided with the White House -- this time splitting from a majority of his Democratic colleagues -- in voting to give the president expedited authority to negotiate the 12-nation Trans Pacific Partnership. "I will do anything to pass trade," he bluntly told *The New York Times* in mid-2015, reflecting the sentiments of several Democratic senators from coastal states that benefit from international trade. Nelson even offered support, albeit tepid, for Obama's steps to normalize diplomatic and trade relations with Cuba at the end of 2014. Nelson had long opposed such a move -- holding up a $410 billion omnibus spending bill in 2009, at the outset of Obama's first term, because of provisions that loosened travel and export restrictions with the island nation. But, five years later, when Obama acted to re-establish diplomatic ties with Cuba, Nelson told the *Associated Press*: "I'm as anti-Castro as they come, but it's time to move on. It's time to get into the 21st century."

At the outset of 2013, Nelson became chairman of the Senate Special Committee on Aging, a politically appealing perch for any Floridian. The panel has no legislative authority but conducts oversight of issues relevant to senior citizens. As a member of the powerful Finance Committee, Nelson emerged as a player in the 2009-2010 debate over the Affordable Care Act, particularly as it related to senior citizens. He amended an early version of the bill to lessen the impact of cuts to Medicare Advantage, a privatized Medicare program. But Republicans castigated it as a backroom deal intended to benefit Florida, and his amendment was killed. He did successfully add an amendment to the Finance version of the bill exempting seniors from a hike in the itemized medical deduction limit. Since then, he has defended "Obamacare" to those seeking its repeal. "Would you like me to repeal the part where you can keep your kid on your family policy until age 26?" he asked an angry constituent at a town hall meeting in 2012. "Would you like me to repeal that part that says that the insurance company can't cancel you when you're in the middle of treatment?"

After returning to the Senate minority in 2015, Nelson turned his attention towards consumer advocacy, using his position as the ranking Democrat on the Senate Commerce, Science and Transportation Committee to question Verizon's use of "supercookies," calling their "snooping" on their customers "outrageous." From 2007 to 2015, when the Democrats controlled the Senate, Nelson was chairman of the Commerce subcommittee with jurisdiction over the space program. Columbia -- the space shuttle on which Nelson once traveled -- disintegrated as it reentered Earth's atmosphere in 2003, killing all seven crew members aboard. Nelson at the time called for accelerated development of a reusable space vehicle to ferry astronauts to the International Space Station. When Obama took office, Nelson sharply criticized the new president's limited commitment to NASA, and got a bill through the Senate providing enough money for another space shuttle flight in 2011, jump-starting NASA's new heavy-lift rocket. In spite of Nelson's boosterism, NASA has struggled in recent years -- as Republicans fought for austerity and the Obama Administration showed limited interest in the program.

In both of his re-election bids to date, Nelson benefited from facing Republican opponents with political baggage. In June 2005, two-term Rep. Katherine Harris announced she would challenge Nelson in 2006. Polling data indicated that Harris' prominent role as Florida secretary of state during the disputed 2000 presidential election had left her too unpopular to win a general election, but she enjoyed celebrity status among many rank-and-file Republican voters, and other big-name Republicans declined to run. Nelson lost in the Panhandle but carried 57 of 67 counties in the state in defeating Harris, 60%-38%, in a good year for Democrats nationally.

In 2012, Rep. Connie Mack IV, son of Nelson's Senate predecessor, emerged from the GOP primary with 60 percent of the vote. Nelson aggressively depicted Mack as a flawed candidate. The Republican had had several past brushes with the law, usually bar fights, as well as problems paying bills while going through a divorce, all of which figured prominently in Nelson's ads. Mack tried to paint Nelson as too liberal, but that line of attack failed to gain traction. Republican groups spent heavily and polling showed a close race for a while, but Nelson won the endorsements of all of Florida's major newspapers and sailed to a 55%-42% win.

While Nelson has kept up collegial relations with most of his state's Republicans, he and Gov. Scott have never gotten along well. Nelson has slammed the governor for refusing to expand the state's Medicaid program and ridiculed him for allegedly banning the term "climate change" in government documents. Nelson weighed a run against Scott in 2014 but eventually deferred to Republican-turned-Democrat former Gov. Charlie Crist, who last narrowly to Scott. In 2016, as the presence of mosquitoes carrying the Zika virus caused alarm in one Miami neighborhood, Scott and Nelson pointed fingers at each other, as legislation containing federal money to combat the virus became bogged down due to unrelated but controversial provisions in the measure. This history could become relevant if they face off in 2018.

Like Trump, Scott is a wealthy businessman who was first elected to office running as an outsider. Scott, in an op-ed piece that ran in *USAToday* in early 2016 prior to the Florida presidential primary, praised Trump and compared his first race for governor in 2010 to Trump's presidential bid. Scott endorsed Trump immediately after the Florida primary, following Rubio's withdrawal from the presidential race, and was among the relatively few top GOP elected officeholders who delivered a speech on Trump's behalf at the Republican National Convention that summer. While Scott could self-fund a campaign -- he spent $90 million of his fortune in his gubernatorial campaign -- he faces obstacles: Early polling shows him trailing Nelson by single digits, and his prospects will be tied closely to how well the Trump Administration fares in its first two years.

Nelson underwent surgery for prostate cancer in 2015, but appears in top shape physically: Shortly before the surgery, he impressed a group of reporters and other onlookers by doing 46 pushups to pay off a bet to Illinois Sen. Dick Durbin when the Tampa Bay Lightning lost the Stanley Cup finals to the Chicago Black Hawks. Nelson may have to deal with a primary challenge from his left, and his age could be a political factor. But, unlike many Florida Democrats, he has demonstrated appeal in all parts of the diverse state, and even some Republicans offer backhanded praise for his staying power. "Except Bill Nelson…we have done pretty well," Palm Beach County Republican County Chairman Michael Barnett told the Fort Lauderdale *Sun-Sentinel* in 2016. "The Democrats don't seem to be able to create superstars within their party like Bill Nelson."

Junior Senator

Marco Rubio (R)

Elected 2010, term expires 2022, 2nd term; b. May 28, 1971, Miami; University of Florida, B.S.; University of Miami (FL), J.D.; Tarkio College (MO), Att.; Santa Fe College (NM), Att.; Roman Catholic; Married (Jeanette Dousdebes); 4 children.

Elected Office: West Miami City Commissioner, 1998-2000; FL House, 2000-2008, Speaker, 2006-2008.

Professional Career: Practicing attorney, 1997-2010; Professor, FL Intl. University, 2009-2010.

DC Office: 284 RSOB 20510, 202-224-3041, Fax: 202-228-0285, rubio.senate.gov.

State Offices: Doral, 305-418-8553; Jacksonville, 904-354-4300; Orlando, 407-254-2573; Palm Beach Gardens, 561-775-3360; Pensacola, 850-433-2603; Tallahassee, 850-599-9100; Tampa, 813-287-5035.

Committees: *Aging*. *Appropriations*: Agriculture, Rural Development, FDA & Related Agencies, DOL, HHS & Education & Related Agencies, Legislative Branch, Military Construction & Veteran Affairs & Related Agencies, State, Foreign Operations & Related Programs. *Foreign Relations*: East Asia, the Pacific & International Cybersecurity Policy, Near East, South Asia, Central Asia & Counterterrorism, State Dept & USAID Mngmnt, Internat'l Ops & Internat'l Dev, West Hem Crime Civ Sec Dem Rights & Women's Issues (Chmn). *Intelligence*. *Joint Congressional-Executive Commission on China*. *Joint Security & Cooperation in Europe*. *Small Business & Entrepreneurship*.

Group Ratings

	ADA	ACLU	AFL-CIO	LCV	ITI	COC	HAFA	ACU	CFG	FRC
2016	-	5%	-	6%	50%	100%	73%	86%	83%	0%
2015	0%	C	9%	0%	C	60%	C	94%	97%	100%

Almanac Ratings 2015

	Economy	Social	Foreign	Composite
Liberal	26%	5%	6%	12%
Conservative	74%	95%	94%	88%

Key Votes of the 114th Congress

1. Keystone pipeline	NV	5. National Security Data	N	9. Gun Sales Checks	N
2. Export-Import Bank	NV	6. Iran Nuclear Deal	Y	10. Sanctuary Cities	Y
3. Debt Ceiling Increase	N	7. Puerto Rico Debt	Y	11. Planned Parenthood	Y
4. Homeland Security $$	N	8. Loretta Lynch A.G	N	12. Trade deals	Y

Election Results

Election	Name (Party)	Vote (%)		Cand. Spent	Ind. Exp. Support	Ind. Exp. Oppose
2016 General	Marco Rubio (R)	4,835,191	(52%)	$21,152,492	$6,102,547	$6,894,783
	Patrick Murphy (D)	4,122,088	(44%)	$8,684,853	$5,145,141	$28,326,406
	Paul Stanton (L)	196,956	(2%)	$19,601		
2016 Primary	Marco Rubio (R)	1,029,830	(72%)			
	Carlos Beruff (R)	264,427	(19%)			

Prior winning percentages: 2010 (49%)

The Spanish word "rubio" translates into "blond" in English -- and when Marco Rubio, the junior senator from Florida, arrived on Capitol Hill following the 2010 election, he was heralded as the figurative fair-haired boy by many within the GOP. Just 39 when sworn into the Senate, he was an eloquent and telegenic public speaker with a compelling biography, and a consistent conservative who had attracted support both from both members of the Republican Party's establishment as well as its insurgent tea party wing. And he was a Latino in a party where many were desperate to make inroads with that rapidly growing demographic group.

But those who envisioned a story with the political version of a fairy tale ending would be disappointed. Rubio -- an impatient personality by his own acknowledgement -- grew frustrated with the pace of the Senate, the proverbial saucer that cools the legislative cup of tea. He skipped votes with increasing frequency: a 10 percent absenteeism rate in 2014, which more than tripled in 2015. By then, he had forsworn a second term in the Senate and was running full bore for the party's presidential nomination. However, his White House hopes died three months before the party's 2016 nominating convention -- in a primary in Rubio's home state, where he was overwhelmed by now-President Donald Trump.

Once regarded as the potential nominee who posed the biggest threat to the Democrats in a general election, some post-mortems attributed Rubio's downfall to factors outside of his control -- an upbeat message at odds with the angry mood of many in the electorate. "America is in the middle of a real political storm, a real tsunami, and we should have seen this coming," Rubio himself was quoted as saying by *Real Clear Politics*. "Look, people are angry and people are very frustrated." But Rubio also committed a series of strategic missteps that contributed to the demise of his presidential hopes. Ultimately, the story would turn out to have an element of back to the future. Seeking to hold on to their Senate majority, Republican leaders convinced Rubio to seek re-election after all. He won a competitive race to secure a second term. And, with the timing uncertain for another crack at his party's presidential nomination, Rubio appeared to be rededicating himself to the work of Capitol Hill as 2017 got underway. "My goal is to be the best senator Florida ever had, and certainly the most consequential," Rubio told *Politico* just after his re-election.

Born in Miami, Rubio was mostly brought up in a working-class neighborhood near the city's Little Havana section; he was the third child of immigrants who had left Cuba in 1956, before Fidel Castro came to power. During his political rise, Rubio often described himself as the "son of exiles" who were forced out by Castro's regime, though he used that characterization less after facing media scrutiny over whether he had embellished the story. His father, a security guard in Havana, worked long days as a hotel bartender after emigrating to Miami, and his mother was a hotel maid with a second job at Kmart. The family moved to follow work; Rubio spent six years in Las Vegas while his parents worked in the hotel industry before returning to Miami for high school. At the encouragement of an aunt, he was baptized a Mormon along with his mother and sister, only to convert back to Catholicism as a teenager.

The young Rubio initially was a Democrat, inspired by Massachusetts Sen. Edward Kennedy's famous "the dream shall never die" speech at the 1980 Democratic National Convention. But he soon joined his beloved grandfather in becoming a staunch Ronald Reagan supporter. "I've been a Republican ever since," Rubio later wrote in his 2012 autobiography, *An American* Son. Rubio played football in high school, and despite his small stature, earned a football scholarship to Tarkio College in Missouri. He returned to Florida after the school went bankrupt, spent a year at a junior college, and got his bachelor's degree at the University of Florida. As an undergraduate, he worked for a couple of leading Cuban-American politicians from the Miami area -- interning for Republican Rep. Ileana Ros-Lehtinen and volunteering for the first campaign of GOP Rep. Lincoln Diaz-Balart. Both legislators wrote letters of recommendation to assist Rubio in being admitted to the University of Miami law school.

In his last year of law school, Rubio ran the Dade County operation for Republican Sen. Bob Dole's presidential campaign in 1996. There, he met future Florida Gov. Jeb Bush, who became a close political ally -- albeit the relationship dissipated into an acrimonious rivalry 20 years later, when both competed for the Republican presidential nod. Bush, who during the 2016 campaign jabbed at Rubio for missed Senate votes, in happier times described him as "the best orator of American politics today … He has managed to find a way to communicate a conservative message full of hope and optimism."

At age 26, Rubio ousted an incumbent city commissioner in West Miami, a small, heavily Cuban town just south of Miami International Airport -- where he still resides today with his wife Jeanette, a one-time Miami Dolphins cheerleader, and their four children. He had been on the city commission only a year when a state House seat opened up. Arriving in Tallahassee, Rubio rose swiftly in the ranks: In 2001, he landed a coveted seat on a special committee created after the 9/11 attacks to look into beefing up security throughout a state where tourism is the top industry. In 2005, he was designated as speaker of the Florida House, making him, at 34, the youngest person and the first Hispanic-American to achieve that position. At a ceremony, Bush presented him with a sword, a symbolic passing of the conservative torch in the state. Rubio formally assumed the speakership a year later, and, meanwhile, toured Florida, holding "idea-raisers" to find budget-neutral ideas to improve the state. The 100 ideas he liked best were bundled into a book, and many of the more incremental proposals passed easily. His personal favorite, replacing the state property tax on primary residences with a sales tax increase, stalled. It did, however, win him praise from a number of activists who became involved in the tea party movement.

Forced out of the state legislature by term limits at the end of 2008, Rubio caught the tea party movement's lightning in its nascent days, and used it to power his upstart primary campaign against then-popular Republican Gov. Charlie Crist for an open Senate seat. Crist, after one term as governor, had been urged by leading national Republicans to run for Senate, and he had a huge cash and name recognition advantage. Initially, Rubio seemed ready to defer to Crist, and was quoted by the *Tampa Bay Times* in early 2009 as saying Crist was the "best candidate" for the job. But Crist (today a Democratic member of the House) was never a favorite of conservatives. His embrace of President Barack Obama's $787 billion economic stimulus bill (and his literal embrace of the president at a public event) infuriated many of them. Announcing in May 2009 for the Senate seat, Rubio received early support from then-Sen. Jim DeMint of South Carolina, a conservative stalwart who was backing insurgent GOP candidates, as well as quiet support from Bush and his allies. By the time Crist realized the conservative base was slipping away, it was too late. On the verge of losing the primary, Crist quit the Republican Party in the spring of 2010 to run as an independent.

In the general election, Rubio faced Crist and the Democratic nominee Rep. Kendrick Meek. Crist started off with an early lead in the polls, but his support plummeted as he got caught in the crossfire from Rubio on the right and Meek on the left, both of whom painted Crist as an opportunist. Crist tried to become the de facto Democratic candidate, but Meek refused to drop out, denying Crist a one-on-one matchup with Rubio. Tea party activists embraced Rubio's campaign and his theme of "Reclaim America," but Rubio was careful not to come off as a firebrand like some of the movement's other stars. He stressed fiscal responsibility, indicating support for raising the eligibility age for Social Security beneficiaries and giving the president the line-item veto over spending bills. He opposed abortion rights and took a more conservative position than Crist on immigration, supporting Arizona's crackdown on illegal immigrants. On Election Night 2010, it was Rubio, 49 percent; Crist, 30 percent; and Meek, 20 percent.

In the Senate, Rubio's voting pattern kept the movement happy; in his first year, he was the 13th most conservative senator, with a perfect conservative score on social issues, according to the *Almanac*'s annual rankings. For 2012 and 2013, he dropped just a few notches, to 17th most conservative. He was one of just eight senators to oppose the New Year's Day 2013 fiscal cliff deal; he contended it would complicate economic growth and job creation because employers would pass the cost of the deal's tax hike for the wealthiest Americans on to their employees. Earlier, in August 2011, Rubio was among 19 Senate Republicans to oppose a deal between the White House and GOP congressional leaders to raise the debt ceiling. "If we simply raise it once again, without a real plan to bring spending under control and get our economy growing, America faces the very real danger of a catastrophic economic crisis," he wrote earlier in the *Wall Street Journal*.

Rubio also sought to offer his party a lifeline on immigration to bolster its low standing among Hispanic-Americans. He began talking about a potential compromise to the stalled DREAM Act aimed at helping children of illegal immigrants. His alternative called for extending legal residency to immigrant children bound for college or the military. The proposal came under sharp attack from the right, and he sought to characterize it as being less about immigration than about humanitarian relief for a group facing deportation. But Rubio's political momentum came to a halt when President Barack Obama used his executive powers to put into place the major elements of Rubio's bill in 2011, leaving the senator grumbling that he deserved some of the credit.

With the 2012 presidential campaign looming, Rubio -- after initially vowing to remain neutral during the primary season -- decided to endorse former Massachusetts Gov. Mitt Romney, and came to Romney's aid on the immigration issue. Rubio blasted another contender, former House Speaker Newt Gingrich, for airing a Spanish-language radio ad that described Romney as "the most anti-immigration candidate," and Gingrich pulled the spot. Romney later told reporters that Rubio was being "thoroughly vetted" as possible running mate, and while the nod eventually went to Wisconsin Rep. Paul Ryan, the speculation benefited the senator: He elevated his national profile while keeping a safe political distance from a candidate many conservatives considered inauthentic. Rubio was chosen to introduce Romney at the Republican National Convention in Tampa, and in his remarks, he criticized Obama for abandoning his positive message of 2008. "Hope and change has become divide and conquer," he complained. "... The story of our time will be written by Americans who haven't yet been born. Let's make sure they write that we did our part." Rubio's speech drew widespread praise, with some pundits deeming it the best of the convention.

Following the 2012 election, Rubio gave several policy-oriented speeches, including one in which he mentioned the phrase "middle class" nearly three dozen times while discussing the need to close "the opportunity gap." As income inequality became an increasingly prominent issue, Rubio worked to come up with a conservative answer, focusing on college affordability. By early 2013, he was being discussed as a presidential contender, and was chosen to give the Republican response to Obama's State of the Union address. Although some commentators mocked him for awkwardly reaching for a water bottle midway through his remarks, he won favorable reviews for weaving elements of his personal into a response in which he criticized the president for an "obsession" with raising taxes.

At the same time, Rubio's impatience with the Senate was becoming increasingly visible, as the partisan divide in government created legislative gridlock for even seemingly modest legislation. The ironically named AGREE Act -- an effort by Rubio to package job growth proposals that had drawn from both sides of the political aisle -- went nowhere after he and Democratic Sen. Chris Coons of Delaware initially introduced it in late 2011. "I don't know that 'hate' is the right word," Rubio said in a 2015 interview with the *Washington Post*, when asked his view of the Senate. "I'm frustrated."

Rubio, after initial hesitation, did decide to get involved in a major legislative initiative following the 2012 election: the so-called "Gang of Eight" negotiations on immigration. It produced a comprehensive bipartisan bill to tighten border security while creating an eventual path to citizenship for many illegal immigrants. The legislation passed the Senate by a wide margin in 2013, but stalled out in the GOP-controlled House. If Rubio won points for statesmanship in some quarters, the blowback from his tea party flank created a political obstacle that was to dog him throughout the 2016 campaign. As right-wing radio turned on its onetime hero, Rubio, who had been leading some early 2016 presidential polls, saw his stock plummet. He retreated to his original stance on immigration, telling a crowd at the 2015 Conservative Political Action Conference that he had learned voters would not approve a pathway to citizenship until it's "proven to them that future illegal immigration will be controlled" -- and that immigration reform should be done in a piecemeal fashion, with border security first.

Rubio formally announced his presidential bid in April 2015, seeking to draw a contrast with both Bush and former Secretary of State Hillary Clinton, the Democratic front-runner. (Bush did not formally announce his candidacy until a couple of months after Rubio, but had clearly been running since late

2014.) "This election is a generational choice about what kind of country we will be," Rubio said in his announcement speech in Miami, while emphasizing his family's modest immigrant roots. At the same time, he continued efforts to distance himself from his association with the "Gang of Eight" -- accusing one rival for the conservative vote, Texas Sen. Ted Cruz, of being insufficiently tough on immigration. But Rubio's ploy backfired: The target of his attack was a Cruz amendment proposed during the immigration bill debate to give legal status to undocumented immigrants, but with no possibility of citizenship. The Cruz amendment was viewed by sponsors of the legislation as a ploy to sink the bill by taking a path to citizenship off the table, and even critics of Cruz suggested that Rubio's attacks were disingenuous.

Rubio finished a strong third in the first contest of the nominating campaign, the Iowa delegate caucuses, and got a boost in the public opinion polls. But he was put on the ropes by another rival, New Jersey Gov. Chris Christie, during a debate just prior to the New Hampshire primary. Rubio seemed to lose his usual oratorical command, resorting to repeated talking points as Christie jabbed at him for his "memorized 25-second speech." Rubio finished a disappointing fifth in New Hampshire. And while he recovered in later debates and finished second in two other early primary states, South Carolina and Nevada, he then made a move for which he later expressed regret -- seeking to match insults with the front-running Trump. "And you know what they say about guys with small hands," Rubio snickered. Trump, master of the snide nickname, later derided Rubio as "Little Marco" in a debate 10 days before their showdown in the Florida primary.

With Rubio scoring a victory in only one statewide delegate contest, Minnesota, and with Bush having fallen along the wayside after South Carolina, it made his home state a must-win. But Trump won by a landslide, 46%-27%, carrying 66 of 67 counties. Some suggested the loss, which forced Rubio's withdrawal from the presidential race, was a byproduct of the ambitious Rubio burning too many bridges at home over the years. "He is extremely skilled and ambitious. He is also extremely not loyal," Tony DiMatteo, a Tampa area GOP leader who helped Rubio launch his 2010 Senate bid, told the *Tampa Bay Times*. More broadly, others attributed Rubio's demise to failing to build on the persona that had gotten him elected to the Senate six years earlier. "He committed the one unforgiveable sin in the 2016 election cycle: He became someone he wasn't," Beverly Hallberg, a Washington-based media consultant, wrote in *The Federalist,* a Web magazine with a conservative tilt. "His brand wasn't built on reciting talking points or resorting to personal attacks. Instead, the Rubio brand was 'the New American Century' that provided opportunity for all no matter their background. In the end, changing his rhetoric to match a polarized electorate instead of using his rhetoric to unite was his downfall. Words matter."

"I have only said like 10,000 times I will be a private citizen in January," Rubio declared in a May 2016 tweet. But, by the end of June, he was a candidate for re-election -- prodded not only by fears among Republican leaders that the seat was in jeopardy without him in the race, but concerns on his part about remaining relevant on the national political scene. Florida's lieutenant governor and two members of Congress bowed out of the GOP Senate race, and Rubio won the August primary with 72 percent of the vote. His victory in November was considered less than a sure bet in a state where Clinton was ahead in many polls. National Democratic leaders lined up behind two-term Rep. Patrick Murphy. For a time, a primary challenge from the left by bombastic Rep. Alan Grayson appeared to be competitive. But Grayson was hit with conflict-of-interest allegations, along with revelations that a former wife had filed domestic abuse complaints. Murphy easily defeated Grayson in the primary, 59%-18%.

In the general election, Murphy, borrowing a page from some of Rubio's presidential rivals, raised the issue of the incumbent's Senate absenteeism rate. The Democrat also sought to tie Rubio to Trump at every turn. But the 33-year old Murphy was hit with media reports showing that he had overstated his resume -- reports that national Republican and conservative independent expenditure groups exploited to boost Rubio. Murphy had significantly less air support: In the closing weeks of the campaign, as they concluded that Murphy had no path to victory, national Democratic groups pulled back on Florida ad buys to concentrate on less expensive media markets in other states where Senate seats were at stake. Rubio won comfortably, 52%-44%, as Trump narrowly bested Clinton in the state, 49%-48%. Exit polls showed Rubio, who tepidly endorsed Trump just before the Republican convention in July, running several points ahead of Trump among women and independent voters, while outdistancing Trump by double digits among Latinos.

Returning to Washington, Rubio refocused on the Foreign Relations Committee, which, prior to his presidential run, he used to heavily criticize Obama while calling for a more muscular, interventionist America -- to the pleasure of conservatives. With Trump now entering the White House, Rubio signaled that he would continue his outspoken posture on the foreign front. Following the 2016 election, he teamed with Democratic Sen. Edward Markey of Massachusetts to urge the new president to strengthen the system of longstanding U.S. strategic alliances -- notably NATO, the subject of several skeptical comments by Trump. "I'm prepared to be a senator that will encourage him to make the right decisions, but also stand up to the bad decisions and the bad policies if he's elected president," Rubio said of Trump.

For a time, it appeared Rubio might be getting ready to derail the confirmation of Trump's secretary of state, Rex Tillerson -- the former Exxon/Mobil chief executive known for his close relationship with Russian President Vladimir Putin. Rubio, who characterized Putin as a "gangster" and "thug" during the presidential campaign, expressed "serious concerns" about the Tillerson pick, and grilled the nominee during Foreign Relations hearings. Hours before the committee vote , Rubio opted to back away from a confrontation with his erstwhile rival for the White House, while taking an indirect swipe at the mercurial Trump. Declared Rubio via Facebook, "Given the uncertainty that exists both at home and abroad about the direction of our foreign policy, it would be against our national interests to have this confirmation unnecessarily delayed or embroiled in controversy."

FIRST DISTRICT

Matt Gaetz (R)

Elected 2016, 1st term; b. May 07, 1982, Hollywood; Florida State University, B.S., 2003; College of William and Mary - Marshall-Wythe Law School (VA), J.D., 2007; Baptist; Not Stated.

Elected Office: FL Senate, 2010-2016.

Professional Career: Practicing attorney .

DC Office: 507 CHOB 20515, 202-225-4136, Fax: 202-225-3414, gaetz.house.gov.

State Offices: Pensacola, 850-479-1183.

Committees: *Armed Services*: Oversight & Investigations, Tactical Air & Land Forces. *Budget*. *Judiciary*: Courts, Intellectual Property & Internet, Regulatory Reform, Commercial & Antitrust Law.

Election Results

Election	Name (Party)	Vote (%)	Cand. Spent	Ind. Exp. Support	Ind. Exp. Oppose
2016 General	Matt Gaetz (R)	255,107 (69%)	$1,037,474	$517,325	$31,131
	Steven Specht (D)	114,079 (31%)	$54,251		
2016 Primary	Matt Gaetz (R)	35,675 (36%)			
	Greg Evers (R)	21,540 (22%)			
	Cris Dosev (R)	20,610 (21%)			
	Rebekah Johansen Bydlak (R)	7,689 (8%)			
	James Zumwalt (R)	7,660 (8%)			

Republican Matt Gaetz was elected to the open seat that was held by Jeff Miller, chairman of the House Veterans' Affairs Committee. When Miller announced his retirement, the chief question in this district was which Republican would win. Gaetz faced a competitive primary. But with superior fundraising and his conservative appeal, he won comfortably.

A Florida native, Gaetz graduated from Florida State University and got his law degree from the College of William and Mary in Virginia. After briefly practicing law with a firm in Fort Walton Beach, he ran in 2010 for an open seat in the state House. He was unopposed that year and in his two reelections. He chaired the House Finance and Tax Committee, where he was an enthusiastic supporter of tax cuts. As a social conservative, he sought to expand the pro-gun "Stand Your Ground" law. The American Conservative Union gave him its "Defender of Liberty" award.

Before Miller announced his retirement, Gaetz had been planning to run for the seat in the state Senate that had been held by his influential father, Senate President Don Gaetz, who was retiring. After the two had a heart-to-heart talk, his father told the *Pensacola News Journal*, "Matt said he didn't like anything that was happening in Washington, and I said, 'Well, Matt, maybe you should go there and do something about it.'" His son was the first to enter the contest.

In the Republican primary, Sen. Greg Evers led in an early poll and had higher favorability scores than Gaetz. Evers gained national attention, mostly negative, when he raffled off a semi-automatic rifle among people in the district who "liked" his Facebook page. He explained that he was trying to highlight the importance of the right to bear arms during a time of rising terrorism. He criticized Gaetz for chairing two political action committees that raised $380,000, which he dissolved three days before he announced his candidacy for Congress and transferred the money to a Super PAC that later spent the money on his behalf. Gaetz drew attention when he said that the Black Lives Matter group was "a terrorist organization," and he criticized Evers for voting to expand Medicaid. Gaetz opposed cuts in the military, which were detrimental to the district. "When the Pentagon gets a cold, we get the flu," he said. Gaetz's advertising called him "the most conservative" candidate. A late-filing candidate was Cris Dosev, a Pensacola businessman and political newcomer. Gaetz spent $1.1 million, compared with $200,000 for Evers. Dosev spent $490,000, of which 80 percent was self-financed. Gaetz won the seven-candidate primary with 36 percent of the vote to 22 percent for Evers and 21 percent for Dosev.

In the general election, Steven Specht, an Air Force veteran, spent $54,000 and attracted scant public attention. Gaetz won, 69%-31%, and ran stronger in the outlying areas of the district than in Escambia. In the House, he got useful assignments with seats on the Armed Services and Judiciary committees.

Western Panhandle: Pensacola, Fort Walton

Population		**Race and Ethnicity**		**Income**	
Total	730,495	White	73.9%	Median Income	$50,667 (246 out of 435)
Land area	4,016	Black	13.0%		
Pop/ sq mi	181.9	Latino	6.0%		
Born in state	39.4%	Asian	2.5%	Under $50,000	49.3%
		Two races	3.9%	$50,000-$99,999	32.6%
Age Groups		Other	0.7%	$100,000-$199,999	14.8%
Under 18	21.7%			$200,000 or more	3.2%
18-34	24.4%	**Education**		Poverty Rate	14.6%
35-64	38.7%	H.S grad or less	38.4%		
Over 64	15.2%	Some college	35.6%	**Health Insurance**	
Work		College Degree, 4 yr	17.1%	With health insurance coverage	85.5%
		Post grad	8.9%		
White Collar	33.7%				
Sales and Service	47.2%	**Military**		**Public Assistance**	
Blue Collar	19.1%	Veteran	17.3%	Cash public assistance income	1.8%
Government	17.1%	Active Duty	3.7%		
				Food stamp/SNAP benefits	13.2%

Voter Turnout			
2015 Total Citizens 18+	556,100	2016 House Turnout as % CVAP	66%
2016 House turnout	369,186	2014 House Turnout as % CVAP	42%

2012 Presidential Vote		
Mitt Romney	242,950	(69%)
Barack Obama	106,824	(30%)

2016 Presidential Vote		
Donald Trump	256,609	(67%)
Hillary Clinton	107,063	(28%)
Gary Johnson	12,770	(3%)

Cook Partisan Voting Index: R+22

The "Redneck Riviera" is the affectionate local name for the Gulf Coast beaches of Florida's Emerald Coast, stretching from Pensacola east to Destin. This has been military country since John Quincy Adams persuaded Spain to sell Florida to the United States in 1819, with the goal of gaining control of the port of Pensacola on the Gulf of Mexico. In October 1861, the Union defeated the Confederates in a battle to control Santa Rosa Island, the outermost spit of land protecting Pensacola Bay. In the 20th century, the Pensacola Naval Air Station was turned into the nation's first naval-aviation training base, giving birth to carrier aviation. About 17,000 people are employed at Eglin Air Force Base, which spreads over three counties. With approximately 100,000 square miles of airspace stretching over the Gulf to the Florida Keys, Eglin is considered the largest air base in the free world. It has been the Air Force center for the development, acquisition, testing, deployment and sustainment of all air-delivered weapons, including the F-35 Joint Strike Fighter.

The western panhandle of Florida is culturally part of Dixie and lies closer to Houston than to Miami. A columnist for the *Pensacola News Journal* once recommended the creation of an independent commonwealth of West Florida. "We don't have much in common with the people inhabiting what I call peninsular Florida," wrote Jerry Maygarden. "I'm convinced that the further south you drive, the further north you get." Until recently, the panhandle was heavily dependent on the military and had little of its own economy. But as the South has become more prosperous, the shore has attracted vacationing and retiring Southerners to its vast, fine-grained, white sand beaches and its pleasant, inlet-dotted bays. It has become a leading spring break destination for sometimes rowdy college students and the site of a large annual gay Memorial Day weekend party. In 2015, visitors to Pensacola spent $849 million, an annual increase of 26 percent.

The economy in the Pensacola area has been strong. In early 2016, the Gulf Power utility began work on a giant solar project at Eglin and two other military facilities on the panhandle, which was expected to yield 120 megawatts of power and could power 18,000 homes. In October 2016, the 18 percent growth in annual home sales in Pensacola was the largest of any metro area in Florida. That same month, construction began at Pensacola Airport on a $46 million aerospace facility that will maintain, repair and overhaul aircraft from around the world.

The 1st Congressional District of Florida runs from Pensacola, adjoining the Alabama border, through Fort Walton Beach and Destin to Santa Rosa Beach. It is so far west, it is in the Central time zone. Inland, the 1st takes in rural Walton and Holmes counties. With 41 percent in Pensacola-based Escambia County, the district population has grown steadily. Young civilians, as well as military retirees, have settled here and raised education and quality-of-life issues. The region has long been culturally and economically conservative, with a strong pro-military bent. Like John McCain in 2008 and Mitt Romney in 2012, who got 67 percent and 69 percent in this district, Donald Trump had his best Florida showing in the district, with a 67%-28% win. Its lines were not changed by the 2016 redistricting.

SECOND DISTRICT

Neal Dunn (R)

Elected 2016, 1st term; b. Feb 16, 1953, New Haven, CT; Washington and Lee University (VA), Bach. Deg.; George Washington University Medical School (DC), M.D.; Catholic; Married (Leah Dunn); 3 children; 3 grandchildren.

Military Career: U.S Army, 1989-2010.

Professional Career: Urologist; Banker.

DC Office: 423 CHOB 20515, 202-225-5235, Fax: 202-225-5615, dunn.house.gov.

State Offices: Panama City, 850-785-0812; Tallahassee, 850-891-8610.

Committees: *Agriculture*: Biotechnology, Horticulture & Research, General Farm Commodities & Risk Management. *Science, Space & Technology*: Energy, Space. *Veterans' Affairs*: Health, Oversight & Investigations.

Election Results

Election	Name (Party)	Vote (%)	Cand. Spent	Ind. Exp. Support	Ind. Exp. Oppose
2016 General	Neal Dunn (R)	231,163 (67%)	$1,948,453	$180,931	$914,714
	Walter Dartland (D)	102,801 (30%)	$130,235		
	Rob Lapham (L)	9,395 (3%)	$15,721		
2016 Primary	Neal Dunn (R)	33,873 (41%)			
	Mary Thomas (R)	32,162 (39%)			
	Ken Sukhia (R)	15,821 (19%)			

Neal Dunn was elected in 2016 to a seat that was significantly changed by redistricting. He joins the several House Republicans who have been physicians, and he also has served in the military — an unusual combination in Congress these days. He won the seat chiefly in a competitive primary, in which he benefited from securing his base in the population center of this sprawling district.

Neal Dunn was born in Boston to a military family. Growing up, he was an Eagle Scout and active in rifle competitions. Dunn received a U.S. Army ROTC scholarship to Washington & Lee University, where he received his bachelor's degree before earning his medical degree from George Washington University. He completed his urological residency at Walter Reed Army Medical Center and served as an attending urologist in the U.S. Army for 11 years, before moving to Panama City and working as a urologist there for 25 years

After leaving his medical practice, Dunn became the chief medical officer for the Advanced Urology Institute in North Florida, which had 45 doctors. In 2014, Florida Senate President Don Gaetz (the father of Dunn's fellow freshman Don Gaetz in the adjacent 1st District) appointed him to serve as the Senate's representative on the Enterprise Florida Board of Directors. Dunn was the founding chairman of Summit Bank in Panama City, which emphasized custom commercial lending.

When first-term Democratic Rep. Gwen Graham decided after redistricting not to seek reelection in 2016 and to focus on a possible run for governor in 2018, the district became a strong Republican pick-up opportunity. The two chief GOP contenders were Dunn and Mary Thomas, a Tallahassee attorney. Panama City-based Bay County had more than 50 percent as many Republicans as did the parts of Tallahassee-based Leon County in the district, giving Dunn an advantage. Former U.S. Attorney Ken Sukhia, a third GOP candidate, also was from Leon. Dunn ran as an "unapologetic conservative Republican" whose top priority was to repeal the Affordable Care Act. That objective required, he said, lawmakers "who have represented patients, not bureaucrats."

Some conservatives criticized Dunn for having made campaign contributions to Florida Democratic Sen. Bill Nelson and to former Gov. Charlie Crist, who switched parties to run successfully for the House in 2016 as a Democrat. Thomas, the former counsel for the Florida Elder Affairs Department, was backed by the conservative Club for Growth, which spent $584,000 on her behalf and called Dunn "a liberal lobbyist." Dunn spent $2 million for his campaign, with Thomas and Sukhia spending $1.1 million and $207,000 respectively.

Dunn defeated Thomas 41.4%-39.3%, a margin of 1,708 votes. Sukhia got 19.3%. Thomas won 11 of the 19 counties. But Dunn won easily in Bay County and oddly took Leon County, which the three candidates split almost evenly. Bay and Leon cast nearly half the total vote. In the general election, Dunn faced Walt Dartland, a former Marine Corps major and state deputy attorney general, who called himself "pretty conservative in terms of fiscal policy." Dartland spent $130,000 and was competitive only in Leon County. Dunn won, 67%-30%.

Dunn got seats on the Agriculture, Veterans Affairs, and Science, Space and Technology committees. His political concerns include a Republican primary with a single opponent and the redistricting scheduled for 2022.

Central Panhandle: Panama City, Parts of Tallahassee

Demographics data for new House districts were not prepared by the Census Bureau prior to our editorial deadline.

Voter Turnout			
2016 House Turnout as % CVAP	N/A	2016 House turnout	343,362

2012 Presidential Vote information unavailable due to recent redistricting.

2016 Presidential Vote		
Donald Trump	234,990	(66%)
Hillary Clinton	108,636	(30%)
Gary Johnson	8,400	(2%)

Cook Partisan Voting Index: R+18

Much of northern Florida is swampy lowlands. Along the 355-mile route across the northern tier of the state from Jacksonville on the Atlantic Coast to Pensacola on the Gulf of Mexico, there are occasional small towns - some of them from the 19th century - and lots of empty land. To outsiders, this is mostly fly-over or drive-through Florida. In a few decades, perhaps this area will become a modern version of central Florida from Orlando to Tampa, or south Florida from Palm Beach to Miami.

For now, there are only two urban centers along the northern tier. By Florida standards, each is small. Tallahassee, inland from the Gulf and relatively isolated, became the state capital when Florida's then-modest population lived mostly along the state's northern tier, placing it, more or less, at its center of gravity. Ralph Waldo Emerson, visiting Tallahassee at the time, called it a "grotesque place, rapidly settled by public officers, land speculators, and desperadoes." Until fairly recently, it remained little more than a Spanish-mossed county seat with a pair of universities and a handsome Creole capitol, which was built in 1845 and preserved opposite its 1977 skyscraper replacement. Since the 1980s, it has spread out and become a middling-sized city, with a tight-knit though sometimes fractious political and legal elite, bringing a taste of newly urbanized Florida to the state's north. In March 2015, the University of Toronto's Martin Prosperity Institute released a study that found Tallahassee the most segregated city in the United States in terms of economics, education and occupation. Tallahassee has not yet attained the critical mass of Sacramento, Austin or Albany, but perhaps it is on its way. There is certainly plenty of room for physical growth.

Panama City is a very different place. What was a popular spring break destination along the state's pretty and underappreciated northwest beaches has become a growing retirement and resort area. This part of Florida had retained one of the highest percentages of native Floridians. But that is changing. The opening of an airport in 2010 near Panama City, the first new international airport in the United States in more than a decade, spurred development. In 2014, Panama City was the 19th fastest-growing metro area in the nation. That future hit at least a short-term glitch in May 2015, when Panama City officials unanimously voted to ban alcohol on the beach during March. In March 2016, that resulted in a 41 percent decline in the city's revenue and a $40 million hit to its economy. Local officials sought to increase revenues from family-oriented summer vacationers.

The new 2nd Congressional District of Florida is an amorphous area whose population center is based in Panama City plus the parts of the Tallahassee area that are not in the new 5th Congressional District. The 5th was radically redrawn as a minority district that extends from Jacksonville to Tallahassee, rather than from Jacksonville to Orlando, as had been the case for more than two decades. Those changes have left the new 2nd with a small minority population and have created a solidly Republican district. Gone are the Democratic parts of Tallahassee plus rural Gadsden County, the state's only black-majority county, though the state capital remains. In their place are seven mostly rural and white counties that curve along the bend of the Gulf with mostly undeveloped beaches and move inland to the outskirts of Ocala in Marion County. The drive from Panama City at the northwest end of the district to Inglis in the southeast is a Texas-sized 251 miles.

The black voting-age population in the new 2nd District has dropped from 19 percent to 10 percent. In its old lines in 2012, Mitt Romney defeated Barack Obama, 52%-47%. With the new lines, Romney would have won, 65%-34%. That explains why Democrats took a pass on a district that was no longer competitive, or even hospitable. Instead, they focused on opportunities that the new map gave them elsewhere, chiefly the Orlando and Tampa areas. In 2016, Donald Trump won this district, 66%-30%. As the *Tallahassee Democrat* newspaper aptly described in July 2016, the odd configurations in that city lack "common sense." The much-lauded Fair Redistricting map seems to have overlooked this area.

THIRD DISTRICT

Ted Yoho (R)

Elected 2012, 3rd term; b. Apr 13, 1955, Minneapolis, MN; Broward Community College (FL), A.A., 1976; University of Florida, B.S., 1979; University of Florida Veterinary College, D.V.M., 1983; Roman Catholic; Married (Carolyn Yoho); 3 children.

Professional Career: Veterinarian, 1983-present.

DC Office: 511 CHOB 20515, 202-225-5744, Fax: 202-225-3973, yoho.house.gov.

State Offices: Gainesville, 352-505-0838; Orange Park, 904-276-9626; Palatka, 386-326-7221.

Committees: *Agriculture*: Biotechnology, Horticulture & Research, Livestock & Foreign Agriculture, Nutrition. *Foreign Affairs*: Asia & the Pacific (Chmn), Western Hemisphere.

Group Ratings

	ADA	ACLU	AFL-CIO	LCV	ITI	COC	HAFA	ACU	CFG	FRC
2016	-	17%	-	3%	83%	100%	83%	96%	77%	100%
2015	10%	C	4%	3%	C	65%	C	100%	95%	92%

Almanac Ratings 2015

	Economy	Social	Foreign	Composite
Liberal	10%	15%	15%	13%
Conservative	90%	85%	85%	87%

Key Votes of the 114th Congress

1. Keystone Pipeline	Y	5. Puerto Rico Debt	N	9. Offenses by Aliens	Y
2. Trade Deals	N	6. Medical Marijuana	Y	10. Troops in Iraq	Y
3. Export-Import Bank	N	7. Sanctuary Cities	Y	11. Homeland Security $$	N
4. Debt Ceiling Increase	N	8. Armor-piercing Bullets	Y	12. Trade Adjustment aid	N

Election Results

Election	Name (Party)	Vote (%)		Cand. Spent	Ind. Exp. Support	Ind. Exp. Oppose
2016 General	Ted Yoho (R)	193,843	(57%)	$754,243		
	Ken McGurn (D)	136,338	(40%)	$599,604		
	Tom Wells (I)	12,519	(4%)	$7,335		
2016 Primary	Ted Yoho (R)		(100%)			

Prior winning percentages: 2014 (65%), 2012 (65%)

Republican Ted Yoho, unexpectedly elected to the House in 2012 as an outsider candidate, gained his proverbial 15 minutes of fame when he emerged as an unlikely candidate for Speaker in January 2015. He received some media buzz and got two votes - one of which was his own. Although his legislative record has been modest, he has been active in conservative groups among House Republicans.

Yoho was born in Minneapolis, the fifth of six sons, and moved with his family at age 11 to South Florida. After a short stint at Florence State University (now the University of North Alabama) on a football scholarship, he soon returned to Florida. He married his high school sweetheart, Carolyn, and decided to become a veterinarian. The couple moved to Gainesville, where he got a bachelor's degree in animal science at the University of Florida, then graduated from its veterinary college. Yoho built a successful large-animal veterinarian practice.

He first became interested in politics during President Bill Clinton's impeachment drama. Over time, he said he got fed up with politicians who either couldn't or wouldn't fix "the mess" in Washington that many of them helped to create. He sold his veterinary practice and launched his campaign. "One political consultant told us this race would be a good 'practice run,'" he recalled with amusement.

In the 2012 Republican primary, Yoho was not nearly as well-known as two of his opponents, 12-term Rep. Cliff Stearns and state Sen. Steve Oelrich of Gainesville. Stearns had a huge cash advantage and had not been considered in jeopardy, but redistricting gave him a district that was more conservative. He committed a few errors, including focusing his attention on Oelrich. With just one paid employee, Yoho stumped aggressively as a Christian (Roman Catholic) and a conservative. He embraced his tea party backing and railed against "career politicians." He emphasized to voters his experience in running a successful small business, where he was on the receiving end of regulations and "garbage legislation" from Washington. He opposed raising taxes, but refused to sign lobbyist and conservative activist Grover Norquist's no-tax pledge on the grounds that a war or other events might leave few alternatives. He said he would serve no more than eight years in the House.

Using humor to show voters that he was a different kind of politician, Yoho ran a campaign ad showing suited "politicians" feeding from a pig trough and a video about an upcoming fundraiser with a President George W. Bush impersonator. Using $50,000 of his own money, he edged out Stearns by just 875 votes, with 34 percent; Oelrich trailed with 19 percent. He had no trouble in the general election, taking 65 percent of the vote.

On his first day in office in January 2013, Yoho joined a protest by a small group of conservatives who refused to back a second term as House Speaker for John Boehner of Ohio. Instead, Yoho cast his vote for Majority Leader Eric Cantor of Virginia. During his first term, he continued to style himself as a tea party leader who was eager to stand up to the political establishment. He advocated the impeachment of President Barack Obama, and said that voting rights should be limited to property owners. When Obama issued his executive order on immigration in 2014, Yoho introduced a bill to rescind the president's authority to stop deportations; the president's action, he later said, would open the door to chain migration into the United States. When Boehner suggested that the House vote on Yoho's bill as a step to keep the government open, conservative Republicans objected that the Speaker's package was not sufficient. As a result, GOP leaders were forced to make additional concessions to scramble for Democratic votes on the omnibus spending bill.

When a floating group of House conservatives, spurred by outside groups, said they would not vote to give Boehner a third term as Speaker, Yoho was the first to volunteer as a candidate. He issued a statement, "Enough of career politicians, enough of political gamesmanship, and enough of the lack of leadership in Washington." But he failed to galvanize the opponents to Boehner. Rep. Daniel Webster, another Florida Republican, later emerged and attracted 12 votes as the leading GOP alternative to Boehner. In addition to his own vote, the other Yoho supporter was Rep. Thomas Massie of Kentucky. Yoho became a founding member of the Freedom Caucus and the Second Amendment Caucus. In November 2016, the House passed his bill to give congressional aides greater access to records of the Veterans Administration to assist in reducing the backlog of claims. *GQ* magazine ranked Yoho among "America's 20 craziest politicians." Tea party advocates continued to embrace him.

In 2016, Yoho was challenged by Democrat Ken McGurn, a local developer. Their spending figures were relatively close: almost $800,000 for Yoho to $600,000 for McGurn, who self-financed about half his contest. With the redistricting changes that decreased the Republican advantage, this was Yoho's most competitive campaign. He won 57%-40% and took five of the six counties. In Alachua, the largest county, McGurn led, 56%-41%. A primary challenge by a Main Street-type candidate from the growing suburbs could be competitive for Yoho.

North Florida: Jacksonville Suburbs, Gainesville

Demographics data for new House districts were not prepared by the Census Bureau prior to our editorial deadline.

Voter Turnout

2016 House Turnout as % CVAP	N/A	2016 House turnout	342,700

2012 Presidential Vote information unavailable due to recent redistricting.

2016 Presidential Vote

Donald Trump	197,478	(56%)
Hillary Clinton	141,362	(40%)
Gary Johnson	9,138	(3%)

Cook Partisan Voting Index: R+9

The flat grasslands of central Florida, once bypassed by southbound tourists heading for the coastal resorts and cities, have become a prime growth area in this high-growth state. Central Florida's economy once depended on farming, on tourists getting off the interstate and on state institutions, most notably the University of Florida in Gainesville. Then retirees began settling in places like the blue-grass country around Ocala, one of America's prime horse-breeding grounds, and the area began to share the development boom, growing by 19 percent from 2000 to 2007. But then the recession hit the region hard, with Ocala's unemployment rate soaring past 14 percent in 2010 and home foreclosures reaching record levels. By 2014, Ocala-based Marion County led the state in economic growth and foreclosures had declined. In October 2016, *Forbes* ranked the Ocala area ninth in the nation for projected job growth in the next two years. CSX plans to develop a major freight rail hub in Ocala. In addition to the university, the Gainesville area has added hundreds of manufacturing jobs since 2010. North-central Florida, including the rapidly growing outskirts of Jacksonville, is more like Georgia than the rest of the state. Its voting patterns have recently solidified for the Republicans and have partly offset the movement toward Democrats in South Florida.

The new 3rd Congressional District of Florida has become centralized in a more compact core of north Florida, with 82 percent of its population in three counties: all of Alachua, which includes Gainesville; all of Clay, which is chiefly Orange Park, Middleburg and other suburbs southwest of Jacksonville; and nearly half of Marion, which includes Ocala. Seven lightly populated and more heavily Republican counties to the west, some of them along the bend of the Gulf of Mexico, have shifted to the 2nd District. With the exception of firmly Democratic Gainesville and its large campus, these areas are comfortably Republican, but in more of a suburban way rather than the previous rural mix. The land area of the new district has shrunk by about 40 percent.

This remains a Republican district, but not quite as solidly as before redistricting. With the previous boundaries, Mitt Romney won the 3rd, 62%-38%; with the new boundaries, his lead would have dropped to 57%-42%. Donald Trump's performance was similar, 56%-40%. What had been the third strongest Republican district in Florida has slipped to 8th.

FOURTH DISTRICT

John Rutherford (R)

Elected 2016, 1st term; b. Sep 02, 1952, Omaha, NE; Florida Junior College, A.A., 1972; Florida State University, B.S., 1974; Catholic; Married (Patricia Rutherford); 2 children; 6 grandchildren.

Elected Office: Sheriff, City of Jacksonville, 2003-2015.

DC Office: 230 CHOB 20515, 202-225-2501, Fax: 202-225-2504, rutherford.house.gov.

State Offices: Jacksonville, 904-831-5205.

Committees: *Homeland Security*: Border & Maritime Security, Emergency Preparedness, Response & Communications. *Judiciary*. *Veterans' Affairs*: Economic Opportunity, Health.

Election Results

Election	Name (Party)	Vote (%)		Cand. Spent	Ind. Exp. Support	Ind. Exp. Oppose
2016 General	John Rutherford (R)	287,509	(70%)	$799,900		$239,760
	David E. Bruderly (D)	113,088	(28%)	$49,320		
	Gary Koniz (I)	9,054	(2%)			
2016 Primary	John Rutherford (R)	38,688	(39%)			
	Lake Ray (R)	20,111	(20%)			
	Hans Tanzler III (R)	18,999	(19%)			
	Bill McClure (R)	9,854	(10%)			

Republican John Rutherford was elected in 2016 to fill the seat of Republican Ander Crenshaw, a quiet insider who was a senior member of the Appropriations Committee. Rutherford, well-known locally as the sheriff of Jacksonville, faced a competitive primary that he won handily. He has shown signs that he would continue Crenshaw's style as a leadership ally.

Rutherford, who has lived in Jacksonville since he was six, earned an associate's degree in police administration from Florida Junior College and a bachelor's degree in criminology from Florida State University. He began his police career as a patrolman in 1974 and was the Jacksonville police department's director of corrections from 1995 until 2003. He was first elected sheriff of Jacksonville in 2003 and served for 12 years.

As sheriff, Rutherford introduced several initiatives to reduce crime, including Operation Safe Streets, gun bounty awards and public awareness programs. In addition to greater community engagement, he focused on better treatment of the mentally ill to reduce their recidivism rate. By the end of his tenure, Jacksonville's violent crime rate was at a 40-year low. He also served as chairman of the Florida Sheriff's Association, where he advocated state legislation that would reduce crime.

After Crenshaw announced his retirement, seven Republicans competed in the primary. In addition to Rutherford, the best-known were state Rep. Lake Ray and Hans Tanzler, son of a former Jacksonville mayor. Tanzler challenged Rutherford's conservative credentials, including the former sheriff's opposition to the death penalty, and his support for higher taxes and for protecting illegal immigrants in Jacksonville. Rutherford charged that Tanzler was a "political insider" who had backed former Republican Gov. Charlie Crist, which resulted in Tanzler getting the position of executive director of the St. Johns River Water Management District board. Republican Sen. John McCain of

Arizona endorsed Tanzler late in the campaign, with praise for the care that Tanzler's father provided for McCain's family while he was a prisoner of war in North Vietnam.

Rutherford spent $833,000 for his campaign. Tanzler reported $814,000, of which half was self-financed. The quieter Ray spent $242,000. Rutherford won 39 percent of the primary vote to 20 percent for Ray and 19 percent for Tanzler; the vote was split evenly across the three counties. The general election was an after-thought. Democrat David Bruderly, who said he welcomed the label of "perennial candidate," spent $50,000. Rutherford won, 70%-28%. He got seats on the Homeland Security and Veterans' Affairs committees.

Parts of Jacksonville and Suburbs

Demographics data for new House districts were not prepared by the Census Bureau prior to our editorial deadline.

Voter Turnout			
2016 House Turnout as % CVAP	N/A	2016 House turnout	409,662

2012 Presidential Vote information unavailable due to recent redistricting.

2016 Presidential Vote		
Donald Trump	261,828	(62%)
Hillary Clinton	143,674	(34%)
Gary Johnson	12,473	(3%)

Cook Partisan Voting Index: R+17

With a metropolitan area of 1.3 million people, Jacksonville has outgrown its reputation as Florida's overlooked city. Not long ago, it was considered a backwater, dominated by insurance companies and smelly paper mills. Jacksonville is now the largest city by land area in the contiguous 48 states, boasting a National Football League franchise, bold new skyscrapers looming above the St. Johns River and a shopping mall that overshadows tiny shotgun houses. Wide freeways sidestep primeval wetlands on their way to huge beachfront subdivisions.

Jacksonville's harbor has grown as a destination for cargo and cruise-line operations, with a total annual economic impact of about $27 billion. With Naval Station Mayport and Naval Air Station Jacksonville - two of the three largest metro-area employers - the city has a significant military employment base. Shipbuilding and repair provide more than 10,000 jobs in the area. Shrewd marketing has lured big-name companies as well. The city is the headquarters of railway giant CSX and hosts major operations such as UPS and Bank of America.

Business leaders are working to make the area into the "Silicon Valley of Logistics" - building on its land, air and sea transportation facilities. New jobs have been especially strong in construction. In June 2016, the Port Authority agreed to dredge 13 miles of the river from 40 feet to 47 feet; this is crucial to the city's long-term growth. In August, Amazon was issued a permit to build a fulfillment center, which would hire 1,500 employees. UPS announced in November a $196 million expansion of its ground hub, which could handle more than 80,000 packages per hour. Also that year, the Navy announced that the base for its new class of 52 littoral combat ships, which will be faster and carry more weapons but with a smaller crew, will be split between Mayport and San Diego. Navy pilots were planning to fly overseas unmanned Triton drone systems from their computers at the naval air station. The air station is one of three bases where the Navy has considered headquartering its East Coast drone operations.

With the new redistricting plan in 2016, the district remained centered in Jacksonville-based Duval County. About 125,000 residents were moved to the African-American majority 5th District, which left the county split about evenly between the two districts. In exchange, the 4th gained to the south 85 percent of St. Johns County, which grew by 54 percent from 2000 to 2010, and has become the second-fastest growing and the wealthiest county in the state. Amid the new construction in much of St. Johns is the well-restored St. Augustine, founded by Spanish colonists as the oldest permanent European settlement in North America - 42 years older than Jamestown, Virginia, and 55 years older than the Plymouth colony in Massachusetts. Remaining in the district is all of rapidly growing Nassau County to the north, including a massive planned community in Yulee between I-95 and state road A1A, where nearly 13,000 people resided in July 2016. The boosterish Jacksonville civic culture and significant military presence make the 4th a pro-business, pro-military and pro-Republican district. With the redistricting changes, Mitt Romney in 2012 would have retained his 66 percent of the vote, his second best in Florida. In 2016, local support for Donald Trump dropped to 62 percent, another example of reduced support for Trump from affluent GOP voters.

FIFTH DISTRICT

Al Lawson (D)

Elected 2016, 1st term; b. Sep 21, 1948, Midway; University of Florida, B.S., 1970; Florida State University, M.S., 1973; Episcopalian; Married (Delores J. Brooks Lawson); 2 children; 2 grandchildren.

Elected Office: FL House, 1982-2000; FL Senate, 2000-2010, Minority Leader, 2008-2010.

Professional Career: Prof. Basketball player & coach, Florida State Univ.; President, Lawson & Assoc. Inc. .

DC Office: 1337 LHOB 20515, 202-225-0123, Fax: 202-225-2256, lawson.house.gov.

State Offices: Jacksonville, 904-354-1652; Tallahassee, 850-558-9450.

Committees: *Agriculture*: Biotechnology, Horticulture & Research, General Farm Commodities & Risk Management, Nutrition. *Small Business*: Agriculture, Energy & Trade, Contracting & Workforce, Health & Technology (RMM).

Election Results

Election	Name (Party)	Vote (%)		Cand. Spent	Ind. Exp. Support	Ind. Exp. Oppose
2016 General	Al Lawson (D)	194,549	(64%)	$340,897		
	Glo Smith (R)	108,325	(36%)	$86,882		
2016 Primary	Al Lawson (D)	39,261	(48%)			
	Corrine Brown (D)	32,157	(39%)			
	L.J. Holloway (D)	11,004	(13%)			

Democrat Al Lawson was elected in 2016 under unusual circumstances. He ran in a district that had been radically altered in a mid-decade redistricting that benefited him. And he defeated Rep. Corinne Brown, a 12-term incumbent who had overcome numerous obstacles during her career, but couldn't survive the combination of adverse redistricting and a criminal indictment. Even with those obstacles, Brown ran a competitive contest and the results reinforced the customary advantages of home turf.

Lawson, a fourth-generation Floridian, was born in Midway. He worked his first job in the Gadsden Community tobacco fields at the age of 8. In high school, he was an accomplished athlete and went on to play basketball at Florida Agricultural and Mechanical University. He received his bachelor's degree in political science, then earned a master's in public administration from Florida State University. He married his college sweetheart, Dr. Delores Brooks, who teaches at Florida A&M University's School of Nursing. Lawson was elected to the Florida House in 1982 and served for 18 years before winning election in 2000 to the state Senate, where he served for another 10 years. He chaired the House Natural Resources Committee, authoring the Preservation 2000 environmental law, which created the largest state-funded land acquisition program in the country. In 2005, Lawson sponsored and passed legislation creating the First Generation Matching Grant scholarship program. Following his departure from the Legislature, he became a lobbyist and insurance agent.

Lawson had twice run for Congress. In 2010, he sought the Democratic nomination in the Tallahassee-based 2nd District, losing narrowly in the primary to seven-term Rep. Allen Boyd. Then, he lost in the 2012 general against Republican Rep. Steve Southerland, who had defeated Boyd two years earlier. In the 2016 primary, Lawson took on yet another incumbent. This time, it was the Democratic primary against Brown, a Florida political legend who had been indicted weeks earlier for corruption. They were running in a radically redrawn district that had two geographic poles: Brown's home town of Jacksonville and Lawson's long-time base in Tallahassee and Gadsden.

Brown, first elected in 1992, focused on constituents in her House work and used the slogan "Corrine Delivers" in her reelection campaigns. Her ability to provide money and other help to her financially ailing district kept her in office, despite a string of controversial comments and ethics issues. She grew up in Jacksonville, taught at a community college, was a guidance counselor, and in 1982, was elected to the Florida House. When she ran for the newly created black-majority district in the 1992 Democratic primary, she faced white talk-radio host Andy Johnson, who called himself "the blackest candidate in the race." But her political base in Jacksonville carried her to a 64%-36% victory in the runoff.

Brown compiled a liberal record on most issues. In her district, many voters work at military bases. She backed high defense spending and argued that the military can be a source of opportunity. On the Veterans' Affairs Committee, she sought additional veterans' cemeteries for Florida, which is the home to more military retirees than any state except California. On Transportation and Infrastructure, Brown worked on legislation to strengthen security at ports. Her long-standing project was a high-speed rail line from Tampa to Orlando and Miami.

Her outspoken, partisan views caused her problems at times. In a dispute in 2008 over the seating of convention delegates from Florida, Brown, who had endorsed Hillary Rodham Clinton for president, said, "If we are not seated, then nobody is going to be seated." The problem was resolved after Barack Obama became the certain nominee. In 2015, she criticized as "hidden racism" the large opposition in the Senate to the confirmation of Loretta Lynch as attorney general.

Despite the ease with which she had been reelected, Brown in 2011 joined Florida Republican Rep. Mario Diaz-Balart in filing a legal challenge to the state's voter-approved Fair District amendment. That amendment to the Florida constitution, approved in a 2010 referendum, called for congressional districts to be drawn more compactly and to be impartial with regard to political party. The two lawmakers said it would have a negative impact on minority voters and the Voting Rights Act guarantee to maximize minority districts. The suit angered Brown's Florida Democratic colleagues and longtime allies such as the NAACP who backed the referendum and called her challenge selfish. In the culmination of the litigation, the state Supreme Court in July 2015 ordered major changes in Brown's 5th District, extending it east-west from Jacksonville to Tallahassee instead of north-south to Orlando. Brown strongly objected and filed court challenges. But she soon ran out of appeals. She reportedly considered seeking reelection in a new Orlando-based district. But she decided to return to her home ground in a contest against Lawson that would test the strength of each candidate's political base.

In a major development eight weeks before the primary, a federal grand jury issued a 22-count indictment of Brown following a lengthy investigation into what prosecutors termed a phony educational charity that she and her chief of staff turned into a personal slush fund with $800,000 in solicitations. Brown pleaded not guilty.

Lawson won the August 30 primary, 48%-39%, with LaShonda Holloway getting 13 percent. Both Lawson and Brown ran well in their home areas, but Lawson did better even though his base had a smaller turnout. In Tallahassee-based Leon County plus adjoining Gadsden, Lawson won 76 percent of the 31,491 votes. In Jacksonville-based Duval County, Brown won 62 percent of the 39,888 votes cast. Those three counties, separated by 160 miles, cast 86 percent of the total votes. Interestingly, Florida election data showed that Duval County had 403,000 residents in the district, compared with only 206,000 for Leon and Gadsden. Brown, a veteran incumbent, spent only $572,000, including a $100,000 personal loan. Lawson spent $356,000 for his campaign.

In the general, Lawson defeated Republican Gio Smith, 64%-36%. Smith, who spent $88,000 and had challenged Brown in the past, won two rural counties.

Northern Florida metro areas: Downtown Jacksonville and Parts of Tallahassee

Demographics data for new House districts were not prepared by the Census Bureau prior to our editorial deadline.

Voter Turnout			
2016 House Turnout as % CVAP	N/A	2016 House turnout	302,874

2012 Presidential Vote information unavailable due to recent redistricting.

2016 Presidential Vote		
Hillary Clinton	191,195	(61%)
Donald Trump	111,891	(36%)
Gary Johnson	5,997	(2%)

Cook Partisan Voting Index: D+12

Before the Civil War, most of Florida was still an uncharted watery wilderness, festooned with exotic greenery, inhabited by unusual animals, a part of the United States so far out of the experience of most

Americans as to seem foreign. As late as 1940, Florida had the smallest population of any Southern state, and most of the people here lived in classic Dixie rural counties with small courthouse towns, where civic affairs were run by the richest white men, and African Americans lived in poorly constructed, unpainted shotgun shacks propped up on blocks, with little money and no vote. This was a land of swamps, lakes and orange groves, and of author Marjorie Kinnan Rawlings' Cross Creek, where she wrote the great children's classic *The Yearling.* The broad St. Johns River, one of the few North American rivers that flows (if only sluggishly) north, meanders through orange-grove country to the port of Jacksonville, which was for many years Florida's largest city. Jacksonville planners have been eager to revitalize the downtown area, which is dominated by shipyards, warehouses and some office buildings. In 2015-16, 15 major downtown development projects were completed at a cost of $221 million; another 25 projects at a cost of $471 million were underway. There are plans to develop the riverfront. In recent years, Jacksonville has benefited from international migration. Filipinos make up the largest group of recent immigrants.

Tallahassee, the seat of state government with many public-sector jobs, has been a source of discomfort for the state's Republican rulers. Its African-American population grew from about 25 percent in the 1990s to 35 percent in 2010. The city's liberal bent is also fueled by its two big universities in the downtown area, Florida State and Florida A&M. In 2016, the city's economic growth was described as slower than in urban areas elsewhere in Florida. This remains a government town, as promises from state leaders of a "new economy" have been mostly unfulfilled. Nearby Gadsden County, the state's only black-majority county, is rural and heavily Democratic. The countryside around Tallahassee is distinctly Dixie and is more reminiscent of southern Georgia than of southern Florida. The landscape is marked by cotton fields, soft pine stands, catfish farms and small towns with big churches.

The new 5th Congressional District is like a barbell that extends more than 160 miles from Jacksonville to Tallahassee. But the barbell is unequal. The Jacksonville-based Duval County territory has 403,000 residents, while the western end in Leon and Gadsden Counties has 206,000 persons. The Jacksonville section of the district includes much of downtown, including the large port, though it stops a few miles short of the Atlantic. The district includes nearly half of Duval County; the remainder is the core of the solidly Republican 4th District. On the western end, the 5th includes close to 60 percent of Leon; the more Republican section is in the realigned 2nd District. Even with its smaller population in the 5th, the Leon County portion can show its weight in elections because its many government employees are more politically connected. Between the two ends of the barbell are five rural counties, each with a population of less than 30,000. For more than 20 years, the district - in various incarnations, some of them like ink spots - had included parts of Jacksonville and Orlando, but not Tallahassee.

The new 5th, like the old one, is the only Democratic district north of Orlando. With the old lines, Barack Obama won in 2012, 73%-26%. Hillary Clinton won in 2016, 61%-36%. Its voting-age population is 50 percent African American and 11 percent Hispanic. It trails only the Miami-based 24thDistrict in the size of its black population.

SIXTH DISTRICT

Ron DeSantis (R)

Elected 2012, 3rd term; b. Sep 14, 1978, Jacksonville; Yale University (CT), A.B.; Harvard University Law School (MA), J.D.; Roman Catholic; Married (Ms. Casey Black).

Military Career: U.S Navy, 2004-2010; Navy Reserves, 2010-present.

Professional Career: Practicing attorney 2004-present.

DC Office: 1524 LHOB 20515, 202-225-2706, Fax: 202-226-6299, desantis.house.gov.

State Offices: DeLand, 386-279-7343; Palm Coast, 386-302-0471; Port Orange, 386-756-9798.

Committees: *Foreign Affairs*: Middle East & North Africa, Western Hemisphere. *Judiciary*: Constitution & Civil Justice, Courts, Intellectual Property & Internet. *Oversight & Government Reform*: Government Operations, National Security (Chmn).

Group Ratings

	ADA	ACLU	AFL-CIO	LCV	ITI	COC	HAFA	ACU	CFG	FRC
2016	-	5%	-	3%	100%	93%	88%	100%	92%	100%
2015	0%	C	0%	0%	C	65%	C	100%	99%	91%

Almanac Ratings 2015

	Economy	Social	Foreign	Composite
Liberal	6%	15%	0%	7%
Conservative	94%	85%	100%	93%

Key Votes of the 114th Congress

1. Keystone Pipeline	Y	5. Puerto Rico Debt	N	9. Offenses by Aliens	Y
2. Trade Deals	Y	6. Medical Marijuana	Y	10. Troops in Iraq	N
3. Export-Import Bank	N	7. Sanctuary Cities	Y	11. Homeland Security $$	N
4. Debt Ceiling Increase	N	8. Armor-piercing Bullets	Y	12. Trade Adjustment aid	N

Election Results

Election	Name (Party)	Vote (%)		Cand. Spent	Ind. Exp. Support	Ind. Exp. Oppose
2016 General	Ron Desantis (R)	213,519	(59%)	$3,681,254	$40,002	
	Bill MCCollough (D)	151,051	(41%)	$39,082		
2016 Primary	Ron DeSantis (R)	41,276	(61%)			
	Fred Costello (R)	16,681	(25%)			
	G.G. Galloway (R)	9,681	(14%)			

Prior winning percentages: 2014 (63%), 2012 (57%)

Republican Ron DeSantis, who was first elected in 2012, embraced the tea party and sought to reduce the federal government's "size, scope, and influence." He managed to find a balance between collaborating with the most conservative Republicans and winning committee leadership assignments from the party establishment. In 2016, he sought to build on that with a run for the Senate. But Marco Rubio changed those plans when he made a late decision to seek reelection to the seat from which he had announced his retirement. DeSantis, whose Senate prospects were not great, decided to retain his House seat.

DeSantis grew up in northeast Florida, where his father installed television ratings devices for Nielsen. A talented baseball player, DeSantis played on a team from Dunedin that made the final four of the Little League World Series in 1991. He went on to captain the squad at Yale, where he majored in history. To help pay for his studies, he held a variety of jobs, including collecting trash, moving furniture and coaching baseball clinics. He earned his law degree at Harvard and became a judge advocate general in the Navy. His military service helped shape his views on national security, including his skepticism of nation-building. While there are a lot of "good people" in Iraq, he said "getting involved in guerilla war doesn't play to our strengths." He has remained a lieutenant commander in the Naval Reserve.

DeSantis ran for office when the new 6th District unexpectedly had no incumbent following the 2012 redistricting. He had written a book, *Dreams From Our Founding Fathers*, whose title is a play on the title President Barack Obama chose for his memoir, *Dreams From My Father*. He argued that Obama and like-minded Democrats "have charted a course that is alien to our Republic's philosophical foundations."

Touting his military experience and strong conservative views, DeSantis easily defeated his six rivals in the August primary, with 39 percent of the vote. He credited old-fashioned retail politics for the win. "I started in February with zero percent name ID, and we'd go door-to-door on a Saturday and Sunday," he said. He also won endorsements from such tea party favorites as former U.N. Ambassador John Bolton and Sen. Mike Lee of Utah, and had a pronounced fundraising advantage. In the general election, Democrat Heather Beaven, a fellow Navy veteran, focused on fixing Florida's hard-hit economy by embracing entrepreneurship and renewable energy. In this Republican district. DeSantis won, 57%-43%.

In the House, DeSantis bonded with conservative Republicans. Unlike several other junior Republicans from Florida, he voted in January 2015 to give John Boehner another term as Speaker, despite pressure from constituents to oppose him. "You've got to have pieces in place and you've got to have good candidates step forward," he responded. He was one of nine founding members of the Freedom Caucus to promote "liberty, safety and prosperity." He was awarded with positions of responsibility. DeSantis became chairman of the National Security Subcommittee of the Oversight and Government Reform Committee, where he pledged to "hold our national security agencies accountable on behalf of the American people." But facing pressure from Majority Whip Steve Scalise to toe the line for the party, he quit as a member of the Republican Whip team.

After Rubio said he would run for President and not seek reelection to the Senate in 2016, DeSantis became the first significant Republican candidate to declare for the seat. "I look forward to offering reforms based on limited government principles that will make our country stronger and more prosperous," he said in May 2015. His plan was to run as the conservative alternative, with extensive support from national advocacy groups such as the Club for Growth and Senate Conservatives Fund. But he faced steep challenges in gaining traction in the wide-open GOP primary, including low name ID outside of his district and the far greater diversity among Florida Republicans than within his constituency.

Even before Rubio responded to pleas from party leaders to re-claim his seat days before the June filing deadline, DeSantis was struggling. Once Rubio made his return official, DeSantis had no choice. But he faced a new problem. State Rep. Fred Costello, the leading Republican candidate for his House seat, was not amenable to stepping outside. A further complication was that Costello in 2012 finished second with 23 percent in the House primary that DeSantis won. "DeSantis' decision to back out of the U.S. Senate race and enter the Congressional District 6 race rather than run in Congressional District 4 where he lives does not in any way change my focus," Costello said in a press release.

Two weeks before the Aug. 30 primary, a reporter for the Daytona Beach *News-Journal* speculated that Costello had potential scenarios for a victory, even though DeSantis was the incumbent and had $3 million in his campaign account; Costello had less than $100,000. But the primary became a blow-out, with DeSantis winning, 61%-25%; in each of the four counties, he more than doubled Costello's support. In November, DeSantis coasted to a 59%-41% victory against Democrat William McCullough, a businessman and political newcomer, who raised $41,000.

Following the election, DeSantis co-authored with Republican Sen. Ted Cruz of Texas a column for *The Washington Post* in support of congressional term limits. Their view that the public had soured on the advantages held by the "permanent political class" likely was a message that rang true among some of DeSantis's constituents - though perhaps not in the way that he intended.

Northeast Florida: Daytona Beach

Demographics data for new House districts were not prepared by the Census Bureau prior to our editorial deadline.

Voter Turnout			
2016 House Turnout as % CVAP	N/A	2016 House turnout	364,570

2012 Presidential Vote information unavailable due to recent redistricting.

2016 Presidential Vote		
Donald Trump	215,940	(56%)
Hillary Clinton	151,453	(40%)
Gary Johnson	8,694	(2%)

Cook Partisan Voting Index: R+7

In 1513, Spanish explorer Juan Ponce de León headed to the New World, hoping to discover the Fountain of Youth. Instead, he found Ponte Vedra Beach, located just south of modern day Jacksonville. A few decades later, as countless students have been taught, Spanish colonists founded St. Augustine, the oldest permanent European settlement in North America. Less well-known is New Smyrna Beach. Another 75 miles down the Atlantic Coast, it was established in 1768 in an attempt by the British to colonize Florida with Greek settlers, whom they believed to be ideally suited to the warm climate. They were not, however, well suited for the brutal wilderness conditions. By 1777, many had abandoned the colony, walking and swimming back to St. Augustine. The area was a popular hideout for rum-runners during Prohibition, and today has become a popular vacation spot and quieter in many ways than nearby and better-known Daytona Beach.

The beaches in Daytona have been attracting sun-seekers for decades, although the city is best known for the Daytona 500 held each February at Daytona International Speedway. Further inland, northeast Florida still retains a taste of "Old Florida." DeLand has a small-town atmosphere centered on Stetson University, whose mascot is, appropriately, the Hatters, after the famous hat-maker who helped build the school that bears his name. In tiny Pierson, known as the "Fern Capital of the World," 54 percent of the population was Latino, according to the 2010 census; many perform the labor-intensive work of trimming the fern fronds. These places are part of Volusia County, much of which has managed to avoid the familiar pattern in Florida of endless high-rise condominiums along the coast - and inland, as well.

Flagler and St. Johns counties, the two coastal counties between Jacksonville and Daytona Beach, were filled with cattle ranches a few decades ago. Between 2000 and 2010, the population in Flagler nearly doubled and St. Johns increased by more than half. As with other parts of Florida, these growth rates slowed dramatically - and reversed, in many cases - during the recession. Since then, there have been signs of a rebound from St. Augustine down to New Smyrna. Tourists returned to the beaches, housing permits ticked up and foreclosure rates dropped.

The 6th District covers the Atlantic coast for nearly 90 miles, more than any other district in Florida, from just south of St. Augustine to the Canaveral National Seashore, which has offered splendid views of NASA lift-offs from the John F. Kennedy Space Center. Other Florida districts along the Gulf or in the Keys offer longer stretches of beachfront, but with fewer towns or people. The 2016 redistricting brought a relatively simple move to the south here: The old 6th included all of St. Johns and most of Volusia down to its southern tip. The new 6th includes only a narrow slice in the south of St. Johns but all of Volusia. Each version has included all of Flagler and a small piece of separate inland counties.

About 71 percent of the population is concentrated in Volusia County, 18 percent in the northern beachfront counties, with the balance in rural Lake County. The redistricting changes reduced the Republican vote by about six percentage points. But Donald Trump did well in the many blue-collar communities of Volusia and got 55 percent of the county vote, compared with only 50 percent for Mitt Romney in 2012. Consequently, Trump's vote in the new district was virtually the same as how Romney fared in the old district.

SEVENTH DISTRICT

Stephanie Murphy (D)

Elected 2016, 1st term; b. Sep 16, 1978, Ho Chi Minh City, Vietnam; College of William and Mary (VA), B.A., 2000; Georgetown University (DC), M.S., 2004; Christian Church; Married (Sean Murphy); 2 children.

Professional Career: Foreign Affairs Specialist, U.S Dept. of Defense, 2004-2008; Businesswoman; Faculty/Instructor, Rollins College, 2014-2016.

DC Office: 1237 LHOB 20515, 202-225-4035, Fax: 202-226-0821, stephaniemurphy.house.gov.

State Offices: Orlando, 888-205-5421; Sanford, 888-205-5421.

Committees: *Armed Services*: Emerging Threats & Capabilities, Readiness. *Small Business*: Contracting & Workforce (RMM), Economic Growth, Tax & Capital Access.

Group Ratings

	ADA	ACLU	AFL-CIO	LCV	ITI	COC	HAFA	ACU	CFG	FRC
2016	-	5%	-	92%	0%	100%	68%	84%	76%	100%
2015	-	C	-	-	C	63%	C	C	C	-

Almanac Ratings 2015

	Economy	Social	Foreign	Composite
Liberal	50%	97%	54%	67%
Conservative	50%	3%	46%	33%

Key Votes of the 114th Congress

1. Keystone Pipeline	Y	5. Puerto Rico Debt	Y	9. Offenses by Aliens	NV
2. Trade Deals	N	6. Medical Marijuana	Y	10. Troops in Iraq	Y
3. Export-Import Bank	Y	7. Sanctuary Cities	N	11. Homeland Security $$	Y
4. Debt Ceiling Increase	Y	8. Armor-piercing Bullets	N	12. Trade Adjustment aid	Y

Election Results

Election	Name (Party)	Vote (%)		Cand. Spent	Ind. Exp. Support	Ind. Exp. Oppose
2016 General	Stephanie Murphy (D)	182,039	(52%)	$1,059,565	$4,056,053	$1,595,995
	John Mica (R)	171,583	(49%)	$1,797,531	$58,266	$2,210,695
2016 Primary	Stephanie Murphy (D)		(100%)			

Democrat Stephanie Murphy, elected in 2016, was one of the few bright spots that year for House Democrats. She narrowly defeated veteran Republican Rep. John Mica, who had chaired the influential Transportation and Infrastructure Committee. At least as significant was Murphy's personal story as a refugee from Vietnam with a remarkably self-made life story in the American immigrant tradition. She is the first Vietnamese-American woman elected to Congress.

At six months, Stephanie Dang fled Vietnam on a refugee boat with her family. After the small craft ran out of fuel and went adrift in the South China Sea, the group was rescued by the U.S. Navy, which provided supplies that aided in the boat reaching Malaysia. The Lutheran Church helped the family to a Malaysian refugee camp in the United States, where they settled in Virginia. She graduated in 2000 from the College of William and Mary. On Sept. 11, 2001, she was working at Deloitte Consulting in Washington. Motivated by a desire for public service, she quit that job to attend graduate school at the Georgetown University School of Foreign Service, where she got a master's degree.

She then served as a national security specialist for the secretary of Defense. She helped to organize the rescue effort for victims of a 2004 tsunami in South Asia. Her work as chief of staff to a global strategic guidance planning effort won her a Defense Department Medal for Exceptional Civilian Service. Later, she was an executive at Sungate Capital, advising on investment decisions and implementing government affairs initiatives. After marrying Sean Murphy, whom she had met while working at Deloitte, they settled in Winter Park, Florida, where his family had been politically active. She taught business and social entrepreneurship at Rollins College. As an advocate of LGBT rights, she was a prominent voice in support of that community following the June 2016 attack at Pulse Nightclub in Orlando, which killed 49.

Murphy got her start in politics in early 2016 when she was advising the Democratic Congressional Campaign Committee, which was looking for a challenger to Mica. After other possible contenders declined or were not credible candidates, the DCCC recruited Murphy to run. Not until mid-June did she register as a Democrat. For the next four months, she had a deep immersion in electoral politics with help from several prominent Democratic women elected officials, including House Minority Leader Nancy Pelosi. She proved a worthy challenger to Mica, who had not faced a serious Democratic opponent since 2002 and had let his campaign skills get rusty. Murphy spent $1.1 million to $1.8 million for Mica, who was slow to take her candidacy seriously. She also received $4.7 million in support from the DCCC and other party affiliates, and at least $3 million more from liberal groups. The National Republican Congressional Committee spent $1.7 million for Mica.

Murphy said that Mica was out of touch with the district, and she criticized his views on gun control, gay rights and women's issues. "He is a career politician who has been part of the problem," she said. Mica highlighted the many benefits, including significant transportation projects, that he had delivered to the district. He ran an ad that negatively featured Pelosi, and said Murphy was "perfect for Washington, D.C., but not for Central Florida."

Donald Trump became an unusual issue in the campaign when Murphy and her allies highlighted the legislative assistance that Mica gave Trump and his business in securing a $3 million annual lease at the Old Post Office Building on Pennsylvania Avenue in Washington as the site for his lavish new Trump International Hotel. Mica had proudly acknowledged his assistance. After the formal opening of the hotel two weeks before the election, the DCCC issued a statement that, "Mica has not only helped Trump line his own pockets, he's stood by Trump every step of the way, even after he was caught bragging about sexual assault."

Murphy became the giant killer, 51.5%-48.5%. Mica got 52.5 percent of the vote in Seminole County. But Murphy prevailed with 58 percent of the vote in Orange County, much of which was tallied in the areas added by redistricting. In the House, she got seats on the Small Business Committee and the Armed Services Committee, which expanded her life-time experiences with the Pentagon. She faced the prospect of a challenging reelection campaign in 2018.

Northern Orlando Suburbs: Seminole, Orange

Demographics data for new House districts were not prepared by the Census Bureau prior to our editorial deadline.

Voter Turnout			
2016 House Turnout as % CVAP	N/A	2016 House turnout	353,655

2012 Presidential Vote information unavailable due to recent redistricting.

2016 Presidential Vote		
Hillary Clinton	186,658	(51%)
Donald Trump	160,178	(44%)
Gary Johnson	11,551	(3%)

Cook Partisan Voting Index: EVEN

For much of the 19th century, central Florida was a sparsely populated region at the southern frontier of the state. The native Timucua tribe had been driven to extinction by war and disease, and only a few towns of any size dotted the state's interior. Steamboats traveled up and down the St. Johns River to supply small trading centers that sprang up at the end of the navigable portions of that waterway on Lake Monroe and Lake Jesup (known for its many alligators) in what is now Seminole County. This state of affairs largely persisted until 1971, when Disney World opened in neighboring Orange County, setting off startling growth and development in the region. Other theme parks followed, tourism flourished, and Seminole County became one of the primary beneficiaries of that explosive development. Its population shot up from 55,000 in 1960 to 449,144 in 2015. The once-quiet county became a collection of largely high-end suburbs with a median income of $59,000, the third-highest in the state. Like much of Florida, the area was hit hard by the housing collapse and the recession. But it has been rebounding. A 2021 completion date has been set for the $2.3 billion reconstruction of a 21-mile stretch of Interstate 4 in Seminole and Orange counties, which will add express lanes through Orlando.

The 7th Congressional District of Florida includes all of Seminole County, which supplies 59 percent of the population, and about one-fourth of Orange County. Seminole has been a key battleground county in one of the nation's key battleground states, and it could become a new bellwether. In 2016, it was a bright spot for Democrats in Florida. The 49%-47% win for Donald Trump in Seminole was notably closer than the 53%-46% county lead for Mitt Romney when he lost the state in 2012. As more apartment complexes have been built, Seminole has become younger and more urban. From 2010 to 2015, the Hispanic population grew from 17 percent to 20 percent. Here, the district takes in the gated neighborhood where Hispanic crime-watch volunteer George Zimmerman touched off a national outcry in early 2012 after he fatally shot Trayvon Martin, an unarmed black teenager who was walking home from a convenience store. A jury found Zimmerman not guilty of second degree murder, and the Justice Department in 2015 found insufficient evidence that he had violated Martin's civil rights.

Redistricting in 2016 made what seemed like modest changes in the 7th, but they had an impact. Removed was a southern slice from Volusia County, including the city of Deltona and surrounding areas, which had about 133,000 people. Added in its place were the remaining 35,000 not previously in the 7th, plus nearly 100,000 more in the northern part of Orange County. This area, largely the eastern side of Orlando, had a significant Hispanic population. The district overall became 21 percent Hispanic and 10 percent black. Already in the 7th from Orange County were such towns as Maitland, Lockhart and Winter Park, the home of Rollins College. As a result of these changes, what had been a 52%-47% win for Romney over President Barack Obama in the district became a virtual tie at 49.4%-49.4%. In 2016, Hillary Clinton took the 7th, 51%-44%, a notable improvement for Democrats.

EIGHTH DISTRICT

Bill Posey (R)

Elected 2008, 5th term; b. Dec 18, 1947, Washington, DC; Brevard Community College (FL), A.A.; Stetson University (FL), Att.; Methodist; Married (Katie Ingram Posey); 2 children; 3 grandchildren.

Elected Office: Rockledge City Council, 1976-1986; FL House, 1992-2000; FL Senate, 2000-2008.

Professional Career: McDonnell Douglas Astronautics Co., 1966-1969; Crawford & Co./Gay & Taylor, 1970-1974; Founder, Posey & Co. Realtors, 1974-present.

DC Office: 2150 RHOB 20515, 202-225-3671, Fax: 202-225-3516, posey.house.gov.

State Offices: Melbourne, 321-632-1776.

Committees: *Financial Services*: Financial Institutions & Consumer Credit, Housing & Insurance. *Science, Space & Technology*: Environment, Oversight, Space.

Group Ratings

	ADA	ACLU	AFL-CIO	LCV	ITI	COC	HAFA	ACU	CFG	FRC
2016	-	17%	-	5%	67%	92%	81%	92%	84%	100%
2015	10%	C	8%	6%	C	60%	C	92%	87%	100%

Almanac Ratings 2015

	Economy	Social	Foreign	Composite
Liberal	9%	0%	13%	7%
Conservative	91%	100%	87%	93%

Key Votes of the 114th Congress

1. Keystone Pipeline	Y	5. Puerto Rico Debt	Y	9. Offenses by Aliens	Y
2. Trade Deals	N	6. Medical Marijuana	N	10. Troops in Iraq	Y
3. Export-Import Bank	N	7. Sanctuary Cities	Y	11. Homeland Security $$	N
4. Debt Ceiling Increase	N	8. Armor-piercing Bullets	Y	12. Trade Adjustment aid	N

Election Results

Election	Name (Party)	Vote (%)		Cand. Spent	Ind. Exp. Support	Ind. Exp. Oppose
2016 General	Bill Posey (R)	246,483	(63%)	$667,952		
	Corry Westbrook (D)	127,127	(33%)	$29,198		
	Bill Stinson (I)	16,951	(4%)	$13,910		
2016 Primary	Bill Posey (R)		(100%)			

Prior winning percentages: 2014 (66%), 2012 (59%), 2010 (65%), 2008 (53%)

Bill Posey, a Republican first elected in 2008, has taken on serious work in Congress, even with occasionally eccentric views. He has pursued his personal interest in finance issues and his district's interest in space issues. He combines extensive experience in business and local government, with a penchant to shake up business-as-usual.

Posey was born in Washington, D.C., and moved several times because of his father's work in the aircraft business. His family landed in Brevard County in 1956. After graduating from high school, Posey took a job with McDonnell Douglas Astronautics at the Kennedy Space Center. He worked on the Apollo 11 Launch Team that in 1969 sent the first men to the moon, and he attended Brevard Community College at night. After Apollo 11, Posey was laid off and went into real estate as founder of Posey & Co. Realtors. Until an accident at an Orlando speedway in 2004 left him with spinal fractures, Posey had been an accomplished stock car racer.

As the first member of his family to register as a Republican, Posey was elected to the Rockledge City Council in 1976 and served a decade. Later, he served eight years each in the state House and Senate. He authored legislation that set new standards for state government accountability. He wrote a book entitled *Activity Based Total Accountability*, detailing his work on the issue.

In 2008, he ran for the open seat. He got endorsements from Rep. Dave Weldon, who was retiring, and state GOP chairman Jim Greer, who called for the party to unite behind Posey. Other Republicans who had been interested fell in line. Democrats were unable to find a strong candidate. Posey faced Democrat Stephen Blythe, a Melbourne family physician, and made government accountability and immigration reform the central themes of his campaign. It was an amiable contest. The candidates expressed mutual admiration and said they would vote for each other if they could not vote for themselves. Posey outspent Blythe by almost 9-to-1 and won 53%-42% in a Democratic year.

Once in Washington, Posey attracted attention when he filed a bill requiring future presidential candidates to file a birth certificate. That came at the height of the 2009 "birther" flap over whether President Barack Obama was born overseas, and the liberal blogosphere made Posey the target of considerable venom. He contended his bill had nothing to do with Obama, but even some of his GOP colleagues publicly expressed their distaste for the proposal. He joined Republicans in opposing Obama's major legislative initiatives, but later showed a willingness to break with his party. He voted with Democrats to extend unemployment benefits and joined a bipartisan bill to double the one-year waiting period before lawmakers who leave their seats can lobby ex-colleagues. His skepticism about the war in Afghanistan made him practically a centrist on foreign policy: In 2011, he was among 16 House Republicans to vote in support of a phased withdrawal of troops.

Posey has continued his quest for more accountability in government. On the Financial Services Committee, he got the results of every committee vote posted on its website within two days. He pushed a proposal to require a 72-hour waiting period before legislation can be brought to the House floor, and he introduced another measure to require state governments to submit fiscal accounting reports as a condition of getting federal money. But he has drawn scorn on several occasions when he has raised the possibility that vaccines cause autism - a contention the scientific community says has no merit. He voiced suspicions that the Centers for Disease Control and Prevention was covering up a link between vaccines and autism. In July 2015, he urged on the House floor an investigation into vaccine-related research. Coincidentally, as with the birther issue, President Donald Trump has voiced similar views.

On the Space, Science and Technology Committee, Posey has worked on behalf of the Kennedy Space Center and the Space Coast to find ways to live with NASA cutbacks. He won praise from the local *Sunshine State News* for using that seat "as a bully pulpit to push private space flight and jab the Obama administration for retreating from space exploration." In endorsing him for reelection in 2016, *Florida Today* praised Posey as a "champion" of the space program and noted that he had cosponsored an enacted measure that ensured the legal rights of private space exploration companies to own and use minerals discovered on asteroids.

His maverick instincts have extended to House leadership contests. In January 2015, Posey voted for fellow Florida Rep. Daniel Webster for Speaker, instead of John Boehner. That October, he again joined the dissidents, as one of nine Republicans who voted for Webster when Paul Ryan was elected to succeed Boehner.

Democrats in 2014 thought that they had a credible challenger with Corry Westbrook, who was the legislative director for the National Wildlife Federation. After she was rocked by accusations that she plagiarized Florida Democratic Rep. Patrick Murphy's campaign website, Westbrook stepped down as a candidate. In 2016, Westbrook ran a weakly funded campaign. Posey won, 63%-33%.

Space Coast/Northern Treasure Coast: Melbourne

Population		**Race and Ethnicity**		**Income**	
Total	711,293	White	76.0%	Median Income	$48,311 (281 out of 435)
Land area	1,752	Black	9.7%		
Pop/ sq mi	406.0	Latino	9.8%		
Born in state	32.8%	Asian	2.0%	Under $50,000	51.5%
		Two races	2.0%	$50,000-$99,999	30.2%
Age Groups		Other	0.6%	$100,000-$199,999	14.6%
Under 18	18.8%			$200,000 or more	3.5%
18-34	18.1%	**Education**		Poverty Rate	14.1%
35-64	39.9%	H.S grad or less	39.1%		
Over 64	23.3%	Some college	33.9%	**Health Insurance**	
		College Degree, 4 yr	16.7%	With health insurance coverage	84.8%
Work		Post grad	10.4%		
White Collar	35.7%				
Sales and Service	46.4%	**Military**		**Public Assistance**	
Blue Collar	17.9%	Veteran	14.4%	Cash public assistance income	2.0%
Government	13.7%	Active Duty	0.2%		
				Food stamp/SNAP benefits	11.9%

Voter Turnout			
2015 Total Citizens 18+	553,996	2016 House Turnout as % CVAP	70%
2016 House turnout	390,561	2014 House Turnout as % CVAP	50%

2012 Presidential Vote		
Mitt Romney	206,074	(57%)
Barack Obama	153,138	(42%)

2016 Presidential Vote		
Donald Trump	234,648	(58%)
Hillary Clinton	151,412	(37%)
Gary Johnson	11,387	(3%)

Cook Partisan Voting Index: R+11

When Cape Canaveral was chosen in the 1940s as the nation's rocket testing site, only 20,000 people lived in all of Brevard County, which stretches along 63 miles of the coast north and south of the cape. It was a quiet, winter-vacation spot that relied on fishing and citrus and its location on the sunny Atlantic Coast. Rockets could be launched eastward so that spent parts fell into the ocean. In 1948, the Brooklyn Dodgers established their spring training home in Vero Beach, 60 miles south of Canaveral in Indian River County. Brevard County had 568,000 people in 2015, although the Dodgers have moved to Los Angeles and their spring home to Arizona. The county is mostly coastal communities and has no major city center. But it has plenty of strip shopping centers along highways, with a white-collar, service economy, knitted together by interest in the space program. The Kennedy Space Center attracts 1.5 million visitors annually, which is fewer than in the days when space flights captured the public's imagination. When the Florida Public Service Commission announced in 1998 that the region needed a new area code, a space enthusiast suggested 321. The North American agency that assigns area codes agreed.

Local uncertainty grew following the retirement of the space shuttle fleet, a move that slashed thousands of aerospace jobs. Officials have sought alternatives. The large share of individuals affiliated with the space program led to a spurt in technological entrepreneurship in sectors as varied as aviation, synthetic materials and clean energy. Harris Corp. - a Fortune 500 company based in Brevard that was purchased by Virginia-based Exelis Inc. - decided in 2015 to keep its headquarters in Melbourne. The company has more than 23,000 employees, including 9,000 scientists and engineers. Northrup Grumman has expanded its Manned Aircraft Design Center of Excellence in Melbourne. The SpaceX company, which operates launch pads at Cape Canaveral Air Force Station and Kennedy Space Center, in November 2016 announced plans for a rocket refurbishing facility in Port Canaveral. Also that year, local business and tourism leaders in the county seat of Titusville reported an increase of more than 1,000 jobs, plus a double-digit increase in tourist revenue.

Proximity to Disney World and Orlando spawned growth in the cruise-line business, which has soared beyond expectations. Port Canaveral in 2015 was the second-largest passenger port in the world, with its 3.9 million annual cruisers trailing only Miami; the port plans to expand its commercial cargo service. Eco-tourism is another promising avenue for growth. The Merritt Island National Wildlife Refuge and Canaveral National Seashore draw wildlife aficionados to view their vast array of flora and fauna. At Jungle Adventures Nature Animal Park, near the town of Christmas, visitors can hold baby alligators and gawk at "Swampy," the 200-foot-long concrete alligator that guards the park. These divergent efforts seem to have paid off.

The 8th Congressional District of Florida starts at the northern edge of Brevard County. It continues along the Atlantic Coast, encompassing all of Brevard and Indian River counties, and makes a nip in the eastern end of Orange County. About 80 percent of the population resides in Brevard. Among the bigger towns are Cocoa Beach, Melbourne, Palm Bay and Vero Beach. The district has become safely Republican. Donald Trump captured 58 percent of the vote here;, Mitt Romney got 57% in 2012. This was a rare district in Florida that had no change in the 2016 redistricting.

NINTH DISTRICT

Darren Soto (D)

Elected 2016, 1st term; b. Feb 25, 1978, Ringwood, NJ; Rutgers University (NJ), B.A., 2000; George Washington University School of Law (DC), J.D., 2004; Catholic; Married (Amanda Soto).

Elected Office: FL House, 2007-2012; FL Senate, 2012-2016, Deputy Minority Whip, 2012-2014.

DC Office: 1429 LHOB 20515, 202-225-9889, Fax: 202-225-9742, soto.house.gov.

State Offices: Kissimmee, 407-452-1171; Orlando, 407-266-7161; Winter Haven, 202-615-1308.

Committees: *Agriculture*: Commodity Exchanges, Energy & Credit, Nutrition. *Natural Resources*: Energy & Mineral Resources, Indian, Insular & Alaska Native Affairs, Oversight & Investigations.

Election Results

Election	Name (Party)	Vote	(%)	Cand. Spent	Ind. Exp. Support	Ind. Exp. Oppose
2016 General	Darren Soto (D)	195,311	(58%)	$1,121,663	$194,429	$327,199
	Wayne Liebnitzky (R)	144,450	(43%)	$29,614		
2016 Primary	Darren Soto (D)	14,487	(36%)			
	Susannah Randolph (D)	11,258	(28%)			
	Dena Grayson (D)	11,116	(28%)			
	Valleri Crabtree (D)	3,090	(8%)			

Darren Soto, elected in 2016, is the first Puerto Rican elected to Congress from Florida, as well as the state's first Hispanic Democrat. He won a competitive primary in which one candidate was the wife of the previous House member, who lost that day in the primary for the Senate. He styles himself as a coalition-builder.

Soto was born in New Jersey to a Puerto Rican father and an Italian-American mother. He worked in finance for Prudential Insurance while he attended Rutgers University, where he graduated with a bachelor's in economics, and got his law degree from George Washington University. Soto practiced as a commercial and civil rights attorney in Central Florida. He joined the Young Democrats club in Orlando, where friends encouraged him to run for the state House. He was successful and served there for six years, and then another four years in the Senate. He passed legislation making it easier for immigrant children with deferred-action status to acquire a driver's license. Gov. Rick Scott vetoed the measure, sparking widespread protests. Soto helped to enact a bill that reduced from five years to one year the statute of limitations for banks to collect foreclosure debt. In 2014, he passed legislation giving the Florida Supreme Court authority to admit immigrant lawyers into the Florida Bar.

When Rep. Alan Grayson ran for the Senate, a leading contender to replace him was Dena Minning, a biochemist who had a medical residency and had a doctorate in molecular cell biology. She married Grayson three months before the primary. Susanna Randolph, the wife of Orange County Tax Collector Scott Randolph, spent hundreds of thousands of dollars for negative ads against Soto. As the frontrunner, Soto discussed the need for better-paying local jobs. He highlighted his efforts in Tallahassee to deliver tens of millions to fight citrus disease in Polk County orchards. He spent $1.2 million for the campaign, compared with $730,000 for Randolph and $620,000 for Minning.

Soto won the primary with 36 percent of the vote; Randolph and Minning each got 28 percent. In Osceola, which cast the most votes, Soto took 44 percent. He ran third with 26 percent in Polk, which had the smallest share of Hispanics. In the general, Soto faced Wayne Liebnitzky, a businessman and retired Navy aviation electrician. The challenger raised $32,000. Soto won, 57%-43%, which was nearly the same as the presidential vote in the district. Soto got a seat on the House Agriculture Committee.

Central Florida: Orlando, Kissimmee

Demographics data for new House districts were not prepared by the Census Bureau prior to our editorial deadline.

Voter Turnout			
2016 House Turnout as % CVAP	N/A	2016 House turnout	339,761

2012 Presidential Vote information unavailable due to recent redistricting.

2016 Presidential Vote		
Hillary Clinton	195,368	(54%)
Donald Trump	149,352	(42%)
Gary Johnson	7,899	(2%)

Cook Partisan Voting Index: D+5

Orlando has become the area with the fastest-growing Puerto Rican population in the United States. Places like Azalea Park in Orange County, as well as Buenaventura Lakes (known as "BVL" to the locals) in neighboring Osceola County, have Puerto Rican-majority populations. One local real estate agent who specializes in the Puerto Rican market called BVL "a Puerto Rican Levittown," referring to the developments that sprung up after World War II near New York City and Philadelphia, where the children of turn-of-the-century immigrants made their first moves into suburban life and the American middle class. Businesses increasingly cater to this emerging "Little Puerto Rico." Banco Popular, a Puerto Rico-based bank, opened branches here in 1997. Goya foods located its central Florida distribution center in nearby Meadow Woods. Non-Hispanic companies such as the supermarket chain Publix have sought to adapt, opening Sabor (Spanish for "taste") stores here, for example. Countless small businesses appealing to the burgeoning Hispanic population line streets as well; small markets move thousands of chickens and plantains a month, and there are car-repair shops, dance clubs, churches, even funeral homes catering to Hispanics.

The Puerto Rican ascendancy in central Florida started in Orlando-based Orange County. As their numbers increased and property became more expensive, many moved to what were the relatively empty and cheaper spaces of Osceola, which has become the fast-growing, heavily Hispanic center of the Puerto Rican community. In 2015, 51 percent of its 324,000 residents were Hispanic. At the same time, 30 percent of the 1.3 million in Orange were Hispanic. The population of those two counties in 1960 was 19,000 and 263,000, respectively. The recent increase in Puerto Ricans has been driven, in part, by islanders escaping the economic collapse in their commonwealth as a result of its severe public debt. "The center of the state, across several counties sprawling outward from Orlando, has been a destination for one of the most significant domestic diasporas in recent American history," Bloomberg News reported in October 2016.

Many of these areas have been rural, but are developing. A national mortgage company ranked the Osceola County seat of Kissimmee as seventh among the nation's boom towns, with surging growth in housing. The share of English-speaking households in Osceola dropped to 51 percent, the Census Bureau reported in 2016. A real-estate consultant in Osceola told the *Orlando Sentinel* that local Puerto Ricans tell their friends, "If you're coming to Florida, come to Osceola County. The schools have ESOL [classes that teach English], a Puerto Rican bakery. It's a comfortable place to live."

The new 9th Congressional District of Florida represents a bow by both political and judicial voices in redistricting to the emerging political realities of central Florida. In 2015, its population of 820,000 (each Florida district was 696,000, following the 2012 redistricting) included 400,000 Hispanics, of whom 235,000 were Puerto Ricans. Black neighborhoods in Orlando were shifted in large numbers from the old 9th to the adjoining new 10th District, which is based entirely in Orange County; blacks are only 12 percent of the new 9th. For its loss of about 195,000 residents to Orange, the district substituted a large section of eastern Polk County, where there has been additional spill-over in development from the Orlando area. The district retains all of Osceola.

Politically, there is an important caveat to those numbers: A relatively small share of Hispanics in the 9th votes. According to official Florida election data, only 166,000 of those Hispanics - about 40 percent - are voting-age population. Many are too young, others choose not to register and some are not legally in the United States (Puerto Ricans are immediately eligible to vote on the mainland). Consequently, it will take time for their political power to catch up to their demographic influence. Plus, Puerto Rican voters in Florida are not a unified voting bloc. Prior to the 2016 election, some Democrat strategists were concerned that lower turnout would jeopardize their party's election prospects. They may have had cause for concern. In 2016, Hillary Clinton won the district, 54%-42%. With the old lines in 2012, President Barack Obama won, 61%-38%.

TENTH DISTRICT

Val Demings (D)

Elected 2016, 1st term; b. Mar 12, 1957, Jacksonville; Webster University (MO), M.P.A.; Southern Police Institute; Florida State University, B.S., 1979; African Methodist Episcopal; Married (Jerry L. Demings); 3 children.

Professional Career: Social worker; Police officer; Commander of Special Operation, FLPD, 2003-2006; Police Chief, FLPD, 2007-2012.

DC Office: 238 CHOB 20515, 202-225-2176, Fax: 202-226-6559, demings.house.gov.

State Offices: Orlando, 321-388-9808.

Committees: *Homeland Security*: Border & Maritime Security, Cybersecurity & Infrastructure Protection. *Oversight & Government Reform*: Intergovernmental Affairs (RMM), National Security.

Election Results

Election	Name (Party)	Vote	(%)	Cand. Spent	Ind. Exp. Support	Ind. Exp. Oppose
2016 General	Val Demings (D)	198,491	(65%)	$10,028	$468,938	
	Thuy Lowe (R)	107,498	(35%)	$45,909		
2016 Primary	Val Demings (D)	23,247	(57%)			
	Geraldine Thompson (D)	8,188	(20%)			
	Bob Poe (D)	6,913	(17%)			
	Fatima Fahmy (D)	2,346	(6%)			

Val Demings was one of three newly elected Orlando-area Democrats in 2016: an African-American woman, a Latino man and a Vietnamese-American woman. Their districts cover 99 percent of Orange County, plus large parts of three surrounding counties in this rapidly growing metropolitan area. Demings, who in 2012 narrowly lost in the previous Republican-leaning version of this district, had a background in police work that made her a prime recruit for House Democrats. She likes to call herself a unifier.

Demings was born in Jacksonville, the youngest of seven children. Her mother was a maid and her father was a janitor. She got a bachelor's degree in criminology from Florida State University, the first in her family to graduate from college. She started as a social worker in Jacksonville, but set her sights on becoming a police officer. After moving to Orlando and enrolling in the police academy, where she was the class president, Demings served with the police department for 27 years, including four years as chief of police. She placed a priority on community engagement to address some of the root causes of violent crime. In 2012, Demings ran in the old 10th District against first-term Republican Rep. Daniel Webster. With the narrow GOP leaning of the district, it was a difficult contest that she lost, 52%-48%.

Following the major changes in the 2016 redistricting, Webster wisely concluded that he could not win the revamped district, took advantage of an open seat in the 11th District to the west, and the GOP largely conceded his old seat. In this now-friendly district, Demings was elected in two relatively easy contests. In the four-candidate Democratic primary, she won 57 percent of the vote against credible opponents. State Sen. Geraldine Thompson, who was runner-up with 20 percent, criticized the national party for giving Demings a speaking slot at the Democratic national convention a month earlier. Bob Poe, the former state Democratic chairman, self-financed his campaign with $2 million; he got 17 percent. In one ad, he said that Demings had condoned police brutality. Demings spent $1.5 million, and benefited from another $538,000 spent on her behalf by the Super PAC financed by Michael Bloomberg, the former New York City mayor and advocate of gun-control measures.

In November, Demings defeated little-known Republican Thuy Lowe, 65%-35%. On the same day, her husband Jerry Demings was reelected to his third term as sheriff of Orange County. In the House, she got seats on the Homeland Security, and Oversight and Government Reform committees.

Central Florida: Lake, Downtown Orlando

Demographics data for new House districts were not prepared by the Census Bureau prior to our editorial deadline.

Voter Turnout			
2016 House Turnout as % CVAP	N/A	2016 House turnout	305,989

2012 Presidential Vote information unavailable due to recent redistricting.

2016 Presidential Vote		
Hillary Clinton	194,934	(61%)
Donald Trump	110,062	(35%)
Gary Johnson	7,205	(2%)

Cook Partisan Voting Index: D+11

Who would have supposed 50 years ago that the most popular tourist destination in the world would rise amid the swamps and orange groves of central Florida? The answer: Walt Disney, and just about no one else. In the mid-1960s, Disney looked at the map and decided that the intersection of Interstate 4 and Florida's Turnpike, the "crossroads of Florida," just a few miles southwest of Orlando, was the perfect place for the vast theme park he was planning. The spirit of the place was established by a man who never lived there but created something now taken for granted. Disney conceived the first theme park in Orange County, California, in 1955, but he perfected it in the 17,000 acres of Florida swamp that his associates stealthily snapped up and where Walt Disney World opened in 1971. With the invention of the theme park, Disney also pioneered sophisticated communications, utility and waste-disposal methods - all out of sight and underground. Disney World is not just an engineering marvel. It required close to 70,000 "cast members" (employees) with know-how and earnest cheerfulness to entertain its 20.4 million visitors in 2015, a 6 percent annual increase. The number of workers is the largest in the world for a company at a single site.

Disney is hardly the only site that has made Orlando one of the world's great tourist destinations. Other popular theme parks here include Sea World and Universal Studios; Cape Canaveral is less than 40 miles away. The technology economy also has moved into Greater Orlando. Defense contractor Lockheed Martin has a "mission system and training" facility southwest of the city, with nearly 7,000 employees. Continuing growth - of the downtown skyline and in the expanding metropolitan region - has spurred what may be uphill efforts to control the sprawl and congestion in one of the nation's booming areas. Amid the growth, Orlando has been the least economically segregated major metro area in the nation. Downtown Orlando was site of the horrific terrorist attack that killed 49 persons at the Pulse nightclub in June 2016.

The new 10th Congressional District of Florida is entirely in Orange County, chiefly its western portion, including the enormous Disney complex. The sections that had been in Republican-friendly Polk and Lake counties have been removed. As a result, the 9 percent black and 11 percent Hispanic shares have grown to 25 and 21 percent, respectively. Many of those minority voters had been in the old 5th District, which was a ribbon from Jacksonville to Orlando. Perhaps the most glaring example of the downsizing of the area's farmlands - because of population gains, on top of devastating frosts -- is that the acreage for the eponymous citrus that gave the county its name dropped by 50 percent from 2005 to 2015, and by more than 95 percent during the past half-century. Not all of the district has been urbanized. It includes smaller black settlements, such as lettuce-producing Zellwood and Eatonville, a town depicted into the stories of Zora Neale Hurston, a preeminent novelist and folklorist. The 10th switched from a district that Mitt Romney in 2012 won, 54%-46%, to one that he would have lost, 61%-38%. In the tally of the 2016 vote, Hillary Clinton won the new district, 61%-35%.

ELEVENTH DISTRICT

Daniel Webster (R)

Elected 2010, 4th term; b. Apr 27, 1949, Charleston, WV; Georgia Institute of Technology; b.E.E., 1971; Baptist; Married (Sandy Jordan); 6 children; 7 grandchildren.

Elected Office: FL House, 1980-1998, speaker, 1996-1998; FL Senate, 1998-2008.

Professional Career: Owner, Webster Air Conditioning & Heating.

DC Office: 1210 LHOB 20515, 202-225-1002, Fax: 202-225-0999, webster.house.gov.

Committees: *Natural Resources*: Federal Lands, Water, Power & Oceans. *Science, Space & Technology*: Energy, Research & Technology, Space. *Transportation & Infrastructure*: Aviation, Railroads, Pipelines & Hazardous Materials, Water Resources & Environment.

Group Ratings

	ADA	ACLU	AFL-CIO	LCV	ITI	COC	HAFA	ACU	CFG	FRC
2016	-	5%	-	0%	83%	100%	73%	91%	80%	100%
2015	5%	C	13%	6%	C	68%	C	88%	68%	100%

Almanac Ratings 2015

	Economy	Social	Foreign	Composite
Liberal	9%	5%	0%	5%
Conservative	91%	95%	100%	95%

Key Votes of the 114th Congress

1. Keystone Pipeline	Y	5. Puerto Rico Debt	Y	9. Offenses by Aliens	Y
2. Trade Deals	N	6. Medical Marijuana	N	10. Troops in Iraq	N
3. Export-Import Bank	N	7. Sanctuary Cities	Y	11. Homeland Security $$	N
4. Debt Ceiling Increase	N	8. Armor-piercing Bullets	Y	12. Trade Adjustment aid	N

Election Results

Election	Name (Party)	Vote (%)	Cand. Spent	Ind. Exp. Support	Ind. Exp. Oppose
2016 General	Daniel Webster (R)	258,016 (65%)	$825,550		
	Dave Koller (D)	124,713 (32%)	$54,140		
	Bruce Ray Riggs (I)	11,990 (3%)			
2016 Primary	Daniel Webster (R)	52,855 (60%)			
	Justin Grabelle (R)	35,516 (40%)			

Prior winning percentages: 2014 (62%), 2012 (52%), 2010 (56%)

Republican Daniel Webster, a staunch conservative, prevailed in contentious elections in 2010 and 2012. He settled into the House with an insider's demeanor, but then unexpectedly became the chief GOP challenger to Speaker John Boehner and, later, Paul Ryan in futile bids by conservatives to register their unhappiness. Webster subsequently was stripped of his prime committee assignment, though he gained a niche among conservatives for his willingness to challenge GOP leaders. His career took an odd turn in 2016 when he switched districts following the 2016 redistricting.

Webster was born in Charleston, West Virginia, and is distantly related to his 19th century namesake, considered one of the greatest senators and orators in history. His family moved to Florida when he was 7 years old because a doctor told them the climate would help cure young Daniel's sinus problems. He graduated from the Georgia Institute of Technology in 1971 with a degree in electrical engineering and began working in his family's heating and air conditioning business in Orlando. Webster eventually took over the family business. He became politically active in 1979, when he led his church's effort to turn a house into a Sunday school, only to be refused a zoning exemption by the county commission.

Webster won a seat in the state House in 1996 and later became the first Republican speaker of the Florida House in 122 years. He sponsored a bill to ban nude performances in bars and another that would have required the legislature to study the impact of proposed laws on families. In 1998, Webster moved to the state Senate, where he pushed to ease gun regulations and to restrict abortion rights, including his bill requiring women to get an ultrasound test and view the results before getting an abortion. He led legislative efforts to prolong the life of Terri Schiavo, a woman in a persistent vegetative state who became a national cause for conservatives.

With the backing of national Republicans, he challenged controversial Democratic Rep. Alan Grayson in 2010. Grayson had become a lightning rod for conservatives because of his harsh rhetoric. His unapologetic liberalism made him a hero to the left, but Webster and Republicans believed that Grayson was a poor fit for the more tempered politics of the swing district. One of Grayson's television ads dubbed Webster "Taliban Dan," and accused him of proposing to make divorce illegal and of believing that women should submit to their husbands. A video clip of Webster in the ad, however, was taken out of context; Webster was asserting the opposite, according to the *Orlando Sentinel*, which endorsed Webster in part because of Grayson's negative campaigning. Webster refused to debate Grayson, or to return his attacks in kind, saying, "We're taking the high road. I'm not getting down in the dirt with him." He focused his campaign on the size of the federal government and the passage of President Barack Obama's health care law. Grayson's strategy energized liberals nationally, and he raked in $6 million for his campaign. The voters turned him out decisively, 56%-38%.

In the newly Republican-controlled House, Webster won a seat on the Rules Committee, a coveted position usually reserved for members whom leaders can trust to hew to the party line. He became the first GOP freshman to get a substantive bill through the House, with a measure aimed at limiting executive bonuses at companies that received financial industry bailout funds. He expressed support for House Budget Committee Chairman Ryan's attempts to rein in spending and overhaul Medicare, a position that earned him national publicity in 2011 after a hostile crowd at a town hall meeting in his district jeered him. In a display of independence, Webster in 2013 voiced conditional support for a comprehensive reform plan that would give illegal immigrants a pathway to citizenship.

In 2012, Grayson talked about a rematch with Webster, but instead ran for - and won – the seat in the solidly Democratic 9th District. Webster was initially considered a reelection shoo-in in his 10th District against Val Demings, the former Orlando police chief, but she outworked and outraised the congressman. The Democrat pulled ahead in the polls and got more than $2 million from New York Mayor Michael Bloomberg's political committee to assist candidates who supported gun control, with the Democratic Congressional Campaign Committee spending another $1.5 million. She accused Webster of using taxpayer money to create a "lobbyists' lounge" when he served in the legislature, a reference to his decision to spend about $100,000 for renovations to the speaker's office suite. He adamantly denied that the remodeling was done to serve lobbyists. The GOP tilt of the district proved decisive and Webster won 52%-48%. In 2014, he had an uncompetitive campaign and won 62 percent of the vote.

As Congress prepared to convene in January 2015, Webster surprised many on Capitol Hill by speaking out against Speaker John Boehner and Republican management of the House. In previous weeks, he had quietly circulated to other Republicans a white paper that was titled "Widgets, Principles and Republicans." It concluded that "Congress is broken, the Republican brand is in trouble, and nothing can change unless congressional processes become less power- and self-preservation driven, and more open to rank-and-file members," the *Orlando Sentinel* reported. "A lot of people liked it," Webster later said. A few lawmakers had told him that he should run for Speaker. When that number grew as others learned of his interest, Webster agreed to enter his name two hours before the vote. He was supported by 12 Republican lawmakers, which was fewer than the number who had told him they would support him, he said. A total of 25 House Republicans did not vote for Boehner. But he won a bare majority of the vote and avoided what could have been a catastrophic second ballot.

With Boehner's allies outraged by Webster's candidacy and urging retribution, the Speaker did not reappoint him and fellow Florida Republican Rick Nugent, who had voted for Webster, to the Rules Committee. Webster issued a conciliatory statement that "my candidacy and vote was not a vote against personalities, policies or even John Boehner," and affirmed his friendship for Boehner. "It was a vote for initiating a process that I know can produce sound public policy for the people who sent us to Washington on their behalf." Boehner took no immediate action to start such a process. But Webster had stirred the pot and Boehner surely was watching Webster more closely and feeling more pressure from conservatives. At the end of September, Boehner had had enough of the internal sniping and he announced that he would step down as Speaker.

Webster and a few of his allies continued to voice unhappiness with Republican leadership. He announced his candidacy to replace Boehner. But he attracted little support, even when Majority Leader Kevin McCarthy abandoned his bid to move up. After most House Republicans rallied behind Ryan, Webster ran and got the votes of nine Republicans.

At home, meanwhile, Webster encountered stormy waves when the Legislature's plan for redistricting turned his district into one that he said would be "impossible" for him to win. He intervened before the state Supreme Court to seek a reversal, but made no progress. Unexpectedly, he was rescued when neighboring Rep. Nugent announced that he would retire from his solidly Republican 11th District. But there was a catch: Nugent's chief of staff Justin Grabelle said he was running for his boss's seat, with the support of Nugent. Webster was disadvantaged because he had little familiarity with the new district, other than parts of Lake County. But he had one big advantage: He was an incumbent, and Grabelle was a first-time candidate. Webster raised more than twice as much money: $1 million to $360,000. He won, 60%-40%, including all five counties. Webster won by more than 2-to-1 in Lake and Marion, where he was more familiar to voters. In distant Citrus County, he won by 296 votes out of nearly 21,000. In this Republican district, Webster breezed to victory in November with 65 percent of the vote, with big leads in all five counties.

Even though Webster had settled into what seemed a secure district, there was another dark cloud on the horizon. His earlier nemesis Grayson - despite his poor showing in the 2016 Senate Democratic primary - left the door open following the election to another congressional run in 2018, with Webster as a possible foe.

Gulf Coast, Central Florida: Ocala, Tampa suburbs

Demographics data for new House districts were not prepared by the Census Bureau prior to our editorial deadline.

Voter Turnout

2016 House Turnout as % CVAP	N/A	2016 House turnout	394,719

2012 Presidential Vote information unavailable due to recent redistricting.

2016 Presidential Vote

Donald Trump	266,257	(64%)
Hillary Clinton	133,448	(32%)
Gary Johnson	7,953	(2%)

Cook Partisan Voting Index: R+15

Over the past quarter-century, Florida's urban areas have grown in almost every direction, occupying the high ground between the swamps that still take up much of the state's peninsula. The pattern of development is evident in counties to the north and east of St. Petersburg and Tampa, where subdivisions, trailer parks and Winn-Dixie supermarkets sprang up in what had been farms and sleepy little towns, with low brick buildings baking in the Florida sun. Drawn by the many inland lakes, greenery and the pleasant climate, retirees from Michigan, Indiana and Ohio flocked to Citrus and Hernando counties by traveling south on Interstate 75 - a pattern distinct from the retirees who drove Interstate 95 from the Boston-Washington corridor to such destinations as Palm Beach, Fort Lauderdale and Miami. The development here has been nothing short of astonishing; the population of Hernando County increased tenfold since 1970, while Citrus County increased at a similar rate, though the growth in both counties has slowed since 2010. The rapid development has created an uneasy tension with environmental concerns. The federal government declared the Crystal River National Wildlife Refuge a restricted manatee refuge after tourists were observed chasing, riding and poking the gentle sea cows.

The new 11th Congressional District of Florida retained much of this rapidly growing area. As with the old 11th, it includes all of coastal Citrus and Hernando counties, where the beach areas are largely undeveloped, plus Sumter County, which contain large tracts of open land. The numbers here offer insight into changing retirement patterns. Sumter County's population is growing rapidly - by 27 percent from 2010 to 2015 - mostly a result of the massive retirement community known as The Villages, with more than 100 miles of golf cart paths and a population that reached 119,000 in 2015. It has been the fastest growing metro area in the nation for the past three years. The median age in Sumter is 66.6 years, which makes it the only county in the nation that exceeds 65. The residents are 90 percent white. With the growth of retirement villages elsewhere, other counties likely will share that distinction.

The remaining 41 percent of the district is in Lake and Marion Counties. Redistricting redrew those boundaries to create nearly equal numbers in each county. Previously, most of those residents had been in Marion. The changes removed most of the Ocala area from the new 11th and added a mostly rural area filled with lakes and state parks. The bulk of the district's population lives inland, in places like Inverness, Spring Hill and Brooksville. This was once politically marginal territory, but it has become reliably Republican of late. Redistricting barely changed the partisan dynamics. Donald Trump took the new district, 64%-32%; in 2012, Mitt Romney won, 59%-40%.

TWELFTH DISTRICT

Gus Bilirakis (R)

Elected 2006, 6th term; b. Feb 08, 1963, Gainesville; Stetson University College of Law (FL), J.D.; University of Florida, B.S.; St. Petersburg Junior College (FL); Greek Orthodox; Married (Eva Lialios Bilirakis); 4 children.

Elected Office: FL House, 1998-2006.

Professional Career: Intern, U.S. President Ronald Reagan, 1983; Intern, NRCC, 1984; Aide, U.S. Rep. Don Sundquist, 1985; Teacher, St. Petersburg College, 1997-2001; Practicing attorney, 1989-2006.

DC Office: 2112 RHOB 20515, 202-225-5755, Fax: 202-225-4085, bilirakis.house.gov.

State Offices: New Port Richey, 727-232-2921; Tarpon Springs, 727-940-5860; Wesley Chapel, 813-501-4942.

Committees: *Energy & Commerce*: Communications & Technology, Digital Commerce & Consumer Protection, Health. *Veterans' Affairs*: Economic Opportunity, Health.

Group Ratings

	ADA	ACLU	AFL-CIO	LCV	ITI	COC	HAFA	ACU	CFG	FRC
2016	-	5%	-	5%	100%	100%	71%	92%	78%	100%
2015	0%	C	4%	0%	C	80%	C	88%	71%	100%

Almanac Ratings 2015

	Economy	Social	Foreign	Composite
Liberal	3%	5%	0%	3%
Conservative	97%	95%	100%	97%

Key Votes of the 114th Congress

1. Keystone Pipeline	Y	5. Puerto Rico Debt	N	9. Offenses by Aliens	Y
2. Trade Deals	Y	6. Medical Marijuana	N	10. Troops in Iraq	N
3. Export-Import Bank	N	7. Sanctuary Cities	Y	11. Homeland Security $$	N
4. Debt Ceiling Increase	N	8. Armor-piercing Bullets	NV	12. Trade Adjustment aid	N

Election Results

Election	Name (Party)	Vote (%)	Cand. Spent	Ind. Exp. Support	Ind. Exp. Oppose
2016 General	Gus Bilirakis (R)	253,559 (69%)	$1,532,701		
	Robert Tager (D)	116,110 (31%)	$57,221		
2016 Primary	Gus Bilirakis (R)	(100%)			

Prior winning percentages: 2014 (100%), 2012 (64%), 2010 (71%), 2008 (63%), 2006 (56%)

Gus Bilirakis, a Republican first elected in 2006 to succeed his father, 12-term Republican Rep. Michael Bilirakis, came into office distancing himself from partisan fights and focusing on his legislative agenda. While gaining seniority, he has sharpened his rhetorical edge. But he was unsuccessful in seeking to chair a House committee. Unlike other Republicans in central and north Florida, the 2016 redistricting caused him no problems.

Bilirakis remembers stuffing envelopes at age 7 for Republican Louis "Skip" Bafalis, who lost his 1970 bid for governor but was elected to five terms in Congress. As an undergraduate at the University of Florida, Bilirakis interned in the Reagan White House and went on to earn a law degree from Stetson University. He later was a probate lawyer and estate planner. In 1998, he was elected to the first of four terms in the Florida House. Bilirakis' career was closely tied to his father's. When Michael Bilirakis decided to retire, his son drew nominal opposition for the Republican nomination. Gus Bilirakis was not shy about running on the family name and his Greek heritage. He touted the relationship on his website, appeared on the ballot as Gus Michael Bilirakis and raised money from many political action committees that supported his father, who served on the Energy and Commerce Committee.

Democrats recruited Phyllis Busansky, a former member of the Hillsborough County Commission and the first executive director of the state's welfare-to-work program. Both candidates were responsive to the district's many senior citizens. Bilirakis pointed to his credentials as a lawyer who specialized in elder law. HIs soft-spoken style contrasted with Busansky's assertive personality. She ran television ads portraying Bilirakis as a follower who relied on his father's reputation. She gained some momentum in October after criticizing Bilirakis for his "deep and lucrative ties" to GOP leaders who had failed to act on knowledge of sexually explicit emails that Republican Rep. Mark Foley of Florida had sent to congressional pages. President George W. Bush, Vice President Dick Cheney, and Speaker Dennis Hastert all stumped for Bilirakis and helped him raise money. In a strongly Democratic year, he outspent Busansky $2.6 million to $1.4 million, and won 56%-44%.

In the House, Bilirakis showed signs of centrism. Soon after taking office, he voted to increase the minimum wage. In 2008, he worked with Rep. Lloyd Doggett, a Texas Democrat, to win House passage of a "silver alert" bill to assist states in finding senior citizens who disappear. He was one of 10 Republicans in 2009 to support a bill to limit executive bonuses in financial companies receiving government bailout money. But his politics shifted, as did those of his party. In 2010, he took the House floor on several occasions to denounce the Democrats' health care overhaul as a "government takeover." On the Foreign Affairs Committee, he followed his father's footsteps in standing up for Greek causes.

After the 2012 election, Bilirakis got a seat on Energy and Commerce, where left-leaning groups attacked him for earlier signing a pledge that he "opposes any legislation relating to climate change that includes a net increase in government revenue." When he worked with Democrats in 2014 to oppose soaring premium hikes for flood insurance coverage, then-Majority Whip Kevin McCarthy bounced him from his whip team. "I have no hard feelings at all, but I had to do what I had to do," Bilirakis told the *Tampa Bay Times*. In December 2014, President Barack Obama signed his bill to promote travel by reauthorizing Brand USA, a public-private partnership that encourages tourists to visit the United States. Some conservatives had opposed the bill as excessive spending. As vice chairman of the Veterans' Affairs Committee, he worked on the 2014 law to overhaul the VA hospital system. That resulted, he said, in the opening of an out-patient clinic in New Port Richey. He enacted bills to offer alternative therapies to veterans. Following the 2016 election, Bilirakis failed in his bid for chairman of the committee. Party leaders gave the post to the less-senior Phil Roe of Tennessee.

In a district that leans Republican, Bilirakis has not faced a serious reelection challenge. In 2016, he was reelected with 69 percent of the vote against token opposition.

Northern Tampa Suburbs: Pasco, Pinellas

Demographics data for new House districts were not prepared by the Census Bureau prior to our editorial deadline.

Voter Turnout			
2016 House Turnout as % CVAP	N/A	2016 House turnout	369,669

2012 Presidential Vote information unavailable due to recent redistricting.

2016 Presidential Vote		
Donald Trump	218,488	(57%)
Hillary Clinton	147,759	(39%)
Gary Johnson	9,918	(3%)

Cook Partisan Voting Index: R+8

In 1873, turtle hunters discovered a large sponge bed off the coast of the Pinellas Peninsula. Soon, boats from Key West began harvesting the sponges, and shortly thereafter, trading outposts were set up at sites that grew into Tarpon Springs and Anclote. Anclote is now just a speck on the map, but Tarpon Springs is a busy city of 25,000. With more than 10 percent of the population, it boasts the highest share of Greek Americans of any place in the United States - descendants of the Greek sponge fishermen who began arriving in the early 1900s. Over the years, Pasco County has become a classic bedroom community as development has moved up the once-empty coast. But population density remains low compared with other parts of Florida. It has been possible to step out of a Dillard's department store and pet a cow grazing in a nearby field.

There have been plans to change this. Two big financial companies - St. Petersburg's Raymond James Financial and Baltimore's T. Rowe Price - had purchased land in Pasco County and each planned to build large campuses for thousands of employees. T. Rowe Price abandoned its plans. Raymond James said in September 2016 that its new buildings will have 750 workers. A month earlier, Meddler Toledo, an international supplier of precision equipment announced that it was closing its facility in Hillsborough and opening a new manufacturing plant in Pasco, with 500 employees. Medical tourism has become a growing industry for patients who travel for treatment they cannot receive in their home states or other nations.

The 12th Congressional District covers an area north and east of Tampa and St. Petersburg. Redistricting in 2016 shifted about 100,000 people from the northern part of Hillsborough County a short distance to the northern part of Pinellas, leaving only a small corner of Hillsborough. In Pinellas County, that extended the 12th beyond Tarpon Springs and the upscale community of Palm Harbor to Dunedin. Two-thirds of the district includes all of Pasco County. This area was largely undeveloped until the 1950s, but now hosts a string of towns along the Gulf of Mexico. Further inland, the district covers older settlements like Land O'Lakes, Dade City, and Zephyrhills, established in 1911 as a retirement center for veterans of the Union Army.

In the 1950s and 1960s, only white-collar retirees could afford to buy new places in Florida, and they were heavily Republican. As Florida retirements became more feasible for people with modest incomes in the 1970s and 1980s, the partisan balance shifted toward Democrats. In the 1990s, young arrivals with professional and technical backgrounds and partisan independence turned this into a politically marginal area. But Republican-drawn redistricting and the modest minority populations have given the 12th District a modest Republican lean.

THIRTEENTH DISTRICT

Charlie Crist (D)

Elected 2016, 1st term; b. Jul 24, 1956, Altoona, PA; Wake Forest University (NC); Florida State University, B.S., 1978; Samford University Cumberland Law School (AL), J.D., 1981; Methodist; Separated; 2 stepchildren.

Elected Office: FL Senate, 1993-1999; FL Education Commissioner, 2001-2003; FL Attorney General, 2003-2007; FL Governor, 2007-2011.

Professional Career: Staff, United States Senator Connie Mack, 1988-1989; FL Deputy Secretary of Business and Prof. Reg., 1999-2001.

DC Office: 427 CHOB 20515, 202-225-5961, Fax: 202-225-9764, crist.house.gov.

State Offices: St. Petersburg, 727-318-6770.

Committees: *Financial Services*: Financial Institutions & Consumer Credit, Monetary Policy & Trade, Oversight & Investigations. *Science, Space & Technology*: Environment, Space.

Election Results

Election	Name (Party)	Vote (%)	Cand. Spent	Ind. Exp. Support	Ind. Exp. Oppose
2016 General	Charlie Crist (D)	184,693 (52%)	$1,976,791	$144,932	$713,320
	David Jolly (R)	171,149 (48%)	$2,168,247	$10,604	$3,363,441
2016 Primary	Charlie Crist (D)	(100%)			

Democrat Charlie Crist was elected in 2016 when he defeated Republican Rep. David Jolly, with a boost from the state's new redistricting plan. His win marked his first victory in a decade-long political odyssey in which he evolved from Republican to independent to Democrat, and that resulted in two statewide defeats after he had served four years as governor. His deep political experience is unusual for a House freshman.

Crist was born in Altoona, Pennsylvania, where his grandfather, a Greek immigrant from Cyprus who arrived in America in 1912, ran a shoe-shine parlor. His family moved to Atlanta before his first birthday, when his father, who shortened the family name from Christodoulos to Crist, was accepted to medical school at Emory University. In 1960, the Crists settled in St. Petersburg. A nearby Greek community and a rising population of retirees made the location a nice fit for a young doctor hoping to build a practice. By the time Charlie was 10, he was campaigning for his father who sought - and won - a seat on the Pinellas County School Board. In high school, Charlie was the starting quarterback and class president. He was a walk-on player at Wake Forest University, which he attended for two years. He transferred to Florida State, where he was student body vice president and homecoming king. He earned his law degree at Cumberland School of Law in Alabama, then worked as general counsel for the minor league division of Major League Baseball.

After an unsuccessful run for the state Senate in 1986, Crist served as state director for Republican Sen. Connie Mack. He ran again for the state Senate and won, serving six years. In the Legislature, he gained the nickname of "Chain Gang Charlie" for taking touch stances on crime. He also gained a reputation as an ambitious, media-savvy pol, always sporting a healthy tan and blessed with retail campaigning skills. He was on the state ballot six times between 1998 and 2014, with three victories. In 1998, he challenged Democratic Sen. Bob Graham but lost, 62%-38%. In the next six years, he was elected state education commissioner, attorney general and then governor in 2006, when he succeeded term-limited Jeb Bush.

Crist brought to the governorship a folksy style and a bipartisan perspective that contrasted with the more cerebral and ideological approach of Bush. The first issue he tackled was insurance. Seven hurricanes had slammed Florida in 2004 and 2005, and property-insurance rates had skyrocketed. Crist denounced insurance companies for being stingy about paying claims, and he expanded the state-owned Citizens Property Insurance until it became the largest wind insurer in Florida. Fiscally, Crist proved to be as conservative as Bush had been. In 2007, he used the line-item veto for $459 million in spending, advocated no tax increase and froze state salaries. His policies seemed to appeal to both conservatives and liberals.

His job ratings were extraordinarily high, including among Democrats and independents. But Republicans didn't rate him as high as Bush. When a Senate seat opened in 2010, Crist said he would seek the GOP nomination. The National Republican Senatorial Committee immediately endorsed him over former Florida House Speaker Marco Rubio. But the conservative Rubio received support from local and national activists. Crist deepened the hostility of Republicans when he endorsed President Barack Obama's $787 billion economic stimulus bill. Plus, his literal embrace of Obama at a public event infuriated many of them. By the time Crist realized the conservative base was slipping away, it was too late. On the verge of losing the primary, Crist quit the Republican Party and ran as an independent.

In the general election, Crist faced Rubio and Democratic Rep. Kendrick Meek. He started with an early lead in the polls, but his support plummeted when he got caught in the crossfire between Rubio and Meek, both of whom painted Crist as a political opportunist. Crist tried to appeal as the de facto Democratic candidate, but Meek got the nomination and refused to bow out. Rubio won with 49 percent of the vote to 30 percent for Crist and 20 percent for Meek.

Crist returned to the campaign trail in 2014 to seek a return as governor - running this time as a Democrat and with the enthusiastic support of Obama. Running against Gov. Rick Scott, Crist adopted the Democratic political playbook and criticized Scott for cutting education and restricting abortion; he vowed to raise the minimum wage. Scott blamed Crist for leaving the state in poor economic shape, and he took credit for the subsequent economic turnaround. In a Republican year, Crist made the contest close. But he lost 48%-47%, a margin of 64,000 votes.

With two statewide losses, most politicians would have called it quits. But Crist gained a new opportunity when redistricting made the 13th District, with his home base of St. Petersburg, an inviting target. Crist secured the support of the Democratic Congressional Campaign Committee. He appeared to lock up the seat after Jolly, a former congressional aide and lobbyist who won his House seat in a special election in March 2014, said it would be "impossible" for a Republican to win the new seat. Jolly decided to run instead for the Senate after Rubio decided to run for president and not seek a second term in the Senate.

That game plan changed in June 2016, a few days before the filing deadline, when Rubio opted to reclaim his Senate seat. Jolly tried to salvage his situation by stepping back to seek reelection to his House seat. He had made his bid even more uphill, when his poor-mouthing of campaign fundraising generally and the National Republican Congressional Committee specifically led the NRCC to deny financial support to Jolly. With money that he had raised for his Senate campaign, Jolly had a fundraising advantage, $3.9 million to $2 million. But Crist was bolstered by $2.6 million in support from the DCCC and other party adjuncts.

The contest turned out closer than most - including Jolly - had expected. A week before the election, the *Tampa Bay Times* headlined the contest as "two nice guys in a not-so-nice congressional race." Democrats, with polls that showed Donald Trump running poorly in the area, sought to tie the presidential nominee around Jolly's neck. Jolly described Crist as an "untrustworthy political opportunist." Jolly, who kept his distance from Trump, said, "Charlie Crist is the Donald Trump of the left. He'll say anything until he gets caught."

Crist won, 51.9%-48.1%. Without redistricting, he almost certainly would have lost. In the House, the experienced freshman got a seat on the Financial Services Committee. As if to corroborate Jolly's critique, Crist said a week after the election that Trump was "pragmatic" and that his plan to increase spending for infrastructure would be a "godsend." Given his political history and the unpredictability of Florida politics, another statewide bid for Crist was not out of the question.

St. Petersburg, Clearwater

Demographics data for new House districts were not prepared by the Census Bureau prior to our editorial deadline.

Voter Turnout			
2016 House Turnout as % CVAP	N/A	2016 House turnout	355,842

2012 Presidential Vote information unavailable due to recent redistricting.

2016 Presidential Vote		
Hillary Clinton	178,892	(49%)
Donald Trump	167,348	(46%)
Gary Johnson	10,022	(3%)

Cook Partisan Voting Index: D+2

When Spanish explorers arrived in what is now St. Petersburg some 500 years ago, they discovered an area covered by a primeval pine forest and teeming with bears, panthers, turkeys and bald eagles. They named the area "Punta Pinal" ("point of pines"), a name that has since been Anglicized into the Pinellas Peninsula. The area remained under-populated - only 50 families lived here when the Civil War broke out - until two events accelerated its development. First, the Orange Belt Railway connected the region to national markets in the 1880s. Second, Dr. W.C. Van Bibber, addressing the American Medical Society convention in 1885, named the peninsula the healthiest place on earth, setting off a stampede of interest. By 1897, the Belleview Hotel was built in Clearwater, and the area began its transition to a major tourist destination - and, later, a retirement community. In the 21st century, St. Petersburg has become a progressive community. In November 2016, the city council voted to make the city the first in Florida to rely 100 percent on renewable energy, with the changes partially financed by the $1 million that the city received in its settlement with BP over the Deepwater Horizon oil spill in 2010. Also that month, ferry service began to downtown Tampa. Local officials have plans to create a Pier District in downtown St. Petersburg.

The population of Pinellas County more than doubled in the 1920s, and did so once more in the 1950s. Mostly from the North and modestly affluent, the newcomers adapted easily to a place whose civic tone was set by the *St. Petersburg Times* (now the *Tampa Bay Times*) and its longtime owners, Nelson and Henrietta Poynter: sober, good-humored and supportive of clean government and civil rights. They also brought with them Republican voting habits, and presaged the political revolution in Florida that would take place as Northern immigrants spread down the coastlines. Democrats had a 56-point registration edge over Republicans here in 1940. By 1950, that edge was only 6 points. In 1954, Pinellas County Republicans elected William Cramer to Congress, the first Republican from Florida since 1882 when Horatio Bisbee Jr. was elected in a district that spanned the eastern half of the peninsula. The Republican tilt faded and Pinellas County is now a swing area of the state. Until 2016, the House seat remained consistently in GOP hands.

The new 13th Congressional District, like the old one, is located entirely within Pinellas County. But redistricting in 2016 made a major shift. It added about 100,000 people in the heavily African-American and Democratic precincts in south St. Petersburg that had been part of the Tampa-based 14th District. In return, the district lost parts of northern Pinellas, including the area surrounding Dunedin. The district retained the remainder of St. Petersburg plus Clearwater, where resorts have grown more upscale and where the Church of Scientology and several buildings of its religious center are headquartered. It also includes many of the beach communities on the barrier islands facing the Gulf of Mexico, including Belleair Beach down to Treasure Island. Inland, it incorporates the new subdivisions of Largo in the center of the peninsula. Almost 20 percent of Clearwater's population is over the age of 65; it once claimed the highest percentage of senior citizens in the nation but has since been eclipsed by other locales in Florida and Arizona. The redistricting shifts had a significant political impact. In the old 13th, President Barack Obama in 2012 led by about 5,000 votes. With the new lines, Obama's lead would have been, 55%-44%. Hillary Clinton won here in 2016 by a narrower 49%-46%. This was one case in which Democrats were the beneficiaries of redistricting.

FOURTEENTH DISTRICT

Kathy Castor (D)

Elected 2006, 6th term; b. Aug 20, 1966, Miami; Emory University - Atlanta (GA), B.A., 1988; Florida State University School of Law, J.D., 1991; Presbyterian; Married (Bill Lewis); 2 children.

Elected Office: Hillsborough County Commissioner, 2002-2006.

Professional Career: Assistant General counsel, FL Department of Community Affairs, 1991-1994; Practicing attorney, 1994-2000.

DC Office: 2052 RHOB 20515, 202-225-3376, Fax: 202-225-5652, castor.house.gov.

State Offices: Tampa, 813-871-2817.

Committees: *Energy & Commerce*: Energy, Health, Oversight & Investigations.

Group Ratings

	ADA	ACLU	AFL-CIO	LCV	ITI	COC	HAFA	ACU	CFG	FRC
2016	-	94%	-	100%	67%	64%	12%	0%	0%	0%
2015	95%	C	100%	91%	C	45%	C	8%	0%	0%

Almanac Ratings 2015

	Economy	Social	Foreign	Composite
Liberal	96%	100%	93%	96%
Conservative	4%	0%	7%	4%

Key Votes of the 114th Congress

1. Keystone Pipeline	N	5. Puerto Rico Debt	Y	9. Offenses by Aliens	N
2. Trade Deals	N	6. Medical Marijuana	Y	10. Troops in Iraq	N
3. Export-Import Bank	Y	7. Sanctuary Cities	N	11. Homeland Security $$	Y
4. Debt Ceiling Increase	Y	8. Armor-piercing Bullets	N	12. Trade Adjustment aid	Y

Election Results

Election	Name (Party)	Vote (%)		Cand. Spent	Ind. Exp. Support	Ind. Exp. Oppose
2016 General	Kathy Castor (D)	195,789	(62%)	$603,841		
	Christine Quinn (R)	121,088	(38%)	$25,341		
2016 Primary	Kathy Castor (D)		(100%)			

Prior winning percentages: 2014 (unopposed), 2012 (70%), 2010 (60%), 2008 (72%), 2006 (70%)

Kathy Castor, a Democrat first elected in 2006, uses her background as an environmental lawyer on behalf of local interests and has staunchly upheld Democratic positions in energy debates. She has worked closely with Republicans to protect her district's sprawling MacDill Air Force Base.

Castor studied political science at Emory University, earned her law degree from Florida State University, and worked as a land-use attorney. Her parents were heavily involved in public service. Her father, Don Castor, sat on the Hillsborough County court for two decades. Her mother, Betty Castor, served in the state Senate, as state education commissioner and as president of the University of South Florida. In 2004, Betty Castor was the Democratic nominee for Senate, but lost 49%-48% to Republican Mel Martinez. Kathy Castor ran unsuccessfully for the state Senate in 2000, but two years later won a four-year term on the Hillsborough County Commission.

In 2006, Kathy Castor ran for the open House seat, benefiting from the family name ID. In a district with a nearly 2-to-1 Democratic advantage, she faced four opponents in the primary. The most formidable was state Senate Minority Leader Les Miller, a veteran African-American legislator. With the support of EMILY's List, Castor raised nearly $1 million before the primary and outspent Miller 3-to-1. She won 54%-34%. In the general election, Castor campaigned for expanded health care for low-income families, stronger ethics and lobbying rules, and a rapid withdrawal of U.S. troops from Iraq. She won, 70%-30%.

In the House, Castor was appointed as the freshman representative to the Democratic Steering and Policy Committee, which determines committee assignments. In 2009, she agreed to serve on the House Ethics Committee, and chaired the subcommittee looking into California Democratic Rep. Maxine Waters' alleged efforts to help get federal bailout money for a bank in which her husband owned stock. Waters was cleared of wrongdoing in 2012. As a reward for her service on the Ethics panel, considered an undesirable posting, Castor got a seat on the Energy and Commerce Committee.

She joined a group of liberals who insisted that any savings from a government-run insurance option in the Democrats' proposed health care overhaul should be used to increase subsidies for low-income persons. She added an amendment to the energy and climate-change bill to allow states to set rates for electricity generated from renewable energy under state incentive programs. Typically a party loyalist, Castor regularly introduced a balanced budget constitutional amendment, normally a GOP priority. In the *Almanac's* 2015 vote ratings, Castor ranked among the liberal half of House Democrats.

Castor was a major player on offshore drilling following the 2010 BP oil spill in the Gulf of Mexico, prodding the company and the Obama administration for more research on the spill's impact. In 2012, she worked to add a provision to a transportation bill directing that most fines collected under the Clean

Water Act should go for Gulf clean-up instead of to the Treasury. Castor has avidly looked out for MacDill, headquarters of the U.S. Central Command and Special Operations Command. When the Air Force in 2016 narrowed the list of air bases to host the Air Force's KC-46 next-generation aerial refueling jet, she advocated MacDill but was unsuccessful.

Castor, whose district has the third-highest number of Cuban Americans in the nation, embraced increased trade and travel to Cuba and was the first House member from Florida to support lifting travel restrictions. She praised President Barack Obama's decision to reopen diplomatic relations with Cuba. In March 2016, she accompanied him when he became the first president to visit the island since 1928. When local officials in Miami objected to suggestions that they could host a Cuban chancery, Castor repeatedly volunteered Tampa as the site. Having urged the addition of Tampa to the list of airports approved to host flights to Havana, Castor in December 2016 praised Southwest Airlines for starting "affordable" service from Tampa to Havana.

In the Republican year of 2010, Castor faced a tougher reelection challenge from Republican Mike Prendergast, a retired Army colonel. She narrowly outspent him and won, but with only 60 percent of the vote, the lowest of her career. In 2016, the additional Republican voters from redistricting left her with a victory margin of 62%-38% in her typically uncompetitive contest. Following the election, she said that Hillary Clinton in her presidential campaign "should have been stronger" on jobs and economic growth issues.

Tampa: Hillsborough County

Demographics data for new House districts were not prepared by the Census Bureau prior to our editorial deadline.

Voter Turnout

2016 House Turnout as % CVAP	N/A	2016 House turnout	316,877

2012 Presidential Vote information unavailable due to recent redistricting.

2016 Presidential Vote		
Hillary Clinton	188,870	(57%)
Donald Trump	128,796	(39%)
Gary Johnson	8,719	(3%)

Cook Partisan Voting Index: D+7

Tampa's history goes back not much more than a century. Its industrial past can be traced to 1886, when Cuban cigar-makers from Key West settled in the city's Latin Quarter, called Ybor City. The city developed along the waterfront, with distinctive architectural touches like the 13 minarets on the Arabian-style Tampa Bay Hotel, built by railroad and real estate tycoon Henry B. Plant in the 1890s and now part of the University of Tampa. For a time, Tampa was Florida's only true industrial city, with a working-class, white population base. Today it has a diverse economy: a service sector, two universities and tourism, led by the Busch Gardens theme park. Tampa's subdivisions and condominiums, office towers, and low-rise commercial buildings have spread inland across swamps and lowlands. Like most of Florida, it was hit hard by the recession. In 2010, the Tampa Bay area's unemployment rate topped 12 percent, the fifth highest among the largest U.S. metropolitan areas. After a slow recovery, business activity has picked up. In October 2016, the *Tampa Bay Times* reported that new real estate in the port area had reached "critical mass" for the $3 billion redevelopment. There has been an increase in commercial cargo at the Port of Tampa, which handles the most cargo of any Florida port. At the international airport, the $1 billion reconstruction includes a 1.4 mile people-mover rail.

Through its history, Tampa has remained a city of families and young people. Senior citizens account for only about 11 percent of the residents here, an unusually low percentage for Florida. It has been an important military center for much of its existence. During the Spanish-American War, when railroads were making their way down Florida's Atlantic Coast, Tampa was a major embarkation point for U.S. troops. MacDill Air Force Base, on the south side of the city and jutting into Tampa Bay, is the vital headquarters of Central Command, which ran the Persian Gulf War and the campaigns in Afghanistan and Iraq. It is also headquarters for Special Operations Command, and the coordinating center for international special operations forces.

The 14th Congressional District is centered on Tampa. With 57 percent of Hillsborough County, it includes most of the city of Tampa and its close-in suburbs, such as Town 'n' Country. In the 2016 redistricting, the 14th lost a thin coastal slice on the eastern side of Tampa Bay plus a more politically vital salient across the Bay, with the heavily African-American and lower-income neighborhoods in St. Petersburg. In exchange for those nearly 100,000 people, the district gained a new area of northern Hillsborough, including additional parts of Tampa. Those changes increased the Republican vote in the district by about seven percentage points, though it remained safely Democratic. More significantly, those neighborhoods in St. Pete were added to the swing 13th District, which gave it a Democratic lean. With the old lines, Democrat Barack Obama won the district with 65 percent of the vote in both 2008 and 2012. The new 14th gave Hillary Clinton a 57%-39% win.

FIFTEENTH DISTRICT

Dennis Ross (R)

Elected 2010, 4th term; b. Oct 18, 1959, Lakeland; Auburn University College of Business (AL), B.S.; Samford University Cumberland School of Law (AL), J.D.; University of Florida, Att.; Presbyterian; Married (Cindy Ross); 2 children.

Elected Office: FL House, 2000-2008.

Professional Career: Practicing attorney, 1987-1989; Counsel, Walt Disney World, 1989; Founder, partner, Ross Vecchio P.A, 1989; President, Greater Lakeland Young Republicans, 1990; Chair, Polk County Republican Executive Committee, 1992-1995.

DC Office: 436 CHOB 20515, 202-225-1252, Fax: 202-226-0585, dennisross.house.gov.

State Offices: Lakeland, 863-644-8215.

Committees: *Financial Services*: Financial Institutions & Consumer Credit, Housing & Insurance, Oversight & Investigations. *Oversight & Government Reform*: Government Operations, Interior, Energy & Environment.

Group Ratings

	ADA	ACLU	AFL-CIO	LCV	ITI	COC	HAFA	ACU	CFG	FRC
2016	-	5%	-	3%	100%	100%	65%	88%	74%	100%
2015	0%	C	8%	0%	C	80%	C	79%	75%	100%

Almanac Ratings 2015

	Economy	Social	Foreign	Composite
Liberal	3%	5%	0%	3%
Conservative	97%	95%	100%	97%

Key Votes of the 114th Congress

1. Keystone Pipeline	Y	5. Puerto Rico Debt	Y	9. Offenses by Aliens	Y
2. Trade Deals	Y	6. Medical Marijuana	N	10. Troops in Iraq	N
3. Export-Import Bank	N	7. Sanctuary Cities	Y	11. Homeland Security $$	N
4. Debt Ceiling Increase	N	8. Armor-piercing Bullets	Y	12. Trade Adjustment aid	N

Election Results

Election	Name (Party)	Vote (%)		Cand. Spent	Ind. Exp. Support	Ind. Exp. Oppose
2016 General	Dennis Ross (R)	182,999	(58%)	$1,195,672		
	Jim Lange (D)	135,475	(43%)	$34,938		
2016 Primary	Dennis Ross (R)		(100%)			

Prior winning percentages: 2014 (60%), 2010 (48%)

Republican Dennis Ross, elected in 2010, has solid conservative views and usually is a reliable team player. He shuns incendiary rhetoric or media attention and is a bit of a loner, rarely attending group events. In his under-stated way, he gained positions in House Republican leadership and as a member of President Donald Trump's transition team.

Ross grew up in Lakeland, Florida, the youngest of five children. He remembers his mother, Loyola Ross, as a strict parent who preached the virtues of hard work. He attended the University of Florida for a year before transferring to Auburn University and graduating with a degree in organizational management. He spent a year working as a legislative aide, installed and sold computers for a short time, then enrolled in law school at Samford University in Birmingham, Alabama. He returned to Lakeland and became an in-house counsel for Walt Disney World, handling workers' compensation claims for the company. With $10,000 borrowed from a neighbor for less than a year, he opened a law firm that grew to seven lawyers and 27 employees. Ross spent three years as chairman of Polk County's Republican Executive Committee. In 2000, he won a seat in the Florida House, where he developed a reputation as a faithful, but not automatic, GOP vote.

When GOP Rep. Adam Putnam ran successfully for agriculture commissioner, Ross jumped into the race for his seat. In the primary, he trounced John Lindsey, a businessman and political neophyte, winning 69 percent of the vote. In the general, he faced Democrat Lori Edwards, the Polk County supervisor of elections. Edwards campaigned as a moderate, saying she would fit in with the Blue Dog Coalition of fiscally conservative Democrats. But Ross ran ads tying her to President Barack Obama and liberal House Speaker Nancy Pelosi, while embracing Putnam's conservatism. Ross spent more than $1 million to Edwards' $657,000. Ross won convincingly, 48%-41%, with 11 percent of the vote going to tea party nominee Randy Wilkinson, a former Polk County commissioner.

In his first year in the House, Ross was unapologetic about his wholehearted opposition to Obama's legislative agenda and his unwillingness to give Republican House Speaker John Boehner much leeway to negotiate a deal to raise the nation's debt ceiling. "I don't view this as clashing," he said. "It's more about slowing down the ship and working to put it in another direction." He joined the Tea Party Caucus and rejected accusations from members of the Congressional Black Caucus that the movement is racist, telling them to "get a grip."

Ross chaired the Oversight and Government Reform subcommittee overseeing federal workforce issues. Ross was highly vocal about reports that federal employees used growing amounts of official time to participate in union activities. He unveiled a proposal that was designed to reduce the federal workforce by 10 percent within four years. On the Financial Services Committee, Ross has filed legislation to create zero-based budgeting for the government, to require federal agency heads to justify their spending.

In 2014, new House Majority Whip Steve Scalise of Louisiana named Ross as one of his five senior whips. After the Republican leadership experienced some legislative failures, Ross offered to resign, especially when he could not support the bill to extend spending for the Homeland Security Department because it failed to block Obama's executive order on immigration. Scalise refused to accept the resignation. The *Almanac* vote ratings for 2015 ranked Ross among the most conservative members of the House.

At home, Ross in 2014 was challenged for reelection by Democrat Alan Cohn, a former local television reporter. Cohn said his views on immigration, taxes and working families were consistent with those of the voters, provided he had enough campaign money to communicate. He had strong backing from organized labor, and criticized Ross' links to big banks and Wall Street. Ross largely ignored Cohn, and benefited from his campaign spending advantage, $1.4 million to $430,000. Ross won 60%-40%, a clear improvement over his initial election.

In 2016, he was challenged by Jim Lange, a political newcomer with a background as a business consultant who had created a non-profit to assist the reconstruction of Haiti following a devastating earthquake in 2010. Before his mother died, Lange said, she asked him to put similar effort into helping Americans. "I'm so disgusted with the shape of the political narrative," he told a reporter for the Florida Politics platform. His agenda included job opportunities for the unemployed and underemployed, and immigration reform. Ross called for improved options for flood insurance, and campaigned on his conservative record and his leadership position. Lange spent only $40,000 and lost 57%-43%.

During the fall campaign, Ross met privately with Trump during an appearance in Lakeland. Following the election, Trump named him to the 12-member executive committee of his transition team-chiefly, to advise on top personnel for the new administration. "The things I have been advocating for years, I will finally have the chance to see them as a reality," Ross told a local reporter. With his ambition, he is well-positioned for an opportunity at home or in Washington.

Central Florida: Tampa Suburbs, Lakeland

Demographics data for new House districts were not prepared by the Census Bureau prior to our editorial deadline.

Voter Turnout			
2016 House Turnout as % CVAP	N/A	2016 House turnout	318,474

2012 Presidential Vote information unavailable due to recent redistricting.

2016 Presidential Vote		
Donald Trump	177,634	(53%)
Hillary Clinton	144,226	(43%)
Gary Johnson	8,906	(3%)

Cook Partisan Voting Index: R+6

The heart of central Florida is Polk County, filled with lakes and small-to-medium-sized cities. Lakeland, with a population of just over 100,000, is the biggest city here and home to the corporate headquarters of the Publix chain of grocery stores, the largest employee-owned supermarket chain in the nation and the second-favorite in a 2016 national consumer survey. With 8,200 employees in the area and a December 2016 plan to add 700 more, Publix is the largest employer in the county. Lakeland-area home prices historically remained below $100,000, making it one of the most affordable areas in the Sunshine State. In November 2016, local real estate agents reported double-digit annual increases in both sales and prices, including a median sales price of $170,000. *U.S. News and World Report* rated the Lakeland area 16th on its list of "Best Places People Are Moving To in the U.S. in 2016"

This is the part of Florida most dependent on agriculture. Strawberries, cattle and citrus are economic mainstays, although periodic freezes in recent years have persuaded some orange growers to move south or to switch to tomatoes. Polk has had a double-digit percentage drop in the number of farms and acreage in the past decade. In 2016, for the first time in 21 years, Polk no longer produced the most citrus in Florida. Due chiefly to the lingering effects of frost and a citrus bacterial disease, St. Lucie became the number-one county for oranges. Proportionately, there have been more manufacturing jobs here than almost anywhere else in Florida (though still not very many). Some new businesses, including distribution centers, have taken advantage of cheap property values to build new plants in Lakeland. One of the few remnants of old Florida, this area has not become a major retiree haven. In Hillsborough, the Plant City area produces close to 90 percent of Florida's strawberry yield. At its annual Strawberry Festival in March, hundreds of thousands of patrons consume at least as many shortcakes.

The new 15th Congressional District is a rural and suburban combo. About 37 percent of the district's population lives in agricultural Polk County, and 52 percent in the rapidly growing suburbs in Hillsborough County east of Tampa. Redistricting removed some suburbs north of Tampa and added farmlands in the southern parts of Lake County. The shifts had scant partisan impact. Overall, the district remains reliably Republican. In 2016, Donald Trump won 53%-43%.

SIXTEENTH DISTRICT

Vern Buchanan (R)

Elected 2006, 6th term; b. May 08, 1951, Detroit, MI; Cleary University (MI); b.B.A., 1975; University of Detroit (MI), M.B.A., 1986; Baptist; Married (Sandy Harris Buchanan); 2 children.

Military Career: MI Air National Guard, 1970-1976.

Professional Career: Taekwondo instructor, 1971-1974; Marketing rep., Burroughs Corporation, 1975-1976; Founder, Vern Buchanan & Association, 1976-1978; Founder & CEO, American Speedy Printing Centers, 1976-1992; Founder & Chairman, Buchanan Automotive Group, 1992-2007; Founder & Chairman, Buchanan Enterprises, 1992-2007.

DC Office: 2104 RHOB 20515, 202-225-5015, Fax: 202-226-0828, buchanan.house.gov.

State Offices: Bradenton, 941-747-9081; Sarasota, 941-951-6643.

Committees: *Ways & Means*: Health, Oversight (Chmn), Social Security.

Group Ratings

	ADA	ACLU	AFL-CIO	LCV	ITI	COC	HAFA	ACU	CFG	FRC
2016	-	11%	-	29%	100%	92%	53%	72%	63%	100%
2015	0%	C	21%	17%	C	90%	C	67%	49%	92%

Almanac Ratings 2015

	Economy	Social	Foreign	Composite
Liberal	14%	16%	6%	12%
Conservative	86%	84%	94%	88%

Key Votes of the 114th Congress

1. Keystone Pipeline	Y	5. Puerto Rico Debt	Y	9. Offenses by Aliens	Y
2. Trade Deals	Y	6. Medical Marijuana	N	10. Troops in Iraq	N
3. Export-Import Bank	Y	7. Sanctuary Cities	Y	11. Homeland Security $$	Y
4. Debt Ceiling Increase	Y	8. Armor-piercing Bullets	Y	12. Trade Adjustment aid	N

Election Results

Election	Name (Party)	Vote (%)	Cand. Spent	Ind. Exp. Support	Ind. Exp. Oppose
2016 General	Vern Buchanan (R)	230,654 (60%)	$886,694		
	Jan Schneider (D)	155,262 (40%)	$53,557		
2016 Primary	Vern Buchanan (R)	53,682 (81%)			
	James Satcher (R)	12,892 (19%)			

Prior winning percentages: 2014 (62%), 2012 (54%), 2010 (69%), 2008 (56%), 2006 50%)

Vern Buchanan, a Republican first elected in 2006, had unusually tough election campaigns. Much of the pain was self-inflicted, with questionable business dealings and campaign finances. But the House Ethics Committee closed its investigation. Buchanan has grown safe at home and has become a subcommittee chairman on the powerful Ways and Means Committee.

Buchanan grew up outside of Detroit, the eldest of six children and the son of a factory foreman. He joined the Michigan Air National Guard and worked his way through college as a tae kwon do instructor. He earned a business degree at Cleary University and later an M.B.A. at the University of Detroit. Buchanan founded American Speedy Printing Centers and made his fortune by selling 700 quick-printing franchises before his 40th birthday. In 1990, he moved his family to Florida, where he found new success as an automobile dealer with franchises throughout the Southeast. Buchanan became active in Republican politics, serving as a top fundraiser for Gov. Jeb Bush and Sen. Mel Martinez. In 2002, he wanted to run for the 13th District House seat, but stepped aside for then-Florida Secretary of State Katherine Harris, who had become a national figure for her role in the 2000 presidential vote recount.

Buchanan got his chance in 2006, when Harris ran for the Senate. His party connections and personal wealth made him the front-runner. In the primary, he stressed his conservative credentials and challenged his chief rival, former Sarasota Republican Party Chairman Tramm Hudson, for his positions on abortion rights and immigration. After spending more than $2 million of his own money, Buchanan won 32 percent of the vote in the five-way primary.

Democratic nominee Christine Jennings, who like Buchanan was a transplanted Midwesterner and a self-made business success, was a bank owner. National Democrats pummeled Buchanan for his business dealings. Buchanan characterized Jennings as a pro-tax liberal. Despite the Republican advantage in the district, Buchanan was hurt by the attacks and the poor political environment for the GOP. This was the most expensive House race in 2006. Buchanan spent more than $8 million, including $5.5 million of his own money. Jennings spent $3 million, with about $2 million from her own pocket. After a recount, Republican election officials certified Buchanan the winner by 369 votes. Jennings alleged voting machine malfunction, but several rounds of testing were inconclusive. Buchanan has been among the wealthiest members of Congress. In 2015, his estimated net worth of $50 million placed him ninth on the list, *Roll Call* reported.

In the House, Buchanan softened his ideological positions. He was one of 19 Republicans who supported most of the Democrats' early legislative agenda when they took control in 2007. He voted for raising the minimum wage, cutting subsidies to industries, and allowing the federal government to negotiate lower drug prices with pharmaceutical companies. "I ran as a conservative, but I also ran as someone who is going to be independent," Buchanan told the *Sarasota Herald-Tribune*. After the BP oil spill in 2010, he pushed for a moratorium on all deep-water drilling permits in the Gulf of Mexico.

He took stances to the right on immigration and terrorism, calling for an English official-language law and using military tribunals instead of civilian courts to try terrorist suspects. The former car dealer voted against the bailout of Detroit automakers in 2008 because, he said, the companies "failed to develop viable restructuring proposals." The industry problems led him to sell several of his dealerships. On Ways and Means, he has been an advocate of corporate tax reform, and joined the bipartisan deal in 2015 to adjust Medicare payments to doctors and extend the Children's Health Insurance Program.

In 2011, Buchanan attracted unwanted attention. The *Sarasota Herald-Tribune* reported that during the past year he had spent almost $1 million in campaign contributions on himself, companies he owned, or family members. Most of the money reportedly was used to repay campaign checks he wrote to himself in 2006. Buchanan had previously faced allegations that business partners and employees of his car dealerships made contributions to his 2006 and 2008 congressional campaigns, and were then reimbursed by Buchanan's companies. He steadfastly denied any wrongdoing, and maintained that the Federal Elections Commission had exonerated him. But in December 2011, the *Herald-Tribune* unearthed FEC documents saying that attorneys investigating the matter found Buchanan to be "less than forthright and at times unbelievable." By 2012, both the Justice Department and the House Ethics Committee were looking into Buchanan's campaign activities.

With ethics questions swirling, his House seat looked to be in jeopardy. Democrat Keith Fitzgerald made Buchanan's integrity the main focus of his campaign and launched a website called the *Buchanan Files*, with links to news stories on the investigations. Then, over the summer, the Ethics Committee said it had ended its probe of Buchanan, though it did not formally conclude until June 2016; in September his office announced that the Justice Department had concluded its investigation without charging him. Buchanan outspent Fitzgerald, $2.7 million to $1.4 million and prevailed, 54%-46%. Since 2012, he has breezed to reelection against weakly funded opposition. Buchanan objected strongly, but to no avail, to the split of Sarasota County in the 2016 redistricting.

Buchanan has eyed other political opportunities, especially after Sen. Marco Rubio said in 2015 that he would not seek reelection, but he has grown more comfortable in the House as he has gained seniority. He has moved into the elite ranks as a subcommittee chairman on Ways and Means. In late 2015, he took over the Human Resources panel. When the Twenty-First Century Cures Act was enacted in December 2016, he claimed credit for a section that removed an accounting flaw from Medicare Advantage plans that jeopardized coverage for many beneficiaries. In the new Congress, he said tax reform was a top priority, including steps to equalize tax rates on small businesses and corporations. In 2017, he switched to chair the Oversight Subcommittee.

Central Gulf Coast: Bradenton, North Sarasota

Demographics data for new House districts were not prepared by the Census Bureau prior to our editorial deadline.

Voter Turnout

2016 House Turnout as % CVAP	N/A	2016 House turnout	385,916

2012 Presidential Vote information unavailable due to recent redistricting.

2016 Presidential Vote		
Donald Trump	213,271	(53%)
Hillary Clinton	170,442	(43%)
Gary Johnson	9,302	(2%)

Cook Partisan Voting Index: R+7

When the Ringling Brothers made a success of the circus they founded in the 1880s, they needed a place for performers and animals to rest during the winter months. They settled on Sarasota: just far enough north to be reachable by railroad and just far enough south to be semitropical so the elephants would stay healthy. John Ringling established the Ringling Museum of Art and a huge sculpture garden, and built his own Venetian palace, the Ca' d'Zan. Next door, his brother, Charles, built a pair of neoclassical revival mansions in pink Georgia marble, which are now part of New College of Florida. But this was still a sparsely populated area until just after World War II, when the balmy Gulf Coast attracted new settlers - affluent, well-educated Republicans from upper-crust suburbs in the North. The population exploded. Manatee and Sarasota counties grew from a combined 64,000 people in 1950 to 770,000 in 2015. Like many Florida cities experiencing boom times, Sarasota was hit hard by the collapse of the housing market. In 2009, one of every 19 homeowners in Manatee and Sarasota counties received a foreclosure notice.

In January 2017, alas, Feld Entertainment announced that the Ringling Brothers Circus was closing in May due to several factors, including a drop in ticket sales and protests by animal-rights groups. Otherwise, the post-recession recovery has been strong, including the 2014 Sarasota opening of the luxury indoor Mall at University. The bayfront area along the Intracoastal Waterway is lined with high-rises and is often clogged with traffic from Bradenton to Sarasota, with record-setting numbers of visitors and revenues from paid lodging in 2016. Though some technology firms diversify the economy, the district as a whole remains reliant on tourists and well-off retirees: People 65 and older are one-third of the population in Sarasota, and one-fourth in Manatee. Now a center for sports tourism, Bradenton has a rowing facility that was a model for the 2020 Olympic Games in Tokyo. The 2017 World Rowing Championships and the 2018 World Sailing annual conference were both scheduled for Sarasota. Reality check: In 2016, Bradenton was the opioid overdose capital of Florida.

The new 16th Congressional District of Florida remains based in Manatee and Sarasota. But instead of being almost the entirety of those two counties, the plan removed the southern part of Sarasota, leaving only 57 percent of that county in the 16th. The district continues to include the idyllic though often busy Sarasota beachfronts from sleepy Anna Maria to pricey Longboat Key and Lido Key and the more casual Siesta Key. Three of the wealthiest census tracts in all of Florida are located on these barrier islands. Besides all of Bradenton-based Manatee, the district swings north along the east coast of Tampa Bay to include the southern edge of Hillsborough. The effect has been to remove Venice and its surrounding beach towns and retirement havens in south Sarasota County, while adding new beach towns from Ruskin and Apollo Beach north to Remlap in Hillsborough. In both Sarasota and southern Hillsborough, Interstate 75 comes within a few miles of the Gulf of Mexico. West of 75, these areas are close to fully developed. East of 75, the lands had been mostly undeveloped until recent years. Some lower-cost subdivisions have opened in those areas, and more have been on the drawing board.

For many years, the 16th District was heavily Republican, though voting results have grown closer. The political impact of the latest redistricting shifts has been virtually nil. Mitt Romney got 54 percent of the vote to 45 percent for President Barack Obama in 2012, and those shares would have remained the same with the redrawing. In 2016, Donald Trump won the district, 53%-43%.

SEVENTEENTH DISTRICT

Tom Rooney (R)

Elected 2008, 5th term; b. Nov 21, 1970, Philadelphia, PA; University of Florida, M.A.; University of Miami Law School (FL), J.D.; Washington and Jefferson College (PA), B.A.; Syracuse University (NY), Att.; Catholic; Married (Tara Rooney); 3 children.

Military Career: U.S Army JAG, 2000-2004; Army Reserves, 2004-2007.

Professional Career: FL Assistant Attorney General, 2004-2005; CEO, Children's Place at HomeSafe, 2005-2006; Practicing attorney, 2006-2008.

DC Office: 2160 RHOB 20515, 202-225-5792, Fax: 202-225-3132, rooney.house.gov.

State Offices: Okeechobee, 863-402-9082; Punta Gorda, 941-575-9101; Sebring, 863-402-9082.

Committees: *Appropriations*: Agriculture, Rural Development, FDA & Related Agencies, Military Construction, Veterans Affairs & Related Agencies, State, Foreign Operations & Related Programs. *Permanent Select on Intelligence*.

Group Ratings

	ADA	ACLU	AFL-CIO	LCV	ITI	COC	HAFA	ACU	CFG	FRC
2016	-	5%	-	3%	100%	92%	71%	77%	74%	82%
2015	0%	C	13%	0%	C	85%	C	79%	76%	82%

Almanac Ratings 2015

	Economy	Social	Foreign	Composite
Liberal	5%	10%	0%	5%
Conservative	95%	90%	100%	95%

Key Votes of the 114th Congress

1. Keystone Pipeline	Y	5. Puerto Rico Debt	N	9. Offenses by Aliens	Y
2. Trade Deals	Y	6. Medical Marijuana	Y	10. Troops in Iraq	N
3. Export-Import Bank	NV	7. Sanctuary Cities	Y	11. Homeland Security $$	N
4. Debt Ceiling Increase	N	8. Armor-piercing Bullets	Y	12. Trade Adjustment aid	N

Election Results

Election	Name (Party)	Vote (%)	Cand. Spent	Ind. Exp. Support	Ind. Exp. Oppose
2016 General	Tom Rooney (R)	209,348 (62%)	$788,714		
	April Freeman (D)	115,974 (34%)	$123,454		
	John Sawyer (I)	13,353 (4%)	$597,260		
2016 Primary	Tom Rooney (R)	(100%)			

Prior winning percentages: 2014 (63%), 2012 (59%), 2010 (67%), 2008 (60%)

Tom Rooney, a Republican elected in 2008, is a former military prosecutor and West Point instructor who holds the firmly conservative views that such a background suggests. In a polarized House, Rooney has been adept on the Appropriations Committee as a deal-maker, including with Democrats. He has been willing to go his own way from his party, without alienating Republican leaders.

The grandson of Pittsburgh Steelers founding owner Art Rooney, he was born in Philadelphia and was a water boy for the team. (Steelers employees were his largest single campaign contributors from 2008 to 2012.) When he was 14, his father moved to Palm Beach Gardens where his family owned the Palm Beach Kennel Club, a racetrack and gambling business. Rooney briefly attended Syracuse University, where he earned a spot as a tight end and deep snapper for the Orangemen. But with no desire for a professional football career, Rooney transferred to the smaller Washington and Jefferson College just outside Pittsburgh, where he played both football and golf. He was a staff assistant for Republican Sen. Connie Mack of Florida for a brief period, then got a law degree from the University of Miami. After graduation, Rooney was a special assistant U.S. attorney at Fort Hood in Texas, and later taught constitutional and criminal law at the U.S. Military Academy at West Point. When then-Republican Charlie Crist became Florida attorney general, he hired Rooney as an assistant attorney general in 2004. Next, he headed a home for abused children and, in 2006, entered private law practice in Stuart.

Rooney ran for the House in 2008, with endorsements from Mack and Crist, who had since become governor. He won the primary by 1,011 votes over state Rep. Gayle Harrell, 36.7%-34.9%. In the general election, Rooney challenged freshman Democratic Rep. Tim Mahoney, who seemed to be preparing for an easy reelection. Mahoney outpaced Rooney in fundraising and had a solid lead in polls. But on Oct. 13, ABC News broke the story that Mahoney had paid a former aide $121,000 to keep quiet about their affair after he ended the relationship and fired her. The incumbent admitted to having "multiple affairs" while in Congress, but asserted he had done nothing to violate his oath of office. Rooney shot up nearly 25 points in the polls. Mahoney declined to end his campaign, even after Democratic House Speaker Nancy Pelosi called for an Ethics Committee investigation into the payment. Mahoney's financial contributions quickly dried up. Rooney won with 60 percent of the vote.

In the House, he joined the Republican whip team and was given a seat on the Intelligence Committee. In 2015, he became chairman of its Subcommittee on NSA and Cybersecurity, an influential position but one that discourages public discussion. Rooney has shown independence and a repeated willingness to challenge GOP leaders. He sponsored a House-passed resolution in 2011 to cut $450 million in Pentagon spending, including a project to build a second engine for the F-35 jet fighter that was based near Republican Speaker John Boehner's Ohio district. Rooney worked with Florida Democrat Ted Deutch — with whom he occasionally plays in a rock band — on a 2011 measure, which became law, to help homeless veterans. And he was the lead sponsor of a bipartisan bill approved by the Judiciary Committee in 2012 to ban the import or interstate trade of Burmese pythons and eight other species of snakes that have decimated native animal populations in the Everglades.

Rooney's bipartisanship has its limits. He was an outspoken critic of efforts to lift the ban on travel and food sales to Cuba. He has taken a strong stand against illegal immigration, introducing a bill to require incarcerated illegal immigrants to be deported as soon as they are released from jail. He pushed a measure in 2011 to deny the Environmental Protection Agency the authority to enforce water pollution rules that agricultural interests deemed overly harsh. "I want to be the environmental congressman for my district," Rooney told EPA Administrator Lisa Jackson at a hearing. "But I also represent a lot of farmers."

On the Appropriations Committee, he has dealt chiefly with military and farm issues. In 2015, he successfully led a bipartisan group of Floridians seeking $7.5 million to fight the citrus greening that has devastated orange crops. In the mostly forgotten tradition of appropriators, Rooney has been outspoken in seeking to limit the ban on earmarks in spending bills. His goal, he said, was to assert congressional prerogatives for water projects under the Army Corps of Engineers and Bureau of Reclamation. He complained that when he formally requests assistance on a critical local project, "They probably look at that letter and put it in the shredder. They don't give a rat's ass what I think." After the 2016 election, his proposed change in House rules gained sufficient support in the Republican Conference that Speaker Paul Ryan unilaterally decided to end the debate and kill it. Rooney likely will seek opportunities to generate additional support for his initiative.

Although redistricting has moved Rooney around, he has not been seriously challenged for reelection. In 2015, he explored running for the Senate after Marco Rubio initially retired. Although he did not follow through, he has remained comfortable in the political spotlight. After the October 2016 release of the 2005 video in which Donald Trump spoke crudely about women, Rooney withdrew his endorsement. Citing his three young sons, he said, "If I support [Trump] for President, I will be telling my boys that I think it's OK to treat women like objects – and I'll have failed as a dad." After the election, Rooney praised Trump's selection of his Cabinet members in national-security posts as "good, solid, conservative leadership-type picks."

South Central Florida: Charlotte, South Sarasota, Okeechobee

Demographics data for new House districts were not prepared by the Census Bureau prior to our editorial deadline.

Voter Turnout

2016 House Turnout as % CVAP	N/A	2016 House turnout	338,675

2012 Presidential Vote information unavailable due to recent redistricting.

2016 Presidential Vote

Donald Trump	220,156	(62%)
Hillary Clinton	123,919	(35%)

Cook Partisan Voting Index: R+13

The population of Charlotte County didn't reach 10,000 until the 1950s. But local histories assure us that the region was anything but quiet before then. In 1886, when railroads reached the convergence of the Peace River and Charlotte Harbor, the area was home to a small fishing center, a port that mostly shipped phosphate, and a few cattle ranches. But the exotic locale - at that point, it was the farthest south one could travel on the rail lines - pleasant climate and emerging sport of tarpon fishing encouraged developers to turn it into a destination for the wealthy. Elizabeth Colt, widow of gun-manufacturer Samuel Colt; John Wanamaker, of the eponymous Philadelphia department store; and other wealthy individuals began annual sojourns to winter in the semitropical paradise. But these riches existed uneasily alongside what remained of a frontier-like culture.

Today, Charlotte County is a very different place. The invention of air conditioning, advances in transportation and the surge of financially secure retirees conspired to drive rapid growth. The county's population doubled in the 1950s, 1960s and 1970s, and nearly did so again in the 1980s. Since then, the gains have slowed. From 2010 to 2015, the population grew from 160,000 to 173,000; Port Charlotte, developed in the 1950s, has become the most populous locale. Punta Gorda maintains a small-town and small-business feel. In 2015 *Kiplinger* listed it as among the top 10 most affordable places in the United States to retire.

The 17th Congressional District of Florida has been based in Charlotte County, with lots of additional pieces. The 2016 redistricting removed the southeast corner of Hillsborough County. In exchange, it substituted the southern part of Sarasota County, chiefly Venice and surrounding beach towns. The district stretches from Buckingham in Lee County north through the Big Cypress Swamp to Bartow in Polk County. The remainder of the population sprawls east and spreads over five lightly populated and mostly rural counties, including Lake Okeechobee. The landscape, largely overlooked by most Floridians, remains dominated by cattle farms and others that produce citrus, tomatoes and vegetables. DeSoto County ranked second in the state in production of oranges. Charlotte and Sarasota each have about 23 percent of the population. The redistricting made little change in what had become comfortable Republican locales. The 62 percent for Donald Trump was his best Florida district south of Orlando.

EIGHTEENTH DISTRICT

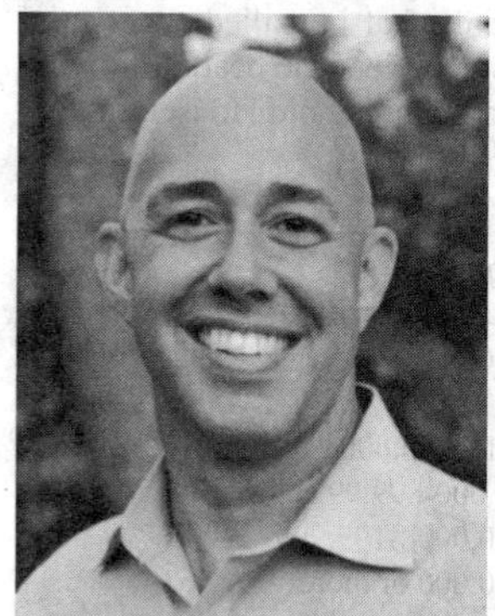

Brian Mast (R)

Elected 2016, 1st term; b. Jul 10, 1980, Grand Rapids, MI; Harvard University, Bach. Deg.; Christian Church; Married (Brianna Mast); 3 children.

Military Career: U.S Army (Afghanistan, WIA) 2000-2011.

Professional Career: Analyst, National Nuclear Security Admin., 2011-2012; Explosive Specialist, U.S Dept. of Homeland Security, 2012-2015.

DC Office: 2182 RHOB 20515, 202-225-3026, Fax: 202-225-8398, mast.house.gov.

State Offices: North Palm Beach, 561-530-7778; Port St Lucie, 772-336-2877; Stuart, 772-403-0900.

Committees: *Foreign Affairs*: Middle East & North Africa, Terrorism, Nonproliferation & Trade. *Transportation & Infrastructure*: Coast Guard & Maritime Transportation, Economic Dev't, Public Buildings & Emergency Management, Water Resources & Environment.

Election Results

Election	Name (Party)	Vote (%)	Cand. Spent	Ind. Exp. Support	Ind. Exp. Oppose
2016 General	Brian Mast (R)	201,488 (54%)	$2,819,457	$985,087	$3,400
	Randy Perkins (D)	161,918 (43%)	$10,817,736		$6,223,404
	Carla Spalding (I)	12,503 (3%)	$17,632		
2016 Primary	Brian Mast (R)	24,060 (38%)			
	Rebecca Negron (R)	16,216 (26%)			
	Carl Domino (R)	7,931 (13%)			
	Rick Kozell (R)	4,329 (7%)			

Republican Brian Mast won an open seat in 2016 to replace Democratic Rep. Patrick Murphy, who ran unsuccessfully for the Senate. Mast, who lost both legs while serving in the Army in Afghanistan, won a nasty contest with a businessman who had recently joined the Democratic Party.

Brian Mast was born in Grand Rapids, Michigan. After graduating from high school there, he followed in his father's footsteps and enlisted in the Army. He served under the elite Joint Special Operations Command as a bomb disposal expert. This meant, he wrote in his campaign bio, "that life was always dangerous and very often deadly." His task was to detect and destroy improvised explosive devices (IEDs). The final one that he found along a roadside in Kandahar, Afghanistan caused catastrophic injuries, including the loss of his legs below the knees, a portion of his forearm and a finger. He received numerous military honors.

As part of his recovery, Mast shared his expertise with the National Nuclear Security Administration's Office of Emergency Operations and the Bureau of Alcohol, Tobacco and Firearms. Following his retirement from the Army, he worked in counter-terrorism and national defense as an explosive specialist for the Transportation Security Administration. He served as a volunteer for the Israel Defense Forces. In 2016, Mast graduated with a degree in economics from Harvard University's online program. Another distinctive characteristic is that he always wears shorts, he said, because his prosthetics legs rip through his pants.

While recovering from his injuries, Mast vowed to serve in Congress. His opportunity came with the House seat in a swing district. He won the six-candidate Republican primary with 38 percent of the vote. The runner-up with 26 percent was Roberta Negron. As the wife of Senate president Joe Negron, she had the support of many Florida Republican leaders and raised $948,000.

The general election was another steep challenge for Mast. Democratic nominee Randy Perkins, who founded a lucrative debris-removal company in Florida following the devastation of Hurricane Andrew in 1992, self-financed $10.1 million of his $10.8 million campaign. In a campaign debate, Perkins showed little subtlety. He asked Mast about the health insurance coverage he receives as a veteran, and why "the sacrifices and service you provided for this country make you capable of solving issues" facing Congress. Mast raised $2.8 million for his campaign and received more than $3.5 million in support from the Congressional Leadership Fund. He won in November, 54%-43%. Mast won by fewer than 1,000 votes in St. Lucie County, but nearly doubled the vote for Perkins in Martin County.

He joined two House committees: Transportation and Infrastructure, where he has sought improvements in the water systems serving Lake Okeechobee to prevent what he called a potential environmental disaster, and Foreign Affairs, where he brought his military experience to bear. Following the election, Murphy said it was "very unlikely" that he would seek to re-claim his old House seat.

Palm Beach, Treasure Coast

Population		**Race and Ethnicity**		**Income**	
Total	717,984	White	69.1%	Median Income	$52,384 (218 out of 435)
Land area	1,513	Black	12.3%	Under $50,000	47.7%
Pop/ sq mi	474.6	Latino	14.8%	$50,000-$99,999	29.5%
Born in state	31.6%	Asian	2.1%	$100,000-$199,999	16.7%
		Two races	1.4%	$200,000 or more	6.0%
		Other	0.3%	Poverty Rate	13.2%
Age Groups		**Education**		**Health Insurance**	
Under 18	19.1%	H.S grad or less	39.0%	With health insurance coverage	84.9%
18-34	17.4%	Some college	31.2%		
35-64	39.6%	College Degree, 4 yr	18.6%		
Over 64	23.9%	Post grad	11.0%		
Work		**Military**		**Public Assistance**	
White Collar	35.5%	Veteran	10.8%	Cash public assistance income	1.6%
Sales and Service	47.4%	Active Duty	0.0%	Food stamp/SNAP benefits	9.0%
Blue Collar	17.1%				
Government	12.3%				

Voter Turnout			
2015 Total Citizens 18+	N/A	2016 House Turnout as % CVAP	N/A
2016 House turnout	375,918	2014 House Turnout as % CVAP	N/A

2012 Presidential Vote		
Mitt Romney	177,300	(52%)
Barack Obama	163,067	(48%)

2016 Presidential Vote		
Donald Trump	203,771	(53%)
Hillary Clinton	168,558	(44%)

Cook Partisan Voting Index: R+5

Urban Florida has fanned far across the swamplands from its original nuclei in beachfront resort communities. Once, metro Palm Beach was a narrow stretch along Lake Worth; now it runs inland almost halfway to Lake Okeechobee, spreading out from its original locus around the posh Breakers Hotel. Old beach towns such as Hobe Sound have become the hub of affluent developments that stretch all the way to Stuart in Martin County. Farther north, near the old town of Fort Pierce, are larger but more modest developments like Port St. Lucie, which had a population of only 330 in 1970. In 2015, it became the eighth largest city in Florida, with a population of 179,413, topping Fort Lauderdale. Of the nearly 300,000 in St. Lucie County, the Hispanic share has grown to 18 percent. Port St. Lucie was hit hard during the 2008 mortgage meltdown, resulting in more than 10,000 properties in foreclosure and an unemployment rate that surpassed 13 percent the following year. But by the end of 2016, the rate was down to 5.7 percent, a bit higher than the rest of Florida and the nation. Farther south, northern Palm Beach County is changing as well. The county, along with the state of Florida, subsidized the Scripps Research Institute's new center in Jupiter. That attracted several other biotechnology businesses to Jupiter. Mayor Todd Wodraska called the city "a biotechnology hub where important scientific advances are realized."

The 18th Congressional District includes all of Martin County, with its affluent towns of Stuart and Hobe Sound, as well as all of more modest St. Lucie County. To the south, about 40 percent of the district's population resides in the northern precincts of Palm Beach County, including Palm Beach Gardens, an area filled with gated communities and home to the Professional Golfers' Association of America. A few miles east of the PGA's official home is Jupiter, where the largest concentration of PGA golfers reside amid lush greenery and plush mansions. At least 28 members of the PGA Tour, plus many retired stars, live in a 20-mile stretch along the Atlantic Ocean, just north of Palm Beach. "Golfers can hardly step out of their mansions without bumping into each other," the *Wall Street Journal* reported in February 2016. Nearby, the $150 million Harbourside Place entertainment complex opened in 2014, including the Woods Jupiter restaurant owned by Tiger Woods.

The 2016 presidential election gave a big boost to the Republican ticket. And that's not because Donald Trump sent his guests and employees to the voting precincts from his Mar-a-Lago estate, which is a few miles down Route 1 -and in the 21st Congressional District. Trump won the 18th by an impressive 53%-44%, compared with Mitt Romney's 52%-48% local win over President Barack Obama in 2012. A notable feature of those numbers was the county breakdown: The Republican performance had a 10-point increase from 2012 to 2016 in its margin in the more-populous St. Lucie County, which more than doubled the change in Martin and the Palm Beach parts of the district. The GOP share of the vote was virtually unchanged in those other two counties. The district lines were not changed by the 2016 redistricting.

NINETEENTH DISTRICT

Francis Rooney (R)

Elected 2016, 1st term; b. Dec 04, 1953, Muskogee, OK; Georgetown University (DC), Bach. Deg., 1975; Georgetown University Law Center (DC), J.D., 1978; Roman Catholic; Married (Kathleen Rooney); 3 children; 2 grandchildren.

Elected Office: U.S Ambassador to the Holy See, 2005-2008.

Professional Career: Owner, Rooney Holdings, Inc.

DC Office: 120 CHOB 20515, 202-225-2536, Fax: 202-226-3547, francisrooney.house.gov.

State Offices: Cape Coral, 239-599-6033; Naples, 239-252-6225.

Committees: *Education & the Workforce*: Health, Employment, Labor & Pensions, Workforce Protections. *Foreign Affairs*: Europe, Eurasia & Emerging Threats, Western Hemisphere. *Joint Economic*.

Election Results

Election	Name (Party)	Vote (%)		Cand. Spent	Ind. Exp. Support	Ind. Exp. Oppose
2016 General	Francis Rooney (R)	239,225	(66%)	$4,831,905	$11,999	$31,399
	Robert Neeld (D)	123,812	(34%)	$12,491		
2016 Primary	Francis Rooney (R)	46,800	(53%)			
	Chauncey Goss (R)	26,520	(30%)			
	Dan Bongino (R)	15,434	(17%)			

Republican Francis Rooney won election in a 2016 contest in which his ample use of personal funds drove away serious competition. After his impressive success in building his own construction companies, and as a deep-pocket political contributor with high-level connections and assignments, he started a new career in the House at age 63.

Born in Oklahoma, Rooney earned his bachelor's and law degrees from Georgetown University. He spent more than three decades in business, serving as founder and chairman of Rooney Holdings Inc. and, after 2008, as chief executive officer of the family-owned Manhattan Construction Group, which is a subsidiary of Rooney Holdings. His many construction projects include the Texas Rangers Stadium with his friend George W. Bush, who was then the managing partner of the team; the presidential libraries in Texas for both Presidents Bush; the underground Capitol Visitors Center on the Capitol grounds, and the International Terminal at Hartsfield-Jackson Airport in Atlanta. He was a contributor to prominent Republican candidates, including seven-figure donations to Bush and Mitt Romney, and has been an active participant in GOP politics. Nominated by Bush, he served three years as the U.S. ambassador to the Vatican. Francis Rooney is not related to Florida Rep. Tom Rooney.

Before deciding to seek the open House seat, Rooney seriously considered in 2016 a bid for the Senate seat that had been opened by Marco Rubio's retirement. "It's very difficult in Florida to win a general Senate election in a presidential year without some coattails from a presidential nominee," he told *Politico* in early June in explaining why he decided not to seek the seat. "And a rational businessman might not want to take that bet." About two weeks later, Rubio changed his mind and was subsequently reelected.

The House seat unexpectedly was opened when Republican Curt Clawson decided in May 2016 not to seek a second term. Rooney's opponents in the primary had political experience: Sanibel councilman Chauncey Goss, whose father Porter Goss had held this House seat, and former Secret Service agent Dan Bongino, who had run for office in Maryland. Other prospective GOP candidates decided not to make the challenge. Rooney took 53 percent of the vote to 30 percent and 17 percent, respectively, for Goss and Bongino. Rooney raised about $3.9 million for the primary, of which $3.2 million was self-financed. The two other contenders raised about $300,000 each.

In the general, Rooney defeated Robert Neeld, 66%-34%. He contributed another $1 million from his pocket to that campaign, while Neeld raised $14,000. In the House, he got seats on the Education and the Workforce, and Foreign Affairs committees. He set as a top priority the use of federal funds to stop contamination of the Caloosahatchee and St. Lucie rivers caused by the release of water from Lake Okeechobee by the Army Corps of Engineers.

Southern Gulf Coast: Fort Myers, Naples

Population		Race and Ethnicity		Income	
Total	738,277	White	71.3%	Median Income	$51,510 (231 out of 435)
Land area	750	Black	7.6%		
Pop/ sq mi	983.9	Latino	18.5%		
Born in state	23.8%	Asian	1.4%	Under $50,000	48.3%
Age Groups		Two races	1.0%	$50,000-$99,999	29.9%
Under 18	17.8%	Other	0.3%	$100,000-$199,999	15.5%
18-34	16.8%	**Education**		$200,000 or more	6.3%
35-64	37.0%	H.S grad or less	40.6%	Poverty Rate	14.8%
Over 64	28.4%	Some college	28.8%	**Health Insurance**	
Work		College Degree, 4 yr	18.6%	With health insurance coverage	82.6%
White Collar	31.7%	Post grad	11.9%		
Sales and Service	50.5%	**Military**		**Public Assistance**	
Blue Collar	17.8%	Veteran	11.7%	Cash public assistance income	1.4%
Government	10.0%	Active Duty	0.0%	Food stamp/SNAP benefits	10.1%

Voter Turnout			
2015 Total Citizens 18+	543,249	2016 House Turnout as % CVAP	67%
2016 House turnout	363,166	2014 House Turnout as % CVAP	45%

2012 Presidential Vote		
Mitt Romney	195,051	(61%)
Barack Obama	124,784	(39%)

2016 Presidential Vote		
Donald Trump	227,096	(59%)
Hillary Clinton	143,001	(37%)
Gary Johnson	8,014	(2%)

Cook Partisan Voting Index: R+13

Florida's Gulf Coast is at the edge of the tropics, a physical environment once teeming with disease and inhospitable to advanced civilization, but now evolved into a model for retirement living. One of the earliest white settlements here was Fort Myers, built in 1850 as an Army post to pursue the Seminole Indians; in 1858, the last of the natives were driven out. For a century after that, this corner of Florida was mostly deserted, save for some small resort communities developed around wide, white-sand beaches with gentle breakers. The inlets and broad estuaries are perfect for boating, and the wetlands are graced with exotic birds. Thomas Edison had his winter home in Fort Myers, Henry Ford used to visit here, and tourists were drawn to beaches thick with seashells on nearby Sanibel and Captiva islands. But the local economy could not support many permanent residents. At the beginning of World War II, there were only 68,000 people living on the Gulf Coast from Bradenton south to Naples.

The climate and environment, and the fact that Florida has no state income or inheritance tax, soon attracted waves of affluent postwar suburbanites from the Midwest and Northeast. Developers such as Barron Collier, who financed the building of the Tamiami Trail across the soggy Everglades and designed Naples with the wealthy in mind, were determined to avoid the high-rise canyons that line the Atlantic from Palm Beach to Miami. Their alternative was to construct low-rise, city-style developments such as the retirement community of Cape Coral, located where the Caloosahatchee River completes its journey from Lake Okeechobee to San Carlos Bay.

When the recession hit in 2008, this Gulf Coast area suffered from a large inventory of housing. Recent home purchasers who were caught up in the housing boom discovered they had overpaid for their properties. The area had the nation's largest number of housing foreclosures, accounting for nearly half of the home sales. Local officials' predictions of a slow recovery initially were borne out: The Cape Coral-Fort Myers area lost more jobs than any other metropolitan area in the state in 2012. Two years later, business conditions had improved notably. A January 2015 business forecast projected Collier as the fastest-growing county in the state, with Lee close behind. From 2010 to 2015, their population had grown by 12 percent. In October 2016, Forbes rated the area number-one in the nation in future job growth with 3.9 percent during the next year. In a cautionary note, the Washington-based Economic Policy Institute ranked the area from Naples to Marco Island as third in the nation for income inequality. The public schools of Collier County have 62 percent of students receiving free or subsidized lunches.

The 19th Congressional District occupies the southern half of the habitable Gulf Coast below Tampa Bay. The 2016 redistricting made no changes. Nearly 30 percent of the residents here are over the age of 65. The 19th includes almost all of Lee County and about half of the population of Collier County, including Naples and Marco Island. The much larger inland portion of Collier is part of the 25th Congressional District, based in Miami-Dade. Over three-quarters of the district's residents live in Lee County, in Fort Myers, Cape Coral and Bonita Springs, and on Sanibel and Captiva islands. In a state where Republican registration rates often understate GOP voting strength, just 27 percent were registered Democrats, the lowest share of any Florida congressional district. The minor downside for Republicans: Donald Trump won 59 percent of the vote here, less than the 61 percent for Mitt Romney in 2012 and a smaller share than he received in five other Florida districts in 2016.

TWENTIETH DISTRICT

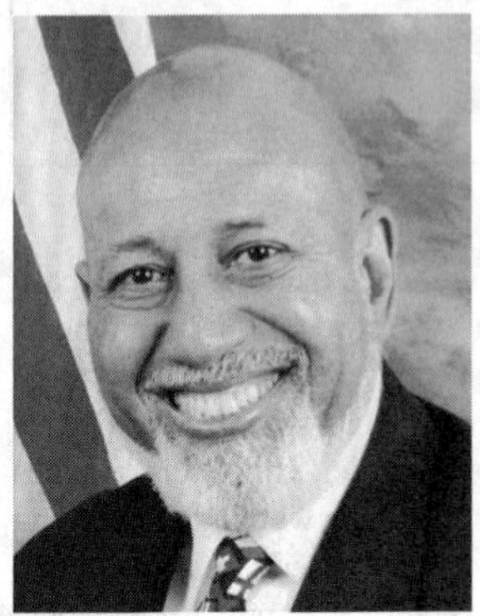

Alcee Hastings (D)

Elected 1992, 13th term; b. Sep 05, 1936, Altamonte Springs; Fisk University (TN), B.A.; Florida Agricultural and Mechanical University College of Law, J.D.; Howard University (DC), Att.; Crooms Academy (FL); African Methodist Episcopal; Divorced; 3 children.

Elected Office: Broward County Circuit Court judge, 1977-1979.

Professional Career: Practicing attorney, 1964-1977, 1989-1992; Federal judge, U.S. District Court, 1979-1989.

DC Office: 2353 RHOB 20515, 202-225-1313, Fax: 202-225-1171, alceehastings.house.gov.

State Offices: Fort Lauderdale, 954-733-2800; Mangonia Park, 561-469-7048.

Committees: *Joint Security & Cooperation in Europe (RMM)*. *Rules*: Legislative & Budget Process (RMM).

Group Ratings

	ADA	ACLU	AFL-CIO	LCV	ITI	COC	HAFA	ACU	CFG	FRC
2016	-	70%	-	37%	25%	58%	17%	0%	12%	0%
2015	90%	C	100%	97%	C	42%	C	4%	0%	0%

Almanac Ratings 2015

	Economy	Social	Foreign	Composite
Liberal	96%	97%	85%	92%
Conservative	4%	4%	15%	8%

Key Votes of the 114th Congress

1. Keystone Pipeline	N	5. Puerto Rico Debt	N	9. Offenses by Aliens	N
2. Trade Deals	N	6. Medical Marijuana	Y	10. Troops in Iraq	Y
3. Export-Import Bank	Y	7. Sanctuary Cities	N	11. Homeland Security $$	Y
4. Debt Ceiling Increase	Y	8. Armor-piercing Bullets	N	12. Trade Adjustment aid	Y

Election Results

Election	Name (Party)	Vote (%)	Cand. Spent	Ind. Exp. Support	Ind. Exp. Oppose
2016 General	Alcee Hastings (D)	222,914 (80%)	$704,269		
	Gary Stein (R)	54,646 (20%)			
2016 Primary	Alcee Hastings (D)	(100%)			

Prior winning percentages: 2014 (82%), 2012 (88%), 2010 (79%), 2008 (82%), 2006 (100%), 2004 (100%), 2002 (77%), 2000 (76%), 1998 (100%), 1996 (73%), 1994 (100%), 1992 (59%)

Alcee Hastings, a personable Democrat first elected in 1992, has shrugged off an assortment of scandals, including his impeachment for bribery and perjury when he was a federal judge in the 1980s. Today he remains a friendly and often candid figure with Democratic colleagues in the House and South Florida constituents.

Hastings had a relatively wide-ranging upbringing in the segregated America of the post-World War II decades. He grew up in a black suburb of Orlando and moved as a child to Jersey City and New York, where his parents worked as domestic servants for a rich Jewish family. He attended a Rosenwald school in Altamonte Springs, one of hundreds established for Southern blacks by Sears executive Julius Rosenwald. He graduated from Fisk University in Nashville and from Florida A&M law school in Tallahassee. From those beginnings, he made a rapid ascent, practicing law in Fort Lauderdale and finishing fourth in the five-candidate Democratic primary when he ran for the U.S. Senate in 1970, at age 34. He became a state judge in Broward County in 1977 and was confirmed as a federal judge in 1979.

Then his career took a sharp turn downward. He was charged with conspiring with a friend to take a $150,000 bribe and give two convicted swindlers light sentences. A Miami jury acquitted Hastings in 1983, but the friend was convicted. The U.S. Court of Appeals for the 11th Circuit called for impeachment in 1987 and referred the case to Congress. Hastings was impeached by the House on a vote of 413-3 and convicted by the Senate, 69-26. In the House, Democratic Rep. John Conyers of Michigan, a senior member of the Congressional Black Caucus, made the case for impeachment. As a footnote, during a 1997 investigation into the Federal Bureau of Investigation crime lab, the Department of Justice found that an agent falsely testified against Hastings. He and Conyers moved to reopen the case, but nothing came of it.

After his removal from the bench, Hastings in 1990 ran an abortive campaign for governor, then lost in a primary for secretary of state. When the 23rd District was created in 1992, he led in the primary 28%-27%. In the October runoff, he faced Palm Beach County legislator Lois Frankel, who blasted Hastings for his record. He responded, "The bitch is a racist." Hastings was helped by a ruling from federal Judge Stanley Sporkin that his removal from office was invalid because the full Senate did not hear the charges. The Supreme Court later ruled to the contrary in a case of another convicted federal judge in 1993, but by that time Hastings was in Congress. He won the runoff 58%-42%, with voting closely following racial lines. He won the general election 59%-31%. (Twenty years later, when Frankel ran successfully in an adjacent district, Hastings endorsed her and offered praise.) Since then, he has not had a serious primary or general election challenge.

In the House, Hastings' voting record has been mostly liberal, and his rhetoric has been proudly so. The *Almanac* vote ratings for 2015 ranked him among the more liberal half of House Democrats. He blasted a GOP-passed defense authorization bill in 2011 for going too far in the name of fighting terrorism. "It commits us to seeing a 'terrorist' in anyone who ever criticizes the United States in any country, including this one," he said. Pro-Israel groups are among his most active campaign contributors, and he has been a strong supporter of the Jewish state. In contrast to many House Democrats who boycotted the March 2015 appearance before Congress of Israeli Prime Minister Benjamin Netanyahu, Hastings said he agreed with Netanyahu that Europe had become increasingly dangerous for Jews.

In 2004, with the support of Republican Speaker Dennis Hastert, Hastings was elected president of the Organization for Security and Cooperation in the pan-European Parliamentary Assembly and served two one-year terms. In 2007, he became chairman of the counterpart U.S. commission. In 2006, the House passed his resolution condemning Iran for hosting a conference on Holocaust denial. The next year, Hastings pressed for the opening of Holocaust archives in Bad Arolsen, Germany, and three weeks later, the archives were opened. However, he drew the attention of ethics investigators in 2010 over whether he exceeded foreign travel stipends. He told the *Wall Street Journal* that he was generous in giving money to people he encountered and said: "You are all concerned about nickels and dimes, and I'm not. You know, in a taxicab in Kazakhstan, I don't have time to get a receipt - I don't speak Kazakh." The investigation was dropped in 2011. In September 2016, *Roll Call* listed Hastings as the second poorest member of Congress. His negative net worth of more than $2 million included many unpaid bills from his impeachment expenses.

Hastings retains a seat on the Rules Committee, an influential post that gives him a hand in discussing the terms for bringing bills to the floor. He irked conservatives in 2010 for his defense of a controversial "deem and pass" strategy for the health care overhaul that was briefly considered. He paraphrased an expression of Thomas Edison's: "There ain't no rule around here; we're trying to accomplish something." Taking an original stand, Hastings in 2008 called for a commission to consider expanding the size of the House beyond 435 members. That number, he pointed out, was established by statute in 1929 and can be changed by an act of Congress. He said there were too many constituents in each district for lawmakers to serve them adequately. In a perhaps less original stand, he noted during a Rules Committee hearing in 2015 that Texas was "a crazy state to begin with." When the Texas Republican delegation demanded an apology, he refused. As co-chairman of the bipartisan Florida delegation, he has worked on behalf of state-related issues.

Hastings has continued to draw - and survive - attention for issues apart from legislating. In December 2014, the House Ethics Committee dismissed charges of sexual harassment against him that had been brought by a Republican congressional aide, but added that his behavior had been "less than professional." Hastings has opened the door to retirement. Following his reelection in 2014, he said that he would seek at least one more term and then will assess the prospects for Democrats regaining control of the House. That opened the door to stepping down in 2018, at age 82. Whenever he exits, he likely won't go quietly. Two weeks before the 2016 election at a rally of Hillary Clinton supporters, he sought to encourage party activists by describing Donald Trump as a "sentient pile of excrement."

Parts of Fort Lauderdale and West Palm Beach

Demographics data for new House districts were not prepared by the Census Bureau prior to our editorial deadline.

Voter Turnout

2016 House Turnout as % CVAP	N/A	2016 House turnout	277,560

2012 Presidential Vote information unavailable due to recent redistricting.

2016 Presidential Vote		
Hillary Clinton	231,595	(80%)
Donald Trump	52,250	(18%)

Cook Partisan Voting Index: D+31

In the morning shadow of the high-rise condominiums that line the Atlantic Ocean, beyond the quiet waters that separate the barrier islands from the mainland, and a few blocks off old U.S. 1, are the African-American neighborhoods of South Florida's Gold Coast. They are clusters of older stucco homes and commercial storefronts, ranging from upper-middle-class enclaves to rundown slums. These neighborhoods, largely populated by the working poor and with relatively few seniors, are bypassed by most tourists.

To the west is a land of swamps and drainage canals, with some farms and citrus groves. Some people live in migrant worker camps, while others live in small towns around Lake Okeechobee. The water quality in the lake has raised alarms on both the southeast and southwest coasts of Florida. Sugar is a big industry throughout this part of Florida. But in 2008, the South Florida Water Management District approved Republican Gov. Charlie Crist's proposal to buy much of the land owned by U.S. Sugar Corp. around Lake Okeechobee for $1.35 billion, with most farming originally scheduled for phase-out within seven years. That would allow water to pass over land from the lake, through the Everglades, to the Gulf of Mexico.

The recession forced the plan to be delayed and scaled back to $197 million. Sugar farmers continued to battle against it, while environmentalists sought its revival. As of November 2016, the start of water storage in the lake was delayed until 2020 and plans for the state to purchase U.S. Sugar have been on hold. Meanwhile, sugar production has been booming. In June 2016, sugar cane growers in Palm Beach County reported the largest crop in their history, the result of record rainfall that disrupted production. The sugar industry in Florida employs more than 14,000 workers, and sugar cane has remained the most valuable field crop in Florida. The Port of Palm Beach has become the fourth-largest container port in Florida. Much of the cargo is sugar-related, and the commerce is largely with Caribbean islands.

The 20th Congressional District of Florida gathers together many of South Florida's black neighborhoods in a geographically contrived, but demographically coherent, constituency. The body of the district is in the Everglades. The bulk of the district's population resides in the two arms that extend east from the Everglades, with one going into West Palm Beach and the other into Fort Lauderdale. These arms embrace most of the 21st and 22nd Congressional Districts.

The top arm moves through northern Palm Beach County, past high-income Wellington and into West Palm Beach and Palm Beach Lakes. In West Palm, a new $144 million home for the Washington Nationals and Houston Astros opened for baseball spring training in 2017. The lower arm of the district reaches into Broward County to take in African American areas in Fort Lauderdale, Lauderhill, North Lauderdale and Pompano Beach. Lauderdale Lakes, after coming close to insolvency in 2011, made progress in reducing its debt and was scheduled to repay it in 2019. Redistricting here made very small tweaks to the 20th: removing nearly half of rural Hendrie County and adding a few precincts in Fort Lauderdale. The population in Broward is about twice that in Palm Beach County.

Overall, the population is 51 percent black and 22 percent Hispanic, and narrowly surpassed the Dade County-based 24th District for the largest black population. President Barack Obama in 2012 won this district, 83%-17%, his second-best in the state behind the 24th District. Hillary Clinton's lead here dropped slightly to 80%-18%.

A week after Donald Trump was elected president, one of his lawyers quietly informed Palm Beach International Airport that Trump had dropped a $100 million lawsuit he had filed in 1995 to re-route airplane traffic and reduce noise over his Mar-a-Lago estate. Palm Beach County said its lawyers had spent $600,000 fighting the lawsuit. The airport is in the 20th District. Mar-a-Lago is in the 21st.

TWENTY-FIRST DISTRICT

Lois Frankel (D)

Elected 2012, 3rd term; b. May 16, 1948, New York, NY (Manhattan); Boston University (MA), B.A., 1970; Georgetown University Law Center (DC), J.D., 1973; Jewish; Divorced; 1 child.

Elected Office: FL House, 1986-1992, 1994-2002; Mayor, West Palm Beach, 2003-2011.

Professional Career: Law clerk, Hon. Judge David Norman, 1973-1974; Assistant public defender, West Palm Beach, 1974-1978; Practicing lawyer, 1978-2003.

DC Office: 1037 LHOB 20515, 202-225-9890, Fax: 202-225-1224, frankel.house.gov.

Committees: *Foreign Affairs*: Middle East & North Africa, Terrorism, Nonproliferation & Trade. *Transportation & Infrastructure*: Highways & Transit, Water Resources & Environment.

Group Ratings

	ADA	ACLU	AFL-CIO	LCV	ITI	COC	HAFA	ACU	CFG	FRC
2016	-	94%	-	100%	67%	57%	14%	4%	4%	0%
2015	90%	C	100%	100%	C	47%	C	4%	0%	0%

Almanac Ratings 2015

	Economy	Social	Foreign	Composite
Liberal	98%	100%	84%	94%
Conservative	2%	0%	16%	6%

Key Votes of the 114th Congress

1. Keystone Pipeline	N	5. Puerto Rico Debt	Y	9. Offenses by Aliens	N
2. Trade Deals	N	6. Medical Marijuana	Y	10. Troops in Iraq	Y
3. Export-Import Bank	Y	7. Sanctuary Cities	N	11. Homeland Security $$	Y
4. Debt Ceiling Increase	Y	8. Armor-piercing Bullets	N	12. Trade Adjustment aid	Y

Election Results

Election	Name (Party)	Vote (%)	Cand. Spent	Ind. Exp. Support	Ind. Exp. Oppose
2016 General	Lois Frankel (D)	210,606 (63%)	$554,941		
	Paul Spain (R)	118,038 (35%)	$25,467		
	Michael Trout (I)	7,217 (2%)			
2016 Primary	Lois Frankel (D)	(100%)			

Prior winning percentages: 2014 (58%), 2012 (55%)

Democrat Lois Frankel won election in 2012 to succeed Republican firebrand Allen West, who ran and lost in what he thought was the more hospitable 18th District. In the minority party, Frankel has made efforts to reach across the aisle, including as co-chair of the Congressional Women's Issues Caucus.

Frankel was born in New York City and raised in Great Neck on Long Island. Her father was in manufacturing, and her mother was a homemaker. Frankel was a tomboy growing up and enjoyed playing sports, especially basketball. She studied psychology at Boston University with the intent of becoming a psychiatrist, but her career plans changed when she became involved in the social movements of the late 1960s. "I was a student activist, and I was involved in antiwar protesting and the women's liberation movement," Frankel told National *Journal*. "There were so many movements … it was all bubbling." She has joked that she "majored in protests."

Frankel got her law degree from Georgetown University and spent a year as a law clerk before moving to West Palm Beach. She became a public defender and advocate for numerous social causes.

Frankel won an open state House seat in 1986 and quickly rose to become the first woman minority leader in Florida. She also wrote the state's first AIDS law, which ensured confidentiality in testing. She ran unsuccessfully against Alcee Hastings for a new House seat in 1992, losing the Democratic primary in a runoff, 57%-43%.

After term limits forced Frankel to leave the Florida House, she thought about challenging Gov. Jeb Bush in 2002, but withdrew before the primary. She ran for mayor of West Palm Beach in 2003 and defeated incumbent Joel Daves. Though she compiled what the *South Florida Sun-Sentinel* described as an "impressive" record, she angered several labor unions when the city laid off workers, and she developed a reputation for being abrasive.

In March 2011, Frankel announced that she would challenge West, a freshman who was an outspoken adherent of the tea party movement. For nearly a year, Frankel and another Democrat, political newcomer Patrick Murphy, struggled to remain financially competitive with West. When West announced that he would run in the neighboring Treasure Coast district, made more GOP-friendly by redistricting, Murphy continued his challenge to West. Instead, Frankel faced a primary with Broward County Commissioner Kristin Jacobs. They had nearly identical stances on issues, but Frankel had the backing of party leaders. She was endorsed by Hastings and got a rare visit from House Minority Leader Nancy Pelosi eight days before the primary. She coasted to a 61%-39% win.

In the general, Frankel attacked Republican nominee Adam Hasner for his support of Wisconsin Rep. Paul Ryan's budget plan, which introduced premium support – vouchers to its critics -- into the Medicare program, and for his stance against abortion rights. An ad by the House Republican "Young Guns" program, later pulled because of inaccuracy, accused Frankel of frivolous spending while mayor. Frankel emphasized her work with small businesses to create incentives for more jobs. As each candidate tried to avoid sounding extreme, the Sun-Sentinel remarked that they had "shed their past personas like pythons in the Everglades." *The Miami Herald* endorsed Frankel, citing her "longer familiarity" with the district. Its Democratic lean helped her pull out a 55%-45% win. Each candidate spent $3.4 million.

Arriving in the House minority, Frankel made alliances with conservative Republicans. During the 2014 State of the Union speech by President Barack Obama, she sought to make a statement of civility by sitting next to Republican Rep. Ileana Ros-Lehtinen of Florida, with whom Frankel worked on foreign affairs issues. On the Transportation and Infrastructure Committee, she served in 2014 on the House-Senate conference committee that reached a final agreement on a water resources bill; it included additional dredging for expansion of Port Everglades plus water conservation and supply in the Everglades swamps. She joined another public works deal in 2016 on a water resources bill that delivered $2 billion for restoration of the Everglades.

Frankel joined two South Florida colleagues among the 25 House Democrats who voted to disapprove of the Obama administration's agreement with Iran on its nuclear program. "It legitimizes Iran's nuclear program after 15 years and gives Iran access to billions of dollars without a commitment to cease its terrorist activity," she said. In 2017, Frankel became co-chair of the bipartisan Congressional Women's Caucus with Republican Rep. Susan Brooks of Indiana, and pledged to find common ground on "issues important to the advancement of women and girls."

When the state Supreme Court redistricting order in August 2015 threw Frankel into the same district with Democratic Rep. Ted Deutch, the two of them pledged to avoid a showdown. For Frankel, the logical choice was to run in the Palm Beach County-based 21st District. That forced Deutch to run in the Broward-based 22nd District, which was a bit less Democratic but included his home in Boca Raton. Each easily won reelection against an under-financed Republican challenger. Frankel had a rematch against Paul Spain, a retired financial adviser, and raised her victory margin to 63%-35%.

Southern Palm Beach County

Demographics data for new House districts were not prepared by the Census Bureau prior to our editorial deadline.

Voter Turnout

2016 House Turnout as % CVAP	N/A	2016 House turnout	335,861

2012 Presidential Vote information unavailable due to recent redistricting.

2016 Presidential Vote		
Hillary Clinton	206,239	(58%)
Donald Trump	137,490	(39%)

Cook Partisan Voting Index: D+9

When the first millionaires came to Palm Beach in the 1920s to winter in their new mansions, there was virtually nothing man-made between Palm Beach and Miami. In 1920, Dade, Broward and Palm Beach counties boasted a mere 66,000 residents. By 1950, the combined population of the three counties had jumped to almost 700,000, and the beachfront areas had largely been incorporated and developed. But the interior regions of the counties, near where Florida's turnpike would soon be laid out, remained marshy, sparsely inhabited and ripe for development. As the coastal areas were filling up, the inland swamps were being drained, abetted by a sequence of canals and levees built by the state in response to flooding from a series of hurricanes in 1947.

More than 3.3 million people inhabited Broward and Palm Beach counties in 2015, an increase from 3.1 million in 2010. Palm Beach has 1.4 million. The Palm Beach area remains, as it has been since the 1920s, the precinct of the very rich. It was the favorite playground of high-stakes swindler Bernard Madoff - and many of his now unhappy former clients. Consider Palm Beach, the great beach resort of the 1920s, where rich WASPs bought Addison Mizner's pseudo-Mediterranean confections as a change of pace from their snow-covered Tudor and Georgian mansions. The top Rolls Royce dealer in the world is in Palm Beach. Wellington is an international site for equestrian events, including polo. High-speed train service from West Palm Beach to Miami, with a new station in West Palm, was expected to start in summer 2017.

The new 21st District is entirely in Palm Beach County. Its ocean-front communities start at the north with Palm Beach, which includes President Donald Trump's Mar-a-Lago club hotel. As the new winter White House, the town has received a tourist boost. John Kennedy was the most recent president in part-time residence here. Palm Beach is separate from the mainland and accessible on two bridges or by continuing to the south on South Ocean Boulevard. To the south, Lake Worth, Boynton Beach and Delray Beach include narrow ocean-front locales, but each of these cities sprawl several miles to the west. Boca Raton, the next city to the south on the ocean, is in the 22nd District. Delray Beach, the site in 1956 of a civil rights showdown over access to the beaches, now hosts international tennis events and has a large Haitian community. The district winds through a series of largely unincorporated residential communities to the west. Subdivisions extend far beyond the Florida Turnpike. This district combines parts of the old 21st and 22nd districts, each of which included substantial parts of both Palm Beach and Broward counties, but with the old 21st to the west and not touching the ocean. The redistricters redrew the lines so that the new 21st has a large section on the ocean, but is entirely in Palm Beach County.

Each of the former districts was solidly Democratic, as are the new ones. The new 21st has voted a bit more Democratic in recent presidential elections than its counterpart. With the new lines, President Barack Obama in 2012 would have won, 60%-39%. Hillary Clinton took the district, 58%-39%. Her vote became a problem for Democrats because they increasingly need to roll up their vote in south Florida to balance setbacks elsewhere in the state.

TWENTY-SECOND DISTRICT

Ted Deutch (D)

Elected 2010, 4th term; b. May 07, 1966, Bethlehem, PA; University of Michigan, B.A., 1988; University of Michigan Law School, J.D., 1990; Jewish; Married (Jill Deutch); 3 children (twins).

Elected Office: FL Senate, 2006-2010.

Professional Career: Practicing attorney, 1991-2010.

DC Office: 2447 RHOB 20515, 202-225-3001, Fax: 202-225-5974, teddeutch.house.gov.

Committees: *Ethics (RMM)*. *Foreign Affairs*: Asia & the Pacific, Middle East & North Africa (RMM). *Judiciary*: Courts, Intellectual Property & Internet, Crime, Terrorism, Homeland Security & Investigations.

Group Ratings

	ADA	ACLU	AFL-CIO	LCV	ITI	COC	HAFA	ACU	CFG	FRC
2016	-	94%	-	100%	50%	57%	12%	0%	4%	0%
2015	85%	C	96%	66%	C	42%	C	0%	0%	0%

Almanac Ratings 2015

	Economy	Social	Foreign	Composite
Liberal	91%	97%	78%	88%
Conservative	9%	4%	22%	12%

Key Votes of the 114th Congress

1. Keystone Pipeline	N	5. Puerto Rico Debt	Y	9. Offenses by Aliens	N
2. Trade Deals	N	6. Medical Marijuana	Y	10. Troops in Iraq	N
3. Export-Import Bank	Y	7. Sanctuary Cities	N	11. Homeland Security $$	Y
4. Debt Ceiling Increase	Y	8. Armor-piercing Bullets	N	12. Trade Adjustment aid	Y

Election Results

Election	Name (Party)	Vote (%)	Cand. Spent	Ind. Exp. Support	Ind. Exp. Oppose
2016 General	Ted Deutch (D)	199,113 (59%)	$1,418,545		
	Andrea Leigh McGee (R)	138,737 (41%)	$18,457		
2016 Primary	Ted Deutch (D)	(100%)			

Prior winning percentages: 2014 (100%), 2012 (78%), 2010 (63%)

Democrat Ted Deutch, who won a special election in 2010, is a liberal with a staunchly pro-Israel posture on foreign policy and a relatively easy-going style. He has become an active legislator, with a knack for making bipartisan deals.

Deutch has working-class roots in Bethlehem, Pennsylvania, where his father ran a small painter contracting company and his mother kept the books. His parents did not go to college and were determined that their five children would. He excelled in high school and was class president for four years. During that period, heart disease forced his father into early retirement and he spent a lot of time watching CNN. Deutch said that sitting next to his dad discussing what was unfolding on the news channel fueled his budding interest in current events. At the University of Michigan, Deutch got his bachelor's in political science and a law degree. He volunteered in political campaigns, including for Democratic presidential candidate Joe Biden in 1987. He caught the eye of an academic advisor who encouraged him to apply for a Harry S Truman Scholarship, which recognizes students such as Deutch with potential for public service careers.

After law school, Deutch specialized in real estate law. That provided his initial entry to Washington, at a firm hired to sell off government assets from the savings and loan crisis. With his wife and their children, they moved to Boca Raton, where Ted's older brother, also a lawyer, hired him to handle his law firm's real estate business. Deutch got active in Florida politics. He worked on issues and raised money for Bill Clinton's two presidential campaigns. He also lobbied for pro-Israel causes. In 2006, he was elected to the Florida Senate. During three years in Tallahassee, he authored two signature measures: a bill putting a surcharge on tobacco products to help pay for smoking prevention programs and cancer research, and a bill barring the state from investing pension funds in any enterprise that aided Iran's effort to attain nuclear weapons or that abetted genocide in the Darfur region of Sudan.

When Democratic Rep. Robert Wexler resigned to head a Middle East think tank, Deutch announced for the seat and seemed a natural successor. His liberal, pro-Israel politics appealed to the area's many Jewish retirees, and his state Senate seat filled half of the congressional district. Deutch faced minimal opposition in the Democratic primary, which was tantamount to election in a district where Democrats outnumbered Republicans 2-to-1. In the general election, his Republican opponent was West Palm Beach business consultant Ed Lynch, who tried to make the race a referendum on the Obama administration and its health care bill. Lynch joined national Republican leaders in calling for repeal. Deutch maintained that the changes would improve access to health care for people without insurance, for those who had been denied insurance because of pre-existing medical problems, and for seniors who rely on Medicare for their prescription drugs. Deutch won 62%-35%, outspending his opponent $1.7 million to $117,000.

With seats on the Foreign Affairs and Judiciary committees, he displayed a savvy legislative instinct, even after Republicans took House control in 2010. He worked across the aisle with fellow Floridian

Tom Rooney on a bill that was enacted to help homeless veterans, and with Scott Rigell of Virginia on a House-passed bill to protect consumers from contaminated drywall. He has drawn attention for his innovative reform proposals. One was a constitutional amendment to ban all corporate money in politics. That later evolved into his Democracy for All Amendment, which would overturn recent Supreme Court rulings that reduced restrictions on money in politics. When a bipartisan group of congressional leaders quietly added a rider to the December 2014 omnibus spending bill that removed some restrictions on campaign contributions to political parties, Deutch sought unsuccessfully to force a House vote.

Deutch has been persistent on foreign policy conflicts. He got a provision in the 2012 Iran sanctions law that required companies to disclose to the Securities and Exchange Commission their business dealings with Iran. As ranking Democrat on the Middle East and North Africa Subcommittee, he has cooperated with Republican Rep. Ileana Ros-Lehtinen of South Florida. Deutch became a go-to guy for his many Jewish constituents and the broader pro-Israel lobby in Washington. In 2014, he helped to write the Iran Threat Reduction Act, which imposed additional transparency and human rights requirements on Iran. He was outspoken after Secretary of State John Kerry concluded the agreement because, Deutch said, it failed to address "too many issues I have long raised as essential to any nuclear deal with Iran." Later, he filed a bill that made it easier to impose sanctions on Iran for violations of the agreement. When many Democrats protested the March 2015 speech to Congress by Israeli Prime Minister Benjamin Netanyahu, Deutch welcomed him as part of the formal committee that escorted him into the House chamber. In September 2016, the House passed a resolution that he filed with Ros-Lehtinen that affirmed the U.S. military-assistance agreement with Israel.

Republicans have not seriously challenged Deutch since he was first elected, though the 2016 redistricting reduced his share of the vote.

Northern Broward, Boca Raton

Demographics data for new House districts were not prepared by the Census Bureau prior to our editorial deadline.

Voter Turnout

2016 House Turnout as % CVAP	N/A	2016 House turnout	337,850

2012 Presidential Vote information unavailable due to recent redistricting.

2016 Presidential Vote		
Hillary Clinton	202,357	(56%)
Donald Trump	146,229	(41%)

Cook Partisan Voting Index: D+6

The barrier islands of Florida's Gold Coast have been developed in spasms of land speculation, not just as vacation places and retirement homes but as embodiments of dreams and fantasies. Addison Mizner built the Boca Raton Resort and Club in 1926. The city of Boca Raton sports the stylish Mizner Park, a collection of upscale stores. Clyde Beatty brought his circus to winter in tiny Fort Lauderdale in the 1930s (locals complained about the roaring lions). Back in the 1950s, many of these beachfront communities were "restricted," which meant no Jews were allowed. Today, the many Jewish retirees in Broward from New York and elsewhere in the Northeast are part of the eighth-largest Jewish community in the nation.

The towns and cities that now populate the western portions of Broward County were generally incorporated in a relatively brief spurt during the late 1950s and early 1960s. This helped fuel yet another boom in Florida real estate, as people flocked to the new developments. It wasn't just retirees and developers who took an interest in the region either. Westinghouse Electric Corp. initially invested in Coral Springs in the 1960s as a sort of "urban laboratory" for products such as central air conditioning, motion detecting lights, security systems and fully electric kitchens. In 1981, IBM developed its first personal computer at a lab in Boca Raton. Also in Broward are the cities of Coral Springs, Margate, Parkland and Deerfield Beach (named for the numerous deer that once roamed the banks of the local river).

Downtown Fort Lauderdale, separated from the beach by miles of canals, is the site of the Museum of Art Fort Lauderdale, the Broward Center for the Performing Arts, and the International Swimming Hall of Fame. Along with neighboring Wilton Manors, it became the home of choice for many gay people. In 2016, the Census Bureau reported that Fort Lauderdale had the highest percentage of same-sex couple households of any mid-sized or large city in the nation; Wilton Manors led the small cities. The housing market collapse hit the area hard and home prices initially were slow to recover. An earlier forecast that the recovery would take until 2030 was accelerated by a decade. *Forbes* reported that Fort Lauderdale in 2016 had an 18 percent increase in the average price of home sales, which was the highest in the nation. In 2016, Port Everglades slipped to third in the world for the number of passengers, behind the port of Miami and Port Canaveral. It has plans to deepen its channel to accommodate larger ships, especially container cargo. Planners envision an increase of 1,500 jobs.

The new 22nd Congressional District of Florida traded large parts of Palm Beach County and received comparable portions of Broward. The district continues to include the southeast corner of Palm Beach, chiefly Boca Raton, where the azure fountains and red-tiled roofs of today's Boca Raton Resort & Club bespeak a vision of a holiday Florida, a bit mannered and antique to today's eye, but still exuberant and benefiting from tasteful refurbishing. After moving through coastal parts of Pompano Beach and Fort Lauderdale, the district includes parts of upscale Plantation but loops around African-American precincts, placed in the 20th District. What was a Republican enclave until the 1990s has become a reliably Democratic district. With the new lines, Democrats have a 14 percentage point registration advantage, and President Barack Obama led Mitt Romney here in 2012, 55%-44%. Hillary Clinton took the new 22nd, 56%-41%, two points lower than her vote in the 21st to the north.

TWENTY-THIRD DISTRICT

Debbie Wasserman Schultz (D)

Elected 2004, 7th term; b. Sep 27, 1966, Forest Hills (Queens), NY; University of Florida, B.A.; University of Florida, M.A.; Jewish; Married (Steve Schultz); 3 children.

Elected Office: FL House, 1992-2000, Minority Leader pro tem., 1999-2000; FL Senate, 2000-2004.

Professional Career: Legislative aide, 1989-1992.

DC Office: 1114 LHOB 20515, 202-225-7931, Fax: 202-226-2052, wassermanschultz.house.gov.

State Offices: Aventura, 305-936-5724; Sunrise, 954-845-1179.

Committees: *Appropriations*: Energy & Water Development & Related Agencies, Legislative Branch, Military Construction, Veterans Affairs & Related Agencies (RMM). *Budget*.

Group Ratings

	ADA	ACLU	AFL-CIO	LCV	ITI	COC	HAFA	ACU	CFG	FRC
2016	-	82%	-	100%	67%	50%	11%	0%	4%	0%
2015	85%	C	95%	89%	C	44%	C	0%	0%	10%

Almanac Ratings 2015

	Economy	Social	Foreign	Composite
Liberal	90%	89%	85%	88%
Conservative	10%	11%	15%	12%

Key Votes of the 114th Congress

1. Keystone Pipeline	N	5. Puerto Rico Debt	N	9. Offenses by Aliens	N
2. Trade Deals	Y	6. Medical Marijuana	N	10. Troops in Iraq	N
3. Export-Import Bank	Y	7. Sanctuary Cities	N	11. Homeland Security $$	Y
4. Debt Ceiling Increase	Y	8. Armor-piercing Bullets	N	12. Trade Adjustment aid	Y

Election Results

Election	Name (Party)	Vote	(%)	Cand. Spent	Ind. Exp. Support	Ind. Exp. Oppose
2016 General	Debbie Wasserman Schultz (D). ...	183,225	(57%)	$3,964,133	$670,231	$230
	Joe Kaufman (R)........................	130,818	(41%)	$104,454		
2016 Primary	Debbie Wasserman Schultz (D).	28,279	(57%)			
	Tim Canova (D)........................	21,504	(43%)			

Prior winning percentages: 2014 (63%), 2012 (63%), 2010 (60%), 2008 (77%), 2006 (100%), 2004 (70%)

Debbie Wasserman Schultz, a hard-charging Democrat elected in 2004, experienced an unexpectedly tumultuous summer of 2016. After she was forced out as chair of the Democratic National Committee as the party convention convened in Philadelphia, she then endured her toughest political challenge in the Democratic primary for her seat, which became an extension of the presidential-primary conflict between Hillary Clinton and Bernie Sanders. Meanwhile, she remains interested in a top leadership post in the House when vacancies open.

Like many of her constituents, Wasserman Schultz was born in Queens. She grew up on Long Island, where she ran for student council every year and always lost. She got bachelor's and master's degrees from the University of Florida. In her last year at school, she sent out 180 resumes to legislators in Florida and New York and got five interviews. Florida State Rep. Peter Deutsch, a Democrat and former New Yorker from Broward County, gave her a summer job and then appointed her as his legislative aide. In 1992, he ran for the House and urged Wasserman Schultz to run for his seat in the legislature. She did, knocking on doors for six months and finishing far ahead of four opponents in the Democratic primary. At age 26, she became the youngest woman elected to the state House. She served eight years there, including two as minority leader, followed by four in the state Senate. She called herself "a pragmatic liberal," and she sponsored a controversial law to require an equal number of men and women on state boards and a bill that failed to pass requiring dry cleaners and some other businesses to charge the same prices for women as for men.

When Deutsch ran in 2004 for the Democratic nomination for an open Senate seat, Wasserman Schultz again moved to replace him. By February 2004, she had lined up endorsements from Minority Leader Nancy Pelosi and six of Florida's seven House Democrats. Wasserman Schultz ultimately collected more than $1 million for what turned out to be a non-contest in the decisive Democratic primary, since no one else filed to run. Wasserman Schultz called for repeal of the Bush-era tax cuts, a reduction in the budget deficit, greater use of diplomacy overseas, improved prescription drug coverage, gay civil rights and abortion rights. Against a Republican who attacked the "homosexual agenda" in the public schools, she won 70%-30%. For the next decade, she did not face a serious challenge, allowing her to channel campaign contributions to her colleagues from a wide spectrum of Democratic interests.

In the House, Wasserman Schultz has had a mostly liberal voting record, although she has been more centrist on foreign policy. She helped found the Cuba Democracy Caucus, a bipartisan group that works to thwart efforts to loosen the U.S. trade embargo with the island nation. She has been one of the Florida delegation's most ardent opponents of offshore oil drilling, declaring after the 2010 BP oil spill in the Gulf of Mexico that "our country needs to run on something other than oil." In 2012, she worked with then-Judiciary Committee Chairman Lamar Smith of Texas to enact a bill giving law enforcement additional authority to combat child pornography while imposing tougher penalties on offenders. The House also passed her bill that year to curb tax-return identity theft.

Her blazing ascension up the leadership ladder began in 2006 when she was appointed co-chairwoman of the Democratic Congressional Campaign Committee's "Red to Blue" program. Working closely with then-Chairman Rahm Emanuel, now Chicago mayor, she became a party spokeswoman and a mentor to Democratic recruits. When Democrats won House control that year, Majority Whip James Clyburn tapped her as a chief deputy whip. She snagged a seat on the Appropriations Committee, and immediately became a "cardinal" as chairwoman of the Legislative Branch Subcommittee. She took charge of the Capitol Visitors Center project, which was plagued by cost overruns, and extracted commitments on costs and completion dates. She pushed successfully for a unionization vote at the Government Accountability Office. In 2017, she became the ranking minority member of the Military Construction and Veterans Affairs Subcommittee.

In the 2008 election season, Wasserman Schultz was criticized by liberal bloggers when she refused to campaign as part of her DCCC duties against the three Cuban-American House Republicans from South Florida. They were facing unusually strong Democratic challenges, and ultimately all three were reelected. Also in 2008, Wasserman Schultz was co-chair of Hillary Rodham Clinton's presidential effort in Florida and nationally, and she was vice chair of the DCCC's incumbent retention program. A *National Journal* poll of party insiders in 2009 predicted she had the brightest political future of anyone on Capitol Hill.

Her success seemed all the more impressive when she announced in March 2009 that for much of the previous year she had been battling breast cancer. Although her tumor was in the early stages, which would typically require only surgery and radiation, she said that she elected to have a double mastectomy after learning that as an Ashkenazi Jew, she had a greater predisposition to recurrence. The mother of three school-aged children, Wasserman Schultz was diagnosed just after turning 40. "I didn't want it to define me," she told *The New York Times* of her illness. "I didn't want my name to be 'Debbie Wasserman Schultz, who is currently battling breast cancer.'"

The foreign policy pursuits of President Barack Obama forced Wasserman Schultz to navigate tricky terrain. As a long-time critic of the Cuban regime, she offered only limited and murky support when the president in December 2014 announced breakthrough initiatives to Cuba. "While I have always been opposed to unearned changes in the status of our relationship with Cuba, I will continue to work with the administration … to support policies that benefit the Cuban people and do not further entrench the Castro regime," she said. When many House Democrats, including some Jewish members, protested the March 2015 speech to Congress by Israeli Prime Minister Benjamin Netanyahu, she carefully said, "Israel is an issue that should not be made partisan." In what became for many a test of party loyalty in September 2015, her decision to support Obama's nuclear deal with Iran led to strong objections from her many Jewish constituents and party contributors, and ultimately caused political backfire for her at home.

In 2011, Wasserman Schultz beat out former Ohio Gov. Ted Strickland to take the helm of the DNC, with Vice President Joe Biden citing "her tenacity, her strength, her fighting spirit, and her ability to overcome adversity." Vowing that the party would be "laser-focused on the economy" as it sought to reelect Obama, she was a ferocious Republican critic. Having once declared that the country needed to run on something other than oil, she blamed the GOP for soaring gasoline prices in May 2011, citing "ridiculous, unacceptable subsidies to oil companies and massive tax breaks that even they have said they don't need." Later, she blasted House Budget Committee Chairman Paul Ryan's budget blueprint because it would "allow insurance companies to deny you coverage and drop you for pre-existing conditions" - a claim that the fact-checking website *PolitiFact* judged to be false. Republicans were outraged in September 2012 when she contended that Israel's U.S. ambassador had said that "what the Republicans are doing is dangerous for Israel," then accused the conservative-leaning *Washington Examiner* newspaper of "deliberately" misquoting her, even though her statement was captured on video.

Wasserman Schultz was frequently deployed in 2012 as a campaign surrogate for Obama, attending hundreds of events across the nation. But she developed a strained relationship with Obama campaign officials, who privately accused her of coming across as too partisan on television. They also reportedly wondered if Obama had made the right decision in selecting her for the DNC. Election Night's results served as her vindication: Not only did Obama win with substantial support from women and Jewish voters, two constituencies that Wasserman Schultz cultivated, but he captured Florida, a state where Republican Mitt Romney enjoyed a sizable lead in pre-election polls. With Pelosi staying on as minority leader, Wasserman Schultz had no apparent promotion in store in the House, and Obama's aides saw little political benefit in dumping a loyal soldier.

After the election, Wasserman Schultz continued her tough talk. As she told *Politico* in 2013: "I don't really do anything halfway." She helped lead the charge that the Republican Party was engaging in a "war on women," an expression meant to highlight the gender gap between the parties. She fiercely challenged attacks on the Affordable Care Act and predicted on CNN in November 2013: "I think actually that Democrats will be able to run on Obamacare as an advantage" in the future. Her comments occasionally landed her in hot water. In a visit to Wisconsin in September 2014, she said GOP Gov. Scott Walker "has given women the back of his hand. ... What Republican tea party extremists like Scott Walker are doing is, they are grabbing us by the hair and pulling us back." After causing a firestorm, she said, "I shouldn't have used the words I used."

Wasserman Schultz also rankled some Democrats. After being reelected as DNC chair in 2013, she ousted the organization's long-time secretary, Alice Germond. When that caused turmoil, she named Germond a "secretary emeritus." The next year, Orlando attorney John Morgan - a major Democratic donor - voiced frustration over her concerns about a medical marijuana proposal that he had worked to put on Florida's ballot. "I know personally the most powerful players in Washington, D.C. And I can tell you that Debbie Wasserman Schultz isn't just disliked. She's despised. She's an irritant," Morgan told the *Miami Herald*. She rejected Morgan's claims.

The most severe test of her mettle came during the 2016 Democratic presidential campaign showdown between Clinton and Sanders. She consistently denied criticisms that her actions as DNC chair had favored Clinton, whom Wasserman Schultz had strongly backed in the 2008 campaign. "I will be frank with you - if I was trying to rig the outcome of the primary, trust me, I could have," she told VICE News following the election. "There are so many things that we - not I - we could have done to enhance the campaign of one candidate over another." But amid the tensions at the July convention in Philadelphia, the demands by combative Sanders allies for a scalp - what she called a scapegoat for their own mistakes -- left her and the Clinton forces little option if they wanted to have a harmonious week. Even after she resigned on the day before the convention opened, she played a behind-the-scenes role in managing the proceedings that she had organized during the past two years.

Following the convention, Wasserman Schultz turned her attention to a vigorous primary challenge from local law professor Tim Canova. As a Sanders backer, he had been criticizing her for months as insufficiently liberal in Congress and too responsive to special interests. He focused on issues such as the U.S. role overseas, international trade and campaign-finance reform, which had been prime topics for Sanders. He called her a "corporate stooge" and sought to exploit the unhappiness of the Sanders forces at the convention. "She's emblematic of an establishment not serving the grass roots," Canova told *The Washington Post*. "I don't think she's loved. I think she's feared."

Sanders endorsed Canova and signed a fundraising letter on his behalf, but failed to make a personal appearance as had been expected. Wasserman Schultz had several factors going her way: Canova's political inexperience; her lengthy and close relationship with constituents; persistence and energy; ample fundraising; and support from many party leaders, including Obama and Clinton. Each candidate had plenty of money: $4 million for Wasserman Schultz to $3.8 million for Canova. She won the primary, 57%-43%. In the general election that was routine and something of an after-thought, Wasserman Schultz won, 57%-40%, against Republican Joseph Kaufman, a writer who had made two earlier challenges.

The political options for Wasserman Schultz have long been a matter of great intrigue. In March 2015, she ruled out a race for Marco Rubio's Senate seat, which might have been a missed opportunity given what turned out to be a weak Democratic field. That decision seemed to confirm that her future is in the House, and with a leadership bid. With the election of Democratic Rep. Chris Van Hollen of Maryland to the Senate, she likely would be a front-runner when a top opening occurs. She would offer strong networking among colleagues, years of political favors, policy gravitas, media savvy and a relentlessness that exceeds even most of her type-A colleagues. That helps to explain why Wasserman Schultz has been the target of usually unattributed criticism -- and, no doubt, jealousy - from would-be rivals. The enmity of Obama aides and allies likely would have little impact, and might even be a plus for her, in a House leadership contest. A lingering question seemed to be whether the controversies linked to her support for Clinton would damage Wasserman Schultz in a battle of insiders within the Democratic Caucus. She appeared to hold a lot of cards.

Southern Broward, Coastal Dade

Demographics data for new House districts were not prepared by the Census Bureau prior to our editorial deadline.

Voter Turnout			
2016 House Turnout as % CVAP	N/A	2016 House turnout	323,120

2012 Presidential Vote information unavailable due to recent redistricting.

2016 Presidential Vote		
Hillary Clinton	209,078	(62%)
Donald Trump	120,967	(36%)

Cook Partisan Voting Index: D+11

When Broward County was created in 1915, its name was to be "Everglades County," reflecting its largely agricultural character, save for a few fledgling beachfront communities like Fort Lauderdale. Development proceeded slowly. Joseph Wesley Young dreamed of building a resort community by the sea and founded Hollywood in 1925. But a hurricane the following year devastated the infant town, people fled in droves, and Young's holdings were eventually auctioned off in 1930. But this prime beachfront real estate could not remain undeveloped for long, and by 1980, the population was exploding. At first, the newcomers were like those who had populated places such as St. Petersburg and Orlando, hailing from Midwestern states and bringing with them a Republican lean. But over time, these new South Florida residents increasingly came from the Northeast, and brought those Democratic politics. They were instrumental in transforming the state's Democratic Party from a rural, Southern party run by the so-called "Pork Chop Gang" of conservative senators into one more closely resembling its Northern counterparts, and eventually helped turn Florida into a swing state.

Today, Broward County is in the midst of another transformation. It is now a minority-majority county, the third largest in the nation (behind Riverside in California and Clark in Nevada), with the non-Hispanic white share of the 1.9 million population dropping to 39 percent in 2015. Blacks are 29 percent and Latinos are 28 percent; each is a big increase since 2000. The most common countries of origin for these newcomers are Haiti, Jamaica and Colombia; almost one in three residents are foreign-born, but many of them are undocumented. While Broward gave Richard Nixon 72 percent of the vote in 1972, 44 years later it was Hillary Clinton's second-strongest county in the state, giving her two-thirds of the vote. The county is developing its own economy. Port Everglades hosts nearly 4 million passengers a year and has annual revenue of about $163 million. In December 2016, Congress approved funding to deepen the channel by six feet to accommodate larger commercial ships that transit the new Panama Canal. In January 2017, five people were killed at Fort Lauderdale-Hollywood Airport when a gunman opened fire in the arrival area with a semi-automatic handgun that he retrieved from his checked bag.

The 23rd District of Florida includes much of southern Broward County. The district is anchored by coastal Hollywood, where huge high-rises house large numbers of retirees from the Northeast, plush new resorts attract vacationers. From there, the district moves inland, with a slight northwestern trajectory. It includes Davie, a former ranching town where the businesses lining downtown all have an "Old Western" motif. The western end of the district is new-growth suburbs, such as Southwest Ranches, where residents have opposed roads and street lights, and Weston, which has a large concentration of Venezuelan Americans. About 90 percent of the district's residents live in Broward, with the remainder occupying a string of barrier islands in northern Miami-Dade County, in North Miami just to the north of Miami Beach. Located here are some of the high-rises along Collins Avenue facing the ocean and Latino neighborhoods north of 88th Street.

Redistricting in 2016 shifted some precincts from Sunrise in the northwest corner to the Pembroke Pines area in the southwest corner of the district. The shift had little impact on the partisan mix or presidential results. The district's voting age population is 55 percent non-Hispanic white. The district overall leans substantially Democratic. In the past two presidential elections, the vote for Barack Obama and Hillary Clinton held steady at 62 percent.

TWENTY-FOURTH DISTRICT

Frederica Wilson (D)

Elected 2010, 4th term; b. Nov 05, 1942, Miami; Fisk University (TN), B.S., 1963; University of Miami (FL), M.Ed., 1972; Episcopalian; Widow; 3 children; 5 grandchildren.

Elected Office: FL House, 1998-2002; FL Senate, 2002-2010.

Professional Career: Teacher; principal; Assistant principal.

DC Office: 2445 RHOB 20515, 202-225-4506, Fax: 202-226-0777, wilson.house.gov.

State Offices: Hollywood, 954-921-3682; Miami Gardens, 305-690-5905.

Committees: *Education & the Workforce*: Early Childhood, Elementary & Secondary Education, Health, Employment, Labor & Pensions. *Transportation & Infrastructure*: Highways & Transit, Railroads, Pipelines & Hazardous Materials, Water Resources & Environment.

Group Ratings

	ADA	ACLU	AFL-CIO	LCV	ITI	COC	HAFA	ACU	CFG	FRC
2016	-	94%	-	95%	67%	67%	13%	0%	0%	0%
2015	100%	C	100%	97%	C	45%	C	5%	2%	0%

Almanac Ratings 2015

	Economy	Social	Foreign	Composite
Liberal	98%	100%	91%	97%
Conservative	2%	0%	9%	3%

Key Votes of the 114th Congress

1. Keystone Pipeline	N	5. Puerto Rico Debt	Y	9. Offenses by Aliens	N
2. Trade Deals	N	6. Medical Marijuana	Y	10. Troops in Iraq	Y
3. Export-Import Bank	Y	7. Sanctuary Cities	N	11. Homeland Security $$	Y
4. Debt Ceiling Increase	Y	8. Armor-piercing Bullets	N	12. Trade Adjustment aid	Y

Election Results

Election	Name (Party)	Vote (%)	Cand. Spent	Ind. Exp. Support	Ind. Exp. Oppose
2016 General	Frederica Wilson (D)...............................	(100%)	$341,366	$2,567	
2016 Primary	Frederica Wilson (D).....................	50,716 (78%)			
	Randal Hill (D).............................	13,968 (22%)			

Prior winning percentages: 2014 (86%), 2012 (86%)

Democrat Frederica Wilson, elected in 2010, is best known for her hundreds of brightly colored, often rhinestone-studded hats. She has compiled a solidly liberal voting record while speaking out on behalf of her low-income constituents, particularly Haitian Americans. She calls herself "a voice for the voiceless."

Wilson's politics were inspired by her father, Thirlee Smith, a native of Timpson, Texas, a town that in his day had an active chapter of the Ku Klux Klan. "He would sit me on his knee and tell me stories of what happened to him in Texas and how people were lynched," she recalled. In Miami, Smith ran a restaurant and a billiard hall, and became active in the civil rights movement, registering voters and pushing for sanitation workers' rights. The couple's three children were sensitized to acts of injustice at a young age. Once, in high school, Wilson spied a new kid in school being teased for wearing torn clothes. Wilson, who weighed about 70 pounds at the time, stepped into the circle of bullies and ordered them to leave the boy alone. She pursued a career in education and eventually politics.

Wilson graduated from Fisk University with a bachelor's degree in elementary education, and got her master's from the University of Miami. She worked as a teacher and then became an assistant educational coordinator for a Head Start program. Following a leave of absence to raise her three children, she returned to a Miami elementary school and later became principal. She served on the Miami-Dade County School Board. In 1984, she joined a campaign to lobby Congress to remove Haitian refugees from a local detention center. The Haitian women in particular, she said, "had no privacy at all, from guards, from visitors, from INS, from no one. When they would take a shower, they had no curtains. They were treating them like animals." The women were eventually released and allowed to remain in Miami.

Wilson was elected to the Florida House in 1998. After four years, she won a seat in the state Senate. In each chamber, she served as minority whip. She worked on immigrants' rights, including a ban on the term "illegal alien" from state documents. In 2004, she led a sometimes bitter fight against Gov. Jeb Bush to scale back the use of standardized testing in schools, which she said had a negative impact on children. Wilson was known in the legislature for her trademark headgear, which was inspired by her grandmother, who wore similar hats as a cultural tradition in her native Bahamas.

When Democrat Kendrick Meek ran unsuccessfully for the Senate, Wilson ran for his House seat. In the nine-candidate Democratic primary, she won with 35 percent of the vote, helped by four candidates splitting Haitian voter support. In the fall, her only competition was lawyer Roderick Vereen, an independent. She won with 86 percent.

In the House, Wilson was barred from wearing her hats in the chamber. She delivered a series of impassioned speeches following the death of local black teenager Trayvon Martin, who in 2012 was shot in Sanford, Florida, by neighborhood watch volunteer George Zimmerman. Wilson said she was "tired of burying young black boys." She called for a civil rights probe into the 2011 spate of shootings by Miami police, involving seven black men over an eight-month period. Wilson founded the 5000 Role Models of Excellence Project, a local version of My Brother's Keeper, to assist at-risk young males. "There is this tension that never goes away between the police and especially black boys," she said. President Barack Obama praised her efforts during a White House event in 2014. After several violent hazing incidents at colleges, Wilson proposed denying federal aid to students who are punished by colleges or convicted for hazing. The North American Interfraternity Conference backed her effort. In the *Almanac* vote ratings for 2015, she had a consistently liberal voting record.

In 2014, the Obama administration adopted Wilson's proposal for a family reunification program for Haitian immigrants who had become separated from their families. The action was part of the U.S. response to a devastating earthquake in Haiti in 2010 that left 1.5 million homeless. Wilson became the most visible advocate for the nearly 300 school girls in Nigeria who had been kidnapped in 2014 by the Boko Haram terrorist group. She traveled to Nigeria to meet on their behalf with Nigerian officials. In December 2016, the House passed her plan for U.S. government assistance.

At home, Rudy Moise, a Haitian-American lawyer and doctor who finished second in the 2010 primary, returned for a rematch in 2012, and this time snagged a rare endorsement from a foreign leader, Haitian President Michel Martelly. Wilson countered with one from Obama and won with 66 percent. Wilson in October 2015 appealed to the state Supreme Court to review the new redistricting plan, which she said created an "apartheid fence" around her district. She was especially unhappy that the district did not include the Port of Miami, but was unsuccessful.

In 2016, her primary challenge came from Randal "The Thrill" Hill, who was a local celebrity as a former football star for the University of Miami and the NFL's Miami Dolphins and became a special agent for the Department of Homeland Security. He criticized Wilson as a career politician who failed to solve problems. "Given her years of leadership, Wilson still deserves to be in the starting lineup," the *Sun Sentinel* wrote in its endorsement. She won the primary, 78%-22%.

Northern Dade, Southern Broward

Population		**Race and Ethnicity**		**Income**	
Total	733,049	White	12.2%	Median Income	$37,700 (411 out of 435)
Land area	102	Black	52.5%		
Pop/ sq mi	7163.6	Latino	32.2%		
Born in state	43.1%	Asian	1.7%	Under $50,000	61.1%
Age Groups		Two races	0.9%	$50,000-$99,999	25.5%
Under 18	23.0%	Other	0.4%	$100,000-$199,999	11.0%
18-34	26.1%	**Education**		$200,000 or more	2.4%
35-64	39.1%	H.S grad or less	51.4%	Poverty Rate	25.1%
Over 64	11.7%	Some college	27.6%	**Health Insurance**	
Work		College Degree, 4 yr	13.4%	With health insurance coverage	72.0%
White Collar	28.1%	Post grad	7.6%		
Sales and Service	52.6%	**Military**		**Public Assistance**	
Blue Collar	19.2%	Veteran	3.2%	Cash public assistance income	2.9%
Government	13.4%	Active Duty	0.0%	Food stamp/SNAP benefits	26.5%

Voter Turnout			
2015 Total Citizens 18+	N/A	2016 House Turnout as % CVAP	N/A
2016 House turnout		2014 House Turnout as % CVAP	N/A

2012 Presidential Vote		
Barack Obama	227,167	(88%)
Mitt Romney	31,651	(12%)

2016 Presidential Vote		
Hillary Clinton	219,784	(82%)
Donald Trump	40,817	(15%)

Cook Partisan Voting Index: D+34

North from downtown, alongside Interstate 95, Miami's main north-south artery, is the largest African-American community in Florida. It stretches from the American Airlines Arena northwest to Overtown - originally called "Colored Town" - where racially restrictive covenants in the rest of Miami forced the city's original African-American laborers to reside. From there the community has spread through Allapattah and Liberty City to the brightly painted minarets and Moorish arches of the city of Opa-Locka, whose name is a shortened version of the Seminole name for the area: Opa-tisha-worka-locka. This has been a kind of frontierland in Miami, where hostilities between the city's blacks and its Cuban-American majority have played out. Many of Miami's African Americans have resented the economic upward mobility and political strength of the Cubans. There is also tension between Cubans and Haitians in Little Haiti as a result of federal policies that give refugee status to Cubans who reach U.S. shores, while Haitians are treated as any other immigrant group with potential for deportation. This animosity is reflected in partisan politics. Cuban Americans have been solidly Republican over the years, though somewhat less so recently. South Florida African Americans have remained largely Democratic, as has the growing Haitian-American community.

The 24th Congressional District covers the historic heart of Miami's black community. Located here are much of northeast Miami-Dade County, including Liberty City and Overtown, Opa-Locka and Miami Gardens, the home of Trayvon Martin, the black teenager whose shooting death near Orlando in 2012 sparked a national debate about racial profiling. Miami Gardens, the third-largest city in Miami-Dade, has suffered from gang violence and drug crime, and numerous incidents of alleged police abuses, especially against blacks. In January 2015, after years of local controversy, the city of Miami reached an agreement with the Justice Department to give the Florida Department of Law Enforcement the authority to investigate police shootings and in-custody deaths. At the southern tip of the district is downtown Miami. In 2016, the film *Moonlight* depicted how residents survive and some thrive amid the gnawing poverty and addiction in Liberty City.

In early 2016, its Wynwood neighborhood was the center of government warnings about the potentially deadly Zika virus from mosquito bites. For several weeks, alarmed tourists stayed away from Miami. Some growing Hispanic neighborhoods in Wynwood have experienced an artistic revival. To the north are heavily Haitian-American towns like Golden Glades, El Portal, Ives Estates and North Miami Beach. On the other side of the Broward County line, about 12 percent of the district resides in fast-growing Pembroke Pines. Redistricting dropped the district's black population to barely 50 percent, while Hispanics increased to 37 percent, though actual Hispanic voter registration and turnout is closer to 25 percent.

The 24th has been among the top 10 most Democrats districts in the nation and the highest in the South. President Barack Obama in 2012 won 88 percent of the vote with the old lines. Hillary Clinton got 82 percent of the new district. In September 2016, the *Miami Herald* reported that some Haitians were hostile toward the candidacy of Clinton because of lingering resentment toward Bill Clinton's trade policies as president that eliminated rice farming, plus her alleged interference in Haitian politics when she was secretary of State.

TWENTY-FIFTH DISTRICT

Mario Diaz-Balart (R)

Elected 2002, 8th term; b. Sep 25, 1961, Fort Lauderdale; University of South Florida, Att.; Roman Catholic; Married (Tia Diaz-Balart); 1 child.

Elected Office: FL House, 1988-1992, 2000-2002; FL Senate, 1992-2000.

Professional Career: A.A., Miami Mayor Xavier Suarez, 1985-1988; Public relations executive.

DC Office: 440 CHOB 20515, 202-225-4211, Fax: 202-225-8576, mariodiazbalart.house.gov.

State Offices: Doral, 305-470-8555; Naples, 239-348-1620.

Committees: *Appropriations*: Defense, State, Foreign Operations & Related Programs, Transportation, HUD & Related Agencies (Chmn). *Budget*.

Group Ratings

	ADA	ACLU	AFL-CIO	LCV	ITI	COC	HAFA	ACU	CFG	FRC
2016	-	5%	-	8%	100%	100%	35%	38%	48%	82%
2015	0%	C	33%	3%	C	95%	C	46%	45%	92%

Almanac Ratings 2015

	Economy	Social	Foreign	Composite
Liberal	12%	35%	14%	20%
Conservative	88%	65%	86%	80%

Key Votes of the 114th Congress

1. Keystone Pipeline	Y	5. Puerto Rico Debt	Y	9. Offenses by Aliens	Y
2. Trade Deals	Y	6. Medical Marijuana	N	10. Troops in Iraq	N
3. Export-Import Bank	N	7. Sanctuary Cities	N	11. Homeland Security $$	Y
4. Debt Ceiling Increase	Y	8. Armor-piercing Bullets	Y	12. Trade Adjustment aid	N

Election Results

Election	Name (Party)	Vote (%)	Cand. Spent	Ind. Exp. Support	Ind. Exp. Oppose
2016 General	Mario Diaz-Balart (R)	157,921 (62%)	$1,397,144		
	Alina Valdes (D)	95,319 (38%)	$34,613		
2016 Primary	Mario Diaz-Balart (R)	(100%)			

Prior winning percentages: 2014 (100%), 2012 (76%), 2010 (67%), 2008 (72%), 2006 (80%), 2004 (73%), 2002 (66%)

Mario Diaz-Balart, a Republican first elected in 2002, has become a pragmatic legislator who has been among the handful of GOP Latinos seeking to nudge their party closer to the political middle on immigration issues. He has been an unswerving hard-liner against Cuba's Castro regime, but has joined Democrats on some national and local issues.

The Diaz-Balart family history has been intertwined with that of Fidel Castro and the rise of communism on the island nation of Cuba. Mario's father, Rafael Lincoln Diaz-Balart, was the majority leader in pre-revolution Cuba's House of Representatives. His uncle and grandfather also served in the Cuban House. The Diaz-Balarts fled Cuba in 1959, shortly after Castro took over and after their house was looted and burned while they were vacationing in Paris. His aunt was briefly Castro's wife and the mother of the dictator's only recognized child. One of Mario's three older brothers is Lincoln Diaz-Balart, who served in the House from 1992 to 2010, then set up a consulting firm. Another brother Jose is an anchorman with Spanish-language Telemundo, and Rafa is an international banker based in Miami.

Mario Diaz-Balart was born in the United States after the family had resettled. He dropped out of the University of South Florida at age 24 to work for former Miami Mayor Xavier Suarez, a Republican. In 1988, he was elected to the Florida House; four years later, at age 31, he became the youngest person elected to the state Senate. Diaz-Balart was chairman of the Senate Ways and Means Committee, where he was a budget hawk. His 1995 call for state agencies to cut spending by 25 percent earned him the nickname "The Slasher" - a moniker he wore with pride. The eight-year term limit forced him from the Senate in 2000, so he again ran for the Florida House and was elected. No ordinary freshman, Diaz-Balart requested and received the chairmanship of the congressional redistricting committee. The resulting plan included a western Miami-Dade district that he tailored for himself. He coasted to victory over largely unknown Democratic state Rep. Annie Betancourt, a former social worker and the widow of a Bay of Pigs veteran. With support from teachers and other unions, Diaz-Balart won 65%-35%.

In the House, Diaz-Balart's voting record has moved from what initially was mostly conservative. His *Almanac* vote ratings for 2015 ranked him near the center of the House for each of the three issue areas. With Republican leaders eager to diversify their caucus, he got a coveted seat on the Appropriations Committee. Seniority has increased his influence and he chairs the subcommittee on Transportation, Housing and Urban Development. He consistently has opposed oil drilling off Florida's coast in the Gulf of Mexico and has used his Appropriations seat to secure funding for the Everglades, local transit and widening of Interstate 75.

Diaz-Balart organized the Congressional Hispanic Conference, a Republican alternative to the Democrats' Congressional Hispanic Caucus, and he has often engaged on immigration issues. With GOP Rep. Ileana Ros-Lehtinen, also of South Florida, he supported a bill to allow children of illegal immigrants to qualify for college aid. After Republican Mitt Romney overwhelmingly lost the Hispanic vote to President Barack Obama in 2012, Diaz-Balart was among those urging support for a broad immigration reform bill, which he has called the "800-pound gorilla." Republicans "cannot pretend there are not millions of people in an underground society," he told the *Orlando Sentinel*. "We can no longer pretend that it's not affecting our ability to be competitive."

He participated in private discussions with many members of each party in an effort to find common ground on immigration. When House Republican leaders in July 2014 declared the issue dead at the time, Diaz-Balart called the result "disappointing and highly unfortunate" and said it was "highly irresponsible not to deal with the issue." A major political setback, he said, was the unexpected Republican primary defeat a month earlier of Majority Leader Eric Cantor of Virginia, who had been spearheading efforts for an immigration bill. In the January 2016 Republican response in Spanish to the State of the Union message, Diaz-Balart remained more conciliatory on immigration than most other Republicans have been. "It's essential that we find a legislative solution to protect our nation, defend our borders, offer a permanent and humane solution to those who live in the shadows, respect the rule of law, modernize the visa system and push the economy forward," he said.

Diaz-Balart adamantly opposed the push by President Barack Obama to resume diplomatic relations with Cuba, and he has continued to resist tourist travel as an important revenue source for the Castro government. "President Obama is the appeaser-in-chief who is willing to provide unprecedented concessions to a brutal dictatorship that opposes U.S. interests at every opportunity," he said in response to Obama's December 2014 actions. Diaz-Balart said that Cuba had not met the terms set by Congress before the embargo could be lifted. Following the 2016 election, he said that economic sanctions on Cuba should continue. When trade restrictions have been relaxed, he added, "the oppression worsens."

In 2008, he faced a serious challenge from Joe Garcia, the Miami-Dade County Democratic chairman and former executive director of the Cuban American National Foundation. Garcia opposed the restrictions on travel and remittances to Cuba and criticized the incumbent for focusing on Cuba rather than on gas prices and the crisis in housing foreclosures. Diaz-Balart won by a narrow 53%-47%. (Four years later, Garcia was elected in the 26th District, then lost his seat in 2014 after one term.)

After his close call, Diaz-Balart in 2010 sought and won his brother Lincoln's seat in a more Republican district when Lincoln retired from the House. Diaz-Balart ended up running unopposed. With redistricting since then, he has returned to the new 25th district that extended across the Everglades and has been easily reelected. That didn't stop him, though, from joining Democratic Rep. Corrine Brown in a lawsuit challenging their state's Fair Districts reforms; they claimed the anti-gerrymandering law unfairly hurt minority voters. Following the failure of their courtroom challenges, Brown lost her seat in 2016.

Diaz-Balart has remained in good shape politically. In 2016, he faced his first major-party opponent since 2008. Little-known Democratic challenger Alina Valdes, a Cuban-born immigrant who became a physician and supported a single-payer health care system, had scant financing of $37,000 and was defeated 62%-38%. During that campaign, Diaz-Balart did not explicitly endorse Donald Trump but said that he would vote for the "Republican nominee." He said Trump needed to provide "clarification" on many issues, including immigration, Cuba, Russia and Israel. Overall, Diaz-Balart has sought a conciliatory approach. In a pre-election interview, he told the *Naples Daily News*, "I'm not a bomb thrower. I don't get bogged down by bitterness. You've got to find those folks that can break through that and achieve results."

Southern Florida: Hialeah, Other Miami Suburbs

Demographics data for new House districts were not prepared by the Census Bureau prior to our editorial deadline.

Voter Turnout			
2016 House Turnout as % CVAP	N/A	2016 House turnout	253,240

2012 Presidential Vote information unavailable due to recent redistricting.

2016 Presidential Vote		
Donald Trump	131,320	(49%)
Hillary Clinton	126,668	(48%)

Cook Partisan Voting Index: R+4

Cuban Americans have proved to be one of America's most dynamic immigrant groups over the past half-century, growing from 50,000 in 1960, the year after Fidel Castro took over Cuba, to well over 1 million today. They almost singlehandedly transformed Dade County from a place that John Kennedy won by 15 percent in 1960 to one that George H.W. Bush won by 11 percent in 1988. Over time, the Cuban-American neighborhoods centered along S.W. 8th Street - Calle Ocho - expanded west to the Florida Turnpike Extension in Fountainebleau and Sweetwater, and northwest to Hialeah. Starting in the 1980s, there was an influx of other Latinos, from Nicaragua, El Salvador, Venezuela and Colombia. In the process, new communities were built and old ones transformed.

The 25th Congressional District remains very much a creature of Miami-Dade, where 70 percent of its residents live. It includes many of the heavily Cuban neighborhoods west and northwest of Miami. To the west in the county, it takes in Doral, home to one of the nation's highest concentration of Venezuelan Americans. Some refer to Doral and its rapidly growing business center just beyond the Miami International Airport as "Doralzuela." Farther north, it includes parts of raffish Hialeah and nearby Miami Lakes, a planned town developed in the 1960s. With 93 percent Spanish-speaking, Hialeah has the largest such concentration in the nation, and the smallest share of English-speaking residents; about 73 percent were foreign-born. In 2016, local plans by developers for a massive $3 billion American Dream Miami retail theme park on land between Interstate 75 and the Florida Turnpike spurred protests from area shopping centers fearful that they would suffer financial losses.

Redistricting in 2016 added the remainder of Hendry County. In 2016, Hendry had two distinctions in Florida: It topped Polk County as the largest producer of oranges and it had the highest unemployment, with 9.1 percent. The farm town of Clewiston has made plans to upgrade its AirGlades Airport to a huge two-way commercial cargo center for both perishable and manufactured goods, with a new 10,000-foot runway. The facility, which opened in 1942 as part of the domestic military response to World War II, would not have commercial service; the plan has raised strong objections from the Miami airport. The district sprawls across the Everglades to the edge of fast-growing Naples in Collier County. Residents of Collier County comprise nearly one-fourth of the district's population; most live in heavily Republican suburbs and exurbs of Naples a few miles from the Gulf of Mexico. The Big Cypress National Preserve, a huge swamp in the Everglades, was created by preservationists and established in 1974 as the first such preserve created in the United States.

Of the three Republican-held districts based in Miami-Dade, the 25th has the most Hispanic voters and it votes the most Republican, but not overwhelmingly so, according to Florida election data. The district's population is 71 percent Hispanic, 37 percent of whom report Cuban origins. Half of the population is foreign-born. The partisan shift from redistricting was minimal. In a district that Mitt Romney took four years earlier, 51%-49%, Donald Trump won, 49%-48%.

TWENTY-SIXTH DISTRICT

Carlos Curbelo (R)

Elected 2014, 2nd term; b. Mar 01, 1980, Miami; Belen Jesuit Preparatory School; University of Miami School of Business (FL); University of Miami (FL), M.P.A., 2011; Roman Catholic; Married (Cecilia Lowell); 2 children.

Elected Office: Miami Dade County School Board, 2010.

Professional Career: Founder, Public & media relations company, 2002-2014; State director, U.S. Sen. George LeMieux, 2009-2011.

DC Office: 1404 LHOB 20515, 202-225-2778, Fax: 202-226-0346, curbelo.house.gov.

State Offices: Florida City, 305-247-1234; Key West, 305-292-4485; Miami, 305-222-0160.

Committees: *Ways & Means*: Human Resources, Oversight.

Group Ratings

	ADA	ACLU	AFL-CIO	LCV	ITI	COC	HAFA	ACU	CFG	FRC
2016	-	29%	-	53%	100%	92%	26%	13%	42%	50%
2015	15%	C	38%	23%	C	95%	C	33%	26%	58%

Almanac Ratings 2015

	Economy	Social	Foreign	Composite
Liberal	18%	55%	18%	30%
Conservative	82%	46%	82%	70%

Key Votes of the 114th Congress

1. Keystone Pipeline	Y	5. Puerto Rico Debt	Y	9. Offenses by Aliens	Y
2. Trade Deals	Y	6. Medical Marijuana	Y	10. Troops in Iraq	N
3. Export-Import Bank	Y	7. Sanctuary Cities	N	11. Homeland Security $$	Y
4. Debt Ceiling Increase	Y	8. Armor-piercing Bullets	Y	12. Trade Adjustment aid	Y

Election Results

Election	Name (Party)	Vote (%)	Cand. Spent	Ind. Exp. Support	Ind. Exp. Oppose
2016 General	Carlos Curbelo (R)	148,547 (53%)	$3,814,131	$1,967,408	$6,059,782
	Joe Garcia (D)	115,493 (41%)	$1,376,820	$1,527,257	$6,237,539
	Jose Peixoto (I)	16,502 (6%)			
2016 Primary	Carlos Curbelo (R)	(100%)			

Prior winning percentages: 2014 (52%)

Republican Carlos Curbelo, who won a face-off in 2014 between two Cuban-Americans to regain the Miami-area 26th District for the GOP, had an unexpectedly good 2016. The redistricting of the 26th turned out to be inconsequential, Democrats created a rematch by nominating a flawed opponent whom party leaders had opposed in the primary and Curbelo was comfortably reelected in one of the most expensive contests of the cycle. As a post-election reward, he got a seat on the Ways and Means Committee.

Curbelo was born in Miami to two Cuban exiles who fled the Castro regime in the 1960s. He earned degrees in business administration and public administration from the University of Miami. In 2002, Curbelo founded Capital Gains, a consulting firm, and worked as a lobbyist and campaign adviser. In 2009, he was state director for appointed Sen. George LeMieux of Florida, advising the GOP lawmaker on Latin American policy and Hispanic issues. In 2010, Curbelo was elected to the Miami-Dade County School Board, a job he said he was inspired to seek after the birth of his first child.

Curbelo faced a primary challenge from former Rep. David Rivera, who had lost his seat to Rep. Joe Garcia in 2012 amid a scandal over a complicated campaign-financing scheme. But Garcia had his own ethical problems, stemming from a fraudulent absentee-ballot scheme during the 2012 election in which his top aide was convicted. The Republican establishment rallied around Curbelo, seeing a strong opportunity to take the seat away from Garcia, who had lost two earlier runs for Congress. Rivera (who had defeated Curbelo by a single vote for the Miami-Dade Republican chairmanship in 2008) suspended his campaign in July. Curbelo won a four-way primary with 47 percent of the vote to 25 percent for runner-up Ed MacDougall. Rivera finished fourth with 8 percent.

The general election pitted two men with similar views on the central issue of immigration and differences on Florida-centric issues. Curbelo was roundly criticized for calling Social Security and Medicare a "Ponzi scheme" - not a vote-getter line in a state with many retirees. Garcia was denounced for saying, in what appeared to be an ironic comment, that "communism works" - not the sort of characterization that played well in a district with Cuban refugees and their descendants. Garcia went after Curbelo for his lobbying activity, accusing him of not disclosing his clients. Garcia denied involvement in the voter-fraud scandal, though two former staffers had been accused of impropriety. Curbelo broke with many Republicans on immigration reform by supporting the "Dream Act" to allow certain children brought to the country illegally by their parents to remain in America. He pledged to work to pass an immigration-reform package, reduce the national debt and create a "consumer-driven" health care system.

In one of the most costly House races in 2014, Garcia outspent Curbelo $3.8 million to $2.3 million, but the national Republican Party spent about $5 million compared with a bit more than $2 million by

Democrats. Curbelo won with 51.5 percent of the vote. He took 52.2 percent in Miami-Dade and 48.2 percent in less populous Monroe County.

In the House, Curbelo won the attention of Republican leaders, who encouraged him to pursue his constituents' desire for coalition-building. During his first weeks in office, he gave the Spanish-language response to the State of the Union message by President Barack Obama. He announced support for comprehensive immigration reform, and created a political action committee to support other Republicans who shared that goal. He was the first Southern Republican to join mostly Democrats in cosponsoring a bill to restore a key part of the Voting Rights Act that the Supreme Court had found unconstitutional. In an op-ed for the *Miami Herald*, Curbelo wrote that climate change is "one of the major challenges of our time," and he sought market-based solutions. He was one of 13 Republicans in April 2015 who voted against repeal of a law in the District of Columbia to protect abortion rights. He wrapped himself in centrism. "The people on either extreme draw a lot of attention to themselves, they make a lot of noise, but they don't get anything done," Curbelo told McClatchy News.

Democrat Annette Taddeo, who ran unsuccessfully for lieutenant governor in 2014 as Charlie Crist's running mate, was the Democrats' early favorite to challenge Curbelo. As a businesswoman with Colombian ancestry who was a favorite of EMILY's List, which provides extensive support to Democratic women who favor abortion rights, Taddeo touched several bases. She had run in 2008 against Rep. Ileana Ros-Lehtinen in the neighboring 27th, and lost 58%-42%. But the Democrats' strategy failed to take into account that the tarnished Garcia wanted another try for his seat, and that he retained voter support. The outcome of the contest between two candidates who had lost a total of five elections since 2008 shocked - and discouraged - many Democrats from outside the district, Garcia won the low-turnout primary by 726 votes, 51.3%-48.7%.

With the unexpected opportunity to remind voters of the ethical problems of an incumbent whom they had ousted two years earlier, Curbelo cited the thin record of Garcia during his two years in Congress and emphasized to Cuban-American voters his disagreement with the actions of President Barack Obama on Cuba. Democrats responded by trying to link Curbelo with Donald Trump, who was unpopular with Hispanic voters. For his part, Curbelo disavowed the "very ugly campaign" by Trump and said he would not vote for either Trump or Hillary Clinton. The money in this rematch was even greater than in 2014. This time, each party spent more than $5 million on behalf of its candidate. Curbelo, as the incumbent this time, raised $3.8 million to $1.2 million for Garcia. Curbelo won by an unexpectedly large, 53%-41% -- all the more surprising given that the same voters gave Clinton a double-digit victory that day.

Following the election, Republican leaders gave Curbelo a seat on the tax-writing Ways and Means Committee, where he said his interests included "the promotion of free and fair trade." In an early initiative, he joined with 22 other members of the House's bipartisan "problem solvers" caucus who invited Trump to join them in rebuilding infrastructure and reforming the tax code.

Southern Florida: Inland Dade, the Keys

Demographics data for new House districts were not prepared by the Census Bureau prior to our editorial deadline.

Voter Turnout

2016 House Turnout as % CVAP	N/A	2016 House turnout	280,542

2012 Presidential Vote information unavailable due to recent redistricting.

2016 Presidential Vote

Hillary Clinton	164,252	(56%)
Donald Trump	117,205	(40%)

Cook Partisan Voting Index: D+6

At the tip of the Florida Keys, a string of islands connected to each other and to mainland Florida by U.S. 1, is Key West, the southernmost city in the continental United States. Over the years, Key West has attracted famous residents - Ernest Hemingway, Tennessee Williams, Jimmy Buffett - and a large gay population, many living in quaint clapboard bungalows called "conch houses." Along the way U.S. 1 stretches 100 miles through small town, parklands and beaches from Key Largo to Key West on a mostly two-lane highway, with several long causeways. With only a 23 percent Hispanic population, the Keys are a stark contrast to most of southern Florida.

On the mainland, an influx of immigrants, first from Cuba and then from other Caribbean nations as well as Central and South America, has filled in the landscape of southern Miami-Dade County.

This immigration surge has created a multicultural pastiche of ethnicities. Tamiami is majority Cuban, but now boasts sizable Nicaraguan, Colombian, Dominican and Venezuelan communities. Homestead, which was leveled by Hurricane Andrew in 1992 but has since been redeveloped, and neighboring Florida City have sizable African-American populations. Fun fact: Key West in 1982 voted to secede from the United States and declared itself the Conch Republic, after U.S. officials tightened security on the Keys as part of the war on drugs. The secession has not been rescinded, but it has been celebrated annually with parades, parties and a drag race.

The 26th Congressional District combines Monroe County (whose residents are mostly on the Keys) with much of southern Miami-Dade County. The large majority of the residents live in mostly Hispanic neighborhoods on the western and southern edges of metropolitan Miami, close to the swamps. Here one can drive out on roads past the subdivisions and find strawberry, tomato and citrus farms. The trees thin out, and then the road just ends at the Everglades - an interconnected sea of wetlands that once covered 8.9 million acres of southern Florida, stretching from Orlando to the peninsula's southern tip. Then, it was a coherent ecosystem, a "river of grass" in which water moved slowly down a gentle slope to the ocean. But the state's white settlers were intent on making the swampland more useful, and in 1948 Congress approved the construction of 1,720 miles of canals and levees to channel and drain the Everglades, making it possible to use the land for agriculture and housing. The Tamiami Trail, one of only two roads that cross swampy southern Florida from coast-to-coast and which took three attempts to build, forms the northern boundary in the eastern half of the district.

Floridians have had second thoughts about taming the Everglades. Since 2000, Congress has approved billions of dollars for Everglades restoration. In 2008, the state proposed buying much of the land owned by U.S. Sugar Corp. around Lake Okeechobee for $1.35 billion, with farming to be phased out in seven years. That would allow water to pass over land from the lake, through the Everglades, to the Gulf of Mexico. The recession forced Gov. Charlie Crist to scale back the project by more than half. Timetables have been delayed by several years, though most state officials say they are committed to the broad objectives. When Congress enacted a water resources bill in December 2016, it included $1.9 billion for Everglades restoration.

Redistricting in 2016 resulted in small tweaks: remaining parts of the leaning-Democrat city of Homestead were added, as were a few black precincts in Miami-Dade on the northern edge of the district, and a few black precincts were removed from the eastern border. Overall, registered Democrats increased by one percentage point, and registered Republicans decreased by two points. The district is 70 percent Hispanic, including 41 percent Cuban American. This is marginal political territory. In 2012, President Barack Obama carried the district 53%-46%. Hillary Clinton in 2016 increased the Democrats' advantage to 56%-40%, though Donald Trump flipped Monroe County to the GOP.

TWENTY-SEVENTH DISTRICT

Ileana Ros-Lehtinen (R)

Elected 1989, 15th term; b. Jul 15, 1952, Havana, Cuba; Florida International University, M.S.; Florida International University, B.A.; University of Miami (FL), Ph.D.; Miami Dade Community College (FL), A.A.; Episcopalian; Married (Dexter Lehtinen); 2 children; 2 stepchildren; 1 grandchild.

Elected Office: FL House, 1982-1986; FL Senate, 1986-1989.

Professional Career: Teacher, principal, & owner, Eastern Acad. Elem. School, 1978-1985.

DC Office: 2206 RHOB 20515, 202-225-3931, Fax: 202-225-5620, ros-lehtinen.house.gov.

State Offices: Miami, 305-668-2285.

Committees: *Foreign Affairs*: Middle East & North Africa (Chmn), Western Hemisphere. *Permanent Select on Intelligence.*

Group Ratings

	ADA	ACLU	AFL-CIO	LCV	ITI	COC	HAFA	ACU	CFG	FRC
2016	-	5%	-	45%	100%	93%	31%	33%	42%	58%
2015	5%	C	35%	14%	C	95%	C	42%	35%	83%

Almanac Ratings 2015

	Economy	Social	Foreign	Composite
Liberal	15%	46%	14%	25%
Conservative	86%	54%	86%	75%

Key Votes of the 114th Congress

1. Keystone Pipeline	Y	5. Puerto Rico Debt	Y	9. Offenses by Aliens	Y
2. Trade Deals	Y	6. Medical Marijuana	Y	10. Troops in Iraq	N
3. Export-Import Bank	N	7. Sanctuary Cities	N	11. Homeland Security $$	Y
4. Debt Ceiling Increase	Y	8. Armor-piercing Bullets	Y	12. Trade Adjustment aid	N

Election Results

Election	Name (Party)	Vote (%)		Cand. Spent	Ind. Exp. Support	Ind. Exp. Oppose
2016 General	Illena Ros-Lehtinen (R)	157,917	(55%)	$3,376,342	$66,540	
	Scott Fuhrman (D)	129,760	(45%)	$887,776		
2016 Primary	Ileana Ros-Lehtinen (R)	30,483	(81%)			
	Maria Peiro (R)	4,447	(12%)			
	David Adams (R)	2,945	(8%)			

Prior winning percentages: 2014 (unopposed), 2012 (60%), 2010 (69%), 2008 (58%), 2006 (62%), 2004 (65%), 2002 (69%), 2000 (100%), 1998 (100%), 1996 (100%), 1994 (100%), 1992 (67%), 1990 (60%), 1989 special (53%)

Republican Ileana Ros-Lehtinen in 1989 became the first Cuban American and the first Hispanic woman elected to Congress. Since then, she has blazed an unusual political trail - generally conservative on fiscal and foreign policy matters with moderate-to-liberal stances on gay rights, immigration, and other social issues that have kept her popular at home. Over time her views have become more centrist across the board. Her fervent hostility toward the Cuban regime has not diminished.

Ros-Lehtinen was born in Havana. She came to Miami at the age of 8 not knowing English, and graduated from Miami Dade Community College and Florida International University. She became a teacher and then was the owner of a private school. In 2004, she got her doctorate in education from the University of Miami - a rare member of Congress who earned a degree while a lawmaker, rather than receiving an honorary degree. Her dissertation was on U.S. House members' views on national testing for high school students. She was elected to the Florida House in 1982, at age 30, and to the state Senate in 1986. While there, she met her husband, Dexter Lehtinen, who also served in both houses of the legislature and as U.S. attorney in Miami during the first Bush administration. She authored Florida's Prepaid College Plan, which became the largest such tuition program in the nation.

In 1989, Ros-Lehtinen ran for the House after the death of Democrat Claude Pepper, one of the most enduring liberals in American politics, though a staunch opponent of Castro. At that time, no Republican and no Cuban American represented Miami or Dade County. Democratic nominee Gerald Richman played on suspicions of Cubans and won the votes of 96 percent of blacks and 88 percent of non-Hispanic whites. But 99 percent of Hispanics, almost all of them Cuban, voted for Ros-Lehtinen. That was enough to give her a 53%-47% victory. In the years afterward, the district became more Hispanic, and she had no serious challenge until 2008.

Ros-Lehtinen's voting pattern moved to the left as the House GOP veered to the right. When Republicans won a House majority in 1995, she refused to sign the party's Contract with America policy manifesto and was a harsh critic of Republican attempts to pass English-only legislation, to cut off welfare benefits for legal immigrants and to reduce the immigration quota for relatives of U.S. citizens. In the 2007 debate on immigration, she pleaded with Republicans not to alienate the growing Hispanic voting bloc. Ros-Lehtinen backed Republican Mitt Romney's presidential bids despite his hard-line immigration stance, saying his position on economic issues mattered far more to her.

She was one of 23 House Republicans to oppose a reauthorization of the Violence Against Women Act in 2012 that Democrats called insufficient, and she abandoned the majority of her party in voting to support an increase in the minimum wage; raise automobiles' fuel-economy standards; tighten food safety; and give the Food and Drug Administration authority to regulate some tobacco products. In 2015, her *Almanac* vote ratings ranked near the center of the House; on social issues, she and Carlos Curbelo of the neighboring 26th District were among the four most liberal Republicans; of the other two, both from the North, one retired and the other was defeated.

Ros-Lehtinen is a longtime supporter of gay rights, backing same-sex marriage and serving as one of the first GOP members of the Congressional LGBT Equality Caucus. LGBT issues are personal to her; her daughter Amanda is now a transgender man named Rodrigo Lehtinen. In an interview with CBS, she had advice for parents of transgenders: "Don't freak out, stay calm and don't be afraid." In May 2016, with her husband and son, she aired a public-service televisions ad in Spanish for a south Florida gay and transgender rights advocacy group.

When Republicans reclaimed control of the House in 2011, Ros-Lehtinen spent two years as chair of the Foreign Affairs Committee until term limits forced her to step down. With the panel's ranking Democrat, Howard Berman of California, she enacted economic sanctions on Iran to discourage its nuclear program. Ros-Lehtinen has been a strong supporter of Israel and a fierce critic of Middle East regimes that are accused of sponsoring terrorism. As chair of the Middle East and North Africa Subcommittee in 2015, she worked with Democrat Ted Deutch of south Florida to launch the bipartisan task force for combating anti-Semitism. In 2016, the two of them won House passage of their bill to make it easier to extend sanctions on Iran.

Ros-Lehtinen strongly backed the 1996 Helms-Burton law that tightened sanctions against Fidel Castro's Cuba, and she has opposed farm-state Republicans who have sought to relax the trade embargo in effect since 1961. In February 2008, after Castro stepped down as head of state, she called for his indictment for shooting down two Brothers to the Rescue planes in 1996. Cuba's state-run newspaper, *Gramma*, once called her "a ferocious wolf disguised as a woman," which she shortened in Spanish to "LOBA FRZ" and proudly put on her license plate. She remained steadfast when Obama opened the door to Cuba. "Raul Castro can continue his dictatorial ways without giving in an inch while the White House gave Mr. Castro all the concessions he wanted," she wrote in a December 2014 op-ed. After Fidel Castro died in November 2016, she criticized world leaders who romanticized the legend of a "thug" and "despot."

In 2008, national Democrats thought Ros-Lehtinen was vulnerable. Democrat Annette Taddeo, owner of the LanguageSpeak translation service, launched a challenge and financed it with $400,000 of her own money. Colombian-born Taddeo favored the embargo on Cuba but wanted to ease travel restrictions. The Democratic Congressional Campaign Committee poured $1.4 million into television ads. Ros-Lehtinen won 58%-42%, even though the district voted 51%-49% for Obama. "If I can make it in this election, I can make it in any election," she told *The Miami Herald*. Her next competitive challenge came in 2016, when Hillary Clinton got 57 percent of her district vote. Democrat Scott Fuhrman, a political newcomer and part of a family fruit-juice bottling business, ran on the message that it was time for change. Ros-Lehtinen ran ads attacking his drunk-driving convictions. She spent $3.4 million, while Fuhrman spent $888,000, 95 percent of which was self-financed. She won, 55%-45%, which was 14 points better than Donald Trump ran in this district. In April 2017, Ros-Lehtinen announced that she will not seek reelection. "I've got to move on," she told *The Miami Herald*. Democrats were gleeful about their prospects for picking up the seat. Republicans conceded that they face an uphill battle, but they likely will be competitive.

Miami

Demographics data for new House districts were not prepared by the Census Bureau prior to our editorial deadline.

Voter Turnout			
2016 House Turnout as % CVAP	N/A	2016 House turnout	287,677

2012 Presidential Vote information unavailable due to recent redistricting.

2016 Presidential Vote		
Hillary Clinton	174,132	(58%)
Donald Trump	115,815	(39%)

Cook Partisan Voting Index: D+5

A century ago, Miami was a tiny tropical village where the Miami River empties into Biscayne Bay. Today, it is a world-class city. The surrealistic high-rises of Brickell Boulevard, the winding lanes of Coral Gables and the shimmer of orange and pink neon signs in the hot night air: This is Miami. It lives on the cusp of two civilizations, North America and Latin America, with different traditions, styles and sensibilities converging in this one place, with the strengths of each despite some frictions. In Miami, where it is easy to fly directly to any part of Latin America, top business and banking services are available to a sophisticated Spanish-speaking, and usually also English-speaking, clientele.

Miami for decades has also been the locus of Cuban America, ever since the first refugees fled Fidel Castro in 1959. Until the 1960s, the tone of Miami civic life was set by the large Jewish community and the liberal voice of *The Miami Herald.* But increasing numbers of Cuban immigrants, implacably opposed to the totalitarian Castro, entered the voting stream as Republicans. Then, Cubans were a noisy minority in the Miami area. Now, they are a dominant voice in a Latino majority in Miami-Dade County (as Dade County was renamed in 1997). But the Latino population has grown more diverse: Little Havana, centered on Calle Ocho (S.W. 8th Street), is now home to many Nicaraguans, Hondurans and Peruvians. Many of these Latino immigrants rose in their adoptive society by going to school at Miami Dade College, the nation's largest community college, or to Florida International University, and then starting businesses or joining professions in Miami's vibrant economy. When Fidel Castro died in November 2016, the celebration in Little Havana went on for hours.

The 27th Congressional District of Florida is one of Miami-Dade's three Hispanic-majority districts. It is 75 percent Hispanic, including 43 percent Cuban, and 8 percent non-Hispanic black. The district follows Calle Ocho from Little Havana west to heavily Hispanic West Miami and Westchester. North of Miami International Airport, which is Florida's busiest airport and an international hub, the district includes Miami Springs and parts of Hialeah. At the southern end of the district are low-income areas along U.S. 1, like Naranja and Homestead, which was leveled by Hurricane Andrew in 1992 but has since been redeveloped.

To the east, the district sweeps up many of metro Miami's high-income residential areas: Coral Gables, with luxurious streets laid out in the 1920s; and Cocoplum, a gated community of huge houses and boat docks for rich Cuban Americans. Off-shore and connected by causeways is Key Biscayne, with its high-rise apartments owned mostly by Latino immigrants and their second-generation offspring. On the southern tip of Miami Beach is its world-famous South Beach, where luxurious art-deco hotels attract the glitziest celebrities of North America, Latin America and Europe. Kendall is the site of the upscale Dadeland Mall, where Spanish is heard more often than English. Many of these places have become hot real estate for Latin Americans seeking a safe investment, which often are made in cash. In February 2016, Associated Press reported that foreigners spent $6.1 billion on Miami-area real estate, which was 36 percent of the total. In the previous year, the average luxury condo price spiked 35 percent to $3.7 million. One topic of concern: With rising tides and less available space, the natural sand on the beaches has been disappearing. Some of it has been replaced by the Army Corps of Engineers, which uses scoops or hoses to move sand from the sea floor and pipe it back to the eroding beach. This is called "renourishment," though the substitute sand is not unlimited.

For years, the district voted Republican, but there have been shifts here. Obama carried the district 53%-47% in 2012. With redistricting in 2016, Republican voter registration dropped from 37 percent to 35 percent. That doesn't fully account for Hillary Clinton's 58%-39% win over Donald Trump.

★ GEORGIA ★

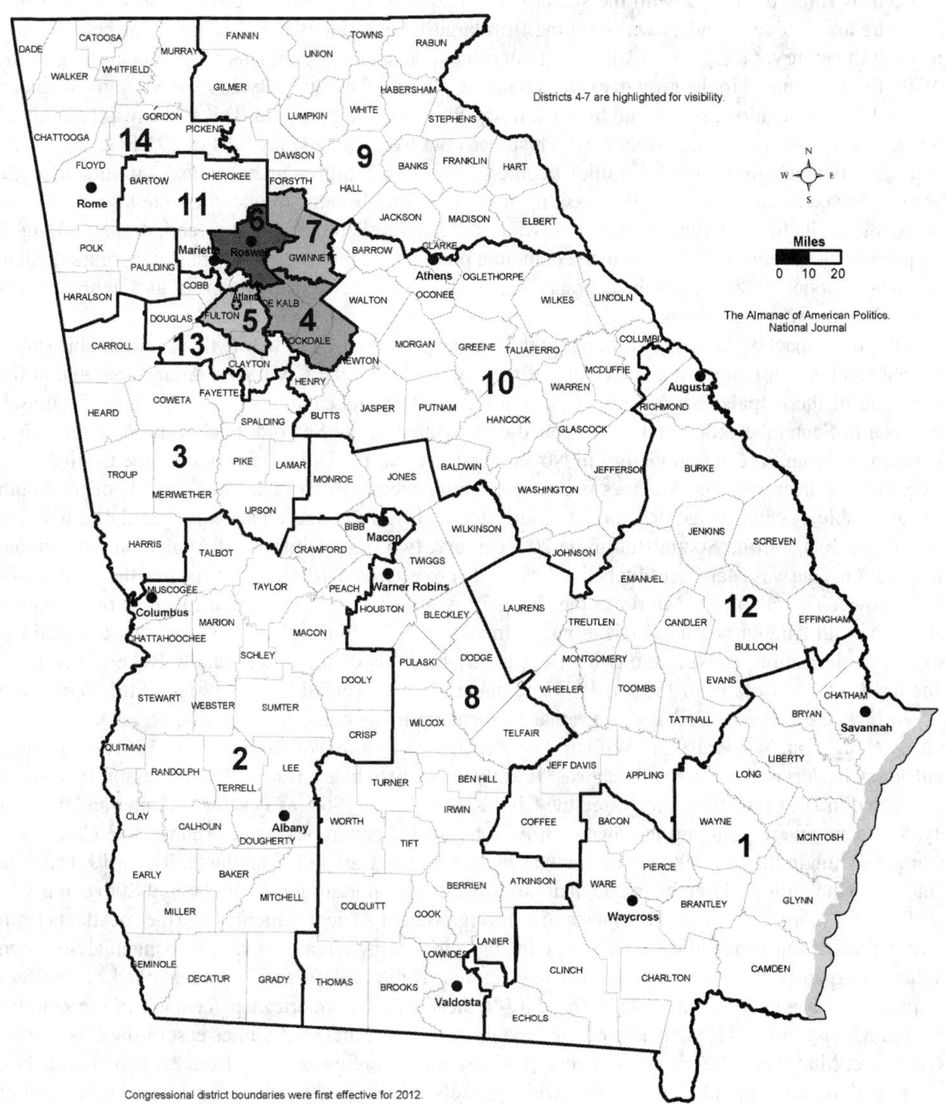
Districts 4-7 are highlighted for visibility.
Miles
0 10 20
The Almanac of American Politics.
National Journal
Congressional district boundaries were first effective for 2012.
Rome
Marietta
Roswell
Atlanta
Athens
Augusta
Macon
Warner Robins
Columbus
Albany
Valdosta
Waycross
Savannah

Georgia, once a Democratic bastion like the rest of the South, has gone heavily for Republicans over the last two decades, in both federal and state races. But changing demographics have given Democrats hope that they can become competitive in the state someday. In 2016, Hillary Clinton had surprising success peeling away affluent, suburban Republicans, though it still wasn't enough to win her the state.

Georgia was the last of the 13 colonies to be founded -- by British Gen. James Oglethorpe in 1733 as an "asylum of the unfortunate," reserved for debtors and other outcasts from England. Oglethorpe, a humanitarian, forbade slavery, but the settlers rebelled and repealed his ban in 1750. In 1790, the first census showed Georgia with the smallest population of any of the original 13 states except tiny Delaware and Rhode Island. It was only the fifth largest slave state when the Civil War began. Early in the 20th century, Georgia was still largely agrarian and sparsely populated. Then, beginning in the 1970s, the state shared in the growth explosion taking place in the South. By 2000, it was ranked among the top 10 most populous states, and by 2012 it was the eighth largest state. This is the result mainly of the stunning growth in metro Atlanta, which spreads out over the red clay hills of 29 of Georgia's 159 counties and which grew from 3.1 million people in 1990 to 4.2 million in 2000 and 5.7 million in 2015. Growth slowed during the 2007-09 recession, and foreclosures became frequent. Unemployment was in the double digits for more than two years - from May 2009 to September 2011 - and, despite falling to 5.4 percent by the end of 2016, it remained about a point above the national average. Georgia's median income was about $6,000 below the national average, but that exceeded all but one of its neighbors (only North Carolina was higher -- narrowly).

Still, the impact of decades of rapid growth remains pervasive. Even before this demographic surge, Atlanta has been in many ways the center of the South. Before the Civil War, Atlanta, located at the south end of the Appalachian chain, was a railroad junction. Its capture by Gen. William Tecumseh Sherman in September 1864 and his scorched-earth March to the Sea did much to produce President Abraham Lincoln's reelection victory in November 1864 and the Union victory over the Confederacy seven months later. Neither Atlanta's rise to world eminence nor its role as the "capital" of the South was inevitable. A century ago, Richmond, Charleston and New Orleans all had stronger claims to being the cultural focus of the South. But in the 20th century, two figures imprinted Atlanta on the national imagination. One was Margaret Mitchell, whose 1936 novel *Gone With the Wind* inspired the eponymous 1939 movie. The other was Martin Luther King Jr., who was based in Atlanta for most of his career and who, with Atlanta-based organizations, ultimately led the civil rights revolution that changed the South and the nation. Linking the two was Atlanta's business community, notably Robert Woodruff, who headed Coca-Cola from 1923 to 1955 and made Coke - invented locally by John Stith Pemberton - a worldwide enterprise. Perhaps aware that a global company could not afford to be associated with racial segregation, Woodruff and William Hartsfield, the city's mayor from 1937 to 1961, cooperated with black leaders and promoted Atlanta as "the city too busy to hate." Hartsfield's successor, Ivan Allen Jr., elected in 1961 and 1965, supported the Civil Rights Act of 1964, as Peachtree Center and the first Hyatt Regency were going up in downtown Atlanta. And if geography made Atlanta, like Chicago, a natural rail hub in the mid-19th century, it was their mayors - Hartsfield in Atlanta, Richard J. Daley in Chicago - who built airports that made their cities major transportation hubs in the mid-20th century.

In recent years, there has been a substantial in-migration of African Americans to metro Atlanta from the big cities of California, the Northeast and the industrial Midwest, attracted by its congenial Southern culture, inexpensive housing and fast-growing suburbs. Today, Georgia is 31 percent black, 10 percent Hispanic and 5 percent Asian. That's the third-highest African-American percentage in the country (behind Mississippi and Louisiana) and the second-lowest percentage of whites east of the Mississippi River (after Maryland). Nearly one of every 10 Georgians is foreign-born, up from 2.7 percent in 1990.

Metro Atlanta's population features wide pockets of prosperity, along with top-flight cultural institutions, a large millennial population and a vibrant LGBT community. African Americans have been moving to middle-class, suburban counties west and southeast of the city, while Hispanics have been clustering along Interstate 85 in Gwinnett County and Interstate 75 in Cobb County to the north. (The FX television show *Atlanta*, a popular and critical hit, has given the diverse region some national cultural cred.) Disadvantaged areas remain, but Atlanta has remained a magnet. This balance came into sharp relief in January 2017, when President-elect Donald Trump attacked one of his critics, civil rights legend and Democratic Rep. John Lewis, by tweeting that Lewis' 5th congressional district, consisting of Fulton County and parts of DeKalb and Clayton counties, was "in horrible shape and falling apart (not to mention crime infested)." In reality, Lewis' district exhibits high rates of educational attainment and is studded with corporate headquarters and universities; *Forbes* has named Atlanta among the best places for businesses, career development, and job growth. The city was aghast at Trump's tweet; the *Atlanta Journal-Constitution* responded with the headline, "Atlanta to Trump: 'Wrong.'"

This new Atlanta grew up amid a mostly rural, deeply segregationist Georgia that, still angry at Sherman's march 96 years before, cast the second-highest Democratic percentage for president in 1960. In the next two elections, Georgia voters swung sharply, voting for Barry Goldwater in 1964 and George Wallace in 1968. Statewide election contests were typically fought out in Democratic primaries that pitted Atlanta-supported moderates against rural-supported segregationists or conservatives, and the latter usually won. Then came change, in the person of Jimmy Carter, a former two-term state senator who was elected governor in 1970 with a rural base. After taking office, Carter proclaimed racial reconciliation and installed a portrait of King in the state Capitol. Carter thus became one of the first politicians from the rural South to celebrate and honor the civil rights movement, and in the process, set himself on the road to being elected president in 1976. Carter was followed by a series of Democratic governors with mostly rural roots - George Busbee, Joe Frank Harris, Zell Miller and Roy Barnes.

In 1976, when every one of Georgia's 159 counties voted for Carter, 44 percent of the state's votes were cast in metro Atlanta. In 2008 and 2012, 57 percent of the votes were cast in metro Atlanta. But countervailing political trends have transformed Georgia from a mostly Democratic state - Bill Clinton carried it narrowly in 1992 and lost it narrowly in 1996 - to a mostly Republican one. Affluent voters in metro Atlanta became generally Republican, while white voters outside metro Atlanta put Sherman and Carter out of their minds and, as in most of the non-metropolitan South, become Republican stalwarts. The upshot is that Georgia swung heavily to the Republicans in the 21st century. George W. Bush carried the state 55%-42% in 2000 and Republican presidential nominees have carried it with between 51 percent and 58 percent of the vote ever since. Barack Obama carried metro Atlanta narrowly in the presidential elections of 2008 and 2012, but he lost Georgia outside metro Atlanta by a 3-to-2 margin. With help from party switchers, Republicans captured the state Senate in 2002 and the state House in 2004 and have kept large majorities in the chambers. And the GOP has dominated statewide and federal races for the better part of two decades.

Democratic efforts to parlay changing demographics and the growing shadow of metro Atlanta into electoral competitiveness have regularly fallen short. In 2014, Republicans defeated highly touted Democrats up and down the ticket by larger-than-predicted margins, and five-term Rep. John Barrow, the delegation's last white Democrat, was ousted, underscoring how, in Georgia as in other southern states, the two parties have sorted racially. But while Trump managed to win Georgia in the 2016 presidential race – by a margin slightly smaller than Mitt Romney's in 2012 -- Hillary Clinton posted some intriguing results after expending some effort in the state during the campaign. Statewide, Trump underperformed Romney by about 10,000 votes, while Clinton exceeded Obama in 2012 by 104,000. The reason? Metro Atlanta. Three metro counties shifted from Romney to Clinton – Gwinnett, with a 17-point swing toward Clinton, Cobb, with a 14-point swing, and Henry, with a seven-point swing. (These three counties still backed incumbent Republican Sen. Johnny Isakson by four points, 11 points and one point, respectively; Isakson won by 14 points statewide.) In addition, Clinton carried several metro counties – including Fulton, Douglas, Rockdale and DeKalb -- by margins that were six to 13 points higher than Obama had managed four years earlier. According to exit polls, Clinton won Georgia's moderates – 36 percent of the vote – by a 57%-37% margin. But while she won nonwhites, 83%-14, Trump took whites, 75%-21%. And while Clinton won Georgians ages 18-29 and 30-44, Trump won older voters convincingly. The unique unpopularity of Trump among educated, affluent suburbanites may have accelerated Democratic gains in the state in 2016, but a more competitive Georgia seems likely in the not-too-distant future, particularly if Hispanics become as strongly Democratic as African-Americans have been.

Population		Race and Ethnicity		Income	
Total	10,006,693	White	54.6%	Median Income	$49,620 (31 out of 50)
Land area	57,513	Black	30.5%		
Pop/ sq mi	174.0	Latino	9.1%	Under $50,000	50.4%
Born in state	55.3%	Asian	3.6%	$50,000-$99,999	29.4%
		Two races	1.7%	$100,000-$199,999	16.1%
Age Groups		Other	0.4%	$200,000 or more	4.3%
Under 18	24.9%			Poverty Rate	18.4%
18-34	20.9%	**Education**			
35-64	39.4%	H.S grad or less	43.0%	**Health Insurance**	
Over 64	11.8%	Some college	28.2%	With health insurance coverage	82.9%
		College Degree, 4 yr	18.1%		
Work		Post grad	10.7%		
White Collar	35.9%			**Public Assistance**	
Sales and Service	41.7%	**Military**		Cash public assistance income	1.9%
Blue Collar	22.4%	Veteran	9.0%		
Government	15.2%	Active Duty	0.6%	Food stamp/SNAP benefits	15.5%

Voter Turnout			
2015 Total Citizens 18+	6,978,660	2016 Pres Turnout as % CVAP	59%
2016 Pres Votes	4,114,732	2012 Pres Turnout as % CVAP	59%

Legislature	
Senate:	18D, 37R
House:	62D, 118R

Presidential Politics

2016 Democratic Primary		
Hillary Clinton (D)	545,674	(71%)
Bernie Sanders (D)	215,797	(28%)
2016 Republican Primary		
Donald Trump (R)	502,994	(39%)
Ted Cruz (R)	305,847	(24%)
Marco Rubio (R)	316,836	(24%)
Ben Carson (R)	80,723	(6%)
John Kasich (R)	72,508	(6%)

2016 Presidential Vote		
Donald Trump (R)	2,089,104	(51%)
Hillary Clinton (D)	1,877,963	(46%)
Gary Johnson (L)	125,306	(3%)
2012 Presidential Vote		
Mitt Romney (R)	2,078,688	(53%)
Barack Obama (D)	1,773,827	(45%)

Georgia has recently been a reliable Republican state in presidential elections. The GOP nominee has carried the state in every election since 1984 except for 1992, when Bill Clinton won the Peach State. But some surveys into the fall of 2016 suggested that Hillary Clinton might have a shot at repeating her husband's accomplishment. Georgia once was part of the Solid South for Democrats and in 1976 native son Jimmy Carter carried all 159 of its counties. Carter won all but 13 in 1980, when Ronald Reagan won a national landslide. Donald Trump kept Georgia in the Republican ranks, defeating Clinton by 51%-46%, not far from the comfortable 53%-45% victory Mitt Romney posted over Barack Obama in 2012. But there were notable differences in the results around Atlanta: Clinton was the first Democrat to carry the two largest suburban counties, Cobb and Gwinnett, since Carter in 1976. Gwinnett, formerly a Republican stronghold, has seen its GOP margins decline as its population became more diverse, especially with an increase in Hispanics. Cobb, once the political base of former Republican House Speaker Newt Gingrich, has an adult population in which 44 percent of adults have a bachelor's degree or higher. Those factors gave Clinton a boost in these traditional GOP suburbs, where Trump's populism and brash style turned off some establishment voters. Overall, Clinton slashed the Republican margin in eight suburban counties that ring Atlanta - Cherokee, Cobb, Douglas, Fayette, Forsyth, Henry, Gwinnett and Walton - from 18 points in 2012 to six points in 2016. Still, that GOP edge, combined with the Republican advantage in the rest of the state, gave Trump his victory. For Democrats, the challenge is how to build on their base in urban Atlanta, Savannah, Augusta, Columbus and Macon, and in the declining rural counties in central Georgia that were once home to cotton plantations. One glaring weakness for Clinton was with Georgia's white population: according to the television network exit poll, she received only 21 percent of their votes.

Georgians like their primary to play an important role in presidential politics. In 1992, Democratic Gov. Zell Miller scheduled it one week before Super Tuesday in order to help Democratic nominee Bill Clinton, and it did: The Dixie victory gave him critical momentum going into the large batch of southern primaries one week later. Clinton swept those contests, and Miller was rewarded with a keynoter slot at the Democratic convention in New York's Madison Square Garden. (Miller would gain notoriety 12 years later in the same spot delivering the keynote address to the Republican convention, eviscerating Democratic standard-bearer John Kerry.) Georgia Secretary of State Brian Kemp was a leader in 2016 in organizing a so-called "SEC primary," named after the South's college football powerhouse Southeastern Conference. Six other southern states - Alabama, Arkansas, Oklahoma, Tennessee, Texas and Virginia - held presidential primaries on March 1. Initially, many observers thought this would give an advantage to Texas Sen. Ted Cruz, but Trump ended up being the main beneficiary as he won all of those states except for Oklahoma and Texas. In Georgia, Trump defeated Florida Sen. Marco Rubio, 39%-24%, with Cruz finishing a close third. Trump won 155 of the state's counties, losing only four to Rubio: Fulton, DeKalb and Cobb in the Atlanta metro, and Clarke, home of the University of Georgia. The Democratic primary was an afterthought. Clinton crushed Vermont Sen. Bernie Sanders, 71%-28%. Sanders won just one tiny rural county, Echols, by four votes. The exit poll reported that 51 percent of the Democratic primary electorate was African-American, 38 percent was white. Clinton won better than four-fifths of those African-American ballots. Democrats saw their presidential primary turnout decline by some 300,000 votes from the record they set in 2008. Republicans set a new record, exceeding the previous high-water mark in 2008 by more than 300,000 votes.

Congressional Districts

115th Congress Lineup	10R 4D	**114th Congress Lineup**	10R 4D

Georgia gained one seat from the reapportionment following the 2010 census, giving it a total of 14; only seven states have more. And unlike in 1991 and 2001, when Democrats drew some of the most convoluted lines in the country, Republicans have gained firm control of redistricting, with boundaries that appear relatively clean while concentrating minority voters. The result in the past two elections, not entirely accidental: 10 Republicans, all of them white; 4 Democrats, all of them African-American.

The Legislature in 2012 achieved the GOP goals with a few partisan tweaks. First, Republicans added a new safe seat thanks to rapid growth along north Georgia's I-85 corridor. Second, they shored up Republican Rep. Austin Scott in south Georgia's 8th District by switching downtown Macon to nearby Democrat Sanford Bishop's 2nd District, which gained an African-American majority. Third, they targeted Democratic Rep. John Barrow, the only remaining white Democrat from the Deep South, by cutting Savannah's black neighborhoods out of his 12th District. Republicans needed a second election cycle before they succeeded on the last count.

For now, Republicans appear secure with their 10-4 advantage in the delegation - a dramatic shift from the Democrats' 9-1 control during most of the 1980s, when backbench Republican Newt Gingrich was plotting historic shifts. In reality, the true partisan balance in Georgia is somewhere between those two ratios. The new map has become so uncompetitive and the state so polarized that, of its 14 House members, seven were reelected in 2014 without major-party opposition and five were in 2016.With the likelihood that Republicans will retain control of redistricting, Georgia could become a battleground for Democratic legal challenges. That likely would require the break-up of black-majority districts to create new, more competitive districts, especially in metro Atlanta. Just as the upscale 6th District became a battleground in the special election during the spring of 2017, the Gwinnett-based 7th District looms as a Democratic opportunity.

Governor

Nathan Deal (R)

Elected 2010, term expires 2019, 2nd term; b. Aug. 25, 1942, Millen, GA; Mercer U., B.A. 1964, J.D. 1966; Baptist; Married (Sandra); 4 children.

Military Career: U.S. Army, 1966-1968.

Elected Office: Hall County Juvenile Court judge, 1971-1972; GA Senate, 1981-1993, President pro tem, 1989-1990 1991-92; U.S. House, 1993-2010.

Professional Career: Assistant District Attorney, NE Judicial Circuit, 1970-1971; Practicing attorney, 1969-1992.

Office: 206 Washington Street, 111 State Capitol, Atlanta, 30334; 404-656-1776; Fax: 404-657-7332; Website: georgia.gov.

Election Results

Election	Name (Party)	Vote (%)
2014 General	Nathan Deal (R)	1,345,237 (53%)
	Jason Carter (D)	1,144,794 (45%)
	Andrew Hunt (L)	60,185 (2%)
2014 Primary	Nathan Deal (R)	430,170 (72%)
	David Pennington (R)	99,548 (17%)
	John Barge (R)	66,500 (11%)

Prior winning percentage: 2010 (53%); House: 2008 (76%), 2006 (77%), 2004 (100%), 2002 (100%), 2000 (75%), 1998 (100%), 1996 (66%), 1994 (58%), 1992 (59%)

Nathan Deal, a Republican, was elected governor of Georgia in 2010 and reelected in 2014. He grew up in Gainesville, graduated from Mercer University, then served in the Army from 1966 to 1968. He returned home to practice "street-level law," always choosing offices located on a ground floor. He was an assistant district attorney, a juvenile court judge, and a county attorney. In 1980, at age 38, he was elected to the state Senate as a Democrat; Jimmy Carter was still president, and the legislature was overwhelmingly Democratic. A capable legislator, Deal was elected Senate president pro tem twice. In 1992, when "Boll Weevil" Democrat Ed Jenkins retired from the House, Deal ran for his seat and defeated a Republican by winning 59 percent of the vote. Deal opposed Clinton policies and was seen as a potential party-switcher, but while campaigning in 1994 he said, "If I choose to switch during the term, I think the honest thing to do is resign and have a special election."

In early 1995, he worked with other Democrats to offer an alternative to the Republicans' welfare reform package. He expressed unhappiness with his party's opposition to tax cuts and with senior Democrats' criticism of Clean Water Act revisions that he had won on a bipartisan committee vote. In April 1995, back home in Gainesville, Deal announced that he was switching to the Republican Party - but he did not resign and run in a special election. He said the national Democratic Party was unwilling to admit it was "out of touch with mainstream America." Democrats were stunned, and the Republican House Speaker, fellow Georgian Newt Gingrich, was delighted. Deal's reward was a seat on the powerful Energy and Commerce Committee.

Deal became chairman of the panel's Health Subcommittee and, after Democrats took control of the House in 2007, he became the ranking Republican. In March 2010, with incumbent Republican Gov. Sonny Perdue term-limited, Deal announced he was running for governor. He resigned his seat immediately, possibly motivated by the fact that he faced an ethics probe into a 20-year business tie with the Georgia state government. The Office of Congressional Ethics found in February 2010 that Deal had intervened with state officials to preserve a state program that earned $300,000 a year for the salvage vehicle business he ran with a partner and that dominated vehicle inspections around Gainesville. He dismissed the charges as a "political witch hunt," and after the ethics office recommended that the House Ethics Committee open an investigation, Deal left Congress to run for governor before the panel could act. (He delayed his resignation from the House from March 8 to March 21 so he could vote against the

Democratic health care bill.) This was not the only cloud over Deal's campaign; it was also revealed that he was rendered insolvent by a $2.3 million debt for which he was liable after co-signing a loan for his daughter and son-in-law to start a sporting goods store. The store failed and they went bankrupt, leaving Deal in the position of having to sell his house to pay the debt.

His financial dealings were an issue in the Republican primary. In a seven-way contest, former Georgia Secretary of State Karen Handel, based in metro Atlanta, finished first with 34 percent, with Deal securing the other spot in the August runoff with 23 percent. The runoff proved highly negative. Gingrich endorsed Deal, saying he stood for "conservative Georgia values," while former Alaska Gov. Sarah Palin campaigned for Handel and dubbed her one of her "mama grizzlies" of 2010. Deal narrowly defeated Handel in the runoff, 50.2% to 49.8% -- 2,519 out of 579,551 votes cast. On the Democratic side, former Gov. Roy Barnes quietly took 66 percent against Attorney General Thurbert Baker's 22 percent. In the general, Barnes criticized Deal for voting against an increase in the federal minimum wage, which Deal called a "state's rights" issue. Deal emphasized his longtime opposition to birthright citizenship for the children of illegal immigrants. The Barnes campaign dubbed Deal "one of the most corrupt members of Congress" and circulated copies of a lien for $4,000 in taxes Deal had failed to pay the city of Gainesville. Deal won convincingly in a strong Republican year, 53%-43%. He did not run much ahead in metro Atlanta - 50%-46% - but he carried the rest of the state overwhelmingly, 58%-39%.

When Deal took office, Georgia, like many states, faced serious fiscal problems. It faced an expected budget shortfall of as much as $1.8 billion -- an especially challenging environment for Deal, who had promised during his campaign to spend more on public education and cut taxes. He signed reductions in how much the HOPE Scholarship Program would cover for students; it had been under fiscal strain due to a failure of lottery funds to keep pace with rising tuition costs and enrollment levels. He also approved a spate of bills that appealed to the conservative base. He signed a hotly debated bill that allowed law enforcement to check and detain those suspected of being in the country illegally; the bill also set penalties for transporting or harboring undocumented immigrants and made it a felony to apply for a job with false documents. Deal turned down Medicaid expansion under the Affordable Care Act and signed a bill to block an insurance-navigator program at the University of Georgia. He signed legislation to test food-stamp applicants suspected of taking drugs (which was opposed by the federal government) and signed one of the nation's strongest measures to expand gun rights, easing laws on the carrying of weapons into churches, bars and some government buildings.

During Deal's 2014 reelection bid, ethics concerns resurfaced. State ethics commission director Holly LaBerge charged that Deal's office had pressured her in 2012 to make ethics complaints against the governor "go away," the *Atlanta Journal-Constitution* reported. In the GOP primary, Deal faced state school superintendent John Barge and former Dalton Mayor David Pennington, who had tea party backing, but the incumbent prevailed with 72 percent of the vote. In the general, he faced Democratic state Sen. Jason Carter, grandson of the former president, and Libertarian Andrew Hunt. Carter was about as strong a challenger as Democrats could have mustered in this shifting state; he had name recognition, legislative experience and some votes with cross-party appeal, such as a vote for the gun bill. Carter led in some pre-election polls, but on a strongly Republican Election Day, Deal won by a larger-than-expected margin of 53%-45%.

After his reelection, Deal won bipartisan passage of one of his legislative priorities - a $1 billion transportation bill, funded by a mix of tax cuts and increases and focused on delayed maintenance projects. He took other steps that pleased many Democrats. In December 2015, Deal signed legislation to legalize medical marijuana, and in March 2016 he vetoed a bill that would have granted protections to critics of same-sex marriage, blocking a measure like the one that had spawned an economic backlash in Indiana after then-Gov. Mike Pence signed it. "In light of our history, I find it somewhat ironic that some in the religious community today feel that it is necessary for government to confer upon them certain rights and protections," Deal said. His veto likely protected the state from an economic backlash similar to Indiana's; reportedly, both Coca-Cola and the National Football League had warned Deal of possible fallout if he signed the bill. Then, in May 2016, Deal vetoed a bill that, with a few exceptions, would have allowed guns on public college grounds. Deal said he vetoed the bill because "colleges have been treated as sanctuaries of learning where firearms have not been allowed." Deal also successfully fought for modest increases in school funding.

Deal's most fear-reaching policy initiative was probably his effort to overhaul the state's criminal justice system. The effort began not long after a Pew study found that Georgia had a higher proportion of its citizens under criminal supervision than any other state, due in large part to passage of one of the nation's stiffest anti-crime laws in the 1990s. The state prison population grew from 20,000 in 1990 to more than 50,000 in 2004, *Fusion* reported; the share of African-Americans prisoners was twice as high as their percentage of the population. Drawing on his years-earlier experience as a juvenile judge, Deal worked with bipartisan legislative majorities to thoroughly rewrite the justice code, including efforts to deemphasize prison for relatively minor offenses and to bolster reintegration prospects following release. Using executive action, Deal also moved to "ban the box" that asked about criminal records on job applications. Since enactment, prison populations in Georgia have declined, drug and mental health treatment opportunities have expanded, and costs have shrunk. "This kind of reform is not a partisan issue," Deal told *Fusion*.

In other areas, Deal stuck to the conservative playbook. He continued to oppose a Medicaid expansion under the Affordable Care Act, and he stocked the state Supreme Court and Court of Appeals with appointees, articularly after the legislature approved an expansion in the number of seats on both. These efforts may have helped keep Deal's approval rating strong despite the same-sex marriage and gun vetoes that angered the GOP base; in January 2017, the *Atlanta Journal-Constitution* found his approval rating at 52 percent. One big disappointment for the governor came with voters' November 2016 rejection of a referendum he'd championed that would have allowed the state to take over its worst-performing schools. The measure attracted concerted opposition from teachers' unions and some African-American groups, and this was enough to outgun conservative school reformers. The race to succeed Deal in 2018 was expected to be wide open on the GOP side, with a surplus of experienced candidates; the Democratic field was expected to include Carter and House Minority Leader Stacey Abrams.

Senior Senator

Johnny Isakson (R)

Elected 2004, term expires 2022, 3rd term; b. Dec 28, 1944, Atlanta; University of Georgia, b.B.A., 1966; Methodist; Married (Diane Davison Isakson); 3 children; 9 grandchildren.

Military Career: U.S Air Force, GA Air National Guard, 1966-1972.

Elected Office: GA House, 1976-1990, Republican Leader, 1983-1990; GA Senate, 1993-1996; U.S. House, 1999-2004.

Professional Career: Northside Realty, 1967-1999, President, 1979-1999; Cochair, Dole GA presidential campaign, 1988, 1996; Chairman, GA Board Of Ed., 1996-1997.

DC Office: 131 RSOB 20510, 202-224-3643, Fax: 202-228-0724, isakson.senate.gov.

State Offices: Atlanta, 770-661-0999.

Committees: *Ethics (Chmn)*. *Finance*: Health Care, International Trade, Customs & Global Competitiveness, Taxation & IRS Oversight. *Foreign Relations*: Africa & Global Health Policy, East Asia, the Pacific & International Cybersecurity Policy, State Dept & USAID Mngmnt, Internat'l Ops & Internat'l Dev (Chmn), West Hem Crime Civ Sec Dem Rights & Women's Issues. *Health, Education, Labor & Pensions*: Employment & Workplace Safety (Chmn). *Veterans' Affairs (Chmn)*.

Group Ratings

	ADA	ACLU	AFL-CIO	LCV	ITI	COC	HAFA	ACU	CFG	FRC
2016	-	11%	-	18%	80%	100%	51%	65%	67%	100%
2015	0%	C	15%	0%	C	93%	C	83%	66%	100%

Almanac Ratings 2015

	Economy	Social	Foreign	Composite
Liberal	28%	0%	0%	9%
Conservative	72%	100%	100%	91%

Key Votes of the 114th Congress

1. Keystone pipeline	Y	5. National Security Data	N	9. Gun Sales Checks	N
2. Export-Import Bank	Y	6. Iran Nuclear Deal	Y	10. Sanctuary Cities	Y
3. Debt Ceiling Increase	N	7. Puerto Rico Debt	Y	11. Planned Parenthood	Y
4. Homeland Security $$	N	8. Loretta Lynch A.G	N	12. Trade deals	Y

Election Results

Election	Name (Party)	Vote (%)		Cand. Spent	Ind. Exp. Support	Ind. Exp. Oppose
2016 General	Johnny Isakson (R)	2,135,806	(55%)	$8,866,720	$1,588,675	
	Jim Barksdale (D)	1,599,726	(41%)	$5,036,206	$4,001	
	Allen Buckly (L)	162,260	(4%)			
2016 Primary	Johnny Isakson (R)	447,661	(78%)			
	Derrick Grayson (R)	69,101	(12%)			
	Mary Kay Bacallao (R)	60,898	(11%)			

Prior winning percentages: 2010 (59%), 2004 (58%); House: 2002 (80%), 2000 (75%), 1999 special (65%)

When Johnny Isakson, now Georgia's senior senator, was first elected to the state legislature four decades ago, he became one of just 19 Republicans in that body -- as compared to 161 Democrats at the time. "Custer had better odds that we had," Isakson wisecracked to *Atlanta Magazine* in early 2016, months before winning a third term in the Senate. Today, the GOP controls both houses of the Georgia Legislature as well as the governorship; including Isakson, 12 of Georgia's 16-member delegation on Capitol Hill are Republicans, too. And Isakson had little trouble keeping his Senate seat in the Republican column in 2016, despite some recent signs of a Democratic comeback in the Peach State and Isakson's disclosure a year earlier that he had been diagnosed with Parkinson's disease.

Isakson, who turned 72 shortly after his latest re-election, is as reliably conservative as other Georgia Republicans on the large majority of issues. But he has exuded afolksy demeanor and a willingness to work across the aisle that-- along with a long-time pragmatic streak -- has led to occasional alliances with his Democratic colleagues. Several of his more recent bipartisan efforts have occurred within the jurisdiction of the Senate Veterans' Affairs Committee, which Isakson -- who spent six years in the Air National Guard after his graduation from college -- has chaired since the Republicans regained a Senate majority in early 2015. The GOP takeover also handed him the chairmanship of the Ethics Committee, making him the only senator to chair two committees.

Isakson credits his career prior to entering politics for teaching him the virtues of negotiation and compromise. "If you want to ever learn how to accept rejection, sell real estate for a few years," he told the *Associated Press* in 2010.Formally christened John Hardy Isakson, he grew up outside Atlanta, in south Fulton County. His father, Ed Isakson, drove a Greyhound bus, and his parents bought old houses, renovated them, and sold them for a profit; Johnny Isakson later recalled living in eight different houses by the time he was six years old. Ed Isakson ultimately helped to found North side Realty, and Johnny Isakson, after graduating from the University of Georgia, went to work for the firm in 1967. He became its president in 1979 and, before relinquishing that position two decades later upon his election to Congress, had built the enterprise into the largest independent real estate brokerage in the southeastern United States.(*Roll Call's* latest survey of congressional wealth, based on 2014 filings, puts Isakson among the 50 wealthiest members of Congress -- ranking 38th.)

In 1974, Isakson made his first bid for elective office, losing a race for the Georgia House. Two years later, he ran again and won, and, in 1983, began an eight year stint as House minority leader. He ran for governor in 1990, losing 53%-45% to Democrat Zell Miller -- whom he would later succeed in the U.S. Senate. Elected to the state Senate in 1992, Isakson made a second run for statewide office in 1996 when he lost the Republican nomination for U.S. Senate to wealthy businessman Guy Millner in a runoff. Millner narrowly lost to Democrat Max Cleland in the general election that year, and, a month later, Gov. Miller appointed Isakson head of the state board of education.

But, just as Isakson's partisan political career seemed over, it was revived by two timely retirements. In November 1998, Newt Gingrich announced that he was stepping down as speaker of the House and that he would resign his seat in Congress. That opened a vacancy in the state's heavily Republican 6th District, which included much of Atlanta's northern suburbs. Isakson was by far the best-known of the six candidates in the February 1999 nonpartisan election. He spent $500,000 of his own money, and won the seat with 65 percent of the vote. In the House, Isakson's committee assignments included the Education and the Workforce panel; he took a leading role in negotiations on President George W. Bush's signature education law, the No Child Left Behind Act, which tied federal funds for schools to test performance. He added a provision requiring that 25 percent of technology funds be used for teacher classroom training.

Isakson passed up a chance to run against Cleland in 2002. But the state's other Senate seat came open in 2004 when Miller announced he would retire after just one term. Isakson had two serious competitors in the Republican primary: Herman Cain, who grew up in a black neighborhood in Atlanta and, starting from low-level jobs, became the owner of Omaha-based Godfather's Pizza (and later ran for president); and Rep. Mac Collins, whose district included the southern edge of metro Atlanta. Cain and Collins were both solid conservatives and abortion rights opponents, and they made abortion a major issue. Isakson also was opposed to abortion, but he had voted against a law preventing the use of foreign aid money to fund abortions overseas and had voted to allow servicewomen to have abortions at their own expense in military hospitals. In the 1996 Senate primary, he irked religious conservatives by running an ad saying, "I will not vote to amend the Constitution to make criminals of women and their doctors. I trust my wife, my daughter, and the women of Georgia to make the right choices." Collins derisively termed him "a certified moderate."

Many observers thought the primary race would end with a runoff. But Isakson won outright in the first round with 53 percent, to 26 percent for Cain and 21 percent for Collins. In the general election campaign, Isakson faced 4th District Rep. Denise Majette, who had served just one term in the House after her upset victory over Cynthia McKinney in the 2002 primary. Isakson attacked Majette's liberal voting record, including her vote against an $87 billion spending bill for the war in Iraq. Majette, seeking to become only the second African-American woman ever elected to the Senate, criticized Isakson for undercutting Bush's education reforms by not voting to fully fund them. Isakson won 58%-40%that year, almost the same margin by which Bush beat Democratic presidential nominee John Kerry in the state. In 2010, Isakson breezed to his first re-election victory over Democrat Michael Thurmond, Georgia's labor commissioner.

Isakson, who sits on the powerful Finance Committee, has shown a willingness to compromise in high-stakes fiscal battles during his Senate tenure. The former real estate broker voted for the Troubled Asset Relief Program (TARP) and to bail out Fannie Mae and Freddie Mac during the 2008-2009 financial crisis. During negotiations over the "fiscal cliff"-when a combination of tax increases and spending cuts were scheduled to kick in on January 1, 2013-Isakson publicly pushed Senate leaders to broker a deal with the White House and keep Bush-era tax cuts for all but the wealthiest Americans. "No one wants taxes to go up on the middle class. I don't want them to go up on anybody, but I'm not in the majority in the United States Senate," Isakson said in late December 2012. Isakson later voted for the bill that extended tax cuts for those making less than $400,000 and postponing spending cuts. In 2013, he was one of only nine Senate Republicans to vote for a bipartisan budget deal -- negotiated by Republican Rep. Paul Ryan of Wisconsin and Democratic Sen. Patty Murray of Washington -- to mitigate some spending cuts and raise some fees. Pressing to reform the much-criticized federal budget process, Isakson in 2015 introduced a bill that called for for two-year, rather than one-year budgets.

On another highly charged issue on Capitol Hill in recent years, immigration reform, Isakson's record of working across the aisle has been mixed. In 2007, he and his in-state Senate colleague, Republican Sax by Chambliss -- who retired in 2014--worked with a bipartisan group of senators on a bill that included a path to legalization for undocumented workers, a guest worker program, and tougher enforcement. He and Chambliss took heat back home: They were booed by hardliners at the May 2007 Georgia Republican convention for their work. A month later, when Senate Democratic leaders brought the bill to the floor, Isakson and Chambliss said they would vote against allowing it to go forward unless a separate appropriation boosting border security was passed. Isakson similarly voted against the Senate's 2013 bipartisan immigration reform bill, which passed that chamber but was killed in the House later that year.

Isakson joined Democrats on the Foreign Relations Committee in supporting the New START arms reduction pact negotiated early in the administration of President Barack Obama. Isakson in December 2010 was among only a dozen Republicans to join Senate Democrats in voting to ratify the agreement, which President Donald Trump -- during a conversation with Russian President Vladimir Putin in early 2017-- reportedly characterized as one of several bad deals negotiated by Obama. Earlier in 2010, Isakson severely rebuked Republican National Committee Chairman Michael Steele when Steele described the Afghanistan conflict as "a war of Obama's choosing." But Isakson was later critical of Obama's 2015 nuclear agreement with Iran, as well as the opening of diplomatic relations with Cuba that year. "He made a deal to give them diplomatic recognition without extracting anything in return," Isakson complained of Obama.

Isakson also took on Obama over a couple of key domestic issues. The Republican senator became entangled in a controversy during the 2009 health care debate when conservatives seized on end-of-life counseling provisions, which former GOP vice presidential nominee Sarah Palin derided as "death panels." Obama responded that one of the leading sponsors of the effort was Isakson, a longtime advocate for end-of-life counseling and assistance in drafting living wills. But Isakson rebutted Obama, contending that he backed a much different policy; the provisions ultimately were dropped from the bill. Near the end of the Obama presidency, in 2016, Isakson led a Senate effort to nullify the so-called fiduciary rule, a controversial Labor Department regulation designed to require that financial advisers act in the best interests of their clients with regard to retirement accounts. Obama vetoed a resolution passed by the Republican-controlled House and Senate to vacate the rule, which opponents argued was overly complex and would increase the cost of obtaining investment advice. Shortly after taking office, Trump instructed the Labor Department to review the rule.

As chairman of the Veterans' Affairs panel, Isakson was present at a 2015 ceremony in which Obama signed a bipartisan bill -- which Isakson helped to pass -- aimed at preventing military veteran suicides. Isakson was among the first legislators to sound alarms about Veterans' treatment, holding a field hearing at Atlanta's VA Medical Center in August 2013. In the spring of 2016, he teamed with the Veterans' Affairs Committee's ranking Democrat, Sen. Richard Blumenthal of Connecticut, to unveil a 400-page bill overhauling practices at the troubled Department of Veterans Affairs. Among other provisions, it sought to make it easier for the VA to hold errant employees accountable. Although backed by a half-dozen Veterans' organizations, it became the subject of intraparty squabbling: The House Veterans' Affairs Committee chairman, Republican Rep. Jeff Miller of Florida, at one point publicly suggested Isakson was overly eager to compromise with the Obama Administration. With others pressing to wait to allow the incoming Trump Administration to weigh in on the issue, the compromise legislation that passed Congress at the end of 2016 omitted the employee accountability provisions while retaining several non-controversial aspects of the original proposal. Isakson gamely praised it as "a down payment on the promise and the debt that we owe to veterans."

Before assuming the Ethics Committee chairmanship in 2015, Isakson spent four years as the senior Republican on the panel, which has an equal number of members from each party. He had a solid working relationship with the panel's top Democrat during that period, California Sen. Barbara Boxer. "I've been impressed with her ability to look through an unfettered lens, and I do the same thing," Isakson said of Boxer in a 2012 *Atlanta Journal Constitution* interview. A year earlier, the committee had investigated Republican Sen. John Ensign of Nevada for trying to cover up an extramarital affair with a campaign aide who was the wife of one of his top staffers. Ensign resigned from the Senate in May 2011, ending the Ethics Committee's direct jurisdiction over the matter. But, a week later,Boxer and Isakson took the rare step of announcing the committee had uncovered evidence that Ensign broke the law, and referred the information to the Justice Department. Boxer and Isakson nonetheless took heat from watchdog groups, which noted that the panel dismissed every case that came before it in 2012 and every new complaint filed in 2013. Boxer and Isakson issued a statement at the end of 2014 asserting that the panel "has significantly increased its efforts to educate and train the Senate community to prevent misconduct and ensure that senators and staff live up to the highest ethical standards."

Boxer retired at the end of 2016, and was replaced as the top Democrat on the Ethics panel by Sen. Christopher Coons of Delaware, with whom Isakson has collaborated on several fronts. Isakson and Coons, who both represent states where poultry is a major industry, founded the Senate Chicken Caucus in 2013. And in late 2016, Isakson co-authored legislation with Coons to prod some of the nation's elite universities. It would require the most selective colleges to either add low-income students or pay a fees to remain in the federal student aid program. Money raised from such fees would be used to help schools that admit a large percentage of low-income students to improve graduation rates. Toward the end of 2016, Isakson teamed with several colleagues from the Finance Committee -- including ranking Democrat Ron Wyden of Oregon and Democratic Sen. Mark Warner of Virginia, as well as Chairman Orrin Hatch of Utah -- to co-sponsor a Medicare reform proposal. Unveiled after months of work, their "Chronic Care Act" was designed to make treatment of Medicare patients for conditions such as heart disease and diabetes more coordinated and cost-efficient.

Isakson had his own health issues to deal when, in June 2015, he revealed that he had been diagnosed with Parkinson's disease. He insisted it would have no impact on his ability to carry out his Senate duties or to seek a third term, while later acknowledging that he had not revealed his condition to anyone other than his wife for the first two years after being diagnosed. "You have a few things in your walk and your gait and some things that become obvious," he said in early 2016. "Then, as an elected official, I owed it to disclose what I had. And I did." Isakson's health issue never was directly raised as an issue during the 2016 campaign, although there were occasional veiled references. Meanwhile, several leading Democrats -- including Atlanta Mayor Kasim Reed and former state Sen. Jason Carter, the party's 2014 nominee for governor and a grandson of President Jimmy Carter --

passed on challenging him. That left the party's Senate nomination to little-known Atlanta investment manager Jim Barksdale. While he spent more than $4.9 million -- including $4.4 millionin loans from his own pocket -- Barksdale was plagued by turnover in his campaign staff, as well as questions about why he had borrowed themes from left-leaning Democratic presidential contender Bernie Sanders for a campaign in a state that remains titled to the GOP.

Although Isakson ledBarksdale by just six points in a *JournalConstitution* poll in August, when Democratic presidential nominee Hillary Clinton seemed competitive with Trump in Georgia, he was never at serious risk. By late October, another poll by the newspaper showed Isakson's lead widening to 15 points -- but with a Libertarian candidate pulling enough support to deny Isakson an absolute majority and force him into a runoff against Barksdale. On Election Day, Isakson won by 55%-41% -- avoiding a runoff as Trump topped Clinton by a 51%-46% margin. Isakson endorsed Trump, while keeping his distance from the top of the ticket. And several leading Georgia Democrats -- including Rep. David Scott, former Sen. Sam Nunn and former Gov. Roy Barnes -- snubbed Barksdale to endorse Isakson, who appealed to Democratic voters with an ad pointing to his role in 2015 bipartisan legislation providing financial compensation for the 52 victims of the 1979-1981 Iranian hostage crisis.

Junior Senator

David Perdue (R)

Elected 2014, term expires 2020, 1st term; b. Dec 10, 1949, Macon; Georgia Institute of Technology, B.S.; Georgia Institute of Technology, Mast. Deg.; Methodist; Married (Bonnie Dunn); 2 children.

Professional Career: Management consultant, Kurt Salmon Associates; Sr. Vice President of Asia operations, Sara Lee; President & CEO, Reebok; Chairman & CEO, Dollar General; Co-founder, Perdue Partners.

DC Office: 455 RSOB 20510, 202-224-3521, Fax: 202-228-1031, perdue.senate.gov.

State Offices: Atlanta, 404-865-0087.

Committees: *Agriculture, Nutrition & Forestry*: Commodities, Risk Management & Trade, Livestock, Marketing & Agriculture Security (Chmn), Nutrition, Agricultural Research & Specialty Crops. *Armed Services*: Cybersecurity, Emerging Threats & Capabilities, Readiness & Management Support. *Banking, Housing & Urban Affairs*: Economic Policy, Financial Institutions & Consumer Protection, National Security & International Trade & Finance. *Budget*.

Group Ratings

	ADA	ACLU	AFL-CIO	LCV	ITI	COC	HAFA	ACU	CFG	FRC
2016	-	11%	-	0%	80%	88%	73%	92%	88%	100%
2015	5%	C	7%	0%	C	71%	C	83%	88%	100%

Almanac Ratings 2015

	Economy	Social	Foreign	Composite
Liberal	11%	0%	9%	7%
Conservative	90%	100%	91%	93%

Key Votes of the 114th Congress

1. Keystone pipeline	Y	5. National Security Data	N	9. Gun Sales Checks	N
2. Export-Import Bank	Y	6. Iran Nuclear Deal	Y	10. Sanctuary Cities	Y
3. Debt Ceiling Increase	N	7. Puerto Rico Debt	N	11. Planned Parenthood	Y
4. Homeland Security $$	N	8. Loretta Lynch A.G	N	12. Trade deals	Y

Election Results

Election	Name (Party)	Vote (%)		Cand. Spent	Ind. Exp. Support	Ind. Exp. Oppose
2014 General	David Perdue (R)	1,358,088	(53%)	$13,796,681	$3,875,475	$5,137,744
	Michelle Nunn (D)	1,160,811	(45%)	$16,063,248	$2,000,453	$12,871,729
2014 Primary Run Off	David Perdue (R)	245,725	(51%)			
	Jack Kingston (R)	237,193	(49%)			
2014 Primary	David Perdue (R)	185,466	(31%)			
	Jack Kingston (R)	156,157	(26%)			
	Karen Handel (R)	132,944	(22%)			
	Phil Gingrey (R)	60,735	(10%)			
	Paul Broun (R)	58,297	(10%)			

Republican David Perdue, Georgia's junior senator, spent most of his professional career in the business world -- as a management consultant and later as an executive at several of the country's major corporations. He is the only former CEO of a Fortune 500 company currently in Congress, by dint of having run the nationwide Dollar GeneralStore chain for four years. He was just short of his 65th birthday when he was elected to the Senate in November 2014, following a race that was his first foray into the electoral arena.In the Senate, he has proven to be the staunchly conservative legislator that he promised to be on the campaign trail. He also campaigned as a political outsider, and, during 2016, emerged as one of the Senate's most enthusiastic backers of another outsider businessman-turned-candidate: Donald Trump. Perdue's closeness to the TrumpWhite House could presage an increasingly influential role for him.

In 2014, Perdue sunk more than $4.3 million of his personal fortune (the most recentranking by *Roll Call* puts him 26th among the wealthiest members of Congress) into winning a crowded GOP primary in which his opponents includedthree members of the House. And while Perdue had the advantage of a familiar surname in Georgia politics, he followed up with a general election victory over a Democratic nominee with an even bigger political name. Along the way, Perdue found the reputation he had built as a turnaround expert for troubled companiesto be a double-edged sword politically, as some of the methods he had usedbecame campaign issues."I've spent my career running toward burning buildings." Perdue told the *Atlanta Journal Constitution* in a 2014 interview. "I've taken risks. They haven't all been five-star successes."

Perdue was born in Macon and grew up in Warner Robins; both of his parents were schoolteachers. After earning a bachelor's degree in industrial engineering and a master's in operations research from Georgia Tech, he launched a career in management consulting.He went on to serve as a senior vice president at three companies with familiar brand names: Sara Lee, Haggar, and Reebok. At Reebok, he rose to become president and CEO of the company's athletic brands, and was credited with reviving the Reebok sneaker line. His tenure was far rockier at Pillowtex, a North Carolina-based textile giantwhere was hired as chairman and CEO in mid-2002 to guide a firm that had recently emerged from Chapter 11 bankruptcy. Perdue was gone nine months later -- and four months after his departure, the firm went under, with a nationwide loss of7,600 jobs.A legal deposition that surfaced during the 2014 campaign, in which Perdue acknowledged that hehad "spent most of my career" at Pillowtex outsourcing jobs, provided ammunition for his foes.Perdue's defenders said he was hamstrung by a $50 million pension liability that did not surface until after he arrived at the firm -- the discovery of which, in turn, prompted the banks that owned Pillowtex to seek to sell the company rather than further invest in it.

Soon after leaving Pillowtex in 2003, Perdue became CEO of another company, Dollar General,that also had been through a troubled period. He streamlined operations, and, while he was forced to close several hundred stores due to competition and changing demographics, the company's stock price doubled and 2,600 new stores were opened during his four-year tenure. Perdue left in 2007, when Dollar General was sold to a private equity firm; his time there made him amultimillionaire, as he receiveda reported $42 million between 2007 and 2008. He also began to contemplate seeking public office during his Dollar General tenure. "I know what it takes to develop economic growth globally, and there are not that many people in Washington who know how to do that," Perdue declared when launching hisSenate candidacy in 2013, after Republican Sen. Saxby Chambliss announced his retirement followingtwo terms. Perdue hoped he would get a boost from his family name: His first cousin, Sonny Perdue, was elected governor in 2002 and served until 2010. (Sonny Perdue, with whom David Perdue formed a global trading firm in 2011, was later named head of the Agriculture Department in the Trump Administration.)

But other Republicans quickly jumped into the Senate primary, all but guaranteeing a runoff -- since no candidate was likely to get to the 50-percent threshold needed to win outright during the first round of voting. Perdue and Rep. Jack Kingston, who had represented southeast Georgia for more than two decades, appeared to be the two early favorites -- with Reps. Paul Broun and Phil Gingrey and former Georgia Secretary of State Karen Handel also in the race. While Perdue had the advantages of personal wealth and a well-known name, Kingston had the support of much of the Washington establishment, including the U.S. Chamber of Commerce.Perdue spent heavily from his own pocket in the first round of the primary, running clever ads painting himself as the only political outsider in the race and depicting his opponents as literal crybabies. Gingrey and Broun ran weak campaigns, and ended up finishing a distant fourth and fifth, respectively. Despite abysmal fundraising, Handel caught fire in the closing weeks of the campaign after a video emerged of Perdue mocking her for not having a college degree. She also was boosted by a late endorsement from formervice presidential nominee Sarah Palin, a tea party favorite.

The final results in May were closer than initially expected, with Perdue and Kingston winning runoff slots with 31 percent and 26 percent, respectively; Handel was third with 22 percent.Kingston led in early polling heading into the six-week runoff period, and he quickly locked in endorsements from both establishment and tea party leaders-including Handel and Gingrey, former House Speaker Newt Gingrich, and RedState.com's Erick Erickson, a leading tea party voice in the state. Kingston hammered Perdue on his business career, slamming him for ties to a national group that supported "amnesty" for undocumented immigrants and for outsourcing at Sara Lee and Haggar. He also took aim at Perdue's experience at Pillowtex. "My friend is telling everyone 'I can fix the problems in Washington,' yet as CEO of Pillowtex, he bankrupted the company and received a million dollars on the way out," Kingston gibed during one debate, referring to $1.7 million in salary and bonuses that Perdue received during his short tenure at the firm. But Perdue spent heavily on ads portraying Kingston as a Washington insider and playing up his independence, andpulled off a 51%-49% win, buoyed by a strong performance in the greater Atlanta media market.

Perdue advanced to face a top Democratic recruit in Michelle Nunn, daughter of former Sen. Sam Nunn, who was as popular at home as he was influential on Capitol Hill during four terms in the Senate. Michelle Nunn was CEO of the Points of Light Foundation, a well-known Atlanta-based charity. Democrats were bullish about her chances despite what was shaping up to be a rough year for the party nationally.While the state had taken a decided turn to the right in the prior two decades, it was seen increasingly in play for the Democrats thanks to changing demographics -- a sharp increase in its Latino residents, on top of greater voter turnout among the 30 percent of its population that is AfricanAmerican. As Kingston had done during the primary, Nunn hammered Perdue on his business career, portraying him as a heartless corporate raider. For a time, Nunn led in the polls, and it appeared the race was headed to a runoff --with a Libertarian candidate siphoning enough of the vote to keep Perdue and Nunn under the 50 percent required for a general electionwin. But Perdue dipped into his fortune once again to run ads tying Nunn to President Barack Obama, who was deeply unpopular in the state. On Election Day, he won by a surprisingly strong 53%-45%, avoiding a runoff.

Arriving on Capitol Hill, Perdue received a seat on the Agriculture Committee, maintaining a decades-long Georgia tradition. He also often followed a hardline conservative path that at times set him apart from many of his Republican colleagues. When a bipartisan deal was reached in early 2015 on long-term legislation to avoid the annual "doc fix" -- which had caused Congressto scramble each year to come up with the money to avoid cutting Medicare reimbursement rates to physicians -- it passed the Senate by 92-8. Perdue was among the handful of opponents, citingcriticism that the measure would add to the long-term federal debt. Later in 2015, as a member of the Judiciary Committee, he joined a core of conservatives who resisted a bipartisan criminal justice reform bill that had the backing of such leading Republicans as Judiciary Committee Chairman Charles Grassley of Iowa and Senate Majority Whip John Cornyn of Texas. The effort was designed to move away from mandatory sentences for non-violent offenders, butPerdue called it a "criminal leniency bill" that was too broad and could lead to the early release of violent felons.(Perdue relinquished seats on Judiciary and Foreign Relations when he was named to the Armed Services and Banking panels in 2017.)

Reflecting the hardline stance against any type of amnesty for illegal immigrants that he took during the 2014 campaign, Perdue -- in a split with a number of other Georgia Republicans, including his in-state colleague, Johnny Isakson -- invoked senatorial prerogative in early 2016 to block a Latino nominee for a federal judgeship. He cited concern about the appointee's membership in the Georgia Association of Latino Elected Officials, which has supported a path to citizenship for illegal immigrants. Ironically, the nominee in question, state court judge Dax Lopez -- althoughtapped by Obama for the federal court slot -- was a Republican who owed his initial judicial appointment to Perdue's cousin, then-Gov. Sonny Perdue. Even tea party leader Erickson, who hosts an Atlanta-based radio program, was among Lopez's supporters, calling him the "best pick you could hope for from [Obama] for Georgia."

Perdue also sits on the Budget Committee, and -- after six months of surveying his Senate colleagues -- in late 2016 unveiled an ambitious plan to fix Congress' dysfunctional budget process, arguing that such a move was essential to restraining growth of the federal debt. The proposal, which would effectively merge Congress' authorizing and appropriations panels, came shortly after the House and Senate had adopted yet another stopgap "continuing resolution" to keep the government running, due to their failure to approveannual appropriations bills. "It's totally embarrassing as a federal government of the largest enterprise in the history of the world that, out of 12 appropriations bills it takes to fund this government, that we've averaged 2.6 [appropriations bills annually] in the last 42 years," Perdue declared. As with past efforts to overhaul the budget process, Perdue's plan encountered significant blowback -- particularly a provision he included to cut the salaries of legislators and their aides if they failed to meet the requirements of the budget process. In response, Perdue said his proposal was not final, and that the goal was to prompt a discussion about what could be done to improve the process.

Perdue enthusiastically endorsed Trump a month before the latter officially became the party's nominee in July 2016, and played a leading role in Trump Georgia campaign in the fall. When Trump hit the ropes in early October as a decade-old video surfaced showing him making lewd comments about women, Perdue allowed that Trump's remarks were "disrespectful" but said he was sticking with nominee. After the election, Perdue met with Trump and was widely seen as a possible Commerce secretary in a Trump Cabinet. With Trump's closest senatorial ally, Alabama's Jeff Sessions, leaving Capitol Hill to head the Justice Department, some saw Perdue emerging as Trump's closest ally in the Senate and a key "go to" figure in relations between the two ends of Pennsylvania Avenue.

In an op-ed piece for *The Washington Post*in the midst of the 2016 campaign, Perdue went to lengths to cast himself in the same mold as Trump. "Two short years ago, I was an outsider businessman campaigning for the first time and endured some of the same criticisms being leveled against Mr. Trump today," he wrote. "In my race, the establishment types said I wasn't Republican enough. They warned the party faithful that I hadn't paid my political dues and that voting for me would be risky. Never mind the fact I had spent my career running major companies and creating jobs, versus running for political office as a full-time job." But, Perdue added, "People listened when I spoke in business terms out on the campaign trail about the national debt and global security crisis – instead of reciting tired old GOP talking points. Instead of the usual Washington Beltway babble, I spoke plainly to people about their concerns with the economy and jobs, and their frustration with Washington."

FIRST DISTRICT

Buddy Carter (R)

Elected 2014, 2nd term; b. Sep 06, 1957, Port Wentworth; University of Georgia School of Pharmacy (GA), B.S.; Young Harris College, A.S.; Methodist; Married (Amy Coppage); 3 children; 2 grandchildren.

Elected Office: Pooler City Council, 1994-1995; Pooler Mayor, 1996-2004; GA House, 2005-2009; GA Senate, 2009-2014.

Professional Career: Pharmacist; Owner, Carter's Pharmacy Inc.

DC Office: 432 CHOB 20515, 202-225-5831, Fax: 202-226-2269, buddycarter.house.gov.

State Offices: Brunswick, 912-265-9010; Savannah, 912-352-0101.

Committees: *Energy & Commerce*: Environment, Health, Oversight & Investigations.

Group Ratings

	ADA	ACLU	AFL-CIO	LCV	ITI	COC	HAFA	ACU	CFG	FRC
2016	-	5%	-	0%	100%	100%	71%	92%	68%	100%
2015	0%	C	13%	0%	C	85%	C	92%	76%	100%

Almanac Ratings 2015

	Economy	Social	Foreign	Composite
Liberal	7%	0%	0%	2%
Conservative	93%	100%	100%	98%

Key Votes of the 114th Congress

1. Keystone Pipeline	Y	5. Puerto Rico Debt	Y	9. Offenses by Aliens	Y
2. Trade Deals	Y	6. Medical Marijuana	N	10. Troops in Iraq	N
3. Export-Import Bank	Y	7. Sanctuary Cities	Y	11. Homeland Security $$	N
4. Debt Ceiling Increase	N	8. Armor-piercing Bullets	Y	12. Trade Adjustment aid	N

Election Results

Election	Name (Party)	Vote (%)	Cand. Spent	Ind. Exp. Support	Ind. Exp. Oppose
2016 General	Buddy Carter (R)	210,243 (100%)	$521,719		
2016 Primary	Buddy Carter (R)	(100%)			

Prior winning percentages: 2014 (61%)

First elected in 2014, Republican Earl "Buddy" Carter survived a fierce primary battle with a tea party candidate. Carter, who fits comfortably in the Main Street wing of the GOP, made effective use of his first term. After winning reelection without major-party opposition, he gained a seat on the influential Energy and Commerce Committee, where he was positioned to deal with issues of interest to himself and his district.

A successful pharmacy owner, his campaign photo featured him in a pharmacist's uniform behind the counter of his small-town drug store. Carter was spurred by his interest in local business issues to run for mayor of Pooler in 1996; he served eight years. He then won election to the state House in 2004 and moved to the state Senate in 2008, securing seats on the appropriations and health panels and eventually rising to deputy whip. The House seat opened when Rep. Jack Kingston made an unsuccessful Senate bid.

The 1st District is solidly Republican, but not as deep-red as other parts of Georgia, thanks in part to northern transplants who have settled there. That may have helped Carter in the primary, when he faced off against a well-funded challenger, surgeon Bob Johnson, who tried to outgun Carter from the right. Carter underscored his legislative and private-sector record, highlighting endorsements from the Chamber of Commerce and local business groups while diving into the wonky details of issues such as flood insurance and port dredging. He tried to shore up his right flank by calling for the repeal of the Affordable Care Act and highlighting his endorsement from the National Rifle Association.

Johnson blasted Carter as a political insider and pledged to adhere to term limits, if elected. He took aim at Carter's ties to pharmacy groups, implying that Carter deliberately delayed the reporting of Medicaid reimbursements to his pharmacies. And he attacked Carter's willingness in 2012 to consider a sales tax for transportation projects. These positions helped Johnson win the backing of the Club for Growth, and he came close in the money race. Carter's more pragmatic message in the May primary secured him a comfortable lead over Johnson, 36%-23%.

In the July runoff, Carter tied himself closely to Kingston, who also was on the runoff ballot, and he took aim at inflammatory comments by Johnson. Each candidate spent more than $200,000 of his own funds. The Club for Growth spent nearly $400,000 against Carter. He prevailed, 54%-46%. Carter took about 60 percent in Savannah-based Chatham County. Johnson led in his base of more-rural Glynn and Camden counties. Democratic nominee Brian Reese was a supervisor for the United Parcel Service. He spent $47,000 against Carter and did not seriously challenge him. Carter won 61%-39%. Reese took 51 percent in Chatham County, with its large African-American population. Carter rolled up the vote in the rural counties. He was not challenged for reelection.

Carter served initially on the Education and the Workforce Committee, where he filed bills to limit intimidating practices of labor unions. As co-chair of the House Community Pharmacy Caucus, he called for lifting the exclusion in federal law that prevents many state and private health-care plans from compensating pharmacists for patient-care services. More broadly, he emphasized his efforts to repeal the Affordable Care Act and replace it with market-oriented solutions. On an issue that has caused local divisions, Carter said he was "very adamant" in his support for off-shore oil exploration and drilling.

In his second term, Carter's seat on the Energy and Commerce Committee gave him an opportunity to apply his drugstore knowledge to health care issues and to advocate more directly for the interests of the local port. *The Atlanta Journal-Constitution* reported that good-government groups had raised concerns that a former pharmacist would face conflicts in handling the committee's agenda. Carter said that he had checked carefully with the House Standards of Official Conduct (Ethics) Committee to avoid problems. "I think it would be irresponsible of me not to use my expertise from years in health care to participate in the discussion of health care," he added. Carter had previously transferred ownership of his businesses to his wife, who then sold two of the pharmacies.

During the first week of the new Congress in 2017, the House passed Carter's bill to enhance the tools of the congressional watchdog, the Government Accountability Office, to oversee federal programs.

Southeast Georgia: Savannah, Brunswick

Population		**Race and Ethnicity**		**Income**	
Total	717,131	White	60.0%	Median Income	$46,243 (321 out of 435)
Land area	7,983	Black	29.1%		
Pop/ sq mi	89.8	Latino	6.5%		
Born in state	56.4%	Asian	1.8%	Under $50,000	53.3%
Age Groups		Two races	2.1%	$50,000-$99,999	29.9%
Under 18	24.4%	Other	0.5%	$100,000-$199,999	13.8%
18-34	25.8%	**Education**		$200,000 or more	2.9%
35-64	37.0%	H.S grad or less	44.1%	Poverty Rate	18.7%
Over 64	12.8%	Some college	31.4%	**Health Insurance**	
Work		College Degree, 4 yr	15.3%	With health insurance coverage	82.5%
White Collar	32.5%	Post grad	9.2%		
Sales and Service	43.6%	**Military**		**Public Assistance**	
Blue Collar	23.9%	Veteran	13.1%	Cash public assistance income	1.4%
Government	19.4%	Active Duty	2.8%	Food stamp/SNAP benefits	14.9%

Voter Turnout			
2015 Total Citizens 18+	521,125	2016 House Turnout as % CVAP	40%
2016 House turnout	210,243	2014 House Turnout as % CVAP	30%

2012 Presidential Vote		
Mitt Romney	145,525	(56%)
Barack Obama	111,903	(43%)

2016 Presidential Vote		
Donald Trump	151,996	(56%)
Hillary Clinton	110,190	(41%)
Gary Johnson	7,382	(3%)

Cook Partisan Voting Index: R+9

In Georgia, the focus is usually on Atlanta, but the state also has some urbane smaller cities with deep roots in the past. One is Savannah, the state's first capital, which by the 1830s was one of America's booming cotton ports. It languished after the Civil War and lived off paper mills and chemical plants for much of the 20th century, while impoverished blacks on the islands a few miles offshore still spoke Gullah dialects. A few decades ago, preservationists began restoring houses and churches on a street grid laid out more than 200 years before.

Today, Savannah is one of the most graciously preserved cities in the country and a prime destination for tourists, who have bolstered the local economy by $2.7 billion annually. The population of the city is 55 percent African American. The region has become a vibrant center for overseas trade. State and local officials have been deepening the port of Savannah to 48 feet and extending the channel of the Savannah River by seven miles, at a cost of $700 million, to attract the next generation of large container ships, which carry more cargo through the widened Panama Canal. The city actively competes with neighboring and equally well-preserved Charleston, South Carolina, not only for tourists but for shipping. Savannah is the fourth-busiest port in the nation and it has the busiest single terminal for container cargo in North America, which expedites fast distribution to customers. Many local officials responded with dismay after the Interior Department in February 2016 reversed the initial decision of the Obama administration a year earlier to open the south Atlantic coast to off-shore oil drilling.

The 1st Congressional District of Georgia covers the state's entire Atlantic coast, including all of Savannah. Also in the 1st are the Sea Islands, with a prospering resort economy and efforts to preserve the African-American Gullah culture and its eponymous West African-originated Creole language. Along the coast south of Savannah is the tiny, historic black settlement of Pin Point. Its citizens are mostly descendants of the first slaves in the area, and its most famous son is U.S. Supreme Court Justice Clarence Thomas. The Pin Point Heritage Museum and the restoration of a seafood factory where his mother once worked were a tribute to him. In October 2016, Hurricane Matthew caused extensive destruction along the coastline, including beach erosion, and an extension of the deadline for voter registration. The district has small cities, including Brunswick, a World War II shipbuilding center that has been revitalized as the gateway to the Sea Islands, and isolated Waycross, a railroad junction and gateway to the Okefenokee Swamp, the largest swamp in North America. Many popular films about the South have been produced in the region, including *Glory* and *Forrest Gump*.

This was Democratic country for a century after Gen. William Tecumseh Sherman's troops marched through Georgia, but voters here are solidly conservative on most issues. For two decades, this part of south Georgia voted for national Republicans but Georgia Democrats. Today it has become more firmly Republican, with the exception of Savannah-based Chatham County, which is the largest population center. The 29 percent African-American population also keeps down the GOP vote. The presidential tally for John McCain, Mitt Romney and Donald Trump has ranged narrowly between 55 percent and 56 percent.

SECOND DISTRICT

Sanford Bishop (D)

Elected 1992, 13th term; b. Feb 04, 1947, Mobile, AL; Emory University - Atlanta (GA), J.D.; Morehouse College (GA), B.A.; Baptist; Married (Vivian Creighton Bishop); 1 child; 1 grandchild.

Military Career: U.S. Army, 1969-1971.

Elected Office: GA House, 1977-1990; GA Senate, 1991-1992.

Professional Career: Primary partner Attorney, Bishop & Buckner, P.C., 1972-1992.

DC Office: 2407 RHOB 20515, 202-225-3631, Fax: 202-225-2203, bishop.house.gov.

State Offices: Albany, 229-439-8067; Columbus, 706-320-9477; Macon, 478-803-2631.

Committees: *Appropriations*: Agriculture, Rural Development, FDA & Related Agencies (RMM), Financial Services & General Government, Military Construction, Veterans Affairs & Related Agencies.

Group Ratings

	ADA	ACLU	AFL-CIO	LCV	ITI	COC	HAFA	ACU	CFG	FRC
2016	-	88%	-	47%	83%	85%	19%	4%	5%	0%
2015	65%	C	92%	54%	C	75%	C	13%	11%	8%

Almanac Ratings 2015

	Economy	Social	Foreign	Composite
Liberal	68%	100%	65%	78%
Conservative	32%	0%	35%	22%

Key Votes of the 114th Congress

1. Keystone Pipeline	Y	5. Puerto Rico Debt	Y	9. Offenses by Aliens	N
2. Trade Deals	N	6. Medical Marijuana	Y	10. Troops in Iraq	N
3. Export-Import Bank	Y	7. Sanctuary Cities	N	11. Homeland Security $$	Y
4. Debt Ceiling Increase	Y	8. Armor-piercing Bullets	N	12. Trade Adjustment aid	Y

Election Results

Election	Name (Party)	Vote (%)	Cand. Spent	Ind. Exp. Support	Ind. Exp. Oppose
2016 General	Sanford Bishop (D)	148,543 (61%)	$1,003,266		
	Greg Duke (R)	94,056 (39%)	$43,252		
2016 Primary	Sanford D. Bishop, Jr. (D)	(100%)			

Prior winning percentages: 2014 (60%), 2012 (64%), 2010 (51%), 2008 (69%), 2006 (68%), 2004 (67%), 2000 (47%), 1998 (57%), 1996 (54%), 1994 (66%), 1992 (64%)

Sanford Bishop, a Democrat first elected in 1992, calls himself a "traditionalist" on cultural issues, and his voting record is among the most conservative in the Congressional Black Caucus - and among House Democrats, more generally. His office web site touts his support for the Second Amendment and his A+ score from the National Rifle Association. On the Appropriations Committee, he has been an advocate for his district's interests in the military and farm programs.

Bishop grew up in Mobile, Alabama, where his father was a college president. He went to Morehouse College in Atlanta, where he was student body president in 1968 and sang at Martin Luther King Jr.'s funeral. "I resolved, after his death, that I would try to follow in his footsteps," he told the Columbus *Ledger-Enquirer* years later. He went to Emory Law School, then served in the Army. After a year in New York, he settled in Columbus to practice law. He was elected to the state House in 1976 at age 29. He served there until 1990, when he was elected to the Georgia Senate. In 1992, he ran for the U.S. House against Democratic Rep. Charles Hatcher, who, with more than 800 check overdrafts, was damaged by the House bank scandal that year; in addition, redistricting changes increased the African-American population of the district. Bishop defeated Hatcher in the runoff 53%-47% and won the general election 64%-36%.

Bishop joined the conservative Blue Dog Democrats and over the years has supported a balanced budget, school prayer, a ban on flag burning and a proposed constitutional amendment to prohibit same-sex marriage. He unsuccessfully sought the chairmanship of the Intelligence Committee after the 2006 election. But he strongly backed the Affordable Care Act, describing it as "a piece of legislation whose time has come. People should not have to choose between going to the grocery store and getting their medicine." In 2013, Bishop joined the "Problem Solvers" coalition of lawmakers who agreed to meet monthly to promote bipartisanship. He has filed bipartisan legislation to repeal the federal estate tax.

With a seat on the Appropriations Committee, Bishop has worked to safeguard and deliver funds to the district's military facilities. In 2013, he became ranking Democrat on the Military Construction, Veterans Affairs and Related Agencies Subcommittee. Following a January 2015 meeting with Veterans Affairs Secretary Robert McDonald, Bishop said he was "hopeful that we can turn over a new leaf and strengthen the VA for the future."

Bishop also looks out for Georgia's peanut farmers. He worked with Republicans on the Freedom to Farm Act to fashion a "market-oriented, no-net cost" program for peanuts. In 2002, he helped to craft the scaled-back program for peanut support, which was designed to phase out quotas and price guarantees. On the 2008 farm bill, he helped design the peanut-rotation program, which he said encourages "a cleaner, greener method of planting while ensuring an affordable and accessible supply to the markets that rely on U.S.-grown peanuts." His clout on farm issues was enhanced when he switched in 2017 to ranking Democrat on the Agriculture Subcommittee of Appropriations.

He has become up-front in separating himself from mainstream Democratic views. He was among the handful of Democrats who did not support the June 2016 House sit-in that protested inaction on gun-control legislation. Bishop objected that the proposals advocated by most Democrats were not "consistent with civil liberties such as due process, equal protection, freedom from unlawful searches and privacy." Later that year, he joined Republicans on the House Appropriations Committee who sought to block a proposal by the Food and Drug Administration to examine the risks from certain tobacco products and e-cigarettes. In 2015, Bishop's *Almanac* vote ratings ranked him among the more conservative House Democrats on economic and foreign policy issues.

Bishop faced serious reelection competition in 2000 from Republican Dylan Glenn, a former aide to President George H.W. Bush. The contest between two African Americans in a rural, then majority-white district was unprecedented, but race was not an issue in the campaign. Bishop largely ignored the challenger and ran on his record, while Glenn offered the perspective of a new generation focusing on economic growth. Bishop won 54%-46%. Bishop has contemplated a run for statewide office, but that has become uphill for any Democrat in Georgia.

In 2010, Bishop found himself in the race of his life when Republicans targeted him for what they called excessive fealty to then-Speaker Nancy Pelosi. His opponent was Mike Keown, a white state representative who highlighted Bishop's support of the Democrats' health care overhaul. In the year's anti-incumbent climate, Keown also got a strong boost from news reports that Black Caucus Foundation scholarships had gone to Bishop's stepdaughter and his wife's niece. Bishop said the scholarships were awarded before rules barring such awards were enacted. He attacked Keown for lacking much of a political record and got a break when a strategist for Keown was indicted in a vote-buying case in Alabama. Bishop prevailed 51%-49%.

Republican-led redistricting in 2012 strengthened Bishop and turned his seat into an African-American majority district, while reinforcing neighboring GOP Rep. Austin Scott. Since then, Bishop has not faced a serious challenge. In 2014 and 2016, Republican challenger Greg Duke spent little money. In each contest, Bishop lost several small rural counties. But he led by more than 2-to-1 in the counties with the three population centers: Macon, Columbus and Albany.

After Democrats lost control of the House in 2010, Bishop refused to back Pelosi for minority leader. He presciently warned that her control would make it difficult to recruit candidates in the South and Republican-leaning states.

Southwest Georgia: Columbus, Macon

Population		**Race and Ethnicity**		**Income**	
Total	692,667	White	40.9%	Median Income	$34,505 (425 out of 435)
Land area	9,626	Black	51.0%	Under $50,000	64.9%
Pop/ sq mi	72.0	Latino	4.9%	$50,000-$99,999	24.5%
Born in state	71.4%	Asian	1.1%	$100,000-$199,999	9.0%
		Two races	1.7%	$200,000 or more	1.7%
		Other	0.5%	Poverty Rate	27.6%
Age Groups					
Under 18	24.5%	**Education**		**Health Insurance**	
18-34	25.0%	H.S grad or less	53.8%	With health insurance coverage	81.4%
35-64	37.3%	Some college	29.6%		
Over 64	13.2%	College Degree, 4 yr	10.2%		
		Post grad	6.4%		
Work					
White Collar	29.2%	**Military**		**Public Assistance**	
Sales and Service	44.7%	Veteran	10.3%	Cash public assistance income	1.9%
Blue Collar	26.1%	Active Duty	2.5%	Food stamp/SNAP benefits	25.5%
Government	21.3%				

Voter Turnout			
2015 Total Citizens 18+	507,939	2016 House Turnout as % CVAP	48%
2016 House turnout	242,599	2014 House Turnout as % CVAP	32%

2012 Presidential Vote		
Barack Obama	153,998	(59%)
Mitt Romney	107,242	(41%)

2016 Presidential Vote		
Hillary Clinton	136,456	(55%)
Donald Trump	107,361	(43%)

Cook Partisan Voting Index: D+6

The hub of central Georgia, Macon is a city proud of its restored houses and its Japanese cherry trees, which it shows off during its annual International Cherry Blossom Festival. It has been the home of music legends Otis Redding, James Brown, Little Richard and the Allman Brothers, and of the Harriet Tubman African-American Museum.

The long shadow of history is felt here. Before the Civil War, the southwest corner of Georgia was mostly plantation country. This is where the Confederate Army ran the Andersonville military prison. About 13,000 of the 45,000 Union soldiers confined there died, and they are remembered at the National Prisoner of War Museum at Andersonville. Today, the U.S. military is a strong presence, and bases in the area have been largely unscathed by several rounds of base closings. Fort Benning, which spreads into Alabama, is the nation's fifth-largest military installation, home of the Army Infantry School and of the Army Armor School. Benning, which provided basic training to 95,000 soldiers in World War II, can now train as many as 16,000 at a time. In recent years, nearly $7 billion has been spent on improvements at the post. In 2015, a Defense Department budget proposal to cut 11,000 jobs at Benning produced a private-sector estimate of a $1 billion hit to the regional economy. During the following year, community leaders in Columbus increased their educational campaign about the adverse impact of a reduction in the nearly $5 billion that Benning annually generates for the local economy,

Much of the rest of this region is farmland. Cotton and peanuts are major crops, and pecans are also grown here. Near the Florida border is Cairo, birthplace of black baseball pioneer Jackie Robinson. Albany, with several factories, also has a civil rights museum and was the site of some of Martin Luther King Jr.'s protests in the 1960s. Not far from Albany, between upland pine stands and bottomland habitats, is the Chickasawhatchee Swamp, one of the Southeast's largest freshwater swamps and home to rare plant species such as the green fly orchid. Plains is the childhood home of President Jimmy Carter, who has said he wants to be buried in his front yard. Plains now has a major biofuels factory. Much of this area remains hardscrabble country that struggles economically. In Decatur County, local officials have encouraged the development of solar-energy farms.

The 2nd Congressional District of Georgia covers the southwestern part of the state. It includes the cities of Columbus, Macon and Albany, as well as Grady and Decatur counties on the Florida border and the counties along the Chattahoochee River border with Alabama. The 2nd District is the slowest-growing district in the state. It is barely a black-majority district and has a Democratic lean, though not nearly as strong as the three black-majority districts in the Atlanta area. Of those four districts, the 2nd was the only one where the Democratic share of the presidential vote fell in 2016. Hillary Clinton won the district 55%-43%, compared with Barack Obama's 59%-41% lead in 2012. Of the 29 counties, she led in 11 - including the three chief population centers. Donald Trump ran strongly in the rural parts of the district.

THIRD DISTRICT

Drew Ferguson (R)

Elected 2016, 1st term; b. Nov 15, 1966, Langdale, AL; University of Georgia, Bach. Deg., 1988; Medical College of Georgia, 1992; Catholic; Married (Elizabeth Ferguson); 4 children.

Elected Office: Mayor of West Point, GA, 2008-2016.

Professional Career: Practicing dentist, Medical College of GA, 1998-2016.

DC Office: 1032 LHOB 20515, 202-225-5901, Fax: 202-225-2515, ferguson.house.gov.

State Offices: Newnan, 770-683-2033.

Committees: *Budget*. *Education & the Workforce*: Health, Employment, Labor & Pensions, Workforce Protections. *Transportation & Infrastructure*: Economic Dev't, Public Buildings & Emergency Management, Highways & Transit, Water Resources & Environment.

Election Results

Election	Name (Party)	Vote	(%)	Cand. Spent	Ind. Exp. Support	Ind. Exp. Oppose
2016 General	Drew Ferguson (R)	207,218	(68%)	$1,186,564	$944,221	$436,326
	Angela Pendley (D)	95,969	(32%)			
2016 Primary	Mike Crane (R)	15,343	(27%)			
	Drew Ferguson (R)	15,277	(27%)			
	Jim Pace (R)	13,198	(23%)			
	Richard Mix (R)	5,165	(9%)			

Republican Drew Ferguson was elected in 2016 to the seat of retiring GOP Rep. Lynn Westmoreland, who was an ally of House leaders. Ferguson, a dentist and the mayor of West Point, won a contentious primary runoff against arch-conservative state Sen. Mike Crane, with support from the business community.

A native of West Point, Ferguson earned his bachelor's degree from the University of Georgia and his doctorate in dental medicine from the Medical College of Georgia. He established a family dental practice and joined the Medical College faculty. Meanwhile, he participated actively in the civic and business life of West Point, which has a population of 4,000. In 2008, Ferguson was elected mayor, with priorities to cut red tape and lower barriers for local businesses.

The retirement of Westmoreland resulted in a seven-candidate Republican primary. The best-known contender was Crane, who was viewed as the most conservative candidate, especially on social issues; he identified himself as close to Texas Sen. Ted Cruz, who made a campaign appearance on his behalf. The Club for Growth endorsed Crane and spent more than $800,000 on his behalf. Ferguson highlighted his record as mayor of West Point, including the economic impact of its Kia auto plant. He won the endorsement of Westmoreland, who said Ferguson was "a strong, conservative voice for hard-working Georgians" who could build political relationships. Ferguson led Crane in the May primary, 27%-26%, a margin of 93 votes. Jim Pace, a successful businessman and consensus-seeker, was third with 23 percent.

In the runoff nine weeks later, Crane said he was "standing for liberty and freedom" against "a bunch of big government, big business, crony-capitalist types masquerading as true conservatives and now they have all lumped themselves together into one group." Ferguson responded that government requires coalition-building, rather than "going up there with a stick of dynamite and blowing it all up." The U.S. Chamber of Commerce spent more than $650,000 on his behalf. Crane's campaign spent about $500,000, almost half of Ferguson's fundraising. Ferguson prevailed 54%-46%. Of the 13 counties, he won 11 - all except Coweta and Fayette. In the general election against Angela Pendley, a political neophyte who did not file a fundraising report, Ferguson won easily, 68%-32%. He took every county except for Henry, where Pendley had 53 percent of the vote.

House Republicans identified Ferguson as one of several mainstream newcomers who defeated party outsiders in heavily GOP districts. He was rewarded with seats on the Budget, Education and the Workforce, and Transportation and Infrastructure committees.

Southern Atlanta Exurbs: Newnan, Carrollton

Population		**Race and Ethnicity**		**Income**	
Total	708,059	White	66.9%	Median Income	$52,082 (222 out of 435)
Land area	3,838	Black	23.4%		
Pop/ sq mi	184.5	Latino	5.5%		
Born in state	61.8%	Asian	1.7%	Under $50,000	48.1%
		Two races	2.0%	$50,000-$99,999	31.5%
Age Groups		Other	0.4%	$100,000-$199,999	17.0%
Under 18	25.1%			$200,000 or more	3.6%
18-34	21.8%	**Education**		Poverty Rate	16.0%
35-64	39.7%	H.S grad or less	45.9%		
Over 64	13.4%	Some college	29.4%	**Health Insurance**	
		College Degree, 4 yr	15.8%	With health insurance coverage	86.0%
Work		Post grad	8.9%		
White Collar	32.6%				
Sales and Service	40.7%	**Military**		**Public Assistance**	
Blue Collar	26.6%	Veteran	10.7%	Cash public assistance income	1.6%
Government	16.1%	Active Duty	0.4%		
				Food stamp/SNAP benefits	15.0%

Voter Turnout			
2015 Total Citizens 18+	512,541	2016 House Turnout as % CVAP	59%
2016 House turnout	303,187	2014 House Turnout as % CVAP	30%

2012 Presidential Vote		
Mitt Romney	195,075	(66%)
Barack Obama	97,748	(33%)

2016 Presidential Vote		
Donald Trump	200,624	(64%)
Hillary Clinton	102,155	(33%)
Gary Johnson	9,085	(3%)

Cook Partisan Voting Index: R+18

South of Atlanta, Henry County has been among the fastest growing areas in the United States, with a leap in population of 71 percent from 2000 to 2010, though the pace slowed to a 7 percent increase in the next five years. The county's flourishing residential, commercial and industrial development, which has become part of Atlanta's exurbs, took root near its Interstate 75 interchanges. West of Henry County is the old courthouse town of Fayetteville, whose Holliday-Dorsey-Fife House is thought to have inspired the columned architecture of Tara in author Margaret Mitchell's classic *Gone With the Wind*. The surrounding area in Fayette County is engulfed by subdivisions spreading out from Atlanta. Sprawl has reached Newnan and Carrollton in Coweta and Carroll counties and spreads farther south to Thomaston. In the old textile town of West Point in Troup County, along the Alabama border, South Korean automaker Kia invested more than $1 billion for a local plant, its first North American facility, which opened in November 2009. With its suppliers, the company said it brought more than 15,000 jobs to the region. By March 2016, Kia reported that it had produced 2 million vehicles at the facility, with the popular Optima and Sorento CUV models; the assembly line had three full shifts during the week. But not all parts of this area are booming. In March 2015, most of the two-block business area of Grantville, a largely abandoned textile town south of Newnan, was put up for sale on eBay. Several weeks later, a former mayor reported that the offer had not generated much interest.

Much of this territory is in the 3rd Congressional District of Georgia. It takes in part of the Atlanta metro area, including southwest and central Henry County and Peachtree City, where many airline pilots live and use the city's famous golf cart paths. Newnan is home of the African-American Museum and the adjacent Farmer Street Cemetery, believed to be the largest slave cemetery in the South. Carrollton made headlines in 2011 when its mayor canceled a local production of the musical *The Rocky Horror Picture Show*, deeming it too risqué. The district stretches south to include LaGrange and part of Columbus. Coweta is the population center of the district, followed by Fayette and Carroll counties. This is conservative country, with a large share of military and tradition-minded families. The ancestral politics of this area was Democratic, but that is as much a part of history now as Tara. The 3rd is a solidly Republican district. After Mitt Romney got 66 percent of the vote in 2012, the vote for Donald Trump dipped to 64 percent - a minor reflection of the more widespread disenchantment with Trump in metro Atlanta Republican districts.

FOURTH DISTRICT

Hank Johnson (D)

Elected 2006, 6th term; b. Oct 02, 1954, Washington, DC; Clark College (GA), B.A., 1976; Texas Southern University, Thurgood Marshall School of Law, J.D., 1979; Buddhism; Married (Mereda Davis Johnson); 2 children.

Elected Office: DeKalb County comm., 2001-2006.

Professional Career: Practicing attorney, 1980-2006; Association judge, DeKalb County magistrate court, 1989-2001.

DC Office: 2240 RHOB 20515, 202-225-1605, Fax: 202-226-0691, hankjohnson.house.gov.

State Offices: Decatur, 770-987-2291.

Committees: *Judiciary*: Courts, Intellectual Property & Internet, Regulatory Reform, Commercial & Antitrust Law. *Transportation & Infrastructure*: Aviation, Economic Dev't, Public Buildings & Emergency Management (RMM), Highways & Transit.

Group Ratings

	ADA	ACLU	AFL-CIO	LCV	ITI	COC	HAFA	ACU	CFG	FRC
2016	-	94%	-	100%	67%	64%	16%	0%	10%	0%
2015	85%	C	96%	100%	C	40%	C	4%	2%	0%

Almanac Ratings 2015

	Economy	Social	Foreign	Composite
Liberal	94%	98%	88%	93%
Conservative	6%	2%	12%	7%

Key Votes of the 114th Congress

1. Keystone Pipeline	N	5. Puerto Rico Debt	Y	9. Offenses by Aliens	N
2. Trade Deals	N	6. Medical Marijuana	Y	10. Troops in Iraq	NV
3. Export-Import Bank	Y	7. Sanctuary Cities	N	11. Homeland Security $$	Y
4. Debt Ceiling Increase	Y	8. Armor-piercing Bullets	N	12. Trade Adjustment aid	Y

Election Results

Election	Name (Party)	Vote (%)		Cand. Spent	Ind. Exp. Support	Ind. Exp. Oppose
2016 General	Hank Johnson (D)	220,146	(76%)	$375,096		
	Victor Armendariz (R)	70,593	(24%)	$7,042		
2016 Primary	Hank Johnson (D)		(100%)			

Prior winning percentages: 2014 (100%), 2012 (74%), 2010 (75%), 2008 (100%), 2006 (75%)

Hank Johnson, a Democrat who won the seat in 2006, has a solidly liberal voting record and a reputation as a thoughtful lawmaker who has sought to broaden debate on legal rights. He has drawn occasional criticism for unusual verbal gaffes and blunt attacks. At home, he has faced competitive Democratic primary challenges.

Johnson was born in Washington, D.C., where his father was director of classifications and paroles for the Bureau of Prisons and his mother was a schoolteacher. He practiced law as a civil and criminal litigator and served 12 years as a magistrate judge in DeKalb County and then five years on the DeKalb County Commission. Although his immediate family members are Presbyterians, he has been a Buddhist since the 1970s; he and Democratic Sen. Mazie Hirono of Hawaii, are the first practicing Buddhists in Congress. "If you could say what drives me, it's the middle ground, the middle way," he told *The Atlanta Journal-Constitution* in 2009, invoking a Buddhist principle.

In 2006, Johnson ousted Democratic Rep. Cynthia McKinney in the primary. McKinney was a controversial incumbent, whose own party lost patience with her after she struck a Capitol police officer who had stopped her at a security checkpoint. In the July primary, McKinney led Johnson, 47%-44%, but her failure to break the 50 percent threshold in the three-candidate field forced a runoff. His fundraising suddenly picked up as donors, including former Democratic Gov. Roy Barnes, weighed in against McKinney. She responded by criticizing Johnson's past financial troubles, which included declaring bankruptcy in the late 1980s. In the runoff, turnout was up and Johnson easily won, 59%-41%. He breezed to victory in the general election.

In the House, Johnson has made eyebrow-raising statements that have landed him atop liberal as well as conservative blogs. After South Carolina Republican Rep. Joe Wilson shouted, "You lie!" at President Barack Obama in 2009 when he unveiled his health care plan to Congress, Johnson suggested that if the House took no disciplinary action against Wilson, "We'll have folks putting on white hoods and white uniforms again." Amid a series of incidents during 2015 in which African Americans had been shot by police, Johnson said, "It feels like open season on black men in America." During a roundtable discussion at the Democratic convention in Philadelphia in July 2016, he apologized for his "poor choice of words" after criticizing Israeli settlements on the West Bank that he said were growing "like termites."

On the Judiciary Committee, as the ranking Democrat on the Regulatory Reform, Commercial and Antitrust Law Subcommittee, Johnson has stirred debate on an array of topics in the legal system. His law enforcement proposals have made scant progress in the Republican-controlled Congress, but they have become part of broader national debates. In 2015, he proposed the Arbitration Fairness Act, to increase consumer protections in arbitration cases. Although the Judiciary Committee took no action, Johnson sparked debate in Congress and elsewhere about inequities that favor business, especially with mandatory arbitration cases without judicial oversight. In response to urban crime problems, he reintroduced a bill with conservative Republican Raul Labrador of Idaho to restrict free Defense Department transfers of surplus military equipment to state and local law enforcement agencies. "Militarizing America's main streets won't make us any safer, just more fearful and more reticent," Johnson said. In response to police malpractice, he has introduced legislation to reform grand jury procedures, including the appointment of special prosecutors in the investigations of police officers for the killing of civilians. That bill would apply to local law enforcement agencies that receive federal funding. In October 2016, he said the Homeland Security Department should have authority over the security of the nation's voting systems to prevent the "destabilization" of democracy.

Johnson also has served on the Armed Services Committee, where he challenged Republican provisions that sought to hamstring the Obama administration, such as basing tactical nuclear weapons in South Korea to counter North Korea.

In 2009, Johnson announced that he had battled hepatitis C, an incurable blood-borne liver disease, for more than a decade. Two Democrats lined up to challenge him in the 2010 primary; one of them, former DeKalb County CEO Vernon Jones, openly questioned his missing a series of debates. Johnson insisted his health was fine and unveiled an endorsement from President Barack Obama, who said the congressman "has done an outstanding job." He won the July primary with 55 percent to 26 percent for Jones and 18 percent for former DeKalb County Commissioner Connie Stokes. He was challenged in 2014 by well-known DeKalb County Sheriff Tom Brown, who criticized Johnson's lack of accomplishments and mocked his 2010 comment that the island of Guam "will become so overly populated that it will tip over and capsize." With another Obama endorsement, Johnson won 55%-45%. He got 55 percent of the vote in DeKalb, which cast 74 percent of the total vote, and led in the three other counties. He faced no primary opposition in 2016. In this district, the general election is a formality.

Eastern Atlanta Suburbs: DeKalb

Population		**Race and Ethnicity**		**Income**	
Total	723,659	White	25.8%	Median Income	$49,343 (265 out of 435)
Land area	497	Black	57.7%		
Pop/ sq mi	1457.2	Latino	9.1%		
Born in state	46.9%	Asian	5.1%	Under $50,000	50.7%
		Two races	1.7%	$50,000-$99,999	31.6%
Age Groups		Other	0.6%	$100,000-$199,999	15.2%
Under 18	26.1%			$200,000 or more	2.6%
18-34	23.5%	**Education**		Poverty Rate	19.0%
35-64	40.8%	H.S grad or less	38.4%		
Over 64	9.7%	Some college	31.7%	**Health Insurance**	
		College Degree, 4 yr	18.9%	With health insurance coverage	80.3%
Work		Post grad	11.0%		
White Collar	34.4%				
Sales and Service	44.2%	**Military**		**Public Assistance**	
Blue Collar	21.3%	Veteran	8.3%	Cash public assistance income	2.0%
Government	15.7%	Active Duty	0.1%		
				Food stamp/SNAP benefits	18.3%

Voter Turnout			
2015 Total Citizens 18+	479,685	2016 House Turnout as % CVAP	61%
2016 House turnout	290,739	2014 House Turnout as % CVAP	34%

2012 Presidential Vote		
Barack Obama	218,428	(74%)
Mitt Romney	76,016	(26%)

2016 Presidential Vote		
Hillary Clinton	224,907	(75%)
Donald Trump	66,433	(22%)
Gary Johnson	7,323	(2%)

Cook Partisan Voting Index: D+24

In 1920, when Gutzon Borglum began sculpting Jefferson Davis, Robert E. Lee and Stonewall Jackson into the side of Stone Mountain - the largest single piece of sculpture in the world - the huge outcropping of granite was a day's drive into the country east of central Atlanta and was soon to become a rallying point for the Ku Klux Klan. Even when the memorial was completed in 1972, suburban development barely reached that far. But today, after some of the most explosive metropolitan growth in the country, DeKalb (pronounced *duh-KAB* by locals) County is at the heart of the Atlanta metropolitan area. And this monument to the Confederate heroes - located along the Stone Mountain Freeway a few miles from the Interstate 285 Perimeter surrounding Atlanta - incongruously sits amid one of the most cosmopolitan and liberal constituencies in the South. In a sign of the times, most of the current visitors to Stone Mountain are African Americans, with many ignoring the Confederate history and enjoying the parkland as a recreational area. The local community has discussed adding to the mountain a monument to Martin Luther King Jr.

South DeKalb County has been transformed from mostly rural territory in the 1970s into one of the nation's largest collections of middle-class African-American neighborhoods, rivaled only by Prince George's County in Maryland. The county was a prime destination for evacuees from New Orleans following Hurricane Katrina in 2005. DeKalb's population grew by 22 percent in the 1990s, and by 4 percent from 2000 to 2010. It is now about 55 percent African American and 9 percent Latino. The county is culturally diverse, with more than 64 languages spoken.

The demographic changes have moved its politics to the left. DeKalb was a Republican county in the 1960s. Now, it is the most heavily Democratic major county in Georgia. In 2004, DeKalb voted 73%-27% for Democrat John Kerry. Hillary Clinton increased that margin to 81%-16% in 2016. As the county has evolved, south DeKalb has become much more African American and its property values have declined compared with north DeKalb. To attract more business, the county has offered tax breaks. In April 2016, *The Atlanta Journal-Constitution* reported that new projects had the potential to add more than 3,000 jobs and nearly $500 million worth of private investment to this lagging area. The county has suffered from government corruption.

The 4th Congressional District includes about half of DeKalb County, with northern and western parts of DeKalb spilling into roughly equal parts of the neighboring 5th and 6th districts. The district takes in a small part of Gwinnett County to the north, all of Rockdale County, and close to half of Newton County. Slightly more than half the voters are in DeKalb, and 20 percent are in Gwinnett. The 4th is a black-majority district and heavily Democratic, though the neighboring 5th District is more urban and even more Democratic.

FIFTH DISTRICT

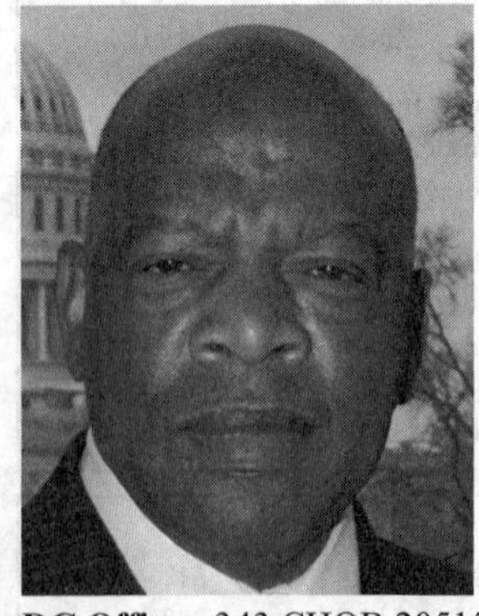

John Lewis (D)

Elected 1986, 16th term; b. Feb 21, 1940, Troy, AL; Western Washington University, Att., 2000; Pike County Training School (AL), 1957; American Baptist Theological Seminary (TN), B.A., 1961; Fisk University (TN), B.A., 1963; Protestant; Widower; 1 child.

Elected Office: Atlanta City Council, 1982-1986.

Professional Career: Chairman, Student Nonviolent Coord. Committee, 1963-1966; Field Foundation, 1966-1967; Community org. Director, Southern Regional Cncl., 1967-1970; Executive Director, Voter Ed. Project, 1970-1976; Director, ACTION, 1977-1980; Community affairs Director, National Consumer Coop. Bank, 1980-1986.

DC Office: 343 CHOB 20515, 202-225-3801, Fax: 202-225-0351, johnlewis.house.gov.
State Offices: Atlanta, 404-659-0116.

Committees: *Ways & Means*: Oversight (RMM).

Group Ratings

	ADA	ACLU	AFL-CIO	LCV	ITI	COC	HAFA	ACU	CFG	FRC
2016	-	88%	-	97%	50%	64%	11%	0%	4%	0%
2015	100%	C	100%	83%	C	40%	C	0%	0%	0%

Almanac Ratings 2015

	Economy	Social	Foreign	Composite
Liberal	98%	100%	100%	99%
Conservative	2%	0%	0%	1%

Key Votes of the 114th Congress

1. Keystone Pipeline	N	5. Puerto Rico Debt	Y	9. Offenses by Aliens	N
2. Trade Deals	N	6. Medical Marijuana	Y	10. Troops in Iraq	Y
3. Export-Import Bank	Y	7. Sanctuary Cities	N	11. Homeland Security $$	Y
4. Debt Ceiling Increase	Y	8. Armor-piercing Bullets	N	12. Trade Adjustment aid	Y

Election Results

Election	Name (Party)	Vote (%)		Cand. Spent	Ind. Exp. Support	Ind. Exp. Oppose
2016 General	John Lewis (D)	253,781	(84%)	$745,920		
	Douglas Bell (R)	46,768	(16%)	$4,111		
2016 Primary	John Lewis (D)		(100%)			

Prior winning percentages: 2014 (100%), 2012 (84%), 2010 (74%), 2008 (100%), 2006 (100%), 2004 (100%), 2002 (100%), 2000 (77%), 1998 (79%), 1996 (100%), 1994 (69%), 1992 (72%), 1990 (76%), 1988 (78%), 1986 (75%)

John Lewis, a Democrat first elected in 1986, made history a half-century ago as a leader of the civil rights movement. That experience has informed his work as a legislator on voting rights and poverty, and made him an iconic figure in American politics. Especially in the House, he carries great moral authority, though modest legislative influence with Democrats in the minority. As he has become more of a rallying force with his party's base, the impact of his actions has been less certain.

A sharecropper's son from Troy, Alabama, Lewis was seized by religious fervor as a child, preaching in the barnyard, determined to be a minister. Lewis was the first in his family to finish high school. He wrote to Rev. Ralph Abernathy for help in suing for the right to enter Troy State College, and he met Rev. Martin Luther King Jr. when he was 18. In 1959, at age 19, he helped organize the first lunch counter sit-in, which was received with open hostility. In 1960, the day after John F. Kennedy was elected president, Lewis sat in the Krystal Diner in Nashville, where a waitress poured cleansing powder down his back and water over his food to get him to leave. The restaurant manager then turned a fumigating machine on him.

In May 1961, he was on the first of the Freedom Rides, in which protesters rode buses through the South to challenge segregation, and were attacked as they went. Lewis was viciously beaten in Rock Hill, South Carolina, and Montgomery, Alabama. He spoke at the 1963 March on Washington, criticizing Kennedy liberals for inaction on civil rights and calling for massive help for the poor. In 1964, he helped coordinate the Mississippi Freedom Project. And in March 1965, he led the Selma-to-Montgomery march to petition for voting rights. During that historic event, he was beaten by policemen, who fractured his skull. Quietly maintaining his poise and sound judgment under harsh circumstances, Lewis was one of the people who risked their lives to make the civil rights revolution happen. He worked for Robert Kennedy's campaign for president in 1968 and was with him in Indianapolis when they heard King had been shot. He recounted his experiences in memoirs: his 1998 autobiography, *Walking with the Wind*; a 2012 book, *Across That Bridge: Life Lessons and a Vision for Change*, in which he describes what he learned in his early years; and *March*, a graphic trilogy that described his life in the civil rights movement and won the 2016 National Book Award.

In Lewis' first foray into electoral politics in 1977, he was defeated by Democrat Wyche Fowler in a special election to succeed Democratic Rep. Andrew Young. After winning a seat on the Atlanta City Council in 1981, Lewis ran again for Congress in 1986. He trailed Julian Bond 47%-35% in the primary, but Lewis won the runoff by assembling a coalition of poor blacks and nearly 90 percent of the whites. "Vote for the tugboat, not the showboat" was his slogan, stressing his work on local issues. He has been reelected easily ever since.

Lewis has been a strong partisan, with a staunchly liberal voting record. Usually quiet, he can speak in the forceful cadences reminiscent of black civil rights-era preachers, as he did in opposition to the Gulf War resolution in 1991 and to the impeachment of President Bill Clinton in 1998. At the dramatic finale of the health care legislation in 2010, Lewis linked arms with House Speaker Nancy Pelosi and walked to the Capitol through a gauntlet of taunting anti-health care reform protesters. In 2001, when Pelosi became Democratic Whip, Lewis initially challenged her, then switched his support to Steny Hoyer of Maryland. Lewis is the senior chief deputy whip in the Democratic leadership, and also the ranking Democrat on the Ways and Means Oversight Subcommittee. He has not been strongly identified with any tax or spending issues at the committee. Only occasionally does he defect from his party, as when he opposed the 1994 crime bill because of his disapproval of capital punishment.

Lewis has worked to commemorate the civil rights revolution in which he played such a large part. He got a federal building in Atlanta named for King and won historic trail designation for the demonstrators' route from Selma to Montgomery. During the 50th anniversary of the 1965 march, he reminisced that the Edmund Pettus Bridge was "almost a sacred site" because of the police attacks that took place there. "That's where some of us gave a little blood and where some people almost died." Since 1998, he has led members of Congress on pilgrimages to civil rights sites. Lewis has stoutly defended racial quotas and preferences. He strongly championed reauthorization of the Voting Rights Act in 2006 when Republicans were the House majority, and his support helped ensure it carried by a large majority over the objections of critics who claimed it was no longer necessary. After the Supreme Court in 2013 limited Justice Department review of voting-law changes in the South, he built bipartisan support to reverse that ruling. But he failed to get a vote on his proposal in the House or Senate in the following three years.

The 2008 presidential campaign was a difficult experience for Lewis. Following extensive pressure from various camps, he endorsed Hillary Clinton in 2007 as "a strong leader," and he defended her from attacks by other civil rights leaders. When Barack Obama won the Georgia primary, Lewis came under local and national pressure to switch to his camp. Some of the pressure came from two challengers in the July primary for his House seat, which Lewis won with 69 percent of the vote. In late February, he endorsed Obama "following a long, hard, difficult struggle" and spoke of Obama's candidacy as a transformational moment. "Something's happening in America, something some of us did not see coming," Lewis said. "It's a movement. It's a spiritual event."

Obama welcomed the switch, and Lewis became an outspoken advocate, perhaps excessively so, as in an October statement when he compared the campaign rhetoric of Republican nominee John McCain to that of former segregationist presidential candidate George Wallace of Alabama. McCain called the comparison "beyond the pale." At the Democratic convention in August, where he was treated as a hero, Lewis broke down in tears as he spoke of Obama's historic candidacy and the 45th anniversary of King's "I Have a Dream" speech. In a dramatic epilogue in February 2009, Elwin Wilson of Rock Hill apologized on national television for slugging Lewis in the Freedom Ride attack, saying, "I am ashamed." Seated next to him, Lewis embraced the 68-year-old man, and said, "I forgive you." Lewis called the apology "amazing, unreal, unbelievable" and said that it showed the "power of reconciliation."

Four years later, Lewis campaigned vigorously for Obama's reelection. During a speech in Florida, he said that Democrats needed to respond to criticism that Obama's supporters are "lost in a sea of despair, that we're disappointed. That's not the way I feel." He complained that voter identification laws and other measures passed by GOP-led state legislatures "constitute the most concerted effort to restrict the right to vote since before the Voting Rights Act." In the 2016 campaign, he actively supported Hillary Clinton, while downplaying in the Democratic primaries the civil-rights record of Bernie Sanders, to the dismay of Sanders supporters. "If there is one person ready to be president Day One, [it's] this woman," he told a Las Vegas rally in February.

Lewis took his protest tactics in a new direction and to a new cause when he organized a sit-in on the House floor in June 2016 for Democrats to object to Republicans' inaction on gun control, following the terrorist attack that killed 49 at the Pulse nightclub in Orlando, Florida. In an extraordinary scene, which ran counter to the rules and precedents of the House, dozens of members initially yelled objections and held protest signs. Following the adjournment that day, they sat on the House floor - many of them surrounding Lewis - to demand that the House vote. Unexpectedly, the sit-in continued for more than 24 hours and attracted national attention, especially on social media, as House Democrats used their cell phones to send personalized video messages. "We have to occupy the floor of the House until there's action," said Lewis, who initially conceived the tactics with Rep. John Larson of Connecticut. Republicans were unmoved, beyond their displeasure over the violation of House decorum. They revised House rules in January 2017 to raise the option of fines or other penalties in an attempt to prevent a recurrence. Some House experts questioned the validity or enforceability of the response.

A few days before the inauguration of Donald Trump in January 2017, Lewis sparked another informal challenge to House traditions when he told a television interviewer that he did not accept the "legitimacy" of Trump's November election. When Trump Tweeted in response that "Congressman John Lewis should spend more time on fixing and helping his district ... rather than falsely complaining about the election results," and that the protests were "All talk, talk, talk – no action or results," several dozen House Democrats responded by boycotting the Inaugural ceremony at the Capitol. Like the gun control sit-in, the boycott expressed the anger of many Democrats and gave some a short-term morale boost. But there was little evidence of a change of Republican strategies or a revival of Democratic fortunes.

Atlanta Metro

Population		**Race and Ethnicity**		**Income**	
Total	725,618	White	28.6%	Median Income	$44,174 (350 out of 435)
Land area	265	Black	57.8%		
Pop/ sq mi	2739.1	Latino	7.4%		
Born in state	53.6%	Asian	4.1%	Under $50,000	54.6%
		Two races	1.7%	$50,000-$99,999	25.5%
Age Groups		Other	0.4%	$100,000-$199,999	13.9%
Under 18	21.0%			$200,000 or more	5.9%
18-34	32.2%	**Education**		Poverty Rate	24.7%
35-64	37.0%	H.S grad or less	36.1%		
Over 64	9.8%	Some college	24.4%	**Health Insurance**	
Work		College Degree, 4 yr	22.9%	With health insurance coverage	81.2%
White Collar	44.0%	Post grad	16.6%		
Sales and Service	40.8%	**Military**		**Public Assistance**	
Blue Collar	15.1%	Veteran	6.2%	Cash public assistance income	2.5%
Government	14.5%	Active Duty	0.1%		
				Food stamp/SNAP benefits	19.5%

Voter Turnout			
2015 Total Citizens 18+	532,286	2016 House Turnout as % CVAP	56%
2016 House turnout	300,549	2014 House Turnout as % CVAP	33%

2012 Presidential Vote		
Barack Obama	241,280	(83%)
Mitt Romney	45,828	(16%)

2016 Presidential Vote		
Hillary Clinton	259,807	(85%)
Donald Trump	36,384	(12%)
Gary Johnson	9,564	(3%)

Cook Partisan Voting Index: D+34

Venture out of the quiet of the Ebenezer Baptist Church or the shade of the Rev. Martin Luther King Jr.'s boyhood home two blocks away and into the steamy heat of the Georgia sun, and one can see, a mile away, downtown Atlanta's atrium skyscrapers. They are evidence of the wealth and vibrant growth of the commercial capital of the South, the metropolis that has grown up where there was little more than a railroad junction at the time of the Civil War. But the human achievement that is downtown Atlanta is overshadowed by the revolution started in large part by a man who grew up on Auburn Avenue. Atlanta's white establishment during King's time, led by Mayors William Hartsfield and Ivan Allen and Coca-Cola's Robert Woodruff, deserve credit for abandoning segregation, but it was King and other civil rights leaders who took the risks that led them to do so. Atlanta's city fathers acted out of goodwill, but also with an eye for the economic growth of the city, having seen the damage that resulted in other Southern cities harmed by violent resistance.

Today, Atlanta is the center of the nation's ninth-largest metropolitan area. From Auburn Avenue, it spreads into two dozen counties of northern Georgia. Its Hartsfield-Jackson Atlanta International Airport is the busiest in the world, with 101 million passengers in 2015. That was a big lead over O'Hare, which was the U.S. runner-up with 70 million. The Chicago airport that year yielded to Atlanta the top slot in the number of flights. Internationally, the runner-up with passengers was Beijing. Business conventions and the airport helped bolster the city's $12 billion hospitality industry. Hotels recovered from the recession, with the fastest annual growth rate in the nation. The three-mile electric streetcar route, which opened in 2014, is part of a broader plan for light rail lines. In November 2016, voters approved a five-year increase in the sales tax to finance new projects for the region's rapid transit system.

Atlanta has vibrant office centers, in downtown, Midtown and Buckhead to the north. Modern sports facilities were built for the 1996 Summer Olympics. The Georgia Dome survived barely 20 more years, when it was demolished and replaced by the palatial Mercedes Benz Stadium on an adjacent lot of the Georgia World Congress Center Authority. The final sports event at the Georgia Dome was the National Football Conference championship in January 2017, which the Atlanta Falcons won. Coca-

Cola's skyscraper headquarters stands as a symbol of Atlanta's most successful worldwide business. The company donated a $10 million parcel of land near Centennial Olympic Park for a $100 million civil rights museum to house King's papers. Atlanta's music scene has flourished in recent years, and *The Guardian* reported that the city remained in 2015 the world capital of hip hop. Hip hop and R&B acts such as Cee Lo Green, Young Jeezy, OutKast and T.I. got their start in Atlanta.

The 5th Congressional District of Georgia includes much of the city of Atlanta and also Forest Park and the smaller communities of Lake City and Morrow in Clayton County. It includes most of the posh and Republican Buckhead. The small population of Buckhead has more financial than political influence in this overwhelmingly Democratic district, where Hillary Clinton got 85 percent of the vote in 2016.

This area unexpectedly became a hot topic of national attention a week before his Inauguration when Donald Trump - angered by criticism of him by its long-time Democratic Rep. John Lewis - tweeted that the 5th District "is in horrible shape and falling apart (not to mention crime infested) …" Trump's criticism surprised many in Atlanta who have proudly lived in the self-styled "city too busy to hate." His reference to local crime had some factual basis. As the Trump transition team noted, Atlanta had the 14th-highest violent crime rate among the nation's cities, though the rate had decreased during the past decade. And like every city, it has had other recent problems. In April 2015, 11 of its chief educators were convicted in a standardized-test cheating scandal. The new stadium, while gentrifying some nearby poor neighborhoods, has had tensions with long-time residents of the Westside.

But based on an array of measures, Trump's criticism fell short, according to a next-day review by *PolitiFact*. Rating Trump's claim as mostly false, the fact-check concluded, "While [the 5th District] has higher unemployment and poverty rates than the national average, it still has a thriving economic hub in Atlanta and higher educational attainment."

SIXTH DISTRICT

Karen Handel (R)

Elected 2017, 1st term; b. Apr 18, 1962, Washington, D.C; Prince George's Community College, Attended; University of Maryland, Attended; married (Steven Handel).

Elected Office: Fulton County Board of Commissioners, 2003-2006; GA Secretary of State 2007-2010.

Professional Career: Businesswoman

State Offices: Roswell, 770-998-0049.

Committees: *Education & the Workforce; Judiciary.*

Election Results

Election	Name (Party)	Vote (%)		Cand. Spent	Ind. Exp. Support	Ind. Exp. Oppose
2017 Special Run Off	Karen Handel (R)	134,595	(52%)	$3,069,138	$532,257	$1,355,237
	Jon Ossof (D)	124,893	(48%)	$21,356,350	$451,995	$117,112
2017 Special	Jon Ossof (D)	92,673	(48%)			
	Karen Handel (R)	38,071	(20%)			
	Bob Gray (R)	20,802	(11%)	$321,028	$989	$105,000
	Dan Moody (R)	17,028	(9%)	$1,865,030		$157,552
	Judson Hill (R)	16,870	(9%)	$356,940		

Republican Karen Handel won the June 2017 special election to fill the seat created by the resignation of GOP Rep. Tom Price. It was the most expensive and one of the most high-stakes House contests ever. She defeated Democrat Jon Ossoff, who led the first round of voting on April 18 but failed to receive a majority of the vote in the traditionally Republican seat.

Price, who had held the seat since 2004, was a prominent House Republican, having served in the GOP leadership and as chairman of the Budget Committee. There had been speculation that he was preparing to run for governor in 2018. His plans were disrupted when Donald Trump selected him as Secretary of Health and Human Services during the presidential transition. That cast an intense spotlight on this suburban district where, ironically, Trump had fared poorly in the election, compared with the customary GOP performance in a district where Newt Gingrich and Johnny Isakson, in addition to Price, had never faced serious Democratic opposition.

In the 18-candidate primary, Ossoff quickly became the frontrunner among the five Democrats, as well as the overall field. In his first campaign, he was little-known in the district. His chief familiarity with Congress had been as an aide to Democratic Rep. Hank Johnson in the neighboring 4th District. Ossoff was embraced by Daily Kos and other progressive organizations, who touted his credentials and helped him to raise huge sums of money that he used for extensive advertising and voter contact. He became a national phenomenon who channeled liberal hostility to Trump. His limited experience became an issue when Republicans, plus news-media fact checkers, claimed that he had exaggerated his work with Johnson as a "national security aide with top-secret clearance."

Handel was one of several Republicans who gained early attention in the contest, either from endorsements or their campaign spending. She emerged from the GOP pack as the candidate with the most experience in local politics and government. She had been Georgia Secretary of State, but lost two statewide bids for office. She earlier was president and CEO of the North Fulton Chamber of Commerce and chaired the Fulton County Board of Commissioners, and described herself as "a life-long conservative who built her career on delivering results in both the public and private sectors."

Prior to the primary, Ossoff had a vast fundraising advantage over Handel - roughly $8 million to $500,000. For that matter, three Republican men in the contest spent more than Handel, but each suffered from political inexperience. With Ossoff's momentum and the divisions among the GOP candidates, Democrats were hopeful that he would secure the majority of the vote in the April primary and avoid a run-off. In a vote count that attracted national attention, Ossoff fell short with 48.1% to 19.8% for Handel in the high-turnout primary. No other candidate received more than 11 percent of the vote.

In the run-off, with a record total of more than $50 million, Ossoff spent more than $30 million, much of it from grass-roots fundraising. Handel got a boost from the Congressional Leadership Fund, the Super PAC supporting House Republicans. Her 52%-48% victory sparked intensive debate about the significance of the outcome, including the ability of GOP candidates to withstand voter unhappiness with Trump, especially in higher-income districts.

Northern Atlanta Suburbs: Fulton, Cobb

Population		**Race and Ethnicity**		**Income**	
Total	724,825	White	61.8%	Median Income	$79,997 (34 out of 435)
Land area	299	Black	12.7%		
Pop/ sq mi	2426.1	Latino	12.5%	Under $50,000	31.8%
Born in state	33.1%	Asian	10.3%	$50,000-$99,999	27.9%
		Two races	2.0%	$100,000-$199,999	26.5%
Age Groups		Other	0.6%	$200,000 or more	13.8%
Under 18	25.0%			Poverty Rate	9.7%
18-34	21.2%	**Education**			
35-64	43.0%	H.S grad or less	20.4%	**Health Insurance**	
Over 64	10.9%	Some college	21.5%	With health insurance coverage	86.3%
		College Degree, 4 yr	36.4%		
Work		Post grad	21.6%		
White Collar	52.7%			**Public Assistance**	
Sales and Service	36.5%	**Military**		Cash public assistance income	0.8%
Blue Collar	10.8%	Veteran	6.2%		
Government	8.0%	Active Duty	0.1%	Food stamp/SNAP benefits	5.0%

2012 Presidential Vote		
Mitt Romney	186,998	(61%)
Barack Obama	114,796	(37%)

2016 Presidential Vote		
Donald Trump	160,029	(48%)
Hillary Clinton	155,087	(47%)
Gary Johnson	16,148	(5%)

Cook Partisan Voting Index: R+8

In the red clay north of Atlanta, an almost wholly new metropolitan quarter has grown up over the past four decades. Affluent Atlanta has spread out past the Perimeter, the local name for Interstate 285, into territory that was once farms, small towns and modest factory cities. Where there were perhaps 100,000 people in the 1950s, there are more than 1 million today. No longer is downtown Atlanta the only focus. The edge city of Perimeter Center is not just for shopping: It is a major office center, exceeding downtown Atlanta in square footage. Along the usually jammed Georgia 400 highway, in the fast-growing northern part of Fulton County, are the affluent suburbs of Sandy Springs, Roswell and Alpharetta.

Home Depot, the nation's second-largest retailer, is based in Sandy Springs. In 2012, Home Depot lobbied Georgia lawmakers for internet sales taxes, arguing that tax loopholes for web retailers put on-the-ground companies at a competitive disadvantage. Georgia Gov. Nathan Deal later signed into law a bill requiring online retailers to collect sales taxes. Sandy Springs has been an innovator in outsourcing basic government services to private industry. In June 2012, *The New York Times* reported that the city "does not have a fleet of vehicles for road repair, or a yard where the fleet is parked. It does not have long-term debt. It has no pension obligations. It does not have a city hall, for that matter, if your idea of a city hall is a building owned by the city. Sandy Springs rents." The city in July 2016 imposed what it said would be a temporary three-year halt to its contract procedures because it feared disruption during a planning and development boom. In the interim, no-bid contracts were permitted. Mercedes-Benz USA had groundbreaking in September 2016 for its new corporate headquarters, which are being moved to Sandy Springs from New Jersey. Alpharetta, the self-styled "Technology City of the South," was rated by NerdWallet in 2015 as the best small city in the nation to start a business.

The 6th Congressional District is based in the northern Atlanta suburbs. It includes the northern sections of DeKalb and Fulton counties and the eastern part of Cobb County. Nearly half of the population is in Fulton. The district has been safely Republican. Mitt Romney and John McCain got 61 percent and 59 percent of the vote, respectively. That changed when Donald Trump won, 48%-47%, one of several upscale suburban districts in the South where the GOP vote dropped precipitously in 2016. The lasting significance of that vote became a matter of great interest to both parties.

SEVENTH DISTRICT

Rob Woodall (R)

Elected 2010, 4th term; b. Feb 11, 1970, Athens; University of Georgia, J.D.; Furman University (SC), B.A.; Methodist; Single.

Professional Career: Clerk, private firm, 1993-1994; Chief of Staff, Legislative aide, Rep. John Linder, 1994-2010.

DC Office: 1724 LHOB 20515, 202-225-4272, Fax: 202-225-4696, woodall.house.gov.

State Offices: Lawrenceville, 770-232-3005.

Committees: *Budget*. *Rules*: Legislative & Budget Process (Chmn). *Transportation & Infrastructure*: Aviation, Highways & Transit, Water Resources & Environment.

Group Ratings

	ADA	ACLU	AFL-CIO	LCV	ITI	COC	HAFA	ACU	CFG	FRC
2016	-	5%	-	3%	83%	100%	66%	88%	79%	100%
2015	5%	C	8%	0%	C	89%	C	91%	71%	83%

Almanac Ratings 2015

	Economy	Social	Foreign	Composite
Liberal	11%	9%	7%	9%
Conservative	89%	91%	93%	91%

Key Votes of the 114th Congress

1. Keystone Pipeline	Y	5. Puerto Rico Debt	Y	9. Offenses by Aliens	Y
2. Trade Deals	Y	6. Medical Marijuana	Y	10. Troops in Iraq	Y
3. Export-Import Bank	N	7. Sanctuary Cities	Y	11. Homeland Security $$	N
4. Debt Ceiling Increase	N	8. Armor-piercing Bullets	Y	12. Trade Adjustment aid	N

Election Results

Election	Name (Party)	Vote (%)	Cand. Spent	Ind. Exp. Support	Ind. Exp. Oppose
2016 General	Rob Woodall (R)........................	174,081 (60%)	$312,292		
	Rashid Malik (D)........................	114,220 (40%)			
2016 Primary	Rob Woodall (R)....................................	(100%)			

Prior winning percentages: 2014 (659%), 2012 (62%), 2010 (67%)

Republican Rob Woodall, elected in 2010, worked the previous 16 years for his predecessor in Congress. His Capitol Hill experience has made him more savvy about how Congress works and less inclined to bash government than other GOP colleagues who entered with him. But he matches them in his activism and fiscal conservatism.

Woodall was born in Athens, where his parents were finishing their studies at the University of Georgia. His father was an entomologist who would take Rob and his older sister on expeditions to collect bugs in swampy areas. The family was of modest means, shopped at Goodwill stores, and drove used cars. "Nobody squeezes a nickel harder than I do," Woodall said. He went to college on an ROTC scholarship and had a summer job on the assembly line at an RC Cola bottling plant. While in law school, he worked for a firm in Washington on issues related to President Bill Clinton's energy policy and Hillary Clinton's health care initiative. He loved being on the frontlines of national policymaking and worked out a deal with the dean of the University of Georgia School of Law to finish his degree in Washington. In 1994, Woodall took a 50 percent pay cut to start work as a legislative aide to Republican Rep. John Linder. He rose to chief of staff in 2000.

He ran for the House after Linder announced his retirement. Eight candidates entered the GOP primary in July. Woodall and radio talk-show host Jody Hice received the most votes, but each fell short of the 50 percent necessary to avoid a runoff. Hice self-funded his runoff campaign and out-spent Woodall. Both candidates courted support from tea party groups. Woodall embraced their principles of limited government, strict constitutional construction and fiscal responsibility. He advocated shifting some of the federal government's powers to the states, repealing the Democratic health care overhaul, and taking tougher steps to deal with immigration. Yet, most local tea party groups backed Hice, especially after he bought billboards sporting a Soviet-era hammer and sickle and depicting Obama as a socialist. Woodall, endorsed by Linder, won the August runoff, 56%-44%. He easily won the general election and has not faced serious opposition since. In 2014, Hice was elected to the neighboring 10th District seat.

Woodall has defined his main issue as the federal tax code, which he calls "a monstrosity" that should be replaced with a national sales tax. He contributed to *The FairTax Book*, which was published by Linder and radio talk-show Neal Boortz and was a best seller. He says the tax code punishes productivity and encourages debt, and that a national sales tax would boost the rate of personal savings. He has regularly filed a Fair Tax bill. By 2016, he had 73 co-sponsors, though the tax-writing committees had taken no action.

In the House, Woodall got seats on the Rules and Budget committees, aided by his familiarity as an ex-staffer with those panels' procedural issues. He joined most other GOP freshmen in opposing the New Year's Day 2013 deal on tax and spending cuts, aimed at averting the so-called fiscal cliff, calling it "all dessert and no vegetables. … Spending is the problem in Washington, not tax revenue."

Woodall has shown occasional independence. On the typically Democratic issue of campaign finance reform, he introduced a bill to bar incumbents from holding onto their campaign money between elections. Politicians' war chests discouraged many would-be challengers, he said. In 2011, he was one of seven Republicans who refused to bar federal funding for National Public Radio and who opposed a measure allowing permit holders to carry concealed weapons across state lines. "If the Second Amendment protects my rights to carry my concealed weapon from state to state to state, I don't need another federal law," he said. Woodall styles himself as vigilant in defending the prerogatives of Congress. In June 2015, he was one of 19 House Republicans who voted for a proposal to remove U.S. troops from fighting the Islamic State until Congress formally authorized such hostilities.

Woodall became chairman of the Republican Study Committee's budget and spending task force. When Louisiana's Steve Scalise stepped down as RSC chairman to become majority whip in June 2014, Woodall was appointed interim chairman. After the 2014 election, he ran for chairman of the Republican Policy Committee, but finished third behind Tom Reed of New York and the winner, Luke Messer of Indiana.

In the 2016 presidential campaign, Woodall initially supported Sen. Marco Rubio for president and later joined what he called the "angst brigade" when Donald Trump became the frontrunner for the Republican nomination. He finally endorsed Trump at the GOP convention in July, and said that he saw a Trump presidency as an opportunity for Congress to assert itself. Given that "Donald Trump has no Capitol Hill constituency," Woodall told *Real Clear Politics*, "we might have members of Congress defending the Constitution, being Article I, doing oversight over the president irrespective of his or her party, rather than being the cheerleader of the president that is the leader of their party."

Northeastern Atlanta Suburbs: Gwinnett, Forsyth

Population		**Race and Ethnicity**		**Income**	
Total	745,461	White	47.7%	Median Income	$64,882 (96 out of 435)
Land area	393	Black	18.6%	Under $50,000	38.0%
Pop/ sq mi	1898.7	Latino	18.8%	$50,000-$99,999	31.5%
Born in state	35.7%	Asian	12.2%	$100,000-$199,999	24.0%
Age Groups		Two races	2.2%	$200,000 or more	6.4%
Under 18	28.4%	Other	0.5%	Poverty Rate	12.0%
18-34	21.5%	**Education**		**Health Insurance**	
35-64	41.6%	H.S grad or less	33.5%	With health insurance coverage	82.1%
Over 64	8.5%	Some college	27.9%	**Public Assistance**	
Work		College Degree, 4 yr	26.4%	Cash public assistance income	1.7%
White Collar	41.0%	Post grad	12.3%	Food stamp/SNAP benefits	9.8%
Sales and Service	40.9%	**Military**			
Blue Collar	18.1%	Veteran	6.1%		
Government	9.2%	Active Duty	0.1%		

Voter Turnout			
2015 Total Citizens 18+	442,958	2016 House Turnout as % CVAP	65%
2016 House turnout	288,301	2014 House Turnout as % CVAP	40%

2012 Presidential Vote		
Mitt Romney	158,741	(60%)
Barack Obama	101,169	(38%)

2016 Presidential Vote		
Donald Trump	150,845	(51%)
Hillary Clinton	132,012	(44%)
Gary Johnson	12,115	(4%)

Cook Partisan Voting Index: R+9

In the past two decades, greater Atlanta has grown out in every direction: south past the airport, west over the Chattahoochee River, north past Perimeter Center, and east and northeast past Stone Mountain. The outer suburbs north of Atlanta have grown fastest of all. Gwinnett County features mature neighborhoods of affluent professionals and entrepreneurs and closer-in communities near Interstate 85 that have been attracting Georgia's largest concentration of Hispanics along with middle-class blacks. The county's rapidly growing school system boasts that its students speak more than 100 languages. Farther out in Lawrenceville, Duluth and Buford, downtown Atlanta seems very far away, both physically - it is 20 to 40 miles, and more than an hour of clogged rush-hour driving, to Peachtree Street - and in state of mind. For many, Atlanta is something off the highway on the way to Hartsfield-Jackson Atlanta International Airport.

The growth and its diversity here are hard to overstate. Gwinnett County's population grew 37 percent from 2000 to 2010, to more than 805,000. In the next five years, it grew to 896,000, despite the slowdown during the recession. Like other metro Atlanta counties, the non-Hispanic white population has been dropping in Gwinnett schools, while the overall student numbers soar. There are Mexicans in

Norcross, Koreans in Duluth and Bosnians in Lawrenceville. The share of the county population who are immigrants increased from 6 percent in 1990 to 32 percent in 2014. In January 2015, the Washington-based Migration Policy Institute estimated that 71,000 immigrants were living illegally in Gwinnett. Overall, the minority population in the county has grown to 28 percent African American, 21 percent Hispanic and 12 percent Asian. In August 2016, civil rights groups filed a lawsuit challenging the district lines and at-large voting in the county, claiming they prevented minority voters from being able to elect candidates of their choosing.

The 7th Congressional District of Georgia comprises about 75 percent of Gwinnett County and 40 percent of Forsyth County to its north, which has been the fastest growing county in Georgia. The 4th District has the southern slice of Gwinnett that is more Democratic. In each county, Donald Trump fared relatively poorly among traditional Republicans in the 2016 presidential election. Gwinnett, which voted 54%-45% for Mitt Romney over President Barack Obama in 2012, backed Hillary Clinton over Trump, 51%-45% -- the first presidential election since 1976 in which the county has voted Democratic. In Forsyth, the 81%-18% vote for Romney dropped to 71%-24% for Trump. Overall, the Republican vote in the district fell to 51%-44% in 2016 from the previous 60%-38%.

EIGHTH DISTRICT

Austin Scott (R)

Elected 2010, 4th term; b. Dec 10, 1969, Augusta; American College (PA); University of Georgia Terry College of Business; b.B.A.; Baptist; Married (Vivien Scott); 2 children.

Elected Office: GA House, 1997-2010.

Professional Career: Owner, Southern Group; Agent, Principal Financial Group, 1993-2010.

DC Office: 2417 RHOB 20515, 202-225-6531, Fax: 202-225-3013, austinscott.house.gov.

State Offices: Tifton, 229-396-5175; Warner Robins, 478-971-1776.

Committees: *Agriculture*: Commodity Exchanges, Energy & Credit (Chmn), General Farm Commodities & Risk Management. *Armed Services*: Emerging Threats & Capabilities, Oversight & Investigations, Readiness.

Group Ratings

	ADA	ACLU	AFL-CIO	LCV	ITI	COC	HAFA	ACU	CFG	FRC
2016	-	5%	-	0%	100%	100%	73%	92%	78%	100%
2015	0%	C	9%	0%	C	84%	C	92%	85%	92%

Almanac Ratings 2015

	Economy	Social	Foreign	Composite
Liberal	6%	0%	0%	2%
Conservative	94%	100%	100%	98%

Key Votes of the 114th Congress

1. Keystone Pipeline	Y	5. Puerto Rico Debt	Y	9. Offenses by Aliens	Y
2. Trade Deals	Y	6. Medical Marijuana	N	10. Troops in Iraq	N
3. Export-Import Bank	N	7. Sanctuary Cities	Y	11. Homeland Security $$	N
4. Debt Ceiling Increase	N	8. Armor-piercing Bullets	Y	12. Trade Adjustment aid	N

Election Results

Election	Name (Party)	Vote (%)		Cand. Spent	Ind. Exp. Support	Ind. Exp. Oppose
2016 General	Austin Scott (R)	173,983	(68%)	$786,076		
	James Harris (D)	83,225	(32%)			
2016 Primary	Austin Scott (R)	34,875	(78%)			
	Angela Hicks (R)	9,982	(22%)			

Prior winning percentages: 2014 (unopposed), 2012 (unopposed), 2010 (53%)

Republican Austin Scott, who defeated a Democratic incumbent in 2010, has been a leader of the large Republican class elected that year. In the rural southern tradition, he has been an active lawmaker on military and agriculture issues who usually operates behind the scenes and doesn't seek attention.

Born in Augusta, Scott's father was an orthopedic surgeon and his mother was a teacher. He graduated from the University of Georgia with a degree in risk management and insurance. After college, he opened an insurance brokerage firm, which he operated for 17 years. Scott was elected to the state House at 26. He sponsored a bill to provide better funding for the state's trauma-care system, championed the expansion of charter schools and supported the right of students to express their religious beliefs in schools. In January 2009, he announced his candidacy for governor. To boost awareness, he went on a 1,000-mile walk around the state, talking to voters. He made his 64-day journey in the height of summer, losing seven pounds in the process. But his campaign failed to gain traction, and he decided to challenge four-term Democratic Rep. Jim Marshall.

Marshall styled himself as a conservative Democrat and voted against President Barack Obama's health care law. But he was vulnerable in 2010 simply because he was a Democrat. Scott promised to reduce the deficit, and he attacked the incumbent for voting for Obama's $787 billion economic stimulus bill. Marshall, unlike most Democrats, was endorsed by the U.S. Chamber of Commerce and the National Rifle Association. In one ad, Marshall showed his driver's license to prove that he wasn't House Speaker Nancy Pelosi, who became a Republican symbol of the reviled Democratic agenda in Congress in much of the South. Still, Scott won the seat, 53%-47%. In the next two elections, he ran without major-party opposition. In 2016, he faced Democrat James Harris, who did not file a campaign spending report and was defeated, 68%-32%

In the House, Scott was elected freshman class president and was regularly asked to explain his boisterous classmates' actions to the news media. They never intended to speak with a single voice, he replied in November 2011: "I think of us as a group of independent thinkers." A year later, he said that their main job was "to play defense against what [President Barack Obama] was going to do. I think we were pretty effective at doing that." Scott has taken a notably low profile.

As a member of the Armed Services Committee, unlike many of the military's boosters on the panel, he has maintained that defense spending must be examined for budget cuts. But he hasn't been reluctant to advocate on behalf of his district. In 2015, Scott collaborated with neighboring 1st District Republican Rep. Buddy Carter to preserve the A10-C Warthog, which provides support for larger aircraft in low-visibility and low-altitude combat and has two squadrons at Moody Air Force Base in Valdosta. He has opposed the Obama administration's request for another round of base closings, which could jeopardize Warner-Robins and Moody. In December 2016, he claimed credit for an amendment to the annual defense spending bill that removed proposed language that might have led to the shift of work from Air Force depots, including Robins. Earlier that year, he filed a bill to prohibit the president from using Air Force One or other government aircraft to transport political candidates to campaign events.

On the Agriculture Committee, he has been chairman of the Commodity Exchanges, Energy, and Credit Subcommittee. In his work to reauthorize the Commodity Futures Trading Commission, he took on the financially complex and often risky derivatives markets and sought a bipartisan solution that struck a balance between market integrity and market access. In June 2015, the House passed his bill to renew the CFTC. Its goal, he said, was to "ensure that our regulatory framework protects the integrity of our markets while not limiting the ability of end users to access these tools to conduct their business.

Elsewhere, Scott introduced a bill to abolish the Legal Services Corporation in 2011 - three days after it became public that its lawyers had won an action against a company in his district that had fired U.S. workers in favor of less-expensive immigrants with visas. In 2016, he filed a bill to limit spending on the federal Lifeline program, which provides telephone and other communications services to low-income consumers at reduced rates.

Scott was a grudging supporter of Donald Trump in the 2016 presidential campaign. He initially endorsed Sen. Marco Rubio and called Trump "a con man." In September, he issued a statement concluding, "I am committed to defeating Hillary Clinton this November," which failed to mention Trump's name.

South-Central Georgia: Warner Robins, Valdosta

Population		**Race and Ethnicity**		**Income**	
Total	700,278	White	60.5%	Median Income	$40,812 (392 out of 435)
Land area	8,712	Black	30.0%		
Pop/ sq mi	80.4	Latino	6.2%		
Born in state	69.1%	Asian	1.4%	Under $50,000	58.3%
		Two races	1.6%	$50,000-$99,999	27.7%
Age Groups		Other	0.3%	$100,000-$199,999	12.0%
Under 18	24.3%			$200,000 or more	2.0%
18-34	23.9%	**Education**		Poverty Rate	22.3%
35-64	38.1%	H.S grad or less	51.8%		
Over 64	13.7%	Some college	28.9%	**Health Insurance**	
		College Degree, 4 yr	11.5%	With health insurance coverage	81.8%
Work		Post grad	7.8%		
White Collar	31.9%				
Sales and Service	42.1%	**Military**		**Public Assistance**	
Blue Collar	26.0%	Veteran	10.7%	Cash public assistance income	1.7%
Government	22.5%	Active Duty	0.8%		
				Food stamp/SNAP benefits	18.4%

Voter Turnout			
2015 Total Citizens 18+	509,480	2016 House Turnout as % CVAP	50%
2016 House turnout	257,208	2014 House Turnout as % CVAP	26%

2012 Presidential Vote		
Mitt Romney	163,908	(62%)
Barack Obama	99,676	(38%)

2016 Presidential Vote		
Donald Trump	168,193	(63%)
Hillary Clinton	91,360	(34%)
Gary Johnson	5,961	(2%)

Cook Partisan Voting Index: R+15

South-central Georgia is a region of farm and forest lands and a collection of small, and some tiny, towns. Twiggs and Wilkinson counties have been among the world's major sources of kaolin, a clay used for china and ceramics. Juliette, along Interstate 75, is an old mill town that's too small for most maps. Scenes from *Fried Green Tomatoes* were filmed in Juliette - an old former hardware store there became the film's Whistle Stop Café. With its Air Logistics Center and testing and repair site for the F-22 Raptor, Robins Air Force Base and the surrounding city of Warner Robins have grown significantly. The sprawling base employed 22,000 people and had an economic impact of $2.7 billion in 2016. Warner Robins was ranked as the most affordable city in Georgia. In April 2016, local organizations promoting the base met with members of the Georgia congressional delegation to promote its future. Earlier that month, a Defense Department report concluded that the Air Force had 32 percent excess capacity overall.

In Pulaski County is Hawkinsville, founded on the banks of the Ocmulgee River and a winter home for harness horse training. Nearby is Tifton, home to the Georgia Museum of Agriculture. Farther south along Interstate 75 is Valdosta, a black-majority city of 55,700 that has the most successful high school football program in the country. No team in the nation has won more games than the Valdosta High School Wildcats, who have a won-loss record of 907-220-34 since 1913; in 2016, the team won its 24th state championship. Valdosta is also where Doc Holliday, made famous by the gunfight at the O.K. Corral, spent much of his youth. The city still has a bit of a wild side: Residents of dry towns in northern Florida frequently cross the Georgia border to buy liquor in Valdosta. Also on the wild side: In 2016, a fake Twitter account for a Rep. Steven Smith of Valdosta, who claimed to represent the 15th District of Georgia, fooled some national reporters.

The 8th Congressional District includes Monroe and Jones counties north of Macon in central Georgia and stretches all the way south to the Florida border. It covers Berrien County, known for its turpentine and bell peppers, and it takes in most of Lowndes County, where Valdosta is located. The district is solidly Republican. Donald Trump won 63 percent of the vote here in 2016, one point higher than Mitt Romney received in 2012.

NINTH DISTRICT

Doug Collins (R)

Elected 2012, 3rd term; b. Aug 16, 1966, Gainesville; North Georgia College and State University (Military College of Georgia) Foundation Inc., B.A.; New Orleans Baptist Theological Seminary (LA), M.Div.; John Marshall University Law School (Atlanta), J.D.; Baptist; Married (Lisa Jordan); 3 children.

Military Career: U.S. Air Force Reserve, 2007-present.

Elected Office: GA House, 2007-2012.

Professional Career: Practicing attorney, 2008-2012; Pastor, Chicopee Baptist Church, 1994-2005.

DC Office: 1504 LHOB 20515, 202-225-9893, Fax: 202-226-1224, dougcollins.house.gov.

State Offices: Gainesville, 770-297-3388.

Committees: House Republican Conference Vice Chairman. *Judiciary*: Courts, Intellectual Property & Internet, Regulatory Reform, Commercial & Antitrust Law. *Rules*: Rules & Organization of the House (Chmn).

Group Ratings

	ADA	ACLU	AFL-CIO	LCV	ITI	COC	HAFA	ACU	CFG	FRC
2016	-	5%	-	0%	83%	100%	79%	92%	74%	100%
2015	10%	C	9%	3%	C	75%	C	96%	82%	100%

Almanac Ratings 2015

	Economy	Social	Foreign	Composite
Liberal	13%	4%	0%	6%
Conservative	87%	96%	100%	94%

Key Votes of the 114th Congress

1. Keystone Pipeline	Y	5. Puerto Rico Debt	Y	9. Offenses by Aliens	Y
2. Trade Deals	N	6. Medical Marijuana	N	10. Troops in Iraq	N
3. Export-Import Bank	N	7. Sanctuary Cities	Y	11. Homeland Security $$	N
4. Debt Ceiling Increase	N	8. Armor-piercing Bullets	Y	12. Trade Adjustment aid	N

Election Results

Election	Name (Party)	Vote (%)	Cand. Spent	Ind. Exp. Support	Ind. Exp. Oppose
2016 General	Doug Collins (R)	256,535 (100%)			
2016 Primary	Doug Collins (R)	52,043 (61%)			
	Paul Broun (R)	18,761 (22%)			
	Roger Fitzpatrick (R)	8,943 (11%)			

Prior winning percentages: 2014 (817%), 2012 (76%)

Republican Doug Collins, elected to a newly drawn seat in 2012, has background in both divinity and the law. He has shown sound legislative skills and likely will gain more attention with his move into the House Republican leadership after the 2016 election..

Collins was born in Gainesville and grew up in Hall County. His father was a state trooper, and his mother worked a variety of jobs in town. In 1988, Collins graduated from North Georgia College & State University, where he studied political science and business. The same year, he met his wife, Lisa, at church. He worked in several jobs in the hazardous-materials industry, but then felt a calling to the ministry. After spending time volunteering as a youth minister, he entered the New Orleans Baptist Theological Seminary. He returned to Gainesville, serving as pastor of Chicopee Baptist Church. In 2002, Collins joined the Air Force Reserve and, in 2008, did a tour in Iraq as a chaplain, an experience that he says gave him "a whole different perspective of what freedom is like and what the lack of it is like." He got a law degree in Atlanta and opened his own practice in Gainesville. He served six years in the state House, including one term as floor leader for Republican Gov. Nathan Deal, whom he had known since high school.

When Georgia got a 14th district following the 2010 reapportionment, Republicans at the State House drew the new 9th District without an incumbent, where they could easily elect one of their own. When Collins decided to run for the seat, his chief primary opponent was Gainesville talk-show host Martha Zoller, a tea party favorite who campaigned as a political outsider. She criticized Collins' role in devising the referendum to raise the sales tax by a penny to address traffic congestion, which was widely rejected in most of the state. Collins touted his legislative experience crafting budgets and his service in Iraq. He also likened her status as a well-known radio host to an "Obama-style celebrity" and hammered her for having once stated that President Barack Obama was "a nice guy."

The two fought to a near-draw in July's primary, with Collins coming out on top, 42%-41%, a difference of just 734 votes. In the runoff, Zoller was endorsed by national figures such as former Alaska Gov. Sarah Palin and 2012 presidential candidates Herman Cain, Newt Gingrich and Rick Santorum. In the final days before the election, Deal recorded a robo-call for Collins; he also had the backing of Georgia House Speaker David Ralston and Zell Miller, a former Georgia governor and senator. Collins played on the local roots of his major endorsers and gathered support with the slogan "We are the 9th District." In the end, Collins outspent Zoller by 3-to-2 and prevailed in the runoff, 55%-45%. In this overwhelmingly Republican district, Collins coasted to victory in November.

In the House, Collins got seats on the Judiciary and Rules committees - good posts for a lawyerly mind. In April 2015, Judiciary Chairman Bob Goodlatte endorsed a resolution filed by Collins to express congressional disapproval of the net neutrality rules that had been approved by the Federal Communications Commission. Collins criticized those rules as "heavy-handed agency regulations that would slow internet speeds, increase consumer prices and hamper infrastructure development," and said that he preferred the alternative of a free and open internet. The committee also approved his proposal to give more authority to state and local governments to enforce national immigration laws. In June 2016, Obama signed into law a Collins bill to guarantee a federal law enforcement officer the right to carry a firearm during a covered furlough from the job. In December 2016, he wrote an op-ed in support of tax incentives for the motion-picture industry, which has a significance presence in Georgia.

Collins broke a two-decade deadlock in his district by adding a provision to the defense spending bill in 2013 that transferred 282 acres of local land from the Forest Service to the U.S. Army, which has used the area for training of Army Rangers. The location in Lumpkin County is near the Military College of Georgia. The Army welcomed the freedom to alter the landscape without the approval of the Forest Service.

Following the 2016 election, Collins defeated Bill Flores of Texas for vice-chairman of the House Republican Conference in a 170-61 vote among House Republicans. Collins said he would focus on the political message that GOP lawmakers take to their home districts. With his seat on the Rules Committee, which schedules bills for the House floor and acts as an arm of the House leadership, Collins has an additional niche as a legislative insider among Republicans.

In one of its first actions in 2017, the House passed a bill filed by Collins to give Congress the right to review major new federal regulations before they take effect. "It's time Congress reasserts its constitutional authority to legislate, rather than letting unelected bureaucrats institute rules that impact the economy to the tune of hundreds of millions of dollars," he said.

Collins faced an unusual challenge in the 2016 primary. Former Rep. Paul Broun, who for nearly eight years had represented the 10th District east of Atlanta and then ran a distant fifth in the 2014 GOP primary for an open Senate seat, ran a quixotic challenge to Collins in this distant district. Broun, whose inflammatory rhetoric endeared him to the far right, raised only $136,000. Collins raised $1.2 million during the cycle, and won the five-candidate primary with 61 percent of the vote. He took each of the 15 counties, while Broun finished second with 22 percent. Collins had no opposition in November.

Northeast Georgia

Population		Race and Ethnicity		Income	
Total	708,458	White	78.0%	Median Income	$46,049 (324 out of 435)
Land area	5,211	Black	6.9%		
Pop/ sq mi	136.0	Latino	12.4%		
Born in state	61.2%	Asian	1.2%	Under $50,000	53.4%
		Two races	1.1%	$50,000-$99,999	29.9%
Age Groups		Other	0.4%	$100,000-$199,999	13.9%
Under 18	23.7%			$200,000 or more	2.7%
18-34	20.4%	**Education**		Poverty Rate	18.0%
35-64	39.5%	H.S grad or less	51.7%		
Over 64	16.4%	Some college	27.4%	**Health Insurance**	
		College Degree, 4 yr	13.2%	With health insurance coverage	82.2%
Work		Post grad	7.7%		
White Collar	29.4%				
Sales and Service	41.3%	**Military**		**Public Assistance**	
Blue Collar	29.4%	Veteran	9.1%	Cash public assistance income	2.2%
Government	13.7%	Active Duty	0.1%		
				Food stamp/SNAP benefits	14.4%

Voter Turnout			
2015 Total Citizens 18+	504,231	2016 House Turnout as % CVAP	51%
2016 House turnout	256,535	2014 House Turnout as % CVAP	36%

2012 Presidential Vote		
Mitt Romney	207,581	(78%)
Barack Obama	54,310	(21%)

2016 Presidential Vote		
Donald Trump	231,194	(77%)
Hillary Clinton	57,468	(19%)
Gary Johnson	8,553	(3%)

Cook Partisan Voting Index: R+31

Northeast Georgia is a land where the coastal plains and cotton fields yield to gently rolling hills and, near the North Carolina border, to the Appalachian Mountains. For most of its history, this was quiet, rural country, with courthouse towns and a few small cities, mostly forgotten by national elites, bypassed even by Union soldiers on their march to the sea. These largely rural areas have been an occasional source of derision and curiosity. James Dickey's 1970 novel *Deliverance* is a thinly disguised portrait of life along the Coosawattee River in Gilmer and Murray counties (although the movie was filmed on the Chattooga River in Rabun County).

Though the area was traditionally agrarian, the northern part of Georgia has undergone a rush of change over two decades. Interstate highways have brought it within easy range of Atlanta. Vacation and retirement communities have sprung up in the mountains and around the lakes. Agribusiness remains important, with huge poultry processors in Hall County around Gainesville. The area around Lake Sidney Lanier, named for the 19th century poet who wrote "The Song of the Chattahoochee," is filled with vacation houses and second homes. Thousands of Latinos from Mexico and other countries have come to the Gainesville area to snap up jobs; the county has grown to 28 percent Hispanic, with 42 percent in the city. The poultry farms have been a target of immigration law-enforcement officers.

The agricultural town of Jefferson transitioned to textiles, and eventually manufacturing. Today the town of Elberton is a large producer of granite monuments, and Royston employs people in the metal and plastics industries. Baseball great Ty Cobb, nicknamed "The Georgia Peach," was born in tiny Narrows in Banks County and played semi-pro ball in Royston, which now houses the Ty Cobb Museum. The University of North Georgia has more than 17,000 students spread over five campuses.

The 9th Congressional District of Georgia covers the northeast corner of the state. The district is anchored by Gainesville's Hall County, and includes the northern slice of fast-growing Forsyth and a small part of Athens-based Clarke County. Georgia Gov. Nathan Deal and Lt. Gov. Casey Cagle launched their careers in Gainesville. The 9th is rural and mostly white. It is the most Republican district in the state and was the third most Republican in the nation following the 2012 and 2016 elections, according to *The Cook Political Report*. Mitt Romney got 78 percent of the vote here in 2012, which was surpassed only by two districts in west Texas. Donald Trump took 77 percent in 2016.

TENTH DISTRICT

Jody Hice (R)

Elected 2014, 2nd term; b. Apr 22, 1960, Atlanta; Pacific Century Fellows Program; Asbury College (KY), B.A.; Southwestern Baptist Theological Seminary (TX), M.Div.; Luther Rice Seminary and University (GA); Southern Baptist; Married (Dee Hice); 2 childre; 4 grandchildren.

Professional Career: Adjunct faculty, Luther Rice University; Pastor; Talk radio host, The Jody Hice Show.

DC Office: 324 CHOB 20515, 202-225-4101, Fax: 202-226-0776, hice.house.gov.

State Offices: Milledgeville, 478-457-0007; Monroe, 770-207-1776; Thomson, 770-207-1776.

Committees: *Natural Resources*: Energy & Mineral Resources, Water, Power & Oceans. *Oversight & Government Reform*: Government Operations, National Security.

Group Ratings

	ADA	ACLU	AFL-CIO	LCV	ITI	COC	HAFA	ACU	CFG	FRC
2016	-	17%	-	0%	83%	100%	91%	96%	88%	100%
2015	0%	C	0%	0%	C	60%	C	100%	96%	92%

Almanac Ratings 2015

	Economy	Social	Foreign	Composite
Liberal	5%	7%	1%	4%
Conservative	95%	93%	99%	96%

Key Votes of the 114th Congress

1. Keystone Pipeline	Y	5. Puerto Rico Debt	N	9. Offenses by Aliens	Y
2. Trade Deals	Y	6. Medical Marijuana	N	10. Troops in Iraq	N
3. Export-Import Bank	N	7. Sanctuary Cities	Y	11. Homeland Security $$	N
4. Debt Ceiling Increase	N	8. Armor-piercing Bullets	Y	12. Trade Adjustment aid	N

Election Results

Election	Name (Party)	Vote (%)	Cand. Spent	Ind. Exp. Support	Ind. Exp. Oppose
2016 General	Jody Hice (R)	243,725 (100%)			
2016 Primary	Jody Hice (R)	(100%)			

Prior winning percentages: 2014 (67%)

Republican Jody Hice, who was elected in 2014 to an open seat, had been a prominent talk-show host who made a career at the forefront of the culture wars. He quickly became a leader of the small-government conservative activists in the House and occasionally created problems for Republican leaders.

Hice was born in Atlanta and grew up in Tucker, Georgia. He graduated from Asbury College, earned his master's degree from Southwestern Seminary and his doctorate from Luther Rice University, a Christian college and seminary in Lithonia. He was the founder of The Culture and Values Network and host of The Jody Hice Show, a conservative talk radio program.

A Baptist minister who served several churches in the metro Atlanta area, he argued in his 2012 book, *It's Now or Never: A Call to Reclaim America*, that supporters of abortion rights are worse than Hitler and that homosexuality causes shorter life spans as well as depression. He got his first taste of political battle in 2003 when he helped lead a campaign against a lawsuit by the American Civil Liberties Union seeking to remove a Ten Commandments display at the Barrow County courthouse. Five years later, he waged a successful effort against the Internal Revenue Service over whether politically active clergy can keep their tax-exempt status. He was a leader of the annual Pulpit Freedom Sunday movement sponsored by the Alliance Defending Freedom, which challenges what the group contends is a provision in the income tax code that censors what pastors can say from the pulpit. In 2010, Hice was the close runner-up to Rob Woodall in the Republican primary for the neighboring 7th District.

When the seat opened in the 10th, Hice jumped in and was among the best-known names in the GOP primary field of seven. The initial favorite was trucking company executive Mike Collins, who played up his success in business and the achievements of his father, former Republican Rep. Mac Collins. Hice slammed Collins as an insider who was too close to Washington because of his father, whom he attacked as well. Collins struck back, painting Hice as an extremist. He cited passages from Hice's book that argued against First Amendment protections for Muslims. Collins also brought up comments Hice made in 2004, when he said women running for office should first consult their husbands. But Collins created his own vulnerability when he equivocated on whether Congress should raise the debt ceiling.

Hice led the May primary by a hair, at 33.5 percent, with Collins 265 votes behind. In the July runoff, Hice had the advantage because he could unify the conservative vote and he defeated Collins, 54%-46%. He easily won in November. Immediately after the election, the liberal website Salon declared Hice "America's worst new congressman."

In the House, Hice joined the newly formed Freedom Caucus of conservatives who often went their own way from Republican leaders. He joined its board after the 2016 election. Much of his focus was on social issues. In January 2015, he introduced the Sanctity of Human Life Act, stating that human life begins with "fertilization, cloning, or its functional equivalent." In September, he pledged to oppose any bill that funded Planned Parenthood. He filed the Nuclear Family Priority Act, which addressed what he called the problem of chain migration, by limiting the assurance that legal status will be granted to extended family members of legal immigrants.

Hice was outspoken in calling for the impeachment of IRS Commissioner John Koskinen. He also was a founding member of the Second Amendment Caucus. In December 2016, President Barack Obama signed his bill that eliminated the filing of eight reports by the Government Accountability Office. Hice said the bill would "ensure that the GAO is better able to focus resources on higher priority areas, making the government more efficient for the American taxpayers."

During his 2014 campaign, Hice had said that he would support "new leadership with a backbone." In explaining his opening-day vote for John Boehner for Speaker, Hice said he had voted against Boehner in the earlier organizational meetings of the Republican Conference, but was "extremely disappointed" that few conservatives joined him. When candidates emerged shortly before the vote for Speaker, but with little debate, Hice concluded that there was no "pathway to victory" and he stayed with Boehner. After Boehner in September 2015 announced that he would step down, Hice was among a group of renegades who backed Rep. Daniel Webster of Florida as the next Speaker. When it became clear that Rep. Paul Ryan had broad support among Republicans, Hice received a minor concession from Ryan and then agreed to support him.

In 2016, Hice was reelected without major-party opposition. Given his earlier controversial campaigns, Hice apparently had found a balance between his conservative advocacy and working with more mainstream Republicans. He made a belated and unenthusiastic endorsement of Donald Trump a month before the November election. "If you are struggling with who to vote for, just remember the platforms the parties are running on," he said in a statement.

East-Central Georgia: Athens, Eastern Atlanta Exurbs

Population		**Race and Ethnicity**		**Income**	
Total	710,214	White	65.5%	Median Income	$47,610 (290 out of 435)
Land area	7,096	Black	24.9%		
Pop/ sq mi	100.1	Latino	5.6%		
Born in state	65.2%	Asian	2.1%	Under $50,000	51.8%
		Two races	1.6%	$50,000-$99,999	29.5%
Age Groups		Other	0.2%	$100,000-$199,999	15.8%
Under 18	23.8%			$200,000 or more	2.8%
18-34	24.6%	**Education**		Poverty Rate	19.4%
35-64	38.6%	H.S grad or less	48.4%		
Over 64	13.0%	Some college	27.5%	**Health Insurance**	
		College Degree, 4 yr	14.4%	With health insurance coverage	85.5%
Work		Post grad	9.6%		
White Collar	33.7%				
Sales and Service	43.0%	**Military**		**Public Assistance**	
Blue Collar	23.3%	Veteran	8.2%	Cash public assistance income	1.6%
Government	18.9%	Active Duty	0.2%		
				Food stamp/SNAP benefits	14.9%

Voter Turnout			
2015 Total Citizens 18+	519,997	2016 House Turnout as % CVAP	47%
2016 House turnout	243,725	2014 House Turnout as % CVAP	38%

2012 Presidential Vote		
Mitt Romney	184,162	(63%)
Barack Obama	107,040	(36%)

2016 Presidential Vote		
Donald Trump	193,029	(61%)
Hillary Clinton	112,691	(36%)
Gary Johnson	9,353	(3%)

Cook Partisan Voting Index: R+15

The north and south wings of General William Tecumseh Sherman's Union Army converged at Milledgeville, wrote author E.L. Doctorow in his novel *The March*: "And then the town of Milledgeville, empty and quiet, sat in its dishevelment, gusts of wind flying paper and brush against the sides of buildings and the leavings of coal fires scuttering in the street." The ghosts of the Civil War never left this region. Baldwin County's Milledgeville was the capital of Georgia from 1804 to 1868, and it is where Georgia legislators decided in 1861 to secede from the Union. Sherman's Army occupied the town and burned the state penitentiary, and the state capital was eventually moved to Atlanta. In nearby Butts County, Sherman's Army burned the courthouse in the county seat of Jackson.

It's no wonder that central Georgia and its tragedies have served as inspiration for several great Southern writers. Alice Walker, author of *The Color Purple*, was born in Eatonton, and her writing draws on family oral histories of life in rural Georgia. Also from Eatonton was Joel Chandler Harris, a freed slave who used the character "Uncle Remus" to write old southern stories with authentic folklore. Southern Gothic writer Flannery O'Connor lived in Milledgeville. Jean Toomer, a writer associated with the Harlem Renaissance, based his classic work *Cane* on his experiences in Hancock County. And Erskine Caldwell's scandalous best-seller, *Tobacco Road*, about an illiterate, Depression-racked farm family, was said to be influenced by his time living in the small town of Wrens in Jefferson County. Monroe was the site in 1946 of what may have been the last mob lynching in the nation; the crime was never prosecuted, though a review of long-ago allegations brought a fresh review in 2015.

Today, the region's economy is dominated by small, high-tech manufacturing, Atlanta's urban sprawl, and the long reach of the University of Georgia in Athens, a campus filled with graceful Greek Revival mansions, boxwood gardens and magnolias. In 2015, local utility companies began to service homes with solar panels. In Walton County, a locally based business opened in 2016 a one-megawatt community solar electricity generation farm. Baxalta, a global biotech firm, was expected to open a $12 billion plasma products manufacturing facility near Covington by 2018, creating about 2,000 jobs.

The 10th Congressional District runs from Barrow, Oglethorpe and Wilkes counties in the north to Baldwin, Washington and Jefferson counties in the south. Rapidly growing and affluent Columbia County is divided between this district and the 12th. The district also takes in toward Atlanta some of fast-growing Henry County and the well-to-do county of Oconee. The Lake Oconee area has more than 100 subdivisions, including gated communities and golf courses that beckon second-home buyers and retirees. Despite the overall economic growth in Georgia, some of the rural counties have been lagging. This district is solidly Republican. Donald Trump's 61 percent of the vote in 2016 was similar to recent GOP presidential performances.

ELEVENTH DISTRICT

Barry Loudermilk (R)

Elected 2014, 2nd term; b. Dec 22, 1963, Riverdale; Wayland Baptist University (TX); Community College of the Air Force (AL); Baptist; Married (Desiree Loudermilk); 3 children; 1 grandchild.

Military Career: U.S. Air Force, 1984-1992.

Elected Office: GA House, 2005-2010; GA Senate, 2011-2013.

Professional Career: Chairman, GA Republican party, 2001-2004; Business owner.

DC Office: 329 CHOB 20515, 202-225-2931, Fax: 202-225-2944, loudermilk.house.gov.

State Offices: Atlanta, 770-429-1776; Cartersville, 770-429-1776; Woodstock, 770-429-1776.

Committees: *Financial Services*: Financial Institutions & Consumer Credit, Oversight & Investigations. *House Administration*. *Science, Space & Technology*: Environment, Oversight.

Group Ratings

	ADA	ACLU	AFL-CIO	LCV	ITI	COC	HAFA	ACU	CFG	FRC
2016	-	11%	-	0%	100%	100%	83%	96%	77%	100%
2015	0%	C	4%	0%	C	70%	C	96%	90%	92%

Almanac Ratings 2015

	Economy	Social	Foreign	Composite
Liberal	2%	15%	0%	5%
Conservative	99%	85%	100%	95%

Key Votes of the 114th Congress

1. Keystone Pipeline	Y	5. Puerto Rico Debt	Y	9. Offenses by Aliens	Y
2. Trade Deals	Y	6. Medical Marijuana	Y	10. Troops in Iraq	N
3. Export-Import Bank	N	7. Sanctuary Cities	Y	11. Homeland Security $$	N
4. Debt Ceiling Increase	N	8. Armor-piercing Bullets	Y	12. Trade Adjustment aid	N

Election Results

Election	Name (Party)	Vote (%)		Cand. Spent	Ind. Exp. Support	Ind. Exp. Oppose
2016 General	Barry Loudermilk (R)	217,935	(67%)	$855,517		
	Don Wilson (D)	105,383	(33%)			
2016 Primary	Barry Loudermilk (R)	29,839	(60%)			
	Daniel Cowan (R)	9,144	(19%)			
	William Llop (R)	4,835	(10%)			
	Hayden Collins (R)	3,234	(7%)			

Prior winning percentages: 2014 (100%)

Republican Barry Loudermilk was elected in 2014 without a Democratic challenger in the open 11th District. With the support of tea party groups that year, he won a lively primary against former Republican Rep. and Libertarian Party presidential nominee Bob Barr. In 2016, the tables turned a bit for Loudermilk. His Republican primary opponents were weak and poorly funded. He then faced a Democrat, and won easily. In this district, that was preferable terrain for him.

Loudermilk was born in Riverdale, and got an associate degree in telecommunications technology from Air Force Community College and a bachelor of science in occupational education and information systems technology from Wayland Baptist University. After serving in the Air Force plus a stint in the cybersecurity business, he turned to politics. He chaired the Georgia Republican Party for four years. His decade as a state legislator included four years in the Senate, where he chaired the science and technology panel. He authored a book, *And Then They Prayed*, which features inspirational stories from American history.

The GOP primary in May drew six candidates. Loudermilk and Barr were the top two vote-getters in the primary, with 37 percent and 26 percent respectively, which forced a runoff in July. Barr, a former federal prosecutor, four-term House member, civil libertarian and Libertarian presidential candidate in 2008, played up his conservative bona fides, including his role in the 1998 impeachment proceedings against President Bill Clinton. Loudermilk, taking a sharp antiestablishment turn, cited Barr's Washington experience as a liability. He called Barr too soft on immigration and criticized him for backing Attorney General Eric Holder's nomination in 2009.

Barr took swipes at Loudermilk, suggesting that he had embellished his Air Force record and that he was involved in an $80,500 settlement that the state Legislature had reached in a racial discrimination suit involving a former Loudermilk staffer. Loudermilk denied both claims. In the end, the attacks did little to slow Loudermilk in the runoff, where he trounced Barr 66%-34%. In the outlying counties, he got 78 percent in Barton and 71 percent in Cherokee. In November, Loudermilk was one of seven members of the Georgia delegation who won without opposition in November, but the only freshman - which once was rare for a newcomer.

When the House Republican Conference met in November to organize for the new Congress and selected John Boehner in a voice vote for another term as Speaker, Loudermilk was one of three Republicans (including fellow Georgia freshman Jodi Hice) who cast what he called a "principled vote" against Boehner. Like Hice, Loudermilk then voted for Boehner in the House roll call vote in January, on the grounds that November was "the time to have that fight," he told the *Cherokee Tribune*. He added that he was "probably punished" by his failure to get the committee assignment he had sought. Instead, he got on Homeland Security and Oversight and Government Reform. By 2017, he had paid his penance and got seats on the Financial Services and House Administration, two committees where House leaders have interests.

Loudermilk had an early conflict with anti-abortion activists when he joined most Republicans in supporting a bill that restricted abortions but allowed exemptions for rape and incest. The leader of Georgia Right to Life complained that Loudermilk had said during the campaign that he would not support such exemptions. Loudermilk explained the challenges that he faced in the House to a political blogger for The Atlanta Journal-Constitution: "You've got 435 egos you have to deal with. And so things are slower. ... But there, if you just go running in headfirst and you don't establish the relationships, establish the credibility with folks, the trust with others, you're not going to get anywhere."

Loudermilk later took some heat from the right, after Boehner stepped down in October and he voted for Paul Ryan as the next Speaker. When Conservative radio host Glenn Beck challenged him for supporting a "Mitt Romney guy," Loudermilk said that Ryan would spend more time leading Republicans to challenge President Barack Obama and assert the congressional power of the purse. He added that the Freedom Caucus, of which he was a member, deserved credit for "where we are today looking for a new Speaker."

The "true problem in Washington is its tendency to govern by crisis," Loudermilk earlier posted on his official website. Inevitably, he added, "Congress would do what Congress does best - kick the can down the road to the next Congress." In contrast, he added, he and other conservatives worked on a long-term vision of where to take the country.

In 2016, Loudermilk got 60 percent of the vote in a five-way Republican primary and won 67%-33% in November. None of his opponents raised enough money to file a federal campaign report. "We made sure the truth was out," he told a reporter following the primary. But he conceded that he was surprised by the size of his victory margin. Following the election, he called for an investigation of alleged Russian interference. Citing his background in cybersecurity, he told a reporter, "Whether it's the Russians, the Chinese or an ally of ours ... you have to have an investigation. It's not an indictment; it's a gathering of facts."

Northwestern Atlanta Suburbs: Cherokee, Cobb

Population		**Race and Ethnicity**		**Income**	
Total	723,473	White	67.6%	Median Income	$63,549 (106 out of 435)
Land area	1,071	Black	15.8%		
Pop/ sq mi	675.4	Latino	11.1%		
Born in state	44.4%	Asian	3.2%	Under $50,000	39.3%
Age Groups		Two races	1.8%	$50,000-$99,999	31.1%
Under 18	24.8%	Other	0.5%	$100,000-$199,999	22.2%
18-34	23.8%	**Education**		$200,000 or more	7.4%
35-64	40.9%	H.S grad or less	33.1%	Poverty Rate	12.0%
Over 64	10.5%	Some college	27.9%	**Health Insurance**	
Work		College Degree, 4 yr	25.6%	With health insurance coverage	84.1%
White Collar	41.1%	Post grad	13.3%		
Sales and Service	41.6%	**Military**		**Public Assistance**	
Blue Collar	17.3%	Veteran	8.1%	Cash public assistance income	1.8%
Government	10.6%	Active Duty	0.1%		
				Food stamp/SNAP benefits	9.0%

Voter Turnout			
2015 Total Citizens 18+	494,070	2016 House Turnout as % CVAP	65%
2016 House turnout	323,318	2014 House Turnout as % CVAP	32%

2012 Presidential Vote		
Mitt Romney	200,863	(67%)
Barack Obama	94,634	(32%)

2016 Presidential Vote		
Donald Trump	198,877	(60%)
Hillary Clinton	116,575	(35%)
Gary Johnson	14,355	(4%)

Cook Partisan Voting Index: R+17

Marietta is one of Atlanta's largest suburbs. Its economic mainstay for many years was defense contractor Lockheed Martin, which built the F-22 jet fighter and the C-130 cargo plane. When the F-22 in 2009 became the first casualty of the Obama administration's decision to cut what it considered unnecessary weapons programs, that assembly line shut down in December 2011. But layoffs at the Marietta plant were limited, chiefly because the Pentagon had ordered additional F-35 fighter jets, parts of which are built there. Prospects for Lockheed Martin and Marietta brightened in August 2016, when the company won a contract for the C-130 Super Hercules airlift plane, which could direct about $10 billion to its local plant.

The WellStar Kennestone Regional Medical Center, a sprawling, 57-acre campus, is another major employer in Marietta. The city retains far more racial and ethnic diversity than nearby counties: 32 percent of Marietta is African American, and 21 percent is Hispanic. In September 2016, civil rights advocates filed a lawsuit against the local school district alleging racial discrimination. Bartow County, to the northwest of Marietta, grew 32 percent from 2000 to 2010, though the growth slowed to 3 percent in the next five years. The county seat of Cartersville hosts the Smithsonian-affiliated Booth Western Art Museum in Cartersville, which has a large collection of Western American and Civil War-era art. The Atlanta Braves in April 2017 moved from downtown to their new Sun Trust Park baseball stadium in close-in Cobb County, a short distance from the busy interchange of Interstates 75 and 285. Over the objections of some citizen groups and with continued uncertainty about costs, the county is paying nearly half the cost.

The 11th Congressional District of Georgia is anchored by Marietta and takes in all of Bartow and Cherokee counties and parts of close-in Cobb, where Marietta is the county seat and the largest city. It includes the northern tip of Fulton County, including part of Buckhead, with the governor's mansion. It has been a solidly Republican district. Closer-in Fulton and Cobb casting a bit more than half the district vote explains why the 67 percent vote for Mitt Romney in 2012 slipped to 60 percent for Donald Trump in 2016. In Bartow and Cherokee combined, Trump drew 74 percent support. In the parts of Cobb and Fulton in the 11th, he got about 50 percent.

TWELFTH DISTRICT

Rick Allen (R)

Elected 2014, 2nd term; b. Nov 07, 1951, Augusta; Auburn University School of Architecture and Fine Arts (GA), B.S.; Methodist; Married (Robin Reeve); 4 children; 12 grandchildren.

Professional Career: Founder, R.W. Allen & Associates, 1976.

DC Office: 426 CHOB 20515, 202-225-2823, Fax: 202-225-3377, allen.house.gov.

State Offices: Augusta, 706-228-1980; Dublin, 478-272-4030; Statesboro, 912-243-9452; Vidalia, 912-403-3311.

Committees: *Agriculture*: Conservation & Forestry, General Farm Commodities & Risk Management. *Education & the Workforce*: Health, Employment, Labor & Pensions, Higher Education & Workforce Development.

Group Ratings

	ADA	ACLU	AFL-CIO	LCV	ITI	COC	HAFA	ACU	CFG	FRC
2016	-	5%	-	0%	100%	92%	76%	92%	77%	100%
2015	0%	C	4%	0%	C	80%	C	88%	71%	100%

Almanac Ratings 2015

	Economy	Social	Foreign	Composite
Liberal	3%	0%	0%	1%
Conservative	97%	100%	100%	99%

Key Votes of the 114th Congress

1. Keystone Pipeline	Y	5. Puerto Rico Debt	N	9. Offenses by Aliens	Y
2. Trade Deals	Y	6. Medical Marijuana	N	10. Troops in Iraq	N
3. Export-Import Bank	N	7. Sanctuary Cities	Y	11. Homeland Security $$	N
4. Debt Ceiling Increase	N	8. Armor-piercing Bullets	Y	12. Trade Adjustment aid	N

Election Results

Election	Name (Party)	Vote (%)		Cand. Spent	Ind. Exp. Support	Ind. Exp. Oppose
2016 General	Rick Allen (R)	159,492	(62%)	$1,023,160		
	Tricia McCracken (D)	99,420	(38%)			
2016 Primary	Rick Allen (R)	46,669	(79%)			
	Eugene Yu (R)	12,437	(12%)			

Prior winning percentages: 2014 (55%)

Republican Rick Allen claimed this increasingly red district for the GOP in 2014 by ousting five-term incumbent John Barrow, the only remaining white Democrat in the House representing a state in the Deep South.

A native of Augusta who still resides there, Allen graduated from Auburn University with a bachelor of science degree in building construction. After spending three years as a project manager with a local builder, he founded R.W. Allen & Associates, a construction company he has operated since 1976 in the Augusta and Athens areas. His experience as a small business owner and job creator, plus his inexperience in government office, formed the centerpiece of his congressional campaign.

Allen had sought the Republican nomination in 2012, but finished second in the primary to state Rep. Lee Anderson, who lost to Barrow 54%-46%. This time around, Allen spent nearly a million dollars of his own money, out of a reported net worth of $21 million. He won the five-way May primary with 54 percent of the vote, avoiding a runoff. In the general election, Allen criticized Barrow - one of the last fiscally conservative Blue Dog Democrats in the House - for hewing too closely to President Barack Obama's agenda, while touting his own conservative credentials. Allen advocated greater fiscal discipline and reductions in government spending, and blasted excessive taxation and regulation as barriers to job creation. Unlike Anderson, who drew criticism in 2012 from local newspapers for his refusal to debate Barrow, Allen debated the congressman, though he drew attention for refusing to do so at an Islamic community center. He called it a "suspect venue," and the location was changed to a government complex.

Although Allen touted his support for the Second Amendment, Barrow boasted an A+ rating and endorsement from the National Rifle Association. Allen won the backing of other traditionally Republican groups, such as the U.S. Chamber of Commerce. With little daylight between the candidates on many issues, the Republican strategy focused instead on the national Democratic Party. The National Republican Congressional Committee bolstered Allen's campaign with ads linking the congressman to Obama. Barrow outspent Allen $3.5 million to $2.5 million, but the nearly $4 million in national GOP assistance more than made up the difference. Allen won handily, 55%-45%. Barrow won Richmond (Augusta), the largest county, with 66 percent of the vote. Bolstered by his party's success in making the contest a national battleground campaign, Allen won 71 percent in adjacent Columbia, the next-largest county, and all but two of the remaining 17 counties.

Allen entered the House with more mainstream Republican views and style than other Georgia GOP freshmen elected in 2014. He was rewarded with assignments to substantive committees: Agriculture, plus Education and the Workforce. With his Main Street business views, he supported extension of the Export-Import Bank. That led to attack ads against him from Americans for Prosperity, an arm of the conservative Koch brothers. But tea party groups failed to wage a significant challenge against him in the 2016 Republican primary.

In April 2016, the House passed his bill to prevent the Internal Revenue Service from targeting citizens who exercise their First Amendment rights. Allen cited recent cases in which tea party and other conservative groups were singled out when they applied for tax-exempt status. In a state where agriculture is heralded as the number-one industry, he claimed credit for winning support of a cost-sharing program for cotton ginning. From the political left, Allen was condemned by gay-rights advocates for delivering at a closed-door meeting of the House Republican Conference an opening prayer that referred harshly to homosexuals.

Democratic challenger Patricia Carpenter McCracken, who raised barely 1 percent of Allen's $1.1 million, made no "known appearances" during the campaign, *The Augusta Chronicle* reported. Allen was reelected, 62%-38%. It is unlikely that Democrats will regain this district any time soon.

East Georgia: Augusta

Population		**Race and Ethnicity**		**Income**	
Total	706,062	White	56.1%	Median Income	$40,684 (394 out of 435)
Land area	8,185	Black	34.5%		
Pop/ sq mi	86.3	Latino	5.7%		
Born in state	67.4%	Asian	1.6%	Under $50,000	58.1%
		Two races	1.6%	$50,000-$99,999	27.4%
Age Groups		Other	0.5%	$100,000-$199,999	12.2%
Under 18	24.3%			$200,000 or more	2.3%
18-34	25.9%	**Education**		Poverty Rate	23.3%
35-64	37.2%	H.S grad or less	51.2%		
Over 64	12.7%	Some college	28.5%	**Health Insurance**	
		College Degree, 4 yr	12.4%	With health insurance coverage	83.1%
Work		Post grad	7.9%		
White Collar	31.8%				
Sales and Service	42.8%	**Military**		**Public Assistance**	
Blue Collar	25.4%	Veteran	10.8%	Cash public assistance income	1.8%
Government	20.1%	Active Duty	1.5%		
				Food stamp/SNAP benefits	18.6%

Voter Turnout			
2015 Total Citizens 18+	518,683	2016 House Turnout as % CVAP	50%
2016 House turnout	258,912	2014 House Turnout as % CVAP	32%

2012 Presidential Vote		
Mitt Romney	148,622	(55%)
Barack Obama	117,131	(44%)

2016 Presidential Vote		
Donald Trump	152,204	(57%)
Hillary Clinton	108,937	(41%)
Gary Johnson	6,534	(2%)

Cook Partisan Voting Index: R+9

Upriver from Savannah is the city of Augusta. Founded in 1735 as a fur-trading post, it has been home since 1835 to the Medical College of Georgia, now part of Georgia Regents University, a public academic health center. It has become a manufacturing hub for big companies like Procter & Gamble, International Paper and Dart Container (formerly Solo Cup).

Many know the city best as the site of Augusta National Golf Club, a private club where the Masters Tournament is held every April, amid azaleas in bloom, reverence for its traditions by both players and spectators, and an annual economic impact in the tens of millions of dollars. Some of that beauty has come at a price. Since about 2000, the Club has spent more than $40 million to buy modest homes in an adjacent neighborhood and has bulldozed them into a parking lot, New Jersey Advance Media reported in April 2016. The exception remains that one stubborn family, which is lonely for 51 weeks a year, likes the location and hasn't succumbed to the offers. When they agree to the inevitable deal, they will pocket a seven-figure payment and several times the price received by the homebuyers who sold early.

The 12th Congressional District takes in Augusta's Richmond County and part of neighboring Columbia County. They include half of the total population for the district. Richmond is 56 percent African American, while Columbia is 17 percent. From 2010 to 2015, Columbia grew from 124,000 to 144,000; Richmond had virtually no change at 201,000. The district has a military presence with the Fort Gordon Army base, which is home to 13,800 troops and the Army Signal Corps. The base is the new headquarters for the cyber command of the Army, plus a National Security Agency facility. They are designed to work with other federal agencies to develop and field cyberspace capabilities, modernize networks and improve sensors and tools for defensive operations, and provide support to combat units. The district also includes the college town of Statesboro, where Georgia Southern University is located, and Vidalia, home of the famous sweet onion. Its 35 percent black population is the largest of any of the 10 Republican-held districts in Georgia. Slightly more than half of the district is rural.

In 2016, Donald Trump won the presidential vote, 57%-41%, a slight increase in the Republican vote from the two previous presidential elections. The two largest counties went in very different directions. Hillary Clinton won Richmond, 65%-32%. But Trump won Columbia, 67%-29%. He won all but one of the other 17 counties in the 12th.

THIRTEENTH DISTRICT

David Scott (D)

Elected 2002, 8th term; b. Jun 27, 1945, Aynor, SC; Florida Agricultural and Mechanical University, B.A.; University of Pennsylvania Wharton School of Business Aresty Institute, M.B.A.; Baptist; Married (Alfredia Aaron Scott); 2 children; 2 grandchildren.

Elected Office: GA House, 1975-1982; GA Senate, 1983-2002.

Professional Career: Founder & President, Dayn-Mark Advertising, 1979-2002.

DC Office: 225 CHOB 20515, 202-225-2939, Fax: 202-225-4628, davidscott.house.gov.

State Offices: Jonesboro, 770-210-5073; Smyrna, 770-432-5405.

Committees: *Agriculture*: Commodity Exchanges, Energy & Credit (RMM), General Farm Commodities & Risk Management. *Financial Services*: Capital Markets, Securities & Investment, Financial Institutions & Consumer Credit.

Group Ratings

	ADA	ACLU	AFL-CIO	LCV	ITI	COC	HAFA	ACU	CFG	FRC
2016	-	82%	-	82%	67%	77%	14%	4%	6%	0%
2015	70%	C	96%	80%	C	68%	C	8%	2%	8%

Almanac Ratings 2015

	Economy	Social	Foreign	Composite
Liberal	77%	97%	54%	76%
Conservative	23%	3%	46%	24%

Key Votes of the 114th Congress

1. Keystone Pipeline	Y	5. Puerto Rico Debt	Y	9. Offenses by Aliens	N
2. Trade Deals	N	6. Medical Marijuana	Y	10. Troops in Iraq	N
3. Export-Import Bank	Y	7. Sanctuary Cities	N	11. Homeland Security $$	Y
4. Debt Ceiling Increase	Y	8. Armor-piercing Bullets	N	12. Trade Adjustment aid	NV

Election Results

Election	Name (Party)	Vote (%)	Cand. Spent	Ind. Exp. Support	Ind. Exp. Oppose
2016 General	David Scott (D)	252,833 (100%)	$837,550		
2016 Primary	David Scott (D)	(100%)			

Prior winning percentages: 2014 (100%), 2012 (72%), 2010 (69%), 2008 (69%), 2006 (69%), 2002 (60%)

Democrat David Scott, first elected in 2002, is distinctly more of a centrist than most other members of the Congressional Black Caucus. He usually gets along well with Republican colleagues and avoids publicly criticizing them. Occasionally, he has endorsed GOP candidates. Scott often works on issues that go beyond race.

Born in rural South Carolina, Scott is the son of a minister and grandson of a deacon. During his middle school years, his family moved to tony Scarsdale, New York, where his parents took jobs as a chauffeur and housekeeper for a wealthy family. Scott was the only African American in his otherwise all-white school. He later graduated from Florida A&M University, then did an internship at the Labor Department in Washington. There he met George Taylor, an authority in labor-management relations who encouraged the bright young man to apply to the prestigious Wharton School at the University of Pennsylvania, which Scott did, earning his MBA. He moved to Atlanta, and in 1974 was elected to the Georgia House. In 1982, he won election to the state Senate, where he served for 20 years and chaired the Rules Committee. From 1979 to 2002, he owned Dayn-Mark Advertising, which creates and places radio, television and print ads. The firm has been operated by his wife and two daughters.

In 2002, Scott ran for the newly created 13th District, which was heavily Democratic. Four other Democrats ran, the best known of whom was former state party Chairman David Worley, who nearly defeated Republican Rep. Newt Gingrich in 1990. Scott was familiar to many voters after more than a quarter-century in the state legislature. And if they didn't know Scott, they certainly knew of his campaign co-chairman: Henry Aaron, the Hall of Fame slugger and Atlanta-area icon, who is Scott's brother-in-law. Scott brought his advertising expertise, plastering the interstate highways with eye-catching billboards. His chief competitors, Worley and state Sen. Greg Hecht of Clayton County, both white, ran ads attacking each other. Scott won the primary with 54 percent of the vote. He won the general election, 60%-40%.

As a freshman in the House, Scott was one of seven Democrats to vote for final passage of President George W. Bush's tax cut, and one of 16 to vote for the prescription drug benefit under Medicare. He split with most of his party by voting for a constitutional amendment to ban same-sex marriage. In recent years, Scott has become a more reliable party vote, but he has had no reluctance to go his own way. In 2014, he embraced a bipartisan approach to the mounting controversy at the Veterans Affairs Department, whose huge hospital in Atlanta encountered major problems. In 2016, he urged President Barack Obama to "stop pussyfooting around, get a sense of urgency and declare war" on Islamic terrorism. "What the hell does it make sense for us to have the most powerful military in the world and we don't use it to protect the American people?" he asked.

On the Financial Services Committee, Scott initially opposed the bailout of the financial markets. After chairman Barney Frank of Massachusetts promised to address the Black Caucus' call for additional protections for homeowners facing foreclosure, Scott switched his vote to support a revised version. In 2015, he joined a bipartisan coalition on the committee that urged Obama to review proposed regulations on financial advisers by the Labor Department. On the Agriculture Committee, he is the second-ranking Democrat on the panel and has been the top Democrat on multiple subcommittees - currently at the Commodity Exchanges, Energy and Credit Subcommittee, which is chaired by fellow Georgia Rep. Austin Scott, a Republican.

In an unusual partisan clash for Scott in 2014, he urged Obama to withdraw his nominations of two federal judgeship nominees for district court seats in Alabama. Those two, Michael Boggs and Mark Cohen, had been recommended by the state's two Republican senators, Saxby Chambliss and Johnny Isakson, and were submitted by Obama after lengthy White House review as a matter of senatorial courtesy. Referring to his pride and love for Obama, Scott said in an interview, "When you are hurt by the one you love, there's no greater pain than that." The Senate confirmed Cohen, but did not act on Boggs because of objections to various rulings that he had issued as a state court judge, including on the state's old flag with its Confederate emblem.

Scott has been an active presence in his district, sponsoring health and job fairs as well as "help for homeowners" events giving constituents the ability to ask questions of federal housing officials. He has been the subject of several unflattering stories about back taxes he owed on his home and business. He attracted both primary and general election challenges in 2008 and 2010. But none of his opponents held Scott below 60 percent of the vote. In 2016, he was reelected without major-party opposition.

He attracted attention at home in 2016 when he endorsed the reelection of Republican Sen. Johnny Isakson. "He's my friend. He's my partner," Scott said in a radio interview. They have known each other since they were junior members in the state House. Perhaps more curious was his $1,000 campaign contribution to first-term Republican Rep. Mia Love of Utah, an African American who was facing a competitive reelection. "Mia has proven herself. She is very smart, very talented," Scott told the *Salt Lake Tribune*. "It is very important for us as African Americans to look at the big picture and realize that we are in a big game here and we have to have alliances." They served together on the Financial Services Committee.

Southwestern Atlanta Exurbs: Clayton, Cobb

Population		**Race and Ethnicity**		**Income**	
Total	723,108	White	28.6%	Median Income	$51,218 (235 out of 435)
Land area	715	Black	55.9%		
Pop/ sq mi	1011.4	Latino	10.7%		
Born in state	51.0%	Asian	2.6%	Under $50,000	48.8%
Age Groups		Two races	1.8%	$50,000-$99,999	32.9%
Under 18	27.7%	Other	0.4%	$100,000-$199,999	15.7%
18-34	22.3%	**Education**		$200,000 or more	2.6%
35-64	40.7%	H.S grad or less	41.3%	Poverty Rate	18.8%
Over 64	9.3%	Some college	31.1%	**Health Insurance**	
Work		College Degree, 4 yr	17.9%	With health insurance coverage	81.0%
White Collar	33.1%	Post grad	9.8%		
Sales and Service	43.5%	**Military**		**Public Assistance**	
Blue Collar	23.5%	Veteran	9.7%	Cash public assistance income	2.1%
Government	15.1%	Active Duty	0.1%	Food stamp/SNAP benefits	18.4%

Voter Turnout			
2015 Total Citizens 18+	480,671	2016 House Turnout as % CVAP	53%
2016 House turnout	252,833	2014 House Turnout as % CVAP	33%

2012 Presidential Vote		
Barack Obama	202,828	(69%)
Mitt Romney	87,742	(30%)

2016 Presidential Vote		
Hillary Clinton	213,805	(71%)
Donald Trump	80,086	(27%)
Gary Johnson	7,136	(2%)

Cook Partisan Voting Index: D+20

Many of the great landmarks of the civil rights movement, and the headquarters of many of its leading organizations, are in the central city of Atlanta. In the 1960s, Atlanta's blacks were clustered in ghetto neighborhoods on the south and west sides of the city. The north side and the suburbs in every direction were heavily white. Today, metro Atlanta's thriving black middle class has moved outward in almost every direction in one of the nation's fastest-growing metro areas - to DeKalb County to the east, to Clayton County directly south of the city, to southwest Fulton County, to Cobb and Douglas counties to the north and west.

The area has had a multi-faceted approach to immigration. Cobb was the first county in the state to be certified for a federal program giving state and local law enforcement the authority to arrest illegal immigrants. The program has been hailed as effective, but it has driven away immigrants seeking friendlier territory. In January 2017, a Fulton County Superior Court judge took a more accommodating approach with a ruling that Georgia residents who had received a reprieve from the deportation program of the Obama administration would be entitled to pay in-state tuition rates.

The Hartsfield-Jackson Atlanta International Airport is the busiest airport in the world, with 101 million passengers arriving and departing in 2015. (Not all of them are on Friday afternoons.) It also has become a huge revenue source for the area, with its many suppliers. In 2016, local interests laid out a blueprint to turn the area surrounding the airport into an "aerotropolis," with an "airport city" that would include a corporate center and a corridor of green trails. Planners envision the area as a central business district, which covers 165 square miles and has 300,000 residents. The transformation could take decades, but planners envision "significant change" in the next 20 years. One of their objectives is to create the kind of development south of Atlanta that has taken place elsewhere in the metro area.

The 13th Congressional District of Georgia is a collection of suburban areas that have attracted Atlanta's African-American middle class. It includes most of Clayton County which is 69 percent African American and 13 percent Latino. It takes in all of Douglas County, and parts of Cobb, Fulton, Fayette and Henry counties. Clayton, Cobb and Fulton each have slightly more than one-fifth of the voters in the 13th. The airport is just across the district line in the 4th. In 2015, Six Flags theme parks in Cobb generated more than $228 million economic impact in the district. Austell is the home of Six Flags over Georgia, which opened in 1967 as the second franchise of the company. In Marietta, the 70-acre Six Flags White Water joined the company in 1999. The 13th is a black-majority district and solidly Democratic. In 2016, Hillary Clinton won the district, 71%-27%, a slight improvement over the 69%-30% victory of President Barack Obama in 2012.

FOURTEENTH DISTRICT

Tom Graves (R)

Elected 2010, 4th term; b. Feb 03, 1970, St. Petersburg, FL; University of Georgia; b.B.A., 1993; Baptist; Married (Julie Howard Graves); 3 children.

Elected Office: GA House, 2003-2010.

Professional Career: Founder, Tough Turf Land Sculpting; Owner, Southern Vision; Real estate developer.

DC Office: 2078 RHOB 20515, 202-225-5211, Fax: 202-225-8272, tomgraves.house.gov.

State Offices: Dalton, 706-226-5320; Rome, 706-290-1776.

Committees: *Appropriations*: Defense, Financial Services & General Government (Chmn), Transportation, HUD & Related Agencies.

Group Ratings

	ADA	ACLU	AFL-CIO	LCV	ITI	COC	HAFA	ACU	CFG	FRC
2016	-	5%	-	0%	83%	100%	79%	84%	72%	100%
2015	0%	C	4%	0%	C	80%	C	91%	89%	92%

Almanac Ratings 2015

	Economy	Social	Foreign	Composite
Liberal	2%	15%	1%	6%
Conservative	99%	85%	99%	94%

Key Votes of the 114th Congress

1. Keystone Pipeline	Y	5. Puerto Rico Debt	Y	9. Offenses by Aliens	Y
2. Trade Deals	Y	6. Medical Marijuana	Y	10. Troops in Iraq	N
3. Export-Import Bank	N	7. Sanctuary Cities	Y	11. Homeland Security $$	N
4. Debt Ceiling Increase	N	8. Armor-piercing Bullets	Y	12. Trade Adjustment aid	N

Election Results

Election	Name (Party)	Vote (%)	Cand. Spent	Ind. Exp. Support	Ind. Exp. Oppose
2016 General	Tom Graves (R)	216,743 (100%)	$745,226		
2016 Primary	Tom Graves (R)	44,224 (76%)			
	Mickey Tuck (R)	7,485 (13%)			
	Allan Levene (R)	6,755 (12%)			

Prior winning percentages: 2012 (73%), 2010 (unopposed), 2010 special (56%)

Republican Tom Graves, who won a special election in June 2010, has been well-regarded by his fellow conservatives but a periodic annoyance to House GOP leaders. His influence has spread as he has moved beyond conservative factionalism and moved up the seniority ladder at the Appropriations Committee.

Graves is from the small town of Ranger, with fewer than 100 people, where he still lives with his wife, Julie Graves, and their three children on a farm. Growing up, he lived in a single-wide trailer on a tar and gravel road, the son of a Georgia Power laborer who told him to "dream big and then work hard." Graves took out loans and worked to pay for college, becoming the first in his family to earn a degree, in business administration from the University of Georgia. After graduation, Graves worked for Federated Department Stores, now Macy's, as an asset recovery specialist. He saved his money and, in 1995, bought a small landscaping business. Graves eventually sold off portions of the company to begin investing in real estate.

He met his future wife at Roswell Street Baptist Church, and she was instrumental in getting him involved in the anti-abortion movement. He has said he opposes abortion "without exception," including cases in which the mother's life is at stake. In 2001, he and Julie, the founding president of the Gordon County Right to Life chapter, successfully opposed the construction of an abortion clinic in the area. The campaign propelled Graves to a seat on the county board and later in the Georgia House, where he served more than seven years. While a state legislator, he supported abortion restrictions and lower taxes. Of his political philosophy, he says, "there is a spectrum of conservatism from fiscal to social ... and I'm a conservative all the way across the board." He said former President Ronald Reagan is the figure he most admires in politics.

In the special election runoff to succeed Nathan Deal, who resigned to run for governor, Graves bested Republican state Sen. Lee Hawkins, 56%-44%, in a June 2010 runoff for the remainder of Deal's term. The two clashed again in the primary for a full term. Graves called for abolition of the departments of Education and Energy and the Environmental Protection Agency. He supported constitutional amendments to balance the budget and to give the president line-item veto power over spending bills. Both Graves and Hawkins supported a conservative proposal to replace the income tax with a national sales tax. Hawkins cast Graves as "out of touch" and attacked him for a bank loan that had gone into default. But he could not overcome Graves' backing by national Republican organizations, House Minority Leader John Boehner and local tea party groups. Graves outraised Hawkins, $1.3 million to $1 million and won the August runoff, 55%-45%, earning a full term without Democratic opposition.

In Washington, Graves joined the Tea Party Caucus. He got a slot on Appropriations. In an unusual move for an appropriator, Graves consistently voted to buck the leadership on spending bills. One of them was a failed 2011 resolution for short-term funding of the government; he was one of 48 Republicans who voted down the measure to protest the addition of $1 billion in disaster relief funds. Senior House Republicans, including some in leadership, reportedly sought to single out Graves for punishment, by stripping his Appropriations seat. But Boehner declined to do so - a favor Graves repaid with another bout of principled obstinacy.

In 2013, Graves led a rebellion against Boehner's strategy over a bill to fund government operations. With the clock ticking toward an Oct. 1 deadline to pass the measure, Graves proposed an amendment to stop funding for the Affordable Care Act, which was in the early stages of implementation. Boehner and other GOP leaders opposed tying the two into one take-it-or-leave-it bill, but Graves drummed up support from 60 fellow conservatives; under pressure, Boehner backed down. As expected, the Democratic-controlled Senate voted 54-44 to strip the health care provision from the government funding bill. The subsequent stalemate led to the first partial government shutdown in 17 years, which exposed Republicans to a public backlash.

"You don't have to threaten to blow the whole thing up if you don't get your way," Obama said as the shutdown began. Even prominent Republicans such as Sen. John McCain of Arizona condemned the strategy as likely to fail. A Quinnipiac University poll showed that voters opposed closing the government to block implementation of the health care law by 72%-22%. The potential fallout for Graves was serious: If the shutdown proved politically damaging for his party, he would shoulder much of the blame. Graves replied that his constituents supported him, and that the Obama administration botched implementation of the new law.

Graves has drawn some negative headlines at home. He was accused of hypocrisy in 2012 when *The Atlanta Journal-Constitution* reported that the Federal Deposit Insurance Corporation bailed out Graves and Georgia Senate Majority Leader Chip Rogers for about half of a $2.3 million loan the two men had received five years earlier to rehabilitate a North Georgia hotel. The dispute was settled privately out of court.

After his easy reelection in 2012, he sought to head the Republican Study Committee and won the endorsement of the group's founders, normally considered key to getting the nod. But the more senior Steve Scalise of Louisiana also sought the job, citing his ability to work with the leadership and his success in passing bills. Scalise petitioned for the full membership to hold a vote and pulled off an upset. For Scalise, that was a big step in his move toward majority whip in 2014.

Graves in 2015 finally played his cards right and gained a different sort of insider position: chairman of the Legislative Branch Subcommittee on Appropriations, where congressional officials approached him to plead for funds. On accepting the position, Graves welcomed the honor and pledged to use it as "a prime opportunity to walk the conservative talk." It was all the more unusual for him to get the position at the start of his third full term. He would not be the first lawmaker to enter as a revolutionary and eventually become House-broken. In May 2016, Graves successfully opposed an amendment to increase public accessibility to reports of the Congressional Research Service. In 2017, he took over as chairman of the Financial Services Subcommittee, where the influential portfolio included the White House and implementation of the Dodd-Frank banking regulatory law.

In the 2016 Republican primary, Graves got 76 percent of the vote against two challengers who complained that he had abandoned his outsider status. He had no Democratic challenger in this GOP bastion. After less than seven years in the House, Graves had settled in as the most senior of the 10 House Republicans from Georgia.

Northwest Georgia: Rome, Dalton

Population		**Race and Ethnicity**		**Income**	
Total	697,680	White	77.7%	Median Income	$45,342 (336 out of 435)
Land area	3,623	Black	8.8%		
Pop/ sq mi	192.6	Latino	10.9%		
Born in state	59.0%	Asian	1.0%	Under $50,000	54.4%
Age Groups		Two races	1.2%	$50,000-$99,999	30.9%
Under 18	25.5%	Other	0.4%	$100,000-$199,999	12.9%
18-34	21.4%	**Education**		$200,000 or more	1.8%
35-64	39.9%	H.S grad or less	55.2%	Poverty Rate	17.6%
Over 64	13.1%	Some college	28.0%	**Health Insurance**	
Work		College Degree, 4 yr	10.4%	With health insurance coverage	82.8%
White Collar	27.4%	Post grad	6.3%		
Sales and Service	40.3%	**Military**		**Public Assistance**	
Blue Collar	32.4%	Veteran	8.6%	Cash public assistance income	3.0%
Government	13.2%	Active Duty	0.1%		
				Food stamp/SNAP benefits	15.7%

Voter Turnout			
2015 Total Citizens 18+	489,866	2016 House Turnout as % CVAP	44%
2016 House turnout	216,743	2014 House Turnout as % CVAP	24%

2012 Presidential Vote		
Mitt Romney	170,385	(73%)
Barack Obama	58,886	(25%)

2016 Presidential Vote		
Donald Trump	191,849	(75%)
Hillary Clinton	56,513	(22%)
Gary Johnson	7,510	(3%)

Cook Partisan Voting Index: R+27

Northwest Georgia was long the home of the Cherokee Nation before the tribe was sent west in the 1830s on the Trail of Tears. It has been manufacturing country for the last century. Hundreds of textile mills and dozens of carpet mills once clustered near the supply of natural cotton and along the railroad lines heading southwest at the base of the southern Appalachian chain. The late 19th-century boosters of the New South hailed factories as the vanguard of technological progress. In fact, the plants produced a higher standard of living than did the farms on this stubborn land. But the mills put scant premium on education or the cultivation of civic virtues and did little to bring in higher-skilled work. All-white hiring practices maintained racial segregation in mostly white north Georgia.

Today, this area has developed a different kind of economy, as metro Atlanta has spread out along highways to the north and west. There are sprawling subdivisions in what once were mill towns. Floyd County is home to an auto parts manufacturing cluster. To the north in Dalton, the traditional craft of tufted bedspread handiwork was transformed into a carpet industry so large that at the turn of the 21st century, four Georgia companies - three of them in Dalton -- produced 80 percent of the nation's tufted carpet. The shortage of workers resulted in the arrival of many Hispanics, many of them illegal immigrants. In recent years, recession and automation have reduced the workforce in the carpet industry. But the industry continues to employ more than 45,000 workers in Georgia, the largest manufacturing sector in the state.

The immigration debate has moved front and center in Dalton. Local business leaders who opposed the policies of President Barack Obama nonetheless welcomed the money that the illegal immigrants have brought to town, *The Wall Street Journal* reported in December 2014. "If these people make more money and feel stability, it will help my business," said a furniture store owner in Dalton. Immigrant advocates said that some employers had been exploiting their workers. Hispanics, though fewer, remain almost half of the population of Dalton. At Dalton State University, Hispanics were 25 percent of the student body in 2016. In May 2016, Floyd County was the subject of a Supreme Court ruling, which overturned a death-penalty conviction on the grounds that prosecutors unlawfully struck all black jurors from the jury pool for the case, in which the defendant was black.

The 14th Congressional District covers the northwest corner of Georgia, including Dalton-based Whitfield County. Chattanooga, Tennessee's metro area has expanded across the state line into places like Chickamauga and LaFayette in Walker and Catoosa counties. It takes in Floyd County and its largest city, Rome, as well as Paulding County, which extends beyond Cobb County in exurban Atlanta. Paulding is the population center with about one-fourth of the voters, followed by Floyd and Whitfield. Politically, the 14th is among the safest Republican districts in the nation. In 2016, Donald Trump won 75 percent of the vote, which was an increase from the 73 percent for Mitt Romney in 2012.

★ HAWAII ★

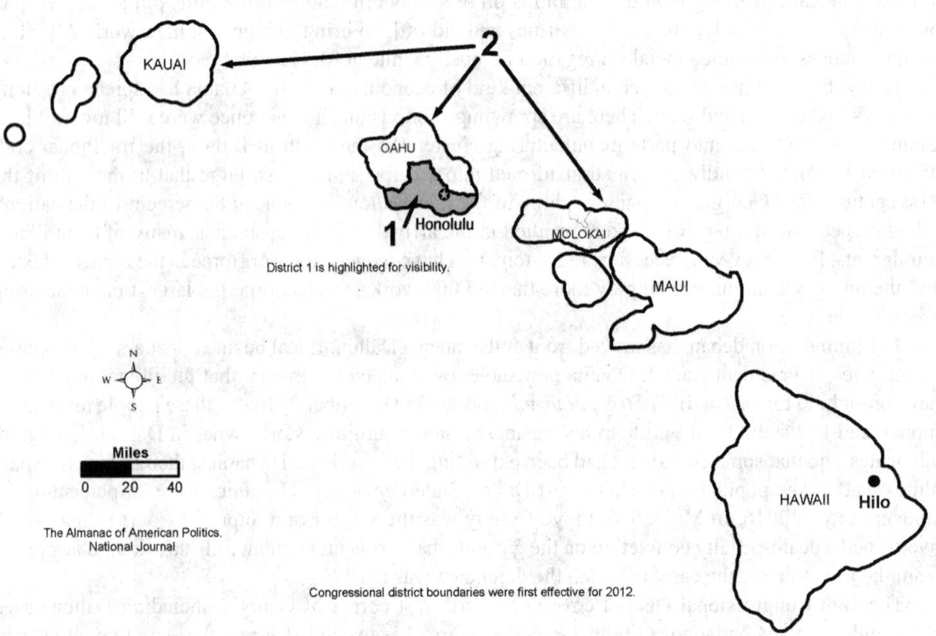
2
KAUAI
OAHU
Honolulu
1
MOLOKAI
MAUI
HAWAII
Hilo
District 1 is highlighted for visibility.
N
W
E
S
Miles
0 20 40
The Almanac of American Politics.
National Journal
Congressional district boundaries were first effective for 2012.

America's state in the Pacific is geographically the most remote archipelago in the world, but it is hardly isolated. It has long been a crossroads of trade between the Asian and American continents, and it has been a vital military base for the United States since before the attack on Pearl Harbor in 1941. Most recently, it has produced a president, Barack Obama.

Thrust up from the ocean by volcanoes, Hawaii is geologically some of the youngest land on earth, and it continues to undergo transformations. Polynesians sailing double-hulled canoes from the Marquesas Islands nearly 2,000 miles away were the first humans to inhabit Hawaii roughly 1,600 years ago. Over time, several small kingdoms developed across the Islands, each ruled by an *ali'i nui* (a grand or great chief). The islands' insulation from the Western world ended when British Captain James Cook, on an exploration to find the Northwest Passage, landed on Kauai in 1778. He would also die in Hawaii on a return visit a year later after a confrontation with natives. Toward the end of the century the most powerful *ali'i nui*, Kamehameha, began a campaign of conquest, and by 1810, all the islands were united into one kingdom under his rule. With unification came foreign trade: Pacific fur traders who stopped off recognized that Hawaiian sandalwood would be popular in the markets of the Far East where it was prized for ornamental use and burning as incense. As king, Kamehameha controlled the harvesting of sandalwood, and by 1811 he was reaching deals with Boston maritime merchants whereby he would receive a hefty share of the profits from their sales. He died in 1819 and his memory is honored by a state holiday-King Kamehameha Day-every June 11.

One year later, two events occurred that would come to define the culture and economy of Hawaii. The first whaling ship arrived in 1820. So did missionaries, led by a New England Congregationalist, Reverend Hiram Bingham. Within a decade, more than a hundred ships were making annual stops in Honolulu, and it quickly became a thriving port. With the Gold Rush and California's admission to the union, shipping between San Francisco and Honolulu grew, strengthening ties to the United States. Mining companies in northern California began importing Hawaiian food and other supplies across the Pacific rather than wait for them to make the difficult trip across the American interior. Meanwhile, the missionaries were converting native Hawaiians to Protestant Christianity. That was steady work after King Kamehameha's successor, Liholiho, abandoned the *kapu* system, the religiously inspired code of taboos that was used to guide and regulate people's lives. But the missionaries' greatest impact on the Islands may have been economic, not spiritual. When they left their religious duties, they took up other avocations and some went into the sugar business. In 1851, after being released from their missionary work, Samuel Northrup Castle and Amos Starr Cooke formed a partnership, Castle & Cooke, which ended up investing heavily in sugar plantations that sprung up on the islands. Samuel Alexander and Henry Baldwin, both sons of missionaries, started the Haiku Sugar Company, which later become Alexander & Baldwin. Both of these partnerships expanded into other commercial enterprises and both became members of the "Big Five" companies that built the sugar industry and associated businesses such as real estate, dominating Hawaii's economy for generations.

The boom in sugar required the importation of labor, because a series of epidemics devastated the native population as it came into increasing contact with Westerners. Soon, contract workers from China and Japan were coming to Hawaii. American sugar interests helped elect King Kalakaua to the Hawaiian throne over the British-leaning Queen Emma in 1874. Kalakaua returned the favor and sought a trade agreement with the United States in 1876 that allowed the duty-free sale of Hawaiian sugar in the states. But American planters and businessmen eventually tired of the caprices of the royal family and in January 1893, with the help of the Marines, ousted Queen Liliuokalani from the Iolani Palace and called on the United States to annex Hawaii. President Grover Cleveland demurred, and Hawaii for five years was a republic until President William McKinley annexed it. This history is a source of regret for some. An *Onipa'a* ceremony remembering Liliuokalani's overthrow was staged by John Waihee, the first governor of Native Hawaiian descent, in January 1993, with the American flag conspicuously absent. Later that year, Congress passed and President Bill Clinton signed an apology for the overthrow of Liliuokalani 100 years before. In 2009, Hawaii staged a commemoration, not a celebration, of the 50th anniversary of statehood.

The Japanese attack on Pearl Harbor led the United States to enter World War II, which brought a massive influx of U.S. armed forces to Hawaii. Military construction boomed. The overall population of the islands doubled to 858,000 in 1944, spurring greater demand for retail services and consumer products. After the war, the economy cooled as the nation demobilized, but with the Korean conflict in the early 1950s, there was another military build-up. The many sailors and troops that transited Hawaii on their way to the front lines, or who were stationed there, invariably shared its charms with family and friends when they returned home. By the 1960s, tourism had displaced sugar, pineapples and other agricultural products as Hawaii's leading industry. From statehood in 1959 to 1990, Hawaii's economic engine roared.

Then Hawaii ran into a trifecta of economic problems. The end of the Cold War brought a decline in military spending; work at the shipyard at Pearl Harbor slowed significantly. But it was Hawaii's traditional bonds across the Pacific that really brought economic woes to the Islands. The early 1990s recession in the United States was particularly severe in California, and it spread to Hawaii as the Golden State sent fewer visitors and less investment its way. And ever since King Kamehameha exploited the sandalwood trade with the Far East, Hawaii has always counted on Asian markets to help boost its bottom line, except during World War II. During Japan's "lost decade," vacationers cut back their trips to Hawaii and Japanese real estate investors stopped bidding up and buying up properties in Oahu. Annual growth in Hawaii sank to about one-third the level in the rest of the United States.

For many years, Hawaii's people did not wall themselves off in ethnic blocs. Asian migrant laborers brought traditions of hard work, family loyalty and group solidarity that found expression most vividly in the performance of the 442nd "Go for Broke" Regimental Combat Team, which was made up mostly of sons of Japanese immigrants and became the most decorated unit in U.S. military history. Once discriminated against, Japanese Americans today have the state's highest annual household incomes. Meanwhile, the Yankee spirit has been evident in Hawaii's commercial success and in its attachment to the rule of Anglo-American law. The Hawaiian spirit is apparent in the vitality of the *aloha* ambience, the welcoming of others despite their differences, and a willingness to absorb the teachings of others while maintaining a certain Polynesian attitude toward life. Hawaii's tolerance inspired segregationist Southern Democrats to block its admission to the Union for years.

Hawaii has seen the demise of its plantation agriculture: Once, one-fifth of the sugar consumed in the United States came from Hawaii. Competition from lower-cost international producers (and occasional environmental concerns closer to home) changed all that. In 2016, the Hawaiian Commercial and Sugar Company closed its doors after 180 years, laying off all 675 workers at its 36,000-acre plantation on Maui and marking a definitive end to the local sugar industry. By then, Del Monte had already picked its last pineapples on the islands, in 2008, with Maui Land & Pineapple shutting down its operations a year later. By 2015, a disused Dole cannery was being prepared for a new, more boutique existence as a 2,000-square-foot factory for processing Waialua-grown cacao, part of a boomlet of artisanal chocolate in the state; only Hawaii among the 50 states has the right climate conditions for growing cacao. If such ventures succeed, they will join such specialty crops as papayas, macadamia nuts, Kona coffee and genetically engineered seeds in a vastly reduced agriculture sector that today contributes less than one-half of 1 percent to the state GDP.

The Great Recession took its toll on the islands. Real estate in Hawaii experienced an even worse downturn than in the country as a whole. Tourism slumped, though it later recovered – and then some. In 2015, Hawaii set a record for visitors with 8.7 million, while the money they spent came close to the 2014 record of $14.7 billion. Japan continues to account for about one-fifth of the state's tourists and, with 1.5 million coming in 2015, Japan is by far the biggest source of visitors from any country other than the U.S. itself. At the same time, tourism from other nations, including Canada, China, Australia and Korea, has grown rapidly. All told, Hawaii's unemployment peaked at only 7.3 percent during the Great Recession and was 3 percent in November 2016 -- well below the national average.

Hawaii, so far removed from any other land, has a particularly fragile ecology, with a profusion of bird and plant species that are vulnerable to invasive predators. Airliners' wheel housings are routinely inspected for the brown tree snakes that have killed off most of the birds in Guam. The oceans around the islands are vulnerable, too. In 2006, President George W. Bush issued an order dedicating the Northwestern Hawaiian Islands Marine National Monument. The area contains 70 percent of the nation's tropical, shallow-water coral reefs, some 7,000 marine species (one-quarter found nowhere else), the endangered Hawaiian monk seal population and threatened species of predatory fish (sharks, groupers and jacks), as well as what remains of the *U.S.S. Yorktown*, which sank during the Battle of Midway in 1942. In 2016, Obama, who spent much of his youth in Hawaii, became the seventh president to preserve the area to one degree or another, expanding the protected area fourfold to more than half a million square miles, including barring commercial fishing and other resource extraction but allowing recreational fishing, scientific study and traditional Hawaiian cultural practices. Hawaii is also losing much of its famed beachfront. The U.S. Geological Survey estimates that chronic erosion is affecting 70 percent of the beaches on Oahu, Kauai and Maui, and a 2015 study by the University of Hawaii found that if current trends continue, the shoreline could recede by an average of 20 feet by 2050. Parts of Waikiki Beach, the birthplace of modern surfing where legendary Olympic athlete Duke Kahanamoku introduced the longboard more than a century ago, are barely ribbons of carbonate sand today.

Fair-weather Hawaii has one of the lowest energy usage rates per capita of any state, but because it has traditionally had to import petroleum, its energy costs are well above the national average. To reverse this pattern, the state has encouraged offshore wind and geothermal power, which have been controversial, as well as solar, which has been wildly popular; installation of rooftop solar panels has enabled consumers to provide energy to the electrical grid and get paid for it. Meanwhile, transmitting electricity through the turbulent channels between the Neighbor Islands to Oahu, where 70 percent of Hawaiians live, poses severe difficulties. Indeed, nature is not always benign. The Kilauea volcano on the Big Island started erupting in 1983 and hasn't stopped. Its slow-moving lava flow has consumed a cemetery and houses, and geologists closely monitor Kilauea for signs of a potential larger seismic event. Nearby Mauna Loa volcano is so forbidding that NASA has been using its environs to isolate researchers for months at a time in preparation for the long journey to Mars.

Only 6 percent of Hawaiians do not have health insurance, just 1 percentage point off the national low, and the state leads the nation in life expectancy. In 2015, Hawaii became the first state to raise the legal age of smoking to 21, reflecting its health-conscious mores and a faith that government knows what's best for its citizens. But while wellness is not a big problem, homelessness is. Driven by an expensive housing market, the number of homeless people grew by 36 percent between 2010 and 2016, the nation's third-biggest increase -- at a time when homelessness was falling nationally by 14 percent.

When Hawaii entered the union, it had a Republican territorial governor, and Democrat John F. Kennedy carried the state in the 1960 presidential election by just 115 votes. From 1962 to 2002, Hawaii's politics were dominated by a Democratic machine that had its beginning in the 1950s, when World War II veterans such as Daniel Inouye, Spark Matsunaga and George Ariyoshi joined forces with former mainlander John Burns, who as a police officer during the war helped prevent persecution of Japanese Americans. They allied themselves with the then-powerful International Longshoremen's and Warehousemen's Union, which represented sugar and pineapple plantation hands as well as dockworkers, cementing the allegiance of Japanese-American voters. The Burns-Inouye alliance built on the grievances against the *haole* (the Hawaiian word for white) owners of the big companies, and triumphed. Over the years this machine built a large government: about a fifth of Hawaii's workers are employed in government, and the state has some of the nation's highest taxes. Voting tended to follow ethnic lines. Japanese Americans were the heart of the Democratic Party, along with Native Hawaiians; whites, with relatively high incomes, leaned Republican. Lower-income Filipinos were heavily Democratic, with Chinese somewhat less so. Inouye, whose grandparents emigrated from Japan to work in Hawaii's sugar fields, was elected to the state legislature in 1954 and died a U.S. senator in 2012. He kept appropriations flowing to the state and kept close tabs on the state's politics.

The political playing field has become particularly lopsided since former two-term governor Linda Lingle, a Republican, left office in 2010 and lost a seemingly competitive Senate race in 2012 by a 2-to-1 margin. In 2008, Hawaii gave native son Obama 72 percent of its presidential vote, and in 2012, he got 70 percent. Hillary Clinton did marginally worse in 2016 – she got 40,000 fewer votes than Obama, while Trump won almost 8,000 more than Mitt Romney had – but she still coasted in the state, 62%-30%, Clinton's widest winning margin in any state. Meanwhile, Democrats have controlled the state House since statehood, and in 2016 won every seat in the state Senate. Few states today are as resiliently blue as Hawaii.

Population		Race and Ethnicity		Income	
Total	1,406,299	White	22.9%	Median Income	$69,515 (5 out of 50)
Land area	6,423	Black	1.9%		
Pop/ sq mi	219.0	Latino	9.9%	Under $50,000	35.3%
Born in state	53.8%	Asian	36.8%	$50,000-$99,999	32.7%
		Two races	19.2%	$100,000-$199,999	25.7%
Age Groups		Other	9.4%	$200,000 or more	6.3%
Under 18	21.9%			Poverty Rate	11.2%
18-34	24.3%	**Education**			
35-64	38.1%	H.S grad or less	36.9%	**Health Insurance**	
Over 64	15.6%	Some college	32.3%	With health insurance coverage	94.1%
		College Degree, 4 yr	20.4%		
Work		Post grad	10.5%		
White Collar	34.0%			**Public Assistance**	
Sales and Service	47.6%	**Military**		Cash public assistance income	3.6%
Blue Collar	18.4%	Veteran	10.4%		
Government	20.6%	Active Duty	3.7%	Food stamp/SNAP benefits	11.3%

Voter Turnout			
2015 Total Citizens 18+	1,001,729	2016 Pres Turnout as % CVAP	43%
2016 Pres Votes	428,937	2012 Pres Turnout as % CVAP	46%

Legislature	
Senate:	25D, 0R
House:	45D, 5R, 1I

Presidential Politics

2016 Democratic Caucus		
Bernie Sanders (D)	23,521	(70%)
Hillary Clinton (D)	10,126	(30%)
2016 Republican Caucus		
Donald Trump (R)	6,805	(43%)
Ted Cruz (R)	5,063	(32%)
Marco Rubio (R)	2,068	(13%)
John Kasich (R)	1,566	(10%)

2016 Presidential Vote		
Hillary Clinton (D)	266,891	(62%)
Donald Trump (R)	128,847	(30%)
Gary Johnson (L)	15,954	(4%)
Jill Stein (G)	12,737	(3%)
2012 Presidential Vote		
Barack Obama (D)	306,658	(71%)
Mitt Romney (R)	121,015	(28%)

Hawaii's presidential voting over the years has been the product of two sometimes countervailing forces. One is the state's historic preference for the Democratic Party. The other is an inclination to support incumbents in a state where many of its citizens were once unjustly questioned and there is a large military presence. It supported Ronald Reagan's reelection bid in 1984 and Richard Nixon's in 1972. They were the only two Republicans to win the islands' votes since the state began casting presidential ballots in 1960. Almost 70 percent of Hawaii's votes come from Oahu; the other islands are even more Democratic-leaning than the most urban island in the archipelago. The 2016 election results were hardly a surprise; Hillary Clinton defeated Donald Trump 62%-30%. In 2008 and 2012, Hawaiians embraced their native son, Barack Obama, and he won each election with more than 70 percent of the vote.

Hawaii chooses presidential delegates by caucus. In 2016, those contests were more eventful than the general election. In a state where whites make up less than a quarter of the population, Hawaii's diversity was no barrier to Trump in the GOP caucuses on March 8: he defeated Texas Sen. Ted Cruz, 43%-32%. Florida Sen. Marco Rubio finished a distant third. None of the GOP candidates campaigned in the state. On the Democratic side, both of the state's Democratic senators backed Clinton, but Rep. Tulsi Gabbard resigned her position as vice chair of the Democratic National Committee to support Sen. Bernie Sanders. More than 33,000 attended the Democratic caucuses and gave the Vermonter a 70%-30% victory over Clinton. Neither Democratic candidate stumped in the state, though Sanders's wife, Jane, made a campaign stop before the March 26 caucuses.

Congressional Districts

115th Congress Lineup	2D	114th Congress Lineup	2D

Hawaii has two congressional districts: The 1st includes urban Honolulu and extends westward to Pearl Harbor and the rural area beyond. The 2nd includes the rest of Oahu and the Neighbor Islands. The 1st District, the only Asian-majority district in the country, is the slightly less Democratic of the two and elected a Republican in 1986, 1988 and briefly in 2010, when Honolulu Councilman Charles Djou won an unusual special election against split Democratic opposition. The lower-income 2nd District has elected only Democrats since it was created in 1971.

Timing and ambition tend to overstep boundaries in Hawaii: In 2010, Democrat Colleen Hanabusa unseated Djou in the 1st District although she lived in the 2nd; in 2012, both major candidates for the open 2nd District lived in the 1st. In 2016, after her unsuccessful primary challenge to Sen. Brian Schatz in 2014, Hanabusa regained her seat following an unexpected vacancy. Given the recent volatility, more changes in the House delegation seem possible. But it remains a heavy lift for Republicans to win a seat here.

Governor

David Y. Ige (D)

Elected 2014, term expires 2018, 1st term; b. Jan. 15, 1957, Honolulu, HI; U of HI –Manoa, B.A., 1979; M.A., 1985; Buddhist; Married (Dawn); 3 children.

Elected Office: HI Senate 1994-2014; U.S. House, appointed 1985.

Professional Career: Electronics engineer, Pacific Analysis Corp.; Senior Administrator, General Telephone & Electronics Hawaiian Telephone, 1981-1999; Project Manager, Pihana Pacific, LLC., 1999-2001; Vice President of Engineering for Net Enterprise, Inc., 2001-2002; Project Manager, R.A. Ige and Associates, Inc., 2003.

Office: Executive Chambers, State Capitol, Honolulu, 96813; 808-586-0034; Fax: 808-586-0006; Website: hawaii.gov.

Election Results

Election	Name (Party)	Vote (%)
2014 General	David Ige (D)	181,065 (50%)
	Duke Aiona (R)	135,742 (37%)
	Mufi Hannemann (I)	42,925 (12%)
2014 Primary	David Ige (D)	157,050 (67%)
	Neil Abercrombie (D)	73,507 (32%)

Democrat David Ige, Hawaii's second Japanese-American governor, serves in the 21st century, but his family history embodies a major story line of 20th century Hawaii. Ige, born and raised in Pearl City, was the fifth of six boys of Japanese-American parents who had settled in Hawaii a generation earlier, at a time when those of Japanese ancestry were widely discriminated against. His father, Tokio, won a Purple Heart and a Bronze Star serving in the famous 100th Battalion, 442nd Regimental Combat Team of the U.S. Army during World War II, which was made up mostly of sons of Japanese immigrants. Hawaii's longtime protector in the Senate, Dan Inouye, was also a member, as were other notable Hawaiians. The veterans cultivated the educational institutions that trained the next generation of leaders, including Ige. "There is no doubt in my mind I would not be governor today if it were not for those war veterans," Ige told the *Wall Street Journal*. After fighting in the war, Ige said, the veterans "felt they deserved to be treated equally."

After studying engineering and business, Ige launched a successful career as an electrical engineer and project manager, working on information technology and telecommunications. Ige wasn't even planning to enter politics in 1985, when Democratic Gov. George Ariyoshi, who was looking for smart young professionals to appoint to vacant seats in the legislature, tapped Ige, who had been recommended by local activists in Pearl City. Ige wasn't even a member of the Democratic Party when Ariyoshi reached out to him. He went on to win reelection four times before advancing to the state Senate in 1994, all while continuing his regular employment.

He brought a novice's sensitivities to his new job and recoiled when he quickly came to understand that the legislative process is often an inside game where knowledge is not always shared and the public is often excluded from decision making. That led to Ige's focus on improving communication with voters (and among his own colleagues) and their access to information. He also joined a faction of lawmakers who were policy oriented and committed to reform called the "Chess Club," and he set about finding ways to increase citizen-involvement with the legislature. Drawing on his experience in the private sector, he often applied technology to the tasks of meeting his goals. Ige took the lead in moving the Senate toward using less paper, and perhaps more importantly, posting draft legislation, hearing notices and budget documents online. To help promote greater awareness of the legislature, he set up an electronic network to involve hundreds of high school students in the legislative process through a primitive form of videoconferencing. Ige wanted to take politics out of the backroom, and he is credited by colleagues with the now common practice in the legislature of holding committee votes in public rather than in closed session. Ige built a reputation as a well-studied policy expert, working on issues ranging from education reform to auto insurance to land conservation. His years of committee work paid off when he rose to chair the state Senate Ways and Means Committee in 2009. He introduced legislation to shore up pension and health care plans for state retirees.

When Ige announced his gubernatorial bid in 2013, it was widely seen as a David-and-Goliath contest. Incumbent Neil Abercrombie had presided over the state's economic revival, with unemployment dropping to 4.4 percent and the state budget swinging into the black by more than $800 million in 2013. Abercrombie outspent Ige by more than 10-to-1, and President Barack Obama, along with most other prominent Hawaii Democrats, endorsed him. What Abercrombie didn't expect was the voters' pushback against his personal style, which was widely viewed as confrontational. Many Asian Americans were unhappy with his decision to appoint Lt. Gov. Brian Schatz, rather than Rep. Colleen Hanabusa, to fill Inouye's seat after his death in 2012. Abercrombie enraged Hawaii's powerful public-sector unions when he proposed ending state reimbursements for federal Medicare Part B premiums for retired public workers. Abercrombie alienated teachers when he imposed a 5 percent pay cut on teachers after contract talks broke down. They would later get a raise, but Abercrombie infuriated them again when he called for a constitutional amendment to allow public funds to be spent on private preschool. It was little surprise when the Hawaii State Teachers Association, which had backed Abercrombie in his primary in 2010, decided to endorse Ige in 2014. Asked by reporters if he anticipated and understood the critical reaction from union leaders, Abercrombie responded: "I am the governor. I'm not your pal. I'm not your counselor. I am the governor."

Ige, by contrast, played up his image of quiet competence. His low-key manner and reputation for collaboration and openness in the legislature persuaded Hawaii Democrats to give him that trust and he won a shocker, defeating Abercrombie in the August primary by a staggering 35 percentage points-the first time that a sitting Hawaii governor had lost a primary since 1962. Ige's challenge in the general against Republican J. "Duke" Aiona was making sure that independent Mufi Hannemann didn't draw away too many centrist voters who would otherwise vote Democratic. Ige took part in 15 debates with his Republican opponent, Aiona, when he might have been tempted to let the state's strong Democratic leanings carry him to victory. In the late summer and early fall, polls showed a fairly tight race. This wasn't surprising, given that Aiona had more name recognition than typical Republican nominees, having served as two-term GOP Gov. Linda Lingle's lieutenant governor and run for the state's top job before, albeit unsuccessfully, against Abercrombie in 2010. But by the closing weeks of the campaign, Ige consolidated his lead and ended up beating Aiona by about a dozen percentage points.

In office, Ige broke with the tendency of most of his predecessors to govern as the *ali'i nui* (the term for a great or grand chief from Hawaii's early days) and began meeting every other week with the leaders of the state House of Representatives and Senate. Ige said he felt that was important because he could remember from his days in the legislature that he was often disappointed in how the governor would implement the measures passed by the lawmakers. But his ties to legislators didn't save his nomination of Carleton Ching to lead the Department of Land and Natural Resources, the state agency charged with protecting Hawaii's wondrous and delicate habitat. Ching was a controversial choice because he had spent 12 prior years as the chief lobbyist for Castle & Cooke, an original member of the elite Big Five that was still one of the state's biggest developers. Critics said that given his background, Ching would face numerous conflicts of interest if approved. But even after the Senate's Water and Land Committee voted 5-2 against Ching, Ige pressed ahead. Only minutes before the full Senate was to vote on the nomination did Ige pull it to avoid what appeared to be a likely narrow defeat. By April, the Senate had unanimously confirmed his second nominee, Suzanne Case, who had more traditional environmental credentials as executive director of the Nature Conservancy since 2001.

During the biennial budget process, Ige and the leaders in the legislature decided with little fanfare or public discussion to allow the temporary hike in the state's top income tax rate to expire. It had been passed to help balance the state's books at the depths of the Great Recession. The move represented as much as a 2.75 percentage point drop in the top rate for Hawaii's joint filers who made more than $400,000 a year. There was some irony in this move because it was the Democratic-controlled legislature in 2009 that overrode then GOP Gov. Lingle's veto of the bill that originally imposed the temporary tax increase. Ige secured a $26 billion biennial budget that generally conformed to his spending proposals. The most far-reaching measure he approved early in his first term was legislation that sets the most ambitious clean energy goal in the country: to make Hawaii self-sufficient in energy and meet 100 percent of its needs with renewable sources. In signing the legislation Ige declared: "Making the transition to renewable, indigenous resources for power generation will allow us to keep more of that money at home, thereby improving our economy, environment and energy security."

Ige signed three bills restricting gun rights. One prevents those charged with stalking or sexual assault from possessing a firearm. Another allows law enforcement to seize guns and ammunition for those disqualified by mental health concerns, while a third requires the entry of Hawaii gun owners' names into a national FBI database. Ige also grappled with the state's continuing challenges of homelessness, issuing an emergency proclamation to extend outreach efforts and urging greater investment in affordable housing during his 2016 State of the State address. He called mental health "the single-most pressing unmet health issue facing our state" and pursued millions in new funding for the Hawaii State Hospital. Ige achieved some success in economic development, working to extend international flights to Kona on the Big Island, rather than just Honolulu International Airport on Oahu, which had been the state's only international commercial airport since 2010. In December 2016, international flights to and from Kona resumed after federal inspection facilities were upgraded. Ige's trickiest challenge, however, was handling a heated and long-running controversy over the $1.4 billion Thirty Meter Telescope project on the Big Island, which would build the world's largest telescope on Mauna Kea, perhaps the best place in the world to study the skies. However, it would be located on land that some Hawaiian Natives consider sacred, and some further worry that the 18-story tall structure is inappropriate for the site. Its construction inspired demonstrations that led to arrests. In December 2015, the state Supreme Court withdrew the project's permit, with its future -- a clash between cutting-edge technology and an ancient culture – remaining to be written.

In April 2017, state legislators requested Executive Branch officials to update plans for coping with a threats of a nuclear attack by North Korea. For reelection in 2018, Ige did not seem to be as vulnerable as Abercrombie was, but Democratic state Sen. Josh Green was weighing a primary challenge.

Senior Senator

Brian Schatz (D)

Appointed Dec. 2012, term expires 2022, 1st full term; b. Oct 20, 1972, Ann Arbor, MI; School for International Training (Kenya), 1992; Pomona College (CA), B.A., 1994, Jewish; Married (Linda Kwok Kai Yun); 2 children.

Elected Office: HI House, 1998-2006; HI Lt. Governor, 2010-2012.

Professional Career: CEO, Helping Hands HI, 2004-2010; Chairman, HI Democratic Party, 2008-2010.

DC Office: 722 HSOB 20510, 202-224-3934, Fax: 202-228-1153, schatz.senate.gov.

State Offices: Honolulu, 808-523-2061.

Committees: *Appropriations*: Commerce, Justice, Science & Related Agencies, Department of Defense, DOL, HHS & Education & Related Agencies, Military Construction & Veteran Affairs & Related Agencies (RMM), Transportation, HUD & Related Agencies. *Banking, Housing & Urban Affairs*: Financial Institutions & Consumer Protection, Housing, Transportation & Community Development, National Security & International Trade & Finance. *Commerce, Science & Transportation*: Aviation Operations, Safety & Security, Communications, Technology, Innovation &

the Internet (RMM), Oceans, Atmosphere, Fisheries & Coast Guard, Space, Science & Competitiveness. *Ethics*. *Indian Affairs*.

Group Ratings

	ADA	ACLU	AFL-CIO	LCV	ITI	COC	HAFA	ACU	CFG	FRC
2016	-	82%	-	100%	80%	38%	5%	0%	0%	0%
2015	95%	C	100%	96%	C	43%	C	4%	0%	0%

Almanac Ratings 2015

	Economy	Social	Foreign	Composite
Liberal	100%	100%	88%	96%
Conservative	0%	0%	12%	4%

Key Votes of the 114th Congress

1. Keystone pipeline	N	5. National Security Data	Y	9. Gun Sales Checks	Y
2. Export-Import Bank	N	6. Iran Nuclear Deal	N	10. Sanctuary Cities	N
3. Debt Ceiling Increase	Y	7. Puerto Rico Debt	Y	11. Planned Parenthood	N
4. Homeland Security $$	Y	8. Loretta Lynch A.G	Y	12. Trade deals	N

Election Results

Election	Name (Party)	Vote (%)		Cand. Spent	Ind. Exp. Support	Ind. Exp. Oppose
2016 General	Brian Schatz (D)	306,604	(74%)	$1,932,020		
	John Carroll (R)	92,653	(22%)	$54,517		
	Joy Allison (C)	9,103	(2%)			
2016 Primary	Brian Schatz (D)	162,905	(86%)			
	Makani Christensen (D)	11,899	(6%)			

When Democrat Brian Schatz, Hawaii's senior senator, was appointed to the Senate at the end of 2012, the move was at odds with the deathbed wishes of his predecessor, Daniel Inouye. In a letter sent to Hawaii Gov. Neil Abercrombie shortly before he died, Inouye -- who had occupied the Senate seat for just weeks short of the half-century mark -- asked that Rep. Colleen Hanabusa, be appointed to succeed him. But Abercrombie opted to name Schatz, his lieutenant governor and running mate from the election two years earlier. A former state legislator and Hawaii Democratic Party chair, Schatz was sworn into the Senate 10 days after Inouye's death -- and, in 2014, narrowly held off Hanabusa in a primary for the special election to fill the remainder of Inouye's term. The situation was far different in 2016, when Schatz faced token opposition in the Democratic primary on his way to election to his first full term in the Senate.

During his Senate tenure, Schatz has demonstrated himself to be an ardent liberal. *National Journal* vote ratings for 2013, his first year in the chamber, showed him in a three-way tie (with now-Minority Leader Charles Schumer of New York and Sen. Chris Murphy of Connecticut) as its most liberal member. Schatz has had an abiding interest in environmental issues, particularly climate change, although he gave up his seat on the Energy and Natural Resources Committee in early 2015 when named to a prized slot on the Appropriations Committee. Given his relative youth and political base in a solidly blue state, Schatz could be around Capitol Hill long enough to acquire the seniority needed to chair the Appropriations panel -- the powerful perch that Schatz's predecessor, Inouye, occupied for three years prior to his death.

Schatz was born in Ann Arbor, Michigan, one of two identical-twin sons of a cardiologist, Irwin Schatz. (Brian Schatz's twin brother, Stephen, is now deputy superintendent of the Hawaii Department of Education, the country's ninth largest school district.) In the mid-1960s, while working at Henry Ford Hospital in Detroit, Irwin Schatz became aware of a decades-long study being conducted by the U.S. Public Health Service in Tuskegee Alabama, in which poor black sharecroppers with syphilis were left untreated in order to study the effects. A letter of protest that he wrote to USPHS officials was ignored at the time, but, when the letter came to light several years later, it helped to spur a public debate that led to new standards governing research on human subjects. When Brian Schatz was two years old, his father accepted a job at the University of Hawaii and the family moved to the state. After high school at the prestigious Punahou School -- which future President Barack Obama had attended a decade earlier -- Schatz went to Pomona College in California, studied abroad in Kenya and received a degree in philosophy. He returned to Hawaii and worked as a community organizer, including heading a beach preservation group.

In 1998, Schatz, then 26, was elected to represent an urban Honolulu district in the Hawaii legislature, where he served for eight years and was eventually appointed majority whip. When Rep. Ed Case decided to challenge Democratic Sen. Daniel Akaka in 2006, Schatz became one of 10 candidates in the Democratic primary for the seat that Case was vacating. Schatz finished a distant sixth, with just 7 percent of the vote -- losing to Mazie Hirono, who at the time was lieutenant governor and is now Schatz's Senate colleague. Schatz then turned his attention to prodding his Punahou School fellow alumnus, Obama, into the presidential race. Schatz joined other Democrats in 2006 in founding a group urging Obama, then a senator from Illinois, to run. Schatz served as spokesman for the state's Obama campaign before being elected state Democratic Party chairman in the spring of 2008. During this period, Schatz was also CEO of Helping Hands Hawaii, a social services agency.

Schatz left both Helping Hands Hawaii and the party chairmanship in early 2010, and announced his candidacy for lieutenant governor. He ran with Abercrombie, who had served for two decades in Congress before seeking the governorship; the Abercrombie-Schatz ticket won by 17 percentage points in November. As lieutenant governor, Schatz worked on energy and climate issues and helped pass same-sex civil unions in the state. When the 88-year-old Inouye fell ill and died six weeks after the November 2012 election, the Hawaii Democratic Party -- as required by state law -- sent Abercrombie three names from among whom to choose a replacement: Hanabusa, former congressional candidate Esther Kiaaina, and Schatz. While Hanabusa was Inouye's choice, Abercrombie, who had a well-publicized rift with Inouye and much of the state's Democratic establishment, chose his ally, Schatz.

Inouye's chief of staff issued a curt statement, saying: "Sen. Inouye conveyed his final wish to Gov. Abercrombie. While we are very disappointed that it was not honored, it was the governor's decision to make. We wish Brian Schatz the best of luck." Schatz sought to be conciliatory, declaring: "No one can fill Sen. Dan K. Inouye's shoes. But together, all of us can walk in his footsteps." Schatz immediately flew to Washington on Air Force One with Obama, who had been spending his Christmas vacation in Hawaii, and was quickly sworn into office as the Senate faced some crucial end-of-year votes, particularly on avoiding the so-called "fiscal cliff" created by a combination of automatic tax increases and spending reductions. The timing made Schatz the state's senior senator by just a few days. The state's other senator, Hirono, who had been elected in November 2012 to replace the retiring Akaka, was not due to be sworn in until January 3, 2013.

Weighing her options for 2014, Hanabusa, after considering a run against Abercrombie, decided to challenge Schatz in the Democratic primary. She sought to depict Schatz, two months past 40 at the time of his Senate appointment, as inexperienced. (Abercrombie was said to have privately cited the 20-year age difference between Schatz and Hanabusa in making his choice, arguing that Schatz was in a position to serve longer and accumulate more congressional seniority, to the benefit of the state.) Hanabusa was backed by the local political networks of Inouye and Akaka, and had financial support from EMILY's List, a national political action committee which backs female Democrats who support abortion rights. Schatz lined up support from the national Democratic establishment, including Obama, then-Senate Majority Leader Harry Reid, and progressive and environmental groups. And he outraised Hanabusa, collecting $4.9 million to her $2.9 million. The contest broke largely along ethnic lines, as Hawaii's primaries often do, with the white Schatz winning with liberal white voters and the Japanese-American Hanabusa performing well with ethnic Hawaiians and Asian-Americans.

Most polling showed Schatz with a lead, but as often happens in Hawaii's difficult-to-forecast environment, the bulk of public opinion surveys proved themselves wildly off the mark. After the Aug. 9 primary election, which came on the heels of a tropical storm that damaged parts of Hawaii and prevented two precincts from voting, Schatz held a tenuous 1,635 vote lead. State election officials said that a make-up election would be held in those areas the following Friday; Hanabusa filed a legal challenge contending those sections were insufficiently recovered to have voters cast ballots, but a judge rejected her argument. After those precincts voted Schatz's lead stood at 1,769 votes out of a statewide total of more than 237,000 ballots cast, for a 49%-48% victory. After that, Schatz's election in November was a cakewalk, as was his election to a full term in 2016. In both cases, Schatz took 70 percent of the vote. Schatz's one-time running mate, Abercrombie, did not fare as well -- losing a 2014 bid for renomination by a 66%-30% margin, with his loss fueled in part by having ignored the dying wishes of Inouye, an iconic figure in Hawaii.

Throughout his relatively brief Senate tenure, Schatz has focused much of his attention on dealing with global warming. In March 2014, he helped organize an all-night "talkathon" to try to draw more attention to the dangers of climate change. In January 2015, his amendment to the Keystone XL oil pipeline bill put lawmakers on record on whether they believe "climate change is real and human activity significantly contributes" to it. The amendment, the first Senate vote on climate change in eight years, got 50 votes in favor, including five from Republicans. Several months earlier, he and Democratic Sen. Sheldon Whitehouse of Rhode Island unveiled a proposed tax on carbon emissions they contended would yield $2 trillion in revenue over 10 years. They sought to attract Republicans by arguing that the money generated could jump-start tax reform, including a lowering of the corporate rate as well as breaks for middle-income taxpayers.

On numerous legislative initiatives, Schatz has teamed up with colleagues, who, like him, are among the more junior and avowedly liberal members of the Senate. Schatz, along with Murphy and Democratic Sen. Martin Heinrich of New Mexico, co-authored a piece in *Foreign Affairs* magazine in June 2015, entitled "Principles For A Progressive Foreign Policy: What Congress Must Do" and advocating steps such as modern-day Marshall Plan. "Now is the time to reinvest in this work, as countries under the economic thumb of Russia or China, and communities seeking protection from extremist groups, are crying out for help that smart, nimble U.S. foreign aid can provide," they declared. Schatz and Murphy were the two youngest members of the Senate at the time, and combined to sponsor legislation aimed at college affordability -- by providing incentives to college administrators to bring down costs. In 2016, Schatz joined with Democratic Sen. Elizabeth Warren of Massachusetts to turn up the heat on those responsible for accrediting for-profit educational institutions.

Like any legislator representing a state separated from the U.S. mainland by 3,000 miles of water, Schatz has spent a great deal of time on issues directly related to Hawaii. And he has often reached across the aisle to senators representing rural, far-flung states with similar issues. In December 2016, Schatz and Utah Republican Orrin Hatch achieved congressional passage of a so-called "telehealth" bill, intended to spur the use of videoconferencing to link teams of specialists to primary care providers in rural and underserved areas for weekly continuing education sessions. On the Commerce, Science and Transportation Committee, he was involved in creating a new subcommittee on tourism policy, which he chaired while the Democrats were in the majority. In September 2016, Obama signed legislation by Schatz and the Commerce Committee chairman, Republican John Thune of South Dakota, intended to foster greater federal involvement in tourism efforts by Native Hawaiian as well as Alaska Native and American Indian communities.

Perhaps Schatz's biggest impact to date has come not through legislation, but rather via an executive order from his fellow Hawaiian, Obama. In late spring of 2016, Schatz wrote to Obama, asking that the Papahanaumokuakea Marine National Monument, which surrounds the uninhabited Northwestern Hawaiian Islands, be quadrupled in size. The marine reserve, initially created by President George W. Bush a decade earlier, is home to 7,000 marine and terrestrial species, a quarter of which are found nowhere else on earth. According to *The Washington Post*, Schatz asked Obama to increase the size of the protected area from just under 140,000 square miles to nearly 583,000 square miles -- an area greater than the state of Alaska. A couple of months later, Obama utilized his power under the 1906 Antiquities Act to accede to Schatz's proposal, making it the largest protected land or ocean conservation area anywhere on earth.

Junior Senator

Mazie Hirono (D)

Elected 2012, term expires 2018, 1st term; b. Nov 03, 1947, Fukushima, Japan; Georgetown University Law Center (DC), J.D.; University of Hawaii, Manoa, B.A.; Buddhism; Married (Leighton Kim Oshima); 1 stepchild.

Elected Office: U.S. House, 2006-2012; HI Lt.Governor, 1994-2002; HI House, 1980-1994.

Professional Career: Deputy HI Attorney General, 1978-1980; Practicing lawyer, 1984-1988.

DC Office: 730 HSOB 20510, 202-224-6361, Fax: 202-224-2126, hirono.senate.gov.

State Offices: Honolulu, 808-522-8970.

Committees: *Armed Services*: Readiness & Management Support, Seapower (RMM). *Energy & Natural Resources*: National Parks (RMM), Public Lands, Forests & Mining. *Judiciary*: Border Security

& Immigration, Oversight, Agency Action, Federal Rights & Federal Courts, Privacy, Technology & the Law. *Small Business & Entrepreneurship*. *Veterans' Affairs*.

Group Ratings

	ADA	ACLU	AFL-CIO	LCV	ITI	COC	HAFA	ACU	CFG	FRC
2016	-	88%	-	100%	80%	38%	7%	0%	0%	0%
2015	100%	C	100%	100%	C	43%	C	0%	0%	0%

Almanac Ratings 2015

	Economy	Social	Foreign	Composite
Liberal	100%	100%	96%	99%
Conservative	0%	0%	4%	1%

Key Votes of the 114th Congress

1. Keystone pipeline	N	5. National Security Data	Y	9. Gun Sales Checks	Y
2. Export-Import Bank	N	6. Iran Nuclear Deal	N	10. Sanctuary Cities	N
3. Debt Ceiling Increase	Y	7. Puerto Rico Debt	Y	11. Planned Parenthood	N
4. Homeland Security $$	Y	8. Loretta Lynch A.G	Y	12. Trade deals	N

Election Results

Election	Name (Party)	Vote (%)	Cand. Spent	Ind. Exp. Support	Ind. Exp. Oppose
2012 General	Mazie Hirono (D)	269,489 (63%)	$5,644,499	$232,692	$585,000
	Linda Lingle (R)	160,994 (37%)	$5,839,282	$1,031,875	$548,596
2012 Primary	Mazie Hirono (D)	134,745 (58%)			
	Ed Case (D)	95,553 (41%)			

Prior winning percentages: House: 2010 (72%), 2008 (76%), 2006 (61%)

When Democrat Mazie Hirono, Hawaii's junior senator, was first elected in 2012, it opened up another crack in the figurative glass ceiling of the world's most exclusive club. Hirono became the first Asian-American woman to serve in the Senate, and only its second non-white woman ever. Hirono is also the first U.S. senator to have been born in Japan, and her status as the Senate's only immigrant member gave the normally low-profile legislator increased visibility throughout the 2016 election year -- as she sharply criticized the immigration policies of Republican presidential nominee Donald Trump on repeated occasions. "My mother brought me to this country to give us a chance at a better life," Hirono said during an appearance on MSNBC in August 2016. "And, believe me, a country with a Donald Trump as president would not be a welcoming country to immigrants like me."

Hirono was born in Fukushima Japan, and immigrated to Hawaii just before her eighth birthday with her mother, Laura, who fled an abusive husband with alcohol and gambling problems. As a child, she shared a single bed in a boarding house room with her mother and older brother, and at age 10 went to work to help support the family. Laura Hirono found work as a typesetter for a Japanese language newspaper. "She was making minimum wage; she had no health coverage," Mazie Hirono said of her mother in an interview in 2007, just after she had been elected to her first term in the House of Representatives. "Our lives were precarious." Speaking only Japanese when she arrived in Hawaii, Hirono mastered English in public school and became a naturalized citizen in 1959, the year that Hawaii became a state.

As a college student, Hirono spent the summer of 1968 working with at-risk youths, and it helped to transform her into an activist with a keen interest in politics. After graduating from the University of Hawaii, Hirono worked as a staffer in the Hawaii legislature and for several campaigns before decamping for Washington, D.C. in 1975. She earned a law degree from Georgetown University and returned to Honolulu to work for the Hawaii attorney general's office. She ran for the state House in 1980 and won, holding the seat until 1994, when she was elected to the first of two terms as lieutenant governor. Hobbled by a bumpy relationship with her running mate, Gov. Ben Cayetano, Hirono barely won her party's nomination for governor in 2002, edging out State House Majority Leader Ed Case by 41%-40%. Her general election campaign was poorly organized and undermined by Democratic Party scandals involving illegal campaign contributions. Despite the state's strongly Democratic tilt, Hirono lost to Republican nominee Linda Lingle, 52%-47%.

Seeking to stay active in politics, Hirono formed a political action committee to assist state-level Democratic women who backed abortion rights; it was named in honor of the late Hawaii Rep. Patsy Mink, who in 1964 became the first non-white woman ever elected to Congress. Hirono got her chance to get back into elected office in 2006, when Case -- by then a member of the House-- gave up that slot to challenge veteran Sen. Daniel Akaka in the Democratic primary. Hirono ran for Case's House seat, and emerged atop a 10-candidate Democratic primary field, with state Senate President Colleen Hanabusa (now the representative from Hawaii's other District) finishing a close second. (Brian Schatz, now Hirono's senior colleague in the Hawaii Senate delegation, finished a distant sixth.) Hirono went on to easily win the general election in a district that had never elected a Republican.

In yet another first, Hirono and Rep. Hank Johnson of Georgia, also elected in 2006, became the first Buddhists ever to serve in Congress. (Hirono would later become the Senate's first Buddhist as well.) As most members of the House placed their hands on the Bible, and Minnesota Rep. Keith Ellison -- elected that year as the House's first Muslim member -- took the oath of office on the Quran, Hirono was sworn in as a member of Congress without a book present. "I don't have a book," Hirono -- who was raised in the Buddhist tradition, but doesn't actively practice the religion -- told *Gannett News Service* at the time. "But I certainly believe in the precepts of Buddhism, and that of tolerance of other religions and integrity and honesty."

Hirono had a solidly liberal voting record and a relatively low profile in the House, where she served on the Education and the Workforce, and the Transportation and Infrastructure committees. Her enthusiastic support of the Democratic agenda led the Hawaii *Tribune-Herald* to say, in endorsing her in 2008, "We wish she'd be a little more independent and less partisan." (Hirono was among only 13 Democratic senators whose voting record rated a 100 percent scores from the liberal Americans for Democratic Action in 2015; the ADA scored her at 100 percent and 90 percent in 2013 and 2014, respectively.) Like the late Hawaii Sen. Daniel Inouye, she was a staunch defender of earmarking of funds for the benefit of the state; and in fiscal 2010, she ranked third among all House members in accumulating special-request spending items, according to Taxpayers for Common Sense. Earmarking has since been curtailed in the House and Senate; Hirono defended the projects she requested as frequently yielding benefits far beyond their local scope.

When Akaka announced his retirement, Hirono was considered the early Democratic favorite, although she faced a primary challenge from former Rep. Case, a party moderate. Meanwhile, Republicans landed their best possible candidate when ex-Gov. Lingle, after months of deliberation, agreed to run. In a rather unusual development, veteran Republican Rep. Don Young of Alaska, who served on the Transportation and Infrastructure with Hirono, endorsed her in the Democratic primary. "While Mazie and I don't see eye to eye on everything, we've done something too many people in Washington refuse to cross the aisle and do: We've worked together," Young declared during a 90-second video in which the two legislators talked about cooperating to preserve native Hawaiian and Native Alaskan education programs -- with Hirono saying she had to fight her own party leadership to do so. Lingle responded by criticizing Young as "controversial" and alluding to ethics issues that had dogged him throughout the prior decade; in the general election, Young returned to the GOP fold to endorse Lingle. By that time, Hirono had defeated Case by 57%-40% in the primary, setting up a rematch of her contest with Lingle a decade earlier.

Lingle initially made the race competitive, campaigning on her successful record as a moderate governor and stressing that she wouldn't be beholden to Senate GOP leaders. She ran an ad criticizing Hirono for not getting any of her own bills signed into law. Democrats eviscerated Lingle for her praise of Sarah Palin during a speech introducing Palin as the party's vice presidential nominee at the 2008 Republican National Convention. Lingle said she would vote for Republican presidential nominee Mitt Romney, which didn't play well in the home state of President Barack Obama. Hirono argued that a vote for Lingle could help put the GOP in the Senate majority, which she claimed would lead to the repeal of Obama's health care reform law and provide more tax cuts for the wealthy. Bringing the argument closer to home, she also asserted that a GOP majority would threaten the influence of Inouye, the Appropriations Committee's top Democrat and an iconic figure to Hawaiians. Hirono opened a double-digit lead by early October and went on to win by a landslide, 63%-37%.

Inouye, 88 and in declining health, died on December 17, 2012, six weeks after Election Day. Democratic Gov. Neil Abercrombie appointed Schatz, his lieutenant governor, as Inouye's immediate replacement. Schatz started his service in the Senate in late December, and so Hirono became the state's junior senator by literally a matter of days. Hirono was said to be unhappy at being leapfrogged by Schatz, and her allies reportedly sought to delay Schatz's swearing-in until the same day as Hirono's. But they were overruled by then-Majority Leader Harry Reid of Nevada, who did not want a seat left vacant as a showdown on the so-called "fiscal cliff" of expiring tax cuts and spending reductions was imminent.

As was the case in the House, Hirono has generally kept a low profile in the Senate, spending much of her time on issues that directly impact Hawaii. Reflecting the emergence of Filipino-Americans as her state's largest ethnic minority, a recent legislative focus for Hirono has been to streamline U.S. immigration procedures for some citizens of the Philippines -- to allow surviving Filipino veterans of World War II living in the United States to be joined by their children. Hirono has served on the Veterans' Affairs Committee as well as the Armed Services Committee, where she is ranking member on the Seapower Subcommittee, since coming to the Senate. In 2015, she joined the Energy and Natural Resources panel, which wields politically significant jurisdiction in a state with a major tourism industry and significant acreage under the control of either the National Park Service or the U.S. Fish and Wildlife Service.

Hirono was named to the Judiciary Committee when first elected, and played an active role in the panel's debate over comprehensive immigration reform legislation in 2013. While the bulk of the amendments she put forth dealt with issues specific to Hawaii, one controversial provision -- which cleared the committee on a party-line vote -- sought to require border agents to ask apprehended individuals whether they were traveling with spouses or children. The intent, Hirono said, was to ensure that families were not separated during the interrogation process, potentially making migrants "more vulnerable by returning them to dangerous places without their family members." The immigration bill passed the Senate with bipartisan support, but was never taken up in the House. Hirono left the Judiciary Committee in early 2015, but returned two years later. The panel "will be on the front lines of fighting to protect Hawaii from the incoming Trump administration's proposals that erode civil rights and target immigrants," she declared.

By all indications, Hirono -- who will turn 71 just prior to Election Day 2018 -- is running for a second term; she actively raised campaign funds. Hawaii has not elected a Republican to the Senate in nearly 50 years, and the GOP does not appear to be in a position to mount a competitive campaign against her. While there has been continuing speculation about a primary challenge to Hirono from Rep. TulsiGabbard, the House member disavowed interest in an insurgent bid in an interview with the Honolulu Star-Advertiser in early 2017, saying she feels Hirono is "doing a good job." In May 2017, Hirono had surgery after doctors discovered kidney cancer.

FIRST DISTRICT

Colleen Hanabusa (D)

Elected 2010, 3rd term; b. May 04, 1951, Wai'anae; St. Andrew's Priory, Att., 1969; Colorado College, Att., 1971; University of Hawaii, Manoa, B.A., 1973; University of Hawaii, Manoa, M.A., 1975; University of Hawaii At Manoa, William S. Richardson School of Law, J.D., 1977; Buddhism; Married (John Souza).

Elected Office: HI Senate, 1999-2010, Majority Leader, 2003-2007, President, 2007-2010.

Professional Career: Practicing attorney, 1978-1998.

DC Office: 422 CHOB 20515, 202-225-2726, Fax: 202-225-0688, hanabusa.house.gov.

State Offices: Honolulu, 808-541-2570.

Committees: *Armed Services*: Seapower & Projection Forces, Strategic Forces. *Natural Resources*: Federal Lands (RMM), Indian, Insular & Alaska Native Affairs. *Science, Space & Technology*: Environment.

Group Ratings

	ADA	ACLU	AFL-CIO	LCV	ITI	COC	HAFA	ACU	CFG	FRC
2016	-	0%	-	100%	-	67%	-	-	-	-

Election Results

Election	Name (Party)	Vote (%)		Cand. Spent	Ind. Exp. Support	Ind. Exp. Oppose
2016 General	Colleen Hanabusa (D)	145,417	(72%)	$485,265		
	Shirlene D. Ostrov (R)	45,958	(23%)			
	Alan Yim (L)	6,601	(3%)			
	Calvin Griffin (I)	4,381	(2%)			
2016 Primary	Colleen Hanabusa (D)	74,013	(80%)			
	Lei Ahu Isa (D)	11,518	(13%)			

Prior winning percentages: 2012 (55%), 2010 (53%)

Democrat Colleen Hanabusa won election in 2016 to the seat that she had held for four years before her unsuccessful run for the Senate in 2014. She unexpectedly returned to the House after first-term Rep. Mark Takai died of cancer in July 2016. She was not seriously challenged and also won a special election to fill the remaining seven weeks in Takai's term. In the interim, she served as chairwoman of the Honolulu Authority for Rapid Transportation.

Hanabusa is a Yonsei, a fourth-generation American of Japanese ancestry. Each of her grandfathers was among the more than 100,000 Japanese Americans forcibly relocated and interned after Japan's attack on Pearl Harbor during World War II. She was raised on a sugar plantation by her maternal grandmother while her parents worked long hours running a gas station in Waianae. While young, she learned ikebana, the Japanese art of flower and plant arrangement that has a strong spiritual component. In ikebana, she says, if the core piece isn't placed well and balanced, the arrangement falls apart. "What I learned from that always has stuck with me," she said.

Hanabusa graduated from the University of Hawaii with a bachelor's degree in economics and sociology and a master's in sociology. She got her law degree from the University of Hawaii's William S. Richardson School of Law, and built a legal practice as a labor lawyer. Elected to the state Senate in 1998, she served 12 years and became Senate president, the first woman to lead either branch of Hawaii's legislature. A signature issue was education, including the creation of charter schools for underserved children and improvement of special education schools.

When 10-term Rep. Neil Abercrombie resigned to run for governor in 2010, Hanabusa was the early favorite of the state's Democratic establishment in the May 2010 wide-open special election. But former Rep. Ed Case also jumped in, disrupting the plans of kingmaker Sens. Daniel Inouye and Daniel Akaka, both long-serving lawmakers who held a grudge against Case for challenging Akaka in the Senate primary in 2006. With Case siphoning off Democratic votes, Hanabusa finished second to Republican Charles Djou. He won 40 percent to 31 percent for Hanabusa and 28 percent for Case.

Djou ran again in November for a two-year term. This time, Case stayed out. Hanabusa sailed to an easy victory in the primary and then had a one-on-one shot in the general election. Both candidates were well-financed, with Djou raising almost $2.7 million to Hanabusa's $2.4 million. Hanabusa was a strong supporter of native-son President Barack Obama's policies during an election when many other Democrats distanced themselves. She was a robust defender of the Affordable Care Act, calling health care a "right" and the legislation a first step toward universal health insurance. Djou attacked wasteful federal spending and supported a constitutional amendment to require a balanced budget. He was more moderate on social issues, and was one of only five House Republicans who backed repeal of the "don't ask, don't tell" legislation for openly gay men and women in the military. This time, Hanabusa won 53%-47%.

During her initial tenure in the House, she unsuccessfully sought to amend a Republican oil-drilling bill to require companies to submit a worst-case oil discharge plan. On the Armed Services Committee, she served on a panel looking at the defense industry's business challenges, and worked to include a recommendation to establish an advocate for small businesses at Pentagon agencies. Djou returned for a rematch in 2012, but faced long odds in a year in which Obama was on the ballot and Hanabusa raised nearly twice as much as he did. She won 55%-45%.

When Inouye died in office in December 2012, he reportedly said on his deathbed that he wanted Hanabusa, who considered the Senate Appropriations Committee chairman her mentor, to take his place. But the iconoclastic Abercrombie, who had a strained relationship with Inouye, instead named Brian Schatz, his lieutenant governor, to the seat. Hanabusa then challenged Schatz in the 2014 Senate primary. She received support from what remained of the Inouye and Akaka political network and from EMILY's List, which backs female Democrats who support abortion rights. As the incumbent, Schatz won support from the Democratic establishment in Washington, including Obama and Senate Majority

Leader Harry Reid, plus progressive and environmental groups. The contest broke along ethnic lines, as Hawaii primaries often do. It turned out to be exceedingly close. Schatz had a 1,635-vote lead after the Aug. 9 primary. But two precincts were prevented from voting because of a tropical storm. In the make-up election in that area, Schatz gained an additional 134 votes.

After Takai won Hanabusa's House seat, the Iraq war veteran focused on military and veterans' issues. In May 2016, he was diagnosed with pancreatic cancer at age 48, and said he would not run for reelection. When Hanabusa announced that she would run for her old seat, Takai endorsed her and she faced minimal competition. In the seven-candidate contest, she won 75% of the vote. Likewise, the general election was a foregone conclusion. Hanabusa defeated Republican Shirelene Ostrov, 73%-22%, and also won the special election that day by a similar margin. Hanabusa raised $972,000 for her campaigns, compared with $41,000 for Ostrov.

Following the election, Hanabusa was sworn into office on Nov. 14. The Democrats' freshman class selected her as their representative to the party leadership.

Honolulu Metro

Population		**Race and Ethnicity**		**Income**	
Total	703,960	White	16.7%	Median Income	$73,598 (58 out of 435)
Land area	209	Black	2.2%		
Pop/ sq mi	3364.7	Latino	8.3%	Under $50,000	32.6%
Born in state	52.8%	Asian	48.9%	$50,000-$99,999	32.6%
Age Groups		Two races	16.4%	$100,000-$199,999	27.6%
Under 18	20.4%	Other	7.5%	$200,000 or more	7.2%
18-34	24.9%	**Education**		Poverty Rate	9.2%
35-64	38.1%	H.S grad or less	34.9%	**Health Insurance**	
Over 64	16.7%	Some college	31.2%	With health insurance coverage	95.0%
Work		College Degree, 4 yr	22.4%		
White Collar	35.9%	Post grad	11.5%	**Public Assistance**	
Sales and Service	47.1%	**Military**		Cash public assistance income	3.2%
Blue Collar	17.0%	Veteran	10.7%		
Government	21.5%	Active Duty	3.8%	Food stamp/SNAP benefits	9.0%

Voter Turnout			
2015 Total Citizens 18+	499,693	2016 House Turnout as % CVAP	40%
2016 House turnout	202,357	2014 House Turnout as % CVAP	36%

2012 Presidential Vote		
Barack Obama	151,023	(70%)
Mitt Romney	62,875	(29%)

2016 Presidential Vote		
Hillary Clinton	132,009	(63%)
Donald Trump	63,916	(31%)
Gary Johnson	7,195	(3%)
Jill Stein	4,431	(2%)

Cook Partisan Voting Index: D+17

The landmarks for visitors to Honolulu are the Joint Base Pearl Harbor-Hickam military facility, the USS *Arizona* monument in Pearl Harbor, the downtown area, with its wondrously Victorian Iolani Palace, and, of course, Waikiki, with its 40-story hotels rising within a few feet of each other. This part of Hawaii is tightly packed with people living between the 3,000-foot Koolau Range and the beaches and harbor, where tropical bungalows and garden apartments house Hawaiians of all incomes. Behind New York, San Francisco and Los Angeles, Honolulu is the densest metropolitan area in the nation. Hawaii's largest shopping centers and its state university are located here. Neighborhoods where the rich overlook the ocean are wedged next to poor enclaves where residents are crammed onto clogged streets. Hawaii's topography jams cars onto just a few freeways and avenues, where traffic slows during rush hour and the *aloha* spirit is sorely tested. But hope may be on the way for relief of traffic congestion. The Honolulu Authority for Rapid Transportation is working on a 20-mile elevated rail line that will serve downtown and outlying communities. The four-car trains will include racks for bicycles and surfboards. By 2016, the costs had increased to $8.6 billion from the $5.2 billion projection in 2012, and the authority debated options to increase taxes or cut back its plans. One option was a city surcharge on the state excise tax. The opening date for the first 10 miles was delayed until at least 2021.

High taxes plus high land and utility costs have limited growth. The recession hit here early, resulting in declining hotel occupancy. Homelessness grew, and Aloha Airlines went bankrupt, ending its passenger service in 2008. But the Honolulu area weathered the recession better than most U.S. cities. The military remains an important presence on Oahu, even as the Naval Base at Pearl Harbor and Hickam Air Force Base merged in 2010. The base still operates Boeing's C-17 Globemaster III cargo jet. Honolulu is key to Hawaii's roaring tourism industry. In 2015, Hawaii attracted a record 8.7 million visitors. Hawaiian Airlines has non-stop flights from Honolulu to several cities on the mainland. In another significant step, a local business plans a delayed completion in 2018 of the Seawater Air Conditioning project, which is designed to produce enough chilled fresh water to supply roughly half of Downtown Honolulu's cooling needs. The project is estimated to reduce the electricity consumption in that area by more than 75 percent.

The 1st Congressional District of Hawaii is entirely in Honolulu, on Oahu. With little land left to develop on the southern part of the island, it is growing less rapidly than the rest of the state. Politically, the neighborhoods around Honolulu's downtown and the university campus are middle and lower-income and usually vote Democratic. To the west, around the harbor, are many military families in modest neighborhoods who vote for candidates from both parties. To the east, around Diamond Head and the Kahala and Koko Head beach areas, is higher-income territory that often votes Republican. Developers have explored plans to combat beach erosion at Waikiki, which is mostly man-made and has exceeded two feet from the public-access staircase to the beach. For the less fortunate, the city has planned a new homeless site on Sand Island off the southern shore of Oahu near the international airport.

Asians are 49 percent of the population in the 1st and 23 percent were foreign-born. In 2016, Hillary Clinton won 63 percent of the vote, compared with 70 percent in 2012 for favorite-son Barack Obama. In local contests, the district has become more competitive.

SECOND DISTRICT

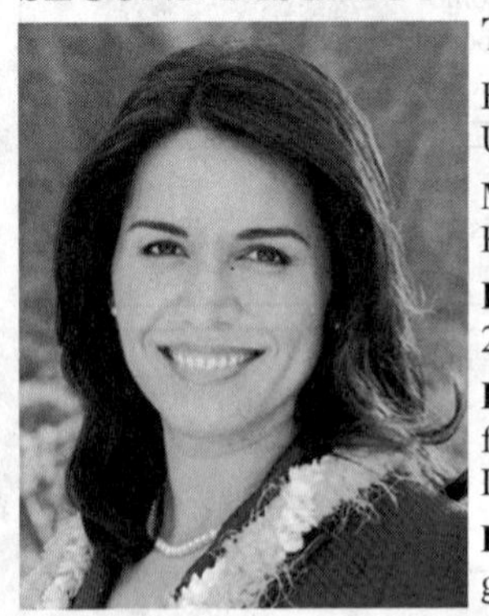

Tulsi Gabbard (D)

Elected 2012, 3rd term; b. Apr 12, 1981, Leloaloa, AS; Hawaii Pacific University, B.A., 2009; Hinduism; Married (Abraham Williams).

Military Career: HI Army National Guard, 2003-present (Iraq, Kuwait).

Elected Office: HI House, 2002-2004; Honolulu City Council, 2010-2012.

Professional Career: Founder, Kanu Productions, 2011-present; Co-founder, Healthy Hawaii Coalition, 2000-present; Legislative aide, Sen. Daniel Akaka, 2006-2007.

DC Office: 1433 LHOB 20515, 202-225-4906, Fax: 202-225-4987, gabbard.house.gov.

State Offices: Honolulu, 808-541-1986.

Committees: *Armed Services*: Emerging Threats & Capabilities, Readiness. *Foreign Affairs*: Asia & the Pacific, Middle East & North Africa.

Group Ratings

	ADA	ACLU	AFL-CIO	LCV	ITI	COC	HAFA	ACU	CFG	FRC
2016	-	94%	-	100%	50%	50%	14%	4%	4%	0%
2015	80%	C	96%	100%	C	50%	C	4%	0%	8%

Almanac Ratings 2015

	Economy	Social	Foreign	Composite
Liberal	87%	100%	72%	86%
Conservative	13%	0%	28%	14%

Key Votes of the 114th Congress

1. Keystone Pipeline	N	5. Puerto Rico Debt	Y	9. Offenses by Aliens	N
2. Trade Deals	N	6. Medical Marijuana	Y	10. Troops in Iraq	N
3. Export-Import Bank	Y	7. Sanctuary Cities	N	11. Homeland Security $$	Y
4. Debt Ceiling Increase	Y	8. Armor-piercing Bullets	N	12. Trade Adjustment aid	Y

Election Results

Election	Name (Party)	Vote (%)		Cand. Spent	Ind. Exp. Support	Ind. Exp. Oppose
2016 General	Tulsi Gabbard (D)	170,848	(81%)	$1,099,789		
	Angela Kaaihue (R)	39,668	(19%)			
2016 Primary	Tulsi Gabbard (D)	80,020	(85%)			
	Shay Chan Hodges (D)	14,643	(16%)			

Prior winning percentages: 2014 (76%), 2012 (77%)

Democrat Tulsi Gabbard, first elected in 2012, was one of the first two female combat veterans and the first Hindu in Congress. A rising star at home and in Washington, she has been outspoken and independent. Her occasional free-lancing on national security issues has generated bipartisan criticism. As a prominent supporter of Bernie Sanders in the 2016 campaign, she clashed with some leading Democratic officials.

The fourth of five children, Gabbard was born in American Samoa and moved with her family to Hawaii at a young age. Her father, Mike Gabbard, serves in the Hawaii Senate, where he chairs the Agriculture and Environment Committee; he switched parties in 2007 because, he said, he thought he would have more influence as a Democrat. Her mother, Carol Gabbard, formerly served on the state Board of Education. Both made names in Hawaii politics as strong opponents of gay marriage, a position their daughter rejects. Gabbard was homeschooled, and with her brothers and sister helped run a family restaurant. She graduated from Hawaii Pacific University with a degree in business administration.

At age 19, Gabbard and her father cofounded the Healthy Hawaii Coalition, an environmental-education nonprofit that teaches elementary students about the ways humans can positively and negatively affect the environment. In 2002, she won a seat representing West Oahu in the state House. At 21, she was the youngest woman ever elected to a state legislature. "A lot of people told me I was crazy and too young, but I really felt the need and passion to do more with my life and be able to make a positive impact for others," she told *National Journal*.

While serving in the legislature, she enlisted in the Hawaii Army National Guard as a private and completed her basic training in South Carolina between legislative sessions. In 2004, her unit was activated for Iraq, but Gabbard was not given orders to deploy. Declaring, "No way would I stay home and watch 3,000 of my brothers and sisters deploy without me," she withdrew from the campaign and voluntarily deployed with the medical unit for 18 months.

In 2007, she went to Fort McClellan's Officer Candidate School in Alabama, and was the first woman to graduate at the top of her class. She deployed again in 2008, to Kuwait as a military police platoon leader training counterterrorism units. In between tours of duty, she worked as a legislative aide to Democratic Sen. Daniel Akaka. Gabbard was elected to the Honolulu City Council in 2010. She said her proudest accomplishments in office included helping to legalize food trucks and organizing an environmental cleanup following a landfill overflow. She indulged an interest in film and television by starting her own film production company, Kanu Productions.

Gabbard was the first of six Democrats to jump into the race for an open House seat, touting herself as a fresh voice for Washington. Her chief primary opponent, who led for most of the race, was former Honolulu Mayor Mufi Hannemann. She called for subsidizing alternative energy projects to diversify Hawaii's tourism-dependent economy, as well as making the state's energy supply more secure. Hannemann held a 3-to-1 lead in a February 2012 poll, but Gabbard steadily closed the gap. Still, her 55%-34% victory over the experienced Hannemann surprised observers. She easily won the general.

In the House, she has shown independence on the Armed Services Committee, a useful assignment for a lawmaker from Hawaii. She often collaborated with Republicans, and grew increasingly critical about President Barack Obama's foreign policy. One of her chief priorities has been to bring all troops home from Afghanistan. In 2014, she said that it "makes no sense" to pursue military action against the Islamic State, and she added that summer that the mission was "lost." She criticized the Obama administration for failing to "recognize that this is about radical Islam." She told Defense Secretary Chuck Hagel that she opposed the swap of Taliban prisoners in exchange for Army Sgt. Bowe Bergdahl, who had abandoned his unit in Afghanistan. She was one of 22 House Democrats who voted with all Republicans to condemn the Obama administration for failing to notify Congress of the Bergdahl exchange. With Republican Rep. Martha Roby of Alabama, Gabbard warned in a letter to other House members in February 2015 that Pentagon spending cuts scheduled to take effect later that year would "undermin[e] our national security, local economies, and the livelihoods of military families." She was a co-founder of a bipartisan House caucus to assist veterans' transition to civilian life. In October 2015, Gabbard was promoted to major in the National Guard.

Gabbard praised the election in 2014 of Prime Minister Narenda Modi of India, and attended a speech that he delivered in New York that she called "electric, inspiring, positive." She met personally with Modi in New York and then in New Delhi. On the House Foreign Affairs Committee, she worked with Republicans in 2015 on legislation to toughen economic sanctions against North Korea. In March 2016, she was one of three House members who voted against a resolution that condemned Syria for war crimes, on the ground that it could result in U.S. military action. On domestic issues, Gabbard joined a bipartisan "No Labels" group of about 70 House members seeking common ground on fiscal policies. "Millennials care less about party labels and blind partisanship, and care more about getting things done," she said. Gabbard also gained attention for joining some Republicans in the House gym for regular sessions of "CrossFit" and circuit training.

In February 2016, Gabbard resigned as a vice chair of the Democratic National Committee and endorsed Sanders. She praised him for understanding "how and when we use our military power - and just as importantly, when we don't use that military power." Earlier, she criticized the DNC's scheduling of presidential debates for favoring Hillary Clinton. At home, Gabbard has coasted to reelection.

During Donald Trump's post-election transition, she met him at his New York headquarters, reportedly to discuss serving as the U.S. representative to the United Nations. They discussed their common ground on the Islamic threat and the need to revamp military interventions overseas. In January 2017, on a fact-finding mission to Syria, she unexpectedly had a meeting with President Bashar al-Assad. She was widely criticized by members of both parties for giving credibility to a leader whose forces have killed hundreds of thousands of Syrians and caused millions of refugees. A few colleagues supported her right to seek information overseas. Gabbard responded that the United States should focus on the more immediate threat from the Islamic state and end its talk of "regime change" in Syria. The impact of her foreign-policy initiatives within Congress and in Hawaiian politics remained to be seen.

Outer Oahu, Other Islands

Population		**Race and Ethnicity**		**Income**	
Total	702,339	White	29.1%	Median Income	$65,239 (91 out of 435)
Land area	6,213	Black	1.6%		
Pop/ sq mi	113.0	Latino	11.5%	Under $50,000	38.1%
Born in state	54.9%	Asian	24.7%	$50,000-$99,999	32.9%
		Two races	22.0%	$100,000-$199,999	23.6%
Age Groups		Other	11.1%	$200,000 or more	5.4%
Under 18	23.5%			Poverty Rate	13.3%
18-34	23.7%	**Education**			
35-64	38.3%	H.S grad or less	38.9%	**Health Insurance**	
Over 64	14.6%	Some college	33.5%	With health insurance coverage	93.1%
Work		College Degree, 4 yr	18.2%		
White Collar	32.0%	Post grad	9.4%	**Public Assistance**	
Sales and Service	48.0%	**Military**		Cash public assistance income	4.1%
Blue Collar	19.9%	Veteran	10.2%		
Government	19.7%	Active Duty	3.5%	Food stamp/SNAP benefits	13.7%

Voter Turnout			
2015 Total Citizens 18+	502,036	2016 House Turnout as % CVAP	42%
2016 House turnout	210,516	2014 House Turnout as % CVAP	36%

2012 Presidential Vote		
Barack Obama	155,635	(71%)
Mitt Romney	58,140	(27%)

2016 Presidential Vote		
Hillary Clinton	134,882	(61%)
Donald Trump	64,931	(30%)
Gary Johnson	8,759	(4%)
Jill Stein	8,306	(4%)

Cook Partisan Voting Index: D+19

The 2nd Congressional District encompasses each island in the Hawaii archipelago, including most of Oahu's acreage beyond the city of Honolulu, which belongs to the 1st District. It takes in Wheeler Army Airfield and some farmlands north of Pearl Harbor, between two jagged chains of mountains that lift the island out of the sea. Over the mountains to the west on Oahu is the Leeward Coast - calm, sultry and lightly populated. Over the mountains to the northeast is the Windward Coast, with many prosperous subdivisions in and around Kaneohe and Kailua.

The 137 islands have distinct personalities. Hawaii, the Big Island, is the size of Connecticut and boasts huge cattle ranches; the active volcano Kilauea, which started erupting in 1983 and has not stopped since; and Mauna Kea, the highest mountain in the world if the count begins at its base far under the ocean. Tourists are told that it is bad luck to take pieces of lava home. On the north shore, with heavy rainfall and tropical foliage, is the old port of Hilo and Hawaii's macadamia nut industry; this is a blue-collar Democratic area in a natural wonderland. On the Kona Coast, where there is little rainfall and the landscape is dominated by lava flows, there are retirement condominiums and a higher-income population. In November 2014, President Barack Obama declared the lava flow a "major disaster," as it threatened to destroy the major road in the town of Pahoa. There has been talk about attempting to divert the flow, but such options would be costly and risky. Scientists are more concerned about the long-term prospects for the volcano.

Maui, favored more by North American than Asian tourists, has dozens of luxury condominiums and upscale resorts. Kauai, much of which was devastated by Hurricane Iniki in 1992, is the least developed and most agricultural of the main islands. Parts of it have the nation's highest rainfall, while others seldom get wet. In August 2016, Obama used his executive authority to create south and west of Hawaii the world's largest protected marine sanctuary, quadrupling the size of the existing refuge.

Despite strong tourism, the local housing market has remained volatile. In 2015, Hawaii had the third-highest foreclosure rate among the 50 states. The expense of transporting fuel from the mainland contributes to some of the highest energy prices in the nation. The electric utility of Hawaii has set a goal of 100 percent renewable energy by 2045. As of 2015, nearly one-fourth of power came from solar and wind. Workers on the islands are employed chiefly in tourism, the military, social services and agriculture.

A fact that has been little-noted by mainlanders: Production of sugar and pineapples has virtually disappeared in Hawaii, chiefly a result of land costs and a higher return for other uses. In 2016, the Hawaiian Commercial and Sugar Company on Maui ended its harvest as the remaining sugar mill in Hawaii and laid off what remained of 650 employees. At one time, the state produced 20 percent of the sugar consumed in the United States. The largest pineapple plantation shut down in 2009. What remains of the large farm workforce - a reminder of what most of Hawaii was like a century ago - remains highly Democratic.

Overall, the district is solidly Democratic. Hillary Clinton's 61%-30% win in the 2nd was tighter than President Barack Obama's 71%-27% performance in 2012. That largely reflected Obama's favorite-son status. In 2000 and 2004, Al Gore and John Kerry each took 56 percent in this district.

★ IDAHO ★

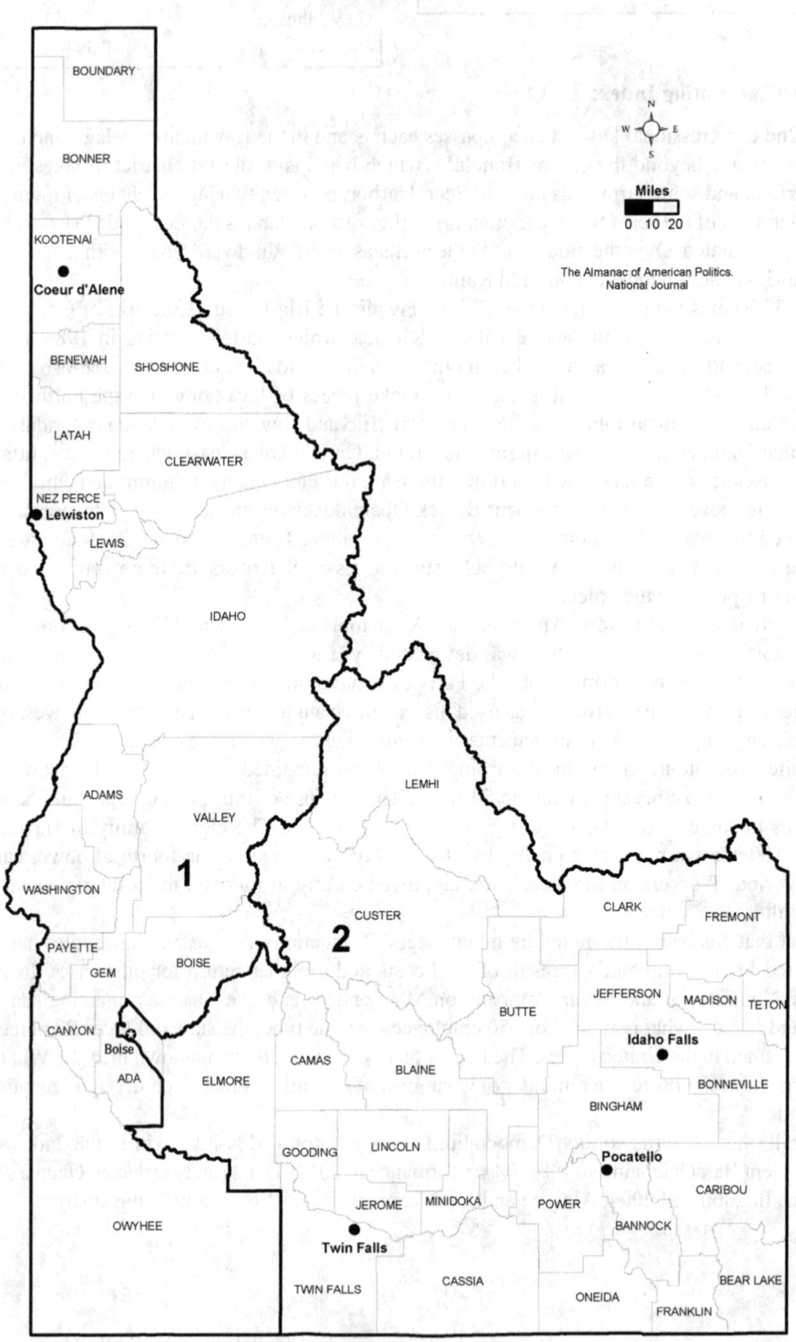

Congressional district boundaries were first effective for 2012.

You may have seen the TV spot: A huge potato on an enormous flatbed truck is driving around the country to promote the consumption of Idaho potatoes. Now that Hawaii has quit producing pineapples in any quantity, no other state is associated so closely with a single crop. But potatoes are not the only product of Idaho. Between 1990 and 2016, the population of this state expanded by more than two-thirds, despite being tucked off near the northwest edge of the continental United States, far from any major metro area. And the flow has not ebbed: From 2015 to 2016 alone, Idaho grew by 1.8 percent, a faster rate than any state but neighboring Utah and Nevada. Population growth has been fed by technological innovation, which in turn has brought increased prosperity and cemented the state's solid support for Republicans.

Back in 1953, an eighth-grade dropout named J.R. Simplot perfected the process of freezing French fries; with a handshake, he sealed a contract with a little restaurant chain called McDonald's and was on his way to becoming the biggest potato processor in the world, and a billionaire. In the 1970s, Simplot was the primary financier of a startup called Micron Technology, which spawned a booming high-tech sector in the state, enabling Hewlett-Packard laser-jet printers. In recent years, Idaho has ranked at or near the top of state rankings for patents per capita. It's a tradition that reaches back into the early years of the 20th century, when a Mormon farm boy from Rigby named Philo T. Farnsworth came up with many of the concepts that laid the basis for the invention of television. The value of Idaho's electronic-component exports now exceeds the value of its potato exports, trading one type of chip for another. Micron remains the state's second-biggest employer and Hewlett-Packard the eighth; Simplot and another Idaho-grown company, grocery retailer Albertsons, rank lower but still in the top 10. The Idaho National Laboratory in the eastern part of the state is one of the nation's major nuclear and cybersecurity outfits following the recession, joblessness fell fast in Idaho. By March 2015, the state's unemployment rate was down to 3.8 percent, almost two full points below the national rate, and it remained that low through the end of 2016. As in other states in America's broad middle, a strong market for agriculture was one reason.

Idaho was the last North American area on which European fur traders set eyes. Then in the 1840s, New England Yankees led by ministers made their way west on the Oregon Trail through southern Idaho. The state's northern panhandle, an extension of Washington's Columbia River Valley, was first settled by miners seeking gold and silver, then by loggers seeking timber. Mormons moving north from Utah settled in the eastern part of the state, while Basque immigrants and their descendants have made a significant impact on Idaho and its politics. Still fresh in family lore are the people who pioneered this state, built the first towns and farms, established the first churches and schools and became its community leaders. Federal water reclamation projects first authorized in 1894 attracted the most settlers; they transformed the barren Snake River Valley into some of the nation's best volcanic, soil-enriched farmland, which along with warm days and cool nights proved ideal for the Burbank russet potato and, more recently, for a fledgling wine industry that has grown from $72 million in revenues to nearly $170 million between 2008 and 2015. Inexpensive hydroelectric power has historically supplied between 60 percent and 80 percent of the state's electricity needs, though more recently drought has reduced that share to about half.

The state is big: The town of Montpelier in the southeast is closer to Farmington, New Mexico, than to Bonner Springs in the northern panhandle. And the wilderness is never far away. Towering over the state Capitol in Boise is the vast peak of Shafer Butte. Not far away are the sharp peaks and broad valleys of the Sawtooth range; the impassable mountains of the Frank Church-River of No Return Wilderness, the largest U.S. wilderness area outside Alaska; and the Salmon River, at 425 miles the longest undammed river in the lower 48 states. Having so much wilderness comes with a downside; according to the EPA, nearly 1 percent of the land in Idaho on average has burned annually since 1984, the highest percentage of any state, and a pattern that is projected to worsen in the coming years. Still, natural beauty is key to the appeal for newcomers. A few highly publicized entertainment personalities and investment bankers have moved to Sun Valley or over the state line from Jackson Hole, Wyoming, and professionals have cropped up in Boise's fertile technology scene. But a much larger number of more conservative-leaning engineers and entrepreneurs have come, from California and all over, for a fresh environment and a fresh start - and fewer cumbersome or expensive regulations. (The one exception to laissez-faire government: a tightly regulated water-rights regime.)

As a result, Idaho has been transformed from a state of farms and small towns, where Boise, the pleasant state capital, was just the largest of them. Today, nearly 60 percent of its people live in just five counties, four of which grew in population between 2010 and 2015 by between 5 percent and 11 percent – Ada (Boise), Bonneville (Idaho Falls), Canyon (Nampa), and Kootenai (Cour d'Alene). About 40 percent of Idahoans live in Treasure Valley around Boise, which accounts for most of the state's recent population growth. The number of Hispanic residents has come close to doubling between 2000 and 2016 and now accounts for 12 percent of Idaho residents. African Americans, at less than 1 percent, are outnumbered by American Indians, 1.7 percent, and Asians, 1.5 percent. Idaho has welcomed not only Americans from other states but those from abroad, including refugees. The state has absorbed more than 20,000 refugees since the 1970s, mostly in Boise and Twin Falls -- first Vietnamese and Cambodians, then Bosnians, and more recently refugees from Iraq, Afghanistan, Sudan, Congo, Eritrea, Nepal and Iran, *The Economist* recently noted. In Twin Falls, just 17 miles from a World War II internment camp for Japanese Americans, this has periodically spawned controversy, but an anti-refugee ballot measure proposal in 2016 failed to secure enough signatures despite swelling anti-refugee sentiment nationally -- including stated opposition to Syrian refugee resettlement by Gov. Butch Otter and all four members of the state's congressional delegation. The Mormon population is widely seen as a reason for the state's tolerant streak, thanks to its international missionary outreach: Idaho has the second highest percentage of Mormons of any state, at 19 percent.

In its early years as a silver-producing state, Idaho backed populism and opposed the gold standard; from 1900 to 1960, it was politically marginal. It used to elect prominent national Democrats such as Sen. Frank Church, an intelligence watchdog and 1976 presidential candidate, and Gov. Cecil Andrus, Jimmy Carter's Interior secretary. But Idaho has become staunchly Republican. Since 1964, no Democratic presidential nominee has won more than 37 percent of the vote here. Idahoans in small counties and in the Treasure Valley see themselves as pioneering entrepreneurs who, rather than seek federal help, want to get a bloated, bossy federal government off their backs. The U.S. government owns 63 percent of Idaho's land, and most Idahoans strongly oppose federal policies that block road-building on one-third of national forestland, limit grazing on public lands, and breach Snake River dams to protect salmon (in the process, depriving potato farmers of water). Social issues, meanwhile, resonate with the state's religious population; legislation to protect LGBT residents has floundered, as have efforts to strengthen statutes against faith healers whose practices lead to child neglect. Idaho has elected only Republicans to the governorship since 1994 and to the Senate starting in 1978, and the GOP has won every election in Idaho's two congressional districts since 1994, except in 2008, when Democrat Walt Minnick beat a fiery freshman in the western 1st District. Minnick was ousted two years later.

The final presidential margins for the 2016 general election broadly mirrored those from 2012, although Donald Trump consistently fared a few percentage points worse than Mitt Romney had, mirroring Trump's relatively weak performance among Mormon Republicans elsewhere. Much of Trump's shortfall flowed to Evan McMullin, a Mormon and an independent Republican who made the ballot in Idaho and won almost 7 percent of the vote. In Boise-based Ada County, the state's largest, Clinton managed to narrow the margin a bit compared with 2012, but she still lost by nine points; today, the city has become substantially Democratic but outlying areas remain solidly Republican. As was the case in 2012, only two Idaho counties – Blaine, which includes the wealthy resort of Sun Valley, and Latah, which includes the university town of Moscow – voted Democratic in the presidential race. Based on such results, Democrats do not look to be competitive in Idaho any time soon.

Population		Race and Ethnicity		Income	
Total	1,616,547	White	83.1%	Median Income	$47,583 (37 out of 50)
Land area	82,643	Black	0.6%		
Pop/ sq mi	19.6	Latino	11.8%	Under $50,000	52.3%
Born in state	47.2%	Asian	1.3%	$50,000-$99,999	31.8%
Age Groups		Two races	2.0%	$100,000-$199,999	13.4%
Under 18	26.6%	Other	1.3%	$200,000 or more	2.6%
18-34	22.8%	**Education**		Poverty Rate	15.5%
35-64	36.9%	H.S grad or less	38.0%	**Health Insurance**	
Over 64	13.8%	Some college	36.1%	With health insurance coverage	85.3%
Work		College Degree, 4 yr	17.7%		
		Post grad	8.2%	**Public Assistance**	
White Collar	33.5%				
Sales and Service	42.1%	**Military**		Cash public assistance income	3.2%
Blue Collar	24.4%	Veteran	10.1%		
Government	15.8%	Active Duty	0.3%	Food stamp/SNAP benefits	12.7%

Voter Turnout			
2015 Total Citizens 18+	1,130,550	2016 Pres Turnout as % CVAP	61%
2016 Pres Votes	690,255	2012 Pres Turnout as % CVAP	61%

Legislature	
Senate:	6D, 29R
House:	14D, 56R

Presidential Politics

2016 Democratic Caucus		
Bernie Sanders (D)	18,640	(78%)
Hillary Clinton (D)	5,065	(21%)
2016 Republican Primary		
Ted Cruz (R)	100,889	(45%)
Donald Trump (R)	62,413	(28%)
Marco Rubio (R)	35,290	(16%)
John Kasich (R)	16,514	(7%)

2016 Presidential Vote		
Donald Trump (R)	409,055	(59%)
Hillary Clinton (D)	189,765	(27%)
Evan McMullin (I)	46,476	(7%)
Gary Johnson (L)	28,331	(4%)
2012 Presidential Vote		
Mitt Romney (R)	420,911	(65%)
Barack Obama (D)	212,787	(33%)

Idaho is one of the most Republican states in presidential politics. No Democratic nominee has come close to carrying it since the 1964 LBJ landslide, when the incumbent Democratic president managed to defeat Barry Goldwater, 51%-49%. It was the fourth best state for both Mitt Romney in 2012, and John McCain in 2008. For Donald Trump, Idaho ranked only 10th in his percentage of the state's presidential vote. But he handily beat Hillary Clinton, 59%-28%, with six third party and independent candidates garnering 13 percent. More than 690,000 Idahoans cast presidential ballots, a record, representing 74 percent of registered voters. Trump was the first Republican nominee not to break 60 percent since Bob Dole took the state in 1996 with 52 percent of the vote. Republican Sen. Mike Crapo, who was up for reelection in 2016 and wavered in his support for Trump during the campaign, was reelected with two-thirds of the vote. The only pocket of Democratic strength is Ada County, home to the state capital and Idaho's largest city, Boise. But even in Ada, Democrats regularly get defeated. The remainder of the state, from the panhandle in the north to the industrial farms and ski resorts in the south, is Republican territory.

Idaho held a GOP presidential primary on March 8, and Texas Sen. Ted Cruz defeated Trump 54%-28%, followed by Florida Sen. Marco Rubio with 16 percent. Ohio Gov. John Kasich finished fourth with 7 percent, even though he had the endorsement of GOP. Gov. Butch Otter. Democrats held a caucus on March 22 and Vermont Sen. Bernie Sanders dominated the local party gatherings, defeating Clinton 78%-21%. Actress Susan Sarandon stumped for Sanders in the state, and he carried every county except for tiny Lewis in the panhandle, which he lost by one vote.

Congressional Districts

115th Congress Lineup	2R	**114th Congress Lineup**	2R

Idaho has two congressional districts, which split Boise between them. It also has a six-member bipartisan reapportionment commission, which probably gives Democrats more of a role in the process than they deserve in a state where roughly four-fifths of state legislators are Republicans. Still, drawing a seat friendly to Democrats is a near-impossible task in Idaho and the commission's tradition has been to simply shift the Boise dividing line between the 1st and 2nd districts slightly west every 10 years to accommodate the 1st District's stronger growth.

In 2011, strong growth in northern Idaho and Boise's western suburbs forced the 1st District to shed about 58,000 residents. Democrats on the commission sought to unite Boise and its small but active liberal community. After a three-month stalemate, one Democratic commissioner folded and agreed to merely move the boundary three miles west. The shift subtly made the 1st District about a point more Republican, shoring up Republican freshman Raul Labrador and perhaps giving 2nd District Republican Mike Simpson a few more moderate primary voters. Simpson easily survived a conservative challenge in the 2014 primary.

Governor

C.L. 'Butch' Otter (R)

Elected 2006, term expires 2019, 3rd term; b. May. 3, 1942, Caldwell, ID; Col. of ID, B.A. 1967; Catholic; Married (Lori); 4 children.

Military Career: ID Army National Guard, 1968-1973.

Elected Office: ID House, 1973-1976; ID Lt. Governor, 1986-2000; U.S. House, 2001-2007; Chairman, Canyon County Republican Party.

Professional Career: Rancher; Director, Food Products Division & President, Simplot Livestock; President, Simplot International, 1963-1993.

Office: State Capitol, PO Box 83720, Boise, 83720; 208-334-2100; Fax: 208-334-3454; Website: gov.idaho.gov.

Election Results

Election	Name (Party)	Vote (%)
2014 General	Butch Otter (R)	235,405 (54%)
	A.J. Balukoff (D)	169,556 (39%)
	John T. Bujak (L)	17,884 (4%)
	Jill Humble (I)	8,801 (2%)
2014 Primary	Butch Otter (R)	79,779 (51%)
	Russell Fulcher (R)	67,694 (44%)

Prior winning percentage: 2010 (59%), 2006 (53%) ; House: 2004 (70%), 2002 (59%), 2000 (65%)

Republican Clement Leroy "Butch" Otter was elected Idaho governor in 2006 and he plans to complete his third and final term in 2018. Though he presides over a deeply Republican state and has shown a flair for attracting media attention, he hasn't always been able to translate his goals into legislative success.

Otter was the sixth of nine children and the first in his family to get a college degree. His father was a journeyman electrician and carpenter and a lifelong Democrat. After high school, Otter entered an abbey to pursue the religious life, but quickly decided that it was not his calling. In 1967, at the age of 25, he graduated from the College of Idaho. He went to work for his then-father-in-law, billionaire J.R. Simplot, at the J.R. Simplot Company, one of the largest potato processors in the world and owner of the largest feedlot in the nation. In 1972, Otter, a credentialed cowboy, won the first of two terms in the state House. He ran for governor in 1978, finishing third in the Republican primary, and in 1986, he was elected lieutenant governor.

His career was put at risk by a drunk-driving arrest. Otter unsuccessfully tried to talk the police officer out of charging him by explaining that he had not been drinking, but chewing tobacco soaked in Jack Daniel's whiskey. The officer didn't buy it. Otter was convicted in 1993 of drunk driving, dashing his hopes of running for governor the following year. Still, he went on to be re-elected lieutenant governor and held the post longer than anyone in Idaho history. He served under three governors before he was elected to Congress in 2000.

Otter has been a big supporter of gun ownership and property rights, but his libertarian political philosophy has at times taken him on a different path than that of social conservatives. In 1992, he won the "Mr. Tight Jeans" contest at the Rockin' Rodeo bar in Boise, and during his tenure in the state legislature Otter voted against an anti-pornography bill by responding "Hell no!" during the roll call. He also questioned the government's right to restrict marijuana use, though in more recent years neighboring Washington and Oregon have gone much further in that regard; in 2015, he vetoed a bill that would have legalized marijuana-based oil to treat seizure disorders, citing uncertainty about the science. Having become a ranch owner after his 1993 divorce, he was acquainted with the government's reach. The Environmental Protection Agency charged him three times with violating the Clean Water Act. In 2001, after fighting the agency for two years, he paid a $50,000 fine for dredging and filling wetlands without a permit.

When he was in Congress, Otter was one of three House Republicans to vote against the USA Patriot Act, a tough anti-terrorism enforcement law, because of what he cited as potential intrusions on privacy and civil liberties. In 2004, he sponsored an amendment with independent Rep. Bernie Sanders of Vermont to prevent authorities from using the act to demand information on book buyers or library users. He lost on a tie vote after Republican leaders held the roll call open for 23 extra minutes to turn the outcome their way.

Otter announced his intention in December 2004 to run for governor, giving him an organizational and fundraising head start over then-Lt. Gov. James Risch, a Republican who was also considering running. In November 2005, Risch decided to run for reelection as lieutenant governor and Otter easily outdistanced three opponents in the 2006 primary, winning with 70 percent. Otter then faced Democrat Jerry Brady, a former publisher of the Idaho Falls *Post Register* who was making his second consecutive bid for governor. Idaho hadn't elected a Democratic governor since 1990, and despite national discontent with the Republican Party, a lackluster campaign and the spirited challenge by Brady, Otter won, 53%-44%. In heavily Mormon eastern Idaho, where Otter's libertarian stands and lifestyle had hurt him in prior statewide elections, he lost just two counties: Bannock, home to Pocatello and Idaho State University, and Teton, which shares a border with Wyoming's tony Jackson Hole.

Soon after taking office, Otter caused a minor controversy by halting construction on a $130 million statehouse expansion that the Republican-controlled legislature had approved the previous year. He objected to the project's cost and the fact that it represented an expansion of government. Negotiations with the legislature produced a compromise. That issue was one of many on which Otter has tangled with lawmakers despite working with a strong Republican majority; other issues early in his tenure included proposed changes to the state's grocery tax credit and a highway funding bill. In 2008, Otter proposed an 11 percent increase in the state's budget, a 5 percent pay raise for state employees, and an increase in vehicle registration fees to fund road repairs, all of which the legislature either modified or rejected outright. As the session came to a close, he criticized legislators publicly for rejecting his proposals, and they in turn accused him of refusing to compromise.

Otter's priority for the 2009 session was providing money for road and bridge construction and maintenance. Despite reservations about increased government spending, he decided to accept $1.2 billion in economic stimulus money from the federal government. Over the course of what became the second-longest legislative session in state history, he and Republican legislators hammered out a deal. Otter had sought a 6-cent increase in Idaho's gasoline tax, but lawmakers adamantly ruled it out. The governor had asked for $174.5 million, but eventually had to settle for $54 million.

Otter drew a challenge to his reelection in 2010 from Keith Allred, a professional mediator and founder of a bipartisan citizens' group called The Common Interest. He decided to run on the Democratic ballot line, though he had a well-earned reputation for being nonpartisan and he put some distance between himself and the Democratic Party. Allred outraised Otter during the early months of 2010, and steadily chipped away at the governor's lead in the polls. But Idaho's staunch Republicanism enabled Otter to win, 59%-33%.

After President Barack Obama's 2012 reelection made it clear that his signature health care law would not be repealed anytime soon by a Republican president, Otter declared he would support setting up a health insurance exchange in Idaho as part of the law. "Obamacare" was exceedingly unpopular in the state, but Otter cast his decision as a states' rights issue, calling an exchange the only alternative to being "at the federal government's mercy" for insurance. Otter faced resistance in the legislature, but he cobbled together enough Democrats and Republicans to enact a state-based marketplace, signing the law in March 2013.

Otter, by then 72, sought a third term in 2014. He attracted a primary challenge - from the right, state Sen. Russ Fulcher, and two others from off the charts - leather-clad biker Harley Brown and Walt Bayes, a homeschooling activist with a prodigious beard and "77 descendants." After a colorful and sometimes baffling debate among the four candidates went viral nationally (to the embarrassment of some state Republicans), Otter prevailed in the primary with a disappointing 51 percent of the vote. In the general election, he faced Democrat A.J. Balukoff. Once again, the state's Republican tilt carried Otter to victory, 54%-39%.

During his third term, Otter encountered friction for negotiating an arrangement with the U.S. Energy Department to accept a modest amount of commercial spent nuclear fuel; two former governors, Democrat Cecil Andrus and Republican Phil Batt, came out publicly against the plan, citing contamination risks that could threaten the state's agriculture industry. Otter also tangled with environmentalists for his aggressive effort to kill wolves that threatened livestock and wildlife. Otter called a special legislative session to pass a bill that earlier had been expected to pass easily - for Idaho to join an agreement on collection of child support payments - but the bill was killed by a House committee after talk that foreign courts and Sharia law might trump Idaho rules. The bill then passed in the special.

In contrast to the libertarianism of his early career, Otter increasingly sided with social conservatives. In 2015, he urged the Supreme Court to overturn the legalization of same-sex marriage in Idaho. The following year, he blasted an Obama administration effort to use federal funding to leverage schools into allowing transgender students to use their preferred bathroom, calling the federal action a "vast overreach." Otter also joined 10 other Republican governors in signing a letter that urged Congress to permit states to test food-stamp beneficiaries for drugs, and he signed a law to allow Idaho adults wide leeway to carry concealed firearms without a permit. Otter bucked conservatives by vetoing a bill to allow the Bible to be taught in public schools, after the state's Republican attorney general cautioned that it could be unconstitutional. And he took flak from both conservatives and liberals for the budget he proposed in 2016, which was criticized as being either spendthrift or insufficient to meet the state's needs, depending on one's perspective.

In the 2016 election, voters seemingly settled one bit of unfinished business: After the issue had ping-ponged from the legislature to the courts, voters disregarded Otter's opposition and approved a ballot measure that allowed the legislature to reject rules enacted by executive-branch agencies. It portended new rounds of sparring between Otter and his fellow Republicans.

In February 2017, Otter confirmed that he would not seek reelection. Lt. Gov. Brad Little, who has been close to Otter, was the early frontrunner to succeed him. In May, Rep. Raul Labrador filed papers for his candidacy.

Senior Senator

Mike Crapo (R)

Elected 1998, term expires 2022, 4th term; b. May 20, 1951, Idaho Falls; Brigham Young University (UT), B.A.; Harvard University Law School (MA), J.D.; Mormon; Married (Susan Diane Hasleton Crapo); 5 children; 8 grandchildren.

Elected Office: ID Senate, 1985-1992, Leader, 1988-1992; U.S. House, 1993-1998.

Professional Career: Clerk, Judge James M. Carter, 1977-1978; Vice Chairman, Bonneville County Republican Comm., 1979-1981; Vice Chairman, ID district 29 Republican Comm., 1982-1984; Practicing attorney, 1978-1992.

DC Office: 239 DSOB 20510, 202-224-6142, Fax: 202-228-1375, crapo.senate.gov.

State Offices: Boise, 208-334-1776; Coeur D'Alene, 208-664-5490; Idaho Falls, 208-522-9779; Lewiston, 208-743-1492; Pocatello, 208-236-6775; Twin Falls, 208-734-2515.

Committees: *Banking, Housing & Urban Affairs (Chmn)*: Economic Policy, Financial Institutions & Consumer Protection, Housing, Transportation & Community Development, National Security & International Trade & Finance, Securities, Insurance & Investment. *Budget*. *Finance*: Energy, Natural Resources & Infrastructure, Social Security, Pensions & Family Policy, Taxation & IRS Oversight. *Indian Affairs*. *Judiciary*: Border Security & Immigration, Constitution, Oversight, Agency Action, Federal Rights & Federal Courts, Privacy, Technology & the Law.

Group Ratings

	ADA	ACLU	AFL-CIO	LCV	ITI	COC	HAFA	ACU	CFG	FRC
2016	-	29%	-	12%	40%	88%	82%	92%	73%	100%
2015	5%	C	7%	0%	C	62%	C	96%	91%	100%

Almanac Ratings 2015

	Economy	Social	Foreign	Composite
Liberal	0%	0%	4%	1%
Conservative	100%	100%	96%	99%

Key Votes of the 114th Congress

1. Keystone pipeline	Y	5. National Security Data	N	9. Gun Sales Checks	N
2. Export-Import Bank	Y	6. Iran Nuclear Deal	Y	10. Sanctuary Cities	Y
3. Debt Ceiling Increase	N	7. Puerto Rico Debt	Y	11. Planned Parenthood	Y
4. Homeland Security $$	N	8. Loretta Lynch A.G	N	12. Trade deals	Y

Election Results

Election	Name (Party)	Vote (%)		Cand. Spent	Ind. Exp. Support	Ind. Exp. Oppose
2016 General	Mike Crapo (R)...........................	449,017	(66%)	$6,461,442		
	Jerry Sturgill (D)...........................	188,249	(28%)	$709,348		
	Ray Writz (C)................................	41,677	(6%)	$2,925		
2016 Primary	Mike Crapo (R)........................	unopposed				

Prior winning percentages: 2010 (71%), 2004 (99%), 1998 (70%); House: 1996 (69%), 1994 (75%), 1992 (61%)

After nearly a quarter of a century on Capitol Hill, Republican Mike Crapo, Idaho's senior senator, began 2017 with his influence considerably enhanced. Already serving in the Senate leadership role of chief deputy majority whip, and with a senior seat on the powerful Finance Committee , the Harvard Law School graduate was assigned to the Judiciary Committee -- just as a contentious confirmation of a Supreme Court nominee was about to get underway. Key to his enhanced clout was his ascension to the chairmanship of the Banking, Housing and Urban Affairs Committee, where -- with the White House and both chambers of Congress in Republican control -- he was laying plans to dismantle mortgage giants Fannie Mae and Freddie Mac, while taking aim at the Dodd-Frank financial services regulation law that was enacted several years earlier over his objections.

Representing a state that has long been a GOP bastion, Crapo is among the most conservative members of the Senate. Vote ratings for 2011 placed him as the third most conservative senator; in 2015, he was one of just three Senators to earn a 100 percent conservative voting score on economic matters. The mild-mannered legislator has a record of reaching across the political aisle to seek consensus. Notably, he served in 2011-2012 as a member of the "Gang of Six" -- a bipartisan group of senators who came up with a plan to reduce the federal deficit by $3.7 trillion over a decade. More than a quarter of that would have come from increased tax revenues, a move that was anathema to many conservatives. "Mike's one of those guys that is a realist and understands that in legislation you don't get everything you want, but the good outweighs the bad," Sen. Jon Tester of Montana, a Banking Committee Democrat who has negotiated with Crapo, told the *Wall Street Journal* in 2016. A decade earlier, then-Senate Democratic Leader Harry Reid singled out Crapo as one of three GOP senators who would make an "outstanding" Supreme Court justice.

On a personal level, his powerful political perch has represented a comeback from earlier adversity. After a battle with cancer early in his Senate tenure, he was arrested for drunken driving in suburban Virginia two years into his third term in an incident that drew national attention. The consumption of alcohol represented a violation of Crapo's Mormon faith, and Idahoans -- nearly 25 percent of whom are Mormon -- were bewildered. *The Lewiston Morning Tribune* ran an editorial headlined, "Is This Mike Crapo the Same Guy We Knew?" Crapo publicly apologized, pleaded guilty to a misdemeanor, and, over a two-year period, held town-hall meetings in all of Idaho's 200 incorporated cities. In 2016, he sought a fourth term, and was overwhelmingly re-elected.

A fourth-generation Idahoan, Crapo was born and grew up in Idaho Falls. His father ran the local post office, and his mother stayed home to care for the family's six children. The couple farmed on 200 acres, growing potatoes and grain. After earning an undergraduate degree from Brigham Young University, Crapo graduated from Harvard Law in 1977. In 1984, the one-time congressional intern was elected to the Idaho Senate at 33. Two years earlier, leukemia had claimed the life of his older brother, Terry, who had been the state House majority leader and a rising star in Idaho politics. The two brothers were close, and Mike Crapo decided to follow his brother's path to the legislature. He became Senate president pro tem in 1988, and in 1992 ran for Congress, campaigning in favor of spending cuts, a balanced-budget amendment, and the line-item veto. He won the primary by better than 2-1. In the general election, "Cowboy Democrat" J.D. Williams, the state controller, ran on a "Put America First" platform on industrial policy and trade. Crapo beat him, 61%-35%.

With a self-professed "passion for reform," Crapo became a Republican freshman class leader and championed institutional reforms, advocating more power for rank-and-file members to bring bills to the floor. Like many Republicans at that time, Crapo favored hard-and-fast rules in the budget process to force tough decisions: He supported across-the-board discretionary spending cuts, excluding Social Security. This approach persisted two decades later, when, in March 2015, Crapo joined other Senate Republicans in opposing a House GOP plan to boost defense spending by sidestepping spending caps. He blasted the maneuver as a "gimmick." On a couple of major international trade deals that came up during his House tenure, Crapo opposed the North American Free Trade Agreement in 1993 but supported normalizing trade relations with China in 2000. Later, he pushed to relax restrictions on agricultural sales to Cuba .

Crapo, who prides himself on returning to Idaho Falls every weekend to be with his family, faced a career choice in 1997. Republican Gov. Phil Batt announced his retirement, and GOP Sen. Dirk Kempthorne said he would run for governor. Within days, Crapo announced he would run for Kempthorne's Senate seat the following year, and was unopposed in the Republican primary. His opponent in the fall was trial lawyer Bill Mauk, a former Democratic state chairman. Despite its large Mormon population, Idaho had never elected a Mormon to the Senate -- but this time it did. Crapo won by 70%-28%, carrying every county. Though he expressed interest in a federal District Court judgeship during the George W. Bush Administration, Crapo sought reelection in 2004 and had no Democratic opponent. In 2010, his margin of victory for a third term was 71%-25%.

In the wake of the 2008 financial industry meltdown, Crapo worked on the Dodd-Frank legislation, but was disappointed with the result -- citing its creation of a new Consumer Financial Protection Bureau and its requirement for commercial banks to spin off most of their derivatives-trading operations. He expressed frustration that the bill would not revamp troubled mortgage giants Fannie Mae and Freddie Mac. "I strongly opposed it when it was being debated on the floor and voted against it," Crapo said of Dodd-Frank in 2016 comments to the *Twin Falls News-Times*. "I have been working to reform its excesses for a long time." At the same time, Crapo praised provisions in the 2010 law that required banks to hold more capital in reserve, saying this had helped to "create a more stable protection against the need for taxpayer bailouts."

When President Barack Obama's 2012 reelection dashed Republican hopes that Dodd-Frank could be repealed, Crapo expressed a desire to reshape parts of it. He took aim at what he considered to be overly broad regulation of derivatives trading: Crapo contended that Congress had intended the rules to apply to financial firms trading derivatives in search of a profit, but that regulators could mistakenly apply them to utilities and other industries that dabble in the derivatives market. In 2014, as ranking member, Crapo teamed with then-Banking Chairman Tim Johnson, a South Dakota Democrat, on a plan to dismantle government sponsored enterprises Fannie Mae and Freddie Mac, while shifting more of the risks of mortgage lending to the private sector. In 2015, Crapo offered a bill to make the Consumer Financial Protection Bureau subject to a 10-year regulatory review; Republicans have complained that the bureau, which receives funding from the Federal Reserve rather than congressional appropriations, is effectively exempt from legislative oversight.

Back in Idaho, Trump's Democratic challenger, businessman Jerry Sturgill, was seeking to make a campaign issue of Crapo's arrest for driving under the influence four years earlier. "The DUI revealed a long cover-up of personal behavior inconsistent with how Sen. Crapo had presented himself as a tee-totaling member of our church, one who had held high office," declared Sturgill, a fellow Mormon -- alluding to the fact that Crapo had become a bishop in the church when he was just 31. On December 23, 2012, Crapo had left his Capitol Hill apartment and driven across the Potomac River to Alexandria, Virginia, where he scored a 0.11 blood-alcohol level on a breathalyzer test after running a red light. (The legal limit in Virginia is .08.) In the police report on the incident, Crapo admitted to having had several shots of vodka. Two weeks after the episode, Crapo pleaded guilty to a misdemeanor and received a $250 fine and a 12-month suspension of his driver's license. "It was a poor choice to use alcohol to relieve stress-and one at odds with my personally held religious beliefs," he said immediately afterward.

In an interview with the *Idaho Statesman* shortly before the 2016 election, Crapo said he had not had a drink since the episode, adding, "I do apologize again for that conduct, one of the worst times of my life, in terms of frankly being disappointed in myself and realizing that I disappointed my constituents." He said that he had worked "really hard" to recommit to his work and earn the support of his constituents, adding, "I think that I have made a strong case for that." The voters appeared to agree: On Election Day 2016, Crapo defeated Sturgill by 66%-28%, a victory margin down only slightly from six years earlier.

Colleagues said Crapo had been feeling overburdened by his responsibilities at the time of the DUI arrest. Nonetheless, his Senate duties expanded significantly in 2013. Crapo was tapped as chief deputy to newly named Senate Minority Whip John Cornyn of Texas; with Cornyn elevated to majority whip when the GOP regained control of the Senate in the 2014 election, Crapo has since served as chief deputy majority whip. In 2017, the term-limited Richard Shelby of Alabama was forced to cede the gavel to Crapo -- to the barely concealed delight of committee Democrats, who had a scratchy relationship with Shelby. "We have a working relationship," the Banking Committee's senior Democrat, Sherrod Brown of Ohio, said of Crapo. "He's way more conservative than I am, but he's straightforward and honorable."

On some high-profile issues, Crapo has found himself siding with some of the most conservative elements in the GOP. At the height of the 2008 recession, he was among a dozen Senate Republicans who voted against the Bush Administration request to create the $700 billion Troubled Asset Relief Program (TARP) aimed at shoring up a number of troubled financial institutions. In 2013, he opposed the bipartisan immigration reform bill that cleared the Senate by a wide margin. In 2015, Crapo joined GOP Sens. James Inhofe and James Lankford of Oklahoma to introduce a bill to prevent the Education Department from setting policies that conflicted with those of local education authorities.

But Crapo has not allowed ideology to get in the way of seeking consensus. He served on the bipartisan Simpson-Bowles debt reduction commission in 2010. He and then-GOP Sens. Tom Coburn of Oklahoma and Judd Gregg of New Hampshire endorsed the commission's final plan, which called for tax increases as well as spending cuts and changes in entitlement programs. It put them at odds with other Republican members of the panel, including then-House Budget Committee Chairman Paul Ryan of Wisconsin. While calling the plan "flawed and incomplete," Crapo and Coburn said in a joint statement that "the time for action is now." Crapo then continued to work over the next two years as a member of the bipartisan "Gang of Six" to forge a budget compromise. He voted in favor of the New Year's Day 2013 budget deal aimed at averting the so-called fiscal cliff of automatic tax increases and spending cuts. But he characterized it as a "missed opportunity to comprehensively address our nation's economic crisis," while highlighting its lack of tax reform.

In 2015-16, Crapo counted seven bipartisan measures he sponsored that Obama signed into law. One of those had a personal dimension for him as a cancer survivor: He had his prostate removed in 2000, and underwent radiation treatment when the cancer recurred five years later. In 2016, Crapo attended a White House ceremony at which Obama signed a reauthorization of the Toxic Substances Control Act (TSCA) containing a provision known as Trevor's Law. The latter, named for Trevor Schaefer of Boise -- who survived a diagnosis of brain cancer at age 13 -- required the tracking of childhood and adult clusters around the nation. Crapo, while a member of the Environment and Public Works Committee, had originally co-sponsored Trevor's Law with that panel's chairwoman, California Democrat Barbara Boxer. Crapo, who has been cancer-free for more than a decade, said his own diagnosis had "accelerated and intensified" his interest in biomedical research, telling the *Idaho Statesman*, "Certainly I believe when one gets the diagnosis that they have cancer, it's a gut-wrencher, and it's an attitude-changer in a lot of ways."

In the 2016 presidential campaign, Crapo initially endorsed GOP nominee Donald Trump. He became one of the first Republicans to withdraw his endorsement after release of the decade-old video showing Trump boasting about groping women. Crapo said Trump's "disrespectful, profane and demeaning" comments made him unfit for the presidency, and suggested Trump be replaced with then-vice presidential nominee Mike Pence. Two weeks prior to the election, Crapo acknowledged that was not going to happen and restored his endorsement of Trump -- citing the stakes in the coming election, particularly the prospect that the next president could have an opportunity to nominate several Supreme Court justices.

Junior Senator

Jim Risch (R)

Elected 2008, term expires 2020, 2nd term; b. May 03, 1943, Milwaukee, WI; University of Idaho, B.S.; University of Idaho, Law School, J.D.; University of Wisconsin, Milwaukee, Att.; Roman Catholic; Married (Vicki L. Choborda); 3 children; 7 grandchildren.

Elected Office: Ada County Prosecuting Attorney, 1970-1974; ID Senate, 1974-1989, 1995-2003, Majority Leader, 1976-1982, pres. pro temp., 1982-1989; ID Lt. Governor, 2003-2006, 2007-2009; ID Governor, 2006-2008.

Professional Career: Rancher; Sr. partner, Risch Goss Insinger Gustavel, 1975-2008.

DC Office: 483 RSOB 20510, 202-224-2752, Fax: 202-224-2573, risch.senate.gov.

State Offices: Boise, 208-342-7985; Coeur d'Alene, 208-667-6130; Idaho Falls, 208-523-5541; Lewiston, 208-743-0792; Pocatello, 208-236-6817; Twin Falls, 208-734-6780.

Committees: *Energy & Natural Resources*: Energy, Public Lands, Forests & Mining, Water & Power. *Ethics*. *Foreign Relations*: East Asia, the Pacific & International Cybersecurity Policy, Europe & Regional Security Cooperation, Near East, South Asia, Central Asia & Counterterrorism (Chmn), State Dept & USAID Mngmnt, Internat'l Ops & Internat'l Dev. *Intelligence*. *Small Business & Entrepreneurship (Chmn)*.

Group Ratings

	ADA	ACLU	AFL-CIO	LCV	ITI	COC	HAFA	ACU	CFG	FRC
2016	-	17%	-	12%	40%	88%	81%	92%	73%	100%
2015	0%	C	7%	0%	C	64%	C	96%	91%	100%

Almanac Ratings 2015

	Economy	Social	Foreign	Composite
Liberal	0%	0%	4%	1%
Conservative	100%	100%	96%	99%

Key Votes of the 114th Congress

1. Keystone pipeline	Y	5. National Security Data	N	9. Gun Sales Checks	N
2. Export-Import Bank	Y	6. Iran Nuclear Deal	Y	10. Sanctuary Cities	Y
3. Debt Ceiling Increase	N	7. Puerto Rico Debt	Y	11. Planned Parenthood	Y
4. Homeland Security $$	N	8. Loretta Lynch A.G	N	12. Trade deals	Y

Election Results

Election	Name (Party)	Vote (%)		Cand. Spent	Ind. Exp. Support	Ind. Exp. Oppose
2014 General	Jim Risch (R)	285,596	(65%)	$1,761,223		
	Nels Mitchell (D)	151,574	(35%)	$357,052		
2014 Primary	Jim Risch (R)	119,209	(80%)			
	Jeremy Anderson (R)	29,939	(20%)			

Prior winning percentages: 2008 (58%)

In 1970, when he was just 27, Republican James Risch -- now Idaho's junior senator -- was elected Ada County prosecutor, a high-profile position in the state's capital and largest city, Boise. He went after the illicit drug trade so aggressively that his enemies tried to plant a bomb in his car. After that incident,

Risch and his wife and political confidant, Vicki, put a piece of tape on the hood of their car every night so they could detect any tampering. Nearly a half-century later, Risch has continued to exhibit his trademark aggressiveness as a member of the Foreign Relations and Intelligence committees, regularly delivering blunt-spoken critiques of foreign policy during the tenure of President Barack Obama.

As Obama left office in early 2017, Risch made little secret of his desire to chair the Foreign Relations Committee. And, with incoming President Donald Trump at one point considering Foreign Relations Committee Chairman Bob Corker of Tennessee to be secretary of state, Risch -- as the panel's second ranking Republican -- seemed within striking distance of his goal. Ultimately, Trump did not choose Corker for the Cabinet, and Risch ended up with a less visible prize: the chairmanship of the Small Business and Entrepreneurship Committee. Risch, whose voting record has made him among the Senate's most conservative members, vowed to use his first committee gavel to reduce the regulatory burden on small business.

From his beginnings in public sector as a local prosecutor, Risch went on to become a leader in the state Senate and lieutenant governor -- and also served a seven-month stint as the state's interim governor prior to arriving on Capitol Hill in 2008. Born in Milwaukee, he attended the University of Wisconsin/Milwaukee before transferring to the University of Idaho, where he earned a bachelor's degree in forestry. He went on to become a successful rancher, and continued to reside on a ranch outside Boise. He earned his law degree from the University of Idaho. Risch has been a successful businessman, and ranks high on ratings of the Senate's wealthiest members. His business interests have included a property management firm, and he is the joint owner of 250 acres in the Boise area. The 2015 *Roll Call* survey of congressional financial assets pegged him as the 20th wealthiest member of Congress. A 2016 assessment by *Money* magazine estimated his net worth at more than $53 million.

In 1974, Risch was elected to the Idaho Senate, where he would serve longer than anyone else in state history. He always carried an index card in his back pocket, one side listing bills that he wanted to pass and the other listing bills he was determined to kill. Quickly eyeing a leadership position, he became majority leader after the 1976 election by defeating a young colleague named Larry Craig -- whom Risch would succeed in the U.S. Senate three decades later. Although popular with some of his colleagues, Risch was seen by some younger senators as a bully who pressured them to vote his way. After six years as majority leader, he spent another six years as Senate president pro tem.

Risch's political career hit a rough patch after he was defeated for re-election by a Democratic challenger in 1988. He ran again for the state Senate in 1994, but this time lost in the GOP primary. A year later, he returned to that chamber when he was appointed to fill a vacancy. Less confrontational this time around, Risch moved back into the ranks of leadership as assistant Republican floor leader. In 2001, he had his eye on the vacant lieutenant governor's job after its previous occupant, C.L. "Butch" Otter, resigned after winning a seat in Congress. Gov. Dirk Kempthorne passed over Risch to appoint state Sen. Jack Riggs to the post. Risch defeated Riggs in the 2002 GOP primary, 35%-28%, with the rest of the vote split among four other candidates.

After three years in the shadow of Kempthorne, Risch assumed the top job when President George W. Bush tapped Kempthorne to be Interior secretary. Risch had just over half a year to serve in what he considered his dream job, and was determined to make the most of it. Within two weeks of taking office, he ordered a reorganization of Idaho's Health and Welfare Department. He created the position of state drug czar to counter the growth in the illicit methamphetamine market in the state. Displeased that the legislature failed to provide property tax relief during its regular session, Risch called the first special session in 14 years. The heavily Republican body obediently passed bills cutting local property taxes by $260 million, raising the sales tax from 5 percent to 6 percent, and cutting state spending by $50 million. The voters approved the tax changes by a nearly 3-1 margin.

In an odd twist, Risch returned to the lieutenant governorship after his stint as governor, because then-Rep. Otter had gotten a head start on the 2006 gubernatorial campaign prior to Kempthorne's elevation to the Cabinet. In November, Risch defeated former Democratic Rep. Larry LaRocco for lieutenant governor, 58%-39%. But another office soon became available: the Senate seat first won by Craig, Risch's old rival, in 1990. Craig was arrested in a Minneapolis airport men's room in 2007 for soliciting sex from an undercover police officer and pleaded guilty to disorderly conduct. He resisted immense pressure from his Senate colleagues to resign immediately, but he then decided against seeking re-election in 2008. Risch announced his intention to run, and had little competition for the Republican nomination. His Democratic opponent was, once again, LaRocco. Risch raised more than twice as much money as his opponent, and cruised to victory by a margin of nearly 25 points.

"I'm reputedly the most conservative member of the Senate," Risch boasted to the Boise Metro Chamber of Commerce during an appearance in early 2016. Statistics appear to back him up: *Almanac* ratings showed that Rich's overall voting score was the most conservative in the Senate in both 2012 and

2013. Risch's aggressive style has at times been a contrast to his more mild-mannered senior colleague, Republican Sen. Mike Crapo, although the two have similar voting records. "Crapo and I are very, very close – we're like brothers," Risch told the *Idaho Statesman*. "I mean, nobody votes the same more than we do: 99.9 percent of the time." Again, statistics bear him out: Risch and Crapo were among two of only three senators whose economic voting records notched 100 percent conservative scores in the 2015 *Almanac* ratings. "I ran for this office as a deficit hawk, and now that I am here, I have moved even further in that direction," Risch told *The Idaho Statesman*.

Risch made his biggest splash as a critic of Obama's foreign policy. He said in 2012 that the Law of the Sea Treaty defining nations' ocean usage and another administration-backed effort to conclude a United Nations treaty on reducing firearms "would push the U.S. away from our constitutional foundations and supplement its authority with judgments from international courts and U.N. bureaucracies." When the Foreign Relations panel sought to take up the New START arms control treaty with Russia in 2010, Risch tried to stop the vote: He cited new intelligence that he said he couldn't reveal in open session, but which had led him to question Russia's intentions. And when the then-Democratic majority Senate approved the pact , Risch unsuccessfully demanded a delay, noting that Russian troops reportedly had stolen five U.S. Humvees used in military exercises.

After the Russian military began working to support rebels in eastern Ukraine in 2014, Risch urged the U.S. government to provide lethal weapons to the Ukrainian government. During a 2014 appearance on Capitol Hill by Secretary of State John Kerry, Risch scolded the one-time Foreign Relations chairman. "I tell you, you can't help but get the impression our foreign policy is just spinning out of control. And we are losing control in virtually every area we are trying to do something in," Risch declared. In 2015, when Risch was one of 47 Senate Republicans to sign on to a letter to Iranian leaders warning that striking a nuclear agreement with the Obama White House without congressional approval could be short-lived, Kerry blasted the move as ignoring "200 years" of precedent in the conduct of foreign policy. Risch shot back calling Kerry's statement "absolute nonsense," according to *The Hill* newspaper; he argued that senators, as elected officials, had the right and responsibility to communicate with foreign officials. Such blunt talk has made Risch a frequent guest of CNN's Wolf Blitzer. "What will keep Risch as a go-to source for Blitzer, and possibly others, is that he's a great interview," observed Idaho journalist Chuck Malloy. While terming Risch only "fair" as a public speaker, Malloy continued: "He knocks out the television interviews. Risch is knowledgeable, engaging, quick on his feet and easy to understand."

On the domestic front, Risch has pushed to rein in the power of the Environmental Protection Agency, telling the *Twin Falls Times-News* in 2011 that he thought it was possible to have clean air and water "without sending out the Gestapo to enforce the thing." But Risch has reached across the aisle in an effort to increase the roles of alternative energy sources, such as biomass and geothermal. He and Crapo joined with Democrats Ron Wyden and Jeff Merkley from neighboring Oregon to pass legislation that would open up public lands to development of geothermal energy. The measure, co-sponsored by Energy and Natural Resources Committee Chairwoman Lisa Murkowski of Alaska, passed the Senate in 2014, andwas part of a broader bipartisan energy bill that Murkowski guided through the Senate in 2016. Efforts to reach a compromise with a House-passed energy bill failed later that year.

In 2014, Risch won a second term in the Senate by a nearly 2-1 margin in one of the most overwhelmingly Republican states in the nation. The seat is likely to remain in Republican hands in 2020, whether or not Risch -- who turns 77 that year -- opts to seek a third term. Risch cited the relative youth of his Senate colleague, Marco Rubio, in backing him for the Republican presidential nomination in 2016. "I am supporting a person for president who has a different view than I do," Risch told the Boise Chamber of Commerce. "But he's three decades younger than I am, and he tells you, 'Our best years are ahead of us, we're Americans and we can do this.' And bless him, I love hearing that." He was a far less enthusiastic backer of Trump in the general election, and his statement following Election Day pointedly omitted mention of the winner -- but rather served to underscore Risch's conservative credo. "Many were surprised by the outcome of Tuesday's election," Risch observed, adding, "Americans have clearly expressed their desire to move in the direction of our founders' vision of freedom from government intrusion and the opportunity for personal success."

FIRST DISTRICT

Raul Labrador (R)

Elected 2010, 4th term; b. Dec 08, 1967, Carolina, PR; Brigham Young University (UT), B.A.; University of Washington School of Law - Seattle, J.D.; Mormon; Married (Rebecca Johnson); 5 children.

Elected Office: ID House, 2007-2010.

Professional Career: Clerk, U.S. Attorney, WA St., 1994; Practicing attorney, 1994-1996; Law clerk, U.S. District Court, District of ID, 1996-1998; Practicing attorney, 1998-2010.

DC Office: 1523 LHOB 20515, 202-225-6611, Fax: 202-225-3029, labrador.house.gov.

State Offices: Coeur d'Alene, 208-667-0127; Lewiston, 208-743-1388; Meridian, 208-888-3188.

Committees: *Judiciary*: Courts, Intellectual Property & Internet, Immigration & Border Security. *Natural Resources*: Federal Lands, Oversight & Investigations (Chmn).

Group Ratings

	ADA	ACLU	AFL-CIO	LCV	ITI	COC	HAFA	ACU	CFG	FRC
2016	-	29%	-	0%	50%	100%	91%	100%	94%	92%
2015	10%	C	10%	6%	C	53%	C	96%	93%	92%

Almanac Ratings 2015

	Economy	Social	Foreign	Composite
Liberal	12%	15%	30%	19%
Conservative	88%	85%	71%	81%

Key Votes of the 114th Congress

1. Keystone Pipeline	Y	5. Puerto Rico Debt	Y	9. Offenses by Aliens	Y
2. Trade Deals	N	6. Medical Marijuana	Y	10. Troops in Iraq	Y
3. Export-Import Bank	N	7. Sanctuary Cities	Y	11. Homeland Security $$	N
4. Debt Ceiling Increase	N	8. Armor-piercing Bullets	Y	12. Trade Adjustment aid	N

Election Results

Election	Name (Party)	Vote (%)		Cand. Spent	Ind. Exp. Support	Ind. Exp. Oppose
2016 General	Raul Labrador (R)	242,252	(68%)	$792,639		
	James Piotrowski (D)	113,052	(32%)	$311,506		
2016 Primary	Raul Labrador (R)	51,573	(81%)			
	Gordon Counsil (R)	6,509	(10%)			
	Isaac Haugen (R)	5,608	(9%)			

Prior winning percentages: 2014 (65%), 2012 (63%), 2010 (51%)

Republican RaÚl Labrador, elected in the GOP tidal wave of 2010, has been a leader among junior conservatives disaffected with the House GOP leadership. He made a futile bid to challenge Rep. Kevin McCarthy for majority leader. Later, he was a founding member of the Freedom Caucus of activist conservatives and he joined in the steps that led to the resignation of John Boehner as Speaker. He participated in extended negotiations on immigration reform, which were unsuccessful. In May 2017, he announced that he was running for governor of Idaho the next year.

Labrador was born in Puerto Rico and raised by his mother, Ana Pastor, who was unmarried. His father, who was married and had five other children, saw RaÚl once a year on his birthday, according to *The Idaho Statesman*. Pastor, a sales representative for the Mars candy company in Puerto Rico, moved to Las Vegas for a new start when RaÚl was a young teenager, taking a job as a change girl in a casino. She joined the city's Mormon Church, which provided help during lean times. A church official became a surrogate father for Labrador, helping pay his way to Brigham Young University, where he earned a bachelor's degree in Spanish and philosophy. He got a law degree from the University of Washington. Labrador spent most of his career in private practice. Before he came to Washington, he was the managing partner of Labrador Law Offices in Nampa, Idaho, which specialized in immigration law.

Labrador was elected to the state House in 2006. He was a steadfast conservative, standing up to GOP Gov. C. L. "Butch" Otter on his plan to raise fuel taxes to pay for new roads. Labrador had a hand in legislation to restore gun rights to those deemed mentally defective by the courts and to exempt Idaho from the federal health care law.

He sought the Republican nomination to challenge conservative Democratic Rep. Walt Minnick in 2010. Marine Maj. Vaughn Ward, a decorated Iraq war veteran, had a 3-to-1 fundraising advantage and the backing of the state and national party establishment. But Ward made a series of gaffes that left him vulnerable, including violation of Pentagon rules prohibiting the use of military uniforms in campaign ads, and failure to disclose his wife's financial assets. Labrador won the primary, 48%-39%.

In the general election, Labrador targeted the first-term Minnick's vote to elect California liberal Nancy Pelosi as House Speaker. He called for large cuts in federal spending and repeal of the Democratic health care law. Minnick, with $2.5 million in the bank and a 5-to-1 money edge, let loose a barrage of attacks, including one that showed a former U.S. marshal criticizing Labrador for running a website that "offers advice to illegal immigrants seeking amnesty." Labrador responded that he in fact advised illegal immigrants to return to their home countries and reapply for admission to the United States through proper channels. The attack ads were not enough to save Minnick in this Republican bastion. Labrador won, 51%-41%.

Labrador pushed for his freshman class to reset the agenda but often fell short. "Why don't we pass the most conservative piece of legislation we can in the House?" he asked at a 2012 news conference. "Instead, we are always passing legislation we know was tacitly approved by [Democratic Senate Majority Leader] Harry Reid." He and 46 other freshmen helped reject a controversial second engine for the F-35 Joint Strike Fighter that was manufactured in Boehner's Ohio district. During negotiations over raising the federal debt limit a few months later, Labrador said he would support an increase as long as Congress passed a balanced budget amendment to the Constitution. His stance led Boehner to add a balanced budget vote to the deal, which passed the House without Labrador's vote; he didn't think it cut spending enough.

Labrador raised eyebrows in Idaho in 2012 when he supported California Republican Tom McClintock's failed amendment to a spending bill to cut funding for the Energy Department's Office of Nuclear Energy, a key funding source for the Idaho National Laboratory. Upset with the news media's portrayal of him and other tea party freshmen, Labrador organized a group called "Conversations with Conservatives," which featured panels of lawmakers taking reporters' questions while sandwiches were served.

When the House convened in 2013, he was among the unhappy Republicans looking to replace Boehner. Their effort stalled when they determined they could not get the 25 GOP votes they needed. When the time came to elect a Speaker, he declined to cast a vote. He later complained to *The New Yorker* that senior House members "want our numbers, but they don't want our input, and they don't want our opinions."

Labrador considered running for Idaho governor in 2014. After telling the *Statesman* that his decision would hinge in part on the fate of immigration reform, he later decided against challenging Otter, telling an August 2013 news conference: "I do not feel that I have yet completed the mission you sent me to Congress to do."

Meanwhile, Labrador worked with a bipartisan "Group of Eight" House lawmakers who quietly met to seek a deal on immigration reform, but abandoned the effort amid disagreements about legalizing undocumented immigrants. In April 2014, Labrador declared he was "disappointed" that Boehner criticized his colleagues for dragging their feet in the negotiations. After President Barack Obama issued his executive order on immigration, Labrador called it "illegal" and said Congress should block related presidential requests. In a September 2016 review of that failed effort, Alec MacGillis of *Pro Publica* termed Labrador an "iconoclast" who stuck to his "doctrinaire conservatism" in limiting the rights of illegal immigrants and abandoned the talks. Labrador, who endorsed Rand Paul and then Ted Cruz for the Republican presidential nomination, said the failure of that legislation is "the reason we have Donald Trump as a nominee."

When Majority Leader Eric Cantor unexpectedly lost his primary in June 2014, forcing a leadership scramble, Labrador entered the race less than a week before the vote on a new leader, when McCarthy, the majority whip, appeared to have the support of a majority of Republicans. "What we've had is kind of a top-down approach where you talk to members of Congress and they feel like they're totally irrelevant," Labrador told Fox News. He lost to McCarthy, but the experience bolstered his stature as a conservative leader. "At the very least, he's shown his party something of what its future might look like," the *American Conservative* wrote of Labrador.

After Boehner resigned under pressure, Labrador was not a contender for a top post, but he worked with allies to impose restrictions on the new party leaders. Ultimately, the Freedom Caucus took no position on whether to endorse Paul Ryan for Speaker and Labrador voted for him. In 2016, Labrador played a constructive role in crafting legislation to create a new federal board to oversee finances for Puerto Rico, which was facing the threat of bankruptcy. "I think this [bill] is one that may have expanded [Labrador's] reputation because he's clearly seen now as somebody who can get in the weeds and do the detail work, " House Natural Resources Committee Chairman Rob Bishop, a Utah Republican, told McClatchy News. "He made it possible. He needs to get credit for it.

In Idaho, Labrador has been reelected easily and remained interested in statewide office. He has clashed frequently with veteran Idaho Rep. Mike Simpson. As Simpson worked on sweeping legislation to designate additional federal lands in Idaho, Labrador said he preferred state management. In 2015, Simpson wrote that the House GOP renegades were an "irresponsible, unrealistic, ineffective segment of the Republican Caucus." He criticized Republicans who had abandoned immigration reform. The column did not explicitly cite Labrador, but many Idaho Republicans understood that he was the target.

Labrador had an awkward start to his campaign for governor when he received extensive national publicity-and second-guessing-after days earlier telling a rowdy town-hall meeting, "Nobody dies because they don't have access to health care." Lt. Gov. Brad Little greeted Labrador with pointed jabs. "I would like to welcome Congressman Labrador back home to the place where we balance our budget and conservative ideals guide us each day," Little said. "Idahoans, including myself, look forward to hearing from Congressman Labrador about the accomplishments he has made while being in Congress for over six years."

Western Idaho: Western Boise, Coeur D'Alene

Population		**Race and Ethnicity**		**Income**	
Total	819,605	White	84.7%	Median Income	$48,617 (274 out of 435)
Land area	39,418	Black	0.4%		
Pop/ sq mi	20.8	Latino	10.4%		
Born in state	43.0%	Asian	1.1%	Under $50,000	51.3%
		Two races	2.1%	$50,000-$99,999	32.7%
Age Groups		Other	2.5%	$100,000-$199,999	13.7%
Under 18	26.0%			$200,000 or more	2.3%
18-34	21.0%	**Education**		Poverty Rate	14.9%
35-64	38.2%	H.S grad or less	39.0%		
Over 64	14.8%	Some college	36.6%	**Health Insurance**	
		College Degree, 4 yr	17.0%	With health insurance coverage	85.4%
Work		Post grad	7.4%		
White Collar	32.6%				
Sales and Service	43.1%	**Military**		**Public Assistance**	
Blue Collar	24.3%	Veteran	10.9%	Cash public assistance income	3.3%
Government	15.7%	Active Duty	0.1%		
				Food stamp/SNAP benefits	12.8%

Voter Turnout			
2015 Total Citizens 18+	585,247	2016 House Turnout as % CVAP	61%
2016 House turnout	355,357	2014 House Turnout as % CVAP	38%

2012 Presidential Vote		
Mitt Romney	213,080	(65%)
Barack Obama	105,645	(32%)

2016 Presidential Vote		
Donald Trump	229,034	(64%)
Hillary Clinton	91,284	(25%)
Evan McMullin	16,087	(5%)
Gary Johnson	14,916	(4%)

Cook Partisan Voting Index: R+21

The 1st Congressional District of Idaho stretches 479 miles from the Nevada border to Canada and includes some of Boise and all of the panhandle. It encompasses two high-growth areas: the western suburbs of Boise and the Coeur d'Alene area in Kootenai County. Coeur d'Alene, which is in the mountains, is a few miles east of Spokane, Washington. With 2,000 employees, its largest employer is the family-owned Hagadone Corp. Headquartered in an 18-story resort hotel on Lake Coeur d'Alene, the company publishes more than 20 newspapers, has its own advertising agency, and offers hospitality and real estate services.

To the south outside of Boise, commercial developers took over land in Nampa that not long ago grew wheat and alfalfa. The population nearly doubled in the 1990s, and it became Idaho's second-largest city. Since 2010, the boom in subdivisions has switched to nearby Meridian, which grew 20 percent from 2010 to 2015 and became the fastest-growing city in the state; with population exceeding 90,000, it surpassed Nampa and was the sixth fastest-growing city in the nation in 2016. Closer-in Meridian is part of Boise-based Ada County, which is split between the state's two districts, with most of Boise in the 2nd. With growth has come urban problems. In Nampa-based Canyon County, the public defender office in 2015 handled 8,000 cases, most of them criminal. Fewer than 10 percent of defendants hired their own attorney. In Boundary County on the Canadian border, Bonners Ferry in March 2015 was included as a target on the "hit list" of the Islamic State, apparently because it was the hometown of many U.S. military personnel.

The growth is these once-rural areas has reinforced, rather than altered, the political landscape. Newcomers routinely say they moved to conservative Idaho to escape from city life, although some old-timers still worry that their communities may become new versions of San Jose or Orange County. Politically, the 1st District of Idaho is overwhelmingly Republican. Kootenai County, once a Democratic stronghold, now leans Republican as much as conservative Canyon County in Boise's suburbs. In the 2016 presidential race, Donald Trump got 67 percent of the vote in Kootenai and 65 percent in Canyon. Northern mining counties were once the district's Democratic base; now that base is the university town of Moscow in Latah County. In 2016, as in 2012, Latah was one of only two counties to vote for the Democratic presidential nominee. Overall, the biggest change in the district vote was the drop on the Democratic side: 64%-25% for Trump, compared with 65%-32% for Mitt Romney in 2012. Independent Evan McMullin and Libertarian Gary Johnson split most of the remainder in 2016.

SECOND DISTRICT

Mike Simpson (R)

Elected 1998, 10th term; b. Sep 08, 1950, Burley; Utah State University, B.S.; Washington University School of Dental Medicine (MO), D.D.S.; Utah State University, Att.; Mormon; Married (Kathy Johnson Simpson).

Elected Office: Blackfoot City Council, 1980-1984; ID House, 1984-1998, speaker, 1993-1998.

Professional Career: Practicing dentist, 1977-1998.

DC Office: 2084 RHOB 20515, 202-225-5531, Fax: 202-225-8216, simpson.house.gov.

State Offices: Boise, 208-334-1953; Idaho Falls, 208-523-6701; Twin Falls, 208-734-7219.

Committees: *Appropriations*: Energy & Water Development & Related Agencies (Chmn), Interior, Environment & Related Agencies, Labor, Health & Human Services, Education & Related Agencies.

Group Ratings

	ADA	ACLU	AFL-CIO	LCV	ITI	COC	HAFA	ACU	CFG	FRC
2016	-	11%	-	13%	100%	100%	43%	52%	57%	100%
2015	10%	C	25%	3%	C	100%	C	48%	36%	92%

Almanac Ratings 2015

	Economy	Social	Foreign	Composite
Liberal	14%	14%	11%	13%
Conservative	86%	86%	90%	87%

Key Votes of the 114th Congress

1. Keystone Pipeline	Y	5. Puerto Rico Debt	Y	9. Offenses by Aliens	Y
2. Trade Deals	Y	6. Medical Marijuana	N	10. Troops in Iraq	N
3. Export-Import Bank	Y	7. Sanctuary Cities	Y	11. Homeland Security $$	Y
4. Debt Ceiling Increase	Y	8. Armor-piercing Bullets	Y	12. Trade Adjustment aid	Y

Election Results

Election	Name (Party)	Vote (%)		Cand. Spent	Ind. Exp. Support	Ind. Exp. Oppose
2016 General	Mike Simpson (R)	205,292	(63%)	$563,706		
	Jennifer Martinez (D)	95,940	(29%)			
	Anthony Tomkins (C)	25,005	(8%)	$1,165		
2016 Primary	Mike Simpson (R)	47,030	(73%)			
	Lisa Marie (R)	17,417	(27%)			

Prior winning percentages: 2014 (61%), 2012 (65%), 2010 (69%), 2008 (71%), 2006 (62%), 2004 (71%), 2002 (68%), 2000 (71%), 1998 (53%)

Mike Simpson, an independent-minded Republican first elected in 1998, would be unusual even if he wasn't an influential lawmaker and didn't represent one of the nation's most right-leaning states. He has used his post on the House Appropriations Committee to deliver huge federal benefits to his district and to enact sweeping federal lands measures. He often reaches out to Democrats on economic and social issues. He easily defeated a primary challenge from the right in 2014.

Simpson grew up in Blackfoot, became a dentist, and joined his father's dental practice. He was elected to the city council in 1980 and to the state House in 1984. In 1993, he became speaker of the Idaho House, while he maintained his dental practice. In the legislature, he was known as a moderate in a conservative chamber, affable and able to get differing sides together. When Republican Gov. Phil Batt announced he would retire in 1998, Simpson wanted to run, but GOP Sen. Dirk Kempthorne's decision to seek the office closed that option. When GOP Rep. Mike Crapo ran for Kempthorne's Senate seat, the House seat opened for Simpson.

The election was hotly contested. In the Republican primary, state Rep. Mark Stubbs called for lower payroll taxes. He opposed nuclear programs at the Idaho National Laboratory, while Simpson - whose hometown is midway between Idaho Falls and Pocatello - wanted more work at the facility. Term limits were the big issue. Simpson refused to take a pledge to serve only three terms, while the other candidates agreed to it. Term-limit advocates spent heavily against Simpson. Angry at the ads, Batt endorsed Simpson five days before the election. Simpson ran ads against "out-of-state folk" interfering with Idaho's elections. He beat Stubbs 47%-41%.

The Democratic nominee was Richard Stallings, a former history professor who was elected to the House in 1984, served four terms, and lost to Kempthorne for the Senate in 1992. Stallings emphasized his conservative voting record in the House, called for more education spending and said he would act to boost falling farm commodity prices. Simpson won 53%-45%, losing Pocatello, Sun Valley and Boise, but carrying just about everywhere else.

Simpson's open-mindedness led *Esquire* magazine in 2008 to call him one of the 10 best members of Congress, saying he "lives by the philosophy that democratic representation is a matter of finding not advantageous positions but common ground." He was one of just 16 House Republicans in March 2012 to back a budget plan along the lines of the bipartisan commission chaired by Alan Simpson (not related) and Erskine Bowles, and he led a bipartisan group of legislators urging budget negotiators to "go big" and look at raising taxes as well as cutting spending. During subsequent negotiations on spending and taxes aimed at averting a so-called fiscal cliff, he told *The Wall Street Journal* that many Republicans likely would accept raising tax rates on households earning more than $500,000 or $1 million as long as Democrats backed substantial entitlement cuts. That proved too ambitious.

When President Barack Obama took office, Simpson supported Democratic bills to rein in credit card companies and housing lenders, and opposed GOP proposals to eliminate the Legal Services Corporation and reduce funding for the National Endowment for the Arts. He has had a contentious relationship with his Idaho GOP colleague Raul Labrador, a hero of the tea party movement. When Labrador reportedly was involved in plotting to oust Simpson's long-time ally John Boehner as Speaker, Simpson told *The Idaho Statesman* that his actions were "irresponsible." Labrador responded by calling Simpson "a bully" and "an old-school legislator that went to Washington, D.C., to compromise."

Simpson has used his seat on the Appropriations Committee to secure funding for the Bureau of Reclamation, the Army Corps of Engineers and the Idaho National Laboratory in his district, which he describes as "the nation's lead nuclear energy research laboratory." As a leading defender of appropriations earmarks, he disagreed with his friend Boehner on restricting them but supported greater transparency in the process. As chairman of the Interior Subcommittee in 2011, he successfully fought a Senate Democratic proposal to cut $150 million from the nuclear energy budget. In 2013, he took over as chairman of the Energy and Water Development Subcommittee, where he promoted the interests of the Idaho Lab and other efforts to spur energy independence for the United States. In March 2015, he played a key parliamentary role on the House floor in successfully breaking the deadlock on funding the Homeland Security Department, even though he did not serve on the subcommittee responsible for that bill.

After easily winning reelection, he encountered problems in 2010, when his support for the rescue of the financial markets and other independent stances drew two primary opponents, state Rep. Russ Mathews and tea party-backed Chick Heileson, a retired heating contractor. They held Simpson to 58 percent, his worst primary showing since 1998. By 2014, Simpson's legislative rating from the conservative group Heritage Action was 45 percent - 17 percentage points below the House GOP average and far below the ratings of his Idaho colleagues. The anti-tax group Club for Growth made him one of its chief targets and spent more than $500,000 on behalf of Bryan Smith, who sought to portray Simpson as a Washington insider who was a captive of special interests. But the U.S. Chamber of Commerce, the National Rifle Association, the National Association of Realtors and other groups responded by pouring in about $4 million on Simpson's behalf; 2012 presidential nominee Mitt Romney appeared in a Simpson ad. Smith ran ads criticizing Simpson as a "supporter of earmarks" and complaining that he "supports a scheme to give amnesty to illegal aliens." In the May primary, Simpson coasted to an easy 62%-38% victory. In November, Stallings made another attempt to return to office and lost 61%-39%.

In August 2015, Simpson gained a legacy victory when Obama signed the Sawtooth National Recreation Area and Jerry Peak Wilderness Additions Act, which included the Boulder-White Cloud Management Area designating 276,000 acres in central Idaho as wilderness area, prohibiting development. He spent more than a decade negotiating the plan with numerous constituencies ranging from mountain bikers to environmentalists, only to run into opposition from fellow Idaho Republicans. Having earlier warned that he would "die trying" to make a deal, Simpson months earlier had filed a scaled-down version to find common ground, and to pre-empt potential unilateral action by Obama to declare the area a national monument. "The threat of a national monument, I think, convinced a lot of people it was better to have an Idaho solution than one imposed by Washington, D.C.," Simpson said.

Despite his idiosyncratic style and the departure of Boehner, Simpson appeared to be more influential and outspoken than ever. In 2016, he defeated routine challenges in the primary and general election. A month before the election, he stated that Donald Trump was "unfit to be president" and reiterated that he had never endorsed him.

Eastern Idaho: Eastern Boise, Idaho Falls

Population		**Race and Ethnicity**		**Income**	
Total	796,942	White	81.3%	Median Income	$46,551 (316 out of 435)
Land area	43,225	Black	0.7%		
Pop/ sq mi	18.4	Latino	13.3%		
Born in state	51.6%	Asian	1.5%	Under $50,000	53.2%
Age Groups		Two races	1.9%	$50,000-$99,999	30.8%
Under 18	27.2%	Other	2.3%	$100,000-$199,999	13.1%
18-34	24.5%			$200,000 or more	2.9%
35-64	35.5%	**Education**		Poverty Rate	16.1%
Over 64	12.8%	H.S grad or less	36.8%		
		Some college	35.6%	**Health Insurance**	
Work		College Degree, 4 yr	18.5%	With health insurance coverage	85.2%
White Collar	34.3%	Post grad	9.0%		
Sales and Service	41.2%	**Military**		**Public Assistance**	
Blue Collar	24.5%	Veteran	9.3%	Cash public assistance income	3.1%
Government	15.9%	Active Duty	0.4%		
				Food stamp/SNAP benefits	12.5%

Voter Turnout			
2015 Total Citizens 18+	545,303	2016 House Turnout as % CVAP	60%
2016 House turnout	326,237	2014 House Turnout as % CVAP	39%

2012 Presidential Vote		
Mitt Romney	207,831	(64%)
Barack Obama	107,142	(33%)

2016 Presidential Vote		
Donald Trump	180,021	(54%)
Hillary Clinton	98,481	(30%)
Evan McMullin	30,389	(9%)
Gary Johnson	13,415	(4%)

Cook Partisan Voting Index: R+17

The 2nd District of Idaho, from Boise east to the Wyoming border, is one of America's most picturesque, with thick forests, mountain ranges, broad river valleys and vacant expanses. It was settled from the east by overland pioneers who stopped in Idaho to establish farms, and from the south by Mormons moving up from Utah to Franklin, Bear Lake and Caribou counties. It has one of the largest concentrations of Mormons among congressional districts.

On Interstate 15, Idaho Falls serves as the modern metropolis for a vast region stretching from West Yellowstone, Montana, to the Salmon River Mountains. Near Idaho Falls, on a windswept, desolate range is Idaho National Laboratory, known locally as "The Site." The Energy Department's leading laboratory for civilian nuclear energy research, development and demonstration, the facility covers 890 square miles and employs 7,500 workers. It has kept the area's economy fairly stable, thanks in part to its work cleaning up Cold War-era nuclear plants. In December 2016, the Naval Nuclear Propulsion Program announced plans for a $1.6 billion facility at the lab to handle spent fuel. Earlier in the year, Utah Associated Municipal Power Systems and the Energy Department announced that INL will host a commercial nuclear reactor plant. In Twin Falls, Greek yogurt maker Chobani operates one of the largest yogurt-processing plants in the world and employs about 1,000 people. Pocatello is an old railroad town, with unionized railroad workers. The city is home to Idaho State University, where the U.S. Justice Department and local police in early 2016 investigated what the university president reported as a few dozen burglaries of students attending the school; most of them were from Saudi Arabia and Kuwait.

To the west, amid the mountains, are Sun Valley and the nearby town of Ketchum. Sun Valley was established as a ski resort in 1936 by business mogul Averell Harriman before he began his political career. Ketchum attracted writer Ernest Hemingway in 1939, and various movie stars followed. In recent years, Blaine County, which includes both Sun Valley and Ketchum, has attracted rich expatriates from the East and West coasts, who have made it the most Democratic county in Idaho. In the 2016 presidential election, Blaine - by 59%-31% -- was one of only two counties in the state to vote for Hillary Clinton. It stands in vivid contrast to the Idaho Falls area, the Mormon country and the farmland along the Snake River, which are among the most Republican areas in the nation.

The 2nd District of Idaho includes most of Boise, where high-tech businesses and tourism have fueled the economy. Boise is home to Micron Technology, which is a leading patent holder and employs 9,500 people. The Hewlett-Packard campus also is in the district. In March 2016, the city ranked sixth in the *U.S. News & World Report* list of the best places to live. The east side of Boise leans Republican but has some Democratic precincts. The district, like the state as a whole, is solidly Republican.

★ ILLINOIS ★

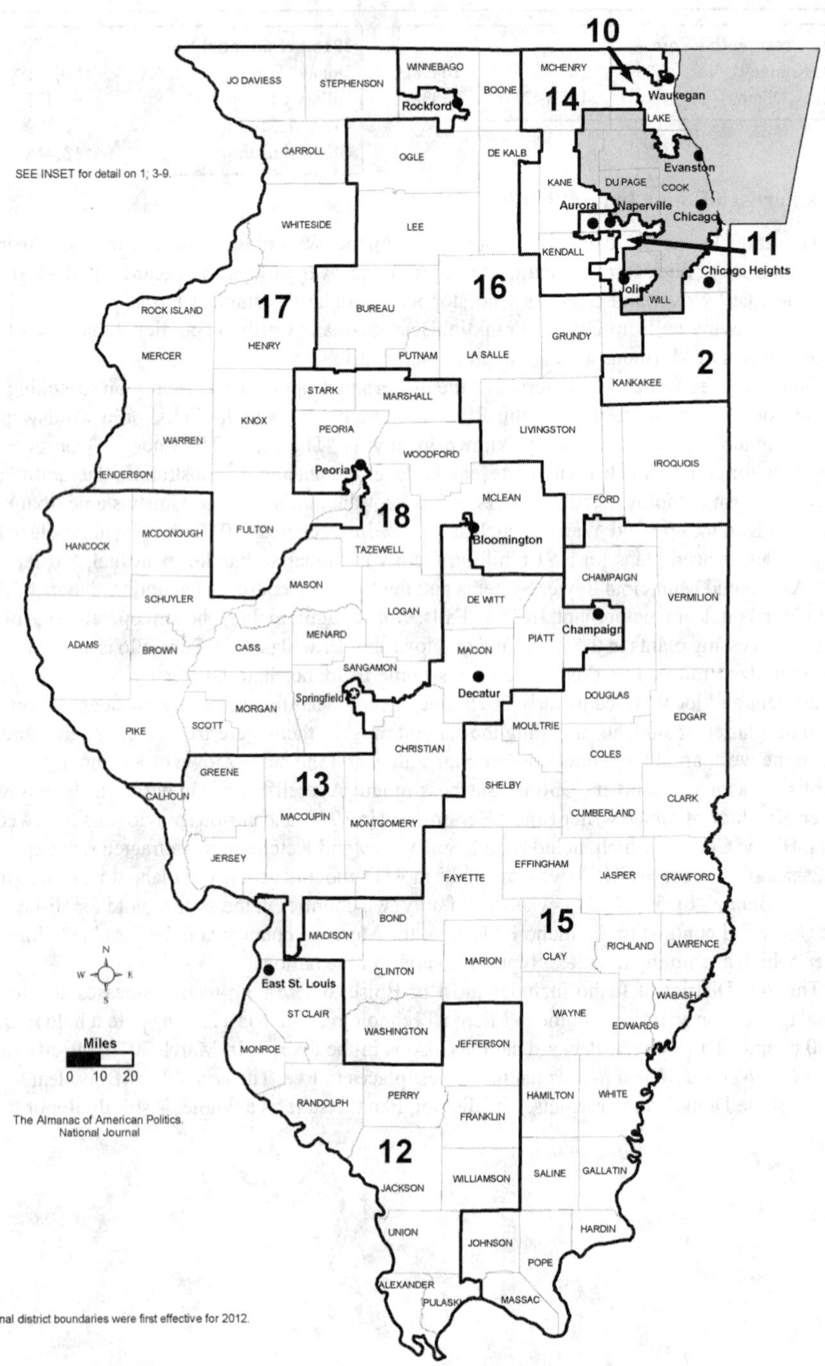
10
14
11
2
16
17
18
13
15
12
JO DAVIESS
STEPHENSON
WINNEBAGO
BOONE
MCHENRY
Rockford
Waukegan
LAKE
CARROLL
OGLE
DE KALB
SEE INSET for detail on 1; 3-9.
KANE
DU PAGE
Evanston
COOK
Aurora
Naperville
Chicago
WHITESIDE
LEE
KENDALL
Chicago Heights
Joliet
WILL
ROCK ISLAND
BUREAU
HENRY
GRUNDY
MERCER
PUTNAM
LA SALLE
KANKAKEE
STARK
MARSHALL
KNOX
PEORIA
LIVINGSTON
WARREN
WOODFORD
IROQUOIS
Peoria
HENDERSON
MCLEAN
FORD
MCDONOUGH
FULTON
Bloomington
HANCOCK
TAZEWELL
CHAMPAIGN
MASON
SCHUYLER
DE WITT
VERMILION
LOGAN
Champaign
MENARD
PIATT
ADAMS
BROWN
CASS
MACON
SANGAMON
Decatur
Springfield
DOUGLAS
MORGAN
EDGAR
PIKE
SCOTT
MOULTRIE
CHRISTIAN
COLES
GREENE
SHELBY
CALHOUN
CLARK
MACOUPIN
CUMBERLAND
MONTGOMERY
JERSEY
EFFINGHAM
JASPER
FAYETTE
CRAWFORD
BOND
MADISON
RICHLAND
LAWRENCE
CLAY
MARION
N
W
E
S
CLINTON
East St. Louis
WABASH
ST CLAIR
WAYNE
EDWARDS
WASHINGTON
Miles
JEFFERSON
MONROE
0 10 20
PERRY
HAMILTON
WHITE
RANDOLPH
FRANKLIN
The Almanac of American Politics.
National Journal
SALINE
GALLATIN
JACKSON
WILLIAMSON
HARDIN
UNION
JOHNSON
POPE
ALEXANDER
PULASKI
MASSAC
Congressional district boundaries were first effective for 2012.

Illinois and the giant city that dominates it, Chicago, have been experiencing the best and the worst of times. On Election Night 2008, a million people thronged to Chicago's lakefront Grant Park to cheer Barack Obama, one of their own. Then, only a month later, the public had a chance to listen to recordings of Gov. Rod Blagojevich demanding recompense for nominating Obama's successor as senator, for which he would be impeached and removed from office, and later convicted and imprisoned. In 2015, amid a budget stalemate between a Republican governor and a Democratic legislature that left programs unfunded for months, Illinois had the lowest credit rating of any state, and Chicago securities were given junk bond status. Chicago's deadly crime wave surged in 2016, as the city saw more murders than New York and Los Angeles combined. A parade of Illinois political notables followed Blagojevich's lead into ethical and legal ignominy, and even native daughter Hillary Clinton lost the presidential race in stunning fashion. The only reason for cheer, it seemed, came that fall, when the Chicago Cubs won their first World Series in more than a century, prompting an estimated 5 million people – half the population of metropolitan Chicago – to attend a celebratory parade.

Illinois has come a long way since May 1860, when Abraham Lincoln was nominated at the Republican National Convention in the 10,000-seat Wigwam convention center in Chicago, less than a mile from Grant Park. That year, Chicago was the nation's ninth largest city, with 112,000 people. Over the next three decades, it grew so rapidly that it became the country's second largest city, with 1.4 million people by the time it hosted the Columbian Exposition in 1893. "Make no little plans," Chicago architect Daniel Burnham exhorted. And the city made enormous plans, building grand parks on the lakefront, erecting America's first downtown of skyscrapers, lining its boulevards with retail palaces, creating a great university from scratch on the Exposition's Midway Plaisance and housing union agitators as well as corporate leaders. Chicago started with the advantage of a great location, where the Great Lakes meet the prairies of the vast Mississippi Valley, and the city's entrepreneurs made it the hub of the nation's railroad network and the center of trade in lumber, grain and meat. Today, Chicago is the nation's third-largest metropolis, a creative, world-class city, the center of a metropolitan area of 9.5 million people with highly educated workers, top-flight universities and ample private capital. In commerce, Chicago has been a prime producer and processor of food products, a major manufacturing center and the strongest service economy between the coasts. In finance, it is the home of the world's greatest commodities exchanges and futures markets. It is a crucial center for rail traffic, and O'Hare International Airport, promoted and nurtured for half a century by both Mayors Richard Daley - father and son served for 43 of the 56 years from 1955 to 2011 - is one of the world's great hubs of commerce.

But job growth in Illinois has trailed the nation's over the past decade, and the state was hit harder by – and recovered more slowly from – the Great Recession than its rivals. The unemployment rate peaked at 11.2 percent, and by December 2016, it was still 5.7 percent, a full point above the national rate. While statewide median income is 7 percent higher than the national average, manufacturing has declined; while some factory sites have been gracefully gentrified, others lay fallow and underused. The state has long experienced fiscal problems, driven by high (and often regressive) taxes, high spending and heavy pension burdens, often worsened by a habit of covering annual budget shortfalls with asset sales and other one-time revenue gimmicks. The fiscal picture reached a nadir after Republican Bruce Rauner won the governorship in 2014 and battled the Democratic legislature in seemingly endless trench warfare that left bills unpaid and optimism elusive. "Illinois' business climate outshines its regional rivals," Moody's Analytics wrote in a study for a state agency in 2017, "but the state's shaky finances have some firms questioning whether they want to expand in the state or elsewhere."

Waves of immigrants moved to Chicago - first Irish and German, then Polish, Italian and Jewish in the Ellis Island years. Then, during the mid-20th century, Chicago became a mecca for African-Americans – a primary destination for the migration of millions of black Americans leaving the rural south for the urban north. The shift in population was sweeping: Journalist Nicholas Lemann was moved to write his landmark book about the migration, *The Promised Land*, after hearing an announcement on a Chicago radio station about a reunion being held locally for a predominantly black high school class from Canton Mississippi. There was no point in holding the reunion in Mississippi; after graduating in 1955, virtually everyone had come north. Later, Chicago attracted hundreds of thousands of Hispanics. A microcosm of that change can be seen in the Chicago neighborhood of Pilsen, also known as the "Heart of Chicago," where Germans and Irish migrated in the 1860s and 1870s, followed later by Poles and Czechs. Bodegas and Mexican bakeries now line its lively commercial center along 18th Street reflecting the influx of Mexicans, and more recently, Guatemalans and Salvadorans. Today, Cook County (Chicago) is 24 percent African American, 25 percent Hispanic and 7 percent Asian. The state as a whole is 15 percent black, 17 percent Hispanic and 6 percent Asian, ranking it among the top 10 states for the percentage of Hispanic and Asian residents. Projections show that a majority of children in Illinois will be minority or mixed-race by 2020. But the state saw a net loss in residents between 2010 and 2016. Most of the decline has come from outside the Chicago metropolitan area, but even the growth rates within Chicagoland during that period have been modest, mostly below 2 percent, depending on the county.

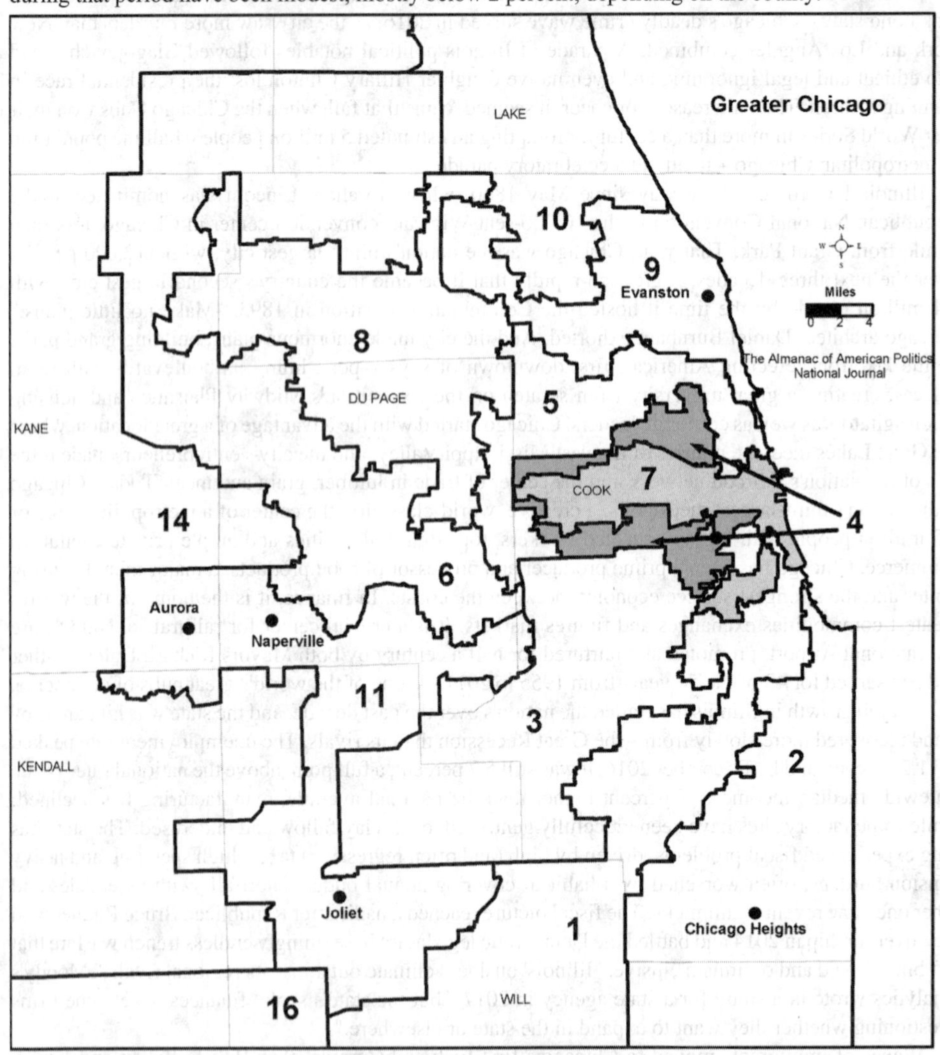

Congressional district boundaries were first effective for 2012.
Districts 4 and 7 are highlighted for visibility.

Chicago has struggled with revenue shortfalls, insolvent pensions, recalcitrant public employee unions and an underperforming school system. Chicago's biggest problem in recent years has been a spiral of gun violence. In 2016, the city had 762 homicides, the most in two decades, as well as 3,550 shootings -- an increase of more than 1,000 over the previous year. The number of guns recovered by police rose by 20 percent in the span of just one year. The violence was most heavily concentrated in five of Chicago's 22 police districts – heavily black, low-income neighborhoods with a significant gang presence – and it did not help that distrust between the police and residents was at a low ebb following the November 2015 release of video showing Laquan McDonald, a 17-year-old African American, being shot 16 times by a white police officer. Protests ensued, and Chicago Police Superintendent Garry McCarthy lost his job. It also led the U.S. Department of Justice to issue a report on the history of excessive use of force by the Chicago police – including its acceptance by senior officials. While Democratic Mayor Rahm Emanuel took steps to ease the crisis and improve prospects within the affected neighborhoods, the rise in crime came to define the city nationally. As president, Donald Trump seized on Chicago as a poster child for his (not always accurate) claims that homicides were soaring nationally. "If Mayor can't do it he must ask for Federal help!" Trump tweeted.

Obama and Emanuel are just the most recent political giants to come from Illinois; the list includes Charles Dawes, Calvin Coolidge's vice president; Chicago lawyer Harold Ickes, a Bull Moose Republican who was Franklin Roosevelt's Interior secretary; Republican House Speaker Joseph Cannon and Senate Minority Leader Everett Dirksen; governor and two-time Democratic presidential nominee Adlai Stevenson; House Ways and Means Chairman Dan Rostenkowski; and perhaps biggest of all, Richard J. Daley, the mayor of Chicago from 1955 to 1976 and a player in national politics. His eldest son, Richard M. Daley, was elected mayor in 1989 and was popular with the city's business elite, ethnic whites and affluent suburbanites (who were not so fond of his father), while also keeping good ties to blacks and Hispanics. The younger Daley was able to forge the kind of consensus politics under the Democratic banner that Obama was able to capitalize on while running for the Senate in 2004 and for president in 2008.

But Illinois political history is rife with machine politics and cronyism. Even Lincoln was no stranger to the Republican machine of his day, which rallied thousands of partisans to cheer him at his debates with Stephen Douglas in 1858 and packed the Wigwam convention hall for him in 1860. Machine politics continued in the 20th century, as politicians in a closely divided state competed for public jobs and as politicians of both parties courted the immigrants streaming into Chicago. "We do not have a few 'rotten apples'," wrote former Chicago alderman Dick Simpson and freelance writer Thomas J. Gradel in the book *Corrupt Illinois*. "We have a rotten apple barrel and a pervasive culture of corruption." With four Illinois governors in the past 50 years having gone to the pokey (including Blagojevich, who's due to be released in 2024), it's hard to argue with them. The ethical swamp has recently extended beyond Cook County: Former Republican House Speaker Dennis Hastert was sentenced to 15 months in a blackmail case that revealed his past sexual abuse of young boys as a wrestling coach, and Republican Aaron Schock from Peoria was forced from the House and indicted on federal charges after remodeling his congressional office as if it were Downton Abbey. The nonchalant attitude in Illinois towards politicians' self-dealing hasn't made lawmakers in Springfield any more diligent in handling the state's purse strings.

Politically, Illinois emerged from the Civil War as a solidly Republican state, with fast-growing Chicago and the northern counties settled by Yankees decisively outvoting the Southern folk from Springfield south to Cairo, which is closer to Mississippi than to Chicago. During the Depression, Chicago became reliably Democratic. In the decades that followed, the suburbs, wary of Chicago, became Republican (and developed machines of their own). But the 2016 election showed how the state's politics are changing. A moderate Republican from the Chicago suburbs, Mark Kirk, was unable to keep Democrat Tammy Duckworth from flipping his Senate seat – one of the two Democratic Senate pickups in that election. In the presidential race, Clinton improved upon Obama's 2012 showing, thanks to a sharp move toward Clinton in Chicagoland, mirroring what happened in urban areas nationally. Clinton's vote haul in Cook County rose by 8 percent over Obama's in 2012, and by 11 percent in the city's five "collar" counties. Trump, as he did elsewhere nationally, ran strongly in rural areas; the GOP's vote margin outside of Cook and the collar counties was almost three times higher in 2016 than 2012, and Clinton's vote total in those areas cratered by 14 percent compared with Obama's. Of the six northernmost counties along the Mississippi River, only Rock Island County voted Democratic in both 2012 and 2016. Among the other previously Democratic river counties, the margin in Whiteside County shifted 23 percentage points toward Trump, Mercer County shifted by 27 points toward Trump, and Henderson County shifted by 40 points toward Trump. Further south along the river, Cairo's Alexander County also flipped from blue to red, shifting 22 points toward Trump. Still, the vote shifts in these counties were outweighed by those in Chicagoland. The percentage margin in Cook County shifted four points toward Clinton, and in four of the five collar counties (DuPage, Lake, Will and Kane), the margin shifted by as much as 13 points in her direction. Only one collar county, McHenry, was red in both elections. All told, 75 percent of the Democratic presidential votes in 2016 came from Cook and the collar counties, up from 71 percent four years earlier – a trend line that seems likely to continue.

Population		Race and Ethnicity		Income	
Total	12,873,761	White	62.5%	Median Income	$57,574 (17 out of 50)
Land area	55,519	Black	14.1%	Under $50,000	43.8%
Pop/ sq mi	231.9	Latino	16.5%	$50,000-$99,999	30.5%
Born in state	67.1%	Asian	5.0%	$100,000-$199,999	19.8%
		Two races	1.7%	$200,000 or more	5.8%
Age Groups		Other	0.2%	Poverty Rate	14.3%
Under 18	23.5%				
18-34	23.5%	**Education**		**Health Insurance**	
35-64	39.5%	H.S grad or less	38.8%	With health insurance coverage	89.0%
Over 64	13.5%	Some college	28.8%		
		College Degree, 4 yr	19.9%		
Work		Post grad	12.4%	**Public Assistance**	
White Collar	36.8%			Cash public assistance income	2.5%
Sales and Service	41.9%	**Military**			
Blue Collar	21.2%	Veteran	6.8%		
Government	12.4%	Active Duty	0.2%	Food stamp/SNAP benefits	13.1%

Voter Turnout			
2015 Total Citizens 18+	8,979,999	2016 Pres Turnout as % CVAP	62%
2016 Pres Votes	5,536,424	2012 Pres Turnout as % CVAP	60%

Legislature	
Senate:	37D, 22R
House:	67D, 51R

Presidential Politics

2016 Democratic Primary		
Hillary Clinton (D)	1,039,555	(51%)
Bernie Sanders (D)	999,494	(49%)
2016 Republican Primary		
Donald Trump (R)	562,464	(39%)
Ted Cruz (R)	438,235	(30%)
John Kasich (R)	286,118	(20%)
Marco Rubio (R)	126,681	(9%)

2016 Presidential Vote		
Hillary Clinton (D)	3,090,729	(55%)
Donald Trump (R)	2,146,015	(38%)
Gary Johnson (L)	209,596	(4%)
2012 Presidential Vote		
Barack Obama (D)	3,019,512	(58%)
Mitt Romney (R)	2,135,216	(41%)

For a century, Illinois was a political bellwether, voting only twice for losing presidential candidates between 1896 and 1996 - in 1916 and 1976, when it went Republican while the nation went Democratic. It picked the winner even when native son Adlai Stevenson was the nominee against Dwight Eisenhower in 1952 and 1956. But starting in the 1990s, Illinois has become significantly more Democratic than the nation. It voted 55 percent for Al Gore and John Kerry in 2000 and 2004 and gave home-stater Barack Obama 62 percent in 2008 and 58 percent in 2012. Hillary Clinton, who was born in Chicago, saw the Democratic number dip in 2016 when she defeated Donald Trump, 56%-39%. But at the same time, the Democratic margin of victory over the Republican nominee actually increased two-tenths of a percentage point over 2012, as the GOP vote in the Chicago collar counties of DuPage, Kane and Lake fell off. That mirrored a national trend where suburban counties of major metropolitan areas leaned more Democratic in 2016. Cook County, home to Chicago and 41 percent of the state's population, was very good to Clinton: more than half of her 2.9 million votes statewide came from the city and its close-in suburban townships. But on the other side of the state, rural counties in the upper Mississippi River basin that had traditionally voted Democratic, sided with Trump. In 2012, 10 such counties backed Obama. In 2016, only Rock Island remained in the Democratic column. Knox County, home to Galesburg, an old railroad center, went from voting for Obama 58%-41% in 2012 to 48-45% for Trump. Despite the state being colored blue on Election Night, the Republican nominee captured 91 of its 102 counties.

The Illinois primary was once a pivotal moment in presidential nominating contests. But as more states have moved their primaries to earlier dates, Illinois has not played a key role in deciding a nomination. That changed in 2016, when the state gave important boosts to both of the major parties' eventual standard-bearers. The Democratic contest was particularly close: Clinton edged out Vermont Sen. Bernie Sanders 51%-49%. Cook County and Chicago delivered again for Clinton, giving her more than 60 percent of her statewide primary total. She had the backing of Chicago Democratic ward bosses who passed out palm cards with Clinton's name on it in the run-up to the primary. Sanders carried all of Chicago's collar counties (except for Lake) and most of rural Illinois, where there are considerably fewer Democratic votes. The Vermonter unsuccessfully tried to tie Clinton to unpopular Chicago Mayor Rahm Emanuel, a former White House aide to Bill Clinton. After suffering an upset loss in the Michigan primary one week earlier, it was vital for Clinton to shut down Sanders' momentum in the industrial Midwest. On the Republican side, Trump defeated Texas Sen. Ted Cruz 39%-30%. Ohio Gov. John Kasich finished third with 20 percent and came in second in Cook County. But he failed to win over enough Republicans in the Chicago suburbs and exurbs, which signaled that his candidacy was unlikely to gain traction. While the GOP turnout in the five suburban collar counties was up by some 135,000 votes over 2012 levels, it exceeded Democratic turnout only by about 27,000. In Lake and Will counties, more voters participated in the Democratic primary than the Republican contest.

Congressional Districts

115th Congress Lineup	7R 11D	**114th Congress Lineup**	8R 10D

Illinois, with its sluggish population growth, lost its 19th seat in the 2010 census; its peak was 27 seats in the 1930s. For 2022, it almost certainly will drop to 17 and perhaps to 16.

In 2011, Democrats controlled the Illinois legislature and governor's office, awarding them their only free hand in the country to give a large state's existing map a total makeover. Under heavy pressure from party leaders desperate to offset Republican gains in other states, Democrats released a map designed to eliminate up to six Republican seats. The state's Republican delegation immediately issued a joint statement calling it "little more than an attempt to undo the results of the elections held just six months ago," and they were largely right.

Illinois Republicans sued to block the map in federal court, alleging Democrats had failed to draw an additional Latino majority seat in Chicago. Democrats mocked Republicans' sudden interest in Latino representation and pointed out that minority-rights groups such as MALDEF had not objected to keeping Chicago's two disparate Latino communities together in the earmuff-shaped 4th District. In December 2011, a three-judge panel upheld the congressional map. In the 2012 election, Democrats swept four of five targets for a 12-6 edge from what had been 11-8 Republican control. Their strategy largely paid off and generated a rare triumph in an otherwise wrenching redistricting year for the party.

But their over-reach backfired when 2014 became a Republican year - in Illinois and across the nation. Their redistricting shifts did not prove strong enough in the "swing" 10th District on Chicago's North Shore and in the long-time Democratic 12th District in the southern part of the state. That narrowed Democratic control of the delegation to 10-8. The 10th swung back to the Democrats in 2016 and it appeared increasingly out of reach for Republicans. Only one of the delegation's Democrats was from downstate.

The next redistricting cycle raises potential alarms for Democrats. If Republican Gov. Bruce Rauner is reelected in 2018, his leverage could restore the kind of bipartisan deal-making that was familiar in past redistricting. With population figures indicating that the 11 districts in Chicagoland will downsize by at least one, the fact that Democrats now control 10 of those seats would pose problems for them. Their biggest challenge may be to preserve the three African-Americans currently in the delegation (two of whom are in their 70s), given that it's unlikely that there will be enough black voters to support three districts on the south and west sides that have stretched farther into the suburbs. If the state loses a second seat following the 2020 census, that could pose risk for a downstate Republican.

Governor

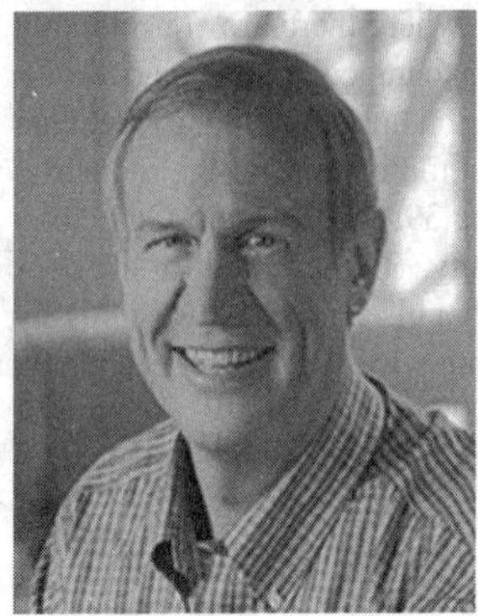

Bruce Rauner (R)

Elected 2014, term expires 2019, 1st term; b. Feb. 18, 1957, Chicago, IL; Dartmouth B.A.; Harvard U., MBA; Episcopalian; Married (Diana); 6 children (3 from previous marriage).

Professional Career: Partner, Golder, Thomas, Cressey (GTCR), 1981-2012; Philanthropist, New Schools for Chicago; Chairman, Chicago Public Education Fund; the Noble Network of Charter Schools; Chicago Communities in Schools; the ACT Charter School.

Office: 207 State House, Springfield, 62706; 217-782-0244; Fax: 217-524-4049; Website: illinois.gov/gov.

Election Results

Election	Name (Party)	Vote (%)
2014 General	Bruce Rauner (R)	1,823,627 (50%)
	Pat Quinn (D)	1,681,343 (46%)
	Chad Grimm (L)	121,534 (3%)
2014 Primary	Bruce Rauner (R)	328,934 (40%)
	Kirk Dillard (R)	305,120 (37%)
	Bill Brady (R)	123,708 (15%)
	Dan Rutherford (R)	61,948 (8%)

Republican Bruce Rauner is a man – a very wealthy one -- taking on a machine. The first-time candidate for elective office captured the Illinois governorship in 2014 running on a platform of economic reform and challenging what he deemed the hidebound political culture of the state dominated by Chicago Democrats. But the irresistible force met the immovable object in the person of Democratic House Speaker Mike Madigan, an old-style machine pol who has survived six governors with his immense powers intact. As the old saying goes, a lot of grass has gotten trampled in the process – specifically, a budget impasse longer than anything seen in the United States in the better part of a century.

Rauner was born in Chicago and grew up in the suburb of Deerfield. He graduated from Dartmouth College with a degree in economics, and got his M.B.A. from Harvard University. After leaving Harvard, Rauner went to work for the private-equity firm now called GTCR, rising to the post of chairman. He left in 2012 to open a self-financed venture-capital firm, R8 Capital Partners. In so doing, he amassed a fortune, much of it from managing public employee pension funds. He has been active in educational issues and chaired the education panel of the Civic Committee of the Commercial Club of Chicago. He backed nonunion charter schools and favored merit pay for principals in Chicago. In the late 1990s, Rauner suggested that future Democratic Chicago Mayor Rahm Emanuel become an investment banker and subsequently hired him on a deal to help GTCR make an acquisition. Emanuel and his family vacationed at Rauner's exclusive ranch in Montana where the two went fly-fishing. (Becoming governor and mayor has tested the relationship.)

Rauner sunk $6 million of his own money - a record for an Illinois governor's race - to secure the GOP nomination in a four-way primary in which his main opposition was Kirk Dillard, a veteran GOP state senator from a suburban Chicago district. Dillard took several not-so-veiled shots at his opponent's wealth and inexperience, saying no one "should be able to buy a political office," and he got some support from labor, but Rauner defeated him 40%-37%. In the general election campaign, Rauner and incumbent Democrat Pat Quinn engaged in a brutal, multi-million dollar air war, with Quinn casting Rauner as a Scrooge who would cut education and other services to pay for tax cuts. In turn, Rauner painted Quinn as having governed "one of the worst-run states in America." Rauner cast himself as a regular Joe with an $18 watch and a 20-year-old Volkswagen bus who would bring his business experience to Springfield, though it came out during the campaign that he belonged to a wine club that charges a $140,000 initiation fee. In any case, that wealth came in handy: The tens of millions that he spent from his own pocket and the millions more he raised helped him defeat Quinn, 50%-46%, becoming the first Republican to win the state's governorship since 1998. As a candidate, Rauner challenged the bedrock belief of many GOP strategists that elections are won by mobilizing the conservative base of the party. He spent many hours campaigning in neighborhoods on Chicago's South Side, wooing the support of black voters and winning some endorsements from black business leaders and prominent pastors. That actually didn't help him attract many extra African-American votes, but it may have helped reassure the kinds of white, suburban swing voters that hard-edged GOP candidates can turn off. Rauner out-performed the losing GOP candidate from four years earlier -- Republican Bill Brady -- by five percentage points in suburban Cook County and seven points in the five collar counties: Lake, McHenry, Kane, DuPage and Will.

In his inaugural address, Rauner took dead aim at the state's political culture. "To the people of Illinois, and the people outside our state who have been reluctant to invest in Illinois because of the insider deals and cronyism," Rauner vowed, "I say this; I'm nobody that nobody sent, and I've come to work for you." (It was a clever play off the famous political phrase uttered by a Chicago Ward boss, "We don't want nobody that nobody sent," to a young Abner Mikva - later a Chicago-area congressman and federal judge - who had just moved to the city and wanted to volunteer in the 1948 campaign.) Thus began a long-running battle between Rauner and Madigan, a protégé of the late Chicago Mayor Richard J. Daley, as well as the state Democratic Party chair, a committeeman for Chicago's 13th Ward, and the longest-serving speaker in any state in two centuries.

Rauner introduced a "turnaround agenda" that included sweeping spending cuts in safety net programs, government worker pensions, state universities and aid to mass transit. Madigan called the plan "reckless" and Emanuel called his proposed cut to the Chicago Transit Authority "bad economics." Rauner, with a political action committee he controls, launched an unprecedented TV ad campaign attacking Madigan by name and accusing him -- "and the politicians he controls" -- of blocking spending cuts and economic reforms in favor of tax increases. The ad blitz wasn't designed to defeat Madigan at the polls: he and his fellow Democrat John Cullerton, the state Senate President, are secure in their Chicago fiefdoms. But the ads were designed to arouse enough public sentiment in the state to force an insular Democratic legislature in Springfield to bend to his will. "To see more people employed at high pay, we need to stop crushing employers. To create good jobs, we need more job creators," Rauner said in his 2016 state of the state address. But Madigan and Cullerton had the votes to block the Rauner initiatives they opposed, including local property tax freezes, legislative term limits, independent redistricting, tort reform and a workers' compensation overhaul. A rare bright spot for Rauner was a 9.1 percent decrease in the inmate population, but his efforts at criminal justice reform were overshadowed by the surge of murders and shootings in Chicago.

The biggest battle was over the budget – or more precisely, the lack of one. For some 18 months, a standoff between Rauner and the Democratic legislature turned Illinois into a fiscal laughingstock, unable to pay its bills and slapped with near-junk-level credit ratings. It took until mid-2016 for the two sides to cut a deal for a six-month stopgap plan that would enable schools, universities and social services to continue, but which did little to pay down a backlog headed past $12 billion or to solve the state's $130 billion-plus unfunded pension liability. "This is not a solution to our long-term challenges," Rauner told reporters. "This is a bridge to reform." During the 2016 campaign, Rauner once again dipped into his personal fortune to try to mold a more amenable legislature. However, his investment of $50 million produced gains of only four seats in Madigan's House and two seats in Cullerton's Senate. As the interim budget expired at the end of 2016, the two sides remained far apart, although existing statutes and court orders were poised to keep large swaths of state spending on autopilot. (Higher education and social services were exceptions.) As his own reelection approached, Rauner had approval ratings as low as the 30s – one of the worst for any governor in the nation. Rauner gave his campaign $50 million in anticipation of possible challenges by a raft of Democratic hopefuls, including Chris Kennedy, a son of Robert F. Kennedy; billionaire businessman J.B. Pritzker; and possibly others. The contest was sure to become a major battle – and an expensive one.

Senior Senator

Dick Durbin (D)

Elected 1996, term expires 2020, 4th term; b. Nov 21, 1944, East St. Louis; Georgetown University (DC), B.S.; Georgetown University Law Center (DC), J.D.; Roman Catholic; Married (Loretta Schaefer Durbin); 3 children (1 deceased); 3 grandchildren.

Elected Office: U.S. House, 1983-1997.

Professional Career: Staff, Lt. Gov. Paul Simon, 1969-1972; Legal counsel, IL Sen. Judiciary Committee, 1972-1982; Professor, S. IL School of Med., 1978-1982.

DC Office: 711 HSOB 20510, 202-224-2152, Fax: 202-228-0400, durbin.senate.gov.

State Offices: Carbondale, 618-351-1122; Chicago, 312-353-4952; Rock Island, 309-786-5173; Springfield, 217-492-4062.

Committees: Senate Minority Whip. *Appropriations*: Department of Defense (RMM), DOL, HHS & Education & Related Agencies, Energy & Water Development, Financial Services & General Government, State, Foreign Operations & Related Programs, Transportation, HUD & Related Agencies. *Judiciary*: Border Security & Immigration (RMM), Constitution, Crime & Terrorism. *Rules & Administration*.

Group Ratings

	ADA	ACLU	AFL-CIO	LCV	ITI	COC	HAFA	ACU	CFG	FRC
2016	-	88%	-	100%	80%	25%	5%	0%	0%	0%
2015	100%	C	92%	100%	C	43%	C	0%	2%	0%

Almanac Ratings 2015

	Economy	Social	Foreign	Composite
Liberal	100%	100%	96%	99%
Conservative	0%	0%	4%	1%

Key Votes of the 114th Congress

1. Keystone pipeline	N	5. National Security Data	Y	9. Gun Sales Checks	Y
2. Export-Import Bank	N	6. Iran Nuclear Deal	N	10. Sanctuary Cities	N
3. Debt Ceiling Increase	Y	7. Puerto Rico Debt	Y	11. Planned Parenthood	N
4. Homeland Security $$	Y	8. Loretta Lynch A.G	Y	12. Trade deals	N

Election Results

Election	Name (Party)	Vote (%)		Cand. Spent	Ind. Exp. Support	Ind. Exp. Oppose
2014 General	Dick Durbin (D)	1,929,637	(54%)	$12,614,224	$22,998	$717,746
	Jim Oberweis (R)	1,538,522	(43%)	$2,416,926	$5,353	$690,250
	Sharon Hansen (L)	135,316	(4%)	$2,367		
2014 Primary	Dick Durbin (D)	Unopposed				

Prior winning percentages: 2008 (68%), 2002 (60%), 1996 (54%); House: 1994 (55%), 1992 (57%),1990 (66%), 1988 (69%), 1986 (68%), 1984 (61%), 1982 (50%

For more than two decades, Richard Durbin -- Illinois' senior senator and the second ranking member of the Senate Democratic leadership -- was the weekday roommate of the man who now sits atop that hierarchy: New York Sen. Charles Schumer. And, for the latter half of the period that the two lived under the same roof, they were also rivals. Beginning when they served in the House of Representatives, Durbin and Schumer were tenants in the Capitol Hill townhouse of former California Rep. George Miller, who sold the residence in late 2014 upon his retirement (but not before it inspired a satirical TV sitcom, *Alpha House)*. The living arrangement did not change when Durbin and Schumer won election to the Senate in the late 1990s, and it remained in place a decade later, when both were elevated to the top rungs of Senate leadership. And that's when the real-life version of *Alpha House* acquired an element of melodrama.

In 2010, Senate Democratic Leader Harry Reid barely survived a re-election bid in his home state of Nevada, sparking persistent chatter among congressional insiders about an eventual Durbin vs. Schumer competition to succeed him as leader -- and, by all accounts, creating strains in what had been a close friendship between the two roommates. In late March 2015, Reid opted to retire rather than seek a sixth term the following year -- but not before endorsing the hard-charging Schumer over the more diplomatic Durbin as his successor. What immediately followed Reid's decision was a late-night conversation on the Senate floor between Durbin and Schumer, whose week-day living arrangement had ended just months earlier. Seeking to put an end to years of behind-the-scenes jockeying, Durbin-according to an account he gave the *Washington Post*-told Schumer, "We've had a lot of good times together. We've had some differences, but I think you've earned this." In response, Schumer is reported to have wept. But what was-or wasn't said-next conspired to keep the Durbin-Schumer plot line going.

Durbin contended that, during their conversation, Schumer agreed to support Durbin staying on as whip. Schumer and his aides denied that any such deals were made. It led to 18 more months of maneuvering, ultimately yielding as happy an ending as Durbin could have hoped for under the circumstances: He was re-elected unchallenged in November 2016 as Democratic whip, a post that he had occupied for a dozen years. But, along the way, there were additional tensions in the already frayed Schumer-Durbin relationship: Schumer, as the incoming party leader, remained silent about his choice for the whip's job, while another veteran Democrat, Sen. Patty Murray of Washington state, for months declined to rule out a challenge to Durbin. Meanwhile, Durbin flirted with the idea of running for governor in 2018, a move that could have brought him back to Springfield -- where he had begun his professional career nearly a half-century earlier.

Durbin grew up in modest circumstances in East St. Louis, the youngest of three brothers. His father, a railroad night watchman, died of lung cancer when Durbin was 14-an event that later prompted him to push for what became one of his signature legislative achievements. He graduated from Georgetown University and its law school while working as an intern for Illinois Democratic Sen. Paul Douglas, who held the seat that Durbin now occupies. Durbin returned to Illinois to join Democrat Paul Simon's staff when Simon was the lieutenant governor from 1969-73. He was a state Senate staff member in Springfield for much of the 1970s, serving for a time as that chamber's parliamentarian-valuable early training for someone who later gained a reputation for expertise in Senate procedures. Durbin lost a race for a state Senate in 1976, and in 1978 was the lieutenant gubernatorial nominee on a losing ticket. But in 1982, he won the nomination to oppose Republican Rep. Paul Findley, who then was among the few members of Congress to criticize Israel publicly and call for a more even-handed policy towards the Palestinians. Durbin had no trouble raising money from well-heeled Israel supporters, and narrowly ousted Findley from the central Illinois district.

In the House, Durbin won a seat on the Appropriations Committee, eventually becoming a member of Capitol Hill's version of the "college of cardinals"-the powerful chairmen of that panel's subcommittees. In 1993, Durbin took over the subcommittee with jurisdiction over agriculture programs as well as the Food and Drug Administration. Years later, in the Senate, he was able to enact major reforms in FDA's food safety inspection powers-but his centerpiece legislative accomplishment in the House was the ban on smoking on domestic airline flights, enacted in 1988. It was an effort inspired by the death of his chain-smoking father. At the time the law was passed, Durbin said he had no idea of the kind of the societal impact it would have. "I didn't realize that would make a difference in terms of whether you could smoke on a train, on a bus, in a building, in a restaurant, in a hospital," he said in a 2015 interview. He followed by pushing to limit tobacco subsidies and to give the FDA authority to regulate tobacco as a health hazard-both accomplished after years of effort.

Finding himself in the minority party in the House following the 1994 election, Durbin announced he would seek the Senate seat being relinquished in 1996 by Simon, his former boss and mentor. Durbin defeated former state treasurer (and future governor) Pat Quinn by better than 2-1 in the primary, and comfortably won the general election with 56 percent. He has not been seriously challenged since: He won re-election in 2002 and 2008 by 60 percent or more, and while held to 54 percent during a difficult year for Democrats in 2014, still defeated Republican businessman Jim Oberweis by a double-digit margin.

Durbin has compiled a voting record that places him solidly in the ranks of the Senate's left wing: In 2015, the *Almanac*'s annual vote rankings put him in a tie for the third most liberal score among Democrats. "He's able to pull off the style of sounding like a moderate or compromiser when he often doesn't act like one," University of Illinois political scientist Brian Gaines said. During negotiations on taxes and spending aimed at averting the so-called fiscal cliff in late 2012, Durbin did exhort Democrats to support a deal that included cuts to entitlement programs. "My liberal friends who say don't touch it (Medicare), they're crazy," Durbin said at the time. Earlier, he served on the bipartisan Simpson-Bowles deficit reduction commission that recommended raising the Medicare eligibility age, and was later part of an informal bipartisan group of senators -- the so-called "Gang of Six" -- that sought unsuccessfully to reach agreement on long-term deficit reduction in 2011.

More recently, Durbin has been part of a bipartisan push for criminal justice reform, using his seat on the Judiciary Committee to team up with the panel's Republican chairman, Charles Grassley of Iowa, on the issue. Their initiative fell short in 2016, but the Durbin and Grassley vowed to try again. On social issues, Durbin has been a death penalty supporter, and, while in the House, favored restrictions on abortion. But Durbin, a Catholic, has opposed most legislation to restrict abortion since coming to the Senate. In 2004, the priest at his home church in Springfield said he wouldn't give Durbin communion as a consequence of his position. Durbin responded by telling a local newspaper: "Is that all this church is about, is one issue? For bishops to announce that they are going to penalize Catholics on certain votes I think is …reaching too far."

Following the 2004 defeat of South Dakota Sen. Tom Daschle, Reid was elevated to succeed Daschle as minority leader. Durbin, named assistant floor leader by Daschle in 2001, moved quickly to secure election to Reid's old job as minority whip. He won by acclamation after one potential opponent counted heads and decided not to challenge him. Durbin's election as whip was but one significant development for him arising out of the 2004 election: He acquired a new junior colleague from Illinois, a former state senator named Barack Obama. In an institution of sizable egos, many senators have tense relationships with home-state colleagues-particularly when the two belong to the same party. It was little secret that Schumer was unhappy at the spotlight continually afforded his junior New York colleague, Hillary Clinton, during her Senate tenure. But Durbin enjoyed a warm relationship with Obama. Rather than chafing at Obama's quick rise and celebrity, Durbin in 2006 urged him to run for president, and later introduced Obama before the latter's acceptance speech at the 2008 Democratic National Convention in Denver. Durbin did not join Obama at the massive 2008 Election Night celebration in Chicago's Grant Park because his 40-year-old daughter had died three days before, but he again introduced Obama at the 2012 party convention.

Often described as the president's closest friend in the Senate during Obama's eight years in office, Durbin frequently appeared on cable talk shows to defend Obama's major legislative achievement, the 2010 Affordable Care Act, and performed the same task during the bruising 2011 debate over raising the federal debt limit. In 2015, it was left to Durbin to lead the campaign to line up Senate support for the Obama Administration's nuclear agreement with Iran, after Schumer came out against the deal and Reid was slow to embrace it. His efforts helped ensure enough Democratic votes to block a resolution of disapproval pushed by Senate Republicans. Earlier that year, Durbin exhibited his tough-talking side when Obama's nomination of Loretta Lynch for attorney general faced a protracted delay by Senate Republicans. At one point, Durbin charged that Republican leaders were putting Lynch at the "back of the bus," an allusion to civil rights icon Rosa Parks. Arizona Republican Sen. John McCain demanded an apology for what he said was Durbin's effort "to use that imagery and suggest that racist tactics are being employed…" Durbin refused to back down, saying he had thought "long and hard" before making his remarks.

Even before Obama became president and sought to advance immigration reform, Durbin was chief sponsor of the DREAM Act, a bill providing a path to citizenship for children of illegal immigrants provisional on completing college or military service. He went to the floor regularly to highlight the stories of the DREAM Act-eligible children, and praised Obama in June 2012 for issuing an executive order -- Deferred Action for Childhood Arrivals (DACA) -- addressing the issue when it became clear that Congress would not act. As President Donald Trump prepared to take office amid campaign promises to roll back DACA, Durbin joined with GOP Sen. Lindsey Graham of South Carolina on legislation to protect nearly three quarters of a million young immigrants who had previously benefited from that initiative.

There were areas on which Durbin and Obama did not see eye-to-eye, notably trade policy. Despite a strongly pro-union voting record, Durbin split with organized labor early in his congressional career to support the North American Free Trade Agreement and normal trade relations with China during the Clinton Administration. In part, his stance reflected Illinois' status as a major exporter. But in 2006, Durbin said he felt "betrayed" by the results of NAFTA and has opposed more recent trade agreements. In 2015, Durbin joined most Democratic senators in opposing Obama's request that Congress grant him expedited authority to negotiate a major trade agreement with Asia.

In 2011, Obama signed a major food safety bill crafted by Durbin which, among other things, allowed the FDA to initiate a mandatory recall of a food product. Perhaps Durbin's most high-profile legislative achievement of his Senate tenure came a year earlier, as Congress considered the so-called Dodd-Frank law to overhaul the nation's financial regulatory structure. As part of Dodd-Frank, he engineered passage of what is widely referred to as the "Durbin amendment," giving the Federal Reserve authority to reduce the "swipe fees" that banks charge merchants for processing debit card transactions. It made Durbin a scourge of the nation's banking industry, which later mounted an extensive lobbying effort to repeal the Durbin amendment. It failed, but the Federal Reserve reduced the fees by less than expected, leaving the retail industry unhappy. As Trump took office vowing to undo the Dodd-Frank law, the banking industry ramped up its attack on the Durbin amendment.

During a legislative battle over Dodd-Frank that stretched out over more than a year, Durbin often delivered lengthy floor speeches criticizing the nation's leading banks. "…The banks-hard to believe in a time when we're facing a banking crisis that many of the banks created-are still the most powerful lobby on Capitol Hill. And they frankly own the place," Durbin fumed in an interview with an Illinois radio station at the time. At the same time, Durbin has not been hesitant to use his clout as a member of the Appropriations Committee to keep an eye out for another major player in the nation's financial marketplace: the Chicago-based commodities exchanges. He has opposed new fees on the exchanges and in 2008, worked behind the scenes to soften the impact of proposed controls on speculators in the oil futures market as gas prices soared.

It is emblematic of how Durbin has utilized his leadership position to look out vigorously for the interests of his home state. In 2010, when the House crafted a multi-year transportation bill whose modified funding formulas would have cost Illinois almost $120 million. Durbin was credited with heading off it off. In late 2012, Durbin helped prod the Justice Department to assist his financially strapped state by buying a former prison, over objections from Republicans who feared it would be used to house inmates from Guantanamo Bay. In January 2013, Durbin assumed the prized chairmanship of Senate Appropriations' Defense Subcommittee, and became its ranking Democrat two years later. He has used the position to fund production of electronic warfare planes for the Navy manufactured at Boeing's St. Louis plant, just across the Mississippi River from Illinois.

If leading banks are no fan of Durbin's, neither are groups pushing for legal tort reform: They have long accused him of aggressively defending the interests of the nation's trial lawyers, and point to $3.4 million in contributions (according to the Center for Responsive Politics) that Durbin received from lawyers and law firms in his last two bids for re-election. Durbin was particularly active within the Judiciary Committee on such issues during his first decade in the Senate. In 2003, he blocked action on a bill to limit damages in medical malpractice suits. In 2006, he helped defeat a proposal that would have replaced a multitude of lawsuits against the asbestos industry with a $140 billion fund to compensate victims of asbestos exposure. In 2015, Durbin introduced legislation to create an online database in which companies manufacturing and handling asbestos would have to file annual reports to the EPA, while listing publicly accessible locations where products with asbestos had been reported in the past year. A spokesman for the American Tort Reform Association dismissed it as an attempt to increase the number of "phony" asbestos lawsuits.

Durbin became majority whip in 2007 following the Democrats' capture of the Senate majority, and resumed the minority whip role in 2015 when the GOP regained control. Respected among colleagues for his willingness to work hard and an ability to articulate his party's themes in everyday language, Durbin is "one of the most skilled debaters we have," a Senate aide said. Others offer a more mixed assessment of Durbin's strengths. "He's a great guy," one long-time Democratic staffer told *Politico.* "But he thinks with his heart, not his head. He's great at communicating ideas, but not at thinking strategically." At a time when he was working to retain the whip's job, Durbin scored points from colleagues for his deft handling of the head count on the Iran nuclear deal. "That's a hard thing to do," Virginia Sen. Tim Kaine told *Roll Call.* "It hasn't really been a whip operation in the traditional sense because this is a big tough issue and people are going to have different points of view."

For much of 2015 and 2016, Durbin claimed sufficient support to remain whip, as Murray refused to rule out a challenge to him throughout that period. Meanwhile, as some leading Illinois Democrats suggested that Durbin would be the strongest challenger to Republican incumbent Bruce Rauner in 2018, Durbin publicly declined to take that option off the table -- while acknowledging that whether he remained whip would "of course" play a role in his decision. A week after Election Day 2016, Durbin was unanimously re-elected as whip, as Schumer crafted a new job -- assistant Democratic leader -- that allowed Murray to move into the No. 3 slot in the party's leadership. "I kept telling people of Illinois, I've got a pretty important job working in the…Senate in the No. 2 Democratic position," Durbin told the *Chicago Tribune* immediately afterward. "It was interesting to me that the day after the election, many of them came up to me and said, 'Stay in the Senate. We need you'." Asked by a reporter whether his choice was to remain on Capitol Hill, Durbin responded, "That's my choice."

His next choice will be whether to seek re-election in 2020, when he will turn 76 shortly after Election Day. Durbin underwent surgery in 2010 for the removal of a small gastrointestinal tumor, later found to be benign. He subsequently dropped 20 pounds after reading a book on how to overcome the effects of aging.

Junior Senator

Tammy Duckworth (D)

Elected 2016, term expires 2022, 1st term; b. Mar 12, 1968; Bangkok, Thailand; Capella University (MN), Ph.D.; University of Hawaii, B.A., 1989; George Washington University Elliot School of International Affairs (DC), M.A., 1992; Northern Illinois University, Att., 2001; Married (Bryan Bowlsbey).

Military Career: U.S Army Reserve, IL Army National Guard (Iraq, WIA), 1992-2014.

Professional Career: Assistant Secretary, U.S Veterans Affairs Department, 2009-2011; Director, IL Veterans Affairs Department, 2006-2009; Mngr., Rotary Intl., 2003-2004.

DC Office: 524 HSOB 20510, 202-224-2854, Fax: 202-228-0618; Website: duckworth.senate.gov.

State Offices: Chicago, 312-886-3506; Springfield, 217-528-6124.

Committees: *Commerce, Science & Transportation*: Aviation Operations, Safety & Security, Communications, Technology, Innovation & the Internet, Consumer Protection, Product Safety, Ins & Data Security, Surface Trans., Merchant Marine Infra., Safety & Security. *Energy & Natural Resources*: Energy, National Parks, Water & Power. *Environment & Public Works*: Clean Air & Nuclear Safety, Fisheries, Water, and Wildlife (RMM), Transportation & Infrastructure. *Small Business & Entrepreneurship*.

Group Ratings (House)

	ADA	ACLU	AFL-CIO	LCV	ITI	COC	HAFA	ACU	CFG	FRC
2016	-	76%	-	95%	67%	58%	13%	0%	0%	0%
2015	85%	C	95%	89%	C	59%	C	0%	0%	0%

Almanac Ratings 2015

	Economy	Social	Foreign	Composite
Liberal	68%	87%	61%	72%
Conservative	32%	13%	39%	28%

Key Votes of the 114th Congress (House)

1. Keystone Pipeline	NV	5. Puerto Rico Debt	Y	9. Offenses by Aliens	NV
2. Trade Deals	N	6. Medical Marijuana	Y	10. Troops in Iraq	N
3. Export-Import Bank	Y	7. Sanctuary Cities	N	11. Homeland Security $$	Y
4. Debt Ceiling Increase	Y	8. Armor-piercing Bullets	N	12. Trade Adjustment aid	Y

Election Results

Election	Name (Party)	Vote	(%)	Cand. Spent	Ind. Exp. Support	Ind. Exp. Oppose
2016 General	Tammy Duckworth (D)	3,012,940	(55%)	$9,000,361	$683,882	$2,061,868
	Mark Kirk (R)	2,184,692	(40%)	$10,513,124	$727,085	$62,499
	Kent McMillen (L)	175,988	(3%)			
	Scott Summers (G)	117,619	(2%)			
2016 Primary	Tammy Duckworth (D)	1,220,128	(64%)			
	Andrea Zopp (D)	455,729	(24%)			
	Napoleon Harris (D)	219,286	(12%)			

Prior winning percentages: House: 2014 (56%); 2012 (55%)

The victory of Tammy Duckworth, now Illinois' junior senator, was a rare bright spot for Democrats in a disappointing 2016 election season. In a year in which the Democrats had hopes of gaining at least five seats to recapture the Senate majority, Duckworth was one of just two candidates nationwide to oust a sitting Republican senator. The offspring of an American father and a Thai mother, Duckworth's election marked a couple of racial and ethnic milestones. She is the first Thai-American senator, while she and her newly elected colleague, Democrat Kamala Harris of California, are only the second and third Asian-American women in Senate history. But perhaps the most precedent-setting aspect of Duckworth's election was the campaign that preceded it: More than a quarter of a century after the passage of the Americans With Disabilities Act, the contest between Duckworth and her opponent, then-Republican Sen. Mark Kirk, marked the first Senate campaign in which both candidates were wheelchair-bound to a significant degree.

In 2004, during the Iraq war, a rocket-propelled grenade struck the Army helicopter that Duckworth was copiloting, costing her both of her legs; on the campaign trail, she alternated between a wheelchair and walking on prosthetic legs with the aid of a cane. Kirk, meanwhile, suffered a severe stroke at the beginning of 2012 that kept him away from Capitol Hill for a year; it left him partly paralyzed on his left side, forcing him to shift between a wheelchair and a cane. Politically, the fact that both candidates suffered from physical handicaps served as an equalizer of sorts: Each felt free to unleash sharp rhetorical attacks without risking a backlash for taking advantage of the other's vulnerability. But if Duckworth campaigned as a wounded warrior demonstrating that a return to a full life was possible after suffering major injuries, Kirk ultimately found his disability to be a political encumbrance: Already fighting an uphill battle in a reliably Democratic state, Kirk faced public and private questions regarding his fitness to serve in the wake of his debilitating illness.

Born in Bangkok, Duckworth spent much of her early life abroad, as her father, a Vietnam War veteran, worked for the United Nations and at several international firms. The family lived in Singapore and Indonesia before settling in Hawaii when Duckworth was 16. Money was tight. "Thank God for the food stamps, public education, and Pell Grants that helped me finish high school and college," she declared during a speech to the 2012 Democratic National Convention. Duckworth studied marine biology at the University of Hawaii, and later earned a master's degree in international affairs at George Washington University while working at the Smithsonian National Museum of Natural History. Her interest in Southeast Asian history, culture, and politics led her to doctoral work at Northern Illinois University.

In 1990, Duckworth -- who often boasts that her family on her father's side has a record of military service that dates back to the American Revolution -- joined the Army Reserve Officers' Training Corps at George Washington University. Two years later, she became a commissioned officer; during her training, she met her future husband, Bryan Bowlsbey, who has become a major in the National Guard. Although Duckworth later said she opposed President George W. Bush's decision to invade Iraq, she felt it was her duty to complete her military service. She became one of the first Army women to fly combat missions in Iraq. The rocket-propelled grenade that hit the Black Hawk helicopter she was copiloting struck the lower half of her body and nearly killed her. "They should have left me behind," she recalled later. Duckworth suffered serious damage to her right arm in addition to the loss of both legs. While recovering at Walter Reed Army Medical Center, she met then-Sen. Barack Obama of Illinois, a member of the Veterans' Affairs Committee, who eventually called her to testify.

Illinois' other senator, Democratic Whip Richard Durbin, urged Duckworth to run for the House in 2006 from an open seat in Chicago's western suburbs. Local Democrats had lined up behind the 2004 nominee, Christine Cegelis, who had mounted a competitive race that year. But then-Rep. Rahm Emanuel, chairman of the Democratic Congressional Campaign Committee (and now Chicago's mayor), weighed in for Duckworth: He felt her background made her the more electable candidate in view of the makeup of the 6th District. Duckworth edged Cegelis in the primary, 44%-40%, but lost narrowly to Republican Peter Roskam in November, 51%-49%. Duckworth, who had undergone numerous surgeries in the wake of the helicopter attack in Iraq two years earlier, later said she that she wasn't fully recovered from her injuries at the time.

Weeks after her loss to Roskam, Duckworth was named director of the Illinois Veterans Affairs Department by Gov. Rod Blagojevich. It was a bumpy experience for Duckworth on several fronts, including a lawsuit that two employees brought against her for alleged workplace retaliation. The suit was settled out of court several months before the 2016 Senate election. While a Duckworth spokesman dismissed the suit as frivolous, it would provide fodder for attacks by Kirk early in the Senate race; he accused Duckworth of hiring "goombahs" at the direction of Blagojevich, now serving a federal prison sentence for trying to sell the appointment to Obama's open Senate seat following the 2008 presidential election. Duckworth received a prominent speaking spot at the 2008 Democratic National Convention in Denver at which Obama was nominated for his first term, and in early 2009 -- shortly after

Blagojevich's arrest -- she left for a job in the Obama Administration, as assistant secretary of public and intergovernmental affairs in the Veterans Affairs Department.

In 2011, Duckworth left the VA to launch a second run for Congress. The 8th District, located in Chicago's northwestern suburbs, had been redrawn by Illinois Democrats to make it more favorable for their party. With another endorsement from Durbin, Duckworth coasted to the March primary victory over New Delhi-born former Illinois Deputy Treasurer Raja Krishnamoorthi, 66%-34%, and again received prime-time exposure at the 2012 convention. Her general election opponent was GOP Rep. Joe Walsh, elected to the House in 2010 on the national tea party wave. He had a reputation for outspokenness but also for damaging political moments, such as failing to make child support payments to his ex-wife and engaging in a tirade at a constituent meeting. Walsh criticized Duckworth for using her military service as a political tool. "She is a hero, and that demands our respect, but it doesn't demand our vote," he told CNN. Redistricting had left Walsh with only a small piece of his old district, and Duckworth won with 55 percent of the vote.

In the House, Duckworth joined the Armed Services Committee, where she filed a bill to extend maternity leave for women serving in the military. Duckworth herself became a mother two weeks after being re-elected by a 56%-44% margin in 2014, giving birth to a daughter. In early 2015, Duckworth scored a legislative victory when Obama signed the Clay Hunt Suicide Prevention for American Veterans Act at a White House ceremony. Designed to improve mental health services for veterans, she co-authored it with Democratic Rep. Tim Walz of Minnesota, a veteran of the war in Afghanistan.

Duckworth announced her challenge to Kirk in March 2015, declaring in an announcement video, "I view my time now as a bonus, and that has allowed me to speak up without fear." She showed her independence soon after, declaring that she would hold former Secretary of State Hillary Clinton "accountable" for erasing emails from her personal server that dealt with the killing of U.S. officials in the 2012 attack on the embassy in Benghazi, Libya; Duckworth was among the Democrats named to serve on the Select Benghazi Committee created by the House GOP majority. Several other Democratic members of the Illinois House delegation opted to take a pass after eyeing the Senate race, and, in the March 2016 primary, Duckworth captured 64 percent of the vote to easily defeat two other candidates: Andrea Zopp, former head of the Chicago Urban League, and state Sen. Napoleon Harris.

Soon after returning to Capitol Hill on the opening day in 2013, Kirk had made clear that his near-fatal stroke would not deter him from seeking a second term. "Now I'm definitely a disabled American with a wheelchair," Kirk told the *New York Times*. "That makes me not quite the demonizable Republican candidate that you would think." Nonetheless, he began the 2016 election cycle as the most endangered Senate incumbent in the nation, a status that likely would have been conferred upon him, even absent the stroke. In 2010, Kirk had won only narrowly over a Democratic opponent with political baggage -- while boosted by the blowback from the pay-to-play scandal that sent Blagojevich to prison. In seeking re-election, he would have to run during a presidential election year in a state that had not cast its Electoral College votes for a Republican in nearly three decades.

In the Senate, Kirk had crafted a record as a fiscal conservative and foreign policy hawk, while well to the left of most of his party on social issues; overall, *Almanac* ratings pegged him as the least conservative Republican senator in 2015. In 2016, he was the first senator to break from the Republican leadership by urging a vote be held on Obama's nomination of Merrick Garland to the Supreme Court. While such positioning served Kirk well politically during the decade that he represented a Republican-leaning congressional district in Chicago's affluent northern suburbs, it alienated a significant number of Republicans statewide without attracting much Democratic support. A poll taken in mid-2015, shortly after both Kirk and Duckworth had announced their candidacies, showed Kirk's disapproval rating outweighing his approval score -- and Duckworth leading a head-to-head matchup by 6 points. Polls throughout the contest showed Duckworth maintaining an edge in the high single digits.

Kirk struggled to raise money (Duckworth outraised him 2-1, by nearly $8 million), and a series of verbal gaffes raised quiet questions about whether the stroke had affected his behavior. He referred to South Carolina GOP Sen. Lindsey Graham, a bachelor, as a "bro with no ho" and suggested that people drive faster through African-American neighborhoods. In October, the state's largest newspaper, the *Chicago Tribune* cited Kirk's health in endorsing Duckworth. "Our reluctant judgment is that, due to forces beyond his control, Kirk no longer can perform to the fullest the job of a U.S. senator," the paper declared. Kirk called it a "sucker punch" -- but less than two weeks before Election Day, he placed the final nail in his candidacy with another gaffe. During a candidate debate, Duckworth again pointed to her family's history of military service going back to the Revolutionary War. Kirk gibed, "I'd forgotten your parents came all the way from Thailand to serve George Washington." Democrats blasted the remark as racist, and Kirk, after his campaign initially declined to offer an apology, later apologized to Duckworth via Twitter. On Election Day, Duckworth won in a 55%-40% landslide, just behind the 56%-39% margin by which Democratic presidential nominee Hillary Clinton took Illinois over GOP opponent Donald Trump -- from whom Kirk had spent most of the campaign trying to separate himself.

While there was mild surprise that Duckworth was not assigned to the Veterans' Affairs panel when she arrived in the Senate, her committees included Commerce Science and Transportation, Environment and Public Works and Energy and Natural Resources. She cited her past in highlighting her assignment to the latter panel, declaring, "I risked my life and limb - as did countless other brave Americans - serving in Iraq, and I saw firsthand the painful price this nation pays because of our reliance on foreign oil."

FIRST DISTRICT

Bobby Rush (D)

Elected 1992, 13th term; b. Nov 23, 1946, Albany, GA; McCormick Theological Seminary (IL), M.Th.; Roosevelt University (IL), B.A.; University of Illinois, M.A.; University of Illinois, Chicago, Att.; Baptist; Widower; 7 children (1 deceased).

Military Career: U.S Army, 1963-1968.

Elected Office: Chicago city alderman, 1983-1992; 2nd ward committeeman, 1984.

Professional Career: Member, Student Non-Violent Coord. Committee, 1966-1968; Co-founder, IL Black Panther Party, 1968; Med. clinic Director, 1970-1973; Ins. agent, 1978-1983.

DC Office: 2188 RHOB 20515, 202-225-4372, Fax: 202-226-0333, rush.house.gov.

State Offices: Chicago, 773-779-2400.

Committees: *Energy & Commerce*: Communications & Technology, Energy (RMM).

Group Ratings

	ADA	ACLU	AFL-CIO	LCV	ITI	COC	HAFA	ACU	CFG	FRC
2016	-	94%	-	82%	50%	50%	18%	0%	14%	0%
2015	90%	C	100%	86%	C	37%	C	0%	0%	0%

Almanac Ratings 2015

	Economy	Social	Foreign	Composite
Liberal	96%	94%	95%	95%
Conservative	5%	6%	5%	5%

Key Votes of the 114th Congress

1. Keystone Pipeline	N	5. Puerto Rico Debt	N	9. Offenses by Aliens	N
2. Trade Deals	N	6. Medical Marijuana	Y	10. Troops in Iraq	Y
3. Export-Import Bank	Y	7. Sanctuary Cities	N	11. Homeland Security $$	NV
4. Debt Ceiling Increase	Y	8. Armor-piercing Bullets	N	12. Trade Adjustment aid	NV

Election Results

Election	Name (Party)	Vote (%)	Cand. Spent	Ind. Exp. Support	Ind. Exp. Oppose
2016 General	Bobby Rush (D)	234,037 (74%)	$586,012		
	August Deuser (R)	81,817 (26%)			
2016 Primary	Bobby Rush (D)	125,633 (71%)			
	Patrick Brutus (D)	33,863 (19%)			
	Howard B. Brookins (D)	16,366 (9%)			

Prior winning percentages: 2014 (73%), 2012 (74%), 2010 (80%), 2008 (86%), 2006 (84%), 2004 (85%), 2002 (83%), 2000 (88%), 1998 (89%), 1996 (87%), 1994 (76%), 1992 (83%)

Once a Black Panther and prison inmate, Democrat Bobby Rush was elected in 1992 and has become an elder liberal statesman of Congress and Chicago's sharp-edged political scene. He will go down in history as the only politician ever to beat Barack Obama in an election. His legislative legacy has been less formidable.

Rush grew up on the North Side, a Boy Scout whose mother was a Republican precinct captain. While in the Army, he became involved in the Student Nonviolent Coordinating Committee in the South, then became disillusioned with the military and went AWOL in 1968. That year, he founded the Illinois Black Panthers, with its "Power to the People" slogan, and recruited Fred Hampton, who became chairman of the organization but was later killed by police in a 1969 raid. The next day, police raided Rush's family's apartment, but he wasn't there. Rush served six months in prison for illegal possession of firearms. During his time with the Black Panthers, he ran a program providing free breakfasts to children and a medical clinic that developed the nation's first mass sickle-cell-anemia testing program. "I don't repudiate any of my involvement in the Panther party. It was part of my maturing," Rush later said. Ordained as a Baptist minister, Rush founded a church in 2002 in the depressed Englewood community, but it struggled financially.

In 1983, he was elected the 2nd Ward alderman on the Chicago City Council and was a strong supporter of Harold Washington, who became the city's first black mayor. While in politics, Rush went back to school and earned master's degrees in political science and theological studies. In 1992, he challenged Democratic Rep. Charles Hayes, an older-generation politician with a union background. Just before the primary, it was revealed that Hayes had 716 overdrafts at the House bank, a practice among lawmakers that blossomed into a national scandal. Rush won 42%-39%.

In the House, Rush has a liberal voting record. His rhetoric has softened over the years, and his more deliberate style contrasts sharply with his days as a Panther. But he sometimes chafes at legislative compromises. He backed the 2010 health care overhaul law, but only after sending mixed signals because of his unhappiness over the removal of a provision that reimburses hospitals for indigent care. He claimed credit for provisions in the law that dealt with women's health and postpartum depression. His *Almanac* vote ratings for 2015 remained solidly liberal.

Gun violence caused great pain to Rush in 1999, when his son, Huey Rich, was murdered by a man wielding a handgun as he returned to his South Side home with his fiancée. After 17-year-old Trayvon Martin was shot dead in Florida in 2012 in an incident that set off a national debate about race, Rush took to the House floor wearing a gray hooded sweatshirt - Martin's garb at the time of his death - in protest. "Just because someone is a young black male and wears a hoodie does not make them a hoodlum," he said.

He has devoted much of his time to the Energy and Commerce Committee, where he chaired the Commerce, Trade and Consumer Protection Subcommittee until Democrats lost control of the House in 2011. Since then, he has been ranking Democrat on the Energy and Power Subcommittee. When gasoline prices soared in early 2012, he called for an investigation into the potential role of Wall Street speculators. He has sought increased job opportunities for minorities throughout the energy industry. After Henry Waxman retired in 2014 as the committee's top Democrat, Rush stepped aside during the intense competition for a successor.

Rush waged a quixotic campaign in 1999 against Richard M. Daley's iron grip on the mayor's office. He was a frequent Daley critic, and during the campaign he attacked the mayor for tolerating police brutality, inadequate mass transit service and cronyism in city government. Only three of the 50 aldermen endorsed him. Rush tried to build a multiracial coalition, but his only chance was with black voters. Daley was popular, and his financial advantage overwhelming. The incumbent won the primary 72%-28%, with nearly 45 percent of the African-American vote and the support of many prominent black ministers.

After that pounding, Rush found himself challenged in his own primary in 2000 by two state senators - Donne Trotter and the then little-known Barack Obama. Obama waged an aggressive campaign, saying at the time that Rush "exemplifies a politics that is reactive, that waits for crises to happen, then holds a press conference, and hasn't been particularly effective at building broad-based coalitions." But Obama came under attack for being absent from the state legislature for two months and missing a vote on a gun control bill while on a family trip to Hawaii, where he was raised. "It was a race in which everything that could go wrong did go wrong," Obama later wrote in his book, *The Audacity of Hope*. Rush was helped by an endorsement from President Bill Clinton. He beat Obama 61%-30%.

Not surprisingly, redistricting in 2002 shifted Obama's Hyde Park home two blocks outside the new lines. Rush has been routinely reelected since then. The *Chicago Tribune*, in endorsing his Republican opponent Donald Peloquin in 2012, complained Rush had become complacent and had not returned calls from mayors in some of his district's small towns. During Obama's pitched battle with Hillary Clinton in the 2008 presidential primary, Rush endorsed Obama, calling it "one of the most difficult decisions I've had to make in politics."

In local politics, Rush usually supports African-American candidates. After Daley announced he wouldn't run for reelection as mayor, Rush in early 2011 joined other black Democratic leaders in backing former Sen. Carol Moseley Braun. The voters gave the job to former Obama White House

Chief of Staff Rahm Emanuel. In the 2015 mayoral election, Rush unexpectedly endorsed Emanuel, and criticized challenger Chuy Garcia for having "cheapened" the legacy of Harold Washington with his claims of building a Latino-black coalition.

The 2016 election offered hints of future elections in this district. Rush had a primary challenge from veteran South Side Alderman Howard Brookins, who raised $200,000 and had the support of Mike Madigan, the powerful Illinois House speaker and state party chairman. Curiously, there were no signs that Madigan issued a prominent statement of support, nor did his organization campaign actively, on behalf of Brookins. The state Board of Elections dismissed a challenge from Brookins that Rush had failed to submit sufficient valid signatures with his campaign filing. Rush won, 71%-19%. Perhaps, Madigan was preparing for who might take the seat following Rush, age 69 at the time. During the campaign, Rush received financial and other help from Emanuel. Of the $586,000 that Rush raised during the cycle, he paid more than $100,000 to family members - in the Chicago tradition. In the uneventful November election that Rush won with 74 percent of the vote, little-known Republican challenger August Deuser took 67 percent in Will County. That suburban area cast only 15 percent of the total vote. Those numbers were a warning that steep population loss on the South Side could jeopardize one of the three African-American districts in Chicago in the 2021 redistricting.

Rush had a brush with cancer in 2008. He spent much of the year recovering from salivary gland cancer and surgery to remove a tumor near his jaw. Doctors later declared him cancer-free. But Rush has slowed down physically and as a player in the House.

Chicago: South Side, Southwest Suburbs

Population		**Race and Ethnicity**		**Income**	
Total	712,393	White	35.5%	Median Income	$48,989 (268 out of 435)
Land area	258	Black	51.1%		
Pop/ sq mi	2757.2	Latino	9.6%		
Born in state	76.3%	Asian	1.9%	Under $50,000	50.7%
		Two races	1.5%	$50,000-$99,999	28.4%
Age Groups		Other	0.3%	$100,000-$199,999	17.4%
Under 18	23.5%			$200,000 or more	3.4%
18-34	23.2%	**Education**		Poverty Rate	19.6%
35-64	39.2%	H.S grad or less	39.7%		
Over 64	14.1%	Some college	33.3%	**Health Insurance**	
		College Degree, 4 yr	16.1%	With health insurance coverage	88.3%
Work		Post grad	10.8%		
White Collar	34.4%				
Sales and Service	46.1%	**Military**		**Public Assistance**	
Blue Collar	19.4%	Veteran	6.5%	Cash public assistance income	3.8%
Government	16.8%	Active Duty	0.0%		
				Food stamp/SNAP benefits	21.3%

Voter Turnout			
2015 Total Citizens 18+	521,096	2016 House Turnout as % CVAP	61%
2016 House turnout	315,862	2014 House Turnout as % CVAP	42%

2012 Presidential Vote			**2016 Presidential Vote**		
Barack Obama	262,936	(79%)	Hillary Clinton	245,945	(75%)
Mitt Romney	67,557	(20%)	Donald Trump	69,913	(21%)

Cook Partisan Voting Index: D+27

The South Side of Chicago has been home to a large urban black community for nearly a century, which is one of the reasons why the metro area has the third largest African-American population in the nation, after New York and Atlanta. A hundred years ago, there were just a few blocks where black families from the South could settle. But the ghetto grew rapidly with the first influx of blacks from the Mississippi Delta in the 1910s. By the 1920s, the South Side was well established as a center of black-owned businesses and of music, from blues to jazz. Politically, the South Side was a heavily Republican constituency throughout those years. The comfortable, white Protestants who settled in solid brick houses here believed in the party of Yankee propriety, while the African-Americans had faith in the party of Lincoln. This Republican Party heartland was represented in the House in the 1920s by Appropriations Chairman Martin Madden. After Madden died in the Appropriations Committee room in 1928, the 1st District elected Republican Oscar De Priest, the first African-American elected to the House in the 20th century. Blacks remained faithful to the party of Lincoln even during the Great Depression, voting for Herbert Hoover and De Priest in 1932.

The New Deal and the racial liberalism of New Dealers like Eleanor Roosevelt and Interior Secretary Harold Ickes attracted blacks to the Democratic Party, and black Democrat Arthur Mitchell defeated De Priest in 1934. The South Side has been Democratic ever since. For 40 years, it was a cooperative part of Chicago's Democratic machine. Then, after the death of longtime Rep. William Dawson, it rebelled against Mayor Richard J. Daley. The South Side seemed to take over the city when Rep. Harold Washington was elected mayor in 1983 and 1987. After he died in November 1987, other black South Side politicians bogged down in infighting, while Chicago's black electorate peaked at about 40 percent.

The 1st Congressional District of Illinois includes about half of Chicago's African-American community on the South Side. It also takes in several black Cook County suburbs and extends about 40 miles (depending on your highway) into conservative-leaning rural parts of Will County, which cover about 15 percent of the district. Overall, its gerrymandered voting population is 51 percent black and 10 percent Hispanic. The 1st has a northern salient that extends to South 26th Street and includes the Gothic spires of the University of Chicago and the mansions of Kenwood, once the home of Chicago's Jewish aristocracy and now a more eclectic and racially integrated mix of well-to-do inhabitants. Kenwood, considered part of the greater Hyde Park community, was home to Barack Obama. Before running for president, he was a regular at the local food co-op and frequent customer at 57th Street Books. After a lengthy competition and review, the leaders of his presidential library decided on a location in Jackson Park, which is on Lake Shore Drive a few blocks east of the University and barely across the line into the 2nd Congressional District. On Jan. 10, 2017, Obama delivered his farewell speech to the nation from McCormick Place, just north of the District.

Several miles to the south, the Woodlawn neighborhood served as the setting for Lorraine Hansberry's 1959 play *A Raisin in the Sun* chronicling a black family's challenges moving into what was then a largely white neighborhood. In Englewood, once the city's second-busiest shopping district before losing half its population after 1970, thousands of homes have been built with federal support in recent years in hopes of creating a new black middle-class community. Some have gone up on vacant land or replaced abandoned buildings that had housed gangs. Despite the persistent poverty in Englewood, a new shopping complex with a Whole Foods opened in 2016 and additional projects were underway. Still, the broader picture for the South Side has remained grim. Even as the population for the entire city increased by 42,000 from 2010 to 2015, the population on the Far South Side away from the lake dropped by 50,000, a loss of 10 percent, according to *Crain's Chicago Business*.

Chicago in recent years has experienced a gang-fueled crime wave. The 762 murder victims in 2016 were more than a 50 percent increase from 2015 and exceeded the combined murder total in the larger cities of New York and Los Angeles. Most of those crimes were gun-related in a city with some of the most restrictive gun laws in the nation; more than half of the guns came from outside of Illinois and were then sold to local gangs. Small consolation: On a per capita basis, the murder rate was lower than in smaller cities such as Detroit, St. Louis and Baltimore. Although incidents of reported crime had dropped in 2013-14, some experts said that Mayor Rahm Emanuel had manipulated the data so he could claim credit before his reelection bid in 2015. The Englewood police district had among the highest rates of serious crimes.

The 1st District is overwhelmingly Democratic. Hillary Clinton prevailed against Donald Trump, 75%-21%, a dip from the 79 percent that hometown President Obama got in 2012. The district vote in 2016 was only the fourth-best Democratic performance in Illinois.

SECOND DISTRICT

Robin Kelly (D)

Elected 2013, 3rd term; b. Apr 30, 1956, New York, NY; Bradley University, M.A.; Bradley University, B.A.; Northern Illinois University, Ph.D.; Christian - Non-Denominational; Married (Nathaniel Horn); 2 children.

Elected Office: IL House, 2002-2007.

Professional Career: Director, minority student services and professional counselor, Bradley University, 1990-1992; Director, community affairs, Village of Matteson, IL, 1992-2006; Chief of Staff, IL Treas., 2007-2010; Chief admin. officer, Cook County Board President, 2010-2012.

DC Office: 1239 LHOB 20515, 202-225-0773, Fax: 202-225-4583, robinkelly.house.gov.

State Offices: Chicago, 773-321-2001; Kankakee, 708-679-0078; Matteson, 708-679-0078.

Committees: *Foreign Affairs*: Europe, Eurasia & Emerging Threats, Western Hemisphere. *Oversight & Government Reform*: Health Care, Benefits & Administrative Rules, Information Technology (RMM).

Group Ratings

	ADA	ACLU	AFL-CIO	LCV	ITI	COC	HAFA	ACU	CFG	FRC
2016	-	82%	-	89%	67%	64%	11%	0%	4%	0%
2015	80%	C	100%	89%	C	42%	C	0%	0%	0%

Almanac Ratings 2015

	Economy	Social	Foreign	Composite
Liberal	94%	97%	89%	93%
Conservative	6%	4%	11%	7%

Key Votes of the 114th Congress

1. Keystone Pipeline	N	5. Puerto Rico Debt	Y	9. Offenses by Aliens	N
2. Trade Deals	N	6. Medical Marijuana	Y	10. Troops in Iraq	Y
3. Export-Import Bank	Y	7. Sanctuary Cities	N	11. Homeland Security $$	Y
4. Debt Ceiling Increase	Y	8. Armor-piercing Bullets	N	12. Trade Adjustment aid	Y

Election Results

Election	Name (Party)	Vote (%)		Cand. Spent	Ind. Exp. Support	Ind. Exp. Oppose
2016 General	Robin Kelly (D)	235,051	(80%)	$609,076	$130	
	John Morrow (R)	59,471	(20%)			
2016 Primary	Robin Kelly (D)	114,122	(74%)			
	Marcus Lewis (D)	24,928	(16%)			
	Charles Rayburn (D)	9,439	(6%)			

Prior winning percentages: 2014 (79%), 2013 special (71%)

Democrat Robin Kelly won a 2013 special election to replace Rep. Jesse Jackson Jr., who resigned amid a criminal investigation and served prison time over his conversion of campaign contributions to personal use. With her clean-government appeal and ardent support for stronger gun-control laws, Kelly has generated a positive response in Democratic circles.

Kelly grew up in New York and moved to Illinois to attend Bradley University in Peoria, where she graduated with a bachelor's degree in psychology and a master's degree in counseling and human development services. She earned a Ph.D. in political science from Northern Illinois University. After working at a youth shelter and a counseling center, she returned to Bradley to become director of minority student services. She then spent 14 years as director of community affairs in Matteson, a village on Chicago's South Side.

In 2002, Kelly won a seat in the Illinois House, where she served three terms. She concentrated on protecting victims of consumer fraud and on extending voter registration, protecting victims of domestic violence and improving public safety in the Chicago area. She resigned her seat in 2007 to become chief of staff to state Treasurer Alexi Giannoulias, who ran unsuccessfully in 2010 for the Senate. Kelly sought to reduce staffing levels in the office as well as return greater amounts of lost cash and assets to Illinois residents and businesses. In 2010, she ran to replace Giannoulias as treasurer, but lost to GOP state Sen. Dan Rutherford, 50%-45%. She became chief administrative officer to Cook County Board President Toni Preckwinkle.

Jackson, the son of civil rights leader Jesse Jackson, had been a popular figure in his district since his election in 1995. In 2012, he became the subject of a federal investigation into possible misuse of campaign funds. Jackson easily won reelection in November, but submitted his resignation two weeks later, citing mental and physical health problems. Three months later, he pleaded guilty to wire and mail fraud after prosecutors said he used about $750,000 in campaign money for personal expenses, including purchasing a fedora worn by singer Michael Jackson. He served nearly two years in prison and was released in September 2015.

Kelly stepped forward for the special election, and won newspaper endorsements and the backing of local Democratic power brokers. "She is not a showboat," the *Chicago Tribune* said in supporting her candidacy. "She won't dazzle you with ebullience. She doesn't grandstand. She just works hard." Kelly was endorsed by New York City Mayor Michael Bloomberg, who created a super PAC to support politicians advocating tougher gun laws. His PAC broadcast ads lauding Kelly for backing universal background checks and a ban on some types of semi-automatic weapons, while criticizing former Democratic Rep. Debbie Halvorson, who had the National Rifle Association's endorsement when she represented a suburban district based in Will County.

Kelly faced criticism after a state inspector general's report and an internal audit alleged she violated timekeeping rules during her failed campaign for state treasurer. "I'm not going to tell you I didn't make a mistake, but I did not do anything wrong," she told the *Tribune*. But it mattered little. She won the February primary with 50 percent of the vote to Halvorson's 24 percent. The general election was largely a formality. "We not only won an election," Kelly said in her victory speech. "We took on the NRA, we gave a voice to the voiceless, and we put our communities on a brand new path to a brighter day."

Kelly has served as chairwoman of the Congressional Black Caucus's Health Braintrust and senior Democrat on the Oversight and Government Reform Subcommittee on Information Technology; with the latter, her interests have included improving cybersecurity, strengthening computer infrastructure and encouraging new technologies. In July 2016, she helped to organize a bipartisan working group to improve relationships between law enforcement officials and the African-American community. Her chief legislative focus has been tighter gun control. Her several bills included a requirement that the surgeon general issue an annual report on the effects of gun violence on public health, and a grant of authority to the Consumer Product Safety Commission to regulate pistols, revolvers and other firearms as consumer products. When the National Rifle Association harshly attacked her as "Assault Gun Kelly," she responded that she was not "anti-gun," but that she favored "common-sense" gun reform that respected "the right of every American to live free from the threat of gun violence." She worked with Rep. John Lewis of Georgia and others to organize the Democrats' June 2016 sit-in of the House to protest inaction on gun-control legislation.

Kelly gave serious consideration to challenging the 2016 reelection of Republican Sen. Mark Kirk, who narrowly defeated Giannoulias in 2010. She criticized Kirk for taking conservative positions contrary to his earlier promises to be a moderate. Before she could challenge Kirk, she faced the prospect of a difficult Democratic primary. Rep. Tammy Duckworth, after declaring her candidacy in March, generated enthusiasm from many Democratic leaders and received the endorsement of EMILY's List, which supports Democratic women candidates who favor abortion rights. Having advised Illinois and Cook County officials and run statewide in her whirlwind political career, Kelly said that she had deeper experience. But Democratic officials leaned toward Duckworth, with her fresher appeal and political base in the suburbs. In June 2015, Kelly said she would seek reelection to the House to work on the "unfulfilled promise" of her district. Following the 2016 election, she voiced early interest in challenging Gov. Bruce Rauner in 2018.

Southeast Chicago, Kankakee

Population		**Race and Ethnicity**		**Income**	
Total	708,498	White	28.8%	Median Income	$45,412 (335 out of 435)
Land area	1,081	Black	55.7%		
Pop/ sq mi	655.6	Latino	13.2%		
Born in state	75.2%	Asian	0.7%	Under $50,000	53.9%
		Two races	1.4%	$50,000-$99,999	29.6%
Age Groups		Other	0.2%	$100,000-$199,999	14.5%
Under 18	24.8%			$200,000 or more	2.1%
18-34	22.0%	**Education**		Poverty Rate	21.0%
35-64	39.4%	H.S grad or less	42.8%		
Over 64	13.8%	Some college	35.3%	**Health Insurance**	
Work		College Degree, 4 yr	13.6%	With health insurance coverage	86.6%
White Collar	29.9%	Post grad	8.2%		
Sales and Service	46.2%	**Military**		**Public Assistance**	
Blue Collar	23.8%	Veteran	7.6%	Cash public assistance income	4.8%
Government	16.4%	Active Duty	0.0%	Food stamp/SNAP benefits	22.4%

Voter Turnout			
2015 Total Citizens 18+	510,293	2016 House Turnout as % CVAP	58%
2016 House turnout	294,522	2014 House Turnout as % CVAP	40%

2012 Presidential Vote		
Barack Obama	250,777	(81%)
Mitt Romney	57,692	(19%)

2016 Presidential Vote		
Hillary Clinton	236,740	(77%)
Donald Trump	58,026	(19%)

Cook Partisan Voting Index: D+29

Chicago is a great center of both commerce and industry. If the city's white-collar offices are heavily concentrated in the Loop, its blue-collar heavy industries are most visible on the far South Side. This part of Chicago, diminished in economic importance today, is historically significant. The remnants of its great hulking factories around Lake Calumet and the nearby rail yards have an undeniable majesty. Thomas Geoghegan wrote in his book, *Which Side Are You On?*, of the fights to win benefits for the workers of shuttered steel mills and of the decline of the labor movement in a place where it got much of its inspiration. This is where the Pullman strike of 1894 was broken by federal troops and where policemen killed 10 union supporters in the Little Steel strike of 1937. Over the years, Chicago grew around the tight ethnic neighborhoods where workers went home at shift break each afternoon or midnight. Today, those workplaces are mostly empty buildings that suburbanites speed past on the Calumet and Dan Ryan expressways. Roseland, once a prosperous home to thousands of mostly white blue-collar workers and later the place where Barack Obama was a young community organizer in the mid-1980s, has had some of the highest murder and unemployment rates in the city.

The 2nd Congressional District of Illinois is a mix of the urban, majority African-American landscape of Chicago's old South Side industrial area and several Cook County suburbs to the south. In the city, the district includes Jackson Park on the lakeshore just to the south of the Museum of Science and Industry, where the Columbian Exposition of 1893 was held and where the Obama presidential library will be built; perhaps coincidentally, a Tiger Woods company in December 2016 unveiled plans to create a championship golf course nearby at Jackson Park. To the south are South Shore, a once heavily Jewish neighborhood and now home to middle-class blacks, and the old industrial area around Lake Calumet. In November 2016, the Chicago Transit Authority began funding for the 5.3 mile Far Red Line rail extension from 95th Street to 130th Street on the Far South Side. Ford Motor Co. announced in January 2017 that it plans to build a new hybrid police vehicle at its assembly plant, where it already had more than 4,200 workers producing Taurus and Explorer vehicles.

From its northern tip, the 2nd District extends more than 60 miles through eastern Will County and all of Kankakee County; combined, those two counties comprise about 24 percent of the district population. The district is one of the most Democratic in the nation. The Chicago portion of the 2nd is overwhelmingly black, though many African Americans, especially young parents fleeing Chicago public schools and crime, are moving into suburbs directly to the south - Harvey, Dolton, Markham, Hazel Crest and Lynwood. Farther south are economically revitalized Homewood and Flossmoor; high-income Olympia Fields; and the still vibrant Park Forest, the post-war planned town where William H. Whyte's *The Organization Man* was set. Farther south, the district takes in Peotone where, with the 2014 reelection defeat of Gov. Pat Quinn, residents may have successfully resisted for now a proposal to build a third Chicago-area airport.

THIRD DISTRICT

Daniel Lipinski (D)

Elected 2004, 7th term; b. Jul 15, 1966, Chicago; Duke University (NC), Ph.D.; Northwestern University (IL), B.S.; Stanford University (CA), M.S.; Catholic; Married (Judy Berkebile Lipinski).

Professional Career: Assistant Professional, University of TN, 2001-2004.

DC Office: 2346 RHOB 20515, 202-225-5701, Fax: 202-225-1012, lipinski.house.gov.

State Offices: Chicago, 773-948-6223; Lockport, 815-838-1990; Oak Lawn, 708-424-0853; Orland Park, 708-403-4379.

Committees: *Science, Space & Technology*: Energy, Research & Technology (RMM), Space. *Transportation & Infrastructure*: Aviation, Highways & Transit, Railroads, Pipelines & Hazardous Materials.

Group Ratings

	ADA	ACLU	AFL-CIO	LCV	ITI	COC	HAFA	ACU	CFG	FRC
2016	-	11%	-	95%	60%	79%	29%	17%	8%	50%
2015	55%	C	92%	86%	C	65%	C	25%	5%	58%

Almanac Ratings 2015

	Economy	Social	Foreign	Composite
Liberal	63%	48%	32%	48%
Conservative	37%	52%	68%	52%

Key Votes of the 114th Congress

1. Keystone Pipeline	Y	5. Puerto Rico Debt	Y	9. Offenses by Aliens	Y
2. Trade Deals	N	6. Medical Marijuana	N	10. Troops in Iraq	N
3. Export-Import Bank	Y	7. Sanctuary Cities	N	11. Homeland Security $$	Y
4. Debt Ceiling Increase	Y	8. Armor-piercing Bullets	N	12. Trade Adjustment aid	Y

Election Results

Election	Name (Party)	Vote (%)	Cand. Spent	Ind. Exp. Support	Ind. Exp. Oppose
2016 General	Daniel Lipinski (D)....................	225,320 (100%)	$569,670		
2016 Primary	Daniel Lipinski (D)....................	(100%)			

Prior winning percentages: 2014 (65%), 2012 (69%), 2010 (70%), 2008 (73%), 2006 (77%), 2004 (73%)

Democrat Daniel Lipinski was first elected in 2004 to replace his father, Bill Lipinski, who represented the district for 22 years. Like his father, the younger Lipinski goes his own way from party leaders and he has focused on transportation and constituent service. He has put his engineering background to work on cyber security and other technology issues.

Daniel Lipinski grew up in Chicago, in the city's 23rd Ward, and first served as a campaign volunteer for his father in 1979. He got engineering degrees from Northwestern and Stanford universities before switching to political science for his doctorate at Duke. He worked as an aide to four House Democrats from Illinois, though not in his father's office, and was an American Political Science Association congressional fellow for the House Democratic Policy Committee. He wrote his doctoral thesis on the topic of congressional newsletters (*Congressional Communication*, published by the University of Michigan Press). At the beginning of 2004, he was an assistant professor of political science at the University of Tennessee in Knoxville.

Lipinski's nomination to run for his father's seat is a case study in Chicago's still-thriving backroom politics. In the summer of 2004, Bill Lipinski denied widespread rumors that he would give up his seat. Then on Aug. 13, he abruptly announced he would not seek reelection in November because he wanted to return to Chicago and "spend more time with my wife." (Not *that* much time, as it turns out, because he later became a transportation lobbyist.) A meeting was scheduled for Aug. 17 for the 19 ward and township Democratic committeemen in the 3rd District. The group consisted of a *Who's Who* of connected Chicago politicians, including Bill Lipinski, the 23rd Ward committeeman. At the meeting, Lipinski proposed the most qualified person he could think of, his son, Daniel, and shortly afterward, he was nominated without opposition. That support was tantamount to election in the 3rd District, and he sailed to victory in November.

In the House, Daniel Lipinski has kept his pledge to be "not really that different from my father," who was the most conservative Democrat in the Illinois delegation. He has opposed same-sex marriage and abortion except when the mother's life is at stake. Showing his continued independence from his party, Lipinski has been among the Democrats who has declined to vote for Nancy Pelosi as their party's leader in the House. In 2011, he cast his vote for Rep. Marcy Kaptur of Ohio, who is the House's most senior woman. Two years later, he backed Rep. Jim Cooper of Tennessee, an outspoken Pelosi critic. In 2015, he voted for Rep. Peter DeFazio of Oregon, the senior Democrat on the Transportation and Infrastructure Committee, where Lipinski serves. Following the 2016 election, he backed Rep. Tim Ryan of Ohio. "The Democratic Caucus needs to take an honest look at the last few elections and recognize that the party's brand does not play well in the House districts we need to pick up to gain the majority," he said. He declined to support the Democrats' health care overhaul, saying that its provision banning federal funds for abortions wasn't strong enough even as other anti-abortion Democrats expressed satisfaction with it. Of the 34 House Democrats who voted against the Affordable Care Act in 2010, he is one of only three who remain in the House. He has continued to press for changes in the law.

As a member of the Science, Space, and Technology Committee, where he has been senior Democrat on the Research and Technology Subcommittee, Lipinski worked with Republican Michael McCaul of Texas to win House passage of a cybersecurity bill in 2012. In 2013-14, he took credit for bipartisan enactment of two bills designed to boost the economy: The American Manufacturing Competitiveness Act, which requires a National Strategic Plan for Manufacturing every four years; and the Cybersecurity Enhancement Act, to protect Americans from cybercrimes.

Lipinski always has an eye on Midway International Airport, which generates the most jobs of any employer in the district. He devotes attention to rail infrastructure and has been a vocal advocate for CREATE, a public-private partnership to improve the Chicago area's passenger and freight rail. In March 2015, he and Rep. Mike Quigley of Chicago's North Side filed a bill to authorize $1 billion over the next five years for rail-safety improvement projects. He noted that his district is home to four commuter rail lines, Amtrak, and six of the nation's seven Class I freight railroads. On the Public Works and Transportation Committee, Lipinski claimed credit for several parts of the water resources bill that was enacted in December 2016, including additional funds for Great Lakes clean-up and harbor improvement, plus "buy American" requirements.

He continues to show independence on other issues. In 2015, he was the only Democrat to join 171 House Republicans in sponsoring the First Amendment Defense Act, which bars the federal government from acting against a business or person who refuses to provide a service for same-sex married couples based on religious or moral objections. He supports an amendment to the Constitution that would prohibit same-sex marriage. The *Almanac* vote ratings for 2015 ranked Lipinski among the most conservative Democrats. On a separate bipartisan initiative, Lipinski joined Republican Rep. Darin LaHood of Illinois on a resolution that called for a joint congressional committee to recommend changes in the legislative process.

Lipinski occasionally has drawn significant primary opposition in his reelection bids. In 2006, John Sullivan, an assistant Cook County state's attorney, made an issue of Lipinski getting the seat in "a backroom deal." Financial planner John Kelly used "no tricks, no fix" as a campaign slogan. Lipinski won with 54 percent, to 26 percent for Kelly and 20 percent for Sullivan. In the 2008 primary, Lipinski faced Cook County Assistant State's Attorney Mark Pera, an abortion rights supporter who criticized Lipinski's support for the war in Iraq and questioned his campaign payments to his father. Liberal interest groups, local reformers, and others contributed to Pera, who spent $770,000. Lipinski prevailed, 54%-25%. He has easily won reelection since then against under-funded GOP challengers and little Democratic opposition. In 2016, he had no major-party opposition. The biggest political threats he is likely to face may be the steady growth of Hispanics in his district and the prospect that Illinois will lose at least one seat in the 2022 redistricting.

Chicago: Southwest Side, West Suburbs

Population		**Race and Ethnicity**		**Income**	
Total	722,289	White	59.4%	Median Income	$61,300 (131 out of 435)
Land area	237	Black	4.5%		
Pop/ sq mi	3045.3	Latino	31.0%		
Born in state	70.1%	Asian	3.9%	Under $50,000	40.6%
		Two races	1.0%	$50,000-$99,999	32.5%
Age Groups		Other	0.2%	$100,000-$199,999	22.1%
Under 18	24.8%			$200,000 or more	4.8%
18-34	22.2%	**Education**		Poverty Rate	12.0%
35-64	39.9%	H.S grad or less	46.2%		
Over 64	13.1%	Some college	27.9%	**Health Insurance**	
		College Degree, 4 yr	16.4%	With health insurance coverage	87.4%
Work		Post grad	9.4%		
White Collar	31.0%				
Sales and Service	43.9%	**Military**		**Public Assistance**	
Blue Collar	25.1%	Veteran	5.6%	Cash public assistance income	2.3%
Government	12.8%	Active Duty	0.0%		
				Food stamp/SNAP benefits	11.4%

Voter Turnout			
2015 Total Citizens 18+	472,631	2016 House Turnout as % CVAP	48%
2016 House turnout	225,411	2014 House Turnout as % CVAP	38%

2012 Presidential Vote		
Barack Obama	143,910	(56%)
Mitt Romney	109,212	(43%)

2016 Presidential Vote		
Hillary Clinton	157,273	(55%)
Donald Trump	113,874	(40%)
Gary Johnson	9,177	(3%)

Cook Partisan Voting Index: D+6

A century ago, humorist Finley Peter Dunne's fictional Mr. Dooley pontificated on matters political in a saloon on Archery Road. This was Archer Avenue on the South Side of Chicago, one of the radial streets that cut across what was once open prairie near the Loop and along the Chicago River. Archer Avenue was one of the paths of outward migration and upward mobility for the children and grandchildren of Chicago's ethnic and cultural groups, and still is. Italians from the river wards along the Chicago Sanitary and Ship Canal moved west, the South Side Irish moved west and south along Cicero Avenue toward Oak Lawn, and the Bohemians (as they were called then; now Czechs) were heavily concentrated in the neat bungalows of industrial suburbs like Berwyn. Today, Latinos are driving these same avenues, up before dawn to arrive at factory jobs, or taking Chicago Transit Authority "El" trains to the Loop or to "edge city" jobs along the expressways. Another transportation center is Midway International Airport, Chicago's main airport from 1927 until O'Hare International Airport opened in 1955, and now a busy discount hub. It has renovated and expanded its congested terminals and parking lots, all squeezed into the heart of a busy commercial area on the Southwest Side. In 2016, local officials made plans for a $248 million redevelopment of the facility.

The 3rd Congressional District of Illinois consists of much of this territory, crisscrossed by grid-pattern streets, the canal, the railroad lines and the switching yards so common in this, the center of the nation's rail network. It is part of Chicago's bungalow belt, with one after another of the ubiquitous peaked brick houses neatly lining every street like Monopoly pieces, the handiwork of Swedish, Italian and Polish masons. In the Archer Avenue neighborhoods, Poles cling to their heritage, with many weekend schools teaching Polish to local kids and adults. A narrow corridor on the near South Side extends to the Bridgeport neighborhood, the lifetime home of the late Mayor Richard J. Daley, father of former Mayor Richard M. Daley, and the storied Irish stronghold that produced four other Chicago mayors. In recent years, Bridgeport has diversified, as Hispanics and Asians have moved in along with artists taking studio space in old warehouses. The neighborhood also has reinvented itself as a commercial and entertainment destination. In June 2016, city officials unveiled a $75 million "advanced manufacturing center" at Richard J. Daley College, with the hope that it will lead to the creation of 14,000 manufacturing jobs within a decade. The ballpark for the Chicago White Sox, a brisk walk away from Bridgeport, opened in 1991 with the iconic Comiskey Park name, evolved 12 years later to U.S. Cellular Field, and in November 2016 transferred its naming rights to Guaranteed Rate, a Chicago-based residential mortgage company; the latest name spawned inevitable jokes about the quality of the South Side team.

The 3rd includes the far southwest edge of Chicago, with its early 20th century, prairie style houses in villages such as the mostly white ethnic Oak Lawn; a few older, affluent suburbs like Western Springs; and middle-income towns like Oak Lawn and Palos Hills. An eastern slice of Will County includes the towns of Orland Park, Lockport and Lemont, home to the large campus of Argonne National Laboratory, which conducts basic and applied research in high energy physics and other disciplines; its presence has sparked numerous private research firms in the area. Only 13 percent of the district is outside Cook County.

The Hispanic voting-age population has grown to about 33 percent, the second largest Hispanic constituency in the state. African Americans are only 5 percent. The district has become decidedly more suburban than urban: In 2010, 39 percent of its votes were cast in the city; in 2012, the vote was 29 percent city and nearly 60 percent in the Cook suburbs. Politically, this area is ancestrally Democratic, culturally conservative, multiethnic and viscerally patriotic. Of the seven congressional districts that include parts of Chicago, the 3rd has cast the highest percentages for Republican presidential candidates. It remains solidly Democratic, but worth monitoring for future political change, including redistricting in 2022. After Barack Obama won 58 percent and 56 percent of the vote here in his two presidential campaigns, Hillary Clinton got 55 percent in 2016. The many Hispanics and millennials here limited the vote for Donald Trump.

FOURTH DISTRICT

Luis Gutierrez (D)

Elected 1992, 13th term; b. Dec 10, 1953, Chicago; Northeastern Illinois University, B.A., 1977; Roman Catholic; Married (Soraida Aracho Gutierrez); 2 children; 1 grandchild.

Elected Office: Chicago city alderman, 1986-1992, President pro tem, 1989-1992.

Professional Career: Teacher, Puerto Rico, 1977-1978; Social worker, Chicago Department of Children & Family Services, 1979-1983; Advisor, Chicago Mayor Harold Washington, 1984-1986.

DC Office: 2408 RHOB 20515, 202-225-8203, Fax: 202-225-7810, gutierrez.house.gov.

State Offices: Chicago, 773-342-0774.

Committees: *Judiciary*: Courts, Intellectual Property & Internet, Immigration & Border Security.

Group Ratings

	ADA	ACLU	AFL-CIO	LCV	ITI	COC	HAFA	ACU	CFG	FRC
2016	-	82%	-	97%	50%	44%	17%	5%	5%	0%
2015	95%	C	100%	89%	C	40%	C	9%	3%	0%

Almanac Ratings 2015

	Economy	Social	Foreign	Composite
Liberal	91%	100%	91%	94%
Conservative	9%	0%	10%	6%

Key Votes of the 114th Congress

1. Keystone Pipeline	N	5. Puerto Rico Debt	N	9. Offenses by Aliens	N
2. Trade Deals	N	6. Medical Marijuana	Y	10. Troops in Iraq	Y
3. Export-Import Bank	Y	7. Sanctuary Cities	N	11. Homeland Security $$	Y
4. Debt Ceiling Increase	Y	8. Armor-piercing Bullets	N	12. Trade Adjustment aid	Y

Election Results

Election	Name (Party)	Vote (%)	Cand. Spent	Ind. Exp. Support	Ind. Exp. Oppose
2016 General	Luis Gutierrez (D)......................	171,297 (100%)	$506,944		
2016 Primary	Luis Gutierrez (D)......................	90,933 (75%)			
	Javier Salas (D).........................	29,938 (25%)			

Prior winning percentages: 2014 (78%), 2012 (83%), 2010 (77%), 2008 (81%), 2006 (86%), 2004 (84%), 2002 (80%), 2000 (89%), 1998 (82%), 1996 (86%), 1994 (77%), 1992 (78%)

Luis Gutierrez, a Democrat elected in 1992 and the only Hispanic to serve from Illinois, has been for years the House's most vocal advocate of comprehensive immigration reform, which he likens to the civil rights struggle. After President Barack Obama's resounding electoral support among Latinos in 2012 led many members of both parties to agree that the issue should be addressed, Chicago Mayor Rahm Emanuel joked that "the rest of America has caught up with Luis Gutierrez." Those expectations were not met during the Obama presidency.

Gutierrez is of Puerto Rican descent and grew up in Chicago. As a student at Northeastern Illinois University in the 1970s, he joined a protest over the lack of basic English classes for students from other countries. Gutierrez after college worked as a teacher for two years in Puerto Rico. When he returned to Chicago, he worked as a cab driver and social worker. In 1983, he ran for 32nd Ward committeeman against Democratic Rep. Dan Rostenkowski and lost decisively. Then he became a staffer for Mayor Harold Washington, the city's first black mayor. He ran for alderman in 1984 and lost. In 1986, he ran again and won in a new Hispanic-majority ward. After Washington died, Gutierrez backed Richard M. Daley in the 1989 mayoral election. Backing winners is a formula that works in Chicago politics. In the 1992 primary for the new House seat, rival and former Alderman Juan Soliz called Gutierrez a machine candidate. Gutierrez won, 60%-40%. Since easily winning a rematch in 1994, he has not had serious competition.

Gutierrez has staked out liberal positions, and is known for his feisty, blunt style. As a freshman, his outspoken opposition to congressional pay raises, including labeling the House "the belly of the beast" in a television interview, got him into hot water with Democratic leaders. "I've gotten my rear end kicked around here," Gutierrez told *The Washington Post*. But he later mended fences with party leaders and got a coveted assignment to the Intelligence Committee.

As a member of the Financial Services Committee, from which he took a leave of absence to join the Judiciary Committee, he proposed higher FDIC charges for big banks and lower fees for community banks in 2009. He sponsored the $200 billion receivership fund (later reduced to $150 billion) for banks, which was included in the financial regulatory changes enacted in 2010.

Gutierrez has traveled the country appearing at rallies and other events - occasionally getting arrested - in support of a path to citizenship for illegal immigrants. Over the years, he has pushed to restore food stamp eligibility for legal immigrants, to grant automatic citizenship to immigrants in military combat, and legal status to immigrants without documentation who make major contributions in the United States. "I want to be a spokesperson for people that are new to this country," he has said. In 2005, he was the lead House Democratic sponsor of an overhaul in immigration policy, which passed the Senate in 2006 but died in the Republican-controlled House.

In March 2010, Gutierrez said he would vote against the Democrats' sweeping health care bill because it barred illegal immigrants from the proposed insurance exchanges; two days before the vote, he switched and then voted in favor. During Obama's first two years, while Democrats had control of the House, he pushed party leaders to no avail to advance comprehensive immigration legislation, leading him to regularly rebuke the president. With Republicans having taken control of the House, he was quick to praise Obama in June 2012 for issuing an executive order allowing people who entered the United States illegally as children to remain and work without fear of deportation for at least two years. "With one swoop of the pen, he has mended a relationship with the Latino community that has been frayed," he told the *Chicago Sun-Times*. Gutierrez blasted Obama's rival, Mitt Romney, an immigration hard-liner, as someone who wanted to turn young children's dreams into "nightmares."

Following the 2012 election, Gutierrez joined a bipartisan group of House members that quietly met, off and on, to draft a proposal on immigration. He began as an optimist, hoping that a friendship he struck with 2012 GOP vice-presidential nominee Paul Ryan - the two worked out together at the House gym - would prove useful. Ryan offered encouragement by joining Gutierrez at an April 2013 lunch meeting of the Chicago City Club where each spoke in positive terms. Gutierrez repeatedly called for action, warning Republicans that if they didn't act, George W. Bush would be "the last Republican president in American history." But Senate passage of a bipartisan bill did nothing to move legislation through the House. "Having given ample time to craft legislation, you failed," he told colleagues in an angry floor speech.

He spread some of the blame to Democratic leaders for their reluctance to compromise. "I just found it extraordinary that every time we reached an agreement on something, then we had to go back to House Democratic leadership to explain it all over again," Gutierrez complained in a lengthy review of the legislative breakdown by the *New York Times Magazine* in September 2016. Some House Republicans praised him for his persistence. Gutierrez had applauded the late 2014 decision by Obama to act unilaterally through an executive order. But a federal judge in Texas barred enforcement of Obama's initiative, and an appeals court and the Supreme Court upheld the ruling.

Gutierrez has weighed in on Puerto Rican issues. He stoutly opposed the Democratic leadership's bill mandating a referendum on the island's commonwealth status and, if that were rejected, giving Puerto Rican voters a choice between the current status and independence. "This bill is not the product of consensus. It does not provide for true self-determination. The two-step process in the bill is designed to craft an artificial majority for statehood," he argued. The House passed the bill 223-169 in April 2010, but it died in the Senate. When the island faced financial crisis and the Republican-controlled Congress responded in 2016 with a plan to create an oversight board, Gutierrez complained that it was inadequate and he demanded that Congress provide more direct aid. But he ran into a stone wall of opposition, including from key House Democrats and Minority Leader Nancy Pelosi, who were backing the bipartisan plan, as did Obama.

Gutierrez has faced occasional ethics problems. In 2008, he was the subject of unflattering news coverage about his dealings with local developers. The *Chicago Tribune* reported that, starting in 2002, he had made about $421,000 by investing in half a dozen real estate deals with campaign supporters and then exiting a short time later. Gutierrez told the newspaper that he had made a profit in five of the deals but lost money on the sixth. During the trial that led to the bribery conviction of the developer, there was testimony that Gutierrez helped him to get a zoning change for a development on the West Side of Chicago. Gutierrez faced another ethics controversy in 2013, when *USA Today* reported that he had made payments for a decade from his official House account to a lobbying firm run by his former chief of staff. Gutierrez denied any wrongdoing, and the House Ethics Committee declined to launch a full-scale investigation.

Though he often plays the rebel, Gutierrez has sometimes built bridges among Chicago's fractious Democratic politicians to maximize Latino influence. In 2015, when the chief challenger to Mayor Rahm Emanuel was Latino community activist Chuy Garcia, Gutierrez joined most of the city's political establishment, including Latino leaders, in support of the mayor, citing his positive actions on immigration issues. He largely ignored Emanuel's reluctance to address those issues during his two years as chief of staff to Obama. "I sincerely believe [Emanuel] has learned, and he has appreciated like never before the kinds of challenges the immigrant community faces," Gutierrez told the *Tribune*.

That loss by Garcia and the independence of Gutierrez led to dissension within the Hispanic community. Spanish radio host Javier Salas, criticizing Gutierrez for what some viewed as a "betrayal," challenged him in the 2016 congressional primary. But Gutierrez raised $560,000 to $44,000 for Salas, and had his customary easy win, 75%-25%. In the presidential primary that year, he endorsed Hillary Clinton and criticized Bernie Sanders for being "absent for the most critical immigration debates." For his future, Gutierrez has announced more than once that he would retire from Congress, only to reverse course before the filing deadline. With the prospect that the election of President Donald Trump and the Republican-controlled Congress might move immigration legislation toward tougher enforcement action, Gutierrez could decide that he has had enough.

Chicago: Parts of North and Southwest Sides

Population		**Race and Ethnicity**		**Income**	
Total	712,139	White	21.1%	Median Income	$44,049 (353 out of 435)
Land area	52	Black	3.9%		
Pop/ sq mi	13577.5	Latino	70.8%		
Born in state	53.1%	Asian	3.0%	Under $50,000	55.5%
		Two races	1.0%	$50,000-$99,999	28.9%
Age Groups		Other	0.2%	$100,000-$199,999	13.2%
Under 18	27.1%			$200,000 or more	2.4%
18-34	28.4%	**Education**		Poverty Rate	21.8%
35-64	36.3%	H.S grad or less	58.5%		
Over 64	8.2%	Some college	21.2%	**Health Insurance**	
		College Degree, 4 yr	13.8%	With health insurance coverage	75.7%
Work		Post grad	6.5%		
White Collar	23.4%				
Sales and Service	45.6%	**Military**		**Public Assistance**	
Blue Collar	30.9%	Veteran	2.6%	Cash public assistance income	4.0%
Government	8.0%	Active Duty	0.0%		
				Food stamp/SNAP benefits	21.2%

Voter Turnout			
2015 Total Citizens 18+	361,683	2016 House Turnout as % CVAP	47%
2016 House turnout	171,297	2014 House Turnout as % CVAP	28%

2012 Presidential Vote		
Barack Obama	137,326	(81%)
Mitt Romney	28,955	(17%)

2016 Presidential Vote		
Hillary Clinton	172,367	(81%)
Donald Trump	27,808	(13%)
Gary Johnson	4,892	(2%)
Jill Stein	4,852	(2%)

Cook Partisan Voting Index: D+33

Just west of the Loop, the Chicago River splits into the North and South Branches, both penetrating the heart of old neighborhoods where immigrants got their start. The South Branch is the guts of Chicago, the site of one of Western civilization's astonishing engineering feats. In 1900, the course of the river was reversed so that sewage flowed downstate through a canal rather than out into Lake Michigan. Just blocks away was Maxwell Street, then thronged with market stalls and long the arrival point for Chicago-bound Jews. Not far away in an Italian-American neighborhood on Halsted Street was Jane Addams' Hull House, the original settlement house, where social workers instructed new immigrants on adapting to American life. To the south were Pilsen, arrival neighborhood for the Bohemians (Czechs), and the Irish neighborhoods along Archer Avenue. To the north was Milwaukee Avenue, the main street of Polish-Americans and Ukrainian-Americans.

Today, many of these places are arrival neighborhoods again, mostly for Chicago's wide variety of Hispanic immigrants. On the South Side, in the old river wards, is Chicago's Mexican-American community, extending west into Pilsen and into the once Bohemian suburb of Cicero, famous as a haven for Al Capone's mobsters in the 1920s. Times have changed: Beginning in the 1980s, Cicero became a transit point for Mexican immigrants, many of whom then made their permanent residences elsewhere in Chicago. Its official census population is 84,000, of whom 87 percent are Hispanic. But town officials believe the actual number is significantly higher because of the influx of undocumented residents. This is by far the largest Latino concentration north of Texas and Florida and between the two coasts. These neighborhoods have suffered serious crime problems. On South Pulaski Street, the police shooting in 2014 of black teenager Laquan McDonald led to the resignation of the Chicago police superintendent and to a U.S. Justice Department civil rights investigation.

The 4th Congressional District of Illinois remains the only majority-Hispanic district in the Midwest. With the South Side Mexican-American areas and the smaller North Side Puerto Rican communities separated by the West Side black ghetto, the solution was the creation of one of the most bizarrely designed congressional districts in the country, shaped like a pair of earmuffs. Essentially these two Latino communities, defined by careful boundaries to maximize the district's Hispanic percentage, are connected by a thin line of territory stretching around the black-majority 7th District at the Cook-DuPage County line. Of the nearly 70 percent of residents who are Hispanic, four-fifths are Mexican-American. The district is entirely in Cook County, with close to 80 percent of the votes cast in Chicago or Cicero.

The district also contains the rapidly gentrifying Northwest Side neighborhoods of Logan Square, famous for its boulevards and spacious mansions, and Humboldt Park, which includes the nation's only museum that focuses on Puerto Rican arts and culture. There, young professionals are moving in, with trendy restaurants, new condominiums and boutique shops locating alongside traditional Latin American *taquerias* and Hispanic churches. The *Chicago Advocate* referred to the area as the "Hipster Mecca of the Midwest." In 2015, the 2.7-mile Bloomingdale Trail for runners, cyclists and others opened in these neighborhoods. The chief downside is for the tenants - many of them Hispanics -- who have been forced out by housing prices that surged 61 percent from 2012 to 2016. Between 2000 and 2014, more than 19,000 Hispanics moved out of the Logan Square neighborhood and 10,000 whites moved in.

FIFTH DISTRICT

Mike Quigley (D)

Elected 2009, 5th term; b. Oct 17, 1958, Indianapolis, IN; Loyola University Law School (IL), J.D.; Roosevelt University (IL), B.A.; University of Chicago (IL), M.PP; Christian - Non-Denominational; Married (Barbara Quigley); 2 children.

Elected Office: Cook County commissioner, 1998-2009.

Professional Career: Cook County aldermanic aide, 1983-1989; Adjunct Professional, Roosevelt University, 2006-2007; Adjunct Professional in political science, Loyola University Chicago, 2002-2009; Practicing attorney, 1990-present.

DC Office: 2458 RHOB 20515, 202-225-4061, Fax: 202-225-5603, quigley.house.gov.

State Offices: Chicago, 773-267-5926; Chicago, 773-267-5926.

Committees: *Appropriations*: Financial Services & General Government (RMM), Transportation, HUD & Related Agencies. *Permanent Select on Intelligence*.

Group Ratings

	ADA	ACLU	AFL-CIO	LCV	ITI	COC	HAFA	ACU	CFG	FRC
2016	-	88%	-	100%	80%	54%	7%	0%	4%	0%
2015	80%	C	96%	97%	C	55%	C	0%	0%	0%

Almanac Ratings 2015

	Economy	Social	Foreign	Composite
Liberal	75%	100%	82%	86%
Conservative	25%	0%	18%	14%

Key Votes of the 114th Congress

1. Keystone Pipeline	N	5. Puerto Rico Debt	Y	9. Offenses by Aliens	N
2. Trade Deals	Y	6. Medical Marijuana	Y	10. Troops in Iraq	Y
3. Export-Import Bank	Y	7. Sanctuary Cities	N	11. Homeland Security $$	Y
4. Debt Ceiling Increase	Y	8. Armor-piercing Bullets	N	12. Trade Adjustment aid	Y

Election Results

Election	Name (Party)	Vote (%)		Cand. Spent	Ind. Exp. Support	Ind. Exp. Oppose
2016 General	Mike Quigley (D)	212,842	(68%)	$541,017		
	Vince Kolber (R)	86,222	(28%)	$50,844		
	Rob Sherman (G)	14,660	(5%)			
2016 Primary	Mike Quigley (D)		(100%)			

Prior winning percentages: 2014 (63%), 2012 (66%), 2010 (71%), 2009 special (69%)

Mike Quigley is a reform-minded Democrat who won a special election in 2009 to succeed Rahm Emanuel, who later became mayor of Chicago. He is both an avid hockey player - he has had more than 300 stitches to prove it - and an ex-political science professor whom *The New York Times* once called "the king of Chicago's public-policy nerds." In the House, he makes the most of his opportunities in the minority party with seats on the Appropriations and Intelligence committees, which tend to be less partisan than other panels.

Quigley grew up in the working-class suburb of Carol Stream in DuPage County. He graduated from Roosevelt University, got a master's in public policy at the University of Chicago and his law degree from Loyola University in Chicago. He practiced criminal law and taught political science part-time at Loyola. He started his career in politics as an aide to Alderman Bernard Hansen and got involved in a community battle to stop the addition of lights for night games at Wrigley Field, which is in the heart of an old, gentrified neighborhood. (He lost that fight, but the Cubs mostly remained a good neighbor.) In 1998, Quigley was elected to the Cook County Board of Commissioners, where he became an independent voice and a frequent nemesis of board President John Stroger. He pushed reforms such as ending patronage jobs at the Cook County Forest Preserve District, promoted environmental action, and sponsored a proposal to allow gay couples to register as domestic partners. In 2005, Quigley decided to challenge Stroger for board president, but later dropped out and backed Forrest Claypool, saying the two would have split the anti-incumbent vote if they had both remained in the race. Claypool repaid the favor by endorsing Quigley for the House seat.

After President Barack Obama plucked Emanuel from the House to serve as his chief of staff, many candidates jumped into the wide-open Democratic primary. State Rep. Sara Feigenholtz was endorsed by EMILY's List, which supports abortion rights. Alderman Patrick O'Connor and state Rep. John Fritchey had local party machine support. The appointment of Roland Burris to the Senate by impeached Democratic Gov. Rod Blagojevich became a campaign issue, with candidates seeking to burnish their credentials as reformers and attacking their opponents for having been associated with the disgraced governor. Fritchey suffered from having defended Burris at a legislative hearing in January 2009. Quigley ran a late ad comparing Feigenholtz to President Richard Nixon, saying she had resorted to unfair campaign charges. That may have extinguished any lingering friendship between Quigley and Feigenholtz, who had dated briefly years earlier.

Quigley received key newspaper endorsements from the *Chicago Sun-Times* and the *Chicago Tribune*, the latter praising him for an "outstanding record of independent, reform-minded performance in office." In a low-turnout event, Quigley won the primary with 20 percent of the vote to 17 percent for Fritchey and 15 percent for Feigenholtz. Quigley breezed to victory in the general election.

In the House, Quigley has been a consistent Democratic vote but one who is unafraid to ruffle feathers. He was among the first Democrats in 2010 to call on Rep. Charles Rangel of New York to give up his Ways and Means Committee chairmanship while battling ethics problems. He cofounded the Congressional Transparency Caucus and introduced legislation requiring lobbyists to disclose the name of each affected executive branch official and each member of Congress and staff with whom they meet. In 2014, he wrote that Supreme Court justices should comply with the same financial disclosure rules that apply to members of Congress and top officials of the executive branch.

He has been a persistent advocate for requiring Congressional Research Service reports to be made public. "Taxpayers have a stake in these reports, providing more than $100 million annually to support the work of the Congressional Research Service," he wrote in *Time*. "Unfortunately, these reports are often made available to just a select few inside the Beltway, leaving everyday citizens out in the dark." In May 2016, the Appropriations Committee defeated his proposal, with opponents objecting that public disclosure would infringe on the information needs of lawmakers. He has worked with other Illinois lawmakers to block former congressmen convicted of corruption from collecting their public pensions. That responded to the conviction of Illinois Gov. Rod Blagojevich, who was the representative for his district prior to Emanuel. He moved into the House hierarchy with a seat on the Appropriations Committee, where he was the only Illinois member from either party; he later joined the Intelligence Committee.In 2017, Quigley became ranking Democrat on the Appropriations Subcommittee on Financial Services-a useful position for the Representative of a city with large financial markets.

Quigley has been active in calling for tighter gun control laws. On two issues of importance to his constituents, he has pushed for an extension of the visa waiver program to Poland, and for review by the Food and Drug Administration of its policy that bans gay and bisexual men from donating blood.

He has been a leader of the LGBT Equality Caucus. To learn more about what his constituents' lives are like, he took a series of temporary work-day jobs ranging from collecting garbage to delivering pizza.

Quigley has coasted to reelection. He toyed with the idea of running in 2011 to succeed retiring Chicago Mayor Richard M. Daley but decided not to join the crowded field that included Emanuel, who went on to be elected mayor.

Chicago: North Side, Cook Suburbs

Population		**Race and Ethnicity**		**Income**	
Total	730,336	White	68.6%	Median Income	$70,734 (71 out of 435)
Land area	96	Black	2.5%		
Pop/ sq mi	7630.7	Latino	19.8%	Under $50,000	35.7%
Born in state	54.8%	Asian	6.9%	$50,000-$99,999	29.7%
		Two races	1.9%	$100,000-$199,999	23.6%
Age Groups		Other	0.2%	$200,000 or more	10.9%
Under 18	18.6%			Poverty Rate	10.4%
18-34	31.5%	**Education**			
35-64	37.9%	H.S grad or less	28.2%	**Health Insurance**	
Over 64	12.0%	Some college	20.8%	With health insurance coverage	88.6%
		College Degree, 4 yr	31.0%		
Work		Post grad	20.0%		
White Collar	48.1%			**Public Assistance**	
Sales and Service	38.3%	**Military**		Cash public assistance income	1.7%
Blue Collar	13.5%	Veteran	3.8%		
Government	9.8%	Active Duty	0.0%	Food stamp/SNAP benefits	6.7%

Voter Turnout			
2015 Total Citizens 18+	529,688	2016 House Turnout as % CVAP	59%
2016 House turnout	313,724	2014 House Turnout as % CVAP	35%

2012 Presidential Vote		
Barack Obama	188,166	(66%)
Mitt Romney	90,715	(32%)

2016 Presidential Vote		
Hillary Clinton	229,944	(70%)
Donald Trump	78,074	(24%)
Gary Johnson	12,645	(4%)

Cook Partisan Voting Index: D+20

Few places in America today have more ethnic and cultural variety than the North Side of Chicago. This has been the destination of one immigrant group after another. Its neighborhoods harbor all manner of successful, middle-class people. Wooden workingmen's cottages from the late 19th century give way to sturdy brick houses from the early 1900s, and then to the prairie bungalows of the 1920s and the white-shuttered, orange-brick colonials of the 1950s. Chicago was America's top immigrant destination for Poles, Lithuanians, Czechs, Slovaks, Ukrainians and Romanians. Something about the heavy, dull clouds of the long winters, the short, hot summers, and a climate suited to potatoes and cabbage and other hardy vegetables may have reminded them of Central and Eastern Europe, with the addition of the bustling Loop. In the 1980s, upwardly mobile immigrants from Mexico and Guatemala, Korea and the Philippines, were moving in.

Family ties, webs of acquaintances that reach back to ancestral villages, have made the North Side of Chicago a natural port of entry for Eastern bloc migrants, even as other newcomers arrive with relationships extending to Latin America and Southeast Asia. The collapse of the Soviet Union encouraged new rounds of immigrants in the 1990s from Poland and Ukraine, and also from Pakistan, India and Bosnia. A couple of blocks from the Chicago River and the Kennedy Expressway is the grand, old St. Stanislaus Kostka Church, a traditional center of the Polish community since the 19th century that now conducts masses in Spanish.

The 5th Congressional District covers an oddly shaped swath across Chicago's North Side and the city's western suburbs, running from the lakefront to, and including, O'Hare International Airport on the north end of the city, and dipping into western suburbs like Elmhurst and affluent Hinsdale. It takes in the old Polish-American and Ukrainian-American neighborhoods and shops around Milwaukee Avenue, and the Italian neighborhoods running west on Grand Avenue. It also includes the gentrified Chicago neighborhoods of Old Town, where Crate & Barrel was founded in 1962, and where old houses and factories are being converted into upscale condominiums, often over the objections of preservationists. Nearby Lincoln Park is the second-richest neighborhood in Chicago (after the Gold Coast); it abounds with boutiques, clubs and restaurants and contains DePaul University, the nation's largest Roman Catholic university. Those commercial activities have substantially reduced the residential population. Chicago Mayor Rahm Emanuel lives in trendy Ravenswood in the district, and he received strong support on the North Side in his 2015 reelection.

The district is home to baseball's famed Wrigley Field, which opened in 1914 and is a protected landmark that has defied the teardown trend in ballparks. The friendly confines finally rewarded the century-long heartbreak of its fans when the Cubs won the World Series in 2016, while in the midst of a $750 million renovation and update of the iconic edifice, which is scheduled for completion in 2018. Just east of Wrigleyville is Boystown, the epicenter of Chicago's gay community; rainbow flags are present on most businesses in the neighborhood. At O'Hare, planning was scheduled to be completed in 2017 for upgrades of two terminals plus additional gates. In June 2016, McDonald's announced that it was abandoning its corporate headquarters in Oak Brook, including renowned Hamburger University, for a new site in Chicago's West Loop area. The 5th District contains the largest white population of the seven districts based in Chicago: The Hispanic share has increased modestly to 20 percent. A scant 3 percent is African-American. While the 5th now has some Republican-leaning western suburbs, it remains a solidly Democratic district. In 2016, Hillary Clinton won, 70%-24%, an increase over the 66%-32% lead for President Barack Obama in 2012.

SIXTH DISTRICT

Peter Roskam (R)

Elected 2006, 6th term; b. Sep 13, 1961, Hinsdale; Illinois Institute of Technology Kent College of Law, J.D.; University of Illinois, B.A.; Anglican; Married (Elizabeth Andrea Gracey Roskam); 5 children (1 deceased).

Elected Office: IL House, 1992-1998; IL Senate, 2000-2006, Minority whip, 2003-2006.

Professional Career: Aide, U.S. Rep. Tom DeLay, 1985-1986, U.S. Rep. Henry Hyde, 1986-1987; H.S. teacher, 1983-1985; Executive Director, Educational Assistance Ltd., 1987-1993; Practicing attorney, 1994-2006.

DC Office: 2246 RHOB 20515, 202-225-4561, Fax: 202-225-1166, roskam.house.gov.

State Offices: Barrington, 847-656-6354; West Chicago, 630-232-0006.

Committees: *Ways & Means*: Health, Tax Policy (Chmn).

Group Ratings

	ADA	ACLU	AFL-CIO	LCV	ITI	COC	HAFA	ACU	CFG	FRC
2016	-	5%	-	3%	100%	100%	67%	67%	67%	100%
2015	0%	C	10%	6%	C	83%	C	65%	69%	100%

Almanac Ratings 2015

	Economy	Social	Foreign	Composite
Liberal	5%	0%	4%	3%
Conservative	95%	100%	96%	97%

Key Votes of the 114th Congress

1. Keystone Pipeline	Y	5. Puerto Rico Debt	Y	9. Offenses by Aliens	Y
2. Trade Deals	Y	6. Medical Marijuana	N	10. Troops in Iraq	N
3. Export-Import Bank	NV	7. Sanctuary Cities	Y	11. Homeland Security $$	N
4. Debt Ceiling Increase	N	8. Armor-piercing Bullets	Y	12. Trade Adjustment aid	Y

Election Results

Election	Name (Party)	Vote (%)		Cand. Spent	Ind. Exp. Support	Ind. Exp. Oppose
2016 General	Peter Roskam (R)	208,555	(59%)	$3,164,019	$17,460	
	Amanda Howland (D)	143,591	(41%)	$55,538		
2016 Primary	Peter Roskam (R)	82,628	(69%)			
	Gordon Kinzler (R)	37,546	(31%)			

Prior winning percentages: 2014 (67%), 2012 (59%), 2010 (64%), 2008 (58%), 2006 (51%)

Peter Roskam, a Republican elected in 2006, is well-regarded among his GOP colleagues as smart, hard-working and fair-minded. He served as chief deputy whip until July 2014, when he sought the whip's job only to lose to the more-conservative Steve Scalise of Louisiana, who had the advantages of hailing from a red state and the South. Roskam remained a go-to player in the House. In 2017, he took the influential chairmanship of the Ways and Means Tax Policy Subcommittee.

A native of DuPage County, Roskam was a varsity gymnast in high school, graduated from the University of Illinois and got his law degree while directing a charitable organization started by his father that used corporate resources to fund college scholarships. He was an aide to widely respected conservative Republican Rep. Henry Hyde, his predecessor. Roskam served six years in the state House, where he was a colleague of Barack Obama, and six years in the state Senate, where he was the Republican whip and floor leader. He ran unsuccessfully in 1998 for an open congressional seat, losing 45%-40% to state House colleague Judy Biggert in the Republican primary.

When Hyde stepped down. Roskam managed to scare off challengers for the GOP nomination, conserving his money for the general election. In the general, he faced Democrat Tammy Duckworth, an Iraq war veteran who was well-known as a Black Hawk helicopter pilot who lost both legs in Iraq after her helicopter was hit by a rocket-propelled grenade and crashed. The two nominees clashed over abortion rights, federal funding for embryonic stem cell research, and expansion of O'Hare International Airport, all of which Roskam opposed. Duckworth criticized Roskam as "a rubber stamp" for the Bush administration. Roskam disparaged Duckworth as the "candidate from the Chicago Democratic machine" because of her ties to Rahm Emanuel, who then chaired the Democratic Congressional Campaign Committee. In one of the few Republican successes in a competitive contest that year, Roskam won 51%-49%. (Duckworth recovered, with election to the 8th District in 2012 and to the Senate in 2016.)

In the House, Roskam opposed Democrats' economic proposals. He accused Obama of being unwilling to deal with Republicans. "You know, in the legislature, Barack Obama was somebody you could sit down and negotiate with. … Now I think the problem is that the president has not shown any bipartisanship," he told *The Daily Beast* website in 2012.

Early in his House career, Roskam cast moderate votes in 2009 to tighten food safety, impose more stringent regulations on credit card companies, and give the Food and Drug Administration authority to regulate some tobacco products. He has styled himself as less centrist since Republicans regained House control in 2011. In the *Almanac* vote ratings for 2015, he ranked among the most conservative House members in each of the three issue categories. As chief deputy whip, he won praise from colleagues. "People like him, he's smart, he's savvy, he understands the policy end and how it relates to the political end," Majority Leader Eric Cantor told the suburban Chicago *Daily Herald* in 2012. It helped that he was a skilled fundraiser, often going to districts of other candidates to assist them. Since 2010, he has taken in more than $12 million through his campaign and political action committees, according to the Center for Responsive Politics.

When Cantor unexpectedly lost his primary in June 2014, Majority Whip Kevin McCarthy of California moved into the majority leader's slot. That left the whip's job open, and Roskam - who had been meeting with colleagues to discuss his future even before Cantor lost - threw his hat in the ring. He met resistance from some Republicans who questioned his conservatism. It didn't help him when the conservative website Breitbart.com reported that he had boasted of receiving praise from Obama on an "Obama Voters for Roskam" website in 2008. Despite his promise to appoint a deputy from a red state, he lost to Scalise.

A year later, when John Boehner resigned as Speaker, Roskam sought to help shape the new Republican leadership team. "We need a plan, not a person," he wrote other Republicans, in calling for wide-ranging discussions. "Simply reshuffling the deck won't serve our members, and it especially won't help our next slate of leaders who will be tasked with producing better results than our leaders have so far been able to achieve." A *National Review* article at the time listed him as a "dark-horse candidate for Speaker." But, as Republicans struggled to find a successor to Boehner, Roskam was not part of the final mix. Instead, the position went to Paul Ryan, another Midwest Republican on Ways and Means, who became the widespread choice. The lack of other openings squelched Roskam's interest in seeking another leadership post.

Roskam has been given assignments, including as leader of the House Democracy Partnership that assists legislatures in emerging democracies. He was a member of the Benghazi investigating committee, where he criticized Hillary Clinton's failure to turn over emails when she was Secretary of State. When she testified before the panel in October 2015, Roskam dramatically tore up sheets of paper to symbolize how she ignored requests for increased diplomatic security for Ambassador Christopher Stevens in Libya. He told her that she should have told Congress in earlier testimony about handling her responsibilities, "We breached our fundamental duty to mitigate [Stevens'] danger and ensure his safety."

With his seat on the powerful Ways and Means Committee, Roskam has made a priority of reforming the tax code, describing the current code as "a mess of loopholes, carve outs, and crony capitalism" that has hindered job growth. In 2015, he helped to prepare a package of bills designed to crack down on allegations of political bias at the Internal Revenue Service. Moving quickly up the seniority ladder, he became chairman of the Tax Policy Subcommittee at a crucial moment when congressional Republicans and President Donald Trump committed themselves to comprehensive reform of the Internal Revenue Code. "We have a once-in-a-generation opportunity to fix our broken tax code and enhance American competitiveness for generations to come. I'm honored to hold this important gavel and look forward to putting it to good use shepherding tax reform across the finish line," he said following his selection.

At home, Sen. Richard Durbin vowed that Democrats would give Roskam a strong challenge in 2008. But Duckworth, the party's top prospect for 2008, decided to stay as head of the Illinois Veterans' Affairs Department. Instead, Democrats nominated another Iraq war veteran, retired Army Col. Jill Morgenthaler, who was the Army spokeswoman during the Abu Ghraib prison scandal. She accused Roskam of having "extreme" views on abortion rights, health care, and the economy. Despite early Democratic hopes that Obama's coattails would reach across Illinois, the national party gave little help to Morgenthaler. Roskam handily won a second term, 58%-42%. Since Illinois Democrats decided in 2012 to pack as many Republicans as possible into his district to create two new neighboring Democratic seats in the Chicago suburbs, he has easily won reelection.

The shrinking Republican vote in his district likely will demand his attention; Democrats identified him an early target for 2018. Otherwise, Roskam may have opportunities for additional influence in the House, where Republicans from Illinois have a long history as party leaders.

West-Central Chicagoland: DuPage, Kane

Population		**Race and Ethnicity**		**Income**	
Total	724,337	White	77.6%	Median Income	$91,507 (15 out of 435)
Land area	379	Black	2.6%		
Pop/ sq mi	1912.3	Latino	9.6%	Under $50,000	25.7%
Born in state	65.6%	Asian	8.5%	$50,000-$99,999	28.4%
		Two races	1.5%	$100,000-$199,999	31.6%
Age Groups		Other	0.1%	$200,000 or more	14.2%
Under 18	24.3%			Poverty Rate	5.8%
18-34	18.8%	**Education**			
35-64	43.5%	H.S grad or less	23.1%	**Health Insurance**	
Over 64	13.4%	Some college	26.5%	With health insurance coverage	93.9%
		College Degree, 4 yr	30.4%		
Work		Post grad	20.1%		
White Collar	48.2%			**Public Assistance**	
Sales and Service	38.4%	**Military**		Cash public assistance income	1.1%
Blue Collar	13.4%	Veteran	5.8%		
Government	10.1%	Active Duty	0.0%	Food stamp/SNAP benefits	4.4%

Voter Turnout			
2015 Total Citizens 18+	510,386	2016 House Turnout as % CVAP	69%
2016 House turnout	352,146	2014 House Turnout as % CVAP	47%

2012 Presidential Vote		
Mitt Romney	179,607	(53%)
Barack Obama	151,760	(45%)

2016 Presidential Vote		
Hillary Clinton	177,549	(49%)
Donald Trump	152,935	(42%)
Gary Johnson	18,336	(5%)

Cook Partisan Voting Index: R+2

Most residents of Chicagoland now live in the suburbs, and increasingly not even in Cook County, but in the collar counties surrounding Cook. DuPage County, straight west of Chicago, had 103,000 residents in 1940; in 2013, there were 934,000, with new subdivisions still springing up at the western edges. This is no longer a one-trick county of bedroom suburbs. It has become an engine of economic growth, containing the Illinois Technology and Research Corridor, one of suburban Chicago's biggest employment hubs. In Oak Brook are the headquarters of Ace Hardware and Federal Signal.

Nearby are graceful, old railroad-commuter towns like Hinsdale and Downers Grove, plus Barrington Hills, known for its country manors and large open areas protected by preservationists. Naperville, once a country village, is now an edge city, with a school district that is top-ranked in science. Wheaton is home to the Illinois landmark Cantigny, a 500-acre public park and recreation area that was once the estate of Col. Robert McCormick, longtime publisher of the *Chicago Tribune*. Wheaton College, known as the "evangelical Harvard," boasts Reverend Billy Graham among its alumni.

Politically, these suburbs were once rock-ribbed Republican, convinced that civic virtues could best be realized by opposing the party of City Hall in Chicago. In the 1990s, they became less Republican, as voters recoiled from the national party's cultural conservatism. After voting for Republicans in every presidential election in the 20th century, DuPage County twice voted for President Barack Obama, giving him a narrow 49.7 percent plurality of the vote in 2012. Hillary Clinton in 2016 increased the Democratic advantage to a more pronounced 54%-40%. The once rural county has become more diverse; foreign-born residents now make up 19 percent of the county-wide population. This increase is part of the broader racial shifts across Chicagoland, which is moving soon to majority-minority status.

The 6th Congressional District of Illinois forms a large C that encompasses a small wedge of Cook County and parts of the collar counties of Kane, McHenry and Lake; a bit more than half the population lives in DuPage, parts of which have been grafted onto five other districts. It takes in towns including Barrington, Wheaton, Winfield, Downers Grove and parts of Naperville. The 6th was designed in redistricting as a Republican bastion, with the solidly GOP Palatine in Cook, St. Charles in Kane, and Crystal Lake in McHenry. The Republican vote here slipped markedly in 2016. What had been a 53%-45% lead for Mitt Romney in 2012 became a 49%-42% lead for Hillary Clinton. Even with that weak performance, this was the best district for Trump in Chicagoland, though the worst vote of the seven Republican-held districts in Illinois.

SEVENTH DISTRICT

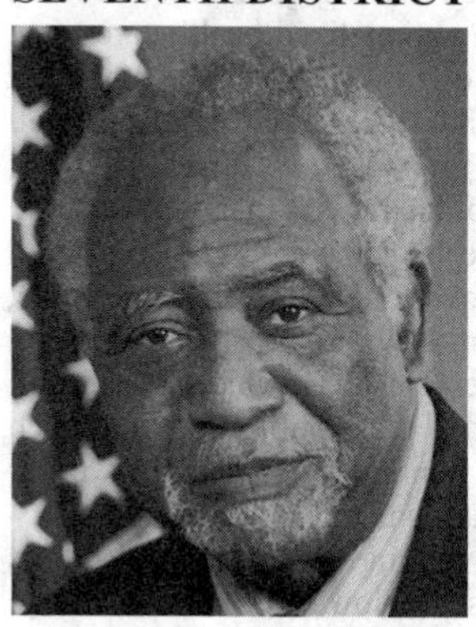

Danny Davis (D)

Elected 1996, 11th term; b. Sep 06, 1941, Parkdale, AR; Arkansas Agricultural and Mechanical College, B.A.; Chicago State University (IL), M.A.; Union Institute & University, Ph.D.; Baptist; Married (Vera G. Davis); 2 children (1 deceased); 4 grandchildren (1 deceased).

Elected Office: Chicago city alderman, 1979-1990; Cook County commissioner, 1990-1996.

Professional Career: Teacher, Chicago Public Schls., 1962-1969; Health care planner, 1969-1979.

DC Office: 2159 RHOB 20515, 202-225-5006, Fax: 202-225-5641, davis.house.gov.

State Offices: Chicago, 773-533-7520.

Committees: *Ways & Means*: Human Resources (RMM), Trade.

Group Ratings

	ADA	ACLU	AFL-CIO	LCV	ITI	COC	HAFA	ACU	CFG	FRC
2016	-	88%	-	97%	50%	64%	13%	0%	0%	0%
2015	95%	C	100%	94%	C	40%	C	0%	0%	0%

Almanac Ratings 2015

	Economy	Social	Foreign	Composite
Liberal	98%	100%	100%	99%
Conservative	2%	0%	0%	1%

Key Votes of the 114th Congress

1. Keystone Pipeline	N	5. Puerto Rico Debt	N	9. Offenses by Aliens	N
2. Trade Deals	N	6. Medical Marijuana	Y	10. Troops in Iraq	Y
3. Export-Import Bank	Y	7. Sanctuary Cities	N	11. Homeland Security $$	Y
4. Debt Ceiling Increase	Y	8. Armor-piercing Bullets	N	12. Trade Adjustment aid	Y

Election Results

Election	Name (Party)	Vote (%)	Cand. Spent	Ind. Exp. Support	Ind. Exp. Oppose
2016 General	Danny Davis (D)	250,584 (84%)	$371,790		
	Jeffrey Leef (R)	46,882 (16%)			
2016 Primary	Danny K. Davis (D)	135,799 (81%)			
	Thomas Day (D)	31,274 (19%)			

Prior winning percentages: 2014 (85%), 2012 (85%), 2010 (82%), 2008 (85%), 2006 (87%), 2004 (86%), 2002 (83%), 2000 (86%), 1998 (93%), 1996 (83%)

Danny Davis, a Democrat first elected in 1996 at age 55, is a liberal who has been eager for political advancement. He waged two unsuccessful campaigns for Chicago mayor and twice flirted with running for president of the Cook County Board of Commissioners. His opportunities to seek other office likely have ended, but he has become a senior statesman in the Congressional Black Caucus.

Davis grew up on a cotton farm in Arkansas, graduated from college in that state, then moved to Chicago and worked as a teacher, assistant principal and guidance counselor in Chicago public schools. For 10 years, he ran a community health project on the West Side. He was elected alderman in the 29th Ward in 1979, and supported Mayor Harold Washington, the city's first black mayor, in his notorious 1980s battles with white machine aldermen dubbed the "Council Wars." In 1990, Davis was elected a Cook County commissioner.

In 1996, when Democratic Rep. Cardiss Collins retired after nearly 24 years in the House, Davis ran for the seat. His major opponents were 3rd Ward Alderman Dorothy Tillman, an ally of Chicago Mayor Richard M. Daley, and 28th Ward Alderman Ed Smith. Davis campaigned as a big-government liberal, calling for a $7.60 minimum wage, affirmative action programs, and a nationalized health care plan. He won with 33 percent and has not faced a serious challenge since. However, he lost his 29th Ward committeeman post to a Daley-backed challenger in 2000 - a political hat that many Chicago elected officials find at least as vital as their government hats.

Davis has a liberal voting record. He has pushed for tax incentives for businesses that create jobs in inner-city communities and distressed rural areas. He has opposed income tax cuts for others, even when advocated by Democratic President Bill Clinton. On the Oversight and Government Reform Committee, where he no longer serves, he was a champion of organized labor as he worked with a bipartisan coalition that in 2006 enacted big changes in the Postal Service. He criticized a new Postal Service overhaul bill that passed the committee under Republican control in 2011, calling it "a glass half-empty approach that creates new bureaucracies, diminished congressional oversight, and continues to attack the worker rights of postal employees." Congressional agreement on a postal overhaul has remained elusive.

His devotion to issues affecting the poor has won him respect even among Republicans. With his wife, Vera, Davis in the mid-2000s supported a local program to increase the low share of black home ownership in his district by offering credit counseling and innovative forms of mortgage financing. With the view that everybody deserves a second chance, Davis has taken a deep interest in the problems of former convicts seeking to transition to the mainstream. He teamed on a bipartisan bill creating tax credits to encourage transitional housing and job training for former prisoners. It evolved into his Second Chance Act, which President George W. Bush signed into law in 2008. Subsequent efforts to expand program benefits have failed. Republican Sen. Rob Portman of Ohio has collaborated with Davis as the chief advocate for the program. Davis also has filed legislation to make available educational Pell Grants to prisoners. That option was eliminated when Congress enacted the 1994 crime bill.

In 2006, Davis sought to become Cook County Board president when incumbent John Stroger suffered a serious stroke. But Democratic committeemen overwhelmingly supported Stroger's son, Todd, for the nomination. After the 2008 election, Davis campaigned publicly for the support of Democratic Gov. Rod Blagojevich to fill Obama's Senate seat. Blagojevich called Davis his top choice, but Davis turned down what was bound to be a tainted appointment after Blagojevich was criminally charged and then convicted for trying to gain politically and personally from his power to make the appointment.

As a consolation prize, House Democratic leaders gave Davis a seat on the Ways and Means Committee. He was an outspoken defender of the committee's chairman, New York Democrat Charles B. Rangel, during his ethics scandal, and called the health care overhaul "good for black America."

In 2009, Davis weighed another bid for the Cook County board but ultimately did not run. After Daley announced in 2010 he would not seek reelection as mayor, Davis jumped into the race, collecting endorsements from 15 African-American aldermen. But with pressure mounting to settle on a single black candidate, he endorsed former Sen. Carol Moseley Braun, who had stressed her fundraising advantage over Davis. She lost to Rahm Emanuel. In 2015, Davis again was on the losing side when he endorsed Chuy Garcia, who challenged Emanuel for reelection.

Following the election of Donald Trump as president, Davis said that he was "not a happy camper." He added, "I think we will struggle for the next four years, but we'll never give up." A week later, the 15-year-old grandson of Davis was shot to death in a dispute over gym shoes. He called for the declaration of a "state of emergency" in high-crime areas of the city to address violence, education, economic development and related problems.

Chicago: Downtown, West Side

Population		**Race and Ethnicity**		**Income**	
Total	724,029	White	27.4%	Median Income	$50,096 (255 out of 435)
Land area	63	Black	50.2%		
Pop/ sq mi	11580.8	Latino	13.9%		
Born in state	63.3%	Asian	6.7%	Under $50,000	50.0%
		Two races	1.5%	$50,000-$99,999	24.9%
Age Groups		Other	0.3%	$100,000-$199,999	16.9%
Under 18	21.7%			$200,000 or more	8.3%
18-34	31.0%	**Education**		Poverty Rate	25.8%
35-64	36.3%	H.S grad or less	38.1%		
Over 64	11.0%	Some college	22.6%	**Health Insurance**	
		College Degree, 4 yr	21.4%	With health insurance coverage	85.8%
Work		Post grad	18.0%		
White Collar	45.0%				
Sales and Service	41.4%	**Military**		**Public Assistance**	
Blue Collar	13.6%	Veteran	4.1%	Cash public assistance income	4.3%
Government	12.3%	Active Duty	0.0%		
				Food stamp/SNAP benefits	22.7%

Voter Turnout			
2015 Total Citizens 18+	513,276	2016 House Turnout as % CVAP	58%
2016 House turnout	297,466	2014 House Turnout as % CVAP	35%

2012 Presidential Vote		
Barack Obama	263,928	(87%)
Mitt Romney	35,595	(12%)

2016 Presidential Vote		
Hillary Clinton	271,156	(87%)
Donald Trump	28,523	(9%)
Gary Johnson	6,759	(2%)

Cook Partisan Voting Index: D+38

An airplane passenger on a cloudless day can get a clear view of the biggest man-made cityscape between the Atlantic and Pacific oceans: Chicago's Loop. Its high rises and parks along Lake Michigan were built a century ago, and the downtown district was named in 1897 for the quadrilateral shape the elevated train forms around the city's center. International School modernists built their most impressive collection of buildings here and along Lake Shore Drive in the years after World War II. The Loop now spreads beyond the elevated train, or the "El" as it's known locally. It reaches west beyond the financial exchanges to the 110-story Willis (formerly Sears) Tower - once the world's tallest building, now fourteenth and second in the United States behind One World Trade Center in New York - situated near the Chicago River. The Loop reaches north and stops at the Gold Coast, the wondrous shopping district along North Michigan Avenue. West of the Gold Coast is the River North neighborhood, which has become one of the city's most vibrant. In October 2016, the vacancy rate for downtown offices was at its lowest since 2000. New construction has remained strong in the Loop and nearby areas.

This is the face Chicago likes to present to the world: giant structures rising where the prairies meet the great lake, a vast concentration of brains and muscle, the nerve center of the nation's commodities markets, and, most recently, a hive of political activity. President Barack Obama's high rise headquarters in 2012 filled a 50,000-square foot floor at One Prudential Plaza. The 2008 campaign office, by comparison, was a 33,000-square foot start-up a few blocks away on Michigan Avenue. South of the Loop sits McCormick Place, the largest convention center in North America; Obama celebrated his reelection victory here in November 2012 and gave his farewell as president in January 2017. At Grant Park, the president delivered his historic 2008 victory speech in front of 240,000 onlookers cheering the election of the nation's first African-American president. The 319-acre park includes several of the city's civic treasures, including the Art Institute, Millennium Park and Buckingham Fountain.

Not far west of the luxurious lakefront neighborhoods are the muscle and sinew, gristle and fat of the city. The West Side of Chicago, the vast acres directly west of the Loop, for years was a grimy and dangerous slum, with some areas almost completely abandoned. The decay spread west almost to the city border with upper-income and racially integrated Oak Park. Many factories that made Chicago the chocolate and candy center of the nation were shuttered, and production went mostly overseas. The West Side began to revive in the 1990s. The United Center, the erstwhile home court of Michael Jordan, sparked commercial development, lower crime rates, and higher land values. Former meatpacking buildings have been turned into art galleries. A massive new downtown dormitory houses students from nearby DePaul University, Roosevelt University and Columbia College.

The 7th Congressional District of Illinois contains the Loop, most of the North Michigan corridor, the Near North Side, and a few South Side neighborhoods. Its heart, demographically and spiritually, is the predominantly African-American West Side, which is more depopulated and socially disorganized than the predominantly black South Side. Like other minority neighborhoods in Chicago, the West Side has suffered from the recent surge in murders and other violence. The district is entirely in Cook County. To preserve its shrinking African-American population, Democratic redistricters drew in additional South Side precincts. A few blocks west of McCormick Place on the South Side is Chinatown, which has retained its ethnic quality while it has grown and avoided gentrification.

Just outside the city limits to the west, but in the district, is Oak Park, the boyhood home of writer Ernest Hemingway and the location of architect Frank Lloyd Wright's home and museum and many of his prairie-style houses. There is also well-heeled River Forest; more modest Maywood, which is a black-majority suburb; Broadview; and Hillside. African Americans now make up 49 percent of the district, with 14 percent Hispanic. It is the most heavily Democratic district in the state. Hillary Clinton got 87 percent of the vote here in 2012, as did Obama in 2012. Unlike Obama, she held her opponent below 10 percent.

EIGHTH DISTRICT

Raja Krishnamoorthi (D)

Elected 2016, 1st term; b. Jul 19, 1973, New Delhi, IN; Princeton University (NJ), Bach. Deg., 1995; Harvard University, J.D., 2000; Hinduism; Married (Priya Krishnamoorthi); 2 children.

Professional Career: Clerk, U.S District Court N. IL, 2000-2002; Staff, Illinois Housing Development Auth., 2005-2007; IL Special Asst. Attorney General, 2006-2007; Deputy State Treasurer of IL, 2008-2009.

DC Office: 515 CHOB 20515, 202-225-3711, Fax: 202-225-7830; Website: krishnamoorthi.house.gov.

State Offices: Schaumburg, 847-413-1959.

Committees: *Education & the Workforce*: Higher Education & Workforce Development, Workforce Protections. *Oversight & Government Reform*: Health Care, Benefits & Administrative Rules (RMM), Information Technology.

Election Results

Election	Name (Party)	Vote (%)		Cand. Spent	Ind. Exp. Support	Ind. Exp. Oppose
2016 General	Raja Krishnamoorthi (D)	144,954	(58%)	$2,484,554	$1,046	
	Pete DiCianni (R)	103,617	(42%)	$162,335	$130	
2016 Primary	Raja Krishnamoorthi (D)	44,174	(57%)			
	Michael Noland (D)	22,593	(29%)			
	Deb Bullwinkel (D)	10,778	(14%)			

Raja Krishnamoorthi, on a second try, was elected in 2016 to the seat vacated by fellow Democrat Tammy Duckworth, who ran successfully for the Senate. In 2012, the two of them competed in the Democratic primary for this seat, which had been significantly redrawn by redistricting. The more politically experienced Duckworth won, 66%-34%. This time, Krishnamoorthi had the easy win. He was one of five Asian Americans who were House Democratic newcomers.

Krishnamoorthi was born in India, came to the United States when he was three months old and was raised in Peoria, Illinois, where his father was a professor of engineering at Bradley University. He earned a bachelor's degree in mechanical engineering from Princeton University and got a law degree from Harvard. Following law school, Krishnamoorthi clerked for a federal judge in Chicago and later became a partner in the law firm of Kirkland & Ellis. In 2004, he served as issues director for the Senate campaign of Barack Obama, and had been a low-level aide in 2000 when Obama ran unsuccessfully for a House seat in Chicago; the two first met at a Chicago reception for lawyers interested in civil rights. In 2008, he was an adviser to Obama's presidential campaign. While practicing law, Krishnamoorthi served as a special assistant attorney general in the state's Public Integrity Unit. He also was a member of the Illinois Housing Development Authority and the Illinois deputy treasurer, where he helped to manage the state's technology venture capital fund.

In the private sector, Krishnamoorthi was president of Sivananthan Labs and Episolar Inc., a group of small businesses that develop and sell national security and renewable industry products. He was co-founder of InSPIRE, a non-profit organization that provides training in solar technology to inner-city students and veterans, and a former vice-chairman of the Illinois Innovation Council. He sought the Democratic nomination for state comptroller in 2010, and lost narrowly. When he first ran for the House two years later, Duckworth was actively supported by Democratic Sen. Richard Durbin and much of the state party establishment.

In the three-way Democratic primary in 2016, Krishnamoorthi benefited from a big fundraising advantage and his previous campaign experience, plus the large Asian - including Indian-American -- population in the district. "Instead of buildings walls, we should be building bridges," an explicit contrast to Republican presidential nominee Donald Trump, was a campaign theme. Most of his views are conventionally liberal, though he adds his background as a business entrepreneur and his interest in bipartisanship. He emphasized his opposition to Trump's hard-line views on immigration, citing his own education experience to encourage more opportunities for foreign students in the United States.

With help from the well-financed national community of Democrats with an Indian heritage, Krishnamoorthi spent $2.6 million for his campaign. The other two candidates were state Sen. Michael Noland, who cited his support for a single-payer health care system and other progressive views during eight years in the Legislature, and Villa Park Village President Deborah Bullwinkel, who called herself the "the regular gal, small-town mayor, middle-class advocate" in contrast to the wealthy connections and contacts of Krishnamoorthi. The *Daily Herald* endorsed Krishnamoorthi, citing his knowledge of the issues and that "he approaches all political issues pragmatically and with an openness that can make him both cooperative and persuasive in conducting the business of a congressman." He won the primary with 57 percent of the vote to 29 percent for Noland, who spent $311,000, and 14 percent for Bullwinkel, who spent $89,000.

In the general, Republican Pete DiCianni, a member of the DuPage County Board and former mayor of Elmhurst, cited the "disappointing" loss of nearly $100 million in mutual funds from the state's college savings program while Krishnamoorthi was deputy treasurer. Krishnamoorthi won, 58%-42%, including 54 percent of the vote in DiCianni's base of DuPage. In the House, he got seats on Education and the Workforce, and Oversight and Government Reform.

Chicago's Northwest Suburbs, DuPage

Population		**Race and Ethnicity**		**Income**	
Total	717,333	White	53.4%	Median Income	$65,222 (92 out of 435)
Land area	206	Black	4.6%		
Pop/ sq mi	3490.3	Latino	27.3%	Under $50,000	37.4%
Born in state	59.0%	Asian	12.8%	$50,000-$99,999	35.5%
		Two races	1.6%	$100,000-$199,999	22.7%
Age Groups		Other	0.4%	$200,000 or more	4.4%
Under 18	24.3%			Poverty Rate	10.2%
18-34	24.2%	**Education**			
35-64	40.3%	H.S grad or less	38.7%	**Health Insurance**	
Over 64	11.2%	Some college	28.3%	With health insurance coverage	86.7%
		College Degree, 4 yr	22.3%		
Work		Post grad	10.7%		
White Collar	33.4%			**Public Assistance**	
Sales and Service	43.2%	**Military**		Cash public assistance income	2.0%
Blue Collar	23.4%	Veteran	4.8%		
Government	8.5%	Active Duty	0.0%	Food stamp/SNAP benefits	9.7%

Voter Turnout			
2015 Total Citizens 18+	440,675	2016 House Turnout as % CVAP	56%
2016 House turnout	248,571	2014 House Turnout as % CVAP	34%

2012 Presidential Vote		
Barack Obama	133,208	(58%)
Mitt Romney	94,944	(41%)

2016 Presidential Vote		
Hillary Clinton	148,277	(58%)
Donald Trump	92,892	(36%)
Gary Johnson	9,851	(4%)

Cook Partisan Voting Index: D+8

Schaumburg may not be nationally known, but it has a long tradition as one of America's major corporate headquarters cities. Sixty years ago, this suburb northwest of Chicago was farmland. Today, Schaumburg - near the intersection of the Northwest Tollway and Interstate 290, and a few miles beyond O'Hare International Airport - is the headquarters of Motorola Solutions and Zurich North American insurance. Nearby are the headquarters of Sears, as well as the Woodfield Mall with 300-plus shops and restaurants, and subdivisions as far as the eye can see. Schaumburg has built a performing arts center, formed an orchestra for young people and built from scratch a traditional downtown district.

Despite those attractions, the area recently has faced challenges. Some large companies are abandoning their suburban mindset, finding that large, isolated corporate campuses breed insularity and make it harder to recruit talent. Chicago Mayor Rahm Emanuel has capitalized on the trend by luring suburban businesses to relocate downtown with financial incentives. Motorola's mobile handset division, after being bought by Google, moved to downtown Chicago's Merchandise Mart. Sara Lee's meat business moved downtown from Downers Grove, while changing its name to Hillshire Brands. AT&T decided to leave its suburban Hoffman Estates office, and moved 500 employees to downtown Chicago, and another 2,500 to nearby suburbs. Financially beleaguered Sears stayed in Hoffman Estates, but its problems extend far beyond its corporate location. From 2006 through 2016, its annual revenues dropped by about half.

"Really, the only thing that's growing is tech, and most of that is downtown. There's not a lot of tech in the suburbs anymore," a suburban real-estate broker told Chicagolandcommercial.com in 2014. Since 2007, more than 50 companies have moved from these suburbs to downtown Chicago. Still, some of the Schaumberg facilities continue to prosper. Motorola has renovated its headquarters, with 1,600 employees. Zurich North America's new building houses nearly 3,000 and meets the highest environmental sustainability standards. Sunstar, an oral-health care company, has a new corporate presence, with 400 employees. In late 2016, the vacancy rate for suburban Chicago offices had dropped to 18.6 percent, the lowest level since 2007.

The 8th Congressional District of Illinois is made up of Schaumburg and the more Democratic communities in Chicago's northwest suburbs, including Carol Stream in DuPage County and nearly majority Hispanic Elgin and Carpentersville in Kane County. About half the population of the 8th resides in the northwest corner of Cook County; most of the remainder are within jagged lines of northern DuPage, plus a few are in a small slice of Kane. It is one of the most Asian-American districts in the Midwest, with a 14 percent Asian-American population. Schaumburg has one of the nation's largest concentrations of Indian Americans, at 11 percent. Once-homogeneous DuPage County has seen an influx of immigrants, and more than a quarter of its residents now speak a first language other than English at home. The area lacks a regional identity, other than the "Northwest Suburbs." The local newspaper, the *Daily Herald* based in Arlington Heights, tried valiantly for a few years to give it a sense of place with a billboard campaign that dubbed it "Herald City." It didn't stick, and the paper abandoned the slogan.

In the past decade, like other parts of the Chicago suburbs, this area has moved toward the Democrats. Like President Barack Obama in 2012, Hillary Clinton carried the district with 58 percent in 2016. But it retains its suburban sensibilities. A moderate Republican could be competitive here.

NINTH DISTRICT

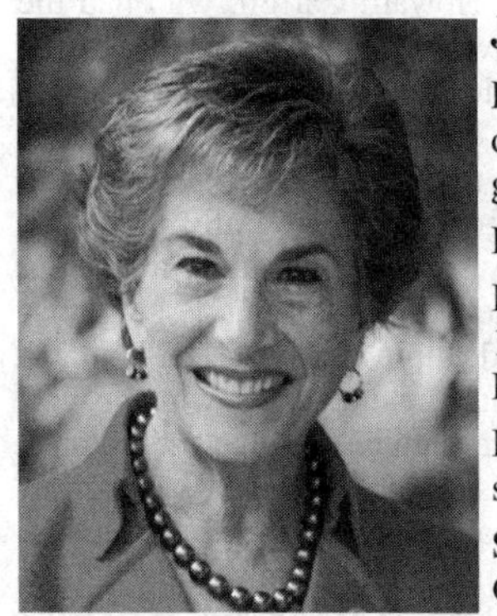

Jan Schakowsky (D)

Elected 1998, 10th term; b. May 26, 1944, Chicago; University of Illinois, B.A.; Jewish; Married (Robert Creamer); 3 children; 6 grandchildren.

Elected Office: IL House, 1990-1998.

Professional Career: Founder, National Consumers Unite, 1969-1973; Prog. Director, IL Public Action, 1976-1985; Executive Director, IL St. Cncl. of Sr. Citizens, 1985-1990.

DC Office: 2367 RHOB 20515, 202-225-2111, Fax: 202-226-6890, schakowsky.house.gov.

State Offices: Chicago, 773-506-7100; Evanston, 847-328-3409; Glenview, 847-328-3409.

Committees: *Budget*. *Energy & Commerce*: Digital Commerce & Consumer Protection (RMM), Health, Oversight & Investigations.

Group Ratings

	ADA	ACLU	AFL-CIO	LCV	ITI	COC	HAFA	ACU	CFG	FRC
2016	-	94%	-	97%	50%	43%	20%	0%	4%	0%
2015	100%	C	100%	100%	C	40%	C	4%	4%	0%

Almanac Ratings 2015

	Economy	Social	Foreign	Composite
Liberal	98%	100%	100%	99%
Conservative	2%	0%	0%	1%

Key Votes of the 114th Congress

1. Keystone Pipeline	N	5. Puerto Rico Debt	N	9. Offenses by Aliens	N
2. Trade Deals	N	6. Medical Marijuana	Y	10. Troops in Iraq	Y
3. Export-Import Bank	Y	7. Sanctuary Cities	N	11. Homeland Security $$	Y
4. Debt Ceiling Increase	Y	8. Armor-piercing Bullets	N	12. Trade Adjustment aid	Y

Election Results

Election	Name (Party)	Vote (%)		Cand. Spent	Ind. Exp. Support	Ind. Exp. Oppose
2016 General	Jan Schakowsky (D)	217,306	(67%)	$989,703		$50,000
	Joan McCarthy Lasonde (R)	109,550	(34%)	$193,649		
2016 Primary	Janice Schakowsky (D)		(100%)			

Prior winning percentages: 2014 (66%), 2012 (66%), 2010 (66%), 2008 (75%), 2006 (75%), 2004 (76%), 2002 (70%), 2000 (76%), 1998 (75%)

Jan Schakowsky, a Democrat elected in 1998, is an outspoken progressive. *The Nation* magazine once called her "the truest heir to Paul Wellstone," the late Minnesota senator and champion of the left, while the more conservative *Chicago Tribune's* editorial page derided her as "one of the most partisan, liberal members of the House." She blends deep policy background with lengthy organizational experience, and has been a stalwart on Nancy Pelosi's Democratic leadership team.

Schakowsky grew up in Rogers Park and worked for two years as a teacher. In 1969, she formed National Consumers Unite to fight for date-of-freshness labels on dairy products and other food. Later she joined Illinois Public Action, a consumer group. In 1985, she became executive director of the Illinois State Council of Senior Citizens, where she organized the pivotal 1989 protest of Democratic Ways and Means Chairman Dan Rostenkowski's Medicare catastrophic health care law for seniors. Television news images of the powerful Rostenkowski fleeing an angry crowd of old people led Congress to repeal the benefit, which many said did not provide adequate coverage. In 1990, Schakowsky was elected to the state House from Evanston and Skokie, and later became Democratic floor leader.

With an open seat in 1998, her strategy was to run from the left - "I don't think I can be defined as too far left in a district like this," she said - and to build a volunteer organization. With ads in college papers, she hired young field organizers to identify Schakowsky voters. She raised $1.4 million, with help from the abortion-rights group EMILY's List. Her opponent was state Sen. Howard Carroll, who had the support of most Democratic ward committeemen and attacked Schakowsky for her opposition to the death penalty. Schakowsky's 1,500 workers, 250 of them from labor unions, helped her to a 45%-34% win. She easily won the general election and has been reelected without difficulty.

In the *Almanac* vote ratings for 2015, Schakowsky had one of the most liberal voting records in the House. She regularly scores perfect ratings from liberal interest groups. A close ally of Pelosi, Schakowsky has worked with Democratic leaders on electoral strategy, including heading a training program for political organizers and encouraging participation by women. She was an early supporter when Pelosi got her start in leadership, and was rewarded with a chief deputy whip post. Her contacts with national liberal groups have helped Schakowsky become a major party fundraiser, drawing heavily from the traditional Democratic constituencies of lawyers, liberal women's interest groups and unions.

In early 2006, she ran for vice chair of the Democratic Caucus. With support from Pelosi, Schakowsky was the early front-runner against New York's Joe Crowley and Connecticut's John Larson. But on the first ballot, she finished third. Schakowsky threw her support to Larson, another Pelosi ally. With Schakowsky's former supporters on board, Larson prevailed. Some Democrats speculated that Schakowsky was hurt by the timing of the contest, which occurred soon after her husband, Robert Creamer, the longtime head of Illinois Public Action Fund, pleaded guilty to bank fraud in a check-kiting scheme. Schakowsky said her husband had "made mistakes," but that she was unaware of his financial problems and that she stood by him. Creamer continued with other controversial campaign tactics. In mid-October 2016, he quit his work with the Democratic National Committee on behalf of Hillary Clinton's campaign when a hidden video suggested that he and other staffers hired people to attend Donald Trump's campaign rallies and incite violence. The incident "put Democrats on defensive about dirty tricks," *The New York Times* headlined.

Schakowsky briefly considered a run for the Senate in 2004 but decided against it. In 2008, she voiced interest in appointment to the remainder of President-elect Barack Obama's Senate term. She was an early backer of Obama for president, giving cover to other prominent Democratic women who may have wanted to back him but felt obliged to support then-New York Sen. Hillary Clinton.

As chairwoman of the Intelligence Oversight Subcommittee, Schakowsky tried to get spy agencies to be more forthcoming in briefing members of Congress about their actions. In 2009, she backed Pelosi's claim that she had not been informed of the use by U.S. interrogators of water boarding. Schakowsky was the only committee member in 2011 to oppose cybersecurity legislation, saying that the measure didn't do enough to safeguard civil liberties. In what she called an "anguished" decision, she boycotted the March 2015 speech to Congress by Israeli Prime Minister Benjamin Netanyahu on the grounds that his actions might jeopardize both nuclear talks with Iran and bipartisan support for Israel. In January 2017, she was one of 76 House Democrats who voted against a measure that attacked the Obama administration for its failure to veto a United Nations Security Council resolution that criticized Israeli settlements.

On the Energy and Commerce Committee, Schakowsky helped to enact in 2008 the child product safety bill, which increased regulations, and she has remained active on consumer issues. In 2009, she was a strong supporter of creating a federally run insurance option in the Democrats' health care bill. The public option provision ultimately was dropped because of opposition from party moderates. Pelosi appointed Schakowsky to the Simpson-Bowles commission on the national debt in 2010, where she opposed ending federal economic stimulus and argued that safety net spending should be exempt from budget cuts. She argued that debt reduction options should include income distribution tables to show who would be hit hardest. She remains outspoken as a critic of income inequality.

As the senior Democrat on the Commerce, Manufacturing and Trade Subcommittee, which handles many consumer issues, Schakowsky has filed legislation to increase funding to train and retain nurses to address shortages. She filed in 2016 the Medicare Fair Drug Pricing Act, which advanced her long-standing demand for transparency and accountability in prescription drug pricing, plus negotiation for the price of certain drugs covered by Medicare.

Chicago: North Side, Northern Cook

Population		**Race and Ethnicity**		**Income**	
Total	716,040	White	64.9%	Median Income	$64,475 (100 out of 435)
Land area	105	Black	8.6%		
Pop/ sq mi	6796.8	Latino	10.9%		
Born in state	53.0%	Asian	13.0%	Under $50,000	40.4%
		Two races	2.3%	$50,000-$99,999	27.6%
Age Groups		Other	0.3%	$100,000-$199,999	21.9%
Under 18	20.3%			$200,000 or more	10.1%
18-34	22.8%	**Education**		Poverty Rate	12.2%
35-64	40.9%	H.S grad or less	26.2%		
Over 64	16.0%	Some college	22.1%	**Health Insurance**	
		College Degree, 4 yr	29.5%	With health insurance coverage	89.3%
Work		Post grad	22.3%		
White Collar	49.0%				
Sales and Service	38.2%	**Military**		**Public Assistance**	
Blue Collar	12.8%	Veteran	4.6%	Cash public assistance income	2.5%
Government	9.8%	Active Duty	0.0%		
				Food stamp/SNAP benefits	9.5%

Voter Turnout			
2015 Total Citizens 18+	497,756	2016 House Turnout as % CVAP	66%
2016 House turnout	326,948	2014 House Turnout as % CVAP	44%

2012 Presidential Vote		
Barack Obama	200,686	(65%)
Mitt Romney	102,728	(33%)

2016 Presidential Vote		
Hillary Clinton	237,984	(69%)
Donald Trump	84,527	(25%)
Gary Johnson	11,494	(3%)

Cook Partisan Voting Index: D+18

"Make no little plans," architect Daniel Burnham once said, and he made no little plans for the Chicago lakefront. The glorious parks he designed are among America's urban jewels, and the row of high-rise apartment buildings - some austere works of masters of the International style, some in traditional styles evocative of some other place and time, some sleek Art Deco works of the 1920s and

1930s - is a splendid accompaniment. Beyond the lakefront is all the diversity of Chicago. In sturdy brick houses, with scarcely a shoehorn's space between them, or in stubby apartment buildings, are ethnic and racial groups of every sort, from Argentinians to Slavs, from Poles to Plains Indians. In the 1970s, the neighborhoods behind the lakefront seemed to be getting seedier and tipping downhill. But since the late 1980s, they have been gentrifying, as young couples and gays, professionals and entrepreneurs renovate old houses and open new businesses. Today, this part of Chicago has as much urban energy and lively diversity as any place in America. In what it describes as the largest capital improvement project in its history, the Chicago Transit Authority is rebuilding the Red Line, its busiest route, and modernizing the Purple Line from the North Side to Wilmette.

The lakefront has long been the most heavily Jewish part of Chicago. The local Jewish community, prominent for more than a century, has never been as much of a political force as it is in New York, or connected to a glamorous industry as in Los Angeles. Yet these Jewish voters' liberal impulses have been strong: the 19th century impulse to resist state authority and the imposition of cultural uniformity, and the 20th century impulse to strive for social fairness. Chicago's North Side Jews have been a solidly Democratic voting bloc, involved with - but mostly keeping at arm's length - the old Democratic machine. In city politics since the 1980s, Jewish voters and lakefront liberals of all backgrounds have been a key swing group. They supported for mayor one of their own, Rahm Emanuel, but have been disappointed with some of his actions.

The 9th Congressional District of Illinois covers the north end of Chicago's lakefront, from just north of Diversey Harbor and the Lincoln Park Zoo past the thriving Asian and Orthodox Jewish communities in West Rogers Park and on to the suburb of Evanston, founded by Methodists to promote temperance (a cause that never prospered in Chicago). Evanston, where the local History Center is in the former home of Charles Dawes, who was vice president for four years with Calvin Coolidge, has moved from Yankee Republicanism to postgraduate Democratic. Northwestern University announced in June 2016 that it planned during the next five years to spend $150 million on computer-science programs. From Evanston and upscale Wilmette, where the only Baha'i Temple in the country - and one of only eight world-wide -- often clogs local streets, the 9th presses inland through heavily Jewish Skokie to Morton Grove and Niles. Skokie made national headlines when Nazi sympathizers got court permission to march there in 1977. Skokie's residents settled the score with the opening in 2009 of the Illinois Holocaust Museum and Education Center; former President Bill Clinton and Nobel Prize-winning author Elie Wiesel attended. Farther out in Des Plaines, the German pharmaceutical company Vetter in July 2016 unveiled plans for a $320 million production center.

The district, which is entirely in Cook County but mostly outside of Chicago, reaches west to incorporate once rock-solid Republican territory - Park Ridge, where Hillary Rodham grew up at 235 Wisner and in 1964 got her first taste of politics in high school as a "Goldwater girl"; the cluster of office buildings and interchanges in Rosemont, next to O'Hare International Airport; and parts of Arlington Heights, developed in the 1950s and 1960s on the Chicago & Northwestern commuter rail line. The 9th's population is 9 percent black, 11 percent Hispanic, and 13 percent Asian, and is solidly Democratic, though less so than most of the districts based in Chicago. As one of at least four hometowns for Clinton, the district gave her 69 percent of the vote in 2016, compared with the 65 percent that President Barack Obama received in his 2012 reelections.

TENTH DISTRICT

Brad Schneider (D)

Elected 2012, 2nd term; b. Aug 20, 1961, Denver, CO; Northwestern University (IL), B.S., 1983; Kellogg Graduate School of Management, Northwestern University (IL), M.B.A., 1988; Jewish; Married (Julie Dann); 2 children.

Elected Office: U.S House, 2013-2015.

Professional Career: Strategic Mgmt Consultant & Founder, Cadence Consulting Group.

DC Office: 1432 LHOB 20515, 202-225-4835, Fax: 202-225-0837, schneider.house.gov.

State Offices: Lincolnshire, 847-383-4870.

Committees: *Foreign Affairs*: Middle East & North Africa, Terrorism, Nonproliferation & Trade. *Judiciary*: Courts, Intellectual Property & Internet, Regulatory Reform, Commercial & Antitrust Law. *Small Business*: Agriculture, Energy & Trade (RMM).

Election Results

Election	Name (Party)	Vote (%)		Cand. Spent	Ind. Exp. Support	Ind. Exp. Oppose
2016 General	Brad Schneider (D)	150,435	(53%)	$4,922,522	$65,222	$2,928,802
	Bob Dold (R)	135,535	(47%)	$5,563,045	$3,058,377	$2,361,937
2016 Primary	Brad Schneider (D)	50,916	(54%)			
	Nancy Rotering (D)	43,842	(46%)			

Prior winning percentages: 2012 (51%)

Democrat Brad Schneider, a business consultant who made a late career move to politics, regained his House seat in 2016 after having earlier served one term. He and Republican Robert Dold had an unusual dance during the past four campaigns in which Dold won two off-year elections and Schneider won the two presidential cycles. Each brought a message of bipartisanship - along with escalating campaign finances. Schneider benefited from Democratic control of redistricting in Springfield. In 2016, the biggest obstacle for Dold was that Donald Trump got only 32 percent of the district vote. Dold found enough ticket-splitters to get to 48 percent - not quite enough.

Schneider was born and raised in Denver, where his parents - an accountant and a real-estate agent - were active Democrats. As a kid, he joined them to canvass for Hubert Humphrey's presidential campaign in 1968. Schneider encountered the Chicago area at Northwestern University, where he received a bachelor's degree in industrial engineering and a masters from the Kellogg Graduate School of Management. After spending a year in Israel working on a kibbutz, he returned to Chicago to take a corporate consulting job. Eventually, he went into business for himself as a consultant, working with small and mid-sized businesses. He did work for the Jewish United Fund in Chicago and served as director of the Business and Professional People for the Business Interest, a local social-justice organization.

Dold, the owner of a pest-control company, eked out a victory in 2010 for the seat of Republican Mark Kirk, who was elected to the Senate that year. As part of their post-census redistricting, Democrats in Springfield responded by removing Dold's Kenilworth home from the district, as well as his best precincts in the high-income towns of Palatine, Northbrook and Winnetka. In the process, they remade the 10th into the most Democratic district represented by a Republican in the House.

In the four-way Democratic primary, Schneider's chief opponent was Ilya Sheyman, a 25-year-old former community organizer who drew staunch support from liberal groups such as MoveOn.org, which launched a "Republicans for Schneider" website to highlight his past support for Kirk and other Republicans. Schneider got the backing of the Democratic establishment, which saw his business experience as the better weapon in this district. He won the primary 47%-39%.

In the general, Schneider portrayed himself as a moderate. He accused Dold of voting in lockstep with GOP leaders on major issues, including women's health and abortion rights. Dold called the charge misleading and cited his dissent from the leadership on such issues as the environment, education and gun control. But the Democratic tide in Illinois proved too much for him to overcome, and he lost

50.6%-49.4%. During his first term, Schneider served on the Foreign Affairs Committee and joined the business-friendly New Democrat Coalition. He joined President Barack Obama in calling for legislative solutions to gun violence, including universal background checks.

Without Obama on the ticket in 2014, Republicans were enthusiastic about Dold's prospects. He stressed his moderate credentials while depicting Schneider as ineffective. Schneider emphasized Dold's past votes in which he sided with the GOP majority, including his support for House Budget Committee Chairman Paul Ryan's blueprint to cut the growth in spending. This was one of the most expensive campaigns in the nation in 2014. Schneider outspent Dold $4.8 million to $3.6 million, while national parties and outside groups spent a total of roughly $10 million more in the contest. This time, Dold won 51.3%-48.7%.

During his second tour in the House, Dold got a break when the resignation of Republican Rep. Aaron Schock of Illinois opened a seat on the powerful Ways and Means, which GOP leaders assigned to Dold as a reelection boost. He filed a bill to foster job creation and innovation in America's economy through reforms to immigration policy and the tax code.

That didn't scare Democrats. Joining Schneider in their primary was Highland Park Mayor Nancy Rotering, an attorney who also had a business background. She had the support of EMILY's List, the political action committee that funds Democratic women who support abortion rights. The two candidates agreed on most issues, with the chief exception of Obama's nuclear deal with Iran. Rotering supported it. Schneider had concerns that Iran might take advantage of loopholes and gain access to nuclear weapons. As was the case in the 2012 primary, liberal activists griped about Schneider. But he prevailed 54%-46%, not all that impressive for a former House member.

Dold moved quickly to disavow Trump - emphasizing his willingness to stand up to his own party and to cooperate with Democrats on occasion. Schneider cited examples of Dold acting as a Republican team player; Obama endorsed him in advertising. The National Republican Congressional Committee ran an ad that praised Dold for his independence from Trump. Once again, both sides spent lavishly: Dold led $5.6 million to $4.9 million. And he had the advantage with outside money on his behalf, about $6 million to $3 million.

Schneider regained the seat by the relatively comfortable 52.4%-47.6%, with similar results in Lake and Cook counties. Dold reasonably might wonder how the outcome would have been affected with a Republican nominee other than Trump. GOP strategists monitored Trump's potential impact on the 2018 campaign, for both the primary and general. Given recent history, Schneider can expect another competitive contest.

Northern Chicagoland: Lake, Northern Cook

Population		**Race and Ethnicity**		**Income**	
Total	713,687	White	59.4%	Median Income	$71,958 (66 out of 435)
Land area	300	Black	6.5%		
Pop/ sq mi	2380.7	Latino	22.3%	Under $50,000	34.6%
Born in state	56.2%	Asian	9.7%	$50,000-$99,999	29.3%
		Two races	1.8%	$100,000-$199,999	24.1%
Age Groups		Other	0.2%	$200,000 or more	12.0%
Under 18	25.3%			Poverty Rate	10.3%
18-34	21.3%	**Education**			
35-64	40.4%	H.S grad or less	32.9%	**Health Insurance**	
Over 64	13.0%	Some college	23.9%	With health insurance coverage	88.6%
		College Degree, 4 yr	25.3%		
Work		Post grad	17.9%		
White Collar	41.2%			**Public Assistance**	
Sales and Service	41.1%	**Military**		Cash public assistance income	2.0%
Blue Collar	17.7%	Veteran	6.0%		
Government	9.6%	Active Duty	1.9%	Food stamp/SNAP benefits	9.8%

Voter Turnout			
2015 Total Citizens 18+	453,519	2016 House Turnout as % CVAP	63%
2016 House turnout	285,996	2014 House Turnout as % CVAP	41%

2012 Presidential Vote		
Barack Obama	157,400	(58%)
Mitt Romney	112,552	(41%)

2016 Presidential Vote		
Hillary Clinton	178,872	(61%)
Donald Trump	94,103	(32%)
Gary Johnson	11,681	(4%)

Cook Partisan Voting Index: D+10

Since 1855, when the Chicago & North Western opened the railroad line from downtown Chicago north along the lakeshore, the North Shore suburbs along Lake Michigan have been home to Chicago's elite. The North Shore starts in Evanston, goes north through Wilmette, Winnetka and Glencoe, and then leaves Cook County and crosses into the eastern Lake County towns of Highland Park and Lake Forest. Each burg has a slightly different personality, each is long established and mightily prosperous, and each exudes a patina of age. These are communities of affluent, well-educated people living in an environment whose natural beauty - the vistas over Lake Michigan, the gentle rolling terrain, and the old trees - is carefully disciplined. Corporate headquarters fit comfortably here, including Baxter Healthcare, Abbott Laboratories and Allstate Insurance. The North Shore suburbs were the setting for the 1980s films *Risky Business, Sixteen Candles* and *Ferris Bueller's Day Off,* which depicted teen angst and lust for adventure among the pampered offspring of the rich.

The exceptions to the atmosphere of gracious high living are Waukegan and the nearby area around the Great Lakes Naval Training Center, where the median income is dramatically lower. The award-winning "Years of Living Dangerously" documentary on the National Geographic Channel in December 2016 described the struggle in Waukegan as the area moved to clean up its coal-fueled power plant. In January 2017, the WalletHub website ranked Waukegan last among 505 cities nationwide in the decrease in its local poverty rate. Farther north along the lake, the small community of Zion has struggled to recover from the shutdown in 1998 of the local nuclear power plant, which was caused by an operational error. Local leaders are also unhappy that the radioactive spent fuel has not been removed, which has discouraged economic development in the area.

The 10th Congressional District of Illinois is the North Shore district. The district starts on the lakefront in Glencoe and runs north in a thin strip all the way to the blue-collar, majority-Hispanic city of Waukegan and on to the Wisconsin border. It moves inland to include most of Lake County, blue-collar territory and some Cook County suburbs west to Wheeling and parts of Mount Prospect. Social disparity ranges from upscale Northbrook and Deerfield to working-class Niles, a suburb featuring the "Leaning Tower of Niles," a half-size replica of Italy's Leaning Tower of Pisa (the landmark was featured in the opening montage of the popular teen movie *Wayne's World*). The district includes Libertyville, near where the Adlai Stevensons, the governor and two-time presidential nominee and his son the former senator, owned a farm. After the family home on the property was donated to Lake County, it was restored in 2008 as the Adlai Stevenson Center on Democracy. Three-fourths of the district is in Lake, with the more Republican parts of that county in the 6th and 14th Districts. Politically, the 10th leans sufficiently Democratic that Hillary Clinton won 61%-32% in 2016 after Barack Obama won 58 percent of the vote in 2012. In non-presidential elections, the area can be competitive locally. But this long-time elite business district has lost favor with the Republican Party.

ELEVENTH DISTRICT

Bill Foster (D)

Elected 2008, 5th term; b. Oct 07, 1955, Madison, WI; Harvard University, Ph.D.; University of Wisconsin, B.A.; Married (Aesook Byon); 2 children.

Elected Office: U.S. House, 2008-2010.

Professional Career: Scientist, Fermi National Accelerator Lab., 1990- 2006; Co-founder, Electronic Theatre Controls, 1975-2007.

DC Office: 1224 LHOB 20515, 202-225-3515, Fax: 202-225-9420, foster.house.gov.

State Offices: Aurora, 630-585-7672; Joliet, 815-280-5876.

Committees: *Financial Services*: Capital Markets, Securities & Investment, Monetary Policy & Trade, Terrorism & Illicit Finance. *Science, Space & Technology*: Energy, Space.

Group Ratings

	ADA	ACLU	AFL-CIO	LCV	ITI	COC	HAFA	ACU	CFG	FRC
2016	-	88%	-	100%	67%	64%	10%	0%	6%	8%
2015	85%	C	100%	97%	C	45%	C	4%	0%	8%

Almanac Ratings 2015

	Economy	Social	Foreign	Composite
Liberal	92%	94%	78%	88%
Conservative	8%	6%	22%	12%

Key Votes of the 114th Congress

1. Keystone Pipeline	N	5. Puerto Rico Debt	Y	9. Offenses by Aliens	Y
2. Trade Deals	N	6. Medical Marijuana	Y	10. Troops in Iraq	Y
3. Export-Import Bank	Y	7. Sanctuary Cities	N	11. Homeland Security $$	Y
4. Debt Ceiling Increase	Y	8. Armor-piercing Bullets	N	12. Trade Adjustment aid	Y

Election Results

Election	Name (Party)	Vote (%)	Cand. Spent	Ind. Exp. Support	Ind. Exp. Oppose
2016 General	Bill Foster (D)	166,578 (60%)	$1,416,496		
	Tonia Khouri (R)	108,995 (40%)	$731,935	$1,249	
2016 Primary	Bill Foster (D)	(100%)			

Prior winning percentages: 2014 (53%), 2012 (59%), 2008 (58%), 2008 special (53%)

Democrat Bill Foster returned to the House in 2012, with a big boost from redistricting. Foster, a physicist, initially won a special election following the resignation of former House Speaker Dennis Hastert, only to lose in 2010 to Republican Randy Hultgren. His new district is a more natural fit in both partisan and professional terms for Foster, who proudly styles himself as the only pure scientist in Congress.

Foster began life as a Washington insider. His parents met on Capitol Hill, where each worked for a senator. His father became a law professor at the University of Wisconsin, and Foster grew up in Madison, graduated from the university, and got his Ph.D. in physics from Harvard University. He was a physicist for 16 years at Fermilab, just outside the 11th District, where he pursued groundbreaking research in elementary particle physics. Foster also ran a theater-lighting business with his younger brother that made each a multimillionaire.

He had not sought public office before volunteering in the 2006 campaign of Patrick Murphy, a Pennsylvania Democrat who ousted a House Republican incumbent. At age 51, Foster then spent five months working on Murphy's Capitol Hill staff. After Hastert resigned in 2007, Foster ran in the Democratic primary against the more liberal Jonathan Laesch, who had lost to Hastert in 2006. Foster won, 50%-43%. In March 2008, he faced Republican Jim Oberweis, a successful dairy owner who had lost numerous statewide campaigns. Amid the clutter of negative charges and countercharges, Foster was boosted by a 30-second endorsement from the Barack Obama presidential campaign. He won, 53%-47%, and defeated Oberweis again to win a full term in November. Foster was the first Democrat to represent the north-central Illinois district since the Great Depression.

In the House, Foster got a seat on the Financial Services Committee, where he supported the bailout of the financial markets. He voted for the $787 billion economic stimulus legislation and the 2010 health care overhaul. He helped to restore $62.5 million in funding for Fermilab. In the 2010 election, Foster did not mention his party affiliation and out-spent Hultgren, $3.7 million to $1.6 million. But Hultgren won, 51%-45% -- one of five Republicans that year who took a Democratic seat (prior to redistricting) in Obama's home state.

Foster soon got another chance. During 2011 redistricting, Democrats carved out a new, Democratic-leaning district that covers Joliet and Aurora and shifts closer to Chicagoland. Foster easily beat two Democratic primary rivals and then faced veteran Rep. Judy Biggert, a moderate Republican. Foster accused Biggert of supporting Social Security privatization, although her campaign maintained that she always opposed full privatization. At a face-to-face meeting with the *Chicago Tribune* editorial board, Foster tried to tie Biggert to President George W. Bush's economic policies that "eviscerated U.S. manufacturing." Biggert snapped back, "You Democrats have never talked about anything that you're going to do. It's always what we did wrong." At the same forum, Foster called for cuts in the federal budget, starting with military aircraft and crop insurance. The race wasn't always pretty, but Foster won convincingly with 59 percent.

In the House, Foster regained his seat on the Financial Services Committee. He warned that Republican bills to strip regulatory authority from the Securities and Exchange Commission would weaken investor protections. He filed a bipartisan bill to require more information from the federal government on "payer states" like Illinois that send more money to Washington than they receive in return. In 2015, he joined the Science, Space and Technology Committee. As the only remaining Ph.D. scientist in Congress, he said, he wanted to counter the "attacks" on science, including the National Science Foundation, that have come from that committee and elsewhere. He cited that background when he voted for a chief priority for Obama: the deal with Iran to limit that nation's access to nuclear material that could be used for a weapon. "After carefully weighing all of the options and possible outcomes I do believe that voting for this deal will make it less likely that Iran will develop a nuclear weapon," said Foster, who added that he had attended 15 technical briefings. "My support of this agreement is informed not just by trust but by science." Some experts disagreed with him. Following the election, he voiced concern that the Trump administration would reduce funding for Argonne and other labs.

Back home, Foster faced competitive contests in his Democratic-friendly district. In 2014, he was a national Republican target when he was challenged by state Rep. Darlene Senger, whom he outspent by more than 2-to-1. The Republican had small leads in DuPage and Cook counties, but Foster rolled up big margins in Will and Kane counties and won 53 percent of the vote. After considering a run for the Senate in 2016, Foster decided not to challenge Republican Sen. Mark Kirk and endorsed Democratic Rep. Tammy Duckworth to avoid a costly primary.

In 2016, DuPage County Board member Tonia Khouri won a three-way Republican primary by 370 votes, 36.9%-36.3%, over Nick Stella, a heart doctor. Khouri owned a landscape company and was the favorite of the party establishment. But her under-performance in the primary led national Republicans to cut back support for her in the general, in which Khouri spent $745,000 to $1.7 million for Foster. Khouri distanced herself from the calls by Republican presidential candidate Donald Trump to deport illegal immigrants, and she said she was offended by his "locker room banter." Foster won, 60%-40%, the most comfortable of his victories.

Southwestern Chicagoland: Aurora, Joliet

Population		**Race and Ethnicity**		**Income**	
Total	722,840	White	52.7%	Median Income	$68,154 (78 out of 435)
Land area	281	Black	10.9%	Under $50,000	35.7%
Pop/ sq mi	2572.8	Latino	26.6%	$50,000-$99,999	33.2%
Born in state	64.7%	Asian	7.3%	$100,000-$199,999	24.7%
Age Groups		Two races	2.2%	$200,000 or more	6.4%
Under 18	27.1%	Other	0.3%	Poverty Rate	11.0%
18-34	23.2%	**Education**		**Health Insurance**	
35-64	39.4%	H.S grad or less	37.7%	With health insurance coverage	88.6%
Over 64	10.3%	Some college	27.8%	**Public Assistance**	
Work		College Degree, 4 yr	21.6%	Cash public assistance income	1.7%
White Collar	36.0%	Post grad	13.0%	Food stamp/SNAP benefits	11.0%
Sales and Service	41.5%	**Military**			
Blue Collar	22.5%	Veteran	5.6%		
Government	10.1%	Active Duty	0.1%		

Voter Turnout			
2015 Total Citizens 18+	456,241	2016 House Turnout as % CVAP	60%
2016 House turnout	275,573	2014 House Turnout as % CVAP	39%

2012 Presidential Vote		
Barack Obama	151,825	(58%)
Mitt Romney	106,532	(41%)

2016 Presidential Vote		
Hillary Clinton	164,664	(58%)
Donald Trump	99,087	(35%)
Gary Johnson	11,728	(4%)

Cook Partisan Voting Index: D+9

Joliet, known as the city of steel and stone, got its start in the mid-19th century as a melting pot of Irish, German, Slovakian, Slovenian, Polish, Croatian and Hungarian immigrants who built the canals and railroads that connected the city with the rest of the state, from the Great Lakes to the Mississippi River. It emerged as the state's largest transportation hub outside Chicago. Workers labored in the stone quarries and steel mill, which by the turn of the century became the economic engine of the manufacturing city. The rails remain relevant to daily life, with officials working to upgrade the safety of the several trains that pass through Aurora each day with freight cars filled with crude oil from North Dakota. Fun fact: The nickname for Aurora is the "city of lights." It was the first in the nation to use electricity to light an entire city. Aurora celebrates an annual Festival of Lights during the month before Christmas.

Job prospects in the area have been mixed. Caterpillar, which had downsized its local plant and shifted jobs to Mexico in recent years, announced in January 2017 that another 800 workers were at risk by the middle of the year, with their work potentially shifted to other U.S. facilities. More encouraging were plans by Amazon to build two large fulfillment centers outside Aurora, which would employ 1,000 workers. In 2015 and 2016, Amazon opened eight other shipping centers, with 7,000 employees. Those sites confirm the central location and prime transportation facilities of the Chicagoland area, plus the plentiful supply of low-cost and less-skilled workers at Amazon. State officials earlier gave tax credits to Amazon in exchange for a guarantee of additional jobs. Hopes have dimmed that Joliet could become an entertainment destination in the otherwise declining Illinois. The landmark Rialto Square Theater, a 1920s-era vaudeville establishment that was a favorite of gangster Al Capone's, was restored as an arts center in a downtown that has been partly revitalized. But the theater then lost millions of dollars and the city began a takeover in 2016. Joliet has been the only city in Illinois with two riverboat casinos, but they experienced steep drops in revenue after the Rivers Casino opened in Des Plaines, which is closer to Chicago.

The 11th Congressional District includes Joliet in Will County, parts of Naperville in southern DuPage County, and Aurora in Kane County. About 27 percent of the district is Hispanic, with 11 percent black and 7 percent Asian. Will County has nearly one-half of the district vote. It is the fastest-growing of the large suburban Chicago counties, jumping from a population of 502,000 in 2000 to 687,000 in 2015, as its Hispanic residents more than doubled and the number of Asian-Americans nearly tripled. Aurora, the state's second most populous city with a long history of manufacturing, saw its population grow 40 percent from 2000 to 2015, also thanks to a large influx of Hispanics.

The district's boundaries run along the technology corridor in DuPage County, and straddle some large engineering facilities. The Argonne National Laboratory, which conducts basic and applied research in disciplines that range from high energy physics to biotechnology, has established a research hub for batteries and energy storage, nicknamed by the lab's director as "Lithium Valley." In December 2016, Argonne officials said they had made progress on the high-energy lithium-ion batteries for electric vehicles, but that additional time might be needed to complete the research. The lab, which employs 3,500, also has been working on a new $200 million super-computer that is expected to be 17 times faster than recent versions. Fermilab, another national laboratory, is just outside the district lines. In 2016, Hillary Clinton won this safely Democratic district, 58%-35%. With growing Hispanic population, the Democratic dominance likely will strengthen in what had been part of the Republican heartland not many years ago.

TWELFTH DISTRICT

Mike Bost (R)

Elected 2014, 2nd term; b. Dec 30, 1960, Murphysboro; University of Illinois; IL Fire Fighter II Academy; Southern Baptist; Married (Tracy Stanton Bost); 3 children; 11 grandchildren.

Military Career: U.S. Marine Corps., 1979-1982.

Elected Office: IL House 1995-2015; Trustee, Murphysboro Township, 1993-1995; Treasurer, Murphysboro Township, 1989-1992; Jackson County Board, 1984-1988.

Professional Career: Cert., Firefighter II Academy, University, of IL, 1993.

DC Office: 1440 LHOB 20515, 202-225-5661, Fax: 202-225-0285, bost.house.gov.

State Offices: Alton, 618-622-0766; Carbondale, 618-457-5787; Granite City, 618-622-0766; Mt. Vernon, 618-513-5294; O'Fallon, 618-622-0766.

Committees: *Agriculture*: Conservation & Forestry, General Farm Commodities & Risk Management. *Transportation & Infrastructure*: Economic Dev't, Public Buildings & Emergency Management, Highways & Transit, Water Resources & Environment. *Veterans' Affairs*: Disability Assistance & Memorial Affairs (Chmn), Oversight & Investigations.

Group Ratings

	ADA	ACLU	AFL-CIO	LCV	ITI	COC	HAFA	ACU	CFG	FRC
2016	-	11%	-	3%	100%	100%	35%	52%	45%	100%
2015	5%	C	46%	3%	C	100%	C	33%	33%	92%

Almanac Ratings 2015

	Economy	Social	Foreign	Composite
Liberal	14%	10%	10%	12%
Conservative	86%	90%	90%	88%

Key Votes of the 114th Congress

1. Keystone Pipeline	Y	5. Puerto Rico Debt	Y	9. Offenses by Aliens	Y
2. Trade Deals	Y	6. Medical Marijuana	N	10. Troops in Iraq	N
3. Export-Import Bank	Y	7. Sanctuary Cities	Y	11. Homeland Security $$	Y
4. Debt Ceiling Increase	Y	8. Armor-piercing Bullets	Y	12. Trade Adjustment aid	Y

Election Results

Election	Name (Party)	Vote (%)		Cand. Spent	Ind. Exp. Support	Ind. Exp. Oppose
2016 General	Mike Bost (R)	169,976	(54%)	$2,106,409	$10,674	$256,017
	C.J Baricevic (D)	124,246	(40%)	$963,929		
	Paula Bradshaw (G)	18,780	(6%)	$3,837		
2016 Primary	Mike Bost (R)		(100%)			

Prior winning percentages: 2014 (53%)

Republican Mike Bost has settled into what had been a safe Democratic seat for decades, giving the GOP one of its most hotly contested and expensive pickups. Democrats sought to run a credible challenge against him in 2016, but they fell further behind. Bost seems to have become secure in the type of seat that Democrats must win to regain the House majority.

Bost was born and raised in Murphysboro and enlisted in the Marine Corps upon graduating from high school. Following his service, he became a firefighter while working in the family trucking business. In 1989, he and his wife opened a beauty shop, the White House Salon, which they have continued to run. In his advocacy of smaller government and lower taxes, Bost often has cited his small-business ownership as the formative experience that drove him into politics. After several stints in local office, Bost was elected to the Illinois House in 1994, and later became Republican Caucus chairman. His work focused on sectors important to the region - especially coal and agriculture - and he became known for tangling with Democrats, who have controlled that chamber since 1996. He won national attention with an outburst on the House floor in 2012 as he protested the rules for a pension bill. After he tossed papers into the air and punched them, he cried out, "Let my people go!" Video of his tirade wound up on YouTube and went viral, attracting more than 430,000 views.

Armed with name recognition - "Meltdown Mike" - that he tried to spin to his advantage, Bost announced in 2013 that he would challenge first-term Democratic Rep. Bill Enyart, a retired two-star general and one of two remaining Illinois Democrats in the House from outside the Chicago metro area. The district's growing divide over coal politics made it a top pick-up priority for the GOP. With neither man facing a primary, the contest escalated into one of the most expensive House races in the country. Bost tried to make the best of his outspoken reputation. "If you want a person who goes and sits and does nothing and not argue on your behalf, then I'm not your guy," he told voters. Each party spent more than $4 million on the contest, an extraordinary amount considering the relatively inexpensive media markets. Enyart out-spent Bost, $1.9 million to $1.2 million. Democrats played up the risk of Bost's temper, while the GOP attacked Enyart as a loyal ally of President Barack Obama, Minority Leader Nancy Pelosi and beleaguered Gov. Pat Quinn.

In the midterm election, Quinn's sagging popularity kept many Democrats at home, while the ad blitz for Bost did enough to motivate GOP voters. Bost won by a surprisingly comfortable 52%-42%, the first Republican to represent St. Clair County since 1942. Enyart took the two largest counties, St. Clair and nearby Madison, but by relatively small margins. Bost won nine of the remaining 10 counties, with margins that exceeded 2-to-1 in some cases, including Carbondale-based Williamson County.

He made increasing local jobs his chief priority. In response to the temporary closing of the local U.S. Steel plant, he urged the Obama administration to enforce international trade laws against unfair practices of other nations. He worked on legislation to protect American companies from trade "dumping" by foreign competitors. He won House passage of a bill requiring the Department of Veterans Affairs to develop a plan to hire directors of its medical centers. With several other House Republicans, he sought to change House rules to permit a return of spending earmarks, but was stymied by the opposition of Speaker Paul Ryan.

In an interview with a St. Louis radio station, Bost offered perspective on his first year in the House. "There are people on each side of the aisle that have a unique personality that might not blend with myself," he said. "And there're also those that probably, whenever they meet me, that have that (same) feeling." He objected, for example, to unnamed House Republicans who "would rather shut down government than govern."

Democrats quickly listed Bost as one of their top campaign targets in 2016. Some talked up former Lt. Gov. Sheila Simon, the daughter of the late Sen. Paul Simon, as a potential challenger. After they failed to recruit a well-known challenger, Democrats rallied behind C.J. Baricevic, a 31-year-old lawyer and first-time candidate.

Baricevic spent an impressive $1 million, to $2.3 million for Bost. His 54%-40% victory margin was similar to 2014: This time, Bost narrowly lost St. Clair and Madison, but rolled up bigger leads in outlying counties.

In the new Congress, Bost became chairman of the Veterans' Affairs Subcommittee on Disability Assistance and Memorial Affairs, which manages national cemeteries. He also got a seat on the Transportation and Infrastructure Committee, a useful assignment for a district that sits at vital national crossroads.

Southwest Illinois: East St. Louis, Carbondale

Population		**Race and Ethnicity**		**Income**	
Total	706,390	White	76.7%	Median Income	$45,018 (341 out of 435)
Land area	5,008	Black	16.6%	Under $50,000	54.0%
Pop/ sq mi	141.0	Latino	3.2%	$50,000-$99,999	29.3%
Born in state	68.7%	Asian	1.1%	$100,000-$199,999	14.4%
Age Groups		Two races	2.1%	$200,000 or more	2.3%
Under 18	22.5%	Other	0.3%	Poverty Rate	18.4%
18-34	22.8%	**Education**		**Health Insurance**	
35-64	39.5%	H.S grad or less	43.1%	With health insurance coverage	90.4%
Over 64	15.2%	Some college	35.5%	**Public Assistance**	
Work		College Degree, 4 yr	13.5%	Cash public assistance income	2.7%
White Collar	31.3%	Post grad	8.1%	Food stamp/SNAP benefits	16.6%
Sales and Service	44.2%	**Military**			
Blue Collar	24.5%	Veteran	11.6%		
Government	17.0%	Active Duty	0.6%		

Voter Turnout			
2015 Total Citizens 18+	538,977	2016 House Turnout as % CVAP	58%
2016 House turnout	313,002	2014 House Turnout as % CVAP	39%

2012 Presidential Vote		
Barack Obama	153,718	(50%)
Mitt Romney	149,165	(48%)

2016 Presidential Vote		
Donald Trump	173,692	(54%)
Hillary Clinton	126,818	(40%)
Gary Johnson	11,115	(4%)

Cook Partisan Voting Index: R+5

Their waters roiling together, the nation's two mightiest rivers, the Mississippi and Missouri, join just a few miles below Alton, Illinois. Its 19th-century buildings recall its turbulent history, when it was the home of antislavery agitator Elijah Lovejoy, who was murdered by a mob. Nearby in Hartford, explorers Lewis and Clark spent five months preparing their team and collecting supplies for their journey westward. More recently, it was the home of conservative crusader and columnist Phyllis Schlafly, who died in September 2016. Farther south along the Mississippi is East St. Louis, situated on the Illinois side of the river, with a view of the Gateway Arch in the larger St. Louis on the Missouri side. It is a terminus for dozens of rail lines and highways that funnel into bridges over the river.

Once a rail and stockyard center second only to Chicago, East St. Louis is now one of America's poorest and most troubled cities, a half-abandoned slum with one of the nation's highest crime rates and a rapidly declining tax base. In 2016, violent-crime data showed that this was the most dangerous city in the United States, with a crime rate that rivals lawless third-world countries. It is dependent on a riverboat casino and an adjacent waterfront hotel for local revenue, but casino taxes have increased and revenues have dipped. After peaking at 82,000 in 1960, its population is now below 27,000 and 98 percent African American, with 46 percent living in poverty. East St. Louis is in St. Clair County, long heavily Democratic.

South of East St. Louis and the industrial area around Belleville, the river counties are lightly inhabited. This was the site of the French Kaskaskia settlement that became Illinois's first capital in

1818, but repeated flooding turned it into an island and reduced its population to nine people and many more egrets. Farther south, the river abuts coal country and is not far from Carbondale, once a coal center but now, as the home of Southern Illinois University, bustling with students.

The southern end of Illinois is sometimes known as Little Egypt, where the Ohio River meets the Mississippi: flat, fertile farmland, protected by giant constructed levees because it is susceptible to yearly floods. The marshy landscape has created the Sinkhole Plain, with more than 10,000 sinkholes. There is more than a touch of Dixie here: The unofficial capital of Little Egypt, Cairo (pronounced *KAY-roh*), is a declining town closer to Memphis than to Chicago. It has been described as a mostly abandoned ghost town, with a population decline from 15,000 in the 1920s, to 6,000 in the 1980s to 2,000 in the latest census. A more enticing locale not far from Cairo is the Shawnee National Forest, which has preserved Native American sites that are 10,000 years old.

The 12th District of Illinois covers all of this Mississippi riverfront from Alton south to Cairo, with some inland territory as well. Slightly more than half its population is in the Metro East area in St. Clair and Madison counties. The largest employer in Southern Illinois is Scott Air Force Base near Belleville, which has a workforce of 12,400 and is home of the 375th Airlift Wing. The private sector continues to struggle. After more than 2,000 workers had been laid off for more than a year by the temporary closing of Granite City's US Steel plant, about 220 went back to work in February 2017.

The district has suffered a steep drop in Democratic support. When he ran for president in 2008, Barack Obama defeated John McCain, 55%-44%. In 2016, Donald Trump won the district, 54%-40%.

THIRTEENTH DISTRICT

Rodney Davis (R)

Elected 2012, 3rd term; b. Jan 05, 1970, Des Moines, IA; Millikin University (IL), B.A., 1992; Roman Catholic; Married (Shannon Davis); 3 children.

Professional Career: Staff assistant, IL Secretary of State, 1992-1996; Projects Director, Rep. John Shimkus, 1997-2012; Executive Director, IL Republican Party, 2011.

DC Office: 1740 LHOB 20515, 202-225-2371, Fax: 202-226-0791, rodneydavis.house.gov.

State Offices: Champaign, 217-403-4690; Decatur, 217-791-6224; Maryville, 618-205-8660; Normal, 309-252-8834; Taylorville, 217-824-5117.

Committees: *Agriculture*: Biotechnology, Horticulture & Research (Chmn), Commodity Exchanges, Energy & Credit, Nutrition. *Commission Congressional Mailing Standards (Chmn)*. *House Administration*. *Transportation & Infrastructure*: Aviation, Highways & Transit, Water Resources & Environment.

Group Ratings

	ADA	ACLU	AFL-CIO	LCV	ITI	COC	HAFA	ACU	CFG	FRC
2016	-	5%	-	3%	100%	100%	41%	56%	56%	83%
2015	0%	C	96%	6%	C	55%	C	42%	37%	75%

Almanac Ratings 2015

	Economy	Social	Foreign	Composite
Liberal	18%	25%	10%	18%
Conservative	82%	75%	90%	82%

Key Votes of the 114th Congress

1. Keystone Pipeline	Y	5. Puerto Rico Debt	N	9. Offenses by Aliens	Y
2. Trade Deals	Y	6. Medical Marijuana	Y	10. Troops in Iraq	N
3. Export-Import Bank	Y	7. Sanctuary Cities	Y	11. Homeland Security $$	Y
4. Debt Ceiling Increase	Y	8. Armor-piercing Bullets	Y	12. Trade Adjustment aid	Y

Election Results

Election	Name (Party)	Vote (%)	Cand. Spent	Ind. Exp. Support	Ind. Exp. Oppose
2016 General	Rodney Davis (R)	187,583 (60%)	$2,102,675	$9,486	
	Mark Wicklund (D)	126,811 (40%)	$21,169		
2016 Primary	Rodney Davis (R)	71,020 (77%)			
	Ethan Vandersand (R)	21,251 (23%)			

Prior winning percentages: 2014 (59%), 2012 (47%)

Republican Rodney Davis, first elected in a tight 2012 contest to replace a veteran GOP incumbent, has become entrenched in this seat - to the surprise of Democrats, including redistricters in Illinois. With the benefit of his experience as a congressional aide, he has been a capable and often bipartisan legislator on his committees.

Davis was born in Des Moines, Iowa, but moved to Taylorville, Illinois, when he was 7 years old, and has never left the area. His parents opened a McDonald's franchise, where Davis pitched in to work before going to college. He said the experience taught him about the challenges facing small business owners. His political science courses at Millikin University spurred an interest in holding public office. After graduating in 1992,

Davis joined Illinois Secretary of State George Ryan's staff. At the time, Ryan's office was engaged in what was later exposed as massive fraud, illegally selling government licenses. Davis denied knowing of the scheme.

He got his first campaign experience at 25, running for the Illinois legislature in 1996. He lost, but returned to the fray quickly, managing Rep. John Shimkus' first reelection bid. With time off to run unsuccessfully for mayor of his hometown in 2000, Davis stayed more than a decade on Shimkus' district office staff. During those years, he was the lawmaker's project coordinator, securing local, federal and private funding for public works projects. "He's great at finding the right mix of funding to move a project forward," Shimkus told the Springfield weekly *Illinois Times*.

When Rep. Tim Johnson announced he was retiring from Congress shortly after winning his primary for reelection in his redistricted seat, a small group of Illinois GOP leaders chose Davis to replace him on the ballot. They were impressed by his fundraising acumen. In 2011, he served as executive director of the Illinois Republican Party and managed to pay off the organization's $300,000 debt. In the general election, Davis faced Democrat David Gill, an emergency room physician and a perennial candidate. Davis promoted his work on the board of education for his local church and as the athletic director of the school his three children attend. He stressed the need to repeal President Barack Obama's health care reform law and to cut government spending, though he made an exception for federal Pell Grants (the district has several colleges and universities). Both men - and their parties - launched fierce negative attacks over the airwaves, prompting Johnson at one point to tell both of them to stop it. Davis outspent Gill $1.4 million to $1.3 million, and eked out a victory by a margin of 1,002 votes -- 46.5%-46.2%. The national parties spent more than $6 million on the contest.

Davis benefited from his experience as the unassuming staffer who did his work without making waves. He has been busy on two committees: Agriculture, and Transportation and Infrastructure. Unusual for a freshman, he served on House-Senate conference committees handling two major pieces of legislation in 2014 and he helped to shape each measure. On the farm bill, he added requirements that the Environmental Protection Administration give farmers a seat at the table when the agency considered new regulations that affect their industry. On the water resources bill, he helped craft language that permits the Army Corp of Engineers to cooperate with private businesses to complete projects needed to improve the nation's waterways. Congress also enacted his bill, the Hire More Heroes Act, to help small businesses hire more veterans.

In 2015, when Congress passed a five-year highway funding bill, Davis took credit for provisions on behalf of pipeline welders and freight auto-haulers and for a provision for new tools to identify underlying causes for repeat behavior in cases of driving while intoxicated. He has shown occasional independence as when he was one of 30 House Republicans who voted in June 2016 to give illegal immigrant "dreamers" the right to join the military. His *Almanac* vote ratings in 2015 placed him near the center of the House in each of the three areas. On Agriculture, Davis has chaired the Subcommittee on Biotechnology, Horticulture, and Research. He also joined the leadership-allied House Administration Committee.

In 2014, Davis survived two significant challenges to his reelection. In the Republican primary, his challenger was Erika Harold, a Harvard Law School graduate and 2003 Miss America, who had tea party support and encouragement from national conservative organizations. *The Weekly Standard* described her as "smart" and "engaging." In her campaign, she said that she represented "the next generation of Republican leadership," and that the GOP needed to reach out to a broader constituency. She ran a credible campaign. But Davis, who largely focused on his record as a freshman, won, 55%-41%.

Democrats initially were enthusiastic about their challenger, Ann Callis, a former chief justice of the Madison County court. Callis took relatively conservative views for a Democrat, including her description of the Affordable Care Act as "a disaster." She referred to Davis as "a Washington politician." On energy issues, Callis won the support of the Sierra Club, while Davis was backed by the United Mine Workers and the coal industry, both of which were unhappy with the Obama administration's hostility to coal. Callis spent a credible $1.9 million, to $3.4 million for Davis. But her national party assistance was limited. Davis won by a robust 59%-41%, and took all of the 14 counties except for university-based Champaign.

In 2016, discouraged Democrats took a pass on a major challenge to Davis. Given Donald Trump's strong local performance, that was probably wise. Still, Davis distanced himself from Trump during the campaign, withdrawing his support following the release of a recording of Trump making lewd comments about women. Citing his role as the parent of three teen-age children, Davis called the behavior "inexcusable and … directly against what I've been doing in Washington to combat assaults on college campuses." Two months earlier, Davis had joined the Trump campaign's agriculture advisory committee. Following the election, Davis became chairman of the House Republicans' Primary Patriot Program to assist GOP members facing a serious primary challenge.

West-Central Illinois: St. Louis exurbs, Champaign

Population		**Race and Ethnicity**		**Income**	
Total	711,498	White	79.3%	Median Income	$48,127 (284 out of 435)
Land area	5,794	Black	11.2%		
Pop/ sq mi	122.8	Latino	3.3%		
Born in state	74.5%	Asian	3.6%	Under $50,000	51.5%
		Two races	2.3%	$50,000-$99,999	30.4%
Age Groups		Other	0.3%	$100,000-$199,999	14.9%
Under 18	20.7%			$200,000 or more	3.2%
18-34	28.6%	**Education**		Poverty Rate	18.9%
35-64	36.4%	H.S grad or less	40.1%		
Over 64	14.3%	Some college	30.3%	**Health Insurance**	
		College Degree, 4 yr	17.8%	With health insurance coverage	91.8%
Work		Post grad	11.8%		
White Collar	37.2%				
Sales and Service	43.1%	**Military**		**Public Assistance**	
Blue Collar	19.6%	Veteran	8.8%	Cash public assistance income	2.1%
Government	19.6%	Active Duty	0.1%		
				Food stamp/SNAP benefits	13.2%

Voter Turnout			
2015 Total Citizens 18+	543,297	2016 House Turnout as % CVAP	58%
2016 House turnout	314,394	2014 House Turnout as % CVAP	39%

2012 Presidential Vote		
Mitt Romney	147,104	(49%)
Barack Obama	146,732	(49%)

2016 Presidential Vote		
Donald Trump	159,013	(49%)
Hillary Clinton	141,540	(44%)
Gary Johnson	14,681	(5%)

Cook Partisan Voting Index: R+3

Springfield, the capital of Illinois, has changed rather little since its great moment in history - when it was the home to Abraham Lincoln, railroad lawyer, elected to the House as a Whig opponent of the Mexican War and later, the 16th president of the United States. Today, beyond the suburban fringe, the prairie countryside outside of Springfield is still mostly farmland with few towns, filled with large industrial farms producing soybeans and corn. Farming technology has changed vastly, but the patterns of cultivation, the contours of the land, even the shape of the ribbons of back country roads, cannot be entirely different from what Lincoln saw as a lawyer making his way from one county seat to another on the circuit. Nor has downtown Springfield changed all that much, at least compared with booming Midwestern capitals, like Columbus, Indianapolis or even Des Moines. Springfield has suffered from continuing job losses on the public payroll under governors of both parties, plus the dispiriting paralysis of state government.

If most of the office fronts and houses captured in old photographs are gone, some remain; and the scale has not changed. Lincoln's clapboard house is still in Springfield, and so is the courtroom where he argued cases before federal judges. The Greek revival downtown block where Lincoln and his partner William Herndon kept their law offices is open for inspection, as is the state Capitol building built here in 1839. The governor's mansion downtown, built in 1855, is the third oldest, continuously occupied residence in the country. Today, Springfield is known more for its dysfunction; four of the state's last 10 governors were sentenced to jail time on corruption charges. The recent delay in approving a state budget has been another form of criminal neglect. In April 2015, on the 150th anniversary of Lincoln's assassination, the state used bad timing to reduce funding and staffing for his tomb.

The 13th Congressional District contains rural, prairie lands from Collinsville, just outside St. Louis, to Champaign-Urbana, a three-hour drive northeast. It includes much of Bloomington, birthplace of former Vice President Adlai Stevenson, who served under Democrat Grover Cleveland, and the hometown of his grandson, Governor Adlai Stevenson II, nominated by Democrats for president in 1952 and 1956. The largest of the towns in the district are anchored by the state's universities: The University of Illinois in Champaign-Urbana, Illinois State University in Bloomington-Normal, and Illinois Wesleyan University, also in Bloomington. Since 2015, those campuses have lost students and funding because of the continuing deadlock over Gov. Bruce Rauner's proposed budget cuts. Decatur is home to politically influential Archer Daniels Midland, one of the world's largest agricultural processors and a major champion of ethanol. Except for youthful Champaign, most of the mid-size cities in downstate Illinois have been suffering population losses.

Politically, the district has been closely divided, with the cultural conservatism of the prairie meshing with the liberal academic population centers and government capital in Springfield. Barack Obama won the district easily in 2008, with 55 percent of the vote. But like the neighboring 12th District, the contests since then have shown a boost for Republicans. In 2016, when Donald Trump won 49%-44%, the result revealed the diminished enthusiasm for Democrats in rural areas plus Trump's working-class appeal.

FOURTEENTH DISTRICT

Randy Hultgren (R)

Elected 2010, 4th term; b. Mar 01, 1966, Park Ridge; Bethel College (IN), B.A.; Chicago-Kent College of Law (IL), J.D.; Wheaton Academy (IL); Evangelical; Married (Christy Hultgren); 4 children.

Elected Office: DuPage County Board, 1994-1998; IL House, 1998-2006; IL Senate, 2006-2010.

Professional Career: Office Manager, Rep. Dennis Hastert, 1988-1990; Vice President., Trust Investment Advisors, 1995-2010; Practicing attorney, 1993-2010.

DC Office: 2455 RHOB 20515, 202-225-2976, Fax: 202-225-0697, hultgren.house.gov.

State Offices: Campton Hills, 630-584-2734; McHenry, 815-679-6352.

Committees: *Financial Services*: Capital Markets, Securities & Investment, Housing & Insurance. *Joint Congressional-Executive Commission on China. Joint Security & Cooperation in Europe. Science, Space & Technology*: Energy, Research & Technology.

Group Ratings

	ADA	ACLU	AFL-CIO	LCV	ITI	COC	HAFA	ACU	CFG	FRC
2016	-	5%	-	0%	100%	100%	76%	88%	86%	100%
2015	0%	C	21%	0%	C	80%	C	88%	81%	100%

Almanac Ratings 2015

	Economy	Social	Foreign	Composite
Liberal	6%	4%	0%	3%
Conservative	94%	96%	100%	97%

Key Votes of the 114th Congress

1. Keystone Pipeline	Y	5. Puerto Rico Debt	N	9. Offenses by Aliens	Y
2. Trade Deals	Y	6. Medical Marijuana	N	10. Troops in Iraq	N
3. Export-Import Bank	N	7. Sanctuary Cities	Y	11. Homeland Security $$	N
4. Debt Ceiling Increase	N	8. Armor-piercing Bullets	Y	12. Trade Adjustment aid	N

Election Results

Election	Name (Party)	Vote (%)	Cand. Spent	Ind. Exp. Support	Ind. Exp. Oppose
2016 General	Randy Hultgren (R)	200,508 (59%)	$879,451	$6,466	
	Jim Walz (D)	137,589 (41%)	$17,973		
2016 Primary	Randy Hultgren (R)	(100%)			

Prior winning percentages: 2014 (65%), 2012 (59%), 2010 (51%)

Randy Hultgren, a Republican who ousted Democratic Rep. Bill Foster in 2010, represents a swath of Chicago's northern and western exurbs that includes Fermi National Laboratory, making him a big advocate for more scientific research money even as he echoes traditional GOP calls for reining in spending. He has been a Main Street Republican, with a focus on business and tax issues.

Hultgren was raised in Wheaton and was the youngest of three children who lived above their family's funeral home. The grandson of a Baptist pastor, Hultgren became the third generation in his family to attend Bethel College (now Bethel University) in Minnesota. After graduation, he headed to Washington, and in 1988, was hired on the staff of Republican Rep. Dennis Hastert of Illinois, who later became House Speaker. Hultgren progressed quickly from intern to office manager for Hastert, and the work persuaded him to return to his hometown to pursue a degree from Chicago-Kent College of Law.

After graduation, Hultgren practiced law with a local firm, and in the mid-1990s, opened his own firm. During that time, he got a stock broker's license so he could serve as an investment adviser. This period also shaped his political career. In 1990, he was elected as a Republican precinct committee member for Milton Township, and four years later, Hultgren won a seat on the DuPage County Board. In 1998, when Hultgren learned that a personal friend, state Rep. Peter Roskam, was planning a bid for Congress, he ran for Roskam's Illinois House seat, which he won. Following that pattern in 2006, he was elected to succeed Roskam in the state Senate after Roskam made a successful run for Congress.

In 2010, Hultgren took on Foster, who had won Hastert's seat in a 2008 special election. In a district that had been in GOP hands since the Great Depression. Hultgren competed in the primary with Ethan Hastert, the son of his former political mentor. In an upset, Hultgren overcame Hastert's high name recognition and political pedigree to win the primary by a comfortable 10 percentage points. The political value of the Hastert name later collapsed after the former Speaker pleaded guilty in 2015 and he was sentenced to a federal prison for failure to comply with federal bank reporting requirements when he withdrew hundreds of thousands of dollars for hush money in a cover-up scheme when he was a high school wrestling coach.

During the general election, Hultgren portrayed Foster as a liberal out of touch with the exurban district. A Harvard-trained physicist, Foster decreed Hultgren to be too "far right" for the district. He raised significantly more money than Hultgren, and conspicuously failed to mention his party affiliation. Hultgren won, 51%-45%. Foster subsequently won election in the 11th District in 2012. The district that each now serves differs markedly from the district where they competed in 2010.

The soft-spoken Hultgren generally avoided hard-right views and he didn't make anti-government waves like many of his freshman colleagues. "I'm never going to be the national media guy," he told *Roll Call* in 2011. He showed his independence within the party by opposing a move by Western conservatives to block the designation of national monuments and another proposal to bar money for government projects that require a union agreement. A member of the conservative Republican Study Committee, he refused to back its aggressive 2011 budget plan, citing its large cuts to Medicare and Medicaid.

His chief committee work has been on Financial Services. In February 2016, the House passed his Capital Markets Improvements Act, which was designed to relax disclosure requirements on issuers of compensatory benefit plans. The bill died in the Senate. In January 2017, Hultgren became vice-chairman of the Capital Markets, Securities and Investments Subcommittee, where he said that his objective was "to unleash the power of small businesses to access the capital they need to hire and expand." When the House passed that month a broader measure to restrict federal regulation, it included Hultgren's proposal for periodic review and termination of many federal regulations. With Democratic Rep. Dutch Ruppersberger of Maryland, he launched the Municipal Finance Caucus to support state and local governments seeking to finance infrastructure projects.

Hultgren helped form the bipartisan Science and National Labs Caucus to raise awareness of Fermilab's physics research. With Foster when he returned to the House, he pushed for additional funding for the labs. With a seat on the Science, Space, and Technology Committee, Hultgren won House passage of his Department of Energy Laboratory Modernization and Technology Transfer Act of 2014 to modernize the national lab system, including a pilot program for cooperation between companies and the labs to develop new technology.

Following redistricting changes that made the district more safely Republican, Hultgren has managed to avoid primary opposition and he has had an easy time in the general election against weakly financed Democrats. Hultgren retained his focus on local problems. At home, he participated in the Starbucks-sponsored "Behind the Bar" program in which local politicians meet with baristas, managers and district managers to discuss the issues that affect them.

Northwestern Chicagoland: McHenry, Kane

Population		**Race and Ethnicity**		**Income**	
Total	723,419	White	79.3%	Median Income	$84,049 (27 out of 435)
Land area	1,598	Black	3.0%		
Pop/ sq mi	452.8	Latino	11.7%	Under $50,000	26.9%
Born in state	70.5%	Asian	4.3%	$50,000-$99,999	32.5%
		Two races	1.5%	$100,000-$199,999	31.7%
Age Groups		Other	0.2%	$200,000 or more	9.0%
Under 18	26.9%			Poverty Rate	6.5%
18-34	18.5%	**Education**			
35-64	43.2%	H.S grad or less	30.4%	**Health Insurance**	
Over 64	11.4%	Some college	31.1%	With health insurance coverage	93.5%
		College Degree, 4 yr	24.4%		
Work		Post grad	14.0%		
White Collar	40.7%			**Public Assistance**	
Sales and Service	40.5%	**Military**		Cash public assistance income	1.3%
Blue Collar	18.8%	Veteran	6.8%		
Government	12.0%	Active Duty	0.1%	Food stamp/SNAP benefits	5.8%

Voter Turnout			
2015 Total Citizens 18+	499,620	2016 House Turnout as % CVAP	68%
2016 House turnout	338,097	2014 House Turnout as % CVAP	44%

2012 Presidential Vote		
Mitt Romney	172,162	(54%)
Barack Obama	140,495	(44%)

2016 Presidential Vote		
Donald Trump	167,327	(48%)
Hillary Clinton	154,058	(44%)
Gary Johnson	17,259	(5%)

Cook Partisan Voting Index: R+5

At the peak of the housing boom, exurban Kendall County southwest of Chicago looked like the city's new suburban frontier. It was rated the fastest-growing large county in the nation by the Census Bureau in 2010. Its population more than doubled in the decade after 2000, as urban flight brought in families attracted by its affordable housing, good schools and low crime rates, all located near job centers in suburban DuPage and Kane counties. Farmland quickly transformed into new housing subdivisions. In effect, Kendall became a suburb of the suburbs. But the downside of the rapid growth became evident during the collapse of the housing finance market, when Kendall posted the highest foreclosure rate in the state. Several newer developments in towns like Yorkville became ghost towns after a sudden halt to building. Kendall County grew only 3.6 percent from 2010 to 2013, barely above the national average;

the next two years may have started a new turnaround, with 4 percent growth. In the exurbs northwest of Chicago, the experience was similar: McHenry County's population dropped by 0.5 percent during those five years, after the population boomed by 19 percent in the previous decade. The area does not depend entirely on residential growth. In June 2016, the Wrigley Co., now owned by the giant Mars Inc., opened its $50 million plant expansion at Yorkville that manufactures Skittles, a popular candy.

The 14th District of Illinois arcs through seven of the Chicago collar counties, including most of solidly Republican Kendall and McHenry and also Republican-leaning chunks of Kane and western Lake County, where little lake communities are surrounded by new suburbs like Wauconda, Deer Park and Volo. Huntley is the site of Del Webb's Sun City; with about 9,500 residents, it claims to be largest retirement community in the Midwest. It also contains smaller parts of Will, DeKalb, and DuPage counties. Also here are parts of the Fox River Valley, including Batavia and the urbane town of St. Charles, which is filled with antique stores and restaurants and sponsors the well-attended Scarecrow Festival. About 55 percent of the voting population resides in McHenry and Kane. Of all the suburban Chicago districts, the 14th is the least ethnically diverse, with a 76 percent white population.

This is the most Republican district in the suburbs, though much of "downstate" has become notably more Republican than the 14th. Still, in a good year Democrats can run competitively here. President Barack Obama narrowly carried it, under the present lines, with 50 percent of the vote in 2008. Donald Trump won here 48%-44% in 2016.

FIFTEENTH DISTRICT

John Shimkus (R)

Elected 1996, 11th term; b. Feb 21, 1958, Collinsville; Christ College (CA), 1989; U.S. Military Academy (NY), B.S., 1990; Southern Illinois University, M.A., 1997; Lutheran; Married (Karen Muth Shimkus); 3 children.

Military Career: U. S Army, 1980-1985; Army Reserves, 1985-2008.

Elected Office: Collinsville Township trustee, 1989-1993; Madison County Treasurer, 1990-1996.

Professional Career: H.S. teacher, 1986-1990.

DC Office: 2217 RHOB 20515, 202-225-5271, Fax: 202-225-5880, shimkus.house.gov.

State Offices: Danville, 217-446-0664; Effingham, 217-347-7947; Harrisburg, 618-252-8271; Maryville, 618-288-7190.

Committees: *Energy & Commerce*: Communications & Technology, Energy, Environment (Chmn), Health.

Group Ratings

	ADA	ACLU	AFL-CIO	LCV	ITI	COC	HAFA	ACU	CFG	FRC
2016	-	5%	-	3%	100%	100%	45%	64%	50%	83%
2015	0%	C	29%	3%	C	95%	C	58%	60%	92%

Almanac Ratings 2015

	Economy	Social	Foreign	Composite
Liberal	6%	14%	11%	10%
Conservative	94%	86%	90%	90%

Key Votes of the 114th Congress

1. Keystone Pipeline	Y	5. Puerto Rico Debt	Y	9. Offenses by Aliens	Y
2. Trade Deals	Y	6. Medical Marijuana	N	10. Troops in Iraq	N
3. Export-Import Bank	N	7. Sanctuary Cities	Y	11. Homeland Security $$	Y
4. Debt Ceiling Increase	N	8. Armor-piercing Bullets	Y	12. Trade Adjustment aid	Y

Election Results

Election	Name (Party)	Vote (%)	Cand. Spent	Ind. Exp. Support	Ind. Exp. Oppose
2016 General	John Shimkus (R)	274,554 (100%)	$2,846,664	$483,569	$273,490
2016 Primary	John Shimkus (R)	75,968 (60%)			
	Kyle McCarter (R)	49,885 (40%)			

Prior winning percentages: 2014 (75%), 2012 (69%), 2010 (71%), 2008 (64%), 2006 (64%), 2004 (69%), 2002 (55%), 2000 (63%), 1998 (61%), 1996 (50%)

John Shimkus, a Republican first elected in 1996, has been an aggressive supporter of business and a fierce critic of regulations he considers overly burdensome. He suffered a setback in December 2016 when he lost his bid to become chairman of the Energy and Commerce Committee, but he retained an influential post as chairman of its Energy Subcommittee. A devout Christian, he uses his official Facebook and Twitter accounts to post daily Bible passages.

Shimkus grew up in Collinsville, in Madison County. His father was an installer for Illinois Bell, and his mother a township trustee. He is of Lithuanian descent, as is his predecessor in the seat, Democratic Sen. Dick Durbin. Shimkus graduated from West Point, trained in the Army as a Ranger and paratrooper, went to college in California, then came back to Collinsville to teach high school. Almost immediately, he began running for local office. In 1988, he ran for the Madison County Board and lost. The next year, he was elected a Collinsville Township trustee. In 1990, he was elected Madison County treasurer. He challenged then-Rep. Durbin in 1992 and lost 57%-43%, a closer margin than in Durbin's previous campaigns.

In 1996, when Durbin ran for the Senate, Shimkus easily won the Republican primary, with 51 percent against seven other candidates. In the general election, he faced state Rep. Jay Hoffman. Both were anti-abortion rights, anti-gun control, and pro-balanced budget amendment. Hoffman raised more money and had the support of the AFL-CIO, but Shimkus won, 50.3%-49.7%.

In the House, Shimkus' voting record is generally conservative. He told *Esquire* magazine in 2010 that he believes President Barack Obama's world view "is of government control, of government solving the inequities of society. And that means big government and higher taxes. ... It's just not what makes this country great." Shimkus can show a centrist streak. He was one of 16 House Republicans in 2012 to back a budget plan along the lines of the bipartisan Simpson-Bowles commission. In the *Almanac* vote ratings for 2015, he ranked toward the center of the House on his social and foreign-policy scores and more conservative on economic issues.

On the Energy and Commerce Committee, Shimkus' ardor has sometimes triggered criticism of what the left describes as hyperbole. When Democrats issued a draft plan to regulate greenhouse gas emissions in 2009, he called it the "largest assault on democracy and freedom in this country that I've ever witnessed." The floods that scientists warn could result from a rapidly changing climate won't happen, Shimkus said, because God promised the Earth would not be destroyed by a flood. During a 2013 hearing with Health and Human Services Secretary Kathleen Sebelius to discuss the Affordable Care Act, he compared her responses to those of an official from North Korea.

Shimkus has been especially vocal about energy production: supporting nuclear power, extending tax credits for ethanol, and giving incentives to coal-to-liquid refineries to help coal-producing areas. In 2005, he helped to pass the law that gasoline must contain a minimum volume of renewable fuels, such as biodiesel and ethanol; that has resulted in what has become known as the Renewable Fuel Standard.

Shimkus has lost two bids to become Energy and Commerce chairman, though in each case he walked away with a significant consolation prize. After 2010, he lost out to the more senior Fred Upton of Michigan. Shimkus was named chairman of the new Environment and the Economy Subcommittee, where he closely monitored the Obama administration's regulatory activities. After several years of painstaking effort and bipartisan compromise, he scored a legislative coup in June 2016 when Obama signed the Chemical Safety for the 21st Century Act, which was an update of the Toxic Substances Control Act. Shimkus was a central player in the extended legislative dealing. He called the new law "a thoughtful approach to protecting people all across the country from unsafe chemical exposure by making long needed improvements to an outdated and ineffective law."

Following the 2016 election, when Upton was term-limited, Shimkus ran again for committee chairman and was challenged by Greg Walden of Oregon. Shimkus this time had the benefit of seniority. But Walden had gained chits with many GOP members as successful chairman of the National Republican Congressional Committee. Speaker Paul Ryan reportedly endorsed Walden - a decisive factor. Instead, Shimkus resumed his role as chairman of the renamed Environment Subcommittee, which expanded its jurisdiction to include the Clean Air Act. He promised to "take the lead on reining in the EPA, dismantling the Obama administration's anti-coal rules and regulations, and reforming the Renewable Fuels Standard." Shimkus continued to push for legislation to store waste from commercial nuclear power plants at Yucca Mountain in Nevada. With the retirement in 2016 of steadfast foe Senate Democratic Leader Harry Reid of Nevada, a major obstacle had been removed.

Coincidentally, Shimkus clashed with Ryan on another House Republican internal conflict, when Shimkus took the lead in seeking to end the House ban on spending earmarks. Previous Speaker John Boehner had pushed for the ban to satisfy critics of excessive federal spending and to avoid occasional abuses. Shimkus decried the abandonment of congressional prerogatives. "All appropriations begin in the House, per the Constitution. So, we've turned over our power of the purse to the executive branch, which can then make their own decisions based on their political whims," he told the Associated Press. Ryan stifled the retreat when Republicans prepared other House rules changes in January 2017, though he left the door open to further review.

As a former high school teacher, Shimkus earlier took what seemed to be a routine assignment as chairman of the House page board. But five weeks before the 2006 election, revelations that Republican Rep. Mark Foley had sent inappropriate and sexually explicit emails to former male pages was a political bombshell for the party, including for Shimkus and then-GOP Speaker Dennis Hastert of Illinois. Both men had known of questionable contacts Foley had with pages and failed to investigate. The House Ethics Committee later found that Shimkus should have shared the information with other House members on the page board, but did not call for sanctions against him.

In 2002, Shimkus had a redistricting-forced contest against Rep. David Phelps, a conservative Democrat. After a spirited contest, in which organized labor spent more than $1.5 million trying to dislodge him, Shimkus won 55%-45%. Since then, he has been reelected easily. When he first ran for the seat, Shimkus said he would limit himself to six terms. But in 2005, he called his pledge "a mistake," and said, "unless everyone plays by the same rules, term limits don't make sense." He has not faced a serious challenge since then.

Eastern South-Central Illinois

Population		**Race and Ethnicity**		**Income**	
Total	705,952	White	90.9%	Median Income	$47,971 (285 out of 435)
Land area	14,696	Black	4.3%		
Pop/ sq mi	48.0	Latino	2.6%		
Born in state	75.7%	Asian	0.6%	Under $50,000	51.7%
		Two races	1.4%	$50,000-$99,999	32.0%
Age Groups		Other	0.3%	$100,000-$199,999	14.2%
Under 18	22.5%			$200,000 or more	2.2%
18-34	21.1%	**Education**		Poverty Rate	14.6%
35-64	39.2%	H.S grad or less	47.0%		
Over 64	17.2%	Some college	34.6%	**Health Insurance**	
		College Degree, 4 yr	12.4%	With health insurance coverage	91.1%
Work		Post grad	5.9%		
White Collar	29.1%				
Sales and Service	41.3%	**Military**		**Public Assistance**	
Blue Collar	29.7%	Veteran	10.0%	Cash public assistance income	2.3%
Government	14.6%	Active Duty	0.0%		
				Food stamp/SNAP benefits	13.5%

Voter Turnout			
2015 Total Citizens 18+	541,394	2016 House Turnout as % CVAP	51%
2016 House turnout	274,554	2014 House Turnout as % CVAP	41%

2012 Presidential Vote		
Mitt Romney	197,262	(64%)
Barack Obama	105,015	(34%)

2016 Presidential Vote		
Donald Trump	226,606	(70%)
Hillary Clinton	78,573	(24%)
Gary Johnson	12,468	(4%)

Cook Partisan Voting Index: R+21

Much of Southern Illinois is a land of prairies, of flat, treeless stretches sloping imperceptibly down to the Ohio and Mississippi rivers. It was settled almost entirely from the south by farmers coming overland from Kentucky, such as Abraham Lincoln's ancestors, who settled in what was then the state capital of Vandalia. Just beyond the Ohio River, they found hilly terrain, some of which turned out to have vast coal deposits. As they traveled farther north, they must have been astonished, after miles of thick forest, to see the great American prairie stretch before them, a vast sea of empty land extending past the horizon. The prairie lands proved wondrously rich and were soon crisscrossed by rail lines taking their produce away and bringing in industrial products from St. Louis, Chicago and points east. About the same time, several mining towns sprouted in Southern Illinois. This was the home turf of John L. Lewis, the imperious leader of the United Mine Workers who for four decades during the middle of the 20th century was one of the most powerful and eloquent figures in American public life.

The mining industry in recent years has become a shadow of itself. In 1990, Illinois produced 62 million tons of coal and employed 10,000 workers in mining; by 2014, 4,500 workers produced 58 million tons. Employers and workers drew some hope - and a few jobs -- from the promises of Donald Trump to revive the production and burning of coal. In Mattoon, General Electric made plans to shut down by August 2017 its Lamp Plant facility. The plant, which once produced flash cubes for camera and employed 1,800 workers, had reduced its payroll to 144 and was manufacturing incandescent and fluorescent lighting.

The 15th Congressional District of Illinois, the largest geographically in the state, extends more than 250 miles up and down, and 150 miles across. Vermilion County and northern Champaign County represent the northern border of the district, which extends along the state's eastern and southeastern borders and to the west along a line that ends with Collinsville in Madison County a few miles from East St. Louis and the Mississippi River. It covers all or part of 33 counties in the rich heartland of Southern Illinois. The old National Road (paralleled by Interstate 70), the traditional boundary between the part of downstate Illinois settled by Southerners and the part settled by Yankees, traverses the district. The city of Effingham, which straddles that line, is where corn and soybean fields give way to hills and valleys with orchards and woodlands. Racial diversity is limited here; in 2012, the district was 93 percent white.

The biggest voting blocs in the 15th are in Madison and Clinton counties (parts of the St. Louis metropolitan area), Coles County (home to Eastern Illinois University), plus Champaign and adjacent Vermilion County on the Indiana border. The district includes sparsely settled areas along the Ohio River, and some prairie counties along U.S. 40. Politically, these prairie lands incline to the party of former House Speaker Joseph (Uncle Joe) Cannon, a Republican from the manufacturing city of Danville (population, 32,977), which is the largest in the district. Traditional Democrats have become hard to find here. In 2016, Trump won 70 percent of the vote and each of the 33 counties in the district except for university-based Champaign. This is the most Republican district in Illinois and has moved significantly in that direction since 2008, when GOP presidential nominee John McCain got 55 percent in the district.

SIXTEENTH DISTRICT

Adam Kinzinger (R)

Elected 2010, 4th term; b. Feb 27, 1978, Kankakee; Illinois State University, Bach. Deg.; Christian Church; Single.

Military Career: U.S Air Force, 2003-present (Iraq, Afghanistan).

Elected Office: McLean County Board, 1998-2003.

Professional Career: Partner, sales rep., STL Technology, 2000-2003.

DC Office: 2245 RHOB 20515, 202-225-3635, Fax: 202-225-3521, kinzinger.house.gov.

State Offices: Ottawa, 815-431-9271; Rockford, 815-708-8032; Watseka, 815-432-0580.

Committees: *Energy & Commerce*: Communications & Technology, Digital Commerce & Consumer Protection, Energy. *Foreign Affairs*: Asia & the Pacific, Middle East & North Africa.

Group Ratings

	ADA	ACLU	AFL-CIO	LCV	ITI	COC	HAFA	ACU	CFG	FRC
2016	-	5%	-	8%	100%	100%	39%	44%	56%	75%
2015	0%	C	38%	6%	C	100%	C	46%	43%	75%

Almanac Ratings 2015

	Economy	Social	Foreign	Composite
Liberal	14%	21%	10%	15%
Conservative	86%	79%	90%	85%

Key Votes of the 114th Congress

1. Keystone Pipeline	Y	5. Puerto Rico Debt	Y	9. Offenses by Aliens	Y
2. Trade Deals	Y	6. Medical Marijuana	Y	10. Troops in Iraq	N
3. Export-Import Bank	Y	7. Sanctuary Cities	Y	11. Homeland Security $$	Y
4. Debt Ceiling Increase	Y	8. Armor-piercing Bullets	Y	12. Trade Adjustment aid	Y

Election Results

Election	Name (Party)	Vote (%)	Cand. Spent	Ind. Exp. Support	Ind. Exp. Oppose
2016 General	Adam Kinzinger (R)	259,722 (100%)	$851,886	$1,130	
2016 Primary	Adam Kinzinger (R)	(100%)			

Prior winning percentages: 2014 (71%), 2012 (62%), 2010 (65%)

Republican Adam Kinzinger, elected in 2010, is a telegenic conservative who has racked up considerable experience in the military and political worlds. A former Air Force pilot, he dispatched a first-term Democratic incumbent, and two years later knocked off 10-term Republican Rep. Don Manzullo in a redistricting-forced primary in 2012. He has been a foreign policy wonk and a harsh critic of President Donald Trump.

Kinzinger was born in Kankakee, but spent the majority of his life in Bloomington. He attributed his interest in public service to his father, who ran a nonprofit homeless shelter, and his mother, a public school teacher. Growing up in a middle-class family with two siblings taught him to spend money prudently. Wanting to stay near home, he got a bachelor's degree in political science from Illinois State University. In 1998, as a sophomore, he took seriously a joking suggestion that he run for the McLean County Board. He did, defeating an incumbent, and served five years. With the September 11 terrorist attacks, "that's when I basically woke up," he recalled. A month later, he joined the Air Force. He worked in the private sector for STL Technology Partners until he started officer and pilot training. He served three tours in Iraq and one in Afghanistan.

In 2006, Kinzinger was returning from the border of Mexico as part of a mission when he witnessed an attempted murder. Seeing a woman whose throat had been slashed running from her knife-wielding aggressor, he wrestled the man to the ground until police arrived. He was awarded the National Guard's Valley Forge Cross for heroism. "During that whole thing, I thought I was going to die," he said. "It really was a life-changing moment about sacrificing yourself for others."

In 2009, following his final tour in Iraq, Kinzinger campaigned for the district based in Will County. Touting his military service, he had important backing from local tea party activists and defeated four opponents in the Republican primary, with 64 percent of the vote. In the fall, he faced first-term Rep. Debbie Halvorson, who had racked up an impressive 58 percent of the vote in 2008. Halvorson attacked Kinzinger's stance on free trade and depicted him as inexperienced. She ran a campaign ad with a senior citizen scolding, "Young man, you have no idea what you're doing." Kinzinger countered with endorsements from former governors and GOP leaders Mitt Romney and Sarah Palin. He won the support of the Chamber of Commerce and the National Federation of Independent Business over Halvorson, who had highlighted her advocacy of small business. He picked up an endorsement from the *Chicago Sun-Times*, which often backs Democrats. Halvorson outspent him $2.5 million to $1.8 million, but Kinzinger won convincingly, 57%-43%.

When he got to Washington, *The New York Times* took him to task in an editorial after Kinzinger held a $5,000-a-head breakfast at the Capitol Hill Club to raise money for his campaign debt. The editorial said it smacked of "business as usual" for a lawmaker who had promised to be different. He became a favorite of GOP leaders, who put him on the whip team and gave him a choice seat on the Energy and Commerce Committee, where he has generally upheld business' interests. He called for dramatically overhauling the tax code to make it friendlier to companies. The House in 2012 passed his bill aimed at helping states streamline certification requirements for veterans with emergency medical technician training who want to continue as civilian EMTs. *Time* named him one of its "40 Under 40" young leaders.

On Energy and Commerce, Kinzinger has focused on the multiple energy sources of interest to his constituents. As he noted on his congressional website, the 16th District "is home to four nuclear power plants, miles of windmills, hydropower plants, and ethanol and biodiesel plants." He has been a major booster of nuclear energy that, he said, "will sustain our economic expansion and keep the lights on while we work to catch up with our international competition." In 2016, Kinzinger won passage of bills to bar the Federal Communications Commission from regulating the rates of internet service providers, streamline procedures for veterans with military emergency medical training and prohibit certain land-use restrictions of amateur radio stations. With Democrat Dan Lipinski of Illinois, he won enactment of the American Manufacturing Competitiveness Act, which requires a national strategy to create U.S. manufacturing competitiveness.

Politically entrenched and with growing seniority, Kinzinger became more activist in the GOP's establishment wing, especially on national security issues. In 2014, he criticized the Pentagon budget-cutting plan of Kentucky Sen. Rand Paul as "devastating for our party." In 2015, he filed a resolution that would grant the president full authority to wage war against the threat posed by the Islamic State. Following the 2016 Republican convention, he cited Donald Trump's criticism of NATO and attacks on Muslims in his decision not to endorse his campaign for president. "Donald Trump is beginning to cross a lot of red lines of the unforgivable in politics. I'm not going to support Hillary, but in America we have the right to skip somebody," Kinzinger said on CNN. Following the election, he said that it was vital for the United States to call Russia to account for its actions to "mess around" with our election systems, and that the response by Trump "to disparage the intel-gathering mechanisms that we have here is not the right answer."

In January 2017, Kinzinger - who has continued to serve in the Air National Guard, as a major -- regained his earlier seat on the House Foreign Affairs Committee, where he said, "I will apply my military service and foreign policy experience in crafting legislation that puts our national security and global relationships at the forefront of our agenda."

At home, Democratic-engineered redistricting in 2012 put Kinzinger in the same district as Manzullo, who was twice his age. The race upended the traditional rules of seniority: Kinzinger won the endorsement of top House GOP leaders, including Majority Leader Eric Cantor and Whip Kevin McCarthy, while Manzullo played up his tea party support and a nod from FreedomWorks PAC, an important financial backer of that movement. Kinzinger touted his combat tours and hit Manzullo for voting to raise the debt limit 12 times in his career. Manzullo fired back, boasting in an ad that he had voted to cut $209 billion more in spending than Kinzinger in the current Congress. Primary voters decided to go with youth and the future over experience and the past, and Kinzinger won 54%-46%. In the fall, he had no trouble, winning with 62 percent over Democrat Wanda Rohl. He faced no major-party opposition in 2016.

North-Central Illinois: Rockford, Ottawa

Population		**Race and Ethnicity**		**Income**	
Total	703,553	White	84.5%	Median Income	$54,976 (184 out of 435)
Land area	7,917	Black	3.8%		
Pop/ sq mi	88.9	Latino	8.7%		
Born in state	77.0%	Asian	1.4%	Under $50,000	45.2%
Age Groups		Two races	1.4%	$50,000-$99,999	33.9%
Under 18	22.9%	Other	0.2%	$100,000-$199,999	17.8%
18-34	21.2%	**Education**		$200,000 or more	2.9%
35-64	40.1%	H.S grad or less	45.3%	Poverty Rate	12.2%
Over 64	15.8%	Some college	33.5%	**Health Insurance**	
Work		College Degree, 4 yr	13.6%	With health insurance coverage	91.5%
White Collar	30.6%	Post grad	7.6%		
Sales and Service	41.1%	**Military**		**Public Assistance**	
Blue Collar	28.3%	Veteran	9.2%	Cash public assistance income	1.9%
Government	12.7%	Active Duty	0.0%		
				Food stamp/SNAP benefits	11.2%

Voter Turnout

2015 Total Citizens 18+	525,232	2016 House Turnout as % CVAP	49%
2016 House turnout	259,853	2014 House Turnout as % CVAP	41%

2012 Presidential Vote

Mitt Romney	160,435	(53%)
Barack Obama	137,749	(45%)

2016 Presidential Vote

Donald Trump	173,068	(55%)
Hillary Clinton	119,529	(38%)
Gary Johnson	15,073	(5%)

Cook Partisan Voting Index: R+8

The third largest city in Illinois is Rockford, on the Rock River, settled by Swedes as well as Yankees, and once a leading furniture and machine tool manufacturer. Rockford's manufacturing base steadily declined after World War II, and by the 1980s, it had a serious unemployment problem. It temporarily rebounded as it moved toward becoming a center for professional services and high technology, but then the recession hit hard. The area's unemployment rate climbed to nearly 20 percent in early 2010 before finally dropping to 6 percent.% at the end of 2016.

Growth has become stagnant in DeKalb County, which had been booming with relatively cheap housing before the recession. In neighboring Boone County, the farming village of Poplar Grove saw its population triple between 2000 and 2010, but growth went flat and thousands of undeveloped lots were left barren after the recession. The Obama administration's auto bailout gave a jump start to the area's economy. The workforce at the big Chrysler plant on 280 acres a few miles east of Rockford in Belvidere had dropped to 200 in 2009, but it rebounded to employ more than 4,000 workers on three shifts, with additional workers at nearby suppliers. The factory and its workers got more good news when Chrysler decided to shift production of its Jeep Cherokee from Toledo, Ohio, to Belvidere, which had manufactured other Jeep models. The retooling began in January 2017 and was expected to take a few months. With completion of the $350 million project, Belvidere planned to produce more than 300,000 vehicles annually, compared with the 220,000 at the shuttered Toledo plant. Jobs at the Belvidere plant were schedule to grow to 4,500, plus more than 2,000 new jobs for local suppliers..

The 16th Congressional District is where downstate Illinois begins, at least where it begins west of Chicago. The elongated district forms a crescent surrounding the exurbs of Chicago as it hooks from the Wisconsin border on the north to the Indiana border on the east. It includes parts of Rockford, the population base of the district, after Democratic redistricters split the city for the first time since 1850 to maximize their House delegation. Farther south, on bluffs above the Illinois River, are the factory towns of Ottawa, LaSalle, and Streator. On the eastern side of the district is DeKalb County, long the world's leading manufacturer of barbed wire. Dixon, to the west, is where Ronald Reagan grew up.

These mostly small towns traditionally were some of the most heavily Republican territory in the country, but they have become more competitive. After the 2010 census, Democrats drew the district to favor Republicans, although in a wave election, Democrats have an opportunity. Barack Obama carried it with 50 percent in 2008, but Donald Trump scored a big turnaround win in 2016, 55%-38%.

SEVENTEENTH DISTRICT

Cheri Bustos (D)

Elected 2012, 3rd term; b. Oct 17, 1961, Springfield; University of Maryland - College Park, B.A.; University of Illinois - Springfield, M.A.; Illinois College - Jacksonville, Att.; Roman Catholic; Married (Gerry Bustos); 3 children; 2 grandchildren.

Elected Office: East Moline City Council, 2007-2011.

Professional Career: Vice President., Iowa Health Systems, 2008-2012; Sr. Director, Trinity Regional Health System, 2002-2008; Reporter, Quad-City Times, 1985-2002.

DC Office: 1009 LHOB 20515, 202-225-5905, Fax: 202-225-5396, bustos.house.gov.

State Offices: Peoria, 309-966-1813; Rock Island, 309-786-3406; Rockford, 815-968-8011.

Committees: *Agriculture*: General Farm Commodities & Risk Management, Livestock & Foreign Agriculture. *Transportation & Infrastructure*: Aviation, Highways & Transit, Railroads, Pipelines & Hazardous Materials, Water Resources & Environment.

Group Ratings

	ADA	ACLU	AFL-CIO	LCV	ITI	COC	HAFA	ACU	CFG	FRC
2016	-	76%	-	95%	83%	64%	14%	0%	0%	0%
2015	65%	C	96%	86%	C	60%	C	0%	0%	0%

Almanac Ratings 2015

	Economy	Social	Foreign	Composite
Liberal	69%	84%	58%	70%
Conservative	31%	16%	42%	30%

Key Votes of the 114th Congress

1. Keystone Pipeline	Y	5. Puerto Rico Debt	Y	9. Offenses by Aliens	Y
2. Trade Deals	N	6. Medical Marijuana	Y	10. Troops in Iraq	N
3. Export-Import Bank	Y	7. Sanctuary Cities	N	11. Homeland Security $$	Y
4. Debt Ceiling Increase	Y	8. Armor-piercing Bullets	Y	12. Trade Adjustment aid	Y

Election Results

Election	Name (Party)	Vote (%)	Cand. Spent	Ind. Exp. Support	Ind. Exp. Oppose
2016 General	Cheri Bustos (D)	173,125 (60%)	$1,822,238	$6,386	
	Patrick Harlan (R)	113,943 (40%)			
2016 Primary	Cheri Bustos (D)	(100%)			

Prior winning percentages: 2014 (56%), 2012 (53%)

Democrat Cheri Bustos, first elected in 2012, took advantage of her roots in Illinois politics - her father was a chief of staff for the late Democratic Sen. Alan Dixon - and the district's Democratic leanings. She has joined her party's leadership team to assert influence as one of the few remaining House Democrats who represent large rural areas.

Bustos grew up in the state capital of Springfield. Her mother was a social worker and preschool teacher, and her father was a journalist before entering government. Her first paid job was selling tacos and lemonade at the Illinois State Fair. As a 10-year-old, she met future Democratic Sens. Paul Simon and Dick Durbin, who at the time was a staffer for then-Lt. Gov. Simon. After attending Illinois College, where she excelled at basketball and volleyball, Bustos graduated from the University of Maryland with a bachelor's degree in political science and history. She earned a master's degree in journalism at the University of Illinois, and became a reporter with the *Quad-City Times*, where she covered city government, corruption, crime, health care and other issues over a 17-year career. Her husband, Gerry, has been a captain in the Rock Island Police Department and commander of the Quad City Bomb Squad.

After leaving journalism, Bustos went into public relations for regional health care providers, including as vice president of public relations and communications for Iowa Health System. Health-related issues are a key concern for her: She lost her uninsured sister-in-law to cancer a few years ago, and her brother to cancer months later, after his insurance refused to cover the medication he needed. President Barack Obama's Affordable Care Act, she said, was "at least in the right direction," but Bustos insists that more is needed to improve what she calls a "broken" system.

She was elected to the City Council in East Moline, and served from 2007 to 2011. Emphasizing economic development, she founded and chaired the East Moline Downtown Revitalization Committee. Democrats in Springfield had used redistricting to make the House district more Democratic for a challenge to freshman Republican Rep. Bobby Schilling. When Bustos entered the race, her friendship with Durbin paid off. He provided a rare primary endorsement and urged other Democrats to exit the race. She won the primary over two other candidates with 54 percent of the vote.

Her race in the fall against pizzeria owner Schilling attracted more than $3 million each from Democratic and Republican party groups, in addition to the more than $2 million that each candidate raised. Bustos received an early endorsement from abortion rights group EMILY's List and was backed by several labor unions. Schilling aligned himself with tea party activists. Bustos called her opponent "extreme" on abortion rights and suggested he didn't care about women's health. National Republicans ran an ad accusing Bustos of voting to spend $625,000 on improvements to the road "connecting her street to her local country club." The ad was debunked - repairs began before Bustos served on the council, and she simply joined other members in approving the project's second phase. And she never belonged to the country club. She won, 53%-47%.

In the House, Bustos enjoyed serving as a deal-cutter. On the Agriculture Committee, she joined the bipartisan coalition that approved a five-year farm bill in 2014. She won approval of a provision to quantify the impact on local agriculture from upgrading the aging locks and dams along the Mississippi and Illinois rivers. On the Transportation and Infrastructure Committee, the bipartisan deal on a water resources bill included her public-private partnership provision for additional financing options to improve the locks and dams. She sided with local farmers and biofuel advocates who opposed a proposal by the Environmental Protection Administration to lower the level of biofuel blended into gasoline. She also called for replacing what she called the "functionally obsolete" I-74 bridge in the Quad Cities.

In June 2016, Bustos made what seemed an unforced error when she filed with Republican Rep. Brett Guthrie of Kentucky, on behalf of professional baseball, a bill to exempt minor league players from overtime pay rules. After some protests, Bustos quickly withdrew her support. Her late father had been a lobbyist for Major League Baseball after leaving politics.

At home, Bustos had a rematch with Schilling. But it proved less competitive than their initial contest. This time, she outspent her opponent $3.1 million to $1.1 million, and Schilling had scant GOP financial support. In an otherwise Republican year in Illinois and elsewhere, Bustos rolled to a 55%-45% win, with 2-to-1 leads in Peoria and Rockford, and 54 percent of the vote in Rock Island County. After the election, she considered a challenge to Republican Sen. Mark Kirk in 2016, but said she did not want to face Democratic Rep. Tammy Duckworth in a primary.

In 2016, Bustos won her first easy election: 60%-40% against Patrick Harlan, a truck driver and local tea party leader. Following the election, Democratic Leader Nancy Pelosi named Bustos as one of three junior members to serve as co-chair of the Democratic Communications and Policy Committee. In December, an aide said that Bustos was giving "serious consideration" to challenging deep-pocketed Republican Gov. Bruce Rauner in 2018. Donald Trump's narrow win in this district in 2016 increased House GOP interest in testing Bustos.

Northwest Illinois: Moline, Rock Island

Population		**Race and Ethnicity**		**Income**	
Total	703,051	White	76.4%	Median Income	$44,116 (352 out of 435)
Land area	6,933	Black	11.2%		
Pop/ sq mi	101.4	Latino	8.9%		
Born in state	72.6%	Asian	1.3%	Under $50,000	55.6%
		Two races	1.9%	$50,000-$99,999	30.6%
Age Groups		Other	0.3%	$100,000-$199,999	12.3%
Under 18	23.0%			$200,000 or more	1.6%
18-34	21.5%	**Education**		Poverty Rate	17.8%
35-64	38.7%	H.S grad or less	48.6%		
Over 64	16.8%	Some college	33.5%	**Health Insurance**	
		College Degree, 4 yr	12.0%	With health insurance coverage	90.4%
Work		Post grad	5.9%		
White Collar	27.7%				
Sales and Service	43.5%	**Military**		**Public Assistance**	
Blue Collar	28.8%	Veteran	9.6%	Cash public assistance income	2.9%
Government	11.9%	Active Duty	0.1%		
				Food stamp/SNAP benefits	16.7%

Voter Turnout			
2015 Total Citizens 18+	522,244	2016 House Turnout as % CVAP	55%
2016 House turnout	287,068	2014 House Turnout as % CVAP	38%

2012 Presidential Vote		
Barack Obama	168,796	(57%)
Mitt Romney	119,789	(41%)

2016 Presidential Vote		
Donald Trump	136,017	(47%)
Hillary Clinton	133,999	(46%)
Gary Johnson	13,457	(5%)

Cook Partisan Voting Index: D+2

Illinois' western prairies are some of America's richest agricultural land. They were first settled by Yankees coming overland from northern Indiana and Ohio and upstate New York. After 1848, Germans left their homeland in search of better opportunities and settled in a place that in many ways resembled the flat, orderly plains of northern Germany. These migrants farmed quarter-sections and built small towns, with banks and stores, community churches and libraries. As farming expanded, so did the need for agricultural equipment. Entrepreneurs and investors built farm-machinery factories, and the Quad Cities of the Mississippi - Davenport and Bettendorf in Iowa, and Rock Island and Moline in Illinois - became one of the nation's biggest agricultural equipment-manufacturing centers. John Deere, a blacksmith from Vermont, set up a "self-polishing plow" shop in 1837 in the small Rock River town of Grand Detour, Illinois. His company, now headquartered in Moline, ranked 97th on the 2016 *Fortune* 500 list of largest American corporations.

The plants were unionized in the 1930s and 1940s, and in post-World War II America wages went up as the demand increased for more sophisticated machines on Midwest farms. But agriculture is a cyclical business. When farm profits vanished and land values declined in the early 1980s, orders for new machinery and equipment dried up. The result was a depression in western Illinois and neighboring Iowa, and a political swing toward the Democrats and away from the Republicans, who had been the ancestral party in most of this area. Although conditions stabilized in the 1990s, long-term challenges remained.

Caterpillar, which fell from 42nd in 2014 on the *Fortune* 500 list to 59th in 2016, has been an iconic Peoria brand that operates around the world. Recent changes in the earth-moving company's business operations and its corporate organization help to explain why its local payroll has shrunk to 12,000 from 35,000 jobs in the 1970s. In 2016, two-thirds of its sales were outside the United States. With a world-wide drop in farm-commodity prices plus a weakening economy in some of those emerging-growth markets, overall sales of farm equipment plummeted. From 2012 to 2016, Cat's annual revenues dropped from $66 billion to $37 billion. In January 2016, a set of company cutbacks included 350 jobs and a factory at the Caterpillar campus in East Peoria. Adding to the local pain, the company announced in January 2017 the move of its corporate headquarters from Peoria to Chicago. "Speed and agility for our senior leadership team to be able to travel around the globe is very important," the company's CEO told the *Peoria Journal Star*. Implicit in his explanation: For many of these top executives, plus their corporate advisers, the location of O'Hare International Airport was only part of the reality that fast-paced Chicago had more appeal than life in Peoria. The overall local impact has been devastating. In the early 1990s, nearly one in four Peoria jobs was in manufacturing; by 2016, that had dropped to one in eight.

In Rockford, the industrial sector got a boost in 2016 when AAR, the largest aircraft maintenance company in North America, began hiring at the local airport for its $40 million jet repair and service center. Executives projected that the facility will provide more than 500 jobs. Local officials said the area was ideal for the facility because it already had more than 250 aviation-related companies and 6,500 aerospace production workers.

The 17th Congressional District links the Illinois portion of the Quad Cities with arms extending to the Democratic-leaning parts of Peoria to the east and Rockford to the north. It takes in the hilly, almost mountainous country in the northwest corner of the state. The shrinking Caterpillar campus in East Peoria along the Illinois River is in the 17th, as is the Mossville campus on the other side of the river The district is steeped in political history: Some 30 miles west of Rockford is Freeport, whose town square hosted 15,000 people coming to hear Abraham Lincoln and Stephen Douglas in one of their seven debates in 1858. Not far away, on a little river once navigable by Mississippi River steamboats, is Galena, the home of Ulysses S. Grant.

The district contains some of the few parts of rural America carried by Barack Obama, who took the district 57%-41% in 2012. Granted, this was his home state. But his local performance was better than his vote in rural southern Illinois. Four years later, with a rhetorical push from Donald Trump, Democratic performance in the 17th was as bad as job numbers in Peoria. Trump led Hillary Clinton 47-46%, a rare bright spot for Republicans in Illinois in what has been the only remaining Democratic-held district in Downstate..

EIGHTEENTH DISTRICT

Darin LaHood (R)

Elected 2015, 2nd term; b. Jul 05, 1968, Peoria; Loras College, B.A.; John Marshall Law School, J.D., 1997; Catholic; Married (Kristen LaHood); 3 children.

Elected Office: IL Senate, 2011-2015.

Professional Career: Staff, U.S Rep. Chalres Jeremy Lewis, 1990-1994; Cook County Prosecutor, 1997-1999; Tazewell County Prosecutor, 1999-2001; Prosecutor, NV U.S Attorney, 2001-2005; Adjunct Professor, Univeristy of Nevada- Las Vegas, 2003-2005.

DC Office: 1424 LHOB 20515, 202-225-6201, Fax: 202-225-9249, lahood.house.gov.

State Offices: Bloomington, 309-205-9556; Jacksonville, 217-245-1431; Peoria, 309-671-7027; Springfield, 217-670-1653.

Committees: *Joint Economic*. *Natural Resources*: Energy & Mineral Resources, Federal Lands, Indian, Insular & Alaska Native Affairs. *Science, Space & Technology*: Energy, Oversight (Chmn), Research & Technology.

Group Ratings

	ADA	ACLU	AFL-CIO	LCV	ITI	COC	HAFA	ACU	CFG	FRC
2016	-	5%	-	0%	100%	100%	68%	84%	76%	100%
2015	0%	C	40%	0%	C	70%	C			100%

Almanac Ratings 2015

	Economy	Social	Foreign	Composite
Liberal	0%	0%	0%	0%
Conservative	0%	0%	0%	0%

Key Votes of the 114th Congress

3. Export-Import Bank	N	4. Debt Ceiling Increase	N	5. Puerto Rico Debt	Y

Election Results

Election	Name (Party)	Vote (%)		Cand. Spent	Ind. Exp. Support	Ind. Exp. Oppose
2016 General	Darin LaHood (R)	250,506	(72%)	$2,072,680	$117,386	$1,350
	Junius Rodriguez (D)	96,770	(28%)	$60,100		
2016 Primary	Darin LaHood (R)		(100%)			

Prior winning percentages: 2015 special (69%)

Republican Darin LaHood won a special election in September 2015, following the resignation of ethics-tarred Republican Aaron Schock. LaHood faced minimal competition in the primary or general election. With his low-profile approach, a notable contrast to his often flamboyant predecessor, he helped to enact two bills during the remainder of the term.

LaHood, who had been a conservative state senator, is the son of former GOP Rep. Ray LaHood, who served seven terms before he retired and became Secretary of Transportation to President Barack Obama. Ray LaHood earlier was an aide to Robert Michel, the long-time House minority leader. Darin LaHood, a Peoria native, earned his bachelor's from Loras College and a law degree from The John Marshall Law School. He spent nine years as a state and federal prosecutor, including with the U.S. attorney's office in Las Vegas, Nevada, where he was recognized for his "outstanding work in fighting terrorism." He returned home to join a law firm in Peoria and was elected to the state Senate in 2010. *National Journal* profiled him as "a media-shy, ethics-focused political scion," a welcome antithesis to his immediate predecessor.

Schock, who was elected in 2008, drew more notice for his youth and buff physique until the focus shifted to his office-decorating tastes and lifestyle. He never faced a serious election challenge and gained little attention for his legislative work, though he sought to make a name for himself on trade and tax reform issues at the Ways and Means Committee. An accumulation of well-publicized controversies involving his use of taxpayer money led him to announce his resignation in March 2015. "The constant questions over the last six weeks have proven a great distraction that has made it too difficult for me to serve the people of the 18th District with the high standards that they deserve and which I have set for myself," he said in a statement. Most notable was a *Washington Post* article about the lavish redecoration of his House office in the style of the popular television series *Downton Abbey*. Although the decorator told the newspaper that she had offered her services for free, Schock repaid the government $35,000 from his personal funds to cover the costs. He was indicted in November 2016 on 24 counts, including wire fraud, false filings of tax returns and Federal Election Commission reports, and theft of government funds. Schock vigorously denied the charges.

After Schock resigned, several other prominent local Republicans considered running in the special election. But they all stepped aside, in apparent recognition of LaHood's strength and the desire of local Republicans to avoid more controversy. His sole primary opponent was little-known Mike Flynn, a libertarian Republican political operative and a former editor of the Breitbart News conservative website. He criticized the LaHoods as career politicians out of touch with the real world, and noted that Ray LaHood had become an ally of the Democratic president. LaHood won the July 7 Republican primary, 69%-28%. Flynn died the following year. The Democratic nominee, Rob Mellon, a high school history teacher and captain in the Army Reserve, raised little money or attention. LaHood won the general, 71%-29%.

LaHood settled into the House with serious purpose and little attention. Befitting his often bipartisan father, he joined with Democratic Rep. Dan Lipinski of Illinois (who served with the elder LaHood, as did his father Rep. Bill Lipinski) to file a resolution calling for a Joint Committee on the Organization of Congress to consider possible reforms. "Every generation or so, Congress has had to reevaluate itself and make big changes in order to be effective and responsive to the American people, LaHood said. The most recent review ended in 1993, prior to the Republican takeover of the House a year later under Newt Gingrich. LaHood also sought to increase transparency and promote ethical behavior in the House.

With his work on the Natural Resources and Science, Space, and Technology committees, LaHood helped to enact two bills during his first term: support for federal computer networking and information technology research; and a provision for fish and wildlife restoration in the Great Lakes that was part of a broader water-resources bill.

LaHood was easily reelected, and was in position to serve a lengthy career in the House. During the campaign, he supported Donald Trump for president as preferable to Hillary Clinton, but he distanced himself from some of Trump's controversial comments. "That's not the kind of Republican I am," he said in August 2016. "And I have publicly talked about how I don't agree with many of the statements that he has made."

West-Central Illinois: Parts of Peoria and Springfield

Population		**Race and Ethnicity**		**Income**	
Total	715,977	White	89.1%	Median Income	$60,016 (142 out of 435)
Land area	10,516	Black	3.6%		
Pop/ sq mi	68.1	Latino	2.6%		
Born in state	77.9%	Asian	2.6%	Under $50,000	41.8%
Age Groups		Two races	1.8%	$50,000-$99,999	33.8%
Under 18	22.5%	Other	0.2%	$100,000-$199,999	20.2%
18-34	21.3%	**Education**		$200,000 or more	4.3%
35-64	39.8%	H.S grad or less	37.7%	Poverty Rate	10.2%
Over 64	16.4%	Some college	31.1%	**Health Insurance**	
Work		College Degree, 4 yr	20.5%	With health insurance coverage	93.7%
White Collar	39.1%	Post grad	10.7%		
Sales and Service	40.0%	**Military**		**Public Assistance**	
Blue Collar	21.0%	Veteran	9.4%	Cash public assistance income	1.6%
Government	15.1%	Active Duty	0.1%		
				Food stamp/SNAP benefits	8.6%

Voter Turnout			
2015 Total Citizens 18+	541,991	2016 House Turnout as % CVAP	64%
2016 House turnout	347,283	2014 House Turnout as % CVAP	45%

2012 Presidential Vote		
Mitt Romney	203,198	(61%)
Barack Obama	125,079	(37%)

2016 Presidential Vote		
Donald Trump	210,530	(60%)
Hillary Clinton	115,441	(33%)
Gary Johnson	17,058	(5%)

Cook Partisan Voting Index: R+15

Old vaudeville bookers, presented with a new act, used to ask, "Will it play in Peoria?" The implication was that if an act went over in this small city on the bluffs above the Illinois River, 154 miles from Chicago and 171 miles from St. Louis, it would go over just about anywhere. In the first half of the 20th century, Peoria seemed pretty typical of America. If its citizens were mostly of British or German descent, with a small percentage of African Americans, that was the image of ordinary America that prevailed through the 1960s. But Peoria's economy has changed, much as America's has changed. This has been a heavy manufacturing town, dominated by big plants that produce farm machinery and earth-moving equipment. Its biggest employer has been Caterpillar, which was founded in 1910 with 12 employees; a century later, it is the world's leading producer of earth-moving and construction equipment, and one of America's major exporters. Memories remain here of the sharp divide between blue collar and white collar, union and management, Democrat and Republican - the basis of the class-warfare politics that was the norm in heavy industrial metropolises of the Great Lakes region.

But the blue-collar workers now are not so numerous and the unions have weakened. The Peoria area suffered terribly in the 1980s, as big farm machinery plants laid off workers and some closed down. Memories of those hard times were revived by the 2007-09 recession. President Barack Obama came to Peoria to stump for his economic stimulus bill, whose enactment was part of the rebound that gave signs of hope for the manufacturing giant. But the revival of Caterpillar, a company that proudly operates around the world, provided less benefit to Peoria: 95 percent of its potential customers live outside the United States, and the company feels a need to manufacture where it sells. By 2016, its local payroll shrunk to less than 12,000 from 35,000 jobs in the 1970s. Adding to the insult, the company decided to move its headquarters from Peoria to Chicago.

Peoria isn't the only industrial engine of the district. Beardstown, a small river town 200 miles southwest of Chicago, is home to a 430,000 square-foot slaughterhouse. Latino and African immigrants have flocked into rural Illinois towns like Beardstown looking for entry-level jobs in manufacturing. In July 2015, the meatpacking giant Cargill sold its local pork division to the U.S. subsidiary of JBS, a Brazilian-based international meat processor. In Normal, Rivian Automotive, an electric vehicle startup, purchased in January 2017 the former Mitsubishi Motors North America facility, and planned to start production of vehicles in 2019

The 18th Congressional District of Illinois, variously configured, has been the Peoria district since the 1940s, and now includes about 60 percent of the city and its suburbs. Much of the downtown area and the Caterpillar campus in East Peoria, with six factory buildings along the Illinois River, are in the 17th District to the northwest. With all or parts of 10 counties, the 18th begins at Quincy along the Mississippi River and runs east through rich farmland to the suburbs of Peoria, Bloomington and Springfield. McLean County is the largest population center, though the Illinois State and Illinois Wesleyan University campuses are in the 13th District.

In addition to President Abraham Lincoln, who served one term in Congress, 1847-49, the 18th has been represented by two national Republican leaders: Everett McKinley Dirksen, who was the Senate Republican leader from 1959-69, and Robert Michel, House Republican leader from 1981-95. It is the home of Eureka College, which dedicated the Ronald Reagan Peace Garden in honor of its 1932 graduate and the end of the Cold War that he helped to achieve. In an attempt to maximize their downstate seats, Democratic redistricters drew this as a heavily Republican district; the 60 percent for Donald Trump in 2016 was his second-best in the state. Since 1994, the best Democratic performance was 41 percent. Overall, the district is still ethnically homogeneous, with a 91 percent white voting-age population.

★ INDIANA ★

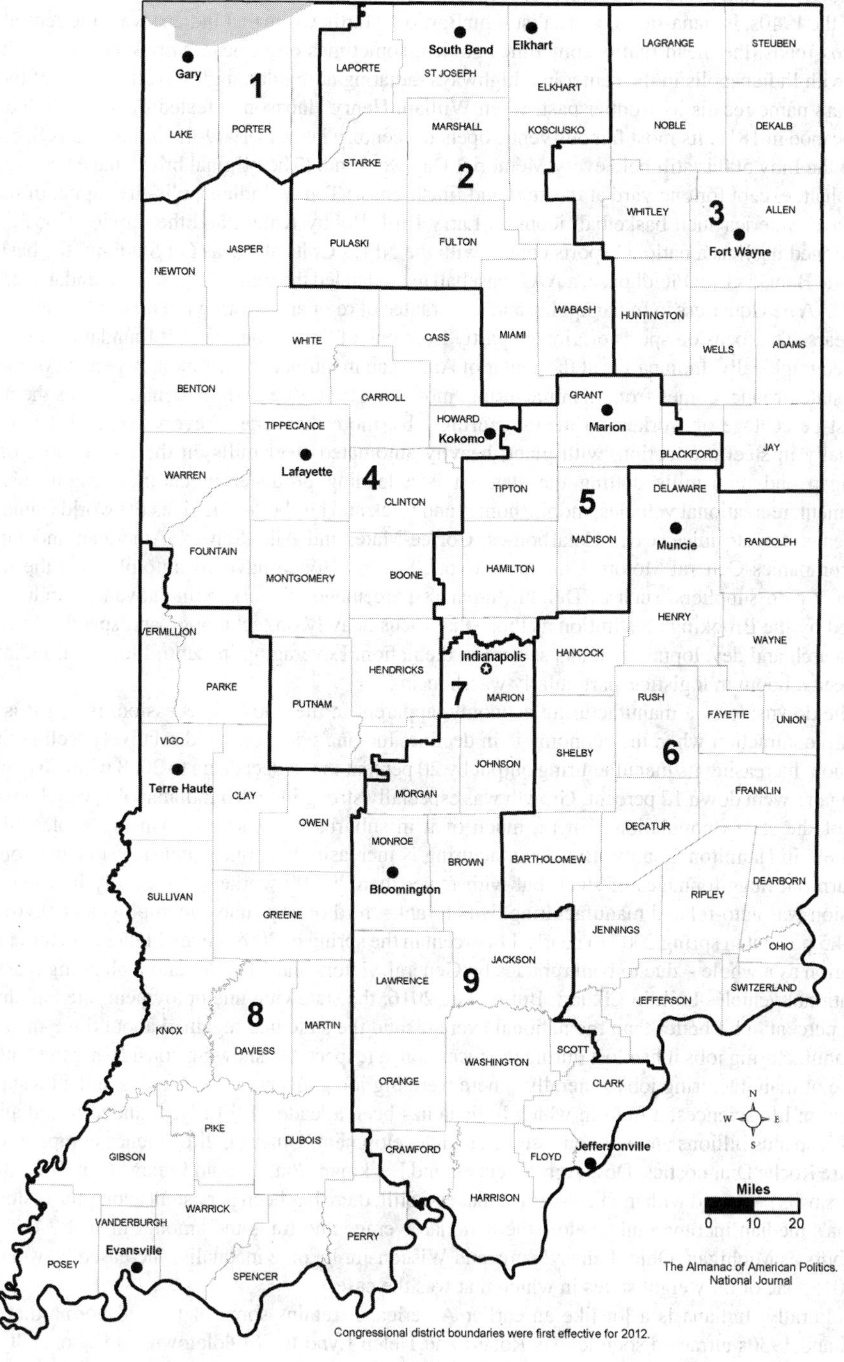

Congressional district boundaries were first effective for 2012.

Indiana, a key manufacturing hub the industrial Midwest, experienced pain during the Great Recession, before recovering along with the rest of the country. But despite economic gains, Indiana – a red state that narrowly voted for Barack Obama in 2008 -- responded eagerly to the angry message of Donald Trump and his running mate, Gov. Mike Pence, eight years later.

In the 1940s, Indiana-raised journalist John Bartlow Martin wrote that Indiana was "the central place, the crossroads, the mean that is sometimes golden, sometimes only mean." Look no further than the map, with Indianapolis in the center and highways radiating at regular angles to all corners of the state. Indiana's name recalls its frontier past, when William Henry Harrison defeated Tecumseh's Indians at Tippecanoe in 1811. Its most famous venue opened a century later, in 1909-the Indianapolis Speedway, where the Indy 500 is still held every Memorial Day weekend. (The original bricks have been replaced by asphalt, except for one yard at the start and finish lines.) Today, Indianapolis-the capital of the state that gave America such basketball icons as Larry Bird, Bobby Knight and the movie "Hoosiers"-has refashioned itself as a national sports center, with the NFL's Colts at Lucas Oil Stadium, the basketball Pacers at Bankers Life Fieldhouse, a AAA baseball team that led the minor leagues in attendance in 2016, the NCAA headquarters in Indianapolis, and a guarantee of regularly hosting Final Four basketball every few years. The focus on sports originated partly from one of the nation's largest foundations, the Lilly

Geographically, Indiana sits at the center of American manufacturing. About 30 percent of Indiana's gross state product comes from manufacturing, more than twice the share nationally; it has the nation's highest percentage of workers in manufacturing jobs, more than one of every six, and it ranks first nationally in steel production, with giant, heavily automated steel mills on the south shore of Lake Michigan and mini-mills dotting the state. It is a leading producer of engines, engine electrical equipment, recreational vehicles, mobile homes and truck and bus bodies. It gives the world canned pork and beans, tomato juice, Coca-Cola bottles, Coffee-Mate, and Alka-Seltzer. American and Japanese auto companies-General Motors, Chrysler, Toyota, Subaru, Honda-have big auto plants in the state, as do many auto suppliers, such as Delphi. Indiana's percentage of workers in "advanced industries" – defined by the Brookings Institution as those that focus heavily on technology and spend significantly on research and development– ranks second in the nation. Leveraging its central location, Indiana has also seen a boom in logistics, particularly warehousing.

The downside of a manufacturing economy, apparent in the 2007-09 recession, is that it is prone to sharp contraction when the economy is in decline. Indiana's economy did relatively well before the recession, increasing its manufacturing output by 20 percent in the decade up to 2008 while, by contrast, Michigan's went down 12 percent. Growth was especially strong in metro Indianapolis, which produced most of the state's population growth, much of it in suburbs like Carmel, Fishers, Noblesville, and Westfield in Hamilton County. But manufacturing is increasingly capital-intensive. Indiana continues to churn out huge tonnages of steel, but with fewer than 20,000 workers. Especially hard-hit by the recession was auto-related manufacturing, which ranks third of any state. Unemployment skyrocketed from 4.5 percent in spring 2007 to nearly 11 percent in the spring of 2009 – even higher than the spike for the nation as a whole – due to bankruptcies by General Motors and Chrysler and a plunging market for recreational vehicles built in Elkhart. But by late 2016, the statewide unemployment rate had dropped to 4.0 percent, a bit better than the national average, and the state had regained about three-quarters of the manufacturing jobs it had lost during the recession, a respectable showing considering the long-term decline of manufacturing jobs generally. There were big job gains not only in autos and auto suppliers but also in life sciences, a field in which Indiana has been a leader. Eli Lilly, founded in Indianapolis in 1876, spends billions annually on research and development. Other big life-science companies in the state are Roche Diagnostics, Dow AgroSciences, and Beckman Coulter. And Indiana from Bloomington to Warsaw is peppered with medical-device makers. Still, there has been persistent economic dislocation. Indiana's median income ranks below the national average and trails the amount in such Midwestern neighbors as Michigan, Ohio, Pennsylvania and Wisconsin. Income inequality increased between 2014 and 2015, one of only eight states in which that was the case.

Culturally, Indiana is a lot like an earlier America. It retains some of the old norms that in the 1920s and 1930s attracted sociologists Robert and Helen Lynd to "Middletown," a fictional "typical" American place (Middletown was actually Muncie). Agriculture -- particularly corn, soybeans and hogs -- accounts for more than $31 billion in direct sales and nearly 107,500 jobs in production and processing. (Orville Redenbacher of popcorn fame hailed from Indiana.) The small-town ethos in the songs of John

Mellencamp stem from his upbringing in Seymour. Ethnically, Indiana seems like an earlier America, too. Except for the steel area around Gary-really an extension of the Chicago metropolitan area-Indiana has relatively few descendants from the 1840-1924 wave of immigration. Its population is 9 percent black, 8 percent Hispanic, and 2 percent Asian. It does have religious diversity, with 109 denominations; according to the Glenmary Research Center, only six states have more. In early 2015, Indiana played host to a high-profile, if brief, national battle between two big, longstanding constituencies within the state-its Christian conservatives and its pragmatic business class. These two camps battled over a religious-freedom law that critics said would make it possible for businesses to discriminate against gays and lesbians. After Pence signed the law, it drew fire not only from liberals but also from much of the state's business establishment, including such athletic mainstays as NASCAR, the NCAA and the NBA. The backlash pushed Pence and legislative leaders to scale back the measure, which in turn led to criticism by religious conservatives.

Indiana's politics have traditionally been shaped by a divide between Yankees from Ohio and New England, and "Butternuts," as they were called in the Civil War years, from Kentucky and the South. Most Yankees became Republicans, and most Butternuts became Democrats, a split that persisted for generations. Indiana was a crucial political target from the Civil War to the New Deal, a big reason why there were Hoosiers on 11 Republican and Democratic national tickets in the 16 elections between 1868 and 1928-more than any other state except New York. Party identification was handed down like religious affiliation. Those enduring traditions enabled Democrats to hold the governorship from 1988 to 2004 and to be competitive in state legislative elections. Democrat Evan Bayh, a former governor and senator, tended to run ahead in Butternut Indiana, whereas Republican former Gov. Mitch Daniels fared well in Yankee Indiana. Two of the three House seats that Democrats captured in 2006 and held in 2008 were in the Butternut south end of the state. But starting in 2010, Republicans picked up every Indiana House seat along the Ohio River from Lawrenceburg to Posey County, and the GOP began picking up the congressional seats.

At the presidential level, Indiana's cultural conservatism and lack of a dovish tradition has generally kept it in the Republican column, ever since it voted 56%-43% for Lyndon Johnson in 1964. Over the next 10 elections, it was so resolutely Republican that it was never a target state for the Democrats, and only one Hoosier, Dan Quayle, was on a national ticket. A main reason was that Indianapolis and the smaller factory towns were not as heavily Democratic as Chicago, Detroit or Cleveland (a trend only reinforced by 1970 consolidation of the city of Indianapolis and Marion County, which brought urban and suburban areas under the same jurisdictional umbrella). Then, in 2008, for the first time in 44 years, Indiana voted Democratic for president. A state that went 60%-39% for George W. Bush in 2004 voted 50%-49% for Barack Obama four years later, the biggest swing in any of the 50 states and was the product of many factors.

But this did not hold true all the way down the ballot. Indeed, Indiana has voted Republican for governor beginning in 2004, when Daniels won, 53%-45%. He was reelected four years later by a solid 58%-40% margin, even as Obama was carrying the state. The victory was all the more remarkable because two of the governor's policies were hugely controversial: the leasing for 75 years of the Indiana Toll Road to an Australian-Spanish consortium (which would hit a major pothole in 2014 when the lease operator declared bankruptcy) and the adoption of Daylight Saving Time (a touchy issue, since Indiana straddles the Eastern and Central time zones). In 2010, Bayh retired from the Senate and left the way open for his predecessor, Republican Dan Coats, to win back the seat handily, while Republicans also picked up the 8th and 9th district House seats and won majorities in both houses of the legislature. By 2012, just four years after Obama won it, Indiana was not even a target state for the incumbent president, and it voted 54%-44% for Republican nominee Mitt Romney, while Pence was elected governor over Democrat John Gregg, 49%-47%. Democratic Rep. Joe Donnelly managed to nab an open Senate seat in 2012 after his opponent, state Treasurer Richard Mourdock, disastrously opined that pregnancy resulting from rape is part of God's plan. But the GOP was able to increase its lead in the House delegation to seven to two with the help of a favorable redistricting plan, and then, in 2014, Republicans increased their legislative majorities to 70 percent in the House and 80 percent in the Senate.

Any notion that the Democrats had an easy path back to competitiveness in Indiana was dashed in 2016. While the presence of Pence on the GOP presidential ticket may have helped, the real attraction was Trump, with his relentless focus on working-class white voters and the Midwestern manufacturing industry, underlined by his post-victory trip to the state to announce that some of Carrier's jobs would remain in the state rather than head to Mexico. Trump -- channeling the bristling charisma of basketball icon Knight, who endorsed him days before the primary -- ended up defeating Hillary Clinton by 19 points, almost twice Romney's margin. The number of Democratic presidential votes statewide fell by 121,000 compared to 2012 and by 341,000 compared to the Obama victory year of 2008. At the same time, Trump increased Republican presidential votes by 134,000 over 2012 and 212,000 over 2008. While Obama won 15 counties in 2008 and nine in 2012, Clinton only managed to win four in 2016, and she came within 10 percentage points in only three others. Clinton's margin in Marion County (Indianapolis) didn't shrink much from 2012, but in Lake County, on the outskirts of Chicago, she won by 21 points, well short of Obama's 31-point margin in 2012. The Trump tide buoyed all GOP boats – Rep. Todd Young beat Bayh for an open Senate seat by double digits, late-entering Lt. Gov. Eric Holcomb notched a somewhat surprising victory over Gregg for the governorship, and the GOP ousted the Democratic superintendent of public instruction, Glenda Ritz. Emblematic of Democratic helplessness in the state was Elkhart, where Obama had visited in 2009 and 2016 – bookends to the Great Recession. During that period, local unemployment fell from 20 percent to just over 3 percent, but Obama got zero credit. In Elkhart County, voters handed Trump a 32-point victory.

Population		**Race and Ethnicity**		**Income**	
Total	6,568,645	White	80.5%	Median Income	$49,255 (35 out of 50)
Land area	35,826	Black	9.0%	Under $50,000	50.7%
Pop/ sq mi	183.3	Latino	6.4%	$50,000-$99,999	31.8%
Born in state	68.4%	Asian	1.8%	$100,000-$199,999	14.7%
		Two races	1.9%	$200,000 or more	2.8%
		Other	0.3%	Poverty Rate	15.4%
Age Groups		**Education**		**Health Insurance**	
Under 18	24.2%	H.S grad or less	46.8%	With health insurance coverage	87.2%
18-34	22.9%	Some college	29.1%		
35-64	39.0%	College Degree, 4 yr	15.4%		
Over 64	13.9%	Post grad	8.7%		
Work		**Military**		**Public Assistance**	
White Collar	32.4%	Veteran	8.6%	Cash public assistance income	2.1%
Sales and Service	40.3%	Active Duty	0.1%	Food stamp/SNAP benefits	12.5%
Blue Collar	27.3%				
Government	11.0%				

Voter Turnout			
2015 Total Citizens 18+	4,801,113	2016 Pres Turnout as % CVAP	57%
2016 Pres Votes	2,734,958	2012 Pres Turnout as % CVAP	56%

Legislature	
Senate:	9D, 41R
House:	30D, 70R

Presidential Politics

2016 Democratic Primary		
Bernie Sanders (D)	335,074	(52%)
Hillary Clinton (D)	303,705	(48%)
2016 Republican Primary		
Donald Trump (R)	591,514	(53%)
Ted Cruz (R)	406,783	(37%)
John Kasich (R)	84,111	(8%)

2016 Presidential Vote		
Donald Trump (R)	1,557,286	(56%)
Hillary Clinton (D)	1,033,126	(37%)
Gary Johnson (L)	133,993	(5%)
2012 Presidential Vote		
Mitt Romney (R)	1,420,543	(54%)
Barack Obama (D)	1,152,887	(44%)

Indiana rarely generates much drama in the race for the White House. In 1968, Robert F. Kennedy upset Eugene McCarthy and Lyndon Johnson's stand-in, Gov. Roger Branigin, in the Democratic primary. In 2008, Barack Obama contested the primary and general election. After organizing for the primary, which Obama narrowly lost to Clinton, his campaign set up 44 offices around the state for the general election and mobilized 80,000 volunteers. Obama carried only 15 of Indiana's 92 counties in the fall, but he got a big vote out of Gary and Indianapolis, cut into traditional GOP margins in the Indianapolis suburbs and exurbs, won blue-collar counties such as Delaware (Muncie) and Madison

(Anderson) and swept college towns to post a 50%-49% win over Arizona Republican Sen. John McCain. Four years later the Obama campaign wrote off the state and Mitt Romney captured it easily, 54%-44%. In 2016, Donald Trump tapped Hoosier GOP Gov. Mike Pence as his running mate, and he increased the Republican margin in the state, defeating Hillary Clinton in November, 57%-38%. Trump's vow to restore manufacturing jobs resonated in the state's blue-collar communities and he won all but four counties: Lake (Gary), Marion (Indianapolis), Monroe (Bloomington and Indiana University) and St. Joseph (South Bend and the University of Notre Dame).

In the May 3 primaries, Indiana served up plenty of excitement. Texas Sen. Ted Cruz said that winning Indiana was critical to the success of his GOP nomination bid. He got a reasonably clear shot at Trump after Ohio Gov. John Kasich stopped campaigning in the state. Pence endorsed the Texan. And Cruz announced that former Republican White House hopeful Carly Fiorina would be his running mate should he capture the nomination. Cruz dropped his gloves and called Trump a "pathological liar" and an unparalleled "narcissist." Trump took up the challenge and waged a vigorous fight. His efforts were rewarded with a 53%-37% victory over Cruz, who won only five counties and announced the suspension of his campaign in his concession speech. Turnout was roughly 1,082,000, a Republican record. The decisive win prompted Republican National Committee Chairman Reince Priebus to take to Twitter that night and declare that Trump was the party's "presumptive nominee." The next day, Kasich withdrew.

The outcome of the Democratic primary was less consequential, but it did sustain Vermont Sen. Bernie Sanders's bid. After losing four East Coast primaries a week earlier, Sanders desperately needed a win to slow Clinton's momentum. The Vermonter campaigned heavily in the state. Clinton nursed her lead and campaign resources, and decided not to spend any money on TV advertising before the primary. Sanders won 52%-48%. Clinton won Marion and Lake counties with their relatively high share of African-American voters, and 17 largely rural counties along the state's southern tier. Democratic turnout was just under 639,000, a big falloff from the 2008 primary vote of 1.3 million. Indiana has no party registration and it's likely that many voters felt the Republican primary was more pivotal, and engrossing, than the Democratic contest.

Congressional Districts

115th Congress Lineup	7R 2D	**114th Congress Lineup**	7R 2D

Indiana law provides that if the House and Senate cannot agree on congressional redistricting, the decision goes to a five-member commission, with the tie-breaking member appointed by the governor. In 2011, Republicans had control of the process. They weakened the 2nd District for the Democrats. When Democratic Rep. Joe Donnelly in 2012 ran for the Senate, Republican Jackie Walorski took his House seat. That gave the GOP a 7-2 majority in the delegation, with Democrats retaining the heavily urban and minority 1st and 7th districts centered on Gary and Indianapolis. A look at the map shows that the nine districts seem to have been drawn logically and without many jagged lines.

For now, Republicans seem entrenched in their seven seats. In recent decades, the delegation has been more evenly balanced and some of its seats often shifted parties. Partisan control of the redistricting map has not always assured success. The 2nd, 8th and 9th districts have been the most competitive, with the greatest likelihood of party switches. Given the overwhelming Republican control of the Legislature, Democrats must either find a way to win the governor's office in the 2020 election or run more competitive candidates for Congress. Another option would be to disperse some Democratic voters in the 1st and 7th districts into the outlying districts and make all of them more competitive.

Governor

Eric Holcomb (R)

Elected 2016, term expires 2021, 1st term; b. May. 2, 1968, Indianapolis, IN; Hanover College, BA; First Church of God; Married (Janet).

Military Career: U.S Navy, 1990-1996.

Elected Office: IN Lt. Governor 2016-2017; Chair, IN Republican Party, 2010-2013.

Professional Career: Staff, U.S Rep. John Holstettler 1997-2000; Chief of Staff, U.S Sen.Dan Coats 2013-2015.

Office: State House, Room 206, Indianapolis, 46204; 317-232-4567; Fax: 317-232-3443; Website: in.gov/gov.

Election Results

Election	Name (Party)	Vote (%)
2016 General	Eric Holcomb (R)	977,362 (53%)
	John Gregg (D)	844,343 (46%)

Eric Holcomb was elected governor of Indiana in 2016, even though he entered the race less than four months before Election Day. On July 26, Holcomb -- who had become lieutenant governor only five months earlier -- became the Republican Party's choice to be its gubernatorial nominee, filling the void left when Donald Trump tapped GOP Gov. Mike Pence as his running mate. Holcomb faced a competitive general-election contest but won by a wider-than-expected margin amid a pro-Trump wave in the state.

Holcomb grew up in Indianapolis and earned a degree in American history from Hanover College, the same school Pence had graduated from nine years earlier. (The two governors belonged to the same fraternity, but didn't overlap.) Holcomb served a six-year stint in the Navy in Jacksonville, Fla., and Lisbon, Portugal, then got involved in Republican politics in Indiana. He ran unsuccessfully for state representative, served as campaign manager and district director for then-Rep. John Hostettler, and worked in several positions, including deputy chief of staff, for Republican Gov. Mitch Daniels between 2003 and 2011. He was also the director of Daniels' Aiming Higher PAC. After working for Daniels, Holcomb served two years as chairman of the Indiana Republican Party. Later, he served as chief of staff to the state's Republican senator, Dan Coats, before resigning in 2015 to run for the seat Coats was vacating. But with weak polling, Holcomb exited the race. Then Lt. Gov. Sue Ellspermann resigned and Pence appointed him as her successor. The legislature approved the appointment in March 2016.

Pence was set to run for a second term as governor in 2016, and despite the state's Republican leanings, the incumbent was facing some headwinds. Pence's proposed launch in 2015 of a state-run news outlet using taxpayer money to compete against for-profit media entities was scrapped after bipartisan opposition within the state and ridicule elsewhere. An even bigger setback came when he signed a religious-freedom law that critics said would enable businesses to discriminate against gay and lesbian customers. Criticism came not only from liberal activists but also much of the state's business establishment, which felt the law would harm the state's image and lead to boycotts. After several days of outcry and a poorly reviewed appearance on national television, Pence and leaders of the Republican-dominated state House and Senate agreed to a legislative fix that clarified that the state would not permit discrimination based on sexual orientation or gender identity. While the change seemed to ease much of the outcry, Pence still faced reelection odds no better than 50-50 against Democrat John Gregg, the former state House Speaker he had defeated narrowly in 2012.

Then, in July, Trump tapped Pence as his running mate, and the gubernatorial contest was thrown into flux. Pence was already the official nominee for governor, and under party rules, it was up to the state party to choose a new nominee. Several well-known Republicans sought the nod, particularly Reps. Susan Brooks and Todd Rokita. Of these, Holcomb was the only one who had never won an election (though he has shot a basketball in a high school gym in all 92 counties in the state). On July 26, the party formally tapped Holcomb, following the lead of Pence, who had endorsed his No. 2 for the nod.

On the issues, Holcomb and Gregg differed more on scale and financing mechanism than on substance. Both nominees supported infrastructure improvements, including completion of I-69 between Indianapolis and Evansville and expansion of high-speed internet statewide, but Gregg backed using direct expenditures and borrowing leverage from the Indiana Toll Road trust fund to do it, whereas Holcomb deferred to a state-appointed task force studying long-term options. On education, both supported expanding pre-kindergarten, but Holcomb backed a modest expansion of a pilot program whereas Gregg wanted to offer it to all students statewide. The two campaigns had enough money to compete – Holcomb was bolstered by generous funding from the Republican Governors Association, while Gregg got a boost from Democratic spending intended primarily to help elect Evan Bayh to Coats' Senate seat – but Gregg seemed to have the edge, with the Democrat up in polls by between four and 12 points as late as October. On Election Day, however, the Trump-led tide in the state was too much for Gregg to overcome. Holcomb won by a narrower margin than Trump's 19-point victory, prevailing 51%-45%, close to Pence's winning margin in 2012. Holcomb flipped six counties: Starke, Madison, Pike, Greene, Crawford and Scott. He was the first Republican gubernatorial candidate since 1980 to win Crawford and Starke, and the first since 1972 to win Pike.

Following his victory, Holcomb named several former Daniels aides to his transition team, and did not include any former aides to Pence, though that may have been because they were otherwise occupied with Pence's own elevation. In his inaugural address, Holcomb promised a state in which residents "can get a good, fulfilling, well-paid job and a world-class education. Where our kids are well-taken care of. Where we have growing opportunities and the freedom to take advantage of them." Holcomb offered more specifics on infrastructure spending, saying he would consider new taxes and fees to pay for road projects, and he proposed a $1 billion plan over 10 years to support homegrown Indiana companies. Holcomb also proposed making the state's schools chief, currently an elected position, an appointed post, and said he wanted to give communities greater flexibility in crafting needle-exchange programs. It remained to be seen whether Holcomb would follow the lead of Daniels, a pragmatist who didn't focus much on social issues, or Pence, who was an active participant in culture-war battles, though early indications suggested Daniels as a more important model for him. Less in doubt is whether Holcomb would be able to add another presidential signature to his collection; prior to Trump's election, he had owned documents signed by 40 of the nation's first 44 presidents.

Senior Senator

Joe Donnelly (D)

Elected 2012, term expires 2018, 1st term; b. Sep 29, 1955, Massapequa (Queens), NY; University of Notre Dame (IN), B.A., 1977; University of Notre Dame Law School (IN), J.D., 1981; Roman Catholic; Married (Jill Donnelly); 2 children.

Elected Office: Mishawaka Marian H.S. Board., 1997-2001, President 2000-2001; U.S. House, 2007-2012.

Professional Career: Practicing attorney, 1981-1996; IN State Election Board, 1988-1989; Owner, Marking Solutions, 1996-2006.

DC Office: 720 HSOB 20510, 202-224-4814, Fax: 202-224-5011, donnelly.senate.gov.

State Offices: Evansville, 812-425-5813; Fort Wayne, 260-420-4955; Hammond, 219-852-0089; Indianapolis, 317-226-5555; Jeffersonville, 812-284-2027; South Bend, 574-288-2780.

Committees: *Aging*. *Agriculture, Nutrition & Forestry*: Commodities, Risk Management & Trade, Conservation, Forestry & Natural Resources, Rural Development & Energy. *Armed Services*: Airland, Strategic Forces (RMM). *Banking, Housing & Urban Affairs*: Economic Policy, Financial Institutions & Consumer Protection, National Security & International Trade & Finance (RMM).

Group Ratings

	ADA	ACLU	AFL-CIO	LCV	ITI	COC	HAFA	ACU	CFG	FRC
2016	-	35%	-	76%	80%	88%	18%	12%	15%	0%
2015	60%	C	100%	68%	C	77%	C	17%	9%	18%

Almanac Ratings 2015

	Economy	Social	Foreign	Composite
Liberal	79%	50%	80%	70%
Conservative	21%	51%	20%	30%

Key Votes of the 114th Congress

1. Keystone pipeline	Y	5. National Security Data	Y	9. Gun Sales Checks	Y
2. Export-Import Bank	N	6. Iran Nuclear Deal	N	10. Sanctuary Cities	Y
3. Debt Ceiling Increase	Y	7. Puerto Rico Debt	Y	11. Planned Parenthood	N
4. Homeland Security $$	Y	8. Loretta Lynch A.G	Y	12. Trade deals	N

Election Results

Election	Name (Party)	Vote (%)	Cand. Spent	Ind. Exp. Support	Ind. Exp. Oppose
2012 General	Joe Donnelly (D)	1,281,181 (50%)	$5,579,171	$1,250,751	$12,320,701
	Richard Mourdock (R)	1,133,621 (44%)	$8,807,000	$5,098,505	$11,653,132
	Andy Horning (L)	145,282 (6%)	$2,923		
2012 Primary	Joe Donnelly (D)	207,715 (100%)			

Prior winning percentages: House: 2010 (48%), 2008 (67%), 2006 (54%)

If the tea party emerged as a major force in recent years by excoriating what it regards as the national Democratic Party's big brother approach to government, it also on occasion has served as the Democrats' unwitting political accomplice-by upending Republican primaries and foisting on the general electorate candidates with controversial pasts and/or prone to making controversial statements. Indiana's junior senator, Democrat Joe Donnelly, in 2012 was a poster child for the benefits of tea party fallout. After three terms in the House, Donnelly started that year as a longshot to reach the Senate. But the seat became very much in play after tea party-backed state Treasurer Richard Mourdock toppled six-term Sen. Dick Lugar in the Republican primary. If the 80-year old Lugar's defeat was attributed more to his having lost touch with GOP voters than to the appeal of Mourdock's hard-line conservatism, it was Mourdock's incendiary comments on rape and abortion during the general election that helped put Donnelly over the top.

Indiana remains the most reliably Republican state in the Northeast-Midwest "Rust Belt," which, combined with the circumstances surrounding Donnelly's unlikely electoral triumph, all but guaranteed that the Republicans would put a political target on his back come 2018. Indeed, the NRSC's first TV ad of the 2017-2018 election cycle took aim at Donnelly, seeking to tie him to such outspokenly liberal colleagues as Senate Democratic Leader Charles Schumer of New York and Massachusetts Sen. Elizabeth Warren. For his part, the low-key Donnelly has spent most of his first Senate term crafting a centrist voting record while focusing on home-state concerns and other issues -- such as improving care for veterans and combating opioid addiction and heroin trafficking -- that don't tend to invite sharp partisan divisions. It is similar to his *modus operandi* during three terms representing a politically marginal district in the northern part of the state.

If Donnelly's ascension to the Senate involved a major stroke of luck, it has capped a political career that got off to a less than successful start. Born in the New York City borough of Queens and raised in nearby Long Island, he was the youngest of five children; a brother, two years older, was the first one in the family to attend college. Donnelly followed in those footsteps when he was accepted at the University Of Notre Dame in South Bend, Ind., where he earned an undergraduate degree in government and later a law degree. He practiced law in the area until 1996, when he opened a printing and rubber stamp company. Donnelly served on the state election board in 1988 and 1989 after a stint as a recount attorney in a 1986 congressional race. But early efforts to run for office himself were disappointing, to say the least. He ran unsuccessfully for the Democratic nomination for state attorney general in 1988, and fell short in a bid for the state Senate in 1990. He also lost his first campaign for Congress in 2004, but held GOP Rep. Chris Chocola to 54 percent. The year 2006 was much more difficult for Republicans nationally, and Donnelly made President George W. Bush's handling of the Iraq war an issue. This time, Donnelly, while outspent 2-to-1, ousted Chocola by 54%-46% in the state's 2nd District.

"In an era of screamers and cable-TV rock stars filling congressional seats, Donnelly has spent his time on Capitol Hill calmly and quietly working on the issues of the day," the *Indianapolis Star* observed during Donnelly's House tenure. Donnelly urged Democratic leaders to advance a moderate agenda in Congress, and joined the fiscally conservative Blue Dog Coalition. He opposed the 2009 bill seeking to create a cap-and-trade system for reducing greenhouse gas emissions, but did support another major priority of national Democrats: the overhaul of the nation's health insurance system. However, he was among the anti-abortion Democrats who withheld their support of the final version until President Barack Obama agreed to issue an executive order reaffirming the government's ban on funding abortion-related services. On the Financial Services Committee, Donnelly backed the 2008 bailout for financial institutions that also covered the nation's automobile companies: Chrysler, whose transmission plants now employ about 7,000 workers in the 2nd District, took a major hit during the Great Recession.

While Donnelly was re-elected by a landslide margin, 67%-30%, in 2008 as Obama was narrowly winning Indiana on his way to a first White House term, in 2010 he hung on, 48%-47%, in a difficult year for Democrats nationally. After the Democrats lost the House majority that year, Donnelly refused to support the avowedly liberal former House Speaker, Nancy Pelosi of California, for minority leader. Indiana Republicans then successfully crafted a redistricting plan to tilt the 2nd District more toward the GOP, prompting Donnelly to announce a run for Senate in 2011 rather than seek reelection. When Mourdock ousted Lugar in the primary a year later, comments made just hours after the polls closed provided Donnelly with a major opening. In several appearances on cable and broadcast television shows, Mourdock suggested he didn't believe in compromise. "I have a mind-set that says bipartisanship ought to consist of Democrats coming to the Republican point of view," Mourdock told the Fox News Channel. The remark allowed Donnelly and fellow Democrats to paint Mourdock as an extremist.

Mourdock worked to tie Donnelly to Obama, calling him "Obama Joe" in TV ads. But in October, Mourdock uttered what may be remembered-along with Missouri Senate candidate Todd Akin's comment about "legitimate rape"-as the most explosive remark of the 2012 campaign. Asked about the right to abortion in cases of rape, Mourdock said: "Life is that gift from God. And I think even when life begins in that horrible situation of rape, that it is something that God intended to happen." Donnelly, while a long-time abortion opponent, took the position that it should be permitted in cases of rape and incest as well as to save the life of the mother. The state's dominant newspaper endorsed Donnelly, and a Democratic poll gave him a 7-point lead. That was about how it came down on Election Day: Donnelly won, 50%-44%.

In his victory speech, Donnelly sought to identify with Lugar, a pragmatic centrist with a reputation for bipartisanship. "I'm not going there as one party's senator or the other party's senator," he declared. Halfway through Donnelly's term, the Lugar Center -- a Washington-based "think tank" founded by Lugar -- issued a "bipartisan index" that found Donnelly to be fourth most bipartisan senator to serve over the previous two decades. That index -- based on how often legislation a senator sponsored attracted co-sponsors from the other political party, and the frequency with which that senator co-sponsored bills proposed by a colleague not of his or her political party -- put Maine Sen. Susan Collins, a moderate Republican who often crosses party lines, in second place. The 2015 *Almanac* vote scores mirror this finding: on economic and social issues, Collins and Donnelly were almost identical in terms of liberal and conservative voting scores. Among Democrats, Donnelly was the ninth most conservative on economic issues, and the most conservative (tied with another red state Democrat, West Virginia's Joe Manchin) on social issues.

Donnelly found himself at odds with the Obama White House on several occasions after joining the Senate at the beginning of Obama's second term. In 2015, he was among the handful of Democrats supporting legislation to build the controversial Keystone XL oil pipeline that Obama vetoed. And, while voting for a major 2013 immigration reform bill that cleared the Senate on a bipartisan vote, Donnelly later joined three fellow moderate Democrats in supporting a Republican move to roll back Obama's 2014 executive order on immigration policy. "I am as frustrated as anyone that Congress is not doing its job, but the president shouldn't make such significant policy changes on his own," Donnelly declared.

While Donnelly voted in favor of the Affordable Care Act as a member of the House, he cosponsored Senate legislation in 2013 and 2015 to revise "Obamacare" by repealing the tax on medical device manufacturers. Obama threatened to veto repeal of the tax, although at the end of 2015 he signed a spending bill that contained a provision suspending the tax for two years. The medical device industry is a significant source of employment in Indiana, with about 16,000 employees. Donnelly also jawboned the Obama administration on behalf of another major Indiana employer: the steel industry. He testified before the International Trade Commission, while urging the Obama Administration to bring World

Trade Organization against China for the "dumping" of steel products. "It is crucial that you use every tool in your toolbox to combat illegal trade because communities in Indiana are relying on it," he told the president in a 2016 letter.

Donnelly joined most Senate Democrats in siding with the White House on the controversial Iranian nuclear agreement in late 2015. And, in one of his first major votes after coming to the Senate, Donnelly-who ran with National Rifle Association support in his House campaigns-supported an unsuccessful effort by the Obama Administration and gun control advocates to expand background checks on those purchasing firearms. It was proposed in response to the 2012 shooting at a Connecticut elementary school that killed 26. Three years later, in the wake of another mass killing -- the June 2016 mass shooting at an Orlando, Fla. nightclub in which 50 died -- Donnelly participated in a Democratic-led filibuster designed to force a vote on gun-control proposals. "I am a supporter of the Second Amendment," Donnelly declared on the Senate floor. "I'm also someone who believes it's reasonable for all of us to consider smart and responsible ways to reduce gun violence. Those things are not in opposition to each other." But while Donnelly voted for the two Democratic-sponsored measures in the wake of that debate, he was virtually alone within his party in also voting for a couple of GOP-sponsored proposals rejected by most Democrats as lacking teeth. Contended Donnelly, "The Democrat [bills] went further, but the Republican votes moved the ball as well."

By early 2017, attorney Mark Hurt, an aide to former Indiana GOP Sen. Dan Coats had announced his candidacy for the nomination to take on Donnelly. Reps. Luke Messer, chairman of the House Republican Policy Committee, and Todd Rokita were both considering bids; GOP strategists anticipated that at least one of them would eventually file for the nomination. . Donnelly clearly lacks the national profile of two other Hoosier Democratic senators of recent decades: Birch and Evan Bayh. But, in a state that has voted Democratic just once in presidential elections since 1964, and which President Donald Trump carried by 19 points in 2016, Donnelly is sure to find himself in the national political spotlight in his coming re-election bid.

Junior Senator

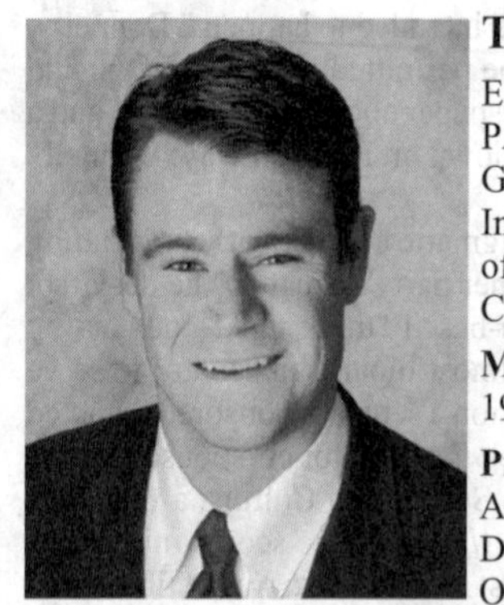

Todd Young (R)

Elected 2016, term expires 2022, 1st term; b. Aug 24, 1972, Lancaster, PA; U.S. Naval Academy (MD), B.S., 1995; University of Chicago's Graduate School of Business, M.B.A., 2000; University of London's Institute of U.S. Studies, M.A., 2001; Leipzig Graduate School of Management, 2001; Indiana University Law School, J.D., 2006; Christian Church; Married (Jennifer B. Young); 4 children.

Military Career: U.S. Navy, 1990-1991; U.S. Marine Corps, 1995-2000.

Professional Career: Staff, Heritage Foundation, 2001; Legislative Assistant, Sen. Richard Lugar, 2001-2003; Adviser, Governor Mitch Daniels, 2004; Management consultant, 2004-2006; Deputy prosecutor, Orange County, 2007-2010.

DC Office: 400 RSOB 20510, 202-224-5623, young.senate.gov.

State Offices: Evansville, 812-350-8956; Fort Wayne, 260-422-7397; Indianapolis, 812-288-3999; New Albany, 812-336-3000.

Committees: *Commerce, Science & Transportation*: Aviation Operations, Safety & Security, Communications, Technology, Innovation & the Internet, Consumer Protection, Product Safety, Ins & Data Security, Oceans, Atmosphere, Fisheries & Coast Guard, Surface Trans., Merchant Marine Infra., Safety & Security. *Foreign Relations*: Africa & Global Health Policy, Internat'l Dev Instit & Internat'l Econ, Energy & Environ Policy (Chmn), Near East, South Asia, Central Asia & Counterterrorism. *Health, Education, Labor & Pensions*: Children & Families, Employment & Workplace Safety, Primary Health & Retirement Security. *Joint Congressional-Executive Commission on China. Small Business & Entrepreneurship.*

Group Ratings (House)

	ADA	ACLU	AFL-CIO	LCV	ITI	COC	HAFA	ACU	CFG	FRC
2016	-	5%	-	5%	100%	100%	58%	72%	85%	92%
2015	0%	C	9%	3%	C	79%	C	82%	74%	91%

Key Votes of the 114th Congress (House)

1. Keystone Pipeline	Y	5. Puerto Rico Debt	Y	9. Offenses by Aliens	Y
2. Trade Deals	Y	6. Medical Marijuana	N	10. Troops in Iraq	N
3. Export-Import Bank	N	7. Sanctuary Cities	Y	11. Homeland Security $$	Y
4. Debt Ceiling Increase	N	8. Armor-piercing Bullets	Y	12. Trade Adjustment aid	Y

Election Results

Election	Name (Party)	Vote (%)		Cand. Spent	Ind. Exp. Support	Ind. Exp. Oppose
2016 General	Todd Young (R)	1,423,991	(52%)	$15,194,428	$3,591,044	$16,862,554
	Evan Bayh (D)	1,158,947	(42%)	$10,886,830	$388,888	$23,884,578
	Lucy Brenton (L)	149,481	(5%)	$483		
2016 Primary	Todd Young (R)	661,136	(67%)			
	Marlin Stutzman (R)	324,429	(33%)			

Prior winning percentages: House: 2014 (62%); 2012 (55%); 2010 (52%)

For much of the latter part of the 20th century, this Senate seat was occupied by two men, Democrat Birch Bayh and Republican Dan Quayle, who went on to achieve national prominence. In the nearly three decades since then, control of the seat has shifted among Hoosiers with close personal and/or political ties to either Bayh or Quayle. The newest occupant, Republican Todd Young, elected as the state's junior senator in 2016, falls within that tradition.

When Quayle was elected vice president in 1988, he was succeeded in the Senate by Republican Dan Coats -- who got his start in politics as an aide to Quayle, and later went on to succeed his mentor in the House of Representatives. Coats opted not to run again for Senate in 1998 in the face of a likely challenge from Democrat Evan Bayh, Birch Bayh's son and a popular former governor in his own right. In 2010, Coats regained the seat after Bayh unexpectedly chose not to seek re-election. And in 2016, when Coats decided to leave for a second time, the Indiana GOP establishment rallied around Young, a fast-rising House member married to Quayle's niece. It ultimately set up a nationally watched general election showdown that was something of a battle of political dynasties -- as Young scored a come-from-behind victory over Evan Bayh, who, after initial hesitation, decided to try to recapture the seat he had given up six years earlier.

At 44, Young -- a U.S. Naval Academy graduate who went on to earn two master's degrees as well as a law degree -- became one of just two GOP freshmen elected to the Senate in 2016. While he was born in Lancaster, Pennsylvania and spent his first 13 years outside Indiana, his family has ties to the Hoosier State stretching back five generations. His father owns a small business that sells heating and air-conditioning equipment; his mother is a registered nurse. Young went to high school in Hamilton County, Indiana, a well-to-do, heavily Republican suburb just north of Indianapolis -- where his prowess as a soccer player helped his school's team win a state championship. He enlisted in the Navy after high school, and, a year later, received an appointment to the U.S. Naval Academy, where he also played on the soccer team. Upon graduation from Annapolis, he opted for service in the Marine Corps, where he worked with unmanned aerial vehicles doing reconnaissance work, including a stint aiding efforts to stem narcotics trafficking in the Caribbean.

Transferred to Chicago to oversee Marine recruiting, Young attended the University of Chicago's business school at night, earning an M.B.A. while becoming a fan of free-market economist Friedrich von Hayek. Young went on to the University of London's Institute of United States Studies, where he received a second master's degree and wrote a thesis on the economic history of Midwestern agriculture. Moving to Washington, he worked at the conservative Heritage Foundation and as a legislative assistant to Indiana GOP Sen. Dick Lugar. In 2004, Young returned to Indiana to work on the gubernatorial campaign of Republican Mitch Daniels.

While attending Indiana University's law school at night, he met his wife, Jennifer Tucker Young. (Her father and Dan Quayle's wife, Marilyn, are brother and sister.) After earning his law degree in 2006, Young and his wife went to work at a law firm established by her great-grandfather in the small southern Indiana town of Paoli, commuting from nearby Bloomington. He and his wife, now the parents of four children, continue to reside in Bloomington -- home of Indiana University's main campus, and an island of liberalism in a red state that has voted Democratic in only one presidential election in more than 50 years. "I'm a Bloomington conservative. My wife and I call it missionary work," Young has occasionally wisecracked on the stump.

In January 2009, Young announced plans to run for the 9th District seat held by Democrat Baron Hill, who was first been elected in 1998. Young narrowly won a three-way primary that also included former Rep. Mike Sodrel -- who had ousted Hill in 2004, only to see Hill regain the House seat two years later. In the 2010 fall campaign, Young campaigned as a fiscal conservative and attacked Hill as a rubber stamp for the Obama Administration. Hill emphasized his Hoosier roots as a former high school basketball star -- in a state in which basketball is a passion in both urban and rural areas -- while seeking to characterize Young as an out-of-touch lawyer who had spent much of his career outside the state. In a year in which House Democrats suffered the loss of more than 60 seats nationwide, Young ousted Hill by 52%-42%.

Young was assigned to the Armed Services and Budget committees and, cultivating ties to House leaders, was awarded a prized seat on the Ways and Means Committee at the beginning of his second term in 2013. The same year, he took over as lead sponsor of a key legislative initiative for Republican conservatives: the REINS Act, requiring congressional approval of federal regulations with an economic impact exceeding $100 million. Unlike some of his more hardline Class of 2010 colleagues, he supported the 2011 compromise to raise the debt limit, saying he wanted deeper spending cuts but that the measure "moves us in the right direction." Despite his avowed desire to work with Democrats, Young at times utilized sharp rhetoric, once calling Senate Democratic Leader Harry Reid "useless" and Reid's House counterpart, Nancy Pelosi, "an irrelevant cheerleader for lost-cause liberalism" at a local GOP event. He had a competitive re-election fight in 2012, defeating his Democratic opponent, Shelli Yoder -- a former Miss Indiana who called for turning the region into a leader in clean energy technologies to produce jobs -- by 55%-45%, but had little trouble winning a third term in 2014.

When Coats announced his retirement in March 2015, Young immediately said he was "very serious" about a race to succeed him, and followed up with a formal announcement in July. Young garnered the support of many GOP officials in the state, as several other House Republicans opted to run for re-election after eyeing the Senate seat. Rep. Marlin Stutzman, who had mounted a tea party-infused insurgency in the primary against Coats six years earlier, ran again for Senate. "The D.C. establishment thinks that they can buy your vote," Stutzman declared in one fundraising appeal, alluding to Young's backing by the U.S. Chamber of Commerce. "They have chosen Todd Young to play as their puppet in this upcoming election."

Initially, it appeared Young's prospects could be complicated by the presence of another party establishment candidate, former state GOP Chairman Eric Holcomb on the ballot. But Holcomb withdrew just days after the filing deadline, opting to become the running mate of then-Gov. Mike Pence. (Pence's nomination as vice president led to Holcomb being chosen as the Republican candidate for governor, and he won that job in November.) Young's next hurdle involved an effort by Indiana Democrats to have him thrown off the primary ballot for not having filed a sufficient number of petition signatures in one congressional district: The Democrats clearly viewed Stutzman as the candidate easier to beat in a general election The national GOP came to Young's aid, and the state election commission rejected the ballot challenge. In the May primary, Young overwhelmed Stutzman, 67%-33%.

Young seemed poised to cruise to victory in the general election against the Democrats' candidate -- none other than Baron Hill, his 2010 opponent. Hill had received the nomination after Evan Bayh turned aside entreaties in early 2015 to run for his old seat. But, in July 2016, Bayh was persuaded to change his mind, and Hill stepped aside. Early public opinion polls showed Bayh -- who had run five times statewide for governor and secretary of state as well as Senate -- with a 20-point lead. National Democrats saw him as a shoo-in who would all but assure a return to the Senate majority.

But it didn't take long for problems to surface for Bayh and the Democrats. Unlike his father -- the author of the 25th and 26th Amendments to the U.S. Constitution -- the younger Bayh never appeared fully comfortable in the Senate. He even considered running for his old job as governor in 2004 before deciding to seek a second Senate term. In early 2010, after forgoing a third term, he professed himself fed up with congressional gridlock in an op-ed column for *The New York Times*, Announcing his retirement, Bayh declared that it was time for him to "contribute to society in another way." By the end of the campaign, Young -- aided by nearly $28 million that poured into Indiana from conservative independent expenditure groups, including more than $3 million from the Koch brothers -- had reframed Bayh's stated desire to contribute to society into a question of how much society had contributed to Bayh during the previous six years.

According to financial disclosure statements, Bayh's net worth had undergone a six-fold increase since he left the Senate, and he was put on the defensive by an *Associated Press* report -- published a month before Election Day -- that disclosed he had numerous meetings and phone calls with headhunters and future corporate employers during his last year in the Senate. The report noted Bayh had been among a small group of Democrats who helped to kill a tax increase on private equity gains. It was a proposal opposed by Apollo Global Management, with whom Bayh had met -- and for whom he went to work after leaving the Senate. Compounding the controversy was that, prior to publication of *AP* report, Bayh had told the *Indianapolis Star* he did not meet with Apollo Global during that period. Bayh's ties to the state since leaving the Senate also came into question: While asserting that he remained an Indiana resident, Bayh was found to have rarely spent time at an Indianapolis condominium he owned, and his voter status was classified as inactive.

Young also hammered away at Bayh's vote for the Affordable Care Act while in the Senate. With the polls tightening in September, a former Indiana Democratic Party chair conceded to *Politico* that the Young campaign had "done a pretty good job of trying to control the narrative." Put another way, Young out-performed Bayh, who seemed to expect that he could win the election without breaking a sweat and was unprepared for the rigors of a competitive campaign. Symptomatic was his failure to recall during a local television interview the correct address of the residence that he had been using during visits to Indianapolis. By mid-October, some polls were showing the race a dead heat. As independent expenditure groups spent nearly $17.5 million in an effort to prop up his struggling candidacy, Bayh released a TV ad seeking to blunt the attacks as the election neared. "Six years ago, I left Congress fed up with the partisanship," he declared. "Yes, I built a good life for my family, spent time with Susan and our boys. … The corrupt interests now falsely attacking me, they're the same ones hurting you." It wasn't enough: The final returns gave Young a 52%-42% win.

FIRST DISTRICT

Pete Visclosky (D)

Elected 1984, 17th term; b. Aug 13, 1949, Gary; Georgetown University Law Center (DC), LL.M.; Indiana University Northwest, B.S.; University of Notre Dame Law School (IN), J.D.; Roman Catholic; Married (Ms. Joanne Royce); 2 children.

Professional Career: Practicing attorney, 1973-1976, 1983-1984; Aide, U.S. Rep. Adam Benjamin, 1977-1982.

DC Office: 2328 RHOB 20515, 202-225-2461, Fax: 202-225-2493, visclosky.house.gov.

State Offices: Merrillville, 219-795-1844.

Committees: *Appropriations*: Defense (RMM), Energy & Water Development & Related Agencies.

Group Ratings

	ADA	ACLU	AFL-CIO	LCV	ITI	COC	HAFA	ACU	CFG	FRC
2016	-	88%	-	100%	67%	57%	14%	4%	0%	0%
2015	90%	C	92%	94%	C	50%	C	0%	7%	0%

Almanac Ratings 2015

	Economy	Social	Foreign	Composite
Liberal	88%	97%	99%	95%
Conservative	12%	4%	1%	5%

Key Votes of the 114th Congress

1. Keystone Pipeline	N	5. Puerto Rico Debt	Y	9. Offenses by Aliens	N
2. Trade Deals	N	6. Medical Marijuana	Y	10. Troops in Iraq	Y
3. Export-Import Bank	NV	7. Sanctuary Cities	N	11. Homeland Security $$	Y
4. Debt Ceiling Increase	Y	8. Armor-piercing Bullets	N	12. Trade Adjustment aid	Y

Election Results

Election	Name (Party)	Vote (%)		Cand. Spent	Ind. Exp. Support	Ind. Exp. Oppose
2016 General	Pete Visclosky (D)	207,515	(82%)	$642,768		
	Donna Dunn (L)	45,825	(18%)			
2016 Primary	Peter Visclosky (D)	77,030	(80%)			
	Willie Brown (D)	19,302	(20%)			

Prior winning percentages: 2014 (61%), 2012 (67%), 2010 (59%), 2008 (71%), 2006 (70%), 2004 (68%), 2002 (67%), 2000 (72%), 1998 (73%), 1996 (69%), 1994 (57%), 1992 (70%), 1990 (66%), 1988 (77%), 1986 (73%), 1984 (71%)

Peter Visclosky, a Democrat first elected in 1984, is a former congressional aide who has found his niche in the House. "I'm an appropriator," he once said. "Money makes policy." In recent years, though, life on the spending side has become more complicated and his career has faced limits.

Visclosky grew up in Lake County. His father was mayor of Gary in the early 1960s, and Visclosky went to college there and to law school at the University of Notre Dame. He practiced law and then worked for six years in Washington for 1st District Rep. Adam Benjamin, a Democrat. Benjamin died of a heart ailment in 1982, and Visclosky returned to Indiana.

In 1984, at age 34, he ran in the Democratic primary against Katie Hall, a black state senator who had been given the 1982 nomination - and thus the election, in this Democratic district - by Gary Mayor Richard Hatcher, who was also the district's party chairman. In their contest, Visclosky pulled out all the stops to reach voters since he couldn't rely on the local Democratic establishment, which was backing Hall. He called himself the "Slovak Kid" to connect with the district's many European ethnic groups, and he held hot dog dinners to attract young people and others not usually involved in local politics. Visclosky narrowly prevailed over Hall with 34 percent of the vote to her 33 percent. He easily won the general election with 71 percent of the vote.

Visclosky has concentrated much of his effort on projects to help the local economy, especially the steel industry. He has a solidly pro-union voting record. He is a leader of the Congressional Steel Caucus and has been vigilant in monitoring surges in steel imports. He has urged the International Trade Commission to maintain trade protections, and has repeatedly introduced bills requiring that federally funded projects use only American-made steel. In a July 2014 appearance before the ITC, he said "there is no higher priority for our domestic steel industry today than the enforcement of our trade laws," and that it was time to take a stand that "we do not allow steel to be dumped here." In 2000, when George W. Bush was elected president with critical help from steel-producing areas, Visclosky had gained leverage and Bush imposed steel import quotas. When the quotas were removed, Visclosky protested that Bush "stabbed the American steelworkers in the back." He opposed the House-passed bill in 2009 establishing a cap-and-trade system to curb greenhouse gas emissions because it "leaves no margin of error as it relates to jobs in the domestic steel industry."

Visclosky, long the dean of Indiana's congressional delegation, has trended moderate on social and foreign policy in his voting record, and he occasionally has shown independence. He broke Democratic ranks to oppose the New Year's Day 2013 budget deal aimed at averting the so-called fiscal cliff, saying that it left too many tax and spending issues unresolved. In 2008, he opposed creation of the Troubled Asset Relief Plan for the ailing financial services industry, although he did back a subsequent proposal to bail out major automakers.

Since 2013, Visclosky has been ranking Democrat on the Defense Appropriations Subcommittee, which has a history of bipartisanship. When Democrats were in the majority, he was chairman of the Energy and Water Development Subcommittee, making him one of the powerful "cardinals" of the House. But he was forced to step aside temporarily in June 2009 after he was subpoenaed as part of a grand jury investigation into possible corruption. In 2007, *The Indianapolis Star* reported that Visclosky had steered more than $12 million to out-of-state defense companies that contributed to his campaign. Much of that money had been secured through the efforts of a lobbying firm, PMA Group, that hired a former top Visclosky aide, Richard Kaelin, the newspaper reported. The House Ethics Committee formally cleared Visclosky and six other Appropriations members in 2010. In 2011, he did not challenge the decision of Democratic leaders to place Nita Lowey of New York - an ally of Nancy Pelosi - as the top Democrat on the full committee, even though she had less seniority than Visclosky.

On Appropriations, Visclosky had been adept at securing federal funding for projects in his district and at doling out such projects to other lawmakers. But those so-called earmarks have been prohibited since 2011. He helped to secure $57 million for expansion of the facility and runway at the Gary airport, which was completed in 2015. In recent years, he echoed President Barack Obama's call for increased federal spending on infrastructure, which he said would help revitalize his district's economy. "I am very big on transformational projects," he has said. But costly economic development projects have not been a priority of the Republican-controlled House.

At home, Visclosky was secure politically until he became a target in the corruption probe. Even then, Republicans had trouble finding a candidate who could compete in the costly Chicago media market, and challenge the Democratic performance in the 1st District. Against weak and poorly financed challengers, Visclosky since 1994 has not dropped below 59 percent in his share of the vote. In November 2016, his sole challenger was from the Libertarian Party. He won the Democratic primary with 80 percent of the vote against Willie Brown, a bus driver in Gary.

Northwest Indiana: Gary, Hammond

Population		**Race and Ethnicity**		**Income**	
Total	718,511	White	63.2%	Median Income	$52,131 (220 out of 435)
Land area	1,157	Black	19.0%		
Pop/ sq mi	621.0	Latino	14.7%		
Born in state	59.2%	Asian	1.3%	Under $50,000	47.7%
		Two races	1.5%	$50,000-$99,999	31.9%
Age Groups		Other	0.3%	$100,000-$199,999	17.5%
Under 18	24.0%			$200,000 or more	2.8%
18-34	21.7%	**Education**		Poverty Rate	16.7%
35-64	40.1%	H.S grad or less	47.4%		
Over 64	14.2%	Some college	31.1%	**Health Insurance**	
		College Degree, 4 yr	14.2%	With health insurance coverage	87.4%
Work		Post grad	7.3%		
White Collar	31.0%				
Sales and Service	42.0%	**Military**		**Public Assistance**	
Blue Collar	27.0%	Veteran	8.5%	Cash public assistance income	2.1%
Government	10.9%	Active Duty	0.0%		
				Food stamp/SNAP benefits	14.4%

Voter Turnout			
2015 Total Citizens 18+	528,175	2016 House Turnout as % CVAP	48%
2016 House turnout	254,583	2014 House Turnout as % CVAP	27%

2012 Presidential Vote		
Barack Obama	182,021	(61%)
Mitt Romney	111,217	(37%)

2016 Presidential Vote		
Hillary Clinton	162,358	(53%)
Donald Trump	124,638	(41%)
Gary Johnson	13,287	(4%)

Cook Partisan Voting Index: D+8

At the southernmost shore of Lake Michigan is a part of America made by steel. In the northwest corner of Indiana, where the water highway of the Great Lakes comes closest to the rail highway of the transcontinental railroads, America's leading capitalists of a century ago identified an ideal site for manufacturing steel. On empty sand dunes, United States Steel, then the nation's largest corporation, founded the city of Gary in 1906 and named it for the company's chairman, Chicago Judge Elbert Gary. For nearly 70 years, the steel mills attracted a diverse and middle-class workforce, more like Chicago than the rest of Indiana: Irish, Poles, Czechs, Ukrainians and blacks from the South.

Politics here has always been turbulent, from the long and unsuccessful steel strike of 1919 to the racially polarized politics of the 1960s and 1970s. The tone of public life - the clash between union stewards and management foremen, between African Americans and Eastern European ethnics, between the stalwarts of different factions vying for control of Gary's massive City Hall - was a clash of steel on steel. Steel brought sudden growth and sudden depression to northwest Indiana. The massive storefronts built on Gary's aptly named Broadway bear witness to the confidence and exuberance of the 1920s. The steel mills went cold during the Depression but were again thronged with workers during World War II. In the years afterward, their massiveness helped create the illusion that a robust economic life in the steel towns of Gary, Hammond and East Chicago would last forever. Today, many of the old mills stand vacant - vandalized, whole blocks burned down - witness to steel layoffs, crime waves and an acute sense of loss. Technological advances replaced increasingly expensive workers with increasingly efficient machines. And the efforts to seal off the U.S. steel market from the world inevitably failed.

The oil crunch of 1979 was the catalyst for change, reducing the demand for large-sized autos, the biggest customer for steel. Steel employed 70,000 workers in northwest Indiana in 1979, but recent employment has dropped by three-fourths. Obsolete mills were closed, old mills modernized and new ones built that cut the number of man hours needed by two-thirds. Just-in-time methods were introduced, and management and highly skilled workers cooperated to engineer higher-quality, less-expensive steel to meet market demands. In the shrinking market, this remained the No. 1 steel-producing state in 2016, as it has been since 1980, with 18,000 industry workers in northwest Indiana. Even with the downsizing, steel remained vital to the local economy. In November 2016, U.S. Steel dealt with a legacy from its past when it settled a Justice Department lawsuit on clean-air violations and agreed to remove and repair aging machinery at its Gary site.

The dramatic decline of the industry left Gary in ruins. A 2012 Federal Reserve Bank of Chicago study categorized Gary as "overwhelmed" by the decline of manufacturing. Nobel Prize-winning economist Joseph Stiglitz in 2006 said the city was saddled with "the same problems facing less-developed countries." White flight to the suburbs has reduced the city's population from a peak of 178,000 in 1960 to 77,000 in 2015, of whom 85 percent are African American. To take advantage of increased taxes in Illinois, Gary and Indiana officials have offered incentives to companies to move to their side of the state border in an intensifying competition. In 2015, the city reelected its first female mayor, Karen Freeman-Wilson, a graduate of Harvard College and Harvard Law School. The epidemic of illegal drugs has consumed much of her attention.

Indiana's 1st Congressional District stretches from Gary and Hammond along the Lake Michigan shoreline east to Michigan City. In majority-white Hammond, the population loss has not been as dramatic as in Gary, and it has had an influx of Hispanic immigrants. The 1st includes Lake and Porter counties. LaPorte County is divided between it and the neighboring 2nd District. In Porter County, Valparaiso is notable for its annual Popcorn Festival honoring Orville Redenbacher. In March 2016, that city opened a $260 million paper recycling mill. Then-Gov. Mike Pence celebrated that Indiana is "the leading manufacturing state in America."

About three-fourths of the vote in the 1st is in Lake County. Like neighboring Chicago, the district has been solidly Democratic. In 2016, Donald Trump's appeal to blue-collar workers and his promise to reduce subsidized imports struck a local chord. He cut nearly in half the 24-point victory of President Barack Obama in 2012. Reduced Democratic support added to the party's woes elsewhere in Indiana. Lake County was one of only four counties that backed Hillary Clinton, albeit with a lower raw vote and percentage than in Indianapolis-based Marion County.

SECOND DISTRICT

Jackie Walorski (R)

Elected 2012, 3rd term; b. Aug 17, 1963, South Bend; Taylor University (IN), B.A.; Liberty Baptist College (VA), Att.; Assembly of God; Married (Dean Swihart).

Elected Office: IN House, 2004-2010.

Professional Career: TV reporter, WSBT-TV, 1985-1989; Executive Director, St. Joseph County Humane Society, 1989-1991; Director of institutional advancement, Ancilla College, 1991-1996; Director of annual giving, IN University, 1997-1998; Founder, Impact Intl., 1999-2003.

DC Office: 419 CHOB 20515, 202-225-3915, Fax: 202-225-6798, walorski.house.gov.

State Offices: Mishawaka, 574-204-2645; Rochester, 574-223-4373.

Committees: *Ways & Means*: Human Resources, Oversight.

Group Ratings

	ADA	ACLU	AFL-CIO	LCV	ITI	COC	HAFA	ACU	CFG	FRC
2016	-	5%	-	3%	100%	100%	63%	84%	66%	100%
2015	0%	C	17%	0%	C	85%	C	83%	70%	100%

Almanac Ratings 2015

	Economy	Social	Foreign	Composite
Liberal	3%	4%	0%	2%
Conservative	97%	96%	100%	98%

Key Votes of the 114th Congress

1. Keystone Pipeline	Y	5. Puerto Rico Debt	Y	9. Offenses by Aliens	Y
2. Trade Deals	Y	6. Medical Marijuana	N	10. Troops in Iraq	N
3. Export-Import Bank	N	7. Sanctuary Cities	Y	11. Homeland Security $$	N
4. Debt Ceiling Increase	N	8. Armor-piercing Bullets	Y	12. Trade Adjustment aid	N

Election Results

Election	Name (Party)	Vote (%)		Cand. Spent	Ind. Exp. Support	Ind. Exp. Oppose
2016 General	Jackie Walorski (R)	164,355	(59%)	$1,987,022		
	Lynn Coleman (D)	102,401	(37%)	$631,829		
	Ron Cenkush (L)	10,601	(4%)			
2016 Primary	Jackie Walorski (R)	77,389	(70%)			
	Jeff Petermann (R)	33,513	(30%)			

Prior winning percentages: 2014 (59%), 2012 (49%)

Republican Jackie Walorski was first elected in 2012 to the seat vacated by now-Democratic Sen. Joe Donnelly. After two close campaigns-one defeat and one victory -- she has solidified her political position and has staked out her legislative niche with mainstream Republican views on farm and nutrition policy plus occasional bipartisanship on military and veterans issues.

Walorski grew up in a working-class family in South Bend, the granddaughter of Polish and German immigrants. Her father was a firefighter, and her mother worked at a hospital. She was the first in her family to attend college, graduating from Taylor University with a bachelor's degree in communications. She didn't become passionate about politics until she heard presidential candidate Ronald Reagan speak, recalling that he said Republicans "believed in smaller government and the power of individuals controlling their own destiny."

Walorski spent her first few years out of college working as a television reporter, and then became an administrator for Ancilla College and Indiana University. In 1999, Walorski and her husband, Dean Swihart, volunteered as Christian missionaries in Romania. The couple eventually set up their own nonprofit organization, Impact International. They were in Romania at the time of the September 11th terrorist attacks, an experience that she said was life-changing. "We sat and watched on the only television we had in Romania. The airspace was closed, we couldn't get back to our country," she said. "We really did not know if we'd ever see our country or family again."

When the couple returned to Indiana, Walorski won a seat in the state House in 2004. She cosponsored the state's voter identification law, which withstood a challenge in the Supreme Court, and worked to establish the Indiana Economic Development Corporation as a public and private cooperative venture.

In what has long been a swing district, Walorski campaigned in tight races. In her 2010 challenge to Donnelly, she had endorsements from Sarah Palin and Newt Gingrich. The National Republican Congressional Committee placed this contest on its priority list, and Walorski got more than $1 million in national party aid. But Donnelly outspent her, $2 million to $1.3 million, and she lost 48%-47%, a margin of 2,538 votes. When Donnelly ran for the Senate, Walorski faced off in the general against Democrat Brendan Mullen, an Army veteran of the Iraq war who campaigned as a pro-gun, anti-abortion rights moderate. Walorski went on the attack, running an ad that accused him of having three homes in Washington, D.C. Mullen said the homes were rental properties, and he criticized Walorski's vote for leasing operations of the Indiana Toll Road as a state lawmaker in 2006. Walorski outspent Mullen, $1.9 million to $1.2 million. The redrawn district's Republican tilt was instrumental in her close win,

49%-48%, a margin this time of 3,920 votes. Walorski was boosted by the strong local performance of Mitt Romney's presidential bid and by Mike Pence's campaign for governor.

In the House, Walorski scored some accomplishments, focused on local issues and avoided the leadership clashes and electoral ambitions of the several other junior Republicans from Indiana. As chair of the Nutrition Subcommittee of the Agriculture Committee, she held hearings on possible changes in the food stamp program, including steps to better serve families and taxpayers. She toured her district's many farm communities and offered assistance in dealing with Washington. On the Armed Services and Veterans' Affairs committees, she worked with veterans' groups to encourage local business opportunities. She filed a bill to require greater accountability by VA hospitals in their prescription practices. In 2013, she enacted her proposal for whistleblower protections to victims of sexual assault in the military and create a safe environment to report attacks. Democrats Amy Klobuchar of Minnesota and Claire McCaskill of Missouri sponsored companion legislation in the Senate.

In 2014, Walorski grew more secure. Her challenger was Joe Bock, a global health professor at Notre Dame. Walorski attacked him for votes to increase his own pay as a member of the Missouri legislature in the 1980s, and suggested that he was a carpetbagger. Bock criticized her as a career politician and for her role in the government shutdown in October 2013. Bock spent more than $800,000 to $1.8 million for Walorski, but this was a bad year for Democrats. The incumbent won 59%-38%. Her similar outcome in 2016 was further evidence that she was growing entrenched. Against Lynn Coleman, a retired police officer and former assistant to the mayor of South Bend, Walorski outspent him $2,1 million to $642,000 and won 59%-37%.

During her campaign, Walorski supported Donald Trump but distanced herself from some of his actions. "I don't think anybody supports everything they've seen in a president," she said. "My job is to represent this district no matter who is in the White House."

North-Central Indiana: South Bend, Elkhart

Population		**Race and Ethnicity**		**Income**	
Total	720,975	White	80.8%	Median Income	$46,905 (309 out of 435)
Land area	3,959	Black	6.8%	Under $50,000	53.1%
Pop/ sq mi	182.1	Latino	9.0%	$50,000-$99,999	32.3%
Born in state	69.0%	Asian	1.2%	$100,000-$199,999	12.3%
		Two races	1.9%	$200,000 or more	2.3%
Age Groups		Other	0.4%	Poverty Rate	16.0%
Under 18	25.2%	**Education**		**Health Insurance**	
18-34	21.7%	H.S grad or less	51.4%	With health insurance coverage	85.4%
35-64	38.6%	Some college	27.6%	**Public Assistance**	
Over 64	14.5%	College Degree, 4 yr	13.2%	Cash public assistance income	2.4%
Work		Post grad	7.7%	Food stamp/SNAP benefits	13.0%
White Collar	28.9%	**Military**			
Sales and Service	38.7%	Veteran	8.2%		
Blue Collar	32.4%	Active Duty	0.0%		
Government	9.4%				

Voter Turnout			
2015 Total Citizens 18+	515,648	2016 House Turnout as % CVAP	54%
2016 House turnout	277,357	2014 House Turnout as % CVAP	28%

2012 Presidential Vote		
Mitt Romney	154,837	(56%)
Barack Obama	116,320	(42%)

2016 Presidential Vote		
Donald Trump	163,539	(58%)
Hillary Clinton	99,496	(36%)
Gary Johnson	12,905	(5%)

Cook Partisan Voting Index: R+11

When the University of Notre Dame was founded in 1842, Catholics were still a rarity in most of America and certainly rare on the limestone-bottomed plains of northern Indiana. This was still farm country and South Bend no more than a crossroads on the banks of the St. Joseph River. But by the 1920s, both the school and the town had grown. Notre Dame, thanks to its football team, the Fighting Irish, was the most famous Catholic university in the land, and South Bend was a significant industrial city, home of Studebaker, Bendix and dozens of other factories. In the past 50 years, Notre Dame has grown in size and reputation, but South Bend, like many Rust Belt cities, diminished in size and reputation. In the 1960s, Studebaker went out of business. In the early 1980s, there were massive factory layoffs.

But these high-profile job losses were accompanied by the much less visible creation of jobs in small factories throughout the region. The work in those facilities required more skill than did the old assembly lines, and the products had to be more responsive to just-in-time prime contractors or computer-inventory retailers. In recent years, many employers have had trouble filling job openings, and the economic base is more secure than when it depended on the fate of two or three big companies. Meanwhile, Notre Dame has led another transition, to a more high technology-focused economy. After acquiring the Midwest Institute for Nanoelectronics Discovery, it has researched the building blocks of the next generation of computers. A priority of the university's roughly $100 million in research projects has been its Environmental Change Initiative, which has explored the related problems of invasive species, land use and climate change, and their synergistic impact on water resources.

Elkhart County is a manufacturing hub that has found creative ways to turn a profit. Local companies there make everything from pharmaceuticals to musical instruments. The county is best known as the nation's manufacturing center for recreational vehicles. The ups and down in gasoline prices, like those in recent years, can have a big impact in Elkhart. The onset of recession strangled demand for big-ticket goods like RVs. In 2008, Elkhart's unemployment jumped to 15 percent, the largest increase of any metropolitan area in the nation, prompting *The New York Times* to call it "the white-hot center of the meltdown of the American economy." Nearly 18,000 jobs disappeared after the RV industry collapsed. The city council passed a law limiting residents to one garage sale per month. President Barack Obama dropped in for a visit in February 2009 to tout his economic recovery plan, including an infusion of federal dollars for Elkhart County. "You can't drive anywhere in Elkhart and not see the stimulus," Democratic Mayor Dick Moore told *The Indianapolis Star* in 2010.

When gas prices dropped, the local economy made an impressive turn-around, as joblessness in Elkhart dropped to 3.5 percent in 2015. Shipments from Elkhart were 321,000 in 2013, nearly double the total in 2009; by 2016, sales spiked again to 400,000. Manufacturing employment rebounded from 28,000 to 38,000. One of every two RVs on the road today was manufactured in Elkhart. Other parts of the auto business have diversified. In Mishawaka, the plant that had manufactured Hummer military vehicles until it shut down in 2009 shifted in 2015 to production of Mercedes sports utility vehicles, which are for sale only in China. When Obama returned to Elkhart in June 2016, he basked in the local turnaround, which he cited as proof that the nation is "the strongest, most durable economy in the world."

The 2nd Congressional District of Indiana is centered on South Bend. This is a blue-collar and ethnic city, with one of the nation's largest percentage of Hungarian Americans, plus a growing community of Mexican Americans. Its Republican base was secured in the latest redistricting. Wabash and Miami counties, plus rural and conservative parts of Kosciusko County, were added to the 2nd District, and it lost parts of Democratic-leaning Porter and LaPorte in the northwest corner of Indiana. But the shifts in the 2nd have resulted more from broader politics than from redistricting. Using the current lines in the 2008 presidential election, Barack Obama and John McCain were separated by 701 votes. That changed dramatically in 2016, when Donald Trump won the working-class district, 58%-36%.

THIRD DISTRICT

Jim Banks (R)

Elected 2016, 1st term; b. Jul 16, 1979, Columbia City; Indiana University, Bloomington, Bach. Deg., 2004; Grace College, M.B.A., 2013; Evangelical; Married (Amanda Banks); 3 children.

Military Career: U.S. Navy Reserves (Afghanistan), 2012-present.

Elected Office: IN Senate, 2010-2016.

DC Office: 509 CHOB 20515, 202-225-4436, Fax: 202-226-9870, banks.house.gov.

State Offices: Fort Wayne, 260-702-4750.

Committees: *Armed Services*: Oversight & Investigations, Tactical Air & Land Forces. *Science, Space & Technology*: Environment, Research & Technology, Space. *Veterans' Affairs*: Disability Assistance & Memorial Affairs, Economic Opportunity.

Election Results

Election	Name (Party)	Vote	(%)	Cand. Spent	Ind. Exp. Support	Ind. Exp. Oppose
2016 General	Jim Banks (R)	201,396	(70%)	$1,497,200	$234,983	$28,078
	Tommy Schrader (D)	66,023	(23%)			
	Pepper Snyder (L)	19,828	(7%)			
2016 Primary	Jim Banks (R)	46,508	(34%)			
	Kip Tom (R)	42,716	(32%)			
	Liz Brown (R)	33,640	(25%)			
	Pam Galloway (R)	9,541	(7%)			

Jim Banks was elected to an open seat in the northeast corner of Indiana. In this safe Republican district, the wide-open primary contest was decisive. Of the six candidates, three were serious contenders. Banks, a commercial real estate broker with extensive military experience in the Navy Reserve, was supported by national conservative groups. The runners-up were a wealthy agri-businessman and a popular state senator. Banks said that he will focus chiefly on military issues.

Banks was born and continued to reside in Columbia City, not far from Fort Wayne. He graduated from Indiana University, where he was president of College Republicans, and got an MBA at Grace College and Seminary. He worked as a real estate broker with the Bradley Co. in Fort Wayne. Elected to the state Senate in 2010, where he claimed the most conservative record, he chaired the Veterans Affairs and the Military Committee. He invoked a state law to take a leave of absence in 2014, while he served for eight months at NATO headquarters in Afghanistan, where he assisted with equipment for the Afghans. He received the Defense Meritorious Service Medal for his military leadership. During that time, his wife, Amanda Banks, was appointed acting state senator.

When Rep. Marlin Stutzman announced that he was running for the open Senate seat, Banks staked out ground among conservative advocacy groups. His political consultant told Banks that he needed to become "less wonky" during the campaign, according to a story in *GQ*. "You don't need to impress people with your intellect," the consultant told him. Affiliates of the Club for Growth and the Senate Conservatives Fund spent more than $700,000 on his behalf. In addition, Brown raised $1.1 million for the primary, compared with $992,000 for farmer Kip Tom, and $338,000 for Elizabeth Brown, a veteran Fort Wayne elected official. He won the primary with 34 percent to 31 percent for Tom and 25 percent for Brown. David McIntosh, the head of the Club for Growth who during the 1990s served in an earlier version of this district, made the election of Banks a top priority and he took credit for playing a "pivotal role" in the victory. In the general, Banks defeated Tommy Schrader, a perennial Democratic candidate, 70%-23%.

Banks got a seat on the Armed Services Committee, where he said that his objective was to "ensure our men and women in uniform receive the resources they need to protect our nation." In March 2017, he filed a bill to authorize the use of force against the Islamic State in Iraq and Syria (ISIS). "The Constitution grants Congress the power of declaring war, and we need to take that obligation seriously,"

Banks said. "Rather than continuing to fight ISIS under an authorization passed by Congress in 2001 to fight al-Qaeda, it is time to pass a new authorization for the use of military force against ISIS."

He showed early insight on the demands of his new job. On the night he won the primary, with his wife and three young daughters standing nearby, he told cheering supporters that he often thought while serving in Afghanistan, "I want to be a better dad and a better husband." After a pause, he added, according to the Fort Wayne *News-Sentinel*, "Then I ran for Congress."

Northeast Indiana: Fort Wayne

Population		**Race and Ethnicity**		**Income**	
Total	730,697	White	84.2%	Median Income	$49,315 (266 out of 435)
Land area	4,180	Black	5.9%		
Pop/ sq mi	174.8	Latino	5.8%		
Born in state	72.4%	Asian	1.9%	Under $50,000	50.8%
		Two races	1.9%	$50,000-$99,999	33.8%
Age Groups		Other	0.3%	$100,000-$199,999	13.1%
Under 18	26.1%			$200,000 or more	2.5%
18-34	21.6%	**Education**		Poverty Rate	14.1%
35-64	38.4%	H.S grad or less	47.6%		
Over 64	13.8%	Some college	30.5%	**Health Insurance**	
		College Degree, 4 yr	14.2%	With health insurance coverage	85.1%
Work		Post grad	7.6%		
White Collar	30.1%				
Sales and Service	37.9%	**Military**		**Public Assistance**	
Blue Collar	32.0%	Veteran	8.2%	Cash public assistance income	2.1%
Government	8.9%	Active Duty	0.1%		
				Food stamp/SNAP benefits	11.2%

Voter Turnout			
2015 Total Citizens 18+	523,439	2016 House Turnout as % CVAP	55%
2016 House turnout	287,247	2014 House Turnout as % CVAP	28%

2012 Presidential Vote		
Mitt Romney	179,629	(63%)
Barack Obama	102,536	(36%)

2016 Presidential Vote		
Donald Trump	189,587	(64%)
Hillary Clinton	87,699	(30%)
Gary Johnson	13,903	(5%)

Cook Partisan Voting Index: R+18

The northeast corner of Indiana was first settled by people of New England Yankee stock, establishing orderly communities with public schools and even colleges. They were joined by German immigrants, who built tidy farms and their own civic institutions. In the northern part of the state, there are hills, lakes and the strange swamp that is the central focus of Gene Stratton-Porter's children's classic, *A Girl of the Limberlost*. The one large city here, Fort Wayne, was built on the flat terrain along the Maumee River that flows to Toledo Ohio. It grew as a factory town, surging ahead and then falling back as large factories, often tied to the auto industry, opened and downsized over the years.

Manufacturing jobs in the Fort Wayne area dropped significantly in the 2000s. The local economy started to revive after a $150 million biodiesel complex opened in Claypool, with the largest soybean processing plant in the United States, which can produce 88 million gallons of fuel annually. In May 2015, General Motors announced that it planned a $1.2 billion expansion of its plant for full-size pickup trucks, which employed 3,800 workers. Kosciusko County, named for the Polish general who served during the Revolutionary War, is renowned for medical supplies. In the town of Warsaw (yes, named for the Polish capital), residents have been making orthopedic devices for more than a century, and the demand keeps growing as baby boomers age. The head of the local Chamber of Commerce expects a big increase in demand for artificial knees: good news for Warsaw, bad news for seniors.

The 3rd Congressional District covers the northeastern part of the state and is centered on Fort Wayne. It is a surprisingly diverse area, with a mix that includes a concentration of Amish, plus Central Americans, Bosnians, Somalis and the nation's largest number of Burmese refugees. In the metro area, only 6 percent of the total population is Hispanic, but the Hispanic share of the population under 18 is much higher. This part of Indiana has been heavily Republican since the Civil War, though it has sometimes veered Democratic in times of economic distress.

The seat sometimes sends its representatives on to higher positions: Dan Quayle, elected here in 1976, was later a senator and vice president. Dan Coats, who succeeded Quayle in the Senate, was ambassador to Germany before winning a second term in the Senate in 2010 and then became Director of National Intelligence with President Donald Trump. In 2016, Rep. Marlin Stutzman tried, but failed, to continue that pattern. He trailed badly in the GOP primary to replace the retiring Coats. In the 2008 and 2012 presidential elections, the 3rd was the most Republican district in Indiana. Donald Trump improved the GOP vote to 64 percent, but that was only his second-highest in the state behind the 6th District.

FOURTH DISTRICT

Todd Rokita (R)

Elected 2010, 4th term; b. Feb 09, 1970, Chicago, IL; Wabash College (IN), B.A.; Indiana University Law School, Indianapolis, J.D.; Roman Catholic; Married (Kathy Rokita); 2 children.

Elected Office: IN Secretary of st., 2003-2010.

Professional Career: Practicing attorney, 1995-1997; General counsel, Office of IN Secretary of St., 1997-2000; IN deputy Secretary of st. 2000-2002.

DC Office: 2439 RHOB 20515, 202-225-5037, Fax: 202-226-0544, rokita.house.gov.

State Offices: Danville, 317-718-0404; Lafayette, 765-838-3930.

Committees: *Budget*. *Education & the Workforce*: Early Childhood, Elementary & Secondary Education (Chmn), Health, Employment, Labor & Pensions. *Transportation & Infrastructure*: Aviation, Railroads, Pipelines & Hazardous Materials, Water Resources & Environment.

Group Ratings

	ADA	ACLU	AFL-CIO	LCV	ITI	COC	HAFA	ACU	CFG	FRC
2016	-	17%	-	0%	100%	100%	70%	92%	89%	100%
2015	0%	C	4%	0%	C	85%	C	92%	77%	100%

Almanac Ratings 2015

	Economy	Social	Foreign	Composite
Liberal	2%	4%	4%	3%
Conservative	99%	96%	96%	97%

Key Votes of the 114th Congress

1. Keystone Pipeline	Y	5. Puerto Rico Debt	Y	9. Offenses by Aliens	Y
2. Trade Deals	Y	6. Medical Marijuana	N	10. Troops in Iraq	N
3. Export-Import Bank	N	7. Sanctuary Cities	Y	11. Homeland Security $$	N
4. Debt Ceiling Increase	N	8. Armor-piercing Bullets	Y	12. Trade Adjustment aid	Y

Election Results

Election	Name (Party)	Vote (%)		Cand. Spent	Ind. Exp. Support	Ind. Exp. Oppose
2016 General	Todd Rokita (R)	193,412	(65%)	$884,562		
	John Dale (D)	91,256	(31%)			
	Steven Mayoras (L)	14,766	(5%)	$1,130		
2016 Primary	Todd Rokita (R)	86,047	(69%)			
	Kevin Grant (R)	38,198	(31%)			

Prior winning percentages: 2014 (67%), 2012 (62%), 2010 (69%)

Republican Todd Rokita, elected in 2010, is a former Indiana secretary of state and devout conservative who has become an energetic partisan. Like other junior Republicans from Indiana, he has been an activist in the House with an impact on budget and education policies. He has shown ambition to move up the ranks and is young enough that further success is a good bet.

Rokita grew up in Munster, which is part of Lake County. His father was a dentist who owned his own practice, and his mother was a dental hygienist. Rokita was president of his high school student body and won a full scholarship to Wabash College. He majored in political science, focusing on political philosophy. A semester at the University of Essex in England reinforced Rokita's already conservative political beliefs. Fellow students told him about long lines and poor service in government-run hospitals, and he noticed the high cost of goods because of a value-added tax. His experience abroad was "a good glimpse into what the future of America would and could be with liberalism on the march here," he said.

After earning his law degree at Indiana University, Rokita worked in private practice for several years. A licensed pilot, Rokita focused on aviation law, among other fields. He also was a volunteer pilot, flying people in need of non-emergency medical care to hospitals and clinics throughout the Midwest. While working on local and state campaigns, he met Indiana's then-Secretary of State Sue Anne Gilroy, who hired him as her general counsel and later made him deputy secretary of state. Rokita worked for George W. Bush's presidential campaign in 2000, training workers to challenge ballots during the historic Florida recount.

When Gilroy was term-limited in 2002, Rokita ran for the Republican nomination to succeed her. He bought a surplus police car and drove across the state, meeting with delegates who would make the selection at a party convention. He won the Republican nomination on the third ballot and went on to win the general election. In office, he fulfilled a campaign pledge to enact a bill requiring a photo ID at polling places to combat voter fraud. Critics of the 2005 law argued that it disenfranchised poor voters who are less likely to have driver's licenses (and are more likely to vote Democratic). A lawsuit challenging the constitutionality of the law reached the Supreme Court, which upheld it in 2008.

Rokita became embroiled in another controversy with civil rights undercurrents. In a 2007 speech, he questioned why 90 percent of blacks vote for Democrats. "How can that be?" Rokita said, according to the Associated Press. "Ninety to 10. Who's the master and who's the slave in that relationship? How can that be healthy?" After African-American leaders condemned his remarks, Rokita apologized. In 2009, he ran into a different political problem when he infuriated the political class with a proposal to make it a felony for lawmakers to draw legislative districts based on political data, such as party registration and where incumbents live - an unpopular idea in both parties.

In 2010, he considered challenging Democratic Sen. Evan Bayh, who eventually decided to retire. Instead, Rokita jumped into the House contest when GOP Rep. Steve Buyer announced his retirement. His main primary opponent was state Sen. Brandt Hershman, Buyer's district director. With high name recognition and solid fundraising, Rokita won 42 percent of the GOP vote to Hershman's 17 percent, while 11 other candidates split the rest. Rokita easily won in November against a Purdue University professor.

Rokita showed early ambition when he was named to the Republican Steering Committee, which makes committee assignments. He recruited fellow freshmen to donate at fundraising events and took in nearly $200,000 through his leadership political action committee for the 2012 election. But he was willing to break ranks with party leaders. He voted against the New Year's Day 2013 budget deal on taxes and spending aimed at averting the so-called fiscal cliff, and he was one of 67 Republicans to oppose Hurricane Sandy relief for the Northeast. "Just as normal American families do, we have to be willing to cut spending on less important things if we want to pay for emergency expenses," he said.

On the Education and the Workforce Committee, he chaired the Early Childhood, Elementary and Secondary Education Subcommittee. As the panel in 2015 rewrote the No Child Left Behind Act, Rokita successfully worked with others to return more school choices to local control. The new law stopped short of his more conservative alternative, the Student Success Act. On another issue, Rokita won the committee's approval of his measure to weaken nutrition requirements for school lunch programs and reduce the number of eligible recipients. The measure generated opposition from Democrats, plus the National Governors Association and nutrition groups. Rokita complained that critics had turned the measure into "a partisan food fight."

On the House Budget Committee, he had served as vice chairman. When Rep. Tom Price of Georgia, the chairman, resigned to become secretary of Health and Human Services in the Trump administration, Rokita sought to succeed Price. But House Republican leaders selected Rep. Diane Black of Tennessee, with whom Speaker Paul Ryan had served as chairman of the Ways and Means Committee. They were under pressure to increase the scant number of women chairing House committees. Rokita remained as vice-chairman of the committee.

Rokita fell short in another behind-the-scenes campaign back home in Indiana. In July 2016, after Donald Trump selected Gov. Mike Pence as his running mate, the state Republican Central Committee scrambled to replace Pence, who had been seeking reelection. Rokita was one of three GOP contenders who actively sought the post. The party chose Eric Holcomb, whom Pence earlier tapped to fill a vacancy as lieutenant governor.

At home, Rokita hasn't had to break a sweat in winning reelection. Despite his setbacks in the two recent back-room contests, Rokita likely will have other opportunities, either statewide or in the House. In early 2017, he explored the possibility of seeking the Republican nomination to oppose Sen. Joe Donnelly in 2018.

West-Central Indiana: Indianapolis Suburbs, Lafayette

Population		**Race and Ethnicity**		**Income**	
Total	736,048	White	86.4%	Median Income	$51,957 (224 out of 435)
Land area	6,353	Black	3.5%		
Pop/ sq mi	115.9	Latino	5.7%		
Born in state	70.2%	Asian	2.6%	Under $50,000	48.0%
		Two races	1.5%	$50,000-$99,999	33.5%
Age Groups		Other	0.3%	$100,000-$199,999	16.0%
Under 18	23.4%			$200,000 or more	2.5%
18-34	24.9%	**Education**		Poverty Rate	13.4%
35-64	38.0%	H.S grad or less	46.2%		
Over 64	13.8%	Some college	29.7%	**Health Insurance**	
		College Degree, 4 yr	15.5%	With health insurance coverage	88.8%
Work		Post grad	8.6%		
White Collar	32.2%				
Sales and Service	38.8%	**Military**		**Public Assistance**	
Blue Collar	29.0%	Veteran	8.7%	Cash public assistance income	1.7%
Government	12.7%	Active Duty	0.1%		
				Food stamp/SNAP benefits	10.1%

Voter Turnout			
2015 Total Citizens 18+	537,730	2016 House Turnout as % CVAP	56%
2016 House turnout	299,434	2014 House Turnout as % CVAP	26%

2012 Presidential Vote		
Mitt Romney	170,244	(61%)
Barack Obama	103,103	(37%)

2016 Presidential Vote		
Donald Trump	194,403	(64%)
Hillary Clinton	91,265	(30%)
Gary Johnson	16,704	(6%)

Cook Partisan Voting Index: R+17

The landscape of central and western Indiana is some of the most prosaic in the United States. It is mostly flat, with neat farms and towns of frame bungalows, looking mostly unchanged from many years ago. Across this landscape have run some of the nation's chief transportation arteries. The earliest was the old National Road, from Baltimore to St. Louis, which was paralleled by U.S. 40 in the 1930s. The region was also crisscrossed by the great east-west rail lines carrying famed passenger trains like the *Wabash Cannonball*. There is no *Cannonball* today. People bounce around the Midwest on commuter airlines from small city to hub, and U.S. 40 has been superseded by Interstate 70. The landscape still looks rural, and there are some large farms, with more than 80 percent of agricultural income from corn and soybeans, and a small slice from hogs. But the economy is more industrial, with small factories in crossroads and courthouse towns.

Tippecanoe County's Lafayette, where the main employer is Purdue University, has been growing and prosperous. It has benefited from a partnership between Toyota and longtime local auto manufacturer Subaru that helped the Lafayette plant's workforce grow to 5,500 people, which is the largest private employer in Tippecanoe. After spending $1.3 billion to expand the facility, which is the company's only factory in North America, Subaru began production at the end of 2016 of its new Impreza model, with plans for 400,000 vehicles annually. In June 2016, Purdue Research Foundation and Browning Investments announced a partnership to create the Purdue Research Foundation, with expected investment of more than $1 billion in West Lafayette. Manufacturing in West Lafayette accounted for roughly 17,000 workers. This is a slice of the country that has had relatively few African Americans or Latinos. The recent spurt in research has led to a boost in the Asian population, with 17 percent in West Lafayette and 6 percent in Tippecanoe.

The 4th Congressional District covers much of west-central Indiana, including Kokomo and western parts of suburban Indianapolis. Each of the 16 counties usually votes Republican. Only Tippecanoe, which is the largest and has about 20 percent of the voters, is competitive. Hendricks County in the Indianapolis suburbs is heavily Republican. In 2016, Donald Trump won 64 percent of the district vote. John McCain, by contrast, had 54 percent of the presidential vote in 2008.

FIFTH DISTRICT

Susan Brooks (R)

Elected 2012, 3rd term; b. Aug 25, 1960, Ft. Wayne; Miami University of Ohio, B.A., 1982; Indiana University Law School, J.D., 1985; Roman Catholic; Married (David M. Brooks); 2 children.

Professional Career: Deputy mayor of Indianapolis, 1998-1999; Practicing attorney, 2000-2001; U.S. Attorney, S. District of IN, 2001-2007; Sr. Vice President., General counsel, Ivy Tech Comm. College, 2007-2012.

DC Office: 1030 LHOB 20515, 202-225-2276, Fax: 202-225-0016, susanwbrooks.house.gov.

State Offices: Anderson, 765-640-5115; Carmel, 317-848-0201.

Committees: *Energy & Commerce*: Communications & Technology, Health, Oversight & Investigations. *Ethics (Chmn)*.

Group Ratings

	ADA	ACLU	AFL-CIO	LCV	ITI	COC	HAFA	ACU	CFG	FRC
2016	-	5%	-	5%	100%	100%	48%	72%	72%	92%
2015	0%	C	23%	3%	C	100%	C	67%	53%	92%

Almanac Ratings 2015

	Economy	Social	Foreign	Composite
Liberal	10%	5%	10%	9%
Conservative	90%	95%	90%	91%

Key Votes of the 114th Congress

1. Keystone Pipeline	Y	5. Puerto Rico Debt	Y	9. Offenses by Aliens	Y
2. Trade Deals	Y	6. Medical Marijuana	N	10. Troops in Iraq	N
3. Export-Import Bank	N	7. Sanctuary Cities	Y	11. Homeland Security $$	Y
4. Debt Ceiling Increase	Y	8. Armor-piercing Bullets	Y	12. Trade Adjustment aid	Y

Election Results

Election	Name (Party)	Vote (%)		Cand. Spent	Ind. Exp. Support	Ind. Exp. Oppose
2016 General	Susan Brooks (R)	221,957	(62%)	$899,635		
	Angela Demareed (D)	123,849	(34%)	$141,954		
	Matthew Wittlief (L)	15,329	(4%)	$7,250		
2016 Primary	Susan Brooks (R)	95,192	(69%)			
	Mike Campbell (R)	21,566	(16%)			
	Stephen MacKenzie (R)	20,400	(15%)			

Prior winning percentages: 2014 (65%), 2012 (73%)

Republican Susan Brooks, first elected in 2012, channels the understated conservatism of the Indianapolis political establishment. Building quickly on her impressive experience in policy and law enforcement, she became chairman in 2017 of the Standards of Official Conduct (Ethics) Committee. Back home, she was unsuccessful in the back-room campaign of the Republican hierarchy to select a new candidate for governor, after Mike Pence became the vice presidential nominee.

Brooks was born in Auburn, Indiana, and raised in Fort Wayne. At Homestead High School, she played basketball, volleyball, and tennis - and was a member of the cheerleading squad. She attended Miami University in Oxford, Ohio, where she pursued a joint degree in political science and sociology and was president of her sorority. She earned a law degree from Indiana University and joined an Indianapolis-based criminal defense practice. That exposed her to what she called the "root causes" of crime, such as domestic strife and mental health problems.

In 1998, Brooks was named deputy mayor of Indianapolis under Republican Mayor Stephen Goldsmith. At his behest, Brooks established the Indianapolis Violence Reduction Partnership, a multiagency collaboration designed to curb homicide, gun assaults and armed robberies. In October 2001, she was appointed U.S. attorney for the Southern District of Indiana by President George W. Bush. Over the next six years, she prosecuted drug kingpins, helped consolidate the Southern District's counter-terrorism apparatus, and drew attention to human trafficking, "something we really weren't talking about in Indianapolis," she said. In 2007, Brooks was appointed senior vice president and general counsel for Ivy Tech Community College, a statewide institution.

In 2012, Brooks and her chief GOP rival, former Rep. David McIntosh, entered the race before veteran Rep. Dan Burton announced his retirement, which may have contributed to his decision to endorse another candidate, Marion Mayor Wayne Seybold. Brooks and McIntosh each raised more than $500,000. McIntosh, who served in the House from 1995 to 2001, received endorsements from Republican power brokers, including former Vice President Dan Quayle and the National Rifle Association.

McIntosh's campaign was undone by questions about his residential status. After relinquishing his seat in Congress to run for governor of Indiana, he moved his family to the Washington area to work as a lobbyist in a large D.C. law firm. But he continued to vote in Indiana, renting area properties to maintain his residency. McIntosh was later absolved of any wrongdoing by a local election board, but not before he had lost the Republican primary. In a crowded field, Brooks prevailed with 30 percent of the vote to 29 percent for McIntosh, a difference of 1,010 votes. Seybold finished fourth with 11 percent. In the general, Democrat Scott Reske, a state legislator and former Marine Corps officer, had a hard time getting traction in the Republican district; Brooks won 58%-38%. Brooks has been reelected without serious competition from either party.

In the House, Brooks co-chaired the Congressional High-Tech Women's Caucus, with an objective to encourage more women to enter the tech industry. The House passed her Social Media Working Group Act, which would codify the Homeland Security Department's social media techniques. She was one of 87 Republicans who voted to end the partial government shutdown in October 2013, which she termed "very much a low point in governing for me." She received leadership assignments to the Ethics Committee and the Select Committee to Investigate Benghazi. She defended the Benghazi panel from charges that its investigation was designed to embarrass Democratic presidential candidate Hillary Clinton. She responded that the panel's review had been "very fact-centric."

After gaining her seat on the influential Energy and Commerce Committee in 2015, Brooks set as a top priority repeal of the medical device tax in the Affordable Care Act - a priority for many businesses in the Indianapolis area. She was part of a bipartisan House group in March 2015 that enacted an extension of the Children's Health Insurance Program, along with changes in Medicare payments to doctors. Also on the committee, she cited her work on the enactment of the Twenty First Century Cures Act, including steps to address mental illness, the opioid epidemic and the development of vaccines.

Following the retirement announcement of Sen. Dan Coats in 2015, Brooks considered running for the seat. She said she concluded that she could have more impact for Indiana by staying in the House.

When Pence accepted the vice-presidential nomination in July 2016, she was one of three candidates in the 10-day campaign for the decision by the 22-member state Republican Central Committee to replace him as the candidate for governor. Brooks reportedly received significant support in the back-room discussions. But Pence's support of Eric Holcomb, whom he had earlier selected as his lieutenant governor, would have made it embarrassing for the state party to defy his wishes after Donald Trump had selected Pence as his running mate.

As the incoming chairman of the Ethics Committee, she unexpectedly became embroiled in a controversial effort by other House Republicans to make the investigations of the largely autonomous

Office of Congressional Ethics more subservient to her committee. Collaborating with Brooks, Speaker Paul Ryan had opposed that internal change on the eve of the convening of the new Congress in January 2017. The two of them initially sought to downplay the impact of the rules revision. Following an overnight uproar inside and outside the House, Republican renegades agreed - at least temporarily - to abandon the change. Still, the controversy made clear the internal challenges that Brooks faced as chairman of the panel that judges and can impose sanctions on other House members. "The House Committee on Ethics has an important role to play in holding members, officers and staff accountable to the American people and to our colleagues," she told a local reporter.

In 2017, she also became co-chair of the bipartisan Congressional Caucus on Women's Issues. "There is more work to be done" with laws such as the Violence Against Women Act and the Children's Health Insurance Program, Brooks said.

Northern Indianapolis Metro

Population		**Race and Ethnicity**		**Income**	
Total	742,679	White	82.4%	Median Income	$62,804 (114 out of 435)
Land area	1,925	Black	7.8%		
Pop/ sq mi	385.9	Latino	4.1%		
Born in state	65.0%	Asian	3.1%	Under $50,000	40.1%
Age Groups		Two races	2.3%	$50,000-$99,999	30.9%
Under 18	24.7%	Other	0.3%	$100,000-$199,999	21.7%
18-34	21.4%	**Education**		$200,000 or more	7.2%
35-64	40.7%	H.S grad or less	30.7%	Poverty Rate	9.6%
Over 64	13.2%	Some college	26.1%	**Health Insurance**	
Work		College Degree, 4 yr	27.1%	With health insurance coverage	90.5%
White Collar	45.2%	Post grad	16.1%		
Sales and Service	39.4%	**Military**		**Public Assistance**	
Blue Collar	15.4%	Veteran	7.8%	Cash public assistance income	2.0%
Government	10.8%	Active Duty	0.1%	Food stamp/SNAP benefits	8.2%

Voter Turnout			
2015 Total Citizens 18+	539,900	2016 House Turnout as % CVAP	67%
2016 House turnout	361,135	2014 House Turnout as % CVAP	30%

2012 Presidential Vote		
Mitt Romney	196,743	(58%)
Barack Obama	139,300	(41%)

2016 Presidential Vote		
Donald Trump	193,018	(52%)
Hillary Clinton	150,083	(41%)
Gary Johnson	20,505	(6%)

Cook Partisan Voting Index: R+9

Indiana's most rapid growth has taken place in the suburban ring counties around Indianapolis, especially in Hamilton County, directly north of the city. This is affluent suburbia, with subdivisions full of spacious houses, shopping centers and office developments in what were not too long ago farm fields. Hamilton County's population increased from 82,000 in 1980 to 182,000 in 2000 and to 275,000 in 2010 - a 50 percent jump in a decade, making it one of the fastest growing counties in the Midwest. The growth continued, and reached 310,000 in 2015. A group of business and civic leaders has developed a mass transit plan that could spur even greater growth.

Hamilton County has drawn many wealthy people from Indianapolis, where they had been concentrated on the north side of the city. Now, they're more likely to be in the former farm communities of Carmel, Fishers and Noblesville. Since the creation of its Midtown development in 2014, wealthy Carmel has attracted new businesses and condominiums. In 2016, the Roche Diagnostics medical-services company completed the first phase of its $300 million expansion in Fishers. Hamilton has the highest median household income in Indiana and is the 35th richest county in the nation, with a population that is nearly 90 percent white. Hamilton is the most Republican of the large counties in

Indiana and is one of the most Republican in the nation. It voted 61%-38% for John McCain in 2008 and 66%-32% for Mitt Romney in 2012. But the county's support for Donald Trump in 2016 dropped to 57%-37%, a common trend in high-income areas across the nation.

The 5th Congressional District is located in the center of the state and includes the northern Indianapolis suburbs. In addition to Hamilton County, which is the core of the district and has about 40 percent of the population, the 5th takes all or part of seven other counties. Some, such as Grant and Tipton, are Republican-leaning. The northern slice of Indianapolis's Marion County is the second largest part of the district and has become Democratic-leaning, even though it remains mostly upscale; the remaining 70 percent of Marion is in the heavily Democratic 7th District. The district also includes the politically mixed Madison County, with its county seat in Anderson, a manufacturing town. The overall makeup of this district is Republican. But the weaker support for Trump in Hamilton reduced Republican presidential vote in the district from 58 percent in 2012 to 52 percent in 2016, ranking as the lowest of the state's seven Republican-held districts.

SIXTH DISTRICT

Luke Messer (R)

Elected 2012, 3rd term; b. Feb 27, 1969, Evansville; Wabash College (IN), B.A.; Vanderbilt University Law School (TN), J.D.; Presbyterian; Married (Jennifer Messer); 3 children.

Elected Office: IN House, 2003-2006.

Professional Career: Legal counsel, Koch Industries, 1995-1996; Staff, Rep. John Duncan Jr., 1997; Press Secretary, Rep. Ed Bryant, 1998; Legal counsel, Reps. Dan Burton & David McIntosh, 1998-1999; Legal counsel, House Government Reform & Oversight Committee, 1999; Executive Director, IN Republican Party, 2001-2005; Practicing attorney, 2006-present; President, Hoosiers for Economic Growth Network, 2010-2012.

DC Office: 1230 LHOB 20515, 202-225-3021, Fax: 202-225-3382, messer.house.gov.
State Offices: Muncie, 765-747-5566; Richmond, 765-962-2883; Shelbyville, 317-421-0704.

Committees: House Republican Policy Committee Chairman. *Education & the Workforce*: Early Childhood, Elementary & Secondary Education, Higher Education & Workforce Development. *Financial Services*: Capital Markets, Securities & Investment, Oversight & Investigations, Terrorism & Illicit Finance.

Group Ratings

	ADA	ACLU	AFL-CIO	LCV	ITI	COC	HAFA	ACU	CFG	FRC
2016	-	5%	-	3%	100%	92%	70%	92%	84%	92%
2015	0%	C	4%	0%	C	89%	C	92%	74%	100%

Almanac Ratings 2015

	Economy	Social	Foreign	Composite
Liberal	9%	4%	4%	6%
Conservative	91%	96%	96%	94%

Key Votes of the 114th Congress

1. Keystone Pipeline	Y	5. Puerto Rico Debt	N	9. Offenses by Aliens	Y
2. Trade Deals	Y	6. Medical Marijuana	N	10. Troops in Iraq	N
3. Export-Import Bank	N	7. Sanctuary Cities	Y	11. Homeland Security $$	N
4. Debt Ceiling Increase	Y	8. Armor-piercing Bullets	Y	12. Trade Adjustment aid	Y

Election Results

Election	Name (Party)	Vote (%)		Cand. Spent	Ind. Exp. Support	Ind. Exp. Oppose
2016 General	Luke Messer (R)	204,920	(69%)	$917,775		
	Barry Welsh (D)	79,135	(27%)	$6,043		
	Rich Turvey (L)	12,330	(4%)			
2016 Primary	Luke Messer (R)	91,366	(78%)			
	Jeff Smith (R)	14,897	(13%)			
	Charles Johnson Jr. (R)	11,370	(10%)			

Prior winning percentages: 2014 (66%), 2012 (59%)

Republican Luke Messer in 2012 took the seat of Mike Pence, who was elected governor that year. After losing in the GOP primary in two runs for Congress during the previous decade, Messer followed in the footsteps of his predecessor, who also had lost two earlier runs for Congress and later won a place in the House leadership. Messer took only two years to be elected chairman of the House Republican Policy Committee, the No. 5 GOP leadership post. Following the 2016 election, Messer made plans for a challenge in 2018 to Democratic Sen. Joe Donnelly.

Messer was born in Evansville, and the family moved to Greensburg when he was 4 years old. A sixth-generation Hoosier, Messer traces his Republican ideology and interest in politics to his family roots. Messer's grandmother, Helen Rotzien, was a ward chairman and secretary of the Marion County Republican Central Committee in the 1960s. He was raised by a single mother. As Messer told *National Journal*, she exemplified hard-working values and taught him that "anyone can come from humble beginnings." Messer attended Wabash College, paying his tuition by working as a waiter and telemarketer and graduating with a major in speech.

After earning a law degree from Vanderbilt University, he held jobs on Capitol Hill with three members of Congress, including Indiana Republican Rep. Dan Burton. In 2000, Messer made his first run for the House in an open-seat contest against Pence and he lost in the GOP primary. He became executive director of the Indiana Republican Party in 2004 and worked in the successful gubernatorial campaign of Mitch Daniels.

With his appointment to a vacancy in the Indiana House, his signature issue was education. His legislation aimed at curbing high school drop-out rates received national attention after Shelbyville High School became a symbol of a national dropout crisis. As highlighted in a *Time* magazine cover story and a special on *The Oprah Winfrey Show*, Messer's 2005 bill required Indiana to raise its minimum dropout age from 16 to 18. After the legislation was implemented, Shelbyville High School's graduation rate increased from 75 percent to 90 percent. Messer was inspired to write a children's book called *Hoosier Heart*. The book, illustrated by his wife, Jennifer, follows the journey of Emma and Ava (named after his daughters) and their friend, Ben, as they discover what it means to be a Hoosier.

In 2010, Messer ran again for the House, this time against 14-term incumbent Burton, his former boss, and lost the Republican primary 30%-28%. The following year, Republicans in charge of redistricting thoughtfully put his home of Shelbyville in the adjacent district, solid GOP turf perfect for Messer. When Pence's run for governor created an open seat, the third time proved the charm for Messer. He publicly aligned himself with Pence's policies. His top competitor was real estate investor Travis Hankins. Hankins ran a competitive grassroots campaign, personally calling more than 19,000 voters and spending the majority of his funds on yard signs to cover the 19-county district. Messer was the choice of the GOP establishment and benefited from a timely endorsement from the popular Daniels days before the primary. Messer defeated Hankins 40%-29%. His $1.1 million overall spending and the Republican lean of the district gave him a 59%-35% victory over Democrat Bradley Bookout, a former Delaware County Council member. He has been easily reelected.

Messer has been a loyal conservative in the House. He immediately impressed his like-minded colleagues, and was a Republican freshman class president. Kentucky GOP Rep. Thomas Massie told *The Indianapolis Star* that Messer was "probably the best listener I have met here in Congress" and that he is "always able to articulate what I think better than what I can." On the Education and the Workforce Committee, Messer has been a vigorous champion of school choice, drawing on his earlier work in Indiana. He formed the Congressional School Choice Caucus, and filed legislation to allow states to use federal education funds to expand school choice programs. "The simple truth is too many kids in America have their destiny determined by zip codes," he wrote in an op-ed column. "That's because too many families live in neighborhoods with bad schools, and they can't afford to do anything about it." On another issue facing education, he introduced with Democratic Rep. Jared Polis of Colorado the Student

Digital Privacy and Parental Rights Act, which was designed to protect the information that computer programs gather on students. Education leaders assisted in the drafting of the bill. Messer also served on the Financial Services Committee, where he crafted a bipartisan bill to reduce banking regulations over critical local infrastructure projects; the House passed the bill in February 2016.

In November 2014, Messer ran for Policy Committee chairman. Playing up support from Pence, who remained highly respected among conservatives in the House, Messer donated money to numerous candidates and promised to expand the Policy Committee's staff to help all GOP members. Messer beat New York's Tom Reed 137-90 after Rob Woodall of Georgia was eliminated on the first ballot. "We need a positive agenda, so we're not defined by just what we oppose," Messer said after he was selected. During the next two years, he promoted conservative policy with working groups on key issue areas, including millennials, law enforcement and women in the 21st century workforce. Following the 2016 election, he pledged to assist House Republicans in reaching common ground with President Donald Trump. In December, he met with aides to Trump to discuss education policy. He reportedly was considered for Education secretary, but the position went to charter-school advocate Betsy DeVos.

After a long struggle to get to Congress, Messer would have other opportunities to move up the political ladder. He passed up possible statewide contests in 2016. But he moved quickly to stake a claim to the Republican nomination to oppose Donnelly, whom Senate Republicans viewed as highly vulnerable following his unlikely win in 2012 and the increasingly Republican bent of Indiana.

Southeast Indiana: Muncie

Population		**Race and Ethnicity**		**Income**	
Total	720,403	White	92.0%	Median Income	$47,178 (301 out of 435)
Land area	6,207	Black	2.4%		
Pop/ sq mi	116.1	Latino	2.5%		
Born in state	70.8%	Asian	1.2%	Under $50,000	52.6%
		Two races	1.6%	$50,000-$99,999	32.4%
Age Groups		Other	0.3%	$100,000-$199,999	13.2%
Under 18	22.8%			$200,000 or more	1.9%
18-34	21.5%	**Education**		Poverty Rate	15.0%
35-64	39.9%	H.S grad or less	52.1%		
Over 64	15.8%	Some college	28.5%	**Health Insurance**	
		College Degree, 4 yr	12.2%	With health insurance coverage	87.7%
Work		Post grad	7.3%		
White Collar	30.3%				
Sales and Service	40.0%	**Military**		**Public Assistance**	
Blue Collar	29.7%	Veteran	9.4%	Cash public assistance income	2.1%
Government	11.7%	Active Duty	0.1%		
				Food stamp/SNAP benefits	12.6%

Voter Turnout			
2015 Total Citizens 18+	545,745	2016 House Turnout as % CVAP	54%
2016 House turnout	296,385	2014 House Turnout as % CVAP	28%

2012 Presidential Vote		
Mitt Romney	172,452	(60%)
Barack Obama	106,365	(37%)

2016 Presidential Vote		
Donald Trump	204,129	(67%)
Hillary Clinton	82,498	(27%)
Gary Johnson	14,897	(5%)

Cook Partisan Voting Index: R+18

Muncie became famous as the "Middletown" where sociologists Robert and Helen Lynd lived and did research for their landmark report in 1924 and 1925. The Lynds were attracted to Muncie because it was typical of "every small city from Maine to California," as *Life* magazine put it. But it wasn't exactly. Muncie was a factory town in a country still almost 50 percent rural in the 1920s, and it was almost entirely Protestant and Northern in a country that was one-fifth Catholic and one-third Southern. Muncie was more typical in that it was culturally homogeneous but economically riven. In the 1920s, when General Motors opened a plant in Muncie, the city celebrated its common values and was loath to admit its economic disparities. In the 1930s, those differences were exposed when Muncie, like much of the industrial Midwest, was unionized, a process that sometimes led to violent clashes. Workers who were joining CIO unions and voting for Democrats fiercely opposed the business elite - local bankers, merchants, GM executives and the Ball family's glass company. Partisan politics took on the sharp, bitter tone of a struggle for wealth between two rival classes whose claims seemed irreconcilable.

Today, the region has remained a story of both sides of the American economic coin. "Local auto parts plants were in many ways the engine that drove the Muncie economy. At its peak in the 1950s, Warner Gear (later BorgWarner Automotive) employed more than 5,000 workers," the Muncie *Star-Press* wrote in a profile of its hometown in 2015. The BorgWarner plant closed in 2009. Earlier, the city was devastated in 2006 by the loss of a General Motors manual transmission plant. But the area regained some of its manufacturing heft with the arrival of a foreign-owned automaker: Honda opened a plant in Greensburg that employed 2,300 workers who annually manufacture 250,000 Civic compact cars. The GM plant was unionized; the Honda plant is not. In March 2016, Honda announced that it will shift its SUV production to Greensburg from Guadalajara, Mexico.

There is one constant in Muncie and the surrounding environs: basketball. It is the civic religion here. Most of the nation's largest high school gyms are in Indiana. The Fieldhouse, in New Castle, near the Indiana Basketball Hall of Fame, is the largest of them all. Tiny Milan High School's 1954 state championship victory over Muncie Central was the basis for the 1986 movie *Hoosiers*.

The 6th Congressional District of Indiana covers most of the east-central and southeast parts of the state. It includes Muncie in the north as well as Richmond, founded by a major branch of American Quakers and home to their Earlham College. Batesville, to the south, is the site of the Batesville Casket Co., which makes the coffins for U.S. military personnel who die in the line of duty. In 2016, the Republican presidential ticket got 67 percent of the district vote, its best showing in the state and a big increase from the 55 percent for John McCain in 2008. The fact that vice presidential nominee Mike Pence represented the 6th from 2001 until 2013 was a boost for Donald Trump in this area.

SEVENTH DISTRICT

Andre Carson (D)

Elected 2008, 5th full term; b. Oct 16, 1974, Indianapolis; Concordia University (WI), B.S.; Indiana Wesleyan University, M.A.; Islam (Muslim); Married (Mariama Carson); 1 child.

Elected Office: Indianapolis/Marion City-County Council, 2007-2008.

Professional Career: Investigator, IN State Excise Police, 1996-2005; Investigator, IN Department of Homeland Security, 2006-2008.

DC Office: 2135 RHOB 20515, 202-225-4011, Fax: 202-225-5633, carson.house.gov.

State Offices: Indianapolis, 317-283-6516.

Committees: *Permanent Select on Intelligence*. *Transportation & Infrastructure*: Aviation, Railroads, Pipelines & Hazardous Materials.

Group Ratings

	ADA	ACLU	AFL-CIO	LCV	ITI	COC	HAFA	ACU	CFG	FRC
2016	-	94%	-	97%	83%	64%	10%	0%	0%	0%
2015	95%	C	96%	94%	C	45%	C	0%	0%	0%

Almanac Ratings 2015

	Economy	Social	Foreign	Composite
Liberal	98%	100%	87%	95%
Conservative	2%	0%	13%	5%

Key Votes of the 114th Congress

1. Keystone Pipeline	N	5. Puerto Rico Debt	Y	9. Offenses by Aliens	N
2. Trade Deals	N	6. Medical Marijuana	Y	10. Troops in Iraq	N
3. Export-Import Bank	NV	7. Sanctuary Cities	N	11. Homeland Security $$	Y
4. Debt Ceiling Increase	Y	8. Armor-piercing Bullets	N	12. Trade Adjustment aid	Y

Election Results

Election	Name (Party)	Vote (%)		Cand. Spent	Ind. Exp. Support	Ind. Exp. Oppose
2016 General	Andre Carson (D)	158,739	(60%)	$786,070		
	Cat Ping (R)	94,456	(36%)	$3,983,789		
	Drew Thompson (L)	11,475	(4%)			
2016 Primary	Andre Carson (D)	69,995	(86%)			
	Curtis Godfrey (D)	8,306	(10%)			

Prior winning percentages: 2014 (55%), 2012 (63%), 2010 (59%), 2008 (65%), 2008 special (54%)

Democrat André Carson won his seat in a 2008 special election to succeed his grandmother, Julia Carson, who died in office. An occasionally outspoken liberal and active in the Congressional Black Caucus, he has expanded his portfolio to include national security issues as a member of the Intelligence Committee.

As a child, Carson studied religion. Originally interested in the priesthood, he later converted to Islam and became the second Muslim elected to Congress, following Democratic Rep. Keith Ellison of Minnesota. Carson also had an artistic side. He wrote poetry as a young man and performed as a rap artist under the name "Juggernaut." With a career in law enforcement, he got a bachelor's degree in criminal justice management from Concordia University and a master's degree in business management from Indiana Wesleyan. Carson spent nine years as a plainclothes officer of the Indiana Excise Police, which enforces alcohol and tobacco laws. "I loved law enforcement," he told *Esquire* magazine in 2010. "But this job sure beats sitting and waiting for something bad to go down at three in the morning."

He recalled that his political interest began in 1984, at age 10, when he attended the Democratic convention in San Francisco and heard civil rights leader Jesse Jackson speak. Carson said his thinking was transformed by reading *The Autobiography of Malcolm X*, and he attended Louis Farrakhan's Million Man March in 1995. In 2007, at age 32, he won a seat on the Indianapolis City-County Council, his first elected office.

After Julia Carson died in December 2007, her grandson faced significant opposition for the Democratic nomination in the special election to fill the remainder of her term. At the January 2008 Democratic caucus, he won a bare majority with 223 of the 439 votes; state Rep. David Orentlicher, a lawyer and doctor, got 123 votes, and Marion County Treasurer Michael Rodman came in third with 27 votes.

Against Republican state Rep. Jon Elrod, a young lawyer, Carson received extensive assistance from the Democratic Congressional Campaign Committee. He called for withdrawing U.S. troops from Iraq, endorsed tax cuts for working families, and said that companies should have incentives to keep them from sending jobs overseas. He won, 54%-43%. Meanwhile, Carson continued campaigning in the May primary for a full term. Running as the incumbent this time and with an endorsement from presidential candidate Barack Obama, Carson won the primary with 47 percent of the vote to 24 percent for former state Health Commissioner Woodrow Myers. Elrod won the GOP nomination, but he soon withdrew and failed to retain his seat in the state House. Carson has faced minimal opposition since, though his vote percentage in the general election is relatively small compared with most other Black Caucus members.

In the House, his voting record has been mostly liberal. He placed near the center of House Democrats in the *Almanac* vote ratings for 2015 He initially opposed the $700 billion bailout of financial markets in 2008, but switched his position after Obama, then the Democratic presidential nominee, urged him to support it. Carson has been a senior whip on Minority Whip Steny Hoyer's team. In 2017, he became first vice chairman of the Black Caucus. Before the final vote on the health care overhaul in March 2010, he claimed that angry protesters outside the Capitol hurled racial epithets at him and civil-rights icon Rep. John Lewis of Georgia.

His biting rhetoric has sometimes gotten him in trouble. At a town hall meeting in August 2011, Carson said that some members of the tea party movement in Congress would love to see blacks "hanging on a tree." A year later, he caused another uproar on the right when he advised at an Islamic convention: "America will never tap into educational innovation and ingenuity without looking at the model that we have in our madrassas, in our schools, where innovation is encouraged, where the foundation is the Koran." He later clarified his remarks by saying that faith-based schools of all religions were models for public education to follow.

Carson has served on the Transportation and Infrastructure Committee. In 2015, he became the first Muslim to get a seat on the Intelligence Committee, which produced protests from some conservative activists. He won committee approval that year of three amendments to increase the transparency of government efforts to counter violent extremism at home and abroad, calling it "critical that we maintain strong oversight of these programs to protect American privacy and civil rights." He is ranking Democrat on the panel's Emerging Threats Subcommittee.

At a press conference in May 2016, Carson voiced concern about what he called anti-Muslim rhetoric by Republican presidential candidate Donald Trump. "That saying about 'Make America Great Again' is a form of meta-messaging to a certain segment, we're talking about our white brothers and sisters, largely blue collar," he said. Earlier, Carson received a death threat at his office days after Trump called for a ban on Muslims entering the United States.

Indianapolis

Population		**Race and Ethnicity**		**Income**	
Total	742,788	White	55.0%	Median Income	$38,600 (405 out of 435)
Land area	304	Black	29.1%		
Pop/ sq mi	2444.7	Latino	10.6%		
Born in state	68.7%	Asian	2.3%	Under $50,000	61.4%
		Two races	2.4%	$50,000-$99,999	27.3%
Age Groups		Other	0.5%	$100,000-$199,999	9.9%
Under 18	26.0%			$200,000 or more	1.4%
18-34	26.5%	**Education**		Poverty Rate	23.9%
35-64	37.1%	H.S grad or less	49.5%		
Over 64	10.4%	Some college	29.1%	**Health Insurance**	
		College Degree, 4 yr	14.4%	With health insurance coverage	83.2%
Work		Post grad	7.0%		
White Collar	28.9%				
Sales and Service	45.6%	**Military**		**Public Assistance**	
Blue Collar	25.5%	Veteran	7.9%	Cash public assistance income	2.7%
Government	10.5%	Active Duty	0.0%		
				Food stamp/SNAP benefits	20.5%

Voter Turnout			
2015 Total Citizens 18+	506,505	2016 House Turnout as % CVAP	52%
2016 House turnout	264,670	2014 House Turnout as % CVAP	22%

2012 Presidential Vote		
Barack Obama	164,902	(63%)
Mitt Romney	92,674	(35%)

2016 Presidential Vote		
Hillary Clinton	156,046	(58%)
Donald Trump	95,656	(36%)
Gary Johnson	12,689	(5%)

Cook Partisan Voting Index: D+11

Indianapolis, radiating outward from the soldiers and sailors statue in Monument Circle, is precisely at the center of Indiana and is the largest and most dominant city in the state. What residents once disparaged as "Nap Town" has become a thriving metropolis, including downtown. The city is the political and governmental capital, industrial and financial hub, and the intellectual center of Indiana as well. It is symmetrically laid out: Just to the west of the circle is the state Capitol, to the north is the American Legion headquarters, to the east is the City-County building, and to the south is the Circle Centre mall and Lucas Oil Stadium, home of the NFL's Indianapolis Colts.

Farther out are some classic and some new Indianapolis institutions: the Indiana University Medical Center, the Eiteljorg Museum of American Indians and Western Art; Bankers Life Fieldhouse, where the NBA's Indiana Pacers play; and the headquarters of the National Collegiate Athletic Association. Indianapolis has fostered its niche as the nation's amateur sports capital, especially for basketball, and it is a popular place for religious conventions. The convention center generated $4.5 billion income in 2015. Home to the iconic Indianapolis 500, the motorsports industry is a prominent business for the state.

Its strong service economy helped Indianapolis do better than most cities during the recession, with its downtown experiencing a multibillion-dollar construction boom. Pharmaceutical giant Eli Lilly & Co. spent $400 million to expand its insulin manufacturing operations, including two insulin cartridge filling lines. After reports in 2012 that the Indianapolis Airport's dwindling number of nonstop flights had hurt the local convention business, the airport highlighted nonstop service to 37 airports.

Indiana's 7th Congressional District takes in most of Indianapolis. The more prosperous northern edge of the city is in the 5th District. In decades past, Indianapolis had robust political competition in local and national races. Republicans held the mayor's office from 1967, when Richard Lugar won it, until 1999. Lugar, who later became a six-term senator, expanded Indianapolis' city limits to include all of Marion County in a new entity called UniGov, which made it a solidly Republican constituency. More recently, affluent young people have been moving to counties farther out. The median income has dropped in Marion County, especially in the 7th. It has become solidly Democratic, though its population remains 66 percent white. In 2016, Hillary Clinton won both the District and county, 58%-36%. In 2012, Barack Obama took the 7th, 63%-35%, and he won Marion, 60%-38%. The District has the largest minority population in the state, but it remains 57 percent white. It is one of only two Democratic districts in the state; the other is the Gary-based 1st.

EIGHTH DISTRICT

Larry Bucshon (R)

Elected 2010, 4th term; b. May 31, 1962, Taylorsville, IL; University of Illinois - Urbana, B.S.; University of Illinois Medical School - Chicago, M.D.; Lutheran; Married (Kathryn Bucshon); 4 children.

Military Career: U.S. Navy Reserve, 1989-1998.

Professional Career: Practicing cardiothoracic surgeon, 1995-1998; Ohio Valley HeartCare, 1998-2010, President, 2003-2010; Chief & Medical Director, St. Mary's Hospital.

DC Office: 1005 LHOB 20515, 202-225-4636, Fax: 202-225-3284, bucshon.house.gov.

State Offices: Evansville, 812-465-6484; Jasper, 812-482-4255; Terra Haute, 812-232-0523; Vincenness, 855-519-1629.

Committees: *Energy & Commerce*: Digital Commerce & Consumer Protection, Energy, Health.

Group Ratings

	ADA	ACLU	AFL-CIO	LCV	ITI	COC	HAFA	ACU	CFG	FRC
2016	-	5%	-	5%	100%	100%	56%	72%	57%	100%
2015	0%	C	21%	3%	C	90%	C	71%	55%	100%

Almanac Ratings 2015

	Economy	Social	Foreign	Composite
Liberal	7%	4%	4%	5%
Conservative	93%	96%	96%	95%

Key Votes of the 114th Congress

1. Keystone Pipeline	Y	5. Puerto Rico Debt	Y	9. Offenses by Aliens	Y
2. Trade Deals	Y	6. Medical Marijuana	N	10. Troops in Iraq	N
3. Export-Import Bank	Y	7. Sanctuary Cities	Y	11. Homeland Security $$	N
4. Debt Ceiling Increase	N	8. Armor-piercing Bullets	Y	12. Trade Adjustment aid	Y

Election Results

Election	Name (Party)	Vote (%)		Cand. Spent	Ind. Exp. Support	Ind. Exp. Oppose
2016 General	Larry Bucshon (R)	187,702	(64%)	$564,319		
	Ron Drake (D)	119,245	(41%)	$8,591		
	Andrew Horning (L)	13,655	(5%)			
2016 Primary	Larry Bucshon (R)	72,507	(65%)			
	Richard Moss (R)	38,974	(35%)			

Prior winning percentages: 2014 (60%), 2012 (53%), 2010 (58%)

Republican Larry Bucshon, elected in 2010, is among the physicians from his party who have been outspoken critics of Democrats on health care. On the Energy and Commerce Committee, he has crafted GOP alternatives and occasionally sought opportunities for bipartisan consensus.

Bucshon was raised in the rural town of Kincaid, Illinois. His mother was a nurse and his father a coal miner; both tended to vote Democratic. He developed his own ideology as an undergraduate at the University of Illinois, and his rightward shift solidified when he became enamored of President Ronald Reagan. In high school, Bucshon decided on a career in medicine, inspired by the surgeons he met at the hospital where his mother worked. After college, he enrolled in medical school at the University of Illinois at Chicago. He completed a residency at the Medical College of Wisconsin, where he specialized in cardiothoracic surgery. Bucshon enlisted with the Naval Reserve, serving for nearly a decade. After three years in private practice in Wichita, Kansas, he joined Ohio Valley HeartCare, a large cardiology and cardiovascular surgery practice in Evansville. In 2003, he became its president.

With a long-time interest in Congress, Bucshon ran when Democratic Rep. Brad Ellsworth sought a Senate seat in 2010. Helped by the National Republican Congressional Committee, Bucshon prevailed over seven other candidates in the May GOP primary, edging out tea party-backed Kristi Risk, 33%-29%. In the general, he faced state Rep. Trent Van Haaften, who fit the centrist mold of Ellsworth. Van Haaften was a prosecutor in rural Posey County, where he was praised for his work fighting a regional methamphetamine epidemic. In the campaign, he emphasized his law-and-order background, while Bucshon campaigned on curbing spending and repeal of the Democrats' health care overhaul. Democrats accused Bucshon of favoring the privatization of Social Security. Bucshon raised and spent $1.1 million, compared with $762,000 for Van Haaften. He won 57%-38%.

Bucshon boasted at the end of his first term that he had voted to cut more than $1.8 trillion "in unnecessary, frivolous spending." He actively opposed the excise tax on medical device equipment, as well as a Medicare cost-control board included in the health care law. "I have been a practicing physician for over 15 years, and I don't think I have seen anything potentially more detrimental to seniors' health care than the Independent Payment Advisory Board," he said. But conservatives criticized his backing the August 2011 increase in the debt limit, unlike other Indiana GOP freshmen. He also broke with them by opposing the Republican Study Committee's fiscal 2012 budget proposal that cut more in spending than House Budget Committee Chairman Paul Ryan's blueprint.

On the Energy and Commerce Committee, he joined in bipartisan support for the 2015 law establishing a permanent fix in Medicare reimbursement of doctor fees. Bucshon cited his cooperation with another doctor, Democratic Rep. Ami Bera of California, on a successful amendment to repeal a complex billing procedure imposed by Medicare officials. With committee Democrats Frank Pallone of New Jersey and Joe Kennedy of Massachusetts, Bucshon filed a bipartisan bill to encourage monitoring programs for prescription drug addiction.

In May 2016, he spearheaded a bipartisan effort to oppose an Obama administration experiment to reduce Medicare funding to doctors who prescribe drugs; the proposal was abandoned later that year. Also in 2016, Bucshon worked with Republican leaders on their priority legislation to treat opioid addiction. They named him to a special panel that investigated the medical procedures and business practices of Planned Parenthood. On Energy and Commerce, he worked on energy legislation to promote his district's large coal resources, and telecommunications topics such as expanded broadband access.

In 2012, tea party candidate Risk mounted another primary challenge to Bucshon but could not come close to competing financially, and the incumbent won 58%-42%. His Democratic challenger in the general election was broadcaster and former state Rep. Dave Crooks, who ran an effective campaign and spent a respectable $980,000. He sought to portray Bucshon as out of touch with regular voters and touted his own culturally and fiscally conservative views. *The Tribune-Star* of Terre Haute endorsed Crooks, saying Bucshon hadn't shown enough willingness to compromise with Democrats on key issues. Bucshon castigated Crooks for being in lockstep with President Barack Obama. He spent $1.4 million and got help from conservative super PACs that ran ads on his behalf in the campaign's closing weeks, eventually notching a solid but hardly overwhelming 53%-43% victory. Since then, Bucshon has faced weakly financed Democratic challengers and he has become entrenched in a district that previously elected a Democrat.

Southwest Indiana: Evansville, Terre Haute

Population		**Race and Ethnicity**		**Income**	
Total	722,271	White	90.8%	Median Income	$46,641 (313 out of 435)
Land area	7,255	Black	4.0%		
Pop/ sq mi	99.5	Latino	2.3%		
Born in state	76.0%	Asian	0.9%	Under $50,000	53.1%
		Two races	1.7%	$50,000-$99,999	31.9%
Age Groups		Other	0.3%	$100,000-$199,999	12.9%
Under 18	22.7%			$200,000 or more	2.0%
18-34	22.2%	**Education**		Poverty Rate	14.8%
35-64	39.5%	H.S grad or less	50.2%		
Over 64	15.6%	Some college	30.6%	**Health Insurance**	
		College Degree, 4 yr	12.3%	With health insurance coverage	88.1%
Work		Post grad	6.9%		
White Collar	29.2%				
Sales and Service	40.2%	**Military**		**Public Assistance**	
Blue Collar	30.6%	Veteran	9.3%	Cash public assistance income	1.9%
Government	11.1%	Active Duty	0.0%		
				Food stamp/SNAP benefits	12.0%

Voter Turnout			
2015 Total Citizens 18+	550,463	2016 House Turnout as % CVAP	54%
2016 House turnout	294,713	2014 House Turnout as % CVAP	31%

2012 Presidential Vote		
Mitt Romney	169,317	(58%)
Barack Obama	114,907	(40%)

2016 Presidential Vote		
Donald Trump	194,208	(64%)
Hillary Clinton	92,844	(31%)
Gary Johnson	13,569	(5%)

Cook Partisan Voting Index: R+15

"Evansville," wrote John Bartlow Martin in 1947, "is the capital of a tri-state area comprising the neglected tag ends of Indiana, Kentucky, and Illinois." It was a factory town then, making car parts and refrigerators, drawing workers from Kentucky, Tennessee and the picturesque but not very fertile hills of Southern Indiana.

Evansville has become a headquarters for midsized companies that offer good-paying, skilled jobs. Car parts still get made here, though it is auto assembly that helps anchor the local manufacturing economy. Toyota in 1998 opened a plant in nearby Princeton that builds SUVs and minivans. With its expansion in 2016, the plant employed more than 5,000 workers. The recovery of the auto industry helped Evansville weather the recession. But the local Whirlpool refrigerator production plant closed in 2010, followed by the shuttering of its refrigeration product design center. Much of that production shifted to Mexico. Only a few years earlier, Whirlpool employed about 1,500 in the Evansville area. In 2016, Alcoa closed its aluminum smelter, with a loss of 600 jobs.

In Vanderburgh County, Evansville is one of two major population centers of the 8th Congressional District, which covers Southwest Indiana. The other, in Vigo County, is Terre Haute, an old manufacturing town and the boyhood home of socialist Eugene Debs. It hosts a maximum-security penitentiary, which includes the only federal death chamber; Oklahoma City bomber Timothy McVeigh was executed there in 2001. The district also takes in Vincennes, now a small town on the banks of the Wabash River but important in Indiana history. Downstream is New Harmony, an early utopian community established by Welsh philanthropist and visionary Robert Owen.

Southern Indiana is ancestrally Democratic, just as northern Indiana is ancestrally Republican. The southern counties were hostile to the Union during the Civil War, and then in New Deal times workers in Evansville moved toward the Democrats. For decades, the result was a very close political balance, and this district was known as the "Bloody 8th" for its tight congressional races. At one point in the 1970s, it sent four different members to the House in four successive elections. In 1984, the state certified the Republican the winner by exactly 34 votes. The Democratic majority in the House investigated and overturned the result, however, in a fight that left many Republican bitter. Since then, the district has flipped between the two parties. As with other rural and blue-collar areas, however, the trend in presidential politics has been away from Democrats. In 2008, John McCain led Barack Obama, 51%-48%. In 2016, Donald Trump swept Hillary Clinton, 64%-31%. Before the May primary, Trump had a rally in Evansville that drew 12,000 supporters. The appeal of Trump showed the challenge facing national Democrats.

NINTH DISTRICT

Trey Hollingsworth (R)

Elected 2016, 1st term; b. Sep 12, 1983, Clinton, TN; University of Pennsylvania, B.S., 2004; Georgetown University (DC), M.PP, 2014; Christian Church; Married (Kelly Hollingsworth).

Professional Career: Small Business Owner.

DC Office: 1641 LHOB 20515, 202-225-5315, Fax: 202-226-6866, hollingsworth.house.gov.

State Offices: Greenwood, 317-851-8710; Jeffersonville, 812-288-3999.

Committees: *Financial Services*: Capital Markets, Securities & Investment, Monetary Policy & Trade, Oversight & Investigations.

Election Results

Election	Name (Party)	Vote	(%)	Cand. Spent	Ind. Exp. Support	Ind. Exp. Oppose
2016 General	Trey Hollingsworth (R)	174,791	(54%)	$3,496,198	$454,340	$2,584,893
	Shelli Yoder (D)	127,869	(40%)	$1,412,705		$1,839,183
	Russell Brooksbank (L)	17,425	(5%)			
2016 Primary	Trey Hollingsworth (R)	40,682	(34%)			
	Erin Houchin (R)	30,298	(25%)			
	Greg Zoeller (R)	26,554	(22%)			
	Brent Waltz (R)	15,750	(13%)			
	Robert Hall (R)	8,020	(7%)			

Republican Trey Hollingsworth was elected in 2016 to the seat that had been held by Todd Young, who ran successfully for an open Senate seat. The contest became more competitive than had been expected, chiefly because of Hollingsworth's ample self-financing and his background of having resided in Tennessee until the previous year. Ultimately, Hollingsworth won handily. His biggest challenge may be to solidify his support among local Republicans and avoid a serious primary challenge.

Hollingsworth was raised in Clinton, Tennessee, a small city near Knoxville, which is about 230 miles from Indiana. At the age of 15, he made news in a *Washington Post* article on his experience at an entrepreneurship camp in Oregon titled, "How I got rich on my summer vacation." He graduated from the University of Pennsylvania in 2004, with a degree in real estate. A decade later, he got a master's degree in public policy from Georgetown University. In the meantime, Hollingsworth became a managing partner and majority owner of his family's fast-growing Hollingsworth Capital Partners, which refurbished vacant factories - including some in Indiana. In 2008, he and a group of partners opened Alexin, an aluminum casting plant in Indiana. According to the *Indianapolis Star*, his company had filed legal papers in five other states that obligated him to live outside of Indiana to represent his business interests. His father earlier considered running for governor of Tennessee, as a Democrat.

In September 2015, after Young had announced his campaign for the Senate, Hollingsworth moved from Tennessee to Jeffersonville Indiana. A month later, he announced his campaign for the open seat.

In the hotly contested five-candidate primary, he spent heavily on campaign ads that touted his business acumen and outsider status. His challengers included Indiana Attorney General Greg Zoeller, and state Sens. Erin Houchin and Brent Waltz. "Mr. Hollingsworth just moved here from Tennessee in the fall of last year trying to buy a congressional seat," Houchin said. Zoeller, who started the contest as the best-known candidate, called Hollingsworth a "political scam artist." Hollingsworth won the primary with 35 percent of the vote, to 25 percent for Houchin and 22 percent for Zoeller.

Shelli Yoder easily won the Democratic nomination. An Indiana native and a former Miss Indiana, who coincidentally lived in Tennessee for 10 years, she returned to her home state in 2009 to teach at Indiana University's Kelley School of Business. In 2012, she challenged Young and lost, 55%-45%. In 2014, she was elected to the Monroe County council. According to the *Star*, which described her as "the quintessential Hoosier," Yoder attacked Hollingsworth for trying to buy the seat with "generic GOP talking points rather than an understanding of Southern Indiana." Hollingsworth attacked Yoder for supporting Hillary Clinton and her policies.

Hollingsworth spent nearly $3.6 million for his campaign, of which $3.1 million was self-financed. His campaign report disclosed that his net worth exceeded $50 million. He also had more than $2.5 million in support from national Republican committees and a Super PAC. Yoder spent $1.4 million and had $1 million support from the Democratic Congressional Campaign Committee. Hollingsworth prevailed, 54%-41%, with his anti-establishment message and business credentials. He won each of the 13 counties except for Monroe, which was Yoder's base and the Democratic stronghold.

In the House, Hollingsworth got a seat on the Financial Services Committee.

South-Central Indiana: Bloomington, Indianapolis Suburbs, Louisville Suburbs

Population		**Race and Ethnicity**		**Income**	
Total	734,273	White	90.0%	Median Income	$50,717 (245 out of 435)
Land area	4,487	Black	2.7%		
Pop/ sq mi	163.7	Latino	3.2%		
Born in state	64.5%	Asian	2.0%	Under $50,000	49.2%
Age Groups		Two races	1.8%	$50,000-$99,999	32.7%
Under 18	22.3%	Other	0.3%	$100,000-$199,999	15.4%
18-34	24.8%	**Education**		$200,000 or more	2.6%
35-64	38.9%	H.S grad or less	46.4%	Poverty Rate	14.7%
Over 64	14.0%	Some college	29.0%	**Health Insurance**	
Work		College Degree, 4 yr	15.0%	With health insurance coverage	88.5%
White Collar	33.9%	Post grad	9.6%		
Sales and Service	40.6%	**Military**		**Public Assistance**	
Blue Collar	25.5%	Veteran	9.1%	Cash public assistance income	1.6%
Government	12.8%	Active Duty	0.2%		
				Food stamp/SNAP benefits	10.6%

Voter Turnout			
2015 Total Citizens 18+	553,508	2016 House Turnout as % CVAP	58%
2016 House turnout	322,843	2014 House Turnout as % CVAP	30%

2012 Presidential Vote		
Mitt Romney	173,433	(57%)
Barack Obama	123,436	(41%)

2016 Presidential Vote		
Donald Trump	198,108	(60%)
Hillary Clinton	110,837	(34%)
Gary Johnson	15,534	(5%)

Cook Partisan Voting Index: R+13

The immense Ohio River is the largest tributary of the Mississippi. In Southern Indiana, it runs along the Indiana-Kentucky border and is an artery of commerce. Utilitarian barges have replaced the old steamers, except for riverboat casinos. Along the river are towns like Corydon, which was the state capital from 1816 to 1825. Charlestown was settled on a hill two miles from the Ohio in 1808. An early visitor to Charlestown was Jonathan Jennings, who moved to the area from Pennsylvania to launch his political career and became Indiana's first governor in 1816. Salem was the home of John Milton Hay, personal secretary to President Abraham Lincoln and later secretary of State in the William McKinley and Theodore Roosevelt administrations. In December 2016, the new $2.3 billion Lewis and Clark Bridge opened on the Ohio River between Jeffersonville and Prospect, Kentucky. In rural Scott County, where many residents continue to live in poverty, Gov. Mike Pence in March 2015 declared a health emergency following an HIV outbreak that was linked to the use of contaminated syringes. He authorized a short-term exchange program for clean needles.

In Indiana's 9th Congressional District, the largest city is Bloomington, where Indiana University and its 48,000 students are based. Since 2015, the university has made plans for a new health campus, hospital and regional academic health center. Bloomington, which is rated second in the Milken Institute's index of best-performing cities for high-tech employment, has developed a technology park near the University campus. In November 2016, officials announced that TASUS Corp., which uses advanced robotics to manufacture automobile components, made a major investment in the development of a design and technical center. Monroe County-based Bloomington is a Democratic stronghold. But its vote usually is overwhelmed - especially by nearby Johnson and Morgan counties, which are growing Republican bastions in the suburbs of Indianapolis. The Louisville, Kentucky, suburbs in Clark and Floyd counties have trended Republican.

For 34 years, the 9th District was represented by Democrat Lee Hamilton, who chaired the House Foreign Affairs and Intelligence committees. Following his retirement in 1998, it frequently switched party control. But like other parts of Indiana, the 9th has become comfortably Republican. The Republican presidential vote increased from 53 percent for John McCain in 2008 to 60 percent for Donald Trump. In 2016, Monroe County voted for Hillary Clinton, 59%-36%. It was the only Indiana county south of Indianapolis that voted Democratic for president.

★ IOWA ★

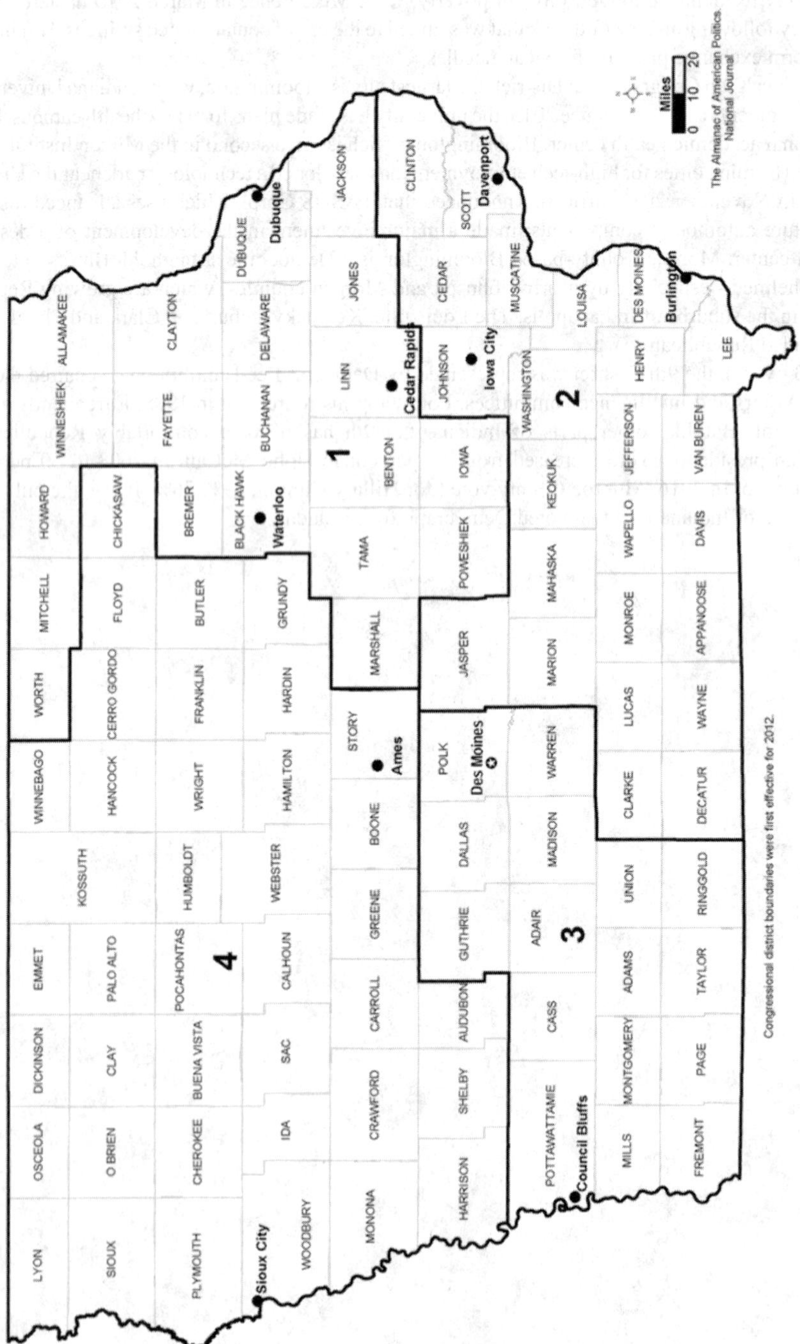

Miles
0 10 20
The Almanac of American Politics
National Journal
1
2
3
4
Dubuque
Davenport
Burlington
Cedar Rapids
Iowa City
Waterloo
Ames
Des Moines
Council Bluffs
Sioux City
JACKSON
CLINTON
SCOTT
DUBUQUE
JONES
CEDAR
MUSCATINE
DES MOINES
LOUISA
ALLAMAKEE
CLAYTON
DELAWARE
LINN
JOHNSON
WASHINGTON
HENRY
LEE
WINNESHIEK
FAYETTE
BUCHANAN
BENTON
IOWA
KEOKUK
JEFFERSON
VAN BUREN
HOWARD
CHICKASAW
BREMER
BLACK HAWK
TAMA
POWESHIEK
MAHASKA
WAPELLO
DAVIS
MITCHELL
FLOYD
BUTLER
GRUNDY
MARSHALL
JASPER
MARION
MONROE
APPANOOSE
WORTH
CERRO GORDO
FRANKLIN
HARDIN
STORY
POLK
WARREN
LUCAS
WAYNE
WINNEBAGO
HANCOCK
WRIGHT
HAMILTON
BOONE
DALLAS
MADISON
CLARKE
DECATUR
KOSSUTH
HUMBOLDT
WEBSTER
GREENE
GUTHRIE
ADAIR
UNION
RINGGOLD
EMMET
PALO ALTO
POCAHONTAS
CALHOUN
CARROLL
AUDUBON
CASS
ADAMS
TAYLOR
DICKINSON
CLAY
BUENA VISTA
SAC
CRAWFORD
SHELBY
MONTGOMERY
PAGE
OSCEOLA
O BRIEN
CHEROKEE
IDA
HARRISON
POTTAWATTAMIE
MILLS
FREMONT
LYON
SIOUX
PLYMOUTH
WOODBURY
MONONA
Congressional district boundaries were first effective for 2012.

Iowa holds a special place in American politics thanks to its presidential caucuses, preceded by months of retail politicking on the snowy prairie. In recent decades, the state has been hotly contested between the two parties. But in 2016, it was transformed from the state that launched Barack Obama into the White House to one that in the general election went sharply for Donald Trump.

The early settlers who founded Iowa could hardly have imagined that their state would one day have more people living in the big city than the small towns. In the 1840s, young Yankee and German farmers streamed across the Mississippi River into the fertile rolling land beyond. Wagon trains headed to the Oregon Trail, and the thousands of Mormons mustered by Brigham Young traveled across Iowa's rolling hills to Council Bluffs on the Missouri River, and then to points further west. Iowa was young and proud of its hundreds of schools and dozens of colleges, sending more than its share of young men back East to fight for the Union. After the Civil War, Iowans built a solid civilization based on farming, farm-machine manufacturing and meat processing that resisted the blandishments of William Jennings Bryan's populism and cheap money. Politically, Iowa became one of the most solidly Republican states in the nation.

Starting around 1900, Iowa's model society stopped attracting new transplants. "If you build it, they will come" was the theme from the movie *Field of Dreams*, set in Iowa. Yet during much of the 20th century, very few people came. The region's commercial and financial center remained the railroad hub of Chicago; Iowa's economy failed to diversify and develop the dense manufacturing base of the Great Lakes states, and its young people started to move east or west to make their fortunes. The state's population, which increased from 674,000 in 1860 to 2.2 million in 1900, did not reach 3 million until 2008. In 1900, Iowa had 11 congressional districts and California had seven. Today, Iowa has four and California 53.

Iowa's great economic achievement has been the development of ever more productive, but also less labor-intensive, agriculture. According to the U.S. Department of Agriculture, Iowa produces one-eleventh of the nation's food supply. Iowa ranks first in the nation in corn, soybean, pork and egg production, and is home to 36 of the largest 100 food processors and manufacturers. Quaker Oats operates the nation's largest cereal mill in the state. Lower prices for commodities such as corn and soybeans have sent the price of farmland dropping by 17 percent since 2013 – the first time farmland prices have fallen for three straight years since the bleak days of the 1980s, when the sector was in crisis. Still, land prices remain well above their 2004 level. That was before the boom in ethanol – an alternative fuel well suited to production in Iowa -- gathered steam.

Politicians in Iowa and elsewhere promoted ethanol-blended gasoline, arguing that it could help address global warming and boost rural economies. In 1998, Republican Sen. Charles Grassley got a tax credit for ethanol extended, and in 2007, a law required a steady increase over time in the use of renewable fuels. Iowa's ethanol industry, the nation's largest, created high-skill positions, and industry leaders and the state's politicians have aggressively guarded federal legislation that benefits the sector (often prompting presidential candidates stumping ahead of the caucuses to back ethanol as well). But amid national opposition by both fiscal conservatives, who see ethanol as a costly and unnecessary additive, and environmentalists, who have poked some holes in the sector's green bona fides, there are signs that ethanol may have peaked. Obama's Environmental Protection Agency proposed slowing the increase in the amount of ethanol in the nation's gasoline supply, and Trump's heads of EPA and the Energy Department are both ethanol skeptics.

The next big thing for Iowa – plainly visible from many rural highways -- is wind energy. Already, wind whipping off the plains supplies almost one-third of Iowa's electricity generation – more than any other state. Quietly, mega-rich investor Warren Buffett's Berkshire Hathaway has spent more than $17 billion on renewable energy since 2004, and he's promised to double that investment in the coming years, including a 2,000-megawatt wind complex in Iowa, *Fortune* reported. As the magazine put it, "Iowa is the Saudi Arabia of wind." The growth in wind energy has, in turn, helped lure data centers that need cheap energy, including facilities for Facebook, Google and Microsoft.

Indeed, while most Americans' mental image of Iowa involves farming, the reality is that agriculture accounts for just 7 percent of the state's economy – well behind manufacturing at 19 percent, including such major employers as John Deere (admittedly agriculture-related) and Pella. Mexican immigrants have moved to smaller cities with meatpacking plants; the state's population is now 8 percent Hispanic. Jobs and small-town life attracted Bosnians and Liberians as well as Congolese, Sudanese and Somali refugees. But Iowa is still a mostly white state – 85 percent – and just 3 percent black and 2 percent Asian. Iowa also ranks among the top 10 states for the size of its 65-and-over population. Iowa lost far fewer jobs in the 2007-09 recession than in the 1980s. Unemployment reached just 6.6 percent in mid-2009 – well below the 10 percent national peak -- and it remained a bit below the national average by late 2016 at 3.8 percent. The state's median income, meanwhile, sits about $3,000 above the national average.

After a stretch of population shrinkage due to farmland woes in the 1980s – Iowa's population shrunk by 4.7 percent between 1980 and 1990, down to the 1960 level – there has been a modest rebound. Iowa has grown by about 3 percent since the 2010 Census -- the longest run of sustained population growth in the state since 1900. Those gains have occurred almost entirely in metropolitan areas; 55 percent of Iowa's population today is concentrated in just 10 of the state's 99 counties. That change is evident around Des Moines, where cornfields are giving way to exurban development. West of the capital city, Clive, Johnston, Waukee and West Des Moines have seen double-digit population growth since 2010. To the north, Ankeny, Altoona and Bondurant have been booming. The state's two major college towns, Iowa City (University of Iowa) and Ames (Iowa State) are also seeing significant population gains. Impeding growth in many rural areas of the state is insufficient high-speed internet that can support multiple devices or run a business.

Iowa has its distinctive political rituals, none more famous than its first-in-the-nation presidential caucuses. One, two, even three years beforehand, White House hopefuls journey to the Iowa State Fair, held every August on the east side of Des Moines, to shake hands, eat a pork chop on a stick, and marvel at the famed butter cow sculpted out of 600 pounds of churned whole milk. Voter turnout levels tend to be among the nation's highest.

For much of the 20th century, Iowa was a culturally and politically counter-cyclical state, headed in the opposite direction of the rest of the nation - determinedly and with confidence in its own chipper rectitude. In the industrial New Deal era, it stayed mostly agricultural and Republican, even as Davenport and Des Moines radio announcer Ronald Reagan became an enthusiastic Roosevelt Democrat before heading to Hollywood. In the 1980s, when Reagan, by then a conservative Republican, was president and Iowa's economy was hit hard, anxiety became the dominant note of Iowa's politics, as voters sought protection from the vagaries of the market. In the 1988 caucuses, Iowa Republicans voted against Reagan's vice president, George H.W. Bush (despite Bush's victory over Reagan in the caucuses eight years earlier), while Iowa Democrats backed populist Dick Gephardt. That fall, Iowa gave Democratic presidential nominee Michael Dukakis his second highest vote percentage of any state. Since then, Iowa and the nation have converged. The state voted twice for Democrat Bill Clinton, for Democrat Al Gore by just 4,144 votes in 2000, and for Republican George W. Bush by 10,059 votes in 2004. Iowa gave Democrat Obama a critical boost in its 2008 caucuses and then gave him its Electoral College votes in 2008 and 2012.

On the state level, Iowans can get comfortable with their elected officials. The state voted for Republican Terry Branstad in 2010 and 2014 just as it had in 1982, 1986, 1990 and 1994, making him the longest-serving governor in the country's history. Democrat Tom Miller is currently serving his ninth term as the state's attorney general, while Michael Fitzgerald, the Democratic state treasurer, has been on the job since 1983. Republicans won majorities in the legislature in the 1990s, lost them in 2004, and regained a state House majority in 2010. The state Senate remained in Democratic hands until the 2016 election.

Iowa's political leanings can confound national expectations. To a greater extent than other states, Iowa has a dovish, isolationist streak, and it is keenly aware of the value of international trade. The Iowa delegation voted for the 1993 North American Free Trade Agreement, for the 1999 normalization of trade relations with China (Mexicans eat lots of corn and the Chinese like pork), and the 2015 measure to give Trade Promotion Authority to Obama. In April 2009, well before same-sex marriage had become more mainstream, the state Supreme Court unanimously ruled that Iowa's limitation of marriage to opposite-sex couples violated the state constitution. The state's high court took another liberal stand in 2015, unanimously striking down a rule by the Iowa Board of Medicine that would have prohibited Iowa doctors from using telemedicine to provide abortion-inducing drugs to rural women. Branstad's second go-round as governor, prior to being nominated as the U.S. ambassador to China in 2017, reflected a mix of conservative principles leavened by pragmatism, particularly when he went further in accepting more aspects of the Affordable Care Act than most of his fellow Republican governors did.

The 2016 presidential election produced profound changes in Iowa's electoral map. Though Iowa had been a general-election battleground for several cycles running, the state received dwindling attention from the candidates as the campaign progressed once it became clear that Trump – on his way to outperforming past Republican nominees among older, white, rural voters – would do well. : In the end, a state that backed Obama by six points in 2012 went for Trump by almost 10. No fewer than 31 counties -- almost one of every three -- shifted from Obama to Trump. The Clinton collapse was especially severe in eastern Iowa, where every county touching the Mississippi River voted for Obama, yet all but one switched to Trump. (Trump came within about 1,300 votes of winning the remaining river county, Scott, which includes Davenport.) The swing in margins were often huge: Jackson County shifted 37 points between 2012 and 2016; in Lee County, the swing was 32, in Clinton County it was 28, and in Muscatine County it was 22. The GOP was also able to take control of the state Senate, which had been controlled for years, though narrowly, by Democrats. Suddenly, Iowa, a disproportionately white, rural, older state, looked a lot less like a presidential battleground than it did just a few years earlier.

Population		Race and Ethnicity		Income	
Total	3,093,526	White	87.4%	Median Income	$53,183 (24 out of 50)
Land area	55,857	Black	3.1%		
Pop/ sq mi	55.4	Latino	5.4%	Under $50,000	46.8%
Born in state	71.4%	Asian	2.0%	$50,000-$99,999	33.7%
Age Groups		Two races	1.6%	$100,000-$199,999	16.2%
Under 18	23.5%	Other	0.5%	$200,000 or more	3.2%
18-34	22.9%	**Education**		Poverty Rate	12.5%
35-64	38.2%	H.S grad or less	40.7%	**Health Insurance**	
Over 64	15.6%	Some college	32.6%	With health insurance coverage	92.7%
Work		College Degree, 4 yr	18.2%		
White Collar	34.5%	Post grad	8.5%	**Public Assistance**	
Sales and Service	39.9%	**Military**		Cash public assistance income	2.4%
Blue Collar	25.6%	Veteran	8.9%		
Government	13.6%	Active Duty	0.1%	Food stamp/SNAP benefits	11.7%

Voter Turnout			
2015 Total Citizens 18+	2,285,126	2016 Pres Turnout as % CVAP	69%
2016 Pres Votes	1,566,031	2012 Pres Turnout as % CVAP	71%

Legislature	
Senate:	20D, 29R, 1I
House:	41D, 59R

Presidential Politics

2016 Democratic Caucus		
Hillary Clinton (D)	70,047	(50%)
Bernie Sanders (D)	69,692	(50%)
2016 Republican Caucus		
Ted Cruz (R)	51,666	(28%)
Donald Trump (R)	45,429	(24%)
Marco Rubio (R)	43,228	(23%)
Ben Carson (R)	17,394	(9%)

2016 Presidential Vote		
Donald Trump (R)	800,983	(51%)
Hillary Clinton (D)	653,669	(42%)
Gary Johnson (L)	59,186	(4%)
Jeb Bush (R)		(3%)
2012 Presidential Vote		
Barack Obama (D)	822,544	(52%)
Mitt Romney (R)	730,617	(46%)

Every four years, in the dead of winter, tens of thousands of Iowans troop to caucuses in nearly 2,000 precincts to begin the formal process of electing a president. The caucuses were scheduled early in the 1972 cycle by liberal Democrats who wanted more leverage for their views, and that year they started George McGovern on his way to the Democratic nomination. But the caucuses have had other, unanticipated consequences. In 1976, Jimmy Carter's chief strategist, Hamilton Jordan, determined that an intensive campaign and a surprise victory could transform a little-known candidate into a national contender. About 50,000 Iowa Democrats caucused and Carter got the boost Jordan anticipated, finishing second to an "uncommitted" slate but winning more votes than any other actual candidate, almost 28 percent. With momentum from Iowa, Carter won the subsequent New Hampshire primary and was on his way to the Democratic nomination. Without the caucuses, Carter might well have just been another former Georgia governor.

Over the next 20 years, the Iowa caucuses were less decisive, but they almost always drew a crowd of White House hopefuls. In 2000, the Iowa caucuses became crucial again for both parties. George W. Bush won the 25,000-strong August 1999 Republican straw poll at Ames, after which Dan Quayle, Lamar Alexander and Elizabeth Dole dropped out, unable to win enough GOP donors who had flocked to Bush. John McCain skipped the straw poll and the caucuses, and staked his candidacy on winning the New Hampshire primary. Bush continued to build his organizational strength and defeated Steve Forbes, 41%-31%. On the Democratic side, the race was between Al Gore and Bill Bradley. In his first White House run in 1988, Gore skipped what he called the "madness" in "the small state of Iowa." But a decade later, he declared, "I love Iowa." With the help of labor unions, he defeated Bradley 63%-37%.

In 2008, both parties had candidates competing in the Iowa caucuses, but the Democratic contest was more vigorous. Hillary Clinton led in initial polls, but her vote for the 2002 Iraq war resolution and her refusal to apologize for it (as John Edwards had in 2005) hurt her with dovish Iowa Democrats. Republican candidates attracted less attention. Mitt Romney outspent all the other Republicans combined and had the most staffers. But Mike Huckabee quietly built a network of evangelical Christians and home-school parents, and on the stump, the former Baptist minister's folksy manner was appealing. Obama won 38 percent of "delegate strength," a clear victory. His victory in a state with a 3 percent black population was pivotal. Through December 2007, polls showed that he had been splitting the black vote with Clinton in South Carolina and in other states. After Iowa, his support from black voters skyrocketed. Her victory in the New Hampshire primary five days portended a long, close race. In retrospect, it's hard to see how Obama could have become president without winning the Iowa caucuses. The result on the Republican side was also important. Three out of five caucus attendees were evangelical or born-again Christians; and nearly half of them voted for Huckabee, who beat Romney, 34%-25%. Romney's defeat eroded his support in New Hampshire, where voters pay attention to what happens in the caucuses, and enabled McCain to revive his candidacy with a victory there and go on to clinch the GOP nomination on Super Tuesday. The Arizonan was the first Republican presidential nominee to have finished lower than third in Iowa.

In 2012, only Republicans had a contest. Romney eschewed extensive campaigning and didn't participate in the Ames straw poll. Tim Pawlenty, from neighboring Minnesota, regarded Iowa as a must-win state and worked to bring voters to Ames. Michele Bachmann, also from Minnesota, attracted support from Tea Party Republicans. Also campaigning hard, and with determined supporters, was libertarian Ron Paul. Bachmann finished first with 29 percent, and Paul second with 28 percent. Pawlenty, running third with 14 percent, withdrew the next morning. In the final weeks before the caucuses, Romney stepped up his efforts. Turnout was 121,000, just a bit higher than in 2008. Romney and Santorum each won 25 percent of the vote, with Paul coming in third at 21 percent. Bachmann finished sixth, with 6,046 votes, not much more than the 4,823 she had won at the straw poll, and she dropped out the next day. But there was ambiguity about who actually won. The counting is done by the Iowa GOP, not state election officials, and initial reports showed Romney ahead of Santorum by a handful of votes; 16 days later, Santorum was declared the winner by 34 votes, though results from eight precincts were still missing. Some Republicans argued for removing the Iowa caucuses as the first nominating contest, but to no avail. To help fend off that criticism, the 16-member central committee of the Iowa GOP voted unanimously in June 2015 to cancel its straw poll, which had begun in 1979.

The 2016 caucuses set records for both parties. The Republican side marked the electoral debut of Donald Trump. The New York billionaire developer eschewed the painstaking retail organizing of Iowans in favor of large raucous rallies. While his chief rival, Ted Cruz, cultivated local evangelical leaders, Trump imported national evangelical figures such as Jerry Falwell Jr. to campaign with him in the run-up to caucus night. Many of the state's religious conservatives viewed Trump with skepticism from the moment he told the Family Leadership Summit in Ames, "Why do I have to repent or ask for forgiveness, if I am not making mistakes?" Still, pre-caucus polls showed him in a position to win even after he abruptly withdrew from the final GOP presidential debate in a spat with Fox News moderators. Trump held a fundraiser for veterans when the rest of the Republican contenders were on the debate stage. Cruz's investment in organization helped the Texan claim a narrow 28%-24% victory over Trump. Florida Sen. Marco Rubio surged at the end of the campaign and finished a close third with 23 percent. Evangelicals demonstrated their importance in the Republican contest and made up nearly two-thirds of the GOP caucus attendees. A plurality, about a third, backed Cruz. None of the other candidates gained any traction and the winnowing process began as Kentucky Sen. Rand Paul, and former winners Huckabee and Santorum promptly withdrew. After Cruz's victory, Trump charged the Texan "stole" the caucuses and committed "voter fraud," with a misleading direct mail piece. Trump said he was considering legal action against Cruz, but never followed through on his threat. One thing that all Republicans cheered was the record GOP caucus turnout, which Associated Press reported was 186,874.

Clinton began her Iowa caucus campaign with a huge lead in the polls over Vermont Sen. Bernie Sanders. But as the campaign wore on, Sanders gained ground, capitalizing on the traditional dovish views and liberal sentiments of Iowa Democrats. In the closing days of the campaign she received the endorsement of the state's leading newspaper, *The Des Moines Register,* and had Democratic Sens. Tim Kaine of Virginia, Cory Booker of New Jersey and Kristen Gillibrand of New York (all potential Democratic presidential contenders in 2020) stumping Iowa on her behalf. The Democratic caucus was the closest on record, in either party: Clinton edged Sanders in "delegate equivalents" by a razor-thin 49.84%-49.59% margin. Iowa Democrats announced that 171,517 participated in their caucuses. The television network news survey of Democratic caucus-goers found that Sanders won millennial voters by a ratio of six-to-one over Clinton.

The general election in Iowa was also bracing. In a state with a relatively small share of minority voters and college graduates, Trump bested Clinton, 51%-42%. The shift toward Republicans since 2012, when Obama beat Romney 52%-46%, was the largest Democratic drop-off in any battleground state.

Iowa's caucuses have come under repeated attack, but they have survived efforts in both parties to end the state's kick-off role in the presidential nominating contests. As David Yepsen, the longtime dean of Iowa political reporters, wrote in September 2008, "Defending the caucuses is a never-ending battle and a never-ending responsibility of political leaders in both parties in Iowa." Critics of the Iowa caucuses will continue to complain that the process is arcane and, like New Hampshire, the state lacks diversity. But don't expect the caucuses to be displaced from the leadoff spot in 2020.

Congressional Districts

115th Congress Lineup	3R 1D	**114th Congress Lineup**	3R 1D

Iowa's congressional district lines are drawn by the nonpartisan Legislative Services Bureau and then approved by the governor and legislature. But it is not entirely apolitical. The bureau is not supposed to take past voting patterns or a legislator's place of residence into account, and in good Iowa fashion they don't. But the governor and legislators can and do.

Iowa lost a House seat in the reapportionment following the 2010 census. The Legislative Services Bureau's plan that was announced in March 2011 resulted in a competitive contest between two incumbents in a Des Moines-based district. Republican Tom Latham defeated Republican Leonard Boswell, and then retired in 2014. That year, Republicans won two open-seat contests. Despite early hopes, Democrats fell short again in 2016. Given the political geography of Iowa, three of its four districts likely will be competitive in the next redistricting, with the exception of the Republican bastion in the northwest 4th District, now held by Rep. Steve King. With anything close to the current lines, Republican Rep. Rod Blum in the northeast 1st District is at greatest risk, if he survives until 2022.

Governor

Kim Reynolds (R)

Assumed office in 2017, term expires 2019, 1st term; b. Aug. 4, 1959, St. Charles, IA; Northwest Missouri State University, att. 1977-1980; Southeastern Community College, att.; Southwestern Community College, att. 1992-1995; Iowa State Univ., BA 2016.; United Methodist; Married (Kevin); 3 children.

Elected Office: IA Senate 2009-2011; IA Lt. Governor, 2011-2017.

Professional Career: Pharmacist assistant; Staff, Clarke County Treasurer.

Office: 1007 E. Grand Ave., Des Moines, 50319; 515-281-5211; Fax: 515-725-3527; Website: iowa.gov.

Iowa Gov. Kim Reynolds, a Republican, was elevated from lieutenant governor in May 2017 following the confirmation of longtime Gov. Terry Branstad as U.S. ambassador to China. Reynolds became the first woman to serve as Iowa's governor, and she ended a 48-year period in which only four people had held the governor's office.

Reynolds hails from rural Iowa; she was born in Truro and raised in St. Charles. Her father worked at a John Deere factory, as did her grandfather and several other family members. Reynolds' father, unlike other family members, did not become a union member; he also farmed on the side. Reynolds attended Northwest Missouri State University, Southeastern Community College, and Southwestern Community College, but had not accumulated enough credits to graduate. She finally rectified that, only days after Branstad's appointment was announced, when she received a bachelor of liberal studies degree from Iowa State University, with concentrations in political science, business management and communications. The speaker at the commencement ceremony was Sen. Joni Ernst, a longtime political ally of Reynolds who had become Iowa's first female U.S. senator.

Reynolds worked as a pharmacist's assistant, and later as a motor vehicles clerk in the Clarke County treasurer's office. When the incumbent county treasurer declined to seek a new term, Reynolds won the seat and was re-elected three times. In 1998, she sought the GOP nomination for a state Senate special election, but despite securing the support of Branstad, she did not win it. Reynolds faced a personal crisis during this period when she was arrested in 1999 and 2000 for drunk driving. "I needed help, and it just took a really devastating thing for me to realize I couldn't do it on my own," she has said. She has been sober since.

In 2008, Reynolds won a seat in the state Senate, and two years later, Branstad tapped her as his running mate. Having just survived a tough primary against Bob Vander Plaats, a strong social conservative, Branstad faced some pressure to consolidate his party's support by choosing a running mate in Vander Plaats' mold. Instead, he settled on Reynolds, a more conventional economic conservative. Branstad's campaign that year represented a political comeback. He had been elected governor in 1982, 1986, 1990 and 1994. Following a decade out of electoral politics, Branstad returned in 2010 to challenge first-term Democratic Gov. Chet Culver. The Branstad-Reynolds ticket prevailed, 54%-43%, and they won reelection in 2014. In December 2015, Branstad became the longest-serving governor in American history.

As lieutenant governor, Reynolds co-chaired the state advisory council on STEM education (science, technology, engineering and math). She also worked on trade promotion, making trips to China, South Korea, Germany, Brazil, Vietnam, the Philippines and Thailand. She considered but eventually declined a chance to run for the seat vacated by longtime Democratic Sen. Tom Harkin in 2014; Ernst eventually succeeded Harkin. Instead, it was Donald Trump who charted the course for Reynolds' political future when he tapped Branstad as ambassador to China. Branstad – an early backer of Trump whose son Eric had served as state director for the Trump campaign -- had a unique and longstanding relationship with Chinese President Xi Jinping. As governor in 1985, Branstad had hosted the future president, then a young rural official, as part of a delegation that came to Iowa to study agricultural practices. As governor, Branstad also promoted China aggressively as a market for Iowa's agricultural products.

Branstad's nomination took longer to surface in the Senate than others that had been announced much later; a hearing was held only in May 2017. That meant that while Reynolds was widely perceived as the governor-in-waiting, it was Branstad who presided over a landmark legislative session in early 2017. The previous fall, as Trump was winning an easy victory in the state, voters had also thrown out the Democratic majority in the state Senate, effectively removing the party's last defense against a conservative agenda. Branstad signed a roll back of public-employee collective-bargaining rights, rewrote workers' compensation laws, restrained medical malpractice awards and lawsuits against livestock producers, enacted a stand-your-ground law, weakened local jurisdictions' rights to establish gun-free zones, allowed teens age 14 and older to use handguns with adult supervision, put in place a strict voter-ID law, cut the number of days for early voting, banned abortion after 20 weeks and required a 72-hour waiting period in cases where it remains legal. He also signed a bill to legalize medical marijuana, though some longtime advocates said the measure was too limited.

As Reynolds awaited her elevation to the governorship, Democratic Attorney General Tom Miller released an opinion that she would not be able to appoint her own lieutenant governor. Miller said, however, that his office would not challenge Reynolds in court if she decided to assert that right. Reynolds is widely expected to seek a term of her own in 2018 -- even before Branstad was tapped for the ambassadorship, she had assembled a $1 million-plus campaign war chest. Assuming she runs, history would be on her side: Culver is the only Iowa incumbent to be denied another term in the last 50 years. Reynolds had solid ratings in the February 2017 *Des Moines Register* poll – 44 percent approval, 24 percent disapproval. Still, several Democrats were considering a run, including state party chair Andy McGuire, state Sen. Rob Hogg, state Rep. Todd Prichard, state Sen. Liz Mathis, former House candidate Jim Mowrer, former state party chair Tyler Olsen and Polk County Conservation Director Rich Leopold. However, none of these Democrats were as well-known as Reynolds. She could also conceivably get a GOP primary challenge from Vander Plaats, Rep. Steve King or Cedar Rapids Mayor Ron Corbett. Another matter remained uncertain: Would Reynolds' husband, soil conservationist Kevin Reynolds, be depicted in doll form at the Iowa state capitol, as all previous first ladies have been? If so, Reynolds joked to the *Register*, her husband's portrayal should be in flannel or hunter's camouflage.

Senior Senator

Chuck Grassley (R)

Elected 1980, term expires 2022, 7th term; b. Sep 17, 1933, New Hartford; University of Iowa Carver College of Medicine; University of Northern Iowa, M.A.; University of Northern Iowa, B.A.; Baptist; Married (Barbara Ann Speicher Grassley); 5 children.

Elected Office: IA House, 1959-1974; U.S. House, 1975-1981.

Professional Career: Farmer; Sheet metal shearer, 1959-1961; Assembly line worker, 1961-1971.

DC Office: 135 HSOB 20510, 202-224-3744, Fax: 202-224-6020, grassley.senate.gov.

State Offices: Cedar Rapids, 319-363-6832; Council Bluffs, 712-322-7103; Davenport, 563-322-4331; Des Moines, 515-288-1145; Sioux City, 712-233-1860; Waterloo, 319-232-6657.

Committees: *Agriculture, Nutrition & Forestry*: Commodities, Risk Management & Trade, Conservation, Forestry & Natural Resources, Livestock, Marketing & Agriculture Security. *Budget. Finance*: Energy, Natural Resources & Infrastructure, Health Care, International Trade, Customs & Global Competitiveness. *Judiciary (Chmn)*: Antitrust, Competition Policy & Consumer Rights, Border Security & Immigration, Oversight, Agency Action, Federal Rights & Federal Courts.

Group Ratings

	ADA	ACLU	AFL-CIO	LCV	ITI	COC	HAFA	ACU	CFG	FRC
2016	-	11%	-	6%	80%	100%	53%	69%	7500%	100%
2015	0%	C	29%	4%	C	79%	C	92%	76%	100%

Almanac Ratings 2015

	Economy	Social	Foreign	Composite
Liberal	11%	0%	18%	10%
Conservative	89%	100%	82%	90%

Key Votes of the 114th Congress

1. Keystone pipeline	Y	5. National Security Data	Y	9. Gun Sales Checks	N
2. Export-Import Bank	Y	6. Iran Nuclear Deal	Y	10. Sanctuary Cities	Y
3. Debt Ceiling Increase	N	7. Puerto Rico Debt	N	11. Planned Parenthood	Y
4. Homeland Security $$	N	8. Loretta Lynch A.G	N	12. Trade deals	Y

Election Results

Election	Name (Party)	Vote (%)		Cand. Spent	Ind. Exp. Support	Ind. Exp. Oppose
2016 General	Chuck Grassley (R)	926,007	(60%)	$10,306,743	$284,077	$37,897
	Patty Judge (D)	549,460	(36%)	$2,189,617	$22,035	$80,410
	John Heiderscheit (L)	41,794	(3%)			
2016 Primary	Chuck Grassley (R)	unopposed				

Prior winning percentages: 2010 (64%), 2004 (70%), 1998 (68%), 1992 (70%), 1986 (66%), 1980 (54%); House: 1978 (75%), 1976 (57%), 1974 (51%)

Republican Charles Grassley, Iowa's senior senator, self-effacingly describes himself as "just a farmer from Butler County," and still climbs aboard his tractor to till land on his family-owned farm. In fact, "Chuck" Grassley has spent a lot more of his career brokering legislative deals and barking at recalcitrant committee witnesses than busting sod: His tenure in elected office goes back almost six decades, including more than 40 years in Congress and stints as chairman of two powerful Senate committees. His time on the tractor on weekends and during congressional recesses is often punctuated by legislative business, courtesy of a cellphone he keeps tucked under his cap. Nonetheless, Grassley's "aw shucks" charm and his reputation for straight talk and accessibility -- he has held meetings in each of Iowa's 99 counties every year he has been in the Senate -- has made him Iowa's most popular politician, regularly re-elected by margins at or exceeding 2-1.

Although he is now the Senate's second oldest member (California Democrat Dianne Feinstein is just three months his senior), Grassley, at 83, was reelected in 2016 to a seventh term in the Senate, an Iowa record. His latest win came by another landslide margin, even as national Democrats --enraged by Grassley's refusal as Judiciary Committee chairman to grant a hearing to Merrick Garland, President Barack Obama's nominee for Supreme Court -- sought to give Grassley his toughest race in more than one-third of a century. Grassley, with a campaign treasury four times as large as his Democratic opponent's, responded with down-home appeal. He ran ads showing him cutting grass with three mowers he welded together, and eating ice cream at one of his favorite hangouts: Dairy Queen.

While the tumult over the Garland nomination showcased his partisan side, perceptions of Grassley on Capitol Hill have evolved significantly since his arrival in the Senate in 1980. His first election was facilitated by the Reagan presidential landslide, which brought a wave of reliable, often hardline conservatives into that chamber. But virtually all of the Senate Republican class of 1980 was gone within a term or two, with several retired involuntarily by an electorate swinging back toward the political center. Grassley is the one of that group who has not only survived, but thrived. He transcended an initial image as a one-dimensional conservative, and has been seen increasingly over the years as a dogged overseer of federal agencies and a hero to government whistleblowers, as well as an independent-minded dealmaker.

Grassley grew up on a farm in New Hartford in northeastern Iowa. His parents were Democrats who switched to the Republican Party when Franklin Roosevelt ran for a third term in 1940. Grassley received his bachelor's degree from the University of Northern Iowa, and while still in graduate school, ran for the Iowa House in 1956, losing by only 70-some votes. Two years later, he ran again and was elected at age 25. While in the state legislature, he worked as a sheet metal shearer and on an assembly line to make ends meet. He won an open House seat in 1974, the hugely successful post-Watergate year for the Democrats: Grassley squeaked in with 51 percent of the vote. Six years later, he garnered 54 percent in ousting Democratic Sen. John Culver. A classmate of the late Massachusetts Sen. Edward Kennedy at Harvard, Culver was among the group of influential liberals-notably George McGovern of

South Dakota, Birch Bayh of Indiana, and Frank Church of Idaho-who dominated the Senate during the 1960s and 1970s, but were swept out of office in the 1980 election.

Grassley was, and remains, a committed fiscal conservative; he was among just eight senators to oppose the 2013 deal aimed at averting the so-called fiscal cliff because, he declared, "Washington has a spending problem, not a taxing problem, and this deal doesn't do anything about the spending problem." He also is a steady conservative on social issues: He opposes abortion and most gun control initiatives. In 2013, he voted to block a compromise measure to expand background checks for gun owners in the wake of the mass shooting at a Connecticut elementary school, in which 26 were killed.

But Grassley is a populist in the Midwestern agrarian tradition, suspicious of concentrations of both public and private power. He has made oversight of bloated, indifferent, or corrupt government agencies a focal point of his Senate career, conducting intensive oversight of the FBI, the Department of Homeland Security, the Centers for Medicare and Medicaid Services, and the Food and Drug Administration. In the mid-1980s, his first major legislative achievement was passage of the Federal False Claims Act, which authorized lawsuits for fraud on behalf of the government; he says it has since returned more than $17 billion to the federal treasury. More recently, in 2015, Grassley sharply criticized the Justice Department over its administration of civil asset forfeiture laws, a position that put him in league with the American Civil Liberties Union. Grassley complained these statutes, as now written, have created a "perverse incentive" for police to seize and sell property without clear evidence that a crime has been committed.

In the populist tradition, Grassley also has shown an inclination to challenge Wall Street. He attacked the Securities and Exchange Commission in 2011 for failing to detail how it handled nearly 20 referrals of suspicious trading at a major hedge fund. A year earlier, he was one of only four Republicans who voted for the Senate version of the Dodd-Frank bill overhauling regulation of the nation's financial markets, although he voted against the final version of the legislation that cleared Congress. The same year, he was the only Republican to vote with Democrats on the Senate Agriculture Committee for sweeping reform of the derivatives market. He supported the government rescue of the financial industry during the final months of the Bush Administration in 2008, a vote for which he faced criticism from Iowa conservatives.

Grassley took the helm of the Judiciary Committee in 2015, after serving as the committee's ranking Republican during the prior two Congresses while the Democrats controlled the Senate majority. Early in Obama's second term, before becoming chairman, Grassley exhibited his partisan side: He came under sharp criticism from Democrats and others for seeking to block votes on many of the president's federal judgeship nominees. During Obama's first term, he voted against the confirmation of Obama's two nominees to the Supreme Court, Sonia Sotomayor and Elena Kagan-marking the first time he had opposed high court nominees. He singled out Sotomayor's views on gun rights as well as property rights.

In February 2016, when the death of Justice Antonin Scalia gave Obama his third opportunity to appoint a member of the Supreme Court, leaders of the Republican-controlled Senate quickly signaled their intention to take no action on filling the seat until after the presidential election. Although it was apparent that Majority Leader Mitch McConnell of Kentucky was the driving force behind this move, the Democrats aimed the bulk of their rhetorical fire at the often independent-minded Grassley -- hoping to force him to hold hearings on Obama's choice, Garland, a federal appeals court judge."As each day passes, the senior senator from Iowa further distinguishes himself as the most political and partisan chairman in history," sniped Minority Leader Harry Reid of Nevada in a Senate floor speech.Vermont Sen. Patrick Leahy, then senior Democrat on the Judiciary panel, sought to needle Grassley into bucking McConnell. "The only option is for the chairman of the committee to say, 'We're going to have a hearing,' " Leahy, flashing a mischievous smile, told *USAToday,* adding pointedly: "I showed a lot of independence when I was chairman of that committee. I held hearings on even controversial things, whether the leadership liked it or not."

Grassley held firm, pointing to comments made by another former Senate Judiciary chairman -- Vice President Joe Biden -- in 1992, when a Republican, President George H.W. Bush, was in office.Citing Biden's advicethat Supreme Court nominees should not be considered in the "cauldron" of an election season, Grassley declared on the Senate floor, "We're not going to drop any nominee into that election-year cauldron." Grassley did ultimately agree to meet overbreakfast with Garland, emerging to tell reporters that it had been "friendly" but did not change his mind about holding hearings. When President Donald Trump took office and nominated another appeals court judge, Neil Gorsuch, for the opening, Democrats were skeptical -- given Trump's campaign promise to appoint "pro-life" judges. Grassley vowed to move the nomination quickly and enthusiastically vouched for Gorsuch's independence. "His grasp on the separation of powers - including judicial independence - enlivens his body of work," Grassley asserted of Gorsuch.

The frictions over the Supreme Court nomination notwithstanding, Grassley has long enjoyed a good relationship with Leahy, who chaired the committee for four years while Grassley was its ranking Republican. "When he's wanted to open an investigation during the time I've been chairman, I just say, 'Fine'," Leahy said of Grassley. "He has that kind of credibility."Grassley and Leahy worked together on such matters as satellite television access and cellphone unlocking technology, and, in 2015, they unveiled legislation -- co-sponsored by a bipartisan group of five other Judiciary Committee members-- addressing the perennial issue of how best to deal with abuses in the current patent system.

Immigration policy also is within the purview of the Judiciary panel, and Grassley has been among the Senate's sharpest critics of the so-called H-1B visa program, which enables the U.S. technology industry to bring in highly skilled labor from overseas. On the committee, Grassley has teamed up with another leading Senate Democrat, Minority Whip Dick Durbin of Illinois, to seek to curb the program-which Grassley contends is being used to replace U.S. workers and reduce wages. As the partisan battle over Garland was playing out, Grassley and Durbin worked together on one of the major bipartisan initiatives of the 114th Congress: criminal justice reform. Their bill, intended to reduce mandatory minimum sentences for those with drug convictions and increase rehabilitation programs for prisoners, cleared the Judiciary panel by a wide margin, but was stalled by objections from a handful of hardline conservatives. Grassley and Durbin vowed to push the measure again in 2017.

Previously, Grassley enjoyed a warm relationship with then-Montana Democratic Sen. Max Baucus when the two men took turns chairing the powerful Finance Committee. Grassley was chairman in the first half of 2001 and from 2003 to the end of 2006. When Democrats took control of the Senate following the 2006 election, Baucus became chairman and Grassley was the panel's ranking Republican until 2010. Grassley held weekly meetings and worked closely with Baucus, to the dismay of conservative Republicans who thought Grassley was too accommodating. But their relationship was crucial to several successful initiatives during the early part of the George W. Bush presidency. Baucus helped Grassley round up bipartisan support for Bush's income tax cuts early on, and later supported the Republican-sponsored Medicare prescription drug program legislation that Grassley was a leader in crafting. By the same token, when Obama became president in 2009 and proposed his signature health care bill, Grassley was one of the Senate negotiators trying to broker a deal, despite pressure from within his party. In the end, Grassley voted against the Affordable Care Act, complaining it would cut funding for Medicare and would neither hold down taxes nor contain costs.

With his populist bent, Grassley has long pursued "fairness" in the tax code. Amid talk that Congress might take up a major tax reform initiative, Grassley publicly mused about trying to reclaim the chairmanship of the Finance panel when it appeared the Republicans were poised to retake the Senate majority following the 2014 election. Under internal party rules, Grassley was compelled to step down as ranking member of the Finance Committee at the end of 2010, prompting him to move to the top slot at the Judiciary panel. However, those same rules made him eligible for one last two-year term as chairman of Finance. But trying to reclaim that post would have likely have created a messy battle within the Republican ranks against Utah Sen. Orrin Hatch, who had taken over as ranking member of Finance in 2010 and was eagerly eyeing the chairmanship. Grassley sidestepped the fight by opting to chair the Judiciary Committee, making him the first non-lawyer ever to head that panel.

Protection of government whistleblowers also has been a continuing legislative passion for Grassley. "Whistleblowers are often treated like skunks at a picnic. It takes guts to put your career on the line to expose waste and fraud, and whistleblowers need senators who will listen and advocate for them," Grassley declared in 2014 in announcing creation of the Senate Whistleblower Protection Caucus. The announcement came on the 25th anniversary of passage of the 1989 Whistleblower Protection Act-which he co-authored. He also helped pass, in late 2012, an update of the whistleblower law that, among other things, created ombudsmen to educate federal agency managers about whistleblower rights.Dating back to Ronald Reagan, Grassley has asked incoming presidents to host a White House Rose Garden ceremony to honor federal agency whistleblowers who identify fraud and abuse. He has yet to convince a new president to do so.

But such efforts have led many frustrated federal workers to turn to Grassley instead of the media, according to former FBI agent Jane Turner. One whistleblower, John Dodson, worked with Grassley's staff in exposing the "Operation Fast and Furious" scandal at the Bureau of Alcohol, Tobacco and Firearms, in which the agency lost track of hundreds of firearms sold to straw purchasers for Mexican drug cartels. "Without Grassley, you would have tenfold more [Edward] Snowdens [and] Wikileaks, because he's the only true hope that whistleblowers have," Turner told the *Des Moines Register*. However, Grassley has kept his distance-rhetorically and otherwise-from Snowden, whose disclosures of information from the National Security Agency's telephone and data mining programs have made him the most visible government whistleblower of recent times. In the wake of that episode, Grassley told *The Hill* that Snowden "surely isn't a hero" and should be prosecuted for what many intelligence experts characterized as one of the most serious information leaks in U.S. history.

In his career as a part-time farmer, Grassley took an 80-acre farm that he inherited in 1960 and added to it over the years; it is now a 710-acre concern producing corn and soybeans that is managed by Grassley's son. In his career as a full-time legislator, Grassley has exhibited his populist skepticism in debates over farm subsidies. He has argued that high payments to individual farmers put the entire agriculture program in political jeopardy, and added an amendment to a 2012 Senate version of the farm bill that would cap payments to farmers along with closing loopholes allowing non-farmers to qualify for payments. When the House and Senate were working on a compromise farm bill a year later, Grassley, writing in an op-ed in *Politico*, declared: "It seems some members want to reduce food stamps while reopening loopholes for multi-million-dollar farming entities. There's bipartisan agreement that the food-stamp program needs reform, but how can we save money in one program and at the same time turn a blind eye to the loopholes that millionaires exploit?"

Grassleyhas utilized his perch at the Finance Committee to look out for the interests of fellow farmers as well as his home state in general. Corn-based ethanol is an important product of Iowa's agribusiness, and Grassley has used his influence to win advantageous tax treatment of ethanol. On another issue important to his state -- wind energy, which provides one-third of Iowa's electricity -- Grassley publicly tangled with both Trump and the 2012 Republican presidential nominee, Mitt Romney. During the 2016 campaign, Trump's criticism -- he complained that the large turbines required were unsightly and killed birds -- prompted speculation he might seek to kill the federal tax credit for wind energy production. Grassley, who authored the credit two decades ago, warned Trump to back off, telling *Yahoo News*, "If he wants to do away with it, he'll have to get a bill through Congress, and he'll do it over my dead body."

Grassley cited the interests of his home state, when, in September 2013, he announced plans to seek reelection to a seventh term. Noting the impending retirement of his veteran Democratic colleague, Tom Harkin, in 2014, he told reporters that "if Iowa had to start over two years from now with two very junior senators, it would hurt Iowans' opportunities to get anything done in the Senate." When asked about his age -- he will be 89 when his current term ends in 2022 -- Grassley told the *Associated Press*, "I think that age isn't a factor or I wouldn't be running for office-or I wouldn't be running this morning." It was a reference to his regular jogging sessions; he runs three miles four times a week after awakening at 4 a.m. He has become a committed Twitter user, regularly using his iPhone to post updates -- distinguished by their abbreviations as well as their occasionally humorous typos and misspellings -- to his121,000Twitter followers. And he isan iron man when it comes to Senate floor votes: He has not missed a vote since July 1993, when he was touring flood damage along the Mississippi River. That streak, which has lasted more than 24 years, is a Senate record.

Initially, Grassley appeared to be cruising to reelection in 2016. But that changed when the controversy over the Garland nomination controversy erupted: Believing Grassley's handling of that issue had created a political opening, national Democrats successfully coaxed former Iowa Lt. Gov. Patty Judge -- previously the state's first female agriculture commissioner -- into the race. Touting herself as "one Judge" that Grassley could not ignore, she sought to use his handling of the Garland matter as evidence that Grassley had grown out of step with Iowa voters. Judge garnered the backing of the DSCC and EMILY's List. But her entry into the contest encountered static among the Iowa Democratic establishment: Many of them were already supporting lesser known state Sen. Rob Hogg for the nomination, and resented what they saw as interference by the national party.In the primary, Judge defeated Hogg by a less than overwhelming 48%-39%.

In the general election, Grassley overwhelmed Judge by 60%-36%. She carried just one of the state's 99 counties: Johnson County, home to the University of Iowa. Grassley ran well ahead of Trump, who defeated Hillary Clinton in the state by 51%-42%. Grassley emphasized his efforts to stay connected to Iowans, while largely ignoring Judge -- agreeing to only one televised debate, in late October. At one point,a frustrated Judge challenged Grassley to four debates in Dairy Queen parking lots in the state's largest media markets. "He's at DQ all the time anyway, so he might as well use the opportunity to talk to Iowans while enjoying 'you know what,'" a Judge spokesman wryly observed. It was a reference to one of Grassley's more infamous tweets when, in 2014, he declared "Windsor Heights Dairy Queen is good place for u kno what." It sparked cyberspace titters -- until the octogenarian senator followed up by explaining in a video that he was referring to nothing more lascivious than indulging in a Blizzard or one of DQ's other trademark offerings.

Junior Senator

Joni Ernst (R)

Elected 2014, term expires 2020, 1st term; b. Jul 01, 1970, Red Oak; Iowa State University (IA), B.S.; Columbus College (IA), M.P.A.; Lutheran; Married (Gail Ernst); 1 child; 2 stepchildren.

Military Career: U.S. Army Reserves (Iraq), 1992-2001; IA National Guard 1992-2015.

Elected Office: IA Senate, 2011-2014.

Professional Career: Auditor, Montgomery County IA, 2005-2011.

DC Office: 111 RSOB 20510, 202-224-3254, Fax: 202-224-9369, ernst.senate.gov.

State Offices: Cedar Rapids, 319-365-4504; Council Bluffs, 712-352-1167; Davenport, 563-322-0677; Des Moines, 515-284-4574; Sioux City, 712-252-1550.

Committees: *Agriculture, Nutrition & Forestry*: Livestock, Marketing & Agriculture Security, Nutrition, Agricultural Research & Specialty Crops, Rural Development & Energy (Chmn). *Armed Services*: Emerging Threats & Capabilities (Chmn), Personnel, Readiness & Management Support. *Environment & Public Works*: Clean Air & Nuclear Safety, Superfund, Waste Management, & Regulatory Oversight, Transportation & Infrastructure. *Small Business & Entrepreneurship*.

Group Ratings

	ADA	ACLU	AFL-CIO	LCV	ITI	COC	HAFA	ACU	CFG	FRC
2016	-	11%	-	0%	60%	100%	60%	88%	7500%	100%
2015	0%	C	21%	0%	C	86%	C	88%	70%	100%

Almanac Ratings 2015

	Economy	Social	Foreign	Composite
Liberal	17%	0%	9%	9%
Conservative	83%	100%	91%	91%

Key Votes of the 114th Congress

1. Keystone pipeline	Y	5. National Security Data	N	9. Gun Sales Checks	N
2. Export-Import Bank	N	6. Iran Nuclear Deal	Y	10. Sanctuary Cities	Y
3. Debt Ceiling Increase	N	7. Puerto Rico Debt	N	11. Planned Parenthood	Y
4. Homeland Security $$	N	8. Loretta Lynch A.G	N	12. Trade deals	Y

Election Results

Election	Name (Party)	Vote (%)		Cand. Spent	Ind. Exp. Support	Ind. Exp. Oppose
2014 General	Joni Ernst (R)	588,575	(52%)	$11,913,212	$12,247,026	$25,196,618
	Bruce Braley (D)	494,370	(44%)	$12,068,095	$4,225,010	$18,841,528
	Douglas Butzier (L)	26,815	(2%)			
2014 Primary	Joni Ernst (R)	88,535	(56%)			
	Sam Clovis (R)	28,418	(18%)			
	Mark Jacobs (R)	26,523	(17%)			
	Matt Whitaker (R)	11,884	(8%)			

When veteran Sen. Tom Harkin announced his retirement from the Senate in early 2013, his fellow Democrats felt good about their chances for holding the seat-notwithstanding the storm clouds gathering over the party's national prospects in the 2014 election. Four-term Democratic Rep. Bruce Braley quickly announced his candidacy to succeed Harkin, while the Republicans struggled for months as several top-tier contenders declined to step up. Consequently, it ranked as one of the one of the biggest-if not the biggest-upset of that election cycle when Republican state Sen. Joni Ernst ended up defeating Braley to become the state'sjunior senator, as well as the first woman ever to represent Iowa in Congress. Ernst's folksy manner on the campaign trail-she highlighted her family's roots in farming, most memorably in a TV that mentioned her experience castrating hogs-helped her prevail amid a fusillade of Democratic attacks on several hard-line conservative positions she had taken. But, even in a swing state that had twice voted for Barack Obama, Democrats were unable to overcome the political damage done by Braley's gaffe-prone candidacy.

Propelled by her surprise victory, Ernst's down-home appeal earned her some high-profile exposure during her first couple of years on Capitol Hill. Less than a month after being sworn into the Senate, Ernst was tapped by Republican leaders to give the GOP response to Obama's State of the Union address. And she was given a prominent speaking role at the 2016 Republican National Convention in Cleveland, where she also was in high demand as a speaker before state delegations. However, in the mold of past senators who have arrived on Capitol Hill with a measure of celebrity but who strived to demonstrate a seriousness of purpose, Ernst -- derided bycritics as "Sarah Palin lite" -- insisted her top prioritieswere representing her home state and acquiring legislative expertise. After meeting with then-Republican nominee Donald Trump in July 2016, amid speculation that she was under consideration as a vice-presidential running mate, Ernst told*Politico*:"I made that very clear to him that I'm focused on Iowa. I feel that I have a lot more to do in the United States Senate…I'm just getting started here."

Born and raised on a farm in Montgomery County (pop. 10,740) in southwest Iowa, Ernst won scholarships to attend Iowa State University, where she majored in psychology, while later earning a master's degree in public administration from Georgia's Columbus State University. She joined the National Guard in 1993 and was deployed to Kuwait during Operation Iraqi Freedom a decade later; she highlighted her status as a veteran and her rank as a lieutenant colonel in the Guard throughout the 2014 campaign, during which national security was high on the list of voter concerns.

Ernst was elected Montgomery County auditor in 2004, serving two terms before winning election to the state Senate in 2010.When a number of better known Republicans wooed by the party strategists-notably then-Rep. Tom Latham-opted against running for Harkin's seat, Ernst became part of a five-way primary. Some establishment Republicans swung behind wealthy businessman Mark Jacobs, after he indicated a willingness to pump several million dollars of his personal fortune into the race. But the "hogs" ad pushed Ernst to front of the pack. "I grew up castrating hogs on an Iowa farm, so when I get to Washington, I'll know how to cut pork.… Washington's full of big spenders, let's make them squeal," she declared in the ad. It was followed by an edgy paid spot showing Ernst, in a black leather jacket, stepping off her Harley-Davidson and firing shots at a shooting-range target as a narrator intoned, "Joni Ernst will take aim at wasteful spending, and once she sets her sights on Obamacare, Joni's gonna unload." If the ads caused some controversy, they delivered by painting Ernst as a political outsider, even as she demonstrated an ability to attract support from the party's establishment as well as the tea party wing: 2012 presidential nominee Mitt Romney endorsed her, as did Palin, the party's 2008 vice-presidential nominee. In the June primary, Ernst easily won with 56 percent.

Meanwhile, Braley, a former trial lawyer first elected to the House in 2006, was beset by a series of self-inflicted wounds -- to the degree that several political publications and handicappers later anointed his as the worst campaign of 2014. In a radio interview during the federal government shutdown in late 2013, he complained about the impact on the House gym. "There's hardly anybody working down there. There's no towel service, we're doing our own laundry…," he griped. Voter perceptions of aloofness intensified several months later, when a dispute erupted over a neighbor's chickens wandering onto Braley's vacation home property. Braley denied he had threatened to sue the neighbor, but a memo from an attorney for the local community association quoted Braley as hinting at legal action. But Braley's biggest gaffe occurred at a private fundraiser of trial lawyers in Texas, when he was caught on tape deriding the prospect of veteran Sen. Charles Grassley chairing the Judiciary Committee if the Republicans regained a Senate majority-characterizing Grassley as "a farmer from Iowa who never went to law school, never practiced law." As then-*Washington Post* politics blogger Chris Cillizza put it: “In the space of two sentences, Braley managed to: (1) insult popular Sen. Chuck Grassley (2) insult farmers and (3) sound as super-arrogant as humanly possible.”

Democrats counterattacked by seeking to portray Ernst in the tea party mold of Palin and former Minnesota Rep. Michele Bachmann: Then-Democratic National Committee Chairwoman Debbie Wasserman Schultz called Ernst "an onion of crazy." Braley and Democratic allies hammered away at Ernst's calls to abolish the Education Department and the Environmental Protection Agency, as well as her opposition to federal minimum wage laws and her support for a "personhood" constitutional amendment to ban all abortions. And a recording of an Ernst appearance at a 2012 National Rifle Association rally surfaced, during which she boasted of owning "a beautiful little Smith & Wesson, 9 millimeter, and it goes with me virtually everywhere." Ernst continued. "…I believe in the right to defend myself and my family-whether it's from an intruder, or whether it's from the government, should they decide that my rights are no longer important." The comments came shortly after 12 people were killed and 58 others wounded in a shooting rampage in a Colorado movie theater. Democrats griped about Ernst being the Teflon candidate of 2014, but she easily triumphed on Election Day, 52%-44%.

Named to the Senate Armed Services Committee as well as the Homeland Security and Governmental Affairs Committee, Ernst moved quickly to focus on fighting terrorism and improving care for her fellow military veterans. In June 2015, an Ernst amendment to a defense authorization bill -- to allow the Obama Administration to sidestep the Iraqi central government and directly arm Kurdish forces fighting the Islamic State (ISIS) -- was defeated by a 54-45 margin. A handful of leading Democratic liberals sided with Ernst, while a few fellow GOP conservatives voted against her. She also joined a push by several senators from both parties for a new authorization for the use of military force against ISIS. Ernst took a more partisan tack in her speech to the 2016 Republican convention, blasting Obama's response to ISIS as "pathetic" and citing FBI reports of an ISIS presence in all 50 states. That speech, focused on military issues, was something of a contrast to her folksy response to Obama's State of the Union address in early 2015, which was heavy on personal retrospective; i.e. "...Growing up, I had only one good pair of shoes. So on rainy school days, my mom would slip plastic bread bags over them to keep them dry."

Ernst could point to a couple of bills she authored involving women veterans that were signed into law by Obama. One measure, the Women Veterans Suicide Prevention Act, authorized additional studies and treatment programs. The other allowed the ashes of women who served in World War II to be buried in Arlington National Cemetery for the first time. At the end of 2015, Ernst retired as a lieutenant colonel after 23 years in the Iowa National Guard,citing both her Senate duties as well as family obligations. Earlier in the year, the left-leaning *Huffington Post*had questioned her claim to being the first female combat veteran elected to serve in the Senate-pointing out that she had commanded a transportation company that never came under fire during her service in Iraq. "It was only by luck and the blessings of God that my soldiers did not encounter an assault," Ernst shot back.

On the domestic front, Ernst continued her attack on a major rhetorical target of her election campaign: the EPA. In early 2016, Obama vetoed an Ernst-sponsored resolution to overturn 2014 Clean Water Act regulations that expanded the EPA's jurisdiction over domestic bodies of water. The resolution passed the Senate and House by margins insufficient to override a veto, but Ernst vowed to continue to look for ways to undermine the so-called Waters of the United States rule. "This rule is not about clean water. Rather, it is about how much authority the federal government and unelected bureaucrats should have to regulate what is done on private land," she declared. At the same time, Ernst has been a vocal advocate of renewable energy, a politically important issue in Iowa -- where about 30 percent of electricity is now produced by wind energy, and where the bountiful corn crop is used to produce ethanol added to gasoline underthe federal Renewable Fuel Standard.

During the October 2016 campaign controversy over lewd comments about women made by Trump in a decade-old video, Ernst was initially the only one of the half-dozen Republican women then in the Senate to stand by the nominee. (A couple of Ernst's GOP female colleagues, after initially suggesting that Trump leave the ticket, later re-endorsed him.) "I am appalled at what he said, his words and the way that he objectified women," Ernst said. "But...I am not fighting for Donald Trump. I am fighting for my country and I don't agree with Hillary Clinton, and so I will support the Republican ticket."A couple of months earlier, Trump had appeared at Ernst's second annual "Roast & Ride" in Des Moines. The senator, attired in black denim jeans and a Harley-Davidson T-shirt, led motorcycle riders in a 40-mile tour before chowing down. Borrowing a page from her Democratic predecessor -- whose yearly Harkin Steak Fry was a must-show for presidential wannabes in the state that selects the first delegates to the national party conventions -- Ernst has turned Roast & Ride into an annual tradition. However, befitting of the TV ad that helped carry her to victory, pork rather than beef has been her menu of choice.

FIRST DISTRICT

Rod Blum (R)

Elected 2014, 2nd term; b. Apr 26, 1955, Dubuque; Loras College; b.B.A.; University of Dubuque, M.B.A.; Episcopalian; Married (Karen Blum); 4 children; 1 stepchild.

Professional Career: Boys basketball coach, Dubuque Senior HS; Columnist, Telegraph Herald; Real estate developer; Owner, Digital Canal Software.

DC Office: 1108 LHOB 20515, 202-225-2911, Fax: 202-225-6666, blum.house.gov.

State Offices: Cedar Falls, 319-266-6925; Cedar Rapids, 319-364-2288; Dubuque, 563-557-7789.

Committees: *Oversight & Government Reform*: Government Operations. *Small Business*: Agriculture, Energy & Trade (Chmn), Investigations, Oversight & Regulations.

Group Ratings

	ADA	ACLU	AFL-CIO	LCV	ITI	COC	HAFA	ACU	CFG	FRC
2016	-	11%	-	3%	83%	100%	73%	84%	72%	92%
2015	0%	C	4%	3%	C	80%	C	96%	89%	83%

Almanac Ratings 2015

	Economy	Social	Foreign	Composite
Liberal	1%	20%	12%	11%
Conservative	99%	80%	88%	89%

Key Votes of the 114th Congress

1. Keystone Pipeline	Y	5. Puerto Rico Debt	N	9. Offenses by Aliens	Y
2. Trade Deals	Y	6. Medical Marijuana	Y	10. Troops in Iraq	Y
3. Export-Import Bank	N	7. Sanctuary Cities	Y	11. Homeland Security $$	N
4. Debt Ceiling Increase	N	8. Armor-piercing Bullets	Y	12. Trade Adjustment aid	Y

Election Results

Election	Name (Party)	Vote (%)		Cand. Spent	Ind. Exp. Support	Ind. Exp. Oppose
2016 General	Rod Blum (R)	206,903	(54%)	$1,615,079	$475,600	$2,318,799
	Monica Vernon (D)	177,403	(46%)	$2,861,310	$291,156	$2,278,043
2016 Primary	Rod Blum (R)		(100%)			

Prior winning percentages: 2014 (51%)

When Republican businessman Rod Blum was narrowly elected in 2014, he scored one of the most surprising upsets on election night to represent what had been the Democratic-leaning 1st District. Following that, his outsider appeal quickly antagonized GOP leaders in the House. Even many Republicans believed that he would have little chance to win a second term. Bolstered by the shifting politics in Iowa, including the success of Donald Trump, he shockingly had a relatively comfortable victory, despite a fundraising disadvantage.

A Dubuque native, Blum has highlighted his working-class roots. His father quit school in 10th grade to enlist in the Navy during World War II and later worked as a foreman at Dubuque Packing Co., while his mother earned extra income cleaning houses. Blum, one of four children, worked his way through college, earning a finance degree at the local Loras College and later an M.B.A. at the University of Dubuque. He worked in the software business, rising to president and CEO of Eagle Point Software before launching his own company. He was a basketball coach at Dubuque Senior High School and worked as a real estate developer.

Blum had dipped a toe into politics in the 1990s, serving two years as the Dubuque County GOP chairman. In 2012 he made a brief bid against Democratic Rep. Bruce Braley - who ran unsuccessfully for the Senate in 2014 - but lost in the GOP primary. Next time around, he relied on a more professional staff and repeatedly declared, "I'm not a career politician." He won a three-way primary with 55 percent of the vote.

His race against former House speaker Pat Murphy, who had spent 25 years in the Legislature, tightened as November neared. Blum advocated lower taxes on businesses, reduced federal spending and repeal of the Affordable Care Act in favor of a free-market approach. He opposed same-sex marriage and supported protection of gun owners' rights. His campaign ran ads featuring footage of "angry career politician" Murphy screaming on the state House floor, followed by a narrator saying that Murphy lied about creating jobs in Iowa. When Murphy blamed congressional Republicans for the government's handling of Ebola because they had not provided enough funding for the Centers for Disease Control and Prevention, Blum responded: "Spoken like a career politician. We never have enough funding in government."

House Speaker John Boehner appeared in Hiawatha to campaign for Blum, and Blum picked up endorsements from the Dubuque and Cedar Rapids newspapers. National Democrats at the end of the race poured $600,000 into an ad campaign. One ad targeted "millionaire Rod Blum," saying he had made a career of putting profits ahead of Iowa workers. But the Republican tide proved too much for Murphy to overcome. "As Braley tanked in the closing weeks to Joni Ernst, he brought Murphy down with him in his own backyard," said David Wasserman of the *Cook Political Report*. Blum was outspent $1.4 million to $1 million, and Murphy had a big advantage with party funds. Blum surprised them all with a victory of 51.1%-48.9%, a margin of 6,617 votes, and took 15 of 20 counties. He narrowly lost the three population centers (Dubuque, Cedar Rapids, Waterloo), but rolled up big margins in the rural areas.

In January 2015, he was one of 25 House Republicans to oppose Boehner for Speaker, casting his vote instead for Florida GOP Rep. Dan Webster. Although he respected Boehner as "a good man," he said that his vote was a statement on behalf of Iowans to "stand up to the status quo in Washington, D.C." He spent his early months trying to change how Congress works. With Democratic Rep. Beto O'Rourke of Texas, he created the Congressional Term-Limits Caucus, with the hope that frequent turnover would stimulate fresh and innovative thinking. He filed a bill that would impose a lifetime ban on former members of Congress lobbying their ex-colleagues. In analyzing prospects for the proposal, *Vox* approvingly wrote that although "Blum's idea may face long odds at the moment, if he and other reformers keep pressing, its moment may one day come." Blum also talked up his support for a balanced budget constitutional amendment. In the *Almanac* vote ratings for 2015, he ranked toward the center on social and foreign-policy votes, and was strongly conservative on economic issues.

Not surprisingly, Blum became an early Democratic target for 2016. Cedar Rapids councilwoman Monica Vernon, who lost the primary to Murphy in 2014, had a rematch with him in the Democratic primary. She had a big lead in fundraising, union endorsements and national Democratic enthusiasm, and won the June primary, 68%-32%. *Roll Call*, the Capitol Hill newspaper, forecast that the contest "leans Democratic." For Blum, the departure of Boehner as Speaker was a plus. Eventually, new Speaker Paul Ryan campaigned for him. But Blum had burned some bridges at the National Republican Congressional Committee, where memories of Boehner remained positive. The *Des Moines Register* reported that he had spent more money on constituent mailers in 2015 than any other member of the House. Vernon, whose contributors ran from the EMILY's List abortion-rights political action committee to business leaders in Cedar Rapids had a $1 million fundraising advantage over Blum. Each received more than $2 million in support from their party and outside groups.

Given Trump's eventual success in the district, Blum oddly kept his distance from him during much of the campaign. "I wish he would get … verbal discipline," Blum told the *Cedar Rapids Gazette* in June 2016. He added that he expected to disagree with Trump on some issues. In his 54%-46% win, Blum took 18 counties and lost narrowly in Black Hawk and Linn. His margin was twice the lead of Trump in the presidential contest.

Northeast Iowa: Cedar Rapids, Dubuque, Waterloo

Population		**Race and Ethnicity**		**Income**	
Total	768,669	White	89.5%	Median Income	$54,028 (198 out of 435)
Land area	12,049	Black	3.3%		
Pop/ sq mi	63.8	Latino	3.6%		
Born in state	75.9%	Asian	1.4%	Under $50,000	45.9%
		Two races	1.7%	$50,000-$99,999	34.9%
Age Groups		Other	0.5%	$100,000-$199,999	16.4%
Under 18	23.1%			$200,000 or more	2.8%
18-34	22.6%	**Education**		Poverty Rate	11.3%
35-64	38.2%	H.S grad or less	42.3%		
Over 64	16.1%	Some college	32.6%	**Health Insurance**	
Work		College Degree, 4 yr	17.1%	With health insurance coverage	93.4%
White Collar	33.3%	Post grad	8.0%		
Sales and Service	40.0%	**Military**		**Public Assistance**	
Blue Collar	26.8%	Veteran	9.3%	Cash public assistance income	2.6%
Government	11.5%	Active Duty	0.0%		
				Food stamp/SNAP benefits	10.8%

Voter Turnout			
2015 Total Citizens 18+	577,570	2016 House Turnout as % CVAP	67%
2016 House turnout	384,977	2014 House Turnout as % CVAP	50%

2012 Presidential Vote		
Barack Obama	225,585	(56%)
Mitt Romney	170,753	(42%)

2016 Presidential Vote		
Donald Trump	190,410	(48%)
Hillary Clinton	176,535	(45%)
Gary Johnson	15,661	(4%)

Cook Partisan Voting Index: D+1

Northeast Iowa, along the Mississippi River and westward, has some of the loveliest landscape in America. Here the Mississippi flows past green bluffs, then broadens out in great quiet pools alongside picturesque towns. A century and a half ago, as settlers surged west of the Mississippi, Germans stopped at the river bluffs reminiscent of their native land and built neat farmhouses and substantial towns. Inland, on the rolling hills portrayed with surprisingly little exaggeration in the paintings of Iowa's Grant Wood, and in the more open territory to the west, New England Yankees and Midwesterners built their characteristic farmhouses, barns, town halls, church spires and small colleges. Railroad companies, headquartered in Chicago, extended their networks of steel rails over the plains and rivers. German Catholics settled Dubuque, whose giant Victorian courthouse looks down on the river.

Dubuque is a self-styled green city that has some large factories but is also proud of its waterfront-generated tourism. *Forbes* magazine in 2010 named Dubuque the best small city in America for families, and the city received All America City awards in 2012 and 2013. Local leaders cite their vision of a "Sustainable Dubuque," which allowed them to transform a rusting city in the 1980s into a successful place that rejuvenated urban life. Among the long-standing employers is John Deere, which employs about 2,000 people and has boosted its output of crawler products, a large and powerful tractor.

Southwest of Dubuque is Cedar Rapids, Iowa's second-largest city. It sports high-tech employers and contemporary office buildings. Unlike most of Iowa, its population boomed in the past two decades, and its per capita income rose. Both Cedar Rapids and Waterloo "built an internet infrastructure in the mid-1990s to draw technology companies to the area," then nurtured small technology companies, the *Des Moines Register* reported. The production of ethanol and other biofuels in Cedar Rapids contributed to its economic health. Although ethanol production has slumped in recent years with the decline in demand for gasoline blends and with the expiration in 2012 of the federal tax credit for ethanol, C.R. continues to produce more ethanol than any other city in the world. It remains the number-one corn-processing city in the world. Traditional industries remain a mainstay: Go down by the river, and you can't miss the smell of cooking oats coming from the Quaker Oats and General Mills factories. The city has a recent history of severe floods from the Cedar River, but has failed to secure federal funding for levees and flood walls. In Waterloo, the John Deere operations employ 4,700. Anamosa, in Jones County just east of Cedar Rapids, was the home of Wood, best known for his famous *American Gothic* painting - the models for the two figures were his dentist and Wood's own sister, who died in 1990.

The 1st Congressional District covers much of northeast Iowa, including the Mississippi riverfront and Cedar Rapids, Dubuque and Waterloo. Politically, this area has leaned Democratic. Dubuque, heavily German Catholic, for years has been Iowa's most Democratic city, unless abortion rights are the issue. But the district had a remarkable swing in the 2016 presidential election. Donald Trump won the 1st, 48%-45%; he led in 18 of the 20 counties, losing only Cedar Rapids-based Linn and Waterloo-based Black Hawk; he won Dubuque by 610 votes. In 2012, President Barack Obama won 56%-42% and took 17 counties, losing only three surrounding Cedar Rapids.

SECOND DISTRICT

Dave Loebsack (D)

Elected 2006, 6th term; b. Dec 23, 1952, Sioux City; Iowa State University (IA), B.S., 1974; Iowa State University (IA), M.A., 1976; University of California, Santa Barbara, Ph.D., 1985; Methodist; Married (Teresa Loebsack); 2 children (2 from previous marriage); 2 stepchildren; 3 grandchildren.

Professional Career: Professor, Cornell College, 1982-2006.

DC Office: 1527 LHOB 20515, 202-225-6576, Fax: 202-226-0757, loebsack.house.gov.

State Offices: Davenport, 563-323-5988; Iowa City, 319-351-0789.

Committees: *Energy & Commerce*: Communications & Technology, Energy.

Group Ratings

	ADA	ACLU	AFL-CIO	LCV	ITI	COC	HAFA	ACU	CFG	FRC
2016	-	88%	-	97%	83%	64%	14%	0%	4%	0%
2015	75%	C	100%	94%	C	60%	C	0%	0%	0%

Almanac Ratings 2015

	Economy	Social	Foreign	Composite
Liberal	74%	86%	74%	78%
Conservative	26%	14%	26%	22%

Key Votes of the 114th Congress

1. Keystone Pipeline	Y	5. Puerto Rico Debt	Y	9. Offenses by Aliens	NV
2. Trade Deals	N	6. Medical Marijuana	Y	10. Troops in Iraq	N
3. Export-Import Bank	Y	7. Sanctuary Cities	N	11. Homeland Security $$	Y
4. Debt Ceiling Increase	Y	8. Armor-piercing Bullets	N	12. Trade Adjustment aid	Y

Election Results

Election	Name (Party)	Vote (%)	Cand. Spent	Ind. Exp. Support	Ind. Exp. Oppose
2016 General	Dave Loebsack (D)	198,571 (54%)	$617,589		
	Christopher Peters (R)	170,933 (46%)	$205,136		
2016 Primary	Dave Loebsack (D)	(100%)			

Prior winning percentages: 2014 (53%), 2012 (56%), 2010 (51%), 2008 (57%), 2006 (51%)

Democrat Dave Loebsack, elected in 2006, is a retired college professor who offsets his liberal leanings by seeking out similarly pragmatic Republicans. Stunningly, he has become the only Democrat in the six-member Iowa delegation. He too has had close races.

A native of Sioux City, Loebsack lived in poverty as a child with his mother, grandmother and three siblings in a two-bedroom house. He worked as a high school janitor to pay for college. He got a master's degree at Iowa State University and went on to the University of California, Davis, to earn a Ph.D. in political science. From 1982 until his election to Congress, he was a professor of international relations at Cornell College in Mount Vernon, a few miles from Cedar Rapids. He had been active in local politics for several years, including a stint as fundraising chairman for Linn County Democrats.

When Loebsack decided to challenge 15-term GOP Rep. Jim Leach in 2006, he insisted that his campaign was not an attack on Leach's three decades in Congress but rather on the GOP leadership in Congress; he called the popular Leach, a moderate and cerebral Republican, an "enabler" for his party leaders. The war in Iraq was a pivotal issue then. Leach was the only member of the Iowa delegation to oppose the war, but Loebsack sought to tie him to President George W. Bush's Defense secretary, Donald Rumsfeld, on the basis that Leach had been an aide to Rumsfeld when he was a House member from Illinois in the late 1960s. Leach refused to disparage his former boss, calling him a friend and insisting that Rumsfeld's ouster would not change the administration's policy in Iraq.

Loebsack raised $522,000, which ordinarily would not have been nearly enough for a competitive House race, and he had little support from the Democratic Congressional Campaign Committee. Leach unwittingly helped Loebsack overcome those obstacles by eschewing modern campaign practices, particularly negative campaigning; he was a notoriously reluctant fundraiser. He refused to accept contributions from political action committees or from sources outside the district and raised only $491,000. Leach was endorsed by the district's major newspapers, but that wasn't enough. Loebsack won, 51%-49%.

In Washington, Loebsack has had a lower profile than most other members of Iowa's congressional delegation. House Minority Whip Steny Hoyer told the *Iowa City Press-Citizen* that he considered him "one of the more thoughtful members" of Congress. One of his first official actions was to sponsor a measure to name the federal building in Davenport the James A. Leach Federal Building; it passed the House in 2007.

Although he initially compiled a liberal voting record, Loebsack has moved steadily to the center since Republicans regained control of the House in 2011. The *Almanac's* ratings for 2015 ranked him among the most conservative House Democrats in each of the three issue areas. He has been among the Democrats joining Republicans in calling for the comptroller general to audit the Federal Reserve, and he joined GOP lawmakers in supporting an end to public subsidies of the national party conventions. He joined the Center Aisle Caucus, an informal group of about 40 House members seeking to establish greater civility between the parties.

On the Armed Services Committee, Loebsack added a provision to the 2012 defense authorization bill to have behavioral health specialists embedded with National Guard and Reserve units during training. He drew praise at home for protecting the Rock Island Arsenal from cutbacks. In January 2015, he made an unusual mid-career switch of committee assignments to Energy and Commerce. On that panel, he pushed for legislation to assist rural areas, including encouragement of regulatory action to promote more broadband in underserved places. He occasionally has shown traces of his earlier activism. In June 2016, he joined the Democrats' sit-in on the House floor to demand votes on gun legislation. "This isn't a stunt," he said in response to criticism from Speaker Paul Ryan. "We're serious about this."

Loebsack has faced competitive campaigns. He won a comfortable reelection, 57%-39%, in 2008 against political neophyte Mariannette Miller-Meeks, a Republican ophthalmologist. She returned for a rematch in 2010, hoping the national political climate favoring her party would give her a boost. She criticized Loebsack's support for the health care overhaul and called for reforming the tax code. She remained roughly even with Loebsack on fundraising, and some polls showed her ahead in the closing weeks. But his work on behalf of flood-stricken communities in the district helped offset his support of Obama's policies, and he won, 51%-46%. When redistricting left Loebsack with a constituency nearly half new, GOP strategists hoped his professorial style might alienate some rural voters and they put up John Archer, a conservative attorney for farm equipment maker John Deere, an iconic company in Iowa. The National Republican Congressional Committee spent more than $760,000 to boost Archer's chances, but Loebsack spent plenty of time back home and won handily, 56%-43%.

In 2014, he was a national Republican target. His opponent again was Miller-Meeks. She spent $1 million from her own campaign and had another million from the NRCC. Loebsack spent $1.7 million, and survived the Iowa Democratic massacre that year, with 52.6 percent of the vote. His 19,600-vote margin in Johnson County exceeded his 14,000-vote overall lead in the district, which should be a warning signal. Loebsack also took the other relatively urban counties, but trailed badly in rural areas. In 2016, he had an easier campaign when his opponent, Christopher Peters, raised only $212,000. Still,

Loebsack's 54%-46% win was a signal that he could be vulnerable, even in the most Democratic district in the state.

Loebsack had criticism for Hillary Clinton after the 2016 campaign. "Iowa could have been taken a little more seriously," he told the *Quad City Times*. He left the door open to a run for governor in 2018..

Southeast Iowa: Davenport, Iowa City

Population		**Race and Ethnicity**		**Income**	
Total	772,811	White	86.8%	Median Income	$51,261 (233 out of 435)
Land area	12,262	Black	3.7%		
Pop/ sq mi	63.0	Latino	5.3%		
Born in state	69.0%	Asian	2.2%	Under $50,000	48.8%
		Two races	1.7%	$50,000-$99,999	32.8%
Age Groups		Other	0.3%	$100,000-$199,999	15.4%
Under 18	22.9%			$200,000 or more	3.0%
18-34	23.6%	**Education**		Poverty Rate	14.1%
35-64	38.2%	H.S grad or less	40.9%		
Over 64	15.4%	Some college	31.9%	**Health Insurance**	
		College Degree, 4 yr	17.3%	With health insurance coverage	91.9%
Work		Post grad	9.9%		
White Collar	34.2%				
Sales and Service	39.5%	**Military**		**Public Assistance**	
Blue Collar	26.3%	Veteran	8.7%	Cash public assistance income	2.6%
Government	15.9%	Active Duty	0.1%		
				Food stamp/SNAP benefits	12.4%

Voter Turnout			
2015 Total Citizens 18+	575,277	2016 House Turnout as % CVAP	64%
2016 House turnout	370,032	2014 House Turnout as % CVAP	47%

2012 Presidential Vote		
Barack Obama	219,946	(56%)
Mitt Romney	168,534	(43%)

2016 Presidential Vote		
Donald Trump	186,384	(49%)
Hillary Clinton	170,796	(44%)
Gary Johnson	13,719	(4%)

Cook Partisan Voting Index: D+1

Southeast Iowa is little-known to outsiders. It is a land of rolling hills and deep river valleys, of undulant farm fields and big skies, of prosperous small towns and grain elevators and factories. Even political writers, who come to Iowa by the thousands for the quadrennial presidential caucuses, tend to hang out in Des Moines and do their reporting there or in the counties within an hour's drive of the city. In the southeastern part of the state, one can find Iowa's contributions to the Quad Cities along the Mississippi River and the Illinois border. Davenport, on the hills over the Mississippi, still has the look of the city where Ronald Reagan got his first radio job. Now, its largest employers are John Deere and the Rock Island Arsenal. Bettendorf is where riverboat gambling was launched in the U.S. in 1991.

West of Davenport is Iowa City, a university town dotted with trendy bookstores and vegetarian eateries. The University of Iowa is known for its Writers' Workshop, which produced the nation's first creative writing degree program and some of its most gifted young authors, including John Irving and Ann Patchett. Iowa City has been ranked among the most gay-friendly cities by various publications. Iowa City resident Zach Wahls cofounded the group Scouts for Equality in 2012 to push the Boy Scouts of America to accept gays. Muscatine County, near the Mississippi River, had the first two towns in Iowa with a Hispanic majority, a legacy of abundant farm work in the area and, more recently, jobs at the Tyson Foods pork processing plant in nearby Columbus Junction. Hundreds of workers who perform grueling jobs at the plant have been Burmese refugees. Since a 2008 raid of an Iowa slaughterhouse, where nearly 400 immigrants were arrested, companies report that they have become more careful about hiring only employees with legal papers. That has become more challenging with the area's unemployment rate, which has been among the lowest in the nation. By 2016, more than 1,000 refugees from Congo recently had settled in Johnson City.

The 2nd Congressional District covers the southeast quadrant of the state, with regularly shaped lines. Its population centers are Davenport and Iowa City, but it also offers up some offbeat claims to fame. Bentonsport, in Van Buren County near the Missouri border, is an artists' and craftsmen's colony. Iowa's newest city, incorporated in 2001, is Maharishi Vedic City, in Jefferson County, where followers of the Maharishi Mahesh Yogi built Maharishi University in 1973 and made the town a magnet for believers in transcendental meditation. Politically, the district usually supports Democrats, thanks in large part to big Democratic majorities in Iowa City, where Bernie Sanders got the largest crowd in his 2016 campaign for the Iowa's Democratic presidential caucuses. But November brought an unexpected shift: Donald Trump won 49%-44% and he won every county except for Iowa City-based Johnson and Davenport-based Scott, which are the two largest counties in the 2nd. Like the rest of the state, its voters don't like to be taken for granted.

THIRD DISTRICT

David Young (R)

Elected 2014, 2nd term; b. May 11, 1968, Van Meter; Drake University (IA), B.A.; Buena Vista University, Att.; Lutheran; Single.

Professional Career: Staff, U.S. Sen. Hank Brown, 1993-1996; Staff, U.S. Sen. James Bunning, 1998-2006; Chief of Staff, U.S. Sen. Charles Grassley, 2006-2013.

DC Office: 240 CHOB 20515, 202-225-5476, Fax: 202-226-1329, davidyoung.house.gov.

State Offices: Council Bluffs, 712-325-1404; Creston, 641-782-2495; Des Moines, 515-282-1909.

Committees: *Appropriations*: Agriculture, Rural Development, FDA & Related Agencies, Financial Services & General Government, Transportation, HUD & Related Agencies.

Group Ratings

	ADA	ACLU	AFL-CIO	LCV	ITI	COC	HAFA	ACU	CFG	FRC
2016	-	5%	-	3%	100%	100%	60%	76%	66%	92%
2015	5%	C	4%	3%	C	85%	C	83%	69%	92%

Almanac Ratings 2015

	Economy	Social	Foreign	Composite
Liberal	5%	9%	5%	6%
Conservative	95%	91%	95%	94%

Key Votes of the 114th Congress

1. Keystone Pipeline	Y	5. Puerto Rico Debt	Y	9. Offenses by Aliens	Y
2. Trade Deals	Y	6. Medical Marijuana	N	10. Troops in Iraq	N
3. Export-Import Bank	N	7. Sanctuary Cities	Y	11. Homeland Security $$	N
4. Debt Ceiling Increase	N	8. Armor-piercing Bullets	Y	12. Trade Adjustment aid	Y

Election Results

Election	Name (Party)	Vote (%)		Cand. Spent	Ind. Exp. Support	Ind. Exp. Oppose
2016 General	David Young (R)	238,983	(61%)	$2,454,046	$331,930	$3,503,981
	Jim Mowrer (D)	155,002	(40%)	$1,940,542	$332,818	$3,668,910
	Bryan Holder (L)	15,372	(4%)			
2016 Primary	David Young (R)	17,852	(85%)			
	Joe Grandanette (R)	3,134	(15%)			

Prior winning percentages: 2014 (53%)

Former Senate aide David Young, elected in 2014, has twice won this competitive seat by surprisingly comfortable margins after an improbable rise from his initial near-defeat in the GOP primary. He showed his Capitol Hill experience by gaining a seat on the Appropriations Committee and quickly settled into an influential position for a first-termer in the House.

A native of Des Moines, Young attended Drake University and worked as a consumer-loan trainee after graduating. He served on the legislative staffs of GOP Sens. Hank Brown of Colorado and Jim Bunning of Kentucky. He spent several years as chief of staff to Sen. Chuck Grassley of Iowa, which can be a productive way to learn about a state and its politics. His pitch to voters relied heavily on his experience, and he vowed to hit the ground running as soon as he was sworn into office. Democrats castigated him as a Beltway insider, which has become a derogatory term. But he seems to have flourished.

In a 2012 post-redistricting battle of veteran incumbents after Iowa had lost a House district, Republican Tom Latham defeated Democrat Leonard Boswell, 52%-44%. That made Latham one of just 17 House Republicans sitting in districts carried by President Barack Obama that year. When Latham decided to retire in 2014, Young ran and placed fifth in a six-way Republican primary. But after nobody received the requisite 35 percent of the vote, he emerged victorious from a special nominating convention that went five ballots, drawing the ire of conservative and libertarian activists. State Sen. Brad Zaun, who led the first round of the GOP primary vote, proposed to rewrite Iowa election law to require that the top two candidates in the primary have a runoff if no one wins more than 35 percent of the vote.

Against Democrat Staci Appel, a former state senator, Young won an endorsement from *The Des Moines Register*, which emphasized his experience on Capitol Hill. Both candidates made a priority of job creation and economic growth. Appel emphasized women's health and Young focused on government reform. Gun control also emerged as an issue in the campaign: Americans for Responsible Solutions PAC, the political arm of the anti-gun-violence group started by former Democratic Rep. Gabby Giffords of Arizona, launched a six-figure ad buy in October criticizing Young, while the National Rifle Association sought to link Appel with former New York City Mayor Michael Bloomberg, a leading NRA critic. Appel outspent Young $2.2 million to $2 million, and they roughly split about $7 million in national party aid. Despite Democrats' initial confidence, Appel proved to be a weak candidate. Young won with unexpected ease, 53%-42%, better than Latham's margin two years earlier. Appel won 48%-47% in Polk County, which cast a bit more than half of the district vote. But Young won every other county, several by more than 2-to-1 margins.

In the House, Young was one of two freshmen Republicans to get a seat on the Appropriations Committee. He said he was helped because he knew committee chairman Hal Rogers of Kentucky from his earlier work with Bunning. Plus, his predecessor Latham was a veteran member of Appropriations. Unlike fellow Iowa GOP freshman Rod Blum, Young voted for John Boehner for Speaker. Having those connections was helpful. More important was Young's ability to utilize them. He spent time with GOP presidential candidates at early Iowa caucus events.

Young also kept busy with legislation. On the House-passed bill in July 2015 to give Congress authority to review all new regulations from the executive branch, he won a roll-call vote on his amendment to require agencies to make available online the data, science, studies and analyses upon which each regulation is proposed. In November 2016, he won enactment of his bill to require that a veteran's call to a crisis hotline be answered in a timely manner by a qualified person.

In 2016, both Zaun and Appel initially discussed a potential re-match with Young, but each failed to follow through. Instead, Young's chief challenge came from another losing candidate in 2014: Democrat Jim Mowrer, who lost to Rep. Steve King, 62%-38%, in the neighboring 4th District. Mowrer, an Iraq war vet, raised $1.9 million to $2.5 million for Young. Each received more than $3 million in support from party committees. Mowrer tightened the margin from Young's initial victory. But, as in 2014, Young won every county except for Polk, which he lost this time by 271 votes out of nearly 210,000 cast.

After the release of Donald Trump's lewd comments in a 2005 video, Young called them "disgusting and indefensible." But he continued to support Trump's presidential candidacy. For now, Young seems secure, at least until the next round of redistricting.

Southwest Iowa: Des Moines, Council Bluffs

Population		**Race and Ethnicity**		**Income**	
Total	791,250	White	84.7%	Median Income	$58,545 (155 out of 435)
Land area	8,790	Black	3.9%		
Pop/ sq mi	90.0	Latino	6.5%		
Born in state	67.8%	Asian	2.7%	Under $50,000	42.4%
		Two races	1.9%	$50,000-$99,999	33.8%
Age Groups		Other	0.4%	$100,000-$199,999	19.3%
Under 18	25.1%			$200,000 or more	4.3%
18-34	22.7%	**Education**		Poverty Rate	11.8%
35-64	38.9%	H.S grad or less	36.7%		
Over 64	13.3%	Some college	31.7%	**Health Insurance**	
Work		College Degree, 4 yr	22.4%	With health insurance coverage	92.9%
White Collar	38.2%	Post grad	9.1%		
Sales and Service	41.3%	**Military**		**Public Assistance**	
Blue Collar	20.6%	Veteran	8.6%	Cash public assistance income	2.4%
Government	12.6%	Active Duty	0.1%	Food stamp/SNAP benefits	13.1%

Voter Turnout			
2015 Total Citizens 18+	566,574	2016 House Turnout as % CVAP	69%
2016 House turnout	390,287	2014 House Turnout as % CVAP	50%

2012 Presidential Vote		
Barack Obama	203,622	(51%)
Mitt Romney	186,645	(47%)

2016 Presidential Vote		
Donald Trump	192,960	(48%)
Hillary Clinton	178,937	(45%)
Gary Johnson	16,693	(4%)

Cook Partisan Voting Index: R+1

Iowa, which today seems very much in the middle of the country, was once part of the West. It was not only the home of sober farmers and pious burghers, but also the eastern terminus of the first transcontinental railroad, a way station for people in a hurry to get across the Great Plains to the Rockies and the Pacific Northwest. Those who stayed behind used the wealth accumulated by methodical husbandry of their fertile farmlands to implant firmly the glories of Western civilization. One can feel that impulse today in Des Moines, looking across the river from downtown to the Victorian capitol, its gold dome above a Corinthian pediment. Terrace Hill, the beautifully restored governor's mansion, sits atop a rise overlooking the Raccoon River.

The city of Des Moines remains classically Middle American, even as it gains a livelier downtown and spreads into the countryside. *Forbes* in 2015 named Des Moines the number-two spot in the country for jobs. The area has become a sanctuary for people looking for a family-friendly urban lifestyle. Insurance, agricultural supply, printing and financial service businesses are expanding in office centers downtown and at freeway interchanges. Principal Financial Group employs more than 7,900 people in the area, and the company also has naming rights to Principal Park, where the city's Iowa Cubs minor league baseball team plays. Kemin Industries, which makes nutritional ingredients, plans to complete in 2017 its multi-phase expansion of its headquarters for $126 million. More than 12,000 Bosnians have settled in Des Moines, many of whom work at meat-packing. Overall, the city's economy is stable, with steady job growth since the recession ended.

Des Moines and the southwest corner of Iowa make up the 3rd Congressional District. The second-most populous city here is Council Bluffs, home to the mansion of Gen. Grenville Dodge, who in 1859 lobbied Illinois lawyer Abraham Lincoln on the need for a transcontinental railroad. Lincoln got it through Congress in 1862, Dodge became its chief engineer, and Council Bluffs became its eastern terminus when it was completed in 1869. Surrounded by beef grazing territory, Council Bluffs looks west across the Missouri River to Omaha, taking on the culturally more conservative tone of Nebraska. The area has developed an economically hip side with a total of six data centers owned by Microsoft,

Facebook and Google, and additional expansions underway that cost billions of dollars. Iowa has become an attractive place for these facilities because of its tax incentives, plenty of cheap land and access to high-speed fiber optics. Also in the district from a slower era is Madison County, famous for the wooden covered bridges that gave their name to a best-selling novel and film.

The small rural towns, where businesses have been struggling, were fertile ground for Donald Trump's campaign. Aside from Des Moines and Polk County, he won the other 15 counties in the 3rd, with an overall win of 48%-45%. President Barack Obama won the district with 52 percent in 2008 and 51 percent in 2012.

FOURTH DISTRICT

Steve King (R)

Elected 2002, 8th term; b. May 28, 1949, Storm Lake; Northwest Missouri State University, Att.; Roman Catholic; Married (Marilyn King); 3 children; 7 grandchildren.

Elected Office: IA Senate, 1996-2002.

Professional Career: Owner, King Construction Co., 1975-2002.

DC Office: 2210 RHOB 20515, 202-225-4426, Fax: 202-225-3193, steveking.house.gov.

State Offices: Ames, 515-232-2885; Fort Dodge, 515-573-2738; Mason City, 641-201-1624; Sioux City, 712-224-4692; Spencer, 712-580-7754.

Committees: *Agriculture*: Livestock & Foreign Agriculture, Nutrition. *Judiciary*: Constitution & Civil Justice (Chmn), Immigration & Border Security. *Small Business*: Agriculture, Energy & Trade, Contracting & Workforce.

Group Ratings

	ADA	ACLU	AFL-CIO	LCV	ITI	COC	HAFA	ACU	CFG	FRC
2016	-	5%	-	3%	83%	100%	75%	88%	71%	100%
2015	5%	C	4%	3%	C	68%	C	87%	87%	100%

Almanac Ratings 2015

	Economy	Social	Foreign	Composite
Liberal	3%	4%	8%	5%
Conservative	97%	97%	92%	95%

Key Votes of the 114th Congress

1. Keystone Pipeline	Y	5. Puerto Rico Debt	N	9. Offenses by Aliens	Y
2. Trade Deals	Y	6. Medical Marijuana	N	10. Troops in Iraq	N
3. Export-Import Bank	N	7. Sanctuary Cities	Y	11. Homeland Security $$	N
4. Debt Ceiling Increase	N	8. Armor-piercing Bullets	Y	12. Trade Adjustment aid	N

Election Results

Election	Name (Party)	Vote (%)	Cand. Spent	Ind. Exp. Support	Ind. Exp. Oppose
2016 General	Steve King (R)	198,658 (54%)	$931,687	$6,977	$18,475
	Kim Weaver (D)	142,993 (39%)	$139,786		
2016 Primary	Steve King (R)	28,858 (65%)			
	Rick Bertrand (R)	15,714 (35%)			

Prior winning percentages: 2014 (62%), 2012 (53%), 2010 (66%), 2008 (60%), 2006 (59%), 2004 (63%), 2002 (62%)

Republican Steve King, who first won his seat in 2002, practices a brand of incendiary, in-your-face conservatism that has been shared by tea party-friendly House colleagues but often is hostile to party leaders. He generates lots of attention with his strongly stated views, especially on immigration. He showed his political influence in 2016 as a top adviser to Sen. Ted Cruz, who won the Iowa caucuses. But he took a low profile after immigration hard-liner Donald Trump locked up the Republican nomination.

King was born in Storm Lake and attended Northwest Missouri State University, though he didn't graduate. In 1975, he founded the King Construction Co. After building up his business, he launched his political career in 1996, with his election to the state Senate, where he quickly gained a reputation as a strong conservative. He opposed abortion rights, racial quotas and preferences, and same-sex marriage. He sponsored Iowa's "God and Country" bill, which required Iowa schools to recognize that the United States "has derived its strength from biblical values," and he was a driving force behind the state's English-only law. On economic matters, King supported repeal of the state's inheritance tax, and backed a 15 percent state income tax cut and a national right-to-work law.

When the House seat came open in 2002, King ran as a full-spectrum conservative and the only rural candidate among the four chief contenders; he called for limiting federal control of local schools. He led in the June primary with 30 percent of the vote. Because no candidate received the required 35 percent, the nomination was determined by a special party convention three weeks later. The 533 voting delegates needed three ballots to select a winner. King led on each ballot and defeated House Speaker Brent Siegrist of Council Bluffs, 272-253, in the final round. The general election outcome was never in doubt.

In the House, King has not been shy about sharing his hyper-partisan views, and he gets national press coverage for controversial remarks. During the January 2015 State of the Union message, he complained on Twitter that an undocumented immigrant seated with first lady Michelle Obama was "deportable." After King filed a bill that intended to keep the courts from ruling on gay-marriage cases, Democratic Rep. Jared Polis of Colorado joked in April 2015 that he planned to file the "Restrain Steve King from Legislating Act." A Carroll, Iowa, *Daily Times Herald* columnist who assembled some of King's quotes into a book, *King Kong Krazy*, called him "maniacally nationalistic."

The conservative super PAC American Crossroads, backed by top GOP political strategist Karl Rove, announced an effort in 2013 to discourage what it considers fringe candidates like King from running in primaries against supposedly more electable Republicans. The group's president, Steven Law, cited King's potential interest in the 2014 Senate race to succeed retiring Democrat Tom Harkin. "We're concerned about Steve King's Todd Akin problem," Law told *The New York Times*, referring to the Missouri conservative whose 2012 Senate campaign self-destructed with his comment that pregnancy cannot result from "legitimate rape." King makes no apologies for his style. "We've got to shoot from the hip sometimes," he said. "It's not always 'Ready, aim, fire.' Sometimes it's just time to fire."

King has been an outspoken proponent of tougher immigration laws. He advocates English as the official language of the United States. In 2008, an Iowa district court judge ruled in favor of King's challenge to state officials who had placed bilingual voting forms on state websites. In 2007, as the ranking Republican on the Judiciary Immigration Subcommittee, King built a model fence on the House floor to show how simple it would be to construct a 2,000-mile fence on the border with Mexico. In a 2013 interview, he said that many illegal immigrants "weigh 130 pounds and they've got calves the size of cantaloupes because they're hauling 75 pounds of marijuana across the desert."

When Republicans took control of the House in 2011, King introduced a bill to end birthright citizenship, an idea that has gained currency in conservative circles but generates strong opposition among Hispanics. "Steve King is positioning our party for disaster," the Latino group Somos Republicans said in a statement. The measure went nowhere. King was in line to serve as chairman of the Immigration Subcommittee, but the gavel went instead to a back-bench representative from California. King blamed Speaker John Boehner, whom he said "isn't very aggressive on immigration." When Democratic Sen. Charles Schumer of New York blamed "the Steve Kings of the world" for the unwillingness of the House to consider immigration legislation in 2014, King challenged Senate Democratic leaders to a duel. With their approach to immigration legislation, he said, "America would be wiped out from a perspective of the rule of law." In a 2014 interview with *The New York Times*, he said that Congress should take the initial steps for an impeachment inquiry against Obama.

King had reelection troubles in 2012. His Democratic opponent was Christie Vilsack; her husband, Tom Vilsack, had been Iowa governor and then served as Obama's secretary of Agriculture. Christie Vilsack scored points by blasting King for failing to sign onto a Democratic measure to force a vote on the stalled 2012 farm bill. With help from popular Gov. Terry Branstad, he escaped with a 53%-45% victory. That was an expensive contest, with King outspending Vilsack $3.8 million to $3.5 million. In the strongly Republican 2014 campaign in Iowa, King breezed with 62 percent of the vote against Jim Mowrer, an Iraq war veteran, who outspent King $2.2 million to $2 million. Democrats turned their attention elsewhere in 2016, and King coasted to a low-cost reelection.

In January 2015, King took a leading role in opposing Boehner for another term as Speaker. "We need a Speaker of the House who carries in his bones the conviction of our oath," he wrote for Breitbart.com. When he voted against the spending bill in March for the Homeland Security Department, King said he suffered "retribution" from the Speaker, who denied him a seat on a House overseas delegation. He told CNN that "the appetite is growing" to oust Boehner as Speaker. Six months later, Boehner resigned under pressure. King threatened to oppose Paul Ryan for Speaker on immigration grounds, but backed down when Ryan won wide support among Republicans.

As national co-chairman of the Cruz campaign, King was instrumental in the narrow victory of Cruz in the Iowa caucuses. He suggested to *Politico* that Donald Trump was using untoward tactics to win support, such as "an unlimited reservoir of resources that he can bring to bear," and called Cruz the "one man that stands out as the courageous conservative whom I believe can restore the soul of America." Despite the often strident views of Trump on illegal immigration, King kept his distance after he became the presidential nominee. During an interview with CNN in July, he voiced concern that Trump was "softening" his view on enforcement of immigration laws. In such a scenario, King warned that he would "push back on that."

In 2017, King became chairman of the Judiciary Subcommittee on Constitution and Civil Justice, after previously having been denied such a perk.

Northwest and Central Iowa: Sioux City, Ames

Population		**Race and Ethnicity**		**Income**	
Total	760,796	White	88.7%	Median Income	$49,790 (259 out of 435)
Land area	22,757	Black	1.4%		
Pop/ sq mi	33.4	Latino	6.3%		
Born in state	73.0%	Asian	1.8%	Under $50,000	50.2%
		Two races	1.3%	$50,000-$99,999	33.5%
Age Groups		Other	0.5%	$100,000-$199,999	13.8%
Under 18	22.8%			$200,000 or more	2.6%
18-34	22.5%	**Education**		Poverty Rate	12.8%
35-64	37.3%	H.S grad or less	43.2%		
Over 64	17.4%	Some college	34.2%	**Health Insurance**	
		College Degree, 4 yr	15.7%	With health insurance coverage	92.5%
Work		Post grad	6.9%		
White Collar	32.1%				
Sales and Service	39.0%	**Military**		**Public Assistance**	
Blue Collar	28.9%	Veteran	9.1%	Cash public assistance income	2.1%
Government	14.3%	Active Duty	0.1%		
				Food stamp/SNAP benefits	10.7%

Voter Turnout			
2015 Total Citizens 18+	565,705	2016 House Turnout as % CVAP	65%
2016 House turnout	370,259	2014 House Turnout as % CVAP	49%

2012 Presidential Vote		
Mitt Romney	204,685	(53%)
Barack Obama	173,391	(45%)

2016 Presidential Vote		
Donald Trump	231,229	(60%)
Hillary Clinton	127,401	(33%)
Gary Johnson	13,113	(3%)

Cook Partisan Voting Index: R+11

Sioux City, one of the oldest market towns on the Great Plains, is nestled in the loess bluffs above the Missouri River. Sioux City has not grown much in the past half century. Its original economic base has become obsolete: The waterfront, once raucous with boatmen and stockyard workers, is now quiet. The stockyards, which employed thousands of people and slaughtered millions of hogs during their peak years in the 1920s, are shuttered. Downtown stores have been replaced by shopping malls at the edge of town, where people spend a day doing a season's shopping and then drive for hours to return to farm communities in one of four nearby states.

There are still plenty of hogs in western Iowa. Instead of meeting sellers in the markets in Sioux City, packers now contract directly with large farms and have built modern slaughterhouses nearby. Tyson

Foods has facilities in Buena Vista and Crawford counties. In 2015, 31 percent of Iowa's energy was based on wind farming and it is second only to Texas in the amount of electricity generated by wind, despite objections from some farmers to the noise and the hazard to birds. Mid-America, which is owned by Warren Buffett's Berkshire Hathaway, built the state's largest wind farm, with 218 turbines, near Primghar. All of this helped Sioux City rank 13th on Forbes' 2014 list of best places for doing business.

Western Iowa is small-town territory. It has some of the world's most productive soil and some of its most creative agricultural scientists and farmers. Ames, in Story County, is home to Iowa State University and had been the host of the Iowa Republican presidential straw poll, which has launched several nomination contests. But after exploring a new site with a much lower fee, Iowa GOP leaders canceled the straw poll as a nationally monitored political event. Republican Gov. Terry Branstad remarked in 2012 that the straw poll had "outlived its usefulness." Ames is part of the growth zone around Des Moines. In Winnebago County near the Minnesota border is Winnebago Industries, which manufactures motor homes and recreational vehicles on computer-controlled assembly lines with robotic equipment. The company has bounced back since the recession by shifting its appeal from retirees to younger consumers, who often prefer less gaudy vehicles. From its headquarters in Forest City, the company employs more than 3,000 employees.

The 4th Congressional District is Iowa's largest geographically, stretching from South Dakota nearly to Illinois. Donald Trump won this 90-percent white district with 60 percent of the vote. In 2008 and 2012, the 4th was the only district in the state Democrats lost. This time, they lost all four.

★ KANSAS ★

The Almanac of American Politics
National Journal

Congressional district boundaries were first effective for 2012.

Kansas is usually depicted as flat, average and uninteresting. It's not really, and in recent years its politics have been anything but. Fiscal conservatives have tried to turn the state into a small-government utopia, with mixed results at best. Meanwhile, one of its most prominent politicians pushed the envelope on policies that seek to crack down on illegal immigration and voter fraud.

The political upheaval of recent years is a reminder that Kansas' history has been punctuated by episodes of anger and rage, sweeping through the tall sheaves like the tornado in the *Wizard of Oz*. The state was born in a moment of violence: the Bleeding Kansas of the 1850s that led proximately to the war that divided the nation. The trigger was the Kansas-Nebraska Act of 1854, which left to local settlers the question of whether the new Kansas Territory would be a free or slave state. Pro-slavery "bushwhackers" rode over the line from Missouri, stealing elections and writing a pro-slavery constitution. But larger numbers of free-soil "jayhawkers," from New England and the Yankee-settled Great Lakes states, put down roots and, despite the massacres perpetrated by John Brown, prevailed and established their own law and order. This was a civil war before the Civil War. Later, Kansas became the birthplace of the Buffalo Soldiers, the African-American units that fought in the Indian Wars; their home base, Fort Leavenworth, is the oldest continuously active military reservation west of the Mississippi River and remains a key facility today.

The ultimate effect of the battle over slavery was calming for Kansas: The anti-slavery majority bent the soil to the plow and built small towns with sturdy networks of schools, churches and colleges. But the rebellious impulse did not entirely die out. Kansans' livelihoods were always at risk: Hailstorms, grasshopper invasions, dry seasons or a drop in world farm prices could mean disaster for thousands of families. The high rainfall of the 1880s attracted hundreds of thousands of new settlers. The low rainfall of the 1890s produced a bust and a populist rebellion. "What you farmers should do," Kansas orator Mary Ellen Lease said, "is to raise less corn and more hell." For a few years in the Populist era of the 1890s and then in the farm rebellions of the 1930s, 1950s and 1970s, Kansans did. But afterwards, the state always returned to jayhawker Republicanism.

Owing to its geography, Kansas was, and remains, a farm state. It is flatter than an IHOP pancake, reported some geographers in 2003, though that flatness is not unrelieved. The Flint Hills between Kansas City and Wichita are irregular uplands, with the Tallgrass Prairie National Preserve hosting bus trips where bison still range. The Kansas City Symphony holds a concert every June in the Flint Hills, and concertgoers sometimes get pelted with rain, a reminder of the imaginary tornado that swept Dorothy and Toto out of Kansas and of the very real 205-mile-per-hour tornado that destroyed the town of Greensburg on the plains in 2007. Kansas can also be afflicted by drought, with seasonal rainfall measured in tenths of inches: A drought in 2011, the worst since the dust storms of the 1930s, lowered the water table while livestock and wildlife died from thirst and reservoirs were drained to keep barges afloat on the Missouri River. In 2014, all but 7 percent of the state was facing severe drought, and the Kansas Water Office noted that the Ogallala Aquifer - the Great Plains' vast underground reservoir - is declining faster than it is recharging and could be 70 percent gone within a half-century.

Kansas does have growing metropolitan pockets. The state's five biggest counties – Johnson (suburbs of Kansas City), Sedgwick (Wichita), Shawnee (Topeka), Wyandotte (Kansas City proper) and Douglas (Lawrence) – accounted for 53 percent of the state's population in 2015, and collectively they grew by 4.2 percent between 2010 and 2015, led by a 6.6 percent spurt in Johnson County. By contrast, the rest of the state shrank slightly in population, putting a new spin on the phrase, "Get the hell out of Dodge," which refers to the frontier town Dodge City in rural, southwestern Kansas. Most Kansans live in or within easy reach of metropolitan Kansas City, the nation's second largest railroad hub, which has a diverse economy that is by no means dependent on farming (though it does produce some of the nation's best barbecue). Wichita is the home base of Koch Industries, a conglomerate that started as an oil refining company and which recently has become a major force in politics, spending lavishly to promote the free-market credo of its owners, Charles and David Koch. But Kansas' trademark industry is aircraft. Beechcraft, Cessna, Lear and Spirit have plants there and Wichita factories produce 40 percent of the world's general aviation planes, though Wichita was hit hard when Boeing announced in January 2012 that it was closing its 97-building operation after 80 years. To the extent there is growth outside of the state's northeastern corner, it has been Kansas State University and the Army's Fort Riley and in the meatpacking towns of southwest Kansas, with large and increasing Hispanic populations in Dodge City, Garden City and the inaptly named Liberal (Donald Trump more than doubled Hillary Clinton's vote there in 2016). Unemployment peaked at only 7.3 percent in the Great Recession and remained slightly better than the national average by late 2016, although median incomes slightly lagged the national average. Supposedly monochrome Kansas has become 12 percent Hispanic, 5 percent black, and 3 percent Asian; Kansas's Hispanic population is now big enough to rank in the top half of states.

Kansas has been reliably Republican in presidential elections and in most congressional contests for years; it has not elected a Democrat to the Senate since 1932. But state politics was dominated for 40 years by a coalition of Democrats and moderate Republicans, according to University of Kansas political scientist Burdett Loomis. That was the case under Republican Gov. Bill Graves, elected in 1994 and 1998, and Democratic Gov. Kathleen Sebelius, elected in 2002 and 2006. When she resigned to become President Barack Obama's secretary of Health and Human Services, she was succeeded by her lieutenant governor, Mark Parkinson, a former Republican state chairman who (like other centrist Republicans) switched parties because of the rightward drift of many in the state GOP. Today, Republican heirs of Alf Landon, Dwight Eisenhower (whose presidential library is in his hometown of Abilene) and longtime Sens. Bob Dole and Nancy Landon Kassebaum have been eclipsed by Republicans with harder-edged conservative views on fiscal and social issues. In 1999, the conservative-led state Board of Education caused a national uproar when it issued guidelines that diminished the classroom role of evolution. After that, a slew of moderate Republicans won primaries, and the guidelines were repealed in 2007. The fiercest fights came over abortion rights. Sebelius vetoed a bill for stricter regulation of abortion clinics favored by conservatives. And abortion opponents were incensed by revelations that Wichita physician George Tiller was performing late-term abortions. Attorney General Phill Kline tried unsuccessfully to indict Tiller, then lost his primary for reelection in 2006. The fight ended in tragedy when Tiller was murdered by an anti-abortion activist in 2009.

By 2010, the tide in Kansas had turned conservative. Parkinson declined to run for a full term and Sam Brownback, after 14 years in the Senate and a brief 2008 run for president, was elected governor. Brownback and the legislature cut spending, abolished three state agencies, closed welfare offices and eliminated arts funding. In 2011, the legislature passed four bills limiting abortion and Brownback set up programs to encourage faith-based counseling on marriage and fatherhood. He returned a federal grant for a health insurance exchange under the national Democrats' health care legislation, and Secretary of State Kris Kobach, who helped write Arizona's laws on illegal immigration, pushed successfully to require voters to show photo identification and proof of citizenship. But Brownback's signature initiative, signed in mid-2012, was a tax cut that, among other things, wiped 330,000 state businesses off the tax rolls. Within months, he and the Koch-backed Americans for Prosperity targeted nine lawmakers for defeat in the August 2012 Republican primary; their candidates won, giving both chambers an even more solid conservative majority.

But the economic returns from the tax cuts were underwhelming, and Standard & Poor's and Moody's slashed the state's credit rating. Throughout 2014, Brownback's approval ratings lagged, but in a solidly Republican mid-term election year -- and with national Republicans going all out for endangered Sen. Pat Roberts -- Brownback beat the odds, winning by four points. The polarizing Kobach won reelection as well. But as Brownback's second term wore on, he posted approval ratings that were among the worst of any governor in the nation. In the 2016 legislative primaries, Brownback-aligned candidates lost a net of two dozen state House and Senate primaries to challengers backed by teachers' unions, roadbuilders and hospitals. Tea party-aligned Rep. Tim Huelskamp also lost his GOP primary. In the general election, the Democrats gained seats in both state legislative chambers, opening up the prospect of an alliance with moderate Republicans that could stymie or even roll back Brownback's initiatives. Voters in 2016 also rejected a conservative-led effort to oust five Supreme Court justices over controversial decisions on crime and other matters.

However, the statewide presidential results were not dramatically different than in 2012: Kansas voted for Donald Trump, 56%-36%, compared with 60%-38% for Mitt Romney. Trump's statewide vote haul shrank by almost 19,000 votes, while Clinton's fell by more than 13,000. (Between them, Libertarian Gary Johnson and Green Party nominee Jill Stein attracted almost 7 percent of the vote.) Only two counties went for Clinton – Wyandotte, a heavily urban, majority-minority area, and Douglas, home of the University of Kansas. The margin in Douglas shifted nine points toward Clinton, but the most notable change was in populous Johnson County, where Romney had won by 17 points but Trump won by fewer than 3 points. Trump won 21,000 fewer votes than Romney had, while Clinton won 19,000 more than Obama had in 2012 – a pattern of suburban shift toward the Democrats that was mirrored in other affluent suburbs across the country.

Population		**Race and Ethnicity**		**Income**	
Total	2,892,987	White	77.0%	Median Income	$52,205 (26 out of 50)
Land area	81,759	Black	5.7%		
Pop/ sq mi	35.4	Latino	11.2%	Under $50,000	47.7%
Born in state	59.0%	Asian	2.6%	$50,000-$99,999	31.9%
		Two races	2.7%	$100,000-$199,999	16.7%
Age Groups		Other	0.9%	$200,000 or more	3.7%
Under 18	25.0%			Poverty Rate	13.6%
18-34	23.7%	**Education**			
35-64	37.4%	H.S grad or less	36.8%	**Health Insurance**	
Over 64	14.0%	Some college	32.2%	With health insurance coverage	88.8%
Work		College Degree, 4 yr	20.0%		
		Post grad	11.0%		
White Collar	36.8%			**Public Assistance**	
Sales and Service	39.7%	**Military**		Cash public assistance income	2.0%
Blue Collar	23.5%	Veteran	9.2%		
Government	15.9%	Active Duty	0.8%	Food stamp/SNAP benefits	9.5%

Voter Turnout			
2015 Total Citizens 18+	2,053,919	2016 Pres Turnout as % CVAP	58%
2016 Pres Votes	1,184,402	2012 Pres Turnout as % CVAP	58%

Legislature	
Senate:	9D, 31R
House:	40D, 85R

Presidential Politics

2016 Democratic Caucus		
Bernie Sanders (D)	26,429	(68%)
Hillary Clinton (D)	12,593	(32%)
2016 Republican Caucus		
Ted Cruz (R)	37,512	(47%)
Donald Trump (R)	18,443	(23%)
Marco Rubio (R)	13,295	(17%)
John Kasich (R)	8,741	(11%)

2016 Presidential Vote		
Donald Trump (R)	671,018	(57%)
Hillary Clinton (D)	427,005	(36%)
Gary Johnson (L)	55,406	(5%)
Jill Stein (G)	23,506	(2%)
2012 Presidential Vote		
Mitt Romney (R)	692,634	(60%)
Barack Obama (D)	440,726	(38%)

Except for 1964, when it narrowly favored Lyndon Johnson over Barry Goldwater, Kansas has voted Republican for president for three-fourths of a century. In the 105 counties, George W. Bush, Mitt Romney and Donald Trump lost only two: Wyandotte, which includes Kansas City and has a majority-minority population; and Douglas, which is home to the University of Kansas in Lawrence. John McCain in 2008 lost one more, by just over 200 votes, Crawford County, home to Pittsburg State University. In 1996, the state legislature voted to cancel the April presidential primary and both parties have held caucuses since. Texas Sen. Ted Cruz handily beat Trump in the 2016 GOP contest, 48%-23%. Cruz's victory, given his campaign's attention to caucuses, was not a surprise. But the turnout was: More than 78,000 attended, compared with 30,377 in 2012. In the Democratic caucuses, Vermont Sen. Bernie Sanders defeated Hillary Clinton 68%-32%. More than 39,000 participated in the Democratic contest, relatively unchanged from the 37,089 in 2008, when Barack Obama overwhelmed Clinton by a nearly 3-1 margin.

Congressional Districts

115th Congress Lineup	4R	**114th Congress Lineup**	4R

In the spring of 2012, a coalition of Democrats and moderate Republicans in the state Senate passed one redistricting plan and the conservative-dominated House passed another; they adjourned in May without reaching agreement. A three-judge federal court took the case, and approved a map that moved Lawrence to the 2nd District, and put Manhattan, home of Kansas State University, and Fort Riley into the western and central 1st district. With the growing Republican dominance of Kansas, including all four seats in its House delegation, redistricting seems less relevant in partisan terms and more important for regional and business interests.

Governor

Sam Brownback (R)

Elected 2010, term expires 2019, 2nd term; b. Sep. 12, 1956, Garnett, KS; KS St. U., B.S. 1978; U. of KS, J.D. 1982; Catholic; Married (Mary); 5 children.

Elected Office: KS Secretary of Agriculture, 1986-1993; U.S. House, 1994-1996; U.S. Senate, 1996-2010.

Professional Career: Radio broadcaster, KKSU, 1978-1979; Practicing attorney, 1982-1986, 1993; Professor, KS State University Law School, 1982-86; Ogden & Leonardville City Attorney, 1983-1986; Fellow, White House Office of USTR, 1990-1991.

Office: 300 S.W. Tenth Ave., Suite 241-S, Topeka, 66612; 785-296-3232; Fax: 785-296-7973; Website: governor.kansas.gov.

Election Results

Election	Name (Party)	Vote (%)
2014 General	Sam Brownback (R)	433,196 (50%)
	Paul Davis (D)	401,100 (46%)
	Keen Umbehr (L)	35,206 (4%)
2014 Primary	Sam Brownback (R)	166,687 (63%)
	Jennifer Winn (R)	96,907 (37%)

Prior winning percentage: 2010 (63%); Senate: 2004 (69%), 1998 (65%), 1996 special (54%) ; House: 1994 (66%)

Kansas Republican Gov. Sam Brownback was elected in 2010 after spending two years in the House and 14 in the Senate. A social conservative who made a short-lived stab at the presidency in 2008, his aggressive exercise of power has put him at the vanguard of activist conservative governors and dismayed the state's Democrats and moderate Republicans, almost leading to his defeat in 2014. He won a second term by just four points in a strongly Republican midterm election, but moderate Republicans and Democrats made gains in 2016, and created a coalition that blunted some of Brownback's earlier agenda.

Brownback grew up on a farm in Anderson County, some 50 miles south of Kansas City; he has family roots in Osawatomie, a center of evangelical abolitionism in Kansas in the 1850s. He was state president of Future Farmers of America while in high school and student body president at Kansas State University. He worked briefly as a farm broadcaster before graduating from law school at the University of Kansas. He practiced law for four years in Manhattan, Kansas, then was appointed secretary of the state Board of Agriculture in 1986, serving until it was abolished in 1993. Brownback was a White House Fellow, working from 1990 to 1991 for Special Trade Representative Carla Hills.

Brownback's path to Congress began in March 1994, when 2nd District Rep. Jim Slattery, a Democrat, ran for governor. Brownback announced his candidacy for the seat, condemning "a welfare system that discourages the work ethic and encourages the disintegration of families, and a government that can't say no to spending or yes to reform." In the general election, Brownback defeated John Carlin, who was governor from 1978 to 1986, by carrying every county in a 66%-34% win. Brownback was among the "revolutionary" Republican freshmen in 1995 who shook up Congress. Brownback played a key role in passage of a bill cracking down on illegal immigration. His legislative director was an ambitious young conservative named Paul Ryan, later to become House Speaker. In 1995, he had a melanoma removed, and this brush with a fatal disease led him toward a deeper faith. An evangelical Christian, Brownback converted to Catholicism, with Sen. Rick Santorum of Pennsylvania as his sponsor. At a prayer breakfast, he apologized to then-Sen. Hillary Clinton of New York for having despised her and her husband years earlier when President Bill Clinton was in office. He also described washing the feet of a staffer at a farewell party to demonstrate respect and humility.

In May 1996, Republican Bob Dole of Kansas, in the midst of his presidential campaign, announced that he would resign from the Senate that June. Two days later, Brownback said he would seek the seat. But Republican Gov. Bill Graves chose a fellow moderate, Lt. Gov. Sheila Frahm, to fill the vacancy until the election, setting up a primary contest. Brownback won the August primary, 55%-42%. In the fall race for the remaining two years of Dole's term, Brownback faced Democrat Jill Docking, a Wichita stockbroker and the wife of a former lieutenant governor whose father and grandfather both served as governor. Brownback won convincingly, 54%-43%.

In the Senate, Brownback had a mostly conservative voting record. He sponsored bills to require doctors to tell women seeking abortions that fetuses can feel pain and to bar doctors from prescribing controlled drugs for use in assisted suicides. With Democratic Rep. John Lewis of Georgia, he worked to authorize the National Museum of African American History and Culture on the National Mall – now a reality -- and with Democratic Sen. Byron Dorgan of North Dakota, he sponsored a resolution apologizing to American Indians for past government misdeeds. To the dismay of many conservatives, Brownback was a leading co-sponsor of the immigration bill that passed in the Senate in 2006 that would have established a guest-worker program. Brownback was elected to a full, six-year term in 1998 after well-known Democrats declined to run. In 2004, Democrats again had a hard time finding a candidate to run against him, and he was reelected, carrying 104 of Kansas's 105 counties. After that election, conservatives encouraged Brownback to run for president. He made several trips to Iowa where, he hoped, his background in agriculture and his strong religious convictions would resonate with Republican caucus-goers. He touted Social Security privatization, but lagging in the polls and in fundraising, he was unable to break out of the pack. At the Iowa straw poll in August 2007, he finished third with 15 percent and soon after withdrew.

By early 2009, Brownback began seeking a different higher office: the governorship. No prominent Democrat rose to the challenge, leaving Brownback to face state Sen. Tom Holland, an information technology consultant, in the general election. Brownback won 63%-32%, becoming the state's first conservative governor in half a century. Early on, Brownback referred to his tenure as a "real live experiment" in conservative governance, a characterization he later said he regretted. He signed a bill banning late-term abortions and another to strip Planned Parenthood of federal family-planning grants. He appointed a secretary of social and rehabilitation services, Robert Siedlecki, who rewrote state contracts to encourage providers of state services to promote fatherhood and pro-family ideals. He drew national attention when he vetoed funding for the Kansas Arts Commission, making the state the only one in the country without an arts agency. He caused further consternation among Democrats, and even some Republicans, when he subsequently announced that he would return a $31.5 million federal grant aimed at helping the state set up health insurance exchanges under the 2010 health care law.

In 2012, Brownback - advised by supply-side guru Arthur Laffer and opposed by Democrats and moderate Republicans - enacted the largest tax cut in Kansas history, trimming more than $1 billion in state revenue. Brownback's ambitions were boosted further that August when a number of moderate GOP lawmakers were ousted in primary elections and conservatives won control of the Senate.

In the run-up to his 2014 reelection bid, Brownback's approval numbers were weak, weighted down not just by controversies surrounding his policy agenda but also by the state's floundering economy. Amid a budget gap of hundreds of millions of dollars and slower growth rates than those of its neighbors, credit agencies downgraded the state's rating, and the poverty rate rose. At the same time, some of Brownback's advisers came under investigation for influence peddling. Brownback won his primary, but his little-known challenger, Jennifer Winn, won a surprisingly large 37 percent of the vote. The state House minority leader, Paul Davis, mounted a challenge and charted the type of moderate course that had succeeded for Democrats in the past, picking up endorsements from more than 100 current and former Republican officials from the party's out-of-favor moderate wing. Polls in mid-2014 showed Davis with a lead, and some forecasters labeled the contest a toss-up. But Brownback, aided by an all-out GOP effort to reelect vulnerable Sen. Pat Roberts, eked out a 50%-46% victory, taking 80 percent of Republicans in a strong year for the party. He became just the second Republican in Kansas to win re-election to the governorship in half a century.

Following the narrow win, Brownback continued moving the state rightward. "Today, thanks in large part to Brownback, the state is a petri dish for movement conservatism, a window into how the national

Republican Party might govern if the opposition vanished," the *New York Times Magazine* wrote in 2015. Brownback signed a measure to limit what welfare recipients could spend money on (from movies to swimming pools to cruises), and he overturned a 2007 executive order by former Democratic Gov. Kathleen Sebelius that had provided protection against job discrimination due to sexual orientation. He also signed a bill authorizing the concealed carry of handguns without a permit, and sought a greater role for the governor in how state judges are chosen.

But the most persistent irritant was a yawning budget gap. In June 2015, Brownback signed a bill that increased the sales tax, eliminated itemized deductions for income taxes, and hiked cigarette taxes. But the budget gap continued unabated, prompting ever-deeper cuts in spending on higher education, health care, highways and children's programs. Arguing that the state's fiscal troubles weren't caused by his tax policy but rather by weakness in such key sectors as oil and gas, Brownback and his allies stood firm against calls to repeal a tax break affecting 330,000 business owners. But with his approval ratings in the dumps, Brownback suffered electoral setbacks in 2016 – first in legislative primaries, as moderate Republicans ousted conservatives and won open-seat primaries, and then, in November, when Democrats gained ground in the legislature. By early 2017, the state faced a $342 million budget gap, with the possibility of a $1 billion shortfall through 2019. Brownback's looming departure after two terms is expected to kick off a wide-open succession battle in 2018 among conservatives, moderate Republicans and Democrats, potentially including Lt. Gov. Jeff Colyer, Attorney General Derek Schmidt, and Secretary of State Kris Kobach on the GOP side, and 2014 challenger Davis and former Wichita Mayor Carl Brewer on the Democratic side.

In June 2017, Brownback suffered a major setback when a bipartisan coalition in the Legislature overrode his veto of the bill to rescind $1.2 billion of his earlier tax cuts during the next two years.

Senior Senator

Pat Roberts (R)

Elected 1996, term expires 2020, 4th term; b. Apr 20, 1936, Topeka; Arizona State University; Kansas State University, B.A.; Methodist; Married (Frankie Fann Roberts); 3 children; 5 grandchildren.

Military Career: U.S Marine Corps, 1958-1962.

Elected Office: U.S. House, 1981-1997.

Professional Career: Co-owner & editor, The Westsider, 1962-1967; A.A., U.S Sen. Frank Carlson, 1967-1968; A.A., U.S Rep. Keith Sebelius, 1968-1980.

DC Office: 109 HSOB 20510, 202-224-4774, Fax: 202-224-3514, roberts.senate.gov.

State Offices: Dodge City, 620-227-2244; Overland Park, 913-451-9343; Topeka, 785-295-2745; Wichita, 316-263-0416.

Committees: *Agriculture, Nutrition & Forestry (Chmn)*: Commodities, Risk Management & Trade, Conservation, Forestry & Natural Resources, Livestock, Marketing & Agriculture Security, Nutrition, Agricultural Research & Specialty Crops, Rural Development & Energy. *Ethics*. *Finance*: Health Care, International Trade, Customs & Global Competitiveness, Taxation & IRS Oversight. *Health, Education, Labor & Pensions*: Children & Families, Employment & Workplace Safety, Primary Health & Retirement Security. *Rules & Administration*.

Group Ratings

	ADA	ACLU	AFL-CIO	LCV	ITI	COC	HAFA	ACU	CFG	FRC
2016	-	11%	-	0%	80%	100%	51%	83%	74%	100%
2015	0%	C	14%	0%	C	93%	C	75%	58%	100%

Almanac Ratings 2015

	Economy	Social	Foreign	Composite
Liberal	29%	0%	4%	11%
Conservative	71%	100%	96%	89%

Key Votes of the 114th Congress

1. Keystone pipeline	Y	5. National Security Data	N	9. Gun Sales Checks	N
2. Export-Import Bank	N	6. Iran Nuclear Deal	Y	10. Sanctuary Cities	Y
3. Debt Ceiling Increase	Y	7. Puerto Rico Debt	Y	11. Planned Parenthood	Y
4. Homeland Security $$	N	8. Loretta Lynch A.G	N	12. Trade deals	Y

Election Results

Election	Name (Party)	Vote (%)	Cand. Spent	Ind. Exp. Support	Ind. Exp. Oppose
2014 General	Pat Roberts (R)	460,350 (53%)	$8,113,419	$3,380,996	$5,794,771
	Greg Orman (I)	368,372 (43%)	$5,702,323	$1,016,961	$7,230,146
	Randall Batson (L)	37,469 (4%)			
2014 Primary	Pat Roberts (R)	127,089 (48%)			
	Milton Wolf (R)	107,799 (41%)			
	D.J. Smith (R)	15,288 (6%)			
	Alvin Zahnter (R)	14,164 (5%)			

Prior winning percentages: 2008 (60%), 2002 (86%), 1996 (62%), House: 1994 (77%), 1992 (68%),1990 (63%), 1988 (100%), 1986 (75%), 1984 (76%), 1982 (68%), 1980 (62%)(62%)

Republican Pat Roberts, Kansas' senior senator, was first elected to his current seat in 1996-just months after the most prominent Kansas politician of recent decades, Bob Dole, resigned from the Senate to pursue an ultimately unsuccessful run for the presidency. Stylistically, Roberts is Dole's political heir: Both gained a reputation on Capitol Hill for direct talk and acerbic wit. But while Dole moved toward the political center as he ascended through the Senate leadership, Roberts has shifted rightward in the latter part of his career, in apparent response to a changing political landscape in his home state. And, unlike Dole, Roberts has shunned the leadership ranks to make his mark on agricultural and national security issues. He has the distinction of having chaired the Agriculture Committee in both houses of Congress.

Besides a sharp tongue, Dole and Roberts share a history as natives of an overwhelmingly rural state in the nation's geographical center who spent most of their adult years working and living in the nation's capital. For Roberts, a perception among many home state voters that he had become more a creature of Washington than of Kansas came close to ending his Senate career in 2014, at the age of 78.

His abolitionist great-grandfather, Roberts likes to say, "arrived in Kansas with a flat-bed press, a six-gun, and a Bible" and founded the state's second-oldest newspaper, the *Oskaloosa Independent.* His father was briefly Republican National Committee chairman during the years when perhaps Kansas' most famous son, Dwight Eisenhower, was president. (Roberts currently chairs the commission leading the effort to erect a memorial to Eisenhower on Washington's National Mall.) Born in Topeka, Roberts graduated from Kansas State University with a journalism degree. He served four years in the Marine Corps, and then spent five years running a weekly newspaper in the suburbs of Phoenix. In 1967, Roberts arrived on Capitol Hill as an aide to Kansas Republican Sen. Frank Carlson. He then served for 12 years as chief aide to Republican Keith Sebelius, who represented Kansas' 1st District and was the father-in-law of future Democratic Gov. Kathleen Sebelius. The relationship between Roberts and Kathleen Sebelius, once friendly, would later become severely strained amid partisan warfare over President Barack Obama's signature health insurance overhaul.

Keith Sebelius had succeeded Dole in the 1st District in 1968 when the latter was elected to the Senate. When Sebelius retired in 1980, Roberts won the GOP primary with 56 percent of the vote in a three-way contest, and went on to easily win the general election. For 14 years, he was in the minority party in the House. Roberts concentrated on farm issues, learning their intricacies and minutiae,while traveling in a van to keep in touch with constituents in the "Big First"-a district that sprawls across central and western Kansas, covering an area so large that it took two weeks to visit every county seat. His voting record was regarded as moderate. In 1996, when Republican Sen. Nancy Landon Kassebaum retired, Roberts ran for her seat, easily defeating his Democratic opponent, 62%-34%.

"When you're from Kansas, you're not appointed to [the Agriculture Committee], you're sentenced to it," Roberts once quipped, displaying his trademark humor. Since 2015, Roberts has been chairman of the Senate Agriculture Committee; he will have a key role in crafting a new farm bill, the omnibus measure that authorizes federal agricultural and nutrition programs. It will replace the current farm bill,which expires in 2018. Roberts was ranking Republican on the committee in 2011-2012, while the Democrats were in the majority. But Mississippi Republican Thad Cochran, term-limited in the ranking spot on the Appropriations Committee, exercised his seniority to bump Roberts in 2013. A year earlier, Cochran opposed a version of the farm bill that Roberts had played a major role in crafting -- but whichfailed to become law. Roberts briefly considered challenging Cochran for the ranking member's slot. He ultimately decided against doing so, but remained on the Agriculture Committee, and opposed theversion of the farm bill signed into law in early 2014.

The 2012 Senate-passed version of the farm bill that bore Roberts' handiwork called for ending a system of target prices as part of a larger shift away from fixed prices and payments for farmers. Roberts joined Democrats, and many Northern Republicans, in arguing that the farm bill shouldn't be about making sure certain groups get the same amount of federal aid they received in the past. But House Republicans and many Southern growers fought the idea: Those farmers contended the private crop insurance called for in the Senate proposal did not work well for crops such as rice and peanuts. Leaders of the House Agriculture Committee, whose membership is more oriented toward the South, reportedly found Roberts difficult to deal with. As 2012 came to a close, it was left toSenate Republican Leader Mitch McConnell of Kentucky to negotiate a nine-month farm bill extension as part of the New Year's Day 2013 deal aimed at averting the so-called "fiscal cliff."

Roberts' experience with the 2012 farm bill in some ways was reminiscent of a battle waged nearly two decades earlier. In 1995, after Republicans won majority control of Congress for the first time in 40 years, Roberts became chairman of the House Agriculture Committee. He had long believed that the huge subsidies of the early 1980s would never return. Faced with tight budget parameters, Roberts drafted the so-called "Freedom to Farm" bill to phase out subsidies over seven years. In September 1995, his bill failed in committee when Southern Republicans, eager to protect cotton, rice and peanut subsidies, opposed it. Two months later, Roberts persuaded Agriculture conferees to include most of his proposal in the 1996 budget reconciliation bill, which President Bill Clinton vetoed. To attract more support, Roberts agreed to changes, including maintaining cotton and rice marketing loans. Still, his legislation was the biggest change in agriculture policy since the New Deal. Roberts' revised bill became law in April 1996-just months before his election to the Senate.

The Freedom to Farm Act worked well in 1997, and farmers seemed to do fine with a diminished government role. But in 1998, crop prices plunged and some farmers demanded a return to the old system. From his new seat in the Senate, Roberts resisted, and bills were passed to accelerate payments and to give farmers an extra $4 billion in disaster aid. In 2000, the pattern continued. Roberts argued that limiting production would not raise prices because the United States accounts for less than one-fifth of world production. The number of family farmers continued to decline in places like western Kansas, yet prices were not sufficient to maintain many operations.Freedom to Farm came up for reauthorization in 2002, when Democrats were in control of the Senate. Roberts acknowledged the Freedom to Farm Act "didn't work out as anybody would have hoped" and, with Cochran, pushed for farm savings accounts. But their proposal was rejected in favor of the Democrats' approach of reviving countercyclical subsidies when crop prices are low, plus a larger Conservation Reserve Program, which paid farmers to leave land fallow to protect environmentally sensitive areas. Roberts argued the legislation that ultimately passed would provide no aid when production was low and crop prices rose, which is what happened when drought struck the Great Plains in the summer of 2002.

Roberts has tried to encourage farm exports in numerous ways: He was a lead sponsor of the 2000 law signed by Clinton that relaxed the embargo on export of food and medicine to Cuba. Roberts was joined by his House successor and now-junior Senate colleague, Republican Jerry Moran, in contending such a move would benefit Kansas farmers, even though moves to normalize relations with Cuba were fought by many of their Republican colleagues.

Roberts' other major sphere of influence has been national security. In 1999, aschairman of the Emerging Threats and Capabilities Subcommittee of Armed Services, he held hearings probing the nation's vulnerability to terrorists and-two years prior to 9/11-presciently asserted that targets would be "selected for their symbolic value, like the World Trade Center in the heart of Manhattan." He was particularly immersed in the issue of intelligence gathering as the Intelligence Committee chairman in 2003-2007. In the summer of 2004, committee members led by Roberts unanimously criticized intelligence-gathering prior to the 2003 start of the Iraq war, and concluded the Central Intelligence Agency had not seriously considered the possibility that Iraqi leader Saddam Hussein had no weapons of mass destruction. Roberts proposed that the Intelligence panel take over from the Armed Services Committee oversight of Defense Department intelligence operations, but the proposal met with predictable resistance on turf-conscious Capitol Hill.

While the criticism of pre-Iraq war intelligence gathering was bipartisan, *The New York Times* touched off a partisan battle in the committee when it reported in December 2005 that the National Security Agency was secretly monitoring contacts between al-Qaida suspects abroad and individuals in the United States. Democrats led by Sen. Jay Rockefeller of West Virginia sought a committee investigation, while Roberts insisted the program was not only within the president's constitutional powers, but "legal, necessary, and reasonable." In March 2006, the committee voted along party lines not to conduct an investigation into the domestic surveillance program, but to establish a seven-member panel charged with that responsibility. Roberts complained that some Democrats "believe the gravest threat we face is not Osama bin Laden and al-Qaida, but rather the president of the United States," referring to George W. Bush.

Roberts rotated off the committee in early 2007, but, after Obama took office, Roberts staunchly opposed shiftingdetainees from Guantanamo Bay, Cuba to Fort Leavenworth in Kansas. "Not in our backyard. Not in Kansas. Not on my watch," he declared. Throughout the Obama Administration, he placed holds on executive branch appointees to the Defense and Justice departments to pressure the Pentagon to block such transfers. His final hold on a nominee was dropped in May 2016, less than a year before Obama left office, after a top Defense Department official assured Roberts that the clock had run out on any effort to bring Guantanamo detainees to Kansas.

Roberts had no Democratic challenger in 2002 when he sought a second Senate term, but in 2008, former Rep. Jim Slattery, who had been working in Washington as a lawyer and lobbyist since losing a race for governor in 1994, returned to the state to challenge him. Slattery ran a vigorous campaign, but Roberts, who routinely visited all 105 Kansas counties, spent nearly $7 million and won, 60%-36%, in a campaign in which he derided Slattery as a lobbyist, "Gucci loafers and all." Six years later, the tables would be turned, and Roberts had to defend himself against efforts to portray him as a captive of the Capital Beltway.Initially, Roberts was considered a safe bet for a fourth term, especially with his home-state colleague, Moran, running the Senate GOP campaign committee. But Roberts almost fell victim to anti-incumbency sentiment and a novice opponent in Milton Wolf, a radiologist who had the strong support oftea-party groups ascendant in Kansas Republican politics.

Wolf-a second cousin to Obama-frequently noted that Roberts had been in Washington as either an aide or legislator for half a century. He based his campaign around his opposition to his cousin's Affordable Care Act.Roberts was hardly a fan of the new law: As a member of the Senate Finance Committee that worked on the legislation prior to its 2010 passage, Roberts declared at the time, "All indications are that this bill will be pulled increasingly toward more cost, more regulations, and more rationing as it continues through this process." When his old friend, HHS Secretary Sebelius, said she would have "zero tolerance" for insurers claiming costs were increased by the bill, Roberts was livid. "She is threatening to shut down private companies for exercising their First Amendment right to free speech," he charged. In October 2013, Roberts went so far as to call for Sebelius' resignation, accusing her of "gross incompetence" in conjunction with the problem-plagued rollout of the Web site for enrolling in "Obamacare." Coincidentally or not, Roberts call for Sebelius' resignation came three days after Wolf announced his primary challenge.

Wolf gained traction in February 2014, when news outlets reported Roberts did not have a home of his own in Kansas, listing as his voting address a Dodge City home belonging to longtime supporters. Roberts' aides responded by noting the senator-who owns a home in Washington's Virginia suburbs-also owned a house in Dodge City, but that it had been rented out. Roberts, seeking to defuse the controversy, did himself little good when he told a local radio station, "Every time I get an opponent-I mean, every time I get a chance, I'm home." But Wolf found himself dealing with an embarrassing controversy of his own: He was discovered to have posted patient X-rays on his Facebook page, accompanying some of them with jokes that many found distasteful. Roberts managed only a 48%-41% primary win.

Roberts's troubles didn't end there. His Democratic opponent dropped out of the race in September, a move thatincreasedthe prospects of Greg Orman, a well-funded independent candidate. Orman, seeking to show how much he disdained both parties, said he would not decide which party he would caucus with in the Senate until it was certain which one held the majority. Republicans blasted Orman's past support for Obama as well as his positions on issues such as abortion and immigration. They also raised questions about his past business dealings.Polls late in the race showed it to be a toss-up, placing Roberts in danger of becoming the first Kansas Republican to lose a Senate race in more than 80 years. It didn't help when media outlets reported in October that the senator had missed two-thirds of the Agriculture Committee meetings since 2000, feeding critics' arguments that he was out of touch. The NRSC sought to take control of Roberts' race by sending Chris LaCivita, a veteran party operative, to Kansas. National Republicans also were forced to pour more than $10 millioninto a race they had thought was over once the primary ended. A barrage of last-minute GOP ads and campaign appearances helped pull in independent voters, and Roberts ended up beating Orman by nearly 11 points.

Following his re-election, Roberts pushed to prohibit the federal government from pressuring states to develop national education guidelines such as the so-called Common Core standards. The latter, while adopted by the overwhelming majority of states, nonetheless had become anathema to conservatives. The Every Student Succeeds Act, which Roberts voted for and Obama signed in 2015, prohibited the secretary of education from forcing states to adhere to a particular set of standards, such as Common Core.

Meanwhile, with Roberts poised to chair the Agriculture Committee, some Democrats-remembering his red-meat rhetoric about food stamps during his bruising re-election bid-worried he might seek to reopen the 2014 farm bill, given his opposition to that measure. But Roberts sought to dampen such speculation, and stressed his desire to talk to panel members of both parties. "No committee chairman will go into the wilderness with a machete and chop left and right," he told *National Journal.* "You've got to check with the committee and calm the waters." While still conservative, his voting record showed signs of moderating: He dropped to the 23rdmost conservative Senator in 2015 in the *Almanac* vote ratings. And in September 2015, he was the only one of the six-member,all-Republican Kansas congressional delegation to support a stop-gap spending bill to avoid a government shutdown. After a third of a century on Capitol Hill, "I'm done voting to shut down the government. I'm just done," Roberts told the *Topeka Capital-Journal.* "I've been through three shutdowns. Every time it was so terribly counter-productive, then to get back up and running it costs even more money…"

As Agriculture chairman,he worked with the panel's ranking Democrat, Michigan Sen. Debbie Stabenow -- who had chaired the panel when Roberts was ranking Republican -- to get a measure to require labeling of genetically modified food signed into law by Obama. Roberts hailed it as the most important farm legislation in 20 years, but a number of consumer groups were unhappy that it mandated the labeling through scan-able smartphone codes rather than text or symbols. Roberts and Stabenow also crafted a compromise on reauthorization of the school meals program,includinglargely maintaining the child nutrition standards that First Lady Michelle Obama had adopted as a signature issue. It cleared their committee, but efforts to enact a bill into law fell short at the end of 2016. "Though our committee passed a good, bipartisan bill – something no one said we could do – it wasn't enough for some," Roberts lamented. While he and Stabenow vowed to try again, coming up with a new child nutrition law was likely to be complicated by a new presidential administration and a committee focus on crafting a new farm bill.

Given that he will be 84 when his current term ends in 2020, it appears that Roberts' long political career is in its final phase. After voicing skepticism about term limits when he first ran for the Senate, Roberts exhibited his trademark humor in a 2015 interview with the *Capital Journal*, declaring, "I promise I will not serve more than two terms." Asked if that pledge was effective with the term he won in 2014, Roberts grinned: "Yeah…I'm new. I've only had the seat a year, not even a year! I think term limits are appropriate now."

Junior Senator

Jerry Moran (R)

Elected 2010, term expires 2022, 2nd term; b. May 29, 1954, Great Bend; University of Kansas, J.D.; University of Kansas, B.S.; Fort Hays State University (KS); Methodist; Married (Robba Addison Moran); 2 children.

Elected Office: KS Senate, 1989-1997, Majority Leader, 1995-1996; U.S. House, 1997-2011.

Professional Career: Operations officer, Consolidated State Bank, 1975-1977; Mgr., Farmers State Bank & Trust Co., 1977-1978; Practicing attorney, 1981-1996; Instructor, Ft. Hays St. University, 1986.

DC Office: 521 DSOB 20510, 202-224-6521, Fax: 202-228-6966; Website: moran.senate.gov.

State Offices: Hays, 785-628-6401; Manhattan, 785-539-8973; Olathe, 913-393-0711; Pittsburg, 620-232-2286; Wichita, 316-631-1410.

Committees: *Appropriations*: Agriculture, Rural Development, FDA & Related Agencies, Department of Defense, DOL, HHS & Education & Related Agencies, Financial Services & General Government, Military Construction & Veteran Affairs & Related Agencies (Chmn), State, Foreign Operations & Related Programs. *Commerce, Science & Transportation*: Aviation Operations, Safety & Security, Communications, Technology, Innovation & the Internet, Consumer Protection, Product Safety, Ins

& Data Security (Chmn), Space, Science & Competitiveness. *Environment & Public Works*: Clean Air & Nuclear Safety, Superfund, Waste Management, & Regulatory Oversight, Transportation & Infrastructure. *Indian Affairs*. *Veterans' Affairs*.

Group Ratings

	ADA	ACLU	AFL-CIO	LCV	ITI	COC	HAFA	ACU	CFG	FRC
2016	-	47%	-	0%	60%	88%	63%	68%	75%	100%
2015	0%	C	36%	0%	C	79%	C	88%	73%	100%

Almanac Ratings 2015

	Economy	Social	Foreign	Composite
Liberal	5%	0%	0%	2%
Conservative	95%	100%	100%	98%

Key Votes of the 114th Congress

1. Keystone pipeline	Y	5. National Security Data	N	9. Gun Sales Checks	N
2. Export-Import Bank	N	6. Iran Nuclear Deal	Y	10. Sanctuary Cities	Y
3. Debt Ceiling Increase	N	7. Puerto Rico Debt	N	11. Planned Parenthood	Y
4. Homeland Security $$	N	8. Loretta Lynch A.G	N	12. Trade deals	Y

Election Results

Election	Name (Party)	Vote (%)		Cand. Spent	Ind. Exp. Support	Ind. Exp. Oppose
2016 General	Jerry Moran (R)	732,376	(62%)	$4,227,284	$529	
	Patrick Wiesner (D)	379,740	(32%)	$34,939		
	Robert Garrard (L)	65,760	(6%)			
2016 Primary	Jerry Moran (R)	230,907	(79%)			
	D.J. Smith (R)	61,056	(21%)			

Prior winning percentages: 2010 (70%); House: 2008 (82%), 2006 (79%), 2004 (91%), 2002 (91%), 2000 (89%), 1998 (81%), 1996 (73%)

In late 2012, as Republicans were looking for someone to lead their effort to regain the Senate majority in the 2014 election, Kansas's junior senator, Jerry Moran-by his own acknowledgment-did not immediately jump to mind. Throughout his tenure on Capitol Hill-14 years in the House prior to election to the Senate in 2010-Moran had established a reputation as a low-key legislator focused on the needs of his constituents. "Most people looking at my time in politics would not think this was a job that I would be willing to do or would pursue," Moran told the *Wichita Eagle*. But after higher profile Republicans -- notably Ohio Sen. Rob Portman -- took a pass onchairing the NRSC, Moran pursued and won the post. He ultimately succeeded in realizing a party goal that had proven elusive during the two prior election cycles-returning the Senate to Republican control.

While accumulating a largely conservative voting record,Moran has demonstrated an independent streak during his years in Congress. Although success in chairing a party's in-house campaign committee has frequently translated into ascending the leadership ladder, Moran, once majority leader of the Kansas Senate, has downplayed any such aspirations on Capitol Hill. "I like my independence. The more that you are part of the leadership, the less flexibility you sometimes have in the positions you take," he told the *Eagle*. At the same time, Moran has acquired a reputation for political caution, to the point of being risk-adverse. Some years ago, Moran's in-state Senate colleague, Pat Roberts -- known for his pointed wit -- stood before a gathering of Kansas Republicans and joked that he had been invited only because pop stars were unavailable."Actually, both Jerry Moran and I received invitations, but he couldn't decide," Roberts was reported to have wisecracked.That cautious side of Moran bumped up against his independent streak in early 2016: Hestrayed from the GOP leadership position against holding hearings on President Barack Obama's nomination of Merrick Garland for the Supreme Court, only to go scrambling back into the party fold when faced with the threat of a primary later that year.

Moran grew up in the tiny town of Plainville on the western plains of Kansas, the son of an oil-field worker. In college, he was a summer intern forGOP Rep. Keith Sebelius, Roberts' predecessor in the House and the father-in-law of future Democratic Gov. Kathleen Sebelius. The job gave Moran a close-up view of the 1974 impeachment hearings of President Richard Nixon. After graduating with a degree in economics from the University of Kansas, Moran worked as a banker before earning a law degree. In 1988, he won election to the state Senate, becoming majority leader in his last term. When Roberts ran for the Senate in 1996, Moran sought the open House seat. He won the primary with 76 percent, tantamount to election in a sprawling rural district as big as the state of Illinois. Moran had no trouble winning reelection a half-dozen times in the "Big First," where he annually held town hall meetings in each of the district's 69 counties.

Since 2000, Moran has cited Kansas farmers in pushing to reopen trade with Cuba, a position that put him at odds with many in his party. In 2007, he won House approval of an amendment to ease restrictions on shipments of food and medicine to the island nation, only to see it removed from the final legislation to avoid a veto by President George W. Bush. In the Senate, Moran inserted a provision into a 2012 appropriations bill to ease agricultural trade by allowing direct cash payments from Cuban buyers to U.S. institutions. Again, it was stripped out of the final legislation. In 2015, after President Barack Obama moved to normalize relations with Cuba, Moran declared in a speech: "...What we have been doing has not worked...because it's a unilateral sanction. When wheat, for example, is not sold to Cuba, it's not that they're not buying wheat, it's that wheat's being purchased from some other place: our competitors."That year, after a group of Kansas agricultural officials visited Cuba to look into trade opportunities, Moran introduced legislation allowing trade using private financing -- sidestepping the need for federal funds to help underwrite the costs. He reintroduced a similar measurein early 2017.

Moran's independence -- and caution -- showed up on other issues during his House tenure. To the dismay of Speaker Dennis Hastert, he was one of 25 House Republicans who opposed the 2003 Republican-sponsored Medicare prescription drug bill. In a memoir, Hastert did not call out Moran by name, but left little doubt about whom he was talking. "Some members had assured me that they would be with us, but when the crunch time came, they weren't," Hastert wrote. "One prairie state member, a fourth-term representative from a solidly Republican district, voted no, then ran and hid. I sent people to find him, they couldn't." Afterward, Moran said the bill did not do enough to lower prescription drug prices, adding that he favored a Democratic proposal to give federal officials negotiating authority to lower drug costs. He later joined Democrats in backing an expansion of the Children's Health Insurance Program.

Moran resisted GOP leaders' pressure to challenge popular Gov. Sebelius in 2006. He decided to run for the Senate in 2010 when Republican Sam Brownback announced he would step aside to run for governor, after Sebelius resigned to become Obama's secretary of health and human services. Moran first had to get by fellow GOP Rep. Todd Tiahrt, who preceded him in the House by two years. The two waged a nasty and expensive primary race, costing nearly $7 million combined. Tiahrt sought to turn the contest into a referendum on who was more conservative, and the candidates battled over endorsements. Former Alaska Gov. Sarah Palin and former Pennsylvania Sen. Rick Santorum were in Tiahrt's camp, while Moran secured the backing of two outspoken Senate conservatives-Tom Coburn of Oklahoma and Jim DeMint of South Carolina. With the endorsement of most of the state's leading newspapers, Moran won by 50%-45%, prevailing on the strength of his base in the state's most Republican district. He won the general election with 70 percent.

In recent years, both Moran and Roberts have found themselves under pressure dueto the increasing role of the tea party within the Kansas GOP.One of Moran's first moves after moving across Capitol Hillwas to join the Senate Tea Party Caucus, a group formed to capitalize on the momentum of tea party activists during the 2010 off-year election. He sounded very much the tea party advocate in lashing out at big government when, in 2012, he slammed the Labor Department for a proposal to prevent children under age 16 from working in dangerous farm jobs. "If the federal government can regulate the kind of relationship between parents and their children on their own family's farm, there is almost nothing off-limits in which we see the federal government intruding in a way of life," he declared. But, notwithstanding the tea party's anti-immigration bent, Moran crossed party lines to work with Democratic Sen. Mark Warner of Virginia on a highly publicized bill that would create a new visa for foreign students receiving graduate degrees from U.S. schools.

Two years into his first term, Moran found himself in a particularly awkward situation when a frail, 89-year old former GOP Sen. Bob Dole-who for three decades had occupied the seat Moran now holds-showed up on the Senate floor in a wheelchair. Dole, who has had limited use of his right arm since being wounded in World War II, in 1990 had engineered passage of the Americans with Disabilities Act; he went to the Senate floor in 2012 to lobby for an international treaty designed to encourage other countries to follow suit. But Moran, after earlier declaring he supported the treaty and would be "standing up for the rights of those with disabilities," cast a key vote to block treaty ratification. In a statement afterward, Moran declared that "foreign officials should not be put in a position to interfere with U.S. policymaking." The statement embraced an argument made by hardline conservatives but adamantly disputed by the treaty's proponents-that it could be used by the United Nations to dictate U.S. policy. In an interview with the *Boston Globe,* Moran contended: "I'm saying I tried to help [the treaty] come to the floor, and had never made a conclusion as to whether I was for or against it, and concluded that it was a bad idea to have the United Nations involved in this."

Moran was given a seat on the Appropriations Committee following the 2010 election, while committing to efforts to ban controversial "earmarks"-funds directed to a legislator's pet projects. Moran sought earmarked funding while in the House, and took heat for it during the primary against Tiahrt. He defended himself by noting he also had sought earmark restrictions while still in the House. In August 2011, he was one of 26 senators to oppose a bipartisan deal to raise the nation's debt limit, noting that the $21 billion in deficit reduction over the first year of the agreement would cover less than a week's worth of borrowing. In December 2014, Moran found himself among a group of 11 Republicans aligned with hardline conservative Texas Sen. Ted Cruz-and at odds with his party's Senate leadership-on a series of votes to stall or derail a $1.1 trillion measure funding federal department and agencies.

As chairman of the NRSC, Moran started the 2013-2014 election cycle with the numbers in his favor: Of the 36 Senate seats up in 2014, the Democrats had to defend 21 of them. But Moran also worked to avoid mistakes that had tripped up his party in the prior two cycles-nomination of poorly vetted, ideologically rigid candidates whose missteps had allowed several imperiled Democrats to survive. "We tried to get all aspects of our party-from tea party to the Chamber of Commerce-to sit in a room and decide on a candidate they could all agree on," he later recalled. Moran reached out to Portman, a member of the GOP's establishment wing, who agreed to serve as the NRSC's vice chairman for finance-while tea party favorite Cruz was appointed vice chairman for grassroots and political outreach. But conservative activists were upset at Moran's efforts back home to help Roberts withstand a serious primary challenge from Milton Wolf, a tea party-backed physician;they lookedfor a candidate to take on Moran in 2016.

In the face of this threat, Moran appeared to tack right. *Almanac* vote ratings pegged him as the fifth most conservative member of the Senate in 2015. He was among a handful of conservatives who voted against the Every Student Succeeds Act, when the Senate adopted it on an 85-12 vote in late 2015.

Two days after the death of Supreme Court Justice Antonin Scalia in February 2016, as Senate Republican leaders made clear their opposition to replacing Scalia until after the coming presidential election, Moran said the Senate had an obligation to consider a nominee put forth by Obama, telling the*Topeka Capital-Journal,* "The Republican-led Senate, which I worked hard to secure, has a constitutional responsibility in the process of determining Supreme Court justices." Moran's stance didn't garner national attention -- to say nothing of triggering a firestorm -- until he repeated it the following month in town meeting with 10 people in the southwestern Kansas town of Cimarron, after Obama had nominated Garland. "I can't imagine the president has or will nominate somebody that meets my criteria, but I have my job to do," Moran, then one of only four Senate Republicans to come out for hearings on the nomination, was quoted as saying by the *Garden City Telegram*. But he added, "I think the process ought to go forward."

Moran found himself under sharp attack from conservative groups, and, while Wolf -- who came within 7 points of ousting Roberts in 2014 -- had been hinting at a primary challenge for months, Rep. Mike Pompeo suggested he might get into the race. A week after his comments at the town hall meeting, Moran retreated, saying through an aide that he "didn't need hearings to conclude" Garland had been rendered "unacceptable to serve on the Supreme Court" as a result of his judicial philosophy. Pompeo (who becameCIA director in the Trump Administration) announced several weeks later he would not run for Senate, citing the limited time until theprimary. But he issued a parting shot at Moran, telling *Politico*, "Filling this vacancy on the U.S. Supreme Court is the transgenerational issue of our time… The Senate cannot fold again on this one. As I watched this waffling up close, I began to contemplate a Senate run."

Wolf ultimately did not file, either, leaving D.J. Smith, who ran a distant third behind Roberts and Wolf in the 2014 Senate primary, as Moran's only intraparty challenger. Moran won the primary by a 4-1 margin, and, in November, was re-elected to a second term by 62%-32% over his thinly fundedDemocratic opponent, Lawrence attorney Patrick Wiesner, in a state that has not elected a Democrat to the Senate since 1932.

FIRST DISTRICT

Roger Marshall (R)

Elected 2016, 1st term; b. Aug 09, 1960, El Dorado; Kansas State University, Bach. Deg., 1982; University of Kansas, M.D., 1987; Christian Church; Married (Laina Marshall); 4 children; 1 grandchild.

Military Career: U.S Army Reserve, 1984-1991.

Professional Career: Physician.

DC Office: 312 CHOB 20515, 202-225-2715, marshall.house.gov.

State Offices: Garden City, 785-714-0104; Salina, 785-829-9000.

Committees: *Agriculture*: Commodity Exchanges, Energy & Credit, Livestock & Foreign Agriculture, Nutrition. *Science, Space & Technology*: Oversight, Research & Technology. *Small Business*: Health & Technology, Investigations, Oversight & Regulations.

Election Results

Election	Name (Party)	Vote (%)	Cand. Spent	Ind. Exp. Support	Ind. Exp. Oppose
2016 General	Roger Marshall (R)	169,992 (66%)	$1,083,608	$727,501	$642,738
	Alan LaPolice (I)	67,739 (26%)	$125,097	$46,750	
	Kerry Burt (L)	19,366 (8%)			
2016 Primary	Roger Marshall (R)	58,808 (57%)			
	Tim Huelskamp (R)	45,315 (44%)			

Republican Roger Marshall was elected in 2016 by defeating Rep. Tim Huelskamp in the GOP primary. The contest attracted national attention and financing as a conflict over the party's direction. Marshall delivered on his promise to get a seat on the Agriculture Committee, which had been stripped from Huelskamp because of his insubordination.

Born in El Dorado, Kansas, Marshall later worked on the family farm after they had moved to town. He got his bachelor's degree in biochemistry from Kansas State University and his medical degree from the University of Kansas. As an obstetrician-gynecologist in Great Bend, he delivered more than 5,000 babies and was chairman of the board of Great Bend Regional Hospital. He served seven years in the Army Reserve, where he was a captain and trained a mobile hospital support unit.

Huelskamp's no-holds-barred conservatism had made him a leader of the House Freedom Caucus and perhaps the most outspoken internal critic of Republican leadership during his three terms in the House. Even after he was stripped of his chief committee assignments in 2012, which reportedly was the first time in more than a century that the local representative did not have a seat on the Agriculture panel, he continued to go his own way - to the detriment of at least some of his constituents. Huelskamp's vulnerability at home became apparent in the 2014 primary, when he was held to 55 percent of the vote against weakly financed challenger Alan LaPolice, who said that Huelskamp had failed to work for his constituents or to find solutions to problems. When LaPolice hesitated about running again, Marshall told reporters in January 2015 that he was considering a challenge.

With the district's many farmers actively engaged in the contest, endorsements had an impact. Perhaps the most significant was the support for Marshall by the Kansas Farm Bureau, which for the first time opposed an incumbent. The bureau's voice had an impact in this district, which is among the leading livestock producers in the nation. Long-ago local hero Bob Dole, at age 92, tweeted his endorsement of Marshall. Also supporting the challenger was the Super PAC organized by the Ricketts family, major players in agri-business, which spent $1.1 million. The U.S. Chamber of Commerce endorsed Marshall and spent about $400,000 on his behalf, despite extensive efforts by Huelskamp at home and in Washington to win the group's support. The state chamber backed Huelskamp, who also benefited from more than $400,000 that the Club for Growth spent on his behalf. Marshall's fundraising was competitive with $1.5 million, of which $300,000 was self-financed. Perhaps the most significant endorsement was one that Huelskamp failed to get - from House Speaker Paul Ryan, who remained neutral and refused the incumbent's request to promise him a return to the Agriculture Committee.

Marshall won the August primary by an unexpectedly large margin, 57%-43%, over Huelskamp. Democrats did not nominate a candidate. LaPolice, who lost the Republican primary in 2014, ran as an independent. He got 26 percent to 66 percent for Marshall. Following his personal request to Ryan, Marshall got a seat on the Ag Committee, and on the Science and Technology Committee, where he advocated on behalf of the giant research facility in Manhattan. He joined the House Republicans' "Doc Caucus." Huelskamp, who said that Ryan was partly to blame for his defeat, opened the door to a possible rematch in 2018.

Central and Western Kansas

Population		**Race and Ethnicity**		**Income**	
Total	718,749	White	77.7%	Median Income	$46,957 (306 out of 435)
Land area	52,543	Black	2.9%		
Pop/ sq mi	13.7	Latino	15.2%		
Born in state	63.5%	Asian	1.6%	Under $50,000	53.1%
		Two races	2.0%	$50,000-$99,999	32.3%
Age Groups		Other	0.6%	$100,000-$199,999	12.4%
Under 18	24.4%			$200,000 or more	2.3%
18-34	25.6%	**Education**		Poverty Rate	14.3%
35-64	34.9%	H.S grad or less	42.3%		
Over 64	15.1%	Some college	34.2%	**Health Insurance**	
		College Degree, 4 yr	15.6%	With health insurance coverage	88.8%
Work		Post grad	8.0%		
White Collar	31.8%				
Sales and Service	39.1%	**Military**		**Public Assistance**	
Blue Collar	29.2%	Veteran	9.3%	Cash public assistance income	1.7%
Government	18.7%	Active Duty	2.2%		
				Food stamp/SNAP benefits	8.9%

Voter Turnout			
2015 Total Citizens 18+	508,285	2016 House Turnout as % CVAP	51%
2016 House turnout	257,971	2014 House Turnout as % CVAP	40%

2012 Presidential Vote		
Mitt Romney	184,232	(70%)
Barack Obama	72,668	(28%)

2016 Presidential Vote		
Donald Trump	183,446	(69%)
Hillary Clinton	64,388	(24%)
Gary Johnson	11,976	(5%)

Cook Partisan Voting Index: R+24

"A prairie is not any old piece of flatland in the Midwest," wrote Kansas-born reporter Dennis Farney. "No, a prairie is wine-colored grass, dancing in the wind. A prairie is a sun-splashed hillside, bright with wild flowers. A prairie is a fleeting cloud shadow, the song of the meadowlark. It is the wild land that has never felt the slash of the plow." The prairie Farney described once covered almost all of Kansas and dipped into Oklahoma. Now only a little virgin prairie can still be found, in the Flint Hills region west and south of Topeka. At the Tallgrass National Prairie Preserve, you can see 30 miles on a clear day and a waist-deep sea of grass waves in the wind as it did when traders and pioneers on the Santa Fe Trail passed through some 150 years ago.

Farther west, near the 100th meridian, begins a region where the Rocky Mountains block moisture from reaching the land, and the prairie gives way to plains. The landscape becomes what Major Stephen Long in 1823 incorrectly called the "Great American Desert." Much of this western area was grazing land, first for buffalo, and then for the cattle driven to Kansas railheads like Abilene and Dodge City in the 1870s and 1880s. That they divided the land into so many counties, many with towns sporting grandiose names like Montezuma, Garden City and Syracuse, is a testament to the big dreams these settlers brought with them.

Today, the area's farm-dependent economy is changing. Big meatpacking plants in Dodge City, Garden City and Liberal (the "Golden Triangle of meatpacking") have attracted large numbers of Hispanic immigrants. As *The Atlantic* reported in July 2016, the Hispanic population in Fort Dodge schools since 1989 grew from 20 percent to 79 percent. Many of the new arrivals are non-English speaking, even in high school. The dairy industry has made a comeback, enticed by inexpensive land and labor and abundant feed stocks. Farmers here face a long-term crisis: Their water is drying up. Parts of Kansas get as much as 90 percent of their supply from the Ogallala Aquifer, which extends from South Dakota to Texas. As its levels have dropped, the local wells pump smaller amounts per hour. In Manhattan, the National Bio and Agro-Defense Facility has been a boost to Kansas State University and the local economy. Surrounding Riley County is one of the few fast-growing areas in the district.

The 1st Congressional District covers all of western and north-central Kansas. It extends more than 300 miles from the Colorado border to the outskirts of Topeka. While the area today is solidly Republican, it was not always so. Farmer uprisings handed the area to the Populists for much of the late 1800s, a Democrat represented southwest Kansas during the farm depression of the 1920s and 1930s, and one did so again in the late 1950s. Republican Bob Dole represented western Kansas from 1961 to 1969. The district takes in almost everything west of the Flint Hills and Abilene, the boyhood home of President Dwight Eisenhower. Just south of Salina, near the center of the state, is Lindsborg, which has one of the highest concentrations of Swedish Americans in the country, and where the biennial Svensk Hyllningsfest celebrates the area's early settlers. It also includes Emporia, where progressive newspaper editor William Allen White published the once-famous *Emporia Gazette*; the paper is still run by the White family.

The district contains 61 full counties and parts of two others. Only Nebraska's 3rd District and South Dakota's at-large seat have more counties. Their average population is about 12,000people. By square miles, the district is the 13th largest in the nation. The 1st is in the top 5 percent of the most Republican districts nationwide. Donald Trump won 69 percent of the vote here in 2016.

SECOND DISTRICT

Lynn Jenkins (R)

Elected 2008, 5th term; b. Jun 10, 1963, Topeka; Kansas State University, A.A.; Weber State College (UT), B.S.; Methodist; Divorced; 2 children.

Elected Office: KS House, 1999-2001; KS Senate, 2001-2003; KS Treasurer, 2003-2008.

Professional Career: C.P.A., 1984-1998.

DC Office: 1526 LHOB 20515, 202-225-6601, Fax: 202-225-7986, lynnjenkins.house.gov.

State Offices: Independence, 620-231-5966; Pittsburg, 620-231-5966; Topeka, 785-234-5966.

Committees: *Ways & Means*: Health, Trade.

Group Ratings

	ADA	ACLU	AFL-CIO	LCV	ITI	COC	HAFA	ACU	CFG	FRC
2016	-	11%	-	3%	100%	100%	73%	86%	79%	89%
2015	0%	C	9%	0%	C	74%	C	96%	82%	100%

Almanac Ratings 2015

	Economy	Social	Foreign	Composite
Liberal	1%	4%	0%	2%
Conservative	99%	96%	100%	98%

Key Votes of the 114th Congress

1. Keystone Pipeline	Y	5. Puerto Rico Debt	Y	9. Offenses by Aliens	Y
2. Trade Deals	Y	6. Medical Marijuana	N	10. Troops in Iraq	N
3. Export-Import Bank	N	7. Sanctuary Cities	Y	11. Homeland Security $$	N
4. Debt Ceiling Increase	N	8. Armor-piercing Bullets	Y	12. Trade Adjustment aid	N

Election Results

Election	Name (Party)	Vote (%)		Cand. Spent	Ind. Exp. Support	Ind. Exp. Oppose
2016 General	Lynn Jenkins (R)	181,228	(61%)	$1,367,578		
	Brittany Potter (D)	96,840	(33%)			
	James Houston Bales (L)	19,333	(7%)			
2016 Primary	Lynn Jenkins (R)		(100%)			

Prior winning percentages: 2014 (57%), 2012 (57%), 2010 (63%), 2008 (51%)

Republican Lynn Jenkins of Kansas, who has served her district since 2008, stepped down as vice chair of the House Republican Conference following the 2016 election. She said that she was exploring a run for governor in 2018. She exercises clout on the Ways and Means Committee, where she has been a reliable conservative vote who has an accountant's familiarity with the tax code. Even with her successes, she has sometimes struggled to bridge the divide with the GOP's tea party wing.

Jenkins was born in Topeka and grew up in the rural town of Holton on a dairy farm. After graduating from college, she worked for nearly 15 years as an accountant. She was elected to the state House in 1998 for one term, and then one in the state Senate. In 2002, Jenkins was elected Kansas treasurer and was reelected four years later. She next set her sights on Democratic Rep. Nancy Boyda, who had pulled off a big upset in 2006 by unseating Republican Jim Ryun.

Jenkins needed to win two competitive contests. In the GOP primary, she faced Ryun, an Olympic silver medalist runner, who had held the seat for a decade. The contest was a clash between the two long-warring wings of the state Republican Party. Ryun was a staunch conservative, while Jenkins had a profile as a pro-business and pro-abortion-rights moderate. Although heavily outspent by Ryun, Jenkins eked out a win by just over 1,300 votes. Eager to quash any bitterness from the contest, Ryun heartily endorsed her. Jenkins still faced an uphill battle. Boyda had carefully crafted a voting record mostly in line with her constituents' views, and sought to distance herself from her party by publicly renouncing support from the Democratic Congressional Campaign Committee. Jenkins tied Boyda to liberal House Speaker Nancy Pelosi every chance she got and accused her of supporting tax increases by voting for Democratic budgets that phased out the Bush-era tax cuts for high-income earners. In a largely Democratic year, though not in Kansas, the strategy paid off. Jenkins won 51%-46%.

Jenkins has become entrenched, though with occasional bumps in the road. After criticizing spending earmarks during the campaign, Jenkins in 2009 submitted requests to the Appropriations Committee for 23 earmarked projects totaling $68 million. The conservative group Club for Growth removed her from its "Sworn off Earmarks" list. She responded that her pledge "only set rigorous standards for how a congressional member must go about requesting those earmarks." Although she was among the initial members of the Tea Party Caucus in 2010, Jenkins had second thoughts. She told a Kansas group in 2011 that members of the movement "don't even like the term compromise. They don't even like the term common ground. … I have always been willing to work with everyone," according to the *Lawrence Journal-World*. In 2013, she joined the "Problem Solvers" coalition of lawmakers who agreed to meet monthly to foster bipartisanship in Congress.

When she joined Ways and Means in 2011, Jenkins joined a Republican effort to overhaul the tax code. As a practitioner, she told the *Washington Examiner* in 2014, tax reform was "something near and dear to my heart." But while awaiting that long-term goal, she proposed her own tax preferences with their complexities. She introduced a bill to extend tax credits to small businesses that hire National Guard members. In September 2015, the committee approved her bill to relax restrictions on the use of health savings accounts. She has been a big supporter of giving trade-negotiating authority to the president, and cited that one in five Kansas jobs results from international trade. Jenkins occasionally cooperated across the aisle. With Democratic Rep. Jim McGovern of Massachusetts, she re-launched the Hunger Caucus in 2015, with their joint appearance at the D.C. Central Kitchen.

Back home, some conservatives have been unhappy with Jenkins' record. State Sen. Dennis Pyle challenged her in the 2010 primary. Without spending much money, he held Jenkins to a 57%-43% win. In 2014, both parties believed that Jenkins might be facing a legitimate threat from Margie Wakefield, a Democratic attorney. But Jenkins won easily, 57%-39%, with assistance from her campaign spending of $3.1 million to $800,000 for Wakefield. Jenkins may have suffered a bit because Republican voters were unhappy with GOP statewide incumbents. During a 2015 speech in Lawrence, she expressed hope that Congress had become less partisan and more productive.

In 2016, Jenkins had a routine reelection. Against Democrat Britani Potter, who did not file a campaign-finance report, Jenkins won 61%-33%. She was intent on reinforcing her more centrist views.

She told a local group that more people were unhappy with government, especially the increase in federal regulations, the *Topeka Capital-Journal* reported. She added that the presidential campaign between Donald Trump and Hillary Clinton had failed to inspire public confidence. "There are a lot of angry people. I get it. I'm ticked off," Jenkins said. "You don't have to be shrill and obnoxious to appeal to the people back home." During the campaign, she typically refused to comment directly about Trump.

When Jenkins stepped down after four years as a Republican leader, she said she wanted to devote more time to her work on Ways and Means, especially with prospective action on tax reform and health care legislation in the new Congress. Another reason for a possible career switch, she told Associated Press after the election, was that she was considering a run to replace term-limited Gov. Sam Brownback in 2018. "Kansas is where my heart is, so whenever there's an opportunity to serve back home, I'm always going to look at it, so that's what I'm going to do," she said. Evidently, her exploration of a campaign for governor was not encouraging. In January 2017, Jenkins announced that she would not seek reelection to the House nor any other office in 2018, and that she would be looking for opportunities in the private sector.

Eastern Kansas: Topeka, Kansas City Suburbs

Population		**Race and Ethnicity**		**Income**	
Total	714,500	White	83.2%	Median Income	$48,818 (271 out of 435)
Land area	14,143	Black	4.3%		
Pop/ sq mi	50.5	Latino	6.2%		
Born in state	63.6%	Asian	1.4%	Under $50,000	51.0%
		Two races	3.5%	$50,000-$99,999	31.8%
Age Groups		Other	1.4%	$100,000-$199,999	14.9%
Under 18	23.3%			$200,000 or more	2.3%
18-34	24.2%	**Education**		Poverty Rate	15.7%
35-64	37.4%	H.S grad or less	40.3%		
Over 64	15.2%	Some college	32.4%	**Health Insurance**	
		College Degree, 4 yr	16.7%	With health insurance coverage	89.2%
Work		Post grad	10.5%		
White Collar	35.2%				
Sales and Service	40.9%	**Military**		**Public Assistance**	
Blue Collar	23.9%	Veteran	10.3%	Cash public assistance income	2.4%
Government	20.2%	Active Duty	0.4%		
				Food stamp/SNAP benefits	10.6%

Voter Turnout			
2015 Total Citizens 18+	533,642	2016 House Turnout as % CVAP	56%
2016 House turnout	297,401	2014 House Turnout as % CVAP	42%

2012 Presidential Vote		
Mitt Romney	163,138	(55%)
Barack Obama	124,401	(42%)

2016 Presidential Vote		
Donald Trump	165,002	(56%)
Hillary Clinton	110,597	(37%)
Gary Johnson	13,250	(5%)
Jill Stein	6,811	(2%)

Cook Partisan Voting Index: R+10

The green plains of eastern Kansas have seen more than their share of American history. In 1827, on bluffs above the Missouri River, the Army built Fort Leavenworth, famous in later years for its war college and military prison and now the oldest U.S. fort west of the Mississippi River. In the 1850s, newly founded towns along the Kansas River and along the Missouri border were the centers of Bleeding Kansas, the name the state took after pro-slavery bushwhackers set up a state capital in tiny Lecompton and anti-slavery New Englanders established their stronghold down the river at Lawrence. These tensions bled into the Civil War; William Quantrill's infamous nighttime raid on pro-Union Lawrence in 1863 resulted in the burning of all but two businesses to the ground and the death of around 200 inhabitants.

Today's Kansas is a much more staid place. The sole capital, Topeka, sits on a low bluff above the Kansas River. The city's system of legal segregation prompted the 1954 landmark case, *Brown v. Board of Education*, which unanimously concluded "separate but equal" is not equal. Topeka has had some success attracting corporate headquarters, including Hill's Pet Nutrition. Population loss is not as large here as in western Kansas. Leavenworth became a controversial national site when President Barack Obama and others considered it as an alternative to house terrorism detainees held at the Guantanamo Bay facility in Cuba. Chelsea Manning was a prisoner at the fort after she was convicted for disclosing classified military information to Wikileaks. In one of his final actions as president, Obama commuted her term.

The area around Lawrence, where the University of Kansas is based, has grown steadily. Farther south of the cities, on the Missouri border, are the hills called "the Balkans," where Eastern European coal miners settled in towns such as Pittsburg and Girard. This area was once a center of American socialism: Clarence Darrow and Upton Sinclair made pilgrimages, and the local paper, *Appeal to Reason*, had a national circulation of 750,000. Recently, coal-bed methane gas wells have provided an economic boost to southeast Kansas. Although its production has declined slightly, oil production has increased.

These disparate areas, Topeka and Lawrence, Fort Leavenworth, the wheat-growing counties, and the Balkans - most of eastern Kansas except the Kansas City metropolitan area - make up the 2nd Congressional District. In recent decades, Democrats have been competitive in state races here, especially in Topeka. For 20 of the years from 1970 to 1994, Democrats held the 2nd District seat. Republicans have held it for all but two years since then. Like Mitt Romney in 2012, Donald Trump won 56 percent of the vote in this district. He got 58 percent in Crawford County, which had remnants of the left-leaning tradition and was the only county outside of the Kansas City area that voted for Obama in 2008.

THIRD DISTRICT

Kevin Yoder (R)

Elected 2010, 4th term; b. Jan 08, 1976, Hutchison; University of Kansas, B.A.; University of Kansas School of Law, J.D.; Methodist; Married (Brooke Yoder); 2 children.

Elected Office: KS House, 2002-2010.

Professional Career: Practicing attorney, 2002-2010.

DC Office: 2433 RHOB 20515, 202-225-2865, Fax: 202-225-2807, yoder.house.gov.

State Offices: Overland Park, 913-621-0832.

Committees: *Appropriations*: Agriculture, Rural Development, FDA & Related Agencies, Financial Services & General Government, Legislative Branch (Chmn).

Group Ratings

	ADA	ACLU	AFL-CIO	LCV	ITI	COC	HAFA	ACU	CFG	FRC
2016	-	11%	-	0%	83%	93%	84%	96%	78%	100%
2015	0%	C	4%	0%	C	80%	C	88%	78%	100%

Almanac Ratings 2015

	Economy	Social	Foreign	Composite
Liberal	3%	0%	6%	3%
Conservative	97%	100%	94%	97%

Key Votes of the 114th Congress

1. Keystone Pipeline	Y	5. Puerto Rico Debt	N	9. Offenses by Aliens	Y
2. Trade Deals	Y	6. Medical Marijuana	N	10. Troops in Iraq	N
3. Export-Import Bank	N	7. Sanctuary Cities	Y	11. Homeland Security $$	N
4. Debt Ceiling Increase	N	8. Armor-piercing Bullets	Y	12. Trade Adjustment aid	Y

Election Results

Election	Name (Party)	Vote	(%)	Cand. Spent	Ind. Exp. Support	Ind. Exp. Oppose
2016 General	Kevin Yoder (R)	176,022	(51%)	$4,072,696	$44,040	$2,185,725
	Jay Sidie (D)	139,300	(41%)	$560,298	$19,506	$799,876
	Steven Hohe (L)	27,791	(8%)			
2016 Primary	Kevin Yoder (R)	37,023	(64%)			
	Greg Goode (R)	21,191	(36%)			

Prior winning percentages: 2014 (60%), 2012 (69%), 2010 (58%)

Republican Kevin Yoder, who won his seat in 2010, has been an energetic star among junior House members. Democrats have seen his district - which they previously held - as a prime pick-up opportunity. In 2016, they went all out to recruit a challenger and spend heavily on his behalf. In the closing weeks of the campaign, they were buoyant about defeating Yoder. The Democrats didn't come close to their expectations. And Yoder emerged following the election with a new sinecure as a House Appropriations subcommittee "cardinal."

Yoder grew up on a farm near the aptly named town of Yoder, founded in 1907 by an Amish settler. His family has been there since the 1880s, and hundreds of Yoders live in the area. His father's farm produces grains, soybeans, corn and meat. His maternal grandfather, William Alexander, who grew up as a poor farmer, was the Republican mayor of Wilmette, Illinois, and president of the Chicago Bar Association. As a child, Yoder recalls visits to his grandfather in downtown Chicago, drawing inspiration from him. Yoder studied English and political science at the University of Kansas, where he was student body president.

He was a registered Democrat before undergoing what he calls his own "personal maturation and growth" and switching to the Republicans. During his senior year in college and into law school, he volunteered in campaigns and interned at the state legislature. He worked as a law clerk at the Pentagon in Washington doing counter-narcotics work. He left a month before the Sept. 11, 2001, terrorist attacks, an event that inspired him to get more involved with politics. Yoder was elected to the Kansas House in 2002 at age 26, and got a seat on the Appropriations Committee, where he had interned in college. He eventually chaired the committee.

When six-term Democratic Rep. Dennis Moore announced he would not seek another term, Yoder jumped into the race. His legislative district, which includes some of Overland Park and the headquarters of Sprint Nextel, gave him access to a large donor base, and his acumen at fundraising forced the early GOP front-runner out of the race. Yoder's primary opponents pointed to his party switch as evidence of flip-flopping on issues. But Yoder managed to win the nine-person contest with 44 percent of the vote.

In the fall, his Democratic opponent was Stephene Moore, the wife of the retiring incumbent and a nurse by trade. She supported President Barack Obama's health care bill while Yoder opposed it. He came out against reinstating the estate tax, which affects many family farms. With a temporary repeal about to expire, Moore favored keeping the tax but at lower rates. Moore seized on a *Topeka Capital-Journal* report that Yoder refused to take a preliminary breath test during a 2009 traffic stop. Yoder pleaded guilty to refusing a law enforcement officer's request and was fined $165. His campaign said that he wasn't drunk and that he refused the test because he had passed a field sobriety test. *The Kansas City Star* endorsed Yoder, calling him "quick-witted and thoughtful," and saying he "could be a force in Congress." He won 58%-39%.

As a freshman, Yoder got a seat on the Appropriations Committee. Though he voted a strongly conservative line, he avoided the anti-government rhetoric of his fellow freshmen and joined the bipartisan Common Ground Caucus. He was among the few Republicans to refuse to sign activist Grover Norquist's pledge never to raise taxes, saying no one can predict the future. In 2011, Yoder introduced a bill to ban the issuing of $1 coins for 15 years as a way of saving money; the Treasury Department later suspended the coins' production.

In 2014, Yoder used his seat on Appropriations to work with a bipartisan group of lawmakers who cut a deal that rolled back a provision in the Dodd-Frank banking law of 2010. He told *Roll Call* that the result was "a minor fix." Critics said removal of restrictions on the ability of banks to trade in certain commodities created a major loophole, which was pushed actively by big Wall Street banks and was strongly opposed by Sen. Elizabeth Warren of Massachusetts. In 2016, he advocated a doubling of research money for the National Institutes of Health, chiefly to seek a cure for cancer, and said that it would become a top priority. With Democratic Rep. Jared Polis of Colorado, Yoder filed the Email

Privacy Act to require law-enforcement officials to get a search warrant before they could access digital records. The House unanimously passed the measure in April 2016.

In August 2012, news accounts reported that during a fact-finding trip to Israel the previous summer, several House freshmen took a late-night swim in the Sea of Galilee, a pilgrimage site for Christians. The other members remained clothed, but Yoder shed his clothing, prompting a rebuke from Majority Leader Eric Cantor and an avalanche of negative publicity. GOP presidential candidate Mitt Romney called the incident "reprehensible," while comic David Letterman turned it into a list of "Top 10 Congressman Kevin Yoder Excuses." A chastened Yoder apologized. In November, he was reelected without major-party opposition. His indiscretion continued as an issue in 2014 when his Democratic opponent, Kelly Kultala, ran an ad that featured a group of nudists talking about Yoder's behavior. Yoder won 60%-40%, which was close to his margin in 2010 and suggested that the Galilee swim after three years had likely run its course.

In 2016, Democrats believed that Yoder had other vulnerabilities, including the potential drag that Donald Trump could create in his district. They made him one of their top campaign targets. The Democratic nominee was Jay Sidie, an investor and former Archer Daniels Midland executive who barely won his primary. Sidie raised nearly $600,000 and benefited from $1.4 million in party spending. Yoder raised $3.2 million and Republicans spent $800,000 on his behalf. Democrats had an early October poll that showed Yoder with only a 44%-40% lead. But Yoder had a comfortable 51%-41% win, even though Trump lost the district.

Yoder got good post-election news when he became chairman of the Legislative Branch Subcommittee of House Appropriations. He promised to "rein in out-of-control federal spending and increase transparency with regard to how we spend taxpayers' hard-earned money," to assure a "streamlined, efficient, and effective legislative branch."

Kansas City Metro

Population		**Race and Ethnicity**		**Income**	
Total	739,564	White	72.8%	Median Income	$66,525 (83 out of 435)
Land area	757	Black	8.6%		
Pop/ sq mi	976.7	Latino	11.6%	Under $50,000	37.5%
Born in state	43.7%	Asian	4.2%	$50,000-$99,999	31.5%
		Two races	2.4%	$100,000-$199,999	23.9%
Age Groups		Other	0.4%	$200,000 or more	7.2%
Under 18	26.2%			Poverty Rate	10.0%
18-34	22.2%	**Education**			
35-64	39.6%	H.S grad or less	26.9%	**Health Insurance**	
Over 64	12.0%	Some college	28.3%	With health insurance coverage	89.5%
		College Degree, 4 yr	28.7%		
Work		Post grad	16.2%		
White Collar	44.5%			**Public Assistance**	
Sales and Service	39.2%	**Military**		Cash public assistance income	1.4%
Blue Collar	16.3%	Veteran	7.8%		
Government	11.3%	Active Duty	0.1%	Food stamp/SNAP benefits	7.0%

Voter Turnout			
2015 Total Citizens 18+	504,788	2016 House Turnout as % CVAP	68%
2016 House turnout	343,113	2014 House Turnout as % CVAP	45%

2012 Presidential Vote		
Mitt Romney	177,886	(54%)
Barack Obama	146,406	(44%)

2016 Presidential Vote		
Hillary Clinton	161,479	(47%)
Donald Trump	157,304	(46%)
Gary Johnson	17,127	(5%)

Cook Partisan Voting Index: R+4

Though its central core is in Missouri, about 40 percent of metropolitan Kansas City's residents live west of the state line in Kansas. Some are in Kansas City, Kansas, or KCK as it is sometimes called, where the low-lying land near the Missouri River used to house one of the nation's largest stockyards. This is still a working-class town with lots of modest frame houses, new Latino neighborhoods that have surpassed in size the African-American community, which lost population between 2010 and 2015, and a Catholic ethnic neighborhood. Kansas City's Wyandotte County has lost 26,000 people since the 1970s, and is now majority-minority: 28 percent Hispanic and 24 percent black. It is one of only four such counties in the state; the other three are in the southwestern corner, where farms and meatpacking plants have attracted immigrants from Mexico.

South of Kansas City and Wyandotte County is Johnson County, which is more affluent and close to four times the size of Wyandotte. The newer neighborhoods are arrayed along the interstates, as subdivisions have replaced croplands. They have grown to the point that Overland Park, Olathe, Shawnee and Lenexa are among the largest cities in the state; Overland Park is the second-largest behind Wichita. Like many suburbs, these towns became more than just residential neighborhoods over the past few decades. Sprint Nextel is headquartered in Overland Park. After Applebee's left Lenexa to cross the river in 2011, city officials responded by convincing SelectQuote Senior Insurance Services to move from the Missouri side two years later. This swap is emblematic of a major problem for the region: Tax incentives are used by states to lure businesses across the tight state borders, producing a net wash in job creation, but a decrease in overall revenues. The local Hall Family Foundation concluded in a 2016 report that the competition during the previous five years had cost the two states more than $200 million in tax revenues, for a net gain of just 414 jobs for Kansas. Local companies have requested officials in both states to find better ways to promote the entire region.

Johnson County, like Wyandotte (and the Missouri suburbs, too), has been diversifying demographically. In 1980, the county was 97 percent white. But the share of non-Hispanic whites dropped to 80 percent of the population in 2015. Wyandotte has an old Democratic machine style of politics, though its influence has been tempered by the consolidation of city and county governments. Johnson, by contrast, has long been heavily Republican, but with plenty of moderate and even liberal voters on cultural issues. It has been a battleground for the fierce fights between moderate and conservative wings of the Kansas Republican Party, which sometimes benefit the Democrats.

The 3rd Congressional District consists of all of Johnson and Wyandotte counties, and a corner of rural Miami County. The 3rd has been comfortably Republican in recent presidential elections. In a notable turnaround, Hillary Clinton led Donald Trump, 47%-46%, in this district, which Mitt Romney won, 54%-44%, over Barack Obama in 2012. Clinton took Wyandotte, 62%-33%. Trump won Johnson County, but only by 48%-45%, in contrast to Romney's 58%-40% advantage.

FOURTH DISTRICT

Ron Estes (R)

Elected 2017, 1st term; b. Jul 19, 1956, Topeka; Tennessee Technology University, B.S.; Tennessee Technology University, M.B.A.; Lutheran; Married (Susan Oliver); 3 children.

Elected Office: Sedgwick County Treasurer, 2004-2010; KS Treasurer, 2010-2017.

Professional Career: Businessman; Farmer.

DC Office: 2452 RHOB 20515, 202-225-6216, Fax: 202-225-3489, estes.house.gov.

State Offices: Wichita, 316-262-8992.

Committees: *Education & the Workforce*: Health, Employment, Labor & Pensions, Higher Education & Workforce Development. *Small Business*: Contracting & Workforce, Investigations, Oversight & Regulations.

Election Results

Election	Name (Party)	Vote (%)	Cand. Spent	Ind. Exp. Support	Ind. Exp. Oppose
2017 Special	Ron Estes (R)	64,044 (53%)	$501,093	$91,722	
	James Thompson (D)	56,435 (46%)	$562,394		$90,000

Republican Ron Estes was elected in April 2017 to the seat vacated by Mike Pompeo, who became director of the Central Intelligence Agency under President Donald Trump. Estes was a long-time businessman and elected official who ran a lackluster campaign. His win was narrower than has been customary in this district for Republicans, who scrambled to avoid potential embarrassment during the final days before the vote.

Estes was born in Topeka, a fifth-generation Kansan. He got a bachelor's in civil engineering and then an MBA, both from Tennessee Technological University. He was a consultant and had management roles in several different industries, including aerospace, automotive, and oil and gas, where he implemented improved efficiencies with financial and other computer systems. He won his first elected office in 2004, as treasurer of Sedgwick County. In 2010, he was elected state treasurer. In each position, he worked to improve operating efficiencies, provide quality customer service and save taxpayers money. He became active in national associations for state treasurers and their various responsibilities and has held several positions in the Republican Party, serving as the Kansas vice chairman.

After Pompeo quit the office, each party selected its candidate at a small nominating convention. That limited the time and financial costs, but it also meant that the candidates had to convince only a small number of party activists. Several Republicans voiced interest in what appeared to be a safe seat in Congress. The chief competitor to Estes was Alan Cobb, a coalitions director for Trump's national campaign; he had been involved in Kansas politics as an aide to former Sen. Bob Dole. At the Republican selection meeting on Feb. 9, Estes cited his experience in government. "I like to solve problems, not create them," he said. On the second ballot, Estes won 66 votes, the requisite majority of the 126 participants. Cobb had 43 votes. Running third with 17 was Todd Tiahrt, who had held the House seat for 16 years until he ran unsuccessfully in 2010 for the Senate seat of Sam Brownback when he was elected governor. Tiahrt apparently left bad feelings when he challenged Pompeo in 2014 and sought to cast his successor as a supporter of the Affordable Care Act because of his votes on several bills that financed the health care law. Tiahrt lost that primary, 63%-37%.

At the Democratic selection meeting two days later, James Thompson won a majority of the 39 Democratic delegates on the second ballot, 21-18. The runner-up was Dennis McKinney, a former state treasurer. Thompson, a civil rights attorney, offered a vigorous approach in what he called a fight for "sanity and justice." He cast the contest in national terms. "Have no doubt that this is going to be a referendum on Trump policies," he told the meeting, *The Wichita Eagle* reported. Thompson cast Estes as "a Brownback clone," a reference to the unpopular governor.

The contest was slow to attract local or national media attention. In the closing days, national Republicans were worried about the outcome. Sen. Ted Cruz of Texas spoke in Wichita at an election-eve get-out-the-vote rally. He described the stakes in the election, including the need to repeal the Affordable Care Act; Estes had said that he opposed an initial version of the repeal measure. Trump and Vice President Mike Pence recorded robo-calls urging Republicans to vote. Democrats apparently were better-organized and benefited from the hostility toward Trump among their supporters. In the early vote of more than 23,000 in Sedgwick County, Thompson got 61 percent. He raised $340,000, which was competitive with the $400,000 that Estes raised before the special election - another sign of grass-roots Democratic enthusiasm in the GOP heartland.

In a district where Trump five months earlier led 60%-33%, Estes won by an unimpressive 53%-46%. He narrowed the gap in Sedgwick so that he lost by only about 1,900 votes, which showed that Republicans were successful with Election Day turnout. He won the other counties in the district, which cast about 30 percent of the vote. "A win is a win," former National Republican Congressional Committee Chairman Tom Davis told the Associated Press. "But this should have been relatively simple and it wasn't."

The outcome signaled that rank-and-file Democrats had been energized. Thompson said that he planned to challenge Estes in 2018. Retrospectively, liberal activists second-guessed a possible missed opportunity in the first federal election during the Trump era. National Democrats "should have put more resources into that election," independent Sen. Bernie Sanders of Vermont said after the vote.

South Central Kansas: Wichita

Population		Race and Ethnicity		Income	
Total	720,174	White	74.6%	Median Income	$50,644 (247 out of 435)
Land area	14,316	Black	6.8%		
Pop/ sq mi	50.3	Latino	11.7%		
Born in state	65.5%	Asian	3.2%	Under $50,000	49.3%
Age Groups		Two races	2.9%	$50,000-$99,999	32.1%
Under 18	26.1%	Other	0.9%	$100,000-$199,999	15.6%
18-34	22.7%	**Education**		$200,000 or more	2.9%
35-64	37.5%	H.S grad or less	38.4%	Poverty Rate	14.5%
Over 64	13.8%	Some college	34.0%	**Health Insurance**	
Work		College Degree, 4 yr	18.6%	With health insurance coverage	87.6%
White Collar	34.6%	Post grad	9.1%		
Sales and Service	39.9%	**Military**		**Public Assistance**	
Blue Collar	25.6%	Veteran	9.5%	Cash public assistance income	2.5%
Government	13.8%	Active Duty	0.5%	Food stamp/SNAP benefits	11.5%

Voter Turnout			
2015 Total Citizens 18+	507,204	2016 House Turnout as % CVAP	54%
2016 House turnout	275,251	2014 House Turnout as % CVAP	41%

2012 Presidential Vote		
Mitt Romney	164,553	(62%)
Barack Obama	96,433	(36%)

2016 Presidential Vote		
Donald Trump	165,266	(60%)
Hillary Clinton	90,541	(33%)

Cook Partisan Voting Index: R+15

With about 390,000 people, Wichita has been a Great Plains metropolis. It is still growing, but it has been falling behind the magnitude of Omaha and Tulsa. It began as a farm market town and grew with local oil and gas discoveries in the 1920s. The aircraft business began in 1911 when Clyde Cessna first flew his plane from a farm in Kingman County. Five years later, Cessna moved his operations to an auto factory in north Wichita. The real impetus for the industry came during World War II and the years just afterward, when aircraft factories sprouted up on the Kansas plains, and Wichita suddenly became the nation's major producer of small aircraft. Workers poured in, many from neighboring Arkansas and Oklahoma, giving the city a taste of Southern culture.

The September 11 attacks were a severe blow to the overall airline industry, with the loss of some 15,000 local jobs, from which the area has not fully recovered. The Navy gave the area a boost in 2004 with a contract for 100 modified 737s to be used to hunt submarines. Then, the 2007-09 recession sparked another wave of layoffs, with Cessna idling more than 1,000 workers; Hawker Beechcraft filed for bankruptcy in 2012. Boeing, once the area's largest employer, shut down its local facilities in 2014; company officials cited cuts in the Pentagon budget and high overhead costs. The local aviation industry never fully recovered. Even with the many cutbacks, Wichita remained the nation's center for general aviation, with more than 20,000 employees in the industry and affiliated businesses. By 2015, business leaders in Wichita were discussing the need for innovation and growth in the local economy. Lower prices for oil and gas and for farm commodities have reduced land values.

The aviation industry is one facet of the local economy, which maintains slow but steady growth. Cargill Inc., the largest privately held corporation in the United States, is based in Wichita and includes 75 businesses. Cargill Meat Solutions, with 800 local workers, announced in 2016 that it would remain in Wichita and build a new headquarters. Koch Industries, owned by the politically active and conservative Koch brothers, has been second only to Cargill as the nation's largest privately held company, which employs about 60,000 in the United States and has revenues of about $100 billion, much of it in agriculture and technology. At a time when the Kochs were battered politically for their well-financed conservative activism and shifting to a softer edge, their company was beloved at home as an employer and philanthropist.

Kansas' 4th Congressional District is centered on Wichita, covering wheat-growing areas to the east and west, but with 70 percent of its people in Wichita and Sedgwick County. It occasionally votes Democratic in local and state contests, and the city elected its first African-American mayor, Democrat Carl Brewer, in 2007. He served two terms and was hailed as a consensus-builder when he stepped down in 2015 and was succeeded by Jeff Longwell, a Republican. In February 2017, Brewer announced that he was running for governor. Politically, the 4th has been solidly Republican in federal elections. Donald Trump got 60 percent of the vote in 2016, compared with 62 percent for Mitt Romney four years earlier.

★ KENTUCKY ★

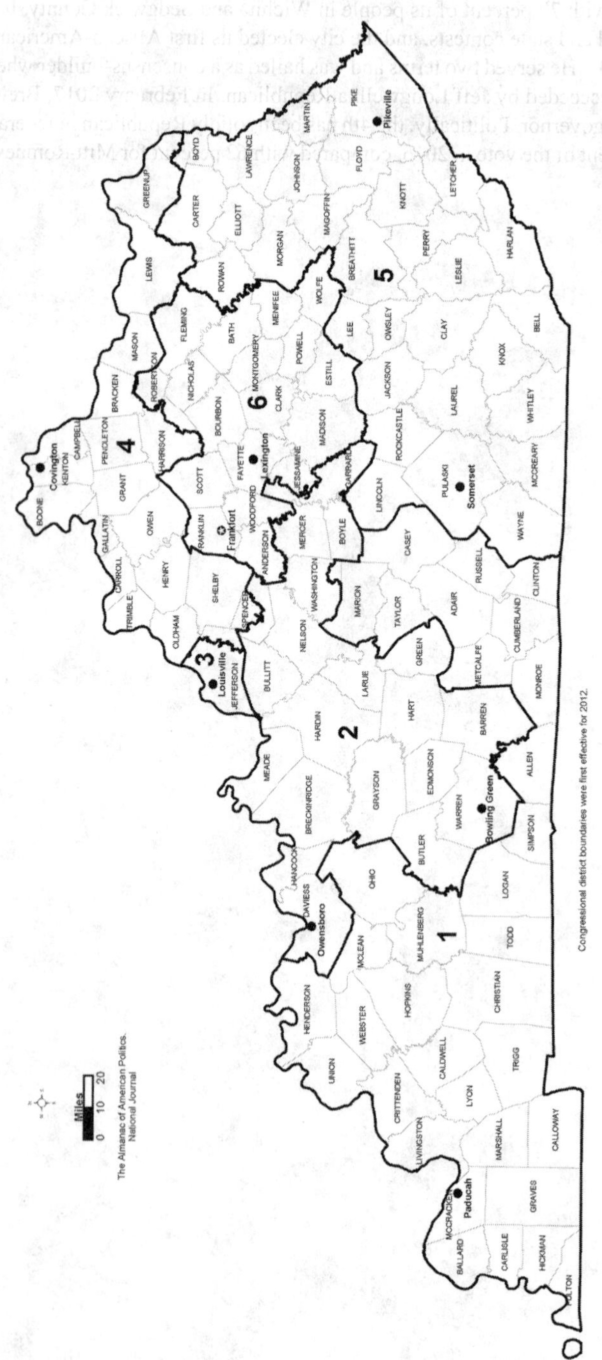
Pikeville
Covington
Lexington
Frankfort
Louisville
Somerset
Bowling Green
Owensboro
Paducah
1
2
3
4
5
6
BOONE
KENTON
CAMPBELL
PENDLETON
BRACKEN
MASON
LEWIS
GREENUP
BOYD
CARTER
LAWRENCE
ELLIOTT
JOHNSON
MARTIN
PIKE
FLOYD
MAGOFFIN
KNOTT
LETCHER
ROWAN
MORGAN
BREATHITT
PERRY
HARLAN
LESLIE
WOLFE
MENIFEE
FLEMING
BATH
ROBERTSON
NICHOLAS
MONTGOMERY
POWELL
LEE
OWSLEY
CLAY
BELL
KNOX
ESTILL
CLARK
BOURBON
HARRISON
GRANT
GALLATIN
OWEN
SCOTT
FAYETTE
JESSAMINE
MADISON
JACKSON
LAUREL
WHITLEY
ROCKCASTLE
GARRARD
LINCOLN
PULASKI
MCCREARY
WAYNE
BOYLE
MERCER
WOODFORD
FRANKLIN
ANDERSON
CARROLL
HENRY
TRIMBLE
OLDHAM
SHELBY
SPENCER
WASHINGTON
MARION
CASEY
RUSSELL
CLINTON
ADAIR
TAYLOR
CUMBERLAND
GREEN
METCALFE
MONROE
NELSON
BULLITT
JEFFERSON
LARUE
HART
BARREN
HARDIN
MEADE
ALLEN
EDMONSON
GRAYSON
BRECKINRIDGE
WARREN
SIMPSON
BUTLER
HANCOCK
OHIO
LOGAN
DAVIESS
MCLEAN
MUHLENBERG
TODD
HENDERSON
WEBSTER
HOPKINS
CHRISTIAN
UNION
CALDWELL
TRIGG
CRITTENDEN
LYON
LIVINGSTON
MARSHALL
CALLOWAY
MCCRACKEN
GRAVES
BALLARD
CARLISLE
HICKMAN
FULTON
Miles
0 10 20
The Almanac of American Politics,
National Journal
Congressional district boundaries were first effective for 2012.

It was a long time coming – perhaps six decades, depending on how you count it – but between 2015 and 2016, Kentucky all but completed its slow-motion transition from Democratic to Republican, a shift supercharged by the decline of one of the state's signature industries, coal.

Kentucky was once part of Virginia. When it was split off and admitted to the union in 1792, it became the first state west of the Appalachian chain. In 1798, Thomas Jefferson, aroused by the Federalists' anti-sedition acts, ghostwrote the Kentucky Resolutions, a defense of self-governance by the states. Kentucky's largest county is named for Jefferson, and its largest city for the monarch to whom he was credentialed as ambassador to France, Louis XVI. Kentucky has a constitution informed by a Jeffersonian suspicion of concentrating power. Its one-term limit on governors was raised to two only in 1992, and until 2001, it limited its state legislature to one 60-day session every two years, with mush important business handled in special sessions. The state has 120 counties – the third most of any state, after the much more populous Texas and Georgia. Kentucky's image remains very much what it was at its beginnings, a Jeffersonian commonwealth built on an agrarian culture: growing tobacco, horses (nine out of 10 Kentucky taxpayers in 1800 owned at least one) and brewing liquor. Later, coal and its extraction became a pillar of the economy.

Kentucky -- home to the Cumberland Gap, the pass through the Appalachian Mountains where Virginia meets Kentucky and Tennessee – remains a logistical hub. The state is within a day's drive of more than half of the U.S. population, and its large air-freight shipping terminals at the Louisville and Cincinnati-Northern Kentucky airports offer access to customers around the world. That was a big reason why Amazon.com opened a fulfillment center in Campbellsville, Kentucky, in 2000. Now the nation's largest online retailer has 11 fulfillment, return and customer service centers in the state, employing some 7,000 full time workers and planning investments worth $25 million. But before Amazon came to Kentucky, the automobile industry arrived, seeking some of the same logistical advantages the state had to offer, as well as a business-friendly environment.

The state is at the center of "auto alley," which runs from the Great Lakes to the Gulf of Mexico. While the nation saw a 30 percent decline in auto parts manufacturing jobs from 1990 to 2013, Kentucky saw an 87 percent increase in employment in that sector. Kentucky is home to four car and truck assembly lines: two Ford plants in Louisville, a Toyota plant in Georgetown, and a General Motors plant in Bowling Green. The University of Louisville Urban Studies Institute estimated that one of every 13 dollars in Kentucky's economy is traceable to the industry, which directly employs more than 85,000 workers in the state. Three of the state's auto plants -- the two in Louisville and the one in Georgetown, just north of Lexington -- are located in the portion of Kentucky known as the "Golden Triangle," the most productive and populous part of the state. The Golden Triangle extends from Jefferson County (Louisville) east to Fayette County (Lexington) and then north to Boone and Kenton Counties (suburban Cincinnati) -- the state's four largest counties by population. They are faster growing and have higher median household incomes than Kentucky as a whole, and several of their adjacent counties are wealthier still and seeing more rapid population growth. Scott County, near Lexington, grew by 11 percent between 2010 and 2015, about five times faster than the state. Oldham County, next door to Louisville, grew by 8 percent over the same period, and it has a median household income of more than $85,000, well above the state average. Such places have helped bolster the state's job market; unemployment was above 10 percent for almost two years during the Great Recession, but by late 2016 was only slightly above the national average.

The Golden Triangle includes the state's famed Bluegrass region, the center of its prized thoroughbred industry. The horse industry – including the Kentucky Derby, run since 1875 on the first Saturday in May -- directly or indirectly employs 55,000 Kentuckians and has an estimated $4 billion economic impact statewide. The Golden Triangle, plus some nearby counties, are also the home of global bourbon production: 95 percent of the liquor is produced in Kentucky, thanks to a combination of calcium-and-magnesium-producing blue limestone, big swings in temperature, and soil favorable to corn production. Employment in distilling has grown notably in recent years.

Outside the Triangle -- and the small metro areas of Bowling Green and Owensboro -- Kentucky is not doing as well. Overall, Kentucky's median income is 25 percent below the national average. The state's 18.5 percent poverty rate in 2015 ranked it in the top five states nationally, and the rate for children was even higher at 25 percent. The Annie E. Casey Foundation found that a third of the state's children live in single-parent households, a fifth of high school students don't graduate on time, and a fifth of pregnant women smoke. An analysis by the Kentucky Center for Economic Policy found that only 28 of the state's 120 counties had more people employed in March 2015 than in March 2007, before the recession began. And in most places beyond the Golden Triangle, population has been stagnant or falling. No fewer than 32 counties east of Lexington have seen population declines since the 2010 Census, and the University of Louisville projects that two-thirds of the state's counties will lose population between 2015 and 2040.

Rural Kentucky counties, particularly those in Appalachia, have seen their economies suffer as manufacturing and coal production decline. In 2016, employment in the state's coal industry fell to its lowest point in 118 years. The increasing popularity of hydraulic fracturing for low-cost natural gas has contributed significantly to the national slowdown in coal production. Tougher federal regulations to protect water quality around mines and higher Environmental Protection Agency emissions standards on coal-burning power plants have exacerbated the downturn. And many coal seams in eastern Kentucky have been stripped of their most accessible product, raising the cost of extraction; coal employment in that region fell by more than two-thirds between 2011 and 2016 alone. (In Western Kentucky, production was not nearly as hard hit; ironically, the higher sulfur content coal from this part of the state once had difficulty coping with clean-air rules, but the installation of scrubbers at many power plants has helped sustain the region's mines.) Even Kentucky itself is increasingly turning to cheaper, out-of-state coal to power electricity generation. Almost 40 percent of the state's coal inputs now come from Ohio, Indiana, Illinois, Colorado and Wyoming.

Another declining product is tobacco. For most of the last century nearly every Kentucky farmer grew at least a small crop of tobacco. But health concerns and more recently social mores gradually took have taken toll. (More than a quarter of Kentuckians smoke.) According to Will Snell, a professor of agricultural economics at the University of Kentucky and a leading expert on the burley leaf, horses overtook tobacco as the state's leading farm product by 1999. The cash payments to farmers who had previously owned tobacco quotas ended in 2014. By now, cattle have replaced tobacco for many Kentucky farmers, and some are anticipating their first hemp crops in 2016.

As in other parts of Appalachia, addiction has spread. When the Centers for Disease Control and Prevention named 220 counties at risk of outbreaks of HIV and hepatitis C from intravenous drug use, 54 were in Kentucky. Life expectancies are significantly lower in the Appalachian portions of the state than in the Golden Triangle, due to a combination of poor education, low income, inadequate nutrition, and smoking, among other factors. When the state – under then-Democratic Gov. Steve Beshear – took advantage of health insurance expansion under the Affordable Care Act, the response was more enthusiastic than in almost any state. And the results were significant: The Commonwealth Fund found that Kentucky had the biggest drop in uninsured, low-income adults of working age.

Kentucky long favored the Democratic Party, which can trace its ancestry at least tenuously back to Jefferson. The Bluegrass region and the western end of the state were slave holding territory and voted Democratic. Louisville, with many German immigrants, was an anti-slavery town, and for years flirted with Republicans, but the city and surrounding Jefferson County has been conspicuously more Democratic than the state in this century. The eastern mountains were pro-Union and remain Republican, except for some counties where the United Mine Workers organized coal miners in the 1930s. But the national Democratic Party has moved to the left on social issues, whereas Kentucky is home to Kim Davis, the elected Rowan County clerk who refused to sign same-sex marriage licenses, and a 300-cubit-long, $100 million Noah's Ark tourist attraction built by Biblical literalists in Williams town, located between Cincinnati and Lexington. The environmental wing of the Democratic Party has also gained ground nationally – a huge problem for voters throughout the state who perceive the party as waging a "war on coal." Partly as a result, Kentucky has gone solidly Republican in the last five presidential elections, and both of its Senators and five of its six House members are Republicans.

For a while, state-level Democrats held on, thanks to incumbency and savvy in navigating the state's politics. But the Democrats' registration lead has eroded, and in the 2015 election, Democrats lost the governorship to tea party-aligned Republican Matt Bevin, who ran on a platform of rolling back Obama care despite its successes in the state. He became only the fourth GOP governor to win in eight decades. (The previous ones were elected in 1943, 1967, and 2003.) Republicans also flipped the offices of state auditor and state treasurer, and they barely fell short of seizing the attorney general's office; Jenean Hampton, Bevin's running mate, became the first African-American to be elected state wide. Then, in

2016, the GOP won control of the state House for the first time since 1920, joining the Senate, which had been in Republican hands since 2000. In fact, bolstered by Donald Trump's candidacy, Republicans exceeded expectations by winning a super majority in the House. In the Senate, Majority Leader Mitch McConnell of Kentucky wielded significant influence with a Republican in the White House.

Kentucky's demographics were a good fit for Trump's strengths. Kentucky is tied for the sixth-whitest state in the country at 85 percent, and only three states (Maine, Vermont and West Virginia) have a smaller Hispanic percentage. It's also the ninth-most rural state at 41.6 percent of the population. While Mitt Romney won Kentucky by 22 points in 2012, Trump won by 30, gaining almost 116,000 more votes than Romney had while Hillary Clinton underperformed Obama's 2012 results by more than 50,000 votes. The fact that she had said "we're going to put a lot of coal miners and coal companies out of business" most certainly did not help. Obama had won just four counties in 2012, but Clinton fared even worse, winning just two – the state's largest, Jefferson (Louisville), where Clinton's margin was two points better than Obama's, and Fayette (Lexington), where she did eight points better. "Far from the metropolitan hubs inhabited by the main beneficiaries of globalization's churn," Roger Cohen wrote in the *New York Times*, "many people feel disenfranchised from both main political parties, angry at stagnant wages and growing inequality, and estranged from a prevailing liberal urban ethos."

Population		**Race and Ethnicity**		**Income**	
Total	4,397,353	White	85.6%	Median Income	$43,740 (46 out of 50)
Land area	39,486	Black	7.8%		
Pop/ sq mi	111.4	Latino	3.3%	Under $50,000	55.4%
Born in state	69.8%	Asian	1.3%	$50,000-$99,999	28.8%
		Two races	1.8%	$100,000-$199,999	13.1%
Age Groups		Other	0.3%	$200,000 or more	2.6%
Under 18	23.1%			Poverty Rate	18.9%
18-34	22.5%	**Education**			
35-64	39.9%	H.S grad or less	49.5%	**Health Insurance**	
Over 64	14.4%	Some college	28.3%	With health insurance coverage	88.6%
		College Degree, 4 yr	13.1%		
Work		Post grad	9.2%		
White Collar	32.9%			**Public Assistance**	
Sales and Service	40.7%	**Military**		Cash public assistance income	2.5%
Blue Collar	26.4%	Veteran	8.8%		
Government	15.1%	Active Duty	0.4%	Food stamp/SNAP benefits	17.3%

Voter Turnout			
2015 Total Citizens 18+	3,297,108	2016 Pres Turnout as % CVAP	58%
2016 Pres Votes	1,924,149	2012 Pres Turnout as % CVAP	56%

Legislature	
Senate:	11D, 27R
House:	36D, 64R

Presidential Politics

2016 Democratic Primary		
Hillary Clinton (D)	212,534	(47%)
Bernie Sanders (D)	210,623	(46%)
2016 Republican Caucus		
Donald Trump (R)	82,493	(36%)
Ted Cruz (R)	72,503	(32%)
Marco Rubio (R)	37,579	(16%)
John Kasich (R)	33,134	(14%)

2016 Presidential Vote		
Donald Trump (R)	1,202,971	(63%)
Hillary Clinton (D)	628,854	(33%)
Gary Johnson (L)	53,752	(3%)
2012 Presidential Vote		
Mitt Romney (R)	1,087,190	(60%)
Barack Obama (D)	679,370	(38%)

It has been 20 years since Democrats won Kentucky in a presidential election. With two Southerners on their ticket, they captured the White House in 1992 and 1996. In 2000, Al Gore initially targeted Kentucky, which is next-door to his home state of Tennessee. But Gore had taken stands viewed as hostile to tobacco, coal and guns, all staples of Kentucky culture. George W. Bush carried the state 57%-41% that year, and Republicans have won by growing margins ever since. In 2012, Barack Obama carried only four of Kentucky's 120 counties, including those containing the state's two largest cities, Louisville and Lexington, and the state capital of Frankfort. He carried only one historically Democratic county in the eastern mountains. By comparison, even when losing by landslide margins, George McGovern carried seven mountain counties in 1972 and Walter Mondale carried 12 mountain counties and seven historically Democratic counties in the west in 1984. After four more years of the Obama administration, tougher regulations on coal extraction and use, and a decline in energy markets, Kentuckians were in no mood to reward the party in power in the White House and Hillary Clinton discovered that when they went to the polls. Trump defeated Clinton 63%-33%. The Democratic nominee carried just two counties, Jefferson (Louisville) and Fayette (Lexington and the University of Kentucky). Of course, Clinton didn't do herself any favors when she told a CNN town hall in February in next-door Ohio, "We're going to put a lot of coal miners and coal companies out of business," in describing her proposals for moving the country toward cleaner energy sources. Democratic Rep. John Yarmouth, a Clinton booster who represents Louisville, told WHAS-11 News, "The first time I heard it, I said, 'Oh my God, that's deadly.'"

Despite that miscue, Clinton managed to eke out a half-point victory over Vermont Sen. Bernie Sanders in the Democratic primary on May 17. One reason for her victory was her decision to shift the discussion to cars and trucks that are produced at four plants around the state, which is also home to many auto parts suppliers. She criticized Sanders for voting against the release of funds from the Troubled Asset Relief Program, a measure primarily designed to benefit the financial sector, but which also included money for the auto bailout. Clinton revved up her television advertising in the state and added numerous stops to her campaign schedule. Every effort was needed - she prevailed by fewer than 2,000 votes. Kentucky Republicans opted to hold a caucus on March 5, at the behest of home-state Sen. Rand Paul, who was seeking the GOP presidential nomination. That was for Paul to get around a state law that forbids a candidate from appearing on two ballots at the same time. Because Paul was up for reelection in 2016, he would have had to choose between the presidential primary and the Senate primary. Paul contributed $250,000 to the state GOP to help defray the costs of conducting the caucus. Unfortunately for Paul, a poor performance in the Iowa caucuses caused him to exit the presidential race before it got to Kentucky. Trump defeated Texas Sen. Ted Cruz, 36%-32%, followed by Florida Sen. Marco Rubio and Ohio Gov. John Kasich, both well back. The earlier date of the caucus when the GOP nominating contest was still in flux may have boosted participation. The caucuses had more than 228,000 attendees, more than the number who voted in either of the past two GOP presidential primaries.

Congressional Districts

115th Congress Lineup	5R 1D	**114th Congress Lineup**	5R 1D

Republicans controlled the state Senate and Democrats the state House after the 2010 censuses. House Democrats presented a plan that would have weakened two Republican incumbents, but acceded to a compromise that made few shifts in congressional district lines. Since then, Republicans have taken control of the House and the governor's office. Democrats have had an edge in party registration in all six districts, but five of them have elected Republicans since 2012. John Yarmuth, the only Democrat, has become entrenched in the formerly marginal 3rd District in Louisville's Jefferson County.

Governor

Matthew Griswold Bevin (R)

Elected 2015, term expires 2019, 1st term; b. Jan. 9, 1967, Denver, CO; Washington and Lee University, BA 1989; Southern Baptist; Married (Glenna); 10 children (4 adopted, 1 deceased).

Military Career: U.S Army, 1989-1993.

Professional Career: Financial Consultant, SEI Investments Company; Vice President, Putnam Investments; President, Bevin Brothers Manfacturing Company.

Office: 700 Capitol Ave., Suite 100, Frankfort, 40601; 502-564-2611; Fax: 502-564-0437; Website: kentucky.gov.

Election Results

Election	Name (Party)	Vote (%)
2015 General	Matt Bevin (R)	511,771 (53%)
	Jack Conway (D)	426,827 (44%)
	Drew Curtis (I)	35,627 (4%)
2015 Primary	Matt Bevin (R)	70,479 (33%)
	James Comer Jr. (R)	70,396 (33%)
	Hal Heiner (R)	57,948 (27%)
	Will T. Scott (R)	15,364 (7%)

Just a year after unsuccessfully challenging Mitch McConnell, the Senate's top Republican, in a GOP primary, Matt Bevin won an underdog bid for the governorship in 2015. He articulated a strongly conservative agenda, targeting state Democrats' embrace of Obamacare, including a big expansion of Medicaid. Bevin is only the fourth Republican to win the governorship in more than eight decades, and his victory came close to completing Kentucky's transition to a solidly Republican state up and down the ballot.

Bevin grew up in Shelburne, New Hampshire, as the second of six children in a family of modest means that lived on their livestock and produce from their garden. He has told audiences that he shared a bedroom with his three brothers in a house without central heat. "It's those stories and the family's history of self-reliance that he says helped form his view that government should just get out of people's way," wrote Joseph Gerth in the Louisville *Courier-Journal*. Bevin was able to attend the Gould Academy, a boarding school in Bethel Maine, and then Washington & Lee University, where he majored in East Asian studies and took part in ROTC. Bevin rose to captain, serving four years of active duty with the 5th Mechanized Infantry Division. After the military, Bevin went into the financial industry and other entrepreneurial ventures, amassing between $13.4 million and $54.9 million in net worth, according to ethics filings. He and his wife Glenna have nine children, four of them adopted from Ethiopia; their eldest daughter, Brittiney, died in a car crash.

In 2014, Bevin decided to challenge McConnell – not only the Senate's leading Republican but the state's political powerhouse – from the right in the GOP primary. Two national conservative groups with deep pockets took an interest in Bevin's candidacy: the Madison Project, which had helped Republican Ted Cruz's successful insurgent Senate bid in Texas, and the Senate Conservatives Fund, a political action committee allied with former South Carolina Sen. Jim DeMint, then-president of the Heritage Foundation and a leader of the conservative wing. McConnell didn't take his opponent lightly; he ran ads calling Bevin an "East Coast Con Man" and "Bailout Bevin." Bevin returned fire, tagging McConnell as a career politician. But Bevin was an inexperienced candidate who made numerous errors - he attended a cock-fighting rally and called it a "state's rights" event - and McConnell crushed him, 60%-35%. After the primary, Bevin refused to endorse McConnell, saying, "You can't punch people in the face, punch people in the face, punch people in the face, and ask them to have tea and crumpets with you and think it's all good."

The election was barely in the rear-view mirror by the time Bevin decided to run for governor. The seat was coming open after being held for two terms by Democrat Steve Beshear, whose most prominent achievement was adding more than 400,000 Kentuckians to the Medicaid rolls. In the primary, Bevin faced three major candidates -- Agriculture Commissioner James Comer, Louisville businessman Hal Heiner and former state Supreme Court Justice Will T. Scott – with the winner expected to take on Democratic Attorney General Jack Conway in the general. The primary was nasty, including allegations by Comer's ex-girlfriend that he had abused her emotionally and physically when they were both in college. The airing of the allegations were linked to the husband of Heiner's running mate, so he was hurt along with Comer. Bevin ran an ad showing two kids in a food fight, representing Heiner and Comer. Somewhat unexpectedly, Bevin came out on top on Election Day – by 83 votes. Bevin and Comer each took 33 percent, with Heiner at 27 percent and Scott at 7 percent.

Heading into the general, Bevin sought to repair ties with McConnell, deleting past tweets critical of his former opponent and making a self-deprecating video about their animosity. McConnell endorsed Bevin, but didn't go far out of his way to offer tangible support. Bevin ran on ending the Common Core educational curriculum, implementing drug testing for recipients of public assistance, enacting a right-to-work law, and, most notable in policy terms, dismantling Kynect, the state's Obamacare health insurance exchange. By mid-2015, Bevin began talking about scaling back the expansion through premiums and work requirements. Conway had put together a mixed record in past elections – notably, he lost to Rand Paul in the 2010 Senate race – but most pre-election surveys found the Democrat with a modest lead. As it turned out, the polls were wrong: Bevin won with relative ease, 53%-44%. He also had coattails, helping eliminate Democratic state auditor Adam Edelen, who would have become a likely 2019 challenger. Ron Fournier, writing in the *Atlantic*, called Bevin's victory "merely the latest warning shot fired at the political status quo, a surge of populism playing out at the edges of both parties." (He wrote that half a year before Donald Trump won the Republican presidential nomination.)

In office, Bevin tapped Heiner, one of his primary rivals, as his secretary of education and workforce. The new governor also signed a bill mandating that women seeking an abortion receive a face-to-face consultation 24 hours before the procedure, and he set about tackling the state's pension underfunding problems, which were among the nation's worst. To start tackling an estimated $30 billion long-term unfunded liability, Bevin promised $1.1 billion in additional funds over two years, funded by a 9 percent cuts in most state agency budgets. As promised, he shuttered the Kynect site and sought a federal waiver to change the benefit structure. The health insurance changes were not the only ways that Bevin tangled with Beshear; he also removed former first lady Jane Beshear's name from the Capitol Education Center. As the two governors traded verbal shots, Beshear's son Andy – elected attorney general on the same day that Bevin won the governorship – clashed with his father's successor on cuts to higher education (the courts sided with Beshear), a reorganization of the state pension board, and Bevin's replacement of the University of Louisville board of trustees. Bevin's first year ended well, as he, McConnell and Trump helped flip the state House to GOP control for the first time since 1920, joining the state Senate, which had been in Republican hands since 2000.

The legislative realignment allowed Bevin an even stronger hand in policy. He signed a pair of abortion bills, including one to ban the procedure at 20 weeks, and another to require a fetal ultrasound to be played audibly for, and in view of, the mother. Bevin carried through on his campaign promise to sign a right-to-work law (Kentucky was the last state in the South to enact one) and he signed a measure allowing charter schools, which had long been blocked by the House when it was in Democratic hands. Bevin also proposed a tax overhaul, floating the elimination or reduction of the income tax, to be replaced by a greatly expanded sales tax. But some of his actions were more heterodox. Citing civil-liberties concerns, Bevin vetoed a bill passed by near-unanimous margins that would have empowered judges to order outpatient treatment for some people who are unable to recognize their own mental illnesses. The legislature overrode him. And he issued an executive order to "ban the box" – removing questions about past criminal convictions from applications for jobs in the executive branch.

Senior Senator

Mitch McConnell (R)

Elected 1984, term expires 2020, 6th term; b. Feb 20, 1942, Tuscumbia, AL; University of Kentucky College of Law, J.D.; University of Louisville (KY), B.A.; Baptist; Married (Elaine Chao); 3 children from previous marriage.

Elected Office: Jefferson County Judge Executive., 1978-1985.

Professional Career: Chief Legislative Assistant, U.S Sen. Marlow Cook, 1968-1970; Deputy Assistant U.S Attorney General, 1974-1975.

DC Office: 317 RSOB 20510, 202-224-2541, Fax: 202-224-2499, mcconnell.senate.gov.

State Offices: Bowling Green, 270-781-1673; Fort Wright, 859-578-0188; Lexington, 859-224-8286; London, 606-864-2026; Louisville, 502-582-6304; Paducah, 270-442-4554.

Committees: Senate Majority Leader. *Agriculture, Nutrition & Forestry*: Conservation, Forestry & Natural Resources, Livestock, Marketing & Agriculture Security, Nutrition, Agricultural Research & Specialty Crops. *Appropriations*: Agriculture, Rural Development, FDA & Related Agencies, Department of Defense, Department of the Interior, Environment & Related Agencies, Energy & Water Development, Military Construction & Veteran Affairs & Related Agencies, State, Foreign Operations & Related Programs. *Intelligence. Rules & Administration.*

Group Ratings

	ADA	ACLU	AFL-CIO	LCV	ITI	COC	HAFA	ACU	CFG	FRC
2016	-	23%	-	12%	80%	88%	40%	69%	74%	0%
2015	5%	C	14%	0%	C	93%	C	75%	62%	91%

Almanac Ratings 2015

	Economy	Social	Foreign	Composite
Liberal	28%	29%	23%	27%
Conservative	72%	71%	77%	73%

Key Votes of the 114th Congress

1. Keystone pipeline	Y	5. National Security Data	N	9. Gun Sales Checks	N
2. Export-Import Bank	Y	6. Iran Nuclear Deal	Y	10. Sanctuary Cities	Y
3. Debt Ceiling Increase	Y	7. Puerto Rico Debt	Y	11. Planned Parenthood	Y
4. Homeland Security $$	Y	8. Loretta Lynch A.G	Y	12. Trade deals	Y

Election Results

Election	Name (Party)	Vote (%)	Cand. Spent	Ind. Exp. Support	Ind. Exp. Oppose
2014 General	Mitch McConnell (R)	806,787 (56%)	$30,435,557	$5,855,598	$10,552,995
	Alison Lundergan Grimes (D)	584,698 (41%)	$18,829,908	$1,481,186	$17,092,419
	David Patterson (L)	44,240 (3%)			
2014 Primary	Mitch McConnell (R)	213,753 (60%)			
	Matt Bevin (R)	125,787 (35%)			

Prior winning percentages: 2008 (53%), 2002 (65%), 1996 (56%), 1990 (52%), 1984 (50%)

If many politicians look in the mirror and see a presidential candidate, Republican Mitch McConnell always aspired to be Senate majority leader-and, in 2015, the senior senator from Kentucky finally realized that ambition after two decades of climbing the leadership ladder. McConnell has not sought to be a household name; he is a dour presence on Sunday TV news shows, with *New York Times* columnist Gail Collins once observing that McConnell has "the natural charisma of an oyster." Rather, his power is derived from his mastery of the Senate's arcane procedures and his close-to-the-vest strategizing, bringing to mind the Capitol Hill power brokers of an era prior to advent of mass media. McConnell must navigate in a modern-day Senate that, with its deep ideological and partisan divisions, bears scant resemblance to the more collegial chamber of an earlier time -- and, since becoming majority leader , he has shown little hesitancy to dispense with tradition to advance his party's agenda.

As minority leader for eight years before the Republicans captured the Senate majority in 2014, McConnell did show his pragmatic side: On several occasions, he skillfully negotiated with Vice President Joe Biden, a former Senate colleague, to head off a crisis when partisanship threatened the ability of the government to function during the Obama Administration. But, for the most part, he made it his quest to lead the opposition to President Barack Obama, who McConnell-in a *Times* interview in early 2015-characterized as "the most left-wing president since Woodrow Wilson, who believed the Founding Fathers kind of got it wrong when they made Congress as strong as it is." McConnell repeatedly criticized Obama's efforts to use the power of the presidency to sidestep Congress in areas such as immigration reform and environmental protection, and, in 2016, took an unprecedented step to restrain presidential power by refusing to vote on -- or even grant a hearing to -- an Obama nominee to the Supreme Court. The following year, when newly elected President Donald Trump moved to fill the vacancy and the Democratic minority filibustered, McConnell responded by invoking the "nuclear option" -- changing the Senate rules to get rid of the 60-vote super majority needed for debate cloture for all presidential appointments.

Inreality, his Democratic predecessor, then-Majority Leader Harry Reid of Nevada, had opened the door in 2013 when Reid invoked the nuclear option to prevent Republican filibusters of Obama's Cabinet nomination and judicial appointees below the Supreme Court level. McConnell all but telegraphed his future intentions that day, warning Reid, "You will regret this, and you may regret it a lot sooner than you think." In contrast to the blunt-spoken Reid -- with whom McConnell dueled for a decade prior to Reid's retirement at the end of 2016 -- McConnell is a highly disciplined speaker who chooses his words carefully. "The idea of an off-the-cuff comment is anathema to him," wrote Louisville *Courier-Journal* columnist John David Dyche in a 2009 biography. But Reid and the Democrats, too, acknowledged during the 2016 campaign their plan to remove the filibuster option for Supreme Court nominees if Hillary Clinton was elected president.

As minority leader, McConnell stressed discipline and cohesion to his GOP colleagues, as he preached how sticking together and playing what he calls "team ball" would give them greater leverage with the Obama White House. In his first two years as minority leader, which intersected with the end of George W. Bush's presidency, McConnell was able to hold 41 or more Republicans together to get Reid to meet his demands, as Republicans conducted a record number of filibusters. McConnell observed that he lived by "an 80/20 rule": He spent 80 percent of his time trying to coax 20 percent of Republican senators to stick with the party. Fellow Republicans also have learned that they cross McConnell at their peril. "There are few things more daunting in politics than the determined opposition of McConnell," Arizona GOP Sen. John McCain once said, perhaps recalling McConnell's ongoing effort to derail the McCain-Feingold campaign law that passed in 2002.

The determined Republican partisan who now controls the Senate agenda began his career on the left wing of his party. Another biographer, *New Republic* writer Alec MacGillis, noted in his 2014 volume that McConnell was both pro-abortion rights and pro-labor-favoring collective bargaining for public employees-in the years prior to his election to the Senate, later moving rightward as his party did so. Christened Addison Mitchell McConnell Jr., he grew up in Alabama, where he overcame polio, and at age 13, moved to Louisville. McConnell has been in politics for virtually all of his adult life. Between college and law school at the University of Louisville, he was an intern for Kentucky Republican Sen. John Sherman Cooper, then a member of what has become an almost extinct bloc in the Senate: moderate Republicans. McConnell later said he admired Cooper for carrying out "his best judgment instead of pandering to the popular view." The young McConnell watched as Cooper helped round up the votes to break the filibuster of the 1964 Civil Rights Act, and accompanied Cooper to the White House when President Lyndon Johnson signed the measure.

Soon after graduating from law school, McConnell became chief legislative assistant to Kentucky Sen. Marlow Cook. He served in the Justice Department during the administration of President Gerald Ford, and then moved back to Louisville. In 1977, at age 35, McConnell won the office that had been Cook's political stepping-stone, Jefferson County judge-executive. He was re-elected in 1981, and in 1984, took on Democratic Sen. Walter (Dee) Huddleston. McConnell ran a clever ad that has become a classic in political advertising circles: It showed bloodhounds sniffing for Huddleston in vacation locales where Huddleston had collected fees for speeches while the Senate was in session. McConnell won by a little more than 5,000 votes out of 1.2 million cast.

In 1990, after winning a second term, McConnell sought to get on the leadership ladder by running for the chairmanship of the NRSC, the Senate GOP's campaign arm. He lost, but tried again in 1996 and won, serving in the post for the 1998 and 2000 election cycles. McConnell's skills as a campaign strategist have been on frequent display since. In a 2009 speech to the Republican National Committee, he warned the GOP to expand its base beyond the South and parts of the Midwest or risk being seen as a "regional party." And he often seeks to shape the party's overall message, repeating poll-tested phrases intended to sway public opinion. After Obama signed his health care legislation into law in 2010, McConnell launched Republicans on the campaign to "repeal and replace" it, which became the byword of the GOP opposition.

In Kentucky, as the state trended increasingly red, McConnell established himself as the behind-the-scenes power in the state Republican Party. But his grip has been loosened in recent years with the rise of the GOP's tea party wing. After helping Republican Jim Bunning win in 1998, McConnell lost faith in Bunning's political skills-and, going into the 2010 election, made it clear he felt that Bunning should not run again. Bunning was livid, calling McConnell a "control freak," but bowed out. The choice of McConnell and other state Republicans to replace Bunning was Kentucky Secretary of State Trey Grayson. Also running was Rand Paul, the son of one-time Libertarian Party presidential candidate Ron Paul, a House Republican from Texas. Bunning endorsed Paul, who also had support from tea party groups. In the May 2010 primary, Paul trounced Grayson, and went on to win in November.

The McConnell-Paul relationship has made for one of the more interesting subplots on Capitol Hill. Facing his own difficult re-election bid in 2014, McConnell sought to reach out to Paul; to make inroads among tea party groups, he hired as his campaign manager Jesse Benton, who had worked for both Rand and Ron Paul. McConnell endorsed Paul for the 2016 Republican nomination for president, even likening him to McConnell's political hero: Kentucky's Henry Clay, the Great Compromiser. "To sum up his significance not only for our state but for our country, in a very short period of time, I can say without fear of contradiction that Sen. Rand Paul is, if he chooses to do this, [our] most credible candidate for president of the United States since Henry Clay," McConnell enthusiastically told a gathering of Kentucky Republicans during the 2014 campaign. By the fall of 2015, however, the Paul presidential campaign was faltering, and -- even before his formal withdrawal in February 2016 -- McConnell was pushing Paul to focus instead on his bid for another Senate term. McConnell had reluctantly assented to Paul simultaneously pursuing both contests, and -- with the Senate majority up for grabs in the 2016 election -- was concerned that Paul's seat could be vulnerable.

The relationship underwent noticeable strain barely five months into McConnell's tenure as majority leader in 2015. McConnell reacted with visible agitation as Paul repeatedly invoked Senate procedures to stall a reauthorization of the USA Patriot Act over the National Security Agency's bulk collection of telephone data from millions of Americans. Paul had made opposition to this controversial practice a major issue in his presidential campaign, and his tactics highlighted a broader challenge for McConnell in his managing the Senate: the presence of four Republicans seeking to promote their own agendas as they sought the presidency, as well as the large contingent of hardline conservatives elected in recent years with tea party support. Meanwhile, opposition Democrats pounced on McConnell for waiting until the 11th hour to bring up the Patriot Act authorization, ultimately causing a brief lapse in the government's post-9/11 surveillance powers before a new bill was signed into law. McConnell had gambled-and lost-on senators fearing the political fallout from such a lapse. McConnell, who had vigorously opposed a House-passed version of the bill that turned the NSA's storage of phone data over to private companies, ended up having to swallow the House bill as the only alternative to continued stalemate.

Following the collapse of Paul's presidential hopes, McConnell kept his distance from the party'seventual nominee -- at times refusing to respond to reporters' questions about Trump during the 2016 campaign. In June, McConnell voiced concerns in a *CNN* interview that Trump's comments about Hispanic Americans could hurt efforts to expand the GOP base, much as presidential candidate Barry Goldwater's vote against the 1964 Civil Right Act had alienated African Americans a half-century earlier. Asked about this immediately after Trump's election, McConnell offered less than a ringing endorsement. "I am not going to relitigate the events of the past," he told reporters. "We have a new president. I would like to see him get off on a positive start." McConnell was more upbeat a month into Trump's presidency, telling the *Times:* "Back during the campaign, there were a lot of questions: Is Trump really a conservative? …But if you look at the steps that have been taken so far, looks good to me." (McConnell's wife, Elaine Chao, whom he married in 1993, was named as Trump's transportation secretary; she was previously labor secretary under President George W. Bush). McConnell did take a harder line on Russia than Trump, calling Russian President Vladimir Putin a "thug," although he turned aside calls from McCain and others for a special Senate panel to probe allegations of Russian interference in the election.

Six years earlier -- in October 2010, just days before the off-year elections -- McConnell, in an interview with *National Journal,* memorably declared: "The single most important thing we want to achieve is for President Obama to be a one-term president." Coming two years prior to Obama standing for -- and winning -- a second term, the quote came to exemplify the impede-at-all costs philosophy that critics saw as McConnell's true colors. McConnell subsequently complained those critics had overlooked a second quote in the interview that followed the first, in which he had said of Obama, "...If he's willing to meet us halfway on some of the biggest issues, it's not inappropriate for us to do business with him." McConnell was somewhat less conciliatory a couple of months earlier when, after having his first one-on-one meeting with the Obama, he expressed limited interest in finding common ground. Asked whether there was too much obstruction in the Senate, he replied, "I think the Senate is operating largely like our founding fathers anticipated it would."

A rare instance of a bipartisan push for a major piece of legislation came in the latter half of Obama's second term when, in May 2015, McConnell-in what he later jokingly referred to as an "out of body experience" -- worked with the Obama White House to pass so-called "fast track" trade negotiating authority. The administration was seeking to expedite negotiation of the Trans Pacific Partnership, a 12-nation Asian trade deal that McConnell supported. After top Senate Democratic leaders opposed to fast track, including Reid and New York Sen. Charles Schumer, dealt the White House an initial defeat, McConnell helped to bring around wavering Democratic senators by promising a series of stand-alone floor votes on several trade-related issues. McConnell and other Senate Republican leaders initially tried to maneuver around Reid and Schumer and cut deals with Democrats supportive of the trade bill. But after Reid and Schumer-borrowing a page from McConnell's old playbook-demonstrated their muscle by holding the Democrats in line and temporarily blocking the fast track bill, McConnell was forced to deal with his counterparts in the Democratic leadership.

Obama's hope of seeing action on the Trans Pacific Partnership (to which both Trump and Democratic presidential nominee Hillary Clinton had come out in opposition) before he left office were dashed in August 2016, when McConnell announced the Senate would not vote on the final deal before January. In a speech to the Kentucky Farm Bureau, McConnell cited "serious flaws" in the agreement. He did not specify the flaws, but they were believed to include a provision in the draft agreement removing legal protections for tobacco interests about which McConnell and other tobacco-state legislators were unhappy. "It can be massaged, changed, worked on during the next administration," McConnell said of the TPP -- from which Trump withdrew the United States days after taking office.

Relations between McConnell and Obama, to say nothing of the partisan atmosphere of the Senate, had taken a major turn for the worse months earlier, following the unexpected death of Supreme Court Justice Antonin Scalia, the court's leading conservative. Determined to prevent Obama from altering the ideological makeup of the court less than a year before the president was due to leave office, McConnell said there would be no confirmation hearings or vote on a replacement until the next president was sworn in. "This nomination will be determined by whoever wins the presidency in the polls," McConnell declared, while urging Obama to reconsider submitting a nominee -- more than three weeks before the president nominated federal appeals court judge Merrick Garland. The GOP leadership and most Republicans refused to even meet with Garland, widely seen as a moderate. McConnell's move was viewed as unprecedented. "What is remarkable is the opposition is not to a particular candidate or even to the notion Obama will only nominate someone too extreme, but that he should not have any right to have a nomination considered," Julian Zelizer, a professor of history and public affairs at Princeton University, told the *Times*.

Senate GOP leaders responded by pointing to 1992 comments by McConnell's long-time Senate colleague, Biden, when the latter chaired the Judiciary Committee. In a floor speech at the time, Biden had urged Republican President George H. W. Bush against making a nomination to the Supreme Court until after that year's presidential election -- which Bush lost to Bill Clinton. No vacancy occurred that year, and aides to the vice president contended that Biden had been talking about a possible vacancy created by a voluntary resignation, not an unexpected death. Asked about Democratic assertions that the so-called "Biden Rule" was irrelevant, McConnell and other GOP leaders laughed in response. Their gamble paid off, as Trump won the presidency and nominated another federal appeals court judge, Neil Gorsuch, considered a solid conservative, less than two weeks after taking office.

As Congress convened in 2017, Reid had retired and was replaced as minority leader by Schumer, who himself had played a significant role in the escalation of partisan warfare over judicial nominations. Early in the presidency of George W. Bush, Schumer, then a junior member of the Judiciary Committee, had devised a strategy that led to Democrats blocking several of Bush's appellate court nominees. In late March, Schumer, as leader of a 48-member minority in which many members remained angry over the treatment of Garland, urged a filibuster of the Gorsuch nomination. According to the *Wall Street Journal*, some Democrats -- to avert the so-called nuclear option -- discussed a possible deal in the party would provide enough votes to confirm Gorsuch in return for a commitment not to change the 60-vote supermajority threshold for future nominees. But such an accord never materialized, while McConnell repeatedly vowed to have Gorsuch confirmed by April. On April 6, all but three Democrats voted against cloture on the nomination, leaving it five votes short. That, in turn, triggered procedural maneuvering in which, on a 52-48 party-line vote, the Senate voted to change the rules and drop the 60-vote threshold -- clearing the way for Gorsuch's confirmation on a 54-45 vote.

Amid the immediate rancor, there were questions about the longer-term impact of McConnell's move on the role of the Senate -- the proverbial "saucer" that cools the "coffee" produced by the House, in George Washington's words. The rules change affected only presidential nominations, not legislation, and McConnell -- who made liberal use of legislative filibusters while in the minority -- vowed there were no plans to change that. "Who would be the biggest beneficiary of that right now? It would be the majority, right?" McConnell told reporters, adding, "There's not a single senator in the majority who thinks we ought to change the legislative filibuster. Not one." Some Republicans, despite having supported McConnell on the rules change, were less certain. "If we continue on the path we are on right now, the very next time there is a legislative proposal that one side of the aisle feels is so important they cannot let their base down, the pressure builds, and then we are going to invoke the nuclear option on the legislative piece, too," Tennessee Sen. Bob Corker warned. As McConnell defended the change in the rule on nominations as good for the Senate, McCain -- in a *Washington Post* interview -- termed the Republican leader an "idiot." McCain, who headed a bipartisan effort that averted changes to the filibuster a decade earlier, declared, "This is a body blow to the institution, and I think we're on a slippery slope."

McConnell started the Trump presidency with a Republican caucus of 52 -- down two from the previous Congress, but a far better position than the one in which he had begun Obama's first term. Democrats emerged from the 2008 election with 58 seats, leaving them just short of the 60 votes needed to overcome a filibuster. Then, Arlen Specter of Pennsylvania, facing a tough battle for renomination the following year, switched parties and joined the Democrats. In July, when Democrat Al Franken was seated in Minnesota after a protracted recount, the Democrats got to the magic 60. During the 2009 debate on Obama's signature Affordable Care Act, with his Republicans united and Democrats divided, McConnell took aim at the option in the bill for a federally run insurance provider, and the so-called public option was eventually dropped. McConnell tried in the spring of 2010 to stop the Dodd-Frank financial regulation bill-a response to the Wall Street financial crash of 2008-but, like health care, it ultimately passed. His ability to hold his caucus together did pay off at some critical moments. With Democrats divided, the Senate stopped in its tracks the bill passed by the House to impose a cap-and-trade system of emission limits on polluters.

After the 2010 election, Obama hoped to strike a deal with congressional Republicans to extend the Bush-era tax cuts for two more years for all households except those earning over $200,000 a year. But Senate Republicans, led by McConnell, rejected any proposal that did not extend the tax cuts for everyone, and Obama was forced to go along. Republicans gained six Senate seats in the November 2010 election, leaving McConnell with 47 GOP votes and Democrats far short of a filibuster-proof majority. Among the new arrivals were independent-minded conservatives who were plugged into the tea party movement and who had beat establishment-backed candidates, including McConnell's new Kentucky colleague, Paul. McConnell indulged the Republican newcomers' appetite for confrontation. He followed the lead of the House, back under GOP control following the election, and brought up repeal of the health care law in February, knowing it would not pass the Senate. He also ceded to the House on other matters, including a ban on budget earmarks.

Next came the drawn-out duel over raising the federal debt ceiling in 2011. McConnell at first sounded an ambitious tone: "Divided government is the best time-and some would argue the only time-where you can do really big stuff," he said in May. When negotiations with the White House over the debt limit stalled, McConnell espoused a more incremental approach in the form of a last-ditch "backup" that would permit a series of debt increases, putting the onus on Democrats to vote for additional borrowing. Members of both parties denounced it as a political solution to a policy problem, while-as the clock ticked toward an economically damaging default-McConnell began warning about the political consequences of failing to act.

He met with Biden-known in the White House as "the McConnell Whisperer," according to Bob Woodward's book *The Price of Politics*-to strike a deal. The final agreement denied Obama any increases in taxes or revenue and foisted the hard budget choices on a bipartisan "super committee." The protracted process over increasing the debt limit, a move made necessary by earlier spending decisions by Congress, greatly disturbed many both on and off Capitol Hill, but McConnell said the debt ceiling had become a highly useful GOP bargaining chip. "I think some of our members may have thought the default issue was a hostage you might take a chance at shooting," he told *The Washington Post.* "Most of us didn't think that. What we did learn is this: it's a hostage that's worth ransoming."

The debt ceiling talks served as a prelude to the "fiscal cliff" negotiations in late 2012, aimed at averting automatic budget cuts and tax hikes that could impair the nation's economic recovery. By then, the super committee had become gridlocked, Obama had won a second term, and Senate Democrats added two seats to their majority. Once again, talks between Obama and congressional Republicans proved fruitless, and again, McConnell reached out to Biden, setting in motion more than a dozen conversations that culminated in a New Year's Day 2013 agreement. The Senate overwhelmingly approved their handiwork, 89-8, and despite conservatives' opposition, it drew sufficient votes to pass in the House as well.

McConnell called the measure "an imperfect solution," but said it was preferable to the large spending cuts that would have immediately kicked in-while vowing not to accept any new revenue in future dealings with Democrats. Still, activists on the right were outraged that it gave Obama his long-desired tax increase on the wealthy. For America Chairman Brent Bozell, in an ad targeting McConnell, charged, "His role as President Obama's bag man in the latest fiscal cliff disaster clearly demonstrates that Sen. McConnell is more interested in the art of the bad deal than standing up and fighting for conservative principles."

Despite the acrimony from the right, political experts said the bipartisanship evident in the agreement probably enhanced McConnell's stature among Kentucky's moderate voters. But the gathering political forces against McConnell in the lead-up to the 2014 election made it far more difficult for him to play the role of deal maker when yet another budget standoff unfolded in October 2013. House Republicans effectively shut down the government by demanding a rollback of the Obama health care law in return for their votes funding routine government operations. The president refused, and unlike the earlier budget battles, there seemed to be little potential for the White House to open quiet, back-channel negotiations with McConnell.

Facing his fifth race for re-election, McConnell took the challenge seriously given that his approval ratings in Kentucky were at or below the 50 percent mark. By the fall of 2013, he had raised more than $13 million. He drew a potentially serious threat in the GOP primary from Matt Bevin, a wealthy businessman favored by the state's potent tea party forces. Two national conservative groups with deep pockets took an interest in Bevin's candidacy: the Madison Project, which helped Republican Ted Cruz' s insurgent and ultimately successful Senate bid in Texas, and the Senate Conservatives Fund, a political action committee allied with former South Carolina Sen. Jim DeMint, then president of the Heritage Foundation and a leader of the no-compromise conservative faction. But Bevin was an inexperienced candidate who made numerous errors, and McConnell crushed him, 60%-35%.

Bitter from his loss, Bevin repeatedly declined repeatedly to endorse McConnell in that year's general election, and, a year later, launched a campaign for governor. After coming out on the losing side in the 2010 primary that Paul had won, McConnell opted to stay out of the 2015 gubernatorial primary. Bevin won narrowly -- and, in a turn-about, actively wooed McConnell's support, including excising a large number of anti-McConnell posts from his Twitter account. It worked. "You don't have to be in love with the guy to know that there's a huge difference...between Matt Bevin and Jack Conway," McConnell told the *Lexington Herald-Leader*, referring to the Democratic nominee. "So I think we need to let bygones be bygones and get together and try to change Kentucky." In November, Bevin was elected to succeed a term-limited Democratic Gov. Steve Beshear.

In the 2014 general election, McConnell faced Democrat Alison Lundergan Grimes, Kentucky's 34-year-old secretary of state. Lundergan Grimes initially was seen as a credible opponent, but she committed several errors, notably refusing to answer a question about whether she had voted for Obama in 2012. It was widely viewed as an opportunistic effort to keep the president, highly unpopular in Kentucky, at a distance. Democrats thought the race would be about which candidate voters liked better, a fight they thought they could win given McConnell's weak approval numbers at the start of the race. Instead, the race became about who voters trusted, and McConnell relentlessly tied Grimes to Obama at every turn. McConnell ended up capturing 56 percent of the vote.

McConnell has seldom had an easy time of it at re-election time. He had spirited competition from former Louisville Mayor Harvey Sloane in 1990, future Gov. Beshear in 1996, and Lois Combs Weinberg, daughter of a former governor, in 2002. Sloane and Beshear held McConnell to 52 percent and 55 percent, respectively. He did much better against Weinberg, winning with 65 percent. In 2008, Democrats, still smarting from former Majority Leader Tom Daschle's defeat for re-election in South Dakota in 2004, were determined to put up a tough opponent against McConnell. They found Bruce Lunsford, a multimillionaire hospital and nursing home operator. Lunsford spent nearly $11 million, more than $7 million of it his own money, and ran a string of negative ads against McConnell. McConnell won with 53 percent, making him the longest-serving senator in Kentucky history.

McConnell became Republican whip after his third re-election victory in 2002. He campaigned for months among his colleagues when the job came open, and his only opponent, Larry Craig of Idaho, dropped out several days before the contest. Then, in December 2002, Republican Leader Trent Lott of Mississippi came under a storm of criticism when he spoke favorably of Strom Thurmond's segregationist campaign for president in 1948 at an event honoring Thurmond's 100th birthday. McConnell was Lott's strongest public defender, threatening retaliation against Democrats if they moved to censure him. But, as the controversy showed no sign of abating, he privately recommended to Lott that he "step down as soon as possible." Ordinarily, McConnell might have been in line for the leader's position, but he did not challenge Tennessee's Bill Frist when Frist-urged on by the Bush White House-ran for Lott's post. Frist became Senate majority leader and McConnell majority whip and a key adviser to Frist, who was relatively unversed in Senate procedures. When Frist retired in 2006, McConnell ran for leader. Republicans ended up losing their majority in 2006, so he became minority leader. A decade later, at the peak of his influence, he had prevailed over numerous opponents.

Junior Senator

Rand Paul (R)

Elected 2010, term expires 2022, 2nd term; b. Jan 07, 1963, Pittsburgh, PA; Baylor University (TX), 1984; Duke University (NC), M.D., 1988; Presbyterian; Married (Kelley Paul); 3 children.

Professional Career: Ophthalmologist, 1993-2010; Founder, S. KY Lions Eye Clinic, 1995.

DC Office: 167 RSOB 20510, 202-224-4343, Fax: 202-228-6917, paul.senate.gov.

State Offices: Bowling Green, 270-782-8303; Crescent Springs, 859-426-0165; Hopkinsville, 270-885-1212; Lexington, 859-219-2239; Louisville, 502-582-5341; Owensboro, 270-689-9085.

Committees: *Foreign Relations*: Africa & Global Health Policy, Europe & Regional Security Cooperation, State Dept & USAID Mngmnt, Internat'l Ops & Internat'l Dev. *Health, Education, Labor & Pensions*: Children & Families (Chmn), Employment & Workplace Safety. *Homeland Security & Government Affairs*: Federal Spending Oversight & Emergency Management (Chmn), Investigations. *Small Business & Entrepreneurship*.

Group Ratings

	ADA	ACLU	AFL-CIO	LCV	ITI	COC	HAFA	ACU	CFG	FRC
2016	-	41%	-	12%	25%	38%	85%	85%	90%	100%
2015	15%	C	50%	8%	C	46%	C	96%	88%	82%

Almanac Ratings 2015

	Economy	Social	Foreign	Composite
Liberal	25%	0%	27%	17%
Conservative	75%	100%	73%	83%

Key Votes of the 114th Congress

1. Keystone pipeline	Y	5. National Security Data	N	9. Gun Sales Checks	N
2. Export-Import Bank	Y	6. Iran Nuclear Deal	Y	10. Sanctuary Cities	Y
3. Debt Ceiling Increase	N	7. Puerto Rico Debt	Y	11. Planned Parenthood	Y
4. Homeland Security $$	N	8. Loretta Lynch A.G	N	12. Trade deals	N

Election Results

Election	Name (Party)	Vote (%)		Cand. Spent	Ind. Exp. Support	Ind. Exp. Oppose
2016 General	Rand Paul (R)	1,090,177	(57%)	$5,994,444	$83,795	
	Jim Gray (D)	813,246	(43%)	$4,665,712	$337,895	$563,868
2016 Primary	Rand Paul (R)	169,180	(85%)			
	James Gould (R)	16,611	(8%)			
	Stephen Slaughter (R)	13,728	(7%)			

Prior winning percentages: 2010 (58%)

Rand Paul benefitted from propitious political timing when he launched his first run for elected office less than a decade ago. While active in the campaign of his father, then-Texas Rep. Ron Paul, for the 2008 Republican presidential nomination, back home in Kentucky Rand Paul was a career ophthalmologist with a limited state wide profile when he announced a Senate bida year later. When a friend asked him to assess his chances of success, Paul reportedly chuckled, "Oh, I guess probably in the 5 percent range." But Paul waded in just in time to catch the rising tide of the tea party movement, enabling him to upset the Kentucky GOP establishment and to win election in 2010 as the Bluegrass State's junior senator. Less than four years later, some polls showed him leading the crowded field of prospects for the 2016 GOP presidential nomination, with a *Time* magazine cover anointing him as "The Most Interesting Man In Politics."

That's when the political timing for him became problematic. Paul had long shared many aspects of the ideology of his father, who temporarily left the GOP to run as the Libertarian Party's presidential candidate in 1988. And hehoped to inherit many of the followers of the elder Paul's 2008 and 2012 bids for the Republican nomination, while extending his outreach to more traditional Republicansin his own pursuit of the White House.But the appeal of Rand Paul's largely non-interventionist -- critics would say neo-isolationist -- foreign policy views fell flat in an election cycle during which the rise of the Islamic State and escalating terror attacks abroad were front and center.And, despite his 2010 election as an outsider -- a status he often reinforced via his tactics on Capitol Hill --Paul found himself eclipsed by an outsider with more celebrity: Donald Trump. "ISIS and Trump fundamentally transformed the dynamic of the race," Chip Englander, Paul's campaign manager, told *Politico* after Paul's presidential hopes came crashing down in early 2016. Paul did manage to salvage re-election to a second Senate term later that year, and he returned to Capitol Hill and his role as a frequent gadfly.

Born in Pittsburgh, Paul was raised in Lake Jackson, Texas, where his father relocated to set up a practice in obstetrics. While stories have circulated that he was named for the iconic Ayn Rand-the writer whose advocacy of laissez-faire capitalism makes her highly popular in libertarian circles-both Paul and his father have denied this. The third of five children, Paul was named Randal at birth and was known as Randy while growing up, switching to Rand as an adult. He attended Baylor University, where he was an active member of the Young Conservatives of Texas. Although he failed to get an undergraduate degree at Baylor, Paul chose to follow in his father's footsteps and become a physician. He received a high score on the medical entrance exam and was admitted to Duke University, where he received his medical degree. Paul subsequently moved to Bowling Green, Kentucky, near his wife's home town, and opened an ophthalmology practice, while establishing an eye clinic to treat low-income patients. Foreshadowing his political career, Paul adopted an outsider stance in the medical profession: Unhappy with the procedures of the American Board of Ophthalmology, which had long certified practitioners of that specialty, Paul mounted an ultimately unsuccessful effort to create a rival certification board.

He mulled entering politics for some time, writing newspaper columns, helping with his father's campaigns -- and founding an anti-tax watchdog group called Kentucky Taxpayers United. When he gave a speech on April 15, 2009-Tax Day-to a tea party group, the energy of the crowd persuaded him that "something enormous was going on," as he later told the *Bowling Green Daily News.* The Senate seat up for election in 2010 was held by two-term Republican Jim Bunning. He had a solid conservative record, but had been barely re-elected six years earlier, and was being pressed by Senate Republican Leader Mitch McConnell -- the *de facto* boss of the Kentucky GOP -- to step down. In July 2009, Bunning announced he would retire, and Paul declared his candidacy a month later. The favorite for the nomination was Kentucky Secretary of State Trey Grayson, who won the backing of McConnell and other leading state Republicans. But Paul had access to his father's devoted network of contributors. Backers eagerly embraced his outspoken views that government should stick to the functions outlined in the Constitution -- that agencies such as the Environmental Protection Agency and the Education Department should be abolished, and the powers of the Federal Reserve drastically curbed.

McConnell appeared in television ads for Grayson, and-foreshadowing criticism that would later confront Paul's presidential bid-Grayson ran spots charging Paul was weak on national security. But Paul, boosted by the accelerating tea party movement,won the primary in a rout, 59%-35%. McConnell made a point of appearing at a victory rally for Paul, who decided to vote for McConnell for Senate Republican leader after previously declining to say whether he would do so. However, Paul's decisive upset was quickly overshadowed by an appearance on MSNBC with talk show host Rachel Maddow. Displaying his libertarian leanings, Paul voiced his opposition in principle to the 1964 Civil Rights Act, arguing that the federal government shouldn't interfere with private businesses. The remarks caused a furor, even after Paul issued a statement saying he did not support repealing the landmark law.

On the Democratic side, Attorney General Jack Conway narrowly defeated Lt. Gov. Dan Mongiardo, 44%-43%, for the Senate nomination. Conway hammered Paul over the comments on the Civil Rights Act, and also seized on Paul's support for raising the Social Security retirement age and opposing federal involvement in drug enforcement. Paul had plenty of material to work with, however, in his attempt to paint Conway as too liberal. In contrast to the anti-abortion Paul, Conway supported abortion rights and also backed the Democrats' health care insurance overhaul, repeal of the ban on being openly gay in the military, and a pro-union bill effectively abolishing the secret ballot in unionization elections. Conway may also have hurt himself with an ad that political insiders considered over the top. In it, the narrator asks, "Why was Rand Paul a member of a secret society that called the Holy Bible a 'hoax'?...Why did Rand Paul once tie a woman up, tell her to bow down before a false idol, and say ... god was Aqua Buddha?" The charges referred to pranks during Paul's college years. *GQ* magazine had reported Paul once belonged to a secret society called the NoZe Brotherhood, which often taunted the school's administration; he and a friend were once accused of blindfolding a female acquaintance and trying to get her to smoke marijuana.

Paul defeated Conway, 56%-44%; upon arriving in the Senate, he established a Tea Party Caucus and quickly sought to use his power to block anything he viewed as government overreach. In September 2011, he utilized Senate procedures to slap a "hold" on a bill to strengthen safety regulations for oil and gas pipelines in the wake of a deadly pipeline rupture near San Francisco the year before. His opposition came despite the fact that the legislation was even supported by pipeline trade associations and the natural gas industry. Paul later dropped his hold on the bill, and it eventually became law. Several months earlier, in May 2011, he tried to block extension of theUSA Patriot Act passed immediately after 9/11. And in 2013 he filibustered for nearly 13 hours to protest the administration's use of lethal drone strikes; the move delayed confirmation of John Brennan as director of the Central Intelligence Agency. Paul later told a student audience in the liberal bastion of Berkeley California that the intelligence community was "drunk with power." Such episodes highlighted the philosophical divide-if not chasm-that has separated Paul from many other Republicans, particularly concerning the United States' role abroad and its use of government surveillanceas a weapon in the war on terrorism.

During the 2011 Patriot Act debate, Paul also offered an amendment to restrict the government's power to obtain gun records, but the measure was overwhelmingly defeated. Paul made national news in January 2012 when he refused a pat-down from the Transportation Security Administration at a Tennessee airport. Five months later, he wanted to relax tough gun control laws adopted by theDistrict of Columbia in exchange for giving the city more budget autonomy-leading Democrats to accuse him of hypocrisy, in light of his hands-off philosophy of government. The following year, he was one of the loudest objectors to President Barack Obama'santi-gun violence proposals unveiled after the December 2012 school massacre in Newtown Connecticut in which more than two dozen were killed. But Paul found common ground with Democrats on other issues relevant to the nation's criminal justice system. In 2013, he teamed up on legislation with Vermont Democratic Sen. Patrick Leahy, then chairman of the Judiciary Committee, to give federal judges greater flexibility on imposing mandatory minimum sentences, while pledging to work with Leahy to eliminate mandatory minimum sentences for marijuana possession.

As the 2016 presidential election approached, Paul aggressively-and deftly-utilized the Senate chamber as a platform to promote his presidential aspirations: It did not endear him to many of his Republican colleagues.In May 2015, Paul conducted an 11-hour filibuster to delay another reauthorization of the Patriot Act, while objecting to the government's bulk collection of phone records under the statute. His procedural tactics not only led to a brief lapse in some government surveillance powers granted under the law;Paul's ployultimately forced McConnell, by then the Senate's majority leader, to swallow House-passed changes in the statute that McConnell at firstvigorously opposed.McConnell, who had worked to build a relationship with Paul-going so far as to embrace his presidential bid-was visibly irritated. In comments aimed at Paul, McConnell decried those spreading "disinformation" about the Patriot Act. And the party's 2008 presidential nominee, Arizona Sen. John McCain-who two years earlier had labeled Paul a "wacko bird"-angrily suggested the Kentucky senator was simply using the issue to help fund his presidential bid. "He obviously has a higher priority for his fundraising and political ambitions than for the security of the nation," McCain gibedas Paul's campaign Web site contained pitches such as "Get your Rand Paul filibuster starter pack!"

The combative Paul-he has acknowledged a need to work "at holding my tongue and holding my temper"-was unapologetic about his actions during that debate, which took place a month after he had formally declared his presidential candidacy. "I'm always concerned about our country's safety and I think that the Constitution is a great and powerful tool for collecting records on people you have suspicion of," he told reporters. "And so I think we should collect more records on terrorists. I just don't want to collect them on innocent Americans." During the Patriot Act debate, he indicated his primary concern was with the erosion of individual liberties. "The people who argue that the world will end and we will be overrun by jihadists are trying to use fear," Paul contended. "Little by little, we've allowed our freedom to slip away." Several days earlier, he sought to put the blame for the growth ofISISsquarely on others in the GOP. "ISIS exists and grew stronger because of the hawks in our party, who gave arms indiscriminately, and most of those arms were snatched up by ISIS," he said during an MSNBC appearance. His comments were widely criticized by leading Republicans: McCain, charged that Paul's reluctance to back U.S. intervention abroad was a step toward a "fortress America."

Paul took some steps to try to assuage his party's interventionist wing in advance of the presidential campaign. In 2014, while continuing to strongly oppose the arming of rebel forces in the Syrian civil war, he expressed support for limited air strikes against ISIS forces. In the April 2015 speech announcing his presidential bid, Paul employed aggressive rhetoric in a not-so-subtle shot against Obama's reluctance to use the term "Islamic terrorism." Declared Paul, "The enemy is radical Islam, and not only will I name the enemy, I will do whatever it takes to defend America from these haters of mankind."

Paul's stance on Israel also provided fodder for critics within the party. In 2012, Paul forced a vote on his proposal to limit aid to Pakistan, Libya, and Egypt. McCain and Graham forcefully opposed it, saying it could limit aid to Israel and other countries as well, and it was resoundingly rejected. In 2014, Paul sought to combat perceptions that he was not sufficiently pro-Israel by introducing a bill to bar the Palestinian government from receiving foreign aid unless it recognized Israel as a state. A libertarian Capitol Hill staffer described the measure to *The New York Times Magazine* as "complete pandering." But a Paul spokesman said the senator never specifically targeted Israel in his calls to cut foreign aid and maintained, "Sen. Paul's position was exactly what Prime Minister [Benjamin] Netanyahu said to Congress on July 10, 1996 and May 24, 2011-Israel will be better off when it does not have to count on anyone else for its protection."Apparent shifts in Paul's positions on policy toward both Israel and Iran yielded a testy, widely reported exchange with NBC "Today" anchor Savannah Guthrie several days after his presidential announcement. "Why don't we let me explain instead of talking over me, OK?" Paul snapped -- two months after he had "shushed" a CNBC anchor pressing him on another issue. It fueled skepticism about Paul's readiness for the scrutiny of a national campaign.

A bigger problem for Paul's presidential campaign, in the view of political insiders, was that, in seeking to appease the GOP's traditional wing, the candidate muddled his message -- alienating portions of his libertarian base without bringing in a lot of new support. "I thinkhe was doing as much following as he was leading," Frayda Levin, a libertarian-leaning GOP donor who sits on the board of the conservative Club for Growth, told *Politico*. "He wanted to win more than he wanted to support the principles."To some extent, such grumbling reflected Paul's moves to make peace with the party's establishment wing: He appeared in ads underwritten by the U.S. Chamber of Commerce during the 2014 mid-term election, and, back home in Kentucky, endorsed McConnell over a tea party challenger -- Matt Bevin, who a year later went on to win election as the state's governor. Such efforts, in turn, complicated Paul's fundraising:By the beginning of 2016, the Paul campaign was effectively broke, as money rolled in to the candidacy of another outsider candidate, Texas Sen. Ted Cruz, who ultimately emerged as the leading alternative to Trump in the race for the GOP nomination.

As he has courted major donors on Wall Street and in Silicon Valley, Paul also sought to reach out to constituencies outside the traditional Republican base-with uneven results. He appeared at the National Urban League conference in July 2014 and pronounced his unequivocal support for the Civil Rights Act. When Ferguson Missouri was swept by rioting that summer after a black teenager was killed by a white police officer, Paul argued for overhauling police departments, writing in *Time* magazine: "If I had been told to get out of the street as a teenager, there would have been a distinct possibility that I might have smarted off. But, I wouldn't have expected to be shot." During the April 2015 riots in Baltimore that followed the death of a black man in police custody, Paul adopted a different tone in speaking to conservative radio talk show host Laura Ingraham. "I am very sympathetic to the plight of the police in this," he said, while noting he had just come through Baltimore by train. "I'm glad it didn't stop," he added, in a wisecrack that raised some eyebrows.

By the beginning of 2016, Paul's sputtering campaign had sunk low enough in the polls that he failed to qualify for a January candidates' debate during prime time.Relegated to the so-called "undercard" debate for second-tier contenders, Paul refused to appear, saying that he was running a "first tier" campaign.In February 2016 -- 10 months after the formal launch of his candidacy -- Paul dropped out of the race, days after the Iowa caucuses chose the first national convention delegates. He came in fifth, winning just 5 percent -- less than a quarter of his father's 21.5 percent showing in Iowa four years earlier -- and was projected to do even worse in the New Hampshire primary a week later.

As he launched his presidential bid, Paul had signaled his intent to simultaneously pursue re-election to the Senate. He took some political heat back home for his two-track candidacy, which he defended at the outset of 2016 in a *Lexington Herald Leader* op-ed."I'm running for president and have been for nearly a year. And I've done my job as your senator every step of the way," Paul declared. "While others simply abandoned their jobs to run, I did mine, working all week in the Senate and campaigning largely on weekends - making 95 percent of my votes, a higher percentage than most senators who weren't running for president." But Paul also faced a legal obstacle, since Kentucky prohibits candidates from appearing on the ballot for two offices in the same election.To get around this, the Republican State Committee -- with the reluctant assentof McConnell -- voted to hold a hold a March 2016 presidential delegate caucus separate from the state's May primary.To win the support of Kentucky Republicans for this maneuver, Paul agreed to provide $250,000 to help cover the increased cost. Moving the presidential vote ahead to March also was seen a providing a potential boost to Paul in the nominating process.

That prospect turned out to be academic, since Paul's presidential bid collapsed prior to the March caucuses. But that collapse was also seen a creating potential vulnerability for him in his re-election bid. He was boosted, however, by Kentucky Democrats' loss of much of their political bench in elections in the fall of 2015 -- including the defeat of state Auditor Adam Edelen, who had been touted as a Paul challenger. Democrats finally found a candidate in Lexington Mayor Jim Gray, who brought personal money and a business background to the contest. Gray had been elected twice as an openly gay candidate in a state where, several months earlier, a county clerk garnered international attention for going to jail rather than issue same-sex marriage licenses. Gray's backers said that was not his biggest political obstacle. Referring to recent polling, former Rep. Ben Chandler told *Roll Call*, "There are numbers that suggest that being allied in any way to President Barack Obama is much more damaging than being gay." Gray acknowledged past votes for Obama, and Paul hammered at him for his support of Obama's choice as a successor, Hillary Clinton. Gray attacked Paul as a do-nothing senator who saw the post as nothing more than a stepping stone. On Election Day, Paul won 57%-43% --finishing behind Trump, who defeated Clinton by 63%-33% in Kentucky.

Returning to Capitol Hill, Paul lost no time in re-establishing himself as a thorn in the side of the Republican leadership -- working with his allies in the House Freedom Caucus to derail an early effort to replace Obama's Affordable Care Act, which they felt did not go far enough in getting the government out of the health care marketplace. As a House committee reviewed details of a possible replacement for "Obamacare" crafted by GOP leaders, Paul showed up outside the closed meeting room. With an aide carrying a miniature copier, Paul asked for a copy of a bill, and a House staff member told him it was still being drafted, according to an account in *The Washington Post*. Turning to a crush of reporters and cameras, Paul proceeded to declare: "We're here today because I'd like to read the Obamacare bill. If you'd recall, when Obamacare was passed in 2009 and 2010, Nancy Pelosi said you'll know what's in it after you pass it. The Republican Party shouldn't act in the same way."

FIRST DISTRICT

James Comer (R)

Elected 2016, 1st term; b. Aug 19, 1972, Carthage, TN; Western Kentucky University, B.S., 1993; Baptist; Married (Tamera Jo (T.J.)); 3 children.

Elected Office: Chairman, Monroe County Republican Party, 1993-1995; Delegate, Republican National Convention, 1996; KY House, 2001-2012; Commissioner, KY Department of Agriculture, 2012-2015.

Professional Career: Businessman; Farmer.

DC Office: 1513 LHOB 20515, 202-225-3115, Fax: 202-225-3547; Website: comer.house.gov.

State Offices: Paducah, 270-408-1865; Tompkinsville, 270-487-9509.

Committees: *Agriculture*: Commodity Exchanges, Energy & Credit, Nutrition. *Oversight & Government Reform*: Interior, Energy & Environment, National Security. *Small Business*: Agriculture, Energy & Trade, Contracting & Workforce.

Group Ratings

	ADA	ACLU	AFL-CIO	LCV	ITI	COC	HAFA	ACU	CFG	FRC
2016	-	0%	-	0%	-	100%	-	-	-	-
2015	-	C	-	-	C	NULL	C	C	C	-

Election Results

Election	Name (Party)	Vote (%)		Cand. Spent	Ind. Exp. Support	Ind. Exp. Oppose
2016 General	James Comer (R)	216,959	(73%)	$963,377	$100,150	
	Sam Gaskins (D)	81,710	(27%)	$10,009		
2016 Primary	James Comer (R)	24,342	(61%)			
	Michael Pape (R)	9,357	(23%)			
	Jason Batts (R)	5,578	(14%)			

Republican James Comer breezed through both the primary and general election to win the open seat in 2016. The victory was a consolation prize of sorts, following Comer's 83-vote loss to Matt Bevin a year earlier in the Republican primary for governor. With some experience in Congress, the ambitious Comer could be positioned for another statewide run in a few years.

Comer grew up in rural Monroe County, Kentucky. He had dreamed of becoming a farmer. After graduating from Western Kentucky University, he borrowed $120,000 from a community bank to purchase his first farm and began his business. It became one of the largest farming operations in south central Kentucky. He had other interests in insurance and restaurant businesses. Comer also started young in politics, winning his first election to the state House at age 28. He served 11 years in what was then the Democratic-controlled House, where he claimed good bipartisan relationships and kept his distance from Republican "party bosses."

In 2011, Comer was elected to a four-year term as Kentucky commissioner of agriculture. He supported legalizing the production of industrial hemp as a potential cash crop for Kentucky farmers. In his 2015 face-off for governor, Comer ran against the more outspoken conservative Bevin, who had taken on veteran Sen. Mitch McConnell in the Republican primary in 2014. "I've fought corruption. I've made government more efficient. I've focused on trying to recruit new industries and good-paying jobs to this state. I've passed legislation," Comer said in a pre-primary interview with the *Lexington Herald-Leader*. The official recanvass of the primary for governor gave 33 percent to each front-runner, with Bevin prevailing by 83 votes.

When 11-term Republican Rep. Ed Whitfield announced his retirement, Comer was the early frontrunner and was not seriously threatened. His chief challenger was Mike Pape, who gained local political connections during his many years as district director for Whitfield. Pape raised $420,000 to the $1 million that Comer raised for the campaign. The U.S. Chamber of Commerce spent another $100,000 on behalf of Comer. He won the four-candidate contest with 61 percent of the vote to 23 percent for

Pape. After more experienced Democrats decided not to run, challenger Samuel Gaskins had a minimal presence. Comer won the general election, 73%-27%.

Because Whitfield had resigned from the House in September 2016 amid allegations of ethical improprieties, Comer also won a special election and took office the week after the Nov. 8 election. His chief committee assignment was Agriculture, where he brought extensive first-hand experience.

Western Kentucky

Population		**Race and Ethnicity**		**Income**	
Total	723,936	White	87.6%	Median Income	$39,108 (403 out of 435)
Land area	12,080	Black	6.8%		
Pop/ sq mi	59.9	Latino	2.8%		
Born in state	69.0%	Asian	0.6%	Under $50,000	60.6%
		Two races	1.7%	$50,000-$99,999	27.9%
Age Groups		Other	0.4%	$100,000-$199,999	10.1%
Under 18	23.0%			$200,000 or more	1.4%
18-34	21.8%	**Education**		Poverty Rate	19.7%
35-64	38.7%	H.S grad or less	55.5%		
Over 64	16.6%	Some college	28.9%	**Health Insurance**	
		College Degree, 4 yr	9.0%	With health insurance coverage	87.4%
Work		Post grad	6.6%		
White Collar	28.3%				
Sales and Service	39.4%	**Military**		**Public Assistance**	
Blue Collar	32.3%	Veteran	9.3%	Cash public assistance income	2.0%
Government	16.1%	Active Duty	1.3%		
				Food stamp/SNAP benefits	17.2%

Voter Turnout			
2015 Total Citizens 18+	549,981	2016 House Turnout as % CVAP	54%
2016 House turnout	299,001	2014 House Turnout as % CVAP	43%

2012 Presidential Vote		
Mitt Romney	197,074	(66%)
Barack Obama	95,273	(32%)

2016 Presidential Vote		
Donald Trump	224,657	(72%)
Hillary Clinton	74,179	(24%)
Gary Johnson	6,920	(2%)

Cook Partisan Voting Index: R+23

The point where the Ohio River flows into the Mississippi - the intersection Huckleberry Finn and Jim missed in the fog - must have struck early settlers as a site for a great city. But no Pittsburgh or St. Louis grew up on the fertile black soil. Instead, the Kentucky land west of the dammed-up Tennessee and Cumberland rivers, bought from the Chickasaw Indians by Gen. Andrew Jackson and Gov. Isaac Shelby in 1818 - the Jackson Purchase - was settled by farmers, mostly from the South. This was one area of Kentucky where public sentiment clearly favored the Confederacy during the Civil War. A group of delegates from western Kentucky and western Tennessee gathered in Mayfield in 1861 and are believed to have voted to join together into a single state in the Confederacy (most of the papers have been destroyed and the record is unclear). The movement was stopped by Tennessee's eventual decision to secede from the Union. Jefferson Davis, the president of the Confederacy, was born in western Kentucky's Christian County, near Hopkinsville. To the east of the Jackson Purchase are the dwindling coalfields and the Pennyrile (after pennyroyal, a common variety of local wild mint), a land of low hills and small farms.

The 1st Congressional District of Kentucky is made up of the Jackson Purchase and much of the Pennyrile. There is a distinctive Southern atmosphere here - in the crops that are grown, in the historically low wages, and in the fact that the big city with the most influence locally is Nashville, not Louisville. The 240 miles from Paducah to the state capital in Frankfort has created more than a physical separation. That's especially true for the four counties that border the Mississippi River, where St. Louis and New Orleans are their frame of reference.

"There is a sense in Western Kentucky that Frankfort ignores them, that policymakers just don't care about them," former state Treasurer Jonathan Miller, who has done public-affairs work for counties in the 1st District, told the *Lexington Herald-Leader* in 2016. "And that sense is even more exacerbated in the river counties, which are even more remote." Paducah, on the Ohio River, has reinvented a large area with an artist relocation program that has boosted development in the Lowertown Arts District. The sprawling Army base at Fort Campbell is home to the 101st Airborne Division, which deployed multiple times during the Iraq and Afghanistan conflicts. The base expected to have about 26,000 troops in 2017 - a drop of about 5,000 in five years, but not as deep a cut as at other large Army facilities.

The Jackson Purchase and the Pennyrile are ancestrally Democratic. Paducah produced one of the most enduring Democratic politicians of the 20th century: Alben Barkley, whose career from 1912 to 1956 included 14 years in the House, 23 in the Senate and four as vice president. This part of the state never elected a Republican to Congress until 1994. But the Republican voting pattern has been firmly established in the 1st District in national elections, and it has continued to grow. The 62%-37% win for John McCain over Barack Obama in 2008 grew to a 72%-24% win for Donald Trump over Hillary Clinton. Strikingly, the two strongest Republican districts in Kentucky are not those in the suburbs or in mid-sized cities. They are the 1st and the 5th Districts, which are the two most rural in Kentucky and that are among the lowest 10 percent of districts nationwide in their median income.

SECOND DISTRICT

Brett Guthrie (R)

Elected 2008, 5th term; b. Feb 18, 1964, Florence, AL; U.S. Military Academy (NY), B.S., 1987; Yale University (CT), M.P.A., 1997; Church of Christ; Married (Elizabeth Clemons); 3 children.

Military Career: U.S. Army, 1987-90; U.S. Army Reserve, 1990-2002.

Elected Office: KY Senate, 1998-2008.

Professional Career: Vice President., Trace Die Cast, 2001-2008.

DC Office: 2434 RHOB 20515, 202-225-3501, Fax: 202-226-2019, guthrie.house.gov.

State Offices: Bowling Green, 270-842-9896; Owensboro, 270-438-6595; Radcliff, 270-438-6599.

Committees: *Education & the Workforce*: Higher Education & Workforce Development (Chmn). *Energy & Commerce*: Communications & Technology, Digital Commerce & Consumer Protection, Health.

Group Ratings

	ADA	ACLU	AFL-CIO	LCV	ITI	COC	HAFA	ACU	CFG	FRC
2016	-	11%	-	0%	100%	100%	67%	96%	78%	100%
2015	0%	C	8%	0%	C	90%	C	79%	64%	100%

Almanac Ratings 2015

	Economy	Social	Foreign	Composite
Liberal	7%	9%	4%	7%
Conservative	93%	91%	96%	93%

Key Votes of the 114th Congress

1. Keystone Pipeline	Y	5. Puerto Rico Debt	Y	9. Offenses by Aliens	Y
2. Trade Deals	Y	6. Medical Marijuana	N	10. Troops in Iraq	N
3. Export-Import Bank	N	7. Sanctuary Cities	Y	11. Homeland Security $$	N
4. Debt Ceiling Increase	Y	8. Armor-piercing Bullets	Y	12. Trade Adjustment aid	Y

Election Results

Election	Name (Party)	Vote (%)	Cand. Spent	Ind. Exp. Support	Ind. Exp. Oppose
2016 General	Brett Guthrie (R)	251,825 (100%)	$892,846		
2016 Primary	Brett Guthrie (R)	(100%)			

Prior winning percentages: 2014 (69%), 2012 (64%), 2010 (68%), 2008 (53%)

Republican Brett Guthrie, elected in 2008, has a military and business background that plays well with constituents, plus a reputation as a loyal party vote that endears him to GOP leaders. He holds a plum seat on the Energy and Commerce Committee, where he has focused on Medicaid and other health care issues and on protecting the state's coal and oil industries.

A graduate of West Point, Guthrie served 14 years in the Army, first in the Reserve, then as a field artillery officer with the 101st Airborne Division at Fort Campbell. After his discharge, Guthrie joined the family business in Bowling Green, Trace Die Cast Inc., a leading supplier of aluminum castings for the automobile industry. His father started the business with his savings and just five employees in the 1980s. Guthrie eventually became vice president. In 1998, he was elected to the state Senate, where he became chairman of the Transportation Committee, helping the state develop its highway budget. Republicans expected him to join their leadership, but Guthrie set his sights on Congress.

When the seat was open in 2008, Guthrie had no opposition for the Republican nomination. The Democratic nominee was state Sen. David Boswell, a 30-year veteran of Kentucky politics. He ran as a conservative Democrat, and the two contenders were virtually indistinguishable on the issues. Both opposed abortion rights and supported gun ownership, and both spoke out against the massive bailout for the financial industry that Congress passed in the fall of 2008. National Democrats made the contest one of their top priorities. Guthrie ran ads tying Boswell to liberal Democrats and their opposition to offshore drilling. He emphasized his military background to the district's large active and retired military population. The Democratic Congressional Campaign Committee ran an ad claiming that Trace Die Cast had sent jobs to Mexico, and former President Bill Clinton stumped for Boswell. Guthrie had a war chest of nearly $1.3 million compared with Boswell's $917,000. He won 53%-47%.

In the House, Guthrie has been a dependable Republican. The House in 2011 passed his bill to water down the Affordable Care Act by converting mandatory funding for teaching health centers to annual congressional spending. Guthrie took a softer line in criticizing the Environmental Protection Agency than other Republicans on Energy and Commerce, telling the *Owensboro Messenger-Inquirer* that the agency needed to strike a better balance between regulation and the economy. "I've been to Mexico City and Beijing," he said. "I don't want to have to wear a mask when I go outside. But I want regulations that don't put companies out of business and cost my district $60,000-a-year jobs." He led a bipartisan working group on how the federal government could more efficiently use wireless spectrum. In 2013, the House enacted his bill to reauthorize the National Center for Missing and Exploited Children. In December 2016, the House passed the bill that he authored with Energy and Commerce Democratic Rep. Kathy Castor of Florida to give companies in the concrete masonry industry more flexibility to research and promote their products.

Guthrie has responsibilities at two key House subcommittees. As vice chairman since 2015 of the Health Subcommittee, he has pledged to achieve "patient-centered health care solutions." He has focused on steps to replace Obamacare and to make the Medicaid program more effective. With Democratic Rep. Paul Tonko of New York, he filed a bill to encourage more effective research to find a cure for Alzheimer's disease. On the Education and the Workforce Committee, Guthrie chairs the Higher Education and the Workforce Subcommittee. In July 2016, the House passed his bill to improve financial counseling for borrowers of student loans. He has filed a bill to revise federal job-training programs.

Guthrie was reelected without opposition in 2016. He and Kentucky Democrat John Yarmuth have led the Congressional Bourbon Caucus. "I have Heaven Hill and Jim Beam in my district," Guthrie told *The Washington Post* in 2012. "I lost Maker's Mark in redistricting." When Kentucky Sen. Rand Paul declared his presidential candidacy in April 2015, Guthrie said he liked that the Bowling Green resident "doesn't blow with the wind," and Guthrie embraced the senator's views on free enterprise, freedom and opportunity. Later in the campaign, he voiced reservations about Donald Trump. The president needs to work with Congress "in a positive way," Guthrie said.

Central Kentucky: Louisville Suburbs, Bowling, Elizabethtown

Population		**Race and Ethnicity**		**Income**	
Total	738,714	White	87.8%	Median Income	$45,631 (333 out of 435)
Land area	7,177	Black	5.4%		
Pop/ sq mi	102.9	Latino	3.2%		
Born in state	71.3%	Asian	1.2%	Under $50,000	53.8%
		Two races	2.0%	$50,000-$99,999	31.3%
Age Groups		Other	0.4%	$100,000-$199,999	12.9%
Under 18	23.7%			$200,000 or more	1.9%
18-34	22.5%	**Education**		Poverty Rate	16.9%
35-64	39.6%	H.S grad or less	52.3%		
Over 64	14.2%	Some college	28.8%	**Health Insurance**	
		College Degree, 4 yr	11.0%	With health insurance coverage	89.5%
Work		Post grad	7.9%		
White Collar	29.4%				
Sales and Service	40.0%	**Military**		**Public Assistance**	
Blue Collar	30.6%	Veteran	10.5%	Cash public assistance income	2.4%
Government	15.5%	Active Duty	0.9%		
				Food stamp/SNAP benefits	15.8%

Voter Turnout			
2015 Total Citizens 18+	551,573	2016 House Turnout as % CVAP	46%
2016 House turnout	251,825	2014 House Turnout as % CVAP	41%

2012 Presidential Vote		
Mitt Romney	186,231	(63%)
Barack Obama	103,410	(35%)

2016 Presidential Vote		
Donald Trump	219,152	(68%)
Hillary Clinton	89,563	(28%)
Gary Johnson	9,269	(3%)

Cook Partisan Voting Index: R+19

In the 1770s and 1780s, Americans began settling the limestone-soil country of central Kentucky, staking out towns like Bardstown and Elizabethtown and starting academies and colleges. They were well-settled when Stephen Foster wrote "My Old Kentucky Home" just before the Civil War. The war tore deeply here. This part of Kentucky gave birth to Abraham Lincoln, and during the conflict it lost thousands of soldiers, both Union and Confederate. The Lincoln family was not immune to this division; Mary Todd Lincoln's brother-in-law, Benjamin Hardin Helm, fought on the side of the Confederacy and rose to the rank of general before dying at the Battle of Chickamauga. Lincoln himself was never particularly popular here prior to his death. Kentucky's most famous son won only 1 percent of the vote in the state in 1860; his home county gave him just three votes. Today, the area hosts several Kentucky landmarks - Fort Knox, the nation's gold depository; some of the nation's largest bourbon distilleries; and Mammoth Cave, the world's largest accessible cavern, which is near Bowling Green. In the small town of Bardstown, site of the My Old Kentucky Home State Park, the annual Kentucky Bourbon Festival draws more than 50,000 visitors to the week-long event.

The 2nd Congressional District of Kentucky consists of much of the territory south and southwest of Louisville, starting with Spencer County and heading south to Bowling Green, where Rand Paul had his eye clinic before he entered politics. That city is the headquarters of apparel giant Fruit of the Loom, and it has a bustling General Motors Corvette assembly plant, the only place in the world where the sleek sports cars have been produced since 1981. The Corvettes had been manufactured in St. Louis, but that city offered little response when Bowling Green offered GM lucrative tax credits to make the move. In July 2016, GM announced plans to invest $290 million in the Bowling Green assembly plant, which produced 40,689 cars during the 2016 model year - more than triple production in 2010. The National Corvette Museum is across the street from the plant. The district jogs west along the Ohio River to Owensboro, a port with warehouses that receive aluminum alloys to make lightweight engine parts. The city has successfully courted new economic development, including the headquarters of U.S. Bank, the fifth-largest commercial bank in the United States, with close to 2,000 employees locally.

Yet Owensboro still tries to preserve the feeling of "Old Kentucky," and hosts an annual international barbecue festival where mutton, a throwback to Welsh shepherds who settled in western Kentucky, remains a favorite. Democrat Wendell Ford, the most famous political son of Owensboro, was the only person to serve as lieutenant governor, governor and senator from Kentucky; he died in 2015.

The district also reaches into the Lexington suburbs, including Lancaster, home of Kentucky's first Republican governor, William O'Connell Bradley, who successfully shepherded an anti-lynching law in 1897. Centre College is located here, in picturesque Danville. Much of the district is rural and small-town country. For many years, it favored the Democrats, but in the 1990s, voters moved to the Republican Party, which better matched their conservative cultural leanings. Donald Trump got 68 percent of the vote in 2016, a boost of a few percentage points over recent Republican presidential performances.

THIRD DISTRICT

John Yarmuth (D)

Elected 2006, 6th term; b. Nov 04, 1947, Louisville; Yale University (CT), B.A., 1969; Georgetown University Law Center (DC), Att., 1972; Jewish; Married (Catherine Yarmuth); 1 child.

Professional Career: Stockbroker, 1969-1971; Sr. aide, U.S. Sen. Marlow Cook, 1971-1975; Publisher, Louisville Today magazine, 1976-1982; Assistant Vice President. of university relations, University of Louisville, 1983-1986; Vice President., Caretenders, 1986-1990; Owner, columnist, & Executive editor, Louisville Eccentric Observer, 1990-2002; Co-host, Yarmuth & Ziegler, 2003; Commentator, Hot Button, 2004-2005.

DC Office: 131 CHOB 20515, 202-225-5401, Fax: 202-225-5776, yarmuth.house.gov.

State Offices: Louisville, 502-582-5129; Louisville, 502-933-5863.

Committees: *Budget (RMM).*

Group Ratings

	ADA	ACLU	AFL-CIO	LCV	ITI	COC	HAFA	ACU	CFG	FRC
2016	-	88%	-	92%	50%	57%	11%	5%	0%	0%
2015	100%	C	100%	91%	C	40%	C	5%	0%	0%

Almanac Ratings 2015

	Economy	Social	Foreign	Composite
Liberal	100%	100%	99%	100%
Conservative	0%	0%	1%	0%

Key Votes of the 114th Congress

1. Keystone Pipeline	N	5. Puerto Rico Debt	Y	9. Offenses by Aliens	N
2. Trade Deals	N	6. Medical Marijuana	Y	10. Troops in Iraq	Y
3. Export-Import Bank	Y	7. Sanctuary Cities	N	11. Homeland Security $$	Y
4. Debt Ceiling Increase	Y	8. Armor-piercing Bullets	N	12. Trade Adjustment aid	Y

Election Results

Election	Name (Party)	Vote (%)	Cand. Spent	Ind. Exp. Support	Ind. Exp. Oppose
2016 General	John Yarmuth (D)........................	212,401 (64%)	$538,374		
	Harold Bratcher (R).....................	122,093 (37%)	$5,792		
2016 Primary	John Yarmuth (D)........................	(100%)			

Prior winning percentages: 2014 (64%), 2012 (64%), 2010 (55%), 2008 (59%), 2006 (51%)

Democrat John Yarmuth, who was first elected in 2006, is a former journalist whose candor and independence sometimes have led him to go off-message in discussing his party's shortcomings. But he also enjoys rebuking Republicans, especially home-state colleague Mitch McConnell, the Senate majority leader. In 2017, Minority Leader Nancy Pelosi awarded Yarmuth the plum of senior Democrat on the Budget Committee, which positioned him as a top party spokesman.

Yarmuth hails from a wealthy Louisville family. His father, Stanley Yarmuth, founded National Industries, a conglomerate that started as a used car business; his maternal grandfather, Samuel Klein, ran the Bank of Louisville. John Yarmuth went to Atherton High School, where he was elected student government president. After graduating from Yale University, he worked briefly as a stockbroker and then as an aide to Republican Sen. Marlow Cook. Yarmuth attended two years of law school but didn't finish his degree.

He founded *Louisville Today* magazine, and served as publisher from 1976 until 1982. He ran unsuccessfully for Louisville alderman in 1975, and for county commissioner in 1981. He worked in public relations from 1983 to 1990 for the University of Louisville and for a health care company. Unhappy with the policies of President Ronald Reagan, Yarmuth switched his party affiliation to Democrat in 1985. (He says he first registered as a Republican as a favor to his father, who was a fundraiser for President Richard Nixon.) In 1990, Yarmuth founded the *Louisville Eccentric Observer*, a free newsweekly popularly known as LEO, and for the next 15 years penned a column called "Hot Coals" that promoted his mostly liberal views. He also did televised political commentary.

In 2006, five-term Republican Rep. Anne Northup was vulnerable in the district. The Democratic Congressional Campaign Committee touted attorney Andrew Horne, an Iraq war veteran and first-time candidate. But Yarmuth raised more money and proved a more formidable candidate than Horne, winning the four-way primary 54%-32%. He called for an immediate pullout of troops from Iraq and referred to Northup as a "rubber stamp" for President George W. Bush. Northup campaigned on Republican tax cuts and her work for the district. She suffered a wrenching tragedy during the campaign when her son died of an undiagnosed heart condition. After suspending her campaign for six weeks, she unleashed an advertising offensive that blasted Yarmuth for his liberal writings, saying he supported removing the phrase "under God" from the Pledge of Allegiance and legalizing marijuana. Northup raised $3.4 million to Yarmuth's $2.3 million, which included $700,000 of his own money. Northup could not overcome a national tide against Republicans that year.

In 2008, Northup returned for a rematch, after losing a primary contest for governor. She criticized Yarmuth for supporting the $700 billion bailout for the financial markets, and attacked his "present" vote on a resolution honoring Christmas, asserting he had lost touch with his constituents. (Yarmuth is Jewish.) Even though Northup raised more money, Yarmuth won much more easily than their first contest, 59%-41%. He has become entrenched in his seat.

Yarmuth told *Esquire* magazine in 2010 that he had trouble adjusting to elected office: "I never had to compromise on my opinion in the column. Suddenly you have to swallow all sorts of compromises, and that's not easy at all." With his journalism background, he joined a "messaging" group that advised Pelosi and other Democratic leaders on media strategy. He snared a seat on the Ways and Means Committee, but lost it after Republicans regained control of the House in 2011. He has pursued occasional bipartisan opportunities. In April 2015, he proposed with Republican Rep. Dave Reichert of Washington the Runaway and Homeless Youth and Trafficking Prevention Act. His "Keeping Our Campaigns Honest Act" would require disclosure of the donors behind super PACs and tax-exempt organizations that flood the airwaves with anonymous ads.

He moved to the Budget and Energy and Commerce committees, where he frequently jabbed at McConnell. The two have clashed since the 1970s. "Mitch McConnell will always do what's in Mitch McConnell's best interest," he has said. Yarmuth goes places rhetorically where most Democrats won't venture. After the House passed the fiscal-cliff budget compromise, he praised House Speaker John Boehner for being "courageous" in sending the Senate-passed deal to the House floor. He told *Roll Call* newspaper that the health care law was the right thing to do policy-wise, but "big picture, politically, it probably wasn't worth it." He told a Louisville radio station after the Senate made changes to the bill, "We couldn't really go to the average American citizen and say, 'Here's what it means to you.'"

In naming Yarmuth as the top Democrat on the Budget Committee after the 2016 election, Pelosi said he "will represent our values in the budget debate, is a master at communicating to the public and has been a leader in advocating the use of social media." Yarmuth described his role: "Budgets are statements of our values, and the Budget Committee provides us the opportunity to show the American people the sharp contrasts between Democratic values and those of Republicans in the House and White House." He acted as a party spokesman during the Democrats' June 2016 House sit-in to protest inaction on gun-control legislation.

Yarmuth finished first among House Democrats - and 14th overall - in *Golf Digest*'s 2016 ranking of the 150 best golfers in Washington's political world. A highlight of his career was when he joined two other House Democrats in an August 2015 round of golf with President Barack Obama at Joint Base

Andrews. Yarmuth said that the foursome did not directly discuss congressional business, though Obama reportedly told his playing partners that he would be "calling." A month later, Yarmuth was among the few Jewish Democrats to vote for Obama's controversial nuclear deal with Iran. A coincidence? Perhaps.

Yarmuth donates his annual salary to charity. He says that the demands of serving in Congress prompted him to scale back his plans to spend a month every year at a home he built near a golf course in Ireland.

Louisville Metro

Population		**Race and Ethnicity**		**Income**	
Total	736,054	White	69.0%	Median Income	$47,714 (288 out of 435)
Land area	319	Black	20.9%		
Pop/ sq mi	2304.9	Latino	4.7%		
Born in state	69.2%	Asian	2.4%	Under $50,000	51.8%
		Two races	2.6%	$50,000-$99,999	29.5%
Age Groups		Other	0.2%	$100,000-$199,999	14.6%
Under 18	22.7%			$200,000 or more	3.9%
18-34	23.6%	**Education**		Poverty Rate	16.8%
35-64	39.6%	H.S grad or less	39.1%		
Over 64	14.1%	Some college	30.2%	**Health Insurance**	
		College Degree, 4 yr	17.9%	With health insurance coverage	89.2%
Work		Post grad	12.9%		
White Collar	36.5%				
Sales and Service	41.4%	**Military**		**Public Assistance**	
Blue Collar	22.1%	Veteran	8.8%	Cash public assistance income	3.0%
Government	11.5%	Active Duty	0.1%		
				Food stamp/SNAP benefits	15.2%

Voter Turnout			
2015 Total Citizens 18+	543,113	2016 House Turnout as % CVAP	62%
2016 House turnout	334,494	2014 House Turnout as % CVAP	45%

2012 Presidential Vote		
Barack Obama	183,015	(56%)
Mitt Romney	140,539	(43%)

2016 Presidential Vote		
Hillary Clinton	186,549	(55%)
Donald Trump	135,714	(40%)
Gary Johnson	9,854	(3%)

Cook Partisan Voting Index: D+6

At the falls of the Ohio River, George Rogers Clark founded one of America's first inland metropolises in 1778: the river port and industrial city of Louisville. It is heavily influenced by the Cavalier culture that the second sons of big landowners from England brought to Virginia in the 17th century - and their heirs brought over the Appalachians to the valleys of Kentucky in the 18th century. When Kentucky decided not to secede from the union in 1861, the decision was not unanimous, and the culture of tidewater Virginia is still evident in the Louisville lawn party. Mint juleps are served on the verandas of mansions, especially (but not only) during Kentucky Derby week in May; horse racing is a preoccupation throughout the year. The last president who owned slaves while in office, Zachary Taylor, is interred at Zachary Taylor National Cemetery.

With 764,000 residents in 2015, Louisville is Kentucky's largest city. Its economy is in many ways "pre-postindustrial:" It produces cigarettes and whiskey, GE appliances and Ford automobiles. Louisville is also the headquarters of Humana health services; the long-term health care facility operator Signature HealthCARE; and several fast food companies, including Yum! Brands, which owns KFC, Pizza Hut, and Taco Bell; Papa John's pizza; and A Great American Brand, which operates Long John Silver's. In March 2015, an iconic business disappeared when the local Hillerich and Bradsby company sold its Louisville slugger baseball bat to Chicago-based Wilson Sporting Goods. But the bats continued to be manufactured at the plant in downtown Louisville. Muhammad Ali, born in Louisville as Cassius Marcellus Clay, has been memorialized by the Muhammad Ali Center, with its interactive exhibits. The

Derby has an annual economic impact of $400 million. Although local economic growth has exceeded that of the nation since 2009, this remains the 11th poorest city in the nation.

The 3rd Congressional District of Kentucky includes all but a handful of precincts in Louisville-Jefferson County. The large African-American population, which is 21 percent of the overall district, resides chiefly in the West End of Louisville. A low-income white population is along the strip highway that leads to Fort Knox. West Buechel, southeast of the city, has one of the highest concentrations of Yugoslavian-Americans in the United States, many of whom were Bosnian refugees relocated by the government. The suburbs to the east tend to be affluent. Small, elite neighborhoods - Mockingbird Valley, Glenview and Ten Broeck - are nestled in the hills above the Ohio River.

The district, like Louisville, has long been an odd duck in Kentucky politics. If its elite were Virginia Cavaliers, many of its burghers were Germans and Pennsylvanians who made the river town a Republican and anti-slavery island in a secessionist and pro-slavery sea. That tradition helps explain how Republican Mitch McConnell won election as Jefferson County judge-executive in 1977 and 1981, when the state was electing Democrats to most other offices. As recently as 2006, the district was held by a Republican. Since the 1990s, Louisville has trended toward the Democrats, even as the rest of Kentucky trended Republican. The Democrats' voter registration advantage over the Republicans has been similar to that in the 1st and 6th districts, but the Democrats here have become much more reliable supporters of Andrew Jackson's party than in the other two. Jefferson County, the largest in the state, was one of only two counties in 2016 to vote for Hillary Clinton - 54%-41%.

FOURTH DISTRICT

Thomas Massie (R)

Elected 2012, 3rd term; b. Jan 13, 1971, Huntington, WV; Massachusetts Institute of Technology, B.S., 1993; Massachusetts Institute of Technology, M.M.E., 1996; Methodist; Married (Rhonda Massie); 4 children.

Professional Career: Founder, Chairman, & chief tech. officer, SensAble Technologies, 1993-2003; Judge Executive, Lewis County KY, 2010-2012; Farmer, 2003-present.

DC Office: 2453 RHOB 20515, 202-225-3465, Fax: 202-225-0003, massie.house.gov.

State Offices: Ashland, 606-324-9898; Crescent Springs, 859-426-0080; LaGrange, 502-265-9119.

Committees: *Oversight & Government Reform*: Government Operations, Intergovernmental Affairs. *Science, Space & Technology*: Energy, Oversight. *Transportation & Infrastructure*: Aviation, Highways & Transit, Water Resources & Environment.

Group Ratings

	ADA	ACLU	AFL-CIO	LCV	ITI	COC	HAFA	ACU	CFG	FRC
2016	-	35%	-	3%	33%	69%	91%	96%	96%	92%
2015	15%	C	13%	11%	C	50%	C	100%	92%	83%

Almanac Ratings 2015

	Economy	Social	Foreign	Composite
Liberal	22%	20%	39%	27%
Conservative	78%	80%	61%	73%

Key Votes of the 114th Congress

1. Keystone Pipeline	Y	5. Puerto Rico Debt	N	9. Offenses by Aliens	Y
2. Trade Deals	N	6. Medical Marijuana	Y	10. Troops in Iraq	Y
3. Export-Import Bank	N	7. Sanctuary Cities	Y	11. Homeland Security $$	N
4. Debt Ceiling Increase	N	8. Armor-piercing Bullets	Y	12. Trade Adjustment aid	N

Election Results

Election	Name (Party)	Vote (%)	Cand. Spent	Ind. Exp. Support	Ind. Exp. Oppose
2016 General	Thomas Massie (R).....................	233,922 (71%)	$346,850	$35,731	
	Calvin Sidle (D).........................	94,065 (29%)			
2016 Primary	Thomas Massie (R).....................................	(100%)			

Prior winning percentages: 2014 (68%), 2012 (62%)

Republican Thomas Massie, first elected in 2012 as a political outsider, has featured his rebellious stripes in Congress. He has been a constant thorn to Republican leaders, who have bypassed him for subcommittee chairmanships. But he has been instrumental in starting up and leading groups of conservative activists in the House, including the Second Amendment Caucus.

Massie has an impressive scientific background. He was raised in Vanceburg, Kentucky, and got his bachelor's degree and master's in engineering at the Massachusetts Institute of Technology. While at MIT, Massie was part of a group that invented the Phantom, a device enabling users to interact with objects in cyberspace through touch. To market the product, he and his wife, Rhonda (his high school sweetheart and also an MIT student), started the firm SensAble Technologies, which raised more than $32 million of venture capital, created 70 jobs, and obtained 29 patents. The hardware and software that he developed has been used to design automobiles, jewelry, shoes, dental prosthetics and reconstructive implants for wounded soldiers. Massie won a $30,000 Lemelson-MIT Student Prize for his work in technology.

Massie left SensAble Technologies in 2003, and returned to Kentucky with his family to run a farm, where he built a timber-frame house that runs on solar energy. He got interested in politics after learning about a proposed tax in rural Lewis County that would fund a building for a local conservation office. After writing a letter to the editor objecting to the tax, "It was probably at that point there was no turning back from my involvement in politics," he later told a gathering in Newport, according to *The Cincinnati Enquirer*. In 2010, he entered politics by winning a campaign for Lewis County judge-executive. In that position, Massie boasted that he eliminated enough wasteful spending in his first nine months to pay three years of his salary.

When he ran for an open seat in 2012, Massie described himself as a "conservative with conviction and common sense." He campaigned on his business background and budget-cutting experience as county official. In an early speech, Massie harkened to his time with SensAble: "For me, the government was one of those entities that was putting land mines in the field that I had to navigate when we started the company." Massie won the all-important support of tea party activists. He had supported tea party favorite Rand Paul in his 2010 Senate race. Paul appeared in a TV ad for Massie, who named a former Paul aide as his campaign manager.

His opponents attacked Massie for benefiting from the largesse of Liberty for All, a Texas-based super PAC that reportedly was bankrolled primarily by James Ramsey, a 21-year-old Texas college student with a hefty inheritance. He provided the group with more than $500,000 to spend on behalf of Massie. Massie effectively portrayed himself as the outsider and won the primary handily, with 45 percent of the vote. His two chief opponents split the establishment vote. In this solidly Republican district, Massie easily won in November. He has not faced a primary challenge since.

In the House, he showed his rebellious streak on his first House vote in 2013, when he opposed John Boehner for a new term as House Speaker. Massie occasionally crossed the aisle to work with Democrats, especially on civil liberties issues where the wings of both parties came together in opposition to Big Government. In May 2015, the House passed a bill that he cosponsored with Democratic Rep. Zoe Lofgren of California to require that the National Security Agency seek a judicial warrant before it could spy on U.S. citizens in its online surveillance. In 2016, the House narrowly defeated a similar amendment days after a suspected Islamic State supporter gunned down 49 persons at a gay club in Orlando, Florida. Massie insisted that the proposal "does not take any tools away from those that want to investigate what happened in Orlando."

With Democratic Rep. Marc Pocan of Wisconsin, he filed a bill to repeal the Patriot Act, the post-9/11 law that has provided broad authority to security agencies. *Buzzfeed* profiled Massie as "Democrats' new go-to Republican." But on most social issues, he remained a solid conservative vote. "Here's the difference between a partisan and an ideologue: An ideologue reads the bill, every word, period and section; a partisan reads the whip recommendation," he told *Buzzfeed*. (He's proudly the former.) In January 2017, he refiled his "Audit the Fed" bill, which he originally introduced with Paul.

The House earlier passed the bill but it died in the Senate, though it was supported by independent Sen. Bernie Sanders.

Massie has worked with other conservatives to channel their opposition to GOP leaders. The House leadership, he said, had become "a significant source of the dysfunction" in the chamber. He has been consistent, and increasingly lonely, in his independence. After Boehner resigned, Massie was one of nine Republicans who voted against Paul Ryan as the new Speaker in October 2015, Then he was the only Republican to vote against Ryan in January 2017. "I'm very concerned about the combination of Donald Trump and Paul Ryan and the implications for our national debt," he told *Reason*, a libertarian magazine.

Massie worked with other members to organize the conservative Freedom Caucus as a way to strengthen their legislative leverage. In December 2016, he revived the Second Amendment Caucus and became its chairman. "The recent election results present us with a new opportunity to advance pro-gun legislation and reverse the erosion of the Second Amendment that's occurred over the last few decade," he said. During his first term, Massie chaired the Technology Subcommittee, a logical assignment for his background. Since then, he has no longer chaired that subcommittee, or any other. Instead, those plums went to more junior Republicans. That seemed a clear message from GOP leaders.

In 2016, he faced Democratic challenger Calvin Sidle, who had twice lost bids for local office in Pikeville, which is in the neighboring 5th District. "Whereas he (Massie) is essentially for non-spending, I am for big spending," said Sidle, who was an Uber driver at night. Massie won, 71%-29%. During the transition to President Donald Trump, Massie made known his interest in serving as a White House science-policy adviser. There was no public indication that he was seriously considered. During the Republican convention, he told the *Washington Examiner* that he was supporting Trump as a "glass is half-full" position. "He's better than 90 percent of the congressmen I serve with," Massie added, with faint praise. He initially was a strong backer of Paul's presidential candidacy.

Northern Kentucky: Cincinnati and Louisville Suburbs

Population		**Race and Ethnicity**		**Income**	
Total	740,371	White	90.5%	Median Income	$55,540 (178 out of 435)
Land area	4,382	Black	3.4%		
Pop/ sq mi	168.9	Latino	3.1%		
Born in state	62.4%	Asian	1.1%	Under $50,000	45.1%
Age Groups		Two races	1.6%	$50,000-$99,999	32.0%
Under 18	24.7%	Other	0.2%	$100,000-$199,999	18.6%
18-34	20.8%	**Education**		$200,000 or more	4.2%
35-64	41.3%	H.S grad or less	44.1%	Poverty Rate	13.9%
Over 64	13.2%	Some college	29.9%	**Health Insurance**	
Work		College Degree, 4 yr	16.3%	With health insurance coverage	90.1%
White Collar	35.9%	Post grad	9.7%		
Sales and Service	40.3%	**Military**		**Public Assistance**	
Blue Collar	23.8%	Veteran	9.2%	Cash public assistance income	2.5%
Government	12.2%	Active Duty	0.1%	Food stamp/SNAP benefits	12.7%

Voter Turnout			
2015 Total Citizens 18+	546,007	2016 House Turnout as % CVAP	60%
2016 House turnout	327,987	2014 House Turnout as % CVAP	41%

2012 Presidential Vote		
Mitt Romney	197,098	(63%)
Barack Obama	108,348	(35%)

2016 Presidential Vote		
Donald Trump	219,749	(65%)
Hillary Clinton	98,664	(29%)
Gary Johnson	11,693	(4%)

Cook Partisan Voting Index: R+18

Along the Ohio River are some very different parts of Kentucky. Ashland, near the West Virginia border, is industrial, the former home of Ashland Inc.; the river here is bound in by tight hills that hold smoke and soot in the air. Farther down the river, the country is more bucolic. This is where Eliza fled across the ice floes in Harriet Beecher Stowe's *Uncle Tom's Cabin*. Farther west, between Louisville and Cincinnati, are counties that look like they're still in the 19th century. But metropolitan growth obtrudes. Oldham County, just upriver from Louisville, has some of Kentucky's oldest homes, and is by far the most affluent county in the state. In rural Williamstown, a group of Christian fundamentalists in August 2016 opened Ark Encounter, a $100 million replica of Noah's Ark, including life-like models of some of the animal creatures. Ken Ham, the founder of the project, prevailed in a lawsuit during the construction that challenged his practice not to employ people who were gay or failed to accept his Christian creed. Ham said the purpose of the ark is not entertainment, but to send a warning of the peril awaiting society because of its errant behavior.

The three Northern Kentucky counties across the river from Cincinnati - Campbell, Kenton and fast-growing Boone - are urban and suburban. Overlooking the suspension bridge built by John Roebling are new buildings on the Covington waterfront. New subdivisions are rising on the hills in Boone County, above the river, near the Cincinnati/Northern Kentucky International Airport. Newport, with its panoramic view of the Cincinnati skyline plus its nightlife, has become a regional hot spot. In October 2016, the Kentucky State Data Center reported that Boone will surpass Kenton by 2035 as the third-largest county in the state, with 50 percent growth by 2040.

The 4th Congressional District of Kentucky is the northernmost district in the state. Much of it is close to Cincinnati Metro, though it's en route to Louisville. It covers 12 counties and 280 miles along the Ohio River and also lightly populated counties just inland. Economically, it runs the gamut from coal mining towns to rich suburbs. The region's clout in state government has been understated because the political focus is more on Cincinnati than on Louisville or Lexington, said former Secretary of State Trey Grayson, a Republican. "There's not a lot of media that people read that cover Kentucky government and politics," he told the *River City News*. The three northern Kentucky counties across the river from Cincinnati, which cast nearly half the district's votes, are heavily Republican; Boone County gave 68 percent of its vote to Donald Trump in 2016. This is a solidly Republican district, though the 65%-29% support for Trump ranked only fourth among the five Republican-held districts in Kentucky.

FIFTH DISTRICT

Hal Rogers (R)

Elected 1980, 19th term; b. Dec 31, 1937, Barrier; University of Kentucky, Bach. Deg.; University of Kentucky College of Law, J.D.; Western Kentucky University, Att.; Baptist; Married (Cynthia Doyle Rogers); 3 children (from a previous marriage).

Military Career: KY & NC Army National Guard, 1957-1964.

Professional Career: Practicing attorney, 1964-1969; Pulaski-Rockcastle Commonwealth's Attorney, 1969-1980.

DC Office: 2406 RHOB 20515, 202-225-4601, Fax: 202-225-0940, halrogers.house.gov.

State Offices: Hazard, 606-439-0794; Prestonsburg, 606-886-0844; Somerset, 800-632-8588.

Committees: *Appropriations*: Commerce, Justice, Science & Related Agencies, Defense, State, Foreign Operations & Related Programs (Chmn).

Group Ratings

	ADA	ACLU	AFL-CIO	LCV	ITI	COC	HAFA	ACU	CFG	FRC
2016	-	5%	-	5%	100%	100%	46%	71%	65%	100%
2015	0%	C	21%	0%	C	100%	C	50%	42%	92%

Almanac Ratings 2015

	Economy	Social	Foreign	Composite
Liberal	12%	10%	11%	11%
Conservative	88%	90%	90%	89%

Key Votes of the 114th Congress

1. Keystone Pipeline	Y	5. Puerto Rico Debt	Y	9. Offenses by Aliens	Y
2. Trade Deals	Y	6. Medical Marijuana	N	10. Troops in Iraq	N
3. Export-Import Bank	N	7. Sanctuary Cities	Y	11. Homeland Security $$	Y
4. Debt Ceiling Increase	Y	8. Armor-piercing Bullets	Y	12. Trade Adjustment aid	Y

Election Results

Election	Name (Party)	Vote (%)	Cand. Spent	Ind. Exp. Support	Ind. Exp. Oppose
2016 General	Hal Rogers (R)	221,242 (100%)			
2016 Primary	Hal Rogers (R)	35,984 (82%)			
	John Burk Jr. (R)	7,669 (18%)			

Prior winning percentages: 2014 (78%), 2012 (78%), 2010 (77%), 2008 (84%), 2006 (74%), 2002 (78%), 2000 (74%), 1998 (78%), 1994 (79%), 1992 (55%), 1988 (100%), 1986 (100%), 1984 (76%), 1982 (65%), 1980 (68%)

Harold Rogers, a Republican first elected in 1980, served six years as chairman of the House Appropriations Committee until he was term-limited in 2016. As the fourth most-senior member of the House, he became chairman of the subcommittee in charge of foreign aid. He is an old-school deal-maker who, in the days before the ban on earmarks, not only defended them but boasted about the prodigious sums he steered back home. *The Lexington Herald-Leader* dubbed Rogers the "Prince of Pork," and he is beloved in his rural district: He regularly is reelected with more than 75 percent of the vote.

Rogers grew up in Wayne County, graduated from the University of Kentucky, served in the National Guard, then practiced law in Somerset before buying the Citizens National Bank in Somerset. In 1969, at age 34, he was elected Pulaski-Rockcastle commonwealth attorney. In 1979, he was the unsuccessful Republican nominee for lieutenant governor. The following year, when there was an open seat, Rogers was one of 11 Republicans in the primary. He got the nomination with 23 percent of the vote and easily won in November.

His toughest race came in 1992, when redistricting combined two districts in eastern Kentucky. At first, his likely opponent was 7th District Rep. Chris Perkins, a Democrat and the son of Rep. Carl Perkins, who had chaired the Education and Labor Committee. Together, they had held the seat for 44 years. But Perkins suddenly retired, just before it was revealed that he had 514 overdrafts at the House bank when such overdrafts were developing into a major Washington scandal. Rogers instead faced state Sen. John Doug Hays of Pike County. Rogers won with 55 percent in a year many Southern Democrats turned out to vote for Arkansas Gov. Bill Clinton for president.

His voting record is mostly, but not always, conservative. The *Almanac* vote ratings for 2015 placed Rogers among the moderate half of House Republicans in each of the three issue areas. His district has long been hungry for federal aid, and Rogers often has found it difficult to maintain an impeccably conservative record on spending issues. He has argued that the federal-state partnership helped to close the gap between the impoverished area and the rest of the country.

During Republicans' initial 12 years in the House majority, Rogers chaired the Commerce, Justice, State Subcommittee starting in 1995, took over the Transportation Subcommittee in 2001, and became chairman in 2003 of the newly created Homeland Security Subcommittee. He helped to increase Kentucky to the fourth-highest state in transportation funding per capita. "The rate of return on highway spending far exceeds most other investments and is a proven engine," Rogers once wrote when he was criticized for his earmarked spending. The Hal Rogers Parkway crosses the Daniel Boone National Forest from London to Hazard.

Rogers over the years has focused on homeland security. Even before the September 11 attacks, he lamented that most airport screeners were not U.S. citizens. After Congress voted to federalize screeners, he kept a close watch on the new agency. In 2010, he challenged the Obama administration's proposals for airport body scanners because he doubted that such a costly and manpower-intensive approach would get results. Rogers questioned the Immigration and Customs Enforcement agency's policy of giving work permits to apprehended illegal immigrants who testify against their employers. The Obama administration, he complained, had practically given up deporting illegal immigrants arrested at work sites in favor of what he derisively called "virtual amnesty."

Controversy over earmarks, the special provisions that lawmakers slip into spending bills for their districts and states, put an unaccustomed spotlight on Rogers and other powerful appropriators, who for years quietly went about their business. When he was criticized for fighting to keep the Transportation

Worker Identification Credential program in Corbin, he replied that it was one of only three government facilities with sufficient security to produce the cards. Rogers has continued raising significant sums of political cash from firms that have won homeland security contracts. He responded, "I've had a lot of fundraisers. Campaign contributions mean nothing on my watch."

Rogers rose to chairman of Appropriations in 2011 after Republicans regained control of the House. He took over just as most House Republicans, especially the 87 freshmen elected in 2010, were determined to end earmarking. Despite his work over the years funding projects at home, he succumbed to the moratorium on earmarks that Speaker John Boehner decreed. As a loyal soldier, he signed on to the program. In 2012, Rogers touted his success in helping to cut wasteful spending. "We've cut the spending Congress does for three years now, which has not happened since World War II," he said. "We've cut $100 billion off the spending Congress appropriates."

Part of the reason for Rogers' continuing clout is his ability to work with Democrats. "He's very approachable," committee Democrat Marcy Kaptur of Ohio said. "He's a matter-of-fact sort of gentleman - I mean, he doesn't spend a lot of time on wasted words, he's terse - but I think very effective." Another source of his influence has been the inability of recent congressional majorities to pass individual appropriations bills. That led to massive omnibus spending bills, something that enabled Republicans to make policy via "riders" on the omnibus legislation. The December 2011 final spending bill included the elimination of more than two dozen federal programs and imposed limits on several key provisions of the Dodd-Frank financial reform law.

Rogers worked well with his Senate counterparts, including Maryland's Democratic Sen. Barbara Mikulski, who in 2013 became chair of the Senate Appropriations Committee. The pair achieved a significant goal in January 2014 when Congress approved an omnibus spending bill - the first time since 2009 that Congress completed appropriations bills that went beyond continuing resolutions.

When President Barack Obama in November 2014 issued an executive order protecting some illegal immigrants, many conservatives vowed to overturn it. But Rogers warned against using the issue to provoke another spending-bill confrontation. "I just don't think it's very smart, wise or prudent to talk about a shutdown scenario," he said. That enraged conservative activists. *National Review Online* ran an article headlined "Hal Rogers, Obama Republican," and talk show host Laura Ingraham demanded that Rogers draw a primary challenger in 2016. "Hal Rogers refuses to consider the sensible process of defunding Obama's executive amnesty and instead throws up all of these false roadblocks to defunding Obama's executive amnesty," she said. When Republicans later sought to use the Homeland Security Department spending bill to try to block the move, Rogers joined his GOP colleagues in criticizing the resistance by Senate Democrats.

In his final year as committee chairman, Rogers sought to deliver a parting gift to his constituents: Legislation to provide $1 billion for mine reclamation projects to revitalize coal communities in his district and nearby areas. The tight budget plus limited congressional action during the presidential year thwarted that goal and resulted in a bare-bones extension of federal spending, though he continued to pursue other options. Despite threats from conservative activists of a competitive primary challenge, Rogers in 2016 won his primary, 82%-18%, against John Burk, and he won without opposition in November.

In January 2017, Rogers became chairman of the State and Foreign Operations Subcommittee at Appropriations. That was an unusual rebuke of an influential and senior House Republican. As McClatchy News reported three months earlier, Rogers wanted to chair the Defense Subcommittee. Instead, that position went to Kay Granger of Texas, who had been an expert on national security issues for many years. At age 80, Rogers could retire in 2018. Republicans would not need to worry about keeping his seat.

Eastern Kentucky

Population		**Race and Ethnicity**		**Income**	
Total	714,056	White	95.9%	Median Income	$31,162
Land area	11,235	Black	1.4%		(434 out of 435)
Pop/ sq mi	63.6	Latino	1.1%		
Born in state	78.6%	Asian	0.3%	Under $50,000	68.9%
		Two races	0.9%	$50,000-$99,999	22.8%
Age Groups		Other	0.3%	$100,000-$199,999	7.5%
Under 18	22.2%			$200,000 or more	0.9%
18-34	21.0%	**Education**		Poverty Rate	27.7%
35-64	41.3%	H.S grad or less	63.6%		
Over 64	15.4%	Some college	24.1%	**Health Insurance**	
		College Degree, 4 yr	6.5%	With health insurance coverage	86.9%
Work		Post grad	5.8%		
White Collar	27.8%				
Sales and Service	42.7%	**Military**		**Public Assistance**	
Blue Collar	29.5%	Veteran	7.1%	Cash public assistance income	2.9%
Government	19.1%	Active Duty	0.0%		
				Food stamp/SNAP benefits	27.6%

Voter Turnout			
2015 Total Citizens 18+	552,250	2016 House Turnout as % CVAP	40%
2016 House turnout	221,242	2014 House Turnout as % CVAP	39%

2012 Presidential Vote		
Mitt Romney	196,192	(75%)
Barack Obama	60,760	(23%)

2016 Presidential Vote		
Donald Trump	221,558	(80%)
Hillary Clinton	48,628	(18%)

Cook Partisan Voting Index: R+31

Mountainous eastern Kentucky has been a unique place since Daniel Boone came through the Cumberland Gap in 1775. Scots-Irish pioneers soon followed him, bringing their assertive egalitarianism, loyalty to family and community, and passionate willingness to defend honor by feuds or violence. Most inhabitants of the mountains today are descendants of the Ulster Protestant and Border Scot families who settled there in the two or three generations after Boone. In the 2010 census, 0 percent of the population of Elliott, Magoffin and Menifee counties reported being foreign-born. Handed down were living memories of the old ways of doing things from an era when there was little contact with the outside world. Even though the demographics have been stable, the politics of the area have gone through much change. The first agent of change here was the Civil War. This was never slave territory - hardly any blacks have ever lived in these mountains, and even today Leslie County is the whitest in the state. The settlers had little use for the party of slavery, and still don't. Today, the counties around Somerset and Corbin in south central Kentucky cast some of the highest Republican percentages in the nation, election after election. Donald Trump won 89 percent of the vote in nearby Jackson County in 2016. The local economic populism, which is well-suited to Trump, differs starkly from the new Republican heartland in places like suburban Georgia and rural Texas. Still, Mitt Romney got 86 percent of Jackson in 2012. Social conservatism remains vocal in many of these places. In September 2015, Rowan County clerk Kim Davis received national attention when she was jailed for refusing to issue marriage licenses to same-sex couples.

Early in the 20th century, vast seams of coal were discovered under the Kentucky mountains, and a new economy sprang up, bringing a new politics. Coal mining was harsh and deadly work, as described in countless country and western songs with titles like "You'll Never Leave Harlan Alive" and "Miner's Prayer." Mine accidents, black lung disease and simple exhaustion killed tens of thousands of miners, while low wages and company stores kept them poor. Then, John L. Lewis's United Mine Workers came in, and open warfare followed, with both mine operators and union organizers willing to use violence. The union mostly won in eastern Kentucky and brought Democratic politics to these counties. In his War on Poverty, President Lyndon Johnson brought attention to this and other parts of Appalachia. He launched his "war" from the front porch of a cabin in the town of Inez in these mountains. But his crusade has been at best a mixed success. A half-century later, high-school graduation rates and life expectancy remained low. Some of these areas have some of the harshest working conditions in the nation: The coal mines have closed and people have left. The number of miners in eastern Kentucky fell from 14,000 in 2009 to below 4,000 in 2016.

The 5th Congressional District of Kentucky includes much of the territory east of the Pottsville Escarpment, which separates the Cumberland Plateau and most of the eastern mountains from the rest of the state. It includes a few counties in the eastern Pennyrile region: small towns like Somerset, Monticello and Mount Vernon. And it takes in Republican areas of the mountains to the east, including Corbin, where Colonel Harland Sanders first served his fried chicken with 11 herbs and spices, birthing fast-food franchise KFC. The northeast section of the district is coal country. There are no major metropolitan areas in the district and few highways go through the mountains; only a handful of towns have a population over 10,000. Overall this district is heavily Republican, among the top 1 percent in the nation: The 80 percent of the vote for Trump was a bit higher than Mitt Romney's 75 percent of the vote in the 5th in 2012.

SIXTH DISTRICT

Andy Barr (R)

Elected 2012, 3rd term; b. Jul 24, 1973, Lexington; University of Virginia, B.A., 1996; University of Kentucky College of Law, J.D., 2001; Episcopalian; Married (Eleanor Carol Leavell); 2 children.

Professional Career: Legislative Assistant, U.S. Rep. Jim Talent, 1996-1998; Instructor, Morehead St. University; Attorney, KY gov.'s office, 2004-2007; Practicing attorney, 2008-2012.

DC Office: 1427 LHOB 20515, 202-225-4706, Fax: 202-225-2122, barr.house.gov.

State Offices: Lexington, 859-219-1366.

Committees: *Financial Services*: Financial Institutions & Consumer Credit, Monetary Policy & Trade (Chmn).

Group Ratings

	ADA	ACLU	AFL-CIO	LCV	ITI	COC	HAFA	ACU	CFG	FRC
2016	-	5%	-	0%	100%	100%	72%	84%	70%	100%
2015	0%	C	4%	0%	C	90%	C	79%	65%	100%

Almanac Ratings 2015

	Economy	Social	Foreign	Composite
Liberal	7%	4%	4%	5%
Conservative	93%	96%	96%	95%

Key Votes of the 114th Congress

1. Keystone Pipeline	Y	5. Puerto Rico Debt	N	9. Offenses by Aliens	Y
2. Trade Deals	Y	6. Medical Marijuana	N	10. Troops in Iraq	N
3. Export-Import Bank	N	7. Sanctuary Cities	Y	11. Homeland Security $$	N
4. Debt Ceiling Increase	Y	8. Armor-piercing Bullets	Y	12. Trade Adjustment aid	Y

Election Results

Election	Name (Party)	Vote (%)		Cand. Spent	Ind. Exp. Support	Ind. Exp. Oppose
2016 General	Andy Barr (R)	202,099	(61%)	$2,362,062		
	Nancy Jo Kemper (D)	128,728	(39%)	$447,122	$5,676	
2016 Primary	Andy Barr (R)	25,212	(85%)			
	Roger Brill (R)	4,608	(16%)			

Prior winning percentages: 2014 (60%), 2012 (51%)

After defeating Democratic Rep. Ben Chandler in their 2012 rematch, Republican attorney Andy Barr secured this seat with 60 percent or more of the vote against two subsequent competitive challengers. He seems well-placed for a successful political career, including a subcommittee chairmanship in the House and perhaps an eventual statewide bid.

Barr grew up in Lexington and graduated from the University of Virginia with a bachelor's degree in government and philosophy. After two years as a legislative assistant for Republican Rep. Jim Talent of Missouri, Barr returned home to earn a law degree from the University of Kentucky. He practiced law, and taught constitutional and administrative law as a part-time instructor at Morehead State University.

Barr served as a deputy general counsel to former Kentucky Gov. Ernie Fletcher. In his 2010 challenge to Chandler, Barr distanced himself from Fletcher, whose tenure was marred by scandal over political hiring of state employees. Chandler and his backers sought to play up those ties, plus Barr's membership in a country club that until 2009 had never admitted an African American. The race went down to the wire. Chandler won by 647 votes. Barr decided against a recount and conceded 10 days after the election.

Barr got an earlier start in his 2012 rematch. But Chandler got help from redistricting, thanks to a last-minute deal in the legislature that excised from the 6th District some southern counties that voted heavily for Barr in 2010 and added traditionally Democratic-leaning counties to the east. Barr attacked the policies of President Barack Obama - especially on coal, an important issue to the district - and aggressively went after his rival, using a picture of his own baby daughter on a campaign mailer that called Chandler a "pro-abortion extremist." Chandler brought up Barr's guilty plea to possession of a fake ID when he was 19, claiming that Barr lied on a job application because he failed to mention the arrest when applying for the position with Fletcher's administration. Barr responded with an ad calling the incident as a teenager a "dumb mistake" and blasting his rival as a "desperate politician scared of losing."

Chandler's campaign attacked one of Barr's ads in which a coal executive was shown as a coal miner, releasing a spot accusing the Republican of playing fast and loose with the truth. Chandler's move proved premature when it was revealed that the executive was a registered miner who was wearing his own hard hat in the spot. This may have been Barr's biggest break in the campaign. Chandler slightly outspent him. But Barr got fundraising help from home-state Sen. Rand Paul and outside Republican groups that helped put him over the top. He won, 51%-47%.

In the House, Barr joined the Financial Services Committee. In March 2015, he filed legislation that would streamline financial regulations, especially affecting community banks and credit unions, which often are important in rural communities. The House passed in 2014 his bill that addressed a similar target. With Democratic Rep. Paul Tonko of New York, he chaired the Congressional Horse Caucus and held a hearing in April 2016 on their proposed Thoroughbred Horseracing Integrity Act.

With the encouragement of Speaker Paul Ryan, Barr in 2016 joined a House Republican task force that proposed changes in federal policy on combatting poverty. Citing what he described as the positive results after the food stamp program allowed more state management of the reorganized Temporary Assistance for Needy Families program, Barr called for increased work requirements in anti-poverty programs. "Work is not a punishment; work is a blessing. It's a ticket to upward mobility," he told the *Lexington Herald-Leader*. "And we think poor people are not liabilities to be managed by some distant welfare bureaucracy in Washington."

Barr's two reelection campaign had similar patterns and positioned him for a lengthy career. In 2014, he faced Elizabeth Jensen, an education advocate and Democratic activist, whom he outspent $2.2 million to nearly $900,000. He coasted to victory with 60 percent of the vote and won all 19 counties. In 2016, Nancy Jo Kemper, former executive director of the Kentucky Council of Churches, advocated a minimum wage increase and campaign-finance reform and said she was "excited to be a Democrat." Barr out-raised Kemper, $2.5 million to $454,000. This time, Barr won 61%-39%. He had a slim lead in Fayette County, 51%-49%, but rolled up big margins elsewhere in the district. The *Leader-Herald* in 2016 endorsed Kemper and said that Barr had "staked out positions that would result in more consumers being exploited by lenders and financial advisers." But its editorial noted that Barr had matured and "seems to have moderated since joining Tea Partiers in 2013."

In January 2017, Barr became chairman of the Financial Services Subcommittee on Monetary Policy and Trade. He planned vigorous oversight of the Federal Reserve System to encourage a stable monetary policy.

Bluegrass Country: Lexington

Population		**Race and Ethnicity**		**Income**	
Total	744,222	White	82.8%	Median Income	$46,883 (310 out of 435)
Land area	4,293	Black	8.6%		
Pop/ sq mi	173.4	Latino	4.5%		
Born in state	68.6%	Asian	1.8%	Under $50,000	52.5%
Age Groups		Two races	2.0%	$50,000-$99,999	29.4%
Under 18	22.4%	Other	0.3%	$100,000-$199,999	14.8%
18-34	25.5%	**Education**		$200,000 or more	3.2%
35-64	39.2%	H.S grad or less	42.4%	Poverty Rate	18.9%
Over 64	12.9%	Some college	27.6%	**Health Insurance**	
Work		College Degree, 4 yr	17.6%	With health insurance coverage	88.6%
White Collar	37.0%	Post grad	12.3%		
Sales and Service	40.9%	**Military**		**Public Assistance**	
Blue Collar	22.0%	Veteran	8.1%	Cash public assistance income	2.1%
Government	17.9%	Active Duty	0.1%	Food stamp/SNAP benefits	15.8%

Voter Turnout			
2015 Total Citizens 18+	554,184	2016 House Turnout as % CVAP	60%
2016 House turnout	330,827	2014 House Turnout as % CVAP	45%

2012 Presidential Vote		
Mitt Romney	170,056	(56%)
Barack Obama	128,564	(42%)

2016 Presidential Vote		
Donald Trump	182,141	(55%)
Hillary Clinton	131,271	(39%)
Gary Johnson	11,074	(3%)

Cook Partisan Voting Index: R+9

With its white picket fences, horse farms and small towns, the rolling plateau of bluegrass in central Kentucky is the part of interior America longest settled by English speakers: Lexington was founded in 1775. Tobacco farming started here in the 1770s, horse racing in 1787, and the Reverend Elijah Craig is often credited with inventing bourbon distilling in 1789 (though many rivals have also affixed stakes to that claim). Tobacco, whiskey and racehorses remained the staples of the economy for six generations, until 1956, when IBM built its typewriter plant in Lexington. The personal computer eventually outclassed the typewriter, and the big employer here became Lexmark International, an IBM spinoff. In 2016, it downsized 6 percent of its 2,300 local employees - now under the control of an Asian investor. Another mainstay is the Toyota plant in Georgetown, a town with early-19th-century houses and lush countryside just one county north of the city. This is the largest Toyota plant in the nation, with more than 7,500 workers and plans for additional expansion, including an engineering campus. In October 2015, Toyota began production of the first U.S.-assembled Lexus, with an additional 750 workers expected to produce 50,000 vehicles annually. The proposed Bluegrass natural gas pipeline in Franklin County has been halted by environmental protests and controversy over land rights.

Lexington, which includes all of Fayette County, grew by a sprightly 25 percent between 2000 and 2013, as its well-educated, young populace - it has the highest percentage of college graduates in the state and Scott County to the north has the youngest population - continued to attract business. Another 30 percent increase is projected by 2040. Lexington voters in 2014 elected construction executive Jim Gray to a second term as mayor. He unsuccessfully challenged Sen. Rand Paul in 2016, but Gray continues to lead the second-largest U.S. city (behind Seattle) with an openly gay chief executive. His sexual orientation has not been an issue in his campaigns. This is the second-largest metropolitan area in the state, after Louisville-Jefferson County. Fayette was the only other county in Kentucky that Hillary Clinton won in 2016.

The 6th Congressional District of Kentucky includes Lexington and the surrounding counties. Lexington casts about 40 percent of its votes. It is the only district in Kentucky that does not border another state. To the northwest is the state capital of Frankfort, platted during the War for Independence by Gen. James Wilkinson, who was also secretly a paid agent of the Spanish Crown and who worked to cede various portions of the United States, including Kentucky, to Spain. This was traditionally a swing area of the state. But Donald Trump carried the district with 55 percent of the vote and Mitt Romney took 56 percent in 2012, clear indications that the 6th has joined the GOP heartland.

★ LOUISIANA ★

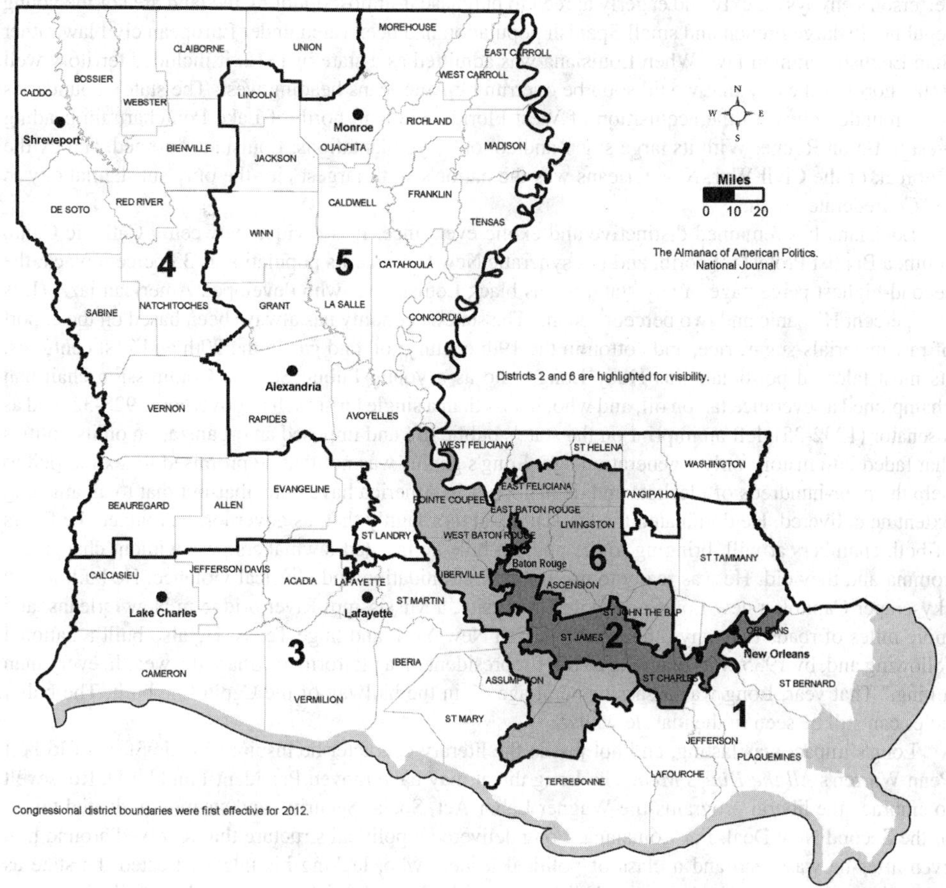
MOREHOUSE
CLAIBORNE
UNION
EAST CARROLL
BOSSIER
WEST CARROLL
CADDO
WEBSTER
LINCOLN
Monroe
RICHLAND
Shreveport
BIENVILLE
OUACHITA
MADISON
JACKSON
N
W
E
S
Miles
0 10 20
DE SOTO
RED RIVER
CALDWELL
FRANKLIN
TENSAS
WINN
4
5
CATAHOULA
The Almanac of American Politics.
National Journal
SABINE
NATCHITOCHES
GRANT
LA SALLE
CONCORDIA
Districts 2 and 6 are highlighted for visibility.
Alexandria
VERNON
RAPIDES
AVOYELLES
WEST FELICIANA
ST HELENA
WASHINGTON
EVANGELINE
EAST FELICIANA
TANGIPAHOA
BEAUREGARD
ALLEN
POINTE COUPEE
EAST BATON ROUGE
LIVINGSTON
WEST BATON ROUGE
ST LANDRY
6
ST TAMMANY
Baton Rouge
CALCASIEU
JEFFERSON DAVIS
ACADIA
LAFAYETTE
IBERVILLE
ASCENSION
ST MARTIN
Lake Charles
Lafayette
ST JOHN THE BAP
ST JAMES
2
ORLEANS
New Orleans
3
IBERIA
CAMERON
ASSUMPTION
ST CHARLES
ST BERNARD
VERMILION
ST MARY
1
JEFFERSON
PLAQUEMINES
LAFOURCHE
TERREBONNE
Congressional district boundaries were first effective for 2012.

In the decade between 2000 and 2010, Louisiana – ravaged repeatedly by hurricanes – was third to last of any state in population growth. But since 2010, Louisiana's population has increased by 3 percent, and by a striking 13 percent in Orleans Parish, home to Louisiana's singular, and singularly resilient, urban gem, New Orleans. The comeback hasn't been perfect, but at least it's a comeback.

Thomas Jefferson once wrote, "There is on the globe one single spot, the possessor of which is our natural and habitual enemy. It is New Orleans, through which the produce of three-eighths of our territory must pass to market." He was writing as Americans were streaming through the narrow gaps of the Appalachian chain, settling land drained by the fast-flowing Ohio and Mississippi rivers. In 1718, the French founded New Orleans on a ridge formed by deposits of silt and declared the Mississippi Valley the colony of Louisiana. It was transferred to Spain in 1763, and after France took possession again, Jefferson sought to buy the city in 1802. When Napoleon offered to sell the entire Louisiana Territory, Jefferson's envoys quickly and eagerly agreed to purchase it-almost doubling the land area of the young republic. Its large French and small Spanish population had been ruled under European civil law rather than English common law. When Louisiana was admitted as a state in 1812, it included territory well to the north of the city that would soon be overrun by Americans heading west. The state's boundaries were rounded out with the acquisition of West Florida, the land north of Lake Pontchartrain heading west to Baton Rouge. With its large sugar and cotton slave plantations, Louisiana boomed, and by the outbreak of the Civil War, New Orleans was the nation's sixth largest city-the only substantial city in the Confederate South.

Louisiana has remained distinctive and exotic ever since. It is divided between a Catholic Cajun south, a Baptist Protestant north, and idiosyncratic New Orleans. Its population is 33 percent black, the second-highest percentage of any state; it was black Louisianans who developed American jazz. (It is five percent Hispanic and two percent Asian.) The state's economy has always been based on the export of raw materials-sugar, rice, and cotton in the 19th century; oil and gas in the 20th and 21st centuries. Its most talented politician was Huey Long, who as a young Public Service Commission chairman championed a severance tax on oil, and who, in less than a single term each as governor (1928-32) and as a senator (1932-35), left an imprint on the state's public life and imposed an organization on its politics that faded into history only a generation ago. Long's genius was not that he promised to tax the rich to help the poor-hundreds of idealists and demagogues in America have done that-but that to an amazing extent he delivered. He dominated the legislature so thoroughly that, as governor, he roamed the floors of both chambers at will, bringing to the podium bills he insisted lawmakers pass without changing a comma-and they did. He was ready to use bribery, intimidation and physical violence. He built a new skyscraper Capitol, a new Louisiana State University, a Mississippi River bridge in New Orleans, and more miles of roads than any other state but rich New York and huge Texas. He also built a national following and, by 1935, was planning to run for president on a platform of "Share the wealth, every man a king." That year, Long was assassinated at age 42 in the hallway of the Capitol he built. The bullet holes can still be seen in the marble walls.

Long's impact was lasting, and not just in the literary character he inspired-Willie Stark of Robert Penn Warren's *All the King's Men*. The Long threat may have moved President Franklin D. Roosevelt to embrace the liberal programs-the Wagner Labor Act, Social Security, and steeply graduated taxes-of the Second New Deal. For Louisiana, Long delivered a political structure that revolved around him even after he was dead-and a class of political leaders who, lacking his talents, treated the state as Long's incompetent doctors had treated his fatal wound, leaving Louisiana with neither a fully developed economy nor a fully competent public sector. For 50 years, until Huey's son, Sen. Russell Long, retired in 1986, Longs and Long protégés held high political office in Louisiana and elections were run along pro- and anti-Long lines. The Long experience strengthened Louisiana's already strong predispositions-tolerance of corruption, disinterest in abstract reform, and a taste for colorful extremists regardless of their short-term means or long-term ends. This has persisted: In 2015, the website FiveThirtyEight tallied the number of public officials with federal corruption convictions in each state. On a per capita basis, Louisiana ranked first.

This has not helped to create a vibrant economy. Louisiana has chronically suffered low incomes, low workforce participation, and low levels of education, with income disparities greater than almost anywhere else in the United States. Louisiana has the nation's highest incarceration rate, the second-biggest gender pay gap in the nation and the fourth-lowest share of female legislators. Its median income is 19 percent below the national average, and its obesity rate – the highest in the nation – has grown from 22.6 percent in 2000 to 36.2 percent in 2015. New Orleans' elite class has been notoriously tight-knit, not venturesome. Louisiana momentarily prospered when oil prices spiked upwards in 1973 and 1979, but then jobs and people flowed out in the 1980s as it failed to develop a diverse economy similar to that of its similarly oil-rich neighbor, Texas. This has made a huge difference over time. Metro New Orleans in 1940 had a population of 564,000; it was about the same size then as metro Houston (610,000) and metro Dallas (624,000). But in 2004, just before Hurricane Katrina struck, metro Houston had 5.1 million people, metro Dallas 5.8 million, and New Orleans just 1.3 million.

Hurricane Katrina, the third deadliest in U.S. history and by far the costliest on record, slammed the Gulf Coast on August 29, 2005, and for several weeks, New Orleans and Louisiana dominated the national spotlight. More than 80 percent of the city was flooded, and hundreds of thousands of residents abandoned their homes for higher ground. All told, Katrina was responsible for some 1,800 deaths and at least $108 billion in property damage. New Orleans mostly withstood the initial winds and storm surge. But then the levees broke, submerging much of the city under water. The 17th Street Canal sprang a 200-foot gash through which much of the water flowed. Levees along the Industrial Canal, in the poverty-stricken 9th Ward, likewise failed to hold back water driven by a wave surge that reached over 20 feet. The Mississippi River Gulf Outlet, built by the Army Corps of Engineers as a shipping channel (though precious few ships ever used it), funneled waters and winds into St. Bernard Parish east of the city and the lowlands of New Orleans, devastating all in its wake. More than half of the 270 miles of federally constructed levees and flood walls in Louisiana were breached or heavily damaged by winds and flood waters. Katrina (with another powerful storm, Rita, less than a month later) also laid bare the state's political and economic frailties. Gov. Kathleen Blanco and Mayor Ray Nagin (who was convicted of bribery charges in 2014) seemed incapable of coping with the disaster.

By July 2006, Louisiana's population declined by 250,000 (mostly in the New Orleans area), although many people eventually returned, as did tourists. In April 2010, disaster struck Louisiana again when BP's Deepwater Horizon oil rig exploded, killing 11 workers and spewing an estimated 4 million barrels of oil into the Gulf of Mexico. The oil slick that spread from the drilling site southeast of the mouth of the Mississippi River to the Mississippi River Delta threatened the state's oyster beds and shrimp fisheries. Volunteers streamed in to tend oil-stained pelicans and herons, while repeated attempts to plug the leak failed until one approach was finally successful in early August; five years later, an estimated 20 species continued to struggle. The federal government imposed a six-month moratorium on offshore drilling, a serious economic setback for the state. In the first five years after the spill, BP spent $27 billion on the recovery, economic claims and fines. But offshore drilling, in operation since 1947, has long been a major part of Louisiana's economy and an estimated 20 percent of the state's jobs depend on it in some form. The resumption of offshore drilling in 2011 and the increasing use of fracking-the extraction of natural gas by hydraulic fracturing-in the Haynesville shale in northwest Louisiana touched off a recovery, with billion-dollar investments in refineries, gas-to-liquid facilities, and liquefied natural gas export terminals. Today, petroleum is the state's biggest industry, ahead of agriculture, chemicals, and processed foods. Unemployment in Louisiana followed an unusual track, peaking at only 8.3 percent in the fall of 2010, but since then improving more slowly than the national average. By late 2016, it was a point and a half above the national average.

Another disaster, a catastrophic flood, struck the Baton Rouge area in August 2016, with as much as 31 inches of rain in 15 hours; the American Red Cross said it ranked as the nation's worst natural disaster since Hurricane Sandy in 2012. The environment is almost certain to be a long-term problem for the state. Low-lying Louisiana is uniquely at risk from rising sea levels. Brett Anderson of the New Orleans *Times-Picayune* has written that if maps of the state rendered wetlands as water and counted only solid "walkable" ground as land, then the very shape of Louisiana-its iconic "boot"-would appear "as if it came out on the wrong side of a battle with a lawnmower's blades."

For more than a century after the Civil War, Louisiana was solidly Democratic, with political divides expressed in Democratic primaries. There were splits between the Cajun Catholic parishes, which cast about 30 percent of the state's votes, and Protestant parishes north of Baton Rouge, which cast about 45 percent. Another division was by income. Low-income voters of both races tended to support Huey Long and his populist successors; higher-income voters often opposed them. So for a long time, Louisiana politics were a struggle between reformist and conservative forces on one side and roguish populists on the other, a struggle waged in lavishly financed campaigns with grandiloquent rhetoric. For more than two decades the lead role in state politics was played by Edwin Edwards, a colorful Cajun populist who was elected governor in 1972 and 1975, sat out 1979 because he was ineligible to run, and then in 1983 won a third term. While in office, he faced corruption charges and was acquitted by a jury in 1986. He lost a bid for reelection in 1987 but ran again in 1991. In Louisiana's all-party system, he won 34 percent of the vote to 32 percent for David Duke, a white supremacist who had won a special election to the legislature as a Republican in 1989. Duke was repudiated by Republican National Committee Chairman Lee Atwater, President George H.W. Bush, and most Louisiana Republicans. Bumper stickers read, "Vote for the crook-it's important," and a majority of voters listened; Edwards won the runoff, 61%-39%. He was convicted on corruption charges in May 2000 and went to prison.

In the years since, Louisiana has become ever more Republican. It voted for Bill Clinton in 1992 and 1996 (the only deep-South state to do so), but has voted solidly Republican ever since. Democratic Sen. Mary Landrieu was elected to three terms starting in 1996, but never with more than 52 percent of the vote, and in 2014, she lost her seat to Republican Bill Cassidy. Republican Sen. David Vitter was elected in 2004 with 51 percent under Louisiana's system of multiparty primaries, and despite scandal in his personal life, was reelected 57%-38% in 2010. Republican Bobby Jindal, defeated for governor 52%-48% by Democrat Blanco in 2003, came back in 2007 and won the multiparty primary with 54% of the vote. The congressional delegation now has five Republicans and one Democrat; the legislature, Democratic since Reconstruction, changed hands as party switchers brought about Republican majorities in the state House in 2010 and the state Senate in 2011.

Jindal, a political wunderkind, came into the governorship as a policy wonk, but he governed more as ideologue than pragmatist. In 2008, he signed a law that, he acknowledged, allows teachers to "teach our kids about creationism." His administration stiffened Louisiana's regulations on abortion clinics, and he clashed with his own state schools superintendent, John White, over the fate of the Common Core school standards. Louisiana, with Jindal's support, had adopted Common Core in 2010, but amid rising national Republican opposition, Jindal became one of his party's most outspoken opponents. Most urgently, Louisiana on his watch was hammered by lower oil prices, which, combined with past tax cuts, meant that Jindal left office with a $943 million budget deficit for his final fiscal year and a projected $2 billion shortfall for 2016-2017. His approval ratings sank to the high 20s -- below even Obama's in the state – and he dropped out of the presidential race several weeks before the Iowa Caucuses. Perhaps most surprising of all, Jindal's rocky tenure enabled a relatively obscure Democrat, West Point graduate John Bel Edwards, to succeed him. Edwards defeated Vitter, the sitting senator, for the governorship by a 56%-44% margin, amid fatigue over Jindal and a re-litigation of Vitter's past scandals. In office, Edwards signed up roughly 400,000 people for Medicaid expansion under the Affordable Care Act, something Jindal had steadfastly refused to do.

In 2016, Donald Trump expanded upon Mitt Romney's 2012 victory in the state, widening the GOP margin from 18 points to 20, thanks to strong backing in rural areas. Trump won about 26,000 more votes than Romney, while Hillary Clinton won 29,000 fewer votes than Obama four years earlier. The Democrats won the same 10 parishes as they did in 2012. Clinton fared about 7,000 votes better in 69% minority Orleans Parish, while neighboring, 41% minority Jefferson Parish voted for Trump by 14 points, down from 18 in 2012. The two other highest-population parishes, East Baton Rouge and Caddo (Shreveport) went for Clinton by similar margins as they had for Obama in 2012. The other notable electoral result from 2016: Duke, the white supremacist, garnered only 3 percent of the primary vote for Vitter's open Senate seat, nowhere near enough to make the runoff.

Population		Race and Ethnicity		Income	
Total	4,625,253	White	59.5%	Median Income	$45,047 (44 out of 50)
Land area	43,204	Black	31.9%		
Pop/ sq mi	107.1	Latino	4.7%	Under $50,000	54.0%
Born in state	78.0%	Asian	1.7%	$50,000-$99,999	27.1%
Age Groups		Two races	1.5%	$100,000-$199,999	15.3%
Under 18	24.1%	Other	0.7%	$200,000 or more	3.5%
18-34	24.3%	**Education**		Poverty Rate	19.8%
35-64	38.3%	H.S grad or less	50.5%	**Health Insurance**	
Over 64	13.2%	Some college	26.9%	With health insurance coverage	84.5%
Work		College Degree, 4 yr	14.8%		
White Collar	32.4%	Post grad	7.7%	**Public Assistance**	
Sales and Service	43.1%	**Military**		Cash public assistance income	1.5%
Blue Collar	24.4%	Veteran	8.1%		
Government	15.5%	Active Duty	0.4%	Food stamp/SNAP benefits	16.3%

Voter Turnout			
2015 Total Citizens 18+	3,410,634	2016 Pres Turnout as % CVAP	59%
2016 Pres Votes	2,029,032	2012 Pres Turnout as % CVAP	61%

Legislature	
Senate:	14D, 25R
House:	42D, 61R, 2I

Presidential Politics

2016 Democratic Primary		
Hillary Clinton (D)	221,733	(71%)
Bernie Sanders (D)	72,276	(23%)
2016 Republican Primary		
Donald Trump (R)	124,854	(41%)
Ted Cruz (R)	113,968	(38%)
Marco Rubio (R)	33,813	(11%)
John Kasich (R)	19,359	(6%)

2016 Presidential Vote		
Donald Trump (R)	1,178,638	(58%)
Hillary Clinton (D)	780,154	(38%)
2012 Presidential Vote		
Mitt Romney (R)	1,152,262	(58%)
Barack Obama (D)	809,141	(41%)

Not many general election presidential campaign ads are going to be taped in Cajun any time soon. Louisiana voted for the Republican nominees by 57 percent, 59 percent, 58 percent and 58 percent in the past four presidential races. The vote in Donald Trump's victory over Hillary Clinton, who received 38 percent, was remarkably similar to the regional results in the state four years earlier when President Barack Obama defeated Mitt Romney: Clinton and Obama both won Orleans Parish with about 80 percent; the Democratic and Republican tickets were essentially tied in the Baton Rouge area, and the Republican nominee won the rest of the state with more than 62 percent of the vote.

Louisiana has rarely played a significant role in presidential primaries and caucuses, with one odd exception. That was 1996, when GOP allies of candidate Phil Gramm of Texas set up a pre-Iowa caucus in Louisiana on Feb. 6. The aim was to jump-start Gramm's campaign. Instead, the caucuses killed it. Only 65,000 Republicans showed up at 42 voting sites (compared with almost 100,000 at 2,000 sites later in Iowa), and conservative commentator Pat Buchanan won more votes than Gramm and took 13 of the 21 delegates. Gramm's candidacy never recovered and he left the race after a dismal fifth-place showing in the Iowa caucuses. In 2016, Trump narrowly defeated Cruz 41%-38% on March 5, but the fighting continued after the ballots were cast: Cruz managed to wrangle an extra 10 delegates in the post-primary selection. After his campaign was outmaneuvered, Trump threatened a lawsuit but never followed through. In the Democratic primary, Clinton trounced Vermont Sen. Bernie Sanders, 71%-23%. She carried 62 of the state's 64 parishes. Like many states in the south, Clinton's overwhelming support from African Americans gave her an advantage in Louisiana, where a majority of the of registered Democrats are black.

Congressional Districts

115th Congress Lineup	5R 1D	**114th Congress Lineup**	5R 1D

Following the 2002 redistricting in Louisiana, five of the seven districts elected House members from each party at some point in the elections from 2002 to 2010. Those politics have changed. The exodus from Louisiana after Hurricane Katrina led to the drop to six House seats after the 2010 census. As recently as 1980, the state had eight seats. Demographically, the 2nd District, centered in New Orleans, suffered the greatest population loss by far. Its black-majority district now extends to parts of Baton Rouge. The latest round of redistricting eliminated a district in Cajun country. With Republican population centers in the New Orleans suburbs, Baton Rouge, the Bayous, Shreveport and the northeast corner, creating a second Democratic or black-majority district would require creative gerrymandering, though breaking up the 2nd could create opportunities for them. The adjacent 4th and 5th Districts in northern Louisiana have 34 percent and 36 percent black population, respectively, which are widely dispersed in small cities and rural areas.

Governor

John Bel Edwards (D)

Elected 2015, term expires 2020, 1st term; b. Sep. 16, 1966, Amite, LA; United States Military Academy, B.S 1988; Louisiana State University Law School, J.D 1999; Roman Catholic; Married (Donna); 3 children.

Military Career: U.S Army, 1988-1996.

Elected Office: LA House, 2007-2015.

Professional Career: Attorney, Edwards & Associates.

Office: PO Box 94004, Baton Rouge, 70804-9004; 225-342-7015; Fax: 225-342-7099; Website: gov.louisiana.gov.

Election Results

Election	Name (Party)	Vote (%)
2015 Primary	John Bel Edwards (D)	444,061 (40%)
	David Vitter (R)	256,105 (23%)
	Scott Angelle (R)	214,907 (19%)
	Jay Dardenne (R)	166,553 (15%)
2015 Run off	John Bel Edwards (D)	646,860 (56%)
	David Vitter (R)	505,929 (44%)

John Bel Edwards, the scion of a law-enforcement and political family, leveraged dissatisfaction with outgoing Republican Gov. Bobby Jindal and his scandal-tarred Republican opponent, then-Sen. David Vitter, to win an upset victory in Louisiana's 2015 gubernatorial race. That enabled Edwards, a Democrat, to become the only Democrat to serve in statewide office in heavily Republican Louisiana, and the only Democratic governor in the Deep South.

Edwards was one of eight children who grew up in Amite, a town of roughly 4,000 residents located 48 miles northeast of Baton Rouge in Tangipahoa Parish. His great-grandfather was the parish sheriff, and his grandfather, Frank Edwards, was a state legislator. His father, Frank Edwards Jr., also served as sheriff, as well as an appointee of then-Gov. Edwin Edwards (no relation). Edwards Jr. was succeeded as sheriff by his son -- Edwards' brother, Daniel Edwards. Another brother, Frank Edwards III, serves as police chief of nearby Independence. The family had such deep political roots that it was inducted collectively into the Louisiana Political Hall of Fame. ("Bel" is his middle name – a family name going back generations – and in informal settings, he is often called "John Bel.")

In high school, Edwards captained the football team and was named class valedictorian. He attended West Point, graduating with a bachelor's degree in engineering, then served for eight years as an airborne ranger. He later earned his law degree from Louisiana State University and became an attorney in private practice in Amite, eschewing criminal cases because of his brother's service as sheriff. In 2007, Edwards was elected to the state House and became a member of its leadership; he served in the chamber until he was elected governor. In the House, Edwards served on the Education Committee, criticizing Jindal's emphasis on charter schools and Republican attacks on teacher tenure.

When Edwards decided to run for governor, he was far from well-known around the state – and he was a Democrat, a toxic label for recent statewide candidates in Louisiana. He gained some traction, though, by running against Jindal's record in office, including a projected $1.4 billion budget deficit and a seeming indifference to state issues while seeking the Republican presidential nomination. Edwards also pledged to raise the minimum wage and expand Medicaid under the Affordable Care Act, which Jindal had steadfastly refused to do. At the same time, Edwards blurred distinctions with Republicans on social issues, supporting gun rights and opposing abortion. (Edwards, a Catholic, ran an ad spotlighting how his family had ruled out an abortion after learning that their unborn daughter had spina bifida. She thrived and was married during Edwards' first year as governor.) In Louisiana's all-party primary, Edwards faced three prominent Republicans: Public Service Commissioner Scott Angelle; Lt. Gov. Jay Dardenne; and Vitter. "Experts roundly predicted Vitter would face Edwards in a classic right-versus-left runoff, drown him in money and trounce him on Election Day," journalists Jeremy Alford and Tyler Bridges wrote in *Louisiana Longshot*, a book about the campaign. "That, in fact, was the heart of Vitter's strategy from Day One." But Vitter was crippled by the resurrection of his 2007 prostitution scandal. Most observers had presumed that the escapade was settled business following Vitter's easy reelection to the Senate in 2010, but Dardenne and Angelle – his Republican rivals -- raised it as an issue, and it gained traction. On Election Day, Edwards, facing minimal Democratic opposition, took 40 percent of the vote, with Vitter barely qualifying for the Nov. 21 runoff with 23 percent. Angelle and Dardenne split the Republican anti-Vitter vote with 19 percent and 15 percent, respectively.

Edwards and his allies kept up the drumbeat on Vitter's past behavior – one ad bluntly compared "John Bel Edwards, who answered our country's call and served as a Ranger" to Vitter, "who answered a prostitute's call." Dardenne endorsed Edwards after the primary rather than back his fellow Republican. (After his victory, Edwards tapped Dardenne for a senior post in his administration.) Late attacks by Vitter on in-state resettlement of Syrian refugees may have moved the needle somewhat, but it was not enough. Edwards won the runoff, 56%-44% -- the biggest Democratic gubernatorial victory in the state since 1991's "Vote for the crook, it's important" race between the ethically challenged Edwin Edwards and white supremacist David Duke. In the 2015 runoff, Edwards was aided by relatively low turnout in Republican northern Louisiana and increased black turnout, noted Julia O'Donoghue in the New Orleans *Times-Picayune*. Vitter's defeat was so thorough that during his concession speech, he announced that he would not seek another term in the Senate.

Once in office, Edwards quickly fulfilled his promise to expand Medicaid. But he faced setbacks, too. By tradition, Louisiana's governor had long played a role in the selection of a House speaker, but in Edwards' case, most House Republicans, joined by one Democrat, rejected his pick for the post, Democrat Walt Leger, and instead chose a Republican, Taylor Barras – a sign, many observers said, that the state's once quirky political alignments were becoming increasingly polarized along national party lines. The speaker vote foreshadowed future sparring between the governor and the legislature over the budget, which was headed toward a $943 million deficit for fiscal 2016 and $2 billion for fiscal 2017, stemming partly from the slump in petroleum prices. In February 2016, Edwards took the unusual step of making a televised budget address, warning of drastic cuts to health care and higher education. "I don't say this to scare you," Edwards said. "But I am going to be honest with you. … No more tricks. No more smoke and mirrors." He proposed hiking the state sales and cigarette taxes; reallocating some of the BP oil spill settlement money; and drawing down the rainy day fund. But Edwards' efforts ran aground. In June 2016, the House Ways and Means Committee – chaired by Rep. Neil Abramson, the one Democrat to oppose Edwards' pick for speaker – narrowly blocked an Edwards-backed tax bill that would have reduced a state income tax break for federal income taxes paid. But Edwards won passage of a higher sales tax through 2018 and a higher cigarette tax.

Edwards faced other setbacks. After issuing an executive order protecting LGBT state employees, Edwards sparred with Republican Attorney General Jeff Landry over its implementation. Landry refused to sign dozens of legal contracts for the state as long as they contained the protections. In December 2016, Edwards' order was overturned in court. But Edwards won plaudits for his handling of two crises.

One was the racial strife in Baton Rouge, which was sparked by the police killing of Alton Sterling, an African-American man, continued with days of protests, and culminated almost two weeks later with the ambush murders of three law enforcement officers. (A few months earlier, Edwards had signed the nation's first "Blue Lives Matter" law, making the killings of police a hate crime.) Louisiana also suffered two rounds of floods – in the northern part of the state in March, and in the southern tier in August, the latter causing an estimated $8.7 billion in damage. In his handling of both episodes, Edwards "was a voice of calm and confidence," Louisiana State University professor Robert Mann wrote. After beginning his term with underwhelming approval ratings, Edwards expanded his popularity, often securing approval ratings in the low 60s as the year went on.

A "fiscal cliff" stemming from $1.4 billion in expiring tax changes, was set to hit on July 1, 2018. So in March 2017, Edwards made another tax proposal, based in part on recommendations of a blue-ribbon panel. He sought to reduce rates for sales, corporate and individual income taxes while eliminating specific tax breaks and extending the sales tax to products not currently covered by it. He also backed creation of a new tax on business sales. In April, a state House committee killed the core of his plan: a commercial activity tax.

Senior Senator

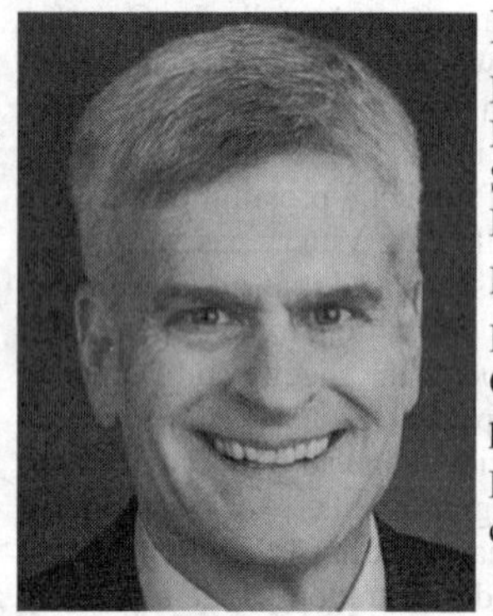

Bill Cassidy (R)

Elected 2014, term expires 2020, 1st term; b. Sep 28, 1957, Highland Park, IL; Louisiana State University, B.S., 1979; Louisiana State University Medical School, M.D., 1983; Christian - Non-Denominational; Married (Laura Layden Cassidy); 3 children.

Elected Office: LA Senate, 2006-2008; U.S. House, 2009-2015.

Professional Career: Physician; Co-founder, Greater Baton Rouge Community Clinic; Association Professor, LSU Medical School, 1990-present.

DC Office: 520 HSOB 20510, 202-224-5824, Fax: 202-224-9735, cassidy.senate.gov.

State Offices: Alexandria, 318-448-7176; Baton Rouge, 225-929-7711; Lafayette, 337-261-1400; Lake Charles, 337-277-5398; Metairie, 504-838-0130; Monroe, 318-324-2111; Shreveport, 318-798-3215.

Committees: *Energy & Natural Resources*: Energy, Public Lands, Forests & Mining, Water & Power. *Finance*: Energy, Natural Resources & Infrastructure, Health Care, Social Security, Pensions & Family Policy (Chmn). *Health, Education, Labor & Pensions*: Children & Families, Employment & Workplace Safety, Primary Health & Retirement Security. *Veterans' Affairs*.

Group Ratings

	ADA	ACLU	AFL-CIO	LCV	ITI	COC	HAFA	ACU	CFG	FRC
2016	-	17%	-	18%	80%	88%	50%	69%	57%	0%
2015	0%	C	14%	0%	C	79%	C	92%	79%	100%

Almanac Ratings 2015

	Economy	Social	Foreign	Composite
Liberal	13%	0%	9%	8%
Conservative	87%	100%	91%	92%

Key Votes of the 114th Congress

1. Keystone pipeline	Y	5. National Security Data	Y	9. Gun Sales Checks	N
2. Export-Import Bank	Y	6. Iran Nuclear Deal	Y	10. Sanctuary Cities	Y
3. Debt Ceiling Increase	N	7. Puerto Rico Debt	Y	11. Planned Parenthood	Y
4. Homeland Security $$	N	8. Loretta Lynch A.G	N	12. Trade deals	Y

Election Results

Election	Name (Party)	Vote (%)		Cand. Spent	Ind. Exp. Support	Ind. Exp. Oppose
2014 General	Bill Cassidy (R)	712,379	(56%)	$14,655,887	$2,345,107	$11,190,682
	Mary Landrieu (D)	561,210	(44%)	$19,969,352	$824,174	$12,479,854
2014 Primary	Mary Landrieu (D)	619,402	(42%)			
	Bill Cassidy (R)	603,084	(41%)			
	Rob Maness (R)	202,556	(14%)			

Prior winning percentages: House: 2012 (79%), 2010 (66%), 2008 (48%)

Smart and telegenic, if low-key by Louisiana standards, Republican Bill Cassidy underscored the state's political shift in recent decades to reliably red when he ousted three-term Democratic incumbent Mary Landrieu in 2014. Currently among three physicians in the Senate, Cassidy won his first term campaigning for repeal of the Affordable Care Act (ACA), while hammering at Landrieu for voting for the law. At the same time, Cassidy, who spent much of his medical career caring for the uninsured and underinsured, has been less hard line than many of his fellow congressional conservatives on the issue. As debate over repeal of "Obamacare" accelerated with the election of President Donald Trump, Cassidy voiced concern in early 2017 over a House Republican plan to replace the ACA after the Congressional Budget Office estimated it could sharply increase the number of Americans without health coverage. He also floated a proposal to allow states to opt to keep "Obamacare."

Once a Democrat, Cassidy has shown a willingness to work across the political aisle, notably on a measure signed into law at the end of 2016 that was hailed as the first major piece of mental health legislation in nearly a decade. A three-term House member before moving to the other side of the Capitol, he became Louisiana's senior senator in 2017 with the departure of GOP Sen. David Vitter. Formally William Morgan Cassidy, he was born in Highland Park, Ill., but grew up in Baton Rouge, the son of a life insurance salesman. He attended Louisiana State University as an undergraduate, and earned a degree from LSU's medical school. During a medical residency in Los Angeles, Cassidy met his wife, Laura, also a physician. The *New Orleans Times-Picayune* has described Laura Cassidy as his "most trusted political adviser." She founded Louisiana Key Academy, a public charter school specializing in children with dyslexic symptoms, after one of their daughters was diagnosed with dyslexia.

In 1990, Cassidy, a gastroenterologist, returned to Baton Rouge and joined the faculty of the LSU Medical School. He also began a nearly 25-year stint treating patients at LSU's Earl K. Long Hospital, part of Louisiana's charity hospital system devoted to the care of uninsured patients. (Laura Cassidy eventually rose to become chief of surgery at Earl K. Long. Cassidy continued working there on a part-time basis after his election to the House in 2008, until the facility closed in 2013.) He went on to co-found the Greater Baton Rouge Community Clinic, which provides free dental and health care to the working uninsured.

In a *Times-Picayune* profile published just prior to his election to the Senate, Cassidy said his own family struggled financially at times when he was growing up, citing that as a major reason he had focused on care of needier individuals rather than working in a more traditional private practice. "It is paying back all those that were nice to me and my family," he said. Several former colleagues at Earl K. Long expressed surprised at his strong opposition to Obamacare, and wondered privately if it was motivated by political expediency. Cassidy brushed aside such suggestions, saying that, after witnessing government-run health care up-close, he had come to the conclusion that the private insurance market is better equipped to provide medical coverage. "I believe my hospital system was one in which the government had all the power, not the patient," he said of his experience at Earl K. Long.

Cassidy had a defining moment when Hurricane Katrina hit in 2005. He created a makeshift field hospital with the help of several other physicians in an abandoned Kmart store. In a PBS documentary, he recalled entering the store after the storm to discover grease covering the floor, no electricity, and no working phone lines. In two days, he and the others transformed the space to be ready to receive patients. He later said the experience played a major role in his decision to run for office. "Katrina hit Louisiana and there was a sense that our leadership had failed. And then, as it turns out, leadership after the storm failed," he said.

In December 2006, Cassidy won a special election to the state Senate as a Republican, and was re-elected in 2007. Several years earlier, as a Democrat, he contributed financially to Landrieu's first re-election bid in 2002. Cassidy never sought office as a Democrat, and he is but one of a number of current Louisiana officeholders (including his junior colleague, Sen. John Kennedy) who switched parties as the once solidly Democratic state transformed into a Republican stronghold. Nonetheless, a couple of the bills Cassidy sponsored in the Louisiana legislature bore a resemblance to elements of Obamacare: One would have established a state-run health exchange, another would have required small businesses to offer insurance coverage for mental illness, alcoholism and drug abuse.

When GOP Rep. Richard Baker resigned his seat to head a Washington trade group, Cassidy passed up the opportunity to compete in the May 2008 special election. But after state Rep. Don Cazayoux narrowly defeated GOP social conservative Woody Jenkins, with a big boost from the Democratic Congressional Campaign Committee, Cassidy vowed to retake the 6th District for the Republicans in November. In that campaign, Cassidy described himself as a "pro-life, pro-gun-rights" social conservative, while highlighting his state Senate record of voting against spending bills and cutting taxes for businesses and for parents with children in private schools. Cazayoux ran an ad criticizing Cassidy for supporting creation of private savings accounts in the Social Security program. State Rep. Michael Jackson, who is African-American, ran as an independent, due in part to unhappiness over national Democrats' early support for Cazayoux in the special election.

Cassidy defeated Cazayoux, 48%-40%, with the rest going to Jackson. He twice coasted to reelection. In the House, Cassidy joined the GOP leadership's whip team. He was given a plum seat on the Energy and Commerce Committee, which has significant jurisdiction over health care, and was called upon to publicly criticize the Obama Administration on that issue. Saying that the government needed to get out of the way of patients, he supported providing incentives for preventive care along with creating health savings accounts. While a reliably conservative vote, Cassidy parted ways with the majority of his party on a few issues. In 2010, when the Democrats controlled the House, Cassidy was one of four Republicans on the Agriculture Committee to vote to end the ban on U.S. travel to Cuba and ease regulations on sale of agricultural exports to the island nation. He backed Democratic bills to extend unemployment benefits, and praised the Teach for America program that established a post-Katrina presence in Louisiana.

Cassidy's impressive re-election margins and his legislative work led Louisiana Republicans to deem him the most formidable potential challenger to Landrieu, the last remaining Senate Democrat from the Deep South. Landrieu had been elected in 1996 by a mere 5,000 votes out of more than 1.7 million cast, and survived re-election in 2002 and 2008 by winning with just 52 percent each time. Over the course of her career, Louisiana slipped politically and demographically away from the Democrats, accelerated by the departure of an estimated 125,000 Democratic voters after Katrina. Cassidy began holding public events in cities outside his district in January 2013, and formally jumped into the race a few months later.

Given aspects of his political past, Cassidy's candidacy initially aroused suspicions among conservative groups about whether he truly was one of them; the Senate Conservatives Fund endorsed tea party-aligned Rob Maness, a retired Air Force colonel. Cassidy responded by making some moves to the right. He repudiated earlier support of the Troubled Asset Relief Program created to prop up financial institutions in 2008, and accepted the backing of Americans for Prosperity, the conservative group affiliated with the Koch brothers, which spent more than $3 million on ads attacking Landrieu. Cassidy also disputed whether climate change was occurring, claiming during one debate -- inaccurately -- that "global temperatures have not risen in 15 years." By mid-2014, polls showed the race a dead heat. Cassidy had to deal with a distraction when he disclosed that his unmarried 17-year-old daughter was pregnant. Still, Landrieu drew just 42 percent of the vote in an eight candidate first-round election in November- short of the majority she needed to avoid a runoff in the Senate "jungle" primary system. Cassidy was just behind with 41 percent; Maness ran a distant third at 14 percent.

With the GOP having won enough seats in November to take over the Senate, the national import of the Landrieu-Cassidy December runoff was diminished. But with the chance to expand the new GOP majority's edge, conservative groups spent an estimated $5.65 million in ads on Cassidy's behalf. In a last-ditch attempt to keep her seat, Landrieu played up her status as the top Democrat on the Energy and Natural Resources Committee and worked to push through a vote on the controversial Keystone XL pipeline, which she ardently supported but which was opposed by most of her party. The measure fell short in the Senate by one vote. With Obama's approval rating in the state at just 39 percent, TV ads backing Cassidy "came down to four words: *Mary Landrieu, Barack Obama*," as Jason Berry, a New Orleans writer, put it. Cassidy rolled to an easy victory, 56%-44%, with exit polls showing only 18 percent of white voters backing Landrieu. His victory left Louisiana without a Democrat elected statewide for the first time since 1876. (That changed the following year, when the Democrats recaptured the governorship.)

Cassidy was named to the Appropriations Committee, along with the Health, Education, Labor and Pensions Committee and Veterans Affairs Committee; he relinquished the Appropriations slot in 2017 when given a coveted seat on the Finance Committee. As promised during the campaign, he was seated on the Energy and Natural Resources panel -- which Landrieu had chaired before her loss, and a politically vital panel for his state's energy resources.

Like the rest of his state's delegation, Cassidy has been an ardent advocate for the oil and gas industry in the House. He butted heads with a fellow Gulf Coast senator: Florida Democrat Bill Nelson, an ardent foe of offshore drilling. In 2016, Cassidy attached to an energy bill a provision increasing the revenues from offshore oil and gas drilling received by Louisiana and three other Gulf states. Nelson, contending Cassidy's proposal would intensify pressure for drilling off the Florida coast, invoked Senate procedures to block the bill. After a weeks-long standoff, Cassidy withdrew his revenue sharing provision; in return, Senate leaders promised him a separate vote on his plan. During the lame duck session in 2016, Cassidy's proposal was again blocked on a procedural vote, but he was optimistic as the Trump Administration took office. "...One thing we're telling folks is that...'President Trump can do a lot of this by executive order'," he told the Lafayette *Advertiser*.

Cassidy urged Senate Republicans to offer a viable alternative to the Affordable Care Act. "It's actually in our nation's interest for people to have insurance," he asserted, but said the law should be voluntary, utilizing tax credits and auto-enrollment with opt-outs. In June 2015, while awaiting a Supreme Court ruling on the legality of providing subsidies to help low- and middle-income residents of states that had not set up their own health insurance exchanges under the ACA, Cassidy floated legislation to convert the subsidies to grants to individuals and families to spend on health care and insurance. The bill did away with most of the ACA's mandates, while giving states flexibility in administering the grants. "It's not an American value to be told what to do by the federal government," Cassidy said in unveiling the measure. But the Supreme Court upheld the subsidies, removing any immediate pressure to move Cassidy's "Patient Freedom Act."

In early 2017, Cassidy, one of the more conservative Republican senators according to 2015 *Almanac* vote ratings, joined with one of the most moderate -- Susan Collins of Maine -- to introduce another version of the Patient Freedom Act. In an effort to appeal to both supporters and critics of Obama's signature legislative accomplishment, they proposed allowing states to decide whether to continue operating under the ACA. In late winter of 2017, as House Republican leaders began moving legislation to replace Obamacare, Cassidy was skeptical. In comments to *The New York Times,* Cassidy noted that Americans over 60 who earn a little too much to qualify for Medicaid would "have a hard time affording insurance" under the House plan, since insurance premiums would rise far higher than modest tax credits being proposed. When the Congressional Budget Office found the House plan could cause a 24 million increase over the next decade in the number of Americans without health insurance, Cassidy responded: "It's awful. It has to be a concern."

Perhaps Cassidy's major legislative achievement to date is the mental health legislation which was included in the 21st Century Cures Act signed by Obama in December 2016. The proposal, which Cassidy co-authored with liberal Democratic Sen. Chris Murphy of Connecticut, strengthened laws requiring parity for mental and physical health care, while providing grants to increase the limited supply of psychologists and psychiatrists across the country. A year earlier, Cassidy voted for the Every Student Succeeds Act after claiming victory in the fight by conservatives to roll back "Common Core" standards. "I campaigned to end federally mandated Common Core. This bill does that," he declared. But he also reached across the aisle to a couple of liberal Democrats. He joined with Democratic Sen. Tammy Baldwin of Wisconsin to push to allow states to evaluate which assessment tests could be eliminated without an adverse effect on education. And he teamed with Minnesota Democrat Al Franken to press for subsidies to low-income students who want to take Advanced Placement exams, and to help low-income schools add teachers who could provide instruction in accelerated courses.

Junior Senator

John Kennedy (R)

Elected 2016, term expires 2022, 1st term; b. Nov 21, 1951, Centreville, MS; Vanderbilt University (TN), B.A., 1973; University of Virginia School of Law, J.D., 1977; Oxford University (England); b.CL, 1979; Methodist; Married (Rebecca (Becky) Ann Stulb Kennedy); 1 child.

Elected Office: Secretary, LA Department of Revenue, 1996-1999; LA Treasurer, 1999-2016

Professional Career: Special Counsel and Cabinet Secretary, Governor Buddy Roemer, 1988-1992; Practicing attorney; Adjunct Professor, Louisiana State University.

DC Office: 383 RSOB 20510, 202-224-4623, Fax: 202-228-0447, kennedy.senate.gov.

State Offices: Alexandria, 318-445-2892; Lafayette, 337-269-5980; Monroe, 318-361-1489.

Committees: *Appropriations*: Commerce, Justice, Science & Related Agencies, Department of Homeland Security, DOL, HHS & Education & Related Agencies, Energy & Water Development, Legislative Branch. *Banking, Housing & Urban Affairs*: Economic Policy, Financial Institutions & Consumer Protection, Housing, Transportation & Community Development. *Budget*. *Judiciary*: Border Security & Immigration, Crime & Terrorism, Oversight, Agency Action, Federal Rights & Federal Courts, Privacy, Technology & the Law. *Small Business & Entrepreneurship*.

Election Results

Election	Name (Party)	Vote (%)	Cand. Spent	Ind. Exp. Support	Ind. Exp. Oppose
2016 General	John Kennedy (R)	536,191 (61%)	$8,886,736	$744,378	$733,207
	Foster Campbell (D)	347,816 (39%)	$8,258,670	$313,915	$978,864

For Republican John Kennedy, the third time was the charm. In 2016, he was elected as Louisiana's junior senator after two failed tries during the prior 12 years -- the first as a Democrat, the second as a Republican. Kennedy finally succeeded campaigning as a "Washington outsider," but he is hardly a newcomer to the political arena: His career as a high-ranking state official dates back almost three decades, including 16 years as Louisiana's elected treasurer. Educated at elite institutions, he has crafted a reputation as a folksy populist -- sometimes coming at it from the left, sometimes from the right, and, in 2016, from both sides. A frequent theme of his ads had Kennedy decrying "too many people at the top getting bailouts, too many people at the bottom getting handouts, and the rest of us in the middle getting stuck with the bill."

He may share the first and last name of another senator elected 70 years earlier who went on to occupy the White House, but not the same middle initial: Born John Neely Kennedy in Centreville, Miss., he grew up in Zachary in Louisiana's East Baton Rouge Parish. After graduating from Vanderbilt University with a triple degree in political science, philosophy and economics, he went on to earn two law degrees -- first from the University of Virginia and then from England's Oxford University. He has remained active in education in recent years as an adjunct professor at Louisiana State University's law school and as a volunteer substitute teacher in East Baton Rouge Parish.

Kennedy worked for a New Orleans law firm until he was named in 1988 as special counsel to Gov. Buddy Roemer, a former member of Congress elected as a reformer in the wake of second tenure of controversial Gov. Edwin Edwards. Kennedy remained with Roemer throughout the latter's four years in office -- adding the responsibilities of Cabinet secretary in 1990 -- and worked with the governor to win legislative approval of the state's first significant campaign finance regulations. "That absolutely changed Louisiana politics," he later told the *New Orleans Times-Picayune*, referring to putting an end to unlimited, unreported contributions.

As Roemer's attorney, Kennedy defended the governor's veto of a restrictive abortion bill that would have made the procedure illegal in cases of rape or incest. He has campaigned in recent years as an opponent of the Supreme Court decision in *Roe v. Wade*, and says he changed his mind on the issue prior to his first bid for Senate in 2004. Kennedy and his wife have a son, and he has said that becoming a father influenced his thinking. But such shifts on policy, as well as his party switch, have provided fodder for opponents -- notwithstanding that Kennedy is among a number of influential Louisiana politicians who have changed parties, as the onetime Democratic stronghold became a reliably red state in recent decades.

After losing his first election -- a race for state attorney general in 1991 -- Kennedy returned to private law practice until he was named secretary of the Louisiana Department of Revenue in 1996 by Gov. Mike Foster, a Republican. Kennedy, however, remained a Democrat, and in 1999 made the first of five successful runs for state treasurer, ousting the incumbent by 56%-44%. He was re-elected as a Democrat in 2003 with no opposition, but switched to the GOP in 2007 before winning a third term, again with no opponent. As treasurer, he was a bipartisan gadfly, criticizing the budget practices of the state's last three governors -- including two Democrats and a Republican. "Some politicians call me a troublemaker, a misfit, a rebel, a square peg in a round hole, because I'm not part of the club," Kennedy declared in announcing his 2016 Senate bid. "My job is to protect taxpayers, not seek the approval of my political peers."

Kennedy's first bid for Senate was as a Democrat, after Democratic Sen. John Breaux announced in December 2003 he would not seek re-election. On economic issues, Kennedy positioned himself to the left of his major Democratic rival, Rep. Chris John, in the state's "jungle" primary. Kennedy criticized the tax cuts enacted by President George W. Bush, while supporting an increase in the minimum wage. He did adopt socially conservative positions supporting gun rights and opposing same-sex marriage as well as abortion. In the first-round of voting in 2004, GOP Rep. David Vitter won 51 percent, avoiding a runoff and becoming Louisiana's first Republican senator in 120 years. John was second with 29 percent; Kennedy trailed with 15 percent.

By the time of Kennedy's next Senate bid in 2008, he was a Republican. His 2007 switch followed a political courtship by Vitter, aided by Bush's chief political strategist, Karl Rove. "For the past several years, it has increasingly been the case that those public servants who have embraced my ideas and my philosophy of trying new approaches are primarily Republicans," Kennedy told supporters in announcing the switch. But he also had grown increasingly at odds with his party over the previous four years, including public disagreements with Gov. Kathleen Blanco and other Democratic elected officials.

Sen. Mary Landrieu was regarded as the most vulnerable Senate Democrat up for re-election in 2008. Kennedy was not the first choice of national GOP strategists to take her on, but emerged after Rep. Richard Baker and Secretary of State Jay Dardenne declined to run. Landrieu outspent Kennedy by more than 2-1, while characterizing him as a "confused politician" whom she charged had mismanaged the treasurer's office. Kennedy stumbled in praising Oklahoma GOP Rep. Tom Coburn for blocking a farm disaster relief bill that Landrieu had pushed after hurricanes Gustav and Ike hit the state in 2008: The bill also was backed by such leading Louisiana Republicans as Vitter and Agriculture Commissioner Mike Strain. Landrieu picked up endorsements from GOP officials in the New Orleans area parishes of Jefferson and St. Tammany, as well as from former GOP Gov. David Treen, and defeated Kennedy, 52%-46%.

Kennedy remained secure in the treasurer's job, winning a fourth term in 2011 with no opposition and a fifth in 2015 with 80 percent of the vote. With Vitter running for governor that year, Kennedy moved to set himself up for a 2016 Senate race -- spending heavily to run TV commercials in his re-election campaign for treasurer, despite the absence of serious opposition. After his upset loss for governor to Democrat John Bel Edwards, Vitter announced he would not seek re-election to the Senate. Ultimately, 24 candidates filed in the primary for the open seat, with the leading Republican contenders including Kennedy and Reps. Charles Boustany and John Fleming. The latter, a founding member of the tea party-aligned House Freedom Caucus, had the backing of such national groups as the Senate Conservatives Fund and the Club for Growth.

But in a year in which two outsiders, Republican Donald Trump and Democrat Bernie Sanders, generated the greatest enthusiasm in the presidential race, Kennedy's populist appeal put him in an unusual position in a Senate race: frontrunner. "He's tapped into what we would call the zeitgeist," Pearson Cross, a political scientist with the University of Louisiana at Lafayette, told the *Times-Picayune*. While hailing Trump as a "change agent," Kennedy declared in one ad, "You can't fix stupid, but you can vote it out." He echoed Trump's hard line on both international trade agreements and President Barack Obama's signature health care law, beginning one commercial by bluntly declaring, "I mean no disrespect, but Obamacare sucks."

While strategists in both parties acknowledged the Louisiana race could be key in a year in which partisan control of the Senate was up for grabs, the contest received limited national attention until August -- when one candidate, former Ku Klux Klan leader David Duke, said he was "100 percent" behind Trump's agenda. As Trump initially bobbled a question about whether he disavowed Duke's support, Kennedy used the final televised debate before the first-round of voting in November to condemn Duke as a "a convicted liar and convicted felon," alluding to Duke's 2002 conviction on tax fraud. But Kennedy focused most of his attention on keeping his more serious Republican opponents, Boustany and Fleming, out of the runoff. Barred by law from transferring money raised for his state treasurer campaigns into his Senate campaign account, Kennedy instead donated $2.4 million to the ESAFund, a so-called "super PAC" that spent nearly $2 million on ads attacking the two House members.

In the first round of voting, Kennedy finished first with 25 percent, followed by Democrat Foster Campbell, a long-time member of the state's elected Public Service Commission supported by Edwards, with 18 percent. Boustany was third with 15 percent, followed by Democrat Caroline Fayard -- a New Orleans attorney supported by Landrieu -- with 13 percent, and Fleming with 11 percent. (Duke finished a distant seventh at 3 percent). Given Trump's 20-point win in Louisiana and the state's increasingly Republican complexion, Kennedy entered the second round as a clear favorite. But in the month before the Dec. 10 runoff, Campbell outraised him, $2.5 million to $1.6 million -- fueled by Democrats around the country stunned by Trump's upset victory and seeking to hit back. (With the Republicans assured of at least 51 seats as a result of the November election, the Louisiana seat was no longer crucial to control.)

Ironically, as Campbell benefited from donations from Democratic liberals outside the state, he emphasized his anti-abortion stance, attacking Kennedy for supporting abortion rights while a Democrat. "He's been a Democrat. He's been a Republican. John Kennedy's been everything but a Baptist preacher," Campbell declared to *Politico*. "John Kennedy's been what's best for John Kennedy." Kennedy sought to tie himself even more closely to Trump, as the president-elect made a campaign stop in Louisiana on Kennedy's behalf. He even borrowed some of Trump's more notable lines, declaring in one TV ad: "I've been with our new president from day one, because I believe we don't have time for political correctness anymore. And the swamp in Washington, D.C., has to be drained." In the Dec. 10 runoff, Kennedy overwhelmed Campbell, 61%-39%.

On Capitol Hill, Kennedy was assigned to the powerful Appropriations Committee (replacing his senior in-state colleague, Republican Bill Cassidy, who shifted to another powerful panel, the Finance Committee) as well as the Banking, Budget and Judiciary panels. Saying his most immediate goal was to secure more federal aid to Louisiana localities ravaged by 2016 flooding, Kennedy also vowed to focus on preventing flood insurance premiums from increasing and ensuring that local officials had a role in drawing future flood maps. After that, he said, his priority would be "jobs, jobs."

FIRST DISTRICT

Steve Scalise (R)

Elected 2008, 5th full term; b. Oct 06, 1965, New Orleans; Louisiana State University, B.S.; Louisiana State University, B.S., 1989; Catholic; Married (Jennifer Letulle Scalise); 2 children.

Elected Office: LA House, 1996-2007, LA Senate, 2008.

Professional Career: Systems engineer, Diamond Data Systems, eVenture Technologies.

DC Office: 2338 RHOB 20515, 202-225-3015, Fax: 202-226-0386, scalise.house.gov.

State Offices: Hammond, 985-340-2185; Houma, 985-879-2300; Mandeville, 985-893-9064; Metairie, 504-837-1259.

Committees: House Majority Whip. *Energy & Commerce*: Communications & Technology.

Group Ratings

	ADA	ACLU	AFL-CIO	LCV	ITI	COC	HAFA	ACU	CFG	FRC
2016	-	5%	-	3%	100%	93%	58%	88%	79%	100%
2015	0%	C	8%	0%	C	95%	C	79%	65%	92%

Almanac Ratings 2015

	Economy	Social	Foreign	Composite
Liberal	10%	5%	14%	10%
Conservative	90%	95%	86%	90%

Key Votes of the 114th Congress

1. Keystone Pipeline	Y	5. Puerto Rico Debt	Y	9. Offenses by Aliens	Y
2. Trade Deals	Y	6. Medical Marijuana	N	10. Troops in Iraq	N
3. Export-Import Bank	N	7. Sanctuary Cities	Y	11. Homeland Security $$	Y
4. Debt Ceiling Increase	Y	8. Armor-piercing Bullets	Y	12. Trade Adjustment aid	Y

Election Results

Election	Name (Party)	Vote (%)		Cand. Spent	Ind. Exp. Support	Ind. Exp. Oppose
2016 General	Steve Scalise (R)	243,645	(75%)	$2,456,943		
	Lee Ann Dugas (D)	41,840	(13%)			
	Danil Ezekiel Faust (D)	12,708	(4%)	$4,273		
	Howard Kearny (L)	9,405	(3%)			

Prior winning percentages: 2014 (78%), 2012 (67%), 2010 (79%), 2008 (66%), 2008 special (75%)

Republican Steve Scalise, who won a special election in 2008, vaulted to House majority whip six years later through a blend of staunch conservatism, Cajun charm and unexpected opportunity. As the third-ranking House Republican leader, and the top Southerner, he was at the center of conflicts and tensions within the GOP. In June 2017, he was critically wounded during a shooting rampage in Alexandria Virginia.

A native of New Orleans, Scalise grew up in Metairie. When his parents gave their son a battery-powered microphone, he played town crier on his neighborhood street, decorating his bicycle in red, white and blue and calling people to the polls — the start of a political career. He majored in computer science at Louisiana State University, where he was twice elected speaker of the student assembly. After college, he settled in Jefferson Parish as a systems engineer. In 1995, at age 30, he was elected to the state House, where he served 12 years before winning a state Senate seat in 2007. He pushed legislation to give incentives to the motion picture industry to produce films in Louisiana, and he helped pass a bill that made it the first state to bar cities from suing gun manufacturers for the actions of criminals. Scalise had considered running for the open seat in the 1st District in 1999 and 2004 but deferred to David Vitter and then to Bobby Jindal; those two were elected to statewide office and then departed public life, leaving Scalise as the last man standing.

In the special election to replace Jindal, the key contest was the Republican runoff between Scalise and state Rep. Tim Burns of St. Tammany. Burns cited Scalise's opposition to a bill banning smoking in restaurants and tried to tie him to special interests. Scalise called for limits on "out-of-control spending" and said he had "the experience to hit the ground running from Day One." Scalise won 58%-42%, capturing 83 percent of the Jefferson Parish vote. The final contest against Democrat Gilda Reed, a college instructor and political neophyte, was never in doubt in this lopsidedly Republican district. Scalise won 75%-23%.

When Scalise ran the following November for his first full term, he faced a bigger challenge. Democrat Jim Harlan, a venture capitalist, sank $1.8 million of his own money into the race and was not shy about throwing mud. In one television ad, he tried to tie Scalise to a local scandal involving a federal investigation of the abuse of tax credits by the Louisiana Institute of Film Technology; Scalise had sponsored the tax credit program in the legislature. Scalise cited his opponent's support of presidential candidate Barack Obama as evidence that Harlan was too liberal for the district. Scalise rolled to a 66%-34% win, taking 71 percent in Jefferson Parish and 68 percent in St. Tammany. Since then, he has coasted to reelection.

Scalise is an ardent Republican with a sharper rhetorical edge than any of his influential predecessors — Jindal, Vitter and former Appropriations Committee Chairman Bob Livingston. He railed against what he called Obama's "radical agenda." In 2009 he joined the powerful Energy and Commerce Committee, a useful assignment for this district. He called for more energy production, including offshore drilling. After the massive BP oil spill in the Gulf of Mexico in 2010, he shepherded colleagues to the region to see the disaster for themselves and was incensed by Obama's moratorium on offshore drilling, calling it "reckless." He later guided through the House and into law the 2012 RESTORE Act, which called for at least 80 percent of fines collected from BP and other parties to be sent directly to areas affected by the disaster, including some bayous and wetlands that he represents. A fierce skeptic of human-caused climate change, he succeeded in amending the House's fiscal 2012 agriculture appropriations bill to bar the Agriculture Department from implementing its climate protection plan.

Before joining the leadership, Scalise showed an occasional willingness to cross it. But he also paid his dues as a rank-and-file member. He opposed the 2011 compromise on raising the debt limit, and he joined most other Louisiana Republicans in refusing to support a relief bill for Hurricane Sandy in January 2013 because it didn't have offsetting cuts in spending. The House in September 2012 passed his bill allowing people to pay extra at tax time to help reduce the deficit. After joining like-minded conservatives in the 62 efforts to repeal or defund the Affordable Care Act, he was instrumental in passage of the January 2016 bill to eliminate the health care law and end government funding for Planned Parenthood. That bill was sent to Obama, who quickly vetoed it. And he joined 80 others in signing a 2013 letter that urged defunding in appropriations bills. Scalise earned some leadership chits as chief recruiter for the National Republican Congressional Committee for the 2012 election.

Scalise has been known for his sense of humor and he is friendly with many Democrats. He plays basketball with 2nd District Democrat Cedric Richmond, an old friend from their days in Baton Rouge, who became chairman of the Congressional Black Caucus in January 2017. After the House Appropriations Committee stripped out $17 million in Louisiana coastal restoration funds from the fiscal 2013 energy and water spending bill, Scalise and Richmond won bipartisan House approval of an amendment restoring $10 million. "Steve is an example of how things used to work in Congress," Republican Rep. Patrick McHenry of North Carolina, a close Scalise ally, told *The Times-Picayune*. "You'd battle it out and afterwards you can sit down and be friendly with one another."

When Ohio Republican Jim Jordan stepped down as chairman of the Republican Study Committee following the 2012 election, Georgia Republican Tom Graves won the endorsement of the group's founders and past chairmen and was set to take his place. But Scalise, who had been managing communications for the group, jumped in and demanded a more democratic method to choose the leader. "From the beginning, I felt like this ought to be a member-driven organization, and the members should decide who's the next chairman," he told *National Journal*. He touted his record of "getting things done," including enactment of his bill limiting the ability of a president to appoint "czars" without Senate approval. Scalise said he won the secret ballot "with votes to spare." That was a vital step in his move up the House GOP leadership ladder.

His next big step came in June 2014. Within hours of Virginia Republican Eric Cantor's shocking primary defeat, Scalise mobilized his bid to join the leadership. Kevin McCarthy of California, who had been whip, faced token opposition to replacing Cantor as majority leader. It helped that as RSC chairman, Scalise had a built-in base of support; it also helped that many Southern Republicans were anxious to see one of their own in a high-ranking post. Another benefit is that he and McCarthy had been friends since long before either was elected to Congress; that stemmed from McCarthy's national leadership of Young Republicans. Scalise left nothing to chance, lobbying many colleagues personally to eventually beat Illinois' Peter Roskam and Indiana's Marlin Stutzman for the job. "He's ... open and direct and he likes it when you're open and direct back to him," Rep. Kevin Brady of Texas, who later became chairman of the House Ways and Means Committee and with whom Scalise shared housing near the Capitol, told *The Times-Picayune*. "But he doesn't take stuff personally. He's friendly, engaging with everyone."

Yet, Scalise can be hard-nosed. When House Financial Services Committee Chairman Jeb Hensarling of Texas balked at passing a flood insurance bill in March 2014, an undaunted Scalise helped engineer enough GOP support for the measure to pass the House on a bipartisan basis — an accomplishment that became a tryout for the whip's job. "We had to build a coalition, and we had to overcome a lot of obstacles," he told *The Advocate* of Baton Rouge. For Scalise, it helped that he was well-versed on the program, which is vital to his district.

His abrupt entry into the leadership posed challenges. Both he and McCarthy lacked Cantor's legislative experience. At a personal level, Scalise had not been close to Speaker John Boehner. Plus, he needed to reassure the Southern base whose support was essential to his victory in the contest for whip. With the relatively limited congressional agenda for the remainder of Obama's presidency, Scalise passed his initial apprenticeship. He faced the challenge of managing the Freedom Caucus, which became the more activist off-shoot of the Republican Study Committee that Scalia had chaired.

The House Republican leadership team remained rocky, notably when Boehner resigned under pressure in October 2015. After McCarthy became the early front-runner to move up, Scalise quickly showed his intentions with a letter to House Republicans that he would seek to replace McCarthy. But that path grew complicated when Rep. Tom Price of Georgia announced his plan to run for majority leader, with the support of Rep. Paul Ryan and other influential Republicans. As it turned out, McCarthy lacked sufficient support to become Speaker, and Republicans eventually turned to Ryan. That left McCarthy in place, with no opportunity for Scalise or Price to move up the ladder.

Scalise faced an unexpected challenge in December 2014 when a Louisiana liberal blogger reported that Scalise had spoken to a group of white supremacists and neo-Nazis in 2002, six years before he was elected to Congress. After the story first broke and a storm of criticism, he expressed his regrets about the appearance and said he had been there to seek support for a tax proposal. He distanced himself from the local group, saying he "wholeheartedly condemned" its views; House GOP leaders as well as other Republicans backed him. A key — and credible — defender was his friend Richmond, the African-American colleague from New Orleans. As part of a damage-control effort, Scalise then spent months meeting with the Congressional Black Caucus and civil rights leaders. Other liberal groups seized on the opportunity to try to depict Republicans as racists. Scalise later called it "a painful time" and "the ugly side of politics," and told *Politico* that he would be "forever grateful" to Richmond for coming to his defense.

Not everyone welcomed Scalise's denials of decade-old connections to the supremacist group. Former Ku Klux Klan leader David Duke, who ran for the 1st District seat in 1999, called Scalise a "sell-out." Duke threatened to challenge him in the 2016 election, but backed off.

More than other congressional Republican leaders, Scalise was a consistent supporter of the presidential campaign of Donald Trump. After Trump took office and posed new challenges for congressional Republicans, Scalise's skills as whip would be crucial to the fate of the Republican program. With uncertainty surrounding how long Ryan would serve as Speaker, plus questions about the depth of Republican support for McCarthy and the departure of Price to become Secretary of Health and Human Services, Scalise seemed well-placed to move to the top of House Republican leadership. But his future was placed in question in June 2017, when he was shot during early-morning practice for the annual congressional baseball game by a Democratic partisan from Belleville Illinois who had posted social-media attacks on Trump and congressional Republicans. Scalise was rushed to a Washington hospital with internal wounds that his surgeon later said had left him at "imminent risk of death."

Following several surgeries, Scalise's condition slowly improved. But he faced the prospect of an extended recovery.

New Orleans Suburbs, Southeast Louisiana

Population		**Race and Ethnicity**		**Income**	
Total	784,820	White	73.2%	Median Income	$54,545 (189 out of 435)
Land area	4,030	Black	13.0%		
Pop/ sq mi	194.7	Latino	8.5%		
Born in state	73.7%	Asian	2.2%	Under $50,000	46.1%
		Two races	1.6%	$50,000-$99,999	29.9%
Age Groups		Other	1.3%	$100,000-$199,999	18.7%
Under 18	23.0%			$200,000 or more	5.4%
18-34	23.3%	**Education**		Poverty Rate	14.3%
35-64	39.6%	H.S grad or less	43.8%		
Over 64	14.2%	Some college	27.9%	**Health Insurance**	
		College Degree, 4 yr	18.4%	With health insurance coverage	86.1%
Work		Post grad	9.9%		
White Collar	35.6%				
Sales and Service	41.9%	**Military**		**Public Assistance**	
Blue Collar	22.5%	Veteran	7.7%	Cash public assistance income	1.1%
Government	12.9%	Active Duty	0.3%		
				Food stamp/SNAP benefits	11.3%

Voter Turnout			
2015 Total Citizens 18+	578,708	2016 House Turnout as % CVAP	56%
2016 House turnout	326,788	2014 House Turnout as % CVAP	42%

2012 Presidential Vote		
Mitt Romney	235,799	(71%)
Barack Obama	89,430	(27%)

2016 Presidential Vote		
Donald Trump	244,906	(69%)
Hillary Clinton	95,170	(27%)
Gary Johnson	9,742	(3%)

Cook Partisan Voting Index: R+24

Founded in 1718 and the nation's sixth-largest city at the outbreak of the Civil War, New Orleans is ancient for an American metropolis. It is still closely girded by the peculiar wilderness of the mushy Delta lands of the sluggish Mississippi River. For decades, you could climb a levee overlooking the Mississippi and see an expanse of water with untidy clumps of trees and disorganized-looking, seemingly abandoned docks - what Mark Twain had in his mind's eye while writing *Life on the Mississippi* in the 1870s. For decades, the river funneled the products of half a continent down to a single port with an international heritage and flair. The New Orleans metropolitan area has lived off that geography and history, with an inward-looking elite preoccupied with who is in which Mardi Gras krewe and interested more in the genealogy of old families than in the geography of the Oil Patch.

That mighty river and its Delta deepened the catastrophe after Hurricane Katrina struck with Category 3 force on Aug. 29, 2005, and devastated many of the area's subdivisions and streetscapes. The city's population plummeted, housing stock was destroyed, some levees were breached, and others were no longer reliable. The last act of nature to have wreaked so much damage on an American city was the San Francisco earthquake of 1906. In Plaquemines and St. Bernard parishes, many people fled the high winds and floodwaters. Some have returned. By 2015, the recovery of St. Bernard's population of 45,000 yielded a 27 percent increase since 2010.

Louisiana's southern coast experienced yet more turmoil with the man-made disaster known as the BP Deepwater Horizon oil spill. The rig exploded on April 20, 2010, and spewed more than 200 million gallons of crude oil into the Gulf of Mexico over three months. Shrimp fishermen, whose profits were already under pressure from aquaculture-raised Asian and Latin American shrimp, were idled as BP and the federal government struggled to seal off the underwater leak. Once the well was finally stemmed in July, the hardest part was yet to come: Cleaning up from the largest marine oil spill in U.S. history, one that caused extensive damage to wildlife and habitats, not to mention Louisiana's coastal economy. About 600 miles of shoreline were affected. Grand Isle, a large commercial fishing area, reopened in December 2014.

The Katrina and BP nightmares exacerbated an ongoing disaster in the Mississippi River Delta. Coastal erosion in the bayous has caused continuing losses in the wetlands, which some experts estimate is the size of a football field for every hour. For many in this swamp land, the ominous future may have been set by the small Native American community on the Isle de Jean Charles, where the land and population largely disappeared due to erosion and sediment mismanagement; in 2016, the federal Department of Housing and Urban Development spent $48 million to move the survivors to a new community on higher ground. If larger communities can be saved, that likely will require a massive coastal restoration that state officials planned to unveil in a new master plan in 2017. As *The Times Picayune* reported in October 2016, their plan envisions projects that will build wetlands and land, build and raise levee systems across the state, and raise or relocate homes and businesses that remain threatened by storm surges and rise in the sea level. The projected 50-year cost could exceed $50 billion. Some of that money would come from the $9 billion the state received from BP in settling litigation. The oil industry, too, has been forced to respond to the rising water. The rising coastline has placed at risk the huge and complex infrastructure of pipelines, refineries, tank farms and ports.

The 1st Congressional District of Louisiana stretches from suburban St. Tammany Parish north of New Orleans to Houma in Terrebonne Parish. The district takes in the vast suburb of Metairie in Jefferson Parish as well as part of western New Orleans. Metairie has remained an attractive place for new businesses, though it faced uncertainties from the unique mix of the local economy with its new and younger citizenry, plus depopulation. Most people in the 1st District live in Jefferson and St. Tammany parishes. Jefferson, which is split between the 1st and the 2nd districts, had almost 436,000 residents in 2015 - down 19,000 from 2000 - but it's still one of the state's most populous. Nearly 75 percent of the homes in St. Tammany were damaged by Katrina, but much of the parish, with the notable exception of Slidell, was spared from the worst effects.

The 14 percent African-American population in the 1st is the lowest of any Louisiana district, and the 9 percent Hispanic is the highest in the state. Even with its setbacks, this is a comfortable, well-educated and heavily Republican district. Donald Trump won 69 percent of the vote, a slight drip from the 71 percent that Mitt Romney received in the 2012 presidential election.

SECOND DISTRICT

Cedric Richmond (D)

Elected 2010, 4th term; b. Sep 13, 1973, New Orleans; Tulane School of Law (LA), J.D.; Morehouse College (GA), B.A.; Harvard University John F. Kennedy School of Government (MA), Att.; Baptist; Married (Raquel Greenup); 1 child.

Elected Office: LA House, 2000-2008.

Professional Career: Practicing attorney, 1998-2010.

DC Office: 420 CHOB 20515, 202-225-6636, Fax: 202-225-1988, richmond.house.gov.

State Offices: Baton Rouge, 225-636-5600; Gretna, 504-365-0390; New Orleans, 504-288-3777.

Committees: *Homeland Security*: Border & Maritime Security, Cybersecurity & Infrastructure Protection (RMM). *Judiciary*: Courts, Intellectual Property & Internet, Crime, Terrorism, Homeland Security & Investigations.

Group Ratings

	ADA	ACLU	AFL-CIO	LCV	ITI	COC	HAFA	ACU	CFG	FRC
2016	-	100%	-	92%	67%	69%	18%	0%	6%	0%
2015	90%	C	100%	80%	C	55%	C	4%	0%	0%

Almanac Ratings 2015

	Economy	Social	Foreign	Composite
Liberal	85%	100%	87%	91%
Conservative	15%	0%	13%	9%

Key Votes of the 114th Congress

1. Keystone Pipeline	Y	5. Puerto Rico Debt	N	9. Offenses by Aliens	N
2. Trade Deals	N	6. Medical Marijuana	Y	10. Troops in Iraq	N
3. Export-Import Bank	Y	7. Sanctuary Cities	N	11. Homeland Security $$	Y
4. Debt Ceiling Increase	Y	8. Armor-piercing Bullets	N	12. Trade Adjustment aid	Y

Election Results

Election	Name (Party)	Vote (%)		Cand. Spent	Ind. Exp. Support	Ind. Exp. Oppose
2016 General	Cedric Richmond (D)	198,289	(70%)	$1,030,187		
	Kip Holden (D)	57,125	(20%)	$42,425		
	Kenneth Cutno (D)	28,855	(10%)			

Prior winning percentages: 2014 (69%), 2012 (55%), 2010 (65%)

Democrat Cedric Richmond, elected in 2010, has formed tight alliances with key senior Congressional Black Caucus members and became chairman in 2017. As the only Democrat in the state delegation, he has worked successfully with Louisiana Republicans to obtain money for the state. He's also become known for his peerless pitching in the annual congressional charity baseball game.

Richmond grew up in eastern New Orleans. His father died when he was 7 years old, and he was raised by his mother, a public school teacher. In his youth, life revolved around an urban park where he loved to play sports and later, while in high school, coached teams of younger boys. He graduated from Atlanta's Morehouse College, the nation's only all-male historically black college, and returned to his hometown to earn a law degree from Tulane University.

Richmond was elected in 2000 at age 26 as the youngest member of the state House. He pushed initiatives such as a redevelopment tax credit for weather-damaged areas, funding for playgrounds, and a ban on certain types of semi-automatic rifles. Richmond ran for the New Orleans City Council in 2005, but was ejected from the race when a judge ruled that he falsified his qualifying papers by failing to meet the residency requirement.

He ran for Congress in 2008, when New Orleans was represented by scandal-plagued Rep. William Jefferson, a Democrat who had been stripped of his committee assignments after being indicted on federal corruption charges. Richmond was one of six Democrats in the contest, and the divided field split the anti-Jefferson vote. Finishing third, Richmond failed to qualify for the runoff. Republican Anh "Joseph" Cao then eked out a 50%-47% general election victory over Jefferson, who was subsequently sentenced to 13 years in jail for bribery.

Two years later, despite having established one of the most independent voting records among House Republicans, Cao was extremely vulnerable given the heavily Democratic makeup of the district. Richmond won the August 2010 primary over three other Democrats, taking 61 percent of the vote. On the campaign trail, he reminded voters of Cao's votes against stimulus legislation and the final version of the Affordable Care Act. His central message was that he would be a more dependable supporter of President Barack Obama's agenda than Cao. The Democratic Congressional Campaign Committee helped Richmond tap campaign funds, though Cao outspent him, \$2.1 million to \$1.1 million. Richmond won easily, 65%-33%. Cao held the challenger's vote down in Jefferson Parish, but got wiped out in Orleans.

In the House, Richmond has been a loyal Democrat, occasionally departing from the party line in deference to his state's needs. He joined the business-friendly New Democrat Coalition. He has worked extensively on curbing youth violence and has seats on the Judiciary and Homeland Security committees. In December 2015, he joined a bipartisan coalition at Judiciary that won approval of criminal justice reforms. In July 2016, Richmond filed with Republican Rep. Garrett Graves, whose district also includes parts of Baton Rouge, a bill to give additional tools to law enforcement in response to the kind of racial conflicts that the city faced.

He also is a friend of his Bayou State Republican colleague Steve Scalise, with whom he has worked on obtaining more disaster-recovery money and other issues. Scalise, now majority whip, said he would be "forever grateful" to Richmond for coming to his defense in December 2014 when a website raised questions about a speech that Scalise had given to a group of white supremacists in 2002. "I don't think Steve Scalise has a racist bone in his body," Richmond said.

When the House is in session, he has regularly had dinner with fellow black Democrats James Clyburn of South Carolina, the assistant minority leader, and Bennie Thompson of Mississippi, the Homeland Security Committee's top Democrat. With Clyburn, Richmond took on voter-mobilization responsibilities for House Democrats in the 2016 campaign. Richmond has been a star in the annual congressional baseball game - both as pitcher and hitter. Even Republicans have agreed that Richmond, who played at Morehouse, had become the "Babe Ruth" of the House. His GOP neighbor Scalise has been a leader of the Republican team.

Richmond had what initially seemed a competitive challenge for reelection in 2016 from East Baton Rouge Mayor Kip Holden, who had served 12 years and was term-limited. When Holden launched his candidacy, he said, "I won't be a Washington-down congressman; I'll be people up." But Holden spent only \$45,000 and he failed to run an active campaign. Richmond spent \$1.2 million and won handily, 70%-20%. He took nine of the 10 parishes, with 80 percent in Orleans and 75 percent in Holden's base of East Baton Rouge.

Following the election, Richmond defeated Democratic Rep. Yvette Clarke of New York to become chairman of the Congressional Black Caucus. When he took over, he passionately described his plans: "We will confront those who seek to divide. We will be clear about our demands on behalf of black people across the globe. …

We will be deliberate in our thoughts and actions and will engage on our own terms." He quickly followed up on that final goal when he voiced unhappiness with the plans of Minority Leader Nancy Pelosi to restructure the Democratic leadership. Some of her changes, Richmond wrote, "may have severe unintended consequences that could diminish [the CBC's] power as a caucus within the Democratic Caucus." His objections included her handling of the assistant leader position that has been held by Clyburn and her failure to adopt reforms suggested by many junior members.

New Orleans Metro, Parts of Baton Rouge

Population		**Race and Ethnicity**		**Income**	
Total	774,078	White	28.2%	Median Income	$36,603 (419 out of 435)
Land area	1,268	Black	61.6%	Under $50,000	61.8%
Pop/ sq mi	610.2	Latino	5.9%	$50,000-$99,999	24.0%
Born in state	79.0%	Asian	2.6%	$100,000-$199,999	11.9%
Age Groups		Two races	1.3%	$200,000 or more	2.4%
Under 18	23.2%	Other	0.4%	Poverty Rate	25.8%
18-34	26.1%	**Education**		**Health Insurance**	
35-64	38.8%	H.S grad or less	50.4%	With health insurance coverage	82.7%
Over 64	11.9%	Some college	27.6%	**Public Assistance**	
Work		College Degree, 4 yr	13.7%	Cash public assistance income	1.8%
White Collar	30.2%	Post grad	8.3%	Food stamp/SNAP benefits	22.4%
Sales and Service	46.5%	**Military**			
Blue Collar	23.3%	Veteran	6.4%		
Government	14.6%	Active Duty	0.2%		

Voter Turnout			
2015 Total Citizens 18+	569,742	2016 House Turnout as % CVAP	50%
2016 House turnout	284,269	2014 House Turnout as % CVAP	38%

2012 Presidential Vote		
Barack Obama	248,947	(76%)
Mitt Romney	74,987	(23%)

2016 Presidential Vote		
Hillary Clinton	247,491	(75%)
Donald Trump	73,779	(22%)

Cook Partisan Voting Index: D+25

Established by the French and ruled by the Spanish from 1763 for almost 40 years, New Orleans was a Creole city - part French, a bit Spanish, more than a touch Caribbean - when the American flag was raised over what is now Jackson Square in 1803. The statue of Andrew Jackson still seems an intrusion in a square set off by the French Market, the Cabildo, the Presbytere, the Pontalba apartments, and St. Louis Cathedral. New Orleans was one of the six largest American cities from 1820 until the Civil War and the only sizable city in the South. It was urbanized, yet poor, with yellow fever epidemics late in the 19th century, even as it was installing electric lights. It had a riot in which Italian immigrants were massacred, even as it was laying streetcar tracks and telephone lines. It also was one of the most corrupt American cities during Reconstruction and the Gilded Age, when its votes were regularly bid for and bought. Like other Southern cities, it became rigidly segregated after 1890.

For a time during the 1970s oil boom, New Orleans seemed to be a fast-growing Sun Belt city. It suffered economically through the 1980s, when it lost substantial port business - oil to Houston and Latin American trade to Miami. By the 1990s, New Orleans was humming again. Crime rates fell and no longer depressed tourism. Incomes went up, and home ownership increased, among African Americans as well as whites. The downtown Superdome was the friendly host of the August 1988 Republican convention.

Then, Hurricane Katrina made landfall early on a Monday morning, Aug. 29, 2005. A nightmarish scene unfolded at the Superdome, the shelter of last resort for more than 20,000 people, many of whom had fled the rising water without food, water or medicine. Conditions worsened when the storm ripped two holes in the roof. A few days later, city officials began to load people on buses for transport to cities better positioned to provide services. The breach of the city's levees led to a surge that churned through the low-income 9th Ward, while the French Quarter, on higher ground, was largely untouched by the floodwaters. Still, 80 percent of New Orleans flooded.

New Orleans was in for a very long recovery. Thousands of government trailers became semi-permanent homes. City residents who had fled the floodwaters only slowly trickled back. It took years to restore regular utility service. Expectations repeatedly were downsized. Then in 2008, the last government trailer parks closed, and the restaurants in the French Quarter were back in business. By

2014, the city's population was 390,000, 15 percent less than in 2000, but more than 80 percent larger than in 2006, indicating an impressive recovery from the storm in many - but not all - parts of the city. Post-recession wages and median household income in the city and suburbs were also on the rise. Still, New Orleans was a relatively poor city before the hurricane and remains so.

The city's post-hurricane recovery and transition suffered when a second disaster struck in April 2010. BP's Deepwater Horizon offshore rig exploded and spewed oil into the Gulf of Mexico at an estimated rate of 60,000 barrels a day. Despite efforts to contain it, the oil slick spread from the drilling site southeast of the mouth of the Mississippi River to the Mississippi River Delta, posing a major threat to the area's oyster beds and fisheries. A federally mandated moratorium on offshore drilling was lifted in October 2010 under pressure from local and state officials and the Louisiana congressional delegation. The fragile regional economy took another serious blow when the 5,000 jobs at the Avondale shipyard in 2010 were all but eliminated. Avondale remained idle and for sale. In December 2016, the *New Orleans Advocate* reported stirrings of hope that some use could be found in an "extensive master planning process" by the Port of New Orleans.

With its unique character and characters, New Orleans remains a popular tourist destination. In the French Quarter - the *Vieux Carré* as it was originally called - are the 19th-century row houses decked out in their island pastels and ornate wrought-iron railings. At street level are restaurants, art galleries, and jazz and blues clubs, and the narrow sidewalks fill up nightly with diners, revelers, and patrons of the tiny voodoo establishments found only in New Orleans. Its storied restaurants serve a cuisine all New Orleans' own - spicy, rich and unaffected by trends in low-fat food.

Upriver from the Quarter is the Central Business District, with its skyscrapers and the Superdome, and the Garden District, with the graceful intact homes of the rich early American settlers lining St. Charles Avenue. A total of 9.8 million tourists visited New Orleans in 2015 and they spent a record-breaking $7 billion. A 2013 University of New Orleans study found that job losses in construction and manufacturing had been offset by gains in educational services, leisure and hospitality. Much to the relief of locals, when Hurricane Isaac hit the Gulf Coast in August 2012, the city's revamped $14.5 billion flood control system worked. Still, amid the optimism, elements of the pre-Katrina reality remained: 27 percent of the city lived in poverty and the city had the second-worst inequality in the nation, Bloomberg News determined.

The 2nd Congressional District of Louisiana includes much of the city of New Orleans. It contains nearly half of Jefferson Parish, most of Orleans Parish, and all or part of eight other parishes between New Orleans and Baton Rouge. More than 100,000 residents in largely black neighborhoods on Baton Rouge's north side were added in the 2012 redistricting to make up for the downsizing in New Orleans. Most of the voters reside in the New Orleans area, and nearly half of them are in Orleans Parish. By including most of the heavily black precincts in south Louisiana, the 2nd is 63 percent African American and one of the most Democratic districts in the South.

THIRD DISTRICT

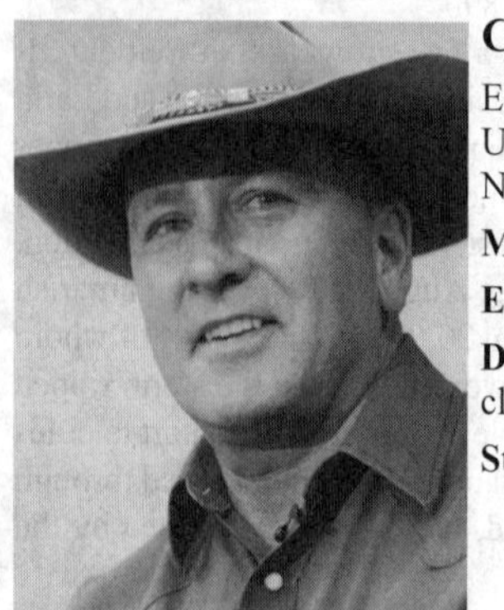

Clay Higgins (R)

Elected 2016, 1st term; b. Aug 24, 1961, New Orleans; Louisiana State University, Att., 1983; Louisiana State University, Att., 1990; Christian - Non-Denominational; Married (Becca Higgins); 4 children (1 deceased).

Military Career: U.S Army Military Police Corps, 1983-1989.

Elected Office: Sheriff, St. Landry Parish, 2008-2016.

DC Office: 1711 LHOB 20515, 202-225-2031, Fax: 202-225-5724, clayhiggins.house.gov.

State Offices: Lafayette, 337-703-6105; Lake Charles, 337-656-2833.

Committees: *Homeland Security*: Oversight & Management Efficiency, Transportation & Protective Security. *Science, Space & Technology*: Environment, Oversight, Space. *Veterans' Affairs*: Health.

Key Votes of the 114th Congress

1. Keystone Pipeline	N	5. Puerto Rico Debt	N	9. Offenses by Aliens	N
2. Trade Deals	N	6. Medical Marijuana	N	10. Troops in Iraq	N
3. Export-Import Bank	N	7. Sanctuary Cities	N	11. Homeland Security $$	N
4. Debt Ceiling Increase	N	8. Armor-piercing Bullets	N	12. Trade Adjustment aid	N

Election Results

Election	Name (Party)	Vote	(%)	Cand. Spent	Ind. Exp. Support	Ind. Exp. Oppose
2016 General	Clay Higgins (R)	77,671	(56%)	$376,659	$34,660	$320,561
	Scott Angelle (R)	60,762	(44%)	$1,739,236	$32,114	$350,681
2016 Primary	Scott Angelle (R)	91,532	(29%)			
	Clay Higgins (R)	84,912	(27%)			
	Dorian Phibian (D)	28,385	(9%)			
	Larry Rader (D)	27,830	(9%)			
	Gus Rantz (R)	25,662	(8%)			
	Greg Ellison (R)	24,882	(8%)			
	Brett Geymann (R)	21,607	(7%)			

Republican Clay Higgins, a political newcomer, unexpectedly won the open seat against a veteran state elected official. Running with elements of Donald Trump's outsider and outspoken appeal but with a modest campaign fund, Higgins - a former captain and spokesman for the St. Landry Parish sheriff's office - ran as an anti-politician and was among the most unlikely winners in the 2016 campaign.

Higgins attended Louisiana State University and had several jobs, including as a police officer and manager of an automobile dealer. His personal life had some sketchy details, including an ex-wife claiming that Higgins owed more than $100,000 in child support. Before his run for Congress, he had gained local attention with "Crime Stopper" videos that he narrated. In a May 2015 profile, *The Washington Post* described him as a "muscled Army veteran and hardened street cop who rarely cracks a smile [who might be] the most irresistibly intimidating man in America." Known as the "Cajun John Wayne," his authentic style with a touch of empathy gained something of a cult following in the bayous and on YouTube. Higgins resigned from the sheriff's office in February 2016, citing an unspecified "matter of principle" that apparently related to an order that he was unwilling to follow. That led to calls for him to run for Congress.

When six-term Rep. Charles Boustany gave up this seat to run for the Senate, there was a wide-open field and no frontrunner. The 12 candidates included eight Republicans and two Democrats. National Democrats paid little attention to the contest in this heavily Republican area. The best-known Republican was Scott Angelle, the chairman of the state Public Service Commission. Angelle had switched parties after he discovered the challenge of running statewide as a Democrat in Louisiana. In 2015, he finished third in the nine-candidate contest for governor, and ran especially well in the Cajun country where he was a native. But Angelle subsequently alienated many Republicans in the bitter contest when he refused to endorse Republican Sen. David Vitter, who lost to Democrat John Bel Edwards in the runoff.

In the nonpartisan Nov. 8 House election, Angelle led Higgins, 29%-27%. Angelle had a big lead in St. Charles, Higgins ran well in the rural areas, and they split Lafayette. In the runoff, which was required because no candidate had won 50 percent of the vote, Angelle highlighted his endorsement by the National Rifle Association and the Louisiana Sheriffs Association. A super PAC organized by friends of Higgins used the slogan, "Make Louisiana Great Again," which was a tweak of Trump's appeal. That group aired an ad that attacked Angelle as a Democrat and a crook; it was produced by a consulting firm that had worked for Vitter. Angelle denied the charges. But with Higgins's background in "reality TV," the facts occasionally were muddled. Angelle spent $1.8 million to $380,000 for Higgins. Outside groups spent about $500,000 in the contest.

Higgins won the runoff, 56%-44%, with local results that were similar to the first round of voting. In the House, he won seats on the Homeland Security, Veterans' Affairs, and Science, Space and Technology committees.

Southwest Louisiana: Lafayette, Lake Charles

Population		**Race and Ethnicity**		**Income**	
Total	770,817	White	68.2%	Median Income	$46,157 (323 out of 435)
Land area	6,983	Black	24.4%		
Pop/ sq mi	110.4	Latino	3.5%		
Born in state	82.7%	Asian	1.4%	Under $50,000	53.1%
Age Groups		Two races	1.9%	$50,000-$99,999	27.4%
Under 18	25.2%	Other	0.4%	$100,000-$199,999	15.8%
18-34	24.0%	**Education**		$200,000 or more	3.8%
35-64	38.1%	H.S grad or less	54.3%	Poverty Rate	17.9%
Over 64	12.7%	Some college	25.9%	**Health Insurance**	
Work		College Degree, 4 yr	13.9%	With health insurance coverage	84.6%
White Collar	30.3%	Post grad	5.9%		
Sales and Service	42.9%	**Military**		**Public Assistance**	
Blue Collar	26.9%	Veteran	7.9%	Cash public assistance income	1.2%
Government	13.1%	Active Duty	0.1%	Food stamp/SNAP benefits	15.4%

Voter Turnout			
2015 Total Citizens 18+	562,683	2016 House Turnout as % CVAP	57%
2016 House turnout	320,454	2014 House Turnout as % CVAP	42%

2012 Presidential Vote		
Mitt Romney	220,490	(66%)
Barack Obama	107,613	(32%)

2016 Presidential Vote		
Donald Trump	231,017	(67%)
Hillary Clinton	100,241	(29%)

Cook Partisan Voting Index: R+20

More than 200 years ago, French-speaking settlers in Canada were forced to leave their land of Acadie, which the British had taken over and renamed Nova Scotia. They made their way to the wetlands of southern Louisiana, called Acadiana. Here, without much notice, they built steep-roofed houses to slough off nonexistent snow and adapted French cuisine to the crawfish and muskrats they found in abundance in the pelican-tended swamps. They are the Cajuns, and the heart of their adopted homeland is around Lafayette, just west of the Atchafalaya Basin, where Mississippi River waters pour through bayous and canals. An 18-mile section of Interstate 10 was built here on elevated stilts. Cajun country has thrived, thanks to the oil and gas that are plentiful on land and just offshore in the Gulf of Mexico. Oil rigs are common, and every once in a while, the swampy foliage parts to reveal a giant refinery or petrochemical plant.

Cajun French has survived decades of efforts to eliminate it. Cajun music - and its black-influenced variant, zydeco - are popular here and nationally; spicy Cajun cooking attracts food lovers, who learn its secrets and then carry them home, in understated form. It's estimated that as many as 200,000 Louisianans speak French as a second language. Lafayette, with its Acadian Village and plethora of oil exploration firms, features an annual *Festivals Acadiens* to celebrate music, food and crafts. Mardi Gras is not just a great party but great for local business - it contributes an estimated $110 million annually to the economy in Lafayette Parish.

In 2005, Hurricane Rita, not Katrina, was the natural disaster with the most devastating local impact. With winds of 120 miles per hour and a storm surge of 15 feet, Rita left a path of destruction 200 miles west of New Orleans. It virtually erased some coastal communities, especially in Cameron Parish. While the nation was spellbound by every development in New Orleans, local residents complained that they were victims of "Rita amnesia." In 2014, three high-tech companies moved to Lafayette, each with hundreds of jobs. But the state-funded Louisiana Immersive Technology Enterprise struggled financially. In December 2016, the University of Louisiana at Lafayette became the manager of the $27 million center, with plans to take control of the facility. Unemployment in Lafayette rose above 6 percent as the low price of oil caused a loss of jobs. West of Lafayette, the economy in Lake Charles was stronger in 2016, with job growth in petrochemicals and engineering. About one-fourth of the residents in each city are black.

The 3rd Congressional District was enlarged during 2011 redistricting, when Louisiana lost a House seat, and it absorbed much of what had been a second district in the bayous. The 3rd covers the southern coast from the Texas border east to St. Mary County, plus much of Cajun country. The population centers are Lafayette Parish and Lake Charles-based Calcasieu Parish, which have about 30 percent and 25 percent of the district's population, respectively. The 3rd District remains very conservative. Donald Trump won 67 percent of the vote, one point and three points more than the Republican presidential nominees took in 2012 and 2008.

FOURTH DISTRICT

Mike Johnson (R)

Elected 2016, 1st term; b. Jan 30, 1972, Shreveport; Louisiana State University, B.S., 1995; Louisiana State University Law School, J.D., 1998; Southern Baptist; Married (Kelly Lary Johnson); 4 children.

Elected Office: LA House, 2015-2016.

Professional Career: Practicing attorney; Talk radio host/columnist.

DC Office: 327 CHOB 20515, 202-225-2777, Fax: 202-225-8039, mikejohnson.house.gov.

State Offices: Bossier City, 318-840-0309; Leesville, 337-392-3146; Natchitoches, 318-357-5731.

Committees: *Judiciary*: Crime, Terrorism, Homeland Security & Investigations, Immigration & Border Security. *Natural Resources*: Oversight & Investigations, Water, Power & Oceans.

Election Results

Election	Name (Party)	Vote	(%)	Cand. Spent	Ind. Exp. Support	Ind. Exp. Oppose
2016 General	Mike Johnson (R).........................	87,370	(65%)	$885,169	$239,824	$132,000
	Trey Baucum (R).........................	46,579	(35%)	$774,059	$12,816	
2016 Primary	Marshall Jones (D).........................	80,593	(28%)			
	Mike Johnson (R).........................	70,580	(25%)			
	Trey Baucum (R).........................	50,412	(18%)			
	Oliver Jenkins (R).........................	44,521	(16%)			
	Elbert Guillory (R).........................	21,017	(7%)			

Republican Mike Johnson was elected in 2016 to an open seat after he led the competitive GOP field in the November vote. Johnson swept the relatively amicable runoff a month later against Democrat Marshall Jones, who largely disavowed his party. "I guess I wasn't able to distinguish myself from the national Democratic party," Jones said following his defeat. In the runoff, each candidate was pro-guns and opposed to abortion. Johnson made his mark in the state House as a social conservative, including support for school prayer and opposition to gay marriage.

Johnson is a native of Shreveport. His father, a local firefighter, was critically burned and disabled in the line of duty. Johnson got his bachelor's in business administration and a law degree at Louisiana State University. In his private practice, he advocated conservative constitutional principles.

He was elected to the state House in 2015, where he had a record as a strong social and economic conservative. He enacted a bill that prohibited a "dismemberment" procedure for second-trimester abortions. He also was the chief sponsor of a religious freedom proposal that would have prohibited local governments from imposing fines or revoking tax benefits from a business based on its owner's views on marriage; his measure was supported by the conservative Family Research Council. An executive of IBM, which was planning to build a technology services center in Baton Rouge that would employ 800 persons, said, "IBM will find it much harder to attract talent to Louisiana if this bill is passed." Johnson criticized IBM and its allies in the Legislature for what he termed their name-calling and added, "Well-intentioned people with different ideologies can still reason together respectfully." In April 2015, a House committee defeated Johnson's bill. But Gov. Bobby Jindal then issued an executive order with similar provisions. Following the 2015 legislative session, Johnson was named an "MVP for Business" by the Louisiana Association of Business and Industry, and "Outstanding Family Advocate" by the Louisiana Family Forum

When Republican Rep. John Fleming ran for the Senate, the contest for his House seat was wide-open on the Republican side. In addition to Johnson, the leading GOP contenders were Johnson, Shreveport cardiologist Trey Baucum and Shreveport City Council member Oliver Jenkins. An Associated Press report on the eve of the November election described the contest as "something of an anomaly, a race that's almost downright genteel." In the first round of voting, Johnson got 25 percent of the total vote; Bracum and Jenkins trailed with 18 and 16 percent. Johnson led the Republican field in 11 of the 15 parishes, including the population centers of Shreveport-based Caddo and Bossier. Elbert Guillory, an African-American Republican from outside of Shreveport, got 7 percent. Democrat Jones was the frontrunner with 28 percent. In the runoff, Johnson consolidated the Republican vote, while Jones had little upside. Johnson won that contest, 65%-35%. The only parish that was close was Caddo, where Johnson took 52 percent of the vote. In his fundraising, Johnson out-paced Jones, $937,000 to $444,000. The three other principal Republicans averaged about $900,000 each.

In the House, Johnson got seats on the Judiciary and Natural Resources committees

Northwest Louisiana: Shreveport, Bossier City

Population		**Race and Ethnicity**		**Income**	
Total	761,080	White	59.0%	Median Income	$41,345 (383 out of 435)
Land area	12,435	Black	33.6%		
Pop/ sq mi	61.2	Latino	3.7%		
Born in state	74.0%	Asian	0.9%	Under $50,000	57.4%
		Two races	1.7%	$50,000-$99,999	26.5%
Age Groups		Other	1.1%	$100,000-$199,999	13.3%
Under 18	24.6%			$200,000 or more	2.7%
18-34	23.6%	**Education**		Poverty Rate	21.1%
35-64	37.5%	H.S grad or less	52.4%		
Over 64	14.3%	Some college	28.2%	**Health Insurance**	
		College Degree, 4 yr	12.7%	With health insurance coverage	84.6%
Work		Post grad	6.8%		
White Collar	30.8%				
Sales and Service	42.8%	**Military**		**Public Assistance**	
Blue Collar	26.5%	Veteran	10.6%	Cash public assistance income	1.9%
Government	18.4%	Active Duty	1.7%		
				Food stamp/SNAP benefits	17.0%

Voter Turnout			
2015 Total Citizens 18+	564,026	2016 House Turnout as % CVAP	51%
2016 House turnout	285,985	2014 House Turnout as % CVAP	37%

2012 Presidential Vote		
Mitt Romney	191,417	(59%)
Barack Obama	128,659	(40%)

2016 Presidential Vote		
Donald Trump	192,977	(61%)
Hillary Clinton	116,599	(37%)

Cook Partisan Voting Index: R+13

Northwestern Louisiana, south of Little Rock and east of Dallas, is part of the Deep South. Unlike in New Orleans, most people here are Protestants, not Catholics. They are often tradition-minded, with names that are English or Scottish, not French. The tone is set not by wide-open Bourbon Street but by smaller Shreveport, which could be just another East Texas oil-patch town, albeit one that has its own, comparatively sedate, Mardi Gras. In 2017, developers planned to complete the upgrade of several entertainment and residential spaces in the downtown area. The countryside is agricultural, though there are some vestiges of large riverfront plantations. Roots here go back a long way. Natchitoches is the oldest town in Louisiana, founded by Louis Antoine Juchereau de St. Denis in 1714, and Shreveport was founded in the 1830s.

Oil fueled much of the region's economic growth in the 20th century. Natural gas took off in the 21st, helping to sustain it during the recession. Gas was discovered in 1870, and the nation's first gas pipeline was built from Caddo Field to Shreveport in 1908. However, it wasn't economical to drill until gas prices soared in 2000. Riverboat gambling and the Port of Caddo-Bossier supplement the local economy. Benteler Steel and Tube opened a billion-dollar steel mill at the port in 2015. It is producing steel pipes for transporting oil and gas. A project to renovate downtown Bossier City was scheduled for completion in mid-2017.

Barksdale Air Force Base in Bossier City, one of the nation's largest airfields, is where President George W. Bush landed on Sept. 11, 2001, and spoke briefly to the nation. In 2009, the Air Force chose Barksdale as home of the Global Strike Command, which combined the nation's land-based nuclear missiles and long-range nuclear bombers under single leadership.

The 4th Congressional District of Louisiana drops down the western side of the state to the bayous. Nearly half of the population is in Caddo Parish and suburban Bossier Parish around Shreveport. The rest is scattered in rural areas. The district overall is 34 percent African American and it has had the lowest Republican support in the past three presidential elections of the five Republican-held districts in Louisiana. Hillary Clinton in 2016 won Caddo with 51 percent of the vote. But Donald Trump took 71 percent in Bossier and 61 percent overall, showing that the 4th is solidly Republican.

FIFTH DISTRICT

Ralph Abraham (R)

Elected 2014, 2nd term; b. Sep 16, 1954, Alto; Louisiana State University, Bach. Deg.; Louisiana State University School of Veterinary Medicine, D.V.M.; Louisiana State University School of Medicine, M.D.; Baptist; Married (Dianne Abraham); 3 children.

Military Career: U.S. Army Reserves; MS Army National Guard Special Forces, 1986-1989; Coast Guard Auxiliary, present.

Professional Career: Flight instructor; General family practitioner; Aviation medical examiner.

DC Office: 417 CHOB 20515, 202-225-8490, Fax: 202-225-5639, abraham.house.gov.

State Offices: Alexandria, 318-445-0818; Monroe, 318-322-3500.

Committees: *Agriculture*: Conservation & Forestry, General Farm Commodities & Risk Management. *Armed Services*: Emerging Threats & Capabilities, Military Personnel, Seapower & Projection Forces. *Science, Space & Technology*: Research & Technology, Space.

Group Ratings

	ADA	ACLU	AFL-CIO	LCV	ITI	COC	HAFA	ACU	CFG	FRC
2016	-	5%	-	3%	100%	100%	67%	84%	70%	100%
2015	0%	C	8%	3%	C	75%	C	83%	69%	100%

Almanac Ratings 2015

	Economy	Social	Foreign	Composite
Liberal	1%	5%	0%	2%
Conservative	99%	95%	100%	98%

Key Votes of the 114th Congress

1. Keystone Pipeline	Y	5. Puerto Rico Debt	N	9. Offenses by Aliens	Y
2. Trade Deals	Y	6. Medical Marijuana	N	10. Troops in Iraq	N
3. Export-Import Bank	N	7. Sanctuary Cities	Y	11. Homeland Security $$	N
4. Debt Ceiling Increase	N	8. Armor-piercing Bullets	Y	12. Trade Adjustment aid	N

Election Results

Election	Name (Party)	Vote (%)		Cand. Spent	Ind. Exp. Support	Ind. Exp. Oppose
2016 General	Ralph Abraham (R)	208,545	(82%)	$386,322		
	Billy Burkette (R)	47,117	(18%)			

Prior winning percentages: 2014 (64%)

Republican Ralph Abraham, a rural doctor and humanitarian pilot elected in 2014, has taken a low profile following the brief and rocky tenure of his predecessor, Vance McAllister. He also was less known than the Republican he defeated that year to advance to the runoff - Zach Dasher, nephew of TV's *Duck Dynasty* star Phil Robertson. Voters preferred Abraham's life experiences to Dasher's ardent tea party views. In the House, he has largely kept to his committee work and has had some legislative success.

Abraham grew up in rural Richland Parish, which remains his home. He trained to be a veterinarian at the LSU School of Veterinary Medicine and practiced for 10 years. But he changed careers in his late 30s, and earned his medical degree at the LSU School of Medicine in Shreveport. He likes to boast he "can treat anything that walks on two or four legs." He was a 1st lieutenant in the Army and remains an aircraft commander in the Coast Guard Auxiliary. He worked as a volunteer pilot with Pilots for Patients, a Monroe group that provides free air transportation to people who need medical assistance and live far from hospitals or doctors.

Abraham was the third Republican elected to this seat in two years. Rodney Alexander took office in 2013 for his sixth term, and served on the Appropriations Committee. He resigned in August 2013 to become head of the Louisiana Department of Veterans Affairs. In the special election, state senator Neil Riser, the initial favorite of the Republican establishment, spent the most money and led the first round of voting with 32 percent of the vote to 18 percent for runner-up McAllister, a political novice who had made money in the oil exploration and production business. McAllister benefited in the runoff from his outsider status and his endorsement by the reality television show family in *Duck Dynasty*. McAllister won the special election, 60%-40%, and appeared to be politically untouchable in a district that gave Mitt Romney 61 percent of the vote in 2012.

In April 2014, a local newspaper published a surveillance video showing the married congressman passionately kissing his office's scheduler. Following the widespread airing of the videotaped embrace with an aide that led him to be dubbed "the Kissing Congressman," McAllister issued a statement saying he had "fallen short," and asked for forgiveness. He rejected leadership suggestions that he should resign. After initially declining to seek reelection, he changed his mind and filed to run.

Abraham, who had never held political office, said he had been considering a run for Congress for several years and felt that the time was ripe. "It's not the America in which we grew up," he told Gannett Newspapers. "Somebody has to step up and change it." He played up his 39-year marriage, pilot experiences and "family values." Dasher drew attention when he argued that atheism has led to moral decay in society. McAllister, an energy businessman who self-financed much of his campaign, claimed that voters were not concerned about his widely publicized kissing incident. The conservative Club for Growth political action committee backed Dasher with $250,000 in advertising that attacked McAllister for his personal issues.

In the November all-party election, Abraham ran a grass-roots campaign and finished first among Republicans with 23 percent of the vote, just 1,861 votes ahead of Dasher's 22 percent and well ahead of McAllister's 11 percent. Abraham ran strongly in Monroe and the northern parishes. Dasher ran strongly in Alexandria and the southern parishes. Abraham had a runoff with the leading vote-getter in the nine-candidate race - Democrat Jamie Mayo, the mayor of Monroe, who got 30 percent of the vote in the first round. That proved to be a no-contest. Abraham outspent Mayo 4-to-1 for the entire campaign, and easily won the runoff, 64%-36%. Of the 24 parishes, Mayo won five; each was on or close to the Mississippi River.

In the House, Abraham has fit comfortably in the GOP establishment wing. On the Veterans' Affairs Committee, he chaired the Subcommittee on Disability Assistance and Memorial Affairs - one of the few freshmen to get a gavel. He complained when VA officials said they wanted to take money from the 2014 law designed to improve benefits and use it to cover nearly $1 billion in cost overruns at their Denver medical center. "That money was designated for those veterans," Abraham told the Monroe *News-Star*. In July 2016, he enacted a bill to give benefit increases to disabled veterans. He passed a bill in the House to give an automatic annual cost-of-living adjustment to veterans. On the Agriculture Committee, Abraham pressed for normalization of trade relations with Cuba, which has been eager to get access to rice from Louisiana.

He won reelection with 82 percent of the vote, the largest share of any member of the Louisiana delegation. His opponent, Billy Burkette, was chairman of the tribe for the Louisiana Band of Choctaw Indians. Given the recent turmoil in the district, Abraham's constituents have welcomed what he called his "steadfast" approach.

Northeast Louisiana: Monroe, Alexandria

Population		**Race and Ethnicity**		**Income**	
Total	753,229	White	60.2%	Median Income	$35,354 (423 out of 435)
Land area	14,453	Black	35.4%		
Pop/ sq mi	52.1	Latino	2.2%		
Born in state	81.0%	Asian	0.7%	Under $50,000	62.4%
		Two races	1.1%	$50,000-$99,999	24.1%
Age Groups		Other	0.5%	$100,000-$199,999	11.3%
Under 18	24.3%			$200,000 or more	2.1%
18-34	23.6%	**Education**		Poverty Rate	25.2%
35-64	37.7%	H.S grad or less	58.4%		
Over 64	14.4%	Some college	24.8%	**Health Insurance**	
		College Degree, 4 yr	11.1%	With health insurance coverage	81.1%
Work		Post grad	5.7%		
White Collar	29.8%				
Sales and Service	44.8%	**Military**		**Public Assistance**	
Blue Collar	25.4%	Veteran	8.5%	Cash public assistance income	2.1%
Government	19.2%	Active Duty	0.1%		
				Food stamp/SNAP benefits	19.9%

Voter Turnout			
2015 Total Citizens 18+	562,409	2016 House Turnout as % CVAP	45%
2016 House turnout	255,662	2014 House Turnout as % CVAP	43%

2012 Presidential Vote		
Mitt Romney	201,058	(61%)
Barack Obama	124,054	(38%)

2016 Presidential Vote		
Donald Trump	205,258	(64%)
Hillary Clinton	110,259	(34%)

Cook Partisan Voting Index: R+15

Northeast Louisiana is perhaps the least known part of the state. Along the Mississippi River and the Red River and their dozens of tributaries, it was plantation country before the Civil War, and there are African-American majorities today in many parishes. Away from the rivers, in the hill country, small farmers scratched out a living on land connected to parish courthouses by dusty lanes. Such was Winn Parish, where Huey P. Long, the transformative figure in modern Louisiana politics, was born in 1893 and from which he began his meteoric political career. Elected governor in 1928 and senator in 1930, he was a national figure when he was assassinated in 1935 in the new high-rise Capitol he had built in Baton Rouge.

The 5th Congressional District of Louisiana contains much of this country, from the hills of Winn Parish to the several small black-majority parishes along the Mississippi. About 36 percent of the population is African American. In this largely rural district, poverty is rampant. Along the river, the health of residents in Concordia is ranked among the "sickest" areas in nation. The median income is in the bottom 3 percent of the nation. The biggest urban areas here are Monroe in the north and Alexandria in the south; each has slightly less than 50,000 people and is majority black. Monroe, in Ouachita Parish, is heavily Protestant. Alexandria, in Rapides Parish, sits at the northern extension of Cajun, Catholic Louisiana and is majority black. The district also includes a few parishes east of the Mississippi River and on the outskirts of Baton Rouge. This is one of the largest row-crop farming districts in the nation, including cotton, rice, corn and soybeans. After the federal government stunned local officials in 2010 by determining that the Red River's levees were no longer certified, which would put much of the area in a flood zone, officials in Rapides Parish used federal disaster relief funds and had repaired about 80 percent of the levees by mid-2015. Near Alexandria, Revolution Aluminum in 2015 announced a new plant in Pineville that could employ more than 1,000. The developers set a completion data of 2020, but they ran into financing problems that could cause delay.

Consistent with his strong showing in other rural districts across the nation, Donald Trump won here, 64%-34%. His vote was slightly higher than those of recent GOP presidential candidates.

SIXTH DISTRICT

Garret Graves (R)

Elected 2014, 2nd term; b. Jan 31, 1972, Baton Rouge; University of Alabama, Att.; Louisiana Tech University, Att.; American University (DC), Att.; Roman Catholic; Married (Carissa Graves); 3 children.

Professional Career: Staff, U.S. Sen. John Breaux; Staff, U.S. Rep. Billy Tauzin; Staff, U.S. Sen. David Vitter; Chairman, Coastal Protection & Restoration Authority of LA; Vice Chairman, Gulf Coast Ecosystem Restoration Task Force, U.S. EPA.

DC Office: 430 CHOB 20515, 202-225-3901, Fax: 202-225-7313, garretgraves.house.gov.

State Offices: Baton Rouge, 225-442-1731; Livingston, 225-686-4413; Thibodaux, 985-448-4103.

Committees: *Natural Resources*: Energy & Mineral Resources, Water, Power & Oceans. *Transportation & Infrastructure*: Coast Guard & Maritime Transportation, Highways & Transit, Water Resources & Environment (Chmn).

Group Ratings

	ADA	ACLU	AFL-CIO	LCV	ITI	COC	HAFA	ACU	CFG	FRC
2016	-	11%	-	8%	67%	100%	71%	88%	85%	100%
2015	0%	C	17%	0%	C	75%	C	96%	74%	100%

Almanac Ratings 2015

	Economy	Social	Foreign	Composite
Liberal	6%	0%	5%	4%
Conservative	94%	100%	95%	96%

Key Votes of the 114th Congress

1. Keystone Pipeline	Y	5. Puerto Rico Debt	Y	9. Offenses by Aliens	Y
2. Trade Deals	Y	6. Medical Marijuana	N	10. Troops in Iraq	N
3. Export-Import Bank	N	7. Sanctuary Cities	Y	11. Homeland Security $$	N
4. Debt Ceiling Increase	N	8. Armor-piercing Bullets	Y	12. Trade Adjustment aid	Y

Election Results

Election	Name (Party)	Vote (%)		Cand. Spent	Ind. Exp. Support	Ind. Exp. Oppose
2016 General	Garret Graves (R)	207,483	(63%)	$1,421,272		
	Richard Lieberman (D)	49,380	(15%)			
	Bob Bell (R)	33,592	(10%)			
	Jermaine Sampson (D)	29,822	(9%)			
	Richard Fontanesi (L)	7,603	(2%)			

Prior winning percentages: 2014 (62%)

Republican Garret Graves was elected in a 2014 runoff against the celebrated 87-year-old former governor and ex-federal convict Edwin Edwards, though the real battle here was for the Republican nomination. Graves won each round handily. With his substantial background on resource issues and as a Capitol Hill aide, he quickly became a player and made an impact in the House, especially on energy and environment issues.

Graves, a native of Baton Rouge, is an experienced politician and policy wonk. He left home for Washington in his early 20s and began his political career as an intern for Democratic Sen. John Breaux. After a couple of months, he joined the office of GOP Rep. Billy Tauzin and worked his way up the ladder. He also worked for the House Energy and Commerce Committee, which Tauzin chaired, and later for Louisiana Sen. David Vitter.

In 2008, newly elected Gov. Bobby Jindal selected Graves to chair the Louisiana Coastal Protection and Restoration Authority and serve as his coastal adviser. Graves won praise for a $50 billion, 50-year master plan to promote coastal restoration and improve hurricane protection, as well as for coordinating the state's response to the 2010 Deepwater Horizon oil spill in the Gulf of Mexico. He was Jindal's point man in a Southeast Louisiana Flood Protection Authority-East lawsuit against more than 100 oil and gas companies, which alleged that decades of drilling and extraction had contributed to wetlands destruction. He said that he was responsible for $18 billion in projects to improve the economic, environmental and community resilience of the state.

After Republican Rep. Bill Cassidy challenged Democratic Sen. Mary Landrieu, Graves stepped down from his state job and dove into the open-seat contest. In the all-party primary, he faced 11 other candidates, including eight Republicans. His best-known opponent was Democrat Edwards, who had been governor for 16 years and served eight years in federal prison on corruption charges. In the first round of voting in November, Edwards took 30 percent of the vote and Graves had 27 percent. Running third was Paul Dietzel II, with 14%.

The colorful past exploits of Edwards vastly increased national attention on the contest, though he had been out of public office since 1996. He ran as a self-described New Deal Democrat and "old relic" who unabashedly favored government spending to help the district. Graves, for his part, voiced surprise at the voters' selection of his runoff opponent. "This was the guy that was a legend or a folklore when I was a kid," he told National Public Radio. "And the fact that he's still around and we were just standing here debating him is really just a surreal experience." Graves supported free-market principles and reduced government, and called for a halt to welfare in favor of incentivized hard work. He worked to convince voters that his familiarity with Washington would be a benefit but that he was not a "Washington insider." He outspent Edwards, $1.5 million to $400,000. No surprise, in this overwhelmingly Republican district, Graves won the run-off, 62%-38%. In East Baton Rouge Parish, which cast nearly one-half of the vote, Graves took 59 percent. Edwards won three small rural parishes.

Even before he was formally elected, House Republican leaders assigned seats to Graves on the Natural Resources, and Transportation and Infrastructure committees, both of which are important to his district. He brought unusually broad experience in dealing with resource issues, especially in a state at the center of many of those conflicts. His willingness to address climate change and its potential problems quickly gave him opportunities among House Republicans. "We have measured sea rise in south Louisiana. For us to stick our heads in the sand and pretend it's not happening is idiotic, and it puts the lives of 2 million people who live in south Louisiana in jeopardy," he told *Bloomberg News*. Later, he criticized the Obama administration for not issuing enough leases for oil and gas drilling in the Gulf of Mexico.

As vice chairman of the Water Resources and Environment Subcommittee, Graves helped to enact in December 2016 the wide-ranging Water Resources Improvement bill. He focused, in particular, on steps to overhaul the Army Corps of Engineers and expedite completion of flood protection projects. He passed amendments to accelerate $150 million in projects in Louisiana, especially in areas that had suffered extensive flood damage a few months earlier. He included in the bill strict deadlines and reporting requirements for Corps' projects designed to mitigate coastal land loss. "We've been waiting decades for the Corps to build projects designed to fix [the Louisiana coast], but all we get is lip service about how it's 'still being considered.' Meanwhile, the coast continues to disappear and our communities become increasingly vulnerable," he said.

Graves won approval by the House Appropriations Committee of his proposal to transfer from a federal agency to a new consortium of five Gulf Coast states, including Louisiana, the authority to set the season for recreational fishing of red snappers. He complained that commercial interests had short-changed recreational fishers with only a 10-day season in the Gulf of Mexico. On another local issue, Graves worked with Democratic Rep. Cedric Richmond of Louisiana to seek federal funds for the families of the three law-enforcement officers who were killed in Baton Rouge in July 2016. The two local representatives also cosponsored a bill to give police federally backed non-lethal weapons and improved training.

In a far less dramatic campaign than his first contest, Graves won reelection with 63 percent of the vote against five challengers. In 2017, he moved up to chairman of the Water Resources Subcommittee, replacing Rep. Bob Gibbs of Ohio, who was term-limited in that position.

Baton Rouge

Population		**Race and Ethnicity**		**Income**	
Total	781,229	White	67.9%	Median Income	$57,884 (158 out of 435)
Land area	4,034	Black	23.6%	Under $50,000	43.8%
Pop/ sq mi	193.7	Latino	4.3%	$50,000-$99,999	31.0%
Born in state	77.7%	Asian	2.1%	$100,000-$199,999	20.9%
		Two races	1.5%	$200,000 or more	4.4%
Age Groups		Other	0.6%	Poverty Rate	14.9%
Under 18	24.3%				
18-34	25.8%	**Education**		**Health Insurance**	
35-64	37.9%	H.S grad or less	44.4%	With health insurance coverage	87.7%
Over 64	12.0%	Some college	27.2%		
		College Degree, 4 yr	19.0%		
Work		Post grad	9.4%	**Public Assistance**	
White Collar	36.7%			Cash public assistance income	1.0%
Sales and Service	40.5%	**Military**		Food stamp/SNAP benefits	12.1%
Blue Collar	22.8%	Veteran	7.4%		
Government	16.0%	Active Duty	0.1%		

Voter Turnout			
2015 Total Citizens 18+	573,066	2016 House Turnout as % CVAP	58%
2016 House turnout	331,098	2014 House Turnout as % CVAP	46%

2012 Presidential Vote		
Mitt Romney	228,507	(66%)
Barack Obama	110,430	(32%)

2016 Presidential Vote		
Donald Trump	230,701	(65%)
Hillary Clinton	110,394	(31%)
Gary Johnson	8,531	(2%)

Cook Partisan Voting Index: R+19

Baton Rouge sits on a cultural fault line in Louisiana, the boundary between the French-speaking, Catholic Cajun country and the heavily Baptist region to the north. Historically, it was part of the Florida Parishes, the territory east of the Mississippi River and north of Lake Pontchartrain that was not included in the Louisiana Purchase in 1803. It still belonged to Spain, until the locals rebelled and declared their own Republic of West Florida in 1810. Then it quickly became part of Louisiana and the United States.

Today, Baton Rouge is the center of a metropolitan area of about 800,000 people, an increase from 700,000 in 2000. It sits on the east bank of the Mississippi and is the largest inland deep-water port located on the river. This is one of the faster-growing parts of Louisiana and did well in coping with the recession. It has been called the "Creative Capital of the South," because of its success in creating public-private partnerships in high-growth sectors, including a new IBM technology center in downtown. New Orleans was long the state's largest city. Baton Rouge, with 229,000 people, grew closer to post-Katrina New Orleans in size, though the recent population return to New Orleans has widened the margin between the two cities. In 2014, its newspaper, *The Advocate*, surpassed the circulation of the *Times Picayune* of New Orleans. Local features are the old Gothic-style capitol, where Huey Long took office, and the 34-story Art Deco capitol, which he had built and where he died at the hands of an assassin in 1935. Also here is Louisiana State University, another Long legacy. The region benefits from the research productivity of LSU's main campus and the Pennington Biomedical Research Center. In 2016, the newly created LSU Industrial Innovation Center made plans to work with area industries to upgrade their huge infrastructure.

The area has suffered more than its share of recent problems. In 2015-16, the parishes south of Baton Rouge lost about 11,000 jobs as the drop in oil prices sparked layoffs and slowdowns throughout the oil industry. The summer of 2016 brought national attention to Baton Rouge for sudden disasters. In July, two police officers responding to an incident at a convenience store fatally shot Alton Sterling, an African American. That led to nearly two weeks of street protests, which culminated in an ambush of law-enforcement officers, three of whom were killed. In August, devastating floods hit the Baton Rouge area; more than 20 inches fell in two days in some areas, and more than 100,000 local residents filed for federal aid. Unusually, the storm was not hurricane-related.

The 6th Congressional District of Louisiana includes the majority of residents in East and West Baton Rouge parishes. Redistricting in 2012 moved Baton Rouge's black neighborhoods into the New Orleans-based 2nd District, reducing the 6th's black population from 35 percent to 24 percent. As a result, the district moved solidly into the GOP camp. The 6th runs from close to the Arkansas border south through part of the bayous and nearly to the Gulf of Mexico. Thibodaux has been ranked by *Smithsonian* magazine as one of the 20 best small towns in the nation to visit.

★ MAINE ★

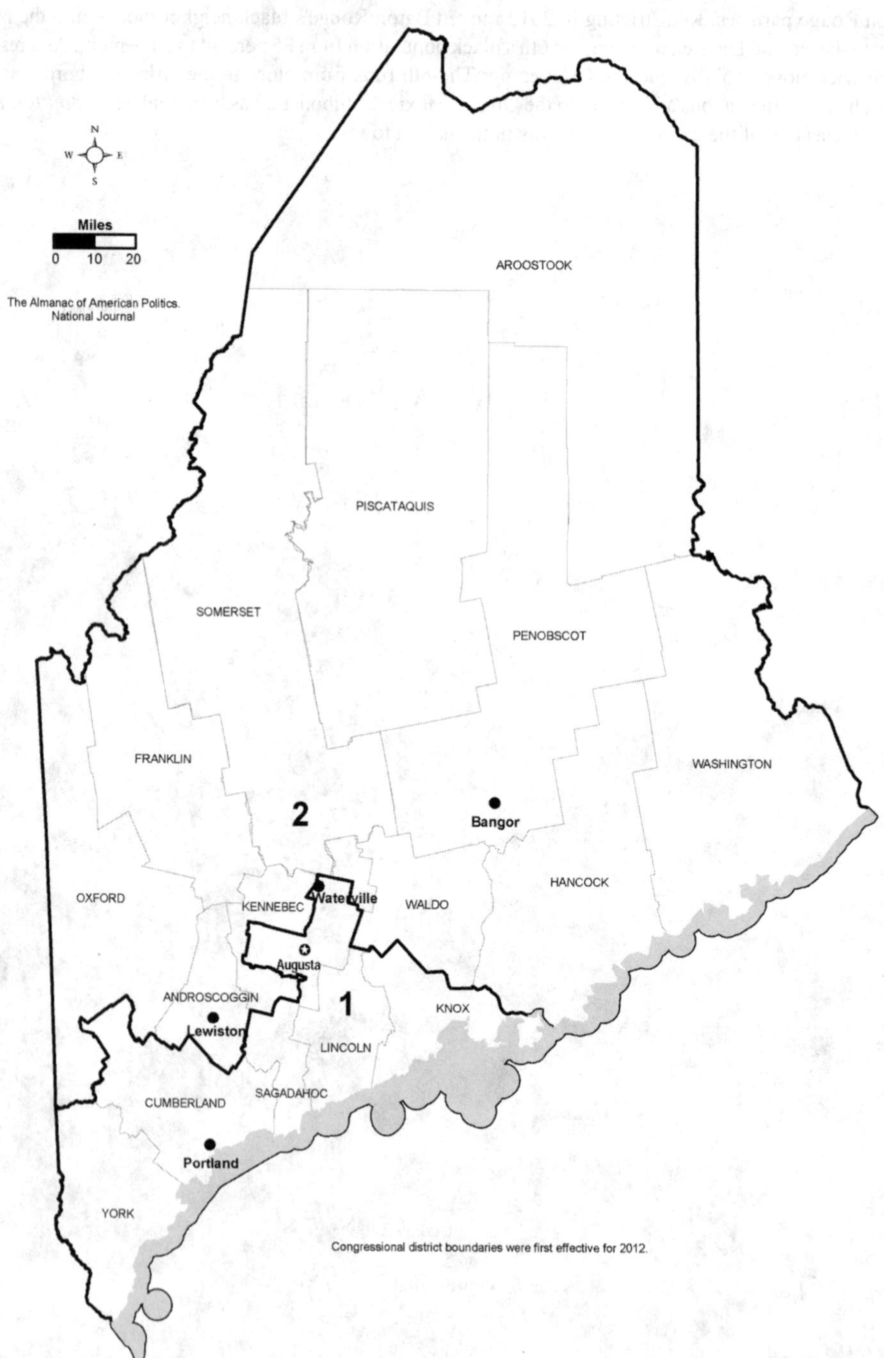
N
W
E
S
Miles
0 10 20
The Almanac of American Politics.
National Journal
AROOSTOOK
PISCATAQUIS
SOMERSET
PENOBSCOT
FRANKLIN
WASHINGTON
2
Bangor
HANCOCK
OXFORD
KENNEBEC
Waterville
WALDO
Augusta
ANDROSCOGGIN
1
KNOX
Lewiston
LINCOLN
SAGADAHOC
CUMBERLAND
Portland
YORK
Congressional district boundaries were first effective for 2012.

The phrase "up in Maine" conveys some of the state's distinctive personality - ornery, contrary-minded, almost bullheaded, and rough-hewn. And its current politics, from its polarizing governor to its stark shift toward Donald Trump in 2016, hews to this stereotype.

In the far northeast corner of the United States, Maine is the state geographically closest to Europe, but it was not heavily settled until the mid-19th century, by people from the South and the West - not the usual direction of American migrations. Maine grew in a rush, and then mostly stopped. There were 600,000 people there in 1860, but the population dipped after the Civil War - many soldiers did not return - and it did not top 1 million until the 1970s. In the urbanizing and rapidly changing country of the early 20th century, Maine was famous for its pointed firs and steady habits, with a few dozen small factory towns and paper-mill hamlets but nothing like a major metropolis.

Despite the Yankee work ethic, Maine has repeatedly found itself at the bottom of various assessments of state business climates. In 2016, Maine was ranked No. 49 on the *Forbes* "Best States for Business" list; the state had been ranked dead last four times in recent years. Part of the negative critiques stem from the state's archaic tax code and relatively high corporate tax rates, but a bigger challenge the state is facing is a demographic one - it's old. In 2015, Maine's population had the highest median age - 44.6 years - of any state, with relatively few young families. A 2016 report by the Maine Development Foundation and the Maine State Chamber warned that the state's ratio of three working people for each retiree will drop to two workers over the next 15 years. Educational attainment also lags the regional average. From 2015 to 2016, the Census estimated that Maine's overall population grew a paltry 0.15 percent, among the lowest rates in the nation. "We will need to attract thousands of additional immigrants to this state to have the workforce that will enable our industries to thrive," said Yellow Light Breen, the foundation's president.

This has put a crimp on economic development. Maine's GDP, when adjusted for inflation, is about where it was before the recession. That's an improvement on the post-recession dip the state experienced, but far below the 9 percent national growth rate over the same period. What expansion there was came primarily from an increase in output in the health care, social assistance and management sectors. Maine spent only 1 percent of its gross state product on research and development in 2011, the most recent year available – well below the 4.4 percent average for New England. Somewhat paradoxically, the state's unemployment rate has tracked a point or two below the national rate since the start of the recession. However, the median household income in 2015 was $51,000 – below the $57,000 national average and much closer to West Virginia ($42,000) than to neighboring New Hampshire ($76,000).

A big part of the reason has been the shrinking of the state's blue-collar job base. Over the past 30 years, Maine has lost jobs in shoe manufacturing, chicken processing, papermaking, leather processing and timber. Scratching small Maine boiling potatoes out of the soil of sprawling Aroostook County has gotten harder, although high schools in northern Maine still shut down at the end of September for "harvest break" for a couple of weeks so farmers can pull their dwindling crop from the ground before it freezes. And while it has a long-term contract to build 21 *Arleigh Burke* Class Navy destroyers, Bath Iron Works, once the state's largest private employer, now trails Hannaford supermarkets, Walmart, L.L. Bean and Maine Medical Center.

Gains have come in tourism, call centers and health care to serve the state' aging population. The most spectacular economic success has come with lobster, a species and an industry that has long been an iconic Maine institution. In 2015, the value of the state's lobster harvest – which accounts for 80 percent of Maine's fishery revenue -- reached a record high for the sixth straight year. The catch currently hovers around 120 million pounds a year, many times what it was in earlier generations. The *Washington Post's* Wonkblog noted that even as Chinese competition has drained an estimated 2 percent of total state employment between 2001 and 2013, much of it in manufacturing, lobster exports to China have risen from virtually nothing to $20 million over the past decade. China's middle class views the crustacean as a dining status symbol; in Chinese culture, the lobster's red hue is considered particularly auspicious. Some suspect climate change, which has pushed cod, herring and northern shrimp toward colder waters, as the cause of the newfound bounty, along with overfishing of competitor species. In effect, there are two Maines - moderately humming coastal Maine and declining interior Maine, one symbolized by the lobster and the other by the moose.

In politics, Maine has a reputation for quirkiness. Until 1958, it held state elections in September, a date originally chosen because it followed the state's early harvest. Starting in 1840, long before the advent of public opinion polls, the election results were taken as a gauge of national sentiment - hence the saying, "As Maine goes, so goes the nation." Actually, Maine didn't vote like the rest of the country most of the time. In 1936, only Maine and Vermont voted for Republican Alf Landon over Democrat Franklin D. Roosevelt, prompting Roosevelt's campaign manager to observe, "As Maine goes, so goes Vermont." Maine was known for its flinty Yankee Republicanism and for Prohibition; it banned liquor in 1851, after which other states enacted "Maine laws." Since voting four times against FDR, it has voted for the loser in the close presidential elections of 1948, 1960, 1968, 1976, 2000, and 2004 - a record equaled by no other state. Maine cast the nation's highest percentages for third-party presidential candidate Ross Perot - 30 percent in 1992 and 14 percent in 1996. In 1974, it elected independent James Longley, a former Republican, as governor; in 1994 and 1998, it elected independent Angus King, a former Democrat, as governor. In 2010, it came close to electing as governor independent Eliot Cutler, who might have won except that early voting allowed many ballots to be cast before it was apparent that support for the Democratic nominee was plummeting. The beneficiary was Republican Paul LePage, who eked out a victory with 38 percent to Cutler's 36 percent. In the past 10 gubernatorial elections, Maine has voted four times for Republicans, four times for Democrats, and twice for independents. In 2012, after moderate Republican Sen. Olympia Snowe retired, King ran for the Senate as an independent. Local and national Democrats, mindful of how LePage won in a split contest, effectively abandoned the Democratic nominee; King beat Republican Charlie Summers by a 53%-31% margin. As expected, in the Senate, King caucused with the Democrats.

Maine has often been a muddle, going back and forth on sanctioning same-sex marriage in the legislature and at the ballot box due to sharply different views in coastal and inland areas. In 2010, in addition to Republican LePage's victory as governor, Republicans gained majorities in both houses of the legislature. Two years later, Democrats recaptured majorities in both houses. When LePage was reelected in 2014, Republicans regained control of the state Senate, but not the House, a lineup that continues.

The 2016 election was dramatic. The state's allocation of electoral votes by congressional district made Maine unusually contested terrain, with both Donald Trump and Hillary Clinton stumping in the state's rural 2nd congressional district. Trump in particular saw promise in the state's heavily white, blue-collar voters; Maine is the nation's whitest state save Vermont, West Virginia and New Hampshire, with which it is tied. "If you are going after a population that is more diverse, that is more highly educated, you are by definition leaving out the vast majority of the voters here in Maine," Democratic strategist Michael Cuzzi told Maine Public Media during the campaign, referring to Clinton's national strategy. The 2nd district has lost jobs to foreign competition for many years and tends to see the government as a distant, even malevolent force. (President Barack Obama's decision during the campaign to unilaterally designate a large chunk of the North Woods as the Katahdin Woods and Waters National Monument, a proposal that had been locally controversial for years, only reinforced this notion.) On Election Day, the 2nd district swung heavily toward Trump. The Republican won nine counties in the state, which was eight more than Mitt Romney won in 2012, and it was enough to secure an electoral vote. The margin in Oxford County shifted 28 points toward Trump; it shifted 25 points in Aroostook, 24 in Franklin, 17 points in Kennebec, which includes Augusta, and 14 in Penobscot. It wasn't just the margins; in these five counties alone, overall turnout rose by 6 percent over 2012. Meanwhile, in the more populous coastal counties, Clinton's margins were either static or narrower than Obama's from 2012. Whereas Obama won the state by 15 points in 2012, Clinton won it by just three; she under-performed Obama by about 44,000 votes while Trump over-performed Romney by about 43,000. It was enough to win Clinton three electoral votes, but narrowly. Meanwhile, voters rejected a ballot measure for tighter gun control while approving a minimum wage hike, marijuana legalization, a high-earner tax hike and ranked-choice voting – the last one an important development given the state's penchant for running three-way elections. In May 2017, the state Supreme Court unanimously ruled unconstitutional the new voting system.

Population		Race and Ethnicity		Income	
Total	1,329,100	White	93.9%	Median Income	$49,331 (34 out of 50)
Land area	30,843	Black	1.1%		
Pop/ sq mi	43.1	Latino	1.5%	Under $50,000	50.6%
Born in state	64.2%	Asian	1.1%	$50,000-$99,999	31.8%
		Two races	1.8%	$100,000-$199,999	14.7%
Age Groups		Other	0.7%	$200,000 or more	3.0%
Under 18	19.7%			Poverty Rate	13.9%
18-34	20.0%	**Education**			
35-64	42.7%	H.S grad or less	41.6%	**Health Insurance**	
Over 64	17.7%	Some college	29.4%	With health insurance coverage	90.0%
Work		College Degree, 4 yr	18.7%		
		Post grad	1.3%		
White Collar	35.4%			**Public Assistance**	
Sales and Service	42.4%	**Military**		Cash public assistance income	4.4%
Blue Collar	22.1%	Veteran	11.2%		
Government	14.1%	Active Duty	0.2%	Food stamp/SNAP benefits	17.1%

Voter Turnout			
2015 Total Citizens 18+	1,048,274	2016 Pres Turnout as % CVAP	71%
2016 Pres Votes	747,927	2012 Pres Turnout as % CVAP	69%

Legislature	
Senate:	17D, 18R
House:	77D, 71R, 3I, 2NV

Presidential Politics

2016 Democratic Caucus		
Bernie Sanders (D)	2,231	(64%)
Hillary Clinton (D)	1,232	(36%)
2016 Republican Caucus		
Ted Cruz (R)	8,550	(46%)
Donald Trump (R)	6,070	(33%)
John Kasich (R)	2,270	(12%)
Marco Rubio (R)	1,492	(8%)

2016 Presidential Vote		
Hillary Clinton (D)	357,735	(48%)
Donald Trump (R)	335,593	(45%)
Gary Johnson (L)	38,105	(5%)
Jill Stein (G)	14,251	(2%)
2012 Presidential Vote		
Barack Obama (D)	401,306	(56%)
Mitt Romney (R)	292,276	(41%)

For most of the past century, Maine was a reliably Republican state. It is one of only two states that voted against FDR in all four of his elections (Vermont was the other). However, since 1992, Maine has voted for a Democratic presidential candidate seven straight times. In 2016 Hillary Clinton defeated Donald Trump 48%-45%, but the Republican still managed to win one of the state's four Electoral College votes. That's because Maine, like Nebraska, allocates one electoral vote to the winner of each of its two congressional districts. The other two go the winner of the statewide vote. The 1st District, which stretches about 120 miles up the state's coast and includes Portland and Augusta, is the more liberal of the two, where Barack Obama won 59 percent of the vote in his elections. Clinton took the 1st District with 54 percent. The 2nd District is more rural, made up of old mill towns, covers the vast interior of the state and includes Bangor and Lewiston. It gave Obama 53 percent of the vote in 2012. But the voters of this mostly economically depressed region were drawn to Trump, just like they were to the blunt and combative GOP Gov. Paul LePage, and switched their allegiance to the Republican ticket in 2016. In Rumford, known for the old Oxford Paper mill on the upper Androscoggin River, voters went from backing Obama 61%-34% in 2012 to siding with Trump 50%-41%. Overall, Trump carried the 2nd District 51%-41%. For the first time since 1972, when Maine's law to divide Electoral votes by district went into effect, it split.

Maine held its first-ever presidential primary on March 5, 1996, in an attempt to attract the candidates' early attention. But the tactic didn't work, and the state abolished its presidential primary for 2004. In 2016, Republicans held their caucus on March 5, a Saturday, and the Democrats caucused the next day. Maine Republicans said their caucus turnout hit 18,650, more than triple from 2012's level, and Texas Sen. Ted Cruz bested Trump, 46%-33%, even though LePage had endorsed the New Yorker. Ohio Gov. John Kasich finished third with 12 percent. Trump won two other contests that day, Kentucky and Louisiana, and joked with supporters in Florida that night that Cruz "should do well in

Maine because it's very close to Canada," a dig at the Texan having been born there. Vermont Sen. Bernie Sanders defeated Clinton 64%-36% in state delegates allocated by the caucuses. Maine Democrats said that 46,000 participated in their caucus.

Congressional Districts

115th Congress Lineup	1R 1D	**114th Congress Lineup**	1R 1D

Maine has a bipartisan advisory commission that draws up a redistricting plan, which the legislature and governor can consider, but a state statute has stipulated that redistricting must be approved by a two-thirds vote in the legislature and delayed until the third year after the census. In practice, this has not made much difference. Since Maine lost its third congressional district following the 1960 census, the lines between the largely rural northern district and the Portland-based southern district have shifted only slightly.

In March 2011, two citizens brought a lawsuit in federal court arguing that the timetable violated the Constitution since it left in place for one election districts that were not of equal population. Although the census showed the two districts' populations differed by only 8,669 people, the court in June ruled for the plaintiffs and ordered a new plan be adopted by January 2012. The Democrats' plan shifted the lines just a bit. The Republicans' plan would have moved six of the 16 counties to a different district and placed the two Democratic incumbents in the same district. The advisory commission voted 8-7 to submit the Democratic plan to the legislature. Harsh words were exchanged, amid threats of a lawsuit if the Republican legislators adopted their plan with less than the two-thirds required by state statute. But when the legislature met, it adopted the Democratic plan with only three dissenting votes and LePage signed it into law. Perhaps the Republicans knew what they were doing. In 2014, the 2nd District elected the state's first Republican to the House in 20 years.

Governor

Paul R. LePage (R)

Elected 2010, term expires 2019, 2nd term; b. Oct. 9, 1948, Lewiston, ME; Husson U., B.S. 1971, U. of ME, M.B.A. 1975; Catholic; Married (Ann); 4 children.

Elected Office: Waterville Mayor, 2003-2011.

Professional Career: CEO, LePage & Kasevich Consulting, 1983-1996; General Manager, Marden's Surplus & Salvage, 1996-2011.

Office: One State House Station, Augusta, 04333-0001; 207-287-3531; Fax: 207-287-1034; Website: maine.gov/governor.

Election Results

Election	Name (Party)	Vote (%)
2014 General	Paul LePage (R)	294,533 (48%)
	Mike Michaud (D)	265,125 (43%)
	Eliot Cutler (I)	51,518 (8%)

Prior winning percentage: 2010 (38%)

"Actions speak louder than words," was one of the reelection slogans of Maine's notoriously blunt-spoken Republican Gov. Paul LePage. If anything, LePage turned up the volume during his second term, with predictably polarizing results.

LePage has a compelling rags-to-riches story. He was the oldest son of 18 children in a poverty-stricken, dysfunctional family. One night in a crowded, dark tenement, he stumbled over the body of his 4-year-old brother, who had fallen and died. After numerous beatings from his alcoholic father, LePage ran away at age 11 and spent two years living on the streets of Lewiston, supporting himself by shining shoes and cleaning horse stables. He slept in hallways, cars and even a strip joint. "Some of those strippers were like surrogate moms," he told *Forbes* magazine in 2010. When he was 13, two families jointly adopted him, and he earned money hauling boxes and washing dishes. He eventually befriended Peter Snowe, a state legislator who later married future Maine Republican Sen. Olympia Snowe. Peter Snowe persuaded officials at Husson University to let LePage take the SAT in French after LePage, who had been raised speaking French in Lewiston's "Little Canada," struggled with the verbal section of the test. LePage was admitted and went on to earn a degree in business administration, followed by an MBA from the University of Maine. He worked in forestry and as a consultant before becoming general manager of Marden's Surplus and Salvage, a Maine-based discount store chain, in 1996.

LePage entered politics in 1998 by running for the City Council in Waterville, a town of about 15,000 between Augusta and Bangor in the middle of the state. He served two terms, then ran for mayor in 2003 and won. He would boast that he lowered taxes 13 percent in six years, improved the city's credit rating, and increased its "rainy day" fund from $1 million to $10 million - all without cutting services and while working with a solidly Democratic council. When he couldn't get Democrats to agree to his ideas, he would make his case to the people through the news media, which earned him the nickname "Front Page LePage."

When LePage entered the 2010 governor's race, he was part of a crowded, seven-candidate Republican field. He cast himself as a solid fiscal and social conservative aligned with the tea party movement. He promised to cut every dollar of state spending he considered wasteful and used his life story to illustrate how that approach could succeed in a Democratic-leaning state. He was the surprise winner of the June GOP primary with 37 percent of the vote, even though he spent less money than all but one other candidate. His victory set up a battle with Democratic state Senate President Libby Mitchell and attorney Eliot Cutler, a former associate director of the Office of Management and Budget under President Jimmy Carter who was running as an independent. Though LePage started out ahead, his campaign ran into obstacles stemming from his take-no-prisoners style. He proposed a five-year limit on welfare benefits and said, "At the end of five years, if you still need welfare, I will personally buy (you) a ticket to Massachusetts so (you) can start over." He also drew criticism when he said at a September forum, "As your governor, you're going to be seeing a lot of me on the front page saying, 'Governor LePage tells [President Barack] Obama to go to hell.'" Cutler narrowed LePage's lead in the polls, but LePage eked out a victory, 38%-36%. Mitchell finished a distant third with 19 percent.

LePage vowed to rectify the state's budget problems, which included a revenue shortfall estimated at $1 billion. Fulfilling a campaign pledge, he unveiled a budget revision that paid down a portion of the state's debt to hospitals. But he continued to show a penchant for controversial remarks. When the NAACP criticized him for declining to take part in Martin Luther King Day events, he said: "Tell them to kiss my butt." In the legislature, LePage enjoyed the luxury of both a Republican-controlled House and Senate. In his first year, he was able to pass a 2011 biennial budget that featured the state's largest-ever tax cut, lowering the top income tax rate from 8.5 percent to 7.95 percent and doubling the estate tax exemption from $1 million to $2 million. In 2013 and 2014, LePage vetoed bills the legislature sent him to expand Medicaid. Indeed, LePage set a record for vetoes in his first term, with 179. He imposed his promised five-year limit on welfare benefits and pushed for investigations of fraud and abuse to prevent Maine from being a "destination state" for welfare seekers.

LePage's pugnaciousness grated on lawmakers. Senate Republicans told him in a closed-door caucus that his bullish style was interfering with legislating. As Obama swept all but one of Maine's 16 counties in the 2012 election, state Democrats used LePage and his record as a foil and picked up six seats in the Senate and 15 in the House to regain control of both chambers. Two embarrassed GOP lawmakers were anonymously quoted by the *Press Herald* as saying that at a 2013 GOP fundraiser they attended with LePage, he said Obama "hates white people." LePage denied he made disparaging comments about the president. It seemed as though Mainers might be growing weary of LePage's no-holds-barred approach, and in 2013 polls found a majority disapproved of how the governor was handling his job.

In his reelection campaign, LePage faced two opponents, Democratic Rep. Mike Michaud and independent Cutler, back for a rematch. Both Michaud and LePage had similar backgrounds: Franco-Americans who came from working class backgrounds. After he got into the race, Michaud disclosed in a *Bangor Daily News* article that he was gay, but it did not come up much in the campaign, and Michaud stressed his ability to work across the aisle in contrast to the governor's confrontational style. LePage emphasized his first-term tax cuts and efforts to rein in state spending, and largely stayed on that message, asking voters to look at his deeds, not his words. He mostly avoided the kind of verbal lunges he was known for, but right before the election, LePage jumped back into the headlines during a scare over Ebola. When a nurse returned to Maine after treating Ebola victims in West Africa and tested negative for the virus, she refused the request of state health officials to remain in her home until the 21-day incubation period for the virus expired. LePage told ABC News that the town where the nurse lived was "scared to death" and state police were stationed outside her home to monitor her movements. State officials sought a court order for a 21-day quarantine, but a Maine judge turned down the request. LePage acquiesced in the ruling, but called it "unfortunate." The voters didn't rebuke LePage, and in a strong Republican midterm election he defeated Michaud by a comparatively comfortable 48%-43% margin, with Cutler winning only 8 percent. LePage carried every Maine county except Cumberland with the state's major metro area, Portland, and Knox, where Rockland is a popular seacoast tourist destination. Michaud was soundly beaten in his former northern Maine congressional district.

In the first year of his second term, the state House, voting on partisan lines, derailed LePage's proposal to present voters with a ballot measure to phase out the state's income tax. The legislature overrode LePage's veto of the state's biennial budget, which had been accompanied by a four-page message that included images of drug trafficking suspects, crying babies and the disabled, all of which, he suggested, would be affected if the legislature didn't back his policies. But acting in bipartisan fashion, the legislature forestalled a government shutdown and enacted a broad-based income-tax cut paid for by the reversal of scheduled sales- and hospitality-tax cuts. In the meantime, LePage dismayed environmentalists by deemphasizing wind power and backing hydropower and natural gas, and he continued his campaign to scale back public assistance, proposing prohibitions on the use of welfare benefits to pay for alcohol, tobacco, lottery tickets and tattoos, and requiring drug-testing for recipients convicted of drug felonies. He also sought to turn over the welfare program to an out-of-state vendor.

LePage did little to tame his shoot-from-the-hip style during his second term. In a radio address, he implied that the state's most famous resident, author Stephen King, had headed off to Florida to avoid paying Maine's state income tax (Florida has no state income tax). King, who owns a winter home in the Sunshine State, denied that allegation and said he and his wife paid $1.3 million in Maine income tax in 2013 and probably a similar amount in 2014. LePage's office amended the governor's remarks, but LePage declined to apologize to King and said the best-selling writer should "just make me the villain of your next book and I won't charge you royalties."

The next ruckus occurred in August 2016, when LePage revealed that he'd been keeping a three-ring binder with mug shots of drug dealers, 90 percent of whom, he said, were black or Hispanic, something official statistics call into question. The ACLU of Maine filed a freedom-of-information request for the binder, and LePage's old antagonist, King, called the governor "a bigot, a homophobe and a racist." Then LePage left state Rep. Drew Gattine a vulgar voice mail, accused the Democrat of calling him a racist – something Gattine denied – and seemed to challenge the lawmaker to a duel. Lawmakers considered whether to censure the governor or even impeach him. LePage took responsibility on a radio show and mused about the possibility of not serving his full term. "If I've lost my ability to help Maine people, maybe it's time to move on," he said, but he later backtracked. "I'm not an alcoholic, and I'm not a drug addict, and I don't have mental issues," he told reporters. "What I have is a backbone." That fall, another politician with a penchant for outrageous comments swung much of rural Maine – LePage's base – in his direction, coming within three points of winning the state in the presidential election. In May 2017, LePage announced that he would not run for the Senate in 2018, removing himself from the political stage at least for a while.

Senior Senator

Susan Collins (R)

Elected 1996, term expires 2020, 4th term; b. Dec 07, 1952, Caribou; St. Lawrence University (NY), B.A.; Roman Catholic; Married (Thomas Daffron).

Professional Career: Legislative aide, U.S Sen. Bill Cohen, 1975-1987, Staff Director, Oversight of Gov. Management SubCommittee, 1981-1987; Professional & Financial Regulation Comm., 1987-1992; New England regional Director, U.S Small Business Admin., 1992; ME deputy treas., 1993; Executive Director, Center for Family Business, Husson College, 1994-1996.

DC Office: 413 DSOB 20510, 202-224-2523, Fax: 202-224-2693, collins.senate.gov.

State Offices: Augusta, 207-622-8414; Bangor, 207-945-0417; Biddeford, 207-283-1101; Caribou, 207-493-7873; Lewiston, 207-784-6969; Portland, 207-780-3575.

Committees: *Aging (Chmn)*. *Appropriations*: Agriculture, Rural Development, FDA & Related Agencies, Commerce, Justice, Science & Related Agencies, Department of Defense, Energy & Water Development, Military Construction & Veteran Affairs & Related Agencies, Transportation, HUD & Related Agencies (Chmn). *Health, Education, Labor & Pensions*: Primary Health & Retirement Security. *Intelligence*.

Group Ratings

	ADA	ACLU	AFL-CIO	LCV	ITI	COC	HAFA	ACU	CFG	FRC
2016	-	35%	-	76%	60%	63%	16%	23%	24%	0%
2015	30%	C	64%	60%	C	71%	C	21%	25%	27%

Almanac Ratings 2015

	Economy	Social	Foreign	Composite
Liberal	80%	49%	22%	50%
Conservative	20%	51%	78%	50%

Key Votes of the 114th Congress

1. Keystone pipeline	Y	5. National Security Data	N	9. Gun Sales Checks	Y
2. Export-Import Bank	N	6. Iran Nuclear Deal	Y	10. Sanctuary Cities	Y
3. Debt Ceiling Increase	Y	7. Puerto Rico Debt	Y	11. Planned Parenthood	N
4. Homeland Security $$	Y	8. Loretta Lynch A.G	Y	12. Trade deals	N

Election Results

Election	Name (Party)	Vote (%)	Cand. Spent	Ind. Exp. Support	Ind. Exp. Oppose
2014 General	Susan Collins (R)	413,505 (67%)	$5,563,101	$1,157,937	$51,797
	Shenna Bellows (D)	190,254 (31%)	$2,335,587	$180,057	
2014 Primary	Susan Collins (R)	unopposed			

Prior winning percentages: 2008(61%), 2002 (58%), 1996 (49%)

Susan Collins, Maine's senior senator, is among the last vestiges of a political breed that, until recent decades, inhabited Capitol Hill in significant numbers: the Northeastern moderate Republican. In 2012, with the retirement of her fellow Maine GOP moderate, Olympia Snowe, and the ouster of Scott Brown of Massachusetts, Collins was left very much on her own regionally. The 2016 defeat of Illinois Republican Mark Kirk left her all but alone nationally in the Senate GOP's centrist wing. But she has been a pivotal swing vote on numerous issues since her initial election in 1996, and, with seniority, has increasingly emerged as a consensus seeker and dealmaker.

Notwithstanding her differences with many in today's GOP, Collins insisted in a 2012 interview with *BU Washington News Service* that she "would never be anything but a Republican." Chuckling, she added: "It's in my DNA. It really is. I come from a part of the country where you're expected to apply independent judgment and that's what I've always tried to do." A couple of votes early in the administration of President Donald Trump underscored her assertion. Collins -- who proclaimed she would not vote for Trump in a *Washington Post* op-ed in August 2016 (she wrote in House Speaker Paul Ryan's name) -- was one of two Republicans to vote against Trump's nomination of school choice advocate Betsy DeVos as education secretary. The defections of Collins and Alaska Sen. Lisa Murkowski forced Vice President Mike Pence to break a 50-50 tie to rescue DeVos. At the same time, Collins came to the defense of another controversial Trump nominee, now-Attorney General Jeff Sessions, whose nomination for a federal judgeship had been derailed three decades earlier amid reports of racist remarks. "I don't know the dynamics of what happened then, but I can speak to Jeff's character in the 20 years that I've known him," declared Collins, elected to the Senate the same year as Sessions.

Collins' handling of both episodes -- according to *Politico*, she held off announcing her opposition until Republicans had lined up enough votes to allow DeVos' nomination to squeak by -- help illustrate why and how she has been able to keep Senate GOP leaders at bay, despite frequent departures from party orthodoxy. Top Republicans are keenly aware as well that Collins' independence has been integral to her winning reelection handily in a state that has given the plurality of its votes to the Democratic nominee for president for the past quarter-century.

Collins grew up in Caribou, in Maine's potato-growing Aroostook County, about as far northeast as you can get in the United States-and closer to the capitals of the Canadian provinces of New Brunswick and Quebec than to the Maine capital of Augusta. Her family has been in the lumber business since 1844 and long involved in politics: Her father was a state senator; her mother was mayor of Caribou and chaired the board of trustees of the University of Maine System. Her introduction to Washington was as a high school senior, when she visited as part of a Senate youth program. In what Collins termed the "highlight of that week," Sen. Margaret Chase Smith, then the Senate's only woman, spent nearly two hours talking with her. Collins today occupies the Senate seat Smith once held, sitting at the desk on the Senate floor that Smith used.

Another role model was Republican William Cohen, her predecessor in the Senate as well as her boss for more than a decade. The lesson that both Cohen and Smith imparted to her, Collins said, is "do what you think is right, no matter the consequences." She interned for Cohen during the summer of 1974, when, as a freshman member of the Judiciary Committee, he joined several other Republicans in voting to impeach President Richard Nixon. Upon her graduation from St. Lawrence University a year later, Cohen hired Collins, and she remained on his staff for 12 years. Cohen moved to the Senate in 1978, and Collins spent six years as staff director of a Governmental Affairs Committee subpanel that Cohen chaired. Two decades later, Collins would find herself chairing the full committee.

After Republicans lost the Senate majority in 1986, Collins returned to Maine to work for GOP Gov. John McKernan, and went on to serve as regional administrator of the Small Business Administration. In 1994, after winning the Republican nomination for governor, she ran third in a three-way general election contest won by independent Angus King-now her Senate colleague. Two years later, Cohen announced his retirement. There was a precedent in Maine for a third-place gubernatorial finisher to be elected senator: Democrat George Mitchell was similarly humiliated in 1974, and then, after being appointed senator in 1980, won election to two full terms. Collins played up her similarities to fellow moderates Cohen and Snowe, while calling for a balanced budget amendment, a line item veto, and term limits. She pledged to serve no more than two terms-broken when she successfully sought a third term in 2008.

Collins was opposed in the general election by former Democratic Gov. Joseph Brennan. He attacked Collins on economic issues and gun control, criticizing Collins for supporting a repeal of the assault weapons ban that had cleared Congress a couple of years earlier. At the time, there were more gun owners per capita in Maine than any state except Alaska, and gun control was anathema in much of the state's rural 2nd Congressional District, where Collins had grown up. But restrictions on firearms were a more popular cause in the state's more densely populated 1st District, which Brennan had represented. Brennan cut into Collins' lead with his attacks on her gun stance-but she outraised him significantly, and ended up winning, 49%-44%.

Years later, in 2013, Collins voted against an assault weapons ban when it was brought before the Senate. But, at the same time, she became one of only four Republicans to break with her party and support a measure to expand background checks on firearms purchases, following the Newtown Connecticut school shooting in which 26 died. After that proposal and subsequent similar ones failed to gain passage, Collins was determined in mid-2016 -- following the Orlando night club shooting in which 49 were killed by a lone gunman -- to broker a compromise that would succeed. Her plan barred sale of guns to terrorism suspects on the government's no-fly or so-called "selectee" list; it was designed to appeal to wavering Republicans by applying the ban to a considerably smaller group than those on the federal terrorist screening database, a list used in a rival Democratic proposal. "I don't want 'Groundhog Day' here," Collins told *The New York Times*. "I don't want us to go through the same thing we went through last year with no result" -- alluding to legislative efforts following the 2014 mass shooting in San Bernardino, Calif. Collins' compromise received solid Democratic support and peeled off seven of her GOP colleagues to gain a Senate majority. But while it survived a procedural vote, it ultimately shared the fate of other previous efforts and failed to advance.

The gun control issue is emblematic of a broader evolution for Collins: While a committed centrist throughout her Senate career, she was at first more conservative than her now-departed Maine colleague, Snowe. But she eventually eclipsed Snowe in the frequency with which she broke with the party. In 2012, their last year in the Senate together, Collins was the second most moderate Republican in the Senate, according to *National Journal*'s annual vote ratings, with Snowe a couple of points behind in fourth place. In 2015, *Almanac* vote rankings showed Collins to again be second most moderate Senate Republican -- bested only by Kirk, who shifted left in the face of a tough reelection campaign. Collins' lifetime score from the conservative Club for Growth through 2015 was 36 percent, by far the lowest of any current GOP senator.

Collins has utilized her status as a swing vote to win concessions: In 2009, she and a moderate Democrat, Nebraska Sen. Ben Nelson, insisted that the price tag of Obama's stimulus package be reduced from $900 billion to $787 billion before providing votes crucial to its passage. But Obama's attempts to win Collins' support for the 2010 Affordable Care Act (ACA) proved fruitless despite months of wooing. She expressed disdain for what she saw as a token effort to include a few Republican ideas in a predominantly Democratic-written measure. While she voted for GOP-sponsored efforts to repeal the ACA that were doomed to failure while Obama was in office, she again found herself at odds with her party in early 2017 -- as Trump entered office and, for the first time, repeal of "Obamacare" was in the realm of reality. She came out in opposition to a House Republican bill backed by Trump to "repeal and replace" the ACA. "This bill doesn't come close to achieving the goal of allowing low-income seniors to purchase health insurance," Collins -- who has chaired the Senate Select Committee on Aging since 2015 -- told the *Portland Press Herald*. "We don't want to in any way sacrifice coverage for people who need it the most." Earlier, she had co-sponsored legislation with Louisiana Republican Sen. Bill Cassidy, a physician, to allow states to opt to continue operating under the ACA.

Collins has joined Democrats on other issues ranging from regulation of the nation's financial markets -- she supported the 2010 Dodd-Frank law, which Trump and many congressional Republicans vowed to roll back -- to gay rights. In 2010, she was the only Republican on the Armed Services Committee to vote to repeal the ban on openly gay people in the military. At a news conference a year later, she held up a postcard she received from an anonymous Army soldier thanking her for her vote. "...I felt so strongly it was the right thing to do," Collins said later, adding that getting the policy repealed "was pretty tough, because even though we ultimately got eight Republican votes [on the Senate floor], I was going up against a person I admire greatly"-Arizona GOP Sen. John McCain, whom Collins calls "a friend and a hero." In 2014, Collins became the fourth Republican senator to publicly support same-sex marriage.

During the 2011-12 debate over avoiding the so-called "fiscal cliff," Collins again found herself at odds with fellow Republicans: She supported a surtax on millionaires to compensate for extending middle-income tax cuts passed early in the administration of President George W. Bush. "They can afford to pay more to help with our deficit, and that's an area where I differ with many in our party," said Collins, the only Senate Republican to vote in favor of implementing the White House's so-called Buffett rule. Inspired by comments from billionaire Warren Buffett, the proposal called for those taking in $2 million or more annually to pay at least 30 percent in taxes.

Similarly in late 2013, Collins led a bipartisan group of 14 senators in an effort to find a solution to a budget crisis that shut down the federal government for 16 days. The crisis was instigated by conservatives in the House, who demanded rollbacks in Obama's health care law in return for their votes on a bill to fund government operations. Collins tried to forge a compromise that called for a two-year delay in the health care law's medical device tax, extended government funding for six months, and raised the debt ceiling through the end of January 2014. But Senate Democrats objected to the continuation of automatic spending cuts that were part of the deal, and it failed to advance.

Collins' efforts were praised for defusing some of the partisan tension that had prevented movement toward a compromise. Days later, Majority Leader Harry Reid and Minority Leader Mitch McConnell reached an agreement that reopened the government, although it was a limited, short-term measure. Shortly after that, Collins was among the Republicans involved in a bipartisan deal in March 2014 to extend expired long-term unemployment benefits. A few months later, she threw herself into an unsuccessful attempt to find a compromise over Democratic demands to raise the minimum wage. She opposed the Democratic calls for it to be set at $10.10 an hour, saying it was "too much and will cost jobs."

Some of Collins' clout comes from her status on the Appropriations Committee, where she chairs the Transportation, Housing and Urban Development Subcommittee. In December 2014, she got a controversial transportation provision attached to a government funding bill eliminating the requirement that truck drivers would have to get two nights' sleep in a row before starting work. The Obama Administration's transportation secretary, Anthony Foxx, warned the measure would "put lives at risk" because of driver fatigue, but Collins contended the rule "presented some unintended and unanticipated consequences" needing more study.

Before stepping down in 2013 due to internal Senate Republican term limits, Collins was for a decade chairwoman or ranking Republican on the Homeland Security and Governmental Affairs Committee, where she had once been a staffer. There, she worked closely with another party outlier, Connecticut Sen. Joe Lieberman, prior to his 2012 retirement. In the wake of 9/11, with Collins in the chair, they collaborated on a reorganization of the intelligence community, creating the Office of the Director of National Intelligence and a new counter-terrorism center. Their friendship extended to the campaign trail: Collins in 2006 endorsed Lieberman when he lost the Connecticut Democratic primary and successfully sought reelection as an independent. Lieberman returned the favor in 2008 when Collins faced a competitive challenge.

DeVos was not the only Trump nominee that Collins opposed in early 2017. With her environmental interests, she was the lone Republican "no" vote on the nomination of Scott Pruitt, decried by some critics as a climate change "denier," to head the Environmental Protection Agency. Seeking a fourth term in 2014, Collins had received the support of several leading environmental groups, who cited her belief in human-caused climate change and her support of rollbacks in allowable levels of carbon emissions. Teaming with Democrat Maria Cantwell of Washington State, Collins introduced a "cap-and-dividend" bill at the end of 2009 to address carbon emissions. Companies would buy carbon shares in auctions, passing on costs to consumers, with 75 percent of the fund paid as dividends to citizens and 25 percent devoted to clean energy research and development. They pressed their bill as an alternative to the Democrats' cap-and-trade legislation, to no avail. In 2011, Collins was the only Senate Republican to oppose an amendment that would have barred the EPA from regulating greenhouse gases.

Collins won reelection in 2014 with 68 percent against her underfunded Democratic opponent, Shenna Bellows, a former director of the Maine chapter of the American Civil Liberties Union. Collins had more formidable opposition in her prior two reelection bids, but won comfortably. In 2002, she was challenged by former state Senate Majority Leader Chellie Pingree, who was known as the sponsor of a state law allowing government negotiations with pharmaceutical companies as a way of lowering prescription drug costs. Pingree ran ads saying Collins was "siding with the big drug companies." Collins cited an amendment she sponsored successfully to make prescription drugs cheaper. She won with 58 percent. Six years later, Pingree was elected to the House seat vacated by Democrat Tom Allen, who decided to take on Collins. Allen made the Iraq war a central issue; Collins voted for the 2002 resolution authorizing the war, and later opposed a Democratic attempt to set a timetable for troop withdrawal. The war became a less salient issue as the success of Bush's troop surge strategy became evident. Collins defeated Allen with 61 percent in the face of a banner year for Democrats nationwide.

In September 2015, Collins observed a milestone: 6,000 consecutive floor votes, extending a streak dating to her arrival in the Senate almost 19 years earlier. Collins, who once twisted an ankle racing to a roll call, has said the streak was inspired by Margaret Chase Smith, who maintained a similar streak for 13 years until surgery forced her to break it. In 2012, Collins married for the first time, at 59. Her husband, government consulting executive Thomas Daffron, then 73, was, like Collins, once a staffer to Cohen, and is also a former chief operating officer of the Baltimore Orioles. The wedding took place in Caribou, and Collins and her husband were said to be spending increasing amounts of time in Maine-fueling speculation that she was aspiring to finish her political career in Augusta, as the state's first woman governor, rather than inside the Beltway.

Talk of a possible 2018 bid by Collins for governor -- after her losing race for that office more than two decades ago -- followed her after she was reelected to a fourth Senate term. Collins acknowledged in early 2017 that she was giving serious consideration to a gubernatorial bid. If she did run, she would not have to give up her Senate seat since she is not up for reelection until 2020. Gov. Paul LePage, an outspoken conservative who is barred by law by running again, has made no secret of his opinion of Collins as a successor. "I think Susan Collins is done in Maine, I think her decision to go against the Maine Republicans really cooked her goose," LePage declared in late 2016. "Some of her moves to come out against Donald Trump are not going to bode well." Neutral observers, however, believe Collins would be a favorite for governor in a general election, but that she could face a primary battle in a state

GOP in which supporters of LePage and Trump have become an increasing presence. After her August 2016 op-ed column -- in which Collins asserted that Trump's "constant stream of cruel comments and his inability to admit error or apologize" made him "unworthy of being our president" -- her popularity among Maine Republican voters took a hit. While a poll by the University of New Hampshire Survey Center found her approval among state GOP voters at a still strong 61 percent, that marked a drop from a 74 percent approval score just weeks before the op-ed appeared.

Junior Senator

Angus King (I)

Elected 2012, term expires 2018, 1st term; b. Mar 31, 1944, Alexandria, VA; Dartmouth College, A.B.; University of Virginia, J.D.; Episcopalian; Married (Mary J. Herman); 5 children; 5 grandchildren.

Elected Office: ME Governor, 1995-2003.

Professional Career: Practicing attorney, 1969-1983, 2003-present; Chief counsel, Sen. William Hathaway, U.S Senate Subcommittee on Alcoholism & Narcotics, 1972-1975; Host, ME Public Television's MaineWatch, 1975-1993; Vice President., General counsel, Swift River/Hafslund, 1983-1989; Founder, President, Northeast Energy Management, 1989-1994; Partner, Independence Wind, 2007-2012.

DC Office: 133 HSOB 20510, 202-224-5344, Fax: 202-224-1946, king.senate.gov.

State Offices: Augusta, 207-622-8292; Bangor, 207-945-8000; Presque Isle, 207-764-5124; Scarborough, 207-883-1588.

Committees: *Armed Services*: Airland (RMM), Seapower. *Budget*. *Energy & Natural Resources*: Energy, National Parks, Water & Power (RMM). *Intelligence*. *Rules & Administration*.

Group Ratings

	ADA	ACLU	AFL-CIO	LCV	ITI	COC	HAFA	ACU	CFG	FRC
2016	-	58%	-	94%	80%	63%	7%	8%	5%	0%
2015	85%	C	100%	100%	C	43%	C	0%	0%	0%

Almanac Ratings 2015

	Economy	Social	Foreign	Composite
Liberal	90%	90%	68%	83%
Conservative	10%	10%	33%	17%

Key Votes of the 114th Congress

1. Keystone pipeline	N	5. National Security Data	Y	9. Gun Sales Checks	Y
2. Export-Import Bank	N	6. Iran Nuclear Deal	N	10. Sanctuary Cities	N
3. Debt Ceiling Increase	Y	7. Puerto Rico Debt	Y	11. Planned Parenthood	N
4. Homeland Security $$	Y	8. Loretta Lynch A.G	Y	12. Trade deals	N

Election Results

Election	Name (Party)	Vote (%)		Cand. Spent	Ind. Exp. Support	Ind. Exp. Oppose
2012 General	Angus King (I)	370,580	(53%)	$2,850,780	$1,314,443	$3,354,401
	Charles Summers (R)	215,399	(31%)	$1,225,838	$345,360	$1,778,522
	Cynthia Dill (D)	92,900	(13%)	$190,528	$204,806	$186,434

Residents of this state in the nation's Northeast tip, with its rocky and sometimes remote terrain, have often demonstrated an independent streak-and, when it comes to politics, Angus King, Maine's junior senator, is Exhibit No. 1. Originally a Democrat, King came to believe that "sometimes the best thing the government can do is get out of the way;" he entered the 1994 governor's race as an independent, criticizing government meddling in business. After serving two terms as Maine's chief executive, King left politics for a decade -- only to emerge as a candidate for an open Senate seat in 2012, while decrying the legislative gridlock in Congress. He again ran as independent, refusing to say during the campaign with which party he would caucus if elected. When he won the seat, King announced he would join the Senate Democratic caucus, a choice that did not surprise those who had watched his political progression in recent years.

He has retained at least a tenuous affiliation with Democrats. In the spring of 2014, with the Republicans given a good chance of retaking the Senate majority in that fall's election, King created a stir when he said he might be willing to caucus with the GOP if he felt the interests of his constituents would be served. But, when the Republicans regained Senate control, King announced the day after the election that he would remain aligned with the Democrats. (Independents are compelled to join one of the two caucuses to secure seats on Senate committees.) "I think it is in Maine's interest to have a senator in each camp," King said, alluding to his senior colleague, Republican Susan Collins. "The reality of the current Senate, whether it is controlled by Democrats or Republicans, is that nothing can or will happen without bipartisan support." In July 2016, he disclosed that he would vote for Hillary Clinton, continuing a pattern of supporting Democratic presidential nominees that goes back more than a decade.

King was raised in the Washington D.C. suburb of Alexandria Virginia, but has spent most of his adult life "Down East." After attending Dartmouth College and the University of Virginia law school, he moved to Maine to work for a legal assistance organization and then became an aide to Maine Sen. William Hathaway, a Democrat. When King was 29, physicians discovered he had an aggressive form of skin cancer during a routine checkup, which he said he would not have scheduled if it weren't free through his insurance. Years later, as a senator, he reacted angrily to a report that opponents of the Obama Administration's health insurance overhaul were urging college students not to sign up under the Affordable Care Act, suggesting those dispensing such advice were "guilty of murder." King told the *Bangor Daily News:* "I think the reason I feel so strongly about this is that if someone had given me that advice when I was 25, I wouldn't be here. I'd be dead."

After leaving Hathaway's office, King returned to Maine to practice law and start an energy conservation business. He sold the latter for $20 million in 1994, just prior to running for governor-a race in which he invested $750,000 of his own money. For 18 years, he had hosted Maine Public Television's *MaineWatch*, making him a well-known figure in the state. King ran a campaign in which he criticized high taxes and called for specific spending cuts; on Election Day, he edged out former Democratic Gov. Joseph Brennan, 35%-34%. Running a distant third was the Republican nominee, now-Sen. Collins.

As governor, King cut the state budget and workforce. He shortened environmental permit delays from nine months to 45 days and opposed the ban on timber clear-cutting. But he signed a bill imposing tight controls on paper mills' dioxin discharges into rivers-celebrating afterward by jumping fully clothed into the Kennebec River. In 1998, with a soaring job approval rating, King won a second term with 59 percent. He then signed legislation to have the state leverage its buying clout to negotiate lower prices for prescription drugs for those without Medicaid or private health insurance. The law was overturned by a federal judge in 2000, but the state won on appeal. Perhaps his best known initiative was to provide middle school students with laptop computers-then a precedent-setting idea. He convinced the legislature to provide $30 million for the effort.

Barred by law from seeking a third term in 2002, there was speculation that King would challenge Collins for the Senate, but he opted to leave politics. His first move after departing the governorship was to embark on a six-month, 15,000-mile road trip through 33 states, as he, his wife and two children lived in a 40-foot recreational vehicle. It produced a book: *Governor's Travels: How I Left Politics, Learned to Back Up a Bus, and Found America.* Later, King lectured at a couple of the state's colleges, worked for a law firm and a mergers-and-acquisitions advisory firm, and formed a wind energy company.

King's reentry into politics, at the age of 68, was almost by accident: Republican Olympia Snowe had been raising money and was expected to seek a fourth term. But, in February 2012, Snowe, a leading Senate moderate, announced her retirement, expressing fatigue over a partisan climate that made passing legislation increasingly daunting. King stepped in, vowing to continue where Snowe had left off. "I can be a broker for common sense. I can speak from the middle," he declared. His campaign headquarters prominently featured two photographs side by side: one of Ronald Reagan and the other of Robert Kennedy. However, the widespread speculation was that King was aligned with Democrats, having revealed he would support President Barack Obama for reelection. He had backed Obama in 2008 and Democratic presidential nominee John Kerry in 2004, although he endorsed the Republican nominee, George W. Bush, while governor in 2000.

National Democrats did little to support their official nominee in the Senate contest, state Sen. Cynthia Dill, figuring that King-who started the race a heavy favorite-would win and end up in their camp. A super PAC with Republican ties ran ads to boost Dill, hoping to siphon enough Democratic votes from King to allow the Republican nominee, Maine Secretary of State Charlie Summers, to win a plurality. The conservative nonprofit Crossroads GPS ran ads blasting King's support of tax hikes as governor, and the NRSC broadcast a spot accusing King of using political connections to win a "sketchy" federal loan guarantee for his wind energy firm-of which he had divested himself before the election-to build an industrial wind farm. While the ad barrage caused some tightening in the polls, King won handily with 53 percent, to 31 percent for Summers and Dill at 13 percent.

Notwithstanding his election as an independent, King voted with a majority of Senate Democrats 94 percent of the time in 2013-2014, according to a *Washington Post* congressional voting database. According to 2015 *Almanac* rankings, King was the 40th most liberal senator, placing him in league with members of the Senate Democrats' centrist wing, but significantly to the left of the Senate GOP's most moderate members, including Collins. King has argued that it is not he, but rather the political landscape, that has shifted since his days in the statehouse. "I've agreed more with the Democrats in part because the Republican Party has moved so far to the right," King said during an interview in late 2013 with *BU Washington News Service*. "When I was an independent in Maine 20 years ago as governor, the Republican Party was a different party."

Others contended that King's floor votes told only part of the story. "...If you look at who is working behind the scenes trying to find compromise, I think he is much more in that bipartisan school than are most of the Democrats and the Republicans," said Colby College government professor Sandy Maisel. A notable instance of King parting company with Democrats came when he helped to craft a Republican-backed student loan deal approved in 2013. The plan linked loan rates more closely to the financial markets, which a number of Democrats contended could create larger long-term financial burdens for borrowers.

King was an active participant in a bipartisan group of 14 Republicans and Democrats that Collins brought together in October 2013 in an effort to end the government shutdown. In 2014, around the time he was suggesting he might switch to the Republican Conference, King joined Republicans in voting to block one of the Democrats' showcase bills, the Paycheck Fairness Act-designed to force employers to prove that salary gaps between men and women employees were based on factors other than gender. In 2015, after affirming his membership in the Democratic caucus, he sided with the Obama White House on sustaining Obama's veto of the Keystone XL pipeline, and bottling up a Republican-sponsored resolution that sought to block the Iran nuclear agreement. King also lined up with most Senate Democrats in opposition to giving Obama expedited authority to negotiate a 12-nation Pacific trade deal, the Trans-Pacific Partnership.

When he entered the Senate and joined the Democratic caucus , King got a seat on the Armed Services Committee, important to Maine given the economic impact of the Portsmouth Naval Shipyard and the Bath Iron Works . On the efforts to combat terrorism through military action against the Islamic State (ISIS), King parted company with the more hawkish members of that panel, notably its chairman, Arizona Sen. John McCain. "We've been in the stamping out business for the last 12 or 13 years and it hasn't worked all that well," King said in early 2015. "Part of the problem is the more we, the U.S. and the West, are active - particularly with troops on the ground - the more it becomes a recruiting tool for the extremists."

On the Energy and Natural Resources Committee, he teamed up with the chairwoman , Alaska Republican Lisa Murkowski, to establish a Senate Arctic Caucus. His move reflected Maine's increasing interest in becoming a gateway to the Northwest Passage -- increasingly navigable due to climate change -- and reaping economic benefits from trade and shipping. Pointing a finger at Senate dysfunction as a roadblock to establishing U.S. policy on the Arctic, he lamented that the Senate had yet to ratify the Law of the Sea Treaty, which established principles and limits on the ocean area that countries may claim. "There's an attitude in the Senate among some people that treaties are an abrogation of U.S. sovereignty," he told the *Bangor Daily News*. "I'm puzzled by that. It puts us on the sidelines."

It bespeaks King's broader continuing frustration about the institution. "About 65 -- two thirds of the senators -- have been here eight years or less," he noted to National Public Radio in 2016. "Most of us have never seen the place work. We're like a football team that's lost every game for the past five years. We don't know how to win...We are getting things done. But on the big issues, the controversial issues, we're just stymied."

Such downbeat sentiments have not deterred King from seeking a second term in 2018, when he turns 74. King disclosed in June 2015 that he had been diagnosed with prostate cancer in its early stages, but said it would not affect his reelection plans. Maine Gov. Paul LePage, a conservative Republican, suggested on a Boston radio show in early 2015 that he might challenge King. The mercurial LePage said a day later he had been joking, but later sounded more serious about it on numerous occasions. Also in the mix was Republican state Sen. Eric Brakey, who spearheaded a successful 2015 push in Maine to allow the carrying of concealed firearms without a permit.

"The only reason I would run against Angus King is I believe he's had a free ride with the people of the state of Maine, despite the fact that he's really not a Mainer, he's from Virginia," LePage declared to a Portland radio station in late 2016. A King spokesman shot back: "I think if you asked most people in Maine, they'd say three successful statewide elections isn't a free pass. And while Sen. King has only been in Maine for 47 years, he has long said he would have preferred to be born in the state, but unfortunately he didn't have much say in the matter and he loves his mother too much to cast blame." LePage announced in May 2017 that he would not run for the Senate in 2018.

FIRST DISTRICT

Chellie Pingree (D)

Elected 2008, 5th term; b. Apr 02, 1955, Minneapolis, MN; University of Southern Maine, Att., 1973; College of the Atlantic (ME), B.A., 1979; Lutheran; Divorced; 3 children (3 from previous marriage); 2 grandchildren.

Elected Office: ME Senate, 1992-2000, Majority Leader, 1996-2000.

Professional Career: Farmer, 1977-1980; Founder & President, N. Island Designs Co., 1981-1992; President & CEO, Common Cause, 2003-2007.

DC Office: 2162 RHOB 20515, 202-225-6116, Fax: 202-225-5590, pingree.house.gov.

State Offices: Portland, 207-774-5019; Waterville, 207-873-5713.

Committees: *Appropriations*: Agriculture, Rural Development, FDA & Related Agencies, Interior, Environment & Related Agencies.

Group Ratings

	ADA	ACLU	AFL-CIO	LCV	ITI	COC	HAFA	ACU	CFG	FRC
2016	-	94%	-	97%	33%	54%	14%	4%	4%	0%
2015	95%	C	100%	100%	C	45%	C	4%	0%	0%

Almanac Ratings 2015

	Economy	Social	Foreign	Composite
Liberal	97%	100%	100%	99%
Conservative	3%	0%	0%	1%

Key Votes of the 114th Congress

1. Keystone Pipeline	N	5. Puerto Rico Debt	Y	9. Offenses by Aliens	N
2. Trade Deals	N	6. Medical Marijuana	Y	10. Troops in Iraq	Y
3. Export-Import Bank	Y	7. Sanctuary Cities	N	11. Homeland Security $$	Y
4. Debt Ceiling Increase	Y	8. Armor-piercing Bullets	N	12. Trade Adjustment aid	Y

Election Results

Election	Name (Party)	Vote (%)		Cand. Spent	Ind. Exp. Support	Ind. Exp. Oppose
2016 General	Chellie Pingree (D)	227,546	(58%)	$267,264		
	Mark Holbrook (R)	164,569	(42%)	$98,631		
2016 Primary	Chellie Pingree (D)		(100%)			

Prior winning percentages: 2014 (58%), 2012 (62%), 2010 (57%), 2008 (55%)

Chellie Pingree, elected in 2008, became the first Democratic woman from Maine in Congress, even though the state has a long history of electing Republican women. A blunt-talking liberal with a long career in public service, Pingree has maintained her popularity by paying close attention to state issues, from ships to seafood. She once ran statewide and has prompted speculation about another such bid.

Pingree grew up in Minnesota, the granddaughter of Scandinavian immigrants who worked as dairy farmers. Her parents moved to Minneapolis, where her father was an accountant and her mother a nurse. The city's anti-war activism during the Vietnam era had a profound influence on Pingree, and she left high school early for alternative education programs on the East Coast. At one program in Worcester,

Massachusetts, she met her future husband and followed him to Maine, where they settled on remote North Haven Island in Penobscot Bay. As disciples of the "back to the land" movement, they lived for years in a cabin without running water or electricity and made their living as organic farmers. Although the couple later divorced, Pingree thrived on the island, both politically and professionally. In 1981, she started her own business selling knitting kits. At its peak, the business, the North Island Designs Co., distributed 100,000 mail-order catalogs. She started her political career in local offices on the island, including serving as tax assessor and on the planning and school boards.

In 1991, Pingree attended a speech by then-Rep. Patricia Schroeder of Colorado, who briefly sought the Democratic presidential nomination in 1988, which inspired her to take her friends' advice and run for an open seat in the state Senate. She went door-to-door in the traditionally Republican district in Knox County and won. Pingree rose to majority leader in 1996. As leader, she fought a challenge from pharmaceutical companies and persuaded reluctant players to agree to a law allowing the state to negotiate prescription drug prices, the first such law in the country.

In 2002, Pingree challenged Sen. Susan Collins, a Republican moderate, who won 58%-42%. Shortly after her loss, she became president of Common Cause, the Washington, D.C., government and campaign watchdog group. She took the reins of the nonprofit organization just after the successful push to overhaul the nation's campaign finance laws. She recalls an often strained relationship with Sen. John McCain of Arizona, the Republican cosponsor of the law, who accused her of injecting partisanship into her work. As president, Pingree also directed Common Cause to lobby against media consolidation in the hands of a few companies.

She left Common Cause in 2007 to run for the House seat that Democrat Tom Allen gave up to run another sacrificial campaign against Collins. Although she had complained for years about the influence of money in politics, Pingree had no trouble raising far more of it than any of her five rivals for the Democratic nomination. She mostly eschewed money from political action committees but enjoyed the backing of EMILY's List, which funds women candidates who support abortion rights. Pingree won the primary with 44 percent of the vote. In the general election, she more than tripled the fundraising of state Sen. Charles Summers. Pingree won 55%-45%.

In the House, Pingree has been a loyal Democrat. In 2013, she gained a plum seat on the Appropriations Committee, where she has looked after her region's defense interests. She has been successful with New Hampshire's Portsmouth Naval Shipyard that virtually straddles the Maine border, and the Pratt & Whitney plant a few miles away that in 2014 got a $1 billion contract to manufacture engines for the F-35 fighter jet. She has taken a strong interest in environmental issues, helping to form the House Sustainable Energy and Environmental Coalition and introducing a bill to force BP to pay royalties on the oil from its massive spill in the Gulf of Mexico in 2010. In June 2016, she joined the House chamber sit-in by Democrats who were demanding action on gun-control legislation - a potentially risky move in a substantially rural state.

She faced a competitive reelection campaign in 2010 against alternative energy company owner Dean Scontras, who got support from tea party activists. The Maine Republican Party ran ads accusing Pingree of taking trips on the corporate jet of her fiancée, hedge-fund billionaire Donald Sussman. (Pingree and Sussman married in 2011.) Scontras also sought to tie her to liberal House Speaker Nancy Pelosi. But Pingree's familiarity with the voters gave her a 57%-43% win. She has handily won reelection since. She has considered running for both the Senate and governor, and has clashed with Republican Gov. Paul LePage on his call for cuts in Medicaid spending.

Her marriage to Sussman, a major donor to Democratic super PACs, increased Pingree's access to big political contributors plus her own donations to other Democrats. He created some controversy when he bought a controlling interest in newspapers in Portland and Augusta. Questions about the influence of her husband disappeared when they announced in September 2015 their plan for a divorce. Pingree is young enough and the state is unpredictable enough that she has an opportunity in 2018, when there will be contests for governor and the Senate. Her daughter Hannah Pingree was speaker of the state House before she was term-limited in 2010.

Southern Maine: Portland

Population		Race and Ethnicity		Income	
Total	670,268	White	93.3%	Median Income	$55,468 (179 out of 435)
Land area	3,286	Black	1.5%		
Pop/ sq mi	204.0	Latino	1.6%		
Born in state	58.1%	Asian	1.5%	Under $50,000	45.1%
		Two races	1.7%	$50,000-$99,999	29.9%
Age Groups		Other	0.4%	$100,000-$199,999	18.0%
Under 18	19.7%			$200,000 or more	4.3%
18-34	19.9%	**Education**		Poverty Rate	11.5%
35-64	43.0%	H.S grad or less	35.7%		
Over 64	17.3%	Some college	28.7%	**Health Insurance**	
		College Degree, 4 yr	22.8%	With health insurance coverage	90.9%
Work		Post grad	12.7%		
White Collar	38.4%			**Public Assistance**	
Sales and Service	42.2%	**Military**		Cash public assistance income	3.7%
Blue Collar	19.4%	Veteran	10.6%	Food stamp/SNAP benefits	13.7%
Government	13.2%	Active Duty	0.2%		

Voter Turnout			
2015 Total Citizens 18+	526,959	2016 House Turnout as % CVAP	74%
2016 House turnout	392,391	2014 House Turnout as % CVAP	58%

2012 Presidential Vote		
Barack Obama	223,040	(59%)
Mitt Romney	143,024	(38%)

2016 Presidential Vote		
Hillary Clinton	212,860	(54%)
Donald Trump	154,399	(39%)
Gary Johnson	18,593	(5%)

Cook Partisan Voting Index: D+8

The 1st District of Maine stretches from southernmost Kittery and nearby Kennebunkport to the craggy-shored, ancestrally Republican counties to the east. From the New Hampshire border, it extends halfway up the Atlantic coast to Canada. The historic center is Portland, Maine's largest city, home to the yuppies and lawyers who have revived and renovated its downtown landmarks. Portland's antique charm, mostly booming economy, and tolerant lifestyle have made it a haven for singles and gays. In a 2013 referendum, Portland voters approved recreational use of marijuana. The more than 100-year-old L.L.Bean is not far away in Freeport. Old mill towns like Biddeford and Sanford have been redeveloped.

The area has a strong defense presence. Base-closing rounds have spared the Portsmouth Naval Shipyard at Kittery, the nation's oldest continually operating naval shipyard. With a workforce of more than 5,300, the future of the yard has improved with billions of dollars in long-term federal contracts to service nuclear-powered submarines. Even though it is the largest such facility on the East Coast, the shipyard's future has always been a topic of worried discussion for locals. Another good omen: In November 2016, the Navy awarded a $29 million contract for repairs at Kittery. Up the coast at Bath Iron Works, which builds destroyers for the Navy for about $4 billion, job cutbacks have loomed because of downsizing of the fleet and competition with the shipyard in Pascagoula Mississippi. Mostly forgotten is the Brunswick Naval Air Station, which closed in 2011, with a big hit to the local economy. In its place, more than 80 businesses and 800 jobs have moved into industrial and commercial space at the overhauled Brunswick Landing.

Portland and several other coastal towns in southern Maine are in the 1st Congressional District. The district includes the five coastal counties from York to Knox, and most of inland Augusta-based Kennebec. About 40 percent of the population is in Portland-based Cumberland. The 1st also takes in several remote islands off the coast, where people enjoy a lifestyle more reminiscent of the Alaska wilderness, shuttling to the mainland on ferries and Cessna aircraft. In the summer, the air traffic includes the families of *Fortune* 500 executives traveling to their estates. In the winter, lobstermen and local business owners board most flights. Lobsters are not just a tradition here but also an economic necessity.

In 2015, the 5,900 licensed lobstermen and women in the state hauled in an estimated 120 million pounds, with a sixth-consecutive record harvest and a recovery from what had been virtually giveaway prices. But local scientists have sounded the alarm that climate change and warmer temperatures in the Gulf of Maine could hurt the lobster population or move them north to colder waters. Warm weather also affected the maple syrup industry during the winter of 2016, with an unusually short season that reduced the supply and the sugar content.

Politically, the 1st District votes like the state as a whole: quirkily, often for independents, and splitting tickets with abandon. In 2008, every county voted for Republican Sen. Susan Collins, and all but one voted for Democratic presidential nominee Barack Obama. While most attention in 2016 focused on the battle for the electoral vote in the 2nd District, Hillary Clinton easily won the 1st, 54%-39%, carrying every county except for Kennebec.

SECOND DISTRICT

Bruce Poliquin (R)

Elected 2014, 2nd term; b. Nov 01, 1953, Waterville; Phillips Academy, (MA), 1972; Harvard University, B.A., 1976; Roman Catholic; Widower; 1 child.

Elected Office: ME Treas., 2011-2013.

Professional Career: Bank employee, 1976; Investment consulting firm, 1978; Business owner & manager; Investor company principal, 1981-1996.

DC Office: 1208 LHOB 20515, 202-225-6306, Fax: 202-225-2943, poliquin.house.gov.

State Offices: Bangor, 207-942-0583; Lewiston, 207-784-0768; Presque Isle, 207-764-1968.

Committees: *Financial Services*: Capital Markets, Securities & Investment, Terrorism & Illicit Finance. *Veterans' Affairs*: Oversight & Investigations.

Group Ratings

	ADA	ACLU	AFL-CIO	LCV	ITI	COC	HAFA	ACU	CFG	FRC
2016	-	11%	-	21%	83%	86%	42%	56%	64%	67%
2015	5%	C	25%	9%	C	95%	C	65%	46%	64%

Almanac Ratings 2015

	Economy	Social	Foreign	Composite
Liberal	23%	16%	16%	18%
Conservative	78%	84%	84%	82%

Key Votes of the 114th Congress

1. Keystone Pipeline	Y	5. Puerto Rico Debt	N	9. Offenses by Aliens	Y
2. Trade Deals	N	6. Medical Marijuana	Y	10. Troops in Iraq	N
3. Export-Import Bank	N	7. Sanctuary Cities	Y	11. Homeland Security $$	Y
4. Debt Ceiling Increase	Y	8. Armor-piercing Bullets	Y	12. Trade Adjustment aid	Y

Election Results

Election	Name (Party)	Vote (%)	Cand. Spent	Ind. Exp. Support	Ind. Exp. Oppose
2016 General	Bruce Poliquin (R)	192,878 (55%)	$3,365,694	$111,923	$5,495,528
	Emily Cain (D)	159,081 (45%)	$3,474,616	$614,108	$4,295,410
2016 Primary	Bruce Poliquin (R)	(100%)			

Prior winning percentages: 2014 (45%)

Republican Bruce Poliquin, elected in 2014, is the only House Republican from New England. In his first term, he pursued his career interest in banking issues, and stayed attuned to his district on international trade. A significant accomplishment was his relatively easy reelection.

Poliquin was born and raised in Waterville and studied at Phillips Exeter Academy and Harvard. After college, he launched a lucrative business career that took him to Chicago and New York, including a stint managing $5 billion in worker pension funds for Bath Iron Works and International Paper, both major Maine employers at the time. He made his first political bid in 2010 when he ran for governor, spending more than $700,000 of his own money. He finished sixth in the seven-candidate field but he mended fences with the winner, GOP Gov. Paul LePage, and was elected state treasurer by the Maine Legislature.

Poliquin's tenure hit a few bumps, including criticism that he had used the office for personal gain in his various holdings and properties. In one case, Democrats charged that he had exploited a tax preference program for forested land to reduce his own property taxes. After striking a deal on the land, he was not charged with wrongdoing. But ethics questions lingered. When he ran in 2012 for the Senate seat of retiring Republican Olympia Snowe, he was second in the five-candidate primary to Charles Summers, 28%-22%.

Poliquin saw his next opening in 2013, when Rep. Michael Michaud left his House seat for an unsuccessful challenge for governor against LePage. In the primary, he won, 57%-43%, over state Sen. Kevin Raye, who had lost two races against Michaud. He faced a strong Democratic challenger in Emily Cain, a 34-year-old rising star who had compiled a long political record, including as state House minority leader, where she had worked across the aisle to cut deals. Despite his positive comments about the tea party during earlier campaigns, Poliquin distanced himself from its supporters. House Speaker John Boehner stumped on Poliquin's behalf in September, tying Cain to President Barack Obama and taking aim at the Affordable Care Act.

The National Republican Congressional Committee spent $1.3 million to help Poliquin, while the Democrats' House Majority PAC countered with a $600,000 ad buy tying him to Wall Street. Poliquin made his case more personal by discussing his wife's tragic death and his life as a single father, which was effective in neutralizing Democratic criticism of him as a Wall Street robber baron. He benefited from a bear-baiting referendum that energized turnout among gun owners. For her part, Cain played up Poliquin's ties to LePage, who has been a polarizing figure in the state. The Democratic Congressional Campaign Committee spent less than $100,000 for Cain. She slightly outspent Poliquin, but supporters said that she faced headwinds on two fronts. One was Obama's unpopularity, which dragged down Democrats. A quirky factor was independent Blaine Richardson, a former Republican and self-styled conservative who played outside the partisan lines and drew 11 percent of voters. Poliquin eked out a plurality, 47%-42%. He was the first Republican to win the seat since Snowe moved to the Senate in 1994.

In the House, Poliquin parlayed his background in banking into a seat on the Financial Services Committee. He said that a top goal was reducing regulations on small banks, with a loosening of restrictions in the Dodd-Frank law, which he said should be used to "catch the big guys." On the panel's task force on terrorism financing, he said it was imperative to investigate how terrorists were receiving funds to carry out their attacks. He said that if federal regulators did not act on natural gas pipeline requests within a year, the projects should be automatically approved. "I'm someone who does not sit back and watch things," he told the *Portland Press-Herald*. "I get involved." Poliquin was a firm opponent of the proposal to provide trade negotiating authority to the president. He cited "unfair and unlawful Canadian subsidies flowing to competing paper mills on the other side of the border" from Maine.

In 2016, Cain ran again. The contest resulted in huge spending in this low-cost media market. Each candidate raised about $3.4 million. This time, the DCCC and other party committees spent more than $4 million on behalf of Cain; their Republican counterparts spent a comparable amount for Poliquin. Democrats accused Poliquin of "flip-flopping" when he was among more than 40 House Republicans who switched a week later their earlier opposition to a measure designed to prevent LGBT discrimination. Cain accused him of trying to "have it both ways" with voters. Poliquin got an unexpected boost from the big vote in the district for Donald Trump, though he dodged questions during the campaign of whether he supported his party's presidential nominee. He won 55%-45%, and took each of the 11 counties except for Hancock along the coast.

Northern and Central Maine, Lewiston, Bangor

Population		Race and Ethnicity		Income	
Total	658,832	White	94.4%	Median Income	$43,404 (358 out of 435)
Land area	27,557	Black	0.7%	Under $50,000	56.2%
Pop/ sq mi	23.9	Latino	1.3%	$50,000-$99,999	129.9%
Born in state	70.5%	Asian	0.7%	$100,000-$199,999	11.3%
		Two races	2.0%	$200,000 or more	1.7%
		Other	0.8%	Poverty Rate	16.4%
Age Groups		**Education**		**Health Insurance**	
Under 18	19.7%	H.S grad or less	47.6%	With health insurance coverage	89.0%
18-34	19.8%	Some college	30.2%		
35-64	42.6%	College Degree, 4 yr	14.5%		
Over 64	17.9%	Post grad	7.7%		
Work		**Military**		**Public Assistance**	
White Collar	32.1%	Veteran	11.7%	Cash public assistance income	5.1%
Sales and Service	42.7%	Active Duty	0.1%	Food stamp/SNAP benefits	20.5%
Blue Collar	25.2%				
Government	15.0%				

Voter Turnout

2015 Total Citizens 18+	521,315	2016 House Turnout as % CVAP	68%
2016 House turnout	352,183	2014 House Turnout as % CVAP	55%

2012 Presidential Vote

Barack Obama	178,266	(53%)
Mitt Romney	149,252	(44%)

2016 Presidential Vote

Donald Trump	181,194	(51%)
Hillary Clinton	144,875	(41%)
Gary Johnson	19,512	(6%)

Cook Partisan Voting Index: R+2

The 2nd District of Maine is heavily forested, rough-hewn and enormous. Covering more than 85 percent of the state, it is larger than the states of New Hampshire, Vermont and Massachusetts combined. The population is not evenly distributed. There are several different Maines represented here: The bays of coastal Maine, with their small fishing towns; the potato fields of far northern Aroostook County; and the mill towns on the fast-running streams of western Maine. Some valleys have more moose than people. The district includes the heavily Democratic mill town of Lewiston and also Eastport. At Belfast on Penobscot Bay, art galleries and boutiques have replaced fish-processing plants. This was one of America's frontiers in the 1850s, when Bangor, on the Penobscot River, was the lumber capital of the world. Today, tiny Bangor is the second-largest city in the district after Lewiston, which was the site a half-century ago where boxer Muhammad Ali famously knocked out Sonny Liston for the heavyweight championship with what many claimed was a "phantom punch." In recent years, the big news from Lewiston, close to Portland, is that the city of 36,000 has become home to 6,000 refugees from Somalia and elsewhere in east Africa.

These parts of Maine have had economic troubles, losing 22,000 jobs to neighboring Canada and other foreign markets with the free-trade agreements in the 1990s. Potato production is less than half what it was in 1960. A once-thriving sardine-canning industry ended with the closing of the last cannery in 2010. Logging, long the largest industry in Maine, has suffered job cutbacks as big paper companies sell off acreage and shut down mills. A movement to set aside yet more acreage in a Maine North Woods National Park, which would be larger than the Yellowstone and Yosemite parks combined, has sparked protests. The proposed park would cover 15 percent of Maine, mostly forests but also including 32,000 miles of rivers and streams. Bumper stickers around the state read: "If you don't like cutting trees, try using plastic toilet paper."

There have been signs of economic life. Washington County's sandy soil produces more than 90 percent of the nation's wild blueberry crop. In Aroostook County, the high schools close for a week in September so teenagers can help harvest the potato crop. In the past decade, acreage has fluctuated slightly, but yield has increased by 10 percent and prices have jumped by 40 percent. About two-thirds of the crop is used for French fries, potato chips and other processed foods. In the North Woods, fishing for wild and native brook trout (in waters that have never been stocked) has become a $300 million annual business and has made the area a world-class destination.

Politically, the district is iconoclastic and permanently enamored of neither major political party. The old 2nd was presidential candidate Ross Perot's strongest district in the nation, with 33 percent in 1992 and 16 percent in 1996. Donald Trump made multiple appearances here during his 2016 campaign, with appeals to its blue-collar and trade-protectionist voters, and handily won its electoral vote, 51%-41%. That was a big switch from 2012, when President Barack Obama won the district, 53%-44%. Trump's success marked the first time that the state's two districts have split in a presidential election.

★ MARYLAND ★

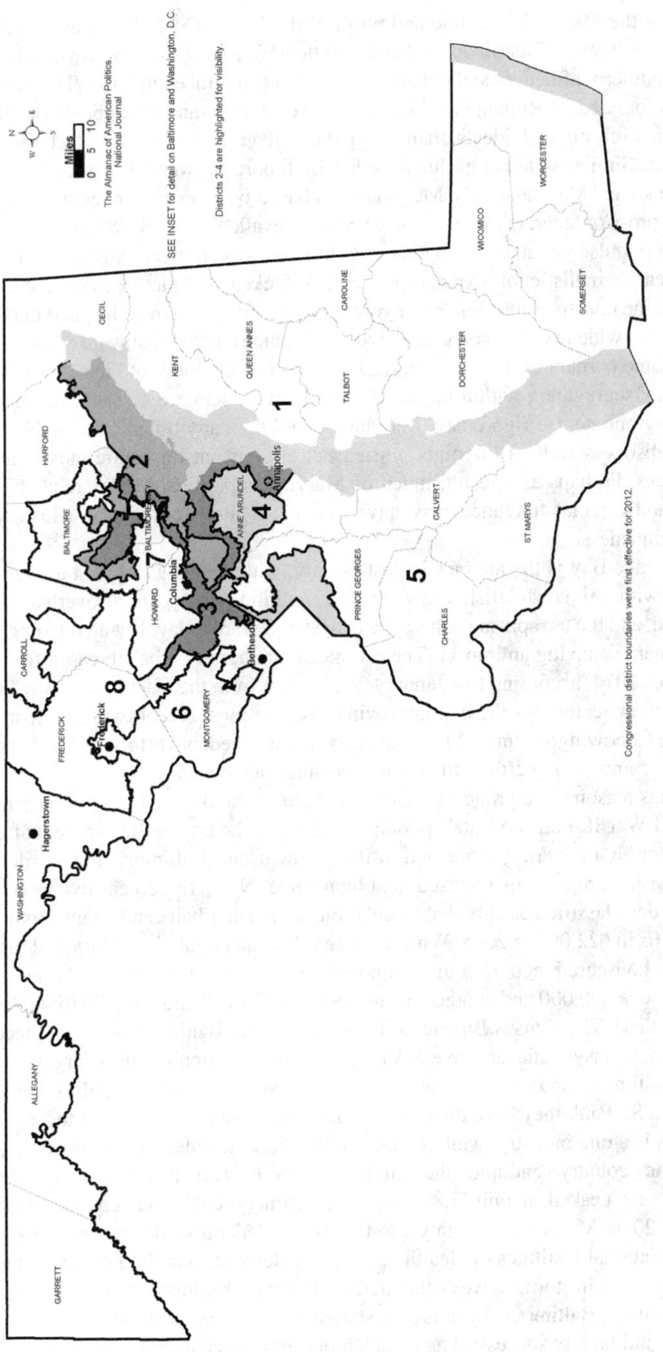
The Almanac of American Politics.
National Journal
Miles
0 5 10
SEE INSET for detail on Baltimore and Washington, D.C.
Districts 2-4 are highlighted for visibility.
Congressional district boundaries were first effective for 2012.
GARRETT
ALLEGANY
WASHINGTON
Hagerstown
FREDERICK
Frederick
CARROLL
MONTGOMERY
Bethesda
HOWARD
Columbia
BALTIMORE
HARFORD
CECIL
KENT
QUEEN ANNES
ANNE ARUNDEL
Annapolis
PRINCE GEORGES
CHARLES
CALVERT
ST MARYS
TALBOT
CAROLINE
DORCHESTER
WICOMICO
SOMERSET
WORCESTER
1
2
3
4
5
6
7
8

Maryland, one of the nation's most Democratic states, serves as a microcosm of the trends shaping today's Democratic Party: continuing lopsided support in ethnically and racially diverse urban areas, increasing Democratic success among affluent, suburban voters, and a waning of the party's influence in rural areas.

Just south of the Mason-Dixon line and north of the Union-Confederate lines during most of the Civil War (and the scene of its bloodiest battle, Antietam), Maryland is a crossroads state, with both Northern and Southern influences and with both industrial and rural economies. This was the only one of the 13 colonies founded by Roman Catholics-the Calvert family-and its embrace of religious tolerance came less from high-minded ideals than from the Calverts' desire to protect their property from religious attacks. Similarly, although hot-blooded Baltimoreans wanted to secede from the Union in 1861 (the state song, "Maryland, My Maryland," is based on a poem condemning Abraham Lincoln's suppression of pro-Confederate rioters), cooler heads prevailed.

The Puritan impulse was never lively here. Prohibition was enforced only laxly in Baltimore, to the delight of its great journalist-cum-lexicographer H.L. Mencken. Slot machines were legal for years in the rural counties of the Eastern Shore, and, after years of controversy and over the pleas of racetrack owners, were legalized statewide in 2007; voters approved table games in 2012, now taxed at the highest rates in the nation. In some corners of the state, segregation was evident well into the 1960s, and longstanding efforts to remedy segregation within the state's university system are still the subject of litigation. By not pursuing any one course rigorously, Maryland could be many things at once-Northern as well as Southern, moralistic as well as libertine, citified but also reliant on nature-mostly leaving people to their own devices. Perhaps as a result, much of Maryland's political history reads like a chronicle of rogues. Maryland's genial tolerance may have given it a little too savory a history, but this state cherishes its uniqueness.

The Chesapeake Bay is the nation's largest estuary, with water saltier than a river but fresher than the ocean, and with unique shellfish and watermen. Pollution and years of overharvesting drastically reduced its yield, and the terrapin and Chesapeake oyster are rare today. But an ongoing statewide Save-the-Bay movement is having an impact. The estimated number of crabs increased from 297 million to 553 million since 2014, according to a January 2017 report from the Chesapeake Bay Foundation, with nine of 13 health indicators for the bay improving over the most recent two-year span. The oozing of sediment on the Conowingo Dam that feeds the Bay has lessened, but efforts to limit agricultural runoff remain a worry, complicating efforts to help oysters make a comeback.

Maryland has reason to be proud of the economy, or economies, it has built over the years. During and after World War II, half the state's population lived in the city of Baltimore and only one-fifth in the suburbs. Then-in a pattern documented in Barry Levinson's Baltimore movie trilogy of *Diner, Tin Men* and *Avalon*-the proportions reversed, and then some. Now, 11 percent live in Baltimore, and 76 percent in counties classified as suburbs. Population in its one urban center sank from about 1 million in the early 1950s to 622,000 in 2015. With its large suburban population, Maryland ranks third among states in median household income, with an amount 30 percent over the national average; four counties have incomes above $90,000 and another six are between $75,000 and $90,000 (though the high cost of living cuts into that). The Census Bureau defines Washington-Baltimore as a combined statistical area that stretches to Pennsylvania and West Virginia; it's the nation's fourth largest, with 9.6 million people. But Baltimore and Washington are not fraternal twins like Dallas and Fort Worth or Minneapolis and St. Paul; they have different histories, economic bases and attitudes.

Washington is a one-industry, white-collar, capital city; the federal government kept it going while the rest of the country endured the Great Recession and a sluggish recovery. Maryland's unemployment rate peaked at only 7.8 percent in February 2010 and remained below the national average by late 2016. Maryland's roughly 145,000-strong federal workforce includes many employees at the massive National Institutes of Health complex in Bethesda and the Food & Drug Administration in Rockville; these, in turn, have generated a thriving health-related and biotech corridor in Montgomery County. Baltimore, by contrast, started off as a port and industrial city and managed to stay diversified and largely successful as it spread out into the countryside from its new central core at the Inner Harbor and the solidly built edifices of its downtown streets. It is home of the popular Oriole Park at Camden Yards (the first of the new-old ballparks of the 1990s) and to Johns Hopkins University, with its Georgian buildings along the affluent corridor that runs directly north from downtown all the way to the developing edge city of Hunt Valley.

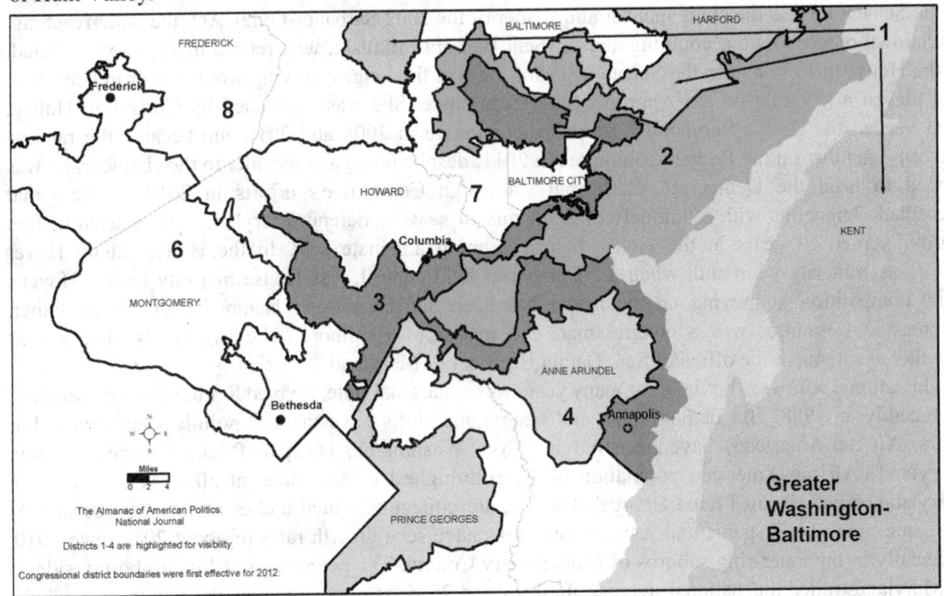

In recent years, though, Baltimore has been better known for its more dystopic elements, painstakingly (and prophetically) chronicled by the celebrated HBO dramatic series *The Wire*. Amid a scourge of drugs and crime, relations between African-American residents and the police soured; between 2011 and 2014, *The Baltimore Sun* revealed, the city paid the staggering sum of $5.7 million for harms inflicted by police with more than 100 victims winning court judgments. And critics have urged reforms of a bail system that "punishes low-income defendants, rewards wealthier defendants and disproportionately detains racial minorities," in the words of former U.S. Attorney General Eric Holder.

Matters exploded in 2015, when Baltimore resident Freddie Gray, 25, died of spinal injuries after being taken into police custody. Rioting, particularly in the Sandtown-Winchester neighborhood, ensued. A curfew was imposed, and eventually charges were filed against six police officers. (None were convicted.) In Sandtown-Winchester, a majority of households earned less than $25,000 a year in 2011, while unemployment in the neighborhood was double the city average, domestic violence was 50 percent higher and bachelor's degrees were one-quarter as common as the city as a whole. While race was a major factor, the reality was more nuanced; the "mayor, city council president, police chief, top prosecutor, and many other city leaders are black, as is half of Baltimore's 3,000-person police force," noted journalist Michael A. Fletcher in the *Washington Post*. In August 2016, the Department of Justice released a report critical of the city's aggressive policing strategy against quality-of-life crimes. "These practices led to repeated violations of the constitutional and statutory rights, further eroding the community's trust in the police," the report said. The turmoil helped torpedo the 2016 presidential candidacy of Martin O'Malley, who had served as mayor when the policing strategy was carried out; later the state's governor, O'Malley quit his White House run after a poor showing in the Iowa caucuses.

Nearly half of Marylanders live in the Baltimore metropolitan area, and its influence is far greater than Washington's on the Eastern Shore and in western Maryland. For years, most of Maryland's successful statewide politicians came from Baltimore, including two mayors who won the governorship, William Donald Schaefer and O'Malley. For three decades, Maryland's senators lived in Baltimore and commuted to Washington. Baltimore has a long Democratic tradition and most of its voters are registered Democrats. Until 2014, Democrats had yielded the governorship only once since 1966-from 2002 to 2006, after Republican Rep. Bob Ehrlich, capitalizing on the unpopularity of two-term incumbent Parris Glendening, won office. O'Malley ousted him in 2006. Democrats outnumber Republicans 7-to-1 in the state's House delegation, an even more extreme discrepancy than voting patterns would suggest, thanks to a redistricting map so aggressive that it has become subject to legal challenge.

Maryland's strong Democratic preferences have helped its members of Congress wield influence over important issues, though it is often quietly exercised. Paul Sarbanes retired in 2006 after 30 years in the Senate; he was the chief sponsor and shaper of the 2002 Sarbanes-Oxley Act, the wide-reaching crackdown on corporate accounting abuses. Sen. Barbara Mikulski, who retired in 2016, was elected to the House in 1976 and to the Senate in 1986; she was the longest-serving woman ever in Congress and played a key role on the Appropriations Committee. She was succeeded by Chris Van Hollen, who headed the House Democrats' campaign committee in 2008 and 2010 and became the ranking minority member on the Budget Committee in 2011; despite being a newcomer to the chamber, he was tapped to head the Democratic Senatorial Campaign Committee's efforts in 2018, a cycle that presented Democrats with a uniquely difficult mix of seats to defend. Maryland's other senator, Ben Cardin, served 20 years in the House before winning a Senate seat. In the House, Steny Hoyer serves as minority whip and, when the Democrats held control, was House majority leader. Hoyer's chief competition in moving up the ladder has been San Francisco's Nancy Pelosi, whose father, Thomas D'Alesandro, was a congressman and mayor of Baltimore. The two rivals once served together as interns in the office of Sen. Daniel Brewster of Maryland.

In national politics, Maryland for many years was a marginal state. It voted Republican for president as recently as 1988. But demographic and geographic shifts have made it solidly Democratic. For years, African-Americans have been moving from Washington, D.C., to Prince George's County; Maryland's African-American population is the fifth-highest of any state, at 30%. Many blacks in Maryland, especially in Prince George's County, are college-educated and economically upscale. At the same time, the Hispanic and Asian populations have seen growth rates of about 20% since 2010, especially in the inner-ring suburbs of Montgomery County. The percentage of foreign-born residents in Maryland trailed the national average until around 2005; it now surpasses the nation as a whole, at about 15 percent. All told, a state that was 80 percent white in 1970 is now essentially a 50-50 split between white and minority residents, making it the fifth least-white state in the country.

Maryland's Democratic gains owe much to the Democratic shift in Montgomery and Prince George's counties, the two collar counties of Washington. In 2016, these counties cast 31% of the two-party presidential vote in the state -- well above the duo of Baltimore city and county, which had 22%. (Another 16% was cast in the Baltimore satellite counties of Anne Arundel and Howard, while 31% was cast elsewhere in the state.) In the 1980s, Montgomery and Prince George's weren't more Democratic than the rest of the state and were sometimes less so. During a generation in which Republicans have backed smaller government and taken conservative cultural stands, and in which the racial composition of the Washington suburbs has grown, Montgomery and Prince George's have become overwhelmingly Democratic. In recent years, minority families have moved further south into once-rural and predominantly white Charles County; it is now Democratic, as well.

Such transformations have helped push Maryland to the left. In 2012, for instance, Maryland voters approved in-state college tuition for children of illegal immigrants and measures in favor of same-sex marriage. But in 2014, voters fired a warning shot at Democratic complacency, electing a little-known Republican activist, Larry Hogan, as governor over Democratic Lt. Gov. Anthony Brown, who had emerged wounded from a tough primary and never attracted much affection statewide. Hogan won amid a strong GOP performance in swingy suburban Baltimore County and weak turnout in traditionally Democratic areas. The GOP also gained seats in the legislature, though the party remains a distinct minority.

The 2016 presidential contest in the state was never in doubt, and the topline results didn't differ much from 2012. Hillary Clinton defeated Donald Trump, 60%-34%, with just one county switching its allegiance -- Anne Arundel (Annapolis), which voted narrowly for Mitt Romney in 2012 and narrowly for Clinton in 2016. The election widened the state's rural-urban chasm -- in most of the state's Republican counties, Trump outperformed Romney's vote totals – and it showed the limits of the post-Obama Democratic coalition. Clinton saw a five-digit vote decline in heavily Democratic and minority Baltimore city. As in other states, Clinton made her biggest gains in affluent counties such as Montgomery, which gave her 34,000 more votes, and Howard, which gave her almost 11,000 more votes.

As governor, Hogan has followed the lesson of recent elections, bucking the national GOP's move to the right, but also acting as a brake on the voters' leftward lurch. Heading into his reelection cycle, he was rewarded with high approval ratings.

Population		**Race and Ethnicity**		**Income**	
Total	5,930,538	White	53.0%	Median Income	$74,551 (1 out of 50)
Land area	9,707	Black	29.1%		
Pop/ sq mi	610.9	Latino	9.0%	Under $50,000	33.2%
Born in state	47.6%	Asian	6.0%	$50,000-$99,999	30.5%
		Two races	2.4%	$100,000-$199,999	27.2%
Age Groups		Other	0.4%	$200,000 or more	9.2%
Under 18	22.7%			Poverty Rate	10.0%
18-34	23.3%	**Education**			
35-64	40.8%	H.S grad or less	36.2%	**Health Insurance**	
Over 64	13.3%	Some college	25.9%	With health insurance coverage	91.0%
		College Degree, 4 yr	20.6%		
Work		Post grad	17.3%		
White Collar	44.6%			**Public Assistance**	
Sales and Service	39.8%	**Military**		Cash public assistance income	2.6%
Blue Collar	15.6%	Veteran	8.9%		
Government	22.3%	Active Duty	0.6%	Food stamp/SNAP benefits	10.9%

Voter Turnout			
2015 Total Citizens 18+	4,182,241	2016 Pres Turnout as % CVAP	67%
2016 Pres Votes	2,781,446	2012 Pres Turnout as % CVAP	68%

Legislature	
Senate:	33D, 14R
House:	91D, 50R

Presidential Politics

2016 Democratic Primary		
Hillary Clinton (D)	573,242	(63%)
Bernie Sanders (D)	309,990	(34%)
2016 Republican Primary		
Donald Trump (R)	248,343	(54%)
John Kasich (R)	106,614	(23%)
Ted Cruz (R)	87,093	(19%)

2016 Presidential Vote		
Hillary Clinton (D)	1,677,928	(60%)
Donald Trump (R)	943,169	(34%)
Gary Johnson (L)	79,605	(3%)
2012 Presidential Vote		
Barack Obama (D)	1,677,844	(62%)
Mitt Romney (R)	971,869	(36%)

Maryland has become one of the most Democratic states in the race for the presidency. In the seven presidential elections since 1992, its Democratic percentages ranked high among the states - second in 1992, sixth in 1996, fourth in 2000 and 2004, fifth in 2008 and 2012 and third in 2016. Only California and Hawaii gave a higher percentage to Hillary Clinton. Two regions drove Clinton's success: the close-in suburbs of Washington, D.C., and Baltimore. Combined, Montgomery and Prince George's counties, which run the spectrum of wealthy white suburbs to working-class African-American communities, gave more than 80 percent of their vote to Clinton. Trump received less than 15 percent. In Baltimore city, Clinton won about 85 percent. The suburbs of Baltimore County went for Clinton, 56%-38%. In the rural eastern and western portions of the state, Trump won a solid majority.

From 1992 to 2004, Maryland held its presidential primaries a week before Super Tuesday to try to get noticed, with limited success. In 2008, the primary was held on Feb. 12, the same day that Virginia and the District of Columbia held primaries. In 2012, the Maryland primary fell back to April 3 and in 2016 it was held on April 26 with four other states and drew little attention. Trump demolished Ohio Gov. John Kasich, 54%-23%, and swept the state's 38 GOP convention delegates. Clinton defeated Vermont Sen. Bernie Sanders 63%-34%. According to the network television exit poll, African Americans made up a plurality, 46 percent, of the Democratic primary voters; 43 percent were white. The former voted by a 3-to-1 margin for Clinton.

Congressional Districts

115th Congress Lineup	1R 7D	**114th Congress Lineup**	1R 7D

Democrats have controlled redistricting since 2000 and have used their power to maximum advantage. Going into the 2002 election, the delegation was divided 4-4 between the two major parties. After the boundaries were changed, the suburban Baltimore 2nd District became inhospitable to Republican Bob Ehrlich, and he decided to run for governor instead, successfully in 2002. Heavily minority areas were added to the Montgomery County-centered 8th district, and Connie Morella, a moderate Republican, lost her reelection bid.

That left only two Republican districts, the 1st and the 6th. In 2011, Gov. Martin O'Malley and Democratic legislators decided to finish one of them off. They made the 1st District more Republican by adding GOP precincts in suburban Baltimore and heavily Republican areas in Carroll County, which had been in the 6th. Republican Andy Harris ended up with a very safe seat, which also covered the Eastern Shore and areas north of Baltimore. At the same time, they made the 6th District in western Maryland far less Republican, chiefly by adding a large chunk of heavily Democratic Montgomery County and subtracting much of Frederick County. These moves made the adjacent 8th District less Democratic, but not enough to put their party in peril. As intended, Republican Rep. Roscoe Bartlett lost in the newly drawn 6th. In order to maintain two black-majority districts - the 4th in metro Washington and the 7th in metro Baltimore - the redistricters had to draw some very convoluted lines that have been prominently featured among the nation's most gerrymandered districts. Although 6th District Democratic Rep. John Delaney had a scare in 2014, that map has been one of the national Democrats' few success stories from the latest redistricting.

That history gave Republican Gov. Larry Hogan an opportunity to decry the partisanship and to demand the creation of an independent redistricting commission. The Democratic-controlled Legislature responded with an alternative that was more form than substance, including a requirement that five neighboring states revise their redistricting procedures; Hogan, whose approach has received broad public approval, vetoed the plan in May 2017 as "phony." If he is reelected in 2018, Hogan likely will have the leverage to force some changes - either in the process or the outcome, or both. That could enhance GOP prospects for one or perhaps two additional seats, including a return of the western Maryland district.

Governor

Larry Hogan (R)

Elected 2014, term expires 2019, 1st term; b. May. 25, 1956, Landover, MD; FL St. U., B.A. 1978; Catholic; Married (Yumi); 3 children.

Professional Career: Founder & President, Hogan Companies, 1985-present; Realtor, Murphy Hogan Commercial Real Estate Services, 1999-2003; MD Secretary of Appointments, Office of Governor, 2003-2007; Founder & Chairman, Change Maryland, 2011-present.

Office: 100 State Circle, Annapolis, 21401; 410-974-3901; Fax: 401-974-3275; Website: maryland.gov.

Election Results

Election	Name (Party)	Vote (%)
2014 General	Larry Hogan (R)	884,400 (51%)
	Anthony Brown (D)	818,890 (47%)
2014 Primary	Larry Hogan (R)	92,376 (43%)
	David Craig (R)	62,639 (29%)
	Charles Lollar (R)	33,292 (16%)
	Ron George (R)	26,628 (12%)

In June 2015, after barely five months in office, Republican Gov. Larry Hogan called a press conference on a hot summer afternoon to share the news that he had just been diagnosed with "a very advanced and very aggressive" form of cancer: non-Hodgkin's lymphoma. It had been discovered in late stage 3, when survival rates for that type of cancer are normally in the 50 to 70 percent range. Seeking to lighten the mood in the room, the affable Hogan wisecracked, "The best news is that my odds of getting through this and beating this are much, much better than the odds I had of beating Anthony Brown," as the audience laughed and aides applauded. The quip underscored that Hogan's surprise victory in deep-blue Maryland over Brown - lieutenant governor under two-term Democratic Gov. Martin O'Malley - ranked as one of the major upsets nationwide in 2014.

Five months after the press conference in which he revealed his illness, Hogan stood in the same room to announce that, after 18 weeks of chemotherapy, "incredibly, as of today I am 100 percent cancer-free." If the news about his physical health has since remained good, his political health has been little short of excellent. A spring 2017 *Morning Consult* survey found him to be the nation's second most popular governor, and home-state polling regularly gave him approval ratings at or above 70 percent in his first two years in office. During and after the 2016 presidential campaign, Hogan maintained a distance between himself and Donald Trump that, figuratively speaking, well exceeded the 35 miles between the White House and Government House in Annapolis. Nonetheless, as Hogan seeks to become the first Maryland Republican governor since Theodore Francis McKeldin in the 1950s to win a second term, Trump's victory has created potential complications for Hogan in a state that cast its vote for Democrat Hillary Clinton by a 26-point margin.

Hogan won over many constituents with his show of stoic courage in dealing with six separate rounds of five-day-a-week, 24-hour-a-day chemotherapy. But the persistence of his popularity speaks to both personal traits and political calculus. Notwithstanding a periodic penchant for confrontation, the former real estate broker generally bears the conciliatory mien of the proverbial nice guy next door. His policy agenda has remained tightly focused on pocketbook issues, consistent with a 2014 campaign in which he tapped into voters' economic unease by pointing a finger at the state's tax structure and repeatedly accusing O'Malley and Brown of imposing "40 consecutive tax increases" (including tolls and fees as well as taxes) over eight years. At the same time, Hogan has studiously avoided riling the state's large bloc of independent voters -- a majority of whom backed him, and who, while often fiscally conservative, tend to be more liberal on social and environmental issues. After promising not to reopen initiatives ranging from strict gun control to repeal of the death penalty enacted on O'Malley's watch, Hogan has frequently opted to allow progressive environmental and social legislation passed by the Democratic-controlled legislature to become law without his signature; he has gone so far as to embrace a few of these proposals, to the consternation of some fellow Republicans.

As he sought to portray himself as the outsider during his uphill bid for governor, Hogan often boasted he wasn't a career politician and had never held elective office. Such self-characterizations underplay the degree to which he grew up immersed in politics. As a teenager in the Washington D.C. suburb of Prince George's County, Hogan often spent weekends on Capitol Hill where his father, Larry Hogan Sr., served in the House. The elder Hogan achieved national attention in 1974 as the only Republican on the Judiciary Committee to vote for all three articles of impeachment against President Richard Nixon, and his son still speaks admiringly of the integrity and political courage his father displayed. (After announcing he would neither endorse nor vote for Trump, the governor wrote in his father's name on his 2016 presidential ballot, six months before the elder Hogan's death at 88.) By the time of the Nixon impeachment proceedings, the younger Hogan was in Florida, where he had moved with his mother following his parents' divorce. He graduated from Florida State University before returning to the Washington area to work briefly as a congressional staffer, and then for his father: The elder Hogan was elected Prince George's County executive in 1978, and the younger Hogan served as his intergovernmental liaison aide.

The fact that Hogan did not hold elected office until being sworn in as governor in January 2015 was not for lack of trying. He took time out from his duties in the Prince George's County executive's office to run in a 1981 special election when his father's former congressional seat came open -- campaigning on a conservative platform that included opposition to abortion. He finished second in a 12-way Republican primary race. The seat was ultimately won by Democrat Steny Hoyer, now the House minority whip. In 1992, he made a second bid for Congress, challenging Hoyer after the latter's district was redrawn to extend beyond Prince George's County. Hoyer came out on top, but by the narrowest margin of his career, 53%-44%.

Hogan's real estate firm foundered in the wake of a series of bank failures in the early 1990s. After declaring personal bankruptcy in 1994, he rebuilt the business, now a success and based in Annapolis. In 2002, he helped Rep. Robert Ehrlich, whom he had known for more than two decades, become the first Republican elected governor since Spiro Agnew in 1966. Hogan took a leave from his business to serve as Ehrlich's secretary of appointments.

Ehrlich was ousted by O'Malley in 2006, and Hogan initially contemplated running in 2010, but stepped aside for Ehrlich. A year later, he began laying the foundation for a 2014 run by founding Change Maryland, an anti-tax group that scrutinized the economic impact of the O'Malley administration's actions. Research funded by the organization helped build the foundation of Hogan's fall campaign against Brown, during which Hogan ran ads complaining that O'Malley and Brown "never met a tax that they didn't like or at least one they didn't hike." . In the face of a nationwide wave for the GOP, President Barack Obama - a classmate of Brown's at Harvard Law School - was more popular in Maryland than many other places, and was brought in to campaign, to no avail. . Brown's collapse was largely attributed to what was seen in Democratic Party circles as one of the most poorly run campaigns in recent state history. Hogan won 51%-47%. Of the state's 24 major jurisdictions, Hogan won 20; tepid turnout in Democratic bastions such as the city of Baltimore and suburban Montgomery County was not enough for Brown to make up for landslide Hogan margins elsewhere. (Brown did capture his home base of Prince George's County, currently two-thirds African-American, by a wide margin; in 2016, he staged a political comeback by winning the Prince George's-based seat in Congress.)

After campaigning with a pledge to roll back taxes, Hogan has made little headway on that front with a Democratic-held General Assembly. He did claim a modicum of success in the fact that the legislature's work product during his first three years did not contain additional tax increases. In his first year, Hogan signed a bill rolling back a requirement passed during O'Malley's tenure that Maryland's 10 most populous jurisdictions collect a storm-water mitigation fee to fund programs to reduce Chesapeake Bay pollution. Republicans had derided the fee as the "rain tax"; it became a frequent applause line during Hogan's campaign. He used executive fiat in 2015 to reduce tolls on the five-mile long bridge that spans the Chesapeake Bay, calling attention to the popular move with special signs. Critics accused Hogan of depriving the state of $50 million annually for road and bridge repair, in return for little economic benefit. Hogan did win legislative approval in 2017 to provide tax breaks to companies that located in Baltimore and depressed rural areas of the state.

Economically troubled Baltimore, the state's largest city, yielded the first major crisis of Hogan's administration when, in April 2015, rioting broke out in the wake of the death of a black man, Freddie Gray, while in police custody. Hogan initially griped that then-Baltimore Mayor Stephanie Rawlings-Blake, a Democrat, failed to return his phone calls for two hours as the rioting spread, causing a delay in sending in the National Guard. When he did reach her, Hogan -- according to an interview with *Washingtonian* magazine nearly two years later -- gave Rawlings-Blake an ultimatum. Hogan told the mayor he had two draft executive orders in front of him -- the first saying he was declaring a state of emergency and deploying the National Guard "at the request of the mayor of Baltimore;" the other that he was doing so on his own authority. "I said, 'I think it's better for you and better for me, and I think PR-wise it's better for you to request for me to come in. But either way, we're coming in'," Hogan recalled telling Rawlings-Blake. The mayor said she needed more time to make a decision, to which Hogan replied, "There's no more time. It's been three hours - the city's on fire." Added Hogan, "She calls back in 14 minutes and she says, 'Since you have a gun to my head and since you are going to do it anyway, I guess I'll ask you to come in'. I go, 'Okay, thank you very much.' Click." Hogan relocated his base of operations to Baltimore for a week and appeared around the city. Democratic strategist Mike Morrill gave Hogan high marks, telling the *Baltimore Sun,* "He's been in the city; he's done what a governor should have done." Rawlings-Blake, who had been talked up as a possible Democratic challenger to Hogan before the riots, saw her political stock take a major hit, as she was criticized for not being sufficiently visible or proactive. Five months after the riots, she announced she would not seek re-election.

Hogan delivered an inaugural speech in January 2015 widely praised for its appeal for bipartisanship and consensus. But the mood in Annapolis went downhill a couple of weeks later, with Democrats complaining that Hogan's first "State of the State" -normally a blueprint for governing in the year ahead-sounded much like a stump speech from the 2014 campaign. In a state in which the constitution gives the governor broad power over the annual budget, Hogan and Democratic legislative leaders often have tussled over spending priorities, with Hogan ultimately refusing to spend nearly $70 million allocated by the General Assembly during his first year to aid school budgets in high cost areas. Hogan charged that the legislature was seeking to divert money needed to shore up the state's pension fund, but critics saw a political motivation - because much of the withheld funding would have gone to heavily Democratic jurisdictions that had not voted for the new governor. The General Assembly responded by making school aid to high cost areas mandatory, taking the matter out of Hogan's hands in the future.

After finding his vetoes overridden on a number of other major pieces of legislation in his first years in office -- ranging from transportation spending to the restoration of voting rights for felons on parole or probation to a requirement that utility companies rely more on renewable energy sources -- Hogan has increasingly sought to pre-empt Democratic moves on high-profile social and environmental issues. During the 2014 campaign, he favored hydraulic fracturing, or "fracking," to tap into natural gas reserves in western Maryland; he said the state was "sitting on an economic gold mine." In 2015, Hogan reluctantly allowed a two-year moratorium on fracking to become law without his signature. But in 2017, he switched and announced he would support a permanent ban even before legislation reached his desk -- making Maryland the third state, after New York and Vermont, to prohibit the practice.

Since November 2016, the Democratic strategy for derailing Hogan's bid for a second term has turned on tying him to Trump, whose approval ratings in Maryland struggled to reach 30 percent in the early months of his administration. Hogan continually sidestepped such questions. "I'm focused on solving Maryland problems," he told a Baltimore radio station with more than a trace of exasperation. "I have 31 different policy proposals and a real agenda to turn our state around, and the only questions we get [are] 'Why aren't you protesting Donald Trump?'…I don't see that as my role." In early 2017, he allowed several General Assembly initiatives aimed at the Trump Administration to become law without his signature.

Some opponents saw a vulnerability when, amid high approval ratings, a *Washington Post* poll in March 2017 found just 41 percent of those surveyed would back Hogan for another term, while 37 percent would prefer a Democrat. But -- unlike O'Malley's ouster of Hogan's one-time boss, Ehrlich, in 2006 -- the Democrats lacked a clear frontrunner going into 2018. Whether Hogan can win a second term is "going to depend on who the Democrats put forward and how much they can attach [Hogan] to what's going on in national politics," University of Maryland government and politics professor Michael Hanmer told *The Washington Post*. Several months into Trump's presidency, Hogan's approval ratings remained high, as the *Baltimore Sun* editorial page -- in the wake of the 2017 General Assembly session -- opined that "Democrats barely laid a glove on him." Concluded the *Sun*: "… Mr. Hogan is in as strong a position as he can be. The 2018 election is his to lose."

Senior Senator

Ben Cardin (D)

Elected 2006, term expires 2018, 2nd term; b. Oct 05, 1943, Baltimore; Baltimore City College (MD), 1961; Baltimore City Public Schools, 1961; University of Pittsburgh (PA), B.A., 1964; University of Maryland School of Law, J.D., 1967; Villa Julie College (MD), LL.D., 2007; Jewish; Married (Myrna Edelman Cardin); 2 children (1 deceased); 2 grandchildren.

Elected Office: MD House, 1966-1986, Speaker, 1979-1986; U.S. House, 1987-2006.

Professional Career: Practicing attorney, 1967-1986; Ways & Means Committee, MD, 1974-1979; Chairman, MD Legal Services Corporation, 1988-1995.

DC Office: 509 HSOB 20510, 202-224-4524, Fax: 202-224-1651, cardin.senate.gov.
State Offices: Baltimore, 410-962-4436; Bowie, 301-860-0414; Cumberland, 301-777-2957; Rockville, 301-762-2974; Salisbury, 410-546-4250.

Committees: *Environment & Public Works*: Clean Air & Nuclear Safety, Fisheries, Water, and Wildlife, Transportation & Infrastructure (RMM). *Finance*: Health Care, Taxation & IRS Oversight.

Foreign Relations (RMM): Africa & Global Health Policy, East Asia, the Pacific & International Cybersecurity Policy, Europe & Regional Security Cooperation, Internat'l Dev Instit & Internat'l Econ, Energy & Environ Policy, Near East, South Asia, Central Asia & Counterterrorism, State Dept & USAID Mngmnt, Internat'l Ops & Internat'l Dev, West Hem Crime Civ Sec Dem Rights & Women's Issues. *Joint Security & Cooperation in Europe (RMM)*. *Small Business & Entrepreneurship.*

Group Ratings

	ADA	ACLU	AFL-CIO	LCV	ITI	COC	HAFA	ACU	CFG	FRC
2016	-	94%	-	100%	60%	50%	9%	0%	0%	0%
2015	100%	C	93%	96%	C	50%	C	0%	0%	0%

Almanac Ratings 2015

	Economy	Social	Foreign	Composite
Liberal	94%	100%	87%	94%
Conservative	6%	0%	13%	6%

Key Votes of the 114th Congress

1. Keystone pipeline	N	5. National Security Data	Y	9. Gun Sales Checks	Y
2. Export-Import Bank	N	6. Iran Nuclear Deal	Y	10. Sanctuary Cities	N
3. Debt Ceiling Increase	Y	7. Puerto Rico Debt	Y	11. Planned Parenthood	N
4. Homeland Security $$	Y	8. Loretta Lynch A.G	Y	12. Trade deals	Y

Election Results

Election	Name (Party)	Vote (%)		Cand. Spent	Ind. Exp. Support	Ind. Exp. Oppose
2012 General	Ben Cardin (D)	1,474,028	(56%)	$6,281,916	$32,091	
	Dan Bongino (R)	693,291	(26%)	$1,767,837	$168,845	
	Rob Sobhani (U)	430,934	(16%)	$8,078,928		
2012 Primary	Ben Cardin (D)	240,704	(74%)			
	C. Anthony Muse (D)	50,807	(16%)			

Prior winning percentages: 2006 (55%); House: 2004 (63%), 2002 (66%), 2000 (76%), 1998 (78%), 1996 (67%), 1994 (71%), 1992 (74%), 1990 (70%), 1988 (73%), 1986 (79%)

Newspaper coverage in the home state of Democrat Ben Cardin, Maryland's senior senator, frequently has referred to him as a centrist or moderate. In fact, according to *National Journal* vote rankings, Cardin has regularly been among the top 10 most liberal senators since being elected to that body a decade ago. (The *Almanac* vote ratings for 2015 put him in 16th place, with a liberal voting score in excess of 95 percent.)The gap between perception and reality does not arise from any marked ideological shift during Cardin's nearly half-century in elected office, but rather appears to be a function of his traditionally low-key style. Throughout his career, Cardin has been an unabashed policy wonk with an agreeable personality, able to work effectively with Republicans because he has shunned partisan sound bites while demonstrating a sincere interest in the nitty-gritty of crafting legislation.

However, it was a sharper tongued, more aggressive Cardin who emerged as President Donald Trump assumed office -- taking on the new administration over numerous aspects of U.S. policy overseasin his role asthe Foreign Relations Committee's ranking Democrat."Equating our country with an authoritarian, murderous regime is outrageous and reprehensible, even for Mr. Trump," Cardin thundered after Trump, in a *Fox News* interview, appeared to put abuses by Russian President Vladimir Putin on the same plane as some past actions by the United States. When Trump's first budget proposed deep cuts in diplomatic and foreign aid programs, Cardin blasted them as "catastrophic," writing in *Time Magazine*: "…The president does not often talk about reaffirming, promoting or funding the American values that have defined our nation since its founding nearly 250 years ago. He does however talk about 'America first' and demonizing immigrants and refugees, and one could surmise that this budget is a reflection of his own personal values…" At the same time, Cardin continued to seek opportunities to act on a bipartisan basis, sponsoringa bill with five Republican and four Democratic colleagues to impose sanctions on Russia over its allegedinterference in the 2016 election via cyberspace. "We have been attacked by Russia," Cardin told a press conference. "That is no longer subject to any debate."

Events in early 2015 conspired to place Cardinmore in the national limelight: In the wake of an indictment on corruption charges, New Jersey Sen. Robert Menendez stepped down as the ranking

Democrat on the Foreign Relations Committee, with Cardin inheriting that slot. While the Democrats were given a significant shot at recapturing the Senate majority in 2016, the party fell three seats short on Election Day -- depriving Cardin of the opportunity to ascend to the chairmanship ofForeign Relations to cap his long career in public office.Although 63 years old when he reached the Senate in 2006, Cardin was once a boy wonder of Maryland politics. Elected to the Maryland House of Delegates at the age of 23-in 1966, six months prior to earning his law degree-he was House speaker by the time he was 35. Just as he later operated in Washington, Cardin gained a reputation in Annapolis as a consensus builder who reached across the political aisle.

The son and nephew of state legislators, Cardin grew up in the Jewish neighborhoods of northwest Baltimore: The area and the era of Cardin's youth were later depicted in Barry Levinson's 1982 movie "Diner." After achieving the top job in the House of Delegates, Cardin's ambitions seemed aimed at moving from the first to the second floor of the Maryland State House-where the governor's office is located. But, when Democrat Barbara Mikulski left her 3rd District House seat to run for the Senate in 1986, Cardin jumped into the congressional race and was easily elected.

In his second term in the House, Cardin obtained a seat on the tax-writing Ways and Means Committee, where he was able to be a productive legislator-even after the Democrats were relegated to the minority following the 1994 elections, with many of his party colleagues lacking the independence or shrewdness to deal with their diminished circumstances. Along with then-Republican Rep. Rob Portman of Ohio, Cardin cosponsored the 1998 Internal Revenue Service reform law and the 2000 bipartisan legislation to expand 401(k) savings and other retirement plans. In 2001, when Congress enacted the Bush tax cut, it included Cardin's provision to increase the limits for maximum IRA and 401(k) contributions. Cardin's hometown newspaper, the *Baltimore Sun* called him a "master of bipartisan lawmaking." But he continued to eye the governorship, and seriously considered giving up his House seat to run in both 1994 and 1998.

Open Senate seats don't come around often in Maryland-and so when Democrat Paul Sarbanes decided to retire in 2006 after three decades in office, Cardin didn't hesitate. He began as the front-runner even though his earnest, somewhat bland demeanor raised questions about his viability as a statewide candidate. Cardin's leading primary opponent was former Democratic Rep. Kweisi Mfume, who resigned his House seat in 1996 to head the NAACP. Mfume and Cardin were friends-both were elected to Congress in 1986-but Mfume and other black leaders warned that the state Democratic establishment's support for Cardin could breed resentment among African-American voters, who by some estimates comprise 40 percent of registered Maryland Democrats. Mfume also had a compelling life story and an abundance of charisma. But Cardin outspent Mfume by 4-1, and won narrowly, 44%-41%. The vote broke down heavily along racial lines: Mfume overwhelmingly carried the majority-black jurisdictions of Baltimore city and Prince George's County, while Cardin won 21 of the 22 remaining counties in the state.

The Republican nominee was Lt. Gov. Michael Steele, the first African-American statewide officeholder in Maryland. Steele ran unconventional ads highlighting his outsider status while Democrats, including Mfume, coalesced around Cardin and portrayed Steele as an inexperienced lightweight. Cardin sought to link Steele to President George W. Bush and criticized him for his support for the Iraq war -- coming out on top, 54%-44%, in a tough year for Republicans nationwide. In contrast to the primary, AfricanAmericans voted overwhelmingly for Cardin. In early 2009, Steele became the first African-American chairman of the Republican National Committee, where he became known for several well-publicized gaffes until his ouster in 2011.

Cardin became the state's senior senator at the beginning of 2017 with Mikulski's retirement; his elevation two years earlier to the role of the Senate Democrats' leading foreign policy spokesman gave that portfolio to someone more supportive of the overseas initiatives of President Barack Obama than his Cardin's predecessor, Menendez. Nonetheless,Cardin, like Menendez, ended up opposing the Iran nuclear agreement -- formally entitled the Joint Comprehensive Plan Of Action, or JCPOA -- that the Obama Administration put forth in 2015. While praising the deal as containing "significant achievements," Cardin, in a *Washington Post* op-ed, complained: "After 10 to 15 years, it would leave Iran with the option to produce enough enriched fuel for a nuclear weapon in a short time. The JCPOA would provide this legal path to a country that remains a rogue state and has violated its international nonproliferation obligations for years." Although one of a handful of Democrats to oppose a deal that the Obama White House considered a major foreign policy breakthrough, Cardin gave Obama a quiet political boost by not announcing his position until after it had become clear that the administration had sufficient votes to block a Senate resolution disapproving the JCPOA.

In contrast to Menendez, Cardin did voice support for the White House when Obama announced in December 2014 that he was moving to restore diplomatic ties with Cuba. "It goes without saying that our previous policy did not achieve the progress that we wanted to see, and so a new approach is needed," Cardin told a committee hearing. In contrast, Menendez, a Cuban-American, continued to resist any engagement with the Castro regime. Asked his opinion of Obama's shift in strategy on the day it was announced, Menendez bluntly told reporters, "I think it stinks."

Obama's new approach was unveiled in conjunction with Cuba's freeing of U.S. government contractor Alan Gross, a Maryland resident, after a five-year imprisonment. Cardin had pressed the State Department to make Gross' freedom a top priority, and condemned his detention as a major human rights violation. As a former co-chair of the U.S. arm of the Commission on Security and Cooperation in Europe, which monitors international human rights issues, Cardin has long been focused on such matters. His recentoutspoken concern about the Trump Administration being overly cozy with the repressive Putin regime is not the first time he has taken on Russia. "My name is well-known in Russia, some places better than in Maryland," Cardin once wryly observed.

One of Cardin's major legislative successes came with the December 2012 passage of a bill that normalized trade relations with Russia after nearly 40 years-but which also required the United States to freeze the assets of, and deny visas to, Russians implicated in human rights abuses. It was entitled the Sergei Magnitsky Rule of Law Accountability Act, for a lawyer who died while in the custody ofRussian authorities; the roster of sanctioned individuals it authorized became known in some quarters as the "Cardin List." The provision so angered Putin that he retaliated by moving to end U.S. adoptions of Russian children, a response Cardin called "embarrassing."At the end of 2016, Obama signed defense legislation that contained the Global Magnitsky Human Rights Accountability Act -- co-authored by Cardin and Armed Services Committee Chairman John McCain of Arizona -- that gives the president the authority to apply the sanctions contained in the earlier law in the case of human rights transgressions by nations other than Russia.

In the spring of 2017, Cardin joined with another GOP colleague, Georgia Sen. David Perdue, to sponsor global anti-corruption legislation: It would require the State Department to compile an annual report rating countries worldwide on their efforts to combat corruption. (The department currently puts together a similar nation-by-nation report on human trafficking.)Cardin's latest move came a couple of months after another of his international anti-corruption initiatives had been stymied. In 2010,Cardin teamed withthen-Indiana Republican Sen. Richard Lugar to attach an amendment to theso-called Dodd-Frank law overhauling regulation of the U.S. financial regulatory system.The Cardin-Lugar amendment required U.S. oil, gas and mining firms to disclose how much they pay to foreign governments -- a move designed to prevent leaders of foreign nations from skimming payments. But, in early 2017, the Republican-controlled Congress, with Trump's support, voted to kill the Obama Administration regulation implementing Cardin-Lugar. The oil industry lobbied for the move, arguing the rule put its members at a disadvantage over foreign competitors. Responded Cardin and Lugar in an op-ed in *The Hill*: "Besides Big Oil, those most eager to repeal Cardin-Lugar are the autocrats, in places like Russia, Iran or Venezuela…who want to keep the money secret from their citizens. Why do their bidding?"

Closer to home,Cardin spent his first four years in the Senate on the Judiciary Committee, and remains involved in a number of issues that fall within that committee's jurisdiction. Two years before rioting broke out in his hometown of Baltimore in April 2015-when the death of a black man in custody brought police-community relations to the boiling point-Cardin introduced legislation to end racial profiling. The legislation would provide training for law enforcement officials in the differences between suspect descriptions and racial profiling. "We can begin to reduce the racial disparities that plague our justice system," Cardin said in 2014, a month after an unarmed black teenager, Michael Brown, was shot and killed by a police officer in Ferguson, Missouri. Brown "did not need to die," Cardin asserted.

Cardin left the Judiciary Committee in 2011 when he won a seat on the influential Finance Committee, a logical segue to his 18 years on the House Ways and Means panel. In late 2014, Cardin exhibited his policy wonk side by introducing a comprehensive overhaul of the nation's tax code. While certain to face daunting political hurdles, the plan garnered attention amid increasing calls on Capitol Hill for tax reform. Cardin's plan would eliminate income taxation-and filing-for households earning less than $100,000, while lowering rates but eliminating many deductions for those above that level. Notably, it would shift the focus of the tax system to a 10-percent levy on consumption, while seeking to encourage exports by rebating that tax on sales of products or services to foreign markets.

Upon his joining the Finance Committee, Senate Democratic leaders put Cardin and Ohio's Sherrod Brown in charge of an effort to shape the party's message on the newly passed Affordable Care Act (ACA). But Cardin also successfully sponsored a 2011 bill with the then-Finance Committee chairman, Montana Democrat Max Baucus, to repeal a much-criticized provision in the health care law that called for businesses to submit forms to the Internal Revenue Service for all purchases above $600. Before joining the committee, Cardin led the fight to include pediatric dental care as an essential benefit under the ACA-an effort prompted by the death of a 12 year-old Maryland boy who suffered a brain infection that started as untreated tooth decay. It was the basis of a campaign ad that ran in the weeks leading up to the April 2012 primary as Cardin was seeking a second term; a young girl recounts the episode and praises Cardin, ending with the tag line, "He's my friend Ben-I hope he's your friend, too."

Other ads in the much-noticed "My Friend Ben" series showed the then 69-year old incumbent helping to load bags onto an airplane and hauling in oysters with Maryland watermen, as narrators highlighted his efforts to land funds for expansion of Baltimore-Washington International Airport as well as restoration of the Chesapeake Bay. To an extent, the ads were an effort to compensate for Cardin's low-key modus operandi, which appeared to have left many Maryland voters with a hazy image of who he was and what he had accomplished in his first term.In the end, Cardin had little to worry about: He turned back a primary challenge from an African-American state senator by nearly 5-1, and, in the general election, he won 56 percent, with the opposition split between the Republican nominee and a wealthy businessman running as a self-financed independent.

Cardin, who turns 75 a month before Election Day 2018,has yet to make an announcement on whether he will seek a third term. But he has been raising campaign funds, and shows no signs of slowing down -- particularly given his new role as the Trump Administration's leading Democratic foreign policy critic. He is reported to be in good health, and is said to make a habit of walking 10,000 steps a day. If he runs for re-election, he is likely to be an overwhelming favorite in a state where Trump lost to the Democratic nominee Hillary Clinton by 26 percentage points. If Cardin decides to call an end to more than 50 years in public life, one potential candidate is Democratic Rep. John Sarbanes, son of Cardin's predecessor, Paul Sarbanes. Democratic Rep. Elijah Cummings, who passed on a bid for the state's other seat in 2016, would also likely be under pressure to run -- in a state that, while 30 percent black, has yet to elect an AfricanAmerican to a Senate seat.

Junior Senator

Chris Van Hollen (D)

Elected 2016, term expires 2022, 1st term; b. Jan 10, 1959, Karachi, Pakistan; Swarthmore College (PA), B.A., 1982; John F. Kennedy School of Government, Harvard University, M.PP, 1985; Georgetown University (DC), J.D., 1990; Episcopalian; Married (Katherine Wilkens Van Hollen); 3 children.

Elected Office: MD House, 1991-1995; MD Senate, 1995-2003; U.S House, 2003-2017.

Professional Career: Practicing attorney; Legislative Assistant, U.S Sen. Charles McC. Mathias, 1985-1987; Staff, U.S Senate Foreign Relations Commission, 1987-1989; Sr. Legislative advisor, Governor William Donald Schaefer, 1989-1991.

DC Office: 110 HSOB 20510, 202-224-4654, Fax: 202-228-0629, vanhollen.senate.gov.
State Offices: Baltimore, 667-212-4610; Hagerstown, 301-797-2826; Rockville, 301-545-1500.

Committees: Senate Democratic Senatorial Campaign Committee Chairman. *Agriculture, Nutrition & Forestry*: Commodities, Risk Management & Trade, Nutrition, Agricultural Research & Specialty Crops, Rural Development & Energy (RMM). *Appropriations*: Commerce, Justice, Science & Related Agencies, Department of the Interior, Environment & Related Agencies, Financial Services & General Government, Legislative Branch, State, Foreign Operations & Related Programs. *Banking, Housing & Urban Affairs*: Financial Institutions & Consumer Protection, Housing, Transportation & Community Development, Securities, Insurance & Investment. *Budget.*

Group Ratings (House)

	ADA	ACLU	AFL-CIO	LCV	ITI	COC	HAFA	ACU	CFG	FRC
2016	-	94%	-	100%	0%	50%	14%	0%	10%	0%
2015	95%	C	100%	100%	C	40%	C	4%	0%	0%

Almanac Ratings 2015

	Economy	Social	Foreign	Composite
Liberal	100%	100%	100%	100%
Conservative	0%	0%	0%	0%

Key Votes of the 114th Congress (House)

1. Keystone Pipeline	N	5. Puerto Rico Debt	Y	9. Offenses by Aliens	N
2. Trade Deals	N	6. Medical Marijuana	Y	10. Troops in Iraq	Y
3. Export-Import Bank	Y	7. Sanctuary Cities	N	11. Homeland Security $$	Y
4. Debt Ceiling Increase	Y	8. Armor-piercing Bullets	N	12. Trade Adjustment aid	Y

Election Results

Election	Name (Party)	Vote (%)		Cand. Spent	Ind. Exp. Support	Ind. Exp. Oppose
2016 General	Chris Van Hollen (D)	1,659,907	(61%)	$32,177,603	$1,758,111	
	Kathy Szeliga (R)	972,557	(36%)	$1,510,202	$462,219	
	Margaret Flowers (G)	89,970	(3%)	$90,437		
2016 Primary	Chris Van Hollen (D)	470,320	(53%)			
	Donna Edwards (D)	343,620	(39%)			

Prior winning percentages: House: 2014 (60%); 2012 (63%); 2010 (73%); 2008 (75%); 2006(77%); 2004 (75%); 2002 (52%)

Six weeks before he was sworn in as Maryland's new junior senator in January 2017, Chris Van Hollen already was a member of his party's Senate leadership -- named to head the DSCC, the counterpart of the House Democrats' campaign arm that Van Hollen chaired a decade earlier. It was the latest example of Van Hollen -- whose quarter-century in elected office includes the Maryland General Assembly as well as both houses of Congress -- quickly climbing the leadership ladder. Elected to the state Senate in 1994 by ousting an incumbent well-liked by Annapolis insiders, he moved to mend fences with the Senate president, and found himself appointed vice chairman of an influential committee. Arriving in the House following the 2002 election, he was chairman of the DCCC by the beginning of his third term and assistant to then-House Speaker Nancy Pelosi by the start of his fourth. In fact, some thought Van Hollen might be on track to succeed Pelosi as Democratic leader -- until he announced in early 2015 for the Senate seat being vacated by Democrat Barbara Mikulski.

Beneath an exterior of Boy Scout-like politeness, Van Hollen is widely credited with possessing both the intellectual curiosity of a policy wonk and the savvy of a master political strategist. He has taken several calculated risks to advance his electoral career -- and inevitably watched them pay off. "Chris has an exquisite sense of timing and opportunity, and that has served him very well," said Virginia Democratic Rep. Gerry Connolly, who has known Van Hollen since they were young Senate aides. "Even when conventional wisdom told him not to, his instincts were better, his timing was superior."

A penchant for risk-taking was evident in Van Hollen at an early age, when his father served as U.S. ambassador to Sri Lanka in the mid-1970s. Family members tell of a teenage Van Hollen who insisted on riding atop jeeps during excursions into the jungle, only to have to scramble quickly inside on occasions when the vehicle was charged by elephants. Van Hollen was born in Pakistan while his father was a Foreign Service officer there (his mother later served as chief of the South Asia division of the State Department's Bureau of Intelligence and Research). While his father's family roots were in Baltimore, Van Hollen largely grew up abroad before returning to the United States to attend boarding school and then Swarthmore College. He earned a master's degree in public policy from Harvard University's John F. Kennedy School of Government, and then a law degree from Georgetown University.

Van Hollen went to work in 1985 for Maryland Sen. Charles Mathias, a liberal Republican who held the seat Van Hollen now occupies. He soon shifted to the staff of the Senate Foreign Relations Committee, where, after a hazardous trip along the Turkish-Iraqi border, he co-authored a report confirming Iraq's use of chemical weapons against its Kurdish minority. Van Hollen seemed headed for a career in the family business of diplomacy, but left the committee in 1989 for a job in Maryland's federal affairs office -- a move clearly aimed at positioning himself for a career in electoral politics. In 1990, he was elected to the state House of Delegates on a candidate slate dubbed the "Choice Team," which pledged to work to codify the U.S. Supreme Court's *Roe v. Wade* decision. In 1994, Van Hollen mounted a primary challenge against the state senator on whose slate he had been elected just four years earlier. His move created some blowback in local political circles, but it paid off: Van Hollen won the primary by a 3-1 margin, thanks to a well-executed campaign and missteps by the incumbent.

In 2002, Van Hollen gambled again -- giving up a safe state Senate seat for an uphill run for Congress. Initially, the odds-on favorite for the Democratic nomination in Maryland's 8th District was a scion of the Kennedy dynasty: state Del. Mark Shriver, son of Sargent and Eunice Kennedy Shriver. But Van Hollen -- bolstered by the grassroots progressive groups with whom he had been allied in Annapolis on environmental and gun control issues, along with the endorsement of *The Washington Post* -- narrowly defeated Shriver in the primary, 44%-41%.

Van Hollen then had only eight weeks to campaign against eight-term Rep. Connie Morella, a liberal Republican. The congenial Morella ran negative ads for the first time, but Van Hollen chose not to directly aim his fire at the popular incumbent. Instead, he argued that Morella's vote with the GOP to organize the House kept in power a conservative majority out of sync with most district voters. Helped by a recent redistricting plan that had made the 8th more favorable to Democrats, Van Hollen won 52%-47%. He was never seriously challenged in six re-election bids.

Notwithstanding his avowedly liberal ideology and his leadership role at the DCCC, Van Hollen's genial personality enabled him to work across the aisle in the House. He notched a legislative victory not long after taking after office when he convinced a majority, including 26 Republicans, to approve his amendment to limit a plan to outsource federal jobs. In 2008, he worked with then-Virginia Republican Rep. Tom Davis to enact a $150 million annual subsidy to the Washington region's subway system. More recently, in 2015, Van Hollen teamed with an unusual ally --- tea party-aligned South Carolina Rep. Mick Mulvaney, now the Trump Administration's director of the Office of Management and Budget -- in an effort to thwart defense spending increases sought by the House Republican leadership.

At the outset of his second term, Van Hollen was selected by then-Rep. Rahm Emanuel of Illinois, chairman of the DCCC, to manage candidate recruitment. In style, Van Hollen presented a stark contrast to the hard-charging, often profane Emanuel, but the two forged a close working relationship -- as Van Hollen traveled to battleground districts for candidate mentoring. After the Democrats captured the House majority in 2006 and Emanuel moved up to chair the House Democratic Caucus, newly installed Speaker Pelosi exhibited her confidence in Van Hollen by naming him to head the DCCC.

Van Hollen's challenging task was to reverse the historical forces that generally produced losses for a winning party after a wave election such as 2006. He ran a skillful in-house research operation, expanded the field program, and performed well in the most important function for a DCCC chairman-fundraising. In the 2008 election cycle, the DCCC outraised the counterpart National Republican Congressional Committee by nearly $50 million. Overall, Democrats gained 21 seats in November 2008, many in traditionally Republican areas, and Van Hollen and the DCCC got much of the credit -- although he was undoubtedly aided by the unpopularity of outgoing Republican President George W. Bush, as well as a cratering economy.

After his 2008 electoral success, Van Hollen contemplated a run for the Democratic Caucus chairmanship, a step up the leadership ladder, after Emanuel was named chief of staff to newly elected President Barack Obama. But the caucus vice chairman, John Larson of Connecticut, was poised to succeed Emanuel, and Pelosi -- to avoid an internal party battle -- persuaded Van Hollen to stay on as DCCC chairman and gave him a newly created leadership post, assistant to the speaker. In the latter post, as well as from a perch on the powerful Ways and Means Committee, he remained active on substantive issues, albeit with an eye to protecting the Democratic majority.

In April 2009, Van Hollen introduced a cap-and-dividend bill on climate change, as an alternative to the Democrats' cap-and-trade legislation; he proposed a carbon tax on coal, oil and gas producers while distributing the proceeds as dividends to citizens. He was concerned about the effect the stricter cap-and-trade bill would have on members in coal states. Climate change legislation passed the House, but died in the Senate. During debate on the Affordable Care Act, Van Hollen cosponsored a successful amendment allowing dependents up to age 26 to stay on their parents' health insurance-a major talking point for Democrats defending the bill in the 2010 campaign. In early 2010, when the Supreme Court ruling in *Citizens United v. FEC* overturned restrictions on corporate involvement in campaign advertising, Van Hollen filed the so-called DISCLOSE Act to increase disclosure requirements for corporations. The House passed a modified version, 219-206. Its passage was blocked in the Senate, although Van Hollen's role would become a flashpoint in his Senate campaign years later.

As he began his second term as DCCC chairman, Van Hollen sensed the national mood turning against incumbents, and cautioned early in 2009 that there would be no "third wave." He identified 41 "endangered species" members, and worked to provide leeway to those with conservative districts to vote against the leadership on the budget. When poll results showed many Democratic incumbents trailing little-known Republican challengers, he warned in August 2010 that Democrats were in for "a very tough campaign season." He contributed $1.6 million of his own campaign funds to others, but acknowledged later that he cut off DCCC funding to nine incumbents who could not be saved -- while sending $12 million to districts where Democrats might win in the final days. "Just on the triage side, we believe we saved 15-20 seats," he told *The New York Times*. Even so, Democrats lost 63 seats in 2010 amid the nationwide tea party revolt.

While the Democrats' loss was larger than either party had experienced in the House since 1948, Van Hollen's own political fortunes were not adversely affected. In fact, in 2011, he gained the plum assignment as ranking Democrat on the Budget Committee, even though he had not previously served on that panel. He established a cordial working relationship with the panel's chairman, Paul Ryan of Wisconsin, another policy wonk who is now House speaker. "He's probably one of the best articulators of the Democrats' position ... but he does it without being too partisan," Ryan told *The Baltimore Sun*. Nonetheless, Van Hollen was a vocal and highly visible critic of Ryan's policy proposals. He argued they would undermine Medicare and relied too heavily on spending cuts and not enough on tax hikes on high-earners.

Van Hollen served as the House Democrats' point man in the 2011 bicameral negotiations over raising the nation's debt limit and was named to the bipartisan "super committee" that unsuccessfully sought to craft a long-term deficit deal. A year later, after Republican presidential nominee Mitt Romney tapped Ryan as his running mate, Obama's reelection team recruited Van Hollen to help prepare Vice President Joe Biden for his debate with Ryan. But Van Hollen was not always in accord with Obama's budgetary ideas. He helped to persuade the president to drop from his proposed budget a move to impose a tax on college savings accounts known as "529 Plans" -- plans popular with many of Van Hollen's middle-class constituents. After he reportedly telephoned Pelosi as she flew with Obama on Air Force One in India, the idea was jettisoned.

Van Hollen's interest in moving to the Senate predated his rise in the House leadership. When Sen. Paul Sarbanes announced his retirement in early 2005, Van Hollen gave serious thought to running. He backed down when it became clear that party leaders were coalescing around Van Hollen's now-senior colleague, Ben Cardin. In March 2015, when Mikulski -- the longest serving woman in congressional history -- decided to retire after 30 years in the Senate, Van Hollen entered the contest within days. He quickly picked up support from much of his state's Democratic leadership as well as Senate Minority Leader Harry Reid, who endorsed Van Hollen as "the best and most effective person for the job."

Ironically, Mikulski's retirement announcement came just as Van Hollen was participating in quiet meetings with fellow House Democrats to discuss a possible plan of succession if and when Pelosi and House Minority Whip Steny Hoyer, both in their mid-70s, decided to leave. "He could have been speaker of the House, if he stuck around," Van Hollen's former Republican colleague, Tom Davis, told *The Washington Post*. But it was anything but clear when the leadership slots would open and Democrats might regain the majority and give Van Hollen, then 57, a shot at that post.

For perhaps the first time in his career, Van Hollen began a race for higher office as the frontrunner, though , his path was not without obstacles. Baltimore-based Rep. Elijah Cummings continued to contemplate running, and some polls showed him leading Van Hollen and the other major primary contender, Rep. Donna Edwards. Finally, after nearly 11 months of declining to rule out a Senate bid, Cummings filed for re-election to his House seat. In the early going, Van Hollen was seemingly a heavy favorite over Edwards, a combative personality who suffered from a rocky relationship with the state party establishment as well as many of her colleagues in the Congressional Black Caucus. She struggled to raise money, with Van Hollen reporting 12-1 advantage at the end of 2015 in terms of cash in his campaign treasury.

But, if Maryland is called "America in miniature" thanks to its varied geography, its 2016 Senate Democratic primary became a mini-version of the Hillary Clinton vs. Bernie Sanders national battle. As Sanders surged in a year of anti-incumbent sentiment, that dynamic aided Edwards -- who was viewed as the outsider, even if there were few policy differences between her and Van Hollen. He sought to turn his insider experience to his advantage. "It's not enough just to cast a vote a certain way," he declared, seeking to reinforce questions about Edwards' effectiveness as a legislator. "At the end of the day, what we all care about in politics is actually delivering results." Cummings' decision left Edwards as the only African American in the contest, and polls showed her with a large lead among black voters in a primary electorate estimated to be 40 percent African American. Edwards' fundraising disadvantage was offset by nearly $3 million spent on her behalf by a "super PAC" tied to EMILY's List -- an investment fueled by the fact that, with Mikulski retiring, a loss by Edwards threatened to leave the Maryland congressional delegation without a woman for the first time in four decades.

With two weeks to go until the April 26 primary, polls showed the race to be tight. Momentum shifted to Van Hollen when Edwards appeared to overplay her hand with a late line of attack. It went back to the

2010 DISCLOSE Act that Van Hollen had authored: Edwards criticized him for exempting the National Rifle Association from the legislation, in an effort to suggest to a liberal-dominated electorate that he was soft on the NRA. Van Hollen, citing his advocacy of gun control dating back to his days as a state legislator, reacted angrily. "I have led the fight against the NRA," he declared during the campaign's final debate. "People should not be misled on the issue." To facilitate passage of the DISCLOSE Act, several large membership-based organizations -- including the Sierra Club and labor unions as well as the NRA -- had been exempted, and Obama had backed the move at the time. The controversy escalated when a super PAC supporting Edwards echoed her criticism of Van Hollen in an ad that contained footage of Obama. The White House publicly called the ad misleading, putting Edwards on the defensive. A late poll showed Van Hollen opening a double-digit lead.

On Primary Day, Van Hollen won, 53%-39%. The vote broke down along racial lines: Edwards carried the black-majority jurisdictions of Baltimore City and Prince George's County, her home base. Van Hollen won 21 of the state's 22 remaining counties, including a nearly 4-1 win in his home base of Montgomery County, the state's most populous jurisdiction. The general election was anti-climactic. The Republicans nominated Kathy Szeliga, minority whip of the House of Delegates. She repeatedly characterized Van Hollen as a "career politician" while associating herself closely with the state's popular Republican governor, Larry Hogan -- and seeking to downplay her socially conservative voting record in a blue state. With polls throughout the fall showing Szeliga trailing by margins approaching 30 points, Van Hollen largely ignored her, agreeing to only two face-to-face debates. On Election Day, he came out on top, 61%-36%, reflecting Clinton's 60%-34% margin over Trump in Maryland.

In part, Senate Minority Leader Charles Schumer's move to put Van Hollen in the DSCC chairmanship reflected a lack of interest in the post by more senior Democrats. Few wanted the task of defending 25 seats in the Democratic Caucus, as compared to only nine Republican seats at risk in 2018. Van Hollen accepted the job only after leveraging it into appointment to the only Democratic vacancy on the powerful Appropriations Committee -- the seat that had been held by Mikulski. As DSCC chairman, Van Hollen sidestepped early questions about whether he could maintain the party's current overall contingent of 48 seats, including 2 Independents. "I'm just saying we have to hold the blue line," he said repeatedly, without talking numbers. He also brushed aside questions of whether success at the DSCC might lead to yet another ascent of a legislative leadership ladder. "I have a full plate right now, and that's my entire focus," he asserted. He wouldn't be the first Democratic senator to reach the top rung on the ladder via the DSCC -- Schumer, to wit.

FIRST DISTRICT

Andy Harris (R)

Elected 2010, 4th term; b. Jan 25, 1957, Brooklyn, NY; Johns Hopkins University Bloomburg School of Hygiene and Public Health (MD), Mast. Deg.; Johns Hopkins University Bloomburg School of Hygiene and Public Health (MD), M.D.; Johns Hopkins University Bloomburg School of Hygiene and Public Health (MD), B.S.; University of Pennsylvania, Att.; Roman Catholic; Widower; 5 children; 2 grandchildren.

Military Career: U.S. Naval Reserve, 1988-2010.

Elected Office: MD Senate, 1998-2010, Minority whip.

Professional Career: Anesthesiologist, Johns Hopkins Hosp., 1980- 2010; Association Professional, Johns Hopkins Med. School, 1984-2010.

DC Office: 1533 LHOB 20515, 202-225-5311, Fax: 202-225-0254, harris.house.gov.
State Offices: Bel Air, 410-588-5670; Chester, 410-643-5425; Salisbury, 443-944-8624.
Committees: *Appropriations*: Agriculture, Rural Development, FDA & Related Agencies, Homeland Security, Labor, Health & Human Services, Education & Related Agencies.

Group Ratings

	ADA	ACLU	AFL-CIO	LCV	ITI	COC	HAFA	ACU	CFG	FRC
2016	5%	11%	4%	0%	100%	100%	88%	100%	95%	100%
2015	5%	C	4%	3%	C	55%	C	100%	90%	100%

Almanac Ratings 2015

	Economy	Social	Foreign	Composite
Liberal	13%	0%	9%	7%
Conservative	87%	100%	91%	93%

Key Votes of the 114th Congress

1. Keystone Pipeline	Y	5. Puerto Rico Debt	Y	9. Offenses by Aliens	Y
2. Trade Deals	N	6. Medical Marijuana	N	10. Troops in Iraq	N
3. Export-Import Bank	N	7. Sanctuary Cities	Y	11. Homeland Security $$	N
4. Debt Ceiling Increase	N	8. Armor-piercing Bullets	Y	12. Trade Adjustment aid	N

Election Results

Election	Name (Party)	Vote (%)		Cand. Spent	Ind. Exp. Support	Ind. Exp. Oppose
2016 General	Andy Harris (R)	242,574	(67%)	$556,923		
	Joe Werner (D)	103,622	(29%)			
	Matt Beers (L)	15,370	(4%)			
2016 Primary	Andy Harris (R)	77,112	(78%)			
	Mike Smigiel (R)	10,597	(11%)			
	Jonathan Goff, Jr. (R)	5,971	(6%)			

Prior winning percentages: 2014 (71%), 2012 (63%), 2010 (54%)

Andy Harris, elected in 2010, is the lone Republican in Maryland's congressional delegation. He juggles working with his Terrapin State colleagues on local matters with advocating for his fervently conservative views. Following the 2016 election, he lost his bid for a powerful niche among House conservatives. At least until the next redistricting, he has no reason to worry about reelection. He has considered running statewide and other possible routes to greater influence.

Harris, a Johns Hopkins University anesthesiologist and professor, was born in Brooklyn, New York, to immigrants from Eastern Europe. His father, a Hungarian anti-communist activist, had been jailed in a Siberian gulag for more than a year for his political views before meeting Harris' mother, who had fled Ukraine, at a displaced persons camp in Austria. Harris credits his parents' escape from communism and the spirited dinner-table conversations they encouraged among their four sons with fostering his fiercely held beliefs in the ills of big government and the sanctity of the private sector. After Harris completed his medical studies at Johns Hopkins, he began to practice and teach there, and lived in a suburb north of Baltimore.

Harris was elected to the state Senate to represent Baltimore County in 1998. In Annapolis, he was one of the most conservative members, and he served as Senate minority whip. He gained a reputation for his artful filibusters - during a fight against a stem cell research bill, he read from a biology textbook on DNA. In 2008, he challenged Rep. Wayne Gilchrest, a moderate Republican, in a bloody primary. When Harris defeated him, Gilchrest refused to concede and then endorsed Frank Kratovil, the Democratic nominee. Kratovil continued Gilchrest's strategy of portraying Harris as too far right for the district and won by fewer than 3,000 votes.

Harris returned for a rematch in 2010. He cast Kratovil as a puppet of President Barack Obama in a year when anti-incumbent feeling was rampant and voters were deeply divided over the president's overhaul of the health insurance system. Pledging not to raise taxes and to repeal the health care overhaul, Harris connected with Republicans in a district where Sen. John McCain got 60 percent of the vote in the presidential race. After his first bid, Harris began to practice medicine a few days a week on the Eastern Shore, which helped deflect the criticism that he was running in an area where he had spent little time. Kratovil attacked Harris for his support of a conservative proposal to replace the income tax with a national sales tax. The freshman Kratovil was swept away by the Republican tide, losing to Harris, 54%-42%.

Harris said the "proudest moment" of his first few months in office was voting for the House-passed omnibus spending bill that cut $61 billion for fiscal 2011. In 2013, he infuriated Maryland Democrats by joining 66 Republicans in voting against $9.7 billion in relief from Hurricane Sandy, which had battered parts of the Eastern Shore. He explained he wanted the bill to strengthen the National Flood Insurance Program instead of writing "another blank check." In 2014, he spurred an investigation by the Health and Human Services Department of how the state had mishandled implementation of the health care law. Later that year, he dropped his bid to be chairman of the Republican Study Committee following the sudden death of his wife, Sylvia. Although he voted for John Boehner for Speaker in January 2015, Harris demanded that Boehner deliver on his promises to conservatives. When he voted for House passage of the 21st Century Cures Act in July 2015, he said, "It's time to accelerate medical innovation and invest in the future of health care."

Harris sought to help the Eastern Shore by introducing a bill in 2011 authorizing federal money to study oxygen-starved "dead zones" in the Chesapeake Bay and the Gulf of Mexico that drive away fish. Some environmentalists criticized the measure, saying it emphasized research instead of action. Harris infuriated residents of the District of Columbia when he sought to use congressional authority to stifle Washington's November 2014 referendum legalizing sales of marijuana. Some suggested a boycott of the Eastern Shore, which would be a major sacrifice in lifestyle for many. "The fact is the Constitution gives Congress the ultimate oversight about what happens in the federal district," Harris responded.

In this district that became solidly Republican after the 2012 redistricting, he has not faced a serious reelection challenge. Kratovil decided against a rematch. His Democratic rival, businesswoman Wendy Rosen, unexpectedly dropped out of the race in September after the state party said she had voted in both Maryland and Florida in two earlier elections. Harris coasted to a win with 63 percent of the vote against a write-in candidate. In 2014, Harris got 70 percent against Democrat Bill Tilghman, a retired lawyer from a longtime Eastern Shore family. Tilghman spent $573,000, but was outspent 2-to-1 and failed to get much traction. In 2015, Harris voiced interest in running for the Senate seat of retiring Democrat Barbara Mikulski. The Democratic lean of the state and his membership on the House Appropriations Committee mitigated against the uphill challenge. Instead, he had three opponents in the Republican primary, including former state delegate Michael Smigiel, a libertarian who had support from groups unhappy with Harris on marijuana in D.C. Harris won the primary with an impressive 78 percent to 11 percent for Smigiel, who raised $32,000 to $1.3 million for Harris. Harris got a majority of the vote in each county.

During the presidential transition, Harris had an interview with Donald Trump about becoming director of the National Institutes of Health. Before the election, Harris had said that Trump's offensive comments about women in 2005 were "wrong," but that Hillary Clinton's handling of the murders of U.S. diplomats in Benghazi Libya plus various Clinton scandals was worse. He had a setback when he was defeated by Rep. Mark Walker of North Carolina for chairman of the Republican Study Committee, which Harris described as "a powerful vehicle for change in Congress." He had the support of conservative activists in the House Freedom Caucus.

Northern Baltimore Suburbs, Eastern Shore

Population		**Race and Ethnicity**		**Income**	
Total	727,304	White	80.4%	Median Income	$69,077 (76 out of 435)
Land area	3,977	Black	11.8%		
Pop/ sq mi	182.9	Latino	3.6%	Under $50,000	36.1%
Born in state	62.1%	Asian	2.1%	$50,000-$99,999	31.7%
		Two races	1.8%	$100,000-$199,999	25.7%
Age Groups		Other	0.2%	$200,000 or more	6.4%
Under 18	21.8%			Poverty Rate	9.8%
18-34	20.2%	**Education**			
35-64	41.3%	H.S grad or less	42.2%	**Health Insurance**	
Over 64	16.6%	Some college	27.5%	With health insurance coverage	92.9%
		College Degree, 4 yr	17.9%		
Work		Post grad	12.3%		
White Collar	38.8%			**Public Assistance**	
Sales and Service	41.2%	**Military**		Cash public assistance income	2.2%
Blue Collar	20.0%	Veteran	9.9%		
Government	18.6%	Active Duty	0.1%	Food stamp/SNAP benefits	10.4%

Voter Turnout			
2015 Total Citizens 18+	552,826	2016 House Turnout as % CVAP	65%
2016 House turnout	362,097	2014 House Turnout as % CVAP	45%

2012 Presidential Vote		
Mitt Romney	214,988	(61%)
Barack Obama	132,286	(37%)

2016 Presidential Vote		
Donald Trump	225,249	(61%)
Hillary Clinton	121,840	(33%)
Gary Johnson	12,919	(4%)

Cook Partisan Voting Index: R+14

Chesapeake Bay is technically not a bay but an estuary. It was the central focus of the most thickly settled of the 13 colonies and today remains a central focus for much of modern Maryland. The first British here were amazed at the Chesapeake's oysters, terrapins, crabs and rockfish. This was an estuary civilization in colonial days, with every little hamlet tied together by the highways of bays and creeks and inlets off the Chesapeake. The streets and docks of Chestertown, Oxford, St. Michaels and Cambridge still look something like they did when George Washington slept there.

In post-colonial times, when most Americans were caught up in the romance of westward movement, these estuaries and peninsulas were mostly forgotten, located too far off the main lines of railroads and highways. In the 160 years between 1790 and 1950, the Eastern Shore counties of Maryland only doubled in population. Since then, much of the Chesapeake has changed beyond recognition. The area has grown vigorously, with second-home buyers, retirees and commuters crossing the Chesapeake Bay Bridge. Now, this is a land of genteel estates fronting the water and of Frank Perdue's thriving chicken empire around Salisbury. In a June 2016 announcement, the more than 2,000 growers that supply Perdue made changes in their breeding and slaughter operations, in response to concerns of animal activists, including fewer drugs and a friendlier ambiance in the chicken houses. Local studies have shown that farmers can make more money per acre from grains and produce than from chicken production.

Easton has a Waterfowl Festival and quaint St. Michaels has an OysterFest, as do other towns on that part of the three-state DelMarVa peninsula. The Asseteague Island National Seashore, with its famous wild ponies, annually supports a $110 million tourism business, including the crowded beaches and boardwalks up the coast in Ocean City. This growth has forced people along the Bay to confront issues that once would have been unimaginable here, such as high-rise condominiums obscuring the sunrise in an old fishing village like Crisfield. Away from the shore, in Harford County, where the population had more than tripled since 1960, the rate has almost flattened since 2010, partly due to job losses, especially among federal contractors. Other rural areas along the Bay have suffered a slow recovery from the recession, due partly to Defense Department cutbacks.

Even more threatening is pollution. Agricultural and suburban runoff have vastly depleted marine populations, and only a few watermen still make their living bringing crabs and oysters to shore. In 2010, the Chesapeake Bay Foundation settled a lawsuit against the Environmental Protection Agency to enforce limits on pollution entering the bay, with increased enforcement of regulations on developers and farmers. In a January 2017 report, the Foundation gave a C- grade to the health of the bay, which was its best since 1998. One result has been a significant increase in the harvest of blue crabs since 2014, when the number of spawning females had dropped to a level that experts said was unsustainable. The health of the bay's oysters improved slightly from 2014, when the oyster harvest was the largest in 30 years.

The 1st Congressional District of Maryland includes all nine counties of the Eastern Shore. At the top of the bay, it takes in parts of the northern Baltimore suburbs of Harford, Baltimore and Carroll counties. Although most people think of this as the Eastern Shore district, nearly half of the votes are cast on the west side of the bay and along the Susquehanna River, chiefly in the solidly Republican suburbs of Harford. The district has some Republican precincts in the outer Baltimore suburbs to maximize Democratic performance in neighboring districts. This is the only district in the state where Republicans hold a voter registration edge, and the only one that presidential nominee Donald Trump carried in 2016 - with 61 percent of the vote, no less. That was about the same as the Republican presidential vote over the previous two elections.

SECOND DISTRICT

Dutch Ruppersberger (D)

Elected 2002, 8th term; b. Jan 31, 1946, Baltimore; University of Baltimore School of Law (MD), J.D.; University of Maryland - College Park, B.A.; Baltimore City College (MD); Methodist; Married (Kay Murphy Ruppersberger); 2 children; 3 grandchildren.

Elected Office: Baltimore County Council, 1986-1994; Baltimore County Executive, 1994-2002.

Professional Career: Clerk, Judge Kenneth C. Proctor, 1970-1972; Assistant state Attorney, Baltimore County, 1972-1980; Partner, Ruppersberger, Clark & Mister, 1980-1994.

DC Office: 2416 RHOB 20515, 202-225-3061, Fax: 202-225-3094, ruppersberger.house.gov.

State Offices: Timonium, 410-628-2701.

Committees: *Appropriations*: Defense, Homeland Security, State, Foreign Operations & Related Programs.

Group Ratings

	ADA	ACLU	AFL-CIO	LCV	ITI	COC	HAFA	ACU	CFG	FRC
2016	-	76%	-	95%	83%	64%	17%	4%	10%	0%
2015	75%	C	100%	80%	C	50%	C	9%	7%	8%

Almanac Ratings 2015

	Economy	Social	Foreign	Composite
Liberal	80%	94%	38%	71%
Conservative	20%	6%	62%	29%

Key Votes of the 114th Congress

1. Keystone Pipeline	N	5. Puerto Rico Debt	Y	9. Offenses by Aliens	Y
2. Trade Deals	N	6. Medical Marijuana	Y	10. Troops in Iraq	N
3. Export-Import Bank	Y	7. Sanctuary Cities	N	11. Homeland Security $$	Y
4. Debt Ceiling Increase	Y	8. Armor-piercing Bullets	N	12. Trade Adjustment aid	Y

Election Results

Election	Name (Party)	Vote (%)		Cand. Spent	Ind. Exp. Support	Ind. Exp. Oppose
2016 General	Dutch Ruppersberger (D)	192,183	(62%)	$989,028		
	Pat McDonough (R)	102,577	(33%)	$217,174		
	Kristin Kasprzak (L)	14,128	(5%)			
2016 Primary	Dutch Ruppersberger (D)		(100%)			

Prior winning percentages: 2014 (61%), 2012 (66%), 2010 (64%), 2008 (72%), 2006(69%), 2004 (67%), 2002 (54%)

Dutch Ruppersberger, elected in 2002 in a district drawn for him, has retained his focus on national security issues. After stepping down in 2015 as ranking Democrat on the House Intelligence Committee, he has shifted his base to the Appropriations Committee, where he continues to seek a bipartisan approach on behalf of a district that he calls "the cybersecurity capital of the world."

Charles Albert Ruppersberger grew up in Baltimore, attended the University of Maryland and graduated from the University of Baltimore School of Law. Working as a Baltimore County assistant state's attorney, Ruppersberger had a near-fatal car accident in 1975 while investigating a drug-trafficking case. When he asked his doctors at the University of Maryland's Shock Trauma Center how he could thank them, he said, they urged him to run for office so he could fund their facility. In 1986, he won a seat on the Baltimore County Council and made good on his promise to help the hospital. In 1994, he was elected Baltimore County executive, a position held in the 1960s by future Republican Vice President Spiro Agnew.

Barred from seeking a third term in 2002, Ruppersberger seriously considered running for governor. But he was dissuaded by state party leaders who felt he was politically vulnerable at the time. In 2000, he had backed a plan to give him the power of eminent domain to redevelop large pieces of the county, but voters rebuked him and rejected it 2-to-1 in a referendum. Compounding the situation for Ruppersberger was a damaging story in *The Baltimore Sun* reporting that he had given county work to a firm to which he had financial ties. Kathleen Kennedy Townsend, the daughter of the late Robert F. Kennedy, became the gubernatorial candidate. She lost. Ruppersberger took advantage of a favorable House district when Democrats redrew the congressional map.

Because he considered his last name to be too long for a bumper sticker, Ruppersberger used his lifelong nickname of "Dutch" in his political campaign. His little-known primary opponent, investment banker Osman Bengur, spent more than $500,000 of his own money. Ruppersberger was backed by the state's Democratic establishment, and he won 50%-36%. In the fall, he faced former Republican Rep. Helen Delich Bentley, who served in the House for a decade until she ran, unsuccessfully, for governor in 1994. Both candidates supported additional dredging of shipping channels in the Chesapeake Bay and increased port security. Ruppersberger won, 54%-46%. His popular-vote margin was more than 13,000 in the small part of the district in Baltimore city, which he carried 79%-21%, and only 3,000 in the rest of the district.

In the House, Ruppersberger has had the least liberal voting record among Maryland Democrats. In the *Almanac* ratings for 2015, his scores in each of the three issue areas ranked near the center of the House. With the help of Baltimore native and Democratic leader Nancy Pelosi, he was appointed to the Intelligence Committee, where he called for expanded oversight of intelligence agencies and for shifting resources from the Iraq war to terrorist "safe havens" in Afghanistan.

Working with Intelligence Committee Chairman Mike Rogers, a Michigan Republican and former FBI agent, Ruppersberger sought to repair the panel's reputation for partisan infighting. "We both focus more on the teamwork," Ruppersberger told *The Washington Post*. The two men traveled together to foreign hot spots, and sat together at classified White House briefings. Ruppersberger did not hesitate to criticize President Barack Obama and his administration. In 2009, he said that he had not been adequately consulted on the White House's plan to buy and launch spy satellites. He added a provision to the 2010 intelligence authorization bill to ensure better oversight of satellite programs. In 2014, he criticized as a "dangerous precedent" the decision by Obama to release five Taliban prisoners of war in exchange for U.S. prisoner of war Bowe Bergdahl.

With Rogers, Ruppersberger signed a report in December 2014 that defended the Pentagon and the Central Intelligence Agency for their handling of the attacks on the U.S. diplomatic compound in Benghazi, Libya. Even after he left the committee, he remained an advocate of the intelligence legislation enacted in 2015 to end the National Security Agency's bulk collection of telephone and email data. The House-passed defense spending bill in 2016 included his provision to create a unified command for cyber operations, based at Fort Meade.

Ruppersberger retained his interest in steps to strengthen cybersecurity, an area that he said had been neglected under Obama. He said in May 2012 that administration leaks of highly classified information - which Republicans sought at the time to turn into an election-year campaign issue - were "about the worst that I've seen." Prompted by concern about the potential sale of shipping operations at the Port of Baltimore to the United Arab Emirates, Ruppersberger helped to enact port-security legislation. After his departure from the Intelligence Committee, where Pelosi had twice extended his term limits, he returned to Appropriations and focused on national security funding. With Republican Rep. Randy Hultgren of Illinois, he launched the Municipal Finance Caucus to assist the financing of local government infrastructure.

Ruppersberger has been reelected easily. His early statewide ambitions dimmed when he passed up opportunities for vacant seats for governor and the Senate, which were won by other Baltimore-area Democrats. He voiced interest in running for the Senate in 2016, but he again deferred - this time, to two Washington-area House Democrats.

Baltimore Metro: Parts of Baltimore County

Population		**Race and Ethnicity**		**Income**	
Total	745,184	White	52.4%	Median Income	$61,839 (123 out of 435)
Land area	349	Black	32.6%		
Pop/ sq mi	2135.9	Latino	6.4%		
Born in state	62.4%	Asian	5.4%	Under $50,000	39.6%
		Two races	2.6%	$50,000-$99,999	33.3%
Age Groups		Other	0.6%	$100,000-$199,999	22.6%
Under 18	23.2%			$200,000 or more	4.4%
18-34	24.9%	**Education**		Poverty Rate	12.3%
35-64	39.7%	H.S grad or less	42.1%		
Over 64	12.2%	Some college	28.5%	**Health Insurance**	
		College Degree, 4 yr	17.6%	With health insurance coverage	91.0%
Work		Post grad	11.9%		
White Collar	39.1%				
Sales and Service	43.1%	**Military**		**Public Assistance**	
Blue Collar	17.7%	Veteran	9.4%	Cash public assistance income	3.5%
Government	20.4%	Active Duty	0.9%		
				Food stamp/SNAP benefits	14.1%

Voter Turnout			
2015 Total Citizens 18+	533,210	2016 House Turnout as % CVAP	58%
2016 House turnout	309,480	2014 House Turnout as % CVAP	36%

2012 Presidential Vote		
Barack Obama	193,834	(63%)
Mitt Romney	107,890	(35%)

2016 Presidential Vote		
Hillary Clinton	193,237	(59%)
Donald Trump	114,460	(35%)
Gary Johnson	8,990	(3%)

Cook Partisan Voting Index: D+11

The spokes of Baltimore's avenues spread out in all directions from the Inner Harbor, connecting the central city with the suburbs, where most residents of metropolitan Baltimore live. The streets reach east to Dundalk and Essex, industrial suburbs where the tone of life was set for years by the giant Sparrows Point steel mill, long the biggest in the country, but which was shuttered in 2012. Northeastward, they extend to charming Havre de Grace and the oldest lighthouse in continuous use on the East Coast, as well as to modest working-class suburbs in Harford County. Aberdeen has generated military and civilian job growth, but the locale is now better known for its Ripken Stadium, home of the Aberdeen IronBirds, a Class A baseball team owned by hometown hero Cal Ripken, the Hall of Fame legend who played 2,632 consecutive games for the Baltimore Orioles. In an arc north of downtown are middle-income towns from Randallstown to Owings Mills. A couple of miles northwest of the Baltimore County seat of Towson is Timonium, the site of the annual Maryland State Fair.

The 2nd Congressional District of Maryland is an irregularly shaped hodgepodge that includes much of this territory. Most of the district is not far from the Chesapeake Bay, including the terminal for the bustling Port of Baltimore, which has been rated as the most efficient container port in the nation. In 2015, it employed 14,600 workers, ranked 9th in the nation for its dollar value of cargo, and moved nearly 800,000 automobiles - the most in the nation. With the widening of the Panama Canal, Baltimore and Norfolk, Virginia, are the only East Coast ports wide and deep enough for post-Panamax cargo ships. A huge redevelopment has been underway to revive Sparrows Point as an international trade hub, with many commercial distribution centers - and salaries about half of what workers received when this was an industrial center.

With its short distance from Washington, D.C., the Baltimore area has become a convenient locale for military work. The Aberdeen Proving Ground tests a wide variety of military weapons. *The Baltimore Sun* has described it as the local "economic lifeblood," with more than 20,000 government and contractor jobs. Down the Baltimore-Washington Parkway is Fort Meade, the sprawling Army post that houses the National Security Agency and supports more than 125,000 jobs in 1,500 buildings and 2,900 homes.

It has evolved from an army base to a cybersecurity center, which now houses more than 100 federal agencies, including the nation's cyber defense operations and the Defense Information Systems Agency. Edward Snowden, who released a trove of secret national security documents before he fled the United States, had been an NSA contractor at Fort Meade.

Like the arms of a Maryland crab, the district angles inland to include some Baltimore County suburbs, residential neighborhoods in northeast Baltimore, an industrial pocket in far southeast Baltimore and a dip south of Baltimore along Interstate 95 to include the NSA headquarters. At that point, the district crosses the Harbor Tunnel to capture the row houses of Brooklyn and Curtis Bay, whose residents are mainly descendants of German and East European immigrants who moved there to work on the docks and in the factories along the Patapsco River and the harbor. About 60 percent of the district's population is in Baltimore County, with 10 percent in Baltimore city, and much of the remainder in Harford County. About one-third of its population is African American. This is a comfortably Democratic district, with some Republican enclaves. In 2016, working-class Dundalk, which has shifted to Republican in recent years, gave 62 percent of its vote to Donald Trump in the general election. Overall in the district, the 59 percent for Hillary Clinton was a slight decrease in the recent Democratic vote.

THIRD DISTRICT

John Sarbanes (D)

Elected 2006, 6th term; b. May 22, 1962, Baltimore; Harvard University, J.D.; Princeton University (NJ), B.A.; Greek Orthodox; Married (Dina Sarbanes); 3 children.

Professional Career: Clerk, Judge Fred Motz, 1988-1989; Practicing attorney, Venable LLP, 1989-2006; Special Assistant MD Schls. Superintendent, 1998-2005.

DC Office: 2444 RHOB 20515, 202-225-4016, Fax: 202-225-9219, sarbanes.house.gov.

State Offices: Annapolis, 410-295-1679; Towson, 410-832-8890.

Committees: *Energy & Commerce*: Energy, Health. *Oversight & Government Reform*: National Security.

Group Ratings

	ADA	ACLU	AFL-CIO	LCV	ITI	COC	HAFA	ACU	CFG	FRC
2016	-	100%	-	100%	50%	43%	14%	0%	10%	0%
2015	95%	C	100%	91%	C	40%	C	0%	0%	0%

Almanac Ratings 2015

	Economy	Social	Foreign	Composite
Liberal	100%	100%	99%	100%
Conservative	0%	0%	1%	0%

Key Votes of the 114th Congress

1. Keystone Pipeline	N	5. Puerto Rico Debt	Y	9. Offenses by Aliens	N
2. Trade Deals	N	6. Medical Marijuana	Y	10. Troops in Iraq	Y
3. Export-Import Bank	Y	7. Sanctuary Cities	N	11. Homeland Security $$	Y
4. Debt Ceiling Increase	Y	8. Armor-piercing Bullets	N	12. Trade Adjustment aid	Y

Election Results

Election	Name (Party)	Vote (%)	Cand. Spent	Ind. Exp. Support	Ind. Exp. Oppose
2016 General	John Sarbanes (D)................... 214,640 (63%)		$592,863		
	Mark Plaster (R)...................... 115,048 (34%)		$560,773		
	Ezr Nnabu (G).......................... 9,987 (3%)				
2016 Primary	John Sarbanes (D).................... 95,405 (87%)				
	John Rea (D)........................... 14,051 (13%)				

Prior winning percentages: 2014 (60%), 2012 (67%), 2010 (61%), 2008 (70%), 2006 (64%)

Democrat John Sarbanes, elected in 2006, is the son of a former five-term senator from Maryland. On the Energy and Commerce Committee, he works on issues ranging from health care to campaign finance reform. His ambition has been to follow his father's path from the House to the Senate. In 2016, he deferred on the opportunity to run in the Democratic primary against two Washington-area House members.

Sarbanes graduated from Princeton University and Harvard Law School, following the academic route taken by his dad, Paul Sarbanes, who retired in 2006 after 36 years in Congress. The younger Sarbanes returned to Baltimore to clerk for a federal District Court judge, then joined the Venable law firm, where he chaired the health care practice and represented nonprofit hospitals and senior-living providers. He spent seven years as special assistant to the Maryland superintendent of schools, serving as liaison to Baltimore schools.

Though his 2006 campaign was his first bid for public office, Sarbanes enjoyed a considerable advantage because of his name recognition. But the primary race was no cakewalk. Openings in the Maryland congressional delegation are rare. So, when Democratic Rep. Ben Cardin announced he was giving up his seat to run for the Senate seat of the senior Sarbanes, eight candidates filed for the primary. Contenders included veteran state Sen. Paula Hollinger and former Baltimore Health Commissioner Peter Beilenson, the son of former Democratic Rep. Anthony Beilenson of California.

Sarbanes issued lengthy, detailed proposals on health care and education, which he called his top two legislative priorities. Beilenson emphasized his experience managing a large government budget. Hollinger was endorsed by the teachers union, and had been an active state lawmaker. Sarbanes, who had a small fundraising advantage, won the Democratic primary with 32 percent to 25 percent for runner-up Beilenson and 21 percent for Hollinger. In the general election, Republican nominee John White, founder and CEO of a marketing company, spent nearly a half-million dollars, most of it from his own pocket. He got little attention in a Democratic year and lost the general election to Sarbanes, 64%-34%.

In the House, Sarbanes has a staunchly liberal voting record. In 2010, he got a provision in an auto safety bill to fund research into new technologies to prevent drunk-driving accidents. Mothers Against Drunk Driving strongly backed the idea, but the American Beverage Institute and some Republicans complained it went too far. He urged the Federal Trade Commission in 2011 to take action against Pfizer for what he described as its attempts to keep consumers away from generic versions of its successful anti-cholesterol drug Lipitor. In the *Almanac* vote ratings for 2015, he had a nearly perfect liberal record.

Sarbanes has promoted a novel 'Government by the People" campaign finance plan that would give contributors tax credits for donations and create a fund to match small donations to "grass-roots" candidates who refuse political action committee money. Although he concedes that its congressional prospects are slim for now, he has been encouraged that some local governments have approved the model. "With Americans fast losing confidence in our democracy, it's time to ring the alarm bells and launch a creative and sustained push to restore the public's faith in government," he wrote in an April 2015 op-ed in *The Baltimore Sun*. "A small-donor matching system would also reinvigorate our democracy by empowering a more diverse pool of candidates who would have the resources to run, compete and win." In November 2016, Howard County voters approved a referendum, which he backed, to authorize a small-donor driven system of financing campaigns.

In 2016, Sarbanes took the lead on legislation that sought to address the growing crisis of opioid addiction, which had become a major problem in Baltimore. The House passed his bill to train doctors to prescribe overdose-reversal drugs when they prescribe pain medication and other opiates. His approach, he said, was to bring together medical professionals, behavioral health experts and law enforcement with local, state and federal officials to improve addiction treatment and expand prevention services. Serving on the House-Senate conference committee that crafted the final details of the 21st Century Cures Act, which was one of the few major bills enacted that year, Sarbanes pushed for the $1 billion that was approved to expand treatment programs.

Like his father, Sarbanes has been an outspoken advocate of Greece and its Hellenic values. Earlier, when he served on the House education panel, Sarbanes won approval of amendments to bolster school instruction on protecting the environment. He got a bill signed into law enabling college graduates to erase student loan debts after 10 years of work in government or the non-profit sector. He has advocated legislative solutions to clean up pollution in the Chesapeake. He unsuccessfully sought in committee in 2012 to prevent offshore drilling near the bay. When House Republicans shot down a proposal to create a national climate change service, he attacked them for their "reckless political stunt of climate change denial."

He has been reelected easily. He says that he drives home to Towson every night. When Sen. Barbara Mikulski announced her retirement in March 2015, Sarbanes initially kept his cards close to his vest. But he soon ruled out a bid for her seat. Perhaps he will seek to succeed Ben Cardin in the Senate, just as he did in the House - though Cardin has shown no signs of retiring.

Baltimore Metro, Annapolis

Population		**Race and Ethnicity**		**Income**	
Total	744,150	White	60.5%	Median Income	$79,173 (41 out of 435)
Land area	304	Black	21.0%		
Pop/ sq mi	2446.7	Latino	8.1%	Under $50,000	31.1%
Born in state	49.3%	Asian	7.1%	$50,000-$99,999	29.9%
		Two races	2.7%	$100,000-$199,999	28.7%
Age Groups		Other	0.5%	$200,000 or more	10.4%
Under 18	21.3%			Poverty Rate	8.2%
18-34	25.7%	**Education**			
35-64	39.3%	H.S grad or less	30.6%	**Health Insurance**	
Over 64	13.7%	Some college	23.3%	With health insurance coverage	91.6%
Work		College Degree, 4 yr	24.6%		
White Collar	50.5%	Post grad	21.5%	**Public Assistance**	
Sales and Service	36.5%	**Military**		Cash public assistance income	2.5%
Blue Collar	12.9%	Veteran	8.5%		
Government	20.4%	Active Duty	1.3%	Food stamp/SNAP benefits	9.0%

Voter Turnout			
2015 Total Citizens 18+	536,380	2016 House Turnout as % CVAP	63%
2016 House turnout	339,675	2014 House Turnout as % CVAP	40%

2012 Presidential Vote		
Barack Obama	205,929	(61%)
Mitt Romney	122,604	(37%)

2016 Presidential Vote		
Hillary Clinton	221,842	(62%)
Donald Trump	113,318	(32%)
Gary Johnson	12,324	(3%)

Cook Partisan Voting Index: D+13

Downtown Baltimore, one of America's major urban centers since the Revolution, has been viewed as one of America's star cities. Its Inner Harbor redevelopment, with a spectacular, multilevel aquarium on the water, and its ballpark at Camden Yards are national models. The local cuisine - crab cakes and steamed crabs spiced a certain way - is known well beyond the watershed of the Chesapeake Bay. In 2009, about half of the city became a National Heritage Area, a designation that boosted tourism and economic development. The minority neighborhoods of Baltimore have had terrible urban problems - high crime, controversial policing, abandoned neighborhoods, poor schools - but the greater Baltimore area that has grown far beyond the city and county lines has fared better and retains a distinctive character. To the south, Annapolis was laid out as a capital in 1694, and the marble-halled Statehouse, built in 1772, is where the Continental Congress ratified the Treaty of Paris and is the oldest state capitol in continuous use. Annapolis is also the home of the U.S. Naval Academy, and the city's gentrified waterfront is both a waterman's and yachter's port.

The 3rd District of Maryland consists of three oddly disjointed pieces of geography that extend from the Inner Harbor area. As it scoops up parts of Baltimore City, Baltimore County, Anne Arundel

County, Howard County, and a small slice of Montgomery County, the 3rd is a leading contender for the most-gerrymandered district in the nation, and was named the ugliest-drawn congressional district by Comedy Central's *The Daily Show with Jon Stewart*. According to *The Washington Post's* Wonkblog, this is the "Praying Mantis" district. From a distance, it seems like an ink spot. But there is a rationale to what some might consider its absurdity. Its boundaries were designed by Democrats with politics in mind: The 3rd borders the majority-black 7th District on three sides. One spoke extends northeast and takes in black city neighborhoods; another extends north and west from the city to the Baltimore County seat of Towson and the heavily Jewish suburbs of Pikesville and Owings Mills. The last crooked spoke extends south to Glen Burnie and the Baltimore-Washington International Thurgood Marshall Airport, where it splits into two tangents: one goes south to Anne Arundel County and all of Annapolis, and the other heads west to Columbia in Howard County, plus rural Olney and Calverton in Montgomery County. About a third of the district's population resides in Anne Arundel, and another quarter is in Baltimore city. Following concerns about the threats posed to illegal immigrants living there by the Trump administration, Howard County officials moved to create a "sanctuary county."

In Baltimore's revived Locust Point industrial neighborhood on the waterfront is the iconic orange Domino Sugars sign glowing from the refinery plant's rooftop - now powered by solar panels. The plant has continued to refine 6.6 million pounds of raw sugar a day, but other industrial land along the water is being redeveloped into upscale residential and commercial properties. The district includes such neighborhoods as Roland Park, and the fabled restaurants and bars of Little Italy and Fell's Point. A water wheel, with solar and water power, periodically removes tons of trash and debris from the Inner Harbor. Like Locus Point, the Inner Harbor neighborhoods have achieved a "critical mass," even as the overall city has continued to lose population, *The Baltimore Sun* reported in January 2017. More construction of apartment buildings has been underway, the first such downtown increase since the 19th century. These sites are close to the troubled neighborhoods of the Baltimore riots that broke out in the spring of 2015 after a black man, Freddie Gray, died in police custody, but those areas are in the 7th District. The solidly Democratic 3rd increased its presidential vote from 61%-37% in 2012 to 62%-32% in 2016.

FOURTH DISTRICT

Anthony Brown (D)

Elected 2016, 1st term; b. Nov 21, 1961, Huntington, NY; Harvard College (MA), B.A., 1984; Harvard University Law School (MA), J.D., 1992; Roman Catholic; Married (Karmen Bailey Walker Brown); 2 children; 1 stepchild.

Military Career: U.S Army, 1984-1994; U.S Army Reserves (Iraq), 1984-present.

Elected Office: Maryland Assembly, 1999-2007; Lt. Governor, 2007-2015.

DC Office: 1505 LHOB 20515, 202-225-8699, anthonybrown.house.gov.

State Offices: Annapolis, 410-266-3249; Largo, 301-458-2600.

Committees: *Armed Services*: Readiness, Tactical Air & Land Forces. *Ethics*. *Natural Resources*: Energy & Mineral Resources, Federal Lands.

Election Results

Election	Name (Party)	Vote (%)		Cand. Spent	Ind. Exp. Support	Ind. Exp. Oppose
2016 General	Anthony Brown (D)	237,501	(74%)	$1,159,571		
	George McDermott (R)	68,670	(21%)			
	Kamesha Clark (G)	9,620	(3%)			
2016 Primary	Anthony Brown (D)	44,712	(42%)			
	Glenn Ivey (D)	36,717	(34%)			
	Joseline Pena-Melnyk (D)	20,392	(19%)			

Anthony Brown of Maryland was elected to the House in 2016. A former lieutenant governor, he was the unsuccessful Democratic nominee for governor in 2014. That made him one of six defeated gubernatorial candidates who became members of his freshman class. With his extensive military background, Brown got a seat on the Armed Services Committee.

Brown is a native of Huntington, New York, where his father was a native of Jamaica and served as a physician on Long Island. He got his bachelor's and law degrees from Harvard University. He joined the Army ROTC program and was commissioned after college as a second lieutenant and served as a helicopter pilot and aviation officer in Germany. Later, in the Army Reserve, he was a lieutenant colonel in the Judge Advocate General's Corps. Following law school, where he was a classmate of Barack Obama, Brown moved to Maryland and clerked for the chief judge of the U.S. Court of Appeals for the Armed Forces.

In 1998, he was elected to the first of four terms in the Maryland House of Delegates and served as majority whip. In 2004, he was deployed to Iraq, where he was a senior consultant to the Iraqi Ministry of Displacement and Migration and worked on refugee problems; he earned the Bronze Star. He was elected lieutenant governor in 2006 as the running-mate of Martin O'Malley and served two terms in that office. He won the Democratic nomination to run for governor in overwhelmingly Democratic Maryland in 2014, but lost to Republican Larry Hogan, 51%-47% after what many considered a lackluster campaign.

When Rep. Donna Edwards ran for the Senate, Brown was the early favorite to succeed her and won endorsements from key local Democratic officials. He ran on a campaign of "redemption" following his setback in 2014, and described himself as a "workhorse not a show horse." His chief opponent was Glenn Ivey, a former prosecutor in Prince George's and a partner in a Washington, D.C., law firm. His wife, Jolene Ivey, a former state delegate, ran for lieutenant governor on the ticket opposing Brown in the close Democratic primary for governor in 2014. Ivey ran more outspoken advertising, pledging to "take on Republicans for all of us."

Brown, who loaned himself nearly $400,000 shortly before the primary, had a fundraising advantage over Ivey of $1.4 million to $1 million, and won the April primary, 42%-34%. State Del. Joseline Pena-Melnuk, who ran as the "progressive fighter" and raised $900,000, was third with 19 percent. In the general election that was a foregone conclusion in this district, Brown defeated businessman George McDermott, 74%-21%.

In addition to the Armed Services Committee, Brown got seats on Natural Resources and on Ethics. The latter is an unusual mark of confidence in a first-term member to deal with often dicey internal problems.

Eastern D.C. Suburbs: Prince George's County

Population		**Race and Ethnicity**		**Income**	
Total	738,944	White	26.7%	Median Income	$75,113 (53 out of 435)
Land area	298	Black	52.3%		
Pop/ sq mi	2481.3	Latino	15.3%	Under $50,000	30.6%
Born in state	30.1%	Asian	3.2%	$50,000-$99,999	33.9%
		Two races	2.1%	$100,000-$199,999	27.9%
Age Groups		Other	0.4%	$200,000 or more	7.6%
Under 18	23.9%			Poverty Rate	9.0%
18-34	24.1%	**Education**			
35-64	40.6%	H.S grad or less	40.0%	**Health Insurance**	
Over 64	11.4%	Some college	28.2%	With health insurance coverage	86.7%
		College Degree, 4 yr	19.0%		
Work		Post grad	12.8%		
White Collar	37.7%			**Public Assistance**	
Sales and Service	44.4%	**Military**		Cash public assistance income	1.7%
Blue Collar	17.8%	Veteran	9.0%		
Government	24.6%	Active Duty	0.5%	Food stamp/SNAP benefits	10.3%

Voter Turnout			
2015 Total Citizens 18+	484,050	2016 House Turnout as % CVAP	66%
2016 House turnout	320,650	2014 House Turnout as % CVAP	39%

2012 Presidential Vote		
Barack Obama	255,226	(78%)
Mitt Romney	69,323	(21%)

2016 Presidential Vote		
Hillary Clinton	256,575	(77%)
Donald Trump	63,390	(19%)

Cook Partisan Voting Index: D+28

In 1696, the proprietors of the colony of Maryland created a new county between the Potomac and Patuxent rivers and named it after the husband of the heir to the throne, Prince George of Denmark. During its 300 years, Prince George's County has not often won national fame - maybe briefly when investigators chased the plotters of Abraham Lincoln's murder here - but it might now. With a population that is nearly two-thirds African American, Prince George's is the home of America's largest black middle class. It is the wealthiest county with a majority black population, and continues fast-growing with an increase in total population from 802,000 in 2000 to 910,000 in 2015.

Historically, Prince George's was tobacco country, dotted by slave plantations and pretty much controlled by its white property owners. A hundred years after the Civil War, the population grew as middle-class blacks moved out of neighboring Washington, D.C., into modest suburbs at the county's edge and affluent subdivisions farther to the east. Its African-American population increased from 14 percent in 1970, to 37 percent in 1980, to 65 percent in 2015, the highest in the state. The county continues to grow, with working-class black and Hispanic residents leaving gentrified Washington for more affordable housing and better schools across the border. As the Hispanic population has climbed above 17 percent, there has been some pushback from black groups over jobs, plus new schools and public facilities in immigrant neighborhoods, including Largo and Langley Park.

With office and shopping mall development, Prince George's County has become more commercially vibrant than adjacent parts of the District of Columbia. Commuters from Virginia travel into the county across the Potomac River on the 12-lane Woodrow Wilson Bridge. Just over the bridge is the National Harbor development area, where a $1.2 billion MGM casino opened in December 2016 with nearly 4,000 employees and $42 million in revenue that month. The Washington Redskins play at FedEx Field in nearby Landover, with occasional protests over the franchise's name and a possible move to a more luxurious stadium elsewhere in the region.

Prince George's County is affluent by national standards, and ranked as the 69th wealthiest county in the nation. The county's median household income of $74,260 easily tops the national median of about $53,889 and is nearly double the $43,300 national median for black households. Slightly more than 31 percent of the county population over 25 holds an undergraduate degree, which is slightly higher than the overall national average. Yet amid this success, considerable problems remain: Prince George's homicide rates are high for a suburban county. Nearly 70 percent of adults are overweight. The recession hit hard at over-extended local homeowners with a disproportionate share of sub-prime mortgages. In 2009, the median value of a home in the county dropped from $343,000 to $245,000. Housing finance continues to plague Prince George's. In September 2016, 26 percent of the homes in the county were underwater, compared with 18 percent in all of Maryland.

The 4th Congressional District of Maryland includes most of Prince George's County inside the Capital Beltway that rings Washington, and a GOP-leaning eastern salient into relatively rural central Anne Arundel County, including Severna Park. This is still a safely Democratic seat; Hillary Clinton carried Prince George's by an extraordinary 89%-8% in 2016 - virtually the same as the 90%-9% in 2012 for President Barack Obama, his fourth-best countywide showing. On certain social issues, however, the district is more conservative: While a 2012 referendum legalizing same-sex marriage in Maryland passed statewide with 52 percent of the vote, it narrowly failed in Prince George's County. The district's biggest employer is the federal government. Suitland, just across the D.C. border, is the home of the Census Bureau, and local and state officials have tried to lure the FBI, which plans to move its longtime headquarters from downtown Washington.

FIFTH DISTRICT

Steny Hoyer (D)

Elected 1981, 19th term; b. Jun 14, 1939, New York, NY; Georgetown University Law Center (DC), J.D.; University of Maryland - College Park, B.S.; Baptist; Widower; 3 children; 3 grandchildren; 2 great-grandchildren.

Elected Office: MD Senate, 1966-1979, President, 1975-1978.

Professional Career: Practicing attorney, 1966-1980; MD Board of Higher Ed., 1978-1981.

DC Office: 1705 LHOB 20515, 202-225-4131, Fax: 202-225-4300, hoyer.house.gov.

State Offices: Greenbelt, 301-474-0119; Waldorf, 301-843-1577.

Group Ratings

	ADA	ACLU	AFL-CIO	LCV	ITI	COC	HAFA	ACU	CFG	FRC
2016	-	100%	-	92%	67%	64%	10%	0%	0%	0%
2015	95%	C	100%	89%	C	47%	C	0%	0%	0%

Almanac Ratings 2015

	Economy	Social	Foreign	Composite
Liberal	92%	100%	85%	92%
Conservative	8%	0%	15%	8%

Key Votes of the 114th Congress

1. Keystone Pipeline	NV	5. Puerto Rico Debt	Y	9. Offenses by Aliens	N
2. Trade Deals	N	6. Medical Marijuana	Y	10. Troops in Iraq	N
3. Export-Import Bank	Y	7. Sanctuary Cities	N	11. Homeland Security $$	Y
4. Debt Ceiling Increase	Y	8. Armor-piercing Bullets	N	12. Trade Adjustment aid	Y

Election Results

Election	Name (Party)	Vote (%)	Cand. Spent	Ind. Exp. Support	Ind. Exp. Oppose
2016 General	Steny Hoyer (D)	242,989 (67%)	$1,693,433		
	Mark Arness (R)	105,931 (29%)	$51,359		
	Jason Summers (L)	11,078 (3%)			
2016 Primary	Steny Hoyer (D)	79,453 (76%)			
	Debbie Wilson (D)	12,556 (12%)			
	Kristin Beck (D)	12,356 (12%)			

Prior winning percentages: 2014 (64%), 2012 (69%), 2010 (64%), 2008 (74%), 2006 (83%), 2004 (69%), 2002(69%), 2000 (65%), 1998 (65%), 1996 (56.9%), 1994 (58.8%), 1992 (53%), 1990 (81%), 1988 (79%), 1986 (81.9%), 1984 (72%), 1982 (80%); 1981 special (56%)

Democrat Steny Hoyer, elected in 1981, is the longest-serving House member from Maryland. He is the minority whip and de facto leader of his party's shrinking moderate wing in the House, and he is at heart a bipartisan deal-cutter despite his role as a public critic of Republicans. He also is part of the aging and entrenched Democratic leadership that seems reconciled to minority status, at least until the 2022 redistricting.

Hoyer is of Danish descent. His first name, he says, was his parents' adaptation of the Danish name Steen. He grew up in New York City, but moved from place to place with his mother and stepfather, who was in the Air Force and, when Steny was in high school, was transferred from Florida to Andrews Air Force Base in Maryland. Hoyer graduated from the University of Maryland, where in 1959 he listened to Democratic presidential candidate John F. Kennedy deliver a campaign speech that inspired him to switch his major from public relations to political science. While working on his law degree at Georgetown University, Hoyer interned one summer with Maryland Sen. Daniel Brewster. Another intern in Brewster's office that summer was Nancy D'Alesandro, daughter of the former mayor of Baltimore and now House Minority Leader Nancy Pelosi.

In 1966, just after graduating from law school, Hoyer was elected to the Maryland Senate at age 27. He was Senate president from 1975 to 1978, the youngest person to hold that post in Maryland history. In 1978, he ran for lieutenant governor on a losing ticket. In 1981, after Rep. Gladys Spellman was incapacitated by a heart attack, the 5th District seat was declared vacant. Hoyer won the special election, edging out Spellman's husband and several other Democrats in the primary and beating a well-financed Republican in the general. The district then was entirely in Prince George's County.

Hoyer was also a fast riser in Congress. He excelled at constituent service and won a seat on the Appropriations Committee, where he worked with Republicans and became a champion for the Washington metro area. He has been an advocate of more spending for education and other social programs, and better pay and benefits for federal workers. He was the chief House sponsor of the Americans with Disabilities Act of 1990, which outlawed discrimination against people with disabilities. He counts that as his greatest legislative achievement, along with the 2002 federal election reform known as the Help America Vote Act. On Sept. 11, 2001, it was Hoyer's idea to have lawmakers gather in front of the Capitol in a show of unity. The group spontaneously sang "God Bless America," an image captured vividly on television on a dark day in U.S. history.

His voting record is relatively moderate among Democrats. In the 2015 *Almanac* vote ratings, he was near the center of House Democrats on economic and foreign issues, but more liberal on social policy. He broke with the party by supporting the balanced budget amendment in 1995. He has backed many of the free-trade initiatives that organized labor opposed, including the North American Free Trade Agreement, though in 2015 he voted against expedited action on the Trans-Pacific Partnership. In 2002, he voted to authorize military action in Iraq and later complained that President George W. Bush "under resourced" the war. He is a former chairman of the Helsinki Commission, and has remained a champion of human rights around the world.

Hoyer won his first leadership post in 1989 as chairman of the Democratic Caucus. When he tried to move up to the job of majority whip in 1991, he lost, 160-109, to David Bonior of Michigan, who had the support of liberals and the committee chairmen. In 2001, Bonior, faced with unfavorable redistricting changes at home, decided to run for governor. Both Hoyer and Pelosi sought to replace him as minority whip. Hoyer argued that he had greater experience in leadership positions and could do a better job of unifying the caucus. Pelosi had more publicly committed votes going into the Caucus election, and she won 118-95.

Although he was a two-time loser of leadership contests, Hoyer was undeterred when Dick Gephardt stepped down as minority leader in 2002. With Pelosi running to succeed Gephardt, Hoyer ran to succeed her as minority whip. He collected commitments for months and was elected unanimously. In that position, it was his job to be partisan, and he often was. As Hoyer said in 2010, as he was being criticized by Republicans, "I think both parties have acted defensively in some respects when they were in the majority."

In the pivotal 2006 campaign, Hoyer worked closely with Illinois Rep. Rahm Emanuel, who chaired the committee to elect a Democratic majority. His September prediction that Democrats would gain 30 seats turned out to be right on the money. Many of the freshmen subsequently credited the help that Hoyer provided, especially those from swing districts where liberal Democratic leaders were not always welcome.

Even so, when it came time to elect leaders to the new Democratic-controlled House, Hoyer had to fight for the position of majority leader against Pennsylvania Rep. John Murtha, who was a close ally of incoming Speaker Pelosi. In spite of their years working together in the leadership, Pelosi and Hoyer still viewed each other with suspicion. Murtha contended that he could work better with Pelosi. Hoyer had little choice but to speak positively about his long-standing relationship with her - he called her a "favorite daughter" of Maryland - and their success in largely unifying an often-unruly party. But he left no doubt about his dismay over her arm-twisting for Murtha.

In spite of Pelosi's efforts for Murtha, Hoyer prevailed 149-86, a powerful endorsement of him for majority leader and a restraint on Pelosi. Democrats responded to his "ability, patience, know-how, and experience," said a Democratic lobbyist. Even more impressive, Hoyer won the support of many California Democrats who previously had been unified behind Pelosi and of numerous prospective committee chairmen who doubted Murtha's ability to do the job. "Nancy thought she could put these people away because of pressure," former Majority Whip Tony Coelho of California told *The New York Times*. Hoyer "has a tremendous capacity for friendship, and when you have that, people don't flake off on you," Coelho said.

As majority leader, Hoyer assumed responsibility for determining the floor schedule, helping guide Democratic initiatives to passage, and holding weekly press briefings. He described his recipe for holding together what had historically been a fractious caucus this way: "First of all, work very hard on communications, find out what people can do and can't do. Secondly, put together a consensus that, while it may not be the first choice of everybody, it is a choice they can live with." And for the most part, the record justifies his boast that House Democrats during their four years in the majority were "the most unified the Democratic Party has been in over half a century." Hoyer kept communications open with the opposition and stayed in close touch with Rep. Roy Blunt of Missouri in the Republican leadership. When Democrats lost their majority in 2010, Pelosi returned to minority leader and Hoyer to whip.

In recent years, Hoyer has found himself at odds with the majority of Democrats on some issues. He voted for military funding in Iraq and against linking war funding to a timetable for withdrawing U.S. troops, earning him criticism from liberal advocates. He worked on the changes in the Foreign Intelligence Surveillance Act, which is a law enforcement tool in catching terrorists, and he backed the release of telecommunications companies from legal liability for complying with government requests for warrantless surveillance of U.S. citizens' communications. Many Democrats did not want to let those companies off the hook.

On domestic issues, Hoyer came out in favor of same-sex marriage in 2012, shortly before his daughter, Stefany Hoyer Hemmer, announced publicly that she is a lesbian. He actively pushed a "Make It in America" package of Democratic bills to boost U.S. manufacturers, with several becoming law. In early 2009, working with Pelosi, Hoyer steered to passage the $787 billion economic stimulus legislation, the first major initiative of the Obama administration. Only 11 House Democrats voted against it, and all of the Republicans opposed it. He had a hand in the Democrats' successful efforts to increase the hourly minimum wage and in the adoption of most of the 9/11 commission's homeland security and intelligence-reform recommendations.

More inclined to defer to committee chairs and hew to regular order than Pelosi, he supported doing away with term limits for committee leaders, which the Republicans imposed when they were in the majority. At his urging, Pelosi agreed to their repeal in late 2008. "I am not for term limits for chairmen," Hoyer said. "It puts intellect on hold." (Term limits work to the advantage of the leadership because they make committee chairs less autonomous.)

Hoyer has fine political instincts, works hard and can speak in an old-fashioned, patriotic style that can be genuinely moving. With Democrats in the minority, he spends much of his time dueling on the House floor. He drew criticism from some conservatives for his rhetoric on the GOP's hardline stance on "fiscal cliff" budget negotiations shortly after the December 2012 school massacre in Newtown, Connecticut. "It's somewhat like taking your child hostage and saying to somebody else, 'I'm going to shoot my child if you don't do what I want done,'" Hoyer said of Republicans. Behind the scenes, though, Hoyer tried to work out a deal, just as he had done on earlier bills. When John Boehner stepped down as Speaker in 2015, Hoyer called it "a bad day for the House" and praised him as a "positive legislator."

Over the years, Hoyer has remained unable to edge out Pelosi in the leadership. As Democrats' prospects to regain majority control have dimmed, speculation occasionally has swirled that Pelosi would give up her party post and Hoyer would become her successor. He told *The Washington Post* that he wasn't fixated on his future. "I'm very comfortable with what I do, very comfortable with the role I play. ... I'm not very anxious about the next step. It'll take care of itself." Pelosi has continued to stay on. She and Hoyer have put aside their differences to form a good working relationship, though some Democrats believe that one reason Pelosi has not walked away is that she does not want Hoyer to take the top spot. Their lengthy leadership reign has frustrated the ambitions of junior House Democrats.

Hoyer again got the better of Pelosi in November 2014 in the internal jockeying among House Democrats to succeed California's Henry Waxman as ranking member on the Energy and Commerce Committee. Pelosi lobbied on behalf of her close friend, fellow Californian Anna Eshoo, while Hoyer backed New Jersey's Frank Pallone. Hoyer mobilized members of the Congressional Black Caucus on Pallone's behalf; caucus members worried that Eshoo's ascension would disrupt the tradition of seniority. Hoyer's ability to count votes is "unmatched," a grateful Pallone said. "Hoyer, he's a shark who never sleeps. ... He's a shark with a killer disposition," Missouri Democrat Emanuel Cleaver, a senior Black Caucus member, told *Politico*.

A month later, Hoyer worked with the unlikely team of Senate Majority Leader Harry Reid of Nevada and House Speaker John Boehner to help President Barack Obama get a massive so-called "cromnibus" spending bill into law. Pelosi and other liberals objected to the measure, in large part because it loosened regulations on Wall Street banks. Hoyer helped to get 57 Democrats to vote for the measure, joining 162 Republicans. Occasionally, he parted company with Obama, including the "sequestration" of defense spending, which he called "totally unacceptable and irresponsible." In a January 2017 vote, he joined the House majority that denounced Obama's decision to abstain from a United Nations vote that condemned Israeli settlements in Jerusalem and the West Bank. Even though he has consistently opposed settlement expansion, Hoyer said the U.N. was not the appropriate forum to raise such concerns.

In his district, Hoyer has pushed for funding Chesapeake Bay cleanup. He has worked shrewdly to maintain and increase jobs at the Goddard Space Flight Center in Greenbelt, at Naval Air Station Patuxent River, and at the Naval Surface Warfare Center at Indian Head. In 2014, he successfully took the side of the air station against a wind energy farm on the other side of the bay that he said "would constitute an unacceptable risk to the security of the United States" and potentially a local loss of Pentagon jobs. In earlier years, he worked for a bill giving the District of Columbia a vote in the House. He sponsored bills allowing more federal employees to work four-day weeks, granting eight weeks of paid parental leave, and raising the government contribution to its employees' health care premiums. In January 2017, he opposed the House rules change that opened the door to cuts in federal salaries, which he said were designed to make "scapegoats" for poor government performance. He kept his hand in other Maryland political campaigns, and usually but not always prevailed.

The last time Hoyer had serious competition in a general election was 1992, the first election after the district was reconfigured to extend beyond Prince George's County. He has won easily since then, and he has gained the loyalty of African-American voters in Democratic primaries. Although he continues to campaign actively for other Democrats, he has publicly been more realistic than Pelosi about their prospects for regaining House control. It remains to be seen whether minority whip will be his final leadership post.

Southern Maryland: Prince George's County

Population		**Race and Ethnicity**		**Income**	
Total	747,788	White	47.7%	Median Income	$91,186 (17 out of 435)
Land area	1,481	Black	37.3%		
Pop/ sq mi	504.8	Latino	7.6%	Under $50,000	24.5%
Born in state	38.5%	Asian	3.9%	$50,000-$99,999	30.8%
		Two races	2.9%	$100,000-$199,999	35.0%
Age Groups		Other	0.5%	$200,000 or more	9.9%
Under 18	23.3%			Poverty Rate	7.4%
18-34	23.4%	**Education**			
35-64	41.8%	H.S grad or less	36.3%	**Health Insurance**	
Over 64	11.6%	Some college	30.0%	With health insurance coverage	92.4%
		College Degree, 4 yr	19.5%		
Work		Post grad	14.2%	**Public Assistance**	
White Collar	43.1%				
Sales and Service	40.3%	**Military**		Cash public assistance income	1.9%
Blue Collar	16.6%	Veteran	11.8%		
Government	30.2%	Active Duty	0.9%	Food stamp/SNAP benefits	8.1%

Voter Turnout			
2015 Total Citizens 18+	537,978	2016 House Turnout as % CVAP	67%
2016 House turnout	360,634	2014 House Turnout as % CVAP	42%

2012 Presidential Vote		
Barack Obama	234,859	(66%)
Mitt Romney	114,536	(32%)

2016 Presidential Vote		
Hillary Clinton	225,989	(63%)
Donald Trump	115,869	(32%)
Gary Johnson	9,375	(3%)

Cook Partisan Voting Index: D+16

Southern Maryland was established as a colony of the British Lords Baltimore, who were seeking a refuge for English Catholics in the New World. The Lords Baltimore, first George and then Cecil Calvert, founded St. Mary's in 1634, not long after the founding of Jamestown and Plymouth. Maryland became one of the two great Chesapeake tobacco colonies, with plantation houses on every inlet off the broad Potomac and Patuxent rivers. For years, the towns of southern Maryland grew slowly, and even today, many of their residents are directly descended from the old families. The region was never Puritan country. Liquor flowed even during Prohibition, and for years, Maryland law specifically allowed slot machines. But tobacco farming is nearing an end, even if the area hasn't completely renounced its tobacco heritage. The highlight of the annual Charles County Fair remains the crowning of Queen Nicotina, who must be a local high school senior.

The area's economic base has owed much to government installations: the Civil War Point Lookout prisoner-of-war camp; the Navy's Patuxent River complex, where many astronauts began their training; and the Naval Air Warfare Center. Metro Washington and Baltimore have been spreading into southern Maryland. The 2010 Census showed rapid growth in Calvert, Charles and St. Mary's counties, though that has slowed since the recession and with zoning changes in Calvert. Charles County has become the new home of many African-American families fleeing crime and troubled schools in Prince George's County. Today, most of Charles County's schoolchildren are black. Its median household income rose to $90,607 in 2015, thanks in part to many two-government-employee families. The economy in St. Mary's has been bolstered by the more than 22,000 employees at the Patuxent River facility.

The 5th Congressional District of Maryland comprises all of Calvert, Charles and St. Mary's counties, plus most of Prince George's County outside the Capital Beltway and a small part of southern Anne Arundel County. Prince George's, with about 40 percent of the population, and Charles, with 20 percent, are the largest and most Democratic counties in the district. The three smaller ones lean Republican. The district takes in College Park, home of the University of Maryland, and nearby Hyattsville, Greenbelt, Beltsville and Bowie. On the Chesapeake Bay, it stops just short of Annapolis. Whites in the rural areas have trended Republican, but African Americans - both new suburbanites and descendants of old southern Maryland families - make up 38 percent of the district's population. The district has been a Democratic stronghold for decades.

SIXTH DISTRICT

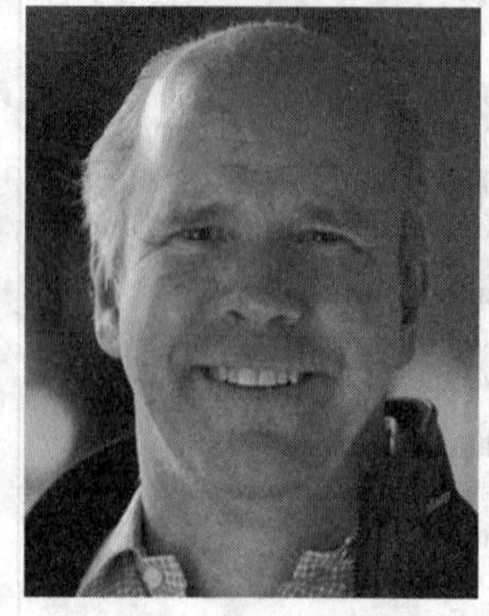

John Delaney (D)

Elected 2012, 3rd term; b. Apr 16, 1963, Wood Ridge, NJ; Columbia University (NY), B.S.; Georgetown University Law Center (DC), J.D.; Roman Catholic; Married (April McClain); 4 children.

Professional Career: Founder, CEO, Health Care Financial Partners, 1993-1999; Founder, Chairman, Capital Source, 2000-2012; Founder, Blueprint MD, 2011-present.

DC Office: 1632 LHOB 20515, 202-225-2721, Fax: 202-225-2193, delaney.house.gov.

State Offices: Gaithersburg, 301-926-0300; Hagerstown, 301-733-2900.

Committees: *Financial Services*: Housing & Insurance, Terrorism & Illicit Finance. *Joint Economic*.

Group Ratings

	ADA	ACLU	AFL-CIO	LCV	ITI	COC	HAFA	ACU	CFG	FRC
2016	-	52%	-	100%	100%	71%	15%	5%	18%	0%
2015	55%	C	88%	89%	C	58%	C	4%	3%	0%

Almanac Ratings 2015

	Economy	Social	Foreign	Composite
Liberal	59%	91%	63%	71%
Conservative	41%	9%	37%	29%

Key Votes of the 114th Congress

1. Keystone Pipeline	N	5. Puerto Rico Debt	Y	9. Offenses by Aliens	Y
2. Trade Deals	Y	6. Medical Marijuana	Y	10. Troops in Iraq	N
3. Export-Import Bank	Y	7. Sanctuary Cities	N	11. Homeland Security $$	Y
4. Debt Ceiling Increase	Y	8. Armor-piercing Bullets	N	12. Trade Adjustment aid	Y

Election Results

Election	Name (Party)	Vote (%)		Cand. Spent	Ind. Exp. Support	Ind. Exp. Oppose
2016 General	John Delaney (D)	185,770	(56%)	$1,847,200		$35,745
	Amie Hoeber (R)	133,081	(40%)	$1,168,964	$3,160,581	
	David Howser (L)	6,889	(2%)			
2016 Primary	John Delaney (D)	63,230	(85%)			
	Tony Puca (D)	10,786	(15%)			

Prior winning percentages: 2014 (50%), 2012 (59%)

Wealthy financier John Delaney was elected in 2012 when he ousted 10-term Republican Rep. Roscoe Bartlett, with a big boost from redistricting. Delaney styled himself as a consensus-builder seeking to restore the nation's competitiveness, and added that he was the only former CEO of a publicly traded company who is serving in the House. He voiced criticisms of Maryland Gov. Larry Hogan, which fueled speculation that Delaney might run against him in 2018.

A native of New Jersey, Delaney was raised by a homemaker mother and an electrician father, who was a member of the International Brotherhood of Electrical Workers. His father had never attended college, but other union members pooled their money for a scholarship fund for his son, allowing Delaney to pursue a degree in biology at Columbia University. He was planning to become a doctor, but eventually switched to business. He received his law degree from Georgetown University.

Delaney founded his first business, HealthCare Financial Partners, in 1993 and served as its chairman for seven years before starting CapitalSource, a Montgomery County-based investment company that lends money to small- and mid-sized businesses. In *Roll Call's* listing in 2015 of the wealthiest members of Congress, Delaney ranked third, with an estimated net worth of $92 million. The $20 million reduction from 2014 resulted from the completion of his sale of CapitalSource, *Roll Call* reported,

In the Democratic primary in the new 6th District, state Senate Majority Leader Rob Garagiola was considered the front-runner. Delaney benefited from some high-powered connections, in addition to his self-financing. A friend of former President Bill Clinton and former Secretary of State Hillary Clinton, he had donated and bundled contributions to her 2008 presidential campaign. Bill Clinton endorsed Delaney in the primary, a decisive moment in the campaign. Delaney, a Catholic and lifelong Democrat, campaigned as a social liberal, championing same-sex marriage and abortion rights, while comparing himself on fiscal issues to more centrist-leaning Democrats like Bill Clinton and Sen. Mark Warner of Virginia. Delaney won a resounding 52%-29% victory in the primary.

In the general election, Delaney had major advantages. Besides the redistricting changes that created a Democrat-leaning territory, the moderate Bartlett was idiosyncratic. A physiologist by training, he chastised conservative Republicans for not accepting the science of climate change. But he was in his mid-80s and he raised almost no money in the early months of the campaign, which led observers to conclude that he would retire. Bartlett picked up the pace a bit after the primary, but it didn't change the perception that Republicans were ceding the seat. Delaney raised $4.4 million (including $2.4 million from his own pocket) to Bartlett's $1.2 million. Delaney won 59%-38%. Bartlett took the three small western counties, but Delaney won Frederick 58%-38% and took Montgomery by an overwhelming 68%-29%.

In the House, Delaney got a seat on the Financial Services Committee. His biggest initiative has been a proposal to create a national infrastructure fund that would be financed by a one-time tax on private companies that bring home the cash they have been sheltering overseas. This so-called repatriation appeared to gain life after the 2016 election when advisers to Donald Trump spoke positively about a similar approach for financing the new president's plans to rebuild the nation's infrastructure.

Delaney has taken an interest in the financial woes of Metro, the transit system serving the Washington metropolitan area. With Republican Rep. Barbara Comstock of Virginia, he prepared legislation to rewrite the agency's charter to strengthen its authority and weaken the veto power of its separate jurisdictions. In addition to Congress, such changes likely would require the approval of the Democratic-controlled Legislature in Maryland, the Republican-controlled Legislature in Virginia and the D.C. City Council. Delaney has not been reluctant to criticize the leaders of either party, including those at the local level. He was harsh on Maryland Democratic officials for the state's bumbling implementation of the Affordable Care Act. In 2015, he said that he was "disappointed" by the decision of Maryland Republican Gov. Larry Hogan to kill the proposed new Red line rail in Baltimore and to reduce state funding for the proposed Purple line in the Washington suburbs.

Delaney denied that he was interested in running for the open seat for governor in 2014, and prepared for what seemed likely to be an easy reelection. Republicans nominated Dan Bongino, a former Secret Service agent with strong conservative roots that helped him to raise $1.5 million. It turned out to be an unexpectedly close contest, despite Delaney including $938,000 of his own money in the $2.6 million that he raised. Bongino ran ads that Delaney was not friendly to business. After two additional days to count the votes, Bongino conceded to Delaney for his 49.7%-48.2% win - a margin of 2,774 votes. As in his first election, Delaney had a big lead in Montgomery, though this time he got only 61 percent of the county vote. Still, this outcome made clear that the redistricting had been vital to the outcome.

After Democrat Barbara Mikulski announced her retirement, Delaney left open the possibility of running for her Senate seat in 2016. But that would have led to a contest with the popular Rep. Chris Van Hollen, who had earlier represented many of Delaney's constituents. Instead, Delaney was challenged for reelection by Amie Hoeber, who was a former top civilian official at the Pentagon, in charge of Army research and development. She criticized defense cutbacks by Democrats, and said that Delaney was not in touch with his constituents. Delaney filed a complaint with the Federal Election Commission about a Super PAC that spent about $3 million on behalf of her campaign and was controlled largely by Hoeber's husband, Mark Epstein. Both candidates ran a barrage of late ads. Hoeber raised $1.2 million for her campaign, while Delaney reported $2 million, of which $350,000 was self-funded. The outcome was close to the result of the presidential campaign in this district, with Delaney winning, 56%-40%. In a familiar pattern, Hoeber won the three western counties, but lost in Frederick and was swamped by more than 2-to-1 in Montgomery County. Hoeber, who would be 76, kept the door open to another run in 2018.

Following the election, Delaney was circumspect about whether he would challenge Hogan in 2018, though he met with Democratic activists and left no doubt of his interest. During the 2016 campaign, he financed a mobile billboard that featured a quote from Delaney asking Hogan, who kept his distance from the presidential election, "Will you support Trump as the Republican nominee?"

D.C. Exurbs, Western Maryland

Population		**Race and Ethnicity**		**Income**	
Total	750,122	White	60.7%	Median Income	$73,619 (57 out of 435)
Land area	1,950	Black	13.0%		
Pop/ sq mi	384.6	Latino	12.4%	Under $50,000	33.7%
Born in state	43.5%	Asian	10.6%	$50,000-$99,999	29.7%
		Two races	2.8%	$100,000-$199,999	26.1%
Age Groups		Other	0.5%	$200,000 or more	10.6%
Under 18	23.9%			Poverty Rate	9.3%
18-34	21.7%	**Education**			
35-64	41.4%	H.S grad or less	34.1%	**Health Insurance**	
Over 64	12.9%	Some college	25.1%	With health insurance coverage	90.9%
		College Degree, 4 yr	21.6%		
Work		Post grad	19.2%		
White Collar	46.6%			**Public Assistance**	
Sales and Service	38.2%	**Military**		Cash public assistance income	2.6%
Blue Collar	15.1%	Veteran	7.8%		
Government	20.1%	Active Duty	0.3%	Food stamp/SNAP benefits	10.6%

Voter Turnout			
2015 Total Citizens 18+	503,275	2016 House Turnout as % CVAP	66%
2016 House turnout	331,973	2014 House Turnout as % CVAP	38%

2012 Presidential Vote		
Barack Obama	176,364	(55%)
Mitt Romney	138,539	(43%)

2016 Presidential Vote		
Hillary Clinton	189,512	(55%)
Donald Trump	134,827	(39%)
Gary Johnson	10,691	(3%)

Cook Partisan Voting Index: D+6

One of America's first frontiers was western Maryland, where the Appalachian ridges that cross the state diagonally from northeast to southwest cut through long sloping fields. The land was settled by Pennsylvania Dutch and Scots-Irish hill people, not Chesapeake Bay tobacco growers. Maryland is where the 19th century's great paths to the interior were staked out: The National Road; the nation's first combined freight and passenger railroad, the Baltimore & Ohio, which crossed the wide valleys of bounteous farms and climbed over the Catoctin Mountains; and the Chesapeake and Ohio Canal, which began operating in 1828, primarily to haul coal from western Maryland to the port of Georgetown in Washington. Towns grew up with narrow streets of row houses that today are overhung with telephone wires. They planted themselves among cornfields, pastureland and ancient mountains.

Across this placid land moved vast armies during the Civil War. In Frederick, city officials paid the Confederates $200,000 not to burn the town, and near Sharpsburg, blue- and-gray-clad soldiers fought the Battle of Antietam on the bloodiest day in American military history. The battle is now commemorated with an annual illumination of 23,000 candles on the battlefield. A century later, without munitions, President Lyndon Johnson unveiled a different kind of War -- on Poverty -- on the steps of City Hall in Cumberland, near the coal-laced hills of Appalachia. Poverty fell here in the 1970s, but conditions worsened in the 1980s with the closure of several large factories. In October 2016, Gov. Larry Hogan showed some love for the area when he held the first-ever regional meeting of a governor and his cabinet in economically hard-hit Washington County (Hagerstown). He noted that his administration had delivered about $700 million to western Maryland in its first two years. Frederick and Washington counties have seen large increases in Hispanics since 2000. The quickly diversifying population has created tensions: Frederick County in 2010 became the first in Maryland to declare English its official language, as county officials struggled to deal with a rise in illegal immigration. But the growing political influence of the Hispanic migrants, plus farm operators who needed the workers, won a repeal of the language measure in 2015. In Montgomery County, by contrast, officials have said that they will not honor federal requests to detain immigrants.

The 6th Congressional District stretches nearly 200 miles from Republican-leaning western Maryland along the West Virginia border to the Washington, D.C., suburbs. Instead of crossing Republican pockets east to Harford County as in the past, redistricters in 2011 dropped the district south from Frederick into Montgomery County. There, it scoops up heavily Democratic Washington suburbs, including most of affluent Potomac, multicultural Gaithersburg, and fast-growing Germantown, whose population increased from about 9,700 in 1980 to 89,826 in 2015. When Bravo TV in 2016 aired the "Real Housewives of Potomac" reality show, the locals complained about its excessive focus on class and etiquette. Half of the district's population lives in suburban Washington. Montgomery County has added diversity: The district has the highest concentration of Asian Americans in the state (11 percent), and Hispanics make up 13 percent of its population. With the district transformed into a Democratic leaning bellwether, Hillary Clinton comfortably carried it 55%-39% in 2016.

SEVENTH DISTRICT

Elijah Cummings (D)

Elected 1996, 11th term; b. Jan 18, 1951, Baltimore; Howard University (DC), B.S.; University of Maryland School of Law, J.D.; Baptist; Married (Maya Rockeymoore); 1 child (1 from previous marriage).

Elected Office: MD House, 1983-1996, speaker pro tem, 1995-1996.

Professional Career: Practicing attorney, 1976-1996; Chief judge, MD Moot Court Board.

DC Office: 2163 RHOB 20515, 202-225-4741, Fax: 202-225-3178, cummings.house.gov.

State Offices: Baltimore, 410-685-9199; Catonsville, 410-719-8777; Ellicott City, 410-465-8259.

Committees: *Oversight & Government Reform (RMM)*: Government Operations, Health Care, Benefits & Administrative Rules, Information Technology, Intergovernmental Affairs, Interior, Energy & Environment, National Security. *Transportation & Infrastructure*: Coast Guard & Maritime Transportation, Railroads, Pipelines & Hazardous Materials.

Group Ratings

	ADA	ACLU	AFL-CIO	LCV	ITI	COC	HAFA	ACU	CFG	FRC
2016	-	88%	-	100%	67%	57%	14%	0%	4%	0%
2015	100%	C	100%	97%	C	40%	C	0%	0%	0%

Almanac Ratings 2015

	Economy	Social	Foreign	Composite
Liberal	100%	100%	99%	100%
Conservative	0%	0%	1%	0%

Key Votes of the 114th Congress

1. Keystone Pipeline	N	5. Puerto Rico Debt	Y	9. Offenses by Aliens	N
2. Trade Deals	N	6. Medical Marijuana	Y	10. Troops in Iraq	Y
3. Export-Import Bank	Y	7. Sanctuary Cities	N	11. Homeland Security $$	Y
4. Debt Ceiling Increase	Y	8. Armor-piercing Bullets	N	12. Trade Adjustment aid	Y

Election Results

Election	Name (Party)	Vote (%)		Cand. Spent	Ind. Exp. Support	Ind. Exp. Oppose
2016 General	Elijah Cummings (D)	238,838	(75%)	$583,452		
	Corrogan Vaughn (R)	69,556	(22%)			
	Myles Hoenig (G)	9,567	(3%)			
2016 Primary	Elijah Cummings (D)	122,299	(92%)			
	Adrian Petrus (D)	10,578	(8%)			

Prior winning percentages: 2014 (70%), 2012 (77%), 2010 (75%), 2008 (80%), 2006(98%), 2004 (73%), 2002 (74%), 2000 (87%), 1998 (86%), 1996 (84%)

Democrat Elijah Cummings, who came to Congress in a 1996 special election, is a liberal who can be blunt in defending his party. As the ranking Democrat on the Oversight and Government Reform Committee, he parried with Republicans on investigations of the Obama administration that Cummings regularly dismissed as "witch hunts." Despite the inevitable tensions resulting from their respective partisan imperatives, he had a relatively positive relationship with the chairman, Jason Chaffetz of Utah. The election of President Donald Trump brought new challenges.

Cummings is the son of sharecroppers from South Carolina who moved north for a better life for their seven children. He grew up in Baltimore, where as an 11-year-old he was one of the first children to integrate a park's swimming pool. "People were throwing bottles, rocks, and screaming, calling us everything but a child of God," he recalled to *Baltimore* magazine. He graduated Phi Beta Kappa from Howard University, and got a law degree from the University of Maryland. He practiced law in Baltimore, and then in 1982, at age 31, he ran successfully for the House of Delegates, where he served 14 years and rose through the ranks to become speaker pro tem.

He ran for the House after Kweisi Mfume resigned to become president of the NAACP. Cummings' main competition was the Rev. Frank Reid III, stepbrother of Baltimore Mayor Kurt Schmoke, who raised $255,000. Cummings had support from local businesses and community-development organizations, and raised $450,000. He won with 37 percent of the vote to 24 percent for Reid. He has not been seriously challenged in a primary or general election since.

Cummings lives in troubled west Baltimore, and he is a crusader against drug abuse, for stricter gun control, and for help for low-income homeowners. When Democrats won the majority in 2006, he became chairman of the Coast Guard and Maritime Transportation Subcommittee at Transportation and Infrastructure, a useful niche for his port-dependent district. The House unanimously passed his bill in 2009 to reform Coast Guard acquisition practices, and a year later he helped get an authorization bill for the agency into law that included some acquisition reforms as well as other changes.

Cummings got the Oversight ranking member slot in 2010 after the Republicans gained control of the House. He took over the job after defeating New York's Carolyn Maloney by a 119-61 vote. Working alongside the energetic and partisan chairman, Californian Darrell Issa, became a challenge for him. Cummings has forcefully pushed back against the GOP on subpoena powers, Democrats' access to records and numerous other matters. But he has won respect from Republicans. "It's not about politics to him; he says what he believes," South Carolina Rep. Trey Gowdy told *The Hill* newspaper. "And you can tell the ones who are saying it because it was in the memo they got that morning and you can tell the ones who it's coming from their soul. And with Mr. Cummings, it's coming from his soul."

Cummings was close to President Barack Obama, having bucked most of the Maryland Democratic establishment in 2007 by announcing his early support for the then-Illinois senator. But he did not spare Obama in his committee work. He took part in several bipartisan investigations in which he rebuked the administration for management deficiencies that led to Secret Service scandals and a lavish General Services Administration conference in Las Vegas. He publicly battled with Edward DeMarco, overseer of government-backed mortgage giants Fannie Mae and Freddie Mac, over debt reduction for homeowners struggling to pay mortgages.

He is a staunch defender of labor unions, which have been his top source of campaign funds throughout his career. In the 2010 campaign, when some Democrats were de-emphasizing their support of Obama's health care overhaul, Cummings was doing just the opposite. "I know the media wants us to apologize for being Democrats," he said at one rally. "They want us to apologize for health care. Why? Because the Democratic Party is the humane party."

One of the biggest flare-ups on the committee came when GOP lawmakers voted in 2012 to hold Attorney General Eric Holder in contempt of Congress for refusing to provide information relating to "Operation Fast and Furious," a botched effort to trace guns to drug cartels and smugglers that instead allowed firearms to cross the border into their hands. Cummings was among Holder's chief defenders, saying the attorney general "acted honorably." When a draft of the contempt citation was leaked to the news media, Cummings sent Issa an angry letter saying the move "suggests that you are more interested in perpetuating your partisan political feud in the press than in obtaining any specific substantive information."

When Republicans subsequently went after the Internal Revenue Service for allegedly targeting conservative groups and Cummings began to speak at a hearing, Issa abruptly adjourned the session, ordering staffers to cut off the Democrat's microphone. The Congressional Black Caucus rose to Cummings' defense to demand that Issa be stripped of his chairmanship and publicly apologize. Issa did apologize to Cummings, who later compared Issa's tactics to those used in the 1950s by Communist-hunting Sen. Joseph McCarthy.

When Chaffetz took over as committee chairman in January 2015, he promised that he would work more cooperatively with Democrats than did his predecessor. Chaffetz earlier spent a day with Cummings in his Baltimore district to get to know him better. "Chaffetz is a good guy," he told local residents. But at the panel's first meeting, Chaffetz pushed through a rules package that Cummings complained was "worse than the rules we had under Chairman Issa." Cummings and other Democrats tried and failed to roll back the chairman's ability to subpoena witnesses or documents without obtaining the prior consent of the ranking member, or putting the subpoena request to a vote of the full committee.

In a sign of the high regard in which he is held by Democrats, including party leaders, Cummings also served as senior Democrat on the House select committee that focused chiefly on former Secretary of State Hillary Clinton as it investigated the administration's handling of the murders of U.S. officials at the diplomatic compound in Benghazi, Libya.

For all of his partisan rhetoric, Cummings has a pragmatic streak that occasionally allows him to work with Republicans in legislative coalitions. He helped secure enactment in 2014 of the DATA Act, which requires federal agencies to publish spending information online in a searchable format. In 2016, he was the chief sponsor of a bill to grant whistleblower protections for federal contractors, which was enacted as part of a broader bill. Cummings earlier worked on a bipartisan bill that reauthorized the White House drug control office and established federal policy to combat rapidly multiplying methamphetamine labs.

The April 2015 death of Freddie Gray and subsequent riots in his home town raised Cummings' profile and increased pressure on him to help resolve conflicts, both immediate and more deep-seated. He joined marches and engaged with protesters, many of whom were his neighbors. "I am telling you we will not rest until we address this and see that justice is done," he said during an emotional speech at Gray's funeral.

Cummings usually wins reelection by landslide margins. He backed Mfume in the Democratic primary for the open Senate seat in 2006, then helped to coalesce Democrats behind the successful nominee, Ben Cardin. A decade later, he was viewed as having considerable influence in the Democratic primary to succeed the retiring Sen. Barbara Mikulski, either as a potential candidate or as a king-maker. Instead, he remained neutral, which many viewed as a boost for Rep. Chris Van Hollen, who ultimately defeated African-American Rep. Donna Edwards. He also turned down the opportunity to run for mayor of Baltimore.

In 2016, Cummings chaired the drafting committee for the Democratic platform, where he had the dicey responsibility of mediating between Hillary Clinton, whom he had supported during the campaign, and Sen. Bernie Sanders. "My approach is not to take us to common ground - it's not good enough this time," Cummings told *The Baltimore Sun*. "I want to take us to higher ground." His work on the platform also gave him the opportunity to continue his role that the *Sun* described as "a kind of defense attorney for the Obama administration." The final platform was largely embraced by most Democrats, though the party faced other problems in the election. That was not the only experience for Cummings in national party politics. In 2015, he teamed with Massachusetts Sen. Elizabeth Warren on a "Middle Class Prosperity Project," a series of public events aimed at trying to bolster the image of their party and Obama with the middle class.

Cummings found numerous opportunities to challenge Trump, especially following his election. After the director of the Office of Government Ethics in January 2017 raised questions about the president-elect's compliance with federal ethics requirements, he attacked Republicans for calling the director to account while failing to investigate any of Trump's "massive global entanglements." Chaffetz and the Trump campaign were "engaged in a blatant, coordinated attack on our nation's top ethics official simply because he is trying to protect against conflicts of interest and constitutional violations by the incoming president," Cummings complained. With Cardin, he urged the creation of an independent commission to review charges of Russian hacking of computer systems during the election. In June 2017, Gowdy replaced Chaffetz as Oversight chairman.

Some Democrats viewed the combative Cummings as a potential contender for a House leadership slot whenever the party's aging leaders step down. But he is not likely to launch such a campaign so long as the minority leader remains a native of Baltimore and the minority whip is from southern Maryland.

Baltimore Metro: Western and Northern Baltimore

Population		**Race and Ethnicity**		**Income**	
Total	725,370	White	33.7%	Median Income	$56,350 (169 out of 435)
Land area	488	Black	53.7%		
Pop/ sq mi	1486.3	Latino	3.6%		
Born in state	62.7%	Asian	6.3%	Under $50,000	45.2%
		Two races	2.1%	$50,000-$99,999	27.3%
Age Groups		Other	0.5%	$100,000-$199,999	19.7%
Under 18	22.0%			$200,000 or more	7.9%
18-34	25.0%	**Education**		Poverty Rate	17.4%
35-64	39.4%	H.S grad or less	38.6%		
Over 64	13.7%	Some college	24.9%	**Health Insurance**	
		College Degree, 4 yr	19.6%	With health insurance coverage	91.6%
Work		Post grad	17.0%		
White Collar	45.7%				
Sales and Service	40.9%	**Military**		**Public Assistance**	
Blue Collar	13.4%	Veteran	7.5%	Cash public assistance income	4.4%
Government	21.8%	Active Duty	0.1%		
				Food stamp/SNAP benefits	19.4%

Voter Turnout			
2015 Total Citizens 18+	533,920	2016 House Turnout as % CVAP	60%
2016 House turnout	318,912	2014 House Turnout as % CVAP	39%

2012 Presidential Vote		
Barack Obama	257,222	(76%)
Mitt Romney	76,446	(23%)

2016 Presidential Vote		
Hillary Clinton	233,796	(74%)
Donald Trump	63,444	(20%)
Gary Johnson	7,795	(3%)

Cook Partisan Voting Index: D+26

At the junction of North and South, Baltimore is a product of both European immigration and the migration of African Americans from the South. Its black community has a rich history. The *Afro-American* newspaper has been published there for more than 100 years, and there was once a black symphony orchestra. Eubie Blake, one of the founders of ragtime music, grew up in Baltimore and now has a museum in his honor on Charles Street. Jazz great Billie Holiday; Cab Calloway, the 1930s and 1940s big band leader; and Thurgood Marshall, the country's first African-American Supreme Court justice, all had roots in Baltimore. Near downtown on the west side is the childhood home of slugger Babe Ruth and the home of writer H.L. Mencken. For years, this side of town had a biracial, bipartisan politics in which Democrats like Gov. Albert Ritchie and Republicans like Gov. Theodore McKeldin competed zestfully for black and white votes. Baltimore overall has been a black majority city since the late 1970s.

In the 1990s, the city was hit by a crime wave, with open drug markets on both the west and east sides. The city's gritty side was vividly depicted in HBO's acclaimed crime drama *The Wire*. In recent years, crime had declined but remained at intolerable levels. The city reported the fifth-highest murder rate among large cities in 2014, and more than 60 percent of the state's prisoners were from Baltimore. In a July 2016 report, the *Baltimore City Paper* found that 85 percent of the more than 2,500 murder victims in Baltimore during the previous decade were African-American males, and 87 percent of them were killed by people using firearms. The city has lost 4 percent of its population since 2000, and is down more than a third from its peak in 1950.

Community anger exploded in April 2015 following the death of Freddie Gray, a young black man who had suffered serious injuries in a police wagon after he had been arrested. The initial response was a series of marches and peaceful protests throughout the west side of the city, especially the Sandtown-Winchester neighborhood. The response turned violent as demonstrators smashed storefront windows, and threw rocks at police and damaged their cruisers as officers made dozens of arrests. The looting intensified after Gray's funeral. Mayor Stephanie Rawlings-Blake cited the difficult "balancing act" that she faced and was slow to increase security before she imposed a curfew on the city for several nights. Gov. Larry Hogan declared a state of emergency and sent in 3,000 National Guard troops following a request from the mayor. Their presence generally restored order. Subsequently, six Baltimore police officers were indicted for their role in the death of Gray. In trials that gripped the attention of the city, the first trial resulted in a hung jury and the next three trials produced acquittals of three police officers. In July 2016, state prosecutor Marilyn Mosby dropped the remaining charges and attributed the outcomes to several factors, including the handling of the police investigation of the event a year earlier. "For those that believe I'm anti-police, it's simply not the case. I'm anti-police brutality," she said.

Questions remained about social conditions, police dealings with the neighborhoods, and the bleak nexus of poverty, race and class that continued to roil many urban centers across the nation. In the local aftermath, Hogan and Rawlings-Blake in January 2016 unveiled a plan to demolish about 4,000 abandoned properties and make available $600 million, mostly state-financed, to encourage redevelopment in the Sandtown-Winchester area. How far such funding could go to fix deep-seated problems in a city with a rich history would take years to determine. In August 2016, *Washington Post* columnist Courtland Milloy visited the area and wrote about alternatives to mass arrests and imprisonment, amid signs "of a neighborhood being transformed, a sense of community beginning to be reborn despite the social and economic problems that linger."

Maryland's 7th Congressional District includes most of Baltimore's west side, plus the heavily African-American suburbs west of the city and extending to Catonsville along the old Baltimore National Pike. It includes much of suburban Howard County. About 40 percent of the district's votes are cast in Baltimore city's precincts, largely north of Pratt Street and including Charles Village, which is home to Johns Hopkins University. Baltimore County and Howard County each cast about 30 percent. Howard County is quite a different area. It grew 32 percent in the 1990s, and another 26 percent since then. Its largest community, Columbia, is a planned town that attracts a culturally liberal population that tends to vote Democratic. In July 2016, Ellicott City was devastated by a "1,000-year flood" that ravaged much of its historic downtown. There is a sharp socioeconomic contrast between these two parts of the district. Howard County is predominantly white and affluent, with the fifth-highest median household income of all counties in the nation. In Baltimore city, only 7 percent of households earn more than $100,000, and almost one-quarter of residents have incomes below the national poverty level.

EIGHTH DISTRICT

Jamie Raskin (D)

Elected 2016, 1st term; b. Dec 13, 1962, Washington, D.C., DC; Harvard College (MA), B.A., 1983; Harvard University Law School (MA), J.D., 1987; Married (Sarah Raskin); 3 children.

Elected Office: MD Senate, 2007-2016, Majority Whip, 2012-2016; MA Assistant Attorney General, 1987-1989.

Professional Career: Law Professor, American University, 1990-2017.

DC Office: 431 CHOB 20515, 202-225-5341, raskin.house.gov.

State Offices: Rockville, 301-354-1000.

Committees: *House Administration*. *Judiciary*: Constitution & Civil Justice, Crime, Terrorism, Homeland Security & Investigations. *Oversight & Government Reform*: Information Technology, Interior, Energy & Environment.

Election Results

Election	Name (Party)	Vote (%)		Cand. Spent	Ind. Exp. Support	Ind. Exp. Oppose
2016 General	Jamie Raskin (D)	220,657	(61%)	$2,057,101	$44,291	
	Dan Cox (R)	124,651	(34%)	$58,212		
	Nancy Wallace (G)	10,930	(3%)	$9,592		
2016 Primary	Jamie Raskin (D)	38,902	(34%)			
	David Trone (D)	31,529	(27%)			
	Kathleen Matthews (D)	27,401	(24%)			
	Ana Sol Gutierrez (D)	6,358	(6%)			

Democrat Jamie Raskin was elected in 2016. In a district that is several miles from the Capitol, he has been familiar with Congress as a law professor and one-time House staffer, and as a veteran Maryland state legislator. His quick start after the election signaled that he will be a freshman worth watching.

A native of Washington, D.C., Raskin got his bachelor's and law degrees from Harvard University, where he was editor of the law review. During college, he was an intern for the House Judiciary Committee. He joined American University's Washington College of Law as a faculty member, specializing in constitutional law. He has written widely about legal topics, including *Overruling Democracy: The Supreme Court versus the American People* and *We the Students: Supreme Court Cases For and About America's Students*. From 2001 to 2005, he chaired the Maryland Higher Education Labor Relations Board. In 2006, he ran for the state Senate and defeated the 32-year incumbent in the Democratic primary. He served as majority whip and spent much of his time building legislative coalitions, which passed proposals such as mandatory minimums for drug sentencing, strict gun control with background checks, and environmental standards for state agencies and institutions to follow in their purchasing and other operations. His wife, Sarah Bloom Raskin, was deputy secretary of the Treasury during the Obama administration.

After Democratic Rep. Chris Van Hollen decided to run for the Senate, Raskin was the early frontrunner for the seat and the one with the deepest policy background. But the Democratic primary became unexpectedly competitive and very expensive. Raskin ran as the progressive candidate with a grass-roots network among the many liberal activists in the Washington suburbs who have an array of interests.

His two chief opponents were both political neophytes in the district, though each had a well-known profile. Kathleen Matthews spent many years as a broadcast-news reporter and anchor, and before that with the Marriott company as a public-relations executive. David Trone launched the Total Wine and More retail stores as a family business, which made him very wealthy. Both Matthews and Trone had a more centrist and business-oriented approach than did Raskin. Matthews also reached out to women, and had the backing of EMILY'S List, which support Democratic women who favor abortion rights.

Trone's self-financing became a major factor in the campaign, as he spent more than $12 million of his own money to introduce himself to voters and to craft his outsider appeal. Matthews used her close connections to the Democratic establishment - abetted by her husband Chris Matthews, the veteran broadcast pundit and writer - to become a prolific fundraiser. Trone raised a record sum for a congressional primary: $13.4 million, all but $7,000 of which came from his own pocket. Matthews raised $2.7 million, including $600,000 in self-financing. Raskin raised $2.5 million for his campaign, with $2,700 of his own money. He mocked the outsider appeal of his two chief opponents, who he said were classic insiders.

Raskin won the April primary, with 34 percent of the vote to 27 percent for Trone and 24 percent for Matthews. In the nine-candidate field, the others all got less than 6 percent of the vote. Trone got a majority of the vote in both Frederick and Carroll counties. But that had little impact in a contest in which Montgomery County Democrats cast more than 80 percent of the total vote. The general election gained scant attention, with little-known Republican Dan Cox raising $73,000, and losing 60%-34%.

In the House, Raskin was tapped as the Democrats' vice-ranking member of the Judiciary Committee, where ranking member Rep. John Conyers of Michigan had been Raskin's boss in the 1980s. He also became a senior whip for House Democrats and vice-chair of the Congressional Progressive Caucus, among other positions. He set infrastructure maintenance and expansion as a top priority, including in his district. And he would serve in the House as "the champion of the Constitution and the Bill of Rights and the separation of powers in Congress," he told *Bethesda* magazine. Even before President Donald Trump took office, Raskin told an interviewer that Trump's personal finances - specifically, a gift or payment from a foreign government - could become an impeachable offense.

Northern D.C. Suburbs: Montgomery County, Frederick

Population		**Race and Ethnicity**		**Income**	
Total	751,676	White	61.8%	Median Income	$96,269 (10 out of 435)
Land area	860	Black	11.5%		
Pop/ sq mi	874.2	Latino	14.6%	Under $50,000	24.3%
Born in state	32.6%	Asian	9.1%	$50,000-$99,999	27.2%
		Two races	2.5%	$100,000-$199,999	32.1%
Age Groups		Other	0.5%	$200,000 or more	16.3%
Under 18	22.5%			Poverty Rate	6.7%
18-34	21.0%	**Education**			
35-64	41.9%	H.S grad or less	26.5%	**Health Insurance**	
Over 64	14.6%	Some college	20.2%	With health insurance coverage	91.2%
		College Degree, 4 yr	24.4%		
Work		Post grad	28.9%		
White Collar	54.0%			**Public Assistance**	
Sales and Service	34.0%	**Military**		Cash public assistance income	1.5%
Blue Collar	12.0%	Veteran	7.1%		
Government	21.7%	Active Duty	0.4%	Food stamp/SNAP benefits	5.3%

Voter Turnout			
2015 Total Citizens 18+	500,602	2016 House Turnout as % CVAP	73%
2016 House turnout	364,324	2014 House Turnout as % CVAP	44%

2012 Presidential Vote		
Barack Obama	222,125	(62%)
Mitt Romney	127,542	(36%)

2016 Presidential Vote		
Hillary Clinton	235,137	(63%)
Donald Trump	112,612	(30%)
Gary Johnson	11,143	(3%)

Cook Partisan Voting Index: D+14

Colonial farmers once rolled barrels of tobacco to the port of Georgetown in Maryland, along an old road that is today the commercial spine of one of America's most affluent and best-educated areas. Wisconsin Avenue begins at the Potomac River in Washington, D.C., traverses the city, and then becomes Rockville Pike after it passes over the Capital Beltway in Montgomery County. The foundation of the economy here is the federal government, with its huge facilities and ongoing construction projects - Walter Reed National Military Medical Center (which merged with Bethesda Naval Hospital), the National Institutes of Health and the Food and Drug Administration. Montgomery is a center of America's biotech industry, the home of firms such as Human Genome Sciences which, with the Human Genome Project, pioneered the study of the human genetic code. Defense contractor Lockheed Martin, with 4,700 employees, is the only manufacturing company among the county's top 10 employers. Marriott International, which plans to move its corporate headquarters a few miles south to downtown Bethesda, employs 5,500.

From the 1960s through the 1980s, Montgomery County ranked at or near the top among counties nationwide in income and education. Downtown Bethesda became a glitzy and popular entertainment and dining destination with expanding high-rise apartment buildings. Its increased urban development and taller office building have diminished the suburban or small-town ambiance, to the dismay of many residents. The county changed gradually as it became a magnet for legal immigrants attracted by the region's strong and stable economy. Today, Montgomery has a diverse population and has been overtaken in affluence regionally by other suburban counties in the metropolitan area. Along with its very upscale neighborhoods, Montgomery now has large Latino communities in areas from Wheaton northwest to Rockville. The county's population in 2015 was 19 percent African American, 19 percent Hispanic, and 15 percent Asian.

Still, the county has the nation's second-highest percentage of adults with graduate school degrees, and it is thoroughly liberal on cultural issues and loyal to the Democratic Party. Montgomery County provided the margin of victory for the 2012 referendum legalizing same-sex marriage in Maryland; it narrowly passed with 52 percent of the statewide vote, but garnered an overwhelming 66 percent in the state's largest county. In 2014, the county passed legislation creating partial public financing of local elections. Perhaps its most unique precinct is Leisure World in Silver Spring, with its 8,500-plus senior citizens and an extraordinarily high voter-turnout rate, mostly Democrats.

The 8th Congressional District of Maryland includes much of the heavily populated parts of Montgomery County (Bethesda, Rockville and Silver Spring). Two-thirds of the voters reside in Montgomery, with the remainder split nearly evenly between Frederick and Carroll counties. To assist Democrats in the 6th District, which now includes 40 percent of Montgomery, it now extends beyond the Washington suburbs to include rural Republican precincts from Frederick and Carroll counties. The presidential retreat of Camp David, where Jimmy Carter brokered the Israeli-Egyptian peace accords, is within the district, outside the small town of Thurmont, though Presidents Barack Obama and Donald Trump each had less interest in the quiet, rural facility than their recent predecessors. The district is reliably Democratic but it's not as overwhelmingly liberal as it was during the previous decade. Hillary Clinton in 2016 won the district, 63%-30%, a slight uptick from the vote for President Barack Obama in his two elections.

★ MASSACHUSETTS ★

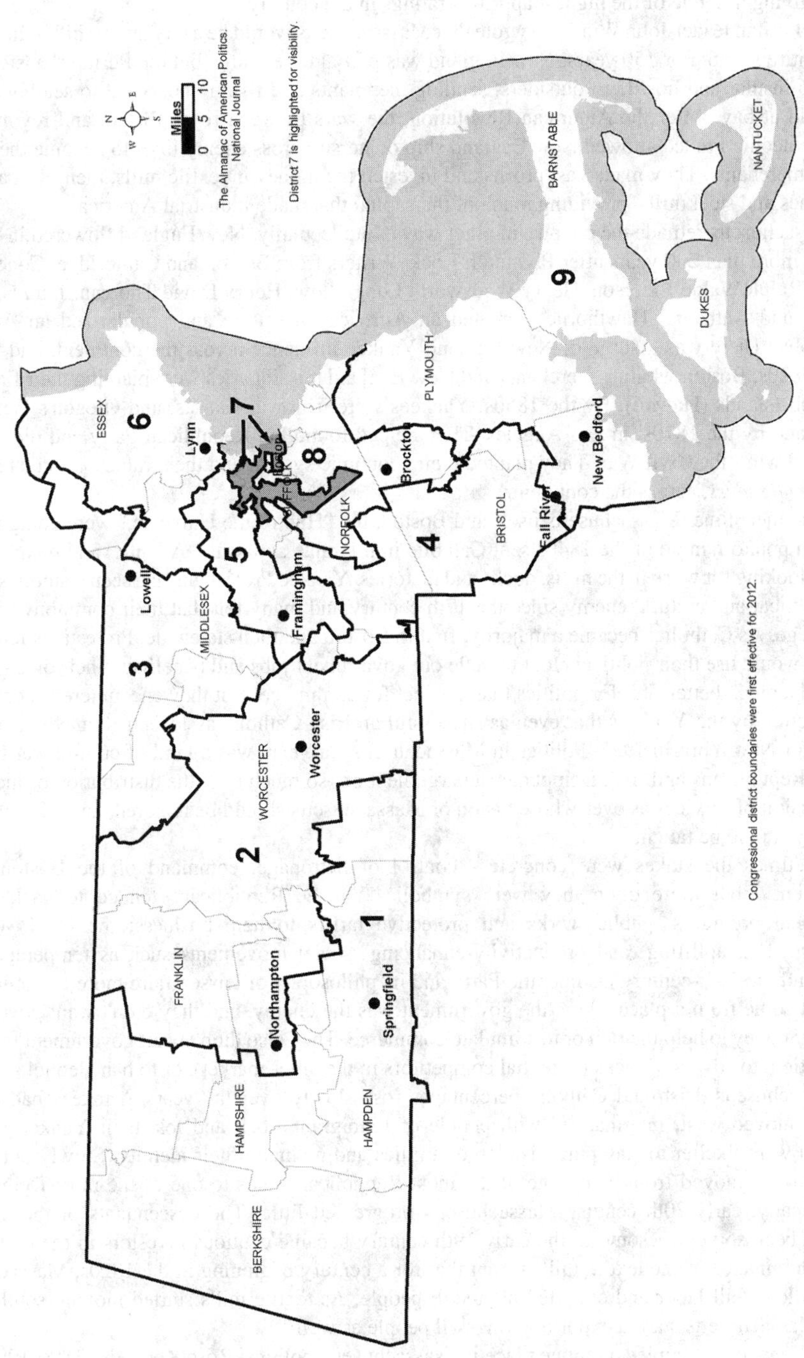

Massachusetts, an affluent, highly educated state at the top of its economic game, is one of the nation's bluest states, but it defies pigeonholing. The Bay State voted for Hillary Clinton by a 27-point margin – yet many of the same voters remained perfectly happy with their Republican governor, Charlie Baker, giving him one of the highest approval ratings in the country.

The Puritan leader John Winthrop wrote that Massachusetts would be a city upon a hill -- an example to the entire world. For 150 years, New England was partial to learning, but the Puritans' austere creed was also insular and hostile to outsiders, sending merchants and fishing boats out to sea but keeping the world at bay. After the American Revolution, the wars between royal Britain and revolutionary and Napoleonic France allowed New England ship owners to cross enemy lines to become the world's leading merchants. They made vast profits and invested the money in textile mills, then railroads, then coal mines and steel mills, providing much of the capital that made industrial America.

Massachusetts remade the country in other ways. Intellectually, New England flowered in the 19th century, more than 200 years after Plymouth Rock. Writers from Boston and Cambridge, Concord and Salem - Ralph Waldo Emerson, Henry Wadsworth Longfellow, Henry David Thoreau, John Greenleaf Whittier and Nathaniel Hawthorne - created an American literature and popularized an American philosophy. There was a surge of New England Yankee influence across the continent, and beyond. By the 1820s, Boston whaling merchants and New England missionaries were planting their flag in the Sandwich Islands (Hawaii). By the 1850s, Yankees were in Iowa, Kansas, and Oregon's Willamette Valley, and by the 1870s, in Los Angeles. They helped found the Republican Party and did much to start - and win - the Civil War. They planted their economic system and their values, articulated in the *McGuffey Readers*, across the continent.

In the meantime, Massachusetts itself and Boston, the "Hub of the Universe," were being remade. The Irish potato famine of the 1840s sent Catholic immigrants across the Atlantic, and many came to Boston, looking for work in the mills, docks and factories. Yankee Protestants had seen Catholics as their great political and cultural enemy since the 17th century and many felt that their commonwealth was under siege. As Catholics became a majority, first in Boston and then statewide, Protestants feared that the Irish would use their political clout to ladle out government jobs and benefits to their own - and the Irish had a much better flair for politics than instinct for commerce. But they encountered such bigotry and rejection by the Yankees that even as successful an Irish Catholic as Joseph Kennedy abandoned Boston for New York in 1927. Politics in Massachusetts for years was a kind of culture war between Yankee Republicans and Irish Democrats, an argument not so much over the distribution of income or the provision of services as over whose vision of Massachusetts should be honored, and whose version of history should be taught.

Sometimes the stakes were concrete - control of patronage, command of the Boston Police Department - but more often they were symbolic. Yankee Republicans tended to back activist government programs: public works and protective tariffs to help business; the Civil War and Reconstruction; uplifting (and productivity-enhancing) social movements such as temperance. The Irish found the 19th-century Democratic Party and its philosophy of laissez-faire more congenial. The Irish had come from a place where the government was the enemy, and they didn't want government spending money to help the rich or to stimulate commerce. They also didn't want government to restrict immigration, to advance blacks (potential competitors in the labor market), or to ban alcohol.

Massachusetts' Irish and Catholic percentages rose slowly over the years. Yankees had smaller families, moved west, intermarried with people of immigrant stock and lost their Yankee identity. The Irish were likelier to stay put, raise large families and maintain their identity. Slowly but surely, Massachusetts moved from being one of the most Republican states to one of the most Democratic. Economically, early-20th century Massachusetts progressed little. The descendants of the Yankees who had been so venturesome in the early 19th century became cautious investors in the early 20th. The predominance of the textile mills meant that for a century beginning in the 1820s, Massachusetts imported low-skill labor and exported high-skill people. As textile mills started moving south in the 1920s, Massachusetts started exporting low-skill people as well.

The Kennedys occupied a unique place in Massachusetts politics. Rose Kennedy (1890-1995) was the daughter of John "Honey Fitz" Fitzgerald, who was elected to Congress at age 32 and served as mayor of Boston in 1906-07 and 1910-14. Her husband, Joseph Kennedy, was chairman of the Securities and Exchange Commission in the 1930s and ambassador to the Court of St. James from 1937 to 1940.

Catholic and uncommonly rich, he was a shrewd and ruthless political operator. Their only residence in Massachusetts after 1927 was their summer home in Hyannis Port. In 1946, Joseph Kennedy moved his oldest surviving son, John, to Boston, and helped steer his election to the House that year, to the Senate in 1952, and to the presidency in 1960. With their elegant manners and charm, the Kennedys were like royalty to the Irish Catholics of Massachusetts. And Catholics across the country, 78 percent of whom voted for John Kennedy, greeted the Democrat's election in 1960 with great pride. Joseph and John Kennedy were, on many issues, conservative or skeptical. But JFK's administration was increasingly identified, even before its tragic end in Dallas, as liberal. His example and that of his brother, Edward Kennedy, who was elected to the Senate in 1962 at age 30, moved Massachusetts Catholics to the left. At the same time, the leftward direction of the state's elite campuses in the 1960s influenced Massachusetts Protestants. The universities also provided the basis for a surging high-tech economy.

In the 1970s and 1980s, Massachusetts had the most liberal governance and outlook on national politics of any state in the country. It was the only state to vote for George McGovern in 1972, although it voted twice for Ronald Reagan, the son of an Irish Catholic. During that span, its senators were Edward Kennedy, liberal Republican Edward Brooke, and Democrats Paul Tsongas and John Kerry. The state also elected liberal governors such as Republican Francis Sargent and Democrat Michael Dukakis. Then in the early1990s, Massachusetts had a momentary political revolution. The 1980s "Massachusetts Miracle" had turned into a curse; the state's tech, real estate and defense economy sagged, and the state government essentially went bankrupt. In 1990, when Dukakis retired as governor, voters embraced big tax cuts and elected patrician Republican William Weld in his place. In time, four different Republicans, fiscally conservative and socially moderate, would hold the governorship for 16 years. The last of the four, Mitt Romney, provided the biggest policy innovation -- the health care plan passed by the legislature in 2006 that required all residents to buy health insurance, levied taxes on employers who did not provide it, and subsidized policies for low-wage earners. Romney's plan became the model for the national health care legislation passed by Congress and signed by President Barack Obama in 2010. But as he prepared to run for the GOP presidential nomination in 2008 (the first of his two presidential bids) Romney turned rightward, alienating voters back home. Democrat Deval Patrick succeeded him, becoming the state's first African-American governor in 2006. But the old model succeeded once again for Republicans in 2014 as Baker -- the cabinet secretary for governors Weld and Paul Cellucci – won the governorship. Baker's pragmatic approach has been a hit with voters even as more liberal candidates – such as Sen. Elizabeth Warren – have won other offices.

Massachusetts' population has grown by 4 percent since 2010, including significant immigration, some from Ireland but also from Brazil; Massachusetts is perhaps the most multi-national part of the United States. The population is 7 percent black, 11 percent Hispanic and 7 percent Asian. The state unemployment rate has typically remained below the national average; it peaked at 8.8 percent in 2009 and by late 2016 it was a strikingly low 2.8 percent, second only to neighboring New Hampshire. The state's median income ranks eighth in the country, 20 percent higher than the U.S. average – and that surely had something to do with the state's No. 1 national rankings in bachelor's and advanced degrees. Calculations by *Governing* magazine rated the state's economy the best-performing in the nation in 2016, and the *Boston Globe* noted that if it were a country, Massachusetts would rank among the richest nations in the world. Manufacturing jobs have been replaced, and then some, by those in technology, health sciences, health care and financial services. CompTIA, a tech-industry association, found that Massachusetts has the highest per capita ranking for patenting, licensing and venture capital. Tech-related sectors are growing so quickly that by 2025, the state's colleges and universities may not be able to churn out enough qualified workers, according to the Massachusetts Department of Higher Education. Such highly prized personnel can opt to work in Silicon Valley, North Carolina's Research Triangle or the great nemesis to the south, New York City.

With its educated electorate, Democratic leanings and mostly moderate Republican governors, cultural liberalism gradually prevailed over conservative Catholic social views in the state. Weld was one of America's first politicians to endorse gay rights, and after the legislature declined to endorse same-sex marriage, the courts in 2004 declared that same-sex couples had the right to marry; within a decade, this policy was widely replicated elsewhere. In 2016, the legislature passed, and Baker signed into law a measure to expand existing protections for transgender people to include public bathrooms, locker rooms and showers. (A petition to repeal it may go to the voters in 2018.) And in November 2016, voters opted to legalize marijuana for recreational use, despite opposition from Baker, Boston Mayor Marty Walsh and Cardinal Sean O'Malley.

The state made its liberal leanings clear in the 2016 presidential election. Amid record statewide turnout, Clinton beat Donald Trump by 27 points, a margin four points wider than Obama's in 2012. Clinton won almost 73,000 votes more than Obama had, while Trump fell 97,000 votes short of Romney's total. Clinton won every county in the state by at least 7 points. Below the surface, Trump outperformed Romney in some places, mainly rural and blue-collar pockets of western Massachusetts; in all, Trump beat Romney's showing in seven counties, four of them by at least seven points. (More than 77,000 voters left the presidential line blank on their ballots, up from 16,000 four years earlier.) The state is expected to be a hotbed of resistance to Trump, led by Warren, the standard-bearer for progressive Democrats and a politician uniquely skilled at getting under the new president's skin.

Population		**Race and Ethnicity**		**Income**	
Total	6,705,586	White	74.3%	Median Income	$68,563 (6 out of 50)
Land area	7,800	Black	6.5%		
Pop/ sq mi	859.7	Latino	10.6%	Under $50,000	37.8%
Born in state	62.2%	Asian	5.9%	$50,000-$99,999	28.3%
		Two races	1.9%	$100,000-$199,999	25.0%
Age Groups		Other	0.7%	$200,000 or more	8.9%
Under 18	20.8%			Poverty Rate	11.6%
18-34	24.1%	**Education**			
35-64	40.6%	H.S grad or less	35.6%	**Health Insurance**	
Over 64	14.7%	Some college	23.9%	With health insurance coverage	96.4%
		College Degree, 4 yr	22.8%		
Work		Post grad	17.7%		
White Collar	44.2%			**Public Assistance**	
Sales and Service	40.1%	**Military**		Cash public assistance income	3.0%
Blue Collar	15.7%	Veteran	6.7%		
Government	12.4%	Active Duty	0.1%	Food stamp/SNAP benefits	12.5%

Voter Turnout			
2015 Total Citizens 18+	4,850,598	2016 Pres Turnout as % CVAP	69%
2016 Pres Votes	3,325,046	2012 Pres Turnout as % CVAP	68%

Legislature	
Senate:	34D, 6R
House:	126D, 34R

Presidential Politics

2016 Democratic Primary		
Hillary Clinton (D)	606,822	(50%)
Bernie Sanders (D)	589,803	(49%)
2016 Republican Primary		
Donald Trump (R)	312,425	(49%)
John Kasich (R)	114,434	(18%)
Marco Rubio (R)	113,170	(18%)
Ted Cruz (R)	60,592	(10%)

2016 Presidential Vote		
Hillary Clinton (D)	1,995,196	(60%)
Donald Trump (R)	1,090,893	(33%)
Gary Johnson (L)	138,018	(4%)
2012 Presidential Vote		
Barack Obama (D)	1,921,290	(61%)
Mitt Romney (R)	1,188,314	(38%)

Massachusetts has been a solidly Democratic state in the past eight presidential elections. True to form, Hillary Clinton defeated Donald Trump in the 2016 race, 60%-33%. What is striking about Massachusetts is how many serious presidential candidates it has produced over the past four decades: Edward Kennedy in 1980, Michael Dukakis in 1988, Paul Tsongas in 1992, John Kerry in 2004 and Mitt Romney in 2008 and 2012. Sen. Elizabeth Warren looms on the horizon as a potential Democratic contender in 2020. Only mega-states California and Texas have produced more serious candidates over that period. Some credit must be given to New Hampshire, which holds the nation's first primary, where most of the residents receive Boston television newscasts and Bay Staters have migrated in search of lower taxes and home prices. But even more credit must go to the hyper-political culture of Boston. Only Chicago seems as preoccupied with its political figures.

The Massachusetts primary in 2016 was held on March 1, the same day as voters in seven Southern states cast ballots. The Bay State's results gave important previews of how both parties' nominating contests were going to unfold. On the Democratic side, Clinton's narrow 50%-49% win over Vermont Sen. Bernie Sanders showed there were limits to the insurgent's appeal. In western Massachusetts, occasionally referred to as the Granola Belt for the fondness that aging hippies and organic farmers have shown the region, Sanders won about 56 percent of the vote. On the South Shore and the old mill towns and manufacturing centers around Route 495, Clinton and Sanders battled to a draw. But Clinton pulled out her victory in Boston and other Democratic strongholds like Newton, Brookline and Cambridge. According to the television network exit polls, she beat Sanders among voters with family incomes of $100,000 or more, 59%-39%. Sanders carried voters who earned less, 55%-45%. In addition to minority voters, Sanders failed to claim the affluent well-educated white liberals who were a key component of Barack Obama's 2008 primary constituency.

On the Republican side, Trump won a near landslide victory, capturing 49 percent of the vote, a higher percentage than he garnered in winning conservative states like Alabama and Arkansas on the same day. Of the 351 towns and cities in Massachusetts, Trump won all but about 20, demonstrating his strong appeal to northern blue-collar working class voters: he won almost two-thirds of the white, non-college voters who cast ballots in the GOP primary. Ohio Gov. John Kasich finished second with 18 percent, about 1,000 votes ahead of Texas Sen. Ted Cruz. Kasich's inability to rally moderate suburban Republicans and independents indicated that he lacked a base to pose a serious challenge to Trump.

Congressional Districts

115th Congress Lineup	9D	114th Congress Lineup	9D

For many years, Massachusetts had some of the most convoluted congressional district boundaries in the nation. It also had a habit of electing moderate Republicans from suburban enclaves. But that practice has disappeared, and the number of House seats fell from 14 in 1960 to nine following the 2010 census. That required the loss of a seat and gave the state legislature a chance to smooth the lines. Because all of the seats had been held by Democrats, it meant a Democratic loss. Any suspense about which district would disappear vanished when the 1st District's John Olver announced he would retire. That was the westernmost district, and its elimination meant that Springfield-based Richard Neal could absorb the heavily Democratic Berkshires and that Worcester-based Jim McGovern would have a district that did not extend all the way east to Fall River. The other districts did not present incumbents with vast swaths of new territory.

In 2012 and 2014, Republican Richard Tisei ran in the 6th District, narrowly losing to ethically scarred incumbent John Tierney and then falling far short against Seth Moulton, who defeated Tierney in the Democratic primary. That continued the state's streak of not having elected a Republican to the House since 1994. The GOP's best opportunity, though still a long shot, probably is the 9th District, which covers Cape Cod and the South Shore. Republicans have no leverage in the Legislature. But if Republican Gov. Charlie Baker is reelected in 2018, he could seek to enhance GOP opportunities in the 6th and 9th.

Governor

Charlie Baker (R)

Elected 2014, term expires 2019, 1st term; b. Nov. 13, 1956, Elmira, NY; Harvard U., B.A. 1979; Northwestern U., M.B.A. 1986; Protestant; Married (Lauren); 3 children.

Elected Office: MA Secretary of Health & Human Services, 1992-1994; Swampscott Board of Selectmen, 2004-2009.

Professional Career: Founder, Pioneer Institute for Public Policy Research, 1988-1991; State Health Undersecretary, 1991-1992; State Administrations & Finance Secretary, 1994-1998; CEO, Harvard Vanguard Medical Associates, 1998-1999; Entrepreneur, 2011-2014.

Office: Massachusetts State House, Room 280, Boston, 02133; 617-725-4005; Fax: 617-727-9725; Website: mass.gov.

Election Results

Election	Name (Party)	Vote (%)
2014 General	Charles D. Baker (R)	1,044,573 (48%)
	Martha Coakley (D)	1,004,408 (47%)
	Evan Falchuk (I)	71,814 (3%)
2014 Primary	Charles D. Baker (R)	116,004 (74%)
	Mark Fisher (R)	40,240 (26%)

Charlie Baker won the Massachusetts governorship in 2014 by tapping two inherent advantages: He's a moderate Republican in a blue state with a history of electing socially liberal, fiscally conservative Republicans to the post. And he was running against Democrat Martha Coakley, the state attorney general who lost in an upset to Scott Brown in the 2010 special election to succeed the late Sen. Edward Kennedy.

Baker was born in Elmira, New York, to a family steeped in politics and public service. His great-grandfather was a federal prosecutor and state assemblyman; his grandfather was a prominent Newburyport politician; his father Charles was a well-connected conservative Republican who had worked for Republican presidents Richard Nixon and Ronald Reagan. His mother was a liberal Democrat, leading to political arguments at the dinner table in Needham, where Baker mostly grew up and went to public schools. He earned a bachelor's degree in English from Harvard University and an MBA from the Kellogg Graduate School of Management at Northwestern University. He married the daughter of a *Fortune* 500 CEO, and delved in policy work as the first executive director of the Pioneer Institute, a conservative think tank in Boston, created in part by Baker's dad.

In 1992, at 36, Baker began his career in public service, when GOP Gov. William Weld appointed him secretary of Health and Human Services, heading up the largest department in state government. Baker, showing efficiency and diligence, was elevated in 1994 to be secretary of Administration and Finance, putting him in charge of the state's budget. Weld's successor, Paul Cellucci, kept Baker in that post, where, among other things, he was the original architect of the financial plan for the Big Dig, the Boston tunnel project plagued by delays and cost overruns. When Baker left government, he became CEO of Harvard Pilgrim Health Care, a nonprofit health benefits organization, from 1999 to 2009. In 2004, Baker was elected to the Board of Selectmen in his home town of Swampscott, an old fishing town on the North Shore of Boston, where the city skyline can be seen in the distance. Despite his high-profile pedigree in state government, Baker was described in a *Boston* magazine story as someone who preferred working in the background on the details of the town budget.

In his first run for governor, Baker took on Gov. Deval Patrick, who was seeking a second term in 2010. Baker came off to some as distant, and he expressed some views that put him at odds with the state's Democratic-leaning electorate. He promised no new taxes, and he was agnostic on climate change, a view that offended many environmentalists. Baker's task in the election was complicated by the presence of a third candidate, former state Treasurer Tim Cahill, who left the Democratic Party to run as an independent. This effectively split the base of the state's fiscally conservative and moderate voters that Baker needed to rally to have any hopes of winning. On Election Day, Patrick defeated Baker, 48%-42% while Cahill captured 8 percent.

When he mounted a second campaign for governor in 2014, Baker was a changed candidate, becoming a more genial - and female-voter-friendly - contender against Democratic nominee Martha Coakley. Baker cast himself as a fiscally responsible businessman, able to use his private-sector fiscal skills to heal what he called a poorly run Democratic administration. He emphasized his liberal take on social issues such as abortion and gay marriage. After stumbling with female voters in 2010, Baker picked a woman, Karyn Polito, as his running mate. The new Baker tweeted out messages on Twitter from Red Sox games and spoke easily about his openly gay brother. While Coakley accused Baker of being weak on gender issues (he downplayed the Supreme Court's *Hobby Lobby* decision on birth control, a statement he later clarified, and called a female reporter "sweetheart," for which he apologized), the strategy did not stick. *CommonWealth* magazine declared, "This is the new Charlie Baker. He's relaxed, he's likable, he's fun to drink beer with." Coakley swept deeply Democratic Suffolk County (Boston) and Berkshire, Hampshire and Franklin counties in Western Massachusetts, with its college towns and resort communities full of liberal artists and former hippies. She also carried Middlesex County, with its mix of wealthy Boston suburbs like Cambridge, Belmont and Newton, heavily ethnic, heavily blue collar towns like Malden and Watertown, and Boston's I-495 exurban ring. But she only did so by a narrow 50%-46% margin. Baker won the rest of the state, including Worcester County, with its classic New England small towns; Essex County, with its Merrimack Valley mill towns and North Shore affluent Boston exurbs; and Norfolk County, with its mix of upper-income Boston exurbs and coastal towns of the South Shore populated by upper-middle-class Irish Catholics.

Baker chose an eclectic cabinet -- traditional pro-business Republicans and some Democrats, even some who disagreed with positions he had taken during the campaign. As secretary of Transportation he appointed Stephanie Pollack, the associate director for research at Northeastern University and a onetime adviser to his Democratic predecessor, Patrick. He named Ronald Walker, a Democratic banker, as secretary of Labor and Workforce Development. And Baker tapped Democratic state Rep. Carlo Basile of East Boston to be his chief secretary and unofficial patronage dispenser. He chose Kristen Lepore, who worked with Baker in the Cellucci administration, as his budget chief and secretary of Administration and Finance, and Marylou Sudders, a respected children's advocate and the former commissioner of the state's Department of Mental Health, as secretary of Health and Human Services. True to his roots as a budgeter, in early 2015 Baker signed a plan offering early retirement to state employees in order to reduce the workforce by up to 5,000 jobs. The Massachusetts General Court gave bipartisan approval to the proposal, a down payment on Baker's efforts to close the state's budget deficit.

At times Baker took right-of-center stances, as when he joined with more conservative Republican governors in November 2015 to urge caution about resettling any more Syrian refugees; this drew criticism from several Democratic members of the congressional delegation. Baker also defied teachers' unions by pushing for a ballot measure to expand charter schools; in November 2016, voters rejected it by a wide margin. He opposed a 2016 ballot measure to legalize marijuana; voters disagreed and passed it. After it passed, Baker signed a bill to delay its enactment by six months. And initially at least, Baker was noncommittal about a bill to protect transgender rights, prompting a pro-LGBT audience to boo him off a stage. But three months later, in July 2016, he switched and signed the transgender law (though critics of the law worked to place a repeal measure on the 2018 ballot). Baker signed a law aimed at achieving equal pay for women by barring employers from forcing applicants to provide their salary history. He helped engineer a deal to bring General Electric's headquarters from Connecticut. And he kept his promise to sign a bill combating opioid addiction; it restricted most initial prescriptions to seven days, required emergency-room evaluations within 24 hours; and mandated that doctors check a state patient database before prescribing opioids.

Perhaps more popular than Baker's policies, however, was his low-key, bipartisan approach – welcome in an increasingly polarized political sphere – and his decision not to vote for his party's presidential nominee, Donald Trump. In mid-2016, Baker registered an approval rating of 72 percent, the highest of any governor in the nation. Some suggested that Massachusetts, with its overwhelmingly Democratic legislature, actually works better with a Republican governor. Lou DiNatale, a senior adviser to Democratic state Senate President Stanley Rosenberg, told the *New York Times* that Democratic lawmakers may have greater leverage over a governor who's Republican. A GOP governor can criticize big spending yet reap the benefits of that spending, since they can't stop it from being enacted. "He'll veto the money, then we override the veto, then he goes and cuts the ribbon on whatever we open," DiNatale said. Baker's popularity gives him a leg up for winning a second term in 2018, though the state's strong Democratic lean – and the chance to punish Trump in the midterm elections – pose risks. So too could a potential primary challenge from the right, and the possibility that boisterous ex-Red Sox star Curt Schilling could share the ballot if he runs for the Senate. Democrats have a strong bench in the state, making it possible that the contest will become a marquee gubernatorial race for 2018.

Senior Senator

Elizabeth Warren (D)

Elected 2012, term expires 2018, 1st term; b. Jun 22, 1949, Oklahoma City, OK; University of Houston (TX), B.A.; Rutgers University (NJ), J.D.; George Washington University (DC), Att.; Methodist; Married (Bruce H. Mann); 2 children; 3 grandchildren.

Professional Career: Professor, University of TX, 1981-1987; Professor, University of PA Law School, 1987-1995; Professor, Harvard Law School, 1992-2013; Chair, Congressional Oversight Panel for the Troubled Asset Relief Program, 2008-2010; Assistant to the President & Special Advisor to Treasury Secretary, 2010-2011.

DC Office: 317 HSOB 20510, 202-224-4543, Fax: 202-228-2072, warren.senate.gov.

State Offices: Boston, 617-565-3170; Springfield, 413-788-2690.

Committees: Senate Democratic Conference Vice Chairman. *Aging*. *Armed Services*: Airland, Personnel, Strategic Forces. *Banking, Housing & Urban Affairs*: Economic Policy, Financial Institutions & Consumer Protection (RMM), Securities, Insurance & Investment. *Health, Education, Labor & Pensions*: Employment & Workplace Safety, Primary Health & Retirement Security.

Group Ratings

	ADA	ACLU	AFL-CIO	LCV	ITI	COC	HAFA	ACU	CFG	FRC
2016	-	94%	-	100%	60%	25%	23%	4%	13%	0%
2015	100%	C	93%	100%	C	29%	C	0%	14%	0%

Almanac Ratings 2015

	Economy	Social	Foreign	Composite
Liberal	98%	100%	100%	99%
Conservative	2%	0%	0%	1%

Key Votes of the 114th Congress

1. Keystone pipeline	N	5. National Security Data	Y	9. Gun Sales Checks	Y
2. Export-Import Bank	N	6. Iran Nuclear Deal	N	10. Sanctuary Cities	N
3. Debt Ceiling Increase	Y	7. Puerto Rico Debt	N	11. Planned Parenthood	Y
4. Homeland Security $$	Y	8. Loretta Lynch A.G	Y	12. Trade deals	N

Election Results

Election	Name (Party)	Vote (%)	Cand. Spent	Ind. Exp. Support	Ind. Exp. Oppose
2012 General	Elizabeth Warren (D)...............	1,696,346 (54%)	$42,211,677	$2,108,019	$724,589
	Scott Brown (R)........................	1,458,048 (46%)	$35,058,354	$687,364	
2012 Primary	Elizabeth Warren (D)................	308,979 (98%)			

Democrat Elizabeth Warren, Massachusetts' senior senator, occupies the seat held for nearly half a century by the late Sen. Edward Kennedy. Just as the traditional liberal wing of the Democratic Party long looked to Kennedy for leadership and inspiration, Warren is now viewed in much the same manner by progressive activists working to push the party to the left. In less than one term in the Senate, the former Harvard Law School professor has emerged as one of its most influential members, thanks to a sharp tongue, the deft use of social media and a large fundraising base. "…She has been a lot more effective than most in communicating an anti-Wall Street message that has been part of the Democratic Party for 80 years…" Charles Geisst, a Manhattan College professor who specializes in Wall Street history, told *Politico*.

Since her election to the Senate in 2012-and even prior to that-Warren has been the subject of seemingly non-stop speculation as a potential presidential candidate. In early 2015, she definitively ruled herself out of the race for the Democratic nomination the following year, but was later vetted as a potential running mate by Hillary Clinton. Although not chosen, Warren became one of Clinton's most effective surrogates in the fall campaign, as she demonstrated an ability to match insults with and get under the skin of Republican candidate Donald Trump. Warren derided Trump as a "small, insecure, money grubber" on the stump, and a "thin-skinned bully who thinks humiliating women at 3 a.m. qualifies him to be president" via Twitter; Trump responded by calling Warren "Pocahontas," a reference to a controversy that erupted during her first Senate race over her claim to Cherokee ancestry. Warren has used her 2018 bid for a second term -- for which she is strongly favored -- to sidestep questions about a possible candidacy to take on Trump in 2020.

If Warren's attitude toward Trump is contemptuous, her relationship with Trump's predecessor, Barack Obama was complicated. "What would Elizabeth Warren say?" Obama White House aides would often ask aloud during policy negotiations, according to *The New York Times,* as they sought to avoid running afoul of Warren and her progressive allies. Obama and Warren share a similar biographical profile: Obama also was a former law school professor who was touted as presidential timber even before his election to the Senate. He helped to launch Warren's meteoric political career when he named her a special adviser to the Treasury Department in 2010, tasking her with setting up the Consumer Financial Protection Bureau created by the Dodd-Frank financial regulatory bill. But, midway through her first Senate term, Warren would derail an Obama Treasury Department appointee and find herself in a very testy public exchange with Obama over a Pacific trade deal that Obama hoped would be one of his legacy achievements.

Opposition to the Trans Pacific Partnership -- from which Trump would withdraw the United States during his first week in office -- highlights an intersection between Warren's left-leaning populism and the conservative brand espoused by Trump. "[Trump] said one thing that was right-because I've said it, too: The system is rigged," Warren observed after Trump's election. "But let's be clear, it is rigged in favor of billionaires like Donald Trump." Warren traces her political convictions to hardscrabble origins as well as academic research. She grew up in Oklahoma City where her teen years were marred when her father, a maintenance man, suffered a heart attack. His lost pay and medical bills imperiled the family's finances; Warren and her mother went to work, with Warren, then 13, waiting tables at her aunt's Mexican restaurant. Betsy, as she was then known, also developed into a champion high school debater; her skills enabled her to win a scholarship and become the first in her family to receive a college diploma.

Warren married a high school sweetheart at 19, had two children, taught elementary school, picked up a law degree from Rutgers University, and went through a divorce-earning an appreciation for working mothers. She developed a specialty in bankruptcy law as a member of the law faculty at three universities before arriving at Harvard in 1992. Along the way, she remarried, to Bruce Mann, who remains a member of the Harvard law faculty. As recently as 1996, Warren was a registered Republican. But she said the families she met in her research into bankruptcy changed her. "These were hard-working, middle-class families who by and large had lost jobs, gotten sick, had family breakups, and that's what was driving them over the edge financially. It changed my vision," Warren said during a 2007 speech.

Warren combined her academic expertise with an ability to translate complicated policy issues into terms that could frame the broader political debate, enabling her to emerge as a leading advocate for consumer interests. In 1995, she became chief adviser to the National Bankruptcy Review Commission and unsuccessfully led the fight against legislation to make it harder for consumers to file for bankruptcy. In the process, she made appearances on the TV talk show circuit and, with her daughter, Amelia Warren Tyagi, co-authored a couple of books on consumer finance aimed at a general audience. The second, *All Your Worth: The Ultimate Lifetime Money Plan,* made *The New York Times* best-seller list in 2005. In 2008, then-Senate Majority Leader Harry Reid named Warren to chair the congressional oversight panel for the $700 billion Troubled Asset Relief Program enacted in the wake of the financial crash.

A year earlier, Warren had written an article in which she proposed a "Financial Product Safety Commission" modeled on the Consumer Product Safety Commission created in the early 1970s. "Financial products should be subject to the same routine safety screening that now governs the sale of every toaster, washing machine, and child's car seat sold on the American market," she wrote. Her idea was incorporated into the 2010 Dodd-Frank law as an agency within the Treasury Department, and Warren was hired by the White House to design and launch the Consumer Financial Protection Bureau. But her barbed criticisms over the years had made her *persona non grata* to many sectors of the nation's financial industry. With Senate Republicans vowing to block her appointment, Obama instead nominated former Ohio Attorney General Richard Cordray as the bureau's first director.

However, the visibility that Warren achieved during her year in the Obama Administration prompted many Massachusetts Democrats, searching for a high-profile candidate to challenge Republican Sen. Scott Brown, to encourage her to run. Not long after leaving her advisory post at the Treasury Department in late 2011, Warren announced her candidacy. She became a national sensation when a speech she gave, exhorting wealthy Americans to recognize the debt they owe to the community and "pay forward for the next kid who comes along," went viral. Warren became a "Doonesbury" cartoon heroine and got a prime-time speaking slot at the 2012 Democratic National Convention in North Carolina.

Brown had shocked Democrats when he won a January 2010 special election to succeed Kennedy. He received substantial support from tea party interests upset about Obama's health care overhaul, but generally steered clear of the tea party in compiling a centrist voting record. Brown's everyman persona made him well-liked among voters, and he pointedly referred to her as "Professor Warren," to drive a wedge between her background at an elite university and the rank-and-file electorate. However, in the last months of the campaign, she frequently asserted a vote for Brown was a vote for a Republican Senate majority, a sentiment that resonated with voters. Brown, recognizing he was vulnerable, repeatedly attacked Warren for claiming she had Cherokee ancestry, an assertion not uncommon among Oklahoma natives. But Brown's backers charged it was a ruse by Warren to exploit affirmative action plans at schools where she had been hired. She denied the allegation, but it provided Trump with rhetorical ammunition four year later. Warren beat Brown, 54%-46%, in one of the most expensive Senate races that cycle: Brown raised $28 million (and spent $35 million), Warren raised and spent $42 million.

Warren was hardly the most liberal member of the Senate in her first year. She placed31st, with a composite liberal score of 73.2 in *National Journal* rankings -- although she shot up to second place, with a 99.2 score, in 2015 *Almanac* rankings. In 2013, she broke with Obama in voting to repeal the Affordable Care Act's medical device tax-a core element to funding the health insurance overhaul. It was an instance of her choosing constituency over party: Many medical device manufacturers are based in Massachusetts. But, as she completed her fourth year in the Senate, she found herself at odds with her home state's large biomedical research industry, as she waged a quixotic battle against a bill to invest $6 billion in public health and medical research over the coming decade. Warren, however, saw the legislation as a giveaway to pharmaceutical companies, declaring, "I will fight it," she declared, "because I know the difference between compromise and extortion." In the end, she was one of just five senators -- and the only member of the Massachusetts congressional delegation -- to vote against the so-called 21st Century Cures Act, the last major piece of legislation that Obama signed into law before leaving office.

Warren has been more successful in exercising influence over the issues and causes that brought her to prominence: reining in the nation's financial industry. At the end of 2014, she mounted an effort to kill a spending bill designed to keep the government running into 2015: She objected to its softening of provisions in the Dodd-Frank law. The measure ultimately passed, but her opposition prompted several dozen House Democrats to break ranks to support her. Before being sworn in, Warren sought a seat on the Banking Committee. Financial industry executives openly crusaded against the idea, but her liberal allies pushed back and she was named to the panel. She pushed to reinstitute the separation between banks and other financial institutions swept away when the Glass-Steagall Act was repealed in the late 1990s, introducing a bill to separate banks that offer checking and savings accounts from riskier financial services. It picked up the support of Arizona Republican John McCain, but other GOP lawmakers wouldn't touch it and it languished. In early 2017, Warren, joined again by McCain, introduced a similar bill, while jawboning Trump -- who voiced support for reviving Glass-Steagall as a candidate -- to back it.

Her jawboning of federal regulators during the Obama Administration often achieved results -- along with visibility for Warren. During her first hearing as a Banking Committee member in early 2013, she pressured federal regulators to take legal action against more of the nation's largest financial institutions. "They can break the law and drag in billions in profits and then turn around and settle, paying out of those profits. They don't have much incentive to follow the law," she complained. She later pressed the Securities and Exchange Commission to seek admission of guilt from corporations found to have violated the law rather than allowing them to pay a fine without admitting or denying guilt-and claimed part of the credit when the policy was changed to do so. Her pointed grilling of top Treasury Department and Federal Reserve officials won her more admiration from the left; *The New Republic* in April 2013 dubbed her a "Regulatory Rock Star."

The strains between Warren and the Obama White House were evident in early 2015, when Antonio Weiss, nominated by Obama as Treasury undersecretary for domestic finance, withdrew his name. He had drawn Warren's fierce opposition: She felt his role as a Wall Street investment banker made him unsuited for a post that involved implementation of the Dodd-Frank law. But the Weiss episode turned out to be a relative skirmish in advance of the battle over the Obama's pursuit of the Trans-

Pacific Partnership. In an op-ed article in February 2015, Warren contended the agreement, by setting up international arbitration panels, would "undermine U.S. sovereignty" and "allow foreign companies to challenge U.S. laws-and potentially to pick up huge payouts from taxpayers-without ever stepping foot in a U.S. court."

The White House issued a response disputing Warren's arguments in detail, but she turned up the heat a couple of months later-just as the Senate was about to vote on a related measure giving Obama so-called "fast track" authority to expedite negotiation of the 12-nation trade accord. Once again, the issue was the future of the Dodd-Frank financial regulatory legislation. Two years prior to the 2016 election, Warren warned that, if the Democrats lost the White House, "a Republican president could easily use a future trade deal to override our domestic financial rules," adding, "A six-year fast-track bill is the missing link they need to make that happen." Obama White House officials again disputed that such a scenario could occur under the terms of the legislation. But, this time, it was clear that Warren had gotten under the skin of the president himself.

In an interview aired by *Yahoo*'s news site, an uncharacteristically blunt Obama called Warren "absolutely wrong" and seemed to question her motives. "The truth of the matter is that Elizabeth is, you know, a politician like everybody else," he declared. "And you know, she's got a voice that she wants to get out there. And I understand that. And on most issues, she and I deeply agree. On this one, though, her arguments don't stand the test of fact and scrutiny." To some, it was a president -- who had taken office vowing to change the ways of Washington, but who ultimately had to bow to political reality -- venting frustration at an adversary who continued to be perceived by many as more a consumer advocate and crusading populist than a politician. "I'll always be an outsider," Warren told the *Washington Post* at the outset of 2015. "That's how I understand the world."

More broadly, it was an argument fueled by longstanding tensions between the Obama White House and a Democratic left wing that believed Obama had spent insufficient political capital on the income equality issues to which Warren had given voice. Such sentiments nourished the Warren for President talk soon after her arrival on Capitol Hill. In spring 2014, she published another best-selling book, *A Fighting Chance*-part autobiography, part packaging of her philosophy. At the liberal Netroots Nation conference that summer, she brought the crowd to its feet with angry denunciations of big business. A draft-Warren movement quickly ramped up; by January 2015, MoveOn.org and Democracy for America collected nearly 250,000 signatures in an online petition urging her to run. But she repeatedly batted away questions about her future by declaring, "I am not running for president." When questioners noted such verbal constructions did not foreclose her running in the future, Warren began using the future tense. "I am not running and I am not going to run," she said in March 2015. By summer, MoveOn.org and Democracy for America announced they were folding their draft-Warren group.

By that point, non-candidate Warren had succeeded in defining the battle lines of the 2016 contest for the Democratic presidential nomination-perhaps as much, if not more so, than if she had run. Her influence was formally recognized when, following the November 2014 election, Senate Minority Leader Harry Reid named her as a member of the Senate Democratic leadership. In her newly created post, "strategic policy adviser" to the Democratic Policy and Communications Committee, she was charged with being an envoy to liberal groups and helping to shape the party's message. (She was elevated to the post of vice chair of the Senate Democratic Conference in 2016 by Reid's successor, Minority Leader Charles Schumer.) Hillary Clinton, preparing to launch her second presidential bid, privately solicited ideas from Warren in a meeting held at Clinton's request at the end of 2014. Clinton's subsequent rhetoric often made her sound much like Warren.

Warren stayed out of the battle for the nomination between Clinton and the party's other leading progressive voice, Vermont Sen. Bernie Sanders -- endorsing Clinton after the primaries had ended and Sanders was preparing to drop out. Speculation about an all-woman, Clinton-Warren ticket intensified, with Reid reportedly pushing the idea in the belief that it could help the Democrats pick up Senate seats in November. Clinton praised Warren as "an incredible public servant, eminently qualified for any role," and a *Bloomberg News* showed the Massachusetts senator with a 2-1 lead over her closest competitor as Democrats' favored vice-presidential nominee. However, the survey also highlighted why many felt a Clinton-Warren ticket wouldn't happen -- the possibility of a running mate who could eclipse the presidential nominee in popularity and enthusiasm. And the Clinton-Warren relationship, never close, had some bumpy history: In a 2003 book, *The Two-Income Trap*, Warren had accused Clinton, as a senator, of doing an about-face on a controversial bankruptcy bill to win favor with the banking industry.

Much as Warren has become a political lightning rod nationally, she has as well in her home state -- where an early 2017 poll by Boston's WBUR-FM showed Warren with a relatively high 37 percent disapproval rating, although 51 percent approved. The same survey found that 44 percent felt she deserved re-election while 46 percent believed it was "time to give someone else a chance." It raised the question of whether she is potentially vulnerable in 2018 in a blue state that, with the exception of Brown?s 2010 special election win, has not elected a Republican senator in nearly five decades. Whether she will attract a competitive challenger in a state with a limited GOP bench remains a question. Former Boston Red Sox pitcher Curt Schilling -- recently fired from ESPN for negative comments about transgender individuals -- expressed interest; a *Globe* poll showed Warren leading him by nearly 35 points.

As Warren did her best to deflect attention away from 2020 and onto her re-election bid, she appeared to be doing the types of things typical of a potential presidential candidate. In 2017, she was given a seat on the Armed Services Committee -- reminiscent of a move that Kennedy made in the early 1980s, as he sought to bolster his foreign policy credentials in advance of a possible White House run. In the spring of 2017, Warren published her 11th book, *This Fight Is Our Fight* -- notable for its absence of post-mortems on the Democratic failures of 2016, and the attendant risk of offending players who could be helpful in the future. "I think it's time to look forward," Warren told the *Globe* in discussing the book.

She got a boost from an unlikely source in early February 2017, when Senate Majority Leader Mitch McConnell -- invoking a little-used Senate rule -- successfully barred her from participating further in the debate over the nomination of Sen. Jeff Sessions of Alabama as attorney general. Warren triggered McConnell's ire by reading from a 30-year old letter by Coretta Scott King, written in opposition to Sessions' nomination to the federal bench at that time. The rule invoked by McConnell, instituted in 1902 following a physical battle between two senators, states that "no senator in debate shall, directly or indirectly, by any form of words impute to another senator or to other senators any conduct or motive unworthy or unbecoming of a senator." McConnell's ploy appeared to be an effort to energize the GOP base by aiming at a figure whom national Republicans are increasingly utilizing as a *bete noire* -- but it also yielded Warren a new round of donations from her fundraising base. And, as with much else that Warren has done since coming to the Senate, the moment went viral: She left the Senate chamber to finish reading King's letter on Facebook, and received 7 million views.

Junior Senator

Ed Markey (D)

Elected 2013, term expires 2020, 1st full term; b. Jul 11, 1946, Malden; Boston College (MA), B.A.; Boston College Law School (MA), J.D.; Roman Catholic; Married (Susan Blumenthal).

Military Career: U.S Army Reserves, 1968-1973.

Elected Office: MA House, 1973-1976; U.S. House, 1976-2013.

DC Office: 255 DSOB 20510, 202-224-2742, Fax: 202-224-8525, markey.senate.gov.

State Offices: Boston, 617-565-8519; Fall River, 508-677-0523; Springfield, 413-785-4610.

Committees: *Commerce, Science & Transportation*: Aviation Operations, Safety & Security, Communications, Technology, Innovation & the Internet, Consumer Protection, Product Safety, Ins & Data Security, Oceans, Atmosphere, Fisheries & Coast Guard, Space, Science & Competitiveness (RMM). *Environment & Public Works*: Clean Air & Nuclear Safety, Fisheries, Water, and Wildlife, Transportation & Infrastructure. *Foreign Relations*: East Asia, the Pacific & International Cybersecurity Policy (RMM), Europe & Regional Security Cooperation, Internat'l Dev Instit & Internat'l Econ, Energy & Environ Policy. *Small Business & Entrepreneurship*.

Group Ratings

	ADA	ACLU	AFL-CIO	LCV	ITI	COC	HAFA	ACU	CFG	FRC
2016	-	94%	-	100%	40%	38%	17%	4%	13%	0%
2015	100%	C	100%	100%	C	31%	C	4%	9%	0%

Almanac Ratings 2015

	Economy	Social	Foreign	Composite
Liberal	96%	100%	100%	99%
Conservative	4%	0%	0%	1%

Key Votes of the 114th Congress

1. Keystone pipeline	N	5. National Security Data	Y	9. Gun Sales Checks	Y
2. Export-Import Bank	N	6. Iran Nuclear Deal	N	10. Sanctuary Cities	N
3. Debt Ceiling Increase	Y	7. Puerto Rico Debt	N	11. Planned Parenthood	N
4. Homeland Security $$	Y	8. Loretta Lynch A.G	Y	12. Trade deals	N

Election Results

Election	Name (Party)	Vote (%)	Cand. Spent	Ind. Exp. Support	Ind. Exp. Oppose
2014 General	Ed Markey (D)	1,289,944 (59%)	$17,857,729	$3,214,292	
	Brian Herr (R)	791,950 (36%)	$118,532		
2014 Primary	Ed Markey (D)	unopposed			

Prior winning percentages: 2013 special (55%), House: 2012(71%), 2010 (66%), 2008 (71%), 2006

When Democrat Edward Markey, Massachusetts' junior senator, arrived in the chamber after winning a June 2013 special election, it was the culmination of a nearly 30-year wait. Back in 1984, Markey, then a four-term House member, had jumped into the Democratic primary for an opening created by the retirement of Sen. Paul Tsongas. But, amid a bumpy reception to his candidacy, Markey reassessed his position, withdrew from the Senate contest and successfully sought re-election to the House. The ultimate winner of the Senate seat that year was then-Lt. Gov. John Kerry, who held onto it until President Barack Obama nominated him as secretary of state at the end of 2012. However, even as Markey accumulated seniority and influence in the House, he continued to eye the Senate seat-hoping it might come open in 2004 if Kerry, then the Democratic presidential nominee, had won the White House. Finally, with Kerry poised to move to the Cabinet, Markey, at age 66, saw his opportunity and grabbed it.

Markey was only 30 when first elected to the House in 1976, and, over the years, became a key player on environmental and telecommunication issues-areas in which he has continued to focus as a senator, while still displaying the barbed rhetoric that has long endeared him to consumer advocates and environmentalists. What makes his move from one side of the U.S. Capitol to the other extraordinary is that there has never before been a House member with Markey's seniority-nearly 37 years-who opted to trade that in to become a freshman senator. In fact, in September 2009, when the death of Democrat Ted Kennedy opened the seat Kennedy had held for nearly five decades, Markey passed on the special election to succeed him. The Democrats then had the House majority, and Markey, in addition to being in third in line for the powerful chairmanship of the Energy and Commerce Committee, was also chairing a special panel tasked with laying the groundwork for legislation to curb global warming. That changed a year later: House Democrats lost their majority in the 2010 election, with no clear prospect of regaining it in the near future, and a high visibility, if junior, Senate slot became significantly more appealing.

Markey grew up in the Boston suburb of Malden, where his father was a milkman. He graduated from Boston College, and was elected to the state House, at age 26, soon after graduating from Boston College's law school. He moved to an open House seat four years later, winning a 12-candidate primary with 22 percent. Markey broke out of the crowded field with a TV ad that remains a classic in Bay State political circles: It played off an episode in which state House leaders removed the furniture from Markey's office to retaliate for a court reform bill he had pushed over their objections. The ad shows a desk in the hallway of the Massachusetts State House, as Markey declares: "The bosses may tell me where to sit, nobody tells me where to stand."

Throughout most of his long career on Capitol Hill, Markey has ranked among the most liberal members of Congress. But, in winning in 1976, Markey favored school prayer and advocated constitutional amendments to end school busing and ban abortion-positions geared to a socially conservative Catholic population in his home base. He subsequently disavowed these positions prior to his brief Senate bid in 1984, but the timing of those reversals became a liability during that short-lived campaign. In recent decades, he has sidestepped questions about the change of position on these matters early in his career, telling the *Boston Globe* in 2013: "For 30 years, I have taken the progressive position, the liberal position, on each and every issue. I just evolved."

In the primary for the 2013 special Senate election, Markey was the establishment favorite and the more traditional liberal against Rep. Stephen Lynch, whose district includes working class neighborhoods in and around south Boston. Lynch was generally regarded as the most conservative of the state's all-Democratic congressional delegation, although he sought to moderate his anti-abortion stance early in the Senate campaign. As a onetime iron worker, he enjoyed substantial labor union support. But Markey's 3-1 cash advantage at the start of the primary helped him to prevail, 57%-43%. Markey had expected his fiercest competition to come in the special general election-from former Republican Sen. Scott Brown, who had lost the state's other seat to Democrat Elizabeth Warren in one of the nation's highest-profile Senate contests of 2012. But Brown opted not to run in the special election, and mounted a competitive but unsuccessful Senate bid in neighboring New Hampshire in 2014.

Instead, Markey faced businessman Gabriel Gomez. A former Navy Seal and a bilingual son of Colombian immigrants, Gomez was no easy target. Markey attacked him on gun control. "Gomez is against banning high-capacity magazines, like the ones used in the Newtown School shooting," one ad charged, referring to the mass shooting at a Connecticut elementary school in December 2012 in which 26 were killed. In response, Gomez mocked the Democratic attack ads, with one Gomez ad sarcastically declaring: "Gabriel Gomez is a very bad man. He kills old people. He hates women. He even leaves the toilet seat up," The ad continued: "This is ridiculous … Markey is everything that's wrong with Congress: 37 years of pay raises, bounced checks, taking millions from people he regulates." But Markey's large campaign treasury again gave him an advantage, allowing him to outspend Gomez by a margin approaching 4-1. He won, 55%-45%, and was easily re-elected to a full six-year term in the 2014 general election, defeating his little-known opponent, businessman and local selectman Brian Herr, 59%-36%.

Markey has comfortably fit in with the Senate's other left-leaning members from the Northeast. For 2015, *Almanac* rankings put him as the 11th most liberal member of the chamber, with a score just a half-point short of his higher-profile Massachusetts colleague, Warren, a leader of the party's progressive wing. But Markey's arrival in the Senate was not the most auspicious: Two months after he was sworn in, when the Foreign Relations Committee voted to authorize Obama's use of force against Syria, Markey voted "present" while most other committee Democrats voted in support. Markey said he was concerned about the "unintended consequences" of a U.S. military attack, which never ended up occurring-but critics saw it as an attempt to sidestep a tough issue. Markey's vote also was regarded as a swipe at his predecessor, Secretary of State Kerry, who had worked to clear the way for Markey to succeed him. *Boston Magazine* afterward captured the widespread reaction in a headline that read, "Ed Markey Annoys Literally Everyone by Voting 'Present' on Syrian Resolution."

Markey's straddling of the issue may have been related to his House vote a decade earlier in favor of the 2002 resolution authorizing the war in Iraq, a decision about which he later expressed strong regret. A year after his "present" vote, in September 2014, Markey joined Warren and eight other Senate Democrats to vote against a bill to fund the federal government through the end of the year due to a provision authorizing the Obama Administration to arm and train Syrian rebels. Markey expressed "grave concerns that American military leaders have not ruled out potential use of ground troops for combat."

Markey also tangled with the Obama White House in early 2016, using a procedural "hold" to stall the nomination of Robert Califf to head of the Food and Drug Administration. "F.D.A. stands for Food and Drug Administration, but over the last 20 years it really stands for 'fostering drug addiction'," Markey gibed on the Senate floor. His primary target was not Califf but what he regarded as the FDA's lax oversight of addictive "opioid" pharmaceuticals. "We have to have an honest discussion about the role that agency is playing," he declared. Califf was ultimately confirmed after the Senate invoked cloture, with Markey one of just four senators to vote against the nomination.

Among those joining in that fight was Connecticut Democrat Richard Blumenthal -- like Markey, a media savvy political veteran who arrived in the Senate late in his career. As members of the Senate Commerce Committee, Markey and Blumenthal teamed up to keep the heat on General Motors in the wake of 2014 revelations of a faulty vehicle ignition switch that the company acknowledged caused at least 124 deaths. And, in early 2016, they introduced legislation to bar airlines from charging fees considered "unreasonable or disproportional to the costs" -- dubbing it the "Forbidding Airlines from Imposing Ridiculous (FAIR) Fees Act." Several of their initiatives were tied to Markey's long-time legislative focus on information technology. This included a bill requiring automobile manufacturers to come up with security standards to prevent hacking of the increasingly computerized systems of today's vehicles. The legislation came on the heels of a June 2015 report by Markey's office entitled "Tracking & Hacking: Security & Privacy Gaps Put American Drivers At Risk." Markey subsequently pressed the nation's airlines for information regarding similar cybersecurity concerns.

In the House, Markey left his most lasting impact on telecommunications and IT policy, where he often worked with Republicans to come up with innovative initiatives. His proposals were frequently inclined toward deregulation, but consumer advocates regarded him as a friend-blaming the skyrocketing cable TV bills of recent years not on Markey's legislation, but on the failure of the industry to produce the level of competition originally promised. Markey's Massachusetts colleague, House Speaker Tip O'Neill, early on put him in a position to be a serious legislator, with a seat on the Energy and Commerce Committee. Impressed by the high-tech boom around Route 128, Markey joined the panel's Telecommunications Subcommittee. In early 1987, after a decade in the House, Markey became chairman of the subcommittee. It was a couple of years after a court ordered the breakup of the old "Ma Bell" monopoly, which put a transformation of the nation's telecommunications industry into motion.

In 1992, Markey crafted a cable television regulation bill with enough support to override President George H.W. Bush's veto. The measure helped to establish today's satellite TV industry. Markey lost the gavel of the Telecommunications Subcommittee when the Republicans captured the House majority in 1994, but continued to exert influence as its ranking Democrat. He was a major player in the passage of the landmark Telecommunications Act of 1996. The legislation, co-authored with Texas Republican Rep. Jack Fields, helped prod cable firms to build the broadband networks integral to the flow of information and images over today's Internet. "Google, Hulu, YouTube-none of it was possible before the 1996 Telecom Act," Markey told the *Globe* years later. "It required broadband in order to make the business models possible."

When the Democrats regained the House in the 2006 election, Markey's other major legislative interest-energy and environmental issues-became his priority. House Speaker Nancy Pelosi chose Markey in 2007 to be chairman of a Select Committee on Energy Independence and Global Warming. It was an attempt to get around Michigan Rep. John Dingell, who as chairman of the Energy and Commerce Committee and representative of an auto manufacturing-dependent district, had resisted efforts to toughen motor vehicle emissions standards. When Dingell strenuously objected, Pelosi announced the select committee would not have authority to propose legislation, but she gave Markey free rein to hold hearings and make the case for a far-reaching bill to curb global warming.

After the 2008 election, Dingell was ousted as chairman of the full Energy and Commerce Committee, and Markey became chairman of the Energy and Environment Subcommittee while retaining the select committee gavel. It gave Pelosi the players she needed to achieve the Democrats' goal of an 85-percent cut in greenhouse gas emissions by 2050, along with a cap-and-trade program to compel companies to buy and sell credits with the goal of reducing emissions. Markey worked with the energy and manufacturing industries to gain their support-or at least to reduce their level of opposition. (When an iceberg four times the size of Manhattan broke off Greenland in 2010, Markey-exhibiting his trademark wit-observed that the development created "plenty of room for global-warming deniers to start their own country.") After fierce negotiations, the bill passed the House, 219-212, in June 2009. Markey hailed its passage as showing that business and consumer interests could cooperate "to create a pathway that works for both." But the Senate never took up the bill, House Republicans used it as a political club in 2010 campaigns, and the issue has since made little headway on Capitol Hill.

Markey was more successful in toughening automobile fuel efficiency standards. In 2007, working closely with Pelosi, he proposed an increase in fuel efficiency standards to 35 miles per gallon by 2018. The domestic auto industry and the United Auto Workers union criticized the plan as extreme, but the bill that became law maintained the 35 miles per gallon standard while pushing the deadline back to 2020. It marked the first increase in the fuel efficiency standards since 1975. In his first bill introduced after his election to the Senate, Markey in late 2013 took aim at electric utilities-proposing a requirement that 25 percent of the power they distribute come from renewable energy sources by 2025. Noting that 30 states had taken similar steps on their own, Markey declared: "There is real bipartisan support for energy efficiency here in the Senate. These are policies that should be embraced and not blocked."

In substance, it was not far from where Markey began his career more than one-third of a century earlier-as a strong foe of nuclear power. At the 1980 Democratic National Convention in New York, anti-nuclear activists threatened to collect enough signatures to put Markey on the ballot for the vice presidential nomination if convention organizers didn't grant him a prime-time speaking slot. The ploy gave the 34-year old Markey 10 minutes to make the case to a national audience to shut down nuclear reactors and increase solar energy. Almost four decades later, Markey is a gray-haired, veteran congressional deal-maker -- but one who has not strayed too far from his rebellious roots. When Obama, during a visit to Hiroshima in May 2016, called for a "moral awakening" and reiterated his hope for a future free of nuclear weapons, Markey took a swipe at the president for what he characterized a "Faustian bargain" in a 2010 arms treaty with Russia -- which allowed for a nuclear weapons modernization plan that Markey said would cost $1 trillion over 30 years.

"This alleged modernization plan is better described as a nuclear weapons expansion plan," Markey declared in a *Globe* op-ed. And, once again demonstrating his agility with the pointed phrase, he added: "If the United States wants other countries to reduce their nuclear arsenals and restrain their nuclear war plans, it must take the lead. It cannot preach nuclear temperance from a bar stool."

FIRST DISTRICT

Richard Neal (D)

Elected 1988, 15th term; b. Feb 14, 1949, Worcester; American International College (MA), B.A.; University of Hartford Barney School of Business (CT), M.P.A.; University of Massachusetts, Att.; Roman Catholic; Married (Maureen Conway Neal); 4 children.

Elected Office: Springfield City Council, 1978-1983; Springfield Mayor, 1984-1988.

Professional Career: Staff Assistant, Springfield Mayor William C. Sullivan, 1973-1978; H.S. & college teacher, 1978-1983.

DC Office: 341 CHOB 20515, 202-225-5601, Fax: 202-225-8112, neal.house.gov.

State Offices: Pittsfield, 413-442-0946; Springfield, 413-785-0325.

Committees: *Ways & Means (RMM)*: Health, Human Resources, Oversight, Social Security, Tax Policy, Trade.

Group Ratings

	ADA	ACLU	AFL-CIO	LCV	ITI	COC	HAFA	ACU	CFG	FRC
2016	-	94%	-	97%	67%	62%	15%	0%	4%	0%
2015	90%	C	100%	97%	C	50%	C	4%	0%	8%

Almanac Ratings 2015

	Economy	Social	Foreign	Composite
Liberal	95%	100%	96%	97%
Conservative	5%	0%	4%	3%

Key Votes of the 114th Congress

1. Keystone Pipeline	N	5. Puerto Rico Debt	Y	9. Offenses by Aliens	N
2. Trade Deals	N	6. Medical Marijuana	Y	10. Troops in Iraq	Y
3. Export-Import Bank	Y	7. Sanctuary Cities	N	11. Homeland Security $$	Y
4. Debt Ceiling Increase	Y	8. Armor-piercing Bullets	N	12. Trade Adjustment aid	Y

Election Results

Election	Name (Party)	Vote (%)		Cand. Spent	Ind. Exp. Support	Ind. Exp. Oppose
2016 General	Richard Neal (D)	235,803	(73%)	$840,656		
	Frederick Mayock (I)	57,504	(18%)			
	Thomas Simmons (L)	27,511	(9%)	$17,395		
2016 Primary	Richard Neal (D)		(100%)			

Prior winning percentages: 2014 (74%), 2012 (78%), 2010 (57%), 2008 (76%), 2006(77%), 2004 (77%), 2002 (77%), 2000 (95%), 1998 (99%), 1996 (72%), 1994 (59%), 1992 (53%), 1990 (68%), 1988 (80%),

The Democrat Richard Neal, first elected in 1988, has established himself as one of his party's leaders on economic policy, with close ties to the insurance and investment industries. In 2017, he became the top Democrat on the powerful Ways and Means Committee, in a position to find common ground with those Republicans open to collaboration. *The Boston Globe* profiled him as "the insider's insider, a veteran relationship-builder on Capitol Hill, a quiet dealmaker."

Neal grew up in Springfield amid the racial tensions of the 1960s. His parents died when he was a teenager, and Neal and his younger sisters received monthly Social Security survivor benefits while being raised by their grandmother and aunt. He graduated from American International College and earned a master's degree in public administration from the University of Hartford. In Springfield, he worked for the mayor; and in 1978, while teaching high school and college history, he was elected to the City Council. As mayor from 1984 to 1988, Neal worked to rehabilitate the downtown area and revitalize neighborhoods.

His congressional predecessor, 36-year incumbent Edward Boland, a longtime pal of Democratic Speaker Tip O'Neill, essentially bequeathed him the House seat. Boland announced his retirement just before the filing deadline - and after Neal had traveled the district for a year. Unopposed in the Democratic primary, Neal won the general election with 80 percent of the vote.

Neal has a generally liberal voting record, especially since Democrats were consigned to the minority in 2011, but has favored enough moderate initiatives to separate himself from more-liberal Massachusetts colleagues. He voted for the 1996 welfare overhaul and supported both the North American Free Trade Agreement and normalization of trade relations with China, although organized labor opposed the pacts. The *Almanac* vote ratings for 2015 gave him solidly liberal scores.

As a senior Democrat at Ways and Means, Neal crusaded for repeal of the alternative minimum tax, which was designed to ensure that the highest earners pay some tax even if they have offsetting deductions but which has been increasingly ensnaring middle-income taxpayers. In 2013, he enacted a permanent "patch" on the tax to keep pace with inflation. He took the lead for House Democrats on a popular proposal to clamp down on companies that incorporate in Bermuda and other offshore havens to avoid U.S. taxes. Neal worked with the Obama administration on a bill to require employers who do not sponsor retirement plans for their workers to automatically enroll them in individual retirement accounts funded by payroll deductions, unless an employee opts out. He has sought to reform the tax code, which he has said is "creaking under its own weight." In 2015, he opposed trade promotion authority for the president - a virtually mandatory position for a senior Democrat in the House.

Neal brings an old-style interest in bipartisanship that may be unfamiliar to many junior Democrats in the House. "I think of him as someone who remembers he's a Democrat but harkens back to the old days where we were able to work across the aisles together," Janice Mays, a former Democratic staff director at Ways and Means, told the *Globe*.

Neal's move to the senior Democrat slot at Ways and Means was a long grind. When Charles Rangel of New York was forced to step down as committee chairman in March 2010 while battling ethics problems, Neal was a possible successor, but the gavel went to the more senior Sander Levin of Michigan. Neal vigorously pushed for the job, arguing that the party needed to shelve its seniority tradition in favor of having a better spokesman in the role. He contended he would be a more business-friendly alternative to Levin and could work more closely with Republicans to get bills passed. He won a 23-22 vote of the Democratic Steering Committee. But he lost to Levin in a vote of the full caucus, 109-78, with many Democrats saying they were not ready to upend seniority.

Following the 2016 election, the 85-year-old Levin decided to cut back his responsibilities. Rep. Xavier Becerra of California quickly voiced interest in replacing Levin, even though he had less seniority than Neal. The following day, Becerra unexpectedly accepted an offer by Gov. Jerry Brown to fill the vacancy as attorney general of California. Neal fulfilled his ambition without a challenge from another Democrat. The more senior Rep. John Lewis of Georgia passed up the opportunity.

On local issues, Neal has focused on the economic problems of Springfield. He has secured funds for renovation of its Union Station, and more than $100 million for high-speed rail service in the region. To help the growing number of craft-beer brewers in his district and elsewhere, he filed a bipartisan bill to cut in half the excise tax on beer. Amid criticism from some consumer groups that the measure would benefit the large MassMutual financial company in his district, Neal filed with Republican Rep. Peter Roskam of Illinois a bill that set guidelines for insurance companies and other investment firms to advise their account-holders.

Neal had serious primary challenges in 1990 and 1992, but won reelection by healthy margins. He ran unopposed in four successive elections before facing a challenge in 2010 from Republican business executive Thomas Wesley, who spent only $144,000 to $2.2 million for the incumbent. Neal campaigned aggressively, but was held to 57 percent of the vote. In 2016, he got 73 percent of the vote against two third-party challengers.

Following the 2016 election, he joined the Democratic advocates of change. "It's time for the Democratic Party to start thinking about a reset," Neal said. "I've been arguing about this for years. That in many ways, the people who voted for Donald Trump, they used to be our people." Even with his independent streak, he remained loyal to Democratic Leader Nancy Pelosi when Rep. Tim Ryan of Ohio challenged her.

Western Massachusetts: Springfield, Pittsfield

Population		**Race and Ethnicity**		**Income**	
Total	731,275	White	74.0%	Median Income	$52,466 (216 out of 435)
Land area	2,350	Black	5.7%	Under $50,000	47.9%
Pop/ sq mi	311.1	Latino	16.4%	$50,000-$99,999	29.7%
Born in state	66.2%	Asian	1.8%	$100,000-$199,999	18.5%
		Two races	1.6%	$200,000 or more	3.8%
		Other	0.3%	Poverty Rate	15.1%
Age Groups		**Education**		**Health Insurance**	
Under 18	21.4%	H.S grad or less	43.5%	With health insurance coverage	96.4%
18-34	22.1%	Some college	28.4%		
35-64	40.5%	College Degree, 4 yr	16.7%		
Over 64	16.0%	Post grad	11.4%		
Work		**Military**		**Public Assistance**	
White Collar	35.5%	Veteran	8.8%	Cash public assistance income	4.3%
Sales and Service	44.5%	Active Duty	0.1%	Food stamp/SNAP benefits	18.8%
Blue Collar	20.0%				
Government	14.8%				

Voter Turnout			
2015 Total Citizens 18+	553,460	2016 House Turnout as % CVAP	58%
2016 House turnout	321,539	2014 House Turnout as % CVAP	31%

2012 Presidential Vote		
Barack Obama	213,423	(64%)
Mitt Romney	114,339	(34%)

2016 Presidential Vote		
Hillary Clinton	194,036	(56%)
Donald Trump	123,953	(36%)
Gary Johnson	14,550	(4%)

Cook Partisan Voting Index: D+12

The stony hills and green mountains of western Massachusetts, which so inspired Henry David Thoreau in the 1840s, look a lot like they did 300 years ago. This was the frontier in the 17th century, where Puritan preachers founded towns in the wilderness, farmed the rocky soil and preached against declension. It remained Yankee New England's western frontier for nearly 200 years. In the 19th century, the area was the home of writers and artists. Edith Wharton lived grandly on her estate in Lenox. Herman Melville struck up a friendship with Nathaniel Hawthorne after purchasing a farm near Hawthorne's Pittsfield home, not far from where the Boston Symphony plays at the Tanglewood Festival each summer. As the 20th century progressed, and trees grew on stony land in the Berkshire hills that were once farmed, much of western Massachusetts returned to its bucolic state. Few giant factories remain along the wide Connecticut River or the country streams. An exception is the Crane & Co. paper mill along the Housatonic River in Dalton, which since 1879 has been the only company to print money for the U.S. Treasury. Armed guards protect the facility's secret plating process, which is the benchmark for producing currency and preventing counterfeiting. In 2015, Crane split its stationery operations from the currency production at its North Adams plant. There no longer are family members in management.

Springfield is the largest city in western Massachusetts and the fourth-largest in New England, far from Boston in mindset and distance but with its own historical cachet. It is the site of the armory where unhappy soldiers mounted the Shays' Rebellion in 1786-87. It is where basketball was invented and where the Webster's unabridged dictionaries (2nd and 3rd editions) were edited and published. Founded by Puritans in the 17th century, Springfield has become home to immigrants from a dozen countries who have worked their way up here. African Americans and Hispanics today account for more than 60 percent of the population; at 30 percent, the poverty rate remains high.

Like other New England city centers, Springfield's downtown has emptied, and its tax base has shrunk in recent decades. Business leaders have tried to revive it, in part with the expansion of the Basketball Hall of Fame. The firearms manufacturer Smith & Wesson is headquartered in Springfield. But the once-robust city has suffered from corruption and serious crime, and in 2004 was forced to submit to state control in a financial bailout. Until 2009, the state board reorganized city government. Springfield had more foreclosures than any other city in Massachusetts in 2010. Other than tourism and academia, the economy in much of the area has remained stagnant. Computer, bio-tech and related industries that have created great wealth in the Boston area have been slow to migrate to these western outposts. The planned 2018 opening of the MGM casino on 14 acres in the South End of Springfield has begun to transform a down-and-out area and created rare hope for the depleted city in the competitive gambling business. Springfield has shown other signs of life, including a rehab of the downtown train station and a $100 million factory in East Springfield that is building rail cars for the Boston-area transit system.

For many years, western Massachusetts was a heartland of the Republican Party - flinty, thrifty and chilly, just like the area's most famous politician, Calvin Coolidge. Frederick Gillett overlapped with President Coolidge for part of his six years as Speaker of the House. The area now contains some of the most liberal precincts of the United States. Progressive MSNBC host Rachel Maddow began as a broadcaster here and still has a home with her partner, Susan Mikula. "We kind of forget we're gay," Mikula told *New York* magazine. "We live in western Mass and New York, and it's very accommodating." Alice's Restaurant in Great Barrington was immortalized by folk singer Arlo Guthrie in his anti-war song of the same name.

The 1st District in western Massachusetts includes Springfield and the old mill towns Chicopee and Holyoke along the river, plus Dalton and Pittsfield in the Berkshires. It stretches east to take in some Worcester County towns such as Charlton and Southbridge. There are year-round, weekend and vacation homes throughout the Berkshires. As recently as 1991, liberal Republican Silvio Conte represented much of this area in Congress. Not anymore. The district votes consistently Democratic, though the local orneriness reduced the presidential vote margin from 64%-34% in 2012 to 56%-36% in 2016.

SECOND DISTRICT

Jim McGovern (D)

Elected 1996, 11th term; b. Nov 20, 1959, Worcester; American University (DC), B.A., 1981; American University (DC), M.P.A., 1984; Roman Catholic; Married (Lisa Murray McGovern); 2 children.

Professional Career: Aide, U.S. Sen. George McGovern, 1981-1984; Sr. aide, U.S. Rep. Joseph Moakley, 1982-1996.

DC Office: 438 CHOB 20515, 202-225-6101, Fax: 202-225-5759, mcgovern.house.gov.

State Offices: Leominster, 978-466-3552; Northampton, 413-341-8700; Worcester, 508-831-7356.

Committees: *Agriculture*: Biotechnology, Horticulture & Research, Nutrition (RMM). *Rules*: Rules & Organization of the House.

Group Ratings

	ADA	ACLU	AFL-CIO	LCV	ITI	COC	HAFA	ACU	CFG	FRC
2016	-	100%	-	97%	33%	46%	14%	4%	4%	0%
2015	100%	C	100%	100%	C	45%	C	4%	0%	0%

Almanac Ratings 2015

	Economy	Social	Foreign	Composite
Liberal	95%	100%	96%	97%
Conservative	5%	0%	4%	3%

Key Votes of the 114th Congress

1. Keystone Pipeline	N	5. Puerto Rico Debt	Y	9. Offenses by Aliens	N
2. Trade Deals	N	6. Medical Marijuana	Y	10. Troops in Iraq	Y
3. Export-Import Bank	Y	7. Sanctuary Cities	N	11. Homeland Security $$	Y
4. Debt Ceiling Increase	Y	8. Armor-piercing Bullets	N	12. Trade Adjustment aid	Y

Election Results

Election	Name (Party)	Vote (%)	Cand. Spent	Ind. Exp. Support	Ind. Exp. Oppose
2016 General	Jim McGovern (D)........................	275,487 (98%)	$600,010		
2016 Primary	Jim McGovern (D)........................	(100%)			

Prior winning percentages: 2014 (72%), 2012 (76%), 2010 (57%), 2008 (75%), 2006(78%), 2004 (67%), 2002 (77%), 2000 (77%), 1998 (57%), 1996 (53%)

Jim McGovern, a liberal Democrat first elected in 1996, though not related to George McGovern, worked for the 1972 presidential nominee and called him "my inspiration, my mentor, my dearest friend" after the former senator's death in 2012. Massachusetts' McGovern is an active progressive on such international causes as human rights and ending hunger while urging his party to embrace a more progressive agenda at home. He is positioned to take over as the top Democrat on an influential House committee.

McGovern grew up in Worcester, where his parents owned a liquor store. He attended American University in Washington and, while in graduate school, he worked in South Dakota Sen. McGovern's office. He ran McGovern's quixotic 1984 campaign in the Massachusetts presidential primary, where the senator finished third with 21 percent of the vote, and nominated him that year at the Democratic convention in San Francisco. He was an aide in Boston-area Rep. Joe Moakley's office and became chief of staff just as Moakley ascended to chairman of the Rules Committee. McGovern was the chief investigator of a 1989 review of the murders of six Jesuits and two lay women in El Salvador, which led to a cutoff of U.S. aid to the country.

In 1994, McGovern ran for the House and lost in the Democratic primary, 38%-30%. In 1996, he ran again, this time with no primary opposition. In the general election, Republican Rep. Peter Blute stressed his independence from then-Speaker Newt Gingrich and attacked McGovern for liberal stands on abortion rights and Cuba. McGovern ran a humorous spot that asked, "If you wouldn't vote for Newt, why would you ever vote for Blute?" At age 36, McGovern won, 53%-45%.

With deft maneuvers reflecting his Capitol Hill experience, McGovern positioned himself as a power broker in the Democratic caucus. In 2001, the dying Moakley personally asked Democratic Leader Dick Gephardt to help McGovern get a seat on Rules, which schedules most legislation for the House floor. As it turned out, the next seat went to Florida's Alcee Hastings, but McGovern got a commitment for the next available Democratic seat, with seniority over Hastings. And, it seems, McGovern is a good boss. A 2013 *Washington Times* study found that he had the lowest turnover among staff of any member of Congress in the previous decade.

On Rules, McGovern started with the advantage of being well-versed in House procedures. With the GOP in the majority, he has shown a sharp partisan edge as he pursued parliamentary maneuvers that led to cries of outrage from House Republicans. When Louise Slaughter of New York, moving into her late-80s, retires, McGovern likely will replace her in the top Democratic post on Rules. With his leverage, he was a party leader on Iraq war policy, though his influence has been more rhetorical than in changing policy. He sponsored an unsuccessful 2007 bill to withdraw U.S. troops from Iraq in six months. Later that year, he proposed a war surtax, but Democratic leaders rejected it. He turned his attention to Afghanistan, and in 2011 nearly succeeded in getting the House to pass a resolution aimed at accelerating troop withdrawals.

McGovern has been outspoken on other overseas issues. On the Cuba Working Group, he called for easing sanctions against the Castro regime. He welcomed the December 2014 announcement by President Barack Obama to open the diplomatic door to Cuba as "a historic, long-overdue day." When he joined the congressional delegation that accompanied Obama to Cuba in March 2016, it was at least his sixteenth visit since he was a college student in 1979. McGovern was the House sponsor of a measure signed into law in 2012 that imposed a visa ban and asset freeze on suspected Russian human rights abusers. Russian President Vladimir Putin protested it was an intrusion into his country's affairs and retaliated by halting U.S. adoptions of Russian children, prompting McGovern to call Putin a "bully."

In November 2015, he joined Nancy Pelosi on a delegation to Tibet and called on China to re-evaluate its policy in the region.

McGovern pushed for a government-run public option in the 2010 health care overhaul bill, but he backed the bill anyway when the public option was dropped under pressure from Democratic moderates. Since the Supreme Court's 2010 *Citizens United* decision, he has introduced bills aimed at diminishing the influence of money in politics. His *Almanac* vote ratings for 2015 gave him consistently high liberal scores. During the official counting of the electoral votes for the 2016 election, he cited reports of Russian interference in the election in his unsuccessful challenge to the proceeding. He refused "to sit quietly when our democratic institutions are under attack," he tweeted.

As chairman of the Congressional Hunger Center, McGovern has pushed for more spending on international nutrition and for less support of biofuels, which he says have driven up food costs. He schedules regular events to publicize his cause, sometimes with Republican allies, including a series of "End Hunger Now" speeches. He branded House GOP efforts to cut domestic funding for food stamps "unconscionable" and "immoral." He has become the ranking Democrat on the House Agriculture Subcommittee on Nutrition. "We know how to end hunger. It's not that hard," he says.

Although Republicans held this seat not long ago, they have all but given up on it. McGovern has run unopposed in seven of the past nine elections, though he was held to 57 percent in the anti-Democratic environment of 2010. Like other old-school Democrats, he is comfortable in setting long-term strategies and pressing until their time returns.

West Central Massachusetts: Worcester

Population		**Race and Ethnicity**		**Income**	
Total	738,797	White	79.2%	Median Income	$63,225 (110 out of 435)
Land area	1,628	Black	4.4%		
Pop/ sq mi	453.8	Latino	9.0%		
Born in state	65.7%	Asian	5.2%	Under $50,000	40.5%
		Two races	1.7%	$50,000-$99,999	30.0%
Age Groups		Other	0.4%	$100,000-$199,999	23.6%
Under 18	20.9%			$200,000 or more	6.1%
18-34	24.7%	**Education**		Poverty Rate	12.8%
35-64	40.6%	H.S grad or less	37.3%		
Over 64	13.8%	Some college	25.8%	**Health Insurance**	
		College Degree, 4 yr	21.3%	With health insurance coverage	96.8%
Work		Post grad	15.6%		
White Collar	42.2%				
Sales and Service	40.4%	**Military**		**Public Assistance**	
Blue Collar	17.4%	Veteran	7.5%	Cash public assistance income	3.0%
Government	15.1%	Active Duty	0.1%		
				Food stamp/SNAP benefits	12.8%

Voter Turnout			
2015 Total Citizens 18+	546,072	2016 House Turnout as % CVAP	51%
2016 House turnout	280,411	2014 House Turnout as % CVAP	32%

2012 Presidential Vote		
Barack Obama	199,549	(59%)
Mitt Romney	133,195	(39%)

2016 Presidential Vote		
Hillary Clinton	197,492	(55%)
Donald Trump	129,437	(36%)
Gary Johnson	17,743	(5%)

Cook Partisan Voting Index: D+9

For more than 200 years, Worcester has been one of the nation's centers of tinkering, contriving and inventing, even though it is one of the few active industrial cities not located on a river, lake or seacoast. In the past, its biggest industries were valentine-making, wire-making, textiles, grinding wheels and envelopes. It is where the birth control pill was invented and where Worcester native and Clark University professor Robert Goddard shot off experimental rockets before relieved locals saw him off to New Mexico.

In the 1970s and 1980s, electronics and computer firms sprouted along Interstate 495 - the circumferential highway 20 miles east of Worcester - just as they had earlier around Route 128, closer to Boston. The high-tech boom brought prosperity, labor shortages, new residents and higher housing prices to central Massachusetts. Then, in the early 1990s, the minicomputer industry slumped, bringing a recession. But Worcester's ingenious entrepreneurs and skilled labor force hustled. Local leaders set up a Biotechnology Research Institute to draw on the city's nine colleges and institutions of higher learning to steer the city back on course.

Just as Worcester's economy has changed, so has its face, with big increases in Asians and Hispanics, mainly from Puerto Rico. The area has also attracted Hmong, Vietnamese, Albanians and Africans, many of whom fled the civil war in Liberia. The second-largest city in New England, Worcester's population has increased 7 percent since 2000. The city population is 71 percent white, though the non-whites are younger and growing faster than the whites. Worcester County has led the state in growth.

The concentration of colleges and universities in the Pioneer Valley west of Worcester brings together a critical mass of scholars and graduate students. The University of Massachusetts in Amherst is the largest, as it has expanded on former farmland. Also nearby are Amherst College, Hampshire College and Smith College in Northampton. Noted abolitionist Thomas Wentworth Higginson was the pastor of the Free Church in Worcester during the 1850s. He also became a literary mentor to a young Emily Dickinson, who lived quietly most of her life in Amherst.

The 2nd Congressional District includes Worcester and part of Pioneer Valley. The population includes 9 percent Hispanics, and 5 percent each of Asians and blacks. To the north, it takes in Connecticut River towns such as Deerfield to the Vermont border. To the west is socially leftist Northampton. To the south, it includes Oxford, birthplace of American Red Cross founder Clara Barton; the Blackstone River Valley town of Millbury; and the mostly rural Sutton. The district extends east to Leominster (pronounced *LEMON-stir*), a western outpost of the Boston suburbs. Many of the small rural towns west of Worcester vote Republican. But the district overall is firmly Democratic.

THIRD DISTRICT

Niki Tsongas (D)

Elected 2007, 6th term; b. Apr 26, 1946, Chico, CA; Michigan State University (MI), Att., 1965; Smith College (MA), B.A., 1968; Boston University School of Law (MA), J.D., 1988; Episcopalian; Widow; 3 children.

Professional Career: Social worker; Practicing attorney; Dean of external affairs, Middlesex Comm. College, 1997-2007.

DC Office: 1714 LHOB 20515, 202-225-3411, Fax: 202-226-0771, tsongas.house.gov.

State Offices: Fitchburg, 978-459-0101; Haverhill, 978-459-0101; Lawrence, 978-459-0101; Lowell, 978-459-0101; Marlborough, 978-459-0101.

Committees: *Armed Services*: Military Personnel, Tactical Air & Land Forces (RMM). *Natural Resources*: Energy & Mineral Resources, Federal Lands.

Group Ratings

	ADA	ACLU	AFL-CIO	LCV	ITI	COC	HAFA	ACU	CFG	FRC
2016	-	100%	-	100%	60%	64%	12%	4%	0%	0%
2015	85%	C	100%	94%	C	40%	C	4%	0%	0%

Almanac Ratings 2015

	Economy	Social	Foreign	Composite
Liberal	98%	100%	99%	99%
Conservative	2%	0%	1%	1%

Key Votes of the 114th Congress

1. Keystone Pipeline	N	5. Puerto Rico Debt	Y	9. Offenses by Aliens	N
2. Trade Deals	N	6. Medical Marijuana	Y	10. Troops in Iraq	Y
3. Export-Import Bank	Y	7. Sanctuary Cities	N	11. Homeland Security $$	Y
4. Debt Ceiling Increase	Y	8. Armor-piercing Bullets	N	12. Trade Adjustment aid	Y

Election Results

Election	Name (Party)	Vote (%)	Cand. Spent	Ind. Exp. Support	Ind. Exp. Oppose
2016 General	Niki Tsongas (D)	236,713 (69%)	$899,047		
	Ann Wofford (R)	107,519 (31%)	$40,193		
2016 Primary	Niki Tsongas (D)	(100%)			

Prior winning percentages: 2014 (60%), 2012 (63%), 2010 (55%), 2008 (75%), 2007 special (52%)

Democrat Niki Tsongas, who won the seat in a 2007 special election, is the widow of Paul Tsongas and now a political force in her own right. She has had less of a media presence than many of her Massachusetts colleagues, but has gained recognition for her work on behalf of women in the military and in expansion of her husband's interest in urban national parks.

Growing up in an Air Force family, Tsongas never had a place to call home thanks to her father's frequent moves. While interning at the Pentagon as an undergraduate at Smith College, she was invited to a party where she met her future husband, who was an intern for 5th District Republican Rep. Brad Morse. On one of their early dates, he told her of his plans to get involved in electoral politics by running for the Lowell City Council. Niki followed him to Lowell in 1968 to help with his successful campaign for city councilor. They were married soon after. Tsongas often stumped for her husband during his various campaigns for office. "I couldn't have run for office if I hadn't spent time campaigning on my own," she said.

Paul Tsongas was first elected to the House in 1974 and to the Senate four years later. After retiring in 1984 with non-Hodgkin's lymphoma, he regained his health and launched a campaign for the 1992 Democratic presidential nomination. Although he won the New Hampshire primary, then-Arkansas Gov. Bill Clinton's surprise second-place finish in the Granite State gave him the momentum to overtake Tsongas, who withdrew in March. The Tsongases moved back to Lowell, and soon thereafter Paul's cancer returned. He succumbed to the disease in 1997.

After graduating from Boston University law school, and while acting as a political adviser to her husband, Tsongas started the first all-woman law firm in Lowell, raised their three daughters, and eventually took a job at Middlesex Community College as the dean of external affairs. When she ran for the open seat, Massachusetts had not had a female House member in 25 years, Tsongas was also motivated by the need for change in Washington and her strong disagreement with the Bush administration on the Iraq war.

Facing four other Democrats in a September primary, Tsongas drew heavily on her ties to Lowell and emphasized her husband's years representing the district. She erred during a debate in saying she spent 10 years in Washington representing the 5th District, a statement that actually described her husband's career. Tsongas' opponents seized on the comment to highlight her lack of elective experience. Tsongas edged out former Lowell mayor Eileen Donoghue, 36%-31%. In the general election, Tsongas faced a Republican with an intensely personal story and a recognizable name in the district. Retired Air Force Lt. Col. Jim Ogonowski's brother, John, was the pilot of the first plane to hit the World Trade Center on Sept. 11, 2001. Ogonowski criticized Tsongas for supporting a path to citizenship for illegal immigrants. Tsongas attacked Ogonowski for not supporting expansion of the Children's Health Insurance Program. Both national parties spent heavily on the race, and EMILY's List worked for Tsongas. Her victory was surprisingly close, 51%-45%. Tsongas handily took Lowell and Lawrence, plus the area closer to Boston.

In the House, Tsongas has been a reliable liberal who has backed her party on major votes. She occasionally goes her own way, including support for pay-as-you-go legislation requiring new spending to be offset, calling it a "critical first step" toward addressing the deficit. She reduced the amount of an excise tax on medical device manufacturers that was included in the health care overhaul law, and later joined Republicans in an effort to repeal it. She said the tax hurts small Massachusetts companies.

On the Armed Services Committee, Tsongas enacted provisions in defense spending bills speeding up development of lightweight body armor and protecting the legal rights of sexual assault victims. She helped persuade the Pentagon in 2012 to have assault cases reviewed by colonels rather than by company commanders, who often know the alleged assailants. Her efforts were featured in the documentary *The Invisible War*, which was nominated for an Academy Award in 2013. In the fiscal 2016 defense bill, she got approval of her provision that the Army should develop a comprehensive policy on breastfeeding for female soldiers. Meanwhile, each branch of the military implemented its own policy for nursing. "It's only when you have women at the table, and women as part of the military, that you force change," Tsongas has said. In 2017, she became ranking Democrat on the Tactical Air and Land Forces Subcommittee.

On the Natural Resources Committee, where she served two years as ranking Democrat on its Federal Lands Subcommittee, Tsongas worked to expand to other communities the concept of urban national parks, which Lowell pioneered. She worried that climate change could have a disastrous impact on traditional national parks, and has advocated more aggressive environmental stewardship of the sites. She filed a bill to assist urban communities to finance efforts to turn blighted environments into public parks or usable green spaces

After her tough contests a year earlier, Tsongas was reelected in 2008 without opposition. In 2010, the GOP nominee was Jon Golnik, a former Wall Street currency trader who enjoyed tea party backing and blasted Tsongas' votes on President Barack Obama's health care bill and other legislation. But he had to compete with the incumbent's overwhelming financial advantage - Tsongas raised more than $1.9 million to his $400,000. She won with 55 percent of the vote. Golnik returned for a rematch in 2012. But in a year in which Obama easily carried Massachusetts, Tsongas coasted with 66 percent. She considered, but ultimately decided against, running for the open Senate seat vacated in 2013 when Democrat John Kerry became Secretary of State. She is the most senior of the three women in the Massachusetts congressional delegation.

North Central Massachusetts: Lowell, Lawrence

Population		**Race and Ethnicity**		**Income**	
Total	749,922	White	69.6%	Median Income	$69,747 (74 out of 435)
Land area	758	Black	2.7%		
Pop/ sq mi	989.5	Latino	17.8%	Under $50,000	37.3%
Born in state	62.2%	Asian	7.5%	$50,000-$99,999	28.3%
		Two races	1.8%	$100,000-$199,999	25.6%
Age Groups		Other	0.6%	$200,000 or more	8.7%
Under 18	23.3%			Poverty Rate	11.9%
18-34	21.6%	**Education**			
35-64	42.3%	H.S grad or less	39.2%	**Health Insurance**	
Over 64	12.8%	Some college	24.5%	With health insurance coverage	96.0%
		College Degree, 4 yr	20.7%		
Work		Post grad	15.7%		
White Collar	42.4%			**Public Assistance**	
Sales and Service	38.4%	**Military**		Cash public assistance income	3.2%
Blue Collar	19.2%	Veteran	6.6%		
Government	11.9%	Active Duty	0.1%	Food stamp/SNAP benefits	13.9%

Voter Turnout			
2015 Total Citizens 18+	522,140	2016 House Turnout as % CVAP	66%
2016 House turnout	344,592	2014 House Turnout as % CVAP	42%

2012 Presidential Vote		
Barack Obama	189,461	(57%)
Mitt Romney	137,869	(41%)

2016 Presidential Vote		
Hillary Clinton	202,952	(57%)
Donald Trump	123,347	(35%)
Gary Johnson	17,580	(5%)

Cook Partisan Voting Index: D+9

When Massachusetts was a kind of maritime republic in the 19th century, with its farmers struggling to scratch out a living from the stony soil, a few clever Yankees used their profits from the sea trade to try to tame the rapidly flowing Merrimack River and build cotton-spinning mills. Creating the cities of Lowell and Lawrence, they built model dormitories and recreation programs for their female workers. This was the center of America's textile industry for more than a century, long after the maritime industry faded. But in the 1920s, the price of labor rose and newly built mills in the Carolinas, much closer to the cotton supply, decimated the local industry that Lawrence and Lowell built. Many residents waited forlornly for an upturn in the local economy.

It came eventually, from an unexpected source. The high-technology industry drove the growth, beginning in the 1960s around the Massachusetts Institute of Technology, then moving out to the Route 128 ring road and eventually to Interstate 495, which passes through once-distant Lowell and Lawrence. Wang, headquartered in Lowell, grew spectacularly, and Democratic Sen. Paul Tsongas - the local kid who made it big before his early death to cancer - spearheaded a historic restoration of the old mill area. This was the Massachusetts miracle of the 1980s. Then came the bust: Sales of Wang's word processors and minicomputers slumped as businesses purchased personal computers and linked them together in networks.

But Lowell revived again. New immigrants provided vitality and entrepreneurial creativity. Cambodians owned many small businesses and are more than 30,000 of the local population, making Lowell second only to Long Beach, California, as a U.S. home for transplanted Cambodians, who fled their homeland following the brutal "killing fields" of the 1970s. Although they have been slow to gain political influence. Their experience in Lowell has helped to preserve Cambodian heritage and culture. Some monks planned to build a Buddhist temple on the Merrimack River. The first Cambodian-American was elected to the state House in 2014. The old Wang buildings have been replaced with health care, banking, telecommunications and internet companies, plus fledgling renewable energy firms. Old mills have been converted to artists' lofts and upscale condos. In 2016, Lawrence ranked as the poorest city in the state.

The 3rd Congressional District of Massachusetts includes Lowell, Lawrence and the high-tech corridor along 1-495. The district includes tony suburbs near the Revolutionary War battleground of Concord, where the Minutemen stood their ground in 1775; rural and old mill towns that never revived in hills along the New Hampshire state line; and small towns west of Lowell. Except for Lowell and Lawrence, the district is ancestrally Yankee Republican. It is culturally liberal, with pockets of big wealth, and it trended Democratic in the early 1970s. Back then, this area produced two Democratic candidates who would later run for president after having succeeded each other in the Senate: Tsongas and John Kerry. Although it went Republican in national and some statewide elections in the 1980s, the district as a whole leans to the Democrats.

FOURTH DISTRICT

Joe Kennedy (D)

Elected 2012, 3rd term; b. Oct 04, 1980, Brighton; Buckingham Browne & Nichols School (MA); Stanford University (CA), Bach. Deg., 2003; Harvard University Law School (MA), J.D., 2009; Roman Catholic; Married (Lauren Birchfield); 1 child.

Professional Career: Peace Corps, 2004-2006; Assistant District Attorney, Cape & Islands, 2009-2011; Assistant District Attorney, Middlesex County, 2011-2012.

DC Office: 434 CHOB 20515, 202-225-5931, Fax: 202-225-0182, kennedy.house.gov.

State Offices: Attleboro, 508-431-1110; Newton, 617-332-3333.

Committees: *Energy & Commerce*: Digital Commerce & Consumer Protection, Energy, Health.

Group Ratings

	ADA	ACLU	AFL-CIO	LCV	ITI	COC	HAFA	ACU	CFG	FRC
2016	-	88%	-	92%	83%	69%	11%	0%	5%	9%
2015	95%	C	100%	100%	C	44%	C	5%	0%	18%

Almanac Ratings 2015

	Economy	Social	Foreign	Composite
Liberal	95%	89%	99%	94%
Conservative	5%	11%	1%	6%

Key Votes of the 114th Congress

1. Keystone Pipeline	N	5. Puerto Rico Debt	Y	9. Offenses by Aliens	N
2. Trade Deals	N	6. Medical Marijuana	N	10. Troops in Iraq	Y
3. Export-Import Bank	Y	7. Sanctuary Cities	N	11. Homeland Security $$	Y
4. Debt Ceiling Increase	Y	8. Armor-piercing Bullets	N	12. Trade Adjustment aid	Y

Election Results

Election	Name (Party)	Vote (%)	Cand. Spent	Ind. Exp. Support	Ind. Exp. Oppose
2016 General	Joe Kennedy (D)........................	265,823 (70%)	$1,770,555		
	David Rosa (R)........................	113,055 (30%)	$13,086		
2016 Primary	Joseph Kennedy III (D)............	(100%)			

Prior winning percentages: 2014 (72%), 2012 (59%)

The election to the House in 2012 of Democrat Joseph (Joe) Kennedy III, the grandson of the late Sen. Robert F. Kennedy, restored a Kennedy to Congress after a brief suspension when Rhode Island Rep. Patrick Kennedy retired in 2010. The third-generation Kennedy, while keeping a low profile as he learned his way, has become an informal leader of junior Democrats.

The son of former Rep. Joe Kennedy II, who represented the Cambridge-based district from 1987 to 1999, Kennedy was born in Brighton, attended the elite Buckingham, Browne and Nichols School and shuffled between his divorced parents' homes in Cambridge and Brighton with his fraternal twin, Matt. Both majored in management science and engineering at Stanford University, where Kennedy was also a starting lacrosse goalie and team co-captain with his brother. His teammates knew him as a committed teetotaler, reportedly ordering milk when they went to bars and nicknaming him "Milkman." After graduating in 2003, Kennedy embarked on two years in the Peace Corps. In the Dominican Republic, he helped to implement an economic development project. Fluent in Spanish, he has remained in touch with people he met there.

Kennedy helped Matt manage their great-uncle Edward Kennedy's 2006 Senate reelection campaign, and he went on to study law at Harvard, where he was active in the Legal Aid Bureau, working as an advocate for tenants facing eviction from foreclosed properties. He worked on the *Human Rights Journal* and started an after-school program for at-risk youth in Boston. After graduating, Kennedy was an assistant prosecutor in the Cape and Islands District Attorney's Office and moved up to assistant district attorney in Middlesex County in 2011.

When Democratic Rep. Barney Frank decided to retire, Kennedy moved to Brookline to run for the seat. The AFL-CIO quickly endorsed him, and other potential candidates decided not to challenge the family name and money. He made economic fairness the central theme of his fall campaign, talking often about the need to create equal opportunity for education and jobs. He also championed abortion rights. Kennedy got help from his family, with grandmother Ethel Kennedy and both of his parents standing on street corners for him. Matt remained his most trusted confidant. "A day doesn't go by when I don't talk to my twin brother," Joe told *National Journal*. Kennedy easily won the September primary with 90 percent of the vote.

Kennedy's Republican opponent, Marine reservist Sean Bielat, argued that Kennedy was running on his name. An October *Boston Globe* editorial echoed Bielat's criticism of Kennedy for not agreeing to more debates. Kennedy characterized Bielat as a rubber stamp for the budget proposals of Republican Rep. Paul Ryan of Wisconsin, including a plan to introduce vouchers into the Medicare program. Kennedy, who outspent Bielat, $3.9 million to $1.1 million, won the seat, 61%-36%, including by margins of 3-to-1 in Newton, and 4-to-1 in Brookline and Fall River.

Kennedy identified his chief priority as boosting economic opportunities in his district through improved education and job training. He was one of several chief sponsors of the Revitalize American Manufacturing Act, which called for a national manufacturing strategic plan and was enacted in 2014. With a coveted seat on the Energy and Commerce Committee, his priorities have included combating drug abuse and reducing energy prices. He has been a vocal advocate for STEM (science, technology, education and mathematics) funding. Even with his liberal voting record, he has styled himself as bipartisan and has reached out to Republicans - in part because that is the only way to get things done in a Republican-controlled House. He worked with Republican Rep. Susan Brooks of Indiana to solicit support for their bill to encourage education for opioid addiction prevention. Kennedy participates in an intense early-morning fitness program led by Republican Rep. Markwayne Mullin of Oklahoma, with whom he serves on Energy and Commerce.

While emphasizing that he was building his own record and not relying on his famous name, he knows that it is unlikely he would have made it to Congress at his age without those connections. Democratic Leader Nancy Pelosi considered Kennedy for chairman of the Democratic Congressional Campaign Committee before selecting Ben Ray Lujan of New Mexico. He has taken advantage of his opportunities, including impressive fund-raising skills. He raised a total of $10 million by 2016, and began the next cycle with a $2.8 million surplus. Against a token Republican challenger in 2016, he got 70 percent of the vote.

In what seemed a revealing acknowledgment, Kennedy said he would "take a look" at a vacant Senate seat if home-state Sen. Elizabeth Warren had been elected vice president in 2016. At the Democratic National Convention that year, he introduced Warren - his former law professor - as "the toughest teacher on campus, but the wait list for her class was a mile long." With both Massachusetts senators eligible for Social Security, it's reasonable to view the latest Kennedy as near the front of the line of that wait list. Another metaphor alert: Since his election to the House, he has run the Boston Marathon.

Western Boston Suburbs, Southern Massachusetts

Population		**Race and Ethnicity**		**Income**	
Total	742,694	White	85.1%	Median Income	$87,821 (22 out of 435)
Land area	668	Black	2.5%		
Pop/ sq mi	1111.4	Latino	4.2%	Under $50,000	29.4%
Born in state	60.8%	Asian	5.8%	$50,000-$99,999	26.3%
		Two races	1.9%	$100,000-$199,999	29.2%
Age Groups		Other	0.4%	$200,000 or more	15.2%
Under 18	23.2%			Poverty Rate	7.1%
18-34	20.1%	**Education**			
35-64	42.4%	H.S grad or less	28.6%	**Health Insurance**	
Over 64	14.3%	Some college	22.2%	With health insurance coverage	97.5%
		College Degree, 4 yr	25.4%		
Work		Post grad	23.8%		
White Collar	50.5%			**Public Assistance**	
Sales and Service	36.1%	**Military**		Cash public assistance income	2.1%
Blue Collar	13.4%	Veteran	6.3%		
Government	11.5%	Active Duty	0.0%	Food stamp/SNAP benefits	7.9%

Voter Turnout			
2015 Total Citizens 18+	537,946	2016 House Turnout as % CVAP	70%
2016 House turnout	379,213	2014 House Turnout as % CVAP	35%

2012 Presidential Vote		
Barack Obama	211,423	(57%)
Mitt Romney	152,699	(41%)

2016 Presidential Vote		
Hillary Clinton	225,976	(58%)
Donald Trump	133,705	(34%)
Gary Johnson	17,360	(5%)

Cook Partisan Voting Index: D+9

The political transformation of Massachusetts is nowhere better illustrated than in the Boston suburbs of Newton and Brookline. These were Yankee enclaves a century ago, with avenues built to resemble the sweep of Haussmann's Grand Boulevards in Paris. Brookline was where the country club (the very first one) was established in 1882, and where Joseph Kennedy, an Irish Catholic, 20-something banker seeking respectability, moved his family in 1914. Brookline and Newton then were solidly Republican, the base of such leading politicians as Christian Herter, the governor of Massachusetts and U.S. Secretary of State in the 1950s. As late as 1960, Brookline, Newton and adjacent wards of Boston were electing a Republican to Congress.

Then came the transformation, personified by the election in 1962 of Michael Dukakis at age 29 to the General Court (the legislature). As Massachusetts' university-educated classes became more liberal, as Jewish populations of Brookline and Newton grew, and as young, liberal-minded families refurbished the graceful old houses, these towns became Democratic bastions. Now there are growing numbers of Russian Jews and Orthodox and Hasidic synagogues. The towns continue to diversify. Brookline is now

19 percent Asian, and nearly half of its school students are non-white. A local public school teaches Mandarin in kindergarten. In 2016, Newton was 31st when *Money* magazine ranked the "Best Places to Live in America." With a median price of $1.6 million, Brookline had the most expensive homes in the state.

The 4th Congressional District of Massachusetts starts with Brookline and Newton at its northern tip. Anchoring the district, they account for about a fifth of its population. About 40 miles away at the southern end of this district are the Bristol County cities of Freetown, Somerset and part of Fall River. Much of the port in Fall River has been rebuilt, chiefly for non-commercial purposes, including Heritage State Park and the boardwalk along the water. The northern and southern ends of the districts are very different sociologically and economically - affluent Boston suburbs suffered relatively little in the recession, the old textile-mill town of Fall River, quite a lot. Connecting them is a corridor with a variety of towns - Foxborough with its Patriots football stadium; Sharon with its Orthodox Jews; Dover, the home of some old-time Boston Brahmins; and Wellesley with its college and high-income residents. Hopkinton is 26 miles, 385 yards from downtown Boston. Politically, these areas historically were mostly Republican but in recent decades they have been, like most of middle-income Massachusetts, Democratic.

FIFTH DISTRICT

Katherine Clark (D)

Elected 2013, 3rd term; b. Jul 17, 1963, New Haven, CT; St. Lawrence University (NY), B.A.; Cornell University Law School (NY), J.D.; Harvard University John F. Kennedy School of Government (MA), M.P.A.; Protestant; Married (Rodney Dowell); 3 children.

Elected Office: MA House, 2008-2011; MA Senate, 2011-2013.

Professional Career: Clerk, Hon. Alfred Arraj, 1990-1991; Prosecutor, Colorado Attorney General office, 1991-1993; General counsel, MA Office of Child Care Svcs.; Policy Division Chief, MA Attorney General.

DC Office: 1415 LHOB 20515, 202-225-2836, Fax: 202-226-0092, katherineclark.house.gov.

State Offices: Cambridge, 617-354-0292; Framingham, 508-319-9757.

Committees: *Appropriations*: Labor, Health & Human Services, Education & Related Agencies, Transportation, HUD & Related Agencies.

Group Ratings

	ADA	ACLU	AFL-CIO	LCV	ITI	COC	HAFA	ACU	CFG	FRC
2016	-	100%	-	100%	50%	50%	12%	0%	4%	0%
2015	100%	C	100%	100%	C	50%	C	4%	0%	0%

Almanac Ratings 2015

	Economy	Social	Foreign	Composite
Liberal	93%	100%	100%	98%
Conservative	8%	0%	0%	3%

Key Votes of the 114th Congress

1. Keystone Pipeline	N	5. Puerto Rico Debt	Y	9. Offenses by Aliens	N
2. Trade Deals	N	6. Medical Marijuana	Y	10. Troops in Iraq	Y
3. Export-Import Bank	Y	7. Sanctuary Cities	N	11. Homeland Security $$	Y
4. Debt Ceiling Increase	Y	8. Armor-piercing Bullets	NV	12. Trade Adjustment aid	Y

Election Results

Election	Name (Party)	Vote (%)	Cand. Spent	Ind. Exp. Support	Ind. Exp. Oppose
2016 General	Katherine Clark (D)......................	285,606 (99%)	$604,532		
2016 Primary	Katherine Clark (D)..................................	(100%)			

Prior winning percentages: 2014 (71%), 2013 special (66%)

Democrat Katherine Clark won a 2013 special election that resulted when previous Rep. Edward Markey, in turn, won a special election six months earlier to fill the Senate seat of John Kerry, who had become Secretary of State. With her policymaking experience in state government and legislative savvy, plus her eagerness to work with more senior Democrats on the party's message, she gained a quick start among liberal advocates.

Clark was born and raised in New Haven, Connecticut, and graduated from St. Lawrence University, where she majored in history. She got her law degree at Cornell University in New York before moving to Chicago and California to practice law. In 1995, Clark relocated to Massachusetts to earn a master's in public administration from Harvard's Kennedy School of Government. She then worked as general counsel for the Massachusetts Office of Child Care Services and as policy chief for Attorney General Martha Coakley. She was elected to the state House in 2008 and two years later to the state Senate, where she chaired the Judiciary Committee.

Markey had represented the 5th District since 1976, and his promotion set off a scramble for the safe Democratic seat among party members with years of pent-up political ambition. In the Democratic primary, Clark competed against six candidates, including Middlesex County Sheriff Peter Koutoujin, and three other state lawmakers. Her early start gave her an edge financially and in the polls. Clark focused her campaign on issues that appealed to her party's base, including equal pay for women and abortion rights. She vowed to fight "extremist Republicans" in Congress who, she said, opposed pay equity and access to women's health care.

Clark wove the stories of her grandmother, a machinist during World War II, and her mother, who was discouraged from pursuing engineering as a young girl, into her TV ads. And she discussed her husband and three young sons to repeatedly make the point that "women's issues are family issues." Clark won the endorsement of Coakley in the primary and received a fundraising boost from the abortion-rights group EMILY's List, which proved a boon in a race where progressive and labor endorsements were fractured. She prevailed in the primary with 32 percent of the vote, to 22 percent for Koutoujin. The sheriff and the other state legislators each won in targeted precincts. Only Clark showed strength across the district. She won easily in the December general election, defeating perennial Republican candidate Frank Addivinola with 66 percent of the vote.

In her early work in the House, Clark gave particular attention to problems facing very young children. Reviewing her first year, she highlighted the enactment, as the result of Senate action, of her proposal to add infant and toddler care improvement to child care block grants to the states. In 2015, she filed a bill to improve education for children up to age 5 who experience higher barriers to learning because of chronic stress or trauma outside of school. With Republican Rep. Steve Stivers of Ohio, she filed a bill to assist hospitals to diagnose and treat the large increase in the number of babies who are born with drug withdrawal, which is referred to as neonatal abstinence syndrome.

Clark played a crucial role in organizing what became an unprecedented sit-in on the House floor in June 2016 by Democrats angered by inaction on gun-control legislation, especially following the terrorist shooting attack at Pulse night club in Orlando, Florida. As she described to *Time*, Clark told Rep. John Lewis of Georgia that the typical moment of silence in the House was not a sufficient response. "I wanted to do something to keep gun violence in the forefront of not only the American people but, more specifically, members of Congress and [Lewis] suggested, in his words, that we do something dramatic, and he suggested having a sit-in, and it really went from there," recalled Clark, who had tried civil rights cases in private practice. "When you have John Lewis, such an icon of the civil rights fight for justice, you know that good things are going to happen." Lewis told *Time* that Clark should be credited for the sit-in idea. In photos of that overnight event, Clark was seated on the House floor next to Lewis - which, as some observers whimsically noted, was a relationship of historical pioneers.

The House sit-in, which was designed to force the hand of Speaker Paul Ryan, had an embarrassing aspect. As Clark described during a subsequent speech to business leaders from New England, her initial conversation with Ryan a few months earlier had been unusually awkward. While engaging in chit-chat at a Washington airport two years after she had been elected to the House, Clark said that she told Ryan that she was Katherine Clark from Massachusetts and that he unknowingly asked her, "So, Katherine, what do you do?" As she told her business audience, Ryan was "horrified" that he initially did not recognize her, according to the report in the Fitchburg *Sentinel and Enterprise*. Ryan subsequently sent her a personal note that she was his "new Democratic best friend." But, she added, "I have tried our friendship since then."

A few days after the 2016 election, Clark tried to gain the attention of Donald Trump by filing a bill that she called the Presidential Accountability Act, which would require the president and vice president to put their assets in a blind trust or disclose to the Office of Government Ethics when decisions are made that would affect their personal finances. Trump did not respond to the proposal. In January 2017, she gained additional influence with a seat on the House Appropriations Committee.

At home, Clark has been reelected twice without opposition and seems entrenched in her seat.

Northern and Western Boston Suburbs

Population		Race and Ethnicity		Income	
Total	749,525	White	73.7%	Median Income	$82,616 (28 out of 435)
Land area	265	Black	4.5%		
Pop/ sq mi	2827.5	Latino	8.4%	Under $50,000	31.3%
Born in state	54.0%	Asian	10.5%	$50,000-$99,999	26.9%
		Two races	2.3%	$100,000-$199,999	28.2%
Age Groups		Other	0.6%	$200,000 or more	13.6%
Under 18	20.1%			Poverty Rate	8.4%
18-34	24.7%	**Education**			
35-64	40.7%	H.S grad or less	27.5%	**Health Insurance**	
Over 64	14.5%	Some college	18.5%	With health insurance coverage	96.8%
		College Degree, 4 yr	26.9%		
Work		Post grad	27.1%		
White Collar	53.5%			**Public Assistance**	
Sales and Service	35.7%	**Military**		Cash public assistance income	1.8%
Blue Collar	10.9%	Veteran	5.0%		
Government	10.3%	Active Duty	0.1%	Food stamp/SNAP benefits	7.4%

Voter Turnout			
2015 Total Citizens 18+	515,129	2016 House Turnout as % CVAP	56%
2016 House turnout	289,807	2014 House Turnout as % CVAP	35%

2012 Presidential Vote		
Barack Obama	235,984	(65%)
Mitt Romney	119,934	(33%)

2016 Presidential Vote		
Hillary Clinton	258,908	(68%)
Donald Trump	95,922	(25%)
Gary Johnson	13,712	(4%)

Cook Partisan Voting Index: D+18

The Yankee Protestants and Irish Catholics who settled Massachusetts arrived by boat, the Yankees to a cold, stony land with a few Indians, the Irish to a crowded city with Yankees who seemed no more welcoming. The Yankees whose ancestors once farmed the soil had, by the early 20th century, founded suburbs filled with solid brick and white frame houses. As the years went on, their local public schools emptied as young people with children moved out, and attendance at Protestant churches fell. The Irish, for decades heavily concentrated in the crowded wards of Boston, started moving out to the suburbs after World War II. There were other ethnic groups here and there (Jews, Italians, French Canadians), but the major conflict - fought out in neighborhood playgrounds, in school committee meetings, and not least in political campaigns - was between Protestant Yankee Republicans and Catholic Irish Democrats. These days, much of the local conflict is among the university towns - Cambridge as the epicenter of Harvard University; Medford, home of Tufts University; and Waltham, home of Brandeis University.

The 5th Congressional District of Massachusetts is made up of northern and western Boston suburbs, where vestiges of the cultural conflict can still be seen. Geographically, the district forms an arc around Boston, starting with the clapboard beach towns of Winthrop and Revere just beyond Logan Airport, going north as far as working-class Woburn (where Charles Goodyear developed the art of vulcanizing rubber) and encompassing Natick and Framingham, the headquarters town of Staples and TJX (T.J. Maxx, Marshalls, HomeGoods). The economy in Framingham has been healthy and diverse; the town also is diverse culturally, with 67 languages spoken in the public schools. In November 2016, Framingham's unemployment rate was just 2.1 percent, the lowest of Massachusetts' metropolitan areas. In 2014, MassBay Community College agreed to a new $60 million campus in downtown Framingham; two years later, it was continuing to search for a location. The long-delayed and over-budget Green Line rapid-transit extension to Medford was scheduled to open in 2018.

The 5th extends south to take in Ashland, Holliston and Sherborn, and west to take in most of Sudbury and Wayland. Sudbury is home to the historic Longfellow's Wayside Inn, which was renamed after Henry Wadsworth Longfellow's 1863 book *Tales of a Wayside Inn* made it a sightseeing attraction. In Lexington, minutemen fired the shots heard 'round the world in 1775. With the universities' presence, high technology and biotechnology have become driving forces of economic growth in the area.

Politically, the district is solidly Democratic. In the 2016 presidential campaign, this was the second strongest Democratic-performing district in Massachusetts, behind only the 7th District. Hillary Clinton led, 68%-25%, a modest increase over the 65%-33% margin for President Barack Obama in his 2012 reelection.

SIXTH DISTRICT

Seth Moulton (D)

Elected 2014, 2nd term; b. Oct 24, 1978, Salem; Phillips Academy, (MA), 1997; Harvard University, B.S., 2001; Harvard Business School (MA), M.B.A., 2011; Harvard University John F. Kennedy School of Government (MA), M.P.A., 2011; Christian - Non-Denominational; Single.

Military Career: U.S Marine Corps, 2002-2008.

Professional Career: Railway managing director, 2011-2012; Health care company president, 2012-2013.

DC Office: 1408 LHOB 20515, 202-225-8020, Fax: 202-225-5915, moulton.house.gov.

State Offices: Salem, 978-531-1669.

Committees: *Armed Services*: Oversight & Investigations (RMM), Seapower & Projection Forces. *Budget*.

Group Ratings

	ADA	ACLU	AFL-CIO	LCV	ITI	COC	HAFA	ACU	CFG	FRC
2016	-	88%	-	100%	67%	64%	12%	0%	4%	0%
2015	90%	C	100%	97%	C	55%	C	0%	0%	0%

Almanac Ratings 2015

	Economy	Social	Foreign	Composite
Liberal	87%	100%	93%	93%
Conservative	13%	0%	7%	7%

Key Votes of the 114th Congress

1. Keystone Pipeline	N	5. Puerto Rico Debt	Y	9. Offenses by Aliens	N
2. Trade Deals	N	6. Medical Marijuana	Y	10. Troops in Iraq	N
3. Export-Import Bank	Y	7. Sanctuary Cities	N	11. Homeland Security $$	Y
4. Debt Ceiling Increase	Y	8. Armor-piercing Bullets	N	12. Trade Adjustment aid	Y

Election Results

Election	Name (Party)	Vote (%)	Cand. Spent	Ind. Exp. Support	Ind. Exp. Oppose
2016 General	Seth Moulton (D)........................	308,923 (98%)	$1,346,691		
2016 Primary	Seth Moulton (D)........................	(100%)			

Prior winning percentages: 2014 (54%)

Democrat Seth Moulton, a former Marine captain and Iraq War veteran, was elected in 2014. With unusual candor in the typically disciplined Democratic Caucus, he was outspoken in demanding explanations and accountability for the 2016 election setbacks. His actions placed him at the forefront of Democrats seeking a post-Nancy Pelosi generation of leadership. His legislative focus has been chiefly on military issues.

Moulton was born in Salem and grew up in Marblehead, the eldest of three siblings. He attended Phillips Academy Andover, an elite boarding school. He got his bachelor's degree in physics from

Harvard University, delivering the Undergraduate English Oration at his commencement in which he focused on the importance of service. He joined the Marine Corps, graduated from Officer Candidate School as a second lieutenant and was among the first soldiers to enter Baghdad at the beginning of the Iraq War. He served four tours of duty from 2004 to 2008, and in 2008 he was a special liaison with tribal leaders in southern Iraq at the request of Gen. David Petraeus. He left the Marines with the rank of captain. He later earned his M.B.A. and master's in public policy from Harvard.

He decided to get involved in politics while still in the Marines. "I actually remember the moment," he told *The Atlantic*. "It was after a difficult day in Najaf in 2004. A young marine in my platoon said, 'Sir, you should run for Congress someday. So this s- doesn't happen again.'" He considered running as an independent candidate in 2012 against embattled Democratic Rep. John Tierney, but decided against it. A close ally of Pelosi, Tierney was under fire because his wife, Patrice, had pleaded guilty to helping her brother file false tax returns; Republicans charged that the congressman must have been aware of the activity. He eked out a 48%-47% victory against Richard Tisei, whose résumé - he is gay and a fiscal conservative who vocally opposed the social policy of his party - made him just the sort of Republican who can win in a part of deep-blue Massachusetts. Tisei ran again in 2014 and appeared well-positioned to take Tierney out.

The Republican plans were foiled when Moulton challenged Tierney in the Democratic primary, secured *The Boston Globe*'s endorsement, and won the nomination 51%-41%. Without the baggage of Tierney, Moulton ran as a progressive Democrat and cast Tisei, who was first elected to the state Legislature in 1984, as a political insider. "We won't get fresh thinking and new leadership by sending someone to Washington who was first elected to office when I was just 6 years old," Moulton said after winning the primary. Tisei offered himself up as an independent thinker who favored limited government and would be a Bay State ambassador to the GOP majority in the House. Moulton won endorsements from Petraeus, retired Army Gen. Stanley McChrystal, and former New York City Mayor Michael Bloomberg. He outspent Tisei $3.3 million to $2 million and won 55%-41%. Each candidate was aided by millions of dollars from national parties and outside groups.

Moulton immediately began drawing attention for his unusual-for-a-Democrat resume. He vowed not to be a typical congressman, saying he told his former Marine buddies to watch him closely. "It's very important when you go to Washington to try and keep yourself grounded," he told *Politico*. "I've asked a few guys in particular to in fact speak up and call me out if I become quote-unquote 'one of them.'"

Following a bumpy transition to the House when Tierney refused to talk to him, Moulton got an opportunity to show his expertise with a seat on the Armed Services Committee, where he has become the ranking Democrat on the Oversight and Investigations Subcommittee. He made three trips to the Middle East, to visit with troops and understand the fight against the Islamic State. He has been outspoken on the need to have a plan to win the peace in Iraq and the Middle East. The key to success, he said, would be "to provide the Iraqi government with diplomatic and political support, and empower Iraqi leaders to take on this fight." In May 2016, he criticized the Obama administration's overall approach, as well as President Barack Obama's refusal to say that American troops deployed to Iraq were on a combat mission. "The bottom line is that we have a military strategy to defeat ISIS, but we don't have any long-term political strategy to ensure the peace." He focused on improving veterans' health care. Obama signed his Faster Care for Veterans Act, which enabled vets to use their phones or computers to schedule medical appointments.

Moulton kept up the criticism with the new president. Donald Trump and his political advisers "use lies to manipulate what Americans think, to pit us against one another, and to pervert our democracy to attain power," he wrote in an op-ed two weeks after Trump took office. "We are at a singularly dangerous point in our nation's history." Concerned about Trump's early refugee and immigration bans, he joined a bipartisan group of House members who were military veterans to urge exceptions for people who risked their lives to aid U.S. forces.

Following the election, he stepped forward with other junior House Democrats in demanding a deeper review of the party's failures and discussion of new directions. In a post-election Tweet, he wrote, "In the Marines, my job was clear: 'You are responsible for everything your platoon does or fails to do.' We need that in Congress." Many colleagues had told him that the status quo and that Democrats had gained only six House seats were unacceptable, he said. He was an early supporter of Rep. Tim Ryan of Ohio in his challenge to Pelosi for minority leader. The lengthy discussions within the Democratic Caucus resulted in some sharing of authority with the rank-and-file, though no changes in specific leadership posts. Despite his distancing from Pelosi, Moulton signed up in 2017 as a senior whip with House Minority Whip Steny Hoyer of Maryland. He also became vice chairman of the informal Bipartisan Working Group.

At home, Moulton was reelected without major-party opposition. Even with his commitment not to become "one of them," he remained ambitious to move up the political ladder - in the House and perhaps beyond. He welcomed news-media speculation that he was thinking about running for President.

North Shore

Population		**Race and Ethnicity**		**Income**	
Total	749,825	White	83.3%	Median Income	$79,695 (37 out of 435)
Land area	527	Black	2.8%		
Pop/ sq mi	1423.4	Latino	8.0%	Under $50,000	32.1%
Born in state	70.7%	Asian	4.0%	$50,000-$99,999	28.2%
		Two races	1.5%	$100,000-$199,999	29.2%
Age Groups		Other	0.4%	$200,000 or more	10.5%
Under 18	21.4%			Poverty Rate	8.0%
18-34	20.1%	**Education**			
35-64	42.4%	H.S grad or less	33.1%	**Health Insurance**	
Over 64	16.1%	Some college	25.3%	With health insurance coverage	97.0%
Work		College Degree, 4 yr	24.9%		
White Collar	44.8%	Post grad	16.8%	**Public Assistance**	
Sales and Service	40.2%	**Military**		Cash public assistance income	2.5%
Blue Collar	15.1%	Veteran	7.4%		
Government	12.4%	Active Duty	0.1%	Food stamp/SNAP benefits	9.5%

Voter Turnout			
2015 Total Citizens 18+	552,185	2016 House Turnout as % CVAP	57%
2016 House turnout	314,055	2014 House Turnout as % CVAP	49%

2012 Presidential Vote		
Barack Obama	212,003	(55%)
Mitt Romney	169,966	(44%)

2016 Presidential Vote		
Hillary Clinton	224,858	(55%)
Donald Trump	153,244	(38%)
Gary Johnson	18,124	(4%)

Cook Partisan Voting Index: D+6

The North Shore of Massachusetts Bay has often been at the leading edge of the nation's economy. In 1640, the Saugus Iron Works was built here - the beginning of American heavy industry. When Europe's great powers were convulsed in international war from 1792 to 1815, American shipowners suddenly became the richest in the world, and traders from Boston and Salem accumulated the capital needed to build textile mills and railroads and to finance much of the American Industrial Revolution. From the small port of Salem, ships left for China, bringing back porcelain and artifacts. Salem had the nation's first millionaire, Elias Hasket Derby. In 1900, it was the richest city per capita in the nation.

Today, the North Shore is less robust economically and more competitive politically than elsewhere in Massachusetts. From Boston Harbor north to the mouth of the Merrimack River, it is a collection of ethnic factory towns from Lynn to Peabody (once one of the world's great leather producers, with more than 100 tanneries) to the former shipbuilding Newburyport. There are a few high-income enclaves, such as Marblehead with its yachts. Coastal towns include artsy Rockport and the fishing center of Gloucester. Salem's House of the Seven Gables is a popular tourist site. Built in 1668, it inspired the novel by Nathaniel Hawthorne and is the oldest surviving wooden mansion in New England. The Salem witch trials are the town's most famous legacy, and local officials have capitalized with Halloween festivities that contribute to Salem's $100 million annual tourism industry.

The 6th Congressional District includes the North Shore from Saugus and Lynn northward to the New Hampshire line, plus towns and cities inland west to Tewksbury and Bedford. The district is mostly based in Essex County, but includes part of Middlesex County. The General Electric jet engine plant, the largest employer in the city, has seen its payroll drop from a peak of 13,000 in 1985 to 2,800 jobs in 2016. It produces helicopter engines for the Black Hawk troop transport and jet engines for the F-18 Super Hornet fighter. In November 2015, Republican Gov. Charlie Baker created a task force to seek options for encouraging development in Lynn, where the poverty rate was twice as high as in the state overall. Revival of the port, with residential housing, has been a priority. In 2014, the state subsidized a seasonal commuter ferry from Lynn to Boston, but the service struggled financially.

While the district is the site of the original gerrymander - named after Elbridge Gerry, who served two terms as governor before winning election as vice president with President James Madison - the current boundaries are hardly grotesque by contemporary standards. The district's high-income Yankee towns historically were liberal Republican, while the old mill towns of Lynn, Salem, Peabody and Merrimac were Irish working-class Democratic. As has been the case elsewhere in reaction to Donald Trump, some of those affiliations have reversed themselves. The 6th has leaned Democratic since the 1960s, although it twice elected a Republican in the 1990s. In 2012, this was President Barack Obama's worst district in Massachusetts, when he won 55%-44%. Hillary Clinton led 55%-38%, which was her second-poorest in the state, behind the 9th District.

SEVENTH DISTRICT

Michael Capuano (D)

Elected 1998, 10th term; b. Jan 09, 1952, Somerville; Dartmouth College, B.A., 1973; Boston College Law School (MA), J.D., 1977; Roman Catholic; Married (Barbara Teebagy Capuano); 2 children.

Elected Office: Somerville alderman, Ward 5, 1977-1979; Somerville alderman-at-large, 1985-1989; Somerville Mayor, 1990-1998.

Professional Career: Chief legal counsel, MA Legislature Taxation Committee, 1978-1984; Practicing attorney, 1984-1990.

DC Office: 1414 LHOB 20515, 202-225-5111, Fax: 202-225-9322; Website: capuano.house.gov.

State Offices: Cambridge, 617-621-6208; Roxbury, 617-621-6208.

Committees: *Financial Services*: Financial Institutions & Consumer Credit, Housing & Insurance, Oversight & Investigations. *Transportation & Infrastructure*: Aviation, Economic Dev't, Public Buildings & Emergency Management, Highways & Transit, Railroads, Pipelines & Hazardous Materials (RMM).

Group Ratings

	ADA	ACLU	AFL-CIO	LCV	ITI	COC	HAFA	ACU	CFG	FRC
2016	-	100%	-	100%	50%	23%	14%	0%	0%	0%
2015	100%	C	100%	97%	C	45%	C	4%	3%	8%

Almanac Ratings 2015

	Economy	Social	Foreign	Composite
Liberal	88%	100%	100%	96%
Conservative	12%	0%	0%	4%

Key Votes of the 114th Congress

1. Keystone Pipeline	N	5. Puerto Rico Debt	Y	9. Offenses by Aliens	N
2. Trade Deals	N	6. Medical Marijuana	Y	10. Troops in Iraq	Y
3. Export-Import Bank	Y	7. Sanctuary Cities	N	11. Homeland Security $$	Y
4. Debt Ceiling Increase	Y	8. Armor-piercing Bullets	N	12. Trade Adjustment aid	Y

Election Results

Election	Name (Party)	Vote (%)	Cand. Spent	Ind. Exp. Support	Ind. Exp. Oppose
2016 General	Michael Capuano (D)...............	253,354 (99%)	$372,394		
2016 Primary	Michael Capuano (D)............................	(100%)			

Prior winning percentages: 2014 (81%), 2012 (74%), 2010 (98%), 2008 (76%), 2006 (79%), 2004 (77%), 2002 (72%), 2000(71%), 1998 (82%)

Blunt-talking liberal Michael Capuano won a 10-candidate brawl in the 1998 Democratic primary and has been safe ever since. His early days as a loyal soldier for Democratic Leader Nancy Pelosi have evolved, as he has failed in his hopes to move to the Senate and voiced doubts that she could lead a Democratic return to the House majority.

Capuano was born and raised in Somerville. His paternal grandfather emigrated from Italy, and his father was the first Italian-American elected official in Somerville. His mother is the granddaughter of Irish immigrants. Capuano graduated from Dartmouth and Boston College Law School. He returned to Somerville to raise his family, practice law and enter politics. By day, he worked for the legislature's Joint Committee on Taxation and practiced law. In off-hours, he served as alderman of the 5th Ward, as his father had. He won election five times as Somerville mayor. For decades an Irish and Italian town, Somerville has become dominated by graduate students and young couples. Capuano seems to have been the right politician for this mix, with deep Somerville roots and a penchant for innovation and reform.

He had a solid base of support to run for the House seat when Joe Kennedy II declined to seek reelection. In a 10-candidate field, Capuano led with 23 percent, with former Boston Mayor Ray Flynn the runner-up at 17 percent. He has not faced a serious challenge since.

In the House, Capuano has been among the most liberal Democrats - a status confirmed by the *Almanac* vote ratings for 2015. He harshly criticized the Bush administration's handling of the war in Iraq, and questioned President Barack Obama's decision in 2011 to order air strikes against Libya without congressional approval. On the Financial Services Committee, he proposed in 2012 the merger of the Securities and Exchange Commission with the Commodities Futures Trading Commission to try to prevent financial disasters like the $1.2 billion loss at derivatives broker MF Global. On the Transportation and Infrastructure Committee, Capuano unsuccessfully sought in 2011 to amend a Federal Aviation Administration reauthorization bill to require greater disclosure of a passenger's baggage fees when a fare is quoted. After years of effort, he got final approval in 2015 of the Green Line rapid-transit extension from Cambridge to Somerville and Medford, which is scheduled for completion in 2018. He is ranking Democrat on the Railroads, Pipelines and Hazardous Materials Subcommittee. During 2016 action on an FAA bill, he won committee approval of his proposal to increase the rest time between work shifts for flight attendants.

Capuano has been close to Pelosi, who shares with Capuano an urban, ethnic political background. After Democrats won the majority in 2006, Pelosi put Capuano in charge of the transition. Tasked with helping to revise party caucus rules and ethics guidelines, Capuano emphasized inclusion and reform. In 2008, the House passed his chief proposal, creating an Office of Congressional Ethics, an independent board that for the first time allowed non-lawmakers to review possible ethics violations by House members; many House members from both parties later complained about the board. While Democrats held the majority, he chaired the Commission on Mailing Standards, which supervises franked mail, another sensitive insider task that requires the trust of House leaders. Republicans groused about possible free speech violations in a Capuano proposal to require House approval of members' postings on outside websites, but he responded that the criticism was "laughably inaccurate."

Capuano has a penchant for taking on the political elite. The *Boston Herald* observed in a 2012 editorial that he "has this unorthodox (for a politician) habit of telling the unvarnished truth." In 2013, he told the leaders of eight banks that took a government bailout, "All or most of you engaged in all or some of the activities that created this crisis. You come here today on your bicycles after buying Girl Scout cookies and helping out Mother Teresa. You're saying, 'We're sorry. We didn't mean it. We won't do it again. Trust us.' America doesn't trust you anymore."

In 2010, before Democrats were swamped in the election, Capuano complained about Obama and his top advisers to *The Daily Beast* website: "They're too disconnected from the grass roots and members of the House close to the grass roots," he said. After Democrats lost their House majority in the election, and despite his alliance with Pelosi, he said that the entire leadership team should step down, telling *Politico*, "If the Red Sox came in and lost every game of the year and they kept the manager at the end of the year, that's a problem. That's what we seem to be on the verge of doing." He nonetheless supported Pelosi for minority leader. His candid advice that she should step down intensified in April 2015. With Democrats' hopes for the majority having faded, he told a Boston public television station, "I think we need leadership that understands that, if something you're doing is not working, change what you're doing." Following the 2016 election, he was among the Democrats who urged a serious autopsy.

After Democratic Sen. Edward Kennedy died in 2009, Capuano entered the special election for the remainder of his term. Pelosi endorsed him and came to his defense when Democratic candidate Martha Coakley, the state attorney general, criticized his vote in 2009 for the health care overhaul that included an amendment banning coverage for abortions in insurance plans receiving federal funds. He emphasized his vote against the Patriot Act and its provision authorizing roving wiretaps. Coakley had superior name recognition and won the primary 47%-28%; she stunningly lost the general election to Republican Scott Brown. Capuano considered running against Brown in 2012, but deferred to progressive folk hero Elizabeth Warren and was an enthusiastic surrogate in her successful challenge. After the election, when Obama named Sen. John Kerry as his Secretary of State, Capuano considered running for Kerry's seat but again deferred, this time to fellow Rep. Ed Markey.

Capuano's days of revived influence seem pegged to the perhaps distant prospect of Democrats regaining House control. In such a scenario, his growing seniority would serve him well.

Boston, Somerville, Cambridge

Population		**Race and Ethnicity**		**Income**	
Total	758,973	White	41.9%	Median Income	$53,401 (208 out of 435)
Land area	63	Black	23.6%		
Pop/ sq mi	12110.6	Latino	20.8%		
Born in state	43.3%	Asian	9.7%	Under $50,000	47.2%
Age Groups		Two races	2.6%	$50,000-$99,999	26.6%
Under 18	17.4%	Other	1.4%	$100,000-$199,999	19.5%
18-34	39.1%	**Education**		$200,000 or more	6.7%
35-64	33.4%	H.S grad or less	39.9%	Poverty Rate	20.9%
Over 64	10.2%	Some college	18.9%	**Health Insurance**	
Work		College Degree, 4 yr	21.8%	With health insurance coverage	94.7%
White Collar	44.3%	Post grad	19.3%		
Sales and Service	43.1%	**Military**		**Public Assistance**	
Blue Collar	12.5%	Veteran	3.2%	Cash public assistance income	4.3%
Government	10.2%	Active Duty	0.1%		
				Food stamp/SNAP benefits	20.1%

Voter Turnout			
2015 Total Citizens 18+	506,428	2016 House Turnout as % CVAP	51%
2016 House turnout	256,911	2014 House Turnout as % CVAP	29%

2012 Presidential Vote		
Barack Obama	233,382	(82%)
Mitt Romney	44,275	(16%)

2016 Presidential Vote		
Hillary Clinton	254,037	(83%)
Donald Trump	36,018	(12%)
Gary Johnson	7,045	(2%)

Cook Partisan Voting Index: D+34

Boston, the most political of cities, has often been the focal point of essential moments in American history. On its streets, originally laid out as narrow 17th century cowpaths with many that still survive, Samuel Adams and Paul Revere plotted revolution, the abolitionist movement helped ignite the Civil War, and various Kennedys opened their campaign headquarters. Today's Boston is different from the Boston of John F. Kennedy's era. Then it was a gray city with no new buildings and dust on every windowsill. The sky was dark with pollution, and the air was thick with ancient Yankee and Irish animosity. The old office buildings were full of Brahmins seeking safe investments for their antique family fortunes. The government was full of Irishmen, scampering after good patronage jobs and regaling one another with political war stories. These days, that Boston is mostly gone.

The new skyscrapers are full of well-educated venture capitalists, lawyers and management consultants, many working for high-tech and bio-tech companies radiating from Cambridge out into the countryside. Boston-Cambridge-Quincy ranks fourth among large U.S. metropolitan areas in the share of residents with college degrees, according to the Brookings Institution. Greater Boston may well have a larger concentration of graduate students and post-graduate hangers-on than any other major American city, and this graduate student community's world is centered in Cambridge, home of Harvard University. Boston's neighborhoods, full of large Irish families - and 95 percent white - when the city reached its peak population of 801,000 in 1950, are now different, with young singles in rowhouse apartments, professionals in waterfront apartment towers and African Americans in old triple-deckers. Today, Boston has had a growth spurt to 650,000 people, and it is 25 percent African American and 19 percent Hispanic.

One of its premier civic events, the fabled Boston Marathon, was the scene of a national tragedy in April 2013 when terrorists detonated two bombs that exploded 12 seconds apart near the finish line, killing three people and injuring more than 170 others. President Barack Obama, who went to Boston soon after the attack and spent three years locally at Harvard Law School, said "Boston is a tough and resilient town. So are its people. I'm supremely confident that Bostonians will pull together, take care of each other and move forward as one proud city." The May 2015 jury verdict that convicted killer Dzhokhar Tsarnaev and gave him the death penalty riveted the city. *Patriots Day*, a 2016 movie about the incident that starred Boston native Mark Wahlberg, was a celebration of that valor. The local civic spirit suffered an embarrassing setback when the U.S. Olympic Committee in January 2015 unexpectedly selected Boston to bid for the 2024 Olympic site, but reversed itself in July amid doubts by some in the business community and grass-roots opposition.

The 7th Congressional District includes most of Boston, although the State House and many of the historic sites in the North End are in the neighboring 8th District. Harvard and much of Cambridge are in the 5th District, but the Massachusetts Institute of Technology is in the 7th, helping to make it an important high-tech center. Boston Children's Hospital enhanced the area's reputation as a leading international center for medical care when it announced in October 2016 a $1 billion expansion. A $2.1 billion Wynn casino on the Mystic River in Everett overcame opposition from Somerville officials and was scheduled to open in 2019 - the largest private-sector development ever in the Boston area.

The 7th takes in Somerville, economically revived Chelsea and many Boston neighborhoods - newly upscale and diverse East Boston around Logan Airport, Brighton and the Back Bay, Fenway, Mattapan, Mission Hill and the South End. It also includes Randolph, where minorities are a majority; and Dorchester, a neighborhood with large numbers of working-class black, Latino, Caribbean Americans and Asian Americans. The Rev. Martin Luther King Jr. lived in Dorchester while he was earning his doctorate at Boston University. As the state's first minority-majority district, it has grown to 27 percent black, 22 percent Hispanic and 10 percent Asian. The 7th is among the most Democratic districts in the nation. Hillary Clinton won here with 83 percent of the vote. Tip O'Neill, who was the most recent Speaker who ably meshed Town and Gown and left the powerful position on his own terms, represented a version of this district from 1953 to 1987.

EIGHTH DISTRICT

Stephen Lynch (D)

Elected 2001, 9th term; b. Mar 31, 1955, Boston; Boston College Law School (MA), J.D.; Harvard University John F. Kennedy School of Government (MA), M.P.A.; Wentworth Institute of Technology (MA), B.S.; Roman Catholic; Married (Margaret Shaughnessy Lynch); 1 child.

Elected Office: MA House, 1995-1996; MA Senate, 1997-2001.

Professional Career: Structural ironworker, 1973-1991; Practicing attorney, 1991-2001.

DC Office: 2268 RHOB 20515, 202-225-8273, Fax: 202-225-3984, lynch.house.gov.

State Offices: Boston, 617-428-2000; Brockton, 508-586-5555; Quincy, 617-657-6305.

Committees: *Financial Services*: Capital Markets, Securities & Investment, Terrorism & Illicit Finance. *Oversight & Government Reform*: Information Technology, National Security (RMM).

Group Ratings

	ADA	ACLU	AFL-CIO	LCV	ITI	COC	HAFA	ACU	CFG	FRC
2016	-	94%	-	100%	83%	43%	16%	4%	4%	0%
2015	90%	C	100%	91%	C	45%	C	0%	0%	0%

Almanac Ratings 2015

	Economy	Social	Foreign	Composite
Liberal	91%	85%	80%	85%
Conservative	9%	15%	20%	15%

Key Votes of the 114th Congress

1. Keystone Pipeline	N	5. Puerto Rico Debt	N	9. Offenses by Aliens	Y
2. Trade Deals	N	6. Medical Marijuana	Y	10. Troops in Iraq	Y
3. Export-Import Bank	Y	7. Sanctuary Cities	N	11. Homeland Security $$	Y
4. Debt Ceiling Increase	Y	8. Armor-piercing Bullets	N	12. Trade Adjustment aid	N

Election Results

Election	Name (Party)	Vote (%)	Cand. Spent	Ind. Exp. Support	Ind. Exp. Oppose
2016 General	Stephen Lynch (D)	271,019 (72%)	$485,707		
	William Burke (R)	102,744 (28%)	$47,381		
2016 Primary	Stephen Lynch (D)	(100%)			

Prior winning percentages: 2014 (77%), 2012 (71%), 2010 (68%), 2008 (76%), 2006 (72%), 2004 (73%), 2002 (71%), 2001 (65%)

Democrat Stephen Lynch, who won a special election in 2001 to succeed the late Joe Moakley, is an ironworker-turned-lawyer who is popular with both blue-collar and white-collar constituents. He is less liberal than his Massachusetts Democratic colleagues, but no less ambitious - he jumped into the 2013 special election for the Senate seat vacated by John Kerry's confirmation as Secretary of State. He marches to his own drummer in the House, with occasional bipartisanship.

Lynch grew up in Boston's housing projects and took pride in making good by following the old ethnic precepts of hard work, family loyalty and personal determination. After graduating from South Boston High School, he joined his father as a full-time ironworker while attending the Wentworth Institute of Technology, where he got a bachelor's degree in construction management. He became the youngest president of the 2,000-member Local 7 of the International Association of Iron Workers. After a fall on the job cut short that career, he graduated from Boston College Law School and opened a legal practice representing working people. As an iron worker, he worked at several large plants that he later said suffered job losses as a result of unfair foreign trade practices. In 1994, he was elected to the state House. Fourteen months later, he won a special election for a seat in the state Senate.

Lynch built a political base in South Boston and had strong union ties, advantages when he pursued the seat after Moakley announced in February 2001 that he would not seek reelection. The ailing Moakley, who was beloved by many House Democrats as a link between the party's old and new generations, died that May. Max Kennedy, son of Robert and Ethel Kennedy, expressed interest in the race but his campaign never gained traction. Lynch became the front-runner. He stumbled after *The Boston Globe* revealed his student loan defaults years earlier, plus a tax lien that was resolved in 1998.

Three other state senators opposed Lynch. The strongest among them was Cheryl Jacques, who was openly gay and had support from EMILY's List and other national feminist groups that criticized Lynch's opposition to abortion rights. Her switch in opposition to capital punishment stirred controversy. Moakley's two brothers, who wielded much influence, endorsed Lynch. Primary Election Day was Sept. 11, 2001, but Republican Gov. Jane Swift decided not to postpone the vote despite the terrorist attacks. Lynch bested Jacques, 39%-29%. In the anti-climactic general election, he defeated another state senator, Jo Ann Sprague, 66%-33%.

In the House, Lynch's views have been right of center in the Democratic Caucus, and he has had the most conservative voting record in the Massachusetts delegation, especially on cultural issues. "That's like being called the slowest of the Kenyans in the marathon," he quipped to the *Boston Herald*. He backed building a fence on the U.S.-Mexico border and was one of three Massachusetts House members to vote for the Iraq war resolution. He moderated his stance on abortion in 2013, saying he believes it is a constitutionally protected right and that as a senator he would oppose anti-abortion Supreme Court nominees. He showed unexpected support for gay rights causes, developing a political alliance with home-state colleague Barney Frank, an openly gay Democrat. In the *Almanac* vote ratings for 2015, his scores were toward the center of the House, though more liberal on economic issues.

On the Oversight and Government Reform Committee, he has taken an interest in helping the financially strapped Postal Service, where his mother was a clerk. He praised a sweeping overhaul that the Senate passed in 2012 but that House Republicans condemned as too costly. As the top Democrat on the Subcommittee on National Security, he said his priority was "defending against threats to America." He was the top Democrat on a Financial Services Committee task force on terrorism financing, which explored the challenges facing counterterrorism officials. In November 2015, he and Rep. William Keating were the only lawmakers from Massachusetts to vote for the bill restricting refugees from Syria, though Lynch backed the admission of some refugees. On behalf of the families of the 9/11 victims, he was a leading proponent of releasing the secret 28 pages from an official report on the role of Saudi Arabia in the attacks. "It may help us at last hold those who are responsible accountable," Lynch said when the document was released in July 2016.

His occasional departures from the party line have mostly been tolerated by the leadership, but Lynch went too far for them in opposing the final health care overhaul bill in 2010. He was one of five Democrats to switch their votes after having backed the initial House version. He cited the Senate's decision to strip an antitrust exemption for insurance companies and the elimination of the government-run public option to compete with private insurers. "In the end, we allowed the insurance companies to prevail," he said. But he has opposed House Republican proposals to repeal the law. During an April 2015 broadcast interview in Boston, he said that Nancy Pelosi should step aside as House Democratic leader. "Nancy Pelosi is not going to lead the Democrats back into the majority," he said. Following the 2016 election, which he called "an epic failure and another lost opportunity," he backed Rep. Tim Ryan of Ohio against Pelosi as more in touch with "lunch-bucket Democrats" rather than the elites.

Lynch has been reelected without great difficulty. His opposition to the health care bill prompted a primary challenge from the left in 2010 from Mac D'Alessandro, a former regional political director for the Service Employees International Union. D'Alessandro drew support from MoveOn.org and other progressive groups. Lynch stressed his independence to voters, outraised his opponent by more than 2-to-1, and won handily, 66%-34%. In 2013, Lynch entered the contest for Kerry's seat, running against Democratic Rep. Ed Markey. "I think what the Senate could use - it's such an elite club - is someone to bring the concerns of the average American people to the U.S. Senate, so they're not so insulated," Lynch said. Markey won the primary, 57%-42%. Lynch led with 56 percent in Norfolk County and 62 percent in Plymouth County, both part of his district, but trailed by more than 2-to-1 in Middlesex and the western part of the state.

Downtown Boston, Quincy, Brockton

Population		**Race and Ethnicity**		**Income**	
Total	752,164	White	75.3%	Median Income	$76,655 (45 out of 435)
Land area	326	Black	8.9%		
Pop/ sq mi	2304.6	Latino	5.4%	Under $50,000	33.9%
Born in state	66.5%	Asian	7.3%	$50,000-$99,999	28.4%
		Two races	2.0%	$100,000-$199,999	27.9%
Age Groups		Other	1.1%	$200,000 or more	9.9%
Under 18	20.2%			Poverty Rate	9.5%
18-34	24.0%	**Education**			
35-64	40.7%	H.S grad or less	32.6%	**Health Insurance**	
Over 64	15.1%	Some college	23.6%	With health insurance coverage	97.1%
		College Degree, 4 yr	26.5%		
Work		Post grad	17.3%		
White Collar	46.9%			**Public Assistance**	
Sales and Service	39.4%	**Military**		Cash public assistance income	2.6%
Blue Collar	13.7%	Veteran	6.8%		
Government	12.7%	Active Duty	0.1%	Food stamp/SNAP benefits	10.2%

Voter Turnout			
2015 Total Citizens 18+	554,549	2016 House Turnout as % CVAP	67%
2016 House turnout	374,265	2014 House Turnout as % CVAP	36%

2012 Presidential Vote		
Barack Obama	213,364	(58%)
Mitt Romney	150,825	(41%)

2016 Presidential Vote		
Hillary Clinton	231,356	(60%)
Donald Trump	131,624	(34%)
Gary Johnson	15,395	(4%)

Cook Partisan Voting Index: D+10

The Irish remain the dominant political tribe here, even as parts of South Boston, long the center of Irish Boston, have gentrified. Southie's influence endures in the memory of two Irish Democrats who represented the area for all but two years from the Great Depression to the start of the 21st century. The first was John McCormack, an old-style, backroom deal-maker who served as House Speaker during the 1960s. The second was Joe Moakley, a close pal of Speaker Tip O'Neill, who chaired the influential Rules Committee before Democrats lost the House majority in 1994.

The 8th Congressional District of Massachusetts has been the most blue-collar district in the Boston suburbs. It takes in South Boston as well as Beacon Hill, the Massachusetts State House, and is a living museum with many of the historic sites in downtown Boston. They include the Paul Revere House; Faneuil Hall and a statue of revolutionary patriot Samuel Adams; the Old State House and the site of the Boston Massacre; the John F. Kennedy Presidential Library and Museum, plus the new Edward M. Kennedy Institute for the United States Senate at Columbia Point.

Completion of the high-dollar Big Dig highway project, with a tunnel under Boston Harbor, transformed economic development in the Financial District and along the waterfront in the port, including office buildings, hotels, condominiums, the John Joseph Moakley Courthouse and a huge convention center. The movie business has followed as well; *Patriots Day* and *Stronger*, two movies about the Boston Marathon bombing, were filmed in South Boston in 2016. The giant General Electric Co., which earlier announced the move of its corporate headquarters from Connecticut with financing assistance from Massachusetts, unveiled in December 2016 plans for a three-building $200 million campus along the Fort Point Channel in Southie. The upscale developments have reduced some of the parochialism but have priced the working class out of their old neighborhoods.

The district takes in Brockton, a once-bustling shoe manufacturing town that has become lined with stretches of empty buildings and has suffered from extensive gun violence. In 2016, the crime and housing foreclosure rates were reduced, though still high. Blacks and Latinos have grown to a 54 percent majority of the city. Also in the district is Braintree, where a 1920 armed robbery and slaying of a shoe factory paymaster and his guard led to the trial and execution of two Italian immigrants blamed for the killings, Nicola Sacco and Bartolomeo Vanzetti, which became one of the most controversial legal disputes in American history.

Ethnically, the 8th remains a heavily Irish congressional district, and also a Democratic one. The annual St. Patrick's Day parade in Southie is preceded by a rowdy political breakfast and roast that is a must-attend for state politicians. The continuing gentrification in parts of the district helps to explain why the Democratic presidential performance improved from 58%-41% in 2012 to 60%-34% in 2016.

NINTH DISTRICT

William Keating (D)

Elected 2010, 4th term; b. Sep 06, 1952, Norwood; Boston College (MA), B.A., 1974; Boston College (MA), M.B.A., 1982; Suffolk University School of Law (MA), J.D., 1985; Roman Catholic; Married (Tevis Keating); 2 children.

Elected Office: MA House, 1977-1984; MA Senate, 1985-1998; Norfolk County District Attorney, 1999-2010.

Professional Career: Practicing attorney, 1999-2010.

DC Office: 2351 RHOB 20515, 202-225-3111, Fax: 202-225-5658, keating.house.gov.

State Offices: Hyannis, 508-771-0666; New Bedford, 508-999-6462; Plymouth, 508-746-9000.

Committees: *Foreign Affairs*: Europe, Eurasia & Emerging Threats, Terrorism, Nonproliferation & Trade (RMM). *Homeland Security*: Counterterrorism & Intelligence, Transportation & Protective Security.

Group Ratings

	ADA	ACLU	AFL-CIO	LCV	ITI	COC	HAFA	ACU	CFG	FRC
2016	-	94%	-	97%	83%	64%	12%	4%	4%	8%
2015	75%	C	96%	91%	C	55%	C	8%	0%	17%

Almanac Ratings 2015

	Economy	Social	Foreign	Composite
Liberal	83%	82%	74%	80%
Conservative	17%	18%	26%	20%

Key Votes of the 114th Congress

1. Keystone Pipeline	N	5. Puerto Rico Debt	Y	9. Offenses by Aliens	N
2. Trade Deals	N	6. Medical Marijuana	N	10. Troops in Iraq	Y
3. Export-Import Bank	Y	7. Sanctuary Cities	N	11. Homeland Security $$	Y
4. Debt Ceiling Increase	Y	8. Armor-piercing Bullets	N	12. Trade Adjustment aid	Y

Election Results

Election	Name (Party)	Vote (%)		Cand. Spent	Ind. Exp. Support	Ind. Exp. Oppose
2016 General	William Keating (D)	211,790	(56%)	$420,477		
	Mark Alliegro (R)	127,803	(34%)	$256,394		
	Paul Harrington (I)	26,233	(7%)	$54,661		
2016 Primary	William Keating (D)		(100%)			

Prior winning percentages: 2014 (53%), 2012 (55%), 2010 (47%)

Democrat William Keating, elected in 2010, is a former prosecutor who has put his experience to work on homeland security and terrorism issues - often in bipartisan ways. He also has sought to resolve maritime-related conflicts in Massachusetts' coastal areas.

A Massachusetts native and life-long public official, Keating followed the path of his father, a police officer and later a veterans' services agent who assisted former soldiers with service-related disabilities. Keating put himself through Boston College by working at a post office. In 1977, at the age of 24, he was elected to the Massachusetts House. One of the first things Keating did was work on a law requiring smoke detectors in houses, after a fire in a nearby town killed a family living in a house without detectors. In 1985, Keating was elected to the state Senate, eventually becoming chairman of the Judiciary Committee and then the Committee on Taxation. He worked on environmental issues, sponsoring a bill to safeguard lakes and streams from pollutants by banning phosphates in household cleaners.

As district attorney for Norfolk County, he became the first in the state to win a murder conviction in the absence of a victim's body. In that case, DNA evidence taken from a saw helped to convict Joseph D. Romano Jr. of murdering and dismembering his wife. Keating worked to curb bullying in schools, a hot-button issue in the state after a teenage girl in western Massachusetts committed suicide after being bullied. He set up facilities for veterans suffering from post-traumatic stress disorder. And he helped create the Norfolk Advocates for Children, an organization for children who have been victimized by sexual assault.

Keating ran for Congress in a district that had been in Democratic hands for more than 30 years, though it is relatively marginal for Massachusetts. It gave Republican Scott Brown 60 percent of the vote in his upset victory in the 2010 special election to fill the seat of the late Democratic Sen. Edward Kennedy. Victoria Reggie Kennedy, Kennedy's widow, said that Keating shared her husband's commitment to universal health care.

Tea party-backed Republican Jeff Perry, a member of the state House, campaigned for smaller government and less spending. Keating's campaign strategy sought to paint Perry, a police officer, as having a "troubled relationship with the truth," pointing to a case in the 1990s in which an officer under Perry's command was involved in illegal strip searches of teenage girls. Perry said he did not know about the searches at the time. Keating had a slight edge in candidate spending, $1.5 million to $1.2 million, and in spending by outside groups, including $1.5 million from the Democratic Congressional Campaign Committee. He provided Democrats a rare, though unimpressive, triumph on an otherwise dismal Election Night for the party in 2010. He won with 45.6 percent of the vote to Perry's 41.3 percent.

In the House, Keating became a persistent inquisitor of Homeland Security officials, with an early interest in failings in perimeter safety at airports. He challenged the Transportation Security Administration on its overly aggressive searches of passengers, and said that the agency's approach was like "locking all the doors on your house but leaving the windows open." With Republican Rep. Michael McCaul of Texas, Keating got the House in 2012 to pass a bill that created independent review of how the Homeland Security Department was ferreting out waste and abuse. In July 2016, the House passed his bill to force TSA to review how it protects airport access points and the perimeters of the nation's airports, and to update its risk assessment for aviation security. The Senate did not complete action on the measure. He sought to decrease opioid abuse by veterans with legislation for more intervention and education by Veterans Affairs Department doctors.

As the top Democrat on the Foreign Affairs Subcommittee on Terrorism, Non-proliferation, and Trade, Keating sought bipartisanship in dealing with the world's trouble spots. With other senior members of the committee, Keating filed in March 2015 a bipartisan anti-terrorism bill to coordinate U.S. efforts to protect historic sites around the world from attacks by the Islamic State and others, and to restrict imports of cultural property illegally trafficked from Syria. Following a December 2016 congressional delegation visit to Asia, he warned that Donald Trump's recent comments about military issues in the Pacific were making American diplomacy in the region more difficult.

Long before the Nuclear Regulatory Commission decided in 2015 to shut down the Pilgrim nuclear power plant in Plymouth until safety issues were addressed, Keating had raised concerns about its licensing. To promote his vision for the South Shore and South Coast as a major maritime industry center, he filed a bill calling for fines from area fishermen to be sent to the New England Fishery Management Council. In June 2016, he filed a bill to ease long-standing friction between federal and local officials in the management of the ocean area in the Monomoy Refuge off Nantucket.

At home, Keating has faced more competition for reelection than has any other current representative from Massachusetts. He amassed an overwhelming financial advantage over his two rivals in 2012 and won comfortably with 59 percent of the vote. His 2014 contest was tighter. GOP attorney John Chapman, a first-time candidate, raised $1 million, to $1.4 million for the incumbent. Keating won 55%-45%, with the benefit of big margins in New Bedford and Fall River. In 2016, he was challenged by Mark Alliegro, a founder of the Upper Cape Tea Party, who raised questions about scientific claims on climate change. Alliegro raised $262,000 to $1.2 million, and lost, 56%-34%; three independent candidates split the remainder of the vote. Keating won all but one town and seemed secure in the district.

Southeast Massachusetts: Cape Cod, Fall River

Population		**Race and Ethnicity**		**Income**	
Total	732,411	White	87.5%	Median Income	$62,099 (120 out of 435)
Land area	1,215	Black	2.7%		
Pop/ sq mi	602.9	Latino	4.8%		
Born in state	71.0%	Asian	1.4%	Under $50,000	41.2%
		Two races	2.1%	$50,000-$99,999	30.0%
Age Groups		Other	1.5%	$100,000-$199,999	23.1%
Under 18	19.8%			$200,000 or more	5.8%
18-34	18.9%	**Education**		Poverty Rate	10.7%
35-64	41.7%	H.S grad or less	39.2%		
Over 64	19.6%	Some college	28.1%	**Health Insurance**	
		College Degree, 4 yr	20.1%	With health insurance coverage	95.9%
Work		Post grad	12.6%		
White Collar	35.8%				
Sales and Service	44.0%	**Military**		**Public Assistance**	
Blue Collar	20.3%	Veteran	9.0%	Cash public assistance income	3.1%
Government	13.4%	Active Duty	0.1%		
				Food stamp/SNAP benefits	12.0%

Voter Turnout			
2015 Total Citizens 18+	562,689	2016 House Turnout as % CVAP	68%
2016 House turnout	379,895	2014 House Turnout as % CVAP	46%

2012 Presidential Vote		
Barack Obama	212,701	(55%)
Mitt Romney	165,212	(43%)

2016 Presidential Vote		
Hillary Clinton	205,581	(52%)
Donald Trump	163,643	(41%)
Gary Johnson	16,509	(4%)

Cook Partisan Voting Index: D+4

The South Shore of Massachusetts Bay, from Boston southward to Plymouth and then down Cape Cod (there is a lot of dispute about which way is up and down on the Cape), is Massachusetts's oldest settled territory. The Pilgrims landed here at Plymouth Rock in 1620. This stony land was farmed by John Adams' father, who was anything but the aristocrat some later members of the Adams family would have had you believe. Daniel Webster lived in the South Shore town of Marshfield, today a high-income suburb of Boston far out on the usually clogged Southeast Expressway.

The Kennedys spent their summers at Hyannis Port on the Cape. As a senator in the 1950s, John F. Kennedy left a lasting legacy by helping to create the 40-mile Cape Cod National Seashore, which preserved much of the beauty, including large sand dunes. Provincetown, at the tip of the Cape, is still a fishing port and also one of the major gay vacation areas in the country. Famed writers Norman Mailer, Eugene O'Neill and Tennessee Williams all spent time in Provincetown. The islands of Martha's Vineyard and Nantucket, rich whaling ports in the early 19th century, are favored summer resorts for the liberal rich of Boston, New York and Washington. The Cape is filled with year-round retirees who enjoy the beauty and quiet pace. Cape Cod Bay supports cranberry growers, who annually produce more than $100 million from more than 14,000 acres of bogs.

The 9th Congressional District of Massachusetts follows the South Shore from Rockland to the Cape and extends west to the famous whaling seaport of New Bedford and to parts of coastal Fall River, both of which have large Hispanic populations. It includes the two tony islands, where the glitterati generated a "not in my backyard" fury over a proposed windmill farm in the nearby channel waters. In October 2015, safety and financial factors led the Entergy Corp. to announce that it would close the Pilgrim nuclear power plant in Plymouth by 2019; state officials raised the possibility of energy shortages. The development of the state-financed offshore wind terminal could offer a long-term solution. With the loss of blue-collar jobs, business growth in the South Shore has been slower than elsewhere in the Boston area.

Politically, the South Shore and the Cape were Republican decades ago. But they have shifted and this district leans Democratic. But it is the most competitive in Massachusetts. Hillary Clinton led Donald Trump in the district, 52%-41%. His 43 percent of the vote in Plymouth was Trump's best county in the state.

★ MICHIGAN ★

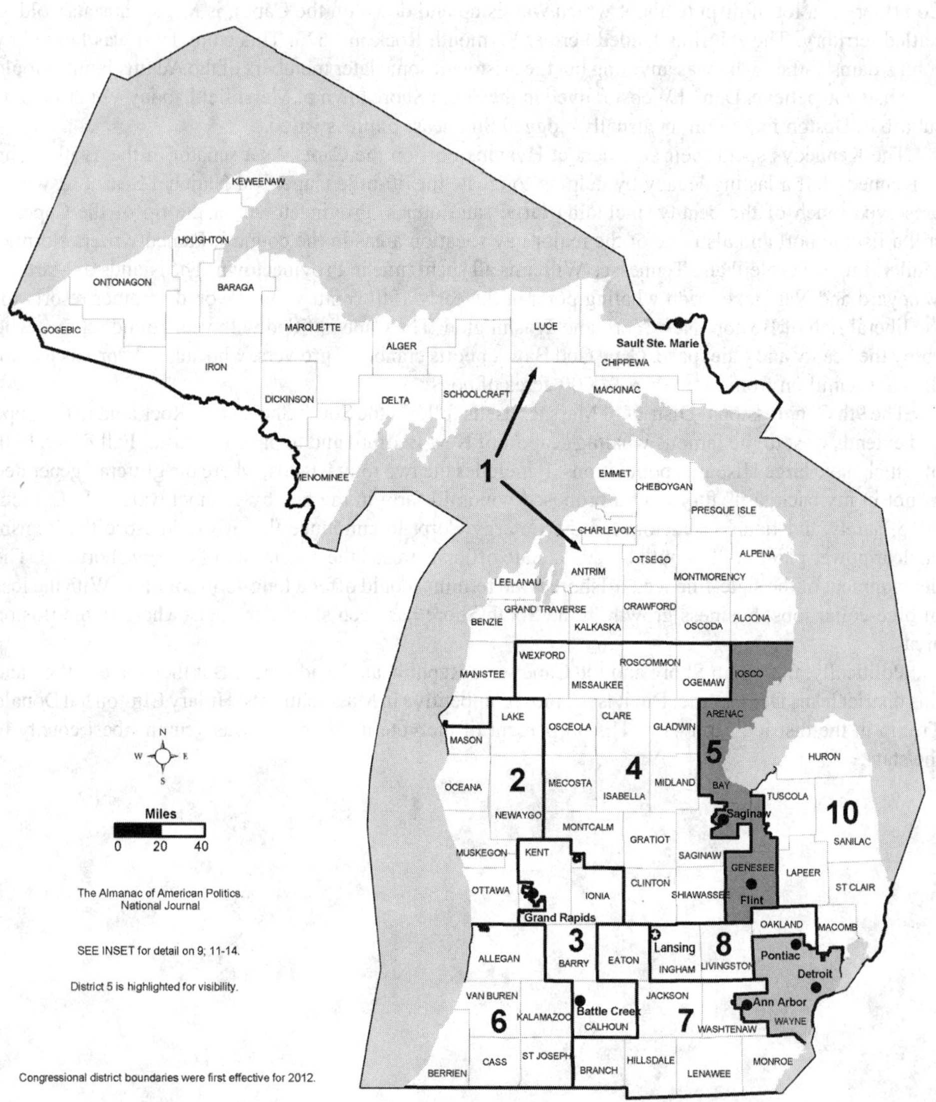
KEWEENAW
HOUGHTON
ONTONAGON
BARAGA
GOGEBIC
MARQUETTE
LUCE
Sault Ste. Marie
ALGER
IRON
CHIPPEWA
SCHOOLCRAFT
MACKINAC
DICKINSON
DELTA
MENOMINEE
1
EMMET
CHEBOYGAN
PRESQUE ISLE
CHARLEVOIX
OTSEGO
ALPENA
ANTRIM
MONTMORENCY
LEELANAU
GRAND TRAVERSE
CRAWFORD
BENZIE
KALKASKA
OSCODA
ALCONA
WEXFORD
ROSCOMMON
MANISTEE
MISSAUKEE
OGEMAW
IOSCO
ARENAC
LAKE
OSCEOLA
CLARE
GLADWIN
MASON
5
HURON
2
4
OCEANA
MECOSTA
MIDLAND
BAY
ISABELLA
TUSCOLA
NEWAYGO
Saginaw
10
MONTCALM
GRATIOT
SANILAC
MUSKEGON
KENT
SAGINAW
GENESEE
LAPEER
CLINTON
OTTAWA
IONIA
SHIAWASSEE
Flint
ST CLAIR
Grand Rapids
OAKLAND
MACOMB
3
Lansing
8
ALLEGAN
BARRY
EATON
INGHAM
LIVINGSTON
Pontiac
Detroit
VAN BUREN
JACKSON
Ann Arbor
Battle Creek
KALAMAZOO
6
CALHOUN
7
WASHTENAW
WAYNE
CASS
ST JOSEPH
HILLSDALE
MONROE
BERRIEN
BRANCH
LENAWEE
N
W
E
S
Miles
0
20
40
The Almanac of American Politics.
National Journal
SEE INSET for detail on 9; 11-14.
District 5 is highlighted for visibility.
Congressional district boundaries were first effective for 2012.

Michigan, though politically competitive in state-level races, hadn't voted Republican for president since 1988 – until 2016, when Donald Trump won it by three-tenths of 1 percent. It was one of the three states -- along with Pennsylvania and Wisconsin -- that enabled him to win the presidency by a healthy Electoral College margin, buoyed by a surge in blue-collar voters in declining industrial areas and apparent indifference from the Hillary Clinton campaign. "Flip Michigan and leave the rest of the map, and Trump is still president-elect," Edward-Isaac Dovere wrote in *Politico*. "But to people who worked in that state and others, how Clinton won the popular vote by 2.8 million votes and lost by 100,000 in states that could have made her president has everything to do with what happened in Michigan."

Nearly 200 years ago, when the French aristocrat Alexis de Tocqueville wanted to visit the American frontier, he boarded a boat and steamed across Lake Erie to visit the Michigan Territory. Tocqueville was not the first Frenchman to travel there. In the 17th century, French explorers and missionaries sailed the Great Lakes and slapped their version of Indian names on the landscape, which is why Michigan's *ch* is pronounced like *sh* and why Mackinac is pronounced with a silent final *c*. (But Michiganders don't carry it to extremes: Detroit ends with a robust English *oit*.) Michigan was not effectively occupied by the United States until 1796 and was bypassed in the initial westward rush into Ohio, Indiana and Illinois. In 1831, Tocqueville was still able to travel through virgin woods occupied by Indian tribes. But later in that decade, Michigan was settled in a rush by Yankee migrants from upstate New York and New England, who cut down trees and built farms and orderly towns complete with schools and colleges. Politically, Michigan was full of Yankee reformers who hated slavery, manned the Underground Railroad, promoted temperance and in 1855 gave Michigan a constitution that banned (as its successors have done to this day) capital punishment. Michigan was one of the birthplaces of the Republican Party, which held its first official meeting in Jackson in 1854, and up through the 1920s, Michigan was one of the most Republican states in the nation.

After the Civil War, Michigan developed an industrial economy. Its Lower Peninsula was mostly covered with trees – even today, half of the state's land area remains forested -- and lumber was the first boom industry on which Michigan relied too much. Forests were clear-cut or swept by blazes such as the 1881 fire that burned out half of Michigan's "Thumb." In the late 1800s, huge copper deposits were discovered on the Keweenaw Peninsula, which juts from the Upper Peninsula into icy Lake Superior. (The state includes 40,000 square miles of the Great Lakes, making almost half of Michigan water; with climate warming, iced-in conditions have declined by more than a week in recent years.) Immigrants from Italy and Finland, Cornwall and Croatia found work in the mines. Then came the auto industry. A combination of accident and shrewdness - the prickly genius of Henry Ford and the willingness of local bankers to finance auto start-ups - ensured that America's fastest-growing industry for the first 30 years of the 20th century was centered in Michigan. Detroit became a boomtown -- the nation's fastest-growing major metropolitan area after Los Angeles, which was then much smaller. The three-county Detroit metro area zoomed from a population of 426,000 in 1900 to 2.2 million in 1930, more than half the 4 million it has today. The auto industry drew labor from outside Michigan, from southern Ontario, and from the farms of Ohio and Indiana. It attracted Poles and Italians, Hungarians and Belgians, Greeks and Jews. During World War II and the two following decades, it attracted whites from the Kentucky and Tennessee mountains and blacks from the cotton country of Alabama and Mississippi.

This influx of a polyglot proletariat eventually changed Michigan's politics. The catalyst was the Great Depression of the 1930s and company managers' desire to use machines efficiently, treating employees as extensions of machines and with great distrust. That culminated in the 1937 sit-down strikes organized by the new United Auto Workers. Management and labor fought, sometimes literally, for pieces of what both sides feared was a shrinking pie. The UAW won and organized most of the companies after Democratic Gov. Frank Murphy refused to send in troops to break the illegal strikes. In the years that followed, autoworkers became more militant, and more militantly Democratic. Michigan politics became a kind of class warfare, conducted with a bitterness that split families and neighbors. The union mostly won, because demographics benefited the Democrats: Autoworkers and post-1900 immigrants were larger in number and produced more children than did outstate Yankees or management. After Walter Reuther's election as UAW president in 1946, voters elected young, liberal G. Mennen Williams as governor in 1948. By 1954, the Democrats, closely tied to the UAW, seemed to have become the natural majority in the state. As growth continued, economic issues became less bitter. By the early 1960s, class warfare had dissipated; in 1964, Henry Ford II joined Reuther in backing

Democrat Lyndon Johnson for president. Republican George Romney, the former American Motors president elected governor in 1962, and his successor, William Milliken, accepted the social welfare policies endorsed by the UAW leadership and the Democrats. The state government was one of the nation's most generous, and not just to the poor and the unemployed. It supported one of the nation's most distinguished and extensive higher-education systems, built state parks and recreation areas, and pioneered efforts to end racial discrimination.

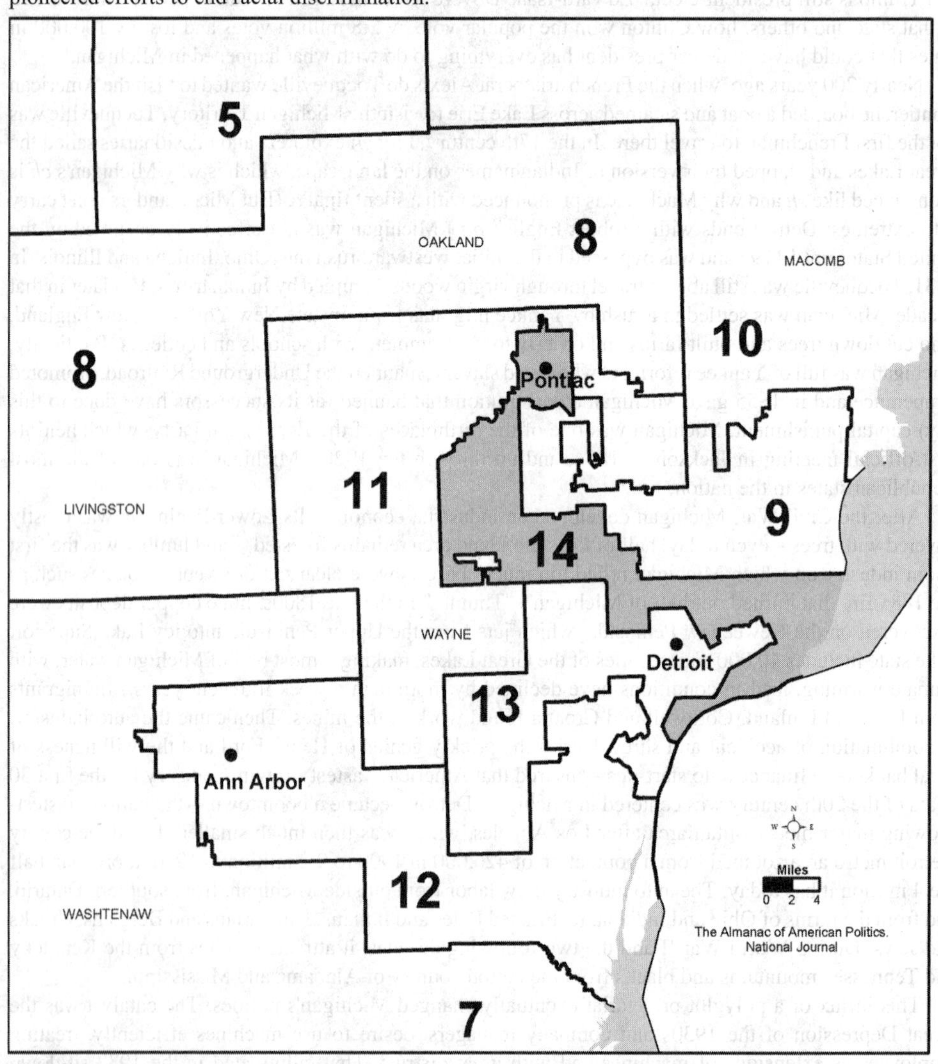

Congressional district boundaries were first effective for 2012. District 14 is highlighted for visibility.

Michigan grew faster than the nation as a whole from 1910 to 1970. Successive censuses and reapportionments increased its House delegation from 12 to 19. But in the four decades from 1970 to 2010, Michigan grew less than one-quarter as fast as the nation, and its House delegation fell back to 14 in 2012. A key turning point may have been the changes in the domestic auto industry. After the UAW's strike against General Motors in 1970, the union won its central demand: "30 and out," retirement after 30 years on the assembly line. That, in turn, led to demands for costlier retiree health benefits on top of those negotiated for active workers. The assumption was that the Big Three - General Motors, Ford, and Chrysler - would continue to dominate the U.S. auto market as they had for decades and could afford top-shelf benefits. The reality turned out to be different. Foreign competitors started producing better and cheaper cars that were more responsive to changes in gas prices and consumer preferences, first in Europe and Japan and then in nonunion plants in the United States. Auto sales plummeted during the oil shock and recession of 1979-82, and Chrysler was saved from bankruptcy by a federal bailout, while GM and Ford foundered.

Politicians woke up to the need for change before the Big Three management or the UAW leaders. Gov. James Blanchard, a Democrat elected in 1982, tried to stimulate high-skill, capital-intensive, flexible manufacturing and used $750 million of state pension funds as venture capital for manufacturers of items ranging from tape drives for microcomputers to fiberglass coffins. Gov. John Engler, a Republican elected in 1990 and reelected twice, cut taxes more than 30 times and slashed welfare rolls by more than two-thirds. He pressed for public school choice and charter schools and changed state pensions from defined benefits to defined contributions. For a time, Michigan's economy boomed. The auto industry became more high-tech, with fewer unionized workers and higher skill requirements. Just-in-time production methods encouraged subcontractors to stay in Michigan near big assembly plants, and the state boasted the nation's highest per capita concentration of engineers. Michigan's population grew 7 percent in the 1990s, and unemployment stayed below the national average. Grand Rapids, Traverse City, and the northern and western Detroit suburbs seemed to be booming. The great exception was the city of Detroit, whose population fell from 1.8 million in 1950 to 713,000 in 2010. Starting with the 1967 rioting, crime rates in Detroit remained intolerably high for 25 years, and much of the city simply vanished - houses were abandoned or burned down, commercial frontage had nearly 100 percent vacancy rates, and the downtown was a beleaguered fortress surrounded by vacant square miles. Detroit's crumbling architecture helped give birth to a subgenre of photography called "ruin porn."

Detroit began rebounding in the 1990s. Crime and welfare rolls were down, new sports stadiums and even some new housing were built downtown, and old theaters were refurbished. But the decade that began in 2000 halted Michigan's economic progress. The Big Three, desperate to generate cash to pay huge costs for workers' and retirees' benefits, squeezed their subcontractors into bankruptcy, and GM and Chrysler followed in 2009; Ford managed to stay afloat only by mortgaging almost all its assets in 2007. Michigan was the only state to lose population between 2000 and 2010, and 631,000 jobs were lost from 2002 to 2009. In June 2009, unemployment peaked at 14.9 percent, the highest of any state, and it remained in double digits for almost three years. During the Great Recession, workers tended to remain unemployed for much longer periods than in the past; median household incomes declined 21 percent in the decade, and net outmigration was higher than from any state except New York. Gov. Jennifer Granholm, a Democrat elected in 2002 and 2006, encouraged redevelopment, arranged for tax breaks for new facilities for the automakers and provided tax breaks to filmmakers who made movies in the state. But any positive effect was overwhelmed by the woes of the Detroit auto companies, with General Motors and Chrysler undergoing arranged bankruptcies in 2009 that protected the benefits of current UAW members even as non-union employees suffered layoffs and pay and benefit cuts.

While Detroit and Flint remained two of the nation's most impoverished cities – the latter afflicted with a manmade water-contamination problem – Michigan did recover along with the rest of the nation. By December 2016, unemployment had fallen to 5.1 percent, not much above the national average. The Big Three started making profits, and GM and Chrysler began buying back government-owned stock. But while manufacturing remained the state's predominant industry, the scars were lasting: Although the manufacturing workforce rose by 38 percent between the depths of the recession and late 2016, it still ended up at only two-thirds the level it was in 2000. The statewide median income remains below average nationally, fed by declines in union membership that were made larger by a right-to-work law that took effect in March 2013. In Detroit, a severe fiscal crisis led to years of governmental and judicial *sturm und drang* before the city emerged from a 17-month bankruptcy in 2014 after striking deals with key creditors. Between 2000 and 2015, Detroit's Wayne County saw its population drop by 3.4 percent, even as the neighboring suburban counties of Oakland and Macomb saw population rises of 3.3 percent and 2.8 percent, respectively. The state's population decline would have been worse without a modest but steady influx of immigrants, who now constitute 6 percent of the population. Michigan leads the nation in residents with Arab ancestry – an estimated 2 percent of the population. It was the nation's second most common destination for Syrian refugees, and the fifth-most common for refugees overall. State figures showed that businesses owned by immigrants produced north of $600 million in income in 2014.

Politically, Michigan was heavily Republican from the 1850s through the 1920s, then developed a partisan equipoise during the 1930s and has mostly maintained it since. A typical result in the class-warfare era was John F. Kennedy's 51%-49% victory in 1960 - Kennedy carried metro Detroit, 62%-38%, while Richard Nixon carried outstate Michigan, 60%-39%. Since then, outstate Michigan has become more Democratic, while whites in metro Detroit have become more Republican. The Grand Rapids area, with its large Dutch-American population and many Christian conservatives, is usually the most Republican part of the state, although the city of Grand Rapids itself is more liberal. Industrial Flint, Saginaw and the Bay City corridor, with their union heritage, have tended to be heavily Democratic, along with the areas around Lansing, the state capital, and Ann Arbor, home of the University of Michigan. The Upper Peninsula, historically Democratic, followed the patterns of rural America, voting for Republicans George W. Bush in 2000 and 2004 and Mitt Romney in 2012. In the relatively prosperous 1990s, Michigan leaned toward Republicans in statewide contests; in the tougher 2000s, the state moved toward the Democrats. In 2010 and 2014, Republican businessman Rick Snyder won as a self-styled "one tough nerd" and the GOP held both legislative chambers.

Just four years after Obama won the state by nine points, Trump won by less than 11,000 votes out of the almost 4.8 million cast. In fact, both Gary Johnson and Jill Stein won more votes than the difference between Trump and Clinton – 172,000 for Johnson and almost 51,000 for Stein. Between 2012 and 2016, the number of Democratic votes for president in the state fell by 296,000, or about 12 percent, while Republican votes increased by about 164,000, or about 8 percent. Obama won 20 counties; Clinton won only eight. In the 12 Obama counties that Clinton lost, the margin shifted in Trump's direction by between seven and 28 points. The most crucial shift was in Macomb County, the ancestral home of "Reagan Democrats," which Obama had won by four points but which Trump won by 12; Trump's margin of victory in Macomb was north of 48,000 votes, which was enough by itself to hand the state to Trump. Even in the counties that Clinton managed to hold, she underperformed Obama in about half of them. In Wayne County (Detroit), her raw vote total dropped by 76,000 and her margin shrank by 10 points. In Genesee County (which includes recently water-hobbled Flint), her margin shrank by 20 points, with Democratic votes for president dropping by one-fifth. In Muskegon County, the Democratic margin of victory shrank by 17 points, and in Marquette on the Upper Peninsula, it shrank by 10 points. The rare bright spots were places such as Oakland County (suburban Detroit), where Clinton's margin roughly matched Obama's, and in Washtenaw County (Ann Arbor), where it increased by five points. The newly elected president touted decisions by Ford, General Motors and Fiat Chrysler to invest in U.S. production, though it was not always clear to what degree the investments had already been in the works before his election. Meanwhile, it remained to be seen whether Trump's skepticism about free trade and his tough stance on immigration would end up helping or hurting the state that did so much to hand him the presidency.

Population		**Race and Ethnicity**		**Income**	
Total	9,900,571	White	75.9%	Median Income	$489,576 (32 out of 50)
Land area	56,539	Black	13.8%		
Pop/ sq mi	175.1	Latino	4.7%		
Born in state	76.7%	Asian	2.7%	Under $50,000	50.3%
		Two races	2.3%	$50,000-$99,999	30.3%
Age Groups		Other	0.6%	$100,000-$199,999	15.8%
Under 18	22.7%			$200,000 or more	3.5%
18-34	22.1%	**Education**		Poverty Rate	16.7%
35-64	40.2%	H.S grad or less	40.3%		
Over 64	14.9%	Some college	32.7%	**Health Insurance**	
		College Degree, 4 yr	16.5%	With health insurance coverage	90.4%
Work		Post grad	10.5%		
White Collar	34.9%				
Sales and Service	41.9%	**Military**		**Public Assistance**	
Blue Collar	23.2%	Veteran	8.2%	Cash public assistance income	3.4%
Government	11.1%	Active Duty	0.0%	Food stamp/SNAP benefits	16.7%

Voter Turnout			
2015 Total Citizens 18+	7,380,136	2016 Pres Turnout as % CVAP	65%
2016 Pres Votes	4,799,284	2012 Pres Turnout as % CVAP	65%

Legislature	
Senate:	11D, 27R
House:	47D, 63R

Presidential Politics

2016 Democratic Primary		
Bernie Sanders (D)	598,943	(50%)
Hillary Clinton (D)	581,775	(48%)
2016 Republican Primary		
Donald Trump (R)	483,753	(36%)
Ted Cruz (R)	329,617	(25%)
John Kasich (R)	321,115	(24%)
Marco Rubio (R)	123,587	(9%)

2016 Presidential Vote		
Hillary Clinton (D)	2,268,839	(47%)
Donald Trump (R)	2,279,543	(47%)
Gary Johnson (L)	172,136	(4%)
2012 Presidential Vote		
Barack Obama (D)	2,564,569	(54%)
Mitt Romney (R)	2,115,256	(45%)

Starting in 1992, Michigan became one of the states that voted for the Democratic presidential nominee in six consecutive elections and became a cornerstone in the so-called "blue wall" that gave the party's standard-bearers a leg up in accumulating 270 Electoral College votes to win the White House. In the 1992 election, the results in Michigan mirrored the national vote for the Democratic and Republican nominees. By 2008, Michigan gave Barack Obama a 16-percentage point margin of victory over John McCain, more than double his national marginal over McCain. Contributing to this Democratic trend was the change in affluent suburban Oakland County, where whites who once voted Republican shifted to the Democrats on cultural issues. Starting in 1996, Oakland voted Democratic in the presidential race and it hasn't deviated from that course since. When Donald Trump smashed through the blue wall in Michigan and defeated Hillary Clinton by 10,704 votes out of 4.8 million cast - an upset that pre-election state polls didn't forecast and very few observers predicted - he did so, in part, by winning blue-collar counties that have eluded Republicans of late.

Exhibit "A" in that regard was Trump's victory in Macomb County, home to the Reagan Democrats. In 2012, Obama won Macomb 16,103 votes. Trump defeated Clinton in Macomb by 48,348, a swing of more than 64,000. Trump also won Saginaw, Bay and Monroe, and came with 1,200 votes of winning Muskegon, all blue-collar counties. Clinton carried white-collar Oakland by a margin of some 1,000 votes more than Obama did in 2012. But in Wayne County, with heavily Democratic Detroit, Clinton's vote trailed Obama's by some 76,000, suggesting an enthusiasm gap in African-American precincts. Meanwhile, Trump picked up about 15,000 votes more than Mitt Romney garnered in 2012, mostly in the western Wayne suburbs of Detroit. With such a narrow defeat, many factors could have caused Clinton's loss. Some Democrats have blamed unions for not getting out their Democratic vote, others blamed Clinton's national team for not supervising a better organization in the Wolverine State. Michigan Democratic Rep. Debbie Dingell, whose district extends from the University of Michigan's cloistered halls in Ann Arbor to auto plants in Dearborn and Flat Rock, wrote a post-election piece in *The Washington Post* in which she argued that while Obama may have helped save the auto industry, many of its workers "don't feel better off." She also recalled, "I predicted that Hillary Clinton was in trouble in Michigan during the Democratic primary."

Indeed, the Democratic primary on March 8 was a rude awakening for Clinton and an embarrassment for the handful of pre-primary polls that showed her with a comfortable double-digit lead over Vermont Sen. Bernie Sanders. But Sanders vigorously stumped the state and highlighted his opposition to trade deals like the North American Free Trade Agreement that Clinton had strongly advocated. Clinton campaigned lightly in the state, seldom outside the Detroit metro area. Clinton carried Wayne, Macomb and Oakland Counties, but lost most of the rest of the state giving Sanders a stunning 50%-48% victory. Trump's anti-trade deal rhetoric also played well among the GOP Michigan primary electorate and he defeated Texas Sen. Ted Cruz 37%-25%. Ohio Gov. John Kasich was a close third taking 24 percent, but he carried only two of the state's 83 counties: Kalamazoo, home to Western Michigan University and Kalamazoo College, and Washtenaw, home to the University of Michigan. Cruz carried only eight counties, most of those around Grand Rapids, where many voters are evangelicals.

The election in Michigan did not end on Election Day. Jill Stein, the Green Party presidential nominee who won 1 percent of the Michigan, vote called for a recount in the state, as well as in

Pennsylvania and Wisconsin. The recount triggered legal battles in state and federal courts over Stein's right to request a recount since she had no chance of carrying the state or winning the presidential election. Ultimately, a federal district judge in Detroit stopped the recount in Michigan, saying Stein failed to qualify as an aggrieved candidate entitled to a recount under state law and that her allegations of voter fraud lacked evidence. But tentative recount efforts uncovered problems with the Michigan vote, most notably in Detroit, where the Wayne County clerk discovered that in 37 percent of the city's precincts the number of ballots cast was different from the number of voters who came to the polls. In roughly two-thirds of those instances, the discrepancy was that more votes were counted than the number of people who were recorded as having voted. A *Detroit Free Press* analysis of 248 precincts found that 782 more votes were tabulated by voting machines than the number of voters recorded as having picked up ballots from precinct poll workers. A Michigan Bureau of Elections audit of the vote found that the discrepancies were due to human error, not illegality.

Congressional Districts

115th Congress Lineup	9R 5D	**114th Congress Lineup**	9R 5D

In 1980, Michigan had 19 House seats and Georgia had 10. Now, each has 14. In 1950, the city of Detroit had five entire congressional districts; today, it has barely enough population for one. But the loss of clout isn't exclusive to Detroit. In 1960, the Upper Peninsula had sufficient residents for 74 percent of a district; that has dropped to just 44 percent of a district. Republicans controlled redistricting in 2011 and were tasked with eliminating one seat. Importantly, they had won control of the Michigan Supreme Court, a key arbiter in determining what Republicans could and could not draw. They squeezed a Democratic district out of the metro Detroit area. In doing so, they barely preserved two black-majority districts, though one of them elected Rep. Gary Peters - who is white -- for one term before he was elected to the Senate in 2014. Despite some challenges in three competitive battlegrounds that Barack Obama had won in 2008, Republicans have been successful in protecting their 9-5 control of the delegation.

It's not impossible to imagine Democrats making a gain or two in Michigan before the next reapportionment. With the state expected to lose yet another seat after the 2020 Census, one of the three white Democratic-held districts could be squeezed, though Republicans in this swing state might be stretched to secure 9-4 control of the delegation. A potentially complicating factor is that blacks may be hard-pressed to preserve both of their seats in Detroit. With Republicans in comfortable control of the Legislature, much may depend on the outcome of the open-seat contest for governor in 2018.

Governor

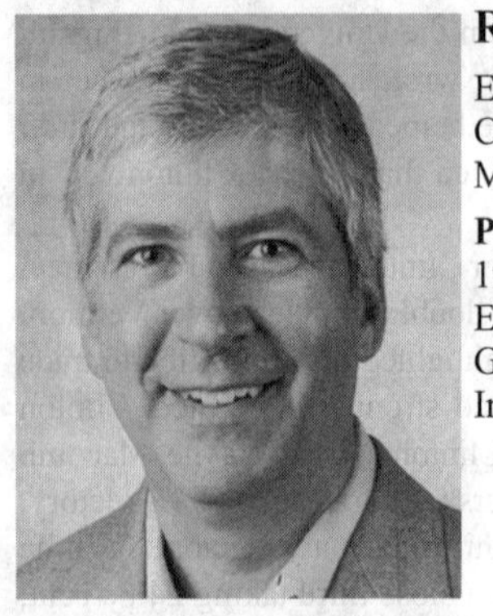

Rick Snyder (R)

Elected 2010, term expires 2019, 2nd term; b. Aug. 19, 1958, Battle Creek, MI; U. of MI, B.A. 1977, M.B.A. 1979; J.D. 1982; Presbyterian; Married (Sue); 3 children.

Professional Career: Adjunct Assistant Professor, University of MI, 1982-1984; Employee & Partner, Coopers & Lybrand, 1982-1991; Executive Vice President, Gateway Inc., 1991-1996; President & COO, Gateway Inc., 1996-1997; Founder & President, Avalon Investments Inc., 1997-2000; Founder, Chairman, & CEO, Ardesta, 2000-2010.

Office: PO Box 30013, Lansing, 48909; 517-373-3400; Fax: 517-335-6863; Website: michigan.gov.

Election Results

Election	Name (Party)	Vote (%)
2014 General	Rick Snyder (R)	1,607,399 (51%)
	Mark Schauer (D)	1,479,057 (47%)

Prior winning percentage: 2010 (58%)

Republican Rick Snyder was elected governor of Michigan in 2010 in his first foray into electoral politics, styling himself as "one tough nerd" able to rise above political gridlock. In his first term. Snyder signed right-to-work legislation that bans unions from requiring non-members to pay dues, but he also won some cross-party support for signing an expansion of Medicaid under the Affordable Care Act. After winning reelection in 2014, Snyder's second term was overwhelmed by a drinking water crisis in Flint for which he bore a measure of broadly shared responsibility.

Snyder grew up in Battle Creek and attended the University of Michigan as an undergraduate, for law school and for business school. He went to work for the accounting firm Coopers & Lybrand, first in Detroit and then in Chicago. In 1991, Snyder joined Gateway, the direct-sales personal computer firm. Gateway was wildly successful in the 1990s, rising to No. 194 on the *Fortune* 500 list. Snyder became president and chief operating officer in 1996; in 1997, he left active management but remained on the board of directors. Exercising options on 2 million shares of stock made him, by age 40, a very rich man.

In 1997, Snyder moved to Ann Arbor and, with $100 million of his own and investors' money, established Avalon Investments. This venture-capital fund had some successes within the state: Esperion Therapeutics in Plymouth and HealthMedia in Ann Arbor. In 2000, he started another $100 million venture-capital firm, Ardesta, to invest in micromechanical technologies and microsystems. Its great success, HandyLab, produced molecular diagnostic testing products, and it eventually sold for $275 million. Gateway fared less well. It struggled to diversify and sent most of its workforce offshore. Snyder came back as CEO in 2006; in 2007, it was sold to a Taiwanese firm for $1.90 a share.

In 1999, Republican Gov. John Engler named Snyder the first head of the Michigan Economic Development Corporation. But he had higher ambitions: He used to tell friends his plan was to be elected governor or senator by the time he was 50. So in July 2009, to little acclaim, Snyder announced his candidacy for governor - at 51, a year behind schedule. Democratic Gov. Jennifer Granholm was term-limited, and her job approval ratings were foundering amid the state's deep recession. He started far behind bigger names such as Attorney General Mike Cox and Rep. Pete Hoekstra, who had chaired the House Intelligence Committee. In February 2010, Snyder ran a 60-second spot during the Super Bowl that unveiled the "one tough nerd" brand, pitching the candidate as a practical man who could turn around Michigan's economy. "Social issues are not on my agenda," Snyder told the *Detroit Free Press*. "If you look at where we're at in Michigan today, it's about our economy, it's about jobs and young people." A shaky campaigner at first, Snyder put $5.9 million of his own money into his campaign, enabling him to dominate television advertising. In August 2010, more than a million people voted in the Republican primary - almost double the typical number - and Snyder won with 36 percent of the vote. Facing Democratic Lansing mayor Virg Bernero – a free-trade skeptic who had pushed for the federal auto bailouts and was sometimes called "America's angriest mayor" for his support of them – Snyder called for replacing the Michigan business tax with a 6 percent corporate profits tax and said he would streamline regulation and switch teachers to defined contribution pensions. Snyder won, 58%-40%, carrying 79 of 83 counties. Snyder made only minor inroads among blacks and college-town voters, but showed major gains among just about every other demographic group.

Snyder quickly found himself in fights over fiscal matters. When he called for an income tax on pensions, thousands of people took to the streets around the Capitol in March 2011, and even some Republican lawmakers expressed doubts. To help Detroit's ailing finances, he proposed a consent agreement that gave the state sweeping power to manage the city; Detroit officials balked. After weeks of intense debate, the City Council agreed to a deal that handed financial oversight to an advisory board, partly appointed by the state. He also signed a bill reducing from 26 to 20 weeks the maximum time for which a person could receive state unemployment benefits, the fewest of any state. Snyder's approval ratings softened, but they stabilized as Michigan's economy brightened. Snyder signed a deal for a new international bridge between Detroit and Windsor, Ontario, with Canadian Prime Minister Stephen Harper.

Depending on the issue, Snyder veered left and right. Snyder surprised his party in July 2012 by siding with Democrats in refusing to sign bills that would have required photo identification for absentee voting, restricted voter registration drives, and mandated a ballot-box affirmation of citizenship. Later that year, just days after the school massacre in Newtown, Connecticut, Snyder vetoed legislation to allow concealed weapons inside public schools, day care centers and hospitals. And with much effort, he successfully expanded Medicaid under the Affordable Care Act, enraging many conservatives but winning him points with Democrats; signups – and costs -- would eventually exceed expectations, with more than 600,000 residents enrolling. On the other hand, when the legislature in December 2012 passed a right-to-work bill, Snyder swiftly signed it, contradicting his promise from the 2010 campaign. Unions and their Democratic allies were outraged at this turn of events in a state with strong historic ties to the labor movement. Meanwhile, in March 2013, Snyder disappointed Democrats by appointing an emergency financial manager for Detroit, which had a deficit topping $325 million.

In 2014, Snyder faced a competitive race against former Democratic Rep. Mark Schauer, who charged the incumbent with favoring the affluent and insufficiently funding education. On a strongly Republican Election Day nationally, Snyder prevailed, 51%-47%, even as Democrat Gary Peters was easily defeating Republican Terri Lynn Land in an open-seat Senate race. In his second term, Snyder pushed hard for a May 2015 ballot measure to raise sales taxes by nearly $2 billion - about two-thirds for roads and one-third for other forms of transportation, schools, local governments and tax cuts for lower-income residents. Voters rejected it by a resounding 4-to-1 margin - the worst outcome for a Michigan constitutional amendment in half a century. In June 2016, Snyder signed a $617 million plan to bail out and restructure the public schools in Detroit, over the objections of Mayor Mike Duggan, other Democrats and teachers unions, who had sought a role for a mayor-appointed commission charged with overseeing traditional and charter schools. And in December 2016, Snyder signed an energy-policy bill he had brokered that stiffened minimum requirements for generating renewable energy and set up a new planning process for the retirement of coal-fired plants.

Snyder's second term was overwhelmed by the water-contamination crisis in the depressed, heavily African-American city of Flint. Its roots lay in a bill Snyder had signed early in his tenure that enhanced the power of the governor to appoint emergency managers to take over financially troubled cities and school districts. (It was later repealed by the voters, but then largely reinstated by the legislature.) Snyder appointed two successive emergency managers for Flint; as a cost-saving measure, they moved the city to switch water suppliers in April 2013. But the new supply, from Lake Huron, was not ready to go, and on an interim basis, an emergency manager decided to have the city draw its water from the Flint River starting in April 2014, without the necessary corrosion-control chemicals being added. Salts in the river water corroded city pipes, a crucial detail not effectively counteracted at the time; the result was foul-looking water with dangerously high levels of lead. Despite complaints from Flint residents and meetings with state officials, use of the water continued until a pediatrician in Flint and a Virginia Tech professor blew the whistle on the lead levels seen in children and the water coming out of residents' faucets. The situation in Flint attracted national attention in late 2015, and efforts to provide safe water and replace lead pipes moved slowly. While local Flint officials, career employees in state government and the federal Environmental Protection Agency all played roles, Snyder's responsibility was considerable and he became the face of the crisis. By the time of his 2016 state of the state address, Snyder accepted part of the blame. "I'm sorry, and I will fix it," he said. "Government failed you at the federal, state and local level. We need to make sure this never happens again in any Michigan city." Attorney General Bill Schuette, a Republican, charged more than a dozen officials, including the city's two emergency managers. The crisis helped send Snyder's approval ratings lower – to the 30s for much of 2016, making him one of the least popular governors in the nation, although he managed to dodge recall efforts.

After Donald Trump won the presidency, Snyder – who had remained at arm's length from the GOP nominee during the campaign – said that he would "continue to encourage people to move here from other states and countries to fulfill their visions and find success." He added that he knows firsthand "the strong economic and entrepreneurial culture that has developed in our state because of the vast number of immigrants who have settled here for generations." With Snyder term-limited, the race to succeed him in 2018 is expected to be competitive. The GOP field could include Schuette and Lt. Gov. Brian Calley, while former state Sen. Gretchen Whitmer could run for the Democrats. It remained to be seen whether the Democrats, after losing the state in dramatic fashion in the 2016 presidential race, could flip the governorship and the state House just 24 months later.

Senior Senator

Debbie Stabenow (D)

Elected 2000, term expires 2018, 3rd term; b. Apr 29, 1950, Gladwin; Michigan State University, M.S.W.; Michigan State University, B.A.; Methodist; Divorced; 2 children; 3 grandchildren.

Elected Office: Ingham County Comissioner, 1975-1978, Chair, 1976-1978; MI House, 1979-1991; MI Senate, 1991-1994; U.S. House, 1997-2001.

Professional Career: Social worker; Consultant & co-founder, MI Leadership Inst., 1995-1996.

DC Office: 731 HSOB 20510, 202-224-4822, Fax: 202-228-0325, stabenow.senate.gov.

State Offices: Detroit, 313-961-4330; East Lansing, 517-203-1760; Flint, 810-720-4172; Grand Rapids, 616-975-0052; Marquette, 906-228-8756; Traverse City, 231-929-1031.

Committees: Senate Democratic Policy and Communications Center Chairman. *Agriculture, Nutrition & Forestry (RMM)*: Commodities, Risk Management & Trade, Conservation, Forestry & Natural Resources, Livestock, Marketing & Agriculture Security, Nutrition, Agricultural Research & Specialty Crops, Rural Development & Energy. *Budget*. *Energy & Natural Resources*: National Parks, Public Lands, Forests & Mining. *Finance*: Health Care (RMM), International Trade, Customs & Global Competitiveness.

Group Ratings

	ADA	ACLU	AFL-CIO	LCV	ITI	COC	HAFA	ACU	CFG	FRC
2016	-	88%	-	100%	80%	63%	5%	0%	8%	0%
2015	85%	C	100%	100%	C	43%	C	4%	0%	0%

Almanac Ratings 2015

	Economy	Social	Foreign	Composite
Liberal	94%	100%	80%	91%
Conservative	6%	0%	20%	9%

Key Votes of the 114th Congress

1. Keystone pipeline	N	5. National Security Data	Y	9. Gun Sales Checks	Y
2. Export-Import Bank	N	6. Iran Nuclear Deal	N	10. Sanctuary Cities	N
3. Debt Ceiling Increase	Y	7. Puerto Rico Debt	Y	11. Planned Parenthood	N
4. Homeland Security $$	Y	8. Loretta Lynch A.G	Y	12. Trade deals	N

Election Results

Election	Name (Party)	Vote (%)	Cand. Spent	Ind. Exp. Support	Ind. Exp. Oppose
2012 General	Debbie Stabenow (D)	2,735,826 (59%)	$13,434,824	$402,183	$1,156,926
	Pete Hoekstra (R)	1,767,386 (38%)	$5,646,406	$330,393	$2,350
2012 Primary	Debbie Stabenow (D)	555,719 (100%)			

Prior winning percentages: 2006 (57%), 2000 (49%); House: 1998 (57%), 1996 (54%)

When Democrat Debbie Stabenow, Michigan's senior senator, found herself in line to chair the Agriculture Committee in early 2011, alarm bells went off among leaders of the nation's farm industry-many of whom viewed Stabenow as an urban liberal interested mainly in two of her state's best-known products: automobiles and cherries. With work about to get underway on a new farm bill reauthorizing the federal government's agriculture and nutrition programs, some were so nervous that they begged then-North Dakota Sen. Kent Conrad to leave his post at the helm of the Senate Budget Committee and use his seniority to take over the Agriculture panel. Conrad advised the farm leaders to keep their powder dry, according to the *Hagstrom Report*, a Washington-based publication that covers agriculture policy.

He assured them that Stabenow, also a Budget Committee member, had been a low-key, mainstream presence in previous budget negotiations, and would do fine.

Indeed, by the time a new farm bill had been enacted into law in early 2014, after a process that stretched over two Congresses, much of the leadership of the agriculture industry had done a political U-turn -- as Stabenow was praised for deftly balancing competing interests in what is invariably one of the most heavily lobbied pieces of legislation to come before Capitol Hill. Stabenow was said to be so persistent that her colleagues began to fear her approach on the Senate floor. "Past farm bills pit regions against regions. I said that we were going to support all of agriculture," Stabenow told *The New York Times* after passage of the bill. That included some enhanced benefits for producers in her home state, best known for so-called specialty crops-such as apples and blueberries in addition to cherries.

Stabenow will confront another reauthorization of the farm bill in 2018, this time as the ranking Democrat on the Agriculture panel working with its current chairman, Kansas Sen. Pat Roberts -- to whom Stabenow turned over the gavel after the Republicans recaptured Senate control in 2014. In the next two years, she and Roberts worked closely to develop compromises on controversial issues within the committee's jurisdiction, ranging from the labeling of food containing genetically modified organisms (GMOs) to nutrition standards for school lunches. The always challenging task of crafting a farm bill in Congress will come as Stabenow could face a significant political challenge back home in 2018, as she seeks a fourth term. President Donald Trump's razor-thin 2016 victory in Michigan put the state in the Republican presidential column for the first time since 1988, and has created further jitters in Democratic circles in a state where both the governorship and state legislature are currently in the hands of the GOP.

Stabenow has been one of the more enduring figures in state politics throughout 40 years of holding elected office: She has a warm, personable demeanor that often causes opponents to underestimate her political toughness. "For nearly four decades, Republicans have sneered at Debbie Stabenow ... then she beats them, every time," Detroit *Metro Times* columnist Jack Lessenberry observed in 2012 -- the year that Stabenow captured 61 of the state's 83 counties to win a third term. Stabenow grew up in the small northern Michigan town of Clare, where her father was an auto dealer (Oldsmobiles) and her mother was a nurse. But her base has long been Lansing and surrounding Ingham County, where Michigan State University is located. She holds a B.A. as well as a master's degree in social work from the latter; she counseled students in public schools and made extra money singing folk songs in coffeehouses. She was politically active, marching in anti-Vietnam War rallies and volunteering for George McGovern's anti-war presidential bid in 1972.

Stabenow was first elected to office at the age of 24: Angered when the Ingham County Commission closed a nursing home, she ran for the commission in 1974 and beat an incumbent who had referred to her as "that young broad." Stabenow was elected to the Michigan House in 1978 when she was just 28, and moved to the state Senate in 1990. Four years later, while running for governor, she was at the center of a storm in state politics. In response to Republican Gov. John Engler's call for changes in financing education, she proposed to zero out the property tax and start over, apparently calculating he would reject such a drastic tax cut. Instead, he accepted her proposal and passed a plan reducing property taxes vastly and increasing the sales tax, which was approved by voters, 70%-30%, in 1994. But, in that year's primary, the state Democratic establishment-including the Michigan Education Association, the United Auto Workers and the AFL-CIO-opposed Stabenow. She won 30 percent of the vote, behind former Rep. Howard Wolpe's 35 percent. She was chosen as Wolpe's lieutenant gubernatorial running mate for the general election, but the ticket lost to Engler by a 3-2 margin.

Undaunted, Stabenow almost immediately began running for Congress, in a district that included Democratic Ingham County and heavily Republican Livingston County to the east. Stabenow raised more than $1 million in individual contributions, and won 54 percent of the vote in 1996 in ousting freshman Republican Rep. Dick Chrysler. In 2000, she challenged first-term Republican Sen. Spencer Abraham, in what turned out to be one of that year's critical Senate races. In the summer, Abraham used his money advantage-he ultimately spent $13 million to Stabenow's nearly $8 million-to run ads spotlighting his own program for prescription drugs for senior citizens, and attacking Stabenow as a free-spending liberal favoring increased bureaucracy and higher taxes, opposing welfare reform, and supporting lenient sentences for criminals. Stabenow hoarded her money for an October ad buy, which turned out to be a wise strategy. She was down by 17 points in polls in mid-October, but answered charges that she was a liberal by citing her House votes for a balanced budget and ending the marriage penalty in the tax code. She attacked Abraham as beholden to corporations and special interests.

On Election Day, Stabenow won 49%-48%, helping the Democrats to gain a 50-50 split of the Senate -- while becoming the first woman ever to represent Michigan in that chamber. Soon after she was sworn in, Senate Democrats moved to help her strengthen her grip on the seat: Capitalizing on a central issue of her election campaign, they named Stabenow head of a task force on prescription drugs, the cost of which was then among the country's hottest issues. She organized bus trips of seniors to Canada, and pressed for measures allowing the importation of U.S. drugs from that country.

Stabenow -- who currently ranks fourth in the Senate Democratic leadership -- has been among the most loyal of Democrats, particularly on economic and social issues. But she joined a number of other leading Democrats in challenging the international trade agenda put forth by President Barack Obama as well as his Republican predecessor, George W. Bush. In early 2015, when Obama was seeking expedited authority in the negotiation of a 12-nation Asian trade deal, Stabenow not only voted against it-but, in the Senate Finance Committee, unsuccessfully proposed an amendment requiring the administration to seek enforceable currency manipulation standards in such a deal. When White House officials called the amendment a "poison pill" that would derail the talks, Stabenow shot back that, if including it meant that a free trade deal might die, it was worth the price. In 2017, Stabenow didn't wait for Trump to fulfill a campaign pledge to withdraw from the agreement, the Trans Pacific Partnership: She introduced legislation a day before he was sworn in to require that he do so. Several days later, Trump signed an executive order withdrawing the United States from the TPP.

Meanwhile, Stabenow sought to bait the new president, with his theme of "America First" theme, into embracing legislation that she has introduced perennially since 2012 -- to provide tax incentives to companies who move jobs back to the United States, while eliminating tax breaks to those firms shifting jobs overseas. "Unfortunately in previous years, Republican colleagues have filibustered it," Stabenow told a press conference in early 2017. Noting she had Obama's backing on the legislation, she added, "I'm hoping the new president will turn to his own party and say this is something he wants to get done." The legislation would eliminate the tax deduction companies normally receive for moving staff if the firm involved is moving jobs abroad, while awarding a new tax credit to companies that shift employment into the United States.

The currency manipulation amendment that Stabenow sought in 2015 was strongly supported by the Big Three domestic automakers, who contended that, without such a provision in a trade agreement, Japanese auto manufacturers could get a big boost from unfair currency intervention. Like other Michigan lawmakers, a significant focus for Stabenow on Capitol Hill has involved pushing the interests of her state's most visible industry. She strongly supported loan guarantees for the automakers and the government acquisition of General Motors and Chrysler in the wake of the 2008 financial crash, and has worked to get the automakers federal assistance to better compete, developing a program to authorize loans to re-equip and expand factories to produce advanced technology vehicles and components. She also worked on a plan that led to the Energy Department announcing two new advanced battery research facilities in Michigan in November 2012, part of a five-year partnership with private companies. Earlier, when the Senate passed the "Cash for Clunkers" program providing government reimbursements for trading in old cars for more fuel-efficient models, Stabenow successfully fended off a proposal by California Democrat Dianne Feinstein for higher mileage standards.

Late in her first term, Stabenow decided to try to gain a toehold in Senate leadership. In 2004, when Barbara Mikulski of Maryland stepped down as secretary of the Democratic caucus, Stabenow called Mikulski to ask for her support, and the two worked the phones. Stabenow got the job, then the No. 4 position in the Democratic leadership. It gave her a voice at leadership meetings, though her impact was limited. Some senior Democrats quietly discussed replacing her after the 2006 election-during which Stabenow won a second Senate term by easily defeating her GOP opponent, Oakland County Sheriff Michael Bouchard, with 57 percent. (Two higher visibility Republicans, Reps. Candice Miller and Mike Rogers, declined to take her on.) Following her re-election, a deal was reached in which Stabenow got a seat on the influential Finance Committee and became chair of the Democratic Steering and Outreach Committee, while Washington Sen. Patty Murray replaced her as caucus secretary. In 2011, Stabenow moved up the leadership ladder as vice chair of the Democratic Policy Committee, now the Democratic Policy and Communications Center. She was elevated to its chairmanship in 2017, succeeding New York Sen. Charles Schumer when the latter became minority leader. The move once again made Stabenow the No. 4 ranking member of the Democratic leadership.

Stabenow also inherited the Agriculture Committee gavel in 2011, becoming the second woman ever to chair the panel, after the first-Arkansas Sen. Blanche Lincoln-was defeated for re-election in 2010. Traditionally, farm bills have favored crops such as corn and wheat that receive big subsidies of various kinds. While such crops continue to benefit heavily in the farm bill rewrite overseen by Stabenow, subsidies for these commodities were cut by about 30 percent over 10 years. Although still a relatively small part of the overall legislation, funding for specialty crops such as fruits, vegetables and nuts -- along with organic farming -- was increased sharply in the bill that Stabenow shepherded to passage. Producers of specialty crops were also given enhanced access to crop insurance programs long utilized by corn and wheat growers. "This is not your father's farm bill," Stabenow repeatedly boasted, as she pointed to savings-notably elimination of a $5 billion a year, much-criticized subsidy that paid farmers whether they grew crops or not.

The House-Senate conference report on the bill contained some concessions to Southern growers from the House version, but most provisions originated in the Senate, making it very much Stabenow's handiwork. It took her close to three years of patient work to pull off. She had to navigate differences between Northern and Midwestern legislators-notably Roberts, later her successor as Agriculture Committee chairman -- and Southern lawmakers. Roberts contended that federal target prices for crops were an out-of-date mechanism to aid farmers, but Southern growers had little experience with the private crop insurance programs envisioned as a replacement. The farm bill version that Stabenow produced in 2012, with Roberts then the ranking member of the Agriculture panel, had no target prices. The issue helped to stall final passage of a new farm bill until 2013, when Mississippi Republican Thad Cochran became ranking member, and insisted on target prices-which were inserted in a new version of the bill. Throughout the jockeying, Stabenow was credited with dealing with such conflicts without allowing them spill out into public view.

On the nutrition titles of the farm bill-which comprise about 80 percent of the funding in the measure-Stabenow asserted herself against House conservatives who wanted to cut $39 billion over 10 years from the Supplemental Nutrition Assistance Program, formerly known as food stamps. This move would have cut several million individuals from SNAP assistance. The initial Senate version of the bill had a far more modest $4 billion cut. In the final agreement, Stabenow refused to go any further than tightening a loophole that some states used to trigger SNAP aid, increasing the estimated savings to $8.6 billion. At one point, House conservatives demanded drug testing for SNAP recipients. According to *The New York Times*, Stabenow told them she would agree only if those receiving farm subsidies were also tested. Anti-hunger advocates remained unhappy, saying the SNAP reductions could reduce benefits an average of $90 per month for hundreds of thousands of households. On the other hand, conservatives felt, despite total budget savings estimated at $17 billion over 10 years, that the latest farm bill remained overly costly. But the final legislation crafted by Stabenow overwhelmingly cleared the Senate on a bipartisan vote, 68-32.

With Roberts taking the chairmanship in 2015, Stabenow worked with him to forge a compromise to require labeling of genetically modified food; it was signed into law by Obama. A number of consumer groups were unhappy that the legislation mandated the labeling be done through scannable smartphone codes rather than text or symbols. At the same time, Roberts was forced to retreat from earlier legislation he favored that would have prohibited states from requiring GMO labels -- a reaction to Vermont's passage of its own labeling law. Roberts and Stabenow also crafted a compromise on reauthorization of the school meals program, including largely maintaining the child nutrition standards that First Lady Michelle Obama had adopted as a signature issue. It cleared their committee unanimously, but efforts to enact a bill into law fell short in the days prior to adjournment. Roberts and Stabenow vowed to try again in 2017, although the task was likely to be complicated by the priority of drafting a new farm bill.

Stabenow won a third term in 2012 against former Rep. Pete Hoekstra, a onetime House Intelligence Committee chairman who had made an unsuccessful stab at Michigan's governorship two years earlier. Early on, she was targeted by what was arguably the most controversial-and ill-advised-TV ad of that election cycle. It ran during the Super Bowl in February 2012, featuring an Asian woman bicycling through a rice paddy and thanking "Sen. Debbie Spend-It-Now" in broken English for sending U.S. jobs to China. The spot caused an uproar, but not in the way Hoekstra intended. Republicans and Democrats alike attacked him for playing on racial stereotypes. Even the actress in the ad apologized. Hoekstra never recovered, and Stabenow bettered her 2006 performance, winning re-election with 59 percent.

As the 2017-2018 election cycle got underway, the senior Republican member of Michigan's House delegation, Republican Fred Upton, was contemplating a challenge to Stabenow. While Upton had accumulated more than three decades of House seniority since his initial election in 1986, party term limit rules forced him to relinquish the chairmanship of the powerful Energy and Commerce Committee at the end of 2016. Some less conventional Republican contenders could also emerge: Ted Nugent, aka the Motor City Madman and one of rock n'roll's few outspoken conservatives, said he was considering a run. As Nugent put it in a tweet: "If these GOP sonsabitches don't get it right this time I will come charging in."

Junior Senator

Gary Peters (D)

Elected 2014, term expires 2020, 1st term; b. Dec 01, 1958, Pontiac; Alma College (MI), B.A.; Michigan State University, M.A.; University of Detroit (MI), M.B.A.; Wayne State University Law School (MI), J.D.; Episcopalian; Married (Colleen Ochoa); 3 children.

Military Career: U.S. Naval Reserve, 1993-2000, 2001-2005.

Elected Office: Rochester Hills City Council, 1991-1993; MI Senate, 1995-2002; U.S. House, 2009-2015.

Professional Career: Assistant Vice President., Merril Lynch, 1980-1989; Vice President., UBS/ Paine Webber, 1989-2003; Chief admin. officer, MI bureau of investments, 2003; Commissioner, MI Lottery Bureau, 2003-2007; Professor, Central MI University, 2007-2008.

DC Office: 724 HSOB 20510, 202-224-6221, Fax: 202-224-7387, peters.senate.gov.

State Offices: Detroit, 313-226-6020; Grand Rapids, 616-233-9150; Lansing, 517-377-1508; Marquette, 906-226-4554; Rochester, 248-608-8040; Saginaw, 989-754-0112; Traverse City, 231-947-7773.

Committees: *Armed Services*: Airland, Emerging Threats & Capabilities, Strategic Forces. *Commerce, Science & Transportation*: Aviation Operations, Safety & Security, Communications, Technology, Innovation & the Internet, Oceans, Atmosphere, Fisheries & Coast Guard (RMM), Space, Science & Competitiveness. *Homeland Security & Government Affairs*: Federal Spending Oversight & Emergency Management (RMM), Investigations.

Group Ratings

	ADA	ACLU	AFL-CIO	LCV	ITI	COC	HAFA	ACU	CFG	FRC
2016	-	88%	-	100%	80%	63%	7%	4%	13%	0%
2015	85%	C	100%	100%	C	38%	C	4%	0%	0%

Almanac Ratings 2015

	Economy	Social	Foreign	Composite
Liberal	94%	100%	80%	91%
Conservative	6%	0%	20%	9%

Key Votes of the 114th Congress

1. Keystone pipeline	N	5. National Security Data	Y	9. Gun Sales Checks	Y
2. Export-Import Bank	N	6. Iran Nuclear Deal	N	10. Sanctuary Cities	N
3. Debt Ceiling Increase	Y	7. Puerto Rico Debt	Y	11. Planned Parenthood	N
4. Homeland Security $$	Y	8. Loretta Lynch A.G	Y	12. Trade deals	N

Election Results

Election	Name (Party)	Vote (%)		Cand. Spent	Ind. Exp. Support	Ind. Exp. Oppose
2014 General	Gary Peters (D)	1,704,936	(55%)	$10,289,555	$5,970,696	$8,040,765
	Terri Lynn Land (R)	1,290,199	(41%)	$12,270,048	$1,960,159	$14,712,548
	Jim Fulner (L)	62,897	(2%)			
2014 Primary	Gary Peters (D)	unopposed				

Prior winning percentages: House: 2012 (82%), 2010 (50%), 2008 (52%)

As Michigan's junior senator, Gary Peters *is* the Democratic freshman class of 2014-the sole Democrat to win an open Senate seat in an election cycle that held few bright spots for his party. While he periodically travels around the Wolverine State aboard a Harley-Davidson Dyna Super Glide -- he has been riding motorcycles since he was a teenager -- Peters is frequently referred to as wonky. He boasts degrees from four different colleges and universities in his home state, and, in the Senate, he often has focused on issues that can only be described as, well, wonky. He has frequently reached across the political aisle to co-author legislation dealing with the working of the inner gears of government. In short, it's not the type of stuff that captures a lot of headlines back home.

So it comes as little surprise that Peters has been described as lacking in charisma, or even a bit stodgy, by those who have questioned his political appeal. Nonetheless, he has had success at the polls going back more than two decades, including three tough races for the House before moving to the Senate. "Peters does get called wonky a lot, because admittedly, he is," Democratic consultant T.J. Bucholz told the *MLive Media Group* during the 2014 campaign. "He's a smart guy, cerebral and thoughtful. But to be fair, this is the race to replace Carl Levin, who is no firebrand either." Levin, another wonky politician, held the seat for more than one-third of a century, ultimately rising to chair the Senate Armed Services Committee.

There is little question that Peters benefited from political serendipity in 2014: In a year in which little went wrong for Senate Republicans in most battleground races, little went right for them in Michigan. Levin announced his retirement in March 2013, and Peters immediately expressed interest. He had the Democratic nomination all but locked up in weeks, as other potential Democratic contenders took themselves out of the running. When the eventual Republican nominee, former Michigan Secretary of State Terri Lynn Land, announced in late spring, her candidacy was met with something short of enthusiasm among party leaders, and Republicans spent months trying to recruit another candidate. When that failed, Land proceeded to run a campaign that alternated between bumbling and bizarre.

Peters' solid, if unspectacular, Senate bid featured ads emphasizing his military service and family history. His family has lived in Oakland County outside Detroit for five generations, and Peters grew up in Pontiac, the son of a public school teacher and a nursing home aide. After college, he spent more than two decades working as a financial advisor for a couple of large investment firms, while earning a law degree and an M.B.A. He enlisted in the U.S. Navy Reserve, becoming a lieutenant commander and serving in the Persian Gulf as part of the military operation enforcing a no-fly zone following the 1991 Gulf War. He left the Navy Reserve in 2000, but re-enlisted following 9/11, and served for another four years. At the beginning of 2017,] Peters was given a seat on the Armed Services Committee -- re-establishing a Michigan presence on the panel that Levin chaired for a total of a decade.

Peters' political career began with his election to the Rochester Hills City Council in 1991, followed by winning a seat in the Michigan Senate in 1994, where he led an effort to ban oil drilling in the Great Lakes. Forced by term limits to give up his Senate seat, Peters mounted a short-lived candidacy for governor before shifting to the state attorney general's race. He lost narrowly in the 2002 election, his only electoral defeat. He then spent nearly five years as the state's lottery commissioner, earning another degree on the side at Michigan State University-an M.A. in philosophy, with a focus on the ethics of development. Peters challenged eight-term Republican Rep. Joe Knollenberg in 2008, and received help from the national Democratic Party and the United Auto Workers. Jack Kevorkian, a physician who garnered national attention as an assisted suicide advocate, was among three other candidates. Peters won with 52 percent, becoming the first Democrat since 1893 to represent the district.

Peters has described himself as a centrist who is pro-business and socially liberal. As a House member, he backed his party on major votes, but showed independence at times. He voted against the 2011 bill to raise the nation's debt limit, saying the measure didn't close tax loopholes. In his freshman term, he was put on the 2010 conference committee that drafted the final version of the landmark Dodd-Frank financial regulatory overhaul; Peters added a provision intended to boost the financing businesses of the nation's automakers. His investment background made him a logical choice for the Dodd-Frank conference committee, although his appointment also appeared designed to bolster him in his first re-election race.

Running for a second term in the traditionally Republican district in 2010, Peters won, 50%-47%, in a year less hospitable to Democrats. In 2012, Michigan lost a congressional seat through reapportionment, and the new map carved up Peters' district. He faced two tough options: challenge long-time Democratic Rep. Sander Levin (Carl Levin's older brother) in another Detroit suburban district, or go up against freshman Rep. Hansen Clarke, an African-American, in a majority-black district encompassing a portion of the city. Peters had some ties to the latter district from his state Senate days, and he courted labor unions and church leaders. He won 47 percent of the vote to Clarke's 35 percent, with another African-American candidate, Southfield Mayor Brenda Lawrence (who captured the seat in 2014) getting 13 percent. Peters went on to easily prevail in the general election.

Entering the Senate race in early 2013, Peters-dubbed "the congressman from Chrysler" in the House for his stalwart defense of the auto industry-sought to emphasize job creation and other middle-class concerns. "I've always believed that the things middle-class families struggle with around their kitchen tables should define my work in Washington," he said in announcing his candidacy. Both Carl Levin and Democratic Sen. Debbie Stabenow endorsed Peters in the late spring of 2013, more than 14 months prior to the primary-in which he ran unopposed. His Republican opponent, Land, also ended up unopposed in the primary, but only after GOP strategists failed to convince a couple of high-profile House members, Reps. Dave Camp and. Mike Rogers, to run.

Polls in early 2014 gave Land a lead, as her campaign benefited from her family's wealth (she ultimately donated $3.35 million in personal funds to a campaign that spent a total of about $12.3 million). But she made a couple of early missteps, and never managed to regain her footing. She launched her TV campaign with what may have been the oddest ad of the election cycle. In it, Land declares: "Congressman Gary Peters and his buddies want you to believe I'm waging a war on women. Really? Think about that for a moment." The rest of the ad is 12 seconds of silence as Land sips from a coffee mug, shakes her head, and looks at her watch. The ad was criticized in Republican circles. Several weeks later, Land put on a lackluster performance before the Detroit Regional Chamber of Commerce, and then all but froze when facing questions from the press. "I can't do this," she declared, as she pushed away a cluster of microphones and departed. The gaffe was compounded by efforts to avoid the media for much of the rest of the campaign, as her organization was often criticized for failing to disclose in advance where she would be appearing. When the NRSC canceled a $1 million TV buy in the closing weeks, it was seen as tantamount to a concession. Peters won easily, 55%-41%, on Election Day.

Three days before the voters went to the polls, Peters became the only 2014 Senate candidate for whom President Barack Obama made a personal appearance. Obama's unpopularity at that point in his presidency had prompted most candidates in battleground states to shun him, and Peters beforehand seemed diffident about the president showing up. But, when Obama appeared at a rally at Detroit's Wayne State University, Peters stressed the bailout of the auto industry, declaring to the crowd, "Thank God, our president stood up for American workers." A little more than two years later, on the Obama Administration's final day in office, it left Peters with something of a farewell present: The site of a former General Motors plant in Michigan's Ypsilanti Township, was designated as proving ground for the development of driverless cars, one of 10 such sites designated nationwide out of 60 that applied. Peters, one of the project's leading advocates, was elated, declaring: "We cannot lose being at the center of this activity for the auto industry. This is critical for our long-term future."

Upon arriving in the Senate, Peters assumed a seat on the Commerce, Science and Transportation Committee, which has jurisdiction over the nation's automakers, as well as the Homeland Security and Governmental Affairs Committee. Lacking Democratic colleagues in the freshman class of 2014, he forged alliances with several GOP freshmen -- largely on issues dealing with government efficiency. With Oklahoma Republican James Lankford, Peters introduced legislation requiring federal agencies to encourage use of remanufactured parts in federal vehicle repairs. The bill, signed into law in late 2015, was spurred by a Government Accountability Office study of the matter requested by Peters. Several months later, Obama signed another Peters-authored bill with a mouthful of a name: the "Making Electronic Government Accountable By Yielding Tangible Efficiencies" Act, or MEGABYTE Act for short. Cosponsored with Louisiana Republican Bill Cassidy, it sought to reduce government waste by improving the management of federal software licenses. "Billions of taxpayer dollars could be saved because federal agencies are now required to keep track of what software they buy," a joint release from the two senators declared.

Peters did receive early recognition on a higher-profile issue: His efforts in a year-long legislative battle to secure federal aid to deal with lead-tainted drinking water in the financially strapped, majority-black city of Flint. The crisis had been precipitated when the city's emergency manager switched the source of the city's drinking water to save money, causing the corrosion of water supply pipes. As a stopgap spending bill to keep the federal government in operation came up just before the Senate's October pre-election recess, Peters and Stabenow used their leverage to block its passage -- conceding only after the House agreed to attach $170 million in aid to Flint to another piece of legislation that Obama later signed into law. Accepting an award for his efforts on behalf of Flint during a 2017 Martin Luther King Day event, Peters observed it had not been easy to convince fellow legislators that a man-made crisis was entitled to the kind of federal aid granted in the case of natural disasters. "If you look into the eyes of a child who's suffering as a result of tainted water, that child doesn't care if it's a man-made problem or a natural problem," he asserted.

FIRST DISTRICT

Jack Bergman (R)

Elected 2016, 1st term; b. Feb 02, 1947, Shakopee, MN; Gustavus Adolphus College, B.A., 1969; University of West Florida, M.B.A., 1975; Lutheran; Married (Cindy Bergman); 5 children; 8 grandchildren.

Military Career: U.S Marine Corps, 1969-1975 & 2002-2009; LA National Guard, 1969-2009.

Professional Career: Commercial pilot; Business owner.

DC Office: 414 CHOB 20515, 202-225-4735, Fax: 202-225-4710, bergman.house.gov.

State Offices: Traverse City, 231-714-4785.

Committees: *Budget*. *Natural Resources*: Federal Lands, Indian, Insular & Alaska Native Affairs, Oversight & Investigations. *Veterans' Affairs*: Disability Assistance & Memorial Affairs, Oversight & Investigations (Chmn).

Election Results

Election	Name (Party)	Vote (%)	Cand. Spent	Ind. Exp. Support	Ind. Exp. Oppose
2016 General	Jack Bergman (R)	197,777 (55%)	$1,343,098	$441,479	$2,653,119
	Lon Johnson (D)	144,334 (40%)	$2,027,392	$18,605	$1,885,036
	Diane Bostow (L)	13,386 (4%)	$4,569		
2016 Primary	Jack Bergman (R)	33,624 (39%)			
	Tom Casperson (R)	27,811 (32%)			
	Jason Allen (R)	25,604 (29%)			

Republican Jack Bergman was elected in 2016 to this district, which Democrats had considered one of their best open-seat opportunities nationwide. In the end, the contest was not particularly close. A retired three-star Marine Corps lieutenant general, Bergman benefited from his party label in what recently had been a swing district.

A native of Minnesota, Bergman said that his ancestors worked in the iron mines of the Upper Peninsula as far back as the 1800s. He got his bachelor's from Gustavus Adolphus College in St. Peter, Minnesota, and a master's of business administration from the University of West Florida. During more than 25 years in the military, he served as commanding general of the Marine Forces Reserve in Louisiana. Bergman also was a pilot for Northwest Airlines and built a business that sold surgical equipment. Although he had no previous experience as a political candidate, he had served on the advisory council for Louisiana Republican Gov. Bobby Jindal. He resided in Watersmeet, a small town in the Ottawa National Forest, at the far western end of the U.P. He ran for a seat in the Michigan state House in 2012, but narrowly lost in the Republican primary.

When Republican Rep. Dan Benishek decided not to seek reelection, Bergman ran as the outsider candidate in the Republican primary against two local political figures: state Sen. Tom Casperson from the U.P., who was a vocal advocate of more wolf hunting, and former state Sen. Jason Allen of Traverse City, who had been an official of the Michigan Veterans Affairs Agency. Bergman benefited from spending more than $270,000 of his own money in the primary campaign. He won with 39 percent of the vote to 32 percent for Casperson and 29 percent for Allen. Lon Johnson, who had chaired the Michigan Democratic Party, easily won the Democratic nomination with 73 percent of the vote against Jerry Cannon, a former county sheriff who lost to Benishek, 52%-45%, in 2014.

Johnson entered the general election as the more successful fundraiser, with a total of $2 million, to $1.4 million for Bergman. Each candidate got more than $2 million of support from national party groups. Johnson emphasized his status as a political outsider against party official Johnson, whose wife Julianna Smoot was national deputy campaign manager for President Barack Obama in 2012 and founded a political consulting firm in Washington, D.C. With neither candidate especially well-known in this sprawling district, the unexpectedly large 22-point victory for Donald Trump in the presidential contest likely provided coattails for Bergman. He took the House contest, 55%-40%.

In the House, Bergman became chairman of the Veterans' Affairs Subcommittee on Oversight and Investigations. He also got seats on the Budget and Natural Resources committees.

Northern Michigan: Upper Peninsula

Population		Race and Ethnicity		Income	
Total	703,859	White	91.4%	Median Income	$43,591 (356 out of 435)
Land area	25,028	Black	1.6%		
Pop/ sq mi	28.1	Latino	1.7%		
Born in state	79.7%	Asian	0.0%	Under $50,000	56.6%
		Two races	2.2%	$50,000-$99,999	30.7%
Age Groups		Other	2.4%	$100,000-$199,999	10.7%
Under 18	19.3%			$200,000 or more	2.0%
18-34	19.2%	**Education**		Poverty Rate	15.3%
35-64	41.1%	H.S grad or less	43.7%		
Over 64	20.4%	Some college	33.2%	**Health Insurance**	
		College Degree, 4 yr	14.6%	With health insurance coverage	89.2%
Work		Post grad	8.5%		
White Collar	30.3%				
Sales and Service	45.0%	**Military**		**Public Assistance**	
Blue Collar	24.7%	Veteran	11.8%	Cash public assistance income	3.0%
Government	14.4%	Active Duty	0.1%		
				Food stamp/SNAP benefits	14.7%

Voter Turnout			
2015 Total Citizens 18+	562,051	2016 House Turnout as % CVAP	64%
2016 House turnout	360,271	2014 House Turnout as % CVAP	44%

2012 Presidential Vote		
Mitt Romney	189,387	(54%)
Barack Obama	160,231	(45%)

2016 Presidential Vote		
Donald Trump	210,816	(58%)
Hillary Clinton	133,239	(36%)
Gary Johnson	13,785	(4%)

Cook Partisan Voting Index: R+9

Michigan's Upper Peninsula, commonly known as the U.P., is a land apart. Surrounded on three sides by frigid Lakes Superior, Huron and Michigan, the U.P. is no farther north than Montreal or Seattle, but there are places here that have some of the coldest climates in settled parts of North America. The winter storms can be legendary: The area surrounding Keweenaw County, which juts into Lake Superior, often ranks high in the nation's heaviest snowfall. These storms can also be cruel. The "gales of November" have caught hundreds of vessels by surprise and sent them to the bottom of the lake, including the SS *Edmund Fitzgerald*, whose loss was memorialized in a Gordon Lightfoot ballad.

With ground too frozen and stony and a growing season too short for most crops, the peninsula was considered a poor consolation prize when much of it was appended to the Michigan Territory in 1836 in exchange for the incipient state giving up its claim to Toledo and its surrounding areas. This ended an occasionally violent feud with Ohio known as the Toledo War. Views on the fairness of the exchange shifted when prospectors found rich veins of ore up north.

The mineral veins of the Keweenaw Peninsula eventually produced more than 13 billion pounds of copper, while the Marquette, Menominee and Gogebic iron ranges produced more than 1 billion tons of iron ore. Immigrants flocked here to work the mines. Most prominent were Finns, who must have found this cold land with its lakes and hills much like home. The western counties of the U.P. remain the only ones in the United States with a plurality of residents of Finnish ancestry. By the early 1900s, the U.P. had become a northern industrial belt with a workforce disposed to radical ideas and union movements.

A major strike in 1913-14 and falling ore prices after World War I accelerated the copper decline. The Empire Mine in Marquette County closed in August 2016 because of limited supply and demand and its final 400 workers lost their jobs. Other industries have taken root. The region's natural beauty - 90 percent of the U.P. is forested - has made tourism a leading economic driver. Skiers can take advantage of the average 200 inches of annual snowfall at several mountain resorts. In October 2016, *Lonely Planet* designated the area as one of its 10 best "value destinations," with abundant outdoor opportunities, including mountain biking and surfing. Population of the U.P. peaked at 332,000 in 1920. In 2014, there were 310,000 "Yoopers," as the locals call themselves, many of whom harbor a strong sense of place. The proposed Soo Locks Modernization Project in the St. Lawrence Seaway has gained the attention of state and national advocates of more infrastructure spending.

The 1st Congressional District of Michigan includes the Upper Peninsula and 16 1/2 northern counties in the Lower Peninsula. Almost half the people live in the U.P. Marquette, with 21,300 people, is the largest city in the district. Mackinac Island, home to a resort area where almost all cars are banned (even UPS delivers packages by bicycle), lies just east of the breathtaking Mackinac Bridge, which connects the two peninsulas. State officials created in April 2015 the Superior Trade Zone to encourage economic cooperation between the two largest cities, Marquette and Escanaba. On the Lower Peninsula, along Lake Michigan, are affluent resort areas around Petoskey and Charlevoix, long summer places for people from Chicago (this is Ernest Hemingway's "Up in Michigan"). There is some agriculture on the district's southern end; the Traverse City area accounts for nearly 50 percent of tart cherry production in the United States.

Politically, the U.P. has a lengthy Democratic tradition, but it has moved toward Republicans in recent years. This is one part of Michigan that has opposed many Democratic environmental and gun control stands. Mitt Romney won the district 54%-45% over President Barack Obama in 2012, a six-point increase over the GOP vote in 2008. That resulted in part from affection for Romney in his home state. When Donald Trump took the mostly blue-collar and low-income district, 58%-36%, it became clear that the partisan shifts were more deep-seated. Marquette was the only county that voted for Hillary Clinton, with 49 percent of the vote.

SECOND DISTRICT

Bill Huizenga (R)

Elected 2010, 4th term; b. Jan 31, 1969, Zeeland; Calvin College (MI), B.A., 1992; Christian Reformed Church; Married (Natalie Huizenga); 5 children.

Elected Office: MI House, 2003-2008.

Professional Career: Realtor, 1991-1996; Aide, Rep. Pete Hoekstra, 1997-2002; Admin., Zeeland Christian Schls., 2009-2010; Co-owner, Huizenga Gravel, 1999-present.

DC Office: 2232 RHOB 20515, 202-225-4401, Fax: 202-226-0779, huizenga.house.gov.

State Offices: Grand Haven, 616-414-5516; Grandville, 616-570-0917.

Committees: *Financial Services*: Capital Markets, Securities & Investment (Chmn), Monetary Policy & Trade.

Group Ratings

	ADA	ACLU	AFL-CIO	LCV	ITI	COC	HAFA	ACU	CFG	FRC
2016	-	5%	-	3%	100%	100%	73%	84%	82%	100%
2015	0%	C	0%	0%	C	80%	C	96%	89%	100%

Almanac Ratings 2015

	Economy	Social	Foreign	Composite
Liberal	3%	0%	4%	2%
Conservative	97%	100%	96%	98%

Key Votes of the 114th Congress

1. Keystone Pipeline	Y	5. Puerto Rico Debt	Y	9. Offenses by Aliens	Y
2. Trade Deals	Y	6. Medical Marijuana	N	10. Troops in Iraq	N
3. Export-Import Bank	N	7. Sanctuary Cities	Y	11. Homeland Security $$	N
4. Debt Ceiling Increase	N	8. Armor-piercing Bullets	Y	12. Trade Adjustment aid	Y

Election Results

Election	Name (Party)	Vote (%)		Cand. Spent	Ind. Exp. Support	Ind. Exp. Oppose
2016 General	Bill Huizenga (R)	212,508	(63%)	$1,187,852		
	Dennis B. Murphy (D)	110,391	(33%)	$12,980		
	Erwin Haas (L)	8,154	(2%)			
2016 Primary	Bill Huizenga (R)		(100%)			

Prior winning percentages: 2014 (64%), 2012 (61%), 2010 (65%)

Republican Bill Huizenga was elected in 2010 to succeed his friend and former boss, Rep. Pete Hoekstra. He upholds the rock-solid conservatism of his western Michigan district and has positioned himself as a key player to overhaul federal regulation of banks and other financial service firms.

Huizenga grew up in Zeeland, and minus a few brief absences, he has lived there all of his life. His grandparents were farmers who started a gravel business by selling the leftover sand and stone that was lying around the farm. In high school, Huizenga was an inattentive student who ultimately transferred to vocational school. His instructors told him he had academic potential and advised him to go to college. Huizenga studied political science at Calvin College. Between his freshman and sophomore years, he made his first real estate investment: With money saved from working in his father's gravel pit, he became the junior stakeholder in a 19-unit housing development. As a young adult, Huizenga indulged his love of travel, taking trips around the world. During anti-government unrest just before the fall of the Berlin Wall, he was chased by riot police and dogs at a pro-democracy rally in Prague.

After college, he worked for a local real estate firm and took over as co-owner in the family business, Huizenga Gravel. As a business owner, he says, he has gained a firm understanding of the regulatory, tax and compliance issues that small businesses face. Hoekstra offered him a job in his district office, and he later became Hoekstra's director of public policy. He won a seat in the Michigan House, where he was chairman of the Commerce Committee.

When Hoekstra ran for Michigan governor, the real contest for his heavily Republican district was the GOP primary. In the seven-way race, former pro-football tight end Jay Riemersma, also of Zeeland, raised $850,000 to Huizenga's $553,000. Huizenga touted his conservative credentials, including his support for replacing the income tax with a 23 percent sales tax and creating private Social Security accounts. Riemersma, the former regional director for the Family Research Council, also ran as an anti-abortion and fiscal conservative. He attacked Huizenga for voting for a state business tax in 2007. Huizenga eked out a victory with a better political organization, built largely on the many contacts that he made with local political and business leaders while on Hoekstra's staff. He prevailed by just 663 votes out of about 106,000 cast. In the general election, he faced nominal Democratic opposition.

Huizenga won quick notice for his facility with the inner workings of Congress. He enacted a bill in 2012 giving taxpayers and businesses who submit information to the Consumer Financial Protection Bureau the same confidentiality protection that other financial regulators are required to provide. After opposing the New Year's Day 2013 budget deal aimed at averting the so-called "fiscal cliff" of tax hikes and spending cuts, he called for providing block grants for Medicare and Medicaid to states while re-examining who qualifies for Social Security. In addition to sharing many fiscal views with now-Speaker Paul Ryan, Huizenga joined Ryan in grueling P90X fitness workouts.

On the Financial Services Committee, Huizenga chaired for two years the Subcommittee on Monetary Policy and Trade, where he used his oversight authority over the Federal Reserve Board to promote more transparent discussion of monetary policy. In 2015, the House passed his Mortgage Choice Act, which he said was designed to remove "technicalities" in qualification requirements for lower and middle-income homeowners. With other House conservatives, he raised questions about the organization of the Export-Import Bank and prevented it from conducting business for several months. But, with strong support for the bank in the business community, its opponents ultimately lost their battle.

Huizenga took over in 2017 as chairman of the Capital Markets, Securities and Investment Subcommittee, where he intensified his campaign to cut back the Dodd-Frank financial regulation law and reduce its impact on businesses. In February 2017, he enacted his bill that repealed Dodd-Frank regulations by the Securities and Exchange Commission that required mining and oil and gas companies to disclose payments that they make to foreign governments. That was the third bill that President Donald Trump signed into law. Huizenga attended high school with the younger brother of Betsy DeVos, and viewed Trump's selection of her as Education Secretary as an inspired choice.

Huizenga has consistently won reelection with more than 60 percent of the vote and seems entrenched in this Republican bastion.

West-Central Michigan: Holland, Muskegon

Population		Race and Ethnicity		Income	
Total	718,740	White	80.0%	Median Income	$49,551 (261 out of 435)
Land area	3,281	Black	6.1%		
Pop/ sq mi	219.0	Latino	9.1%		
Born in state	79.0%	Asian	0.0%	Under $50,000	50.4%
		Two races	2.2%	$50,000-$99,999	33.2%
Age Groups		Other	0.5%	$100,000-$199,999	14.3%
Under 18	24.3%			$200,000 or more	2.2%
18-34	23.7%	**Education**		Poverty Rate	14.8%
35-64	38.1%	H.S grad or less	42.7%		
Over 64	13.8%	Some college	32.8%	**Health Insurance**	
		College Degree, 4 yr	16.6%	With health insurance coverage	91.1%
Work		Post grad	7.9%		
White Collar	30.8%				
Sales and Service	40.6%	**Military**		**Public Assistance**	
Blue Collar	28.7%	Veteran	8.0%	Cash public assistance income	3.7%
Government	9.4%	Active Duty	0.0%	Food stamp/SNAP benefits	15.6%

Voter Turnout			
2015 Total Citizens 18+	523,262	2016 House Turnout as % CVAP	65%
2016 House turnout	339,328	2014 House Turnout as % CVAP	40%

2012 Presidential Vote		
Mitt Romney	184,732	(56%)
Barack Obama	142,077	(43%)

2016 Presidential Vote		
Donald Trump	193,201	(55%)
Hillary Clinton	132,467	(38%)
Gary Johnson	15,127	(4%)

Cook Partisan Voting Index: R+9

When the glaciers receded from Michigan some 16,000 years ago, they left behind piles of boulders, sand and clay. Over time, the lake winds eroded the boulders, while waves ground up glacial drift deposited in the lake and washed it ashore. The end result is a lakeshore that today is home to the largest collection of freshwater dunes in the world, located in several state parks along the western rim of the state.

In the late 19th century, the river ports on this shoreline were choked with logs and full of lumbermen from Norway and Sweden, Ireland and Scotland, Quebec and New England. During the timber boom, the shoreline was the locus of the country's largest migration from the Netherlands and today still has the nation's largest concentration of Dutch-Americans. Wooden shoes are now seen only at the Tulip Festival in the town of Holland, but conscientious Dutch work habits have produced many highly skilled workers. This is a busy manufacturing area, with products ranging from baby food at Gerber in Fremont to office furniture at Herman Miller in Zeeland and Haworth in Holland. Away from the shore is fruit-growing country, with some of the nation's largest cherry orchards to the north and blueberry patches to the south.

The 2nd Congressional District of Michigan occupies four counties on the Lake Michigan shoreline, plus a tier of inland counties. It stretches from the old lumber port of Ludington south to Holland. About a fifth of the district's residents live in an arc of suburbs surrounding Grand Rapids in Kent County. The 2007-09 recession hit this area hard, with unemployment close to 20 percent. Since then, the economy in western Michigan (including Grand Rapids) has diversified and has had the strongest growth in the state. Holland-based Ottawa, the most populous county in the district, grew by 17 percent from 2000 to 2015; its unemployment rate in December 2016 dropped to 3.1 percent. The more industrial Muskegon grew by only 2 percent during that period. Alcoa, which had been the largest industrial employer in Muskegon with 2,200 jobs, spun off its non-aluminum operations to Arconic, a new company, in 2016.

For years, Dutch-American voters have been strongly Republican and fast-growing. Heavily Dutch Ottawa County gave native-son Mitt Romney 67 percent of the vote in 2012; Donald Trump got 62 percent in 2016. The chief exception to Republican voting patterns comes from the old industrial centers in Muskegon County. Hillary Clinton under-performed in Muskegon, 48%-46%, compared to the 58 percent that President Barack Obama got in 2012. In 2008 and 2012, the 2nd was the most Republican district in the state. Trump's lead of 55%-38% in 2016 ranked only fourth highest.

THIRD DISTRICT

Justin Amash (R)

Elected 2010, 4th term; b. Apr 18, 1980, Grand Rapids; University of Michigan, B.A.; University of Michigan Law School, J.D.; Grand Rapids Christian H.S.; Eastern Orthodox; Married (Kara Amash); 3 children.

Elected Office: MI House, 2008-2010.

Professional Career: Practicing attorney, 2006-2007; Consultant, MI Industrial Tools, 2005-2010.

DC Office: 114 CHOB 20515, 202-225-3831, Fax: 202-225-5144, amash.house.gov.

State Offices: Battle Creek, 269-205-3823; Grand Rapids, 616-451-8383.

Committees: *Oversight & Government Reform:* Information Technology National Security

Group Ratings

	ADA	ACLU	AFL-CIO	LCV	ITI	COC	HAFA	ACU	CFG	FRC
2016	-	41%	-	8%	33%	64%	91%	83%	100%	75%
2015	20%	C	17%	20%	C	35%	C	96%	97%	83%

Almanac Ratings 2015

	Economy	Social	Foreign	Composite
Liberal	30%	15%	51%	32%
Conservative	70%	85%	49%	68%

Key Votes of the 114th Congress

1. Keystone Pipeline	N	5. Puerto Rico Debt	N	9. Offenses by Aliens	Y
2. Trade Deals	N	6. Medical Marijuana	Y	10. Troops in Iraq	
3. Export-Import Bank	N	7. Sanctuary Cities	Y	11. Homeland Security $$	N
4. Debt Ceiling Increase	N	8. Armor-piercing Bullets	Y	12. Trade Adjustment aid	N

Election Results

Election	Name (Party)	Vote (%)		Cand. Spent	Ind. Exp. Support	Ind. Exp. Oppose
2016 General	Justin Amash (R)	203,545	(60%)	$733,256		
	Douglas Smith (D)	128,400	(38%)	$24,583		
2016 Primary	Justin Amash (R)		(100%)			

Prior winning percentages: 2014 (58%), 2012 (53%), 2010 (60%)

Justin Amash, a Republican elected in 2010, has been one of the most iconoclastic members of the House. A persistent thorn in the side of GOP leaders with his libertarian views, he lost his seat on the Budget Committee in 2012 for his refusal to toe the party line. When John Boehner resigned in October 2015, Amash voted for the new House Speaker, Paul Ryan. But he and his allies continued their independence.

Amash was born in Grand Rapids, the son of a wealthy Palestinian tool importer who immigrated to the United States with the sponsorship of a Christian church. He began high school at the time of the Republican tidal wave of 1994 and graduated as class valedictorian. He majored in economics and graduated magna cum laude at the University of Michigan, then earned a degree from its law school. He counts himself as an admirer of both the 19th-century author Frederic Bastiat, who argued against taxing people to pay for schools or roads, and the 20th-century writer Friedrich Hayek, a favorite of the tea party movement who strongly opposed government intervention in the economy. Amash kept Hayek's portrait on the wall of his congressional campaign offices.

He has been a consultant to his family's tool-import business, and served as a corporate lawyer for a year before he was elected to the Michigan House in 2008. He fought to eliminate state taxes on businesses. *The Grand Rapids Press* reported in July 2010 that Amash was the only "no" vote on 59 bills in his first term.

Amash entered the 3rd District race, he said, because he was fed up with the moderate voting record of eight-term GOP incumbent Vern Ehlers. When Ehlers announced his retirement, that opened the door for other Republican candidates, including former Kent County Commissioner Steve Heacock, whom Ehlers personally asked to run. In the primary race, Amash outraised both Heacock and state Sen. Bill Hardiman, and he was endorsed by the anti-tax group Club for Growth. He won the primary, getting 40 percent of the vote to Heacock's 26 percent and Hardiman's 24 percent. In the general election, Democratic lawyer Pat Miles accused Amash of exporting jobs to China through his ownership of Dynamic Source International, a Chinese company that supplied industrial tools to his father's tool-import business. Amash accused Miles of supporting taxpayer-funded abortions because he backed the Democrats' health care overhaul. He won, 60%-37%.

Amash immediately displayed his independence by refusing to vote in favor of House legislation he believed was unconstitutional or that he was not given adequate time to consider, voting "present" on numerous bills. He was one of 22 Republicans in July 2011 to oppose Boehner's bill to raise the federal debt limit. He explained to *The New York Times* how he votes: "I follow a set of principles, I follow the Constitution. And that's what I base my votes on. Limited government, economic freedom and individual liberty."

Amash introduced a balanced budget amendment that would limit spending to the federal government's average annual revenues for the previous three years. He deployed his Facebook page to detail his reasons for all of his actions and got into a "Facebook feud" with the National Rifle Association for opposing legislation that granted reciprocity for state concealed weapons permits. He said the measure subverted federalism.

In 2012, Democrats thought they had a chance to defeat Amash by drawing alienated GOP moderates from him, and nominated Steve Pestka, a former state representative, prosecutor and judge. He criticized Amash for his contrarian votes and began climbing in the polls after loaning his campaign more than $1 million. Amash beat Pestka by a not overwhelming 53%-44%. Pestka edged Amash in Calhoun County, but Kent County hewed to its historic Republican tendency.

Returning to Washington for a lame-duck session, Amash learned that the Boehner-controlled Republican Steering Committee had taken him off the Budget Committee, making him one of four Republicans to receive such punishment. He called it "a slap in the face" to the GOP's expanding libertarian faction. He was a central figure in an attempt to persuade fellow Republicans to vote against Boehner for Speaker in January 2013, but the effort collapsed shortly before the vote when the group could not secure sufficient votes.

Amash defended former National Security Agency contractor Edward Snowden after Snowden leaked details of the agency's domestic surveillance efforts. He managed to unite the Republican leadership and the Obama White House against himself when he proposed an amendment to strip funding for an NSA phone-surveillance program; it fell short by just 12 votes. In 2015, when the House overwhelmingly voted to end the meta-data phone collection program, he voted against the bill because he said "it actually expands the statutory basis for the large-scale collection of most data." In 2016, he helped to defeat a House bill that would strengthen the terrorism-fighting Patriot Act by encouraging banks to alert federal authorities about possible illicit financing. Amash was instrumental in forming the Freedom Caucus, a group of libertarian-minded conservatives who have sought to reduce the control of Republican leaders and to make the House a more open institution. That has given the Freedom Caucus - and Amash - occasional veto power in the House. Following the 2016 election, he helped to form the Second Amendment Caucus on behalf of pro-gun legislation.

Establishment Republicans challenged Amash in the 2014 primary. Their candidate was Brian Ellis, who served on the East Grand Rapids school board and drew support from local and national Chamber of Commerce-types. Ellis criticized what he called Amash's "bizarre" voting record. Amash's allies in the Club for Growth ran ads bashing Ellis for "leaving massive deficits" on the school board. Amash and his allies cried foul at an attack ad calling the congressman "al-Qaida's best friend in Congress." Citing his Palestinian-American heritage, Amash called the ad "disgusting." He prevailed in the August primary, 57%-43%, and lashed out at former Michigan Rep. Pete Hoekstra, who supported the challenger. "I want to say to lobbyist Pete Hoekstra, you're a disgrace," Amash said. He easily defeated Democrat Bob Goodrich in November, 58%-39%.

In the 2016 presidential campaign, Amash supported Rand Paul and then Ted Cruz for the Republican nomination; he said that he would not support Donald Trump. After the election, Amash voiced concern about Trump's expansion of presidential powers and federal spending. "He may even go beyond what President Obama did in terms of violating our rights." In January 2017, he was one of nine Republicans who voted against a procedural step to repeal the Affordable Care Act. He voiced concern about huge increases in the federal debt. He also criticized what he viewed as the excesses in Trump's executive orders to limit immigrants and refugees.

West-Central Michigan: Grand Rapids Metro

Population		**Race and Ethnicity**		**Income**	
Total	720,096	White	79.8%	Median Income	$51,780 (226 out of 435)
Land area	2,629	Black	8.4%		
Pop/ sq mi	273.9	Latino	7.1%		
Born in state	78.4%	Asian	0.0%	Under $50,000	48.3%
		Two races	2.5%	$50,000-$99,999	32.3%
Age Groups		Other	0.5%	$100,000-$199,999	16.0%
Under 18	24.9%			$200,000 or more	3.5%
18-34	22.8%	**Education**		Poverty Rate	15.6%
35-64	39.0%	H.S grad or less	38.8%		
Over 64	13.3%	Some college	32.1%	**Health Insurance**	
Work		College Degree, 4 yr	19.0%	With health insurance coverage	91.1%
White Collar	34.3%	Post grad	10.1%		
Sales and Service	40.4%	**Military**		**Public Assistance**	
Blue Collar	25.3%	Veteran	8.1%	Cash public assistance income	4.5%
Government	9.4%	Active Duty	0.1%	Food stamp/SNAP benefits	15.9%

Voter Turnout			
2015 Total Citizens 18+	521,172	2016 House Turnout as % CVAP	66%
2016 House turnout	342,365	2014 House Turnout as % CVAP	42%

2012 Presidential Vote		
Mitt Romney	177,772	(53%)
Barack Obama	153,052	(46%)

2016 Presidential Vote		
Donald Trump	180,341	(51%)
Hillary Clinton	147,335	(42%)
Gary Johnson	15,803	(5%)

Cook Partisan Voting Index: R+6

Grand Rapids is Michigan's second-largest city and the center of its most prosperous metropolitan area. It grew as a center for turning the hardwood forests of northern Michigan into furniture. By the early 20th century, Grand Rapids was the leading furniture manufacturer in the nation. The Great Depression knocked the bottom out of the residential furniture market, and many manufacturers moved to North Carolina, where labor was cheaper. So Grand Rapids reinvented itself. It went into office furniture, and today three of the nation's largest office furniture manufacturers - Steelcase, Haworth and Herman Miller - are located in its metropolitan area.

It also capitalized on a knack for sales. Rich DeVos and Jay Van Andel started Amway, the direct sales empire, which has had about 90 percent of its sales abroad. With nearly $10 billion in revenues in 2016, Amway was the largest direct-selling company in the world; China has been its largest market. DeVos's son Dick later ran the business and was the unsuccessful Republican nominee for governor of Michigan in 2006. Dick's wife Betsy DeVos became active in state and national Republican politics and the charter-school movement before she became Education Secretary for President Donald Trump. The Grand Rapids area is a center for machine tools, Hush Puppies shoes, and Bissell carpet sweepers. Fifty years ago, Grand Rapids and its up-and-coming businesses were outshone by Detroit and the auto industry. Today, while Detroit struggles to stay afloat, more diversified Grand Rapids chugs along. The metropolitan area had the nation's ninth-fastest growing economy in 2014 and has led the state.

Politically, the Grand Rapids area has been the center of Michigan Republicanism for much of the last century; cultural conservatism and a belief in market economics run deep among the descendants of the pious Dutch immigrants who settled in western Michigan in the 1870s. It has also produced national

Republican leaders. The conversion of Sen. Arthur Vandenberg from isolationism to internationalism during World War II provided key support for the foreign policies of Franklin D. Roosevelt and Harry Truman; he chaired the Senate Foreign Relations Committee in 1947-48. Another was Gerald Ford, who rose to House Republican leader in 1965, vice president in 1973, and then president after Richard Nixon resigned in 1974. A Democratic win in the special election to replace Ford - the first for a Democrat here since 1910 - was part of a string of five special election pickups for the Democrats in early 1974 that helped convince Republicans that Nixon needed to resign, and which presaged the Democratic landslide later that year. The election of the local Democrat did not last long.

The 3rd Congressional District of Michigan can be thought of in three distinct parts. The first is the city of Grand Rapids itself, which constitutes about 25 percent of the population and has become heavily Democratic. The second includes most of the remainder of Kent, Ionia and Barry counties, and a small portion of Montcalm County. This part of the district, which includes a majority of its residents, is heavily Republican. The third part of the district is Calhoun County, which tends to vote close to the national average and is centered on Battle Creek, where sanitarium operator W.K. Kellogg invented corn flakes as a health food and where the Air National Guard base has become a prominent site for the Defense Department's cybersecurity operations. The net result is a district that leans Republican; Donald Trump won 51%-42% in 2016. He had his final rally of the campaign in Grand Rapids, after midnight on Election Day.

FOURTH DISTRICT

John Moolenaar (R)

Elected 2014, 2nd term; b. May 08, 1961, Midland; Hope College (MI), B.S., 1983; Harvard University, M.P.A., 1989; Christian - Non-Denominational; Married (Amy Moolenaar); 6 children.

Elected Office: Midland MI City Council, 1997-2000; MI House, 2003-2008; MI Senate, 2011-2014.

Professional Career: Chemist, Dow Chemical; Director, Middle MI Development Corporation Small Business Cntr.; School admin., Midland Academy of Ad-vanced & Creative Studies.

DC Office: 117 CHOB 20515, 202-225-3561, Fax: 202-225-9679, moolenaar.house.gov.

State Offices: Cadillac, 231-942-5070; Midland, 989-631-2552.

Committees: *Appropriations*: Financial Services & General Government, Labor, Health & Human Services, Education & Related Agencies, Legislative Branch.

Group Ratings

	ADA	ACLU	AFL-CIO	LCV	ITI	COC	HAFA	ACU	CFG	FRC
2016	-	5%	-	3%	100%	100%	58%	88%	72%	100%
2015	0%	C	17%	3%	C	90%	C	71%	67%	100%

Almanac Ratings 2015

	Economy	Social	Foreign	Composite
Liberal	7%	10%	11%	9%
Conservative	93%	90%	90%	91%

Key Votes of the 114th Congress

1. Keystone Pipeline	Y	5. Puerto Rico Debt	Y	9. Offenses by Aliens	Y
2. Trade Deals	Y	6. Medical Marijuana	N	10. Troops in Iraq	N
3. Export-Import Bank	Y	7. Sanctuary Cities	Y	11. Homeland Security $$	Y
4. Debt Ceiling Increase	N	8. Armor-piercing Bullets	Y	12. Trade Adjustment aid	Y

Election Results

Election	Name (Party)	Vote (%)		Cand. Spent	Ind. Exp. Support	Ind. Exp. Oppose
2016 General	John Moolenaar (R)	194,572	(62%)	$944,381		
	Debra Wirth (D)	101,277	(32%)	$10,552		
	Leonard Schwartz (L)	8,516	(3%)			
2016 Primary	John Moolenaar (R)		(100%)			

Prior winning percentages: 2014 (57%)

Republican John Moolenaar was elected in 2014 after winning a spirited three-way primary, with outspoken views on the economy. Conservative credentials and endorsements trumped cash in the contest. Moolenaar usually supported House Republican leaders and was rewarded with a seat on the Appropriations Committee.

Born in Midland, Moolenaar earned his bachelor's in chemistry from Hope College in Holland, Michigan. He got his master's in public administration from Harvard. He was a chemist and director of business development for MITECH+ and Dow Chemical, where he helped develop new product markets. He was an administrator at the Midland Academy of Advanced and Creative Studies. In 2002, he was elected to the state House. Later in the Senate, he chaired the Veterans, Military Affairs and Homeland Security Committee, and was vice-chair of the Appropriations Committee. A Democratic foe sought to recall Moolenaar in 2011 because he voted for a bill allowing taxation of public employee pensions. The effort failed when the petition did not attract enough signatures.

The retirement of Rep. Dave Camp, who chaired the House Ways and Means Committee, led to a battle among three GOP primary contenders: Moolenaar, businessman Paul Mitchell, and software consultant Peter Konetchy. Mitchell vastly outspent his opponents, dumping $3.6 million of his own money - several times what Moolenaar and Konetchy had raised, combined - into his campaign to finance an aggressive TV ad blitz. He attacked Moolenaar as insufficiently conservative, accusing the state lawmaker in an ad of enabling the Affordable Care Act by voting to expand Medicaid. Moolenaar, who signed a pledge to repeal the health care law, had voted for an overall state health agency budget that included federal dollars for Medicaid expansion.

Moolenaar turned Mitchell's campaign cash advantage against him, saying in a GOP primary debate that "quite frankly, I don't think this seat is up for sale." He had key Republican endorsements, including from Camp. Moolenaar questioned Mitchell's conservative credentials, including his contribution to the 2006 campaign of Democratic Sen. Debbie Stabenow. Moolenaar won the nomination with 52 percent of the vote, to 36 percent for Mitchell and 11 percent for Holmes. He scored especially well in his base of Midland, where he got 67 percent. In the general, Democrat John Holmes said that he did not want to repeal the health care law, which he argued was helping many people. Instead, Holmes preferred to improve the law. Moolenaar's more conservative views played far better in the GOP-friendly district. He won 57%-39%, and led in 14 of the 15 counties. He won Camp's district, but not his committee gavel.

During his first term, Moolenar was vice chair of the Science, Space and Technology Subcommittee on Research and Technology. In July 2016, the House passed his bill to designate the National Institute of Standards and Technology in the Commerce Department to serve as the president's principal adviser on standards for technological competitiveness and innovation ability. The effect of the legislation, he said, was to "provide small manufacturers like those here in Michigan with the expertise and advice they need when investing in new technologies." Working with Democratic Rep. Dan Kildee in 2016, he helped to enact $170 million to fix the badly contaminated drinking water system in Flint, Michigan. He cited failures in local, state and national governments that contributed to the crisis.

As a new member of Appropriations in 2017, Moolenaar became the first Republican from Michigan to serve on the panel since 2009.

Central Michigan: Midland

Population		Race and Ethnicity		Income	
Total	702,929	White	91.8%	Median Income	$44,960
Land area	8,458	Black	1.8%		(342 out of 435)
Pop/ sq mi	83.1	Latino	3.0%		
Born in state	85.6%	Asian	0.0%	Under $50,000	54.9%
		Two races	1.7%	$50,000-$99,999	30.3%
Age Groups		Other	0.7%	$100,000-$199,999	12.5%
Under 18	21.2%			$200,000 or more	2.3%
18-34	22.7%	**Education**		Poverty Rate	17.5%
35-64	39.2%	H.S grad or less	45.6%		
Over 64	16.9%	Some college	33.8%	**Health Insurance**	
		College Degree, 4 yr	13.0%	With health insurance coverage	89.9%
Work		Post grad	7.6%		
White Collar	31.0%				
Sales and Service	42.4%	**Military**		**Public Assistance**	
Blue Collar	26.6%	Veteran	9.2%	Cash public assistance income	3.0%
Government	13.2%	Active Duty	0.0%		
				Food stamp/SNAP benefits	15.9%

Voter Turnout			
2015 Total Citizens 18+	546,474	2016 House Turnout as % CVAP	58%
2016 House turnout	315,751	2014 House Turnout as % CVAP	40%

2012 Presidential Vote		
Mitt Romney	171,862	(53%)
Barack Obama	146,088	(45%)

2016 Presidential Vote		
Donald Trump	195,303	(59%)
Hillary Clinton	113,817	(35%)
Gary Johnson	14,062	(4%)

Cook Partisan Voting Index: R+10

Flat and treeless for miles, the central reaches of Michigan's Lower Peninsula are farm country, exposed to bitter winds and snowdrifts in winter and shining sun for precious weeks in summer. Like the steppes of Eastern Europe, these are farmlands that produce hearty crops: potatoes, navy beans, sugar beets. The cities here are often small factory towns, with neat, tree-lined streets that end at bare fields. Midland in 1891 was a declining lumber town when Herbert Dow perfected an electrolytic process to extract chemicals from northern Michigan's extensive brine wells. That was the start of Dow Chemical, still headquartered in this now upscale town and today a large producer of pesticides and agricultural biotech products. In 2015, Dow merged with another chemical giant; the resulting DowDuPont company retained a major local presence. Also that year, Dow completed its acquisition of Corning, a silicon-based materials company. With a cutback of about 700 jobs in the latter transaction, the company retained about 6,000 jobs in the Midland area. Owosso was the birthplace of Thomas E. Dewey, later New York governor and Republican nominee for president in 1944 and 1948. It was also the home of novelist James Oliver Curwood and the location of his Curwood Castle writing studio. Mount Pleasant, to the north, is the home of Central Michigan University, the third largest public university in the state. The economy recently has been steady: better than Detroit, but not as strong as Grand Rapids.

The 4th Congressional District of Michigan, geographically the state's second-largest, includes much of this territory north of Lansing and Grand Rapids and west of Flint and Saginaw. Two-thirds of its populace lives in rural areas. It stretches north up the highways, rarely venturing outside U.S. 131 to the west and Interstate 75 to the east. The rolling country around Houghton Lake was once lumber country and is now a retirement and resort area, with condominiums and knotty-pine cottages clustered around icy green lakes. This is historically Republican territory, having sent only one Democrat to Congress since it was created in 1912. This was another part of Michigan that out-performed Republican expectations in the 2016 presidential election. After Barack Obama won by one percentage point in 2008 and Mitt Romney carried the district with 53 percent of the vote in 2012, Donald Trump in 2016 won, 59%-35%. That was more than enough to account for his victory in the state. When Trump spoke in

Grand Rapids in December 2016, Dow announced that it was adding 200 research and development jobs at an innovation center in Midland.

FIFTH DISTRICT

Dan Kildee (D)

Elected 2012, 3rd term; b. Aug 11, 1958, Flint; University of Michigan, Flint, Att.; Central Michigan University, B.S.; Roman Catholic; Married (Jennifer Kildee); 3 children; 2 grandchildren.

Elected Office: Flint MI Board of Education, 1977-1985; Genesee County Board Of Commissioner, 1985-1997; Genesee County Treasurer, 1997-2009.

Professional Career: Youth specialist, Whaley Children's Center, 1976-1985; Founder, Genesee County Land Bank; Co-founder & CEO, Center For Comm. Progress, 2009-2012.

DC Office: 227 CHOB 20515, 202-225-3611, Fax: 202-225-6393, dankildee.house.gov.

State Offices: Flint, 810-238-8627.

Committees: *Financial Services*: Housing & Insurance, Monetary Policy & Trade, Terrorism & Illicit Finance.

Group Ratings

	ADA	ACLU	AFL-CIO	LCV	ITI	COC	HAFA	ACU	CFG	FRC
2016	-	100%	-	100%	67%	62%	14%	0%	11%	0%
2015	80%	C	96%	94%	C	41%	C	0%	0%	0%

Almanac Ratings 2015

	Economy	Social	Foreign	Composite
Liberal	94%	100%	99%	97%
Conservative	6%	0%	1%	3%

Key Votes of the 114th Congress

1. Keystone Pipeline	N	5. Puerto Rico Debt	Y	9. Offenses by Aliens	N
2. Trade Deals	N	6. Medical Marijuana	Y	10. Troops in Iraq	Y
3. Export-Import Bank	Y	7. Sanctuary Cities	N	11. Homeland Security $$	Y
4. Debt Ceiling Increase	Y	8. Armor-piercing Bullets	N	12. Trade Adjustment aid	Y

Election Results

Election	Name (Party)	Vote	(%)	Cand. Spent	Ind. Exp. Support	Ind. Exp. Oppose
2016 General	Dan Kildee (D)	195,279	(61%)	$447,165		
	Al Hardwick (R)	112,102	(35%)			
	Steve Sluka (L)	7,006	(2%)			
2016 Primary	Dan Kildee (D)		(100%)			

Prior winning percentages: 2014 (57%), 2012 (55%)

Democrat Dan Kildee, elected in 2012, followed in the footsteps of his uncle Dale Kildee, who retired after 36 years in the House: a quiet and usually reliable party man, who focused chiefly on local issues. In 2016, he earned prominence for helping to secure a congressional response to the contaminated water crisis in his district

The younger Kildee grew up in a close-knit neighborhood in Flint. There were six children in his family, and so many in the neighborhood that they formed their own football team, the Genesee Jets. He carried that athleticism into high school and became captain of the hockey team. But his real interest was in hanging out at Democratic headquarters. He worked on his uncle's campaigns for the state legislature and for Congress, distributing yard signs and doing other tasks.

After high school, Kildee enrolled at the University of Michigan's Flint campus and worked part-time at a treatment facility for emotionally disturbed children. That job became full-time, and Kildee dropped out of college, although he returned decades later to Central Michigan University to earn a bachelor's degree in administration. At age 19, Kildee was elected to the Flint Board of Education. "I'd go to visit the schools and I'd quite literally get asked for a hall pass," he said. During his more than seven years on the board, he fought unsuccessfully for a ban on corporal punishment, which the state legislature outlawed soon after he left the post.

Kildee served as a commissioner in Genesee County for 12 years before becoming county treasurer for another 12 years, during which time he founded a local land bank. His method for tackling abandoned properties - getting rid of them - brought him national attention. Though he saw the idea as "a common-sense approach to urban planning in an age of decline," others viewed it as "a radically un-American idea that embraces defeat and limited horizons," according to a 2010 profile of Kildee in *Slate*. That year, he entered the Michigan governor's race but dropped out after less than a month, saying that he wanted to avoid a fractious primary fight.

When Uncle Dale announced his retirement, Kildee was instantly a strong contender, given his family name and his years of public service. Several prominent Democrats, including former Rep. James Barcia, considered a challenge. But Kildee won the primary unopposed. He had little trouble dispatching Republican former state Rep. Jim Slezak in the general, 65%-31%.

In the House, Kildee got a seat on the Financial Services Committee. His first bill focused on cleaning up blight in Flint. He eventually got $100 million in federal funds for local demolition. With a bipartisan group of House members, he filed a resolution seeking to prevent any threat to the Great Lakes from a proposed Canadian nuclear waste site. In 2015, he became chairman of the Frontline program of the Democratic Congressional Campaign Committee, which assists vulnerable incumbents. House Democrats had other problems in November 2016. But Kildee evidently did his job. Only one Democratic incumbent lost reelection to a Republican.

When it became clear that the Flint water crisis would require a congressional response, the Senate took the lead and overwhelmingly approved emergency assistance. In the House, Republican leaders deferred action to await broader legislation on water projects, partly due to fear that many conservatives would object to the Flint aid. Kildee complained about the delay and pressed for House action, but he didn't burn bridges. Teaming with first-term Republican Rep. John Moolenaar of the neighboring district, he helped to put together with Speaker Paul Ryan and other House leaders a bipartisan back-room deal for $170 million.

That success opened other doors for Kildee. He made known his interest in running in 2018 for the open seat for governor, though he again said that he was reluctant to join a Democratic primary contest. In May 2017, he said that he would run for reelection and focus on the challenges posed by Republicans. In the House, he was tapped for the Democrats' new position of vice ranking member at the Financial Services panel. He has been a vice chair of the LGBT Equality Caucus.

Kildee has been reelected easily.

East-Central Michigan: Flint, Bay City

Population		**Race and Ethnicity**		**Income**	
Total	691,727	White	74.2%	Median Income	$41,545 (379 out of 435)
Land area	2,349	Black	17.2%		
Pop/ sq mi	294.5	Latino	4.7%		
Born in state	83.9%	Asian	0.0%	Under $50,000	58.4%
Age Groups		Two races	2.5%	$50,000-$99,999	28.9%
Under 18	23.0%	Other	0.5%	$100,000-$199,999	11.1%
18-34	20.6%	**Education**		$200,000 or more	1.7%
35-64	40.1%	H.S grad or less	45.6%	Poverty Rate	20.4%
Over 64	16.3%	Some college	35.8%	**Health Insurance**	
Work		College Degree, 4 yr	11.9%	With health insurance coverage	91.0%
White Collar	29.3%	Post grad	6.6%		
Sales and Service	46.0%	**Military**		**Public Assistance**	
Blue Collar	24.7%	Veteran	9.1%	Cash public assistance income	4.8%
Government	11.2%	Active Duty	0.0%	Food stamp/SNAP benefits	22.5%

Voter Turnout			
2015 Total Citizens 18+	527,387	2016 House Turnout as % CVAP	61%
2016 House turnout	319,291	2014 House Turnout as % CVAP	42%

2012 Presidential Vote		
Barack Obama	205,804	(61%)
Mitt Romney	129,896	(38%)

2016 Presidential Vote		
Hillary Clinton	162,982	(49%)
Donald Trump	148,953	(45%)
Gary Johnson	10,880	(3%)

Cook Partisan Voting Index: D+5

The flat plains south of Saginaw Bay, the inlet of Lake Huron that separates Michigan's Thumb (people really call it that) from the mitten of the Lower Peninsula, was once one of America's top industrial areas. Some 130 years ago, it was the nation's premier lumber country, with huge stands of virgin trees feeding 36 sawmills in Bay City. When the trees were gone, farmers took over, and the land was sown with beans and sugar beets. Then, a century ago, came the automobile. Flint, a small town on a minor branch of the Saginaw River, was the home base of W.C. Durant, the investor who merged several young auto firms to form General Motors in 1908. GM put its Chevrolet and Buick factories in Flint and its power steering facility in Saginaw, chosen because it was already a center of precision machinery manufacturing.

From 1910 through the 1950s, Flint grew lustily as it built Chevys and Buicks. Miners from the east Kentucky coal fields, mountain folk from eastern Tennessee and farmers from the Black Belt of Alabama found their way to Flint. Before long, Southern accents were common in an area settled by New England Yankees. Labor strife followed industrialization. In January 1937, Flint was the scene of the great sit-down strike that began when workers noticed GM preparing to move the dies that were used to stamp cars out of its plant - a potential prelude to a move to the South - and ended with GM recognizing the United Auto Workers as the bargaining agent for its workers.

Economic disaster struck with the energy crisis of the 1970s. Imports, especially from Japan, that were higher quality and lower priced than American cars, took an increasing share of the market. In 1979, GM employed more than 70,000 workers in its Flint plants, a huge share of the labor force in a metropolitan area of 430,000 people. Eventually, GM closed 13 of its 15 factories, and by the late 2000s, the GM payroll had fallen below 12,000. In June 2009, the company filed for bankruptcy.

By 2010, more than 40 percent of Flint households were in poverty, and many skilled workers had fled what *Forbes* magazine called one of "America's fastest-dying cities." Only two other U.S. cities - Cleveland and Detroit - lost more people in 2009. Michael Moore, the liberal filmmaker, has used his hometown of Flint as the locale for much of his work about rust-belt hardships. There have been some flickering signs of hope: Since General Motors emerged from bankruptcy in 2010, it has kept open a Flint engine plant and added a third shift at its truck assembly facility, which is the oldest GM factory in the nation. In April 2015, GM announced that its old Chevrolet plant, where Chevrolet Avenue crosses the Flint River, will be turned into an automotive research area with the local Kettering University. The company plans to complete in 2018 a new $900 million body shop that will improve the efficiency between its local assembly plant and its metal center. Since 2010, GM has invested or committed to $270 million to upgrade its plant in Bay City. Even with its recent improvements, the economy in the Flint area is 7 percent smaller than in 2007. Unemployment fell below 6 percent in 2016. Total jobs dropped from 208,000 in 2000 to 176,000 in 2015, though that was an improvement from 162,000 in 2010.

In April 2015, Gov. Rick Snyder announced the end of the 41-month "financial emergency" in Flint, and the restoration of authority to the mayor and city council. But a new crisis hit Flint later that year: the belated discovery of lead contamination in its drinking water system. In a city that was 57 percent African-American and with a median household income one-half of the average for the total state, the local government had turned to the Flint River as its water source while it was building a new pipeline to Lake Huron. Despite a state-ordered cleanup of the river's watershed, a lawsuit revealed that the Environmental Quality Department had failed to treat the river with an anti-corrosive agent, which resulted in severe health risks. According to an October 2016 report by the inspector general at the Environmental Protection Agency, that federal agency also was slow to respond.

The 5th Congressional District includes Flint and surrounding Genesee County - which are about 60 percent of the district - Saginaw and eastern Saginaw County, Bay City and most of Bay County, rural Arenac and Iosco counties along Lake Huron, and a strip of rural Tuscola County. Flint, evenly divided between the parties during the sit-down strikes, is now heavily Democratic, Saginaw and Bay City somewhat less so. This is the only Democratic district in the state that is not located at least partly in Wayne or Oakland counties, and it overall has been strongly Democratic. But Hillary Clinton fared poorly in this low-income, 74 percent white district. Her lead of 49%-45% in 2016 was a big drop from 2012, when President Barack Obama won 61%-38%. That was one of many factors in her narrow loss of Michigan.

SIXTH DISTRICT

Fred Upton (R)

Elected 1986, 16th term; b. Apr 23, 1953, St. Joseph; Shatluck School (MN); University of Michigan, B.A.; Congregationalist; Married (Amey Rulon-Miller Upton); 2 children.

Professional Career: Project Coordinator, U.S. Rep. David Stockman, 1975-1980; Legislative affairs, O.M.B., 1981-1983, Director, 1984-1985.

DC Office: 2183 RHOB 20515, 202-225-3761, Fax: 202-225-4986, upton.house.gov.

State Offices: Kalamazoo, 269-385-0039; St. Joseph, 269-982-1986.

Committees: *Energy & Commerce*: Digital Commerce & Consumer Protection, Energy (Chmn), Health.

Group Ratings

	ADA	ACLU	AFL-CIO	LCV	ITI	COC	HAFA	ACU	CFG	FRC
2016	-	5%	-	13%	100%	100%	37%	48%	59%	75%
2015	0%	C	29%	3%	C	100%	C	58%	42%	75%

Almanac Ratings 2015

	Economy	Social	Foreign	Composite
Liberal	10%	32%	11%	17%
Conservative	90%	68%	90%	83%

Key Votes of the 114th Congress

1. Keystone Pipeline	Y	5. Puerto Rico Debt	Y	9. Offenses by Aliens	Y
2. Trade Deals	Y	6. Medical Marijuana	Y	10. Troops in Iraq	N
3. Export-Import Bank	N	7. Sanctuary Cities	Y	11. Homeland Security $$	Y
4. Debt Ceiling Increase	Y	8. Armor-piercing Bullets	Y	12. Trade Adjustment aid	Y

Election Results

Election	Name (Party)	Vote (%)	Cand. Spent	Ind. Exp. Support	Ind. Exp. Oppose
2016 General	Fred Upton (R)	193,259 (59%)	$2,540,042	$100,002	
	Paul Clements (D)	119,980 (36%)	$1,098,956	$12,000	
	Lorence Wenke (L)	16,248 (5%)	$8,909		
2016 Primary	Fred Upton (R)	(100%)			

Prior winning percentages: 2014 (56%), 2012 (55%), 2010 (62%), 2008 (59%), 2006 (61%), 2004 (65%), 2002 (69%), 2000 (67.9%), 1998 (70%), 1996 (68%), 1994 (74%), 1992 (62%), 1990 (58%), 1988 (71%), 1986 (62%)

Fred Upton, an affable Republican first elected in 1986, chaired the House Energy and Commerce Committee for six years. Term-limited at that post in 2016, he took over as chairman of the Energy Subcommittee. His voting record has been unusually moderate for a Republican committee chairman.

He has offset his centrism by regularly aligning with the interests of business against what he considers excessive government regulation.

The grandson of one of the founders of Whirlpool, Upton grew up in St. Joseph. He attended the University of Michigan and worked for David Stockman, first on Stockman's congressional staff, then at the White House in the Office of Management and Budget from 1981 to 1985. Upton returned home and ran in the 1986 Republican primary against Rep. Mark Siljander, a conservative and evangelical Christian, and won 55%-45%, going on to win the seat handily in the general election.

Upton's family fortune puts him in the upper echelon among members of Congress in wealth, but he has a regular-guy image. He is well known for insisting that everyone, from reporters to staffers to fellow lawmakers, call him "Fred," and says he personally reads and signs all of his legislative mail. He is a devoted Chicago Cubs fan, rarely missing an Opening Day at Wrigley Field, and has a bat from ex-Cubs slugger Sammy Sosa in his office. His niece, Kate Upton, is a supermodel who has graced the covers of *Sports Illustrated*'s swimsuit issues. After the initial issue appeared, Upton said colleagues jokingly asked him, "Fred, are you adopted?"

Early in his House career, Upton was known for his amendments to force across-the-board cuts in appropriations. As a leader of the moderate Republicans' Tuesday Group, he also was outspoken about the need to find middle ground. He freely exercised his independence when his party controlled the House from 1995 to 2006, and he occasionally caused heartburn for GOP leaders. He sought, with limited success, to reduce the tax cuts of the Bush era. He backed increases in the minimum wage, increased funding for Amtrak, and Democratic measures to expand government medical insurance for poor children. He also voted with Democrats to preserve the Endangered Species Act.

On Energy and Commerce, Upton has been more of a party regular. When he chaired the Telecommunications Subcommittee, he supported a bill to allow regional telephone companies to provide broadband service more easily, and he pushed for larger fines against broadcasters for indecent programming. President George W. Bush signed his bill to create a "safe playground for kids" on the internet, free of pornography and other inappropriate material.

Upton made an aggressive bid for the Energy and Commerce gavel after the 2010 election, contributing thousands of dollars to Republican challengers. The contest heated up when conservative talk radio host Rush Limbaugh came out against Upton, and pundit Glenn Beck called him "all socialist." The GOP Steering Committee, heavily influenced by fellow Midwestern Speaker John Boehner, chose Upton. In his House voting patterns, Upton became more conservative as he was courting Republican leaders for the chairmanship in 2010. In 2015, when he no longer faced an internal House Republican contest to remain as chairman, the *Almanac* vote ratings ranked him near the center of House Republicans on economic issues but toward the left on social and foreign policy.

Taking the helm of Energy and Commerce in 2011, he was under pressure to show fellow Republicans that he was more than the squishy moderate that had been emblematic of his career. He confidently predicted that "a significant number of Democrats" would join his party's efforts to overturn President Barack Obama's 2010 health care law, which he dismissed as "a massive new government program that does real and lasting damage to our current system and all those covered under it." It turned out, though, that the repeated repeal votes never drew more than a handful of Democrats in support.

Many of Upton's other initiatives as chairman got through the House on largely party-line votes and were left for dead in the Senate. They included legislation to overturn the Environmental Protection Agency's authority to regulate greenhouse gas emissions blamed for global warming. Another bill overturned Federal Communications Commission's net neutrality rules designed to prevent internet providers from creating tiered pricing structures. He and other Republicans, with support from the cable television industry, said net neutrality rules are unnecessary and were enacted without the proper authority. On the investigative front, his panel dug into the Obama administration's loan guarantees to the failed solar company Solyndra Corp., which became a prominent GOP campaign issue in 2012.

Upton's efforts delighted fellow Republicans, who once had derided him as "Red Fred" for his bipartisan tendencies. But the Sierra Club and other environmental groups began running ads against him at home. And some Michiganders wondered what had happened to the politician who had championed a bill to ban incandescent light bulbs as part of the 2007 energy bill, and then voted four years later to undo the measure. "The old Upton who five, six, eight years ago would have been more moderate on votes and parted company with his party, that old Upton is gone," Bill Ballenger, editor of the newsletter *Inside Michigan Politics* told *The Chicago Tribune.*

With Republicans in control of the Senate in 2015, Upton expressed hope that some of his efforts to block federal environmental regulations could at least clear Congress, if not get signed into law. But the Senate failed to act on most of those initiatives. Instead, he had an unexpectedly productive two years in enacting major bipartisan legislation. He worked with Democratic Rep. Diana DeGette of Colorado to accelerate innovative medical treatments and devices. Their 21st Century Cures Act easily passed the House in July 2015. It gained additional health-policy initiatives in the Senate - including funds to fight opioid addiction and to research cures for cancer - and was enacted after the 2016 election. Upton worked with Rep. Frank Pallone of New Jersey, the senior Democrat on Energy Commerce, to overhaul the outdated chemical safety law. That measure, too, had overwhelming bipartisan support.

Upton has been an election target from both the left and right. In 2010, former state Rep. Jack Hoogendyk ran against him in the GOP primary, criticizing Upton for voting for the bailout of the financial industry and for the Republicans' Medicare prescription drug bill in 2003. Upton vastly outspent Hoogendyk and won 57%-43%, not a robust outcome for a longtime incumbent. Hoogendyk came back for another challenge in 2012. Upton took him more seriously this time, conducting outreach to tea party groups and winning with ease, 67%-33%. His Democratic opponent that year was Mike O'Brien, a former Marine and office furniture company manager making his first run for elective office, who blasted Upton's support for the Republican spending plan. The $294,000 that O'Brien raised was no match for Upton's $4.7 million, contributions that are readily available to the Energy and Commerce chairman. Upton won, 55%-43%, the smallest margin in his career. He took every county, though the race in Kalamazoo County, the district's largest, was a virtual tie.

In 2014, Upton drew a better-funded Democratic challenger - Paul Clements, a Western Michigan University political scientist who decided to run after becoming dismayed by Upton's reversal on climate change. Clements received help from Harvard law professor Lawrence Lessig's Mayday political action committee, which spent more than $2 million to portray Upton as a captive of oil and drug companies. Lessig cultivated and received extensive media attention, but his influence with Michigan voters seemed limited. Upton denied the allegations from Lessig, and responded that he continued to work on a bipartisan basis to steer clear of the Washington dysfunction. Upton spent $3.9 million to $800,000 for Clements and won, 56%-40%, in a good year for Republicans. Clements ran again in 2016, and appeared to have a chance to close the gap with the higher turnout in a presidential election year. Clements raised $1.2 million this time, again with help from Lessig's network, but his appeal faded. Upton won more comfortably, 59%-36%.

During the 2016 campaign, Upton remained neutral on Donald Trump and the presidential campaign. Upton said that Trump should consider "stepping away from the ticket," following the early October release of the 2005 video with Trump's lewd comments about women. "It's a new low. It's outrageous. ... I urge him to think about our country over his own candidacy." Following the election, Upton congratulated Trump and offered a guarded, "We've got a lot of work to do." Following Trump's initial executive orders on travel bans for refugees and immigrants, Upton criticized the plan for creating "real confusion for travelers and those who enforce the laws. When House Republicans took up their bill to revise the Affordable Care Act, he objected that the proposal did not continue coverage of pre-existing conditions. In negotiations with House GOP leaders and later with President Trump, who were desperate for his vote, he agreed to join the party ranks after they added to the bill a small fund designed to assure coverage of those illnesses.

At Energy and Commerce, Upton became chairman of the Energy Subcommittee and said that he was eager to promote bipartisan "all of the above" strategies. In February, a spokesman said Upton was considering a challenge in 2018 to Democratic Sen. Debbie Stabenow. If Upton creates an open seat in his district, that could prompt the fierce challenges in each party that recently have been lodged against Upton.

Southwest Michigan: Kalamazoo

Population		**Race and Ethnicity**		**Income**	
Total	710,981	White	81.3%	Median Income	$47,498 (293 out of 435)
Land area	3,547	Black	8.2%		
Pop/ sq mi	200.5	Latino	5.7%		
Born in state	69.8%	Asian	0.0%	Under $50,000	52.1%
Age Groups		Two races	2.7%	$50,000-$99,999	31.1%
Under 18	23.2%	Other	0.5%	$100,000-$199,999	14.1%
18-34	22.7%	**Education**		$200,000 or more	2.6%
35-64	38.9%	H.S grad or less	41.0%	Poverty Rate	16.9%
Over 64	15.1%	Some college	33.0%	**Health Insurance**	
Work		College Degree, 4 yr	16.1%	With health insurance coverage	90.0%
White Collar	33.0%	Post grad	10.0%		
Sales and Service	40.3%	**Military**		**Public Assistance**	
Blue Collar	26.7%	Veteran	8.5%	Cash public assistance income	3.2%
Government	10.2%	Active Duty	0.0%	Food stamp/SNAP benefits	15.7%

Voter Turnout			
2015 Total Citizens 18+	529,146	2016 House Turnout as % CVAP	62%
2016 House turnout	329,552	2014 House Turnout as % CVAP	40%

2012 Presidential Vote		
Mitt Romney	163,306	(50%)
Barack Obama	158,963	(49%)

2016 Presidential Vote		
Donald Trump	170,320	(51%)
Hillary Clinton	142,293	(43%)
Gary Johnson	14,034	(4%)

Cook Partisan Voting Index: R+4

The southwest corner of Michigan was settled by New England Yankees and Upstate New Yorkers in the 1830s and 1840s. They built small towns with schools, churches and colleges; supported temperance; and opposed capital punishment. And in 1854, they joined the newly formed Republican Party. There are towns in southwest Michigan that still recall proudly their past as termini of the Underground Railroad, and there are black families whose ancestors made their way north out of slavery to freedom.

Later, big industries transformed some of the small towns into significant cities. Kalamazoo, started by Dutch Americans who introduced celery to this country, became the home of Upjohn pharmaceuticals, which is now part of Pfizer. The pharmaceutical giant generated $2.2 billion in economic activity and more than 5,600 jobs (direct and indirect) for the area, according to an October 2016 research report. Predominantly black and struggling Benton Harbor and predominantly white and prosperous St. Joseph are small towns that sit across from each other where the St. Joseph River empties into Lake Michigan. In April 2015, a columnist for the local newspaper described the contrasts in their school systems as a "sad tale of educational apartheid." Benton Harbor had been known as the headquarters for Whirlpool. But Whirlpool closed its plant in 2010, and many other local companies and famous industrial names such as Gibsŏn Guitars have moved out of the area, taking their thousands of jobs. In December 2016, citing "the business risks of continued operation," Entergy Corp. announced plans to close in October 2018 its nuclear power plant in Covert Township.

Kalamazoo, plus nearby Grand Rapids and Muskegon, have been the only parts of Michigan to recover to pre-recession economic strength, as of January 2017. The city has had some success keeping its young people in school with the Kalamazoo Promise program, funded by anonymous philanthropists, that pays college tuition for all public high school students who graduate; it has stabilized enrollment and racial balance and has resulted in higher test scores. In July 2016, other donors created the Foundation for Excellence, with $70 million for local projects. Michigan's southwest corner is heavily influenced by Chicago, which is much closer than is Detroit; people here watch Chicago television and root for the Cubs (especially in 2016, when they won the World Series) or White Sox rather than the Detroit Tigers.

The 6th Congressional District occupies the southwest corner of Michigan. It takes in five counties and most of a sixth. Kalamazoo is the largest, with nearly 40 percent of the population. The counties in the far southwest of the state - Cass, Berrien and Van Buren - are part of the so-called "cabinet counties," named, respectively, for Andrew Jackson's secretary of War, attorney general, and vice president. For many decades, this was arch-Republican territory. Its tradition was to elect conservative congressmen who deplored federal spending and welfare-state measures: New Deal opponent Clare Hoffman (1935-63), Nixon defender Edward Hutchinson (1963-77), and Reagan-era Office of Management and Budget Director David Stockman (1977-81). Since the 1990s, while continuing with Republican representation, the district, in particular Kalamazoo, has trended toward the Democrats. Barack Obama took 53 percent in 2008 and 49 percent in 2012. Hillary Clinton slipped in 2016, trailing Donald Trump 51%-43%.

SEVENTH DISTRICT

Tim Walberg (R)

Elected 2006, 5th term; b. Apr 12, 1951, Chicago, IL; Western Illinois University, Att.; Taylor University (IN), B.S.; Wheaton College (IL), M.A.; Moody Bible Institute (IL), Att.; Fort Wayne Bible College; b.R.E., 1975; Protestant; Married (Susan Walberg); 3 children; 2 grandchildren.

Elected Office: MI House, 1983-1998; U.S. House, 2007-2009.

Professional Career: Minister, 1973-1982; President, Warren Reuther Center, 1999-2000; Div. Manager, Moody Bible Inst., 2000-2005.

DC Office: 2436 RHOB 20515, 202-225-6276, Fax: 202-225-6281, walberg.house.gov.

State Offices: Jackson, 517-780-9075.

Committees: *Education & the Workforce*: Health, Employment, Labor & Pensions (Chmn). *Energy & Commerce*: Energy, Environment, Oversight & Investigations.

Group Ratings

	ADA	ACLU	AFL-CIO	LCV	ITI	COC	HAFA	ACU	CFG	FRC
2016	-	5%	-	3%	100%	100%	68%	88%	78%	100%
2015	0%	C	17%	0%	C	85%	C	96%	79%	100%

Almanac Ratings 2015

	Economy	Social	Foreign	Composite
Liberal	3%	0%	4%	2%
Conservative	97%	100%	96%	98%

Key Votes of the 114th Congress

1. Keystone Pipeline	Y	5. Puerto Rico Debt	N	9. Offenses by Aliens	Y
2. Trade Deals	Y	6. Medical Marijuana	N	10. Troops in Iraq	N
3. Export-Import Bank	N	7. Sanctuary Cities	Y	11. Homeland Security $$	N
4. Debt Ceiling Increase	N	8. Armor-piercing Bullets	Y	12. Trade Adjustment aid	Y

Election Results

Election	Name (Party)	Vote (%)		Cand. Spent	Ind. Exp. Support	Ind. Exp. Oppose
2016 General	Tim Walberg (R)	184,321	(55%)	$2,559,943		$712,480
	Gretchen Driskell (D)	134,010	(40%)	$2,480,500	$123,604	$309,196
	Ken Proctor (L)	16,476	(5%)			
2016 Primary	Tim Walberg (R)	43,064	(75%)			
	Doug North (R)	14,228	(25%)			

Prior winning percentages: 2014 (54%), 2012 (53%), 2010 (50%), 2006 (50%)

Republican Tim Walberg, first elected in 2006, is an ardent social and fiscal conservative who has been active in the health care debate. He narrowly lost his first reelection bid to Democrat Mark Schauer and then reclaimed the seat in 2010 in another close election. Since then, the victory margin for Walberg has grown as he has relied on his conservative base, with boosts from redistricting and the shift to Republicans outside of Metro Detroit.

Walberg was born in Chicago, growing up on the city's South Side. He worked in a steel mill to get through college and got his bachelor's degree from Fort Wayne Bible College and a master's from Wheaton College. He was a minister for 10 years before running for office. In 1982, he won a seat in the Michigan House by beating a moderate GOP incumbent. In his 16 years as a state legislator, Walberg had a reputation as a tireless advocate for gun rights and an opponent of abortion rights. He belonged to a group dubbed the "No" caucus for its unflinching opposition to tax hikes and increased spending. Term limits put an end to his tenure, and from 1998 to 2005, he was president of a conservative education foundation and a division manager for the Moody Bible Institute of Chicago.

Walberg ran for an open seat in 2004. He placed third in a GOP primary field crowded with other conservatives; moderate Joe Schwarz won the primary with 28 percent of the vote and went on to win the general election. Two years later, Walberg tried again. He ran on a record of having never once voted for a tax increase in the legislature. The well-funded anti-tax Club for Growth took notice and poured $500,000 into television ads attacking Schwarz. The national GOP backed the incumbent, and Schwarz had a spending advantage of 2-to-1. Walberg prevailed 53%-47%, and went on to defeat a weak Democratic opponent, 50%-46%. He became a prime target for Democrats in 2008.

That year, Democrats nominated Schauer, the Michigan Senate's minority leader and a former community organizer. With unemployment rising, Schauer focused on the economy and secured an endorsement from Republican Schwarz. Schauer benefited from the favorable national environment for Democrats. The Club for Growth again spent heavily for Walberg, but Schauer had strong union support and won narrowly, 49%-46%.

Walberg came back for a rematch in 2010 in a much more favorable climate for his party. In August, he won a three-way Republican primary with 57 percent of the vote. In the general election, Walberg and his allies attacked Schauer for his vote for Obama's $787 billion economic stimulus, saying that he was part of the problem of deficit spending in Washington. Schauer and his backers portrayed Walberg as too far right for the district, highlighting his support for creating private accounts in Social Security. They spotlighted a September radio interview in which Walberg said he didn't know whether Obama is an American citizen. "We don't have enough information about this president," he said. By day's end, he reversed course and acknowledged that Obama is "certainly an American citizen." Schauer outspent Walberg, $3.3 million to $1.6 million, and outside groups and national parties showered more than $7 million on the race. Walberg regained the seat, 50%-45%.

Walberg has had a solidly conservative voting record. In the *Almanac* vote ratings for 2015, he tied with Rep. Bill Huizenga for the most conservative scores in Michigan. His amendment proposing to cut National Endowment for the Arts funding by more than $20 million narrowly passed the House in 2011 but went nowhere in the Democratic-controlled Senate. On the Oversight and Government Reform Committee, Walberg expressed the view of many conservative activists that the botched "Operation Fast and Furious" operation intending to trace guns actually was designed to take away gun owners' rights.

As chairman of the Education and the Workforce Subcommittee on Workforce Protections, Walberg argued that the Obama administration's proposal giving home-care workers minimum wage and overtime protections would result in reduced hours for workers and higher costs for taxpayers. He later helped block a Labor Department proposal to ban youths younger than 16 from working on family farms. At a hearing of his subcommittee, Walberg voiced concern that the Equal Employment Opportunity Commission had been overstepping its authority. In 2014, the House passed Walberg's Senior Executive Service Accountability Act, which makes it easier for federal agencies to suspend or fire their top managers, for sufficient cause.

In 2017, he took over as chairman of the Health, Education, Labor and Pensions Subcommittee at Education and the Workforce, where he said that fixing the health care system was one of his chief priorities. He gained a seat on the Energy and Commerce Committee, which gave him an additional niche to restore what he called "patient-centered health care."

Schauer declined a rematch in 2012 after Michigan's GOP redistricters moved his Battle Creek home into the 3rd District. In Republican-leaning 2014, against Democrat Pam Byrnes who spent $1.4 million but had little outside assistance, Walberg won 54%-41%. In 2016, he faced Gretchen Driskell, who was mayor of Saline for 14 years and then served in the state House. In her broadcast ads, she labelled Walberg as "Trade Deal Tim" because of his support for international trade agreements;

Walberg responded that he was "a free and fair trader" and that he opposed the Trans-Pacific Partnership. Driskell was well-financed with $2.5 million in campaign funds and another $655,000 in support from Democratic allies. She evidently was hoping to benefit from coattails in the presidential campaign. But it turned out that Hillary Clinton performed poorly in this district and elsewhere in Michigan, and Driskell lost badly, 55%-40%.

His largest victory margin in six campaigns indicated that Walberg had become more secure in this district, with its growing Republican lean.

Southern Michigan: Jackson, Monroe

Population		**Race and Ethnicity**		**Income**	
Total	704,416	White	88.5%	Median Income	$52,732 (214 out of 435)
Land area	4,228	Black	4.1%		
Pop/ sq mi	166.6	Latino	4.1%		
Born in state	74.2%	Asian	0.0%	Under $50,000	47.4%
		Two races	1.9%	$50,000-$99,999	33.1%
Age Groups		Other	0.4%	$100,000-$199,999	16.8%
Under 18	22.7%			$200,000 or more	2.9%
18-34	20.0%	**Education**		Poverty Rate	13.0%
35-64	41.8%	H.S grad or less	42.5%		
Over 64	15.5%	Some college	34.7%	**Health Insurance**	
		College Degree, 4 yr	14.4%	With health insurance coverage	91.5%
Work		Post grad	8.4%		
White Collar	31.9%				
Sales and Service	41.3%	**Military**		**Public Assistance**	
Blue Collar	26.8%	Veteran	9.2%	Cash public assistance income	3.1%
Government	12.5%	Active Duty	0.0%		
				Food stamp/SNAP benefits	13.6%

Voter Turnout			
2015 Total Citizens 18+	537,263	2016 House Turnout as % CVAP	62%
2016 House turnout	334,807	2014 House Turnout as % CVAP	42%

2012 Presidential Vote		
Mitt Romney	169,310	(51%)
Barack Obama	158,963	(48%)

2016 Presidential Vote		
Donald Trump	189,677	(55%)
Hillary Clinton	131,552	(38%)
Gary Johnson	14,136	(4%)

Cook Partisan Voting Index: R+7

The small cities and towns nestled in and around southern Michigan's Irish Hills, near where the major glaciers stopped their southward crawl in the last ice age, have been incubators of innovation since they were settled by Yankees from New England 150 years ago. Hillsdale, a picture book old town south of Jackson, is home to Hillsdale College, founded about the same time as the Republican Party, by likeminded people. It has been proudly admitting African Americans and women since the 1850s while refusing all forms of federal aid.

Southern Michigan mostly rejected New Deal tinkering and was hostile to the United Auto Workers union. But the people here were receptive to moral claims made by later 20th-century reformers challenging racial segregation, the Vietnam War and the Watergate cover-up. In the past 100 years, the congressional district for the region has tended to elect Democrats only in presidential wave years: in 1912, 1932, 1964, and 2008.

Jackson, an old industrial town named for a founder of the Democratic Party and site of Michigan's first prison, is one of five towns that claim to have been the birthplace of the Republican Party in 1854. Today, Jackson is a city in decline. It ranked 324th out of 381 cities in economic health in 2015, according to *Policom*. It has lost 3,200 residents since 2000, nearly 9 percent of its total population. It is down almost 40 percent from its peak in 1930.

The district has had some positive developments. General Motors completed in June 2016 a $583 million retooling and expansion project at its Lansing Delta Township assembly plant. That assembly plant had about 3,200 workers. Clemens Food Group planned to open in late 2017 a $255 million pork processing plant in Branch County, which will employ more than 800. In May 2015, the federal Nuclear Regulatory Commission approved a construction license for a nuclear reactor near Monroe, though prospects remained unclear in early 2017.

The 7th Congressional District takes in six counties in southern Michigan plus parts of another. The district includes three of the so-called "cabinet counties," named for members of President Andrew Jackson's administration (Jackson presided over Michigan's admission to the Union): Branch County, named for Jackson's secretary of the Navy; Eaton County, for his first secretary of War; and Jackson County, for the president himself. The city of Jackson votes Democratic, as do the parts of Lansing in Eaton County. The district includes the outer townships of Washtenaw County, which lean Republican; more than two-thirds of Washtenaw is in the Democratic 12th District. The 7th has leaned Republican, though not overwhelmingly so. As with other Republican-held districts in Michigan, it had a big boost in Republican presidential support in 2016. Donald Trump won, 55%-38%, compared with the 51%-48% edge for Mitt Romney in 2012. Jackson County had its largest Republican presidential vote since Ronald Reagan in 1984.

EIGHTH DISTRICT

Michael Bishop (R)

Elected 2014, 2nd term; b. Mar 18, 1967, Almont; University of Michigan, B.A.; Michigan State University College of Law, J.D.; Universidad de Sevilla (Spain); Cambridge University, England; University of Paris; Congregationalist; Married (Cristina Bishop); 3 children.

Elected Office: MI House, 1999-2003; MI Senate, 2003-2011, Majority Leader, 2007-2011.

Professional Career: Practicing attorney; Chief legal officer, Int'l Bancard Corporation; Instructor, Thomas M. Cooley Law School.

DC Office: 428 CHOB 20515, 202-225-4872, Fax: 202-225-5820, mikebishop.house.gov.

State Offices: Brighton, 810-227-8600.

Committees: *Ways & Means*: Human Resources, Oversight.

Group Ratings

	ADA	ACLU	AFL-CIO	LCV	ITI	COC	HAFA	ACU	CFG	FRC
2016	-	5%	-	5%	100%	100%	60%	84%	69%	100%
2015	0%	C	17%	3%	C	90%	C	92%	73%	92%

Almanac Ratings 2015

	Economy	Social	Foreign	Composite
Liberal	6%	10%	10%	9%
Conservative	94%	90%	90%	91%

Key Votes of the 114th Congress

1. Keystone Pipeline	Y	5. Puerto Rico Debt	Y	9. Offenses by Aliens	Y
2. Trade Deals	Y	6. Medical Marijuana	N	10. Troops in Iraq	N
3. Export-Import Bank	N	7. Sanctuary Cities	Y	11. Homeland Security $$	Y
4. Debt Ceiling Increase	Y	8. Armor-piercing Bullets	Y	12. Trade Adjustment aid	Y

Election Results

Election	Name (Party)	Vote (%)	Cand. Spent	Ind. Exp. Support	Ind. Exp. Oppose
2016 General	Michael Bishop (R)	205,629 (56%)	$1,563,235	$30,044	
	Suzanna Shkreli (D)	143,791 (39%)	$767,050		$1,422,224
	Jeff Wood (L)	9,619 (3%)			
2016 Primary	Michael Bishop (R)	(100%)			

Prior winning percentages: 2014 (55%)

Republican Mike Bishop, elected in 2014, was the party establishment favorite to fill an open seat. He got the nod over a tea party challenger in the primary, and had a relatively easy time in November. With his legislative experience, he comfortably fit the House Republicans' leadership wing. He faced a well-funded but disorganized Democratic challenge in his initial reelection. In 2017, he took a seat on the powerful Ways and Means Committee.

Bishop, a life-long resident of Oakland County, got his bachelor's degree at the University of Michigan and his law degree from Michigan State. He had his own Oakland County law firm. A licensed real estate broker, he worked as chief legal officer for International Bancard and as an adjunct professor at Thomas M. Cooley Law School. He served four years in the Michigan House before filling a state Senate seat previously held by his father, Donald Bishop, and rising to majority leader. Bishop sponsored legislation to create the Michigan Child Protection Registry to shield children from receiving pornography, tobacco and other unsuitable materials. He authored a state law that established identity theft as a felony. Term limited in 2010, he ran for and lost the Republican nomination for attorney general that year.

In the abbreviated campaign following the retirement announcement by Rep. Mike Rogers, Bishop presented himself as the classic conservative option, pledging to secure the border, promote a strong military and reform Social Security. He was challenged by state Rep. Tom McMillin, who was a more active social conservative and known for his outspoken opposition to gay rights as well as for graphic images of late-term abortions in his campaign literature. Bishop quickly won the endorsement of Rogers. "I'm here supporting Mike Bishop because I think he will not embarrass this district," Rogers said succinctly. Speaker John Boehner, a friend of Rogers, gave Bishop a pre-primary contribution. Bishop won the primary 60%-40%.

In the general election, Democratic nominee Eric Schertzing, the treasurer of Ingham County, faced an uphill battle, especially after the Democratic Congressional Campaign Committee in early October canceled ads that it had planned to run on his behalf. Schertzing criticized his opponent for participating in two government shutdowns in Michigan while he served in the Senate, and for comments about not supporting the federal bailout of the auto industry. Bishop outspent Schertzing 2-to-1, and was elected, 55%-42%. Bishop was held to 35 percent of the vote in Ingham, but he took 65 percent in Livingston and 67 percent in his base of Oakland.

During his first term, Bishop had seats on the Judiciary Committee, plus Education and the Workforce. The wide-ranging measure that was enacted in July 2016 to fight opioid abuse included his provision to give state and local governments increased authority to mandate child-proof containers for prescription drugs. On another bipartisan measure, he took the lead in winning an extension of the Perkins program of low-interest loans to needy students. He was a freshman representative on the Republican Steering Committee, which makes committee assignments.

Democrats grew enthusiastic about their reelection challenge to Bishop, when Hollywood actress Melissa Gilbert stepped forward as their prime contender. Gilbert, who had been a star in television's "Little House on the Prairie," had settled with her family in Livingston County and was receiving large contributions from Hollywood celebrities as part of her $800,000 in fundraising. Her campaign suffered a setback when *The Detroit News* reported that she owed $470,000 in back taxes to the IRS and to California. In May 2016, she ended her candidacy when she said that her doctor diagnosed her with migraine headaches after having suffered two concussions.

Forced to scurry for a new contender, Democrats tapped Suzanna Shkreli, a 29-year-old assistant prosecutor in Macomb County. She accused Bishop of trying to "hide" his support for Republican presidential nominee Donald Trump and raised $780,000, compared with $1.6 million for Bishop. In October, following the release of Trump's lewd comments about women in an *Access Hollywood* video, Bishop said that he was "appalled" and that he would not talk further about Trump, though he did not withdraw his endorsement. This proved to be another district in Michigan where Trump performed better than expected and Democratic hopes were deflated. Bishop won 56%-39%, with better than 2-to-1 margins in Oakland and Livingston County though Shkreli took Ingham with 56 percent of the vote.

Following his reelection, Bishop got a seat on Ways and Means, where he pledged to "simplify our tax code, create more jobs and replace Obamacare with a health care law that works for more hardworking Americans."

South-Central Michigan: Detroit Exurbs, Lansing

Population		**Race and Ethnicity**		**Income**	
Total	719,666	White	82.9%	Median Income	$63,541 (107 out of 435)
Land area	1,503	Black	5.3%		
Pop/ sq mi	478.8	Latino	4.7%		
Born in state	75.2%	Asian	0.0%	Under $50,000	39.8%
Age Groups		Two races	2.6%	$50,000-$99,999	31.0%
Under 18	22.6%	Other	0.3%	$100,000-$199,999	23.0%
18-34	23.9%	**Education**		$200,000 or more	6.0%
35-64	40.6%	H.S grad or less	28.3%	Poverty Rate	12.4%
Over 64	12.9%	Some college	32.9%	**Health Insurance**	
Work		College Degree, 4 yr	22.9%	With health insurance coverage	92.9%
White Collar	42.4%	Post grad	15.8%		
Sales and Service	40.3%	**Military**		**Public Assistance**	
Blue Collar	17.3%	Veteran	7.2%	Cash public assistance income	2.2%
Government	13.6%	Active Duty	0.0%		
				Food stamp/SNAP benefits	10.7%

Voter Turnout			
2015 Total Citizens 18+	532,086	2016 House Turnout as % CVAP	69%
2016 House turnout	366,968	2014 House Turnout as % CVAP	46%

2012 Presidential Vote		
Mitt Romney	183,510	(51%)
Barack Obama	172,131	(48%)

2016 Presidential Vote		
Donald Trump	189,891	(50%)
Hillary Clinton	164,436	(44%)
Gary Johnson	15,205	(4%)

Cook Partisan Voting Index: R+4

Lansing is Michigan's state capital, chosen in 1847 because of its geographic position halfway between Lake Huron and Lake Michigan - and away from the border with Canada and the threat of invasion by British forces. The only drawback was fewer days with sunshine than anywhere else in the state. It is a tidy and pleasant city with more than its share of amenities. It has a beautifully restored Capitol, a fine state history museum, and is neighbor to Michigan State University in East Lansing, founded in 1855 as America's first land grant college.

Its Oldsmobile plant stimulated growth in the first half of the 20th century, and state government did the same in the second half. GM closed its Olds line and two other Lansing plants in 2004. Two GM assembly plants have been constructed in the Lansing area. At the Grand River plant, the third shift shut down in January 2017, with a remaining payroll of close to 2,000 employees. The Lansing Delta Township plant was not affected. As public employee unions have grown in membership and strength, Lansing, like other state capitals, has become heavily Democratic, as are East Lansing and surrounding Ingham County. In October 2016, East Lansing voters approved the legalization of marijuana - for the possession, use or transfer of up to one ounce for people over 21 on private property. Use or possession of marijuana remained illegal on the Michigan State campus. Also that month, *Crain's Detroit Business* reported a "development boom" in Lansing, with GM and Jackson National Life Insurance expanding locally, and the University an "economic powerhouse."

Just east of Ingham is quite another part of Michigan, Livingston County. (Most of the counties in these parts were named for members of President Andrew Jackson's Cabinet: Livingston was secretary of State and Ingham secretary of the Treasury.) Forty years ago, Livingston County was mostly rural, known mainly for its many lakes. Then, subdivisions, schools and shopping malls sprouted up. (The community of Hell is located here, too; the average high temperature in the area is below 32 degrees Fahrenheit in January, so one assumes it freezes over regularly.) Most of these people are conservatives, happy to leave behind the urban problems of Detroit, unhappy about high taxes, and hewing to traditional religious faiths. They have made Livingston one of Michigan's fastest-growing counties - its population rose 19 percent from 2000 to 2015 - and one of its most Republican.

The 8th Congressional District of Michigan includes virtually all of exurban Ingham and Livingston counties and the northern, more rural parts of Oakland County, which has slightly more than one-third of the vote. With the two outlying counties more-or-less canceling each other out politically (Democratic-leaning Ingham has a bit higher turnout), the tie-breaker in recent presidential elections has been in Oakland, in places like Republican-leaning Rochester and Rochester Hills, and farther out in Springfield and Oxford. In 2016, Donald Trump took the district, 50%-44% -- a slight GOP improvement from Mitt Romney's 51%-48% lead in 2012 and a larger shift from Barack Obama's 52%-46% lead in 2008.

NINTH DISTRICT

Sander Levin (D)

Elected 1982, 18th term; b. Sep 06, 1931, Detroit; Columbia University (NY), M.A.; Harvard University Law School (MA), LL.B.; Harvard University John F. Kennedy School of Government (MA); University of Chicago (IL), B.A.; Jewish; Married (Victoria Schlafer Levin); 4 children; 10 grandchildren.

Elected Office: Oakland Board of Supervisors, 1961-1964; MI Senate, 1965-1970, Minority Leader, 1969-1970.

Professional Career: Practicing attorney, 1957-1964, 1970-1976; Fellow, Harvard JFK School of Government, 1975; Assistant admin., U.S. Agency for Intl. Devel., 1977-1981.

DC Office: 1236 LHOB 20515, 202-225-4961, Fax: 202-226-1033, levin.house.gov.

State Offices: Roseville, 586-498-7122.

Committees: *Ways & Means*: Health (RMM), Trade.

Group Ratings

	ADA	ACLU	AFL-CIO	LCV	ITI	COC	HAFA	ACU	CFG	FRC
2016	-	94%	-	100%	67%	57%	16%	100%	7%	0%
2015	95%	C	100%	97%	C	45%	C	0%	0%	17%

Almanac Ratings 2015

	Economy	Social	Foreign	Composite
Liberal	95%	89%	93%	92%
Conservative	6%	11%	7%	8%

Key Votes of the 114th Congress

1. Keystone Pipeline	N	5. Puerto Rico Debt	Y	9. Offenses by Aliens	N
2. Trade Deals	N	6. Medical Marijuana	N	10. Troops in Iraq	N
3. Export-Import Bank	Y	7. Sanctuary Cities	N	11. Homeland Security $$	Y
4. Debt Ceiling Increase	Y	8. Armor-piercing Bullets	N	12. Trade Adjustment aid	Y

Election Results

Election	Name (Party)	Vote	(%)	Cand. Spent	Ind. Exp. Support	Ind. Exp. Oppose
2016 General	Sander Levin (D)	199,661	(58%)	$704,106		
	Christopher Morse (R)	128,937	(37%)			
	Matt Orlando (L)	9,563	(3%)			
2016 Primary	Sander Levin (D)		(100%)			

Prior winning percentages: 2014 (60%), 2012 (62%), 2010 (61%), 2008 (72%), 2006 (70%), 2004 (69%), 2002 (68%),2000 (64%), 1998 (56%), 1996 (57%), 1994 (52%), 1992 (53%), 1990 (70%), 1988 (70%), 1986 (76%), 1984 (100%), 1982 (67%)

Sander Levin, first elected in 1982, stepped down in January 2017 as the ranking Democrat on the Ways and Means Committee, having briefly served as its chairman before Republicans regained the majority in 2011. At age 85, he acknowledged that his unexpected move was a response to pressure by younger Democrats for a generational shift of power. Like his younger brother, retired Sen. Carl Levin, he has been an old-school liberal and one of his party's most respected voices on tax and trade matters.

Sander Levin grew up in Detroit and got degrees from the University of Chicago, Columbia University and Harvard Law School. In college, Levin sat at a lunch counter in protest with black students as they were denied service together. He later studied village democracy in India. "I was essentially trained by World War II vets who combined a progressive view of life with a deep distrust of anything authoritarian," he told *National Journal*.

He settled in the suburb of Berkley after school, joined the Oakland County Board of Supervisors at age 30, and was elected to the state senate, where he served two years as minority leader. In 1970 and 1974, he ran for governor and lost narrowly each time to Republican William Milliken. During the Carter administration, he was a top appointee at the Agency for International Development.

In 1982, a House seat opened after redistricting when two incumbents retired. Levin won a spirited primary and has held the seat since, with shifts of geography. The 1992 redistricting moved him east, into Macomb County, and placed him in the same district with another Democrat, who retired. Levin had serious competition in the next two elections from Republican retired Army Col. John Pappageorge and won by just 53%-46% in 1992 and 52%-47% in 1994. Since then, he has won easily.

Levin is a hard worker and a details man, willing to spend endless hours with others working out solutions. He has played an important role on significant issues. On welfare reform, Levin helped to shape the 1996 overhaul that introduced more work requirements for welfare beneficiaries. In 2005, as the ranking Democrat on the Social Security Subcommittee, his outspoken opposition to personal retirement accounts put Republicans on the defensive and helped stop the proposal. "He led us in the winning strategy, which was an inside-outside strategy, that we would mobilize people around the country, and two, that we would not offer an alternative - that was absolutely key," said Rep. Jan Schakowsky of Illinois, a fellow liberal.

For years, he has been at the center of trade debates, seeking ways, as he has put it, to shape globalization. He favored the 1980s free trade agreement with Canada, which helped the auto industry. He was a strong opponent of the North American Free Trade Agreement in 1993, but supported normal trade relations with China, playing an instrumental role in crafting details with the Clinton administration. With many union leaders, Levin pushed for trade agreements to contain provisions on workers' rights, ways of settling workers' disagreements and environmental protection. He insisted on changes in provisions on workers' rights and environmental protections in the agreements that the Bush administration negotiated with Peru, South Korea, Colombia and Panama.

As House Speaker and Minority Leader, Nancy Pelosi tended to defer to Levin as support for free trade pacts in the Democratic Caucus declined dramatically. Levin pressed hard for China to allow its currency to rise in value and introduced a bill to authorize the Commerce Department to decide whether an undervalued currency is an export subsidy. He worked with Senate Finance Committee Chairman Max Baucus of Montana on a 2010 tax bill to extend unemployment benefits, boost oil company payments for spills and create a tax credit for electric vehicle technology development. Levin's customary standard is that taxes should be "fair and progressive."

While Democrats were still in power, Levin got the gavel at Ways and Means after Charles Rangel became mired in an ethics scandal and resigned the chairmanship in March 2010. Pelosi initially installed the next most senior Democrat, her neighbor Pete Stark of northern California, in the post. But prominent Democrats privately expressed concerns about the flamboyant Stark. Next in line in seniority after Stark was the level-headed Levin, who quickly became an acceptable replacement. After the 2010 election, Levin was challenged for the ranking minority position by Richard Neal of Massachusetts, who has worked more comfortably with business groups. The Democratic Steering Committee voted 23-22 for Neal. Levin, having gained some chits by giving $570,000 to other Democrats during the election season, took his case to the full Democratic Caucus and prevailed over Neal on a 109-78 vote.

In 2016, Levin was reelected with 58 percent of the vote, his smallest share since 1998. When he decided after the election to step down from his senior Democratic post at Ways and Means, he said, "It is imperative that we support younger members as they seek to fully assume the mantle of leadership in the four years ahead." He threw his support to Rep. Xavier Becerra of California as his successor. Unexpectedly, Gov. Jerry Brown of California announced the next day the selection of Becerra as the state's attorney general. Finally, Neal became the top Democrat at Ways and Means. Levin took over as the ranking Democrat on the Health Subcommittee. Meanwhile, Republicans identified Levin - and his district - as a target in 2018 for the first time in two decades. Although he insisted that his health was fine, his office confirmed in December 2015 that he had fainted during a meeting at the Capitol and was suffering from dehydration.

Northern Detroit Suburbs: Southern Macomb, Eastern Oakland

Population		**Race and Ethnicity**		**Income**	
Total	713,802	White	79.2%	Median Income	$51,550
Land area	184	Black	11.8%		(230 out of 435)
Pop/ sq mi	3888.0	Latino	2.2%		
Born in state	76.8%	Asian	0.0%	Under $50,000	48.4%
		Two races	2.3%	$50,000-$99,999	31.3%
Age Groups		Other	0.5%	$100,000-$199,999	16.6%
Under 18	20.8%			$200,000 or more	3.8%
18-34	22.2%	**Education**		Poverty Rate	14.2%
35-64	41.2%	H.S grad or less	39.3%		
Over 64	15.8%	Some college	32.0%	**Health Insurance**	
		College Degree, 4 yr	17.6%	With health insurance coverage	90.0%
Work		Post grad	11.1%		
White Collar	37.0%				
Sales and Service	42.3%	**Military**		**Public Assistance**	
Blue Collar	20.8%	Veteran	7.6%	Cash public assistance income	3.0%
Government	8.8%	Active Duty	0.1%		
				Food stamp/SNAP benefits	15.3%

Voter Turnout			
2015 Total Citizens 18+	536,642	2016 House Turnout as % CVAP	64%
2016 House turnout	344,775	2014 House Turnout as % CVAP	43%

2012 Presidential Vote		
Barack Obama	199,625	(57%)
Mitt Romney	146,185	(42%)

2016 Presidential Vote		
Hillary Clinton	183,085	(51%)
Donald Trump	155,597	(44%)
Gary Johnson	12,101	(3%)

Cook Partisan Voting Index: D+4

The flat expanse of land just north of Eight Mile Road, Detroit's northern city limit, was mostly vacant in the years just after World War II. A string of suburbs in Oakland County ran along Woodward Avenue from the Detroit city limits to the National Shrine of the Little Flower Catholic Church in Royal Oak, where Father Charles Coughlin in the 1930s made his radio broadcasts opposing Franklin D. Roosevelt and denouncing bankers and Jews. In the 1950s and 1960s, Woodward was one of America's greatest cruising highways, where teenagers drove big Detroit cars up and down the eight lanes and where the lights were timed at 42 miles per hour. Since 1994, the annual Woodward Dream Cruise of old cars has commemorated that era with a celebration drawing more than 1 million spectators. To the east, in Macomb County, was some industrial development along rail lines, but this too was mostly empty land in the 1950s.

Then Polish Americans began migrating out Van Dyke Avenue from Hamtramck to Warren. Italian Americans headed out Gratiot Avenue from Detroit's east side to Roseville and Clinton Township. Belgian Americans from the Mack corridor moved out farther to St. Clair Shores. Today, half of metro Detroit's population is north of Eight Mile, as African Americans and other minorities have joined whites in moving to the suburbs. In 2015, 14 percent of Oakland County residents and 11 percent of Macomb County residents were black. Freddie Kennedy, who moved to Macomb County a few years earlier, summed up his reasons for *The Detroit News*: "Everything's better in Warren. You call the police, and they respond."

The 9th Congressional District covers this suburban territory, with about two-thirds of its population in Macomb County. On the Oakland County side are Royal Oak and Ferndale, which have been economically revitalized, attracting singles and gays as well as traditional families. The Macomb side includes the more Democratic neighborhoods in the southern part of the county: Warren and much of Sterling Heights, site of the General Motors Technical Center, a big Fiat Chrysler plant, and the M-1 tank plant, which helps make metro Detroit a major defense manufacturer. In 2016, auto manufacturers had 69,000 jobs in Macomb; half of them were with GM, Ford and Chrysler. GM planned to complete in 2018 a $1 billion expansion and renovation of its Tech Center, with about 21,000 employees and contractors. In January 2017, Chrysler said it would spend several hundred million dollars at its Warren plant to upgrade manufacturing of Wagoneer SUVs.

Farther east are the blue-collar communities of Macomb: Eastpointe (formerly known as East Detroit, it voted to change its name to make it sound less like Detroit and more like tony Grosse Pointe); Roseville; St. Clair Shores; Clinton Township; and Mount Clemens. Overall, the district is Democratic, although not overwhelmingly so, the least partisan of the four Democratic-held districts in metro Detroit. Barack Obama twice won the 9th by at least 15 percentage points. In 2016, Hillary Clinton won by only seven points. Donald Trump took Macomb, 54%-42%. In 2012, Obama won the county, 52%-48%. In Oakland, both Clinton and Obama won by eight points.

TENTH DISTRICT

Paul Mitchell (R)

Elected 2016, 1st term; b. Nov 14, 1956, Boston, MA; Michigan State University (MI), Bach. Deg., 1978; Protestant; Married (Sherry Mitchell); 6 children.

Elected Office: St. Clair City Council.

Professional Career: Businessman.

DC Office: 211 CHOB 20515, 202-225-2106, Fax: 202-226-1169, mitchell.house.gov.

State Offices: Shelby Township, 586-997-5010.

Committees: *Education & the Workforce*: Health, Employment, Labor & Pensions, Higher Education & Workforce Development. *Oversight & Government Reform*: Health Care, Benefits & Administrative Rules, Information Technology. *Transportation & Infrastructure*: Aviation, Highways & Transit, Railroads, Pipelines & Hazardous Materials.

Election Results

Election	Name (Party)	Vote (%)		Cand. Spent	Ind. Exp. Support	Ind. Exp. Oppose
2016 General	Paul Mitchell (R)	215,132	(63%)	$3,915,980		$27,311
	Frank Accavtti Jr. (D)	110,112	(32%)	$47,145		
	Lisa Gioia (L)	10,612	(3%)			
2016 Primary	Paul Mitchell (R)	30,114	(38%)			
	Phil Pavlov (R)	22,019	(28%)			
	Alan Sanborn (R)	12,639	(16%)			
	Anthony Forlini (R)	7,885	(10%)			

Republican Paul Mitchell was elected in 2016 to an open seat in Michigan. He paid for 90 percent of his $4 million campaign with his own contributions and loans. In 2014, he self-financed $3.6 million in an unsuccessful campaign for another House seat in Michigan. He had a successful career in business before he became active in conservative causes, including as chairman of the Faith and Freedom Coalition of Michigan.

Mitchell grew up in Oakland County in Michigan and graduated from Michigan State University. Much of his business career was with Ross Education, where he was in charge of educational programs that aided welfare recipients and eventually became its chief executive officer. His contracts included the welfare-to-work program in Detroit. He said that his business trained 6,000 persons annually for health care jobs, WDET radio reported. Mitchell served as a commissioner with the Accrediting Bureau of Health Education Schools and as a board member of the Michigan Association of Career Colleges and Schools. His 2014 House bid was for an open seat in the 4th District, where he got 36 percent of the vote in the Republican primary to 52 percent for John Moolenaar. During a debate in the primary, Moolenaar said, "quite frankly, I don't think this seat is up for sale."

In 2015, Mitchell got involved in state politics when he led the fight to defeat the Proposal 1 increases in the sales and gas taxes. The ballot initiative, which was opposed by 80 percent of the voters, had been initiated by highway construction and contracting companies and was backed by Republican Gov. Rick Snyder and state legislative leaders.

Mitchell's run for the 10th District opened when Republican Rep. Candace Miller announced her retirement. She was elected in 2016 as public works commissioner in Macomb County. His chief opponents were state Sen. Phil Pavlov and former state Sen. Alan Sanborn. During a campaign debate, Mitchell compared himself to Donald Trump in that he "stood up to the club, funded his own primary and he kicked their backside," the MLive website reported. "It is my money to do as I wish with." Mitchell won the primary with 38 percent of the vote to 28 percent for Pavlov and 16 percent or Sanborn. In contrast to Mitchell's $4 million, they spent about $410,000 and $60,000, respectively.

In the general election, Mitchell faced former Democratic state representative Frank Accavitti, who had served as mayor of Eastpointe and as a Macomb County commissioner. Accavitti spent $48,000 and did not pose a serious challenge in this Republican-leaning district. Mitchell won, 63%-32%, including 61 percent in Macomb. In the House, he got assignments to three committees: Transportation and Infrastructure, Education and the Workforce, and Oversight and Government Reform.

Detroit Northern Exurbs, "The Thumb": Macomb, St. Clair

Population		**Race and Ethnicity**		**Income**	
Total	709,685	White	90.5%	Median Income	$57,011 (163 out of 435)
Land area	4,140	Black	2.9%		
Pop/ sq mi	171.4	Latino	3.1%		
Born in state	83.5%	Asian	0.0%	Under $50,000	43.7%
Age Groups		Two races	1.7%	$50,000-$99,999	33.0%
Under 18	22.7%	Other	0.3%	$100,000-$199,999	20.0%
18-34	18.7%	**Education**		$200,000 or more	3.1%
35-64	43.0%	H.S grad or less	42.7%	Poverty Rate	10.9%
Over 64	15.6%	Some college	35.1%	**Health Insurance**	
Work		College Degree, 4 yr	14.2%	With health insurance coverage	91.4%
White Collar	33.6%	Post grad	8.0%		
Sales and Service	40.5%	**Military**		**Public Assistance**	
Blue Collar	26.0%	Veteran	8.7%	Cash public assistance income	2.8%
Government	10.4%	Active Duty	0.1%		
				Food stamp/SNAP benefits	12.3%

Voter Turnout			
2015 Total Citizens 18+	534,231	2016 House Turnout as % CVAP	64%
2016 House turnout	340,983	2014 House Turnout as % CVAP	43%

2012 Presidential Vote		
Mitt Romney	187,660	(55%)
Barack Obama	148,425	(44%)

2016 Presidential Vote		
Donald Trump	228,190	(64%)
Hillary Clinton	113,045	(32%)
Gary Johnson	11,997	(3%)

Cook Partisan Voting Index: R+13

Macomb County, just northeast of Detroit, has been one of the nation's most closely watched political battlegrounds, a place where it once seemed the electoral fate of Michigan and even the entire country might be determined. It owes much of that to its reputation as blue-collar suburbia. These suburbanites were often from the east side of Detroit and were typically Catholic, at least modestly well-off, and ancestrally Democratic. They accepted the New Deal as part of their natural heritage. In 1960, Macomb County was the most Democratic major suburban county in the nation, voting 63 percent for the first Catholic president, John F. Kennedy. But these Democrats resented the efforts of Detroit politicians to tax them to pay for welfare programs and were fearful of the city's crime problem. Over the next three decades, Macomb moved away from national Democrats. From 1980 to 1992, no Democratic presidential candidate got more than 40 percent of the vote here. In 1996, after great effort and with the advice of pollster Stan Greenberg, who had studied Macomb closely, Bill Clinton carried the county by a solid 50%-39%.

Lately, central and northern Macomb County have been filling up with fast-growing and expensive subdivisions that are not as culturally liberal as the affluent parts of Oakland County. More people hold white-collar jobs than blue-collar jobs these days, and there is far less work in auto plants than during earlier generations. Republican George W. Bush carried it 50%-49% in 2004. Democrat Barack Obama defeated John McCain handily in Macomb in 2008, 53%-45%, and he beat Mitt Romney in 2012, 51%-47%. But in between the Democratic victories, Republican Gov. Rick Snyder racked up 61 percent of the vote in Macomb in 2010 and 54 percent in his tighter 2014 reelection. The 54 percent vote for Donald Trump in 2016 suggested that Macomb has gone back to the future. The setback for Hillary Clinton in Macomb was further evidence of the unpopularity of her husband's trade deals. Support for Obama may have been an exception, perhaps due to his more skillful political team.

The recession hit Macomb every bit as hard as Detroit - between 2007 and 2009, the number of people in poverty jumped nearly a third in the county, while median income dropped from $68,000 in 1999 to $49,000 in 2010. But the recovery has been relatively strong, with median income climbing back to $54,600 in 2015 (in inflation-adjusted dollars). In 2015, Macomb had 865,000 people, compared with 185,000 residents in 1950. It continues to grow, as farms convert to subdivisions. Chesterfield Township, along Lake St. Clair, has become busy with commercial development. Those seeking optimism about the future of Macomb can point to Ford and Fiat Chrysler each spending more than $1 billion on their assembly plants at Sterling Heights.

The 10th Congressional District of Michigan centers on the northern tier of Macomb, and encompasses nearly half of the county's population. It includes Lapeer County and most of Michigan's "Thumb," where population declined over the past decade. The second-largest county is St. Clair, with Port Huron and its Blue Water Bridge to Canada; Students for a Democratic Society drafted its famous Port Huron Statement just north of here in Lakeport in 1962, setting the stage for the counterculture movement. Northern Macomb has become increasingly Republican, Lapeer and St. Clair have leaned Republican, and the Thumb has long been very Republican. Half of the voters are in Macomb.

The district has voted Republican in recent presidential elections, but with notable swings in outcome. In 2016, Trump increased GOP support to 64%-32%, which made the 10th the most Republican district in the state. That margin was a remarkable shift in eight years from McCain's 50%-48% tight lead over Obama.

ELEVENTH DISTRICT

David Trott (R)

Elected 2014, 2nd term; b. Oct 16, 1960, Birmingham; University of Michigan, B.A.; Duke University (NC), J.D.; Roman Catholic; Married (Kathleen (Kappy) Trott); 3 children.

Elected Office: Bingham Farms Village Council, 1989-1991.

Professional Career: Practicing attorney, Trott & Trott, P.C.; MI St. Building Authority Board of Trustees, 2011-2015.

DC Office: 1722 LHOB 20515, 202-225-8171, Fax: 202-225-2667, trott.house.gov.

State Offices: Troy, 248-528-0711.

Committees: *Financial Services*: Financial Institutions & Consumer Credit, Housing & Insurance, Oversight & Investigations.

Group Ratings

	ADA	ACLU	AFL-CIO	LCV	ITI	COC	HAFA	ACU	CFG	FRC
2016	-	5%	-	5%	100%	100%	53%	79%	65%	100%
2015	0%	C	21%	3%	C	95%	C	75%	63%	92%

Almanac Ratings 2015

	Economy	Social	Foreign	Composite
Liberal	6%	10%	11%	9%
Conservative	94%	90%	90%	91%

Key Votes of the 114th Congress

1. Keystone Pipeline	Y	5. Puerto Rico Debt	Y	9. Offenses by Aliens	Y
2. Trade Deals	Y	6. Medical Marijuana	N	10. Troops in Iraq	N
3. Export-Import Bank	N	7. Sanctuary Cities	Y	11. Homeland Security $$	Y
4. Debt Ceiling Increase	N	8. Armor-piercing Bullets	Y	12. Trade Adjustment aid	Y

Election Results

Election	Name (Party)	Vote (%)		Cand. Spent	Ind. Exp. Support	Ind. Exp. Oppose
2016 General	David Trott (R)	200,872	(53%)	$1,338,710		
	Anil Kumar (D)	152,461	(40%)	$1,112,084		
	Kerry Bentivolio (I)	16,610	(5%)	$30,851		
	Jonathan Osment (L)	9,545	(3%)			
2016 Primary	David Trott (R)		(100%)			

Prior winning percentages: 2014 (56%)

Republican David Trott, elected in 2014, brought some stability to this district following the cartoonish behavior of his two GOP predecessors. Despite his controversial background as a foreclosure lawyer, he made few waves as he settled into the House. In his second term, he gained a seat on the Financial Services Committee.

Trott, who was born in Birmingham, got his bachelor's from the University of Michigan and his law degree from Duke. He returned home to the family law firm, which he later chaired. In a campaign ad, he said that he expanded the company from six people to 1,200. The business became the largest foreclosure law firm in Michigan and one of the largest in the country.

Trott initially challenged first-term Republican Rep. Kerry Bentivolio - a part-time reindeer rancher and Santa Claus impersonator in a traveling Christmas show before coming to Congress. Bentivolo had become the accidental congressman in 2012 when the district's seemingly entrenched five-term GOP congressman, Thaddeus McCotter, who ran a baffling presidential campaign in 2008, was found not to have enough valid signatures on his nominating petitions to qualify for the ballot. To the embarrassment of local Republicans, that left Bentivolio as the only Republican on the primary ballot after the filing deadline. A write-in campaign in the Republican primary proved to be too little and too late. With tea party support, Bentivolio got the nomination with 66 percent of the vote. The general election that year proved uneventful.

Trott styled himself as an innovative and problem-solving businessman who had lived the American Dream. His background with the economic woes of Michigan left him uniquely prepared to provide job-creating measures in Congress, he said. For the most part, he avoided discussion of the work of his law firm. Bentivolio launched a negative campaign, calling Trott the "Foreclosure King." A real-life campaign ad featured a 101-year-old Detroit woman who had lived in the family home for 65 years and lost it to a foreclosure handled by Trott's firm. The woman's son, without her knowledge, had taken out a reverse mortgage and hidden eviction notices from her. That saga resulted in a media outcry, and the woman soon returned to her home. "While I served my country in two wars, he was serving foreclosure notices," Bentivolio said of Trott. In an interview with the *Detroit Free Press*, Trott defended his business, saying, "I'm just doing my job for my clients." In a contest that *Mother Jones* headlined "Santa vs. Scrooge," voters went with Scrooge. Trott won 66%-34%.

Missing an opportunity to run an experienced local political figure, Democrats nominated Bobby McKenzie, a former counterterrorism adviser to the State Department. He attacked Trott for his foreclosure practice, but Trott's solid conservatism - he pledged to repeal the Affordable Care Act, secure the border, and defend gun rights - played well with voters. "What you see is what you get," he promised on his campaign website. "I will not tell you one thing and do another." National Democratic and liberal groups stayed away from this contest. Trott overwhelmed McKenzie, as he did Bentivolio, with his free-spending $5 million budget, of which $3.3 million came from his own deep pocket. He won the general election 56%-40%. A limited and late-starting write-in campaign on behalf of Bentivolio yielded an inconsequential 1,411 votes. McKenzie spent a total of $815,000, and Bentivolio spent $747,000.

During his first term, Trott got seats on the Foreign Affairs and Judiciary committees. In April 2015, he joined a presidential delegation to Armenia for the centennial observance of the Armenian genocide. Michigan has 15,000 residents of Armenian descent. From the Judiciary Committee, he filed a bill that he called the Financial Institution Bankruptcy Act of 2016 - an apt subject for a foreclosure lawyer. The bill "protects taxpayers by reforming the process of how failing banks go through bankruptcy proceedings," Trott told the House. "It will also result in a transparent judicial process instead of there being a group of bank CEOs and regulators that meets in a back room in order to decide how to save a failing bank." The House passed the bill on a voice vote and with virtually no debate. Trott and the other House members from both parties who discussed the legislation did not identify the failing bank.

In his 2016 reelection, Trott faced Anil Kumar, a urologist who founded a surgical center and was a faculty member at Michigan State University. Trott led in fundraising, $1.3 million to $1.1 million, including Kumar's $750,000 loan to his campaign. Kumar appealed to his South Asian culture. But that wasn't enough in this campaign. Trott won, 53%-40%. Bentivolio ran again as an independent and got 4 percent of the vote. During the campaign, Trott wrote in *The Detroit News* that Donald Trump was popular with voters because his "message has given a voice to millions of Americans who are fed up with Washington and disgusted with the continued failures of career politicians running this country."

With his seat on Financial Services in 2017, Trott said that his objective was "allowing Michiganders to take charge of their financial independence."

Central Detroit Suburbs: Southern Oakland, Western Wayne

Population		**Race and Ethnicity**		**Income**	
Total	714,349	White	80.2%	Median Income	$74,873 (55 out of 435)
Land area	419	Black	5.1%		
Pop/ sq mi	1703.8	Latino	3.4%	Under $50,000	32.5%
Born in state	71.3%	Asian	0.0%	$50,000-$99,999	31.6%
		Two races	2.0%	$100,000-$199,999	27.0%
Age Groups		Other	0.4%	$200,000 or more	8.9%
Under 18	22.8%			Poverty Rate	7.0%
18-34	19.5%	**Education**			
35-64	43.5%	H.S grad or less	25.9%	**Health Insurance**	
Over 64	14.2%	Some college	28.6%	With health insurance coverage	92.9%
		College Degree, 4 yr	26.6%		
Work		Post grad	18.8%		
White Collar	48.5%			**Public Assistance**	
Sales and Service	37.2%	**Military**		Cash public assistance income	1.5%
Blue Collar	14.4%	Veteran	6.9%		
Government	8.9%	Active Duty	0.0%	Food stamp/SNAP benefits	6.8%

Voter Turnout			
2015 Total Citizens 18+	515,961	2016 House Turnout as % CVAP	74%
2016 House turnout	379,488	2014 House Turnout as % CVAP	49%

2012 Presidential Vote		
Mitt Romney	199,308	(52%)
Barack Obama	178,768	(47%)

2016 Presidential Vote		
Donald Trump	194,245	(49%)
Hillary Clinton	177,143	(45%)
Gary Johnson	14,960	(4%)

Cook Partisan Voting Index: R+4

While Detroit has struggled with seemingly endemic urban decay, many of its suburbs have shown more resilience than the city that spawned them - and a more youthful adaptability to economic change. Sixty years ago, Livonia had 18,000 people. By 2015, it had 95,000. Battery maker A123 Systems has a large lithium ion factory in Livonia, and Ford is building a new transmission plant for its F-150 pick-up trucks. A University of Michigan-Dearborn study ranked the city among the state's top communities for fostering business development and local entrepreneurship.

Novi, in Oakland County, is a high-income suburb that grew 24 percent between 2000 and 2015. Its Asian-American population was 16 percent in 2010, and it is now nicknamed "Little Tokyo." Many of these newcomers have work visas and participate in research and development, as Japanese automotive suppliers increasingly build their products in the United States; the city has adapted by offering multilingual instruction in its hospitals, workplaces and schools. In partnership with Fiat-Chrysler, Google has built a self-drive development center in Novi.

The 11th Congressional District of Michigan covers several suburbs west and northwest of Detroit. About three-fifths of the district is in southern Oakland County, including Troy, Birmingham and Novi, plus Bloomfield Hills and Waterford to the north; the remainder are in western Wayne County, with Northville and Plymouth plus Livonia. The district has 10 percent Asians, which is the largest minority group in the 80 percent white district. Livonia was long closely divided between the two major parties, but the recent affluent influx into this part of Wayne County has made it more Republican. In contrast to other Republican-held districts in Michigan, the upscale 11th had little change in the 2016 presidential contest. Donald Trump won 49%-45%. In 2012, Mitt Romney won 52-47%.

TWELFTH DISTRICT

Debbie Dingell (D)

Elected 2014, 2nd term; b. Nov 23, 1953, Detroit; Georgetown University (DC), B.S.; Georgetown University (DC), M.S., 1998; Roman Catholic; Married (Hon. John D. Dingell Jr.); 4 children.

Elected Office: Wayne State U. Board of Governors, 2007-2014.

Professional Career: President, sr. Executive public affairs, GM Foundation; Founder, Chairman, Nat'l Women's Health Resource Cntr. & the Children's Inn, Nat'l Inst. of Health; Co-host, Detroit public TV show "Am I Right."

DC Office: 116 CHOB 20515, 202-225-4071, Fax: 202-226-0371, debbiedingell.house.gov.

State Offices: Dearborn, 313-278-2936; Ypsilanti, 734-481-1100.

Committees: *Energy & Commerce*: Communications & Technology, Digital Commerce & Consumer Protection, Environment.

Group Ratings

	ADA	ACLU	AFL-CIO	LCV	ITI	COC	HAFA	ACU	CFG	FRC
2016	-	100%	-	97%	67%	69%	14%	0%	8%	0%
2015	90%	C	100%	97%	C	47%	C	4%	0%	0%

Almanac Ratings 2015

	Economy	Social	Foreign	Composite
Liberal	96%	95%	99%	96%
Conservative	5%	5%	1%	4%

Key Votes of the 114th Congress

1. Keystone Pipeline	N	5. Puerto Rico Debt	Y	9. Offenses by Aliens	N
2. Trade Deals	N	6. Medical Marijuana	Y	10. Troops in Iraq	Y
3. Export-Import Bank	Y	7. Sanctuary Cities	N	11. Homeland Security $$	Y
4. Debt Ceiling Increase	Y	8. Armor-piercing Bullets	N	12. Trade Adjustment aid	Y

Election Results

Election	Name (Party)	Vote (%)	Cand. Spent	Ind. Exp. Support	Ind. Exp. Oppose
2016 General	Debbie Dingell (D)	211,378 (64%)	$825,876		
	Jeff Jones (R)	96,104 (29%)	$1,222,538		
	Tom Bagwell (L)	7,489 (2%)			
2016 Primary	Debbie Dingell (D)	(100%)			

Prior winning percentages: 2014 (65%)

Democrat Debbie Dingell, elected in 2014, has been a longtime power player and the wife of former Rep. John Dingell, the Dean of the House who retired after 59 years. Her victory constituted a historic level of political continuity and she became the first wife of a sitting member to take a seat while the spouse remained alive. She created her own niche: less cantankerous and more of a team player than her husband, but willing to hold Democrats accountable.

During the long era that her husband was a powerful member of Congress, Debbie Dingell was a well-known figure in her own right following their marriage in 1981, the year he became chairman of the Energy and Commerce Committee. She grew up in a family with close ties to General Motors. Her grandfather cofounded Fisher Body, an early and important GM acquisition. After completing college at Georgetown, she joined GM as a lobbyist in 1977. That year, she met her future husband. After they married, she gave up her lobbying but remained a senior executive until 2009, managing its public affairs operation and heading the GM Foundation.

As an influential operative, Dingell developed an extensive network with a hand in high-stakes political activities. A member of the Democratic National Committee, she ran Al Gore's Michigan campaign in 2000 and took on the same role for John Kerry four years later. She promoted women's health issues and Michigan economic development through her work with foundations.

Dingell considered a run for the Senate when Democratic Sen. Carl Levin announced he would retire in 2014. She decided against it and Rep. Gary Peters ran instead. When her husband said that he would end his tenure as Congress' longest-serving member, she became his likely successor. Not only is the district solidly blue, but it's a place where close ties to GM help rather than hurt.

Dingell faced token opposition in the August primary, which she won with 78 percent of the vote. Against Republican Terry Bowman, a Ford autoworker whom she outspent 38-to-1, Dingell coasted to a 65%-31% victory in November, roughly the margin of her husband's recent victories. After her win, she said, "I am more interested in finding solutions than looking for fights." With her husband and his father John Dingell Sr., a Dingell family member has represented the Detroit area in the House non-stop since 1933.

As a freshman in the minority party, Dingell wielded tools of influence that often were rhetorical or political. She was named a senior whip by Minority Whip Steny Hoyer, who was a long-time ally of her husband. She was vice-chair of the seniors' task force for the Democratic Caucus, and co-chair of a Democratic Congressional Campaign Committee project to recruit more women candidates. A few days before the 2016 election, she said that one of the "worst things" with the Affordable Care Act is that Democrats passed it without any Republican votes. She added that the two parties should cooperate to fix it - a clear rebuke to President Barack Obama and Democratic Leader Nancy Pelosi.

Two days after the election, she wrote an op-ed in *The Washington Post* that she had repeatedly warned campaign officials for Hillary Clinton that they were taking her state for granted. "I was the crazy one. I predicted that Hillary Clinton was in trouble in Michigan during the Democratic primary. I observed that Donald Trump could win the Republican nomination for president. And at Rotary Clubs, local chambers of commerce, union halls and mosques, I noted that we could see a Trump presidency."

Dingell showed nuances in her support for gun rights when she praised Michigan Gov. Rick Snyder for vetoing a bill that would have permitted concealed-weapon permits for individuals with a history of domestic violence. During the June 2016 House sit-in when Democrats demanded action on gun control, she recounted her experience growing up with a risk of gun violence. "I lived in a house with a man that should not have had access to a gun," Dingell said in a speech on the House floor. "I know what it is like to see a gun pointed at you and wonder if you were going to live. And I know what it is like to hide in the closet and pray to God 'do not let anything happen to me.'"

In January 2017, Dingell got a seat on Energy and Commerce. For a junior member, she joined the committee with deep familiarity with its history, practices and tensions, not least with policies affecting the auto industry.

Southern Detroit Suburbs, Ann Arbor

Population		**Race and Ethnicity**		**Income**	
Total	704,504	White	75.6%	Median Income	$52,447
Land area	403	Black	10.4%		(217 out of
Pop/ sq mi	1747.2	Latino	5.5%		435)
Born in state	69.1%	Asian	0.0%	Under $50,000	47.8%
		Two races	2.9%	$50,000-$99,999	30.0%
Age Groups		Other	0.4%	$100,000-$199,999	18.3%
Under 18	21.9%			$200,000 or more	3.8%
18-34	27.3%	**Education**		Poverty Rate	17.8%
35-64	38.1%	H.S grad or less	36.6%		
Over 64	12.7%	Some college	30.4%	**Health Insurance**	
Work		College Degree, 4 yr	17.5%	With health insurance coverage	91.4%
		Post grad	15.4%		
White Collar	39.5%				
Sales and Service	40.6%	**Military**		**Public Assistance**	
Blue Collar	19.9%	Veteran	6.8%	Cash public assistance income	3.0%
Government	14.1%	Active Duty	0.0%		
				Food stamp/SNAP benefits	15.1%

Voter Turnout			
2015 Total Citizens 18+	515,560	2016 House Turnout as % CVAP	64%
2016 House turnout	328,542	2014 House Turnout as % CVAP	40%

2012 Presidential Vote		
Barack Obama	217,542	(66%)
Mitt Romney	107,632	(33%)

2016 Presidential Vote		
Hillary Clinton	205,953	(60%)
Donald Trump	116,719	(34%)
Gary Johnson	10,293	(3%)

Cook Partisan Voting Index: D+14

The American-made automobile may be a vanishing breed elsewhere, but it still reigns supreme in Dearborn, the home of Ford Motor Co.'s headquarters. At the far eastern edge of Dearborn is Ford's famous River Rouge complex, which initially produced anti-submarine ships for use in World War I and which at one point contained almost all of the equipment needed to manufacture an automobile from raw materials through finished product.

The 12th Congressional District of Michigan covers southern and central Wayne County and is a predominantly white, blue-collar district centered on Dearborn. South of Dearborn, the district swings around heavily African-American Romulus and Inkster (which are in the 13th District), taking in several working-class Detroit suburbs known collectively as the "Downriver" area: Taylor; Southgate; Woodhaven, the site of another big Ford plant; and Flat Rock, home to a joint Ford-Mazda auto plant, one of the few Japanese plants in Michigan. In January 2017, Ford announced its plan to spend $700 million on a manufacturing and innovation center at Flat Rock, which will work on electric cars. In 2016, Ford made long-term commitments to Dearborn, with an upgrade of its headquarters campus plus additional office space on the west side of town. The district takes in Ypsilanti, where the U.S. Transportation Department in the closing days of the Obama administration announced its financing of an $80 million driverless car testing facility.

Also in the 12th is two-thirds of Washtenaw County, which centers on the University of Michigan and Ann Arbor, one of the nation's largest university towns. It is oriented to the university but also is home to auto executives and young families who like a town with plenty of bookstores, coffeehouses and liberal neighbors. In 2006, Ann Arbor landed the headquarters of Google's AdWords unit, which operates the company's "pay-per-click" advertising method, Google's main revenue source. After the recession postponed the initial plan for Google to have a local workforce of 1,000, company officials in 2015 said they would double their office space and move to a new corporate campus near the university.

The district is Democratic territory. In 2016, Hillary Clinton won 60 percent of the vote, which was a drop from the 66 percent that President Barack Obama won in 2012. The Washtenaw County portion includes about 40 percent of the district and is its center of Democratic strength, where Obama won almost 80 percent in 2008.

THIRTEENTH DISTRICT

John Conyers (D)

Elected 1964, 27th term; b. May 16, 1929, Detroit; Wayne State University Law School (MI), LL.B.; Wayne State University (MI), B.A.; Baptist; Married (Monica Ann Esters Conyers); 2 children.

Military Career: MI National Guard, 1948-1950; U.S. Army, 1950-1954 (Korea); U.S. Army Reserve, 1954-1957.

Professional Career: Legislative Assistant, U.S. Rep. John Dingell, 1958-1961; Practicing attorney, 1959-1964; Referee, MI Workmen's Comp. Department, 1961- 63; Executive bd., Detroit NAACP, 1963-present; Executive Board Member, Detroit ACLU, 1964-present.

DC Office: 2426 RHOB 20515, 202-225-5126, Fax: 202-225-0072, conyers.house.gov.

State Offices: Detroit, 313-961-5670; Westland, 734-675-4084.

Committees: *Judiciary (RMM)*: Constitution & Civil Justice, Courts, Intellectual Property & Internet, Crime, Terrorism, Homeland Security & Investigations, Immigration & Border Security, Regulatory Reform, Commercial & Antitrust Law.

Group Ratings

	ADA	ACLU	AFL-CIO	LCV	ITI	COC	HAFA	ACU	CFG	FRC
2016	-	100%	-	97%	40%	58%	14%	0%	8%	0%
2015	95%	C	100%	94%	C	40%	C	0%	0%	0%

Almanac Ratings 2015

	Economy	Social	Foreign	Composite
Liberal	100%	93%	99%	97%
Conservative	0%	7%	1%	3%

Key Votes of the 114th Congress

1. Keystone Pipeline	N	5. Puerto Rico Debt	Y	9. Offenses by Aliens	N
2. Trade Deals	N	6. Medical Marijuana	Y	10. Troops in Iraq	Y
3. Export-Import Bank	Y	7. Sanctuary Cities	N	11. Homeland Security $$	Y
4. Debt Ceiling Increase	Y	8. Armor-piercing Bullets	NV	12. Trade Adjustment aid	Y

Election Results

Election	Name (Party)	Vote (%)		Cand. Spent	Ind. Exp. Support	Ind. Exp. Oppose
2016 General	John Conyers (D)	198,771	(77%)	$545,915	$11,051	
	Jeff Gorman (R)	40,541	(16%)			
	Tiffany Hayden (L)	9,648	(4%)			
2016 Primary	John Conyers, Jr. (D)	30,922	(61%)			
	Janice Winfrey (D)	19,956	(39%)			

Prior winning percentages: 2014 (80%), 2012 (83%), 2010 (77%), 2008 (92%), 2006 (85%), 2004 (84%), 2002 (83%), 2000 (89%), 1998 (87%), 1996 (86%), 1994 (82%), 1992 (82%), 1990 (89%), 1988 (91%), 1986 (89%), 1984 (89%), 1982 (97%), 1980 (95%), 1978 (93%), 1976 (92%), 1974 (91%), 1972 (88%), 1970 (88%), 1968 (100%), 1966 (84%), 1964 (84%)

John Conyers is the ranking Democrat on the Judiciary Committee and the longest-serving current member of Congress. He remains a soft-spoken yet stubborn counterweight to the panel's numerous conservatives. First elected in 1964, on the eve of the Voting Rights Act, Conyers was a founder of the Congressional Black Caucus and has been among the most liberal members of the House.

The son of a UAW operative, Conyers grew up in Detroit. He played cornet at Northwestern and Cass Technical High Schools and watched jazz greats at Baker's Keyboard Lounge. He served in the Army in

Korea, got his bachelor's and law degrees from Wayne State University, practiced law, then worked on the staff of a young Rep. John Dingell, the longest-serving member of Congress, who retired in 2015.

Conyers was one of six African Americans in the House when he was first elected. Conyers won his primary, in which 60,000 votes were cast, by 108 votes. Civil rights heroine Rosa Parks, who by then had moved to Detroit, worked on his 1964 campaign and then in his Detroit office until her retirement in 1988. When she died, Conyers sponsored the resolution paving the way for her to lie in state in the Capitol Rotunda, the first woman so honored. He sponsored the original Martin Luther King Jr., holiday bill just days after the civil rights leader was assassinated in 1968 and he persevered until it passed in 1983. Since 1989, he has sponsored legislation to establish a commission to examine slavery and its lingering effects and to consider whether reparations should be paid to descendants of slaves. He has been wary of crime legislation that strengthens the power of law enforcement and he opposed the welfare changes of the 1990s. "Through the course of my career, I've had a straightforward aim - to live out Martin Luther King Jr.'s vision of a society oriented toward jobs, justice and peace," he told the *Michigan Chronicle* in 2015.

Gun control has long been one of Conyers' chief causes. He supports banning high-capacity ammunition magazines, requiring background checks for all gun sales, and toughening penalties for the transfer of multiple firearms to anyone forbidden to own guns, such as convicted felons. On immigration, he railed against the Republicans' emphasis on enforcement, calling it "a race to the bottom," and has compared the issue to the struggle for civil rights. "Like the civil rights movement, the journey may be long and the path uneven, but the result will be a stronger and more just America," he wrote in a 2012 op-ed column.

Conyers has shown that he is capable of bipartisanship. In the tense weeks after the September 11 attacks, Conyers, as Judiciary's ranking member, worked hand-in-hand with the Republican chairman, conservative Jim Sensenbrenner of Wisconsin, on anti-terrorism legislation. They agreed that the government could detain immigrants suspected of terrorism without bringing charges, but only for seven days, and they introduced the anti-terrorism bill together. Over time, Conyers worked with Sensenbrenner on other issues, despite their deep ideological differences.

Conyers rose to Judiciary chairman in 2007 after Democrats won control of the House. He favored bringing a censure motion against President George W. Bush and Vice President Dick Cheney for allegedly misleading Congress and the American people on the rationale for invading Iraq in 2003. He called for creation of a special committee to investigate. But House Speaker Nancy Pelosi, in an effort to calm partisan tensions after the 2006 elections, ruled out an investigation. Still, Conyers examined the Bush presidency, including the use of presidential signing statements that he said went beyond the terms of the legislation. He pushed contempt charges against Bush White House Chief of Staff Joshua Bolten and former counsel Harriet Miers after they refused to give sworn testimony about the firings of U.S. attorneys across the country.

Taking a hand in the huge government bailout of the financial sector in 2008, Conyers pushed to allow bankruptcy judges to lower mortgage rates or the principal for homeowners who go bankrupt. He achieved one of his longtime goals in 2010 when he won enactment of a law reducing the sentencing disparities between crack and powder cocaine, something he and other civil rights activists had argued for years was unfair to African Americans. But he has been unable to advance another priority, requiring radio stations to pay performers a fee for playing their music on air.

He has had his differences with current Chairman Bob Goodlatte of Virginia, though they have sought common ground on legislation to address police practices. "Our country has been plagued by unrest due to a series of tragic incidents related to police-involved violence. In far too many cases, we have experienced situations that are further dividing communities and law enforcement," Conyers said at a May 2015 hearing, where he voiced appreciation to Goodlatte for his willingness to work on the issue. In July 2016, the two of them announced the creation of a working group to hold roundtables to examine police strategies. Earlier, Conyers reintroduced with Democratic Sen. Ben Cardin of Maryland his bill to prohibit racial profiling by law-enforcement officers.

In recent years, Conyers has been the subject of negative news stories at home. In 2003, the *Detroit Free Press* reported that Conyers assigned his congressional staff to work on his political campaigns and also made them run personal errands and babysit his two children. In 2006, the House Ethics Committee concluded an investigation of the allegations by saying Conyers must take "a number of additional, significant steps to ensure that his office complies with all rules and standards regarding campaign and personal work by congressional staff." In 2009, his wife, Detroit City Council President Pro Tem Monica Conyers, pleaded guilty to taking bribes for helping a company called Synagro Technologies get a sludge-hauling contract with the city. She was released in 2013 following her three-year sentence, and got a job in neighborhood legal services. She later filed for divorce, but they reconciled and renewed their marital vows in 2016.

Nevertheless, Conyers - described by *The Detroit News* as "part showman, part junkyard dog, part evangelist" - has been reelected mostly without difficulty, relying on his longevity to cover other political weaknesses. "He's a terrible campaigner and doesn't raise much money, but he's an institution," Bill Ballenger, editor of *Inside Michigan Politics* newsletter, told the *Free Press* in 2012. He made two runs for mayor of Detroit, in 1989 and 1993. But he waged desultory campaigns, and trailed far behind in each.

Some political observers thought Conyers might be vulnerable in 2012 with significantly redrawn lines that included Downriver and western Wayne County. He drew four Democratic primary challengers. All of them castigated Conyers for being out of touch and unresponsive to constituents, but none of them had much money. Conyers won the primary with 55 percent of the vote, ensuring his reelection in November.

Conyers faced more drama in 2014, when the county clerk and secretary of state ruled that hundreds of signatures gathered by his reelection campaign were invalid. He was struck from the ballot, and his aides discussed the possibility of a write-in campaign. But a federal judge subsequently ordered him on the ballot after the congressman's lawyers joined civil rights activists in contending the law setting requirements for people gathering signatures was itself unconstitutional.

Before the judge's ruling, Detroit's *Metro Times* columnist Jack Lessenberry suggested that Conyers gracefully retire. "When the votes are cast, when it comes to anything that matters, he is nearly always on the side of the angels," Lessenberry wrote. "But here's something else you should know about John Conyers: Increasingly, he isn't the man he once was." Rev. Horace Sheffield, his opponent in the 2014 primary, questioned "whether or not he's capable at this point." Still, his constituents remained supportive, and he won the primary 74%-26%. In 2016, Detroit City Clerk Janice Winfrey mounted a serious challenge in the Democratic primary. She drew a contrast to Conyers, but she seemed careful not to directly criticize him. Her campaign, she said, was "solely based on my commitment to serve and to address the neglect of the district." She raised $84,000 to $605,000 for Conyers. He won, 61%-39%, a signal that his political clout may be weakening and that Winfrey might be positioning herself as a potential successor.

By virtue of his long tenure and his committee position, Conyers carries authority, even though he may be a voice from another era. As the new House dean, he said that his priorities remained "justice and peace," including a $15 hourly minimum wage. That goal is unlikely to be enacted in a House with a Republican Speaker, but Conyers and his allies have been successful in other forums. Following the election of Donald Trump as president, he wrote in *Time* magazine of his "fear that our nation may again be veering towards a constitutional crisis, but with far fewer safeguards than we have had in the past." In February 2017, he joined a quiet protest march to the Senate by a handful of House Democrats who objected to the confirmation of Jeff Sessions as Attorney General.

Detroit Metro West

Population		**Race and Ethnicity**		**Income**	
Total	690,748	White	33.8%	Median Income	$31,393 (433 out of 435)
Land area	185	Black	55.5%		
Pop/ sq mi	3736.8	Latino	7.0%		
Born in state	76.4%	Asian	0.0%	Under $50,000	68.2%
		Two races	1.9%	$50,000-$99,999	23.3%
Age Groups		Other	0.6%	$100,000-$199,999	7.6%
Under 18	24.9%			$200,000 or more	0.8%
18-34	23.7%	**Education**		Poverty Rate	33.0%
35-64	38.7%	H.S grad or less	52.5%		
Over 64	12.7%	Some college	33.4%	**Health Insurance**	
		College Degree, 4 yr	9.2%	With health insurance coverage	85.2%
Work		Post grad	5.0%		
White Collar	23.8%				
Sales and Service	48.6%	**Military**		**Public Assistance**	
Blue Collar	27.6%	Veteran	7.0%	Cash public assistance income	5.8%
Government	9.1%	Active Duty	0.0%		
				Food stamp/SNAP benefits	34.6%

Voter Turnout			
2015 Total Citizens 18+	496,735	2016 House Turnout as % CVAP	52%
2016 House turnout	257,797	2014 House Turnout as % CVAP	34%

2012 Presidential Vote		
Barack Obama	249,656	(85%)
Mitt Romney	41,911	(14%)

2016 Presidential Vote		
Hillary Clinton	209,105	(78%)
Donald Trump	48,111	(18%)

Cook Partisan Voting Index: D+32

Detroit's early auto factories - Packard, Hudson, Ford Highland Park, Dodge Main, Briggs, Ford Rouge, Cadillac, Kelsey-Hayes, Chrysler, Plymouth, DeSoto - were built between 1905 and 1925 about five miles from the city's center and at what was then the edge of urban development. Almost instantly, the flat farmlands all around were platted in streets arranged in a grid and built up with wooden bungalows and brick prairie-style houses. Detroit's neighborhoods filled up with factory workers and civil servants, professionals and maintenance men, corner-store owners and management personnel, Catholics and Protestants and Jews: a middle-class melting pot. With one exception: Detroit in those days had few blacks. They did not begin in earnest their great migration here from the South until around 1940, when defense plants began hiring African Americans in large numbers. In 1910, blacks made up 1 percent of Detroit's population; in 1970, the share had risen to 44 percent. Today, Detroit is 83 percent black.

The history of the city is one of conflict and uplift, inspiration and tragedy. The wartime mixture of Appalachian whites and Deep South blacks proved volatile. During the war years, blacks were pent up in a few severely overcrowded neighborhoods like the Black Bottom, most of it now covered by the Chrysler Freeway; whites opposed any attempt to expand black neighborhoods, sometimes with violent measures. This tinderbox erupted in June 1943 after a fight started on a beach on Belle Isle. Rumors spread among blacks that a white man had thrown a black woman and her baby off a bridge, while a competing rumor spread among whites that a white woman had been raped and murdered on the bridge. The ensuing race riot lasted three days and resulted in 34 deaths.

After 1945, when African Americans began moving outward, real estate agents played on racial fears. In the 1950s, whole square miles of Detroit changed racial composition in a matter of months. The 1960s started with hope that the civil rights movement, encouraged by Walter Reuther's United Auto Workers union, would improve matters. In fact, many black Detroiters found good jobs and made good incomes. Then came the riots of July 1967, followed by extensive white flight and steep increases in crime. Detroit's first African-American mayor, Democrat Coleman Young, elected in 1973, pressured major employers like the Big Three auto companies to build facilities in Detroit and raised taxes to expand city services. But economic conditions continued to deteriorate and violent crime became a part of everyday life.

Detroit took on a garrison atmosphere. Crime reduced the value of much residential real estate to near zero, and the city's population fell from 1.7 million in 1960 to a still-declining 677,000 in 2015. The public sector took a larger share of residents' income than almost anywhere else in the country and served citizens poorly. Turnaround began belatedly when Democratic Mayor Dennis Archer, elected in 1993, worked to fight crime and encourage private-sector growth. Incomes rose, as did median housing value, from $32,000 to $71,000. The city later made some small progress under Mayor Dave Bing, a former NBA star with the Detroit Pistons. The downtown and midtown areas have increasingly attracted young professionals, students, and empty nesters. The occupancy rates for rentals here approach 100 percent, a Whole Foods grocery market opened in 2013, and the Pistons planned to return to downtown in late 2017 at the new Little Caesars Arena on Woodward Avenue.

The auto industry's fortunes have brightened since the government takeover of General Motors and Chrysler in 2009. Despite some salutary trends, the city remained largely blighted. In March 2013, Republican Gov. Rick Snyder declared the city in a state of financial emergency, and he appointed an emergency manager to try to steer the city to fiscal stability. In December 2014, Detroit emerged from bankruptcy. But that transition marked only the start of the long-term revival of the city, under Mayor Mike Duggan (who was elected as the city's first white mayor in a half-century) and a rapidly changed population. Local finances remained subject to oversight by a commission with a majority of its members appointed by the state. In 2015, Wayne County gave to Cook County, Illinois, its mark as the county with the largest annual population loss. But it continued to fall, including its black population. Poverty in Metro Detroit remained the worst in the nation.

The 13th Congressional District of Michigan covers much of the western half of the city. Republican redistricters had dual objectives: Maintain two black majority districts even though there are barely enough blacks to achieve those numbers, and maximize Republican strength in the neighboring suburban districts. The 13th, based entirely in Wayne County, covers an area stretching from Highland Park to the east side of downtown Detroit. One salient to the southwest takes in parts of "Mexicantown," with its growing Hispanic population, as well as the cities of Ecorse, River Rouge and Melvindale. Another swings south through white-majority neighborhoods, such as Dearborn Heights, Garden City and Westland, to take in heavily African-American Inkster and Romulus, which is the home of Detroit's Metro Airport. Plans to open in 2016 a $100 million Outlets of Michigan mall in Romulus were delayed by the uncertain economy. Overall the district is about 55 percent African American and one of the most strongly Democratic in the country. President Barack Obama won 85 percent of the vote in 2012. Hillary Clinton got a still strong 78 percent in 2016. But in a state that Donald Trump won by barely 10,000 votes, each dent in the Democratic turnout made a big difference in the outcome.

FOURTEENTH DISTRICT

Brenda Lawrence (D)

Elected 2014, 2nd term; b. Oct 18, 1954, Detroit; Central Michigan University, B.S.; University of Detroit (MI), Att.; Christian - Non-Denominational; Married (McArthur Lawrence); 2 children.

Elected Office: Southfield Board of Education, 1992-1996; Southfield City Council, 1997-2001, President, 1999; Southfield Mayor, 2002-2015.

Professional Career: Manager, USPS.

DC Office: 1213 LHOB 20515, 202-225-5802, Fax: 202-226-2356, lawrence.house.gov.

State Offices: Detroit, 313-423-6183; Southfield, 248-356-2052.

Committees: *Oversight & Government Reform*: Government Operations. *Transportation & Infrastructure*: Aviation, Highways & Transit, Water Resources & Environment.

Group Ratings

	ADA	ACLU	AFL-CIO	LCV	ITI	COC	HAFA	ACU	CFG	FRC
2016	-	94%	-	100%	50%	58%	12%	0%	11%	0%
2015	90%	C	100%	94%	C	45%	C	4%	0%	0%

Almanac Ratings 2015

	Economy	Social	Foreign	Composite
Liberal	96%	100%	99%	98%
Conservative	4%	0%	1%	2%

Key Votes of the 114th Congress

1. Keystone Pipeline	N	5. Puerto Rico Debt	Y	9. Offenses by Aliens	N
2. Trade Deals	N	6. Medical Marijuana	Y	10. Troops in Iraq	Y
3. Export-Import Bank	Y	7. Sanctuary Cities	N	11. Homeland Security $$	Y
4. Debt Ceiling Increase	Y	8. Armor-piercing Bullets	N	12. Trade Adjustment aid	Y

Election Results

Election	Name (Party)	Vote (%)		Cand. Spent	Ind. Exp. Support	Ind. Exp. Oppose
2016 General	Brenda Lawrence (D)	244,135	(79%)	$534,862	$12,727	
	Howard Klausner (R)	58,103	(19%)			
2016 Primary	Brenda Lawrence (D)	55,433	(87%)			
	Vanessa Moss (D)	5,235	(8%)			

Prior winning percentages: 2014 (78%)

Democrat Brenda Lawrence, elected in 2014 in the diversifying 14th District, pursued her interest in transportation issues. With her seat on the Transportation and Infrastructure Committee, she pressed for more information on the water crisis in Flint.

Lawrence was born and raised in Detroit, earned a bachelor's degree in public administration from Central Michigan University, and started her career in the U.S. Postal Service. As her children went through the public school system in Southfield, she was drawn to education issues and was elected to the school board. Later, she won a seat on the City Council and was elected mayor in 2001. As the city's first African American or woman to hold that post, she was reelected three times. She underscored Southfield's resilience as a corporate hub that held up well despite the economic collapse of Detroit.

Lawrence's long tenure as mayor was slow to translate to other political victories. She fell short in her run for Oakland County executive in 2008, and then for lieutenant governor in 2010 with gubernatorial candidate Virg Bernero. In 2012, she made her first bid for the House in the redrawn 14th District, running against two sitting House Democrats: Reps. Gary Peters and Hansen Clarke. That primary became a contentious debate over race. Clarke, a biracial candidate who claimed African-American ancestry, came under criticism amid questions over whether he was truly "black." Later, a local media outlet, with an assist from Lawrence's campaign, reported that the death certificate of Clarke's mother listed her as white. That skirmishing gave Peters a chance to stay above the fray, and he won the primary handily, with 47 percent of the vote to 35 percent for Clarke and 13 percent for Lawrence. Clarke dominated the vote in Wayne County, but Peters did even better in his base of Oakland County.

Lawrence got another chance in 2014 when Peters announced his Senate bid. State Rep. Rudy Hobbs, who was endorsed by Detroit Mayor Mike Duggan, was the early Democratic front-runner. Lawrence gained an edge with endorsements from unions and local business groups. Clarke jumped into the race, hoping to win back his seat. Lawrence made the best of her ground operation and won the primary by 2,391 votes. This time, she got 36 percent to 32 percent for Hobbs and 31 percent for Clarke. She got 41 percent of the vote in Oakland County but only 32 percent in Wayne. In the general election in the heavily Democratic district, she won 77 percent of the vote and ended her losing streak.

In the House, Lawrence styled herself as a strong advocate for improved roads, bridges and regional transit. "My goal is to help make 8 Mile a major thoroughfare that is the 50-yard line of the congressional district that I represent, not a line that demarcates the haves and the have-nots," she wrote in the *Detroit Free-Press.* She joined the Transportation Committee in her second term and urged "opportunities for economic growth and job creation." With Democratic Rep. Alan Lowenthal of California, she filed a bill that provides dedicated funding to upgrade freight-related railroad infrastructure. On the Oversight and Government Reform Committee, she doggedly pursued more details of the Flint water crisis from Michigan Gov. Rick Snyder. In 2017, she became a vice-chair of the Congressional Caucus on Women's Issues.

Her reelection in 2016 was uneventful, with no Democratic primary and a Republican challenger who did report any campaign finances. She seemed well-positioned politically, at least until redistricting in 2022.

Detroit Metro North and East

Population		**Race and Ethnicity**		**Income**	
Total	695,069	White	31.3%	Median Income	$41,234 (388 out of 435)
Land area	186	Black	56.8%		
Pop/ sq mi	3742.4	Latino	4.7%		
Born in state	71.0%	Asian	0.0%	Under $50,000	57.3%
		Two races	2.6%	$50,000-$99,999	24.9%
Age Groups		Other	0.4%	$100,000-$199,999	13.5%
Under 18	23.7%			$200,000 or more	4.3%
18-34	22.1%	**Education**		Poverty Rate	25.6%
35-64	39.5%	H.S grad or less	39.7%		
Over 64	14.7%	Some college	30.7%	**Health Insurance**	
		College Degree, 4 yr	16.3%	With health insurance coverage	87.1%
Work		Post grad	13.3%		
White Collar	36.7%				
Sales and Service	45.5%	**Military**		**Public Assistance**	
Blue Collar	17.8%	Veteran	6.4%	Cash public assistance income	4.5%
Government	10.8%	Active Duty	0.0%		
				Food stamp/SNAP benefits	26.6%

Voter Turnout			
2015 Total Citizens 18+	502,166	2016 House Turnout as % CVAP	62%
2016 House turnout	310,974	2014 House Turnout as % CVAP	41%

2012 Presidential Vote		
Barack Obama	273,273	(81%)
Mitt Romney	62,794	(19%)

2016 Presidential Vote		
Hillary Clinton	252,387	(79%)
Donald Trump	58,179	(18%)

Cook Partisan Voting Index: D+30

Few central cities in America were as vibrant in the 20th century as Detroit, the nation's fourth-largest city during the middle decades, then in a class shared or surpassed only by New York, Chicago, Philadelphia and Los Angeles. Few have been as diminished as Detroit, which now stands as the nation's 18th-largest city, behind Fort Worth and just ahead of El Paso, both of which continue to grow. This was America's first automobile city, not just because it manufactured so many cars but also because it was built to automobile scale. Detroit started the 20th century about the size of Milwaukee, with fewer than half a million people and extending no farther than four or five miles from the site where the French built Fort Pontchartrain on the Detroit River in 1701. As the Motor City boomed, it grew outward along wide avenues and, starting in the 1950s, along freeways. Metro Detroit eventually expanded to 4 million people, each generation moving out in all directions, leaving behind the previous generation's neighborhoods and civic institutions.

Today, large parts of Detroit are literally empty. Formerly iconic buildings in the downtown area have been demolished, and others are all but vacant, while officials struggle to create new population centers and reestablish a business district. On the positive side, GM bought, for $72 million, the 70-story Renaissance Center, built in the 1970s for $350 million, and the company moved several thousand employees there. Quicken moved more than 10,000 employees from the suburbs to downtown and began to restore some of the landmark buildings in the city; Microsoft made plans for its tech center to become a tenant. But beyond these well-policed enclaves lie acres of vacant lots and half-empty blocks where there were once five-story apartment buildings and brick houses. In 2016, violent crime rates had fallen, but were still high.

In March 2013, Gov. Rick Snyder declared the city in a state of financial emergency and appointed an emergency manager to try to steer the city into the black. When that control ended nearly two years later, Detroit's finances were nominally in better shape. In 2017, Mayor Mike Duggan ran for reelection, with legitimate claims for having promoted the turnaround but was still struggling to provide routine services such as trash pick-up. Both the city and its nearby suburbs, plus state officials in Lansing, faced continuing crises about the direction of the metropolitan area. That future likely would be nothing like the good times - or the bad - of the past half-century.

The 14th Congressional District of Michigan is an amalgamation of heavily minority areas in metro Detroit. Its serpentine shape offers testimony to the difficulty of maintaining majority-minority districts as African Americans increasingly move out of compact neighborhoods in inner cities. The district takes in Hamtramck and the Grosse Pointes, both white majority areas, and also the northern neighborhoods of Wayne County, which became heavily African American following the flight of whites in the 1970s and 1980s. It includes the newest frontiers in African-American migration in southern Oakland County; Southfield was 0.1 percent black in the 1970 census and 70 percent black in the 2010 census, while Oak Park went from being 0.2 percent black to 57 percent in the same period. To the north and east, the district takes in majority-black Pontiac, where the police department was disbanded in 2010 during a fiscal emergency. The Oakland County sheriff department took control the next year, and crime incidents dropped. The resulting district is 56 percent African American and is overwhelmingly Democratic. It is split almost evenly between Wayne and Oakland counties, with their separate political networks.

★ MINNESOTA ★

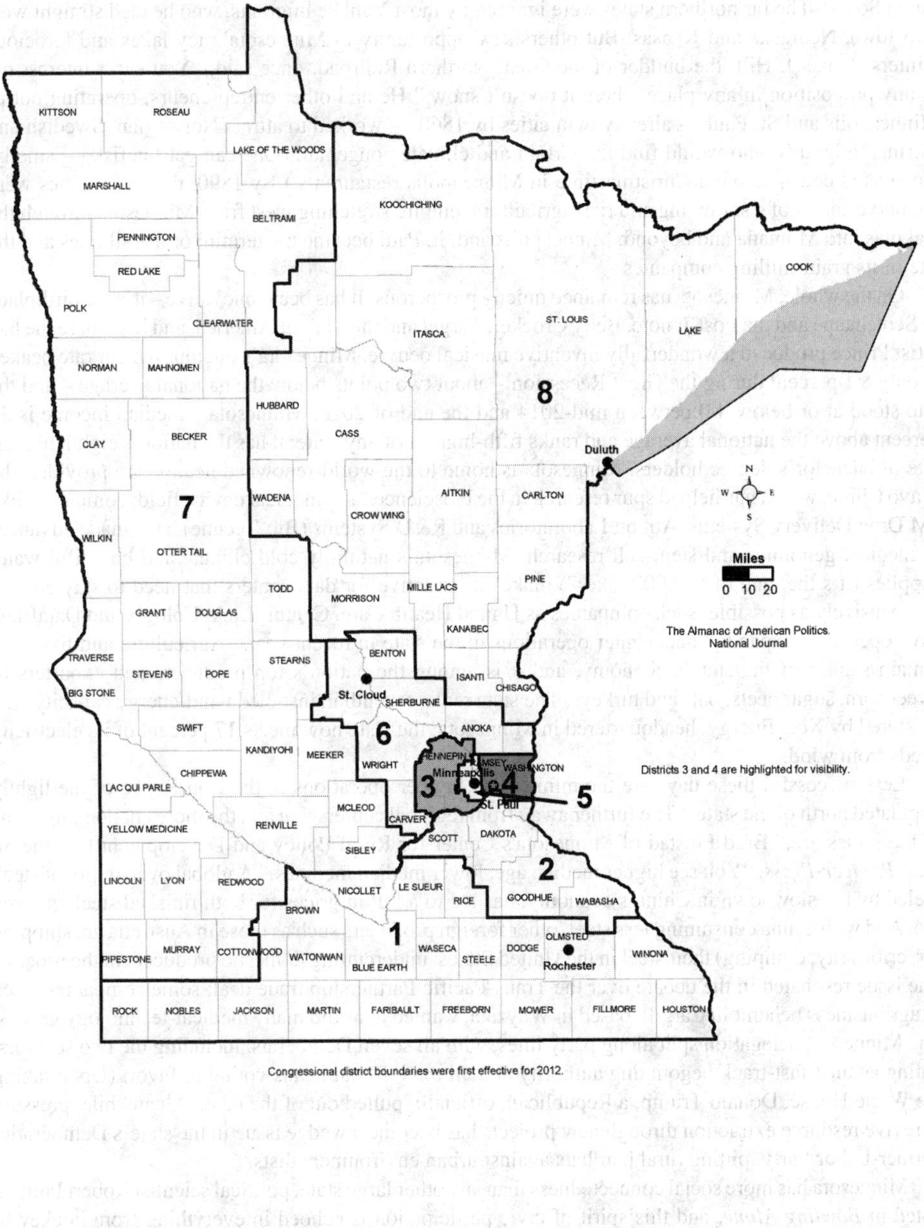

Districts 3 and 4 are highlighted for visibility.

Miles
0 10 20

The Almanac of American Politics.
National Journal

Congressional district boundaries were first effective for 2012.

Minnesota hasn't voted Republican for president since Richard Nixon's landslide in 1972. (The quirk of having native son Walter Mondale on the ballot against Ronald Reagan in 1984 kept it from going Republican that year.) But 2016 was a wake-up call for national Democrats: Minnesota was the state Hillary Clinton won with the narrowest margin save New Hampshire, and rather surprisingly, Minnesota's final margin ended up closer than the margin in states that saw far more 2016 campaign action, such as North Carolina, Ohio and Nevada.

Minnesota began as the node of the transcontinental railroads that linked the winter wheat fields of the northern prairies to the great grain-milling center of Minneapolis and to the bustling Pacific ports of Puget Sound. The far northern states were ignored by most Yankee migrants, who headed straight west into Iowa, Nebraska and Kansas. But others saw opportunity in Minnesota's icy lakes and ferocious winters. James J. Hill, the builder of the Great Northern Railroad, once said, "You can't interest me in any proposition in any place where it doesn't snow." He and other entrepreneurs, operating out of Minneapolis and St. Paul — already twin cities by 1860 — worked to attract Norwegian, Swedish and German migrants who would find the terrain and climate congenial. (One can get lutefisk — smelly, lye-soaked cod — around Christmastime in Minneapolis restaurants.) By 1890, the Twin Cities were the nerve center of a sprawling and rich agricultural empire stretching west from Minnesota through the Dakotas into Montana and beyond. Minneapolis and St. Paul became the termini of its rail lines and the site of its grain-milling companies

On the whole, Minnesota has remained quietly prosperous. It has been innovative – it's the birthplace of Scotch tape and the Post-It note, Betty Crocker, Target and the Mall of America, and it's where the late artist Prince produced a wonderfully inventive musical oeuvre. Minnesota's unemployment rate peaked at only 8.1 percent during the Great Recession – about two points below the national average – and the rate stood at or below 4.0 between mid-2014 and the end of 2016. Minnesota's median income is 22 percent above the national average and ranks fifth-highest of any state; it has the nation's eighth highest rate of bachelor's degree holders. Minnesota is home to the world-renowned health care provider, the Mayo Clinic, which has helped spur research in the biosciences and medical device field; companies like 3M Drug Delivery Systems, Abbott Laboratories and R&D Systems (Bio-Techne) have made advances in medical genomics and stem-cell research. Minnesota's naturally cold climate and bountiful water supplies (it's the land of "10,000 lakes") makes it attractive for data centers that need to stay cool as inexpensively as possible; such companies as United Health Care, CenturyLink, Cologix and DataBank have opened or expanded data center operations in the state in recent years. Agriculture and livestock remain staples of the state's economy, and it is among the nation's top producers and exporters of sweet corn, sugar beets, oats and turkeys. The state ranks seventh in installed wind-energy capacity and, bolstered by Xcel Energy, headquartered in Minnesota, the state now meets 17 percent of its electricity needs from wind.

Less successful these days are the mining and lumber operations in the Iron Range of the lightly populated north of the state. "The further away from regional centers you are, the more challenging some of the issues are," Brad Finstad of Minnesota's Center for Rural Policy and Development told the *St. Paul Pioneer-Press*. "You see higher median age, lower median incomes." A global oversupply of steel, fueled by the slowdown in China's economy, has led to a fall in prices for both finished steel and iron ore. And with China consuming less steel, other foreign producers such as those in Australia are shipping (or, critics say, dumping) their steel in the United States, undercutting domestic producers in the process. The issue resonated in the debate over the Trans-Pacific Partnership trade deal; some companies, such as agribusiness behemoth Cargill, based in Wayzata, wanted it, as did many medical-technology groups. The Minnesota delegation split along party lines, with all seven Democrats, including the two senators, voting against fast-track negotiating authority and all three Republicans voting in favor. (Upon taking the White House, Donald Trump, a Republican, officially pulled out of the deal.) Meanwhile, pressure to revive resource extraction through new projects has become a wedge issue in the state's Democratic-Farmer-Labor Party, pitting rural hardhats against urban environmentalists.

Minnesota has more social connectedness than any other large state, political scientist Robert Putnam noted in *Bowling Alone,* and this spirit of civic participation is echoed in everything from hockey to the party precinct caucuses and conventions. The Twin Cities boast of having more museums than any other city but Chicago and Washington; the Minnesota Historical Society was founded in 1849, nine years before statehood (when there wasn't much Minnesota history yet). Beyond the Twin Cities, you can visit the Spam Museum in Austin, the Judy Garland Museum in Grand Rapids, and the Laura Ingalls Wilder Museum in Walnut Grove, near the banks of Plum Creek.

Today, Minnesota is 81 percent white – the whitest state of any in the Midwest except for Iowa. It's 6 percent black, 5 percent Hispanic and 5 percent Asian. But the state's overall population has grown only modestly -- 4 percent higher than when the 2010 census was taken – and every year, more than 9,000 more 18-to-24-year-olds leave the state than move in. As a result, the population is aging: More Minnesotans are expected to retire in the next decade or so than in the previous six, and by 2020, the state is forecast to have a shortage of more than 100,000 workers. As a result, the minority and foreign-born share of Minnesota's population has become increasingly important for the state's economic future. The state has the largest Somali population on the continent, along with large Hmong and Vietnamese communities. Almost one of every six children born in Minnesota has one or more immigrant parents. This has created some tensions, and in 2010 the Justice Department indicted Somali immigrants in Minneapolis for allegedly raising money for the Islamist militant group Al-Shabaab. But such incidents have been the exception. After Trump issued an executive order tightening immigration, Minnesota became one of the first states to sue.

As in Wisconsin and North Dakota, a strong third-political party developed in Minnesota in the years after the Populist era. Alarmed by the concentration of economic power and wealth in the hands of a few identifiable millionaires who lived on St. Paul's Summit Avenue or on the hill above Minneapolis's Hennepin Avenue, the immigrants from Scandinavia drew on their native traditions of cooperative activity and bureaucratic socialism. The Farmer-Labor Party elected senators in the 1920s and came to dominate state politics when Floyd B. Olson was elected to three two-year terms as governor beginning in 1930. Prior to that, Republicans had held the Minnesota governorship for 63 of the 73 years that the state had been in the union. Midway through his tenure, Olson had secured a lengthy list of reforms that would become the foundation for modern and progressive Minnesota, including the state's first income tax, municipally owned liquor stores, large appropriations for relief, a two-year moratorium on farm foreclosures, a ban on injunctions in labor disputes and a limit on hours worked by women in industrial jobs to 54 per week. Hurt by ties to communists, the Farmer-Laborites were beaten by Gov. Harold Stassen's Republicans in 1938. But this was still a New Deal state, and by 1944 the bedraggled local Democrats merged with the anti-communist faction of Farmer-Laborites to form the Democratic-Farmer-Labor Party, a name that persists to this day. Hubert Humphrey, the mayor of Minneapolis in 1945 and the premier advocate of the civil rights plank at the 1948 Democratic National Convention, played a key role in this progression. Humphrey's DFL — idealistic, civic-minded, closely tied to labor unions, backed by many farmers and shorn of communists — attracted dozens of talented politicians, including Eugene McCarthy, Orville Freeman and Mondale. Humphrey was elected to the Senate at age 37. In the years that followed, the DFL dominated Minnesota politics as a series of progressive businesses led the development of a strong, diversified economy.

After the Humphrey breakthrough in 1948, the Republican Party in Minnesota was barely an afterthought and was practically wiped out in the 1974 Watergate mid-term elections. As part of its rehabilitation effort, the Republican Party of Minnesota became the Independent-Republican Party, a moniker that lasted until 1995, by which time a more conservative wing had taken over. By this time, the DFL had slowly begun to weaken, as well. In 1998, three contenders in the Democratic "my three sons" gubernatorial primary were Hubert Humphrey III, Mike Freeman and Ted Mondale. Humphrey won a divisive primary and faced St. Paul GOP mayor Norm Coleman, but former professional wrestler and suburban mayor Jesse Ventura ran as an independent and won with a plurality. Ventura's tenure initially seemed promising -- his selections for a multi-partisan cabinet were widely admired -- but he became isolated from lawmakers, picked fights with the media and succumbed to celebrity distractions. In 2002, he decided not to run again, and the Twin Cities exurbs — the area just outside the Hennepin (Minneapolis) and Ramsey (St. Paul) core — went heavily Republican, helping Tim Pawlenty win the governorship in another three-way race in which former Democratic Rep. Tim Penny ran on Ventura's old ballot line. In the Senate race that year, Coleman defeated the elder Mondale, whom Democrats had turned to after two-term DFL incumbent Sen. Paul Wellstone died in a plane crash. Eventually, the DFL regained the upper hand: Amy Klobuchar won an open Senate seat in 2006 by a huge margin, and in 2008, DFL nominee Al Franken held Coleman to a 42%-42% tie; after eight months of contentious ballot recounts and court challenges, Franken was certified as the winner in July 2009. Since the 2010 election, every partisan, statewide elected post has been in DFL hands. The legislature, by contrast, has seesawed back and forth.

Minnesota, though not typically included in national analysts' lists of top battleground states, has actually been more closely divided in recent presidential races than is popularly remembered. In 2012, Obama won Minnesota by a bit under eight percentage points, a smaller margin than he'd mustered in Michigan and not much larger than his margins in such states as Iowa, Nevada and Wisconsin. In 2016, Hillary Clinton was able to win the state by only 1.5 percentage points. The narrower margin had less to do with Trump's gains compared with 2012 GOP nominee Mitt Romney – Trump added only a few thousand additional votes statewide in 2016 – but rather because Clinton's vote total fell short of Obama's by more than 178,000. Obama won 28 Minnesota counties, Clinton won only nine. Many of the counties that shifted from blue to red were small, but the shifts were often massive: A half-dozen counties saw their margins of victory shift toward Trump by between 20 and 36 percentage points. Even some counties that remained Democratic in both elections saw their margins shift sharply toward Trump, including St. Louis County (Duluth), with an 18-point swing, and Carlton County (on the outskirts of Duluth), with a 25-point shift to the GOP. Clinton's salvation was her continued edge in the more populous Twin Cities region. The margin in Hennepin shifted eight points in Clinton's direction, and in Ramsey, it shifted toward her by four points; suburban Washington and Dakota counties also remained Democratic, by marginally wider margins. (The regional exception was Anoka County, which went for Romney by two points and Trump by nine.) Both 2016 candidates saw lower raw-vote totals in the five Twin Cities counties, but Trump's decline was three times as big as Clinton's. Outside of the Twin Cities, it was a different story: The Democratic vote haul in these predominantly rural areas fell by 155,000, while the GOP's rose by 82,000. This divide has been quietly fed by partisan divergence on social issues. Ultimately, the election showed how dependent on the Twin Cities the DFL had become – whereas 57 percent of Democratic presidential votes in 2012 came from the Twin Cities, that figure rose to 63 percent in 2016. Expect Minnesota to become an increasingly contested battleground state in the near future.

Population		**Race and Ethnicity**		**Income**	
Total	5,419,171	White	81.7%	Median Income	$61,492 (10 out of 50)
Land area	79,627	Black	5.4%		
Pop/ sq mi	68.1	Latino	5.0%	Under $50,000	40.6%
Born in state	68.2%	Asian	4.4%	$50,000-$99,999	33.1%
Age Groups		Two races	2.3%	$100,000-$199,999	21.1%
Under 18	23.6%	Other	1.1%	$200,000 or more	5.2%
18-34	23.1%	**Education**		Poverty Rate	11.3%
35-64	39.6%	H.S grad or less	33.6%	**Health Insurance**	
Over 64	14.0%	Some college	32.6%	With health insurance coverage	93.0%
Work		College Degree, 4 yr	22.5%		
White Collar	39.5%	Post grad	11.2%	**Public Assistance**	
Sales and Service	39.7%	**Military**		Cash public assistance income	3.6%
Blue Collar	20.9%	Veteran	8.3%		
Government	11.9%	Active Duty	0.0%	Food stamp/SNAP benefits	8.9%

Voter Turnout			
2015 Total Citizens 18+	3,950,807	2016 Pres Turnout as % CVAP	75%
2016 Pres Votes	2,944,813	2012 Pres Turnout as % CVAP	77%

Legislature	
Senate:	33D, 34R
House:	57D, 77R

Presidential Politics

2016 Democratic Caucus		
Bernie Sanders (D)	126,229	(61%)
Hillary Clinton (D)	78,381	(38%)
2016 Republican Caucus		
Marco Rubio (R)	41,397	(36%)
Ted Cruz (R)	33,181	(29%)
Donald Trump (R)	24,473	(21%)
Ben Carson (R)	8,422	(7%)
John Kasich (R)	6,565	(6%)

2016 Presidential Vote		
Hillary Clinton (D)	1,367,825	(46%)
Donald Trump (R)	1,323,232	(45%)
Gary Johnson (L)	112,984	(4%)
2012 Presidential Vote		
Barack Obama (D)	1,546,167	(53%)
Mitt Romney (R)	1,320,225	(45%)

Minnesota has the longest consecutive streak of voting Democratic for president of any state, but that run was severely tested in 2016. The last time Minnesota voted for the Republican nominee was in 1972, and even then it gave Richard Nixon his lowest percentage margin over George McGovern. Before 1932 and the New Deal, the state voted Republican in every presidential race except 1912, when it went for Teddy Roosevelt, a Republican-turned-Bull Moose candidate. Close races in 2000 and 2004 gave Republicans encouragement, but after Barack Obama won the state handily in 2008 and 2012, few thought it would be a battleground in 2016. But with relatively few minority voters and large swaths of rural territory, the Democratic bastion was a competitive contest and Hillary Clinton defeated Donald Trump by just 46%-45%. Trump won the three most rural congressional districts in the state, the, 1st, 7th and 8th, which also reelected Democratic members of Congress. Meanwhile, Clinton captured the 3rd District, which encompasses the southern suburbs of the Twin Cities and contains no rural population, according to the Census. In that district, GOP Rep. Erik Paulsen was also reelected. So, in half of the state's districts, Minnesota voters split their tickets between president and Congress, the highest percentage of split-ticket districts of any state in the country. Clinton won just nine of the state's 87 counties: the two largest vote producers, Hennepin and Ramsey, home to Minneapolis and St. Paul, respectively; Dakota and Washington, two Democratic suburban counties outside the Twin Cities; four counties on the Iron Range; and Olmsted County, home to the Mayo Clinic and the University of Minnesota at Rochester. The Democratic-Farmer-Labor Party base, formerly prairie populists, Scandinavian farmers and blue-collar workers from industrial communities, is now more likely to be the cultural liberals who cluster in comfortable neighborhoods in Minneapolis and St. Paul. Some 33 counties that voted for Obama in either 2008 or 2012 voted for Trump in 2016, many in rural areas of the state.

Minnesota has a tradition of selecting national convention delegates in caucuses. In the March 1 GOP caucuses, Florida Sen. Marco Rubio defeated Texas Sen. Ted Cruz 36%-29%. Trump finished third with 21 percent. Rubio likened Trump to former Reform Party Gov. Jesse Ventura, the professional wrestling celebrity and political rookie who served one term and left office -- and left the state with a \$4.5 billion deficit. Rubio carried five districts. Cruz carried the 6th, 7th and 8th. It was the only state that Rubio carried in the nominating contest. He also won the Puerto Rico primary and the Washington, D.C., convention. More than 114,000 Republicans attended the caucuses, a record, and more than double the roughly 49,000 who participated in 2012. In the Democratic contest, Vermont Sen. Bernie Sanders defeated Clinton 62%-38% and swept all eight congressional districts. Turnout was more than 204,000, not far from the 214,000 who attended the 2008 caucuses when Obama swamped Clinton 66%-32%. Sanders was endorsed by three Democratic members of Congress: Reps. Keith Ellison, Rick Nolan and Collin Peterson, more than he garnered from any other state.

Congressional Districts

115th Congress Lineup	3R 5D	114th Congress Lineup	3R 5D

Minnesota was on the cusp of losing a House seat in the reapportionment following the 2010 census. But under the statutory formula, it qualified for the 435th House seat by a margin of about 9,000 people, narrowly edging out North Carolina, which missed gaining a 14th seat. As a result, Minnesota kept its eight House seats. Democratic Gov. Mark Dayton followed through on his promise to veto any map that lacked broad bipartisan support, and a five-judge special judicial panel took over the process. The judges made only minor changes to the congressional layout. Freshman Republican Chip Cravaack lost handily in the Iron Range 8th District. The Democrats' gain gave them a 5-3 edge in the delegation - not quite the bipartisan outcome that Dayton had supposedly endorsed.

Minnesota is expected to lose its eighth seat in the reapportionment following the 2020 Census. Given growing Republican strength in the outlying 7th and 8th Districts, it's difficult to see how Democrats could retain each of those seats, if one or both had not already switched to the Republicans. The flip side is that Republicans may be strained to retain their suburban 2nd and 3rd District seats, if they had not already lost either before the 2022 election. In any case, once-placid Minnesota seems likely to remain a congressional battleground both before and after the next redistricting. With Republicans in control of the Legislature, the stakes will be high for Democrats to retain the governor's office in 2018, when Dayton is term-limited.

Governor

Mark Dayton (D)

Elected 2010, term expires 2019, 2nd term; b. Jan. 26, 1947, Minneapolis, MN; Yale U., B.A. 1969; Presbyterian; Divorced; 2 children.

Elected Office: MN Auditor, 1990-1994; U.S. Senate, 2001-2007.

Professional Career: Teacher, N.Y. City Public Schools, 1969-1971; Counselor & Administrator, Social Service Agency, Boston, MA, 1971-1975; Legislative Assistant, U.S. Sen. Walter Mondale, 1975-1976; Aide, MN Governor Rudy Perpich, 1977-1978; MN Commission of Economic Development, 1978-1982; MN Commission of Energy & Economic Development, 1983-1986; Founder & President, Vermillion Investment Co., 1987-90, 1995-1997.

Office: 130 State Capitol, 75 Rev. Dr. Martin Luther King Jr. Blvd., St. Paul, 55155; 651-201-3400; Fax: 651-797-1850; Website: mn.gov/governor.

Election Results

Election	Name (Party)	Vote (%)
2014 General	Mark Dayton (D)	989,113 (50%)
	Jeff Johnson (R)	879,257 (45%)
	Hannah Nicollet (I)	56,900 (3%)
2014 Primary	Mark Dayton (D)	177,849 (93%)

Prior winning percentage: 2010 (44%) Senate: 2000 (49%)

As a candidate, Mark Dayton has freely spent from his $1 billion-plus family wealth to win elections. In 2010, he reclaimed the Minnesota governorship for the Democratic-Farmer-Labor Party for the first time since the mid-1980s, and retained it for the DFL in 2014. Dayton has signed some significant pieces of legislation, but at times he has seemed beleaguered as a chief executive, often facing hostile GOP majorities in the legislature.

Dayton grew up in Minnesota, the son of Bruce Dayton, longtime head of the department store chain Dayton Hudson (now Target). He graduated from Yale University in 1969 - he was a Delta Kappa Epsilon fraternity brother of future President George W. Bush - and taught ninth-grade science in a New York school in the Bowery for two years. He then worked as a counselor and administrator for a Boston crisis center for teenage runaways. He was a conscientious objector during the Vietnam era and was active in the anti-war movement; his name found its way, presumably because of his family and that of his then-wife, a Rockefeller, onto President Richard Nixon's enemies list. In 1975 and 1976, he worked for Democratic Sen. Walter Mondale. Dayton then returned to Minnesota to work for DFL Gov. Rudy Perpich. In 1979, after Perpich lost, Dayton spent $400,000 funding a nonprofit agency to spur development in rural Minnesota. Dayton's first run for elected office came in the 1982 DFL primary for

Senate; he spent $7 million of his own money against former Sen. Eugene McCarthy and won 69%-24%. He lost the general election, 53%-47%, to Republican incumbent David Durenberger. In 1990, Dayton was elected state auditor. In 1998, he ran in the DFL primary for governor, spending $2 million of his own money, but finished fourth, far behind the winner, Skip Humphrey, with 18 percent of the vote.

In 2000, Dayton challenged Sen. Rod Grams, the most vulnerable Republican senator up that year. Grams' staunchly conservative voting record was out of line with Minnesota opinion on many issues, and he lacked significant legislative accomplishments. To call attention to the issue of high prescription drug prices, Dayton accompanied busloads of senior citizens to Canada to buy medicine at lower prices than in the United States. Dayton once again spent his own money and, after winning the primary, offered voters a clear contrast to Grams. He favored universal government-run health insurance, called for the federal government to lower prescription drug prices, and advocated doubling the $500 per child tax credit. The $11.6 million he spent doubled the previous Minnesota record he had set 18 years earlier. Grams raised only half as much, and Dayton won, 49%-43%. In the Senate, Dayton successfully spearheaded an amendment giving Congress the right to a separate vote on any trade agreement provision that would weaken U.S. anti-dumping laws -- a priority on the state's Iron Range. In October 2004, after Congress had recessed for the election, Dayton attracted national attention when he announced that he was closing his Washington office because of security threats. No other member took such action, and the Minneapolis *Star Tribune* ran a critical editorial that said, "In staking out this Cassandra position, Dayton has added considerably to unfortunate aspects of his reputation: loner, loose cannon, flake." Dayton responded, "I still believe in my soul I made the necessary and wise decision to protect my staff and constituents who might visit my office." Still, the episode hurt his reelection prospects in 2006, and he announced he would not seek a second term.

Four years after leaving the Senate, Dayton ran for governor, aware that he would have to answer for some personal baggage. He told the *Star Tribune* in December 2009 that he was a recovering alcoholic; he revealed that he had lapsed late in his term as a senator and had entered a treatment program in February 2007, a month after his term expired. In addition, he said that he had been treated for mild depression during most of his adult life, though he said he was able to control it with diet, exercise and medication. In his gubernatorial bid, Dayton promised to reverse the policies of two-term Republican Gov. Tim Pawlenty, who had blocked DFL plans for tax increases and who had tried to advance a socially conservative agenda. Dayton declined to compete in the DFL precinct caucuses or state convention, making it clear that he would run in the primary against the party-endorsed candidate. In the August primary, he faced House speaker and convention endorsee Margaret Anderson Kelliher and former House Minority Leader Matt Entenza, who spent $5 million of his family money on the campaign and cast himself as a centrist. Dayton spent $3 million of his own money and targeted Duluth and the Iron Range, bolstered by his choice of running mate, state Sen. Yvonne Prettner Solon from a blue-collar Duluth-Iron Range district. Dayton edged Kelliher, 41%-40%, with Entenza a distant third. In the general, Dayton faced conservative state Rep. Tom Emmer. Dayton called for higher taxes on upper-income Minnesotans and more spending on education; Emmer called for lower taxes, less regulation and scaling back state government. Dayton outspent Emmer by nearly 2-1 and won by just 8,770 votes, with Independence Party candidate Tom Horner getting 12 percent.

Dayton faced a legislature with unexpectedly solid Republican majorities - 37-30 in the Senate, 72-62 in the House -- that closed ranks against Dayton's tax increases. He vetoed the first budget sent to him in February 2011, and lashed out at Republicans a month later for proposing cuts that he said would close state parks and end meat and restaurant inspections while cutting taxes for the highest earners. He and GOP lawmakers remained deadlocked for months, and by July 1 Minnesota became the only state that year to experience a government shutdown. After two weeks and considerable national publicity, the two sides struck a compromise to raise $1.4 billion in revenue. In the meantime, the NFL's Minnesota Vikings wanted the state's help in building a new stadium. Some lawmakers said the public had no business taking on most of the costs of a new facility for a profitable sports team. Dayton played up the job-creation potential, and after a hard-fought battle, he signed an agreement in May 2012 to build the Vikings a $975 million stadium at the downtown Minneapolis site of the team's existing home, the Metrodome. On another front, Dayton sought $775 million for school and transportation construction projects, but GOP lawmakers balked at the price tag and he eventually signed a bill providing $496 million, saying that it was better than nothing.

With a popular Democratic president on the ballot, Minnesota's political winds in 2012 shifted, and the state Senate and House DFL caucuses reestablished their majorities in both legislative chambers, thanks in part to voter ID and anti-same-sex-marriage constitutional amendments on the ballot, both of which were defeated. With unified Democratic control in St. Paul, Dayton scored some notable victories: To help close a budget shortfall in 2013, Minnesota lawmakers approved his request to raise the state's top income tax rate to 9.85 percent. In 2014, Dayton signed legislation increasing the minimum wage from $6.15 per hour to $9.50 by 2016 and indexing it to inflation; it passed the legislature with only Democratic votes. Taking a cue from the voters' rejection of the 2012 ballot measure, the legislature moved to legalize same-sex marriage. With those accomplishments in hand, as well as falling unemployment rates and a recovering economy, Minnesota's Democrats headed into the 2014 elections confident about their prospects. Dayton faced off against Republican Jeff Johnson, the Hennepin County commissioner, and Independent Hannah Nicollet. Dayton said he would push for increases in education spending in his second term, but he declined to say whether he would raise taxes to help pay for them. Johnson pledged to reform the state's tax code and said he would consider expanding the sales tax. Voter turnout was the lowest since 1986, and Dayton won, 50%-45%, carrying the urban Twin Cities and the Iron Range; Johnson held every suburban and exurban county that rings the Twin Cities, along with much of the rest of the state. The silver lining for Republicans was retaking control of the state House.

Dayton began his second term with a $1 billion state budget surplus, a far cry from the nearly $6 billion budget deficit in 2011 that had prompted the 21-day government shutdown. He announced that he would not seek elective office again and considered himself freed from political constraints. He sought a $10 billion transportation plan funded by a gas tax hike, as well as state-funded, universal, all-day Pre-K programs for 4-year-olds that would apply to some 57,000 children. But the new GOP House majority had different goals, and Dayton didn't help his prospects when he called Senate Majority Leader Tom Bakk, a fellow Democrat, a "back stabber" for freezing pay hikes Dayton had approved for state commissioners. The budget battle turned into a stalemate and nearly caused another shutdown. Ultimately, Dayton failed to secure his transportation plan or universal pre-K, although he did win a significant funding increase for existing education programs. Working around the legislature and farm groups, Dayton issued an executive order in 2016 that limited certain pesticides suspected by scientists of harming the bee population.

The biggest issue of 2016 proved to be health care, particularly involving the quarter-million Minnesotans who buy individual insurance under the state's portion of the Affordable Care Act; many faced premium increases of 50 percent or more for 2017, and Blue Cross and Blue Shield of Minnesota, the state's biggest insurer, eliminated one of its popular offerings from the state exchange. Minnesota's commerce department issued a report that noted the "dramatic rate increases" and calling them "unsustainable and unfair." Dayton added his voice just weeks before the 2016 presidential election when he said the ACA was "no longer affordable to increasing numbers of people." National Republicans seized on Dayton's remarks, and the governor quickly expressed "regret" that his words were being politicized, though he didn't back off on the substance of the remark. With voters feeling uneasy over health care – and with an underperforming presidential campaign in the state by Hillary Clinton – the Democrats lost control of the state Senate as the GOP gained six seats and expanded its lead in the House to 19 seats.

The new session began on a positive note, as the two sides worked together to enact a $21 million tax cut estimated to affect about 200,000 residents – a down payment on the governor's proposal for $300 million in tax cuts. While giving the 2017 state of the state address, Dayton suffered a sudden, stunning collapse, hitting his head on the lectern before being caught by aides and ending his speech early. He later disclosed that he was being treated for prostate cancer. The parties continued working together, passing health insurance premium relief by wide margins just days before the open-enrollment period closed. The measure would spend $310 million in taxpayer money to cut premiums for qualifying enrollees by about 25 percent. During the rest of the session, Dayton pledged to seek higher funding for K-12 and higher education, children's programs, a rural broadband expansion and transportation projects. His agenda was destined to clash with those of the GOP majorities, and indeed, tensions flared in June 2017 when Dayton vetoed the legislative branch's funding and the legislature responded by filing a lawsuit seeking to overturn his veto. Meanwhile, attention was also turning to the open-seat gubernatorial race in 2018. Declared and potential Democratic candidates included Representative Tim Walz, St. Paul Mayor Chris Coleman, state Auditor Rebecca Otto, Lt. Gov. Tina Smith and former state House Majority Leader state Rep. Erin Murphy. The Republican field was more in flux, but given the partisan currents in the state, the general election was expected to be competitive.

Senior Senator

Amy Klobuchar (D)

Elected 2006, term expires 2018, 2nd term; b. May 25, 1960, Plymouth; University of Chicago (IL), J.D.; Yale University (CT), B.A.; Congregationalist; Married (John Bessler); 1 child.

Elected Office: Hennepin County Attorney, 1998-2006.

Professional Career: Practicing attorney, 1985-1998.

DC Office: 302 HSOB 20510, 202-224-3244, Fax: 202-228-2186, klobuchar.senate.gov.

State Offices: Minneapolis, 612-727-5220; Moorhead, 218-287-2219; Rochester, 507-288-5321; Virginia, 218-741-9690.

Committees: Senate Democratic Steering Committee Chairman. *Agriculture, Nutrition & Forestry*: Conservation, Forestry & Natural Resources, Livestock, Marketing & Agriculture Security, Rural Development & Energy. *Commerce, Science & Transportation*: Aviation Operations, Safety & Security, Communications, Technology, Innovation & the Internet, Consumer Protection, Product Safety, Ins & Data Security, Surface Trans., Merchant Marine Infra., Safety & Security. *Judiciary*: Antitrust, Competition Policy & Consumer Rights (RMM), Border Security & Immigration, Crime & Terrorism, Oversight, Agency Action, Federal Rights & Federal Courts. *Rules & Administration (RMM)*.

Group Ratings

	ADA	ACLU	AFL-CIO	LCV	ITI	COC	HAFA	ACU	CFG	FRC
2016	-	82%	-	100%	80%	63%	5%	4%	5%	0%
2015	90%	C	100%	100%	C	43%	C	0%	0%	0%

Almanac Ratings 2015

	Economy	Social	Foreign	Composite
Liberal	94%	100%	80%	91%
Conservative	6%	0%	20%	9%

Key Votes of the 114th Congress

1. Keystone pipeline	N	5. National Security Data	Y	9. Gun Sales Checks	Y
2. Export-Import Bank	N	6. Iran Nuclear Deal	N	10. Sanctuary Cities	N
3. Debt Ceiling Increase	Y	7. Puerto Rico Debt	Y	11. Planned Parenthood	N
4. Homeland Security $$	Y	8. Loretta Lynch A.G	Y	12. Trade deals	N

Election Results

Election	Name (Party)	Vote (%)		Cand. Spent	Ind. Exp. Support	Ind. Exp. Oppose
2012 General	Amy Klobuchar (D)	1,854,595	(65%)	$8,532,377	$31,565	
	Kurt Bills (R)	867,974	(31%)	$955,342	$24,162	
	Stephen Williams (I)	73,539	(3%)			
2012 Primary	Amy Klobuchar (D)	183,766	(91%)			

Prior winning percentages: 2006 (58%)

Although she has not attracted the national media attention of some of her female colleagues-notably Massachusetts' Elizabeth Warren and New York's Kirsten Gillibrand-Democrat Amy Klobuchar, Minnesota's senior senator, is widely seen as aiming for bigger things. First elected in 2006, Klobuchar-who turned 57 in 2017-has been variously mentioned as a potential Cabinet appointee or Supreme Court nominee, to say nothing of a future presidential candidate. Since the beginning of 2015, she has been a member of the Senate Democratic leadership as chair of the Steering and Outreach Committee, tasked with keeping in touch with key party constituencies and developing a policy agenda. And, if Klobuchar is sometimes dinged by critics for not taking on the difficult, controversial issues associated with her Minnesota Senate forebearers-ranging from Hubert Humphrey to Eugene McCarthy to Paul Wellstone-the one-time prosecuting attorney can claim a solid record of legislative accomplishment, keyed to consumer protection as well criminal justice matters.

"I tend not to be a spear-thrower," Klobuchar told the Minneapolis *Star Tribune* in 2013. "To some people, that means I'm being overly careful. I am careful with how I say things…I don't complain about the state of things. I don't do it in my speeches, and I don't do it one-on-one. I try to look for solutions." Unlike the other Democratic women senators mentioned as presidential contenders, Klobuchar represents a state that has become a political battleground in recent years. While she has been a fairly reliable Democratic vote in the Senate, she has exhibited centrist tendencies; the 2015 *Almanac* vote rankings place her as the 27th most liberal senator, nearly in the middle of the Senate Democratic caucus. Klobuchar has regularly sought to reach across the political aisle -- Republican John Hoeven from neighboring North Dakota is a good friend -- to the point that some home-state liberals have been known to take pokes at her as "the last moderate Republican in Minnesota."

Representing a battleground state, Klobuchar also has paid particular attention to constituent service, visiting all 87 Minnesota counties annually. It prompted her junior in-state colleague and former "Saturday Night Live" regular, Democrat Al Franken, to wisecrack to a Minneapolis audience several years ago: "Amy wanted to be with us tonight, but she discovered there was one county in Minnesota where her popularity was below 70 percent. So, she's up there pumping gas and cleaning windshields." Although Klobuchar may lack Franken's professional comedic experience, she had developed a reputation as a resident wit before he joined her on Capitol Hill in 2009. She was a hit as a speaker at a national press dinner in 2009, producing howls of laughter when she quipped: "I raised $17,000 from ex-boyfriends - true story! … I know that is the record in the Senate, but in the House, it's held by Barney Frank" -- the Massachusetts Democrats who at the time was among the House's handful of openly gay members.

Klobuchar was born in the Minneapolis suburb of Plymouth, the daughter of longtime *Star Tribune* columnist Jim Klobuchar. On her father's side, Klobuchar is the descendant of Slovenian immigrants who settled in northern Minnesota's Iron Range; her grandfather worked in the iron mines along with many others of Eastern European ancestry. Today, Klobuchar serves *potica*, a traditional Slovenian holiday nut roll, at the weekly Thursday meetings she holds for visiting Minnesota constituents when the Senate is in session. Growing up, Klobuchar helped her father recover from alcoholism, a battle that both of them later documented in memoirs. She graduated from Yale, where she wrote a paper on the machinations behind the building of Minneapolis' Hubert H. Humphrey Metrodome. She earned a law degree from the University of Chicago, and returned home to work as a lawyer and a lobbyist. In 1998, Klobuchar ran successfully for Hennepin County prosecuting attorney, serving two terms. She spearheaded a crackdown on gun crimes and was credited with securing nearly 300 homicide convictions.

Hennepin County is the center of a media market that includes much of the state's population, providing Klobuchar an excellent springboard when Democrat Mark Dayton (now the state's governor) announced he would not seek reelection to the Senate in 2006. Republican Rep. Mark Kennedy, victorious in three consecutive highly competitive House races, made it clear he was running for Senate. While the GOP establishment quickly united behind him, it took the Democratic-Farmer-Labor Party field time to shake out. Klobuchar declared her candidacy in April, as several prominent DFLers subsequently announced they would not run. Minneapolis Heart Institute Foundation President Ford Bell did run, but dropped out after Klobuchar received the DFL endorsement at the state convention in June. In the general election, Kennedy sought to distance himself from the Iraq war and President George W. Bush, but it did little good in what turned out to be a strong Democratic year. Klobuchar slammed Kennedy as a "rubber stamp" for Bush while advocating middle-class tax relief and a minimum wage increase. She touted her record as a prosecutor, even as Kennedy sought to highlight the increasing rate of violent crime in Minneapolis. Klobuchar consistently led in polls and easily won, 58%-38%, to become the first woman ever to represent Minnesota in the Senate.

Klobuchar serves on the Commerce Committee, where a primary focus of her work has been on consumer protection. She got a number of provisions to toughen airline safety into the Federal Aviation Administration reauthorization that became law in February 2012. She also has pushed for several measures aimed at giving cell phone users more clout in dealing with telecommunications companies. Shortly after her initial election, in 2007, when a six-year-old sustained serious injuries from a swimming pool drain in a Minneapolis suburb, Klobuchar and Minnesota Republican Rep. Jim Ramstad sponsored a bill, ultimately signed into law, banning swimming pool covers that fail to meet entrapment safety standards and requiring automatic drain shutoffs. The next year, after news stories described the discovery of lead in children's toys made in China, Klobuchar sponsored provisions in a child safety bill -- which became law -- that banned lead in children's products and required that toys contain batch numbers to make recalls easier.

As part of a continuing effort to promote tourism, Klobuchar in 2012 teamed with Republican Sen. Roy Blunt of Missouri to win passage of a measure eliminating redundant baggage screening for travelers arriving from airports that participate in the United States' preclearance program. (Klobuchar and Blunt share more than legislation in common: They were tied for first place as the Senate's best cooks in the 2014 version of the annual survey of congressional staffers conducted by *Washingtonian* magazine.) That legislation is among several bipartisan bills and initiatives in which Klobuchar has been involved during the course of her Senate tenure. After gasoline prices spiked in the summer of 2008, she joined a bipartisan group pushing coastal states to allow offshore drilling-although she coupled that with support for a windfall profits tax on oil companies. When the Dodd-Frank financial industry regulation overhaul passed in 2010, Klobuchar and Texas Republican Kay Bailey Hutchison won a provision to maintain regional Federal Reserve banks' supervision of community banks.

More recently, Klobuchar was part of the bipartisan group organized by Maine moderate Republican Susan Collins-seven Republicans, six Democrats and an independent-that helped pave the way for an end to the stalemate that caused a 16-day government shutdown in late 2013. Speaking to a political event in early 2015, Klobuchar noted that half of that 2013 bipartisan group were women, notwithstanding that women comprised only 20 percent of the overall Senate. "Women have gotten things done," she declared.

Klobuchar's fans among Republicans include *New York Times* columnist David Brooks, who wrote in 2012: "She represents the modern senator to me. Not some big-hair blowhard, but a happy regular person with an independent streak." But other Republicans have suggested she has concentrated on popular, easy-to-support legislative matters while avoiding the tougher ones; former Minnesota GOP Gov. Arne Carlson once called her "the great avoider." Responding to such criticism in 2012, Klobuchar told the *Star Tribune:* "I've worked on things that have actually passed and gotten done, that have helped people," while noting that present-day partisan divisions that have intensified the difficulty of moving legislation on many controversial issues.

Klobuchar's centrist tendencies have prompted griping from the left as well. Gay activists complained that she should have been quicker to support ending the military's "don't ask, don't tell" ban on openly gay service members, and environmentalists were angered at her efforts to remove Minnesota wolves from the federal endangered species list and her support for a new bridge over the St. Croix River. Outside of Minnesota, Klobuchar ran afoul of teen-pop sensation Justin Bieber in 2011 when she introduced a bill making it a felony to profit from streaming unlicensed content online. "She needs to be locked up, put away in cuffs," asserted Bieber, who gained fame when his music got exposure on YouTube. Bieber and other critics notwithstanding, polls at home have regularly put Klobuchar's approval rating at 60 percent or above, and she is widely regarded as the state's most popular politician. Seeking a second term in 2012, she crushed her Republican opponent, state Rep. Kurt Bills, 65%-31%, after several better-known Republicans passed on challenging her.

In late 2014, two years into her second term, Klobuchar -- who also serves on the Judiciary Committee -- was floated as a possible successor to Eric Holder as the Obama Administration's attorney general. Klobuchar quickly moved to shoot down the speculation, declaring in a statement: "I intend to continue my work for the people of Minnesota as their senator. We have a lot of work ahead in Congress in the next year and I want to be there to do it." Part of that work was a bill that Klobuchar co-authored to combat human trafficking -- which ended up becoming politically entangled with President Barack Obama's nomination of Loretta Lynch to succeed Holder in the spring of 2015.

The bipartisan, seemingly noncontroversial trafficking bill sailed through the Judiciary Committee; it was only when the measure was poised to be taken up on the Senate floor that several Democrats noticed a provision expanding the scope of the so-called Hyde Amendment, which bars federal dollars from being spent on abortions. Until a deal was ultimately reached in late April, the abortion language prompted the Democrats to repeatedly block the bill from advancing-with Senate Majority Leader Mitch McConnell, under heat from GOP conservatives over the Lynch nomination, refusing to move on Lynch until the human trafficking bill passed. It ended up creating a six-week long controversy that stalled the confirmation of Lynch and caused strains among Senate Democrats. During one closed-door Senate luncheon, there was reportedly a suggestion that Klobuchar was being unfairly blamed by male senators for the error involving the abortion language. Klobuchar, meanwhile, raised eyebrows among some colleagues by seeking to shift blame to a staff aide for failing to alert her to the anti-abortion provision. Asked later about the personal toll of the episode, Klobuchar told *Politico:* "Not the most pleasant."

At the outset of the administration of President Donald Trump, Klobuchar was part of her party's solid opposition to the confirmation of her colleague, Alabama Republican Sen. Jeff Sessions, as the next attorney general. She in particular pointed to Sessions' position on the Violence Against Women Act, first passed in 1994 and reauthorized three times since then. "The 2013 reauthorization of the Violence Against Women Act was supported by the vast majority of senators as well as every Democratic and Republican woman senator ... Sen. Sessions voted against it," Klobuchar noted. She was also part of the solid bloc of Democrats to support a filibuster of the Supreme Court nomination of Neil Gorsuch. However, Klobuchar sided with a number of Rust Belt Democrats in the confirmation of another Trump nominee, Commerce Secretary Wilbur Ross -- due in part to home state concerns. At a Commerce Committee hearing, Klobuchar praised Ross for his stand against the "dumping" of Chinese steel in the United States -- a practice widely blamed for a sharp decline in production of domestic steel, and consequent layoffs and plant shutdowns in Minnesota's Iron Range.

The road to the White House has run through the state house far more than through the Senate over the past half-century, and -- looking ahead to 2018 -- many in Minnesota's DFL urged Klobuchar to run for governor to succeed the retiring Dayton. But Klobuchar, in an interview with the *Star Tribune* at the end of 2016, turned aside the gubernatorial entreaties and said she would instead seek a third term in the Senate. "I really looked at the moment in history and I feel like my job is there," said Klobuchar. "The fact that I've been able to get through the gridlock many, many times means that you can't just walk away when it's an ugly time. It means you have a duty and obligation to keep doing your job. It may sound Pollyanna but it's what I decided." Klobuchar starts out as a prohibitive favorite for re-election in a state that remained blue in the 2016 presidential election, with the Republicans expected to concentrate their energies on the vacancy in the governor's office.

Beyond that, Klobuchar has utilized the traditional political sidestep when asked about her longer-term future. "We just got through a presidential race, and I love my job and what I do now, and more than ever we need people in the Senate that can work across the aisle," she told a Minnesota television station in late 2016. Klobuchar lined up behind Hillary Clinton's candidacy two years prior to Election Day 2016, was among more than three dozen names floated as a vice-presidential running mate in a leaked email from Clinton's campaign chair, and was given a high-profile speaking spot at that year's Democratic National Convention in Philadelphia to tout Clinton's record of battling human trafficking. But that didn't prevent Klobuchar from doing the kinds of things that future presidential contenders often do.

During the 2013-2014 election cycle, she traveled to a dozen states, delivering keynote speeches and raising campaign funds for fellow Democrats. During that period, she made four trips to Iowa-Minnesota's neighbor to the south, but also where the first delegates to presidential nominating conventions are chosen. "I feel at home here. Maybe people from other states don't feel at home here. I feel at home here," Klobuchar gushed during an Iowa Jefferson-Jackson Day dinner speech in the fall of 2014. Earlier, at an Iowa delegation breakfast at the 2012 Democratic National Convention in North Carolina, she flashed her trademark wit, tweaking former Alaska Gov. Sarah Palin's infamous statement about her state's proximity to Russia. Exclaimed Klobuchar, "I can see Iowa from my porch!" And, literally borrowing a page from other presidential wannabes, Klobuchar in August 2015 released her autobiography, entitled *The Senator Next Door: A Memoir from the Heartland.*

Junior Senator

Al Franken (D)

Elected 2008, term expires 2020, 2nd term; b. May 21, 1951, New York, NY; Harvard University, B.A.; Jewish; Married (Franni Bryson Franken); 2 children; 1 grandchild.

Professional Career: Writer, network comedy show; Radio talk show host.

DC Office: 309 HSOB 20510, 202-224-5641, Fax: 202-224-0044, franken.senate.gov.

State Offices: Duluth, 218-722-2390; Moorhead, 218-284-8721; Rochester, 507-288-2003; St. Paul, 651-221-1016.

Committees: *Energy & Natural Resources*: Energy, Public Lands, Forests & Mining, Water & Power. *Health, Education, Labor & Pensions*: Children & Families, Employment & Workplace Safety

(RMM). *Indian Affairs*. *Judiciary*: Antitrust, Competition Policy & Consumer Rights, Border Security & Immigration, Constitution, Oversight, Agency Action, Federal Rights & Federal Courts, Privacy, Technology & the Law (RMM).

Group Ratings

	ADA	ACLU	AFL-CIO	LCV	ITI	COC	HAFA	ACU	CFG	FRC
2016	-	94%	-	100%	60%	50%	7%	4%	1400%	0%
2015	100%	C	100%	100%	C	43%	C	0%	0%	0%

Almanac Ratings 2015

	Economy	Social	Foreign	Composite
Liberal	100%	100%	100%	100%
Conservative	0%	0%	0%	0%

Key Votes of the 114th Congress

1. Keystone pipeline	N	5. National Security Data	Y	9. Gun Sales Checks	Y
2. Export-Import Bank	N	6. Iran Nuclear Deal	N	10. Sanctuary Cities	N
3. Debt Ceiling Increase	Y	7. Puerto Rico Debt	Y	11. Planned Parenthood	N
4. Homeland Security $$	Y	8. Loretta Lynch A.G	Y	12. Trade deals	N

Election Results

Election	Name (Party)	Vote (%)		Cand. Spent	Ind. Exp. Support	Ind. Exp. Oppose
2014 General	Al Franken (D)	1,053,205	(53%)	$31,908,222	$867,752	$471,547
	Mike McFadden (R)	850,227	(43%)	$7,026,515	$23,620	$1,215,810
	Steve Carlson (I)	47,530	(2%)			
2014 Primary	Al Franken (D)	182,720	(95%)			
	Sandra Henningsgard (D)	10,627	(6%)			

Prior winning percentages: 2008 (42%)

In 1999, just four years out from his lengthy stint as a regular on NBC's "Saturday Night Live," Al Franken authored a satirical novel entitled "Why Not Me?" -- chronicling a fictitious celebrity campaign that put him in the White House. Fast forward ahead a couple of decades, and, with Franken now Minnesota's real-life junior senator, some voices in the progressive wing of the Democratic Party were starting to ask -- in all seriousness -- "Why Not Al?" in 2020. A "Draft Al Franken" Website appeared shortly after Election Day 2016, and a number of political analysts stopped well short of dismissing the notion out of hand. "Why 'Al Franken for president' isn't as crazy as you might think," read a *Washington Post* headline. "Perhaps the SNL writer-turned-progressive pugilist is the ideal Democratic politician for the Trump era. Like the president-elect, he excels at insult comedy," wrote CBS political analyst Will Rahn shortly before President Donald Trump was sworn in. Franken, added Rahn, "has a comic's natural ability to notice and exploit weaknesses. In the Age of Trump, those will be particularly [advantageous] skills for any Democrat."

When he first arrived on Capitol Hill in 2009, Franken did his best to obscure the very comedic skills that are now serving him so well. He went to lengths not to exhibit a sense of humor in public, and studiously avoided the spotlight -- declining to talk to the national media for much of his first term. Members of the Capitol Hill press corps recounted stories of Franken telling a joke to his Senate colleagues, only to stop in mid-sentence when a reporter got within earshot. Meanwhile, he dived into issues ranging from health care to consumer privacy to the reauthorization of federal farm programs. It was all part of a conscious strategy by Franken to demonstrate he could be serious as well as funny. The gambit worked, much as it did for other new senators in the past-ranging from Bill Bradley to Hillary Clinton-who had initially gained celebrity in another role. "I had to show people that I was taking the job seriously, and I had come here for serious purposes," he told *The Washington Post* in early 2017. But, as he neared the halfway mark of his second term, he said he felt "a little freer to be myself, and so every once in a while, something comes out."

It's been more than "once in a while" as of late. He was nearly five years into his first term before he agreed to appear on a Sunday news show, but is now a regular guest -- as he cracks jokes on national TV as well as on the Senate floor. (Franken's staff, monitoring Senate floor votes via C-SPAN. is said to keep track of where he is by the sound of his rollicking laugh.) "You know, sometimes students ask me 'How do you become a U.S. senator?'" Franken deadpanned on "CBS This Morning" in the spring of 2015. "And I say 'Do comedy for about 35 years and then run for the Senate. It works every time'." His speech to the 2016 Democratic National Convention in Philadelphia was a mixture of satire and stand-up comedy, as he opened with: "I'm Al Franken: Minnesotan, senator, and world-renowned expert on right-wing megalomaniacs: Rush Limbaugh, Bill O'Reilly, and now Donald Trump." The buzz around Franken intensified in early 2017 -- the result of not only his piercing humor, but his demonstrated ability to pose probing questions that put several Trump Cabinet appointees on the spot during confirmation hearings. "Welcome to the new Al Franken. Al Franken is funny and fierce, Al Franken is on a path to be one of the lead Democratic critics of the Trump administration," University of Minnesota political science professor Lawrence Jacobs told a Minneapolis TV station.

Franken's reticence to exhibit this side of himself when he first arrived in the Senate was related to the torturous path he had to travel to get there. He was not sworn into office until six months after the opening of the 111th Congress, when a protracted court battle ended with his being declared the victor by a mere 312 votes out of more than 2.86 million cast. Formally Alan Franken, he was born in New York City, but his family moved when he was four to St. Louis Park, a heavily Jewish suburb of Minneapolis; his father was a printing salesman and his mother a real estate agent. From a young age, Franken reconciled competing political and comedic impulses by combining them. As a seventh grader, he ran for class president as "Honest Al" and hung posters in the hallways picturing himself with a fake beard and a stovepipe hat.

After graduating from Harvard in 1973, Franken took a writing job in New York for "Saturday Night Live" when it was launched in 1975. For most of the next 20 years, he helped to define the program's sense of humor, as it evolved from a fledgling variety show into a pop culture mainstay. Franken also frequently appeared on the program, most memorably as Stuart Smalley, an obnoxious self-help guru. Franken left the show in 1995 and began working as a political commentator while writing four books, including "Rush Limbaugh Is a Big Fat Idiot". In 2004, he joined the new liberal Air America Radio network with a daily, three-hour show that ran in the same time slot as Limbaugh's program. Franken spent the next three years excoriating conservatives of every stripe, from Bush Administration officials to former Fox News personality O'Reilly, whom Franken singled out in his 2003 book *"Lies and the Lying Liars Who Tell Them: A Fair and Balanced Look at the Right"*. Fox sued Franken over use of "fair and balanced" in the title, but a judge denied its request for an injunction, and the network dropped the suit.

Franken began thinking about returning to Minnesota to run for the Senate after Democratic Sen. Paul Wellstone, a hero to many liberals, died in a plane crash in October 2002 while running for a third term against former St. Paul Mayor Norm Coleman. Democrats chose former Vice President Walter Mondale to replace Wellstone on the ballot at the 11th hour, but, despite Mondale's prominence and long political history in the state, Coleman won, 50%-47%. Franken moved his radio talk show in 2006 from New York to Minneapolis, and in February 2007, announced he would seek the Democratic-Farmer-Labor nomination to take on Coleman. For a time, Franken appeared to have a clear shot at the party nod, but damaging revelations on the eve of the DFL convention in June 2008 threatened to derail him. A sexually explicit satirical article he wrote for *Playboy* in 2000 about a virtual sex institute diminished enthusiasm for him among feminist groups. Franken apologized for the article and won the DFL endorsement, but polling showed him looking increasingly weak against Coleman.

Franken slowly won over skeptical Democrats and kept pace with Coleman in fundraising; each ended up spending more than $19 million. The dynamics of the race shifted considerably in July, when former Sen. Dean Barkley-appointed to fill the few months remaining in Wellstone's term in 2002-entered the race as the Independence Party candidate. Franken attacked Coleman for reportedly receiving free suits and below-market rent in Washington from political benefactors. But Franken was embarrassed by disclosures that he owed $70,000 in back taxes, and he paid a $25,000 fine to New York State for failing to carry workmen's compensation insurance for his employees. As the returns came in on Election Night, the race was exceedingly tight, with 42 percent each for Coleman and Franken and 15 percent for Barkley.

On Nov. 18, the Minnesota Canvassing Board showed Coleman with a 206-vote lead. A recount began the next day, and the board ultimately concluded Franken was 225 votes ahead. Coleman went to court to contest the results. On March 31, a three-judge court issued an order designating 400 absentee ballots for review; 351 were opened and counted. Finally, on April 13, the judges ruled Franken had received the highest number of votes by a margin of 312. Coleman appealed to the state's highest court, and conceded the contest after it ruled in Franken's favor. Each side ended up spending $6 million on the recount process. Franken was sworn into the Senate on July 7, 2009.

With Franken's arrival, Senate Democrats had the 60 votes they needed to prevent Republicans from using the legislative filibuster, notably with regard to President Barack Obama's signature health insurance overhaul. Franken may have had the greatest legislative impact of his first term on the Affordable Care Act. In September 2009, he introduced a bill requiring that at least 90 percent of health insurance premiums be spent directly on improving the quality of health care. The percentage ultimately was lowered to 85 percent, but the idea was incorporated as a provision of the new law.

In *Almanac* vote ratings, he took over first place in 2015 as one of only three senators (along with Ohio's Sherrod Brown and Vermont's Patrick Leahy) to show a 100 percent liberal voting score. While he supported the Obama administration on most issues-his 2014 Republican opponent accused Franken of voting with Obama more than 97 percent of the time-Franken sometimes did so reluctantly. In January 2010, after a trip to Afghanistan (where he did exhibit his comic side to entertain the troops) Franken told the *St. Paul Pioneer Press* that Obama's plan for a temporary surge in U.S. troops was "probably the best of a series of options that weren't so great." The newly minted senator showed little reluctance to take on top White House aides in private: At a White House meeting in February 2010, he excoriated Obama adviser David Axelrod for failing to set a clear course on health care legislation, and later reportedly got into a profanity-laden exchange with economic adviser Gene Sperling about taxes.

Franken is among the few non-lawyers on the Judiciary Committee, and, as a veteran of television, has taken a particular interest in mergers and acquisitions in that industry. He was an early critic of the plan by Comcast to acquire Time Warner Cable, and some analysts said his outspoken opposition helped lead to the collapse of the deal in early 2015. At the outset of 2017, he led a dozen of his Democratic colleagues in writing to AT&T to question the consumer benefits of its proposed merger with Time Warner. (It represented a rare point of agreement between Franken and Trump, who had expressed opposition to the merger.) Several years earlier, Franken also opposed the AT&T takeover of T-Mobile, breaking with organized labor to do so; that $39 billion takeover collapsed in late 2011. Franken chaired the Judiciary Privacy, Technology and the Law Subcommittee, and remains its ranking member with the Republicans in majority. He has used the panel as a platform to go after Uber, the ride-sharing app, over allegations it was misusing data collected on where customers travel-and in mid-2016, amid the Pokemon Go craze, questioned the makers of that app about the sharing of users' information without their consent.

But perhaps Franken's most visible moment as a Judiciary Committee member came in early 2017, when Trump's nominee for attorney general, Alabama Sen. Jeff Sessions, came before the panel for a confirmation hearing. "If there is any evidence that anyone affiliated with the Trump campaign communicated with the Russian government in the course of this campaign, what will you do?" Franken asked -- in an apparent effort to see if Sessions would recuse himself from any Justice Department investigation into allegations that Russia sought to influence the outcome of the 2016 U.S. election. Replied Sessions, a leading Trump backer during the campaign: "I'm not aware of any of those activities. I have been called a surrogate at a time or two in that campaign and I did not have communications with the Russians, and I'm unable to comment on it." Sessions later did recuse himself from any probe of interaction between Russia and the Trump campaign after *The Washington Post* reported that he met twice with the Russian ambassador to the United States in 2016 -- but had not disclosed those meetings when questioned by Franken.

It was not the only occasion in which Franken caught a Trump nominee in an embarrassing moment. When Trump's pick for education secretary, Betsy DeVos, who came before the Health, Education, Labor and Pension Committee, Franken questioned her about a longstanding debate in the education community: whether proficiency, which relates to how much a student knows about a given subject, or growth, relating to how much a student has improved, should be used to judge test scores. DeVos was clearly confused in responding to the question, prompting Franken to correct her. The episode heightened existing concerns about whether DeVos -- confirmed by the full Senate only after Vice President Mike Pence stepped in to break a tie -- was qualified for the post.

If such moments have tended to reinforce Franken's reputation as a partisan, he also has sought to reach across the aisle on numerous occasions throughout his tenure. His first bill after being elected, to provide 200 service dogs for wounded veterans, was co-sponsored by three Republicans and became law. He worked with Maine GOP moderate Olympia Snowe to let women in the military have access to emergency contraception. And he joined Indiana Republican Richard Lugar on funding for diabetes prevention, Arkansas Republican John Boozman on rural veterans' health care, and Iowa Republican Charles Grassley on improving student loan forms. "He's surprised me," Grassley told *Politico* in May 2014, as Franken was preparing to seek re-election "He's taken very seriously doing the work of a senator…I think he's shown he's a senator and not a comedian."

Grassley, who became chairman of the Judiciary panel in 2015, was less charitable after Franken put Sessions on the spot. At a later hearing, he accused Franken of asking a "gotcha" question, which Franken denied -- while pointedly advising Grassley during a heated exchange to "look at the tape." Franken sought to smooth things over at the end of the hearing, declaring: "I have incredible respect and regard for the chairman and dare I say affection. The chairman has co-sponsored my legislation more than any other Republican."

Franken's celebrity has made him a magnet for campaign donors, prompting Senate Democratic leaders to ask him to chair the Democratic Senatorial Campaign Committee during the 2011-2012 cycle. Franken declined, saying he needed to stay focused on Minnesota issues. Even so, he frequently traveled to stump for Senate candidates that year, including Massachusetts' Elizabeth Warren -- a frequent guest on his old radio talk show. Given his narrow victory margin in 2008, Franken was an early GOP target in 2014, with Republican strategists hoping Obama's unpopularity in the state would have a negative effect on his candidacy. But Coleman declined to seek a rematch, and at least two GOP members of the Minnesota House delegation opted not to run. Absent a top-tier Republican challenger, Franken became the clear favorite. While his opponent, businessman Mike McFadden, sought to tie him closely to Obama, Franken focused as much as possible on Minnesota and as little as possible on the president. Franken spent nearly $32 million, four times as much as McFadden-while sharply attacking McFadden's business record. He charged the Republican was behind business deals resulting in large layoffs and relocation of corporations overseas to avoid taxes. Amid a nationwide GOP wave, Franken won comfortably, 53%-43%.

If stopping short of Shermanesque statements, Franken has sought to dampen speculation that he might opt for a presidential bid in place of a run for a third term in 2020. "No. No," he told *The Washington Post*. "I really like this job. I like representing the people of Minnesota. I feel like I'm really beginning to know this job." Plus, a presidential run could put him on a collision course with his more centrist home-state senior state colleague, Democrat Amy Klobuchar -- herself the subject of 2020 chatter. Franken and Klobuchar are said to enjoy a warm friendship, in contrast to past pairs of ambitious senators from the same party who have shared representation of a state.

While his comfortable re-election victory may have liberated him to return to his comedic roots -- and yield political prominence in the process -- Franken wasn't always able to suppress such instincts during his first term. There was the time in 2010 when Franken, exercising the freshman duty of presiding over the Senate, was seen making dismissive faces and hand gestures as Republican Leader Mitch McConnell delivered a floor speech. "This isn't 'Saturday Night Live,' Al," snapped the dour McConnell, prompting Franken to later write an apology note. As for SNL, Franken, while gone for more than two decades, is hardly forgotten. In a case of art imitating life imitating art, cast member Alex Moffat in early 2017 portrayed Franken in a skit involving the Judiciary Committee. A quarter of a century earlier, the show had featured a skit involving the Judiciary panel, with then-Illinois Sen. Paul Simon being played by -- yup, Franken.

FIRST DISTRICT

Tim Walz (D)

Elected 2006, 6th term; b. Apr 06, 1964, West Point, NE; Saint Mary's University of Minnesota; Chadron State College (NE), B.S., 1989; Minnesota State University, Mankato, M.S., 2001; Lutheran; Married (Gwen Whipple Walz); 2 children.

Military Career: U.S Army National Guard, 1981-2005.

Professional Career: Teacher, Pine Ridge Indian Reservation, SD, 1984; Teacher, People's Republic of China, 1989-1990; Founder, Educational Travel Adventures, 1991-2006; H.S. teacher, 1989-2006.

DC Office: 2313 RHOB 20515, 202-225-2472, Fax: 202-225-3433, walz.house.gov.

State Offices: Mankato, 507-388-2149; Rochester, 507-388-2149.

Committees: *Agriculture*: Conservation & Forestry, General Farm Commodities & Risk Management. *Joint Congressional-Executive Commission on China. Veterans' Affairs (RMM).*

Group Ratings

	ADA	ACLU	AFL-CIO	LCV	ITI	COC	HAFA	ACU	CFG	FRC
2016	-	88%	-	82%	83%	71%	19%	0%	17%	0%
2015	70%	C	92%	77%	C	55%	C	4%	0%	0%

Almanac Ratings 2015

	Economy	Social	Foreign	Composite
Liberal	75%	93%	63%	77%
Conservative	25%	7%	37%	23%

Key Votes of the 114th Congress

1. Keystone Pipeline	Y	5. Puerto Rico Debt	N	9. Offenses by Aliens	N
2. Trade Deals	N	6. Medical Marijuana	Y	10. Troops in Iraq	N
3. Export-Import Bank	Y	7. Sanctuary Cities	N	11. Homeland Security $$	Y
4. Debt Ceiling Increase	Y	8. Armor-piercing Bullets	Y	12. Trade Adjustment aid	Y

Election Results

Election	Name (Party)	Vote (%)	Cand. Spent	Ind. Exp. Support	Ind. Exp. Oppose
2016 General	Tim Walz (D)	169,074 (50%)	$1,546,286		
	Jim Hagedorn (R)	166,526 (50%)	$339,139		
2016 Primary	Tim Walz (D)	(100%)			

Prior winning percentages: 2014 (54%), 2012 (58%), 2010 (49%), 2008 (63%)

Tim Walz, a Democrat first elected in 2006, has survived competitive elections in his rural district, including a narrow escape in 2016. He has had some legislative success in seeking to balance strong support for farmers, military veterans and gun owners with a commitment to his party's main economic planks.

Walz grew up in Nebraska and joined the Army National Guard when he was 17. When he retired from the Guard 24 years later, in 2005, he held the rank of command sergeant major. Walz earned his teaching degree in Nebraska, taught school in China for a year through a Harvard University program, and later established an educational travel company that helped high school students study in China. He and his wife moved to Minnesota in 1996 to take teaching jobs in Mankato. There, he taught high school geography and coached the football team to two state championships.

Walz got into politics relatively late in life - he was 42 when he ran for Congress. In 2004, President George W. Bush made an appearance in the area as part of his reelection campaign. Walz took two students to the event, where Bush campaign staffers demanded to know whether he supported the president and barred the students from entering after discovering one had a sticker for Democratic candidate John Kerry. Walz suggested that it might be bad PR for the Bush campaign to bar an Army veteran, and he and the students were allowed in. Walz said the experience sparked his interest in politics, first as a volunteer for the Kerry campaign and then as a congressional candidate. "I don't know if I'd necessarily call it an epiphany, but it was definitely one of those things that pushed me into" politics, Walz said.

In 2006, Walz challenged six-term Republican Rep. Gil Gutknecht, an affable conservative who was not considered especially vulnerable. The district had sent Republicans to Washington for 102 of the previous 114 years. Walz was not a polished campaigner. But he struck a chord with his message in opposition to declining middle-class wages and tax cuts for high earners, plus Congress's failure to hold Bush accountable on the Iraq war. He supported abortion rights and opposed a ban on same-sex marriage. Walz ran as a political outsider and painted Gutknecht as too closely tied to Bush. His military experience and football coaching gave an aura of authenticity to his campaign that made him harder to attack. Walz won, 53%-47%, and became the highest-ranking enlisted soldier ever to serve in Congress.

Walz has established a mostly centrist voting record. In the *Almanac* vote ratings for 2015, he ranked toward the center of the House in each of the three issue categories. He opposed the creation of the Troubled Asset Relief Program to assist the financial services industry because he said it didn't do enough to protect homeowners from foreclosure. His championing of gun owners' rights has earned him the National Rifle Association's endorsement. He voted for the Keystone XL pipeline, to the dismay of environmental groups. But he backed most of President Barack Obama's chief initiatives, including health care reform and the cap-and-trade bill to reduce carbon emissions. In calling for more domestic renewable energy to replace oil imports from countries hostile to the United States, Walz likes to say, "We export $1 billion a day to countries who hate us. They'll hate us for free."

On the Agriculture Committee, Walz secured increased access to credit and conservation opportunities for farmers in the 2008 farm bill. In the debate over the 2012 farm bill, he urged House Republicans to take up the committee-passed version instead of seeking a better bill. "Perfect is what you get in heaven," he said. "The U.S. House of Representatives is closer to hell." Walz has introduced numerous good-government bills. In 2012, the House passed a version of his bill barring the use of inside information by lawmakers to make financial trades and requiring members to disclose their investments. The measure had languished for five years, but picked up momentum after it was featured in a *60 Minutes* story.

Walz has had a continuing interest in veterans' issues, including suicide prevention and improving the treatment of traumatic brain injuries. In 2012, he and Republican Rep. Jeff Denham of California enacted a bill to make it easier for veterans to find jobs using skills acquired through military training. In 2016, he enacted a bill to provide annual evaluations of mental health care for all veterans and to create suicide prevention programs in the VA. In 2015, Walz sought the top Democratic slot on the Veterans Affairs Committee and had support from several veterans' organizations. But he lost to Corrine Brown of Florida, who benefited from seniority and the support of Democratic leaders. Instead, Pelosi tapped Walz to chair her quarterly roundtables on veterans' issues. In 2017, after Brown had been indicted and then was defeated in the Democratic primary, Walz finally took the senior Democratic post on the committee. He said that he would bring "a soldier's perspective to ... working with veterans, the VA and my colleagues to uphold our nation's promises to those who have served and sacrificed." He and Republican Rep. Phil Roe of Tennessee, an Army vet and the committee's new chairman, had co-chaired the Invisible Wounds Caucus, which focused on veterans' issues.

Walz has faced competitive reelections in his historically Republican district. In 2010, farmer and state Rep. Randy Demmer slammed Walz's support of the Democratic agenda. Walz highlighted a video of his opponent seeming receptive to partially privatizing Social Security, and won 49%-44%. In 2014, pro-business Republican Jim Hagedorn, whose father Tom Hagedorn represented the district in the 1970s, won the primary 54%-46% over convention-endorsed Aaron Miller, a social conservative. Walz outspent Hagedorn in the general, $1.6 million to $239,000. The challenger took six counties in the western part of the district. Walz took Rochester-based Olmsted County 54%-46%, and won the district by the same margin.

His biggest election scare came in 2016 in a rematch. Hagedorn again suffered on fundraising, with Walz having more than a 4-to-1 advantage, and the national parties paid little attention to this contest. Unexpectedly, Hagedorn became a late threat by linking himself closely to the presidential campaign of Donald Trump, whose message of change proved to be popular in rural Minnesota. "Hillary Clinton and Tim Walz are four more years of Obama policies," Hagedorn said. He vowed to take a harder line against "Islamic supremacists" and criticized the influx of immigrants and refugees, including to the 1st District. This time, Walz won, 50.3%-49.6%, a margin of 2,547 votes. His 53%-47% lead in Olmsted proved to be decisive. The turnout in heavily rural counties went disproportionately to Trump and Hagedorn. Hagedorn said that he planned a third bid in 2018.

Walz announced in March that he will run in 2018 for the open governor's seat. Democratic primary opposition from the Twin Cities area could pose a big obstacle for him, unless multiple candidates divide the liberal, urban vote. Whether or not a statewide contest is a convenient escape from his competitive congressional district, this district seems certain to be competitive in 2018.

Southern Minnesota: Rochester

Population		Race and Ethnicity		Income	
Total	667,238	White	87.2%	Median Income	$56,192 (171 out of 435)
Land area	11,974	Black	2.6%		
Pop/ sq mi	55.7	Latino	6.0%		
Born in state	68.7%	Asian	2.5%	Under $50,000	44.5%
Age Groups		Two races	1.4%	$50,000-$99,999	34.6%
Under 18	23.2%	Other	0.3%	$100,000-$199,999	17.3%
18-34	23.2%	**Education**		$200,000 or more	3.5%
35-64	37.8%	H.S grad or less	39.6%	Poverty Rate	11.8%
Over 64	15.8%	Some college	22.1%	**Health Insurance**	
Work		College Degree, 4 yr	17.9%	With health insurance coverage	93.2%
White Collar	35.6%	Post grad	9.0%		
Sales and Service	38.6%	**Military**		**Public Assistance**	
Blue Collar	25.8%	Veteran	8.8%	Cash public assistance income	2.8%
Government	11.1%	Active Duty	0.0%	Food stamp/SNAP benefits	8.3%

Voter Turnout			
2015 Total Citizens 18+	492,067	2016 House Turnout as % CVAP	68%
2016 House turnout	335,877	2014 House Turnout as % CVAP	46%

2012 Presidential Vote		
Barack Obama	170,377	(49%)
Mitt Romney	165,720	(48%)

2016 Presidential Vote		
Donald Trump	181,647	(53%)
Hillary Clinton	130,831	(38%)
Gary Johnson	13,881	(4%)
Evan McMullin	6,915	(2%)

Cook Partisan Voting Index: R+5

The Mississippi River flows majestically southeast from Minneapolis and St. Paul, cutting through rolling hills and, where it widens, forming calm lakes. This far north, the westward tide of Yankee migrants thinned out; most settlers following the railroads on the flood plains west of the river after the Civil War were Germans and Scandinavians, bringing their families to a terrain much like the Rhineland and to the rolling uplands beyond, which resemble the northern European plain.

Along the Mississippi River, tourism spiked upward after the old St. Paul and Milwaukee Railroad was converted to a hiker-biker nature trail in the 1990s. A little to the west is Rochester, home to the renowned Mayo Clinic, founded in 1863 when English-born physician William Mayo set up a practice to examine inductees into the Union Army. Today, 135,000 people annually visit the clinic for cancer treatment and other illnesses. With more than 33,000 people employed at Mayo, Rochester is prosperous and has been the fastest-growing metropolitan area in Minnesota. That growth will continue, with Mayo's $6.5 billion plan for a high-tech medical center that will compete for what has been called the "global medical tourism industry" and is expected to double the local population in 20 years. In 2016, state officials abandoned a plan for a high-speed rail link to Minneapolis-St. Paul. Mayo and community leaders were concerned in early 2017 about the impact for employees and patients of President Donald Trump's executive orders to limit immigration and refugees.

In Mower County, Austin is the headquarters of the Hormel meatpacking firm, which produces "miracle meat" Spam, Hormel chili and Dinty Moore stew. The expanded museum provides free "Spamples" for visitors. Farther west is flat farmland. This was the southern locus of the 1862 Dakota Uprising, which resulted in the simultaneous hangings of 38 Dakota warriors at Mankato. Many of the bodies were dug up at night by doctors - including William Mayo - for use in medical study. To the north is Le Sueur, where Minnesota Valley Canning Co., later renamed Green Giant, was founded; a 55-foot statue of the iconic giant was erected in 1978 in Blue Earth. The farther west you go, the more frequently you find communities with a German heritage, like New Ulm, where the "Hermann the

German" monument guards the town. Many small towns in Southern Minnesota are now filling up with Hispanic farmworkers. The Somali community in Rochester exceeds 4,000 persons. Still, the overall minority population in the area remains small.

The 1st Congressional District of Minnesota includes most of the state's two southern tiers of counties. It stretches over 250 miles, from the South Dakota border to the Wisconsin border. This historically was a political borderland, with Civil War Republicans in the east and Farmer-Laborites more common in the west, but the traditions have been upended. Rochester had long been a Republican stronghold, but like many Northern white-collar areas, it has trended Democratic. With its working-class tradition, Austin has remained solidly Democratic-Farmer-Labor. To the west, the population-losing farm counties between Mankato and the South Dakota border now vote solidly Republican. In 2015, the 1st ranked ninth in the nation in farm production. This is one of three Democratic-held, mostly rural districts in Minnesota that has had double-digit percentage drops in the Democratic presidential vote: In the 1st, it went from 49 percent for Barack Obama in 2012 to 38 percent for Hillary Clinton in 2016.

SECOND DISTRICT

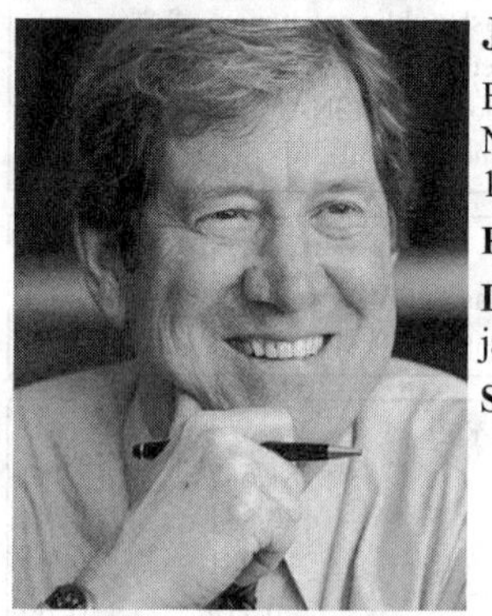

Jason Lewis (R)

Elected 2016, 1st term; b. Sep 23, 1955, Waterloo, IA; University of Northern Iowa, B.A., 1979; University of Colorado at Denver, M.A., 1992; Catholic; Married (Leigh Lewis); 2 children.

Professional Career: Radio/ television host.

DC Office: 418 CHOB 20515, 202-225-2271, Fax: 202-225-2595, jasonlewis.house.gov.

State Offices: Burnsville, 651-846-2120.

Committees: *Budget*. *Education & the Workforce*: Health, Employment, Labor & Pensions, Higher Education & Workforce Development. *Transportation & Infrastructure*: Aviation, Coast Guard & Maritime Transportation, Railroads, Pipelines & Hazardous Materials.

Group Ratings

	ADA	ACLU	AFL-CIO	LCV	ITI	COC	HAFA	ACU	CFG	FRC
2016	-	5%	-	97%	50%	100%	86%	0%	4%	-
2015	-	C	-	-	C	40%	C	0%	C	-

Key Votes of the 114th Congress

1. Keystone Pipeline	N	5. Puerto Rico Debt	N	9. Offenses by Aliens	N
2. Trade Deals	N	6. Medical Marijuana	N	10. Troops in Iraq	N
3. Export-Import Bank	N	7. Sanctuary Cities	N	11. Homeland Security $$	N
4. Debt Ceiling Increase	N	8. Armor-piercing Bullets	N	12. Trade Adjustment aid	N

Election Results

Election	Name (Party)	Vote	(%)	Cand. Spent	Ind. Exp. Support	Ind. Exp. Oppose
2016 General	Jason Lewis (R)	173,970	(47%)	$1,007,328	$299,669	$4,293,753
	Angie Craig (D)	167,315	(45%)	$3,962,556	$56,416	$2,287,504
	Paula Overby (I)	28,869	(8%)	$2,818		
2016 Primary	Jason Lewis (R)	11,642	(49%)			
	Darlene Miller (R)	7,310	(31%)			
	John Howe (R)	3,253	(14%)			
	Matthew Erickson (R)	1,617	(7%)			

Jason Lewis, elected in 2016, unexpectedly held this open seat for Republicans. This was one of the most discouraging setbacks that year for House Democrats, who amply touted and financed their candidate, Angie Craig. Their attempts to link Lewis to Donald Trump turned out to be not such a wise strategy when Trump narrowly won the district.

Lewis is a native of Waterloo Iowa, and graduated from the University of Northern Iowa. He began his career with a family business, Lewis Motor Supply Inc. It was sold in the mid-1980s after "the government put an eminent domain project through the warehouse," he said. While working on his master's degree in political science at the University of Colorado, Lewis ran for Congress in 1990 against Democratic Rep. David Skaggs in the Boulder-area district. He lost 61%-39%. Lewis subsequently returned to his mother's home state of Minnesota and built a devoted audience for more than two decades as a nationally syndicated conservative radio talk show host, based in the Twin Cities area. He also was co-host of a public affairs program on Minnesota Public Television. In 2010, he wrote a book, *Power Divided is Power Checked*, on the importance of states' rights. Over the years, he made countless controversial comments, which made him a rich target for opposition researchers. As examples, the Associated Press in August 2016 wrote that Lewis "called young women 'non-thinking' for their passion for contraceptive and abortion access, and seemed to question in a book of his whether it was the government's role to ban slavery."

After Republican Rep. John Kline, chairman of the Education and the Workforce Committee, announced his retirement, he threw his support in the primary to Darlene Miller, a local businesswoman. She raised nearly $400,000 but ran a disappointing campaign and lost to Lewis, 49%-31%. Craig, a first-time candidate who won the Democratic nomination without opposition, was president of the St. Jude Medical Foundation; she was a lesbian with a wife and four children. When a spokeswoman for the Democratic Congressional Campaign Committee said that Lewis was "going to be forced to defend every sexist, racist, misogynistic and outrageous comment he's ever made," Lewis responded dismissively to AP, "There's already chronic fatigue on that stuff." Some Republican campaign aides initially were skeptical of his prospects in the general election.

Lewis happily modeled himself after Trump. In a story about the campaign, headlined "Meet Minnesota's Mini-Trump," *The Atlantic* described Lewis as "a hard-right radio provocateur turned internet activist famous for racist, misogynistic, and generally from-the-fringe rants that make Donald Trump sound like Mitt Romney." Craig was a superior fundraiser, with $4 million (including nearly $1 million of self-financing) to $1 million for Lewis. Democrats and their allies spent a bit more than $3 million on her behalf, while Republicans spent nearly $3 million for Lewis. Defying expectations, Lewis won, 47%-45.2%. Craig led in the population center of Dakota County by about 6,000 votes. But Craig won the far less populous Scott County by almost 12,000 votes.

In anticipation of a likely tough Democratic reelection challenge, Republican leaders gave Lewis prime committee assignments: Budget, Education and the Workforce, and Transportation and Infrastructure.

Twin Cities' South Suburbs

Population		**Race and Ethnicity**		**Income**	
Total	681,358	White	82.9%	Median Income	$75,564 (50 out of 435)
Land area	2,438	Black	3.9%		
Pop/ sq mi	279.5	Latino	5.6%	Under $50,000	31.1%
Born in state	67.6%	Asian	4.5%	$50,000-$99,999	34.1%
		Two races	2.5%	$100,000-$199,999	28.1%
Age Groups		Other	0.5%	$200,000 or more	6.7%
Under 18	25.7%			Poverty Rate	7.4%
18-34	21.3%	**Education**			
35-64	41.3%	H.S grad or less	29.30%	**Health Insurance**	
Over 64	11.7%	Some college	21.70%	With health insurance coverage	94.0%
		College Degree, 4 yr	26.20%		
Work		Post grad	11.30%		
White Collar	41.1%			**Public Assistance**	
Sales and Service	39.8%	**Military**		Cash public assistance income	2.7%
Blue Collar	19.1%	Veteran	8.3%		
Government	11.3%	Active Duty	0.1%	Food stamp/SNAP benefits	5.8%

Voter Turnout			
2015 Total Citizens 18+	484,065	2016 House Turnout as % CVAP	77%
2016 House turnout	370,514	2014 House Turnout as % CVAP	51%

2012 Presidential Vote		
Mitt Romney	184,576	(49%)
Barack Obama	184,802	(49%)

2016 Presidential Vote		
Donald Trump	176,088	(46%)
Hillary Clinton	171,396	(45%)
Gary Johnson	16,565	(4%)

Cook Partisan Voting Index: R+2

Drive south from the Twin Cities and one encounters big-box stores, catering to the youngish families that live nearby in new housing developments and who work in managerial, business and technical careers. Many come from elsewhere, attracted by Minnesota's strong economy and pleasant living (provided they can tolerate its cold winters). They have turned places such as Eagan, Lakeville, Apple Valley, Mendota Heights and Burnsville in Dakota County into fast-growing suburbs. The upscale suburbs of Scott County grew by an impressive 58 percent since 2000. Dakota, which with 415,000 remains about triple the size of Scott, has grown by 17 percent during that time. In recent years, these suburban areas have begun to see an influx of lower-income residents, attracted by the good schools and low crime rates. *Money* magazine listed Northfield among the nation's best places to retire. In his book *Shot All to Hell*, Mark Gardner wrote about Northfield's previous claim to fame, when it was the site in 1876 of the final bank robbery attempt of Jesse James and his gang.

This area has been attractive to the corporate world. After Lockheed Martin closed its Eagan plant in 2013, several prominent businesses filled the space, including the headquarters of the Minnesota Vikings in the NFL. Tech support company Stream Global Services relocated its office from Boston in 2012, and was purchased in 2014 by Cincinnati-based Convergys, a corporate rival. Drive farther south on Interstate 35 and U.S. 52 - a little farther every year - and suddenly you are in farm country. This area is the home of Carleton College and its late professor-turned-liberal-senator, Paul Wellstone.

These suburbs and hamlets make up the 2nd Congressional District of Minnesota. Like several districts in the state, this has become a battleground. Dakota County, just south of St. Paul, casts about 60 percent of the votes in the district; historically, Dakota was marginally Democratic, although today it is more of a swing county. Neighboring Scott County has the highest median income in the state, and is rapidly growing and heavily Republican, though it casts about one-third as many votes as Dakota. Donald Trump won this district by one percentage point-more than 4,000 votes. In 2012, President Barack Obama took the district by 226 votes.

THIRD DISTRICT

Erik Paulsen (R)

Elected 2008, 5th term; b. May 14, 1965, Bakersfield, CA; Saint Olaf College (MN), B.A.; Lutheran; Married (Kelly Paulsen); 4 children.

Elected Office: MN House, 1995-2008, Majority Leader, 2002-2006.

Professional Career: Marketing analyst, Target Corporation.

DC Office: 127 CHOB 20515, 202-225-2871, Fax: 202-225-6351, paulsen.house.gov.

State Offices: Eden Prairie, 952-405-8510.

Committees: *Joint Economic*. *Ways & Means*: Health, Trade.

Group Ratings

	ADA	ACLU	AFL-CIO	LCV	ITI	COC	HAFA	ACU	CFG	FRC
2016	-	5%	-	18%	100%	100%	52%	76%	72%	83%
2015	0%	C	17%	9%	C	95%	C	83%	64%	92%

Almanac Ratings 2015

	Economy	Social	Foreign	Composite
Liberal	6%	9%	10%	9%
Conservative	94%	91%	90%	91%

Key Votes of the 114th Congress

1. Keystone Pipeline	Y	5. Puerto Rico Debt	Y	9. Offenses by Aliens	Y
2. Trade Deals	Y	6. Medical Marijuana	N	10. Troops in Iraq	N
3. Export-Import Bank	N	7. Sanctuary Cities	Y	11. Homeland Security $$	Y
4. Debt Ceiling Increase	N	8. Armor-piercing Bullets	Y	12. Trade Adjustment aid	Y

Election Results

Election	Name (Party)	Vote (%)		Cand. Spent	Ind. Exp. Support	Ind. Exp. Oppose
2016 General	Erik Paulsen (R)	223,077	(57%)	$5,711,991	$445,265	$3,961,019
	Terri Bonoff (D)	169,243	(43%)	$1,969,678	$938,474	$1,521,630
2016 Primary	Erik Paulsen (R)		(100%)			

Prior winning percentages: 2014 (62%), 2012 (58%), 2010 (59%), 2008 (49%)

Erik Paulsen, first elected in 2008, is a serious-minded Republican on the Ways and Means Committee who focuses on tax and trade issues that boost Minnesota businesses. In 2016, Democrats talked up their first serious reelection challenge to Paulsen in his suburban district. Instead, he distanced himself from Donald Trump and won easily, while three House Democrats in rural districts in Minnesota survived much tougher contests.

Raised in the Twin Cities suburbs, Paulsen attended nearby St. Olaf College, where he met his wife, Kelly, in a math class. After graduation, Paulsen worked for a summer in Yellowstone National Park, then returned to begin a career in marketing. He later took a job in Rep. Jim Ramstad's Washington office, where he worked for a year and a half before returning to Minnesota to manage the district office. He was elected to the Minnesota House of Representatives, rising to majority leader, and was a leading supporter of Republican Gov. Tim Pawlenty's no-new-taxes policy. While in the legislature, Paulsen worked as a business analyst for the Minneapolis-based Target Corp.

When Ramstad retired, Paulsen faced no Republican competition and got an early fundraising lead. Democratic newcomer Ashwin Madia, an Iraq war veteran, was his opponent in the general election. Madia had upset better-known state Sen. Terri Bonoff to secure the Democratic-Farmer-Labor nomination, and he pulled even with Paulsen in the polls. Paulsen called himself "one of a new generation of Republican reformers." On the stump, he emphasized his differences with Madia on taxes, contrasting his support for making the Bush-era tax cuts permanent with Madia's position allowing them to expire for people with annual incomes over $250,000.

The campaign turned highly negative. Democrats ran ads that attempted to link Paulsen to a Republican fundraiser at a Las Vegas strip club. Paulsen parried with ads accusing Madia of lying about his voting record. Republicans ran an ad in the final days of the campaign that the Madia camp said deliberately depicted Madia's skin tone as darker than it is. Madia is of Indian descent. The two candidates each spent about $2.7 million. A third candidate, businessman David Dillon, ran as an independent. In this competitive district, Paulsen withstood the national Democratic wave with 48 percent to Madia's 41 percent. Dillon picked up 11 percent, drawing support in areas where Madia should have been strong.

Paulsen usually has been a reliable Republican vote, which helped him to snag a prized seat on Ways and Means. He filed a bill to repeal the medical device tax that was included in the 2010 health care overhaul, calling it "a tax on innovation" that hurt several Minnesota companies. The measure passed the House in 2012 and went nowhere in the Senate under Democratic control, but Paulsen remained persistent. A devout free-trade enthusiast, he co-chaired a GOP working group on South Korea to seek bipartisan votes on trade deals. "Our constituents expect us to be results-oriented," he told the *Minneapolis Star-Tribune*. He co-chaired the House Medical Technology Caucus, where he advocated on behalf of the industry's jobs. In 2016, two of his tax bills were enacted: permitting the disclosure of certain tax return information for the investigation of missing or exploited children, and excluding compensation for surviving dependents of a public safety officer who died from an injury sustained in the line of duty.

When he served on the Financial Services Committee, Paulson tried without success in 2009 to strip the Treasury Department of the power to extend the Wall Street bailout program for another year. He showed independence by joining with Democrats on expansion of the Children's Health Insurance Program, a credit card overhaul bill and a measure giving the Food and Drug Administration authority to regulate tobacco products. He showed his moderate credentials when he backed a measure adding sexual orientation and gender identity to federal hate crimes statutes. In 2015, his *Almanac* vote ratings became relatively conservative and in the center of House Republicans.

During House debate in 2017 to replace the Affordable Care Act, Paulsen won approval of his plan to repeal the medical device tax. A proposal to enact a border tax, strongly opposed by Target and other retailers, placed Paulsen in a difficult position and led him to seek middle ground.

Following his first election, Paulsen was not seriously challenged for reelection. In 2016, Bonoff, who continued to style herself as a moderate in the Legislature, finally got the opportunity to face him directly and criticized his conservative record as out of step with the district. She raised $2 million and had $3.3 million in support from Democrats. Paulsen rose to the occasion by raising $5 million and had $1.3 million in party support. Democratic advertising emphasized, "We need to step up and stand up to Donald Trump." In early October, following the release of the 2005 video in which Trump made lewd comments about women, Paulsen called the remarks "disgusting and offensive" and said, "I will not be voting for him." But 2016 was a tough year for Democrats in Minnesota. Paulsen defeated Bonoff, 57%-43%. He drew 55.7 percent in Hennepin, with a higher vote in the outlying areas.

Twin Cities: West Suburbs

Population		**Race and Ethnicity**		**Income**	
Total	688,465	White	79.4%	Median Income	$79,517 (38 out of 435)
Land area	527	Black	6.8%		
Pop/ sq mi	1306.3	Latino	4.2%	Under $50,000	30.2%
Born in state	62.5%	Asian	6.7%	$50,000-$99,999	31.1%
		Two races	2.3%	$100,000-$199,999	27.6%
Age Groups		Other	0.5%	$200,000 or more	11.2%
Under 18	24.0%			Poverty Rate	6.5%
18-34	20.1%	**Education**			
35-64	42.5%	H.S grad or less	23.00%	**Health Insurance**	
Over 64	13.4%	Some college	20.70%	With health insurance coverage	94.3%
Work		College Degree, 4 yr	31.30%		
White Collar	46.8%	Post grad	15.70%	**Public Assistance**	
Sales and Service	38.8%	**Military**		Cash public assistance income	2.7%
Blue Collar	14.3%	Veteran	7.3%		
Government	8.6%	Active Duty	0.1%	Food stamp/SNAP benefits	5.7%

Voter Turnout			
2015 Total Citizens 18+	492,132	2016 House Turnout as % CVAP	80%
2016 House turnout	393,464	2014 House Turnout as % CVAP	55%

2012 Presidential Vote		
Barack Obama	199,093	(50%)
Mitt Romney	195,802	(49%)

2016 Presidential Vote		
Hillary Clinton	201,833	(50%)
Donald Trump	164,259	(41%)
Gary Johnson	16,012	(4%)
Evan McMullin	8,348	(2%)

Cook Partisan Voting Index: D+1

Over the past half century, Minnesota's two-headed metropolis has spread out from the neat streets inside the city limits of Minneapolis and St. Paul into the countryside all around. People have sorted themselves out geographically. In the lower lands along the Mississippi and Minnesota rivers, where rail lines fan out from the Twin Cities, are the blue-collar suburbs, with modest houses and warehouses and factories near the tracks. Inland, around the lakes Minnesota is so proud of, in subdivisions with curved streets hugging the hills, are more affluent neighborhoods, quiet and unflashy in the Minnesota way but comfortable whether blanketed with snow or with a nearby lake glinting in the summer sun.

In between are the freeway interchanges where some of the Twin Cities' innovations can be seen - Southdale shopping center in Edina, the first enclosed mall; huge indoor water parks; and the giant Mall of America in Bloomington, with its 5.6 million square feet, 520-plus stores, 85 eating options, 14 movie screens, 25 rides, and 11,000 year-round employees. The mall attracts 40 million people annually. Phase Two, with another 5.6 million square feet and a scheduled opening in 2018, was planned to appeal to upscale patrons who travel a greater distance. To the west is Eden Prairie, which *Money* magazine in 2010 named the best medium-sized U.S. city. For years, this was a high-growth area, but there are some signs that the trend has changed; 26 suburbs in the Twin Cities area lost population in the 2010 census, including many in the 3rd District: Coon Rapids, Corcoran, Dayton, Deephaven, Minnetonka, Orono and Shorewood.

The 3rd Congressional District of Minnesota consists mostly of the Hennepin County suburbs of the Twin Cities. Less than 20 percent of the district is in parts of Anoka and Carver counties. On the north side of the district is working-class Brooklyn Park, long a Democratic-Farmer-Labor Party stronghold, where professional wrestler-turned-governor Jesse Ventura began his political career as mayor. On the south is middle-income Bloomington. To the west are Edina, Plymouth, Wayzata and other towns around Lake Minnetonka, all traditionally Republican. The 3rd is the home of Minnesota's traditional Republican establishment. Like many Northern suburban districts, it has moved toward the Democrats in recent years. Overall, the district is close to evenly matched in presidential contests, with consistent outcomes. Barack Obama twice won it narrowly: 51 percent in 2008, 50 percent in 2012. In 2016, Hillary Clinton led by a wider margin, 50%-41%.

FOURTH DISTRICT

Betty McCollum (D)

Elected 2000, 9th term; b. Jul 12, 1954, Minneapolis; College of St. Catherine (MN), B.S., 1986; Roman Catholic; Divorced; 2 children.

Elected Office: N. State Paul City Council, 1986-1992; MN House, 1992-2000.

Professional Career: Teacher; Retail Sales & Management.

DC Office: 2256 RHOB 20515, 202-225-6631, Fax: 202-225-1968, mccollum.house.gov.

State Offices: St. Paul, 651-224-9191.

Committees: *Appropriations*: Defense, Interior, Environment & Related Agencies (RMM), Legislative Branch.

Group Ratings

	ADA	ACLU	AFL-CIO	LCV	ITI	COC	HAFA	ACU	CFG	FRC
2016	-	100%	-	100%	67%	57%	12%	0%	0%	0%
2015	100%	C	96%	91%	C	40%	C	0%	4%	0%

Almanac Ratings 2015

	Economy	Social	Foreign	Composite
Liberal	96%	96%	99%	97%
Conservative	5%	4%	1%	3%

Key Votes of the 114th Congress

1. Keystone Pipeline	N	5. Puerto Rico Debt	Y	9. Offenses by Aliens	N
2. Trade Deals	N	6. Medical Marijuana	Y	10. Troops in Iraq	Y
3. Export-Import Bank	Y	7. Sanctuary Cities	N	11. Homeland Security $$	Y
4. Debt Ceiling Increase	Y	8. Armor-piercing Bullets	N	12. Trade Adjustment aid	Y

Election Results

Election	Name (Party)	Vote (%)		Cand. Spent	Ind. Exp. Support	Ind. Exp. Oppose
2016 General	Betty McCollum (D)	203,299	(58%)	$722,431		$10,000
	Greg Ryan (R)	121,032	(34%)	$46,103		
2016 Primary	Betty McCollum (D)	33,107	(94%)			
	Steve Carlson (D)	2,105	(6%)			

Prior winning percentages: 2014 (61%), 2012 (62%), 2010 (59%), 2008 (68%), 2006 (70%), 2004 (58%), 2002 (62%), 2000 (48%)

Democrat Betty McCollum, first elected in 2000, has been an ally of Minority Leader Nancy Pelosi of California, whom she calls a mentor. With her partisanship and liberal views, McCollum can be an assertive voice. As a senior member on the Appropriations Committee, she sometimes works with Republicans.

McCollum grew up in North St. Paul and graduated from the College of St. Catherine. She was a substitute social studies teacher, while working as a retail sales manager at a Sears department store and raising two children. After her daughter suffered a fractured skull in a fall from a slide in a city park, McCollum worked with local officials to add sand to soften the area around the slide. She ran for the North St. Paul City Council and was elected on her second try. In 1992, she was elected to the state House after defeating incumbents in both the primary and general election.

When the congressional seat opened, McCollum was endorsed by the Democratic-Farmer-Labor Party. She faced three opponents in the primary. With the DFL's backing, McCollum won 50 percent to 23 percent for state Sen. Steve Novak. Republicans nominated state Sen. Linda Runbeck, a vigorously anti-abortion candidate. McCollum opposed cutting taxes before Congress paid down the national debt. Runbeck, who took conservative positions on health care and education, attacked McCollum and her Democratic allies for running "hateful, vicious attack ads." Former Ramsey County prosecutor Tom Foley, a longtime DFLer, ran on Gov. Jesse Ventura's Independence Party. Once again, McCollum won unexpectedly easily, 48%-31%, with 21 percent for Foley.

McCollum has a staunchly liberal voting record. Her *Almanac* vote ratings for 2015 ranked her among the most liberal 10 percent of the House. On the Appropriations Committee, she is the top Democrat on the Interior-Environment Subcommittee. That panel has jurisdiction over one of her long-time interests: funding for Indian tribes across the nation, especially for school construction. She has worked with GOP subcommittee Chairman Ken Calvert of California to build support for that goal. "I don't make headlines," she told the *Pioneer Press*. "A lot of stuff I work on is not visible to the public." She has sought to limit cutbacks at the Environmental Protection Agency and the National Park Service, including spending for the National Mall. McCollum has advocated major changes in Appropriations operations, which are not likely to gain the approval of Republicans but might help Democrats to define their own views. She wants to end the practice of adding policy-focused "riders" to spending bills. She would reinstate "earmarks" for specific projects rather than continue to yield control to the executive branch. She also sought to end the budget "sequestration" that has restrained discretionary spending. With Republican Rep. Tom Cole of Oklahoma in 2016, she enacted a bill that created a commission to address the needs of Native American children.

McCollum raised her profile when she sought to end military sponsorships in sports - including NASCAR, a passion in the Republican-dominated South. She later told *The New York Times*, "The Defense Department said it didn't have anything that could be cut. Seven million dollars to sponsor a car and we're cutting cops, we're cutting teachers, we're cutting programs for homeless vets?" The move triggered hate mail and angry blog posts, but the Army joined the Navy and Marine Corps in 2013 in abandoning the sponsorships. In 2015, she highlighted splits among Minnesotans, including Democrats, when she proposed to restrict most copper-nickel mining in the national forest near Minnesota's Boundary Waters Canoe Area Wilderness.

An important local project for McCollum was the light-rail link between downtown St. Paul and Minneapolis, which was completed in 2014. She had secured an initial $2 million for the project and was incensed when conservative Republicans targeted additional funding as pork barrel spending. Republican Gov. Tim Pawlenty objected to her insistence that he sign a statement supporting congressional funding for the project. McCollum helped to keep it alive by securing $20 million in the 2009 spending bill to cover the final design work.

Encouraging lawmakers to view the World Bank more positively, McCollum founded a caucus advocating more dialogue with the global financier. She has noted that Congress and the bank participate in many of the same overseas efforts, including fighting poverty and AIDS.

McCollum has been reelected easily. In a routine challenge from Republican Greg Ryan in 2016, she got twice as many votes as him in Ramsey County. But they were even in Washington County, which cast only one-fourth of the total vote.

St. Paul Metro

Population		**Race and Ethnicity**		**Income**	
Total	687,656	White	68.9%	Median Income	$62,153 (119 out of 435)
Land area	332	Black	9.4%	Under $50,000	40.9%
Pop/ sq mi	2068.2	Latino	6.4%	$50,000-$99,999	30.9%
Born in state	61.3%	Asian	11.5%	$100,000-$199,999	22.0%
		Two races	3.1%	$200,000 or more	6.3%
		Other	0.6%	Poverty Rate	13.8%
Age Groups		**Education**		**Health Insurance**	
Under 18	23.8%	H.S grad or less	30.10%	With health insurance coverage	92.3%
18-34	25.2%	Some college	19.60%		
35-64	38.3%	College Degree, 4 yr	25.70%		
Over 64	12.7%	Post grad	16.10%		
Work		**Military**		**Public Assistance**	
White Collar	44.4%	Veteran	6.9%	Cash public assistance income	4.7%
Sales and Service	39.6%	Active Duty	0.1%	Food stamp/SNAP benefits	11.3%
Blue Collar	16.0%				
Government	13.5%				

Voter Turnout			
2015 Total Citizens 18+	486,724	2016 House Turnout as % CVAP	72%
2016 House turnout	351,944	2014 House Turnout as % CVAP	49%

2012 Presidential Vote		
Barack Obama	231,511	(62%)
Mitt Romney	131,521	(35%)

2016 Presidential Vote		
Hillary Clinton	223,803	(61%)
Donald Trump	111,163	(30%)
Gary Johnson	13,513	(4%)

Cook Partisan Voting Index: D+14

Above the Mississippi River bluffs stand St. Paul's two most distinctive landmarks: the Minnesota State Capitol and Archbishop John Ireland's Cathedral of St. Paul. The city's origins are more colorful than its pious name and status as state capital might imply. Its original name was "Pig's Eye," after the tavern set up by the first European settler in the area, Pierre "Pig's Eye" Parrant. It almost wasn't the capital; the territorial legislature in 1857 passed a bill moving the capital to St. Peter, near Mankato. But a legislator hid the physical bill, keeping the governor - who owned the land on which the new capitol building was slated to be built - from signing it, thus preventing the move. The area was settled mainly by Catholic Irish and German immigrants in the 1850s, as opposed to the Protestant Swedes and Yankees who settled Minneapolis.

St. Paul became a major transportation hub, a railroad center and river port, while Minneapolis, upriver at the Falls of St. Anthony, became the nation's largest grain milling center. Both industries stoked the ire of farmers in the Dakotas who were forced to deal with them to make a living. With the large curve in the river, St. Paul borders a longer stretch of the Mississippi than any other city. Beneath the Capitol and the cathedral, the skywalk-linked downtown is home to the Ordway Center for the Performing Arts, the headquarters of Minnesota Public Radio; Garrison Keillor's "Prairie Home Companion" ended its 42-year run in 2016.

Beyond the cathedral is Summit Avenue, on which capitalists like the Great Northern Railway's James J. Hill built grandiose Romanesque houses. Along with Monument Avenue in Richmond and Meridian Street in Indianapolis, it remains one of America's grand 19th century residential boulevards.

The parallel Grand Avenue is home to a pleasant commercial strip with a walkable, urban feel. The Minnesota state fairgrounds are in nearby Falcon Heights, where each year a new "Princess Kay of the Milky Way" is crowned; she and the other finalists sit in a walk-in cooler for six hours while their effigies are carved into 90-pound blocks of butter.

Businesses in the area range from multinational conglomerates like 3M, formerly known as Minnesota Mining and Manufacturing Co., to small enterprises like the William Marvy Co., the last makers of barber poles in the United States. Economic development got a boost with the 11-mile Green Line light rail, which shares 5 stations with the Blue Line in downtown Minneapolis. The area has become home to Hmong immigrants, some of whom were recruited by the Central Intelligence Agency during the Vietnam War and resettled here after Laos fell to the communists in 1975. From 2010 to 2015, the Asian population of Ramsey County grew by 29 percent, while the white population grew by 1 percent. More than 30,000 in the county spoke Hmong. A spacious indoor marketplace on St. Paul's east side called Hmong Village caters to their shopping. The city and Ramsey County face pressure for redevelopment, but they have scant available land. Ramsey County grew 6 percent from 2010 to 2015, a notable increase from the previous decade. The increase in Hmongs has had an unexpected consequence: Declining use of the 13 hockey rinks (most of them aging) in the county.

Minnesota's 4th Congressional District is based in St. Paul. Even before the Democratic-Farmer-Labor Party was formed in 1944, St. Paul was a firmly Democratic part of Minnesota. The 4th includes all of Ramsey County, which hasn't voted for a Republican presidential candidate since it narrowly went for Calvin Coolidge in 1924. In 2016, it was the strongest Democratic county in the state. To the north, it takes in two-thirds of Washington County, which is more evenly balanced politically. To the east are the St. Croix River and Wisconsin. The vote for Hillary Clinton in 2016 was consistent with recent Democratic performance.

FIFTH DISTRICT

Keith Ellison (D)

Elected 2006, 6th term; b. Aug 04, 1963, Detroit, MI; University of Minnesota Law School, J.D.; Wayne State University (MI), B.A.; Islam (Muslim); Divorced; 4 children.

Elected Office: MN House, 2002-2006.

Professional Career: Practicing attorney, 1990-2002.

DC Office: 2263 RHOB 20515, 202-225-4755, Fax: 202-225-4886, ellison.house.gov.

State Offices: Minneapolis, 612-522-1212.

Committees: *Financial Services*: Capital Markets, Securities & Investment, Financial Institutions & Consumer Credit, Oversight & Investigations.

Group Ratings

	ADA	ACLU	AFL-CIO	LCV	ITI	COC	HAFA	ACU	CFG	FRC
2016	-	94%	-	87%	33%	62%	14%	0%	11%	0%
2015	100%	C	100%	100%	C	35%	C	4%	6%	0%

Almanac Ratings 2015

	Economy	Social	Foreign	Composite
Liberal	94%	100%	97%	97%
Conservative	6%	0%	4%	3%

Key Votes of the 114th Congress

1. Keystone Pipeline	N	5. Puerto Rico Debt	Y	9. Offenses by Aliens	N
2. Trade Deals	N	6. Medical Marijuana	Y	10. Troops in Iraq	Y
3. Export-Import Bank	Y	7. Sanctuary Cities	N	11. Homeland Security $$	Y
4. Debt Ceiling Increase	Y	8. Armor-piercing Bullets	N	12. Trade Adjustment aid	Y

Election Results

Election	Name (Party)	Vote (%)	Cand. Spent	Ind. Exp. Support	Ind. Exp. Oppose
2016 General	Keith Ellison (D)	249,964 (69%)	$1,723,544		
	Frank Nelson Drake (R)	80,660 (22%)			
2016 Primary	Keith Ellison (D)	40,380 (92%)			

Prior winning percentages: 2014 (71%), 2012 (75%), 2010 (68%), 2008 (71%), 2006 (56%)

Democrat Keith Ellison, first elected in 2006, was the first Muslim to serve in Congress and the first black representative from Minnesota. With his outspoken progressive views, including his early endorsement of Sen. Bernie Sanders in the 2016 presidential campaign, he ran after the election to chair the Democratic National Committee. Although he won the support of many elected Democratic officials and union officials, he narrowly lost to Tom Perez, who had been Labor Secretary for President Barack Obama. Ellison returned to the House, from which he had said he would have resigned if he had won the DNC position.

Ellison was raised Catholic in Detroit, the son of a psychiatrist and the third of five boys. (Four became lawyers and the fifth a doctor.) Ellison studied economics at Wayne State University, and it was there that he converted to Sunni Islam. He moved to Minnesota in 1987 to study law at the University of Minnesota, worked in private practice, and ran a nonprofit criminal defense firm while also hosting a public affairs radio show. Ellison won the first of two terms in the state House in 2002.

When the seat opened in 2006 for the first time since 1978, it unleashed a torrent of pent-up political ambition. The chief contenders were Ellison, former state Sen. Ember Reichgott Junge and Mike Erlandson, who had been an aide to retiring Rep. Martin Olav Sabo. Ellison attracted support from Iraq war opponents and backers of the late Democratic Sen. Paul Wellstone of Minnesota, who died in the crash of a small airplane in the final days of his 2002 reelection campaign. Ellison easily won the DFL endorsement, but Erlandson and Reichgott Junge competed in the seven-way September primary.

Ellison had to overcome several unhelpful personal revelations: Unpaid parking tickets and moving violations had led to multiple suspensions of his driver's license, and he once owed $25,000 in back taxes. Most damaging were his ties to the controversial Nation of Islam leader Louis Farrakhan, and Farrakhan's anti-Semitic pronouncements. Ellison said his association with the group was limited to the 18 months he spent helping organize the 1995 Million Man March in Washington, D.C., although his writings about Farrakhan were traced back to his law school days. Ellison won the primary with 41 percent, followed by Erlandson with 31 percent and Reichgott Junge with 21 percent.

In the general election, Republican Alan Fine described Ellison as "an embarrassment to our district, our state, our country, and our world." Ellison won with 56 percent of vote, while Fine and Independence Party candidate Tammy Lee each got 21 percent. He has not been seriously challenged since then, although controversy has continued to dog him. A conservative commentator stirred up opposition to his plan to take the oath of office with the Quran, rather than the Bible. In a politically adept move, Ellison borrowed a Quran from the Library of Congress that Thomas Jefferson once owned.

Ellison has been frequently called on as a spokesman for his faith. (Indiana Democratic Rep. André Carson joined him in 2008 as another Muslim in Congress.) When Homeland Security Committee Chairman Peter King of New York held hearings to explore al-Qaida's attempts to radicalize American Muslims, Ellison offered examples of Muslims who had thwarted several plots by reporting them to law enforcement officials. In 2011, he broke into tears as he testified before the King panel, recounting the death of a Muslim-American firefighter on September 11. "The best defense against extreme ideologies is social inclusion and civic engagement," Ellison said. "I fear these hearings may undermine our efforts in this direction." In 2008, he was the first member of Congress to make the Hajj pilgrimage to the Muslim holy city of Mecca, later describing it as a "transformative" experience.

Ellison has had a strongly liberal voting record, which was confirmed by the *Almanac* vote ratings for 2015. As co-chair of the Congressional Progressive Caucus, he led efforts to end racial profiling and voter ID laws that he said were thinly veiled attempts to suppress minority voting. He continued to be a target for conservatives. Republican Rep. Allen West of Florida in 2011 called Ellison "the antithesis of the principles upon which this country was established." Ellison has mostly ignored the criticism, and has won recognition for his legislative work.

On the Financial Services Committee, Ellison challenged lending practices and foreclosures by credit card and mortgage companies, which he said "have torn holes in the fabric of neighborhoods." On the 2009 bill to overhaul credit card practices, he added a provision to stop companies from raising rates on people with unrelated debt problems. He introduced a bill in 2012 to replace the mortgage interest tax deduction with a 20 percent flat rate tax credit, which he said would bring in $27 billion in new federal revenue while increasing the number of homeowners. In 2015, he filed a bill to raise billions of dollars by taxing Wall Street financial transactions. His measure, which was described as modern-day Robin Hood by robbing the rich to give to the poor, spurred vigils across the country by community activists.

In a 2014 interview with *New York* magazine, Ellison explained the significance of the broad opposition to the "cromnibus" spending bill that Congress narrowly approved that month. "The lesson is that there are at least 206 members of Congress and at least 40-some members of the Senate who have finally realized that a government of, by, and for the people should be on the side of the people," Ellison said. "You're seeing a realignment, an adjustment of substantial portions of the Congress in alignment with the American people. Congress is finally catching up on fighting for the interests of working people. We're going to dig in."

As the 2016 election approached, he moved his focus to national politics. In October 2015, he became the second member of Congress to endorse the presidential candidacy of Sanders. "He is talking about the issues that are important to American families," Ellison said, with references to bills that the two of them had introduced to raise the minimum wage and ban private prisons. He shared the objective of Sanders to increase grass-roots organizing, which they said Hillary Clinton had abandoned in her presidential campaign. In the drafting of the platform for the 2016 Democratic convention, Sanders designated Ellison among his five supporters in the negotiations. When the agreement was reached, Ellison said, "We've made some substantial moves forward."

Following the disastrous election results for Democrats, Ellison was the first candidate to announce for the DNC chairmanship, with what he called a "bottom-up" campaign. Early supporters included Sanders and incoming Senate Democratic Leader Charles Schumer, the Jewish New Yorker who helped Ellison allay concerns about his Islamic religion. Ellison said he would quit his seat in the House if he won the DNC post, which was an implicit rebuke of Rep. Debbie Wasserman Schultz, who had previously chaired the DNC while serving in the House. He sought to depict Perez as a surrogate for Democratic presidential nominee Hillary Clinton, whose campaign had disappointed many Democrats, especially with her failure to reach working-class voters in the battleground states of Michigan, Pennsylvania and Wisconsin. Perez benefited from several factors, including his support from many allies of President Barack Obama and the prospect that he would be the first Latino to chair the DNC. Perez won on the second ballot, 235 to 200. In the spirit of reconciliation, Perez named Ellison as DNC deputy chair.

Minneapolis Metro

Population		**Race and Ethnicity**		**Income**	
Total	687,435	White	63.7%	Median Income	$53,964 (201 out of 435)
Land area	136	Black	15.9%		
Pop/ sq mi	5067.3	Latino	9.2%		
Born in state	55.6%	Asian	6.1%	Under $50,000	46.4%
		Two races	3.8%	$50,000-$99,999	29.7%
Age Groups		Other	1.2%	$100,000-$199,999	18.6%
Under 18	21.1%			$200,000 or more	5.3%
18-34	31.1%	**Education**		Poverty Rate	17.7%
35-64	36.7%	H.S grad or less	29.40%		
Over 64	11.1%	Some college	19.10%	**Health Insurance**	
		College Degree, 4 yr	27.70%	With health insurance coverage	90.2%
Work		Post grad	16.00%		
White Collar	46.2%				
Sales and Service	39.7%	**Military**		**Public Assistance**	
Blue Collar	14.2%	Veteran	6.0%	Cash public assistance income	6.0%
Government	11.5%	Active Duty	0.0%		
				Food stamp/SNAP benefits	13.4%

Voter Turnout			
2015 Total Citizens 18+	490,435	2016 House Turnout as % CVAP	74%
2016 House turnout	361,882	2014 House Turnout as % CVAP	47%

2012 Presidential Vote		
Barack Obama	274,635	(73%)
Mitt Romney	89,643	(24%)

2016 Presidential Vote		
Hillary Clinton	273,402	(73%)
Donald Trump	68,535	(18%)
Gary Johnson	12,558	(3%)
Jill Stein	7,522	(2%)

Cook Partisan Voting Index: D+26

From almost nowhere in Minneapolis today can you see the geographic feature that created the city: the Falls of St. Anthony, where rapids still course beneath low downtown bridges. In olden days, every riverboat had to stop here - these are the only significant waterfalls on the upper Mississippi River - and the waterpower generated by the falls was the energy source first for the pioneers' grist mills and then for the giant grain mills that processed northern Great Plains wheat into food for the United States. By 1890, Minneapolis and St. Paul made up one of America's largest urban areas, living mainly off grain. Today, grain is still important to Minneapolis; after all, the headquarters for General Mills is located in nearby Golden Valley. But Minneapolis is also a center of high technology, banking and finance. In a lengthy story in the March 2015 issue of *Atlantic*, headlined "The Miracle of Minneapolis," writer Derek Thompson argued that "fiscal equalization" accounts for the success. "By spreading the wealth to its poorest neighborhoods, the metro area provides more-equal services in low-income places, and keeps quality of life high just about everywhere."

The city of Minneapolis and a few of its older suburbs make up the 5th Congressional District. In the southwest corner are the affluent neighborhoods around Lake Calhoun and Lake Harriet -- long built-up and proudly maintained, amid trees that turn golden in early autumn. Not far away are Minneapolis' skywalk-laced downtown skyscrapers, the museum quarter on the hill above Hennepin Avenue. In 2016, the National Football League's Vikings moved into the new U.S. Bank Stadium, which will host the Super Bowl in February 2018; the state financed about half the cost of the new facility, whose location in the renamed East Town spurred many nearby residential and office tower projects in the urban area three blocks from the river. Straddling the Mississippi is the University of Minnesota, which has fostered the area's cutting-edge biotechnology research and medical innovations, and nearby Dinkytown, a student area where Robert Zimmerman discovered folk music and reinvented himself as Bob Dylan. The Witch's Hat Water Tower in Prospect Park is believed to be the inspiration for Dylan's classic "All Along the Watchtower." Left-leaning in its politics, the area is a product of Minneapolis's unique brand of liberalism, which is drawn from the Yankee tradition of clean government, the Scandinavian tradition of cooperative enterprise, and the industrial-labor tradition of economic redistribution.

Most of the 5th District is low on the income scale. Except for a small section of Anoka County near Coon Rapids, all of the district is in Hennepin. Many of the working-class neighborhoods of small frame houses and ample parks are now kept up by new immigrants, and more than a third of the district is nonwhite, the highest percentage in the state. To the northeast, behind the railroad and warehouse district along the Mississippi, are many Hmong from Laos. Hennepin County is also home to the largest number of African immigrants in the state, and Brooklyn Center has a large concentration of Liberians. The Jewish community here also has increased with immigrants from the former Soviet Union. The resulting district is the most heavily Democratic in the state. Hillary Clinton won 73 percent of the vote in 2016, precisely the same as the vote for Barack Obama in his two runs for president.

SIXTH DISTRICT

Tom Emmer (R)

Elected 2014, 2nd term; b. Mar 03, 1961, South Bend, IN; William Mitchell College of Law (MN), J.D.; University of Alaska, Fairbanks, B.A.; Saint Thomas Academy (MN); Boston College (MA), Att.; Roman Catholic; Married (Jacqueline (Jacquie) Samuel); 7 children.

Elected Office: Independence City Council, 1995-2002; Delano City Council, 2003-2004; MN House, 2004-2010 (Deputy Minority Leader, 2007-2008).

Professional Career: Attorney; radio talk show host.

DC Office: 315 CHOB 20515, 202-225-2331, Fax: 202-225-6475, emmer.house.gov.
State Offices: Otsego, 763-241-6848.

Committees: *Financial Services*: Capital Markets, Securities & Investment, Monetary Policy & Trade, Terrorism & Illicit Finance.

Group Ratings

	ADA	ACLU	AFL-CIO	LCV	ITI	COC	HAFA	ACU	CFG	FRC
2016	-	11%	-	0%	83%	100%	66%	76%	72%	83%
2015	0%	C	17%	3%	C	80%	C	83%	72%	92%

Almanac Ratings 2015

	Economy	Social	Foreign	Composite
Liberal	1%	32%	11%	15%
Conservative	99%	68%	89%	85%

Key Votes of the 114th Congress

1. Keystone Pipeline	Y	5. Puerto Rico Debt	N	9. Offenses by Aliens	Y
2. Trade Deals	Y	6. Medical Marijuana	Y	10. Troops in Iraq	N
3. Export-Import Bank	N	7. Sanctuary Cities	N	11. Homeland Security $$	Y
4. Debt Ceiling Increase	N	8. Armor-piercing Bullets	Y	12. Trade Adjustment aid	Y

Election Results

Election	Name (Party)	Vote (%)		Cand. Spent	Ind. Exp. Support	Ind. Exp. Oppose
2016 General	Tom Emmer (R)	235,380	(66%)	$1,550,608	$7,691	
	David Snyder (D)	123,008	(34%)			
2016 Primary	Tom Emmer (R)	13,548	(69%)			
	A.J. Kern (R)	5,217	(27%)			

Prior winning percentages: 2014 (56%)

Republican Tom Emmer, a former state representative and conservative talk-show host, was elected in 2014 to the seat vacated by Michele Bachmann, the tea party leader and one-time presidential contender. An ardent conservative, he settled in comfortably and sought far less attention than his predecessor. His occasional cooperation with party leaders was rewarded with a seat on the Financial Services Committee and a niche at the National Republican Congressional Committee.

Emmer was born in South Bend, Indiana, where his father was completing a degree at Notre Dame, and grew up in Edina. He got his bachelor's degree in political science at the University of Alaska, and his law degree from William Mitchell College. His great-grandfather founded a lumber business in Minneapolis that his family continued to run, under the name of Viking Forest Products. Emmer practiced law at his own firm, and served on the city councils of Independence and Delano before winning election to the state Assembly. His GOP colleagues voted him deputy majority leader.

In 2010, Emmer easily won the Republican nomination for governor and challenged Democrat Mark Dayton. He staked out one of the most conservative platforms that this blue-leaning state had seen in decades. Along with calls to cut spending, slash taxes and promote socially conservative values, he proposed a constitutional amendment requiring a supermajority in the Legislature to approve any federal law before it could take effect in the state. The national Republican wave was not quite strong enough to lift him over Dayton, who won by 8,770 votes of the 2.1 million cast. Emmer subsequently launched a conservative radio talk show in the Twin Cities.

After Bachmann announced her retirement in 2013, Emmer was the first Republican to declare. He gave up his radio slot to raise money and rack up endorsements, including from the local GOP. He outraised his opponent, Anoka County Board Chair Rhonda Sivarajah, by 20-to-1, and coasted to his primary victory with 73 percent of the vote in a low-turnout race. In the general election against DFL nominee Joe Perske, which was not seriously contested, Emmer had close to a 10-to-1 fundraising advantage. He won, 56%-38%, and took all eight counties.

Emmer quickly showed that he intended to be a player in Congress. A week after his election, he said that he was impressed with the leadership style of Speaker John Boehner. "I am being very - and I will be very - deliberate," he told *USA Today*. "I'm here to accomplish something." With Democratic Rep. Grace Meng of New York, he filed a bill to accelerate the visa process for physicians from overseas to work in U.S. hospitals. He joined dozens of House colleagues who attended the commemoration of the 50th anniversary of the march in Selma, Alabama, and noted that all Americans deserve "equal protection under the law." With California Rep. Mimi Walters, he led an effort by freshmen House Republicans to send a letter to President Barack Obama with their support for approval of the Trans-Pacific Partnership. Following his trip in April 2015 on a House delegation to Ethiopia and Kenya, Emmer said that it opened his eyes about the value of foreign aid. In March 2016, he joined the bipartisan congressional delegation that accompanied Obama to Cuba. Citing the potential market for agricultural exports from Minnesota, he called for lifting the U.S. trade embargo on Cuba.

In his first term, Emmer got a seat on the Financial Services Committee. In April 2016, the House passed his bill to reduce the regulatory requirements imposed by the Financial Stability Oversight Council, which the Dodd-Frank banking law created in 2010. "Over the years, Congress has given much of its authority to unelected bureaucrats, but this legislation returns the Constitutional 'power of the purse' back to Congress," he said.

Emmer disagreed with conservatives who opposed funding the Homeland Security Department because of the conflict over immigration policy, and warned that the threatened government shutdown was a bad idea. "Two wrongs don't make a right," he said. The leader of the Minnesota Tea Party Alliance responded that he was "very disappointed" by his early votes. Emmer defended what he called his incremental approach, and seemed to make a pointed and informed jab at Bachmann, his erstwhile ally, about how to succeed in Congress. "If you want to go out there and make a lot of noise, maybe you're going to get people from all across the country to send you a lot of money, and that's great because then you can increase your own brand. But you'll never change the inside of the building," he told the *St. Cloud Times*.

Emmer was reelected easily. He got 69 percent of the GOP primary vote against two opponents, including an outspoken critic of immigration policy, and 66 percent in the general. In 2017, he became one of two deputy chairs of the NRCC, where he was assigned to focus on its future operations. The move by Emmer toward the more establishment wing of his party could position him for another run for statewide office, perhaps an eventual bid for the Senate.

Twin Cities Exurbs, St. Cloud

Population		**Race and Ethnicity**		**Income**	
Total	681,284	White	90.4%	Median Income	$71,558 (68 out of 435)
Land area	2,882	Black	2.3%		
Pop/ sq mi	236.4	Latino	2.6%	Under $50,000	32.7%
Born in state	78.0%	Asian	2.2%	$50,000-$99,999	36.4%
		Two races	2.0%	$100,000-$199,999	26.6%
Age Groups		Other	0.4%	$200,000 or more	4.2%
Under 18	26.2%			Poverty Rate	8.1%
18-34	22.2%	**Education**			
35-64	40.9%	H.S grad or less	33.90%	**Health Insurance**	
Over 64	10.7%	Some college	24.60%	With health insurance coverage	94.6%
		College Degree, 4 yr	20.40%		
Work		Post grad	8.10%		
White Collar	35.9%			**Public Assistance**	
Sales and Service	39.9%	**Military**		Cash public assistance income	2.5%
Blue Collar	24.3%	Veteran	8.5%		
Government	11.3%	Active Duty	0.0%	Food stamp/SNAP benefits	6.8%

Voter Turnout			
2015 Total Citizens 18+	492,201	2016 House Turnout as % CVAP	73%
2016 House turnout	358,924	2014 House Turnout as % CVAP	48%

2012 Presidential Vote		
Mitt Romney	205,652	(56%)
Barack Obama	151,238	(41%)

2016 Presidential Vote		
Donald Trump	218,546	(59%)
Hillary Clinton	123,329	(33%)
Gary Johnson	15,314	(4%)

Cook Partisan Voting Index: R+12

The earliest settlers of Minneapolis and St. Paul lived within walking distance of the mills and factories and rail yards where they worked. As the first streetcars and then automobiles allowed them to live farther from their jobs, they spread out in the Twin Cities and then all around the lake-strewn countryside. The flatlands are bleak here when the winter sun struggles to pierce gray clouds, but even so, the creativity and productivity of Minnesotans have turned the countryside into some of the nation's most pleasant suburbs. Taking maximum advantage of their lakes, they refurbished old towns and farmhouses and built comfortable homes in new subdivisions.

The 6th Congressional District of Minnesota is a suburban and exurban area north of St. Paul and Minneapolis. It is a mix of upscale and working-class suburbs, based in Anoka County, which has about one-third of the voters. (Small parts of closer-in Anoka are in the 3rd and 5th Districts.) To the northwest, along the Mississippi River, are Wright, Sherburne and Benton counties, which have nearly doubled from a combined total of 141,000 people in 1990 to more than 263,000 in 2015. Those counties have accounted for much of the recent job growth in the metro area.

The district includes the eastern half of St. Cloud-based Stearns County, a heavily German-Catholic area and a stronghold of anti-abortion rights sentiment. St. Cloud is the headquarters of the Electrolux Co., which has expanded beyond vacuum cleaners to other appliances and kitchen products. The city is 85 percent white, but its demographics have changed. The 1990s brought an influx of Vietnamese, Chinese and Japanese immigrants. Since 2000, several thousand Somalis have moved in and started businesses or worked at local meat-processing plants. Many of them have settled in St. Cloud from elsewhere in the United States after learning of the tight-knit local Somali community. Federal and local investigators have reviewed charges that Somalis in the public schools of St. Cloud have suffered civil rights violations, and there have been allegations of bullying of young Somalis. Business leaders have sought to educate local citizens about the Somali culture. Six Somalis were arrested in 2015 and charged with trying to travel to Somalia to join the al-Shabab terrorist group. In September 2016, there were new tensions following a knife attack in which a Somali injured 10 at a local mall before he was shot and killed by an off-duty police officer.

The district is solidly Republican. Mitt Romney's 56%-41% lead in 2012, his largest Minnesota margin, increased to an overwhelming 59%-33% win for Donald Trump in 2016.

SEVENTH DISTRICT

Collin Peterson (D)

Elected 1990, 14th term; b. Jun 29, 1944, Fargo, ND; Moorhead State University (MN), B.A., 1966; Lutheran; Single3 children.

Military Career: U.S Army National Guard, 1963-1969.

Elected Office: MN Senate, 1976-1986.

Professional Career: Accountant, 1966-1990.

DC Office: 2204 RHOB 20515, 202-225-2165, Fax: 202-225-1593, collinpeterson.house.gov.

State Offices: Detroit Lakes, 218-847-5056; Marshall, 507-537-2299; Montevideo, 320-235-1061; Willmar, 320-235-1061.

Committees: *Agriculture (RMM)*: Biotechnology, Horticulture & Research, Commodity Exchanges, Energy & Credit, Conservation & Forestry, General Farm Commodities & Risk Management, Livestock & Foreign Agriculture, Nutrition.

Group Ratings

	ADA	ACLU	AFL-CIO	LCV	ITI	COC	HAFA	ACU	CFG	FRC
2016	-	29%	-	18%	83%	93%	34%	21%	29%	33%
2015	25%	C	71%	14%	C	85%	C	33%	25%	75%

Almanac Ratings 2015

	Economy	Social	Foreign	Composite
Liberal	36%	40%	40%	39%
Conservative	64%	60%	60%	61%

Key Votes of the 114th Congress

1. Keystone Pipeline	Y	5. Puerto Rico Debt	N	9. Offenses by Aliens	Y
2. Trade Deals	N	6. Medical Marijuana	Y	10. Troops in Iraq	N
3. Export-Import Bank	Y	7. Sanctuary Cities	N	11. Homeland Security $$	Y
4. Debt Ceiling Increase	Y	8. Armor-piercing Bullets	Y	12. Trade Adjustment aid	Y

Election Results

Election	Name (Party)	Vote (%)	Cand. Spent	Ind. Exp. Support	Ind. Exp. Oppose
2016 General	Collin Peterson (D)	173,589 (53%)	$493,626	$17,500	
	Dave Hughes (R)	156,952 (47%)	$16,425		
2016 Primary	Collin Peterson (D)	(100%)			

Prior winning percentages: 2014 (54%), 2012 (60%), 2010 (55%), 2008 (72%), 2006 (70%), 2004 (66%), 2002 (65%), 2000 (69%), 1998 (72%), 1996 (68%), 1994 (51%), 1992 (50%), 1990 (54%)

Collin Peterson, first elected in 1990, is one of the few conservative "aggies" left in an increasingly liberal and metropolitan Democratic caucus. He has the dubious honor of holding the Democratic seat that leans most heavily Republican and he often has stymied the hopes of GOP political operatives. He is the top Democrat on the Agriculture Committee, where he works well with like-minded lawmakers in both parties representing rural regions. "I am just a country boy, and I am doing the best I can," he once said.

Peterson grew up on a farm in Baker, just across the Red River of the North from Fargo, North Dakota. He graduated from Moorhead State College and then started a certified public accounting business in Detroit Lakes. In 1976, he was elected to the state Senate. In 1982, he ran for the House but lost in the Democratic-Farmer-Labor Party caucus, then set out to prove that he's nothing if not persistent. He tried three more times, losing to Republican Arlan Stangeland in 1984 and 1986 (by only

121 votes that year) and losing a DFL primary in 1988. In 1990, when the *St. Cloud Times* reported that Stangeland made 341 credit card calls to a woman who was not his wife, Peterson won with a robust 54 percent of the vote.

In office, Peterson has been known as a free spirit, wearing cowboy boots and playing guitar in a bipartisan rock band called the Second Amendments. He has performed with Willie Nelson at Farm-Aid concerts and he co-chairs the Rock and Roll Caucus with Democratic Rep. Marcia Fudge of Ohio. He is candid with Capitol Hill reporters, sometimes revealing more about the thinking of Republicans than do GOP lawmakers themselves. He has acted as his own campaign consultant and pilot, flying his single-engine plane to stops around the district.

Peterson had the most conservative voting record of any House Democrat in 2015, according to the *Almanac* vote ratings. On environmental issues, Peterson takes the view of his constituents, who hunt and fish as a way of life and often see environmentalists' policies as hindrances. He has supported lifting trade restrictions on Cuba, a move favored by farmers eager for another export market. He backs labor unions, a vital Democratic constituency. He has supported Minority Leader Nancy Pelosi on the theory, he said, that only a liberal can tell liberals what to do. Pelosi accepted Peterson's invitation to attend Farmfest in Redwood County in August 2006, where she ate pork chops on a stick and got a warm reception.

When Democrats controlled the House, Peterson chaired Agriculture. "There were people in my party who were skeptical of me taking that position. I was seen as a renegade, a maverick," he told *National Journal* in 2013. He had been a skeptic of the Republicans' 1996 Freedom to Farm Act and he joined the bipartisan majority that restored market controls when the farm program was renewed in 2002. In the mid-2000s, Peterson called for extending the Conservation Reserve Program to keep millions of additional acres of farmland idle to produce switch grass and plant waste that could be used to make ethanol.

Peterson worked with Republicans to achieve many of his goals on the farm bill enacted in 2008. It was not easy. It took six short-term extensions of the bill and two votes to override President George W. Bush's veto. Peterson sought an income limit of $900,000 annually for subsidy payments, and the final deal set a ceiling of $750,000 for farmers receiving direct payments. It also barred payments to persons with more than $500,000 in nonfarm income. He finally got his permanent disaster fund so that farmers could get their aid more quickly following a drought or flood. Peterson boosted the subsidy for cellulosic ethanol to $1 per gallon, while reducing the subsidy for corn ethanol from 51 cents to 45 cents per gallon.

With demands for new acreage, especially from the large fruit and vegetable states of Florida and California, the committee reduced the Conservation Reserve Program from 39 million acres to 32 million acres. Peterson, the former accountant, proved adept at figuring the costs of commodity programs.

Many of Peterson's views are a throwback to earlier political times. A fiscal conservative and founding member of the Blue Dog Coalition, Peterson has shown a bit more loyalty to his party since it lost the majority in 2011. But in his Republican-leaning district, he oppose many of President Barack Obama's major initiatives. He voted against the New Year's Day 2013 budget deal aimed at averting the so-called "fiscal cliff" and supports a balanced-budget constitutional amendment. He opposes abortion rights and gun control. Peterson voted against both the 2009 economic stimulus bill and the Affordable Care Act, and in favor of dozens of GOP attempts to repeal the latter.

Peterson has been cooperative on a few big issues, but generally only after extracting legislative concessions. He said in 2009 that the Democrats' cap-and-trade bill to limit carbon emissions was "an urban-dominated bill" that catered to the environmental lobby. As part of his support for the deal, Peterson insisted that the Agriculture Department, rather than the Environmental Protection Agency, oversee the carbon emissions offset program for farmers. The bill passed the House, but it died in the Senate. When the EPA announced it would move on its own to begin regulating carbon emissions under the Clean Air Act, Peterson cosponsored a bill to block the move.

In 2010, on the major financial industry regulatory bill, Peterson struck an agreement with Financial Services Chairman Barney Frank of Massachusetts that preserved for the Commodity Futures Trading Commission some oversight of agricultural commodities trading. The deal stopped Frank's committee from grabbing jurisdiction of the commission.

Peterson had hoped a five-year farm bill could be passed in 2012, but declared in March that House Budget Committee Chairman Paul Ryan's GOP budget blueprint made that task impossible because it called for unacceptably steep reductions while ending direct payments to farmers. Another complication arose over Peterson's desire to come up with a new program for the dairy industry. His proposal would let the government manage the milk supply by setting production limits for farmers enrolling in a market-stabilization program. Republicans said his measure would only worsen what House Speaker John Boehner derided as "Soviet-style" management of the farm program.

House Republicans brought up a five-year bill in June 2013 that they hoped could win at least 40 Democratic votes with Peterson's help. But the White House, angered that the measure cut food-stamp programs by more than $20 billion, mobilized Democrats against it. Peterson could attract only 23 members of his party to back it. Boehner was enraged. "The Democrats walked away from this," he told *The Hill*. In 2014, Congress cleared a bill with bipartisan support that cut about $9 billion.

Republicans have been eager for Peterson to retire, which they believe would make it nearly certain that they would take his seat. He typically has won reelection easily. Despite the Republican wave in 2010, Peterson prevailed 55%-38%. Four years later, Republicans were confident they could finally beat him. The National Republican Congressional Committee recruited state Sen. Torrey Westrom, who is legally blind, and outside groups poured millions into ads depicting Peterson as out of touch for his use of a taxpayer-subsidized plane to get around his district. Peterson touted his work on the farm bill and won, 54%-46%, his closest margin in 20 years. Each party spent more than $4 million on the contest. Peterson was not intimidated. "They [Republicans] energized me last time, they got me fired up," he told the *Star Tribune*. Their threats to target him again make him less likely to retire, he said, showing his independent streak. In 2016, against lightly financed David Hughes, the margin tightened to 53%-47%. Hughes, a former Air Force officer, said he planned to run again in 2018.

Western Minnesota

Population		**Race and Ethnicity**		**Income**	
Total	663,049	White	89.7%	Median Income	$51,591 (229 out of 435)
Land area	33,429	Black	1.0%		
Pop/ sq mi	19.8	Latino	4.3%		
Born in state	73.1%	Asian	0.8%	Under $50,000	48.3%
		Two races	1.5%	$50,000-$99,999	34.7%
Age Groups		Other	2.7%	$100,000-$199,999	14.6%
Under 18	23.4%			$200,000 or more	2.5%
18-34	20.5%	**Education**		Poverty Rate	12.0%
35-64	37.8%	H.S grad or less	43.10%		
Over 64	18.2%	Some college	22.90%	**Health Insurance**	
		College Degree, 4 yr	15.30%	With health insurance coverage	92.4%
Work		Post grad	5.80%		
White Collar	32.4%				
Sales and Service	38.3%	**Military**		**Public Assistance**	
Blue Collar	29.3%	Veteran	9.5%	Cash public assistance income	3.2%
Government	13.8%	Active Duty	0.0%		
				Food stamp/SNAP benefits	9.1%

Voter Turnout			
2015 Total Citizens 18+	497,682	2016 House Turnout as % CVAP	66%
2016 House turnout	330,848	2014 House Turnout as % CVAP	48%

2012 Presidential Vote		
Mitt Romney	180,334	(54%)
Barack Obama	147,750	(44%)

2016 Presidential Vote		
Donald Trump	208,215	(61%)
Hillary Clinton	104,566	(31%)
Gary Johnson	12,523	(4%)

Cook Partisan Voting Index: R+12

The fabled Mississippi River begins modestly in Minnesota's Itasca State Park, 2,552 miles from the Gulf of Mexico. At that point, it can be crossed by foot on stepping-stones. The lake-strewn country in which the river begins has made its own contributions to American literature. More than a century ago, Sinclair Lewis grew up in the town of Sauk Centre, which provided grist for his critical but affectionate portrayals of small-town America in *Main Street* and *Babbitt*. In those years, this seemingly placid country was seething with rage, as WASP nationalists banned German from schools, renamed sauerkraut "liberty cabbage," and boycotted German-American businesses. This was also once prime logging country. Although that industry is in long-term decline here, Bemidji is still home to giant statues of Paul Bunyan and Babe the Blue Ox. In April 2015, the Bemidji city council agreed to new plaques that described the atrocities committed against local Indian tribes. To the west, on the North Dakota border, is

Moorhead, the largest city in the district (pop. 39,000). Moorhead was the planned destination of Ritchie Valens, Buddy Holly and J.P. "The Big Bopper" Richardson when their airplane took off from Iowa in a snowstorm in 1959; the plane crashed, and Feb. 3 would be committed to the ages by singer/songwriter Don McLean as "the day the music died." In 2017, Moorhead gained a new distinction when it became the only city of its size in Minnesota with a woman as mayor and a female majority on the city council.

Farther south is great farming country, the start of the wheat fields that sweep across the Dakotas and into Montana. Even today, farmers toil against the elements to make a profitable living, although many acres have been taken out of production by the federal Conservation Reserve Program. Farmers have turned to corn and soybeans, which have more markets and uses. This area is the nation's leading producer of sugar beets and a leading supplier of turkeys.

On the banks of Plum Creek, near Walnut Grove, is where Laura Ingalls Wilder's family came on the way west to South Dakota in the *Little House* books. After all their struggles, Wilder's family left the farm for town as soon as they could. Their pain would be all too familiar to contemporary residents along the Red River of the North, which overflowed its banks in 1997, inundating East Grand Forks and Grand Forks, North Dakota, dislocating 50,000 people - America's largest mass evacuation between the Civil War and Hurricane Katrina. Southwest of Walnut Grove is Pipestone National Monument. Native Americans have used rocks collected from the quarries here to make ceremonial pipes for centuries. In 2016, Pipestone County approved a permit for the largest solar project in Minnesota.

The 7th Congressional District of Minnesota covers almost all of the western part of the state. Its southeastern corner extends to 30 miles from Minneapolis. From the Canadian border to the southern end of the district is roughly a 400-mile drive. It takes in the wheat-farming plains adjoining North Dakota as well as the German Catholic areas, with their farm villages named for saints. This is the fourth most productive farm district in the nation.

The 7th's political history could have been on Garrison Keillor's *Lake Wobegon Days*: In 1958, DFL Rep. Coya Knutson was defeated for reelection when her husband, Andy, issued a plaintive statement urging her to come home from Washington and make his breakfast again. She was the only incumbent Democrat to lose in that heavily Democratic year; they divorced shortly thereafter. This has become a prime marginal district. After Mitt Romney won the district in 2012 with 54 percent, Donald Trump took it, 61%-31%, the most Republican district in the state and the most Republican district in the nation that elected a Democrat in 2016.

EIGHTH DISTRICT

Richard Nolan (D)

Elected 2012, 3rd term; b. Dec 17, 1943, Brainerd; St. John's University (MN), Att., 1964; University of Minnesota, B.A., 1966; University of Maryland - College Park, 1967; St. Cloud State College (MN), Att., 1969; Roman Catholic; Married (Mary Nolan); 4 children.

Elected Office: U.S. House, 1974-1980; MN House, 1969-1973.

Professional Career: President, Emily Forest Products, 1994-2011; President, MN World Trade Center Corporation, 1987-1994; President, U.S. Export Corporation, 1981-1986; Teacher, 1968-1969; Head Start ed. Director, 1968; Staff Assistant, Sen. Walter Mondale, 1966-1968.

DC Office: 2366 RHOB 20515, 202-225-6211, Fax: 202-225-0699, nolan.house.gov.

State Offices: Brainerd, 218-454-4078; Center City, 218-491-3131; Chisholm, 218-491-3114; Duluth, 218-464-5095.

Committees: *Agriculture*: Conservation & Forestry, General Farm Commodities & Risk Management (RMM). *Transportation & Infrastructure*: Aviation, Highways & Transit, Railroads, Pipelines & Hazardous Materials.

Group Ratings

	ADA	ACLU	AFL-CIO	LCV	ITI	COC	HAFA	ACU	CFG	FRC
2016	-	100%	-	89%	67%	64%	14%	4%	0%	0%
2015	75%	C	100%	80%	C	56%	C	4%	0%	0%

Almanac Ratings 2015

	Economy	Social	Foreign	Composite
Liberal	83%	100%	84%	89%
Conservative	17%	0%	16%	11%

Key Votes of the 114th Congress

1. Keystone Pipeline	Y	5. Puerto Rico Debt	N	9. Offenses by Aliens	N
2. Trade Deals	N	6. Medical Marijuana	Y	10. Troops in Iraq	Y
3. Export-Import Bank	Y	7. Sanctuary Cities	N	11. Homeland Security $$	Y
4. Debt Ceiling Increase	Y	8. Armor-piercing Bullets	N	12. Trade Adjustment aid	Y

Election Results

Election	Name (Party)	Vote (%)	Cand. Spent	Ind. Exp. Support	Ind. Exp. Oppose
2016 General	Richard Nolan (D)	179,098 (50%)	$2,819,971	$1,662,861	$7,859,380
	Stewart Mills (R)	177,089 (50%)	$3,575,337	$45,650	$7,708,151
2016 Primary	Richard Nolan (D)	(100%)			

Prior winning percentages: 2014 (49%), 2012 (54%), 1978 (55%), 1976 (60%), 1974 (55%)

Democrat Rick Nolan returned to the House in 2013 after an unusual 32-year absence. When he quit in 1981, Nolan told *The Washington Post*, "Congress is relatively impotent to make the changes the country needs." But he returned, a full generation later, confident that he could get things done in a district that had limited overlap with his old one. He is the only surviving member of the 1974 freshman class, though others had much longer and more influential careers during his lengthy break.

Nolan grew up as the middle of three children in the old railroad town of Brainerd, Minnesota. When he was a teenager, his aunt, Eleanor Nolan, was appointed Minnesota's first female district judge. He calls her his biggest political influence growing up. He got his bachelor's degree at the University of Minnesota, and did graduate study in public policy at the University of Maryland and later in education at St. Cloud State University. He campaigned for antiwar candidate Eugene McCarthy in the 1968 presidential race before serving two terms in the Minnesota House and later was an aide to Sen. Walter Mondale.

In 1974, Nolan was elected to the House from southwest Minnesota, and compiled a liberal voting record. He made his mark in 1979 when he traveled to Cuba to secure the release of American prisoners. Nolan and Cuban leader Fidel Castro bonded over fishing, and Castro - after agreeing to the prisoners' release - extended an invitation for him to return for some deep-sea angling. Nolan battled what he saw as the federal government's favoritism of large farms and pushed legislation for education programs, equipment loans and tax-code changes to benefit small farmers.

Frustrated with his party's leadership, Nolan broke ranks and joined five House colleagues to lobby Sen. Edward Kennedy of Massachusetts to challenge Jimmy Carter for the 1980 Democratic nomination for president. He left Congress, calling himself a "liberal idealist unhappily turned wiser and more realistic," and returned to Minnesota.

When the Minnesota World Trade Center Corp., or WTC, launched in 1983, Nolan was appointed as an unpaid chairman by then-Democratic Gov. Rudy Perpich, and in 1987 he went on the payroll as the organization's president. Nolan claims to have created 326,000 Minnesota jobs through his work at the organization, a public-private initiative to help Minnesota businesses expand into international markets. His Republican foes criticized his $70,000 salary, which they considered high for a civil servant at the time, and the budget deficits the company ran up. In 1994, Nolan became president of Emily Forest Products, a sawmill and pallet manufacturer. He is an avid hunter, fisherman and farmer; he harvests wild rice and makes his own maple syrup.

The lack of local jobs, he says, inspired him to return to Washington at age 69 to push for small business tax breaks and infrastructure spending. In 2012, national Democrats targeted tea party-backed freshman Republican Chip Cravaack, who scored a big upset in 2010 by beating 18-term Rep. Jim Oberstar, then chairman of the Transportation and Infrastructure Committee. Nolan, who first entered the

House with Oberstar in the huge Democratic class of "Watergate babies," beat two other candidates in the Democratic primary with 38 percent of the vote, setting up a confrontation with Cravaack in the fall.

Cravaack dismissed Nolan as "a big-government, more-taxes, more-spending, more-regulation kind of guy." Nolan played up his support for small business and blasted Cravaack for backing House Budget Committee Chairman Paul Ryan's plans to introduce vouchers into Medicare. Cravaack outspent Nolan, $2.4 million to $1.2 million. Outside spending on the contest totaled more than $8 million, which was closely divided between the two sides. Nolan won 54%-46%.

On a local conflict with national implications, Nolan strongly opposed a bill filed by fellow Minnesota Democratic Rep. Betty McCollum that would limit mining in the watershed of the Boundary Waters, which is in Nolan's district. "This bill is a duplicative, overlapping regulatory scheme designed to prohibit mining on the Iron Range," he objected. After the Forest Service during the final days of the Obama administration launched a review that could lead to a 20-year ban on mining in the watershed, Nolan pleaded for a reversal from the new Trump administration - over the objections of McCollum. "Denying any business activity before you know what it is – and what kind of pollution abatement technology they will use or how effective it will be – lacks common sense and subverts the good, thorough and elaborate environmental review process we have in place," Nolan said. On the Agriculture Committee, he was the senior Democrat on the General Farm Commodities and Risk Management Subcommittee.

Reminiscing with constituents about how Congress had changed between his two stints, Nolan said he was frustrated by repeated votes to repeal the Affordable Care Act, without having the opportunity to discuss the law in more detail. A proponent of single-payer health care, he conceded that the 2010 law had "plenty of room for improvement." Republican attacks on environmental regulation were also frustrating, he said, because of the huge improvements during the previous 40 years in air pollution, water pollution and chemical waste. Nolan found that the news media overstated the extent of gridlock in Congress. "I've had a Republican partner on everything I have done," he said, according to the *Chisago County Press*.

Some Democratic campaign insiders have criticized Nolan for his unwillingness to adjust to modern campaign realities, including the need for constant fundraising. "Rick is an old-school politician and doesn't believe in a lot of the things that members of Congress have to do in tight districts," a Minnesota Democratic strategist told *Roll Call*, a Capitol Hill newspaper, during the 2014 campaign. With his objections to modern campaign techniques, Nolan somewhat concedes the point. "Money has become a terribly corruptive influence in our politics," he said, while explaining his proposed "We The People" constitutional amendment that would eliminate First Amendment speech protections for corporations.

Nolan's reelection campaigns have been very competitive. In each case, his Republican opponent was Stewart Mills, a wealthy heir and executive of his family's Mills Fleet Farms stores. With his good looks and long blond hair, Republicans called their candidate the "Brad Pitt of the GOP." In 2014, each candidate spent about $2 million, and outside groups this time spent more than $10 million on the contest. Nolan won, 48.5%-47.1%, a margin of 3,732 votes. Nolan led by about 15,000 votes in St. Louis County, which cast about 30 percent of the votes, while Mills led in the remainder of the district by 11,500 votes. Mills returned two years later, clean-shaven and with an apparent boost from local support for Republican presidential nominee Donald Trump. The candidates and the parties roughly split the astounding total of more than $20 million in this low-cost district. The outcome grew even closer. Nolan won by 2,009 votes. With close to a 50 percent increase in overall turnout, he took St. Louis County by more than 26,000 votes.

Following the election, Nolan considered but rejected a bid in 2018 for the open governor's seat.

Nolan and his district likely will remain high on the Republicans' target list.

Northeastern Minnesota: Duluth, Northern Twin Cities

Population		**Race and Ethnicity**		**Income**	
Total	662,686	White	92.3%	Median Income	$50,464 (250 out of 435)
Land area	27,908	Black	1.0%		
Pop/ sq mi	23.7	Latino	1.5%		
Born in state	79.0%	Asian	0.7%	Under $50,000	49.4%
		Two races	2.0%	$50,000-$99,999	33.5%
Age Groups		Other	2.5%	$100,000-$199,999	14.7%
Under 18	21.5%			$200,000 or more	2.2%
18-34	19.9%	**Education**		Poverty Rate	13.0%
35-64	40.5%	H.S grad or less	41.50%		
Over 64	18.1%	Some college	24.80%	**Health Insurance**	
		College Degree, 4 yr	15.10%	With health insurance coverage	92.7%
Work		Post grad	7.10%		
White Collar	31.2%				
Sales and Service	43.1%	**Military**		**Public Assistance**	
Blue Collar	25.7%	Veteran	11.0%	Cash public assistance income	3.8%
Government	14.8%	Active Duty	0.1%		
				Food stamp/SNAP benefits	10.4%

Voter Turnout			
2015 Total Citizens 18+	515,501	2016 House Turnout as % CVAP	69%
2016 House turnout	356,979	2014 House Turnout as % CVAP	52%

2012 Presidential Vote		
Barack Obama	186,761	(52%)
Mitt Romney	166,977	(46%)

2016 Presidential Vote		
Donald Trump	194,779	(54%)
Hillary Clinton	138,665	(38%)
Gary Johnson	12,618	(4%)

Cook Partisan Voting Index: R+4

In the 1860s, prospectors in Minnesota's Arrowhead region, northwest of Lake Superior in the low hills of the Mesabi Range, happened upon one of the nation's largest veins of iron ore. They moved on, looking for gold. But in the 1880s, Duluth banker George Stone and Philadelphia financier Charlemagne Tower started mining the Iron Range. Rail lines were built from the Range south to the port of Duluth, where the average low temperature is below freezing six months of the year. Duluth, with its signature aerial lift bridge traversing its shipping channel, is nestled on dramatic bluffs over the always-cold and often frozen waters of Lake Superior - one of the most beautiful settings for a city in North America, though also one of the most isolated. Duluth was a grain shipping rival of Chicago and the premier iron ore port. Its city plan was drawn up by architect Daniel Burnham, who also planned Chicago, and its splendid turn-of-the-century buildings still celebrate the triumph of technology and civilization over wilderness and the elements. Millions of tons of ore have been dug out of the Range and loaded into railcars for the ride to Duluth, and into Great Lakes freighters for shipment to Chicago, Gary, Detroit, Cleveland, Pittsburgh and Buffalo.

For most of the 20th century, about 100,000 people lived on the Iron Range and another 100,000 in Duluth, most of them descendants of America's 1880-1924 wave of immigration: Italians, Poles, Serbs, Croats, Swedes, Finns and Eastern European Jews. In this punishing environment, they built solid houses with reliable central heating, and wore layers of warm clothing to survive the brutal winter. The work was hard, the hours long and the pay low. The churches, a separate one for each ethnic group, were the main community institutions. Living conditions improved vastly in the booming growth after World War II. But periods of economic distress persisted. More efficient iron mines and steel mills needed fewer workers. Employment is well below its 1970s peak.

The new airport terminal in Duluth was dedicated in October 2015 in honor of former local Democratic Rep. Jim Oberstar, who served 36 years and chaired the Transportation and Infrastructure Committee, from which he steered much of the financing for the project. The terminal has spurred economic development, including resorts for adventure tourists. The new sports competition included the winter ultra-marathon, a 135-mile endurance contest of walking, running, cycling and skiing from International Falls to Tower. Revenue from a tourism tax in hotels and restaurants doubled in the decade ending in 2016. The port still ships large quantities of grain, and in the late 1990s, a new taconite and steelmaking factory was built - the first big new plant in more than 20 years. Rising commodity prices brought new mining companies to the area to explore the possible extraction of copper, nickel and other nonferrous metals.

The 8th Congressional District of Minnesota includes Duluth and the Iron Range, plus much of the state's north woods and lake country to the west and south. Duluth-based St. Louis County is the largest in the district, with about 30 percent of the voters. The population of about 200,000 in the county and 86,000 in Duluth has remained flat for the past quarter century. The district extends south to the boundaries of the Twin Cities metro area, to Isanti and Chisago counties, where young families are building new homes in pleasant old lakeside towns. Those fast-growing exurban and largely Republican counties have become an increasingly dominant part of the district, even as the Duluth area remains Democratic. From 1946 through 2008, the district elected only two congressmen, both Democrats. The second one had worked for the first. Although Duluth and the Iron Range remain Democratic, issues like gun control and environmental regulation have sometimes moved those areas toward the Republicans. The 8th has leaned Democratic, but only marginally. As with the two other rural districts in Minnesota that surround the Twin Cities metro area on three sides, the 2016 election brought a huge shift. In a district that President Barack Obama in 2012 took, 52%-46%, Donald Trump won by a 54%-38% margin.

★ MISSISSIPPI ★

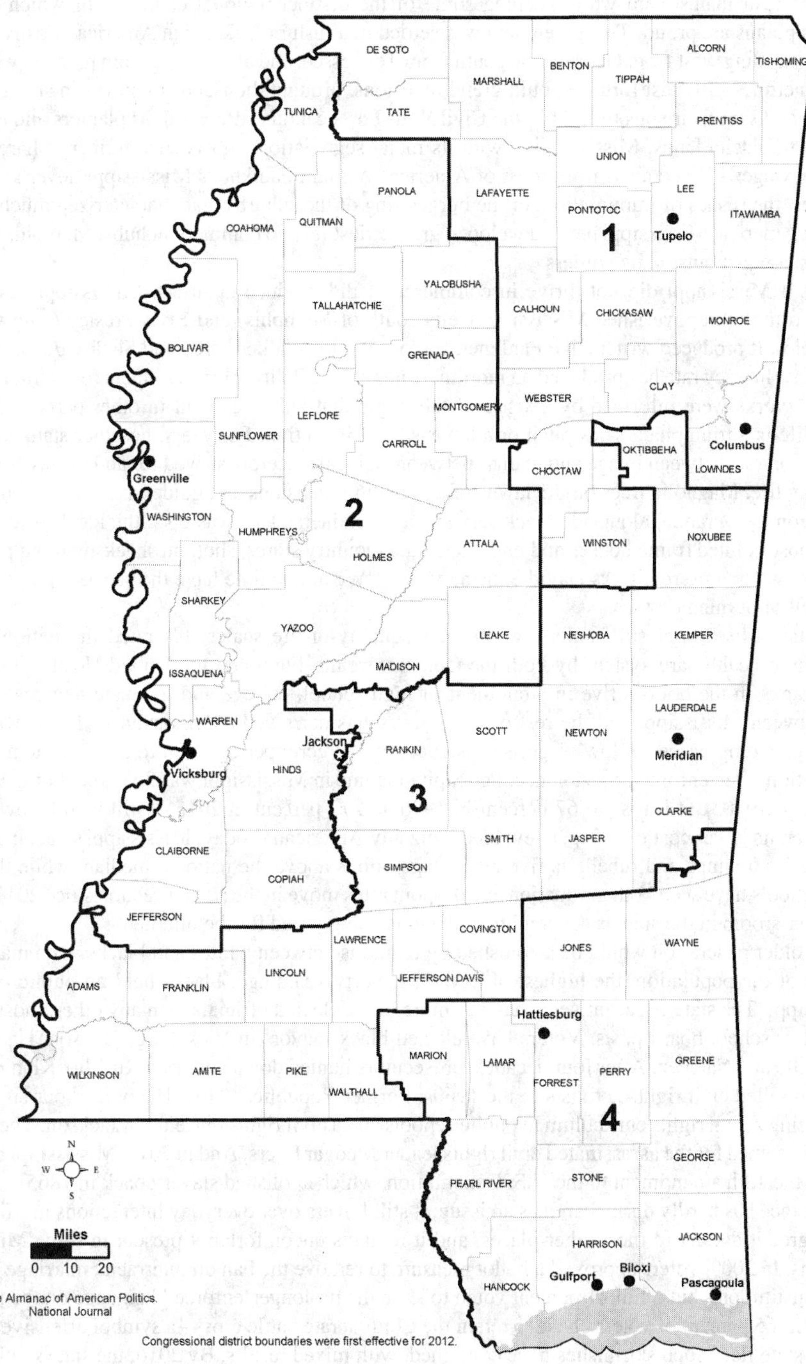

Tragedy and pride: These are two strains that run through Mississippi's history and through Mississippi today. The state has long lagged behind almost all others in just about every leading indicator. But now, half a century after the success of the civil rights movement, it has in many ways entered the American mainstream while keeping some of the distinct regional character of which so many Mississippians are proud. This green land was settled in a rush in Jacksonian America, mostly by small farmers heading west from Georgia and south from Tennessee, and also by a few big planters who made, and sometimes lost, vast fortunes, built grand mansions, brought thousands of slaves in ship holds and coffles, and sent their sons to fight in the Civil War. For a century afterward, as planters and engineers drained the Delta lands, Mississippi -- with its racial segregation, subsistence farmers, sharecroppers and low wages -- lived apart from most of America. William Faulkner's Mississippi never knew giant factories, the rushes of immigration, or the burgeoning of the suburbs that characterized much of 20th-century America. Mississippi never developed great cities: Its two commercial hubs, Memphis and New Orleans, are just outside its borders.

But if Mississippi did not thrive in commerce, it did produce great art. Mississippi gave us the blues (from the impoverished Mississippi Delta south of Memphis) and Elvis Presley (who was born in Tupelo). It produced writers like Faulkner, Eudora Welty, Walker Percy and Shelby Foote. The state with a low literacy rate has produced an inordinate number of Pulitzer Prize winners for literature. These authors' works were informed by a sense of the tragic that is less evident in other parts of America, where life is a triumphant sales pitch or a labor-saving invention. For years, no other state had such a painful contrast between image and reality, between an ideal sincerely strived for and the tawdry facts of everyday life. Magnolia trees on the lawns of antebellum mansions and golden-haired women in white dresses on the veranda, alongside black servants and retainers: This was once the ideal. And behind it stood loose-jointed frame houses and unpainted back-country stores, shotgun shacks without plumbing, and poor white crossroads. As David Sansing wrote, "We at one time have the scent of magnolias and the smell of burning crosses."

Today, Mississippi still ranks low on many quality-of-life scales. It's rated the nation's worst-performing health care system by both the Commonwealth Fund and the United Health Foundation, and it ranks in the bottom five in attainment of high school, college and graduate degrees. Still, the gulf between Mississippi and the rest of the country has narrowed enormously. In 1940, Mississippi had an economy based on low-wage, subsistence, or sharecropper agriculture and a system of racial segregation often enforced by violence. Per capita income in Mississippi was 36 percent of the national average in 1940. But it rose to 67 percent in 1990 and 73 percent in 2015 -- still well below average but, given its lower cost of living, a level recognizably American. Today, Mississippi's vaccination rate for measles, mumps and rubella is five percentage points above the national median, while the state's K-12 schools have seen both graduation and dropout rates move in the right direction since 2011. Nearly every classroom in the state is air-conditioned and is being wired for the internet.

An older generation would be astonished by relations between whites and blacks, who make up 38 percent of the population, the highest of any state. Forty years ago, blacks held no public offices in Mississippi. The state in recent years has had more black elected officials than any other, most of them in local or school board posts. Voters have elected black mayors in Vicksburg, Jackson, Hattiesburg, Greenville and Natchez. After four decades, prosecutors hunted down and tried Ku Klux Klan members who had killed civil rights activists in the 1960s. Former Republican Gov. Haley Barbour signed bills authorizing a civil rights curriculum in public schools and a civil rights museum in Jackson. The Jackson airport is named for the assassinated civil rights leader Medgar Evers. And in 2013, Mississippi belatedly ratified the 13th amendment to the U.S. Constitution, which abolished slavery back in 1865.

But race has hardly disappeared as an issue; it still hovers over everyday interactions in Mississippi to a degree it doesn't in most other places, and it remains uncomfortably present in some Mississippi elections. In 2000, voters approved a ballot measure to remove the ban on interracial marriage from the state constitution - but a full 41 percent voted to keep the no-longer-enforced language on the books. A year later, 65 percent of voters chose to retain the Confederate battle cross - a symbol offensive to many - in the state flag. Such skirmishes have continued, with mixed results. By 2016, the state's universities had all removed the flag from their campuses. But the same year, a federal judge dismissed a lawsuit that sought to have the Confederate emblem on the state flag declared unconstitutional, and the month after that, an effort to remove the Confederate design from the flag failed to gain enough signatures to make the ballot. Meanwhile, the same year, Republican Gov. Phil Bryant issued a proclamation designating April as Confederate Heritage Month -- without mentioning slavery.

Mississippi's economy once depended on cotton, but no longer; in the mid-20th century, mechanization spawned a mass migration of African Americans from Mississippi to northern industrial cities like Chicago, profoundly changing both. Manufacturing jobs have declined here as elsewhere in recent years, but northeast Mississippi around Tupelo remains the center of the nation's upholstered furniture industry and is the site of a $1.3 billion plant where workers began assembling Corollas in November 2011 after the state offered Toyota $296 million in incentives; in 2015, the plant built its 500,000th Corolla sedan. Growth has also been rapid around a Nissan auto plant that opened in 2003 in Canton, just north of Jackson. The company has invested more than $3 billion there; the state and local governments have given hundreds of millions of dollars in assistance and tax breaks. After little more than a decade, the automobile manufacturing and supply sector employs tens of thousands of (non-union) workers. Continental Tire is building a plant near Jackson, again with generous tax breaks provided. Growth is most rapid in DeSoto County, just south of Memphis, in Jackson and its suburbs in Rankin and Madison counties, and along the Gulf Coast and to the north around Hattiesburg.

The Gulf Coast has big military installations, with Air Force intelligence units and the Navy's Seabees, as well as the Stennis Space Center. The huge Ingalls shipyard is in Pascagoula, and many of the military's and CIA's unmanned aerial vehicles are built on the Gulf Coast or in Columbus. In the mid-1960s, the United States even conducted a pair of nuclear tests in salt domes 28 miles southwest of Hattiesburg, the only such blasts east of the Rockies. Then there is gambling. Mississippi approved it in 1990, and big companies have built more than two dozen casinos, in economically struggling Tunica County south of Memphis, on riverboats on the Mississippi River, and on the Gulf Coast. The coastal casinos have been more resilient, despite Hurricane Katrina, but they are threatened by the possible expansion of gambling in neighboring states. All told, gambling brings an estimated $2 billion a year in direct revenues, though the state has fallen from third to seventh nationally in casino gaming revenue since 2007.

Mississippi's economy has faced other travails over the last decade. The main force of Hurricane Katrina made landfall in Hancock County, where in 2005 it wiped out the towns of Waveland and Bay St. Louis. In a few hours, waves up to 55 feet high destroyed one-quarter of the structures in Biloxi and Gulfport; floodwaters swept 10 miles inland, and the storm ultimately killed 238 people in Mississippi. The congressional delegation, headed by Senate Appropriations Chairman Thad Cochran, delivered aid and Barbour administered grants and low-interest loans to home and business owners who suffered uninsured losses. More quickly than New Orleans, Mississippi set about rebuilding its coast, though eight years later almost $1 billion in federal recovery money still hadn't been spent and in 2016 the federal government suspended reimbursement of almost $30 million of recovery funds due to insufficient state oversight. During the Great Recession, unemployment peaked at 10.8 percent; by late 2016, it had fallen to 5.6 percent, but that was still above the national average. Further disaster struck with major floods in 2011 and a massive tornado outbreak in 2014 that killed 14 and destroyed hundreds of structures. Since 2010, the population has increased by less than 1 percent, and it actually shrunk slightly from 2014 to 2015 and from 2015 to 2016.

Once almost unanimously Democratic but ready to support segregationist presidential candidates like Strom Thurmond in 1948 and George Wallace in 1968, Mississippi is now reliably Republican. It was Richard Nixon's No. 1 state in 1972, Ronald Reagan gave a high-profile speech at the Neshoba County Fair in 1980, and it has been solidly Republican in presidential elections starting in 1980. Republicans have held both U.S. Senate seats since John Stennis retired in 1988. On the federal level, Democrats now have only the black-majority district the party has held since 1986 and which Rep. Bennie Thompson has represented since 1993; it includes the Delta and much of metro Jackson. Even Democrats as conservative Gene Taylor, who held the Gulf Coast House district from 1989 to 2010, are out of luck. (In 2014, Taylor switched to the GOP and lost in a primary.) Among the 50 states, Gallup found, Mississippi is tilted most heavily conservative.

A turning point in the state's shift from Democratic to Republican leadership came in 2003, when Haley Barbour, emphasizing his Yazoo City roots over his decades as a Washington powerbroker, unseated Democratic Gov. Ronnie Musgrove. Barbour was re-elected 58%-42% in 2007, and by 2011, both chambers of the legislature had switched from Democratic to Republican control. That same year,

Lt. Gov. Phil Bryant beat Hattiesburg Mayor Johnny DuPree, the first black Democratic gubernatorial nominee, 61%-39%, and Republicans won all statewide offices except attorney general. Bryant easily won reelection in 2015; the strongest potential Democratic opponents, Attorney General Jim Hood and Public Service Commissioner Brandon Presley, passed on running against him.

Voting in Mississippi runs along racial lines, with whites heavily Republican in most contests and blacks heavily Democratic. (At 3 percent, Mississippi has the smallest percentage of Hispanics in the South.) Perhaps spurred by memories of the franchise denied, black turnout percentages in Mississippi have exceeded white turnout in some recent elections. Black voters also showed their muscle in the hard-fought Senate primary runoff contest between Cochran and tea party-aligned Chris McDaniel in 2014, arguably carrying the aging and comparatively moderate senator to a seventh term. And on some issues, there is consensus. In a state with the highest percentage of "very religious" residents - almost 61 percent - Mississippians in 2004 voted by 86 percent to ban same-sex marriage, and abortion is widely opposed by blacks and whites alike.

Mississippi has often sought to enact a cutting-edge conservative agenda. In 2016, Bryant signed legislation to allow guns to be carried in belt and shoulder holsters without a permit, and to let churches allow certain parishioners to carry concealed weapons on their premises. That same year, Bryant signed a law to allow businesses to refuse services to same-sex couples. The courts, however, haven't always agreed. A federal judge ruled the LGBT law unconstitutional, and judicial decisions have kept open the one abortion clinic in the state despite state laws that had tightened regulatory requirements in a way that threatened to close it.

In the 2016 campaign, Mississippi was a key element of Hillary Clinton's minority-backed firewall strategy to defeat Democratic primary challenger Bernie Sanders; she won the Mississippi primary, 83%-17%. And Donald Trump campaigned in the state as late as the last week of August. But as usual, Mississippi was not considered a serious battleground state in the general election. Trump ended up winning by 18 points – seven points better than Mitt Romney's margin in 2012. : Both candidates actually collected fewer votes compared with their party's nominees in 2012 – 10,000 fewer votes for Trump and 78,000 fewer for Clinton, with Clinton's drop likely linked to the absence of Obama, an African American, on the ballot. The only bits of good news for Democrats were the narrow victory by Jim Kitchens, the Democratic-favored candidate in a nonpartisan state Supreme Court race, and the election of another Democrat, Cecil Brown, to the Public Service Commission. Overall, though, Democrats can continue to expect an extraordinarily uphill battle in Mississippi, as long as voters keep dividing decisively along racial lines.

Population		**Race and Ethnicity**		**Income**	
Total	2,988,081	White	57.4%	Median Income	$39,665 (50 out of 50)
Land area	46,923	Black	37.2%		
Pop/ sq mi	63.7	Latino	2.9%	Under $50,000	59.5%
Born in state	71.5%	Asian	1.0%	$50,000-$99,999	27.0%
		Two races	1.0%	$100,000-$199,999	11.3%
Age Groups		Other	10.4%	$200,000 or more	2.2%
Under 18	24.6%			Poverty Rate	22.5%
18-34	23.4%	**Education**			
35-64	38.2%	H.S grad or less	47.9%	**Health Insurance**	
Over 64	13.9%	Some college	31.4%	With health insurance coverage	84.2%
		College Degree, 4 yr	12.9%		
Work		Post grad	7.7%		
White Collar	31.1%			**Public Assistance**	
Sales and Service	41.4%	**Military**		Cash public assistance income	2.8%
Blue Collar	27.5%	Veteran	8.2%		
Government	18.5%	Active Duty	0.5%	Food stamp/SNAP benefits	18.3%

Voter Turnout			
2015 Total Citizens 18+	2,210,424	2016 Pres Turnout as % CVAP	55%
2016 Pres Votes	1,209,357	2012 Pres Turnout as % CVAP	60%

Legislature	
Senate:	20D, 32R
House:	48D, 74R

Presidential Politics

2016 Democratic Primary		
Hillary Clinton (D)	187,334	(82%)
Bernie Sanders (D)	37,748	(17%)
2016 Republican Primary		
Donald Trump (R)	196,659	(47%)
Ted Cruz (R)	150,364	(36%)
John Kasich (R)	36,795	(9%)
Marco Rubio (R)	21,885	(5%)

2016 Presidential Vote		
Donald Trump (R)	700,714	(58%)
Hillary Clinton (D)	485,131	(40%)
2012 Presidential Vote		
Mitt Romney (R)	710,746	(55%)
Barack Obama (D)	562,949	(44%)

Mississippi voted for Jimmy Carter in 1976 and came within 12,000 votes of doing so again in 1980. But starting in 1984, Democratic presidential nominees have won between only 37 and 44 percent here. Presidential voting is racially polarized. The state's Delta region with its heavy African-American population hugs the Mississippi River and votes Democratic. The rest of the state stretching from Tupelo in the north, to the suburban Jackson counties of Madison and Ranking to Biloxi on the Gulf Coast, votes Republican. While some pre-election polls in 2016 suggested the state might be competitive, Mississippi followed its historical norm and Donald Trump defeated Hillary Clinton 58%-40%. One of Trump's more enthusiastic backers and surrogates, GOP Gov. Phil Bryant, shared the Republican nominee's views on the political process, telling radio talk show host Paul Gallo before November, "The election is rigged. Any Republican has to have an overwhelming majority of the vote [to prevail]."

Mississippi has held a presidential primary in the second week of March since 1988, a surprising consistency given the jockeying for position that many states have engaged in over that time. The March 8 GOP contest saw a record turnout of 416,270 votes, with Trump defeating Texas Sen. Ted Cruz, 47%-36%. Ohio Gov. John Kasich finished a distant third. Trump won 75 of the state's 82 counties to seven for Cruz. On the Democratic side, African Americans accounted for more than 70 percent of the primary electorate, and their overwhelming support gave Clinton an 83%-17% victory. In the 2nd and 3rd districts, Sanders didn't break the 15 percent threshold needed to qualify for convention delegates. Democratic turnout was 227,164, barely half of the 434,000-plus record Democratic turnout in 2008.

Congressional Districts

115th Congress Lineup	3R 1D	114th Congress Lineup	3R 1D

Redistricting in Mississippi following the 2010 census was relatively simple, though with an unusual procedural twist. The state retained its four seats and after the 2010 wave election, Republicans held all three white-majority districts while Democrat Bennie Thompson held the black-majority 2nd District. Republicans held the governorship and state Senate, but some were fearful that the Obama Justice Department would deny preclearance to any map that didn't create a second African-American seat. So they filed suit asking federal judges to step in, because any map drawn by a federal court doesn't need to win Justice Department pre-approval.

The end-around worked. A three-judge federal panel gave the legislature until December 2011 to draw its own map. When the legislature failed to meet its deadline, the court put its own proposal into place. The map made only minor changes, shifting racially mixed Grenada, Panola and Yalobusha counties from the northeastern 1st District, which contains fast-growing DeSoto County in the Memphis suburbs, to the 2nd District, which was underpopulated by 73,000 residents. The African-American share of the Delta 2nd ticked down only two percentage points, from 66 percent to 64 percent, ensuring Thompson's continued safety. The three other districts range from 23 percent to 35 percent black. Elsewhere, the courts simply smoothed out existing boundaries, reducing the number of counties split from eight to four statewide.

Governor

Phil Bryant (R)

Elected 2011, term expires 2020, 2nd term; b. Dec. 9, 1954, Moorhead, MS; U. of Southern MS, B.S. 1977, MS Col., M.S. 1988; Methodist; Married (Deborah); 2 children.

Elected Office: MS House, 1991-1996; State Auditor, 1999-2008; MS Lt. Governor, 2008-2011.

Professional Career: Deputy Sheriff, Hinds County Sheriff's Office, 1976-1981; Insurance investigator, 1981-91; State auditor appointee, 1996-1999.

Office: PO Box 139, Jackson, 39205; 601-359-3150; Fax: 601-359-3741; Website: governorbryant.ms.gov.

Election Results

Election	Name (Party)	Vote (%)
2015 General	Phil Bryant (R)	476,697 (66%)
	Robert Gray (D)	231,643 (32%)
2015 Primary	Phil Bryant (R)	254,779 (92%)
	Mitch Young (R)	22,628 (8%)

Prior winning percentage: 2011 (61%)

Mississippi's Gov. Phil Bryant, elected in 2011 and reelected four years later, is a Republican who succeeded term-limited Haley Barbour. Bryant had served as lieutenant governor under Barbour, and he has pleased conservatives with his willingness to go even further to the right than his patrician predecessor on social issues.

Bryant was born in Moorhead in the Mississippi Delta. His father was a diesel mechanic and his mother a homemaker. His family eventually relocated to South Jackson, where Bryant finished high school. He worked in a tire store to earn extra money and decided that he needed more schooling. "Changing tires five-and-a-half days a week made me decide I would check out community college," Bryant told the Biloxi-based *Sun Herald*. He later earned a bachelor's degree in criminal justice from the University of Southern Mississippi. Bryant worked for the local police as a deputy sheriff and later spent time in the private sector as an insurance investigator.

Bryant first ran for office in 1991, winning a state House seat representing Rankin County. In 1996, he was appointed state auditor by Republican Gov. Kirk Fordice. Bryant was elected to two full terms as auditor in 1999 and 2003 before being elected on the Barbour ticket as lieutenant governor in 2007. He became a favorite of tea party groups for his tough stance on illegal immigration. Bryant presided over the state Senate, which put him in the middle of some heated legislative battles, including redistricting in 2011. With Barbour term-limited, Bryant sought to succeed him. Despite his ties to the popular incumbent, Bryant had to fight off four other candidates in the Republican primary. He won with 59 percent, exuding more of a common touch than Barbour but less national influence. In the general election, Bryant faced Democrat Johnny DuPree, mayor of Hattiesburg and the state's first African-American gubernatorial nominee. The campaign was relatively low-key and congenial, but Bryant won easily, 61%-39%.

As governor, Bryant quickly distanced himself from Barbour's controversial decision, shortly before leaving office, to pardon more than 200 inmates, including more than 20 convicted of murder, manslaughter or homicide. Bryant's state budget proposal called for cutting his own office expenses, and he later sold the state jet, which Barbour had used extensively, for $2 million (though he kept a prop plane). On social issues, he signed into law a bill requiring all physicians at abortion clinics to be board-certified gynecologists and to have admitting privileges at a local hospital, an effort widely perceived as being aimed at shutting down the state's only remaining clinic. (The courts later moved to keep the clinic open.) Amid unemployment rates persistently above the national average, Bryant was a tireless promoter of economic development, and he used conservative talk radio to promote his agenda.

On health care, Bryant squabbled for months with state Insurance Commissioner Mike Chaney over whether to establish an insurance exchange under the Affordable Care Act, but ultimately, Bryant's position - that the state not set up an exchange - won out. Then, after the Supreme Court allowed states to opt out of the law's Medicaid expansion provision, Bryant pushed passionately against expanding Medicaid in Mississippi, despite the state's 50th-place ranking for health in several national studies and the possibility that 137,800 uninsured residents – many of them able-bodied adults with no children -- could have received Medicaid coverage, according to Kaiser Family Foundation estimates.

In 2014, Bryant signed three bills curbing organized labor, which was already weak in the state. "Just to be blunt about it: We just don't want unions involved in our businesses or our public sector," Bryant said upon signing the bills. He also signed a bill to allow residents to carry concealed guns without a license. On criminal justice, he signed a bill requiring convicts to serve at least 50 percent of their sentence, and at least 25 percent for those convicted of a nonviolent offense - a less stringent requirement than previously, and with added flexibility for judges to impose sentences that don't include incarceration. The aim was to reduce the cost of a corrections budget that had been rapidly expanding.

In 2015, Bryant burnished his conservative credentials, criticizing the federal government for its "troubling" decision to send roughly 200 of the 30,000 unaccompanied children who crossed the U.S.-Mexico border to family members or guardians in Mississippi, and vetoing a bill critical of Common Core educational standards because it wasn't tough enough. Bryant was already coasting to a reelection victory in 2015 when the Democratic primary produced a stunner – Robert Gray, a truck driver and political novice who had barely campaigned, managed to beat the establishment-backed candidate, trial lawyer Vicki Slater, by 20 points. In November, Bryant won, 67%-32%, in a race mostly overshadowed by the battle over a ballot measure that would have stiffened enforcement of a law that required higher education funding. The measure failed.

After winning reelection, Bryant called for tax cuts, expanded school choice and infrastructure spending. Within months, he signed a tax cut totaling $415 million over 12 years, including a phase-out of the state's corporate franchise tax, an increase to the threshold for paying income taxes, and cuts to self-employment taxes. He also pursued a solidly conservative social agenda, including a law allowing businesses to deny services to LGBT couples that had drawn objections from some business leaders; in October 2016, a federal court found the law unconstitutional. Meanwhile, Bryant said he would "do everything humanly possible to stop any plans from the Obama administration to put Syrian refugees in Mississippi," and he built ties to Donald Trump. Bryant was one of a handful of sitting governors to campaign for Trump and he raised money for the GOP nominee in Mississippi.

As Trump was settling in at the White House, Bryant kicked off 2017 by instituting his fourth round of budget cuts or withdrawals from the state's "rainy day" fund in two years. He also had to grapple with rising costs for Medicaid. The fiscal pressures led Bryant to mull the possibility of starting a state lottery. He pledged to pursue tougher penalties for attacks on law enforcement and said that fixing the state's troubled foster care system would be a top priority. Despite the challenges, Bryant seemed to be in a strong position going into his final three years in office.

Senior Senator

Thad Cochran (R)

Elected 1978, term expires 2020, 7th term; b. Dec 07, 1937, Pontotoc; Trinity College, University of Dublin (Ireland), Att.; University of Minnesota, B.A.; University of Mississippi School of Law, J.D.; U.S. Navy School of Justice (RI); Baptist; Married (Kay Webber); 2 children; 3 grandchildren.

Military Career: U.S. Navy, 1959-1961.

Elected Office: U.S. House, 1973-1978.

Professional Career: Practicing attorney, Watkins & Eager, 1965-1972.

DC Office: 113 DSOB 20510, 202-224-5054, Fax: 202-224-5321, cochran.senate.gov.

State Offices: Gulfport, 228-867-9710; Jackson, 601-965-4459; Oxford, 662-236-1018.

Committees: *Agriculture, Nutrition & Forestry*: Commodities, Risk Management & Trade, Conservation, Forestry & Natural Resources, Rural Development & Energy. *Appropriations (Chmn)*: Agriculture, Rural Development, FDA & Related Agencies, Commerce, Justice, Science & Related Agencies, Department of Defense (Chmn), Department of Homeland Security, Department of the Interior, Environment & Related Agencies, DOL, HHS & Education & Related Agencies, Energy & Water Development, Financial Services & General Government, Legislative Branch, Military Construction & Veteran Affairs & Related Agencies, State, Foreign Operations & Related Programs, Transportation, HUD & Related Agencies. *Rules & Administration*.

Group Ratings

	ADA	ACLU	AFL-CIO	LCV	ITI	COC	HAFA	ACU	CFG	FRC
2016	-	11%	-	24%	80%	100%	30%	60%	56%	0%
2015	5%	C	14%	0%	C	93%	C	58%	54%	100%

Almanac Ratings 2015

	Economy	Social	Foreign	Composite
Liberal	48%	9%	19%	25%
Conservative	52%	91%	82%	75%

Key Votes of the 114th Congress

1. Keystone pipeline	Y	5. National Security Data	N	9. Gun Sales Checks	N
2. Export-Import Bank	N	6. Iran Nuclear Deal	Y	10. Sanctuary Cities	Y
3. Debt Ceiling Increase	Y	7. Puerto Rico Debt	Y	11. Planned Parenthood	Y
4. Homeland Security $$	Y	8. Loretta Lynch A.G	Y	12. Trade deals	Y

Election Results

Election	Name (Party)	Vote (%)	Cand. Spent	Ind. Exp. Support	Ind. Exp. Oppose
2014 General	Thad Cochran (R)	378,481 (60%)	$7,868,305	$2,435,395	$3,779,663
	Travis Childers (D)	239,439 (38%)	$668,975	$20,305	
	Shawn O'Hara (Ref)	13,938 (2%)			
2014 Primary Run Off	Thad Cochran (R)	194,932 (51%)			
	Chris McDaniel (R)	187,265 (49%)			
2014 Primary	Chris McDaniel (R)	157,733 (50%)			
	Thad Cochran (R)	156,315 (49%)			

Prior winning percentages: 2008 (61%), 2002 (85%), 1996 (71%), 1990 (100%), 1984 (39%), 1978 (45%), House: 1976 (76%), 1974 (70%), 1972 (48%)

Republican Thad Cochran, Mississippi's senior senator, was elected in 1972 to the House and in 1978 to the Senate, where he sits at Jefferson Davis's old desk. He personifies an all-but-vanished breed of Southern Republicans-amiable to all, conservative but not rigidly so, a devoted institutionalist, and a proficient procurer of funding for his poor, rural state. With the help of the national GOP establishment and his state's black voters, he escaped an embarrassing defeat in a 2014 primary runoff. He returned the next year as chairman of the Appropriations Committee. The panel struggled to assert its customary influence, as key spending decisions were made elsewhere.

Cochran grew up in small towns in northern Mississippi, the son of a principal and a mathematics teacher. Cochran was athletic in high school, lettering in football, basketball, and baseball. He was also valedictorian of his senior class and a talented musician; he sometimes relaxes by playing a baby grand piano in his Senate office. Cochran excelled academically at Ole Miss; he was also a cheerleader, which was not uncommon for men at that time and was considered an honor. (Former Mississippi Sen. Trent Lott was one as well.) Cochran went on to get a law degree from Ole Miss, served in the Navy, spent a year abroad, and then practiced law in Jackson.

In 1968, he worked on the Nixon-Agnew presidential campaign in Mississippi, where Richard Nixon ran third. Four years later, when President Nixon was sweeping Mississippi, Cochran ran for Congress and was elected from the Jackson-area district with a plurality against a white Democrat and a black independent. When segregationist Sen. James Eastland, a Democrat and long-time chairman of the

Judiciary Committee, retired, Cochran jumped into the race and again won with a plurality over a white Democrat and a black independent.

In the House and in the Senate, Cochran managed for years to amass a generally conservative record with little controversy or acrimony. His courtly demeanor, his refusal to engage in racial politics, and his Republican Party label-in a state where most whites have been voting Republican for president for four decades-have made him acceptable to voters at home. Until 2014, his toughest race came in 1984, when he was opposed by popular former Democratic Gov. William Winter. Winter could make a case for himself, but not against Cochran. Cochran outraised him $2.7 million to $738,000, and won 61%-39%.

Cochran competed for years with Lott to climb the leadership ladder, and he usually lost. In 1990, Cochran was elected as chairman of the Senate Republican Conference, the No. 3 position. Although he had less seniority, Lott set his sights higher and challenged Wyoming's Alan Simpson for majority whip, the No. 2 position. Cochran pointedly endorsed Simpson, but Lott won anyway, with the support of junior Senate conservatives, and leapfrogged over Cochran. Then in 1996, when Kansas Republican Bob Dole stepped down as Majority Leader and ran for president, Cochran and Lott both entered the race. Lott wrapped up the vote quickly. Cochran stayed in the contest and lost, 44-8.

Cochran played an important role in shaping very different farm bills. In 1996, he supported the Republican initiative to phase out most crop subsidies, although he insisted on maintaining the cotton marketing loan plan that he had written. In 2002, he helped to revive annual crop payments and to vastly increase the Conservation Reserve Program. In 2005, Cochran defeated on the Senate floor Iowa Republican Charles Grassley's move to cap subsidies to individual farmers at $250,000. And in 2008, he supported the farm bill that passed over the veto of President George W. Bush, who said the bill was too costly and did not go far enough to curb subsidies.

Cochran has made his biggest mark on the Appropriations Committee. He regularly incensed reformers with his additions to spending bills for Mississippi projects. He takes a particular interest in his state universities' research needs and casts a wide net. He first chaired the panel from 2005 to 2007, when Republicans controlled the Senate. At the time, Cochran promised to get appropriations bills passed on time, rather than rolling multiple bills into large "omnibus" measures, which had become the practice as Congress was unable to agree on individual spending bills. Earmarks and discretionary spending became major issues.

When Hurricane Katrina struck in August 2005, causing massive damage in Mississippi, keeping tight controls on spending suddenly was no longer the chairman's prime concern. Cochran viewed the devastation by helicopter two days later, and then persuaded the Senate to immediately vote for $10.5 billion in disaster relief. A week later, he persuaded it to vote for $52 billion more. In late October, when Bush called for an additional $17 billion. Cochran, working closely with Republican Gov. Haley Barbour, pushed for $35 billion, with community development block grants (CDBG) available for homeowners and businesses with uninsured losses. This was a new policy. Congress passed a $29 billion bill, with Mississippi receiving $5 billion of the $11.5 billion CDBG funds.

The following year brought more spending vagaries, with Bush's request for sizable additional money for the war in Iraq. The president's request was sweetened with nearly $20 billion in additional funds for hurricane recovery. Cochran sought some controversial provisions: $700 million for a CSX rail line inland, to replace the line on the Gulf Coast; $500 million for Northrop Grumman, which was in litigation with the insurers of its Pascagoula shipyard; and $1 billion for Katrina housing. House GOP leaders called the bill a "special-interest shopping cart." But Cochran prevailed in the Senate, 50-47. Ultimately, Congress agreed to the aid for Iraq and for Katrina recovery, although it rejected the railroad line. Cochran continued to defend earmarking. But when Republicans announced an earmark moratorium in 2011, he reluctantly went along. Despite the moratorium, he secured funding for his priorities, including his state's NASA Stennis Space Center and the Coast Guard.

Cochran gave up his position as Appropriations' ranking Republican in 2013 to take the same position on the Agriculture Committee, using his seniority to bump Pat Roberts of Kansas from the post. He faced the added challenge of trying to find middle ground between the Democratic-controlled Senate and House Republicans who sought big cuts in spending on food stamp and nutrition programs. With Democratic Sen. Debbie Stabenow of Michigan and Republican Rep. Frank Lucas of Oklahoma, the two committee chairmen, Cochran was part of the conventional farm-bill coalition that found middle ground, with a mostly status quo approach on the farms sand few spending cuts in social programs.

After the GOP took back the Senate in 2014, Cochran returned to the Appropriations gavel with the backing of Majority Leader Mitch McConnell, a fellow appropriator. Cochran has often partnered with his Mississippi Senate colleague Roger Wicker, a Republican whose ascension in the Senate-to succeed Lott-was a welcome change for Cochran. He also had a long relationship with Maryland's Barbara Mikulski, the panel's top Democrat, who sought his help on getting national security and other spending for her state before she retired at the end of 2016. One of Cochran's most notable habits in recent years has been a willingness to abandon his party on floor votes. He worked to expedite the disaster recovery process in the aftermath of Hurricane Sandy, and he was the first GOP senator to back President Barack Obama's choice of former Republican Sen. Chuck Hagel for secretary of Defense.

Cochran continued to find opportunities to send money to Mississippi for military projects, even when the Pentagon had not requested the funds. That was the case with the year-end spending bill in 2015, which included $640 million for a Coast Guard cutter that would be built at the shipyard in Pascagoula. The Office of Management and Budget criticized the spending as "an unnecessary acquisition." Cochran responded that the Obama Administration was "based on dated assessments and is insufficient to meet current or future requirements." An obstacle to Cochran's influence was that the chief spending deal in 2015 was crafted by bipartisan congressional leaders working with the Budget Committees. That measure raised congressional spending caps for two years but left few major decisions for the appropriators. The status quo budgeting continued in 2016 when Congress extended spending levels as it awaited the outcome of the election.

For the 76-year-old Cochran, questions surfaced about whether he would run again in 2014. The ensuing bitter primary unexpectedly propelled Cochran into the national spotlight. He drew a challenge from outspoken state Sen. Chris McDaniel, who with the support of tea party groups, the Club for Growth and the Senate Conservatives Fund, mounted a full-throttle assault on Cochran as insufficiently conservative for the deeply red state. McDaniel held Cochran barely below the 50-percent mark in the June primary, forcing a runoff, which the challenger entered as a modest favorite. The race's ugliest moment came when a McDaniel supporter took photos of Cochran's long-ailing wife Rose in bed at a nursing home and posted them online without her consent; she died in December 2014. McDaniel denied any connection with the incident, in which four men were arrested. One of the men committed suicide; another pleaded guilty to conspiracy.

In the three-week runoff, Cochran staged a remarkable political comeback. He re-introduced himself to voters via advertisements, running one spot that listed 20 institutions or companies he had helped by procuring funds. The Republican establishment, led by McConnell and business groups, leapt into action by writing checks and providing other assistance. Most strikingly, Cochran's campaign took a calculated risk by reaching out to Democrats-most of whom were African Americans-who were eligible to vote in the runoff. The strategy paid off: Amid unexpectedly high turnout, Cochran eked out a victory in the runoff, 51%-49%. Harry Enten of fivethirtyeight.com concluded that, based on county-level results, "traditionally Democratic voters provided Cochran with his margin of victory." A furious McDaniel filed a formal challenge alleging thousands of voting irregularities; a judge dismissed it. Not that Cochran faced any trouble in the general: He beat former Democratic Rep. Travis Childers, likely the strongest candidate Democrats could have run, by 23 points.

After Cochran's victory, members of the Congressional Black Caucus said he owed them one. "Absolutely we have expectations," Democratic Rep. Marcia Fudge of Ohio told *Politico*. In his new term, Cochran was one of 10 Republicans who voted to confirm Obama's pick for attorney general, Loretta Lynch. But he didn't need much encouragement. In December 2016, he was part of a bipartisan coalition that agreed to the nationwide water-resources bill, which included more than $400 million in disaster assistance for the lower Mississippi River valley in response to extensive flooding early that year

In March 2017, President Donald Trump posed a challenge to Cochran and other appropriators when he proposed large cuts in domestic spending to help pay for additional funds for the military.

Junior Senator

Roger Wicker (R)

Appointed Dec. 2007, term expires 2018, 1st full term; b. Jul 05, 1951, Pontotoc; University of Mississippi, J.D.; University of Mississippi, B.A., Baptist; Married (Gayle Long Wicker); 3 children; 4 grandchildren.

Military Career: U.S. Air Force, 1976-1980; U.S. Air Force Reserve, 1980-2004.

Elected Office: Tupelo city judge pro temp., 1986-1987; MS Senate, 1988-1994; U.S. House, 1995-2007.

Professional Career: Staff, U.S House Rules Committee, 1980-1982; Practicing attorney, 1982-1994; Lee County public defender, 1984-1987; Board Of Visitors, U.S Naval Academy, 2005.

DC Office: 555 DSOB 20510, 202-224-6253, Fax: 202-228-0378, wicker.senate.gov.

State Offices: Gulfport, 228-871-7017; Hernando, 662-429-1002; Jackson, 601-965-4644; Tupelo, 662-844-5010.

Committees: *Armed Services*: Airland, Emerging Threats & Capabilities, Seapower (Chmn). *Commerce, Science & Transportation*: Aviation Operations, Safety & Security, Communications, Technology, Innovation & the Internet (Chmn), Oceans, Atmosphere, Fisheries & Coast Guard, Surface Trans., Merchant Marine Infra., Safety & Security. *Environment & Public Works*: Clean Air & Nuclear Safety, Fisheries, Water, and Wildlife, Transportation & Infrastructure. *Joint Security & Cooperation in Europe (Chmn)*. *Rules & Administration*.

Group Ratings

	ADA	ACLU	AFL-CIO	LCV	ITI	COC	HAFA	ACU	CFG	FRC
2016	-	17%	-	12%	80%	100%	52%	72%	68%	100%
2015	5%	C	14%	0%	C	93%	C	75%	61%	100%

Almanac Ratings 2015

	Economy	Social	Foreign	Composite
Liberal	27%	0%	0%	9%
Conservative	73%	100%	100%	91%

Key Votes of the 114th Congress

1. Keystone pipeline	Y	5. National Security Data	N	9. Gun Sales Checks	N
2. Export-Import Bank	N	6. Iran Nuclear Deal	Y	10. Sanctuary Cities	Y
3. Debt Ceiling Increase	Y	7. Puerto Rico Debt	N	11. Planned Parenthood	Y
4. Homeland Security $$	N	8. Loretta Lynch A.G	N	12. Trade deals	Y

Election Results

Election	Name (Party)	Vote (%)		Cand. Spent	Ind. Exp. Support	Ind. Exp. Oppose
2012 General	Roger Wicker (R)	709,626	(57%)	$8,646,288		
	Albert N. Gore Jr. (D)	503,467	(41%)			
2012 Primary	Roger F. Wicker (R)	254,936	(89%)			
	Robert Maloney (R)	18,857	(7%)			

Prior winning percentages: 2008 (55%), House: 2006 (66%), 2004 (79%), 2002 (71%), 2000 (70%), 1998 (67%), 1996 (68%), 1994 (63%)

Roger Wicker was appointed in late 2007 to serve as Mississippi's junior senator, filling the vacancy created by the resignation of Trent Lott, a powerful Mississippian who had served as both majority and minority leader. Wicker won comfortably in a state that has not elected a Democrat to the Senate since 1982. He entered the GOP leadership ranks in 2015 as chairman of the NRSC and performed capably under difficult political circumstances. He was rewarded after the election when Majority Leader Mitch McConnell tapped Wicker as a counsel and gave him a seat at the GOP leadership table.

Wicker grew up in Pontotoc, the same north Mississippi town where his senior colleague in the Senate, Republican Thad Cochran, spent part of his childhood. Wicker's father was a conservative Democrat, a state senator, and a circuit judge. He attended public schools and as a teenager became interested in Republican politics. From then on, his career was intertwined with the two senior Mississippians, Lott and Cochran. He was a page in the House and he campaigned door-to-door for Cochran in his first race for Congress. At Ole Miss, Wicker served in student government and got his bachelor's and law degree. He spent four years in the Air Force Judge Advocate General Corps.

Wicker worked for Lott on the House Rules Committee. After he returned to Mississippi, he served as the public defender in his wife's hometown of Tupelo. In 1987, he was elected to the state Senate, the first Republican from northern Mississippi since Reconstruction. He helped to draft the state's strict abortion law and was a leading advocate of government-sponsored vouchers for private school tuition.

In 1994, Democratic Rep. Jamie Whitten momentously retired after having been the longest-serving member of the House and the powerful chairman of the Appropriations Committee, leaving big shoes to fill in Mississippi's 1st District. Pent-up demand produced crowded primaries, attracting six Republicans and three Democrats. On the strength of support from Tupelo, Wicker finished first in the GOP primary, 27%-19%. He won the runoff against Grant Fox, a young former aide to Cochran, 53%-47%, then easily defeated Democratic state Rep. Bill Wheeler, 63%-37%, in the general election. A district that had been held by a leading Democrat for five decades thus shifted to the GOP.

Wicker compiled a solidly conservative voting record in the House. He got a seat on Appropriations, an unusual prize for a freshman. In those days, appropriators retained an atmosphere of bipartisan cooperation, and Wicker worked quietly in subcommittees to get funding for his low-income district, with Yalobusha River flood control and an interstate highway through DeSoto County. He delivered research dollars to Mississippi universities, and he worked with Lott, by then a Senate leader, to attract defense technology firms to the state. Citizens Against Government Waste gave him the dubious distinction of No. 1 earmarker in the House for securing $176 million in projects, most of it for his district. "I am a fiscal conservative, and I believe in keeping spending low," Wicker said later. "But once the national budget is set, I think it is only fair to fight for our fair share for Mississippi." He reluctantly supported the GOP's earmark ban starting in 2011.

In November 2007, Lott announced his resignation from the Senate. Wicker wanted the seat, but so did 3rd District GOP Rep. Chip Pickering and Netscape founder James Barksdale. Gov. Haley Barbour appointed Wicker and said that the election for the remainder of Lott's term would be held the next November. Mississippi Democrats had not seriously contested a Senate race in 20 years. President Bush's low poll ratings, enthusiasm among African-American voters for Democratic presidential nominee Barack Obama, and a victory by Democrat Travis Childers in Wicker's old House district combined to give them hope. The Democratic nominee was former Gov. Ronnie Musgrove, who Barbour had ousted in 2003. It was a battle between old friends: Wicker and Musgrove had both been elected to the state Senate for the first time in 1987 and they roomed together in Jackson.

Musgrove criticized Wicker for his support of earmarks and called him a "poster child" for a moratorium on pork-barrel spending. Musgrove also criticized him for opposing increases in the minimum wage. Musgrove even hinted at ethical misconduct, criticizing Wicker for securing a $6 million earmark, not sought by the Pentagon, for Aurora Flight Sciences to build unmanned aerial vehicles in north Mississippi, as company executives were contributing $17,000 to his campaign and hiring Wicker's former chief of staff to lobby for the project. Wicker said the effort was all about bringing high-paying jobs to Mississippi. Wicker outspent Musgrove, $6.2 million to $5.3 million, though the DSCC pumped in more than enough money to compensate. Wicker won, 55%-45%, with 82 percent of whites backing Wicker and 92 percent of blacks supporting Musgrove.

Wicker has voted to the right of Cochran, especially on social issues. In the *Almanac* vote ratings for 2015, he had perfect conservative scores on social and foreign issues. He drew widespread attention in 2015 when he cast the lone "no" vote against Democrat Sheldon Whitehouse's amendment to get Republicans to acknowledge on record that climate-change is actually occurring. Wicker called it a "gag" and said he agreed "with the more than 31,000 American scientists who do not believe the science on this matter is settled." He has repeatedly introduced legislation to overturn *Roe v. Wade.* He called repeal of the Affordable Care Act the "great fight for…maybe our lifetimes" and filed a bill to enable state officials to challenge the law. After Congress voted in 2010 to repeal the "don't ask, don't tell" ban on openly gay service members, Wicker cosponsored a bill forbidding same-sex marriages on military bases.

In his legislative work, Wicker often has had a home-state focus. As chairman of the Armed Services Seapower Subcommittee, he secured funding in the 2016 defense spending bill for a new Naval destroyer and a big-deck amphibious ship. At the Commerce, Science and Transportation Committee, he chaired the subpanel on technology and the Internet and sought more broadband access for rural areas. He complained that the Federal Communications Commission was setting Internet speed artificially high. He was the lead sponsor of a bill to extend a Safe Drinking Water Act program to assist public water systems in small and rural communities, which was enacted in 2015.

At home, Wicker faced far fewer headwinds in winning a full term in 2012, defeating Albert Gore, a retired United Methodist minister and distant relative of the former vice president who ran a bare-bones campaign. Wicker spent more than $8 million and won 57%-41%. Wicker poked fun at his fundraising chops at a Washington fundraiser for the Shakespeare Theater Company; he played "Super PAC Man," using his checkbook to taunt others.

In 2014, Wicker helped Cochran survive, when he faced an aggressive challenge from tea party-backed Chris McDaniel. Neither Cochran nor McDaniel reached 50 percent in the primary; in the runoff, Cochran narrowly edged McDaniel amid outreach to African-American voters, an unusual effort that may have put Cochran over the top. "I think we did the country a favor, and certainly the party a favor, because we got a good man back in office," Wicker said.

His assistance for Cochran aided his bid for the NRSC chairmanship. When seeking the post, one of his first calls was to Lott, who told him, "Golly, Roger, why would you want that job? It's the toughest job in the Senate leadership," *CQ-Roll Call* reported. As chairman, he faced a formidable task, with Republicans defending 24 seats to 10 for the Democrats. GOP incumbents lost only two seats: in Illinois and New Hampshire; Donald Trump was defeated in each state. Defying initial expectations, Republicans prevailed in tough contests in Florida, Indiana, Pennsylvania and Wisconsin. They survived unexpected challenges in Missouri and North Carolina. Wicker worked with other Senate Republicans to determine a campaign balance with Donald Trump. "Republicans won because we had better candidates, ran better campaigns, invested early and starting on day one made every preparation to run in an uncertain and volatile political environment," Wicker said on Election Night.

Preparing for his own reelection campaign in 2018, the chief concern that Wicker faced was the possibility that McDaniel could reprise the primary opposition that he posed to Cochran in 2014. Wicker would be better prepared for such a challenge, including his fundraising.

FIRST DISTRICT

Trent Kelly (R)

Elected 2015, 2nd term; b. Mar 01, 1966, Union; University of Mississippi Business School, LL.B.; University of Mississippi Law School, LL.B.; U.S. Army War College (PA), Mast. Deg.; Methodist; Married (Sheila Kelly Hampton); 3 children.

Military Career: MS Army National Guard, 1987-present (Iraq).

Elected Office: Tupelo City Prosecutor, 1999-2011; 1st Circuit Judicial District Attorney, 2012-2015.

Professional Career: Practicing attorney, 1995-1999.

DC Office: 1721 LHOB 20515, 202-225-4306, Fax: 202-225-3549, trentkelly.house.gov.

State Offices: Columbus, 662-327-0748; Corinth, 662-687-1525; Eupora, 662-258-7240; Hernando, 662-449-3090; Tupelo, 662-841-8808.

Committees: *Agriculture*: Conservation & Forestry, Livestock & Foreign Agriculture. *Armed Services*: Military Personnel, Readiness, Tactical Air & Land Forces. *Small Business*: Economic Growth, Tax & Capital Access, Investigations, Oversight & Regulations (Chmn).

Group Ratings

	ADA	ACLU	AFL-CIO	LCV	ITI	COC	HAFA	ACU	CFG	FRC
2016	-	17%	-	0%	100%	100%	72%	92%	84%	100%
2015	0%	C	20%	0%	C	70%	C	71%	71%	100%

Almanac Ratings 2015

	Economy	Social	Foreign	Composite
Liberal	13%	0%	15%	14%
Conservative	87%	0%	85%	86%

Key Votes of the 114th Congress

2. Trade Deals	Y	4. Debt Ceiling Increase	N	10. Troops in Iraq	NV
3. Export-Import Bank	N	5. Puerto Rico Debt	N	12. Trade Adjustment aid	NV

Election Results

Election	Name (Party)	Vote (%)		Cand. Spent	Ind. Exp. Support	Ind. Exp. Oppose
2016 General	Trent Kelly (R)	206,455	(69%)	$946,957		
	Jacob Owens (D)	83,947	(28%)			
2016 Primary	Trent Kelly (R)	95,049	(89%)			
	Paul Clever (R)	11,397	(11%)			

Prior winning percentages: 2015 special (70%)

Republican Trent Kelly in 2015 won a competitive primary in a special election, following the death of Rep. Alan Nunnelee. Appointed to the Armed Services Committee to take advantage of his lengthy military experience, Kelly has quietly settled into his seat.

Kelly graduated from the business school and law school at the University of Mississippi. He got a master's degree in strategic studies from the U.S. Army War College in Carlisle, Pennsylvania. Kelly has been in the National Guard since the mid-1980s as an engineer, and achieved the rank of colonel. He served in Iraq during the Gulf War, then had two tours of duty during the Iraq War, where he commanded 670 troops. He received two Bronze Stars and numerous other military awards. He became city prosecutor in Tupelo in 1999, and held that position for 12 years before he was elected district attorney for seven rural counties in the northeast corner of the state.

After Nunnelee died, 13 candidates filed for the special election. Of the 12 Republicans, not one was from DeSoto County, which is the population center of the district. That led to a wide-open contest, with none of the candidates a big fundraiser. Mike Tagert, the northern Mississippi transportation commissioner, started with important political support as an ally of former Republican Gov. Haley Barbour, according to the *Cook Political Report*. Kelly received contributions from Nunnelee's campaign fund, assistance from his former consultant and an aide, and an important endorsement from his widow Tori, who said that nobody "respected the men and women who defend this country more than" her late husband. In the "jungle primary," Walter Zinn, the only Democrat, led with 17.4 percent, Kelly got 16.3 percent, and Tagert finished third with 12.7 percent. Given the Republican tilt of the district, it was no surprise that Kelly won the runoff with 70 percent of the vote.

In Kelly's first year, the House passed his bill to make it easier for Small Business Administration representatives to review contract requests from small businesses. The measure later was included in the House version of the annual defense spending bill. He developed a working relationship with neighboring Democratic Rep. Bennie Thompson, including their joint opposition to a Senate resolution to switch the regulation of catfish from the Agriculture Department to the Food and Drug Administration. Catfish farming is big business in Mississippi.

In 2017, Kelly achieved his objective of a seat on the Armed Services Committee. He also became chairman of the Oversight and Investigations Subcommittee at Small Business, where he planned to examine how the SBA and other federal agencies could operate programs that affect small businesses in a more cost-effective manner. In an interview with the *Jackson Clarion-Ledger*, he said that what bothers him most about the House is, "There are so many opportunities where we as members like each other - we just disagree on policy."

Kelly in 2016 won an uneventful reelection, 69%-28%. During the campaign, he said that neither party's presidential candidate was "perfect." But, he added, Donald Trump would be "much better than Hillary" at leading the nation.

Northeast Mississippi: Memphis area, Tupelo

Population		**Race and Ethnicity**		**Income**	
Total	752,701	White	67.8%	Median Income	$41,858 (373 out of 435)
Land area	10,573	Black	26.9%		
Pop/ sq mi	71.2	Latino	3.2%		
Born in state	63.4%	Asian	0.7%	Under $50,000	57.6%
		Two races	1.2%	$50,000-$99,999	28.8%
Age Groups		Other	0.2%	$100,000-$199,999	11.6%
Under 18	24.6%			$200,000 or more	2.0%
18-34	22.8%	**Education**		Poverty Rate	18.8%
35-64	38.4%	H.S grad or less	49.6%		
Over 64	14.2%	Some college	31.7%	**Health Insurance**	
		College Degree, 4 yr	12.3%	With health insurance coverage	85.5%
Work		Post grad	6.5%		
White Collar	29.3%				
Sales and Service	39.7%	**Military**		**Public Assistance**	
Blue Collar	31.0%	Veteran	7.6%	Cash public assistance income	3.1%
Government	15.1%	Active Duty	0.2%		
				Food stamp/SNAP benefits	16.0%

Voter Turnout			
2015 Total Citizens 18+	557,543	2016 House Turnout as % CVAP	54%
2016 House turnout	300,423	2014 House Turnout as % CVAP	27%

2012 Presidential Vote		
Mitt Romney	197,980	(62%)
Barack Obama	118,435	(37%)

2016 Presidential Vote		
Donald Trump	203,135	(65%)
Hillary Clinton	100,780	(32%)

Cook Partisan Voting Index: R+16

The university town of Oxford - the "Jefferson" of William Faulkner's fictional Yoknapatawpha County - sits on a divide between the hill country of Mississippi and the flat farmlands of the Mississippi Delta. Named for Oxford, England, it is home to the University of Mississippi, where violence broke out in 1962 when James Meredith became the school's first black student. Ole Miss, as it is known, now houses Meredith's papers in its library. Under student pressure, the university in 2015 removed the state flag because it featured the Confederate battle flag within its design. To the west is the Delta, with a large African-American majority, and DeSoto County, just south of Memphis and Mississippi's fastest-growing county, including a 7 percent increase from 2010 to 2015. The relatively affluent DeSoto has become a magnet for Memphis commuters looking for affordable housing, better schools and lower taxes across the state line. DeSoto has become very aggressive in economic development, and has taken business from Memphis. East of Oxford is the hill country, which stretches to where the Tennessee River nicks the northeast corner of Tishomingo County. This was traditional farming country, but it is now more engaged in small manufacturing.

The Golden Triangle in the Starkville area has become a center for aerospace research, including work on unmanned air vehicle designs for surveillance and communications. The biggest town in the area is Tupelo, home to an upholstered furniture industry that has survived more prosperously than furniture centers elsewhere. Tupelo was also the birthplace of Elvis Presley in 1935, and the family's two-room house today is open to visitors. The town produces many Christian conservatives, the kind of townsfolk who were shocked by Presley's music and hip-swirling dance moves in the early days of rock 'n' roll. Donald Wildmon's American Family Association, a prominent Christian conservative organization, is based there. The Tupelo region got a big economic boost when Toyota in 2011 started operations at a new assembly plant. Five years later, its workforce of 2,000 had produced its 1 millionth Corolla, a rate of one every 71 seconds. Several Toyota suppliers have sprung up nearby, with employment of another 2,000 people. Clay County has become a tire-manufacturing center.

The 1st Congressional District of Mississippi includes Southaven, the district's biggest city, Oxford, Tupelo and most of the hill country. It is the descendant of the district represented by Jamie Whitten, the longtime Democratic chairman of the Appropriations Committee, who held office 53 years, until January 1995. This once-conservative Democratic territory has become solidly Republican in national politics. Even with rural Clay and Marshall counties voting for Hillary Clinton, Donald Trump got 65 percent of the district vote. As with the other two Republican districts in Mississippi, Trump surpassed the local vote for Mitt Romney in 2012.

SECOND DISTRICT

Bennie Thompson (D)

Elected 1993, 13th term; b. Jan 28, 1948, Bolton; Jackson State University (MS), M.S.; Tougaloo College, B.A.; Methodist; Married (London Johnson Thompson); 1 child; 2 grandchildren.

Elected Office: Bolton Board of Aldermen, 1968-1972; Bolton Mayor, 1973-1980; Hinds County supervisor, 1980-1993.

DC Office: 2466 RHOB 20515, 202-225-5876, Fax: 202-225-5898, benniethompson.house.gov.

State Offices: Bolton, 601-866-9003; Greenville, 662-335-9003; Greenwood, 662-455-9003; Jackson, 601-946-9003; Marks, 662-326-9003; Mound Bayou, 662-741-9003.

Committees: *Homeland Security (RMM)*: Border & Maritime Security, Counterterrorism & Intelligence, Cybersecurity & Infrastructure Protection, Emergency Preparedness, Response & Communications, Oversight & Management Efficiency, Transportation & Protective Security.

Group Ratings

	ADA	ACLU	AFL-CIO	LCV	ITI	COC	HAFA	ACU	CFG	FRC
2016	-	100%	-	97%	67%	64%	14%	0%	0%	0%
2015	100%	C	96%	86%	C	40%	C	4%	6%	0%

Almanac Ratings 2015

	Economy	Social	Foreign	Composite
Liberal	92%	97%	89%	92%
Conservative	8%	4%	12%	8%

Key Votes of the 114th Congress

1. Keystone Pipeline	N	5. Puerto Rico Debt	Y	9. Offenses by Aliens	N
2. Trade Deals	N	6. Medical Marijuana	Y	10. Troops in Iraq	Y
3. Export-Import Bank	Y	7. Sanctuary Cities	N	11. Homeland Security $$	Y
4. Debt Ceiling Increase	Y	8. Armor-piercing Bullets	N	12. Trade Adjustment aid	N

Election Results

Election	Name (Party)	Vote (%)		Cand. Spent	Ind. Exp. Support	Ind. Exp. Oppose
2016 General	Bennie Thompson (D)	192,039	(67%)	$967,057		
	John Bouie II (R)	83,122	(29%)			
2016 Primary	Bennie Thompson (D)		(100%)			

Prior winning percentages: 2014 (68%), 2012 (67%), 2010 (62%), 2008 (69%), 2006 (64%), 2004 (58%), 2002 (55%), 2000 (65%), 1998 (71%), 1996 (60%), 1994 (54%)

Bennie Thompson, who was elected in 1993, has been a liberal Democratic fixture in an otherwise deeply conservative Republican state. He is the longest-serving African-American elected official in Mississippi. His official bio says that he "has spent his entire life giving a voice to the voiceless." Since 2005, he has served as the top Democrat on the Homeland Security Committee, where he deals with a panel and issues that did not exist when he entered the House.

Thompson grew up in Bolton, in Hinds County outside Jackson, and graduated from Tougaloo College and got a master's degree from Jackson State University. He was elected alderman in Bolton in 1969, at age 21, and elected mayor four years later. A longtime volunteer firefighter, he got the first fire engine for Bolton and also a street named after the Rev. Martin Luther King Jr. In 1980, he became a Hinds County supervisor. A lifelong grass-roots activist and labor organizer, he led voter-registration drives and successfully encouraged other African Americans to run for office. He organized associations of Mississippi black mayors and supervisors.

After Democratic Rep. Mike Espy exited Congress to become President Bill Clinton's Agriculture secretary, Thompson ran for the seat in an all-party primary. He came out ahead of Henry Espy, Mike Espy's brother and mayor of Clarksdale, 28%-20%. Hayes Dent, an aide to Gov. Kirk Fordice, led Republicans with 34 percent. Voting in the runoff was largely along racial lines, and Thompson won 55%-45%, with his margin coming mostly from Hinds County.

Thompson has a staunchly liberal voting record. He initially made little attempt to win white votes in his district, making roughly as few concessions across the racial divide as white lawmakers had earlier made. In time, he moderated his votes and reached out to whites, including some of the district's large farmers. He backs expansion of Medicaid, and accused Republican Gov. Phil Bryant of refusing to go along with the health care plan of President Barack Obama "just because a black man created it," *Buzzfeed* reported. Thompson publicly supported GOP Sen. Thad Cochran in his successful June 2014 runoff against tea party favorite Chris McDaniel, then urged Cochran to expand efforts to assist the black community.

A few months earlier, Thompson drew widespread attention for comments in an interview with a New Nation of Islam radio show in which he called Supreme Court Justice Clarence Thomas an "Uncle Tom" and accused Senate Republican leader Mitch McConnell of being racist toward Obama. For years he has eaten dinner every night that Congress is in session with James Clyburn of South Carolina and Cedric Richmond of Louisiana, also black and the only Democrats in the House from their states. "It's tough being the lone voice of reason from your state," Thompson told *USA Today*. "You got to have some solace with talking to somebody."

The locus of his legislative activity has been the Homeland Security Committee. As both chairman and ranking minority member, Thompson has focused on the needs of first responders. He has been vocal about the threat of computer-based attacks and successfully pushed back in 2012 against Republican calls to scale back the Homeland Security Department's role in favor of defense and intelligence agencies. He also has criticized the GOP's desire to replace Transportation Security Administration (TSA) workers with private screeners at airports. "On September 11th, screeners at our airports were employed by private companies; a return to a pre-9/11 status for screeners would not improve aviation security or assist national security," he said in 2012.

For years, Thompson had a sometimes-productive relationship with the top committee Republican, Peter King of New York. The two worked together to restructure the Federal Emergency Management Agency after FEMA's failures in the aftermath of Hurricane Katrina in 2005. House Republicans wanted it to become an independent agency. Thompson and King called for keeping it within the Homeland Security Department, but with the kind of autonomy the Coast Guard has. They came to an agreement, but when Thompson demanded an additional $3 billion to improve state and local communications capability, King declined and the deal foundered.

Taking over as chairman in 2007, Thompson shepherded through the House one of the new Democratic majority's "first 100 hours" bills, which was to adopt the unfinished recommendations of the 9/11 commission. He enacted a requirement to screen all passenger jet and ship cargo. In 2009, Thompson unsuccessfully pushed to centralize House oversight of Homeland Security under his committee, seeking to end the sharing of jurisdiction across dozens of panels. He worked with King to pass annual Homeland Security authorization bills, only to have the Senate ignore them.

Back in the minority after Republicans regained control of the House, Thompson was named a vice chair of a House Democratic task force on gun violence formed after the December 2012 school massacre in Newtown Connecticut. He regularly gets "F" ratings from the National Rifle Association, but Thompson is an avid hunter and says the ratings don't reflect sportsmen's views. In June 2016, he joined the Democrats' sit-in on the House floor to protest the inaction on gun-control legislation. Earlier that month, Republican leaders blocked his proposal to ban Confederate imagery in the Capitol.

In 2012, *The Washington Post* reported that Thompson obtained a $900,000 earmark to resurface about two dozen Mississippi roads, including those in a neighborhood where he and his daughter owned two homes. He said it was up to the county to decide where the work should be done. "I didn't say, 'Do the street that I live on,'" he said. The Ethics Committee had exonerated Thompson and several colleagues of wrongdoing. In January 2017, his long-time chief of staff Isaac Lanier Avant was sentenced to four months in prison after he pleaded guilty to failing to file a tax return for five years.

Thompson has encountered occasional campaign opposition. In 2002, he was reelected by a less than impressive 55%-43% against Republican challenger Clinton LeSueur, a consultant to the Yazoo

Community Action Agency. State Rep. Chuck Espy, nephew of the former representative, challenged him in the 2006 primary, but Thompson prevailed 64%-35%. He has faced no serious challengers since then. He did not attend the Inaugural ceremony in January 2017, stating that the criticism by President Donald Trump of Democratic Rep. John Lewis was "far beneath the dignity of the Office of the President."

Mississippi Delta, Jackson

Population		Race and Ethnicity		Income	
Total	729,410	White	31.6%	Median Income	$32,064 (432 out of 435)
Land area	15,552	Black	64.8%		
Pop/ sq mi	46.9	Latino	2.2%		
Born in state	83.6%	Asian	0.6%	Under $50,000	67.1%
		Two races	0.6%	$50,000-$99,999	23.3%
Age Groups		Other	0.3%	$100,000-$199,999	8.3%
Under 18	25.5%			$200,000 or more	1.4%
18-34	24.0%	**Education**		Poverty Rate	30.2%
35-64	37.4%	H.S grad or less	51.5%		
Over 64	13.1%	Some college	30.3%	**Health Insurance**	
		College Degree, 4 yr	11.4%	With health insurance coverage	82.9%
Work		Post grad	6.8%		
White Collar	29.2%				
Sales and Service	44.0%	**Military**		**Public Assistance**	
Blue Collar	26.9%	Veteran	6.6%	Cash public assistance income	4.2%
Government	22.4%	Active Duty	0.0%		
				Food stamp/SNAP benefits	24.8%

Voter Turnout			
2015 Total Citizens 18+	535,902	2016 House Turnout as % CVAP	53%
2016 House turnout	286,626	2014 House Turnout as % CVAP	28%

2012 Presidential Vote		
Barack Obama	219,273	(66%)
Mitt Romney	109,180	(33%)

2016 Presidential Vote		
Hillary Clinton	185,501	(64%)
Donald Trump	102,159	(35%)

Cook Partisan Voting Index: D+14

"The Mississippi Delta," wrote native David Cohn, "begins in the lobby of the Peabody Hotel in Memphis and ends on Catfish Row in Vicksburg." For centuries, the flooding Mississippi and Yazoo rivers left their sediments here, producing a fertile, dark soil. Ironically, what may well be America's richest agricultural land has been home for more than a century to many of its poorest people. Crisscrossed by rivers and famously disease-ridden, the Delta wasn't much settled until after the Civil War. Then, Reconstruction-era profit-seeking operators used late-19th-century technology to drain the land, line the river with levees and build railroads on tracks above the rise of the river. Black sharecroppers and field hands worked here in conditions little better than bondage. From this episode of industrial farming came both great misery and great art: Clarksdale in Coahoma County, where Martin Luther King in 1958 held the first meeting of the Southern Christian Leadership Conference, was the real birthplace of blues music, the home of W.C. Handy and Muddy Waters, John Lee Hooker, Ike Turner and Sam Cooke. In May 2015, B.B. King was buried in his home town of Indianola. Greenville on the Mississippi has produced writers of the caliber of Walker Percy and Shelby Foote. Yazoo City produced author Willie Morris and bluesman Skip James. Today, Vicksburg's antebellum mansions and battlefield monuments are popular tourist attractions.

Twentieth-century technology changed life in the Delta. The mechanical cotton-picking machine, invented in 1944, came along just as Northern factories were seeking low-wage workers. The great exodus to Chicago and other Northern cities accelerated, and the Delta's population has been declining ever since. In the decade ending in 2010, each of the 16 counties in the Delta suffered a double-digit population loss. Income levels remain very low, the teen pregnancy rate high and infant mortality at Third World levels. Yet there are signs of hope. Soybeans have become a big-dollar crop here and poultry farms have become a major enterprise. The Delta produces most of the nation's catfish, although excessive summer heat has driven up production costs. In 2015, the Agriculture Department imposed closer regulation and import limits on the soaring supplies of a catfish-like product from Vietnam, which had cut jobs in the local industry by more than half in the prior decade. Imports have grown to 70 percent of the U.S. catfish supply, though 39,000 acres of catfish remained in Mississippi.

Not far from Memphis, Tunica County is one of the nation's poorest counties, its struggling economy dependent on the area's eight casinos, which help to generate 10 million visitors and 15,000 tour buses annually. The casinos have increased local per capita income, but there is still a gulf between rich and poor. GreenTech Automotive, a clean energy startup chaired by Virginia Gov. Terry McAuliffe, opened in 2014 a 300,000-square-foot plant, which produces its two-seat battery-powered MyCar electric vehicle for use chiefly at stadiums and on large campuses. Just north of the affluent suburbs of Jackson, Nissan operates a 6,400-employee factory in Canton. The company planned to complete by 2017 a major expansion in its production line for Altima sedans, which was expected to increase annual production to about 500,000 vehicles. The United Auto Workers has made several costly bids to unionize the plant, but all have failed, most recently in 2014. Subsequently, the National Labor Relations Board during the Obama administration investigated alleged violations of workers' rights.

The 2nd Congressional District of Mississippi includes the entire Delta, with the Mississippi riverfront from Tunica almost to Natchez. It includes most of heavily African-American Jackson and surrounding Hinds County except for the affluent Belhaven neighborhood. Nearly one-third of the population is in Hinds, which is 71 percent African American. This black-majority district includes a few counties in the east that are majority white and vote Republican. But the political tone of the district is set by the African-American neighborhoods in Jackson and the Delta counties. In 2016, the 2nd was the only Mississippi district to vote for Hillary Clinton. She got 64 percent of the vote, two points less than Barack Obama got in 2012.

THIRD DISTRICT

Gregg Harper (R)

Elected 2008, 5th term; b. Jun 01, 1956, Jackson; Mississippi College, B.S.; University of Mississippi School of Law, J.D.; Baptist; Married (Sidney Harper); 2 children.

Professional Career: Practicing attorney, 1981-present; City prosecutor, Brandon, Richland; Chmn, Rankin County Republican Party, 2000-2007.

DC Office: 2227 RHOB 20515, 202-225-5031, Fax: 202-225-5797, harper.house.gov.

State Offices: Brookhaven, 601-823-3400; Meridian, 601-693-6681; Pearl, 601-932-2410; Starkville, 662-324-0007.

Committees: *Energy & Commerce*: Digital Commerce & Consumer Protection, Energy, Environment. *House Administration (Chmn)*.

Group Ratings

	ADA	ACLU	AFL-CIO	LCV	ITI	COC	HAFA	ACU	CFG	FRC
2016	-	11%	-	0%	100%	100%	64%	79%	67%	100%
2015	0%	C	17%	3%	C	89%	C	67%	52%	100%

Almanac Ratings 2015

	Economy	Social	Foreign	Composite
Liberal	11%	9%	4%	8%
Conservative	90%	91%	96%	92%

Key Votes of the 114th Congress

1. Keystone Pipeline	Y	5. Puerto Rico Debt	Y	9. Offenses by Aliens	Y
2. Trade Deals	Y	6. Medical Marijuana	N	10. Troops in Iraq	N
3. Export-Import Bank	Y	7. Sanctuary Cities	Y	11. Homeland Security $$	N
4. Debt Ceiling Increase	Y	8. Armor-piercing Bullets	Y	12. Trade Adjustment aid	Y

Election Results

Election	Name (Party)	Vote (%)		Cand. Spent	Ind. Exp. Support	Ind. Exp. Oppose
2016 General	Gregg Harper (R)..........................	209,490	(66%)	$1,081,658		
	Dennis Quinn (D)...........................	96,101	(30%)			
2016 Primary	Gregg Harper (R)...........................	87,997	(89%)			
	Jimmy Giles (R).............................	10,760	(11%)			

Prior winning percentages: 2014 (69%), 2012 (80%), 2010 (68%), 2008 (63%)

Gregg Harper, a Republican elected in 2008, is a dependable conservative vote who impressed his party's leaders, and he has shown a desire to join them in the leadership. In 2017, Speaker Paul Ryan named Harper as chairman of the House Administration Committee, a position described as the Mayor of Capitol Hill

Harper was born in Jackson, where his father was a petroleum engineer and his mother was a homemaker. The family moved frequently because of his father's job, but always returned home to Mississippi. Harper became a Christian after attending a youth rally in high school, and later met his wife, Sidney, at a church function. Their adult son Livingston suffers from a developmental disorder called fragile X syndrome..

Harper graduated from Mississippi College and got his law degree from the University of Mississippi. He has long experience in politics. He chaired the Rankin County Republican Party and worked on several local and state campaigns. When the 2000 presidential election hinged on results in Florida, he volunteered as a legal observer for George W. Bush's recount efforts. Until 2008, he was the prosecuting attorney for the cities of Brandon and Richland.

When Harper ran for the open seat in 2008, his toughest Republican competitors were state Sen. Charlie Ross, considered the early favorite, and businessman David Landrum. Ross rolled up endorsements from local leaders and national groups such as the anti-tax Club for Growth, and both he and Landrum outspent Harper. Harper rallied a hardworking core of young volunteers and family members for door-to-door campaigning. He got a key endorsement from former Senate Majority Leader Trent Lott, who remained active in Mississippi politics. Ross led the primary with 33 percent, and Harper finished second with 28 percent. In the runoff, Ross portrayed Harper as too inexperienced for the job, but Harper emphasized his conservative stances against abortion rights and same-sex marriage. He won the runoff 57%-43%. In the general election, Democrat Joel Gill, a rancher and a Pickens alderman, ran folksy ads that referred to him as "Joel the Cattleman." Still, a catchy ad was not enough in this GOP district. Harper won with 63 percent of the vote and has not been seriously challenged since.

As a freshman, he joined the Republican Steering Committee and got a slot on the House Administration Committee, which oversees election laws and internal housekeeping tasks. When the chairmanship opened in 2012, he expected to get the committee gavel, but GOP leaders instead gave it to Candice Miller of Michigan. Harper remained a loyal soldier, and became chairman in 2016 after Miller retired. He pledged that the House would run in "an effective and efficient manner" as it enacts "real change." He listed as an early priority the protection of Congress from cybersecurity threats, with increased training about attacks by foreign governments such as malware in email.

Harper has sought to eliminate the Election Assistance Commission, a group that sets voluntary voting system guidelines for states. Harper said the commission had been intended as a temporary panel to assist with a 2002 voter registration law. The House passed an earlier version of that bill in 2011, but the Senate was not receptive. Following the 2016 election, he criticized Green Party presidential candidate Jill Stein for seeking to cast the outcome as illegitimate. Harper and his committee likely would have a role in consideration of proposals to revise campaign-finance laws.

With his plum seat on the Energy and Commerce Committee, Harper frequently blasted the health care overhaul law and called for more domestic energy production while beseeching President Barack Obama to approve the Keystone XL pipeline from Canada. "If he cared about jobs and the energy independence in this country, it's a no-brainer," he said in 2012. In 2014, Obama had a White House signing ceremony for a bill introduced by Harper to increase funding for pediatric medical research, especially for cancer. With Mississippi playing a leadership role in the development of telemedicine, he has filed legislation to expand those payments. In January 2017, he filed a bill that would guarantee that individuals would be permitted to retain the health insurance plan that they had prior to the enactment of the Affordable Care Act.

With his son in mind, Harper has been bipartisan on governmental aid to children with special needs. Harper chairs the Fragile X Caucus, which has sought to increase awareness of the genetic disorder and has secured funding at the Centers for Disease Control and Prevention for adults with intellectual disabilities. He also has made the disorder eligible for Defense Department medical research. In 2012, he included a provision in the bipartisan pharmaceutical user fee agreement to extend market exclusivity for drugs that treat fragile X syndrome, autism and other neurological disorders.

South Central Mississippi: Jackson Suburbs

Population		**Race and Ethnicity**		**Income**	
Total	748,654	White	60.0%	Median Income	$41,730 (375 out of 435)
Land area	12,754	Black	35.0%		
Pop/ sq mi	58.7	Latino	2.2%		
Born in state	76.6%	Asian	1.0%	Under $50,000	57.2%
		Two races	0.8%	$50,000-$99,999	26.5%
Age Groups		Other	1.0%	$100,000-$199,999	13.3%
Under 18	24.2%			$200,000 or more	3.1%
18-34	23.3%	**Education**		Poverty Rate	20.9%
35-64	38.2%	H.S grad or less	44.8%		
Over 64	14.3%	Some college	30.0%	**Health Insurance**	
		College Degree, 4 yr	15.3%	With health insurance coverage	86.1%
Work		Post grad	9.8%		
White Collar	35.8%				
Sales and Service	39.3%	**Military**		**Public Assistance**	
Blue Collar	25.0%	Veteran	7.6%	Cash public assistance income	2.1%
Government	19.3%	Active Duty	0.2%		
				Food stamp/SNAP benefits	14.8%

Voter Turnout			
2015 Total Citizens 18+	556,901	2016 House Turnout as % CVAP	57%
2016 House turnout	316,445	2014 House Turnout as % CVAP	31%

2012 Presidential Vote		
Mitt Romney	204,232	(60%)
Barack Obama	133,114	(39%)

2016 Presidential Vote		
Donald Trump	198,768	(61%)
Hillary Clinton	118,805	(37%)

Cook Partisan Voting Index: R+13

The Neshoba County fair has been held every August since 1889 in the town of Philadelphia. What started as a farmer's picnic has become the traditional place where Mississippi politicians announce their candidacies, with the crowds watching to take their measure. Devotees call it "Mississippi's Giant House Party," and many stay for the entire week. The crowds are also there to watch the races on the state's only legal horse track. But nationally, Philadelphia and Neshoba County are known for something less harmonious. There is no memorial, except engraved stones at two African-American churches, to mark the events of the summer of 1964, when three civil rights workers, two white and one black, were murdered for the crime of urging black American citizens to register to vote. It wasn't until June 2005 that a jury of nine whites and three blacks convicted Edgar Ray Killen, by then an 80-year-old preacher and sawmill operator, of manslaughter and sentenced him to three life sentences. In November 2014, President Barack Obama commemorated the 50th anniversary when he awarded a posthumous presidential Medal of Freedom to James Chaney, Andrew Goodman and Michael Schwerner.

The 3rd Congressional District of Mississippi has its population centers in the Jackson suburbs in Rankin County and south Madison County, plus the affluent neighborhoods of northeast Jackson in Hinds County. East and north of Jackson, subdivisions, shopping centers and office complexes have sprouted in the countryside. In late 2016, Rankin had the lowest unemployment rate in the state.

Demographers predict big increases in Asian and Latino population in this area during the coming decades. A different kind of wealth opened along the southern border of the district in 2014, as oil gushers burst forth from fracked wells.

From the Jackson suburbs, the 3rd stretches north to Starkville, home of Mississippi State University, and south almost to Laurel. In the southwest, which extends to the Louisiana border, it includes Natchez, where 668 antebellum mansions and other properties with live oaks sit atop bluffs overlooking the Mississippi River. Natchez -- settled in 1716, two years before New Orleans - was ranked second by *Lonely Planet* in 2016 as the most exciting destination to visit in the United States. In the middle of the district are Neshoba County and Meridian, home of Peavey Electronics Corp., whose electric guitars and powerful amplifiers are popular with rock stars. The plant suffered layoffs in early 2015; the company denied reports that it was moving its manufacturing operations overseas. The district's political tradition remained Democratic for decades, but its preference has become strongly Republican, even with its 35 percent black population. In 2016, Donald Trump won the district, 61%-37%, virtually the same as recent Republican presidential performances.

FOURTH DISTRICT

Steven Palazzo (R)

Elected 2010, 4th term; b. Feb 21, 1970, Gulfport; University of Southern Mississippi; b.B.A.; University of Southern Mississippi, M.S.; Roman Catholic; Married (Lisa Palazzo); 3 children.

Military Career: U.S. Marine Corps Reserve, 1988-1996 (Persian Gulf); MS Army National Guard, 1997-present.

Elected Office: MS House, 2007-2010.

Professional Career: FO, Biloxi Housing Authority; Owner, Palazzo & Co. PLLC.

DC Office: 2349 RHOB 20515, 202-225-5772, Fax: 202-225-7074, palazzo.house.gov.

State Offices: Biloxi, 228-864-7670; Hattiesburg, 601-582-3246.

Committees: *Appropriations*: Agriculture, Rural Development, FDA & Related Agencies, Commerce, Justice, Science & Related Agencies, Homeland Security.

Group Ratings

	ADA	ACLU	AFL-CIO	LCV	ITI	COC	HAFA	ACU	CFG	FRC
2016	-	11%	-	0%	100%	100%	76%	88%	66%	100%
2015	0%	C	13%	0%	C	80%	C	83%	77%	100%

Almanac Ratings 2015

	Economy	Social	Foreign	Composite
Liberal	2%	0%	0%	1%
Conservative	99%	100%	100%	99%

Key Votes of the 114th Congress

1. Keystone Pipeline	Y	5. Puerto Rico Debt	N	9. Offenses by Aliens	Y
2. Trade Deals	Y	6. Medical Marijuana	N	10. Troops in Iraq	N
3. Export-Import Bank	N	7. Sanctuary Cities	Y	11. Homeland Security $$	N
4. Debt Ceiling Increase	N	8. Armor-piercing Bullets	Y	12. Trade Adjustment aid	N

Election Results

Election	Name (Party)	Vote (%)	Cand. Spent	Ind. Exp. Support	Ind. Exp. Oppose
2016 General	Steven Palazzo (R)	181,323 (65%)	$474,070		
	Mark Gladney (D)	77,505 (28%)	$59,540		
	Rick McClusky (L)	12,710 (5%)			
2016 Primary	Steven Palazzo (R)	(100%)			

Prior winning percentages: 2014 (70%), 2012 (64%), 2010 (52%)

Republican Steven Palazzo, who unexpectedly won his seat in 2010, is a fervent fiscal and social conservative representing an area where Hurricane Katrina caused severe damage and imposed huge costs. He drew considerable attention for voting against paying Hurricane Sandy claims on the East Coast without offsetting cuts. He struggles to satisfy what may be irreconcilable elements among local Republicans. As a member of the Appropriations Committee, he has become more familiar with the benefits of spending.

Palazzo was born and raised in Gulfport, where five generations have called south Mississippi home. After graduating from high school and enrolling for a semester at his local community college, Palazzo enlisted in the Marine Corps. From 1988 to 1996, Palazzo was assigned to the 3rd Force Reconnaissance Company, gathering intelligence and taking tours of duty in Kuwait and Saudi Arabia during the Persian Gulf War. He remained active in the military following his full-time service, joining the Mississippi Army National Guard and supporting base operations at Camp Shelby for Operation Iraqi Freedom. After he returned from the Persian Gulf War, Palazzo earned his bachelor's and master's degrees in accounting from the University of Southern Mississippi. He worked in accounting positions at various firms, primarily in the construction industry. In 2001, he and his wife, Lisa Belvin, started the accounting practice Palazzo & Co., which grew into an international firm specializing in individual income tax returns for expatriates.

In 2007, Palazzo was elected to the state House. Two years later, he decided to challenge veteran Blue Dog Democrat Gene Taylor, who was almost a folk hero in Coastal Mississippi. Taylor lost his home to Katrina, was in good stead with the National Rifle Association, had one of the most conservative voting records among House Democrats, and had spoken out against many of his party's major initiatives, including health care reform.

But even Taylor, once viewed as a safe Democrat in the House, had reason to sweat in the anti-incumbent environment of 2010. Although it was difficult to attack Taylor's conservative voting record, Palazzo portrayed him as an enabler of the Democratic agenda for his vote for Nancy Pelosi of California as House Speaker, which he said showed Taylor's support for a "liberal socialist agenda." That vote was, implicitly at least, a trade-off for Taylor to chair an Armed Services subcommittee. Taylor couldn't count on much help from national Democrats, whom he had often bucked over the years. Taylor touted his conservative positions and even boasted to his local newspaper that he voted for Republican John McCain for president in 2008. It wasn't enough, not in 2010. Palazzo won 52%-47%.

In the House, Palazzo joined the Tea Party Caucus and shared the insistence of his large freshman class for sharp reductions in spending. He opposed the New Year's Day 2013 budget deal aimed at averting the so-called fiscal cliff, saying it failed to cut enough. That year, he added an amendment to the Pentagon spending bill to ban same-sex marriage ceremonies on military bases; it was dropped in the Senate. Palazzo found ways to protect some spending. Opposing a proposal in 2012 by Democratic Rep. Betty McCollum of Minnesota to end military sponsorships of NASCAR and other sports, he said there was "no reason Congress should be telling the Department of Defense where and how to spend money." He added money to a defense spending bill to buy land to expand a National Guard facility in his district, as well as for ship design and feasibility studies at Ingalls Shipbuilding in nearby Pascagoula. Recalling his attacks on Taylor for pork-barrel spending, Democrats and watchdog groups accused Palazzo of hypocrisy.

Following the 2012 election, Palazzo drew the most attention of the 67 House Republicans who voted against the bill with $9.7 billion in government borrowing to pay claims from Superstorm Sandy, which did considerable damage in the Northeast. He contended the measure should have made offsetting spending cuts. Most other GOP lawmakers from coastal areas backed the bill, prompting the *Sun Herald* of Biloxi to say of Palazzo, "Seldom has a single vote in Congress appeared as cold-blooded and hard-headed." Aware of the political damage, Palazzo toured Sandy-stricken areas and then co-signed a letter calling on colleagues to support a larger aid bill. He continued to pursue the interests of his district, including $1 billion in the 2015 defense spending bill for the Navy's LPD-28 amphibious assault ship, which would be built at Ingalls; he also got a provision to discourage downsizing at Keesler Air Force Base.

In 2014, Palazzo survived an unusual reelection contest when Taylor changed parties and challenged him in the Republican primary. Having determined that it was "impossible" for a Democrat to win, Taylor offered himself as the candidate best-equipped to deliver for the 4th District. Palazzo barely avoided a run-off, with 50.5% to 43% for Taylor.

But internal tensions remained. After more than one hour of a "man to man" conversation with John Boehner the evening before the vote, Palazzo decided that he was "willing to give the Speaker and his team a last chance to put us back on a conservative path for America." Southern Mississippi Tea Party Chairman Barry Neyrey responded angrily that Palazzo was a "coward" and had "betrayed us;" Neyrey promised Palazzo to "work tirelessly to see that you don't get another term." Two months later, Palazzo got a coveted seat on the Appropriations Committee following the death of home-state Republican Alan Nunnelee. He styled himself as an insider. "Serving as an appropriator is a privilege and a tremendous responsibility that I don't take lightly," he said. It was highly unlikely that he would have won that seat if he had voted against Boehner.

Although he and other conservatives sought a stronger conservative for the new Speaker, they had little serious option other than Paul Ryan. That did not stop Palazzo from pursuing his own conservative agenda. In January 2016, he filed a resolution to censure President Barack Obama for his executive order to restrict private gun sales. In April, he voiced his support when the Mississippi Legislature went on record in opposition to the U.S. Supreme Court's recognition of same-sex marriages.

Palazzo did not face a conservative challenge in the 2016 election. In January 2017, he called attention to his new seat on the Appropriations Subcommittee on Homeland Security, where he said he would work "to secure and fortify our borders, combat amnesty and illegal immigration," in addition to protecting the nation against terrorism and natural disasters.

Southeast Mississippi: Gulfport/Biloxi, Hattiesburg

Population		**Race and Ethnicity**		**Income**	
Total	757,316	White	69.3%	Median Income	$42,042 (370 out of 435)
Land area	8,044	Black	23.2%		
Pop/ sq mi	94.1	Latino	4.0%		
Born in state	62.9%	Asian	1.5%	Under $50,000	57.2%
		Two races	1.6%	$50,000-$99,999	29.2%
Age Groups		Other	0.4%	$100,000-$199,999	11.6%
Under 18	24.3%			$200,000 or more	2.0%
18-34	23.5%	**Education**		Poverty Rate	20.6%
35-64	38.3%	H.S grad or less	46.1%		
Over 64	13.8%	Some college	33.5%	**Health Insurance**	
Work		College Degree, 4 yr	12.7%	With health insurance coverage	82.2%
White Collar	29.9%	Post grad	7.7%		
Sales and Service	43.1%	**Military**		**Public Assistance**	
Blue Collar	27.0%	Veteran	11.1%	Cash public assistance income	1.9%
Government	17.9%	Active Duty	1.3%		
				Food stamp/SNAP benefits	18.1%

Voter Turnout			
2015 Total Citizens 18+	560,078	2016 House Turnout as % CVAP	50%
2016 House turnout	278,779	2014 House Turnout as % CVAP	28%

2012 Presidential Vote		
Mitt Romney	199,354	(68%)
Barack Obama	92,127	(31%)

2016 Presidential Vote		
Donald Trump	196,652	(69%)
Hillary Clinton	80,045	(28%)

Cook Partisan Voting Index: R+21

Coastal Mississippi has gone through several transformations in its history. French explorers founded Biloxi in 1699, before New Orleans or St. Louis, and made it the capital of an empire extending across the Rocky Mountains. Two hundred years later, rich people from New Orleans came to this section of the Gulf Coast in the summer to get away from yellow fever and to rest on Victorian verandas. Six American presidents have vacationed here. There is also a military flavor to the Gulf Coast. Biloxi's Keesler Air Force Base, one of the elite bases in the world, trains 28,000 airmen annually. Pascagoula, the largest military shipbuilder in the nation and the largest private employer in the state, is home to 11,500 workers over 800 acres at Ingalls Shipyard, whose gray, hangar-like buildings and skeletons of ships under construction loom over the landscape.

The region's economic growth was put on hold for several years after these coastal communities took a direct hit from Hurricane Katrina on Aug. 29, 2005. From Waveland to Pascagoula, about 80 miles were obliterated: Beachfront cottages, fishing villages, hotel casinos, oil-drilling platforms, and refineries all were either cruelly swamped or swept away. Status meant nothing. The homes of Confederate President Jefferson Davis in Biloxi and former Senate Majority Leader Trent Lott in Pascagoula were destroyed. The eye of the monster storm passed over the region, and in an instant, countless livelihoods were gone and property losses reached tens of billions of dollars.

If there was a saving grace, many of the communities were left with a clean slate to start over, with more control over the building of high rises and strip malls that had started to overwhelm more distinctive properties. As the cleanup wore on, important decisions were made, especially in Biloxi. Condominium projects were more carefully managed, and shrimp boaters got docks for their boats and places to sell their catch. The state got $560 million in hurricane recovery money for a planned $1.6 billion expansion of the Port of Gulfport. In February 2016, the Topsail company agreed to create 1,000 jobs to build vessels to service offshore drilling rigs. That was a significant down payment on the port's promise of 1,300 jobs. Following the setback that the gulf areas suffered with the massive BP oil spill in 2010, the huge fines from the recovery helped the state to set more rigorous standards to restore the coast and its facilities.

This is the heart of the 4th Congressional District. The three Gulf Coast counties, which include more than 40 percent of the population, experienced growth from 2000 to 2010. The rest of the district's people live inland, in farm counties or around Hattiesburg and Laurel. It has long been Republican territory. A different configuration of the district gave President Richard Nixon his highest percentage of any congressional district in 1972, and it voted five times against fellow Southerners Jimmy Carter, Bill Clinton, and Al Gore. In 2016, the district gave 69 percent of the vote to Donald Trump, one point more than Mitt Romney received in 2012. The district, which has the smallest African-America population in Mississippi, has become the most Republican in the state.

★ MISSOURI ★

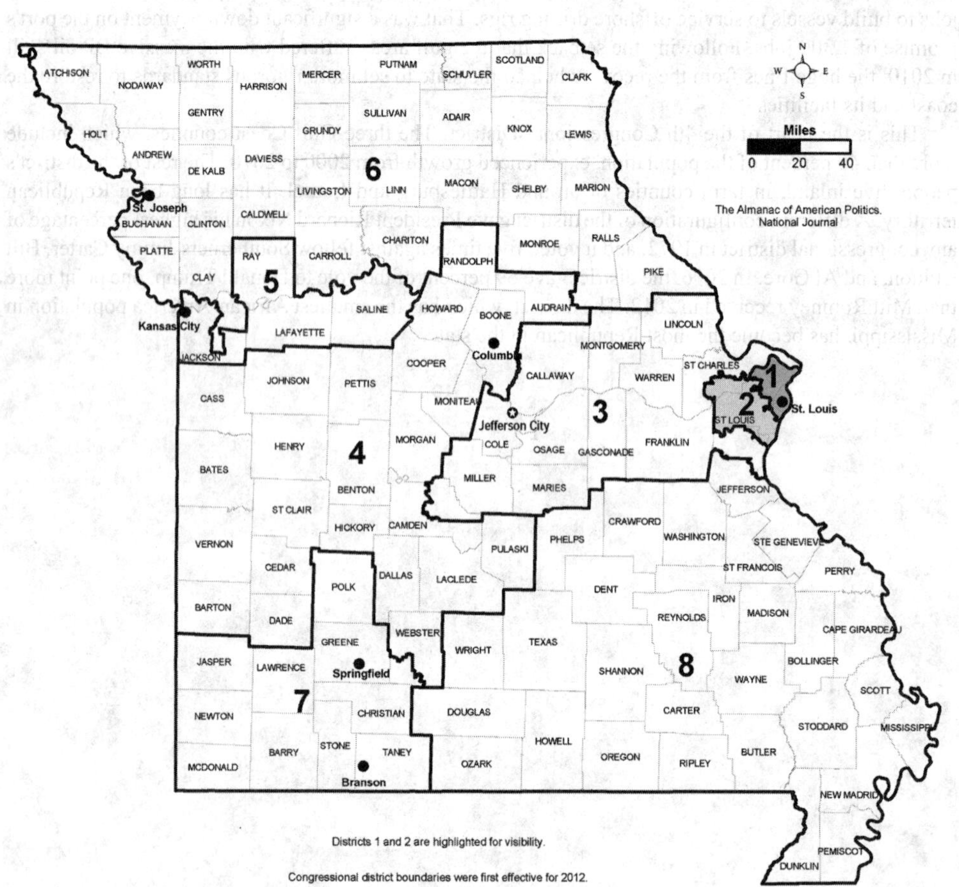

Districts 1 and 2 are highlighted for visibility.

Congressional district boundaries were first effective for 2012.

For a century, Missouri was one of America's political bellwether states. It voted for every presidential winner but one from 1904 to 2004; the exception came in 1956, when it narrowly backed Adlai Stevenson. As recently as 2008, John McCain defeated Barack Obama by fewer than 4,000 votes in the state. But those days are gone. In 2012, Mitt Romney defeated Obama by 10 percentage points. Four years later, Donald Trump won by almost 19 points, inspiring a wave that swept Republicans into every statewide office on the ballot, four of them previously held by Democrats. "Missouri has just become quite a Republican, conservative state," said St. Louis University political scientist Ken Warren.

The Gateway Arch, rising gracefully over the Mississippi River, is a worthy tribute to St. Louis and Missouri as the gateway to the American West, but it is no longer a gleaming symbol of the state's vigor and prosperity. This land was part of France's thinly settled North American empire; St. Louis, just below the swirling confluence of the Missouri River and the Mississippi, was founded by Pierre Laclède and Auguste Chouteau in 1764, while further south in Missouri, the French began mining in the Old Lead Belt as early as 1720. All this and much more was acquired by the United States as part of the Louisiana Purchase of 1803, and on May 14, 1804, at Thomas Jefferson's direction, Meriwether Lewis, William Clark and the Corps of Discovery set out from St. Louis on their expedition to the Pacific. St. Louis was then the one well-established city in America's interior, with an aristocracy of French merchants, a brawling bourgeoisie of Yankee and Southern frontiersmen and fur traders, and a proletariat of black slaves. Statehood came in 1821, and for years thereafter the frontier democracy was a passage for westward expansion, captured in the paintings of George Caleb Bingham. West of St. Louis, new areas were settled: St. Joseph was the eastern terminus of the Pony Express; Westport, now part of Kansas City, was the starting point of the Santa Fe Trail; Independence, identified by Joseph Smith as the site of the Second Coming, was settled by Mormons who left after Gov. Lilburn Boggs ordered them "exterminated"; and Hannibal, on the Mississippi River, was where a boy named Sam Clemens engaged in pranks and watched the early steamboats that he would later chronicle as Mark Twain.

Missouri was also a focus of the furious battle over slavery. It was the northernmost slave state in the 1850s, when Missouri ruffians rode across the border and killed antislavery settlers in the Kansas Territory. The state had its own bloody civil war in the hilly counties along the Missouri River and in the southwest. After the war, in 1874, the Eads Bridge opened, one of the few spans on the Mississippi; St. Louis' Cupples Station was then the largest rail hub in the world. At the turn of the 20th century, Missouri was the fifth-largest state, and St. Louis was the fourth-largest city, site of the 1904 World's Fair, and one of the few cities with two Major League Baseball teams, the Cardinals and the Browns. Missouri was also the national center of the mule trade (Harry Truman's father's line of work), an important business at a time when half of Americans lived on farms and motorized tractors had not yet been invented.

After the 1900 census, Missouri had 16 congressional districts, twice the number it has now. In the 20th century, Americans increasingly headed toward the coasts, to the big cities of the East and West, and eventually to Florida and Texas (as did the baseball Browns, who moved to Baltimore in 1954, and Kansas City's Athletics, who decamped to Oakland in 1968; the football Cardinals, who moved to Phoenix in 1988; and their NFL successor the Rams, who moved back to Los Angeles in 2016). Missouri was the geographic center of the nation's population in the 2010 census: An imaginary, flat map of the United States population, if everyone weighed the same, would balance in Texas County, Missouri. However, Missouri has had below-average population growth since 1900, and today it is the 18th-largest state. Since the 2010 census, the state has grown by 1.7 percent, below average by national standards. Inside its narrow 19th century boundaries, the city of St. Louis had 856,796 in 1950 and 622,000 people in 1970 but only 315,685 in 2015. St. Louis County, which does not include the city's population, has been pretty stable: 952,000 people in 1970 and 1,003,000 in 2015. The three suburban-exurban counties around St. Louis County -- Franklin, Jefferson and St. Charles – have grown by between 1 and 3 percent since the 2010 census. The long-term growth of St. Charles County, a key Republican-leaning county, has been notable, growing from 93,732 in 1970 to 385,590 in 2015. But the state's fastest-growing area is the Lake of the Ozarks region in central and southwest Missouri, around the country music center of Branson. Taney County, which includes Branson, has grown by 5.7 percent since 2010, fed by an influx of modest-income retirees looking for traditional lifestyles and inexpensive recreation.

Missouri's recovery from the Great Recession has closely tracked the national comeback, with unemployment peaking at 9.8 percent and declining to 4.4 percent by December 2016. Median income is 5.6 percent above the national average. Transportation manufacturing remains important in Missouri, employing tens of thousands of workers at plants owned by Boeing, Ford, General Motors and the auto supply firms Yanfeng USA and TG Missouri, among others. Far more jobs are found in the hospital industry, which includes some of the state's largest employers, BJC HealthCare and Mercy Health Systems. St. Louis is home to Express Scripts, the largest pharmacy benefit manager in the country. Major companies native to the state - McDonnell Douglas, TWA, Ralston Purina, May Department Stores, Monsanto, Anheuser-Busch - have been acquired by outside competitors and multinational corporations. In recent years, GDP and job growth has been modest, and farmers have had to deal with severe flooding on the Missouri River in 2011, drought conditions in 2012, and then flooding again in 2016. Meanwhile, local law enforcement agencies have cracked down on the scourge of methamphetamine, with some success, seen in a declining number of lab seizures.

Overall, the state is 80 percent white, 11 percent African American, 4 percent Hispanic and 2 percent Asian. Missouri has some tough immigration laws, even as it has attracted relatively few immigrants; less than 4 percent of residents are foreign-born. This relatively small minority population has had a profound influence on the state's political direction. Unlike states such as Colorado and Nevada, Missouri has not been pushed toward the Democrats by a growing minority population, leaving rural, conservative and largely white areas – with farms and small towns thick with churches and modest shopping centers and laced with man-made lakes and boat launches -- to flex their political muscle. Only one city outside the two big metro areas, Springfield, has a population over 150,000, and in the state's rural heartland, life - and politics - seem not to have changed much over the past half-century. Missouri has permissive gun laws, including the right to carry a concealed weapon without a permit, and it has only one remaining abortion provider. A bill to enable businesses to avoid serving same-sex weddings passed the state Senate in 2016 before failing in the state House amid pressure from business and sports groups, who feared boycotts like those launched in North Carolina and elsewhere. The victory in 2016 by Republican Eric Greitens in an open-seat gubernatorial race – succeeding Democrat Jay Nixon – opened additional possibilities for enacting socially conservative legislation from the supermajority Republican legislature, as well as traditional Republican priorities like the state's new right-to-work measure, among the first bills Greitens signed into law.

Once-obscure Ferguson, a city of 21,000 in St. Louis County where two-thirds of the population is African American, attracted intense national attention when it was rocked by riots in 2014 following the shooting of an unarmed black teenager, Michael Brown, by a white police officer who was later cleared of criminality by a Justice Department investigation. A St. Louis County grand jury had previously declined to indict the officer. Brown's death became an inspiration for the Black Lives Matter movement, which led protests and marches in cities across the country. A Justice Department probe found that the Ferguson police department engaged in abusive policing. The Missouri legislature responded in 2015 by enacting a law to curb the use of traffic fines as a revenue stream to fill municipal coffers, a practice that disproportionately affects the poor and that had inflamed tensions. Those tensions continued into late 2015 at the University of Missouri, where months of protests, including a threatened walkout by the football team, led to the resignation of the university system president, the voluntary demotion of the chancellor of the main campus, and difficulties recruiting minority athletes.

Politically, Missouri was not only a mixture of urban and rural, but its Civil War political divisions still held: Democrats dominated in Little Dixie in the northeast, first settled by Virginians, and in the northwest, settled by southerners. Republicans held sway in the Ozarks in the southwest, which was pro-Union, and the southeast was split, like next-door downstate Illinois. (This is the only state whose name is pronounced two ways, depending on where you're from. In metro St. Louis, they say "Mizuree." In the rest of the state it's "Mizuruh.") But by 2000, these political patterns were being overridden. The large metro areas became even more Democratic as the remainder of the state turned Republican as Civil War loyalties gave way to cultural conservatism. For a while, the parties were evenly matched: In the state's 10 contests for president, senator, and governor between 2000 and 2008, only two were decided by wide margins: Republican Sen. Christopher Bond's reelection in 2004 and Democratic Gov. Jay Nixon's election in 2008. In the eight other contests, Republicans got between 47 percent and 53 percent of the vote, Democrats between 46 percent and 50 percent.

That balance shifted to a strong GOP tilt over the next eight years, led by a relatively large contingent of evangelical voters. This culminated in Trump's sweeping victory. He won 112,000 more votes in the state than Mitt Romney had four years earlier, as Hillary Clinton was winning 153,000 fewer votes than

Obama had in 2012. In both elections, the county-by-county map was a sea of red, with both Obama and Clinton winning only St. Louis city, St. Louis County, Jackson County (Kansas City), and Boone County (Columbia, home of the University of Missouri). In the Democrats' four winning counties, the margins were relatively stable between 2012 and 2016, changing by only two to four percentage points, but the cumulative losses in those counties only accounted for about one-tenth of the Democrats' raw-vote decline in the state. The rest occurred in counties that were red in both elections. Even a suburban county like Jefferson near St. Louis saw its Republican margin expand from 13 percentage points in 2012 to 35 points in 2016, with GOP candidates winning every contested race in the county, including legislative seats, county offices and judicial positions. Even more worrisome for Democrats, a number of its statewide candidates for 2016 had seemed strong until Election Night, notably Jason Kander, who lost a bid against GOP Sen. Roy Blunt despite an impressive television ad showing him assembling a firearm blindfolded. The lesson of 2016 was that the old model for Democratic success – a centrist approach that played well enough outside the big cities to put the party over the top when combined with a strong urban vote – is now a thing of the past.

Population		**Race and Ethnicity**		**Income**	
Total	6,045,448	White	80.2%	Median Income	$48,173 (36 out of 50)
Land area	68,742	Black	11.4%		
Pop/ sq mi	87.9	Latino	3.9%	Under $50,000	51.6%
Born in state	66.2%	Asian	1.7%	$50,000-$99,999	30.4%
		Two races	2.1%	$100,000-$199,999	14.8%
Age Groups		Other	0.6%	$200,000 or more	3.2%
Under 18	23.2%			Poverty Rate	15.6%
18-34	23.0%	**Education**			
35-64	38.9%	H.S grad or less	42.9%	**Health Insurance**	
Over 64	14.9%	Some college	30.0%	With health insurance coverage	87.8%
Work		College Degree, 4 yr	16.9%		
		Post grad	10.2%		
White Collar	35.2%			**Public Assistance**	
Sales and Service	42.7%	**Military**		Cash public assistance income	2.4%
Blue Collar	22.1%	Veteran	9.8%		
Government	12.7%	Active Duty	0.4%	Food stamp/SNAP benefits	13.5%

Voter Turnout			
2015 Total Citizens 18+	4,525,035	2016 Pres Turnout as % CVAP	62%
2016 Pres Votes	2,808,605	2012 Pres Turnout as % CVAP	62%

Legislature	
Senate:	9D, 24R, 1V
House:	46D, 117R

Presidential Politics

2016 Democratic Primary		
Hillary Clinton (D)	312,285	(50%)
Bernie Sanders (D)	310,711	(49%)
2016 Republican Primary		
Donald Trump (R)	383,631	(41%)
Ted Cruz (R)	381,666	(41%)
John Kasich (R)	94,857	(10%)
Marco Rubio (R)	57,244	(6%)

2016 Presidential Vote		
Donald Trump (R)	1,594,511	(57%)
Hillary Clinton (D)	1,071,068	(38%)
Gary Johnson (L)	97,359	(3%)
2012 Presidential Vote		
Mitt Romney (R)	1,482,440	(54%)
Barack Obama (D)	1,223,796	(44%)

Before 1904, Democratic strength in Missouri outside of its big cities made the state more Democratic in presidential races than the nation. Since 2000, Republican strength in the numerous rural counties outside the two big metro areas has made it more Republican than the nation. Missouri was a battleground in 2008, and John McCain's 3,903-vote margin might have sparked a challenge but for the fact that it would not affect the election of Barack Obama. Before Missouri's more recent form as a reliably Republican state, it was a swing state and a bellwether: from 1904 to 2004, it voted for the winning presidential candidate in every election except for 1956. In 2016, voters in the Show Me State favored Donald Trump over Hillary Clinton, 57%-38%. In eight years, the state went from a toss-up to one that gave the Republican nominee a 19 point victory margin. Clinton carried only St. Louis and three of the state's 114 counties: Boone, home to the University of Missouri at Columbia; Jackson, Kansas City; and St. Louis County, the largest vote producer in the state and also home to Ferguson, the site of 2014 racial unrest. Some political observers say that Trump's law-and-order rhetoric played well in the aftermath. "Across the state of Missouri, I think the predominant opinion is that the governor did not crack down enough on protests, and I think that's unfortunately an attitude that has taken hold," St. Louis African-American alderman Antonio French told Huffingtonpost.com a month before the election.

Missouri provided two of the closest presidential primaries of the 2016 campaign. In the March 15 Republican primary, Trump edged out Texas Sen. Ted Cruz by 1,965 votes out of more than 920,000 cast - essentially a 41%-41% tie. Trump carried the St. Louis metropolitan area and most of the rural counties in the state, while Cruz won the Kansas City metro, where he had advertised heavily, the Columbia metro, Springfield, Joplin and several surrounding Ozark Mountain counties where many evangelical voters reside. On the Democratic side, Clinton squeaked out a 50%-49% victory over Vermont Sen. Bernie Sanders in which the margin was 1,574 votes out of some 630,000 cast. She won St. Louis County and the city, as well as Jackson (Kansas City), while Sanders won Boone and Greene (Missouri State University) counties and suburban-exurban counties around Kansas City and St. Louis. They split rural counties, with Clinton winning along the Mississippi River and Sanders taking more counties in the western part of the state. But it was Clinton's 18,000-vote margin in St. Louis County that contributed most to her victory.

Congressional Districts

115th Congress Lineup	6R 2D	**114th Congress Lineup**	6R 2D

Slow population growth cost Missouri its ninth seat in the 2010 census. Republicans badly wanted to expand their 6-3 advantage into a 6-2 edge by eliminating Democratic Rep. Russ Carnahan's district in the St. Louis suburbs. The sole Democratic obstacle was Gov. Jay Nixon. Republicans held a sufficient majority in the state Senate (26-8) but not quite in the state House (106-57) to override a veto. In April 2011, the Republican legislature passed a plan folding much of Carnahan's 3rd District into African-American Democrat William Lacy Clay's 1st District based in St. Louis. As expected, Nixon vetoed the map, but did so seemingly halfheartedly. Some Democrats contended Nixon could have helped Carnahan more by delaying his veto and reducing Republicans' window to override. Nonetheless, it was up to Republicans to find the 109 votes to override, and in soap opera fashion they did. Four African-American Democrats, under private pressure from Clay and Kansas City 5th District Democrat Emanuel Cleaver, then chairman of the Congressional Black Caucus, ultimately broke ranks to provide the decisive votes. One, Kansas City state Rep. Jonas Hughes, held his tearful face in his hand afterwards, explaining "[Cleaver] asked me to."

In this example of how underlying tension between black and white Democrats often helps Republicans on redistricting, Cleaver and Clay, eager to keep the strong African-American constituencies the Republican map offered them, didn't mind throwing Carnahan under the bus. Carnahan reacted by, reportedly, swearing at Clay on the floor of the House, then mounting a weak and uphill primary challenge to him in the 1st District.

Since then, Republicans have easily retained their six districts, despite considerable geographic shifts within them. The state's once-influential centrist Democrats in the House have become a relic of the past. If Republicans retain the governorship they won in 2016, Democrats in the next redistricting will be hard-pressed to find a third district beyond St. Louis and Kansas City. Ironically, their best opportunity might be in the 2nd District, which is the surviving seat in the St. Louis suburbs. That prospect would increase if Clay changed his approach and relinquished some of his base in the heavily Democratic 1st.

Governor

Eric Greitens (R)

Elected 2016, term expires 2021, 1st term; b. Apr. 10, 1974, St. Louis, MO; Duke University (Rhodes Scholar, Truman Scholar), 1996; Oxford University, D.Phil 2000; Jewish; Married (Sheena); 2 children.

Military Career: U.S Navy SEAL, 2001-2017.

Professional Career: White House Fellow 2005-2008, Non-Profit Founder, Author

Office: PO Box 720, Jefferson City, 65102-9500; 573-751-3222; Fax: 573-526-3291; Website: mo.gov.

Election Results

Election	Name (Party)	Vote (%)
2016 General	Eric Greitens (R)	1,424,730 (51%)
	Chris Koster (D)	1,261,110 (45%)
2016 Primary	Eric Greitens (R)	236,481 (35%)
	John Brunner (R)	169,620 (25%)
	Peter Kinder (R)	141,629 (21%)
	Catherine Hanaway (R)	136,521 (20%)

Eric Greitens, whose sterling resume includes years of service as a Navy SEAL and founder of a veterans' group, was elected governor of Missouri in 2016 running as a political outsider. Greitens, who prevailed in a bitter four-way GOP primary, trailed his opponent, Democratic Attorney General Chris Koster, for most of the general-election campaign. But he closed the gap thanks to a strong wave of support for Donald Trump.

Greitens grew up in a Jewish family in suburban St. Louis County; his mother was an early childhood special education teacher, and his father worked for the state Agriculture Department. While attending Duke University, Greitens traveled extensively. In China, he studied kung fu (he was already a boxer) and taught English. He also provided humanitarian services for Bosnian, Rwandan and Bolivian children. He continued such activities in India and Albania as a Rhodes Scholar at Oxford University.

Greitens joined the Navy in January 2001. After graduating from officer candidate school, he was assigned to train as a SEAL and eventually served four tours of duty overseas, including stints in Afghanistan and Iraq. On his final tour of duty, he served in Fallujah, Iraq, commanding a group tasked with targeting mid- to senior-level al-Qaida leaders. While there, his team was hit by a suicide truck bomb. Greitens received a Combat Action Ribbon, a Purple Heart and a Bronze Star. Upon his return home, he remained a reservist and founded a veterans' assistance group called the Mission Continues. President George W. Bush gave Greitens the President's Volunteer Service Award, and *Time* magazine included him on its list of 100 influential people in the world.

Greitens grew up in a Democratic household, and he attended the Democratic National Convention in 2008. Two years later, the Democratic Congressional Campaign Committee courted him to run for Congress, but he declined. He said his military service and work with veterans has made him a conservative -- "not by birth but by conviction." In 2015, Democratic Gov. Jay Nixon was winding down his second and final term in office, and Greitens announced that he was running in the Republican primary to succeed him. The other three main primary candidates were all better known, and two of them had more extensive experience in politics. Peter Kinder was first elected to the state Senate in 1992; he became Senate president in 2001 and was elected lieutenant governor in 2004, 2008 and 2012. Catherine Hanaway was a former state House speaker and U.S. attorney for the Eastern District of Missouri; her campaign was supported by wealthy donor Rex Sinquefield and advised by Jeff Roe, who had managed Texas Sen. Ted Cruz's presidential campaign. Businessman John Brunner, meanwhile, competed with Greitens for the outsider mantle, touting his experience as the CEO of Vi-Jon, a personal-care products company.

All of the four candidates positioned themselves in opposition to Nixon, particularly his handling of the fatal August 2014 shooting of unarmed black teenager Michael Brown by a white police officer in Ferguson, a predominantly black city of 21,000 in St. Louis County. The Republican candidates sharply criticized Nixon for a lack of leadership as the nonviolent protests turned into rioting and looting. "For many people in Missouri, especially the approximately 600,000 Republicans who expect to vote in the GOP primary Tuesday, the lesson of Ferguson is not that the police used too much force, it's that it used too little," Maggie Severns wrote in *Politico*. "Ferguson, to them, was an embarrassment: preventable chaos that tarnished the name of the otherwise orderly St. Louis suburbs." The GOP primary candidates also promised to enact a wide variety of conservative initiatives that had been vetoed by Nixon; during his tenure, Nixon successfully handed down 283 vetoes, with 96 others overridden.

Greitens' biography and his positioning as an outsider resonated. "We have a political class of corrupt consultants, well-paid lobbyists and career politicians who have been in Jefferson City for decades," he said when announcing his run. "They have produced nothing for us but embarrassment and failure." Greitens proposed term-limiting all statewide offices and banning gifts from lobbyists to legislators. Spending by outside groups proliferated in the primary, and the attacks between Brunner and Greitens became particularly contentious. Brunner hit Greitens for taking $1 million from a California man who had been accused of sexual assault; the donor hit Brunner with a defamation suit. Greitens posed enough of a threat that the Democratic Governors Association spent a half million dollars before the primary on attack ads targeting him. In the end, Greitens won the nomination by a larger-than-expected margin – he got 35 percent, to 25 percent for Brunner, 21 percent for Kinder and 20 percent for Hanaway.

That set up a race, as the *Kansas City Star* noted, "between a Republican who used to be a Democrat and a Democrat who used to be a Republican." The latter would be Koster, who had been a Cass County prosecutor and then a Republican state senator. In 2007, saying that "Republican moderates are all but extinct," he switched parties, and the following year he was elected attorney general for the first of two terms. Koster, a centrist similar to Nixon, became the obvious Democratic hopeful to succeed him; he skated through the primary without significant opposition, allowing him to amass a sizable war chest. Koster managed to get endorsements from the National Rifle Association and the Farm Bureau – a coup for a Democrat running in an increasingly red state, and useful talking points as he tried to separate himself from the unpopular Democratic standard bearer, Hillary Clinton.

Koster led Greitens in the polls for most of the campaign, but on Election Day, Greitens won by five points – a much more modest victory than Trump's dominating 19-point win in the state, but an 18-point swing from 2012, when Nixon had won a second term by 13 points. Whereas Nixon won more than three dozen counties, Koster prevailed in only three (St. Louis, Jackson and Boone) plus St. Louis city. Greitens flipped four of the biggest seven counties in the state – St. Charles and Jefferson in the St. Louis area, Clay in metro Kansas City, and Greene (Springfield). Each of these four counties saw their margins shift by between 12 and 25 points toward the GOP candidate, and even in the big counties that remained blue, Koster's margins shrank by five to nine percentage points compared with Nixon's in 2012. The Trump wave also pushed Republicans to victory in the races for lieutenant governor, treasurer, secretary of state and attorney general.

At his inauguration, Greitens said, "To those who would trouble this house for their own selfish and sinful gain, hear me now: I answer to the people, and I come as an outsider to do the people's work." That day, he signed an executive order banning lobbyist gifts to executive branch employees. In short order, he signed a right-to-work bill and a temporary freeze on new regulations, though he also faced budgetary problems – a projected $40 million shortfall by the end of the fiscal year. Still, as the first Missouri Republican governor to serve with GOP supermajorities in both legislative chambers, Greitens had reason to expect a productive legislative season. And success as governor could vault him to a national profile.

Senior Senator

Claire McCaskill (D)

Elected 2006, term expires 2018, 2nd term; b. Jul 24, 1953, Rolla; University of Missouri Law School, J.D.; University of Missouri, B.S.; Roman Catholic; Married (Joseph Shepard); 3 children; 4 stepchildren; 8 grandchildren.

Elected Office: MO House, 1982-1988; Jackson County Legislature, 1990-1992; Jackson County prosecutor, 1992-1998; MO auditor, 1998-2006.

Professional Career: Law clerk, MO Court of Appeals, 1978; Assistant Jackson County prosecutor, 1978-1982; Practicing attorney, 1983-1992.

DC Office: 503 HSOB 20510, 202-224-6154, Fax: 202-228-6326, mccaskill.senate.gov.

State Offices: Cape Girardeau, 573-651-0964; Columbia, 573-442-7130; Kansas City, 816-421-1639; Springfield, 417-868-8745; St. Louis, 314-367-1364.

Committees: *Armed Services*: Airland, Cybersecurity, Personnel. *Finance*: International Trade, Customs & Global Competitiveness, Taxation & IRS Oversight. *Homeland Security & Government Affairs (RMM)*: Federal Spending Oversight & Emergency Management, Investigations, Regulatory Affairs & Federal Management.

Group Ratings

	ADA	ACLU	AFL-CIO	LCV	ITI	COC	HAFA	ACU	CFG	FRC
2016	-	70%	-	82%	80%	75%	5%	12%	15%	0%
2015	65%	C	57%	76%	C	64%	C	4%	9%	0%

Almanac Ratings 2015

	Economy	Social	Foreign	Composite
Liberal	66%	100%	75%	80%
Conservative	34%	0%	25%	20%

Key Votes of the 114th Congress

1. Keystone pipeline	Y	5. National Security Data	Y	9. Gun Sales Checks	Y
2. Export-Import Bank	N	6. Iran Nuclear Deal	N	10. Sanctuary Cities	N
3. Debt Ceiling Increase	Y	7. Puerto Rico Debt	Y	11. Planned Parenthood	N
4. Homeland Security $$	Y	8. Loretta Lynch A.G	Y	12. Trade deals	Y

Election Results

Election	Name (Party)	Vote (%)		Cand. Spent	Ind. Exp. Support	Ind. Exp. Oppose
2012 General	Claire McCaskill (D)	1,494,125	(55%)	$21,264,093	$2,384,795	$1,220,150
	Todd Akin (R)	1,066,159	(39%)	$6,165,888	$2,626,339	$6,653,741
	Jonathan Dine (L)	165,468	(6%)			
2012 Primary	Claire McCaskill (D)	289,481	(100%)			

Prior winning percentages: 2006 (50%)

Democrat Claire McCaskill, Missouri's senior senator, is among the moderate Democrats who have prepared for a tough reelection contest in 2018. As the campaign cycle began, she faced the challenge in her diverse state of demonstrating her independence from partisan pressures while responding to pressure from liberal Democrats to take a hard line in opposing President Donald Trump and the Republican-controlled Congress. She gave an early signal in April 2017 when she voted against the confirmation of Neal Gorsuch to the Supreme Court, while three other Democratic senators facing tough reelection contests in 2018 voted for Gorsuch.

With Missouri growing more conservative and McCaskill having become the only remaining Democrat elected statewide, it was unlikely that she would enjoy the good fortune that boosted her to a second term in 2012. In that race, she helped to make her own big break when her general election opponent, Republican Rep. Todd Akin, committed a disastrous gaffe, with his infamous remark about "legitimate rape." McCaskill had run advertising during the GOP primary that bolstered Akin among conservatives. Once he was nominated, national Republicans soon fled from his candidacy and enabled the once politically endangered McCaskill to cruise to a 16-point win, even as GOP presidential nominee Mitt Romney scored a 9-point victory over President Barack Obama in the Show-Me State.

While Akin and other Republicans sought to hammer McCaskill as a liberal during the 2012 campaign, her Senate voting record has been decidedly centrist, even as the blunt-spoken former prosecutor has not hesitated to take on controversial issues and situations, on which she displayed her independence. In the *Almanac* vote ratings for 2015, she ranked as the fifth most-conservative Democrat in the Senate; on economic and foreign-policy issues, she was No. 2. She was among eight Democrats to join all Republican senators in a vote to override President Obama's veto of legislation to move ahead on the Keystone XL Pipeline project. When she voted to give Obama so-called fast track authority to expedite negotiation of a 12-nation Asian trade deal, it pitted her against the large majority of her Democratic colleagues and most labor unions. No doubt, McCaskill drew lessons from the unexpectedly narrow reelection in 2016 of Sen. Roy Blunt, her Republican colleague, who was repeatedly attacked for losing touch at home.

McCaskill was born in Rolla, about halfway between St. Louis and Springfield. Her father, William, later served as state insurance commissioner, and her mother became the first female city council member in the university town of Columbia after the family moved there. McCaskill earned degrees from the University of Missouri and its law school, and worked as an assistant prosecutor. In 1982, she was elected to the Missouri House, where she was the first member to have a baby while in office. Ten years later, she became Jackson County (Kansas City) prosecutor.

In 1998, she was elected state auditor, and halfway through her second term, in 2004, she challenged incumbent Democratic Gov. Bob Holden. Holden's administration had started off on the wrong foot, holding a $1 million inaugural that wound up $417,000 in debt. As a tough economic climate necessitated deep spending cuts, Holden battled with the legislature. McCaskill responded to the many Democrats who felt the party needed a stronger candidate to survive a Republican challenge, defeating Holden in the primary, 52%-45%. In the general election, McCaskill sought to take advantage of the youth and government inexperience of her opponent, 33-year old Secretary of State Matt Blunt, boasting she would not need on the on-the-job training. Blunt, the son of McCaskill's junior Senate colleague, won, 51%-48%. It was not the first election between the Blunt and McCaskill families. In 1978, McCaskill's mother, Betty, lost a race to Roy Blunt's father, Leroy, for a seat in the Missouri House.

Despite that narrow loss, McCaskill, with three statewide races under her belt, was a prize Senate recruit for the national party in 2006. That seat had changed partisan hands twice in the previous six years. In 2000, term-limited Democratic Gov. Mel Carnahan took on Republican incumbent John Ashcroft and was elected, even though Carnahan was killed in a plane crash just days before the polls opened. Carnahan's widow, Jean, was appointed to fill the seat, and served until 2002, when former GOP Rep. Jim Talent was elected to fill the remaining four years of the term. McCaskill announced her candidacy against Talent on the steps of the Houston feed mill where her father once worked. It was a backdrop that telegraphed her focus on the rural counties, where her weak showing cost her the governor's election. She denounced tax breaks for oil companies, called for an increase in the minimum wage, and said she would push tax credits for first-time home purchases as well as for child care and college education.

McCaskill linked Talent to President George W. Bush, whose popularity was sinking. The controversial issue of embryonic stem cell research generated the most attention. A proposed state constitutional amendment forced both candidates to address whether they supported more government funding for the research. McCaskill supported it, with Talent opposed. Missouri Republicans were split: State business leaders backed the proposal in hopes of attracting biomedical research, while religious conservatives opposed it, regarding use of surplus human embroyos as tantamount to abortion. In October, Talent targeted McCaskill's family's finances, demanding that her husband, Joseph Shepard, a developer of low income housing financed by government loans, release his tax returns-filed separately from his wife's. Talent suggested the couple hadn't paid all of their taxes, and accused Shepard of owning an offshore tax shelter. McCaskill won 50%-47%, the third consecutive election for the seat with a party switch that was decided by fewer than 50,000 votes. As in the governor's race, McCaskill won big margins in the Kansas City and St. Louis metro areas, but unlike 2004, she held her own in outstate Missouri and carried 11 rural counties she lost earlier.

McCaskill has consistently sought to emphasize her independence in the Senate, including with her voting record. She did vote in 2010 with all Senate Democrats for the Affordable Care Act, but later said she would consider changing its individual mandate requirement. That year, she joined other moderates in questioning the party's support for additional extensions of expanded unemployment benefits. "At some point, it starts to look like another entitlement program," she observed. Earlier, she opposed an immigration bill that created a guest worker program and a path to citizenship for illegal immigrants.

After Democrats across the country were portrayed as pork-barrel spenders in the 2010 election, McCaskill joined with conservative Republican Sen. Tom Coburn of Oklahoma to push for a ban on spending earmarks, historically used by influential members of Congress to direct money to favored projects back home. Their move failed on a procedural vote. Early the next year, Appropriations Committee Chairman Daniel Inouye announced an earmark moratorium, which was extended a year later-even as McCaskill and Republican Sen. Pat Toomey of Pennsylvania failed in their bid to make the earmark ban permanent. Arguments that a permanent ban would impede congressional power were "horseradish," McCaskill declared in the folksy vernacular that has become a trademark. Her blunt-spoken style has helped to win points with Democratic colleagues, such as when she declared in 2011 that Republican Leader Mitch McConnell had "lost his mind" by allowing political considerations to take precedence over striking a deal to raise the federal debt limit. She continued her fight against earmarks in an interview following the 2016 election. "If this election stood for anything, it's that the voters are not going to put up with business as usual," she told McClatchy News.

The earmark battle has been consistent with her focus, as a former state auditor, on government reform. The crowning achievement of her first term was a provision included in the fiscal 2013 defense spending bill. It required government agencies to prove that money will not be wasted on projects before they allocate funds, while at the same time strengthening the powers of inspectors general investigating fraud and abuse. The bill established a clear chain of authority for contracting oversight in the Defense Department, State Department, and Agency for International Development. But McCaskill's image as a watchdog suffered a blow in 2011 with news reports that she had spent $76,000 in taxpayer funds to fly on a private plane she co-owned with her husband. She contended it was a minor oversight, and sought to extinguish the controversy by reimbursing the Treasury. But the situation-dubbed "Air Claire"-became more embarrassing when McCaskill acknowledged she had failed to pay more than $287,000 in personal property taxes on the plane. She later paid $88,000 to the government to cover all costs associated with the flights and sold the plane.

Amid the "Air Claire" flap and Missouri's increasingly conservative leanings, McCaskill headed into the 2012 election high on the list of Senate Democrats seen as vulnerable, with approval rating back home stuck just above 40 percent. Republican groups such as American Crossroads had poured more than $15 million into attack ads against her. Besides Akin, who had a record in the House for vehement social conservatism, the primary field included more moderate Republicans such as former state Treasurer Sarah Steelman and St. Louis businessman John Brunner. McCaskill made no secret of her desire to avoid a more centrist candidate. With the help of the Democratic Party and its allies, she sought to boost Akin's prospects by airing an ad that branded Akin the "true conservative." The DSCC followed with ads that aired on conservative talk radio stations. The gambit worked: Akin won with 36 percent, with Brunner and Steelman running second and third in an eight-person Republican field. McCaskill's tactic has since been emulated by other Democratic campaigns without much success.

As she had in the prior campaign, McCaskill pressed for a minimum wage increase, while vowing to protect Social Security. But she also refused to cede rural areas, driving to small towns to highlight how often she had differed with her party. While early polls gave Akin a lead, the race abruptly changed two weeks after the August primary, when Akin appeared on St. Louis TV station KTVI. Asked if women who had been raped should be afforded the option of abortion, he dropped a bombshell: "If it's a legitimate rape, the female body has ways to try to shut that whole thing down." Realizing the disaster on their hands, Republicans from Romney on down called on Akin to withdraw from the race. NRSC Chairman John Cornyn of Texas said he would no longer provide Akin financial help (although it was later revealed the NRSC provided $760,000 in the race's closing days). Akin refused to get out, and on Election Day, it wasn't even close, with McCaskill winning, 55%-39%. Akin won most of the small rural counties, but MacAskill won several other counties that she had lost in 2006, including St. Charles County in the St. Louis suburbs, which had been considered an Akin stronghold.

McCaskill attracted media attention in 2013 as she and Democratic Sen. Kirsten Gillibrand of New York lobbied their colleagues on behalf of rival proposals for dealing with an increasingly high-profile issue: Sexual assault in the military. Both women, members of the Armed Services Committee, sought to address complaints that the military was not dealing seriously enough with such transgressions. Gillibrand wanted to remove sexual assault cases from the military chain of command, while McCaskill advocated for a more incremental approach that limited the discretion of military commanders without removing court-martial proceedings from their jurisdiction.

As a former prosecutor, McCaskill reportedly spent hundreds of hours meeting with military and civilian prosecutors and others involved in the issue. Her approach was backed by the Defense

Department, while victims' groups favored Gillibrand's alternative. McCaskill was said to be enraged when one victims' group took out newspaper ads in Missouri attacking her. In 2014, the Senate voted in favor of McCaskill's plan. The two senators later put aside their differences to work together on combating sexual assault on college campuses. In response to criticism, McCaskill said that their bill provided due process to anyone who was accused, transparency for the process and training for the colleges.

In 2014, McCaskill was a high-profile presence in the wake of unrest in the St. Louis suburb of Ferguson that followed the shooting death of a black teenager, Michael Brown, by a white police officer. While suggesting much of the violence that followed Brown's death was the work of outsiders, McCaskill criticized the response of the Ferguson police to nightly demonstrations. "I think most Americans were uncomfortable watching a suburban street in St. Louis with vivid images of a war zone," McCaskill told a hearing of the Senate Homeland Security and Governmental Affairs Committee, on which she serves. "Those lawful, peaceful protesters did not deserve to be treated like enemy combatants." She was critical of a Defense Department program that provided surplus military equipment to local police forces, some of which was used in Ferguson, and advocated "demilitarization." She filed a bill to require that local police be trained in the use of such equipment, along with providing federal grants to help municipalities equip police with body cameras.

Amid the unrest, McCaskill said via social media that she had made "dozens" of calls "to de-escalate the tense and unacceptable situation in Ferguson." It highlighted her status as one of Congress' most avid users of Twitter, where she has attracted nearly 200,000 followers by regularly tweeting political and personal tidbits.

After the Democrats lost the Senate majority in the 2014 election, McCaskill was among a handful of Democrats from Republican-leaning states to oppose Nevada Sen. Harry Reid remaining as Senate Democratic leader. She told reporters that the loss of nine Senate seats was a message that change was needed at the top of the Senate leadership. Her comments brought speculation that McCaskill was growing frustrated on Capitol Hill and looking homeward to a possible run for governor. But in early 2015, to the relief of Senate Democrats, McCaskill said she would not run in 2016 to succeed term-limited Democratic Gov. Jay Nixon. "I look at the makeup of the current U.S. Senate and I see what might be possible in terms of me helping forge some… compromises, and at the end of the day the work is too important, the job is too rewarding and too fulfilling," she told KCUR Radio in Kansas City.

In 2017, McCaskill took over as the ranking Democrat on the Homeland Security Committee, where the focus on government process is a good match for her interests. When President Donald Trump issued his initial ban on travel by refugees and some immigrants to the United States, she led committee Democrats in demanding that the Homeland Security Department provide details and a legal analysis of the action. "The gathering of the appropriate officials to actually put guidance out and make this work didn't begin until the order was signed – so no wonder it was as chaotic and rocky as it was," she said, following a classified briefing. On her vote against Gorsuch, she said that it was "a really difficult decision" and that she was not comfortable with either choice that she had. His views "reveal a rigid ideology that always puts the little guy under the boot of corporations," she said, while adding, "I remain very worried about our polarized politics."

As Republicans prepared to challenge her in 2018, McCaskill said that she was "very familiar" with being the underdog. In July 2017, Rep. Ann Wagner surprisingly decided not to run. Rep. Vicky Hartzler and Attorney General Josh Hawley remained possibilities. In early 2016, McCaskill had three weeks of treatment for breast cancer. She said that her doctors concluded that her prognosis was "very good." She has been able to make the most of the challenges that she faces.

Junior Senator

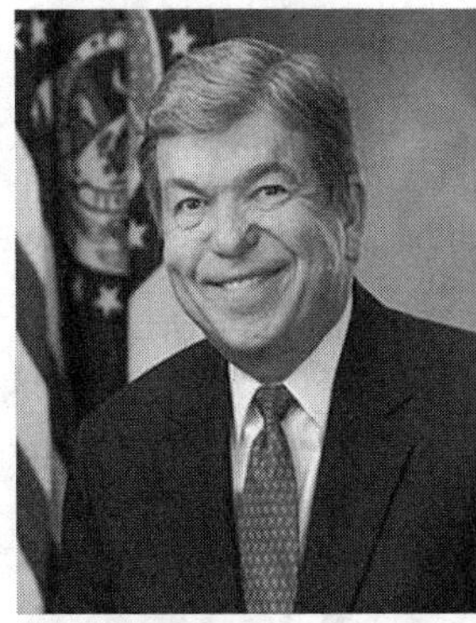

Roy Blunt (R)

Elected 2010, term expires 2022, 2nd term; b. Jan 10, 1950, Niangua; Southwest Baptist University (MO), B.A.; Southwest Missouri State University, M.A.; Baptist; Married (Abigail Blunt); 4 children; 6 grandchildren.

Elected Office: MO Secretary of State, 1984-1993; U.S. House, 1997-2011.

Professional Career: H.S. teacher, 1970-1973; Greene County clerk, 1973-1985; Adjunct instructor, Drury College, 1976-1982; President, SW Baptist University, 1993-1996.

DC Office: 260 RSOB 20510, 202-224-5721, Fax: 202-224-8149, blunt.senate.gov.

State Offices: Cape Girardeau, 573-334-7044; Clayton, 314-725-4484; Columbia, 573-442-8151; Kansas City, 816-471-7141; Springfield, 417-877-7814.

Committees: Senate Republican Conference Vice Chairman. *Appropriations*: Agriculture, Rural Development, FDA & Related Agencies, Department of Defense, Department of the Interior, Environment & Related Agencies, DOL, HHS & Education & Related Agencies (Chmn), State, Foreign Operations & Related Programs, Transportation, HUD & Related Agencies. *Commerce, Science & Transportation*: Aviation Operations, Safety & Security (Chmn), Communications, Technology, Innovation & the Internet, Consumer Protection, Product Safety, Ins & Data Security, Surface Trans., Merchant Marine Infra., Safety & Security. *Intelligence. Rules & Administration.*

Group Ratings

	ADA	ACLU	AFL-CIO	LCV	ITI	COC	HAFA	ACU	CFG	FRC
2016	-	11%	-	24%	80%	100%	47%	60%	54%	100%
2015	0%	C	21%	4%	C	92%	C	83%	68%	100%

Almanac Ratings 2015

	Economy	Social	Foreign	Composite
Liberal	21%	0%	0%	7%
Conservative	79%	100%	100%	93%

Key Votes of the 114th Congress

1. Keystone pipeline	Y	5. National Security Data	N	9. Gun Sales Checks	N
2. Export-Import Bank	N	6. Iran Nuclear Deal	Y	10. Sanctuary Cities	Y
3. Debt Ceiling Increase	N	7. Puerto Rico Debt	Y	11. Planned Parenthood	Y
4. Homeland Security $$	N	8. Loretta Lynch A.G	N	12. Trade deals	Y

Election Results

Election	Name (Party)	Vote	(%)	Cand. Spent	Ind. Exp. Support	Ind. Exp. Oppose
2016 General	Roy Blunt (R)	1,378,458	(49%)	$13,690,121	$1,619,549	$15,738,323
	Jason Kander (D)	1,300,200	(46%)	$12,867,419	$6,305,759	$21,999,506
	Jonathan Dine (L)	67,738	(2%)			
2016 Primary	Roy Blunt (R)	481,444	(73%)			
	Kristi Nichols (R)	134,025	(20%)			

Prior winning percentages: 2010 (54%), House: 2008 (69%), 2006 (67%), 2004 (70%), 2002 (75%), 2000 (74%), 1998 (73%), 1996 (65%)

Republican Roy Blunt, Missouri's junior senator, won a second term after an unexpectedly close contest in 2016 with Secretary of State Jason Kander, a former Army intelligence officer who emphasized his own youth and Blunt's excessive ties with Washington and lobbyists. Blunt won his contest by 3 percentage points, while Donald Trump won his race in Missouri by 19 points-a clear indication that Blunt survived because of presidential coattails. Although his stature in Washington might not have provided much benefit at home, Blunt is among the handful of legislators to serve as a party leader in both the House and Senate. After serving in the House as both majority and minority whip-and, for several months in 2005, as acting House majority leader-Blunt, just a year after his 2010 election to the Senate, was chosen as vice chairman of the Republican Conference. Blunt has added to his influence as chairman of the Rules and Administration Committee, whose jurisdiction includes the internal management of the Senate. He has been an occasional spokesman for Senate Republicans.

As Kander and the Democrats described in the 2016 campaign, Blunt has presided over a family with many connections to the lobbying community, which have occasionally prompted public interest groups to raise conflict-of-interest questions. Blunt's second wife, Abigail, is the head of governmental affairs for Kraft Foods, and was previously a lobbyist for the Altria Group, parent company of the Philip Morris tobacco giant. The Blunts insist they don't mix business with family matters: Abigail Blunt formally abstained from lobbying the House when her husband served there, and filed disclosure forms in 2011 saying she would not lobby the Senate. The family's lobbying connections extended to two sons from Blunt's first marriage. His oldest son, Matt, who was Missouri's governor from 2004-2008, is president of the American Automotive Policy Council, which represents the Big Three automakers. His son Andrew runs a Missouri-based lobbying firm, whose clients have included AT&T, American Airlines, MillerCoors and Motorola. He has managed each of his father's Senate campaigns.

Roy Blunt grew up on a farm in Niangua, near Springfield in southwest Missouri. His father Leroy, who died in 2016, was a dairy farmer who won election as a state representative in 1978 by defeating the mother of Democratic Sen. Claire McCaskill, now Roy Blunt's senior Missouri colleague. By then, the younger Blunt's political career was well underway. In 1970, he graduated from Southwest Baptist University, teaching high school classes in history and government while earning his master's degree in 1972. He got his start in politics the same year, volunteering in the unsuccessful congressional campaign of Republican John Ashcroft-who went on to become governor, senator, and U.S. attorney general. In 1973, then-GOP Gov. Christopher (Kit) Bond named the 23-year-old Blunt as Greene County clerk. In 1980, Republican Sen. John Danforth asked Blunt to run for lieutenant governor, but Blunt lost. Four years later, he was elected Missouri secretary of state, the first Republican to win that office in half a century, and served two terms. In 1992, he ran for governor and narrowly lost the Republican primary, and took a respite from politics to become president of Southwest Baptist University, his alma mater.

In 1996, Blunt ran for the open House seat in the Springfield area and won with two-thirds of the vote. The district has been solidly Republican, and Blunt was reelected easily in his following six terms. In his 14 years in the House, Blunt had a mostly conservative voting record, with intermittent moves toward the center on social issues. In 2006, he won passage of his Combat Meth Act, the first comprehensive approach to fighting the supply of methamphetamine. He sponsored a measure creating an Internet database of federal spending: The sponsor of the Senate companion bill: a young Illinois Democrat named Barack Obama. Blunt's greater impact in the House was in his leadership roles, which gave him a say in shaping the major legislation produced by the Republican majority.

In 1999, Blunt was one of 10 original members of then-Texas Gov. George W. Bush's presidential exploratory committee. Bush called him "a leader who knows how to raise his sights and lower his voice." Blunt's rise in leadership began in 1999, when Majority Whip Tom Delay, a Texas Republican, plucked him from the ranks of deputy whips and made him chief deputy whip, an important leadership stepping stone. In contrast to DeLay, nicknamed "the Hammer," Blunt had a reputation as a good listener with a light touch. On numerous issues, Blunt's job was to make certain that bills the leadership hoped to pass were palatable to conservatives. He also paid attention to party moderates, then a larger share of the House GOP Conference. Blunt spent a good deal of time meeting with lobbyists and organizing groups around issues such as trade, taxes, and energy, while raising substantial sums for GOP candidates. When DeLay moved up to replace Majority Leader Dick Armey of Texas in 2002, Blunt took the whip post.

As whip, he met his toughest challenge in passing the 2003 bill to create a prescription drug benefit as part of the Medicare program. In a highly controversial vote in which the roll call was held open for three hours, he was able to persuade two Republicans to switch their votes. But there were rocky moments. In 2003, the House leadership was embarrassed by disclosures in *The Washington Post* that Blunt, the previous fall, had quietly sought to insert into a homeland security bill a provision benefiting Philip Morris. At the time, Blunt was dating his future wife, then a Philip Morris lobbyist (the couple married in 2003) and Blunt's son, Andrew, was doing work for Philip Morris in Missouri. Blunt defended the provision, dropped after other House leaders objected to it, as "good policy" aimed at curbing bootlegged cigarette sales. He said it was a "serious homeland security issue" because such sales had become a source of terrorist financing. But the flap came on the heels of another episode for which Blunt took heat: According to the *Wall Street Journal*, he was behind a last-minute effort to block a German-owned competitor of United Parcel Service-another client of his son's-from expanding in the United States.

In 2005, Blunt temporarily held two leadership posts, as acting majority leader as well as whip-when DeLay was forced to step down as leader after being indicted by a Texas grand jury for election law violations. It was a heavy burden for Blunt, particularly when the House was dealing with the devastating impact of Hurricane Katrina in the South. During the next three months, House Republicans struggled to pass bills. In January 2006, after DeLay announced he would permanently give up his post as leader, Blunt positioned himself to take over permanently and, after a week of lobbying his colleagues, claimed he had the votes to win. John Boehner of Ohio aggressively campaigned against him, and the multiple DeLay controversies involving well-heeled lobbyists indirectly hurt Blunt, himself viewed as being overly cozy with Washington's vaunted K Street. Blunt led on the first ballot in the Republican Caucus, coming within a half-dozen votes of the needed majority. On the second ballot, Boehner prevailed, 122-109. Blunt suffered the double indignity of losing his bid and looking like a whip who couldn't count votes.

Blunt remained majority whip and developed a smooth working relationship with Boehner. When House Republicans lost their majority in 2006, Blunt became minority whip. In September 2008, Boehner gave him the thankless task of negotiating the $700 billion financial bailout bill, which proved to be wildly unpopular with fellow Republicans. After the 2008 election, Blunt stepped down as whip to make way for his chief deputy, Rep. Eric Cantor of Virginia. "Ten years of asking people to do things they don't want to do is a long time," Blunt told reporters, adding he had promised himself-after the Republicans lost the House majority in 2006-that he would only serve two more years as whip unless the GOP recaptured the House. Even if they regained the majority, Blunt's path to becoming House speaker had become permanently obstructed.

In February 2009, Bond-who had helped to launch Blunt's political career almost four decades earlier-announced he would not seek reelection to a fifth Senate term, and Blunt began to focus on a campaign to succeed him. A couple of potentially competitive primary opponents opted out. State Sen. Chuck Purgason appealed to tea party activists, but Blunt easily prevailed in the August primary with 71 percent. The fall campaign was the real contest. Blunt faced Secretary of State Robin Carnahan, heir to a Missouri Democratic dynasty whose surname brought her instant name recognition. Blunt did his best to tie Carnahan to President Obama and Democratic policies unpopular with conservative voters. His opposition to the Affordable Care Act played well for him, and his ads featured images of Carnahan with Obama at a Kansas City fundraiser.

Carnahan tried to paint Blunt as the insider in the race. But her family ties made it a stretch for voters to see her as an outsider: Her father was a popular governor, her mother had served two years as an appointed senator, and both her grandfather and brother served in the House. Carnahan sought to link Blunt to corruption, with one ad featuring a Fox News clip in which anchor Chris Wallace mentioned Blunt inserting the provision favorable to Philip Morris into the homeland security legislation. It mattered little to Missouri voters in a year in which Obama's popularity sharply dropped. The race began as a close contest, but Blunt eventually prevailed, 54%-41%.

Just months after taking office, when a tornado devastated the town of Joplin, and killed 159 people, Blunt pushed for a strong federal relief effort to help the battered community. (Blunt represented Joplin while in the House.) When Cantor, by then majority leader with Republicans back in House control, suggested that the disaster relief aid should be offset with other budget cuts, Blunt told *Politico*, "We need to prioritize spending, and this needs to be a priority."

Blunt didn't wait long to seek a Senate leadership position. In late 2011, he ran for an open slot as the vice chairman of the Republican Conference against Wisconsin Sen. Ron Johnson, another freshman, with the race portrayed as a battle of the establishment and tea party wings of the GOP. Despite Johnson's efforts to pitch himself as a fresh conservative face, Blunt prevailed in a secret ballot that reportedly went 25-22 in his favor. His victory came shortly after Republican presidential aspirant Mitt Romney selected him as his primary liaison to win support from House and Senate lawmakers. Blunt's wife became one of the Romney campaign's "bundlers" to gather checks from other supporters.

Blunt sponsored in 2012 an amendment that would allow employers to exclude any insurance benefit under the new health-care law that they deemed immoral. His action came after Obama proposed a new contraception coverage rule in response to complaints from religious groups. Blunt and other supporters tried to frame the issue as one of religious freedom. The move mobilized women's groups, who charged the amendment would allow employers to choose women's health care options based on an employer's moral beliefs. The amendment was narrowly defeated.

An issue later that year was a personal one for Blunt: When Russian President Vladimir Putin announced in 2012 that he would ban U.S. adoptions of Russian children in retaliation for a law enabling the Obama Administration to target Russian human rights violators, Blunt led an effort to persuade Putin to allow adoptions that had been completed. He related the story of how he and his wife had adopted a son born in a Russian orphanage in late 2004.

On the Appropriations Committee, when Republicans regained the majority following the 2014 election, Blunt became chairman of the subcommittee with jurisdiction over the Labor, Health and Human Services, and Education departments-giving him an influential voice in how a large portion of the federal government's domestic discretionary budget is allocated. In May 2016, he won bipartisan approval of his plan for $1.1 billion to prevent, control and treat the spread of Zika virus, which he called a "public-health emergency." After months of partisan bickering with the House and the Obama Administration, the funds were enacted that September in the government-wide spending bill. Earlier, Blunt led an unsuccessful Senate fight to tie continued funding for the Homeland Security Department to a move to block implementation of President Obama's 2014 executive order on immigration policy. He voted against the nomination of Loretta Lynch for attorney general, to protest Obama's attempt to usurp Congress on immigration. Blunt was also among just five senators who opposed the nomination of Ashton Carter as defense secretary, accusing Obama of micromanaging the Pentagon without laying out a clear national security strategy against the radical Islamic group known as ISIS.

As he prepared for reelection in 2016, Blunt followed other establishment Republican senators who have veered to the right to pre-empt a tea party primary challenge. Former Republican Rep. Todd Akin, whose comments about "legitimate rape" in his 2012 campaign against McCaskill set off a national firestorm, briefly considered a challenge to Blunt before backing off. Blunt remained the subject of grumbling among some conservative groups, although his *Almanac* vote ratings in 2015 were in the top fifth of the most conservative Senate Republicans. In the GOP primary, he got 73 percent of the vote against three challengers.

In the general, the 35-year-old Kander said that "Washington is broken" and he ran as an outsider, though he had served eight years in elected office. He drew many contrasts to Blunt, including generational and his service in Afghanistan with the Army National Guard. Blunt, 66, did not serve in the military. As Jennifer Duffy wrote in the *Cook Political Report*, "Trump's anti-insider, 'drain the swamp' message is not helpful for an incumbent who has been in Washington for 20 years, is married to a lobbyist, has children who are lobbyists and owns a lovely home in Georgetown." Blunt's ads described Kander as "too liberal for Missouri" and he said that the challenger shared the views of Hillary Clinton. Kander ran a widely-viewed ad that showed him assembling a rifle while he was blindfolded and discussing his support for gun rights. *Politico* described him as "the break-out candidate of 2016." Kander won only 5 of the 114 counties, compared to 3 for Hillary Clinton, though he significantly improved Democratic performance in rural areas. Blunt won, 49%-46%.

As Senate Rules Committee chairman, Blunt officiated at the Inaugural ceremony for President Donald Trump. He had been largely supportive of Trump throughout the campaign, and largely dismissed the candidate's various controversies.

FIRST DISTRICT

Lacy Clay (D)

Elected 2000, 9th term; b. Jul 27, 1956, St. Louis; University of Maryland - College Park, B.S.; John F. Kennedy School of Government; Harvard University; Roman Catholic; Divorced; 2 children.

Elected Office: MO House, 1983-1990; MO Senate, 1991-2001.

Professional Career: Assistant doorkeeper, U.S. House, 1976-1983; Paralegal, 1988-1998; Real estate agent, 1986-2000.

DC Office: 2428 RHOB 20515, 202-225-2406, Fax: 202-226-3717, lacyclay.house.gov.

State Offices: Florissant, 314-383-5240; St. Louis, 314-367-1970; St. Louis, 314-669-9393.

Committees: *Financial Services*: Financial Institutions & Consumer Credit (RMM), Housing & Insurance. *Natural Resources*: Oversight & Investigations. *Oversight & Government Reform*: Government Operations.

Group Ratings

	ADA	ACLU	AFL-CIO	LCV	ITI	COC	HAFA	ACU	CFG	FRC
2016	-	70%	-	100%	67%	62%	12%	0%	6%	-
2015	100%	C	100%	86%	C	50%	C	4%	3%	-

Almanac Ratings 2015

	Economy	Social	Foreign	Composite
Liberal	93%	100%	78%	90%
Conservative	7%	0%	22%	10%

Key Votes of the 114th Congress

1. Keystone Pipeline	N	5. Puerto Rico Debt	Y	9. Offenses by Aliens	N
2. Trade Deals	N	6. Medical Marijuana	Y	10. Troops in Iraq	N
3. Export-Import Bank	Y	7. Sanctuary Cities	N	11. Homeland Security $$	Y
4. Debt Ceiling Increase	Y	8. Armor-piercing Bullets	N	12. Trade Adjustment aid	Y

Election Results

Election	Name (Party)	Vote (%)	Cand. Spent	Ind. Exp. Support	Ind. Exp. Oppose
2016 General	Lacy Clay (D)	236,993 (76%)	$642,646		
	Steven Bailey (R)	62,714 (20%)			
	Robb Cunningham (L)	14,317 (5%)			
2016 Primary	William Lacy Clay (D)	55,847 (63%)			
	Maria Chappelle-Nadal (D)	23,940 (27%)			
	Bill Haas (D)	9,395 (11%)			

Prior winning percentages: 2014 (73%), 2012 (79%), 2010 (74%), 2008 (88%), 2006 (73%), 2004 (73%), 2002 (70%), 2000 (75%)

Democrat William Lacy Clay was first elected in 2000 to the seat that his father, Bill Clay, held for 32 years. In recent years, he has survived serious conflicts in his St. Louis district and in his political life. The half-century lock that the Clays have held on the district is second only to the six-decade control by spouses John and Debbie Dingell of their suburban Detroit district.

Born in St. Louis, Clay, who goes by "Lacy," moved to the Washington area at age 12 after his father's election to the House. He attended public schools in suburban Silver Spring, Maryland and then the University of Maryland, studying by night for seven years while he worked as a House staffer by day. He had started law classes at Howard University when he returned to St. Louis for a special election to the state House in 1983. Party leaders appointed him the Democratic nominee. Eight years later, party leaders again chose him to run in a special election for a safely Democratic state Senate seat.

In 1999, his father announced that he would retire from Congress, after helping to enact many labor and education laws. Clay wanted to take his father's place, but he had a serious primary contest. St. Louis Councilman Charlie Dooley, an African American with a base of support in the mostly white suburbs of St. Louis County, raised nearly $400,000. Dooley said that the office should not be "inherited," and he attacked what he called Clay's old-style tactics of political threats and bossism. The St. Louis Labor Council and Missouri AFL-CIO, long allied with Bill Clay, declined to endorse his son, but more than 30 locals did. The candidate played up his father's name and revved up the still reliable machine. He won the primary 61%-28% over Dooley, winning St. Louis City 76%-12% and the county, where twice as many votes were cast, 49%-39%. In the general election, Clay won 75%-22%, and has won reelection since then by comparable margins.

In the House, Clay has had a mostly liberal voting record, though his foreign-policy scores were more centrist in the *Almanac* vote ratings for 2015. He is active in the Congressional Black Caucus, where his father had been a founding member. He can show his partisanship, as he did in 2012 when he denounced a House Republican vote to hold Attorney General Eric Holder in contempt of Congress as a "disgraceful political witch hunt." Clay is usually low-key and can be diplomatic in resolving differences among other lawmakers. "He's a peacemaker," fellow Missouri Democratic Rep. Emanuel Cleaver told the *St. Louis Post-Dispatch*. "He has just the right personality to take the temperature up, or bring it down." Clay also can be a deal-maker. He agreed to support Nancy Pelosi over Steny Hoyer for Democratic whip in 2001 only after securing a promise of $5 million to clean up contaminants at an Army plant in his district.

Clay has worked to protect voting rights for blacks and is the main proponent of creating a national Civil Rights Trail, with markers linking important sites in the civil-rights movement, including those in St. Louis. On the Financial Services Committee, Clay is the ranking Democrat on the Financial Institutions and Consumer Credit Subcommittee. In 2015, he proposed the Small Bank Exam Cycle Reform Act, which doubled to $1 billion the size of insured depository institutions eligible for 18-month on-site examination cycles. He was a leading advocate for continuing the authority of the Export-Import Bank, which supported $339 million in exports from his district, Clay said. In January 2017, he ran into an unusual conflict when House Republicans objected to a Clay-sponsored painting in an exhibit in the Capitol as anti-police and personally returned it to him. Clay objected to the repeated removal and said that the conflict was "about defending the Constitution" and the First Amendment rights of his constituent.

The riots that followed the police shooting in August 2014 of an unarmed black man in Ferguson, a city in his district, raised Clay's profile. He criticized police for a "heavy-handed" approach to peaceful demonstrations and said that law enforcement organizations needed more diversity in their ranks. He called on the federal government to take over the investigation into the shooting, which he called a "murder," saying in a radio interview: "I have absolutely no confidence in the Ferguson police, the county prosecutor. I know we won't get a fair shake there." Clay defended Missouri Gov. Jay Nixon for his handling of the emergency, and said on Twitter that Nixon was trying to protect civil rights and public safety. In 2015, he filed legislation that called for more "sensitivity training" for local police, and threatened the loss of federal law-enforcement funds to cities that don't require independent investigations when police use deadly force. He also sought reforms in the police use of military equipment.

After Missouri lost a seat in the 2010 reapportionment, Republicans eliminated the neighboring district of Democratic Rep. Russ Carnahan, who decided to challenge Clay. The newly drawn 1st District included 70% of Clay's old district and just 30% of Carnahan's. Clay ran a radio ad featuring representatives of two prominent black churches urging listeners to stand behind "leaders like Lacy Clay and President Obama." The *Post-Dispatch* endorsed Carnahan, saying that Clay "has coasted on the organization that his father and predecessor built but without being as deeply and continuously involved in local issues as Bill Clay was." Clay won the primary, 63%-34%. Reflecting the demographic shifts in the area, Clay ran more strongly in St. Louis County, where he got 66% of the vote, than in the city, where he had 60%.

Clay faced a competitive primary challenge in 2016 from state Sen. Maria Chappelle-Nadal, a supporter of Sen. Bernie Sanders in the presidential primary and a leader of the protests in Ferguson in 2014. During a debate, she told the audience, "You must ask yourself a question: Is 48 years too long for one family?" After President Barack Obama endorsed him, she responded that Clay was "quite accustomed to riding on someone else's coattails to win elections." Clay had a huge fundraising advantage over Chappelle-Nadal, who raised only $78,000. He won the primary, 63%-27%, with similar advantages in both the city and county.

St. Louis Metro

Population		**Race and Ethnicity**		**Income**	
Total	744,066	White	42.0%	Median Income	$40,514 (395 out of 435)
Land area	225	Black	48.8%		
Pop/ sq mi	3301.7	Latino	3.2%		
Born in state	69.7%	Asian	2.8%	Under $50,000	58.9%
Age Groups		Two races	2.8%	$50,000-$99,999	27.4%
Under 18	22.4%	Other	0.4%	$100,000-$199,999	11.1%
18-34	27.2%	**Education**		$200,000 or more	2.5%
35-64	38.0%	H.S grad or less	38.7%	Poverty Rate	21.6%
Over 64	12.4%	Some college	31.6%	**Health Insurance**	
Work		College Degree, 4 yr	17.1%	With health insurance coverage	85.5%
White Collar	36.2%	Post grad	12.7%		
Sales and Service	46.9%	**Military**		**Public Assistance**	
Blue Collar	16.9%	Veteran	7.9%	Cash public assistance income	2.8%
Government	11.5%	Active Duty	0.0%	Food stamp/SNAP benefits	20.9%

Voter Turnout			
2015 Total Citizens 18+	553,358	2016 House Turnout as % CVAP	57%
2016 House turnout	314,024	2014 House Turnout as % CVAP	30%

2012 Presidential Vote		
Barack Obama	280,194	(80%)
Mitt Romney	66,286	(19%)

2016 Presidential Vote		
Hillary Clinton	246,107	(77%)
Donald Trump	60,136	(19%)
Gary Johnson	7,948	(3%)

Cook Partisan Voting Index: D+29

For a century or more, St. Louis seemed the center of America: the starting point for the Lewis and Clark expedition in 1804, the locus half a century later of the *Dred Scott* slavery case, and the site of the 1904 World's Fair, which introduced the hotdog and the ice cream cone and got 19 million people to *Meet Me in St. Louis*. Its 630-foot-high Gateway Arch is just below the point where the waters of the Missouri surge into the Mississippi, about halfway between Lake Superior and New Orleans, between the Atlantic and the Pacific. This was the first major American city west of the Mississippi River, the final resting place of Daniel Boone, and for many years, Chicago's rival as the transportation hub of America. It was a heavily German city, with a Teutonic solidity and orderliness that distinguished it from the surrounding Southern-accented rural terrain. From *Mitteleuropa* came the founders of St. Louis's great businesses-the Anheuser-Busch brewery, May Company department stores, Joseph Pulitzer's *St. Louis Post-Dispatch*-and its first great politician, Carl Schurz, the senator and Interior secretary. There is almost a European aura to Forest Park, the site of the 1904 fair, and the mansion-lined private streets nearby.

St. Louis has dropped below Denver as the 20th largest metro area in the nation. It does not occupy as central a place in the national consciousness and the central city itself has largely emptied out. The German order that made so many people comfortable living in close quarters and commuting by streetcar has yielded to an American desire for suburban spaces and the less restrictive automobile. St. Louis' population peaked at 856,000 in 1950; now it is at its lowest level since the late 19th century-315,685 in 2015, a nine percent decrease from 2000. In recent years, downtown St. Louis has been spruced up: A new Busch Stadium opened in 2006 with a panoramic view of the Arch and downtown, part of more than $4.5 billion that has been spent on a variety of projects since 1999. In 2008, local icon Anheuser-Busch was taken over by Belgium-based InBev. The Anheuser-Busch InBev corporate offices and factory operations have remained along the Mississippi just south of the Arch, though the worldwide headquarters are in Belgium and a U.S. commercial strategy office has shifted to New York City. The city suffered a civic blow, though it may have avoided a ruinous financial deal, when the St. Louis Rams of the National Football League returned to Los Angeles in 2016 after the city failed to satisfy the team owner's demand for a new stadium. A larger economic threat came in January 2017, when shareholders of St. Louis-based Monsanto agreed to a purchase by the German-based Bayer chemical company.

About 10 miles up Interstate 70 from the Arch is the suburb of Ferguson, which became a center of riots and heated discussion of police practices following the shooting death in August 2014 of Michael Brown, an unarmed 18-year-old, by police officer Darren Wilson. A short time earlier, Brown and a friend had been videotaped in a local convenience store, apparently stealing cigars. The next day, the county police chief said that Brown had assaulted Wilson. Like other parts of St. Louis County, Ferguson (pop. 21,059) has a majority-black population, 67% in this case. But the minority white population had managed to keep control of the local government and the police department. As the details of Brown's death spread, there were growing protests and then riots in the streets of Ferguson, with police using tear gas and arresting dozens of persons. A week after the incident, Gov. Jay Nixon ordered a state of emergency and a curfew in Ferguson, then deployed the National Guard. A fragile calm eventually was restored until November, when the county prosecutor announced that a grand jury had decided not to indict Wilson, which resulted in additional protests.

News accounts described how several municipalities in St. Louis County, including Ferguson, had profited from poverty and from police and court actions that resulted from often petty offenses, which added to the economic and social dislocation. In a March 2015 report requested by President Barack Obama, a panel of outside experts working with the Justice Department found persistent racial bias by

Ferguson authorities, who had used arrest warrants to raise large sums for the operation of the city. Many of those officials resigned, and voters replaced two white members of the city council with African Americans, though more activist candidates were defeated. In April 2016, a federal judge approved a consent decree to resolve a civil rights lawsuit that the Justice Department had brought against Ferguson. The city agreed to major changes in local laws and police practices, though it failed to meet deadlines in January 2017.

The 1st District takes in all of St. Louis, plus about two-fifths of the people in suburban St. Louis County. It includes all of the predominantly African-American suburbs north of the city, including Ferguson, plus Bellefontaine Neighbors, Spanish Lake and Black Jack. It includes working-class St. Ann, part of Bridgeton and, west of the city, the affluent suburb of University City, which has a significant Jewish population. African Americans, a 49 percent plurality in the district, account for far more than half the votes in Democratic primaries. Given that the population of St. Louis city is 47 percent black, the portion of the district that is in St. Louis County has a slight majority of blacks. Overall, the county is 27 percent black; St. Louis and Clay (Kansas City) counties are the two reliably Democratic counties in Missouri. The 1st is heavily Democratic, although the party organization has been weakened by the loss of patronage and by state approval of term limits. After Obama twice won 80 percent of the vote in this district, Hillary Clinton got a comfortable 77 percent.

SECOND DISTRICT

Ann Wagner (R)

Elected 2012, 3rd term; b. Sep 13, 1962, St. Louis; University of Missouri, B.S., 1984; Roman Catholic; Married (Raymond T. Wagner Jr.); 3 children.

Professional Career: Manager, Hallmark Cards; Manager Ralston Purina; MO Director, George H. W. Bush reelection campaign, 1992; Chair, MO Republican Party, 1999-2005; Co-chair, Republican National Committee, 2001-2005; U.S. ambassador to Luxembourg, 2005-2009; Chairwoman, Roy Blunt for Senate campaign, 2009-2010.

DC Office: 435 CHOB 20515, 202-225-1621, Fax: 202-225-2563, wagner.house.gov.

State Offices: Ballwin, 636-779-5449.

Committees: *Financial Services*: Capital Markets, Securities & Investment, Oversight & Investigations (Chmn). *Foreign Affairs*: Asia & the Pacific, Middle East & North Africa.

Group Ratings

	ADA	ACLU	AFL-CIO	LCV	ITI	COC	HAFA	ACU	CFG	FRC
2016	-	11%	-	5%	100%	100%	63%	88%	74%	100%
2015	0%	C	14%	0%	C	89%	C	74%	64%	100%

Almanac Ratings 2015

	Economy	Social	Foreign	Composite
Liberal	3%	12%	4%	6%
Conservative	97%	88%	96%	94%

Key Votes of the 114th Congress

1. Keystone Pipeline	Y	5. Puerto Rico Debt	Y	9. Offenses by Aliens	Y
2. Trade Deals	Y	6. Medical Marijuana	N	10. Troops in Iraq	N
3. Export-Import Bank	N	7. Sanctuary Cities	Y	11. Homeland Security $$	N
4. Debt Ceiling Increase	N	8. Armor-piercing Bullets	Y	12. Trade Adjustment aid	Y

Election Results

Election	Name (Party)	Vote (%)		Cand. Spent	Ind. Exp. Support	Ind. Exp. Oppose
2016 General	Ann Wagner (R)	241,954	(59%)	$1,417,754		$875
	Bill Otto (D)	155,689	(38%)	$456,728		
	Jim Higgins (L)	11,758	(3%)			
2016 Primary	Ann Wagner (R)	76,731	(83%)			
	Greg Sears (R)	16,204	(17%)			

Prior winning percentages: 2014 (64%), 2013 (60%)

A former Republican National Committee co-chair and fundraiser, Ann Wagner was elected in 2012 by overpowering her opponents financially and with her political expertise. She quickly became a favorite of GOP leaders, and seemed to have a bright future. In July 2017, she unexpectedly decided against a challenge in 2018 to Democratic Sen. Claire McCaskill.

Wagner grew up in the St. Louis suburbs, where her father ran a carpet store and her grandfather owned a paint business. At an all-girls Catholic school, she acted in musicals, playing the female roles at all-boys' schools. Her father wanted to see his daughter get a business degree. She graduated with one from the University of Missouri, then went to work for Hallmark Cards and Ralston Purina. Her involvement in politics began in 1989 when her husband, Raymond, took a job with John Ashcroft, then governor of Missouri. She oversaw Missouri's redistricting after the 1990 census, and ran the Missouri campaign for President George H.W. Bush in 1992, which he lost both nationally and in the state. In 1999, Wagner became chairman of the Missouri GOP. Both chambers of the General Assembly went Republican in 2002, for the first time in 54 years. President George W. Bush named her ambassador to Luxembourg, and for four years she rotated her family between Missouri and the tiny European nation.

It wasn't until 2012-with two of her children out of the house, the third a high school senior, and a Democratic administration that she charged was "mortgaging" her children's future-that she decided to run for office. After GOP Rep. Todd Akin announced his ill-fated bid for the Senate, she announced for his seat, quickly raising money, with substantial contributions from employees of St. Louis-based Enterprise Rent-A-Car, where her husband was an executive. Some Republicans accused Enterprise of essentially buying her the seat, but her campaign said the donations merely reflected the employees' trust in her. Initially, Wagner seemed likely to have a fight on her hands. But Republican Ed Martin, who had unsuccessfully challenged Democratic Rep. Russ Carnahan in 2010, dropped out of the race. And Carnahan, whose district had been dismantled in redistricting, decided to challenge fellow Democrat William Lacy Clay rather than run against Wagner. That left Democrat Glenn Koenen, a former food pantry executive director, who faced insurmountable odds. Wagner won, 60%-37%. She spent $2.5 million, compared to a paltry $60,000 by Koenen.

Wagner has had a conservative voting record on economic and foreign issues and has ranked more centrist on social issues, according to the *Almanac* ratings for 2015. As one of four House members from Missouri to serve on the Financial Services Committee, she has tended to their home state's large financial community. In September 2016, the House passed on a largely party-line vote her bill to increase access to capital for small businesses. She filed a bill that would delay so-called "fiduciary standards," dealing with financial advisers, which were mandated by the 2010 Dodd-Frank banking law. She complained that the proposed rules would adversely affect access for low-income groups. In February 2017, she applauded the executive order by President Donald Trump for agencies to review Dodd-Frank, including the fiduciary rule; she stood next to him in the Oval Office during the signing ceremony. As the new chairman of the Oversight and Investigations Subcommittee at Financial Services, she said that her plan was to "expose the damage the old administration caused to our national economy while detailing what the new and hopeful administration will do to restore the American family." Outside of her committee work, the House passed in 2015 her bill to prevent advertisements that might be used for sexual trafficking.

Wagner has found roles within the House GOP. She was chosen leader of the freshman class, and played a prime role in the recruitment of candidates by the National Republican Congressional Committee. When Rep. Steve Scalise of Louisiana became whip in June 2014, he selected Wagner as one of five senior deputy whips. She had become politically close to Scalise since her 2012 campaign, when he subbed at a campaign appearance for her on the day after her father died. After she decided not to run in 2016 for chairman of the NRCC, she became vice-chair for fundraising.

She has been reelected easily, though her victory in 2016 fell to 59%-38% against lightly financed Democrat Bill Otto. Following the release of the controversial "Access Hollywood" video in October

2016, she withdrew her endorsement of Trump and said that Mike Pence should replace him at the top of the ticket. A few days before the election, she said that she would vote for Trump. Following the election, she said that she looked forward to working with Trump. During the spring of 2017, sources close to her said that they expected Wagner to challenge McCaskill and that she led in private polls. Her surprising announcement in July that she would not run for the Senate left questions of whether her concern was a primary or the general election.

St. Louis Suburbs

Population		Race and Ethnicity		Income	
Total	757,785	White	87.7%	Median Income	$75,308 (51 out of 435)
Land area	466	Black	3.7%	Under $50,000	32.0%
Pop/ sq mi	1627.0	Latino	2.6%	$50,000-$99,999	31.3%
Born in state	66.1%	Asian	4.2%	$100,000-$199,999	27.0%
		Two races	1.6%	$200,000 or more	9.6%
Age Groups		Other	0.2%	Poverty Rate	5.9%
Under 18	22.4%				
18-34	19.2%	**Education**		**Health Insurance**	
35-64	41.6%	H.S grad or less	25.0%	With health insurance coverage	94.0%
Over 64	16.8%	Some college	27.4%		
		College Degree, 4 yr	28.5%		
Work		Post grad	19.0%	**Public Assistance**	
White Collar	48.4%			Cash public assistance income	1.1%
Sales and Service	39.0%	**Military**		Food stamp/SNAP benefits	4.5%
Blue Collar	12.6%	Veteran	8.6%		
Government	8.0%	Active Duty	0.0%		

Voter Turnout			
2015 Total Citizens 18+	566,807	2016 House Turnout as % CVAP	73%
2016 House turnout	413,296	2014 House Turnout as % CVAP	40%

2012 Presidential Vote		
Mitt Romney	235,374	(57%)
Barack Obama	170,786	(42%)

2016 Presidential Vote		
Donald Trump	220,727	(52%)
Hillary Clinton	177,731	(42%)
Gary Johnson	16,078	(4%)

Cook Partisan Voting Index: R+8

Just as the geographic center of the U.S. population has moved west from St. Louis to rural Texas County, so has the center of metropolitan St. Louis moved farther west from the Gateway Arch on the Mississippi River. Now the midpoint is suburban St. Louis County, established in 1876 when the city, tired of paying for dusty back roads, separated itself from the sticks. That year, there were 350,000 people in the city and 31,000 in the county. In 2015, there were about 315,000 in the city and 1 million in St. Louis County. The area's office center is fast moving out along the Daniel Boone Expressway (U.S. 40) to Chesterfield. Near the city-county border is Grant's Farm, where Ulysses S. Grant lived in the 1850s and where Anheuser-Busch bred the Budweiser Clydesdales.

The 2nd Congressional District of Missouri consists of central and western St. Louis County, part of St. Charles County across the Missouri River, and a small sliver of Jefferson County to the south. Along the expressway, in the center of St. Louis County, are long-settled suburbs: Kirkwood, LaDue, and high-income Town and Country, where one-acre lots for sale remain common. In Chesterfield, Pfizer in November 2016 announced expansion of its large research and development center, and Monsanto has grown its sprawling research center and had more than 5,000 jobs prior to the uncertainties of its conditional January 2017 purchase by German chemical giant Bayer. Chesterfield has the most expensive housing in the area, and upscale shopping. Ballwin is a growing center for immigrants with biotech and health care jobs. For the district, more than four-fifths of the population is in St. Louis County, which has had a big increase in racial minorities. But they are mostly in the 1st District. The 2nd is 89 percent white.

These are all Republican areas, more so in the newer family-oriented subdivisions than in the leafy precincts of the older enclaves. Fast-growing St. Charles County, where the supply of available land and affordable housing has tightened, has more people and casts more votes than the city of St. Louis, though its Republican vote has become smaller than in the more outlying counties of the St. Louis exurbs. From 2000 to 2010, it gained nearly 27,000 jobs, even as the number of jobs in St. Louis city dropped by 14%. This district voted for Donald Trump in 2016, 52%-42%, a four-point drop from Mitt Romney's performance in 2012. Of the six Republican-held districts in Missouri, this is the most suburban, wealthiest and best-educated, and the only one where the Trump vote was below 63% and the GOP share fell from 2012.

THIRD DISTRICT

Blaine Luetkemeyer (R)

Elected 2008, 5th term; b. May 07, 1952, Jefferson City; Lincoln University (MO), B.A.; Catholic; Married (Jackie Luetkemeyer); 3 children; 4 grandchildren.

Elected Office: MO House, 1999-2005.

Professional Career: Bank examiner, State of MO, 1974-1976; Loan officer, Bank of St. Elizabeth, 1978-2008; President, Luetkemeyer Ins. Agency, 1978-2008; Director, MO div. of tourism, 2007-2008.

DC Office: 2230 RHOB 20515, 202-225-2956, Fax: 202-225-5712, luetkemeyer.house.gov.

State Offices: Jefferson City, 573-635-7232; Washington, 636-239-2276; Wentzville, 636-327-7055.

Committees: *Financial Services*: Financial Institutions & Consumer Credit (Chmn), Housing & Insurance. *Small Business*: Agriculture, Energy & Trade, Health & Technology.

Group Ratings

	ADA	ACLU	AFL-CIO	LCV	ITI	COC	HAFA	ACU	CFG	FRC
2016	-	5%	-	0%	100%	100%	59%	84%	70%	100%
2015	0%	C	13%	3%	C	95%	C	71%	54%	92%

Almanac Ratings 2015

	Economy	Social	Foreign	Composite
Liberal	11%	9%	4%	8%
Conservative	90%	91%	96%	92%

Key Votes of the 114th Congress

1. Keystone Pipeline	Y	5. Puerto Rico Debt	NV	9. Offenses by Aliens	Y
2. Trade Deals	Y	6. Medical Marijuana	Y	10. Troops in Iraq	N
3. Export-Import Bank	Y	7. Sanctuary Cities	Y	11. Homeland Security $$	N
4. Debt Ceiling Increase	Y	8. Armor-piercing Bullets	Y	12. Trade Adjustment aid	Y

Election Results

Election	Name (Party)	Vote	(%)	Cand. Spent	Ind. Exp. Support	Ind. Exp. Oppose
2016 General	Blaine Luetkemeyer (R)	249,865	(68%)	$696,899		
	Kevin Miller (D)	102,891	(28%)			
	Dan Hogan (L)	11,962	(3%)			
2016 Primary	Blaine Luetkemeyer (R)	84,265	(74%)			
	Cynthia Davis (R)	30,436	(27%)			

Prior winning percentages: 2014 (68%), 2012 (64%), 2010 (77%), 2008 (50%)

Republican Blaine Luetkemeyer, first elected in 2008, has a firm political grip on a large swath of suburban and rural Missouri. He once worked in the banking business and has been a conservative advocate of the industry on the Financial Services Committee, where he became chairman of a key banking subcommittee in 2017.

Luetkemeyer has Missouri roots that stretch back five generations. He grew up in St. Elizabeth, where his father worked as an insurance agent and then owned a bank. Luetkemeyer was a star high school baseball player, but his Major League tryouts were unsuccessful. He graduated from Lincoln University, a historically black college in Jefferson City, with a degree in political science. He and his wife settled on his great-grandfather's farm in St. Elizabeth. In addition to farming, he joined his family's banking operations and founded the Luetkemeyer Insurance Agency.

Luetkemeyer was elected in 1999 to the state House of Representatives, where he developed a reputation as a thoughtful legislator. He campaigned for Missouri treasurer in 2004 but lost in the Republican primary. In 2007, Luetkemeyer was appointed director of the Missouri Division of Tourism.

The House seat opened when Republican Rep. Kenny Hulshof ran unsuccessfully for governor. Luetkemeyer was the Republican favorite in a five-way GOP primary. The conservative anti-tax group Club for Growth endorsed GOP state Rep. Bob Onder, but Luetkemeyer gained a critical endorsement from Missouri Right to Life. Luetkemeyer led the field with 40 percent to 29 percent for Onder. In the general election, he faced state Rep. Judy Baker, a health care consultant from Columbia. Luetkemeyer emphasized his farming background to the district's largely rural constituency. He raised $2.8 million, two-thirds of it his own money; Baker raised $1.7 million. In the election, Baker carried populous Boone County (Columbia), but Luetkemeyer won the rural counties and those west of St. Louis. In a Democratic year, he won 50%-47.5%.

Luetkemeyer joined the Tea Party Caucus and established himself as a devout fiscal and social conservative. He dismissed President Barack Obama's economic stimulus as a "large-scale failure," but the liberal think tank Center for American Progress noted that he later joined Missouri lawmakers in requesting $100 million in stimulus money for a road project. He successfully amended a House-passed bill in 2011 to bar the United States from contributing to the United Nation's Intergovernmental Panel on Climate Change, which he said engaged in "dubious science." Luetkemeyer introduced a bill in 2012 barring the Health and Human Services Department from forcing organizations to provide contraceptive and sterilization coverage in violation of their religious beliefs.

On the Financial Services Committee, he scorned the Democrats' Dodd-Frank Wall Street reform law as detrimental to small banks, writing in a *Washington Times* op-ed, "People on Main Street understand that community banks did not cause the financial crisis and that they already carry daunting regulatory burdens." He and Democratic Rep. David Scott of Georgia enacted a bill in 2012 eliminating the physical fee-warning notices on automatic-teller machines in favor of having them displayed on-screen. He organized conservative support for the reauthorization of the Export-Import Bank, which many on the right opposed as unnecessary government intervention. In December 2016, he won House passage of his bill to strip the Dodd-Frank automatic coverage of any bank with at least $50 billion. The regulations, he said, had led to "unintended" restrictions of some small and mid-sized banks. In a speech to bankers, he called Massachusetts Democratic Sen. Elizabeth Warren the "Darth Vader of the financial services world." (She replied that she saw herself "more as a Princess Leia-type.")

As chairman of the Housing and Insurance Subcommittee in 2015-16, he said that the Housing and Urban Development "suffers from not only misguided policy but also mismanagement." He was especially unhappy with the inadequate funding of the mutual mortgage insurance fund, which he said might require another bailout.

Luetkemeyer had a notably productive two years as Housing Subcommittee chairman. He worked closely with Democratic Rep. Emanuel Cleaver of Missouri to enact in 2016 what he called "comprehensive legislation which represents real reforms to our nation's housing programs." In February 2016, the House passed his bill to end the Obama Administration's controversial Operation Choke Point, which was designed to investigate consumer fraud but allegedly had terminated legitimate banking accounts that had supported industries such as guns and tobacco that it disliked. The House unanimously approved in April his bill to open the door for the first time to federal acceptance of private flood insurance policies.

In January 2017, Luetkemeyer moved up in seniority and became chairman of the Financial Institutions and Consumer Credit Subcommittee, where he said that his goal was to "to ensure all Americans have access to the tools they need to reach financial independence."

Luetkemeyer has breezed to reelection every two years. Redistricting in 2011 removed Columbia, the home of the University of Missouri, and made his district more Republican. Despite encouragement from some Republicans, he decided not to run for governor in 2016.

East-central Missouri: St. Louis area

Population		**Race and Ethnicity**		**Income**	
Total	763,567	White	91.4%	Median Income	$55,440 (180 out of 435)
Land area	6,852	Black	3.3%		
Pop/ sq mi	111.4	Latino	2.4%		
Born in state	74.5%	Asian	0.9%	Under $50,000	44.3%
		Two races	1.6%	$50,000-$99,999	34.9%
Age Groups		Other	0.4%	$100,000-$199,999	18.0%
Under 18	24.0%			$200,000 or more	2.8%
18-34	21.7%	**Education**		Poverty Rate	11.5%
35-64	40.2%	H.S grad or less	44.6%		
Over 64	14.0%	Some college	31.6%	**Health Insurance**	
		College Degree, 4 yr	15.8%	With health insurance coverage	90.1%
Work		Post grad	7.9%		
White Collar	32.7%				
Sales and Service	42.3%	**Military**		**Public Assistance**	
Blue Collar	25.0%	Veteran	10.1%	Cash public assistance income	2.2%
Government	12.4%	Active Duty	0.1%		
				Food stamp/SNAP benefits	10.3%

Voter Turnout			
2015 Total Citizens 18+	571,654	2016 House Turnout as % CVAP	64%
2016 House turnout	368,333	2014 House Turnout as % CVAP	34%

2012 Presidential Vote		
Mitt Romney	218,926	(62%)
Barack Obama	127,104	(36%)

2016 Presidential Vote		
Donald Trump	254,321	(67%)
Hillary Clinton	106,245	(28%)
Gary Johnson	13,524	(4%)

Cook Partisan Voting Index: R+18

Missouri was the first state settled west of the Mississippi, and the folks who settled it were a picture of pioneer diversity. Virginians and other Southerners made their way to counties north of the Missouri River, while Germans settled around the small capital, Jefferson City. A taste of that diversity can be found in the Capitol, with its mural by Thomas Hart Benton, great-grandnephew of one of Missouri's first senators, who championed hard money and westward expansion for 30 years and lost his seat for opposing the expansion of slavery. The painting depicts dance hall girls, black coal miners, and a mother diapering an infant. Fulton is the home of Westminster College, where former Prime Minister Winston Churchill, accompanied by President Harry Truman, told the world in 1946: "From Stettin in the Baltic to Trieste in the Adriatic, an iron curtain has descended across the continent." In the small town of Washington, Meerschaum Co. remains the largest and oldest manufacturer of corn cob pipes in the world. It has been continually operating in its brick factory since 1869 and now produces close to 800,000 pipes annually. A few decades ago, it shipped up to 25 million pipes each year.

The 3rd Congressional District covers east-central Missouri, stretching from Jefferson City to the western St. Louis exurbs of St. Charles and Jefferson counties, and extends like a claw to the Mississippi Rivers both north and south of St. Louis County and city. Its population base is in the western parts of fast-growing St. Charles County, which has about one-third of the voters. The economic growth in these exurbs has been noted as a sharp distinction from beleaguered St. Louis city and riot-scarred Ferguson. In 2015, General Motors added a third shift and 750 employees at its Wentzville plant, where it produced the Chevy Express and GMC Savana vans plus the new GMC Canyon midsize pickup. The GM expansion has been a boon to parts suppliers, which had been hurt by the closing of Ford and Chrysler plants in the area.

The district is solidly Republican, with every county voting for Donald Trump in 2016. His 67%-28% win was a notable increase over the 56%-43% margin by which John McCain led Barack Obama in 2008.

FOURTH DISTRICT

Vicky Hartzler (R)

Elected 2010, 4th term; b. Oct 13, 1960, Harrisonville; University of Missouri, B.S., 1983; Central Missouri State University, M.S., 1992; Evangelical; Married (Lowell Hartzler); 1 child.

Elected Office: MO House, 1995-2001.

Professional Career: Teacher, 1983-1994; Spokeswoman, Coalition to Protect Marriage, 2004; Appointee, MO Women's Cncl., 2005-2010; Owner, Hartzler Equipment Co.

DC Office: 2235 RHOB 20515, 202-225-2876, Fax: 202-225-0148, hartzler.house.gov.

State Offices: Columbia, 573-442-9311; Harrisonville, 816-884-3411; Lebanon, 417-532-5582.

Committees: *Agriculture*: Livestock & Foreign Agriculture, Nutrition. *Armed Services*: Oversight & Investigations (Chmn), Readiness, Seapower & Projection Forces.

Group Ratings

	ADA	ACLU	AFL-CIO	LCV	ITI	COC	HAFA	ACU	CFG	FRC
2016	-	5%	-	0%	100%	100%	69%	96%	71%	100%
2015	0%	C	17%	0%	C	90%	C	75%	64%	100%

Almanac Ratings 2015

	Economy	Social	Foreign	Composite
Liberal	9%	0%	0%	3%
Conservative	91%	100%	100%	97%

Key Votes of the 114th Congress

1. Keystone Pipeline	Y	5. Puerto Rico Debt	N	9. Offenses by Aliens	Y
2. Trade Deals	Y	6. Medical Marijuana	N	10. Troops in Iraq	N
3. Export-Import Bank	Y	7. Sanctuary Cities	Y	11. Homeland Security $$	N
4. Debt Ceiling Increase	Y	8. Armor-piercing Bullets	Y	12. Trade Adjustment aid	N

Election Results

Election	Name (Party)	Vote	(%)	Cand. Spent	Ind. Exp. Support	Ind. Exp. Oppose
2016 General	Vicky Hartzler (R)	225,348	(68%)	$583,410	$694	
	Gordon Christensen (D)	92,510	(28%)	$210,664		$596
	Mark Bliss (L)	14,376	(4%)			
2016 Primary	Vicky Hartzler (R)	73,807	(73%)			
	John Webb (R)	28,012	(28%)			

Prior winning percentages: 2014 (68%), 2012 (60%), 2010 (50%)

Republican Vicky Hartzler was elected in 2010 when she defeated Democrat Ike Skelton, the powerful chairman of the Armed Services Committee. A former activist who led the movement to ban same-sex marriage in Missouri, she has been an energetic social and fiscal conservative. She has shown influence on Armed Services as chairman of the Oversight and Investigations Subcommittee.

Hartzler has spent her entire life in rural Cass County, where she grew up on the family farm. After getting her bachelor's degree in education at the University of Missouri, she worked as a high school home economics teacher for 11 years. Later, she got her master's in education at the University of Central Missouri. She and her husband, Lowell, resided on a 1,600-acre farm outside of Harrisonville, where they raised corn, soybeans and cattle and ran the Hartzler Equipment Co., which sold farming equipment. Her career changed in 1994 when she got a phone call from a friend while she was grading papers, urging her to run for state representative. "He asked me to think about it and pray about it, and I did," Hartzler said. "After 30 days, I knew I was supposed to run." She served three terms in Missouri's House, where she overhauled the state's adoption law. With the adoption of her daughter, she had a special interest in the topic.

In 2004, Hartzler headed the Coalition to Protect Marriage in Missouri, a campaign to add an amendment to the state's constitution banning same-sex marriage. Despite being outspent 17-to-1 by opposition groups, her group passed the amendment with 71 percent of the vote. She wrote the book *Running God's Way: Step by Step to a Successful Political Campaign*, a detailed guide for Christian candidates. The liberal magazine *Mother Jones* headlined an article about her in October 2010, "Is Vicky Hartzler the Most Anti-Gay Candidate in America?"

Her bid to unseat Skelton in 2010 drew the interest of tea party groups. In the conservative district, Skelton had relied on crossover GOP voters during his 17 terms in the House. In an election year that went from bad to worse for Democrats, Hartzler's message resonated. She assailed Skelton on his votes with "the liberal leadership" for the $787 billion economic stimulus bill and an energy bill imposing caps on carbon emissions. "I don't have a 'To Do list,' I have an 'Undo list'," she said. "We have to undo all these destructive policies." Hartzler tried to turn Skelton's image as a wise legislative elder into a negative,, "So many people in Washington [are] removed from rural America. Ike's lost touch," she said. Skelton raised $3 million and outspent Hartzler 3-to-1. She won, 50%-45%.

Republican leaders made good on their promise to give Hartzler a seat on Armed Services so that she could continue Skelton's stewardship of the district's military bases. She used that platform to pursue her advocacy of social issues. She added a provision to the defense bill in 2011 defining marriage as a union between a man and a woman for the purpose of military benefits and policy. The provision was dropped in conference with the Senate. She filed a bill preventing military veterans convicted of sexual abuse of children from being buried in Arlington National Cemetery.

As chairman of Oversight and Investigations, she pledged to ensure accountability by the Pentagon. The interests of her district remained paramount. In its annual defense spending bill, the House in 2015 approved her provision for construction at Whiteman Air Force Base of a Consolidated Stealth Operations and Nuclear Alert Facility. She took credit for approval of 12 additional F/A-18F Super Hornet aircraft, which she said would be built in Missouri.

After supporting Budget Committee Chairman Paul Ryan's budget-cutting efforts, defense-hawk Hartzler found that the tight-budget demands of fiscal hawks can be objectionable. She opposed the New Year's Day 2013 bipartisan deal aimed at averting the so-called "fiscal cliff." In 2015, she urged Congress to end budget "sequestration" and warned that automatic cuts in Defense Department spending threatened "impending devastation to our military."

Continuing her work on social issues, Hartzler in 2015 joined the special House committee charged with investigating abortion providers, including Planned Parenthood, following the release of controversial undercover videos about the group. "The horrific videos showing a disregard for human life raise issues of great public importance," she said. Also that year, she filed a resolution to veto a law passed by the District of Columbia that would ban discrimination against LGBT students attending religious schools, which she said, "infringed on the fundamental right of religious freedom."

At home, Hartzler absorbed Democratic-leaning Columbia in her district after the 2011 redistricting, which was drawn to make other Republican districts safer. She was compensated with more of her home base in Cass County, and the 4th remained solidly conservative. She has not been seriously challenged for reelection. Since 2014, she has won Columbia-based Boone County. In 2016, Hartzler said that some comments by Donald Trump were "undefendable," but that she supported him because of the policies that he advocated. Following the election, she was among the Republicans exploring a challenge in 2018 to Democratic Sen. Claire McCaskill.

West-central Missouri: Columbia

Population		Race and Ethnicity		Income	
Total	758,907	White	87.2%	Median Income	$45,124 (340 out of 435)
Land area	14,401	Black	4.5%		
Pop/ sq mi	52.7	Latino	3.6%		
Born in state	62.6%	Asian	1.4%	Under $50,000	54.5%
		Two races	2.7%	$50,000-$99,999	31.0%
Age Groups		Other	0.6%	$100,000-$199,999	12.7%
Under 18	22.8%			$200,000 or more	2.0%
18-34	25.6%	**Education**		Poverty Rate	17.7%
35-64	36.6%	H.S grad or less	46.3%		
Over 64	14.9%	Some college	29.4%	**Health Insurance**	
		College Degree, 4 yr	14.9%	With health insurance coverage	87.1%
Work		Post grad	9.4%		
White Collar	34.2%				
Sales and Service	41.2%	**Military**		**Public Assistance**	
Blue Collar	24.6%	Veteran	11.3%	Cash public assistance income	2.6%
Government	18.2%	Active Duty	2.7%		
				Food stamp/SNAP benefits	13.5%

Voter Turnout			
2015 Total Citizens 18+	573,008	2016 House Turnout as % CVAP	58%
2016 House turnout	332,234	2014 House Turnout as % CVAP	31%

2012 Presidential Vote		
Mitt Romney	201,702	(61%)
Barack Obama	119,932	(36%)

2016 Presidential Vote		
Donald Trump	222,141	(65%)
Hillary Clinton	99,858	(29%)
Gary Johnson	13,316	(4%)

Cook Partisan Voting Index: R+17

Roughly equidistant from St. Louis and Kansas City, Columbia in central Missouri has emerged as an economic hub in its own right. Nicknamed the Athens of Missouri, Columbia surpassed Independence in 2015 to become the fourth-largest city in the state, with a population that increased 9 percent since 2010. With a nearly 33,000-person student body, the University of Missouri is the biggest employer in the city and helped the town survive the recession. A number of graduates stay in the city to work in the health care and insurance industries. In 2015, allegations of racism plus multiple budget cuts led to widespread campus protests, including by its football team, and resulted in the resignation of the university president. Improved service at Columbia Regional Airport doubled the passenger load from 2009 to 2014. The city council in 2016 pursued plans for a new terminal..

The 4th Congressional District occupies Columbia and rural west central Missouri. Columbia's Boone County includes about one-fourth of the district's voters. It was one of just three counties in the state to support Hillary Clinton in 2016, 49%-43%. South of Kansas City, the district includes fast-growing Belton and Raymore in ancestrally Democratic Cass County, where Donald Trump got 65 percent in 2016. The southern portion, toward Springfield, is predominantly Republican. There are two big military bases here: Fort Leonard Wood in Pulaski County, where Marines, sailors, and airmen train in joint exercises with Army troops; and Whiteman Air Force Base, near Knob Noster in Johnson County, from which B-2 bombers have flown to drop precision-targeted bombs in Afghanistan. In 2014, the Air Force announced plans to upgrade its B-2 fleet.

The district overall has become safely Republican, despite its Democratic heritage. Like other non-urban parts of Missouri, Trump scored a big increase in Republican support in the 4th to 65%-29%, from the 57%-42% lead that John McCain had in 2008.

FIFTH DISTRICT

Emanuel Cleaver (D)

Elected 2004, 7th term; b. Oct 26, 1944, Waxahachie, TX; Murray State College (OK), Att., 1964; Prairie View Agricultural and Mechanical University (TX), B.S., 1972; St. Paul School of Theology, Kansas City (MO), M.Div., 1974; Methodist; Married (Dianne Cleaver); 4 children (twins); 3 grandchildren.

Elected Office: Kansas City Council, 1979-1991; Mayor, Kansas City, 1991-1999.

Professional Career: Pastor, 1970-present; Radio talk-show host, 2002-2004.

DC Office: 2335 RHOB 20515, 202-225-4535, Fax: 202-225-4403, cleaver.house.gov.

State Offices: Higginsville, 660-584-7373; Independence, 816-833-4545; Kansas City, 816-842-4545.

Committees: *Financial Services*: Housing & Insurance (RMM), Oversight & Investigations.

Group Ratings

	ADA	ACLU	AFL-CIO	LCV	ITI	COC	HAFA	ACU	CFG	FRC
2016	-	76%	-	95%	60%	64%	9%	0%	0%	0%
2015	100%	C	100%	91%	C	59%	C	0%	0%	8%

Almanac Ratings 2015

	Economy	Social	Foreign	Composite
Liberal	97%	86%	88%	90%
Conservative	3%	14%	12%	10%

Key Votes of the 114th Congress

1. Keystone Pipeline	N	5. Puerto Rico Debt	Y	9. Offenses by Aliens	N
2. Trade Deals	N	6. Medical Marijuana	N	10. Troops in Iraq	N
3. Export-Import Bank	Y	7. Sanctuary Cities	N	11. Homeland Security $$	Y
4. Debt Ceiling Increase	Y	8. Armor-piercing Bullets	NV	12. Trade Adjustment aid	Y

Election Results

Election	Name (Party)	Vote (%)		Cand. Spent	Ind. Exp. Support	Ind. Exp. Oppose
2016 General	Emanuel Cleaver (R)	190,766	(59%)	$117,308		
	Jacob Turk (D)	123,771	(38%)	$755,412		
	Roy Welborn (L)	9,733	(3%)			
2016 Primary	Emanuel Cleaver (D)	48,352	(88%)			
	Robert Gough (D)	6,491	(12%)			

Prior winning percentages: 2014 (52%), 2012 (61%), 2010 (53%), 2008 (64%), 2006 (64%), 2004 (55%)

Democrat Emanuel Cleaver, first elected in 2004, is an ordained minister who is known for his leadership of the Congressional Black Caucus and his work on housing issues, as well as his efforts to improve civility to Congress. "I am convinced, irreversibly, that the lack of civility is causing most of the problems we have in our government," he said in 2011.

Cleaver grew up in Waxahachie Texas, in a three-room shack with no plumbing or electricity. He graduated from Prairie View A&M University, moved to Kansas City and earned a divinity degree, and then became pastor of St. James United Methodist Church. He was elected to the city council in 1979 and as mayor in 1991. In city hall, Cleaver voiced support for the Clinton administration's changes in welfare policy, which he described as "corrective surgery." He backed expansion of downtown's Bartle Hall Convention Center and supported renovation of the deteriorating Liberty Memorial, the country's largest World War I memorial. After leaving office, he hosted a radio talk show.

In December 2003, Democratic Rep. Karen McCarthy announced that she would not run for reelection, and Cleaver was widely expected to succeed her. His road to Congress was tougher than expected. In the primary, he faced former National Security Council aide Jamie Metzl, who raised substantial funds. Metzl hammered Cleaver on ethics issues, questioning the propriety of a loan that Cleaver took out to purchase a car wash and his failure to pay $36,000 in back taxes on the business. Cleaver won the primary by 60%-40%.

In the general election, Cleaver faced Republican businesswoman Jeanne Patterson, who had $3 million of her own money to spend. Like Metzl, she made an issue of Cleaver's ethics, emphasizing bribery and fraud convictions of his allies, though there was no evidence that he was involved in any crimes. He said that Patterson was politically inexperienced and was trying to buy the seat. Cleaver won 55%-42%.

In the House, Cleaver's voting record initially was near the center of the Democrats. The *Almanac* vote ratings for 2015 show that he has moved leftward, particularly on economic matters. Despite his religious background, he disdains injecting religion into politics. In his first term, he was one of 22 members, all Democrats, who opposed a Republican House-passed resolution expressing support for Christmas that he dismissed as a sop to social conservatives. He opposed the 2011 deal to raise the federal debt limit, describing it to an audience back home as a "sugar-coated Satan sandwich" that would cost jobs and hurt the poor. He later advocated means-testing of Medicare as part of a deficit reduction deal, calling it far preferable to across-the-board cuts. He has sponsored bills to promote financial literacy and to make it easier for students to vote. Speaker Nancy Pelosi designated Cleaver to act as a liaison with mayors and faith communities on those issues.

He proposed changing House rules to require members to lease energy efficient vehicles in their districts. "The public would rather see a sermon than hear one," said Cleaver, whose own taxpayer-leased car ran on used cooking grease. (He drew criticism in 2009 when it was revealed that the car's $2,900 monthly cost was higher than that of any other House member.) On the Financial Services Committee, Cleaver initially opposed the creation of the Troubled Assets Relief Program to bail out the financial industry, but backed a revised version in the face of constituents' anger.

As ranking member of the Housing and Insurance Subcommittee since 2015, Cleaver has made affordable housing his priority. With Republican Rep. Blaine Luetkemeyer of Missouri, who chaired the subcommittee, he enacted in 2016 what they described as the most significant changes in federal housing programs in a quarter-century. The measure included a streamlining of the inspection and income review process for families living in Section 8 housing, improved condo ownership opportunities and increased access to rural housing loans.

Cleaver chaired the Black Caucus in 2011-12 at a time when members often expressed dissatisfaction with President Barack Obama for failing to do more to help low-income minorities. Cleaver, who had backed Hillary Clinton over Obama for the 2008 nomination, tried to walk a fine line between joining in the criticism and working to ensure the reelection of the nation's first black president. "With 14% [black] unemployment, if we had a white president, we'd be marching around the White House. ... The president knows we are going to act in deference to him in a way we wouldn't to someone white," he told *The Root* in September 2012. He led a Black Caucus job creation initiative featuring public events in several cities that caucus members said led to as many as 2,000 people getting work.

Cleaver periodically has taken the spotlight on issues involving race. When then-House Budget Committee Chairman Paul Ryan of Wisconsin made comments about poverty in March 2014 that some African-American lawmakers said were highly offensive, Cleaver said Ryan ended up in "a mouth trap" because of his lack of experience with inner-city issues. After the August 2014 fatal police shooting of an unarmed black teenager in Ferguson Missouri touched off riots there, he defended Obama's decision not to visit the city, even as he told MSNBC that it "resembles Fallujah" because of the militarized law-enforcement presence, which he called "un-American." Cleaver filed a bill in 2015 to make it a civil rights violation for police to set criminal or traffic violations for the purpose of raising local revenue, and he urged passage of police reform legislation.

Cleaver and West Virginia Republican Rep. (and now Senator) Shelley Moore Capito in 2011 resurrected their idea for a "Civility Caucus," and Cleaver issued regular pronouncements to colleagues stressing the importance of collegiality. "Bees cannot sting and make honey at the same time; they have to make a choice," he said.

Questions about his car wash have continued to hound Cleaver. Bank of America sued him and his wife in 2012 over outstanding debt, late fees and interest costs for a loan used to buy the business. The Small Business Administration guaranteed 75% of the loan, and local newspapers pointed out that if the Cleavers defaulted, taxpayers could be responsible. In February 2014, the Jackson County court clerk issued an order to withhold part of Cleaver's salary to repay more than $1.3 million that he and his wife owed the bank. News organizations have reported that he is one of the poorest members of Congress.

In the 2016 election, Cleaver faced Republican Jacob Turk for the sixth time. After having run their closest campaign in 2014, a 52%-46% win for Cleaver, the incumbent regained his more customary victory margin in 2016, 59%-38%. Cleaver raised $1.1 million to $124,000 for Turk, who called himself "an ordinary citizen." Cleaver won by 4-to-1 in Kansas City, which cast about 40% of the vote, and more narrowly in Clay. Turk won the four outlying counties.

Following the election, Cleaver successfully urged the Democratic Caucus to delay its organization for the new Congress to engage in "a season of introspection" following their setbacks and prepare to "strengthen [Pelosi] for these final two years as she moves into probably the most difficult time she's had in caucus leadership." Cleaver voted for Pelosi, but he said that the leadership challenge of Rep. Tim Ryan of Ohio was a welcome message that "Hold on, change is coming." Cleaver said that he attended the January 2017 inauguration of President Donald Trump "out of respect for the peaceful transfer of power," despite Trump's innuendoes of Democratic Rep. John Lewis of Georgia, "a man of unsurmountable courage and strength."

Kansas City Metro

Population		**Race and Ethnicity**		**Income**	
Total	754,804	White	64.7%	Median Income	$44,911 (343 out of 435)
Land area	2,425	Black	21.6%		
Pop/ sq mi	311.3	Latino	8.7%		
Born in state	61.1%	Asian	1.7%	Under $50,000	54.6%
		Two races	2.4%	$50,000-$99,999	30.2%
Age Groups		Other	1.0%	$100,000-$199,999	12.9%
Under 18	23.5%			$200,000 or more	2.3%
18-34	24.2%	**Education**		Poverty Rate	18.2%
35-64	38.3%	H.S grad or less	43.1%		
Over 64	14.0%	Some college	30.9%	**Health Insurance**	
		College Degree, 4 yr	16.6%	With health insurance coverage	85.2%
Work		Post grad	9.4%		
White Collar	33.9%				
Sales and Service	44.7%	**Military**		**Public Assistance**	
Blue Collar	21.4%	Veteran	9.0%	Cash public assistance income	3.1%
Government	12.3%	Active Duty	0.0%	Food stamp/SNAP benefits	14.9%

Voter Turnout			
2015 Total Citizens 18+	554,401	2016 House Turnout as % CVAP	58%
2016 House turnout	324,270	2014 House Turnout as % CVAP	28%

2012 Presidential Vote		
Barack Obama	198,356	(59%)
Mitt Romney	132,632	(39%)

2016 Presidential Vote		
Hillary Clinton	179,354	(55%)
Donald Trump	130,051	(40%)
Gary Johnson	12,098	(4%)

Cook Partisan Voting Index: D+7

Kansas City, named after a state it isn't in and a river it doesn't touch, is the center of one of America's largest metro areas, the biggest on the central Great Plains. The first settlers here started little towns on the bluffs above the Missouri River-Independence, Kansas City, Westport-that coalesced a few decades later. Here, traders on the Santa Fe Trail set out to cross the Sand Hills of Kansas to reach Mexican territory, and pioneers headed for Oregon and California. Kansas City was a rail center and, in the 1920s, had one of the largest stockyards in the country, a major commercial center with lean skyscrapers, and the Country Club Plaza, the first shopping center in America. Harry Truman grew up on a farm now in the suburb of Grandview and lived in his wife's family's house in Independence, the old county seat just to the east. The city is famous for its National Negro Leagues Baseball Museum, its historic jazz district that has been home to musicians like Scott Joplin, Charlie Parker and Count Basie, and for its much-praised barbecue. The redevelopment downtown includes the Kauffman Center for the Performing Arts.

More than 20,000 people live downtown, most of them millennials. That increase has been accompanied by a small reduction in the black population, which reduced the black total in the city from 31 percent in 2000 to about 29 percent in 2015. (Kansas City, Kansas is about one-third the size of its counterpart.)

Overall, Kansas City fared better than most cities during the recession. City leaders designated a 150-block area as a Green Impact Zone, a national model of sustainable living which used federal economic stimulus money. The initiative drew criticism from conservatives who said that its benefits did not translate on a wide scale. In February 2014, *Time* magazine asked what had been the impact. "Less than folks had hoped," wrote David von Drehle. The Green Impact Zone quietly closed its office in early 2014. A 2.2 mile downtown streetcar, which started service in May 2016, had modest ridership, though it was greater than planners had expected. That spurred discussion of a more ambitious 3.5 mile extension to the University of Missouri's Kansas City campus. Some development has been encouraging. As the launch city for Google Fiber, Kansas City had moved "to the front of the line in the innovation economy," the *Kansas City Star* reported in 2015.

The 5th Congressional District of Missouri includes most of Kansas City, the largest city in Missouri, plus Grandview and the bulk of Independence. On Election Night 1948, when just about everyone thought he would lose, Truman was not far away in the resort town of Excelsior Springs. Most of the Kansas City area's landmarks, including the Truman home, are here, but much of the metropolitan area's growth has been across the state line in Kansas. About 40% of the voters live in Kansas City, which is overwhelmingly Democratic. Another 40% live in surrounding Jackson County, which leans a bit Republican; one-fourth of Jackson has been drawn into the heavily Republican 6th District. 22% of the district's residents are African-American, the second highest percentage among Missouri districts. Politically, the seat leans Democratic, though not nearly so much as the St. Louis-based 1st District. Hillary Clinton got 55% of the vote, compared to the 59% for President Barack Obama in 2012.

SIXTH DISTRICT

Sam Graves (R)

Elected 2000, 9th term; b. Nov 07, 1963, Tarkio; University of Missouri, B.S., 1986; Baptist; Married (Lesley Graves); 3 children.

Elected Office: MO House, 1992-1994; MO Senate, 1994-2000.

Professional Career: Farmer.

DC Office: 1135 LHOB 20515, 202-225-7041, Fax: 202-225-8221, graves.house.gov.

State Offices: Hannibal, 573-221-3400; Kansas City, 816-792-3976; St. Joseph, 816-749-0800.

Committees: *Armed Services*: Strategic Forces, Tactical Air & Land Forces. *Transportation & Infrastructure*: Aviation, Highways & Transit (Chmn), Railroads, Pipelines & Hazardous Materials.

Group Ratings

	ADA	ACLU	AFL-CIO	LCV	ITI	COC	HAFA	ACU	CFG	FRC
2016	-	11%	-	0%	100%	100%	57%	74%	45%	100%
2015	5%	C	35%	3%	C	89%	C	65%	56%	100%

Almanac Ratings 2015

	Economy	Social	Foreign	Composite
Liberal	11%	4%	4%	6%
Conservative	89%	96%	96%	94%

Key Votes of the 114th Congress

1. Keystone Pipeline	Y	5. Puerto Rico Debt	Y	9. Offenses by Aliens	Y
2. Trade Deals	Y	6. Medical Marijuana	N	10. Troops in Iraq	N
3. Export-Import Bank	Y	7. Sanctuary Cities	Y	11. Homeland Security $$	N
4. Debt Ceiling Increase	N	8. Armor-piercing Bullets	Y	12. Trade Adjustment aid	Y

Election Results

Election	Name (Party)	Vote	(%)	Cand. Spent	Ind. Exp. Support	Ind. Exp. Oppose
2016 General	Sam Graves (R)	238,388	(68%)	$1,195,444		
	David Blackwell (D)	99,692	(28%)			
	Russ Monchil (L)	8,123	(2%)			
2016 Primary	Sam Graves (R)	62,758	(76%)			
	Christopher Ryan (R)	11,685	(14%)			
	Kyle Reid (R)	7,909	(10%)			

Prior winning percentages: 2014 (67%), 2012 (65%), 2010 (69%), 2008 (59%), 2006 (62%), 2004 (64%), 2002 (63%), 2000 (51%)

Republican Sam Graves, first elected in 2000, chairs the influential Highways and Transit Subcommittee and was instrumental in the enactment in 2015 of the first long-term highway bill in more than a decade. He earlier headed the Small Business Committee, where he battled Democrats over federal regulations on business.

Graves is a lifelong resident of Tarkio in the northwest corner of the state. An Eagle Scout, he regularly played "Taps" on his bugle at local cemeteries, a practice he has continued in his district each Memorial Day. He graduated from the University of Missouri with a degree in agronomy, farmed with his father and brother, and joined the Farm Bureau. He ran for the state House in 1992 and beat a longtime Democratic incumbent. Two years later, he was elected to the state Senate. He attracted attention with a five-hour filibuster against a school desegregation bill that he said put rural areas at a disadvantage, but the bill eventually passed.

Graves ran for the House when Democratic Rep. Pat Danner dropped her bid for reelection just minutes before the filing deadline. Not by accident, the immediate favorite to succeed her was her son, state Sen. Steve Danner, also a Democrat. Graves entered the race within the short window provided by state law and drew support from national Republicans. Teresa Loar, a moderate Republican on the Kansas City Council, attacked Graves as the darling of extremist party leaders, but Graves beat her in the primary, 68%-17%. In the general, Danner billed himself as a conservative Democrat and switched from being pro-abortion rights to opposing abortion. In an editorial endorsing Graves, *The Kansas City Star* said that Danner's campaign switch on abortion showed that he "engaged in raw opportunism at the slightest opportunity." Graves won 51%-47%.

Graves has mostly been a rock-solid conservative, though his *Almanac* vote ratings for 2015 showed that has deviated on some economic issues. He was 1 of just 9 Republicans to vote in 2011 against reinstituting a school voucher program for District of Columbia students. He was 1 of 54 to oppose barring the use of funds to administer the Davis-Bacon Act, which requires prevailing union wages on federal projects. He has remained a hard-liner on immigration. He amended a fiscal 2013 spending bill to stop the Obama administration's family unity waiver system, which allowed illegal immigrants who are married to U.S. citizens to remain with their spouses while their green-card status is reviewed. His measure died in the Democratic-controlled Senate.

On the Small Business Committee, he was a regular critic of the Obama administration. He held hearings on the Environmental Protection Agency's failure to comply with a law requiring agencies to analyze the effects of regulations on small entities and to consider less burdensome alternatives. In 2014, he filed a bill to stop all new regulations by the EPA. He opposed an effort to make more businesses eligible for a tax credit under the 2010 health care law; the credit was designed to help businesses afford health insurance for their workers. Graves worked with Democrats to pass a series of bills in 2012 aimed at fixing small business contracting problems. In December 2014, he told the Associated Press that he had made the committee "relevant" and forced the administration to analyze the burdens that regulations placed on small business. More changes are needed in federal contracting to encourage small businesses, he added.

With his new focus on transportation programs, Graves said that a long-term solution was needed for funding shortfalls in the highway trust funds. On a bipartisan basis, he and Transportation and

Infrastructure Committee chairman Bill Shuster of Pennsylvania secured enactment in 2015 of the five-year Fixing America's Surface Transportation (FAST) Act, which gave states the flexibility to focus on the safety needs and permitted the development of user-funded tools as an alternative to gasoline taxes to finance the highway trust fund; the new law required that each state spend at least 15 percent of its funds to maintain and repair rural bridges. That left the door open for action on a more sweeping infrastructure bill, which President Donald Trump has advocated. Graves has doubted that an increase in the gasoline tax would receive much support and he has said that public-private partnerships for new highways are worth exploring, though he objects to toll roads.

An experienced private pilot, Graves co-chairs the House's General Aviation Caucus and contends that government needs to better understand the impact of its aircraft regulations. His work on highway and aviation issues, plus his district's borders on both the Missouri and Mississippi Rivers, could position Graves to jump over more senior Republicans and seek the chairmanship of the parent Transportation and Infrastructure Committee after Shuster is term-limited in 2018.

On local issues, Graves has sought to compel the Army Corps of Engineers to emphasize flood control on the Missouri River, telling the *St. Joseph News-Press* that the agency's focus on environmental recovery over levee operations and maintenance was "out of whack." In 2005, the House passed his amendment to the transportation bill to preempt state laws governing liability for damages involving rental cars, a measure of interest to St. Louis-based Enterprise Rent-A-Car.

Graves was the subject of an ethics investigation for his role in arranging testimony before his committee by a family friend. The matter touched off a public squabble in 2009 between the new Office of Congressional Ethics and the House Ethics Committee. OCE recommended that the case be investigated further, but the Ethics Committee found deficiencies in the office's handling of the matter and voted unanimously to clear Graves. He and other Republicans in January 2017 reportedly cited that experience to make the case for a House rules change to restrict the powers of the OCE, which Speaker Paul Ryan short-circuited.

In 2008, national Democrats were excited when former Kansas City Mayor and St. Joseph native Kay Barnes announced she would challenge Graves. But Graves attacked Barnes for "San Francisco values" and supporting "a homosexual agenda" because her picture had appeared in a gay magazine; he won, 59%-37%. His recent victory margins have exceeded 2-to-1.

Northern Missouri: Kansas City suburbs

Population		**Race and Ethnicity**		**Income**	
Total	757,302	White	88.4%	Median Income	$53,473 (206 out of 435)
Land area	18,199	Black	4.0%		
Pop/ sq mi	41.6	Latino	3.8%		
Born in state	65.1%	Asian	1.2%	Under $50,000	46.8%
Age Groups		Two races	2.0%	$50,000-$99,999	32.5%
Under 18	24.1%	Other	0.5%	$100,000-$199,999	17.5%
18-34	21.7%	**Education**		$200,000 or more	3.1%
35-64	39.5%	H.S grad or less	44.4%	Poverty Rate	12.8%
Over 64	14.8%	Some college	29.4%	**Health Insurance**	
Work		College Degree, 4 yr	17.2%	With health insurance coverage	89.2%
White Collar	34.7%	Post grad	9.1%		
Sales and Service	40.9%	**Military**		**Public Assistance**	
Blue Collar	24.4%	Veteran	9.9%	Cash public assistance income	2.2%
Government	14.1%	Active Duty	0.1%	Food stamp/SNAP benefits	10.3%

Voter Turnout			
2015 Total Citizens 18+	565,086	2016 House Turnout as % CVAP	62%
2016 House turnout	350,444	2014 House Turnout as % CVAP	33%

2012 Presidential Vote		
Mitt Romney	205,798	(60%)
Barack Obama	130,512	(38%)

2016 Presidential Vote		
Donald Trump	226,783	(64%)
Hillary Clinton	110,474	(31%)
Gary Johnson	14,252	(4%)

Cook Partisan Voting Index: R+16

The rolling fields along the Missouri River in northwest Missouri were settled in a rush in the late 19th century. These lands lost people for most of the 20th century as fewer hands were needed on farms. But increased efficiencies lately have led to resurgent production. In 1940, northern Missouri had one of the largest meatpacking operations in the world. In recent years, the business has expanded in St. Joseph and has drawn many Hispanics. Barge traffic on the Missouri reopened in late 2014, following an increase in water levels and record corn and soybean crops. Two years later, the river transportation was proclaimed a success. In 2008, Rock Port in the northwest corner became the first town in the country to get all of its energy from wind power. Other local utility companies joined the move. In October 2016, the Missouri Public Service Commission planned a hearing on the application of the Grain Belt Express Clean Line, which would provide cheaper energy from wind farms in Kansas and had the support of 38 utilities and nearly 70 local governments. Some farmers in northern Missouri have objected that transmission lines for wind power interfere with their crops or reduce property values. The overall economy of northern Missouri remained sluggish. Twenty local counties lost population from 2000 to 2010.

Across the state is Little Dixie, the swath of Missouri along the Mississippi River. This area was settled by Southerners from Kentucky and Virginia. Its most famous native son is Mark Twain, born Samuel Langhorne Clemens in Hannibal, then as now a little town on bluffs overlooking the river. Hannibal was the thinly disguised St. Petersburg of Twain's classics, *The Adventures of Tom Sawyer* and *The Adventures of Huckleberry Finn*.

Hannibal is on the eastern edge of the 6th Congressional District, which takes in all or parts of 36 counties in northern Missouri, stretching more than 200 miles from Kansas and Nebraska to Illinois. On the western edge is the river town of St. Joseph, the biggest city north of Kansas City, which was the starting point for the Pony Express and its roughly 10-day transport of mail to Sacramento. The 6th also takes in the Kansas City suburbs of Clay and Platte and a sliver of eastern Jackson County. That area casts about half of the district's vote. The historic political tradition here was mostly Democratic. But the rural vote here, as across the nation, has been tempered by dislike for national Democrats' cultural liberalism and has moved solidly Republican. The Kansas City suburb of Clay County traditionally was a reliable national bellwether, but it has swung the GOP's way too: Democrat Al Gore won in 2000 by one vote. Republican Donald Trump carried Clay by 12 percentage points in 2016, and the overall district, 64%-31%.

SEVENTH DISTRICT

Billy Long (R)

Elected 2010, 4th term; b. Aug 11, 1955, Springfield; University of Missouri, Att.; Indiana University, Bloomington, Att.; Missouri Auction School; Presbyterian; Married (Barbara Long); 2 children.

Professional Career: Talk show host, 1999-2006; Realtor, 1978-2010; Owner, Billy Long Auctions.

DC Office: 2454 RHOB 20515, 202-225-6536, Fax: 202-225-5604, long.house.gov.

State Offices: Joplin, 417-781-1041; Springfield, 417-889-1800.

Committees: *Energy & Commerce*: Communications & Technology, Energy, Health.

Group Ratings

	ADA	ACLU	AFL-CIO	LCV	ITI	COC	HAFA	ACU	CFG	FRC
2016	-	5%	-	0%	100%	100%	75%	92%	80%	100%
2015	0%	C	17%	0%	C	80%	C	91%	74%	100%

Almanac Ratings 2015

	Economy	Social	Foreign	Composite
Liberal	5%	8%	7%	7%
Conservative	95%	92%	93%	94%

Key Votes of the 114th Congress

1. Keystone Pipeline	Y	5. Puerto Rico Debt	N	9. Offenses by Aliens	Y
2. Trade Deals	Y	6. Medical Marijuana	N	10. Troops in Iraq	N
3. Export-Import Bank	Y	7. Sanctuary Cities	Y	11. Homeland Security $$	NV
4. Debt Ceiling Increase	N	8. Armor-piercing Bullets	Y	12. Trade Adjustment aid	N

Election Results

Election	Name (Party)	Vote	(%)	Cand. Spent	Ind. Exp. Support	Ind. Exp. Oppose
2016 General	Billy Long (R)	228,692	(68%)	$1,590,981	$5,000	
	Genevieve Williams (D)	92,756	(27%)	$12,838		
	Benjamin Brixey (L)	17,153	(5%)			
2016 Primary	Billy Long (R)	67,001	(62%)			
	Mary Byrne (R)	14,067	(13%)			
	Matthew Canovi (R)	9,538	(9%)			
	Matthew Evans (R)	5,345	(5%)			

Prior winning percentages: 2014 (64%), 2012 (64%), 2010 (63%)

Republican Billy Long, elected in 2010, succeeded Roy Blunt who was elected to the Senate and brought a new style to the House. His orientation has been tea party and rural rather than K Street, and his campaign motto was an anti-Beltway "Fed Up!" He has forged occasional alliances with Democrats.

Long grew up in Springfield, where he developed an interest in Republican politics at an early age. When he was 9 years old, he told the *Springfield News-Leader*, he would ride his bike to pass out bumper stickers for a Greene County sheriff's candidate who was the brother of a family friend. After briefly attending the University of Missouri to study business, he became interested in real estate and attended auction school, eventually starting a company that would conduct as many as 200 auctions a year. He spent six years as a morning-drive talk show host for an AM station covering southwest Missouri.

When Blunt sought the Senate seat, Long ran as a plain-talking conservative who would clamp down on federal spending and set Congress straight. He billed his lack of government service as a plus. "We have enough political experience in Washington, D.C., to choke a horse," he told the Associated Press. "That's exactly the problem." In the GOP primary, he defeated seven other candidates, including two veteran state senators, with more than 37% of the vote. In the fall, former Democratic gubernatorial aide Scott Eckersley sought to make an issue of racist remarks that Long was accused of making at a bar that featured strippers and illegal gambling tables-a claim that Long dismissed as a "flat-out lie." Long advocated a constitutional amendment to limit the federal government's taxation powers and for repeal of the Democrats' health care law. He wore a cowboy hat and inveighed against "elitist politicians." In this Republican bastion, Long won 63%-30%.

Long has made good on his promise to try to change Washington's ways. He voted against several spending resolutions and for a conservative budget alternative with deeper cuts than the version by Budget Committee Chairman Paul Ryan. A Long bill that attracted widespread support, but did not move, called for ensuring that the Environmental Protection Agency does not impose regulations intended for hazardous-waste cleanups on livestock operations. He adamantly opposed President Barack Obama's 2013 proposals intended to reduce gun violence, including limiting the sale of ammunition clips to those holding 10 rounds or fewer. "If you're lying in bed at 4 in the morning and four people kick your door in, would you like to be restricted to five shots or six shots?" he asked the *News-Leader*. He said that the Democrats' 2016 sit-in on the House floor to demand action on gun control was "a sheer publicity stunt."

On the Energy and Commerce Committee, Long won bipartisan support for his amendment to the 21st Century Cures bill to improve information to consumers about new pharmaceuticals. He generated conservative enthusiasm for his Taxpayer Transparency Act, which required executive branch agencies to disclose when there are expenses in their advertising or promotional material. Similar disclosure requirements apply to congressional materials, such as newsletters. On the water resources bill that was enacted in December 2016, he got a provision to end a freeze on construction permits for docks on Table Rock Lake, which is near Branson.

Long's lack of polish showed at times. He drew widespread criticism in 2011 for a tweet comparing the spending habits of Congress with singer Amy Winehouse, who died from drug and alcohol addictions. He later apologized. But he won bipartisan praise for his role in the disaster response to the deadly Joplin tornado, working closely with the Obama administration to provide funding to the ravaged area. "It was a lot heaped onto a freshman," Missouri Democratic Rep. William Lacy Clay told the *News-Leader*. "But you could see him right before our eyes grow into the job and grow into his responsibility."

Some of Long's votes-such as supporting a raise in the federal debt limit and reauthorizing the Export-Import Bank-annoyed conservatives back home, and he has drawn primary challengers in his three reelection bids. Long has been held to between 60 and 65 percent of the vote in each case, enough to get his attention but not to force big changes. In a 2014 campaign ad, Long spoke to the camera and said that he remained "fed up," especially with political ads. "I approve this message because I'm still fed up with Obama's agenda, and all these ads," he closed.

In October 2016, Long "deplored" 11-year-old comments by Donald Trump about groping women. But he criticized Republicans such as Speaker Ryan who distanced themselves from Trump. "If everyone backs away from our nominee for president, that's going to spell disaster down-ticket," Long said. "No one's seen anything like this election before. It's a movement."

Western Ozarks: Springfield, Joplin

Population		**Race and Ethnicity**		**Income**	
Total	761,206	White	88.9%	Median Income	$42,002 (372 out of 435)
Land area	6,273	Black	1.8%		
Pop/ sq mi	121.3	Latino	4.7%		
Born in state	57.7%	Asian	1.2%	Under $50,000	57.9%
		Two races	2.4%	$50,000-$99,999	29.5%
Age Groups		Other	0.9%	$100,000-$199,999	10.6%
Under 18	23.1%			$200,000 or more	2.0%
18-34	23.7%	**Education**		Poverty Rate	17.5%
35-64	37.3%	H.S grad or less	45.1%		
Over 64	15.9%	Some college	31.6%	**Health Insurance**	
		College Degree, 4 yr	15.3%	With health insurance coverage	84.7%
Work		Post grad	8.0%		
White Collar	31.5%				
Sales and Service	44.9%	**Military**		**Public Assistance**	
Blue Collar	23.6%	Veteran	10.4%	Cash public assistance income	2.2%
Government	11.5%	Active Duty	0.1%		
				Food stamp/SNAP benefits	13.8%

Voter Turnout			
2015 Total Citizens 18+	570,447	2016 House Turnout as % CVAP	59%
2016 House turnout	338,607	2014 House Turnout as % CVAP	29%

2012 Presidential Vote		
Mitt Romney	220,146	(66%)
Barack Obama	98,889	(30%)

2016 Presidential Vote		
Donald Trump	240,700	(70%)
Hillary Clinton	84,415	(25%)
Gary Johnson	12,163	(4%)

Cook Partisan Voting Index: R+23

One of the biggest tourist destinations in America today is Branson Missouri, something almost no one would have predicted 30 years ago. Branson has only 11,000 year-round residents, but it thrives thanks to the surging popularity of country and western music. It has more than 50 theaters and 57,000 seats-more than Broadway and equaling Las Vegas-and has become a hub for nonstop, low-cost entertainment, attracting 8 million visitors a year. As *The Kansas City Star* put it, each attraction is "more church-loving, more family-friendly, more country than the next." The 150-feet high Ferris wheel that had operated at Chicago's Navy Pier opened in Branson in June 2016.

Nearby are fishing, boating and plenty of shopping. These diversions have made southwest Missouri the fastest-growing part of the state, generating new businesses and attracting retirees as well as vacationers. Branson even got its own privately financed small airport in 2009, a new concept in the United States but more familiar elsewhere. Southwest and Frontier Airlines left the market in 2014, but start-up Via Airlines planned to begin service in mid-2017. The Spirit of 76 master plan that was approved in 2014 will upgrade much of the commercial center, with the prospect of more tourist attractions on the strip.

Springfield is the biggest city in southwest Missouri and the self-styled "buckle of the Bible Belt." It is home to more than 200 churches, including the headquarters of the Assemblies of God, one of the nation's largest and fastest-growing Protestant denominations. In April 2015, 51 percent of voters agreed in a referendum to repeal the city's prohibitions on LGBT discrimination. Advocates of the anti-discrimination provisions fought back and restored the earlier prohibitions in a June 2016 referendum, which also got 51 percent. Southwest Missouri is dairy country and home to a growing poultry industry; the state ranks fourth in the nation for turkey production. Latinos have been moving into McDonald County to work in chicken-processing plants; roughly 1,000 of the 1,600 employees at the Tyson Foods chicken plant in Noel were minorities, including about 500 from Somalia. The number of languages spoken in the Noel Elementary School increased from 6 in 2008 to 11. In a town of fewer than 2,000 residents that had been known as the "Canoe Capital of the Ozarks," the influx has diversified Noel, including its cultural and dining opportunities, but housing and social services remain scarce.

In Jasper County, the city of Joplin (pop. 51,818) has been mostly rebuilt following a devastating May 2011 tornado that killed 158 people and heavily damaged or destroyed 2,000 buildings, including a hospital and schools. With winds exceeding 200 miles per hour, it was the deadliest tornado in the United States since 1950. By 2014, more businesses were operating locally than before the disaster.

The 7th Congressional District of Missouri includes Springfield and Joplin. This area has been Republican territory since 1861, when it opposed secession. Pro-union Springfield changed hands several times as Missouri staged its own civil war. Its conservative response to the big-spending government of the 1960s and cultural liberalism of the 1970s reinforced its allegiance to the GOP, and now it is the most Republican part of Missouri. In 2016, Donald Trump won all of the counties here, many by 2-to-1 margins. He took the district, 70%-25%, a big Republican increase from the 63%-35% for John McCain in 2008.

EIGHTH DISTRICT

Jason Smith (R)

Elected 2013, 3rd term; b. Jun 16, 1980, St. Louis; Trinity College, Cambridge (England); Missouri State University, B.S., 2001; Oklahoma City University Law School (OK), J.D., 2004; Assembly of God; Not Stated.

Elected Office: MO House, 2005-2013.

Professional Career: Farmer, practicing Attorney, 2004-2013.

DC Office: 1118 LHOB 20515, 202-225-4404, Fax: 202-226-0326, jasonsmith.house.gov.

State Offices: Cape Girardeau, 573-335-0101; Farmington, 573-756-9755; Poplar Bluff, 573-778-6679; Rolla, 573-364-2455; West Plains, 417-255-1515.

Committees: House Republican Conference Secretary. *Budget. Ways & Means*: Human Resources, Social Security.

Group Ratings

	ADA	ACLU	AFL-CIO	LCV	ITI	COC	HAFA	ACU	CFG	FRC
2016	-	11%	-	0%	100%	100%	82%	96%	85%	100%
2015	0%	C	9%	0%	C	75%	C	95%	83%	100%

Almanac Ratings 2015

	Economy	Social	Foreign	Composite
Liberal	0%	9%	3%	4%
Conservative	100%	91%	97%	96%

Key Votes of the 114th Congress

1. Keystone Pipeline	Y	5. Puerto Rico Debt	N	9. Offenses by Aliens	Y
2. Trade Deals	Y	6. Medical Marijuana	N	10. Troops in Iraq	N
3. Export-Import Bank	N	7. Sanctuary Cities	Y	11. Homeland Security $$	NV
4. Debt Ceiling Increase	N	8. Armor-piercing Bullets	Y	12. Trade Adjustment aid	N

Election Results

Election	Name (Party)	Vote	(%)	Cand. Spent	Ind. Exp. Support	Ind. Exp. Oppose
2016 General	Jason Smith (R)	229,792	(74%)	$1,092,188		
	Dave Cowell (D)	70,009	(23%)			
	Jonathan Shell (L)	9,070	(3%)			
2016 Primary	Jason Smith (R)	65,441	(68%)			
	Hal Brown (R)	15,337	(16%)			
	Todd Mahn (R)	11,561	(12%)			

Prior winning percentages: 2014 (67%), 2013 special (67%)

Republican Jason Smith won a special election in 2013 to replace Republican Jo Ann Emerson, who resigned to become president of the National Rural Electric Cooperative Association. Smith is a fervent advocate of limited government who is far more conservative than his predecessor. He moved quickly to show his influence on tax and regulatory policy.

Smith grew up as the son of a church pastor in Salem Missouri, and he still runs the family farm that his great-grandfather started. At the University of Missouri, he received degrees in agricultural economics and business administration. He earned his law degree from Oklahoma City University. After returning to run the family farm and practice law, he became alarmed by "the harm that the overbearing government was inflicting on Missourians and our economy," according to his campaign website. He won a seat in the state House in 2005 and rose to majority whip and speaker pro tempore. He sought to amend the state constitution to protect farmers' rights, which he said was necessary to protect Missouri farmers from out-of-state animal rights groups and "environmental extremists." He joined social conservatives on gun rights and abortion-related legislation.

A former co-chair of the House GOP's centrist Tuesday Group, Emerson was a veteran of the Appropriations Committee and its Agriculture Subcommittee, where she fought to add money for food stamp programs. Smith, by contrast, ran a campaign that centered on his opposition to President Barack Obama's health care law and other issues of strong interest to the GOP's right-wing base. "Voters do not want Obamacare, they are tired of burdensome and costly regulations and they know our $16 trillion national debt is a ticking time bomb," he said.

Steve Hodges, a state representative with pro-gun rights and anti-abortion views, won the Democratic nomination at a February convention on the sixth ballot over Lt. Gov. Peter Kinder, who suffered from controversial allegations on his use of campaign funds and his connection with a stripper and former *Penthouse* Pet. Hodges made an issue of Smith's missed state legislative votes during the special election campaign, and he tried to criticized his support for an unpopular state sales tax hike. But Hodges got little help from national Democrats, and Smith touted himself positive ads as a "common-sense conservative." Smith raised just over $500,000, more than double what Hodges took in. The result wasn't close. Smith won 67%-27%, and took all 30 counties except for two in the bootheel. He has been reelected with ease.

At age 32 when he entered the House, Smith was its fifth-youngest member. On the Natural Resources Committees, he sought to defend the interests of rural America: opposed to excessive regulations, in search of new markets for farmers and ranchers, and protecting his constituents' way of life. At a 2014 hearing of the panel, he strongly objected to tentative plans by the National Park Service to restrict recreational use of the Ozarks National Scenic Riverways, and vowed to fight "tooth and nail" to resist any change.

In January 2015, Smith gained a seat on the Ways and Means Committee, at the risk of confusion with another Smith (Adrian) on Ways and Means who is a young policy nerd from neighboring Nebraska.

In a column for *The Hill*, Jason Smith criticized the lack of clarity in the tax code, and said that Congress needed to move on tax reform, in part, "to provide our small-business owners, farmers and entrepreneurs with the assurances they need to grow the economy."

In its opening week in January 2017, the House passed Smith's Searching for and Cutting Regulations that are Unnecessarily Burdensome (SCRUB) bill, which would create a bipartisan panel to review all federal regulations and identify those that should be repealed. He filed a bill that week to make it no longer mandatory to sign up for some form of health insurance coverage. And he proposed legislation that would deprive highway trust fund money to places that declared themselves "sanctuary cities" and refused to enforce immigration laws. Smith praised the numerous executive orders that President Donald Trump issued during his opening days in office for having "done more to help working-class Americans" than President Barack Obama did in eight years.

Southeast Missouri

Population		**Race and Ethnicity**		**Income**	
Total	747,811	White	90.9%	Median Income	$38,153 (409 out of 435)
Land area	19,901	Black	4.6%		
Pop/ sq mi	37.6	Latino	1.8%		
Born in state	73.2%	Asian	0.6%	Under $50,000	62.2%
		Two races	1.6%	$50,000-$99,999	27.1%
Age Groups		Other	0.4%	$100,000-$199,999	9.3%
Under 18	22.9%			$200,000 or more	1.4%
18-34	20.7%	**Education**		Poverty Rate	20.3%
35-64	39.4%	H.S grad or less	56.7%		
Over 64	16.9%	Some college	28.3%	**Health Insurance**	
		College Degree, 4 yr	9.4%	With health insurance coverage	86.3%
Work		Post grad	5.8%		
White Collar	27.4%				
Sales and Service	42.6%	**Military**		**Public Assistance**	
Blue Collar	30.0%	Veteran	10.9%	Cash public assistance income	2.8%
Government	15.1%	Active Duty	0.1%		
				Food stamp/SNAP benefits	19.4%

Voter Turnout			
2015 Total Citizens 18+	570,274	2016 House Turnout as % CVAP	54%
2016 House turnout	308,871	2014 House Turnout as % CVAP	28%

2012 Presidential Vote		
Mitt Romney	201,522	(66%)
Barack Obama	97,982	(32%)

2016 Presidential Vote		
Donald Trump	239,652	(75%)
Hillary Clinton	66,884	(21%)
Gary Johnson	7,980	(3%)

Cook Partisan Voting Index: R+24

The southeast quadrant of Missouri is part river valley, part industrial mining and part agriculture. For years, there has been a population outflow from the Missouri Bootheel, as machines replaced low-wage farm workers and crops shifted from cotton to rice, corn and soybeans. Dairy cattle, pigs, apples and berries, plus some timber, are among the area's other products. The area is also home to Missouri's Lead Belt, a mining region rich in ore minerals such as lead, zinc, copper, silver and cadmium. Reynolds and Iron counties produced about 70 percent of the nation's lead, but many of the local mine recently have closed because of environmental contamination. Ste. Genevieve County has the nation's largest cement plant, which sparked a mini-economic boom after it opened at a huge limestone quarry in 2009 and initially produced four million metric tons per year. The area has suffered industrial shutdowns. Doe Run Resources Corp., the largest lead producer in the country, closed its smelter in 2013 following an agreement with Missouri and the Environmental Protection Agency, but continued to produce metal from recycled lead. The Noranda Aluminum smelting plant in New Madrid, which had 850 local jobs, declared bankruptcy in February 2016 and closed its operations following lower aluminum prices. It sold its smelter to Switzerland-based ARG International.

Carrying many of these industrial goods to market is the Mississippi River, which Mark Twain might not recognize today. The river is hidden behind levees, which ordinarily screen small towns and river roads from rows of barges tethered together, full of coal and corn and soybeans. The Mississippi today is an industrial waterway. But it was never really all that romantic. Twain's steamboats, as he was at pains to point out, were dangerous, noisy contraptions, forever blowing up or getting embedded in roots and branches in the river currents. This is one of the oldest settled parts of the United States. French pioneers founded such Missouri towns as Cape Girardeau in the late 1700s. The poverty rate in the Bootheel is the highest in the state. New Madrid has had some of the most powerful earthquakes in the nation; the most famous was in 1811-12.

The 8th District, the largest in Missouri, covers its southeast corner, including rural Ste. Genevieve County, the site of Missouri's oldest permanent settlement, and takes in southern Jefferson County in the suburbs of St. Louis. It includes Plato, the tiny Missouri village named the population midpoint of the country based on 2010 census data. Cape Girardeau is heavily Republican and the hometown of conservative commentator Rush Limbaugh. The Bootheel was once solidly Democratic, though the mining counties have mostly lost their traces of Democratic sentiment and Republicans have held it since 1980. In 2016, it surpassed the 7th District with the largest Republican vote in Missouri. Donald Trump won here, 75%-21%, a marked increase from John McCain's 60%-38% lead over Barack Obama in 2008.

★ MONTANA ★

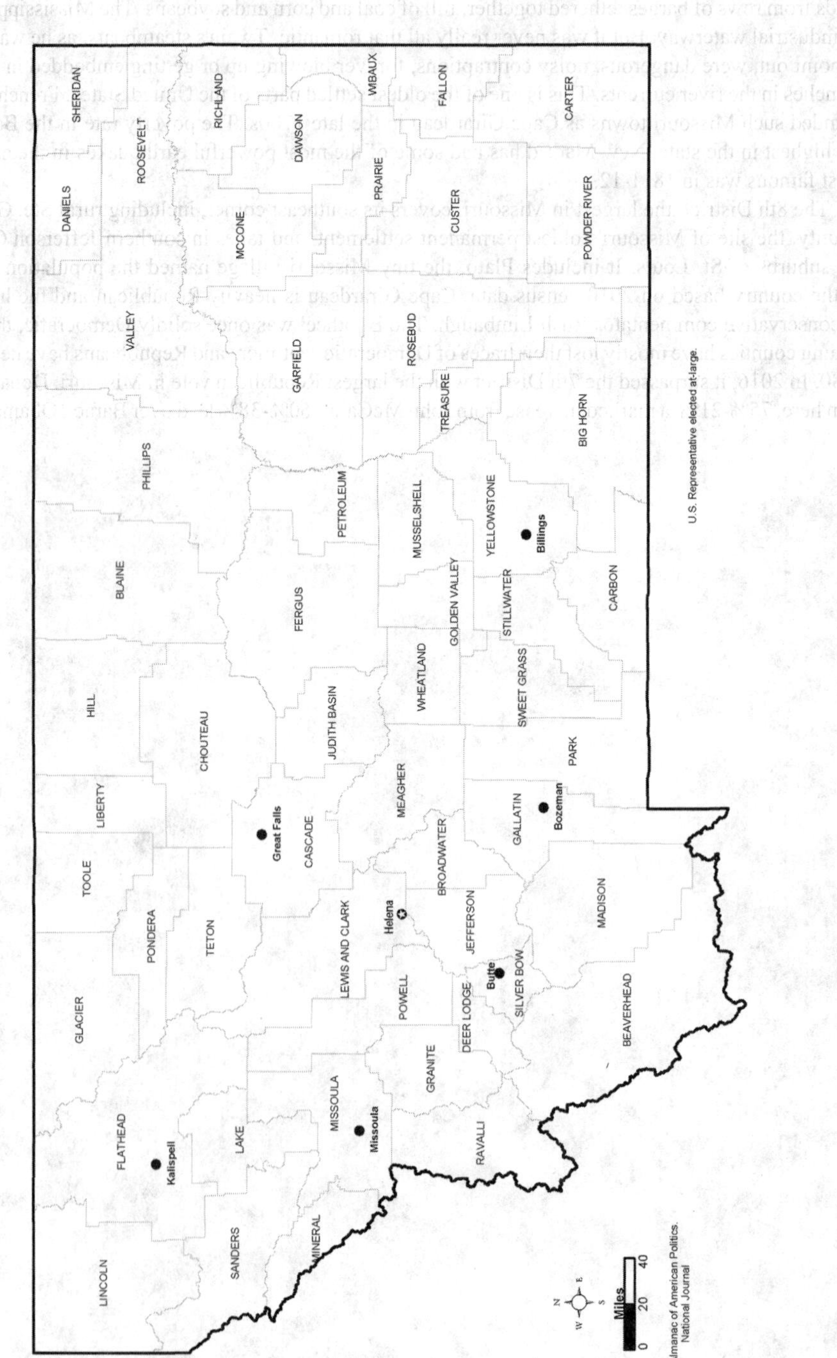
SHERIDAN
DANIELS
ROOSEVELT
RICHLAND
WIBAUX
DAWSON
FALLON
CARTER
PRAIRIE
MCCONE
CUSTER
POWDER RIVER
VALLEY
GARFIELD
ROSEBUD
TREASURE
BIG HORN
PHILLIPS
PETROLEUM
MUSSELSHELL
YELLOWSTONE
Billings
BLAINE
FERGUS
GOLDEN VALLEY
STILLWATER
CARBON
WHEATLAND
SWEET GRASS
HILL
CHOUTEAU
JUDITH BASIN
PARK
LIBERTY
MEAGHER
GALLATIN
Bozeman
Great Falls
CASCADE
BROADWATER
TOOLE
PONDERA
TETON
LEWIS AND CLARK
Helena
JEFFERSON
MADISON
GLACIER
POWELL
DEER LODGE
Butte
SILVER BOW
BEAVERHEAD
GRANITE
MISSOULA
Missoula
FLATHEAD
Kalispell
LAKE
RAVALLI
MINERAL
SANDERS
LINCOLN
U.S. Representative elected at-large
N
E
S
W
Miles
0
20
40
The Almanac of American Politics.
National Journal

Montana prides itself as "The Last Best Place," with 77 percent of residents believing that their state is either the best or one of the best possible in which to live, tying it with Alaska for the highest percentage in the nation. Montana's population grew by 13 percent in the 1990s and another 10 percent between 2000 and 2010; in the half-decade since 2010, it has increased by another 5.4 percent. But Montana is the fourth-largest state in area and it ranks third from the bottom in population density. So while the state's natural beauty and open spaces have drawn a steady stream of newcomers, the state still isn't close to filling up. In recent years, many have bought up ranchlands and condominiums, but Montana is still a land of great empty vistas, with mountains in the west and vast plateaus and plains in the east.

In April 1805, Meriwether Lewis, William Clark and their pirogues wended up the Missouri River just past the Yellowstone River into what now is Montana. To celebrate July 4, 1976, the historian Stephen E. Ambrose (who would retire to Helena and write the Lewis and Clark history *Undaunted Courage*) took his family to Lemhi Pass, where Lewis was the first U.S. citizen to cross the Continental Divide. Ambrose noted that the terrain was little changed from when Lewis and Clark passed through. Even earlier, dinosaurs roamed, their remains scattered more densely and uncovered more frequently than in any other state. Almost nowhere is the wilderness out of sight. It has the Lower 48's largest population of grizzly bears and bison - the "department store of the plains" to the Native Americans who used every last part. Montana sits atop the spine of the continental United States, spanning the Rockies so that on Interstate 15 one can cross the Continental Divide three times.

The first settlers here were itinerant trappers seeking fur and miners seeking gold, silver and copper. They built ramshackle towns and, in a few cases, gained sudden wealth, which made them kings not of their barren homestead but of the metropolises back East. Then came the workers who built and serviced the Northern Pacific and Great Northern railroads, followed by wheat farmers and ranchers. Statehood arrived in 1889, less than a century after Lewis and Clark. On the verge of statehood, dozens of millionaires lived in Helena; in today's dollars, roughly $3.6 billion in gold was taken from the city's fabled Last Chance Gulch.

Montana's mining economy gave the state a radical, class-warfare political tradition. On one side was the Anaconda Mining Co., which until 1959 owned five of Montana's six daily newspapers, the Montana Power Co., and, in effect, many of the state's politicians. The company had strong allies in the Stockgrowers Association and the Farm Bureau. On the other side were progressives like Sen. Thomas Walsh, who exposed the Teapot Dome scandal, and Sen. Burton Wheeler, a New Dealer who broke with President Franklin D. Roosevelt over court-packing and isolationism. Allied with them were the labor unions (Montana has no right-to-work law and has been the most pro-union Rocky Mountain state) and pork-barrel beneficiaries (for a while in the 1930s, Montana received more federal money per capita than almost any other state). In 1912, Montana voters passed the Corrupt Practices Act to curb influence in elections, striking a major blow against the Copper Kings. The act stood for a century until plaintiffs cited the *Citizens United* decision in a successful U.S. Supreme Court challenge. But the impetus remained; in 2015, Gov. Steve Bullock signed a bipartisan law that requires "dark money" groups to disclose their spending in state races, and it has so far been upheld in the courts.

For years, the focus of the skirmishing was Butte, with its gold and copper mines on "The Richest Hill on Earth," with its gamblers, bootleggers and millionaires; its company goons, union thugs and IWW organizers. Butte and surrounding Silver Bow County had 60,000 people in 1920 - the fourth highest in the Rocky Mountain states, behind only the counties containing Denver, Salt Lake City and Phoenix - but only 34,000 in 2015. The mines are mostly closed, their ore depleted; the stone temples of commerce are grim. Most spectacular is Butte's Berkeley Pit - a disused open copper mine more than a mile in diameter that's now filled with a toxic brew of contaminated groundwater.

As mines gradually closed after Butte's population peak in 1920, agriculture - wheat growing and cattle grazing - became the mainstay of Montana's economy. Class warfare died down. Other towns grew, although only Billings has ever topped 100,000. Other growth areas recently have been the university towns of Missoula and Bozeman, Kalispell near Flathead Lake, and the state capital of Helena. The lasting muscular tone of the state can be traced to the mountain men, the miners and the cowboys who drove herds of Texas longhorns across the open range. Hunting and fishing opportunities abound; development in the small cities and resort areas has not been enough to drive the game away. Montana's libertarian streak persists: For a stretch in the 1990s, the state had no speed limit and after one was reimposed by the courts, lawmakers raised it to 80 miles per hour in 2015, becoming only the fifth state with a limit that high. Montana has no state limits on using handheld devices while driving.

Over the past quarter-century, Big Sky Country attracted at first a trickle and then a flood of affluent Americans who purchased second homes here - high-visibility movie stars and billionaires like CNN founder Ted Turner, but also just ordinary people buying small spreads near Big Sky, McLeod or Bozeman, or around Flathead Lake, Big Timber and Whitefish. Some newcomers, from California and other urban states, are putting down roots, as the internet makes it possible for entrepreneurs to run businesses from Montana, far from their customers and clients, but in an environment they love - and not far from the coffee houses and gambling parlors one finds along every highway. These new Montanans have added a spark of energy and inventiveness to a population that had consisted of people left behind when others moved elsewhere. There has been little immigration – the state is less than 1 percent black, and the biggest minority group is Native Americans, at 6.6 percent. (The Hispanic population has climbed fairly quickly from a small base, from 2.9 percent to 3.6 percent between 2010 and 2015.)

The state's economy, fueled by construction and strong agricultural commodity and energy prices, produced 3.1 percent percent unemployment in 2006, a historic low. Unemployment peaked at just 7.4 percent in early 2010, well below the national average, and by late 2016 it was hovering around 4 percent, a bit better than the nation as a whole. Median income was not as impressive, at 9 percent below the national average, and over the long term the state's population dynamics, notably an aging population, pose challenges. The state's job market is on track to lose 120,000 baby boomers to retirement in the next decade, compared to between perhaps 90,000 younger people entering the workforce. In this regard, the state's low unemployment poses a threat because companies could have trouble finding enough workers to produce sustainable economic growth.

The boom in the Bakken shale oil field near the North Dakota border helped the state's economy for a while. Montana Democrats as well as Republicans have been big boosters of building the Keystone XL pipeline south from Alberta through Montana to Oklahoma. But the boom has since been followed by a bust, with the number of active drilling rigs falling almost to zero in the eastern part of the state. The state's sizable coal reserves also face increasing difficulty due to national shifts in how electricity is generated and environmental regulations. The fossil-fuel economy has had other drawbacks for the state: To the west, occasional accidents have spilled tens of thousands of gallons of crude oil into the Yellowstone River. In recent years, the state has tentatively begun to harness its abundant renewable energy resources, particularly the wind on the sparsely populated plains. A $1 billion, 400-megawatt project in the central part of the state received a license in 2016; it would store power from wind turbines. Under President Barack Obama, the Interior Department settled with Devon Energy to cancel oil and gas leases on federal lands sacred to the Blackfeet Tribe. But under a Trump administration – and his Interior Secretary Ryan Zinke, who was previously Montana's at-large congressman -- extraction and pipeline-building are expected to get a boost.

Sometimes newcomers are startled by the hardness of Montana life. The DeLorme Montana Road Atlas gives advice on what to do if you should encounter a bear. There are lively political arguments over the grizzly bears and gray wolves reintroduced to Montana in the 1990s. Wolf hunting is now allowed, and some wildlife experts say the grizzlies have gotten used to human beings and vice versa, which might be bad for both. The great outdoors is big business in Montana. Revenue from tourism overtook mining as early as 1970, and in 2015, 11.7 million visitors from out of state visited Montana, while the number of visitors to both Glacier and Yellowstone national parks hit records. The American Prairie Foundation, funded by Manhattan and Silicon Valley millionaires, is buying up land in the northern plains to create a 500,000-acre reserve, where eventually 5,000 buffalo can roam and also attract tourists and hunters. In 2014, Obama signed a measure to increase wilderness area by 250,000 acres, the first such additions in the state in more than three decades.

Montana's senators have often had an impact in Washington far greater than the state's share of the national population, going back to the days of Walsh and Wheeler. Mike Mansfield, who was born to Irish immigrants in 1903 and became a Far Eastern history professor, was elected to the Senate in 1952. He rose to Senate majority leader in 1961 and held the job until his retirement in 1976, after which he was appointed ambassador to Japan by President Jimmy Carter. Max Baucus was scion of the family that owns the Sieben Ranch. He was elected to the House in 1974 at age 32 and to the Senate in 1978; in 2001, he became ranking Democrat on the Senate Finance Committee and held that position or the chairmanship until his retirement in 2014. Montana lost its second House seat in the reapportionment following the 1990 census. Its population grew in the 2000s but came up just short in the reapportionment following the 2010 census. Its at-large seat in the House has the largest population of any House district in the country. Census Bureau projections show that the state is on the cusp of regaining its second seat following the reapportionment in 2020.

From 1952 to 1988, Montana elected only Democrats to the Senate, and from 2006 to 2014, it had two Democratic senators again. Montana has also often elected Democratic governors, most recently the feisty populist rancher Brian Schweitzer in 2004 and 2008 and state Attorney General Steve Bullock in 2012 and 2016. Increasingly, though, Montana has favored conservatives' fierce opposition to higher taxes and federal government dictates. Montana has not elected a Democrat to the House since 1996, and other than Bill Clinton's victory 1992, it has been reliably Republican in presidential races. Since 1993, Democrats have won the outright majority in the state House or Senate only once. In 2016, with President Donald Trump on the ballot, Bullock narrowly won reelection, but Republicans successfully flipped three other statewide offices that had been held by the Democrats – secretary of state, auditor and superintendent of public instruction. Party activists were disappointed that Montana Democrats did not nominate a stronger candidate for the May 2017 special election to replace Rep. Ryan Zinke, who resigned to become Secretary of Interior for Trump.

With his 21-point win, Trump exceeded the statewide margins of Mitt Romney in 2012 (13 points)and John McCain in 2008 (3 points). Trump increased the number of Republican votes over 2012 by 11,000 but Clinton fared 24,000 votes worse than Obama did four years earlier; some of those missing Democratic votes may have gone to third-party candidates Gary Johnson and Jill Stein, who collectively took 7.8 percent of the state's presidential vote. Trump improved GOP performance by between four and 13 points in four of the state's six most populous counties – Yellowstone (Billings), Flathead (Kalispell),Cascade (Great Falls) and Lewis and Clark (Helena). Clinton won the other two. In Missoula County, her margin declined somewhat compared with Obama in 2012, though in Gallatin (Bozeman), the voters backed Clinton by one point after supporting Romney by five points in 2012. Montana's population may be expanding and changing, but not in ways that look likely to boost the Democrats' prospects by much in the immediate future.

Population		**Race and Ethnicity**		**Income**	
Total	1,014,699	White	87.0%	Median Income	$47,169 (39 out of 50)
Land area	145,546	Black	0.4%		
Pop/ sq mi	7.0	Latino	3.3%	Under $50,000	52.4%
Born in state	54.5%	Asian	0.7%	$50,000-$99,999	30.7%
		Two races	2.2%	$100,000-$199,999	13.9%
Age Groups		Other	6.4%	$200,000 or more	2.9%
Under 18	22.1%			Poverty Rate	15.2%
18-34	22.4%	**Education**			
35-64	39.3%	H.S grad or less	37.3%	**Health Insurance**	
Over 64	16.2%	Some college	33.2%	With health insurance coverage	84.5%
		College Degree, 4 yr	20.0%		
Work		Post grad	9.5%		
White Collar	35.9%			**Public Assistance**	
Sales and Service	41.8%	**Military**		Cash public assistance income	2.3%
Blue Collar	22.3%	Veteran	11.4%		
Government	18.1%	Active Duty	0.4%	Food stamp/SNAP benefits	10.7%

Voter Turnout			
2015 Total Citizens 18+	781,250	2016 Pres Turnout as % CVAP	64%
2016 Pres Votes	497,147	2012 Pres Turnout as % CVAP	64%

Legislature	
Senate:	18D, 32R
House:	41D, 59R

Presidential Politics

2016 Democratic Primary		
Bernie Sanders (D)	65,156	(52%)
Hillary Clinton (D)	55,805	(44%)
2016 Republican Primary		
Donald Trump (R)	115,594	(74%)
Ted Cruz (R)	14,682	(9%)
John Kasich (R)	10,777	(7%)

2016 Presidential Vote		
Donald Trump (R)	279,240	(56%)
Hillary Clinton (D)	177,709	(36%)
Gary Johnson (L)	28,037	(6%)
2012 Presidential Vote		
Mitt Romney (R)	267,928	(55%)
Barack Obama (D)	201,839	(42%)
Gary Johnson (L)	14,165	(3%)

Cook Partisan Voting Index: R+11

Usually Montana, with its three electoral votes and remote location, doesn't see much of presidential candidates. But it was a close state in 1992, when Democrat Bill Clinton carried it by three percentage points, and in 1996, when he lost by the same margin, and again in 2008. Montana, which had voted 59%-39% for President George W. Bush in 2004, voted only 50%-47% for John McCain. Montana was not vigorously contested in 2012 and Republican Mitt Romney carried it 55%-42%. In 2016, the state swung further in the GOP direction and Donald Trump defeated Hillary Clinton 57%-38%. Trump won 50 of the state's 56 counties. Clinton carried Glacier, home to a huge Blackfeet Indian reservation; Missoula, home to the University of Montana; Silver Bow, Butte, once known as "the Gibraltar of unionism;" next-door Deer Lodge, home to what was once the largest copper smelter in the world, now the largest in size superfund site in the country; Big Horn, home to a substantial Crow Indian Reservation; and Gallatin, home to Montana State University in Bozeman. Trump carried relatively fast-growing Flathead County, with its affluent new migrants; and Lewis and Clark County, with its government employees who work in the state capital of Helena.

Montana holds its presidential primaries in June, at the end of the primary season when nominations have usually long since been decided. In 2016, the Republican primary was a non-event - Trump had already captured the GOP nomination and won 74 percent of the vote. The Democratic contest was much more spirited. Vermont Sen. Bernie Sanders defeated Clinton 52%-42%. The Vermonter, who campaigned in the state while Clinton did not, carried the two major university counties, Missoula and Gallatin, and his advantage there more than accounted for his statewide margin of victory.

Congressional Districts

115th Congress Lineup	1R	114th Congress Lineup	1R

Governor

Steve Bullock (D)

Elected 2012, term expires 2021, 2nd term; b. Apr. 11, 1966, Missoula, MT; Claremont McKenna Col., B.A. 1988; Columbia U., J.D. 1994; Catholic; Married (Lisa); 3 children.

Elected Office: MT Attorney General, 2008-2012.

Professional Career: Chief legal counsel, MT Secretary of State, 1996-1997; Executive Assistant Attorney General, MT Deptartment of Justice, 1997-2001; Practicing attorney, 2001-2004, 2005-2008; Adjunct professor, George Washington University School of Law, 2001-2004; Acting chief deputy, MT Department of Justice, 2001.

Office: PO Box 200801, Helena, 59620-0801; 406-444-3111; Fax: 406-444-5529; Website: governor.mt.gov.

Election Results

Election	Name (Party)	Vote (%)
2016 General	Steve Bullock (D)	255,933 (50%)
	Greg Gianforte (R)	236,115 (46%)
	Ted Dunlap (L)	17,312 (3%)

Prior winning percentage: 2012 (49%)

Democrat Steve Bullock was elected governor of Montana in 2012 to succeed term-limited Democrat Brian Schweitzer. A popular state attorney general, he beat former Rep. Rick Hill narrowly and was reelected four years later despite the headwinds of Donald Trump's rout in the state.

Bullock, 51, was born in Missoula and raised in Helena, where his newspaper delivery route included the governor's mansion. He received his undergraduate degree from Claremont McKenna College and his law degree from Columbia University. After a brief stint at a law firm following his graduation from law school, Bullock returned to his home state in 1996 to be the chief legal counsel to Democratic Secretary of State Mike Cooney (whom he would tap two decades later as a replacement lieutenant governor). Bullock rose through the ranks in the state Justice Department and ran for attorney general in 2000. He lost in the Democratic primary and then moved to Washington, D.C., to join the law firm of Steptoe & Johnson and to teach as an adjunct professor at George Washington University Law School. He returned to Montana in 2004 to work in private practice in Helena.

Bullock did better in his second try for attorney general in 2008, winning a three-way Democratic primary with 42 percent and taking 53 percent in the general election. He created a state prescription drug registry and a 24/7 sobriety program, which holds repeat DUI offenders accountable by requiring them to submit to, and pay for, regular blood alcohol tests. He also developed a Children's Justice Center to improve law enforcement's ability to track down and prosecute child predators. He supported Montana's century-old ban on corporate campaign contributions, fighting for it until it was struck down by the U.S. Supreme Court. And he became known for teaming with Schweitzer's administration on public-lands access laws.

In 2012, Bullock ran for governor to succeed Schweitzer, who had developed a national reputation as a folksy, bolo-tie-wearing, maverick with a touch of populism and a flair for the dramatic. While Bullock had a more buttoned-down style, he portrayed his candidacy as a continuation of Schweitzer's work. After the primary, he told the *Missoulian* that the race is about "what sort of progressive Montana we want this to be." After eight years of Democratic control of the governorship, Montana Republicans felt they were in a solid position to pick up the governor's office, but they first had to get through an acrimonious seven-way primary. Hill won the nomination but had to work to unite the party behind his candidacy and to replenish his campaign coffers, and that gave Bullock a head start in the general election. Hill was also hobbled by campaign-finance revelations down the stretch. And Republicans faced another problem: the presence of a Libertarian candidate on the general election ballot. Libertarians have long been a presence on statewide ballots in Montana, but they generally get substantially less support than pre-election polls suggest and rarely affect the outcome of the race. This time, however, Libertarian candidate Ron Vandevender won 3.76 percent of the vote on Election Day, and his 18,160 votes may have cost Hill the election. Bullock came out on top by 7,571 votes, or 48.9%, to Hill's 47.3%.

In his initial State of the State speech in January 2013, Bullock appealed to lawmakers for cooperation, saying, "We need each other if we are going to make progress." This olive branch stood in contrast to Schweitzer's antagonistic relationship with the GOP-led legislature, sometimes punctuated by his use of red-hot "veto" branding irons in front of the capitol. But Bullock ended up using the veto almost as much as his predecessor. He vetoed three tax-relief bills that were high on the GOP's agenda, arguing that they would put the state's $300 million surplus at risk. He also vetoed GOP-backed firearm bills, including a measure to allow most adults to carry a concealed weapon without a permit. Meanwhile, the GOP legislature worked to stymie many of Bullock's initiatives, including an expansion of Medicaid under the Affordable Care Act and a $37 million proposal for state-funded preschools. Bullock was unafraid to take a few other liberal positions, including support for overturning the state's ban on same-sex marriage and for efforts to oppose a possible transfer of federal land to the state, which was seen by environmentalists and others as a way to turn over public resources to industry.

One setback for Bullock was his selection of Lt. Gov. John Walsh as the temporary successor for the retiring Democratic Sen. Max Baucus in 2014. Walsh was the underdog in the race for a full-six year term later that year, but revelations about plagiarism in a paper he had written at the Army War College pushed him out of the race entirely. Bullock said he had no knowledge of this part of Walsh's background when he appointed him. The Walsh fiasco continued to reverberate, as Bullock's handpicked successor as lieutenant governor, Angela McLean, left her post amid reports of acrimony between her and Bullock. To fill the post, Bullock chose his old mentor, Cooney, who was praised as an experienced, safe choice.

Bullock's efforts on health care and campaign finance had happier endings, despite facing solid Republican majorities in the legislature. As was the case in 2013, the legislature in 2015 tabled his Medicaid expansion proposal. But Bullock worked with moderate Republicans to draft a compromise expansion plan that won approval in the legislature and eventually enabled tens of thousands of Montanans to sign up for the program. Meanwhile, after the Supreme Court put the kibosh on the state's century-old campaign finance law, Bullock worked with Republican and Democratic lawmakers to craft a bill that required disclosure by "dark money" groups spending on state races. He signed it into law in 2015, and it was upheld in the courts the following year. Bullock also negotiated a water-rights compact with the Confederated Salish and Kootenai Tribes. But for the second straight cycle, the governor and the legislature were unable to agree on terms of an infrastructure package, and Bullock's proposal for a statewide preschool program was dead on arrival.

Bullock began his 2016 re-election bid in a position of national prominence as chairman of the Democratic Governors Association for the 2015-2016 cycle. But winning the governorship in a red state was no easy task. Greg Gianforte, a Bozeman tech entrepreneur, won the GOP primary and sought to paint Bullock as a captive of the national Democratic Party. Gianforte spent more than $6 million from his own pocket and ran more television ads than were aired in any 2016 gubernatorial race, according to the Center for Public Integrity. But with the DGA's help, Bullock raised enough money to remain competitive. Polls showed a narrow contest, and election night proved to be a seesaw affair. Ultimately, Bullock defeated Gianforte by just under 19,000 votes. The incumbent won 12 counties, twice the number Hillary Clinton did on the same ballot, and generally with much larger margins. This was no small feat for Bullock, considering Trump's strength in the state; on the same night, the GOP flipped three other statewide offices and solidified their legislative margins. (Gianforte made an unexpectedly quick return to state politics the following spring, when he won the special election for Montana's open House seat. He got far more national attention during that contest than when he ran for governor, particularly when he body-slammed a reporter, which led to an arrest and misdemeanor guilty plea.) The 2017 session was expected to include continued sparring over the state budget and whether or how to implement infrastructure improvements.

In May 2017, Bullock vetoed a key measure that would have eased regulation of water wells in suburban and rural housing developments

Senior Senator

Jon Tester (D)

Elected 2006, term expires 2018, 2nd term; b. Aug 21, 1956, Havre; University of Great Falls (MT), B.S.; Congregationalist; Married (Sharla Tester); 2 children; 1 grandchild.

Elected Office: Big Sandy School Board, 1983-92, Chariman 1986-91; MT Senate, 1998-2006, Minority Leader, 2003-05, President, 2005-2006.

Professional Career: Operations Management, Procter & Gamble, 1984- 97; Vice President., Clair Daines Construction, 1997-2000; Gen. Manager/Vice President., Right-Now Technologies, 2000-2012.

DC Office: 311 HSOB 20510, 202-224-2644, Fax: 202-224-8594, tester.senate.gov.

State Offices: Billings, 406-252-0550; Bozeman, 406-586-4450; Butte, 406-723-3277; Glendive, 406-365-2391;Great Falls, 406-452-9585; Helena, 406-449-5401; Kalispell, 406-257-3360; Missoula, 406-728-3003.

Committees: *Appropriations*: Agriculture, Rural Development, FDA & Related Agencies, Department of Defense, Department of Homeland Security (RMM), Department of the Interior, Environment & Related Agencies, Energy & Water Development, Military Construction & Veteran Affairs & Related Agencies. *Banking, Housing & Urban Affairs*: Financial Institutions & Consumer Protection, Securities, Insurance & Investment. *Homeland Security & Government Affairs*: Investigations. *Indian Affairs*. *Veterans' Affairs (RMM)*.

Group Ratings

	ADA	ACLU	AFL-CIO	LCV	ITI	COC	HAFA	ACU	CFG	FRC
2016	-	94%	-	88%	40%	50%	12%	4%	12%	0%
2015	85%	C	100%	84%	C	50%	C	8%	4%	0%

Almanac Ratings 2015

	Economy	Social	Foreign	Composite
Liberal	83%	100%	84%	89%
Conservative	17%	0%	16%	11%

Key Votes of the 114th Congress

1. Keystone pipeline	Y	5. National Security Data	Y	9. Gun Sales Checks	Y
2. Export-Import Bank	N	6. Iran Nuclear Deal	N	10. Sanctuary Cities	N
3. Debt Ceiling Increase	Y	7. Puerto Rico Debt	N	11. Planned Parenthood	N
4. Homeland Security $$	Y	8. Loretta Lynch A.G	Y	12. Trade deals	N

Election Results

Election	Name (Party)	Vote (%)	Cand. Spent	Ind. Exp. Support	Ind. Exp. Oppose
2012 General	Jon Tester (D)	236,123 (49%)	$13,347,866	$1,683,327	$11,624,934
	Denny Rehberg (R)	218,051 (45%)	$9,526,859	$575,574	$10,924,254
	Dan Cox (L)	31,892 (7%)			
2012 Primary	Jon Tester (D)	88,720 (100%)			

Prior winning percentages: 2006 (49%)

Democrat Jon Tester was elected in 2006 and won a tough reelection fight in 2012. With his signature $8 flattop haircut and his plain-spoken Western manner inveighing against "D.C. politicians," he doesn't come across like a typical Democrat, but he takes his party's side on key votes often enough to satisfy party leaders. His campaign prowess landed him the chairmanship of the DSCC for the crucial 2016 cycle, when his party had a favorable map and high hopes of retaking the chamber.

Tester grew up in a farming family, on the same prairie land his grandparents homesteaded almost a century ago near the small town of Big Sandy, home of Big Bud 747, the largest farm tractor in the world. His family ran a custom butcher shop behind their barn; at the age of 9, Tester lost three fingers from his left hand in a meat grinder. The accident, he says, changed him from a saxophone player to a trumpet player. He earned a music degree from the University of Great Falls and later taught music at a local elementary school before devoting himself to farming. He has raised wheat, hay, alfalfa, barley, buckwheat, lentils, millet, and peas, and served on the local Soil Conservation Service Committee. He then switched to organic farming. "In the eighties, we realized we had to do something to add value to our product, to make it more marketable, to get a better price for it. That's when we made the conversion to organic," He told *Esquire* magazine. "It's been a blessing for us. Before we converted, when we sprayed weeds, I just planned on being sick for about a week."

Tester's political career began on the Big Sandy school board, where he served for a decade. In 1998, when his neighbor, a Republican state senator, decided not to run for reelection, Tester ran for the seat and won. In 2002, he became minority leader, then Senate president in 2005 after Democrats won a majority. In that role, he helped pass a budget that cut taxes for small businesses and middle-class families while increasing funding for public education. When the 2005 legislative session adjourned, Tester announced he would challenge three-term Republican Sen. Conrad Burns.

He was one of five Democrats seeking the party nomination; his only significant opposition came from two-term state Auditor John Morrison, a former president of the Montana Trial Lawyers Association and the son of a state Supreme Court justice. Morrison outspent Tester nearly 2-1, but in a campaign that focused on Burns's ethics, Morrison was weakened by the disclosure that he had an extramarital affair in 1998 with the fiancée of a businessman who was later investigated by the auditor's office. Running as an unabashed populist, Tester gained support from Daily Kos and other progressive Internet activists, and in Montana he assembled a formidable grassroots operation with hundreds of volunteers. He beat Morrison, 61%-35%.

Tester was taking on the only Republican senator Montana voters had ever reelected. But by 2006, the 71-year-old conservative incumbent had two serious problems. The first was his connection to disgraced and later convicted lobbyist Jack Abramoff. He was the largest congressional recipient of campaign donations from Abramoff's clients, and he faced campaign accusations that he "sold his vote" and betrayed Montana's American Indian population by earmarking funds for Abramoff's Indian clients in other states. Burns's second handicap was a gaffe-prone style, which was ill-suited for the *YouTube* era. In 2006, while discussing the war on terrorism, he spoke of enemies who "drive taxicabs in the daytime and kill at night."

It was a bare-knuckled campaign. Burns spent $9 million, $3.5 million more than Tester, and argued that Tester was too liberal for Montana because of his opposition to the Bush-era PATRIOT Act anti-terrorism law and his links to "radical environmentalists" and left-wing bloggers. But Tester was not so easily caricatured. His haircut, highlighted in a television ad filmed at the Riverview Barbershop in Great Falls, combined with his beefy farmer's build, his 3,000 acre farm, his size 12-C cowboy boots and his down-to-earth style (he's fond of saying, "You have two ears and one mouth; act accordingly.") worked to temper the criticism. The race was decided by just 3,562 votes. In Washington, Democrats hailed Tester's victory as a signal of a new political direction in the Mountain West.

Arriving in Washington, Tester stressed the importance of transparency and accountability in government, distancing himself from the questionable practices that hurt his predecessor. He cosponsored a Republican bill to ban former members of Congress from ever lobbying, and he joined a group of senators seeking to ban secret holds on legislation and nominations, a longtime Senate practice. Tester drew notice for his practice of prominently posting his daily schedule on the Internet, a Senate first. In 2015, his bill to streamline the federal hiring process for its civil servants was signed into law by President Obama. He was distinctive in other ways, hauling to Washington in his luggage a supply of beef he'd butchered himself.

Tester supports abortion rights and same-sex marriage, but takes a Westerner's attitude on firearms. He cosponsored with Republican Sen. John McCain of Arizona an amendment to repeal the District of Columbia's gun control laws, which effectively stopped legislation to give D.C. a voting representative in Congress. Early in Barack Obama's presidency, Tester and fellow Montana Democratic Sen. Max Baucus also made it clear they would oppose any notion of reinstating the ban on military-style assault weapons. But after 2012 school massacre in Newtown Connecticut, Tester expressed a willingness to listen to proposals dealing with assault weapons, and was one of the few red-state Democrats to back the bipartisan legislation from Democratic Sen. Joe Manchin of West Virginia and Republican Sen. Pat Toomey of Pennsylvania to tighten background check laws. But he voted against a 2016 proposal to close the "gun show loophole" in background checks because it didn't have an exemption for sales and gifts between family members.

Tester also holds more Western, libertarian views on surveillance issues. He was one of eight senators led by GOP Sen. Rand Paul of Kentucky to participate in a standing filibuster against ending debate on PATRIOT Act's reauthorization in 2015, though he backed the eventual compromise legislation after some changes to please civil libertarians. More recently, he voted against President Donald Trump's pick to run the CIA, former GOP Rep. Mike Pompeo of Kansas, over concerns about Pompeo's views on surveillance and "enhanced interrogation."

Baucus' departure to become Ambassador to China in early 2014 opened other top Senate posts and gave Tester the chairmanship of the Indian Affairs Committee. In his first few months he impressed tribal observers with his energy, getting 15 bills through the panel dealing with housing, education, water rights and a legislative remedy for a 2009 Supreme Court decision that limited the Interior Department's ability to take lands into trust for tribes. *Indian Country Today* praised Tester's "shoe leather diplomacy," including visits to Native American communities to gauge education, health and environmental programs. He called for protection of the Badger-Two Medicine area near Glacier National Park in Montana, a place sacred to the Blackfeet Tribe but long a bone of contention with oil and gas companies. Tester, along with Montana's junior senator, Republican Steve Daines, has repeatedly won committee-level approval of federal recognition for the Little Shell Tribe of Chippewa Indians, though the measure has yet to pass the Senate.

On the Banking, Housing, and Urban Affairs Committee, Tester worked on the credit card regulation act signed into law in 2009, banning certain fees and deadlines and providing an extra week for paying bills. In May 2010, he sponsored a successful amendment requiring large banks to pay higher Federal Deposit Insurance Corporation fees. He and Tennessee Republican Sen. Bob Corker sought to block new limits on the "swipe fees" that banks and credit card companies charge stores for debit card transactions, arguing that the fee limits would hurt small rural banks. Their amendment in June 2011 drew 54 votes, six short of the 60 needed. Tester was named in 2013 to chair the Banking panel's Securities, Insurance, and Investment Subcommittee, which is responsible for overseeing computerized high-speed traders and efforts to rein in technological snafus that hurt investor confidence in the markets. Tester is also on the

Homeland Security and Governmental Affairs Committee; in that capacity, he authored a bill, signed into law in December 2014, to simplify Customs and Border Protection's overtime pay practices. Tester also voiced criticism of how political scientists from Stanford and Dartmouth were able to send a "voter guide" to 100,000 Montanans to test theories about how voters respond to nonpartisan contests; Tester said that "using the people of Montana as their guinea pigs is bad enough, but the truth is that elections should not be a lab for political experiments."

At times, Tester tested the boundaries of party loyalty. He was one of only two Democrats in October 2011 to join Republicans in a filibuster of Obama's jobs bill, contending it contained "tax gimmicks" that did not address deficit reduction. He aroused the ire of left-wing bloggers in December 2010 when he voted against the DREAM Act, which would provide a path for citizenship for the children of illegal immigrants who attend college or serve in the military. Even though Montana has one of the lowest percentages of immigrants, legal or illegal, of any state, Tester said, "Illegal immigration is a critical problem facing our country, but amnesty is not the solution." The Daily Kos' Markos Moulitsas, a staunch Tester backer in 2006, said he would do whatever he could to defeat him in 2012. In 2015, Tester again raised liberals' ire with his complaint, on Montana Public Radio, that "every logging sale in Montana right now is under litigation." Under fire, his staff revised the claim not once but twice, but the *Washington Post* Fact Checker still gave Tester Four Pinocchios, its worst rating, saying he was "wildly off the mark."

Tester envisioned a tough reelection battle even before Republican Denny Rehberg, Montana's sole House member, announced in February 2011 that he would run for the seat in 2012. In 1996, Rehberg had given Baucus his closest race ever, losing by just 50%-45%. By October 2011, the nonpartisan Center for Responsive Politics found that Tester, despite running as an outsider, had accepted more campaign contributions from lobbyists than any other member of Congress. Republicans also pointed to Tester's financial support from large banks on the swipe-fee issue as evidence of his hypocrisy.

Rehberg relied on the familiar Republican strategy of attacking Tester as a liberal Obama ally, citing his vote in favor of the president's health care law, though that strategy took a hit when it was revealed that the NRSC had photoshopped Tester's face onto a man embracing Obama in one of its ads. (it was obviously not Tester, as the body had all its fingers.) Tester defended his Obamacare vote as "about being able to get health care without breaking the bank." He took a page from the national Democratic playbook in sowing doubt about Rehberg's support for Social Security and Medicare. Although Rehberg got outside GOP money, national Democratic interests from labor and women's groups came into the state to assist Tester, organizing a get-out-the-vote effort that proved effective. The senator also got help from an unlikely source, the Seattle grunge-rock group Pearl Jam. He used his friendship with bassist Jeff Ament, a Big Sandy native, to raffle off to campaign donors a prize of two onstage reclining concert seats, along with dinner with Tester and Ament.

Republican Mitt Romney had carried Montana with 55 percent of the vote, and election forecaster Nate Silver determined that Tester had just a 34 percent chance of winning. Yet Tester ended up winning, 49%-45%, with 7% for Libertarian Dan Cox.

Tester's campaign-trail acumen helped him overcome his occasional breaks with Senate leadership to win him the DSCC job, where he had to defend just 10 seats, compared to 24 for the GOP. Despite Tester's acknowledged misgivings about the job's intense fundraising demands, he helped the committee out-raise the NRSC by $180 million to $138 million for the cycle. But Democrats failed to recapture Senate control despite its advantages, picking up just two seats in a disappointing election cycle and losing races where they once appeared to have the edge in Wisconsin and Pennsylvania. Few Democratic Senate candidates managed to run ahead of Hillary Clinton at the top of the ticket, a sign of a weak class of recruits, and Donald Trump's surprising election night victory doomed Senate Democrats' chances at retaking the chamber.

That disappointing showing has a silver lining for Tester, who faces reelection in 2018 and could face a tough fight. It will likely be easier for him to run as an independent voice for the state with Trump in the White House than with Clinton, though Trump won the state by 20 percentage points, a big swing from Obama's two-point loss there in 2008. Trump removed what many believed to be Tester's biggest reelection threat when he chose Republican Rep. Ryan Zinke to become his Interior Secretary. Tester gleefully introduced Zinke at his committee confirmation hearing and voted for his confirmation, though he voted against most of Trump's more controversial cabinet selections.

In 2017, Tester became Democrats' ranking member on the Senate Veterans Affairs Committee, where he could play a key role in negotiating any Veterans Affairs reforms pushed by the Trump Administration.

Junior Senator

Steve Daines (R)

Elected 2014, term expires 2020, 1st term; b. Aug 20, 1962, Van Nuys, CA; Montana State University, Bozeman, B.S.; Presbyterian; Married (Cindy Daines); 4 children.

Elected Office: U.S. House, 2013-2015.

Professional Career: Music teacher, F.E. Miley Elementary, 1978-1980; Custom butcher, T-Bone Farms, 1978-1998; Farmer, T-Bone Farms, 1978-present.

DC Office: 320 HSOB 20510, 202-224-2651, Fax: 202-228-1236, daines.senate.gov.

State Offices: Billings, 406-245-6822; Bozeman, 406-587-3446; Great Falls, 406-453-0148; Hardin, 406-665-4126; Helena, 406-443-3189; Kalispell, 406-257-3765; Missoula, 406-549-8198; Sidney, 406-482-9010.

Committees: *Agriculture, Nutrition & Forestry*: Commodities, Risk Management & Trade, Conservation, Forestry & Natural Resources (Chmn), Livestock, Marketing & Agriculture Security, Rural Development & Energy. *Appropriations*: Department of Defense, Department of the Interior, Environment & Related Agencies, Financial Services & General Government, State, Foreign Operations & Related Programs, Transportation, HUD & Related Agencies. *Energy & Natural Resources*: Energy, National Parks (Chmn), Public Lands, Forests & Mining. *Homeland Security & Government Affairs*: Investigations, Regulatory Affairs & Federal Management. *Indian Affairs*. *Joint Congressional-Executive Commission on China*.

Group Ratings

	ADA	ACLU	AFL-CIO	LCV	ITI	COC	HAFA	ACU	CFG	FRC
2016	-	64%	-	12%	60%	100%	77%	92%	81%	100%
2015	5%	C	21%	0%	C	79%	C	92%	83%	100%

Almanac Ratings 2015

	Economy	Social	Foreign	Composite
Liberal	4%	0%	34%	13%
Conservative	96%	100%	66%	87%

Key Votes of the 114th Congress

1. Keystone pipeline	Y	5. National Security Data	Y	9. Gun Sales Checks	N
2. Export-Import Bank	Y	6. Iran Nuclear Deal	Y	10. Sanctuary Cities	Y
3. Debt Ceiling Increase	N	7. Puerto Rico Debt	N	11. Planned Parenthood	Y
4. Homeland Security $$	N	8. Loretta Lynch A.G	N	12. Trade deals	Y

Election Results

Election	Name (Party)	Vote (%)		Cand. Spent	Ind. Exp. Support	Ind. Exp. Oppose
2014 General	Steve Daines (R)	213,709	(58%)	$6,668,759	$377,362	$303,790
	Amanda Curtis (D)	148,184	(40%)	$968,388	$39,751	$43,265
	Roger Roots (L)	7,933	(2%)			
2014 Primary	Steve Daines (R)	110,565	(83%)			
	Susan Cundiff (R)	11,909	(9%)			
	Champ Edmunds (R)	10,151	(8%)			

Prior winning percentages: House: 2012 (53%)

Republican Steve Daines was elected Montana's junior senator in 2014, coasting to the win after appointed Democratic Sen. John Walsh's candidacy imploded over a plagiarism scandal. Shifting into politics following a successful career in business, Daines became the first Republican to hold the seat since Joseph M. Dixon in 1913, when senators were still appointed by state legislatures. He has been a reliably Republican vote who is further right on energy and social issues but less so on foreign policy. He pays particular attention to the energy and land use issues important to Montana.

Daines grew up in Bozeman, where his father started a home-construction business. He went on to study chemical engineering at Montana State University, and during his senior year, he became one of the youngest delegates at the 1984 Republican National Convention. When he graduated, Daines spent 13 years with consumer goods giant Procter & Gamble. After seven years managing operations in the United States, he moved his young family overseas for a six-year stint with the company in Hong Kong and China. In 1997, Daines left P&G to join the family construction business in Bozeman. Three years later, he got a call from local entrepreneur Greg Gianforte, founder of RightNow Technologies, asking him to come on board as vice president of customer service. Daines has since returned the favor, supporting Gianforte in his failed 2016 gubernatorial run and helping to convince him to make his successful run for Congress a few months later, when Rep. Ryan Zinke was appointed President Trump's Interior Secretary.

Daines dipped into local politics in 2007 when he and his wife, Cindy, founded *Giveitback.com,* a nonprofit organization that pushed for the return of the state's $1 billion budget surplus to taxpayers. Not long after that, former Arkansas Gov. Mike Huckabee asked Daines to serve as Montana state chairman for his presidential campaign. Daines also chaired Montana's delegation to the 2008 Republican National Convention. That same year, he ran for lieutenant governor on a ticket with former state Sen. Roy Brown, but they failed to oust Democratic Gov. Brian Schweitzer.

Two years later, Daines announced his intention to challenge Democrat Jon Tester for his Senate seat. But when Rep. Denny Rehberg said in February 2011 that he would run against Tester, Daines dropped out of the Senate race to vie for Rehberg's vacated House seat instead. He ended up winning with 53 percent of the vote.

In the House, Daines compiled a conservative voting record, especially on foreign policy issues, but was not as far to the right as other recent GOP arrivals. Daines bucked some in his party by ultimately voting to end the government shutdown and to reauthorize the Violence Against Women Act. He also sponsored a bill to bar energy development on the North and Middle forks of the Flathead River, and worked with Tester to push for federal recognition of the Little Shell Tribe of Chippewa Indians. The former tech executive led successful efforts to expand broadband and cell phone coverage, with the FCC approving expanded wireless broadband access for 1 million people in Montana and Wyoming due to Daines' work.

Daines took a variety of conservative stands as well, supporting the budget crafted by Wisconsin Rep. Paul Ryan, and voting for a measure to make abortion illegal after 20 weeks. The House in 2013 passed his bill to expand hydropower production in Montana, and he successfully amended several other bills to include provisions specific to his state's energy production.

Daines's rise to the Senate included some good fortune. Rehberg left politics after losing the 2012 race to Tester. The state's other Democratic senator, Max Baucus, announced his retirement and subsequently resigned his seat early when President Barack Obama named him Ambassador to China. Daines jumped into the race, just 14 months after his election to the House. After former Gov. Brian Schweitzer declined to run, the Democrats turned to Walsh, who had been tapped by Democratic Gov. Steve Bullock to succeed Baucus. But in June, the *New York Times* published a bombshell story saying that Walsh had plagiarized large portions of his master's thesis at the U.S. Army War College. A muddled response by Walsh and his staff only made matters worse, and in August, shortly before the ballot deadline, Walsh exited the race. The party chose state Rep. Amanda Curtis to take his place, but a race that had already favored the well-funded Daines increasingly looked like a rout in the making. On Election Day, Daines defeated Curtis, 58%-40%-making this one of the key races that helped the GOP take over the chamber.

Daines took seats on two panels of special interest to Montana-Energy and Natural Resources and Indian Affairs-as well as Appropriations and Commerce, Science and Transportation. The first Senate bill he introduced was the Balanced Budget Accountability Act, which would force lawmakers to balance the budget or give up their salaries. He urged approval of the Keystone XL pipeline and decried federal regulations that curbed timber harvests.

In 2017, Daines was awarded spots on the Agriculture and Homeland Security committees, while giving up his spot on Commerce. He chairs Agriculture's Conservation subcommittee, and the Energy Committee's National Parks subcommittee (his hometown of Bozeman is a short drive, by western standards, from Yellowstone National Park and Glacier National Park). He chairs the Western Caucus, a coalition of western Republicans focused on land use and energy issues.

REPRESENTATIVE-AT-LARGE

Greg Gianforte (R)

Elected 2017, 1st term; b. Apr. 17, 1961, San Diego, CA; Stevens Institute of Technology, B.Eng, MS, 1983; Christian; married (Susan Gianforte); 4 children.

Professional Career: Engineer; Businessman; Co founder, Brightwork Development Inc.; Founder, RightNow Technologies.

Committees: *Natural Resources; Oversight & Government Reform.*

Election Results

Election	Name (Party)	Vote (%)		Cand. Spent	Ind. Exp. Support	Ind. Exp. Oppose
2017 Special	Greg Gianforte (R)	189,473	(50%)	$2,536,047	$262,392	$87,705
	Rob Quist (D)	166,483	(44%)	$2,558,602	$350,339	$3,255,994
	Mark Wicks (L)	21,509	(6%)			

Republican Greg Gianforte won a special election in May 2017 for the seat vacated by Republican Rep. Ryan Zinke, who President Donald Trump selected as Secretary of Interior. The contest received a disproportionate amount of national attention and dollars in the intense political environment that followed Trump's election. It was capped by an unusual election-eve incident at Gianforte's headquarters in Bozeman, when he slammed to the floor a reporter for a British newspaper who asked his views about changes in the Affordable Care Act.

In the subsequent 24 hours, prominent state newspapers withdrew their endorsements of Gianforte and he was charged with a misdemeanor by the local sheriff. The impact on voters appeared to be negligible and Gianforte apologized to the reporter as he delivered his victory speech. National Republicans initially seemed dumbfounded by the incident. House GOP leaders said there was no justification for the incident, though there were no immediate congressional sanctions. Whether they would support Gianforte for reelection remained to be seen. He won the election, 50%-44%.

The special election was triggered when the Senate, on a 68-31 vote, confirmed Zinke on March 1. The major parties selected their nominees in conventions four and five days later at the same hotel in Helena. A former Navy SEAL, who was first elected in 2014, Zinke had served on the Natural Resources Committee, where he had shown interest in conservation issues.

Democrats nominated Rob Quist, a musician with a local wood band, whose public service included 11 years on the Montana Arts Council and as an ambassador for Montana to its sister state in Japan. Quist, who rarely was seen without a cowboy hat, won on the fourth ballot in a field of eight candidates, including two state representatives. He highlighted his support during the 2016 presidential campaign for Sen. Bernie Sanders of Vermont, who made campaign appearances on his behalf.

Gianforte was well-known locally from his 2016 campaign as the GOP nominee against Gov. Steve Bullock, who was reelected, 50%-46%. He got a majority of the GOP convention votes on the first ballot against five other candidates. Gianforte was a New Jersey transplant who moved to Montana and started the technology firm RightNow Technologies, which he sold to Oracle for $1.8 billion. During the special election, he enthusiastically supported Trump, who won the Montana presidential vote, 56%-36%, on the same day Gianforte lost his contest for governor.

Despite its GOP lean in presidential elections and the party's control of the state Legislature, Montana Democrats have won their share of statewide contests for governor and the Senate, though Republicans have controlled the House seat since 1996. With Quist as the nominee, the Democratic Congressional Campaign Committee concluded that his prospects were dim and they gave him little financial support. That dismayed many party activists who saw an opportunity to take a Republican-held seat, especially with the contentious national politics during the Trump era.

As was the case with lavish grass-roots funding for the Democratic nominee in other House special elections during the spring of 2017, Quist reported that he raised more than $6 million for his campaign - a huge amount for a two-month contest in a state with low advertising costs. Gianforte also raised millions of dollars, including $1 million in self-financing. The two candidates benefited from a total of more than $7 million in outside spending, chiefly by national party groups and their allies; a majority of those funds were spent on behalf of Gianforte, largely for negative ads on Quist.

Gianforte ran into problems during the campaign in clarifying his view on what action Congress should take on health care reform. When asked whether he would support the recent House-passed Republican plan, he earlier said that he would not respond until the Congressional Budget Office had issued its analysis. The CBO issued its report on the day before the Montana election. That led Ben Jacobs, a Washington-based reporter for the Guardian newspaper, to cite the CBO in seeking Gianforte's reaction. The candidate later acknowledged that he reacted poorly to Jacob's questioning. After Gianforte threw him to the floor, Jacobs showed that his glasses had been broken and he went to a local hospital for X-rays.

House Speaker Paul Ryan the next morning told reporters in Washington that Gianforte should issue an apology, which he did that evening during his celebration in Montana. "There's no call for this, no matter what - on any circumstance," Ryan said.

★ NEBRASKA ★

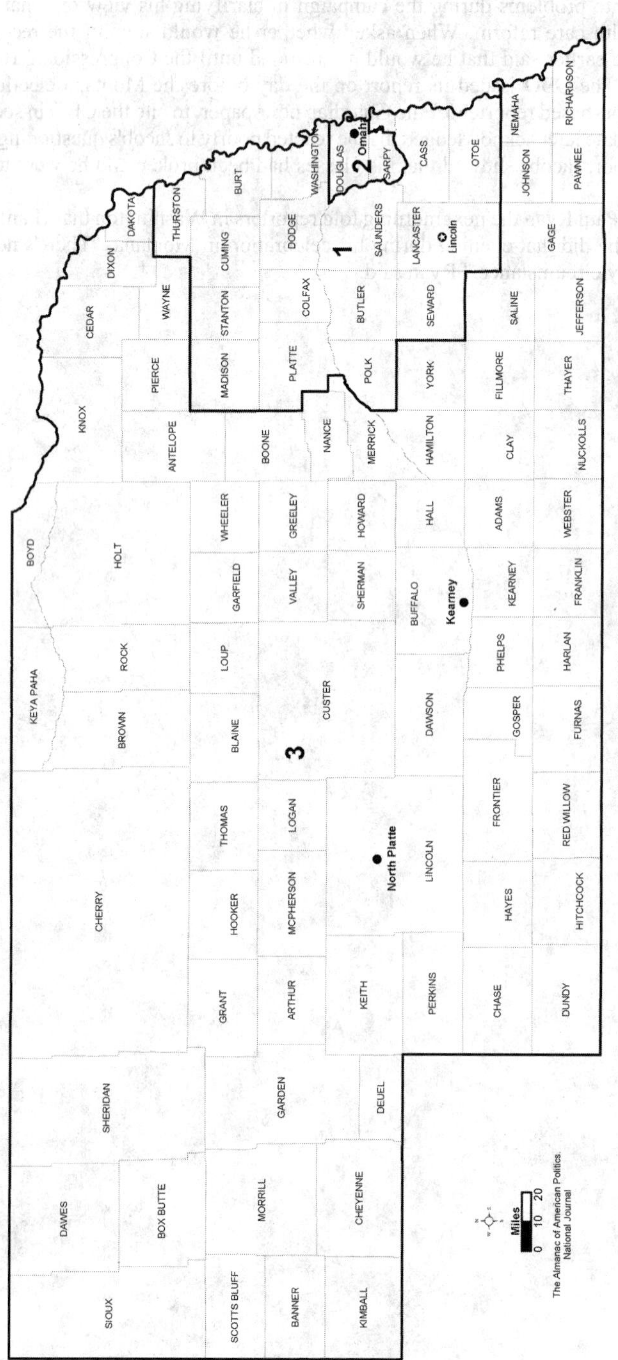
RICHARDSON
NEMAHA
PAWNEE
JOHNSON
OTOE
CASS
SARPY
2
Omaha
DOUGLAS
WASHINGTON
BURT
THURSTON
DAKOTA
DIXON
CEDAR
WAYNE
CUMING
DODGE
SAUNDERS
LANCASTER
Lincoln
1
GAGE
JEFFERSON
SALINE
SEWARD
BUTLER
COLFAX
STANTON
MADISON
PLATTE
POLK
YORK
FILLMORE
THAYER
PIERCE
KNOX
ANTELOPE
BOONE
NANCE
MERRICK
HAMILTON
CLAY
NUCKOLLS
WEBSTER
ADAMS
HALL
HOWARD
GREELEY
WHEELER
HOLT
BOYD
GARFIELD
VALLEY
SHERMAN
BUFFALO
Kearney
KEARNEY
FRANKLIN
HARLAN
PHELPS
DAWSON
CUSTER
LOUP
ROCK
KEYA PAHA
BROWN
BLAINE
3
GOSPER
FURNAS
FRONTIER
RED WILLOW
LINCOLN
North Platte
LOGAN
THOMAS
CHERRY
HOOKER
MCPHERSON
HAYES
HITCHCOCK
DUNDY
CHASE
PERKINS
KEITH
ARTHUR
GRANT
GARDEN
DEUEL
SHERIDAN
DAWES
BOX BUTTE
MORRILL
CHEYENNE
SIOUX
SCOTTS BLUFF
BANNER
KIMBALL
Congressional district boundaries were first effective for 2012.
Miles
0 10 20
The Almanac of American Politics.
National Journal

Nebraska – America's top beef exporter and fifth-biggest agricultural exporter overall – has long been, and remains, one of the most Republican states in the nation. But Nebraska's largest and fastest-growing metropolitan area, Omaha, is politically marginal and, thanks to the state's eccentric Electoral College rules, it gave one of its five electoral votes to Barack Obama in 2008 and came within two percentage points of doing so again for Hillary Clinton in 2016, even as Donald Trump was winning the state with 60 percent of the vote.

The first travelers on the Oregon Trail in the 1840s called what they saw when they crossed the Missouri River and moved west along the Platte River "the sea of Nebraska." The state's ruggedly beautiful sandhills, a blanket of grass tucked roughly over submerged sand dunes, bloom atop the Ogalalla Aquifer and cover about a quarter of the state. In Nebraska, you can see nothing but rolling fields for miles on end, sectioned off here and there by barbed wire fences and perhaps, in the distance, a grain elevator towering over a tiny town and its railroad depot. The Platte is not actually a single river, but a braid of streams that weaves a silver chain around sandbars and islands, flooding the level floor of the Nebraska plain - a mile wide, the saying goes, and six inches deep. Settlers in Nebraska sliced the top level of earth to prepare for planting, using the layers of sod to construct rustic but practical homes.

The state was mostly settled in a single rush in the 1880s, when its population increased from 452,000 to 1 million. Omaha became a major railroad center and farming and food products reigned as the main businesses. Czechs, Germans and Danes came to work the factories in Omaha and farms on the Plains - Willa Cather tells the story beautifully in her novels. Nebraska was a major destination for Volga Germans, ethnic Germans who had settled in Russia; they bequeathed runza, a meat-in-bread delicacy kept alive in the state by a popular chain of casual restaurants of that name. For about a century, Nebraska remained pretty much the same. From 1890 to 2010, its population rose from 1 million to just 1.8 million. This is not what its founders envisioned. They hoped that Nebraska would develop a diversified farming, industrial and commercial economy like the ones that emerged in Illinois, Missouri and Ohio. But climate is hard to predict. Rains were plentiful in the 1880s, but the 1890s were years of drought, and Nebraska abruptly stopped growing. Many rural counties, and even Omaha, lost population. Nebraska exported people for 100 years: 48 percent of Nebraskans in 1890 were children, but in 2010 only 25 percent were. For a long time, the creative energies in the American economy seemed to have skipped over the Great Plains and moved west.

Since 1990, Nebraska has been growing relatively robustly for the first time in decades. Its population grew 16 percent between 1990 and 2010 - more than the increase in the previous 60 years combined - and since 2010, it has risen by another 4.4 percent. Between 2015 and 2016, Nebraska ranked in the top third of states for population growth. Growth has been concentrated in the Omaha region – Douglas County, which includes Omaha, and its suburban neighbor Sarpy County – as well as Lancaster, which includes the state capital of Lincoln. Sarpy County alone has grown at double-digit rates in recent years; combined, these three counties now account for 54 percent of the state's population. A big reason for the population uptick in the state has been an influx of Hispanics. The Hispanic share of the population rose from 2 percent in 1990 to 11 percent today, a higher share of the population than in such diverse states as Virginia, Georgia, Pennsylvania and Michigan. Many came from Texas and Mexico to work in meatpacking factories in such places as Colfax County (Schuyler), which is 44 percent Hispanic, and Dawson County (Lexington), which is 33 percent Hispanic. Meanwhile, the state's Asian population is growing quickly (though starting from a small base) because of an influx of South Asians from such places as Bhutan, Myanmar (Burma), Nepal and Thailand. As a result, Nebraska's population is no longer quite so elderly. Today, Nebraska has more than 120,000 residents born outside the United States, and 73 percent of them are of working age, compared with less than 50 percent of the native-born population.

Nebraska, without a housing bubble and with an economy based on agriculture, escaped the worst of the Great Recession. The unemployment rate in Nebraska was at 3.3 in December 2016 – the ninth-best of any state -- and it hasn't even touched 4.0 percent since May 2012. While farm income has weakened despite the national economic recovery, the state's median income remains 7 percent higher than the national average, and those dollars can go further with the state's low cost of living. Measured by the value of its exports, Nebraska ranks first in the country for beef and veal, first in hides and skins, third in corn, third in feed grains, and seventh in pork. Nebraskans cheered when Japan opened its market to U.S. beef in January 2013 and when China said it would do so in September 2016. Omaha has been thriving economically, and not just because America's second-richest man, Warren Buffett, lives there. Omaha is home to four Fortune 500 companies: Buffett's Berkshire Hathaway, Union Pacific, the construction, engineering and mining giant Kiewit, and Mutual of Omaha, though it lost a fifth, ConAgra, to Chicago in October 2015. The Omaha area also harbors such large employers as Green Plains Renewable Energy, TD Ameritrade and Valmont Industries, which manufactures linear irrigation equipment and windmill support structures. Lincoln, with its skyscraper state Capitol and University of Nebraska, has a solid economic base as well. On Saturdays during the fall, when the 'Huskers (Nebraskans don't say Cornhuskers) play in Lincoln, nearly all the 92,000 seats at Memorial Stadium are filled, which equates to roughly one out of every 20 people in the state. The economy has been growing more slowly outside metropolitan Omaha and Lincoln, though Trump's decision to green-light the Keystone XL pipeline, which crisscrosses the state, has given reason for optimism.

The sudden boom of the 1880s and the bust of the 1890s produced the most colorful - and atypical - politics of Nebraska's history: the populist movement and William Jennings Bryan, the "silver-tongued orator of the Platte." Bryan was only 36 when he delivered his "Cross of Gold" speech at the 1896 Democratic National Convention and was swept to the nomination. "From the first sentence, the audience was with me," recalled Bryan in his memoirs. But the country wasn't. Bryan was so radical that Democratic President Grover Cleveland wouldn't support him, although he still won 47 percent of the popular vote in the first of his three attempts at the presidency. Since Bryan's time, Nebraska's most notable politician has been George Norris. In 1934, Norris spurred adoption of the state's unicameral, nonpartisan legislature, in which every bill gets a public hearing where anyone can speak. In Washington, Norris sponsored the Norris-LaGuardia Anti-Injunction Act, the first federal pro-union legislation, and the Tennessee Valley Authority Act. But most Nebraskans were repelled by the New Deal, which they believed threatened their way of life.

Although it has sometimes elected Democratic governors and senators – James Exon, Bob Kerrey and Ben Nelson each served in both offices -- Nebraska over the past half-century has been strongly Republican, and in recent years it has been growing increasingly so. The state hasn't elected a Democrat to statewide office in more than a decade, although unusually for a strongly Republican state, the Nebraska legislature voted to abolish the death penalty in 2015. Republican Gov. Pete Ricketts vetoed the bill, but the legislature overrode him. Then, with Ricketts' support, a measure to reject the legislature's move qualified for the ballot, and in 2016, the measure passed with 57 percent of the vote.

In the presidential race, Trump widened Mitt Romney's margin in the state by three points, winning 21,000 more votes statewide than Romney had as Clinton lagged Barack Obama's 2012 total by 18,000 votes. Nebraska is one of only two states (along with Maine) that allocate electoral votes by congressional district, and Clinton nearly nabbed one from the 2nd district. After having made an unusual campaign stop in Omaha alongside Buffett 99 days before the election, Clinton lost the district to Trump by two percentage points and slightly less than 6,000 votes. That was an improvement from Obama's 2012 showing in the district, when he lost by 7 points. After Obama won the 2nd district in 2008, the legislature -- officially nonpartisan but unofficially Republican-leaning -- redrew the district's lines to expand into fast-growing Sarpy County. In 2016, Clinton beat Trump in the Douglas County portion but Trump won the Sarpy precincts by an almost 2-to-1 margin. Douglas County was one of only two that Clinton won, the other being Lancaster County (Lincoln), by about 300 votes; Romney had won both in 2012. All told, 62 percent of Clinton's votes in the state came from those two counties – an indication that the vast sea of red in the rest of Nebraska is not about to change its hue any time soon.

Population		Race and Ethnicity		Income	
Total	1,869,365	White	80.8%	Median Income	$52,997 (25 out of 50)
Land area	76,824	Black	4.6%		
Pop/ sq mi	24.3	Latino	10.0%	Under $50,000	46.9%
Born in state	65.3%	Asian	2.0%	$50,000-$99,999	32.9%
		Two races	1.8%	$100,000-$199,999	16.8%
Age Groups		Other	0.9%	$200,000 or more	3.5%
Under 18	24.9%			Poverty Rate	12.7%
18-34	23.6%	**Education**			
35-64	37.5%	H.S grad or less	36.8%	**Health Insurance**	
Over 64	14.2%	Some college	33.8%	With health insurance coverage	89.7%
Work		College Degree, 4 yr	19.6%		
		Post grad	9.7%		
White Collar	35.6%			**Public Assistance**	
Sales and Service	40.7%	**Military**		Cash public assistance income	2.1%
Blue Collar	23.6%	Veteran	9.5%		
Government	14.1%	Active Duty	0.3%	Food stamp/SNAP benefits	9.0%

Voter Turnout			
2015 Total Citizens 18+	1,333,860	2016 Pres Turnout as % CVAP	63%
2016 Pres Votes	844,227	2012 Pres Turnout as % CVAP	61%

Presidential Politics

2016 Democratic Primary		
Hillary Clinton (D)	42,692	(53%)
Bernie Sanders (D)	37,744	(47%)
2016 Republican Primary		
Donald Trump (R)	122,327	(61%)
Ted Cruz (R)	36,703	(18%)
John Kasich (R)	22,709	(11%)
Ben Carson (R)	10,016	(5%)

2016 Presidential Vote		
Donald Trump (R)	495,961	(59%)
Hillary Clinton (D)	284,494	(34%)
Gary Johnson (L)	38,946	(5%)
2012 Presidential Vote		
Mitt Romney (R)	475,064	(60%)
Barack Obama (D)	302,081	(38%)

Over the past 50 years, Nebraska has voted an average of 60 percent Republican in presidential elections, more than any other state except Utah, Idaho and Wyoming. In 2016, Donald Trump came close to hitting that mark defeating Hillary Clinton 59%-34%. Nebraska is one of two states (Maine is the other) that allocate two of its Electoral College votes to the statewide winner and the others to the winners in each of the congressional districts. In 2008, Barack Obama managed to carry the 2nd District, Omaha and its suburbs, 50%-49%, by just 3,370 votes out of 277,809 cast. John McCain carried the state overall, 57%-42%. Thus, one Nebraska Electoral Vote went to Obama, the first time a Democrat picked up any of the state's Electoral College votes since 1964. The Clinton campaign aired television ads in the Omaha media market in hopes of repeating Obama's 2008 coup. She also campaigned with Omaha investment billionaire Warren Buffett. The 2nd was close, but Trump bested Clinton there, 49%-45%. Trump won 91 of the state's 93 counties, all but Douglas (Omaha) and Lancaster (the University of Nebraska at Lincoln).

The May 10 GOP primary came shortly after Trump became the de facto Republican nominee, but Texas Sen. Ted Cruz, who had withdrawn from the race after he lost the May 3 Indiana primary, mischievously said he might get back into the GOP contest if Nebraska Republicans rejected Trump. No such thing happened and Trump captured 62 percent of the vote to 18 percent that in protest went for Cruz. Then Republican Gov. Pete Ricketts endorsed Trump after he became the presumptive nominee. His father, who co-founded TD Ameritrade based in Omaha and bought the Chicago Cubs, donated millions of dollars to Our Principals PAC, which had earlier run anti-Trump ads in the primaries. (Rickets later contributed at least $1 million in the general election campaign to a pro-Trump PAC.) Trump nominated Gov. Ricketts brother, Todd, to be the deputy secretary of Commerce, but he withdrew after difficulties arose untangling his financial holdings sufficiently to satisfy federal ethics rules. In the March

5 Democratic caucuses, Vermont Sen. Bernie Sanders defeated Clinton, 57%-43%. But Clinton defeated Sanders in the non-binding Democratic primary two months later, 53%-47%.

Congressional Districts

115th Congress Lineup	3R	**114th Congress Lineup**	2R 1D

Nebraska has had three congressional districts since the 1960 census. Boundaries can generate strong feelings in Nebraska if only because it has been one of just two states where Electoral College votes are apportioned by congressional district. The unicameral legislature is technically nonpartisan, but in reality, Republicans have long controlled the process. With the tight presidential vote in the 2nd District in 2016, plus its competitive congressional battleground, Republicans have added incentive to eliminate the Electoral College anomaly.

As the sparse western two-thirds of the state has shed residents, the western 3rd District has needed to expand, and the Lincoln-based 1st District and Omaha-based 2nd District have needed to shrink. In 2011, Republicans' obvious top priority was to shore up the 2nd. So, the legislature passed a map trading politically mixed Bellevue and Offutt Air Force Base south of Omaha to the 1st District in exchange for the deeply Republican western half of Sarpy County, making the 2nd about a percentage point safer overall. To give neighboring Republican Jeff Fortenberry extra insurance, legislators shifted very conservative Platte County from the 3rd to the 1st. To offset the move, the "Big Third" now stretches from Wyoming to Missouri and Iowa and includes all or part of 75 counties, more than any other seat in the country. That helped Republicans in 2012. But the 2nd then resumed its highly competitive status, with House incumbents ousted the next two cycles. Unless Republican redistricters want to divide Omaha, which seems unlikely, their options are limited.

Governor

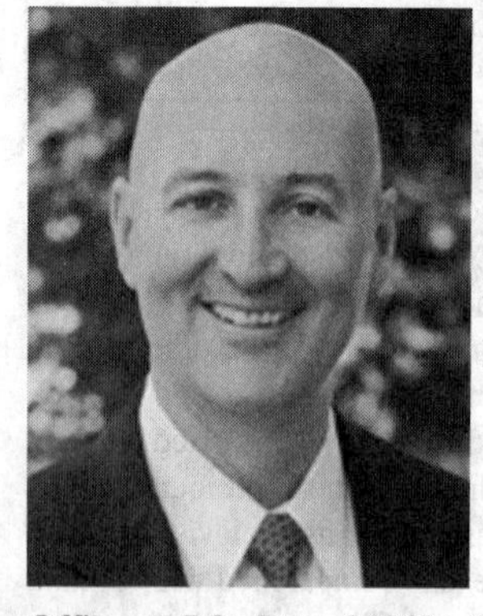

Pete Ricketts (R)

Elected 2014, term expires 2019, 1st term; b. Aug. 19, 1964, Nebraska City, NE; U. of Chicago, B.A., M.A.; Catholic; Married (Susanne); 3 children.

Professional Career: Customer Services, Senior VP Strategy & Business Devel., Senior Vice President of Product Development, Senior Vice President of Marketing, COO at Ameritrade, 1993-2005; Founder, Drakon, LLC.

Office: PO Box 94848, Lincoln, 68509-4848; 402-471-2244; Fax: 402-471-6031; Website: governor.nebraska.gov.

Election Results

Election	Name (Party)	Vote (%)
2014 General	Pete Ricketts (R)	308,751 (57%)
	Chuck Hassebrook (D)	211,905 (39%)
	Mark G. Elworth Jr. (L)	19,001 (4%)
2014 Primary	Pete Ricketts (R)	58,671 (27%)
	Jon Bruning (R)	56,324 (26%)
	Beau McCoy (R)	46,196 (21%)
	Mike Foley (R)	42,394 (19%)

Republican Pete Ricketts's last name was well known in Nebraska before he ever tried for public office. His father, Joe, had founded the company that became TD Ameritrade, based outside of Omaha, and the family owns Major League Baseball's storied franchise, the Chicago Cubs. Ricketts worked to burnish his image as more than a candidate with deep pockets when he ran for governor in 2014, and to fend off constant criticism that he - and his politically engaged father - were trying to buy the governor's mansion. He has found some success in that, despite a rocky relationship with a legislature that has often overridden his vetoes.

Ricketts is one of four children, and the eldest son. On the campaign trail, he told voters that growing up in Omaha, he and his siblings were latchkey kids in a middle-class home where both parents worked and his father built a financial empire. He graduated from Westside High School in Omaha and attended the University of Chicago, earning a bachelor's degree in biology and an MBA. After college, Ricketts joined the family business, rising to president and chief operating officer. He left TD Ameritrade in 2005 to run for the Senate against incumbent Democrat Ben Nelson in 2006. Republicans were not looking for a wealthy scion to be their standard-bearer against Nelson, who was a former two-term governor born in the small plains town of McCook that had also produced Nebraska icon George Norris. But after a number of other notable Republicans, including Gov. Dave Heineman, former Gov. Mike Johanns, and Reps. Lee Terry and Tom Osborne all passed on the race, Republicans rallied around Ricketts, who could self-fund his campaign. Running on a platform of tax cuts and smaller government, Ricketts won the primary, but in the general election he backed a guest-worker program for immigrants, enabling Nelson to run to his right and call for securing the border. Ricketts, with his investment background, also came out in favor of private Social Security accounts, something Nelson opposed. Ricketts supported a ban on congressional earmarks in the federal budget, which Nelson had directed to Nebraska communities for years. Ricketts plowed almost $12 million of his own money into the race and outspent Nelson almost 2-to-1. But on Election Day, he lost by a nearly 2-to-1 margin.

For the next five years, Ricketts served on the Republican National Committee, building his connections to the party establishment, grassroots activists in Nebraska and GOP political players around the country. He also invested in startups, served on various boards, and developed philanthropic interests. He founded Drakon LLC, based in Omaha, a management firm that supports local entrepreneurs and new growth companies, and the Platte Institute for Economic Research, a conservative think tank based in Omaha. As he ran for governor in 2014, Ricketts got endorsements from Wisconsin Gov. Scott Walker, Indiana Gov. Mike Pence, 2012 vice presidential nominee Rep. Paul Ryan of Wisconsin, and Sen. Ted Cruz of Texas, among others – potential White House hopefuls who may have been looking to woo Ricketts' father and his super PAC, as well as his brothers Todd and Tom. (Pete Ricketts' sister Laura was the exception; she was one of 27 high-profile gay and lesbian "bundlers" for President Barack Obama in 2012.) During the GOP primary, Republican challengers criticized Ricketts for highlighting his opposition to same-sex marriage and for distancing himself from the Cubs' sponsorship of gay-pride events; he frequently had to explain how he disagreed with Laura over same-sex marriage, though he always added, "I love her." Ricketts' main rival for the GOP nod was Attorney General Jon Bruning, who had lost a 2012 Senate primary to longshot Deb Fischer, thanks in part to a last-minute TV ad blitz for Fischer that was funded by Joe Ricketts. Bruning repeatedly accused the Ricketts family of using its wealth to buy another victory, but in a field of six candidates, Ricketts was able to edge Bruning, 27%-26%. Ricketts' Democratic opponent, Center for Rural Affairs executive director Chuck Hassebrook, took a few stabs at making his family fortune an issue, but it went nowhere; Ricketts overwhelmed Hassebrook, 57%-39%, as he carried 89 of the state's 93 counties. Ricketts' campaign spent roughly $7 million, including almost $1 million from his personal checkbook and more than $1 million from his family members - more than twice what Hassebrook spent. The Democrat's largest contribution, of $100,000, came from Berkshire Hathaway CEO Warren Buffett.

Entering office, Ricketts enjoyed a state budget surplus and a favorable economy, but that did not help him prevail in a number of tests with the legislature in 2015. First, Nebraska lawmakers overrode Ricketts's veto of a gas-tax hike. Ricketts said the increase would hurt "hard-working Nebraskans," but the legislature wanted the estimated $75 million generated annually by the tax increase for state road repair and maintenance. The legislature voted to override Ricketts' veto of a bill that would allow immigrants who were brought into the country illegally as children to get a driver's license; the governor called the measure "an inappropriate benefit to non-citizens." Most spectacularly, the legislature overrode his veto of a bill to end the state's death penalty, becoming the first conservative state in more than four decades to do so. On this issue, the governor was ultimately successful – with his support, voters qualified a ballot measure to reinstate the death penalty, and in 2016, it passed easily.

The veto overrides continued in April 2016 with a bill that would allow children who were brought to the country illegally by their parents to acquire occupational licenses. The bill had been supported by business leaders – another indication that Ricketts and the business community were not always on the same page. (Opposing a business-supported effort to protect LGBT workers was another example.) A happier outcome was a $450 million transportation bill that Ricketts signed; the bill was designed to complete the state's 600-mile expressway system by 2033. Ricketts also courted business in Japan, China, Hong Kong and Macau -- potential consumers for Nebraska beef. In January 2016, Ricketts initially declined to meet President Barack Obama during his first presidential visit to the state, then reversed course after an outcry and greeted him at the airport. During the 2016 presidential campaign, Ricketts backed Trump, despite other members of his family having opposed him in the GOP primary. In 2016, Ricketts took the unusual step of financially supporting several challengers to members of the legislature who had voted to override one or more of his vetoes. Even though the unicameral legislature is officially nonpartisan, the targeted lawmakers are widely considered to be unofficial Republicans, and Ricketts' offensive did not play well in some GOP circles. A few of the winners he backed went on to have conflicts with more moderate lawmakers. For 2017, Ricketts proposed cuts to income and property taxes, a spending slowdown and regulatory reform. He also announced his intention to run for a second term in 2018. With approval ratings in the 50s, it seems unlikely that any Democrat will be able to keep him from winning.

In May 2017, the Legislature sustained vetoes by Ricketts of $56.5 million of social spending in the two-year budget.

Senior Senator

Deb Fischer (R)

Elected 2012, term expires 2018, 1st term; b. Mar 01, 1951, Lincoln; University of Nebraska, Lincoln, B.S.; Presbyterian; Married (Bruce G. Fischer); 3 children; 1 grandchild.

Elected Office: NE Legislature, 2005-2012; Valentine Rural High School Board of Education, 1990-2004.

Professional Career: Rancher, 1972-2012.

DC Office: 454 RSOB 20510, 202-224-6551, Fax: 202-228-1325, fischer.senate.gov.

State Offices: Kearney, 308-234-2361; Lincoln, 402-441-4600; Norfolk, 402-200-8816; Omaha, 402-391-3411; Scottsbluff, 308-630-2329.

Committees: *Aging*. *Armed Services*: Cybersecurity, Emerging Threats & Capabilities, Strategic Forces (Chmn). *Commerce, Science & Transportation*: Aviation Operations, Safety & Security, Communications, Technology, Innovation & the Internet, Consumer Protection, Product Safety, Ins & Data Security, Oceans, Atmosphere, Fisheries & Coast Guard, Surface Trans., Merchant Marine Infra., Safety & Security (Chmn). *Environment & Public Works*: Clean Air & Nuclear Safety, Fisheries, Water, and Wildlife, Transportation & Infrastructure. *Rules & Administration*.

Group Ratings

	ADA	ACLU	AFL-CIO	LCV	ITI	COC	HAFA	ACU	CFG	FRC
2016	-	5%	-	6%	60%	100%	64%	88%	7400%	100%
2015	0%	C	21%	0%	C	71%	C	92%	76%	100%

Almanac Ratings 2015

	Economy	Social	Foreign	Composite
Liberal	6%	0%	9%	5%
Conservative	94%	100%	91%	95%

Key Votes of the 114th Congress

1. Keystone pipeline	Y	5. National Security Data	N	9. Gun Sales Checks	N
2. Export-Import Bank	Y	6. Iran Nuclear Deal	Y	10. Sanctuary Cities	Y
3. Debt Ceiling Increase	N	7. Puerto Rico Debt	Y	11. Planned Parenthood	Y
4. Homeland Security $$	N	8. Loretta Lynch A.G	N	12. Trade deals	Y

Election Results

Election	Name (Party)	Vote (%)	Cand. Spent	Ind. Exp. Support	Ind. Exp. Oppose
2012 General	Deb Fischer (R)	455,593 (58%)	$5,146,461	$1,500,923	$1,806,421
	Bob Kerrey (D)	332,979 (42%)	$6,116,555	$257,359	$1,811,313
2012 Primary	Deb Fischer (R)	77,594 (41%)			
	Jon Bruning (R)	68,796 (36%)			
	Don Stenberg (R)	35,984 (19%)			

As the only Republican in the country in 2012 to pick up a Senate seat that had previously been in Democratic hands, Deb Fischer, now Nebraska's senior senator, was one of the national GOP's bright spots in a year that saw President Barack Obama re-elected and Democrats increase their Senate majority. A state senator from a rural town who lacked a statewide profile when the contest began, Fischer stunned political observers when she beat two better-known Republicans in the May primary. She went on to defeat Democrat Bob Kerrey in the general election, derailing his bid to reclaim the Senate seat he gave up in 2000.

Since arriving in Washington, Fischer has been a reliably conservative vote and voice on most matters. But she has sought to reach out to Democrats on some issues, while maintaining a relatively low profile as a nuts-and-bolts legislator. She declined an invitation to speak at the 2016 Republican National Convention -- not because of concerns about the nominee-in-waiting, Donald Trump, but rather because convention organizers were looking for a "more political speech" than she wanted to give. "...I do realize it's a political convention - but I'm kind of known as a policy person, so I wanted to focus on that," Fischer told the *World Herald*. But it was politics that gave her a rare moment in the national spotlight a couple of months later: After a decade-old recording of Trump making lewd comments about women surfaced, Fischer initially called upon Trump to resign from the ticket, only to reverse herself days later.

Fischer grew up in Lincoln, the state capital, where her mother, Florence Strobel, was an elementary school teacher and her father, Jerry Strobel, spent many years as an engineer in the Nebraska Department of Roads, finishing his career heading the department in the late 1980s. Issues related to transportation funding would later be a legislative focus for Fischer at the state and federal level. She attended the University of Nebraska, where she met her husband, Bruce Fischer. She left school to marry him, and the couple settled on the Fischer family ranch in Valentine, in northern Nebraska. Despite growing up in what she described as the "big small town" of Lincoln, Fischer said she had little trouble adjusting to ranching life. She honed one talent often associated with farm wives. "She's infamous for her pie-making," her husband told the *World Herald* shortly after Fischer was nominated for the Senate. "She doesn't do it very often, but it's a darn-sure treat when she does." As her three sons grew older, Fischer returned to the University of Nebraska in Lincoln to finish her undergraduate work, earning a degree in education in 1988.

Her first run for elected office came two years later, when she won a seat on the Valentine Rural High School Board of Education. She went on to become president of the Nebraska Association of School Boards and serve on the Nebraska Coordinating Commission for Postsecondary Education, the state's oversight agency for higher education institutions. In 2004, Fischer won a seat in Nebraska's unicameral legislature, representing a district that sprawled across a dozen counties -- an area the size of the state of New Jersey. She was unopposed for a second term in 2008. During her first term, an upheaval in the legislature gave Fischer the chairmanship of the Transportation and Telecommunications Committee. Among her biggest achievements was helping to win passage of legislation to shift about $70 million of the state's sales tax revenues to road construction on an annual basis.

Fischer said she was initially drawn to the Republican Party by its focus on limited government, and this philosophy was evident as she placed her imprint on several issues. In 2007, she joined in a move to filibuster a bill to ban smoking statewide for indoor worksites and other public places. She was somewhat mollified when the bill was amended to allow cities and council to vote to opt out of the restrictions. A year earlier, responding to a 2005 U.S. Supreme Court decision, she won passage of legislation barring use of eminent domain for government-backed economic development projects. But some of Fischer's constituents were said to be less than happy with her support of the Keystone XL pipeline, which cut across Nebraska on its route from Canada to the Gulf of Mexico. Some questioned how her support of the pipeline jibed with her criticism of eminent domain, a legal option being utilized by the company seeking to build the pipeline. Later, as a senator, Fischer joined all of her GOP colleagues in an unsuccessful attempt in 2015 to override an Obama veto of a bill to move ahead on the Keystone pipeline.

Barred by law from seeking a third term in the state legislature in 2012, Fischer entered the race to succeed retiring Democratic Sen. Ben Nelson. Nelson, like Kerrey, had served as governor before winning a Senate seat. While he had accumulated one of the most conservative voting records among members of his party, he took intense political heat for his crucial 2009 vote in favor of Obama's health insurance overhaul-particularly after it was disclosed he had cut a side deal with then-Senate Majority Leader Harry Reid to relieve his home state of millions in Medicaid payments required under the law. The deal backfired: Republicans derided it as "the Cornhusker Kickback," and Nelson ultimately renounced it as his approval ratings in Republican-dominated Nebraska hit the skids. His decision to retire averted what would have been an uphill battle to win a third term.

Fischer began her Senate bid as the underdog in a primary against state Attorney General Jon Bruning and state Treasurer Don Stenberg. Bruning enjoyed the support of the GOP establishment, while tea party leaders rallied behind Stenberg. Fischer, however, steadily gained traction as Stenberg and Bruning turned their fire on each other. She also benefitted from the endorsement of one tea party favorite, 2008 vice presidential nominee Sarah Palin, along with a last-minute television ad blitz funded by wealthy businessman Joe Ricketts, founder of the Omaha-based TD Ameritrade stock brokerage. (Ricketts son, Pete, would be elected governor in 2014.) Fischer won the primary with 41 percent, followed by Bruning with 36 percent and Stenberg with 19 percent.

In the general election, Kerrey-having held office as governor and senator throughout the 1980s and 1990s-was considered the Democrats' best hope in a state where nearly half of voters identify as Republicans, while only about one-third register as Democrats. But, although Kerrey was a household name, many voters were turned off by the fact that he had been living out of state since leaving the Senate in 2000; he served as president of the New York City-based New School University from 2001-2010. He responded by pointing to his continuing Nebraska ties, including several businesses he owned in the state. After initially sending conflicting signals about whether he would get back into politics, Kerrey in early 2012 said he would run to reclaim the seat.

Fischer campaigned vowing not to serve more than two terms in the Senate, and backed a constitutional amendment for congressional term limits. She also stressed her family's ranching background and her work in the legislature on issues important to rural Nebraska. However, in light of her criticisms of the scope of the federal government's reach, Kerrey tried to make an issue of her family's use of grazing rights on 11,000 acres of federal land, calling her a "welfare rancher." He also dubbed her a "bad neighbor" for suing an elderly couple in the 1990s in a dispute over ownership of more than 100 acres along the scenic Snake River, and suggested Fischer had used her influence in the legislature to try to bar the couple from later selling the land in question to the state. Fischer's campaign called such attacks a "transparent act of desperation"; the charges were contained in an ad that Kerrey launched in mid-October, as polls showed him trailing by double digits. On Election Day, Fischer came out ahead, 58%-42%. While Kerrey carried the state's two most populous counties around Omaha and Lincoln, Fischer won all but a handful of counties throughout the rest of the state. She began the 2018 election cycle as a heavy favorite for a second term, with no Democratic opponent in sight in a state that Trump won by 25 points.

One of Fischer's first votes upon arriving in the Senate in early 2013 was to join most of her Republican colleagues in voting against Obama's nomination of another former Nebraska senator, Republican Chuck Hagel, as secretary of defense. She cited what she termed Hagel's "confusing and contradictory" testimony before the Armed Services Committee, of which she was then a newly appointed member. In opposing Hagel, Fischer parted company from Republican Mike Johanns, then Nebraska's senior senator, whom Fischer had called a role model. Few were particularly surprised by her vote since Hagel, who served in the Senate from 1996-2008, had backed Kerrey in the fall election.

Fischer's philosophy has put her in the conservative Republican mainstream on issues ranging from taxes to abortion rights (she is a strong abortion opponent, saying it should be allowed only in cases where necessary to save the life of the mother). She had the Senate's sixth most conservative voting record in 2015, according to *Almanac* rankings and has used her seat on the Environment and Public Works Committee to excoriate the Environmental Protection Agency for what she has termed "extreme overreach" in its regulatory regimen. But she has shown a pragmatic streak, declining to go as far as other conservatives who have called for abolishing the EPA and the Education Department. "I've always said…that if I would stand up and say we should abolish the Department of Education, and we should abolish the EPA, many people in the crowd would stand up and applaud," Fischer said during the 2012 campaign. "Those of you who know me know that I have a more thoughtful approach. I believe we need to look at the programs that are involved in the department, and [ask] if they are effective, if they are meeting their purpose."

Fischer was named a member of the Senate Republican leadership in 2015 -- with the title of counsel to the majority leader -- and has been called upon to promote GOP alternatives on issues such as pay equity and family leave. In 2017, Fischer reintroduced legislation -- which she originally proposed in 2014 -- to provide tax incentives to businesses offering two weeks of paid family leave annually. "I think it's an issue that to be honest, that we as a party have not taken a high profile on," she acknowledged in an interview with *Politico*. But advocacy groups for paid leave criticized Fischer's legislation because it was optional -- and not as generous as the leading Democratic bill, which proposed guaranteeing workers two-thirds of their pay for up to 12 weeks.

The Republican recapture of the Senate majority in the 2014 election gave Fischer the chairmanship of the Commerce Committee's subpanel with jurisdiction over surface transportation. The first long-term reauthorization of surface transportation funding in more than a decade passed at the end of 2015, but still left the federal highway trust fund with solvency issues arising from diminishing fuel tax revenues. Drawing from her experience in the Nebraska legislature, Fischer identified a dedicated funding source -- and, in early 2017, introduced legislation to redirect $107 billion to the highway trust fund over a five-year period from Customs and Border Patrol fees collected on freight cargo and passengers. While addressing the trust fund solvency issue, a potential sticking point in the proposal was that the Custom and Border Patrol fees are currently used as general fund revenue -- and redirecting them to the highway trust fund could translate into cuts elsewhere.

As a Commerce Committee member, Fischer has reached out to Democratic colleagues on several technology-related fronts. She and Florida Democrat Bill Nelson sponsored legislation allowing manufacturers to put warranties online; it was signed into law in late 2015. It was a follow-on to a bill that Fischer got passed a year earlier allowing manufacturers of radio frequency equipment to utilize the option of electronic labeling in place of affixing physical labels to equipment. Fischer also has joined with a bipartisan group of senators seeking to promote the economic potential of the so-called "Internet of Things," an expanding market of consumer products in which information can be transmitted without the need to consult a computer. She stuck to her philosophy of limited government regulation, claiming that legislation she proposed had prompted the Food and Drug Administration to back off from regulating FitBit and other wearable devices that are part of the Internet of Things.

By all indications, Fischer has had a good working relationship with her in-state junior colleague, the more outspoken and avowedly conservative Ben Sasse, since he succeeded Johanns in early 2015. But Sasse's adamant opposition to Trump as the party's nominee -- he went so far as to advocate a third-party conservative alternative -- created some awkward moments. At the Nebraska Republican convention in May 2016, delegates overwhelmingly approved a resolution -- aimed at Sasse -- that condemned a possible third-party candidacy. The force behind the resolution was Sam Fischer, a state political operative who is Deb Fischer's nephew. Sam Fischer and an aide to the senator denied she had any involvement in the resolution. But *Politico* reported that the view in state political circles was that the nephew would not have acted without his aunt's tacit approval. In comments two months prior to the state convention, Fischer rejected Sasse's third-party strategy, telling the *World Herald*: "I don't know how any Republican or conservative can support that. We've seen this story before. We saw it in '92 with the election of Bill Clinton because of a third party. And I certainly don't want to see it in 2016 and have the election of another Clinton because of a third party."

Fischer did join at least a dozen of her GOP Senate colleagues in urging that Trump step down or be removed from the national ticket following the October 2016 release of the "Access Hollywood" tape. She took some criticism when she became the first of that group to reverse herself and say she would support him after all. Three days after her call for Trump to resign from the ticket, she told a Nebraska radio station, "I put out a statement ... with regard to Mr. Trump's comments. I felt they were disgusting. I felt they were unacceptable and I never said I was not voting for our Republican ticket." Fischer's original statement, via Twitter, had declared: "It would be wise for [Trump] to step aside and allow Mike Pence to serve as our party's nominee." During the radio interview, she added: "He decided he would not step aside. I respect his decision. I support the Republican ticket."

Junior Senator

Ben Sasse (R)

Elected 2014, term expires 2020, 1st term; b. Feb 22, 1972, Plainview; Harvard University, A.B.; Saint John's College (MD), M.A.; Yale University (CT), Ph.D.; Oxford University (England); Yale University (CT), M.A.; Yale University (CT), M.Phil; Lutheran; Married (Melissa Sasse); 3 children.

Professional Career: Chief of Staff, U.S Department of Justice Office of Legal Policy, 2004-2005; Chief of Staff, U.S Rep. Jeff Fortenberry, 2005; Assistant Professor, University of TX-Austin 2005-2006; Counselor to secretary, Health & Human Services; Assist. Assist. Sec. Health & Human Services, 2007-2009; President, Professor University of TX-Austin, 2009; Midland University 2010-2014.

DC Office: 136 RSOB 20510, 202-224-4224, sasse.senate.gov.

State Offices: Kearney, 308-233-3677; Lincoln, 402-476-1400; Omaha, 402-550-8040; Scottsbluff, 308-632-6032.

Committees: *Armed Services*: Airland, Cybersecurity, Personnel. *Banking, Housing & Urban Affairs*: Financial Institutions & Consumer Protection, National Security & International Trade & Finance (Chmn), Securities, Insurance & Investment. *Judiciary*: Constitution, Crime & Terrorism, Oversight, Agency Action, Federal Rights & Federal Courts (Chmn).

Group Ratings

	ADA	ACLU	AFL-CIO	LCV	ITI	COC	HAFA	ACU	CFG	FRC
2016	-	5%	-	0%	60%	63%	94%	100%	100%	100%
2015	0%	C	0%	0%	C	57%	C	100%	98%	91%

Almanac Ratings 2015

	Economy	Social	Foreign	Composite
Liberal	0%	0%	0%	0%
Conservative	100%	100%	100%	100%

Key Votes of the 114th Congress

1. Keystone pipeline	Y	5. National Security Data	N	9. Gun Sales Checks	N
2. Export-Import Bank	Y	6. Iran Nuclear Deal	Y	10. Sanctuary Cities	Y
3. Debt Ceiling Increase	N	7. Puerto Rico Debt	N	11. Planned Parenthood	Y
4. Homeland Security $$	N	8. Loretta Lynch A.G	N	12. Trade deals	Y

Election Results

Election	Name (Party)	Vote (%)		Cand. Spent	Ind. Exp. Support	Ind. Exp. Oppose
2014 General	Ben Sasse (R)	347,636	(64%)	$5,864,653	$1,681,914	$297,050
	Dave Domina (D)	170,127	(32%)	$1,227,205		$18,597
	Jim Jenkins (I)	15,868	(3%)	$354,598		
2014 Primary	Ben Sasse (R)	110,802	(49%)			
	Sid Dinsdale (R)	50,494	(23%)			
	Shane Osborn (R)	47,338	(21%)			
	Bart McLeay (R)	12,840	(6%)			

In 2015, in his first year on Capitol Hill, Republican Ben Sasse -- Nebraska's junior senator -- was the only member of the Senate with a perfect 100 conservative voting score, according to *Almanac* rankings. If Sasse is one of the most conservative members of that chamber, in background and style he is also among its most unusual, and, perhaps, its quirkiest. He is the holder of no less than four degrees from a couple of elite East Coast universities (Harvard and Yale) who, with his wife, homeschools their three children. He's a tea party-backed, self-described "constitutionalist" who propounds a very limited role for the federal government. But he also has considerable experience working inside the Beltway, to the extent that a leading primary opponent sought to portray Sasse as a creature of Washington during his first run for Senate in 2014.

Sasse spent most of his first year in the Senate under the radar, conducting "interviews" with colleagues. While most freshman senators deliver their "maiden" floor speeches within days or weeks of being sworn in, Sasse -- reverting to Senate tradition prior to the electronic age -- waited 10 months to do so. He more than made up for his relative silence in his second year, utilizing a steady stream of tweets and a couple of lengthy manifestos via Facebook to blister the Republican presidential frontrunner, Donald Trump, and question both Trump's conservative credentials and personal behavior. "You brag abt many affairs w/ married women. Have you repented?" Sasse asked Trump via Twitter in late January 2016, prior to the Iowa caucuses. Sasse's vow not to support Trump as the party's nominee made him a leading member of the "Never Trump" movement within the Republican Party -- and earned him a rebuke from the Nebraska GOP. At the state convention in late spring, delegates condemned Sasse's call for a third-party conservative alternative to Trump. Sasse was undeterred. "I don't know where it's written that fighting for what you believe in will always be popular with 51 percent," he told *The New York Times*.

Sasse (pronounced Sass) is a fifth-generation Nebraskan who, growing up, spent summers working in soybean and corn fields; he bears a scar on his forehead from a boyhood fall from a hayloft. He was born in the small town of Plainview in northeastern Nebraska, and was raised and went to high school in the nearby city of Fremont. Sasse, who turned 45 in 2017, spent nearly two decades away from the state before returning in 2009 to head a struggling university. He was recruited by Harvard, thanks to his prowess as a high school wrestler. ("@BenSasse looks more like a gym rat than a U.S. Senator. How the hell did he ever get elected?" Trump would later tweet in response to Sasse's criticisms.) Sasse earned his Harvard undergraduate degree while spending a junior year abroad at the University of Oxford in England, and then worked for a year at the Boston Consulting Group -- the financial firm where Mitt Romney had gotten his start -- before returning to school. He collected a master's degree from St. John's College in Annapolis, Maryland (he tutored and proctored House pages on Capitol Hill during that time), followed by two more master's degrees from Yale University on his way to earning a Ph.D. in American history from Yale in 2004. That led to a teaching post at the University of Texas' Lyndon B. Johnson School of Public Affairs.

But Sasse spent most of the five years after earning his Ph.D. working in Washington, first for the Justice Department and then briefly as chief of staff to Nebraska Republican Rep. Jeff Fortenberry, followed by consulting for the Homeland Security Department. He was at the Health and Human Services Department the last two years of the administration of George W. Bush, first as a counselor to the secretary and later, following Senate confirmation, as HHS assistant secretary for planning and evaluation. At the end of the Bush Administration, Sasse returned to his hometown of Fremont to become president of Midland University, a 130-year-old school affiliated with the Evangelical Lutheran Church that had been beset by financial difficulties. At 37, he was among the youngest college presidents in the country; during the 2014 campaign, he boasted of successfully executing a "turnaround job" that has now made Midland University what he termed "one of the fastest growing in the Midwest." He ended lifetime tenure for professors, convinced some to take buyouts, and helped bring about a takeover of a rival school.

In early 2013, Republican Mike Johanns, a former Nebraska governor and U.S. secretary of agriculture, announced he would retire from the Senate after just one term. Sasse said in July 2013 he would run for the seat, about a month after former state Treasurer Shane Osborn had announced he would run. Before his political career, Osborn was a Navy pilot detained by the Chinese briefly in 2001 after a midair collision with a Chinese fighter jet forced him to make an emergency landing. In the primary, Osborn sought to cast Sasse as not only as too close to Washington, but also insufficiently conservative: Sasse had penned a column in 2009 for *U.S. News and World Report* calling Medicare Part D, the prescription-drug benefit passed by a GOP-controlled Congress during the Bush Administration, "enormously successful" and a "viable model for reform." But conservative groups rallied around Sasse as he headed to the top of the polls, and the Club for Growth and the Senate Conservatives Fund spent heavily on his behalf. Campaign visits by Sen. Ted Cruz of Texas and former Alaska Gov. Sarah Palin helped cement Sasse as the conservative choice in the primary. In January 2014, Sasse was featured on the cover of the conservative *National Review* as a "rising conservative star."

Foreshadowing his verbal assault on Trump, Sasse showed little hesitancy to aim at major political targets. In the fall of 2013, Sasse posted a video, complaining about federal taxpayers underwriting health care insurance premiums for members of Congress and their staffs. "It is time for every Republican in Washington, starting with Minority Leader Mitch McConnell, to show some actual leadership on this issue by voluntarily giving up their healthcare subsidy," Sasse declared. The video was said to have enraged McConnell, now majority leader, who was himself trying to turn back a conservative primary challenger in his own re-election bid in Kentucky. According to a *National Review* account, Sasse subsequently visited McConnell in an effort to clear the air, and to deny rumors he had secretly vowed to oppose McConnell's election as leader if he won the Senate seat. But the session reportedly did little to assuage McConnell-who was upset not only about the video, but also by Sasse's support from the Senate Conservatives Fund and his interaction with leaders of that organization. McConnell had long been at odds with the group, which was supporting McConnell's conservative challenger in the Kentucky primary. McConnell ultimately won his primary and a sixth term, and there is no indication he sought to quietly work against Sasse in retaliation.

In the May 2014 Nebraska primary, a late surge by wealthy bank executive Sid Dinsdale, who ran a largely self-funded campaign, raised the prospect of an upset if the conservative vote divided between Sasse and Osborn. But Dinsdale met with attack ads from the Club for Growth and others hitting him as being too liberal. Sasse finished with 49 percent, followed by 23 percent for Dinsdale and 21 percent for Osborn. National Democrats made no attempt to seriously contest the seat in November; Sasse defeated Democrat Dave Domina, an Omaha attorney who had last sought public office three decades earlier, by 64%-32%.

A month before his November 2015 maiden Senate speech, Sasse -- amid watching a football game at home --- tweeted: "New to politics & in deference to tradition I've spent first 9mos in Senate keeping head down, interviewing older members/listening/learning." However, he promptly raised eyebrows when, during the same Twitter session, he suggested Arthur Brooks -- president of the conservative-leaning American Enterprise Institute -- as the new speaker of the House, in the wake of the resignation of John Boehner of Ohio. (Under the Constitution, the speaker does not have to be an elected member of the House.) "Next speaker needs to have the ideas of Jack Kemp, work ethic of Mike Rowe, resolve of Margaret Thatcher, & wit of Larry the Cable Guy," Sasse observed, adding later: "I'm not saying @arthurbrooks is definitely the best communicator in America; I'm just saying: If you know of a better one…Tell me. I'll wait."

In his first floor speech, attended by about three dozen of his colleagues, Sasse bemoaned "a real institutional decline in the Senate in recent decades," while placing the blame on both parties. "When you're interviewing senators in private, it is amazing how much of a shared understanding there is about what things are broken; it's just that we don't talk about it in public because one party wants to pretend when they're in charge it works well and the other party when they're in charge it works well," he said. (Sasse was even blunter in a Facebook post in May 2016, declaring, "These two national political parties are enough of a mess that I believe they will come apart.") In his speech, he asked: "If the Senate isn't going to be the venue for addressing our biggest national problems, where should we tell people that venue is? Where should they look for long-term national prioritization if it doesn't happen on this floor?"

Underlying this process-oriented critique was an apparent conviction that the long-term priorities the Senate ought to be debating involve the basic role of the federal government -- which Sasse feels needs to be sharply curtailed. "What the federal government exists to do is provide for national security and the common defense of the people," Sasse said in an interview with the *Atlantic* prior to the speech. "Almost everything else in life could conceivably be solved by some other institution or some other level of government." His votes against proposals that he feels exceed the scope of the federal government -- including those broadly embraced by both parties -- has exasperated even some fellow Republicans. In March 2016, Sasse was on the losing end of a 94-1 vote in favor of a bill to combat opioid abuse, a version of which later became law. When asked for comment by *The New York Times* on Sasse's vote, New Hampshire GOP Sen. Kelly Ayotte, a sponsor of the measure, rolled her eyes and replied, "Whatever, dude."

At the end of February 2016, Sasse posted a lengthy "Open Letter to Trump Supporters" likening Trump and President Barack Obama in their view of executive power. "Much like President Obama, he displays essentially no understanding of the fact that, in the American system, we have a constitutional system of checks and balances, with three separate but co-equal branches of government." Sasse declared of Trump. "The law is king, and the people are boss. But have you noticed how Mr. Trump uses the word "Reign" – like he thinks he's running for King? It's creepy, actually." In another long Facebook post in late May, when Trump and Democrat Hillary Clinton had sewn up their respective parties' nominations, Sasse gibed, "There are dumpster fires in my town more popular than these two 'leaders'." Meeting with Senate Republicans prior to the party's national convention, Trump reportedly singled out three senators -- including Sasse -- who had been critical of his candidacy, and predicted they would lose their reelection bids. Asked for comment afterward, a Sasse spokesman told the *Omaha World Herald*: "Mr. Sasse continues to believe that our country is in a bad place and, with these two candidates, this election remains a dumpster fire. Nothing has changed."

Sasse's push for a third-party conservative alternative to Trump prompted speculation about the senator as a possible candidate, but he repeatedly disavowed interest -- citing his family and Senate duties. (There has since been speculation that Sasse will take a serious look at running for the Republican nomination in 2020 or 2024.) When efforts failed to produce a national candidacy of the type advocated by Sasse, he announced he would write in Trump's running mate, now-Vice President Mike Pence, for president in November. Sasse greeted Trump's election with a mixture of restrained rhetoric and lowered profile. "Starting today, I will do everything in my power to hold the President to his promises: to fight for an ethics reform package that upends cronyism and enacts term limits; to lead on repealing and replacing Obamacare; and to nominate judges who reject law-making by unelected courts," Sasse said.

Several months after taking office, Sasse had introduced the "Winding Down Obama Care Act," which was seen as a potential Republican fallback position if the Supreme Court had failed to uphold a key provision of the Affordable Care Act-subsidies to the federal health insurance exchange-in June 2015. Sasse's bill proposed to do away with the current subsidies under ACA, replacing them with general tax credits that would disappear within 18 months. He argued this would give the Republican-controlled Congress time to come up with an alternative to the ACA. But, as the debate over repeal of the law was joined in earnest in early 2017, Sasse -- once hailed as "Obamacare's Nebraska Nemesis" by the *National Review* -- was playing a secondary role. "I'm trying to figure out how to add value, wherever I can, in that fight," Sasse, who does not sit on committees with jurisdiction over health care, told the *World Herald.*

Sasse's committee assignments changed significantly at the outset of the 115th Congress: He moved to the Armed Services Committee, where his senior in-state colleague, Republican Deb Fischer, was already serving, as well as the Judiciary Committee. In the process, Sasse gave up his seat on the Agriculture Committee -- marking the first time in nearly a half-century a Nebraskan would not be sitting on that panel. Nebraska ranks fourth among the 50 states in receipts from agricultural output, and its lack of Agriculture Committee representation caused consternation among some state farm groups, particularly as debate on a new farm bill was set to get underway in 2017. "I will engage in no less activity in listening to Nebraska farmers and producers about their priorities and concerns," Sasse vowed to the *Lincoln Journal Star*. Fischer, whose family operates a ranch in northern Nebraska, offered something short of a full-throated defense of Sasse's decision to leave the Agriculture panel. "Senator Sasse made his own committee selections. Any questions regarding his choices should be directed to him," she told the newspaper. It was not the only recent bit of bumpiness in the relationship between Sasse and Fischer, considered a more pragmatic conservative: The move to condemn Sasse's advocacy of a third-party alternative at the 2016 state GOP convention was instigated by Fischer's nephew.

FIRST DISTRICT

Jeff Fortenberry (R)

Elected 2004, 7th term; b. Dec 27, 1960, Baton Rouge, LA; Franciscan University (OH), M.Th.; Louisiana State University, B.A., 1982; Georgetown University (DC), M.PP, 1986; Franciscan University (OH), M.A., 1996; Roman Catholic; Married (Celeste Gregory Fortenberry); 5 children.

Elected Office: Lincoln City Council, 1997-2001.

Professional Career: Staffer, U.S. House Comm. on Ag., 1986; Research Association, Gulf South Research Inst., 1987-1989; Assistant Director, Baton Rouge Downtown Dev. District, 1989-1992; Sales rep., Sandhills Publishing, 1995-2004.

DC Office: 1514 LHOB 20515, 202-225-4806, Fax: 202-225-5686, fortenberry.house.gov.

State Offices: Fremont, 402-727-0888; Lincoln, 402-438-1598; Norfolk, 402-379-2064.

Committees: *Appropriations*: Energy & Water Development & Related Agencies, Military Construction, Veterans Affairs & Related Agencies, State, Foreign Operations & Related Programs.

Group Ratings

	ADA	ACLU	AFL-CIO	LCV	ITI	COC	HAFA	ACU	CFG	FRC
2016	-	5%	-	16%	67%	100%	58%	60%	67%	100%
2015	0%	C	17%	9%	C	90%	C	61%	54%	100%

Almanac Ratings 2015

	Economy	Social	Foreign	Composite
Liberal	5%	11%	10%	9%
Conservative	95%	89%	90%	91%

Key Votes of the 114th Congress

1. Keystone Pipeline	Y	5. Puerto Rico Debt	Y	9. Offenses by Aliens	Y
2. Trade Deals	Y	6. Medical Marijuana	N	10. Troops in Iraq	N
3. Export-Import Bank	N	7. Sanctuary Cities	Y	11. Homeland Security $$	N
4. Debt Ceiling Increase	Y	8. Armor-piercing Bullets	Y	12. Trade Adjustment aid	Y

Election Results

Election	Name (Party)	Vote (%)	Cand. Spent	Ind. Exp. Support	Ind. Exp. Oppose
2016 General	Jeff Fortenberry (R).....................	189,771 (70%)	$295,632		
	Daniel Wik (D)............................	83,467 (31%)			
2016 Primary	Jeff Fortenberry (R)................................	(100%)			

Prior winning percentages: 2014 (69%), 2012 (68%), 2010 (71%), 2008 (70%), 2006 (58%), 2004 (54%)

Republican Jeff Fortenberry, elected in 2004, has a reputation as a brainy policy expert who has evolved into a centrist. In the tradition of many Nebraskans (including former Sens. Chuck Hagel and Bob Kerrey), Fortenberry takes a strong interest in foreign policy.

Fortenberry grew up in Baton Rouge, Louisiana, where his father was a life insurance salesman and his mother worked as a 4-H Club extension agent. When Fortenberry was 12, his father was killed in a car accident. "It taught me a hard lesson that you wouldn't want to wish on any other child - you have to figure out a lot of things on your own," he told *Esquire* magazine. Fortenberry got the political bug early as a page to a Democratic state senator, but switched to the Republican Party after he graduated from Louisiana State University. He earned one master's degree in theology from Franciscan University of Steubenville, Ohio, and another in public policy from Georgetown University. For a time, he studied for the priesthood.

In 1995, Fortenberry moved to Nebraska to take a public relations position with Sandhills Publishing, a publisher of trade magazines for the trucking, aircraft and computer industries. He later got into the sales end of the business. In 1997, he won a seat on the Lincoln City Council. He served for four years, focusing on neighborhood concerns and on an increase in the police force.

When the House seat opened in 2004, three candidates mounted competitive campaigns for the Republican nomination: Fortenberry; Curt Bromm, the speaker of the state's unicameral legislature; and Greg Ruehle, a former executive vice president of the Nebraska Cattlemen Association. The moderate Bromm lost momentum after a barrage of negative television ads financed by the Club for Growth, a national anti-tax group that supported Ruehle. Fortenberry, a social conservative, drew criticism from his opponents as a single-issue candidate, but his superior grassroots operation and fundraising carried him to victory. Fortenberry won with 39 percent of the vote, to 33 pecent for Bromm and 21 percent for Ruehle. In Lincoln's Lancaster County, which cast 43 percent of the vote, he got 52 percent.

In November, Fortenberry faced state Sen. Matt Connealy, a farmer from Decatur who sought to exploit GOP divisions. Bromm refused to endorse Fortenberry after the primary and characterized him as a stranger to Nebraska farm issues, a potent charge in a state where one in four jobs is agriculture-related. Fortenberry promised to improve trade policies for farmers and to support ethanol development. He focused on socially conservative themes: opposition to abortion rights, support of capital punishment and a ban on same-sex marriage. Fortenberry won 54%-43%, losing only two American Indian reservation counties.

In the House, Fortenberry has moved over time to the ideological center. His *Almanac* vote ratings for 2015 ranked him among moderate Republicans on social and foreign policy issues. He backed the 2011 compromise to raise the federal debt limit as well as the New Year's Day 2013 budget deal aimed at averting the so-called "fiscal cliff." He was one of a handful of Republicans who signed a Democratic "discharge petition" seeking to force a floor vote on a stalled farm bill. In 2011, he praised President Barack Obama's speech outlining his approach in the Middle East and North Africa, which conservatives panned. He noted that both he and Obama won Lincoln in 2008. "People here pride themselves on independence," he told *Esquire*. Earlier, he supported President George W. Bush on the war in Iraq, won

House approval of an increase in visas for Iraqi translators, and enacted a bill barring U.S. assistance for governments using children as soldiers.

His legislative work has been chiefly on the Appropriations Committee, where his subcommittee assignments have been on foreign operations, military construction and veterans, plus energy and water projects. He has moved up the seniority ladder and is close to gaining a subcommittee chairmanship. He supported extension of the Export-Import Bank of the United States on the basis that "we don't have a perfect world." As evidence of his continuing interests overseas, he co-chairs the Caucus on Religious Minorities in the Middle East, the Congressional Study Group on Europe and the Nuclear Security Working Group. In March 2016, the House unanimously passed a resolution that he authored with Democratic Rep. Anna Eshoo of California that labeled Islamic State atrocities against Christian groups in Syria and Iraq as "genocide." Later, he called for the creation of a nation for Christians in the Middle East.

In 2006, Fortenberry's first reelection campaign was against former Democratic Lt. Gov. Maxine Moul, who made the Iraq war an issue. Even with ample fundraising, Moul's campaign did not catch fire. Fortenberry won 58%-42%. He hasn't been held below 68 percent since.

During the 2016 campaign, he expressed some ambivalence about Donald Trump. After initially urging Trump to withdraw as the presidential nominee following the early October release of the *Access Hollywood* video with his lewd comments on women, Fortenberry said a few days later that he would vote for Trump. When his 17-year-old daughter in tears earlier told Fortenberry, "Daddy, you've got to do something - Trump hates women," he relayed the story to vice-presidential nominee Mike Pence during a meeting with other House Republicans and urged the Trump campaign to reach out to women. After the meeting, Pence privately thanked him for his comment, said Fortenberry, who has five daughters.

Eastern Nebraska: Lincoln

Population		**Race and Ethnicity**		**Income**	
Total	627,284	White	83.5%	Median Income	$53,758 (202 out of 435)
Land area	8,879	Black	2.8%		
Pop/ sq mi	70.6	Latino	8.3%		
Born in state	66.7%	Asian	2.4%	Under $50,000	46.2%
Age Groups		Two races	1.9%	$50,000-$99,999	33.6%
Under 18	24.3%	Other	1.1%	$100,000-$199,999	17.1%
18-34	25.2%	**Education**		$200,000 or more	3.1%
35-64	36.8%	H.S grad or less	35.3%	Poverty Rate	12.5%
Over 64	13.7%	Some college	35.1%	**Health Insurance**	
Work		College Degree, 4 yr	19.7%	With health insurance coverage	90.3%
White Collar	35.1%	Post grad	9.8%		
Sales and Service	40.9%	**Military**		**Public Assistance**	
Blue Collar	23.9%	Veteran	10.1%	Cash public assistance income	2.4%
Government	16.6%	Active Duty	0.6%	Food stamp/SNAP benefits	8.6%

Voter Turnout			
2015 Total Citizens 18+	452,948	2016 House Turnout as % CVAP	60%
2016 House turnout	273,238	2014 House Turnout as % CVAP	39%

2012 Presidential Vote		
Mitt Romney	152,021	(57%)
Barack Obama	108,082	(41%)

2016 Presidential Vote		
Donald Trump	158,576	(56%)
Hillary Clinton	100,106	(36%)
Gary Johnson	14,025	(5%)

Cook Partisan Voting Index: R+11

The eastern half of Nebraska, between the Missouri River and the 98th parallel, was laid out in relentless Midwestern mile-square grids and became some of America's prime farmland during the 1880s. Here the Plains have completed most of their gentle decline from the Rockies to sea level, and the land has contours just regular enough, and weather just favorable enough, to make farming economically viable. The area was settled by Yankee-descended farmers from the Midwest and immigrants from Germany and other countries. Traces of the immigrant heritage can still be found. Many people from Luxembourg, for example, settled along the Platte River in Butler County, where St. Mary's Presentation Parish still has a statue of Our Lady of Luxembourg. Not far away are villages with names that recall other immigrant groups - Prague (Czechs), Malmo (Swedes), Aloys (Germans).

Today, a new wave of immigrants is coming to eastern Nebraska, including Latinos from Mexico and the southwest United States, to work in the region's meatpacking factories. Fremont, a town of 26,000 northwest of Omaha that is about 12 percent Hispanic, made national news in 2010 when voters overwhelmingly approved an ordinance mandating immigration background checks for anyone seeking to rent an apartment or house. A few thousand refugees from Vietnam settled in Lincoln and organized community groups.

The 1st Congressional District of Nebraska comprises 16 counties and parts of two others in the eastern slice of the state. It surrounds but does not take in Omaha-based Douglas County, which is in the 2nd District. Taking up almost half of the district is Lancaster, home to Lincoln and the main campus of the University of Nebraska, which has many scientific units that receive large research grants. Growing and affluent, Lincoln has above-national average income and its unemployment rate - 2.8 percent in December 2016 - has been among the lowest in the nation. The city is home to more than 100 companies and government agencies with 250 or more workers, including a strong manufacturing sector. In the smaller towns, there are many farm equipment and meatpacking factories. A few miles from Omaha, the district includes the eastern part of fast-growing Sarpy County and the city of Bellevue, home of Offutt Air Force Base, headquarters of the top-secret Strategic Air Command. Offutt got good news in June 2016, with the Pentagon announcement that it will make a $55 million repair of its runway. In September, the base was selected as one of five finalists to house a drone wing mission control unit.

Politically, Lincoln is fond of moderate Democrats but is still, on balance, Republican in national contests. In 2016, Lancaster was one of two counties - along with Douglas - that voted for Hillary Clinton, but by a scant 310 votes. The remaining counties were secure for Donald Trump, who took 56 percent of the district vote, compared with 57 percent for Mitt Romney in 2012. The district has not elected a Democrat to Congress since 1964. In January 2017, hundreds of protesters gathered outside the state capital to rally against Trump's executive order that limited immigration and refugees.

SECOND DISTRICT

Don Bacon (R)

Elected 2016, 1st term; b. Aug 16, 1963, Momence, IL; Northern Illinois University, B.A., 1984; Officer Intelligence School (CO), 1986; Squadron Officer School (AL), 1989; Navigator/Electronic Warfare School (CA), 1992; University of Phoenix, Mast. Deg., 1995; Air Command and Staff College (AL), 1998; National War College (DC), Mast. Deg., 2004; Massachusetts Institute of Technology, 2006; Eckerd College Leadership Development Institute (FL), 2009; University of Virginia Darden School of Business, 2009; Christian - Non-Denominational; Married (Angie Bacon); 4 children.

Military Career: U.S Air Force (Iraq), 1985-2014.

Professional Career: Military Advisor, Rep. Jeff Fortenberry, 2014-2015; Assistant Professor, University of Bellvue , 2014-2017.

DC Office: 1516 LHOB 20515, 202-225-4155, bacon.house.gov.

State Offices: Omaha, 402-938-0300.

Committees: *Agriculture*: Biotechnology, Horticulture & Research, General Farm Commodities & Risk Management. *Armed Services*: Military Personnel, Tactical Air & Land Forces. *Small Business*: Agriculture, Energy & Trade, Investigations, Oversight & Regulations.

Election Results

Election	Name (Party)	Vote (%)		Cand. Spent	Ind. Exp. Support	Ind. Exp. Oppose
2016 General	Don Bacon (R)	141,066	(49%)	$1,566,768	$1,988,785	$1,184,800
	Brad Ashford (D)	137,602	(48%)	$2,501,765	$2,882,464	$3,918,365
	Steven Laird (L)	9,640	(3%)			
2016 Primary	Don Bacon (R)	31,639	(66%)			
	Chip Maxwell (R)	16,294	(34%)			

Republican Don Bacon, elected in 2016 to this usually reliable Republican district in Nebraska, was the only GOP candidate nationwide who defeated a Democratic incumbent. His high-level military career was apt for this district and he had some experience with Congress, though this was his initial election campaign. He was well-prepared for his seat on the Armed Services Committee.

Bacon grew up on a farm in Illinois. He got his bachelor's degree in political science at Northern Illinois University in 1984. The following year, he joined the Air Force, where he served for nearly 30 years and retired as a brigadier general. He specialized in electronic warfare, intelligence, reconnaissance and public affairs. He deployed four times to the Middle East, and commanded an electronic warfare squadron during the invasion of Iraq. In 2009, he was selected as Europe's top Air Force wing commander and later commanded Offutt Air Force Base outside of Omaha. After leaving the Air Force, Bacon worked for Republican Rep. Jeff Fortenberry of Nebraska as his military adviser and focused on Offutt. He received two master's degrees, from the University of Phoenix in Arizona and the National War College in Washington D.C. As an assistant professor at Bellevue University, he taught courses on leadership and American values.

In 2016, he challenged Rep. Brad Ashford, who was one of two Democrats in 2014 to oust a House Republican incumbent. Ashford had taken advantage of his own nonpartisan - or multi-partisan - background, plus the occasional gaffes of veteran Republican Rep. Lee Terry. With this district's slightly Republican lean, Ashford immediately became a top GOP target for 2016. With his superior fundraising, Bacon became the frontrunner for the Republican nomination against Chip Maxwell, a more outspoken conservative who had been an editorial writer for the *Omaha World-Herald* and later was elected to county and state offices. In 2014, Maxwell collected signatures to run against Terry as an independent, but he did not follow through.

The primary was unusually robust. Maxwell accused the National Republican Congressional Committee of siding with Bacon, and cited a fundraising letter for Bacon that NRCC deputy chairman Steve Stivers of Ohio sent to other House Republicans. During the primary, the Democratic Congressional Campaign Committee spent more than $400,000 in ads that extolled Maxwell's conservative credentials, which revealed their concern about Bacon. That may have backfired. Running as a political outsider, even with the informal party endorsements, Bacon won the primary, 66%-34%.

In the general, Ashford and Bacon discussed foreign policy at length and criticized each other's ads, including references to the Islamic State and claims of improper uses of U.S. military photos. In a debate, Ashford separated himself from President Barack Obama on his nuclear deal with Iran and the efforts to close the U.S. prison in Guantanamo Bay. He supported a U.S.-backed no-fly zone in Syria. Bacon parted company with the criticism of NATO by Republican presidential nominee Donald Trump. "I'm not a blank check for party or president," Bacon said. In August, House Speaker Paul Ryan spoke at a fundraising lunch for Bacon in Omaha. The outcome was tight. Ashford led by nearly 9,000 votes in Douglas County. Bacon won on the basis of his 60 percent of the vote in Sarpy, even though that county cast less than 20 percent of the total vote. He won overall, 48.9%-47.7%, a margin of 3,464 votes.

In the House, Bacon got special attention from Republican leaders, including seats on the Armed Services and Small Business Committees, plus the Agriculture panel, where he can protect the agribusiness interests of his largely urban district. He likely will get a different kind of attention from Democrats in 2018.

Greater Omaha

Population		Race and Ethnicity		Income	
Total	634,595	White	73.7%	Median Income	$58,344 (157 out of 435)
Land area	510	Black	9.8%		
Pop/ sq mi	1244.9	Latino	10.7%		
Born in state	60.3%	Asian	2.9%	Under $50,000	43.1%
		Two races	2.3%	$50,000-$99,999	31.6%
Age Groups		Other	0.6%	$100,000-$199,999	20.5%
Under 18	26.4%			$200,000 or more	4.9%
18-34	25.0%	**Education**		Poverty Rate	13.0%
35-64	37.7%	H.S grad or less	31.1%		
Over 64	10.9%	Some college	31.2%	**Health Insurance**	
		College Degree, 4 yr	24.6%	With health insurance coverage	89.7%
Work		Post grad	13.0%		
White Collar	40.3%				
Sales and Service	42.0%	**Military**		**Public Assistance**	
Blue Collar	17.7%	Veteran	8.7%	Cash public assistance income	1.9%
Government	11.2%	Active Duty	0.3%		
				Food stamp/SNAP benefits	9.9%

Voter Turnout			
2015 Total Citizens 18+	436,302	2016 House Turnout as % CVAP	66%
2016 House turnout	288,308	2014 House Turnout as % CVAP	39%

2012 Presidential Vote		
Mitt Romney	140,976	(53%)
Barack Obama	121,889	(46%)

2016 Presidential Vote		
Donald Trump	137,564	(47%)
Hillary Clinton	131,030	(45%)
Gary Johnson	13,245	(5%)

Cook Partisan Voting Index: R+4

Omaha is the commercial heart of Nebraska and the largest city on the Great Plains north of Kansas City and west of Minneapolis. It got its start from the government, when President Abraham Lincoln picked it as the eastern terminus of the Union Pacific railroad, from which emerged the stockyards and livestock exchange that made it a thriving town. Over the years, Omaha filled up with cattle hands and European immigrants, especially Germans and Czechs. It developed fine civic institutions, from the Joslyn Art Museum to Boys Town, an orphanage founded by the Rev. Edward Flanagan in 1917 and the subject of a 1938 movie. Today, the facility is a gender-neutral home for troubled youth. While Norfolk to the west became known for launching late-night TV host Johnny Carson, a number of Hollywood legends had roots in Omaha: Fred Astaire, Marlon Brando, Montgomery Clift and Henry Fonda.

Though a major city by the 1880s, Omaha has remained small enough to be intimate. One doesn't feel distant, physically or psychologically, from the other side of town. The older, less affluent part of Omaha is on the Missouri River across from Council Bluffs, Iowa. Downtown and the riverfront have experienced substantial growth and development; the Tower at First National Center is the tallest structure between Minneapolis and Denver. To the west, the city has flourished with the rise of upscale neighborhoods and shopping malls. Omaha has entered the Wall Street vernacular as the place where investor Warren Buffett - ranked by *Forbes* in December 2016 as the world's second-richest person, with $74 billion in net worth, behind Microsoft founder Bill Gates - lives and works. Buffett was a high-profile supporter of President Barack Obama and his so-called "Buffett Rule" - that wealthy people should pay a greater share of taxes - became a frequent Democratic talking point.

Omaha was largely spared from the recession. It has recently experienced a construction boomlet, with a $370-million cancer center with more than 4,600 employees at the University of Nebraska Medical Center, a $2 billion sewer separation project, and expansions into new buildings of the headquarters of Omaha-based TD Ameritrade and Tenaska, an energy company. While Omaha's economy remains dependent on overseas sales of food, it has also become the headquarters of more than 30 insurance companies and the nation's telecommunications hub, employing more than 20,000 people at more than two dozen telemarketing centers. Millennials have been 38 percent of this expanding workforce. Its 6 percent increase in millennials between 2005 and 2015 was the fifth-highest percentage increase among major U.S. cities. The city has become more ethnically diverse: It's about 14 percent African American and 13 percent Hispanic.

The 2nd Congressional District includes Omaha and all of Douglas County. Omaha has long had competitive politics, with Democrats strong on the south side around the stockyards and the northeast and Republicans strong on the west side. As Omaha and Nebraska have boomed, they have become more Republican, and increasingly the Republican primary decides elections. The district includes nearly two-thirds of more-conservative Sarpy County, but not its Offutt Air Force Base, which is in the 1st District. Obama scored an impressive achievement when he won the district in 2008 by 50%-49%, ensuring him one elector from Nebraska as a consequence of the state's proportional division of Electoral College votes. Four years later, he lost the district 53%-46% and came up empty handed. In 2016, Hillary Clinton won Douglas County, 48%-46%. But, with his big lead in Sarpy, Donald Trump prevailed in the district, 47%-45%. This has been the least conservative district in Nebraska and Democrats can prevail in local elections under the right circumstances.

THIRD DISTRICT

Adrian Smith (R)

Elected 2006, 6th term; b. Dec 19, 1970, Scottsbluff; University of Nebraska, Lincoln, B.S.; Liberty University (VA), Att.; Evangelical; Married (Andrea Smith).

Elected Office: Gering City Council, 1994-1998; NE Legislature, 1998- 2006.

Professional Career: Realtor, Buyer Realty, 1997-2006; Owner, My Other Garage, 2003-2006.

DC Office: 320 CHOB 20515, 202-225-6435, Fax: 202-225-0207, adriansmith.house.gov.

State Offices: Grand Island, 308-384-3900; Scottsbluff, 308-633-6333.

Committees: *House Administration*. *Ways & Means*: Health, Human Resources (Chmn).

Group Ratings

	ADA	ACLU	AFL-CIO	LCV	ITI	COC	HAFA	ACU	CFG	FRC
2016	-	5%	-	0%	60%	100%	72%	88%	72%	100%
2015	0%	C	4%	3%	C	80%	C	96%	86%	92%

Almanac Ratings 2015

	Economy	Social	Foreign	Composite
Liberal	6%	0%	5%	3%
Conservative	94%	100%	95%	97%

Key Votes of the 114th Congress

1. Keystone Pipeline	Y	5. Puerto Rico Debt	Y	9. Offenses by Aliens	Y
2. Trade Deals	Y	6. Medical Marijuana	N	10. Troops in Iraq	N
3. Export-Import Bank	N	7. Sanctuary Cities	Y	11. Homeland Security $$	N
4. Debt Ceiling Increase	N	8. Armor-piercing Bullets	Y	12. Trade Adjustment aid	Y

Election Results

Election	Name (Party)	Vote (%)	Cand. Spent	Ind. Exp. Support	Ind. Exp. Oppose
2016 General	Adrian Smith (R)	226,720 (100%)	$422,483		
2016 Primary	Adrian Smith (R)	(100%)			

Prior winning percentages: 2014 (75%), 2012 (74%), 2010 (70%), 2008 (77%), 2006 (55%)

Republican Adrian Smith, elected in 2006, is an unwavering conservative who uses his seat on the Ways and Means Committee and his low-key style to focus intently on the rural issues important in his district. In 2017, he became chairman of its Human Resources Subcommittee.

Smith hails from a politically active family; his father is a former county Republican chairman, and his mother has been the state GOP secretary. But the most significant political influence in Smith's life was President Ronald Reagan. When he was in fourth grade, Smith recalls, adults around him were weighing Reagan's attributes against that of Democrat Jimmy Carter's, and it sunk into the boy's head that Reagan favored a strong defense. "It just made sense to me that we needed a strong military," said Smith, whose congressional office is filled with portraits of the former president. In college, Smith served as an intern in the Nebraska governor's office and as a page in the state's unicameral legislature.

At 23, shortly after graduating from the University of Nebraska, he won election to the City Council in his hometown of Gering. Four years later, he knocked off a Democratic incumbent to win the first of two terms in the legislature. There, Smith devoted his efforts to opposing abortion rights, protecting Nebraskans' right to bear arms, fighting tax increases and blocking efforts to expand casino gambling. He also worked as a real estate agent and owned a storage business.

In May 2005, Smith joined the race for the open seat of retiring Rep. Tom Osborne. Leading the crowded Republican primary field were Grand Island Mayor Jay Vavricek and John Hanson, who had been Osborne's district director. Smith championed tax incentives to attract new residents and encourage local investment. He promised to expand global markets for Nebraska farmers. Smith's opponents charged that he betrayed rural Nebraska by accepting more than $300,000 in contributions from members of the Club for Growth, a national anti-tax group that opposes farm subsidies. Smith, who supported caps on subsidies, parried by touting his support from the Nebraska Farm Bureau. Smith won the nomination with 39 percent of the vote. Hanson finished second with 29 percent, while Vavricek got 27 percent.

In the general election, Democrats fielded an unusually strong nominee: Yale-educated cattle rancher Scott Kleeb, who called for changes in farm policy to emphasize niche markets, and accused Smith of "distorting the truth" about the Club for Growth's opposition to farm subsidies. Smith portrayed Kleeb as a political carpetbagger who grew up overseas on military bases and attended schools in Colorado and Connecticut before settling in Nebraska on a family-owned ranch. Kleeb was competitive financially and kept the race close in the polls. Still, Smith won 55%-45%. He has easily won reelection since. In 2016, for the first time, he was reelected without opposition.

In Washington, Smith has been more conservative than his Nebraska colleagues in the House. He is a member of the Tea Party Caucus, and he once answered a survey from the conservative Heritage Foundation about what makes him happy by responding, "Having the freedom to pursue opportunities relating to my faith while upholding the ideals of our Founding Fathers."

With his coveted assignment on Ways and Means, Smith has focused on agriculture and trade issues. He sought to ensure that agriculture was part of the talks held by a U.S.-European Union working group that met to consider a free trade agreement. He was a leading voice in calling for repeal of the estate tax, which was eliminated for all but a few thousand wealthy taxpayers in the New Year's Day 2013 budget compromise. He has advocated lower corporate tax rates to keep the United States more competitive in the world economy, and he contends that free-trade agreements are good for the nation's overall economy, especially agriculture. When President Donald Trump formally abandoned U.S. participation in the Trans-Pacific Partnership three days after he was inaugurated, Smith responded, "Our country should be a leader in writing the rules of the global economy, rather than allowing other world powers to take our place."

As co-chairman of the Congressional Rural Caucus, Smith has pushed to preserve federal grants for tiny airports. He urged President Barack Obama to create a new Office of Rural Affairs. In 2009, Smith got the House to pass his bill setting up a grant program to relieve veterinarian shortages. As founder and co-chairman in 2015 of the Modern Agriculture Caucus, Smith promoted scientifically based policies to move agriculture forward and to educate other lawmakers about the issues that farmers face. During the June 2016 House approval of the annual defense spending bill, Smith won approval of his amendment to prevent the exclusion of meat from the Defense Department's food service program manual.

When he took the gavel at the Human Resources Subcommittee in January 2017, Smith said he would seek "to improve our country's anti-poverty programs by demanding positive results which break the cycle of government dependency and empower people through freedom and economic opportunity."

Central and Western Nebraska

Population		**Race and Ethnicity**		**Income**	
Total	607,486	White	85.3%	Median Income	$48,573 (276 out of 435)
Land area	67,435	Black	1.1%		
Pop/ sq mi	9.0	Latino	10.9%		
Born in state	68.9%	Asian	0.7%	Under $50,000	51.4%
		Two races	1.2%	$50,000-$99,999	33.4%
Age Groups		Other	0.8%	$100,000-$199,999	12.8%
Under 18	23.8%			$200,000 or more	2.4%
18-34	20.4%	**Education**		Poverty Rate	12.7%
35-64	37.8%	H.S grad or less	44.1%		
Over 64	17.9%	Some college	35.3%	**Health Insurance**	
		College Degree, 4 yr	14.4%	With health insurance coverage	89.2%
Work		Post grad	6.2%		
White Collar	31.2%				
Sales and Service	39.1%	**Military**		**Public Assistance**	
Blue Collar	29.6%	Veteran	9.7%	Cash public assistance income	1.9%
Government	14.6%	Active Duty	0.0%	Food stamp/SNAP benefits	8.7%

Voter Turnout			
2015 Total Citizens 18+	444,610	2016 House Turnout as % CVAP	51%
2016 House turnout	226,720	2014 House Turnout as % CVAP	42%

2012 Presidential Vote		
Mitt Romney	182,067	(70%)
Barack Obama	72,110	(28%)

2016 Presidential Vote		
Donald Trump	199,821	(74%)
Hillary Clinton	53,358	(20%)
Gary Johnson	11,676	(4%)

Cook Partisan Voting Index: R+27

West of Grand Island, Nebraska is wheat and livestock country. For miles on end there are rolling brown fields, only occasionally interrupted by barbed wire fences. The wind, rain and tornadoes that come suddenly remind you that the original settlers likened this part of the country to an ocean and thought themselves in their wooden wagons almost as helpless as passengers at sea in a rowboat. Settlers passed through here on the Oregon, California and Mormon trails in the 1840s, and then set down roots in the 1880s. But the rain they hoped for fell too unreliably, and wheat lands gave way to pasture and open range. It is a beautiful but hard land, exacting much from its people, as the novels of western Nebraska's Willa Cather make poignantly clear. Chimney Rock - a clay and sandstone spire that marked a good camping spot and offered reliable spring water for travelers and their animals - was the landmark that travelers on the way west most frequently mentioned in their journals. This symbol of westward expansion now graces the Nebraska issue of the U.S. quarter.

Dozens of small counties in the region today have fewer people than they did in 1900. Severe droughts in recent years have seemed a kind of end point for some, as the grasslands turned dry and brown, reservoirs and aquifers began to run dry, and ranchers sold off their thinning herds. Still, many farmers have found ways to adapt. The $17.7 billion value of farm production sold in this large area was higher than any other congressional district in the nation, according to the most recent Census of Agriculture in 2012. That total included $7.7 billion for cattle. Economic life also sets records in other industries. In North Platte, according to Union Pacific, Bailey Yard is the world's largest railroad classification yard, covering 2,850 acres and handling 14,000 rail cars every 24 hours. The 103-mile Union Pacific line from North Platte east to Gibbon is the busiest freight rail corridor in the world, with 139 trains a day passing through. The railroads employ about 8,000 people in Nebraska. The booming economy in North Platte has recently led to a shortage of housing.

The town of Sidney is home to Cabela's, a large mail order and internet business for hunting, fishing and camping gear. The company and Sidney entered into a $400 million partnership in 2012 to build 800 new homes in the area. In October 2016, Missouri-based Bass Pro Shops took control of Cabela in a $5.5 billion merger. Despite initial reassurances by Bass, the move raised fears about the future of the small town near the Colorado line, where 2,000 were employed by Cabela. When the Keystone XL oil pipeline was proposed to go through the environmentally sensitive Sandhills area in north central Nebraska, many Cornhusker politicians pushed to have the pipeline rerouted. President Barack Obama rejected the company's application in early 2012 in part, he said, because of concerns about this region. That set off a new round of review in Nebraska, with the state Supreme Court in January 2015 upholding the decision by Gov. Dave Heineman to approve the route. Obama rejected the application in November 2015, contending that it was not in the national interest. Four days after he took office, President Donald Trump reversed that decision and approved completion of the final segment for Keystone. Opponents responded with court challenges.

The 3rd Congressional District is geographically massive, reaching roughly 460 miles from the Wyoming border to the Iowa border and larger than the state of New York. The district takes in all or part of 75 counties, more than any other district in the nation. This is among the top 5 percent of the most conservative districts. In 2016, it became even more solidly Republican. Donald Trump won the district, 74%-20%, an increase from Mitt Romney's 70%-28% lead over Obama in 2012.

★ NEVADA ★

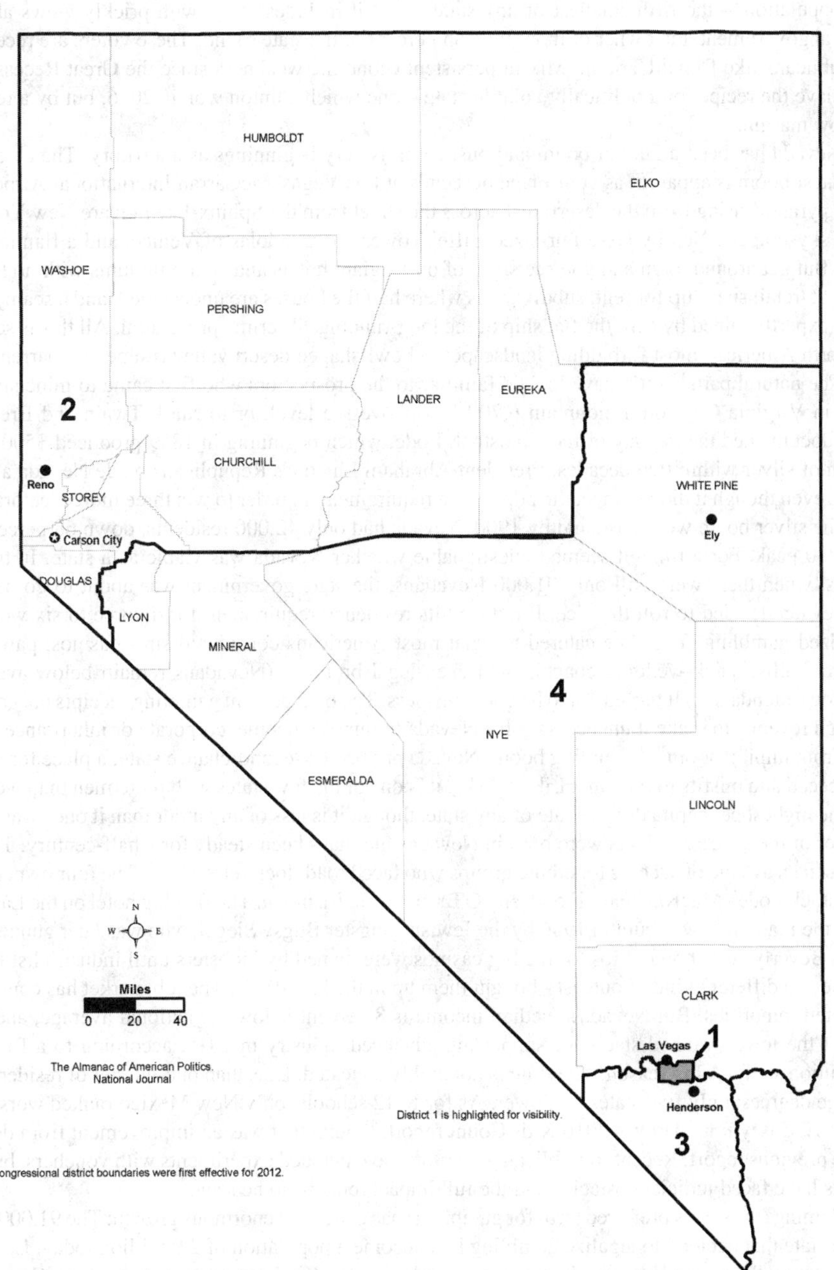
HUMBOLDT
ELKO
WASHOE
PERSHING
LANDER
EUREKA
2
CHURCHILL
WHITE PINE
Reno
STOREY
Ely
Carson City
DOUGLAS
LYON
MINERAL
4
NYE
ESMERALDA
LINCOLN
N
W
E
S
Miles
0
20
40
CLARK
1
Las Vegas
Henderson
3
The Almanac of American Politics.
National Journal
District 1 is highlighted for visibility.
Congressional district boundaries were first effective for 2012.

Nevada fuses two important, and divergent, demographic groups in today's political scene – minorities and blue-collar whites. The state is 28 percent Hispanic (the fifth highest of any state), 9 percent black and 8 percent Asian (tied for fourth highest) – prime voting groups for Democratic candidates like Hillary Clinton. Nevada's white population, meanwhile, accounts for just 50 percent of the population -- the fifth smallest of any state -- but it includes many with prickly views about the federal government, the owner of more than 85 percent of the state's land. These voters are receptive to Republicans like Donald Trump. Mix in persistent economic weakness since the Great Recession and you have the recipe for a politically volatile state – one which Clinton won in 2016, but by a relatively narrow margin.

Nevada has been a land of boom and bust from its very beginnings as a territory. The evidence of the latest boom is apparent as your plane descends at Las Vegas' McCarran International Airport. You see a pyramid rising from the desert; just across the street from the Sphinx-like lion are New York City-style skyscrapers. Nearby are a fair-sized Eiffel Tower, the gondolas of Venice, and a flaming pirate ship. But get around town and you see signs of bust - giant hotels and condominiums with no lights on at night, retail space up for rent, subdivisions where half the houses are unoccupied, and a seamy side of town expertly mined by *CSI*, the flagship of the long-running TV crime procedural. All this is set in one of North America's most forbidding landscapes, a bowl-shaped desert valley rimmed by barren peaks.

The natural parts would have looked familiar to the prospectors who first came to mine silver and gold in Virginia City, on a mountain 6,700 feet above sea level, or to Mark Twain and Bret Harte, who documented the heyday of the Comstock Lode, which beginning in 1859 produced $500 million worth of silver within two decades. President Abraham Lincoln's Republicans made Nevada a state in 1864, even though it did not meet the population requirement, in order to win three more electoral votes. But the silver boom went bust, and by 1900, Nevada had only 42,000 residents, down 68 percent from its 1880 peak. For a time, it seemed questionable whether Nevada was viable as a state. In the early 1930s, when there were still only 91,000 Nevadans, the state government was about to go bankrupt. So Nevada decided to roll the dice. It reduced its residency requirement for divorce to six weeks and legalized gambling. The state catered to what most Americans considered sin - casinos, pawnshops, divorce mills, quick-wedding chapels, and even legal brothels. (Nevadans remain below-average in religious attendance.) It turned out to be good business. The 6.75 percent gambling receipts tax generated enough revenue to make it unnecessary for Nevada to impose income, corporate or inheritance taxes.

From mining boom to gambling boom, Nevada has been a second-chance state, a place for outcasts to succeed and misfits to rebound. Like Alaska, it is one of the few states with more men than women. It has the highest per capita divorce rate of any state, though it is less of an outlier than it once was. Only a quarter of the state's residents were born in Nevada, and that's been steady for a half-century. The state has been an avenue of success for ethnic groups who faced roadblocks elsewhere. The four owners of the Comstock Lode - MacKay, Fair, Flood, and O'Brien - were Irishmen. The first big hotel on the Las Vegas strip, the Flamingo, was built in 1946 by the Jewish gangster Bugsy Siegel, who was later gunned down in his Beverly Hills home. Most of the big casinos were owned by mobsters until industrialist Howard Hughes - a different kind of outcast - bought them up in the late 1960s. The job market has consistently attracted minorities. But Nevada's median income is 8 percent below the national average, and it was one of the lowest-ranked states for supporting advanced industry in 2015, according to a Brookings Institution study. A big reason: The state is not highly educated. Less than one-quarter of residents have college degrees; only five states are lower. As for K-12 schools, only New Mexico ranked worse in the Annie E. Casey Foundation's 2016 Kids Count report, though that was an improvement from dead last in the previous report. Recent Republican governors have pursued experiments with vouchers, but some efforts have faced judicial obstacles and the full impact remains to be seen.

Gaming (the state's preferred term for gambling) has generated enormous growth: The 91,000 people in the state that decided to legalize gambling had become a population of 2.9 million today. Las Vegas was a dot on the map when gambling became legal, a one-traffic-light crossroads in Clark County with 8,532 people county-wide. Now, Clark County has 2.1 million. Las Vegas' 23,000 hotel rooms in 1973 mushroomed into roughly 150,000 today. Reno, once known as "the biggest little city in the world," now has roughly 425,000 people in its metro area. Nevada was America's fastest-growing state in the 1960s, 1970s, 1980s, and 1990s and from 2000 to 2007. For a long time, gaming was a good economic bet. But in 2007, gaming revenues declined even before the national economy fell into recession. Nevada suddenly went bust, with the decline in gaming revenues cascading into a housing and construction crash. Nevada's unemployment rate peaked at 13.7 percent in late 2010 and was in double digits for more than four years straight. Nevada recorded the nation's steepest fall in homeownership rates between 2004 and 2012. Foreclosure rates peaked at nearly 10 percent of households, and more people left the state than moved there from other states from 2008 to 2011 - in all, a sharp reversal of fortune.

As the nation began to recover, so did Nevada. Las Vegas' Clark County has grown in population by 9 percent since 2010, operating with a revised business model. With some form of gambling available in all of the lower 48 states and with neighboring California now dotted with Indian casinos, Las Vegas promoted itself as a family destination, not just a gambling den. While gaming accounted for 50 percent of Las Vegas Strip revenues in 1998, it was only 38 percent by 2011. The Strip became a luxury shopping center with world-class restaurants. The casinos continue to cater to high rollers, even sending private planes to fly them in, but they face increasing competition for rich Chinese and Japanese players; Macau's gaming revenues, despite recent backsliding, are bigger than Las Vegas'. Las Vegas has become a major player for convention business, and in 2016 the legislature approved a financing plan for a $1.9 billion domed stadium to house the NFL's Oakland Raiders, expected to arrive in 2020. Reno's challenge has been trickier. Without Las Vegas' luxury attractions, it has sunk in the gaming rankings. But the Reno area has a lower cost of living than coastal California and a pleasant combination of sun and slopes; population has increased by 6 percent in Washoe County, and economic diversification is proceeding with a big push from the state. Apple received $89 million in tax breaks to build a data center in Reno; then, electric automaker Tesla accepted $1.3 billion in state incentives to build the biggest battery factory in the world outside Reno, directly employing a projected 6,500 workers. It is also expanding the factory to produce parts for its Model 3 sports car. Still, the state's recovery has been modest compared with past booms. By late 2016, the unemployment rate was 5.1 percent – much improved, but still higher than the national average. As late as 2015, Nevada continued to rank among the top five states for foreclosures, and more than half of those were underwater - the highest rate in the nation and well above the national average of 35 percent.

For all its distinctiveness, Nevada has been similar to the nation politically. A silver-producing state, it voted three times for the free-silver populism of William Jennings Bryan, but since his final candidacy in 1908, Nevada has voted only twice for the loser of a presidential election - Gerald Ford in 1976 and Clinton in 2016. Nevada twice provided Bill Clinton and George W. Bush narrow victories and, with its increasingly Hispanic electorate, twice provided somewhat bigger margins for Barack Obama. Since 2000, it has elected one Democratic and one Republican senator and has produced divided House delegations. Backing from the big casino owners helped elect Democratic Gov. Bob Miller in 1990 and 1994 and Republican Gov. Kenny Guinn in 1998 and 2002. In the Democratic year of 2006, it elected a Republican governor, Jim Gibbons, whose messy divorce - his wife disputed his right to occupy the governor's mansion - and acerbic style antagonized voters. He was beaten in the 2010 Republican primary by former state Attorney General Brian Sandoval, who went on to be elected in the fall.

For years, this sparsely populated desert sent politically shrewd Democrats to Washington and kept them there to protect the interests of a state heavily dependent on the federal government. The most enduring figure in recent Nevada politics has been Harry Reid. He was elected lieutenant governor way back in 1970, then headed the Nevada Gaming Commission from 1977 to 1981; his life was threatened and he indignantly turned down an offer of a bribe. In 1982, he won election to the House and in 1986 ran for the Senate and won. He became majority leader in 2007. Keeping him in this position was of immense importance to the gaming industry and to the Culinary Union, which represents many casino employees and has a crackerjack political organization. When the federal government planned to build a national nuclear waste repository at Yucca Mountain, a scant 90 miles from Las Vegas, Reid fought it mightily - and successfully. In 2014, Reid lost his Senate majority, suffered a serious accidental injury and decided to retire. Two years later, Democrat Catherine Cortez Masto narrowly won the race to succeed Reid, becoming the first Latina senator. Another Hispanic politician playing a leading role in the state is Sandoval, a Republican who has staked out enough maverick stances to generate crossover appeal. A different kind of power rests with Sheldon Adelson, a casino magnate, who has been a Republican mega-donor and since 2015 the owner of the *Las Vegas Review-Journal*.

In 2014, a strong Republican midterm election nationally, the GOP flipped control of the state legislature (the first time they managed to win both chambers since 1985) and won every statewide office. In 2016, the Democrats staged a comeback, aided by a strong early-voting push. They won back both chambers of the legislature as Hillary Clinton was winning the state's electoral votes. Support from nonwhites proved crucial to Clinton's victory. Trump ran strongly among white voters – well enough to cut Obama's six-point margin in 2012 down to less than three points against Clinton. A solid ground game helped the Democrats net 8,000 more votes than in 2012, but Trump beat Mitt Romney's 2012 showing by six times that – 48,000 votes. Even in Clark County, the Democratic nominee's winning margin shrank from 14 points to 10. In Washoe (Reno), the only other county Clinton won, the Democratic margin shrank from four points to just one. Nevada Democrats can take comfort in their 2016 victories and the state's demographic direction, but this is a state that should remain competitive for the near future.

Population		**Race and Ethnicity**		**Income**	
Total	2,798,636	White	52.0%	Median Income	$51,847 (27 out of 50)
Land area	109,781	Black	8.1%		
Pop/ sq mi	25.5	Latino	27.5%	Under $50,000	48.1%
Born in state	25.5%	Asian	7.5%	$50,000-$99,999	32.1%
		Two races	3.2%	$100,000-$199,999	16.3%
Age Groups		Other	1.7%	$200,000 or more	3.5%
Under 18	23.6%			Poverty Rate	11.4%
18-34	23.4%	**Education**			
35-64	39.4%	H.S grad or less	43.1%	**Health Insurance**	
Over 64	13.6%	Some college	33.8%	With health insurance coverage	81.7%
		College Degree, 4 yr	15.2%		
Work		Post grad	7.9%		
White Collar	27.7%			**Public Assistance**	
Sales and Service	53.8%	**Military**		Cash public assistance income	3.2%
Blue Collar	18.5%	Veteran	10.4%		
Government	12.3%	Active Duty	0.4%	Food stamp/SNAP benefits	12.1%

Voter Turnout			
2015 Total Citizens 18+	1,863,799	2016 Pres Turnout as % CVAP	60%
2016 Pres Votes	1,125,385	2012 Pres Turnout as % CVAP	58%

Legislature	
Senate:	11D, 9R, 1I
House:	27D, 15R

Presidential Politics

2016 Democratic Caucus		
Hillary Clinton (D)	6,440	(53%)
Bernie Sanders (D)	5,785	(47%)
2016 Republican Caucus		
Donald Trump (R)	34,531	(46%)
Marco Rubio (R)	17,940	(24%)
Ted Cruz (R)	16,079	(21%)

2016 Presidential Vote		
Hillary Clinton (D)	539,260	(48%)
Donald Trump (R)	512,058	(46%)
Ben Carson (R)		(5%)
Gary Johnson (L)	37,384	(3%)
2012 Presidential Vote		
Barack Obama (D)	531,373	(52%)
Mitt Romney (R)	463,567	(46%)

After going heavily Republican in the 1980s, Nevada voted narrowly, by a margin of three-tenths-of-one percent, for Bill Clinton in 1992. Since then, it has been a battleground in every presidential election and has voted for the winner in each race - until 2016, when Hillary Clinton defeated Donald Trump 48%-46%. Clinton's victory came by winning Clark County (Las Vegas), which regularly accounts for about two-thirds of the state's total vote. Her 82,170-vote margin in Clark was more than triple her 27,202 statewide winning margin. (Barack Obama beat Mitt Romney by 67,806 votes in 2012.) Clinton also carried Washoe County (Reno), but by less than 3,000 votes. Trump won the state's other 15 counties, once referred to as the "cow counties" for their cattle-grazing, which vote heavily Republican. The growing number of Hispanic voters in Nevada - many of whom live in Clark - is another asset for Democratic presidential candidates. Hispanics comprised 15 percent of the Nevada electorate in 2008, 19 percent in 2012, and 18 percent in 2016, according to the television networks' exit poll. The network voter survey found that Hispanics voted 60%-29% for Clinton over Trump. But that Clinton advantage among Hispanics was less than Barack Obama's margins in both of his presidential races in Nevada. Both campaigns spent heavily to contest the state, and overall turnout jumped by more than 100,000 votes from 2012. The *Las Vegas Review-Journal*, owned by casino magnate GOP donor Sheldon Adelson, was one of a handful of newspapers that endorsed Trump in the general election. Adelson, along with his wife Miriam, gave more than $20 million to various entities to help elect Trump. The only other major metro daily to endorse Trump was the Jacksonville *Florida Times-Union*.

A significant change in Nevada politics took place in 2008: For the first time, it became an important part of the presidential nominating process. The Democratic National Committee, under heavy pressure from then Senate Majority Leader Harry Reid, chose Reid's home state as one of four allowed to hold early contests, along with Iowa, New Hampshire and South Carolina. Republicans went along with the idea to give regional balance to the opening salvo of the nominating race. Both parties agreed to conduct caucuses. In 2016, Trump scored a huge victory in the GOP caucuses, defeating Florida Sen. Marco Rubio 46%-24%. Texas Sen. Ted Cruz finished third with 21 percent. Cruz won two of the cow counties, Elko and Lincoln, and Trump won the other 15. Rubio was the runner-up to Trump in Clark and Washoe. Turnout soared above the 75,000-mark, more than double the nearly 33,000 who attended the 2012 GOP caucuses. On the Democratic side, Clinton held off Vermont Sen. Bernie Sanders, winning 53 percent of the county delegates to 47 percent for Sanders. Democratic turnout was estimated to be 84,000, down from more than 117,000 who attended in 2008 when Clinton beat Obama, 51%-45%. Clinton handily won Clark, where the largest number of delegates was at stake, and five other counties. Both parties are entertaining the idea of changing state law to provide for a presidential primary in 2020 instead of a caucus. In 2015, legislation to adopt a primary passed the state Senate but died in the Assembly without a vote.

Congressional Districts

115th Congress Lineup	1R 3D	**114th Congress Lineup**	3R 1D

Nevada's population surged 66 percent in the 1990s and 35 percent in the 2000s, leading the nation each time. The boom may finally be subsiding, but the state has rocketed from one district in 1980 to four in 2012. In 2011, partisan control was split and tension ran high. Democrats in charge of the legislature, including several eyeing a promotion to Congress, passed maps creating one safely Republican seat in northern Nevada and three Democratic-leaning seats in Clark County. Republican Gov. Brian Sandoval vetoed the maps on the grounds that Latinos had accounted for 46 percent of the state's growth between 2000 and 2010 and deserved a majority Latino seat based in the northeast quadrant of metro Las Vegas. Democrats decried Sandoval's position as a veiled attempt to pack Democratic voters and create three Republican-leaning seats in the process. The debate fractured Latino advocacy groups, and the legislature adjourned in a stalemate.

Carson City District Judge James Todd Russell appointed three independent special masters - a county elections administrator, a former state legislative research director and a lawyer - to draw a map. The trio submitted a diplomatic plan that created a safely Democratic, 43 percent Latino 1st District and preserved a Republican-leaning 2nd District in the north. They created a slightly more Republican 3rd District including Henderson to the south, and a new Democratic-leaning 4th District linking substantially Latino North Las Vegas with several rural counties to the north. The result in 2012 was an even 2-2 split.

Since then, multiple developments have increased the stakes for the next round of redistricting. In 2016, Democrats gained two seats to take 3-1 control of the delegation. Nevada was the only state where either party gained more than one House seat. Democrats also regained control of the Legislature. That increased the importance of the 2018 election for governor, which may be the Republicans' last chance to assure themselves a seat at Nevada's increasingly Democratic table. It's a safe bet that both national parties will be spending more time than ever in Vegas.

Governor

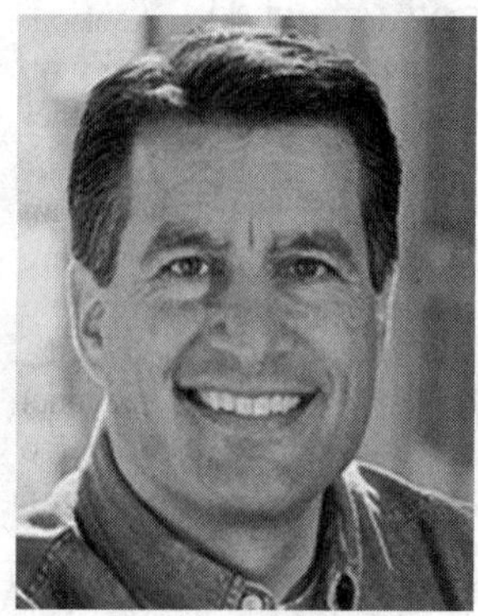

Brian Sandoval (R)

Elected 2010, term expires 2019, 2nd term; b. Aug. 5, 1963, Redding, CA; U. of NV, Reno, B.A. 1986; OH St. U., J.D. 1989; Catholic; Married (Kathleen); 3 children.

Elected Office: NV Assembly, 1994-1998; NV Attorney General 2002-2005.

Professional Career: NV Gaming Commission, 1998-2001; Tahoe Regional Planning Authority, 1998-2001; Judge, U.S. District Court, 2005-2009.

Office: 101 N. Carson St., Carson City, 89701; 775-684-5670; Fax: 775-684-5683; Website: nv.gov.

Election Results

Election	Name (Party)	Vote (%)
2014 General	Brian Sandoval (R)	386,340 (71%)
	Robert Goodman (D)	130,722 (24%)
	David Lory VanderBeek (I)	14,536 (3%)
2014 Primary	Brian Sandoval (R)	105,857 (90%)

Prior winning percentage: 2010 (53%)

Republican Brian Sandoval was elected Nevada's first Latino governor in 2010. Handsome and telegenic, Sandoval has been heralded as a trailblazer in Republican circles, having previously been Nevada's first Hispanic elected to statewide office as attorney general and the first Hispanic to take the bench as a U.S. District Court judge. But since the passage of a tax hike to fund education in 2015, Sandoval has found himself "somewhat lonely on the Republican stage," Politico's Ben Wofford wrote in 2016. "He is in the unenviable position of being seen as an ideological apostate," thanks to un-Republican stances on such issues as abortion, immigration, and tort reform. Wofford wrote that Sandoval is "living proof that today's Republicanism looks very different depending on whether you are running for president or governing on the state level."

Sandoval was born in Redding, California, and his family moved to Fallon Nevada, when he was five. He grew up in Sparks, just east of Reno. His mother worked as a legal secretary for the U.S. attorney and for a magistrate judge; as a teenager, Sandoval worked at the cafeteria at Reno's federal courthouse. He attended the University of Nevada-Reno and went to law school at Ohio State University, then went into private practice. After five years, he ran for a seat in the state Assembly and won. He served two terms, developing a reputation as a moderate. He left office to take over the gaming commission, a powerful post that former Senate Majority Leader Harry Reid once held. In three years in that job, the commission adopted regulations to limit neighborhood gambling, prohibit child-themed slot machines, and enhance protections for problem gamblers.

Sandoval quit the commission to run for attorney general in 2002 and won easily. In the job, he was thrust into the legal fight over storing commercial nuclear waste at Yucca Mountain, which was a priority for the Bush administration. Sandoval also created the state's first public integrity unit to prosecute corrupt lawmakers. Midway through his term, in 2005, an opening came up on the U.S. District Court in Las Vegas. Reid reached out to Sandoval, and he accepted the offer to become, at 42, one of the youngest federal judges in the country. (Conveniently for Reid, the arrangement also removed Sandoval as a potential Senate challenger in 2010.)

Meanwhile, Nevada GOP Gov. Jim Gibbons, a former House member, was elected in 2006 but was in office when the Great Recession hit and was caught in a seemingly endless loop of scandals. When Sandoval decided to challenge Gibbons in the GOP primary in 2010, he had no trouble raising money, although with tea party activists gaining strength, Sandoval began shifting his emphasis from consensus-builder to that of a committed conservative. He backed neighboring Arizona's stringent new immigration law that allowed law enforcement officials to hold people detained on other charges whom they suspected of being in the country illegally. In the June 2010 primary, Sandoval defeated Gibbons,

56%-27%, setting up a fall matchup with Rory Reid, a Clark County commissioner and the son of Harry Reid. Sandoval went on Spanish-language TV to remind Hispanic voters of the historic nature of his candidacy. He promised to maintain Nevada's low-tax climate, to add as much as $2 million in state spending on economic development and to privatize some state services. He steered clear of divisive issues such as immigration, and Sandoval ended up winning by a comfortable 53%-42% margin, dominating rural counties while topping his opponent by 7,000 votes in Clark County, Reid's home turf.

In marked contrast to Gibbons, Sandoval was active and engaged with legislators, meeting personally with all 63 during his first 100 days. He cheered fellow Republicans by hewing to his promise not to raise taxes under any circumstances and by appointing GOP Rep. Dean Heller in April to serve the unexpiredSenate term of John Ensign, who had resigned amid a sex scandal. But Democrats were less impressed, and by May activists had set up "Sandoville," a tent encampment near the state Capitol in protest. To help balance the $6 billion budget, the governor borrowed a tactic from the previous administration and siphoned money from a local sewer district, a move that the Nevada Supreme Court said was improper. Calling the ruling a "game-changer," Sandoval reversed himself on his no-new-taxes pledge, prompting outrage from conservatives. He managed to quiet the storm by scaling back his initial pronouncement and eventually reached agreement with lawmakers for temporarily reauthorizing $620 million in taxes that had been set to expire June 30.

Through his legislative battles, Sandoval remained relentlessly upbeat, earning the nickname "Governor Sunny" and racking up some of the highest approval ratings of any governor in the country. Increasingly, he hewed to the center. He angered conservatives by agreeing to establish a state health-insurance exchange under the federal health care law and to expand Medicaid - two policies most other GOP governors resisted. (Technical problems eventually forced Nevada, along with a number of other states, to abandon their state exchanges for the federal marketplace.) He also expressed moderate-to-liberal views on abortion and same-sex marriage. In his 2014 re-election bid, Sandoval was never in danger; his Democratic opponent, Bob Goodman, was an octogenarian businessman so obscure that he won his party's nod only by finishing second to "none of the above" - a ballot line that is a quirk of Nevada's election law. Sandoval won, 71%-24%. Bolstered by Sandoval's rout, Republicans rolled to victory up and down the ballot, sweeping statewide offices and taking control of the legislature - the GOP's first unified control of state governance since 1929.

For 2015, Sandoval proposed an aggressive agenda -- hiking a range of taxes to provide an additional $1.1 billion for education, an area where the state fares poorly in national rankings. Veteran Nevada political commentator Jon Ralston called Sandoval's proposals a "nearly perfect combination of rhetoric and substance" as well as "visionary and controversial." The plan drew immediate opposition from the tea party wing of the GOP, which had gained ground in the 2014 sweep. After several legislative twists and turns, the legislature approved a revised version of his plan. Sandoval also signed several other education measures that expanded programs on literacy, pre-kindergarten education and English as a second language, along with a school choice bill that's among the nation's most far-reaching. On immigration, Sandoval broke with others in his party; he opposed the decision by newly elected Republican Attorney General Adam Laxalt to join the successful multi-state lawsuit against President Barack Obama's executive actions on immigration. Sandoval also made another daring move by shepherding $1.3 billion in incentives for Tesla Motors to build a "gigafactory" for electric car batteries near Reno. The plant would "change Nevada forever" by creating a projected 20,000 jobs and $100 billion in economic activity, Sandoval argued, but skeptics wondered whether subsidies of perhaps $190,000 per job were warranted.

Such efforts raised Sandoval's national profile as a Latino rising star. But even though Nevada was a hotly contested primary and general-election state in 2016, his imprimatur wasn't highly valued, at least within the party. One adviser to Texas Sen. Ted Cruz called Sandoval "a total piece of toxic waste" and "the kiss of death for any conservative," *Politico* reported. He passed up a chance to run for Reid's old seat in the Senate (Catherine Cortez Masto ended up holding the seat for Democrats). The Obama White House floated Sandoval's name as a possible Supreme Court nominee prior to settling on Merrick Garland, but most observers considered it no more than a feint, given Republican concerns about his ideology and Democratic concerns about his partisan affiliation. In the 2016 election, Hillary Clinton won the state and the Democrats took back both chambers of the legislature. Perhaps reflecting the state's new partisan lineup, Sandoval proposed in early 2017 to boost the state budget by 10 percent, including increases for education and workforce development; conservatives consoled themselves with a continued push for school vouchers. After Trump's victory, Sandoval was one of several GOP governors who had acted to expand coverage under Obama's health care law to write to House Republicans to share their concerns about repealing the law. But he vetoed in June 2017 a measure from the Democratic-controlled Legislature that would have made Medicaid available to all Nevadans, regardless of income. He called the proposal "an undeveloped remedy to an undefined problem." The race to succeed Sandovalin 2018 could include Laxalt and state Treasurer Dan Schwartz on the Republican side and Clark CountyCommission Chair Steve Sisolak on the Democratic side. Given the back-and-forth nature of recentelections in the state, it is expected to be a competitive contest.

Senior Senator

Dean Heller (R)

Appointed May. 2011, term expires 2018, 1st full term; b. May 10, 1960,Castro Valley, CA; University of Southern California, B.A., 1985, Mormon; Married (Lynne Heller); 4 children; 1 grandchild.

Elected Office: NV Assembly, 1990-1994; NV Secretary of State, 1994-2006, U.S. House, 2007-2011.

Professional Career: Stockbroker, 1983-1988; Chief Deputy State Treasurer, 1988-1990; Public funds rep., Bank of America, 1990-1995.

DC Office: 324 HSOB 20510, 202-224-6244, Fax: 202-228-6753, heller.senate.gov.

State Offices: Elko, 775-738-2001; Las Vegas, 702-388-6605; Reno, 775-686-5770.

Committees: *Banking, Housing & Urban Affairs*: Financial Institutions & Consumer Protection, Housing, Transportation & Community Development, Securities, Insurance & Investment (Chmn). *Commerce, Science & Transportation*: Aviation Operations, Safety & Security, Communications, Technology, Innovation & the Internet, Consumer Protection, Product Safety, Ins & Data Security, Surface Trans., Merchant Marine Infra., Safety & Security. *Finance*: Energy, Natural Resources & Infrastructure (Chmn), Health Care, International Trade, Customs & Global Competitiveness. *Veterans' Affairs*.

Group Ratings

	ADA	ACLU	AFL-CIO	LCV	ITI	COC	HAFA	ACU	CFG	FRC
2016	-	70%	-	24%	80%	100%	55%	77%	77%	100%
2015	25%	C	21%	8%	C	92%	C	71%	68%	60%

Almanac Ratings 2015

	Economy	Social	Foreign	Composite
Liberal	23%	10%	58%	30%
Conservative	77%	91%	42%	70%

Key Votes of the 114th Congress

1. Keystone pipeline	Y	5. National Security Data	Y	9. Gun Sales Checks	N
2. Export-Import Bank	N	6. Iran Nuclear Deal	Y	10. Sanctuary Cities	Y
3. Debt Ceiling Increase	N	7. Puerto Rico Debt	N	11. Planned Parenthood	Y
4. Homeland Security $$	Y	8. Loretta Lynch A.G	N	12. Trade deals	Y

Election Results

Election	Name (Party)	Vote (%)		Cand. Spent	Ind. Exp. Support	Ind. Exp. Oppose
2012 General	Dean Heller (R)	457,656	(46%)	$9,192,588	$1,234,469	$13,098,190
	Shelley Berkley (D)	446,080	(45%)	$11,624,756	$1,258,783	$12,389,046
	David Lory VanderBeek (I)	48,792	(5%)			
2012 Primary	Dean Heller (R)	88,958	(86%)			
	Sherry Brooks (R)	5,356	(5%)			

Prior winning percentages: 2012 (46%); House: 2010 (63%), 2008 (52%), 2005 (50%)

Republican Dean Heller was appointed Nevada's junior senator in May 2011 and went on to win the seat in the 2012 election, defeating a scandal-plagued opponent even as Democratic President

Barack Obama easily carried Nevada. Reflecting the Democratic trend of his state Heller has amassed a relatively centrist voting record since joining the Senate, breaking with his party on some major issues. He is expected to face a bruising reelection campaign in 2018.

Heller was a political fixture in Carson City long before he won his first House contest in 2006. He got a taste of politics during childhood when his newspaper route included deliveries at the state capitol. He graduated from the University of Southern California in 1985 with a degree in business administration, and then worked as a stockbroker trading on the Pacific Stock Exchange. In 1990, he won the first of two terms in the Nevada House, and in 1994, he was elected to the first of three terms as Nevada secretary of state. During his 12-year tenure, Heller streamlined the corporation registration process, increasing revenues tenfold. He supported more public access to government records and greater transparency in the state campaign finance system. Nevada was seen as a national model in 2004, when it became the first state to create a paper trail for its electronic voting machines. Heller declined to use his office to boost his party during the razor-close 1998 Senate contest, affirming incumbent Democrat Harry Reid's defeat of Republican John Ensign, then a House member, by about 400 votes. At times, Democrats even hoped he might switch parties.

But Heller remained a Republican, and he made his move in 2006 when five-term Republican Rep. Jim Gibbons gave up his 2nd District seat to run for governor. Heller faced competition for the Republican nomination from Assemblywoman Sharron Angle and former Assemblywoman Dawn Gibbons, the outgoing congressman's wife. Gibbons' underfunded candidacy never took off, but Angle, a Christian conservative, emerged as a serious primary rival after she picked up the endorsement and financial support of the deep-pocketed and fiscally conservative Club for Growth. In the primary, Heller barely edged Angle by 421 votes. (Angle later ran a spectacularly bad campaign against then-Senate Majority Leader Harry Reid, likely costing Republicans the seat in 2010).

His campaign treasury depleted, Heller entered the general election campaign against Democrat Jill Derby, an 18-year veteran of the Nevada Board of Regents. While Republican candidates elsewhere considered President George W. Bush a liability in 2006, Heller got Bush to stump twice for him, helping motivate the traditionally Republican-leaning rural vote. Heller defeated her, 50%-45%, and won reelection with ease in 2008 and 2010.

In the House, Heller was enough of a loyalist to land a coveted seat on Ways and Means in 2009, although he found little success securing passage of amendments. In early 2011, he was chosen to succeed the fast-unraveling Ensign. In selecting Heller to replace Ensign, Republican Gov. Brian Sandoval cited the need for an "experienced voice" in Washington. Nevada was among the states hardest hit by the 2007-09 recession; by March 2011, unemployment had soared to 13.2 percent, the nation's highest.

Heller's electorate "shifted overnight from the domain of staunch, mostly white conservatives ... to an increasingly Democratic one that is projected to be majority-minority by 2030," Nevada journalist Steve Friess wrote. Perhaps as a result, Heller has taken some maverick stances for a Republican. On the Energy and Natural Resources Committee, he called for an end to some of the same subsidies to large oil companies that Democrats have sought to repeal. He was the only GOP senator to support a Democratic balanced-budget plan in December 2011, and one of just five Republicans in October 2011 to join Democrats in rejecting an amendment that would have limited the taxpayer liability for mortgage giants Fannie Mae and Freddie Mac. He was among the first in the party to publicly distance himself from 2012 GOP presidential nominee Mitt Romney's secretly recorded speech saying that 47 percent of voters wouldn't support him because they were reliant on the government. He was one of 12 GOP senators in January 2013 to support raising the federal debt limit. The latter measure incorporated his bill to cut off the salaries of House and Senate members in years they do not meet deadlines to pass a budget or individual spending bills. He also voted for the Senate immigration bill in 2013.

As majority leader, Reid tangled openly with Heller, even though he had avoided feuding with Ensign. Most prominently, Reid squawked about Heller's role in a bill legalizing online poker that both supported. Reid accused Heller in September 2012 of "a failure of leadership" for failing to round up the 15 Senate votes needed for passage; Heller responded that Reid deliberately waited until close to the Nov. 6 election to bring up a vote on Internet gaming, knowing that it would not pass. In Heller's bid for a full term in 2012, Democrats made the race a priority. His general election rival was Rep. Shelley Berkley, an outspoken Democrat who had served with him on Ways and Means. Berkley hitched her wagon to Obama's, aware that the president would make an all-out effort to win a state that he had captured in 2008. In one of the cycle's nastiest races, Berkley and other Democrats attacked Heller for his support of House Budget Committee Chairman Paul Ryan's budget plan. But Berkley had a significant piece of political baggage-she was the subject of a House ethics committee investigation into whether she had used her position to benefit the financial interests of her husband, a physician who operates dialysis centers in Nevada.

Heller also sought to raise broader questions about Berkley's ethics, running ads that questioned her real estate investments and a 2008 taxpayer-funded trip to Italy after attending a conference in neighboring Slovenia. He got considerable financial help from conservative casino mogul Sheldon Adelson, who had a history of feuding with Berkley. Heller eked out a 45.9%-44.7% victory, with Independent American Party candidate David VanderBeek drawing 5% and the state's "none of these candidates" option registering 4.5%. Heller won his native Washoe County, which includes Reno, with 51 percent, and he held Berkley to 50 percent in her stronghold of Las Vegas-based Clark County.

After his reelection, Heller considered siding with gun-control advocates but ultimately decided to join with almost all Republicans and some Democrats to vote against legislation that would have banned assault weapons, limited magazine capacity, and expanded background checks for gun sales. But on another issue, Heller bucked key players in his party-in the fall of 2013, he supported the Employment Non-Discrimination Act, which bars discrimination against gays in the workplace. It had been stalled in the Senate for lack of a 60th vote to break a threatened filibuster. Heller, noting that Nevada already had a similar law, issued a statement saying he would vote for the bill, giving Democrats a sufficient number of Republican votes for passage. The federal bill passed, 64-32, with Heller joining 10 Republicans voting yes.

In 2014, Heller worked with Democratic Sen. Jack Reed of Rhode Island to push legislation to retroactively provide unemployment compensation. "I believe there ought to be a safety net," he said, "and that safety net needs to be solid." He joined Democratic Sens. Claire McCaskill of Missouri and Kirsten Gillibrand of New York in backing a measure to hold universities more accountable to students who are raped. He's long worked with New Mexico Democrat Martin Heinrich to repeal Obamacare's "Cadillac Tax," which taxes expensive healthcare plans and is set to take effect in 2018.

With the GOP takeover in the November 2014 elections-and the demotion of Reid to minority leader-Heller saw his influence rise. He became the first Nevada senator to chair a subcommittee on the influential Finance Committee (Social Security, Pensions, and Family Policy), and he took the reins of a subcommittee on Banking, Housing, and Urban Affairs. He lost a closed-door election against Mississippi Sen. Roger Wicker to head the National Republican Senatorial Committee, perhaps because of his low-key role in Reid's tight 2010 reelection bid against Angle, but he did get the consolation prize of becoming one of three vice chairs. With Reid out of the Senate, Heller took on growing responsibility for defending the state against activation of the planned, but long-delayed, Yucca Mountain nuclear waste site northwest of Las Vegas. In March 2015, Heller joined with several fellow Nevada lawmakers to introduce a bill to give the state veto power over Yucca. And when President Trump's proposed 2017 budget included a proposal to restart licensing for the repository, Heller worked across the aisle with newly elected Democratic Sen. Catherine Cortez Masto to scuttle those efforts. "Yucca is dead and this reckless proposal will not revive it," he declared. "We will not be the nation's nuclear waste dump."

As a member of the majority, Heller continued to take an eclectic mix of stances - he was ranked the seventh least conservative Republican senator in the *Almanac's* 2015 vote ratings. As a member of the majority, Heller continued to take an eclectic mix of stances. He secured passage of an amendment that would require extra training for airport and border agents in detecting possible human trafficking. He signed on to a bipartisan measure to remove marijuana from Schedule I of the Controlled Substances Act, the most stringent level. And as "the senator from the only state where sports betting is legal," Heller urged a thorough investigation of the "deflate-gate" charges against the New England Patriots. In 2017 he introduced bipartisan legislation with Ohio Democrat Sherrod Brown to support free tax preparation and filing services, and along with Michigan Democrat Debbie Stabenow put forward legislation aimed at keeping homeowners from having to pay taxes on forgiven mortgage loan debt (the foreclosure crisis continues to reverberate in Nevada).

Heller was the chief Senate sponsor of the INSPIRE Women Act, aimed at encouraging young women to pursue careers in science, technology, engineering and math fields. It received broad bipartisan support and was signed into law in early 2017. He also introduced a resolution with Republican Sens. Marco Rubio of Florida and Ted Cruz of Texas to move the U.S. embassy in Israel to Jerusalem, a pet issue of Las Vegas-based mega-donor Sheldon Adelson.

Heller backed Rubio for president and remained strongly critical of then-candidate Donald Trump throughout the campaign, refusing to say if he voted for Trump or not after floating the possibility that he may vote "none of these" (Nevada is the only state in the nation with that option on the ballot). "I'm not happy with some of the comments that he's made about women, about minority groups, about the disabled, about veterans. I mean, we can go down the list," Heller told the *Reno Gazette-Journal* in August 2016.

But at least early on in the Trump Administration, Heller made few breaks with the president. He voted to confirm all of Trump's first 19 cabinet nominees. That included a vote for Treasury Secretary Steve Mnuchin, who as former CEO of OneWest bank had made huge profits as his bank foreclosed on thousands of Nevadans during the housing crisis and who Heller had given a tough grilling in during his Senate Banking Committee confirmation hearing. He was one of a number of GOP senators who harshly criticized early Republican legislation to repeal Obamacare, but said later that spring at a private meeting with conservatives that he "will do everything I can to get to a yes" on a repeal bill.

After publicly toying with the idea of a 2018 run for governor, Heller announced in late 2016 that he'd run for reelection. He's expected to face a tough campaign in a state that's gone from Republican-leaning to Democratic-leaning in the last decade due to large growth in its Hispanic and Asian-American communities.

And Heller didn't help himself with a few early missteps, including declaring during a hostile town hall that "I will protect Planned Parenthood" and "I have no problems with federal funding for Planned Parenthood," forcing his staff to clarify that he still opposed federal funding for the organization. The moment was somewhat reminiscent of a 2014 controversy he generated for praising those who rallied to support Nevada rancher Cliven Bundy, who was in the midst of an armed standoff with federal law enforcement officers. "What Sen. Reid may call domestic terrorists, I call patriots," Heller said. But after Bundy was caught on video making racist comments, Heller backtracked, saying, "I am very quick in calling American citizens 'patriots,' maybe in this case, too quick."

Heller is the only Republican in a state Trump lost who faces reelection in 2018, making him Democrats' top target. But Democrats will need a top-tier candidate, and the state's Democratic bench took some major blows in a rough 2014 election wave. Possible Democratic challengers include former state Treasurer Kate Marshall, former state Secretary of State Ross Miller, Rep. Dina Titus, and former Rep. Steven Horsford. By late spring, Reid and Senate Democrats had rallied around first-term Rep. Jacky Rosen as the most likely challenger to Heller. Whoever is the Democratic nominee, Heller faced a costly and competitive challenge.

Junior Senator

Catherine Cortez Masto (D)

Elected 2016, term expires 2022, 1st term; b. Mar 29, 1964, Las Vegas; University of Nevada, Reno, B.S., 1986; Gonzaga University School of Law, J.D., 1990; Catholic; Married (Paul Masto).

Elected Office: NV Attorney General, 2007-2015.

Professional Career: Federal Prosecutor, U.S Attorney's Office DC; Chief of Staff, NV Governor Bob Miller.

DC Office: 204 RSOB 20510, 202-224-3542; Website: cortezmasto.senate.gov.

State Offices: Las Vegas, 702-388-5020; Reno, 775-686-5750.

Committees: *Aging*. *Banking, Housing & Urban Affairs*: Financial Institutions & Consumer Protection, Securities, Insurance & Investment. *Commerce, Science & Transportation*: Communications, Technology, Innovation & the Internet, Consumer Protection, Product Safety, Ins & Data Security. *Energy & Natural Resources*: Energy, Public Lands, Forests & Mining. *Indian Affairs*. *Rules & Administration*.

Election Results

Election	Name (Party)	Vote (%)		Cand. Spent	Ind. Exp. Support	Ind. Exp. Oppose
2016 General	Catherine Cortez Masto (D)	521,994	(47%)	$17,148,576	$6,552,180	$42,462,146
	Joe Heck (R)	495,079	(45%)	$11,707,759	$12,978,487	$38,915,182
2016 Primary	Catherine Cortez Masto (D)	81,971	(81%)			
	Allen Rheinhart (D)	5,650	(6%)			

Catherine Cortez Masto became the first Latina senator in U.S. history by winning a hard-fought 2016 election that turned into a proxy battle between outgoing Democratic Senate Minority Leader Harry Reid and the right-wing billionaire Koch brothers.

Cortez Masto is a lifelong Nevadan whose grandfather emigrated to the state from Mexico (the other side of her family is Italian). Her father, Manny Cortez, was a major player in Las Vegas and Nevada politics, who, as head of the powerful Las Vegas Convention and Visitors Authority, worked tirelessly to improve and expand the city's crucial tourism industry. Cortez Masto followed in his footsteps, earning her undergraduate degree in business administration the University of Nevada-Reno before getting her law degree from Gonzaga University.

After practicing law in Las Vegas, Cortez Masto served Democratic Gov. Bob Miller's chief of staff and as an assistant to the United States attorney general. Both of those positions ended in 2002, and she became an assistant county manager for Clark County on issues relating to juvenile detention alternatives and child services. She became Nevada's attorney general after a landslide 2006 win, receiving more votes than any other statewide candidate, and easily won reelection against a weak candidate in 2010,.

As attorney general, Cortez Masto focused on combating meth manufacturing and sale, elder abuse, and strengthening laws against sex trafficking and violence against women. She mostly received plaudits for her investigations into national banks for predatory lending and foreclosure practices after the state was rocked by the housing meltdown, including a $750 billion settlement she negotiated with Bank of America. But she took heat for her 2009 decision to prosecute then-Lieutenant Gov. Brian Krolicki, a Republican who at the time was mulling a run against Reid (her husband, a retired Secret Service agent, was scheduled to host a fundraiser for a Democrat running for Krolicki's office just days after she announced the investigation). The charges that Krolicki had mishandled the Nevada College Savings Fund were thrown out in late 2009.

Cortez Masto, long viewed as a rising political star in the state, was term limited out of office in 2014 and declined to run against popular Republican Gov. Brian Sandoval that year. But she wasn't out of the game for long. When the powerful and Machiavellian Reid decided to retire in early 2015 after sustaining major injuries in a freak accident while exercising, he was quick to throw his support behind Cortez Masto. "She has a great résumé," Reid told radio station KNPR just hours after announcing his plans to retire. "Her dad and I were friends many years ago. She has a background that really is significantly powerful. I hope she runs, and if she does I will help her."

Reid's strong support helped Cortez Masto clear the primary field (Democratic Rep. Dina Titus backed down after a brief flirtation with a run), setting her up for a slog of a race against Republican Rep. Joe Heck, a doctor and Iraq War veteran who'd won a number of tough races in previous years in a highly competitive district encompassing much of suburban Las Vegas.

The race quickly turned into a proxy war where both disciplined politicians were largely at the whims of larger forces. Reid, the puppet master of the Nevada Democratic Party machine, looked to cement his legacy by helping Democrats recapture races up and down the ballot with a heavy emphasis on keeping his famous ground game clicking on all cylinders and working behind the scenes to back his preferred candidates. He had a particular interest in seeing his seat filled by the first Latina in the Senate, a tidy way to close the loop on his decades-long efforts to bring Hispanic and other immigrant communities into the Democratic party in the state.

But his longtime nemeses, the billionaire conservative Koch brothers, had other ideas, as did national Republicans who saw the race as their only pickup opportunity in 2016. After failing to defeat Reid in 2010 and facing years of harsh criticism at the hands of the Democratic leader, the Kochs were eager to sully his record in the state. "It would certainly be poetic justice to see Harry Reid, who for so long has waged an unhinged personal vendetta against people we care a lot about, to see his seat go to someone who supports limited government, free speech," Tim Phillips, the president of the Koch-funded Americans for Prosperity, told the *New York Times* in August 2016.

Cortez Masto outspent Heck on the race by $19 million to $12 million, but that was a small sum compared to an outside spending deluge from Koch Brothers-backed organizations and other groups on both sides - more than $90 million in total.

But it was another billionaire who set the tone for the race. Then-candidate Donald Trump's harsh words about immigrants and other controversies were a big problem for Heck in the fast-diversifying state. Heck held a narrow lead in polls for much of the election cycle and tried to keep Trump at arm's length, actively avoiding Nevada's early-state caucuses and endorsing him only after he'd sewn up the nomination. After an *Access Hollywood* video of Trump bragging about sexually assaulting women surfaced, he unendorsed his party's nominee. "I cannot in good conscience continue to support Donald

Trump," Heck said at a rally, getting booed by some Republicans in the crowd. But as Trump recovered in the campaign's closing week Heck backed off that demand, calling Trump "qualified" to be president and refusing to say how he'd vote.

Cortez Masto ran as a mainline Democrat, promising to push for immigration reform, college affordability, women's rights, environmental protections, a liberal Supreme Court justice and a higher minimum wage. Her ads touted her family's immigrant roots and her work to help Nevadans who'd faced foreclosures and featured endorsements from Obama, who'd won the state twice, and Vice President Joe Biden. Heck heavily touted his experience as a military doctor and ran as a law-and-order candidate, attacking Cortez Masto for the state's rising violent crime rates, while taking a centrist tone on entitlement programs and immigration. But Cortez Masto ran ad after ad tying him to Trump and showing his earlier endorsement of the GOP presidential candidate.

Cortez Masto, a disciplined politician, remained fairly circumspect throughout the race and permitted Reid to be her attack dog as he repeatedly painted Heck as a lackey of the Koch Brothers. "Heck is an absolute stooge for these right-wing nut cases," he told the *Times*.

While Trump recovered enough to pull off a stunning electoral college victory, he failed to win Nevada - and likely dragged Heck down with him. Hillary Clinton won the state by 47.9%-45.5%, while Cortez Masto edged Heck by a very similar 47.1%-44.7%.

In the Senate, Cortez Masto secured spots on the Energy & Natural Resources and Banking, Housing & Urban Affairs Committees, both of which have jurisdiction of substantial parts of Nevada's economy, including its growing renewable wind and solar energy industries, and still struggling housing sector. She sought a lower profile than some other newly elected senators, and voted for 11 of Trump's first 21 cabinet nominations, more than most other Democrats - even those from swing states. But she was a vocal critic of Trump's immigration moves. She participated in the Women's March to protest Trump the day after his inauguration and was one of just 11 Democrats who voted against confirming Department of Homeland Security Secretary John Kelly.

The first bill she introduced in the Senate aimed at undoing Trump's executive orders that made almost all undocumented immigrants priorities for deportation and sought block funding for so-called "sanctuary cities" that don't fully cooperate with immigration authorities. "When he's talking about bad hombres, he's talking about my family," she told MSNBC during a fight between Trump and Mexico's president shortly after she took office. "Really, the only bad hombre in this scenario is the one who's sitting in the White House." She also railed against the confirmation of Treasury Secretary Steve Mnuchin, who made a lot of money heading a bank that foreclosed on thousands of Nevadans during the housing crisis. She joined Republican Sen. Dean Heller, her in-state colleague, to fight against Trump's plan to restart the planning process to open a nuclear waste repository at Yucca Mountain, calling the plan "unacceptable."

FIRST DISTRICT

Dina Titus (D)

Elected 2008, 4th term; b. May 23, 1950, Thomasville, GA; College of William and Mary (VA), A.B., 1970; University of Georgia, M.A., 1973; Florida State University, Ph.D., 1976; Greek Orthodox; Married (Thomas Clayton Wright).

Elected Office: U.S. House, 2008-2010; NV Senate, 1988-2008.

Professional Career: Professor, University of NV, Las Vegas, 1977-2011; Professor, N. TX St. University, 1975-1976.

DC Office: 2464 RHOB 20515, 202-225-5965, Fax: 202-225-3119, titus.house.gov.

State Offices: Las Vegas, 702-220-9823.

Committees: *Foreign Affairs*: Asia & the Pacific, Terrorism, Nonproliferation & Trade. *Transportation & Infrastructure*: Aviation, Highways & Transit, Water Resources & Environment.

Group Ratings

	ADA	ACLU	AFL-CIO	LCV	ITI	COC	HAFA	ACU	CFG	FRC
2016	-	94%	-	95%	83%	50%	12%	0%	4%	0%
2015	80%	C	100%	94%	C	55%	C	0%	0%	0%

Almanac Ratings 2015

	Economy	Social	Foreign	Composite
Liberal	83%	100%	99%	94%
Conservative	17%	0%	1%	6%

Key Votes of the 114th Congress

1. Keystone Pipeline	N	5. Puerto Rico Debt	Y	9. Offenses by Aliens	N
2. Trade Deals	N	6. Medical Marijuana	Y	10. Troops in Iraq	Y
3. Export-Import Bank	Y	7. Sanctuary Cities	N	11. Homeland Security $$	Y
4. Debt Ceiling Increase	Y	8. Armor-piercing Bullets	N	12. Trade Adjustment aid	Y

Election Results

Election	Name (Party)	Vote (%)		Cand. Spent	Ind. Exp. Support	Ind. Exp. Oppose
2016 General	Dina Titus (D)	116,537	(62%)	$534,682	$15,193	
	Mary Perry (R)	54,174	(29%)	$27,366		
	Reuben D'Silva (I)	13,185	(7%)	$22,618		
2016 Primary	Dina Titus (D)	15,549	(82%)			
	Jose Solorio (D)	1,774	(9%)			
	Patrick Boylan (D)	1,552	(8%)			

Prior winning percentages: 2014 (57%), 2012 (64%), 2008 (47%)

Democrat Dina Titus was elected to Nevada's 1st District House seat in 2012 after losing reelection two years earlier in a more competitive district. An open seat gave her an opportunity to move to a liberal, Las Vegas-based district that was safe for a Democrat. A political science professor, she has continued to welcome political challenges.

Raised in Tifton, Georgia, Titus retained her thick Southern drawl. "I get teased a lot because I haven't lost the accent, but that's kind of become part of how people know me," she told *National Journal*. Her upbringing gave her a strong interest in politics. She recalls listening to local politicians talk shop at her grandfather's Greek restaurant across from the courthouse. Her father ran for city council, and her Republican "black sheep" uncle, as she puts it, served in the Georgia Legislature.

Titus attended the College of William and Mary, where she majored in political science; she later obtained a master's degree from the University of Georgia and a doctorate from Florida State University. After teaching at the University of North Texas, she joined the faculty at the University of Nevada, Las Vegas. She taught there for 34 years, until she retired in 2011. Titus has authored two nonfiction books, *Bombs in the Backyard: Atomic Testing and American Politics*, and *Battle Born: Federal-State Relations in Nevada During the Twentieth Century*. Her husband, Tom Wright, is a Latin American history professor at UNLV. In 1988, Titus put her political knowledge to use and was elected to the Nevada Senate, where she was minority leader for 16 years. She became an advocate for people with disabilities and her work was recognized when a Las Vegas affordable-housing complex for the disabled was named after her. In 2006, she lost a run for governor to Republican Jim Gibbons.

In 2008, Titus ran successfully for the House, defeating Republican incumbent Jon Porter. That tenure was short-lived. She was swept out of office by the Republican wave in 2010, losing a bruising battle to Republican Joe Heck by 1,748 votes out of more than 314,000 cast. She ran in 2012 in the 1st District, with its 2-1 Democratic edge in voter registration. Democratic state Sen. Ruben Kihuen also got in the race but withdrew after Titus significantly outraised him. In November, she largely avoided engaging Republican Chris Edwards, a Navy officer making his first foray into politics. Abortion rights groups NARAL Pro-Choice America PAC and EMILY's List endorsed Titus. She won, 64%-32%.

Following her return to the House, Titus was the ranking Democrat on the Veterans' Affairs Subcommittee on Disability Assistance and Memorial Affairs. She filed bills that would overturn the VA's prohibition on doctors signing off on marijuana for patients and to permit same-sex couples to be eligible for veterans' benefits. In 2017, she left the Veterans panel to join the Foreign Affairs Committee. On the Transportation and Infrastructure Committee Titus has been an enthusiastic advocate of reopening rail service from Las Vegas to Los Angeles, perhaps with a private partner. Amtrak shut down the line in 1997. She has strongly opposed creating a nuclear waste dump at Yucca Mountain, and has been a staunch ally of the casinos.

Titus voiced interest in a 2016 run for the Senate seat of retiring Majority Leader Harry Reid. But Reid, with whom Titus had a distant relationship, was firmly behind former state Attorney General

Catherine Cortez-Masto for the Democratic nomination. Titus decided "I just love representing Nevada's 1st District." Having lost two elections in the past decade, she was circumspect about giving up her safe seat in the House. She has breezed to reelection. She kept her options open on a possible challenge to Republican Sen. Dean Heller in 2018.

Las Vegas

Population		**Race and Ethnicity**		**Income**	
Total	675,450	White	33.8%	Median Income	$38,241 (408 out of 435)
Land area	105	Black	9.9%		
Pop/ sq mi	6463.6	Latino	44.4%		
Born in state	8.5%	Asian	8.0%	Under $50,000	62.7%
		Two races	2.7%	$50,000-$99,999	26.5%
Age Groups		Other	1.2%	$100,000-$199,999	9.2%
Under 18	23.2%			$200,000 or more	1.6%
18-34	25.1%	**Education**		Poverty Rate	22.7%
35-64	39.3%	H.S grad or less	56.1%		
Over 64	12.4%	Some college	29.0%	**Health Insurance**	
		College Degree, 4 yr	10.3%	With health insurance coverage	73.6%
Work		Post grad	4.5%		
White Collar	17.4%				
Sales and Service	62.5%	**Military**		**Public Assistance**	
Blue Collar	20.2%	Veteran	8.2%	Cash public assistance income	4.3%
Government	88.1%	Active Duty	0.1%		
				Food stamp/SNAP benefits	19.3%

Voter Turnout			
2015 Total Citizens 18+	395,506	2016 House Turnout as % CVAP	48%
2016 House turnout	188,352	2014 House Turnout as % CVAP	20%

2012 Presidential Vote		
Barack Obama	123,205	(65%)
Mitt Romney	60,812	(32%)

2016 Presidential Vote		
Hillary Clinton	121,321	(62%)
Donald Trump	64,233	(33%)
Gary Johnson	5,406	(3%)

Cook Partisan Voting Index: D+15

Las Vegas, that garish and improbable city, had a fittingly colorful beginning. It began as a Paiute Indian settlement that in the late 1700s served as a watering stop for Spanish priests making the 1,200-mile trek between New Mexico and California. By the 1800s, the Old Spanish Trail, as it came to be known, was used by horse and mule smugglers, by explorers like John C. Fremont, and by Mormon emigrants heading west. Las Vegas was still a small crossroads when Nevada, its mining industry a shambles, legalized gambling in the 1930s. The WPA Guide to Nevada, published in 1940 when the city had 10,000 people, describes a prim Las Vegas: "Relatively little emphasis is placed on the gambling clubs and divorce facilities - though they are attractions to many visitors - and much effort is being made to build up cultural attractions."

All that changed big-time after World War II, when gangster Bugsy Siegel built the Flamingo hotel and casino on what became the Strip south of the city limits. Pseudo-romantic architectural themes became the order of the day (flamingos are found in the waters of Florida, not in the deserts of Nevada), and one casino followed another. Organized crime provided much of the money and muscle for Las Vegas, and investment capital came from Teamsters pension funds. In the late 1960s, eccentric billionaire Howard Hughes moved into the Desert Inn, bought most of the casinos, and hired Mormons to run them. After Hughes abruptly left town, most of his hotels eventually were torn down, and other operators built casinos like Caesars Palace, Circus Circus, the Mirage, Excalibur, the lavish Bellagio and the Venetian, which remains the largest. In the 1970s, the casinos were the haven of flashy high rollers, of Frank Sinatra and showgirls.

By the 1990s, diversification became the buzzword. Las Vegas began to produce more family-oriented entertainment, shopping, and even high art, with the Bellagio's museum-quality collection on view. Las Vegas also built the biggest convention center in the country. But the city has not neglected its core clientele: people who fly in from elsewhere to be entertained, and to be, for a weekend, maybe even a little naughty. "What happens in Vegas stays in Vegas," remained the unofficial motto. In 2016, gambling had dropped to 34 percent of casino revenue on the Strip (compared with 58 percent in 1990), with increasing amounts of money spent on food, beverages and all sorts of entertainment. The scent of the underworld has not entirely disappeared. The flashy Oscar Goodman, a former mob lawyer, was elected mayor and actively promoted the city. Barred from seeking a fourth term in 2011, his wife, Carolyn, succeeded him and won a second term in April 2015. She continued his habit of taking scantily clad showgirls to events promoting the city.

Because of the city's dependence on leisure-time spending, the recession hit hard here and persisted long after other areas recovered, with gambling down, joblessness up and many new homes unsold. The unemployment rate climbed above 14 percent in 2010, higher than in any other metropolitan area. In December, it had dropped to 5.1 percent, slightly above the national average. The recovery in the housing market remained very slow. In 2011, the average home value had declined a staggering 58 percent since 2006. Finally, in May 2016, the *Las Vegas Sun* headlined a story, "Las Vegas housing market rising from the grave." Homeowners with underwater mortgages had dropped to 21 percent from 71 percent in 2012. There also was good news on the strip. In 2016, casinos reported their first profits since 2008. They had record revenues of $26 billion and attendance of 43 million visitors. Gambling accounted for only 34 percent of casino revenue, down from 58 percent in 1990. The new visitors were more interested in shopping, concerts and nightlife. At Planet Hollywood, resident entertainer Britney Spears was grossing nearly $500,000 per show. The newest big business in Vegas has become professional sports. The Oakland Raiders made plans to move their NFL franchise into the desert. After extended debate, the state Legislature approved increased hotel taxes to support bonds for Clark County to build a huge new stadium to house the team. An expansion franchise was scheduled to join the National Hockey League in October 2017.

The 1st Congressional District of Nevada consists of the inner core of Las Vegas that visitors are most likely to see. They cross into it as soon as they drive their rental cars out of the lot at McCarran International Airport. On the three-mile Strip are the nation's 11 largest hotels, each with thousands of rooms that extend far back on their properties. The District is 47 percent Hispanic, the highest proportion in the state, and is the only solidly Democratic district in Nevada. Even with the vaunted Democratic machine across the state, the 62 percent vote for Hillary Clinton in 2016 fell from 65 percent for President Barack Obama in 2012.

SECOND DISTRICT

Mark Amodei (R)

Elected 2011, 4th term; b. Jun 12, 1958, Carson City; University of the Pacific McGeorge School of Law (CA), J.D.; University of Nevada, Reno, B.A.; Presbyterian; Divorced; 2 children.

Military Career: U.S. Army JAG, 1983-1987.

Professional Career: NV Assembly, 1997-1998; NV Senate, 1999-2010.

DC Office: 332 CHOB 20515, 202-225-6155, Fax: 202-225-5679, amodei.house.gov.

State Offices: Elko, 775-777-7705; Reno, 775-686-5760.

Committees: *Appropriations*: Financial Services & General Government, Interior, Environment & Related Agencies, Legislative Branch.

Group Ratings

	ADA	ACLU	AFL-CIO	LCV	ITI	COC	HAFA	ACU	CFG	FRC
2016	-	5%	-	3%	100%	100%	54%	76%	66%	92%
2015	0%	C	9%	3%	C	80%	C	67%	69%	92%

Almanac Ratings 2015

	Economy	Social	Foreign	Composite
Liberal	13%	11%	0%	8%
Conservative	88%	90%	100%	92%

Key Votes of the 114th Congress

1. Keystone Pipeline	Y	5. Puerto Rico Debt	Y	9. Offenses by Aliens	Y
2. Trade Deals	NV	6. Medical Marijuana	N	10. Troops in Iraq	N
3. Export-Import Bank	Y	7. Sanctuary Cities	Y	11. Homeland Security $$	N
4. Debt Ceiling Increase	N	8. Armor-piercing Bullets	Y	12. Trade Adjustment aid	N

Election Results

Election	Name (Party)	Vote	(%)	Cand. Spent	Ind. Exp. Support	Ind. Exp. Oppose
2016 General	Mark Amodei (R)	182,676	(58%)	$785,552		
	Chip Evans (D)	115,722	(37%)	$204,748		
2016 Primary	Mark Amodei (R)		(100%)			

Prior winning percentages: 2014 (66%), 2012 (58%), 2011 special (62%)

Republican Mark Amodei won a 2011 special election to fill the seat of now-GOP Sen. Dean Heller. A former state Senate president pro tempore and state party chairman, Amodei is a small-government conservative whose governing experience has allied him with the party establishment in pushing for legislation on multiple fronts.

Amodei grew up in Carson City, Nevada's capital, the son of an Italian immigrant father who worked for the state Forestry Division and a mother who was a physician. He attended the University of Nevada at Reno, where he joined ROTC, and earned a law degree from the University of the Pacific's McGeorge School of Law. He joined the Army and became a prosecutor for the Judge Advocate General Corps, handling criminal matters.

After opening a law practice in his hometown, Amodei was elected to the state Assembly and then to the state Senate, where he chaired the Judiciary Committee and then took his leadership post. In 2003, Amodei worked on a comprehensive tax bill that would have raised $900 million in taxes over two years, which drew criticism when he later ran for Congress. In 2007, Amodei became president of the Nevada Mining Association. He said that he saw no conflict of interest with his work as a senator, but a year and a half later he stepped down from the organization because, he said, he didn't want to have a "distracting" dual role during the legislative session.

In 2009, Amodei announced a challenge to powerful Senate Majority Leader Harry Reid, portraying himself as a common-sense conservative who could appeal to independent voters. He dropped out of the contest six months later, explaining that he was able to raise only about $80,000, a pittance compared to Reid's multimillion-dollar war chest.

When Heller was appointed to the Senate in May 2011 to replace Republican John Ensign, who resigned amid a sex scandal with the wife of one of his former aides, Amodei announced his bid for Heller's seat and won the nomination with ease during a meeting of the GOP state Central Committee members. In the special-election matchup, Democratic state Treasurer Kate Marshall boasted of support from the National Rifle Association and said that she would have voted against increasing the federal debt ceiling, which Amodei also opposed. Amodei played up his conservative credentials, calling for tax cuts, passage of a balanced-budget amendment to the Constitution and opening more public lands to domestic oil and gas production. He used an ad with his mother to deflect the Medicare attacks. The National Republican Congressional Committee pumped in more than $600,000 to pummel Marshall, and the Democratic Congressional Campaign Committee never came to her rescue. Amodei won, 58%-36%.

Amodei has been an often pragmatic conservative in the House, who emphasizes spending discipline. He has brought a home-spun approach to his job, and believes that lawmakers need to talk more with each other. When Amodei is on the House floor, said Republican Rep. James Renacci of Ohio, "Everybody knows him and sees him as someone they can work with." Democratic Rep. John Garamendi of California told the *Reno Gazette-Journal* that Amodei "knows the legislative process," and they have worked together on issues related to Lake Tahoe. In December 2016, Amodei and Garamendi joined with others to enact the Lake Tahoe Restoration Act to "keep Tahoe blue."

On the Appropriations Committee, he won approval of his provision to protect the water rights of private land-holders. He has been vice chairman of the Legislative Branch Subcommittee. As vice chairman of the Western Caucus, Amodei has concentrated on natural resource issues. In contrast to the hardline opposition of many in Nevada, he said that the Yucca Mountain proposed burial site for high-level nuclear waste storage should be examined instead as a potential home for nuclear reprocessing and research. Nevada could become "the world-wide leader in reprocessing the fuel so it becomes a commodity instead of trash," he told the *Nevada Appeal* in July 2016. With Heller, he filed legislation in January 2017 to expedite the permitting process for mines in Nevada and across the country.

In a May 2015 interview with the *Sparks Tribune*, Amodei said that the problems of immigration are "eminently solvable," except that "everybody's got a political angle." In his view, "I'd rather be criticized for trying to do something because I'm tired of defending nothing." He reached across the aisle to Democrat Jared Polis of Colorado to seek common ground on the topic. Following the 2016 election, he said, "If you're going to put immigration on the table, well, we're coming to dinner."

Amodei quickly ruled out running for Reid's open Senate seat in 2016. But he kept the door open to run for attorney general in 2018. During the final weeks of the 2016 contest, while he was the Nevada campaign chairman for Donald Trump, he said that some of the criticism and outrage over Trump's comments about women were "appropriate and deserved." But he stood by Trump. "I am genuinely concerned about the future of our country, and who will set the tone," Amodei said. "The present political wars have accomplished nothing. I want to try a new direction."

Northern Nevada: Reno

Population		**Race and Ethnicity**		**Income**	
Total	690,426	White	67.7%	Median Income	$53,988 (200 out of 435)
Land area	55,830	Black	1.8%	Under $50,000	46.6%
Pop/ sq mi	12.4	Latino	21.6%	$50,000-$99,999	31.8%
Born in state	5.9%	Asian	3.9%	$100,000-$199,999	18.0%
Age Groups		Two races	2.6%	$200,000 or more	3.8%
Under 18	22.8%	Other	2.5%	Poverty Rate	14.6%
18-34	22.6%	**Education**		**Health Insurance**	
35-64	39.7%	H.S grad or less	39.1%	With health insurance coverage	83.6%
Over 64	14.9%	Some college	35.8%	**Public Assistance**	
Work		College Degree, 4 yr	16.1%	Cash public assistance income	3.2%
White Collar	31.3%	Post grad	9.0%	Food stamp/SNAP benefits	10.4%
Sales and Service	46.4%	**Military**			
Blue Collar	22.2%	Veteran	11.3%		
Government	78.0%	Active Duty	0.3%		

Voter Turnout			
2015 Total Citizens 18+	486,894	2016 House Turnout as % CVAP	64%
2016 House turnout	313,336	2014 House Turnout as % CVAP	38%

2012 Presidential Vote		
Mitt Romney	155,186	(53%)
Barack Obama	131,540	(45%)

2016 Presidential Vote		
Donald Trump	169,631	(52%)
Hillary Clinton	129,317	(40%)
Gary Johnson	13,966	(4%)

Cook Partisan Voting Index: R+7

Outside of metro Las Vegas, huge, empty and mountainous Nevada has only one sizable population center, a cluster of small cities and towns near the border with California: the casino cities of Reno and Sparks, the small capital of Carson City, the restored Comstock Lode boomtown of Virginia City, and the resort areas that surround (and endanger) the deep, impossibly blue waters of Lake Tahoe. Reno is so remote from Las Vegas that the only quick way to get there is by air; it takes more than nine hours to drive (although the spectacularly stark scenery makes it time well spent). Ghost towns that once bustled with miners dot the parched, sand-swept deserts, and in some places the land remains distinctly rutted from the wagon trains that crossed here more than 100 years ago. Today, Nevada's small towns survive on mining, ranching and, in some cases, servicing the human sins of greed and lust: Nevada's legal brothels are generally found in the small, desert counties. Another distinction is the Basque influence. Immigrant Basque shepherds once tended their flocks in remote portions of northern Nevada; Basque festivals, social clubs and restaurants can still be found in Winnemucca and Elko.

The military has holdings in the Nevada interior, including the Fallon Naval Air Station, home to the Navy Fighter Weapons "Top Gun" School. Many places in Nevada depend on other federal government programs: The Newlands Irrigation Project near Fallon was among the first of its kind. Nevada's gold-mining operations, booming since 2000, do not have to pay royalties to the government, thanks to the Mining Act of 1872. The spread of legalized gambling throughout the country has hurt Reno. In 2016, it had only 7 per cent of the casino revenues in Nevada. Instead, economic diversification has come with solar and wind-energy enterprises and high-precision technologies. Northern Nevada planned to add about 50,000 jobs - many of them tech-related -- between 2014 and 2019, the Economic Planning Indicator Committee reported. Electric-car manufacturer Tesla Motors planned to complete in 2018 a huge factory near Sparks, with lower-cost cell production for its batteries. The facility, which it called the Gigafactory, will produce more lithium ion batteries annually than were produced worldwide in 2013. In January 2017, Apple announced plans for a joint venture with the utility NV Energy to build a massive solar plant in Nevada to power its huge data centers in the Reno area.

The 2nd Congressional District of Nevada takes in Reno and Carson City in territory that covers nearly the northern half of Nevada. It includes Churchill, Pershing, Humboldt and Elko counties. Washoe County, which includes Reno and Sparks, has nearly two-thirds of the district's population. Washoe was an important swing county in the 2016 presidential election; Hillary Clinton won it, 46%-45%. Donald Trump won each of the outlying counties with more than 60 percent of the vote and took the 2nd comfortably, 52%-40%. This was the only Nevada district where he won a majority of the vote.

THIRD DISTRICT

Jacky Rosen (D)

Elected 2016, 1st term; b. Aug 02, 1957, Chicago, IL; University of Minnesota, B.A., 1979; Jewish; Married (Larry Rosen); 1 child.

Professional Career: Business Owner; Computer programmer/ software developer.

DC Office: 413 CHOB 20515, 202-225-3252, Fax: 202-225-2185, rosen.house.gov.

State Offices: Las Vegas, 702-963-9500.

Committees: *Armed Services*: Military Personnel, Tactical Air & Land Forces. *Science, Space & Technology*: Energy, Research & Technology.

Election Results

Election	Name (Party)	Vote (%)		Cand. Spent	Ind. Exp. Support	Ind. Exp. Oppose
2016 General	Jacky Rosen (D)	146,869	(47%)	$1,670,325	$910,601	$7,986,608
	Danny Tarkanian (R)	142,926	(46%)	$1,914,432	$841,133	$8,051,158
2016 Primary	Jacky Rosen (D)	14,219	(62%)			
	Jesse Sbaih (D)	2,928	(13%)			
	Barry Michaels (D)	2,218	(10%)			
	Steven Schiffman (D)	1,237	(5%)			

Democrat Jacky Rosen was elected in 2016 to an open seat that was one of the closest and most expensive House campaigns in the nation. A political newcomer, she prevailed with a low-profile appeal amid better-known and more controversial candidates during the campaign in Nevada.

Rosen was raised in Chicago and got her bachelor's degree in psychology from the University of Minnesota. She was the first in her family to graduate from college. She discovered an affinity for computer science and developed her skills independently in the school's math lab during her free time.

Her parents had moved to Las Vegas while she was in college. So Rosen moved west too, where she worked at Summa Corp. as a computer programmer. Eventually, she started her own consulting firm. She was actively involved with her faith-based community, as president of Congregation Ner Tamid in Henderson. During that time, Rosen worked on issues such as energy conservation, senior taxes and homelessness.

When Republican Rep. Joe Heck decided to run for the Senate, both parties had wide-open primaries. Rosen was unknown to most Nevadans, according to the *Las Vegas Review Journal.* She took mostly conventional Democratic views and was backed by Senate Majority Leader Harry Reid, who was a native of Searchlight in this district and had failed to convince other candidates to run in the contest. She had a relatively easy time in the Democratic primary, with 62 percent of the vote against five other candidates. Danny Tarkanian, a businessman, outspoken conservative and son of legendary UNLV basketball coach Jerry Tarkanian, had previously lost four election campaigns, including two bids for Congress, and had a tougher challenge in his seven-candidate Republican primary. He got 32 percent to 24 percent for runner-up Michael Roberson, who had been a leader in the state Senate and was backed by much of the GOP establishment, including Gov. Brian Sandoval.

In the general election, Rosen continued to have low name identification with the voters. "Democrats don't need to know" who Rosen is, Reid said in an interview with *The Las Vegas Sun* two weeks before the election. "They know who Tarkanian is. They're going to be fine." In fact, Democratic groups and their allies spent more than $6 million to assist the voters, including extensive advertising that described Tarkanian's business practices as shady. Tarkanian largely failed to respond to the charges. "I don't have the bandwidth to fight that, and I don't want to be on the defensive," he told a campaign event. But Republican groups spent more than $9 million on his behalf. Rosen and Tarkanian each raised nearly $2 million of their own. Democrats were counting on coattails from their presidential nominee Hillary Clinton, though it turned out that she narrowly trailed in this district. In contrast to other Republican candidates in Nevada, Tarkanian remained loyal to GOP presidential nominee Donald Trump. Rosen proved successful with what the *Sun* described as her "under the radar" strategy. She won, 47.2%-46.0%, a margin of 3,943 votes.

Rosen got a seat on the House Armed Services Committee, which will be helpful in advocating the interests of the Nellis and Creech Air Force Bases in Nevada (though they are north of her district), plus an assignment to the Science, Space and Technology Committee. By June 2017, Democrats in Nevada and Washington said that Rosen was making plans to challenge Republican Sen. Dean Heller, who was the prime Senate Democratic target for 2018. Rosen might find herself in another contest as a "generic Democrat" against an unpopular Republican.

Southern Las Vegas area: Henderson

Population		**Race and Ethnicity**		**Income**	
Total	723,741	White	58.6%	Median Income	$63,360 (109 out of 435)
Land area	2,849	Black	6.7%		
Pop/ sq mi	254.0	Latino	16.6%		
Born in state	5.7%	Asian	12.8%	Under $50,000	37.8%
		Two races	4.0%	$50,000-$99,999	35.4%
Age Groups		Other	1.4%	$100,000-$199,999	21.2%
Under 18	22.3%			$200,000 or more	5.6%
18-34	22.7%	**Education**		Poverty Rate	9.4%
35-64	40.8%	H.S grad or less	33.0%		
Over 64	14.2%	Some college	35.4%	**Health Insurance**	
		College Degree, 4 yr	20.8%	With health insurance coverage	87.0%
Work		Post grad	10.8%		
White Collar	33.9%				
Sales and Service	52.9%	**Military**		**Public Assistance**	
Blue Collar	13.2%	Veteran	9.9%	Cash public assistance income	2.0%
Government	84.0%	Active Duty	0.1%		
				Food stamp/SNAP benefits	6.3%

Voter Turnout			
2015 Total Citizens 18+	515,536	2016 House Turnout as % CVAP	60%
2016 House turnout	310,963	2014 House Turnout as % CVAP	28%

2012 Presidential Vote		
Mitt Romney	138,238	(49%)
Barack Obama	140,501	(49%)

2016 Presidential Vote		
Donald Trump	154,814	(48%)
Hillary Clinton	151,552	(47%)
Gary Johnson	9,971	(3%)

Cook Partisan Voting Index: R+2

Las Vegas, "The Meadows" in Spanish, began as a stop along the Old Spanish Trail trading route between Santa Fe and California in the 1830s. Water from artesian wells had created vast grasslands in the area and let traders replenish their supplies. In the early 20th century, Las Vegas was a terminus of the Las Vegas & Tonopah Railroad, a link to Nevada's silver mines. Even at the end of the 1930s, soon after gambling was legalized in Nevada, it was still a town of less than 10,000. Then came decades of amazing growth, as Las Vegas became America's destination for gambling and entertainment. From 2000 to 2008, the Las Vegas metropolitan area grew by 36 percent, to 1.9 million, making it one of the five fastest-growing metropolitan areas in America. It spread across the desert in every direction from the few blocks around Fremont Street that it occupied in the 1930s, and today it is an exuberant, undisciplined and chaotic city. Following the fast pace of building, Las Vegas was particularly hard hit by the crisis in the credit markets, and the red-hot real estate market tanked. The metro area had the highest foreclosure rate in the nation in 2010, according to *RealtyTrac*. In 2014, the foreclosures remained high enough that Henderson created a registry to monitor abandoned properties.

The 3rd Congressional District covers the southern part of Clark County and several Las Vegas suburbs. It includes retiree communities, small blue-collar towns such as Blue Diamond, and a variety of planned, and often gated, areas like Summerlin South, where young families have sought job opportunities and retired baby boomers have purchased vacation homes. Gypsum Resources has planned to build thousands of homes near Blue Diamond, but local groups have stalled the project with the County Commission because of their concern about damage to the ecosystem. Southeast of Las Vegas, the district takes in the population hub of Henderson, and Boulder City, originally built for federal workers at Hoover Dam. (Under an old agreement with the federal government, Boulder City is the only place in Nevada where gambling and prostitution are prohibited.) After the dam was completed, many of the workers unexpectedly decided to stay in the hot desert. The sale of liquor was legalized in 1969. Interstate 11 was scheduled to open in 2018 with a by-pass around Boulder City, through the Eldorado Mountains overlooking Lake Mead. Henderson resumed its rapid growth following the recession and has a population of 285,000. Fun fact: Henderson provides tours of its "Artisan Booze" district.

The 3rd includes the Nevada half of Lake Mohave on the Arizona border, plus the state's southernmost tip, including Searchlight, the hometown of former Senate Majority Leader Harry Reid. Amid a local gold rush, Reid in 2014 sold his home and 110 acres of land, plus the water and mining rights, to a mining company for $1.75 million. The 3rd, with a growing 17 percent Latino population, is politically competitive. After President Barack Obama twice won the district, Donald Trump in 2016 took it, 48%-47%.

FOURTH DISTRICT

Ruben Kihuen (D)

Elected 2016, 1st term; b. Apr 25, 1980, Guadalajara, JL; Community College of Southern Nevada (CCSN); University of Nevada - Las Vegas, B.S.; University of Oklahoma (OK); Catholic; Single.

Elected Office: NV Assembly, 2007-2010; NV Senate, 2011-2016, Majority Whip, 2013-2014, Minority Whip, 2016.

Professional Career: Academic adviser, College of Southern Nevada; Staff, Sen. Harry Reid, 2004-2006.

DC Office: 313 CHOB 20515, 202-225-9894, Fax: 202-225-9783; Website: kihuen.house.gov.

State Offices: North Las Vegas, 702-274-1707.

Committees: *Financial Services*: Housing & Insurance, Terrorism & Illicit Finance.

Election Results

Election	Name (Party)	Vote (%)	Cand. Spent	Ind. Exp. Support	Ind. Exp. Oppose
2016 General	Ruben Kihuen (D)	128,985 (49%)	$2,203,305	$4,146,541	$5,516,253
	Cresent Hardy (R)	118,328 (45%)	$1,863,757	$492,374	$2,760,022
	Steve Brown (L)	10,206 (4%)			
2016 Primary	Ruben Kihuen (D)	12,220 (40%)			
	Lucy Flores (D)	7,848 (26%)			
	Susie Lee (D)	6,405 (21%)			
	Morse Arberry (D)	1,900 (6%)			

Democrat Ruben Kihuen was one of six challengers who defeated House Republican incumbents in 2016. Widely acclaimed by Democrats as a rising star, the 36-year-old had already served 10 years in the Nevada Legislature and earlier made an aborted bid for Congress. But his victory was narrow and he might face a competitive challenge in 2018.

Kihuen was born in Guadalajara, Mexico, and moved to the United States when he was a child. His father, who had been a school teacher, left the family to find work across the border as a farmworker. Two years later, his mother accompanied the remainder of the family to reunite with their husband and father; she took a job as a housekeeper in a hotel. They eventually settled in Las Vegas and became citizens. Kihuen said that he first became interested in running for public office while attending Rancho High School, when he volunteered his time to talk door-to-door with Nevada residents. He graduated from the University of Nevada, Las Vegas, with a bachelor's in education. He served four years in the state Assembly and was elected to the Senate in 2010, where he served for six years. One of the youngest senators ever elected in Nevada, he worked with Republicans to enact need-based grants for low-income Nevadans seeking college degrees.

In the 2012 campaign, Kihuen was an early candidate for the open seat in the Las Vegas-based 1st District. But he withdrew in February as former Rep. Dina Titus significantly outraised him. Titus took the primary without opposition and easily won the general election.

In 2016, Kihuen challenged first-term Republican Rep. Cresent Hardy, who was an unexpected winner in 2014 against freshman African-American Democratic Rep. Steven Horsford. Hardy had taken advantage of growing discontent with President Barack Obama and a low turnout among Democratic voters. He became a top Democratic target for 2016. This time, Kihuen got early support from Democratic leaders in Nevada, chiefly Senate Democratic Leader Harry Reid, whom Kihuen had once served as a junior aide. Unlike 2012, he had no problem raising money. In the eight-candidate primary, his chief competitor was Lucy Flores, a former member of the Assembly who had backed Bernie Sanders in the presidential primary. Kihuen won the low-turnout primary, with 40 percent to 26 percent for Flores.

Against Hardy, Kihuen spent time telling his life story. "He is an embodiment of the dream our members have for their children," former Culinary Union political director Yvanna Cancela told the *Las Vegas Sun*. Hardy distanced himself from some of the harder-edge Republican views, including their opposition to Obama's efforts to stop deportation of children of undocumented immigrants. His supporters tried to depict Kihuen as a policy lightweight. But Hardy faced an uphill battle, especially with turnout that was more than double the total vote in his 2014 victory. In addition to the roughly $2 million that each candidate raised, both parties spent heavily on this contest: more than $6 million by Republicans and $5 million by Democrats and their allies. Kihuen won, 48.5%-44.5%. The outcome for Kihuen was close enough that " he's not a lock for a second term," wrote David Wasserman of the *Cook Political Report*.

Kihuen got a seat on the influential Financial Services Committee. When his appointment was announced, he recounted that he was among the many who had their home foreclosed in Las Vegas during the 2008 recession. "As a Latino, I'll fight to make sure undeserved communities can benefit from the nation's economic recovery by increasing access to capital for minority-owned businesses," he said. He was eager to support legislation for a path to citizenship for undocumented immigrants who worked in the United States.

Central Nevada: Northern Las Vegas area

Population		**Race and Ethnicity**		**Income**	
Total	709,019	White	47.3%	Median Income	$53,073 (209 out of 435)
Land area	50,998	Black	13.8%		
Pop/ sq mi	13.9	Latino	28.4%		
Born in state	6.9%	Asian	5.3%	Under $50,000	46.7%
		Two races	3.5%	$50,000-$99,999	34.4%
Age Groups		Other	1.6%	$100,000-$199,999	16.2%
Under 18	26.2%			$200,000 or more	2.7%
18-34	23.2%	**Education**		Poverty Rate	15.7%
35-64	37.7%	H.S grad or less	45.8%		
Over 64	13.0%	Some college	34.8%	**Health Insurance**	
		College Degree, 4 yr	12.7%	With health insurance coverage	82.1%
Work		Post grad	6.7%		
White Collar	26.9%				
Sales and Service	54.0%	**Military**		**Public Assistance**	
Blue Collar	19.1%	Veteran	12.0%	Cash public assistance income	3.6%
Government	80.0%	Active Duty	1.1%		
				Food stamp/SNAP benefits	13.1%

Voter Turnout			
2015 Total Citizens 18+	465,863	2016 House Turnout as % CVAP	57%
2016 House turnout	265,846	2014 House Turnout as % CVAP	28%

2012 Presidential Vote		
Barack Obama	136,124	(54%)
Mitt Romney	109,329	(44%)

2016 Presidential Vote		
Hillary Clinton	137,070	(50%)
Donald Trump	123,380	(45%)
Gary Johnson	8,041	(3%)

Cook Partisan Voting Index: D+3

A vast majority of the land in Nevada is owned by the federal government - a constant source of tension with local officials, ranchers, loggers and miners. Their pursuits, frequently solitary and often ornery, shaped Nevada's culture from its earliest days. On the desolate frontier, speculation runs wild: Art Bell used to broadcast his popular radio show about the paranormal, aliens and other unexplained phenomena from tiny Pahrump. The federal government's top-secret aviation experiments at places like Area 51 on the Nellis Air Force Gunnery Range have stoked UFO lore to the point that adjoining Route 375 was rededicated as the Extraterrestrial Highway in 1996.

Anti-establishment views also flourish here in more mainstream ways. Nevada residents and most of its politicians have long opposed a nuclear waste repository 1,000 feet beneath Yucca Mountain, 90 miles northwest of Las Vegas. Congress finally approved the project in 2002. President Barack Obama shelved it and a commission recommended alternative storage options. With the arrival of President Donald Trump, Republicans - including some in Nevada - considered new options. Another controversy was the December 2015 agreement by the Legislature to provide more than $200 million in tax incentives to the Farraday Future company to build an electric-car plant in north Las Vegas. Construction was unexpectedly suspended in November 2016. Executives of the firm, which was financed by a Chinese billionaire, assured state officials that their plans were proceeding.

The vast interior away from Las Vegas includes the 3-million-acre Nellis Air Force range. Also found here is the Energy Department's Nevada National Security Site, which was created by President Harry Truman. More than 800 underground tests of nuclear weapons were conducted here, as well as 100 above ground tests, before they ended in 1962. The explosions left the Rhode Island-sized facility pockmarked with unstable "subsidence craters" as far as the eye can see. In a potentially significant twist, Nye County officials in 2015 approved the shipment of uranium waste from the Oak Ridge National Laboratory in Tennessee to a landfill at the nuclear site. Yucca Mountain also is located in Nye County.

As of the 2010 census, the 4th District is a rural and suburban mix that sprawls across most of southern Nevada. It contains much of North Las Vegas and stretches north into the state's interior. The northern part of Clark County, as well as Esmeralda, Mineral, White Pine (and the city of Ely), Nye and Lincoln counties are in the district. Clark County, which dropped from 61 percent non-Hispanic white in 2000 to 45 percent in 2015, has become one of the largest majority-minority counties in the nation, with 31 percent Hispanic, 12 percent black and 10 percent Asian. Nearly 90 percent of the district vote is cast in Clark. Democrats had a voter registration edge of 46%-33% and Hillary Clinton took the 4th in 2016 by four percentage points. President Barack Obama won it by 10 points in 2012 and 15 points in 2008. The district, which is 28 percent Hispanic and 15 percent black, has become competitive.

★ NEW HAMPSHIRE ★

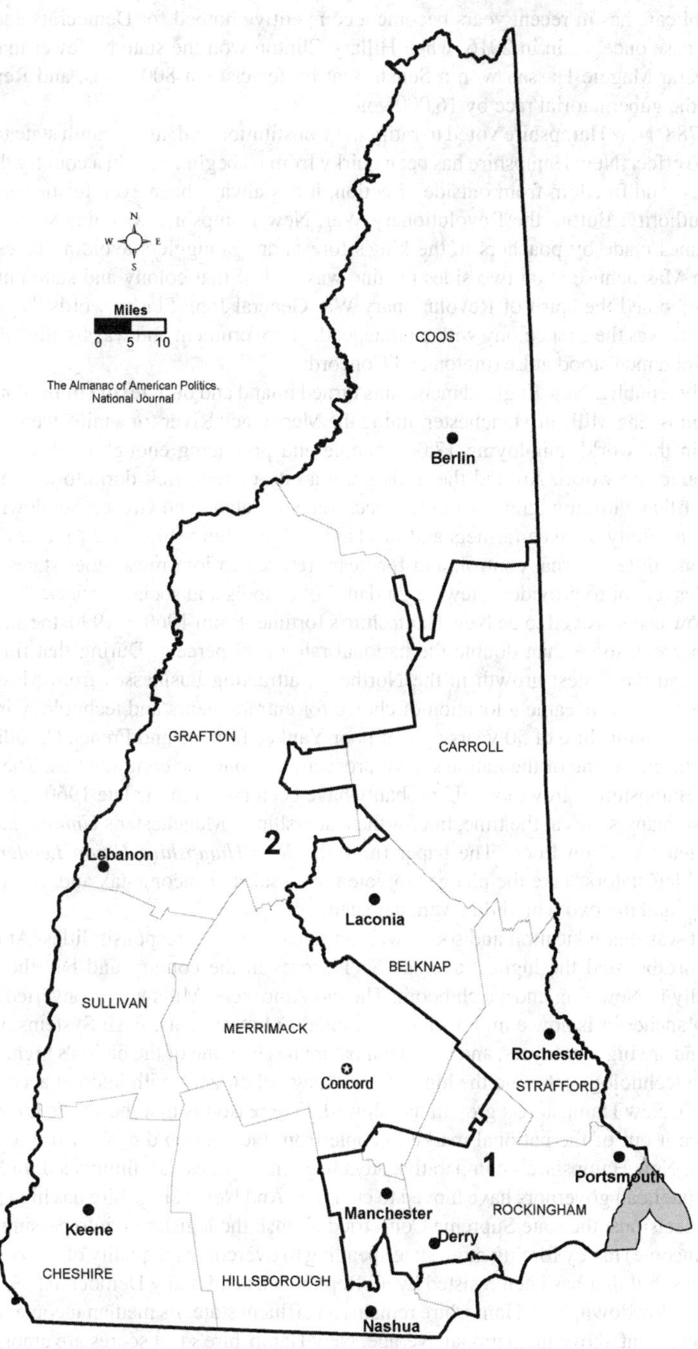

Congressional district boundaries were first effective for 2012.

Though it is home to just .41 percent of the nation's population, New Hampshire becomes the center of the political universe every four years -- the place where the contest for the American presidency is temporarily focused, where every vote is avidly sought, handshake by handshake. The state, once solidly Republican, has in recent years become a competitive hotbed for Democrats and Republicans. This was the case once again in 2016, when Hillary Clinton won the state by fewer than 3,000 votes, fellow Democrat Maggie Hassan won a Senate seat by fewer than 800 votes, and Republican Chris Sununu won the gubernatorial race by 16,000 votes.

In June 1788, New Hampshire voted to ratify the Constitution and, as the ninth state to do so, put the document into effect. New Hampshire has been quirky from its beginnings. In a country that prides itself on its feistiness and freedom from outside direction, it has always been even feistier and more lightly fettered by authority. Before the Revolutionary War, New Hampshire was almost an outlaw colony, its great fortunes made by poachers in the king's forests and smugglers avoiding taxes. Boxed-in by bossy Puritan Massachusetts on two sides (Maine was part of that colony and state until 1820), New Hampshire embodied the spirit of Revolutionary War General John Stark's words, "Live free or die." New Hampshire was the first colony with an independent government and was fighting the British even before the Minutemen stood at Lexington and Concord.

In the early republic, New England merchants turned inland and built textile mills along fast-flowing rivers. The Amoskeag Mills in Manchester, lining the Merrimack River for a mile, were once the largest cotton mills in the world, employing 17,000 people and producing enough cloth every two months to extend around the world. Around the mills grew a city of red-brick dormitories and three-family frame houses filled with immigrants from Quebec, Ireland, Poland and Greece, set down amid villages of dirt roads and flinty Yankee farmers and mechanics. New Hampshire held to its traditions of local government and little external control, and for years refused to join most other states in enacting an income or sales tax, or to provide statewide guidance of schools and social services.

Instead, low taxes proved to be New Hampshire's fortune. From 1960 to 1990, the state's population grew by 83 percent, more than double the national rate of 39 percent. During that time and through the 1990s, it had the fastest growth in the Northeast, attracting businesses from Massachusetts and other high-tax states. It became a location of choice for entrepreneurs and technology innovators. The bedraggled New Hampshire of 50 years ago, of poor Yankee farmers and French Canadian mill hands, has been overtaken by one of the nation's most prosperous economic communities. The low taxes that spurred New Hampshire's growth would probably have been raised in the late 1960s or early 1970s, as they were in so many states at the time, but for the leadership of Manchester's *Union Leader* newspaper and its proprietor William Loeb. The paper (now the *New Hampshire Union Leader*) insisted that governors and legislators "take the pledge" to vote for no sales or income tax and, from 1970 to 1998, almost all did - and the two who didn't were defeated.

The result was that education and social welfare remained local responsibilities. At the same time, New Hampshire boasted the highest average SAT scores in the country and had the brainpower to participate fully in New England's tech boom. The old Amoskeag Mills were converted to offices, and once-grimy Manchester is now a high-tech center. Fidelity Investments, BAE Systems, Liberty Mutual and Timberland are big employers, and New Hampshire has had one of the nation's highest growth rates in information technology jobs and the highest percentage of citizens with internet access.

Since 1990, New Hampshire's growth has slowed. One reason is that the state's housing costs have tended to price it out of the national market; people from the heartland can't afford to relocate there. Another is that New Hampshire's comparative advantage in tax rates has diminished. In Massachusetts, voters and Republican governors have moved to cut rates. And New Hampshire has high property taxes. In a series of decisions, the state Supreme Court tried to push the legislature into passing a broad-based (i.e., sales or income) tax by forcing more state spending to overcome inequality of resources in different cities and towns, but that has been resisted by all Republicans and many Democrats.

Despite the slowdown, New Hampshire remains an affluent state. Its median income ranks highest in the nation, 36 percent above the national average. New Hampshire's test scores are among the top three nationally in the National Assessment of Educational Progress. And the unemployment rate peaked at only 6.6 percent in mid-2009; by January 2017, it had fallen to a nation-leading 2.7 percent. This was not problem-free: Such a tight labor market poses problems for employers. In addition, New Hampshire faces a "silver tsunami" – it has the second-oldest population measured by median age in 2015, equal to Vermont and trailing only Maine. The biggest concern recently has been a sharp rise in opioid use. New Hampshire ranked third nationally in per capita overdose deaths, behind only West Virginia and New Mexico -- two significantly less affluent states. And the death toll has been increasing each year.

New Hampshire's political architecture is quirky. The state House has 400 members - one representative for every 3,337 residents, with each lawmaker paid just $100 a year. (California, by comparison, has one Assembly member for every 475,518 residents, and they are paid $104,115 a year.) Meanwhile, there's a five-member, elected "executive council" that is essentially a fourth branch of government - one that's able to stymie the governor, who as a result is structurally one of the nation's weakest. There's little impetus among voters to change the way the government works. "We've never had a major scandal, there's no widespread corruption and it's pretty transparent," Tom Rath, a former state attorney general and former Republican National Committee member, told *Governing*. "It works, sometimes in spite of itself, but it works. It fits with who we are."

The lever with which this small state has sometimes moved the political world is its first-in-the-nation presidential primary. In many ways, the state is atypical demographically – it is 91 percent white (tied for third nationally), 1 percent black (one of only six states with such a small percentage), 3 percent Hispanic and 3 percent Asian. But residents are well-schooled in politics, are willing to show up in the snow for town halls, and take the process seriously. The state fiercely defends its first-in-the-nation prerogative, led for decades by Secretary of State Bill Gardner, whose intense advocacy for keeping New Hampshire's primary the nation's earliest has made him arguably the safest incumbent in the nation, appointed by the legislature regardless of party since 1976. New Hampshire gave a huge boost to Dwight Eisenhower's candidacy in 1952 and prompted the retirement of Lyndon Johnson in 1968. It helped launch Jimmy Carter in 1976, Ronald Reagan in 1980, George H.W. Bush in 1988, and Bill Clinton in 1992, who had his "Comeback Kid" moment in the Granite State. That said, New Hampshire has not always picked winners. Primary victors Al Gore, John Kerry, John McCain and Mitt Romney all lost in November.

New Hampshire has some Democratic roots: It voted for Andrew Jackson over John Quincy Adams, and its only president, Franklin Pierce, was a Democrat (and a coddler of slaveholders). But from 1856 to World War II and beyond, New Hampshire voted mostly Republican, with Yankee Protestant farmers outvoting Irish and French-Canadian Catholic mill workers. Manchester and Nashua, formerly Democratic, trended toward Republicans. In the presidential elections from 1972 to 1988, it voted on average 8 percent more Republican than the nation.

Over the past two decades, the state has become much more Democratic and has become important in presidential elections not just as a primary state but as a target in the general election, albeit one with a small number of electoral votes. The shift began when local housing prices crashed in the early 1990s. In 1992, Bill Clinton beat incumbent George Bush, 39%-38%, with 23 percent for Ross Perot. In 1996, Clinton carried the state, 49%-39%, and Democrat Jeanne Shaheen was elected to the first of three two-year terms as governor. (New Hampshire and neighboring Vermont are the last states with two-year gubernatorial terms.) Much of New Hampshire is part of the Boston metro area, and like most non-Southern metro areas, it has trended Democratic in response to the Republicans' conservative stands on cultural issues. And if New Hampshire voters don't like broad-based taxes, many don't much like politicized religion either. In the 2016 general-election exit poll, just 15 percent of New Hampshire respondents identified as born-again or evangelical Christians, below the national percentage of 26 percent.

New Hampshire went for George W. Bush in 2000 but for John Kerry in 2004 and Barack Obama in 2008 and 2012; the two George W. Bush elections were close. Below the presidential level, too, the state has been one of the nation's swingiest, with governor's offices, Senate seats, House seats and legislative chambers switching parties on a semi-regular basis. The state made history in 2012 when all five of its full-time politicians were women - Gov. Maggie Hassan, Sen. Jeanne Shaheen, Sen. Kelly Ayotte, and Reps. Carol Shea-Porter and Ann Kuster.

In 2016, Donald Trump bounced back from a loss in the Iowa caucuses with a big win in New Hampshire. Trump didn't prevail in November, but he came extraordinarily close, losing to Clinton by less than half a percentage point, the second-closest state in the nation percentage-wise, and close enough that it took six days to officially call a winner. (Only Michigan was closer and decided later.)Libertarian Gary Johnson won 4.1percent in New Hampshire and Green Party nominee Jill Stein won early 1 percent;

in raw votes, Johnson's share was 10 times bigger than Clinton's winning margin, and Stein's was triple. Clinton's showing represented a decline from Obama's showing in 2012, when he won the state by six points. All told, Clinton's vote total was down by more than 21,000 from Obama's, while Trump's was up by almost 16,000. Three of the state's counties (Hillsborough, Coos and Sullivan) shifted from blue to red between 2012 and 2016. Even more strikingly, every single one of the state?s10 counties saw their winning margins shift toward Trump in 2016, including the four that remained blue. In those four counties (Cheshire, Grafton, Merrimack, and Strafford), Clinton's winning margin was between one and 10 percentage points smaller than Obama's had been. Meanwhile, with a victory in the gubernatorial race, the Republicans took full control of state government for the first time since 2002. Still, in early 2017, the state House killed an effort to pass right-to-work legislation, suggesting that New Hampshire's knife's edge political environment would keep the state from lurching rightward.

Population		**Race and Ethnicity**		**Income**	
Total	1,324,201	White	91.4%	Median Income	$66,779 (7 out of 50)
Land area	8,953	Black	1.2%		
Pop/ sq mi	147.9	Latino	3.2%	Under $50,000	37.2%
Born in state	42.3%	Asian	2.4%	$50,000-$99,999	32.6%
		Two races	1.6%	$100,000-$199,999	24.1%
Age Groups		Other	0.2%	$200,000 or more	6.1%
Under 18	20.5%			Poverty Rate	5.6%
18-34	21.0%	**Education**			
35-64	43.1%	H.S grad or less	36.5%	**Health Insurance**	
Over 64	15.3%	Some college	28.6%	With health insurance coverage	90.7%
		College Degree, 4 yr	21.8%		
Work		Post grad	13.0%		
White Collar	39.8%			**Public Assistance**	
Sales and Service	40.0%	**Military**		Cash public assistance income	2.8%
Blue Collar	20.2%	Veteran	10.2%		
Government	13.5%	Active Duty	0.1%	Food stamp/SNAP benefits	8.0%

Voter Turnout			
2015 Total Citizens 18+	1,020,130	2016 Pres Turnout as % CVAP	73%
2016 Pres Votes	744,296	2012 Pres Turnout as % CVAP	71%

Legislature	
Senate:	10D, 14R
House:	173D, 226R, 1L

Presidential Politics

2016 Democratic Primary		
Bernie Sanders (D)	152,193	(60%)
Hillary Clinton (D)	95,355	(38%)
2016 Republican Primary		
Donald Trump (R)	100,735	(35%)
John Kasich (R)	44,932	(16%)
Ted Cruz (R)	33,244	(12%)
Marco Rubio (R)	30,071	(11%)
Jeb Bush (R)	31,341	(11%)
Chris Christie (R)	21,089	(7%)

2016 Presidential Vote		
Hillary Clinton (D)	348,526	(47%)
Donald Trump (R)	345,790	(46%)
Gary Johnson (L)	30,777	(4%)
2012 Presidential Vote		
Barack Obama (D)	369,561	(52%)
Mitt Romney (R)	329,918	(46%)

Before Donald Trump won the 2016 election, New Hampshire had lost a bit of its kingmaker status: the three previous presidents all captured the White House without first winning the state's revered primary. New Hampshire began conducting the first-in-the-nation primary in 1920, and since 1952, when candidates' names were first put on the ballot; it has often exerted inordinate influence on the presidential selection process. The arguments for having early contests in small states is that they provide a venue in which candidates meet voters in person, listen to them, share their vision for the country, and allow citizens to gauge their character. Like Iowa, New Hampshire's retail politics offers little-known candidates the ability to propel themselves into the national spotlight. In the 1970s, the national Democratic Party tried to confine primaries to a "window" in which New Hampshire would have competition. But New Hampshire, with its don't-tread-on-me tradition, insisted it would hold its primary before the window if necessary, confident that candidates and reporters would still pay it heed even if its small delegation was not seated at the national convention as punishment. In 1996, Iowa Gov. Terry Branstad and New Hampshire Gov. Steve Merrill, both Republicans, threatened voter retaliation against candidates who took part in caucuses or primaries held before those in their states. Democratic and Republican leaders in both states have developed a pact to work together to maintain their states' unique political rituals at the beginning of the presidential nominating calendar. New Hampshire Secretary of State William Gardner has been in his job since 1976 and has the unilateral authority to select a primary date, a power he has wielded effectively to thwart any state that might attempt to crowd New Hampshire on the primary starting line.

New Hampshire has long had more registered Republicans than Democrats, but "undeclared" registrants are the largest bloc of voters in the state, eclipsing the 400,000 mark in the last election. They can vote in either party's presidential primary and on occasion they have provided the margin of victory for both Democratic and Republican winners. Once upon a time, the state's registered Democrats were mill workers in Manchester and other factory towns, ethnics who rejected the state's Yankee Republican establishment. Those days are long gone. The two largest cities, Manchester and Nashua, lean Democratic but can vote Republican. Democratic strength is more pronounced in the state capital of Concord and in clusters of towns around universities including, the area around Durham (University of New Hampshire), Keene (Keene State College) and Hanover (Dartmouth College). The New Hampshire counties across the Connecticut River from Vermont are Democratic — a sort of East Vermont. Republican support can be found in the small towns and suburbs around Nashua and Manchester that many commuters to Boston area jobs moved to from Massachusetts in search of lower real estate prices and tax bills.

In 2008, despite the Republican registration advantage, there was higher turnout on the Democratic side — a harbinger of the November results. Hillary Clinton trailed Barack Obama after his win in the Iowa caucuses, but shortly before the primary, at a coffeehouse in Portsmouth, Clinton was asked how she was withstanding the rigors of campaigning, and in response she seemed to tear up as she talked about her hopes for the country. Her vulnerability generated sympathy and Clinton edged Obama 39%-36%. On the Republican side the winner was McCain who edged Mitt Romney 37%-32%, on his strength among independent voters. The victory revived McCain's candidacy, which had nearly collapsed just six months before.

In 2012, New Hampshire was the site of intensive GOP campaigning. For Romney this was a must-win state: Voters knew him from his 2008 run, and he also owned a summer home in the Lake Country in Wolfeboro. But New Hampshire Republicans nevertheless flirted with Texas Gov. Rick Perry, businessman Herman Cain, and former House Speaker Newt Gingrich, who was endorsed by *The New Hampshire Union Leader*. Former Utah Gov. Jon Huntsman stayed out of Iowa and staked his whole campaign on New Hampshire. Romney won the primary 39%-23% over Texas Rep. Ron Paul, whose flinty libertarianism helped him run strongest in the North Country. Huntsman came in third with 17 percent, running strongest around Concord and the Connecticut River Valley counties.

The 2016 primary was a memorable one for the state's voters who turned to firebrands in both parties. In a GOP debate on the eve of the primary New Jersey Gov. Chris Christie savaged Florida Sen. Marco Rubio for his rote performance. Ohio Gov. John Kasich skipped the Iowa caucuses and lavished his attention on New Hampshire, holding more than 100 town hall meetings in the state. Former Florida Gov. Jeb Bush brought his mother, former First Lady Barbara Bush to his town halls to help draw crowds. Trump campaigned vigorously in the state after his defeat in the Iowa caucuses. His raucous rallies that attracted thousands seemed to mock the state's tradition of meet-and-greets with earnest voters in living rooms. Moreover, Trump engaged in a public fight with *The Union-Leader*, the venerable voice of conservatism in the New Hampshire, calling its publisher a "low-life." The paper endorsed Christie and ran front-page editorials attacking Trump. (The animosity persisted into the general election when the paper broke a century-long streak of endorsing GOP nominees and backed Libertarian Gary Johnson.) But the celebrity billionaire's brashness appealed to Republican primary-goers of all stripes and Trump defeated Kasich 35%-16%. In the top 25 wealthiest towns in New Hampshire based on their median household income, Trump's average vote was 31 percent. In the bottom 25 downscale towns (excluding the tiny burgs of Ellsworth, Millsfield and Wentworth's Location), Trump's average vote was 40 percent.

On the Democratic side, Clinton started out with a substantial lead, but by the fall of 2015, Sanders pulled ahead in the pre-primary polls. His popularity among young voters and his attacks on Wall St. fueled his 60%-38% victory over Clinton. Until the 1992 election, political reporters left New Hampshire the day after the primary and never returned in the fall, since it was assumed that the state would go Republican. But in six of the seven elections between 1992 and 2016, New Hampshire has voted Democratic. It has often been close: Bill Clinton in 1992, George W. Bush in 2000, and John Kerry in 2004 won the state by just one point. Hillary Clinton defeated Trump by less than 3,000 votes, or three-tenths of 1 percent. Clinton's margin was about five percentage points lower than Obama's margin over Romney in 2012. The falloff in Democratic votes was notable in working class and old mill towns, more than 10 points in Berlin, Claremont, Franklin and Rochester (an old shoe-making center). Obama captured all four in 2012. In 2016, Trump won the latter three and Clinton narrowly carried Berlin, but the Democratic vote there fell by almost 20 percentage points.

Congressional Districts

115th Congress Lineup	2D	**114th Congress Lineup**	1R 1D

New Hampshire's two congressional districts have had roughly the same boundaries since 1881, neatly separating the Merrimack River mill towns of Manchester and Nashua, the state's largest cities, along a mostly north-south line. That was originally done to split the Catholic Democratic vote, and for years the arrangement helped Republicans hold both districts. But lately, New Hampshire's movement away from its Yankee Republican roots and its high share of independent voters have led to wild gyrations: Both seats swung to Democrats in the wave of 2006, then to Republicans in 2010, and back to Democrats in 2012 and again in 2016. The flinty 2nd District along Vermont's border has crept more Democratic than the eastern 1st District, with its tax-averse Massachusetts exiles, but it remains competitive.

In the 1st District, the four consecutive contests between Republican Frank Guinta and Democrat Carol Shea-Porter, which have resulted in four consecutive defeats of the incumbent, may have reached the end with Guinta's ethics-scarred defeat, albeit narrowly, in 2016. With the added volatility of Republicans in control of state government, but with a two-year term for governor, probably the only predictability in the next redistricting is that it will be unpredictable.

Governor

Chris Sununu (R)

Elected 2016, term expires 2019, 1st term; b. Nov. 5, 1974, Salem, NH; Massachusetts Institute of Technology, BS 1998; Catholic; Married (Valerie); 3 children.

Elected Office: NH Executive Councilor, 2011-2017.

Professional Career: Engineer 1998-2006; Owner and Director, Sununu Enterprises 2006-2010

Office: 107 N. Main St., Concord, 03301; 603-271-2121; Fax: 603-271-7640; Website: governor.nh.gov.

Election Results

Election	Name (Party)	Vote (%)
2016 General	Chris Sununu (R)	307,342 (49%)
	Colin Van Ostern (D)	294,946 (47%)
	Max Abramson (L)	26,483 (4%)
2016 Primary	Chris Sununu (R)	34,137 (31%)
	Frank Edelblut (R)	33,149 (30%)
	Ted Gatsas (R)	22,840 (21%)
	Jeanie Forrester (R)	19,716 (18%)

Chris Sununu, a member of one of New Hampshire's most durable political families, won a Democratic-held open gubernatorial seat in 2016. It marked the first time a Republican had won the New Hampshire governorship since 2002, and only the second time since 1994. Despite a general drift away from Republicans in recent years, New Hampshire became the fourth of the six New England states to have a Republican as governor by early 2017. Sununu also had the distinction of entering office as the nation's youngest governor.

Sununu's father is John H. Sununu, the former three-term governor of New Hampshire and chief of staff to President George H.W. Bush, and his mother is Nancy Sununu, a former chairwoman of the New Hampshire Republican Party. He is also the brother of former Sen. and Rep. John E. Sununu. His father was legendary for his prickly nature. "Unlike the reserved Yankee reputation of many New England pols, the Sununu family brings a different brand to elected politics: combat," James Pindell wrote in the *Boston Globe*. Though Chris Sununu was a native of Salem, New Hampshire, he graduated from a suburban Virginia high school because his father was working in Washington at the time. As youngster, Sununu attended National Governors Association meetings and hung out with Chelsea Clinton, whose father, future president Bill Clinton, was then the governor of Arkansas. At the Massachusetts Institute of Technology, Sununu earned a degree in civil and environmental engineering, and for a decade he worked as an environmental engineer. He also served as CEO of Waterville Valley Ski Resort. His father didn't think that Chris, among his eight children, would end up going into politics, the *Concord Monitor* reported. But in 2010, Sununu won a seat on the state's executive council, an unusual "fourth branch of government" whose five members must approve most state contracts and confirm gubernatorial appointees. Sununu was reelected in 2012.

He set his sights higher when Maggie Hassan, the state's two-term Democratic governor, decided to challenge Republican Sen. Kelly Ayotte rather than run for reelection in 2016. Sununu joined a GOP primary field that included state Rep. Frank Edelblut, state Sen. Jeanie Forrester, and Manchester Mayor Ted Gatsas. The September primary ended up being mainly a race between Sununu and Edelblut, who ran an insurgent campaign to Sununu's right. In the end, Sununu edged Edelblut by fewer than 1,000 votes – 31% for Sununu, 30% for Edelblut, 21% for Gatsas, and 18% for Forrester. Meanwhile, on the Democratic side, the easy winner was Colin Van Ostern, who like Sununu was an incumbent member of the executive council. Van Ostern had also worked for Stonyfield Yogurt, Southern New Hampshire University and Dartmouth College.

The two nominees shared an opposition to a state sales or income tax – a third-rail of New Hampshire politics – but Sununu proposed shrinking the size of government and instituting a right-to-work law, while Van Ostern supported making the state's Medicaid expansion permanent. Sununu irritated people on both sides of the abortion divide by voting as an executive councilor against renewing a state contract with Planned Parenthood in 2015 and then later voting to restore the funding. Sununu endorsed Donald Trump for president and, unlike many other GOP candidates and elected officials, did not walk back his support following the release of a videotape that had recorded Trump bragging about groping women. (He did call the remarks "repugnant, unacceptable and offensive.") During the short sprint to Election Day, polls showed the race to be competitive, with both candidates trading off leads in the low- to mid-single digits.

On Election Day, Sununu won by two percentage points, or a little over 12,000 votes. That would ordinarily be considered a close race – but in the context of the other statewide contests that year, it was a veritable landslide. In the presidential contest, Hillary Clinton won by fewer than 3,000 votes, while in the Senate race, Hassan won by just over 1,000 votes. Though the Democrats won the presidential and Senate races in the state as well as both House seats, Sununu showed electoral strength, particularly compared to Hassan's reelection two years earlier. Whereas Hassan won by a 15-point margin in 2014, Sununu prevailed by two points, a swing of 17 points toward the GOP. Republican votes for governor rose by more than 123,000 between 2014 and 2016 while Democratic votes fell by more than 83,000, and while Hassan had won seven of the state's counties in 2014, Van Ostern won just four. The state's two most populous counties, Hillsborough and Rockingham, both went red in 2014 and 2016. Indeed, in every single county in the state – even those that remained in the Democratic camp-- the vote margin for governor shifted in the GOP's direction, by as much as 25 points.

Entering office, Sununu proposed cutting business taxes and temporarily curbing new business regulations. Sensitive to the state's opioid abuse crisis, he urged the establishment of more rehab programs.

He also pledged to improve the Division for Children, Youth and Families, which had been taken to task in a recent independent report. One notable development was Sununu's appointment of Edelblut, his former primary rival, as state education commissioner; Edelblut had home-schooled his seven children and had aggressively opposed the Common Core curriculum. Sununu proposed a budget that would expand full-day kindergarten, as well as services for residents with developmental disabilities and charter schools. His budget would also boost infrastructure projects at community colleges. However, it was silent on family and medical leave policy and on the future of the state's Medicaid expansion under the Affordable Care Act. Working with a Republican-led legislature, Sununu signed a bill to get rid of licensing requirements for carrying a concealed pistol or revolver. But Sununu saw right-to-work legislation he favored hit a roadblock in the state House, thanks to more than two dozen Republicans siding with Democrats and labor unions.

Senior Senator

Jeanne Shaheen (D)

Elected 2008, term expires 2020, 2nd term; b. Jan 28, 1947, St. Charles, MO; Shippensburg University (PA), B.A.; University of Mississippi, M.S.; Protestant; Married (William Shaheen); 3 children; 7 grandchildren.

Elected Office: NH Senate, 1990-1996; NH Governor, 1997-2003.

Professional Career: Teacher, 1969-1971; A.A., University of NH, 1973-1974; Parents' Association Program Coordinator, 1982-1986; Manager, seasonal retail business, 1973-1976; Campaign Manager, Carter/Mondale NH presidential campaign, 1979- 80; Hart, NH pres. campaign, 1983-1984; McEachern, NH Governor campaign, 1986-1988.

DC Office: 506 HSOB 20510, 202-224-2841, Fax: 202-228-3194, shaheen.senate.gov.
State Offices: Berlin, 603-752-6300; Claremont, 603-542-4872; Dover, 603-750-3004; Keene, 603-358-6604; Manchester, 603-647-7500; Nashua, 603-883-0196.

Committees: *Appropriations*: Commerce, Justice, Science & Related Agencies (RMM), Department of Homeland Security, DOL, HHS & Education & Related Agencies, Energy & Water Development, State, Foreign Operations & Related Programs. *Armed Services*: Emerging Threats & Capabilities, Readiness & Management Support, Seapower. *Ethics*. *Foreign Relations*: Europe & Regional Security Cooperation, State Dept & USAID Mngmnt, Internat'l Ops & Internat'l Dev (RMM), West Hem Crime Civ Sec Dem Rights & Women's Issues. *Joint Security & Cooperation in Europe*. *Small Business & Entrepreneurship (RMM)*.

Group Ratings

	ADA	ACLU	AFL-CIO	LCV	ITI	COC	HAFA	ACU	CFG	FRC
2016	-	88%	-	100%	100%	75%	2%	4%	5%	0%
2015	95%	C	79%	96%	C	57%	C	0%	5%	0%

Almanac Ratings 2015

	Economy	Social	Foreign	Composite
Liberal	83%	100%	80%	88%
Conservative	17%	0%	20%	13%

Key Votes of the 114th Congress

1. Keystone pipeline	N	5. National Security Data	Y	9. Gun Sales Checks	Y
2. Export-Import Bank	N	6. Iran Nuclear Deal	N	10. Sanctuary Cities	N
3. Debt Ceiling Increase	Y	7. Puerto Rico Debt	Y	11. Planned Parenthood	N
4. Homeland Security $$	Y	8. Loretta Lynch A.G	Y	12. Trade deals	Y

Election Results

Election	Name (Party)	Vote (%)		Cand. Spent	Ind. Exp. Support	Ind. Exp. Oppose
2014 General	Jeanne Shaheen (D)	251,184	(52%)	$16,436,371	$1,402,045	$10,104,403
	Scott Brown (R)	235,347	(48%)	$9,163,652	$3,913,621	$13,027,425
2014 Primary	Jeanne Shaheen (D)	Unopposed				

Prior winning percentages: 2008 (52%); Governor: 2000 (49%), 1998 (66%), 1996 (57%)

Democrat Jeanne Shaheen, New Hampshire's senior senator, is the first woman in U.S. history to be elected both governor and senator, as well as the first in New Hampshire history elected to either of those offices. She has been a political fixture in the Granite State for four decades, first coming to notice not as a candidate but as a behind-the-scenes political operative-engineering victories for Jimmy Carter and Gary Hart in the state's first-in-the-nation presidential primary.

Since being elected to the Senate in 2008, Shaheen has been a reliable Democratic vote: She was hammered during her first bid for re-election for voting with President Barack Obama 99 percent of the time. As a result, she came close to being upset in 2014 by former Massachusetts Republican Sen. Scott Brown, who had moved across the border to take her on. But Shaheen, has been adept at balancing partisan loyalties with the reality that she represents a state that has become a hypersensitive political bellwether. She once taught a university course on how elected officials can overcome partisanship, and she has sought to put those lessons into practice by reaching across the aisle in her legislative efforts.

Shaheen grew up in the suburbs of St. Louis, where her father was in the shoe manufacturing business and her mother was a secretary at their local church. She graduated from Shippensburg College in Pennsylvania with a degree in education; after teaching for a couple of years, she earned a master's degree in political science from the University of Mississippi. Shaheen was raised in a Republican family, and cast her first presidential vote for Richard Nixon in 1968. But she registered as a Democrat while still an undergraduate at Shippensburg, where her activities reflected the campus activism of the era: She successfully challenged a curfew that applied to women but not to men. While in Mississippi, she came to admire Carter, then governor of Georgia, for his efforts to foster racial integration.

She moved to New Hampshire in 1973, where she worked as a teacher and ran a seasonal silver and leather business with her husband, attorney William Shaheen, a New Hampshire native who himself has been a behind-the-scenes political power in the state. In December 2007, as Jeanne Shaheen was preparing to make a second bid for the Senate, William Shaheen-in his capacity as co-chairman of Hillary Clinton's national and New Hampshire presidential campaigns-told reporters that Republicans would attack one of Clinton's rivals, Obama, for admitting in his autobiography that he "got into drinking" and experimented with drugs. The next day, Clinton apologized, and Shaheen resigned his position in the Clinton campaign. (In the 2016 contest, Jeanne Shaheen endorsed Clinton almost six months before the New Hampshire primary, and, during the fall campaign, became the first senator to call for hearings into allegations of Russian interference in the presidential race.)

Decades earlier, William and Jeanne Shaheen were among Carter's earliest New Hampshire supporters when, in 1975, the former Georgia governor began laying the groundwork for his longshot bid for the presidency. Carter won the 1976 New Hampshire primary, and, with Carter in the White House, William Shaheen was appointed U.S. attorney for New Hampshire. In 1980, Jeanne Shaheen was named Carter's state director in New Hampshire, and guided the incumbent to a 10-point win in the presidential primary over the insurgent candidacy of Massachusetts Sen. Edward Kennedy. Four years later, another longshot presidential hopeful, Colorado Sen. Gary Hart, recruited Shaheen to manage his New Hampshire primary campaign. Hart defeated the Democratic frontrunner, Walter Mondale, by 9 points.

At the time, Democrats had limited success in winning statewide office in then-solidly Republican New Hampshire. Shaheen oversaw two unsuccessful efforts to elect Democrat Paul McEachern as governor. The first time, McEachern failed to oust incumbent John Sununu, later White House chief of staff for President George H.W. Bush; the second time, McEachern lost an open seat race to then-GOP

Rep. Judd Gregg, who later went on to serve three Senate terms. In 1990, Shaheen became a candidate herself -- winning election to the state Senate, where she supported expanded health care coverage and term limits on federal and state legislators.

In 1996, she ran for governor. She had no serious primary opposition, while the Republicans had a close race between Rep. Bill Zeliff and Board of Education Chairman Ovide Lamontagne, a strong conservative who won the nomination. Shaheen took what is referred to in New Hampshire as "The Pledge," to oppose an income or sales tax. Such a vow had long been politically sacrosanct in a jurisdiction that has prided itself as the only state in the nation not to impose a broad-based tax. Shaheen won, 57%-39%, becoming only the fourth Democrat in more than 70 years to serve as the Granite State's governor.

As governor, Shaheen won more funding from the legislature for kindergarten programs and signed a bill creating a needle exchange pilot program. She vetoed bills that would have abolished the estate tax and the death penalty. A 1997 state Supreme Court ruling that outlawed New Hampshire's system of local school financing provided a continuing challenge. Shaheen proposed increasing state revenues through slot machine gambling and a hike in the tobacco tax, but the court invalidated her plan in 1998. That year, when her two-year term was up, Shaheen was reelected by 66%-31%. But she then abandoned her pledge to oppose an income or sales tax and was reelected in 2000 by only 49%-44%. The controversy over school funding continued, and the GOP-controlled legislature refused to pass either an income or sales tax.

Shaheen ran for the Senate in 2002, as Republicans faced a divisive primary in which Rep. John Sununu, son and namesake of the former governor and White House chief of staff, defeated the incumbent, Robert Smith, 53%-45%. Smith had angered GOP leaders when, after a failed bid for the 2000 Republican presidential nomination, he temporarily left the party. During the general election campaign, Shaheen backed President George W. Bush's tax cuts and the authorization of military force in Iraq passed by Congress in October 2002. But her abandonment of the tax pledge came back to haunt her, and Sununu won 51%-46%. In the 2004 election season, Shaheen served as the national chairman of Democrat John Kerry's presidential campaign, and was credited with reviving his campaign in the early primaries -- including helping to orchestrate a victory in New Hampshire. After Kerry's loss in the general election, Shaheen became director of the Kennedy School of Government's Institute of Politics at Harvard. (Earlier, at Tufts University, she taught a course in 2003 called "Governing in a Partisan Environment.")

Shaheen insisted she had no interest in running for office again. But after the 2006 election, which returned both houses of Congress to Democratic control, New Hampshire Democrats pressed her to seek a rematch with Sununu in 2008. A July 2007 poll showed her far ahead in a theoretical matchup. In September, Shaheen quit her job at Harvard and announced she was running again for Senate.

While the 2008 Senate campaign had the same candidates as six years earlier, it took place in a very different political atmosphere. In 2002, Shaheen had emphasized areas where she agreed with Bush and congressional Republicans; in 2008, she emphasized her disagreements with them. She attacked Sununu for votes against changing the tax treatment of oil companies and was supported by environmental groups. Shaheen led in polls throughout the campaign, but Sununu rebounded after gas prices reached $4 a gallon, and he criticized Shaheen's opposition to offshore oil drilling. He also attacked her for doubling state spending in her six years as governor. But he lost ground in October 2008, when he voted for a $700 billion government bailout for the financial industry, which Shaheen, like many non-incumbent candidates in both parties, opposed. The outcome was a reversal of 2002: Shaheen won, 52%-45%, for the first Democratic Senate victory in New Hampshire since 1974.

On Capitol Hill, Shaheen has acquired a reputation as a disciplined politician who tends to stay on message and refrain from headline-grabbing sound bites. And while her loyalty to her party was rewarded with a seat on the Appropriations Committee in 2013, her commitment to reaching across the aisle was underscored by the four-year legislative journey of an energy efficiency bill she co-authored with Ohio Republican Sen. Rob Portman. The original legislation, introduced in 2011, sought to increase energy efficiency in buildings by offering mortgage incentives and getting the federal government more involved in working with manufacturers. Finally, in the spring of 2015, a stripped-down version of the bill was passed and signed into law by Obama.

Although a modest policy achievement, the Shaheen-Portman measure was highlighted as a rare victory over the partisan gridlock that has plagued Capitol Hill. First, the bill failed in September 2013 after it became entangled in divisive debates over the two high-profile controversies: the Affordable Care Act and Keystone XL pipeline. It failed again in May 2014 when Republicans insisted on being able to offer amendments to it, including proposals to oppose Obama Administration regulations on future power plants. "On the bill's merits-creating jobs, saving consumers money and reducing pollution-it was never a hard sell," Shaheen told *The New York Times* after the measure was enacted. "The tough part was convincing Washington to not play politics with a good idea."

Shaheen also worked with a bipartisan group that sought to enact many of the recommendations made by Obama's deficit commission in 2010, and, in 2013, was part of the group of 14 senators (seven Republicans, six Democrats and an independent) brought together by Maine Republican Sen. Susan Collins to find a way out of the budget stalemate that had led to a government shutdown. In addition, Shaheen sought ways to avoid the frustrations many former governors experience once in the Senate -- witness the slow pace and limited volume of accomplishment. Borrowing an idea from her days as a chief executive, she introduced a bill with Georgia Republican Sen. Johnny Isakson in 2011 to move to a two-year budget cycle

As the Affordable Care Act was debated during Shaheen's first year on Capitol Hill, she got several provisions into the final bill, including one to close a loophole allowing drug companies to avoid competition with generic drugs. On another health issue, Shaheen's interest has been personal: Her granddaughter has Type 1 diabetes and participated in a medical trial for an artificial pancreas. The senator has been involved in numerous efforts to highlight the problems associated with juvenile diabetes, and has worked actively to persuade the Food and Drug Administration to issue "clear and reasonable guidance" on artificial pancreas devices.

Despite representing a state where Republicans still hold a registration edge, Shaheen has not shied away from the culture wars. She has been an outspoken critic of efforts to cut off funding for Planned Parenthood. "I don't believe that the Republican leadership in the House or in the Senate for that matter got a mandate in the last election to defund Planned Parenthood," Shaheen declared in early 2017, as many congressional Republicans redoubled their efforts to cut off funding for that organization as the Trump Administration took office. In March 2011, more than four years before the U.S. Supreme Court paved the way for same-sex marriage across the country, Shaheen signed on to cosponsor a bill to repeal the Defense of Marriage Act and allow the federal government to provide benefits to same-sex married couples. As a member of the Armed Services Committee, she got provisions into the fiscal year 2013 defense authorization bill to repeal a policy denying military women abortion coverage in cases of rape or incest.

Shaheen picked up the Armed Services seat in 2011, where she keeps an eye on the Portsmouth Naval Shipyard, an important employer in eastern New Hampshire. On another local matter, Shaheen used her Appropriations perch to get funding for a new federal prison in upstate Berlin. Congress had tried to cut $276 million for the facility, but Shaheen argued it would supply 332 jobs and put $40 million annually into the stagnant economy of northern New Hampshire.

With a WMUR/University of New Hampshire poll in February 2013 giving her a 59-percent approval rating, Shaheen was an early favorite to win re-election the following year. But the dynamics of the race changed when Brown announced an exploratory committee in March 2014 and declared his candidacy a month later. In early 2010, Brown had capitalized on public unease over passage of the Affordable Care Act to win a special election to fill the Senate seat left vacant by Kennedy's death in solidly blue Massachusetts. Despite receiving substantial tea party support in 2010, Brown compiled a moderate voting record. But in 2012, he was soundly defeated 54%-46% by Democrat Elizabeth Warren, as the Bay State's Democratic voters came out in force to reelect Obama.

After his loss to Warren, Brown and his wife sold their Massachusetts residence and moved to New Hampshire, where they long had owned a vacation home. His campaign got off to a rocky start, but picked up steam after he won the endorsement of part-time New Hampshire resident Mitt Romney and was joined on the campaign trail by Arizona Sen. John McCain, who twice won the New Hampshire presidential primary. Brown gained traction by relentlessly seeking to tie Shaheen, a co-chair of the 2012 Obama campaign and a leading surrogate Obama campaigner that year, to the president -- including continual use of the statistic that she had voted with Obama's position 99 percent of the time. (That figure came from a *CQ/Roll Call* analysis of Shaheen's 2013 voting record.) Obama, despite having won the state in both 2008 and 2012, had seen his popularity nosedive: Polls were showing fewer than 40 percent of New Hampshire voters approved of the job he was doing.

A WMUR poll in August 2014 shocked political observers when it showed Shaheen with a 46%-44% lead, within the poll's margin of error. A month earlier, a WMUR poll had Shaheen leading by 12 points. Shaheen's campaign professed itself to be unfazed, saying it had been prepared for a tough race. Although polls showed Brown within a hair of the incumbent heading into Election Day, she managed to win with 52 percent-narrowly blocking his bid to become the first person in 135 years to represent two different states in the Senate. It was a rare bright spot for national Democrats, as they lost control of the Senate amid a nationwide 2014 Republican electoral wave.

Returning to Capitol Hill, Shaheen focused her attention to a problem that had reached epidemic proportions in her home state: opioid addiction. (New Hampshire officials reported that, during 2014, deaths from heroin overdoses had surpassed traffic fatalities in the state.) At the end of 2015, Shaheen called for an emergency appropriation of $600 million to address what she called a "national public health emergency" through treatment programs and prevention education. But a move by Shaheen in March 2016 to attach the money to a bill funding continued government operations fell short. While the Comprehensive Addiction and Recovery Act (CARA), sponsored by Shaheen and her then-junior colleague, GOP Sen. Kelly Ayotte, was signed into law by Obama in July 2016, it contained no immediate funding. "CARA is good legislation but without funding, it's like a life preserver with no air in it," Shaheen declared. However, most of CARA's initiatives were funded about six months later, when Obama, as one of his last major acts in office, signed the 21st Century Cures Act that included $1 billion to combat opioid addiction and abuse over a two-year period.

Several of Shaheen's efforts early in her second term were focused on issues of particular concern to women. She got wording into the fiscal 2016 defense authorization bill to increase access to birth control for women covered by military health programs. "Almost 15 percent of our military are now women, but the military has not developed a comprehensive program to make sure they have access to family planning, contraception and counseling," Shaheen declared. Another measure signed by Obama in late 2016 -- authored by Shaheen and two other New England Democrats, Sens. Richard Blumenthal of Connecticut and Patrick Leahy of Vermont -- required that sexual assault evidence collection kits in criminal cases be preserved for the entire relevant statute of limitations, and that victims be notified in writing 60 days before the kit is destroyed. While the requirement applied only to federal cases, the legislation included incentives for states to give survivors more information at the time they report sexual crimes.

On a more upbeat note, Shaheen in April 2015 gave a push to a campaign to put a woman on the face of the $20 bill in 2020, the centennial of the women's suffrage. Her legislation directed the Treasury Department to establish a panel to decide the matter. A month later, the "Woman on the 20s" campaign announced that Harriet Tubman had won its online poll to replace Andrew Jackson on the $20. When Treasury officials voiced a preference for putting a woman on a $10 bill since it was already slated for design, Shaheen introduced another bill to put Tubman on the $10. But, after protests by fans of the current face on the $10 -- Alexander Hamilton, first secretary of the Treasury and the subject of a hit Broadway musical -- the Treasury reverted to its original proposal to put Tubman on the $20. Noting that she serves on the Foreign Relations as well as the Armed Services and Appropriations panels, Shaheen observed Congress has a responsibility "not only to deal with life and death issues, but to also deal with the ways in which we value" the achievements of Americans.

Junior Senator

Maggie Hassan (D)

Elected 2016, term expires 2022, 1st term; b. Feb 27, 1958, Boston, MA; Brown University (RI), A.B., 1980; Northeastern University Law School (MA), J.D., 1985; United Church of Christ; Married (Thomas (Tom) Hassan); 2 children.

Elected Office: NH Governor, 2013-2016; NH Senate, 2004-2010, Majority Leader, 2008-2010.

Professional Career: Practicing attorney, 1996-2009; Association General counsel, Brigham & Women's Hosp., 1993-1996; Practicing attorney, 1985-1992; Information officer, MA Department of Social Services, 1980-1982.

DC Office: 330 HSOB 20510, 202-224-3324, Fax: 202-228-0581, hassan.senate.gov.

State Offices: Manchester, 603-622-2204; Portsmouth, 603-433-4445.

Committees: *Commerce, Science & Transportation*: Aviation Operations, Safety & Security, Communications, Technology, Innovation & the Internet, Consumer Protection, Product Safety, Ins & Data Security, Space, Science & Competitiveness, Surface Trans., Merchant Marine Infra., Safety & Security. *Health, Education, Labor & Pensions*: Children & Families, Primary Health & Retirement Security. *Homeland Security & Government Affairs*: Federal Spending Oversight & Emergency Management, Regulatory Affairs & Federal Management.

Election Results

Election	Name (Party)	Vote (%)		Cand. Spent	Ind. Exp. Support	Ind. Exp. Oppose
2016 General	Maggie Hasan (D)	354,649	(48%)			
	Kelly Ayotte (R)	353,632	(48%)	$17,281,997	$5,671,191	$52,308,296
	Aaron Day (I)	17,742	(2%)			
2016 Primary	Maggie Hassan (D)	unopposed				

Prior winning percentages: Governor: 2014 (53%), 2012 (55%)

When, after months of effort, national Democrats persuaded Gov. Maggie Hassan to forgo a bid for a third term in favor of a run against Republican Sen. Kelly Ayotte, it marked one of their biggest recruiting coups of the 2016 election cycle. Ayotte and Hassan were regarded as perhaps New Hampshire's most popular politicians, and convincing Hassan to run was key to the Democratic strategy of putting enough seats in play to retake the Senate majority. While the party fell short of the latter goal, the recruitment of Hassan paid off, as she became one of just two Democrats nationwide to win a Senate race against an incumbent Republican on Election Day 2016.

Ayotte vs. Hassan was one of just two all-woman Senate races in 2016, along with the contest in California. There have been only 16 such matchups over the past 70 years, according to Rutgers University's Center for American Woman and Politics. Another historical milestone accompanied Hassan's initial election as governor in 2012: New Hampshire became the first state to have a woman governor in addition to an all-female congressional delegation. Hassan grew up steeped in politics. Raised in the upscale Boston suburb of Lincoln, she is the daughter of Robert C. Wood, a MIT political science professor who played a leading role in the creation of the Department of Housing and Urban Development under President Lyndon Johnson; Wood later served as president of the University of Massachusetts and superintendent of the Boston school system. Hassan earned her undergraduate degree at Brown University and her law degree at Northeastern University, and then practiced law in Boston -- including a stint as a corporate attorney for Brigham and Women's Hospital.

Hassan and her husband, Tom Hassan, met as undergraduates at Brown. Her connection to New Hampshire dates back to the late 1980s when her husband was appointed to the faculty of the Phillips Exeter Academy, an elite prep school. (He later became head of the school.) The couple has two children, one of whom, a son now in his late 20s, has cerebral palsy. Maggie Hassan credits him with inspiring her career in public service, which began in 1999 when then-Gov. (now senior Sen.) Jeanne Shaheen appointed Hassan as a citizen advisor on an education panel. Hassan earlier had become involved in disability rights activism while working to ensure the elementary school attended by her son, Ben, could accommodate his needs. "I had a moment when he was 3," Hassan recalled in an interview with the *New England Cable Network*. "The school bus came to pick him up for the first day of pre-school, and it was a mainstream pre-school here in town ... and I found myself thinking, 'You know, he's going to school in his hometown and he's going to have a chance to make friends and a chance to learn.' " Ben Hassan was featured in the first TV ad of his mother's 2016 Senate campaign.

Hassan's first race for elected office was in 2002. She lost a state Senate contest to incumbent Republican Russell Prescott, but came back two years later and beat him -- serving six years until he reclaimed the seat in 2010. During her three terms, Hassan held several leadership positions, culminating with majority leader. As leader, she proposed a bill in 2010 to set up a government commission to regulate health care costs. As the Affordable Care Act -- "Obamacare" -- was being debated in Washington, New Hampshire Republicans jabbed at the idea as "Maggie Care". The bill that passed did establish the commission, but without the authority to limit rates. A year earlier, Hassan was more successful on the issue of gay marriage. Several of her Democratic colleagues were reluctant to tackle the subject, but Hassan convinced them to move ahead -- and she played an integral role in New Hampshire becoming one of the first states in the country to legalize same-sex marriage, six years before the U.S. Supreme Court ruling that recognized such unions nationwide.

After Democrat John Lynch -- the longest serving governor in New Hampshire history -- announced in September 2011 that he would not seek a fifth two-year term, Hassan got into the race a month later. She focused on boosting growth through investment in higher education, promising to restore $50 million in funding for the University System of New Hampshire that the legislature had cut in exchange for a two-year tuition freeze. She also backed a proposed casino on the Massachusetts border to raise revenue in a state that stands alone in its lack of a broad-based tax.

Hassan easily won a three-way Democratic primary with 54 percent. Her Republican opponent in the general election was attorney Ovide Lamontagne, a hardline conservative who had run unsuccessfully for governor in 1996 against Shaheen and then lost to Ayotte in the 2010 Republican Senate primary. Hassan sought to portray Lamontagne as a rubber stamp for the GOP-controlled legislature, saying that her "New Hampshire way" was preferable to his "tea party way." Lamontagne branded Hassan as a tax-and-spend liberal who lacked his "real world business experience." Polls in the campaign's final weeks showed a close race, but President Barack Obama's strong showing-he beat Republican Mitt Romney in the state, even though the former Massachusetts governor has a vacation house there-helped Hassan to a 55%-43% victory.

Taking office with a House that had been returned to Democratic control but a Senate that remained in Republican hands, Hassan stressed the need for bipartisanship: It paid off when the two-year budget that she signed her first year passed the Senate unanimously and cleared the 400-member House with fewer than 20 dissenting votes. She made good on one campaign promise when her first budget restored the cuts made to the university system during the Republicans' 2011-2012 control of the legislature; subsequent budgets under her watch lowered tuition at the community college system and froze it at state universities in some years. But Hassan was unable to deliver on another key campaign vow; she fell short in efforts during her first term to legalize casino gambling, at a time when neighboring Massachusetts and Maine were moving to do so.

In her second year in office, Hassan secured bipartisan support to expand Medicaid under the Affordable Care Act. The Medicaid expansion allowed 50,000 low-income New Hampshire residents to receive subsidized health care, while also covering substance abuse treatment in a state that has been besieged by heroin and opioid addiction. Other legislation passed and signed into law in the final year of her initial term included the state's first gas-tax increase in more than two decades and a bill to prevent employers from barring workers from talking about their compensation. On the criminal justice front, Hassan signed legislation to boost mental-health resources in the wake of a Department of Justice-backed class-action lawsuit, as well as enacting a series of laws aimed at curbing domestic violence and human trafficking, preventing sexual abuse and limiting the parental rights of rapists. She did veto a bill intended to protect public employees from on-the-job bullying, saying the language was too broad and subjective.

In the 2014 gubernatorial election, Hassan faced Republican Walt Havenstein, the former CEO of defense contractor BAE Systems -- an international firm with a significant presence in New Hampshire. Havenstein proposed cutting the state's corporate tax from 8.5 percent to 7.4 percent. He opposed Hassan's stand on gambling, backed a right-to-work law, and charged that, under Hassan, the state's economic recovery had lagged that of its neighbors. He pumped $2 million of his own money into his bid. But many of Hassan's policy achievements had received bipartisan support, and she benefited from incumbency-it's rare for a one-term New Hampshire governor to be ousted. Havenstein managed to close the gap from 20 points in June to nearly a dead heat by Election Day, but Hassan prevailed, 53%-47%-a point better than Shaheen notched in her higher-profile Senate win that day against former Massachusetts GOP Sen. Scott Brown.

Hassan had a bumpier second term, as she faced an all-Republican legislature (the GOP had taken back the House) as well a Republican majority on the state's Executive Council, which approves the governor's picks for agencies and judgeships as well as major state contracts. Hassan stood up to Republicans by vetoing bills that would have curbed the Common Core education standards and allowed the concealed carrying of firearms without a license. She also had to deal with a protracted budget impasse with the GOP-controlled legislature in her second year. On an issue that had brought her into politics, she signed the nation's first law banning sub-minimum wages for people with disabilities.

A WMUR/University of New Hampshire survey in the spring of 2015 showed Hassan with a 55 percent approval rating, and a string of favorable poll results in a hypothetical Senate matchup fueled continuing speculation throughout the spring and summer that she would forgo another term as governor to challenge Ayotte. Republicans seemed to have little doubt about Hassan's intentions; by the end of summer, GOP-allied outside groups had spent more than $2 million in ads seeking to weaken her political standing. Hassan remained publicly silent on her future, with a spokesman telling *Roll Call* at the end of August that the governor was "focused on her efforts to reach a fiscally responsible, bipartisan budget compromise," and that "there is no timetable for any decisions related to 2016." But, by early September, the Democratic-aligned Senate Majority PAC was up with a second ad aimed at countering the Republican media effort against Hassan, and, a month later, Hassan formally announced her Senate candidacy. Polls would show the race between the two women neck-and-neck for much of the following year, although Ayotte struggled continually to achieve a political equilibrium with regard to the controversial candidacy of Donald Trump.

Ayotte, first elected in the Republican wave year of 2010, was facing the voters again in a decidedly purple state that had trended Democratic in presidential years over the previous quarter-century. During her first term, Ayotte's voting record took a turn to the center. She was the 17th most conservative member of the Senate in 2011, but dropped to 35th in 2013, according to *National Journal* rankings. By 2015, she was down to 50th, and placed among the five least conservative Senate Republicans in *Almanac* rankings. While disgruntled conservatives talked of mounting a primary challenge, Ayotte was easily renominated with 80 percent. Heading into the general election, she sought to play up her parting of the ways with her party's leadership on issues ranging from immigration reform to air pollution. In a July 2016 interview with *Boston Magazine*, Ayotte characterized herself as "independent" four separate times and boasted repeatedly of working "across the aisle." But she also had taken heat in her home state for a 2013 vote in which she joined most Senate Republicans to oppose expanded background checks on gun purchasers; a gun control group founded by former Arizona Rep. Gabrielle Giffords spent $2.5 million in 2016 in an effort to defeat her.

Ayotte's playing up her independence was an effort to draw distinction with Hassan. "I'm not hesitant to take on my party or the other side. I don't see that same level of independence from her," declared Ayotte. Hassan, in turn, pointed to her dealing with legislatures partly or totally under Republican control. "I have a real record of working with members of the opposite party, having disagreements with them, to be sure, but then getting results," Hassan told *USA Today*. She also cited disagreements with Obama ranging from the Trans-Pacific Partnership trade deal to allowing more Syrian refugees into the United States as proof her willingness to buck her own party. Hassan endorsed the presidential candidacy of Hillary Clinton even before announcing her Senate bid, and while Clinton lost the first-in-the-nation New Hampshire primary to Bernie Sanders by a wide margin, polls throughout the summer and fall gave Clinton a significant lead over Trump in the Granite State's general election. Trump, on the other hand, had comfortably won the New Hampshire primary. As Hassan relentlessly sought to tie Ayotte to Trump, Ayotte was bedeviled by trying to thread the needle between assuaging Trump's base of GOP supporters and appealing to the independents who make up an estimated 40 percent of the state's voters -- a larger bloc than either registered Democrats or Republicans.

When it became apparent Trump would be the Republican nominee, the Ayotte campaign initially said she would "support" Trump but not "endorse" him -- a semantical exercise greeted in political circles with at best, puzzlement, and, at worst, ridicule. In early June, when Trump questioned a judge's integrity because of his Mexican heritage, Ayotte initially remained silent, but later told the *Washington Post* that Trump's comments were "offensive and wrong." A couple of months later, Ayotte blasted Trump for his criticism of the parents of an American Muslim soldier who had died in service, following their appearance at the Democratic National Convention. "I am appalled that Donald Trump would disparage them and that he had the gall to compare his own sacrifices to those of a Gold Star family," Ayotte, whose husband is a military veteran, declared. But Ayotte stuck by her support of Trump, even as Trump took public swipes at her. It gave Hassan -- who, if sometimes criticized as lacking spontaneity, is nothing if not disciplined -- another opening to pounce. She declared that that Ayotte's decision "...to continue to stand by Trump as he reinforces every day just how temperamentally unfit he is to serve as president - raises serious questions about her judgment."

Ayotte's Trump-related complications escalated in early October during a debate with Hassan. Asked by the moderator whether she would "tell a child to aspire to be like Donald Trump," Ayotte initially dodged the question. When pressed on whether she would "point to [Trump] as a role model," Ayotte responded, "Well, I think certainly there are many role models that we have. And I believe he can serve as president, and so absolutely, I would do that." Immediately after the debate, Ayotte said she had "misspoke," adding, "While I would hope all of our children would aspire to be president, neither Donald Trump nor Hillary Clinton have set a good example and I wouldn't hold up either of them as role models for my kids." Days later, the "Access Hollywood" tape with Trump making lewd comments about women emerged, prompting Ayotte to disavow the nominee and saying she would write in the name of GOP vice presidential nominee Mike Pence for president. Ayotte backers hoped her action would finally undercut Democratic efforts to use Trump as a weapon, but the fusillade from Hassan and her allies only increased. An outside group aligned with Clinton ran an ad accusing Ayotte of "running away [from Trump] to save her political career."

While a WMUR/University of New Hampshire poll in the wake of those developments gave Hassan an 8-point lead, the Ayotte camp could take heart from a *Bloomberg News* survey showing New Hampshire with the largest percentage of ticket-splitters among eight swing states: Nearly 10 percent indicated they planned to vote for both Clinton and Ayotte. On Election Day, it turned out to be nearly a dead heat. Hassan came out on top by just over 1,000 votes out of more than 708,000 cast. Geographically, the voting patterns mirrored those in the Clinton-Trump contest, which was much closer than pre-election polls had foreseen: Clinton won by barely half a percentage point, with exit polls showing New Hampshire independents evenly split in both the presidential and Senate contests.

Hassan's margin of victory -- one-tenth of a percentage point -- was close enough to trigger a recount, but Ayotte conceded a day after the polls closed. Early in the campaign, the two sides had fenced over proposals to limit spending, without an agreement. By the time it was over, spending had reached $130 million, more than double the $55 million spent during the 2014 hotly contested race between Shaheen and Brown. In part, it reflected New Hampshire's heavy reliance on the expensive Boston TV market. Spending by the candidates themselves exceeded $38 million, with Ayotte spending about $1 million more than Hassan. But Hassan enjoyed about a $10 million advantage in the nearly $92 million pumped in by outside groups, according to the Center for Responsive Politics. On Capitol Hill, Hassan was named to the committees on Commerce; Health, Education, Labor and Pensions; and Homeland Security and Governmental Affairs. Her arrival marked another historical first: Hassan and Shaheen are the first instance of two former woman governors serving together to represent a state in the Senate.

FIRST DISTRICT

Carol Shea-Porter (D)

Elected 2006, 4th term; b. Dec 02, 1952, Brooklyn, NY; University of New Hampshire, B.A., 1975; University of New Hampshire, M.P.A., 1979; Roman Catholic; Married (Gene Porter); 2 children.

Elected Office: U.S House, 2007-2011, 2013-2015.

Professional Career: Presidential Campaign Staff, General Wesley Clark, 2004.

DC Office: 1530 LHOB 20515, 202-225-5456, Fax: 202-225-5822, shea-porter.house.gov.

State Offices: Dover, 603-285-4300.

Committees: *Armed Services*: Military Personnel, Readiness. *Education & the Workforce*: Health, Employment, Labor & Pensions, Workforce Protections.

Election Results

Election	Name (Party)	Vote	(%)	Cand. Spent	Ind. Exp. Support	Ind. Exp. Oppose
2016 General	Carol Shea-Porter (D)	162,080	(44%)	$1,513,386	$62,784	$599,108
	Frank Guinta (R)	157,176	(43%)	$1,516,432	$651,470	$73,044
	Shawn O' Connor (I)	32,939	(9%)	$1,467,385	$11,369	
2016 Primary	Carol Shea-Porter (D)		(100%)			

Prior winning percentages: 2012 (50%), 2008 (52%), 2006 (51%)

In an ongoing seesaw battle, Democrat Carol Shea-Porter in 2016 for the second time reclaimed the seat she held before Republican Frank Guinta had ousted her. They have met four consecutive times since 2010, when Guinta prevailed with 54 percent of the vote. Shea-Porter, who was the first woman from New Hampshire elected to Congress in what has become an all-female delegation, won the latest contest over her ethically scarred foe, 44.3%-43.0%. With five switches in the past six elections, and another competitive contest likely in 2018, this district might earn an award for being a ping pong ball.

Shea-Porter was born in New York City and moved to New Hampshire at age 14. Her mother, Margaret (Peggy) Shea, was an antique appraiser and a descendent of John Stark, a general in the Continental Army who coined the term "Live Free or Die" that would become New Hampshire's motto. Shea-Porter got her bachelor's and earned her master's degree in public administration at the University of New Hampshire. She moved to Colorado with her husband, an officer stationed at an Army medical center. There, she witnessed soldiers returning from the Vietnam War in need of medical and psychological care, an experience that would contribute to her antiwar candidacy decades later. She went to New Orleans, where she worked as a social worker, then relocated to the Washington area. At that time, she taught politics and history at a community college and a retirement facility.

Returning to New Hampshire in 2001, she worked on retired Gen. Wesley Clark's 2004 presidential campaign and served as chair of the Rochester Democrats, cultivating a network of liberal activists.

Preparing to run for a House seat in 2006, she started following Republican Rep. Jeb Bradley from event to event, asking pointed questions about the issues. She got the media's attention in February 2005, when she was escorted from a town hall meeting hosted by President George W. Bush. She removed her sweater to reveal a T-shirt that read, "Turn your back on Bush." The Democratic Congressional Campaign Committee, not for the final time, questioned her viability in a general election against Bradley and backed state House Minority Leader Jim Craig in the four-way primary. But Shea-Porter pulled off an upset. Against Bradley, she campaigned on an anti-Iraq war platform and advocated the creation of a federal institute dedicated to reducing dependence on foreign oil. Bradley defended Bush on Iraq and argued that withdrawing troops would destabilize the Middle East. Shea-Porter eked out a win, 51%-49%.

With a centrist voting record among Democrats, she sought major changes in the Bush administration's No Child Left Behind law, which she compared to a "beautiful-looking car (that) doesn't start." In 2010, she drew a challenge from Guinta, a former Manchester mayor who cut taxes and spending and developed a reputation as a pragmatic, bipartisan official. Guinta had to overcome a contentious GOP primary battle that sullied his reputation when he failed to disclose a bank account worth at least $250,000. He blamed a paperwork error for the lack of disclosure. He called for government hiring freezes and cast Shea-Porter as a big spender. In a favorable year for Republican, he won by an impressive 54%-42%.

In their 2012 rematch, the candidates debated entitlements and the effectiveness of the 2009 stimulus bill, which Shea-Porter supported. That was a stronger year for Democrats, and Shea-Porter took back the seat 50%-46%. She subsequently moderated some of her liberal positions. In 2013, she voted for GOP Rep. Fred Upton's bill to allow health insurance policyholders to keep their current plan even if it did not meet the Affordable Care Act's regulations. In 2014, Shea-Porter attacked Guinta for "being funded by the billionaire Koch brothers." But, again, she could not turn around voters' discontent with President Barack Obama in the mid-term election. This time, Guinta's victory margin was 51.7%-48.1%. Both candidates, especially Guinta, received extensive national party and interest-group assistance.

In May 2015, Guinta was jolted by a politically damaging incident when he agreed to a settlement of charges by the Federal Election Commission that he had accepted $355,000 in illegal campaign contributions from his parents, which he had described as a loan in 2010. After the FEC required that he repay the money, Guinta agreed to resolve the charges that he said had become "distractions." Some New Hampshire Republicans viewed the action as a mortal wound to his political future and demanded that he resign immediately. That included Sen. Kelly Ayotte, who faced reelection in 2016. The conservative *Manchester Union-Leader* joined the call for his resignation. Rich Ashooh, his chief opponent in the GOP primary and a former aerospace executive, was backed by a Super PAC to which prominent Republicans contributed. Still, Guinta pushed ahead. In the four-candidate primary, Guinta led Ashooh, 47.7%-46.4%, a margin of 722 votes. Post-primary polls showed that he trailed by double digits in the general election.

Shea-Porter hardly waltzed to victory. Computer-hacked documents from the Democratic Congressional Campaign Committee revealed efforts by House Democrats to recruit another candidate for the 2016 contest. She initially faced a contentious primary against businessman Shawn O'Connor, who threatened to file a lawsuit against the state Democratic Party with allegations of defamation. In June 2016, O'Connor, a supporter of Sen. Bernie Sanders in the presidential campaign, withdrew from the primary and decided to run as an independent. In the fall campaign, each of the three candidates spent $1.5 million; O'Connor mostly self-financed. National Republicans spent $1.3 million on behalf of Guinta, with the hope that he would benefit from voter support for Donald Trump. In the unexpectedly close outcome, Shea-Porter led by 4,904 votes out of nearly 366,000 cast. O'Connor received 34,735. For the third time, she was assigned a seat on the Armed Services Committee.

Eastern New Hampshire: Manchester

Population		**Race and Ethnicity**		**Income**	
Total	665,132	White	91.5%	Median Income	$67,706 (80 out of 435)
Land area	2,464	Black	1.4%		
Pop/ sq mi	270.0	Latino	3.2%	Under $50,000	36.3%
Born in state	41.9%	Asian	2.2%	$50,000-$99,999	32.7%
Age Groups		Two races	1.6%	$100,000-$199,999	24.8%
Under 18	20.4%	Other	0.2%	$200,000 or more	6.2%
18-34	21.5%	**Education**		Poverty Rate	8.7%
35-64	43.1%	H.S grad or less	35.5%	**Health Insurance**	
Over 64	15.0%	Some college	29.1%	With health insurance coverage	90.4%
Work		College Degree, 4 yr	22.4%		
White Collar	39.5%	Post grad	12.8%	**Public Assistance**	
Sales and Service	40.9%	**Military**		Cash public assistance income	3.0%
Blue Collar	19.6%	Veteran	10.0%		
Government	6.5%	Active Duty	0.2%	Food stamp/SNAP benefits	8.0%

Voter Turnout			
2015 Total Citizens 18+	512,905	2016 House Turnout as % CVAP	69%
2016 House turnout	353,451	2014 House Turnout as % CVAP	48%

2012 Presidential Vote		
Barack Obama	179,148	(50%)
Mitt Romney	173,419	(48%)

2016 Presidential Vote		
Donald Trump	179,259	(48%)
Hillary Clinton	173,344	(46%)
Gary Johnson	15,994	(4%)

Cook Partisan Voting Index: R+2

The greatest growth in New Hampshire over the past two decades has been in the southeast and south-central parts of the state - the Seacoast and the Manchester area. Manchester was once famous for the Amoskeag Mills, the world's largest textile mill complex. In the first half of the 20th century, it was the quintessential mill town, with a few mansions for mill owners and managers and closely packed neighborhoods of frame houses for mill workers, many of them immigrants - from Quebec, Ireland and Greece. By the beginning of the 21st century, it was something quite different: a high-tech city, with big shopping malls at freeway interchanges, a spiffy new airport and downtown arena, spruced-up neighborhoods, and growth extending to the wooded suburbs all around. A quarter of New Hampshire residents claim French or French-Canadian ties, and racial minorities are sparse here. Manchester had participated in a State Department program to resettle refugees - more than 60 languages are spoken in the school system - but the city's Republican mayor halted the program, citing the strain on public services.

The Seacoast, within easy commuting distance of Massachusetts, is a collection of towns of ancient pedigree and high-tech growth along the 18-mile coastline. The biggest city on the coast is Portsmouth, the colonial capital of New Hampshire, with its busy naval shipyard and old seaport with well-preserved houses and a solid local economy that includes many art galleries and bars. Pease Air Force Base, shuttered in 1991, has been successfully redeveloped as Pease International Tradeport, with office buildings and an airplane runway, resulting in more than 250 businesses and nearly 10,000 jobs on the Seacoast. In Stratham, Swiss chocolate maker Lindt has a major facility, and Exeter is home to Phillips Exeter Academy, the elite boarding school.

The 1st Congressional District of New Hampshire includes the Manchester area and the Seacoast from Manchester and next-door Bedford, its affluent suburb, east to Portsmouth. It extends north to include Laconia and gentrifying Lake Winnipesaukee, studded with summer resorts and new mansions, including former Massachusetts Gov. Mitt Romney's $10 million vacation home in Wolfeboro. In 2015, Portsmouth opened an African Burying Ground Memorial to commemorate slaves who arrived in New Hampshire in the 18th century. Politically, this is the slightly more Republican of New Hampshire's two congressional districts. It has been the destination of many people fleeing high taxes in Massachusetts. Manchester, the largest city in the state, is a politically competitive bellwether and provides scenic backdrops for campaign events. During primary season, Saint Anslem College has regularly hosted presidential debates for both parties. In June 2016, Donald Trump spoke outside a shuttered factory to call for changes in international trade.

Portsmouth, with its trendy coffee shops, is Democratic, as are Durham, home of the University of New Hampshire, and nearby Dover, once a mill town and now the second fastest-growing city in the state. Most of the smaller towns on the Seacoast and to the north have been solidly Republican, though that is changing. Donald Trump won this swing district in 2016, 48%-46%, after Romney had lost his home ground to President Barack Obama, 50%-48%, in 2012.

SECOND DISTRICT

Ann Kuster (D)

Elected 2012, 3rd term; b. Sep 05, 1956, Concord; Dartmouth College, A.B., 1978; Georgetown University Law Center (DC), J.D., 1984; Christian Church; Married (Brad Kuster); 2 children.

Professional Career: Owner, Newfound Strategies, 2011-2013; Practicing lawyer, 1984-2010; Legislative aide, U.S. Rep. Pete McCloskey, 1978-1981.

DC Office: 137 CHOB 20515, 202-225-5206, Fax: 202-225-2946, kuster.house.gov.

State Offices: Concord, 603-226-1002; Littleton, 603-444-7700; Nashua, 603-595-2006.

Committees: *Agriculture*: Commodity Exchanges, Energy & Credit, Conservation & Forestry. *Veterans' Affairs*: Health, Oversight & Investigations (RMM).

Group Ratings

	ADA	ACLU	AFL-CIO	LCV	ITI	COC	HAFA	ACU	CFG	FRC
2016	-	82%	-	95%	83%	57%	14%	0%	4%	0%
2015	75%	C	96%	94%	C	58%	C	4%	0%	0%

Almanac Ratings 2015

	Economy	Social	Foreign	Composite
Liberal	80%	94%	62%	79%
Conservative	21%	6%	38%	21%

Key Votes of the 114th Congress

1. Keystone Pipeline	N	5. Puerto Rico Debt	Y	9. Offenses by Aliens	Y
2. Trade Deals	N	6. Medical Marijuana	Y	10. Troops in Iraq	Y
3. Export-Import Bank	Y	7. Sanctuary Cities	N	11. Homeland Security $$	Y
4. Debt Ceiling Increase	Y	8. Armor-piercing Bullets	N	12. Trade Adjustment aid	Y

Election Results

Election	Name (Party)	Vote (%)		Cand. Spent	Ind. Exp. Support	Ind. Exp. Oppose
2016 General	Ann Kuster (D)	174,371	(50%)	$1,938,804	$13,801	
	Jim Lawrence (R)	158,825	(45%)	$99,764		
	John Babiarz (I)	17,525	(5%)			
2016 Primary	Annie Kuster (D)		(100%)			

Prior winning percentages: 2014 (61%), 2012 (50%)

Democrat Ann McLane Kuster, elected in 2012, has had four hard-fought contests and won the last three. In doing so, she toppled veteran Rep. Charlie Bass, one of the House's few remaining GOP moderates. She has achieved some legislative success in dealing with opioid addiction and veterans' health issues.

Kuster was born in Concord and is part of a prominent political family in the Granite State. Her great-grandfather John McLane served as governor of New Hampshire from 1905 to 1907, while her father, Malcolm McLane, was mayor of Concord and an unsuccessful gubernatorial candidate in 1972. Her mother, Susan McLane, was a Republican state legislator for 25 years. "Politics was sort of a way of life in our family," Kuster said. She published a 2004 memoir based on interviews with her mother called *The Last Dance*. It dealt with Susan McLane's struggles with Alzheimer's disease.

Kuster worked on the 1972 presidential campaign of Republican Rep. Pete McCloskey of California, an anti-Vietnam War candidate who launched a quixotic challenge against President Richard Nixon. Kuster later graduated from Dartmouth College and worked in McCloskey's Washington office for three years. During that time, she specialized in foreign policy. Kuster earned her law degree from Georgetown University and returned to Manchester to practice law.

She spent many years in Concord as a lobbyist and adoption lawyer. "I represented women with unplanned pregnancies from age 14 to 40, and they ranged from living in their car to living in the nicest neighborhoods in town," she said. "Unplanned pregnancy is an equal-opportunity affliction." Kuster also became immersed in politics, and toured New Hampshire with Barack Obama during his 2008 presidential campaign.

In 2010, Kuster faced off against Bass, and was the underdog in a strong year for Republicans. She criticized his role in securing tax rebates for wood-pellet stove buyers before investing in a wood-pellet stove company himself, New England Wood Pellet. Bass denied any wrongdoing, but the issue gave her momentum. Kuster came under fire over an anecdote she repeated on the campaign trail about a New Hampshire firm that lost 4,000 jobs to outsourcing; a local newspaper found that no such company existed. The incumbent Bass was outspent 2-to-1, but he eked out the victory 48%-47%.

Kuster had a rematch with Bass and a more favorable political climate two years later. Kuster called for a return to the Clinton-era income tax rates and Bass favored an extension of the Bush-era tax cuts. Kuster supported Obama's 2010 health care overhaul, and Bass called the law a "bureaucratic boondoggle." Kuster again outspent Bass by more than a million dollars and had a comparable advantage in the outside money that was spent on the contest. This time she won, 50%-45%.

Kuster has had several accomplishments as a member of the Veterans' Affairs Committee. During her first term, the House passed her bill to improve health care options for veterans. In 2015, she cooperated with home-state Republican Rep. Frank Guinta on health issues, including veterans' access to care. As ranking Democrat on the Veterans Affairs' Oversight and Investigations Subcommittee, she has had opportunities to work on those issues. In March 2016, the subcommittee held a field hearing in New Hampshire on the problem of opioid prescriptions and pain management practices by the VA.

Her interest in opioid addiction extended to the community. As parts of broader legislation, she enacted two proposals that sought additional treatment for addiction that related to mental health or substance abuse. She enacted another bill that assured federal jurisdiction over offenses committed by U.S. personnel stationed in Canada for border-security initiatives

Kuster has continued to have competitive campaigns. In 2014, she faced a reelection challenge from state Rep. Marilinda Garcia, a young conservative Latina activist. Kuster called her opponent "naïve," and won 55%-45%. Kuster outspent Garcia 3-to-1, and outside groups flooded the contest with more than $7.5 million. The contest was "much fiercer than the final margin would seem to suggest," according to House elections expert David Wasserman, who added that Garcia's campaign gained wide attention among national conservatives. Against underfunded Republican challenger Jim Lawrence in 2016, Kuster was held to a 50%-45% win. In the New Hampshire tradition, her district remains a swing seat.

Kuster gained unusual attention in October 2016 following the revelations by Donald Trump of his groping of women. In interviews with New Hampshire reporters, she described publicly for the first time how she had been assaulted as a young woman, including an incident four decades earlier when she was working for McCloskey. While seated during a lunch on Capitol Hill next to famed South African heart-transplant surgeon Christian Barnard, who died in 2001, she said she realized that his hand was underneath her skirt. "I was just shocked. I didn't feel anything. I didn't know what to do. I was in the middle of a meeting. I didn't have the presence of mind to leave," Kuster told the *Manchester Union Leader*.

Western New Hampshire: Nashua, Concord

Population		**Race and Ethnicity**		**Income**	
Total	659,069	White	91.3%	Median Income	$65,822 (88 out of 435)
Land area	6,489	Black	1.0%		
Pop/ sq mi	101.6	Latino	3.2%	Under $50,000	38.2%
Born in state	42.6%	Asian	2.5%	$50,000-$99,999	32.5%
		Two races	1.7%	$100,000-$199,999	23.4%
Age Groups		Other	0.3%	$200,000 or more	6.0%
Under 18	20.6%			Poverty Rate	9.1%
18-34	20.6%	**Education**			
35-64	43.3%	H.S grad or less	37.5%	**Health Insurance**	
Over 64	15.5%	Some college	28.1%	With health insurance coverage	90.9%
		College Degree, 4 yr	21.2%		
Work		Post grad	13.3%		
White Collar	40.1%			**Public Assistance**	
Sales and Service	38.9%	**Military**		Cash public assistance income	2.6%
Blue Collar	20.9%	Veteran	10.4%		
Government	7.4%	Active Duty	0.0%	Food stamp/SNAP benefits	8.1%

Voter Turnout			
2015 Total Citizens 18+	507,225	2016 House Turnout as % CVAP	69%
2016 House turnout	350,189	2014 House Turnout as % CVAP	47%

2012 Presidential Vote		
Barack Obama	190,413	(54%)
Mitt Romney	156,499	(44%)

2016 Presidential Vote		
Hillary Clinton	175,182	(48%)
Donald Trump	166,531	(45%)
Gary Johnson	14,783	(4%)

Cook Partisan Voting Index: D+2

Political reporters covering New Hampshire's first-in-the-nation primary usually stay in Manchester, the state's largest city and within an hour's drive of the rest of the state except for the North Country. Yet there are other noteworthy cities and towns in New Hampshire. Concord, north of Manchester, is the state capital. On one side of Main Street is the handsome, small, granite Capitol, and on the other you can usually find the headquarters of the two political parties and many candidates: an entire state's politics within 100 yards. Nashua, south of Manchester and on the Massachusetts line, is twice the size of Concord and the state's second-largest city, a technology and financial services center that has been mostly booming for three decades.

To the east is prosperous and growing Salem, first chartered in 1750 and the largest of the border suburbs. To the west near the Vermont border, past the pleasant country around Mount Monadnock, is Keene (pop., 23,265), the hub of southwest New Hampshire, and the largest city in the state north or west of Concord. To the north are towns along the Connecticut River; some are mill towns, and some are vacation enclaves. Hanover, home of Dartmouth College, is a tiny, picturesque town set in the mountains. Every political reporter's itinerary has to include a trip, usually by plane, to the little lumber mill city of Berlin in the middle of the North Country, where the last paper mill has closed, and perhaps also to Dixville Notch in the White Mountains, where the town's handful of voters cast their ballots at a minute past midnight and provide the first reported returns in every presidential election. Hillary Clinton led Donald Trump, 4-2, in 2016, which perhaps signaled that she would win New Hampshire. (Or not.)

The 2nd Congressional District of New Hampshire includes Concord, Nashua, Salem, Keene, the Connecticut River counties, Hanover, Berlin and Dixville Notch. It includes Mount Washington, with its spectacularly violent weather and winds that have been measured up to 231 miles per hour; entrepreneurs have considered wind power plants, but the manager of its state park said the location was too windy and icy to be practical. The district takes in the Bretton Woods resort, where the world monetary system was established at a conference in 1944.

Politically, this region is mixed, though it has become the more Democratic of New Hampshire's two congressional districts. Nashua is more Democratic than Manchester, Salem more Republican. The area between Mount Monadnock and Keene and the territory running north along the Connecticut River to Hanover and Dartmouth has become very Democratic, much like Vermont across the river. In 2016 Hillary Clinton led Donald Trump by only 48%-45%, a significant tightening of the 13 and 10 percentage point leads that Barack Obama had in 2008 and 2012. A state map shows that many of the interior towns had moved from blue to red.

★ NEW JERSEY ★

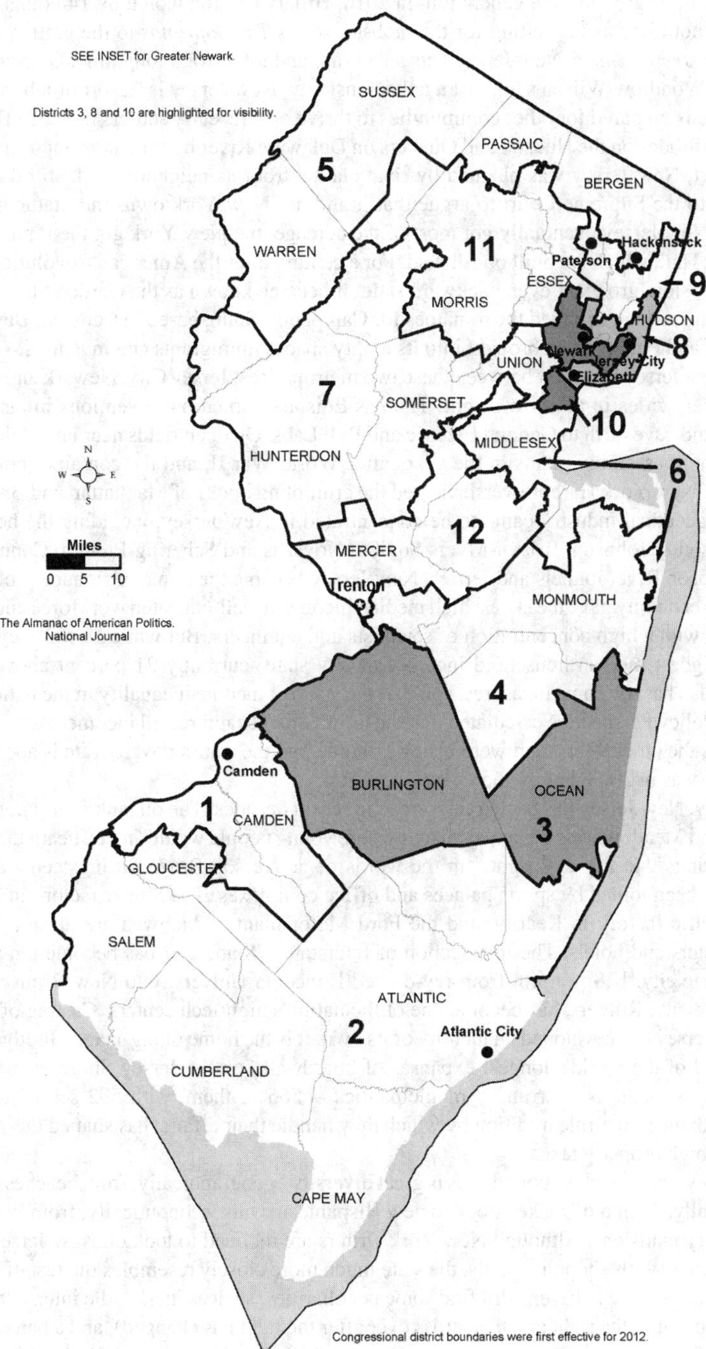
SEE INSET for Greater Newark.
Districts 3, 8 and 10 are highlighted for visibility.
SUSSEX
PASSAIC
BERGEN
5
11
WARREN
Paterson
Hackensack
ESSEX
9
MORRIS
HUDSON
Newark
Jersey City
8
UNION
Elizabeth
7
SOMERSET
10
HUNTERDON
MIDDLESEX
6
Miles
0 5 10
12
MERCER
Trenton
MONMOUTH
The Almanac of American Politics.
National Journal
4
Camden
BURLINGTON
OCEAN
1
CAMDEN
3
GLOUCESTER
SALEM
ATLANTIC
2
Atlantic City
CUMBERLAND
CAPE MAY
Congressional district boundaries were first effective for 2012.

New Jersey leaned Republican from the 1940s through the 1980s, but over the past two decades, it has become a Democratic bastion due to a growing immigrant population and the presence of many affluent suburbanites who reject the GOP's conservative stands on cultural issues. The state hasn't been a presidential battleground for a generation; in 2016, Hillary Clinton won it by 14 points.

From its notoriety as the setting for the mobster series *The Sopranos* to the grating stereotypes of its citizens on *Jersey Shore*, New Jersey gets a bad rap, and it has for a long time. During his two years as governor, Woodrow Wilson said, just a tad defensively, New Jersey is "a sort of laboratory in which the best blood is prepared for other communities to thrive on." Its early settlers included Dutch in towns behind the Palisades on the Hudson and Quakers on Delaware River bottomlands opposite Philadelphia. From the start, New Jersey was plagued by rival claims from its neighbors and, still defensive in the 1980s, went to the Supreme Court to argue that it and not New York owns the Statue of Liberty and Ellis Island. New Jersey eventually got most of the acreage, but New York got the immigrant museum and the Great Hall, which are built on fill land. For a century after the American Revolution, New Jersey was a modest, slow-growing, even backward state. It became known as the Garden State because of its vegetable farms, which supplied the tomatoes for Campbell's Soup, based in Camden. But its proximity to New York and Philadelphia brought into its empty spaces immigrants and inventors.

While New Jersey is caught between these two metropolises, Jersey City, Newark and Camden grew to be significant cities in their own right. Thomas Edison churned out inventions in his laboratory at Menlo Park and gave birth to General Electric and Bell Labs. On open fields near large labor pools, U.S. automakers built assembly plants in the years after World War II, and the container port on the New Jersey side of New York Harbor overshadowed the crumbling docks of Manhattan and Brooklyn. Much of the pharmaceutical industry came to be concentrated in New Jersey, including the headquarters of Merck, Johnson & Johnson, Bristol-Myers Squibb, Novartis and Schering-Plough. Connected to Wall Street by Hudson River tunnels and ferries, New Jersey became the home of finance professionals and lawyers. This economy gave the state a high median income, a well-educated workforce and a prosperous middle class, with a high concentration of scientists and engineers. But while New Jersey has long had one of the highest median household incomes of any state -currently 21 percent above the national average – it also has, by some measures, some of the starkest income inequality in the nation. The group New Jersey Policy Perspective calculated that the top 1 percent captured all income growth from 2009 to 2013, even as the other 99 percent were losing ground. And the state's poverty rate is about one-quarter higher than it was in 2008, before the Great Recession.

Physically, New Jersey has been transformed in recent decades. The oil tank farms, concrete ribbons of turnpike and Meadowlands swamps - places where young people would "meet 'neath that giant Exxon sign / that brings this fair city light," in the words of native son Bruce Springsteen - are still there, but they have been joined by sports palaces and office complexes. The Singer factory in Elizabeth, the Western Electric factory in Kearny, and the Ford Motor plant in Mahwah are all gone, replaced by shopping centers and hotels. The intersection of Interstates 78 and 287 has become a major shopping and office edge city. U.S. 1 north from ivy-draped Princeton University to New Brunswick, home of the state university, Rutgers, has become one of the nation's high-tech centers. Casting off its suburban image, New Jersey has developed an identity of its own. It is the home of big-league football and hockey franchises and of the world's longest expanses of boardwalk, on the Jersey Shore from Cape May to Sandy Hook. The state is overrun by municipalities -- 565 of them, with 592 school districts. This, combined with the home-rule tradition by which they handle their affairs, has shaped the state's politics, including its high property taxes.

Within New Jersey's close boundaries is great diversity - geographically, from beaches to mountains; demographically, from old Quaker stock to new Hispanic arrivals; economically, from inner-city slums to hunt-country mansions. Although New York writers are inclined to look on New Jersey as a land of 1940s diners and 1970s shopping malls, the state much more closely resembles the rest of America than does Manhattan, although drivers will find some peculiarities, such as jug-handle intersections (to make a left turn, you exit to the right and then cross over after the light has changed), and a ban on self-service gas stations. The row houses one used to encounter upon emerging from the Holland Tunnel are now joined by office and apartment towers and, a few miles further out, the skyscrapers of Newark and its performing arts center. Farther out are comfortably packed middle-income suburbs and the horse country around Far Hills, old industrial cities such as Paterson and Trenton (also the state capital), and dozens of suburban towns and small factory cities. Among them are commuter towns such as Middletown, whose commuter trails lead to Lower Manhattan. In South Jersey is the desolate expanse known as the pine barrens, where Christopher Moltisanti and Paulie ("Walnuts") Gualtieri of *The Sopranos* spent an uncomfortable winter's night trying to dispose of a Russian mobster.

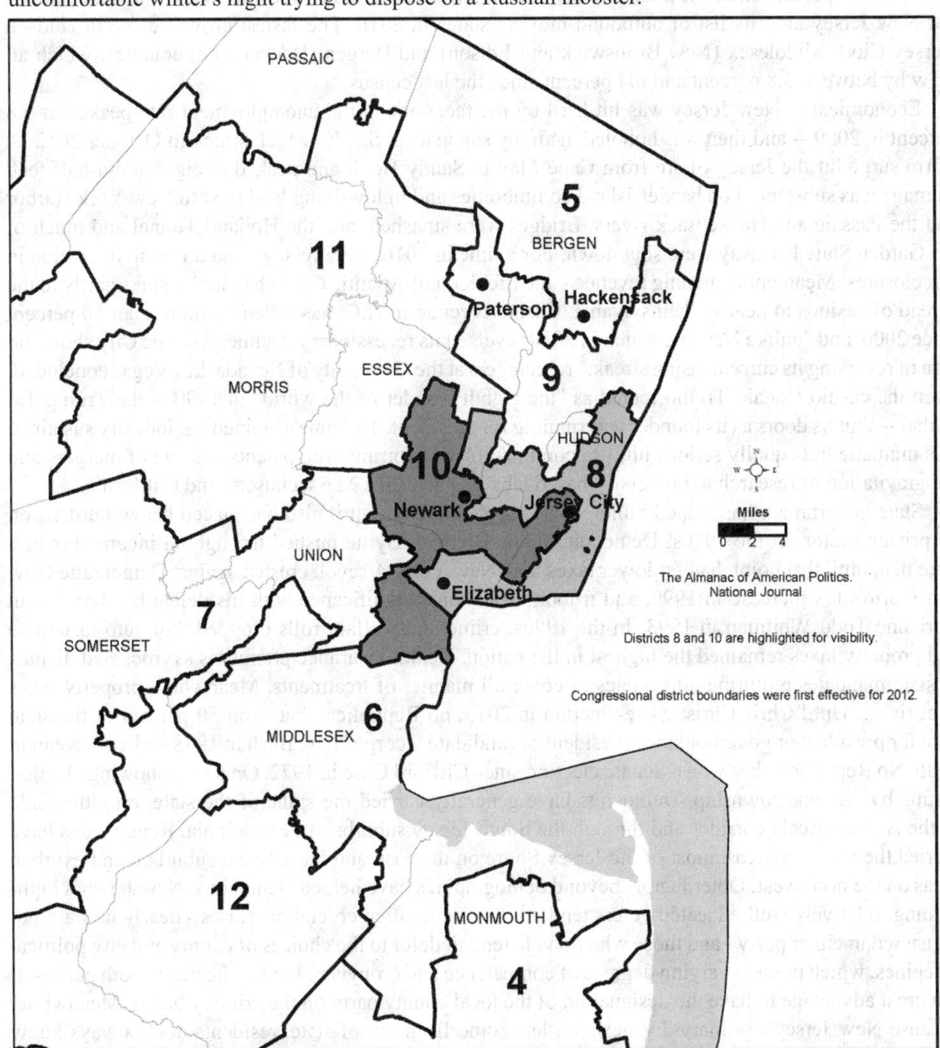

Regardless of which state holds legal title to Ellis Island, New Jersey has long been a magnet for immigrants. In its post-World War II years of rapid growth, the state was a quilt pattern of WASPs, Irish, Italians, Jews and Hungarians (the nation's largest concentration of the latter was in Middlesex County). Small-town-like suburbs centered on Dutch Reform or Episcopal churches became heavily Catholic or Jewish. Immigrant growth has been concentrated in North and Central Jersey, within range of New York City. (South Jersey, as in adjacent Philadelphia, has few communities of recent immigrants.) New Jersey's population is 13 percent black, 18 percent Hispanic (ranking eighth nationally), 11 percent Asian (third behind Hawaii and California), and 56 percent white (ranking among the bottom 10 states). Hudson County, which includes Jersey City opposite Manhattan, was the home of hundreds of thousands of Irish, Italian, Polish and Jewish immigrants in the early 20th century, and it is now 43 percent Hispanic, a grouping that includes Cubans, Puerto Ricans, Dominicans and Mexicans, 16 percent black and and 14 percent Asian. Immigrants are also plentiful in the small middle-American towns of Bergen County: Filipinos in Bergenfield, Guatemalans in Fairview, Koreans in Leonia, Indians in Lodi, and Chinese in

Palisades Park. The old industrial cities of Elizabeth and Paterson are majority Hispanic, and Newark is majority black.

For all its strengths, New Jersey has faced difficulties in the new century. The state's population has grown by 1.7 percent since the 2010 census, but it fell from 2015 to 2016. United Van Lines calculations put New Jersey atop its list of outbound-moving states in 2016. The fastest growth came in Hudson (Jersey City), Middlesex (New Brunswick and Edison) and Bergen (Hackensack) counties, which all grew by between 3.8 percent and 6.4 percent since the last census.

Economically, New Jersey was hit hard by the recession -- the unemployment rate peaked at 9.8 percent in 2009 -- and then was hobbled again by superstorm Sandy, which struck in October 2012. A storm surge hit the Jersey Shore from Cape May to Sandy Hook and peaked at eight-and-a-half feet. Damage was substantial on barrier-island communities and in low-lying land next to New York Harbor and the Passaic and Hackensack rivers. Bridges were smashed, and the Holland Tunnel and much of the Garden State Parkway were shut down. For a time in 2016, New Jersey ranked first in the nation in foreclosures. Meanwhile, gaming revenue – the lifeblood of Atlantic City – has sunk thanks partly to the spread of casinos to nearby Pennsylvania. Casino revenue in A.C. has fallen by more than 50 percent since 2006, and "unlike Nevada, which in 2010 reversed its recessionary decline, Atlantic City shows no sign of reversing its current losing streak," researchers at the University of Nevada-Las Vegas concluded. Even the casino Donald Trump touted as "the eighth wonder of the world" in 1990 -- the Trump Taj Mahal -- shut its doors as its founder was running for president. The state's biomedical industry sustained less dramatic but equally serious hits – a combination of expiring drug patents, a spate of mergers and the gravitation of research to university-based labs in places like Massachusetts and California.

State government has helped build New Jersey's identity, but it also has placed heavy burdens on its private sector. In the 1970s, Democratic Gov. Brendan Byrne pushed through an income tax in a state that, until that point, had far lower taxes than New York. A revolt crested against Democratic Gov. Jim Florio's tax increase in 1990, and it took on national significance with his defeat by Republican Christine Todd Whitman in 1993. In the 1990s, crime and welfare rolls dropped, but auto insurance and property taxes remained the highest in the nation. Health insurance premiums skyrocketed, thanks to state mandates requiring all policies to cover all manner of treatments. Meanwhile, property taxes kept rising. Until Chris Christie's re-election in 2013, no Republican had won 50 percent of the state vote for president or governor since presidential candidate George H.W. Bush in 1988 and Tom Kean in 1985. No Republican has won a Senate election since Clifford Case in 1972. On a map showing election results by city and township, Democrats have generally carried the spine of the state, on either side of the Amtrak Acela corridor and through the South Jersey suburbs of Philadelphia. Republicans have carried the outlying areas, most of the Jersey Shore on the east, and the affluent suburban and exurban areas on the northwest. Other factors beyond demographics have helped Democrats. New Jersey's high-earning, relatively well-educated voters tend not to vote in often crucial primaries - nearly half are not registered in either party - and those who do vote tend to defer to the choices of county and city political machines, which possess varying degrees of competence and cronyism. For candidates in both parties, it is a great advantage to have the designation of the local county party on the primary ballot. Meanwhile, because New Jersey's primary TV news outlets come from out-of-state, residents don't always know what's going on in Trenton. It also makes it expensive to run a statewide campaign because New York and Philadelphia are among the nation's priciest media markets.

Christie won the governorship in 2009. As U.S. attorney, he had secured the convictions of dozens of political figures from both parties. New Jersey government, he argued, was bloated and overly expensive, and he promised not to raise taxes. Christie's first term produced bipartisan successes on public-employee pensions and the state budget, and in 2013 Christie rolled to a second term. But his tendency to speak bluntly and act aggressively, often a positive in a state that champions the tough guy, was also polarizing. That made it harder for him to inspire sympathy when his administration, shortly after he was re-elected, faced investigations into the closing of a lane on the George Washington Bridge, which some suspected was a way to punish Christie's political detractors. Other stumbles piled up – his presidential bid cratered, voters back home got restless about the time he spent away from the state, and eyebrows were raised when he became the first establishment Republican to back Trump (only to be purged from the transition team after Trump won).

Christie's endorsement aside, New Jersey remained solidly blue in 2016, though the race was slightly closer than in 2012 – a 14-point Democratic margin rather than 17. Clinton won 22,000 more votes than Obama had in 2012, but Trump exceeded Mitt Romney's showing by an even heftier 123,000. Two counties switched from blue to red—Gloucester, a small county where the margin shifted almost 12 points in Trump's direction, and Salem, the state's smallest, with a 16-point shift to Trump. Most of the counties that went Republican in both elections saw Trump improve on Romney's performance, except for two wealthy counties -- Morris, where the GOP's winning margin slipped from 11 points to four, and Hunterdon, where it fell from 18 points to 14. Among counties that went Democratic in both elections, Clinton improved on Obama's vote hauls in some of the more urban and suburban counties near New York City, including Bergen. Combined with Christie's meteoric decline in popularity, Trump's failure to make the state genuinely competitive suggests that New Jersey won't be promising territory for Republicans anytime soon.

Population		**Race and Ethnicity**		**Income**	
Total	8,904,413	White	57.2%	Median Income	$72,093 (3 out of 50)
Land area	8,729	Black	12.7%		
Pop/ sq mi	1,020.1	Latino	19.0%	Under $50,000	35.7%
Born in state	52.5%	Asian	9.0%	$50,000-$99,999	28.3%
		Two races	1.6%	$100,000-$199,999	25.9%
Age Groups		Other	0.5%	$200,000 or more	10.1%
Under 18	22.7%			Poverty Rate	8.2%
18-34	21.7%	**Education**			
35-64	41.2%	H.S grad or less	40.0%	**Health Insurance**	
Over 64	14.4%	Some college	23.2%	With health insurance coverage	88.4%
		College Degree, 4 yr	22.8%		
Work		Post grad	14.0%		
White Collar	40.9%			**Public Assistance**	
Sales and Service	41.4%	**Military**		Cash public assistance income	2.8%
Blue Collar	17.6%	Veteran	5.7%		
Government	13.8%	Active Duty	0.1%	Food stamp/SNAP benefits	9.1%

Voter Turnout			
2015 Total Citizens 18+	6,053,893	2016 Pres Turnout as % CVAP	64%
2016 Pres Votes	3,874,046	2012 Pres Turnout as % CVAP	62%

Legislature	
Senate:	24D, 16R
House:	52D, 28R

Presidential Politics

2016 Democratic Primary		
Hillary Clinton (D)	566,247	(63%)
Bernie Sanders (D)	328,058	(37%)
2016 Republican Primary		
Donald Trump (R)	360,212	(80%)
John Kasich (R)	59,866	(13%)
Ted Cruz (R)	27,874	(6%)

2016 Presidential Vote		
Hillary Clinton (D)	2,148,278	(55%)
Donald Trump (R)	1,601,933	(41%)
2012 Presidential Vote		
Barack Obama (D)	2,125,101	(58%)
Mitt Romney (R)	1,477,568	(41%)

In the second half of the 20th century, New Jersey was a close state in close presidential races. In the 1980s, the vast suburban expanses leaned toward Republicans. But since 1992, Democrats have won all seven presidential elections. Lately, GOP nominees have just cleared the 40 percent mark. The suburbs, with many secular and Jewish voters, reject GOP positions on cultural issues, and rising immigrant communities, including Asians in Bergen County, have generally voted Democratic. As a result, New Jersey, which had voted 56%-43% for George H. W. Bush in 1988 (a race where he carried 18 of the state's 21 counties), voted 54%-36% for Bill Clinton in 1996 (he won 16 counties) and 56%-40% for Al Gore in 2000. In 2004, George W. Bush's campaign strategists kept an eye on New Jersey's polls to see whether September 11 had had enough impact on voters to make the state worth contesting. It didn't and Democrat John Kerry won the state 53%-46%. In 2008, Barack Obama carried New Jersey 57%-42%, the best Democratic showing since 1964. In 2012, it was one of five states where Obama increased his percentage, to 58%-41%. This may have been the result of Hurricane Sandy: Turnout was down everywhere, but down most in Republican Ocean and Monmouth counties on the Jersey Shore. Obama visited the devastation before the election and GOP Gov. Chris Christie praised the president for his pledge to steer federal relief to the Garden State. In 2016, Hillary Clinton dispatched Donald Trump, 56%-41%. Trump won the northwestern section of New Jersey that includes the state's two fastest growing counties, Hunterdon and Somerset, home to the Trump National Golf Club in Bedminster. Those counties and Morris are among the wealthiest in the country. Trump ran close to Clinton in South Jersey, with its working class suburbs of Philadelphia, farms around Vineland and Millville, and beach communities in Atlantic, Cape May and Ocean counties. Clinton rolled up her biggest margins in Jersey City, Newark and Union City. She also ran well in Passaic and Paterson, old industrial centers that attracted immigrants from Italy and Eastern Europe in the early 1900s, but now have large Hispanic populations.

For years, New Jersey held its presidential primary in early June, but it was usually overshadowed by the California primary on the same day. In April 2007, the legislature rescheduled the primary for Feb. 5, 2008, Super Tuesday. But New Jersey again got lost in the shuffle. Democratic turnout was 1.1 million, nearly double the previous record, and Clinton beat Obama 54%-44%. She carried Jewish and Latino voters, while Obama carried blacks and did well in high-income suburbs, except those with large Jewish populations. Turnout on the Republican side was 566,000, more than ever before but only half the number of Democrats who voted. John McCain defeated Mitt Romney by a surprisingly large 55%-28% margin. In 2012, New Jersey went back to the June primary. By then the race was over, and Romney won 81 percent. In 2016, Trump was the de facto GOP nominee and rolled up 80 percent of the vote in the June 7 primary. The night before the primary, the Associated Press and CNN reported that Clinton had acquired enough delegates to claim the Democratic nomination. The next day she defeated Vermont Sen. Bernie Sanders, 63%-37%.

Congressional Districts

115th Congress Lineup	5R 7D	**114th Congress Lineup**	6R 6D

Since 1991, New Jersey has employed a bipartisan redistricting commission, made up of 12 members - six Democrats and six Republicans - appointed by party leaders in the legislature. The members pick a tie-breaking arbiter, and in both 1991 and 2001, they chose Rutgers University professor Alan Rosenthal. In 1991, Rosenthal picked the Republicans' plan, with grotesquely shaped districts, but New Jersey's trend toward Democrats in the 1990s reduced Republicans to six of the state's 13 seats by 2000. In 2001, the 13 incumbents agreed on a bipartisan, if contorted, map and submitted it to the commission. Rosenthal liked the incumbent-protection plan, and over the next 10 years, only the South Jersey 3rd District switched parties.

The 2010 census cost New Jersey a House seat, raising the stakes and rendering protection of all seven Democratic and six Republican incumbents impossible. In 2011, the commission appointed former state Attorney General John Farmer as its 13th member, and then the sides retreated to their war rooms. (Rosenthal died in 2013.) Democrats argued that the state's Democratic drift made a 7-5 partisan split logical, with the unwieldy Republican-held 7th District ripe for the chopping block. Republicans contended the urban northeastern corner of the state had grown the slowest, and while the black-majority 10th District and Hispanic-majority 13th District were sacrosanct, the nearby Democratic-held 8th and 9th districts were logical choices to merge.

Farmer let it be known that he preferred considering population over party breakdown. Farmer chose the Republicans' proposal, pitting Steve Rothman against Scott Garrett in a more Republican seat. The plan stuffed most of Rothman's political base into Bill Pascrell's district. Rather than face Garrett, Rothman opted to primary Pascrell and was trounced. But Garrett's hard-line conservative views made him increasingly vulnerable in his moderate district. Democrat Josh Gottheimer styled himself as a centrist and defeated Garrett in 2016. With Gottheimer an obvious target in 2018 and Democrats salivating over their opportunities against other GOP incumbents, the map has become volatile. The state's tradition of incumbent protection in redistricting, plus the prospect of Democratic control in Trenton, raise the possibility that a deadlocked delegation has become a relic.

Governor

Chris Christie (R)

Elected 2009, term expires 2018, 2nd term; b. Sep. 6, 1962, Newark, NJ; U. of DE, B.A. 1984; Seton Hall U., J.D. 1987; Catholic; Married (Mary Pat); 4 children.

Elected Office: Morris County freeholder, 1994-1998; Director, Freeholder Board, 1997.

Professional Career: Practicing attorney & Partner, Dughi Hewit & Palatucci, 1987-2001; U.S. Attorney for NJ, 2002-2008.

Office: PO Box 001, Trenton, 08625; 609-292-6000; Fax: 609-292-3454; Website: nj.gov/governor.

Election Results

Election	Name (Party)	Vote (%)
2013 General	Chris Christie (R)	1,278,932 (60%)
	Barbara Buono (D)	809,978 (38%)
2013 Primary	Chris Christie (R)	205,666 (92%)
	Seth Grossman (R)	18,095 (8%)

Prior winning percentage: 2009 (48%)

Chris Christie, a Republican, was elected governor of New Jersey in 2009 and quickly became lionized in his party as the archetypal "Jersey guy" for his confident, cut-the-crap persona. But a home-grown scandal and economic challenges for the state helped torpedo his 2016 presidential bid and brought his approval ratings down as low as the teens.

Christie grew up in Livingston, a comfortable suburb 10 miles west of Newark, the son of an accountant who was an ardent Republican, and a Sicilian-American mother who was a lifelong Democrat. He was president of his class throughout middle school and high school and was selected for student leadership programs in Washington. In 1977, when he was 15, he volunteered in Republican Thomas Kean's race for governor, and Kean became his role model. He graduated from the University of Delaware and Seton Hall Law School. After law school, Christie joined a firm in Cranford, where he specialized in corporate securities law and appellate work, making partner in 1993. His wife, Mary Pat Christie, pursued a career in investment banking. One of Christie's law partners, Bill Palatucci, was state coordinator for George H.W. Bush's campaign in 1992 and the two together raised money in 2000 for his son, George W. Bush. In 1994, Christie was elected as a Republican to the Morris County Board of Chosen Freeholders. In 1995, he ran for the Assembly but lost the primary to candidates favored by the county Republican organization. He remained a freeholder, but in 1997, he was defeated for reelection in the Republican primary.

Christie's political spadework paid off when President George W. Bush appointed him U.S. attorney for New Jersey in 2002. This was a critical position in a state known for its corrupt politics. Ordinarily, U.S. attorneys are chosen by the president in consultation with a state's senators. In this case, both were Democrats, and Bush evidently wanted to bypass the county Republican organizations in order to appoint someone not indebted to them. The selection was strongly criticized in the state's legal circles as political patronage; Christie had no experience in criminal law. But he ultimately silenced his critics with a string of successful cases against corrupt public officials, street gangs, child pornographers and terrorists. He was best known for a crackdown on public corruption that yielded 130 convictions of both Democrats and Republicans, including that of a former state Senate president and a former Newark mayor.

In 2008, Christie resigned as U.S. attorney to challenge Gov. Jon Corzine, a former U.S. senator and chief executive officer of Goldman Sachs. Republicans had not won a statewide race in New Jersey since 1997. Corzine had deep pockets, having spent more than $100 million of his own money on his 2000 and 2005 campaigns. But Corzine also had problems. The state had dizzying budget shortfalls, and Corzine had been unable to fulfill his campaign pledge of lowering property taxes in a state with the highest rates in the nation. Christie campaigned as a middle-class native of the state, a father of four children under the age of 15, and a Mets baseball fan. He said he played New Jersey native Bruce Springsteen's song "Prove It All Night" to get psyched before press conferences. (All told, he attended 141 Springsteen concerts through August 2016.) Christie was endorsed by most Republican county organizations and he won the June primary. Corzine spent $27 million of his own money on the campaign, while Christie was limited by New Jersey's public financing law to spending $11 million. One ad supporting Corzine depicted the corpulent Christie struggling to emerge from a car with the suggestion that as U.S. attorney, he had "thrown his weight around" during a traffic stop. By mid-October, Corzine and Christie were running about even, with Christopher Daggett, a former Republican running as an independent, polling as high as 20 percent, seemingly splitting the anti-Corzine vote. But despite a rally for Corzine headlined by President Barack Obama, the incumbent was hurt by the arrests (by Christie's office) of 44 people, including several Democratic politicians, on such charges as corruption and money-laundering. Christie ended up winning, 48%-45%, with 6 percent for Daggett.

Structurally, New Jersey's governor is perhaps the nation's most powerful, and Christie used his authority aggressively. In May 2010, he refused to reappoint Supreme Court Justice John Wallace, as previous governors had routinely done, because of what he called "out of control" activism on the court. Democratic Senate President Stephen Sweeney refused to let the Senate vote on Christie's nominee to fill the post. In October 2010, he canceled proposed rail tunnels to Manhattan, citing cost overruns. During the 2011 legislative session, Christie vetoed Democratic bills taxing millionaires to pay for schools and to provide tax relief for low-income workers. He also vetoed $7.5 million for family planning clinics, but redirected those dollars toward Federally Qualified Health Centers, which provide some of the same services but do not provide abortions. Christie used his line-item veto to cut $900 million from a Democratic spending plan and avert a government shutdown. He signed legislation allowing non-public schools to be converted into charter schools.

Yet Christie did not totally cut off relations with New Jersey Democrats, including Newark Mayor (and later Sen.) Cory Booker and Essex County Executive Joseph DiVincenzo. Christie's most fruitful relationship was with Sweeney, a moderate with blue collar cred - he served as an organizer of the International Association of Ironworkers. Their relationship was stormy - Christie once enraged Sweeney so much that he called the governor a "rotten prick" - but together they produced legislation requiring public employees to pay more for their pensions and health insurance, in exchange for higher payments to pension funds to make up for past short contributions. Christie won bipartisan praise for his call for drug courts, which take a more treatment-oriented approach. A measure to cut business taxes passed both chambers unanimously, and lawmakers backed his plan to hand control over most of New Jersey's University of Medicine and Dentistry to Rutgers University. "He knows all the tools and knows how to use them," Tom Wilson, a former state GOP chairman told *Governing*. "He has a deep appreciation that political capital does not have a long shelf life, and that it's best appreciated by spending it."

Christie's big personality helped make his achievements possible, but his tendency to shoot from the hip has also gotten him in trouble. Irritated by criticism from Assemblyman Reed Gusciora about Christie's opposition to gay marriage, he called the state's first openly gay lawmaker "numbnuts." Challenged at a town meeting by Rutgers law student Bill Brown, Christie called the former Navy SEAL an "idiot." He called a nonpartisan legislative analyst "a joke," a "handmaiden" for the majority and "the Dr. Kevorkian of numbers." In a video, Christie explained his confrontational style: "I have an Irish father and I had ... a Sicilian mother. For those of you who have been exposed to the combination of Irish and Sicilian, it has made me not unfamiliar with conflict."

In 2012, Christie threw himself into campaigning for GOP presidential nominee Mitt Romney, though in his Republican convention keynote he focused on his own accomplishments, a decision that drew some criticism for seeming to place his own political career over Romney's. In the closing days of the 2012 campaign, Superstorm Sandy ravaged New Jersey's coastline. Christie accompanied Obama to damaged areas and heaped praise on the president's responsiveness – a decision that came to haunt him with Republican primary voters. He further irked conservatives when he announced an expansion of the state's Medicaid program. By 2013, Christie was strong politically (and perhaps a bit slimmer, following weight-loss surgery). Nine months before election day, a Quinnipiac University poll gave Christie an approval rating of 74% - the highest that poll had found in 17 years of testing New Jersey governors. Nearly half of Democrats surveyed - 48% - felt that he deserved another term. On Election Day, he won 60 percent of the vote against underfunded Democratic state Sen. Barbara Buono.

But within weeks came "Bridgegate." In September 2013, two of the three local access lanes to the tolls on the George Washington Bridge linking Fort Lee to New York City had been closed to morning rush-hour traffic. Streets were backed up for several days until the Port Authority - citing a potential danger to lives - reopened the lanes. Christie adamantly denied knowing anything about the lane closures, joking at a news conference in December, "Unbeknownst to anyone, I was working the (traffic) cones." There was considerable speculation that the closures were done to retaliate against Fort Lee Mayor Mark Sokolich, a Democrat who had refused to endorse Christie's re-election. And in January he apologized to Fort Lee, the people of the state and the Legislature for his staffers' actions; several Christie aides resigned, and the governor fired his deputy chief of staff, Bridget Anne Kelly, after an email surfaced saying it was "time for some traffic problems in Fort Lee." Christie was booed at a Super Bowl ceremony and even his beloved Springsteen mocked him in song alongside Jimmy Fallon on *The Tonight Show* ("highways jammed with pissed off drivers with no place left to go," went their parody of "Born to Run.") Christie hired a law firm to investigate and it issued a report clearing him of any wrongdoing; the legal costs to taxpayers ran to at least $10 million. In May 2015, a former senior Christie appointee, David Wildstein, pleaded guilty to conspiracy in the Bridgegate matter, saying the closings were political punishment against Sokolich. Then, in November 2016, Kelly and former Port Authority Deputy Executive Director Bill Baroni were found guilty of charges including conspiracy to misuse Port Authority resources and civil rights infringements. Their depiction of Christie on the stand was withering; Wildstein testified that he and Baroni had told the governor about the lane closures in real time, and that Christie had laughed. But Christie received good news in January 2017, when the Bergen County prosecutor announced that he would not bring charges personally against the governor.

Bridgegate was not Christie's only setback. Credit agencies lowered the state's ratings 10 times during his tenure, he faced continuing budget strain, and a gambling implosion in Atlantic City forced him to appoint an emergency manager for the city. In anticipation of his presidential run, Christie positioned himself well to the right of most New Jersey voters. He said Common Core school standards - which he had implemented in 2010 - are "simply not working." And Christie continued to oppose same-sex marriage. But he forged ahead on the national stage. As chairman of the Republican Governors Association in 2014, he spearheaded an outstanding election night for GOP governors. He announced his bid for president in June 2015, saying, "I am not going to be the most popular guy who looks into your eye every day and says what you want to hear." He focused most intensively on New Hampshire, where it seemed like voters might respond well to his pragmatic streak. But he ended up finishing sixth in the GOP field and quit the race.

Not long after, he dropped a bombshell – that he would be endorsing Donald Trump, becoming the first major establishment Republican to do so. New Jersey voters, already irritated at the long stretches he had spent away from the state campaigning, did not respond well to his support for Trump, who was not popular in the state. By December 2016, Christie's approval rating had fallen to an anemic 18 percent in a Fairleigh Dickinson University poll. In January 2017, *Governing* rated the New Jersey governorship the most likely to flip control in the 2017-18 election cycle, with Phil Murphy, a former Goldman Sachs executive, ambassador to Germany and party fundraiser, the leading Democratic candidate. Adding to Christie's woes, his alliance with Trump didn't work out as planned. After months of assembling a transition plan during the campaign, Christie was purged from that role after Trump won, just weeks before the inauguration. The saddest cut of all, however, was probably his widening rift with Springsteen. In September 2015, Christie told Fox News' Sean Hannity that he was no longer friends with the musician; he was, however, friends with Jon Bon Jovi.

Senior Senator

Robert Menendez (D)

Appointed Jan. 2006, term expires 2018, 2nd full term; b. Jan 01, 1954, New York, NY; Rutgers University Law School (NJ), J.D.; St. Peter's College (NJ), B.A., Roman Catholic; Divorced; 2 children.

Elected Office: Union City Board of Education, 1974-1982, CFO, 1978-1982; Union City Mayor, 1986-1992; NJ Assembly, 1987-1991; NJ Senate, 1991-1992; U.S. House, 1993-2006.

Professional Career: Practicing attorney, 1980-1992.

DC Office: 528 HSOB 20510, 202-224-4744, Fax: 202-228-2197, menendez.senate.gov.

State Offices: Barrington, 856-757-5353; Newark, 973-645-3030.

Committees: *Banking, Housing & Urban Affairs*: Economic Policy, Housing, Transportation & Community Development (RMM), Securities, Insurance & Investment. *Finance*: Energy, Natural Resources & Infrastructure, Health Care, Taxation & IRS Oversight. *Foreign Relations*: Europe & Regional Security Cooperation, Near East, South Asia, Central Asia & Counterterrorism, West Hem Crime Civ Sec Dem Rights & Women's Issues (RMM).

Group Ratings

	ADA	ACLU	AFL-CIO	LCV	ITI	COC	HAFA	ACU	CFG	FRC
2016	-	88%	-	100%	60%	50%	9%	4%	13%	0%
2015	95%	C	100%	100%	C	43%	C	0%	6%	0%

Almanac Ratings 2015

	Economy	Social	Foreign	Composite
Liberal	97%	100%	79%	92%
Conservative	3%	0%	21%	8%

Key Votes of the 114th Congress

1. Keystone pipeline	N	5. National Security Data	Y	9. Gun Sales Checks	Y
2. Export-Import Bank	N	6. Iran Nuclear Deal	Y	10. Sanctuary Cities	N
3. Debt Ceiling Increase	Y	7. Puerto Rico Debt	N	11. Planned Parenthood	N
4. Homeland Security $$	Y	8. Loretta Lynch A.G	Y	12. Trade deals	N

Election Results

Election	Name (Party)	Vote (%)	Cand. Spent	Ind. Exp. Support	Ind. Exp. Oppose
2012 General	Robert Menendez (D)	1,985,783 (59%)	$16,226,545	$1,053,060	
	Joe Kyrillos (R)	1,329,405 (39%)	$4,559,919	$479,304	
2012 Primary	Robert Menendez (D)	272,201 (100%)			

Prior winning percentages: 2006 (57%), House: 2004 (76%), 2002 (78%), 2000 (79%), 1998 (80%), 1996 (79%), 1994 (71%), 1992 (64%)

Robert Menendez, New Jersey's senior senator, has been facing an uncertain future stemming from a federal corruption probe that has overshadowed his longtime work on foreign policy and immigration. The former chairman of the Foreign Relations Committee was forced to step aside as the committee's ranking Democrat in the spring of 2015, when he became only the 12th sitting senator in history to be indicted for a crime. His trial was scheduled to begin in September 2017, just over a year before his 2018 reelection, leaving his political future in doubt.

The indictment-which charged both the senator and Salomon Melgen, a Florida eye surgeon whom Menendez has characterized as a friend and political supporter-followed allegations that first surfaced as Menendez was assuming the chairmanship of Foreign Relations. A Justice Department spokesman described it as "a bribery scheme in which Menendez allegedly accepted gifts from Melgen in exchange for using the power of his Senate office to benefit Melgen's financial and personal interests." The gifts that Menendez allegedly received include luxury vacations, pricy golf outings and more than $750,000 in campaign contributions. Menendez has asserted his innocence while vowing to fight the charges, and has continued to speak out regularly on foreign policy and immigration issues. But Menendez's court case raises questions about the future of a political career that dates back more than 40 years - especially after Melgen was found guilty of Medicare fraud in April 2017.

Ironically, Menendez first gained political prominence in the early 1980s when he agreed to testify at a corruption trial against Union City Mayor William Musto, a political mentor. Menendez, the child of Cuban immigrants who arrived in the United States prior to his birth, grew up in Union City and got into politics at an early age. He was elected to the school board in 1974, at age 20, and worked for Musto before quitting and testifying against the mayor; Menendez wore a bulletproof vest for protection during the trial because of death threats. Menendez himself went on to be elected in 1986 as mayor of Union City, located in an area that is home to the largest concentration of Cuban Americans in the United States outside of Miami. He was also elected to the New Jersey Assembly in 1987 and later the state Senate in 1991; he served simultaneously as mayor and state legislator, which was common practice in New Jersey politics. As head of the Democratic Party organization in Hudson County, which has the third-highest number of registered Democrats of any county in the state, he was a major player in state politics well before winning a Senate seat.

In 1992, when new congressional district lines were drawn and incumbent Frank Guarini retired, Menendez was elected to Congress, winning both the primary and general election by 2-1 margins. He was the first Hispanic American to represent New Jersey in the House. When Democratic Sen. Frank Lautenberg announced his retirement in 1999, Menendez was widely expected to run for the seat. But support was not forthcoming from New Jersey Sen. Bob Torricelli, the Democratic Senatorial Campaign Committee chairman, who preferred Jon Corzine, a wealthy former investment banker who could self-finance his campaign. (Three years later, when Torricelli was forced to abandon a run for reelection amid controversy over his acceptance of gifts from a businessman who had pleaded guilty to violating federal election laws, Lautenberg stepped in to win a second Senate stint.) Menendez decided to stay in the House and try to help Democrats recapture the majority (and elevate his own power in the chamber), raising $4 million for the 2002 cycle, but Democrats fell short.

Ambitious and hard-driving, Menendez has been admired-if not always warmly regarded-for his prodigious fundraising as well as his strategic savvy. In 2002, California's Nancy Pelosi defeated Maryland's Steny Hoyer in a race for party whip, House Democrats' No. 2 leadership position, opening up the job of caucus chairman, the No. 3 leadership position. Menendez, with Hoyer's support, ran and defeated Pelosi-backed Rosa DeLauro of Connecticut by a secret-ballot vote of 104-103.

Later, following his election to the Senate, Menendez got some negative attention for blocking a promotion for a prosecutor investigating Puerto Rican Gov. Aníbal Acevedo Vilá, a friend of his, who, as the non-voting delegate from Puerto Rico in the House had cast a decisive vote for Menendez in the caucus chairman race. The prosecutor was in line to become the U.S. attorney in Puerto Rico and, at the time, was investigating Acevedo Vilá's fundraising practices. The prosecutor got the appointment in the end, and Acevedo Vilá was indicted for violating campaign finance and tax laws in 2008.

When Corzine was elected New Jersey governor in 2005, Menendez made it known that he would run for Corzine's Senate seat. He had amassed more than $4 million for a statewide campaign, enough to scare Reps. Robert Andrews and Frank Pallone away from challenges and clearing the primary field in spite of Democratic concerns about Menendez's Hudson County political baggage and his efforts to steer lobbying and consulting work to former aide Kay LiCausi. Nonetheless, Corzine appointed Menendez to his Senate seat in January 2006.

In the general election, Menendez faced state Sen. Tom Kean Jr., son and namesake of popular former Republican Gov. Thomas Kean. Menendez campaigned against the Iraq war, while Kean said he would have voted for the Iraq war resolution, while opposing a timetable for withdrawing U.S. troops.

Kean also sought to call attention to Menendez's activities and influence in Hudson County. In September 2006, then-U.S. Attorney Chris Christie subpoenaed records from a lease arrangement between Menendez and an anti-poverty group for which Menendez had sought federal funding, and that paid him some $300,000 in rent on a building he owned in Union City. (A subsequent U.S. attorney closed the case in 2011 after Christie was elected governor.) Menendez counterattacked with an attack ad linking Kean to contributors with ethics problems. Then it was revealed that the Kean campaign's opposition researchers had contacted former Hudson County Executive Robert Janiszewski, who was serving time in federal prison on corruption charges. Menendez struck back with a television ad accusing Kean of a smear campaign: "Federal prisoner 25038-050. He's Tom Kean Jr.'s newest adviser." Polls late in the season showed Menendez with only a slight lead, but he won by 53%-44%.

Menendez has a voting record consistent with most other Democrats from the Northeast; The *Almanac's* 2015 vote ratings found he was the 25th most liberal senator, in the middle of the Democratic caucus. He's consistently liberal on social and environmental issues, but more to the center on economic policies - and is one of the most hawkish Democrats on foreign policy, which in the Obama years led to conflicts with the White House on issues ranging from Cuba to Iran to Russia and Ukraine. (Menendez supported Hillary Clinton for the 2008 and 2016 Democratic presidential nomination.) These differences were accentuated when Menendez became chairman of the Foreign Relations panel in 2013.

Reflecting both his own background and his constituent base, Menendez has been a strong supporter of anti-Fidel Castro legislation since his election to the House. In 2009, he placed a hold on two of Obama's nominees to administration jobs to protest a provision easing travel restrictions to Cuba that was included in an appropriations bill. His refusal to vote for the spending bill prevented it from getting the needed 60-vote super majority to move until he was offered assurances by the administration that the Cuba rider would have little impact. When the Obama Administration moved in late 2014 to open diplomatic relations with Cuba, Menendez angrily charged that Obama's move had "vindicated the brutal behavior of the Cuban government." When Castro died in late 2016, Menendez said Castro's "oppressive legacy will haunt the Cuban regime and our hemisphere forever," and warned that "recent lopsided concessions in U.S. policy towards Cuba have not led to an iota of positive changes in the way the regime rules or the Cuban people live."

Menendez pressed for a more aggressive response to Russia's aggression in Ukraine from 2014 on, urging increased sanctions on the former and increased military assistance for the latter. As the controversy over President Trump's alleged ties with Russia heated up in early 2017, he called for an independent investigation into the connections, and voted against confirming Secretary of State Rex Tillerson, calling Tillerson's lack of specifics on Russia policy "intensely troublesome." As the Obama Administration began negotiation with Iran in early 2015 to prevent that country from developing nuclear weapons, Menendez-as the Foreign Relations panel's ranking Democrat-said he would give Obama two months before defying a veto threat and voting for new sanctions against Iran. When asked by The New York Times whether the White House had lobbied him for the reprieve, Menendez responded, "I don't get calls from the White House," a seeming acknowledgment of his rift with Obama. He was one of only four Democrats to vote against the Iran nuclear treaty in late 2015. Later, he was one of only two Democrats to vote for President Donald Trump's pick for ambassador to Israel, David Friedman, in early 2017.

Menendez's foreign relations work has been overshadowed in recent years by his ethical troubles, however. News outlets reported in early 2013 that he had possibly violated Senate rules by accepting two round-trip flights to the Dominican Republic in 2010 from Melgen, whose Florida medical offices had been raided by the FBI. After a New Jersey Republican lawmaker filed a complaint with the Senate Ethics Committee, Menendez paid the estimated $58,500 cost of the flights and related expenses. He explained that the issue "unfortunately fell through the cracks."

Later news accounts said the senator's staff had thwarted U.S. donations of cargo-screening equipment to the Dominican government because the equipment could have jeopardized a port security contract benefiting Melgen. In addition, *The Washington Post* reported that Menendez spoke with top federal health officials in 2009 and 2012 about a finding that Melgen had overbilled Medicare by almost $9 million. The paper later reported that a federal grand jury in Miami was investigating the senator's dealings with Melgen. At the same time, conservative news websites trumpeted allegations from an anonymous tipster that Menendez had hired prostitutes in the Dominican Republic. The FBI said it could not substantiate the allegations, and Dominican police later said an attorney there paid three women to make up the stories.

The senator denied any wrongdoing, and later blamed the Castro government for orchestrating a smear campaign. However, both *The New York Times* and *The Star-Ledger* of Newark called for Menendez to relinquish his Foreign Relations chairmanship while the Ethics Committee addressed his dealings with Melgen, although the senator initially refused to do so. When he was indicted by the Justice Department in early 2015 he relinquished his status as ranking member on the committee, a move he described as temporary, but ignored the call for him to resign from the Senate. Some supporters in the New Jersey Cuban-American community suggested it was payback by the Obama Administration for Menendez's hardline stances on Cuba and Iran-although Menendez himself publicly disavowed such suggestions. After multiple delays in the trial as Menendez fought to get his case dismissed, the Supreme Court in March 2017 denied his request to dismiss many of the 14 counts against him, setting up a September trial that could end his political career. The charges include bribery, conspiracy and making false statements. Menendez is accused of intervening with senior federal officials to help Melgen in a multi-million dollar billing dispute over Medicare charges, protect a $500 million port security contract with the Dominican Republic and to obtain U.S. visas so Melgen's three foreign girlfriends could visit in exchange for political support. Melgen was found guilty of 67 counts of Medicare fraud in April and was sentenced to 15-20 years in prison, another blow to Menendez that is likely to impact how their joint trial plays out later in the year.

Menendez has been a major player on immigration issues. He took part in bipartisan discussions on a comprehensive immigration bill in 2007 but walked out of the talks , complaining that Democrats had made too many concessions and that the bill would "tear at the fabric of family reunification." After that bill died, he defended tax rebates to illegal immigrants in the 2008 economic stimulus bill, and introduced comprehensive immigration legislation in 2010. One of its components-the DREAM Act, offering children of illegal immigrants a path of citizenship-failed to become law in 2010, but was put into policy by a 2012 Obama executive order. When immigration became a front-burner issue during the 2012 election season, Menendez was part of a bipartisan group of eight senators that secretly crafted a comprehensive reform proposal. It passed the Senate by a wide margin in 2013 but was never taken up by the House. He took up the issue again when the Trump Administration dramatically accelerated deportations of undocumented immigrants, leading the battle to help a Union City grandfather stay in the country. That prompted a Menendez bill to repeal Trump's immigration executive orders, give due process rights to undocumented immigrants, and make racial profiling illegal. ""Families have already been torn apart by the Trump administration's overzealous deportation policy," he said announcing the policy.

Menendez won a coveted slot on the Finance Committee in 2009. In that role, he backed two attempts in the committee to add a government-run "public option" to the health insurance overhaul legislation, but both failed. His stance on that issue, immigration and other Democratic priorities incensed New Jersey tea party activists. In early 2010, they launched a recall effort. Menendez dismissed the recall as an unconstitutional "political stunt" appealed to the state Supreme Court to stop their actions, which sided with him.

Menendez took over the chairmanship of the DSCC in the 2010 election cycle, giving him the fourth-ranking leadership position in the Senate Democratic majority. His low-key approach contrasted sharply with that of his frenetic and publicity-driven predecessor, New York Democrat Chuck Schumer. But the economic downturn and the public's discontent with the Democrats' health care bill worked heavily against him, and his party was shocked by Republican Scott Brown's upset win in Massachusetts in a January 2010 special election. An anonymous White House aide was quoted as blaming the loss on Menendez, adding to strains in the Obama-Menendez relationship.

Under Menendez, the DSCC outraised its Republican counterpart, $130 million to $115 million. Even though Democrats lost six Senate seats, many in the party were relieved the damage wasn't worse. Several vulnerable incumbents, including Majority Leader Harry Reid of Nevada and Colorado's Michael Bennet, hung on to win. And it marked the first time in 100 years that the party in power had held onto the Senate while losing control in the House. "The windstorm he was walking into, it wasn't just 30 miles per hour winds with gusts up to 40 miles per hour; it was a hurricane," Reid said of Menendez to *The Record* of Hackensack.

Republicans hoped to defeat Menendez in 2012, but struggled to find a top-tier challenger. The task fell to state Sen. Joe Kyrillos, a good friend of Christie's whose best weapon became the governor accompanying him to campaign events. Kyrillos took in $4.6 million, but Menendez again demonstrated his fundraising prowess by bringing in more than $17 million. Menendez won, 59%-39%.

Menendez's future - and those of a number of ambitious politicians in the state - remain murky as his corruption trial plays out. National Democrats quietly fret that his legal troubles could put his seat in play in 2018 even if he wins his case, and while he's adamantly opposed calls for his resignation, a guilty verdict would likely force him from office. If that happens before his term is up in 2018, a special election would be called to elect a successor. The potential field in such a race is currently unclear, particularly since an open gubernatorial contest in 2017 will play out beforehand. If Menendez is found guilty and resigns his seat before Christie leaves office in January 2018, then he will appoint a placeholder until the special election. However, if the trial drags on but still ends in a guilty verdict, the new governor would name the placeholder. Pallone, who has eyed a Senate seat for more than a decade, is now ranking Democrat on the powerful House Energy and Commerce Committee. But he could run in a special election without giving up his House seat. Other possible candidates on the Democratic side include former Rep. Rush Holt-who, like Pallone, ran unsuccessfully in the 2013 special primary won by now-Sen. Cory Booker-and state Rep. Donald Norcross. Torricelli, who has been in private business since leaving office in 2002 after being formally admonished by the Senate Ethics Committee over gifts he accepted, in mid-2015 gave an interview to *The Star Ledger* saying he would like to get back into politics, and Democrats believe he's still interested. On Republican side, Kean and Kyrillos, Menendez's challengers in 2006 and 2012, respectively, are possibilities in a state that has not elected a GOP senator since 1972, as is New Jersey Lt. Gov. Kim Guadagno if she doesn't win her 2017 gubernatorial race. If Menendez does run again in 2018 he could draw a serious challenger, even if he is found innocent in his court case.

Democrats who express an interest in the seat ran the risk of offending the still influential Menendez, who continues to express confidence he will prevail in court, reassume his Foreign Relations Committee post, and remain New Jersey's senior senator for the foreseeable future. "Look, I have fought my entire life for what I believe in and for everything I have ever achieved-and most of the time, against some pretty tough odds," he told *The Washington Post* in June 2015. "So that's just who I am."

Junior Senator

Cory Booker (D)

Appointed Oct. 2013, term expires 2020, 1st full term; b. Apr 27, 1969, Washington, DC; Stanford University (CA), B.A.; Stanford University (CA), M.A.; The Queens College, University of Oxford (UK); Yale Law School (CT), J.D.; Baptist; Single.

Elected Office: City Council, 1998-2002; Newark Mayor 2006-2013.

Professional Career: Practicing attorney.

DC Office: 359 DSOB 20510, 202-224-3224, Fax: 202-224-8378, booker.senate.gov.

State Offices: Camden, 856-338-8922; Newark, 973-639-8700.

Committees: *Commerce, Science & Transportation*: Aviation Operations, Safety & Security, Communications, Technology, Innovation & the Internet, Consumer Protection, Product Safety, Ins & Data Security, Oceans, Atmosphere, Fisheries & Coast Guard, Surface Trans., Merchant Marine Infra., Safety & Security (RMM). *Environment & Public Works*: Fisheries, Water, and Wildlife, Superfund, Waste Management, & Regulatory Oversight. *Foreign Relations*: Africa & Global Health Policy (RMM), Near East, South Asia, Central Asia & Counterterrorism, State Dept & USAID Mngmnt, Internat'l Ops & Internat'l Dev. *Small Business & Entrepreneurship*.

Group Ratings

	ADA	ACLU	AFL-CIO	LCV	ITI	COC	HAFA	ACU	CFG	FRC
2016	-	94%	-	100%	60%	50%	16%	4%	13%	0%
2015	95%	C	100%	100%	C	43%	C	4%	9%	0%

Almanac Ratings 2015

	Economy	Social	Foreign	Composite
Liberal	98%	100%	100%	99%
Conservative	2%	0%	0%	1%

Key Votes of the 114th Congress

1. Keystone pipeline	N	5. National Security Data	Y	9. Gun Sales Checks	Y
2. Export-Import Bank	N	6. Iran Nuclear Deal	N	10. Sanctuary Cities	N
3. Debt Ceiling Increase	Y	7. Puerto Rico Debt	N	11. Planned Parenthood	N
4. Homeland Security $$	Y	8. Loretta Lynch A.G	Y	12. Trade deals	N

Election Results

Election	Name (Party)	Vote (%)		Cand. Spent	Ind. Exp. Support	Ind. Exp. Oppose
2014 General	Cory Booker (D)	1,043,866	(56%)	$16,871,163	$1,452,027	$534,109
	Jeff Bell (R)	791,297	(42%)	$599,118	$86,711	
2014 Primary	Cory Booker (D)	Unopposed				

Prior winning percentages: 2014 (56%), 2013 special (55%)

Cory Booker is New Jersey's junior senator, a telegenic and social media-savvy politician with a national political profile who has generated widespread speculation about a possible 2020 presidential run. He has long emphasized civil rights issues and has a mostly liberal voting record, though he's shown a willingness to work across the aisle that's drawn both praise and scorn.

Booker was a force in national Democratic politics even before he was sworn in as New Jersey's junior senator following an October 2013 special election. For the seven years prior to moving to Capitol Hill, the former Rhodes Scholar was the high-profile mayor of Newark, the state's largest municipality- and long a national poster child for the problems and challenges that confront urban America. From his gritty political base, Booker built an impressive network of celebrity friends and acquaintances in the technology, finance and entertainment sectors - contacts that yielded huge sums for Newark's schools and bountiful coverage of Booker in the national media. However, such star power at times has proven to be a double-edged sword: From his first run for mayor through his time in the Senate, Booker often faced criticism for traveling the country to tend to his influential network and build his national profile at the expense of dealing with the problems of his constituents back home. And his well-heeled connections (and some votes to protect New Jersey's pharmaceutical and banking industries) have led some progressives to question his liberal bona fides, painting him as too cozy to Wall Street and too interested in getting in front of the cameras.

Booker is not only New Jersey's first African-American senator; he is one of only six African Americans elected to the Senate since Reconstruction, a group that also includes former Illinois Sen. Barack Obama - another Ivy League-educated lawyer turned community activist who Booker was often compared to early in his career. (Two other African-Americans have been appointed to the Senate in recent years to fill unexpired terms, but did not stand for election.) Booker was born in Washington, D.C., but was raised in the affluent, predominantly white New York City suburb of Harrington Park, New Jersey. It was less than a decade after the passage of the Civil Rights Act of 1964, and, according to Booker, housing rights activists helped the family buy their first home after they initially faced hurdles due to racial bias. His parents were IBM business executives active in the civil rights movement. Booker attended top schools, earning both a bachelor's and master's degree at Stanford University, where he played varsity football. He studied modern history at England's Oxford University as a Rhodes Scholar before attending Yale Law School, graduating in 1997.

A year later, in 1998, Booker ran successfully for the city council in Newark, about 25 miles to the south of where he had grown up. Booker made waves by moving into Brick Towers, one of the city's poorest and most violent housing projects, to call attention to the problems of drug-dealing and crime there, along with the lack of consistent utility service and a functioning elevator. He lived there until the Newark Housing Authority razed the building in 2006, the year he was elected mayor. He then bought a home in Newark's predominantly African-American Central Ward, where he now resides.

In 2002, he challenged longtime Mayor Sharpe James, a fellow Democrat and also an African American. On one level, it was a generational battle: The 33-year old Booker was half the age of his rival. The bitterly negative race increased tensions in the violence-prone city, and the federal government sent in observers on Election Day to prevent fraud. The campaign became the subject of a documentary film called "*Street Fight*" that portrayed Booker as an idealistic political newcomer taking on a ruthless establishment fighting to hang onto power. The film was nominated for an Oscar-and helped make Booker a rising political star. After his narrow loss, 53%-47%, he practiced law and worked for nonprofit civic organizations, as he geared up for rematch against James in 2006. But, after serving five terms-and perhaps glimpsing what the future had in store for him-James declined to run again in 2006. He was indicted the following year on corruption charges. (When Booker was elected to the Senate, the city's newspaper, the *Star-Ledger*, wryly observed he deserved kudos for "being the first mayor in 45 years not to leave City Hall under the shadow of an indictment.")

Booker easily defeated a former James deputy with 72 percent of the vote, and his coattails helped to elect a slate of political allies to the city council. During the campaign, Booker promised nothing short of a renaissance of one of the most troubled cities in the United States. He succeeded on several fronts. The city achieved a balanced budget for the first time in a decade, opened new parks, and spent more money for mass transit. Two new office towers went up in the business district and a $150 million educational complex opened downtown. Booker raised $400 million for philanthropic efforts in the city, including $100 million for the public school system from a member of his celebrity network, Facebook co-founder Mark Zuckerberg, which was matched by $100 million more in other public funds and private donations. Booker, Zuckerberg and Chris Christie, New Jersey's Republican governor, announced the big donation on The Oprah Winfrey Show to great fanfare, though some local education experts complained they'd been left out of the process. He persuaded electronics manufacturer Panasonic to relocate to Newark, and other companies opened offices. But the successes came with some noteworthy failures, topped by his inability to make a lasting dent in Newark's notorious crime problem. As Booker was poised to depart for Capitol Hill, a *Star-Ledger* story noted that the city had 83 homicides and about 2,850 other violent crimes in 2003 under James-as compared to 95 homicides and 3,220 violent crimes in 2012, the last full year of the Booker Administration.

His high-profile push to revamp Newark's struggling schools has been met with mixed reviews. The effort has doubled the number of kids going to public charter schools, which unlike in national comparisons, do outperform local public schools by a significant margin. But the overall changes didn't show the widespread success many had hoped, as $1,000-per-day consultants made lot of money off the efforts while teachers didn't get much of a promised boost in pay. Zuckerberg largely abandoned his plan to use Newark as a national model for education reform after uneven results amid criticism that the top-down approach pushed by the well-heeled donors and politicians with national aspirations like Booker and Christie struggled to achieve its goals. Former *Washington Post* reporter Dale Russakoff, who spent years writing "The Prize," a book on the efforts, told NPR that while Booker had an "incredible talent" at "framing issues and getting the nation to pay attention to them," he struggled with the "patient, tedious, kind of unglamorous work of taking those promises and hammering them out into a different reality."

Still, Booker enjoyed approval ratings that routinely topped 60 percent, and he easily won reelection in 2010. His persona as the city's savior gained novel-like dimensions after he shoveled an elderly resident's walk when a city plow failed to show up, and when he rescued a neighbor from a burning house in 2012. (Booker and his security detail got the woman out of the house before the fire department arrived, and Booker was treated for smoke inhalation.) Meanwhile, his national profile increased with positive coverage of Newark's accomplishments in the national media and his friendship with Obama as well as such entertainment luminaries as producer Jerry Weintraub, actors Ben Affleck and Matt Damon, and talk show impresario Oprah Winfrey. He was a featured speaker at the 2012 Democratic National Convention.

Even some longtime political allies groused about the amount of time he spent on the road, while failing to follow up on important city projects. Booker created a particularly embarrassing moment for Obama during the 2012 presidential campaign when, on a national news program, he criticized Democratic attacks on Republican opponent Mitt Romney's business dealings at Bain Capital as "crap" and "nauseating." Booker was less defending Romney than sticking up for the private equity industry, which is important to New Jersey. Still, he was roundly criticized within his party, and the comments continue to be used by progressives to question whether he's really one of them.

Booker was often mentioned as a possible candidate for higher office: The only question was when. In January 2013, he announced plans to seek the Senate seat held by Democrat Frank Lautenberg when it came open in 2014. The 89-year old Lautenberg had suffered health problems, and was seen as all but certain to retire. But, after a 30-year career on Capitol Hill, he bristled at what he regarded as a lack of deference by Booker, whom he publicly likened to a disrespectful child who needed to be spanked. While Lautenberg announced shortly thereafter that he would not seek reelection, Booker's eagerness created some political fallout when Lautenberg's death from viral pneumonia in June 2013 triggered a special election and members of the Lautenberg family endorsed a Booker rival, Rep. Frank Pallone, in the Democratic primary, saying in a statement that "gimmicks and celebrity status won't get you very far in the real battles that Democrats face in the future."

Christie appointed his attorney general, Jeffrey Chiesa, as a temporary senator, while scheduling an Oct. 13, 2013 special election to fill the seat. The special election could have as easily been held during New Jersey's regularly scheduled general election that November, at a savings to the state of $24 million. Politically, the move was viewed as Christie's way of avoiding having the popular Booker on the ballot when Christie himself was up for reelection. First, Booker had to get through a crowded August primary. Pallone attracted labor backing, including from the state's teachers, who ardently opposed Booker's support of charter school expansion and push to change teacher tenure laws. Also filing in the primary were Rep. Rush Holt, a former research physicist, and state Assembly Speaker Sheila Oliver.

With the aid of greater name recognition and a larger campaign treasury, Booker had little trouble winning the primary, garnering 59 percent - nearly three times the 20 percent captured by Pallone; Holt trailed with 17 percent, with Oliver at 4 percent. Booker collected political dents along the way, notably a *New York Times* report disclosing that, while full-time mayor of a struggling city, he had founded an internet start-up on the side - with money raised from friends such as Winfrey and Google executive Eric Schmidt. The site, Waywire, was designed to make it easier to collect and share Web videos. To put the controversy behind him, Booker stepped down from the company's board and donated his ownership interest to charity.

Booker's general election opponent was Steve Lonegan, a former Republican mayor of Bogota, and state director of the tea party-affiliated Americans for Prosperity. Lonegan's right-wing profile made him a decided underdog in a state with 700,000 more registered Democrats than Republicans, and which had not elected a Republican to the Senate since 1972. Booker overwhelmed Lonegan in fundraising, taking in more than $11 million to $1.3 million for his opponent. Lonegan managed to capitalize on Booker's vulnerabilities and a bad national climate for Democrats to make it a closer race than many had expected. He hammered at Newark's stubbornly high crime rate as well as Booker's ties to Obama, whose approval ratings in New Jersey were following a national downward trend. Lonegan made some political headway with radio ads that highlighted Booker's post-primary trips to Los Angeles and Silicon Valley to raise money, as he sought to paint his rival as being more interested in boosting himself on a national stage than being around New Jersey voters.

Booker also created some problems on his own, with ill-conceived Twitter messages to a dancer at a strip club and questionable claims about his relationship with a drug dealer he called T-Bone, who turned out to not actually exist. Booker described him as an "archetype" of Newark's many problems. But while Lonegan cut into Booker's lead in polls, the Democrat still pulled off a solid victory, 55%-44%. He won a full term in 2014, defeating conservative activist and public affairs consultant Jeffrey Bell, who in 1978 defeated moderate Republican Sen. Clifford Case in the primary, and then lost the general election to Democrat Bill Bradley. After a few polls showed a close race, Booker went on the attack and ended up winning by 56%-42%, similar to his margin a year earlier.

Like other high-wattage figures who have been elected to the Senate-notably Bradley, who in 1978 won the seat Booker now occupies following a professional basketball career-Booker initially sought to keep a low profile and focus on state-specific issues. "He represents a new type of Democrat-fiscally conservative, socially progressive," George Norcross, a southern New Jersey Democratic power broker who backed Booker in the primary, told the *Associated Press*. Striving to show his bipartisanship, he even sought to make friends with arch-conservative Texas Sen. Ted Cruz, meeting him for a three-hour dinner that Booker later described to a local Fox News station as "one of the best constitutional law discussions since I got out of law school." But he soon began taking on national issues. He joined with another tea party standard-bearer, Kentucky Sen. Rand Paul, on a bill to overhaul the criminal justice system, in part by encouraging states to change policies to steer children away from being tried as adults.

He later worked closely with South Carolina Republican Sen. Tim Scott, the Senate's only other black lawmaker at the time, to craft comprehensive criminal justice reform that would reduce mandatory minimum sentences for nonviolent criminals including drug offenders, limit mandatory sentences to serious felonies, ban solitary confinement for juveniles and boost reentry programs for those getting out of prison. The effort received bipartisan praise and had the backing of a broad coalition of lawmakers including members of leadership in both parties. That included making some compromises to win over Judiciary Committee Chairman Chuck Grassley of Iowa, who originally was deeply skeptical of the legislation. Advocates ranged from the liberal American Civil Liberties Union to the Libertarian-conservative Koch Brothers. The bill stalled out during the 2016 presidential campaign. While Booker promised to redouble his efforts to pass the legislation, that could prove much harder under President Donald Trump.

In early 2015, Paul and Booker joined forces on another bill to remove the threat of federal prosecution against medical marijuana patients in states where it is legal. Booker told ABC News in mid-2014 that the two had bonded via Twitter once Booker arrived in the Senate. The apparent starting point of their bond: an affinity for Festivus, the made-up holiday popularized on TV's long-running "Seinfeld." Booker's knack for social media had earned him more than 2.8 million Twitter followers as of April 2017, second-most of any senator behind 2016 presidential candidate Bernie Sanders of Vermont, who had 6.1 million followers.

Just 44 years old when elected to the Senate, Booker immediately faced speculation about his future beyond Capitol Hill-similar to the speculation that accompanied Obama's arrival in Washington a decade earlier. Following the 2013 special election, Booker told reporters that he "absolutely… unequivocally" was not interested in running for president or vice president in 2016. But he was quite happy to be on Hillary Clinton's short list for vice president that year after working hard to be in her good graces, and campaigned vigorously for her around the country.

He again got a prime speaking slot at the 2016 Democratic National Convention, and delivered a soaring speech slamming Trump and touting a hopeful America that earned comparisons to the stirring, star-making speech Obama delivered at the 2004 DNC, both for the passion of the delivery, the sweep of the narrative and for speculation about his national ambition. "My fellow Americans, we cannot be seduced by cynicism about our politics, because cynicism is a refuge for cowards, and this nation is and must always be the home of the brave," Booked bellowed as the speech closed. "We are the United States of America. We will not falter or fail. We will not retreat or surrender our values. We will not surrender our ideas. We will not surrender the moral high ground."

He was tied for the fourth most liberal senator in the *Almanac's* 2015 vote ratings. But Booker's sometimes-centrist economic streak hasn't completely disappeared: In early 2017 he earned scorn from liberals when he was one of just 13 Democrats to vote against a symbolic amendment to import prescription drugs from Canada (New Jersey is home to a large number of pharmaceutical companies and the industry is a major donor to Booker).

As Booker has shifted left, he emerged as one of President Trump's harshest critics, taking on a hard partisan edge rarely seen earlier in his career as he made his national ambitions more obvious. He led the charge against Trump's nomination of then-Alabama Sen. Jeff Sessions as Attorney General because of what he described as Sessions' long, controversial record of "hostility" towards minorities, becoming the first senator in history to testify against a fellow senator's cabinet confirmation.

He was one of only five Democrats to vote against at least 16 of Trump's 19 initial cabinet nominees (only New York's Kirsten Gillibrand voted against more), including opposition to Betsy DeVos's confirmation for Education Secretary, surprising some given her role in pushing the Newark school reform experiment he helmed. Along with Wisconsin Democrat Tammy Baldwin, he introduced legislation in 2016 to create a new transitional jobs grant program at the Department of Labor and expand Earned Income Tax Credits.

In 2017 Booker added a spot on Senate Foreign Relations Committee to his portfolio, shoring up his foreign policy credentials.

All those moves led to strong speculation that he was gearing up for a 2020 presidential bid. "He obviously is interested in running for president, and he's decided to position himself as vocally anti-Trump. There's certainly an appetite for that," veteran Democratic strategist Bob Shrum told *Politico* in early 2017. "He's obvious, and I don't find anything wrong with being obvious." Booker's youthful charisma, strong fundraising ability and fierce opposition to Trump (as well as his social media savvy and appeal to African-American and Millennial voters) could help make him a serious player. But it's unclear if he can win over enough of a Democratic base that is increasingly populist, uncompromising on economic issues and skeptical of anyone with Wall Street ties.

FIRST DISTRICT

Donald Norcross (D)

Elected 2014, 2nd full term; b. Dec 13, 1958, Camden; Camden County College (NJ), A.S., 1979; Lutheran; Married (Andrea Doran); 3 children; 2 grandchildren.

Elected Office: NJ Assembly, 2010; NJ Senate, 2010-2014.

Professional Career: Electrician; Assistant business Manager, Local 351, Int'l Brotherhood of Electrical Workers; President, Southern NJ AFL-CIO.

DC Office: 1531 LHOB 20515, 202-225-6501, Fax: 202-225-6583, norcross.house.gov.

State Offices: Cherry Hill, 856-427-7000.

Committees: *Armed Services*: Seapower & Projection Forces, Strategic Forces. *Education & the Workforce*: Health, Employment, Labor & Pensions, Workforce Protections.

Group Ratings

	ADA	ACLU	AFL-CIO	LCV	ITI	COC	HAFA	ACU	CFG	FRC
2016	-	82%	-	100%	67%	64%	15%	4%	0%	0%
2015	70%	C	100%	91%	C	60%	C	0%	0%	0%

Almanac Ratings 2015

	Economy	Social	Foreign	Composite
Liberal	77%	100%	49%	75%
Conservative	23%	0%	52%	25%

Key Votes of the 114th Congress

1. Keystone Pipeline	Y	5. Puerto Rico Debt	N	9. Offenses by Aliens	N
2. Trade Deals	N	6. Medical Marijuana	Y	10. Troops in Iraq	N
3. Export-Import Bank	Y	7. Sanctuary Cities	N	11. Homeland Security $$	Y
4. Debt Ceiling Increase	Y	8. Armor-piercing Bullets	N	12. Trade Adjustment aid	Y

Election Results

Election	Name (Party)	Vote (%)		Cand. Spent	Ind. Exp. Support	Ind. Exp. Oppose
2016 General	Donald Norcross (D)...................	183,231	(60%)	$1,964,002	$214,627	
	Bob Patterson (R)........................	112,388	(37%)	$204,109		
2016 Primary	Donald Norcross (D).................	46,826	(70%)			
	Alex Law (D).............................	20,333	(30%)			

Prior winning percentages: 2014 (57%), 2014 special (57%)

Democrat Donald Norcross, who was first elected in 2014, is the brother of South Jersey's chief political boss. He became a usually reliable ally of Democratic leaders and organized labor and was rewarded with prime committee assignments.

Norcross graduated from Camden County College. He started his career as an electrician, who installed power lines in refineries and on the top of bridges. Later, he became a business manager for the International Brotherhood of Electrical Workers, and president of the Southern New Jersey AFL-CIO. Norcross jumped into politics in 2009, when he won election to the state Assembly. A year later, he was appointed to fill a state Senate seat. He was a leading backer of the state's constitutional amendment to raise the minimum wage as well as a bill providing tax incentives to businesses that operate in hard-hit areas. On some social issues - notably charter schools - Norcross has staked out more centrist positions.

Norcross got his opening when Democratic Rep. Robert Andrews resigned to take a job at a Philadelphia law firm. At the time, Andrews was facing an ethics probe into alleged misuse of campaign funds. Under congressional rules, such inquiries must end when a member retires. Andrews denied any connection between the probe and the decision to step away from his seniority and influence.

Norcross was primed to run from the start. With Andrews' backing, he lined up endorsements from key Democrats across South Jersey. Not only was he the favored Democrat in a blue district, but his brother, George Norcross III, has been a longtime power broker in the state and owned a majority stake in *The Philadelphia Inquirer*. (George Norcross divested his interest in the newspaper soon after his brother's campaign began.) Norcross's two primary opponents, Frank Minor and Frank Broomell, tried to play up his entrenched political ties as a liability. But he handily defeated them with 72 percent of the primary vote.

Republican Garry Cobb, a local talk-radio personality and former Philadelphia Eagles linebacker, faced an uphill battle in a district where President Barack Obama won 66 percent of the vote in 2012. He emphasized that he was an outsider who was not part of the "Norcross machine" and that he wanted to clean up politics in South Jersey, but he was outspent $2.1 million to $108,000. Norcross won with a comfortable, though less than overwhelming, 57%-39%. He won a special election the same day and filled the remaining seven weeks of his predecessor's term.

Norcross has seats on the Armed Services plus Education and the Workforce committees. His *Almanac* vote ratings in 2015 were toward the center of the House on economic and foreign issues, but solidly liberal on social issues. He pledged support for the military installations based in New Jersey and occasionally has gone his own way on key votes. He supported approval of the Keystone XL pipeline, which has been strongly backed by many labor unions but opposed by most Democrats. And he opposed Obama's nuclear deal with Iran, saying that "a better deal can be achieved." He served on the leadership-controlled House Democratic Steering and Policy Committee.

Norcross filed the Toxics by Rail Accountability and Community Knowledge (TRACK) Act, which would improve safety measures for rail shipments of hazardous materials and was based on recommendations that followed a 2012 train derailment in Paulsboro. "I was an electrician for many, many years, and understanding some of the complex issues in trying to get the economy growing is something I deal with every day," he said.

In 2016, he faced a primary challenge from Alex Law, a 25-year-old political newcomer and supporter of Sen. Bernie Sanders in the presidential campaign who had been a consultant for IBM. Law ran against the "Norcross machine," which he said had been "marked by corruption and political cronyism." Norcross out-spent him more than 20-to-1 and got 70 percent of the vote. He breezed through the general election, 60%-37%, against Bob Patterson, who had been a policy adviser to former Republican Gov. Tom Corbett of Pennsylvania.

Philadelphia suburbs: Camden

Population		Race and Ethnicity		Income	
Total	731,683	White	64.1%	Median Income	$64,779 (97 out of 435)
Land area	350	Black	16.0%		
Pop/ sq mi	2090.4	Latino	12.6%	Under $50,000	39.8%
Born in state	54.3%	Asian	5.0%	$50,000-$99,999	30.2%
		Two races	1.9%	$100,000-$199,999	24.7%
Age Groups		Other	0.4%	$200,000 or more	5.3%
Under 18	23.0%			Poverty Rate	12.0%
18-34	22.6%	**Education**			
35-64	40.4%	H.S grad or less	43.5%	**Health Insurance**	
Over 64	14.1%	Some college	27.1%	With health insurance coverage	90.3%
		College Degree, 4 yr	19.4%		
Work		Post grad	10.1%		
White Collar	38.7%			**Public Assistance**	
Sales and Service	43.1%	**Military**		Cash public assistance income	3.9%
Blue Collar	18.2%	Veteran	7.1%		
Government	14.4%	Active Duty	0.1%	Food stamp/SNAP benefits	11.4%

Voter Turnout			
2015 Total Citizens 18+	535,846	2016 House Turnout as % CVAP	57%
2016 House turnout	305,473	2014 House Turnout as % CVAP	30%

2012 Presidential Vote		
Barack Obama	212,236	(66%)
Mitt Romney	110,377	(34%)

2016 Presidential Vote		
Hillary Clinton	199,386	(60%)
Donald Trump	118,880	(36%)
Gary Johnson	6,512	(2%)

Cook Partisan Voting Index: D+13

The closely built streets of Camden, across the Delaware River from Philadelphia, have seen a fair amount of history. This was where the poet Walt Whitman lived when he wrote some of the versions of his *Leaves of Grass*. It was an immigrant-jammed industrial city then, with tinkerers and inventors. In 1894, a Camden machinist named Eldridge Johnson produced the Victor Talking Machine, the birth of the recorded music industry and a company that became RCA Victor in 1929. A few years later, the new Campbell Soup Co. began producing condensed soups. Camden remained for years a major industrial locus on the New Jersey side of the Delaware River, not the broadest and certainly not the most picturesque of Atlantic estuaries, but probably the East Coast's premier industrial waterway, with a concentration of steel mills, chemical plants, and oil tank farms equal to any in the country. The flatlands all around, mostly ignored in the 19th century, had easy access to cheap water transportation and plenty of skilled labor from the Philadelphia area. For a quarter-century starting in the 1940s, this was one of the country's fastest-growing industrial areas.

In the 1980s and 1990s, Camden emptied out. Many of its factories had closed, and fewer than 10,000 manufacturing jobs remained. Its neighborhoods were beset by crime, its mostly minority residents were heavily dependent on public assistance and its mayor was convicted of doing favors for Philadelphia's organized crime leaders. Camden continues to struggle. Census figures released in 2012 showed Camden with a poverty rate of 42 percent, the highest in the nation. Since then, an influx of jobs modestly lowered the rate. In 2015, its average household income of $25,000 compared with $72,000 for the state. From 2002 to 2010, the state controlled its finances and government. In 2011, the mayor laid off almost half the police department, citing a $26.5 million deficit. The following year, a new county force took over police functions for the city. According to FBI data, Camden had the highest crime rate in the nation in 2012. Gov. Chris Christie and local officials have cited a dramatic drop in violent crime since then, though it remains high. In 2014, the privately compiled data of NeighborhoodScout continued to rate Camden the most violent city in the nation, by several measures.

Camden has had some recent bright spots: a redeveloped riverfront park, the New Jersey aquarium and a state-of-the-art amphitheater. Campbell in 2010 opened an addition to its world headquarters, and in 2012, Rowan University opened a $139 million medical school in the city, the first new medical college in New Jersey in 35 years. The port of Camden rebounded from the recession, spurred by Del Monte's large fruit-processing plant and increased steel imports. In 2015-16, Christie and Mayor Dana Redd had several bullish announcements about business moves into the city. Subaru broke ground on its new corporate headquarters. That was followed by further development on Subaru's 13 acre site, which *The Philadelphia Inquirer* described as "a self-contained city in what is now a desolate part of Camden." The governor and mayor unveiled a nearly $1 billion project for investment along the waterfront. Critics pointed out shortcomings, including that Subaru and some of the other new businesses were moving from nearby sites chiefly because of huge tax incentives, there was no guarantee of new jobs for residents of Camden, and the leases might be as short as 15 years. Still, almost any progress in Camden has been radical change.

The 1st Congressional District is greater Camden, the Delaware riverfront from Palmyra south to a point across the river from the Delaware state line. The district includes two-thirds of adjacent Gloucester County, an area that is about one-third of the district, plus a small slice of Burlington County. The 1st is traversed by Black Horse Pike and White Horse Pike, which connect Philadelphia to its South Jersey suburbs. Many of the nearby boroughs and townships developed over the past half-century as a result of flight from Camden. Haddonfield, an old-fashioned community filled with galleries and shops, was once described by *The Inquirer* as "a Norman Rockwell picture come to life." The district is 16 percent black and 13 percent Hispanic; those two groups comprise nearly equal shares of virtually all of Camden's population. Democratic-leaning Cherry Hill is more affluent. Politically, the district remains safe for Democrats. Hillary Clinton led Donald Trump, 60%-36%. That was a drop from the Democratic performance in 2012, when President Barack Obama took the district, 66%-34%, against Mitt Romney. This is the only Democratic-held seat in New Jersey that does not reach into the New York City suburbs.

SECOND DISTRICT

Frank LoBiondo (R)

Elected 1994, 12th term; b. May 12, 1946, Bridgeton; St. Joseph's University (PA), B.A., 1968; Catholic; Married (Tina Ercole); 2 children (2 from previous marriage).

Elected Office: Cumberland County Board of Chosen Freeholders, 1985- 87; NJ Assembly, 1988-1994.

Professional Career: Operations Manager, LoBiondo Bros. Motor Express Inc., 1968-1994.

DC Office: 2427 RHOB 20515, 202-225-6572, Fax: 202-225-3318, lobiondo.house.gov.

State Offices: Mays Landing, 609-625-5008.

Committees: *Armed Services*: Emerging Threats & Capabilities, Tactical Air & Land Forces. *Permanent Select on Intelligence*. *Transportation & Infrastructure*: Aviation (Chmn), Coast Guard & Maritime Transportation, Highways & Transit.

Group Ratings

	ADA	ACLU	AFL-CIO	LCV	ITI	COC	HAFA	ACU	CFG	FRC
2016	-	11%	-	50%	83%	93%	33%	32%	45%	67%
2015	25%	C	67%	23%	C	85%	C	33%	30%	75%

Almanac Ratings 2015

	Economy	Social	Foreign	Composite
Liberal	35%	27%	11%	24%
Conservative	65%	73%	90%	76%

Key Votes of the 114th Congress

1. Keystone Pipeline	Y	5. Puerto Rico Debt	N	9. Offenses by Aliens	Y
2. Trade Deals	N	6. Medical Marijuana	Y	10. Troops in Iraq	N
3. Export-Import Bank	Y	7. Sanctuary Cities	Y	11. Homeland Security $$	Y
4. Debt Ceiling Increase	Y	8. Armor-piercing Bullets	Y	12. Trade Adjustment aid	Y

Election Results

Election	Name (Party)	Vote (%)	Cand. Spent	Ind. Exp. Support	Ind. Exp. Oppose
2016 General	Frank LoBiondo (R)..................... 176,338	(59%)	$1,541,382	$12,000	
	David Cole (D).............................. 110,838	(37%)	$126,068		
2016 Primary	Frank LoBiondo (R)...................................	(100%)			

Prior winning percentages: 2014 (62%), 2012 (58%), 2010 (66%), 2008 (59%), 2006 (62%), 2004 (65%), 2002 (69%), 2000 (66%), 1998 (66%), 1996 (60%), 1994 (65%)

Republican Frank LoBiondo, first elected in 1994, is one of his party's most moderate members, especially on labor and environmental matters. "LoBo," as he is known to colleagues, has quietly climbed the seniority ladder on the Transportation and Infrastructure Committee. Behind closed doors, including on the Intelligence Committee, he apparently speaks his mind.

LoBiondo grew up in Vineland, on the vegetable farm his grandparents established after leaving Sicily. His father started transporting his produce to market in a used truck, and as Atlantic City boomed in the early 20th century, he made a good living transporting the produce of other farmers as well. He created LoBiondo Brothers Motor Express, where his son worked when he was young. After getting his bachelor's degree in business administration from St. Joseph's University in Philadelphia, he joined the family business.

LoBiondo was first elected to public office in 1984 with the Cumberland County Board of Chosen Freeholders. He served in the New Jersey Assembly, where he stoutly opposed new taxes and gun control laws. In 1992, he ran against veteran Democratic Rep. William Hughes and lost 56%-41%. After Hughes retired two years later, LoBiondo ran again. In the primary, he competed with state Sen. William Gormley, whom LoBiondo portrayed as favoring tax increases and gun control. LoBiondo won 54%-35%, and easily took the general, 65%-35%.

In the House, LoBiondo has retained his conservative stance on gun rights but has often bolted his party on other issues. In 2009, he was one of eight Republicans who joined Democrats on energy legislation creating a "cap and trade" system on greenhouse-gas emissions. He backed an expansion of the Children's Health Insurance Program, and food safety legislation. He cosponsored the so-called "card check" bill aimed at making it easier to organize work sites by eliminating the secret ballot in union elections.

LoBiondo was among the New Jersey lawmakers incensed at Speaker John Boehner in January 2013 for initially delaying a vote on disaster relief following Hurricane Sandy. New Jersey news outlets reported that the two men got into an angry confrontation. "I've never been this angry. ... This could have been a poster child for bipartisanship; instead, this is what we have," LoBiondo told the website *PolitickerNJ.* He took to the House floor to blast colleagues from disaster-prone areas for failing to be supportive. "Shame on you!" he said. "What does the misery index have to get to for our constituents?" With Democratic Rep. Frank Pallone of New Jersey, he has been the senior co-chairman of the bipartisan Congressional Coastal Communities Caucus.

As chairman of the Transportation and Infrastructure Subcommittee on Aviation, LoBiondo has helped the William J. Hughes Technical Center near Atlantic City, the Federal Aviation Administration's national scientific testing base. "I've said repeatedly that our tech center is a premier site ... and for whatever reason, they've been under-recognized and under-appreciated," he told *The Press of Atlantic City*. His district also is home to the TSA Security Lab and the Federal Air Marshal training facility. He worked to implement the FAA's Next Generation Air Transportation System, commonly known as NextGen, which is aimed at making air travel more efficient as it moves from a radar-based to a satellite-based system. LoBiondo opposes oil drilling within 125 miles of the Jersey coast, and helped to enact the Delaware River Protection Act, increasing the liability for single-hull oil tankers that pollute. In 2015, his *Almanac* vote ratings were among the most liberal for House Republicans, especially on economic and social issues.

On the Armed Services Committee, LoBiondo expressed reservations about the Iraq war, but he opposed efforts to set a timetable for troop withdrawals. He opposed trying terrorists in civilian courts, and lamented that homeland security became "lost in the mix" of debates during the Obama administration. On the Select Intelligence Committee, he has chaired the subcommittee with oversight of the CIA. In December 2015, the House passed his bill requiring the Director of National Intelligence to file a report every six months with congressional committees on the flow of foreign fighters to and from terrorist safe havens.

When he was first elected, LoBiondo promised to serve no more than 12 years, but has since broken that pledge. Still, he routinely wins reelection by comfortable margins. In 2014, he faced William Hughes Jr., a lawyer with an Atlantic City law firm and the son of the congressman to whom LoBiondo initially lost. His $2.4 million more than tripled the spending of Hughes, who had little party assistance. What had been viewed as potentially a close contest turned out to be a surprisingly easy victory for the incumbent, 61%-37%. LoBiondo remains a good fit for his district. Democrats have suffered recruiting setbacks. With his easy reelection in 2016, he set a record for longevity in this seat. During the campaign, he distanced himself from Donald Trump. Earlier, when Trump was a major business figure in the district, LoBiondo was the top recipient of his campaign contributions.

South Jersey: Atlantic City, Philadelphia exurbs

Population		**Race and Ethnicity**		**Income**	
Total	732,697	White	66.2%	Median Income	$58,584 (153 out of 435)
Land area	2,092	Black	12.1%		
Pop/ sq mi	350.2	Latino	15.5%		
Born in state	59.4%	Asian	3.9%	Under $50,000	43.1%
		Two races	2.0%	$50,000-$99,999	30.9%
Age Groups		Other	0.3%	$100,000-$199,999	21.5%
Under 18	22.1%			$200,000 or more	4.7%
18-34	20.6%	**Education**		Poverty Rate	13.2%
35-64	40.9%	H.S grad or less	49.6%		
Over 64	16.4%	Some college	26.1%	**Health Insurance**	
Work		College Degree, 4 yr	16.3%	With health insurance coverage	88.8%
White Collar	32.5%	Post grad	7.9%		
Sales and Service	47.0%	**Military**		**Public Assistance**	
Blue Collar	20.5%	Veteran	8.1%	Cash public assistance income	3.8%
Government	17.6%	Active Duty	0.2%		
				Food stamp/SNAP benefits	11.9%

Voter Turnout			
2015 Total Citizens 18+	534,697	2016 House Turnout as % CVAP	56%
2016 House turnout	297,795	2014 House Turnout as % CVAP	33%

2012 Presidential Vote		
Barack Obama	166,908	(54%)
Mitt Romney	141,480	(46%)

2016 Presidential Vote		
Donald Trump	162,486	(50%)
Hillary Clinton	147,656	(46%)
Gary Johnson	6,596	(2%)

Cook Partisan Voting Index: R+1

The builders of the Camden & Atlantic Railroad in 1852 may not have known it, but when they extended their line to the little inlet town of Absecon, they were launching one of America's first beach resorts, Atlantic City. Like all resorts, it was a product of developments elsewhere - of industrialization and spreading affluence. In the years after the Civil War, Atlantic City and the Jersey Shore, from Brigantine to Cape May, became a seaside resort, and Atlantic City developed its characteristic features: the boardwalk in 1870, the amusement pier in 1882, the rolling chair in 1884, salt water taffy in the 1890s, and the Miss America pageant in 1921. In the book *Boardwalk Empire*, author Nelson Johnson argues that in order to attract tourists, a powerful alliance of local politicians and racketeers allowed gambling, prostitution and Sunday liquor laws to be flouted. "Nothing could interfere with the visitors' fun or they might stop coming," he writes. But a long period of decline came after World War II, and by the early 1970s Atlantic City was grim, featuring a bedraggled convention hall (site of the 1964 Democratic National Convention), empty hotels and bleak streets.

Then in 1977, New Jersey voters legalized casino gambling in Atlantic City, and gleaming new hotels sprang up, big-name entertainers came in, and the resort became more stylish than it had been in 90 years. But it hasn't been that way for everyone: Casino and hotel jobs tend to be low-wage, and decrepit neighborhoods begin just feet from the casinos' massive parking lots. For years, its dozen casinos had net annual revenues nearly as high as Las Vegas' casinos. Then, the recession hit the entertainment sector hard. From 2005 until 2016, casino revenues dropped more than 50 percent, to a bit more than $2 billion. As *The Washington Post* wrote in October 2016, Donald Trump helped to orchestrate this "casino-industry bubble," during which he had three corporate bankruptcies, the final one in 2010. His hundreds of millions of dollars in losses helped him to offset income elsewhere. To protect the region, Republican Gov. Chris Christie in 2011 signed legislation easing regulatory oversight of the casinos, which angered watchdog groups that said it was unfair to single out gambling for special treatment. But five of the 12 casinos closed from 2013 to 2016, and others sought tax relief as gambling revenues continued to drop and the local economy struggled. In the first quarter of 2016, Atlantic County retained the highest foreclosure rate of any metropolitan area in the nation.

Other beach resorts lie south of Atlantic City. There is Wildwood, with its refurbished 1950s motels, and also Cape May, with its lovingly preserved Victorian houses. In 2015, Cape May was rated among the top 10 family beaches in the nation by a TripAdvisor site. Commercial and residential properties in Ocean City and Sea Isle City suffered major damage from Hurricane Sandy in 2012. West of the Jersey Shore are swamps and flatlands, the Pine Barrens and abundant vegetable fields that gave New Jersey its "Garden State" nickname. The number of farms decreased 10 percent between 1997 and 2012, though agriculture remained the third largest sector of the state's economy. The Northeast's high-tech and service economy boom has not reached this far south in Jersey.

The 2nd Congressional District covers the southern end of New Jersey. Atlantic is the largest county, with more than 35 percent of the population. Politically, it has Democratic leanings in the chemical industry towns along the Delaware River and in Vineland and a strong Republican presence in Cape May County. In 2016, Trump won this home-town district, 50%-46%, an improvement over the Republican vote of 45 percent and 46 percent in 2008 and 2012. The 2nd was one of three New Jersey districts where he got a majority, all of them south of the New York City suburbs.

THIRD DISTRICT

Tom MacArthur (R)

Elected 2014, 2nd term; b. Oct 16, 1960, Hebron, CT; Hofstra University, B.A.; Episcopalian; Married (Debbie MacArthur); 3 children (1 deceased).

Elected Office: Randolph City Council, 2011-2013; deputy Mayor, Randolph, 2012; Randolph Mayor, 2013-2014.

Professional Career: Insurance adjuster; Chmn & CEO, York Risk Services Group, 1999-2010.

DC Office: 506 CHOB 20515, 202-225-4765, Fax: 202-225-0778, macarthur.house.gov.

State Offices: Marlton, 856-267-5182; Toms River, 732-569-6495.

Committees: *Financial Services*: Capital Markets, Securities & Investment, Housing & Insurance.

Group Ratings

	ADA	ACLU	AFL-CIO	LCV	ITI	COC	HAFA	ACU	CFG	FRC
2016	-	0%	-	13%	75%	100%	42%	42%	38%	82%
2015	5%	C	38%	6%	C	95%	C	46%	31%	92%

Almanac Ratings 2015

	Economy	Social	Foreign	Composite
Liberal	26%	24%	11%	20%
Conservative	74%	76%	90%	80%

Key Votes of the 114th Congress

1. Keystone Pipeline	Y	5. Puerto Rico Debt	Y	9. Offenses by Aliens	Y
2. Trade Deals	N	6. Medical Marijuana	N	10. Troops in Iraq	N
3. Export-Import Bank	Y	7. Sanctuary Cities	N	11. Homeland Security $$	Y
4. Debt Ceiling Increase	Y	8. Armor-piercing Bullets	Y	12. Trade Adjustment aid	Y

Election Results

Election	Name (Party)	Vote (%)	Cand. Spent	Ind. Exp. Support	Ind. Exp. Oppose
2016 General	Tom MacArthur (R)................... 194,596	(59%)	$1,562,831	$2,401	
	Fred LaVergne (D)...................... 127,526	(39%)			
2016 Primary	Tom MacArthur (R).................	(100%)			

Prior winning percentages: 2014 (54%)

Republican Tom MacArthur, elected in 2014, did not shy away from a fight - or a lawsuit - as he battled to win his seat in competitive contests. He showed similar tenacity as he helped to lead the New Jersey congressional delegation in protecting the future of Joint Base McGuire and, in early 2017, as he negotiated with other House Republicans to reach consensus on revision of the Affordable Care Act. His efforts on health care revealed major splits among Republican moderates.

MacArthur grew up in Hebron, Connecticut, and lives in Toms River. He earned his bachelor's from Hofstra University and spent 28 years working in the insurance industry, including 11 years as chairman and CEO of York Risk Services Group. In 2011, he became a Randolph Township councilman, and was deputy mayor and mayor of Randolph. MacArthur and his wife, Debbie, created and funded the St. Peter's Sandy Relief Fund to help victims of Superstorm Sandy. Their In God's Hands Charitable Foundation distributed 1,600 wheelchairs worldwide, the campaign said, in honor of the couple's special-needs daughter Grace, who died at age 11. He lived 90 miles away in Morris County before he launched his congressional campaign in the south Jersey district.

In the campaign to succeed Republican Rep. Jon Runyan, both the primary and general campaigns were divisive. In both cases, MacArthur pushed back with a lawsuit or the threat of one. In the primary, MacArthur faced Steven Lonegan, a conservative activist who in October 2013 lost the special-election Senate race to Democrat Cory Booker. Lonegan accused MacArthur's insurance firms of underpaying or denying payment to wildfire victims in California. MacArthur's campaign responded that the few claims were not only dismissed, but settled after MacArthur left the company. MacArthur was endorsed by the GOP organization in each county and took the primary, 60%-40%, with a similar margin in each county.

In the general election, MacArthur styled himself as a self-made businessman focused on job creation. He earned endorsements from the United Brotherhood of Carpenters and the Laborers' International Union of North America. MacArthur criticized Democratic nominee Aimee Belgard, a Burlington County freeholder (and a lawyer who also had worked in the insurance industry) for failing to denounce an ad that MacArthur claimed was untrue. The Democratic Congressional Campaign Committee ad featured a firefighter who accused MacArthur's insurance company of denying injury claims from firefighters. MacArthur threatened to sue, noting he had sold the company a year before the claims mentioned in the ad, and the DCCC pulled the spot. MacArthur raised $5.7 million in the overall campaign, of which $5 million was a loan from himself, compared with $1.8 million for Belgard. The two candidates benefited from more than $3 million in additional spending by national party and interest groups. MacArthur won by an unexpectedly comfortable margin, 54%-44%. MacArthur took a huge 63 percent in Ocean. Burlington was virtually even. His victory marked the first time since the 1930s that a Republican has replaced another Republican in the 3rd District.

On the Armed Services Committee, MacArthur had many meetings at Joint Base McGuire and with Pentagon officials in attempts to show his support for the base and to avert a potential shutdown. He attacked "outrageous" maneuvering by the Obama administration to seek ways to shut down military facilities if Congress did not agree to a base-closing review. "Shuttering our military installations devastates local economies and harms tight-knit communities, and I won't let that happen in South Jersey," MacArthur warned. The annual defense spending bill that was enacted in November 2015 included a provision he authored with Democratic Rep. David Norcross of New Jersey that prevented the Pentagon from spending money to retire the KC-10 refueling tanker planes stationed at the base.

When the Air Force announced in January 2017 that new KC-46 tankers would be housed at the Joint Base, he exalted, "Over 42,000 New Jersey residents in my district who are employed at the base and the thousands of additional jobs in the surrounding area that rely on its survival can breathe easy knowing the Joint Base will remain our nation's premier air mobility installation." During his first term, he had a relatively moderate voting record. His *Almanac* vote ratings for 2015 ranked near the center of the House in each of the three issue areas.

In the new Congress, MacArthur switched his chief committee assignment to Financial Services. He became one of three co-chairs of the Tuesday Group, a coalition of more than 50 center-right House Republicans. He said that the group would work in "a responsible, solutions-oriented way." Days later, he was one of nine Republicans who voted against a revised budget plan to expedite House action on revisions to the Affordable Care Act. He said that the House needed to take sufficient time to assure a careful review.

Following the initial failure of House Republicans to find majority support for their proposal, MacArthur reached out to White House officials and to Freedom Caucus chairman Mark Meadows of North Carolina with his proposal to relax the requirement for coverage of pre-existing illnesses. That led to House passage of the bill in early May. His move caused major dissension within the Tuesday Group, which led MacArthur to resign as co-chair. In a barbed reaction, MacArthur told *The Washington Post*, "What has rankled my Tuesday Group colleagues the most is that I negotiated with the House Freedom Caucus. I'm not going to stop doing that. To me, not to work with one part of our party is ridiculous."

South Central New Jersey

Population	
Total	736,043
Land area	900
Pop/ sq mi	818.1
Born in state	60.2%
Age Groups	
Under 18	21.2%
18-34	19.3%
35-64	41.5%
Over 64	18.0%
Work	
White Collar	39.4%
Sales and Service	43.2%
Blue Collar	17.3%
Government	18.4%

Race and Ethnicity	
White	76.3%
Black	10.2%
Latino	7.4%
Asian	3.5%
Two races	2.2%
Other	0.4%
Education	
H.S grad or less	40.5%
Some college	27.5%
College Degree, 4 yr	21.3%
Post grad	10.8%
Military	
Veteran	10.2%
Active Duty	0.6%

Income	
Median Income	$73,485 (59 out of 435)
Under $50,000	33.6%
$50,000-$99,999	31.6%
$100,000-$199,999	27.5%
$200,000 or more	7.3%
Poverty Rate	6.7%
Health Insurance	
With health insurance coverage	92.7%
Public Assistance	
Cash public assistance income	1.9%
Food stamp/SNAP benefits	5.9%

Voter Turnout			
2015 Total Citizens 18+	558,834	2016 House Turnout as % CVAP	59%
2016 House turnout	328,060	2014 House Turnout as % CVAP	33%

2012 Presidential Vote		
Barack Obama	179,028	(52%)
Mitt Romney	163,204	(48%)

2016 Presidential Vote		
Donald Trump	187,703	(51%)
Hillary Clinton	165,090	(45%)
Gary Johnson	7,639	(2%)

Cook Partisan Voting Index: R+2

The Pine Barrens of New Jersey are one of the last vacant spots on the eastern seaboard - not quite terra incognita, but still not thickly populated. Encroached on by the Philadelphia suburbs of South Jersey and the Delaware River on the west and burgeoning retirement developments of the *Jersey Shore* on the east, the 1 million acres of heavy forest and white sand, with their unusual plant life, are crossed mostly by narrow two-lane roads. For years, the Pine Barrens was seen as a barrier to development. Only recently have environment-minded Jerseyites come to see the relatively unspoiled area as a natural treasure. There are a few small towns here, plus Joint Base McGuire-Dix-Lakehurst, the giant amalgamation of an Air Force base, Army military reservation and training site, and Navy air station. In a major long-term victory for the facility, the Air Force announced in the final days of the Obama administration that the Joint Base will house 24 of Boeing's KC-46A air-refueling tankers. Starting in 2020, the new planes will replace the base's older-model KC-10 refueling planes currently at the Joint

Base. In 2014, Lockheed Martin, a big employer with its naval electronics and surveillance system plant, opened in Moorestown the Surface Navy Innovation Center to develop new technologies. In December 2016, the Joint Base announced that it is building the largest military solar energy installation in the Northeast, with more than 50,000 solar panels.

East of the Pine Barrens is Ocean County, including the barrier islands from Mantoloking south to Stafford, with older communities on the beachfront and larger clusters of new subdivisions and condominiums inland. Here you can find the house in Seaside Heights where several seasons of MTV's Jersey Shore were set. Ocean County has been the fastest-growing part of New Jersey, a kind of Frost Belt Florida, with many retirees from New York and North Jersey eager to leave urban crime and high taxes. But it hasn't been all paradise lately; Hurricane Sandy in 2012 damaged more than 40,000 buildings in the county, its 20-foot waves smashing boardwalks and flooding dunes. Four years later, parts of the county were still receiving tens of millions of dollars in recovery assistance from the state.

The 3rd Congressional District of New Jersey spans the Pine Barrens and thousands of acres of farmland, plus the Joint Base. It includes large parts of Burlington and Ocean counties, including several suburban Philadelphia townships. In Toms River, the largest city in the district, the city council in February 2016 imposed a five-year ban on real-estate solicitors. Parts of the city had felt besieged by demands that they believed were on behalf of a burgeoning orthodox Jewish community in nearby Lakewood. Nearly 60 percent of the population resides in Burlington; Ocean County is more Republican-leaning. The 3rd is comfortable, but not affluent, suburban territory. Donald Trump in 2016 won the district, 51%-45%, after President Barack Obama got 52 percent in 2012. This is likely to remain a swing district.

FOURTH DISTRICT

Chris Smith (R)

Elected 1980, 19th term; b. Mar 04, 1953, Rahway; Worcester College (England), 1974; Trenton State College (NJ), B.A., 1975; Roman Catholic; Married (Marie Hahn Smith); 4 children.

Professional Career: Sales Executive, family-owned sporting goods business, 1975-1980; Executive Director, NJ Right to Life, 1976-1978.

DC Office: 2373 RHOB 20515, 202-225-3765, Fax: 202-225-7768, chrissmith.house.gov.

State Offices: Freehold, 732-780-3035; Hamilton, 609-585-7878; Plumsted, 609-286-2571.

Committees: *Foreign Affairs*: Africa, Global Health, Global Human Rights & Internat'l Orgs (Chmn), Western Hemisphere. *Joint Congressional-Executive Commission on China. Joint Security & Cooperation in Europe.*

Group Ratings

	ADA	ACLU	AFL-CIO	LCV	ITI	COC	HAFA	ACU	CFG	FRC
2016	-	5%	-	45%	83%	79%	51%	48%	49%	100%
2015	15%	C	63%	23%	C	70%	C	48%	50%	100%

Almanac Ratings 2015

	Economy	Social	Foreign	Composite
Liberal	15%	17%	10%	14%
Conservative	85%	83%	90%	86%

Key Votes of the 114th Congress

1. Keystone Pipeline	Y	5. Puerto Rico Debt	Y	9. Offenses by Aliens	Y
2. Trade Deals	N	6. Medical Marijuana	N	10. Troops in Iraq	N
3. Export-Import Bank	N	7. Sanctuary Cities	Y	11. Homeland Security $$	Y
4. Debt Ceiling Increase	N	8. Armor-piercing Bullets	Y	12. Trade Adjustment aid	Y

Election Results

Election	Name (Party)	Vote (%)		Cand. Spent	Ind. Exp. Support	Ind. Exp. Oppose
2016 General	Chris Smith (R)	211,992	(64%)	$574,754	$2,401	
	Lorna Phillipson (D)	111,532	(34%)	$187,042		
2016 Primary	Chris Smith (R)	41,658	(92%)			
	Bruce MacDonald (R)	3,629	(8%)			

Prior winning percentages: 2014 (68%), 2012 (64%), 2010 (69%), 2008 (66%), 2006 (66%), 2004 (67%), 2002 (66%), 2000 (63%), 1998 (62%), 1996 (64%), 1994 (68%), 1992 (62%), 1990 (63%), 1988 (66%), 1986 (61%), 1984 (61%), 1982 (53%), 1980 (57%)

Republican Chris Smith, first elected in 1980, combines outspoken opposition to abortion with an equally passionate commitment to human rights, whoever the perpetrator may be. Such independence does not always sit well with Republican leaders, but Smith's tenacity has made him one of the most successful legislators at guiding bills into law. Even though he is tied for the third-senior Republican in the House, his independence has led to struggles in his quest for a committee chairmanship.

Smith grew up in the Trenton area, worked in his family's sporting goods business, and, after graduating from the College of New Jersey with a degree in business administration, he became executive director of the New Jersey Right to Life Committee in 1976. Four years later, he ran for the House in the Trenton-centered district and defeated 26-year Rep. Frank Thompson, a Democrat convicted in the Abscam bribery scandal.

He has won enactment of more than 50 bills since he took office, according to congressional websites. Smith "has a gift for embracing issues that touch nerves and generate publicity," Bob Braun, a columnist for *The Star-Ledger* of Newark, once wrote. His recent successes include the International Religious Freedom Act of 2016, which clarifies that religion is understood to protect theistic and non-theistic beliefs, and the Global Food Security Act of 2016, which reforms foreign aid programs for developing countries to reduce global poverty and hunger.

A devout Roman Catholic, Smith is best known for his unwavering fight against legalized abortion. He has worked to stop abortions in military hospitals, and he persuaded the George W. Bush administration to reinstate Reagan-era restrictions denying federal funds to family-planning organizations that promote abortions abroad. (In 2009, President Barack Obama rescinded the restrictions during his first week in office. Three days after President Donald Trump took office, he rescinded Obama's executive order and reimposed the earlier restrictions.) Smith was a prime mover of legislation to ban "partial birth" abortions. After Republicans regained control of the House in 2011, Smith passed a bill taking away tax benefits from employee-sponsored health insurance plans that offer abortion coverage. Critics said his bill was a step toward outlawing abortions outright. He sought to add the word "forcible" to a long-standing exemption for rape, drawing angry criticism from abortion-rights advocates, who said the change could exclude statutory rape or rapes where the victim was drugged or unconscious. He later agreed to remove the word.

Smith has long crusaded for his Unborn Child Pain Awareness Act, which would require doctors to inform pregnant women that some experts say that a fetus can feel pain after 20 weeks of gestation. The House passed the bill in 2015, after agreeing to limits to accommodate several House GOP women. He has a bill to revoke the Food and Drug Administration's approval of the abortifacient RU-486, which Smith calls "baby pesticide." He has opposed federal funding for embryonic stem cell research, which uses excess embryos from in vitro fertilization, but he has been a champion of other stem cell research. In 2005, Congress enacted his Stem Cell Therapeutic and Research Act, which funds research and therapy using umbilical cord stem cells plus cells from bone marrow transplants. In the 2016 campaign, Smith was a co-chair of the Pro-Life Coalition for Trump.

Smith has brought his strong moral views to his work against human rights abuses abroad. He has sharply criticized China for its forced sterilizations and abortions, and its persecution of Christians and other religious minorities. As a result, he opposed normalizing trade relations with the country. Smith has condemned Russia for barring entry of foreign Catholic priests, and he criticized the Saudis for treating foreign servants as slaves. In 2000, Congress enacted his legislation to combat sex trafficking around the world, including requiring yearly reports on each nation's record. At one point, Smith learned of Ukrainian girls being held against their will in brothels in Montenegro; he personally called the country's prime minister, who ordered a raid on the operation.

He often has traveled great distances on behalf of his principles. On the eve of the Olympics in 2008, Smith tried to meet human rights lawyers in Beijing, but they were placed under house arrest. He unsuccessfully urged President George W. Bush not to attend the Olympic opening ceremonies. Less than a year later, he flew to Brazil to reunite a New Jersey man with his 8-year-old son whose Brazilian mother had taken him out of the United States in defiance of a court order.

Overall, Smith has been one of the most moderate members of the House GOP. In 2009, he was one of eight Republicans to support the Waxman-Markey energy bill imposing a cap-and-trade system to limit greenhouse gas emissions. He cosponsored the so-called "card check" bill aimed at making it easier for unions to organize work sites by eliminating secret-ballot elections. In recent years, he usually has voted with Republicans on major votes such as budget blueprints.

Earlier, he dramatized his willingness to buck his party for the sake of his beliefs and to accept the consequences when, as chairman of the Veterans' Affairs Committee, Smith angered budget conservatives by pushing expanded benefits for veterans. In a major breach of party protocol, he voted for the Democratic spending plan because it contained more money for veterans. In 2005, the Republican Steering Committee booted Smith from his chairmanship. Veterans groups expressed outrage, to no avail. Smith's bid to chair the Foreign Affairs Committee in 2013 was thwarted when GOP leaders chose the more reliably conservative Ed Royce of California. Instead, Smith took the chairmanship of the tailor-made Subcommittee on Africa, Global Health, Global Human Rights and International Organizations. Royce is term-limited in 2018, which could give Smith an opportunity to convince a new leadership team of his credentials to succeed him.

Smith's devotion to principle and his reputation for tending to constituent problems have made him popular in the 4th District, which has become safely Republican. Since 1984, he has received at least 61 percent of the vote. In 2008, Democratic challenger Joshua Zeitz, a first-time candidate, accused him of being a resident of Virginia because Smith owned a home there and his daughter paid in-state Virginia tuition. Smith rents a townhouse in Hamilton Township. He was reelected that year 66%-33%.

Central New Jersey: Monmouth and Ocean Counties

Population		**Race and Ethnicity**		**Income**	
Total	738,191	White	78.1%	Median Income	$76,071 (46 out of 435)
Land area	692	Black	6.3%		
Pop/ sq mi	1066.9	Latino	10.0%	Under $50,000	33.9%
Born in state	59.2%	Asian	4.0%	$50,000-$99,999	27.6%
		Two races	1.4%	$100,000-$199,999	27.6%
Age Groups		Other	0.2%	$200,000 or more	10.8%
Under 18	24.8%			Poverty Rate	9.6%
18-34	18.5%	**Education**			
35-64	39.5%	H.S grad or less	36.4%	**Health Insurance**	
Over 64	17.2%	Some college	25.6%	With health insurance coverage	91.6%
		College Degree, 4 yr	23.8%		
Work		Post grad	14.2%		
White Collar	42.1%			**Public Assistance**	
Sales and Service	42.3%	**Military**		Cash public assistance income	1.7%
Blue Collar	15.7%	Veteran	7.4%		
Government	15.1%	Active Duty	0.1%	Food stamp/SNAP benefits	6.4%

Voter Turnout			
2015 Total Citizens 18+	518,802	2016 House Turnout as % CVAP	64%
2016 House turnout	332,684	2014 House Turnout as % CVAP	34%

2012 Presidential Vote		
Mitt Romney	180,437	(55%)
Barack Obama	148,621	(45%)

2016 Presidential Vote		
Donald Trump	198,859	(55%)
Hillary Clinton	146,191	(41%)
Gary Johnson	7,184	(2%)

Cook Partisan Voting Index: R+8

An invisible and not-well-defined line divides North Jersey and South Jersey. North of the line, people watch New York television stations, eat hero sandwiches and root for the Yankees. South of the line, they watch Philadelphia television, eat hoagies and root for the Phillies. The state capital of Trenton lies south of the line, which passes east somewhere around Six Flags Great Adventure in the

Pine Barrens and heads southeast past Lakewood and Brick to the Jersey Shore. On both sides of the line, a stronger New Jersey identity has developed. The big cities - New York and Philadelphia - are not all that close, particularly when traffic is heavy, which is often. The economy of central New Jersey has its own character, with big pharmaceutical companies and the consolidated Joint Base McGuire-Dix-Lakehurst. (The German zeppelin Hindenburg exploded while docking in 1937 at what was then called Lakehurst Naval Air Station.)

No less a true New Jersey persona than Bruce Springsteen was raised in Freehold Borough, the subject of his bleak portrayal in "My Hometown." Freehold Township, which grew 15 percent from 2000 to 2010, is now a city of 36,000. Nearby Ocean County was smashed by Hurricane Sandy in the fall of 2012; of the nearly 72,000 buildings damaged in the storm, more than half were in Ocean County. As of 2015, the state housing agency had made $360 million in loan commitments for 18 affordable-housing projects in Ocean and Monmouth counties. Lakewood, the area's biggest town, has become home to the nation's largest population of Orthodox Jews outside of Brooklyn -- they live in crowded housing and account for more than 60 percent of Lakewood's population of 100,000. The community caused some tension when some of its members sought to become aggressive home-buyers in nearby Tom's River. A sagging economy led to the creation of a Lakewood-area "Tent City," filled with teepees and shanties for the homeless. In July 2014, it finally closed as county officials found temporary housing for those who remained and then destroyed the remaining structures. In 2015, environmentalists sued Six Flags over its plan to level 90 acres of trees to support its planned solar-power facility. After the project was reduced to 66 acres, developers won local approval in October 2016 and planned to clear thousands of trees.

The Fourth Congressional District of New Jersey is based in Monmouth County, which has about 55 percent of its population, with parts of Mercer County and the fast-growing exurban Ocean County making up the rest. The district has become relatively safe for Republicans. Donald Trump got 55 percent of the vote here in 2016, the same as Mitt Romney got in 2012. In each case, the 4th was the best GOP district in New Jersey.

FIFTH DISTRICT

Josh Gottheimer (D)

Elected 2016, 1st term; b. Mar 08, 1975, Livingston; University of Pennsylvania, B.A., 1977; Harvard University Law School (MA), J.D., 2004; Jewish; Married (Marla Brooke Tusk Gottheimer); 2 children.

Professional Career: Special Assitant and Speechwriter, President Bill Clinton, 1998-2001; Senior Counselor, Federal Communications Commission, 2010-2012.

DC Office: 213 CHOB 20515, 202-225-4465, Fax: 202-225-9048, gottheimer.house.gov.

State Offices: Glen Rock, 201-389-1100; Newton, 973-814-4078; Ringwood, 973-814-4076; Washington, 973-814-4076.

Committees: *Financial Services*: Capital Markets, Securities & Investment, Oversight & Investigations, Terrorism & Illicit Finance.

Election Results

Election	Name (Party)	Vote	(%)	Cand. Spent	Ind. Exp. Support	Ind. Exp. Oppose
2016 General	Josh Gottheimer (D)	172,587	(51%)	$4,678,611	$1,935,706	$30,000
	Scott Garrett (R)	157,690	(47%)	$4,261,529	$315,712	$5,220,641
	Claudio Belusic (L)	7,424	(2%)			
2016 Primary	Josh Gottheimer (D)		(100%)			

Democrat Josh Gottheimer was elected in 2016 by defeating a veteran Republican incumbent who appeared to have lost touch with key parts of his upscale district. As the first Democrat elected in a version of this district since 1978, Gottheimer became an early Republican target for the 2018 campaign. He deliberately styled himself as a centrist in anticipation of the challenge.

Born and raised in New Jersey, Gottheimer was introduced to politics as a high school student, when he served as a page for Democratic Sen. Frank Lautenberg. He got his bachelor's at the University of Pennsylvania and then became a Thouron Fellow at Oxford University in England. After working on the rapid response team for Bill Clinton during his 1996 reelection campaign, he joined the Clinton administration as a speechwriter from 1998 until 2001. Gottheimer attended law school at Harvard University, while working for the 2004 presidential campaigns of Wesley Clark and then John Kerry. Following that election, Gottheimer worked for the Ford Motor Co. and later became executive vice president for Burson-Marsteller and an official for Microsoft. On the staff of the Federal Communications Commission, he was its first director of public-private initiatives.

His race against incumbent Scott Garrett was heavily funded on both sides as Democrats fought to unseat Garrett, a seven-term Republican who was the most conservative member of New Jersey's congressional delegation. His uncompromising views on reining in federal spending and banking regulation made him a player on the House Budget and Financial Services committees and as a founder of the conservative Freedom Caucus, but they set him apart from his Garden State colleagues. He attracted largely negative attention in his district when he said that he would not support the National Republican Congressional Committee because it was financing candidates who are homosexual. Later, he sought to clarify that he would not support GOP candidates who backed same-sex marriage. But the damage was done, especially with many of Garrett's Wall Street contributors.

Gottheimer talked about governing from the center with a broad coalition of support in his Republican-leaning district. He supported tax cuts and fewer regulations and he opposed President Barack Obama's nuclear deal with Iran. Garrett had won his seat after two unsuccessful primaries against moderate Republican Rep. Marge Roukema, who then retired; but he never secured her Bergen County-based voters, who had been moving to the left in any case. Gottheimer benefited from record fundraising for a House candidate from New Jersey -- $4.8 million that he raised, plus another $6 million in support from Democratic groups and allies. Garrett raised $2.4 million and had less than $1 million in outside support. In the onslaught of ads, which were disproportionately on behalf of Gottheimer, the northjersey.com website said that the truth was "stretched, bent or broken." Gottheimer accused Garrett of raising the already high local taxes by failing to secure sufficient support from federal programs.

Gottheimer won 51%-47%, a margin of about 15,000 votes, with a 56%-42% lead in Bergen. In Garrett's base of Sussex and Warren counties, the turnout and Garrett's lead were too small to make a difference. In an unusual but not unprecedented scenario, Garrett refused to cooperate in the post-election transition.

In some ways, Gottheimer followed Garrett's model once in office: He took a seat on the Financial Services Committee, and was one of nine House Democrats in January 2017 to vote for a bill that restricted the Securities and Exchange Commission. He moved in a different direction when he became co-chair of the bipartisan Problem Solvers Caucus in the House. The National Republican Congressional Committee identified Gottheimer as a "top offensive target" in 2018.

Northern New Jersey: Bergen County

Population		**Race and Ethnicity**		**Income**	
Total	741,254	White	70.9%	Median Income	$92,550 (12 out of 435)
Land area	991	Black	4.6%		
Pop/ sq mi	747.8	Latino	13.0%	Under $50,000	26.6%
Born in state	51.9%	Asian	9.9%	$50,000-$99,999	26.8%
Age Groups		Two races	1.2%	$100,000-$199,999	31.8%
Under 18	22.6%	Other	0.4%	$200,000 or more	14.8%
18-34	18.1%	**Education**		Poverty Rate	5.8%
35-64	43.6%	H.S grad or less	32.0%	**Health Insurance**	
Over 64	15.6%	Some college	22.6%	With health insurance coverage	91.9%
Work		College Degree, 4 yr	28.4%		
		Post grad	17.1%		
White Collar	46.2%			**Public Assistance**	
Sales and Service	39.2%	**Military**		Cash public assistance income	1.5%
Blue Collar	14.6%	Veteran	5.8%		
Government	12.6%	Active Duty	0.0%	Food stamp/SNAP benefits	4.3%

Voter Turnout			
2015 Total Citizens 18+	526,132	2016 House Turnout as % CVAP	64%
2016 House turnout	337,701	2014 House Turnout as % CVAP	36%

2012 Presidential Vote		
Mitt Romney	172,451	(52%)
Barack Obama	162,318	(49%)

2016 Presidential Vote		
Donald Trump	178,058	(48%)
Hillary Clinton	173,969	(47%)
Gary Johnson	8,014	(2%)

Cook Partisan Voting Index: R+3

The northern edge of New Jersey was settled three centuries ago by the Dutch, for whom this plateau of land behind the Hudson River Palisades seemed a natural part of Nieuw Amsterdam. The Dutch influence is seen in old, steep-roofed farmhouses and in many of the place names - Bergen County, Cresskill, Closter. But overall, northernmost New Jersey has the well-settled look of so many northeastern suburbs, with touches of both affluence and small-town hominess, crisscrossed at its edges with limited-access highways and shopping centers. Since the late 1950s, Paramus has been transformed from celery farms to the site of three shopping malls and numerous shopping centers that do more than $5 billion a year in retail sales. Recently, some local mall executives have begun to reconsider the most effective use of their space, with possibilities such as office, hotel or residential use, or sites for online deliveries. After 15 years of delay, the American Dream mega-mall was scheduled to open in 2018, with a 16-story indoor ski hill and the largest indoor theme park in the Western Hemisphere.

Not far away are Saddle River and Franklin Lakes, with million-dollar houses on multi-acre lots, and Park Ridge, with office buildings and condominiums. This area may look like WASP suburbia on the surface, but in fact it is home to successful people of all ethnic groups, many of them descended from those who first saw the Statue of Liberty from steerage. Bergenfield has many people of Filipino descent, and it's known locally as "Little Manila." In Bergen County overall, the population has grown to 19 percent Hispanic and 17 percent Asian. Bergen is the last urban county in the nation that widely complies with "Blue Law" limitations on Sunday retailing. An advocacy group, Modernize Bergen County, has taken steps on a referendum to challenge the practice. But its supporters have been unable to obtain sufficient signatures for a referendum, and many small business owners prefer not having to worry about the malls on one day during the week.

The 5th Congressional District of New Jersey comprises most of northern Bergen County, plus a swath of North Jersey stretching west to the upper reaches of the Delaware River. Nearly three-fourths of its population is in Bergen County. Farther west are exurban and heavily Republican Sussex and Warren counties. Redistricting changes added more of Bergen County and reduced John McCain's local vote of 54 percent to 51 percent. Though the district still favors Republicans, it has become more competitive. In 2016, Donald Trump took the district, 48%-47%.

SIXTH DISTRICT

Frank Pallone (D)

Elected 1988, 15th term; b. Oct 30, 1951, Long Branch; Middlebury College (VT), B.A., 1973; Tufts University Fletcher School of Law and Diplomacy (MA), M.A., 1974; Rutgers University Law School (NJ), J.D., 1978; Roman Catholic; Married (Sarah Hospodor Pallone); 3 children.

Elected Office: Long Branch City Council, 1982-1988; NJ Senate, 1983-1988.

Professional Career: Assistant Professional, Rutgers University, 1979-1980; Practicing attorney, 1981-1983; Instructor, Monmouth College, 1984-1986.

DC Office: 237 CHOB 20515, 202-225-4671, Fax: 202-225-9665, pallone.house.gov.

State Offices: Long Branch, 732-571-1140; New Brunswick, 732-249-8892.

Committees: *Energy & Commerce (RMM)*: Communications & Technology, Digital Commerce & Consumer Protection, Energy, Environment, Health, Oversight & Investigations.

Group Ratings

	ADA	ACLU	AFL-CIO	LCV	ITI	COC	HAFA	ACU	CFG	FRC
2016	-	100%	-	100%	40%	50%	12%	0%	4%	0%
2015	100%	C	100%	100%	C	40%	C	4%	0%	0%

Almanac Ratings 2015

	Economy	Social	Foreign	Composite
Liberal	98%	100%	92%	97%
Conservative	2%	0%	8%	3%

Key Votes of the 114th Congress

1. Keystone Pipeline	N	5. Puerto Rico Debt	Y	9. Offenses by Aliens	N
2. Trade Deals	N	6. Medical Marijuana	Y	10. Troops in Iraq	Y
3. Export-Import Bank	Y	7. Sanctuary Cities	N	11. Homeland Security $$	Y
4. Debt Ceiling Increase	Y	8. Armor-piercing Bullets	N	12. Trade Adjustment aid	Y

Election Results

Election	Name (Party)	Vote (%)	Cand. Spent	Ind. Exp. Support	Ind. Exp. Oppose
2016 General	Frank Pallone (D)	167,895 (64%)	$1,298,951		
	Brent Sonnek-Schmelz (R)	91,908 (35%)	$75,012		
2016 Primary	Frank Pallone (D)	(100%)			

Prior winning percentages: 2014 (60%), 2012 (63%), 2010 (55%), 2008 (67%), 2006 (69%), 2004 (67%), 2002 (66%), 2000 (68%), 1998 (57%), 1996 (61%), 1994 (60%), 1992 (52%), 1990 (49%), 1988 (52%), 1988 special (52%)

Democrat Frank Pallone, elected in 1988, became the ranking Democrat on the Energy and Commerce Committee in 2015. His first two years in that position had several bipartisan achievements during a mostly unproductive time in Congress. He has been one of his party's chief messengers on health care and environmental issues.

Pallone is the son of a disabled Long Branch policeman. He became an environmentalist in 1969, when as a Middlebury College freshman in Vermont he worked for that state's first-in-the-nation bottle deposit law. After getting a master's degree in international relations from Tufts University and a law degree from Rutgers, he was elected to the Long Branch City Council at age 31, and to the New Jersey Senate a year later.

Pallone ran for an open House seat that a Democrat had long held. The district leaned Republican, but residents were angry about untreated sludge, plastic containers and medical waste washing up on the beach. Pallone's bumper sticker, which didn't mention party affiliation, said, "Stop Ocean Dumping." That, combined with his conservative views on taxes and crime, helped him to win 52 percent of the vote.

His environmental interest resulted in a continuing focus on measures to protect the New Jersey shoreline. In 2006, he won passage of a bill to reduce and prevent debris in the marine environment. Two years later, he was the lead sponsor of a bipartisan bill to rebuild American fisheries, in part by requiring a review of factors that lead to over-fishing. Pallone was the chief sponsor of a new law in 2015 that placed restrictions on the sale or distribution of personal care products that contain synthetic plastic microbeads, which can pollute waterways. New Jersey earlier passed its own law to ban the products.

As chairman of Energy and Commerce's Subcommittee on Health when President Barack Obama took office in 2009, Pallone helped steer to passage the Democrats' expansion of the Children's Health Insurance Program, which he called "a down payment to ensuring that all Americans have access to affordable health care." On the Democrats' economic stimulus bill, he backed an increase in the federal matching rate for Medicaid as a step to reduce the program's financial burden on states. During the health care overhaul debate, he shuttled among various factions of Blue Dogs and progressives to try to get them to be flexible. After the bill passed in 2010, and Republicans tried to repeal it, Pallone was among its most outspoken defenders. "The fact of the matter is, that if we pass these defunding amendments in the guise of budget austerity, (Republicans) are one step towards repealing the largest deficit-cutter passed in the last decade, and that's the Affordable Care Act," he said in 2011. Pallone got a bill through the subcommittee that set guidelines for the time period student athletes must be benched after suffering concussions.

Pallone clashed with Obama on New Jersey coastal issues. After the BP oil spill in the Gulf of Mexico in 2010, he and other Democrats implored Obama to oppose oil and gas drilling off the East Coast. After criticizing as "unthinkable" an initial plan by Obama for partial approval of drilling, Pallone welcomed the administration's later reversal, including a five-year moratorium. During his final weeks in office, Obama took regulatory action to prohibit drilling in canyons in the Atlantic Ocean between Massachusetts and Virginia. Pallone continued to urge a permanent ban on offshore drilling anywhere in the Atlantic. He criticized the administration's response to Superstorm Sandy, which damaged many of his district's coastal communities in 2012. He repeatedly demanded that the Federal Emergency Management Agency provide mobile homes for thousands of stranded residents, then criticized the agency when it came through with just 50 trailers. To improve local communications during emergencies, Pallone crafted Securing Access to Networks in Disasters (SANDY) Act, which the House passed in January 2017.

He has channeled the interests of his district's large Asian population. In a bow to the many persons of Armenian descent, Pallone helped push congressional approval of normalizing trade relations with Armenia. He sponsored the resolution that labeled the 1915 killing of Armenians by Ottoman Turks as genocide, which Turkey vehemently opposed. He has been active on issues involving India and has introduced a resolution condemning violence against the Hindus known as Kashmiri Pandits.

When Rep. Henry Waxman retired in 2014 as ranking Democrat on Energy and Commerce, Rep. Anna Eshoo was actively supported by her long-time friend, Minority Leader Nancy Pelosi, as his successor. The Pelosi-controlled Democratic Steering and Policy Committee had endorsed Eshoo for the position, 30-19. But Eshoo was edged out by Pallone, 100-90, in secret balloting by the Democratic Caucus. Pallone highlighted that he had four years more seniority than Eshoo, which appealed to many in the Congressional Black Caucus and other traditionalists. He acknowledged the big boost that Minority Whip Steny Hoyer gave him.

After moving into his new position, Pallone made progress in reducing the fractiousness on the panel. In 2016, the committee was instrumental in enacting the bipartisan Twenty First Century Cures Act, which advanced a series of medical-research innovations. Also that year, the committee was at the center of successful efforts to complete the long-delayed update of chemical safety laws. The new law resolved numerous manufacturing and public-health issues related to New Jersey and gave new authority to the Environmental Protection Agency to evaluate existing and new chemicals.

Since 1994, Pallone has been reelected with at least 60 percent of the vote, with two exceptions. In 1998, he faced a tough challenge from 28-year-old Republican Mike Ferguson, an ally of former GOP Gov. Thomas Kean. An insurance group unhappy with Pallone's support of President Bill Clinton's plan to regulate health maintenance organizations spent nearly $2 million on Ferguson's campaign. But Pallone won 57%-40%. Ferguson won a neighboring district two years later and served eight years. In 2010, Pallone drew another formidable opponent in Republican Anna Little, the mayor of Highlands. With strong tea party backing, Little took socially conservative positions and blasted Pallone's efforts to pass the health care bill. Pallone was bolstered by a series of newspaper endorsements and kept his seat, 55%-44%.

He has pursued opportunities to run for the Senate. When Democratic Sen. Jon Corzine ran for governor in 2005, Pallone endorsed him. Corzine was elected, but he disappointed Pallone by appointing Rep. Robert Menendez to his Senate seat. After Democratic Sen. Frank Lautenberg died in 2013, Pallone ran in the special election and appealed to party regulars in the Democratic primary. Newark Mayor Cory Booker easily prevailed with 59 percent to 20 percent for Pallone, the runner-up.

East-Central New Jersey: Middlesex and Northern Monmouth Counties

Population		Race and Ethnicity		Income	
Total	743,854	White	49.2%	Median Income	$75,968 (48 out of 435)
Land area	216	Black	9.3%		
Pop/ sq mi	3451.0	Latino	21.2%	Under $50,000	33.4%
Born in state	50.0%	Asian	18.3%	$50,000-$99,999	29.6%
Age Groups		Two races	1.7%	$100,000-$199,999	27.7%
Under 18	22.2%	Other	0.3%	$200,000 or more	9.3%
18-34	25.1%	**Education**		Poverty Rate	10.5%
35-64	40.5%	H.S grad or less	39.8%	**Health Insurance**	
Over 64	12.2%	Some college	22.3%	With health insurance coverage	87.5%
Work		College Degree, 4 yr	23.1%		
White Collar	41.1%	Post grad	14.7%	**Public Assistance**	
Sales and Service	39.9%	**Military**		Cash public assistance income	2.0%
Blue Collar	19.0%	Veteran	4.5%		
Government	12.8%	Active Duty	0.0%	Food stamp/SNAP benefits	7.4%

Voter Turnout			
2015 Total Citizens 18+	482,338	2016 House Turnout as % CVAP	55%
2016 House turnout	263,435	2014 House Turnout as % CVAP	25%

2012 Presidential Vote		
Barack Obama	163,428	(62%)
Mitt Romney	99,564	(38%)

2016 Presidential Vote		
Hillary Clinton	162,858	(56%)
Donald Trump	117,679	(40%)

Cook Partisan Voting Index: D+9

For generations, great transportation arteries have brought people out of the huge central cities of New York and Philadelphia and into the flatlands and hills of New Jersey - to vacation, to raise families, to work toward affluence and to build communities. The railroads of the late 19th century created the towns of the Jersey shore. After 1874, when the first train from New York City reached Long Branch, the shore became the summer home of seven presidents from Grant to Wilson (James Garfield, convalescing after he was shot, died there in 1881), and of New York racehorse owners and socialites. Over time, the ambiance degraded, and the fishing pier and much of the boardwalk went up in flames in 1987. A shopping and dining complex took its place. In 2016, the city awarded a contract for the design of a pier and terminal for a commuter ferry to Manhattan.

The freight rail lines in the New York-Philadelphia corridor sparked electrical and chemical industries here - many of them building on the inventions of Thomas Edison, produced in his Menlo Park laboratory just off the rail lines. Today, a 131-foot tower stands as a memorial to the inventor. The same corridor was the site of America's first cloverleaf intersection, at the junction of U.S. 1 and U.S. 9. The New Jersey Turnpike roars past oil tank farms and petrochemical plants, major rail lines and the oily waters of Raritan Bay. Superstorm Sandy devastated much of this area in 2012. Five years later on Raritan Bay, Union Beach planned to start work on a $273 million flood plan, which included a 12,000-foot wall to protect some properties.

The 6th Congressional District inelegantly ties together these great transportation nodes, and the upward mobility that has taken place around them. The district is shaped like a backward capital F, with a string of towns running from Piscataway down the Atlantic coast to Long Branch and Asbury Park. Middlesex County accounts for 69 percent of the district's population, with the remainder in Monmouth County. The two largest localities are Woodbridge and Edison Township - an industrial area that has housed some of America's great research and development facilities. Asbury Park, which began as a Christian resort, is plagued by a 32 percent poverty rate and was immortalized in the music of Bruce Springsteen. The district has become majority-minority: 22 percent Latino, 19 percent Asian and 10 percent black. It has the third-largest share of Asians of any district on the East Coast, behind two in New York City. The largest and fastest-growing group is Indians, who have a major presence in Edison.

This is a safe Democratic district. The presidential contest tightened in 2016, when Hillary Clinton led Donald Trump, 56%-40%. In 2012, President Barack Obama won the district, 62%-38%.

SEVENTH DISTRICT

Leonard Lance (R)

Elected 2008, 5th term; b. Jun 25, 1952, Easton, PA; Lehigh University (PA), B.A., 1974; Vanderbilt University Law School (TN), J.D., 1977; Princeton University Woodrow Wilson School of Public and International Affairs (NJ), M.P.A., 1982; Roman Catholic; Married (Heidi A. Rohrbach); 1 child.

Elected Office: NJ Assembly, 1991-2002; NJ Senate, 2002-2008, Minority Leader, 2002-2008.

Professional Career: Clerk, Warren County Court, 1977-1978; Assistant counsel, Gov. Thomas H. Kean, 1983-1990.

DC Office: 2352 RHOB 20515, 202-225-5361, Fax: 202-225-9460, lance.house.gov.

State Offices: Flemington, 908-788-6900; Westfield, 908-518-7733.

Committees: *Energy & Commerce*: Communications & Technology, Digital Commerce & Consumer Protection, Health. *Ethics*.

Group Ratings

	ADA	ACLU	AFL-CIO	LCV	ITI	COC	HAFA	ACU	CFG	FRC
2016	-	5%	-	13%	100%	100%	56%	64%	70%	83%
2015	0%	C	25%	11%	C	80%	C	71%	71%	92%

Almanac Ratings 2015

	Economy	Social	Foreign	Composite
Liberal	5%	10%	6%	7%
Conservative	95%	90%	94%	93%

Key Votes of the 114th Congress

1. Keystone Pipeline	Y	5. Puerto Rico Debt	N	9. Offenses by Aliens	Y
2. Trade Deals	Y	6. Medical Marijuana	N	10. Troops in Iraq	N
3. Export-Import Bank	N	7. Sanctuary Cities	Y	11. Homeland Security $$	Y
4. Debt Ceiling Increase	N	8. Armor-piercing Bullets	Y	12. Trade Adjustment aid	N

Election Results

Election	Name (Party)	Vote (%)		Cand. Spent	Ind. Exp. Support	Ind. Exp. Oppose
2016 General	Leonard Lance (R)	185,850	(54%)	$1,196,285	$1,000	
	Peter Jacob (D)	148,188	(43%)	$294,166		
2016 Primary	Leonard Lance (R)	31,018	(54%)			
	David Larsen (R)	18,857	(33%)			
	Craig Heard (R)	7,643	(13%)			

Prior winning percentages: 2014 (59%), 2012 (57%), 2010 (59%), 2008 (50%)

Leonard Lance is a wonky, self-styled "Eisenhower Republican" elected in 2008. His moderate stances have drawn primary challenges from the right, but his pattern of pragmatic fiscal conservatism and social liberalism has proven popular in a suburban district that, politically, has many voters who still like Ike. Lance hasn't changed much, though he faces the tension that his once-centrist views have shifted to the left of the GOP but sometimes fall to the right in his suburban district. Democrats have targeted his reelection in 2018.

Lance's English-German ancestors lived in Hunterdon County for 300 years, and he and his twin brother, James, grew up there in the small town of Glen Gardner. Politics is in Lance's blood. His father, Wesley Lance, was a state senator and eventually rose to Senate president. The younger Lance went to Lehigh University to get his bachelor's degree, then headed south to Vanderbilt University for a law degree. He returned to New Jersey to pursue a master's from Princeton University. One of his early jobs was as Republican Gov. Thomas Kean's assistant counsel for county and municipal matters. In 1990, he was elected to the New Jersey legislature, where he made a name for himself as a budget hawk and independent thinker. He opposed a spending plan by GOP

Gov. Christie Whitman, a move that cost him the Budget Committee chairmanship.

In 2008, GOP Rep. Mike Ferguson did not seek reelection after narrowly holding his seat two years earlier against Democratic Assemblywoman Linda Stender. Lance got into the primary race against six other candidates. He was the establishment Republicans' pick, but he faced tough competition from Whitman's daughter, Kate Whitman, who outraised him and questioned his fiscal bona fides. After spending nearly all of his funds early, he won the primary by a surprisingly large margin, 39%-20%, over Whitman.

Lance started the general election campaign seriously outmatched by Stender, who ran again and outspent him 2-to-1. She criticized Lance for opposing her legislation to make it mandatory for pharmacies to fill prescriptions for birth control pills, including emergency contraception. Lance said he voted against the bill because he believed that mom-and-pop pharmacies should have the right to decide whether to fill such prescriptions. Both political parties pulled out all the stops for this seat. Lance did better than expected, winning 50%-42%.

In his first term, Lance showed some bipartisan colors. He was one of eight Republicans to support energy legislation that included a cap-and-trade program aimed at reducing greenhouse gas emissions, and one of three to back the Lilly Ledbetter Fair Pay Act, which made it easier to sue over alleged wage discrimination. He held firm against most of President Barack Obama's big-spending agenda, voting against the stimulus bill even as he touted a flood control project in his district that was ready for stimulus money. He was a critic of the Dodd-Frank Wall Street reform law, saying he was especially troubled by its reliance on unused government bailout funds.

When Republicans took the House majority, Lance became more of a party regular. He voted in favor of New Jersey Republican Rep. Scott Garrett's budget proposal that cut spending even further than Budget Committee Chairman Paul Ryan's blueprint, and for a measure to repeal the ban on incandescent light bulbs established in the 2007 energy law. In 2015, he introduced a constitutional amendment to require a balanced budget. Despite his backing of abortion rights, he has voted with Republicans to cut off public funding for Planned Parenthood. In January 2017, he voted for a proposal by abortion-foe Rep. Chris Smith of New Jersey to prevent funding for any federal insurance plan that provides abortion coverage. Lance also has looked for opportunities to cross the aisle. On the Energy and Commerce Committee in 2016, he collaborated with Democratic Rep. Frank Pallone of New Jersey on a proposal to increase the authority of the Food and Drug Administration to regulate cosmetics. That measure had support from local businesses.

Lance has drawn regular primary challenges from tea party-backed candidate David Larsen, who has called his rival "totally disconnected from the people." A lightly funded businessman in home construction who had no experience in elected office, he cited as a model neighboring Rep. Garrett, who lost his seat in 2016 to big-spending Democratic challenger Josh Gottheimer. Lance won 61%-39% in 2012. Two years later, his victory over Larsen narrowed to 54%-46%; Lance attributed that outcome to low turnout. In 2016, the turnout more than doubled and Lance comfortably won the three-candidate primary, 54%-33%, against runner-up Larsen. Lance took every county. The closest was Morris, where the vote total was fourth among the six counties.

In the 2016 general, against Peter Jacob, a progressive but politically inexperienced social worker, Lance was held to his closest win since he was first elected, 54%-43%. Lance won each county except Essex, which had the smallest turnout. He raised $1.1 million to $320,000 for Jacob. Neither had much independent financial support. Compared to Garrett, Lance has seemed more politically adept.

Despite their failure to take this district seriously in recent years, House Democrats featured Lance on their early target list for 2018. They were hoping that significant local protests of President Donald Trump would fuel opposition to Lance, who sought to emphasize his independence. Lance criticized as "rushed and poorly implemented" Trump's initial executive order restricting the entry of immigrants and refugees, though he added that new policies were needed. If a more robust challenge from Democrats pulls Lance to the left, conservatives could pursue another primary contest.

North-Central New Jersey: Somerset, Union and Hunterdon Counties

Population	
Total	740,850
Land area	970
Pop/ sq mi	763.6
Born in state	56.8%
Age Groups	
Under 18	23.9%
18-34	17.0%
35-64	45.0%
Over 64	14.1%
Work	
White Collar	50.1%
Sales and Service	36.7%
Blue Collar	13.2%
Government	12.5%

Race and Ethnicity	
White	73.0%
Black	4.3%
Latino	11.8%
Asian	9.2%
Two races	1.3%
Other	0.5%
Education	
H.S grad or less	28.5%
Some college	20.7%
College Degree, 4 yr	29.1%
Post grad	21.6%
Military	
Veteran	5.4%
Active Duty	0.0%

Income	
Median Income	$1,02,551 (5 out of 435)
Under $50,000	22.9%
$50,000-$99,999	25.5%
$100,000-$199,999	31.8%
$200,000 or more	19.8%
Poverty Rate	4.7%
Health Insurance	
With health insurance coverage	93.1%
Public Assistance	
Cash public assistance income	1.7%
Food stamp/SNAP benefits	3.7%

Voter Turnout			
2015 Total Citizens 18+	514,844	2016 House Turnout as % CVAP	67%
2016 House turnout	343,635	2014 House Turnout as % CVAP	33%

2012 Presidential Vote		
Mitt Romney	178,318	(53%)
Barack Obama	157,285	(47%)

2016 Presidential Vote		
Hillary Clinton	180,525	(48%)
Donald Trump	176,386	(47%)
Gary Johnson	9,794	(3%)

Cook Partisan Voting Index: R+3

The transportation arteries beneath First Watchung Mountain played a large role in New Jersey's development. The rail lines of the late 19th century opened up commuter suburbs. In the 1940s, the four lanes of U.S. 22 made those communities readily accessible by car. Next, Interstate 78, completed in the mid-1980s, put Newark only an hour's distance from the Pennsylvania line. The interstate stimulated development of an edge city called Bridgewater Commons halfway between Philadelphia and Manhattan. An enormous shopping mall and office development, which included the headquarters of AT&T, rose up in the horse country around Far Hills and Bernardsville, where the likes of Malcolm Forbes and Charles Engelhard owned huge estates. (New Jersey claims more horses per square mile than any other state.) These towns are in Somerset County, with a median household income in 2014 of $99,020, the eighth highest among U.S. counties. In Essex County, Short Hills had the second highest median income (behind Scarsdale, New York) of any town in the nation, the luxury publication *Veranda* reported in 2016.

Nearby, fast-growing Hunterdon County has the nation's fourth highest median household income, at $105,000. Hunterdon lost about 2 percent of its population between 2010 and 2015, chiefly because some of its kids have grown up and moved away. To the east, Diamond Nation in Flemington is a 35-acre baseball and softball complex and the site of many tournaments. Flemington was also the setting of the "trial of the century," in the kidnapping and murder of the 20-month-old son of aviator Charles Lindbergh. In January 2017, Mayor Phil Greiner said that it was time for Flemington to move beyond Lindbergh and to be "cool again."

The 7th Congressional District of New Jersey covers several generations of suburban development. It crosses the breadth of the state, from the edge of Pennsylvania's Lehigh Valley in the west to parts of Union County in the east. It is an agglomeration of places, and includes parts of five counties and all of Hunterdon. The largest slice of population is the 32 percent in Somerset County, with 25 percent in Union County and about 18 percent in Hunterdon County. The district usually favors Republicans, but not overwhelmingly. Mitt Romney took 53 percent in 2012. But Donald Trump in 2016 had less appeal in these upscale precincts. He trailed Hillary Clinton, 48%-47%. This was the only one of the five Republican-held districts in New Jersey where Clinton led, albeit narrowly.

EIGHTH DISTRICT

Albio Sires (D)

Elected 2006, 6th term; b. Jan 26, 1951, Bejucal, Cuba; St. Peter's College (NJ), B.A., 1974; Middlebury College (VT), M.A., 1985; Roman Catholic; Married (Adrienne Sires); 1 stepchild.

Elected Office: West New York Mayor, 1995-2006; NJ Assembly, 2000-2006, speaker, 2002-2006.

Professional Career: H.S. Spanish & ESL teacher, 1975-1985; Special Assistant, NJ Department of Comm. Affairs, 1985; Part-owner, A.M. Title Agency, 1986-2006.

DC Office: 2342 RHOB 20515, 202-225-7919, Fax: 202-226-0792, sires.house.gov.

State Offices: Elizabeth, 908-820-0692; Jersey City, 201-309-0301; West New York, 201-558-0800.

Committees: *Foreign Affairs*: Europe, Eurasia & Emerging Threats, Western Hemisphere (RMM). *Transportation & Infrastructure*: Economic Dev't, Public Buildings & Emergency Management, Highways & Transit, Railroads, Pipelines & Hazardous Materials.

Group Ratings

	ADA	ACLU	AFL-CIO	LCV	ITI	COC	HAFA	ACU	CFG	FRC
2016	-	94%	-	92%	67%	69%	14%	4%	0%	0%
2015	85%	C	100%	94%	C	60%	C	4%	6%	0%

Almanac Ratings 2015

	Economy	Social	Foreign	Composite
Liberal	79%	100%	67%	82%
Conservative	21%	0%	33%	18%

Key Votes of the 114th Congress

1. Keystone Pipeline	Y	5. Puerto Rico Debt	NV	9. Offenses by Aliens	N
2. Trade Deals	N	6. Medical Marijuana	Y	10. Troops in Iraq	Y
3. Export-Import Bank	Y	7. Sanctuary Cities	N	11. Homeland Security $$	Y
4. Debt Ceiling Increase	Y	8. Armor-piercing Bullets	N	12. Trade Adjustment aid	Y

Election Results

Election	Name (Party)	Vote	(%)	Cand. Spent	Ind. Exp. Support	Ind. Exp. Oppose
2016 General	Albio Sires (D)	134,733	(77%)	$386,710		
	Agha Khan (R)	32,337	(19%)			
2016 Primary	Albio Sires (D)	44,944	(87%)			
	Eloy Delgado (D)	6,703	(13%)			

Prior winning percentages: 2014 (77%), 2012 (78%), 2010 (74%), 2008 (75%), 2006 (78%)

Democrat Albio Sires, who won a special election in 2006, is the only Cuban-American Democrat in the House. He is an old-style political boss who remains a player in Hudson County. He concentrates on local issues, and on foreign policies that affect his district, including his continued tough stance against Cuba's Castro regime that has shown his willingness to go his separate way from other Democrats.

Sires, who was born in Cuba, remembers the book-burning following the Communist revolution there. His family fled Fidel Castro's regime in 1962 when he was 10. He attended St. Peter's College on a four-year basketball scholarship - he is 6-feet-4-inches tall -then earned a master's degree from Middlebury College. He became a high school Spanish teacher.

On his fourth try, he was elected mayor of West New York as a Republican in 1995, and held that post until 2006. He focused on the creation of more affordable housing in the small but densely populated town and won praise for merging the fire department with three neighboring departments. He switched parties in 1999 and, with the support of his new party's leaders, defeated a veteran Democratic incumbent in the primary to win a state House seat. With strong support from Democratic Gov. Jim McGreevey in 2002, he became speaker of the Assembly.

After Democratic Gov. Jon Corzine appointed Rep. Robert Menendez as his replacement in the Senate, Sires became the front-runner for the House seat. In the primary, he faced a fierce challenge from Joe Vas of Perth Amboy, who likewise was a state House member and a mayor. Vas assailed Sires as a puppet of the Hudson County Democratic machine. Sires responded by depicting Vas as soft on crime and won the support of most leading Democrats, except for his longtime rival Menendez, who remained neutral. Vas carried his home base of Middlesex County 76%-24%, but Sires crushed him 80%-20% in Hudson County, which cast 74 percent of the total vote. Overall, Sires won 72%-28%. Sires won the general, 78%-19%, and has been reelected easily since.

In the House, Sires established a voting record that has placed him toward the middle of the House on economic and foreign issues and with occasional independence from the Obama administration, according to the 2015 *Almanac* vote ratings. He allied himself with South Florida members who have wanted to keep U.S. sanctions on Cuba in place, including travel and economic aid. As the ranking Democrat on the Foreign Affairs Committee's Western Hemisphere panel, he opposed President Barack Obama's opening to Cuba in 2014 as "naïve and disrespectful," and said that the effort to "encourage a form of Cuban glasnost is a dangerous miscalculation." He remained a harsh critic of the steps to establish diplomatic relations with Cuba, and he advocated retention of the embargo. In 2015, Sires opposed Obama's agreement with Iran on nuclear fuel. He said that the timeframe for the agreement was too short and he objected that Iran would be "allowed to enhance its nuclear and weapons capabilities."

On the Transportation and Infrastructure Committee, he was successful in convincing the Army Corps of Engineers to raise the Bayonne Bridge's height to accommodate larger ships. The result will provide an additional 64 feet of clearance plus access for all container ships to the port, with the delayed completion scheduled for 2019. He introduced legislation to revitalize urban parks, and to help commuters find alternative ways to get to work. In 2015, he was one of 28 House Democrats who opposed Obama and sided with some unions in support of the Keystone XL pipeline.

In the 2010 election, Sires was a vice chair of the Democratic Congressional Campaign Committee, in charge of member participation and outreach. After Democrats lost their majority, he called for Speaker Nancy Pelosi to step down. His comments didn't endear him to Democratic leaders, nor did the fact that he raised significantly less money than other DCCC leaders. Sires has seemed to value his independence.

Jersey City/Newark Area

Population		**Race and Ethnicity**		**Income**	
Total	762,276	White	25.5%	Median Income	$54,261 (193 out of 435)
Land area	55	Black	8.6%		
Pop/ sq mi	13938.1	Latino	54.9%		
Born in state	37.1%	Asian	8.3%	Under $50,000	46.7%
		Two races	1.2%	$50,000-$99,999	28.0%
Age Groups		Other	1.5%	$100,000-$199,999	18.5%
Under 18	22.0%			$200,000 or more	6.7%
18-34	29.8%	**Education**		Poverty Rate	18.4%
35-64	38.4%	H.S grad or less	50.7%		
Over 64	9.8%	Some college	19.3%	**Health Insurance**	
		College Degree, 4 yr	18.9%	With health insurance coverage	77.0%
Work		Post grad	11.0%		
White Collar	32.6%				
Sales and Service	42.3%	**Military**		**Public Assistance**	
Blue Collar	25.0%	Veteran	2.3%	Cash public assistance income	4.4%
Government	9.6%	Active Duty	0.0%		
				Food stamp/SNAP benefits	16.4%

Voter Turnout			
2015 Total Citizens 18+	415,257	2016 House Turnout as % CVAP	42%
2016 House turnout	174,889	2014 House Turnout as % CVAP	19%

2012 Presidential Vote		
Barack Obama	161,443	(79%)
Mitt Romney	42,896	(21%)

2016 Presidential Vote		
Hillary Clinton	173,834	(75%)
Donald Trump	49,336	(21%)

Cook Partisan Voting Index: D+27

Standing in New York Harbor since 1886, the Statue of Liberty has been the symbol of America's receptiveness to immigrants. The statue is on the New Jersey side of the harbor, and so is, as the U.S. Supreme Court ruled in 1998, most of Ellis Island, where immigrants once were processed. So it's natural that the towns atop the granite and gneiss ridge of Hudson County, overlooking the harbor, became immigrant territory. Many children and grandchildren of Irish and Italian immigrants stayed in Hudson County, living in the same neighborhoods, working on the same docks or in the factories, and voting the dictates of the same political machine. Hudson County was the setting of one of America's classic political machines, undisciplined by any metropolitan elite. From 1917 to 1949, the boss of Hudson County was Frank ("I am the law") Hague. His machine chose governors and U.S. senators, prosecutors and judges, and had influence in the White House of Franklin D. Roosevelt. Hague collected high taxes from industries clustered here, which then passed them on to consumers. In return, he gave them an orderly city, free of most crime and vice, and a workforce insulated against racketeers and militant unions. Hague's successor, John V. Kenny, was boss from 1949 to 1971 - continuous power for 54 years.

Hudson County has changed. New immigrants were coming in - refugees from Fidel Castro's Cuba, and other Latinos and Asians. Union City, once predominantly Cuban, has gained a mix of Colombian, Ecuadoran, Peruvian, Dominican and Filipino immigrants. Starting in the 1980s, huge new condominium and office developments went up in Jersey City, housing big banks, securities firms and, later, internet businesses. Upscale young singles looking for lower rents moved into Hoboken's five-story Victorians; they were a quick commute through the PATH tubes to Wall Street or Greenwich Village. In Hoboken, the home of Frank Sinatra and the Oreo cookie, shopping and apartment complexes have taken up the waterfront sites where factories were common (and where the classic movie *On the Waterfront* was filmed). Hoboken continues to attract urban professionals plus a growing number of families seeking affordable housing; the city grew by 39 percent from 2000 to 2015. A commuter train crashed into the Hoboken rail terminal in September 2016 and caused major damage. In 2015, Jersey City officials reported an unprecedented amount of construction, with a high and growing skyline. Jersey City is "emerging as a destination of choice," *The New York Times* wrote in February 2016. Since 2010, the 6.4 percent population increase in Hudson made it the fastest-growing county in the state.

Hudson County, which seemed to be dying a generation ago, is now more vibrant. But challenges remain: The county suffered double-digit unemployment well after the recession. Hurricane Sandy in the fall of 2012 did severe damage in Hoboken. Bayonne has become a cruise ship port. Its 5,780-foot-long bridge, built in 1931, is being raised from 151 feet to 215 feet high so that it is tall enough for super-sized container ships.

The 8th Congressional District includes much of Hudson County, plus most of the immigrant entry ports along the water and the bustling docks along the Hudson River and New York Bay. It takes in Hoboken and Elizabeth, now 64 percent Hispanic; nearly half of Newark; West New York and Weehawken; parts of Jersey City and Bayonne; working-class Harrison, an aging factory town where European immigrants have been replaced by Hispanic immigrants; and part of industrial Kearny. The district is 55 percent Hispanic, by far the largest percentage in the state; 44 percent of the population is foreign-born. About 70 percent is in Hudson, as are sections of Essex and Union and a thin slice of Bergen County. The district lines in Hudson and Essex counties were drawn like pieces of a jig-saw puzzle to assure that the 8th District is heavily Hispanic and the 10th District is heavily black. This is easy territory for Democrats to defend. In 2016, Hillary Clinton got 75 percent of the vote.

NINTH DISTRICT

Bill Pascrell (D)

Elected 1996, 11th term; b. Jan 25, 1937, Paterson; Fordham University (NY), B.S., 1959; Fordham University (NY), M.A., 1961; Roman Catholic; Married (Elsie Marie Botto Pascrell); 3 children; 3 grandchildren.

Military Career: U.S Army, 1961-1962; U.S. Army Reserves, 1962-1967.

Elected Office: President, Paterson Board of Education, 1979-1982; NJ Assembly, 1988-1997, Minority Leader pro temp; Paterson Mayor, 1990-1996.

Professional Career: H.S. teacher, 1960-1974; Director, Paterson Department of Public Works, 1974-1977; Director, Paterson Department of Policy, 1977-1987.

DC Office: 2370 RHOB 20515, 202-225-5751, Fax: 202-225-5782, pascrell.house.gov.

State Offices: Englewood, 201-935-2248; Lyndhurst, 201-935-2248; Passaic, 973-472-4510; Paterson, 973-523-5152.

Committees: *Ways & Means*: Social Security, Trade (RMM).

Group Ratings

	ADA	ACLU	AFL-CIO	LCV	ITI	COC	HAFA	ACU	CFG	FRC
2016	-	100%	-	97%	67%	64%	12%	0%	0%	0%
2015	90%	C	100%	97%	C	50%	C	4%	0%	0%

Almanac Ratings 2015

	Economy	Social	Foreign	Composite
Liberal	97%	100%	86%	94%
Conservative	3%	0%	14%	6%

Key Votes of the 114th Congress

1. Keystone Pipeline	N	5. Puerto Rico Debt	Y	9. Offenses by Aliens	N
2. Trade Deals	N	6. Medical Marijuana	Y	10. Troops in Iraq	Y
3. Export-Import Bank	Y	7. Sanctuary Cities	N	11. Homeland Security $$	Y
4. Debt Ceiling Increase	Y	8. Armor-piercing Bullets	N	12. Trade Adjustment aid	Y

Election Results

Election	Name (Party)	Vote (%)	Cand. Spent	Ind. Exp. Support	Ind. Exp. Oppose
2016 General	Bill Pascrell (D)	162,642 (70%)	$978,658		
	Hector Castillo (R)	65,376 (28%)	$99,695		
2016 Primary	Bill Pascrell (D)	(100%)			

Prior winning percentages: 2014 (69%), 2012 (74%), 2010 (63%), 2008 (71%), 2006 (71%), 2004 (70%), 2002 (67%), 2000 (67%), 1998 (62%), 1996 (51%)

Bill Pascrell, elected in 1996, is kind of a Democratic version of Gov. Chris Christie: He shares Christie's feisty Jersey-guy demeanor as a local boss. And he can be candid about expressing his displeasure with his party on the national scene, where he often operates as an old-style, favor-trading pol.

He grew up in Paterson, the grandson of Italian immigrants. His father worked for the railroad, and Pascrell was the first one in his family to graduate from college. He worked his way through Fordham University, served in the Army, then taught high school for 14 years. From there Pascrell went into politics, first as director of Paterson's public works department, and then as school board president. In 1987, he was elected to the New Jersey Assembly. In 1990, Pascrell was elected mayor of Paterson but continued to serve in the Assembly - a common practice in New Jersey until the legislature voted in 2007 to stop the practice.

In 1996, Pascrell challenged first-term Republican Rep. Bill Martini, whom Pascrell portrayed as the tool of an "extremist" House leadership; his ads showed Martini's face on a puppet being manipulated by House Speaker Newt Gingrich. Despite Martini's support from the Sierra Club and labor unions, Pascrell won 51%-48%.

Pascrell has compiled a liberal voting record, especially on economic issues. He has voted for some restrictions on abortion, including a parental notification requirement. In 2002, he voted to authorize the use of force in Iraq, and, on the Homeland Security Committee, he was a voice for improved communications among first responders. "How is it we can talk to people on the moon, but we can't talk one block away?" Pascrell asked. He authored the Firefighter Investment and Response Enhancement (FIRE) Act in 2001, and has fought regularly to increase grants to local fire departments. Pascrell is a big supporter of the Community Oriented Policing Services (COPS) office. After the program was targeted for budget cuts, Pascrell and Republican Rep. Dave Reichert of Washington in 2011 won House passage of a measure to restore $199 million to the office.

As a member of the powerful House Ways and Means Committee, Pascrell has worked with labor and consumer groups to promote "fair trade," and to expand the Trade Adjustment Assistance program for workers who have lost their jobs. He has become an increasingly harsh critic of international trade agreements. During his early days in the House, he had a bumper sticker hanging in his office that said "NAFTA is Shafta," a caustic reference to the North American Free Trade Agreement. Despite pleas from Obama administration officials, Pascrell strongly opposed giving authority to the president to negotiate the Trans-Pacific Partnership and later praised President Donald Trump for withdrawing the proposal. In January 2017, he became the ranking Democrat on the Trade Subcommittee, where he vowed to shape trade policy "for the benefits of American workers as well as industry."

Pascrell has been successful with some pet projects. A bill to designate Paterson's Great Falls as a 120-acre national park was enacted in 2009. The following year, the House passed his bill calling for development of a new set of concussion-management guidelines for student athletes. That bill was part of his focus on research for traumatic brain injuries, which he calls the "silent epidemic," especially among military members as well as athletes. In January 2017, he joined Republican Rep. Leonard Lance in filing legislation to support a New Jersey project for a thin blue line between the double yellow lines on a highway in honor of law-enforcement officials. Showing that "all politics is local," he objected to a proposal to place a woman on the $10 bill in place of local icon Alexander Hamilton. Instead, he suggested that a woman go on the $20 bill in place of Andrew Jackson.

As his party's political fortunes declined in 2010, Pascrell was among the Democrats who were open in venting frustrations. When White House spokesman Robert Gibbs speculated that the Democrats' House majority was in doubt in the 2010 election, Pascrell told *The Washington Post*, "What the hell do they think we've been doing the last 12 months? We're the ones who have been taking the tough votes." During the debt ceiling standoff in the summer of 2011, Pascrell criticized House Minority Leader Nancy Pelosi, his one-time ally, for refusing to accept any deal with cuts to entitlement programs.

The 2011 round of redistricting put his comfortable House seat in jeopardy. The new 9th District included his home base of Paterson, but it contained a large share of Democratic colleague Steve Rothman's former Bergen County-based district. Rothman moved to Englewood to run in the 9th, setting up a primary showdown against Pascrell. Throughout the campaign, Pascrell hammered Rothman for running against him rather than taking on Republican Scott Garrett in the new 5th District. (Garrett was defeated in 2016.) Rothman attacked Pascrell's record on abortion rights, while Pascrell touted his work on the 2010 Affordable Care Act. Former President Bill Clinton endorsed Pascrell. Although Obama officially remained neutral, his top political adviser David Axelrod campaigned for Rothman. In the end, the race was not close. In a battle of turnout, Pascrell's Passaic County machine outmatched Rothman's Bergen County team and he won 61%-39%.

In the 2012 general election, Pascrell had an easy time against Republican Shmuley Boteach, a celebrity rabbi who wrote a best-selling book for couples entitled *Kosher Sex*. Billionaire casino magnate Sheldon Adelson seemed to waste $1 million on super PAC ads promoting Boteach. Pascrell won 74%-25%. (Later, there were news reports in New Jersey that Adelson was exploring options to build a casino in the Meadowlands. But Christie and other officials opposed new competition to the flagging casinos in Atlantic City.) Since then, Pascrell's campaigns have been uneventful. William Pascrell III, an attorney with a Passaic firm and the counsel to Passaic County, reportedly has been groomed for when his father, who turned 80 in January 2017, decides to step down.

Northeast New Jersey: Southern Bergen County, Paterson

Population		**Race and Ethnicity**		**Income**	
Total	749,137	White	40.3%	Median Income	$60,930 (135 out of 435)
Land area	95	Black	9.7%		
Pop/ sq mi	7857.5	Latino	35.4%		
Born in state	44.1%	Asian	12.9%	Under $50,000	42.5%
		Two races	1.3%	$50,000-$99,999	27.8%
Age Groups		Other	0.5%	$100,000-$199,999	22.6%
Under 18	23.1%			$200,000 or more	7.3%
18-34	23.2%	**Education**		Poverty Rate	15.2%
35-64	40.3%	H.S grad or less	47.2%		
Over 64	13.4%	Some college	20.9%	**Health Insurance**	
		College Degree, 4 yr	20.9%	With health insurance coverage	82.7%
Work		Post grad	11.1%		
White Collar	36.0%				
Sales and Service	41.5%	**Military**		**Public Assistance**	
Blue Collar	22.4%	Veteran	3.5%	Cash public assistance income	3.0%
Government	10.7%	Active Duty	0.0%		
				Food stamp/SNAP benefits	14.1%

Voter Turnout			
2015 Total Citizens 18+	464,864	2016 House Turnout as % CVAP	50%
2016 House turnout	233,242	2014 House Turnout as % CVAP	26%

2012 Presidential Vote		
Barack Obama	173,070	(69%)
Mitt Romney	77,988	(31%)

2016 Presidential Vote		
Hillary Clinton	177,953	(64%)
Donald Trump	91,696	(33%)

Cook Partisan Voting Index: D+16

Paterson is one of the few American cities that has turned out pretty much as planned. It was the brainchild of Alexander Hamilton, who in the 1790s journeyed 20 miles from Manhattan to the Great Falls of the Passaic River in New Jersey. Watching the water surge down 72 feet - the highest falls along the East Coast - he predicted an industrial city would rise on the site. Hamilton formed the Society for Establishing Useful Manufactures, which opened a calico factory in 1794, and got Pierre L'Enfant, the designer of Washington, D.C., to design Paterson (named after then-Gov. William Paterson). In 1836, Samuel Colt began manufacturing revolvers there. One of the first American locomotives, the Sandusky, was built in Paterson in 1837. Paterson ultimately became America's "Silk City," employing 25,000 silk mill workers before the great strike of 1913 led by the radical Industrial Workers of the World. Throughout, Paterson attracted immigrants from England, Ireland and, after 1890, Italy and Poland.

The city continues to attract immigrants today, even if its economy produces more service jobs than manufacturing jobs. It has a lively artists' community in its postindustrial setting, and downtown's "Little Palestine" reflects the city's sizable Arab community - Palestinians, Lebanese, Jordanians; Syrian refugees have settled here since their civil war in 2011, despite the opposition of Gov. Chris Christie to the resettlement program of the Obama administration. Like Paterson, the surrounding area is a melting pot. Old towns like Rutherford have enclaves of Americans of Polish, German and Italian descent. Blue-collar Palisades Park has a large concentration of Korean Americans. Englewood is home to middle-class blacks and Orthodox Jewish families.

The 9th Congressional District is based chiefly in the urban parts of Bergen and Passaic counties. It also takes in the leafy suburbs of Englewood, Palisades Park and fast-growing Edgewater, where dwellers in luxury apartment houses brag about their views of New York City. The high-rise towers of Fort Lee became famous in 2013 when top aides to Gov. Chris Christie decided to slow traffic to the George Washington Bridge, an incident that led to felony convictions. The district also takes in East Rutherford and the Meadowlands Sports Complex, which is along Interstate 95. Once 8,400 acres of wetlands and home to thousands of species of animals and plants, the Meadowlands was developed in the 1970s. A generation later, the state built the $1.6 billion MetLife Stadium at that site for the National Football League's Giants and Jets.

A bit more than half of the voters reside in Bergen County, with about 40 percent in Passaic and the remainder in a small slice of Hudson. This was a growth area in the 1950s and 1960s, as New Yorkers moved out of the city. It lost population in the next two decades, as young people moved farther out. Now, the population is rising with the influx of new immigrants, many of them low-income. Home prices in blue-collar neighborhoods plunged during the recession, and sales figures in early 2015 showed that they had not recovered. From 2000 to 2015, the number of Hispanics in Bergen County nearly doubled to 178,000 (now, 19 percent of 938,000), and in Passaic County, the Latino population grew to 40 percent of the 510,000 residents. With 37 percent Hispanic and 14 percent Asian, the 9th has become a minority enclave, though Democrats' share of the presidential vote has remained roughly 65 percent.

TENTH DISTRICT

Donald Payne (D)

Elected 2012, 3rd full term; b. Dec 17, 1958, Newark; Kean College (NJ), Att., 1978; Baptist; Married (Bea Payne); 3 children (triplets).

Elected Office: Freeholder-at-large, Essex County, 2005-2012; At-large rep., Newark City Council, 2006-2012, President 2010-2012..

Professional Career: NJ highway authority, 1990-1996; District leader, Newark's South Ward, 1992-2013.

DC Office: 132 CHOB 20515, 202-225-3436, Fax: 202-225-4160, payne.house.gov.

State Offices: Hillside, 862-229-2994; Jersey City, 201-369-0392; Newark, 973-645-3213.

Committees: *Homeland Security*: Emergency Preparedness, Response & Communications (RMM), Transportation & Protective Security. *Transportation & Infrastructure*: Aviation, Railroads, Pipelines & Hazardous Materials.

Group Ratings

	ADA	ACLU	AFL-CIO	LCV	ITI	COC	HAFA	ACU	CFG	FRC
2016	-	88%	-	95%	75%	82%	11%	4%	0%	0%
2015	70%	C	100%	77%	C	43%	C	5%	3%	0%

Almanac Ratings 2015

	Economy	Social	Foreign	Composite
Liberal	85%	100%	93%	93%
Conservative	15%	0%	7%	8%

Key Votes of the 114th Congress

1. Keystone Pipeline	N	5. Puerto Rico Debt	NV	9. Offenses by Aliens	N
2. Trade Deals	N	6. Medical Marijuana	Y	10. Troops in Iraq	Y
3. Export-Import Bank	NV	7. Sanctuary Cities	N	11. Homeland Security $$	Y
4. Debt Ceiling Increase	Y	8. Armor-piercing Bullets	N	12. Trade Adjustment aid	NV

Election Results

Election	Name (Party)	Vote (%)	Cand. Spent	Ind. Exp. Support	Ind. Exp. Oppose
2016 General	Donald Payne (D)........................ 190,856	(86%)	$428,767		
	David Pinckney (R)..................... 26,450	(12%)			
2016 Primary	Donald Payne (D)...................................	(100%)			

Prior winning percentages: 2014 (85%), 2012 (88%), 2012 special (97%)

Donald Payne Jr., elected in 2012, succeeded his father, Rep. Donald Payne Sr., who served 23 years and died of cancer. He has been a reliable Democratic vote and has made few waves as he focused on homeland security issues, which are vital to his metropolitan region.

A Newark native, Payne became involved in politics as a teenager when he founded and became president of the Newark South Ward Junior Democrats. He attended Kean College (now Kean University) and studied graphic arts, but did not graduate. At 21, he began working in the tolls division of the New Jersey Highway Authority; a back injury prompted him to give up the job a few years later. In 1996, at the age of 27, he became a school bus monitor with the Essex County Educational Services Commission, and went on to become director of student transportation for the county. In 1992, Payne was elected by local Democrats to the party position of South Ward leader in Newark. In 2006, Payne was elected to the Newark Municipal Council and was its president from 2010 to 2012. He co-founded Embracing Arms, a nonprofit youth-advancement organization that sponsors public service projects for young people.

Following his father's death, Payne entered the Democratic primary. His family pedigree made him a heavy favorite. Not only was his father the first African-American member of Congress to represent New Jersey, but his uncle, William Payne, served in the New Jersey General Assembly for 10 years. Payne Jr. had the backing of the powerful Democratic Party machines in Essex, Hudson and Union counties.

Political opponents and journalists raised questions about his readiness for Congress. In an editorial board meeting with *The Star-Ledger* before the election, Payne named creating jobs as his chief priority, but declined to provide specific details. He was vague about how he would deal with several other issues, including ensuring the future of Medicare and Social Security and solving the Israeli-Palestinian conflict. On the latter issue, he said, "I have people in Congress that are looking forward to helping me understand." The newspaper editorialized, "The dispiriting truth is that his claim to the seat is based entirely on his last name. He has only the vaguest grip on key federal issues. He is simply not ready for the job, and hasn't done his homework." Payne won the primary election with 60 percent of the vote, beating out fellow Newark Councilman Ron Rice and state Sen. Nia Gill. He got 88 percent in the general election in the solidly Democratic district, and appears to have become entrenched with little difficulty.

Payne has focused his legislative work at Homeland Security, where he is the ranking Democrat on the Emergency Preparedness, Response and Communications Subcommittee. He has noted that the area surrounding Exit 13A of the New Jersey Turnpike, which provides access to Elizabeth and the Newark Airport, has been described by homeland security officials as the "most dangerous two miles in America" because of its cluster of industrial and transportation infrastructure. In 2014, Payne won House passage of the bipartisan SMART Grid Study Act of 2014, which seeks to examine ways to upgrade and strengthen the nation's electric grid to protect critical infrastructure from natural disasters and cyberattacks. He won enactment of his DHS Interoperable Communications Act of 2015, legislation to improve emergency communications capabilities for first responders. The annual defense spending bill that was enacted in December 2016 included Payne's provision that required decision-makers in disaster-response planning to gain a complete understanding of a community's vulnerabilities so that homeland security grants can have appropriate priority.

In January 2017, Payne got a seat on the Transportation and Infrastructure Committee - an apt assignment, given the extensive air, rail, port and highway services in his district. With Republican Rep. Markwayne Mullin of Oklahoma, Payne created and co-chairs the Congressional Men's Health Caucus. He has called attention to his father's death from colo-rectal cancer and the need for cancer screenings.

Newark/Jersey City area

Population		**Race and Ethnicity**		**Income**	
Total	738,622	White	20.7%	Median Income	$47,148 (303 out of 435)
Land area	76	Black	51.3%	Under $50,000	51.9%
Pop/ sq mi	9729.0	Latino	18.3%	$50,000-$99,999	26.9%
Born in state	50.6%	Asian	7.1%	$100,000-$199,999	16.6%
Age Groups		Two races	1.6%	$200,000 or more	4.6%
Under 18	23.4%	Other	1.0%	Poverty Rate	19.5%
18-34	25.4%	**Education**		**Health Insurance**	
35-64	39.8%	H.S grad or less	47.1%	With health insurance coverage	83.0%
Over 64	11.4%	Some college	25.9%	**Public Assistance**	
Work		College Degree, 4 yr	17.4%	Cash public assistance income	5.6%
White Collar	33.3%	Post grad	9.5%	Food stamp/SNAP benefits	17.2%
Sales and Service	47.2%	**Military**			
Blue Collar	19.5%	Veteran	4.0%		
Government	16.2%	Active Duty	0.0%		

Voter Turnout			
2015 Total Citizens 18+	476,727	2016 House Turnout as % CVAP	47%
2016 House turnout	222,771	2014 House Turnout as % CVAP	24%

2012 Presidential Vote		
Barack Obama	240,052	(88%)
Mitt Romney	31,352	(12%)

2016 Presidential Vote		
Hillary Clinton	233,822	(85%)
Donald Trump	35,111	(13%)

Cook Partisan Voting Index: D+36

Newark was once the heart of New Jersey. All of the main transportation arteries led there, and its corporate headquarters buildings were the tallest in the state. In 1930, 442,000 people lived in Newark, one of every nine in New Jersey. The city fell on hard times in the latter half of the 20th century. Whole sections of the city were dominated by criminals and deserted by most law-abiding residents. By the year 2000, there were just 273,000 people left in Newark, representing one in every 30.

In recent years, Newark has been attempting a turnaround. Population was up to 282,000 in 2015; new office buildings have joined the Prudential and Public Service Enterprise Group headquarters; and the New Jersey Performing Arts Center has been popular with city-dwellers seeking a less expensive experience than Manhattan. There are new restaurants and trendy bars, plus a new downtown arena. The young and charismatic mayor, Democrat Cory Booker, brought energy to the city and declared war on street gangs before he was elected to the Senate in 2013. Ras Baraka, his successor, reached out to gang members in 2014 to try to reduce crime, and he hired more police.

Facebook founder Mark Zuckerberg in 2010 gave $100 million to Newark public schools - conditioned on matching grants. But his program ran into bureaucratic problems, including with state officials, and it fell short of expectations, as described by writer Dale Russakoff in her 2015 book, *The Prize*. Crime remained intolerably high and downtown office buildings had plenty of empty spaces. In 2015, a survey by WalletHub ranked Newark last among 150 cities as the best place to start a business. Still, there recently have been positive developments. With Baraka's leadership, city and business officials announced in January 2017 expansive plans for a new commercial center and public park in downtown. After two decades of state control of local schools, Gov. Chris Christie and Baraka spearheaded a plan to restore local control in late 2017.

There has been some industrial development around Newark Liberty International Airport, a glass and aluminum facility that has been greatly expanded for international carriers and is prospering as a hub for United Airlines. To accommodate the increased passenger load, plans were underway for a $2.3 billion replacement of Terminal A. Port Newark-Elizabeth Marine Terminal is part of the larger Port of New York and New Jersey, the busiest container port on the East Coast.

The 10th Congressional District of New Jersey is centered in Essex County, with about 60 percent of its total population, including the majority of Newark. Other parts of Essex extend to Republican suburbs. Smaller parts of the 10th take in Hudson and Union counties. The district includes the predominantly African-American city of East Orange, plus parts of Bloomfield, West Orange, Jersey City and Bayonne. It is a 51 percent black-majority district and one of the most heavily Democratic in the nation. Hillary Clinton took 85 percent of the vote in 2016, after President Barack Obama won 88 percent in 2012.

ELEVENTH DISTRICT

Rodney Frelinghuysen (R)

Elected 1994, 12th term; b. Apr 29, 1946, Manhattan, NY; Trinity College (CT); Hobart College (NY), B.A., 1969; Episcopalian; Married (Virginia Robinson Frelinghuysen); 2 children.

Military Career: U.S. Army, 1969-1971 (Vietnam).

Elected Office: Morris County Board of Freeholders, 1974-1983, dir., 1980; NJ Assembly, 1983-1994.

Professional Career: Coordinator & admin. Assistant, Morris County Board of Freeholders, 1972-1974.

DC Office: 2306 RHOB 20515, 202-225-5034, Fax: 202-225-3186, frelinghuysen.house.gov.

State Offices: Morristown, 973-984-0711.

Committees: *Appropriations (Chmn)*: Agriculture, Rural Development, FDA & Related Agencies, Commerce, Justice, Science & Related Agencies, Defense, Energy & Water Development & Related Agencies, Financial Services & General Government, Homeland Security, Interior, Environment & Related Agencies, Labor, Health & Human Services, Education & Related Agencies, Legislative Branch, Military Construction, Veterans Affairs & Related Agencies, State, Foreign Operations & Related Programs, Transportation, HUD & Related Agencies.

Group Ratings

	ADA	ACLU	AFL-CIO	LCV	ITI	COC	HAFA	ACU	CFG	FRC
2016	-	11%	-	8%	100%	100%	45%	64%	69%	83%
2015	0%	C	21%	3%	C	100%	C	46%	48%	83%

Almanac Ratings 2015

	Economy	Social	Foreign	Composite
Liberal	10%	17%	11%	13%
Conservative	90%	83%	90%	87%

Key Votes of the 114th Congress

1. Keystone Pipeline	Y	5. Puerto Rico Debt	Y	9. Offenses by Aliens	Y
2. Trade Deals	Y	6. Medical Marijuana	N	10. Troops in Iraq	N
3. Export-Import Bank	N	7. Sanctuary Cities	Y	11. Homeland Security $$	Y
4. Debt Ceiling Increase	Y	8. Armor-piercing Bullets	Y	12. Trade Adjustment aid	Y

Election Results

Election	Name (Party)	Vote (%)		Cand. Spent	Ind. Exp. Support	Ind. Exp. Oppose
2016 General	Rodney Frelinghuysen (R)	194,299	(58%)	$1,192,167		
	Joseph Wenzel (D)	130,162	(39%)			
2016 Primary	Rodney Frelinghuysen (R)	43,427	(76%)			
	Rick Van Glahn (R)	13,546	(24%)			

Prior winning percentages: 2014 (63%), 2012 (59%), 2010 (67%), 2008 (62%), 2006 (62%), 2004 (68%), 2002 (72%), 2000 (68%), 1998 (68%), 1996 (66%), 1994 (71%)

Republican Rodney Frelinghuysen, first elected in 1994, has a record as a foreign policy conservative and a fiscal moderate. His takeover in 2017 as chairman of the Appropriations Committee moved him into the elite power brokers of the House. Although the spending process has broken down in recent years, he took a crucial post in allocating federal funds, making requisite deals and assuring that bills would be enacted. Earlier, as chairman of the Defense Subcommittee, he faced challenges in balancing a tight budget with the many conflicting demands.

Frelinghuysen is the scion of one of New Jersey's most durable political families. The Frelinghuysens emigrated from Germany near the Dutch border in 1720 and settled in what is now the 11th District. Four Frelinghuysens served as senators from New Jersey, starting in 1793 and as recently as 1923. Theodore Frelinghuysen was the candidate for vice president in 1844 (spawning the memorable chant, "Hurrah! Hurrah! The country's risin,' for Henry Clay and Frelinghuysen"). Frederick Frelinghuysen was President Chester Arthur's Secretary of State. Peter Frelinghuysen, Rodney's father, was elected to the House in 1952 and served until his retirement in 1974. "He was always my role model," he told *The Star-Ledger* of Newark after his father's death in 2011.

History tends to repeat itself, and Frelinghuysens have been involved in every presidential impeachment. Rodney Frelinghuysen's great-great-grandfather Frederick voted to convict Andrew Johnson in 1868, and his father, Peter, after the revelations of July 1974, would have voted to impeach Richard Nixon if the president had not resigned. The current-generation Frelinghuysen voted to impeach Bill Clinton in December 1998.

As a child, Rodney Frelinghuysen lived in the large brick house on Georgetown's N Street that was later owned by The Washington Post editor Ben Bradlee and his wife, Sally Quinn. He attended St. Albans preparatory school with the future Democratic vice president, Al Gore. After graduating from Hobart College, he completed Army basic training at Fort Dix and served in Vietnam, where he built roads in the Mekong Delta. In 1972, he was an aide to Morris County Freeholder Dean Gallo, who was later elected to Congress. Frelinghuysen was a freeholder himself from 1974 to 1983. He was elected to the state Assembly in 1983, and had two tours as chairman of the Appropriations Committee. He ran for Congress in 1990 in a nearby district, but lost the primary to Dick Zimmer. In 1994, Gallo retired from Congress because of illness, and Frelinghuysen was chosen to be the Republican nominee at a September party convention. He was elected with 71 percent of the vote. In November 2015, *Roll Call* newspaper reported that Frelinghuysen ranked 18th among the wealthiest members of Congress.

Frelinghuysen has taken moderate and even liberal stands on some social and foreign-policy issues, though he generally aligns with his party on economic policy, as shown by the *Almanac* vote ratings for 2015. He refused to join three fellow New Jersey Republican moderates who supported in 2009 the cap-and-trade bill aimed at reducing greenhouse gas emissions, calling it a "job-killer." But he was one of seven House Republicans that year who voted to protect federal funding for Planned Parenthood, which led to anti-abortion protests outside his New Jersey office. In 2012, he joined Democrats in opposing GOP measures to open the Arctic National Wildlife Refuge to oil drilling, to eliminate the Economic Development Administration and Legal Services Corporation, and to double the number of oil and gas drilling leases on federal land. In 2015, he was one of four Republicans who voted against the House-passed bill to ban abortions after 20 weeks of pregnancy. He has cited numerous objections to the Affordable Care Act, and has supported its repeal among the chief Republican priorities.

Frelinghuysen has been known nationally as the sponsor of the "Know Your Caller" law, which bars telemarketers from interfering with Caller ID systems of customers seeking to avoid such solicitations. Another of his pet projects has been environmental cleanup in his district, which has a large number of Superfund sites. He has toured the sites annually with environmental and local officials to get updates on cleanup progress.

While still a freshman, he secured a seat on the Appropriations Committee. As Frelinghuysen gained seniority, he claimed the gavel of the Energy and Water Development Subcommittee in 2011. The energy and water bill he got through the House in 2012 reduced President Barack Obama's proposed spending for energy efficiency and renewable energy programs by $886 million. The bill was eventually rolled into a continuing resolution that maintained funding at current levels.

Following the death of veteran Appropriations Republican Rep. Bill Young of Florida in October 2013, Frelinghuysen became chairman of the Defense Subcommittee. When he took the position, he described the responsibility to "provide for a strong national defense and support the men and women who provide for that defense each and every day." He made numerous trips to Afghanistan and the Mideast to monitor how the military is spending its money. Following an April 2015 trip to that region, he reported "growing concern about Iran's aggressive behavior," and the need for a "clear comprehensive strategy" to take on the growing threat posed by the Islamic State. "The Middle East is truly on fire and the United States needs to demonstrate our clear support for our allies and partners," he concluded. In December 2015, congressional negotiators agreed to an omnibus spending bill that gave the Pentagon most of what the Obama administration had been seeking.

As his official biography notes, Frelinghuysen "is well known for championing the important work being done at New Jersey's vital military installations," including McGuire Air Force Base and Fort Dix, whose future has been a concern to many officials in New Jersey. As Appropriations chairman, Frelinghuysen has been an influential booster of those facilities. His experience as a veteran has made him a strong defender of Veterans Affairs medical centers, in New Jersey and elsewhere. Because New Jersey currently has no senator on the Appropriations Committee, and no Democrat on House Appropriations, Frelinghuysen has become the go-to guy for the entire delegation on projects benefiting New Jersey. In past years, he has concentrated on big projects: construction of the Hudson-Bergen light rail, dredging of channels in the Port of New York and New Jersey, and slowing erosion on the Jersey Shore.

With Hal Rogers of Kentucky term-limited as Appropriations chairman after the 2016 election, Frelinghuysen was next in line in Republican seniority and succeeded him without controversy. After he formally received the assignment, he responded that he took seriously the constitutional "power of the purse" and that he would "put members back in charge of funding decisions." As chairman, he began to receive far more media attention, compared to the low profile that he had kept with reporters. After President Donald Trump outlined big cuts in non-military spending that would permit additional funds for the Pentagon, Frelinghuysen responded that those other programs were "vital to our national security" and that cuts in entitlement spending such as Medicare and Medicaid should be considered. "Those are the real cost drivers," he said.

Frelinghuysen has not been seriously challenged for reelection. In 2014, he faced a primary challenge from Rick von Glahn, a home-improvement contractor who wanted to rein in federal spending. Frelinghuysen won, 67%-33%. In 2016, he was reelected, 58%-39%, against Democrat Joseph Wenzel, who did not report raising any campaign money. That was the lowest winning percentage of his career. Democratic campaign strategists were hoping that Frelinghuysen's additional responsibilities as Appropriations chairman would make him a more vulnerable target in 2018. His support for the election of Trump had seemed reluctant, at best. In an interview two weeks before the election, he told the editorial board of *The Record* (Bergen County), "While I'm offended by a lot of things he said and continues to say, I think he would be a strong leader, especially in the areas that I work in, in national defense." He added that he disagreed with Trump's muddled call during the campaign to ban Muslims from entering the United States. Soon after Trump's inauguration, constituent groups - with apparent assistance from liberal activists - pressured Frelinghuysen to participate in more frequent "town hall" meetings in his district.

North-Central New Jersey: Morris and Essex Counties

Population		**Race and Ethnicity**		**Income**	
Total	741,282	White	75.2%	Median Income	$1,00,923 (7 out of 435)
Land area	505	Black	3.5%		
Pop/ sq mi	1468.0	Latino	10.1%	Under $50,000	22.5%
Born in state	59.5%	Asian	9.4%	$50,000-$99,999	26.8%
		Two races	1.7%	$100,000-$199,999	32.3%
Age Groups		Other	0.2%	$200,000 or more	18.2%
Under 18	21.9%			Poverty Rate	4.4%
18-34	18.3%	**Education**			
35-64	43.4%	H.S grad or less	29.0%	**Health Insurance**	
Over 64	16.3%	Some college	19.9%	With health insurance coverage	93.5%
		College Degree, 4 yr	30.6%		
Work		Post grad	20.6%		
White Collar	51.1%			**Public Assistance**	
Sales and Service	37.5%	**Military**		Cash public assistance income	1.1%
Blue Collar	11.3%	Veteran	5.6%		
Government	13.4%	Active Duty	0.0%	Food stamp/SNAP benefits	2.8%

Voter Turnout			
2015 Total Citizens 18+	537,305	2016 House Turnout as % CVAP	62%
2016 House turnout	334,992	2014 House Turnout as % CVAP	33%

2012 Presidential Vote		
Mitt Romney	183,427	(53%)
Barack Obama	163,183	(47%)

2016 Presidential Vote		
Donald Trump	185,696	(48%)
Hillary Clinton	182,334	(47%)
Gary Johnson	7,911	(2%)

Cook Partisan Voting Index: R+3

Morris County in New Jersey, west of the Watchung Mountains, was one of the first parts of the United States west of the seaboard to be settled. It has long been a place of comparative wealth, the home of skilled craftsmen working in the water mills and iron forges in the 19th century. But only in the late 20th century did it come into its own, as one of the most affluent parts of the United States. With its $100,000 median household income, Morris County was among the 10 wealthiest counties in the nation in 2016.

The very rich have lived here for many decades, connected to Manhattan by commuter rail. But starting in the 1970s, new residents rushed out through the newly completed interstates. Prompted by court-required zoning changes, old farms and woods were cleared to make way for new subdivisions. This is not just a bedroom community. New Jersey's economic energy, entrepreneurial creativity and research expertise are found in office complexes and corporate headquarters. Large forested areas of state parkland remain, and preservation of the state's Highlands region, a 1,000-square-mile forest- and lake-filled oasis, has been a priority. The Highlands Council, tasked with protecting the area from development, has been led by a pro-business ally of Republican Gov. Chris Christie who has criticized local land-use restrictions. Local environmentalists have battled constantly with Christie.

The 11th Congressional District of New Jersey takes in about three-fourths of Morris County, including the county seat of Morristown, Randolph and Rockaway. Half of the district is in Morris, one-fourth is in western Essex, and there are small parts of Passaic and Sussex. Among the seven Fortune 500 companies based here are Toys 'R Us and Automated Data Processing. In 2016, *Money* Magazine ranked Parsippany-Troy Hills fifth in the nation among the best places to live. This area is family territory, with relatively few singles. It is predominantly white, though the minority population has grown to 12 percent Hispanic and 10 percent Asian. The 11th still leans Republican, with a moneyed caste. In 2016, Donald Trump won 48%-47%, a drop from the 52 percent that the GOP presidential candidates took in the two previous elections.

TWELFTH DISTRICT

Bonnie Watson Coleman (D)

Elected 2014, 2nd term; b. Feb 06, 1945, Camden; Thomas Edison State College, B.A.; Rutgers University (NJ), Att.; Baptist; Married (William E. Coleman Jr.); 1 child; 2 stepchildren; 3 grandchildren.

Elected Office: NJ Assembly, 1998-2014, Majority Leader, 2006-2009.

DC Office: 1535 LHOB 20515, 202-225-5801, Fax: 202-225-6025, watsoncoleman.house.gov.

State Offices: Ewing, 609-883-0026.

Committees: *Homeland Security*: Emergency Preparedness, Response & Communications, Transportation & Protective Security (RMM). *Oversight & Government Reform*: Government Operations, Health Care, Benefits & Administrative Rules.

Group Ratings

	ADA	ACLU	AFL-CIO	LCV	ITI	COC	HAFA	ACU	CFG	FRC
2016	-	100%	-	100%	50%	57%	16%	4%	10%	0%
2015	100%	C	100%	100%	C	40%	C	4%	0%	0%

Almanac Ratings 2015

	Economy	Social	Foreign	Composite
Liberal	98%	100%	89%	96%
Conservative	2%	0%	11%	4%

Key Votes of the 114th Congress

1. Keystone Pipeline	N	5. Puerto Rico Debt	Y	9. Offenses by Aliens	N
2. Trade Deals	N	6. Medical Marijuana	Y	10. Troops in Iraq	Y
3. Export-Import Bank	Y	7. Sanctuary Cities	N	11. Homeland Security $$	Y
4. Debt Ceiling Increase	Y	8. Armor-piercing Bullets	N	12. Trade Adjustment aid	Y

Election Results

Election	Name (Party)	Vote (%)	Cand. Spent	Ind. Exp. Support	Ind. Exp. Oppose
2016 General	Bonnie Watson Coleman (D)	181,430 (63%)	$725,281		
	Stven Uccio (R)	92,407 (32%)			
2016 Primary	Bonnie Watson Coleman (D)	66,029 (94%)			
	Alexander Kucsma (D)	4,463 (6%)			

Prior winning percentages: 2014 (61%)

Democrat Bonnie Watson Coleman was easily elected in 2014 to an open seat. A well-regarded state legislator and active partisan, she is the first African-American woman to represent New Jersey in Congress, and the first woman that her state sent to Capitol Hill since 2002. She has been an activist for liberal causes, and gained recognition for her legislative skills at the Homeland Security Committee.

Watson Coleman grew up in a political family, with her father, a state assemblyman, often guiding debates at the dinner table. She graduated from Thomas Edison State College. Her public service began in 1966, when she went to work for the state public safety department's civil rights division. She later headed the civil rights office of the state's Department of Transportation before taking on senior roles at the Department of Community Affairs. In 1997, she was elected to the General Assembly, where she rose through the ranks to become majority leader. She was the first African-American woman to chair the State Democratic Committee.

In the Assembly, Watson Coleman promoted staunchly liberal positions on issues such as gun safety, the minimum wage and women's health care funding, and worked to reduce recidivism among state prisoners. She took an active role in legislation on identity-theft protection and the expansion of urban enterprise zones. In 2014, she joined the panel investigating GOP Gov. Chris Christie's role in the 2013 George Washington Bridge slowdown, but she stepped down after she came under fire for having said earlier that Christie should resign.

When Democratic Rep. Rush Holt, a leading progressive in Congress, said that he would step down, Watson Coleman announced her bid. She got a boost from the Progressive Change Campaign Committee, major unions and liberal women's groups such as EMILY's List. In the June primary, only state Sen. Linda Greenstein posed any real competition. Watson Coleman topped the field with 43 percent to 28 percent for Greenstein, who ran relatively close only in her Middlesex County base. Watson Coleman breezed in November with 61 percent against Republican Alieta Eck, who sought to become the first woman physician among House members but was outspent 6-to-1.

Watson Coleman focused her committee work on Homeland Security, where she was ranking Democrat on the oversight subcommittee. In May 2015, the House-passed Cybersecurity Protection Advancement Act included her amendment to encourage public awareness and education on personal cybersecurity issues. The House passed in June her Homeland Security Drone Assessment and Analysis Act, whose goal was "clarifying the framework for drone manufacturers and enthusiasts alike," she said. In January 2017, Watson Coleman became the vice-ranking member of that committee, a new position that the Democratic Caucus created at each House committee to give additional influence to junior members.

With Democratic Reps. Robin Kelly of Illinois and Yvette Clark of New York, Watson Coleman founded the Congressional Caucus on Black Women and Girls. Its objective was to create public policy that "eliminates significant barriers and disparities experienced by black women." Following the election of Donald Trump as president, she became outspoken in leading protest marches and political mobilization. "Trump's unrelenting misogyny and lack of apparent empathy toward women is unfathomable," she wrote in an October 2016 column for the *Star Ledger*, which she co-authored with former Assembly Speaker Sheila Oliver.

Central New Jersey: Middlesex County, Trenton

Population		**Race and Ethnicity**		**Income**	
Total	748,524	White	48.6%	Median Income	$79,328 (40 out of 435)
Land area	412	Black	17.0%		
Pop/ sq mi	1815.8	Latino	15.9%	Under $50,000	31.7%
Born in state	47.1%	Asian	15.9%	$50,000-$99,999	28.4%
Age Groups		Two races	1.5%	$100,000-$199,999	27.6%
Under 18	22.4%	Other	1.0%	$200,000 or more	12.2%
18-34	22.0%	**Education**		Poverty Rate	9.5%
35-64	41.6%	H.S grad or less	35.6%	**Health Insurance**	
Over 64	14.0%	Some college	21.4%	With health insurance coverage	88.8%
Work		College Degree, 4 yr	23.6%		
White Collar	45.5%	Post grad	19.3%	**Public Assistance**	
Sales and Service	39.1%	**Military**		Cash public assistance income	2.3%
Blue Collar	15.3%	Veteran	4.9%		
Government	14.0%	Active Duty	0.0%	Food stamp/SNAP benefits	7.0%

Voter Turnout			
2015 Total Citizens 18+	488,247	2016 House Turnout as % CVAP	59%
2016 House turnout	288,634	2014 House Turnout as % CVAP	30%

2012 Presidential Vote		
Barack Obama	198,155	(67%)
Mitt Romney	96,520	(33%)

2016 Presidential Vote		
Hillary Clinton	204,660	(65%)
Donald Trump	100,043	(32%)

Cook Partisan Voting Index: D+16

New Jersey politics is centered in Trenton. The city has been a manufacturing mecca since the 19th century, when it was the setting for the Lenox and Boehm china factories and the old Roebling ironworks, which produced parts for many of the great American bridges. Its lifeline today is U.S. 1, on any day crowded with cars taking high-salaried workers and clerical help to one of the East Coast's thickest concentrations of office buildings. The highway also is now a locus of telecommunications and pharmaceutical research, and a vital artery to the brain centers of Princeton and Rutgers.

The 12th Congressional District includes Trenton, which is 52 percent African American and 34 percent Hispanic. It stretches east to East Brunswick, with a significant Asian population, and South River, a city that has attracted Polish, Russian and Portuguese immigrants. It is home to Princeton University, which provides $1.6 billion in economic output for New Jersey and supports more than 13,000 jobs. Since 1865, the iconic "Dinky" train has connected the town of Princeton with nearby Princeton Junction, ferrying passengers such as Albert Einstein and Woodrow Wilson. In Trenton, the weak economy has forced continuing cutbacks in operations. Its poverty rate of 28 percent is close to that of Newark, and contrasts with a statewide rate of 11 percent.

In the north, the district takes in Plainfield, Scotch Plains and modest-income suburbs such as Franklin, which made *Money* magazine's list of 50 best small cities to live in for 2014. Much of the district's population is in Middlesex County and the more heavily Democratic and Princeton-based Mercer County. Somerset and Union counties have small slices of the district. As recently as two decades ago, with different boundaries, this was a highly competitive district that House Republicans frequently won. Back then, it had a small minority population, in contrast to the latest and growing 18 percent African American and 17 percent Hispanic. The district has become safe for Democrats. Hillary Clinton got 65 percent of the vote in 2016. President Barack Obama - whose wife Michelle Robinson was a 1985 graduate of Princeton - got 66 percent in 2008 and 67 percent in 2012.

★ NEW MEXICO ★

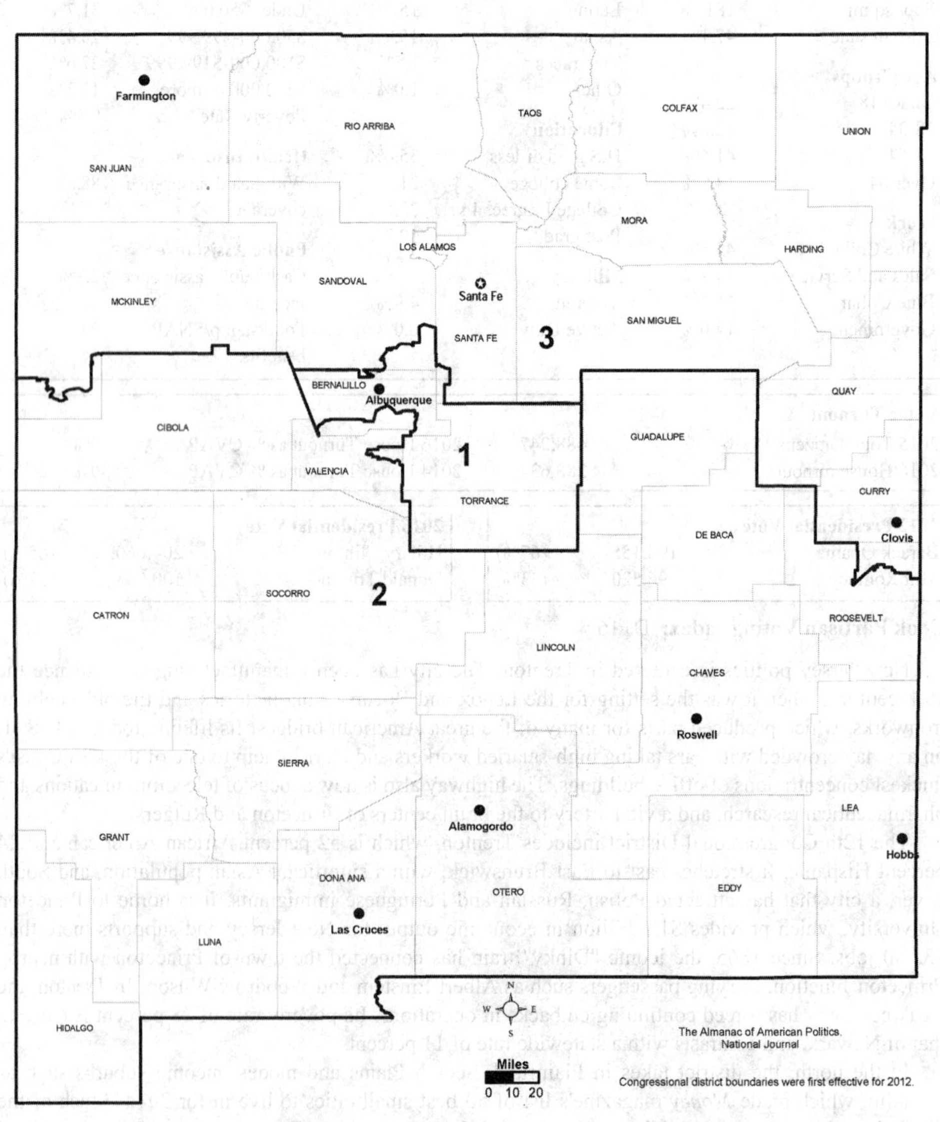
Farmington
SAN JUAN
RIO ARRIBA
TAOS
COLFAX
UNION
MORA
HARDING
LOS ALAMOS
SANDOVAL
MCKINLEY
Santa Fe
SANTA FE
3
SAN MIGUEL
BERNALILLO
Albuquerque
QUAY
CIBOLA
GUADALUPE
1
VALENCIA
TORRANCE
CURRY
DE BACA
Clovis
SOCORRO
2
CATRON
ROOSEVELT
LINCOLN
CHAVES
Roswell
SIERRA
LEA
Alamogordo
GRANT
Hobbs
DONA ANA
OTERO
EDDY
Las Cruces
LUNA
HIDALGO
N
W
E
S
The Almanac of American Politics
National Journal
Miles
0 10 20
Congressional district boundaries were first effective for 2012.

New Mexico has a higher percentage of Latino residents than any other state, and that has shaped its political transition in recent decades. The state was won by Republican presidential candidates in every election from 1968 to 1988, but since then, Democrats – on the strength of a strong edge with nonwhite voters -- have won it every four years except for 2004. Though the state was decided by 366 votes in 2000 and fewer than 6,000 votes in 2004, it has barely been a battleground state in ensuing elections.

New Mexico has some of the oldest settlements in America and some of its newest technologies, often in surrealistic proximity to one another. The oldest permanently inhabited city in the United States is not Plymouth Massachusetts, or Jamestown Virginia or St. Augustine, Florida; it is probably Acoma, which thrived in what is now New Mexico long before the Spanish conquistadors arrived in 1540, and has been continuously inhabited for more than 470 years since. While the settlers of Jamestown and Plymouth were building flimsy wood houses, the Indians in New Mexico were living in extensive dwellings hundreds of years old, made with the adobe that is still the characteristic building material here. They used small pebbles as mulch to retain scarce moisture on the rocky desert land.

Nearly five centuries later, much of what makes New Mexico distinctive derives from centuries of indigenous architecture and artistic traditions. The cultures in other states are mostly an outgrowth of what early European settlers brought to the land. The number of Native American people sharply declined, either killed off by disease or maltreatment or driven onto reservations. History took a different course in New Mexico, the northernmost salient of the great Indian-Spanish civilizations of the Cordillera, the mountain chain that extends south to Mexico and through Central and South America to the southern end of Chile. The Spanish settled in Santa Fe in 1609 and while their imprint remains, their hold on the town was often tenuous. There are still 19 Indian pueblos in New Mexico today, plus the reservations of the Navajo and the Jicarilla Apache and the Mescalero Apache. A substantial minority of today's New Mexicans are descendants of those Indians, or the Spanish, or both. New Mexico's population is 44 percent Hispanic – highest of any state – and almost 11 percent Native American. It's 38 percent white, second lowest in the nation, and 2 percent black, the lowest of any state in the lower half of the United States. Relatively few Hispanics are immigrants -- only about 10 percent of the state population is foreign born – and relations with Mexico are arguably less fraught than they are in other border states, owing to the relatively short length of the border and the sparse population nearby.

Modern New Mexico got a boost from science and technology. It was to a remote mesa called Los Alamos that Gen. Leslie Groves brought his Manhattan Project scientists during World War II to build a secret town and develop a secret weapon that would, in two explosions, end the war and change the course of history. Los Alamos is still a government laboratory crucial to producing U.S. nuclear weapons, and in 2016, the federal government took steps toward restarting production of plutonium "pits" for the nuclear arsenal. New Mexico has other high-tech sites as well: the White Sands Missile Range near Alamogordo, where the first atomic bomb was detonated in July 1945, and Sandia National Laboratories, near Albuquerque, run by Lockheed Martin, a non-nuclear weapons research facility with one of the fastest computers in the world, used to simulate nuclear explosions. But science has limits. At the federal Waste Isolation Pilot Plant (WIPP) near Carlsbad, where the U.S. deposits transuranic radioactive waste, a 55-gallon drum of nuclear waste buried in a salt mine cavern burst apart in 2014, shutting down the disposal site. By late 2016, the facility was moving toward restarting, but the incident gave ammunition to critics who question the Department of Energy's management of nuclear waste; a DOE report said workers at the Los Alamos National Laboratory improperly prepared the waste for disposal. At the western edge of White Sands in Sierra County is Spaceport America, an 18,000-acre facility in the New Mexico desert built with more than $215 million in state and local tax dollars to support space tourism. The bipartisan list of boosters included former Democratic Gov. Bill Richardson and Republican Gov. Susana Martinez. Billionaire Richard Branson predicted that his Virgin Galactic would be ferrying passengers on space tours by 2014 for up to $250,000 a ticket. Those hopes were dashed in October 2014, when Virgin Galactic's SpaceShipTwo rocket plane broke up on a test flight and crashed in the Mojave Desert, killing one pilot and seriously injuring another. The effort goes on, but without a date certain for a maiden launch.

New and old New Mexico intermingle in varying proportions in this land of majestic vistas. Historic Acoma shares its nickname, "Sky City," with a nearby casino. The Hispanic and Indian cultures predominate north and west of Albuquerque, with picturesque old towns and active pueblos, low-income Indian reservations, and lavish gambling resorts. Varieties of chili peppers grow today just as they did centuries ago. "Little Texas" in the south and east has small cities, plenty of oil wells, vast cattle ranches and desolate military bases; the region resembles, economically and culturally, the adjacent West Texas high plains. In the middle of the state is Albuquerque, which, with the arrival of air conditioning, grew from a small desert community of 35,000 in 1940 into a Sun Belt metropolitan area of more than 908,000 today. The city's economy is based on technology, especially nuclear power, and there, as everywhere in New Mexico, government is a prime employer. This high-tech New Mexico, however, coexists with hardship, a dichotomy expertly mined by the acclaimed TV series *Breaking Bad*, set in the office parks and grimy neighborhoods of Albuquerque. Prior to the Great Recession, statewide unemployment hovered around 4 percent, but it rose quickly and peaked above 8 percent. Unlike the rest of the country, unemployment remained stuck around 6.5 percent in 2015 and 2016. Meanwhile, the state's median income ranks sixth from the bottom, 20 percent lower than the national average. New Mexico's 20.4 percent poverty rate in 2015 ranked second-highest to Mississippi, and the state ranked highest in child poverty and third-highest in the child hunger rate. Homelessness has been a stubborn problem in Albuquerque. One bright spot is tourism, which has hit record highs for four straight years. Wealthier migrants are attracted by the destination golf courses built by Indian tribes next to their reservation casinos. The arts are another bright spot; over the years, the state's stunning scenery and unique culture have attracted writers such as D.H. Lawrence and painters such as Georgia O'Keeffe, and industries linked to arts, culture and heritage are estimated to represent nearly one of every 10 jobs, more than construction and manufacturing combined. Santa Fe and Taos are particular magnets in this regard.

Statewide population is up by 1.1 percent since 2010, but there's been a divergence between major metro areas and rural regions. The four biggest counties -- Bernalillo (Albuquerque), DoÑa Ana (Las Cruces), Santa Fe (Santa Fe), and Sandoval (the northern suburbs of Albuquerque, including Rio Rancho) – collectively grew by 2.7 percent from 2010 to 2015, but the rest of the state was down by almost 1 percent over the same period. Suburban Sandoval County alone grew by 6 percent. New Mexico's population of Hispanic millennials is the nation's highest at 52.9 percent and ranks second to Alaska in Hispanic millennials, according to the Brookings Institution.

For many years, New Mexico politics was a somnolent business. Local bosses - first Republican, later Democratic - controlled the large Hispanic vote. Elections in many counties featured irregularities that would have made a Chicago ward committeeman blush. Politics was a family business in New Mexico that could rival the House of Windsor. Members of the extended Luján family - distant cousins - represent two-thirds of the state's House seats: Democrat Michelle Luján Grisham holds the Albuquerque-based 1st District, and Democrat Ben Ray Luján represents the northern 3rd District seat that includes Santa Fe. Ben Ray Luján's father was speaker of the state House, and the grandfather of Michelle Luján Grisham was chief justice of the state Supreme Court. Her uncle, Manuel Luján Jr., was a longtime GOP congressman for the 1st District as well as Secretary of Interior for President George H.W. Bush. Manuel Luján's father was mayor of Santa Fe.

In the 2016 presidential election, Hillary Clinton's margin of victory (8 points) was slightly smaller than Barack Obama's four years earlier (10 points). Democratic votes for president fell by 30,000, while Republican votes fell by 16,000. (Gary Johnson, the Libertarian candidate who had previously served two terms as the state's Republican governor, took 9.3 percent, his best showing of any state.) Clinton lost a handful of counties Obama had won, but all were small. The four most populous counties remained blue, and the margins in both elections were strikingly consistent – no big falloffs or surges, a contrast with other states. In the meantime, the Democrats ended a two-year GOP run at controlling the state House, and they maintained their grip on the state Senate. After Trump's victory, the state had reason to worry: a federal hiring freeze; tensions with Mexico, which has become a major trading partner; and the possibility of a border wall, which could disrupt that trade. How much leverage this increasingly Democratic state will have to stave off such developments remained an open question.

Population		**Race and Ethnicity**		**Income**	
Total	2,084,117	White	39.2%	Median Income	$44,963 (45 out of 50)
Land area	121,298	Black	1.8%	Under $50,000	54.5%
Pop/ sq mi	17.2	Latino	47.4%	$50,000-$99,999	28.2%
Born in state	52.7%	Asian	1.3%	$100,000-$199,999	14.5%
		Two races	1.6%	$200,000 or more	3.0%
Age Groups		Other	8.7%	Poverty Rate	21.0%
Under 18	24.3%				
18-34	23.3%	**Education**		**Health Insurance**	
35-64	37.6%	H.S grad or less	42.2%	With health insurance coverage	83.6%
Over 64	14.8%	Some college	31.4%		
		College Degree, 4 yr	14.8%		
Work		Post grad	11.5%	**Public Assistance**	
White Collar	35.4%			Cash public assistance income	2.7%
Sales and Service	44.0%	**Military**			
Blue Collar	20.5%	Veteran	10.5%		
Government	22.2%	Active Duty	0.5%	Food stamp/SNAP benefits	16.2%

Voter Turnout			
2015 Total Citizens 18+	1,457,632	2016 Pres Turnout as % CVAP	55%
2016 Pres Votes	798,319	2012 Pres Turnout as % CVAP	56%

Legislature	
Senate:	26D, 16R
House:	38D, 32R

Presidential Politics

2016 Democratic Primary		
Hillary Clinton (D)	111,334	(52%)
Bernie Sanders (D)	104,741	(48%)
2016 Republican Primary		
Donald Trump (R)	73,908	(71%)
Ted Cruz (R)	13,925	(13%)
John Kasich (R)	7,925	(8%)

2016 Presidential Vote		
Hillary Clinton (D)	385,234	(48%)
Donald Trump (R)	319,667	(40%)
Gary Johnson (L)	74,541	(9%)
2012 Presidential Vote		
Barack Obama (D)	415,335	(53%)
Mitt Romney (R)	335,788	(43%)
Gary Johnson (L)	27,788	(4%)

New Mexico was a battleground state in the first two presidential elections in this century, but fell off the list in the third. In 2000, after some ragged vote counting, the state gave a 366-vote margin to Al Gore. In 2004, it reported a 5,988-vote margin for George W. Bush. Then-GOP Sen. Pete Domenici worked the phones with television network news officials in the early morning hours after Election Day, insisting that the state was going to tip into the GOP column.

The 2008 contest was another story, with Barack Obama deploying a superior campaign organization in the state and beating John McCain 57%-42%. In 2012, former Republican Gov. Gary Johnson was running on the Libertarian ticket and won 4 percent in his home state, while Obama posted a 53%-43% victory over Mitt Romney. Johnson more than doubled his Libertarian vote to 9 percent when he ran again in 2016, and Hillary Clinton defeated Donald Trump, 48%-40%. Clinton handily won the three largest vote-producing counties in the state: Bernalillo (Albuquerque), Santa Fe, and Donna Anna (Las Cruces, home to New Mexico State University), and = narrowly carried the fourth largest, Sandoval (suburban and exurban Albuquerque), which contains several Native American Indian reservations. Trump carried the eastern part of the state, which includes "Little Texas," where cattle ranching, cotton farming and oil drilling exert a conservative influence that makes this the most Republican region in the state.

New Mexico traditionally held its presidential primary in June; long after every major party nomination was clinched from 1984 to 2004. For 2008, with former Democratic Gov. Bill Richardson as a candidate, New Mexico scheduled its Democratic primary for February 5, Super Tuesday. By that time, Richardson had withdrawn, but the race between Barack Obama and Hillary Clinton was close, and ittook nine days to count all the votes, including 17,000 provisional ballots. Clinton won 49%-48%. The Republicans did not hold their primary until June, when no one was paying attention. McCain won 86 percent of the vote. In 2012, the primary was again in June, and Romney won 73 percent. The June

7 primary in 2016 saw Trump roll up a 71 percent victory as all his rivals had withdrawn from the GOP race. The Democratic contest was spirited. Vermont Sen. Bernie Sanders narrowly carried the four-county Albuquerque region, but Clinton won the rest of the state and the primary, 52%-48%.

Congressional Districts

115th Congress Lineup	1R 2D	**114th Congress Lineup**	1R 2D

New Mexico's three congressional districts have remained substantially the same since the state gained a third seat in 1982: one heavily Hispanic and Democratic district in Santa Fe and the north, one more rural and Republican district in the south, and a competitive Albuquerque seat in the middle. Both parties have held all three seats at various points. As Albuquerque's 1st District has moved away from Republicans, the prevailing balance has shifted from a 2-to-1 Republican edge to a 2-to-1 Democratic advantage.

New Mexico grew faster than the national average between 2000 and 2010, but fell far short of gaining a fourth seat. Control was split between a Democratic legislature and a Republican governor, and Democrats couldn't agree on an approach. The state Supreme Court assigned the matter to retired Judge James Hall, who in December 2011 adopted a compromise plan supported by both Republican Gov. Susana Martinez and a band of Democratic legislators. The new map shifted part of Valencia County from the 1st District to the 2nd to balance population, but bore little partisan consequence. Democrats have regained control of the Legislature and have a good chance to win the governor's office in 2018. If they are in control of redistricting in 2021, Republican control of the 3rd could be at risk, though that likely would require extensive changes in the current relatively orderly map.

Governor

Susana Martinez (R)

Elected 2010, term expires 2019, 2nd term; b. Jul. 14, 1959, El Paso, TX; U. of TX, El Paso, B.A. 1981; U. of OK, J.D. 1986; Catholic; Married (Chuck Franco); 1 child.

Elected Office: District Attorney, Dona Ana Cnty., 1996-2010
Professional Career: Prosecutor, Dona Ana County, 1986-1997

Office: 490 Old Sante Fe Trail, Room 400, Santa Fe, 87501; 505-476-2200; Fax: 505-476-2226; Website: governor.state.nm.us.

Election Results

Election	Name (Party)	Vote (%)
2014 General	Susana Martinez (D)	293,443 (57%)
	Gary King (R)	219,362 (43%)

Prior winning percentage: 2010 (53%)

Republican Susana Martinez became the first Hispanic woman governor of a state when she was elected in 2010, and from that point on she was seen as a rising GOP star. While she jousted with Democratic state legislators, and occasionally Republicans, she easily won reelection in 2014 as a pragmatist. But like another Hispanic governor of a purple-to-blue state, Nevada's Brian Sandoval,

Martinez by 2016 found herself out of step with a national GOP newly led by Donald Trump, with whom she sparred during the campaign.

Martinez was born and raised in El Paso, Texas, the daughter of a sheriff's deputy who started a successful security business with his wife. She helped to care for her developmentally disabled older sister while working part-time as a security guard and going to school. After graduating from the University of Texas at El Paso, she went on to law school at the University of Oklahoma. Martinez joined the Dona Ana County district attorney's office in Las Cruces, an hour's drive north of El Paso, and mainly handled prosecution of crimes against children.

In 1996, she decided to run for district attorney. Although she was a registered Democrat, she agreed to meet with local Republicans who hoped to recruit her - an idea she said she initially disdained. "I remember telling my husband, 'We're going to be very polite. We're going to say thank you very much, and we're going to leave,'" she told the *Los Angeles Times*. But she said the meeting influenced her thinking, and recalled her reaction, "We got in the car, we looked at each other and said, 'Oh my God, we are Republicans! Now what do we do?'" Martinez switched parties and did not expect to win in an area where registered Democrats outnumber Republicans by about 3-to-1. But she managed to attract enough support from her old party to capture the office with nearly 60 percent of the vote. She went on to win reelection easily three times. As district attorney, she gained a reputation for being driven and meticulous. She went after members of Mexico's drug cartels and prosecuted a number of high-profile child abuse cases herself. She also developed a habit of generously rewarding her staff; the *Albuquerque Journal* reported in August 2010 that she gave out around $477,000 in bonuses from fiscal years 2006 to 2010, more than three times as much as any other district attorney in the state.

In July 2009, Martinez announced her candidacy for governor, vowing to "remove pay-to-play in this state." She drew the attention of the Republican Governors Association, which saw the merits of having a female Hispanic join its ranks. The organization steered money to her campaign and helped line up a coveted endorsement from former Alaska Gov. Sarah Palin. She won the June 1 GOP primary with 51 percent over four other candidates, including longtime New Mexico Sen. Pete Domenici's son, Pete Domenici Jr., and Allen Weh, a former state Republican chairman. Her victory set up a battle with Lt. Gov. Diane Denish, whom Martinez wasted no time linking with outgoing Democratic Gov. Bill Richardson, whose image had been eroded by an unsuccessful 2008 presidential bid and a federal investigation into state billing practices (which didn't result in any charges against him). The national Republican tide was strong in 2010 and Martinez won, 53%-47%. In addition to winning her home county of Dona Ana, she edged out Denish in Bernalillo County, the state's most populous.

Taking office, Martinez signed executive orders to enhance public access to state records, a sharp contrast to Richardson, whose administration was criticized for invoking executive privilege to deny records requests. She ordered the sale of the state's jet and fired two personal chefs at the governor's residence. Her first budget of $5.4 billion provided more money for public school classrooms while cutting spending for colleges, universities and local education administrators. She also pulled the state out of a federal program to reintroduce Mexican gray wolves into the Southwest, and tried to suspend regulations aimed at reducing greenhouse gas emissions blamed for global warming, though the state Supreme Court overruled her. She showed a populist streak that helped keep her approval rating at high levels. When record-low temperatures led to natural gas shortages, she dispatched National Guardsmen to help the gas company relight the pilot lights of freezing homeowners.

She occasionally rankled Democratic lawmakers by avoiding negotiations on many of her initiatives. She further angered them when her political action committee aggressively went after two of the legislature's top Democrats and helped to unseat one of them in the November 2012 elections - Senate President Pro Tem Tim Jennings, a veteran conservative Democrat popular among his GOP colleagues. "It's her way or the highway," Jennings told the Santa Fe *New Mexican*. But she also broke with party orthodoxy. Although she had opposed the Affordable Care Act as a candidate for governor, in 2013, Martinez approved a state expansion of Medicaid under the law. She told the state Legislature, "My job is not to play party politics, but to implement this law in a way that best serves New Mexico." Unlike many of her GOP counterparts, Martinez defended the Common Core public education standards and comprehensive immigration reform.

Democrats were hopeful they could derail Martinez's 2014 reelection bid with an established political figure, Attorney General Gary King, who had been elected in 2006 after a dozen years in the state House. His father, Bruce King was the longest-serving governor in the state's history, winning terms in 1970, 1978 and 1990. But the son lacked his dad's folksy, glad-handing, cowboy persona; Martinez's charisma outshined the state's economic troubles, and her campaign war chest overwhelmed King's. She even ran an ad featuring praise from the liberal American Civil Liberties Union for signing a law promoting equal pay for women. Martinez won easily, 57%-43%, carrying 28 of the state's 33 counties, and her victory aided the GOP's takeover of the state House of Representatives, the first time that had happened in 60 years.

As her second term began, Martinez signed a long-term gaming agreement between the state and five tribal governments that designated a portion of casino revenues for gambling addiction services. She approved a $295 million capital infrastructure improvement bill and a package of tax incentives to stimulate economic growth targeting investors, high-tech employers and New Mexicans who had incurred major out-of-pocket medical expenses. In addition, she approved a law sharply restricting the practice of civil asset forfeiture, a policy that critics say denies citizens due process and gives a financial incentive to law enforcement to seize property. But the biggest story of 2015 came at an annual holiday party in December at a Santa Fe hotel, when police were dispatched to check on a noise complaint at a room rented by Martinez's staff. The governor demanded to know who had complained, and she told police that there was no need to investigate. Some law-enforcement officers believed her to have been inebriated, something she denied. Martinez later apologized for the incident.

In 2016, she signed a compromise bill that ended a lingering controversy over drivers' licenses; under the new law, undocumented immigrants would continue to be able to obtain licenses if they submitted their fingerprints, but legal residents would be able to get a higher-level license that was compliant with federal REAL ID standards. Immigrant-rights groups called the law a loss for Martinez, who had tried to eliminate licenses for undocumented immigrants. She also signed a bill to tighten prescription monitoring for opioids and to expand access to the anti-overdose drug naloxone. Martinez's difficult relationship with Trump cast a shadow. After Martinez, a Marco Rubio supporter, said she was too busy to attend a Trump event in her state, the future nominee lashed out at her on her own turf, saying, "Your governor has got to do a better job. She's not doing the job." These tensions were especially awkward since Martinez was chairing the Republican Governors Association, the group charged with electing GOP governors nationwide. After the election, Martinez released a statement saying, "I may have taken issue with some of the rhetoric on the campaign trail, but I believe that President-elect Trump was a better choice than Hillary Clinton, and I congratulate him on his hard-fought victory."

Repairing ties with a Trump-led Washington was just one of the challenges Martinez faced heading into the final two years of her tenure. She sparred with the legislature – fully in Democratic hands again after the 2016 election – over a budget shortfall exacerbated by hard times in the oil and gas industry. And she tried again to reinstitute the death penalty, which had been eliminated in 2009; however, the Democrats' gains in the legislature only made the odds longer. In addition to her difficulties with national Republicans, Martinez saw her approval ratings back home sink to 42 percent in late 2016, down from 69 percent four years earlier. The race to succeed her in 2018 was expected to be competitive, with a Democratic field that includes Rep. Michelle Lujan Grisham and may add Attorney General Hector Balderas. The GOP field could include Albuquerque Mayor R.J. Berry, Lt. Gov. John Sanchez and Rep. Steve Pearce.

Senior Senator

Tom Udall (D)

Elected 2008, term expires 2020, 2nd term; b. May 18, 1948, Tucson, AZ; Cambridge University (England), LL.B.; Prescott College (AZ), B.A.; University of New Mexico Law School, J.D.; Mormon; Married (Jill Z. Cooper Udall); 1 child.

Elected Office: NM Attorney General, 1990-1998; U.S. House, 1998-2008.

Professional Career: Clerk, 10th Circuit Court of Appeals, 1977; Assistant U.S Attorney, Dist. of NM, 1978-1981; Practicing attorney, 1981-1983, 1985-1990; Chief counsel, NM Health & Environment Department, 1983-1984.

DC Office: 531 HSOB 20510, 202-224-6621, Fax: 202-228-3261, tomudall.senate.gov.

State Offices: Albuquerque, 505-346-6791; Carlsbad, 575-234-0366; Las Cruces, 575-526-5475; Portales, 575-356-6811; Santa Fe, 505-988-6511.

Committees: *Appropriations*: Agriculture, Rural Development, FDA & Related Agencies, Department of Defense, Department of the Interior, Environment & Related Agencies (RMM), Energy & Water

Development, Military Construction & Veteran Affairs & Related Agencies. *Commerce, Science & Transportation*: Aviation Operations, Safety & Security, Communications, Technology, Innovation & the Internet, Consumer Protection, Product Safety, Ins & Data Security, Space, Science & Competitiveness, Surface Trans., Merchant Marine Infra., Safety & Security. *Foreign Relations*: Africa & Global Health Policy, Internat'l Dev Instit & Internat'l Econ, Energy & Environ Policy, State Dept & USAID Mngmnt, Internat'l Ops & Internat'l Dev, West Hem Crime Civ Sec Dem Rights & Women's Issues. *Indian Affairs*. *Joint Security & Cooperation in Europe*. *Rules & Administration*.

Group Ratings

	ADA	ACLU	AFL-CIO	LCV	ITI	COC	HAFA	ACU	CFG	FRC
2016	-	94%	-	100%	60%	38%	9%	4%	5%	0%
2015	95%	C	100%	92%	C	43%	C	0%	4%	0%

Almanac Ratings 2015

	Economy	Social	Foreign	Composite
Liberal	100%	100%	84%	95%
Conservative	0%	0%	16%	5%

Key Votes of the 114th Congress

1. Keystone pipeline	N	5. National Security Data	Y	9. Gun Sales Checks	Y
2. Export-Import Bank	N	6. Iran Nuclear Deal	N	10. Sanctuary Cities	N
3. Debt Ceiling Increase	Y	7. Puerto Rico Debt	Y	11. Planned Parenthood	N
4. Homeland Security $$	Y	8. Loretta Lynch A.G	Y	12. Trade deals	N

Election Results

Election	Name (Party)	Vote (%)	Cand. Spent	Ind. Exp. Support	Ind. Exp. Oppose
2014 General	Tom Udall (D)	286,409 (56%)	$8,736,822	$154,367	$173,814
	Allen Weh (R)	229,097 (44%)	$3,630,413	$70,867	
2014 Primary	Tom Udall (D)	Unopposed			

Prior winning percentages: 2008 (61%) House: 2006 (75%), 2004 (69%), 2002 (100%), 2000 (67%), 1998 (53%)

Democrat Tom Udall, New Mexico's senior senator, belongs to a political clan sometimes referred to as the "Kennedys of the West." His father, Stewart Udall, was a member of the House of Representatives from Arizona from 1955 to 1961, when he resigned to become interior secretary in the administrations of Presidents John F. Kennedy and Lyndon Johnson. His uncle, Morris Udall, then took over the Arizona House seat and held it for 30 years, while mounting a competitive bid for the Democratic presidential nomination in 1976. For 16 years of his nearly two decades on Capitol Hill, Tom Udall served with his first cousin, Mark Udall (Morris Udall's son) when the latter represented Colorado in the House and Senate. And, unlike the Kennedys, this dynasty has a bipartisan component: Republican Gordon Smith, whose mother was a Udall, represented Oregon in the Senate for two terms (1997-2009). Smith, now president of one of Washington's major trade/lobbying groups, the National Association of Broadcasters, is a second cousin. So is current Utah Republican Sen. Mike Lee, a tea party favorite.

Tom Udall -- for the most part, a reliably liberal vote from a state that at times has been a political battleground -- grew up in Tucson and then in McLean Virginia, a well-to-do Washington, D.C., suburb. He attended Prescott College in Arizona for his undergraduate work, and then earned two law degrees: a bachelor of laws at Cambridge University in England in 1975, and a doctor of jurisprudence from the University of New Mexico Law School two years later. He worked as a law clerk for a federal appellate court judge, a prosecutor in the criminal division of the U.S. attorney's office, and chief counsel to the New Mexico Department of Health and Environment before going into private practice.

Since Udall had grown up in politics -- he was six when his father was elected to Congress for the first time -- it seemed a question of when, not if, he ran for public office. In 1982, when New Mexico's 3rd District was newly created, the then-34-year-old Udall sought the Democratic nomination and finished last among four candidates, with 13 percent of the vote. The winner was Democrat Bill Richardson, who went on to become New Mexico's governor. In 1988, he tried again and ran in the Albuquerque-based 1st District to succeed long-time GOP Rep. Manuel Lujan, who was retiring. Udall won the Democratic nomination, but lost the general election to Republican Steven Schiff, the Bernalillo County district attorney, 51%-47%. Two years later, Udall scored his first election victory in a race for state attorney general, winning a four-way primary and coming out on top in November by a 2-1 margin. He focused on the environment and consumer protection, and successfully sued the federal government to delay the planned opening of the Waste Isolation Pilot Plant, the nation's first deep underground nuclear waste burial site, located in far southeastern New Mexico. He was reelected easily in 1994.

In 1997, when Richardson resigned the 3rd District seat to become the Clinton Administration's United Nations ambassador, Republican Bill Redmond, a Christian minister from Los Alamos, won in an upset, assisted by a Green Party nominee who siphoned 17 percent of the vote in the special election. In 1998, Udall decided he had a shot at the seat, given the district's heavy ratio of Democrats to Republicans. Drawing on fellow lawyers, the arts community and friends of the Udall family, he raised impressive sums. The Sierra Club and the League of Conservation Voters criticized Redmond and ran waves of ads against him. As for the third-party threat, Udall said, "I intend to make peace with the Greens." He succeeded, and won with 53 percent of the vote. Redmond got the same 43 percent he had won 18 months before, while Green Party nominee Carole Miller saw her 17 percent evaporate to 4 percent. Udall easily won reelection four times in the 3rd District, which sprawls across 14 counties in northern New Mexico.

His cousin, Mark Udall, was elected to the House for the first time as well in 1998, from a district that stretches north and east of Denver. Tom Udall was given a seat on the House Natural Resources Committee, on which his father had served and which his uncle had chaired. He helped to enact a bill to explore establishment of a national historical park at Los Alamos, the birthplace of the Atomic Age. He won passage in 2006 of a ban on oil drilling in the Valle Vidal area of the Carson National Forest, located north of Los Alamos.

After Democrats took control of the House in 2007, Udall secured a seat on the powerful Appropriations Committee. He sponsored an amendment to an energy bill that year requiring 15 percent of electricity to be generated from renewable sources other than nuclear power by 2020. The House Democratic leadership supported this amendment, and the bill passed 220-190. But the Senate refused to accept Udall's proposal, and it was dropped from the final legislation. In the wake of the 9/11 attacks, Udall opposed several of the Bush Administration's major initiatives: He voted against the 2002 Iraqi war resolution, as well as the USA Patriot Act, which gave law enforcement greatly expanded powers to investigate terrorists. He proposed revisions in the act to limit police authority to obtain search warrants, and to restore civil liberty protections for libraries and bookstores.

When Republican Sen. Pete Domenici announced he would not run for reelection in 2008, Republican Reps. Heather Wilson and Steve Pearce immediately jumped into the race; several Democrats, including moderate Albuquerque Mayor Martin Chavez, considered it as well. Udall was urged to run by Gov. Richardson and Democratic Senatorial Campaign Committee Chairman Charles Schumer of New York, and his entry into the race quickly cleared the Democratic field. Domenici endorsed Wilson, a long-time political protégé, over Pearce a few days before the June primary. Pearce narrowly won, 51%-49%.

The primary depleted Pearce's war chest, and Udall outspent him by more than $3 million. Pearce painted Udall as captive to the liberal wing of the Democratic Party and its "hippie" traditions. A former oil executive, Pearce hammered Udall for his opposition to energy exploration in environmentally sensitive areas. Udall responded that he was for a "do-it-all" approach to energy. It was apparent long before November that this wasn't much of a contest. Udall won 61%-39%, running about 4 points ahead of Democratic presidential nominee Barack Obama --and carrying the entire state except for its southeast and northwest corners.

Once again, the Udalls moved in tandem: Mark Udall was elected to represent Colorado in the Senate the same day that Tom Udall won his seat. They worked together closely, but tried to avoid serving on the same committees so they could "branch out" and cover a greater range of issues, Tom Udall said. Tom Udall was generally the more faithful Democrat of the two. In a nod to his state's rural leanings, however, Udall has not supported all of the gun control measures backed by other liberals -- although he did back Democratic-sponsored efforts to expand background checks for gun purchases in 2013 and, in 2016, to bar those on the federal terrorist watch list from buying firearms.

Udall is amiable and avoids fierce rhetoric, which enables him to work with senators on the other side of the ideological spectrum. He teamed in 2012 with conservative Republican Jon Kyl of Arizona on a measure to study the Energy Department's much-criticized National Nuclear Security Administration and with libertarian Rand Paul of Kentucky in 2011 in calling for a faster troop withdrawal from Afghanistan. Udall and his cousin, Utah's Mike Lee, teamed up with two other senators on a 2015 letter to top Obama Administration officials urging an end to the program to train and equip Syrian opposition fighters. In a statement, they contended the effort had "endangered Americans and further escalated conflict in the region."

Perhaps Udall's most notable bipartisan effort was as the lead Democratic negotiator in talks to update the nation's chemical-safety laws -- picking up the mantle from the late New Jersey senator, Frank Lautenberg. Prior to his death in 2013, Lautenberg worked for years to improve the much-criticized Toxic Substances Control Act, which had remained largely unchanged since its enactment in 1976. As Udall worked closely with conservative Louisiana Republican David Vitter, the measure in 2015 won approval from the Environment and Public Works Committee, 15-5, with the backing of industry groups as well as some environmental organizations. Still, other environmental groups criticized it as doing little to improve the *status quo*, and Udall's role stoked the ire of some Democrats, notably California Sen. Barbara Boxer, a former chairwoman of the committee who wanted a bill that took a tougher line on the industry. She all but threatened a filibuster, but later was assuaged after winning some changes to the final legislation .

Environmentalists and consumer advocates who favored the legislation praised it for strengthening the Environmental Protection Agency's oversight of hazardous chemicals. "For the first time in 40 years, the United States of America will have a chemical safety program that works…and protects families from dangerous chemicals in their daily lives," Udall declared. Industry officials, who complained about having to comply with a hodgepodge of state laws, were pleased that, going forward, they would be dealing with a single federal regimen. The bill cleared the Senate by voice vote and was signed by Obama in June 2016.

Udall's legislative interests have ranged widely. He gave up his Environment and Public Works Committee seat in 2015 to sit on the Commerce, Science and Transportation Committee, where he had served earlier. In 2013, he was named to the Appropriations Committee, a vital position for a state as dependent on federal spending as New Mexico. In his work on the Foreign Relations Committee, Udall sponsored a bipartisan measure to boost agricultural sales to Cuba. In November 2014, he and Republican Sen. Jeff Flake of Arizona met with Alan Gross, an American prisoner in Cuba. Gross was released a month later, in a move that foreshadowed Obama's efforts to re-establish diplomatic ties with the island nation. During his earlier stint on the Commerce panel, Udall pushed the Federal Trade Commission to investigate misleading safety claims for football helmets, and introduced a bill requiring new cars to have "black box" data recorders to help investigate crashes. He introduced a bill to crack down on the use of performance-enhancing drugs in horse racing. The legislation gained some attention following a *New York Times* exposé that showed rampant abuses at racetracks, but did not advance.

Udall serves on the Indian Affairs Committee, of which he became ranking Democrat in 2017. New Mexico, where more than 10 percent of residents are of American-Indian ancestry, ranks second behind Alaska in the percentage of Native Americans in the state population. In conjunction with Pearce (who returned to the House in the 2010 election) and Democratic Rep. Ben Ray Lujan, Udall and his in-state colleague, Democratic Sen. Martin Heinrich, sponsored a bill to reauthorize a federal program to preserve Native American Languages. Udall has taken up other issues of special interest at home. He and Heinrich also introduced a bill to expand federal compensation for those in close proximity to above-ground nuclear tests, including some carried out decades ago in New Mexico.

While a supporter of Hillary Clinton in the 2016 Democratic presidential primaries, Udall has teamed with Clinton's erstwhile rival, Vermont Sen. Bernie Sanders, to introduce a long-shot constitutional amendment explicitly allowing Congress and the states to "set reasonable limits on the raising and spending of money by candidates and others to influence elections," including distinguishing between "natural persons and corporations." It is aimed at the 2010 Supreme Court decision that opened the way for unlimited spending by corporations and labor unions in federal elections. Udall has repeatedly introduced a constitutional amendment since the 2010 ruling. When Democrats controlled the Senate, it attracted 54 votes, but failed to get the 60 needed to advance amid a Republican filibuster.

Like a number of other senators who have come over from the House, Udall dislikes the frequent use of filibusters to delay or block pending legislation, and has devoted significant effort to altering the way the Senate conducts business. In 2011, he offered a plan to bar use of the filibuster on the initial motion to begin debate, but permit lawmakers to filibuster a final bill if they remained on the floor during debate. His plan included elimination of secret "holds" used to delay nominations of executive branch officials. Udall's proposed changes came up short of the votes needed to advance. In 2013, Majority Leader Harry Reid did invoke the so-called "nuclear option" and eliminate the filibuster for executive branch and most judicial appointments. But, in 2015, Udall pointed to protracted delays in considering Obama's attorney general nominee, Loretta Lynch, as evidence that additional changes were needed.

Udall, a popular figure in New Mexico, easily won re-election in 2014 by 56%-44% over businessman Allen Weh, a retired Marine who largely self-funded his campaign. His victory was bittersweet: It came as the Democrats lost the Senate majority amid a Republican electoral wave, in which his cousin, Mark Udall, was among the political casualties. Soon after the 2016 election, Tom Udall, a resident of the state capital of Santa Fe, acknowledged he was "considering" a run for governor in 2018, when term-limited Republican Susana Martinez was due to retire. "I've heard from many New Mexicans who are urging me to run for governor," Udall, who turned 68 in 2016, said. "I'm flattered by their support." A month later, he decided against it, citing his seniority and the Democrats' upcoming battles with the new Trump Administration. "This is not the time to weaken our position in Washington," Udall told the *Albuquerque Journal*, noting that "New Mexico depends significantly more on federal funding than it does on state revenue."

Junior Senator

Martin Heinrich (D)

Elected 2012, term expires 2018, 1st term; b. Oct 17, 1971, Fallon, NV; University of Missouri, B.S.; University of New Mexico, Att.; Lutheran; Married (Julie Heinrich); 2 children.

Elected Office: Albuquerque City Council, 2003-2007, President 2005-2006; U.S. House, 2009-2013.

Professional Career: Contractor, Phillips Laboratories; Executive Director, Cottonwood Gulch Foundation, 1997-2002; NM natural resources trustee, 2006-2008.

DC Office: 303 HSOB 20510, 202-224-5521, Fax: 202-228-2841, heinrich.senate.gov.

State Offices: Albuquerque, 505-346-6601; Farmington, 505-325-5030; Las Cruces, 575-523-6561; Roswell, 575-622-7113; Santa Fe, 505-988-6647.

Committees: *Armed Services*: Emerging Threats & Capabilities (RMM), Strategic Forces. *Energy & Natural Resources*: Energy, National Parks, Public Lands, Forests & Mining. *Intelligence*.

Group Ratings

	ADA	ACLU	AFL-CIO	LCV	ITI	COC	HAFA	ACU	CFG	FRC
2016	-	88%	-	100%	80%	38%	12%	4%	5%	0%
2015	85%	C	100%	96%	C	43%	C	8%	4%	0%

Almanac Ratings 2015

	Economy	Social	Foreign	Composite
Liberal	94%	100%	80%	91%
Conservative	6%	0%	20%	9%

Key Votes of the 114th Congress

1. Keystone pipeline	N	5. National Security Data	Y	9. Gun Sales Checks	Y
2. Export-Import Bank	N	6. Iran Nuclear Deal	N	10. Sanctuary Cities	N
3. Debt Ceiling Increase	Y	7. Puerto Rico Debt	Y	11. Planned Parenthood	N
4. Homeland Security $$	Y	8. Loretta Lynch A.G	Y	12. Trade deals	N

Election Results

Election	Name (Party)	Vote (%)		Cand. Spent	Ind. Exp. Support	Ind. Exp. Oppose
2012 General	Martin T. Heinrich (D)	395,717	(51%)	$6,692,326	$937,245	$2,657,362
	Heather Wilson (R)	351,260	(45%)	$7,108,688	$771,629	$1,702,707
	Jon Barrie (I)	28,199	(4%)	$26,483		
2012 Primary	Martin Heinrich (D)	83,432	(59%)			
	Hector Balderas (D)	58,128	(41%)			

Prior winning percentages: House: 2010 (52%), 2008 (56%)

Democratic Rep. Martin Heinrich was elected New Mexico's junior senator in 2012 after a campaign in which he portrayed himself as a younger version of the man he succeeded: five-term Democratic Sen. Jeff Bingaman, who retired after spending three decades as a centrist Democrat representing a battleground state that trended from red to blue during his tenure. Like Bingaman, Heinrich has established a voting record that largely puts him in the ideological middle of the Senate Democratic Caucus, while focusing on issues relating to energy and technology -- issues of particular interest to New Mexico, home to several large federal government laboratories.

Heinrich was born in Fallon Nevada, the son of a utility company lineman and a factory worker. He grew up not far from Columbia, Missouri, where he attended the University of Missouri and earned a degree in mechanical engineering. He arrived in New Mexico in 1995 -- where he took a job doing mechanical drawings at an Albuquerque laboratory, but soon went to work for AmeriCorps, President Bill Clinton's public service initiative for recent college graduates. He went on to serve as executive director of the Cottonwood Gulch Foundation, which runs adventure programs in the Southwest, and to start a political consulting business. Elected to the Senate when he was 41, Heinrich has enjoyed a swift political ascent, starting with his election to the Albuquerque City Council nine years earlier, in 2003. His signature issue was increasing New Mexico's minimum wage in 2006, when, as council president that year, he worked with the city's business leaders and community activists to produce compromise legislation mandating a gradual increase.

Encouraged by then-Democratic Gov. Bill Richardson, Heinrich announced he would challenge six-term GOP Rep. Heather Wilson for the 1st District seat in 2008. National Democrats backed Heinrich's candidacy, and he won 44 percent of the primary vote to defeat three other Democratic hopefuls -- including former New Mexico Secretary of State Rebecca Virgil-Giron and Michelle Lujan Grisham, the current representative. Meanwhile, in 2007, Wilson had announced her intention to give up the seat to run for the Senate. (She lost in the primary.) Republicans fielded a strong replacement in Bernalillo County Sheriff Darren White. Heinrich tied White to the unpopular incumbent president by reminding voters that White had served as George W. Bush's Bernalillo County reelection chairman in 2004. White, in turn, questioned Heinrich's business practices, charging that although nonprofit groups paid him for advocacy work, he didn't register as a lobbyist. Heinrich maintained the law had not required him to register when he was a political consultant from 2002 to 2005 for the Coalition for New Mexico Wilderness -- in conjunction with a successful effort to gain federal protection for the Ojito Wilderness, 35 miles from Albuquerque. Thanks in part to that year's national Democratic wave, which included the election of President Barack Obama, Heinrich won easily, 56%-44%.

While supporting many of Obama's major initiatives, including the 2010 Affordable Care Act,

Heinrich sought to avoid being a down-the-line Democrat during his two terms in the House. He endorsed spending cuts in some appropriations bills and, like many Western lawmakers, backed gun owners' rights. The National Rifle Association, which had stayed out of his House race in 2008, endorsed Heinrich for reelection in 2010 -- citing his vote for an amendment to allow guns in national parks. During debate on the Affordable Care Act, Heinrich pushed successfully to include provisions of long-sought legislation to improve Indian health care, and later counted this among his major achievement in the House. "That was something that had been out there for 12-14 years in Congress," Heinrich told the *Albuquerque Journal*. "The negotiations to get that passed as part of health reform was a real coup for New Mexico." More than 10 percent of New Mexico's population is American Indian; the state ranks second only to Alaska in its percentage of Native American residents.

Like Bingaman -- who chaired the Senate Energy and Natural Resources Committee -- Heinrich advocated expanding energy production through a broad range of sources. As a member of the House Natural Resources Committee, he introduced a bill in 2009 aimed at creating clean energy jobs by providing a dedicated funding stream for the Bureau of Land Management to process a backlog of clean energy project applications. To help his district's Sandia National Laboratories, Heinrich worked to raise the percentage of money spent on high-tech research and development at national labs. He also added a provision to the fiscal 2011 defense bill for a pilot program in which military bases and the labs work together on developing new electric power systems. Heinrich withstood the nationwide Republican wave of 2010 to win reelection, 52%-48%, over GOP challenger Jon Barela, a former president of the Albuquerque Hispano Chamber of Commerce. Heinrich did a solid favor for Tom Udall, his future Senate colleague, by sponsoring a measure to name the Interior Department building for Udall's father, Stewart, who was interior secretary during the Kennedy and Johnson administrations. The measure was signed into law; in the Senate, Heinrich and Udall would collaborate frequently on issues.

New Mexico's Democratic establishment was eager for Heinrich to run for Bingaman's seat as soon as the senator announced his retirement. Heinrich drew a competitive Democratic primary opponent in state Auditor Hector Balderas, who hoped to tap into the state's sizable Hispanic vote. But the party rallied around the more politically experienced Heinrich, and he won the primary with 59 percent. That set up a general election matchup against Wilson. It was a contest between two well-regarded candidates. A former Air Force officer (she was later named Air Force secretary by President Donald Trump) and National Security Council staffer, Wilson was the political protégé of popular former GOP Sen. Pete Domenici. With the help of Domenici's network of supporters, she won several close House reelection races before losing to Rep. Steve Pearce in the 2008 GOP primary to succeed Domenici in the Senate.

In taking on Heinrich, Wilson stressed her independence from her party, running a biographical ad that played up her military record without mentioning she was a Republican. She got outside financial help from conservative groups, including Crossroads GPS. (After leaving Congress, she served on Crossroads' board for six months.) Heinrich benefited from the Obama reelection campaign's heavy presence in the state and touted his connection to the president. Wilson consistently trailed Heinrich in polls, eventually prompting national Republicans to turn their attention elsewhere. Heinrich defeated Wilson, 51%-45%. He won their mutual home base in Bernalillo County, 54%-43%. Heinrich was assigned to the Energy and Natural Resources Committee and the Intelligence Committee, as well as the Joint Economic Committee -- of which he became the ranking Democrat in 2017. He later picked up a seat on the Armed Services Committee.

On the Intelligence Committee, Heinrich emerged as a sharp critic of what he considered the Obama administration's overly broad use of surveillance. After it was first revealed in 2013, he charged that the National Security Agency's bulk collection of phone records was "a major invasion of Americans' privacy and has done little if anything to further the fight against terrorism." The program was curtailed in the 2015 reauthorization of the Patriot Act. Heinrich voted to confirm John Brennan as the Central Intelligence Agency director soon after joining the panel. But in mid-2014, he called for Brennan's resignation after revelations that CIA officials had hacked into computers used by Intelligence Committee staff who were investigating controversial interrogation techniques used on terrorism suspects in the wake of 9/11. Heinrich pushed for the panel to release the staff's full 6,700-page report on the matter, declaring, "This was a dark and regrettable chapter in our country's history and betrayed the American values of respecting and upholding the dignity and human rights of all people. The American people deserve a full accounting of what happened, so that they can come to terms with what has been done in their name." But then-Intelligence Chairman Dianne Feinstein overruled Heinrich and several other members, opting to release a 500-page summary of the report.

In the *Almanac* vote ratings for 2015, his scores put him in the ideological middle of the Senate Democratic Caucus -- although he has shifted left on at least one issue. After receiving the backing of the NRA six years earlier, Heinrich appeared on the Senate floor in June 2016 in support of an effort by Connecticut Democratic Sen. Chris Murphy to force a vote on a proposal to deny the sale of firearms to those on the government's terrorist watch list. Describing himself as a "law abiding gun-owning American," Heinrich declared: "This is about separating the law abiding from the terrorists and criminals. So what could be more common sense?" He noted that the proposal gave those who felt wrongly placed on the terrorist watch list the ability to contest their status. Heinrich joined most of his Democratic colleagues in voting for the plan, which failed on a largely party-line vote.

As a camping and hunting enthusiast, Heinrich has zeroed in on land issues as a member of the Energy and Natural Resources panel. He worked to ensure hunting and fishing access to lands owned by the federal government, while criticizing calls to transfer federal land to state-government control. In tandem with Udall, he has pushed to create two new wilderness areas -- the Cerro del Yuta Wilderness and Rio San Antonio Wilderness -- within the 242,500 acre Rio Grande del Norte National Monument in northern New Mexico. Also on the home front, Heinrich -- in conjunction with Utah Republican Orrin Hatch and Hawaii Democrat Brian Schatz -- won passage at the end of 2016 of a so-called "telehealth" bill. Intended to spur videoconferencing to link teams of specialists to primary care providers in rural and underserved areas for weekly continuing education sessions, the new law uses an effort by the University of New Mexico School of Medicine as a nationwide model.

Despite his lack of seniority, the telegenic Heinrich has attracted a measure of attention in the chamber on several non-legislative fronts. He has shown up on *The Hill* newspaper's "50 Most Beautiful" list as a senator and House member, and was deemed the runner-up for "hottest senator" (behind South Dakota Republican John Thune) by *Washingtonian* magazine. In contrast, Heinrich ends up at the bottom of lists when it comes to the financial assets of individual members of Congress: *Roll Call's* latest survey pegs him as the eighth poorest member of Congress, with a negative net worth of nearly $725,000.

Heinrich, who slept on a camping mat in his office while serving in the House, was embarrassed in 2015 when *USAToday* reported that he had been reimbursed with public funds for $1,900 in personal taxi and ride sharing costs over a two-year period. An apologetic Heinrich attributed the errors to problems in his office's accounting system, and repaid the money.

His biggest splash, so to speak, came from a Discovery Channel reality show he starred in with Jeff Flake, his Arizona Republican colleague. *Rival Survival* featured the bipartisan duo spending six days with minimal supplies on the isolated island of Eru, located in a shark sanctuary halfway between Hawaii and Australia. The trip took place weeks prior to the 2014 election. The pair later tried to adapt the bipartisan approach by holding a Senate lunch for members of both parties; typically, the parties hold their luncheons separately. "We wanted to show that Republicans and Democrats can get along and survive together," Flake told *The Washington Post*. "Then we approached Discovery because they have a number of survivor shows and they said, 'Well, we like the idea, but how about you let us come film it?'"

Heinrich is seeking a second term in 2018, and began the election cycle as a solid favorite. Republican Gov. Susana Martinez is term-limited in her current job, but has expressed little interest in a move to Washington. At least three other Republican office holders in the state -- Pearce, Lt. Gov. John Sanchez, and Albuquerque Mayor Richard Berry -- are seen as possible candidates for higher office. One or more of them may opt to go for the gubernatorial seat that Martinez is vacating.

FIRST DISTRICT

Michelle Lujan Grisham (D)

Elected 2012, 3rd term; b. Oct 24, 1959, Los Alamos (NM); University of New Mexico; b.E., 1981; University of New Mexico, J.D., 1987; Roman Catholic; Widow; 2 children.

Elected Office: Commissioner, Bernalillo County, 2010-2012.

Professional Career: Director, NM State Agency on Aging, 1991-2002; Secretary, NM Aging & Long-Term Services Department, 2002-2004; Secretary, NM Department of Health, 2004-2007; Co-owner, Delta Consulting Group, 2008-present.

DC Office: 214 CHOB 20515, 202-225-6316, Fax: 202-225-4975, lujangrisham.house.gov.

State Offices: Albuquerque, 505-346-6781.

Committees: *Agriculture*: Biotechnology, Horticulture & Research (RMM), Nutrition. *Budget*.

Group Ratings

	ADA	ACLU	AFL-CIO	LCV	ITI	COC	HAFA	ACU	CFG	FRC
2016	-	82%	-	100%	83%	64%	16%	0%	4%	0%
2015	80%	C	95%	80%	C	58%	C	0%	6%	0%

Almanac Ratings 2015

	Economy	Social	Foreign	Composite
Liberal	80%	97%	71%	82%
Conservative	20%	3%	30%	18%

Key Votes of the 114th Congress

1. Keystone Pipeline	N	5. Puerto Rico Debt	Y	9. Offenses by Aliens	N
2. Trade Deals	N	6. Medical Marijuana	Y	10. Troops in Iraq	N
3. Export-Import Bank	Y	7. Sanctuary Cities	N	11. Homeland Security $$	Y
4. Debt Ceiling Increase	Y	8. Armor-piercing Bullets	N	12. Trade Adjustment aid	Y

Election Results

Election	Name (Party)	Vote (%)	Cand. Spent	Ind. Exp. Support	Ind. Exp. Oppose
2016 General	Michelle Lujan Grisham (D)..... ...	181,088 (65%)	$1,517,608		
	Richard Priem (R)......................	96,879 (35%)			
2016 Primary	Michelle Lujan Grisham (D).....	(100%)			

Prior winning percentages: 2014 (59%), 2012 (59%)

With her election in 2012, Democrat Michelle Lujan Grisham joined a state family dynasty. Her grandfather, Eugene Lujan, was the Supreme Court's first Latino chief justice; her uncle, Manuel Lujan Jr., was a GOP congressman and Interior secretary; her apparently distant cousin, Rep. Ben Ray Luján, represents the 3rd District. In 2017, she raised her political profile in Congress and at home.

The daughter of a dentist, Lujan Grisham was born in Los Alamos and attended high school in Santa Fe. After earning bachelor's and law degrees from the University of New Mexico, she was named director of the State Bar of New Mexico's Lawyer Referral for the Elderly Program, which provides basic legal services to seniors. In 1991, then-Gov. Bruce King appointed Lujan Grisham director of the New Mexico State Agency on Aging. She remained in that position for the next 13 years, serving under a Republican as well as two Democratic governors - a point she later stressed when she ran for the House to contend that she can be bipartisan.

In 2004, Lujan Grisham's college sweetheart and husband of 22 years, Gregory Alan Grisham, collapsed while jogging and died the next day from a ruptured cerebral aneurysm. Three years later, Lujan Grisham filed a wrongful death lawsuit, seeking damages from an Albuquerque physician who had misdiagnosed him with migraines, but the suit was dismissed. After her husband's death, Lujan Grisham was named secretary of the New Mexico Department of Health, which had 3,800 employees and a $440 million budget. In 2007, the Justice Department filed a lawsuit against New Mexico in response to substandard conditions and practices at the state-run Fort Bayard Medical Center. A settlement was reached in four days. Lujan Grisham resigned a month later, telling the *Albuquerque Journal* that overseeing the Department of Health was the "hardest job on the planet."

Lujan Grisham made an unsuccessful run in 2008 for the 1st District seat, placing third in the Democratic primary. Two years later, she was elected a commissioner of Bernalillo County. When Rep. Martin Heinrich ran for the Senate, Lujan Grisham started as a long-shot candidate to replace Heinrich. She maintained that her real-life hardships gave her insight into voters' problems. "As a widow and a caregiver and a single mother, I'm living the experience that New Mexicans are," she told the *Journal*. She conserved cash while her rivals for the Democratic nomination, state Sen. Eric Griego and former Albuquerque Mayor Marty Chavez, attacked each other and did not take her seriously until it was too late. Lujan Grisham won the primary with 40 percent of the vote to 35 percent for Griego and 25 percent for Chavez. She cruised to victory over Republican former state Rep. Janice Arnold-Jones, 59%-41%. She was reelected easily.

On the Agriculture Committee, Lujan Grisham was ranking Democrat on the Conservation and Forestry Subcommittee, where she focused on healthier forest reserves and stronger watershed programs. Those issues are important to New Mexico, which has more than 9 million acres of Forest Service land. She filed a proposal to create Care Corps, a national organization that would help seniors and people with disabilities continue to live independently and also provide support to family caregivers. In 2017, she became ranking Democrat on the Biotechnology, Horticulture and Research Subcommittee.

Following the 2016 election, Lujan-Grisham took on new partisan dimensions. In the House, she became chairwoman of the Congressional Hispanic Caucus, which has been open only to Democrats. Her goal, she said, was to "develop a strong economic agenda to highlight the economic impact of Hispanic communities and create more opportunities for Hispanic-owned business and entrepreneurs." The election of President Donald Trump increased the need for the Caucus to combat his "dangerous rhetoric and regressive policies … aimed to tear families apart and hurt the communities we represent," she added. In December 2016, she announced her candidacy for governor of New Mexico. Republican Susana Martinez is term-limited in 2018. Democrats were likely to hold her House seat, though Republicans could make the contest competitive.

Albuquerque Area

Population		Race and Ethnicity		Income	
Total	693,273	White	40.8%	Median Income	$47,001 (305 out of 435)
Land area	4,600	Black	2.4%		
Pop/ sq mi	150.7	Latino	48.9%		
Born in state	51.8%	Asian	2.1%	Under $50,000	52.4%
Age Groups		Two races	1.8%	$50,000-$99,999	28.3%
Under 18	22.7%	Other	4.0%	$100,000-$199,999	15.6%
18-34	24.3%	**Education**		$200,000 or more	3.6%
35-64	38.9%	H.S grad or less	36.9%	Poverty Rate	19.8%
Over 64	14.0%	Some college	31.4%	**Health Insurance**	
Work		College Degree, 4 yr	17.3%	With health insurance coverage	85.2%
White Collar	39.6%	Post grad	14.5%		
Sales and Service	43.4%	**Military**		**Public Assistance**	
Blue Collar	16.9%	Veteran	10.3%	Cash public assistance income	2.5%
Government	20.0%	Active Duty	0.4%	Food stamp/SNAP benefits	15.5%

Voter Turnout			
2015 Total Citizens 18+	491,897	2016 House Turnout as % CVAP	57%
2016 House turnout	277,967	2014 House Turnout as % CVAP	37%

2012 Presidential Vote		
Barack Obama	155,915	(55%)
Mitt Romney	111,749	(40%)

2016 Presidential Vote		
Hillary Clinton	147,250	(52%)
Donald Trump	100,132	(35%)
Gary Johnson	30,767	(11%)

Cook Partisan Voting Index: D+7

New Mexico's past and future come together in its single metropolis, Albuquerque. The city's Spanish and Indian past is memorialized in its name (for a 17th-century Spanish nobleman), its age (founded in 1706) and its quaint Old Town. But Albuquerque's future is decidedly high-tech. For decades, the Sandia National Laboratories, Kirtland Air Force Base and the University of New Mexico have attracted scientists and engineers to Albuquerque and promoted private-sector technology growth. The city's minor-league baseball team is the Isotopes, named in part to honor the area's association with the Atomic Age. When rocket scientist Robert Goddard moved here in 1930 and nuclear scientist J. Robert Oppenheimer reconnoitered the site in 1940, Albuquerque was still a town of 35,000 at the junction of the Rio Grande River and old U.S. 66, which paralleled the Santa Fe Railroad. "A dirty, red sod-hut tortilla desert highway city," novelist Tom Wolfe wrote.

Now, metro Albuquerque, spreading out from Bernalillo County into Sandoval and Valencia counties, has more people - 908,000 in 2016 - than all of New Mexico did when the scientists first arrived. Bill Gates founded a little company called Microsoft here in 1975, although the software maker moved its 13 employees to Bellevue, Washington, in 1979. The University of New Mexico has become a magnet for biotechnology, with more than a dozen local startups working to commercialize UNM's biomedical discoveries. In a warning sign of the limits of the local tech-based economy, the workforce at Intel's facility in Rio Rancho dropped from 3,300 in 2013 to 1,900 in 2016; its advanced chip-making has lost market share. The city's prosperous neighborhoods have climbed the gently rising heights to the east; poorer residents have spread north and south along the Rio Grande. Hemmed in by the Sandia Mountains and by federal installations, growth is moving west and north. In June 2015, the county narrowly approved the master plan for Santolina, a planned 22-square-mile development west of Albuquerque that within a few decades might house 90,000 persons and create 75,000 jobs, according to the developers; some skeptical community groups were concerned about sprawl and scant water resources.

In the Old Town centered on the plaza, some of the adobe buildings date to the 18th century. Albuquerque has seen modest growth in tourism. Every October, it hosts the International Balloon Fiesta, which features more than 500 hot-air balloons and many resident balloonists. The annual Gathering of Nations typically attracts more than 700 tribes plus 100,000 participants and spectators. The city has a large public sector - nearly 24 percent of its workforce have been employed by government, but those numbers declined after 2007. The AMC television series *Breaking Bad* was set and filmed here for five years until 2013 and explored issues prevalent in the Southwest: drug trafficking, economic instability, immigration and porous borders.

The 1st Congressional District includes almost all of Albuquerque and some of its suburbs. It is 49 percent Hispanic and takes in most of Bernalillo County, all of sparsely populated Torrance County in the desert, and small corners of Sandoval, Santa Fe and Valencia counties. More than 90 percent of the vote is in Bernalillo. Until 2008, the district elected only Republicans to Congress. With additional Latino voters, it has grown more Democratic. Republican Susana Martinez won Bernalillo County in each of her campaigns for governor. But the Democratic presidential candidates in 2012 and 2016 had double-digit wins in the county. The third-party candidacy of former New Mexico Gov. Gary Johnson reduced each party's vote across the state in 2016. President Barack Obama's 55%-40% win in the 1st District in 2012 was reduced to a 52%-35% win for Hillary Clinton in 2016.

SECOND DISTRICT

Steve Pearce (R)

Elected 2002, 7th term; b. Aug 24, 1947, Lamesa, TX; New Mexico State University; b.B.A., 1970; Eastern New Mexico University, M.B.A., 1991; Baptist; Married (Cynthia Pearce); 1 child.

Military Career: U.S Air Force, 1970-1976 (Vietnam).

Elected Office: NM House, 1997-2000; U.S. House, 2003-2009.

Professional Career: Owner, Lea Fishing Tools.

DC Office: 2432 RHOB 20515, 202-225-2365, Fax: 202-225-9599, pearce.house.gov.

State Offices: Alamogordo, 855-473-2723; Hobbs, 575-393-6995; Las Cruces, 575-522-0771; Los Lunas, 855-473-2723; Roswell, 575-622-6200; Socorro, 575-835-8979.

Committees: *Financial Services*: Housing & Insurance, Terrorism & Illicit Finance (Chmn). *Natural Resources*: Energy & Mineral Resources, Federal Lands.

Group Ratings

	ADA	ACLU	AFL-CIO	LCV	ITI	COC	HAFA	ACU	CFG	FRC
2016	-	11%	-	0%	83%	100%	73%	86%	83%	100%
2015	5%	C	17%	6%	C	75%	C	79%	70%	100%

Almanac Ratings 2015

	Economy	Social	Foreign	Composite
Liberal	13%	0%	0%	4%
Conservative	87%	100%	100%	96%

Key Votes of the 114th Congress

1. Keystone Pipeline	Y	5. Puerto Rico Debt	N	9. Offenses by Aliens	Y
2. Trade Deals	N	6. Medical Marijuana	N	10. Troops in Iraq	N
3. Export-Import Bank	NV	7. Sanctuary Cities	Y	11. Homeland Security $$	N
4. Debt Ceiling Increase	N	8. Armor-piercing Bullets	Y	12. Trade Adjustment aid	N

Election Results

Election	Name (Party)	Vote (%)	Cand. Spent	Ind. Exp. Support	Ind. Exp. Oppose
2016 General	Steve Pearce (R)	143,515 (63%)	$838,509		
	Merrie Lee Soules (D)	85,232 (37%)	$378,698		
2016 Primary	Steve Pearce (R)	(100%)			

Prior winning percentages: 2014 (64%), 2012 (59%), 2010 (55%), 2006 (59%), 2004 (60%), 2002 (56%)

Republican Steve Pearce, first elected to the House in 2002, abandoned the seat for an unsuccessful Senate race in 2008 and then reclaimed it two years later in the Republican landslide. He has moved further rightward since then and has joined up with the GOP's anti-leadership activists. He has had occasional bipartisan moments.

Pearce grew up in Hobbs, near the Texas line, graduated from New Mexico State University and received an MBA from Eastern New Mexico University. He served in the Air Force and flew 518 hours of missions as a combat pilot during the Vietnam War. He returned to Hobbs and became wealthy after he started an oil-field service company. In 1996, he was elected to the state House, where he chaired the Republican Caucus. Pearce became the frontrunner when the U.S. House seat opened in 2002. He won the primary over two competitors and then defeated Democratic state Sen. John Arthur Smith, 56%-44%.

During Pearce's first stint in the House, he was chairman of the National Parks subcommittee and made park accessibility a priority. He proposed giving states and counties broad authority over rights of way on federal land, but made little progress on the measure before Democrats won majority control in 2006.

After he returned in 2011, Pearce voted increasingly with conservatives. On the Financial Services Committee, he joined in GOP attacks on the Consumer Financial Protection Bureau, created under the 2010 Dodd-Frank financial services overhaul. He lambasted Federal Reserve Chairman Ben Bernanke in 2013 for keeping interest rates low, depriving senior citizens of income. Pearce has been an enthusiastic supporter of hydraulic fracturing for oil and gas extraction, and said that federal and state regulators had not documented a single case of contaminated underground drinking water at such sites.

He has had conflicts with Republican leaders. In January 2013, he was one of nine Republicans to oppose John Boehner of Ohio for another term as Speaker. Pearce's spokesman said the congressman was upset by Boehner's deal with President Barack Obama to avert the so-called "fiscal cliff," in part, by raising taxes on high-income earners. When Pearce voted for Boehner for Speaker in 2015, he issued a statement that said, somewhat elliptically, "I will fight the hard fight." The next step came in June when Majority Whip Steve Scalise removed Pearce and two other Republicans from the GOP whip team because they abandoned the party on a key procedural vote dealing with an international trade agreement. Pearce responded that he would continue to "vote on principle." When Boehner stepped down under pressure in October, Pearce said he would support Rep. Daniel Webster as the next speaker because of his experience as speaker of the Florida House and because of what he called the relative inexperience of Majority Leader Kevin McCarthy, who was the initial heir apparent for the post. When McCarthy couldn't get sufficient support and Rep. Paul Ryan of Wisconsin stepped forward as an alternative, Pearce supported him.

Pearce was one of a handful of Republicans who moved to change House rules to weaken the Office of Congressional Ethics in January 2017. Ryan stifled their efforts, at least for the time being. That didn't stop Pearce from becoming chairman of the new Financial Services Subcommittee on Terrorism and Illicit Finance, whose chief objective was to identify ways to shut off terror financing. He also regained a seat on the Natural Resources Committee. Pearce was mostly a supporter of Donald Trump during the 2016 campaign and after he became president. When Trump's lewd comments about women were revealed, Pearce said that the words were "horrid," but he stood by Trump because he could "never support" Hillary Clinton.

Pearce has made efforts to cross the aisle. In 2014 he joined with Democratic Rep. Beto O'Rourke of Texas on a bill to improve training for Border Patrol officers. An aide to Pearce, who represents an adjoining district along the border, reportedly said, "He trusts O'Rourke and O'Rourke trusts him." In 2015, he filed a bill with California Democratic Rep. Eric Swalwell of California to seek ways for House members, especially from the West, to limit their travel to Washington for committee hearings.

When Republican Sen. Pete Domenici retired in 2008, Pearce jumped into the race along with the more moderate GOP Rep. Heather Wilson. Pearce attacked Wilson for supporting the Democrats' expansion of the Children's Health Insurance Program, which he called "socialized medicine," and for voting to raise taxes. Domenici endorsed Wilson a few days before the June primary, but Pearce won, 51%-49%. The primary drained Pearce's war chest. Democratic Rep. Tom Udall outspent Pearce, $7.8 million to $4.6 million and won the seat, 61%-39%.

Harry Teague took advantage of the national Democratic wave in 2008 to capture Pearce's House seat. In 2010, Pearce challenged Teague for his old job, attacking him for his vote in favor of the 2009 cap-and-trade bill to reduce carbon emissions, which Pearce argued would hurt the region's oil and gas industry. He ran ads calling Teague "one of the richest men in Congress," as a fellow owner of an oil-field service company, while neglecting to mention his own personal fortune. Bolstered by the national Republican tide, Pearce won easily, 55%-45%. He turned down the opportunity to run for another open Senate seat in 2012. Since then, he has easily won reelection.

Southern New Mexico: Las Cruces

Population		**Race and Ethnicity**		**Income**	
Total	699,589	White	38.4%	Median Income	$40,962 (390 out of 435)
Land area	71,739	Black	1.7%		
Pop/ sq mi	9.8	Latino	52.9%		
Born in state	50.3%	Asian	0.7%	Under $50,000	58.7%
		Two races	1.2%	$50,000-$99,999	27.4%
Age Groups		Other	5.1%	$100,000-$199,999	11.8%
Under 18	25.3%			$200,000 or more	2.0%
18-34	23.8%	**Education**		Poverty Rate	23.0%
35-64	35.6%	H.S grad or less	48.8%		
Over 64	15.3%	Some college	30.9%	**Health Insurance**	
		College Degree, 4 yr	12.2%	With health insurance coverage	83.4%
Work		Post grad	8.1%		
White Collar	28.9%				
Sales and Service	45.5%	**Military**		**Public Assistance**	
Blue Collar	25.6%	Veteran	10.8%	Cash public assistance income	3.0%
Government	23.1%	Active Duty	0.7%		
				Food stamp/SNAP benefits	18.9%

Voter Turnout			
2015 Total Citizens 18+	473,665	2016 House Turnout as % CVAP	48%
2016 House turnout	228,813	2014 House Turnout as % CVAP	32%

2012 Presidential Vote		
Mitt Romney	119,168	(52%)
Barack Obama	103,438	(45%)

2016 Presidential Vote		
Donald Trump	117,212	(50%)
Hillary Clinton	93,362	(40%)
Gary Johnson	18,903	(8%)

Cook Partisan Voting Index: R+6

Southeastern New Mexico is a disparate landscape: endless sagebrush-strewn acreage and then, suddenly, 9,000-foot mountain peaks rising along the Continental Divide. (The Robledo Mountains, says the Smithsonian Institution, are the world's greatest repository of pre-dinosaur-era fossil tracks.) The eastern part of this region - places like Lovington and Hobbs - speaks with a Texas twang rather than a northern New Mexico lilt. In Little Texas, as southeastern New Mexico is known, oil has been the economic mainstay. Cattle ranching is common, and cotton is grown on irrigated land. Roswell, the site of a supposed flying saucer landing in 1947, is now home of the International UFO Museum and Research Center. Farther west is White Sands National Monument, with its immaculate gypsum dunes and specially evolved animals with white coloration that allows them to elude predators in the harsh environment.

Virgin Galactic, a company started by billionaire Richard Branson, leased land near White Sands to build the nation's first commercial spaceport (called Spaceport America). By early 2011, more than 400 people had put down deposits to travel to the edge of space. But those plans have become dubious. The $218 million facility "sits largely vacant," *The Wall Street Journal* reported in 2014. The focus for commercial space flight had moved to Cape Canaveral, Florida, and the SpaceX program led by electric-car entrepreneur Elon Musk. State officials have been trying to sell the New Mexico facility. Close by is Alamogordo, not far from where the first atomic bomb was exploded in the empty land at 5:29:45 a.m. Mountain War Time on July 16, 1945.

Las Cruces, New Mexico's second-largest city, has grown at rates well above the statewide average, thanks to migrants from Mexico coming up the Rio Grande. For decades, Anglo and Mexican ranchers across the border spoke "the common language of cattle," and communities frequently shared public services with their cross-border neighbors, not hindered by a wall or other major barrier. Rapid development after the 1993 North American Free Trade Agreement, a surge in illegal immigration and a sharp uptick in drug trafficking posed new challenges. Still, the New Mexico portion of the largely empty 150-mile U.S.-Mexico border remains sleepier than elsewhere.

As in many places on America's high plains, population here is thinning and old economic pillars are crumbling. Once reliant on potash mining, Carlsbad aggressively sought the Waste Isolation Pilot Plant, a nuclear waste repository that after 1999 buried shipments of plutonium-contaminated garbage from the nation's Energy Department weapons factories. But the repository shut down following a "radiation event" and fire in February 2014. East of Carlsbad, a uranium enrichment plant was built in Eunice, the first such facility licensed by the Nuclear Regulatory Commission.

The 2nd Congressional District of New Mexico covers the southern part of the state, reaching to Albuquerque's southern suburbs. Demographically and politically, it is diverse. It includes most of Little Texas - majority Anglo and solidly conservative - but also politically marginal Las Cruces and the Indian country around the pueblos, which is strongly Democratic. The district is 54 percent Hispanic and 5 percent Indian. Las Cruces-based Dona Ana County has about one-third of the voters. Many Latinos here are migrant workers and not part of an organized, Democratic voting bloc. The district in 2016 voted for Donald Trump, 50%-40%, a wider margin than the GOP wins in the two previous presidential elections.

THIRD DISTRICT

Ben Lujan (D)

Elected 2008, 5th term; b. Jun 07, 1972, Santa Fe; New Mexico Highlands University, B.A.; University of New Mexico, Att.; Roman Catholic; Single.

Elected Office: NM public reg. comm., 2004-2008, Chairman, 2005-2007.

Professional Career: NM deputy state treas., 2002-2003; Director admin. services, CFO, NM Cultural Affairs Department, 2003-2004.

DC Office: 2231 RHOB 20515, 202-225-6190, Fax: 202-226-1528, lujan.house.gov.

State Offices: Farmington, 505-324-1005; Gallup, 505-863-0582; Las Vegas, 505-454-3038; Rio Rancho, 505-994-0499; Santa Fe, 505-984-8950; Tucumcari, 575-461-3029.

Committees: House Democratic Congressional Campaign Committee Chairman. *Energy & Commerce*: Digital Commerce & Consumer Protection, Health.

Group Ratings

	ADA	ACLU	AFL-CIO	LCV	ITI	COC	HAFA	ACU	CFG	FRC
2016	-	94%	-	100%	67%	54%	14%	0%	0%	0%
2015	90%	C	96%	94%	C	45%	C	0%	3%	0%

Almanac Ratings 2015

	Economy	Social	Foreign	Composite
Liberal	90%	100%	99%	96%
Conservative	10%	0%	1%	4%

Key Votes of the 114th Congress

1. Keystone Pipeline	N	5. Puerto Rico Debt	Y	9. Offenses by Aliens	N
2. Trade Deals	N	6. Medical Marijuana	Y	10. Troops in Iraq	Y
3. Export-Import Bank	Y	7. Sanctuary Cities	N	11. Homeland Security $$	Y
4. Debt Ceiling Increase	Y	8. Armor-piercing Bullets	N	12. Trade Adjustment aid	Y

Election Results

Election	Name (Party)	Vote (%)	Cand. Spent	Ind. Exp. Support	Ind. Exp. Oppose
2016 General	Ben Lujan (D)............................	170,612 (62%)	$1,303,290		
	Michael Romero (R)....................	102,730 (38%)	$135,305		
2016 Primary	Ben Ray Lujan (D)..................................	(100%)			

Prior winning percentages: 2014 (62%), 2012 (63%), 2010 (57%), 2008 (57%)

Democrat Ben Ray Luján, who was elected in 2008, has ascended in his party's ranks. In 2015, Minority Leader Nancy Pelosi selected him as chairman of the Democratic Congressional Campaign Committee. Democrats were mostly unhappy that they gained only six seats in 2016, but Lujan largely avoided the blame and he retained his position.

A seventh-generation New Mexican, Luján is the son of Ben Luján, a former state House speaker and legendary figure in state politics. The younger Luján has sought to establish his own niche by focusing on complex topics important to the state, especially energy and technology. He was born in Santa Fe and grew up on his family's farm, where he and his three siblings helped raise cattle, sheep and chickens. After graduating from high school, Luján worked as a card dealer in a casino while attending classes at New Mexico Highlands University. After he graduating, he had several state jobs, including deputy treasurer, and chief financial officer and director of administrative services at the Department of Cultural Affairs.

Luján launched into electoral politics in 2004, when he was elected to the New Mexico Public Regulation Commission, which regulates utilities, telecommunications, insurance and transportation. His fellow commissioners elected him chairman. The most pressing issue was the failure of Qwest Communications to invest a promised $788 million in its New Mexico communications network. Under Luján's leadership, the PRC ordered Qwest to invest in infrastructure or refund the money to customers. Qwest refused, and Democratic Gov. Bill Richardson advocated a settlement. But Luján and the PRC steadfastly rejected Qwest's settlement offer, opting instead to take the company to the New Mexico Supreme Court. In 2006, the court sided with the commission, and Qwest finally agreed to spend $270 million in the state over three years. He worked with other regulatory commissioners from the West to create regional solutions to climate change.

When Rep. Tom Udall gave up his House seat to run for the Senate, Luján courted the local Democratic establishment. New Mexico developer Donald Wiviott also ran. At the Democratic convention, Luján got 40% of the vote and Wiviott 30%; since both passed the 20% threshold, their names were on the primary ballot. Also on the ballot was Benny Shendo, former head of the New Mexico Indian Affairs Department. The primary race quickly turned negative. Wiviott ran ads claiming Luján's father had helped him secure his job as deputy state treasurer. Luján responded with ads claiming that Wiviott's Texas trailer parts company had been charged by the Federal Trade Commission with price-fixing. Shendo caused the race's biggest controversy when he implied at a candidate forum that Luján was gay. Shendo drew criticism from local gay rights groups.

Luján picked up endorsements from Richardson, local labor unions and the Sierra Club. Wiviott spent almost $1.6 million of his own money in the campaign; Luján spent less than $800,000, and won with 42% of the vote to Wiviott's 26%; Shendo got 16%. The general election was a foregone conclusion. Luján led Republican building contractor Daniel East, 57%-30%. He has not faced serious competition since.

Luján has a liberal voting record, but with some moderate strokes. He sided with northern New Mexico ranchers in 2011 in their fight against the U.S. Forest Service over reducing cattle-grazing allotments within the Santa Fe and Carson National Forests, a position that dismayed state environmental groups. Luján has pushed several bills aimed at preserving wilderness areas and settling some high-profile water rights disputes in his state. He has filed legislation to authorize additional money for victims of diseases caused by uranium mining and nuclear tests, many of whom are citizens of the Navajo nation. He supports the natural gas industry, which has a strong presence in the northwest Four Corners region.

On the Energy and Commerce Committee, he has a prominent perch from which to work on two of his pet causes: alternative energy and Los Alamos National Laboratory's non-nuclear weapons scientific research. He called for moving federal funding directly to the labs instead of through the Energy Department. In a 2015 speech to the New Mexico Legislature, Luján urged creation of a public-private consortium for the state's two national labs to bid on federal contracts. Earlier, he organized the bipartisan Technology Transfer Caucus to funnel research from the labs to the private sector. In 2016, his work on

Energy and Commerce included the far-ranging legislation that was enacted to treat and prevent opioid abuse, which had become a crisis in New Mexico.

Luján expressed interest in running for the open Senate seat in 2012. National Democrats made it clear that Rep. Martin Heinrich was their preferred choice. Luján stepped aside. In 2013, he became a chief deputy Democratic whip and was elected to the Hispanic Caucus's No. 2 post. He has used his leadership niches to seek immigration reform. He received his biggest reward following the 2014 election when, in a surprise move, Pelosi chose him to head the DCCC over higher-profile House Democrats who had advocated their case. His selection highlighted Democrats' continued outreach to progressives and Hispanics. Pelosi described Luján as "a dynamic and forward looking leader with fresh energy and ideas." He promised to go "on the offensive to put the majority in play."

But the 2016 campaign revealed little change in DCCC strategy and resulted in widespread disappointment. Democrats grumbled that Pelosi and her close team of operatives remained in control, that they failed to put enough House seats in play in a competitive cycle and that they ran cookie-cutter campaigns that failed to connect with voters, especially in swing states that were not in their favored coastal constituencies. Like the presidential campaign of Hillary Clinton, House Democrats fell short in reaching out to unhappy voters to whom Donald Trump appealed. Starting the cycle with their smallest number of seats since 1928, they regained only six House seats. In election post mortems, Democrats questioned and second-guessed the campaign strategy.

Luján acknowledged those shortcomings in a December 2016 letter to House Democrats. "We have honed in on critical improvements that can be made to form a more inclusive messaging strategy, the need for more member-driven recruitment, and an interest in setting up a regional structure to better tap the expertise of our members," he wrote. He gained another term at DCCC without opposition, and sought to harness the grass-roots anger toward Donald Trump. His first campaign test was the high-profile special election for the Atlanta-area seat that Republican Rep. Tom Price had vacated to join Trump's Cabinet.

Northern New Mexico: Santa Fe

Population		**Race and Ethnicity**		**Income**	
Total	691,255	White	38.4%	Median Income	$47,274 (298 out of 435)
Land area	44,959	Black	1.5%		
Pop/ sq mi	15.4	Latino	40.2%		
Born in state	56.2%	Asian	1.2%	Under $50,000	52.4%
Age Groups		Two races	1.7%	$50,000-$99,999	28.6%
Under 18	24.9%	Other	17.2%	$100,000-$199,999	15.7%
18-34	21.7%	**Education**		$200,000 or more	3.3%
35-64	38.6%	H.S grad or less	41.5%	Poverty Rate	20.2%
Over 64	14.8%	Some college	32.0%	**Health Insurance**	
Work		College Degree, 4 yr	14.7%	With health insurance coverage	82.1%
White Collar	36.9%	Post grad	11.9%		
Sales and Service	43.4%	**Military**		**Public Assistance**	
Blue Collar	19.7%	Veteran	10.3%	Cash public assistance income	2.4%
Government	23.6%	Active Duty	0.5%	Food stamp/SNAP benefits	14.3%

Voter Turnout			
2015 Total Citizens 18+	492,070	2016 House Turnout as % CVAP	56%
2016 House turnout	273,342	2014 House Turnout as % CVAP	37%

2012 Presidential Vote		
Barack Obama	155,983	(58%)
Mitt Romney	104,871	(39%)

2016 Presidential Vote		
Hillary Clinton	144,622	(52%)
Donald Trump	102,323	(37%)
Gary Johnson	24,871	(9%)

Cook Partisan Voting Index: D+8

"The dancing ground of the sun" is what the Pueblo Indians called the land of northern New Mexico, where the long vistas, dotted with low-lying scrub, are painted in pastel hues in the cold light and clear air. For 100 years, artists have been coming here, attracted by the scenery and by a unique civilization that is part Indian, part Anglo, part Spanish, and a little Mexican. (Northern New Mexico was under Mexican control from 1821-46.) The Indians were here first and built adobe pueblos, including some of the world's earliest apartment buildings. The Spanish conquistadors and priests brought the Catholic religion, the baroque architectural accents, and the Spanish language. The Palace of the Governors, built in Santa Fe in 1610, is now a museum on Santa Fe's Plaza and is the nation's oldest extant public building. Zoning laws vigorously enforce the height and adobe-like appearance of buildings in the historic district.

Along the back roads in Rio Arriba or Taos counties, one can find a religion that mixes Catholicism with adaptations of Indian festivals, buildings not that much different from the old pueblos, and a standard of living reminiscent of the Indian past, sometimes punctuated by high rates of drug abuse and alcoholism. It's quite a contrast with the ski lodges in the Taos Valley, the high-security research facilities of Los Alamos-which has the second-highest median income of any city in the nation (behind Washington D.C.) and has among the most PhDs per capita, thanks to Los Alamos National Laboratory-and the affluent, bohemian lifestyles of modern-day Santa Fe.

The 3rd Congressional District of New Mexico contains most of the state's historic Spanish-speaking and Indian regions. This district, similar in size to Pennsylvania though smaller than New Mexico's 2nd District to the south, runs from the High Plains along the Texas border, past the haunting Sangre de Cristo Mountains, through the vast ridges and isolated buttes in the center, to the windy and dusty desert-like plains. With 94,000 residents, Rio Rancho began as a retirement community in the 1960s and has become the district's most populous city. But the artsy state capital of Santa Fe, which has the most museums of any city in the nation except New York, remains its most lively and dominant. The economy in Santa Fe has remained strong, though it has been a "gray" growth as the number of persons 65 and older has come close to surpassing those 18 and younger. The district's Hispanic population is 41%, the lowest of the state's three districts. Another 18% of the population is Indian, the highest in the state. Concentrated in and around the Navajo reservation in the west, many of the district's Indians live in abject poverty.

The politics of northern New Mexico have been unique. For years, votes were bartered in Spanish by Republicans and Democrats, often cynically, sometimes corruptly. Loyalties ran to families and communities more than to principles or parties. Those traditions evolved. Hispanics and Indians are solidly Democratic. In Santa Fe and Taos, the upscale and many elderly migrants have produced a strong liberal tilt, and the 3rd District leans strongly Democratic. In 2016, Hillary Clinton took the district, 52%-37%.

★ NEW YORK ★

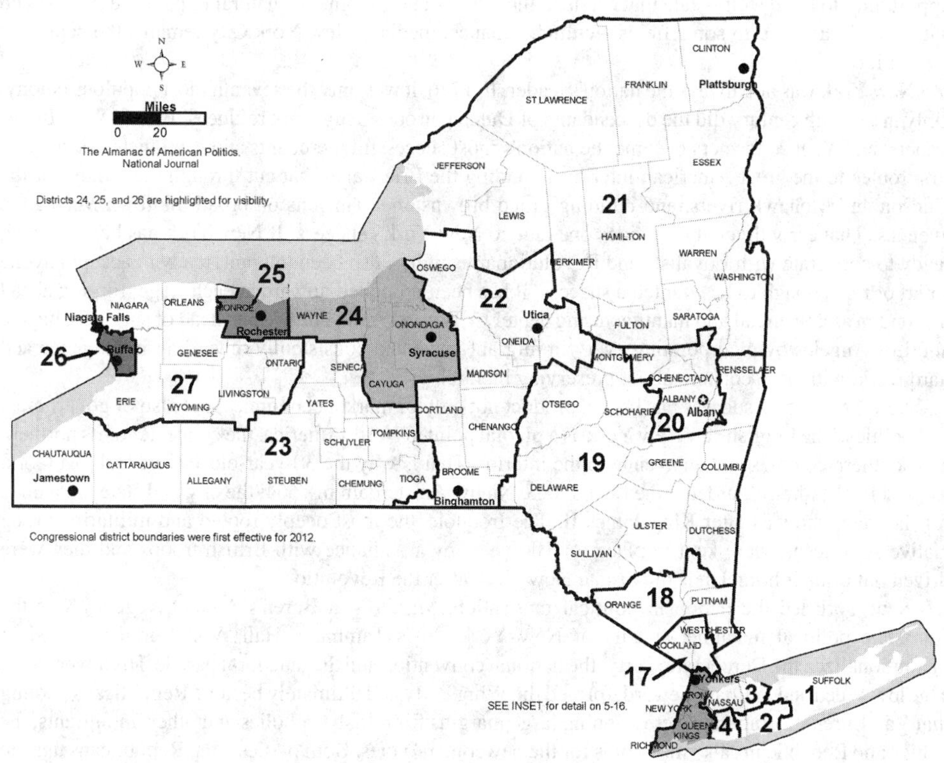
N
W
E
S
Miles
0
20
The Almanac of American Politics.
National Journal
Districts 24, 25, and 26 are highlighted for visibility.
CLINTON
Plattsburgh
FRANKLIN
ST LAWRENCE
JEFFERSON
ESSEX
21
LEWIS
HAMILTON
WARREN
WASHINGTON
OSWEGO
HERKIMER
25
22
NIAGARA
ORLEANS
MONROE
Niagara Falls
Rochester
WAYNE
24
ONONDAGA
Utica
SARATOGA
FULTON
ONEIDA
Syracuse
26
Buffalo
GENESEE
ONTARIO
SENECA
MADISON
MONTGOMERY
SCHENECTADY
RENSSELAER
CAYUGA
27
ERIE
LIVINGSTON
WYOMING
YATES
CORTLAND
OTSEGO
SCHOHARIE
ALBANY
Albany
20
TOMPKINS
CHENANGO
CHAUTAUQUA
23
SCHUYLER
19
CATTARAUGUS
GREENE
COLUMBIA
Jamestown
ALLEGANY
STEUBEN
CHEMUNG
TIOGA
BROOME
DELAWARE
Binghamton
ULSTER
DUTCHESS
Congressional district boundaries were first effective for 2012.
SULLIVAN
18
ORANGE
PUTNAM
WESTCHESTER
ROCKLAND
17
Yonkers
SUFFOLK
3
1
SEE INSET for detail on 5-16.
BRONX
NASSAU
NEW YORK
4
2
QUEENS
KINGS
RICHMOND

New York may no longer be the giant among states it once was, but it still packs plenty of heft in American politics. Its governor, Andrew Cuomo, has long been considered presidential timber; its senior U.S. senator, Charles Schumer, is his party's minority leader; and its junior senator, Kirsten Gillibrand, is a potential future presidential hopeful. Until Justice Antonin Scalia's death, four Supreme Court justices hailed from New York City. And the newly elected President of the United States, Donald Trump, lived in a luxury skyscraper in midtown Manhattan.

"Even old New York was once *Nieuw Amsterdam*," the old song goes. Today's New York - America's largest city, financial capital, artistic and media center, and largest immigrant destination - seems far removed from once tiny, rough-hewn *Nieuw Amsterdam*. But this is a city with a certain enduring character that goes back to its birth. Less than 2 percent of today's New Yorkers are descended from the Dutch of *Nieuw Amsterdam*, but the character of the place, including its tolerance, endures in daily life and in its great institutions and helps explain its miraculous growth. Combine Amsterdam and America, Dutch character with British-born political freedoms and American military strength, and you have the opportunity to build a city-state that can lead the world - and become the natural target of terrorists who hate that civilization. In some fields – culture, finance, media -- New York City remains the capital of the world.

New York was not always the nation's leader. In 1776, it was only the seventh most populous colony. Only in the 19th century did the descendants of Dutch patroons, Huguenot refugees, British West Indies traders, and Yankee farmers become the nation's most successful merchants and capitalists, forging the first routes to the great American interior, including the Erie Canal that cut through the valleys of the Hudson and Mohawk rivers, and building grand brownstone mansions on broad midtown Manhattan avenues. That early diversity provides one clue to New York's success. If New York has been cynical, ready to cooperate with Loyalists and Revolutionaries, it has also been tolerant, ready to accept anyone smart or rich enough to be counted a success. It has been propelled upward at each stage, forging ahead of London as a financial and manufacturing center by World War I and staying ahead of surging Chicago and Los Angeles by incorporating every immigrant wave and consistently rewarding intelligence and hard work, with little concern about preserving hierarchies.

New York state's success has been a product not only of market economics, but also of government and politics. The English saw New York as a pivotal point in North America, the connecter of its northern and southern colonies and an avenue to the interior. That is why the 30-year-old James, Duke of York, as Lord High Admiral, ordered the fleet to take Nieuw Amsterdam in 1664; the city and state are named for the man who was later King James II. The Iroquois, the most deeply rooted and militarily strong Native Americans, were kept in place for 100 years by an alliance with British troops and then were driven out of their homelands in Upstate New York after the Revolution.

New York led the nation in political innovation. Martin Van Buren's Albany Regency was the first state political machine, an ally of New York City's Tammany Hall. Van Buren invented or institutionalized the Democratic Party, the national convention and the inaugural parade. His adversaries, Thurlow Weed and William Seward, formed the Whig Party and ultimately became Republicans. Noting that Van Buren's Democrats were winning large margins from Irish Catholics and other immigrants, the Whigs and Republicans also made bids for the newcomers' votes. Both parties – the Republicans upstate and the Democrats downstate -- served the function of mediating between the divergent interests of the urban masses and the farmers and burghers upstate. This conflict is still evident in New York -- city and country, immigrant and native, Catholic and Protestant, the Big Apple and the apple-knockers.

Both parties also worked to protect New Yorkers against the untrammeled workings of free economic and political markets. Tammany Democrats embarked on an unprecedented, labor-intensive campaign to build infrastructure - the bridges and tunnels that made Greater New York possible. The tradition carried on from the time of Mayor Abram Hewitt, elected in 1886 over the single-taxer Henry George and the 27-year-old Theodore Roosevelt, up through the time of Gov. Al Smith in the 1920s and his protégé Robert Moses, who built bridges, tunnels, highways, beaches and the World's Fairs of 1939 and 1964, laying the groundwork for modern-day New York City but also embedding infrastructure with a more mixed legacy for urban planning and the environment. Progressive Republicans, from Theodore Roosevelt through Elihu Root and Henry Stimson, worked to create civil service laws and bureaucratized purchasing and spending to protect taxpayers from corrupt party machines. The Democratic Tammany machine led by Charles F. Murphy and the talented young men he advanced, Smith and Robert Wagner, responded to the shocking 1911 Triangle Shirtwaist fire - when hundreds of women jumped 11 floors to their death because fire escapes were blocked - by passing labor and safety laws. The results included minimum wages, maximum work hours, working-condition regulations, encouragement of unions and state-owned electric utilities - the prototype of the New Deal. In later years, New York pioneered public housing and fair housing laws, industry-wide unions (in the garment trades), rent control and dairy price controls to help both New York City tenants and Upstate farmers.

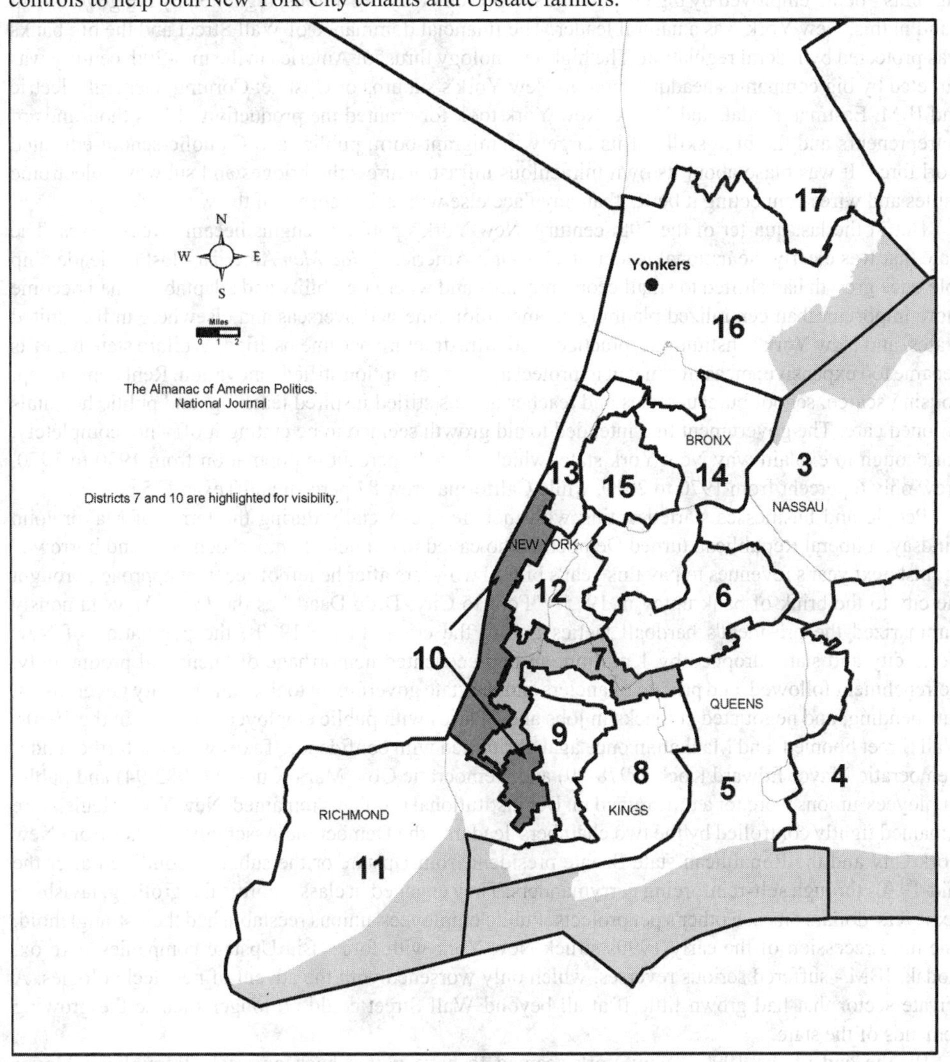

Congressional district boundaries were first effective for 2012.

Statewide elections were exceedingly close, with Democrats carrying the New York City Catholic vote and Republicans winning Upstate Protestants. Swing votes were cast by more than 1 million Jewish immigrants, who supported a generous welfare state but mistrusted the Tammany machine and valued civil rights. The politician who combined these appeals most cannily was Fiorello LaGuardia, a nominal Republican but almost a socialist, an Episcopalian who was half Jewish as well as Italian, and the man who, as mayor of New York City from 1933 to 1945, built much of the public housing and many of the civic monuments that still stand. Incensed that New York had no airport, he built what is now LaGuardia within a year. Both parties produced politicians whose positions appealed to these swing voters. At a time when the national media was much more concentrated in Manhattan than in Washington, D.C., many became nationally prominent and often presidential candidates: Democrats

Smith, Wagner, Franklin D. Roosevelt and Averell Harriman; Republicans Thomas Dewey, Wendell Willkie and Nelson Rockefeller. Dwight Eisenhower, then president of Columbia University, was a New Yorker when he won the presidency in 1952.

The polity that these men built was productive, generous, tolerant and closely regulated, in large part because its roaring economy allowed it to be. The country was becoming accustomed to working in big units - being employed by big corporations, represented by big unions, regulated by big government - and in this, New York was a natural leader. The financial dominance of Wall Street and the big banks was protected by federal regulation. The high-technology thrust of America in the mid-20th century was directed by big companies headquartered in New York's suburbs or Upstate: Corning, General Electric and IBM, Eastman Kodak and Xerox. New York took for granted the productivity of its thousands of entrepreneurs and the high skills of its largely immigrant-born, public- and Catholic-school-educated workforce. It was blasé about its own miraculous infrastructure - the bridges and subways, electronic cables and wires connecting it better than anyplace else with every corner of the world.

But in the last quarter of the 20th century, New York's public strengths became weaknesses. The state that was clearly the national leader of a big-unit America - *Mad Men* America - lost the leadership role once growth had shifted to small economic units and where flexibility and adaptability had become more important than centralized planning. Competition emerged overseas and elsewhere in the United States, and New York's institutions, practices and infrastructure became ossified. Welfare state benefits became too expensive; measures meant to protect against corruption stifled innovation. Rent control kept housing scarce, school bureaucracies and teacher unions stifled inspired teaching, and public hospitals rationed care. The government that intended to aid growth seemed to be cutting it off - not completely, but enough to explain why New York state, which grew 45 percent in population from 1930 to 1970, grew only 6 percent from 1970 to 2010, while California grew 87 percent and Texas 125 percent.

People and businesses started voting with their feet, especially during the terms of Mayor John Lindsay, a liberal Republican turned Democrat who caved to municipal unions' demands and borrowed against next year's revenues to pay this year's bills. Two years after he left office, that approach brought the city to the brink of bankruptcy in 1975 - "Ford to City: Drop Dead," as the *Daily News* famously summarized the president's hardball tactics during the crisis. In the 1970s, the population of New York, city and state, dropped by 1 million, an unprecedented hemorrhage of talent and productivity. Retrenchment followed, and private financiers and the state government took control of city government, cut spending, and negotiated cutbacks in jobs and salaries with public employees' unions. In the 1980s, Wall Street boomed, and Manhattan once again brimmed with confidence. Taxes were cut further under Democratic Mayor Edward Koch (1978-89) and Democratic Gov. Mario Cuomo (1982-94) and public employees' unions were for a time reined in. But institutional problems remained. New York's legislature remained tightly controlled by the two chambers' leaders - the Democratic Assembly speaker from New York City and the Republican state Senate president from Upstate or the suburbs, solidified after the mid-1970s through self-reinforcing gerrymanders. They engaged in classic political logrolling, lavishing taxpayers' dollars on each other's pet projects. Public employees' unions reestablished their stranglehold. The mild recession of the early 1990s struck New York with force. Big Upstate companies - Xerox, Kodak, IBM - suffered serious reverses, which only worsened with the advent of new technologies. A private sector that had grown little if at all beyond Wall Street could no longer finance the growing demands of the state.

By the end of the 1990s, New York seemed to have gotten back on track. Republican Mayor Rudolph Giuliani, first elected in 1993, cut crime and welfare rolls in half and cut hard deals with the unions, though with a swagger that was polarizing. Republican Gov. George Pataki, first elected in 1994, imposed huge tax and spending cuts in 1995. Wall Street and the financial services industry boomed in the late 1990s, to the point that the jobs lost in the early-1990s recession were replaced. Then came September 11, 2001.

It was a beautiful late-summer morning, the sunshine lighting a blue sky above the skyscrapers of Manhattan, commuters hurrying through the streets and subways to work. At 8:46 a.m., the first plane hit the North Tower of the World Trade Center. When the second plane hit the South Tower 17 minutes later, it was clear that America was under attack, at war, even as office workers fled the burning buildings and New York firefighters streamed in. The terrorists had chosen to attack the seat of government in Washington - the Pentagon and a second target saved by the heroes of United Flight 93 - and the seat of commerce in New York to inflict the maximum possible damage. The people of New York, like those at the Pentagon and on United 93, responded with courage and determination. Firefighters, police officers, and rescue workers risked death to help others. Strangers helped strangers. People who had no experience with disaster figured out how to cope and help others. Millions volunteered to give blood, send money, and provide food and supplies. In less than a week, the New York Stock Exchange reopened.

Giuliani and Pataki performed well in the national spotlight. But New York faced an economic downturn and a turn in the course of government. Despite heroic efforts at recovery, Manhattan and New York lost 200,000 jobs in 2001 and 2002. Downtown real estate values tumbled as financial services firms decentralized and sought office space elsewhere. Giuliani was term-limited, and all the leading contestants were well to his left. Media billionaire Michael Bloomberg, previously a Democrat, became a Republican and spent $70 million of his own money on his way to victory. The financial industry boomed as never before, generating revenues far beyond expectations - until the underlying driver of the boom, mortgage-backed securities, imploded in September 2008, with repercussions internationally, nationally and locally.

In the first decade of the 21st century, when Bloomberg won a third term, New York City's economy grew largely because of the boom in financial services, while its population growth was fueled almost entirely by immigration. The city's population grew 2 percent from 2000 to 2010, to nearly 8.2 million, and the four close-in suburban counties grew 3 percent. But this small change masked much greater movements. The elderly moved out, heading to Florida and other warmer climes, and middle-income workers and young blue-collar workers headed to lower-cost and lower-tax states like the Carolinas, Georgia and Florida. Moving in, meanwhile, were immigrants who streamed into outer-borough neighborhoods and created new businesses, churches, and neighborhood institutions - Afro-Caribbeans in Flatbush; Chinese in Flushing, Borough Park, and on Staten Island; Colombians and Mexicans in Corona; Pakistanis and Bangladeshis in Jackson Heights; Greeks in Astoria; Russians in Brighton Beach; and Dominicans in Washington Heights and much of the Bronx. At the same time, the city's black population declined; Hispanics now outnumber blacks in every borough except Brooklyn. More than one-quarter of the residents of Queens are Asians; nationally, New York state ranks fourth for its percentage of Asian residents.

Today's immigrants are arriving in a different sort of city. New York has long since lost most of its manufacturing jobs, and many corporate headquarters have moved elsewhere. The financial-services industry pays enormous salaries and bonuses to those at the very top and generates service jobs for those who tend to the needs of the rich. But finance was sent reeling by the meltdown of 2008, and although it has rebounded, it's not clear whether the cornucopia will be as bounteous as before. Wall Street firms cut jobs by 8 percent between 2007 and 2015 even as other private industries were growing, and for a quarter century, New York City has been bleeding finance-sector jobs to other states, including Texas and Pennsylvania. Statewide unemployment peaked at 8.9 percent in 2009 and, after a dip, rose again to 8.7 percent in 2012; by late 2016, it was back down to 4.6 percent, right around the national average. The outer boroughs, particularly Brooklyn, started to experience a revival during the Bloomberg years, as artisanal-minded, latte-swilling hipsters helped gentrify older neighborhoods; these areas became iconic through HBO's *Girls* and other depictions in the media. Hillary Clinton ran her 2016 presidential campaign from Brooklyn. The liberal drift was made clear by the 2013 mayoral victory of Bill de Blasio to succeed Bloomberg as mayor. It came amid slackening support for Bloomberg's anti-crime stop-and-frisk policy, particularly among minorities most at risk from the strategy. Questions about the death of Eric Garner, a black man in Staten Island, after being put in a police chokehold on July 17, 2014, raised tensions over policing; the tensions were only intensified after the claimed revenge killing of NYPD officers Wenjian Liu and Rafael Ramos later that year.

In the suburbs, the problems stemmed from having much higher property taxes than those in the city. The high property taxes are in effect tuition to good suburban school districts -- New York spends more per pupil than any other state, at about 85 percent above the national average -- but the burden becomes heavy when the kids go off to college. Places like Levittown, buzzing with young families moving from Brooklyn in the 1950s, aged and lost population. Immigrant communities coalesced in low-income suburbs whose first residents had departed. But New York's suburbs have not necessarily been attractive to new businesses - the hedge-fund sector bloomed across the state line in Greenwich, Connecticut.

Upstate New York, despite some successes in agricultural products such as Greek yogurt, has even deeper problems. Medicaid mandates have forced Upstate counties to drastically raise property taxes, which now rank as the nation's highest compared to property values. Large, formerly paternalistic companies have been shedding jobs. Buffalo, once one of the nation's great steel producers, has become a center for the debt-collection industry. Since the 2010 census, the state as a whole has seen 2 percent population growth, but it was bifurcated -- up by a healthy 4.6 percent in New York City and by less than 1 percent elsewhere. In this decade, both Upstate and the city have been dealt blows by the elements. In August 2011, Hurricane Irene came roaring through Upstate New York, causing record flooding and damage. And in late October 2012, superstorm Sandy - not technically a hurricane - struck the beaches of New Jersey, New York City and Long Island. Houses were smashed and swept away on the Rockaway Peninsula, and subway tunnels were flooded. A major electric power station blew, leaving Manhattan below 34th Street without power for days. On Staten Island, thousands remained homeless for weeks, and the rebuilding effort dragged on and on.

In races for statewide office, New York has been voting heavily Democratic in recent years. The Republican Party remains a factor only in the state Senate, which the GOP controlled from 1965 to 2008, in part because the heavily Democratic Assembly and the Senate Republicans agreed to draw their own chamber's district lines. Republicans won the majority back in 2010 and, have generally controlled the chamber through a shifting series of alliances with renegade Democrats. Albany's long-festering problems with ethics and corruption have come to a head in recent years. Eliot Spitzer, elected governor in 2006, visited high-end prostitutes, got caught and resigned; his successor, David Paterson, had such low job approval ratings that he decided not to seek a full term. During their tenures, the state Senate was often laid low by power plays and petty maneuverings, often by lawmakers just one step ahead of legal or ethics problems. Various observers called Albany the most dysfunctional state government in America.

The election of Cuomo in 2010 represented a turn toward improved political stability and stronger public support. Cuomo earned the gratitude of liberals by securing the legalization of same-sex marriage, including decisive votes from Republican state senators, while appealing to moderates with a more conservative approach on fiscal issues. But longtime power players in both chambers - Assembly Speaker Sheldon Silver, a Democrat, and Senate Majority Leader Dean Skelos, a Republican - were indicted on separate federal corruption charges and convicted, pending appeals.

In the 2016 presidential election, Clinton won New York state easily, though with a margin a few percentage points smaller than Obama's four years earlier. Both Clinton and Trump improved their party's performance in the state: Clinton secured 70,000 more votes than Obama had in 2012,while Trump won about 329,000 more votes than Mitt Romney had. Trump won 19 counties that had voted for Obama in 2012, and in some of them, the shifts were massive. Franklin (on the Canadian border) and Oswego (along Lake Ontario) both shifted by more than 30 points towards the GOP. Five other counties shifted between 20 and 29 points, while another nine shifted between 10 and 19 points, including Niagara (Niagara Falls), Orange (Newburgh), Rensselaer (Troy), and Staten Island. Even many counties that remained blue between 2012 and 2016 saw diminished Democratic margins, although the Democratic margin of victory in the affluent suburb of Westchester County did increase significantly, from 25 points to 34 points. Clinton improved the Democratic vote haul in the five boroughs by 169,000, on Long Island by 29,000 and in Westchester by 32,000, but her vote totals in every other part of the state fell by a cumulative 161,000. Trump, meanwhile, increased the number of GOP votes by 128,000 in Staten Island, Nassau and Suffolk alone, and by 182,000 outside the City, Long Island and Westchester.

The election results illustrated the growing split between metro and rural areas. The cumulative share of Democratic votes from New York City, Long Island and Westchester increased from 63 percent in 2012 to 67 percent in 2016. "While the geographic reach of the Trump vote looks impressive on a map," wrote the *National Review's* Dan McLaughlin, "the parts of the state he dominated are outnumbered and dying, and with them the competitiveness of Republicans in New York for the foreseeable future."

Population		Race and Ethnicity		Income	
Total	19,673,174	White	56.8%	Median Income	$59,269 (15 out of 50)
Land area	47,126	Black	14.4%		
Pop/ sq mi	417.5	Latino	18.4%	Under $50,000	43.3%
Born in state	63.4%	Asian	7.9%	$50,000-$99,999	28.3%
		Two races	1.7%	$100,000-$199,999	20.9%
Age Groups		Other	0.7%	$200,000 or more	7.5%
Under 18	21.6%			Poverty Rate	15.7%
18-34	24.4%	**Education**			
35-64	39.7%	H.S grad or less	41.1%	**Health Insurance**	
Over 64	14.3%	Some college	24.7%	With health insurance coverage	90.3%
		College Degree, 4 yr	19.4%		
Work		Post grad	14.8%		
White Collar	39.2%			**Public Assistance**	
Sales and Service	44.1%	**Military**		Cash public assistance income	3.4%
Blue Collar	16.8%	Veteran	5.4%		
Government	15.6%	Active Duty	0.1%	Food stamp/SNAP benefits	15.4%

Voter Turnout			
2015 Total Citizens 18+	13,531,404	2016 Pres Turnout as % CVAP	57%
2016 Pres Votes	7,721,453	2012 Pres Turnout as % CVAP	54%

Legislature	
Senate:	31R, 23D, 8I.Dems, 1I
House:	105D, 44R, 1I, 2V

Presidential Politics

2016 Democratic Primary		
Hillary Clinton (D)	1,133,980	(58%)
Bernie Sanders (D)	820,256	(42%)
2016 Republican Primary		
Donald Trump (R)	554,522	(60%)
John Kasich (R)	231,166	(25%)
Ted Cruz (R)	136,083	(15%)

2016 Presidential Vote		
Hillary Clinton (D)	4,556,142	(59%)
Donald Trump (R)	2,819,557	(37%)
Gary Johnson (L)	176,600	(2%)
2012 Presidential Vote		
Barack Obama (D)	4,485,741	(63%)
Mitt Romney (R)	2,490,431	(35%)

With two New Yorkers as the major party nominees in 2016 - the first time that had happened since 1944 when Franklin D. Roosevelt faced Thomas E. Dewey - it's not surprising that the Empire State saw a jump in turnout of about 10 percent. Nonetheless, the state was largely an afterthought in the general election. In the first half of the 20th century, New York was the dominant state in presidential politics. It had the most electoral votes, and of all the large states, it was usually the most evenly divided between the two parties. Dewey, then the GOP governor, came within five percentage points of FDR in 1944. He would carry the state four years later against Harry Truman. But in the 21st century, New York has seen its Electoral College clout drop from 33 in 2000 to 29 in 2016 - tied with Florida (and likely to trail the Sunshine State after the 2020 reapportionment) - while becoming a heavily Democratic large state. In 1988, Republican George H.W. Bush was beaten by only 52%-48%.

In the past six elections, Democratic presidential nominees have won 59%, 60%, 58%, 63%, 63% and 59% of New York's votes. How did this Democratic dominance come to pass? One reason is that Jewish voters, who did not identify strongly with either major party in the first half of the 20th century, became strong Democrats in the second. Increases in the percentages of black, Hispanic and Asian voters also raised the Democratic percentage. White Catholic voters took conservative positions on cultural issues like crime in the 1970s and 1980s, but today, these voters and their descendants are more likely to take liberal stands on cultural issues such as gun control, abortion and gay rights. Republican allegiance in the New York City suburbs - on Long Island and in the upscale commuter towns of Rockland and Westchester counties - faded away starting in 1992. In 2012, the only county in the New York City metropolitan area that was still casting its ballots for GOP presidential hopefuls was tiny Putnam.

Hillary Clinton defeated Donald Trump, 59%-37%, but the Republican managed to win back some old GOP turf. Trump captured Suffolk County; the first time a Republican carried that suburban enclave since President Bush in 1992. In the Hudson River Valley, Trump won back exurban Orange County, as well as Rensselaer and Saratoga. Upstate, he won blue-collar Oswego, Niagara -- which includes suburbs of Buffalo -- and several other rural central New York counties. But that couldn't offset Clinton's huge advantage in New York City, where she lost only the Borough of Staten Island.

Typically, the New York Republican presidential primary draws little attention. In 2008, John McCain beat Mitt Romney 52%-28%, carrying every county and congressional district. In 2012, New York did not vote until May 24, when the GOP race was effectively over. Turnout was an exceptionally low 189,000, and Romney won with 63 percent of the vote. In 2016, Texas Sen. Ted Cruz wooed Orthodox Jewish voters in Brooklyn, but Trump reminded his home state that the Texan had once disparaged "New York values," in a presidential debate. Ohio Gov. John Kasich repeatedly indulged in deli cuisine in the Big Apple. But Trump easily won the April 19 GOP primary, swamping Kasich 60%-25%, winning 61 of the state's 62 counties. Kasich won Manhattan where Trump resides, but only by some 1,000 votes. The victory restored Trump's momentum, which had taken a slight hit with a loss in the Wisconsin primary two weeks earlier. From this convincing victory, Trump's march to the GOP nomination was virtually unimpeded.

The Democratic race was an equally important moment for Clinton. In the run-up to New York, she had lost one primary (Wisconsin) and four caucuses to Vermont Sen. Bernie Sanders. Clinton had easily captured the 2008 Democratic presidential primary over Barack Obama, 57%-40%, carrying 26 of the 29 congressional districts. Still, Sanders was a native of Brooklyn, many of state's Democratic primary voters are die-hard liberals, and the rough-and-tumble tabloid media culture of New York City can throw even experienced candidates off stride. But it was Sanders who ran into a political buzz saw. First, an editorial board interview with the *New York Daily News* went poorly and Sanders offered few details on how he planned to break up the big banks on Wall Street, one of his signature issues. Then Sanders blasted Clinton on whether she was qualified to serve as president, a charge that seemed implausible to many New Yorkers who had elected her to the Senate twice. Reporters repeatedly forced Sanders to defend his assertion; he eventually backed off of it. Sanders predicted he would win the New York primary and then days before the balloting he flew off to Rome to attend a conference at the Vatican and score a brief meeting with Pope Francis. Clinton campaigned as a confident veteran with the support of the entire New York Democratic establishment and handily defeated Sanders 58%-42%, even though the Vermonter had outspent her on television advertising. Turnout was just shy of 2 million, eclipsing the previous record of 1.9 million in 2008. Clinton won 21 of the state's 27 congressional districts, losing six relatively rural ones upstate.

Congressional Districts

115th Congress Lineup	9R 18D	**114th Congress Lineup**	9R 18D

When John F. Kennedy was elected president in 1960, New York elected 43 members, California 30, and Florida eight. In 2012, New York and Florida each elected 27 members and California 53. Texas has been the largest-growing state, with 36 seats. Reapportionment has been carnage time for New York: the state lost five districts in the 1980 census, three in 1990, and two each in 2000 and 2010. In 2022, it's a virtual certainty that Florida will gain at least one seat and New York will lose another one, cementing its status as the fourth-largest state.

New York has more than 200 state legislators, but legislative decisions have been made by three power brokers: the state Senate president, Assembly speaker, and a veto-wielding governor. Traditionally, the trio starts crafting a redistricting deal only when courts threaten to take over the process, and House incumbents have no choice but to hire expensive and well-wired Albany lobbyists to preserve their seats. In 2012, Democrats held the governorship and state Assembly, but Republicans clung to a tiny majority in the state Senate. New York needed to trim two seats, and this time it was clear Upstate and Downstate would split the loss. But the "old way" of deal-cutting hit two snags. First, Democratic Gov. Andrew Cuomo, along with late New York City Mayor Ed Koch, had made major redistricting reform a signature issue. In 2010, Cuomo threatened to "veto any redistricting plan in 2012 that reflects partisan gerrymandering." Second, in January 2012, a federal court ruled New York would need to move up its federal primary from September to June to prevent disenfranchisement of overseas voters, further compressing the tortoise-like legislature's timeline.

Republican state Senate President Dean Skelos cleverly responded to Cuomo and Koch's entreaties for a nonpartisan commission by gaining Senate passage of a constitutional amendment creating one - in time for 2020. As the partisan deadlock continued, a federal three-judge panel appointed U.S. Magistrate Judge Roanne Mann as special master in charge of implementing a map should the legislature fail. Mann released her proposal, drawn up by hired consultant and law professor Nathaniel Persily, which morphed the state's 29 existing contorted districts into 27 geographically compact seats. In a past era, indignant House incumbents might have browbeaten the legislature into halting such a rearrangement. But in 2012, the court map was largely met with reluctant acceptance. The plan even-handedly eliminated retiring Democrat Maurice Hinchey's Upstate seat and the Queens seat of Republican special election winner Bob Turner, who hadn't expected to win reelection anyway. In November 2012, Democrats netted a single seat: Republican freshmen in Syracuse and the Hudson Valley lost their seats, but Democrat Kathy Hochul also lost after her Western New York district was made more Republican. Five other incumbents - three Republicans and two Democrats - survived by less than 6 percentage points.

Republicans have performed notably better since then and have taken three Democratic seats: one on the eastern end of Long Island, and two in the northeast region Upstate. That left the delegation with an 18-9 Democratic edge; Republicans held six of the nine House seats north of the New York City suburbs and two of the four Long Island seats east of the city. With the state's population lagging Upstate, that Republican advantage could turn against them when it comes time to eliminate a seat in redistricting. If a second district needs to be eliminated, it likely would come from the 18 current seats in Greater New York and Long Island.

Governor

Andrew Cuomo (D)

Elected 2010, term expires 2019, 2nd term; b. Dec. 6, 1957, Queens, NY; Fordham U., B.A. 1979; Albany Law Schl., J.D. 1982; Catholic; Divorced; 3 children.

Elected Office: NY Attorney General, 2006-2010.

Professional Career: Assistant District Attorney, Manhattan, 1984-1985; Practicing attorney, Blutrich Falcone & Miller, 1985-1988; Founder, Housing Enterprise for the Less Privileged, 1988-1993; Assistant Secretary, Department of Housing & Urban Development, 1993-1997; U.S Secretary, Department of Housing & Urban Development 1997-2001.

Office: Executive Chambers, Albany, 12224; 518-474-8390; Fax: 518-474-1513; Website: governor.ny.gov.

Election Results

Election	Name (Party)	Vote (%)
2014 General	Andrew Cuomo (D)	2,069,480 (54%)
	Rob Astorino (R)	1,536,879 (40%)
	Howie Hawkins (G)	184,419 (5%)
2014 Primary	Andrew Cuomo (D)	361,380 (63%)

Prior winning percentage: 2010 (63%)

Democrat Andrew Cuomo was elected governor in 2010 and rapidly piled up a record of accomplishments that, along with soaring approval ratings, led many to wonder if he would compete for the White House. Cuomo is a former state attorney general and secretary of the U.S. Department of Housing and Urban Development – an atypical path to governor in the state -- and he is the son of the late three-term Gov. Mario Cuomo. He won reelection in 2014, but his star dimmed somewhat, especially among liberals, casting further doubt about whether he might someday run for president.

Cuomo was born in Queens and grew up in the middle-class neighborhood of Hollis, the second of five siblings. At the time, his father was a lawyer in Brooklyn who assisted journalists such as Pete Hamill and the late Jimmy Breslin and Jack Newfield in exposing and addressing injustices on city issues such as housing policy. The younger Cuomo showed an early aptitude for repairing and building automobiles. "If Andrew gets a car, it's about (him) making the car," his brother Chris Cuomo, a journalist for CNN, told *Esquire*. "It's really a metaphor for what he does in government - he does it himself, he fixes things." He graduated from Fordham University in 1979, one year after his father was elected lieutenant governor, and from Albany Law School in 1982.

He began working for his father's campaign for governor that year and received credit for masterminding his come-from-behind primary victory against popular New York City Mayor Ed Koch. However, some critics said the younger Cuomo was too willing to engage in dirty politics. "Andrew Cuomo was his father's id, aggressive where Mario was cerebral - the muscle that helped win Mario three terms as governor of New York," as *New York* magazine put it. He spent several years as an aide to his father, working for $1 a year, as the governor's national profile skyrocketed in the wake of his eloquent – and ineffective -- denunciation of President Ronald Reagan's policies as keynote speaker at the 1984 Democratic National Convention.

After a short stint in the Manhattan district attorney's office, Cuomo in 1986 founded the Housing Enterprise for the Less Privileged (HELP USA), a nonprofit organization dedicated to helping the homeless. He left his private law practice in 1989 to run the group, which became a national model for its formula of offering shelter but also job training, education, drug treatment and other assistance. Two years later, he married Kerry Kennedy, the daughter of Robert F. Kennedy, in a widely publicized union that was described as a merger of two Democratic political dynasties.

Cuomo's work at HELP caught the attention of Arkansas Gov. Bill Clinton, who asked Cuomo to serve on his transition team after being elected president in 1992 and then as assistant secretary of community planning and development at HUD. After Clinton's reelection in 1996, Cuomo took over as secretary of the department. He won praise for his energetic efforts to make housing more affordable, but he also adopted policies to broaden home ownership for low-income Americans that contributed to the housing crisis a decade later. One of those policies was a dramatic rise in the number of loans that government-sponsored mortgage giants, Fannie Mae and Freddie Mac, were required to buy. HUD also produced rules that explicitly forbade imposing new reporting requirements on the two enterprises.

Cuomo returned to New York in 2001 with the intention of running for governor the following year. But he did himself in with some brash and ill-advised remarks. He said that Republican Gov. George Pataki had done little after 9/11 other than hold New York Mayor Rudy Giuliani's coat. He also angered African Americans who had been looking to State Comptroller Carl McCall as their party's "next in line" candidate. Cuomo dropped out of the race before the primary, and McCall lost to Pataki. Around the same time, Cuomo became engaged in a bitter public divorce and child custody battle with Kennedy.

Cuomo largely disappeared from the public eye for the next several years. In 2006, he came back to run for New York attorney general when the incumbent in that job, Eliot Spitzer, ran for governor. He patched up his differences with Democrats and won the primary with ease, then easily beat the Republican nominee, former Westchester District Attorney Jeanine Pirro, 58%-40%. He conducted investigations into alleged misdeeds within the financial industry, something that had propelled Spitzer to the governorship. At the same time, he looked into the student loan industry's allegedly deceptive marketing practices, uncovered fraud among health insurers, and crusaded against online child pornography. He also ended up investigating Spitzer for using the state police to gather information about then-state Senate Majority Leader Joseph Bruno. Cuomo's popularity rose.

When Spitzer resigned in disgrace in 2008 over revelations that he had been the client of a prostitution ring, Lt. Gov. David Paterson took over. He took some bold budget stands and inspired many with his ability to overcome blindness, but by March 2009, Paterson's job ratings were the lowest in state history. He eventually acceded to the demands of the Obama White House and decided not to run for a full term. In May 2010, Cuomo announced his candidacy, declaring the state had slipped from being a "national model" under his father to a "national disgrace." In the general election, Cuomo faced Carl Paladino, a real estate executive who self-funded his campaign. The New York tabloids dubbed Paladino "Crazy Carl" for his sometimes outrageous statements (he also became close to Donald Trump). Cuomo had little trouble rolling to a landslide 63%-33% victory.

Cuomo warned in his initial inaugural address that the state was spending too much and receiving too little in return. He promised that his fiscal plan would not involve new borrowing or higher income taxes, a stand that irked some state lawmakers. Just days before the March 31 deadline, he was able to strike a deal with the legislature's leaders on a $132.5 billion budget that reduced year-to-year spending by about 2 percent without raising taxes. He agreed to add $250 million for schools, education, human services, and prescription drugs for the elderly. News of the deal outraged New York City Mayor Michael Bloomberg, who said the cuts would disproportionately affect the city even though it was responsible for generating much of the state's revenue. The two men later reportedly settled their differences. Cuomo's efforts to win cooperation from unions - a problem confronting governors in many states - brought strong criticism from labor groups. The public, however, gave him high approval ratings, and he even won praise from Republican Sen. Mitch McConnell of Kentucky.

Cuomo was more liberal on issues beyond fiscal policy. He decided to use his political capital on an ambitious undertaking: legalizing same-sex marriage, which the state Senate had defeated two years earlier. He met with wealthy Republican campaign donors, asking them to insulate GOP senators from conservative attacks. To avoid infighting among gay rights activists, he had them merge into a single coalition and hire a consultant with ties to his office. He repeatedly assured wavering lawmakers that he had their back, and he successfully tamped down opposition from the Catholic Church. In the end, six senators who had voted against a legalization bill in 2009 voted for one in June 2011, including three Republicans, and New York became the largest state yet to permit such unions. Political commentators of all stripes said the governor's maneuvering was masterful, and national gay activists as well as prominent liberals began opening their wallets to him in gratitude. (Some of his Republican allies on the issue met an unhappier fate at the ballot box.) Other accomplishments followed, including the implementation of a 2 percent annual cap on property taxes, which were unpopular among local jurisdictions, and a rewrite of the state tax code in which the wealthy paid higher rates while middle-income earners saw theirs go down.

Cuomo entered 2012 with his highest job-approval rating as governor - 62 percent in the Siena poll, along with a 73 percent favorability rating. He did not shirk from another confrontation with public employee unions, proposing a teacher evaluation system and limiting pension benefits for future government workers. He was able to strike a deal the next month on evaluations that blocked positive ratings for teachers who failed to at least minimally boost their students' performance. And he won a new fund fueled by $1.2 billion in additional state and federal spending for infrastructure. His name began popping up on the early lists of 2016 presidential prospects; even his father stoked speculation at his 80th birthday party. In 2013, Cuomo called for raising New York's minimum wage, decriminalizing small amounts of marijuana, and a Women's Equality Act that would promote pay equity, outlaw pregnancy discrimination, and toughen human-trafficking laws. But the proposal that drew the most attention was his call for action on gun control in the wake of the Newtown, Connecticut, school massacre. He proposed tightening the definition of so-called assault weapons and lowering the maximum magazine capacity. He quickly got the legislation into law, which caused his job-approval rating to dip below 60 percent. While downstate Democrats remained in his corner, his support among Republicans, and voters Upstate generally, suffered.

Cuomo dealt with controversy over the Common Core educational standards in 2014. The standards, which were designed to improve classroom instruction, ran into substantial opposition from conservatives across the country - and from moderates in New York - who regarded them as being overly inflexible and intrusive. Cuomo acknowledged flaws in the implementation of Common Core and later struck a compromise with legislators to delay and restrict certain elements of the program, such as testing and teacher evaluations. He scoffed at de Blasio's call to impose a city tax on the rich to finance universal pre-kindergarten. The mayor eventually received $300 million from the state for the program, less than the $340 million he had sought, and the state adopted a number of provisions dealing with charter schools that de Blasio opposed.

But those controversies were overshadowed by an even larger one. *The New York Times* reported in July that his administration had sought to thwart the progress of the independent commission he had established to investigate corruption after the panel began delving into issues that involved him and his political supporters. Cuomo said he disbanded the panel when an ethics law was passed in March that strengthened anti-bribery laws and achieved roughly nine of its 10 goals. But the unmet goal, a system of publicly financed campaigns that cut off unlimited donations, was seen by the governor's critics as the most important. The episode helped Cuomo draw a Democratic primary challenge from Zephyr Teachout, a Fordham University law professor. *The Times* refused to endorse either candidate, calling Cuomo's failings and his rival's lack of experience equally dispiriting. "As he has repeatedly shown, Mr. Cuomo knows how to bend lawmakers to his will, especially when it serves his political interest," the newspaper said in an editorial. "But he has repeatedly failed to do so when it comes to cleaning up Albany." By the numbers, Cuomo prevailed easily, 63%-34%, but Teachout's showing was stronger than expected. In the general election against Westchester County Executive Rob Astorino, Cuomo used his 9-to-1 fundraising advantage to pull out a victory, but with just 54 percent, well below the 65 percent figure with which his father won a second term.

Observers saw a duality in Cuomo's first term: Substantive tactical achievements, undercut by political mistakes that led to sinking popularity. As *New York* magazine noted, Cuomo's first term had strong accomplishments on paper, including the gun restrictions and same-sex marriage law. "The state has gone from a $10 billion deficit in 2010 to a projected $6 billion surplus. He's restored functionality, if not total rationality, to a state government that had become a national embarrassment," including the passing of four on-time budgets and the state's highest credit rating in more than four decades. Yet Cuomo "underestimated the anger of the state's left wing" and, on the ethics issue, acted in ways that "fueled the perception that he views himself as above the democratic process."

In 2015, the legislative landscape experienced an earthquake, as Assembly Speaker Sheldon Silver, a Democrat, and Senate Majority Leader Dean Skelos, a Republican, were both arrested on federal corruption charges; ultimately, both were convicted. Cuomo's on-time budget streak ended (technically - the bill passed only three hours late) but it included key education provisions he backed, including tougher personnel rules for teachers and consequences for low-performing schools, as well as enhanced disclosure rules for state lawmakers. The liberal wing of his party bemoaned that the budget deal didn't include a minimum wage hike (Cuomo supported a $10.50 rate, smaller than the $15 many liberals wanted) and critics called the ethics reforms insufficient. Within weeks, Cuomo went around the Legislature to set in motion a minimum wage boost for fast-food workers, and he traveled to Havana to promote engagement and trade with Cuba.

The year also brought a string of personal and professional challenges. Cuomo's father died at 82, and the governor's girlfriend, Food Network cooking show host Sandra Lee, was diagnosed with breast cancer. (She was later declared cancer free.) Cuomo was on the hot seat after the escape of two murderers from the state prison at Dannemora, with the assistance of prison staff; it was a top-tier national story until one escapee was killed by police and the other was captured. Meanwhile, by summer, Cuomo was mired in a loud feud with de Blasio, with the mayor criticizing the governor for, among other things, his handling of public-housing funds and mayoral control of the city's public schools. "What we've often seen is if someone disagrees with him openly, some kind of revenge or vendetta follows," the mayor told the NY1 network; he even made a point of calling reporters into his office to tell them about their strained relationship. In 2015, a string of polls showed Cuomo's approval ratings falling into the low-to-mid 40s - record lows for his tenure. (Of cold comfort were the similarly weak ratings for de Blasio.)

In 2016, Cuomo faced criticism of Start-Up New York, an economic development program to give tax breaks to companies located near academic technology centers; it spent more than $50 million on marketing in its first two years but had created just 408 jobs. Under pressure from legislators and fiscal watchdogs, the program changed its name to the Excelsior Business Program and refocused on true start-up companies. Meanwhile, ethics reemerged as an issue in November 2016 when Joe Percoco, an aide to Cuomo, and Alain Kaloyeros, the former president of SUNY Polytechnic Institute, were indicted in an alleged bribery scheme; a lobbyist with ties to Percoco, Todd Howe, had decided to cooperate with prosecutors. As Cuomo prepared for an expected reelection campaign in 2018, he proposed college tuition assistance for low- and middle-income residents as well as tax cuts for middle-income taxpayers, though the funding mechanism, a three-year extension of a high-earner surtax, faced uncertainty in the state Senate. He also backed a second phase of his Buffalo Billion initiative, an economic-development effort to aid the Buffalo-Niagara area. His party's progressive wing, and even some establishment Democrats, urged Cuomo to become more active in corralling or ousting renegade Democrats who have provided the GOP with a working Senate majority for several sessions running, something he had traditionally stayed away from.

The election of Donald Trump as president offered a foil for Cuomo to win back some disgruntled progressives and a chance to move past his feuding with de Blasio by facing down a common enemy. In the wake of Trump's election, Cuomo established an emergency call-in network to report alleged bias crimes. The two men "now seem to be elevating their longstanding rivalry to one for the role of progressive opponent in chief," wrote the *New York Times'* Ginia Bellafante. By early 2017, Cuomo looked like a favorite to win a third term, barring a primary challenge from a high-profile opponent such as Attorney General Eric Schneiderman or state Comptroller Thomas DiNapoli. Any serious shot at the presidency two years later, however, would likely require a victory margin more like his first election than his second – something that, a little more than two years from Election Day, looked conceivable but unlikely.

Senior Senator

Chuck Schumer (D)

Elected 1998, term expires 2022, 4th term; b. Nov 23, 1950, Brooklyn; Harvard University, J.D.; Harvard University, B.A.; Jewish; Married (Iris Weinshall); 2 children.

Elected Office: NY Assembly, 1975-1980; U.S. House, 1981-1999.

DC Office: 322 HSOB 20510, 202-224-6542, Fax: 202-228-3027, schumer.senate.gov.

State Offices: Albany, 518-431-4070; Binghamton, 607-772-6792; Buffalo, 716-846-4111; Melville, 631-753-0978; New York, 212-486-4430; Peekskill, 914-734-1532; Rochester, 585-263-5866; Syracuse, 315-423-5471.

Committees: Senate Minority Leader. *Intelligence. Rules & Administration.*

Group Ratings

	ADA	ACLU	AFL-CIO	LCV	ITI	COC	HAFA	ACU	CFG	FRC
2016	-	88%	-	100%	80%	25%	9%	4%	5%	0%
2015	100%	C	100%	100%	C	43%	C	0%	6%	0%

Almanac Ratings 2015

	Economy	Social	Foreign	Composite
Liberal	100%	100%	83%	94%
Conservative	0%	0%	17%	6%

Key Votes of the 114th Congress

1. Keystone pipeline	N	5. National Security Data	Y	9. Gun Sales Checks	Y
2. Export-Import Bank	N	6. Iran Nuclear Deal	Y	10. Sanctuary Cities	N
3. Debt Ceiling Increase	Y	7. Puerto Rico Debt	Y	11. Planned Parenthood	N
4. Homeland Security $$	Y	8. Loretta Lynch A.G	Y	12. Trade deals	N

Election Results

Election	Name (Party)	Vote (%)		Cand. Spent	Ind. Exp. Support	Ind. Exp. Oppose
2016 General	Chuck Schumer (D)	5,221,967	(71%)	$13,854,876	$100,000	$39,600
	Wendy Long (R)	2,009,380	(27%)	$685,926	$3,003	
2016 Primary	Chuck Schumer (D)	unopposed				

Prior winning percentages: 2010 (66%), 2004 (71%), 1998 (55%); House: 1996 (75%), 1994 (73%), 1992 (89%), 1990 (80%), 1988 (78%), 1986 (93%), 1984 (72%), 1982 (79%), 1980 (77%)

When he was just out of Harvard Law School, Democrat Charles Schumer, New York's senior senator, began immediately running for a seat in the New York Assembly—over the objections of his mother. "Don't run, you'll never win," she is said to have advised her son. (She wanted him instead to accept a job offer from a leading New York City law firm.) Not only did Schumer win; he has not lost an election in the intervening four decades. Just months prior to her 89th birthday in early 2017, Selma Schumer saw her son installed as the first New Yorker to assume party leadership in the Senate since the roles of majority and minority leader were formally created a century ago.

The 2016 election made Schumer the national Democratic Party's most influential figure, if not its *de facto* leader. It was not the role, however, that he had hoped for. He had aspired to begin his tenure as the top Senate Democrat serving as majority -- not minority -- leader, working alongside his one-time New York Senate colleague, Hillary Clinton, to enact the White House's policy initiatives. .On top of Clinton's surprise loss of the presidential race, the Democrats fell three seats short of regaining the Senate majority they had surrendered just two years earlier. And so Schumer instead found himself in a delicate balancing act between disparate factions of his party, as he searched for a workable strategy to confront another ambitious New Yorker, President Donald Trump.

As the new Congress convened, the party's left wing and its Senate allies were in no mood to offer anything but massive resistance to the conservative agenda of a president whom they regarded as little more than an Electoral College fluke. Grassroots activists even organized rallies outside Schumer's apartment in the New York City borough of Brooklyn, waving signs reading, "Grow a spine, Chuck" and chanting, "Filibuster everything!" Squeezing Schumer from the other side was the political predicament of several Senate Democratic centrists up for reelection in 2018 in states that Trump won by landslide margins -- and whose preservation was key to the party regaining control of the Senate in the foreseeable future, giving Schumer the power to control the Senate agenda that he had sought in the 2016 election.

First elected to the Senate in 1998 after nearly two decades in the House, Schumer began his rise in the leadership as chairman of the Democratic Senatorial Campaign Committee -- helping to engineer the Senate majority in the 2006 election that his party maintained for the next eight years. He reprised the DSCC role in the 2008 election campaign, then ascended to the No. 3 slot in the leadership (vice chairman of the Democratic Conference) and later assumed responsibility for Senate Democrats? policy and political messaging. When Harry Reid of Nevada, the Senate Democratic leader since 2004, announced his retirement in February 2015, he anointed Schumer over another would-be successor, Democratic Whip Richard Durbin of Illinois. Reid's move put an end to a years-long, behind-the-scenes rivalry between Schumer and Durbin, friends who for a dozen years were weekday housemates in a Capitol Hill townhouse -- a living arrangement that inspired a satirical TV sitcom, *Alpha House*.

The image of Schumer that accompanied him in throughout the early part of his career -- part brash partisan, part publicity hound -- persists in many quarters. Former Senate Majority Leader Bob Dole once famously wisecracked that the most dangerous place to be in Washington was between Schumer and a television camera. Fellow New York lawmakers often upstaged by Schumer came up with a verb to describe the experience: "Schumed." But those who know him well say he has changed. "Most people don't evolve. He is someone who has, in ways that enable him to be more successful than he would have been," Howard Wolfson, a top New York political operative who worked on Schumer's first Senate race two decades ago, told *The New York Times* in late 2016. Added Wolfson, "If you think about him circa 1998, he was very focused on press, somewhat parochial in his view of the world and very partisan. He has evolved into someone who is very focused on results rather than flash, and very much able and interested in working with the other party to get things done." The current-day Schumer sometimes appears to have his antiquated flip phone attached to the side of his head as he traverses the Senate corridors, reaching out to his colleagues to cajole and to cut deals.

Schumer grew up in and around Flatbush Brooklyn, where his father had a small exterminating business. (Another Schumer with a knack for media attention, comedian and film star Amy Schumer, is his cousin's daughter.) He graduated first in his class at James Madison High School, also the *alma mater* of Supreme Court Justice Ruth Bader Ginsburg and Sen. Bernie Sanders of Vermont -- the erstwhile presidential contender whom Schumer installed as a member of the Senate leadership team in late 2016. Schumer graduated from Harvard College as well as Harvard Law School, but never practiced law. With his law degree fresh in hand in 1974, he won an open New York Assembly seat . At 23, he was the state's youngest member of the Assembly since Theodore Roosevelt was elected in the early 1880s.

In 1980, he was elected to an open seat in the House. His career was threatened almost as soon as it started. Due to the 1980 reapportionment, New York stood to lose five House seats and, under the requirements of the Voting Rights Act, the state was under pressure to create a second majority-minority district in Brooklyn. Consequently, the district of the newly arrived Schumer was widely regarded as being on the chopping block. But, exhibiting the fundraising prowess that would later help him climb the Senate leadership ladder, Schumer quickly accumulated a large campaign treasury. It saved him and his district: The neighboring district of a more senior House member, albeit a legislator with a far thinner campaign bankroll, was eliminated instead.

Schumer obtained a seat on the House Banking Committee, recognizing its importance to Wall Street, located just across the East River from Schumer's home borough. He served on the Judiciary Committee and chaired the Crime Subcommittee. Schumer sponsored the 1994 crime bill that banned assault weapons and created "three strikes" mandatory life terms for repeat violent criminals. He was House sponsor of the Brady bill, which created waiting periods for handgun purchases. It passed over the strong opposition of the National Rifle Association.

In early 1997, Schumer considered seeking the governorship. But Republican Gov. George Pataki's strong job approval ratings instead persuaded him to run against GOP Sen. Alfonse D'Amato. It was by no means obvious that Schumer would win, despite New York's Democratic tilt. D'Amato's initial win in 1980 had been considered something of a fluke, as he benefitted from a three-way split in the general election. But he had won reelection twice, thanks to his assiduous constituent service and his ability to dominate the tabloid wars that are a mainstay of metropolitan New York political campaigns. As chairman of the Banking Committee in the GOP-controlled Senate, he excelled at raising money.

Schumer started off largely unknown outside Brooklyn, and faced serious primary opposition from Geraldine Ferraro, the 1984 vice presidential nominee, and Mark Green, the New York City public advocate. With little difference between his rivals on social issues, Schumer focused on pocketbook concerns. By summer, he was much better financed . In September, he won the primary with 51 percent; Ferraro was a distant second with 26 percent. Schumer immediately launched an attack on D'Amato, saying the incumbent had told "too many lies for too long," which echoed D'Amato's earlier criticisms of his opponents as "too liberal for too long." By mid-October, most polls put the race within the margin of error. Late in the campaign, D'Amato suffered self-inflicted damage after it leaked out that, in a closed meeting before a Jewish group, he had called Schumer a "putzhead," Yiddish slang for "jerk." Schumer was the beneficiary of two visits from President Bill Clinton and no fewer than four from first lady Hillary Clinton. Although outspent, Schumer won, 55%-44%.

When Hillary Clinton was elected senator two years later upon the retirement of long-time Democratic Sen. Daniel Patrick Moynihan, speculation centered around how well the ambitious Schumer would take to being overshadowed by a junior colleague regarded as a potential presidential candidate. At times, Schumer did appear irked by the wattage from Clinton's celebrity. "It took a while for us; we're both Type-A personalities," Schumer recalled in a *Washington Post* interview during Clinton's 2016 White House campaign. "We had to learn — which we did in about a year — that working together was a lot better than working separately." Schumer endorsed Clinton in her 2008 unsuccessful bid for the party's presidential nomination against Barack Obama, and her subsequent appointment as Obama's secretary of state made him indisputably New York's lead senator—while underscoring his paramount role in New York politics. When Democratic Gov. David Paterson dithered over appointing a successor to Clinton, Schumer weighed in on behalf of Rep. Kirsten Gillibrand, who received the appointment. Schumer has since helped Gillibrand blossom into a formidable political player in her own right.

Conscious of New York's traditional upstate/downstate political divide, Schumer vowed when first elected to visit all of the state's 62 counties annually, and constant travel upstate has made him as well-known there as in New York City. In his first reelection, in 2004, his fundraising skills enabled him to raise more than $27 million and win easily, 71%-24%, exceeding the 67%-31% record set by Moynihan in 1988. (Schumer's record was later eclipsed, when Gillibrand received 72 percent when she won in 2012.) With the Senate under Democratic control for only an 18-month period during his first term in the chamber, Schumer again eyed a run for governor in 2006—when Pataki's retirement left that job open. But the issue was settled when Reid named Schumer as DSCC chairman in 2005, with a seat on the influential Finance Committee as an enticement to remain on Capitol Hill.

The task facing Schumer in the 2006 election appeared formidable: The lineup of Senate seats up for grabs left Republicans with more target seats than Democrats. But he persuaded four Democratic Senators from states that President George W. Bush carried in 2004 not to retire. He then demonstrated his pragmatic side as he worked on getting strong challengers to Republican incumbents. In Pennsylvania, Schumer -- who had campaigned for the Senate as a strong supporter of abortion rights -- aggressively recruited state Treasurer Robert Casey, Jr., son of the late governor known for his vocal opposition to abortion rights. In Virginia, Schumer backed Jim Webb, a decorated Vietnam veteran who served as Reagan's Navy secretary, over liberal lobbyist Harris Miller; Webb won a narrow victory in the primary and went on to defeat the heavily favored GOP incumbent, George Allen.

During the campaign, Schumer wrote a book, *Positively American: Winning Back the Middle-Class Majority One Family at a Time*, in which he urged Democrats to offer 50 percent solutions—increase math and reading scores by 50 percent, cut property taxes by 50 percent, and reduce illegal immigration by 50 percent. Schumer's success in helping to win a Democratic majority prompted Reid to ask him to stay on as head of the DSCC in the 2008 election season. On top of the six seats picked up in 2006, the Democrats saw a net gain of eight in 2008, while losing none of their own in either election: A 45-seat minority had become a 59-seat majority in the span of a little over two years. Seldom had one senator made such a difference in the partisan composition of the body.

In return for Schumer agreeing to remain DSCC chairman, Reid created a leadership position for him as vice chairman of the Democratic Conference. Schumer effectively became the confidential adviser to the new majority leader, putting Schumer—himself known for private flashes of temper over the years—in the position of counseling the hot-tempered and difficult Reid. If the Schumer-Durbin rivalry was long a subject of chatter among congressional insiders, so was the unlikely bond of the New York City-bred, Harvard-educated Schumer with Reid, a one-time amateur boxer who grew up in a small Nevada mining town. While they shared a strategic savvy and an intense drive to succeed, Reid was as uncomfortable in front of the cameras as Schumer is at ease. Two weeks after the 2010 election, which saw the Democratic majority diminished by a half-dozen seats, Reid assigned Schumer more legislative scheduling and communications duties – as chairman of the Democratic Policy and Communications Center, with the role of sharpening the party's appeal to the middle class.

Schumer has established a solidly liberal voting record, which was displayed in the *Almanac* vote ratings for 2015. But, in his leadership role, his pragmatism has won him strong support among the Senate Democrats' moderate wing. Following the Democrats' loss of the Senate majority in 2014, several moderates—who ended up voting against Reid's reelection as Democratic leader—were reported to have privately urged Schumer to challenge Reid, according to *Politico*. But Schumer, four months before Reid announced his retirement and anointed Schumer, rebuffed the moderates' pleas, citing loyalty. "Reid made me [who I am]," Schumer is reported to have said. Upon succeeding Reid, Schumer did expand the Democratic leadership team to include Sanders, a self-styled socialist, but also Joe Manchin of West Virginia -- whose voting scores have pegged him as the most conservative Senate Democrat in recent years.

If Schumer was frequently a key congressional ally for Obama's policy agenda, there were some highly visible differences with the White House. In the spring of 2015, when Obama sought so-called "fast track" negotiating authority to expedite a 12-nation Asian trade deal, Reid and Schumer opposed the president—who ultimately had to rely heavily on Republicans to pass the measure. "I don't believe in these agreements anymore," Schumer told the *Wall Street Journal*. "I've changed." Also in 2015, Schumer opposed the Iran nuclear deal negotiated by the Obama Administration on the grounds that it eventually would permit Iran to have a nuclear weapon. "After 10 years, if Iran is the same nation as it is today, we will be worse off with this agreement than without it," Schumer said. Notably, he did not actively lobby against the agreement, which garnered enough Democratic votes to allow it to go into force; his opposition was widely seen as a bow to the politics of New York, whose Jewish population is the largest in the nation.

After the Democrats' drubbing at the polls in 2014, Schumer drew wide attention when he gave a National Press Club speech chastising his party for pushing the Affordable Care Act after getting the $787 billion economic stimulus law through in 2009. "Unfortunately, Democrats blew the opportunity the American people gave them," Schumer said, while making clear he still backed Obama's signature legislative achievement. "We took their mandate and put all of our focus on the wrong problem—health care reform." He has been a proponent of focusing Democratic efforts on the middle class; he often says his political reference point is an imaginary Long Island couple convinced that politicians devote too much attention to the very rich and very poor. A number of Schumer's fellow liberals, however, were incensed at the speech, pointing out the law didn't help only lower-income patients.

In the aftermath of 2016, Schumer voiced the view prevalent among leading Democrats that the party had failed to appeal to voters struggling economically -- and he set out to reverse that in advance of the 2018 mid-term elections. "…We did not have a sharp, strong, populist enough economic message," he told the *New Yorker*. "If you ask average voters, 'What did we stand for?', they say we weren't Trump. It wasn't good enough."

Schumer's relationship with Trump has resembled the roller coaster at Coney Island, on the southern edge of Schumer's Brooklyn. Indeed, efforts to define their relationship often begin by noting they both grew up in New York City's outer boroughs, albeit Trump was raised in a Queens neighborhood considerably tonier than Schumer's home turf. The two men fit the stereotype of the aggressive New Yorker widely held west of the Hudson River: Both crave the spotlight, and won't shy away from the political equivalent of a street brawl. How close they were prior to their current roles appears to be -- like much else between them -- a matter of dispute. They talked several times by phone in the weeks following the election, with Trump declaring during a January MSNBC interview, "Hey look, I think I'll be able to get along well with Chuck Schumer. "I was always very good with Schumer. I was close to Schumer in many ways." But Schumer weeks earlier disputed that the two were ever close. "He was not my friend. We never went golfing together, even had a meal together," Schumer told *Politico*. During his days as a frequent Democratic campaign donor, Trump did hold a DSCC fundraiser at his Florida estate when Schumer chaired the DSCC in 2008; the event raised $230,000.

Schumer did offer early olive branches. "If he is going to agree on issues like trade and transportation infrastructure in a very real way with us, we have an obligation to pursue it," Schumer told *The New York Times* shortly after Trump's election. But, following blowback from his left wing, Schumer took a harder line. "The only way we're going to work with [Trump] is if he moves completely in our direction and abandons his Republican colleagues," Schumer told CNN in January 2017. After voting to confirm the first couple of Trump Cabinet nominations, Schumer voted against of 14 of the next 18 Cabinet-level appointees. "This Cabinet is the most extreme…as well as the most conflict-of-interest-laden Cabinet,

I think, in the history of America," Schumer later told the *New Yorker*, adding, "It means there are almost no areas where we can compromise with Trump—or 'work together' is a better word." Trump, aggravated by the Democrats' resistance, responded by calling Schumer the Democrats' "head clown" via Twitter. When Schumer teared up at a press conference criticizing Trump's effort to ban immigration from Muslim nations, the president sneered: "I noticed Chuck Schumer yesterday with fake tears. I'm going to ask him who is his acting coach." Later Trump tweets referred to "Cryin' Chuck Schumer."

During his first major test as leader -- Trump's nomination of federal judge Neil Gorsuch to the Supreme Court -- Schumer sought to restrain the more hardline members of his caucus, as he constructed a strategy to ramp up opposition to Gorsuch while seeking to avoid charges of obstructionism. With many Senate Democrats still fuming over Majority Leader Mitch McConnell's refusal to hold hearings or a vote on Obama's nomination of appeals court judge Merrick Garland a year earlier, Oregon Sen. Jeff Merkley in January -- before Gorsuch's nomination was unveiled -- announced plans to filibuster any Trump nominee to succeed the late Justice Antonin Scalia. According to *Politico*, Schumer later buttonholed Merkley to chide him for his comments and to warn him not to make the fight about retribution for Garland. While warning publicly that the Democrats would fight any high court nominee who wasn't "mainstream," Schumer privately urged his caucus members to hold off on full-scale opposition until a nominee was selected and the nominee's record had been vetted via hearings. Once that process was completed, Schumer did call for a filibuster a couple of weeks before a scheduled vote on Gorsuch.

The final outcome was not a happy one for Schumer and his caucus, as McConnell invoked the so-called "nuclear option," changing the Senate rules so that all presidential nominations would no longer be subject to filibuster. It allowed Gorsuch to be confirmed, while diminishing the leverage of the Democratic minority if future Supreme Court openings arose under Trump. Defenders of McConnell's move pointed a finger at Reid, who, in 2013, had executed a similar rules change. Reid's move, in response to GOP resistance to Obama Administration nominees, changed the rules to end the filibuster for presidential appointments -- except for the Supreme Court. Weeks before McConnell invoked the so-called nuclear option in 2017, Schumer expressed regret that Reid had opened the door to it four years earlier. "I will say it was a mistake," he told the *New Yorker*.

The once icy relationship between Schumer and Arizona Sen. John McCain, the 2008 Republican presidential nomination, thawed during the discussions to save the filibuster. The two again combined in the bipartisan "Gang of Eight" that produced a comprehensive immigration reform package in 2013. Schumer has had a longstanding interest in immigration policy reform, going back to his days on the House Judiciary Committee, when he contributed key provisions to immigration laws passed in 1986 and 1990. Although a comprehensive bill was not high on Obama's agenda at the outset of his first term, Schumer worked with Republican Lindsey Graham of South Carolina to establish concepts for later legislation.

When immigration moved to the political front burner in 2013, Graham as well as McCain and Schumer were part of the Gang of Eight— which came up with a plan that offered a legalization pathway for illegal aliens, a new system for employers in a variety of industries to hire guest workers, and stringent border-security provisions. Schumer sought 70 votes for the measure, and ended up falling just two short: It passed 68-32 in July 2013, with 14 Republicans joining the entire Democratic caucus in backing it. He and other Gang of Eight members succeeded in building a coalition of interest groups to support the bill, including the Republican-leaning U.S. Chamber of Commerce; Schumer believed that the Chamber's support would help to neutralize the furor of far-right conservatives. But the Republican-controlled House refused to take up the bill or pass anything that would satisfy the then-Democratic-controlled Senate.

In January 2015, Schumer became co-chairman of another bipartisan working group -- this one on tax reform, with Ohio Republican Sen. Rob Portman as the other co-chairman. The group was convened amid talk of the potential for a bipartisan deal that could open the way for the policy goals of both parties: a more business friendly tax code sought by Republicans, and revenue for new domestic infrastructure advocated by Democrats. Schumer's interest in tax reform appeared to be a shift from recent years: When House and Senate negotiators sought a deal on taxes and spending to avoid the so-called "fiscal cliff" in 2012, he dismissed the idea of a tax code overhaul as "little more than happy talk." Republicans reacted angrily, and an overhaul never made it into the final legislation.

As a member of the Banking Committee, Schumer has been a steadfast ally of a major home state constituency, Wall Street, which has come under sharp attack from the party's increasingly vocal liberal populist wing led by Sanders and Massachusetts Sen. Elizabeth Warren. In 1999, Schumer supported the Gramm-Bliley-Leach bill eliminating the barriers between banks and investment banks, a measure that Warren has pushed to roll back. Schumer has fought increasing tax rates on so-called carried interest;

such a move would fall heavily on the hedge fund operators and private equity firms based in New York's financial district and surrounding areas. He did shift to support greater oversight and stricter regulation of the industry following the 2008 financial crisis.

In 2015, Schumer passed on asserting his seniority to become the ranking Democrat on the Banking Committee, allowing the less-senior Sherrod Brown of Ohio to assume that position. Until he became minority leader, Schumer was the top Democrat on the Rules and Administration Committee, where, as chairman in January 2013, he played a high-profile role in the arrangements for Obama's second term inauguration. He was said to be furious at superstar singer Beyoncé Knowles for lip-synching "The Star-Spangled Banner" without first informing anyone.

The Sept. 11, 2001 attacks hit home for Schumer more than for most members of Congress: Growing up in Brooklyn in the 1960s, he watched the World Trade Center towers rise in the distance while under construction. Six weeks before his election to Congress in 1980, he was married in the "Windows on the World" restaurant, which was located on the 107th floor of the north tower. (Schumer's wife, Iris Weinshall, was transportation commissioner from 2002-2007 under New York City Mayor Michael Bloomberg, and is now chief operating officer of the New York Public Library.) When the hijacked planes struck the World Trade Center on 9/11, the older of his two daughters, Jessica, was attending high school near the twin towers, and it was several hours before Schumer and his wife could determine that she was all right. (Jessica Schumer served as chief of staff and general counsel to the White House Council of Economic Advisers during Obama's second term, and, during the 2016 campaign, was policy director for the Democratic vice-presidential nominee, Virginia Sen. Tim Kaine.)

Schumer played a major role in shepherding recovery money through Congress after 9/11. He immediately requested $20 billion in aid for New York, which Bush approved. The Bush Administration then turned to Schumer to rally support for its centerpiece anti-domestic terrorism law, the USA Patriot Act. In 2010, he opposed Obama administration plans to try Khalid Sheikh Mohammed, considered by U.S. intelligence sources to be the mastermind of the 9/11 attack, in New York. "My advice to the president is, with a great deal of respect, take New York off your radar screen," Schumer declared. The plan to try Mohammed in New York was subsequently scrapped. In another break with Obama, Schumer in late 2016 led the effort to override Obama's veto of a bill that allowed families of 9/11 victims to sue Saudi Arabia for possible involvement in the attack. Schumer teamed with a fellow Judiciary Committee member, Senate Republican Whip John Cornyn, in what was the first time that Congress overrode an Obama veto.

Schumer easily won a third term in 2010: He raised $19 million and overwhelmed Republican Jay Townsend, owner of a market research firm, 66%-32%. Running for a fourth term in 2016, Schumer overwhelmed Wendy Long, a Manhattan attorney active in conservative circles, by 71-27%. Schumer spent nearly $13 million on the campaign -- more than 18 times what Long spent -- and transferred another $6 million to the DSCC to assist candidates in competitive races.

After his re-election, Schumer headed off an intraparty leadership battle. According to published accounts, Reid's decision in late February 2015 to anoint Schumer as the next leader was followed by a late-night conversation between Schumer and Durbin on the Senate floor. Durbin is reported to have told his long-time friend that he had earned the leadership mantle, and Schumer, in response, is said to have wept in gratitude. But what was, or wasn't, said next remained unclear. The Durbin camp contended that, during the conversation, Schumer agreed to support Durbin staying on as whip. But Schumer and his aides denied that any such deal was made, and Washington Sen. Patty Murray, another member of the Democrats' leadership team, eyed a challenge to Durbin. Not eager for an intraparty fight in the wake of the 2016 results, Schumer split the proverbial baby: Durbin stayed on as whip, while Murray was elevated to the new post of assistant Democratic leader, No. 3 in the hierarchy.

Of perhaps greater significance was Schumer's relations with McConnell, who had headed the Republican caucus for a decade. "If they were looking for 10 different ways to get off to a bad start, this would be 11," Tennessee GOP Sen. Lamar Alexander, a friend of both Schumer and McConnell, observed to *The Washington Post* in early 2017. It started with the Democrats slow-walking the confirmation of Trump's Cabinet nominees, with Schumer pointedly one of just six Democrats to vote against confirming Transportation Secretary Elaine Chao -- McConnell?s wife. And then the filibuster of Gorsuch had prompted McConnell to retaliate with a party-line vote on ending super-majority thresholds for all nominees.

Some worried that the legislative filibuster was next for extinction. McConnell insisted there were no such plans, and that his caucus was united in opposing such a move. But even some Republicans worried that there was now a precedent for changing the legislative filibuster rule the next time a high-stakes piece of legislation came along. "Let us go no further down this road," Schumer urged. "I hope the Republican leader and I can find a way to build a firewall around the legislative "filibuster. Let's find a way to further protect the 60-vote rule for "legislation." As he began his long-sought position as Democratic leader, Schumer voiced concern that the erosion of the "filibuster "will make this body a more partisan "place." Alluding to the purported conversation between George Washington and Thomas Jefferson depicting the Senate as the saucer that cools the figurative hot coffee generated by the House, Schumer added, "It will make the cooling saucer of the Senate considerably hotter."

Junior Senator

Kirsten Gillibrand (D)

Appointed Jan. 2009, term expires 2018, 1st full term; b. Dec 09, 1966, Albany; Dartmouth College, B.A.; University of California, Los Angeles, J.D., Roman Catholic; Married (Jonathan Gillibrand); 2 children.

Elected Office: U.S. House, 2007-2009.

Professional Career: Practicing attorney, 1991-2006; Special counsel, HUD, 2000.

DC Office: 478 RSOB 20510, 202-224-4451, Fax: 202-228-0282, gillibrand.senate.gov.

State Offices: Albany, 518-431-0120; Buffalo, 716-854-9725; Lowville, 315-376-6118; Mahopac, 845-875-4585; Melville, 631-249-2825; New York, 212-688-6262; Rochester, 585-263-6250; Syracuse, 315-448-0470.

Committees: *Aging*. *Agriculture, Nutrition & Forestry*: Commodities, Risk Management & Trade, Livestock, Marketing & Agriculture Security (RMM), Nutrition, Agricultural Research & Specialty Crops. *Armed Services*: Cybersecurity, Personnel (RMM). *Environment & Public Works*: Clean Air & Nuclear Safety, Fisheries, Water, and Wildlife, Transportation & Infrastructure.

Group Ratings

	ADA	ACLU	AFL-CIO	LCV	ITI	COC	HAFA	ACU	CFG	FRC
2016	-	88%	-	100%	75%	25%	12%	4%	0%	100%
2015	100%	C	100%	100%	C	43%	C	0%	6%	0%

Almanac Ratings 2015

	Economy	Social	Foreign	Composite
Liberal	100%	100%	96%	99%
Conservative	0%	0%	4%	1%

Key Votes of the 114th Congress

1. Keystone pipeline	N	5. National Security Data	Y	9. Gun Sales Checks	Y
2. Export-Import Bank	N	6. Iran Nuclear Deal	N	10. Sanctuary Cities	N
3. Debt Ceiling Increase	Y	7. Puerto Rico Debt	Y	11. Planned Parenthood	N
4. Homeland Security $$	Y	8. Loretta Lynch A.G	Y	12. Trade deals	N

Election Results

Election	Name (Party)	Vote (%)	Cand. Spent	Ind. Exp. Support	Ind. Exp. Oppose
2012 General	Kirsten Gillibrand (D)..............	4,822,330 (72%)	$14,257,872	$18,122	$3,515
	Wendy Long (R).......................	1,758,702 (26%)	$742,747	$963,484	
2012 Primary	Kirsten Gillibrand (D).............	Unopposed			

Prior winning percentages: 2010 special (63%); House: 2008 (62%), 2006 (53%)

Democrat Kirsten Gillibrand, New York's junior senator, was appointed in 2009 to fill the Senate seat vacated by Hillary Clinton when the latter was named secretary of state-and, in the years since, Gillibrand signaled that she would eventually like to follow Clinton in pursuit of national office as well. Like most future presidential hopefuls, Gillibrand, who turned 50 at the end of 2016, is coy about such ambitions-saying in 2014 she would consider the White House "someday." After being dogged for months by questions from reporters, she said in May of 2017 that she was ruling out a run in 2020, but many political observers didn't believe her, given that she wanted to focus on her re-election in 2018. There are other New Yorkers in line ahead of her, notably Gov. Andrew Cuomo, for whom Gillibrand once worked. But Gillibrand has taken many of the steps followed by members of Congress seeking to raise their national profiles, including a memoir and a leadership PAC where the money raised has gone to encourage and aid other women candidates. And, in early 2017, she was embraced by the party's left wing as she voted against and spoke out in opposition to all but a couple of the President Donald Trump's top appointees -- even as the so-called "Trump Resistance Movement" was vocally pushing her senior New York colleague, newly named Minority Leader Charles Schumer, to take a harder line against the White House.

It was merely the latest wrinkle in the often surprising evolution of an ambitious and aggressive politician who, prior to arriving in Congress, was a private attorney defending Big Tobacco -- and who joined the Blue Dog Caucus, a group of conservative Democrats, after first being elected to the House a decade ago. Gillibrand comes from a politically wired family with bipartisan connections. Her father, Douglas Rutnik, is an attorney and lobbyist with close ties to a number of leading New York Republicans, including former Sen. Alfonse D'Amato, for whom Gillibrand interned while in college. Her grandmother, Polly Noonan, was a prominent Democratic activist in Albany and longtime companion of Albany Mayor Erastus Corning, who held that office for more than 40 years as part of the political organization run by the legendary Daniel O'Connell. Rutnik also was close to Corning, who was a frequent hunting companion. Gillibrand attended the exclusive all-girls Emma Willard School in Troy, just across the Hudson River from Albany, and graduated from Dartmouth College, where she majored in Asian studies and attained fluency in Mandarin; she was among the first Dartmouth students to visit China after the country was opened to students from the United States.

Gillibrand graduated from law school at the University of California, Los Angeles, and did a United Nations internship in Vienna, Austria. After law school, she clerked for Roger Miner, an Albany-based federal appeals court judge appointed by President Ronald Reagan, but spent most of the 1990s working for Davis, Polk & Wardwell, a prominent New York City-based law firm. Her clients there included tobacco giant Philip Morris, then the subject of numerous criminal probes and civil lawsuits. Shortly after her Senate appointment in 2009, *The New York Times* reported that her work for Philip Morris included helping to defend the firm against allegations that it lied about the existence of internal research on the health effects of smoking. Gillibrand served toward the end of the Clinton Administration as special counsel to Cuomo while he was secretary of the Department of Housing and Urban Development, and then joined another major New York law firm, Boies, Schiller & Flexner.

Gillibrand raised money for Clinton's first Senate campaign in 2000, and five years later, launched what appeared to be a quixotic campaign against four-term Rep. John Sweeney in the upstate Albany-Troy region where she had grown up. In 2005, Sweeney was considered a rising Republican star with a seat on the Appropriations Committee. He had never faced a serious reelection challenge in a district that, for the previous century, had elected Democrats on only the rarest of occasions. As late as August, polls showed Sweeney with a solid lead. However, Gillibrand, aided by a national Democratic wave that enabled the party to regain control of both the House and the Senate, ultimately triumphed in what turned into one of that year's nastier races.

Sweeney called Gillibrand a carpetbagger who lived not in the Hudson Valley-based district but in a Manhattan high-rise, and contrasted his working class background with Gillibrand's prep school pedigree. He accused her campaign of making anonymous and intimidating phone calls to his wife. In turn, Gillibrand demanded that Sweeney release police reports from arrests in 1977 and 1978, and from a 2001 automobile accident. Sweeney was buffeted by a couple of unflattering revelations in the closing weeks of the campaign. In October, it was revealed that he had traveled to the Northern Mariana Islands with an associate of disgraced lobbyist Jack Abramoff, who pleaded guilty to conspiracy charges in a scandal that involved several congressional junkets to the islands. Then, a week before the election, the Albany *Times Union* reported Sweeney's wife had called the police in December 2005 to complain the legislator was "knocking her around." Sweeney's campaign at first insisted the report was "false and concocted by our opposition," but Sweeney eventually conceded that the police had been called to his home. Gillibrand won, 53%-47%.

When she arrived in the House, Gillibrand began posting a "Sunlight Report" of her daily schedule, including meetings with lobbyists; she asserts on her current Web site that she was the first member of Congress to post such information daily. Reflecting her district, her voting record had a conservative tilt. She won a 100-percent voting score from the National Rifle Association, as Gillibrand said she kept two rifles under her bed, while boasting she "always believed in protecting hunters' rights" as she grew up in a family of hunters. Gillibrand also opposed drivers' licenses for illegal immigrants. Defending the seat in 2008, Gillibrand faced a strong opponent in state Republican Chairman Sandy Treadwell, who spent nearly $6 million of his own money. But she raised $4.6 million, and her moderate-to-conservative stands on issues paid off as she won, 62%-38%.

When Clinton was named President-elect Barack Obama's choice for secretary of state, Gillibrand was hardly the first person to spring to mind as a successor. New York Gov. David Paterson considered appointing Cuomo, then state attorney general, which would have removed him as a possible primary opponent to Paterson in 2010. (Cuomo later was nominated and elected governor after Paterson opted not to run.) Paterson also gave serious thought to appointing Caroline Kennedy, the daughter of President John F. Kennedy. But after Kennedy performed poorly in an interview with *The New York Times* and during an upstate "listening tour," she withdrew. Two days later, Paterson announced he was appointing Gillibrand, a surprise pick considering that several more senior House members were interested. Arguing in Gillibrand's favor was her moderate politics, as Paterson, a New York City resident elevated to the governorship when Eliot Spitzer resigned amid scandal in 2008, hoped to win upstate support as he considered seeking election in his own right.

On Jan. 23, 2009, Gillibrand, then 42, was announced as Paterson's choice, making her the youngest senator at the time. Things were bumpy for her literally from the start: A picture taken as her appointment was announced showed a beaming D'Amato looking on, irking a number of leading Democrats. The reaction to the appointment by *El Diario*, New York City's dominant Spanish language newspaper, was an unflattering photo of Gillibrand with the headline: "Anti-immigrante." Gillibrand quickly moved to modify some of her positions that were out of step with the statewide Democratic Party, particularly on immigration and gun control. The day after her appointment, she attended a rally in Harlem, where she won applause by vowing flexibility on gun control. "I was somebody who was not as focused on this, as I should have been, as a House member," she told *Politico* years later, tearfully describing encounters with families victimized by gun violence. "Meeting these families devastated me, broke my heart." Gillibrand subsequently opposed Senate amendments that would have allowed licensed gun owners to carry concealed firearms across state lines and would have repealed the District of Columbia's tough gun laws; in the House, she had supported a bill lifting gun restrictions in the District.

Several Democratic House members-Rep. Carolyn Maloney and then-Reps. Steve Israel and Carolyn McCarthy-began mulling primary challenges to Gillibrand. The motivations were a combination of pique at being passed over for the appointment in favor of a colleague with less congressional seniority, as well as concern over Gillibrand's past issue stances. But the three House members dropped out as potential Senate primary candidates in the ensuing months, with Maloney the last to go. At the end of 2009, another possible candidate surfaced: former Tennessee Rep. Harold Ford, who had moved to New York to become an adviser to Merrill Lynch after losing a 2006 bid for a Senate seat in his home state.In March 2010, after a statewide tour, he, too, ruled out running.

Throughout this maneuvering, Gillibrand benefited from the assistance of two powerful patrons: Obama and Schumer, by then a member of the Senate Democratic leadership. The White House, fearing an expensive primary could cost the Democrats a seat in the 2010 general election, mounted a full-court press to clear the field for Gillibrand, with both the president and Schumer personally lobbying would-be challengers to stay out. At the same time, Schumer-who was known for being less than thrilled at having to often share the spotlight with Clinton-seemed to delight in taking his new colleague under his wing. He pressed Senate leaders to give her the committee assignments she desired, put her name next to his on project funding announcements in the state, and introduced her to deep-pocketed Democratic donors.

With her path seemingly cleared for election to the final two years of Clinton's term, Gillibrand turned her focus to legislating. The reauthorization of the Child Nutrition Act, passed into law in the lame-duck session of 2010, included a number of her proposals, such as banning junk food from schools. But the issue that initially brought Gillibrand the most attention was her call for repeal of the 17-year-old "don't ask, don't tell" policy barring openly gay military service members. She introduced legislation in July 2009 at a time when interest in the issue was lagging, as it leading champion, Sen. Edward Kennedy of Massachusetts, was dying of cancer. In subsequent months, she lobbied former House colleagues as well as fellow senators, pushed for hearings and set up a website featuring videos of gay and lesbian veterans telling their stories. "If you care about national security, if you care about our military readiness, then you will repeal this corrosive policy," she said in an emotional floor speech shortly before it passed the Senate. It became law soon thereafter, earning her widespread praise from progressive and gay rights groups.

Gillibrand's poll numbers remained lackluster throughout 2009, giving some Republicans hope . But by April 2010, she had amassed a $6 million war chest, and the leading potential GOP contenders, New York Mayor Rudy Giuliani and former Gov. George Pataki, took a pass. The Republicans nominated former Rep. Joseph DioGuardi -- who had not held public office since a 1985-1989 stint representing suburban Westchester County, and had been unsuccessful in several subsequent attempts to return to Congress. Despite a rough year for the Democrats nationally, Gillibrand had no trouble winning, 63%-35%. In 2012, she was up for a full six-year term. Wendy Long, a Manhattan lawyer active in conservative circles, got the Republican nod. Gillibrand spent more than $14 million -- nearly 20 times as much as Long -- and won a commanding 72%-26% victory. It was a record margin in a New York Senate race, slightly eclipsing the 71 percent of the vote that Schumer garnered in winning re-election in 2010 and again in 2016.

While tending to her home base-visiting all of the Empire State's 62 counties-Gillibrand also began burnishing her national image by starting an effort, Off the Sidelines, to mobilize female candidates. It was organized as a leadership PAC, a device that allows members of Congress to raise money to increase their visibility, promote their ideas-and collect political chits. Gillibrand cemented her reputation as a fundraising powerhouse: In two election cycles, Off the Sidelines distributed more to candidates than any other Senate leadership PACs, according to the nonpartisan Center for Responsive Politics. The PAC funneled more than $500,000 to candidates in 2014, and nearly $675,000 in 2016.

Since winning election in her own right, Gillibrand has continued her leftward shift. In addition to calling in 2011 for Obama to begin withdrawing troops from Afghanistan, she introduced a bill to repeal the federal Defense of Marriage Act and appeared in a video backing gay marriage. She pleased good-government advocates in early 2012 when she pushed the Senate version of a bill to require more public disclosure of stock transactions by lawmakers. A year later, Gillibrand introduced the Family and Medical Leave (FAMILY) Act with Democratic Rep. Rosa DeLauro of Connecticut to guarantee workers at least two-thirds pay for up to 12 weeks annually for health-related leave. Modeled on existing programs in three states, the bill made little progress in the legislative process -- it was reintroduced in 2015 and again in 2017 -- but served to tout the national Democratic Party's stance on the issue. She was in a tie for sixth most liberal Senator in 2015, according to *Almanac* vote ratings.

Combating sexual assault is the issue with which Gillibrand has become most identified; it has been her major focus since 2013. She introduced a bill to remove the military chain of command from handling sexual assault cases. Gillibrand waged a high-profile effort for her proposal, telling Illinois voters during one trip there that they needed to pressure their senator, Democrat Richard Durbin, to sign on as a sponsor. (Durbin, the party's Senate whip, was reportedly irked by the move, but eventually did so.) The issue pitted Gillibrand against Missouri Democrat Claire McCaskill. As members of the Armed Services Committee, both aggressively lobbied their colleagues on behalf of rival approaches. Gillibrand's proposal fell five votes short of the 60 needed to overcome a Republican filibuster in March 2014; McCaskill's more incremental alternative, to reform the process for handling sexual assault allegations while keeping them within the military chain of command, passed the Senate unanimously with the support of the Defense Department.

Gillibrand has refused to concede on the matter, even though her approach fell 10 votes short when it came up again in 2015. In 2016, she was "deeply upset" that the annual defense authorization bill was brought to a vote without her proposal being debated. "Today is a setback in our fight on survivors' behalf, but it is no more than that," Gillibrand told *Newsday*. "Whether it is this president and Congress or the next, we will not give up." In January 2017, she was the only dissenter in the 98-1 Senate vote to confirm former Marine Corps General James Mattis to head the Department of Defense. Gillibrand said her opposition arose out of concern for civilian control of the military: Mattis had been retired from the military for only four years, and required a waiver to serve as defense secretary. But a conservative online publication, *Independent Review Journal*, suggested Gillibrand was carrying a "vendetta" because Mattis had been among the generals who resisted removing sexual assault cases from the military chain of command.

Despite disagreements on adjudicating sexual assault charges in the military, Gillibrand and McCaskill forged an alliance on legislation to deal with the problem on college campus. A bill initially introduced in 2014 would require schools to establish a standardized process to respond to sexual assaults, with penalties for colleges that did not comply. The legislation was reintroduced in 2015, and attracted more than one-third of the Senate as co-sponsors. Also that year, they headed off legislation that would have prevented universities from investigating cases of sexual assault, and mandating instead that they be reported to law enforcement. When the two women senators, both members of sororities as undergraduates, learned that national organizations representing fraternities and sororities were lobbying for the bill, they summoned representatives of these groups and convinced them to withdraw their support. "Every campus administrator needs to be able to keep his or her campus safe. What we're offering in our legislation is the tools to do that," Gillibrand told *Elle* magazine.

In 2014, playing off the name of her leadership PAC, Gillibrand published a memoir: *Off the Sidelines: Raise Your Voice, Change the World*, about her efforts to help get women into politics. The book deviated from the usual tomes on the subject by offering self-help and diet advice, and drew attention when Gillibrand wrote about how some unnamed male colleagues commented about her weight. One expressed concern that she might become "porky," while another assured her that she was attractive even when she was heavier. (Early in her Senate tenure, fitness magazines took note of her 40-pound weight loss.) In the book, she also confronted the lurking doubts about her intellectual heft that accompanied her arrival in the Senate, bluntly acknowledging that she was seen by some as a "parakeet" without original thoughts. She said she sought to learn from such critics rather than exact revenge. "I was new at my job, and I needed to address my inexperience and weaknesses head-on," she wrote. "She often underwhelms people at first sight," former Vermont Gov. Howard Dean observed of Gillibrand in a 2013 *Politico* interview. But Dean -- whose 2004 bid for the presidential nomination mobilized the Democratic left, the wing of the party recently drawn to Gillibrand -- added, "…When you look under the hood, you find a first-class political mind and someone who has a great deal of skill."

FIRST DISTRICT

Lee Zeldin (R)

Elected 2014, 2nd term; b. Jan 30, 1980, East Meadow; State University of New York (Albany), Bach. Deg., 2001; Albany Law School, J.D., 2003; Jewish; Married (Diana Zeldin); 2 children (twins).

Military Career: U.S. Army, 2003-2007 (Iraq); U.S. Army Reserve, 2007-present.

Elected Office: NY Senate, 2011-2014.

Professional Career: Practicing attorney.

DC Office: 1517 LHOB 20515, 202-225-3826, Fax: 202-225-3143, zeldin.house.gov.

State Offices: Patchogue, 631-289-1097.

Committees: *Financial Services*: Housing & Insurance, Oversight & Investigations, Terrorism & Illicit Finance. *Foreign Affairs*: Middle East & North Africa, Terrorism, Nonproliferation & Trade.

Group Ratings

	ADA	ACLU	AFL-CIO	LCV	ITI	COC	HAFA	ACU	CFG	FRC
2016	-	11%	-	8%	83%	93%	59%	60%	63%	75%
2015	5%	C	42%	14%	C	85%	C	54%	53%	75%

Almanac Ratings 2015

	Economy	Social	Foreign	Composite
Liberal	14%	9%	0%	8%
Conservative	86%	91%	100%	92%

Key Votes of the 114th Congress

1. Keystone Pipeline	Y	5. Puerto Rico Debt	N	9. Offenses by Aliens	Y
2. Trade Deals	N	6. Medical Marijuana	Y	10. Troops in Iraq	N
3. Export-Import Bank	N	7. Sanctuary Cities	Y	11. Homeland Security $$	N
4. Debt Ceiling Increase	N	8. Armor-piercing Bullets	Y	12. Trade Adjustment aid	N

Election Results

Election	Name (Party)	Vote (%)	Cand. Spent	Ind. Exp. Support	Ind. Exp. Oppose
2016 General	Lee Zeldin (R)............................	188,499 (58%)	$4,005,848	$616,527	$1,219,494
	Anna Throne-Holst (D)............	135,278 (42%)	$3,805,436	$798,318	$1,026,768
2016 Primary	Lee Zeldin (R)..	(100%)			

Prior winning percentages: 2014 (53%)

Republican Lee Zeldin, elected in 2014 against a Democratic incumbent whom he derided as a "backbencher," brought a burst of energy to the House. In 2016, perhaps with some benefit from the coattails of Donald Trump, he coasted to reelection against a well-financed challenger.

Zeldin was raised in Shirley, New York, and received his bachelor's degree from the State University at Albany before earning his law degree at Albany Law School. He received an Army commission as a second lieutenant, spent four years on active duty, and deployed to Iraq in 2006 with an infantry battalion of paratroopers from the 82nd Airborne Division; he remained in the Army Reserve, as a major. Zeldin opened a law practice, and in 2010 won election to the state Senate, where he led an effort to fund a pilot program for soldiers suffering from post-traumatic stress disorder. He also led a bid to scale back a transportation-authority payroll tax and sought to end fees for saltwater fishing.

The national Republican Party sought for years to make inroads in this eastern Long Island swing district. Democrat Tim Bishop, who had served since 2003, defeated Zeldin in 2008 by 58%-42%, but the party gap subsequently narrowed. President Barack Obama carried the district by only 1,593 votes in 2012. In his second challenge to Bishop, Zeldin said that he would no longer be dragged down by voter fatigue with George W. Bush's presidency and the Iraq War. In the GOP primary, he defeated perpetual candidate George Demos, who outspent him by more than 3-to-1.

In the general election, a September poll showed Bishop with a 10-point lead. The American Action Network and the National Republican Congressional Committee spent nearly $4 million accusing Bishop of being a corrupt Washington insider. Bishop aired two ads to tell voters he was not under FBI investigation for helping a donor secure a fireworks permit for a bar mitzvah. Bishop struck back by attacking Zeldin for accepting contributions from industries that he said were polluting New York. Democrats and their allies spent a similar amount to attack Zeldin as a conservative Albany insider. From their own campaign funds, Bishop outspent Zeldin, $3 million to $1.8 million. Zeldin scored a key endorsement from *Newsday*, which said that Bishop "does not have a significant voice in Congress" and that "Long Island needs this seat at the Republican table." Zeldin got 54 percent of the vote and won with surprising ease. He became the House's lone Jewish Republican, a status held by Majority Leader Eric Cantor of Virginia before his primary loss and subsequent resignation in 2014.

Preparing for a likely tough reelection, Zeldin kept a busy pace. In February 2015, the House gave voice-vote approval to his amendment to permit states to refuse to comply with Common Core education standards; it subsequently became law. On the Transportation and Infrastructure Committee, he worked with Democratic Rep. Sean Patrick Mahoney of New York to gain approval of their Safe Bridges Act as part of the sweeping highway bill in 2015. Their proposal restored funding to the highway trust fund specifically for bridges and overpasses. As co-chairman of the House Republican Israel Caucus, he said that Obama's conflicts with Israeli Prime Minister Benjamin Netanyahu were an opportunity for House Republicans to increase their Jewish ranks. "President Obama is operating as if he doesn't grasp who truly are America's friends and enemies in that region of the world," he told Bloomberg News. In 2017, Zeldin joined the Financial Services Committee.

National Democrats designated Zeldin as a top target for 2016. For their challenger, local Democrats quickly fell in line behind Anna Throne-Holst, who had served six years as Southampton town supervisor. She criticized his opposition to a bill prohibiting gun sales to individuals on the "no fly" lists. She sought to link Zeldin to Donald Trump. That might not have been the best strategy, given Trump's double-digit victory in the district on Nov. 8. Zeldin said that he occasionally disagreed with Trump but supported him as "a better candidate by far than Hillary Clinton," and that Throne-Holst had distorted his position on guns. Both candidates were lavishly funded, with more than $5 million available for each side. Even with a turnout that was nearly twice as large as in 2014, Zeldin won with unexpected ease, 59%-41%. The history of this district suggests that it will take time before he is safe for reelection.

Eastern Long Island

Population		**Race and Ethnicity**		**Income**	
Total	723,323	White	76.1%	Median Income	$87,272 (23 out of 435)
Land area	650	Black	4.7%		
Pop/ sq mi	1112.8	Latino	13.7%	Under $50,000	27.8%
Born in state	78.3%	Asian	3.9%	$50,000-$99,999	28.8%
Age Groups		Two races	1.3%	$100,000-$199,999	32.4%
Under 18	22.0%	Other	0.4%	$200,000 or more	10.8%
18-34	20.3%	**Education**		Poverty Rate	7.2%
35-64	42.1%	H.S grad or less	37.6%	**Health Insurance**	
Over 64	15.5%	Some college	27.9%	With health insurance coverage	92.2%
Work		College Degree, 4 yr	18.5%		
White Collar	39.1%	Post grad	16.0%	**Public Assistance**	
Sales and Service	42.7%	**Military**		Cash public assistance income	1.9%
Blue Collar	18.3%	Veteran	6.9%		
Government	20.5%	Active Duty	0.1%	Food stamp/SNAP benefits	5.9%

Voter Turnout			
2015 Total Citizens 18+	524,078	2016 House Turnout as % CVAP	62%
2016 House turnout	323,890	2014 House Turnout as % CVAP	33%

2012 Presidential Vote		
Barack Obama	146,708	(50%)
Mitt Romney	145,115	(49%)

2016 Presidential Vote		
Donald Trump	183,233	(54%)
Hillary Clinton	141,900	(42%)
Gary Johnson	7,217	(2%)

Cook Partisan Voting Index: R+5

Long Island - "the Island" to most New Yorkers - is the largest and most populous island in the mainland United States. It stretches 118 miles, from the two-century-old Montauk Point lighthouse on a crumbling bluff to Fort Hamilton at the foot of the Verrazano-Narrows Bridge. Ranging from 12 to 20 miles wide, Long Island is ringed by gentle hills and cliffs above Long Island Sound and sand-spit beaches that front the Atlantic Ocean. Including the populations of Brooklyn and Queens, some 7.7 million people live there, more than in all but 12 states. Brooklyn, at the island's western end, is urban and thickly settled, while the Hamptons in the east are manicured countryside, preserved as a playground for the New York elite.

More important economically - and politically - are the areas immediately west of the Hamptons: the suburbs created in the post-World War II migration out of the city. Developers looking for cheaper land for aircraft factories, shopping centers, subdivisions and office parks found them first in Nassau County, just east of Queens, and then farther out in Suffolk County. Suffolk attracted young families of Irish and Italian descent looking for more space and less crime. Over the past 30 years, the island's economy soured as defense plants were decimated by the end of the Cold War, and young people fled older suburbs for jobs elsewhere. In January 2017, the Long Island Power Authority approved a plan to build a 15-turbine wind farm at sea and run cables from Rhode Island to Montauk, with a 2022 target date for completion. More recently the county has been attracting Latinos, who have grown to 19 percent of the population (compared with 8 percent black in Suffolk) and include Salvadorans and Puerto Ricans in lower-income areas. In a sign that some urban problems have accompanied them, Latino advocates in 2015 filed a class-action suit against Suffolk County, contending that they were the victims of police discrimination and harassment. Outside of "the city," Suffolk is the largest county in the state.

The 1st Congressional District of New York consists of the eastern end of Long Island and Suffolk, with about half of the county's population. It runs as far west as Smithtown on the North Shore and Patchogue on the South Shore. It includes Shelter Island, located between the north and south forks of Long Island's "fishtail," and Plum Island. It takes in Brookhaven National Laboratory, a physics research lab. Also in the 1st are the Hamptons and most of Fire Island National Seashore, the only federal wilderness area in New York state and a magnet for gay vacationers for decades. Suffolk County was long one of the most conservative parts of New York - Richard Nixon won 70 percent of the vote here in 1972 - but it has not been very conservative by today's national standards. Democratic registration has drawn almost even with Republican in recent years. The district voted solidly for Democrat Al Gore in 2000 and went for Republican George W. Bush in 2004 by less than 1 percent - a September 11 effect. It narrowly backed Democrat Barack Obama in 2008 and 2012. Donald Trump was popular here, with a 54%-42% win. Other than Staten Island, Suffolk was the only county that Trump won in New York City or its suburbs (including Connecticut and New Jersey). Like the two adjacent districts, each of which includes parts of Suffolk, this has been a classic swing district under most scenarios.

SECOND DISTRICT

Peter King (R)

Elected 1992, 13th term; b. Apr 05, 1944, New York; University of Notre Dame Law School (IN), J.D.; St. Francis College (NY), B.A.; Roman Catholic; Married (Rosemary Wiedel King); 2 children; 2 grandchildren.

Military Career: U.S Army NY National Guard, 1968-1974.

Elected Office: Hempstead Town Council, 1977-1981; Nassau County comptroller, 1981-1992.

Professional Career: Practicing attorney, 1968-1972, 1978-1981; Deputy Attorney, Nassau County, 1972-1974; Executive Assistant, Nassau County Executive, 1974-1976; General counsel, comptroller, 1977.

DC Office: 339 CHOB 20515, 202-225-7896, Fax: 202-226-2279, peteking.house.gov.

State Offices: Massapequa Park, 516-541-4225.

Committees: *Financial Services*: Capital Markets, Securities & Investment, Oversight & Investigations. *Homeland Security*: Counterterrorism & Intelligence (Chmn), Transportation & Protective Security. *Permanent Select on Intelligence*.

Group Ratings

	ADA	ACLU	AFL-CIO	LCV	ITI	COC	HAFA	ACU	CFG	FRC
2016	-	5%	-	13%	100%	100%	38%	46%	52%	100%
2015	10%	C	50%	9%	C	95%	C	33%	87%	83%

Almanac Ratings 2015

	Economy	Social	Foreign	Composite
Liberal	14%	42%	11%	22%
Conservative	86%	58%	90%	78%

Key Votes of the 114th Congress

1. Keystone Pipeline	Y	5. Puerto Rico Debt	Y	9. Offenses by Aliens	Y
2. Trade Deals	Y	6. Medical Marijuana	Y	10. Troops in Iraq	N
3. Export-Import Bank	Y	7. Sanctuary Cities	N	11. Homeland Security $$	Y
4. Debt Ceiling Increase	Y	8. Armor-piercing Bullets	N	12. Trade Adjustment aid	Y

Election Results

Election	Name (Party)	Vote (%)	Cand. Spent	Ind. Exp. Support	Ind. Exp. Oppose
2016 General	Peter King (R)	181,506 (62%)	$967,583		
	DuWayne Gregory (D)	110,938 (38%)	$370,578	$12,455	
2016 Primary	Peter King (R)	(100%)			

Prior winning percentages: 2014 (65%), 2012 (52%), 2010 (71%), 2008 (54%), 2006 (53%), 2004 (54%), 2002 (65%), 2000 (51%), 1998 (58%), 1996 (47%), 1994 (49%), 1992 (43%)

Republican Pete King, first elected in 1992, has grown from a loquacious maverick to a serious player on domestic security matters. His penchant for quotable quips has made him a constant presence on cable television. His New York accent and intensity have grown out of place in the increasingly conservative Republican Conference. But he gained new opportunities with a like-minded ally in the White House.

King grew up in Sunnyside, Queens. His parents were Irish immigrants and Democrats, his father a New York City police detective. He went to St. Francis College and law school at the University of Notre Dame, and he clerked one summer at former Republican President Richard Nixon's law firm with a Long Islander named Rudolph Giuliani. After law school, he followed the trek to the suburbs and became part of the Nassau County Republican machine. He worked as a lawyer and staffer in county government. He was elected to the Hempstead town council in 1977, and to county comptroller in 1981. When the seat opened in 1992, King ran and won the GOP primary. In the general election, King ran as a fiscal conservative and abortion rights opponent. He won by just 50%-46% but hasn't had a close reelection since then.

King's voting record ranks him near the ideological center of the House, as the *Almanac* vote ratings for 2015 confirmed. He is more conservative on foreign policy, but with distinctive interests. He is far to the left of most Republicans on gun control, declaring after the Newtown, Connecticut, school massacre that Americans "don't need assault weapons" and has filed a bill with Democratic Rep. Mike Thompson of California to expand background checks for firearm purchases at gun shows. On immigration issues, King is an outspoken conservative. He opposes racial quotas and preferences, as well as bilingual education. He supports English-only laws and opposes aid to illegal immigrants. He moved back to the center in 2012 when he challenged anti-tax activist Grover Norquist's never-raise-taxes pledge. Norquist angrily accused him of trying to "weasel out" of an agreement; King called Norquist "a lowlife."

King has been an ardent supporter of the Irish Republican Army. He had a role in 1998 peace negotiations, carrying messages between the IRA and the Irish government. His activism on the issue led to an unusually close bipartisan relationship with President Bill Clinton, who helped broker the agreement. But in 2005, after the suspected involvement of Sinn Féin, the IRA's political arm, in a bank robbery and a highly publicized murder, King called for the IRA to disband. He has written three novels about politics and diplomacy in Northern Ireland. In one of them, *Deliver Us From Evil*, a thinly disguised Long Island congressman is the protagonist. "Maybe after I retire from Congress, or get thrown out of Congress, or whatever, I'll be a writer because as I've seen from some newspaper columnists, almost anyone can be a writer," he told the *Long Island Sentinel.*

After the September 11 attacks, in which 160 of his constituents died, King became more of a Republican regular and focused on legislation to prevent a repeat of the attacks. In 2005, GOP leaders tapped King to be chairman of the Homeland Security Committee. The following year, he was the first House Republican to attack the Bush administration's plan to give control of six major U.S. ports to a company in Dubai in the United Arab Emirates, and he subsequently helped to enact tighter controls on port security.

King sharpened his rhetoric on terrorist threats following the election of President Barack Obama. He said excessive concerns about alleged discrimination against Muslims had hamstrung authorities in the case of Army Maj. Nidal Malik Hasan, who went on a killing rampage at Fort Hood in Texas. When the Homeland Security Department issued a report in April 2009 about domestic right-wing extremism, King complained that the agency "has never put out a report talking about 'look out for mosques.'" The Council on American-Islamic Relations called his remarks "bigoted."

After Republicans regained House control in 2010, King held hearings on "the radicalization of the American Muslim community and homegrown terrorism." Islamic leaders said they feared a witch hunt, and King acknowledged that his stance carried risks. "It is controversial," he told *The New York Times.* "But to me, it is something that has to be discussed." The hearings opened in 2011 amid massive publicity and round-the-clock security for King following reports of threats against him. Some Muslim groups accused him of a double standard. King responded, "The fact is, the IRA never attacked the United States. And my loyalty is to the United States."

Under House GOP rules, King was term-limited to chair the committee after 2012. He settled for the chairmanship of its Counterterrorism and Intelligence Subcommittee. Praising Obama's willingness to kill terrorist leaders with unmanned drone attacks, he gave the president credit in 2012 for preventing another September 11. But in 2014, he blasted Obama for withdrawing troops from Iraq and accused him of helping foster the rise of the Islamic State of Iraq and the Levant (ISIL). He said that the terrorist group was more powerful than al-Qaeda was on September 11 and described the president's handling of Iraq as "shameful." In 2015, the House passed his bill to assist first responders to prepare for an anthrax attack. King won House approval in 2016 and again in January 2017 of his bill to tighten defenses against insider threats at the Homeland Security Department.

Over the years, King has been a provocative and frequent presence on radio and television chat shows. When Republican leaders abruptly pulled from the House floor a $60 billion relief bill for Superstorm Sandy in January 2013, two months after the storm ravaged the East Coast, King declared on CNN, "There's some dysfunction in the Republican leadership." He suggested on Fox News that New York and New Jersey residents stop donating to his party. After the legislation passed easily, King told *Newsday* that he has felt like a "second-class citizen in the Republican caucus" as it became more Southern-oriented.

King picked fights with Texas GOP Sen. Ted Cruz, even before he became a presidential candidate. When Cruz attempted to defund the Affordable Care Act, prompting a partial government shutdown in October 2013, King told MSNBC: "We have to start going after him by name. ... It's really time to speak out against him." If Cruz had won the Republican nomination, King said, "I think that I'll take cyanide." In March 2015, he said that Republicans who threatened to shut down the Homeland Security Department to challenge Obama's executive actions on immigration were "delusional." After Speaker John Boehner resigned under pressure in October 2015, King said, "the crazies have taken over the party."

National and New York Democrats vowed to challenge him following the 2010 redistricting. But their top recruit, Nassau County Prosecutor Kathleen Rice, opted not to run in 2012. Instead, she was elected in the 4th District two years later.

Despite his Queens background and friendship with Trump ally Giuliani, King did not endorse Trump until he wrapped up the nomination. "He has real challenges and he has real opportunities," King told *Newsday* at the time. "But he's got to find a way to turn it around on his negative numbers." He criticized Trump's campaign suggestion that Japan and South Korea might need to develop nuclear weapons. During the presidential transition, King met with him at Trump Tower and urged him to consider a Muslim domestic surveillance program. When Trump issued an executive order a few days after he took office that imposed a temporary immigration ban on several Muslim-majority countries with records of supporting terrorism, King said that it was "overdue."

South-Central Long Island

Population		**Race and Ethnicity**		**Income**	
Total	723,479	White	63.8%	Median Income	$88,543 (20 out of 435)
Land area	182	Black	9.2%		
Pop/ sq mi	3974.9	Latino	22.2%	Under $50,000	26.8%
Born in state	75.9%	Asian	3.1%	$50,000-$99,999	29.6%
Age Groups		Two races	1.3%	$100,000-$199,999	33.8%
Under 18	22.8%	Other	0.4%	$200,000 or more	9.7%
18-34	21.8%	**Education**		Poverty Rate	6.3%
35-64	41.8%	H.S grad or less	44.2%	**Health Insurance**	
Over 64	13.6%	Some college	27.1%	With health insurance coverage	91.1%
Work		College Degree, 4 yr	17.0%		
White Collar	33.6%	Post grad	11.6%	**Public Assistance**	
Sales and Service	45.4%	**Military**		Cash public assistance income	2.8%
Blue Collar	21.0%	Veteran	6.0%		
Government	16.9%	Active Duty	0.0%	Food stamp/SNAP benefits	7.3%

Voter Turnout			
2015 Total Citizens 18+	499,817	2016 House Turnout as % CVAP	59%
2016 House turnout	292,595	2014 House Turnout as % CVAP	28%

2012 Presidential Vote		
Barack Obama	140,817	(52%)
Mitt Romney	128,791	(47%)

2016 Presidential Vote		
Donald Trump	165,908	(53%)
Hillary Clinton	137,680	(44%)

Cook Partisan Voting Index: R+3

At the end of World War II, Suffolk County was largely given over to potato fields. It was also directly in the path of one of the major suburban migrations of our day. On the highways that Robert

Moses built to connect his parks to the middle-class parts of New York City came tens of thousands of young veterans and their families, forsaking the row house neighborhoods where they had grown up for comparatively spacious lots and single-family houses. The first wave of postwar migration moved into Nassau County, starting in 1947, when 300 families moved into 750-square-foot houses that sold for $6,990, with no money down for veterans. The location was Levittown - America's first mass-produced suburb, where delivery trucks dropped off piles of prefabricated materials 60 feet apart, to be picked up by roving teams of specialized workers with power tools. By the time the final house was sold for $9,500 in 1951, Levittown, a former potato field, had become synonymous with instant suburbanization. This wave represented a cross-section of all but the poorest New Yorkers: almost half Catholic, about one-quarter Jewish, and one-quarter Protestant. As Long Island developed its own employment base, the next wave of migration came, this time as far out as Suffolk County. This second wave was more Catholic and less Jewish, more blue-collar (aircraft manufacturers were big Suffolk employers) and less white-collar, more Democratic in ancestral politics.

The 2nd Congressional District of New York takes in Massapequa and Levittown, where the median house is now worth $382,000 after having dipped below $300,000 following the recession. These areas in the eastern part of Nassau County are generally Republican, but only about one-third of the district's population resides in Nassau. Most of its residents live in more Democratic areas in the southwest corner of Suffolk County, where the district stretches from Amityville and Babylon east through Bay Shore and Islip to Sayville and Bayport - one community after another strung out along the Sunrise Highway. The district takes in Brentwood, which is two-thirds Hispanic and has a per capita income barely half of the average in Suffolk. The state laid double-track to improve service on the Long Island Railroad in the Islip area, which previously had only one track. Also near Islip, state and local officials have considered options for bolstering MacArthur Airport, possibly with international service. In Amityville, which became famous for a book and movies about the "The Amityville Horror" murders at a family home, the supposedly haunted 5,000 square foot residence was sold in November 2016.

President Barack Obama twice won this district by a few percentage points. As with other Suffolk-based districts, Donald Trump strengthened Republican support, with a 53%-44% win in 2016.

THIRD DISTRICT

Tom Suozzi (D)

Elected 2016, 1st term; b. Aug 31, 1962, Glen Cove; Boston College (MA), B.S., 1984; Fordham University School of Law (NY), J.D., 1989; Roman Catholic; Married (Helene Suozzi); 3 children.

Elected Office: Glen Cove Mayor, 1994-2001; Nassau County Executive, 2002-2009.

Professional Career: CPA; Practicing Attorney.

DC Office: 226 CHOB 20515, 202-225-3335, Fax: 202-225-4669, suozzi.house.gov.

State Offices: Huntington, 631-923-4100; Little Neck, 718-631-0400.

Committees: *Armed Services*: Oversight & Investigations, Tactical Air & Land Forces. *Foreign Affairs*: Africa, Global Health, Global Human Rights & Internat'l Orgs, Middle East & North Africa.

Election Results

Election	Name (Party)	Vote	(%)	Cand. Spent	Ind. Exp. Support	Ind. Exp. Oppose
2016 General	Tom Suozzi (D)	171,775	(53%)	$2,355,543	$59,180	$774,114
	Jack Martins (R)	152,304	(47%)	$1,134,807		$285,114
2016 Primary	Tom Suozzi (D)	6,532	(36%)			
	Steve Stern (D)	4,069	(22%)			
	Jon Kaiman (D)	4,060	(22%)			
	Anna Kaplan (D)	2,815	(15%)			

Tom Suozzi, elected to the House in 2016, won a peculiar contest to succeed Rep. Steve Israel, a House Democratic leader who retired. The victory was a political comeback for Suozzi, once a boy wonder on Long Island, who had not been elected to any office in more than a decade.

A native of Glen Cove, Suozzi graduated from Boston College and got his law degree from Fordham University. He was the mayor of Glen Cove, a position that his father once held, and then served eight years in the more powerful office of Nassau County Executive, the first Democrat to hold that position in three decades. In 2004, he spearheaded FixAlbany.com, an initiative that targeted corruption in New York state politics and sought to enact a limit on local Medicaid expenses. Not surprisingly, the initiative ruffled some Democratic chieftains, as well as Republicans, in Albany. Since then, he had more than his share of political setbacks. From 2006 until 2013, he lost three campaigns: an uphill Democratic primary for governor against Eliot Spitzer, followed by two unexpected defeats for county executive. In private life, he led a state commission that proposed the first statewide cap on property taxes, which subsequently was enacted. He worked as a senior adviser at the investment bank Lazard Freres and as a litigator at the Shearman & Sterling law firm.

When Israel announced his decision to step down, Suozzi quickly voiced interest in a run. His extensive credentials did not clear the Democratic field. The contenders included three other office-holders, two from Nassau and one from Suffolk. North Hempstead councilwoman Anna Kaplan had the support of EMILY's List, which supports Democratic women who back abortion rights. She raised $750,000, including $365,000 in self-financing. Suozzi and Steve Stern, a Suffolk County legislator, each raised about $800,000 for the primary, and former North Hempstead supervisor Joe Kaiman raised $400,000. The late June primary had a low turnout of about 20,000 voters. Suozzi won with 35 percent to 22 percent for Stern (who got more than half the vote in Suffolk), 22 percent for Kaiman and 16 percent for Kaplan.

In the general, Suozzi faced Jack Martins, a construction businessman who served six years in the state Senate and earlier was the mayor of Mineola. The campaign took an unusual turn when a federal judge ruled in August that another Republican candidate had been improperly excluded from the primary ballot. When the judge scheduled a new GOP primary for Oct. 6, Martins sought to delay the general election until Dec. 6. There was speculation that Martins believed that it would be an advantage for him not to appear on the ballot with Donald Trump and Hillary Clinton. Shortly before Labor Day, the judge denied Martins' motion. Then, on Sept. 14, a federal appeals court canceled the rescheduled primary. Martins accused the Democrats of encouraging the shenanigans. The result, wrote David Wasserman of the Cook Political Report, was that the National Republican Congressional Committee "cooled" its enthusiasm and shifted its attention elsewhere. The NRCC supported Martins with $844,000. But Suozzi doubled the fundraising of Martins and he won, 53%-47%. Martins got 51 percent of the vote in Suffolk, but he lost narrowly in Nassau and by nearly 2-to-1 in Queens.

With that blemished victory, the NRCC placed Suozzi on its early target list for 2018. It remained to be seen whether Republicans would find and support a credible challenger. Suozzi got seats on the Armed Services and Foreign Affairs committees and became co-chair of the bipartisan Congressional Problem Solvers Caucus.

Northern Long Island, Eastern Queens

Population		**Race and Ethnicity**		**Income**	
Total	723,457	White	70.4%	Median Income	$1,01,806 (6 out of 435)
Land area	255	Black	3.1%		
Pop/ sq mi	2838.0	Latino	10.4%	Under $50,000	24.2%
Born in state	70.5%	Asian	14.2%	$50,000-$99,999	24.9%
		Two races	1.4%	$100,000-$199,999	30.8%
Age Groups		Other	0.6%	$200,000 or more	20.2%
Under 18	21.9%			Poverty Rate	5.5%
18-34	17.5%	**Education**			
35-64	42.2%	H.S grad or less	28.1%	**Health Insurance**	
Over 64	18.4%	Some college	20.8%	With health insurance coverage	94.2%
		College Degree, 4 yr	27.2%		
Work		Post grad	23.9%		
White Collar	50.0%			**Public Assistance**	
Sales and Service	38.7%	**Military**		Cash public assistance income	1.1%
Blue Collar	11.3%	Veteran	5.5%		
Government	14.8%	Active Duty	0.0%	Food stamp/SNAP benefits	3.7%

Voter Turnout			
2015 Total Citizens 18+	518,125	2016 House Turnout as % CVAP	63%
2016 House turnout	324,254	2014 House Turnout as % CVAP	32%

2012 Presidential Vote		
Barack Obama	155,451	(51%)
Mitt Romney	147,617	(48%)

2016 Presidential Vote		
Hillary Clinton	178,288	(51%)
Donald Trump	156,942	(45%)

Cook Partisan Voting Index: D+1

The North Shore of Long Island is "Gatsby country," where peninsulas jutting out into the Sound are covered with vast green lawns leading to the mansions of America's great capitalists. Nineteenth-century millionaires commuted by steam yacht from Manhattan to their estates in what is now Queens or Nassau County. In the early 20th century, the richest people in business and show business spent their leisure time here, playing croquet while their servants unloaded bootleggers' boats at their private docks. Inland, behind the expansive lawns, Long Island was still farm country, with little villages clustered at railroad stations, occasional colonial-era houses, and acres of billboard-strewn wasteland on the highways to New York City. But as the city grew outward, affluent neighborhoods developed in Douglaston on the water, just beyond the middle-class Flushing area of Queens inland, and the Great Neck peninsula became a very affluent, mostly Jewish suburb. Farther out, on Sands Point and Oyster Bay, old estates alternated with more modest homes originally built for servants and newer subdivisions. The Sagamore Hill home of President Theodore Roosevelt at Oyster Bay was restored for $10 million and reopened in 2015. Oyster Bay and Huntington were listed in 2016 in *Money Magazine's* 50 Best Places to Live. A few miles to the west in Glen Cove, developers in January 2017 began a planned $1 billion in building along the waterfront, with parks, marinas and an amphitheater, plus 1,100 residences.

The 3rd Congressional District of New York ties together a disparate collection of New York City neighborhoods and suburbs. About one-third of its votes are cast in Suffolk County, where the political leanings are more conservative than elsewhere in the district. A bit more than 10 percent live at the western extreme of the district, in upscale neighborhoods of Queens near the Throgs Neck and Bronx-Whitestone bridges to the Bronx and points north: Douglaston, Bellaire and Beechurst. This area is more affluent than other portions of Queens and is heavily Democratic. In the middle - politically, as well as geographically - is northern Nassau County. Roughly half of the district's population lives here, many in the posh neighborhoods abutting or near Long Island Sound. This affluence largely continues inland; the median household incomes in Jericho exceeded $150,000 per year. The district has been politically competitive. In 2012, Barack Obama defeated Mitt Romney, 51%-48%. Even with Donald Trump's improved performance in the Suffolk part of the district, Hillary Clinton raised Democratic performance elsewhere and led, 51%-45%.

FOURTH DISTRICT

Kathleen Rice (D)

Elected 2014, 2nd term; b. Feb 15, 1965, New York City; Catholic University of America (DC), B.A., 1987; Touro Law Center, J.D., 1991; Roman Catholic; Single.

Elected Office: Nassau County District Attorney, 2006-2015.

Professional Career: Assistant District Attorney, Brooklyn; Assistant U.S. Attorney, 1999-2005.

DC Office: 1508 LHOB 20515, 202-225-5516, Fax: 202-225-5758, kathleenrice.house.gov.

State Offices: Garden City, 516-739-3008.

Committees: *Homeland Security*: Counterterrorism & Intelligence (RMM), Oversight & Management Efficiency. *Veterans' Affairs*: Economic Opportunity, Oversight & Investigations.

Group Ratings

	ADA	ACLU	AFL-CIO	LCV	ITI	COC	HAFA	ACU	CFG	FRC
2016	-	82%	-	89%	83%	64%	9%	0%	7%	0%
2015	60%	C	87%	97%	C	60%	C	0%	5%	0%

Almanac Ratings 2015

	Economy	Social	Foreign	Composite
Liberal	75%	100%	56%	77%
Conservative	25%	0%	44%	23%

Key Votes of the 114th Congress

1. Keystone Pipeline	N	5. Puerto Rico Debt	Y	9. Offenses by Aliens	N
2. Trade Deals	Y	6. Medical Marijuana	Y	10. Troops in Iraq	N
3. Export-Import Bank	Y	7. Sanctuary Cities	N	11. Homeland Security $$	Y
4. Debt Ceiling Increase	Y	8. Armor-piercing Bullets	N	12. Trade Adjustment aid	Y

Election Results

Election	Name (Party)	Vote (%)	Cand. Spent	Ind. Exp. Support	Ind. Exp. Oppose
2016 General	Kathleen Rice (D)	186,423 (60%)	$1,644,373		
	David Gurfein (R)	126,438 (40%)	$433,120		
2016 Primary	Kathleen Rice (D)	(100%)			

Prior winning percentages: 2014 (51%)

Democrat Kathleen Rice, a veteran Nassau County prosecutor who built a reputation for being tough on drunken drivers, won an open seat in 2014. For a junior lawmaker, she has shown an unusual willingness to challenge authority - namely, that of Minority Leader Nancy Pelosi. Whether or not it's a coincidence, her assignments have been on second-tier committees. She has made the most of her opportunities and she could be well-positioned in a post-Pelosi Democratic Caucus.

Born in Manhattan and raised in Garden City, Rice was one of 10 children borne by an only-child mother. She graduated from Catholic University in Washington, D.C., and got her law degree from Touro Law Center in Central Islip, Long Island. Rice registered as a Republican in 1984 and did not vote until 2002, *Newsday* reported in 2010. She responded that her lack of voting was a "mistake."

She began her legal career as an assistant district attorney in Kings County, prosecuting burglaries, robberies, and sexual assaults. For six years, she was an assistant U.S. attorney in Philadelphia, where she handled white-collar crimes, corporate fraud, gun and drug cases, and public corruption. Rice was elected Nassau County's district attorney in 2005, defeating a Republican who had held the job for three decades, and quickly developed a reputation for prosecution of drunken drivers. She worked to pass legislation imposing harsher penalties on drunken drivers who had children in the car or who injured other motorists. Rice went after cheating on college admission tests, working to improve test security. She was co-chair of the Moreland Commission to Investigate Public Corruption in New York State, and was president of the state's District Attorneys Association.

As she increased her political ambition, Rice ran in the five-candidate Democratic primary for state attorney general in 2010. She trailed eventual winner Eric Schneiderman, 34%-32%, though she led in counties outside of New York City. In Nassau, she was the only countywide Democrat to win reelection in 2013.

In her campaign for Congress, Republican nominee Bruce Blakeman ran negative ads against Rice, accusing her of being anti-woman for her workplace policies as district attorney and her refusal to fire a staffer who made sexist and racially offensive comments on Twitter. As a new D.A., Rice had told part-timers (many of them women caring for children) that they had to become full-timers or leave the office. She told *Newsday* at the time that the county "deserves victims' advocates that are full time." Rice won the support of numerous women's groups. Blakeman questioned her role on the Moreland Commission, which itself was a target in a state corruption investigation, though there had been no evidence of wrongdoing by Rice. She won the election, 53%-47%. Prior to her predecessor Carolyn McCarthy, who won the seat in 1996, Republicans held this district consistently since 1952. Rice won reelection with 60 percent of the vote in a contest that got little attention.

During her first two years, Rice was the senior Democrat on the Homeland Security Subcommittee on Transportation Security, where the chairman was another freshman from New York, Republican John

Katko. In July 2015, the House passed her bill that directed the Transportation Security Administration to develop and implement preventive maintenance for security-related technology at airports. In 2017, she became ranking Democrat on the Counterterrorism and Intelligence Subcommittee. The chairman was Republican Rep. Peter King from her neighboring district on Long Island.

On the Veterans Affairs Committee, she had success with two of her bills. In May 2015, the House passed a measure that she cosponsored with Republican Rep. Paul Cook of California that would give preference to companies with high numbers of veterans when awarding Veterans Affairs contracts; the House passed that bill again in February 2017. Rice enacted a bill that provided dental insurance courage for veterans and their survivors and dependents. That bill was included as part of broader veterans legislation. Rice bucked the Obama administration when she voted against its nuclear agreement with Iran. "Here, the president is displaying an admirable political vision and optimism, but I just don't trust the progress of that social experiment [in Iran] enough to pay the cost of this gamble's security risk," she wrote in an op-ed.

Following the 2016 election, Rice was on the front line in questioning the poor campaign results for House Democrats and, especially, the leadership of Pelosi. As an early supporter of Rep. Tim Ryan of Ohio in his challenge to Pelosi's post, she wrote, "I believed it was important to delay House Democratic leadership elections so that we had time to learn from this loss … [and] have some tough conversations about how we got here and what strategy we can unite behind to give ourselves a realistic chance of retaking control of Congress." Ryan, she added pointedly, was "the one forcing us to ask the tough questions about our party's future, and he's the one providing real answers." During the vote for Speaker in January 2017, Rice took the unusual step of voting for Ryan. She was one of four Democrats who did not vote for Pelosi, the party nominee.

Southern Nassau County: Hempstead

Population		**Race and Ethnicity**		**Income**	
Total	721,286	White	58.7%	Median Income	$94,770 (11 out of 435)
Land area	111	Black	13.9%		
Pop/ sq mi	6506.9	Latino	19.3%	Under $50,000	26.6%
Born in state	70.7%	Asian	6.2%	$50,000-$99,999	26.0%
		Two races	1.3%	$100,000-$199,999	33.2%
Age Groups		Other	0.5%	$200,000 or more	14.4%
Under 18	22.5%			Poverty Rate	7.3%
18-34	21.1%	**Education**			
35-64	41.2%	H.S grad or less	35.7%	**Health Insurance**	
Over 64	15.3%	Some college	24.4%	With health insurance coverage	91.2%
		College Degree, 4 yr	22.1%		
Work		Post grad	17.8%		
White Collar	41.4%			**Public Assistance**	
Sales and Service	43.7%	**Military**		Cash public assistance income	1.7%
Blue Collar	14.9%	Veteran	5.0%		
Government	17.0%	Active Duty	0.1%	Food stamp/SNAP benefits	6.1%

Voter Turnout			
2015 Total Citizens 18+	495,558	2016 House Turnout as % CVAP	63%
2016 House turnout	313,000	2014 House Turnout as % CVAP	35%

2012 Presidential Vote		
Barack Obama	165,876	(56%)
Mitt Romney	129,049	(43%)

2016 Presidential Vote		
Hillary Clinton	179,845	(53%)
Donald Trump	147,469	(44%)

Cook Partisan Voting Index: D+4

Nassau County has long been on the cutting edge of American suburban life. It is the home of one of the earliest suburbs: Garden City, founded in 1869 with wide avenues and single-family homes. After World War II, it pioneered large-scale suburban development, as freeways replaced highways, and shopping centers sprang up at intersections. Many of the middle- and upper-income residents continue to depend on the Long Island Railroad to speed them to jobs in New York City. Prominent sites include the county seat of Mineola; Hofstra University in Hempstead, which has held a presidential debate during the past three general elections; and Roosevelt Field, where Charles Lindbergh took off for Paris in 1927. The fate of this historic airstrip perhaps typifies the extent of suburbanization in Nassau County: It's now the site of an upscale shopping mall, with a long-standing conflict over the exact spot of Lindbergh's departure, either at an escalator in the shopping center or just behind a parking garage near a Best Buy.

The 4th Congressional District of New York comprises Garden City and the towns around it. It is one of six districts in the state that is wholly included within a single county. The 4th takes in several suburbs along the Jericho Turnpike - New Hyde Park, Mineola, Westbury - as well as a large swath of southern Nassau County. This territory includes Hempstead, Uniondale, Rockville Centre and part of ethnically diverse Valley Stream, as well as most of the predominantly Jewish "Five Towns" - the railway suburbs of Lawrence, Cedarhurst, Hewlett and Woodmere; Inwood is in the neighboring 5th District. In January 2017, the Long Island Railroad began review of a $2 billion plan to build a third track between Floral Park and Hicksville, with underground stations that would increase the frequency of service and reduce traffic jams on the streets. Jones Beach, a state park with more than six miles of an expansive ocean beachfront and 2,400 acres for maritime entertainment, hosts about six million annual visitors. In 2015, the New York Islanders professional hockey team abandoned the 43-year-old Nassau Coliseum and had a reverse migration to the full-service Barclays Center in rejuvenated Brooklyn. It didn't take long before speculation ensued that the team might return to the coliseum, following its $260 million renovation.

Nassau County was traditionally Republican, and Garden City remains that way. Now, the county is on the cutting edge of American suburban life as it has become more diverse and more Democratic. Hempstead typifies these emerging changes. Once swing territory that served as the political base of Republican Sen. Alfonse D'Amato, non-Hispanic whites in the village make up just 6.6 percent of the population. In December 2016, developers broke ground on a $2.5 billion redevelopment in downtown Hempstead. Nearby Roosevelt is only 2 percent non-Hispanic white. These towns, plus Freeport, combined to give Barack Obama 86 percent of the vote in 2008. The district includes the old resort areas around Lido Beach and Long Beach and suburban Merrick, Bellmore and Wantagh; these areas are more marginal. Following Obama's two double-digit wins, Hillary Clinton won the district, 53%-44%. Overall, she got 52 percent of the vote in Nassau.

FIFTH DISTRICT

Gregory Meeks (D)

Elected 1998, 10th term; b. Sep 25, 1953, Harlem; Adelphi University (NY), B.A., 1975; Howard University Law School (DC), J.D., 1978; African Methodist Episcopal; Married (Simone-Marie Meeks); 3 children.

Elected Office: NY Assembly, 1992-1998.

Professional Career: Assistant District Attorney, Queens County, 1978-1983; NY St. Commission of Investigations, 1984-1985; Judge, NY St. Workers' Compensation Board, 1985-1992.

DC Office: 2234 RHOB 20515, 202-225-3461, Fax: 202-226-4169, meeks.house.gov.

State Offices: Arverne, 347-230-4032; Jamaica, 718-725-6000.

Committees: *Financial Services*: Capital Markets, Securities & Investment, Financial Institutions & Consumer Credit, Monetary Policy & Trade. *Foreign Affairs*: Europe, Eurasia & Emerging Threats (RMM), Western Hemisphere.

Group Ratings

	ADA	ACLU	AFL-CIO	LCV	ITI	COC	HAFA	ACU	CFG	FRC
2016	-	94%	-	92%	83%	69%	13%	0%	6%	0%
2015	90%	C	84%	89%	C	50%	C	0%	0%	0%

Almanac Ratings 2015

	Economy	Social	Foreign	Composite
Liberal	79%	97%	84%	87%
Conservative	21%	3%	16%	13%

Key Votes of the 114th Congress

1. Keystone Pipeline	N	5. Puerto Rico Debt	Y	9. Offenses by Aliens	N
2. Trade Deals	Y	6. Medical Marijuana	Y	10. Troops in Iraq	N
3. Export-Import Bank	Y	7. Sanctuary Cities	N	11. Homeland Security $$	NV
4. Debt Ceiling Increase	NV	8. Armor-piercing Bullets	N	12. Trade Adjustment aid	Y

Election Results

Election	Name (Party)	Vote (%)	Cand. Spent	Ind. Exp. Support	Ind. Exp. Oppose
2016 General	Gregory Meeks (D)	199,815 (85%)	$929,249		
	Michael O'Reilly (R)	30,312 (13%)	$39,032		
2016 Primary	Gregory Meeks (D)	5,981 (82%)			
	Ali Mirza (D)	1,327 (18%)			

Prior winning percentages: 2014 (80%), 2012 (75%), 2010 (76%), 2008 (67%), 2006 (70%), 2004 (70%), 2002 (65%), 2000 (69%)

Democrat Gregory Meeks, first elected in 1998, is a liberal who is more sympathetic to business than are other New York City Democrats - sometimes to the unhappiness of organized labor. In part, that reflects the commercial interests of his international district. Ethics controversies have dogged him in recent years. With the retirement in 2016 of Rep. Charlie Rangel, Meeks became the senior African-American in the delegation.

Meeks grew up in public housing projects in Harlem. He was inspired by his mother, who went back to school when her four children were older and who encouraged community service volunteerism. Meeks' childhood hero was Supreme Court Justice Thurgood Marshall. After graduating from Adelphi College and Howard University law school, Meeks moved to Far Rockaway. He became an assistant district attorney and a workers' compensation judge. He was elected to the state Assembly in 1992 and became an ally of Democratic Rep. Floyd Flake, a minister whose Allen African Methodist Episcopal Church congregation grew from 1,400 members in 1976 to more than 20,000 members.

When Flake resigned, Meeks won a majority of Democratic committee members at a January 1998 endorsement meeting and thus became the party's nominee in a special election. Democratic state Sen. Alton Waldon and Assemblywoman Barbara Clark ran as independents. With the support of Flake and civil rights leaders, Meeks won 57 percent of the vote, to Waldon's 21 percent and Clark's 13 percent. Since then, he has had only token opposition.

Meeks has a voting record toward the center of House Democrats. The *Almanac* vote ratings for 2015 ranked him as more conservative on economic issues and liberal on social issues. He has been active in the commerce-oriented New Democrat Coalition. On the Financial Services Committee, he has been an ally of Wall Street interests and has joined African-American members in seeking to ensure that legislation addresses minorities' issues. He has backed numerous free-trade agreements. In 2015, he was one of the few outspoken Democratic supporters of President Barack Obama's Trans-Pacific Partnership. These agreements promised new opportunities for JFK airport and its many auxiliary businesses.

Meeks has been ranking Democrat on the Foreign Affairs Subcommittee on Europe, Eurasia and Emerging Threats, where he has talked about the need for "working with allies" and contrasted the approach of President Donald Trump who, Meeks said, "has us stepping back from the world stage." With Republican Rep. Joe Wilson of South Carolina in February 2017, he created the European Union Caucus to promote shared values of freedom and democracy.

On local issues, Meeks worked with Republicans in 2012 to enact a bill authorizing construction of natural gas pipelines in the state's portion of the Gateway National Recreation Area. He sought to help constituents facing foreclosure. "The worst thing that I've seen is families in my office crying because they are about to lose their house," he said at a town hall meeting.

His financial ethics have become fodder for New York's major dailies in recent years. The Federal Election Commission in 2006 reprimanded him for using more than $6,000 in 2004 campaign funds for a personal trainer and other expenses. In 2010, *The New York Times* wrote that despite acknowledging that he has no more than a few thousand dollars in his savings account, he "lives a life worthy of a jet-setter," staying in luxury hotels, driving a taxpayer-leased $1,000-a-month Lexus and buying a $1 million house built by a developer who was a campaign contributor. He told the newspaper that he observed all campaign finance laws, and that "I am not going to raise the money in my district that I need to be a player here in Washington." Meeks blamed the negative attention on conservative groups out to undermine Democrats.

The New York Post reported in 2013 that Meeks had ties to several people who were either in jail or under indictment. One friend facing sentencing in a mortgage-fraud scheme, Edul Ahmad, gave Meeks $40,000 in 2007. The congressman said the money was a loan but did not pay it back until after the FBI inquired about it. The House Ethics Committee cleared Meeks of wrongdoing in the matter. A Queens immigration lawyer, Albert Baldeo, who was arrested for campaign finance fraud in a 2010 special-election bid to serve on the city council, told *The Post* he gave Meeks a break on rent for office space in a building he owned because he wanted the congressman to have a presence in his area. House rules prohibit members from receiving below-market rent. Meeks told the newspaper, "My office complied with the law and continues to do so." In 2015, Baldeo was sentenced to 18 months in prison for witness tampering.

The support by Meeks for the Trans-Pacific trade deal led some national unions to threaten a primary challenge in 2016. Democratic state Sen. James Sanders, an ally of organized labor, filed to challenge him but dropped out of the primary shortly before the filing deadline. "I wanted to rid the complacency, mediocrity and ethical lapses from yet another elected seat that has been preventing real improvements from being enacted in our neighborhoods," Sanders said. He changed his mind, he said, so he could work with other Democrats to secure a majority in the state Senate. Instead, Meeks faced Ali Mirza, a little-known businessman from Elmont, and won with 82 percent of the vote in a low-turnout contest.

Southeast Queens, Western Nassau

Population		**Race and Ethnicity**		**Income**	
Total	765,409	White	10.9%	Median Income	$61,312 (130 out of 435)
Land area	52	Black	48.0%		
Pop/ sq mi	14753.5	Latino	19.6%		
Born in state	49.1%	Asian	13.3%	Under $50,000	41.2%
		Two races	3.1%	$50,000-$99,999	31.3%
Age Groups		Other	5.2%	$100,000-$199,999	23.2%
Under 18	23.1%			$200,000 or more	4.4%
18-34	24.5%	**Education**		Poverty Rate	13.8%
35-64	39.9%	H.S grad or less	49.2%		
Over 64	12.5%	Some college	27.0%	**Health Insurance**	
Work		College Degree, 4 yr	15.7%	With health insurance coverage	87.4%
White Collar	28.0%	Post grad	8.2%		
Sales and Service	52.1%	**Military**		**Public Assistance**	
Blue Collar	19.9%	Veteran	3.3%	Cash public assistance income	4.2%
Government	18.1%	Active Duty	0.0%		
				Food stamp/SNAP benefits	18.9%

Voter Turnout			
2015 Total Citizens 18+	475,358	2016 House Turnout as % CVAP	49%
2016 House turnout	233,853	2014 House Turnout as % CVAP	17%

2012 Presidential Vote		
Barack Obama	200,004	(90%)
Mitt Romney	22,026	(10%)

2016 Presidential Vote		
Hillary Clinton	211,667	(85%)
Donald Trump	31,322	(13%)

Cook Partisan Voting Index: D+37

A half-century ago, there was a small black community in southern Queens, near Jamaica Bay. Since then, many African-American families have bought houses and raised their families in neighborhoods that fan east from there. They fought to maintain the relatively spacious streets, relishing the plenitude of natural light, safe schools and good neighborhood stores. There is block upon block of low-rise, frame and brick houses, built mostly from the 1920s to the 1950s, in the neighborhoods of Springfield Gardens and Laurelton, St. Albans and Rosedale, Cambria Heights and Queens Village. This part of Queens today is home to New York City's largest concentration of middle-class black homeowners, with a median income higher than white households in Queens. Showing the community's economic strength, multiple developers have launched plans for new residential towers and retail space. Some of them are near the Jamaica rail terminal, which is about a 15-minute ride from JFK Airport. On Wareham Place, in the small upper middle class neighborhood of Jamaica Estates, is the Tudor home, built by Fred Trump, where Donald Trump lived from his birth until he was four years old. It reportedly was sold at auction during the week of Trump's inaugural by a seller who had purchased it a month earlier and was hoping to make a quick profit.

The 5th Congressional District of New York contains all of these southeast Queens neighborhoods, plus other less affluent sections of southern Queens. It is bounded on the north, more or less, by Grand Central Parkway, and a line running just east of Cross Bay Boulevard to the west. To the east, the Nassau County line has melted away as the unofficial boundary between black and white Long Island. The district now takes in some precincts in southwestern Nassau, with about 15 percent of the district voters: Inwood, Valley Stream and Elmont, which is the home of the Belmont Stakes, the third jewel in horse racing's annual Triple Crown. To the south, it includes Rockaway Peninsula, much of which is occupied by vast swaths of government-financed housing that were planned by Robert Moses in the 1950s and 1960s but never completely rebuilt. The beach and its boardwalk were reopened in July 2016 following $140 million in repairs and restoration that were required following the devastation of Superstorm Sandy in 2012. In the middle of all this is John F. Kennedy International Airport, the largest international gateway for air travelers entering the United States. The airport has generated 230,000 jobs in the area, and businesses there have reported more activity - a hopeful sign for New York's economy. Airlines have invested billions of dollars in upgrading terminals, some of which had sunk to third-world levels. In January 2017, New York Gov. Andrew Cuomo announced a $10 billion plan to further modernize the terminals at the airport and improve its transportation systems.

Richmond Hill and Ozone Park, just northwest of JFK, were previously white ethnic neighborhoods, but now have sizable numbers of Latinos and Asians. South Ozone Park is home to many immigrants from Jamaica, Haiti, the Dominican Republic, and Trinidad and Tobago. The 5th District is 49 percent African American, 21 percent Hispanic, and 13 percent Asian. Politically, it has been in the top 2 percent of the country's most-Democratic districts. President Barack Obama got 90 percent of the vote here in 2012. The vote in 2016 for Hillary Clinton dropped to 85 percent. Perhaps some of Trump's former neighbors remained loyal to him.

SIXTH DISTRICT

Grace Meng (D)

Elected 2012, 3rd term; b. Oct 01, 1975, Queens; University of Michigan, B.A.; Yeshiva University Benjamin N. Cardozo School of Law (NY), J.D.; Christian Church; Married (Wayne Kye); 2 children.

Elected Office: NY Assembly, 2009-2012.

Professional Career: Practicing attorney, 2003-2013.

DC Office: 1317 LHOB 20515, 202-225-2601, Fax: 202-225-1589, meng.house.gov.

State Offices: Flushing, 718-358-6364; Forest Hills, 718-358-6364.

Committees: *Appropriations*: Commerce, Justice, Science & Related Agencies, State, Foreign Operations & Related Programs.

Group Ratings

	ADA	ACLU	AFL-CIO	LCV	ITI	COC	HAFA	ACU	CFG	FRC
2016	-	100%	-	100%	67%	54%	12%	0%	4%	0%
2015	80%	C	100%	94%	C	50%	C	0%	0%	0%

Almanac Ratings 2015

	Economy	Social	Foreign	Composite
Liberal	95%	100%	85%	93%
Conservative	5%	0%	15%	7%

Key Votes of the 114th Congress

1. Keystone Pipeline	N	5. Puerto Rico Debt	Y	9. Offenses by Aliens	N
2. Trade Deals	N	6. Medical Marijuana	Y	10. Troops in Iraq	N
3. Export-Import Bank	Y	7. Sanctuary Cities	N	11. Homeland Security $$	Y
4. Debt Ceiling Increase	Y	8. Armor-piercing Bullets	N	12. Trade Adjustment aid	Y

Election Results

Election	Name (Party)	Vote (%)	Cand. Spent	Ind. Exp. Support	Ind. Exp. Oppose
2016 General	Grace Meng (D)	136,506 (72%)	$589,816		
	Danniel S. Maio (R)	50,617 (27%)			
2016 Primary	Grace Meng (D)	(100%)			

Prior winning percentages: 2014 (72%), 2012 (60%)

Democrat Grace Meng, elected to the House in 2012 as the first Asian American from New York, became a rising political star among Asian Americans in Congress and in the Democratic Party. In 2017, she joined the Appropriations Committee, which gave her more opportunity to deliver funds to her district.

Meng was born and raised in Queens. Her parents had left Taiwan for the United States in the early 1970s. After debating whether to become a teacher or a lawyer, she chose law, studying history at the University of Michigan and getting her law degree from Yeshiva University's Cardozo School of Law. She did pro bono work for Sanctuary for Families, and joined a law firm. She worked as a volunteer on several New York political campaigns, including Hillary Clinton's reelection to the Senate in 2006.

Her father, Jimmy Meng, served one term in the state Assembly and did not seek reelection following reports of legal problems in his campaign. In 2006, she sought to take his place but residency issues forced her out of the race. She then defeated his successor, Assemblywoman Ellen Young. During her four years in Albany, Meng enacted a measure to eliminate the word "Oriental" - a term critics say is outdated and offensive - from state documents referring to people of Asian descent. She worked to protect senior citizens from higher property taxes.

When she ran for the open seat, Meng received the backing of the Queens Democratic Party and several Asian-American advocacy groups as well as the powerful New York Hotel and Motel Trades Council. She easily won the Democratic primary against three other contenders, with 53 percent of the vote to 25 percent for runner-up Assemblyman Rory Lancman, who appealed to the district's sizable Jewish constituency. In the small turnout, Meng in effect was elected by the 14,825 votes she received in the primary.

She had little trouble in the general election against Republican Daniel J. Halloran, a member of the New York City Council. The contest became raucous after Halloran accused Meng of running a campaign of "ethnocentrism" based on her roots, referred to her as a "Chinese national" and falsely accused her of having dual citizenship. She won, 68%-31%, and has not been seriously challenged since then. Meng persevered through an embarrassing episode, when her father was arrested in 2014 and accused of soliciting $80,000 from a friend facing criminal charges, claiming he could bribe prosecutors. After she was reelected without opposition, Jimmy Meng pleaded guilty to wire fraud and was sentenced to one month in prison.

In the disaster-relief measure following Superstorm Sandy, she won a provision to permit disaster funds to be used for rebuilding houses of worship damaged or destroyed by the storm. Much of her work has reflected the international interests of her district. On the Foreign Affairs Committee, she filed a bill with Republican Rep. Tom Emmer of Minnesota to direct the State Department to speed up visa approvals for international physicians who are slated to work at U.S. hospitals. Following the devastating Nepal earthquake in 2015, she worked with New York Democratic colleague Joe Crowley to grant protected immigration status on a temporary basis to Nepali nationals residing in the United States so they were not forced to return home to harmful and unsafe conditions. In 2016, she enacted a law modeled on her New York statute to remove from U.S. law "Oriental," a word that she called "insulting and outdated," and replace it with "Asian Americans." In July 2015, Meng was the first House

Democrat to oppose the Obama administration's nuclear agreement with Iran, which she described as "simply too dangerous for the American people."

In 2016 and again in January 2017, the House passed her bill to prohibit a practice known as "spoofing," which has been described as deliberately changing one's cell phone ID when texting another person - a practice used to steal money and personal information. She was a founder and co-chair of the Kids' Safety Caucus. When she gained a seat on Appropriations in 2017, she described it as an opportunity "to improve the lives of all Americans – particularly here in Queens."

Meng became one of five vice-chairs of the Democratic National Committee after Rep. Tulsi Gabbard of Hawaii resigned in 2016 to become an active supporter of Bernie Sanders for the Democratic presidential nomination. In February 2017, Meng won a full term in that position.

Central Queens: Forest Hills, Flushing

Population		**Race and Ethnicity**		**Income**	
Total	727,625	White	36.1%	Median Income	$58,575 (154 out of 435)
Land area	30	Black	3.4%		
Pop/ sq mi	24433.3	Latino	19.0%		
Born in state	42.8%	Asian	38.7%	Under $50,000	43.1%
Age Groups		Two races	2.0%	$50,000-$99,999	30.4%
Under 18	18.8%	Other	0.7%	$100,000-$199,999	21.4%
18-34	22.8%	**Education**		$200,000 or more	5.0%
35-64	42.8%	H.S grad or less	41.5%	Poverty Rate	13.9%
Over 64	15.6%	Some college	22.0%	**Health Insurance**	
Work		College Degree, 4 yr	22.2%	With health insurance coverage	85.4%
White Collar	38.3%	Post grad	14.3%		
Sales and Service	45.8%	**Military**		**Public Assistance**	
Blue Collar	15.9%	Veteran	2.5%	Cash public assistance income	2.5%
Government	13.1%	Active Duty	0.0%	Food stamp/SNAP benefits	10.3%

Voter Turnout			
2015 Total Citizens 18+	445,126	2016 House Turnout as % CVAP	43%
2016 House turnout	189,433	2014 House Turnout as % CVAP	12%

2012 Presidential Vote		
Barack Obama	125,495	(68%)
Mitt Romney	57,455	(31%)

2016 Presidential Vote		
Hillary Clinton	134,970	(65%)
Donald Trump	66,487	(32%)

Cook Partisan Voting Index: D+16

A half-century ago, most of the neighborhoods in New York's outer boroughs were virtually all-white. Most of these areas have filled with descendants of the great mass of immigrants who came from eastern and southern Europe between 1890 and 1924 and from northern Europe earlier - Irish and Italians, Jews and Hungarians, Poles and Czechs and Greeks. This hodgepodge produced many cultural icons of the last half-decade: Paul Simon, the Ramones, Michael Landon and Donna Karan all trace their roots to Forest Hills. A few parts of Queens were WASPy and high-income. Forest Hills in Queens, with its famous tennis stadium and large Tudor houses, was a notable example.

But the only thing permanent in New York is change. The 1960s saw pitched battles of city politics between John Lindsay, a liberal Manhattan Republican, and his mostly outer-borough opponents. During Lindsay's reign as mayor, middle-class New Yorkers fled the city's high taxes and crime-addled neighborhoods, while Forest Hills was the site of sometimes violent protests when Lindsay attempted to place low-income housing projects in the neighborhood. The result was a drop in population; Queens had four congressional districts and large portions of two others at the end of the 1960s, while today it is barely entitled to three. Some of this neighborhood change would have happened anyway. Neighborhoods settled by immigrants in the 1920s were full of old people, and increasing numbers of African Americans were eager to move from the old ghettoes. After Mayor Bill DeBlasio in 2014 moved homeless families - many of them African-American - into Elmhurst and sparked protests, chiefly by Chinese Americans. They criticized the growing numbers and his excessive use of hotels as shelters. The mayor defended his attempts to address the problem. By 2016, the overall picture in Queens seemed bright. The 10 largest property sales that year in the Borough, mostly residential, totaled more than $1 billion.

The 6th Congressional District is the only district that is entirely in Queens. It begins near the border of Nassau County, at Fresh Meadows, and runs west through Pomonok and the old rail suburbs of Kew Gardens and Forest Hills. It continues west to Rego Park, which has many 1950s high-rise apartments; Middle Village; Glendale; and part of Maspeth. Across Flushing Bay from LaGuardia Airport (which is in the 14th District), it takes in Flushing, long a modest-income white ethnic neighborhood and now about 70 percent Asian, with several Chinese dialects. The New World Mall in downtown Flushing is the largest indoor Asian mall on the East Coast. West of 138th Street, Queens is dominated by Taiwanese and ethnic Chinese from Malaysia, Vietnam, and Thailand. Shops have an urban "Chinatown" feel and feature a wide variety of delicacies. (New York City has three Chinatowns - one each in Manhattan and Brooklyn, with the largest in Queens.) The area east of 138th Street is predominantly Korean. With more than 130 languages spoken in Queens, some call it the "Borough of Diversity."

The district has grown to 40 percent Asian American, with 19 percent Latino and only 4 percent black. While there are pockets of Republican voting, especially around Middle Village and Kew Gardens Hills, it is solidly Democratic. Hillary Clinton led Donald Trump, 65%-32%. As was the case for President Barack Obama, that was her lowest share of the vote in the 10 Democratic-held districts in New York City.

SEVENTH DISTRICT

Nydia Velazquez (D)

Elected 1992, 13th term; b. Mar 28, 1953, Yabucoa, PR; New York University, M.A.; University of Puerto Rico (Rio Piedras), B.A.; Roman Catholic; Married (Paul Bader).

Elected Office: NY City Council, 1984-1986.

Professional Career: Faculty, University of PR, 1976-1981; Adjunct Professional, Hunter College, 1981-1983; Special Assistant, U.S. Rep. Edolphus Towns, 1983; Migration Director, PR Department of Labor & Human Resources, 1986-1989; Director, PR Department of Community Affairs in the U.S., 1989-1992.

DC Office: 2302 RHOB 20515, 202-225-2361, Fax: 202-226-0327, velazquez.house.gov.

State Offices: Brooklyn, 718-599-3658; Brooklyn, 718-222-5819; New York, 212-619-2606.

Committees: *Financial Services*: Financial Institutions & Consumer Credit, Housing & Insurance. *Small Business (RMM)*.

Group Ratings

	ADA	ACLU	AFL-CIO	LCV	ITI	COC	HAFA	ACU	CFG	FRC
2016	-	100%	-	100%	33%	57%	14%	0%	4%	0%
2015	100%	C	100%	100%	C	40%	C	0%	0%	0%

Almanac Ratings 2015

	Economy	Social	Foreign	Composite
Liberal	98%	100%	94%	98%
Conservative	2%	0%	6%	3%

Key Votes of the 114th Congress

1. Keystone Pipeline	N	5. Puerto Rico Debt	Y	9. Offenses by Aliens	N
2. Trade Deals	N	6. Medical Marijuana	Y	10. Troops in Iraq	Y
3. Export-Import Bank	Y	7. Sanctuary Cities	N	11. Homeland Security $$	Y
4. Debt Ceiling Increase	Y	8. Armor-piercing Bullets	N	12. Trade Adjustment aid	Y

Election Results

Election	Name (Party)	Vote (%)		Cand. Spent	Ind. Exp. Support	Ind. Exp. Oppose
2016 General	Nydia Velazquez (D)	172,146	(91%)	$693,782	$5,076	
	Allan E. Romaguera (R)	17,478	(9%)			
2016 Primary	Nydia Velazquez (D)	9,565	(62%)			
	Yungman Lee (D)	4,302	(28%)			
	Jeff Kurzon (D)	1,573	(10%)			

Prior winning percentages: 2014 (83%), 2012 (79%), 2010 (79%), 2008 (67%), 2006 (73%), 2004 (10%), 2002 (55%), 2000 (63%), 1998 (64%), 1996 (83%), 1994 (58%), 1992 (55%)

Nydia Velázquez, first elected in 1992, is the ranking Democrat on the Small Business Committee and the first Puerto Rican woman elected to Congress. Sometimes called *La Luchadora* - "The Fighter" -- she is a senior member of the Financial Services Committee, which oversees companies with many employees who are her constituents. With the changes in her district, her constituents increasingly include entrepreneurs and managers, in addition to blue-collar workers.

She grew up in Puerto Rico as one of nine children of sugar-cane field workers. Although her father never finished elementary school, he was a political leader in her hometown of Yabucoa and inspired her to pursue politics as a career. She studied political science at the University of Puerto Rico and taught there in the 1970s. After graduate school in New York City, she went to work for local Democratic Rep. Edolphus Towns. In 1983, she became the first Hispanic woman elected to the New York City Council.

When the new district was created in 1992, Velázquez was a major contender in the Democratic primary. She had to overcome nine-term Rep. Stephen Solarz, who had decided to run in the new district rather than challenge Rep. Charles Schumer. Velázquez was endorsed by Mayor David Dinkins and civil rights leader Jesse Jackson. In a light turnout, she beat Solarz 34%-28%. After the primary, confidential hospital records leaked to a New York City tabloid indicated that Velázquez had attempted suicide in September 1991, was hospitalized and underwent counseling. Evidently, voters had little concern. She won in November with 77 percent of the vote.

Velázquez has a solidly liberal voting record, with occasional pro-business votes on economic issues. Velázquez has been a leading voice on issues related to Puerto Rico and the ongoing debate over changing the commonwealth's status. She favors a process that would allow the people of Puerto Rico to determine the status of the island, and has filed legislation authorizing a constitutional convention that would produce a recommendation that would then be subject to a referendum. The results would be submitted to Congress for approval. During the House debate in June 2016 on debt relief for Puerto Rico, she was unhappy about the anti-union measures in the bill. "The reality is that Republicans are in control and we have no choice but to compromise," she said in a statement. Following enactment of the bill, she was named to the bipartisan Congressional Task Force on Economic Growth in Puerto Rico. Its unanimous December 2016 report was optimistic about the future of the island, but concluded, "the people of Puerto Rico deserve a strong, stable and diversified economy."

As chairwoman of the Hispanic Caucus in 2009, Velázquez lauded President Barack Obama's choice of a woman with a Puerto Rican background, Sonia Sotomayor, to be the Supreme Court's first Latina justice. She repeatedly pressed him to move comprehensive immigration reform higher on his agenda. When vehement GOP opposition made clear that such a battle was unwinnable, she worked to separate the DREAM Act, a bill providing a path to legal status for the children of illegal immigrants who attend college or serve in the military. The House approved that bill in late 2010, but Senate supporters could not reach the 60-vote threshold to overcome a filibuster. Later, the Senate passed comparable measures but they went nowhere in the Republican-controlled House.

Much of her legislative work has focused on the Small Business Committee. During the Bush administration, Velázquez joined with Republicans to reinstate an SBA loan program that had guaranteed lenders a 75 percent payback if a borrower defaulted on loans of up to $750,000. The White House insisted on abolishing the SBA subsidy and funding the program with higher fees to borrowers and lenders. Velázquez initiated an annual scorecard to show whether the federal government had met its goal of granting 23 percent of contracts to small businesses. Velázquez charged that the SBA repeatedly fell short of its goal of granting 5 percent of loans to women. After a government report pointed to chaotic service and a loan approval process that lagged behind demand, she called on SBA Administrator Hector Barreto to resign, and in 2006, he did.

As the panel's chairwoman in 2009, Velazquez praised the Obama administration for requiring the nation's largest banks to report monthly on how much they lend to small businesses. She criticized an administration proposal to give $30 billion of the Troubled Asset Relief Program to community banks for small business, but without any conditions that the money actually be used for small business loans. "Taking $30 billion and simply handing it to banks - in the hopes that they will make loans - is not sound policy," she said. The administration dropped the idea of using TARP money.

Following the recession, she sought to ensure that small businesses get attention in the recovery. She sponsored legislation aimed at helping women-owned small businesses secure federal contracts, and she filed another bill to reopen the Small Business Administration's disaster loan program. In 2015, *The Washington Post* reported that Velázquez was miffed that the SBA had launched new programs to assist entrepreneurs and had taken the funds from existing programs without informing Congress. "This makes no sense," she said. SBA officials defended their approach as a better way to assist emerging businesses. Later in 2015, she enacted a bill to improve the disaster-assistance programs of the SBA. Republican David Vitter was the chief sponsor in the Senate.

A longtime combatant in New York City's political wars, Velázquez has won reelection easily every two years, often without major-party opposition. In the 2016 primary, she faced a credible challenger: Yungman Lee, a banker in Chinatown, who raised $417,000, which was about half of the total for Velazquez. In the three-candidate contest, Lee got her attention by taking half of the vote in Manhattan, though that borough cast only one-fourth of the total vote. Velazquez got 69 percent in vote-heavy Brooklyn and defeated Lee overall, 62%-27%.

Northern Brooklyn, Lower East Side of Manhattan

Population		**Race and Ethnicity**		**Income**	
Total	745,005	White	28.8%	Median Income	$46,584 (315 out of 435)
Land area	16	Black	7.8%		
Pop/ sq mi	46101.8	Latino	42.6%		
Born in state	46.2%	Asian	18.4%	Under $50,000	52.3%
		Two races	1.6%	$50,000-$99,999	24.7%
Age Groups		Other	0.8%	$100,000-$199,999	16.1%
Under 18	23.6%			$200,000 or more	6.9%
18-34	30.2%	**Education**		Poverty Rate	27.2%
35-64	36.5%	H.S grad or less	53.5%		
Over 64	9.7%	Some college	16.3%	**Health Insurance**	
		College Degree, 4 yr	18.8%	With health insurance coverage	84.5%
Work		Post grad	11.4%		
White Collar	36.2%				
Sales and Service	46.9%	**Military**		**Public Assistance**	
Blue Collar	17.0%	Veteran	1.7%	Cash public assistance income	4.5%
Government	9.5%	Active Duty	0.0%		
				Food stamp/SNAP benefits	27.3%

Voter Turnout			
2015 Total Citizens 18+	425,588	2016 House Turnout as % CVAP	45%
2016 House turnout	189,890	2014 House Turnout as % CVAP	15%

2012 Presidential Vote		
Barack Obama	156,860	(89%)
Mitt Romney	18,378	(10%)

2016 Presidential Vote		
Hillary Clinton	177,664	(86%)
Donald Trump	21,198	(10%)

Cook Partisan Voting Index: D+38

In 1957, amid a vast wave of Puerto Rican migration to New York, Leonard Bernstein wrote the music for *West Side Story*, which featured Romeo as an Italian American and Juliet as a Manhattan Puerto Rican. Before World War II, there were 60,000 Puerto Ricans in New York City. Three decades later, with cheap airfares and no need to go through passport control, there were 800,000. But as the city's industrial base grew stagnant, the number declined, and young New Yorkers of Puerto Rican descent increasingly returned there or moved to Florida. By the late 1990s, New York City was experiencing a large influx of Latinos from places not under the U.S. flag. Even though New York still has the largest Puerto Rican population outside of that island, most arriving Hispanics in the city today come from the Dominican Republic, Colombia, Mexico, Panama and Peru.

The 7th Congressional District of New York was designed to stitch together many of these diverse people. About 70 percent of the district's population is in Brooklyn, with the remainder split between Queens and Manhattan. Each borough runs along the East River. Overall, the district is 41 percent Hispanic and 19 percent Asian (mostly Chinese). Of the Hispanics, one-third are Puerto Rican. Chinese, predominantly in Brooklyn, have joined Dominicans as the largest foreign-born groups in the city. But this is New York, so it takes in many other ethnicities as well.

In Brooklyn, the district hugs the upscale Brooklyn Heights waterfront, with its stunning views of Lower Manhattan, and nearby Carroll Gardens, with young professionals intermingled with Italian immigrants. Inland is Downtown Brooklyn (originally called *Breuckelen* by the Dutch), which has attracted a critical mass of business and residential development to become a "city that never sleeps" in its own right. To the south is Sunset Park, once the home of Irish, Polish and Norwegian immigrants, and now filled with Chinese, Puerto Ricans, Colombians and Ecuadorans. The Brooklyn Nets, who moved into the Barclays Center in Downtown in 2012, opened a basketball practice facility in Sunset Park in 2015.

North of Brooklyn Heights is DUMBO (Down Under the Manhattan Bridge Overpass), with artists in old industrial lofts that have become hot real estate. Just above that is Vinegar Hill. Gentrification has caused housing prices to spike in recent years, and rents for the average studio apartment in DUMBO and Williamsburg have grown higher than the average in Greenwich Village, the Financial District or the Upper East Side of Manhattan. The old Brooklyn Navy Yard, which built ships more than two centuries ago and employed 70,000 during World War II, now houses a vibrant and rapidly growing industrial park, including the largest movie and television production complex outside of Hollywood. Williamsburg has many Orthodox Jews and recent Latino arrivals as well as the young and hip. Inland, the district takes in Bushwick, a former slum that is now the latest beachhead in Brooklyn's urban renewal and multi-ethnic Cypress Hills. A new center of attention is the Red Hook area in the southwest corner of Brooklyn, where rapid gentrification has supplanted public housing. Planners have envisioned a 246-acre waterfront development with perhaps 45,000 residential units, which would be twice the size of Battery Park City in lower Manhattan.

In Manhattan, the 7th District includes parts of the Lower East Side, East Village, Chinatown and Little Italy. The small salient in Queens includes Woodhaven. The 86 percent of the vote for Hillary Clinton in 2016 ranked the 7th as the most Democratic in Brooklyn and Queen and in the top 2 percent of the most Democratic districts in the nation.

EIGHTH DISTRICT

Hakeem Jeffries (D)

Elected 2012, 3rd term; b. Aug 04, 1970, Brooklyn; State University of New York, Binghamton, B.A.; Georgetown University (DC), M.PP; New York University Law School, J.D.; Baptist; Married (Kennisandra Jeffries); 2 children.

Elected Office: NY Assembly, 2007-2012.

Professional Career: Clerk, Judge Harold Baer, 1997-1998; Practicing attorney, 1999-2003; Counsel, Viacom, 2004-2005; Assistant General counsel, CBS Broadcasting, 2006.

DC Office: 1607 LHOB 20515, 202-225-5936, Fax: 202-225-1018, jeffries.house.gov.

State Offices: Brooklyn, 718-373-0033; Brooklyn, 718-237-2211.

Committees: *Budget. Judiciary*: Courts, Intellectual Property & Internet, Crime, Terrorism, Homeland Security & Investigations.

Group Ratings

	ADA	ACLU	AFL-CIO	LCV	ITI	COC	HAFA	ACU	CFG	FRC
2016	-	100%	-	95%	67%	69%	12%	4%	4%	0%
2015	100%	C	100%	100%	C	45%	C	0%	0%	0%

Almanac Ratings 2015

	Economy	Social	Foreign	Composite
Liberal	98%	100%	93%	97%
Conservative	2%	0%	7%	3%

Key Votes of the 114th Congress

1. Keystone Pipeline	N	5. Puerto Rico Debt	Y	9. Offenses by Aliens	N
2. Trade Deals	N	6. Medical Marijuana	Y	10. Troops in Iraq	Y
3. Export-Import Bank	Y	7. Sanctuary Cities	N	11. Homeland Security $$	Y
4. Debt Ceiling Increase	Y	8. Armor-piercing Bullets	N	12. Trade Adjustment aid	Y

Election Results

Election	Name (Party)	Vote (%)	Cand. Spent	Ind. Exp. Support	Ind. Exp. Oppose
2016 General	Hakeem Jeffries (D)	214,595 (93%)	$509,379		
	Daniel Cavanaugh (C)	15,608 (7%)			
2016 Primary	Hakeem Jeffries (D)	(100%)			

Prior winning percentages: 2014 (81%), 2012 (78%)

Democrat Hakeem Jeffries, elected in 2012, has brought energy and a spirit of consensus-building to his office. In December 2016, he won a new mid-level House Democratic leadership slot. He turned down urgings that he run for mayor in 2017. But the ambitious Jeffries remained a bright prospect for increased influence in Congress.

Jeffries was born and raised in the Crown Heights neighborhood of Brooklyn and graduated from the State University at Binghamton. He pledged Kappa Alpha Psi, the predominantly African-American fraternity, where he received the nickname "Kool Ha," for his measured speech. As a senior in college, he solidified his commitment to public service after the not-guilty verdict for two police officers accused in the beating of Los Angeles motorist Rodney King. He went to Georgetown University for a master's degree in public policy and later earned a law degree from New York University. He clerked for a federal judge, and worked for Paul, Weiss, Rifkind, Wharton & Garrison, a law firm known for launching the careers of prominent New York Democrats such as former Gov. Eliot Spitzer and former Rep. Elizabeth Holtzman.

After two unsuccessful campaigns against an entrenched incumbent in the state Assembly, Jeffries won an open seat in 2006. Within a few years, Jeffries appeared in *City and State* magazine's list of 40 rising political stars under 40. In the legislature, he worked on affordable housing issues and got a bill signed into law forcing the elimination of the New York City Police Department's "stop-and-frisk" database, which contained personal information from each police stop since 2004. He took on political reforms and introduced legislation to establish an independent congressional redistricting process.

When the House seat opened, Jeffries faced another African-American politician, New York City Councilman Charles Barron, in the Democratic primary. A former Black Panther, Barron had a history of making inflammatory statements against Israel; Jeffries voiced support for Israel and, as a result, benefited from national campaign donations. Jeffries spent $1.4 million and won the primary in a rout, defeating Barron 72%-28%. That was tantamount to victory in the heavily Democratic district. The Democratic Congressional Campaign Committee tapped him as a fundraising "all-star," asking him to help campaign around the country in other congressional races.

On the Judiciary Committee, Jeffries has focused much of his time on law-enforcement issues. In 2015, President Barack Obama enacted the Slain Officer Family Support Act, which Jeffries introduced with Republican Rep. Peter King of New York. The bill extended the tax deadline for charitable deductions of contributions to the families of two Brooklyn police officers who were killed in Bedford-Stuyvesant in December 2014. Following protests against alleged police excesses in several cities, including Brooklyn, he filed a bill to bar the use of chokeholds, which he called a deprivation of civil rights. "It's not sufficient simply to ban a policy through departmental practice. We've got to elevate it, embed it in law, if we really and truly want to end it," he told CNN. To a group sponsored by Al Sharpton's National Action Network in May 2015, Jeffries criticized New York Mayor Bill de Blasio for the city's continued enforcement of the "broken windows policing" of minor violations. In July 2016, he joined an informal congressional task force exploring the relationship between law enforcement and minority communities.

Jeffries has twice been reelected without major party opposition. Following the 2016 election, with the public support of Democratic Leader Nancy Pelosi, he was selected as one of three co-chairs of the House Democratic Policy and Communications Committee. "Jeffries has quickly become a national voice for our party and our Caucus," she wrote. Following the inauguration of Trump, he told an audience in Brooklyn, "Some folks down in Washington, D.C., want us to step back. But I'm here today to make it clear we plan to fight back." In February 2017, he told *Politico* that he was not running for mayor. "The stakes are so high in Washington, D.C., right now, and I want to be part of the effort to turn the situation around. It would be a dereliction of duty to abandon ship at the moment when times are tough," he said. Prior to a scheduled meeting between the Congressional Black Caucus and President Donald Trump at the White House, he said that Trump strategist Steve Bannon should not be included because he was "a stone cold racist and a white supremacist sympathizer."

Brooklyn: Bedford-Stuyvesant

Population		**Race and Ethnicity**		**Income**	
Total	744,271	White	22.7%	Median Income	$44,700 (344 out of 435)
Land area	30	Black	52.4%		
Pop/ sq mi	25093.4	Latino	17.9%		
Born in state	53.0%	Asian	4.9%	Under $50,000	53.6%
		Two races	1.4%	$50,000-$99,999	25.6%
Age Groups		Other	0.7%	$100,000-$199,999	16.7%
Under 18	22.4%			$200,000 or more	4.0%
18-34	26.4%	**Education**		Poverty Rate	24.0%
35-64	38.3%	H.S grad or less	47.5%		
Over 64	13.0%	Some college	23.7%	**Health Insurance**	
		College Degree, 4 yr	17.9%	With health insurance coverage	89.5%
Work		Post grad	10.8%		
White Collar	36.3%				
Sales and Service	48.7%	**Military**		**Public Assistance**	
Blue Collar	15.0%	Veteran	2.9%	Cash public assistance income	5.5%
Government	19.1%	Active Duty	0.0%		
				Food stamp/SNAP benefits	26.2%

Voter Turnout			
2015 Total Citizens 18+	495,887	2016 House Turnout as % CVAP	46%
2016 House turnout	230,203	2014 House Turnout as % CVAP	17%

2012 Presidential Vote		
Barack Obama	209,422	(89%)
Mitt Romney	23,861	(10%)

2016 Presidential Vote		
Hillary Clinton	215,689	(84%)
Donald Trump	34,356	(13%)

Cook Partisan Voting Index: D+36

African Americans began settling in Brooklyn's Bedford-Stuyvesant neighborhood in the 1930s, with the opening of the subway line that was celebrated in Duke Ellington and Billy Strayhorn's "Take the 'A' Train." After World War II, the pace accelerated, as crime and crowding in Harlem - as well as a large influx of African Americans from the South - drove black New Yorkers to the aging but solid brownstones of "Bed-Stuy." When job growth slowed, Bed-Stuy faced more than its share of poverty and crime. But after a 1966 visit by New York's two senators, Democrat Robert F. Kennedy and Republican Jacob Javits, Bed-Stuy won a Model Cities designation, which brought federal development funds and the establishment of the Bedford-Stuyvesant Restoration Corporation, the first such community development organization in the United States.

Even as the black community expanded across Brooklyn, Bed-Stuy became almost as powerful a symbol of black New York as Harlem, thanks in part to the films of Spike Lee, a Brooklyn native. His *Do the Right Thing*, shot on Stuyvesant Avenue between Lexington Avenue and Quincy Street, succinctly captured the racial tensions then brewing in the old neighborhood. The neighborhood also gave birth to rappers Jay-Z and Notorious B.I.G., two of the most influential hip hop artists. With smart planning, Bed-Stuy remained in better shape than many other areas of Brooklyn. The neighborhood's stately, Hopperesque architecture largely avoided the wrecking ball, and community vigilance kept the streets maintained. The revitalized residential area developed a Caribbean flavor that, combined with handsome brownstones and new shops and galleries, led to a wave of gentrification. In 2016, Bed-Stuy had the largest increase in the sale of million-dollar homes of any neighborhood in the entire city. The median home sales price rose from $600,000 in 2013 to $800,000 in 2016. Spike Lee has hosted an annual block party in Bed-Stuy. The owners of the nearby Barclays Center set a 2019 completion to expand the large Paramount Theater, a surviving Jazz Age movie house on Flatbush Avenue. In January 2017, New York University announced plans to invest $500 million in Brooklyn, including a science and engineering center.

The 8th Congressional District of New York takes the shape of a sideways "U" as it rambles across Brooklyn. It begins in Fort Greene, a rising arts area, and from there runs southeasterly through Clinton Hill, Bed-Stuy and East New York. Less than 10 percent of the district is in Queens, taking in Lindenwood and Howard Beach, an Italian neighborhood that was the home of Mob boss John Gotti and has remained remarkably unaffected by the demographic shifts elsewhere in the borough. The district runs along the Belt Parkway and the edge of Jamaica Bay through Spring Creek and Canarsie, which have become substantially black neighborhoods mainly due to Caribbean immigrants who prized the backyards and single-family homes.

The 8th takes in parts of heavily African-American Flatlands and the equally heavily white neighborhoods of Bergen Beach, Marine Park and Mill Basin. It includes the Coney Island peninsula, which was an island before the city filled in Coney Island Creek. Today, it is a diverse collection of neighborhoods and home to the famous theme park, which opened in June 2016 an amphitheater for year-round entertainment. Brighton Beach, part of Coney Island, has more Russian Jewish immigrants than any other district in the nation. These factors, plus the gentrification, have increased the population of the district and slightly reduced the minorities to 53 percent black and 18 percent Hispanic. Hillary Clinton, with 84 percent of the vote in 2016, showed that this remains one of the most Democratic districts in the nation.

NINTH DISTRICT

Yvette Clarke (D)

Elected 2006, 6th term; b. Nov 21, 1964, Brooklyn; State University of New York - Medgar Evers College; Oberlin College (OH), 1986; African Methodist Episcopal; Single.

Elected Office: NY City Council, 2002-2007.

Professional Career: Childcare specialist, Erasmus Neighborhood Fed., 1987-1989; Legislative aide, Sen. Velmanette Montgomery, 1989-1991; Executive Assistant, NY Workers' Compensation Board, 1992-1993; Youth program Director, Hospital League/Local S.E.I.University 1199 Training & Upgrading Fund, 1993-1997; Business Development Director, Bronx Overall Development Corporation, 1997-2001.

DC Office: 2058 RHOB 20515, 202-225-6231, Fax: 202-226-0112, clarke.house.gov.
State Offices: Brooklyn, 718-287-1142.

Committees: *Energy & Commerce*: Communications & Technology, Digital Commerce & Consumer Protection, Oversight & Investigations. *Ethics*. *Small Business*: Contracting & Workforce, Economic Growth, Tax & Capital Access.

Group Ratings

	ADA	ACLU	AFL-CIO	LCV	ITI	COC	HAFA	ACU	CFG	FRC
2016	-	100%	-	100%	50%	50%	14%	0%	4%	0%
2015	100%	C	100%	100%	C	45%	C	0%	0%	0%

Almanac Ratings 2015

	Economy	Social	Foreign	Composite
Liberal	98%	91%	100%	97%
Conservative	2%	9%	0%	4%

Key Votes of the 114th Congress

1. Keystone Pipeline	N	5. Puerto Rico Debt	Y	9. Offenses by Aliens	N
2. Trade Deals	N	6. Medical Marijuana	Y	10. Troops in Iraq	Y
3. Export-Import Bank	Y	7. Sanctuary Cities	N	11. Homeland Security $$	Y
4. Debt Ceiling Increase	Y	8. Armor-piercing Bullets	NV	12. Trade Adjustment aid	Y

Election Results

Election	Name (Party)	Vote (%)	Cand. Spent	Ind. Exp. Support	Ind. Exp. Oppose
2016 General	Yvette Clarke (D)	214,189 (92%)	$504,343		
2016 Primary	Yvette Clarke (D)	(100%)			

Prior winning percentages: 2014 (81%), 2012 (78%), 2010 (85%), 2008 (69%), 2006 (75%)

Democrat Yvette Clarke, elected in 2006, is a liberal who concentrates on immigration and other issues important to her diverse constituency. She has been a leader of the Congressional Black Caucus, though she lost to Rep. Cedric Richmond of Louisiana in her bid to become its chairman following the 2016 election.

She was born in the Flatbush section of Brooklyn to immigrant parents from Jamaica. As a young girl, she tagged along to political meetings and events with her mother, Una Clarke, who in 1991 became the first Jamaican elected to the New York City Council. Yvette Clarke attended Oberlin College in Ohio but fell short of graduating by six credit hours. She returned to New York, helped train child care workers, worked as a state legislative aide, and served as business development director for the Bronx Overall Economic Development Corporation. In 2001, when term limits forced her mother off the City Council, Clarke defeated four other candidates to succeed her in the predominantly Caribbean area of Flatbush and East Flatbush.

From its creation in 1968 until 2006, the district had been represented by just two people, both Democrats - trailblazer Shirley Chisholm, the first black woman elected to Congress and a 1972 presidential candidate, and Major Owens, who succeeded her in 1982. Clarke's mother had run unsuccessfully against Owens, an African American, in the 2000 Democratic primary, a bitter contest that exposed divisions between the local Caribbean-American community and the African-American community. Four years later, Yvette Clarke and fellow City Councilwoman Tracy Boyland challenged Owens in the Democratic primary. The incumbent won the low-turnout primary with an unimpressive 45 percent, to 29 percent for Clarke and 22 percent for Boyland. Owens soon retired.

In the 2006 primary for the open seat, Clarke had to navigate a competitive primary field. New York City Councilman David Yassky, who is white, jumped in and was called a "colonizer" for running in a majority-black district by Chris Owens, a health industry administrator and son of the retiring lawmaker. By the end of August, Yassky had raised more than $1.3 million, exceeding the other three candidates' combined fundraising. Clarke's status as the only woman in the contest and her support among Caribbean Americans were helpful. She stumbled when she was forced to backtrack from her claim that she had graduated from Oberlin. With the endorsement of the Service Employees International Union's powerful Local 1199, which turned out votes, Clarke defeated Yassky 31%-27%; Owens got 19 percent.

Clarke has had a staunchly liberal voting record. In the *Almanac* vote ratings for 2015, she fell short of perfect liberal ranking because of her scores on social issues. She joined some Black Caucus members who expressed frustration with what they considered President Barack Obama's lack of focus on helping minorities. "What we are asking for is that the president use his bully pulpit to look at a more far-reaching, deeper-penetrating jobs initiative. … The level of unemployment in our communities is unacceptable," she told National Public Radio in 2010. In 2014, she was more aggressive than other Black Caucus members in calling for an investigation of reports that House Majority Whip Steve Scalise of Louisiana spoke to a white supremacist group. Notably, Scalise was defended by Richmond, who two years later defeated Clarke for the CBC chair. With Reps. Bonnie Coleman Watson of New Jersey and Robin Kelly of Illinois, Clarke in 2016 organized a Caucus on Black Women and Girls to bring "a balance in the dialogue about black Americans."

One of Clarke's priorities has been immigration, specifically the DREAM Act providing in-state college tuition breaks and other benefits to children of illegal immigrants. In 2008, the House passed her bill to create an appeals process for individuals alleging denial of rights in homeland security investigations. She traveled to Alabama in 2011 to focus attention on the state's aggressive new immigration law, which she blasted as "just a step below apartheid." In 2015, she was "deeply disappointed" when a federal judge in Texas delayed the Obama administration plan that would have permitted illegal Caribbean immigrants to apply for work permits. In February 2017, she filed a bill to block President Donald Trump's executive actions that targeted sanctuary cities. "Without sanctuary in New York City, undocumented immigrants are forced to live with the fear that any contact with the government - even a call to the local police precinct to report a crime - could result in deportation," she said.

In 2015, Clarke joined the powerful Energy and Commerce Committee. She worked on legislation to urge the Federal Communications Commission to encourage small businesses to participate in spectrum auctions. In October 2016, she complained about the FCC's failure to promote more aggressively diversity in minority-focused programming.

She drew attention in 2012 when she said on Comedy Central's *Colbert Report* that Brooklyn blacks lived in slavery in 1898, more than three decades after emancipation and 71 years after New York State abolished slavery. She said that the Dutch, who last controlled the city three centuries earlier, were responsible. Her spokeswoman said her boss was just trying to be humorous. It hasn't mattered to voters. In both 2014 and 2016, she was reelected without major-party opposition.

Brooklyn: Flatbush, Crown Heights

Population		**Race and Ethnicity**		**Income**	
Total	740,868	White	30.7%	Median Income	$48,507 (277 out of 435)
Land area	16	Black	48.9%		
Pop/ sq mi	47674.9	Latino	11.4%		
Born in state	47.0%	Asian	6.7%	Under $50,000	50.8%
		Two races	1.7%	$50,000-$99,999	27.7%
Age Groups		Other	0.6%	$100,000-$199,999	16.3%
Under 18	22.8%			$200,000 or more	5.1%
18-34	26.1%	**Education**		Poverty Rate	19.8%
35-64	38.4%	H.S grad or less	43.0%		
Over 64	12.7%	Some college	22.4%	**Health Insurance**	
		College Degree, 4 yr	20.5%	With health insurance coverage	88.7%
Work		Post grad	14.2%		
White Collar	38.9%				
Sales and Service	47.6%	**Military**		**Public Assistance**	
Blue Collar	13.5%	Veteran	2.3%	Cash public assistance income	4.5%
Government	16.6%	Active Duty	0.0%	Food stamp/SNAP benefits	22.5%

Voter Turnout			
2015 Total Citizens 18+	465,649	2016 House Turnout as % CVAP	50%
2016 House turnout	232,094	2014 House Turnout as % CVAP	20%

2012 Presidential Vote		
Barack Obama	202,361	(85%)
Mitt Romney	33,045	(14%)

2016 Presidential Vote		
Hillary Clinton	211,812	(83%)
Donald Trump	36,600	(14%)

Cook Partisan Voting Index: D+34

Brooklyn. Just saying the word in a comedian's monologue used to elicit laughter. It evoked an accent of twisted English, a raucous, in-your-face style, a sense of humor with an edge, and the chip-on-the-shoulder assertiveness of those sure they will always be in second place. As its name testifies, Brooklyn was a separate community from the 17th century on, and in the 19th century, it was one of the largest cities in the country, with its own celebrities - Henry Ward Beecher, Walt Whitman, John Roebling. By 1898, when the five boroughs were welded into Greater New York, 1 million people lived in Brooklyn. In 1913, a transit agreement was struck to link the city's then-independent lines and triple the track to

619 miles. The agreement helped Brooklyn expand well beyond its established neighborhoods near the Brooklyn Bridge.

Suddenly, Manhattan factory workers no longer had to live in the crowded Lower East Side tenements that social reformer Jacob Riis had exposed in the 1890s. They moved in droves into neighborhoods of three- to five-story apartments and four-family houses. Brooklyn grew from 1.1 million in 1900 to 2.6 million in 1930; in 1900 its population was 63 percent of Manhattan's, and by 1930, it had surpassed its neighbor. The old Brooklynites were mostly Protestant - Dutch, Yankee and German, plus some Catholic Irish. The new Brooklynites were heavily Italian and Jewish, and they populated the sports and entertainment businesses for a long generation, making their hometown nationally famous. Now, its population of 2.6 million exceeds the 1.6 million of Manhattan, though the thin island is twice as densely populated.

Around the time Jackie Robinson suited up for the Brooklyn Dodgers in 1947 as the first black player in Major League Baseball, Brooklyn was experiencing an influx of African Americans into Brownsville and Crown Heights near Ebbets Field. Just as rapid was the flight of ethnic whites, driven away by "blockbusting," in which unscrupulous real estate brokers stoked white fears, then bought homes cheaply and re-sold them for higher prices. After "Dem Bums" left for Los Angeles in 1958 and Ebbets Field was knocked down and replaced by an apartment complex, Brooklyn's African-American neighborhoods continued to grow.

Today, Kings County, which is coterminous with Brooklyn, is New York's largest county, the nation's eighth largest -- ranked between Miami-Dade and Dallas. Some of its old neighborhoods were ravaged by crime, but there has been great vitality among upwardly mobile Hispanic, Asian, Caribbean and Russian immigrants, among middle-class blacks, and among new generations of Italians and Jews. A change in zoning laws in 2004 resulted in a burst of new residential and office construction that reinvigorated Brooklyn's commercial district. In 2016, Brooklyn had the distinction of the county with the least affordable housing in the nation: the median sales price as a share of average wages. Some builders have moved to modular construction to reduce housing costs.

The 9th Congressional District of New York begins southeast of Downtown Brooklyn. At the far northwestern tip is the Barclays Center, a large arena that is home to basketball's Brooklyn Nets and the New York Islanders hockey franchise that moved in 2015 from Nassau County, though there has been speculation that the hockey team might make an early exit, partly due to lagging attendance. Deeper into the district are some of Brooklyn's jewels: the Grand Army Plaza, the Parisian-style Eastern Parkway (the world's first six-lane parkway), and Prospect Park, home to the Brooklyn Public Library, the Brooklyn Museum, and the Brooklyn Botanic Garden, with its Japanese landscaping and placid duck ponds.

Park Slope, on Prospect Park's west side, has become affluent, filling up with young professionals who welcome the easy commute to Manhattan. On the east side of Prospect Park is Crown Heights, with its mix of modest apartment buildings and nicely restored row houses. Prospect Park South, also adjoining the park, is an upscale neighborhood whose stately late Victorian era mansions contrast sharply with the vibrant Caribbean street life just around the corner on Flatbush's Church Avenue. At the southern end of the district are Midwood, Homecrest and Sheepshead Bay, mostly white communities with substantial Jewish populations. Most of these neighborhoods have great diversity. The district's population is 50 percent black and 12 percent Hispanic. Politically, the 9th is overwhelmingly Democratic, though it ranked barely behind three other Brooklyn and Queens-based districts - the 5th, 7th and 8th- in support for Hillary Clinton in 2016, as was also the case with President Barack Obama in 2012.

TENTH DISTRICT

Jerrold Nadler (D)

Elected 1992, 13th term; b. Jun 13, 1947, Brooklyn; Columbia University (NY), Bach. Deg., 1969; Fordham University School of Law (NY), J.D., 1978; Jewish; Married (Joyce L. Miller); 1 child.

Elected Office: NY Assembly, 1977-1992.

Professional Career: Legislative Assistant, NY Assembly, 1972; Law clerk, 1976.

DC Office: 2109 RHOB 20515, 202-225-5635, Fax: 202-225-6923, nadler.house.gov.

State Offices: Brooklyn, 718-373-3198; New York, 212-367-7350.

Committees: *Judiciary*: Constitution & Civil Justice, Courts, Intellectual Property & Internet (RMM). *Transportation & Infrastructure*: Highways & Transit, Railroads, Pipelines & Hazardous Materials.

Group Ratings

	ADA	ACLU	AFL-CIO	LCV	ITI	COC	HAFA	ACU	CFG	FRC
2016	-	88%	-	95%	50%	50%	17%	0%	4%	0%
2015	100%	C	100%	100%	C	42%	C	0%	4%	0%

Almanac Ratings 2015

	Economy	Social	Foreign	Composite
Liberal	95%	100%	99%	98%
Conservative	5%	0%	1%	2%

Key Votes of the 114th Congress

1. Keystone Pipeline	N	5. Puerto Rico Debt	Y	9. Offenses by Aliens	N
2. Trade Deals	N	6. Medical Marijuana	Y	10. Troops in Iraq	Y
3. Export-Import Bank	Y	7. Sanctuary Cities	N	11. Homeland Security $$	Y
4. Debt Ceiling Increase	Y	8. Armor-piercing Bullets	N	12. Trade Adjustment aid	Y

Election Results

Election	Name (Party)	Vote (%)		Cand. Spent	Ind. Exp. Support	Ind. Exp. Oppose
2016 General	Jerrold Nadler (D)	192,371	(78%)	$1,061,297		
	Phillip Rosenthal (R)	53,857	(22%)	$65,230		
2016 Primary	Jerrold Nadler (D)	25,527	(90%)			
	Mikhail Oliver Rosenberg (D)	2,949	(10%)			

Prior winning percentages: 2014 (79%), 2012 (70%), 2008 (63%), 2006 (74%), 2004 (64%), 2002 (55%), 2000 (64%), 1998 (71%), 1996 (66%), 1994 (67%), 1992 (60%)

Democrat Jerrold Nadler, first elected in 1992, is among the House's most vehement liberals, with a strong civil libertarian bent. He has become increasingly vocal in economic debates and is an outspoken advocate of large public works projects, especially for New York City. If Democrats regain the House majority in the next several years, Nadler would be well-positioned on his two committees to drive major legislation.

Nadler was born in Brooklyn and moved around with his family as a child. His parents bought a chicken farm in New Jersey, but the business failed, and they moved back to the city. His father ran a gas station on Long Island and owned an auto parts store. Interested in politics from a young age, Nadler campaigned for Democrat Eugene McCarthy for president in 1968 while at Columbia University, where he roomed with Dick Morris, who would later become a top adviser to President Bill Clinton.

After getting his law degree from Fordham University, Nadler ran for the New York Assembly in 1976, at age 29. In the primary, he beat Ruth Messinger, the Democratic nominee for mayor in 1997, by 73 votes. In 1992, he suddenly had the opportunity to run for Congress. Representative Ted Weiss, long an Upper West Side icon, died the day before the September primary, which he won posthumously.

The nomination was decided by a convention of almost 1,000 county Democratic committee members. Nadler won 62 percent of the votes to secure the nomination and thus the election.

Nadler's leftward leanings are evident in his open fondness for the New Deal. He told a New York audience in 2012 that President Franklin Roosevelt's economic program "put into practice regulations on corporations and banks to prevent economic catastrophes - regulations that worked until they were dismantled, starting in the 1980s." He said Republicans have been misguided in cutting social programs and in letting large corporations pay little or no taxes. After Superstorm Sandy ravaged New York and other states in October 2012, he said the Federal Emergency Management Agency under President Barack Obama was ill-equipped to handle large urban disasters and that New York City needed higher seawalls and waterproofed electric power facilities.

With Ground Zero from the 9/11 attacks as part of his district, Nadler has had a continuing focus on the consequences and the clean-up. In late 2010, he helped steer into law a long-delayed post-September 11 measure providing more than $4 billion in compensation to first responders suffering health problems - a development he called "without a doubt the proudest moment of my 34-year career in government." In 2015, he was the original sponsor of the bill that Congress enacted to assure lifetime health benefits for 9/11 survivors. "I am proud of my country today for fulfilling our commitment to never leaving the wounded on the battlefield," he said.

As the number-two Democrat on the Judiciary Committee, Nadler has been a counterweight to lawmakers of both parties seeking expanded police powers to crack down on terrorism. Nadler insists that is not unsympathetic to their cause. But he has worked to protect detainees' habeas corpus rights. When the House voted in 2012 to extend a warrantless wiretapping program, he bemoaned how much power it gave to presidents. A vigorous opponent of the USA Patriot Act, the Bush administration's centerpiece anti-terrorism law, he was a leader of the bipartisan coalition that crossed ideological lines as it narrowed the law's scope and limited the collection of bulk data by the National Security Administration. The renamed USA Freedom Act, which the House enacted in 2015, was "the first significant reform of government surveillance carried out by the federal government since 1978," he said.

On domestic issues, he led the fight in the House against conservative proposals to ban same-sex marriage and has blasted the National Rifle Association's resistance to gun control legislation. He called suggestions for putting armed guards in schools "ludicrous and insulting." As the top Democrat on the Judiciary Subcommittee on Courts, Intellectual Property and the Internet, he filed in 2015 with Republican Rep. Marsha Blackburn of Tennessee the "Fair Play, Fair Pay" proposal to require that radio stations pay royalties to the record companies that own copyrights to records that are played over the airwaves.

Nadler has been an activist on district-related issues at the Transportation and Infrastructure Committee. He has fought to add rail service east of the Hudson and to subsidize Amtrak. His biggest idea has been a rail-freight tunnel under the Hudson. Lack of such a line has meant that New York gets only a tiny share of its freight by rail; a new line could mean cheaper freight and therefore lower prices. Nadler has been a strong proponent of high-speed passenger rail, which many Republicans have rejected as a boondoggle. He has been an enthusiastic advocate of the new Second Avenue subway line and the Moynihan rail terminal at Penn Station. In the 1990s, he successfully fought developer Donald Trump's attempts to alter the West Side Highway to accommodate his proposed luxury housing project in rail yards. Trump in turn called Nadler a "hack."

On foreign policy, Nadler opposed the Iraq war resolution in 2002. Regarding Afghanistan, he said in 2010, "An intelligent policy is not to try to remake a country that nobody since Genghis Khan has managed to conquer." He was among the Democrats who criticized Obama in 2011 for intervening militarily in Libya without congressional approval. In 2015, he supported Obama's nuclear agreement with Iran, a difficult vote for many of his Jewish constituents. "My conclusion is that this deal - of the available alternatives to us, not what might or should have been - is the best," he told *The New York Times*.

Nadler faced unusual competition for reelection in 2016, which he easily survived. In the primary, Oliver Rosenberg, a 30-year-old former investment banker, called his vote for the Iran nuclear deal "disastrous." Rosenberg, who self-financed $367,000, said that Nadler was out of touch with younger voters. The outcome suggested otherwise. Nadler won the primary with 89 percent. The vote was nearly even in the Brooklyn part of the district, but it cast only 10 percent of the total vote. The general election was a reprise of sorts. Republican Philip Rosenthal said that Nadler's Iran vote was "an existential threat" to both Israel and to New York City. A lawyer with a business in data analytics, Rosenthal raised only $74,000. Nadler, who raised $1.6 million for the campaign, won 78%-22%, including 57 percent in Brooklyn.

Following the election, Nadler was quick to confront his long-time adversary Trump. To examine the new president's alleged conflicts of interests, Nadler filed a "resolution of inquiry," which would have required the Justice Department to provide to the House documents related to Trump's finances. In March 2017, the Judiciary Committee rejected his resolution in a series of party-line votes.

Manhattan West Side, Brooklyn Borough Park

Population		**Race and Ethnicity**		**Income**	
Total	731,519	White	63.7%	Median Income	$79,425 (39 out of 435)
Land area	14	Black	3.5%		
Pop/ sq mi	51334.7	Latino	12.6%	Under $50,000	35.2%
Born in state	44.5%	Asian	17.8%	$50,000-$99,999	22.9%
Age Groups		Two races	1.8%	$100,000-$199,999	22.9%
Under 18	19.5%	Other	0.5%	$200,000 or more	19.1%
18-34	29.5%	**Education**		Poverty Rate	16.8%
35-64	37.7%	H.S grad or less	27.8%	**Health Insurance**	
Over 64	13.3%	Some college	13.0%	With health insurance coverage	92.1%
Work		College Degree, 4 yr	30.3%		
White Collar	59.0%	Post grad	29.0%	**Public Assistance**	
Sales and Service	32.9%	**Military**		Cash public assistance income	2.1%
Blue Collar	8.1%	Veteran	2.3%		
Government	7.7%	Active Duty	0.0%	Food stamp/SNAP benefits	11.5%

Voter Turnout			
2015 Total Citizens 18+	482,731	2016 House Turnout as % CVAP	51%
2016 House turnout	246,525	2014 House Turnout as % CVAP	22%

2012 Presidential Vote		
Barack Obama	173,487	(74%)
Mitt Romney	58,970	(25%)

2016 Presidential Vote		
Hillary Clinton	205,114	(78%)
Donald Trump	49,179	(19%)

Cook Partisan Voting Index: D+26

Over the course of the 20th century, New York City spread so far beyond its original boundaries in Lower Manhattan that, for a while, it became easy to forget how pivotal the southern end of the island had been in making the city what it is today. That changed in an instant on the morning of Sept. 11, 2001, when al-Qaida terrorists flew two hijacked jets into the twin towers of the World Trade Center, killing nearly 3,000 people and laying waste to 13 city blocks. The terrorists struck the tallest buildings in the nation's biggest city, toppling a complex whose name embodied American capitalism. The city, nation and world were forever altered.

Lower Manhattan has long been home to Wall Street and the Financial District. Over the years, it has represented America's striving spirit in other ways as well. The Brooklyn Bridge, begun in 1869 just a few blocks east of the Twin Towers site and completed in 1883, was half again as long as any bridge then standing and seven times higher than any building in the adjoining boroughs. The Holland Tunnel, built in 1927, was the first underwater vehicular tunnel built anywhere in the world. Just offshore are Ellis Island, now split between New York and New Jersey, where members of the great immigration wave first set foot on American soil, and the Statue of Liberty, the symbol of freedom they saw as they sailed in.

The 10th Congressional District of New York includes all of these places. From the Battery, at the southern tip of Manhattan, the 10th runs north up the island's west side, covering the Financial District and many neighborhoods. Battery Park City has attractive, modern apartments and parks. Sophisticated TriBeCa has artists' lofts and an annual film festival that has spurred economic and cultural revitalization. Art galleries have thrived in Chelsea, and SoHo has become an international shoppers' paradise. Greenwich Village, home of New York University, has long had a taste for the radical, though some of its ideas have become mainstream: Led by Jane Jacobs, its successful fight against the proposed Lower Manhattan Expressway popularized historic preservation and urbanism. A leading antagonist at the time was the local builder, Donald Trump. Clinton is the economically diverse incarnation of the old slum known as Hell's Kitchen. In Midtown, the district boundary is mostly along Eighth Avenue. At 57th Street, it cuts east to Fifth Avenue and includes most of Central Park, then continues north along Amsterdam Avenue as it excludes Harlem. The Upper West Side is home to Lincoln Center, while the northern end of the district at 122nd Street takes in Morningside Heights, site of Columbia University.

The venerable apartment buildings along Central Park West, West End Avenue and Riverside Drive, and the brownstones on the cross streets, house some of the country's most dedicated liberals. These professional people were satirized on *Seinfeld*, the long-running sitcom that resonated far beyond Manhattan. In the 1950s, West Siders took up the reform banner and finally killed off the ancient and ailing Tammany Hall Democratic machine. In 2016, editors of *Bicycling* magazine ranked the city fourth-best in the nation for cyclists. In a post-9/11 building spree, the famous Manhattan skyline has gained many new towers. The parts in Manhattan include about three-fourths of the district's voters.

The slice of the 10th District in Brooklyn includes a very different set of neighborhoods. Borough Park has one of the nation's largest Orthodox Jewish communities, with Yiddish-language ATMs and Russian bathhouses. Jews have a long history in the city. After World War I, as many as 400,000 disembarked each year at Ellis Island until a 1924 law virtually shut down immigration. Their children moved up faster than those of any new group, despite the widespread prejudice against them in the professions and in educational institutions. Today, New York has the largest Jewish population of any city other than Tel Aviv. The political attitudes of Brooklyn's Jews are quite different from those of most American Jews, who are liberal on cultural and economic issues. The Russians, many of whom live close to poverty, are anti-socialist. The Hasidic Jews of Borough Park are conservative and hostile to racial preferences, and they favor tough police treatment of crime. Even with these conservative enclaves, the district remains at the cultural and financial heart of national liberalism. Hillary Clinton got 78 percent of its vote in 2016, slightly higher than the vote for President Barack Obama in his two elections.

Infrastructure remains a local preoccupation. Repairs of the Brooklyn Bridge began in 2010, with costs that have escalated at least 60 percent to more than $800 million and the initial completion date of 2014 moved back to 2017, though additional repairs have been planned. The Port Authority Bus Terminal on the West Side, originally opened in 1950 and generously described as decrepit, has generated plans for billions of dollars of renovation and expansion to accommodate greatly increased demand. The Hudson Yards, a massive web of rail tracks on 34th Street near the Hudson River, has become the platform for ambitious real-estate development that is envisioned as a new neighborhood of skyscrapers. In the continuing aftermath of the World Trade Center catastrophe, Congress in December 2015 enacted lifetime health care benefits for survivors of September 11. That bill was named for James Zadroga, a city police officer who died in 2006 from toxins at the site. In September 2016, Congress overrode President Barack Obama's veto of a bill to permit 9/11 survivors to file lawsuits against Saudi Arabia for the terrorists attacks that day.

ELEVENTH DISTRICT

Daniel Donovan (R)

Elected 2015, 2nd term; b. Nov 06, 1956, Staten Island; Saint John's University (NY); Fordham University School of Law (NY), J.D.; Roman Catholic; Single.

Elected Office: District Attorney, Richmond County, 2003-2015.

Professional Career: Investigator; Youth counselor; Assistant District Attorney, 1989-1996; Chief Staff, borough President Guy Molinari, 1996-2002; Deputy borough President, Staten Island, 2002-2003.

DC Office: 1541 LHOB 20515, 202-225-3371, Fax: 202-226-1272, donovan.house.gov.

State Offices: Brooklyn, 718-630-5277; Staten Island, 718-351-1062.

Committees: *Foreign Affairs*: Africa, Global Health, Global Human Rights & Internat'l Orgs, Middle East & North Africa. *Homeland Security*: Cybersecurity & Infrastructure Protection, Emergency Preparedness, Response & Communications (Chmn).

Group Ratings

	ADA	ACLU	AFL-CIO	LCV	ITI	COC	HAFA	ACU	CFG	FRC
2016	-	11%	-	21%	75%	100%	35%	44%	43%	83%
2015	10%	C	56%	11%	C	93%	C	35%	32%	57%

Almanac Ratings 2015

	Economy	Social	Foreign	Composite
Liberal	33%	61%	5%	33%
Conservative	67%	39%	95%	67%

Key Votes of the 114th Congress

2. Trade Deals	N	5. Puerto Rico Debt	Y	8. Armor-piercing Bullets	N
3. Export-Import Bank	N	6. Medical Marijuana	Y	10. Troops in Iraq	N
4. Debt Ceiling Increase	Y	7. Sanctuary Cities	N	12. Trade Adjustment aid	Y

Election Results

Election	Name (Party)	Vote (%)		Cand. Spent	Ind. Exp. Support	Ind. Exp. Oppose
2016 General	Daniel Donovan (R)	142,934	(62%)	$1,752,735	$130,428	
	Richard Reichard (D)	85,257	(37%)	$27,825		
2016 Primary	Daniel Donovan (R)		(100%)			

Prior winning percentages: 2015 special (59%)

Republican Dan Donovan won a special election in May 2015 after Republican Rep. Michael Grimm pleaded guilty to tax fraud. Donovan has prevailed easily, despite widespread criticism of his role as Staten Island prosecutor in handling charges against police officers in a choke-hold death of a black man. Donovan became an active legislator on homeland security issues.

A native of Staten Island, Donovan got a bachelor's degree in criminal justice from St. John's University and a law degree from Fordham University. With his working-class roots, he paid his way through those schools with various jobs. He began his career as a prosecutor with eight years in the office of the Manhattan D.A., where he handled major narcotics cases. He moved to the political world as chief of staff to Staten Island President (and former Rep.) Guy Molinari. In 2002, he became deputy borough president. A year later, he was elected Richmond County district attorney, becoming the first Republican elected D.A. in New York City in more than 50 years. He easily won two additional terms, and became a leader in state and national associations of district attorneys.

Donovan entered the national spotlight on rocky terms during a period of controversial deaths of black youths at the hands of the police. Eric Garner, who was notably overweight, had been stopped in 2014 by police who were suspicious that he was selling loose, untaxed cigarettes. As two officers sought to arrest him, Garner resisted. One of the officers applied a choke-hold for an estimated 15 seconds, a move that was barred by NYPD procedures. Garner gasped, "I can't breathe." As a bystander filmed the incident, Garner fell to the ground, where he remained for several minutes until he was taken to a hospital. He died prior to arrival. As prosecutor, Donovan investigated the police conduct and presented the results to a grand jury. He decided not to bring charges.

Meanwhile, Grimm was indicted in April 2014 on federal charges that he had lied to federal investigators about having hired undocumented immigrants for his Manhattan health-food restaurant, Healthalicioius. The Republican Party largely abandoned him, but he decided to seek reelection. Although widely viewed as an underdog, he won 57%-43% over Democratic challenger Domenic Recchia, a former city councilman from Brooklyn. In December, Grimm pleaded guilty to a single count and he soon agreed to resign.

In the special election to replace Grimm, Donovan was the preferred choice of most Republicans. Democrats selected Vincent Gentile, a city council member from Brooklyn who had represented Staten Island in the state Senate. The Garner case was rarely mentioned by either candidate or their supporters. Donovan cited grand jury secrecy rules and minimized his role. Gentile faced multiple problems, including scant fundraising, a brief campaign, the unpopularity of Democratic Mayor Bill de Blasio and the predominantly Staten Island electorate. He focused chiefly on economic issues and largely avoided discussion of the Garner case, apparently because it would not be politically helpful in the special election. Symptomatic of their widespread failure to recruit top-flight candidates, Democrats threw in the towel on a district that they had held four years earlier. Donovan easily won, 59%-40%. Gentile got 60 percent of the vote in Brooklyn, but it cast only 22 percent of the total.

In the House, Donovan reached out to his local Democratic colleagues, though some of them had harshly criticized his handling of the Garner case. He took a bipartisan approach on many issues, defended the Affordable Care Act, and opposed the Trans-Pacific Partnership plan and accompanying legislation. He passed three bills in the House from the Homeland Security Committee, where he became chairman in 2017 of the Emergency Preparedness, Response and Communications Subcommittee. They included a counter-terrorism measure to improve the capabilities of first responders, security assistance to public transit authorities and local preparedness for cyber attacks.

The Democratic Congressional Campaign Committee, after having made Donovan a leading campaign target for 2016, failed to find a credible opponent. Donovan raised $2 million to $31,000 for Richard Reichard, a retired city employee who had never run for office. Donovan won, 62%-37%. The Justice Department opened an investigation into possible civil rights violations during the Garner controversy, but brought no action before President Barack Obama left office.

During the campaign, Donovan endorsed Donald Trump for president with limited enthusiasm and what he described as "60 percent" agreement with the nominee. "I don't agree with him on his positions on Muslims, I don't agree with his position on women and I don't agree with him on his position on immigration, but there are other things I do agree with him on," Donovan said in May 2016. "I think that he loves this country and he would be a better president than Hillary Clinton." After Trump took office, Donovan agreed with his executive orders to suspend admission of refugees and some immigrants. Mayor de Blasio said that Donovan had been "very, very helpful to New York City" in seeking reimbursement of police expenses in protecting Trump during the transition. In February 2017, small groups of anti-Trump protesters rallied outside Donovan's Brooklyn office.

Staten Island, South Brooklyn

Population		**Race and Ethnicity**		**Income**	
Total	731,365	White	61.9%	Median Income	$65,480 (90 out of 435)
Land area	66	Black	7.0%		
Pop/ sq mi	11109.9	Latino	16.2%	Under $50,000	39.6%
Born in state	63.4%	Asian	13.2%	$50,000-$99,999	29.2%
Age Groups		Two races	1.3%	$100,000-$199,999	24.8%
Under 18	22.2%	Other	0.4%	$200,000 or more	6.5%
18-34	22.8%	**Education**		Poverty Rate	14.1%
35-64	40.5%	H.S grad or less	43.7%	**Health Insurance**	
Over 64	14.6%	Some college	23.6%	With health insurance coverage	91.7%
Work		College Degree, 4 yr	19.8%		
White Collar	39.0%	Post grad	12.8%	**Public Assistance**	
Sales and Service	44.0%	**Military**		Cash public assistance income	3.3%
Blue Collar	17.0%	Veteran	4.3%		
Government	18.8%	Active Duty	0.1%	Food stamp/SNAP benefits	14.4%

Voter Turnout			
2015 Total Citizens 18+	498,083	2016 House Turnout as % CVAP	47%
2016 House turnout	232,317	2014 House Turnout as % CVAP	22%

2012 Presidential Vote		
Barack Obama	110,088	(52%)
Mitt Romney	100,811	(47%)

2016 Presidential Vote		
Donald Trump	133,232	(53%)
Hillary Clinton	108,807	(44%)

Cook Partisan Voting Index: R+3

Staten Island is part of New York City, yet is a land apart, closer geographically and culturally to New Jersey than to the city's other boroughs. Its inclusion in Greater New York as part of the great 1898 consolidation was something of an afterthought. It was connected to the rest of the city only by ferry or through Bayonne, New Jersey, until the Verrazano-Narrows Bridge - one of Robert Moses' last and most impressive infrastructure achievements - opened to traffic in 1964. Hilly Staten Island (or Richmond

County) is the state's southernmost county, one-tenth as densely populated as Manhattan. That's after it grew 25 percent between 1990 and 2015, one of the largest increases in New York state. Its rate of home ownership, 70 percent, is double that of New York City as a whole.

Ethnically, Staten Island has the highest percentage of residents of Italian ancestry in the nation. The signs on coffee shops read *Caffe* and on delicatessens, *Salumeria.* The Staten Island Ferry docks at St. George, where the Staten Island Yankees, nicknamed the "Baby Bombers," were the first minor league baseball team in New York City. The north and south shores that spread out from there are notable for their pleasant Victorian homes, while the island's west shore is industrial marshland, with development underway on the 2,200-acre Freshkills park - more than twice as large as Central Park - on top of the former landfill that collected more than 50 years of the city's trash. Staten Island's interior consists of scrubland that has become blocks of suburbia for New Yorkers who like a small-town ambience. In St. George, Empire Outlets, a $350 million shopping and entertainment complex with extensive waterfront and the first outlet mall in New York City, was scheduled to open in late 2017. Population growth, plus limited public transit, has brought significant traffic congestion to the island, which depends on cars more than the other boroughs. Construction of a $579 million seawall and 20-foot levy on the eastern shore of the island that were designed to limit or delay a repeat of the devastating floods in 2012 from Superstorm Sandy was scheduled for completion in 2021.

Culturally, Staten Islanders are more conservative than people from the other boroughs, particularly those from Manhattan, which is a 20-minute ferry ride away. Not many people here read *The New York Times*; the local paper is the *Staten Island Advance.* Fed up with the city's high income taxes and social programs, Staten Island residents voted in 1993 for secession, but the legislature never carried out their wish. In that same election, Staten Islanders provided the margin of victory for Republican Mayor Rudy Giuliani. His agenda of cutting crime and welfare rolls soothed the secessionist fervor. The Giuliani years contributed a new ferry terminal, additional shops, and hundreds of new houses near cleaned-up beaches. The Wall Street crisis in 2008 reverberated strongly in this land of commuters, heavily dependent on jobs off the island.

The 11th Congressional District of New York is made up of Staten Island plus neighborhoods with similar demographics in the southwest corner of Brooklyn. These include heavily Catholic and Italian Bay Ridge, Dyker Heights and part of Bensonhurst, middle-class enclaves with large single-family brownstones that are nowhere near a subway stop and largely impervious to the gentrification spreading across Brooklyn. The entertainment industry has found some memorable characters in these neighborhoods: The Three Stooges (Moe, Curly and Shemp) grew up in Bensonhurst, which also was the home to the fictional Ralph Kramden of *The Honeymooners*. John Travolta danced to fame in the film *Saturday Night Fever* on the streets of Bensonhurst and Bay Ridge. The northern shore of Staten Island has gained African-American population centers on the corners of the island, with a large Hispanic community in between.

Staten Island overall remains New York's whitest borough, with the fewest immigrants. It was 18 percent Hispanic, 12 percent black and 9 percent Asian in 2015. As a whole, the district is 17 percent Hispanic, 14 percent Asian and 8 percent black. Not surprisingly, Donald Trump won this district, 53%-44%, a notable shift from the 52%-47% win by President Barack Obama in 2012. In the county itself, Trump won 56 percent of the 177,000 votes. The county cast only 6 percent of the total city vote. But Staten Island was twice the size of the next largest county in the state that Trump won: Niagara, in the northwest corner.

TWELFTH DISTRICT

Carolyn Maloney (D)

Elected 1992, 13th term; b. Feb 19, 1946, Greensboro, NC; Greensboro College (NC), Bach. Deg.; University Dijon, Paris (France); New School for Social Research (NY); Presbyterian; Widow; 2 children.

Elected Office: NY City Council, 1982-1992.

Professional Career: Community affairs Coordinator, Board of Ed. Welfare ed. program, 1972-1975; Staff, Board of Ed. cntr. for career & occupational ed., 1975-1976; Sr. program analyst, NY Assembly committee, 1977-1979; Legislative aide, NY Assembly & NY Senate, 1979-1982.

DC Office: 2308 RHOB 20515, 202-225-7944, Fax: 202-225-4709, maloney.house.gov.

State Offices: Astoria, 718-932-1804; Brooklyn, 718-349-5972; New York, 212-860-0606.

Committees: *Financial Services*: Capital Markets, Securities & Investment (RMM), Financial Institutions & Consumer Credit, Terrorism & Illicit Finance. *Joint Economic*. *Oversight & Government Reform*: Government Operations.

Group Ratings

	ADA	ACLU	AFL-CIO	LCV	ITI	COC	HAFA	ACU	CFG	FRC
2016	-	94%	-	97%	67%	57%	12%	0%	10%	0%
2015	90%	C	100%	97%	C	53%	C	0%	0%	0%

Almanac Ratings 2015

	Economy	Social	Foreign	Composite
Liberal	91%	100%	83%	91%
Conservative	9%	0%	17%	9%

Key Votes of the 114th Congress

1. Keystone Pipeline	N	5. Puerto Rico Debt	Y	9. Offenses by Aliens	N
2. Trade Deals	N	6. Medical Marijuana	Y	10. Troops in Iraq	Y
3. Export-Import Bank	Y	7. Sanctuary Cities	N	11. Homeland Security $$	Y
4. Debt Ceiling Increase	Y	8. Armor-piercing Bullets	N	12. Trade Adjustment aid	Y

Election Results

Election	Name (Party)	Vote (%)	Cand. Spent	Ind. Exp. Support	Ind. Exp. Oppose
2016 General	Carolyn Maloney (D)	244,358 (83%)	$1,698,409		
	Robert Ardini (R)	49,399 (17%)			
2016 Primary	Carolyn Maloney (D)	13,389 (90%)			
	Pete Lindner (D)	1,654 (10%)			

Prior winning percentages: 2014 (77%), 2012 (72%), 2010 (71%), 2008 (66%), 2006 (76%), 2004 (81%), 2002 (61%), 2000 (60%), 1998 (66%), 1996 (61%), 1994 (59%), 1992 (42%)

Democrat Carolyn Maloney, first elected in 1992, is known for her forceful efforts on behalf of women and consumers and has been a prolific legislator on Capitol Hill. Like other New York lawmakers, her seniority has positioned her for the top Democratic positions on her committees.

Born and educated in North Carolina, she visited New York at the age of 22, loved it, and "just stayed." She taught adult-education classes in East Harlem and, from 1977 to 1982, was an influential legislative staffer in Albany. She was elected to the New York City Council in 1982. Redistricting in 1992 made the Silk Stocking district more Democratic, and Maloney ran against incumbent Bill Green, an independent Republican who shared Manhattan's cultural liberalism. But he was poorly positioned to appeal to voters in the outer-borough neighborhoods that had been added to the district, who preferred Republicans to be conservative on cultural issues but liberal on economics. Maloney lost the Manhattan part of the district 50%-44% but carried Queens heavily, winning 50%-48% overall.

Maloney has a mostly liberal voting record. She is a senior member of the Financial Services Committee, where she has been a leading voice on banking issues. She had a hand in crafting the Dodd-Frank Wall Street overhaul in 2010, working with Democratic Sen. Richard Durbin of Illinois to achieve a compromise on interchange fees charged on consumers' debit cards. The fees had been an area of contention between merchants worried about their high rates and the financial industry's worries that lower fees would not cover their costs. She worked to enact her bill to promote more transparent practices by credit card companies and to restrict abusive lending practices. She called the 2009 law "a much-needed correction to a market that is out of balance."

Even though she has many constituents in banking, Maloney had tough rhetoric for bankers who took millions of dollars in bonuses after their firms received federal bailout money in 2008. But she opposed in early 2010 a proposed .25% tax on stock transactions above $100,000. In earlier years, she worked to keep banks from controlling other businesses, sought more oversight of the Federal Reserve, and added privacy provisions to financial modernization bills. She helped to craft reforms tightening rules for foreign investment.

A leader of the Women's Caucus, Maloney drew national attention in 2012 for walking out of an Oversight and Government Reform Committee hearing on contraception and religious protection after pointing out its all-male witness list. "What I want to know is, where are the women?" she asked. She also blasted GOP efforts to bar funding for Planned Parenthood and prenatal care. When conservatives that year removed expanded protections for lesbians and Native Americans in a reauthorization of the Violence Against Women Act, Maloney called it "as chilling and callous as anything I have seen come before this Congress in modern times." Earlier, she demanded that the Food and Drug Administration permit over-the-counter sales of morning-after birth-control pills, and she opposed separating men and women in basic training in the military. With Republican Rep. Marsha Blackburn of Tennessee, she filed a proposal for a commission to study a national women's museum in Washington; the House approved the bill in 2014.

In 2007, with Sen. Edward Kennedy of Massachusetts, Maloney initially introduced the Women's Equality Amendment, a latter-day version of the Equal Rights Amendment, which had fallen three states short of constitutional ratification in the 1970s. The House passed her 2008 bill to give eight weeks of paid leave to federal employees for the birth or adoption of a child. Also that year, she published a book called, *Rumors of Our Progress Have Been Greatly Exaggerated: Why Women's Lives Aren't Getting Any Easier - And How We Can Make Real Progress for Ourselves and Our Daughters.* In 2017, she reached out to first daughter Ivanka Trump to seek common ground on paid-leave legislation.

With part of her district in Lower Manhattan and close to Ground Zero, Maloney has been heavily involved in the government response to the September 11 attacks. She was outspoken in urging President George W. Bush to quickly send New York the $20 billion that Congress approved for cleanup and recovery. In 2010, she and several other New York members steered into law a long-delayed measure to compensate September 11 first responders with health problems. "It is so fair, it is so right, it should have passed nine years ago," she said. In 2015, she took the lead in extending those benefits to cover the entire life of survivors. When gun violence became a prominent topic following the Newtown, Connecticut, school massacre, she introduced a bipartisan bill to make firearms trafficking a federal crime and to impose stronger penalties for straw purchasers buying guns for convicted felons. In 2015, she filed a bill to require gun owners to have liability insurance.

Maloney made a bid for the top Democratic slot on Oversight and Government Reform after Democrats lost the House majority in 2010. She lost to the less senior Elijah Cummings of Maryland, 119-61, in the Democratic Caucus. Cummings reportedly had the pivotal backing of Minority Leader Nancy Pelosi. She has been ranking Democrat on the Joint Economic Committee and the Financial Services Subcommittee on Capital Markets and Government Sponsored Enterprises.

Maloney has a firm lock on the district. She was bitterly disappointed when Democratic Gov. David Paterson appointed the less-seasoned Rep. Kirsten Gillibrand to the Senate seat vacated by Hillary Clinton in 2009. Maloney publicly questioned Gillibrand's stances on issues such as gun control and curbing illegal immigration, and she began raising money for a primary challenge in 2010. Gillibrand quickly moved left in the Senate, and in August 2009 Maloney heeded the calls of Obama and senior New York Democrats to give her a clear path to the nomination.

As the number-two Democrat on each of her House committees, she is positioned to gain additional influence.

Manhattan's East Side, Queens Astoria

Population		**Race and Ethnicity**		**Income**	
Total	723,973	White	66.3%	Median Income	$91,414 (16 out of 435)
Land area	15	Black	4.4%	Under $50,000	29.6%
Pop/ sq mi	48950.2	Latino	13.4%	$50,000-$99,999	23.6%
Born in state	41.5%	Asian	13.0%	$100,000-$199,999	25.3%
Age Groups		Two races	2.3%	$200,000 or more	21.4%
Under 18	11.5%	Other	0.6%	Poverty Rate	11.8%
18-34	36.2%	**Education**		**Health Insurance**	
35-64	37.9%	H.S grad or less	16.5%	With health insurance coverage	91.7%
Over 64	14.4%	Some college	12.9%	**Public Assistance**	
Work		College Degree, 4 yr	38.8%	Cash public assistance income	1.6%
White Collar	65.2%	Post grad	31.8%	Food stamp/SNAP benefits	6.3%
Sales and Service	30.0%	**Military**			
Blue Collar	5.0%	Veteran	2.8%		
Government	7.2%	Active Duty	0.0%		

Voter Turnout			
2015 Total Citizens 18+	542,629	2016 House Turnout as % CVAP	54%
2016 House turnout	294,071	2014 House Turnout as % CVAP	21%

2012 Presidential Vote			**2016 Presidential Vote**		
Barack Obama	205,662	(77%)	Hillary Clinton	255,601	(82%)
Mitt Romney	57,489	(22%)	Donald Trump	41,384	(13%)

Cook Partisan Voting Index: D+31

The Upper East Side of Manhattan is home to people with more accumulated wealth than anywhere else in the world. Its western border was established at Fifth Avenue in 1857, when work began on Central Park; originally a swampy, rocky slum, it was completed in 1873. During the 1880s, the avenues - Fifth, Madison, Park, Lexington, Third, Second, First - were paved, and rich New Yorkers as well as many who had made their money elsewhere, built mansions on Fifth Avenue. With its elevated train line, Third Avenue was lined with walk-ups for working-class commuters. The side streets off Fifth Avenue were filled with massive brownstones shielded from the industrial haze along the East River.

The Upper East Side began taking on its present character in 1913, when Grand Central Terminal opened and the New York Central rail line was buried under Park Avenue. What had been a filthy railroad cut became a broad boulevard lined with grand apartment buildings. The federal income tax, passed the same year, had the unintended consequence of encouraging New York's rich to dispense with grand mansions and live, quietly and out of sight, in apartment buildings where doormen protected their privacy. Although New York has been transformed by gleaming postmodern skyscrapers, its most enduring landmarks are products of the first half of the 20th century: the Flatiron Building, built in 1902; Grand Central, in 1913; the Chrysler Building, in the 1920s; and the Empire State Building and Rockefeller Center, in the 1930s. The United Nations headquarters, the world's first glass-fronted skyscraper, went up after World War II. The Upper East Side remains a world apart from ordinary folks. The neighborhood is overwhelmingly white as well as expensive, with only a 2.7 percent non-Hispanic black population in 2010. On New Year's Eve 2016, the first phase of the long-awaited Second Avenue subway line opened, with a price tag of $4.4 billion and the prospect of a jump in local rents.

The 12th Congressional District of New York includes the Upper East Side. It begins at East 96th Street, the historic dividing line between Manhattan's wealthiest and poorest neighborhoods, and runs south through Murray Hill and Gramercy Park all the way to Houston Street, with a few salients protruding further south. It takes in Alphabet City, with its unique lettered avenue names, almost all of the East Village, with its pricey lofts and busy nightlife, and much of the Lower East Side. In August 2016, a survey by a local real-estate brokerage found that Murray Hill had become the most popular residential locale for young business professionals. Average monthly rent for a one-bedroom apartment was $3,300. The district's cultural landmarks are among the world's finest: the Museum of Modern Art, the Guggenheim, the Whitney Museum of American Art, and the Frick Collection. Midtown Manhattan's skyscrapers and the Garment District are also here, along with Times Square and the Theatre District. Roosevelt Island, once dubbed Welfare Island and home to massive hospital and prison complexes, was renamed and transformed in the 1970s into an ethnically diverse residential neighborhood. Nearly 80 percent of the district resides in Manhattan.

Across the East River in Queens, the 12th encompasses Long Island City and vibrant, historically Greek Astoria, now with many Asians, Latinos and Arabs. In the northwest corner of Brooklyn, another 10 percent of the district takes in parts of trendy Williamsburg, gritty East Williamsburg, and working-class yet gentrifying Greenpoint.

The district historically has been dominated by its affluent and highly educated voters, leaders in securities, publishing, advertising, entertainment, broadcasting and communications. Historically, they mistrusted the city's usually Democratic immigrant masses. But as the Republican Party increasingly took on cultural conservatism and its Southern accents, the attitude of the Manhattan elite shifted from its "silk stocking" liberal Republican to leftish Democratic, and the Upper East Side's 10021 zip code was the nation's top zip code for Democratic campaign contributions from 2004 to 2010. In 2016, the zip code slipped to 22nd on the list of big contributors, with about two-thirds going to Democrats and their allies.

In recent years, a new local address has consumed the business and political worlds: Trump Tower, on Fifth Avenue, two blocks south of Central Park. Trump purchased the property in 1979 and created what his publicists describe as the first super-luxury high-rise property in New York to include high-end retail shops, office space and residential condominiums. Its distinctive five-story atrium gained renown when he launched his campaign at the bottom of an escalator. During the presidential transition, reporters and camera crews camped out in the lobby to monitor the latest visitors taking a private elevator to the executive suites of the Trump Organization. Its location in the heart of one of the world's busiest and most expensive shopping areas created a costly and disruptive security nightmare. Government security officials took offices in the building, and paid high rent to the landlord - and their new boss.

This district, one of the wealthiest in the nation, gave 82 percent of its vote in 2016 to Hillary Clinton. That was a few percentage points higher than its support for President Barack Obama in his two elections. Trump likely did not expect a thumbs-up from these neighbors.

THIRTEENTH DISTRICT

Adriano Espaillat (D)

Elected 2016, 1st term; b. Sep 27, 1954, Santiago, Dominican Republic; New York University and Rutgers University Leadership for Urban Executives Institute; University of New York Queens College (NY), B.S., 1978; Roman Catholic; Married (Marthera Madera Espaillat); 2 children.

Elected Office: NY Assembly, 1996-2010; NY Senate, 2010-2016.

Professional Career: Coordinator, New York City Criminal Justice Agency, 1980-1988; Director, Washington Heights Victim Services Community Office, 1992-1994; Director, Project Right Start, 1994-1996.

DC Office: 1630 LHOB 20515, 202-225-4365, espaillat.house.gov.

State Offices: Bronx, 718-450-8241; New York, 888-216-6147; New York, 212-663-3900.

Committees: *Education & the Workforce*: Health, Employment, Labor & Pensions, Higher Education & Workforce Development. *Foreign Affairs*: Western Hemisphere. *Small Business*: Health & Technology.

Election Results

Election	Name (Party)	Vote (%)		Cand. Spent	Ind. Exp. Support	Ind. Exp. Oppose
2016 General	Adriano Espaillat (D)	207,194	(89%)	$625,487	$59,509	
	Robert A. Evans Jr. (R)	16,089	(7%)			
	Daniel Rivera (G)	10,454	(5%)			
2016 Primary	Adriano Espaillat (D)	15,735	(37%)			
	Keith Wright (D)	14,499	(34%)			
	Clyde Williams (D)	4,665	(11%)			
	Adam Clayton Powell (D)	2,664	(6%)			

Adriano Espaillat, elected to the House in 2016 after narrowly losing two primary challenges to Democratic Rep. Charlie Rangel, took the open seat after Rangel retired. In addition to following two legendary lawmakers who held this Harlem-based district for a total of 72 years, Espaillat's Dominican background marked the gentrification of Harlem and the shift of the district to a Hispanic majority.

Espaillat was born in Santiago, Dominican Republic. He arrived in the United States with his mother and sister at the age of nine and overstayed his visa. He described himself as the first undocumented immigrant elected to Congress, though he became a citizen in his late 20s. He graduated from Bishop Dubois High School, a Roman Catholic school in Harlem, and got his bachelor's from Queens College. He took graduate courses in public administration at New York University and Rutgers University. He got involved in legal services, as a courts coordinator for the New York City Criminal Justice Agency and later as a certified resolution mediator for the Washington Heights Inwood Conflict Resolutions and Medication Center. In Washington Heights, he was the director of Project Right Start, a national initiative designed to combat substance abuse by educating parents.

In 1996, Espaillat successfully challenged a 16-year Assemblyman in the Democratic primary and became the first Dominican-American elected to a state legislature. He chaired the New York State Black, Puerto Rican, Hispanic and Asian Legislative Caucus. After 14 years, he was elected to an open seat in the state Senate. His two challenges to Rangel were bitter affairs, reflecting the changes in the minority community and the ethical problems that Rangel had experienced in his later years, which resulted in his censure by the House, which required him to step aside in 2010 as chairman of the tax-writing Ways and Means Committee.

Espaillat argued that Rangel had overstayed his welcome in Congress, but Rangel's surrogates maintained that his seniority and experience were valuable to the district. In 2012, Rangel spent $1.6 million, while former Bill Clinton aide Clyde Williams spent $418,000 and Espaillat spent $328,000. Rangel won by 1,086 votes, 44.5 percent to 42 percent for Espaillat and 10 percent for Williams. In 2014, Rangel appeared to be in greater jeopardy in his primary rematch. Espaillat had become more familiar to voters and was more competitive financially, spending $716,000 for the campaign to $1.5 million for Rangel. But the outcome yielded little change in two years. In the four-candidate primary, Rangel won the contest 48%-43%. Espaillat got 51 percent of the vote in the Bronx, but that borough cast only 14 percent of the vote.

When Rangel retired in 2016, he endorsed influential state Assemblyman Keith Wright, his long-time protégé.

The large number of serious African-American contenders in the June primary benefited Espaillat. With nine Democratic candidates, Espaillat won 36 percent of the vote to 34 percent for Wright, 11 percent for Williams and 7 percent for Adam Clayton Powell IV, a former city councilman who had earlier challenged Rangel. Wright led by 159 votes in Manhattan, but Espaillat got nearly half of the vote in the Bronx. Espaillat raised $800,000 for his campaign, compared with $930,000 for Wright. His victory in November was a formality.

Espaillat promised to be an assertive advocate on immigration and a critic of President Donald Trump. "I will be a strong voice for those people that are in the front lines that could get hit by a tsunami," he told *Real Clear Politics*. In a February 2017 interview with CNN, he cited his own experience as a young boy living in the big city without any legal documents as he criticized Trump's deportation plans. "What I find is many people are afraid. I hear in my district office people calling in concerned. ... They don't know how these new guidelines will apply to them. People are afraid to go out during the daytime. I heard of folks that only go out at nighttime."

Manhattan's Upper West Side: Harlem, Washington Heights

Population		**Race and Ethnicity**		**Income**	
Total	759,136	White	13.3%	Median Income	$36,412 (420 out of 435)
Land area	10	Black	25.5%		
Pop/ sq mi	74062.0	Latino	54.3%		
Born in state	46.4%	Asian	4.6%	Under $50,000	61.1%
		Two races	1.7%	$50,000-$99,999	25.0%
Age Groups		Other	0.6%	$100,000-$199,999	11.0%
Under 18	20.9%			$200,000 or more	2.9%
18-34	30.4%	**Education**		Poverty Rate	29.1%
35-64	37.6%	H.S grad or less	49.7%		
Over 64	11.1%	Some college	21.1%	**Health Insurance**	
		College Degree, 4 yr	17.4%	With health insurance coverage	85.7%
Work		Post grad	11.7%		
White Collar	33.2%				
Sales and Service	52.6%	**Military**		**Public Assistance**	
Blue Collar	14.2%	Veteran	2.3%	Cash public assistance income	5.5%
Government	12.6%	Active Duty	0.0%		
				Food stamp/SNAP benefits	32.9%

Voter Turnout			
2015 Total Citizens 18+	461,520	2016 House Turnout as % CVAP	51%
2016 House turnout	233,737	2014 House Turnout as % CVAP	17%

2012 Presidential Vote		
Barack Obama	219,319	(95%)
Mitt Romney	10,558	(5%)

2016 Presidential Vote		
Hillary Clinton	232,925	(92%)
Donald Trump	13,727	(5%)

Cook Partisan Voting Index: D+43

Harlem, for many years America's most famous black ghetto, has turned from grim times to major social evolution. In the late 19th century, Harlem was a commuter neighborhood, first for Germans and then for Jews and Italians. After the turn of the century, real estate speculators began constructing blocks of impressive brownstones, hoping to capitalize on the impending arrival of the subway. Overbuilding led to high vacancy rates. Some landlords agreed to rent to African Americans, as long as they were willing to pay a premium. After generations of being shunted from one neighborhood to the next as the city developed, black residents were willing, and the neighborhood soon turned into the locus of New York City's African-American community. Harlem expanded from its nucleus around Lenox Avenue and 125th Street, while the neighborhood to the east grew outward from 116th Street and Pleasant Avenue. Many great Americans - W. E. B. DuBois, Thurgood Marshall, Ralph Ellison, Joe Louis - lived in Harlem's Sugar Hill.

For a long moment in history, Harlem was a center of writers, professionals and entertainers. The rosters of the Apollo Theater on 125th Street in the 1920s and 1930s were filled with the names of great artists. Then, the *WPA Guide* described Harlem as "the spiritual capital of Black America." Starting with a riot in the summer of 1964, Harlem endured deterioration. Hundreds of brownstones were abandoned or pulled down. As successful black families moved out, Harlem's population shifted increasingly toward welfare dependency and criminal gangs. Its population declined by a third between 1970 and 1990.

In the 1990s, Harlem began to recover. The federal government provided $300 million in investment capital, and the huge drop in crime under Mayor Rudy Giuliani made Harlem real estate valuable again. Brownstones were renovated, vacant city buildings sold off, neighborhood schools upgraded and arts spaces opened. Harlem became an enterprise zone, with favorable federal and state tax treatment. Younger African Americans returned. Visitors of all races flocked from overseas for historical tours in the area, prompting a boomlet in niche hotels and guest houses. The façade of the Apollo Theater was restored, a new Harlem pier constructed, supermarkets and chain stores opened. In 2001, former President Bill Clinton opened his post-presidential office at 55 West 125th Street in Harlem.

Politically, Harlem has been heavily Democratic since the 1930s, when blacks switched from the Republican Party of Abraham Lincoln to the Democratic Party of Franklin Roosevelt. Harlem got its own congressional district in 1944 and elected Adam Clayton Powell Jr., minister at the Abyssinian Baptist Church and a brilliant orator. He was instrumental as chairman of the Education and Labor Committee when it crafted many of the Great Society programs, but lost his power when the House refused to seat him because of ethical issues.

Today, the 13th Congressional District of New York includes not just Harlem but all of Upper Manhattan, south to 122nd Street on the far west side and lower into Manhattan along both sides of Central Park. On the west side, the district includes portions of the liberal Upper West Side. On the east side, it's East Harlem, once known as Spanish Harlem. This area had been Italian and was Fiorello LaGuardia's political base, before it became Puerto Rican. Today, it is dominated by Mexicans and Dominicans and gentrifying whites, some of whom like the close-in location but have had conflicts with local preservationists and residents who want to keep their low rents and worry about "whitewashing." In the final quarter of 2016, prices for condos and co-ops in northern Manhattan (including Harlem) had a 9.5 percent yearly increase to $575,000. At the northern tip of Manhattan, the district takes in Washington Heights and Inwood, both heavily Latino, with lower incomes and more affordable housing; nearly half of their population of about 220,000 are immigrants, with two-thirds of them Dominican. Across the Harlem River in the Bronx, the district includes Marble Hill and heavily Hispanic Kingsbridge. Those neighborhoods in the Bronx are about 20 percent of the district.

Overall, the district is 54 percent Hispanic and 29 percent African American, figures that testify to decades of black flight from Harlem and the continuing inflow of immigrants from the Western Hemisphere. These changes have altered the identity of Harlem and the 13th. For now, this remains overwhelmingly Democratic territory. President Barack Obama had his second-best showing in the nation in the district in 2012 when he got 95 percent of the vote. It trailed only the adjacent 15th District in New York. In 2016, Hillary Clinton took 92 percent.

FOURTEENTH DISTRICT

Joseph Crowley (D)

Elected 1998, 10th term; b. Mar 16, 1962, Queens; Queens College (NY), B.A.; Roman Catholic; Married (Kasey Nilson Crowley); 3 children.

Elected Office: NY Assembly, 1986-1998.

DC Office: 1035 LHOB 20515, 202-225-3965, Fax: 202-225-1909, crowley.house.gov.

State Offices: Bronx, 718-931-1400; Queens, 718-779-1400.

Committees: House Democratic Caucus Chairman. *Ways & Means*: Oversight, Social Security.

Group Ratings

	ADA	ACLU	AFL-CIO	LCV	ITI	COC	HAFA	ACU	CFG	FRC
2016	-	94%	-	95%	50%	62%	12%	0%	4%	0%
2015	95%	C	100%	89%	C	50%	C	4%	0%	0%

Almanac Ratings 2015

	Economy	Social	Foreign	Composite
Liberal	93%	100%	94%	96%
Conservative	7%	0%	6%	4%

Key Votes of the 114th Congress

1. Keystone Pipeline	N	5. Puerto Rico Debt	Y	9. Offenses by Aliens	N
2. Trade Deals	N	6. Medical Marijuana	Y	10. Troops in Iraq	N
3. Export-Import Bank	Y	7. Sanctuary Cities	N	11. Homeland Security $$	Y
4. Debt Ceiling Increase	Y	8. Armor-piercing Bullets	N	12. Trade Adjustment aid	Y

Election Results

Election	Name (Party)	Vote (%)		Cand. Spent	Ind. Exp. Support	Ind. Exp. Oppose
2016 General	Joseph Crowley (D)	147,587	(83%)	$2,408,876		
	Frank Spotorno (R)	30,545	(17%)	$95,321		
2016 Primary	Joseph Crowley (D)		(100%)			

Prior winning percentages: 2014 (75%), 2012 (71%), 2010 (73%), 2008 (63%), 2006 (64%), 2004 (59%), 2002 (49%), 2000 (51%), 1998 (50%)

Joseph Crowley, an ambitious and garrulous Democrat first elected in 1998, continued his extended path up his party's leadership ranks in 2016 by becoming Democratic Caucus chairman. Once a moderate who chaired the centrist New Democrat Coalition, he has moved leftward in recent years and become an energetic fundraiser. Ranked behind a trio of party leaders in their mid-70s, he is an old-style coalition builder who is positioned to help lead the next generation of a Caucus that emphasizes its diversity.

Crowley grew up in Woodside, where his family was involved in politics. His uncle, Walter Crowley, was elected to the New York City Council in 1984. When he died in 1985, Joseph Crowley wanted to succeed him, at age 23. But Tom Manton, the boss of the efficient Queens County Democratic Party, chose his chief of staff instead. (Walter's daughter and Joseph Crowley's cousin, Elizabeth, now has a council seat from Queens. She lost a congressional bid in the 6th District in 2012.) Fresh from Queens College, Crowley ran and won, with support from Manton, when an Assembly seat opened the following year. Crowley was interested in Irish affairs and sponsored the law that requires public school students to be taught about the Irish potato famine. He played guitar and sang tenor with the Budget Blues Boys, a group of assemblymen who performed on cold Albany nights. He still loves to sing, and once did a version of Bruce Springsteen's "Pink Cadillac" at a USO concert with Springsteen's guitarist, Nils Lofgren.

When political boss Manton decided in 1998 that it was time to transfer his seat in Congress, Crowley was the beneficiary. Manton had filed for reelection to the House by the July 16 deadline. Then at 11 a.m. on July 21, he convened a meeting of Queens Democratic committeemen, announced that he was retiring, and got them to vote for Crowley as the Democratic nominee. Manton shrewdly concluded that Crowley, at 36, was in a position to accumulate seniority and power in Washington. Other potential candidates were not notified beforehand and were naturally miffed, but resigned to reality. Crowley said, "What you're hearing is not so much about the process, but sour grapes. What happened here is simply that I was offered an ice cream cone, and I took it." His Republican opponent had no money and no chance. Crowley won in November, 69%-26%.

Once elected, Crowley voted as a centrist Democrat. He was the freshman Democrats' class president that year. After the September 11 attacks, Crowley was especially active on homeland security issues. His district lost many firefighters at the collapse of the World Trade Center, including his first cousin, who was a battalion chief. He won passage of an amendment to issue the Public Safety Officers Medal of Valor to the 414 first responders who died that day.

Over time, he changed his views. He switched his position from opposing abortion rights to favoring them, a stance in line with the party. After Republicans reclaimed control of the House, he became much more of a loyalist across the board. When Republicans called for repeal of the Democrats' 2010 health care overhaul, Crowley organized an effort asking GOP lawmakers who backed repeal to forgo their taxpayer-subsidized health insurance as a matter of principle. In his early years, he had worked with Republicans on behalf of business interests to gain approval of bilateral free trade agreements. But he sided with most House Democrats in 2015 in opposing President Barack Obama's planned Trans-Pacific Partnership. In 2015, his *Almanac* vote ratings were among the most liberal, virtually tied with Minority Leader Nancy Pelosi.

His eventual move into party leadership compensated for two earlier failures. In 2005, he sought the chairmanship of the Democratic Congressional Campaign Committee and highlighted his fundraising connections to Wall Street. As an ally of Minority Whip Steny Hoyer, he was on the wrong side of Pelosi. The DCCC appointment went to Rep. Rahm Emanuel of Illinois, who led Democrats to House control.

After the 2006 election, Crowley sought to move up to caucus vice chairman. But Pelosi ally John Larson of Connecticut prevailed, 116-87. Crowley did some bridge-building with Pelosi and her allies, serving as chief deputy whip and DCCC vice chairman for finance. When the caucus vice chairmanship opened again after the 2008 election, he expressed interest but deferred when Pelosi backed Rep. Xavier Becerra of California.

For a time, Crowley held sway as head of the New Democrat Coalition, a group of moderate Democrats. Crowley worked chiefly on economic issues and sought closer cooperation with the leadership than did the more confrontational Blue Dog Coalition. He cited his group's success in reshaping elements of the financial regulatory reform bill that passed the House in 2009 and became law a year later. Crowley found himself fighting allegations that he was the object of a lobbyists' fundraiser right before a vote on the financial bill. The House Ethics Committee ultimately cleared him and two other lawmakers in 2011. The coalition lost about a third of its members in the 2010 election. With Republicans in control of the House, its influence waned.

In 2012, Crowley finally became caucus vice chairman after his two rivals, Barbara Lee of California and Jared Polis of Colorado, dropped their bids. He was helped by his new-found alliance with Pelosi. Fundraising has been one of Crowley's chief duties. He concentrated his attention on junior Democrats in tough campaigns. He also has used his seat on the tax-writing Ways and Means Committee to serve as an attack dog against Republicans, including their efforts to investigate the Internal Revenue Service for allegedly targeting conservative groups.

Crowley has focused on immigration to bolster his standing with Hispanics and Asians. In 2013, he was one of eight lawmakers arrested at an immigration rally on the National Mall that urged Congress to permit individuals who were illegally in the United States to apply for citizenship. When protesters on social media objected in January 2015 to the appointment of Democratic Rep. Andre Carson of Indiana to the House Select Intelligence Committee, Crowley urged Democrats to support Carson. "We will never be able to grow as a society if we allow this kind of hatred and division to go unchecked," he said. His interest in immigration has played well at home, where nearly half of his constituents are foreign-born.

He has worked on many foreign policy issues, from extending economic sanctions against Burma's earlier military regime to criminalizing the removal of girls from the United States for the purpose of genital mutilation, a practice common across Africa and elsewhere. He has co-chaired the House Ad Hoc Committee on Irish Affairs.

He has not faced serious reelection opposition. After Manton died in 2006, Crowley became Queens Democratic chairman, a job that has enabled him to weigh in on important grass-roots political issues. His handling of responsibilities at home and in Washington is reminiscent of old-time political bosses.

When Becerra was term-limited as caucus chairman in 2016, Crowley faced no opposition to become his successor. During the post-election turmoil among Democrats, he rejected suggestions that he challenge Pelosi for party leader after initially showing an open mind in internal discussions. Following the inauguration of President Donald Trump, Crowley became an outspoken critic of his fellow native of Queens and worked with other Democrats to determine how they should position themselves. "I've never seen my party more unified in a single goal: fighting to prevent President Trump and Congressional Republicans from hurting all Americans," he said at a February 2017 issues conference with Democrats. They were not looking to "get dragged down into the mud and to the pettiness of Donald Trump," he added, but if Trump "wants to mix it up, we'll go there too."

Crowley's patient move up the leadership ladder may have been well-timed to seek a more influential House Democratic post. He appears to be prepared.

Eastern Bronx, Northern Queens

Population	
Total	728,916
Land area	28
Pop/ sq mi	25765.9
Born in state	44.0%
Age Groups	
Under 18	20.6%
18-34	28.3%
35-64	39.2%
Over 64	12.0%
Work	
White Collar	27.7%
Sales and Service	50.9%
Blue Collar	21.3%
Government	11.5%

Race and Ethnicity	
White	23.5%
Black	9.7%
Latino	48.2%
Asian	16.7%
Two races	1.3%
Other	0.5%
Education	
H.S grad or less	53.4%
Some college	21.3%
College Degree, 4 yr	16.6%
Post grad	8.8%
Military	
Veteran	2.5%
Active Duty	0.0%

Income	
Median Income	$51,215 (236 out of 435)
Under $50,000	48.8%
$50,000-$99,999	31.0%
$100,000-$199,999	17.2%
$200,000 or more	3.0%
Poverty Rate	18.2%
Health Insurance	
With health insurance coverage	80.5%
Public Assistance	
Cash public assistance income	4.1%
Food stamp/SNAP benefits	17.7%

Voter Turnout			
2015 Total Citizens 18+	400,809	2016 House Turnout as % CVAP	44%
2016 House turnout	178,323	2014 House Turnout as % CVAP	14%

2012 Presidential Vote		
Barack Obama	136,783	(81%)
Mitt Romney	30,978	(18%)

2016 Presidential Vote		
Hillary Clinton	151,407	(77%)
Donald Trump	38,560	(20%)

Cook Partisan Voting Index: D+29

Like Brooklyn, the Bronx derives its name from its original European settlements. In this instance, the name comes from the surname of Jonas Bronck, a Swede who emigrated to the New World, started a farm, and once wrote that his new homeland was "a veritable paradise and needs but the industrious hand of man to make it the finest and most beautiful region in the world." His name was given to a nearby river, then to a borough, and it became a county in 1914.

Real growth began in 1910, when the subways started connecting these neighborhoods with job sites in Manhattan. The Bronx was rapidly transformed by hundreds of thousands of immigrants flooding to the open spaces northeast of the Harlem River. They established neighborhoods called East Bronx, Morris Park, Schuylerville and Throgs Neck. Today, these neighborhoods are filling with Latinos, with more Mexicans than Puerto Ricans, and many from the Dominican Republic and elsewhere in the Caribbean and Latin America.

Out past Eastchester Bay is City Island, a Cape Cod-like resort area with boat makers and plenty of seafood restaurants that still looks like it did half a century ago. Across the bridges in Queens is College Point, a middle class neighborhood. Further south and west are Jackson Heights, home to Little India and a sizable Latino community; East Elmhurst; and Woodside, a long-settled enclave with recent immigrants. Corona was once predominantly Italian and African American (Louis Armstrong, Duke Ellington, and Malcolm X lived here), but it has become home to Dominican and Ecuadorian immigrants and many Asians. Also in northern Queens is Ditmars, increasingly popular with professionals, as well as Steinway, where the plant that makes pianos for North and South American distribution is still located. Prominent locales include the Bronx Zoo and New York Botanical Garden in the Bronx, and the New York Mets home at Citi Field in Queens. Gov. Andrew Cuomo promised to upgrade LaGuardia Airport, which has struggled with short runways and poor commuter access, into a "21st century airport," with plans for two new terminals by 2020. Under discussion was an AirTrain connection from LaGuardia to subway and Long Island Railroad lines at Willets Point, near Citi Field.

These Bronx and Queens neighborhoods make up the 14th Congressional District of New York. The district is a polyglot; it is 48 percent Hispanic, 18 percent Asian and 11 percent black. Nearly two-thirds of the voters reside in Queens. Not long ago, Republicans were competitive here. George H.W. Bush twice held his Democratic opponent to under 60 percent of the vote in an earlier iteration of this district. Redistricting and demographic changes reversed GOP expansion. Hillary Clinton won the district with more than three-fourths of the vote, as Barack Obama did twice.

FIFTEENTH DISTRICT

Jose Serrano (D)

Elected 1990, 14th term; b. Oct 24, 1943, Mayaguez, PR; City University of New York - Herbert H. Lehman College, Att., 1961; Roman Catholic; Divorced; 5 children.

Military Career: U.S. Army Medical Corps, 1964-1966.

Elected Office: District 7 School Board, 1969-1974; NY Assembly, 1975-1990.

Professional Career: Banker, 1961-1969.

DC Office: 2354 RHOB 20515, 202-225-4361, Fax: 202-225-6001, serrano.house.gov.

State Offices: Bronx, 718-620-0084.

Committees: *Appropriations*: Commerce, Justice, Science & Related Agencies (RMM), Energy & Water Development & Related Agencies, Financial Services & General Government.

Group Ratings

	ADA	ACLU	AFL-CIO	LCV	ITI	COC	HAFA	ACU	CFG	FRC
2016	-	100%	-	97%	33%	57%	12%	0%	4%	0%
2015	100%	C	100%	100%	C	40%	C	0%	0%	0%

Almanac Ratings 2015

	Economy	Social	Foreign	Composite
Liberal	98%	100%	100%	99%
Conservative	2%	0%	0%	1%

Key Votes of the 114th Congress

1. Keystone Pipeline	N	5. Puerto Rico Debt	Y	9. Offenses by Aliens	N
2. Trade Deals	N	6. Medical Marijuana	Y	10. Troops in Iraq	Y
3. Export-Import Bank	Y	7. Sanctuary Cities	N	11. Homeland Security $$	Y
4. Debt Ceiling Increase	Y	8. Armor-piercing Bullets	N	12. Trade Adjustment aid	Y

Election Results

Election	Name (Party)	Vote (%)		Cand. Spent	Ind. Exp. Support	Ind. Exp. Oppose
2016 General	Jose Serrano (D)	165,688	(95%)	$224,348		
	Alejandro Vega (R)	6,129	(4%)			
2016 Primary	Jose E. Serrano (D)	8,343	(89%)			
	Leonel Baez (D)	990	(11%)			

Prior winning percentages: 2014 (90%), 2012 (86%), 2010 (86%), 2008 (75%), 2006 (76%), 2004 (75%), 2002 (65%), 2000 (73%), 1998 (74%), 1996 (71%), 1994 (68%), 1992 (64%), 1990 (66%)

Democrat José Serrano, who won his seat in a 1990 special election, is known for his jesting about everything from Republicans to his thick mustache. He has wielded influence as a senior member of the Appropriations Committee, where he has taken a new assignment as the top Democrat to oversee spending for several federal agencies that handle law enforcement, immigration and other areas.

Born in Mayagüez, Puerto Rico, he grew up in the Mill Brook project in Mott Haven. After serving in the Army, he worked at a bank and as a school administrator. Serrano moved up while other Bronx politicians fell by the wayside because of corruption. He was elected to the New York Assembly in 1974 and chaired its Education Committee. In 1985, he ran for Bronx borough president, bucking the Democratic organization, and nearly won. Then in 1990, Rep. Robert García was convicted of accepting money from the minority contractor Wedtech. His conviction was later reversed, but his resignation paved the way for Serrano's election to the House.

Serrano once described himself as being "to the left of the left." The *Almanac* vote ratings for 2015 ranked him among the top 2 percent of the most liberal members of the House. Serrano was the only House member from New York City who voted in 2008 against the federal bailout for banks and other financial services companies. He said he couldn't justify giving money to the wealthy people he believed created the problem. A big local priority for Serrano has been the environmental restoration of the Bronx River, and he delivered more than $30 million for the effort. (When the river progressed to the point where it could support wildlife, a beaver appeared for the first time in 200 years and was dubbed "José" in honor of Serrano's work.) With Republicans in control of the House, he said he sees one of his chief goals as "trying to avoid as much harm as possible" in spending cuts in the federal budget.

On Appropriations, where he had spent the previous decade as the top Democrat on the Financial Services Subcommittee, he took over in 2017 as senior Democrats on the Commerce, Justice, Science Subcommittee, where he can focus on spending and enforcement issues for his economically struggling district. "I will do everything in my power to ensure adequate funding for these agencies, which guarantee that our fundamental constitutional rights are respected and protected," he said. With the election of Donald Trump as president, Serrano said that he would oppose any effort to cut federal spending for "sanctuary cities" that refuse to cooperate with federal law-enforcement authorities.

If Democratic Rep. Nita Lowey, who represents a nearby district in New York, steps down as the top Democrat at Appropriations, Serrano could be positioned to replace her atop the full committee. The next two senior Democrats on the panel have been passed over in the past.

Another of his issues has been statehood for Puerto Rico, which he has called an American "colony." A proponent of a long-stalled referendum to determine the island's status, he got a bill through the House in 2010 calling for a two-step process. Unlike fellow Puerto Rican New York Democrat Nydia Velázquez, he saw great significance in the 2012 vote of islanders in favor of statehood, even though Congress did not authorize the process. "It will demand the attention of Congress, and a definitive answer to the Puerto Rican request for change," he said.

In 2016, with the island's finances in disarray, he supported the Puerto Rico Oversight, Management, and Economic Stability Act, which was designed to approve debt reorganization and encourage financial stability. Noting that he had found it "disheartening and difficult" as Congress ignored earlier pleas for action, he said that the legislation was not the bill that he would have written. But, he added, "In a Republican-led Congress, this compromise legislation is the only one with a possibility of getting to the president's desk. There is no realistic alternative." The House approved his amendment to the bill that created a commission to investigate the legitimacy of Puerto Rico's debt. Serrano said that the financial crisis had demonstrated that as a Commonwealth, Puerto Rico had been "treated unfairly and unequally," and that debate was needed on the two best alternatives -- statehood or independence.

Serrano's attempts to join the Democratic leadership were stymied. In 1998, he ran for Democratic Caucus vice chairman as "the candidate who refuses to raise money to buy your vote for leadership." He lost out to the less-senior Robert Menendez of New Jersey, who later became a senator. Serrano briefly toyed with running against newly appointed Sen. Kirsten Gillibrand in the 2010 primary because of concerns over her centrist voting record. He passed, and Gillibrand moved left once she was in the Senate.

Serrano had become "alienated from the Bronx political establishment" and Democratic officials had sought another candidate for his seat, the New York *Observer* reported in 2015. But there has been no sign of a recent political challenge to Serrano, or an attempt to demonstrate his unpopularity. In the low-turnout 2016 primary, he won 89 percent of the vote against political newcomer Leonel Baez, a community activist.

South Bronx

Population		**Race and Ethnicity**		**Income**	
Total	739,618	White	2.5%	Median Income	$25,213 (435 out of 435)
Land area	15	Black	28.2%		
Pop/ sq mi	50867.8	Latino	65.9%		
Born in state	51.3%	Asian	1.8%	Under $50,000	75.1%
		Two races	0.8%	$50,000-$99,999	18.5%
Age Groups		Other	0.8%	$100,000-$199,999	5.7%
Under 18	28.6%			$200,000 or more	0.7%
18-34	27.8%	**Education**		Poverty Rate	40.0%
35-64	34.7%	H.S grad or less	64.3%		
Over 64	8.9%	Some college	23.1%	**Health Insurance**	
		College Degree, 4 yr	9.1%	With health insurance coverage	84.7%
Work		Post grad	3.4%		
White Collar	17.4%				
Sales and Service	62.2%	**Military**		**Public Assistance**	
Blue Collar	20.4%	Veteran	2.2%	Cash public assistance income	9.7%
Government	12.4%	Active Duty	0.0%		
				Food stamp/SNAP benefits	49.0%

Voter Turnout			
2015 Total Citizens 18+	384,508	2016 House Turnout as % CVAP	45%
2016 House turnout	174,036	2014 House Turnout as % CVAP	14%

2012 Presidential Vote		
Barack Obama	171,364	(97%)

2016 Presidential Vote		
Hillary Clinton	179,454	(94%)
Donald Trump	9,371	(5%)

Cook Partisan Voting Index: D+44

It may not quite be "the beautiful Bronx," as borough historian Lloyd Ultan calls it, but the Bronx has rebounded from rock bottom. The borough began its modern development in 1906 with the arrival of the first subway, which allowed the children of immigrants to move from grim Lower East Side tenements to spacious walk-up apartments flooded with light. The population grew from 200,000 in 1900 to 1.2 million in 1930. Its population hit nearly 1.5 million in 1950. Four years later, Supreme Court Justice Sonia Sotomayor was born in a South Bronx tenement before her family moved into the nearby Bronxdale Houses public housing project. The years prior to mid-century were the peak days for the Bronx, when Babe Ruth, Lou Gehrig and Joe DiMaggio knocked home runs out of Yankee Stadium, art deco apartment buildings were built along the Grand Concourse, and shoppers thronged Tremont Avenue stores.

In the mid-1960s, several factors led to the destruction of Bronx neighborhoods. Rent control guaranteed that many owners of low-rent property wouldn't maintain it. Once empty, buildings were torched for the insurance money, sometimes as many as four blocks a week. A decline in low-skill jobs in Manhattan and the Bronx led to a rise in welfare dependency and crime, and empty building shells became the perfect venue for drug dealing. The 13-year, $250 million effort to build the Cross-Bronx Expressway - a brainchild of Robert Moses that crossed 113 streets and avenues, hundreds of utility mains and 10 mass-transit lines - made things worse. A vicious cycle emerged: Crime drove away jobs, which produced more crime. When Tom Wolfe imagined the "wrong turn" that sank a high-flying Wall Street career in *Bonfire of the Vanities*, he set it in the South Bronx.

The borough's eventual saviors were churches and creative community groups that built single-family bungalows and small-scale apartment projects for the elderly, single-parent families and the homeless. In the 1980s, a building spree created the Bronx's first new cluster of private residences since the 1930s. As immigrants from the Dominican Republic, Jamaica, Ecuador and Central America settled in, the population began to rise. After a quarter-century of deterioration, its population grew by almost 11 percent in the 1990s and another 9 percent since then. Today, nearly 1.5 million people live in the Bronx, as new immigrants revive neighborhoods that had been given up for dead. Charlotte Street, a former slum, is now Charlotte Gardens, with owner-occupied houses. Businesses - warehouses, distribution centers and small industrial parks - have begun to move back in. The new Yankee Stadium, at $1.5 billion the most expensive baseball stadium ever built, focused attention on the area's economic renewal. In 2016, the Bronx led the other boroughs in new homes and apartments authorized for construction. A promising development has been the city's plans to improve 30 blocks of the waterfront along the Bronx side of the Harlem River. Yet, incomes remain low in the South Bronx, with many people on public assistance, and check-cashing outlets are still easier to find than banks.

The 15th Congressional District of New York includes most of the South Bronx. It is bounded by the Harlem River on the west; the East River on the south; the Hutchinson River, Cross Bronx Expressway, and Bronx Park (home of the Bronx Zoo) on the east; and it goes just past Fordham Road on the north. It includes the gentrifying Belmont to the north, the industrial flatlands of Bruckner Boulevard, and Hunts Point, where meat and produce markets supply the city's tony restaurants, with some new housing. The district is 31 percent black, and it has the highest share of Hispanics - 66 percent - of any New York district; it is perhaps 1 percent white. It has long had New York's largest concentration of Puerto Ricans, but about 69 percent of Hispanics are now from other parts of Latin America. Poverty here remains endemic. The 15th District has the lowest median income in the nation. As longstanding Democratic territory, it is extreme in other ways. The 15th was the most Democratic district in the nation in 2012, giving Barack Obama almost 97 percent of the vote. The 94 percent for Hillary Clinton in 2016 took the same prize .

SIXTEENTH DISTRICT

Eliot Engel (D)

Elected 1988, 15th term; b. Feb 18, 1947, Bronx; Hunter-Lehman College (NY), B.A., 1969; City University of New York - Herbert H. Lehman College, M.S., 1973; New York University Law School, J.D., 1987; Jewish; Married (Patricia Ennis Engel); 3 children.

Elected Office: NY Assembly, 1977-1988.

Professional Career: Teacher, guidance counselor, NYC Public Schools, 1969-1977; Bronx Democratic District ldr., 1974-1977.

DC Office: 2462 RHOB 20515, 202-225-2464, Fax: 202-225-5513, engel.house.gov.

State Offices: Bronx, 718-796-9700; Bronx, 718-320-2314; Mount Vernon, 914-699-4100.

Committees: *Energy & Commerce*: Communications & Technology, Health. *Foreign Affairs (RMM)*: Africa, Global Health, Global Human Rights & Internat'l Orgs, Asia & the Pacific, Europe, Eurasia & Emerging Threats, Middle East & North Africa, Terrorism, Nonproliferation & Trade, Western Hemisphere.

Group Ratings

	ADA	ACLU	AFL-CIO	LCV	ITI	COC	HAFA	ACU	CFG	FRC
2016	-	88%	-	97%	67%	64%	12%	4%	5%	0%
2015	95%	C	100%	94%	C	50%	C	4%	0%	0%

Almanac Ratings 2015

	Economy	Social	Foreign	Composite
Liberal	90%	100%	78%	89%
Conservative	10%	0%	22%	11%

Key Votes of the 114th Congress

1. Keystone Pipeline	N	5. Puerto Rico Debt	Y	9. Offenses by Aliens	N
2. Trade Deals	N	6. Medical Marijuana	Y	10. Troops in Iraq	N
3. Export-Import Bank	Y	7. Sanctuary Cities	N	11. Homeland Security $$	Y
4. Debt Ceiling Increase	Y	8. Armor-piercing Bullets	N	12. Trade Adjustment aid	Y

Election Results

Election	Name (Party)	Vote (%)	Cand. Spent	Ind. Exp. Support	Ind. Exp. Oppose
2016 General	Eliot Engel (D)	209,857 (94%)	$894,624		
2016 Primary	Eliot Engel (D)	(100%)			

Prior winning percentages: 2014 (72%), 2012 (66%), 2010 (69%), 2008 (66%), 2006 (68%), 2004 (60%), 2002 (55%), 2000 (70%), 1998 (72%), 1996 (67%), 1994 (61%), 1992 (60%), 1990 (52%), 1988 (55%)

Democrat Eliot Engel, elected in 1988, has remained popular at home by relentlessly staying on top of constituent service and working on issues of interest to his district's foreign-born and low-income residents. As ranking Democrat on the Foreign Affairs Committee, he is one of three New York Democrats (and the youngest) to hold a top committee post. He has backed many downtrodden ethnic groups and has been a stalwart defender of Israel.

Engel is the son of a welder and grew up in the Bronx. He graduated from Hunter-Lehman College, got a master's in guidance and counseling from the City University of New York, then taught and was a guidance counselor in the New York City public schools. After 14 years, he returned to school for a law degree from New York Law School. In 1977, at age 30, he was elected to the New York Assembly in a special election to replace a convicted incumbent. He won election to the House in 1988, replacing Democratic Rep. Mario Biaggi, who also had been convicted of bribery.

Engel's once strongly liberal voting record has become more moderate, especially on foreign policy, if only because his party has shifted to the left. The *Almanac* vote ratings in 2015 demonstrated this pattern. He is limited in what he can accomplish in the minority on Foreign Affairs, which has a far lower profile than its Senate counterpart. He has forged a good working relationship with California Republican Ed Royce, the committee's chairman and a fellow staunch supporter of Israel, and they have issued many joint news releases. In 2014, they won committee support of their bill to require that the Voice of America actively support U.S. policy. That measure ran into trouble when VOA journalists objected to restraints on their work. They appeared together on CNN in 2014 to call for greater action against the Islamic State after the group released a video depicting the beheading of an American hostage. Failure to act against ISIS, Engel warned, would lead to "many more September 11ths." With Royce's Foreign Affairs predecessor, Ileana Ros-Lehtinen of Florida, Engel worked on legislation to rein in Syria's weapons program and promote human rights there. She called him "a principled man ... an incredible freedom fighter."

He makes a point of displaying his bipartisanship. When a senior Obama administration official was quoted in *The Atlantic* in 2014 comparing Israeli Prime Minister Benjamin Netanyahu to poultry excrement, Engel issued a statement calling it "counterproductive and unprofessional for administration officials to air their dirty laundry in such a public way." When Netanyahu in 2015 addressed a joint session of Congress, many Democrats boycotted the speech because they said it would undermine U.S. negotiations on Iran's nuclear program. Engel cautioned, "the U.S.-Israel relationship is bigger than any of the personalities involved at a given time."

Engel occasionally sought to deflect Republican criticism of the Obama administration. At a 2013 hearing at which committee members sharply questioned outgoing Secretary of State Hillary Clinton about security flaws that led to the attack on the U.S. consulate in Benghazi, Libya, Engel noted that House Republicans had cut diplomatic security funding. Engel has written laws relating to Albania and Kosovo, Cyprus and Irish affairs, and co-authored a law that addressed child slave labor in the cocoa fields of Africa. He was successful in encouraging some collaboration between Obama and Republicans, including enactment in 2016 of laws that encouraged engagement with nations in the Caribbean and sought to preserve international cultural antiquities.

Engel is not a 1970s-style dove. He supported the Gulf War resolution in 1990, the bombing of Serbia to get a settlement in Bosnia, and the use of force in Iraq in 2002, though he criticized President George W. Bush's handling of that conflict. As chairman of the Western Hemisphere Subcommittee in 2008, he criticized socialist Venezuelan President Hugo Chávez for "provocation" of the United States. He was one of three lawmakers to participate in a 2011 documentary, *Iranium*, which sounded alarms about Iran's pursuit of nuclear weapons. After the agreement was reached in 2015, he was an outspoken opponent and said that the deal might "strengthen Iran's position as a destabilizing and destructive influence across the Middle East."

On the Energy and Commerce Committee, Engel has worked on a wide range of subjects, from climate change to cell phone theft. He joined a bipartisan group of lawmakers who sponsored a 2009 measure requiring half of all new cars sold in the U.S. to be flex-fuel vehicles capable of burning any combination of ethanol, methanol and gasoline. The automobile industry fought the measure, and it was not added to the House-passed energy bill that year. In 2010, he enacted a bill that made it illegal to use false caller IDs to trick people into revealing personal information. Following a skit on *Saturday Night Live*, he learned that there are no restrictions on flamethrowers in all but two states. In January 2016, he filed a bill that would regulate them like machine guns.

Engel had a personal tradition of staking out an aisle seat many hours before the start of the annual State of the Union address so he can shake the president's hand or occasionally give him a hug. In February 2009, CNN anchor Anderson Cooper called Engel "pathetic" for waiting more than 12 hours for President Barack Obama's address to Congress. Engel replied that Cooper was "pathetic" for failing to share his enthusiasm. He later told *The Journal-News* that constituents loved him for it: "It'll be September, October and people will say they saw me on TV." But he abandoned that practice when President Donald Trump made his first address to Congress in February 2017. "Unfortunately, since Jan. 20, the new administration has shown no interest in working with the Congress on both sides to tackle problems," he told the House. "That's why I've decided not to stand on the aisle of the House chamber to shake the president's hand during this joint session of Congress."

Engel has had a handful of spirited election opponents. In the 2000 primary, Assemblyman Larry Seabrook attacked Engel for living in suburban Maryland. Engel won 50%-41%. After redistricting made his district more suburban in 2002, Engel had vigorous competition from Rockland County Executive Scott Vanderhoef, a Republican who criticized Engel for voting against tax cuts and defense spending. Engel won 63%-34%. He has not faced major-party opposition in his secure district since 2012.

Southern Westchester County, North Bronx

Population		**Race and Ethnicity**		**Income**	
Total	737,824	White	38.1%	Median Income	$64,064 (102 out of 435)
Land area	78	Black	30.5%		
Pop/ sq mi	9414.6	Latino	24.1%		
Born in state	56.9%	Asian	4.8%	Under $50,000	40.7%
		Two races	1.6%	$50,000-$99,999	26.7%
Age Groups		Other	0.8%	$100,000-$199,999	21.2%
Under 18	22.9%			$200,000 or more	11.4%
18-34	21.7%	**Education**		Poverty Rate	13.3%
35-64	39.9%	H.S grad or less	38.3%		
Over 64	15.4%	Some college	23.3%	**Health Insurance**	
Work		College Degree, 4 yr	20.3%	With health insurance coverage	90.2%
White Collar	41.4%	Post grad	18.1%		
Sales and Service	44.7%	**Military**		**Public Assistance**	
Blue Collar	13.9%	Veteran	4.2%	Cash public assistance income	3.5%
Government	15.7%	Active Duty	0.0%	Food stamp/SNAP benefits	14.6%

Voter Turnout			
2015 Total Citizens 18+	481,415	2016 House Turnout as % CVAP	46%
2016 House turnout	222,230	2014 House Turnout as % CVAP	21%

2012 Presidential Vote		
Barack Obama	197,364	(74%)
Mitt Romney	68,373	(26%)

2016 Presidential Vote		
Hillary Clinton	212,644	(75%)
Donald Trump	63,590	(22%)

Cook Partisan Voting Index: D+24

The northeastern Bronx wasn't settled until the early 20th century, when it became a collection of middle-class neighborhoods clustered around subway stops, places where the children of immigrants left behind Manhattan's gloomy tenements and walk-ups and basked in the sunlight, wide avenues, and hilly vistas. Different ethnic groups collected here: Irish in Kingsbridge; well-to-do WASPs and Jews in Riverdale; and middle-class blacks in Williamsbridge. When neighboring areas in the South Bronx began to deteriorate, many residents fled to Westchester County.

The 16th Congressional District of New York includes the bulk of these Bronx neighborhoods, as well as southern Westchester County. It is divided roughly into three parts. South of the Westchester County line and west of the Bronx River Parkway, the area is about 70 percent white and heavily Democratic. This portion has the century-old Van Cortlandt Park, at 1,146 acres, New York City's fourth-largest park. It includes Riverdale and leafy Woodlawn, still a magnet for Irish immigrants. The second section of the district is the southern edge of Westchester. It extends from Yonkers, which is the most populous city in the county and 35 percent Hispanic, across the Bronx River Parkway into Mount Vernon, which is 63 percent African American. The sprawling Co-op City is here, consisting of 35 buildings that house more than 50,000 residents in 15,000 apartments that were built by a consortium of labor unions in the late 1960s. Yonkers has suffered from high debt and taxes, and has received additional state aid. After an environmental clean-up along the waterfront, development has increased.

The district's third section, to the north in Westchester, stretches from Hastings-on-Hudson eastward to Mamaroneck on Long Island Sound. This section pushes well into Westchester County suburbs, all the way to a touch short of the Connecticut border. It includes a number of affluent suburbs, many within easy reach of Grand Central via the Metro North rail lines - Bronxville, Tuckahoe, Eastchester, New Rochelle, Scarsdale, Larchmont, Mamaroneck and Rye. In October 2016, New Rochelle began work on $4 billion in downtown redevelopment.

Historically, Westchester was a Republican county, with a successful GOP machine and an electorate of white-collar professionals who naturally preferred the political party that opposed the big city political bosses and labor union leaders. But today, party registration in Westchester is majority-Democratic, after an influx of racial and ethnic minorities and of Jews who broke down many barriers to residence after World War II. Overall, the parts of the richly diverse 16th have had a major transformation. It is 33 percent African American and 28 percent Hispanic - and solidly Democratic, with an increase to 75 percent for Hillary Clinton in 2016.

SEVENTEENTH DISTRICT

Nita Lowey (D)

Elected 1988, 15th term; b. Jul 05, 1937, Bronx; Mount Holyoke College (MA), B.S., 1959; Jewish; Married (Stephen Lowey); 3 children; 8 grandchildren.

Professional Career: Assistant for Econ. Devel. & Neighborhood Preservation, NY Secretary of st.; Deputy Director, Div. of Econ. Opportunity, 1975-1985; NY Assistant Secretary of st., 1985-1987.

DC Office: 2365 RHOB 20515, 202-225-6506, Fax: 202-225-0546, lowey.house.gov.

State Offices: New City, 845-639-3485; White Plains, 914-428-1707.

Committees: *Appropriations (RMM)*: Agriculture, Rural Development, FDA & Related Agencies, Commerce, Justice, Science & Related Agencies, Defense, Energy & Water Development & Related Agencies, Financial Services & General Government, Homeland Security, Interior, Environment & Related Agencies, Labor, Health & Human Services, Education & Related Agencies, Legislative Branch, Military Construction, Veterans Affairs & Related Agencies, State, Foreign Operations & Related Programs (RMM), Transportation, HUD & Related Agencies.

Group Ratings

	ADA	ACLU	AFL-CIO	LCV	ITI	COC	HAFA	ACU	CFG	FRC
2016	-	100%	-	100%	67%	57%	14%	0%	0%	0%
2015	90%	C	100%	100%	C	50%	C	0%	3%	0%

Almanac Ratings 2015

	Economy	Social	Foreign	Composite
Liberal	87%	100%	85%	91%
Conservative	13%	0%	15%	9%

Key Votes of the 114th Congress

1. Keystone Pipeline	N	5. Puerto Rico Debt	Y	9. Offenses by Aliens	N
2. Trade Deals	N	6. Medical Marijuana	Y	10. Troops in Iraq	N
3. Export-Import Bank	Y	7. Sanctuary Cities	N	11. Homeland Security $$	Y
4. Debt Ceiling Increase	Y	8. Armor-piercing Bullets	N	12. Trade Adjustment aid	Y

Election Results

Election	Name (Party)	Vote (%)	Cand. Spent	Ind. Exp. Support	Ind. Exp. Oppose
2016 General	Nita Lowey (D)	214,530 (99%)	$803,509		
2016 Primary	Nita Lowey (D)	(100%)			

Prior winning percentages: 2014 (54%), 2012 (58%), 2010 (65%), 2008 (58%), 2006 (63%), 2004 (57%), 2002 (51%), 2000 (57%), 1998 (55%), 1996 (57%), 1994 (53%), 1992 (52%), 1990 (59%), 1988 (53%)

Democrat Nita Lowey, first elected in 1988, is a formidable insider among House Democrats. A usually close ally of Minority Leader Nancy Pelosi, she has been since 2013 the Appropriations Committee's ranking Democrat, the first woman to hold that slot. During the 2016 presidential campaign, at age 79, Lowey was enthusiastic about the prospect that her constituent Hillary Clinton would be elected president. There has been speculation that Chelsea Clinton could be Lowey's successor.

Lowey was born in the Bronx. After graduating from Mount Holyoke College with a degree in marketing, she moved to Queens, where she became a homemaker raising three children. She got involved in politics when her neighbor, Mario Cuomo, got Lowey to assist his 1974 campaign for lieutenant governor. He lost that race but was appointed New York secretary of state and hired Lowey as his assistant in 1975. She remained a top official in his administration until she ran for Congress.

In the Democratic primary for the open seat, Lowey faced Hamilton Fish III, who was politically well connected but, as a former publisher of *The Nation*, was considerably to the left of Lowey. She won 44%-36%. In the general election, two-term Republican Rep. Joseph DioGuardi was dogged by charges of illicit contributions. Lowey won 50%-47%, while spending $657,000 of her own money.

Lowey's voting record is liberal, although she has been more moderate on foreign policy. She has been a strong advocate of aid to Israel and voted for the 2002 Iraq war resolution. Her ties to Pelosi were evident in 2012 when she defeated Marcy Kaptur of Ohio for the ranking Democratic slot on Appropriations, even though Kaptur had more seniority. As ranking Democrat on the State and Foreign Operations Subcommittee, Lowey worked closely with Texas Republican Kay Granger, who was that panel's chairwoman until 2017. They warned the Palestinian Authority that any unilateral moves toward statehood jeopardized its U.S. funding. Lowey opposed GOP proposals to cut U.S. contributions to international financial organizations, arguing that American companies' access to foreign markets would be impaired.

On an overseas topic separate from her work at Appropriations, Lowey has won passage of two of her bills designed to promote education around the world: the Education for All Act that is designed to help the 263 million children, adolescents and young adults who are not enrolled in school, which the House approved in September 2016; and the Reinforcing Education Accountability in Development (READ) Act, which was passed in January 2017. "We cannot build the world we want for ourselves, and for future generations, without making education the center of our efforts," Lowey said.

On domestic issues, Lowey has been a big supporter of biomedical research and helped increase spending on cancer research at the National Institutes of Health. She became a vigorous crusader against skin cancer after watching two close friends undergo surgeries and chemotherapy for melanoma, calling for better guidelines on sunscreen. She worked to combat drunken driving, advocating the increased use of ignition interlock devices to impede repeat offenses. Pursuing her interest in feminist issues, she has backed funds for international family planning, including abortion. She has actively supported the National Endowment for the Arts. During Appropriations Committee debate in 2016 on the Homeland Security bill, the panel defeated her "no fly, no buy" amendment to use the FBI's no-fly list to disqualify people from purchasing firearms; opponents criticized its lack of due process.

Lowey reportedly played a key behind-the-scenes role in loosening restrictions on derivatives in the 2010 Dodd-Frank financial industry overhaul law that would have negatively affected New York's banking industry. That provision became a controversial part of the 2014 year-end omnibus spending bill when Lowey - working with Sen. Barbara Mikulski of Maryland - cut a deal with Republican appropriators to permit an exemption for big banks from derivatives regulation. In exchange, Lowey got an additional $185 million in spending for banking regulators. That agreement raised major objections from Pelosi and Democratic Sen. Elizabeth Warren of Massachusetts, but the appropriators held firm. Obama went along with the agreement.

Since Lowey first won, the boundaries of her district have been radically altered three times by redistricting but she has been reelected by wide margins. She thought about a Senate bid in 2000, but deferred to first lady Hillary Clinton, and she was an enthusiastic supporter of Clinton's two presidential campaigns. Her party loyalty and avid fundraising led Minority Leader Dick Gephardt to appoint her to chair the Democratic Congressional Campaign Committee for the 2002 election. That year, the GOP's six-seat gain was an acute disappointment to Lowey. In 2008, she was mentioned as a possible Senate successor after Clinton became Secretary of State, but the plum fell to Democratic Rep. Kirsten Gillibrand.

When redistricting in 2012 gave Lowey a district in which just over half of her constituents were new to her, she drew a stronger GOP candidate in Rye Town Supervisor Joe Carvin. But she won 64 percent of the vote and bolstered her bid to become the senior Democrat at Appropriations by donating nearly $700,000 to colleagues before the election. In the more Republican-leaning 2014 cycle, Lowey got 56 percent against Republican Chris Day, a retired Army captain who served in Iraq and Afghanistan, whom she outspent by more than 10-to-1. In 2016, she was reelected without major-party opposition.

If Lowey steps down from the seat, Republicans could run a competitive campaign, building on their recent successes in upstate New York. Such a contest would be all the more interesting, given widespread speculation that Chelsea Clinton and her family have had their eye on the seat.

Northern Westchester, Rockland Counties

Population		**Race and Ethnicity**		**Income**	
Total	735,374	White	60.7%	Median Income	$89,680 (18 out of 435)
Land area	383	Black	9.8%		
Pop/ sq mi	1921.9	Latino	21.5%	Under $50,000	29.6%
Born in state	62.4%	Asian	5.8%	$50,000-$99,999	25.0%
		Two races	1.6%	$100,000-$199,999	29.2%
Age Groups		Other	0.4%	$200,000 or more	16.2%
Under 18	24.8%			Poverty Rate	10.8%
18-34	20.5%	**Education**			
35-64	39.9%	H.S grad or less	33.4%	**Health Insurance**	
Over 64	14.8%	Some college	21.5%	With health insurance coverage	90.4%
		College Degree, 4 yr	23.5%		
Work		Post grad	21.6%		
White Collar	45.5%			**Public Assistance**	
Sales and Service	41.6%	**Military**		Cash public assistance income	1.5%
Blue Collar	13.0%	Veteran	4.6%		
Government	14.6%	Active Duty	0.0%	Food stamp/SNAP benefits	7.7%

Voter Turnout			
2015 Total Citizens 18+	473,480	2016 House Turnout as % CVAP	46%
2016 House turnout	216,585	2014 House Turnout as % CVAP	37%

2012 Presidential Vote		
Barack Obama	167,884	(57%)
Mitt Romney	123,125	(42%)

2016 Presidential Vote		
Hillary Clinton	186,437	(58%)
Donald Trump	122,339	(38%)

Cook Partisan Voting Index: D+7

Blessed with some of America's loveliest scenery and easily accessible from Manhattan by train, Westchester County has some of America's earliest suburbs, where grand estates were built by millionaires - Jay Gould's Gothic revival Lyndhurst and John D. Rockefeller's spectacular Kykuit. Today, Westchester still looks suburban, but with the patina of age. It has little commuter railroad stations across from faux Tudor drugstores, soda fountains and cobblestone post offices. But it also has shopping malls and plenty of corporate headquarters, from IBM to Pepsi. In recent years, Westchester also has been drawing biotech companies; a former Union Carbide site in Tarrytown - which writer Washington Irving fictionalized into Sleepy Hollow while sending his headless horseman on a chase for schoolmaster Ichabod Crane - has become a bustling hub. Development slows north of White Plains, where Westchester is crossed by the first of several mountain ridges - the closest the Appalachians come to the ocean. In Ossining, on the Hudson River, looms the famed Sing Sing maximum security prison.

The 17th Congressional District of New York contains northern and western sections of Westchester County: Port Chester, White Plains, Tarrytown, Armonk and Chappaqua, where former President Bill Clinton and 2016 presidential nominee Hillary Clinton have a home. Facebook Chairman and CEO Mark Zuckerberg was born in White Plains and grew up in Dobbs Ferry, now the southernmost town in the district on the east bank of the Hudson River. Also here are Yorktown Heights and Peekskill, where George Pataki was mayor before becoming governor. At the Rockefeller State Park Preserve, sheep have been preserved as part of a land study. *Westchester* magazine in 2014 described White Plains, the county seat, as the heart of the county that "combines a suburban environment with urban sophistication for a great living and working experience." In February 2017, a developer unveiled plans to expand the city's popular restaurant row. The twin Indian Point nuclear reactors were scheduled to shut down by 2021, largely because of fears about the safety risk to New York City.

Across the Tappan Zee - a stretch in the Hudson River so wide that Henry Hudson believed he had finally discovered the Northwest Passage to the Pacific Ocean upon entering it - the district takes in all of Rockland County, which comprises about 40 percent of the residents of the 17th and is the second fastest-growing county in the state. First settled by Dutchmen, Rockland was studded by little towns that grew up as if they were 1,000 miles from Gotham, but which eventually thrived on their proximity to the city once the Palisades Interstate Parkway and Tappan Zee Bridge were built in the 1950s.

Today, Rockland is a triangular stretch of suburbia, wedged among New Jersey, the Hudson River and the Appalachians. Its demographics have changed; Haverstraw, on the banks of the Hudson, has a large share of Dominicans; Kaser, a village in the inland town of Rampao, has a large community of Romanians. Orangetown is the site of several large high-tech data centers. The new twin-span, eight-lane 3.1 mile bridge to replace the deteriorating Tappan Zee was scheduled to open in 2018. The total cost of $4 billion is expected to be paid from future toll revenue of the New York Thruway.

The 17th District is 22 percent Hispanic and 11 percent black. In her home district, Hillary Clinton won, 58%-38%, a bit higher than President Barack Obama's 57%-42% win in 2012.

EIGHTEENTH DISTRICT

Sean Maloney (D)

Elected 2012, 3rd term; b. Jul 30, 1966, Sherbrooke, Canada, QC; Georgetown University (DC), Att., 1986; University of Virginia, B.A., 1988; University of Virginia Law School, J.D., 1992; Roman Catholic; Married (Randy Florke); 3 children.

Professional Career: Practicing attorney, 1993-1997, 2004-2006, 2009-present; Staff Secretary, President Bill Clinton, 1997-2000; Founder & COO, Kiodex, 2000-2003; First deputy Secretary, Gov. Eliot Spitzer, 2007-2008.

DC Office: 1027 LHOB 20515, 202-225-5441, Fax: 202-225-3289, seanmaloney.house.gov.

State Offices: Newburgh, 845-561-1259.

Committees: *Agriculture*: Commodity Exchanges, Energy & Credit, General Farm Commodities & Risk Management, Nutrition. *Transportation & Infrastructure*: Aviation, Highways & Transit, Water Resources & Environment.

Group Ratings

	ADA	ACLU	AFL-CIO	LCV	ITI	COC	HAFA	ACU	CFG	FRC
2016	-	70%	-	97%	67%	57%	15%	4%	4%	0%
2015	70%	C	96%	86%	C	65%	C	13%	7%	8%

Almanac Ratings 2015

	Economy	Social	Foreign	Composite
Liberal	61%	94%	32%	62%
Conservative	40%	6%	68%	38%

Key Votes of the 114th Congress

1. Keystone Pipeline	Y	5. Puerto Rico Debt	Y	9. Offenses by Aliens	Y
2. Trade Deals	N	6. Medical Marijuana	Y	10. Troops in Iraq	Y
3. Export-Import Bank	Y	7. Sanctuary Cities	N	11. Homeland Security $$	Y
4. Debt Ceiling Increase	Y	8. Armor-piercing Bullets	N	12. Trade Adjustment aid	Y

Election Results

Election	Name (Party)	Vote (%)		Cand. Spent	Ind. Exp. Support	Ind. Exp. Oppose
2016 General	Sean Maloney (D)	162,077	(56%)	$1,901,323		
	Phil Oliva (R)	129,383	(44%)	$223,946		
2016 Primary	Sean Maloney (D)		(100%)			

Prior winning percentages: 2014 (48%), 2012 (49%)

Elected in 2012, Sean Patrick Maloney of New York was a staffer on both of Bill Clinton's presidential campaigns and was a West Wing aide. Later, he was a top state official in Albany. The former president's brand of centrism and his endorsement have been helpful in this swing district. Maloney has been a productive legislator and has taken an interest in House Democrats' campaign strategy.

Maloney was born in Quebec, Canada, where his father worked in the lumber industry. He grew up in Hanover, New Hampshire, attended Georgetown University for two years and then transferred to the University of Virginia, where he got a bachelor's in international relations and stayed on to earn a law degree. Maloney delayed taking the bar exam to work on Clinton's 1992 campaign as a deputy to Susan Thomases, then the chief scheduler. In the 1996 reelection campaign, he was director of surrogate travel. After that, he snagged a job in the White House as the No. 3 official under Chief of Staff John Podesta. Maloney later became staff secretary, responsible for coordinating the flow of information to the president.

After Bill Clinton left office, Maloney worked as the chief operating officer at Kiodex, a firm that developed risk management tools. He made his first bid for office in 2006, when he lost badly to Andrew Cuomo in the Democratic primary for attorney general. Maloney became first deputy secretary to Gov. Eliot Spitzer and, after Spitzer resigned, to David Paterson. Maloney came under a cloud for possible obstruction of justice following a scheme to release damaging information about then-Senate Majority Leader Joseph Bruno's travel. Bruno was convicted on federal corruption charges in December 2009, but he was later acquitted in a retrial.

When Maloney ran for the House seat in 2012, his role in Albany became an issue in the five-way Democratic primary. Although his defenders insisted that was not involved in the Bruno affair, *The New York Times* editorial board said that during law-enforcement review of the charges, Maloney "appeared to be most interested in holding back the staff's personal emails from investigators." Still, he won the primary handily. He led his closest competitor, Cortlandt Town Council Member Richard Becker, 48%-32%.

In his general election challenge to first-term Rep. Nina Hayworth, Maloney and Democratic allies painted Hayworth as a tea party extremist, citing her votes for Rep. Paul Ryan's budget and for cutting funding for Planned Parenthood. Maloney argued that his moderate politics better suited the district. Hayworth outraised Maloney $3.3 million to $2.3 million and had a comparable edge in outside assistance. Maloney eked out a win, 52%-48%.

Maloney, who is gay, married in 2014 his longtime partner, Randy Florke, a prominent Realtor and interior designer. After his initial election, the front page of *The Times* featured a photo of Maloney taking his oath of office alongside Florke and their three children. He has co-chaired the Congressional LGBT Equality Caucus. He has been an active legislator, though with occasional embellishment. In summarizing his work during his first term, Maloney claimed credit for introducing 10 bills that were signed into law. In most of those cases, he appeared to have been a co-sponsor of legislation, which often was changed prior to enactment. The official listing of the bills that he introduced in 2013-14 showed that the only one enacted was the naming of a post office in his district.

Maloney sparked a furor in the House in May 2016, when he offered an amendment to prevent federal contractors from engaging in job discrimination on the basis of sexual orientation. The proposal lost, 213-212, after Republican leaders used strong-arm tactics to urge some of their members to switch their votes. Following Democratic shouts of "Shame!" and other protests, Maloney again offered his amendment the following week and it easily passed, though his provision died in the Senate. He was successful on two other initiatives in 2016. The Federal Aviation Administration reauthorization included his amendment to hire more air traffic controllers, with priority to military veterans. The House passed his bill to require an advisory committee of the Food and Drug Administration to recommend procedures for use of certain new drugs that are opioids. Later that year, Congress approved comprehensive legislation dealing with opioids.

In 2014, Maloney won a rematch with Hayworth. This time, Maloney outraised his opponent, $4.3 million to $3.5 million, and assistance from super PACs gave him another $2 million. In a Republican year, he won 49.7%-47.9%, and led in three of the four counties, losing only Putnam. In an unusual move, Republican state Sen. Greg Ball, whose district included much of Putnam County, crossed party lines to endorse Maloney. Ball, who retired in 2014, said that he had "no stronger ally" on veterans' issues than Maloney. A spokesman for Hayworth said that Ball's action was "revenge" because she "scared him out of running" when Hayworth was elected to the seat in 2010. In 2016, his opponent Phil Oliva, an aide to the Westchester County executive, accused Maloney of exaggerating or lying about his legislative successes. Oliva raised only $224,000 to Maloney's $3.6 million and was limited in getting his message out. Maloney won, 56%-44%.

Following the election, Maloney raised questions about the operations of the DCCC during the campaign, including its strategy and financing of candidates. He decided not to seek the committee's chairmanship after House Democrats tapped him to lead an independent review of its activities. In February 2017, Maloney told *The Washington Post*, "We can win [in districts] where we used to struggle, and we're struggling a bit where we used to win." Whether the DCCC would make internal reforms remained to be seen.

Lower Hudson Valley

Population		**Race and Ethnicity**		**Income**	
Total	720,822	White	69.9%	Median Income	$78,021 (42 out of 435)
Land area	1,353	Black	8.6%	Under $50,000	32.7%
Pop/ sq mi	532.6	Latino	15.9%	$50,000-$99,999	28.4%
Born in state	70.8%	Asian	3.1%	$100,000-$199,999	28.9%
		Two races	2.0%	$200,000 or more	9.9%
Age Groups		Other	0.4%	Poverty Rate	10.3%
Under 18	24.3%				
18-34	20.7%	**Education**		**Health Insurance**	
35-64	41.5%	H.S grad or less	36.7%	With health insurance coverage	92.3%
Over 64	13.5%	Some college	28.4%		
		College Degree, 4 yr	19.8%	**Public Assistance**	
Work		Post grad	15.0%	Cash public assistance income	2.3%
White Collar	39.3%			Food stamp/SNAP benefits	9.4%
Sales and Service	43.5%	**Military**			
Blue Collar	17.2%	Veteran	7.2%		
Government	18.0%	Active Duty	0.8%		

Voter Turnout			
2015 Total Citizens 18+	511,358	2016 House Turnout as % CVAP	57%
2016 House turnout	291,527	2014 House Turnout as % CVAP	35%

2012 Presidential Vote		
Barack Obama	149,610	(51%)
Mitt Romney	137,144	(47%)

2016 Presidential Vote		
Donald Trump	152,142	(49%)
Hillary Clinton	146,188	(47%)
Gary Johnson	7,930	(3%)

Cook Partisan Voting Index: R+1

The great interior of America can be said to begin where the Hudson River squeezes through a series of Appalachian ridges at the Hudson Highlands. This chokepoint became a barrier to British military power during the Revolutionary War, when American forces put a chain across the river to keep the British from sailing north. Benedict Arnold betrayed his country over control of this part of the Hudson, and the new nation built its Military Academy high on the cliffs at West Point. The Hudson was the impetus for the builders of the Erie Canal and the water-level New York Central Railroad, two great projects that made New York City the port of the American interior.

The 18th Congressional District of New York covers much of the southern Hudson Valley, sprawling across four counties. West of the Hudson, the district includes all of Orange County, which takes in about half of the voters in the district and trails only Rockland as the state's fastest-growing county outside of New York City, with an 11 percent increase between 2000 and 2015. There, old farming villages like Warwick adjoin mountains, farms and new middle-income subdivisions on the nation's biggest deposit of muck soil outside the Everglades. Orange County includes Kiryas Joel, a Hasidic Jewish settlement with 20,000 residents, many of whom moved from Brooklyn to find room for their large families. In November 2016, the county approved plans for a $500 million Legoland theme park. Opposition by community groups had killed plans to locate the park in Rockland. Also in Orange, the heirs to railroad baron E.H. Harriman battled Caesars Entertainment moguls over plans to locate a large casino and resort complex next to their parkland. The state awarded the license to a site in adjacent Sullivan County. Plans to expand service at Stewart International Airport got a boost in February 2017 when low-cost carrier Norwegian Air Shuttle announced service to Europe.

East of the river, the 18th takes in all of Putnam County and nearly 60 percent of Dutchess County, including Poughkeepsie, home of Vassar College, and Wappingers Falls. In Poughkeepsie, which has suffered many years of economic hard times, robust economic development was underway along the Hudson after officials in 2015 approved a booming waterfront plan. Putnam has become popular with first-time home buyers, who make an 80-minute commute to Grand Central Station. The district takes in the lightly populated northeastern reaches of Westchester County, around Somers, North Salem and Lewisboro.

The region has proved attractive to middle- and higher-income white-collar workers seeking reasonably priced housing in low-crime areas. This has led to robust population growth at a time when many other areas of the state are losing residents. Politically, Putnam County is reliably Republican; the rest of the district is swing territory or leans slightly Democratic, resulting in a district that tends to end up near the national average. Donald Trump won the district, 49%-47%, after President Barack Obama twice won here narrowly.

NINETEENTH DISTRICT

John Faso (R)

Elected 2016, 1st term; b. Aug 25, 1952, Massapequa, L.I.; State University of New York at Brockport, B.A., 1974; Georgetown University Law Center (DC), J.D., 1979; Roman Catholic; Married (Mary Frances Faso); 2 children.

Elected Office: NY Assembly, 1986-2002.

Professional Career: Staff, United States House of Representatives Government Operations Committee, 1979-1981; Staff, NY Senate, 1981-1983; NY Legislative Bill Drafting Commission, 1983-1986; Buffalo Fiscal Stability Authority, 2003-2006.

DC Office: 1616 LHOB 20515, 202-225-5614, Fax: 202-225-1168, faso.house.gov.

State Offices: Delhi, 607-746-9537; Kinderhook, 518-610-8133; Kingstown, 845-514-2322.

Committees: *Agriculture*: Commodity Exchanges, Energy & Credit, Nutrition. *Budget*. *Transportation & Infrastructure*: Economic Dev't, Public Buildings & Emergency Management, Highways & Transit, Railroads, Pipelines & Hazardous Materials.

Election Results

Election	Name (Party)	Vote (%)		Cand. Spent	Ind. Exp. Support	Ind. Exp. Oppose
2016 General	John Faso (R)	166,180	(54%)	$2,863,268	$96,588	$4,301,204
	Zephyr Teachout (D)	141,231	(46%)	$4,955,144	$173,636	$6,203,022
2016 Primary	John Faso (R)	9,967	(68%)			
	Andrew Heaney (R)	4,607	(32%)			

Republican John Faso, elected in 2016 to an open seat, brought extensive experience as a state lawmaker and later as a lobbyist in both Albany and Washington. His comfortable victory followed three unsuccessful campaigns during the previous decade. As a practical politician, he initially had a comfortable fit in the House, with committee assignments that gave him opportunities for early influence.

Faso was born in Massapequa on Long Island, graduated from high school in Queens and got his bachelor's from the State University of New York at Brockport. He was a grants officer for Nassau County before he went to Georgetown University, where he got his law degree. He stayed in Washington as an aide to New York Republican Rep. John Wydler and then for the Washington office of the New York State Senate. For three years, he worked for the New York State Legislature Bill Drafting Commission. Faso was elected in 1986 to the State Assembly, where he served 16 years, including four years as minority leader.

Faso left the legislature for an unsuccessful run for state comptroller. He then became a partner in the national law firm of Manatt, Phelps and Phillips, where he did lobbying in Washington. In 2006, he made another statewide run, this time for governor against Elliot Spitzer. As the 2008 *Almanac* wrote, Faso was "little known and attracted little financing." He lost badly, 70%-29%. He was an early candidate in 2009 for the special election to fill the House seat of Kristen Gillibrand, who had been appointed to the Senate. Faso withdrew from that contest prior to the Republican primary; the GOP nominee lost the competitive contest by 726 votes.

When Republican Rep. Chris Gibson retired, Faso decided to make another bid for the House. He was endorsed by Gibson and won the GOP nomination. Oddly, he postured himself as an outsider against the "ivory tower intellectuals and bureaucrats in Washington who think they know better than we do." He won the primary against Andrew Heaney, a businessman who founded a website that was a marketplace for propane sales; Heaney spent $1.8 million, including $600,000 in self-financing. Faso easily won the low-turnout primary with 68 percent of the vote. Democrats had recruiting failures with several familiar local officials. Their nominee, Zephyr Teachout, a law professor at Fordham University in New York City, seemed like less than a perfect fit for the Upstate district. She was an academic scholar on corruption and campaign financing, and had proposed sweeping reforms. Her academic website described her "rich background in laws governing political behavior." In her challenge to Gov. Andrew Cuomo in the 2014 Democratic primary, she got 34 percent of the vote.

This was a high-dollar contest, with the ironic twist of campaign reformer Teachout out-spent lobbyist Faso, $5 million to $2.9 million. In a sign that each party viewed this as a close contest, Republican groups spent $7 million on behalf of Faso and Democrats spent more than $3 million for Teachout. The outcome was not particularly close. Faso won 54%-46% and took every county except for Ulster, which was the most urban.

Faso got seats on the Agriculture, Budget, and Transportation and Infrastructure committees. After showing some independence from Donald Trump during the campaign, he was an early critic of the new president on several fronts, calling his executive orders to limit immigrants and refugees "not well-implemented." He criticized Trump's handling of his job, including his "ill-advised" tweeting. "We need a little more Ronald Reagan and a little less P.T. Barnum," Faso told his district's *Times-Journal* newspaper in a February 2017 interview.

Central Hudson Valley, the Catskills

Population		**Race and Ethnicity**		**Income**	
Total	710,732	White	85.5%	Median Income	$57,566 (160 out of 435)
Land area	7,937	Black	4.0%		
Pop/ sq mi	89.5	Latino	6.8%		
Born in state	75.5%	Asian	1.6%	Under $50,000	43.6%
		Two races	1.9%	$50,000-$99,999	32.1%
Age Groups		Other	0.2%	$100,000-$199,999	20.1%
Under 18	19.4%			$200,000 or more	4.2%
18-34	20.7%	**Education**		Poverty Rate	12.4%
35-64	42.5%	H.S grad or less	42.9%		
Over 64	17.4%	Some college	29.8%	**Health Insurance**	
		College Degree, 4 yr	14.7%	With health insurance coverage	91.8%
Work		Post grad	12.5%		
White Collar	36.7%				
Sales and Service	41.7%	**Military**		**Public Assistance**	
Blue Collar	21.7%	Veteran	8.6%	Cash public assistance income	2.7%
Government	19.5%	Active Duty	0.1%		
				Food stamp/SNAP benefits	10.9%

Voter Turnout			
2015 Total Citizens 18+	554,882	2016 House Turnout as % CVAP	55%
2016 House turnout	307,614	2014 House Turnout as % CVAP	37%

2012 Presidential Vote		
Barack Obama	157,279	(52%)
Mitt Romney	138,384	(46%)

2016 Presidential Vote		
Donald Trump	162,266	(50%)
Hillary Clinton	140,517	(44%)
Gary Johnson	10,235	(3%)
Jill Stein	6,434	(2%)

Cook Partisan Voting Index: R+2

The Hudson River, an avenue of commerce in colonial days and an inspiration to artists in the early republic, is still one of America's great sights, although it is no longer central to the nation's consciousness and politics. The classic mansions overlooking the river, like Clermont, built by Robert Livingston, who financed the first steamboat, are reminders of the cool serenity of the 18th century mind and the daring nature of its spirit. The Hudson was also a center of American culture during the Romantic era. From Frederick Church's Moorish mansion, Olana, one can see the still-unspoiled river landscape that inspired his art and that of others of the Hudson River School of painters.

The Hudson gave birth to America's passionate party politics. On a visit to this area in the 1790s, James Madison and Aaron Burr welded the Virginia-New York alliance that changed the course of American political history. Nearby is Kinderhook, the home of Martin Van Buren, the innkeeper's son, who in concert with Andrew Jackson, invented the torchlight parade, the national party convention, and, many argue, the Democratic Party. Later in the 19th century, the Hudson was lined with the palaces of the nation's first great millionaires and the comfortable country homes of New York's gentry. One of the latter, Springwood in Hyde Park, was the birthplace and home of Franklin Roosevelt, who, even as president, was most comfortable looking out over his sloping lawn to the river, where he liked to go iceboating in the winter. To the north is the charming town of Rhinebeck, site of the 2010 wedding of Chelsea Clinton and Marc Mezvinsky.

On the other side of the Hudson, the Catskills loom, where Rip Van Winkle was said to have fallen asleep for 20 years after drinking with nine pipe-playing dwarfs. Eventually, the area became part of a great pathway west, along the Erie Lackawanna and Delaware & Hudson railroad lines, with engines steaming over giant viaducts and along narrow river valleys through the mountains. Later in the 19th century, huge kosher hotels were built in Sullivan County in the Catskills, the resort area popularly known as the Borscht Belt. These thrived when Jews were excluded from other resorts but fell on hard times in the late 20th century. Today, there is little passenger train service, and the Catskills are bypassed by major airlines.

The sprawling 19th Congressional District of New York connects these two regions into a single district. Like most of the Upstate districts, its boundaries are relatively straight, in contrast to past gerrymanders. It includes seven full counties (Schoharie, Delaware, Sullivan, Ulster, Otsego, Columbia and Greene) and parts of four others (Rensselaer, Dutchess, Montgomery and Broome). It is a collection of small towns and villages, some suburban in nature, and some rural. The largest locale is Kingston (pop. 23,436) and only one other place, Hyde Park, has more than 20,000 residents. It bends around the Albany metropolitan area in the north, taking in a bit of the Mohawk Valley, and the Baseball Hall of Fame in Cooperstown. In Ulster is Bethel, where the 1969 Woodstock music festival took place. Many of the local populations have been declining. In 2014, state-imposed restrictions stifled local interests in Schoharie County that advocated hydraulic fracturing of natural-gas deposits. A huge new casino, with more than 2,000 jobs, was scheduled to open in Sullivan County in 2018.

Ulster, the largest county, is solidly Democratic at the national level. Like most of Upstate New York, Republicans fare better at the local level and even control the county legislature. The district was once solidly Republican, part of a tradition that dated to the Civil War (Franklin Roosevelt never carried his home territory except when he ran for the state Senate in 1910). Today, it is swing territory: Donald Trump won here, 50%-44%. Barack Obama carried the district twice, with vote totals close to his national averages.

TWENTIETH DISTRICT

Paul Tonko (D)

Elected 2008, 5th term; b. Jun 18, 1949, Amsterdam; Clarkson University (NY), B.S., 1971; Roman Catholic; Single.

Elected Office: Montgomery County Board of Supervisors, 1976-1983, Chairman, 1981; NY Assembly, 1983-2007.

Professional Career: NY Department of Transportation, 1972-1974; NY Department of Public Service, 1974-1983; President & CEO, NY St. Energy Research & Devel-opment Authority, 2007-2008.

DC Office: 2463 RHOB 20515, 202-225-5076, Fax: 202-225-5077, tonko.house.gov.

State Offices: Albany, 518-465-0700; Amsterdam, 518-843-3400; Schenectady, 518-374-4547.

Committees: *Energy & Commerce*: Energy, Environment (RMM), Oversight & Investigations. *Science, Space & Technology*: Energy.

Group Ratings

	ADA	ACLU	AFL-CIO	LCV	ITI	COC	HAFA	ACU	CFG	FRC
2016	-	100%	-	97%	67%	50%	14%	8%	4%	0%
2015	95%	C	100%	100%	C	45%	C	4%	0%	0%

Almanac Ratings 2015

	Economy	Social	Foreign	Composite
Liberal	94%	95%	99%	96%
Conservative	6%	5%	1%	4%

Key Votes of the 114th Congress

1. Keystone Pipeline	N	5. Puerto Rico Debt	Y	9. Offenses by Aliens	N
2. Trade Deals	N	6. Medical Marijuana	Y	10. Troops in Iraq	Y
3. Export-Import Bank	Y	7. Sanctuary Cities	N	11. Homeland Security $$	Y
4. Debt Ceiling Increase	Y	8. Armor-piercing Bullets	N	12. Trade Adjustment aid	Y

Election Results

Election	Name (Party)	Vote (%)		Cand. Spent	Ind. Exp. Support	Ind. Exp. Oppose
2016 General	Paul Tonko (D)	213,018	(68%)	$677,747		
	Francis J. Vitollo (R)	100,740	(32%)			
2016 Primary	Paul Tonko (D)		(100%)			

Prior winning percentages: 2014 (59%), 2012 (64%), 2010 (57%), 2008 (55%)

Democrat Paul Tonko, elected in 2008, came to Congress with an extensive background in energy issues and parlayed his expertise into a seat on the powerful Energy and Commerce Committee, where he has dealt with similar issues. He has had some bipartisan accomplishments.

The grandson of Polish immigrants, Tonko was born in the old mill town of Amsterdam, New York, where he still lives. He graduated from Clarkson University with a degree in engineering. Attracted from a young age to public service, he built his career in state government, first at the New York Department of Transportation and then as an engineer at the Department of Public Service, the state's utilities regulator. His working-class background gave him an appreciation for the "underdog" that remains the underpinning of his political beliefs.

In 1974, at age 26, he became the youngest person elected to the Montgomery County Board of Supervisors, and later became board chairman. Tonko won a seat in the state Assembly in 1983 and served for nearly a quarter century. He won passage of a law requiring health insurers to cover most mental illnesses and another requiring social workers to report all cases of suspected child abuse to the state. He exercised his greatest influence over state energy policy, serving as chairman of the Assembly's energy committee for 15 years, until he resigned to head the state's Energy Research and Development Authority.

When the House seat opened, Tonko in the primary faced Phil Steck, an Albany County legislator, and Tracey Brooks, a former staffer for Democratic Sen. Hillary Clinton. Both enjoyed a head start raising money. But most of the local Democratic establishment lined up behind Tonko. He won important union endorsements, plus the backing of the Working Families Party. With few differences between the candidates on major issues, the local support likely made the difference. Outraised and outspent by both opponents, Tonko sailed to victory with 40 percent of the vote to 30 percent for Brooks. In the general, Tonko faced Republican Jim Buhrmaster, a Schenectady County legislator who made an appeal to independents to overcome the registration advantage for Democrats in the district. But Tonko won with 62%-35%.

Tonko has focused on the issue he knows best, energy policy. Even as a freshman, while Democrats controlled the House, Tonko was quick to exploit his policy expertise. He got a bill through the House in 2009 creating an $800 million research program in wind energy technologies, which would benefit GE in his district. Another of his bills, which passed the same year, created a research program to improve the efficiency of gas turbines used in power generation systems that convert heat into energy. In 2010, following the BP disaster in the Gulf of Mexico, Tonko got a provision in a House-passed bill to speed up the response to future oil spills.

On Energy and Commerce, he has been ranking Democrat on the Environment and the Economy Subcommittee, where he was at the vanguard of defending the Environmental Protection Agency against frequent GOP attacks. He has co-chaired the Sustainable Energy and Environment Coalition. On spending bills, he has sought to protect EPA's authority to regulate carbon emissions. He worked to undo Republican cutbacks to the Weatherization Assistance Program, which improves home energy efficiency through insulation and superior equipment. On the Science, Space and Technology Committee, he worked in 2015 to protect federal research funds that had been directed at upstate New York's manufacturing facilities. In 2016, the House passed his bill to encourage citizen activities in the federal government to accelerate scientific research. It was enacted as part of a broader package of innovation measures.

On other issues, Tonko worked to expand low-income children's access to healthy meals. He has sought to promote mental-health parity, as he did in Albany. His efforts to rein in pay for government contractors have won him some attention. The *Almanac* vote ratings for 2015 ranked Tonko among the most liberal members.

Tonko has had little trouble winning reelection. Albany *Times Union* columnist Marv Cermak described him in 2011 as "a super-duper campaigner who shows up all over the place," and said "If there is a chink in his armor, colleagues and media types agree it's his penchant for long-winded speeches." He is one of only three Democrats in the nine New York districts north of Poughkeepsie.

Capital Region: Albany, Schenectady

Population		**Race and Ethnicity**		**Income**	
Total	723,568	White	77.8%	Median Income	$60,765 (139 out of 435)
Land area	1,231	Black	8.6%		
Pop/ sq mi	587.7	Latino	5.9%		
Born in state	76.7%	Asian	4.4%	Under $50,000	41.5%
		Two races	2.6%	$50,000-$99,999	32.0%
Age Groups		Other	0.6%	$100,000-$199,999	21.9%
Under 18	20.4%			$200,000 or more	4.7%
18-34	24.9%	**Education**		Poverty Rate	12.7%
35-64	39.6%	H.S grad or less	35.0%		
Over 64	15.1%	Some college	29.1%	**Health Insurance**	
		College Degree, 4 yr	19.5%	With health insurance coverage	94.1%
Work		Post grad	16.4%		
White Collar	42.2%				
Sales and Service	42.9%	**Military**		**Public Assistance**	
Blue Collar	14.8%	Veteran	7.6%	Cash public assistance income	2.8%
Government	21.9%	Active Duty	0.2%		
				Food stamp/SNAP benefits	11.8%

Voter Turnout			
2015 Total Citizens 18+	554,260	2016 House Turnout as % CVAP	57%
2016 House turnout	313,939	2014 House Turnout as % CVAP	37%

2012 Presidential Vote		
Barack Obama	186,460	(59%)
Mitt Romney	122,230	(39%)

2016 Presidential Vote		
Hillary Clinton	175,384	(53%)
Donald Trump	131,557	(40%)
Gary Johnson	12,538	(4%)

Cook Partisan Voting Index: D+7

As readers of novelist William Kennedy know, Albany is an antique city. Its solid row houses recall its 19th-century prosperity. Its once-teeming lumberyards, railroad car shops, restaurants and hotels have the patina of age and the accumulated grime of decades of coal smoke burned during six-month-long winters. Its history dates to 1609, when Dutch traders from Henry Hudson's ship *Half Moon* set up a fur trading post. Hudson, his son, and seven crew members were set adrift amidst a mutiny in James Bay, Canada, two years later and never seen again, but the trading post endured. The Dutch built Fort Orange on the banks of the Hudson in 1624 so seagoing ships could dock at the edge of the great, gloomy forests near the confluence of the Hudson and the Mohawk. Albany became one of America's biggest lumber towns in addition to serving as New York's state capital.

A few miles upriver, Troy was a steel town rivaling Pittsburgh in the 1840s, greatly advantaged by its proximity to the mouth of the Erie Canal. That is where meat-packer Samuel Wilson supplied beef rations to soldiers during the War of 1812; we know Wilson today as "Uncle Sam." Lately, a gentrified Troy has been bustling with antique shops. Schenectady, a few miles up the Mohawk, was the site of Charles Steinmetz's fabled General Electric laboratories and long remained a GE town.

In addition to state government, Albany had one of the nation's most famed Democratic political machines, dating to 1921, when Daniel O'Connell, his brothers, and local aristocrat Edwin Corning took control of City Hall. Democrats have lost only a handful of congressional elections here since. The machine was sustained by legions of city and county employees, by a certain creativity when it came to counting votes, and by the raffish atmosphere of the speakeasies during Prohibition. Curiously, the machine made possible the transformation of Albany into the shinier metropolis it is today. Mayor Corning and Republican Gov. Nelson Rockefeller collaborated on a smorgasbord of civic improvement projects: the Empire State Plaza with 11,000 employees in 10 government buildings on 98 acres; the distinctive, ovoid performing arts center known as the Egg; and a renovated Union Station.

The economy in the Capital Region has been stronger than elsewhere in Upstate, with a population gain of 11,000 in Albany between 2010 and 2015. The area has remained vibrant with renewable energy jobs and high-tech manufacturing. GE has new plants producing digital X-ray equipment and advanced batteries. In January 2017, the port of Albany announced a $50 million expansion to move additional cargo. Notably, the only recent drag on the local economy has been government.

The 20th Congressional District of New York includes most of the Albany metropolitan area: all of Albany and Schenectady counties, which take in nearly two-thirds of the district population; most of Montgomery County, including Amsterdam; parts of Rensselaer County, including Troy; and much of Saratoga County. The horse-race track at Saratoga Springs, operating since 1863 and reportedly the oldest sports venue in the nation, planned to complete a major upgrade in its facility for the 2017 racing season. Politically, Democratic voters in Albany and Troy outweigh the Republican tilt of the outer counties and make this a comfortably Democratic district. As in other Upstate districts, the Democratic presidential vote fell in 2016. Hillary Clinton got 53 percent of the vote, compared with 59 percent for President Barack Obama in 2012.

TWENTY-FIRST DISTRICT

Elise Stefanik (R)

Elected 2014, 2nd term; b. Jul 02, 1984, Albany; Harvard University, B.A.; Roman Catholic; Engaged (Matthew Manda).

Professional Career: Staff, President George W. Bush, 2006-2009; Staff, Vice President. candidate Paul Ryan, 2012; Director Communications, Foreign Policy Initiative; Sales, marketing & mgmt operations, Premium Plywood Products.

DC Office: 318 CHOB 20515, 202-225-4611, Fax: 202-226-0621, stefanik.house.gov.

State Offices: Glens Falls, 518-743-0964; Plattsburgh, 518-561-2324; Watertown, 315-782-3150.

Committees: *Armed Services*: Emerging Threats & Capabilities (Chmn), Readiness. *Education & the Workforce*: Higher Education & Workforce Development, Workforce Protections. *Permanent Select on Intelligence*.

Group Ratings

	ADA	ACLU	AFL-CIO	LCV	ITI	COC	HAFA	ACU	CFG	FRC
2016	-	23%	-	29%	100%	93%	29%	40%	45%	75%
2015	0%	C	33%	9%	C	100%	C	33%	36%	67%

Almanac Ratings 2015

	Economy	Social	Foreign	Composite
Liberal	14%	27%	10%	17%
Conservative	86%	73%	90%	83%

Key Votes of the 114th Congress

1. Keystone Pipeline	Y	5. Puerto Rico Debt	Y	9. Offenses by Aliens	Y
2. Trade Deals	Y	6. Medical Marijuana	Y	10. Troops in Iraq	N
3. Export-Import Bank	Y	7. Sanctuary Cities	Y	11. Homeland Security $$	Y
4. Debt Ceiling Increase	Y	8. Armor-piercing Bullets	Y	12. Trade Adjustment aid	Y

Election Results

Election	Name (Party)	Vote (%)	Cand. Spent	Ind. Exp. Support	Ind. Exp. Oppose
2016 General	Elise Stefanik (R)	177,886 (65%)	$2,614,416	$233,870	
	Mike Derrick (D)	82,161 (30%)	$1,225,772		$379,334
	Matt Funiciello (G)	12,559 (5%)	$14,727		
2016 Primary	Elise Stefanik (R)	(100%)			

Prior winning percentages: 2014 (53%)

Republican Elise Stefanik, elected to an open seat in 2014 that had been Democratic-held, has taken advantage of her opportunities. The politically adept Stefanik - the youngest woman ever elected to Congress - has become a rising and prominent Republican star. With good connections to House leaders, she has worked to entrench herself politically, with apparent success.

Born and raised in Albany, Stefanik grew up among entrepreneurs, with both parents running a wholesale plywood business. She became politically engaged during her college years at Harvard, and upon graduation she landed a job with the Bush administration's Domestic Policy Council. She worked in the White House chief of staff's office, and later joined Tim Pawlenty's presidential campaign as policy director. After Pawlenty withdrew, she worked for Rep. Paul Ryan of Wisconsin when he became the running mate for Mitt Romney, advising him on vice presidential debate preparation.

After Blue Dog Democratic Rep. Bill Owens announced his retirement, Stefanik unveiled her House bid and got the backing of the National Republican Congressional Committee's "Young Guns" program, which supports new talent. With nearly $800,000 in help from Karl Rove's American Crossroads - making a rare intervention in a GOP primary, mostly through negative ads - Stefanik dispatched Republican Matt Doheny in the June primary, 61%-39%. A Wall Street investment banker, Doheny had run twice against Owens, and lost each time by two percentage points.

Democrats faced problems in recruiting, and their nominee, Aaron Wolff, was a film-maker who was a resident of Brooklyn. His only claim to the North Country was that his family owned some land. In the general, Stefanik moderated from the customary GOP line on some issues. She signaled willingness to compromise on raising the minimum wage, and proposed expanding Medicare as part of an alternative to the Affordable Care Act. She refused to sign Grover Norquist's anti-tax pledge, arguing that she was beholden to voters, not lobbyists. Her campaign came under criticism for lacking a district address and for property-tax delinquency in Washington. Stefanik benefited from nearly $2 million in party-related assistance, far more than Democrats spent for Wolff, who also suffered from an active campaign by Green Party candidate Matt Funicello. Stefanik pulled away to a surprisingly comfortable win, with 55 percent of the vote to 34 percent for Wolff and 11 percent for Funicello. She won nine of the 12 counties, losing three in the northeast corner of the state.

Stefanik has drawn considerable publicity, nearly all of it favorable. CBS News featured her with an online story headlined, "Is Elise Stefanik the future of the GOP?" She told the network: "I think we need to have a tone that reaches out to women, and that's something that I've been very focused on. I also think that we need to do a better job of listening." She recounted that she took the advice of Speaker Paul Ryan that "you have one mouth and two ears. Use them in that ratio."

With her chief assignment on the Armed Services Committee, Stefanik in 2015 was the only freshman appointed to the House-Senate conference committee on the annual defense spending bill, where she included language to protect Fort Drum from cutbacks and backed steps to reverse the overall reduction in troop levels. In January 2017, she was promoted to chair the Emerging Threats and Capabilities Subcommittee, which oversees counterterrorism programs and the proliferation of weapons of mass destruction. Stefanik also began her second term with a plum assignment to the Intelligence Committee. As a member of the Education and the Workforce Committee, she worked with Democratic Rep. Cheri Bustos of Illinois to provide more flexible access to student assistance under Pell Grants.

Stefanik has had multiple party assignments. Freshman Republicans selected her as their representative on the GOP Policy Committee. In 2017, she became co-chair with Rep. Charlie Dent of Pennsylvania of the Tuesday Group of moderate Republicans, which has emphasized the need for bipartisanship. At the National Republican Congressional Committee, she became vice chair for recruitment, the first woman to hold that position.

In 2016, Democrats ran a credible challenger - Mike Derrick, a retired Army colonel who had taught at the U.S. Military Academy. He raised $1.2 million, though he received virtually no party assistance. Stefanik showed her fundraising strength, with $3.1 million, and she coasted to victory, 65%-30%, with 5 percent for Funicello, who ran again as the Green Party candidate. The outcome indicated that Stefanik had locked down a district that Democrats had held for the previous six years.

Stefanik kept her distance from Donald Trump during the campaign, when she voiced occasional criticism and said that she would be "an independent voice for the district." After he became president, she criticized Trump for his handling of the immigration and refugee bans, which she said was "rushed and overly broad."

Northern New York: Glens Falls, Watertown

Population		**Race and Ethnicity**		**Income**	
Total	718,502	White	90.5%	Median Income	$51,255 (234 out of 435)
Land area	15,115	Black	2.9%	Under $50,000	48.7%
Pop/ sq mi	47.5	Latino	3.2%	$50,000-$99,999	33.4%
Born in state	77.1%	Asian	0.9%	$100,000-$199,999	15.6%
Age Groups		Two races	1.6%	$200,000 or more	2.3%
Under 18	21.2%	Other	1.0%	Poverty Rate	14.6%
18-34	23.3%	**Education**		**Health Insurance**	
35-64	40.1%	H.S grad or less	47.2%	With health insurance coverage	91.8%
Over 64	15.5%	Some college	30.5%	**Public Assistance**	
Work		College Degree, 4 yr	12.4%	Cash public assistance income	3.1%
White Collar	32.4%	Post grad	9.9%	Food stamp/SNAP benefits	14.8%
Sales and Service	44.3%	**Military**			
Blue Collar	23.3%	Veteran	10.5%		
Government	21.4%	Active Duty	2.0%		

Voter Turnout			
2015 Total Citizens 18+	555,274	2016 House Turnout as % CVAP	49%
2016 House turnout	272,606	2014 House Turnout as % CVAP	32%

2012 Presidential Vote		
Barack Obama	138,889	(52%)
Mitt Romney	122,471	(46%)

2016 Presidential Vote		
Donald Trump	150,481	(53%)
Hillary Clinton	111,760	(39%)
Gary Johnson	11,620	(4%)
Jill Stein	5,577	(2%)

Cook Partisan Voting Index: R+4

Some early 19th century visionaries believed that the North Country of Upstate New York - a battleground in both the Revolutionary War and the War of 1812 - was the land of the future. Financier Gouverneur Morris, French slave trader James LeRay, and Dutch silver speculator David Parish bought up thousands of acres between the Adirondacks and the St. Lawrence River and tried to unload them on farmers unaware of the shortness of the growing season and the unnavigability of the river. These developers left behind grand mansions, but their hopes for huge profits were frustrated when the Erie Canal turned the stream of settlement westward, and Canadians built their new capital of Ottawa far north of the river. But northern New York was not without its business successes: It was in Watertown in 1878 that 26-year-old Frank Woolworth put a sign over a table of odds and ends that read "Any Article 5 Cents," starting America's first retail chain and inventing the concept of discount stores.

More recently, the North Country has looked to government for help. The St. Lawrence Seaway proved too small for most oceangoing freighters and remains frozen three months of the year. Plan 2014, a binational agreement with Canada to return the St. Lawrence River to more natural flowing patterns, took effect in 2016. Fort Drum, despite the Army's preference for warm-weather training sites, has been the home since 1985 of the 10th Mountain Division, a 10,000-person light infantry division near Watertown. The unit performed valiantly in difficult environs in Afghanistan and Iraq. Reflecting nationwide trends, the number of soldiers and economic impact of Drum fell annually from 2012 to 2016. Private developers have built big malls in Watertown and Massena, with the cheap dollar attracting Canadian tourism and shopping, as even New York taxes are lower than Ontario's. Plans were underway to harvest the wind, which is in plentiful supply, for multiple wind farms.

The 21st Congressional District of New York covers most of the North Country, starting at Lake Champlain, running westward along the St. Lawrence Seaway and over the Adirondacks Forest Preserve to Lake Ontario. Lake Placid is here, site of the 1980 Olympic Games and the famous "Miracle on Ice," when a heavily favored Soviet hockey team was upset by an upstart American squad. It stretches to the edges of Saratoga Springs to the southeast, and near Oswego and Syracuse to the southwest. The district has only a few population centers, including Plattsburgh on Lake Champlain, Watertown near Lake Ontario, and Gloversville and Glens Falls in the south. Each is smaller than 30,000 residents, with population declining from 2010 to 2015. Warren County is known as "catheter valley" because of its many medical-device companies that make such products. In 2014, the state of New York reached a tentative land settlement with the St. Regis Mohawk tribe, contingent on agreement by the local counties. As of January 2017, Franklin and St. Lawrence were still negotiating. The North Country captured national attention for three weeks in June 2015 when two convicted murderers escaped a maximum-security prison in Clinton, along the Canadian border. Federal border agents and state police killed one in the woods and captured the other along a street.

Geographically it is the largest district in New York and one of the largest in the East. It is ancestrally Republican but more inclined toward moderates than conservatives and increasingly divided in its partisan loyalties. Clinton, Franklin and St. Lawrence counties in the northeast corner along the Vermont border have been solidly Democratic since the 1990s. The southwestern counties are more heavily Republican. Overall, the district is competitive. Barack Obama twice won the presidential contest with 52 percent, which approximated his wins nationally. In 2016, Donald Trump ran well beyond his national performance, with a 53%-39% win.

TWENTY-SECOND DISTRICT

Claudia Tenney (R)

Elected 2016, 1st term; b. Feb 04, 1961, Utica; Colgate University, B.A., 1983; University of Cincinnati, J.D., 1987; Presbyterian; Divorced; 1 child.

Elected Office: NY Assembly, 2011-2016.

Professional Career: Practicing attorney; Founder, Tenney Media Group.

DC Office: 512 CHOB 20515, 202-225-3665, Fax: 202-225-1891; Website: tenney.house.gov.

State Offices: Binghamton, 607-376-6002; New Hartford, 315-732-0713.

Committees: *Financial Services*: Financial Institutions & Consumer Credit, Monetary Policy & Trade, Oversight & Investigations.

Election Results

Election	Name (Party)	Vote (%)		Cand. Spent	Ind. Exp. Support	Ind. Exp. Oppose
2016 General	Claudia Tenney (R)	129,444	(47%)	$877,054	$405,700	$3,885,431
	Kim Myers (D)	114,266	(41%)	$1,645,271	$393,671	$1,936,481
	Martin Babinec (Ref)	34,821	(13%)	$3,008,241	$46,374	$1,772,732
2016 Primary	Claudia Tenney (R)	8,876	(42%)			
	Steve Wells (R)	7,214	(34%)			
	George Phillips (R)	5,303	(25%)			

Republican Claudia Tenney, elected in 2016, has emphasized her conservative pedigree. She took a big step toward winning this seat during her close primary in 2014 with moderate Republican Rep. Richard Hanna. Tenney kept running, Hanna retired and Democrats had high hopes for recapturing what had become a swing district. Both parties spent heavily on this contest, which was complicated by a big-spending independent candidate. Tenney won with unexpected ease, aided in part by Donald Trump's strong local performance.

Tenney, the daughter of a New York State Supreme Court justice, was born in New Hartford. She got her bachelor's from Colgate University and a law degree from the University of Cincinnati. Working for the Consulate General of Yugoslavia, she served as an intermediary between ABC Sports and the Yugoslavian government prior to the 1984 Winter Olympics in Sarajevo. She started the Tenney Media

Group, where she served as publisher and corporate counsel, and was the moderator of a radio television show called "Common Cents."

She was elected to the state Assembly in 2010 in a district that covered parts of Oswego and Oneida counties, and then was reelected. In 2014, she challenged Hanna, who advocated bipartisan compromise and had a voting record that ranked him among the most moderate Republicans in the House. Tenney criticized Hanna's support for gay marriage, and his votes to increase the debt ceiling and oppose delay of implementation of the Affordable Care Act. She raised only $187,000, of which $112,000 came from loans that she made to her campaign. Tenney had backing from the tea party and conservative talk-show hosts Laura Ingraham and Sean Hannity. Hanna, who ran without Democratic opposition in 2014, spent $862,000 during the cycle, and he had $665,000 support from a Super PAC backed by billionaire investor Paul Singer. Hanna took five of the eight counties and won 53.5%-46.5%.

Facing another tough primary challenge from Tenney, Hanna announced his retirement in December 2015. Tenney had competitive primary challenges from businessman Steve Wells and Broome County legislator George Phillips, who had run against veteran Democratic Rep. Maurice Hinchey in 2010 and was defeated, 51%-46%. Unexpectedly, the American Conservative Union ran ads that questioned Tenney's voting record in Albany, and supported Phillips. Hanna endorsed Wells and warned that Tenney could not win in November. In the primary with a turnout of 23,000 votes, Tenney won with 41 percent to 34 percent for Wells and 25 percent for Phillips. Tenney got a majority of the votes in Oneida; Phillips did likewise in Broome.

That seemed to give a big opportunity to Democrats, who agreed that Tenney was too conservative for the district. But they encountered recruiting setbacks, as had become a growing problem for Democrats in Upstate districts. After more experienced officials decided not to run, Democrats turned to Broome County legislator Kim Myers, the daughter of the founder of Dick's Sporting Goods. Also running in November was Martin Babinec, a deep-pocket venture capitalist who ran as the "Upstate Jobs" Party candidate. Tenney raised the least money of the three candidates: $1 million to $1.7 million for Wells and $3 million that Babinec self-financed. The National Republican Congressional Committee spent $3 million on behalf of Tenney, while Wells benefited from $3.7 million from national Democrats. With likely boosts from Trump and Babinec, Tenney proved the skeptics wrong. She got 47 percent of the vote to 41 percent for Wells and 12 percent for Babinec.

Tenney got a seat on the Financial Services Committee, where she set a priority of rolling back banking regulations. She joined with Sen. Kirsten Gillibrand of New York on a bill to fight elder abuse. Tenney became an early Democratic target for 2018.

Central New York: Utica, Binghamton

Population		**Race and Ethnicity**		**Income**	
Total	711,202	White	88.2%	Median Income	$48,499 (278 out of 435)
Land area	5,077	Black	3.6%		
Pop/ sq mi	140.1	Latino	3.5%		
Born in state	80.4%	Asian	2.6%	Under $50,000	51.1%
		Two races	1.8%	$50,000-$99,999	31.3%
Age Groups		Other	0.3%	$100,000-$199,999	15.1%
Under 18	21.0%			$200,000 or more	2.3%
18-34	23.0%	**Education**		Poverty Rate	16.1%
35-64	39.3%	H.S grad or less	45.4%		
Over 64	16.7%	Some college	31.0%	**Health Insurance**	
Work		College Degree, 4 yr	13.5%	With health insurance coverage	93.0%
White Collar	34.6%	Post grad	10.1%		
Sales and Service	43.3%	**Military**		**Public Assistance**	
Blue Collar	22.1%	Veteran	9.3%	Cash public assistance income	3.7%
Government	19.0%	Active Duty	0.1%	Food stamp/SNAP benefits	16.2%

Voter Turnout			
2015 Total Citizens 18+	548,105	2016 House Turnout as % CVAP	51%
2016 House turnout	278,531	2014 House Turnout as % CVAP	24%

2012 Presidential Vote		
Mitt Romney	136,500	(49%)
Barack Obama	135,172	(49%)

2016 Presidential Vote		
Donald Trump	158,913	(54%)
Hillary Clinton	114,016	(39%)
Gary Johnson	12,349	(4%)

Cook Partisan Voting Index: R+6

One of the first American frontiers was the Mohawk River Valley of Upstate New York. But from the establishment of Fort Orange in 1624 in what is now Albany until the Revolutionary War, white settlers did not dare move west along the Mohawk. The British used their Iroquois allies as a buffer against the French and in turn kept New England Yankees from moving westward. Only after the French were driven from North America in 1759 did the pressures for westward settlement prevail. Once the Revolutionary War started, Iroquois dominion ended. The later digging of the Erie Canal was an engineering feat that hastened the westward push. In 1811, it cost more to ship goods 30 miles inland from New York City than to send them to England. But after eight years of work by 9,000 men, the canal opened in 1825, ahead of schedule and on budget, effectively tying together the nation and guaranteeing the preeminence of New York City in America's economy.

When the New York Central built its water-line rail route to the west, the Mohawk Valley became one of the nation's early industrial centers. The little Oneida County hamlets of Utica and Rome, where the canal builders had to dig through the route's highest ground, became sizable factory towns. The utopian Oneida Community, with its believers in plural marriage and communal ownership, operated a stainless steel factory. First settled by New England Yankees, these towns attracted a new wave of immigration from the Atlantic coast in the early 20th century, including many Italian and Polish Americans.

The 22nd Congressional District of New York drops from Lake Ontario to the Pennsylvania border in a strip east of Syracuse, as it sprawls through all or parts of eight counties in central New York, most of them lightly populated. The biggest cities are Utica and Rome in Oneida County and Binghamton in Broome County. Each county takes in about 30 percent of the district. This part of Upstate New York has been bypassed by economic growth for decades. Oneida County's population has dropped 15 percent since it peaked in the 1970 census. A similar pattern applied in Broome, which has lost about 10 percent of its population since 1970, plus 16,000 jobs in the past decade. From 2010 to 2015, each county lost another 2 percent of its population. With these losses, it's no surprise that Oneida has become a popular spot for refugees and immigrants from across the world; the recent arrivals have accounted for as much as 20 percent of the local population. In a once economically dynamic area, the largest employer in central New York has become Oneida Nation's Turning Stone Resort Casino, which operates a huge retail outlet and entertainment complex with 4,600 employees. State government has completed dredging for Utica Harbor, which is the successor to the Erie Canal in Utica, though barge traffic is not a growth industry.

Politically this part of Upstate New York had been Republican since the party came into existence in the 1850s, and the GOP maintains a registration advantage in every county except for Broome. The Republican advantage had become broad, not deep, as shown in the 2008 and 2012 elections, when President Barack Obama and his GOP opponent got 49 percent each time. That outcome shifted significantly in 2016, when Donald Trump won the district, 54%-39%, and took each of the eight counties in the 22nd. In Oneida, where Mitt Romney led 52%-46% in 2012, Trump won 57%-37%.

TWENTY-THIRD DISTRICT

Tom Reed (R)

Elected 2010, 4th term; b. Nov 18, 1971, Joliet, IL; Ohio Northern University College of Law, J.D.; Alfred University (NY), Bach. Deg.; Roman Catholic; Married (Jean Reed); 2 children.

Elected Office: Corning Mayor, 2008-2010.

Professional Career: Clerk, private firm, 1995; Association Attorney, private firm, 1996-1999; Owner, Law Office of Thomas W. Reed II.

DC Office: 2437 RHOB 20515, 202-225-3161, Fax: 202-226-6599, reed.house.gov.

State Offices: Corning, 607-654-7566; Geneva, 315-759-5229; Ithaca, 607-222-2027; Jamestown, 716-708-6369; Olean, 716-379-8434.

Committees: *Ways & Means*: Health, Human Resources, Trade.

Group Ratings

	ADA	ACLU	AFL-CIO	LCV	ITI	COC	HAFA	ACU	CFG	FRC
2016	0%	17%	33%	8%	83%	100%	39%	63%	58%	58%
2015	0%	C	33%	6%	C	100%	C	46%	36%	67%

Almanac Ratings 2015

	Economy	Social	Foreign	Composite
Liberal	14%	9%	4%	9%
Conservative	86%	91%	96%	91%

Key Votes of the 114th Congress

1. Keystone Pipeline	Y	5. Puerto Rico Debt	N	9. Offenses by Aliens	Y
2. Trade Deals	Y	6. Medical Marijuana	Y	10. Troops in Iraq	N
3. Export-Import Bank	Y	7. Sanctuary Cities	Y	11. Homeland Security $$	N
4. Debt Ceiling Increase	Y	8. Armor-piercing Bullets	Y	12. Trade Adjustment aid	Y

Election Results

Election	Name (Party)	Vote (%)		Cand. Spent	Ind. Exp. Support	Ind. Exp. Oppose
2016 General	Tom Reed (R)	161,050	(58%)	$3,054,679	$262,657	$71,763
	John Plumb (D)	118,584	(42%)	$1,621,769	$1,000	$299,900
2016 Primary	Tom Reed (R)		(100%)			

Prior winning percentages: 2014 (58%), 2012 (49%), 2010 special (53%)

Republican Tom Reed, who took office in 2010, is a pragmatic and low-key centrist. On the Ways and Means Committee, he has worked on tax and trade issues. He failed in a party leadership bid, but has promoted efforts for more bipartisanship.

Reed was born in Joliet, Illinois, the youngest of 12 children. His father was an Army veteran and Silver Star recipient who fought in World War II and Korea, but he accidentally died of carbon monoxide poisoning while working on his car when Reed was two years old. Reed's surviving family soon moved to Corning, New York, where his mother had grown up. She stayed home to take care of the children, relying on her late husband's military death benefits and Social Security checks for financial support. Reed opted to stay close to home, and got his bachelor's at Alfred University in western New York. He went to law school at Ohio Northern University College, then worked at a law firm in Rochester before he returned to Corning to start his own firm. He was elected mayor in 2007.

He first ran for a vacant seat after the Democratic incumbent resigned following inappropriate behavior with staff aides. Reed was unchallenged for the Republican nomination. Democratic nominee Matthew Zeller, an Afghanistan combat veteran, argued that he would protect Social Security and create jobs more effectively than would Reed, who focused his message on reducing the deficit and shrinking government. Zeller raised $457,000, compared with Reed's $1 million. By capitalizing on voter angst over excessive spending and on the Republican wave that resulted, Reed won handily, 57%-43%.

Reed has mostly stuck with his party on major legislation, though his *Almanac* vote ratings for 2015 ranked him near the center of House Republicans. He impressed House leaders by getting the support of colleagues for free trade agreements with Colombia, Panama and South Korea. In 2011, he got a prized seat on Ways and Means, rare for a freshman. Later that year, he was one of six GOP members chosen as conferees in payroll tax-cut negotiations. In 2015, he backed a change that Republicans made in House rules to prevent a transfer of funds from the Social Security retirement system as "a short-term Band Aid" to fix the serious financial shortfall in the federal disability program. Later that year, he enacted his Trade Facilitation and Trade Enforcement Act, which was largely a law-enforcement measure that overhauled the Customs and Border Protection agency.

After the 2014 election, Reed ran against two other candidates for chairman of the House Republican Policy Committee, which has been viewed as a stepping-stone to higher leadership positions. He said that he wanted the committee to play a more formal role in working with Republicans on legislation. On the showdown second ballot, he lost to Luke Messer of Indiana, 137-90.

On local issues, Reed added an amendment to the House-passed fiscal 2013 energy and water spending bill to increase money for cleanups at sites such as his district's West Valley Demonstration Project, a former nuclear fuel reprocessing facility. In Ithaca, which is the solitary Democratic bastion in the district, Reed may have found an acceptance level, at least on his terms. On his House website, a photograph of a shirt-sleeved Reed smiling among a group of mostly young constituents from Ithaca is accompanied by his comment: "Listening to people is what representation is all about. We may not always agree on every issue, but we are always willing to listen and have a conversation."

Reed has faced competitive reelection challenges from the Ithaca-based eastern edge of his district. In 2012, the energetic Democratic challenger was Nate Shinagawa, the 28-year-old vice chairman of the Tompkins County Legislature. He attacked Reed for his support of hydraulic fracturing for natural gas, contending it would endanger tourism and agriculture in the Finger Lakes region. Reed said he supported an exemption for drilling in the Finger Lakes. He raised more than $2 million to Shinagawa's $829,000 and eked out a win, 52%-48%. In 2014. Martha Robinson, chairwoman of the Tompkins Legislature, challenged Reed. She advocated liberal views in strong opposition to fossil-fuel production in New York and to changes in the Social Security cost-of-living adjustment. She raised more money than Shinagawa, but was outpaced, $3.4 million to $2.3 million. Reed won overwhelmingly, 62%-38%, an indication that he had become entrenched in his seat.

His opponent in 2016 was J.D. Plumb, a former Pentagon and National Security Council aide who returned to his native Jamestown area to run for Congress. Plumb raised $1.7 million, but he seemed to have scant connection to the district or to Democratic operatives. In a familiar pattern, Reed took every county except for Tompkins and won 58%-42%.

Reed was one of more than two dozen vice-chairmen on Donald Trump's presidential transition committee, where he managed to avoid controversy. In January 2017, Reed was enthusiastic about taking over as Republican co-chair of the bipartisan Problem Solvers Caucus. The nearly 40-member group "will be fighting for common sense principles that impact all Americans – Democrat, Republican, independent – everyone," he said. "It's a new day in Washington and now is the time for us to work together with new energy to get things done for the American people."

Southern Tier: Jamestown, Ithaca

Population		Race and Ethnicity		Income	
Total	713,070	White	88.9%	Median Income	$47,266 (299 out of 435)
Land area	7,372	Black	2.7%		
Pop/ sq mi	96.7	Latino	3.6%		
Born in state	74.7%	Asian	2.3%	Under $50,000	52.3%
		Two races	1.8%	$50,000-$99,999	31.0%
Age Groups		Other	0.7%	$100,000-$199,999	14.1%
Under 18	20.7%			$200,000 or more	2.4%
18-34	24.2%	**Education**		Poverty Rate	16.7%
35-64	38.8%	H.S grad or less	45.3%		
Over 64	16.3%	Some college	29.8%	**Health Insurance**	
		College Degree, 4 yr	12.8%	With health insurance coverage	91.5%
Work		Post grad	12.0%		
White Collar	34.8%				
Sales and Service	41.1%	**Military**		**Public Assistance**	
Blue Collar	24.2%	Veteran	9.6%	Cash public assistance income	3.2%
Government	16.6%	Active Duty	0.0%		
				Food stamp/SNAP benefits	14.8%

Voter Turnout			
2015 Total Citizens 18+	550,568	2016 House Turnout as % CVAP	51%
2016 House turnout	279,735	2014 House Turnout as % CVAP	33%

2012 Presidential Vote		
Mitt Romney	137,307	(50%)
Barack Obama	133,940	(48%)

2016 Presidential Vote		
Donald Trump	158,158	(54%)
Hillary Clinton	115,014	(39%)
Gary Johnson	11,749	(4%)

Cook Partisan Voting Index: R+6

The Southern Tier of New York is one of the nation's forgotten stretches of territory, yet it has an interesting and distinctive history. Elmira was the hometown of Mark Twain's beloved wife, Olivia, and it is where Twain is buried. On Lake Chautauqua, not far from Lake Erie, a training camp for Methodist Sunday school teachers was founded in 1874. In summers, on wide green lawns and in Victorian-style gazebos, some 25,000 people heard educational talks and inspirational lectures from the likes of William Jennings Bryan. The area has an Indian presence, with small reservations as wells as the Seneca-Iroquois National Museum in Salamanca, plus miles and miles of dairy farms. Sheltered by hills, the lands at the edge of Upstate New York's deep lakes constitute the nation's largest grape-growing area outside of California and are the home of New York wineries.

Corning is the headquarters of Corning Glass Works, a company successful over the years not only in manufacturing but also in its artistic distinction, which is showcased at a well-visited glass museum. Its long-term prospects have improved dramatically, with heavy demand for its fiber optics and other high-tech components. The *Fortune* 500 company makes key components of the liquid crystal display (LCD) glass used in flat-screen televisions and computers. But the company produces and sells much of that display glass overseas, including in Beijing. The growing demand for the glass has fueled local hope that Corning will create a new facility at its old plant. The state of New York has tried to improve the region's fortunes, with economic development grants. Many local residents criticized as a missed job-creating opportunity the 2014 decision by Gov. Andrew Cuomo to ban hydraulic fracturing in this area, which is believed to have large deposits of natural gas. In Jamestown, where it employs 1,400 workers, the Cummins Co. in late 2016 began manufacturing a new, more efficient line of engines for its heavy-duty trucks.

The 23rd Congressional District of New York is centered on the state's Southern Tier, extending from Chautauqua near the Pennsylvania line almost to Binghamton, more than halfway to the Massachusetts line. To the north, it includes the central Finger Lakes: giant gorges torn into the Earth's crust by expanding glaciers, and then naturally dammed up by the debris deposited when the glaciers retreated.

Nearby Seneca Falls was the birthplace of the women's rights movement in 1848, when Boston transplants Elizabeth Cady Stanton and Lucretia Mott produced a Declaration of Sentiments that initiated the push for suffrage. The town is believed to be the inspiration for Bedford Falls in the classic film, *It's a Wonderful Life*. In the small town of Celoron, a statue was constructed to honor Lucille Ball, the hometown native who became a renowned comedian. Its un-Lucy-like features so frightened many local residents that they demanded its removal. In August 2016, the town unveiled a new, more felicitous statue of Lucy.

The towns here have long had a Democratic tilt, reflecting the Irish and Italian Catholics who settled there, but the countryside was traditionally Protestant and Republican. The addition to the district of the heavily Democratic university town of Ithaca helped turn this into true swing territory at the federal level; Republicans still perform well at the state and local levels. President Barack Obama lost this district by two percentage points in 2012, after winning it by one point in 2008. In 2016, Donald Trump won the district by 15 points and took every county by a double-digit margin except for Ithaca-based Tompkins, where he lost nearly 3-to-1.

TWENTY-FOURTH DISTRICT

John Katko (R)

Elected 2014, 2nd term; b. Nov 09, 1962, Syracuse; Niagara University, Bach. Deg.; Syracuse University - College of Law (NY), J.D.; Roman Catholic; Married (Robin Katko); 3 children.

Professional Career: Sr. trial Attorney, U.S. Securities & Exchange Comm., 1991-1995; Prosecutor, NY Northern District U.S. Attorney office; Assistant U.S. Attorney, U.S. Justice Department, 1995-2013.

DC Office: 1620 LHOB 20515, 202-225-3701, Fax: 202-225-4042, katko.house.gov.

State Offices: Auburn, 315-253-4068; Lyons, 315-423-5657; Oswego, 315-423-5657; Syracuse, 315-423-5657.

Committees: *Homeland Security*: Cybersecurity & Infrastructure Protection, Transportation & Protective Security (Chmn). *Transportation & Infrastructure*: Highways & Transit, Railroads, Pipelines & Hazardous Materials, Water Resources & Environment.

Group Ratings

	ADA	ACLU	AFL-CIO	LCV	ITI	COC	HAFA	ACU	CFG	FRC
2016	-	23%	-	26%	83%	100%	33%	33%	35%	42%
2015	5%	C	54%	14%	C	95%	C	33%	25%	67%

Almanac Ratings 2015

	Economy	Social	Foreign	Composite
Liberal	31%	28%	14%	24%
Conservative	69%	72%	86%	76%

Key Votes of the 114th Congress

1. Keystone Pipeline	Y	5. Puerto Rico Debt	Y	9. Offenses by Aliens	Y
2. Trade Deals	N	6. Medical Marijuana	N	10. Troops in Iraq	N
3. Export-Import Bank	Y	7. Sanctuary Cities	Y	11. Homeland Security $$	Y
4. Debt Ceiling Increase	Y	8. Armor-piercing Bullets	Y	12. Trade Adjustment aid	Y

Election Results

Election	Name (Party)	Vote (%)	Cand. Spent	Ind. Exp. Support	Ind. Exp. Oppose
2016 General	John Katko (R)	182,761 (61%)	$2,373,980	$881,815	$1,594,720
	Colleen Deacon (D)	119,040 (39%)	$1,471,309	$50,334	$2,284,315
2016 Primary	John Katko (R)	(100%)			

Prior winning percentages: 2014 (58%)

Republican John Katko, first elected in 2014, has had two notable political accomplishments. His reelection in 2016 was the first time in a decade that anybody in this district has won consecutive terms. His capture of at least 60 percent of the vote in each campaign surprised Democrats who ran well-financed campaigns in this competitive battleground. Katko has focused his legislative attention on transportation security.

Katko grew up in Onondaga County, then attended Niagara University and Syracuse University's law school. He worked for a D.C. law firm before taking a position at the Securities and Exchange Commission. In two decades at the Justice Department, he was a federal prosecutor in Virginia's Eastern District and worked for the narcotics and dangerous drugs section of the criminal division. During that time, he joined multiple organized crime and drug enforcement-related prosecutions with the U.S. Attorney's Office in Syracuse. He contends that his successful prosecution of a major gang case led to a significant drop in the violent crime rate in Syracuse.

Katko retired from the Justice Department to challenge Democratic Rep. Dan Maffei, who was elected in 2008 and again in 2012 - albeit with just 49 percent of the vote, as President Barack Obama won 57 percent in the district. Maffei had an unusual streak of participating in five consecutive elections with alternating party control of the seat. As with his previous Republican opponents, Katko tried to depict Maffei as an out-of-touch Beltway insider. He pointed to his purchase of a $700,000 house in the Washington area.

Maffei emphasized his moderate stripes and nonideological pragmatism. He tried to poke holes in Katko's record as a prosecutor, criticizing him for his handling of a local mayor's sex-offender case as well as for an incident involving a gun that was stolen from Katko in 2000 and used in a robbery that left two people dead. Katko complained that such campaign attacks "destroyed my character." Katko won with surprising ease, 60%-40%, and he took all four counties. Onondaga was the tightest, with 53 percent for Katko. Maffei became a member of the Federal Maritime Commission.

In the House, Katko chaired the Transportation Subcommittee on the Homeland Security Committee. He passed several bills, which later were enacted as part of the reauthorization of the Federal Aviation Administration. Those measures called for a review of the Transportation Security Administration's security and staffing procedures, enhanced the security of overseas flights and revised TSA's expedited security program. He also took the leadership of a bipartisan Task Force on Combating Terrorist and Foreign Fighter Travel.

In February 2017, he joined another task force on denying terrorists entry into the U.S.

He showed occasional independence from the House GOP leadership, as when he voted in 2015 to oppose both the final version of the annual budget plan and a plan to overturn a District of Columbia law that banned workplace discrimination over employees' reproductive decisions but provided no faith-based exemptions. Katko's *Almanac* vote ratings in 2015 placed him in the center of the House, though he was a bit more conservative on foreign policy issues.

Katko emphasized that his chief priorities were at home. When he issued a report on his first 100 days in office, each of his top 10 highlights dealt with Central New York. He undoubtedly was mindful that he would face a serious reelection challenge.

After Syracuse Democratic Mayor Stephanie Miner decided not to challenge him, Democrats rallied around Colleen Deacon, who had been the Syracuse district director for Sen. Kirsten Gillibrand. She got 50 percent of the vote in a low-turnout primary with two other candidates. During a debate, she suggested that Katko had misled voters into believing that he was more independent of Republicans than was the case. "When the chips are down, he stands with his do-nothing Republican colleagues on the issues that matter," Deacon said. Katko responded that she was a tool of Democratic leaders. "She is 100 percent in the tank with not only her party, but Hillary Clinton," he said. Following the October release of the video in which Donald Trump made lewd comments about women, Katko said that he should step aside as a candidate. Katko later said that he would not vote for Trump.

Both candidates were well-financed in their cheap-media market. Katko outraised Deacon, $2.7 million to $1.5 million. National Republicans spent more than $2 million on the contest, twice the amount by national Democrats. In an outcome that was similar to 2014, Katko won 61%-39%, with a narrow lead in Onondaga. In 2017, Democrats said they planned early organizational and communications steps to prepare for their 2018 challenge to Katko.

North-Central New York: Syracuse Metro

Population		**Race and Ethnicity**		**Income**	
Total	715,530	White	82.5%	Median Income	$53,034 (210 out of 435)
Land area	2,389	Black	8.0%		
Pop/ sq mi	299.6	Latino	4.1%		
Born in state	79.5%	Asian	2.5%	Under $50,000	47.3%
Age Groups		Two races	2.2%	$50,000-$99,999	31.6%
Under 18	21.9%	Other	0.7%	$100,000-$199,999	17.7%
18-34	23.0%	**Education**		$200,000 or more	3.4%
35-64	40.0%	H.S grad or less	40.2%	Poverty Rate	15.2%
Over 64	15.1%	Some college	30.4%	**Health Insurance**	
Work		College Degree, 4 yr	16.6%	With health insurance coverage	92.8%
White Collar	37.8%	Post grad	12.8%		
Sales and Service	42.4%	**Military**		**Public Assistance**	
Blue Collar	19.7%	Veteran	8.2%	Cash public assistance income	3.8%
Government	17.1%	Active Duty	0.1%		
				Food stamp/SNAP benefits	14.2%

Voter Turnout			
2015 Total Citizens 18+	542,001	2016 House Turnout as % CVAP	56%
2016 House turnout	302,115	2014 House Turnout as % CVAP	37%

2012 Presidential Vote		
Barack Obama	171,502	(57%)
Mitt Romney	123,534	(41%)

2016 Presidential Vote		
Hillary Clinton	151,021	(49%)
Donald Trump	139,763	(45%)
Gary Johnson	13,090	(4%)

Cook Partisan Voting Index: D+3

Syracuse is a Middle American city in the middle of Upstate New York, halfway between Albany and Buffalo on the Erie Canal and the old New York Central Railroad, which were for years the nation's major east-west transportation routes. Built on a swamp that was a salt spring, Syracuse is the home of many practical-minded inventions - the dental chair, Stickley mission furniture, the drive-in bank teller, and the serrated knife. It is the site of the New York State Fair, which attracts 1 million visitors annually; of Syracuse University, which plays basketball and football inside the Carrier Dome, the largest domed stadium on a college campus; and of the Museum of Automobile History, home to the largest private collection of automobiles and automobile-related objects in the world.

Nearby, the agricultural hinterland is rich with specialty crops like wine grapes, and its industrial jobs are mostly high-skill. Still, with the decline in manufacturing, there are 25,000 fewer jobs here than there were in the mid-2000s. Poverty in Syracuse remains deep-seated, with 45 percent of children living below the poverty line. The good news is that housing in Syracuse is among the most affordable in the nation, with a median home value of $84,000. With more than one-fourth of its residents foreign-born, the growing communities of immigrants and refugees have been driving the limited economic growth.

The 24th Congressional District of New York centers on Syracuse and surrounding Onondaga County, which takes in two-thirds of the voters in the 24th. From 1990 to 2015, the city lost 12 percent of its population, while the county remained even. West of Syracuse is territory that dips south from Lake Ontario, with all of Cayuga County, home of abolitionist Harriet Tubman. Near Rochester, in Wayne County, is the village of Palmyra, where Joseph Smith had his vision of the angel Moroni and received the golden tablets that led him to found the Mormon Church. To the north, the district includes part of Oswego County, including the city of Oswego, whose port facilities on Lake Ontario have made it an attractive tourist destination. Both Oswego and Auburn, the next-largest after Syracuse, are smaller than 30,000 and have been slowly decreasing in size.

Historically, Syracuse was Republican, partly out of antipathy to New York City. Like much of Upstate, this has become a politically competitive area. In the 1990s, economically ailing Upstate New

York trended sharply toward national Democrats even as it voted for Republican Gov. George Pataki. The 24th district has leaned Democratic. But it has shown competitive tendencies. Following President Barack Obama's double-digit victory margins in his two elections, the 2016 election narrowed to a 49%-45% win for Hillary Clinton.

TWENTY-FIFTH DISTRICT

Louise Slaughter (D)

Elected 1986, 16th term; b. Aug 14, 1929, Lynch, KY; University of Kentucky, M.S.; University of Kentucky, B.S.; Episcopalian; Widow; 3 children; 7 grandchildren.

Elected Office: Monroe County Legislature, 1976-1979; NY Assembly, 1982-1986.

Professional Career: Regional Coordinator, NY Department of St., 1976-1979; Regional Coordinator, Lt. Gov. Mario Cuomo, 1979-1982.

DC Office: 2469 RHOB 20515, 202-225-3615, Fax: 202-225-7822, louise.house.gov.

State Offices: Rochester, 585-232-4850.

Committees: *Rules (RMM)*: Rules & Organization of the House (RMM).

Group Ratings

	ADA	ACLU	AFL-CIO	LCV	ITI	COC	HAFA	ACU	CFG	FRC
2016	-	88%	-	100%	50%	50%	14%	0%	4%	0%
2015	90%	C	100%	91%	C	37%	C	4%	0%	0%

Almanac Ratings 2015

	Economy	Social	Foreign	Composite
Liberal	96%	95%	92%	94%
Conservative	4%	5%	9%	6%

Key Votes of the 114th Congress

1. Keystone Pipeline	N	5. Puerto Rico Debt	Y	9. Offenses by Aliens	N
2. Trade Deals	N	6. Medical Marijuana	Y	10. Troops in Iraq	Y
3. Export-Import Bank	Y	7. Sanctuary Cities	N	11. Homeland Security $$	Y
4. Debt Ceiling Increase	Y	8. Armor-piercing Bullets	N	12. Trade Adjustment aid	Y

Election Results

Election	Name (Party)	Vote (%)	Cand. Spent	Ind. Exp. Support	Ind. Exp. Oppose
2016 General	Louise Slaughter (D)	182,950 (56%)	$1,571,582	$1,288	
	Mark Assini (R)	142,650 (44%)	$217,336		
2016 Primary	Louise Slaughter (D)	(100%)			

Prior winning percentages: 2014 (49%), 2012 (56%), 2010 (61%), 2008 (63%), 2006 (67%), 2004 (61%), 2002 (58%), 2000 (61%), 1998 (63%), 1996 (56%), 1994 (58%), 1992 (55%), 1990 (63%), 1988 (57%), 1986 (54%)

Democrat Louise Slaughter, elected in 1986, is the only woman who has chaired the powerful Rules Committee. She has a long history of working on issues important to liberal women and was one of the original authors of the 1994 Violence Against Women Act. In an election rematch in 2016, she won comfortably after barely survived in 2014. Slaughter is the second-oldest member of Congress, trailing John Conyers of Michigan by a few months.

A coal miner's daughter and a descendant of Daniel Boone, she grew up in Kentucky and still speaks with the distinctive phraseology of the mountains. She wound up in New York in the 1950s when she moved there with her husband. Her involvement in community issues led to a career in government. Slaughter became a staffer for Mario Cuomo when he was lieutenant governor in the 1970s, and she won a seat in the Monroe County Legislature in 1976. She was elected to the New York Assembly in 1982.

Four years later, she beat one-term conservative Republican Rep. Fred Eckert, 51%-49%, after charging that he did nothing to free Associated Press reporter Terry Anderson, a Rochester native held hostage in Lebanon for nearly seven years. She carefully tended to local problems and earned the support of area businesses and the local *Democrat and Chronicle* newspaper.

As a loyal lieutenant of House Speaker Nancy Pelosi, who once called Slaughter "the best politician that I have ever seen," Slaughter helped to bring the first legislation to the House floor for the new Democratic majority in 2007: an overhaul of House rules, largely dictated by Pelosi and her lieutenants. Slaughter hailed the result as "a Congress people can be proud of again." Republicans quickly cried foul when Democrats next moved to the floor six bills from their campaign agenda, without committee action and with no opportunity for amendments.

During the 2009 health care debate, she was a major advocate of including a government-run insurer to compete with private companies and was sharply critical of the Senate's decision to jettison this so-called public option. When the final compromise reached the House in March 2010, Slaughter wrote a rule for the floor vote that attempted to get around the Senate by deeming the Senate version passed by the House once the House approved a "corrections bill" making changes to the other body's version. Outraged Republicans dubbed the move the "Slaughter Solution," even as Slaughter noted that the GOP occasionally used the strategy in the majority. Her idea eventually was scrapped. Back in the minority, she seeks to represent the parliamentary interests of House Democrats at the majority-dominated Rules Committee.

A microbiologist by training, Slaughter opposed proposals to ban human cloning and was an outspoken proponent of federal support for embryonic stem cell research. She introduced a bill in 2009 to limit the non-therapeutic use of pharmaceuticals in livestock. The bill did not move, but hearings on it drew widespread attention. The Food and Drug Administration released guidelines recommending a halt to the use of antibiotics to promote animal growth, a move Slaughter hailed as a step in the right direction.

Slaughter has a staunchly liberal voting record. She drew widespread attention in 2011 when she said at a rally that a GOP bill blocking federal financing of abortions had documentation requirements that were "sort of like an old German Nazi movie: 'Show me your papers.'" She is a fiery opponent of international trade agreements that she contends have put Americans out of work. In 2015, she said the proposed Trans-Pacific Partnership agreement would kill jobs and hurt the middle class. "I have yet to see a trade bill that benefited the American manufacturer and the American worker," she said.

She has scored occasional legislative successes on pet causes. In 2012, Obama signed her bill banning insider stock trading by lawmakers, a cause she had championed for years. In 2008, Slaughter capped a years-long campaign by enacting her bill to bar discrimination in employment or health insurance based on the use of genetic information.

Slaughter has faced occasional challenges at home. In 2002, redistricting placed her in district that stretched to Buffalo, with Democratic Rep. John LaFalce, the party's ranking member on the Banking Committee. Luckily for Slaughter, LaFalce decided to retire. After the 2012 redistricting placed her in a more balanced district, popular Monroe County Executive Maggie Brooks challenged her. Questions arose about whether it was time for Slaughter to make way for someone younger. Brooks hammered her opponent for being a "Washington insider," but she failed to offer a compelling reason for replacing Slaughter. The incumbent won, 57%-43%.

In 2014, no one expected her to be in trouble. But a lackluster local economy and dissatisfaction with Democratic Gov. Andrew Cuomo adversely affected Democrats in her region. In contrast to 2012, when Slaughter outspent Brooks $2.5 million to $1.4 million, Slaughter and Gates Town Supervisor Mark Assini combined spent one-third that total. Slaughter won narrowly with a margin of 871 votes and 50.2%. She told reporters that she had trouble with "messaging," not performance. Assini ran again in 2016 with his "time for a change" message, and was taken more seriously by his own party and by Slaughter. But he raised only $227,000, which is a small amount for a House campaign, even in an inexpensive market such as Rochester. This time, Slaughter won, 56%-44%.

Rochester Metro

Population		**Race and Ethnicity**		**Income**	
Total	722,333	White	70.8%	Median Income	$52,046 (223 out of 435)
Land area	510	Black	14.9%		
Pop/ sq mi	1415.8	Latino	8.1%		
Born in state	74.3%	Asian	3.6%	Under $50,000	48.2%
Age Groups		Two races	2.0%	$50,000-$99,999	30.1%
Under 18	21.6%	Other	0.5%	$100,000-$199,999	17.9%
18-34	24.6%	**Education**		$200,000 or more	3.7%
35-64	38.7%	H.S grad or less	35.0%	Poverty Rate	15.5%
Over 64	15.1%	Some college	29.0%	**Health Insurance**	
Work		College Degree, 4 yr	20.1%	With health insurance coverage	93.9%
White Collar	41.8%	Post grad	15.9%		
Sales and Service	42.4%	**Military**		**Public Assistance**	
Blue Collar	15.7%	Veteran	6.8%	Cash public assistance income	4.7%
Government	12.4%	Active Duty	0.0%	Food stamp/SNAP benefits	15.0%

Voter Turnout			
2015 Total Citizens 18+	542,393	2016 House Turnout as % CVAP	60%
2016 House turnout	325,831	2014 House Turnout as % CVAP	35%

2012 Presidential Vote		
Barack Obama	187,753	(59%)
Mitt Romney	125,897	(39%)

2016 Presidential Vote		
Hillary Clinton	182,896	(55%)
Donald Trump	128,955	(39%)
Gary Johnson	12,514	(4%)

Cook Partisan Voting Index: D+8

Rochester, with a metropolitan area of just over 1 million, is a major city of Upstate New York and was one of America's first boomtowns. Here, the Genesee River descends in a 100-foot drop known as High Falls, which powered the city's early industries. Rochester became known as Flour City for the mills that served western New York farmers. Rochester was also the home base of women's suffrage leader Susan B. Anthony and abolitionist Frederick Douglass, and a popular center of 19th century tent revivals.

It became one of the early high-tech cities, after a bank clerk named George Eastman marketed the first still camera and film for Thomas Edison's motion picture camera. Later, Bausch & Lomb developed its lens business in Rochester. The optics and imaging industry continues to be a significant regional employer. The industries it has produced - Bausch & Lomb, Eastman Kodak and Xerox, which started here as Haloid before moving its headquarters to Connecticut in 1969 - thrived on technical innovation, precision workmanship, high reliability and customer service. They gave Rochester an affluent and well-educated population as well as fine civic institutions, including the George Eastman House, one of the world's leading repositories of photographic and motion picture history.

In recent decades, Rochester's big employers have fallen on hard times, and young professionals have been leaving the area. Kodak was hard hit by competition from digital cameras, and although it locally employed 1,700 people (of 6,000 worldwide) in early 2017, the workforce was down from 60,000 people in 1981. In 2012, it filed for bankruptcy and reemerged a year later as what it called "a technology company focused on imaging for business." In a February 2017 interview with the local public radio station, CEO Jeff Clarke said that the chief focus of the company has shifted to commercial printing and packaging, with advanced technologies, and that the company made a profit in 2016. Kodak continues to make film for motion pictures. In a back-to-the-future step, the company has returned its famed Ektachrome film to the consumer market, with a different chemical mix. Xerox has continued to decline in size but maintained a significant presence in the area, with a payroll of about 6,000. The city's population - 332,000 in 1950 - has dropped in each census since then, to 210,000 in 2015; the overall metropolitan area has grown by less than 10 percent in the past 40 years.

The 25th Congressional District of New York is a compact district that is entirely within Rochester's Monroe County. All but a small northwest corner of the county is in the 25th. Heavily Democratic areas in Rochester mix with more marginal suburbs in a district that is comfortably but not overwhelmingly Democratic. Hillary Clinton performed better here than in other Upstate districts, with a 55%-39% win over Donald Trump. That was close to the roughly 20-point margin that President Barack Obama had in his two campaigns.

TWENTY-SIXTH DISTRICT

Brian Higgins (D)

Elected 2004, 7th term; b. Oct 06, 1959, Buffalo; Buffalo State College (NY), M.A.; Buffalo State College (NY), B.S.; Harvard University John F. Kennedy School of Government (MA), M.A.; Catholic; Married (Mary Jane Hannon); 2 children.

Elected Office: Buffalo City Council, 1988-1994; NY Assembly, 1999-2004.

Professional Career: Chief of Staff, Erie County Leg., 1994-1998; Lecturer, Buffalo St. College, 2000-2003.

DC Office: 2459 RHOB 20515, 202-225-3306, Fax: 202-226-0347, higgins.house.gov.

State Offices: Buffalo, 716-852-3501; Niagara Falls, 716-282-1274.

Committees: *Budget*. *Ways & Means*: Health, Trade.

Group Ratings

	ADA	ACLU	AFL-CIO	LCV	ITI	COC	HAFA	ACU	CFG	FRC
2016	-	94%	-	100%	67%	64%	14%	4%	4%	0%
2015	95%	C	100%	97%	C	55%	C	4%	0%	0%

Almanac Ratings 2015

	Economy	Social	Foreign	Composite
Liberal	91%	94%	99%	94%
Conservative	9%	6%	1%	6%

Key Votes of the 114th Congress

1. Keystone Pipeline	N	5. Puerto Rico Debt	Y	9. Offenses by Aliens	Y
2. Trade Deals	N	6. Medical Marijuana	Y	10. Troops in Iraq	Y
3. Export-Import Bank	Y	7. Sanctuary Cities	N	11. Homeland Security $$	Y
4. Debt Ceiling Increase	Y	8. Armor-piercing Bullets	N	12. Trade Adjustment aid	Y

Election Results

Election	Name (Party)	Vote (%)	Cand. Spent	Ind. Exp. Support	Ind. Exp. Oppose
2016 General	Brian Higgins (D)	215,289 (75%)	$385,228		
	Shelly Shratz (R)	73,377 (25%)			
2016 Primary	Brian Higgins (D)	(100%)			

Prior winning percentages: 2014 (68%), 2012 (75%), 2010 (61%), 2008 (74%), 2006 (79%), 2004 (51%)

Democrat Brian Higgins, elected in 2004, devotes his energies to reviving the Buffalo area's economy. After a six-year hiatus, he has welcomed a return to the House Ways and Means Committee, with its work on tax and trade issues.

Higgins grew up in Buffalo, the son of a skilled tradesman who was prominent in local politics, serving on the Buffalo City Council and later as commissioner of the New York State Workers Compensation Board. His mother was a schoolteacher. Higgins graduated from Buffalo State College, where he later became an instructor, and got a master's degree in public administration from Harvard. A political junkie, he launched his career in government with staff jobs in the Erie County sheriff's office, the state Assembly, and the county legislature. In 1993, after six years on the Buffalo City Council, he ran for county comptroller and lost. In 1998, he was elected to the Assembly and served three terms. In a district crowded with unionized workers, Higgins reminded voters that his father and uncle were bricklayers and he stressed his Irish heritage.

When the House seat opened after Republican Rep. Jack Quinn retired, five Democrats battled for their party's nomination. Higgins was the favorite of local and national Democratic leaders, organized labor and *The Buffalo News*, which called him "an unusually productive member of a largely dysfunctional legislative body" in Albany. He won the primary with 44 percent of the vote. In the contentious general election, Higgins reminded voters that Republican nominee Nancy Naples, a former Merrill Lynch executive in Manhattan and a popular local figure with strong name recognition, supported many of President George W. Bush's policies and accused Republicans of shifting the tax burden from the rich to the middle class. He ran on a platform of making health care more widely available. Naples criticized Higgins for supporting tax increases in Albany. Higgins won 51%-49%, about a 3,800-vote victory, in a district that was far more competitive than the current lines.

After spending his first years on efforts for his district, he was rewarded with a seat on the powerful Ways and Means Committee in 2009. He initially opposed the 2010 deal to extend the expiring Bush-era tax cuts because it would not extend the Renewal Communities program, which had brought $150 million in development to the district. But he voted for the deal and said, "The cost of inaction would be far worse for western New York families and seniors." After the Republican takeover of the House in 2011 reduced the number of Democratic seats on Ways and Means, Higgins was forced off the committee and served on the Homeland Security and Foreign Affairs panels.

He asserted his seniority to regain the Ways and Means seat in 2017. "This is a great opportunity for an expanded role in shaping economic development policies and issues that reach the heart of life quality for our seniors and working families," he said. His priorities included the New Markets Tax Credit program, the solar investment tax credit and tax simplification for middle-class families. He cosponsored the Social Security 2100 proposal to expand benefits and pay for them with increased withholding taxes on higher-income earners.

Hoping to kick off a debate about the importance of infrastructure, he introduced a bill in 2012 calling for $1.25 trillion to be spent over five years to rebuild roads, bridges, railroads, ports and airports. "This isn't a stimulus bill, it's a nation-building bill," he said. "It's rebuilding this country as we've rebuilt other countries - Iraq and Afghanistan - in recent years." He helped create, and co-chaired, a Revitalizing Older Cities Task Force and has sought tax credits to transform older neighborhoods. In 2015, he updated his transportation proposal and criticized Congress for its failure to approve long-term action to address the "deplorable status of our infrastructure investment." In 2016, the House passed his bill to require a terrorism threat assessment regarding the transportation of chemical, biological, nuclear and radiological materials.

In the debate over gun control, Higgins once sided with gun owners, voting in favor of a 2011 amendment to block federal efforts to demand reports from gun dealers on sales of multiple semi-automatic rifles. After the Newtown Connecticut, elementary school massacre in 2012, he called for "meaningful reforms" to gun laws. He joined the Democrats' sit-in on the House floor in June 2016. His *Almanac* vote ratings for 2015 ranked him consistently among House liberals.

Since developing skin cancer, Higgins has worked on cancer research, introducing bills to establish a national cancer trust fund and pushing for money for Buffalo's Roswell Park Cancer Institute. He helped to broker an agreement with the New York Power Authority for local financial aid, including waterfront improvements, in exchange for its long-term right to operate the Niagara Power Project. The issue strained his relationship with Rochester-area Democratic Rep. Louise Slaughter, who disagreed with his strategy.

Higgins has been reelected easily in what has become a safe district. The declining population of Buffalo could prove perilous during the next redistricting.

Buffalo Metro

Population		Race and Ethnicity		Income	
Total	715,616	White	70.0%	Median Income	$44,159 (351 out of 435)
Land area	219	Black	17.8%		
Pop/ sq mi	3265.7	Latino	5.9%		
Born in state	79.3%	Asian	3.7%	Under $50,000	54.7%
		Two races	2.1%	$50,000-$99,999	29.0%
Age Groups		Other	0.6%	$100,000-$199,999	14.0%
Under 18	20.7%			$200,000 or more	2.3%
18-34	25.5%	**Education**		Poverty Rate	19.2%
35-64	37.9%	H.S grad or less	40.1%		
Over 64	16.0%	Some college	30.5%	**Health Insurance**	
		College Degree, 4 yr	16.2%	With health insurance coverage	93.6%
Work		Post grad	13.3%		
White Collar	36.2%				
Sales and Service	46.6%	**Military**		**Public Assistance**	
Blue Collar	17.3%	Veteran	8.1%	Cash public assistance income	3.8%
Government	16.3%	Active Duty	0.1%		
				Food stamp/SNAP benefits	20.4%

Voter Turnout			
2015 Total Citizens 18+	543,159	2016 House Turnout as % CVAP	53%
2016 House turnout	288,679	2014 House Turnout as % CVAP	31%

2012 Presidential Vote		
Barack Obama	193,362	(64%)
Mitt Romney	103,743	(34%)

2016 Presidential Vote		
Hillary Clinton	175,336	(58%)
Donald Trump	115,558	(38%)
Gary Johnson	8,632	(3%)

Cook Partisan Voting Index: D+11

With its massive 1920s City Hall overlooking the Niagara River and Lake Erie, Buffalo declares itself to be a city of substance. The butt of jokes about the snow from Lake Erie that supposedly keeps it immobilized half the year, Buffalo also can claim credit for building a heavy industrial base in the late 19th and early 20th centuries, as America's No. 1 grain milling center and as a major steel producer. By 1910, it had installed the first electric street light, produced the world's largest office building (Ellicott Square), and erected one of the earliest skyscrapers. It also played a part in producing two presidents: Grover Cleveland was mayor of Buffalo, and Millard Fillmore worked in nearby East Aurora. Today, the area still benefits from cheap hydroelectric power, but the Lackawanna steel mills are shuttered and grain milling waned after the St. Lawrence Seaway opened in the 1950s. Buffalo was eclipsed by the larger Great Lakes industrial cities of Chicago, Detroit and Cleveland.

Buffalo was the nation's 15th-largest city in 1950, when it had a population of 580,000. By 2018, it was 78th-largest, with a population reduced by more than half to about 258,000. As a further insult, right across Buffalo's Peace Bridge is the richest part of Canada, the "Golden Horseshoe," from Niagara Falls through Hamilton to Toronto. Still, Buffalo retains considerable assets: a high-skill labor force, inexpensive real estate, including a gentrified and handsome waterfront on a now-cleaner Lake Erie, and some impressive cultural institutions. The area has had some encouraging economic developments. In December 2016, General Motors said that it will spend $296 million on equipment for engine production at its Tonawanda plant. Panasonic announced a new business opportunity when it said that it will join the electric-car company Tesla to make solar cells and modules at Tesla's SolarCity factory in south Buffalo, which the two companies said would create 1,400 jobs by 2018. The SolarCity factory was built by the state as part of Gov. Andrew Cuomo's Buffalo Billion economic development initiative. In January 2017, Cuomo sought support for the $500 million second phase of his plan, though he insisted on keeping the funding out of the Legislature's control.

The 26th Congressional District of New York includes all of Buffalo and the cities and townships abutting it, and almost two-thirds of Erie County overall. To the north, it takes in a small slice of Niagara

County with Niagara Falls and North Tonawanda. About 90 percent of the district is in Erie County. The large number of Eastern European settlers, many of whom hailed from Poland, gave Buffalo a Democratic tilt early on. Unlike much of Upstate New York, it began electing Democrats with some regularity in the 1860s, and almost exclusively after the 1930s. Today, the district is solidly Democratic. Hillary Clinton got 58 percent of the vote in 2016, which was a dip of a few percentage points in the recent Democratic presidential vote. Barack Obama won here twice with almost two-thirds of the vote. Local voters can be quirky: independent presidential candidate Ross Perot won 28 percent of the vote in Buffalo in 1992 - his best showing in any urban center.

TWENTY-SEVENTH DISTRICT

Chris Collins (R)

Elected 2012, 3rd term; b. May 20, 1950, Schenectady; North Carolina State University, B.S.; University of Alabama, Birmingham, M.B.A.; Roman Catholic; Married (Mary Sue Collins); 3 children; 3 grandchildren.

Elected Office: Erie County Executive, 2007-2011.

Professional Career: Westinghouse Electric, 1972-1983; Founder & CEO, Nuttall Gear Corporation, 1983-1997; Entrepreneur, 1998-2007.

DC Office: 1117 LHOB 20515, 202-225-5265, Fax: 202-225-5910, chriscollins.house.gov.

State Offices: Geneseo, 585-519-4002; Williamsville, 716-634-2324.

Committees: *Energy & Commerce*: Communications & Technology, Health, Oversight & Investigations.

Group Ratings

	ADA	ACLU	AFL-CIO	LCV	ITI	COC	HAFA	ACU	CFG	FRC
2016	-	5%	-	0%	83%	100%	49%	83%	59%	82%
2015	5%	C	33%	6%	C	85%	C	65%	46%	75%

Almanac Ratings 2015

	Economy	Social	Foreign	Composite
Liberal	25%	20%	10%	18%
Conservative	75%	80%	90%	82%

Key Votes of the 114th Congress

1. Keystone Pipeline	Y	5. Puerto Rico Debt	Y	9. Offenses by Aliens	Y
2. Trade Deals	N	6. Medical Marijuana	Y	10. Troops in Iraq	N
3. Export-Import Bank	Y	7. Sanctuary Cities	Y	11. Homeland Security $$	Y
4. Debt Ceiling Increase	Y	8. Armor-piercing Bullets	Y	12. Trade Adjustment aid	N

Election Results

Election	Name (Party)	Vote (%)	Cand. Spent	Ind. Exp. Support	Ind. Exp. Oppose
2016 General	Chris Collins (R)	220,885 (67%)	$442,876		
	Diana Kastenbaum (D)	107,832 (33%)			
2016 Primary	Chris Collins (R)	(100%)			

Prior winning percentages: 2014 (67%), 2012 (49%)

Republican Chris Collins, a self-made multimillionaire, was elected in 2012 by narrowly defeating first-term Democratic Rep. Kathy Hochul, who had won a special election. Following a quiet three years, he became the first member of Congress to endorse Donald Trump for president. The result, as the *Buffalo News* wrote, turned Collins "from back-bencher to power broker."

As a child, Collins' family moved around the country with his father's job transfers at General Electric. After high school in Hendersonville, North Carolina, he earned a bachelor's degree in mechanical engineering from North Carolina State and a master's in business administration from the

University of Alabama at Birmingham. He went to work for Westinghouse in Buffalo and planned to spend his career climbing the corporate ladder there, as his father did at GE. Westinghouse promoted him to take over its plant, where he already was the general manager of the industrial gear division. He ran the Nuttall Gear Corp., which eventually reverted to private ownership after he sold it.

Former local Rep. Bill Paxon, a House Republican leader in the 1990s, persuaded Collins to get into politics. He challenged veteran Democratic Rep. John LaFalce in 1998, hoping to benefit from dissatisfaction with the local economy, but Collins lost, 57%-41%. He returned to business as an entrepreneur, spending the next 10 years working on almost two dozen financially distressed and bankrupt companies in the Buffalo area.

In 2007, New York Republicans again tapped Collins, this time to run for Erie County executive. "Erie County was effectively bankrupt, and I was now known as a fix-it guy," Collins told *National Journal*. He ran as an independent on a platform of business know-how and won with 64 percent of the vote. He lost reelection in 2011 in this Democratic county. The defeat became a positive break for his career. Collins said his experience at the county level inspired him to head to Washington, where he hoped to apply his budget experience. "If there's ever anything that's broken, it is Congress," Collins said.

In 2012, he thought that redistricting gave him a chance. Democrats accused Collins of neglecting the county's infrastructure, but he stayed focused on his business background. "Unlike my opponent and President Obama, who think we can tax our way to prosperity, I'm saying we need to grow our way to prosperity, by having a balanced budget and having some certainty for business on the financial side," Collins said. He benefitted from heavy campaign spending from outside GOP groups and beat Hochul, 51%-49%. He hass been reelected with token opposition.

With a seat on the Energy and Commerce Committee, Collins has styled himself as a pragmatic problem-solver. As part of the bipartisan 21st Century Cures Act, he won committee support for his plan to simplify the approval of new medical treatments for the market, with adaptive clinical trials that monitor patients. Calling the measure "common sense," he said that his proposal "makes sure these drugs come through the [Food and Drug Administration] process faster." Collins promoted hydraulic fracturing for natural gas in New York.

Collins showed occasional independence. In 2015, the *Buffalo News* praised him as one of 75 House Republicans who supported the plan to keep open the Homeland Security Department rather than engage in "a suicide charge" against President Barack Obama's proposed easing of immigration enforcement. "I didn't come here to lurch from crisis to crisis," Collins said. In June, he joined most House Democrats, and abandoned Obama and most House Republicans, when he voted against a plan to expedite congressional action on the president's proposed Trans Pacific Partnership. He objected that the trade deal failed to stop overseas currency manipulation.

When Collins decided to endorse Trump in February 2016, he instructed his staff to ask the campaign whether he should seek media attention. "A few hours later he was surprised to receive a voicemail from Trump thanking him for his support and encouraging him to go big," *Politico* reported. Collins saved the message on his phone. He organized a small number of House members into the "Trump Caucus." They were a "pretty lonely group," he recounted. He became Trump's chief salesman to other lawmakers. Following the election, Collins became a go-to person on behalf of the new president and his team. Trump responded with appreciation. Among his initial steps as he prepared to deal with Congress, Trump requested Speaker Paul Ryan to designate Collins as his liaison to lawmakers. Ryan called Collins that night to say that it was a done deal. "Mr. Trump, I have come to find out, very much values loyalty," Collins told *Politico*.

Collins turned down the opportunity to join the new administration. Instead, in the heady days of the transition, he became a "clearinghouse for everything coming out of Congress" about the new president and his team, Collins said to the *News*. He was especially interested in appointments of federal officials in western New York.

Not surprisingly, Collins agreed with Trump on virtually every issue. When many colleagues in Congress criticized Trump's executive orders limiting access to the United States by refugees and immigrants, Collins responded, "These are people who just need to get some backbone." One exception was his strong opposition to Trump's call for biometric tests at border crossings, which Collins said would "significantly delay" access from Canada, including in the Buffalo area.

His high visibility on behalf of Trump increased local attention. When critics threatened protests, Collins said that he never held town-hall meetings and never would. "Because what you get are demonstrators who come and shout you down and heckle you," Collins told a local TV station. "They are not what you hope they would be, which is a give and take from people actually interested in getting some facts." Such an approach would be hazardous in other congressional districts, but probably not for Collins.

Northwestern New York: Buffalo and Rochester Suburbs

Population		**Race and Ethnicity**		**Income**	
Total	719,351	White	92.0%	Median Income	$59,941 (143 out of 435)
Land area	3,973	Black	2.4%		
Pop/ sq mi	181.1	Latino	2.6%		
Born in state	85.1%	Asian	1.1%	Under $50,000	41.6%
Age Groups		Two races	1.2%	$50,000-$99,999	33.4%
Under 18	21.0%	Other	0.7%	$100,000-$199,999	21.1%
18-34	19.3%	**Education**		$200,000 or more	3.9%
35-64	43.1%	H.S grad or less	40.1%	Poverty Rate	9.3%
Over 64	16.6%	Some college	31.4%	**Health Insurance**	
Work		College Degree, 4 yr	16.1%	With health insurance coverage	94.3%
White Collar	36.6%	Post grad	12.4%		
Sales and Service	40.7%	**Military**		**Public Assistance**	
Blue Collar	22.6%	Veteran	9.0%	Cash public assistance income	2.2%
Government	16.6%	Active Duty	0.1%	Food stamp/SNAP benefits	9.2%

Voter Turnout			
2015 Total Citizens 18+	559,043	2016 House Turnout as % CVAP	59%
2016 House turnout	328,809	2014 House Turnout as % CVAP	36%

2012 Presidential Vote		
Mitt Romney	180,681	(55%)
Barack Obama	140,136	(43%)

2016 Presidential Vote		
Donald Trump	206,867	(59%)
Hillary Clinton	122,106	(35%)
Gary Johnson	13,162	(4%)

Cook Partisan Voting Index: R+11

The destination of the Erie Canal, the great engineering project that made New York the Empire State, is Lake Erie. The final 100 miles of the canal passed through the rolling countryside of western New York when it was scarcely occupied, except by American Indians. The appropriately named Lockport was founded as a site for locks on the canal. Later, the land was settled mostly by New England Yankees, with cultural folkways quite different from those of New York City. By the end of the 19th century, much of the farmland found here had become dominated by heavy industry, especially in Buffalo, where the Yankees were joined by Irish, Italian and Polish immigrants who came to work in the factories. For most of its history, western New York had an economy more prosperous than that of the rest of the country, as is visible in the solid houses and schools, stores and factories built to weather the Upstate winters. But in recent decades, economic growth has lagged behind the rest of the nation. Many of Buffalo's factories have closed. The slow growth and population decline have frequently spilled over to the suburbs that sprang up around the city in outer Erie County. In some ways, the region has a Midwest flavor, culturally as well as economically. People speak not in the pungent accents of New York City, but in flat Midwestern tones.

The 27th Congressional District of New York covers much of western New York. It extends from the suburbs that surround Buffalo to suburbs southeast of Rochester, plus the northwest corner of Monroe County. In between are rural areas and small towns, including Attica, scene of a terrible prison uprising in 1970. The district has elected influential national Republicans such as Jack Kemp and Bill Paxon. With population changes, the size of the district has expanded. Erie and Niagara counties have been reduced to 60 percent of the district, though Erie remains its heart. Politically, these suburbs are ancestrally Republican country, based on Upstaters' general distrust of New York City. It is the most Republican district in the state by most measures. Donald Trump's 59%-35% win in 2016 was his best performance in his home state.

★ NORTH CAROLINA ★

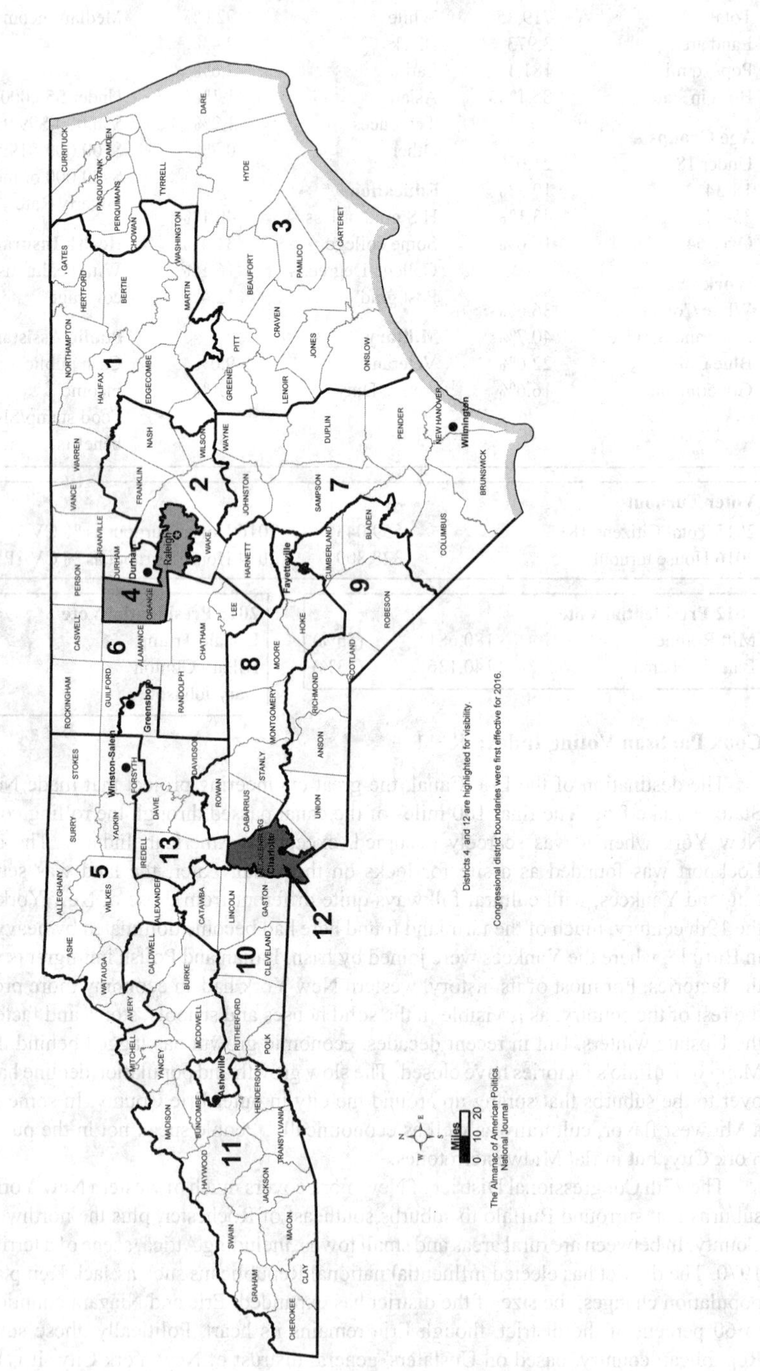

In few states today is the political climate more polarized between Democrats and Republicans, and between urban and suburban areas, than in North Carolina. Bolstered by rapid population growth from other states, North Carolina has become a hard-fought presidential battleground, but skirmishes over the direction of the state government have proven to be even more intense.

In the early republic, when Virginia and South Carolina produced statesmen and spokesmen, and had grand plantation cultures, North Carolina was often called a valley of humility between two mountains of conceit. It joined the Confederacy only after those two neighbors did so. After the Civil War, North Carolina developed its tobacco industry and enticed textile mills south from New England, while its hardwood forests produced raw material for furniture factories. Textile mills were prevalent in the Piedmont region as owners saw in the South an opportunity for cheap land, cheap labor, and state governments eager to foster pro-business, anti-union climates. In the following decades, the industry continued to expand and drastically improved the economy of the South. The mill industry became the main source of industrial paid labor for white southerners, and while it was one of the lowest paying manufacturing industries, the jobs were valued because there were few other employment options other than agricultural or service work.

The tobacco-textile-furniture trio enabled North Carolina to grow faster than the national average in the 1920s and 1930s, but the state began to lag in the 1950s. Then, two developments transformed the state. In 1959, Gov. Luther Hodges established Research Triangle Park between Raleigh and Durham. With synergy from near-by universities - Duke, North Carolina, and North Carolina State - the region became one of the leading research centers in the United States. The second development was Charlotte's emergence as the No. 2 city in financial assets, behind only New York, which owes much to the state's expansive banking laws. NationsBank and Wachovia set up headquarters on Tryon Street. NationsBank bought Bank of America and took its name, while during the financial crisis, Wachovia was acquired by Wells Fargo, which kept many of its operations in Charlotte.

These twin developments explain how North Carolina has become one of the fastest-growing and largest states. Its population essentially doubled between 1970 and 2016, from 5.1 million to 10.1 million. In the same period, the city of Charlotte grew from 241,000 to 827,000 and Raleigh grew from 123,000 to 451,000. Since the 2010 census, the state as a whole has grown by a healthy 6.4 percent, but several populous counties have expanded by rates even higher than that: Wake County (Raleigh) grew by 16.2 percent, Mecklenburg County (Charlotte) by 14.7 percent, Durham County (Durham) by 13.4 percent, Buncombe County (Asheville) by 7.4 percent, and Guilford County (Greensboro) by 6.7 percent. As the state has shifted from old-line manufacturing in textiles and furniture to fast-growing industries, including pharmaceuticals and aerospace, so have its exports. Fitting for a state that was home to the first flight at Kitty Hawk, the state's top export is now civilian aircraft engines and parts. North Carolina ranks highly in biotech employment, and the Triangle - as the Raleigh-Durham area is commonly known - is one of the world's leading pharmaceutical, medical device and telecommunications centers. High-tech firms are also sprouting farther west in the Piedmont Triad of Greensboro, Winston-Salem and High Point. State officials continue to tout their business-friendly ways, and *Site Selection* magazine ranked North Carolina the No. 1 state in the country in 2017 for its business climate. The state has the nation's second-least unionized labor force, trailing only neighboring South Carolina. Highly skilled people from the Northeast have flocked to the state – Cary, in the Triangle and jokingly referred to as "Containment Area for Relocated Yankees," has grown by 18 percent since 2010. Immigrants seeking jobs in construction and in meat and chicken factories have driven the Hispanic population to 11 percent.

Urban, affluent, high-tech North Carolina, however, is not the only North Carolina: The state ranks second to Texas in its number of rural residents with 3.2 million. North Carolina's agriculture sector is significant -- the state is the nation's top producer of poultry and eggs, and it ranks second in hog production, with big feedlots in the southeastern portion of the state. Ashe County is the country's top grower of Christmas trees. The psychic draw of rural North Carolina runs deep: If Charlotte is proud of its downtown bank towers and modern art museum, it is also proud of its Billy Graham Museum and the NASCAR Hall of Fame. But all is not well in this North Carolina; the Census Bureau found in 2016 that 41 percent of communities in the state lost population over the previous year, many of them hurt by the declines of former economic mainstays. The textile industry largely moved offshore, and the federal government's 2004 buyout of tobacco quotas greatly diminished that sector. Between 1992 and 2012, the textile and apparel industry in North Carolina lost almost 87 percent of its employees -- more than 200,000 jobs in all. High Point still hosts annual furniture industry shows, but much of the production has gone elsewhere, including China. Unemployment peaked at 11.3 percent in February 2010, and it didn't fall below 9 percent until almost three years later. The statewide unemployment rate had returned to the vicinity of the national average by March 2017, but median income still lagged the nation as a whole by 10 percent.

North Carolina has grown with the aid of both its progressive and tradition-minded citizens. Liberal progressivism has provided an impetus toward building good schools and universities, as well as highways and amenities like the nation's first state-funded symphony and state high schools for science, mathematics, and the arts. Religious conservatism, meanwhile, has provided a communitarian spirit and charitable impulses, and a moral undertone that anchors those who might go astray. The state's racial conflicts were never as intense as they were in Alabama or Mississippi, though the Greensboro sit-ins in 1960 were a pivotal, and effective, moment in the civil rights movement. In a state with an African-American population of 21 percent -- the seventh-highest of any state -- the legacy of segregation persists. Racial tensions divided Durham in 2006, when its prosecutor wrongly accused three white Duke lacrosse players of raping an African-American dancer. Race has been an issue in the state's moves to tighten its voting procedures, and the police shooting of Keith Lamont Scott in Charlotte heightened tensions in 2016.

From these two strands of North Carolina tradition, a polarized, increasingly party-line politics evolved, waged partly on economic issues but even more on cultural attitudes. This politics was built on historic partisan patterns. Coastal North Carolina settlers tended to be British Anglicans who became Methodists and slaveholders, supported the Confederacy, and voted Democratic. Piedmont settlers, by contrast, tended to be Scots-Irish Presbyterians, with a scattering of German sects, coming overland from the Northeast through the Shenandoah Valley of Virginia. They were Union men in 1861 and Republicans ever after. Over the past four decades, Republicans tended to win federal elections in North Carolina, and Democrats tended to do well in state elections. The exemplars of these traditions were Republican Sen. Jesse Helms and Democratic Gov. Jim Hunt, each of whom were elected to statewide office five times and, in 1984, faced off against each other in what was then the most expensive Senate race in U.S. history. Helms won, but Hunt returned to the governorship for two terms in the 1990s.

In 2008, Barack Obama's organization spotted North Carolina's potential early and targeted it in the general election. Blacks who had not previously voted, Hispanics who had recently become citizens and upscale professionals who had recently moved from elsewhere flocked to the polls, and Obama narrowly won North Carolina's 15 electoral votes, 49.7%-49.4%. For 2012, Obama chose Charlotte as the location for the Democratic National Convention. But conservatives fought back. Aided by Democratic sales- and income-tax increases in 2009, the Great Recession and fatigue from 20 years of Democratic government, the Republicans achieved big legislative majorities in the 2010 election, the first period of GOP control since Reconstruction. Two years later, Republican Pat McCrory was elected governor. He ran as a centrist, pro-business mayor of Charlotte, but the legislature produced a virtual assembly line of conservative legislation and dared McCrory to use his veto. Despite some tensions and a few vetoes, McCrory mostly acceded to their wishes. Over the course of several years, the GOP enacted a partisan redistricting map, a constitutional amendment to ban same-sex marriage, cuts to unemployment benefits, a tax overhaul that eliminated elements of progressivity in the code, a law requiring voters to show ID along with a shorter early-voting period, an increase in the waiting period for abortions, and a repeal of a state law to commute the death penalty if racial bias in sentencing could be shown. It didn't take long for a liberal backlash to coalesce – a running series of protests known as "Moral Mondays," led by Rev. William Barber III of the state NAACP. In the meantime, federal court decisions invalidated all or part of some of the laws passed by the GOP, including the redistricting and voting measures.

The backlash mushroomed in March 2016, when Republicans passed a bill known as H.B. 2. The measure had been spurred by Charlotte's enactment of a non-discrimination ordinance on sexual orientation. The state bill preempted local ordinances such as this one and, in so doing, required people to use bathrooms that coincided with one's birth gender. This time, allies of the LGBT community peeled off sizable portions of the business community, who feared, with reason, that national groups would boycott the state. Indeed, PayPal and Deutsche Bank were among those to pull out of projects in the state, and the NCAA and NBA canceled major events; the Associated Press projected the full economic hit to be $3.76 billion over 12 years. Democrats – including McCrory's Democratic challenger, attorney general Roy Cooper – hammered away at Republicans for recklessly inviting economic hardship. In time, the law became an albatross for McCrory, and after the election, the two sides explored ways to repeal the law. Following one failed attempt in December 2016, the GOP legislature and Cooper – who defeated McCrory after an extended recount -- finally agreed to repeal the bill in March 2017, though the replacement law's continued three-year clampdown on local ordinances drew fire from LGBT advocates and many Democrats.

But Trump ended up winning, doubling Mitt Romney's two-point winning margin in2012 to four points. Clinton won 11,000 more votes than Obama, but Trump won 92,000 more votes than Romney, thanks to a strong showing in rural areas. Seven counties --- mostly smaller ones – switched from Obama to Trump, with shifts as large as 21 points in the GOP's direction. Clinton made gains in the more populous counties. Her margin in Wake County was eight points higher than it had been for Obama; it was seven points higher in Mecklenburg and Durham counties, and two to four points higher in Buncombe, Guilford and Forsyth (Winston-Salem). Cooper, for his part, didn't beat McCrory by much, but he did improve on the Democrats' 2012 gubernatorial performance by 377,000 votes, while McCrory underperformed his 2012 election result by 142,000 votes.

The 2016 down-ballot contests were also close and showed mixed results – Democrats held the attorney general seat Cooper had vacated and secretary of state, and they seized a majority on the nominally nonpartisan Supreme Court. However, Republicans held the lieutenant governorship and flipped the state treasurer's office. The GOP-led legislature flexed its muscles after Cooper's victory, which was declared on Dec. 5. McCrory, a lame duck, signed bills to curb the incoming governor's powers over cabinet appointments, to reduce the number of gubernatorial appointments, and to make Supreme court seats explicitly partisan. Such moves foreshadowed a continued period of bitter partisan conflict in this politically volatile state.

Population		**Race and Ethnicity**		**Income**	
Total	9,845,333	White	64.2%	Median Income	$46,868 (41 out of 50)
Land area	48,618	Black	21.2%	Under $50,000	52.7%
Pop/ sq mi	202.5	Latino	8.8%	$50,000-$99,999	29.2%
Born in state	57.5%	Asian	2.5%	$100,000-$199,999	14.4%
		Two races	1.9%	$200,000 or more	3.6%
Age Groups		Other	1.4%	Poverty Rate	17.4%
Under 18	23.2%				
18-34	23.0%	**Education**		**Health Insurance**	
35-64	39.6%	H.S grad or less	40.9%	With health insurance coverage	85.6%
Over 64	14.2%	Some college	30.8%		
		College Degree, 4 yr	18.4%		
Work		Post grad	9.9%	**Public Assistance**	
White Collar	36.2%			Cash public assistance income	1.9%
Sales and Service	41.1%	**Military**		Food stamp/SNAP benefits	14.6%
Blue Collar	22.7%	Veteran	9.3%		
Government	14.9%	Active Duty	1.1%		

Voter Turnout			
2015 Total Citizens 18+	7,107,998	2016 Pres Turnout as % CVAP	67%
2016 Pres Votes	4,741,564	2012 Pres Turnout as % CVAP	67%

Legislature	
Senate:	15D, 25R
House:	46D, 74R

Presidential Politics

2016 Democratic Primary		
Hillary Clinton (D)	622,915	(55%)
Bernie Sanders (D)	467,018	(41%)
2016 Republican Primary		
Donald Trump (R)	462,413	(40%)
Ted Cruz (R)	422,621	(37%)
John Kasich (R)	145,659	(13%)
Marco Rubio (R)	88,907	(8%)

2016 Presidential Vote		
Donald Trump (R)	2,362,631	(50%)
Hillary Clinton (D)	2,189,316	(46%)
Gary Johnson (L)	130,126	(3%)
2012 Presidential Vote		
Mitt Romney (R)	2,270,395	(50%)
Barack Obama (D)	2,178,391	(48%)

Republicans have carried North Carolina in 10 of the last 12 presidential elections. The only Democratic victories came in 1976, when Southerner Jimmy Carter won the state and 2008, when Barack Obama's campaign built an organization that was able to take advantage of a 2007 state law permitting same-day voter registration and the growing appeal of early voting to mobilize large numbers of college students and African Americans.

The recent arrivals of many Hispanics - 9 percent of the population in 2015 - and affluent professionals in the state's Research Triangle provided opportunities for Democrats to compete in the GOP-leaning state. In his 2012 reelection bid, Obama was unable to repeat his success in the Tar Heel State, but Democrats were optimistic that the state was winnable in 2016. After Republican lawmakers passed and the governor signed into law in early 2016 legislation to restrict the use of public bathrooms to people's biological gender, a backlash further roiled the state's politics. But on Nov. 8, Donald Trump defeated Hillary Clinton, 50%-46%. North Carolina was vigorously contested on both sides and saw more television ads than any state other than Florida and Ohio. Trump's 173,000-vote victory was helped by higher GOP margins in rural counties in both the eastern and western parts of the state. Turnout of black voters was off from its 2008 and 2012 levels. Clinton captured 24 of the state's 100 counties. She performed well in the Research Triangle, Durham (Duke University), Orange (University of North Carolina at Chapel Hill) and Wake (Raleigh) counties. She boosted the Democratic vote in Mecklenburg (Charlotte) as well. And she carried Forsyth (Winston-Salem) and Guilford (Greensboro). But GOP numbers leapt in places like Burke, Caldwell, Haywood, McDowell, Rutherford, Surry and Wilkes counties in the Blue Ridge and Smokey Mountain region of the western part of the state. Those small town, rural and largely white counties were Republican to begin with, but in some cases Trump's vote reached 76%. Much has been made of the Democrats' ability to turn out their supporters before Election Day, and indeed, Clinton won the early vote in North Carolina (in-person plus absentee-by-mail) by almost 78,000 votes. But Trump beat Clinton by more than 251,000 votes cast on Election Day (including provisional ballots). Even though a three-judge panel on the U.S. Court of Appeals for the 4th Circuit had suspended North Carolina's stricter voter ID and voter-access law three months before the election, some Democrats still complained that the measure somehow had a chilling effect on minority voting.

North Carolina's presidential primary, held on the same day in May as its state primary, has occasionally played a role in presidential politics. In 1976, after five straight losses, Ronald Reagan won his first major victory over Gerald Ford in the Republican primary, reenergizing his campaign that went all the way to the convention in Kansas City. After Obama trounced Clinton in the 2008 primary the venerated political observer Tim Russert of NBC News declared that the Democratic nomination race was decided for the first-term Illinois senator. In 2012, North Carolina's May primary was too late to have much impact. Mitt Romney won with 66 percent of the vote. But in 2016, the state moved its primary up to March 15, a day that hosted four other important primaries: Florida, Illinois, Missouri and Ohio. Even in that mix, North Carolina got attention. In the GOP primary, Trump narrowly defeated Texas Sen. Ted Cruz, 40%-37%. Forecasting the future, Trump carried dozens of rural and small town counties in the west and east. Cruz won the Research Triangle as well as Winston-Salem and Greensboro metros. Clinton beat Sanders 55%-41%, and carried 83 of 100 counties.

Congressional Districts

115th Congress Lineup	10R 3D	**114th Congress Lineup**	10R 3D

North Carolina is projected to gain the 14th House seat that it fell barely short of taking after the 2010 census, when that seat instead remained with Minnesota. The history of North Carolina redistricting virtually guarantees an extended battle. Since the 1990s, the state has been the epicenter of race-based redistricting litigation, including controversy over a long, skinny new black-majority 12th District that went to the U.S. Supreme Court four times. Throughout these battles, Democrats managed to retain partisan control of the delegation.

That ended in 2011, when North Carolina was the site of Democrats' worst redistricting devastation, the seeds of which were sown 15 years prior. In 1996, Democrats in charge of the General Assembly exempted redistricting matters from new gubernatorial veto powers, reasoning they would always hold the legislature but voters might occasionally elect a Republican governor. In the ultimate tale of unintended consequences, Republicans shocked even themselves by taking over the legislature by large margins in 2010 (31-19 in the Senate, 67-52-1 in the House), rendering Democratic Gov. Bev Perdue helpless to foil their map makeover. Republicans quickly released and passed a new plan that unraveled and reversed the Democrats' 2002 map, and then some. They packed Democratic voters into just three of the state's 13 seats: an African-American majority 1st District covering parts of rural northeastern counties and heavily black neighborhoods in Durham, an almost comically gerrymandered and liberal 4th District connecting via tentacles the academic haven of Chapel Hill, black neighborhoods in Raleigh and faraway Fayetteville, and an even more tightly packed African-American majority 12th District knifing along the I-85 corridor in a strip from Charlotte to Winston-Salem and Greensboro. Republicans drew the other 10 seats at least 10 percentage points more Republican than the national average. They were all comfortably Republican, but balanced enough in sharing GOP voters that none of them were in the top 20 percent of the nation's most Republican districts.

Their handiwork eviscerated four of the state's seven Democrats. The map double-bunked Chapel Hill Democrat David Price and Raleigh Democrat Brad Miller in the 4th District. It carved the burgeoning progressive mountain mecca of Asheville out of Democrat Heath Shuler's western 11th District, and black neighborhoods in Charlotte and Fayetteville out of Democrat Larry Kissell's southern tier 8th District. Republicans even purged Democrat Mike McIntyre's Robeson County home base, as well as black neighborhoods in Wilmington, from his southeastern 7th District. Republican freshman Renee Ellmers, who had defeated Democrat Bob Etheridge in the suburban Raleigh 2nd District in 2010, received a much safer seat. A furious state Democratic Party and the NAACP sued in state court to block the map. But the Justice Department's preclearance of the lines undercut the groups' claims of racial gerrymandering, and a state panel ruled the map could proceed. Miller and Shuler opted to retire, while Kissell lost 53%-45% in the 8th District. McIntyre beat the odds in a radically redrawn 7th District. Democrats won a majority of the state's votes in House races, but just four of 13 seats. In the 2014 cycle, McIntyre bowed to the inevitable and retired, and a Republican won in a rout. The only remaining Carolina blue were the two African-American districts and Price's liberal bastion.

The redistricting battles have continued . In 2015, the litigation resulted in yet another new map, with the gross gerrymanders largely eliminated. The GOP-controlled legislature was given the opportunity to redraw the districts. With their lengthy experience in litigation and demographics, the map-drawers found a way to ensure 10 secure Republican districts. One Republican was severely disadvantaged. Ellmers had her district sliced up and ran at a big disadvantage against Republican Rep. George Holding. The former Ellmers district morphed into a new and safely Republican seat with an entirely new constituency, west of the Research Triangle.

In May 2017, in yet another North Carolina case, the Supreme Court ruled, 5-3, that racial implications could be reviewed in the context of partisan considerations. That had the effect of finding that the African-American majority 1st and 12th Districts were unconstitutional gerrymanders. But the actual impact of this ruling was not immediately clear. For one thing, those districts were from the original 2011 map and they were substantially redrawn in the 2016 redistricting. The GOP-controlled Legislature has gained considerable dexterity in revising maps to achieve its partisan goals. In addition, the Republican takeover in Washington plus changes in the Supreme Court and the lower courts raise questions about the future of the current legal activism.

In drawing the new 14th district after the 2020 census, even the Republicans would be hard-pressed to draw themselves a secure 11th seat. With the prospect that the courts will continue to intervene,

Democrats likely will have an opportunity to gain at least one seat. Given population trends, an option could be a new "fair-fight" district in the state's growing capital region.

Governor

Roy Cooper (D)

Elected 2016, term expires 2021, 1st term; b. Jun. 13, 1957, Nashville, NC; Univ. of North Carolina Chapel Hill, BA 1979; Univ. of North Carolina, JD 1982; Presbyterian; Married (Kristin); 3 children.

Elected Office: NC House 1987-1991; NC Senate 1991-2000; NC Attorney General 2001-2017

Office: Office of the Governor, 20301 Mail Service Center, Raleigh, 27699-0301; 919-814-2000; Fax: 919-733-2120; Website: governor.nc.gov.

Election Results

Election	Name (Party)	Vote (%)
2016 General	Roy Cooper (D)	2,309,190 (49%)
	Pat McCrory (R)	2,298,927 (49%)
	Lon Cecil (L)	102,986 (2%)
2016 Primary	Roy Cooper (D)	710,658 (69%)
	Ken Spaulding (D)	323,774 (31%)

Roy Cooper, a Democrat who had served four terms as North Carolina's attorney general, narrowly ousted Republican Gov. Pat McCrory in 2016 amid public dissatisfaction with H.B. 2, a bill that preempted local non-discrimination ordinances on sexual orientation, requiring, among other things, that people use bathrooms corresponding with their birth gender.

Cooper was born and raised in a rural portion of east-central North Carolina. He earned a bachelor's degree in psychology and political science and a law degree at the University of North Carolina. While Cooper was still in law school, then-Gov. Jim Hunt, a Democrat, named him to a state goals and policy board. Upon graduation, Cooper joined the family law firm, handling civil suits and personal injury and insurance cases; he also served as a Sunday school teacher and deacon at his Presbyterian church. Cooper served in the state House from 1987 to 1991, and in the state Senate from 1991 to 2001 -- part of that time as majority leader. In 2000, Cooper ran for attorney general against Republican Dan Boyce. It was a hard-fought race, with Cooper airing ads accusing Boyce of overbilling in a class-action lawsuit against the state. (The overbilling allegation prompted a 14-year legal battle that ended with Cooper apologizing.) After outspending Boyce four-to-one, Cooper won the race by five points. He later won reelection three times, serving a total of 16 years. As attorney general, Cooper oversaw the increased use of DNA testing and sought tougher sentences for child predators and pornographers. He took over the hot-button Duke lacrosse rape case after Durham District Attorney Mike Nifong recused himself; Cooper re-investigated the allegations and cleared the players of all charges. However, his tenure was undercut by problems with improper handling of cases by the state crime lab.

In 2013, Cooper actively opposed a voter-ID and election overhaul law driven by the Republican legislature. This and other stances made it increasingly clear that Cooper was aiming for a gubernatorial run against McCrory in 2016. McCrory, a seven-term mayor of Charlotte, had run for governor in 2012 touting a pragmatic, "middle way" philosophy based on pro-business policies and little emphasis on social issues – an approach that had worked for him as a Republican serving on the city level, and that embodied the kind of centrism that had historically carried both Republicans and Democrats to the governor's mansion. (Indeed, Cooper's rise to prominence came as a mirror image to McCrory's – he was a moderate Democrat able to win rural and small-town votes.) In 2012, McCrory won office on frustration with the Great Recession and opposition to a tax hike passed under Democratic Gov. Bev Perdue. Once in office, however, McCrory had to work with a Republican-dominated legislature that had little interest in pragmatic centrism and a strong desire to control the agenda, which often included socially conservative issues. The GOP legislative majority had a two-year head start in crafting its platform, and leaders expressed little deference to their fellow Republican in the governor's chair. As a result, McCrory sometimes clashed with GOP legislators and vetoed their bills. More often, though, he signed them, including the election overhaul bill (later overturned in the courts), a tax overhaul that took away progressivity, and an abortion waiting period. Such moves drew intense opposition from "Moral Monday" protests at the state legislative building.

The biggest threat to McCrory's hopes for reelection came from H.B. 2. The types of business interests who had historically aligned with McCrory were unhappy, fearing boycotts and economic pullouts that indeed materialized within weeks. In the campaign, Cooper made opposition to H.B. 2 – and particularly its effect on the state's economy – a cornerstone of his message. He also advocated increased funding for K-12 education. Cooper's approach resonated – at least enough to narrowly defeat McCrory by a little over 10,000 votes. Donald Trump carried the state in the presidential election, but McCrory underperformed the top of the ticket in some of the industrial areas of the Piedmont and western North Carolina; in such places, Trump's message resonated especially well, while McCrory's "Carolina comeback" theme didn't. Still, the results were close enough that it wasn't clear on Election Night who had won; in the succeeding days, the McCrory camp raised the specter of election fraud, but election boards headed by Republicans disagreed. In December, the incumbent finally conceded.

Even then, it wasn't over. Before Cooper took office, Republican legislators, many ensconced in safe districts, felt comfortable enough to pass laws to strip some of Cooper's powers. They cut the number of gubernatorial appointees, ended the edge of the governor's party on election boards, required cabinet members to be confirmed by the state Senate, and curbed the governor's power to appoint trustees of University of North Carolina institutions. In previous decades, both parties had occasionally made such moves to poke the opposition, but the increased ideological polarization meant that these changes would not be seen as simply business as usual. In December 2016, true to the ongoing partisan tensions, the two sides failed to come to agreement on how to repeal H.B. 2.

In his inaugural address, Cooper said, "I don't think anyone believes that North Carolina families sit around the kitchen table every night, thinking that their lives would change for the better if only the legislature would spend its time on the hot-button social issue of the day." In his budget, Cooper proposed increasing pay for teachers. When he tried to expand Medicaid under the Affordable Care Act, the legislature filed suit, saying the governor couldn't do so unilaterally. And he continued seeking an H.B. 2 repeal, calling it a "dark cloud hanging over our state of promise." Finally, in March 2017 – after the Associated Press had estimated that the state would suffer $3.76 billion over 12 years in lost business – the two sides agreed to a repeal, but with a provision sought by Republicans that continued for three years a restriction on the types of local ordinances that had precipitated H.B. 2 in the first place. The three-year moratorium was a bitter pill for LGBT advocates, and Cooper signed it unhappily, saying it wasn't his "preferred solution." But facing a unified Republican legislature, such victories might be the only ones Cooper can look forward to, at least during his first two years in office.

Senior Senator

Richard Burr (R)

Elected 2004, term expires 2022, 3rd term; b. Nov 30, 1955; Charlottesville, VA; Wake Forest University (NC), B.A.; Methodist; Married (Brooke Fauth Burr); 2 children.

Elected Office: U.S. House, 1995-2005.

Professional Career: National sales Manager, Carswell Distributing, 1978-1994.

DC Office: 217 RSOB 20510, 202-224-3154, Fax: 202-228-2981, burr.senate.gov.

State Offices: Asheville, 828-350-2437; Rocky Mount, 252-977-9522; Wilmington, 910-251-1058; Winston-Salem, 336-631-5125.

Committees: *Aging. Finance*: Energy, Natural Resources & Infrastructure, Health Care, Taxation & IRS Oversight. *Health, Education, Labor & Pensions*: Children & Families, Employment & Workplace Safety, Primary Health & Retirement Security. *Intelligence (Chmn)*.

Group Ratings

	ADA	ACLU	AFL-CIO	LCV	ITI	COC	HAFA	ACU	CFG	FRC
2016	-	17%	-	24%	60%	75%	40%	62%	61%	100%
2015	5%	C	29%	4%	C	79%	C	79%	63%	91%

Almanac Ratings 2015

	Economy	Social	Foreign	Composite
Liberal	32%	0%	0%	11%
Conservative	68%	100%	100%	89%

Key Votes of the 114th Congress

1. Keystone pipeline	Y	5. National Security Data	N	9. Gun Sales Checks	N
2. Export-Import Bank	N	6. Iran Nuclear Deal	Y	10. Sanctuary Cities	Y
3. Debt Ceiling Increase	N	7. Puerto Rico Debt	Y	11. Planned Parenthood	Y
4. Homeland Security $$	N	8. Loretta Lynch A.G	N	12. Trade deals	Y

Election Results

Election	Name (Party)	Vote (%)	Cand. Spent	Ind. Exp. Support	Ind. Exp. Oppose
2016 General	Richard Burr (R)	2,395,376 (51%)	$12,398,612	$2,293,659	$26,170,688
	Deborah Ross (D)	2,128,165 (45%)	$20,299,019	$3,001,651	$28,311,467
	Sean Haugh (L)	167,592 (4%)	$4,298		
2016 Primary	Richard Burr (R)	627,354 (61%)			
	Greg Brannon (R)	257,331 (25%)			
	Paul Wright (R)	86,940 (9%)			

Prior winning percentages: 2010 (55%), 2004 (52%); House: 2002 (70%), 2000 (93%), 1998 (68%), 1996 (62%), 1994 (57%)

Republican Richard Burr, North Carolina's senior senator, occupies the seat once held by the late Democrat Sam Ervin -- who, near the end of his two decades in the Senate, secured a place in history as chairman of the special committee that investigated the Watergate scandal. Burr, newly reelected to a third term that he says will be his last, could find his legacy defined in a similar manner. As chairman of the Senate Intelligence Committee, he was tasked when Congress convened in 2017 with probing allegations of Russian interference in the 2016 presidential election -- including suspicions of collusion between the Russians and the campaign of the newly inaugurated Republican president, Donald Trump. It placed Burr, regarded as a hard-working and consistent conservative, in an unfamiliar setting: the spotlight. First elected to the Senate in 2004 after 10 years in the House, he had not previously achieved the national profile of many other senators. But his ascension to the chairmanship of the Senate Intelligence panel in 2015 offered him a chance to shape debates over surveillance and terrorism -- before the controversy over the 2016 presidential election emerged.

Burr's own political fortunes were very much intertwined with that contest. Initially considered a heavy favorite in 2016 after well-known Democrats opted not to challenge him, he nonetheless found himself in a struggle to win re-election in a purple state that has become a major battleground in recent presidential elections. A distant relative of Vice President Aaron Burr, Richard Burr grew up a minister's son in Winston-Salem, was a star football player in high school and later at Wake Forest University. He then spent the better part of two decades in sales for Winston-Salem-based Carswell Distributing, a wholesaler of lawn and garden equipment and home heating appliances. His first run for office was in 1992, against nine-term Democratic Rep. Steve Neal. Although outspent 3-1, he lost by a relatively narrow 53%-46%. Neal retired in 1994 and Burr ran again, this time winning a solid 57 percent of the vote in a Republican wave year in which the GOP captured a House majority for the first time in four decade. Burr did not have a serious challenge in four re-election bids.

Named to the influential Energy and Commerce Committee, Burr's early cause was streamlining the Food and Drug Administration's drug and medical device approval process, which he argued would speed lifesaving products to the market. With broad bipartisan support, his FDA Modernization Act became law in 1997. He also helped to set up the National Institute for Biomedical Imaging and Bioengineering at the National Institutes of Health. With an eye toward his home constituency, Burr sought a crackdown on illegal textile imports -- but backed President George W. Bush's request for so-called "fast track" authority to expedite the negotiation of trade agreements, after securing promises that the local textile industry would have a seat at the table. He called it a difficult vote, but said it could help make U.S. textiles more competitive internationally -- although the North Carolina textile industry has since seen a steep decline. A decade later, with the other party in the White House, Burr was more skeptical: He voted against giving President Barack Obama fast-track authority for the Trans-Pacific Partnership, the only Republican on the Senate Finance Committee to do so.

In 2004, his last year in the House, a major issue for Burr was a plan to end the tobacco quota system in place since 1938 with a government buyout of quota holders. The entire North Carolina delegation favored it; tobacco quotas had been cut back in recent years, and seemed likely to be again. At issue was whether the buyout should be coupled with FDA regulation of tobacco. Burr favored the buyout without FDA regulation, arguing that the toxicity of cigarettes should be regulated by the Centers for Disease Control and Prevention and that package labeling should fall under the Federal Trade Commission. Burr was appointed to the conference committee, where he held out for the buyout without FDA regulation; Senate conferees yielded, and the bill was enacted to reflect his preferences.

Burr had promised to serve only five terms in the House and by the early 2000s, wanted to run for the Senate. In 2002, when five-term GOP Sen. Jesse Helms retired, Burr deferred to fellow Republican Elizabeth Dole, who had the backing of the Bush White House. Two years later, Democratic Sen. John Edwards opted to run for president over seeking re-election, and Burr had the shot he was waiting for. He had serious opposition from Erskine Bowles, a White House chief of staff under President Bill Clinton, who had lost the 2002 Senate race 54%-45% to Dole. Bowles had deep roots in North Carolina: His father, Hargrove "Skipper" Bowles had been the Democratic nominee for governor in 1972. As Clinton's top aide, Bowles negotiated the 1997 legislation that helped produce a balanced federal budget for the first time in years.

Each candidate spent about $13 million. Bowles started running ads in May and led in the polls until September, while Burr held back on ads until then and, having conserved resources, had a money advantage in the final two months. Bowles touted his ability to work with both parties while depicting Burr as a captive of special interests, especially the pharmaceutical and tobacco companies. For his part, Burr linked Bowles to Clinton's policies on tax increases, welfare for immigrants, and trade with China. On Election Day, Bush carried North Carolina 56%-44% in his bid for a second term, and Burr beat Bowles, 52%-47%. Later, when he co-chaired President Barack Obama's fiscal commission, Bowles had kind words for Burr: "I think by the grace of God we both ended up in the exact right jobs for North Carolina ... I can tell you from firsthand experience nobody works harder or is smarter than this guy in Washington."

In the Senate, Burr has shown little interest in calling attention to himself. He told *The Charlotte Observer* in 2009: "I tend to be more of a policy guy than I am a guy who shows up on the 24-hour talk shows or a guy who goes to the floor and speaks." He has leaned conservative on cultural issues and initially toward the center on foreign policy, although he has moved further to the right in that area after Obama became president. His voting record places him somewhere in the middle of the Senate Republican caucus: He was the 21st most conservative senator overall in 2015, according to the *Almanac* vote ratings.

Taking over as the Intelligence chairman, Burr's relationship with the panel's ranking member, Dianne Feinstein of California -- who was chairman from 2009 until the Democrats lost the Senate majority at the end of 2014 -- was bumpy at times. Feinstein had commissioned a staff investigation of the Central Intelligence Agency's use of harsh interrogation techniques in the wake of 9/11. It produced a critical report of more than 6,700 pages, although only a 500-page summary was declassified and released publicly. Burr lambasted the report's conclusions that the CIA's torture program had proven ineffective, calling the report "fiction" and arguing in a letter with his GOP committee colleagues that the program "was an effective means of gathering significant intelligence information and cooperation from a majority of these CIA detainees." Burr fought declassification of the report, and, after becoming chairman, wrote to Obama asking that copies of the full classified report sent to the White House and other parts of the executive branch be returned -- apparently fearing the report could become available under the Freedom of Information Act. Feinstein wrote to Obama opposing Burr's request, later telling the *New Yorker*, "I was surprised and somewhat suspicious about who put him up to it." The White House declined to return or destroy copies of the report.

Burr resisted reining in the power of intelligence agencies in the face of domestic snooping revelations, and fought hard to turn back attempts at greater openness when sections of the USA Patriot Act came up for reauthorization. "If I had my way, with the exception of nominees, there would never be a public intelligence hearing," he told reporters in 2014. A year later, as Intelligence chairman, Burr helped lead the charge to reauthorize the full Patriot Act, fighting against bipartisan efforts to curtail the program's bulk collection of Americans' phone records. He and Senate Majority Leader Mitch McConnell did all they could to renew the act without making changes, even after the House passed a bill with reforms by overwhelming bipartisan margins. After an attempt to force a short-term extension of the law failed and the Patriot Act expired on June 1 -- thanks in large part to a filibuster by McConnell's home-state colleague, libertarian-minded Republican Rand Paul -- McConnell relented and allowed a vote on the House-passed measure. Burr was among 32 senators to vote against the reforms. "I am disappointed in the final bill and, quite frankly, am very concerned about the new system's ability to keep up with the threats we face," he declared.

In 2016, Burr got behind Trump in May, when it was clear that the New York businessman would be the party's nominee; at one point, the usually low-key senator compared himself to the bombastic billionaire. "He's a very non-traditional candidate, and he's run a very non-traditional campaign," Burr told reporters during the Republican National Convention in Cleveland. "Most in Washington would probably say that describes me to a T, and so I can associate with Donald Trump very well." He later signed on as a national security adviser to the Trump campaign, while downplaying the possibility of Russian interference in the election to benefit Trump. "I have yet to see anything that would lead me to believe that's the case," Burr told *Foreign Policy* magazine in early October. He called his congressional colleagues' warnings "probably incorrect," adding, "They give the impression there's one cyber-problem in the world: Russia and the elections, and that's a huge understatement." But Burr vowed impartiality as his panel's investigation of Russian interference -- and possible collusion between Moscow and the Trump campaign -- got underway in early 2017. "I'll admit that I voted for [Trump]," Burr said. "... But I've got a job in the United States Senate, and I take that job extremely seriously. It overrides any personal beliefs that I have or loyalties that I might have."

In addition to the Finance and Intelligence panels, Burr serves on the Health, Education, Labor and Pensions Committee. One of his most significant legislative achievements came in 2005, his first year in the Senate, when he won enactment of a bill to create the Biomedical Advanced Research and Development Authority to develop vaccines and other countermeasures to biological terrorism or a pandemic; he cosponsored reauthorization of the bill in 2009 with the late Democratic Sen. Edward Kennedy of Massachusetts. It was a continuation of Burr's efforts in the House, where he sponsored laws to improve defenses against bioterrorism in the wake of the 9/11 attacks. It also was among several notable instances of Burr reaching across the political aisle. In 2013, he was part of a bipartisan group of senators that struck a deal to keep down student loan interest rates by tying those rates to the government's cost of borrowing. It passed the Senate by 81-18 vote and was signed into law.

In December 2010, Burr surprised his conservative supporters when he voted to end the "don't ask, don't tell" ban on openly gay service personnel. In 2015, he voted to give legally married same-sex spouses Social Security and veterans' benefits they have earned. Burr occasionally has shown a willingness to take on far-right colleagues; he said in July 2013 that talk of shutting down the federal government over opposition to the Affordable Care Act was "the dumbest idea I've ever heard." A year later, he worked with Republicans Orrin Hatch of Utah and Tom Coburn of Oklahoma on a comprehensive alternative to the ACA that retained many of the law's most popular elements, but guaranteed coverage to those with pre-existing medical conditions only if they maintained "continuous coverage."

One area where Burr has taken a strong conservative line is immigration. In 2006, he voted against an immigration overhaul because he said it would lead to "blanket amnesty" for illegal immigrants. During negotiations on a compromise bill the following year, Burr supported the "touchback" amendment that would have forced illegal immigrants to return to their home countries before applying for visas. When the amendment was voted down, he voted against allowing the compromise measure to advance. He vowed to keep an open mind as a bipartisan group of his colleagues drafted a comprehensive immigration reform proposal in 2013. But he ultimately voted against the bill, saying it didn't do enough to secure the border.

As ranking Republican on the Veterans' Affairs Committee in 2014, after a scandal erupted at the Veterans' Affairs Department over mismanagement and overly long wait times for treating patients, Burr -- who represents a state with more than 800,000 veterans -- found himself at the center of an acrimonious spat. He wrote an open letter charging that the staff at various veterans groups "has ignored the constant VA problems expressed by their members and is more interested in their own livelihoods and Washington connections than they are to the needs of their own members." His comments produced an outraged reaction; an official at Disabled American Veterans said the senator "shows no interest in pursuing serious policy solutions, preferring instead to launch cheap political attacks on the integrity of leaders of veterans' organizations that do not agree with him."

During the financial crisis in 2008, Burr voted for the $700 billion government rescue of the financial industry, but later had reservations and opposed release of the second half of the money from the Troubled Asset Relief Program. He attracted unfavorable attention during the crisis when he said he had advised his wife to withdraw as much cash as possible out of ATMs. In 2012, when a bill aimed at banning insider trading by members of Congress was brought up on the Senate floor, there was little doubt it would pass; the legislation gained momentum after a *60 Minutes* exposé on the practice. It passed the Senate on a 96-3, with Burr one of the three dissenters -- and on the receiving end of widespread criticism. The left-leaning *Huffington Post* reported that Burr stood to gain from his natural gas tax-credit bill because he had personal investments in the natural gas industry. Burr denied any attempt to profit from past legislation, and contended that insider trading bans were already on the books.

Burr has sought to move up the Senate leadership ladder. In 2007, he lost a bid for Republican Conference chairman to Lamar Alexander of Tennessee. In January 2009, he was named chief deputy whip. In October 2011, Burr said he intended to run for Senate Republican whip, the No. 2 slot in the GOP leadership chain, after the then-whip, Jon Kyl of Arizona, announced his retirement. Burr changed his mind in March 2012 and said he would rather focus on legislation, clearing the way for Texas' John Cornyn to take the job.

When he came up for reelection in 2010, there was speculation Burr could encounter serious opposition, considering Obama's victory in North Carolina in 2008 and Dole's defeat for reelection to the Senate that year. Moreover, polls showed Burr had a low profile in the state. But the strongest possible Democratic challenger, state Attorney General Roy Cooper, declined to run. (Cooper is now the state's governor.) North Carolina Secretary of State Elaine Marshall emerged from the Democratic primary with little money. Burr raised $11 million, nearly four times as much as his opponent. Marshall hit him for supporting the 2008 financial bailout and dubbed him "Bank Run" Burr for his ATM advice to his wife. None of this got much traction, and Burr won, 55%-43%.

Democrats also had recruiting difficulties when Burr came up for reelection to a third term in 2016. Former Sen. Kay Hagan, narrowly ousted by Burr's junior colleague, Republican Thom Tillis, in 2014, declined to take on Burr -- as did Obama Secretary of Transportation Anthony Foxx, a former Charlotte Mayor. Former state Rep. Deborah Ross, a Raleigh attorney, announced her candidacy in late 2015, and was soon embraced by the state Democratic establishment. In the March 2016 primary, Ross outdistanced three rivals, winning 62 percent. Burr was renominated with 61 percent in a four-way field, with his chief competition coming from tea party-aligned Greg Brannon.

Initially, the Burr-Ross faceoff did not appear to be high on the list of competitive Senate races, but a *Wall Street Journal/Marist* poll in early August, showing Ross ahead by 46%-44%, helped to change that perception. The same poll showed Trump trailing Democratic presidential nominee Hillary Clinton by 9 points, underscoring the degree to which the fate of the Senate candidates was tied to the top of the ticket in the battleground state. Burr was weighed down by a couple of other factors beyond his control: the unpopularity of GOP Gov. Pat McCrory, who ended up losing to Cooper, and the so-called "bathroom bill" passed by the North Carolina General Assembly -- which required transgender individuals to use bathrooms in government buildings consistent with the gender on their birth certificates. Ross accused Burr of failing to speak out forcefully against the measure; Burr sought to distance himself from the law, telling the *Huffington Post:* "The legislature botched what they were trying to do. It was far too expansive."

Burr also created some problems for himself. To the frustration of GOP officials, Burr only began to campaign in earnest in late September, after Congress had adjourned for the election. When he was on the campaign trail, his tongue got him in trouble. In the leaked audio of a private campaign gathering, Burr was heard referring to an edition of the *American Rifleman*, the magazine of the National Rifle Association, with a picture of Clinton on the cover. "I was a little bit shocked that they didn't have a bullseye on it," Burr wisecracked -- in a remark for which his campaign later apologized. (Burr promised on the same recording to block all Supreme Court nominees if Clinton was elected.) Ross sought to paint Burr as a Washington insider, while accusing him of voting to privatize Medicare and cut Social Security benefits -- charges that Burr disputed. Meanwhile, Burr and his GOP allies sought to characterize Ross as "too extreme for North Carolina." They sought to tie her to several unpopular stances taken by the state chapter of the American Civil Liberties Union, of which Ross was a former director.

Burr pulled out a 51%-45% win on Election Day -- similar to the 50%-46% margin by which Trump captured the state. Ross won the state's major cities -- Charlotte, Fayetteville, Greensboro and Raleigh

-- along with the Research Triangle and the black-majority counties. Burr, as was the case in his two prior victories, scored heavily in rural counties in the Piedmont and the mountains. Although short of the $111 million spent in the Hagan-Tillis contest in 2014, spending in the Burr-Ross race approached $84 million. The candidates themselves spent about $24 million, with Ross outspending the incumbent by $4 million -- but that was dwarfed by nearly $60 million pumped into the state by outside expenditure groups.

Months before the votes were counted, Burr proclaimed that, if he won, it would be his last term. "It's real simple: I'm beginning to get old," Burr, who turned 61 in 2016, told reporters at the Republican National Convention. "I still look forward to getting back into the private sector before retirement even comes into the picture. I never envisioned retiring out of the Congress."

Junior Senator

Thom Tillis (R)

Elected 2014, term expires 2020, 1st term; b. Aug 30, 1960, Jacksonville, FL; University of Maryland University College, B.S.; Catholic; Married (Susan Tillis); 2 children.

Elected Office: Board of Commissioners, Cornelius, NC, 2003-2005; NC House, 2007-2014.

Professional Career: Life insurance company consultant, 1981-1982; Executive and Manager, PricewaterhouseCoopers, IBM, 1983-2009.

DC Office: 185 DSOB 20510, 202-224-6342, Fax: 202-228-2563, tillis.senate.gov.

State Offices: Charlotte, 704-509-9087; Greenville, 252-329-0371; High Point, 336-885-0685; Raleigh, 919-856-4630.

Committees: *Aging*. *Armed Services*: Airland, Personnel (Chmn), Seapower. *Banking, Housing & Urban Affairs*: Economic Policy, Housing, Transportation & Community Development, Securities, Insurance & Investment. *Joint Security & Cooperation in Europe*. *Judiciary*: Antitrust, Competition Policy & Consumer Rights, Border Security & Immigration, Oversight, Agency Action, Federal Rights & Federal Courts, Privacy, Technology & the Law. *Veterans' Affairs*.

Group Ratings

	ADA	ACLU	AFL-CIO	LCV	ITI	COC	HAFA	ACU	CFG	FRC
2016	-	17%	-	18%	80%	100%	47%	69%	67%	100%
2015	5%	C	14%	4%	C	86%	C	79%	65%	91%

Almanac Ratings 2015

	Economy	Social	Foreign	Composite
Liberal	28%	0%	9%	12%
Conservative	72%	100%	91%	88%

Key Votes of the 114th Congress

1. Keystone pipeline	Y	5. National Security Data	N	9. Gun Sales Checks	N
2. Export-Import Bank	Y	6. Iran Nuclear Deal	Y	10. Sanctuary Cities	Y
3. Debt Ceiling Increase	Y	7. Puerto Rico Debt	N	11. Planned Parenthood	Y
4. Homeland Security $$	N	8. Loretta Lynch A.G	N	12. Trade deals	Y

Election Results

Election	Name (Party)	Vote (%)		Cand. Spent	Ind. Exp. Support	Ind. Exp. Oppose
2014 General	Thom Tillis (R)	1,423,259	(49%)	$10,513,963	$13,033,391	$37,000,532
	Kay Hagan (D)	1,377,651	(47%)	$24,851,013	$7,789,136	$20,462,687
	Sean Haugh (L)	109,100	(4%)			
2014 Primary	Thom Tillis (R)	223,174	(46%)			
	Greg Brannon (R)	132,630	(27%)			
	Mark Harris (R)	85,727	(18%)			

Republican Thom Tillis, North Carolina's junior senator, benefited from Republicans' 2014 wave election -- pulling off a narrow win over Democratic Sen. Kay Hagan in what was, up to that point, the most expensive Senate campaign in history. Prior to arriving on Capitol Hill, Tillis was speaker of the North Carolina House -- a portion of his tenure overlapping with a period that, with a Republican governor and GOP-controlled saw public policy in the Tarheel State take a sharp right turn. But, with North Carolina increasingly a political battleground, Tillis has sought to adopt a centrist tone as a senator, as he looks ahead to the prospect of reelection in the presidential year of 2020.

"Since the election, I've heard some of my fellow Republicans claim that the party received a decisive mandate from voters," Tillis noted in an op-ed page column published in the *Charlotte Observer* following the 2016 election. But he went on to declare: "Let's be clear: the American people didn't give the GOP a stamp of approval or a mandate to ram through an ideologically-driven, far-right agenda. If the election was a mandate for anything, it was for elected officials in both parties to break through the gridlock to finally start producing results." Tillis' column appeared two months after a split electoral decision in his home state: North Carolina voters, while giving President Donald Trump a 50%-46% victory, also ousted the incumbent GOP governor.

Tillis was born in Jacksonville Florida, one of five siblings. By the time he was 17, his family had moved 20 times as his parents sought work, at one point living in a trailer park. While he graduated near the top of his high school class, he and his siblings "weren't wired to go to college," he told an interviewer shortly after becoming House speaker. Instead, he took a job as a warehouse records clerk -- later earning a bachelor's degree in technology management, at the age of 36, through University of Maryland-University College, an online institution. By that time, he was a partner at the international accounting and consulting firm of PriceWaterhouseCoopers, after earlier working for now-defunct Wang Laboratories. He remained at PriceWaterhouseCoopers after it was taken over by IBM, advising banks and other corporations. It was his work for Charlotte-based NationsBank -- which later became Bank of America after a merger with the latter -- that brought him to North Carolina in 1998.

After settling in Cornelius, a Charlotte suburb, his political rise was little short of meteoric. From a start as the president of the PTA at his daughter's high school, he served as a town commissioner before winning election to the state House in 2006. Four years later, the House flipped to a Republican majority and Tillis was chosen as the fifth GOP speaker in state history. He touted his business background in winning election to the House and later managing it. "A democratic institution is by definition not a business. But there is the business of running the Legislature, which I think we're doing pretty well," he told *North Carolina Business* in 2012. Critics on the left, however, suggested a contradiction between Tillis' initial political image and his later persona. "He goes to the General Assembly as a business conservative and then votes for or enables some of the most far-right legislation in our state's history," Chris Fitzsimon, executive director of the liberal N.C. Policy Watch, told the *Observer* during Tillis' campaign for Senate.

As a business-oriented conservative, Tillis helped to enact laws that included restructuring North Carolina's tax code to reduce personal and business income taxes, eliminating the estate tax, and capping the gasoline tax. But on his watch, state House Republicans also passed bills to allow guns in bars and on college campuses, and to require women to watch a narrated ultrasound of their live fetuses before having abortions. (The abortion measure was later struck down by a federal judge.) In 2013, the Tillis-led House created outrage among civil rights groups when it repealed a law allowing citizens to register and vote on the same day, while adopting a requirement that voters had to present one of six state-approved ID cards at the polls. Democrats attacked Tillis for those moves, as well as for cutting funds from the University of North Carolina system and dragging his feet on teacher pay increases-charges that became a prominent feature in Hagan's Senate campaign ads. Nonetheless, some on the right griped that Tillis wasn't going far enough in pushing changes through the General Assembly.

Indeed, Tillis faced resistance from his right after he decided to take on Hagan in 2014. While a programmatic social and fiscal conservative, he was not a fire-breather -- and had no trouble picking up the support of the state's GOP establishment. That helped him to prevail in an eight-way primary with 46 percent of the vote, more than the 40-percent threshold necessary to avoid a runoff. Greg Brannon, a tea party-aligned acolyte of former Rep. Ron Paul of Texas, was second with 27 percent, followed by Mark Harris, an evangelical preacher who had led the state's referendum against gay marriage, with 18 percent. But for two months after the May primary, pressure from conservatives in the statehouse kept Tillis more focused on his day job than was helpful for a candidate in a nationally targeted race. After months of debate over state budget proposals that pitted Tillis against the more hardline conservatives running the state Senate, he finally wrapped up a special legislative session in July and was able to turn his full attention to Hagan.

Hagan was high on national Republican lists of pickup opportunities: She had ousted Republican Sen. Elizabeth Dole in 2008, a good year for Democrats when Barack Obama became only the second Democratic presidential nominee in more than four decades to carry North Carolina. Despite a reputation as a cautious centrist, Hagan was willing to back Obama on his chief legislative priorities. Tillis's main campaign objective was to tie Hagan to Obama, highlighting her support for the Affordable Care Act. He accused his rival of skipping an Armed Services Committee hearing on the threat of the Islamic State (ISIS) to raise campaign money, a particularly potent attack in a state with two large military bases and 800,000 veterans statewide. If tea party activists in the state remained lukewarm at best toward his candidacy, Tillis had the support of major outside groups such as Americans for Prosperity as well as American Crossroads and the U.S. Chamber of Commerce. These independent expenditures organizations spent months and multiple millions of dollars attacking Hagan in television ads.

Hagan responded by campaigning against what she characterized as Tillis' extreme agenda on issues ranging from abortion to education to taxes. "At every opportunity he has fought for policies that are taking our state backwards," Hagan charged during an October debate. "Speaker Tillis feels that those who have the most should get the most help." Hagan also emphasized her opposition to a statewide ban on same-sex marriage, which Tillis said he would continue to defend. The North Carolina constitution's ban on same-sex marriage was overturned in 2014 by a federal judge, prompting Tillis to charge during the October debate, "We're in a dangerous time in this country where the president has appointed liberal activist judges - and Sen. Hagan has endorsed them or confirmed them - that are literally trying the legislate from the bench."

Democrats had the edge in the race in public and private polling for much of the year, but the last few weeks of the 2014 election featured a notable shift to Republicans nationwide. As Hagan turned her attention toward turning out her base -- focusing on equal pay legislation for women as well as Tillis' opposition to a minimum wage increase and North Carolina Republicans' push to constrain ballot access -- Tillis tightened his message: He hammered Hagan on national security issues such as ISIS and the Ebola virus, as well as problems at the Veterans' Administration. Tillis edged Hagan by 48.8%-47.2%, the Republicans' closest win of the election cycle -- a margin of 45,000 votes out of more than 2.9 million cast. Polls showed neither candidate was well-liked by Election Day-but Obama's low popularity in the state likely was the crucial blow for Hagan. The contest stood as the most expensive Senate race in history -- until 2016, when it was supplanted by that year's Pennsylvania Senate battle. In North Carolina, total spending in the Hagan-Tillis face-off came to $111 million, with more than two-thirds of that, $77 million, from outside groups. Hagan outspent Tillis by more than 2-1 in terms of their campaign committees; without the outside groups' heavy support, it is questionable whether Tillis would have been able to remain competitive throughout the race.

Tillis' committee assignments included two of particular political importance given the military presence in the state: the Armed Services and Veterans Affairs panels. His Senate debut was choppy : Tillis became a late-night comedy punch line in February 2015 for arguing the government should not require food workers to wash their hands after using the bathroom, saying "the market will take care of that" by causing businesses that didn't to fold. The *Daily Show*'s Jon Stewart jumped on the comments, jabbing at Tillis as "Sen. Dunghands Von Fecalfingers."

In some of his early actions, Tillis appeared much the same lawmaker who had steered the North Carolina House sharply to the right. He backed a state push to add anti-abortion "choose life" license plates and called the Department of Justice's investigation into the restrictive voting laws and gerrymandered congressional map he had helped pass in the state House a "waste of resources." He voted against Obama's nomination of Loretta Lynch, a North Carolina native, to be attorney general in the spring of 2015. But he did vote for a bill to give legally married same-sex spouses Social Security and veterans' benefits they had earned, despite his opposition to same-sex marriage. He was the 27th most conservative senator in 2015, according to *Almanac* vote ratings, putting him squarely in the middle of the Republican caucus.

He actively reached out to Democrats, seeking to hit the reset button in an effort to dispel the image he had brought with him to Capitol Hill. "When you're in a race like mine … you come up here, the first thing you want to do is dispel any myths about what you may be like," Tillis said told the *Observer* in 2016. "The only way you do that is just by building good personal relationships. Now what I'm trying to do is figure out how we continue to translate that into legislative initiatives." Just weeks into his term, he became the only Republican to join 13 Democratic senators on a bill to create a mechanism for monitoring conflicts worldwide and detecting early warning signs that might enable the United States to prevent genocides. He also co-authored legislation with Delaware Democratic Sen. Tom Carper to ensure payments made to eugenics victims did not affect their eligibility for federal benefits such as Medicaid and food stamps. The measure, signed by Obama in late 2016, was aimed at protecting the victims of compulsory sterilization programs that operated in 33 states as recently as the 1970s. The eugenics legislation was a follow-on to a bill that Tillis got through the North Carolina General Assembly in 2013 that made that state the first in the nation to provide compensation for those sterilized as a result of eugenics programs.

Meanwhile, Tillis carefully kept his distance from another piece of state legislation -- the so-called "bathroom bill" that passed the General Assembly more than a year after his departure. He called it a matter for the city of Charlotte and the state to settle. The bill, which required transgender individuals to use bathrooms based on their gender at birth, was repealed in 2017 after causing a national furor, with a number of organizations vowing to boycott North Carolina as a location for future events.

Tillis initially endorsed his colleague, Florida Sen. Marco Rubio, for the 2016 Republican presidential nomination, but was a steadfast supporter of Trump from late spring -- when Trump had clearly secured the nomination -- through the election. "Anybody who doesn't support the Republican nominee ... is a RINO," Tillis asserted, referring to the acronym "Republican In Name Only." He added: "We have to recognize that more than anything else, we have to unite. At the end of the day, we're all Republicans." In his *Observer* op-ed following the election, he cautioned: "Republicans should remember that when Trump campaigned, he wasn't holding up a conservative manifesto at every rally. Instead, his message was simple: cut deals and deliver results." Added Tillis: "I, for one, have no intention of sitting down and watching another re-run of the same divisive partisanship we see year after year…I'll be reaching across the aisle to find opportunities to work with Democrats on the issues that desperately need to be addressed."

When, early in his presidency, Trump issued an executive order imposing a temporary ban on immigration from seven predominantly Muslim countries, Tillis joined Missouri Democrat Claire McCaskill and New Hampshire Democrat Jeanne Shaheen in a letter to the Defense Department -- protesting the treatment of two Iraqis who had aided U.S. forces, but were detained at New York's Kennedy International Airport. Tillis, while saying he supported tighter screening of refugees, complained that "there is a lot of confusion surrounding the order," and that it needed to be "refined." A month later, he disclosed he had been meeting with Republican and Democratic colleagues to come up with a comprehensive plan on immigration and border security. "You will never satisfy the far extremes on the left and the right," Tillis told *Fox News*, saying his aim was "to get something to the president's desk that he will sign."

In late 2016, Tillis suggested that he might not seek re-election unless a bipartisan criminal justice reform measure -- within the jurisdiction of the Judiciary Committee, of which Tillis is a member-- became law. The bill, intended to reduce mandatory minimum sentences for those with drug convictions and increase rehabilitation programs for prisoners, had cleared the Judiciary panel by a wide margin , but was then stalled by objections from a handful of hardline conservatives. It returned to the committee's agenda in 2017 . Tillis, who pushed a criminal justice reform measure through the state House in his first year as speaker, has made the issue one of his top priorities . "I don't run again until 2020, and if we're not able to get things like this done, I don't have any intention of coming back," he declared to applause at a juvenile justice forum. "It is time to tell the far-left and the far-right to get productive or get out of the way because we need to solve this problem." Asked later whether he was serious about not running again, Tillis replied, "I came here to get things done."

Amid his overtures across the political aisle, Tillis has not abandoned his more partisan instincts. In advance of the 2010 election in which Republicans gained control of the North Carolina House, he crisscrossed the state recruiting candidates and raising money. Likewise, for much of 2016, he pursued a leadership role at the NRSC, the Senate GOP's campaign arm. For a time, Tillis and Colorado Sen. Cory Gardner -- also elected in 2014 from a purple state -- floated the idea of co-chairing the NRSC. Tillis ultimately threw his support behind Gardner to chair the panel in the 2018 cycle; he said he expected to play a role in NRSC finances, but wanted to focus on his prospective reelection in 2020, in view of North Carolina's rapidly changing politics.

If Tillis seems to be carefully treading a political pathway, he is something of a daredevil on terrain outside of politics. He is an avid mountain biker, although, now in his late 50s, his most adventurous days may be behind him -- after two cracked helmets and a broken collar bone.

FIRST DISTRICT

G.K. Butterfield (D)

Elected 2004, 7th term; b. Apr 27, 1947, Wilson; North Carolina Central University, B.A.; North Carolina Central University School of Law, J.D.; Baptist; Divorced; 3 children.

Military Career: U.S Army, 1968-1970.

Elected Office: NC Superior Court, 1988-2001, 2002-2004; NC Supreme Court, 2001-2002.

Professional Career: Practicing attorney, 1974-1988.

DC Office: 2080 RHOB 20515, 202-225-3101, Fax: 202-225-3354, butterfield.house.gov.

State Offices: Durham, 919-908-0164; Wilson, 252-237-9816.

Committees: *Energy & Commerce*: Communications & Technology, Energy, Health.

Group Ratings

	ADA	ACLU	AFL-CIO	LCV	ITI	COC	HAFA	ACU	CFG	FRC
2016	-	100%	-	89%	67%	62%	12%	0%	0%	0%
2015	100%	C	100%	91%	C	45%	C	0%	0%	0%

Almanac Ratings 2015

	Economy	Social	Foreign	Composite
Liberal	94%	100%	87%	94%
Conservative	6%	0%	13%	6%

Key Votes of the 114th Congress

1. Keystone Pipeline	N	5. Puerto Rico Debt	Y	9. Offenses by Aliens	N
2. Trade Deals	N	6. Medical Marijuana	Y	10. Troops in Iraq	N
3. Export-Import Bank	Y	7. Sanctuary Cities	N	11. Homeland Security $$	Y
4. Debt Ceiling Increase	Y	8. Armor-piercing Bullets	N	12. Trade Adjustment aid	Y

Election Results

Election	Name (Party)	Vote (%)	Cand. Spent	Ind. Exp. Support	Ind. Exp. Oppose
2016 General	G.K Butterfield (D)	240,661 (69%)	$651,182		
	H. Powell Dew (R)	101,567 (29%)	$19,767		
	J.J Summerell (L)	8,471 (2%)	$21,419		
2016 Primary	G.K. Butterfield (D)	(100%)			

Prior winning percentages: 2014 (73%), 2012 (75%), 2010 (59%), 2008 (70%), 2004 (64%)

Democrat G.K. (George Kenneth) Butterfield, who won a special election in 2004, rarely makes headlines but has been a key behind-the-scenes strategist for Democratic leaders and the Congressional Black Caucus. As CBC chairman in 2015-16, he quietly sought to maintain its role as "conscience of the Congress" on issues such as gun control and economic diversity.

Butterfield grew up in Wilson County, where his father was a dentist and the first black elected official in Wilson in the 20th century; he lost his seat in 1957 when the white majority switched voting procedures to at-large elections. His mother was a schoolteacher for 48 years. In 1963, young Butterfield joined his father in Washington when Martin Luther King Jr. delivered his "I have a dream" speech. He got his bachelor's and law degrees from North Carolina Central University and participated in many registration drives after enactment of the Voting Rights Act. As a civil rights lawyer, Butterfield took on voting rights cases. He joined hospital employees at Duke University in their drive to organize a union. As a Superior Court judge for 12 years, he handled thousands of civil and criminal cases in 46 counties until 2001, when Democratic Gov. Michael Easley appointed him to the state Supreme Court. After Butterfield lost election in 2002 to a full term, Easley appointed him as a special Superior Court judge.

In the special election that resulted when the first-term incumbent resigned due to a combination of ethical and health problems, party caucuses selected the nominees and the six-week contest in the safe

Democratic district received little local or national attention. Butterfield said that his priorities would be strengthening the rural economy and halting U.S. job losses. He won 71%-27% and has not been seriously challenged since.

Butterfield has a solidly liberal voting record, as shown by his *Almanac* vote ratings in 2015 for each of the three issue areas. He has focused on an array of racial-discrimination issues. He helped to settle claims of up to 74,000 African-American farmers who were discriminated against when applying for Agriculture Department loans and programs between 1983 and 2010. He lobbied to include an exhibit in the Capitol Visitor Center on the slave labor that was employed in building the Capitol and on the careers of the 22 African Americans who served in Congress during and after Reconstruction. He pressed Obama administration officials for the appointment of an African American to fill a vacancy for federal judge in North Carolina's Eastern District.

A longtime friend of Democratic Rep. James Clyburn of South Carolina, Butterfield managed his successful campaign for majority whip in 2006. Butterfield became a chief deputy whip under Clyburn and has retained the position with Democrats in the House minority. A long-time leader of the Black Caucus, he was less confrontational toward President Barack Obama than were other CBC members. Along with Clyburn, he was among the few who supported funding of the wars in Iraq and Afghanistan.

As caucus chairman, Butterfield led a delegation to Ferguson, Missouri in 2015 to call for "transformative changes" nationwide in police practices. During a meeting of CBC members with Obama, he told the president that "black America continues to be in a state of emergency." Separately, Obama pressed hard for him to support his Trans-Pacific Partnership trade initiative; Butterfield opposed trade negotiating authority for the president, as did all but three CBC members. He met with leaders of Silicon Valley to demand more diversity in the tech industry. During the June 2016 House sit-in by Democrats demanding action on gun control, Butterfield was a chief organizer.

With his connections to Democratic leaders, Butterfield has a seat on the influential Energy and Commerce Committee, where he has worked to prohibit states from passing on their Medicaid costs to counties. In his low-income district, many counties spend more of their property-tax revenues on Medicaid than on public schools. When the House passed in 2009 the Democrats' proposed cap-and-trade system of carbon emissions swapping, he got assurance that more of the revenue would be used to help low-income areas. That bill stalled in the Senate. He worked with Republican Rep. Michael McCaul of Texas to enact in 2012 a bill allowing pharmaceutical companies to receive faster Food and Drug Administration reviews of profitable drugs in return for developing treatments for rare pediatric diseases.

Although redistricting in 2016 had a major impact on other East Carolina districts, it caused little political change for Butterfield.

Northeastern North Carolina: Durham, Greenville

Demographics data for new House districts were not prepared by the Census Bureau prior to our editorial deadline.

Voter Turnout

2016 House Turnout as % CVAP	N/A	2016 House turnout	350,699

2012 Presidential Vote information unavailable due to recent redistricting.

2016 Presidential Vote		
Hillary Clinton	240,217	(67%)
Donald Trump	108,565	(30%)
Gary Johnson	7,041	(2%)

Cook Partisan Voting Index: D+17

In colonial days, the eastern portion of North Carolina was a smaller version of the Chesapeake Bay colonies of Virginia and Maryland. A fertile land laced by rivers and inlets, it had tobacco plantations and farms with docks on waterways accessible to the ocean and so to London. In 1890, James B. Duke founded the American Tobacco Co. in Durham, and began mass production of cigarettes. Today, East Carolina survives with remnants of Tobacco Road and is still largely inhabited by the descendants of the original white settlers and black slaves of 250 years ago. They live in small towns and cities. Tobacco was a labor-intensive crop that for many years produced yields of $4,000 an acre; a family lucky enough to have a tobacco quota could make a living off 40 acres. In 2004, Congress enacted a $10 billion buyout of quota holders.

North Carolina's tobacco production dropped from 454 million pounds in 2014 to 332 million pounds in 2016 and the industry's political influence has diminished, though its yield remained larger than that of the next six states combined. More of the local business in this area has turned to hog farming, where its $1.5 billion in sales make North Carolina the largest-producing state on the East Coast. Food-processing plants have replaced textile mills. Reser's Fine Foods began operations locally in 1950 with a potato-salad recipe, and now has nearly 5,000 employees who produce deli foods and salads at 12 facilities in the United States and one in Mexico, with its headquarters in the tiny town of Halifax. In February 2017, the CSX rail company announced plans for a $270 million cargo hub in Rocky Mount that will extend to Greenville.

The 1st Congressional District of North Carolina covers much of the old tobacco country of East Carolina. The new redistricting has significantly straightened out its boundaries, which had been ranked among the most gerrymandered districts in the nation and was described as a misshapen ostrich placing its head in the sand. As with the old district, the chief population center is Durham, where the district takes in Duke University. Duke is an anchor for the Research Triangle area, whose facilities attract scientists from across the globe in a wide variety of studies and were ranked fourth in the nation in 2015 for tech jobs. The district includes about 90 percent of Durham County, which is the chief urban area in the district and totals about one-third of its residents. The population of the county grew by 37 percent between 2000 and 2016, when it reached 306,000. Durham is overwhelmingly Democratic. Hillary Clinton took 79 percent of the presidential vote in 2016. The only other urban area in the district is Greenville-based Nash County, nearly half of which is in the 1st with the remainder in the 3rd District.

The rest of the district is a swath of mostly rural, heavily African-American counties in the northeastern portion of the state. These are Democratic precincts in a variety of cities and small towns along North Carolina's coastal plain, including Roanoke Rapids, Tarboro, Wilson and parts of Albemarle Sound, but none of the Outer Banks. No longer in the district are Elizabeth City, Goldsboro, New Bern and half of Rocky Mount. Even with robust Durham, the mostly rural district is among the lowest in the nation in its median income. The district is 52 percent African American overall. In a mark of the skill of the redistricters, this is one of three solidly Democratic North Carolina districts where Hillary Clinton got an identical 67 percent of the presidential vote in 2016. President Barack Obama received a similar share in the three districts in each of his campaigns.

SECOND DISTRICT

George Holding (R)

Elected 2012, 3rd term; b. Apr 17, 1968, Raleigh; Wake Forest University (NC), B.A., 1991; University of Saint Andrews (Scotland), Att., 1992; Wake Forest University (NC), J.D., 1996; Baptist; Married (Lucy E. Herriott); 4 children.

Professional Career: Practicing lawyer, 1996-1999; Legislative aide, Sen. Jesse Helms, 1999-2001; Practicing lawyer, 2001-2002; Assistant U.S. Attorney, E. District of NC, 2002-2006; U.S. Attorney, E. District of NC, 2006-2011.

DC Office: 1110 LHOB 20515, 202-225-3032, Fax: 202-225-0181, holding.house.gov.

Committees: *Ways & Means*: Oversight, Tax Policy, Trade.

Group Ratings

	ADA	ACLU	AFL-CIO	LCV	ITI	COC	HAFA	ACU	CFG	FRC
2016	-	5%	-	0%	100%	100%	89%	96%	95%	100%
2015	0%	C	0%	0%	C	65%	C	100%	90%	100%

Almanac Ratings 2015

	Economy	Social	Foreign	Composite
Liberal	0%	0%	0%	0%
Conservative	100%	100%	100%	100%

Key Votes of the 114th Congress

1. Keystone Pipeline	Y	5. Puerto Rico Debt	N	9. Offenses by Aliens	Y
2. Trade Deals	Y	6. Medical Marijuana	N	10. Troops in Iraq	N
3. Export-Import Bank	N	7. Sanctuary Cities	Y	11. Homeland Security $$	N
4. Debt Ceiling Increase	N	8. Armor-piercing Bullets	Y	12. Trade Adjustment aid	N

Election Results

Election	Name (Party)	Vote (%)		Cand. Spent	Ind. Exp. Support	Ind. Exp. Oppose
2016 General	George Holding (R)	221,485	(57%)	$2,558,940	$216,847	
	John McNeil (D)	169,082	(43%)	$76,995	$1	
2016 Primary	George Holding (R)	16,999	(53%)			
	Renee Ellmers (R)	7,527	(24%)			
	Greg Brannon (R)	7,320	(23%)			

Prior winning percentages: 2014 (57%), 2012 (57%)

Former federal prosecutor George Holding, elected in 2012, has been blessed with many good breaks in his political career. Redistricting that year all but guaranteed Republican success and led five-term Democratic Rep. Brad Miller to retire. Another redistricting in 2016 created an unusual clash in the middle of the decennial cycle. Holding survived the kind of contest that many House members most fear: a redistricting-forced matchup with a member from the same party. His challenge was from the more senior and outspoken Rep. Renee Ellmers. Instead, she faced numerous obstacles. The biggest plus for Holding was that the new district contained far more of his former 13th District than of Ellmers's former 2nd District. He won in a rout.

Holding grew up in Raleigh in a wealthy family. He gave his first public speech at age 11 to dedicate a statue of his recently deceased father, a prominent banker. He entered Massachusetts' prestigious Groton School and graduated from Wake Forest University. During those years, Holding developed an interest in conservative ideas and worked as a summer intern for his state's conservative Republican Sen. Jesse Helms. After Holding graduated from Wake Forest law school, he clerked for a federal judge and worked at a law firm. He re-joined Helms as a legislative counsel, where he concentrated on business, tax and tobacco issues.

In 2006, President George W. Bush nominated him as U.S. attorney for eastern North Carolina, an office where Holding had served as assistant U.S. attorney. His territory included Raleigh, which led to prosecution of numerous politicians, including former Gov. Mike Easley for campaign finance irregularities, and former state House Speaker Jim Black for accepting illegal funds. His most prominent case was that of former Democratic Sen. John Edwards, and the nearly $1 million that his supporters paid to Edwards' mistress, Rielle Hunter, during his 2008 presidential campaign. Holding initiated the prosecution against Edwards but resigned to run for Congress before the case was argued in court. In June 2012, a jury deadlocked on five of the six felony counts, prompting the Justice Department to drop the charges. Holding, defending the prosecution, said that Edwards' conduct called out for action.

His campaign for the open House seat turned acrimonious. Holding's chief opponent in the primary was Wake County Commission Chairman Paul Coble, a nephew of Helms. Coble accused Holding of politicizing Edwards' indictment and set up a website accusing Holding of taking "dirty money" from trial lawyers who supported President Barack Obama's Affordable Care Act. Holding's massive financial advantage of more than 6-to-1, including $319,000 in self-financing, helped him notch a victory, 44%-34%.

In the general election, Democrat Charles Malone accused Holding of being "surrounded by wealth" and therefore out of touch. Malone raised only $18,000, about 1 percent of his opponent's $1.7 million, and his message had little resonance. Holding won, 57%-43%.

Holding fit comfortably in the Republican establishment. His *Almanac* vote ratings for 2015 ranked him among the five most conservative members of the House. He took an interest in India, meeting there with President Narendra Modi, and became co-chairman of the India Caucus. In a significant career move, he won a seat on the Ways and Means Committee and set tax reform as a top priority, "including closing loopholes and stopping fraud." In April 2015, the House approved by voice vote his IRS Bureaucracy Reduction and Judicial Review Act, which he said would streamline Internal Revenue Service reviews by "allowing groups to declare their tax-exempt status rather than wait for endless amounts of time to gain approval." He called the IRS "an agency in turmoil." In February 2017, he wrote that reshuffling the IRS was a major part of the Republican plan to fix the tax code. "Taxpayers deserve an IRS that is responsive, transparent, and above all, accountable," he wrote on the Breitbart website.

When the Republican-controlled state Legislature in late February 2016 approved the new redistricting plan for North Carolina, in response to a court order, it postponed the House primaries until early June. At another time, Ellmers had a political biography that might have been successful. She entered the House following her victory in 2010 over Democratic Rep. Bob Etheridge and quickly became a Republican leadership ally, with several prime assignments.

Instead, Holding must have been amazed at his good fortune. Ellmers confronted a nightmarish set of circumstances: no obvious district in which to run, a brief interval for the campaign, her occasional splits with Republican dogma, Holding's $1.4 million fundraising advantage plus more than $1 million in support from GOP and conservative groups. In addition, Rep. Walter Jones of North Carolina a few months earlier had spurred a notably public whisper campaign about an alleged affair between Ellmers and House Majority Leader Kevin McCarthy, which each of them denied.

Ellmers got a late and uneventful endorsement from Donald Trump, who was the presumptive GOP presidential nominee at that time. She had earlier endorsed his candidacy.

The campaign dynamics created an unexpectedly easy victory for Holding, who got 53 percent of the vote to 24 percent for Ellmers and 23 percent for Greg Brannon, a physician and tea party favorite who had lost primaries to each of the state's GOP Senators. Ellmers led slightly in her base of Harnett County. In the five other counties, the vote for Holding exceeded the combined total for his two opponents. In the general election, he ran TV ads that called his little-known Democratic opponent, Marine Corps veteran John McNeil, an "odd duck" who raised chickens and supported Bernie Sanders for president. Holding led in each county and won, 57%-43%. He has an apparently safe seat, at least until the next redistricting.

East-Central North Carolina: Raleigh Metro, Rocky Mount

Demographics data for new House districts were not prepared by the Census Bureau prior to our editorial deadline.

Voter Turnout

2016 House Turnout as % CVAP	N/A	2016 House turnout	390,567

2012 Presidential Vote information unavailable due to recent redistricting.

2016 Presidential Vote

Donald Trump	210,842	(53%)
Hillary Clinton	172,612	(43%)
Gary Johnson	12,564	(3%)

Cook Partisan Voting Index: R+7

A generation ago, Raleigh was a sleepy state capital, moderately prosperous but not very big or showy, while the small cities to the east, such as Rocky Mount, had economies built around tobacco and textile factories, the railroad and later Interstate 95. Just a few miles from the center of town, farm fields started, dotted by country towns with barbecue restaurants and churches. Today, the booming metropolitan areas of North Carolina have spread far beyond the old city and county lines into the adjacent counties. Wake County, which includes Raleigh, grew 67 percent between 2000 and 2015, a population exceeding 1 million; Raleigh is about 45 percent of the total and also is fast-growing. Once-rural roads are clogged in the morning with commuters headed for jobs in new office parks, and income levels have risen far above what they once were. Raleigh is 29 percent African American, compared with 21 percent for the county.

Much of this territory makes up the 2nd Congressional District of North Carolina. Nearly half of its residents live in Wake County. Republican redistricters revised its lines in 2012 (when it was the 13th District) and again in 2016 to remove downtown Raleigh and add Republican areas outside Wake County. Roseville is a fast-growing boom town in northern Wake County, where farmlands have been converted in a few years into subdivisions and commercial development. Raleigh has long had an active Lebanese community, which celebrates an annual cultural festival. Zebulon is a growing business area, including the pharmaceutical firm GlaxoSmithKline that employs about 1,000 and produces respiratory drugs and inhalers. The new 2nd draws in the affluent Republican suburbs and exurbs that surround Raleigh, such as Wake Forest and Holly Springs. In the 2012 redistricting, about two-thirds of the residents were in Wake.

The district extends to a collection of crossroads towns such as Smithfield in Johnston County and Dunn in Harnett. The new 2nd absorbed suburban Harnett County and the southwest corner of Wake from the old 2nd, but little else from that district. Rocky Mount in Nash County is in the 2nd; the eastern part of Rocky Mount, in Edgecombe County in the 1st District, has more poverty and a lower per capita income. Overall, the district's voters lean solidly Republican, as is the case with each of the state's 10 re-drawn GOP-held districts. In 2016, Donald Trump won 53 percent. The GOP presidential nominees got 54 percent in 2008 and 56 percent in 2012, when this was the modestly different 13th District.

THIRD DISTRICT

Walter Jones (R)

Elected 1994, 12th term; b. Feb 10, 1943, Farmville; Hargrave Military Academy (VA), 1961; North Carolina State University, Att., 1965; Atlantic Christian College (NC), B.A., 1966; Catholic; Married (Joe Anne Whitehurst Jones); 1 child.

Military Career: NC National Guard, 1967-1971.

Elected Office: NC House, 1982-1992.

Professional Career: Manager, Walter B. Jones Office Supply Co., 1967- 73; Salesman, Dunn Association, 1973-1982; President, Benefit Reserves Inc., 1989- 94; President, Judson Co., 1990-1994.

DC Office: 2333 RHOB 20515, 202-225-3415, Fax: 202-225-3286, jones.house.gov.

State Offices: Greenville, 800-351-1697; Havelock, 252-565-6846; Jacksonville, 252-565-6846.

Committees: *Armed Services*: Military Personnel, Tactical Air & Land Forces.

Group Ratings

	ADA	ACLU	AFL-CIO	LCV	ITI	COC	HAFA	ACU	CFG	FRC
2016	-	35%	-	21%	20%	75%	85%	96%	94%	92%
2015	40%	C	25%	17%	C	20%	C	88%	76%	67%

Almanac Ratings 2015

	Economy	Social	Foreign	Composite
Liberal	45%	20%	42%	36%
Conservative	55%	80%	58%	64%

Key Votes of the 114th Congress

1. Keystone Pipeline	Y	5. Puerto Rico Debt	N	9. Offenses by Aliens	Y
2. Trade Deals	N	6. Medical Marijuana	Y	10. Troops in Iraq	Y
3. Export-Import Bank	N	7. Sanctuary Cities	Y	11. Homeland Security $$	N
4. Debt Ceiling Increase	N	8. Armor-piercing Bullets	Y	12. Trade Adjustment aid	N

Election Results

Election	Name (Party)	Vote (%)		Cand. Spent	Ind. Exp. Support	Ind. Exp. Oppose
2016 General	Walter Jones (R)	217,531	(67%)	$616,701	$17,004	
	Ernest Reeves (D)	106,170	(33%)			
2016 Primary	Walter Jones (R)	15,722	(65%)			
	Phil Law (R)	4,929	(20%)			
	Taylor Griffin (R)	3,599	(15%)			

Prior winning percentages: 2014 (68%), 2012 (63%), 2010 (72%), 2008 (66%), 2006 (69%), 2004 (71%), 2002 (91%), 2000 (61%), 1998 (62%), 1996 (63%), 1994 (53%)

Republican Walter Jones, first elected in 1994, has survived as one of his party's leading iconoclasts against campaigns by party regulars to take him out. An evangelical Christian and devout social conservative, he has been the GOP's most fervently antiwar House member and happens to represent many military members and retirees. As party leaders often treat him as an outcast, Jones has shown little regret.

Jones grew up in eastern North Carolina, attended North Carolina State and Atlantic Christian College, and served in the National Guard. His father, Walter Jones Sr., was a Democratic representative with a similar district. The senior Jones served for a quarter-century and chaired the Merchant Marine and Fisheries Committee. The younger Jones, then a Democrat, was elected in 1982 to the state House, where he often broke with party leaders.

In 1992, he ran in the new black-majority 1st District after his father retired. He led the primary with 38 percent but lost the runoff to Democrat Eva Clayton, an African American who got 55 percent to Jones' 45 percent. In April 1993, the resourceful Jones switched to the Republican Party to run in the 3rd District. This pitted him against four-term Rep. Martin Lancaster, a Democrat who had worked earnestly on local projects. But Lancaster voted for President Bill Clinton's budget and tax bills and his crime legislation, while failing to persuade Clinton to drop the cigarette tax from health care legislation. Jones ran an ad showing Lancaster jogging with Clinton, with the voiceover message: "How'd Martin Lancaster get so out of touch? Well, look who he's running around with in Washington." Jones won 53%-47%.

Jones' voting record began consistently conservative and hawkish, but over the years has moderated. In the *Almanac* vote ratings for 2015, he ranked as the second-most liberal Republican in the House, behind Rep. Bob Dold of Illinois, who lost reelection. Jones underwent a remarkable reversal on the war in Iraq. He voted in 2002 to authorize the use of force in Iraq, as did all but six House Republicans. Not long afterward, he was profoundly affected by a local Marine's funeral, setting the stage for an unlikely conversion to passionate war critic.

As the war dragged on, Jones supported Democratic proposals for a timetable to withdraw troops from Iraq, and he opposed President George W. Bush's troop surge. He drew the line at a Democratic plan to attach conditions to future war funding, saying that attempts to "starve" the war to bring it to a close were wrong. Jones began writing letters to the families of every soldier killed in Iraq and Afghanistan, calling them his "mea culpa to my Lord" for voting for the war.

His independence from his party has cost him top Republican posts on the Armed Services Committee. After punishment by GOP leaders, Democrats approached Jones about switching parties, but he declined, saying his opposition to abortion rights would make him ill at ease in the party. House Republican leaders, again exasperated with Jones, kicked him off the Financial Services Committee after the 2012 election; GOP leadership aides said it wasn't because of ideology but because he had not raised enough campaign money for the party. Jones retained his seat on Armed Services, but without a subcommittee chairmanship.

If anything, his political independence has increased. Jones twice refused to support John Boehner for House Speaker, casting his vote in 2013 for former Comptroller General David Walker, a deficit hawk, and in 2015 for Republican Rep. Dan Webster of Florida. After the Supreme Court's *Citizens United* decision on campaign finance, he co-sponsored a bill backed by President Barack Obama aimed at restricting corporate spending on campaign ads. When Majority Leader Kevin McCarthy ran for Speaker in October 2015 after Boehner announced his decision to resign, Jones went public with unproven allegations that McCarthy had had an affair with Rep. Renee Ellmers of North Carolina. "I have had many people in the district tell me I did the right thing," Jones told *Politico*. Ellmers lost the Republican primary in 2016. In February 2017, he was the only Republican to join House Democrats in backing a bipartisan commission to investigate charges of Russian interference in the 2016 presidential election.

He took a variety of steps to voice his anti-war concerns. In 2011, he got the Pentagon to investigate substandard mental health treatment for soldiers returning from Iraq and Afghanistan to Camp Lejeune. With Democratic Rep. Jim McGovern of Massachusetts, Jones organized a constitutional war study group to promote discussion of congressional powers. In 2015, they urged House action on Obama's request for an authorization of military force against the Islamic State. In February 2017, he was the only Republican to sign a Democratic letter stating that continued military action against the Islamic State should require a congressional vote.

At home, Jones occasionally has joined battles on local cultural matters. He called for the state school superintendent to remove from an elementary school a book about two gay princes who get married, and he complained in 2013 about a federal grant to Craven Community College to acquire 25 books and a DVD series educating Americans about Muslim culture.

His outspoken criticism of the Iraq war brought Jones a serious primary challenge in 2008 from Onslow County Commissioner Joe McLaughlin, a former Army Ranger. McLaughlin called Jones "a poster boy for the Left." Jones seemed to benefit from Iraq fatigue among voters, even among military families; he won, 59%-41%. In the 2014 primary, he faced Taylor Griffin, a native of eastern North Carolina who worked more than a decade in Washington, both in government and as a lobbyist, and returned home to challenge Jones as too close to Obama in his views. The margin narrowed to 51%-45%. Two years later, Phil Law, a supervisor for Hewlett-Packard who earlier served four years in the Marines, joined Griffin in challenging Jones. The two both ran active campaigns and raised a total of nearly $500,000; Jones raised $673,000. A month before the vote, Jones told a Washington reporter for McClatchy that the contest would be "close – but I think we're going to be OK." Jones won an unexpectedly large 65 percent of the vote, and led the combined vote of his two opponents in each of the 17 counties.

Coastal North Carolina: Jacksonville, Outer Banks

Demographics data for new House districts were not prepared by the Census Bureau prior to our editorial deadline.

Voter Turnout			
2016 House Turnout as % CVAP	N/A	2016 House turnout	323,701

2012 Presidential Vote information unavailable due to recent redistricting.

2016 Presidential Vote		
Donald Trump	198,972	(60%)
Hillary Clinton	120,964	(37%)
Gary Johnson	8,490	(3%)

Cook Partisan Voting Index: R+12

Nearly 500 years ago, Giovanni da Verrazzano, a Florentine explorer under the flag of France, sailed past the Gulf Stream and landed on a sand-spit island he thought was the outer edge of China. It was the Outer Banks of North Carolina. These are probably America's most unstable barrier islands, constantly changing shape and cut by new inlets as they are battered by ocean currents and storm winds. The islands were settled early by Europeans. Sir Walter Raleigh's Roanoke colony was founded here in 1587, near present-day Manteo, then vanished shortly thereafter when supply ships diverted themselves to loot Spanish galleons rather than deliver their badly needed cargo. Edward Teach, better known as Blackbeard, and other pirates lurked in Pamlico and Albemarle sounds behind the islets.

History is very much alive on the Outer Banks. An antique form of English is spoken by some on Ocracoke Island, reachable only by ferry and largely insulated from the commercialization of the upper islands. A pack of about 100 feral horses - believed to be the last remaining descendants of late-16th century Spanish mustangs - roams free in a 12,000-acre sanctuary in Corolla; fears of their extinction have led the Fish and Wildlife Service to OK the introduction of other horses. The 208-foot lighthouse on Cape Hatteras, America's tallest, looks out on some of the most treacherous currents in the Atlantic. The sands along Kitty Hawk, with their winds, brought the Wright brothers to the Outer Banks to undertake mankind's first heavier-than-air flight in December 1903. The Outer Banks are prime vacation and retirement country, with affluent beachfront communities on both the coastal and sound side. Kill Devil Hills has the most millionaires per capita in the state. In 2016, the Obama administration made plans for off-shore wind leases near Kitty Hawk. In February 2017, the largest wind farm in the Southeast began operations on land near Elizabeth City, with 104 turbines. Rising sea levels on the Outer Banks have raised concerns by residents and activists worried about climate change.

Inland, vestiges of the area's 18th-century past can be seen in New Bern with its reconstructed Tryon Palace, the governor's house when this was the capital, and in the tiny, well-preserved town of Edenton on Albemarle Sound, where 51 women in 1774 protested the taxing of tea and cloth. It is considered the first women's political protest on American shores. Further south, amid swamps outside of Jacksonville, is the Marine Corps' Camp Lejeune. With its 14 miles of beachfront and 80 live-fire ranges, it is home base for about 40,000 enlisted Marines and officers, and the Corps' largest base. On the other side of the Croatan National Forest is Cherry Point, the world's largest Marine Corps air station.

The 3rd Congressional District of North Carolina covers the Outer Banks and the coastal plain of North Carolina from the Virginia border nearly to Wilmington. With straighter boundaries in the coastal plain, redistricting in 2016 added Elizabeth City and Washington; the 3rd no longer has minority communities in Wilmington. The three largest counties are inland: Onslow, Craven and Pitt (which is shared with the 1st District). The redistricting shifts had little impact on the presidential vote, which has been about 60 percent Republican in the past two elections.

FOURTH DISTRICT

David Price (D)

Elected 1996, 15th term; b. Aug 17, 1940, Erwin, TN; Mars Hill College (NC), Att., 1959; University of North Carolina, Chapel Hill, B.A., 1961; Yale University (CT); b.D., 1964; Yale University (CT), Ph.D., 1969; Baptist; Married (Lisa Kanwit Price); 2 children; 2 grandchildren.

Elected Office: U.S. House, 1986-1994.

Professional Career: Legislative aide, U.S. Sen. Bartlett, 1963-1967; Professor, Yale University, 1969-1973, Duke University, 1973-1986, 1995-1996; Executive Director, NC Dem. Party, 1979-1980, Chairman, 1983-1984; Staff Director, DNC Comm. on President Nominations, 1981-1982.

DC Office: 2108 RHOB 20515, 202-225-1784, Fax: 202-225-2014, price.house.gov.

State Offices: Chapel Hill, 919-967-7924; Raleigh, 919-859-5999.

Committees: *Appropriations*: Homeland Security, State, Foreign Operations & Related Programs, Transportation, HUD & Related Agencies (RMM).

Group Ratings

	ADA	ACLU	AFL-CIO	LCV	ITI	COC	HAFA	ACU	CFG	FRC
2016	-	100%	-	100%	67%	54%	10%	96%	0%	0%
2015	100%	C	100%	100%	C	50%	C	4%	0%	0%

Almanac Ratings 2015

	Economy	Social	Foreign	Composite
Liberal	95%	100%	93%	96%
Conservative	6%	0%	7%	4%

Key Votes of the 114th Congress

1. Keystone Pipeline	N	5. Puerto Rico Debt	Y	9. Offenses by Aliens	N
2. Trade Deals	N	6. Medical Marijuana	Y	10. Troops in Iraq	N
3. Export-Import Bank	Y	7. Sanctuary Cities	N	11. Homeland Security $$	Y
4. Debt Ceiling Increase	Y	8. Armor-piercing Bullets	N	12. Trade Adjustment aid	Y

Election Results

Election	Name (Party)	Vote (%)	Cand. Spent	Ind. Exp. Support	Ind. Exp. Oppose
2016 General	David Price (D)	279,380 (68%)	$517,549	$1	
	Sue Googe (R)	130,161 (32%)	$76,273		
2016 Primary	David Price (D)	(100%)			

Prior winning percentages: 2014 (75%), 2012 (75%), 2010 (57%), 2008 (63%), 2006 (65%), 2004 (64%), 2002 (61%), 2000 (62%), 1998 (57%), 1996 (54%%),1992 (65%), 1990 (58%), 1988 (58%), 1986 (56%)

Democrat David Price was first elected in 1986, lost the seat in 1994, and regained it in 1996. Since his return, he has distinguished himself as an influential spender and a thoughtful voice on education and science issues. A long-time political science professor, Price has remained a working scholar who has shared his insights on Congress. He is among the 15 longest-serving House Democrats.

Price grew up in East Tennessee, the son of a school principal and an English teacher. He is an interesting blend of political scientist, practical politician and lay Baptist preacher. He attended the University of North Carolina at Chapel Hill, worked as a young aide on Capitol Hill, earned a degree in divinity and a doctorate in political science at Yale University, and taught there for four years. In 1973, he became a political science professor at Duke. He was executive director of the North Carolina Democratic Party in the 1980 election season and chairman in 1983-84. With Democratic Gov. Jim Hunt, Price helped develop North Carolina's robust straight-ticket politics.

In 1986, he ran for the House and beat Republican freshman Rep. Bill Cobey. In 1994, Price lost the seat, 50.4%-49.6%, to Fred Heineman, a former New York City police officer and Raleigh police chief in the 1970s. Two years later, Price outspent Heineman in a rematch, winning 54%-44%.

Price has written four books about Congress, including *The Congressional Experience*, which focuses on his life as a lawmaker. That book was first published in 1992, with two subsequent editions. The polarization of the two chambers has made him pessimistic about finding agreement to solve the nation's fiscal problems. "Our capacity to take them on in the bipartisan fashion that history teaches us is almost always necessary is far weaker" than it was in the 1990s, he said in 2010. Circumstances subsequently proved him correct, and they have worsened.

His Education Affordability Act, which he considers his proudest achievement, was folded into the 1997 Balanced Budget Act. It made interest on student loans tax-deductible and allowed penalty-free withdrawals from individual retirement accounts for education expenses. Price founded and has served as the senior Democrat on the House Democracy Partnership, a bipartisan, 20-member commission that seeks to strengthen democracy by mentoring 14 legislatures across the world.

From 2007 through 2010, Price chaired the Homeland Security Appropriations Subcommittee. He sought higher levels of spending for homeland security measures, like support for first responders, than were requested by the Bush administration. In 2007, the House passed Price's bill establishing a code of conduct for private security contractors in Iraq and Afghanistan. A target of the bill was North Carolina-based Blackwater, whose controversial activities in Iraq included the shooting of 17 people in a Baghdad square. After President Barack Obama took office, Price crafted spending bills that rejected the administration's proposal to hold criminal trials for terror suspects in New York City and restored budget cuts that the administration had made to the Coast Guard. In 2010, he called increased drug trafficking and violence on the U.S. border "an emergency" that merited as much attention as the wars in Afghanistan and Iraq. He became the subcommittee's ranking member with Democrats in the minority.

In 2015, Price switched to ranking Democrat on the Transportation, HUD Appropriations Subcommittee. He joined a bipartisan group of senior appropriators who strongly opposed a proposal from the Transportation and Infrastructure Committee to create a separate air traffic organization outside of the Federal Aviation Administration and removed from the annual appropriations process. The oversight and funding role of Congress, they wrote, was critical "in the operation of our nation's air traffic system." In December 2016, Price took credit for extensive disaster-relief aid for North Carolina following the devastation of Hurricane Matthew. Otherwise, he said, the enactment of a continuing resolution for the next four months was "an unfortunate decision by House Republican leadership to abandon the appropriations bills we negotiated on a bipartisan basis in favor of yet another stopgap measure."

Price has been active on campaign finance law. He sponsored the "stand by your ad" requirement for candidates to appear in the full frame of television ads reading their disclaimers on the air, so they would more likely be held responsible for negative ads. His proposal was enacted in the 2002 campaign reform law. He has sought a similar requirement for internet ads and said the Supreme Court's *Citizens United* decision allowing unlimited spending by corporations, labor unions and wealthy individuals contributed to the flow of misleading ads. "The least we can do is inform viewers who has bought the ads they are seeing," he said. In a 2015 column co-authored by Democratic Rep. Chris van Hollen of Maryland, Price promoted their bill to clarify and strengthen the ban on candidate coordination with outside spending groups. "The unchecked and rapid rise of new organizations solely designed to circumvent campaign finance law should be a call to action for Congress," they wrote in *The Hill*.

Price has nurtured local projects for appropriations support, including $272 million for a new Environmental Protection Agency complex in Research Triangle Park, plus defense- and technology-related programs for colleges in his district. He helped to get the Obama administration's support for $545 million in North Carolina's Raleigh-to-Charlotte high-speed rail corridor. He voiced regret that such funding has become more difficult to secure. Speaking to UNC researchers in 2014, he said, "I've never seen things so locked up in terms of some people just having the ideology that will not let them bend. That's pretty unusual in American politics," the *Daily Tarheel* reported. In 2016, he took the lead in seeking to relax restrictions on the Centers for Disease Control and Prevention to conduct research on gun violence.

Since his return to the House in 1996, Price has been reelected by wide margins. After Democratic Rep. Brad Miller decided to retire rather than face Price in a primary following the 2012 redistricting, he had a secure seat, at least until the redistricting in 2022.

Research Triangle: Raleigh, Chapel Hill

Demographics data for new House districts were not prepared by the Census Bureau prior to our editorial deadline.

Voter Turnout

2016 House Turnout as % CVAP	N/A	2016 House turnout	409,541

2012 Presidential Vote information unavailable due to recent redistricting.

2016 Presidential Vote

Hillary Clinton	281,535	(67%)
Donald Trump	116,368	(28%)
Gary Johnson	14,632	(4%)

Cook Partisan Voting Index: D+17

Back in the 1950s, few people would have predicted that the countryside around Raleigh and Durham would become one of America's high-tech boom areas. But Democratic Gov. Luther Hodges did, and he started the 6,900-acre Research Triangle Park as a research and development industrial park between the musty state capital of Raleigh and the Lucky Strike-manufacturing city of Durham. With the drawing power of three universities - North Carolina State in Raleigh, Duke in Durham, and the University of North Carolina in Chapel Hill - Research Triangle Park slowly began attracting top R&D organizations, which in turn spawned a dynamic entrepreneurial sector. Today, this is among the top tech centers in the nation, with big-name employers that include IBM, Cisco Systems, GlaxoSmithKline, Fidelity and RTI International. Nearly half of the 2,000 employers are in biotech or life sciences. A sleepy metro area that once trailed the nation in income is now a vibrant, affluent metropolis and the prime engine of North Carolina's growth. The Triangle has one of the highest concentrations of Ph.D.s in the nation, many earning livelihoods in academia, the sciences, and social services. After years of planning, local officials revised the new transit system for the area from light-rail to diesel, and added bus service in dedicated lanes. In 2011, voters in Durham approved a half-cent sales tax to help pay for it. Voters in Wake County narrowly approved a similar tax hike in 2016.

Still, the region prides itself on its homier touches. Barbecue is a serious business here. The state is split between proponents of Eastern Carolina barbecue (vinegar-based) and Lexington style (vinegar-plus-tomato), and controversy engulfed the statehouse when bills were introduced to declare the Lexington Barbecue Festival the state's official festival. The all-you-can-eat buffet at Bullock's in Durham is a regular stop for celebrities and politicians. College basketball is the other major preoccupation here, and UNC, N.C. State, and Duke (in the neighboring 1st District) have fielded more March Madness contenders than any similarly sized area. UNC has reached the Final Four more often than any other team, and claimed its sixth national title in 2017.

The combination of upscale and down-home has proved to be a popular draw. From 1990 to 2014, the Raleigh-Durham-Cary "combined statistical area" (in new Census Bureau jargon) more than doubled in population, from 855,000 to 2.1 million. Many of the new arrivals are from the North; locals joke that the fast-growing town of Cary is an acronym for "Containment Area for Retired Yankees." The new arrivals are changing the politics of the region as well. Just as Northern immigrants helped bring Republicanism to the South in the 1950s and 1960s, today they have made this the most heavily Democratic region in the state.

The 4th Congressional District of North Carolina is the core of the Research Triangle, with almost two-thirds of Raleigh-based Wake County, a small tuck in the southern part of Durham County and all of Orange County, which includes Chapel Hill. About four-fifths of the residents are in Wake, which grew 16 percent from 2010 to 2016. In 2015, Raleigh was the 16th fastest-growing metro area in the nation. The new redistricting made the district more compact, as it removed arms that had extended north into Burlington and south to the Democratic portions of Fayetteville. The 4th -- 32 percent black and 12 percent Hispanic -- is the most heavily Democratic district with a non-Hispanic white majority population in the South. The district elects the only white House Democrat in a coastal state between northern Virginia and Orlando. Like the minority-majority 1st and 12th districts, the latest version of this district has continued to accentuate its Democratic vote, though it is far less gerrymandered. The vote for President Barack Obama in 2012 dropped from 72 percent under the old lines to 65 percent with the new lines. Hillary Clinton increased the Democratic vote to 67 percent in 2016.

FIFTH DISTRICT

Virginia Foxx (R)

Elected 2004, 7th term; b. Jun 29, 1943, Bronx, NY; Lees McRae College (NC), 1961; Appalachian State Teachers College (NC), Att., 1963; University of North Carolina, Chapel Hill, Bach. Deg., 1968; University of North Carolina, Chapel Hill, M.A., 1972; University of North Carolina, Greensboro, Ed.D., 1985; Roman Catholic; Married (Thomas A. Foxx); 1 child; 2 grandchildren.

Elected Office: Watauga Board of Education, 1976-1988; NC Senate, 1994-2004.

Professional Career: Owner, Grandfather Mountain Nursery, 1976-2004; Professor, Assistant Dean of General College, Appalachian St. University, 1976-1985; President, May-land CC, 1987-1994.

DC Office: 2262 RHOB 20515, 202-225-2071, Fax: 202-225-2995, foxx.house.gov.
State Offices: Boone, 828-265-0240; Clemmons, 336-778-0211.
Committees: *Education & the Workforce (Chmn). Oversight & Government Reform*: Intergovernmental Affairs, National Security.

Group Ratings

	ADA	ACLU	AFL-CIO	LCV	ITI	COC	HAFA	ACU	CFG	FRC
2016	-	17%	-	0%	100%	100%	67%	96%	86%	100%
2015	0%	C	0%	0%	C	75%	C	83%	73%	100%

Almanac Ratings 2015

	Economy	Social	Foreign	Composite
Liberal	3%	0%	0%	1%
Conservative	97%	100%	100%	99%

Key Votes of the 114th Congress

1. Keystone Pipeline	Y	5. Puerto Rico Debt	Y	9. Offenses by Aliens	Y
2. Trade Deals	Y	6. Medical Marijuana	N	10. Troops in Iraq	N
3. Export-Import Bank	N	7. Sanctuary Cities	Y	11. Homeland Security $$	N
4. Debt Ceiling Increase	N	8. Armor-piercing Bullets	Y	12. Trade Adjustment aid	N

Election Results

Election	Name (Party)	Vote (%)		Cand. Spent	Ind. Exp. Support	Ind. Exp. Oppose
2016 General	Virginia Foxx (R)	207,625	(58%)	$1,176,774		
	Josh Brannon (D)	147,887	(42%)		$1	
2016 Primary	Virginia Foxx (R)	17,083	(68%)			
	Pattie Curran (R)	8,035	(32%)			

Prior winning percentages: 2014 (61%), 2012 (58%), 2010 (66%), 2008 (58%), 2006 (57%), 2004 (59%)

Republican Virginia Foxx, first elected in 2004, is a vocal conservative who has been savvy in gaining influence. She held a Republican leadership position for four years, and moved up in 2017 as chair of the House Education and the Workforce Committee. A former teacher and university administrator, she pledged to cut back on federal rules and return education policy to a more traditional state-federal relationship. Although liberal critics dismiss her as a loose cannon, she has raised herself by the boot straps and moved into a position to influence major social–policy changes.

Foxx grew up in the hardscrabble hollows of western North Carolina; she lived in a home that didn't have running water or electricity until she was 14. She got her bachelor's in English from the University of North Carolina in Chapel Hill and her doctorate in education from UNC-Greensboro, and had a diverse background before she was elected to Congress. She owned with her husband a nursery and landscape company, and she taught sociology and was assistant dean of the General College at Appalachian State University. Later, she was president of Mayland Community College. She served 12 years on the Board of Education of Watauga County. In 1994, Foxx was elected to the state Senate, where she served 10 years and sponsored a constitutional amendment to ban same-sex marriage and a bill to deny Social Security benefits to undocumented immigrants. She actively supported gun rights and home schooling, and she opposed abortion rights.

In 2004, Foxx was one of five candidates in a hotly contested Republican primary for an open seat. Winston-Salem Councilman Vernon Robinson, a retired Air Force officer who campaigned as "the black Jesse Helms," finished first with 24 percent of the vote. Foxx was second, with 22 percent, just 511 votes ahead of Ed Broyhill, the son of former Republican Sen. James Broyhill. In a hard-fought, four-week runoff campaign, Robinson aired several controversial ads highlighting his tough position on illegal immigrants. Foxx warned voters that Robinson's aggressive style would make him a weak general election candidate who would lose the district for the GOP. She won 55%-45%. In the general election, Foxx won relatively easily, 59%-41%.

Foxx has been close to House GOP leaders and has a solidly conservative voting record. Her *Almanac* vote ratings in 2015 were one vote short of a perfect conservative. She was elected Republican Conference secretary in 2012 when she defeated Rep. Jeff Denham of California to become one of three women to take leadership roles as the party was smarting from its losses on the gender gap in the elections that year.

Foxx has not been afraid to speak her mind in her home-spun style. She was one of only 11 House members who voted against a $52 billion relief bill following Hurricane Katrina in 2005 because, she said, there was too little accountability in how the money would be spent. During the health care debate in 2009, she remarked that the public had more to fear from the legislation than from terrorists. In 2011, she attached an amendment to a House-passed health bill forbidding medical schools from teaching doctors how to perform abortions as a condition of the schools receiving federal grant money. During debate on a hate crimes bill named for Matthew Shepard, a Wyoming man tortured and murdered allegedly because of his sexual orientation, she said naming the bill for Shepard was "a hoax" because, she argued, he wasn't gay. She later apologized. Republican leaders saw her as a useful attack dog and put her on the Rules Committee.

On the Education Committee, Foxx chaired the Higher Education Subcommittee. She has said the Education Department imposes burdensome regulations on colleges. Foxx is an advocate of for-profit colleges and community colleges. Appearing on G. Gordon Liddy's radio show in 2012, she expressed her disdain for people taking out student loans. "I have very little tolerance for people who tell me that they graduate with $200,000 of debt or even $80,000 of debt, because there's no reason for that." President Barack Obama later repeated her remarks at a campaign stop at the University of North Carolina. "Can you imagine saying something like that?" he asked. Despite the rhetoric from both sides, Foxx found common ground with Obama in 2013 during renewal of the student-loan program. They tied the rate to the 10-year Treasury bond in what Foxx termed a "market-based approach."

When Rep. John Kline was term-limited as chairman of the committee and retired in 2016, Rep. Joe Wilson of South Carolina was next in line in seniority. But he said that he was more interested in his work at the Armed Services Committee. Wilson may have seen the handwriting on the wall. Foxx was eager to take the post, had curried favor with GOP leaders and Republicans were about to lose their only woman chair. During the 2016 campaign, Speaker Paul Ryan had tapped her to write the House GOP's "Better Way" campaign platform and she represented House Republicans in the drafting of the party platform at the Republican convention. Foxx won the position without opposition. (As it turned out, Rep. Diane Black of Tennessee unexpectedly became chairwoman of the Budget Committee at the same time as Foxx moved up in January 2017.)

Foxx was unabashed in describing her plans at the committee. In an interview with McClatchy News, she referred to the federal bureaucracy as "the fourth branch of government" and that it needed to be tamed regardless of which party controlled the White House. "Republicans are not anti-government," she said. "We want reasonable rules." She told Politico, "I'm going to push to diminish the role of the federal government in everything it's in that isn't in the Constitution." Her targets have included overtime rules at the Department of Labor, plus restrictions imposed by the National Labor Relations Board. During her first week with the gavel, she filed with Democratic Rep. Henry Cuellar of Texas a bill that required federal regulators to provide more information on possible unfunded mandates imposed on local governments and private-sector employers. The legislation, she said, would "hold Washington bureaucrats accountable for the true cost - in dollars and in jobs - that federal dictates pose to the economy." In March 2017, Foxx was one of three House chairs who brought the leadership-drafted

American Health Care Act to the House floor, where it was pulled because Republican were divided on how to replace Obamacare. After additional tinkering, the bill passed in early May.

In her safely Republican district, Foxx has been reelected by modest margins against low-profile opponents. In 2012, The Winston-Salem Journal, the largest newspaper in her district, endorsed her Democratic challenger, Elisabeth Motsinger. The newspaper said Foxx "has accomplished little" for the district and "represents the calcification of the political process and is therefore an impediment to reasoned political compromise." Regardless, she has remained popular with her political base. In 2016, she was challenged in the Republican primary by Pattie Curran, who said that Foxx had moderated her views. "She's establishment and I'm not," Curran told a local reporter. Foxx won 68 percent of the vote and easily took every county.

Northwest North Carolina: Winston-Salem

Demographics data for new House districts were not prepared by the Census Bureau prior to our editorial deadline.

Voter Turnout

2016 House Turnout as % CVAP	N/A	2016 House turnout	355,512

2012 Presidential Vote information unavailable due to recent redistricting.

2016 Presidential Vote

Donald Trump	205,332	(57%)
Hillary Clinton	142,369	(39%)
Gary Johnson	10,302	(3%)

Cook Partisan Voting Index: R+10

From the Atlantic Ocean, the terrain of North Carolina rises slowly through the Piedmont, a transitional land of modest hills that lies between the coastal plain and the Blue Ridge Mountains. The Blue Ridge, named for the mysterious blue haze that blankets it, provides the headwaters of the New River - somewhat ironically named given that it is the oldest river in North America - which cuts majestic crevasses as it flows north to West Virginia. The lower Piedmont lands of North Carolina were first settled by independent-minded Scots-Irish farmers and by followers of British and German sects like the Moravians. This was hardscrabble farm country before the Civil War, with few slaves. By the late 19th century, it was becoming industrialized, with textile mills alongside streams, furniture factories not far from hardwood forests, and R.J. Reynolds' cigarette factories in the growing city of Winston-Salem.

Today, the Winston-Salem area's pharmaceutical companies, banking institutions and high-skill Piedmont factories have largely supplanted the tobacco industry. At a former R.J. Reynolds Tobacco plant, the booming Wake Forest Innovation Quarter focuses on medical education and biotech research. A smaller and more urban version of the Research Triangle less than 100 miles to the east, it is a broad partnership among the city, state, university and the private developer, with 3,500 workers in more than 60 companies, four colleges with 5,000 students, 650 apartments and lofts, and more growth underway. "The park has transformed from a place of abandoned factories and far-off dreams into a real, tangible work place that's full of multi-million dollar projects," *Winston-Salem Monthly* wrote in August 2016. Arts and entertainment sites are nearby on Trade Street. In August 2016, Caterpillar announced that it would "repurpose" its giant plant from mining to rail equipment. Also headquartered in Winston-Salem is Krispy Kreme Doughnuts.

Aside from Winston-Salem, the region has remained rural. Places of interest include chicken-raising Wilkes County, the remnants of the socks-manufacturing plant of Hanes-Brand in Mount Airy, and Appalachian State University in Boone (named for Daniel), which has become a center for resurgent pride in the culture of Appalachia, a region often the target of either pity or condescension.

All of these places are in the 5th Congressional District. The new 5th includes all of Forsyth County and Winston-Salem, whose minority population previously had been part of the black-majority and Democratic 12th District. Nearly half of the district's residents reside in Forsyth, which is 27 percent black. Hillary Clinton in 2016 won the county, 54%-43%. To the west, the remainder of the district takes in nine counties and a small part of Catawba, with small cities and towns in the heavily Republican Piedmont and mountain areas, none of which accounts for more than 10 percent of the 5th. With the inclusion of the entirety of Forsyth, the district no longer includes the Democratic precincts of

Statesville and Hickory. The only other area of Democratic strength is in Watauga County, with the university. These rural areas have sparse minority population. The district, as a whole, is 13 percent black. Redistricting reduced the Republican presidential vote by about 2 percent, but it remains a solidly GOP district. Donald Trump won 57 percent of the vote in 2016, the same as Mitt Romney four years earlier.

SIXTH DISTRICT

Mark Walker (R)

Elected 2014, 2nd term; b. May 20, 1969, Dothan, AL; Trinity Baptist College (FL), Att., 1988; Houston Community College System, Att., 1990; Piedmont International University (NC), B.A., 1999; Baptist; Married (Kelly Walker); 3 children.

Professional Career: Sales & business Manager, automotive company, 1991-1996; Church minister & official, 1998-2014.

DC Office: 1305 LHOB 20515, 202-225-3065, Fax: 202-225-8611, walker.house.gov.

State Offices: Asheboro, 336-626-3060; Graham, 336-229-0159; Greensboro, 336-333-5005.

Committees: *House Administration. Oversight & Government Reform*: Health Care, Benefits & Administrative Rules, Intergovernmental Affairs.

Group Ratings

	ADA	ACLU	AFL-CIO	LCV	ITI	COC	HAFA	ACU	CFG	FRC
2016	-	11%	-	0%	100%	100%	85%	96%	95%	100%
2015	5%	C	0%	0%	C	65%	C	100%	92%	92%

Almanac Ratings 2015

	Economy	Social	Foreign	Composite
Liberal	5%	9%	0%	5%
Conservative	95%	91%	100%	95%

Key Votes of the 114th Congress

1. Keystone Pipeline	Y	5. Puerto Rico Debt	Y	9. Offenses by Aliens	Y
2. Trade Deals	Y	6. Medical Marijuana	N	10. Troops in Iraq	N
3. Export-Import Bank	N	7. Sanctuary Cities	Y	11. Homeland Security $$	N
4. Debt Ceiling Increase	N	8. Armor-piercing Bullets	Y	12. Trade Adjustment aid	N

Election Results

Election	Name (Party)	Vote (%)		Cand. Spent	Ind. Exp. Support	Ind. Exp. Oppose
2016 General	Mark Walker (R)	207,983	(59%)	$607,140		
	Pete Glidewell (D)	143,167	(41%)	$87,384		$1
2016 Primary	Mark Walker (R)	16,787	(78%)			
	Chris Hardin (R)	4,745	(22%)			

Prior winning percentages: 2014 (59%)

Republican Mark Walker was elected to an open seat in 2014 as an ordained minister who framed his campaign in religious terms and ran as a Washington outsider. He became an influential player as chairman of the Republican Study Committee.

Walker was born in Dothan, Alabama, and grew up in Pensacola, Florida, where his father was a minister. He got his bachelor's degree in religious studies at Piedmont Baptist College. Most of his professional career was spent serving churches in the Greensboro region. He devoted time to helping local and state Republicans in campaigns, and engaging in civic affairs.

The firmly GOP open seat attracted a scrum of nine Republican candidates. The initial front-runner was Phil Berger Jr., the district attorney for Rockingham County and son of a state senator. Boosted by name recognition and endorsements from the GOP establishment, including retiring Rep. Howard Coble, Berger topped the primary field at 34 percent of the vote, with Walker at 25 percent.

In the runoff, Walker built up his campaign base in Guilford County while underscoring his outsider credentials. He rejected signing on to activist Grover Norquist's anti-tax pledge because he said he did not want to be beholden to "a guy in Washington." The race was unusual in that Walker aimed to get the edge on the ground with door-to-door contacts rather than to seek support of national tea party groups, and he pledged to decline money from political action committees. Berger took a more negative approach with his ads, which may have cost him support. With turnout low and much of the vote from the defeated candidates in the primary turning toward the insurgent, Walker won 60%-40%. He took 65 percent in Guilford County, which cast a bit more than half of the vote in the runoff.

The general election was a breeze for Walker in this Republican stronghold. Democratic challenger Laura Fjeld took three counties at the eastern end of the district, but Walker won 59%-41%. Fjeld spent nearly $900,000, which was slightly more than the total that Walker spent in his three contests. Her money appeared to do little more than attract the Democratic base vote.

Walker has seats on the Oversight and Government Reform Committee, and on House Administration, where party leaders typically make sure they can rely on its members to perform housekeeping tasks. Walker was the first freshman Republican to pass a bill in 2015, when the House passed his Human Traffic Detection Act. It was designed to improve the training of workers at the Homeland Security Department to intercept human traffickers and their victims. "We must act to end this unconscionable industry," said Walker, who added that North Carolina was a leading state for the illicit trade.

Walker became an active member of the Republican Study Committee, the mainstream group of House conservatives that has worked more closely with GOP leaders than has the Freedom Caucus. Following the 2016 election, he was successful in an insurgent campaign to chair the group, even though the group's board members initially sided with more experienced Rep. Andy Harris of Maryland. Walker described his ambitious plans: "Looking at the election results, it is clear the American people want to reclaim constitutional principles and reinvigorate our economy. It is unacceptable for us not to deliver on the faith the voters have invested in us."

In an interview about his RSC plans with McClatchy News, Walker said that conservatives should take their message "into places and communities that haven't heard our voices." He pointed out his cooperation with Democratic Rep. Alma Adams of North Carolina to assist historically black colleges and universities. He emphasized the need for Republicans to repeal - and replace - the Affordable Care Act. In those early discussions, he was more cooperative than fellow North Carolina Republican Rep. Mark Meadows, the head of the Freedom Caucus.

In his reelection campaign, Walker got 78 percent of the vote in the Republican primary against Chris Hardin, who criticized "broken campaign promises" by Walker, including his vote in 2015 for John Boehner for House Speaker. In November, Walker faced Pete Glidewell, a textile sales executive who campaigned on his familiarity with the problems of local workers. Walker out-raised Glidewell nearly 10-to-1, and won, 59%-41%. Glidewell won narrowly in Guilford and Chatham counties.

North-Central North Carolina: Greensboro, The Piedmont

Demographics data for new House districts were not prepared by the Census Bureau prior to our editorial deadline.

Voter Turnout			
2016 House Turnout as % CVAP	N/A	2016 House turnout	351,150

2012 Presidential Vote information unavailable due to recent redistricting.

2016 Presidential Vote		
Donald Trump	201,385	(56%)
Hillary Clinton	148,693	(41%)
Gary Johnson	8,741	(2%)

Cook Partisan Voting Index: R+9

The rolling hills of the Piedmont, which are really the foothills of the long ridges of the Appalachian Mountains, are a geographic feature that helped define North Carolina politically. The Piedmont was settled not by the aristocratic planters who typified the Southern lowlands, but by the more hardscrabble Scots-Irish who colonized the Appalachian regions. These settlers clustered in small towns, usually around a mill or a factory. Even today, there isn't a large population center between High Point and the ancient sand dunes in the Sandhills region toward Fayetteville. Instead, the landscape is a collection of small towns, places like Asheboro and Siler City, burial place of Francis Bavier, best known as Aunt Bee on *The Andy Griffith Show*. Wyeth Vaccines is the largest employer in Sanford. Chatham County has ambitious development plans near Pittsboro, including a brewery, hotel and senior housing. Some of these areas have faced hard times. Medical device manufacturer Teleflex had a sizable presence in Asheboro, but it has downsized and planned to shut down in 2017. In Rockingham County, the MillerCoors brewery and the affiliated Ball Cannery were scheduled to close.

The 6th Congressional District of North Carolina takes in these Piedmont towns plus the eastern parts of greater Greensboro, which collectively contain more than half of its residents. Much of Greensboro's downtown has shifted to the 13th District, including the site of the Woolworth's where, on Feb. 1, 1960, four young black men sat down at a segregated lunch counter and asked for coffee. They were refused service, and the ensuing sit-ins helped desegregate the department store's eateries that year. Greensboro-based Guilford County is the chief part of the district that is politically competitive. The remaining residents of the 6th live in Alamance and in a tier of three largely rural counties stretching along the Virginia border from Person in the east to Rockingham in the west.

The redistricting changes reduced the Republican presidential vote in 2008 and 2012 by about two percentage points. This was once a swing area of the state, but now the Piedmont, where about one-third of the district's population lives, is solidly Republican, especially Randolph County. In 2016, Donald Trump got 56 percent, about the same as the vote for Mitt Romney in 2012.

SEVENTH DISTRICT

David Rouzer (R)

Elected 2014, 2nd term; b. Feb 16, 1972, Landstuhl, Germany; Fund for American Studies; North Carolina State University, B.S., 1994; North Carolina State University, B.A., 1994; Southern Baptist; Single.

Elected Office: NC Senate 2009-2012.

Professional Career: PAC coordinator, 1996; Congressional aide, 1996-2000, 2001-2005; University official, 2000-2001; Administrator, U.S. Department of Agriculture, 2005-2006; Owner, consulting company, 2006-present; Owner, cleaning products business, 2009-present.

DC Office: 424 CHOB 20515, 202-225-2731, Fax: 202-225-5773, rouzer.house.gov.

State Offices: Bolivia, 910-253-6111; Four Oaks, 919-938-3040; Wilmington, 910-395-0202.

Committees: *Agriculture*: Biotechnology, Horticulture & Research, Livestock & Foreign Agriculture (Chmn), Nutrition. *Natural Resources*: Federal Lands, Water, Power & Oceans. *Transportation & Infrastructure*: Coast Guard & Maritime Transportation, Highways & Transit, Water Resources & Environment.

Group Ratings

	ADA	ACLU	AFL-CIO	LCV	ITI	COC	HAFA	ACU	CFG	FRC
2016	-	5%	-	0%	100%	100%	75%	96%	83%	100%
2015	0%	C	8%	0%	C	80%	C	92%	75%	100%

Almanac Ratings 2015

	Economy	Social	Foreign	Composite
Liberal	3%	0%	0%	1%
Conservative	97%	100%	100%	99%

Key Votes of the 114th Congress

1. Keystone Pipeline	Y	5. Puerto Rico Debt	N	9. Offenses by Aliens	Y
2. Trade Deals	Y	6. Medical Marijuana	N	10. Troops in Iraq	N
3. Export-Import Bank	N	7. Sanctuary Cities	Y	11. Homeland Security $$	N
4. Debt Ceiling Increase	N	8. Armor-piercing Bullets	Y	12. Trade Adjustment aid	N

Election Results

Election	Name (Party)	Vote (%)	Cand. Spent	Ind. Exp. Support	Ind. Exp. Oppose
2016 General	David Rouzer (R)........................ 211,801	(61%)	$643,022	$218	
	J. Wesley Casteen (D)............... 135,905	(39%)	$14,173		
2016 Primary	David Rouzer (R).....................................	(100%)			

Prior winning percentages: 2014 (59%)

With his election to an open seat in 2014, Republican David Rouzer became the first Republican to represent southeastern North Carolina since the late 19th century. He came close to defeating the Democratic incumbent in 2012, losing by 654 votes. He styled himself as an expert in public relations and legislative strategy, tools that appear to have aided him in becoming quickly entrenched in the district. He benefited from the failure of Democrats to seriously compete.

Rouzer was born in Landstuhl, Germany, and was raised in Durham, North Carolina. He attended North Carolina State University's College of Agriculture, where he received his bachelor's degree in three majors: agricultural business management, agricultural economics and chemistry. He spent much of his career in Washington as an aide to two home-state Republican senators, Jesse Helms and Elizabeth Dole; as a Bush administration appointee in the Agriculture Department; and as a lobbyist for tobacco companies.

During four years in the state Senate, Rouzer co-chaired the Agriculture and Environment Committee. He became known for his vocal support of a North Carolina law banning the state's use of scientific predictions of how much the sea level will rise in developing coastal policy. The law, passed in 2012, drew criticism from environmental groups, which said it amounted to denial of scientific evidence of climate change.

Centrist Democratic Rep. Mike McIntyre was targeted by the GOP in 2014. The independent and once-untouchable incumbent barely survived the 2012 challenge from Rouzer, who had more than $4 million in support from party groups; McIntyre had $1.9 million in party assistance, and spent $2.3 million of his campaign funds. When he announced his retirement after nine terms, the seat became an easy pickup for Republicans, despite a Democratic voter-registration advantage. The real contest was in the primary, where Rouzer's chief opponent was attorney Woody White. They agreed on many issues. Not surprisingly given the stakes, the campaign got nasty: White accused Rouzer of being a Beltway lobbyist, and Rouzer derided White's work as a trial lawyer. With more money, more establishment support and more name recognition, Rouzer won, 53%-40%.

In the general, Rouzer campaigned as an unabashed conservative. As in 2012, Rouzer argued for a strong military, less regulation and a simplified tax code, preferably a flat tax. Democratic nominee Jonathan Barfield, a commissioner in New Hanover County and a local real estate agent, said he did not want to see U.S. boots on the ground in Syria. National Democrats and their allies had no presence in their long-time bastion. Rouzer spent nearly $1.5 million for the entire campaign, compared with $60,000 for Barfield, and won 59%-37%.

Rouzer got a rare chairmanship for a freshman at the Agriculture Subcommittee on Livestock and Foreign Agriculture, which was well-suited to his background. With the current farm bill expiring in September 2018, that panel focused chiefly on oversight and planning during his first term. In 2017, Rouzer picked up the pace. During early hearings, he talked up export promotion and "the overarching benefits that market development funding brings the U.S. agricultural industry as a whole." With livestock, he highlighted the challenges posed by federal regulations and explored modifications that could reduce the harm to farmers. He noted growing concerns about devastating animal diseases and "the linkages between agriculture and national security."

On other issues, Rouzer talked up familiar proposals from the conservative arsenal: shutting down the Education Department and requiring drug tests for welfare recipients. In April 2016, the House passed his bill to prevent the IRS from hiring employees who have failed to meet their own tax obligations.

Rouzer breezed to a routine reelection in 2016 against Wesley Canteen, a CPA and attorney in Wilmington who was uncontested for the Democratic nomination. Casteen had run in the 7th as an independent in 2014 and got 4 percent of the vote. This time, he rallied the Democratic base vote, but little more. Rouzer outraised him nearly 100-to-1 and won, 61%-39%.

Southeast North Carolina: Wilmington, Goldsboro

Demographics data for new House districts were not prepared by the Census Bureau prior to our editorial deadline.

Voter Turnout

2016 House Turnout as % CVAP	N/A	2016 House turnout	347,706

2012 Presidential Vote information unavailable due to recent redistricting.

2016 Presidential Vote

Donald Trump	206,192	(57%)
Hillary Clinton	142,782	(40%)
Gary Johnson	8,950	(3%)

Cook Partisan Voting Index: R+9

At the end of the 19th century, North Carolina's lengthy attachment to the Democratic Party and white supremacy seemed to be weakening. A fusion ticket of Populists and Republicans had taken over the state legislature in 1894, and the state elected a rotund, racially egalitarian Republican named Daniel Russell as governor two years later. At the epicenter of this not-so-quiet revolution was Wilmington, a bustling majority-black city then. It was truly revolutionary, but the changes fell short. The run-up to the 1898 elections was marked by increasing violence and assertion of racial supremacy by many whites. In the ensuing vote, Democrats recaptured the statehouse, though a biracial governing coalition was elected in Wilmington. That, too, was short-lived. A white mob instigated a violent protest, and hundreds of African Americans fled to the nearby woods and swamps. The biracial government was forced to resign at gunpoint in the only violent *coup d'état* in American history. Wilmington became a majority-white city, which it remains to this day.

The coastal counties of southern North Carolina recently have grown smartly. The military has kept things afloat, as have tourism and growing retirement communities. South of Wilmington, the Army runs the 16,000-acre Military Ocean Terminal at Sunny Point, the Army's main deep-water port on the East Coast. It is the largest military ammunition port in the world, and often is referred to as "the FedEx of the sea" because it is almost always open. From 1990 to 2015, the population of Wilmington-based New Hanover County increased by about 75 percent, and Brunswick County to the south more than doubled. In 2015, New Hanover planners projected 56 percent growth by 2040. The region has some of the busiest movie and television production facilities outside Los Angeles, with more than a dozen credits, including the popular teenage TV drama series *One Tree Hill* and *Dawson's Creek*.

Inland, hogs outnumber humans by more than 30-to-1 in Duplin County. Smithfield Foods in Tar Heel runs the largest pork production plant in the world. The smell of hog manure, some of it stored in open-air pits, is a big problem. Farther north in Wayne County is Goldsboro, a former railroad crossing in the exurbs of Raleigh that has been losing jobs and population. Goldsboro had a 26 percent drop in median income between 2000 and 2014, among the worst in the nation, the Pew Research Center reported.

The 7th Congressional District of North Carolina covers much of this territory. It is ancestrally Democratic, and it was the final white-majority district in the state that hadn't elected a Republican since Reconstruction. Redistricting in 2012 made the 7th the second-most Republican district in the state, and that anomaly was resolved in 2014. The latest redistricting restored the minority communities of the Wilmington area to the new 7th and added Goldsboro. New Hanover and Brunswick include half of the voters in the 7th. The redistricting shifts reduced by about three percentage points the GOP presidential vote in 2008 and 2012. Even though the new district dropped to fourth statewide in its party vote, the area has remained comfortably Republican. Donald Trump won it in 2016, 57%-40%.

EIGHTH DISTRICT

Richard Hudson (R)

Elected 2012, 3rd term; b. Nov 04, 1971, Franklin, VA; University of North Carolina, Charlotte, B.A., 1996; Methodist; Married (Ms. Renee Hudson); 1 child.

Professional Career: Deputy chief of Staff, Rep. Robin Hayes, 2000-05; Chief of Staff, Rep. Virginia Foxx, 2005-2006; Chief of Staff, Rep. John Carter, 2006-2008; Chief of Staff, Rep. Mike Conaway, 2008-2011; President, Cabarrus Marketing Group, 2011-present.

DC Office: 429 CHOB 20515, 202-225-3715, Fax: 202-225-4036, hudson.house.gov.

State Offices: Concord, 704-786-1612; Fayetteville, 910-997-2070.

Committees: *Energy & Commerce*: Energy, Environment, Health. *Joint Security & Cooperation in Europe*.

Group Ratings

	ADA	ACLU	AFL-CIO	LCV	ITI	COC	HAFA	ACU	CFG	FRC
2016	0%	5%	0%	0%	100%	100%	82%	96%	84%	100%
2015	0%	C	0%	0%	C	76%	C	95%	90%	100%

Almanac Ratings 2015

	Economy	Social	Foreign	Composite
Liberal	7%	4%	4%	5%
Conservative	93%	97%	96%	95%

Key Votes of the 114th Congress

1. Keystone Pipeline	Y	5. Puerto Rico Debt	N	9. Offenses by Aliens	Y
2. Trade Deals	Y	6. Medical Marijuana	N	10. Troops in Iraq	N
3. Export-Import Bank	N	7. Sanctuary Cities	Y	11. Homeland Security $$	N
4. Debt Ceiling Increase	NV	8. Armor-piercing Bullets	Y	12. Trade Adjustment aid	N

Election Results

Election	Name (Party)	Vote (%)	Cand. Spent	Ind. Exp. Support	Ind. Exp. Oppose
2016 General	Richard Hudson (R)	189,863 (59%)	$2,248,096	$40,671	
	Thomas Mills (D)	133,182 (41%)	$394,856	$1	$600
2016 Primary	Richard Hudson (R)	16,305 (65%)			
	Tim D'Annunzio (R)	8,943 (35%)			

Prior winning percentages: 2014 (65%), 2012 (53%)

Republican Richard Hudson, elected in 2012, has used a boost from redistricting to take control of a formerly Democratic-held seat. A former senior congressional staffer and usually a party regular, Hudson secured a prized seat on the Energy and Commerce Committee, where he has worked on health and energy issues.

Hudson grew up in the Charlotte area, and has a good political blood line. He helped his grandfather run for the Roanoke Rapids City Council, where he served for 30 years. He put up yard signs for another role model, conservative Republican Sen. Jesse Helms. Hudson was student-body president at the University of North Carolina at Charlotte, where he got a bachelor's degree. After college, he worked in Washington, as chief of staff to GOP Reps. Mike Conaway and John Carter of Texas and Virginia Foxx of North Carolina. He was deputy chief of staff for local Rep. Robin Hayes, who lost this seat to Democrat Larry Kissell in 2008. In November 2011, two months after moving back to the district, Hudson said he had a sense that God had a higher purpose for his life and was calling him to run for Congress.

Republicans made Kissell's seat a top 2012 takeover target after the favorable work of GOP mapmakers. After Hayes passed on a bid, Hudson led the first round in the five-candidate primary with

32 percent, setting up a runoff with former Iredell County Commissioner Scott Keadle. When Keadle tried to portray Hudson as a Washington insider out of touch with the district, Hudson maintained that his experience on Capitol Hill created connections that would allow him to be more effective than most freshmen. He cruised to a runoff win, 64%-36%.

In the general, Hudson turned the tables by painting Kissell as the Beltway insider. He blamed the incumbent for moving the country toward "skyrocketing debt" and for "out-of-control spending." To find work for laid-off textile workers, he promised to work for full funding of job retraining programs. He accused Kissell of flip-flopping to try to save his seat. "I don't know where my opponent stands on many issues, it depends which day of the week it is," he told *The Fayetteville Observer*. Kissell stressed his vote against the Affordable Care Act and touted a provision he inserted into the economic stimulus bill requiring federal purchase of U.S.-made uniforms. But styling himself as a conservative Blue Dog who was distant from Obama alienated black voters. Hudson took the seat, 53%-45%.

On Energy and Commerce, he has sought to unleash the energy resources of North Carolina and to replace the Affordable Care Act with "a health care system that puts patients first." He helped to form the Atlantic Offshore Energy Caucus, which was designed to promote policies that explore and expand energy production on the Outer Continental Shelf. Hudson showed his sensitivity to the rural Carolina culture when he filed a bill in March 2016 to stifle a proposal by the Environmental Protection Agency in the Obama administration that would have regulated the engines or exhaust modifications in automobiles used in competitive races. In January 2017, the House unanimously passed his bill to allow emergency medical technicians to dispense medications, subject to general approval of local medical directors.

In the *Almanac* vote ratings for 2015, Hudson ranked consistently conservative in each of the three issue areas. During his first term, he claimed credit for enacting two bills from the Homeland Security Committee, on which he served. One was designed to promote greater transparency and accountability at the TSA. The other limited to $11.20 per round-trip the passenger security fee on airline flights. He chaired the agriculture policy group of the House Republican Policy Committee.

He breezed to reelection in 2014 with 65 percent of the vote against Democratic challenger Antonio Blue, the mayor of tiny Dobbins Height (pop. 855). In 2016, redistricting created more robust challenges for Hudson in the primary and general, with opponents who had credible financial support. Hudson won each contest comfortably, though he struggled in the new parts of the district. In the Republican primary, he faced Tim D'Annunzio, a former Army paratrooper who went into the military-equipment business. D'Annunzio, who had run for Congress during the previous three cycles, self-financed most of his $239,000 campaign. He won narrowly in Cumberland, Hoke and Moore counties. Hudson had big margins in the western counties, including 82 percent of the vote in Cabarrus, and won 65%-35%.

In the general, Hudson faced Tom Mills, a veteran Democratic consultant in the area who founded the website, *politicsnc.com*, where he posted blog posts about the necessity of long-shot challengers in elections. The candidates shared doubts about new international trade agreements and agreed on the need to protect U.S. citizens from the Islamic State. They disagreed on other issues, including gun control and immigration. Hudson raised $2 million overall to $400,000 for Mills. The national parties and their allies spent little money here. In the two biggest counties, each of which cast about 90,000 votes, Hudson got 62 percent in Cabarrus and Mills got 60 percent in Cumberland. Hudson took four other counties with margins of up to 78 percent and won overall, 59%-41%. After the election, Mills wrote a scathing piece for *Politico* in which he ripped the Democratic Congressional Campaign Committee for its failure to give attention to him or his campaign. "Over time, the DCCC has lost much of its innovative spirit and edge - which is evident in the fact that, today, support seems to be available only to a select group of targeted races," Mills wrote. "The organization charged with getting Democrats back in the majority should do much better. Now, more than any time in my lifetime, our country needs a better class of politicians and better qualified operatives."

Following the 2016 election, Hudson advised Donald Trump on firearms issues, including his proposal to guarantee holders of concealed-carry permits the right to have a gun outside their home state, so long as the gun-holder abides by local laws. His wife, Renee Hudson, shared his background as a senior House aide. In February 2017, she moved to the White House as chief of staff to presidential counselor Kellyanne Conway.

South-Central North Carolina: Eastern Charlotte Suburbs, Fayetteville

Demographics data for new House districts were not prepared by the Census Bureau prior to our editorial deadline.

Voter Turnout			
2016 House Turnout as % CVAP	N/A	2016 House turnout	323,045

2012 Presidential Vote information unavailable due to recent redistricting.

2016 Presidential Vote		
Donald Trump	185,920	(56%)
Hillary Clinton	136,191	(41%)
Gary Johnson	9,128	(3%)

Cook Partisan Voting Index: R+8

In the Carolina Piedmont, from Atlanta to Durham along Interstate 85, lie the remnants of America's once-mighty textile industry. These sites included Concord and Kannapolis, the latter named for its founding company, Cannon Mills. While eastern Carolina was settled by Englishmen, the Piedmont was settled mainly by Scots and diverse groups like Quakers and Moravian sects, coming down the Blue Ridge from Pennsylvania through Virginia. These migratory patterns were reflected in Civil War divisions and continue to some degree in current voting habits. The textile mill towns along the interstate were anti-secession and are now Republican.

To the east is military-focused Fayetteville, which is centered on Fort Bragg. The Army base styles itself as the largest military base in the world, which has had more than 50,000 active-duty military personnel. This is the home of the famed 82nd Airborne Division, which specializes in forcible-entry operations. In 2014, the 82nd lost its "airborne" status because of the high cost of maintenance plus injuries to the paratroopers and others. A nearly 10 percent reduction in troops from 2011 to 2016 slowed the local economy. The area is home to 100,000 Army retirees and family members.

These separate areas are the end points of the 8th Congressional District, which stretches across the southern part of the state with five mostly rural and heavily Republican counties between them. They recently have moved in very different directions. Cabarrus County, which includes the southern end of the textile corridor around Kannapolis and Concord, has been fed by migration from Charlotte and has moved beyond its small-town roots to become a booming exurban county. The county grew by 54 percent from 2000 to 2015. Concord, with an influx of technology jobs, was the ninth-fastest growing city in the nation from 2009 to 2015 and the third-fastest in the small city category. In August 2016, city officials in Kannapolis approved a $60 million downtown economic revitalization. Cabarrus casts one-fourth of the district's votes. Fayetteville-based Cumberland County is less robust economically, with growth of only 8 percent since 2000. It leans Democratic, with about three-fourths of it in the 8th.

The new redistricting added Cumberland from the Raleigh-based 4th District and lost to the new 9th District a string of counties from Union to Robeson along the South Carolina border. What had been a political swing area prior to 2012 has become a much more Republican district. The latest changes in the 8th reduced the Republican presidential vote in 2008 and 2012 by about three percentage points. But the area remained safely Republican. Donald Trump in 2016 led, 56%-41%.

NINTH DISTRICT

Robert Pittenger (R)

Elected 2012, 3rd term; b. Aug 15, 1948, Dallas, TX; University of Texas, B.A.; Protestant; Married (Suzanne Bahakel); 4 children; 9 grandchildren.

Elected Office: NC Senate, 2003-2008.

Professional Career: Assistant to the President, Campus Crusade for Christ, 1970-1985; Owner, Robert Pittenger Co., 1989-present.

DC Office: 224 CHOB 20515, 202-225-1976, Fax: 202-225-3389, pittenger.house.gov.

State Offices: Charlotte, 704-362-1060; Fayetteville, 910-303-0669; Monroe, 704-917-9573.

Committees: *Financial Services*: Financial Institutions & Consumer Credit, Monetary Policy & Trade, Terrorism & Illicit Finance. *Joint Congressional-Executive Commission on China.*

Group Ratings

	ADA	ACLU	AFL-CIO	LCV	ITI	COC	HAFA	ACU	CFG	FRC
2016	-	5%	-	0%	100%	100%	69%	88%	74%	100%
2015	0%	C	4%	0%	C	90%	C	83%	69%	100%

Almanac Ratings 2015

	Economy	Social	Foreign	Composite
Liberal	7%	5%	10%	7%
Conservative	93%	95%	90%	93%

Key Votes of the 114th Congress

1. Keystone Pipeline	Y	5. Puerto Rico Debt	Y	9. Offenses by Aliens	Y
2. Trade Deals	Y	6. Medical Marijuana	N	10. Troops in Iraq	N
3. Export-Import Bank	N	7. Sanctuary Cities	Y	11. Homeland Security $$	Y
4. Debt Ceiling Increase	Y	8. Armor-piercing Bullets	Y	12. Trade Adjustment aid	Y

Election Results

Election	Name (Party)	Vote (%)		Cand. Spent	Ind. Exp. Support	Ind. Exp. Oppose
2016 General	Robert Pittenger (R)	193,452	(58%)	$1,077,157	$45,861	
	Christian Cano (D)	139,041	(42%)	$55,460		$600
2016 Primary	Robert Pittenger (R)	9,268	(35%)			
	Mark Harris (R)	9,126	(34%)			
	Todd Johnson (R)	8,118	(31%)			

Prior winning percentages: 2014 (94%), 2012 (52%)

Republican Robert Pittenger, first elected in 2012, has used his experience as a real estate entrepreneur as a member of the Financial Services Committee and has been more of a party regular than some other junior members from North Carolina. He barely survived the redistricting shifts that moved his district beyond its Charlotte core and encountered additional problems with investigations of his personal finances.

A Texas native, Pittenger's father was a lawyer and real estate agent. After graduating from the University of Texas with degrees in psychology and political science, he served 10 years as assistant to the president for Campus Crusade for Christ, an evangelical Christian organization. As a public relations officer for the group, he helped to organize Explo, a weeklong conference that attracted nearly 100,000 high school and college students and became known as the "Christian Woodstock." Pittenger trekked to Africa, Asia and South America to promote Campus Crusade's work. He and his wife, Suzanne, moved to her hometown of Charlotte, where he started a real estate business and invested in growth opportunities across the Sunbelt. In the state Senate for six years, Pittenger was a strong conservative advocate on economic and social issues. On his first day, he introduced legislation to reform medical liability laws; 3,000 doctors rallied in support. The Democratic-controlled Senate proved challenging for him, and the nonpartisan North Carolina Center for Public Policy in 2007 ranked his effectiveness as 49th out of 50. In 2008, Pittenger ran unsuccessfully for lieutenant governor.

When the House seat opened, Pittenger partially financed his campaign with $2.3 million from his fortune. He poured $324,000 into ads on a single day, nearly equaling the amount that his chief Republican opponent, former Mecklenburg County Sheriff Jim Pendergraph, spent on his entire campaign. In their bruising primary runoff, Pittenger accused Pendergraph of being a Democrat and Pendergraph supporters accused Pittenger of buying the election. They highlighted Pittenger's 2003 vote in the state legislature on a land annexation that benefited his real estate company. An independent ethics committee in the Senate had reviewed the issue, but brought no charges. Pittenger won the runoff, 53%-47%. In the general, Pittenger under-performed when he defeated Democrat Jennifer Roberts, a Mecklenburg County commissioner, 52%-46%. His vote share was four points less than GOP presidential nominee Mitt Romney received in the district that day. Roberts led 50%-47% in Mecklenburg, which cast 72 percent of the vote, but Pittenger won suburban Union and Iredell by 2-to-1 margins.

Pittenger's *Almanac* vote ratings placed him in the center of House Republicans. On the Financial Services panel, he was vice chairman of its Task Force to Investigate Terrorism Financing. Its bipartisan 191-page report in December 2016 examined how criminals and terror groups exploit corrupt governments and extort money worldwide, and called for a national strategy to curb terrorism finances and increase surveillance. "I look forward to implementing the recommendations found in this report as we continue efforts to defeat radical Islamic terrorism," Pittenger said. He earlier co-chaired the Congressional Task Force on Terrorism and Unconventional Warfare, which met with international security experts to advocate increased global cooperation on security and intelligence. In July 2016, he helped to pass three bills in the House that gave the Treasury Department new methods to crack down on illicit funds of the Islamic State. Critics said that legislation over-reached and infringed on privacy rights.

He won House approval of his bipartisan bill to strengthen the voice of small businesses in the actions of federal banking regulators. Following up on his interest in religious issues, he has served on the Congressional-Executive Commission on China, which monitors human rights and the rule of law in China. He defended Israeli Prime Minister Benjamin Netanyahu against complaints about his disagreements with the Obama administration. "He is the Winston Churchill of the day, warning the world about Iran," Pittenger said. He has co-chaired the bipartisan United Solutions Caucus, whose mostly junior members have sought to move forward on fiscal issues, including entitlement spending and tax reform.

Pittenger has encountered more than his share of personal problems. In September 2016, he apologized for saying that protesters of police misconduct in Charlotte "hate white people because white people are successful and they're not." Local critics called him racist. He later told another interviewer that the comment "doesn't reflect who I am." The Justice Department and House Ethics Committee investigated his alleged continuing ties with his real estate company, including a possible loan to his campaign. In January 2017, *The Charlotte Observer* reported that witnesses appeared before a grand jury on the case.

In 2014, Pittenger won the Republican primary with 68 percent of the vote against tea party challenger Michael Steinberg. He had no Democratic opposition. Two years later, he faced two credible GOP challengers: Mark Harris, a Charlotte pastor who had been a leader in seeking to ban same-sex marriages statewide, and Todd Johnson, a former Union County commissioner. Both criticized Pittenger as a "Washington insider." More than 84 percent of the primary vote was cast in Mecklenburg, where Pittenger won 48 percent, and in Union, where he ran third with 27 percent. He got 35 percent of the total vote and won by 142 votes over Harris following a recount. In the general, Democratic political newcomer Christian Cano cited the "need to bring undocumented immigrants out of the shadows." Pittenger outraised him 20-to-1, and won, 58%-42%. Cano won three of the rural counties.

Southern Charlotte Suburbs, Southern North Carolina

Demographics data for new House districts were not prepared by the Census Bureau prior to our editorial deadline.

Voter Turnout			
2016 House Turnout as % CVAP	N/A	2016 House turnout	332,493

2012 Presidential Vote information unavailable due to recent redistricting.

2016 Presidential Vote		
Donald Trump	186,926	(54%)
Hillary Clinton	147,162	(42%)
Gary Johnson	9,841	(3%)

Cook Partisan Voting Index: R+8

"An agreeable village but in a damn rebellious country," recorded British Revolutionary War Gen. Charles Cornwallis when, before the unpleasantness at Yorktown, he visited Charlotte. Settled by Scots-Irish and German colonists who came down from Pennsylvania along the Blue Ridge Mountains, Charlotte has been a rapidly growing metropolitan area and the largest in North Carolina. Before the California gold rush, Charlotte was the gold-mining capital of the country; in 1837, the U.S. Mint established a branch here. And the city continues its preoccupation with the financial sector today. It is headquarters to one of the nation's biggest banks, Bank of America, though it was not immune to the tumult in the financial markets. Charlotte-based Wachovia, which was the area's second-largest employer, was taken over in early 2009 by San Francisco-based Wells Fargo, a move that likely saved Wachovia from failure.

The 9th Congressional District has been a microcosm of the changes that have taken place in the South in the past century. In 1928, it elected Republican Charles A. Jonas to Congress. It was considered a fluke - he lost two years later - but in truth it was a precursor of trends in urban areas across the region. In 1952, the congressman's son, Charles R. Jonas, won the Charlotte district, and this time held it for another nine elections; Republicans haven't given it up since. As Charlotte and other urban areas moved toward Republicans, the party became competitive across the South.

Although redistricting in 2016 radically changed the 9th, the Republican portions of Charlotte remained the constant factor. What had been a relatively compact district that stretched north and south of Charlotte has evolved so that its population base is in the southern parts of Charlotte in Mecklenburg County, plus rapidly growing Union County. Union increased from 124,000 in 2000 to 227,000 in 2016. Matthews, whose population doubled to 31,000 from 1990 to 2015, has been among the hot real-estate markets south of Charlotte. These areas include about 60 percent of the voters in the district. The remainder of the 9th sprawls east in an area, new to the district, which includes four mostly rural counties that extend east along the South Carolina border and then hooks north to Bladen and a small share of Fayetteville-based Cumberland County. Robeson County, which is the home of the Lumbee Tribe, leans Democratic. Scotland County had the lowest household income in the state. Redistricting in 2016 moved the heavily Democratic urban core of Mecklenburg to the 12th District. The black population in the new 9th increased from 13 percent to 20 percent. But its political leaning showed little change. Donald Trump in 2016 got 54 percent of the vote, compared with 56 percent for Mitt Romney in 2012.

TENTH DISTRICT

Patrick McHenry (R)

Elected 2004, 7th term; b. Oct 22, 1975, Charlotte; Belmont Abbey College (NC), B.A.; North Carolina State University, Att.; Roman Catholic; Married (Giulia Cangiano McHenry); 1 child.

Elected Office: NC House, 2002-2004.

Professional Career: Real estate broker, 2000-2002; Special Assistant to the U.S. Secretary of Labor, 2001.

DC Office: 2334 RHOB 20515, 202-225-2576, Fax: 202-225-0316, mchenry.house.gov.

State Offices: Black Mountain, 828-669-0600; Gastonia, 704-833-0096; Hickory, 828-327-6100.

Committees: House Chief Deputy Whip. *Financial Services*: Capital Markets, Securities & Investment, Oversight & Investigations.

Group Ratings

	ADA	ACLU	AFL-CIO	LCV	ITI	COC	HAFA	ACU	CFG	FRC
2016	-	5%	-	3%	100%	100%	60%	92%	78%	100%
2015	0%	C	4%	0%	C	95%	C	83%	66%	92%

Almanac Ratings 2015

	Economy	Social	Foreign	Composite
Liberal	10%	5%	14%	10%
Conservative	90%	95%	86%	90%

Key Votes of the 114th Congress

1. Keystone Pipeline	Y	5. Puerto Rico Debt	Y	9. Offenses by Aliens	Y
2. Trade Deals	Y	6. Medical Marijuana	N	10. Troops in Iraq	N
3. Export-Import Bank	N	7. Sanctuary Cities	Y	11. Homeland Security $$	Y
4. Debt Ceiling Increase	Y	8. Armor-piercing Bullets	Y	12. Trade Adjustment aid	Y

Election Results

Election	Name (Party)	Vote (%)	Cand. Spent	Ind. Exp. Support	Ind. Exp. Oppose
2016 General	Patrick McHenry (R)	220,825 (63%)	$1,708,235		
	Andy Millard (D)	128,919 (37%)	$277,834		
2016 Primary	Patrick McHenry (R)	14,770 (79%)			
	Jeff Gregory (R)	2,268 (12%)			

Prior winning percentages: 2014 (61%), 2012 (57%), 2010 (71%), 2008 (58%), 2006 (62%), 2004 (64%)

Patrick McHenry, a Republican first elected in 2004, has evolved from a highly partisan GOP guerilla fighter in his early years in the House into a leadership insider seeking to move the party's agenda. As the chief deputy to Majority Whip Steve Scalise, McHenry is perhaps the junior Republican best-positioned for future influence. After Scalise was critically wounded during a June 2017 shooting in Alexandria Virginia, McHenry took the Whip's reins, at least temporarily.

McHenry grew up in Cherryville as the youngest of five children and graduated from Belmont Abbey College, where he was president of the state College Republicans. After school he worked as a real estate broker. As a young conservative, he cut his political teeth on his strenuous opposition to the Clintons. He once dressed up in an Abraham Lincoln costume at a North Carolina appearance by Bill Clinton after Clinton was accused by Republicans of rewarding big contributors with overnight stays in the Lincoln Bedroom in the White House. McHenry worked on several Republican campaigns in North Carolina and was appointed to a job in the Labor Department. In 2002, he was elected to the state House.

When McHenry ran for an open seat, his chief competition in the Republican primary was Catawba County Sheriff David Huffman. Both made conservative Christian values their main issue. After Huffman finished first with 35 percent and McHenry second with 26 percent, the four-week runoff campaign took a negative turn. Huffman questioned McHenry for hosting noisy late-night parties at his house, which also served as a residence for his campaign staff, a claim rebutted by McHenry's neighbors. McHenry accused Huffman of campaign finance irregularities. He ran an energetic, door-to-door grassroots campaign, billing himself as a "pro-life, pro-gun, anti-gay-marriage" Christian conservative. He won the runoff by just 85 votes after a recount. Huffman carried Catawba County 59%-41%. But McHenry rolled up huge majorities in the counties close to his Gaston County home. In a solidly Republican district, he easily won the general election.

At age 29, McHenry arrived as the youngest member of the House. Instead of keeping a low profile and doing constituent work to sew up his seat, he made repeat appearances on talk shows to serve up red meat and sound bites. On the House floor, he took on Democrats no matter how powerful or senior. In 2007, he accused Speaker Nancy Pelosi of California of abusing her office by using military jets to fly home to San Francisco during congressional recesses. In 2009, he sidled up to the "birther" movement by saying at a town hall forum that "I haven't seen evidence one way or the other" of President Barack Obama's U.S. citizenship. He backed away from the comment the next day.

His political style soon softened. When Republicans took control of the House in 2011, he became chairman of a new subcommittee specializing in government bailouts, such as the Troubled Asset Relief Program for the financial industry. He told *The Charlotte Observer* that TARP was "a very uneven response from the federal government," with some banks bailed out and others, notably Charlotte-based Wachovia, forced to merge. He got into a hostile exchange at a 2011 hearing with Elizabeth Warren, then a Harvard professor who helped create the Consumer Financial Protection Bureau as part of the Dodd-Frank financial services overhaul. The two squabbled over the amount of time she was supposed to testify, with McHenry snapping at one point, "You're making this up, Ms. Warren." Supporters of Warren, a liberal Democrat who was later elected to the Senate from Massachusetts, posted thousands of angry comments on McHenry's Facebook page.

He has remained active on the Financial Services Committee, where he has been an ally of Chairman Jeb Hensarling. In 2011, he won enactment of his bill allowing financial institutions involved in multiple transactions to combine them into one contract, something helpful to the banking industry in Charlotte. His district is on the outskirts of the city, and his constituents include many banking executives. The House passed his measure that year to terminate the Home Assistance Mortgage Program, which assists eligible homeowners with mortgage loan modifications. The bill drew a veto threat from the White House, and the Senate never took it up. McHenry passed a provision in the jobs bill enacted in 2012 that allowed companies to more easily raise equity through social media and online platforms. In September

2016, he filed a bill to expedite regulatory approval of their new products for financial technology companies.

As he has become more effective as a legislator, others have taken notice. McHenry in 2012 was named one of *Time* magazine's "40 Under 40" civic leaders who is "at work trying to fix a broken system" and restore public faith in government. Behind the scenes, he helped his friend Scalise win election as chairman of the Republican Study Committee, the caucus of the House's most conservative members.

When the Louisiana Republican became majority whip in the fallout from Eric Cantor's surprise primary defeat in 2014, he repaid the favor, replacing chief deputy Peter Roskam of Illinois - who had unsuccessfully challenged Scalise for the whip's job - with McHenry. Like Scalise, McHenry spent much of his time courting his long-time conservative allies, not always successfully. The North Carolina delegation has included troublemakers for GOP leaders, including Rep. Mark Meadows, who represents the district adjacent to McHenry's and was instrumental in the decision by John Boehner to step down as Speaker in October 2015. For his new job, McHenry abandoned his earlier presence on the media circuit and went underground, *The Wall Street Journal* reported. "Some [lawmakers] know on day one how to be effective in this institution; others, it takes time - and I was in that camp," McHenry told the *Journal* in May 2015.

McHenry's *Almanac* rating in 2015 ranked him near the center of House Republicans, another sign of his mellowing. Given the economic plight of the textile industry, McHenry often voted against free trade deals, as he did in 2005 on a pact proposed with Central America and in 2010 on a Haiti trade relief bill. His leadership post created a new twist in 2015 as he engaged in countless discussions to rally support from GOP members for the trade promotion authority request from Obama. His growing experience at the leadership table highlighted a comment that he made in an earlier interview with the *Raleigh News-Observer*: "The opportunity to shape outcomes is what is meaningful."

McHenry has had little trouble at election time. He faced GOP primary challengers in 2010, 2012 and again in 2016 who accused him of being insufficiently conservative, but won each contest easily. In the 2012 general election, he beat Democrat Patsy Keever with 57 percent of the vote. In 2016, he got 63 percent against Andy Millard, a financial planner who raised nearly $300,000 for his campaign. Each voiced reservations about international trade. Millard called for changes on guns and immigration.

Following the election, McHenry's responsibilities to help win enactment of the agenda of President Donald Trump and congressional Republicans created additional tensions with his neighbor Rep. Meadows, who had taken over as chairman of the rebellious Freedom Caucus. Although each earlier denied reports that McHenry had sought Republican primary opposition for Meadows, the colleagues from western North Carolina had clearly moved to competing tracks for influence in the House. The June 2017 shooting of Scalise left McHenry with new responsibilities for legislative management of the fractious House Republicans.

West-Central North Carolina: Gastonia, Asheville

Demographics data for new House districts were not prepared by the Census Bureau prior to our editorial deadline.

Voter Turnout			
2016 House Turnout as % CVAP	N/A	2016 House turnout	349,744

2012 Presidential Vote information unavailable due to recent redistricting.

2016 Presidential Vote		
Donald Trump	216,943	(60%)
Hillary Clinton	129,104	(36%)
Gary Johnson	9,088	(3%)

Cook Partisan Voting Index: R+12

In 1790, one of the most important decisions in North Carolina's history was made - in Pennsylvania. That was when 19-year-old Michael Schenck decided to leave his family farm in Lancaster and settle in western North Carolina. In 1813, on a small creek west of Lincolnton, Schenck built the first cotton mill south of the Potomac River. In 1816, he brought in investors and erected the Lincoln Cotton Mills on the South Fork of the Catawba River, which operated until the Civil War. The North Carolina textile industry was born and soon dominated in an area that had specialized in corn, cotton and whiskey production. After the Civil War, the surfeit of cheap labor and fast-flowing streams on the Piedmont made it a perfect locus for manufacturing. By the end of the 19th century, North Carolina had more textile plants than

Connecticut, Maine or Vermont. These companies relied on the "Rhode Island model" of development, where towns were put up around the mills and whole families were placed in small, company-owned homes. These towns spread across the Piedmont; some grew into substantial cities, while others remained hamlets.

Ground zero for the industry was Gaston County and nearby towns. By the 1930s, there were 570 mills within a 100-mile radius of Gastonia. The relationship between workers and management was often uneasy. Gastonia was the site of a massive strike at Loray Mills in the late 1920s, led by the communist-dominated United Textile Workers, which erupted in violence and resulted in the deaths of the local police chief and Ella May Wiggins, the unofficial balladeer of the union who penned tunes such as "A Mill Mother's Song" and "The Big Fat Boss and the Workers." Today, the textile industry is in decline and Gastonia has the slowest growth in the area surrounding Charlotte. Still, the western Piedmont continues to excel in making things. The Wuxi Taiji Paper Industry Co., which makes spiral-wound cardboard tubes, put a plant in Conover. Tenowo expanded nonwoven textile production at its Lincoln County plant. Developers have found new uses for abandoned mills. Asheville has had a spurt of technology-related manufacturing plus craft breweries.

The 10th Congressional District of North Carolina is centered on Gastonia, where a little more than a quarter of the district's votes are cast. To the north, it takes in Lincoln County and most of Hickory's Catawba County. To the west are Cleveland and Rutherford counties. In the 2011 redistricting, the 10th gained most of heavily Democratic Asheville, a popular artistic and retirement mecca with its well-preserved historic structures in styles ranging from Gothic Revival to Art Deco. Those new lines reduced the Republican advantage in the 10th, but the district retained a strong GOP tilt. The 2016 redistricting made a small tweak in Catawba. Asheville-based Buncombe is a blue island in a red sea. The other seven counties remain solidly Republican. Donald Trump took 60 percent here in 2016, his second-best performance in the state and a slight increase in the recent GOP vote.

ELEVENTH DISTRICT

Mark Meadows (R)

Elected 2012, 3rd term; b. Jul 28, 1959, Verdun, French Republic; University of South Florida, A.A., 1980; Christian Church; Married (Debbie Meadows); 2 children; 1 grandchild.

Professional Career: Director, customer relations & public safety, Tampa Electric, 1983-1986; Owner, sandwich shop, 1986-1990; Real-estate developer, 1990-2012.

DC Office: 1024 LHOB 20515, 202-225-6401, Fax: 202-226-6422, meadows.house.gov.

State Offices: Hendersonville, 828-693-5660; Lenoir, 828-426-8701; Spruce Pine, 828-765-0573; Waynesville, 828-452-6022.

Committees: *Foreign Affairs*: Africa, Global Health, Global Human Rights & Internat'l Orgs, Middle East & North Africa. *Oversight & Government Reform*: Government Operations (Chmn), Health Care, Benefits & Administrative Rules. *Transportation & Infrastructure*: Aviation, Highways & Transit, Railroads, Pipelines & Hazardous Materials.

Group Ratings

	ADA	ACLU	AFL-CIO	LCV	ITI	COC	HAFA	ACU	CFG	FRC
2016	-	11%	-	0%	67%	100%	90%	96%	96%	100%
2015	10%	C	9%	3%	C	63%	C	100%	80%	92%

Almanac Ratings 2015

	Economy	Social	Foreign	Composite
Liberal	18%	0%	1%	7%
Conservative	82%	100%	99%	93%

Key Votes of the 114th Congress

1. Keystone Pipeline	Y	5. Puerto Rico Debt	N	9. Offenses by Aliens	Y
2. Trade Deals	N	6. Medical Marijuana	N	10. Troops in Iraq	N
3. Export-Import Bank	N	7. Sanctuary Cities	Y	11. Homeland Security $$	N
4. Debt Ceiling Increase	N	8. Armor-piercing Bullets	Y	12. Trade Adjustment aid	N

Election Results

Election	Name (Party)	Vote (%)	Cand. Spent	Ind. Exp. Support	Ind. Exp. Oppose
2016 General	Mark Meadows (R)	230,405 (64%)	$437,847	$56,303	
	Rick Bryson (D)	129,103 (36%)	$44,042	$1	
2016 Primary	Mark Meadows (R)	(100%)			

Prior winning percentages: 2014 (63%), 2012 (57%)

Businessman and longtime Republican activist Mark Meadows, elected in 2012, has emerged from the pack of junior Republicans from North Carolina and elsewhere. After voting against John Boehner for Speaker in 2015 and making other maverick moves that alienated party leaders, he was temporarily stripped of his subcommittee chairmanship. An angry rank-and-file reaction restored his post a few days later, following which Meadows played a key role in Boehner's September decision to resign. With that taste of influence and his leadership role in the Freedom Caucus, Meadows helped to shape the House Republicans' early 2017 response to the Affordable Care Act. That dismayed some moderate Republicans and, for a time, President Donald Trump.

Meadows was born in the 42nd Army Field Hospital in Verdun, France, while his father was stationed abroad. His father was a draftsman; his mother, a surgical nurse. He attended high school in the Tampa area and went on to get a degree in business management from the University of South Florida. After college, he worked for Tampa Electric, but he and his wife, Debbie, whom he met in Tampa, dreamed of living in North Carolina. They said to each other, "Wouldn't it be great to retire to the mountains one day?" Instead of retiring, they just moved there in 1986. They started a small sandwich shop in the resort town of Highlands, and ran it for a few years before they sold it and turned to real estate investments.

A self-described history buff, Meadows was drawn to conservative politics by his observations of history and experiences as a businessman. He was the only person who showed up for a precinct meeting of his local Republican Party in rural North Carolina, thus becoming precinct chairman and eventually county chairman. He worked on behalf of GOP candidates for 25 years and was a delegate to party conventions.

In 2010, Republicans captured control of North Carolina's General Assembly for the first time since Reconstruction. In redistricting, Rep. Heath Shuler was one of four Democrats who were targeted. His 11th District was revamped to become significantly more conservative. Shuler, who had challenged Nancy Pelosi for minority leader following the 2010 elections, decided to retire. Meadows faced six Republicans in the May primary. He led with 38 percent of the vote. In the runoff campaign, where both candidates stressed their opposition to increases in federal spending and regulations, Meadows trounced tea party activist Vance Patterson, 76%-24%.

In November, Meadows faced Shuler's former chief of staff, Hayden Rogers, who received significant financial backing from local business and labor interests. A moderate western North Carolina native, Rogers ran ads espousing his "mountain values" and sought to depict his opponent as wealthy and out of touch. He spent $726,000, but received little national party assistance. Meadows played up his business background; his ads, which focused heavily on opposition to President Barack Obama, struck a chord with district voters. He took 12 of the 17 counties and won his first elected office, 57%-43%.

In the House, Meadows joined other conservative activists. In 2015, he was one of nine founding members of the Freedom Caucus, which pressed House Republicans to pursue a more conservative agenda. Also that month, he was one of 25 Republicans who did not vote for Boehner for Speaker; he explained that he was reflecting the widespread view of his constituents that they wanted a new direction. Meadows took an interest in investigative work, and he became chairman in 2015 of the Oversight and Government Reform Subcommittee on Government Operations, whose jurisdiction includes federal employees. He created a "tip line" for them to report problems. In March 2015, the committee approved his bill to prohibit government workers from using their computers to surf pornographic websites. He investigated the Patent and Trademark Office and cited a report that the patent examiners engaged in widespread fraud with their time and attendance records. Meadows said he was alarmed that "internal controls are lacking" to monitor fraud.

After taking some steps toward becoming a team player, Meadows took several other steps that offended House Republican leaders. His June 2015 vote against a rule for debating trade legislation - on top of his vote against Boehner plus his failure to pay dues to the National Republican Congressional Committee - led Oversight and Government Reform Chairman Jason Chaffetz of Utah to strip his subcommittee chairmanship. After angry conservatives threatened retaliatory moves to weaken his control of the committee, Chaffetz quickly reversed himself and Meadows regained his gavel. On the eve of the August recess, he stirred the pot by filing a resolution designed to oust Boehner. Meadows said that he hoped for a "family discussion." But when Republicans returned in September, it became clear to Boehner that he could not defeat the resolution if Meadows insisted on a vote under arcane House procedures. At the end of the month, Boehner announced that he would step down as Speaker.

The election of Donald Trump as President raised doubts about the influence of the Freedom Caucus, as Republicans prepared for what they expected would be a busy and productive legislative agenda. "Certainly it's easier to fight the president when it's someone from the opposing party," Meadows told *The Atlantic* in December 2016, as he became the group's chairman.

As it turned out, Meadows became an outspoken critic of the initial House Republican plan to revise the Affordable Care Act, and he played a prominent role in making changes that further reduced the scope of President Barack Obama's landmark law. Trump targeted Meadows for the initial setback, with a caustic Tweet that the Freedom Caucus had "saved Planned Parenthood & Ocare." And he not so jokingly threatened Meadows at a White House meeting with conservatives, "I'm coming after you," if the House failed to pass a bill. Reinforced by grass-roots conservative encouragement to hold firm, Meadows resumed negotiations for his approach. He reached agreement with Republican Rep. Tom MacArthur of New Jersey on a key provision, which became the trigger for the House-passed agreement. In a review of how Meadows handled the deal, *Yahoo* headlined the outcome: Under Mark Meadows, the Freedom Caucus discovers the power of 'yes'

At home, Meadows twice won easy reelection. Democrats appear to have thrown in the towel on this district and he faced no primary opposition. That apparently did not mean that all Republicans were happy with him. In September 2015, a few days before Boehner announced his resignation, *The Hill* reported that some local Republicans were discussing the possibility of a primary challenge, with national party encouragement. GOP Rep. Patrick McHenry, who represents the district adjacent to Meadows, acknowledged the rumors but denied that he had anything to do with them. In any case, no opponent stepped forward.

Western North Carolina: Asheville

Demographics data for new House districts were not prepared by the Census Bureau prior to our editorial deadline.

Voter Turnout

2016 House Turnout as % CVAP	N/A	2016 House turnout	359,508

2012 Presidential Vote information unavailable due to recent redistricting.

2016 Presidential Vote		
Donald Trump	230,018	(62%)
Hillary Clinton	123,790	(34%)
Gary Johnson	10,246	(3%)

Cook Partisan Voting Index: R+14

Steeped in the hues that gave them the name Blue Ridge, the heavily wooded mountains of North Carolina seem placid and ancient. Geologically, they are some of the oldest ranges in the world; they began forming 400 million years ago, when plant life was just beginning to spread across the continents. In the early 20th century, this hardscrabble country, around the county seats of Lenoir and Morganton, became a manufacturing area. Textile mill owners moved their operations from New England to western North Carolina for its low-wage workforce. After the collapse of the residential furniture industry in Grand Rapids, Michigan, during the Great Depression, furniture manufacturing took hold in the region because of the abundance of hardwood forests.

Textiles are a low-wage industry that typically represent the first stage in industrial development, migrating to cheaper venues when wages rise. And furniture has faced competition from Asia. So the region has increasingly turned to technology. In the 1990s, the boom industry in the Catawba Valley was fiber optics, with new factories that helped reduce unemployment. Google built a $600 million data center in Lenoir. In November 2015, Google announced that it was the first customer of a Duke Energy program to bring renewable power from a nearby solar farm. Tourism has become a major local business. The Blue Ridge Parkway is the main route that feeds into the Great Smoky Mountains, which cross into Tennessee. In 2015, they were the most popular site and the most popular park in the National Park Service.

The 11th District of North Carolina includes the Catawba Valley and consists of small, mountainous counties in far western North Carolina. The local politics had been volatile. From 1978 through 2012, the western North Carolina district switched between the parties seven times and threw out six incumbents. Republicans redistricters after the 2010 census worked hard to make sure that it wouldn't switch again anytime soon. About a third of the district's residents live in the stretch of counties along the Tennessee border. These include some of the most reliably Republican locales in the nation. Another third of the district comes from the Asheville and Hendersonville areas, but redistricters have removed most of the Democratic precincts in Asheville and kept Republican areas of Buncombe County. Retiree-friendly Henderson County - which, like Buncombe, grew by 7 percent from 2010 to 2016 -- is heavily Republican. Avery County, which has never voted for a Democratic presidential candidate since it was created in 1912, was moved to the 5th District by the 2016 redistricting, part of the minor tweaks to the 11th. In 2016, Donald Trump got 62 percent in the 11th, which remained the strongest GOP-performing district in North Carolina.

TWELFTH DISTRICT

Alma Adams (D)

Elected 2014, 2nd full term; b. May 27, 1946, High Point; North Carolina A&T State University, B.S., 1969; North Carolina A&T State University, M.S., 1972; Ohio State University, Ph.D., 1981; Baptist; Divorced; 2 children; 4 grandchildren.

Elected Office: Guilford Cty., School Board, 1984-1986; Greensboro City Council, 1987-1994; NC House, 1994-2014.

Professional Career: Professor, Bennett College, 1972-2012.

DC Office: 222 CHOB 20515, 202-225-1510, Fax: 202-225-1512, adams.house.gov.

State Offices: Charlotte, 704-344-9950; Greensboro, 336-275-9950.

Committees: *Agriculture*: Nutrition. *Education & the Workforce*: Higher Education & Workforce Development, Workforce Protections. *Joint Economic*. *Small Business*: Investigations, Oversight & Regulations (RMM).

Group Ratings

	ADA	ACLU	AFL-CIO	LCV	ITI	COC	HAFA	ACU	CFG	FRC
2016	-	100%	-	100%	80%	62%	11%	0%	4%	0%
2015	100%	C	100%	97%	C	47%	C	5%	0%	0%

Almanac Ratings 2015

	Economy	Social	Foreign	Composite
Liberal	98%	83%	85%	89%
Conservative	2%	17%	15%	11%

Key Votes of the 114th Congress

1. Keystone Pipeline	N	5. Puerto Rico Debt	Y	9. Offenses by Aliens	N
2. Trade Deals	N	6. Medical Marijuana	NV	10. Troops in Iraq	Y
3. Export-Import Bank	Y	7. Sanctuary Cities	NV	11. Homeland Security $$	Y
4. Debt Ceiling Increase	Y	8. Armor-piercing Bullets	NV	12. Trade Adjustment aid	Y

Election Results

Election	Name (Party)	Vote (%)		Cand. Spent	Ind. Exp. Support	Ind. Exp. Oppose
2016 General	Alma Adams (D)	234,115	(67%)	$811,253	$1	
	Leon Threatt (R)	115,185	(33%)	$36,163		
2016 Primary	Alma Adams (D)	12,356	(43%)			
	Malcolm Graham (D)	8,414	(29%)			
	Tricia Cotham (D)	6,151	(21%)			

Prior winning percentages: 2014 (75%), 2014 special (75%)

Democrat Alma Adams, elected in 2014, has pursued a relatively moderate approach, with occasional bipartisanship. When redistricting in 2016 removed her home base, she showed flexibility.

Adams arrived in Washington as a rarity: a lawmaker with a fine-arts background. She grew up in New Jersey, with her single mother who did domestic work. She got her bachelor's degree from North Carolina A&T State University, a master's and her doctorate in art education and multicultural education from Ohio State University. Until 2012, she taught art history at Bennett College, a historically black women's college. She got her first taste of politics in the 1980s, with election to the Guilford County School Board and the Greensboro City Council; she was the first African-American woman elected to the school board. A single mother from a working-class African-American community, she focused on educational and housing disparities. She helped to organize Greensboro for the 1988 presidential campaign of Jesse Jackson.

In 1994, Adams was appointed to the state Assembly, where she chaired the Legislative Black Caucus and became known as "the minimum-wage lady" because of her advocacy. Adams is known for her hats; she said she had 903 of them. "It's a part of my wardrobe," she told National Public Radio in 2015. "I started wearing hats because I was sick a lot. And I remember my grandmother telling me, 'Cover your noggin; you'll stay healthy.'"

The departure of Rep. Melvin Watt, who held the seat from 1993 until President Barack Obama nominated him to head the Federal Housing Finance Agency, set off a scramble. Seven Democrats jumped into the race. With her political experience, Adams was in a strong position for contributions, endorsements and name recognition. She was backed by progressive and abortion-rights organizations that funneled at least $186,000 to super PACs that took aim at her top Democratic rival, Malcolm Graham, a former Charlotte city council member and state senator. Organized labor was another major ally.

In a heavily Democratic district, the candidates largely agreed on the core issues: supporting the Affordable Care Act, opposing the decision of Republican Gov. Pat McCrory to block Medicaid expansion, and taking aim at Republican efforts to curtail early voting. Adams emphasized her role as a legislator in the Democratic pushback against the GOP majority in a state where partisan politics had become fractious. Her tactics paid off. She easily topped the field in the primary with 44 percent to 24 percent for Graham. Her victory in the general election was a foregone conclusion. She got 75 percent against Republican Vince Coakley.

She displayed her activism on numerous issues. With Republican Rep. Bradley Byrne of Alabama, she founded the Historically Black Colleges and Universities Caucus. In July 2016, the House passed their bill with improvements in capital financing of HBCUs. Adams introduced with Democratic Rep. Rosa DeLauro the Paycheck Fairness Act for gender equality on wages, and she filed a measure to raise the federal minimum wage to $12 hourly by 2020. She said that voting must be made easier for all Americans, and claimed that mandatory voter ID laws did the opposite. During the House Democrats' June 2016 sit-in to demand House action on gun control, she said that the National Rifle Association needed to "get the hell out of the way."

As the Democrats' vice ranking member on the Small Business Committee and the ranking Democrat on the Investigation, Oversight and Regulations Subcommittee, Adams filed the Small and Disadvantaged Businesses Act, which called for a review of government purchasing procedures. That measure was enacted as part of the defense spending bill in 2016. Earlier, the House approved her amendment calling on the Pentagon to assure that service members have enough resources and treatment for post-traumatic stress disorder.

When redistricting reduced her district to only Mecklenburg County, Adams claimed that she picked up roots from her home in Greensboro to run in the Democratic primary. Graham ran again. *The Charlotte Observer*, saying that it preferred "someone with a better grounding in Charlotte's history, culture and neighborhoods," endorsed him, and cited his "deep varied local experience." Graham ran an ad with the slogan, "A house is not a home." Also running in the primary was state Rep. Tricia Cotham, who said that Adams was "intentionally deceiving" voters by claiming that she had changed her residence. Adams had a big fundraising advantage, including contributions from EMILY's List, the abortion-rights group that supports Democratic women. Memos that had been hacked from the computers of the Democratic Congressional Campaign Committee revealed its assistance for Adams, who raised more than $900,000, to about $100,000 for each of her chief challengers. In another seven-candidate primary, Adams got 43 percent to 29 percent for Graham and 21 percent for Cotham. She won the general with 67 percent of the vote, which was an after-thought in this district. Still, the outcome of the primary was evidence that she had not locked down the district.

Charlotte

Demographics data for new House districts were not prepared by the Census Bureau prior to our editorial deadline.

Voter Turnout			
2016 House Turnout as % CVAP	N/A	2016 House turnout	349,300

2012 Presidential Vote information unavailable due to recent redistricting.

2016 Presidential Vote		
Hillary Clinton	243,693	(67%)
Donald Trump	101,178	(28%)
Gary Johnson	11,425	(3%)

Cook Partisan Voting Index: D+18

"This is perhaps the Negro's temporary farewell to Congress," began the peroration of the last speech given by George White, an African-American lawyer from Tarboro, North Carolina, and a Republican, in his last days in the House in 1901. Segregation was being imposed by law, and blacks were informally but effectively driven from the voting rolls in the rural South. The conclusion of White's speech proved prophetic: "Phoenix-like, he will rise up some day and come again. These parting words are in behalf of an outraged, heart-broken, bruised, and bleeding, but God-fearing people, faithful, industrious, loyal people - rising people, full of potential force." When White said his farewell, most North Carolina blacks lived on farms or in tiny towns. Through the 20th century, few moved to the textile towns, where most mills hired only whites, but some moved to its larger cities. After the Voting Rights Act of 1965, their "potential force" began to be felt as they elected members to the state legislature. Some blacks won in white-majority constituencies, notably Charlotte Mayor Harvey Gantt. No African American from North Carolina succeeded White in Congress until the Democratic legislature after the 1990 census drew two irregularly shaped black-majority districts. That resulted in the election in 1992 of Eva Clayton in the mostly rural and small-town 1st District and of Melvin Watt in the mostly urban 12th District.

Charlotte-based Mecklenburg County and Raleigh-based Wake include about one-fifth of the population in North Carolina, but they accounted for half of the population gain in 2015. Charlotte, which is about 80 percent of Mecklenburg, has a respectable share of *Fortune* 500 companies. Nine are headquartered in the Charlotte area, including Bank of America, Lowe's, Family Dollar Stores and Duke Energy. The city has a boosterish pride in its capacity for accommodation. The downside of this rapid growth is that the city has had the worst sprawl of 15 fast-growing metro areas. Construction by a private contractor of two toll lanes in each direction for 26 miles on Interstate 77 was scheduled for completion in late 2018. Charlotte has promoted cultural development and entertainment worthy of its growing business stature. It boasts the NASCAR Hall of Fame and a $50 million performing arts center across from the 60-story Bank of America tower. In March 2017, an investment firm unveiled plans for a 75-acre warehouse and distribution center just north of downtown.

The 12th Congressional District of North Carolina has been the most litigated district in the country since the 1990s and has been the focus of no fewer than four cases that went to the Supreme Court. It originally comprised a series of black precincts connected in some places by nothing wider than the lanes of Interstate 85, and it stretched 160 miles from Gastonia to Durham. Over the years, it grew a bit shorter, though the Republican-drawn version in 2012 remained a snake-like agglomeration that roughly paralleled I-85 and included parts of Charlotte, Greensboro, Winston-Salem, Salisbury, Lexington and High Point. The district, among the most gerrymandered in the nation, concentrated Democratic strength of any color, helping to make nearby districts more Republican. Finally, in the 2016 redistricting, the 12th took on regular lines and was entirely in Mecklenburg. The outcome was the same: The district remained a Democratic island that bordered four Republican-held districts, with three others nearby in western North Carolina.

The district, including the major banking center in downtown Charlotte, is 37 percent black and 14 percent Hispanic - compared with 54 percent and 15 percent in the old 12th. The Hispanic share is the largest of any district in the state. The remaining blacks from the old 12th have been apportioned to other districts. The changes reduced the vote in 2012 for President Barack Obama from 79 percent, among the highest in the nation in 2008, to 68 percent. In 2016, Hillary Clinton won 67 percent here, the same as her vote in the two other Democratic-held districts in North Carolina.

THIRTEENTH DISTRICT

Ted Budd (R)

Elected 2016, 1st term; b. Oct 21, 1971, Winston-Salem; Appalachian State University (NC), B.S., 1994; Dallas Theological Seminary (TX), M.Th., 1998; Wake Forest University (NC), M.B.A., 2007; Christian - Non-Denominational; Married (Amy Kate); 3 children.

Professional Career: Investment analyst; Business owner.

DC Office: 118 CHOB 20515, 202-225-4531, budd.house.gov.

State Offices: Advance, 336-998-1313.

Committees: *Financial Services*: Capital Markets, Securities & Investment, Housing & Insurance, Terrorism & Illicit Finance.

Election Results

Election	Name (Party)	Vote	(%)	Cand. Spent	Ind. Exp. Support	Ind. Exp. Oppose
2016 General	Ted Budd (R)	199,443	(56%)	$550,632	$501,219	
	Bruce Davis (D)	156,049	(44%)	$54,938	$1	
2016 Primary	Ted Budd (R)	6,308	(20%)			
	John Blust (R)	3,293	(10%)			
	Hank Henning (R)	3,270	(10%)			
	Julia Howard (R)	3,230	(10%)			
	Matthew McCall (R)	2,859	(9%)			
	Andrew Brock (R)	2,788	(9%)			
	Jason Walser (R)	2,309	(7%)			
	Dan Barrett (R)	2,284	(7%)			

Ted Budd was elected in 2016 to a newly created seat in a contest that received little attention, either locally or nationally. A political newcomer, he owns a gun store and range. He has set a limit for himself of three terms in the House.

Budd grew up on a 300-acre cattle and commercial chicken farm and he continues to reside there in the town of Advance, which had a population of 1,138 in the 2010 census. His father built a janitorial supply house into a facility-services company that employs 3,400 people in 10 states, *The Charlotte Observer* reported. He graduated from Appalachian State University, where he worked on phone banks for Republican Sen. Jesse Helms. He got graduate degrees in theology from Dallas Theological Seminary and in business administration from Wake Forest University. Budd met his wife, Amy Kate, while they were on a mission trip to the former Soviet Union. He worked for his father's company and owned his gun store and shooting range, which he called ProShots. He opposes gun control, and he views terrorism and mental health problems as the chief causes of gun-related violence.

The Republican primary included 17 candidates, none of whom spent sizable amounts of money. Budd raised about $150,000 for the primary, which was more than any of the next three candidates in the contest. He got a big boost from the Club for Growth, which viewed him as a true outsider and spent $500,000 on his behalf, with ads that highlighted his conservative values and firm resolve. In a remarkably low-turnout contest, Budd got 6,340 votes and won the primary with 20 percent. Three other candidates were next in line with 10 percent each: John Blust, Hank Henning and Julia Howard. Budd won Davie and Davidson counties, finished second in Iredell, third in Guilford, which cast about one-third of the vote, and fourth in Rowan, which had the lowest vote.

In the general election, Budd faced Democrat Bruce Davis, a Marine Corps veteran who owned a child development center in High Point and served 12 years as a Guilford County commissioner. In 2014, Davis ran for the House from the 6th District and lost the Democratic primary, 56%-44%. The two candidates had similar views on several issues, including support of gun ownership, opposition to the Trans-Pacific Partnership, and the need to address Islamic extremism. Davis disagreed with Budd's support for a wall on the southern border to keep out illegal immigrants. Davis raised only $91,000 and had scant opportunity to get his message out compared with Budd, who raised nearly $600,000 overall. On November 8, Budd won, 56%-44%. Davis won 60 percent in Guilford, which cast slightly more than half of the vote. Budd won Davie, Davidson and Iredell by margins of more than two-to-one, and more narrowly in Rowan.

In the House, he got a seat on the Financial Services Committee, where he said he would be "using my real world experience to roll back the restrictive regulations that strangle job creation in this country." The redistricting and low voter turnout that created unusual campaign circumstances in 2016 could make Budd vulnerable to a well-organized challenge for reelection.

North-Central North Carolina: Greensboro, High Point

Demographics data for new House districts were not prepared by the Census Bureau prior to our editorial deadline.

Voter Turnout			
2016 House Turnout as % CVAP	N/A	2016 House turnout	355,492

2012 Presidential Vote information unavailable due to recent redistricting.

2016 Presidential Vote		
Donald Trump	193,990	(53%)
Hillary Clinton	160,204	(44%)
Gary Johnson	9,678	(3%)

Cook Partisan Voting Index: R+6

For more than half a century, furniture store managers and owners from all over the country twice a year have converged on the huge Furniture Mart in High Point, the center of the U.S. furniture business. The giant trade show put on by manufacturers has attracted about 75,000 visitors and 2,000 exhibitors. The furniture business grew here early in the 20th century because of the hardwoods in the mountains not far to the west and the abundance of low-wage labor in the flatlands not far to the east. For many years, the furniture business has proven more resilient than textiles and tobacco. Recently, it has faced serious competition from China, though *Forbes* reported in May 2016 that the Furniture Capital had made a comeback. Projections from the North Carolina Commission on Workforce Development, showed that it stood to lose more than 3,000 jobs between 2012 and 2016. Attendance at the May 2016 trade show was down about 1 percent, probably due in part to the state's controversial "bathroom bill," which was opposed by the High Point Market Authority.

The Triad area - Greensboro, High Point, and Winston-Salem - has scrambled for new sources of economic growth to keep pace with booming Raleigh-Durham and Charlotte. In 2009, FedEx opened a hub at Piedmont Triad International Airport, between Winston-Salem and Greensboro, which was followed in 2011 by a new "super hub" ground sorting facility that handled up to 24,000 packages per hour. That has led other firms to plan distribution centers to utilize the "aerotropolis," otherwise known as a city built around an airport.

The new 13th Congressional District has no overlap with the old 13th, which was east of Raleigh. It was formed with pieces of five districts under the old map, from west of Raleigh and north of Charlotte. Nearly half its population is in Greensboro-based Guilford County, which had been the center of the old 6th. The population in the new 6th shifted closer to Raleigh. Along with two-thirds of Guilford, the district includes all of Davie and Davidson, most of Iredell and one-third of Rowan. Iredell has had rapid growth as the Charlotte metro area has expanded deeper into the suburbs.

Politically, the 13th is divided into two distinct parts. Guilford, which has a bit more than half of the population, leans Democratic. Hillary Clinton got 59 percent in the county, which is 41 percent black. The five counties to the west are comfortably Republican with large white majorities. When the district was created, it had the lowest Republican presidential support of the 10 GOP-leaning districts in North Carolina. John McCain got 51 percent of the vote in 2008 and Mitt Romney had 53 percent in 2012. In 2016, Donald Trump led, 53%-44%.

★ NORTH DAKOTA ★

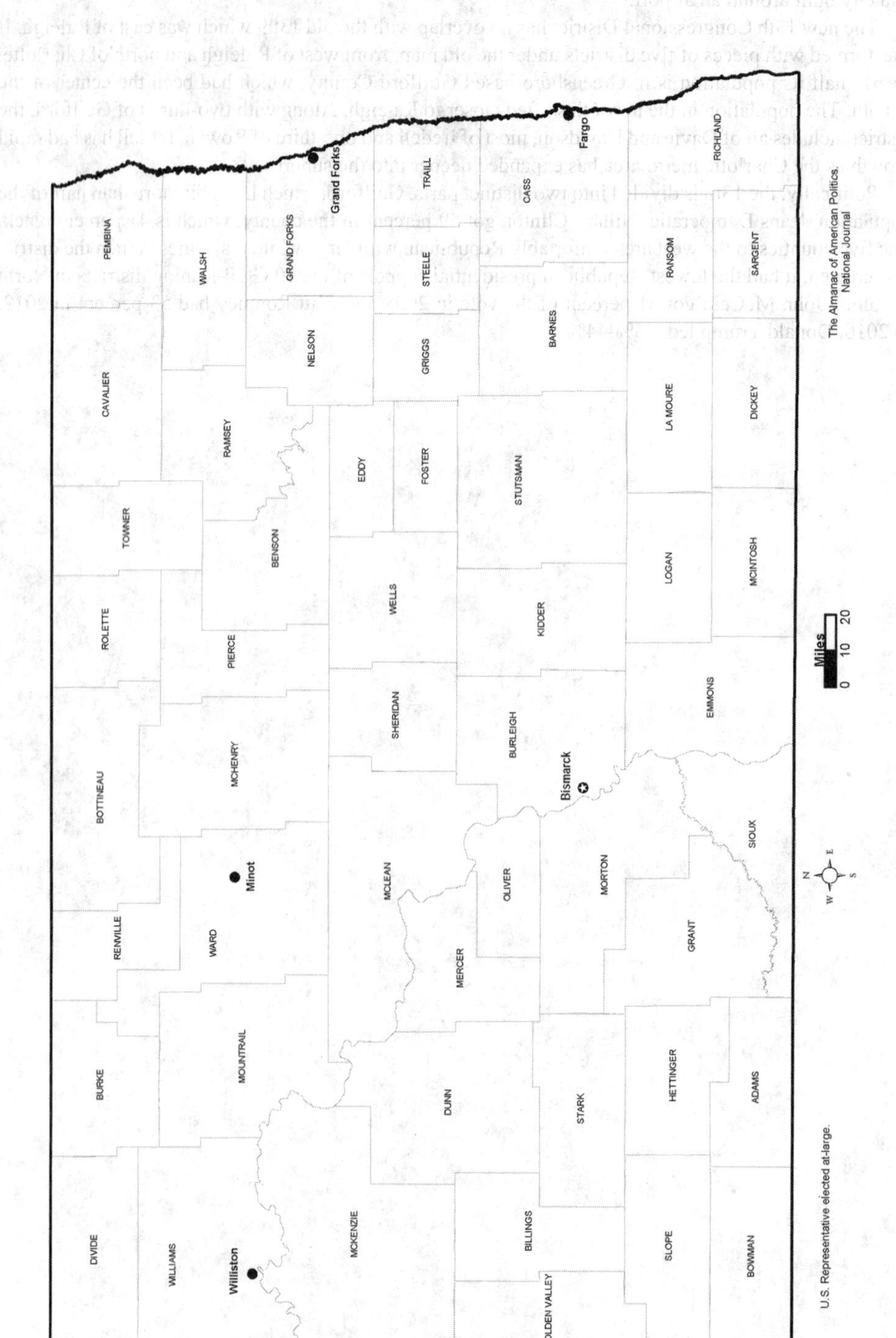

For a state that is one of the most remote in the Lower 48, North Dakota has been much in the news recently – first for a shale-oil boom that, at least for a while, transformed the western part of the state, and then for protests by Native Americans against the Dakota Access Pipeline. Amid the ferment and turmoil, North Dakota was strengthening its already solid Republican leanings.

In late 1804, members of the Lewis and Clark Expedition paddled up the Missouri River and reached what is now North Dakota. The explorers bivouacked for the winter across the river from where the state capital of Bismarck now stands, and spent 146 nights in North Dakota. On the Lewis and Clark Trail, you can still see traces of the pristine landscape the expedition encountered - a vast unfenced land where the Indians built a civilization based on the buffalo and the horse, a Spanish import. Less than a hundred years later, railroads crisscrossed the prairie and the Sioux were herded onto reservations; it was from Fort Abraham Lincoln, built on the site of an old Mandan Indian village in central North Dakota, that the post's commander, George A. Custer, rode out to his death at Little Bighorn. Theodore Roosevelt owned a ranch in the late 19th century. By the time he visited the state as president in 1903, he needed perseverance to find a buffalo to shoot. North Dakota is relentlessly flat, its lush, green farmland pockmarked in places by placid blue "prairie pothole" lakes carved by glaciers; its flatness encourages flooding, as in the massive Grand Forks flood in April 1997 as well as the creeping expansion of Devils Lake, which for a while in the 1990s threatened to overwhelm the eponymous city.

North Dakota was admitted to the Union in 1889, on the same day as South Dakota -- no one knows which is the 39th state and which is the 40th, thanks to some quick paper shuffling by President Benjamin Harrison's Secretary of State -- and settlers poured in. Its prairies turned out to be some of the best wheat-growing acreage in the world, and while wheat - mostly spring wheat but also durum (used in pasta) - remains the biggest crop, it is not the only one. North Dakota ranks high in the production of dry edible beans, oats, dry peas, sunflowers, barley, sugar beets and rye. There is also plenty of cattle ranching on the arid plains in the western half of the state. While North Dakota's cold climate discouraged many Americans from settling this far north, it was no deterrent to emigrants from Germany, Norway, Bohemia (now the Czech Republic), Iceland and Russia. North Dakota's population shot up from 191,000 in 1890 to 319,000 in 1900 and to 647,000 in 1920. For the next nine decades, its population oscillated in the 600,000s, until it began to rise dramatically after 2007, reaching 757,952 in the Census estimate for 2016. Just a decade after worries about an emptying-out of the northern plains, North Dakota saw the fastest-growing population of any state. All told, the population has risen by 12.7 percent since the 2010 census

Behind those numbers are two stories. The contraction owed to the state's dependence on an agriculture sector growing ever more productive and efficient, and thus requiring less labor. The subsequent rise came from a newer economic engine: oil and natural gas from the Bakken shale formation in the western part of the state. North Dakota had seen energy booms before. In the 1970s, it developed lignite coal just west of Bismarck, which bequeathed six electric power plants and a coal gasification facility. But that paled in compared to Bakken. Discovered in 1951 and named after a Williston-area farmer, it remained untapped for many years. Then, in 2006, oil producers began using extended-reach horizontal drilling to reach more deposits, along with hydraulic fracturing to break up the shale in which the oil is embedded. "Satellite photos of western North Dakota at night, aglitter like a metropolis with lighted rigs and burning flares, crystallized its rapid transformation from tight-knit agricultural society to semi-industrialized oil powerhouse," the *New York Times* wrote at the peak of the region's production. After a twenty-fold increase in six years, North Dakota surged to No. 2 in the nation in petroleum production; natural gas output rose as well. At its peak in 2014, oil production contributed $50 million a day to North Dakota's economy, with more than $11 million daily in oil and gas taxes for the state, according to the North Dakota Petroleum Council. Unemployment peaked at a ridiculously low 4.3 percent and was below 3 percent between May 2013 and November 2015. After a bump to 3.3 percent in early 2016, it sank again to 3 percent in late 2016, fourth best in the nation.

Fueling this boom has been a surge of men (and fewer women) to western North Dakota, lured by annual earnings of $100,000; many lived in RVs or modular living pods lined up on farm fields, because Williston, improbably, had become the nation's highest average rent for an entry-level apartment. Ten counties in the region registered double-digit population increases in the first half-decade after the 2010 census, led by Williams County (58 percent) and McKenzie County (102 percent). In what is the sixth-whitest state in the country, the share of African Americans and Hispanics essentially doubled, from a small base, largely due to the new work available for qualified out-of-staters. Trucks carrying water in for fracking and oil out for refining jammed the two-lane roads and buckled the pavement; there were long lines at stores and fast-food takeout lanes, and schools were strained. In Williston, "the first thing you see leaving the Amtrak station is two strip clubs that cater to the wave of men coming into town from the oil fields, their pockets stuffed with cash," NPR reported. This milieu has spawned human and drug trafficking, organized crime and homicides - a situation worrisome enough that the FBI opened an office there.

But the energy sector is volatile, and beginning in 2015, with lower prices on the global market, production began to decline. This didn't necessarily show up in the unemployment figures – workers would often leave the state when work dried up – but the number of operating rigs fell by three quarters. This had an immediate impact on the state budget, which in February 2016 faced a $1 billion hole over two fiscal years. The environmental impact caused worries as well. In 2013, a pipeline spilled more than 20,000 barrels of crude into a wheat field; later that year, a mile-long train carrying crude exploded into a giant fireball after colliding with a grain-hauling train and derailing. In 2014, 1 million gallons of saltwater produced by oil extraction leaked from a pipeline and headed toward a Native American reservation. Worker deaths spiked, and the lack of government regulation has been questioned. The *New York Times* calculated that North Dakota regulators have collected just one-thirtieth the fines on industry that Texas collected over the same period.

Another potential casualty of the oil boom was Native American culture and resources. For 10 months starting in 2016, the Standing Rock Sioux, joined by the Cheyenne River Sioux and a small group of celebrities, camped out to oppose the $3.7 billion Dakota Access Pipeline, which would run for 1,170 miles from North Dakota to Illinois. Living in teepees and rallying behind the cry "Mni wiconi!" – "water is life" – they said the pipeline would threaten drinking water supplies and harm ancestral lands. Work was temporarily halted by the Obama administration, but President Donald Trump reversed that decision as one of his first actions. The remaining demonstrators were cleared in February 2017 after burning some of their teepees as a final act of protest (and leaving tons of trash behind); tensions between the protest camp and nearby ranchers had become so heated that one state lawmaker proposed a bill to legalize running over protesters in the road as long as it was done accidentally. (The bill was defeated in the state House.) For Native Americans – the state's largest minority group – choosing between economic growth and cultural and environmental protection was often wrenching. "We would like to see more drilling," Indian official Gene McCowan told Reuters. "But we are caught in a bind because people are concerned about fracking and how that will affect the earth and water."

Until recently, dependence on agriculture, not oil, shaped North Dakota's politics. When farm prices are high, it is often because of low production; when they are low, farmers seek protection. The boosterish optimism of the first settlers was soon followed by cries, reverberating with varying intensity, for government protection against market forces. Since commodity prices tend to fall during periods of economic growth, there was often a countercyclical force at work in North Dakota politics - a tendency to vote against the national trends and a radical strain going back to the 1910s. That strain also owes much to the Scandinavian and German origins of many of the state's early settlers, who produced orderly small towns and grain cooperatives and supported the Nonpartisan League, which operated as an independent force from its founding in 1915 until its alliance with the Democratic Party in 1956.

The NPL appealed to marginal farmers, cut off in many cases from the wider American culture by language barriers and seemingly at the mercy of the grain millers in Minneapolis, the railroads in St. Paul, the banks in New York City, and the commodity traders in Chicago. The NPL's program was socialist - government ownership of railroads and grain elevators - and its members, like most North Dakota ethnics, opposed going to war with Germany in 1917 and in 1940-41. The NPL often determined the outcome of the usually decisive Republican primary, but sometimes swung its support to the otherwise heavily outnumbered Democrats, instituting reforms and creating the state-owned Bank of North Dakota and a state grain elevator. Such Democratic politicians as Sens. Quentin Burdick, Kent Conrad and Byron Dorgan and Rep. Earl Pomeroy championed a politics of NPL lineage: supportive of government farm programs, wary of if not hostile to American military involvement abroad, and a cheerful championing of the little guy from North Dakota against out-of-state corporations.

One reason Democrats thrived for years while the state steadily voted Republican for president is that politics is personal in a place where most everyone knows everyone else. For years voter registration has been automatic because people spotted anyone who was not eligible. (In a sign of the times, the

GOP-led state government tightened its voter ID law in 2013, though three years later a federal judge barred the state from enforcing it.) North Dakota's combination of light taxation and regulation on the one hand and the state-owned Bank of North Dakota on the other has encouraged business start-ups. But communal closeness has produced an innate cultural conservatism. Bills to ban discrimination based on sexual orientation have been rejected four times since 2009; the state joined a suit to challenge the Obama administration's transgender schools policy; and Republican Gov. Jack Dalrymple signed what was widely regarded as the nation's strictest anti-abortion law. (The law was overturned by the courts, and North Dakota voters separately rejected a ballot measure in November 2014 that would have defined life as beginning at conception.)

With rare exceptions – such as Democrat Heidi Heitkamp's narrow Senate victory in 2012 – North Dakota has become a solidly Republican state. Donald Trump – who visited the state to tout his pro-fossil-fuel energy agenda – was able to expand Mitt Romney's 2012 winning margin of 19 points to a 36-point victory in 2016, with Republican votes climbing by 29,000 and Democratic votes tumbling by 31,000 between the two elections. Whereas Obama had won six counties in 2012, but Hillary Clinton won just two in 2016, both of them small. Each of the four counties that switched from Obama to Trump shifted their margins heavily in the GOP's direction – Steele (a 20-point shift toward Trump), Benson (21 points), and Ransom and Sargent (both 28 points).In contrast to many states, North Dakota's most populous counties – Cass (Fargo), Burleigh (Bismarck), Ward (Minot), and Grand Forks -- all voted Republican in both 2012 and 2016. Even more strikingly, each of these four populous counties shifted their margins towards Trump by between seven and 16 percentage points. Today, Democrats – including Heitkamp, who is up for reelection in 2018 – face stiffer odds than ever in North Dakota.

Population		**Race and Ethnicity**		**Income**	
Total	721,640	White	87.0%	Median Income	$57,181 (18 out of 50)
Land area	69,001	Black	1.6%		
Pop/ sq mi	10.5	Latino	2.9%	Under $50,000	44.2%
Born in state	65.7%	Asian	1.2%	$50,000-$99,999	32.4%
		Two races	2.0%	$100,000-$199,999	18.9%
Age Groups		Other	5.2%	$200,000 or more	4.6%
Under 18	22.6%			Poverty Rate	11.5%
18-34	26.9%	**Education**			
35-64	36.3%	H.S grad or less	35.7%	**Health Insurance**	
Over 64	14.2%	Some college	36.6%	With health insurance coverage	90.9%
		College Degree, 4 yr	20.1%		
Work		Post grad	7.6%		
White Collar	35.0%			**Public Assistance**	
Sales and Service	39.4%	**Military**		Cash public assistance income	1.7%
Blue Collar	25.6%	Veteran	9.3%		
Government	16.4%	Active Duty	1.0%	Food stamp/SNAP benefits	7.7%

Voter Turnout			
2015 Total Citizens 18+	546,486	2016 Pres Turnout as % CVAP	63%
2016 Pres Votes	344,360	2012 Pres Turnout as % CVAP	63%

Legislature	
Senate:	9D, 38R
House:	14D, 80R

Presidential Politics

2016 Democratic Caucus		
Bernie Sanders (D)	253	(64%)
Hillary Clinton (D)	101	(26%)

2016 Presidential Vote		
Donald Trump (R)	216,794	(63%)
Hillary Clinton (D)	93,758	(27%)
Gary Johnson (L)	21,434	(6%)
2012 Presidential Vote		
Mitt Romney (R)	188,163	(58%)
Barack Obama (D)	124,827	(39%)

Cook Partisan Voting Index: R+16

In the past 20 presidential elections North Dakota has voted only once for a Democratic nominee: Lyndon Johnson in 1964. So it came as no surprise that Donald Trump defeated Hillary Clinton here, 63%-27%. Clinton carried just two of the state's 53 counties, Rolette and Sioux, where the Native American population exceeds 75 percent. The latter county was also the site of the Standing Rock Sioux Tribe protests against the Dakota Access Pipeline. North Dakota was the state that turned most Republican in the 2016 election: Trump's margin over Clinton was 36 percentage points, a whopping 16-point increase from Mitt Romney's margin over Barack Obama in 2012. No other state saw such a large jump. Democrats can be competitive in North Dakota if they win Cass (Fargo) and Grand Forks (home to the University of North Dakota) counties, which have a relatively high share of white-collar workers. Republican strength is in the central and western part of the state where oil and natural gas production from the Bakken shale formation has had a significant impact on the state's economy.

North Dakota Democrats and Republicans use caucuses to help select their national convention delegates. In 2016 the state GOP declined to include a presidential preference poll at the first stage of its caucuses, opting to elect individuals its state party convention, who would then select a delegation to the national Republican confab in Cleveland that was technically unbound to any candidate. When the state convention was held April 3, Texas Sen. Ted Cruz's campaign, as it had in other states with similar formats, was able to get many of his supporters elected as national convention delegates. However, after Cruz suspended his campaign, many of the Cruz delegates switched their allegiance to Trump. The Democratic caucuses were held June 7, overshadowed by primaries in California, New Jersey and other states. But Vermont Sen. Bernie Sanders campaigned in Bismarck and won 64 percent of the county delegates selected to the state convention to Clinton's 26 percent, with 10 percent uncommitted.

Congressional Districts

115th Congress Lineup	1R	**114th Congress Lineup**	1R

Governor

Doug Burgum (R)

Elected 2016, term expires 2016, 1st term; b. Aug. 1, 1956, Arthur, ND; North Dakota State University, BA 1978; Stanford University, MBA 1980; Married (Kathryn); 3 children.

Professional Career: CEO, Great Plains Software 1983-2001; Senior Vice President, Microsoft Business Solutions Group,2001-2007; Founder, Arthur Ventures.

Office: 600 E. Boulevard Ave., Bismarck, 58505-0001; 701-328-2200; Fax: 701-328-2205; Website: governor.nd.gov.

Election Results

Election	Name (Party)	Vote (%)
2016 General	Doug Burgum (R)	259,863 (77%)
	Marvin Nelson (D)	65,855 (19%)
	Marty Riske (L)	13,230 (4%)
2016 Primary	Doug Burgum (R)	68,042 (59%)
	Wayne Stenehjem (R)	44,158 (39%)

Doug Burgum, a successful software entrepreneur, was elected governor of North Dakota in 2016 after winning the state primary as an underdog and then prevailing easily in the general election. North Dakota voters, who have not voted Democratic for governor since 1988, made Burgum the third out of the state's four most recent governors to ascend to the office without having held a lower elective office. Burgum took the reins of a state that has grown substantially from oil and gas production, but which more recently has suffered budgetary challenges stemming from declining drilling.

Burgum grew up near tiny Arthur, northwest of Fargo, and attended North Dakota State University, where he was a cheerleader. He earned an MBA at Stanford before returning to North Dakota. In 1983, he mortgaged the family farm to get into the computer business. He became CEO of Fargo-based Great Plains Software, expanded the company, took it public in 1997, then sold it to Microsoft for $1.1 billion in 2001, when it had 1,200 local employees. Burgum then led Microsoft Business Solutions for six years before founding a group to revitalize downtown Fargo and establishing a venture-capital firm.

After Gov. Jack Dalrymple announced that he would not seek another term, Burgum announced his intention to run for the seat in January 2016. With a deep Republican bench in the state, others were ahead of him in the establishment queue, notably long-serving state Attorney General Wayne Stenehjem. Burgum seized the outsider's mantle, touting his business experience ("when I think about the governor's job, I like it because it's a CEO position," Burgum told *Fortune*) and announcing that he would forgo his gubernatorial salary if elected. He was dealt a setback in the state Republican convention in April, when he finished a distant third behind Stenehjem and state Rep. Rick Becker. Moving onto the primary, Stenehjem had the endorsements of Dalrymple, Sen. John Hoeven and most Republican state lawmakers. But amid a $1.6 billion state budget shortfall and the Republican surge for Donald Trump, Burgum's outsider approach was more effective with rank-and-file voters in the June primary. Burgum endorsed Trump in May and spoke more favorably about him than Stenehjem did. Burgum defeated Stenehjem, 60%-38%, carrying 49 of North Dakota's 53 counties.

The general election was anticlimactic, as the Democrats put up under-funded state Rep. Marvin Nelson. Much of Burgum's time was spent trying to heal rifts with fellow Republicans. On Election Day, Burgum won, 77%-19%. That 58-point margin was double Dalrymple's already substantial 29-point victory in 2012. Nelson won only two counties, down from the six won by the Democratic nominee in 2012. Strikingly, Burgum increased the GOP's winning margins from 2012 by roughly double digits in each of the state's four most populous counties – Cass (Fargo), Burleigh (Bismarck), Ward (Minot) and Grand Forks.

Upon taking office, Burgum kept most of Dalrymple's cabinet and sought more extensive spending cuts in order to square the state's budget with declining tax revenues from oil and gas. Drawing from his own background, Burgum touted the role of technology in economic growth and the diversification of the state's economy. In his first state of the state address, he choked up while telling the story of a young man he had met in Fargo who was homeless, suffering from addiction to methamphetamine, and facing a parole violation. "Jail time without rehab is not a cure for addiction," Burgum said. "We need to start treating addiction like the chronic disease it is, and by moving these services upstream we will save lives and we will save taxpayer money."

Burgum supported the Dakota Access Pipeline, which had drawn intense protests on environmental and cultural grounds from the Standing Rock Sioux tribe and a band of celebrity allies. However, Burgum offered a "fresh start" to critics of the pipeline, which was eventually green-lighted by Trump. "This is not an issue that will simply go away after the pipeline is completed," Burgum said in his state of the state address. "Trust has been eroded, and it will take time, effort and leadership to rebuild." Beyond policy, Burgum pushed the envelope in at least one stylistic way: by wearing blue jeans to his inauguration. However, his sartorial choice got him in to trouble later when he was ejected from the floor of the state Senate for wearing insufficiently formal attire.

In April 2017, the Legislature approved a bill that allowed Burgum to fulfill his campaign pledge to not accept a salary.

Senior Senator

John Hoeven (R)

Elected 2010, term expires 2022, 2nd term; b. Mar 13, 1957, Bismarck; Dartmouth College, Hanover (NH), B.A.; Northwestern University Kellogg School Management (IL), M.B.A.; Roman Catholic; Married (Mikey Hoeven); 2 children; 3 grandchildren.

Elected Office: ND Governor, 2000-2010.

Professional Career: Executive Vice President., First Western Bank, 1986-1993; President & CEO, Bank of ND, 1993-2000.

DC Office: 338 RSOB 20510, 202-224-2551, Fax: 202-224-7999, hoeven.senate.gov.

State Offices: Bismarck, 701-250-4618; Fargo, 701-239-5389; Grand Forks, 701-746-8972; Minot, 701-838-1361; Williston, 701-580-4535.

Committees: *Agriculture, Nutrition & Forestry*: Commodities, Risk Management & Trade, Nutrition, Agricultural Research & Specialty Crops, Rural Development & Energy. *Appropriations*: Agriculture, Rural Development, FDA & Related Agencies (Chmn), Department of Homeland Security, Department of the Interior, Environment & Related Agencies, Energy & Water Development, Military Construction & Veteran Affairs & Related Agencies, Transportation, HUD & Related Agencies. *Energy & Natural Resources*: Energy, National Parks, Public Lands, Forests & Mining. *Homeland Security & Government Affairs*: Federal Spending Oversight & Emergency Management. *Indian Affairs (Chmn)*.

Group Ratings

	ADA	ACLU	AFL-CIO	LCV	ITI	COC	HAFA	ACU	CFG	FRC
2016	-	17%	-	12%	100%	100%	40%	69%	64%	100%
2015	5%	C	14%	0%	C	93%	C	79%	67%	100%

Almanac Ratings 2015

	Economy	Social	Foreign	Composite
Liberal	29%	0%	22%	17%
Conservative	71%	100%	78%	83%

Key Votes of the 114th Congress

1. Keystone pipeline	Y	5. National Security Data	Y	9. Gun Sales Checks	N
2. Export-Import Bank	N	6. Iran Nuclear Deal	Y	10. Sanctuary Cities	Y
3. Debt Ceiling Increase	N	7. Puerto Rico Debt	Y	11. Planned Parenthood	Y
4. Homeland Security $$	N	8. Loretta Lynch A.G	N	12. Trade deals	Y

Election Results

Election	Name (Party)	Vote (%)	Cand. Spent	Ind. Exp. Support	Ind. Exp. Oppose
2016 General	John Hoeven (R)	268,788 (78%)	$2,055,899		
	Eliot Glassheim (D)	58,116 (17%)	$32,799		
	Robert Marquette (L)	10,556 (3%)			
2016 Primary	John Hoeven (R)	unopposed			

Prior winning percentages: 2010 (76%)

When initially elected in 2010, North Dakota's senior senator, John Hoeven, became the first Republican sent to the Senate from that state in 30 years. His election heralded the political evolution of a jurisdiction in which a majority of voters, while not supporting a Democratic presidential candidate since Lyndon Johnson in 1964, nonetheless had consistently sent Democrats to Capitol Hill to represent them in the intervening years. But, in 2010, amid an oil and gas boom that transformed North Dakota into one of the nation's most economically flourishing states, the Republican tilt at the top of the ticket spread to the congressional delegation. Hoeven, who had presided over the state's new prosperity during a decade as governor, was elected to the Senate by better than a 3-1 margin, and voters also chose a Republican to fill the state's at-large House seat for the first time since 1978.

The overwhelming popularity that Hoeven enjoyed as governor did not fade during his first term in the Senate: In 2016, he was re-elected to a second term by a margin that exceeded 4-1. However, outside of North Dakota, Hoeven's ascension in early 2017 to the normally low-profile chairmanship of the Senate Indian Affairs Committee stirred controversy among progressive activists -- arising from his outspoken condemnation of the months-long protest against an oil pipeline slated to run through an Indian reservation in the southern part of his state.

Ironically, the man credited with helping to put North Dakota firmly in the red state column publicly declared himself a Democrat as recently as four years before his 2000 election as governor. In a 1996 letter to a local newspaper, Hoeven, then president of the Bank of North Dakota-the only state-owned bank in the country-declared, "I have always been moderate in my political views, but now that I am considering elective office, I realize I must join a political party and stick to it." He continued, "I have decided to join the Democratic-NPL Party because I believe that is the best fit for my views." The bank that Hoeven was running at the time had been created in 1919 at the initiative of the Nonpartisan League, a coalition of reformers and radicals that was a major force in North Dakota for the first half of the 20th century (and which merged with state Democrats in 1960 to create what is now known as the Democratic-NPL Party).

When the letter surfaced during Hoeven's 2010 Senate bid, his campaign manager, Don Larson, told *Talking Points Memo* that, shortly after writing the letter, Hoeven "realized his views were more in line with the Republicans than the Democrats. So he got involved with the Republican Party, became a Republican district chairman, helped Republican candidates around North Dakota, and then ran for and won the governorship. Before that, he had not been involved in politics at all, either as a Republican or a Democrat." Throughout his tenure as governor and senator, Hoeven has been in the conservative Republican mainstream on most social issues, ranging from abortion to gun control. But, unlike his colleagues in the Senate Republicans' tea party wing, Hoeven has been open to committing increased funds for education and infrastructure; while he was governor, the state budget increased dramatically, with much of the added spending directed toward those categories.

Hoeven was born in Bismarck and grew up in Minot. His father was a banker who in 1969 took over the First Western Bank & Trust of Minot, which became a family business. John Hoeven started working there as a bookkeeper at age 15. He graduated from Dartmouth College and went on to earn his master's degree in business administration from Northwestern University. In 1981, he returned home to become First Western Bank's executive vice president. In 1993, he was chosen to head the Bank of North Dakota by a board that included his predecessor as governor, Republican Ed Schafer, and Attorney General Heidi Heitkamp, a Democrat who is now the state's junior senator. Under Hoeven's stewardship, the bank's worth rose from $990 million to $1.6 billion, and its loan portfolio increased from $200 million to $1 billion. Hoeven's banking career, combined with successful investments he has made, have placed him among the 25 wealthiest members of the House and Senate, according to *Roll Call*'s latest survey of congressional assets. Financial disclosure forms show him with a net worth of at least $17 million and possibly as much as $73 million.

In 2000, after Schafer retired as governor, Hoeven ran for the post against Heitkamp. He cited his work attracting and retaining local jobs and organizing the effort to keep Minot Air Force Base off the government's base closure list. He called for economic development in the state with an emphasis on the technology industry and on improving education, and he pledged more money for teacher training and salaries. He won 55%-45%, as Heitkamp was compelled to all but forfeit the campaign after she was diagnosed with breast cancer.

As governor, Hoeven used North Dakota's burgeoning state revenues to fund programs to stimulate economic development. In his first years, he combined several state agencies into a Commerce Department. In 2002, he announced an ambitious research and development program, borrowing $50 million for university projects to help commercialize new technology. From 2005 to 2007, more than $40 million in state funds and double that amount in private funds were invested in the Center of Excellence in Life Sciences and Advanced Technologies and other research centers. Much of this was aimed at exploiting North Dakota's considerable energy resources, including oil, coal, ethanol, wind, and hydrogen. In 2002, Hoeven announced his EmPower North Dakota energy plan, aiming to build three new biodiesel plants by 2015 and to have wind supply 10 percent of the state's electricity by 2015. (By the end of 2014, wind energy was actually supplying 17.5 percent of electricity generated in North Dakota, according to the U.S. Department of Energy.)

During his second term, Hoeven submitted budgets with reductions in local property taxes that also provided for big increases in education spending, with the latter targeted at raising teachers' salaries. He had no trouble winning a second term in 2004 over former state Sen. Joseph Satrom, 71%-27%, and national Republicans were hoping that he would take on one of the state's two Democratic senators.

But he opted not to challenge Sen. Kent Conrad in 2006 and, in November 2008, won re-election to a third term by easily defeating state Sen. Tim Mathern, capturing nearly 75 percent of the vote. Before the 2008 election, Hoeven brushed aside speculation that he would run against the state's other senator, Democrat Byron Dorgan or at-large Democratic Rep. Earl Pomeroy in 2010, but did not pledge to serve out his third term.

One poll, at the end of 2009, showed Hoeven with a stratospheric 87-percent approval rating, with the same poll showing him leading Dorgan by a 58%-36% margin in a hypothetical matchup. By all indications, Dorgan was planning to run for a fourth term-he had been raising money for the campaign-until he stunned Senate colleagues in January 2010 by saying he had decided to retire after reflecting over the Christmas holidays. Shortly thereafter, Hoeven announced he was running for the newly open Senate seat, criticizing President Barack Obama's economic agenda and what he called an overly bureaucratic overhaul of the health care system. He didn't have to campaign very hard. Both Pomeroy and Heitkamp declined to run for the Senate seat, leaving the Democrats without a top-tier candidate. The eventual Democratic nominee, Tracy Potter, a state senator from Bismarck, struggled to raise money and achieve any momentum. Hoeven spent $4 million to just $28,000 for Potter, and won by 76%-22%.

Upon his arrival on Capitol Hill, Hoeven was given a prized slot on the Senate Appropriations Committee, and also was named to the Agriculture Committee, where he was a conferee on the 2014 farm bill that renewed federal agriculture and nutrition programs for five years. Hoeven supported an earlier version of the bill that cleared the Senate in June 2012, which ended direct payments to farmers but included a new form of crop insurance favored by farm state senators outside the South. Both of these features were included in the final farm bill that was approved in 2014. Hoeven also worked to ensure that the legislation contained an extension of the sugar program contained in past farm bills-important to North Dakota, one of the nation's leading producers of sugar beets, but controversial among critics who complain it has made sugar significantly more expensive for U.S. consumers.

In early 2015, as the Agriculture Committee was preparing to reauthorize the 2010 Healthy Hunger-Free Kids Act, Hoeven found himself on a potential collision course with first lady Michelle Obama and her campaign to reduce childhood obesity. Hoeven introduced a measure that would relax Agriculture Department rules for schools with regards to serving whole grain products and reducing sodium levels. "We all want to work with the spirit of the Healthy Hunger-Free Kids Act," Hoeven told a gathering of the School Nutrition Association. "But we've got to have the flexibility to do it right." Efforts to reach a compromise on a new authorization of the Healthy Hungry-Free Kids Acts fell short at the end of 2016, bumping the issue into the 115th Congress.

As a member of the Energy and Natural Resources Committee, Hoeven continued his focus while governor on energy issues, advocating efforts to develop a national energy plan similar to EmPower North Dakota -- an approach that encompasses renewable as well as traditional energy resources. With regard to the latter, Hoeven was an outspoken critic of Obama's decision to block construction of the Keystone XL oil pipeline designed to run from Canada to the Gulf Coast-while carrying a projected 100,000 barrels a day produced in the oilfields of western North Dakota and neighboring Montana. In March 2012, Hoeven offered a bill to reinstate the project, and, while 11 Democrats crossed over to support the measure, it failed to reach the 60-vote threshold needed to end a threatened filibuster. With the Senate in Republican control following the 2014 election, Hoeven sponsored the bill and led the effort to allow the pipeline to move ahead-which, this time around, cleared both the House and Senate. Pipeline advocates fell five votes short in March 2015 of the two-thirds majority needed to override Obama's veto. Hoeven's cause ultimately prevailed in early 2017, when newly inaugurated President Donald Trump reversed his predecessor's decision, with administration officials issuing a permit to complete the project.

It was not the only pipeline controversy in which Hoeven played a leading role during his first term. In 2016, members of the Standing Rock Sioux Tribe launched protests against allowing the Dakota Access Pipeline -- being built to transport 470,000 barrels of oil daily from North Dakota to Illinois -- to run through their reservation. Tribal opponents of the project contended it violated a nearly 170-year old treaty with the U.S. government, and that a leak in the pipeline -- routed to run under reservoir adjacent to the reservation -- could have disastrous consequences for drinking water supplies. As the Sioux were joined by thousands of Native American allies during the latter part of the year in and around the community of Cannon Ball, North Dakota, the protests attracted international attention as a symbol of the continuing fight for Native American rights. But Hoeven sharply criticized the protests as often violent and disruptive of the economic livelihood of farmers and ranchers in the area.

After unsuccessfully seeking congressional approval in September to direct $6 million in federal funds to state and local law enforcement authorities dealing with the protests, Hoeven wrote to Obama in late November asking the president to "provide federal law enforcement resources immediately to state and local agencies in order to maintain public safety, which has been threatened by ongoing - and oftentimes violent - protest activity." In a Senate floor speech, Hoeven complained, "More than 500 protesters have been arrested for breaking the law, and over 90 percent of them are from out of state – many if not most are not Native American. They are environmental activists from other parts of the country." He also dismissed the arguments against the pipeline as specious, noting, "Twice challenged and twice upheld – including by the Obama Administration's own appointees – the federal courts found that the Army Corps had followed the appropriate process, the Standing Rock Sioux Tribe was properly consulted, and the project could lawfully proceed." However, while Obama was still in office, the Army Corps of Engineers in December, denied an easement to allow pipeline builders to burrow under the reservoir. As with the Keystone pipeline, the Trump Administration reversed that decision and granted the easement, although tribal leaders vowed to continue to fight it.

While he has targeted federal regulations that he feels have stifled innovation and are onerous for state and local governments, Hoeven is no conservative absolutist. After Hurricane Irene hit the East Coast in the summer of 2011, he was one of 10 Republicans to support a $6.9 billion increase in Federal Emergency Management Agency funding. He showed a willingness to cross party lines when he joined 14 other Republicans to vote for a reauthorization of the Violence Against Women Act in April 2012. In the early months of 2013, Hoeven expressed support for the idea of bipartisan immigration reform being pushed by Republican Sens. Marco Rubio of Florida and John McCain of Arizona, and, during the same period, was one of just 12 Republicans to vote for a successful measure to raise the limit on how much debt the government can acquire. At the end of 2013, he was one of only nine Senate Republicans to back a budget deal crafted by the chairmen of the Senate and House Budget committees-Washington Democrat Patty Murray and Wisconsin Republican Paul Ryan, respectively-that was criticized by conservative groups as permitting too much spending.

Continuing his efforts as governor to spur economic development through commercialization of new technology, Hoeven again reached across the aisle to join New Jersey Democrat Cory Booker on legislation in 2015 to set guidelines for unmanned aircraft systems (UAS) -- in an effort to promote increased commercial use of so-called drones. A year later, from his Appropriations Committee perch, Hoeven worked to insert funding and language for UAS research at several federal agencies. At the end of 2016, he helped to gain approval from the Federal Aviation Administration for a UAS test site in Grand Forks to oversee unmanned aircraft operations that go beyond the line of sight of the operator. The North Dakota test site became the first in the nation to have such beyond-line-of-sight operability -- the dearth of which has prompted U.S.-based firms such as Amazon and Google to experiment with drones in overseas locations.

In the 2016 campaign, Hoeven spent a little over $2 million -- about half of what he spent six years earlier -- against Democrat Eliot Glassheim, a member of the North Dakota House. Glassheim, owner of a Grand Forks used bookstore called Dr. Eliot's Twice Sold Tales, spent a mere $33,000. Hoeven won in a 78%-17% blowout, running 15 points ahead of Trump in the state. He took 52 of the state's 53 counties: Glassheim won only Sioux County, the one county in North Dakota located entirely within the boundaries of the Standing Rock Sioux reservation.

Junior Senator

Heidi Heitkamp (D-NPL)

Elected 2012, term expires 2018, 1st term; b. Oct 30, 1955, Breckenridge, MN; University of North Dakota, B.A.; Lewis & Clark College (OR), J.D.; Roman Catholic; Married (Darwin Lange); 2 children.

Elected Office: ND Attorney General, 1992-2000; Tax Commissioner, 1986-1992.

Professional Career: Director, Dakota Gasification, 2001-2012; Attorney, ND Tax Commissioner Office, 1981-1986; Attorney, U.S Environmental Protection Agency, 1980-1981.

DC Office: 516 HSOB 20510, 202-224-2043, Fax: 202-224-7776, heitkamp.senate.gov.

State Offices: Bismarck, 701-258-4648; Dickinson, 701-225-0974; Fargo, 701-232-8030; Grand Forks, 701-775-9601; Minot, 701-852-0703.

Committees: *Agriculture, Nutrition & Forestry*: Commodities, Risk Management & Trade (RMM), Livestock, Marketing & Agriculture Security, Rural Development & Energy. *Banking, Housing*

& Urban Affairs: Economic Policy (RMM), Housing, Transportation & Community Development, National Security & International Trade & Finance. *Homeland Security & Government Affairs*: Investigations, Regulatory Affairs & Federal Management (RMM). *Indian Affairs*. *Small Business & Entrepreneurship*.

Group Ratings

	ADA	ACLU	AFL-CIO	LCV	ITI	COC	HAFA	ACU	CFG	FRC
2016	-	70%	-	53%	100%	100%	9%	15%	30%	0%
2015	60%	C	71%	40%	C	93%	C	13%	10%	0%

Almanac Ratings 2015

	Economy	Social	Foreign	Composite
Liberal	62%	70%	80%	71%
Conservative	38%	30%	20%	29%

Key Votes of the 114th Congress

1. Keystone pipeline	Y	5. National Security Data	Y	9. Gun Sales Checks	N
2. Export-Import Bank	N	6. Iran Nuclear Deal	N	10. Sanctuary Cities	N
3. Debt Ceiling Increase	Y	7. Puerto Rico Debt	Y	11. Planned Parenthood	N
4. Homeland Security $$	Y	8. Loretta Lynch A.G	Y	12. Trade deals	Y

Election Results

Election	Name (Party)	Vote (%)	Cand. Spent	Ind. Exp. Support	Ind. Exp. Oppose
2012 General	Heidi Heitkamp (D)	161,163 (50%)	$5,493,544	$1,175,717	$6,236,825
	Rick Berg (R)	158,282 (49%)	$6,344,251	$1,896,755	$7,730,094
2012 Primary	Heidi Heitkamp (D)	57,246 (100%)			

Democrat Heidi Heitkamp, North Dakota's junior senator, was one of the more surprising success stories of the 2012 election: Her victory enabled the Democrats to hang onto a seat that, at the beginning of the cycle, was widely regarded as a prime Republican pickup opportunity due to the retirement of long-serving Sen. Kent Conrad. In narrowly winning in a red state, Heitkamp kept her distance from President Barack Obama -- and ran 11 points ahead of him on Election Day -- while vowing to place pragmatic legislating above politics in a Congress beset by partisanship and legislative gridlock.

Heitkamp arrived on Capitol Hill in early 2013 to join a group of nearly a dozen Democratic senators with centrist leanings representing traditionally Republican states. But a combination of retirements and defeats in 2014 cut this number in half, while reducing the Democrats to a Senate minority -- and prompting Heitkamp to eye a run for governor, a job she had sought a decade and a half earlier. She ultimately decided to remain in the Senate, but, after the 2016 election, Heitkamp met with President-elect Donald Trump amid widespread speculation that she was being considered for agriculture secretary to give a bipartisan patina to a Trump Cabinet. Once again, it didn't happen, and Heitkamp returned to Capitol Hill, where she broke with her party to vote to confirm several of Trump's appointees -- notably Neil Gorsuch to the Supreme Court --while confronting the prospect of a 2018 re-election campaign in a state that Trump won by a 36-point margin.

Born in Breckenridge Minnesota, Heitkamp (her formal given name is Mary Kathryn) grew up just over the state line in Mantador, North Dakota (population 64 in 2010). Her mother was the school cook and custodian, and her father held a series of jobs ranging from truck driver to construction worker. Heitkamp was the fourth of seven children. "Being right in the middle of seven bossy people-does that prepare me for being bipartisan, collaborative, and a compromiser?" she asked rhetorically in a 2014 interview with the *Daily Beast*. "I've been compromising and collaborating all my life."

Heitkamp studied political science at the University of North Dakota and then earned a degree from the Lewis & Clark College Law School in Portland, Oregon. She briefly worked for the Environmental Protection Agency as an attorney before moving to the North Dakota State Tax Commissioner's Office. It was there that she met Conrad, then tax commissioner. He became her political mentor, and, when he left to successfully run for Senate in 1986, she subsequently ran for tax commissioner in 1988 "with a push" from him. (She had previously waged an unsuccessful bid for state auditor.) She won the tax commissioner's post with 66 percent of the vote and served until 1992, running for attorney general when that office became open. She captured 62 percent, and was easily reelected four years later. As attorney general, Heitkamp was best known for leading the state's legal efforts against tobacco companies that ultimately produced a national settlement in 1998. She also has cited efforts to revamp the state's juvenile justice system and to improve the anti-domestic violence system as highlights of her tenure.

Heitkamp hoped to parlay those accomplishments into becoming governor in 2000, but lost to Republican John Hoeven-now her senior colleague in the Senate-by 55%-45%. Her ability to compete was hindered by a diagnosis of breast cancer in August of the election year. She took a month off the campaign trail to undergo treatment and has been in remission since, but that time away eroded whatever advantage she had in the contest. After that disappointing race, Heitkamp took a job as a director for Dakota Gasification, a company that operates a synthetic fuels plant, and sometimes filled in for her brother, Joel, a former state senator, as host of his weekday radio talk show in Fargo.

When long-time Democratic Sen. Byron Dorgan retired in 2010, opening the seat easily won by Hoeven, Heitkamp was urged to run, but declined. "My life, my family and my friends are here in North Dakota. In the final analysis, I simply could not compete for a job that would require me to spend so much time in Washington…," Heitkamp said. Many in the state's political establishment took it as an indication that Heitkamp was eyeing a run for governor in 2012. But she was urged by Conrad to change her mind and run to succeed him, prompting her to announce for Senate in November 2011. Prior to her announcement, potential Democratic Senate candidates included former Rep. Earl Pomeroy, who had lost his at-large House seat in 2010 after almost two decades in Congress. Pomeroy had been ousted by Republican Rick Berg, a former majority leader of the North Dakota House. Berg's upset of Pomeroy-coupled with Hoeven's election to an open Senate seat the same year-cemented North Dakota's status as a red state. Just months after being sworn in as a freshman member of the House, Berg announced in May 2011 that he would run for Senate.

Given the evolving politics of a state undergoing an oil and gas boom, Berg initially was seen as a strong favorite. But he was hurt by what was widely viewed as a poorly run campaign-and, just as he worked to tie Heitkamp to Obama, she in turn sought to link him to a Congress whose approval ratings were even lower than the president's. Meanwhile, Heitkamp stressed her independence from her national party on issues such as energy, including her support for the controversial Keystone XL pipeline, and spending, where she backed a constitutional balanced budget amendment. Heitkamp walked a fine line on Obama's health care legislation, which was unpopular in the state. In a widely noticed TV ad, she said the law contained "good and bad" and "needs to be fixed," but rebuked her opponent for voting to repeal it. "Rick Berg voted to go back to letting insurance companies deny coverage to kids, or for pre-existing conditions," she said. "... I don't ever want to go back to those days." The ad contained a pointed reference to her own struggles: "I'm Heidi Heitkamp, and 12 years ago I beat breast cancer. When you live through that, political attack ads seem silly."

If Heitkamp had developed a reputation for what is referred to in the state as "North Dakota nice," she did not hesitate to take off the gloves in what became one of the nastiest political contests in state history. Berg was among the wealthiest members of Congress thanks to his real estate holdings, and Heitkamp called attention to his ties to a company that owns and manages rental housing-and which had drawn numerous tenant complaints and been cited for fire safety violations. When Berg contended he had "absolutely no involvement" with the management of the company, Heitkamp's campaign released an ad listing documents it said tied him to the firm, and asking whether he could be trusted on other issues. "Maybe it shouldn't be a surprise that Rick Berg would use his business experience to privatize Social Security," Heitkamp asserted in the ad. "He's voted time and again to risk Social Security funds in the stock market. Rick Berg, treating seniors the same way he treats his tenants." Privately, even some Democratic consultants considered the ad to be a stretch, *Politico* reported.

Heitkamp maintained a lead in the polls during the summer of 2012, and although the race tightened as Election Day approached, she held on to win the closest Senate race in the country that year, 50.23% to 49.33%, just under 3,000 votes out of nearly 321,000 cast. Berg carried most of the state's central and western counties, but Heitkamp won the county that includes Fargo along the border with Minnesota, and dominated the eastern side of the state. She became the first woman elected to the Senate from North Dakota (the widow of Democratic Sen. Quentin Burdick had filled the seat by appointment for three months following his death in 1992).

Her voting record on Capitol Hill has put her in the middle of the Senate and on the right edge of the Democratic Caucus: *Almanac* vote ratings for 2015 pegged Heitkamp as the third most conservative Democrat that year. As a partisan budget stalemate led to a 16-day government shutdown toward the end of her first year in the Senate, Heitkamp was part of a 14-member bipartisan group organized by Maine moderate Republican Susan Collins; the group's efforts were credited with helping to bring an end to the standoff.

As on the campaign trail, Heitkamp distanced herself from Obama. She joined a bipartisan effort seeking quick action on the Keystone pipeline, siding with seven other Democrats and all Republicans in an unsuccessful effort in early 2015 to override Obama's veto of a bill allowing the pipeline to go forward. She blasted the president's opposition as "purely driven by politics that ignored the facts." Later that year, Heitkamp was among just three Democrats to support a GOP-sponsored effort to nullify Obama-promulgated Clean Water Act rules expanding the Environmental Protection Agency's jurisdiction over domestic bodies of water.

Shortly after arriving on Capitol Hill, Heitkamp told ABC News she was concerned that Obama was taking his focus off the economy to address not only environmental issues such as climate change, but social concerns such as gun control as well. "The one thing that has gotten lost by everyone is, one of the best ways that we can perform here is by getting people back to work, making sure that this economic recovery, slow as it is, gets amped up and moves forward," she declared. While an early supporter of Hillary Clinton's presidential candidacy -- Heitkamp urged Clinton to run as early as 2013, and formally endorsed her at the end of 2015 -- the North Dakotan was also reported to have been critical of the Clinton campaign's focus on turnout among the presidential nominee's urban and suburban base at the expense of white rural voters. A month after Clinton's loss to Trump, Heitkamp hosted a dinner of Senate Democratic moderates for an informal strategy session, amid complaints that Clinton had helped to do herself in by underplaying the economy and overemphasizing cultural issues. Heitkamp later praised the Trump Administration's "razor-like focus on getting people to work."

Earlier in her tenure, Heitkamp won praise for her self-deprecating remarks at a media-sponsored dinner in Washington. "You're asking yourself, 'How did this middle-aged, red-headed Democrat win a United States Senate seat in a red state that the president lost by 21 points?'" she deadpanned. "To you, I'm like a unicorn …You just wanted to tell your family that you saw me in person, and I am the last of my species." But not many Democrats were laughing when Heitkamp, after three months on Capitol Hill, joined three other red state Democratic senators in voting to block compromise legislation that would have expanded background checks for gun owners. The measure was brought up in the wake of the December 2012 Connecticut school shooting in which two dozen were killed by a deranged gunman. Largely due to the Democratic defections, it fell five votes short of the 60-vote supermajority needed to proceed.

Writing in *The Washington Post* two days later, an outraged William Daley, a former Obama White House chief of staff, accused Heitkamp of buckling to the gun lobby and said he wanted his $2,500 donation to her campaign returned. "…She struck me as strong-willed, principled and an independent thinker. But this week, Heitkamp betrayed those hopes," declared Daley, son and brother of former mayors of Chicago-a city wracked by gun violence. Heitkamp voted against the measure even though it had been crafted by West Virginia Sen. Joe Manchin, a fellow Democratic moderate from a red state. While praising Manchin for having "worked very hard to forge a compromise," Heitkamp told *The Daily Beast*, "I made a judgment call that [the proposed law's] main purpose was to put more restrictions on law-abiding gun owners as opposed to really capturing criminals." Heitkamp has remained adamant in her opposition to new restrictions on gun ownership: In 2016, she was the only Democrat to join most Republicans in opposing a ban on firearm purchases by those on the federal terrorist watch list.

On a less controversial issue of importance to her home state, Heitkamp -- whose committee assignments include the Indian Affairs Committee -- pushed for measures to assist Native Americans; nearly 6.5 percent of the North Dakota population consists of American Indians. She introduced a bill when Congress to create a commission on Native American children and explore solutions to the challenges they face; it was signed into law by Obama toward the end of 2016. But, along with her senior colleague Hoeven, she found herself at odds with her state's Standing Rock Sioux Tribe over plans to run the Dakota Access Pipeline through their reservation. After tribal protests against the project gained international attention in the latter part of 2016, she advised the tribe to abandon the fight as unwinnable after Trump's victory. When the Obama Administration in December 2016 denied an easement to build the pipeline underneath a reservoir adjacent to the Sioux reservation, Heitkamp matter-of-factly stated that the decision would be reversed when Trump took office -- which is precisely what happened.

In alliance with other lawmakers from oil-producing states, Heitkamp succeeded in late 2015 in winning approval for a provision attached to a spending bill that repealed a 40-year old ban on exporting U.S.-produced oil. The plan was pushed by the U.S. oil industry, amid rising energy production and decreasing gasoline prices domestically. Perhaps Heitkamp's major legislative initiative to date is a bill to increase incentives for so-called "carbon capture and storage," or CCS. It involves technologies that can strip carbon dioxide from processes such as steel manufacturing and coal burning, and store it beneath the ground for use in energy extraction. CCS legislation that Heitkamp introduced in 2016 attracted 11 Democrats and eight Republicans, including Majority Leader Mitch McConnell. She contended the plan was key to addressing global warming in nations reliant on coal. "People who think that the United States of America taking single action without developing technologies will solve what they perceive to be a climate problem globally, that's just a formula for failure," Heitkamp declared.

Four of Heitkamp's red state Democratic colleagues were defeated for re-election in 2014, prompting a number of the remaining moderates-including Heitkamp-to vote against Nevada Sen. Harry Reid continuing as Senate Democratic leader. (Reid announced his retirement the following spring.) "The clearest message from the recent election is that Congress needs to change and get to work. We need to show the American people that we hear them by implementing real, tangible changes to help restore trust," Heitkamp said. A couple of the other moderates who voted against Reid, Manchin and McCaskill, contemplated runs for governor in 2016 but opted to remain in Washington. Heitkamp also looked homeward for much of 2015.

Speaking to the *Fargo Forum* editorial board in early 2015, Heitkamp conceded "the proof is in the past" regarding her desire to be governor, a reference to her failed 2000 bid. She also called the governor's post "the greatest honor that you can have from the people of North Dakota." But even after GOP Gov. Jack Dalrymple disclosed in late August that he would not seek re-election, allowing Heitkamp to run for an open seat, she announced in early September that she had decided against a gubernatorial run. "I think how difficult it would be to run a very competitive governor's race and be as aggressive as I've been on all these issues that affect North Dakota's economy and North Dakota's people," she told the *Forum*, while acknowledging she had been urged to remain in Washington by fellow centrists. "They said, 'We think we will be weaker as conservative or moderate Democrats if you leave'," Heitkamp said.

National Democratic strategists were also heaving sighs of relief: As Heitkamp contemplated the governorship, a bill passed by the Republican-controlled North Dakota Legislature changed state law, effective August 2015, so that future Senate vacancies would be filled by special election rather than gubernatorial appointment. It would have barred Heitkamp from appointing her successor if she were elected governor, while giving the Republicans a good shot at grabbing her Senate seat in a special election.

The prospect of an additional Republican Senate seat also appeared to be in mind as reports surfaced that Heitkamp was under consideration as Trump's agriculture secretary after she and the president-elect met in New York in December 2016. But, according to *Politico*, Heitkamp's potential appointment was strongly opposed by Trump's rural advisers, who regarded it as a slap in the face to farm-state Republicans who stuck by the GOP nominee during times when he was politically besieged during the campaign. Perhaps with these factors in mind, Heitkamp downplayed the prospect of ending up in the Trump Cabinet.

"I'm not saying 'never never'," she said during an appearance on her brother's radio show. "But I will tell you that I'm very, very honored to serve the people of North Dakota and I hope that no matter what I do, that will always be my first priority." She did praise Trump's advisers for their "willingness to listen to a different perspective," while adding that they "don't come as establishment Republicans" -- which she said boded well for bipartisan cooperation. While not officially announcing for a second term, Heitkamp was actively raising campaign funds in early 2017. "I'm taking the steps to prepare to run, but am still in the process of making a decision," she said. Without her in the race, the contest would be a likely pickup for the GOP. If she runs, a strong Republican challenger would have an opportunity. But Heitkamp has shown that she can win, even without incumbency, albeit narrowly and against a flawed opponent. Rep. Kevin Cramer, who occupies the state's single at-large seat, has come under pressure to run from party leaders. However, some Republicans, concerned about Cramer's periodic penchant for controversial comments, eyed state Sen. Tom Campbell, who has personal wealth. Also expressing interest on the Republican side was state Rep. Rick Becker.

REPRESENTATIVE-AT-LARGE

Kevin Cramer (R)

Elected 2012, 3rd term; b. Jan 21, 1961, Rolette; Concordia College (MN), B.A.; University of Mary (ND), Mast. Deg.; Evangelical; Married (Kris Neumann); 5 children; 3 grandchildren.

Elected Office: ND Public Service Commission, 2003-2012.

Professional Career: Director, Harold Schafer Leadership Foundation, 2001-2003; Director, ND tourism, 1993-1997; Chairman, ND Republican Party, 1991-1993.

DC Office: 1717 LHOB 20515, 202-225-2611, Fax: 202-226-0893, cramer.house.gov.

State Offices: Bismarck, 701-224-0355; Fargo, 701-356-2216; Grand Forks, 701-738-4880; Minot, 701-839-0255.

Committees: *Energy & Commerce*: Communications & Technology, Energy, Environment.

Group Ratings

	ADA	ACLU	AFL-CIO	LCV	ITI	COC	HAFA	ACU	CFG	FRC
2016	-	5%	-	3%	100%	100%	53%	84%	65%	100%
2015	0%	C	21%	0%	C	100%	C	65%	47%	83%

Almanac Ratings 2015

	Economy	Social	Foreign	Composite
Liberal	14%	9%	12%	12%
Conservative	86%	91%	88%	88%

Key Votes of the 114th Congress

1. Keystone Pipeline	Y	5. Puerto Rico Debt	Y	9. Offenses by Aliens	Y
2. Trade Deals	Y	6. Medical Marijuana	Y	10. Troops in Iraq	N
3. Export-Import Bank	Y	7. Sanctuary Cities	Y	11. Homeland Security $$	N
4. Debt Ceiling Increase	Y	8. Armor-piercing Bullets	Y	12. Trade Adjustment aid	Y

Election Results

Election	Name (Party)	Vote (%)	Cand. Spent	Ind. Exp. Support	Ind. Exp. Oppose
2016 General	Kevin Cramer (R)	233,980 (69%)	$980,783		
	Chase Iron Eyes (D)	80,377 (24%)	$208,176		
	Jack Seaman (L)	23,528 (7%)	$2,319		
2016 Primary	Kevin Cramer (R)	(100%)			

Prior winning percentages: 2014 (56%), 2012 (55%)

Republican Kevin Cramer was elected to the House in 2012 in his fourth attempt to win North Dakota's at-large seat. A former state GOP chairman and a strong conservative, Cramer serves on the Energy and Commerce Committee, where he tends to his home-state's oil and gas interests. During the uncertainties of the transition to President Donald Trump, Cramer made clear his interest in moving to the Senate - under the right circumstances - and Senate Republicans encouraged him.

Cramer grew up in Kindred, southwest of Fargo. Throughout high school, Cramer worked for the same electric cooperative as his father. He got his bachelor's from the Lutheran Church-owned Concordia College in Minnesota, where he was a pre-seminary student majoring in social work. Cramer was inspired to get involved in politics by Ronald Reagan, whom he described as a "joyful conservative." He was a campaign aide to Sen. Mark Andrews in his failed 1986 reelection bid and worked for the state Republican Party, where he rose to executive director. At age 30, he was the youngest-ever state party chairman. As a self-professed leader of a GOP "youth movement," he was courted by national party bigwigs. Looking back, Cramer said, he was "naïve enough" to be "quite bold - you might say reckless, even."

After serving as state tourism director, he ran for the House in 1996. Cramer lost to Democratic Rep. Earl Pomeroy, 55%-43%. After the loss, Cramer became the state's economic development director. He ran for the House seat a second time, but again lost to Pomeroy, with 41 percent of the vote. He later called that run a political mistake that cost him the state party's endorsement when he ran for the seat in 2010. That year, in his third try, he dropped out before the GOP primary. From 2003 to 2012, he served on North Dakota's public service commission, helping to oversee an energy-driven boom in the state economy. He worked for a foundation offering faith-based training for students at the University of Mary in Bismarck, where he got a master's in management.

When Republican Rep. Rick Berg ran for the Senate, Cramer tried again, spurning the state party's endorsement and taking his campaign directly to the primary. He edged out party-backed Brian Kalk, a fellow public service commissioner, 55%-45%. Against Democrat Pam Gulleson, a former state House member, Cramer ran in the general as a strong social conservative, saying on his campaign website, "I hope you know that my public service is an extension of my service to Christ." He called himself "a strong advocate for the free market system." Gulleson was competitive financially, but the state's Republican tilt gave the win to Cramer, 55%-42%.

Cramer advocated on behalf of a host of North Dakota interests. He often said "you're welcome" to President Barack Obama for the huge economic boost to the nation from oil and gas drilling in North Dakota, most of which is on private or state land, and he urged Obama to open more federal lands to production. He was one of the few congressional Republicans to support Obama on normalizing relations with Cuba. In addition to the opportunity for farm sales, he said that the move was "an opportunity to influence an oppressed country." In 2016, he enacted a bill to set procedures for criminal background checks of adults working in foster care or tribal social service agencies. His *Almanac* voting record for 2015 ranked him toward the center of the House.

On Energy and Commerce, Cramer took an interest in proposals designed to protect electricity consumers from higher costs imposed by Environmental Protection Agency regulation of power plants. He was an enthusiastic advocate for the completion of the Dakota Access Pipeline, and he criticized the "political expediency" of the Obama administration for its delay in the face of court challenges. "I can't wait for the adults to be in charge on Jan. 20," Cramer said after the 2016 election.

In 2014, Cramer faced a competitive contest with Democratic state Sen. George Sinner, the son of former Gov. George Sinner. The challenger complained that Cramer's campaign ads were dishonest and he proposed "truth in politics" legislation. Cramer responded that his ads were true and that Sinner's proposal would violate the free-speech guarantee of the First Amendment. Cramer won 56%-39%. His next reelection campaign was routine.

As one of seven House members who serve single-district states, Cramer was well-positioned to run for the Senate when opportunity knocked. He had been viewed as a prospect to challenge Democratic Sen. Heidi Heitkamp if she sought reelection in 2018 in this increasingly Republican state. When Heitkamp showed interest in joining Trump's Cabinet following the 2016 election, he quickly gained notice. Cramer had a well-publicized meeting with Senate Republican Leader Mitch McConnell to discuss the possibility that he would run in the special election for a vacant seat. At about the same time, he had his own meeting with Trump in New York City to discuss the possibility of becoming Secretary of Energy. During the campaign, he had written a white paper for Trump about energy policy and his skepticism about climate change. When neither Heitkamp nor Cramer was selected for the Cabinet, the possibility remained that they would face off in 2018.

★ OHIO ★

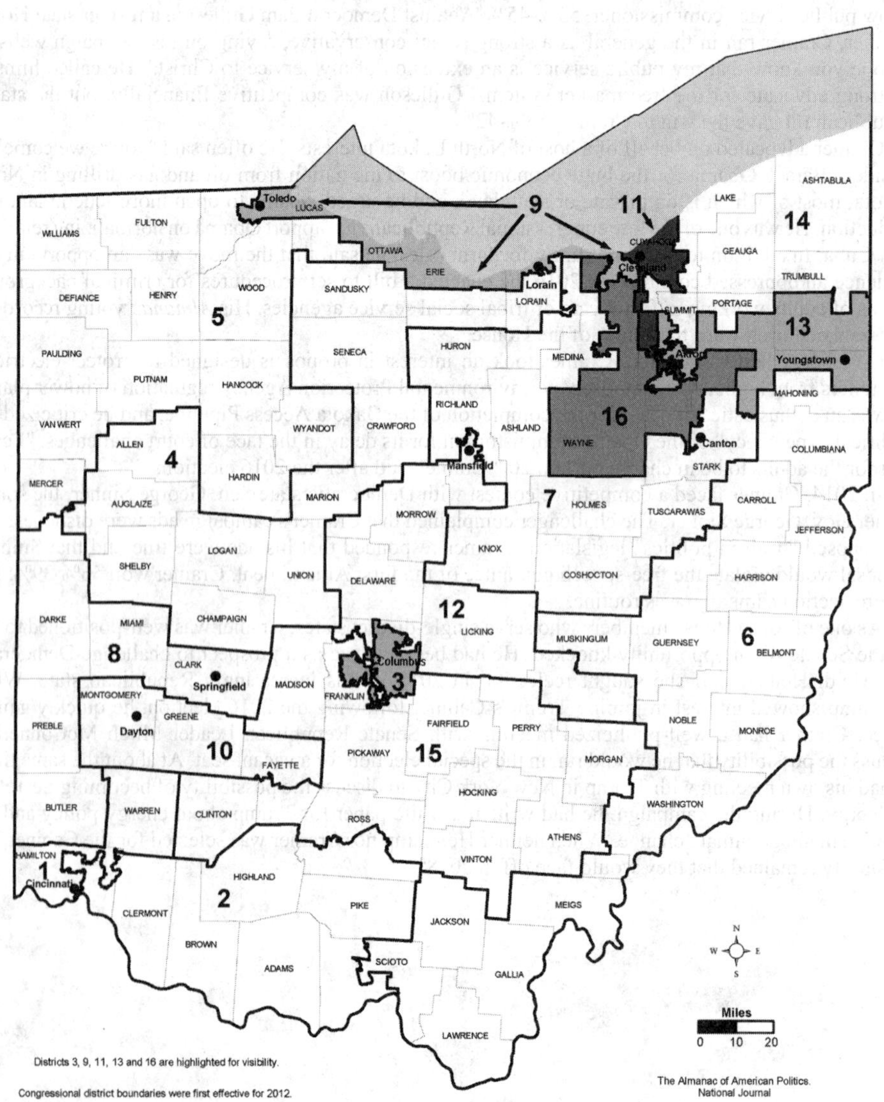

Districts 3, 9, 11, 13 and 16 are highlighted for visibility.

Congressional district boundaries were first effective for 2012.

The Almanac of American Politics.
National Journal

Ohio, a crossroads of the Midwest, has long been a bellwether state politically – it has not voted for a presidential loser since 1960. True to form, Ohio shifted by a double-digit margin from supporting Barack Obama in 2012 to backing Donald Trump in 2016. But Ohio's role as a bellwether could be in jeopardy if the Trump-era Republican Party can consolidate gains among working-class white workers.

Ohio was the first entirely American state. The original 13 started as British colonies, and the next three - Vermont, Kentucky and Tennessee - were spun off from them. But Ohio sprang, Athena-like, from the head of Congress, as the first state formed from the Northwest Territory. The Northwest Ordinance of 1787 established 6-mile-square townships, which imposed geometric order on diverse new American landscapes to the west. It set aside one square mile per township for public schools, and the land was soon peppered with schoolhouses and small colleges, the foundation stones of a literate republic. The ordinance prohibited slavery at a time when most northern states still had it, opening the way for free labor to clear fields, raise crops, and build mills and factories. In less than half a century, the former wilderness wrested from British-aided Indian control only in 1796 was one of the most productive parts of the young republic. In the years after the Civil War, Ohio became one of the great industrial states, the original headquarters of John D. Rockefeller's Standard Oil, the site of major steel mills along the narrow Cuyahoga and Mahoning rivers, and the location of the biggest soap companies, machine tool makers, and tire manufacturers. Dayton was the home of the Wright brothers, who developed the airplane; Akron was the home of Harvey Firestone, B. F. Goodrich and F. A. Seiberling - the great tire manufacturers. Cincinnati was and is the headquarters of Procter & Gamble.

Ohio was settled by New Englanders in the northeast (in the Western Reserve) and by Virginians in the south, creating a split between the Southern-accented counties south of the National Road and U.S. 40 and the Yankee-accented cities and towns to the north. In the middle were the Amish, who moved west from Pennsylvania. (By 2013, Ohio was home to more than 65,000 Amish in 485 congregations, the most in the country; they form a near majority in Holmes County, where their horse-drawn buggies are a common sight.) The state was also similarly split between Butternut and Copperhead territory that didn't want to fight the Civil War and Yankee territory that fiercely prosecuted the war. This split heritage was an early reason why Ohio became a closely divided state politically - and a nationally pivotal one. Ohio produced the winning candidate for president in 1896 and 1900, William McKinley, who inaugurated a 34-year period of mostly Republican national majorities. McKinley's Republicans were for high tariffs and hard money and had a friendly regard for workers and even some unions, but they had no patience with large unions. They preached a nationalist Americanism tempered by wariness about making major commitments abroad. Republicans were the majority in this increasingly industrial Ohio, losing rural Butternut counties but carrying the big industrial cities of the north.

Then came the Great Depression of the 1930s, and Ohio became the scene of class warfare, with sit-down strikes and victories for industrial unions in autos, steel, and tires. CIO cities - Cleveland, Akron, Youngstown, and Toledo - moved sharply toward the Democrats, while places with fewer union members, such as Cincinnati and Columbus, stayed Republican. The political fighting was fierce, and the stakes were high. CIO leaders hoped to organize the entire workforce, but Republican leaders like Ohio Sen. Robert Taft feared union control of business would imperil freedoms and throttle the economy. In the 1930s and 1940s, unions made great gains, but Taft held them off, reducing union power with the Taft-Hartley Act of 1947 and his own reelection after hotly contested campaigns in 1944 and 1950. Ohio thrived in the industrial economy after World War II, with new auto and auto-parts plants going up and its population rising. In those years it was often said that Ohio was a great test market, close to the national average in income levels, urban-rural balance, and ethnic mix, as well as partisan proclivities. The typical American voter, wrote Richard Scammon and Ben Wattenberg in 1970, was a Dayton housewife whose brother-in-law was a machinist and who was hoping one of her children might go to college.

But Ohio is not so typical today: It remains industrial in an increasingly post-industrial country. In Ohio, manufacturing accounted for 18 percent of state GDP in 2015, compared with 12 percent for the nation as a whole. The ArcelorMittal steel mill in Cleveland – once again operating after being closed in 2002 – makes specialized, advanced-technology steel that allows it to compete against cheaper foreign competitors. But like other industrial operations in an era of automation, the mill employs far fewer employees than it once did. Indeed, for years, Ohio's manufacturing economy has been shrinking relative to other sectors of the economy. Manufacturing accounted for 18.2 percent of Ohio's employment in 2000 but just 12.7 percent in 2015, while the number of manufacturing workers in the state declined by

334,000 during that span. Such losses helped drive the unemployment rate to 11 percent in late 2009, and even after the Great Recession had passed, median income in the state was parked 6 percent below the national average.

Still, Ohio was slowly adapting to new economic realities. The recovery of the auto industry after the Great Recession boosted Ohio: In 2011, Chrysler committed $500 million to its Jeep plant in Toledo, and General Motors announced $343 million in upgrades to its transmission plant there a few months later. Akron, once hailed as the tire and rubber capital of the world, has attracted new jobs in polymers, information technology and biomedical engineering and its joblessness rate has fallen below the state average. The development of the Marcellus and Utica shale formations that lie under much of eastern Ohio, horizontal drilling and hydraulic fracturing - fracking - enabled drillers to tap into huge reservoirs of oil and natural gas, stimulating demand for steel pipe that the French firm Vallourec makes at a new mill in Youngstown. In 2014, General Electric announced that it would open a new U.S. Global Operations Center in the Cincinnati area with up to 2,000 high-salaried jobs in human resources, accounting and information technology - the single biggest business expansion in the state in a decade. The growth in health services is underscored by the economic impact of the world-renowned Cleveland Clinic, which has helped midwife hundreds of biomedical firms, including Invacare, Philips Healthcare and Steris. Agriculture remained a significant industry; Ohio ranks second nationally in egg production and in the top 10 states for soybeans, corn and hogs. By June 2015, the unemployment rate hit 5 percent, and it stayed at that level or lower through at least early 2017. That came despite a slump in the energy sector amid low global energy prices; in 2015, Vallourec had to shut down its Youngstown plant for three weeks and offered a six-month voluntary layoff.

The state's population has stagnated in recent decades. Between 1970 and 2010, Ohio's population grew by only 8 percent, a lower rate than any other state except New York, West Virginia, Pennsylvania and Iowa. Since the 2010 Census, Ohio's population has grown by less than a percentage point. During that period, six of the state's 10 biggest counties lost population, and of the others, only one grew by more than 2.6 percent – Franklin County (Columbus), which grew by a healthy 8.7 percent. Part of the reason for Ohio's slow population growth has been a relative lack of Hispanics – it ranks in the bottom 10 states for the percentage of residents who are Hispanic. The percentage of foreign-born residents in Ohio is about 4 percent, far below the national average of 13 percent (though immigrants represent a disproportionate 13.9 percent of all scientific, technological, engineering and mathematics workers in the state, according to the group New American Economy). African-Americans make up 12 percent of the population, a reflection of the great northward migration of 1940-65

Despite challenges – including a 2015 consent decree to impose new standards and monitoring on the use of force by the city's police department – Cleveland has moved past its days as the "mistake by the lake" in the 1960s and '70s. Downtown Cleveland has blossomed – a clear lesson that visitors and media took away from the 2016 Republican National Convention, the first major party gathering in the city since the GOP nominated Alf Landon there in 1936. Indeed, 2016 was a banner year for the city, even beyond the convention. The city opened the renovated Public Square, transforming the asphalt-heavy, traffic-snarled plaza into a lush urban park designed by landscape architect James Corner, who had designed Manhattan's celebrated High Line. In the spring, the NBA's Cleveland Cavaliers, led by local hero LeBron James, won the championship in dramatic, comeback fashion and prompted a massive victory parade. Then in the fall, the Cleveland Indians made it to the World Series, losing in extra innings in the seventh game to the Chicago Cubs.

Post-New Deal, Ohio has had two politically distinct regions. Traditionally, Northeast Ohio - centered on Cleveland and extending west to Toledo and south and east to the factory towns of Akron and Canton, Youngstown and Warren - has been the state's Democratic heartland, with the highest percentages of union members and African Americans. The other part of Ohio - south and west of the industrial belt and including Columbus, Cincinnati and Dayton - was never as heavily unionized and in national elections has tended to vote Republican, much like most of Indiana, although not always by wide margins. These patterns began shifting in recent years. Metro Columbus has trended Democratic and provided key votes for Barack Obama in 2008 and 2012. At the same time, the hill country along the Ohio River - coal country and now shale oil country - has trended Republican.

These recent shifts only intensified in the 2016 presidential election, but more strongly in the Republican direction. It became clear during the campaign that, given its demographics, Ohio was ripe for Trump to flip to the GOP column, though as late as mid-October, polls showed the state leaning slightly toward Hillary Clinton. On Election Day, it was a romp: A four-point winning margin for Obama in 2012 became an eight-point margin for Trump in 2016. Clinton's raw vote total fell by a stunning 433,000 compared with Obama in 2012, as Trump outperformed Mitt Romney by 180,000. Clinton won eight counties, about half as many as Obama.

The shifts were particularly strong in the state's blue-collar northern tier: In seven of the Obama counties that Trump was able to flip, the margins shifted toward the GOP by between 12 and 32 points. Even in some of the counties that remained blue, the Democratic margins narrowed significantly, shrinking by 25 points in Mahoning County (Youngstown), by 16 points in Lorain County (west of Cleveland), by 14 points in Lucas County (Toledo), and by seven points in Summit County (Akron). In many places, Trump outperformed Romney robustly, such as Stark County (Canton), where a virtual tie in 2012 became a 17-point Trump win in 2016. Clinton improved on Obama's showing in several of the state's biggest urban and suburban areas. In Columbus' Franklin County, she took an additional 5,000 votes; in Hamilton County (Cincinnati), she increased the winning Democratic margin from seven points to 11; and in the Columbus suburbs of Delaware County, Clinton got within 16 points of Trump, where Obama had lost by 23 points to Romney. (An exception: Clinton had poor returns in Cuyahoga County, tallying 49,000 fewer votes than Obama had in 2012.) On the whole, though, Clinton's improvements were dwarfed by Trump's; the impact such patterns will have on the state's status as a political bellwether remains to be written.

Population		**Race and Ethnicity**		**Income**	
Total	11,575,977	White	80.3%	Median Income	$49,429 (33 out of 50)
Land area	40,861	Black	12.0%	Under $50,000	50.4%
Pop/ sq mi	283.3	Latino	3.4%	$50,000-$99,999	30.5%
Born in state	75.1%	Asian	1.9%	$100,000-$199,999	15.6%
Age Groups		Two races	2.2%	$200,000 or more	3.4%
Under 18	22.9%	Other	0.2%	Poverty Rate	15.8%
18-34	22.2%	**Education**		**Health Insurance**	
35-64	40.0%	H.S grad or less	45.0%	With health insurance coverage	90.3%
Over 64	15.1%	Some college	28.9%	**Public Assistance**	
Work		College Degree, 4 yr	16.4%	Cash public assistance income	3.2%
White Collar	35.1%	Post grad	9.7%	Food stamp/SNAP benefits	15.0%
Sales and Service	41.5%	**Military**			
Blue Collar	23.5%	Veteran	9.1%		
Government	12.5%	Active Duty	0.1%		

Voter Turnout			
2015 Total Citizens 18+	8,709,050	2016 Pres Turnout as % CVAP	63%
2016 Pres Votes	5,496,487	2012 Pres Turnout as % CVAP	65%

Legislature	
Senate:	9D, 24R
House:	33D, 66R

Presidential Politics

2016 Democratic Primary		
Hillary Clinton (D)	696,681	(56%)
Bernie Sanders (D)	535,395	(43%)
2016 Republican Primary		
John Kasich (R)	933,886	(47%)
Donald Trump (R)	713,404	(36%)
Ted Cruz (R)	264,640	(13%)

2016 Presidential Vote		
Donald Trump (R)	2,841,006	(51%)
Hillary Clinton (D)	2,394,169	(43%)
Gary Johnson (L)	174,498	(3%)
2012 Presidential Vote		
Barack Obama (D)	2,827,709	(51%)
Mitt Romney (R)	2,661,437	(48%)

In the last 31 presidential elections, Ohio has sided with the winner in all but two: 1944, when it cast its votes for Thomas Dewey over Franklin D. Roosevelt; and 1960, when it sided with Richard Nixon over John F. Kennedy. No Republican has ever captured the White House without carrying Ohio. No Democrat, given recent electoral vote arithmetic, can be sure of winning without it. The critical role that Ohio plays in this electoral calculus was reflected in the intensity of campaigning there in 2016. Second only to Florida, Ohio saw the biggest barrage of television ads during the general election season. Hillary Clinton pulled out all the stops in her quest to corral the state's 18 electoral votes In the closing days of the campaign, Beyonce and Jay Z headlined a concert in Cleveland. And at a separate campaign rally, basketball superstar LeBron James of the NBA's Cleveland Cavaliers introduced Clinton. Trump campaigned vigorously too, but without the support of one of his chief rivals for the GOP nomination, Ohio Gov. John Kasich, who never endorsed him. And after Trump's taped comments about groping women were released in early October, a number of Ohio Republicans, including Sen. Rob Portman and State Auditor Dave Yost, repudiated their support. Yet amid all that strife, Trump handily defeated Clinton, 52%-44%. Clinton won just eight of the state's 88 counties: Athens (Ohio University), Cuyahoga (Cleveland), Franklin (Columbus), Hamilton (Cincinnati), Lorain (working-class Cleveland suburbs), Lucas (Toledo), Mahoning (Youngstown) and Summit (Akron). It was a remarkable turnaround from the 2008 and 2012 presidential elections, when Barack Obama won the pivotal battleground state. In dozens of counties, the falloff in the percentage of voters who cast ballots for Clinton compared with the percentage who voted for Obama was dramatic. Agricultural counties like Marion and Tuscarawas where Obama was competitive with Romney in 2012 became more than 30-point Trump blowouts. Blue-collar counties like Ashtabula, Ottawa, Sandusky and Trumbull, all carried by Obama in 2012, flipped to Trump in 2016. Trump's criticism of trade deals like NAFTA - a striking policy departure from recent GOP presidential nominees - and his vow to restore manufacturing jobs played particularly well in these depressed Rust Belt counties. Ashtabula went from a 12-point Obama victory to a 19-point Trump win. Obama won Trumbull by 22 points; Trump beat Clinton there by six.

In 1996, Ohio switched its presidential primary from May to March, the month where it would remain on the nominating calendar. In 2008, the Republican contest was effectively over when Ohio voted on March 4. Mike Huckabee remained an active candidate, but John McCain beat him 60%-31%, carrying all 88 counties. There was a spirited contest on the Democratic side, with Clinton besting Obama 53%-45%. She ran well in the Mahoning Valley steel country around Youngstown (Mahoning County) and Warren (Trumbull County), and the Democratic-leaning smaller industrial counties along the Ohio River. Clinton got as much as 80 percent of the primary vote in some counties (places that soundly rejected her in the 2016 general election). In 2012, the March 7 GOP primary was a pivotal contest between Mitt Romney and Rick Santorum. Romney won narrowly, 38%-37%, and secured his path to the GOP nomination.

In 2016, the March 15 GOP presidential primary featured a spirited Trump-Kasich faceoff. Trump accused Kasich of being an "absentee governor," and blasted him for voting for NAFTA when he was in the House. On the eve of the primary Trump scheduled an extra stop in the state to stump in Youngstown, symbol of industrial decline. Kasich, who was fond of saying he ran an "unwavering, positive" campaign, nonetheless noted the "toxic atmosphere" at Trump rallies and told a town hall before the primary. "Ohio is going to send a message that we don't accept those kind of tactics," he said. Buckeye voters sided with their governor and gave him a 47%-36% victory. But the GOP results pointed toward Trump's strength in the state in the fall: he won 32 of the state's counties, most of which were in an arc from the Mahoning Valley in the northeast corner through the Appalachian region and along the Ohio River to the outskirts of Cincinnati. Kasich's victory coupled with Florida Sen. Marco Rubio's primary loss in his home state primary to Trump on the same day meant that Kasich became the lone remaining establishment candidate in the GOP race. But the Ohioan was unable to consolidate that wing of the party, and after finishing a distant third in the Indiana primary two months later he ended his White House run. The Democratic primary took on added significance after Vermont Sen. Bernie Sanders upset Clinton in the March 8 Michigan primary. A subsequent loss in Ohio could have seriously wounded her candidacy. Clinton rallied party regulars and cruised to a 56%-43% victory. She enjoyed the backing of the state's senior Democrat, Sen. Sherrod Brown, and three of Ohio's House Members, Reps. Joyce Beatty, Marcia Fudge and Tim Ryan. The fourth, Rep. Marcy Kaptur, endorsed Sanders. Clinton handily carried the five counties she lost in the 2008 Democratic primary: Cuyahoga, Delaware, Franklin, Hamilton, and Montgomery. In Cuyahoga and Hamilton, she was boosted by strong support from African Americans. She won 72 counties in all. Turnout in the Republican primary was 1,988,960, close to double 2008. In the 2016 Democratic contest, 1,241,478, slightly more than half the 2008 vote. Ohio does not have partisan registration, so voters are free to choose which party primary they participate in. Combining the results of the GOP and Democratic primaries, Kasich won the highest number of votes in 53 counties, Trump won the most in 29, Clinton won the most in five and Sanders won the most in one. That was a warning sign that Ohio would be a challenge for the Democrat nominee in the fall.

Congressional Districts

115th Congress Lineup	12R 4D	**114th Congress Lineup**	12R 4D

Ohio is projected to lose one seat in the next reapportionment. As was the case following the most recent redistricting, Republicans may find that they again are victims of their own success.

Following the 2010 census, the state lost two House seats in the reapportionment reducing the delegation to 16 members, the fewest since Ohio was frontier country in the 1820s. During the previous decade, the map had been somewhat competitive: Democrats won a 10-8 majority in 2008 and Republicans a 13-5 majority in 2010. Even with their complete control of redistricting, GOP strategists conceded that they had too many Democrats to allocate if they wanted to keep all 13 of their seats. To resolve the dilemma, they forced one pair of Democrats to run against each other in the Cleveland-Toledo area, and they weakened another Democrat by creating a heavily Democratic seat in the Akron-Youngstown corridor that favored Rep. Tim Ryan. Furthermore, for decades, Republicans had cracked Columbus into multiple districts to shortchange Democrats. But the state capital was growing and attracting progressive-minded voters at such a rate that neither the Republican-held 12th nor 15th might hold until 2020. So, under the watchful guidance of House Speaker John Boehner of Ohio, Republican legislative aides hatched an innovative scheme. Republicans would pack Democrats into a new Columbus 3rd District. The creation of a Columbus Democratic vote sink would produce a beneficial ripple effect, allowing Republicans to shore up their freshmen and keep a 12-4 advantage.

The legislature and Gov. John Kasich easily approved the plan. To attract enough support to achieve the two-thirds support required to avoid a veto referendum in the next election, Republicans plotted minor changes designed to appease enough Democrats. Chiefly, those were allies of Toledo-based Marcy Kaptur, who got the better draw of the new district with Cleveland-based (and former presidential candidate) Dennis Kucinich. In the subsequent primary, Kucinich appealed to his left-leaning national fundraising network, but was steamrolled by Kaptur's loyal supporters. Republican Mike Austria, a low-key sophomore, retired, given the option of running in a district that favored Dayton-based Republican Mike Turner. Republicans got the 12-4 delegation they envisioned in a state that Barack Obama twice won. In addition, voters defeated by 63%-37% a seemingly benign ballot initiative to transfer future redistricting authority to an independent citizens' commission.

Reforms of Ohio's redistricting procedures gained support after the 2014 election. Spurred by Republican Secretary of State Jon Husted, a bipartisan coalition voted for a compromise plan that transferred redistricting authority from a handful of statewide elected officials to a broader group that would require support from both parties. The plan, which was approved by 71 percent of voters in a November 2015 referendum, has limitations. At Boehner's urging, the new procedures did not apply to the state's congressional map, at least initially. The revisions had become a work in progress.

Even if Republicans retain control of congressional redistricting, their House delegation again may have maxed out. Since the current map took effect in 2012, none of the current 12 GOP members has been seriously challenged for reelection. If that continues through 2020, Republicans may discover that they face a situation comparable to a decade earlier when they had to sacrifice one of their own members in order to secure their remaining seats. If they are unable to squeeze enough Democratic voters into three districts, one option is that the 12th Republican who has drawn the short straw could be matched in a "fair fight" with one of the three Democrats in northeast Ohio - though the African-American majority 11th District likely would be protected. In that scenario, the Republicans facing the greatest jeopardy would be those in the 6th, 7th, 14th and 16th districts. Many of the remaining Republicans in the Ohio delegation would find their districts moved a bit to the east.

In May 2017, a proposed constitutional amendment for new congressional redistricting procedures was approved for a statewide referendum, assuming supporters get enough signatures.

Governor

John Kasich (R)

Elected 2010, term expires 2019, 2nd term; b. May. 13, 1952, McKees Rocks, PA; OH St. U., B.A. 1974; Christian; Married (Karen); 2 children.

Elected Office: Republican National Committee, 1993-2002; OH Senate, 1978-1982; U.S. House, 1983-2001.

Office: 77 S. High St., 30th Floor, Columbus, 43215; 614-466-3555; Fax: 614-466-9354; Website: governor.ohio.gov.

Election Results

Election	Name (Party)	Vote (%)
2014 General	John Kasich (R)	1,944,848 (64%)
	Ed FitzGerald (D)	1,009,359 (33%)
	Anita Rios (G)	101,706 (3%)

Prior winning percentage: 2010 (49%); House: 1998 (67%), 1996 (64%), 1994 (66%), 1992 (72%), 1990 (70%), 1988 (80%), 1986 (73%), 1984 (70%), 1982 (50%)

John Kasich had a long career in the House of Representatives before winning Ohio's governorship twice, in 2010 and 2014. Then, in 2016, he ran for president and outlasted 15 rivals before conceding the nomination to Donald Trump. Traditionally a conservative, Kasich staked out a moderate image to differentiate himself from his more conservative rivals. Unlike most sitting governors who have run for president, Kasich returned home with his political reputation intact and he remains a potential leader of an establishment wing of the party if it ever decides that its embrace of Trump was wrongheaded.

Kasich has spent much of his adult life in politics. He grew up the son of a mail carrier in working-class McKees Rocks, Pennsylvania, and is of Hungarian, Czech and Croatian ancestry. After graduating from Ohio State University with a bachelor's in political science, he worked for a state legislator. In 1978, at age 26, Kasich ran a strenuous door-to-door campaign and beat a Democratic state senator, becoming the youngest person ever elected to that chamber. He ran for the House four years later and, with the help of a favorable redistricting plan, ousted Democrat Bob Shamansky, who was the only Democratic House incumbent to lose in a midterm election that was mostly tough for Republicans nationally. As a brash new member of Congress, Kasich caused his first commotion on the Armed Services Committee, where he was the leading Republican opponent of the B-2 bomber and teamed with California Democrat Ron Dellums in drastically reducing its production. Although he was raised a Catholic, after a drunk driver killed his parents in 1987, he turned to evangelical Christianity.

Kasich got a seat on the Budget Committee in 1989 and won the ranking Republican spot four years later with the help of Rep. Newt Gingrich of Georgia, then an ascendant figure in the GOP. In that Democratic Congress, Kasich led the Republicans' charge to "cut spending first," which laid the groundwork for the defeat of Clinton's 1993 economic stimulus legislation. He advanced a budget alternative with no tax increases or Social Security cuts, but it did contain means-testing and cuts in discretionary spending. In 1994, he and Democrat Tim Penny of Minnesota put together spending cut bills that the House narrowly defeated. He offended some conservatives by supporting the ban on certain classes of semi-automatic rifles in the 1994 crime bill. The serious and detailed work Kasich did on the budget was an indispensable ingredient in his successes in 1995 and 1996 after Republicans regained control of Congress. Kasich and House Republicans pushed to curb discretionary spending, and their persistence helped lead to the Balanced Budget Act of 1997, a sweeping deal that combined tax cuts with reductions in Medicare and Medicaid payments to health care providers and added money for higher education assistance and the creation of the State Children's Health Insurance Program. Kasich remained popular in his Columbus-area district, winning reelection eight times. In 1999, Kasich explored a presidential bid but faced huge obstacles, including fundraising and a personal reputation for prickliness, and he abandoned his bid by July of that year. He left the House in 2001 and later worked at financial giant Lehman Brothers – whose spectacular failure at the outset of the Great Recession would become an issue in his later gubernatorial and presidential bids – and he hosted a Fox News talk show until 2007.

Ohio's dire economic situation during the Great Recession helped lure Kasich back into politics. In June 2009, he announced his challenge to Democratic Gov. Ted Strickland, who just a year earlier had been popular enough to be considered a potential running mate for Barack Obama. Kasich cited the need to balance the state budget and cut bureaucracy that he said was hampering business growth, and he jumped to an early lead in the polls. His lead in the polls shrank by October. In the end, though, he was able to pull out a 49%-47% victory.

As governor, Kasich immediately made clear his willingness to break with the previous administration. He rejected a passenger rail line through the state that Strickland had pushed, calling it a waste of taxpayer money. He joined other new GOP governors in seeking to curtail the influence of public employee unions, calling for a ban on strikes by teachers and embracing a limit on collective bargaining. And he drew opposition to his proposed $55.5 billion budget, which called for sharing services among agencies, pooling health care costs and reducing prevailing-wage requirements on public construction contracts. It also called for a 25% reduction in local government funding. Rather than go on the defensive, an upbeat Kasich sought to sell his approach to closing an $8 billion budget gap as being done "with no smoke and mirrors" and promoting growth over the long term. He mostly got his way. The national media began recognizing him as a successful example of the new crop of young GOP state chief executives.

Amid polls showing strong public opposition to his move to limit collective bargaining with public-sector unions, including police and firefighters, Kasich and fellow Republicans offered to meet with unions to discuss a compromise that would keep the issue off the ballot as a referendum that November. But the unions, who were firmly opposed to the concept, rebuffed him. Voters overwhelmingly voted down Kasich's collective-bargaining law, 62%-38%. Kasich seized the moment and, with a touch of humility, told reporters after the defeat, "I respect what the people have to say in an effort like this. And as a result of that, it requires me to take a deep breath and to spend some time to reflect on what happened here."

Kasich tried a new budgetary tack in 2012, calling for a higher tax on oil and gas companies that extract from wells using the controversial method of hydraulic fracturing. Most of the tax revenue would fund an across-the-board income tax reduction. State GOP lawmakers, however, balked at the idea. Kasich departed from his fiscally conservative record in 2013 by embracing Medicaid expansion over the opposition of the Republican legislature. The state's improving economy corresponded with a rise in his job approval rating, but surveys also indicated that a successful reelection bid was far from assured. Kasich responded by taking some steps that proved popular. He created JobsOhio, a private non-profit economic development entity to be funded with state liquor proceeds, and he signed a bipartisan law that reformed criminal sentencing laws to ease prison overcrowding. In 2014, he helped craft a compromise on state mandates on utility companies that froze, rather than eliminated, the requirements that they use renewable sources to generate a portion of their power.

Democrats were initially hopeful for their 2014 nominee, Cuyahoga County Executive Ed FitzGerald, a former FBI agent. But FitzGerald stumbled through a series of embarrassing disclosures, notably a police report from 2012 that said he had been in a car at 4:30 a.m. with a woman who was not his wife. This, in turn, led to a records check that found that FitzGerald had been driving without a valid license for 10 years. Several senior staffers left his campaign, and he struggled raising funds. FitzGerald's meltdown enabled Kasich to ignore his Democratic opponent. The two didn't debate-the first time since 1978 there wasn't at least one gubernatorial debate in Ohio-and Kasich pitched himself as a recovery Republican with a record of success. Kasich won a sweeping reelection victory with 64 percent of the vote, capturing majorities even in normally Democratic Cuyahoga County (Cleveland) and Franklin County (Columbus). He lost only two of the state's 88 counties, both rural ones along the Ohio River. He even won a majority of union household members – a group that had fiercely fought his labor reform initiative just three years earlier.

In 2015, Kasich signed a budget bill that continued his Medicaid expansion, cut the state's top personal income tax rate to just below 5 percent, provided tax relief to small businesses, raised cigarette taxes 35 cents a pack and boosted state aid to K-12 education by $955 million over two years. He failed to win approval for his proposed tax increase on oil-and-gas drillers and he had initially sought a $1-a-pack hike in cigarette taxes along with a broader reduction in income taxes. He made use of his line-item veto, cutting more than 40 provisions in the budget, including several specific benefits lawmakers had sought for business and industry, including power plants, big-box retailers and nursing homes. The bill also included new restrictions on abortion clinics.

In July 2015, Kasich announced his bid for president – the second to last among the unusually large field seeking to succeed Barack Obama. As a candidate, Kasich did not seek to out-conservative his rivals to woo the party's base, and he couldn't have done so plausibly anyway. Instead, Kasich articulated the out-of-fashion view that expertise matters, that practical solutions can be achieved, and that the party needs to serve the needs of those society had left behind – people "in the shadows," such as the drug addicted, the mentally ill and the imprisoned. Equally uncharacteristic of its time was Kasich's style – he ran as the proudly unflashy candidate in a race that would eventually elect the most outrageous presidential nominee in American history. In addition to targeting votes in his midwestern base, Kasich focused intensively on New Hampshire, courting establishment Republicans in a state that has relatively few evangelical party members. Kasich held more than 100 town hall meetings in New Hampshire, and his combination of bluntness and wonkiness won over many voters there. Kasich ended up finishing second to Trump in the Granite State, giving him enough momentum to soldier on.

It was something of a tightrope walk for Kasich: Shortly after the South Carolina primary, where he finished a weak fifth, Kasich was presented with a bill prohibiting the state from contracting with abortion providers such as Planned Parenthood. He signed the bill – but he didn't trumpet it. The balancing act between conservative and pragmatic ultimately proved unsustainable once the battle moved to areas where the electorate was a weak fit for his approach, both ideologically and temperamentally. As Trump was rallying crowds against illegal immigration, Kasich was asking, "Do the Republicans actually think that they can win an election by scaring every Hispanic in this country to death?" Kasich hung on, but won only his home state of Ohio, which bolstered the fading hopes of senior party figures who were eager for a more conventional alternative to Trump. On May 4, the day after Trump won the Indiana primary, Kasich quit the race. He was the last candidate other than Trump in the race, slightly outlasting Texas Sen. Ted Cruz.

Even after the nomination was settled, the Trump and Kasich camps found themselves at odds. Awkwardly, the GOP had scheduled its convention for Cleveland, meaning that Kasich would be the nominal host for a nominee who he was not that fond of. Kasich declined an offer to address the convention, instead making the rounds of satellite events where he usually touted Republican themes without promoting the party's candidate. Paul Manafort, then Trump's campaign manager, complained on MSNBC on the eve of the convention that Kasich "is hurting his state. He's embarrassing his state, frankly." Matt Borges, the Ohio GOP chair and a Kasich ally, fired back on Twitter: "Manafort still has a lot to learn about Ohio politics." Kasich reportedly rebuffed the Trump campaign's eccentric offer to make him the "most powerful vice president in history," and after the October leak of a tape of Trump boasting about groping women, Kasich reiterated his distaste. "I've long had concerns with Donald Trump that go beyond his temperament," he said. "We have substantive policy differences on conservative issues like trade, our relationship with Russia, and the importance of balancing the federal budget." When he cast his early vote for president, Kasich wrote in Sen. John McCain's name rather than casting a ballot for Trump, a spokesman said.

After the election, Kasich sought to maintain his national profile. He wrote a book, *Two Paths: America Divided or United*, and some of his allies created a new group named after the book's title to promote some of his key issues, although Kasich himself would not be directly involved. Demonstrating his pragmatic streak, Kasich trekked to Washington to see if he could win over White House officials on a proposal to expand Medicaid. With a bipartisan group of governors, he laid out principles for a blueprint that, he wrote, "can result in an improved health insurance system that is available and affordable for every American." Back in Ohio, Trump-allied officials ousted Borges as state Republican chairman. Then, when Trump fired FBI Director James Comey in May 2017, Kasich quickly blasted the move, saying he was "extremely troubled" by it and emphasized the need for "full and fair investigations into Russia's efforts to influence our election."

The Trump-Kasich friction foreshadowed sharp elbows within a crowded and well-credentialed Republican field to succeed him as governor in 2018. The GOP field included Attorney General Mike DeWine, Secretary of State Jon Husted, Rep. Jim Renacci and Lt. Gov. Mary Taylor. The pool of potential Democratic candidates, by contrast, was wide but shallow, particularly after Rep. Tim Ryan – who had sought unsuccessfully to oust House Minority Leader Nancy Pelosi – decided not to run for governor. Possible Democratic candidates included Ohio Supreme Court Justice William O'Neill, state Sen. Joe Schiavoni, former U.S. Rep. Betty Sutton, former state Rep. Connie Pillich, Dayton Mayor Nan Whaley, and, most intriguingly to some observers, former state attorney general and Consumer Financial Protection Bureau Director Richard Cordray.

Senior Senator

Sherrod Brown (D)

Elected 2006, term expires 2018, 2nd term; b. Nov 09, 1952; Mansfield; Ohio State University, M.P.A.; Ohio State University, M.A.; Yale University (CT), B.A.; Lutheran; Married (Connie Schultz); 2 children; 2 stepchildren; 2 grandchildren.

Elected Office: OH House, 1974-1982; OH Secretary of State, 1982-1990; U.S. House, 1993-2007.

Professional Career: Professor, OH St. University Mansfield, 1979, 1981, 1991.

DC Office: 713 HSOB 20510, 202-224-2315, Fax: 202-228-6321, brown.senate.gov.

State Offices: Cincinnati, 513-684-1021; Cleveland, 216-522-7272; Columbus, 614-469-2083; Lorain, 440-242-4100.

Committees: *Agriculture, Nutrition & Forestry*: Commodities, Risk Management & Trade, Nutrition, Agricultural Research & Specialty Crops, Rural Development & Energy. *Banking, Housing & Urban Affairs (RMM)*: Economic Policy, Financial Institutions & Consumer Protection, Housing, Transportation & Community Development, National Security & International Trade & Finance, Securities, Insurance & Investment. *Finance*: Health Care, Social Security, Pensions & Family Policy (RMM). *Veterans' Affairs*.

Group Ratings

	ADA	ACLU	AFL-CIO	LCV	ITI	COC	HAFA	ACU	CFG	FRC
2016	-	88%	-	100%	60%	50%	7%	0%	0%	0%
2015	95%	C	100%	96%	C	46%	C	0%	4%	0%

Almanac Ratings 2015

	Economy	Social	Foreign	Composite
Liberal	100%	100%	100%	100%
Conservative	0%	0%	0%	0%

Key Votes of the 114th Congress

1. Keystone pipeline	N	5. National Security Data	Y	9. Gun Sales Checks	N
2. Export-Import Bank	N	6. Iran Nuclear Deal	N	10. Sanctuary Cities	N
3. Debt Ceiling Increase	Y	7. Puerto Rico Debt	N	11. Planned Parenthood	N
4. Homeland Security $$	Y	8. Loretta Lynch A.G	Y	12. Trade deals	N

Election Results

Election	Name (Party)	Vote (%)	Cand. Spent	Ind. Exp. Support	Ind. Exp. Oppose
2012 General	Sherrod Brown (D)	2,762,766 (51%)	$24,576,288	$3,447,764	$16,227,889
	Josh Mandel (R)	2,435,744 (45%)	$18,868,809	$7,226,232	$11,782,303
	Scott Rupert (NP)	250,617 (5%)	$6,337		
2012 Primary	Sherrod Brown (D)	522,827 (100%)			

Prior winning percentages: 2006 (56%); House: 2004 (67%), 2002 (69%), 2000 (65%), 1998 (62%), 1996 (60%), 1994 (49%), 1992 (53%)

He has yet to achieve the national profile of such like-minded colleagues as Massachusetts' Elizabeth Warren and Vermont's Bernie Sanders, but Sherrod Brown, Ohio's senior senator, has emerged as an outspoken and influential member of the Democrats' liberal populist wing. Brown was vetted as a vice-presidential running mate by Hillary Clinton in 2016 -- as someone who could appeal to those who voted for Sanders during the latter's battle with Clinton for the Democratic nomination. For his part, Brown, who has spent all but a couple of the past 40 years in elective office, has insisted he has "zero interest" in trying to move up further. "I don't think you can do your job well in the Senate if you're looking over your shoulder wanting to be president," he told *The Washington Post* in early 2015. That has not stopped the buzz surrounding Brown as a possible presidential contender in 2020.

First, however, Brown must win reelection to his Senate seat in a battleground state that voted for President Donald Trump by an 8-point margin, Consequently, as he gears up to seek a third term in 2018, Brown has adopted a tactical approach at odds with many of his fellow progressives --who have urged hardline resistance to any cooperation with the Trump Administration. In public comments as well as communications with Trump and White House officials, Brown has offered his cooperation in such areas as trade -- Brown has long shared Trump's distaste for the North American Free Trade Agreement (NAFTA) -- and infrastructure improvement. "I'll work with him when he's right for Ohio, and I'll oppose him when he's wrong for Ohio," Brown told *Politico* during a visit to his home turf in the spring of 2017 -- even as he hammered Trump for appointment of Cabinet officials whose "life's goal" is "a rollback of protection for workers."

The Senate seat that Brown has occupied since his initial 2006 election was held for nearly two decades by the late Howard Metzenbaum, to whom Brown is sometimes compared. Metzenbaum, a self-made multimillionaire, was often dubbed "the last angry liberal." But he positioned himself as a populist whose frequent attacks on big business and other powerful interests gave him an appeal that transcended ideological lines in a swing state. Like his predecessor, Brown can be rhetorically combative; in a March 2011 floor speech, he likened the GOP's push in some states to restrict collective-bargaining rights to the anti-union efforts of Adolf Hitler and Joseph Stalin, a remark for which he later apologized. Behind such rhetoric is a personal style that is often cheerful and informal. Brown loves to chat about baseball; he has a personal email address that begins with "DamnYankees", and he took his wife to Chicago's Wrigley Field on their honeymoon. In addition to his fondness for wearing sneakers (American-made) with his suits, he is known for a voice that sounds perpetually hoarse and a mop of tousled hair that frequently appears in need of a comb. Brown is so often described as "rumpled" that it sometimes appears to be part of his given name. He also is known as an energetic cheerleader for his state, dropping the names of Ohio localities in his floor speeches, while amassing a solid constituent service record.

Brown grew up in Mansfield in north central Ohio, halfway between Cleveland and Columbus. The son of a physician, he graduated from Yale in 1974, and went directly to the campaign trail, winning a seat in the Ohio House that November as he was turning 22. He earned a master's degrees in education and public administration from Ohio State University while serving in the legislature. In 1982, he was elected Ohio secretary of state and worked to increase voter registration and turnout. After serving two terms, he lost that office in 1990 to Republican Bob Taft, a scion of Ohio's most famous political family and later the state's governor. It didn't take long for Brown to make a political comeback, winning an open House seat in 1992. The district stretched from the western suburbs of Cleveland south to Akron; with solid labor support, Brown campaigned hard against NAFTA, which would come before Congress in 1993, while championing universal health care. He won 53%-35%. He had a close call in the Republican wave year of 1994, winning by only 49%-46%, but, after that, was regularly re-elected with more than 60 percent of the vote.

For many years, Brown wore a self-designed lapel pin of a canary in a cage, to commemorate underground miners who were at risk back in the days before labor unions and government safety inspections. (In late 2016, he and West Virginia Sen. Joe Manchin led a group of coal state senators who threatened to block a funding bill needed to keep the government in operation unless a program providing health care benefits to miners was extended.) Brown had a consistently liberal voting record in the House. On trade, he was one of the most voluble pro-labor and "fair trade" members from the Great Lakes area, attacking the string of trade agreements and free trade policies that followed NAFTA. In 2005, he helped to lead the effort to defeat the Central American Free Trade Agreement, which cleared the House by just two votes. One of two books he published during his House years was entitled *Myths of Free Trade: Why American Trade Policy Has Failed.* (The other was *Congress on the Inside: Observations from the Majority and the Minority*, reflecting his experiences before and after the House switch to Republican control in 1994.) During a period of widespread calls to allow import of Canadian pharmaceuticals to drive down prices in the United States, Brown sponsored bus trips to Canada for consumers to buy prescription drugs.

Brown had had his eye on a return to statewide office, but, in 2005, he initially said he would not challenge two-term Republican Sen. Mike DeWine, who had won the seat in 1994 when Metzenbaum retired. That left Iraq War veteran Paul Hackett as the Democratic frontrunner. Hackett was an attractive candidate, but there were questions about whether he could raise enough money, and his shoot-from-the-hip style aroused concerns about how he would play statewide. Brown reconsidered and entered the race in October 2005. Although incensed, Hackett withdrew from the race, and Brown breezed to the Democratic nomination.

DeWine, meanwhile, was seeking reelection in a hostile political environment: There was an undertow from various scandals associated with the Republican-controlled state government, plus the drag from the unpopular administration of President George W. Bush. Brown charged that DeWine was a "rubber stamp" for Bush and tied him to Bush's Iraq policy. DeWine focused on his accomplishments and his ability to work across party lines, hoping to heighten the contrast between himself and the more sharply partisan Brown, whose legislative effectiveness had been limited under Republican House rule. Brown won 56%-44%, dominating nearly all of Ohio's population centers. He also carried everything east of Interstate 77, where his high-profile opposition to free trade resonated in the coal and steel counties.

In the Senate, Brown's voting record has been as unfailingly liberal as it was in the House, even though he now represents a state that, as a whole, has long been politically marginal. In 2015, *Almanac* vote rankings put Brown in a tie (with Minnesota's Al Franken and Vermont's Patrick Leahy) for the Senate's most liberal voting record. Of the 15 most liberal senators in 2015, Brown was one of just two whose home state voted for Trump a year later. As in the House, his focus has been on trade issues. "In a place like Mansfield, Ohio, where I grew up, which used to have six or eight major manufacturers and five dozen small manufacturers, most of them are gone. The rest of them, by and large, will be gone, if we don't take care of worker enforcement on trade law and if we don't help those workers that lose their jobs," he told the *Huffington Post* in a 2015 interview. When he sought reelection in 2012, a sign posted outside his Columbus campaign headquarters was less nuanced: "Only vehicles assembled by union workers in North America are welcome in this parking lot."

At the beginning of the term of President Barack Obama, as Congress passed a $787 billion measure-which Brown felt should be even larger-he fought to include requirements that the money be used on U.S.-made goods. The provision was included in the versions of the bill that passed the House and Senate, but the final legislation allowed goods to be purchased from some of America's largest trading partners. Also in 2009, Brown called on Obama to take a tougher stance with China on trade, saying the White House should prod the Chinese government to allow its currency to float rather than keep it pegged to the dollar, a change that would have the effect of raising prices for Chinese goods. He led a subsequent effort in 2012 to persuade Obama to file a series of trade cases against China, accusing Beijing of unfairly subsidizing Chinese auto parts makers.

Immediately after the 2016 election, Brown reached out to the Trump transition team on trade, offering to work with the incoming president on his campaign pledge to alter NAFTA. "He's got a lot of resistance from his own party, but people like me will stand with him on renegotiation of [NAFTA]," Brown told the *Cleveland Plain Dealer*. He later sent Trump a letter urging such a renegotiation, with a note back from Trump reading: "Great letter. I will never let our workers down. Best wishes!" Brown's letter also asked Trump to withdraw from the Trans-Pacific Partnership, a 12-nation trade negotiated by Obama -- Trump did so within a week of taking office -- as well as to "overhaul" U.S.-China trade relations.

When the fight was joined in the spring of 2015 over granting Obama so-called "fast track" negotiating authority to pursue the TPP, Brown showed up as a member of the Finance Committee with no less than 88 amendments in an effort to both modify the measure and slow down its progress. The fast track measure ultimately cleared the Senate, but Brown could claim a small victory when his "Level the Playing Field Act" made it into both the House and Senate bills to reauthorize the U.S. Customs Service and Border Patrol. The measure was intended to strengthen the hand of the Commerce Department and International Trade Commission against foreign producers selling in the United States below market price or receiving subsidies from their home nations; Brown complained enforcement of anti-dumping and countervailing duty statutes had been weakened through court challenges by foreign producers.

At the outset of 2015, when New York's Charles Schumer passed on becoming the ranking Democrat on the Banking Committee to concentrate on his duties in the Senate leadership, the slot went to Brown. While Brown and Schumer share a voting record that puts them on the left end of the Senate spectrum, Schumer-reflecting the presence of Wall Street in his home city-has been supportive of the nation's financial industry. Brown, on the other hand, has sided with Warren in favor of reinstituting some of the barriers between banks and other financial institutions dropped in 1999 when the Depression-era Glass-Steagall Act was repealed. Prior to the 2014 election, with control of the Senate in the balance, one bank executive anonymously told *The Washington Post* that the prospect of Brown becoming committee chairman was "frightening," complaining the senator had showed no interest in finding common ground with large banks.

The 2015-16 period in Congress was not a productive one for the Banking panel, amid a bumpy relationship between Brown and the chairman, Alabama Republican Richard Shelby. The two men produced competing bills on the 2010 Dodd-Frank financial industry regulation law, targeted for a significant rollback by Republican congressional leaders. Shelby's bill cleared the Banking Committee in June 2015 but went no further, amid the prospect of a Democratic filibuster if it was brought to the

Senate floor. Brown was clearly happy to see Idaho Republican Mike Crapo replace Shelby as chairman at the end of 2016 due to GOP term limit rules. "We have a working relationship," Brown said of Crapo, according to *The Hill* newspaper. "He's way more conservative than I am, but he's straightforward and honorable." Brown and Crapo have a history of working across the aisle: They previously teamed up on a bill to loosen a Dodd-Frank rule on credit card companies, while leading a Senate Finance Committee tax-reform working group on savings and investment. In early 2017, it appeared that Crapo and Brown were poised to pursue a bipartisan approach to changes in Dodd-Frank, starting with regulatory relief for smaller community banks and credit unions -- a move favored by many Democrats.

Brown worked on Dodd-Frank when it was first enacted, and unsuccessfully pushed a proposal to limit the size of banks deemed "too big to fail" in the wake of the government bailout of financial firms during the 2008 crash. He called for capping banks at holdings of no more than 2 percent of the gross domestic product or 10 percent of insured bank deposits nationally. The cap would have affected three large banks: Bank of America, Wells Fargo, and JP Morgan Chase. His attitude toward large financial institutions guided Brown's actions on a couple of Obama's major appointments. In 2013, Brown got 20 fellow Democrats to sign a letter supporting Janet Yellen as the next chair of the Federal Reserve; she was ultimately appointed. Obama's preferred choice, former Treasury Secretary Larry Summers, was seen by Brown and other progressive Democrats as overly close to Wall Street. Similar objections prompted Brown to oppose confirmation of Mary Jo White as chair of the Securities and Exchange Commission earlier that year In May 2017, Brown joined three dozen Democratic colleagues in voting against the confirmation of Trump's choice of Jay Clayton as White's successor, declaring, "Americans deserve a chair who will run the SEC on their behalf, not for the benefit of Wall Street banks and big corporations."

Brown says one of his proudest legislative achievements was a bill passed with the help of the late Massachusetts Sen. Edward Kennedy. During reauthorization of the Food and Drug Administration in 2009, Brown won passage of an amendment creating incentives for pharmaceutical companies to produce drugs for diseases common in the developing world. Within weeks of it going into effect, an international aid group reported a flood of new TB drugs on the market.

Closer to home, as a liberal from a coal-producing state, Brown has tread carefully on environmental issues -- while again seeking to protect U.S. interests in the international marketplace. In early 2011, when Obama announced the Environmental Protection Agency would issue new regulations for carbon emissions, Brown said he would insist on protections for U.S. manufacturers. A year earlier, as a negotiator on a climate change bill that the Senate worked on but failed to pass, he was point man for a bloc of Democrats who dubbed themselves the "Brown Dogs"-and likewise refused to support the bill without protections for U.S. firms. Brown surprised environmental groups in 2007 when he said nuclear power is safe and should be an option; more recently, he has worked to make Ohio a leader in wind energy production.

In the 2012 election, Brown was the target of one of the most expensive outside efforts to date to defeat a member of Congress, as conservative groups poured $40 million into attacking him. His Republican opponent was 35-year-old Josh Mandel, who broke a pledge to serve a full term as state treasurer by challenging Brown less than two years into his tenure. Mandel raised $19 million on his own and served up plenty of stinging rhetoric, calling Brown's support for the auto industry bailout "un-American" and labeling the senator "a liar" during a debate. Brown and his allies accused Mandel of not being ready for the Senate, pointing to Mandel statements that fact-checking watchdogs had labeled as false. The senator called his rival "the king" of "Pants on Fire," a reference to the website *PolitiFact's* lowest rating for truthfulness. (Brown later had his own problems on this front, thanks to *The Washington Post*'s counterpart to *PolitiFact*. During the 2015 trade debate, the *Post* awarded Brown "four Pinocchios" for repeatedly attributing a quote to former President George H.W. Bush that Bush had never made.)

Brown's campaign and outside liberal groups came up with $35 million, and, boosted by Obama's substantial political investment in Ohio, turned what was a neck-and-neck race in August into a 51%-45% win. Mandel won most counties, but Brown dominated the major population centers, winning 69 percent in Cleveland's Cuyahoga County and 61 percent in Columbus' Franklin County. He ran slightly ahead of Obama, who carried the state over Republican Mitt Romney, 50%-48%.

The 2018 contest initially shaped up as a Brown-Mandel rematch, as Mandel announced in December 2016 that he would make a second run at the incumbent. Mandel has been vocally supportive of Trump, adopting some of the same phrases as the president -- "rigged system" and "drain the swamp" in his announcement video. Eight-term Rep. Pat Tiberi explored a Senate run before announcing in May 2017 that he had decided to seek re-election to the House, where he sits on the Ways and Means Committee. "I believe I could have been the best candidate to win a seat in November of 2018 on our side," Tiberi told the *Columbus Dispatch*, adding that he "does not have the baggage of losing to the current incumbent already" -- a not-so-subtle jab at Mandel.

The 2012 campaign caused professional complications for Brown's wife, Pulitzer Prize-winning columnist Connie Schultz, whom he had married in 2004 (his second marriage). In 2011, Schultz resigned after 18 years with the *Cleveland Plain Dealer*, telling colleagues that "in recent weeks, it has become painfully clear that my independence, professionally and personally, is possible only if I'm no longer writing for the newspaper that covers my husband's Senate race on a daily basis." She remains a nationally syndicated columnist. Schultz apologized for failing to mention earlier that, during a tea party event at which she was present, Mandel had attended and she had videotaped him. Schultz had taken a leave of absence from the paper during Brown's first Senate campaign in 2006. Her experiences provided material for a book, published in 2007, entitled *...And His Lovely Wife: A Memoir From the Woman Beside the Man.*

Brown supported Clinton during the 2016 primaries, but, responding in March to speculation about him as a possible running mate, he told the *Toledo Blade*: "I do not want to be vice president. I feel lucky to be Ohio's senator, and working for our state is the only job I want." However, talking with reporters at the Democratic National Convention in Philadelphia, Brown indicated that it had been a more serious prospect than originally thought: He said he went through an "arduous" 32-day vetting process, culminating in a 90-minute meeting with Clinton, with only a single aide in attendance. Then-Senate Democratic Leader Harry Reid was cool to the possibility of Brown on the ticket, because a potential vacancy would be filled by Ohio's Republican governor. Brown himself voiced concern about that scenario in an interview with MSNBC two months prior to the convention, declaring: "If I were on the ticket and Hillary were to win, that John Kasich would nominate and would appoint my successor, and that bothers me so."

Junior Senator

Rob Portman (R)

Elected 2010, term expires 2022, 2nd term; b. Dec 19, 1955, Cincinnati; Cincinnati Country Day School, 1974; Dartmouth College, B.A., 1979; University of Michigan Law School, J.D., 1984; Methodist; Married (Jane Portman); 3 children.

Elected Office: U.S. House, 1993-2005.

Professional Career: White House Legislative Affairs Director, 1989-1991; U.S trade rep., 2005-2006; Director, Office of Management & Budget, 2006-2007; Practicing attorney, 1984-1988, 2007-2010.

DC Office: 448 RSOB 20510, 202-224-3353, Fax: 202-224-9075, portman.senate.gov.

State Offices: Cincinnati, 513-684-3265; Cleveland, 216-522-7095; Columbus, 614-469-6774; Toledo, 419-259-3895.

Committees: *Energy & Natural Resources*: Energy, National Parks, Water & Power. *Finance*: Health Care, Social Security, Pensions & Family Policy, Taxation & IRS Oversight (Chmn). *Foreign Relations*: Europe & Regional Security Cooperation, Internat'l Dev Instit & Internat'l Econ, Energy & Environ Policy, Near East, South Asia, Central Asia & Counterterrorism, State Dept & USAID Mngmnt, Internat'l Ops & Internat'l Dev. *Homeland Security & Government Affairs*: Investigations (Chmn), Regulatory Affairs & Federal Management.

Group Ratings

	ADA	ACLU	AFL-CIO	LCV	ITI	COC	HAFA	ACU	CFG	FRC
2016	-	17%	-	35%	60%	100%	28%	48%	40%	0%
2015	15%	C	31%	8%	C	86%	C	71%	65%	64%

Almanac Ratings 2015

	Economy	Social	Foreign	Composite
Liberal	44%	19%	9%	24%
Conservative	56%	81%	91%	76%

Key Votes of the 114th Congress

1. Keystone pipeline	Y	5. National Security Data	N	9. Gun Sales Checks	N
2. Export-Import Bank	N	6. Iran Nuclear Deal	Y	10. Sanctuary Cities	Y
3. Debt Ceiling Increase	N	7. Puerto Rico Debt	N	11. Planned Parenthood	Y
4. Homeland Security $$	N	8. Loretta Lynch A.G	Y	12. Trade deals	Y

Election Results

Election	Name (Party)	Vote (%)		Cand. Spent	Ind. Exp. Support	Ind. Exp. Oppose
2016 General	Rob Portman (R)	3,118,568	(58%)	$33,851,658	$3,264,568	$15,540,944
	Ted Strickland (D)	1,996,913	(37%)	$10,231,752	$4,827,629	$34,525,870
2016 Primary	Rob Portman (R)	1,336,686	(82%)			
	Don Elijah Eckhart (R)	290,268	(18%)			

Prior winning percentages: 2010 (57%), 2004 (72%), 2002 (74%), 2000 (74), 1998 (76%), 1996 (72%), 1994 (77%), 1993 special (70%)

For Republican Rob Portman, Ohio's junior senator, election to the Senate in 2010 was the latest stop for a consummate insider whose career has alternated between the two ends of Pennsylvania Avenue in official Washington: Capitol Hill and the White House. After service in the administration of President George H.W. Bush-to whom Portman occasionally has been compared, in terms of both his center-right views and even-keeled modesty-Portman won a Cincinnati-based House seat in a 1993 special election, only to head back up Pennsylvania Avenue a dozen years later when he was appointed head of the Office of the U.S. Trade Representative and later director of the Office of Management and Budget by President George W. Bush. For a time following his arrival in the Senate, it appeared that another White House stint might be in Portman's future: He was on a short list of possible running mates to Republican presidential nominee Mitt Romney in 2012, and, early in the 2016 election cycle, Portman made the requisite visits to Iowa and New Hampshire, where the earliest contests for national convention delegates take place, as he mulled a presidential bid himself. But in December 2014, Portman cited the newly acquired GOP majority in the Senate as a key factor in announcing his decision not to seek the presidency.

While some questioned how saleable Portman might have been in a GOP presidential nominating contest given some of his more moderate views, his decision was good news for Republicans looking to hang onto a Senate seat in the battleground state of Ohio. Portman's reelection appeared very much at risk early in the 2015-16 cycle, as some polls showed him trailing the likely Democratic nominee, former Gov. Ted Strickland, by nearly double digits. But Portman ran a well-executed campaign in which he adeptly kept his distance from his party's controversial nominee, now-President Donald Trump, while, by his own admission, borrowing some of the sophisticated voter targeting tactics utilized by the campaigns of Trump's Democratic predecessor, Barack Obama. The result was that Portman ended up cruising to victory over Strickland. "I very much believe - no offense to anyone - that Rob Portman ran the best campaign in America," Ohio Republican Chairman Matthew Borges boasted to *The New York Times*. By the same token, Portman reaped the benefit of a problem-plagued Strickland campaign effort that produced private consternation in Democratic Party circles.

Portman grew up in Cincinnati, where his father in 1960 started a forklift distribution company employing five people. The privately held Portman Equipment Co. eventually grew into a 350-person operation before being sold to a Dutch conglomerate in 2004. On his mother's side, Portman's grandfather in 1926 had purchased the Golden Lamb Inn in the Cincinnati suburb of Lebanon, which opened in 1803 and is considered to be Ohio's oldest continuously operated business. (A dozen presidents have stayed at the hotel, which today is owned by Portman and his siblings.) In his youth, Portman worked summers at his father's equipment firm, sweeping floors and grinding old paint off trucks. While at Dartmouth College, he hung out with a crowd nicknamed the "Granola Gang" known for its love of the outdoors; many of its members later volunteered for the Peace Corps or went to work in the field of renewable energy. He took a semester off to work for Cincinnati-area Rep. Willis Gradison, whom Portman would later succeed.

After graduating from Dartmouth, Portman worked for George H.W. Bush's 1980 campaign for the Republican presidential nomination as part of the advance team. It was the beginning of a long association with the Bush family. Portman earned a law degree at the University of Michigan in 1984, and was hired by a leading Washington lawyer/lobbying firm, Patton, Boggs and Blow, as a trade attorney. He returned to Cincinnati in 1987 to practice law before coming back to Washington in 1989 as an associate White House counsel and then head of the Office of Legislative Affairs under George H.W. Bush. Portman was back practicing law in Cincinnati when, in January 1993, Gradison resigned his House seat to become head of a Washington-based trade association. Portman ran to fill the vacancy, and had help from former first lady Barbara Bush, who made a radio ad for him. He won a seven-candidate primary with 36 percent to 30 percent for the second place-finisher: former Rep. Bob McEwen, who had been ousted in a neighboring district in 1992. The special general election in the predominantly Republican district was anticlimactic; Portman won with 70 percent. He was easily reelected six times from 1994 through 2004.

In the House, Portman got on the Ways and Means and Budget committees and became known for his fiscal conservatism and his ability to work across the aisle. He co-chaired the National Commission on Restructuring the Internal Revenue Service and won broad support for repeal of the 3 percent excise tax on telephone service. He worked with Democrats, notably his current Senate colleague, Ben Cardin of Maryland (then a House member also serving on Ways and Means), on issues ranging from land conservation to welfare reform to pensions. He helped revise 401(k) rules to make it easier for small businesses to offer pension plans, but he got nowhere with a 2002 attempt to repeal the alternative minimum tax. He also sponsored the bill to create a National Underground Railroad Museum in Cincinnati; Portman's ancestors include Quaker abolitionists who were active in Underground Railroad.

In 2005, President George W. Bush nominated Portman as trade representative, making him the administration's top negotiator in efforts to reduce trade barriers. A year later, Bush appointed him OMB director, a position that requires immersion in the arcana of federal spending and regulation. Bush nicknamed him "The Mule," in tribute to his persistence. Portman succeeded in pushing the budget more toward balance, although he later told *The Hill* newspaper that he was frustrated he couldn't do more. "I wanted to offer a balanced budget over five years, and a lot of people didn't," he said. He left the agency in 2007 and returned to the Cincinnati area, where he joined a law firm and taught a class at Ohio State University's John Glenn School of Public Affairs. (He now occupies the Senate seat held by Glenn for 24 years.)

Just after Republican Sen. George Voinovich announced in January 2009 that he would not run for a third term, Portman entered the contest. The timing of his candidacy did not seem propitious. Despite his stint in two Cabinet-level positions, he had virtually no name recognition beyond the Cincinnati media market. And Obama had just been sworn in as president, after moving Ohio into the Democratic column in 2008. Soon, two Democratic officials who had run statewide joined the race: Lt. Gov. Lee Fisher and Secretary of State Jennifer Brunner. Polls showed Portman trailing both. Unfazed, he campaigned around the state in blue jeans and a windbreaker, putting out a six-point jobs program and opposing the Democrats' $787 billion stimulus bill and their health care overhaul-albeit doing so affably. Portman raised serious money, $16.5 million, and he also benefited from a fractious Democratic primary in May 2010, which Fisher won, 56%-44%.

In the fall campaign, Fisher derided Portman's long association with the Bush family, telling *The Columbus Dispatch*, "Rob Portman had his hands on the steering wheel as George W. Bush drove us off the cliff and into the deepest economic ditch in most of our lives." But Fisher had little money-much of the $6.4 million he raised was spent on the primary-and his position as Strickland's "jobs czar" in 2007 and 2008 proved to be a political liability. Portman asserted that Ohio lost 400,000 jobs while Fisher held the post. Portman fended off criticism of his work as trade representative by saying he would make enforcement of trade laws a high priority. He was not a particular favorite of tea party activists, but they didn't campaign against him. By October, the race was off everyone's list of competitive contests. Fisher lost to Portman, 57%-39%. Portman carried 82 of the state's 88 counties, and ran even in usually Democratic northeast Ohio.

In the Senate, Portman's government experience and personable demeanor quickly earned him respect as well as affection from members of both parties. In an institution where some adults have a reputation for exhibiting juvenile behavior, Portman is regularly described as a "grownup." It's a description he self-deprecatingly waves off, quipping, "When your hair starts to turn more gray, as mine has been, people are going to call you a grownup." His voting record has been conservative, but not extremely so. He attracted widespread attention in March 2013 when he reversed his opposition to same-sex marriage after he disclosed that his 21-year-old son, Will, had come out as gay. It made Portman the first Republican senator to support same-sex marriage. Some conservatives vowed to oppose him for renomination in 2016, but a serious primary challenger did not emerge.

In a 2014 interview with the *Associated Press* -- a year before the Supreme Court ruling that legalized same-sex marriage nationwide -- Portman said, "I feel very comfortable in taking a position of respecting people for who they are, which is what I think ultimately same-sex marriage is about." Also present for that interview was Portman's wife, Jane, who grew up in a Democratic family in North Carolina

-- and has a resume that includes an internship in Jimmy Carter's White House and a stint as a staffer to South Dakota Democratic Sen. Tom Daschle in the mid-1980s. She has laughingly referred to the "consolidation agreement" when she and Rob Portman married: She agreed to become a Republican and he agreed to become a Methodist.

Just months after Portman was sworn into the Senate, a standoff between the Obama White House and Republican leaders on Capitol Hill over raising the federal debt limit resulted in a deal that created the Joint Committee on Deficit Reduction-the so-called "Supercommittee"-consisting of 12 members of the House and Senate, evenly divided between the two parties. Portman was one of three Senate Republicans appointed to the panel, which was charged with finding an additional $1.5 trillion in budget savings over a 10-year period. As the late November 2011 deadline for the committee to act approached, efforts to come up with an agreement faltered. Portman and Massachusetts Sen. John Kerry-a Democratic member of the panel who later was named secretary of state-are devoted cyclists, and took numerous bike rides together as they informally discussed ways to move forward. But the deadline passed with the panel in a partisan deadlock.

In the wake of that experience, Portman teamed with Montana's Jon Tester on a 2012 bill to end the practice of government shutdowns. He was still trying five year later. Portman organized an ideologically diverse group of fellow Republicans in the spring of 2017 to sponsor a bill calling for an automatic "continuing resolution" at current spending levels if Congress fails to meet the deadline for enacting annual appropriations bills. After the first 120 days, spending in the continuing resolution would be cut by 1 percent every 90 days, as an incentive for Congress to reach a deal. "Almost everybody hates government shutdowns…They don't get our fiscal house in order and they disrupt critical government programs that have a big impact on people's lives," Portman told *Roll Call*.

A highlight of Portman's bipartisan collaborations was a four-year legislative effort, in tandem with New Hampshire Democratic Sen. Jeanne Shaheen, to pass legislation to encourage more energy efficient buildings. Finally, it met with success in early 2015, when Obama signed a scaled-down version of the legislation. The bill was initially brought to the floor in September 2013, but become entangled in debates over two perennial flashpoints: the Affordable Care Act and Keystone XL pipeline. It faltered again in May 2014 after Republicans insisted on being able to offer controversial amendments to block environmental regulations.

Portman and Shaheen teamed up again in 2016 on what had become an epidemic in their respective states: heroin and opioid abuse. (Statistics for Ohio were showing a death from an overdose every three hours.) In March, Portman was among five Republicans to back an effort led by Shaheen to add $600 million for treatment and prevention programs to a bill funding continued government operations. The move failed due to opposition from Republican leaders. But Obama later that year signed the 21st Century Cures Act, which included $1 billion to combat opioid addiction and abuse over a two-year period. Portman's push for additional funding was later highlighted in ads run during his re-election campaign.

Portman was urged to seek the chairmanship of the NRSC for the 2013-2014 cycle, but declined. He did agree to serve as one of two vice chairs of the committee, and played an active role in the successful effort to gain a Republican Senate majority. In 2012, Portman had thrown his Ohio organization behind Romney before the state's crucial March 6 Republican primary, which the former Massachusetts governor won by just over 10,000 votes. He and Romney got along well, and Portman later took on the role of Obama in Romney's debate preparation sessions, having earlier portrayed other Democrats in similar mock debates. But Portman's close association with the unpopular George W. Bush was probably a mark against him in the vice presidential sweepstakes, along with the perception that his personality is-well, bland. Those who know him say such characterizations are off the mark; in fact, he has a reputation as a prankster, and his outdoor exploits include smuggling a kayak into China in the 1980s to paddle the Yangtze River.

As trade moved to the front of the congressional agenda in 2015, Portman found himself having to navigate between his high-profile past as a negotiator of trade agreements and the widespread skepticism toward such deals in his home state -- where "free trade" is widely blamed for reduced employment and a shrinking manufacturing base. He was at odds with members of his own party as he pushed an amendment to Obama's request for so-called "fast track" negotiating authority to expedite the Trans-Pacific Partnership. Teaming with a fellow Finance Committee member, Michigan Democrat Debbie Stabenow, Portman unsuccessfully sought an amendment to require the White House to establish "enforceable rules" to combat currency manipulation. "We need a more level playing field," Portman told the *Cincinnati Enquirer*. His amendment was backed by the nation's domestic automakers, who have charged that they are being undercut by Japan's undervaluing of the yen. But Portman's currency amendment was strongly opposed by the committee chairman, Utah Republican Orrin Hatch. The *Wall*

Street Journal's conservative editorial page called the proposal a "killer amendment"-a charge strongly disputed by Portman-while suggesting the senator was "abandoning his policy chops in favor of re-election politics."

The currency amendment was later proposed on the Senate floor, and defeated, 51-48, with Portman and 11 other Republicans joining a majority of Democrats in supporting it. If Portman took heat from fellow Republicans for pushing the currency proposal, he was criticized by Democrats for supporting the final passage of the measure to give the president fast-track negotiating authority. Among the critics: Strickland, who said he would have voted against giving the president such authority. In February 2016, despite a history of advocating trade deals, Portman came out against the TPP agreement negotiated by the United States and other involved countries. "I cannot support the TPP in its current form because it doesn't provide that level playing field," Portman said, adding, "I will continue to urge the Obama Administration to support American workers and address these issues before any vote on the TPP agreement." Portman's position helped attract labor support to his campaign, as the Ohio Teamsters later cited his opposition to TPP in endorsing him. Ultimately, the TPP deal never came before Congress for a vote, and Trump withdrew the United States from the agreement days after entering the White House.

A month before coming out against the TPP, Portman -- after earlier suggesting he would not make an endorsement in the 2016 race for the GOP presidential nomination -- threw his support behind his home-state governor, John Kasich. It was something of a surprise, given Portman's ties to the Bush family and the presence of former Florida Gov. Jeb Bush in the race, but it presumably helped to solidify Portman's home state party base as polls showed his reelection in jeopardy. In May, when Trump emerged as the all-but-certain nominee, Portman endorsed him, but said little more about it. Strickland sought to tie the incumbent to Trump, and reporters repeatedly pelted him with questions -- but Portman, unlike Republicans in some other targeted races, succeeded in minimizing the issue. "I would give the same succinct answer: This race isn't between Donald Trump and Hillary Clinton, it's between Rob Portman and Ted Strickland," Portman told *The New York Times* following his reelection. Portman did disengage himself from Trump after the October disclosure of the "Access Hollywood" tapes in which Trump is heard making lewd comments about women. "While I continue to respect those who still support Donald Trump, I can no longer support him," said Portman, adding that he would write in the party's vice-presidential nominee, Mike Pence, for the top spot.

National Democrats initially thought they had scored a coup in recruiting Strickland, who scored a nearly 3-1 Democratic primary victory over Cincinnati City Councilman P.G. Sittenfeld in March 2016. While he was 75 years old and had been ousted by Kasich in 2010, Strickland enjoyed greater name ID than Portman; a Quinnipiac College survey in mid-2015 showed him with an approval rating nearly 20 points higher than his disapproval score. The same poll gave him a 6-point lead over Portman. But Portman -- who, during his first term, raised more for the NRSC than any other freshman senator -- again demonstrated his fundraising prowess. By July 2016, he had raised more than $15 million, more than twice as much as Strickland, and entered the homestretch with a campaign treasury nearly four times as large as his opponent. It allowed Portman to go on air during the summer with negative ads, to which the Strickland campaign was slow to respond. In a reprisal of charges he had lobbed at Strickland's lieutenant governor, Fisher, six years earlier, Portman's spots declared that the state had lost hundreds of thousands of jobs while Strickland was in office, with one ad breaking down the job loss by regions of the state. The ads also accused Strickland of poor management of state finances.

When the Strickland campaign finally went on air, it was with an ad that sought to rebut Portman's attacks by attributing the state's difficult situation to the Great Recession. "They say I lost jobs and drained the rainy-day fund," Strickland says to the camera in opening the ad, thereby giving Portman's charge additional exposure -- and causing some Democratic operatives to wince.

While Portman has been viewed with suspicion by the tea party wing, he got a big assist from the billionaire Koch brothers, the tea party's financial angels -- who were determined to see the Senate remain in Republican control. Groups aligned with the Kochs poured nearly $12 million for advertising into the Ohio Senate race, with the large majority of this coming prior to the official Labor Day start of the campaign. By that time, the advertising blitz had sliced Strickland's favorability ratings in half, and a Monmouth College survey showed him trailing Portman by 8 points -- even as Hillary Clinton led Trump in the state at that point. National Democratic strategists appeared to confirm their fading prospects in the Ohio Senate race when both the Democratic Senatorial Campaign Committee and the Senate Majority PAC, tied to Senate Democratic leaders, pulled large ad buys scheduled for the first part of September.

Ultimately, $90 million was spent on the contest, with $53 million coming from outside groups and Republican-aligned groups enjoying a 2-1 advantage. Portman's campaign committee spent $26.5 million, compared with $10.5 million for Strickland, in winning 84 of the state's 88 counties. Portman scored a 58%-37% win, as Trump took the state by 51%-43% over Clinton. Like Clinton, Strickland captured the counties in which Columbus, Cleveland and Toledo -- three of the state's four largest cities -- are located. But in several other counties won by Clinton, Portman's attention to independents and ticket-splitters paid off. In Summit County, where Akron, the fifth largest city is located, Portman won by 50%-45% -- running 7 points ahead of Trump, who lost to Clinton, 52%-43%. The ticket-splitting was particularly notable in Portman's home base: Hamilton County, which contains Cincinnati, the state's third largest city. It went to Portman by 54%-42%, almost the mirror image of Clinton's 53%-42% win -- a 12-percent advantage for Portman over his party's presidential nominee.

FIRST DISTRICT

Steve Chabot (R)

Elected 1994, 11th term; b. Jan 22, 1953, Cincinnati; College of William and Mary (VA), B.A.; Northern Kentucky University Salmon P. Chase College of Law (KY), J.D.; Roman Catholic; Married (Donna Chabot); 2 children; 1 grandchild.

Elected Office: Cincinnati City Council, 1985-1990; Hamilton County Commission, 1990-1994; U.S. House, 1995-2009.

Professional Career: Teacher, St. Joseph School, 1975-1976; Practicing attorney, 1978-1994.

DC Office: 2371 RHOB 20515, 202-225-2216, Fax: 202-225-3012, chabot.house.gov.

State Offices: Cincinnati, 513-684-2723; Lebanon, 513-421-8704.

Committees: *Foreign Affairs*: Asia & the Pacific, Middle East & North Africa. *Judiciary*: Courts, Intellectual Property & Internet, Crime, Terrorism, Homeland Security & Investigations. *Small Business (Chmn)*.

Group Ratings

	ADA	ACLU	AFL-CIO	LCV	ITI	COC	HAFA	ACU	CFG	FRC
2016	-	11%	-	0%	100%	100%	78%	92%	88%	100%
2015	0%	C	4%	0%	C	75%	C	96%	84%	100%

Almanac Ratings 2015

	Economy	Social	Foreign	Composite
Liberal	3%	0%	0%	1%
Conservative	97%	100%	100%	99%

Key Votes of the 114th Congress

1. Keystone Pipeline	Y	5. Puerto Rico Debt	Y	9. Offenses by Aliens	Y
2. Trade Deals	Y	6. Medical Marijuana	N	10. Troops in Iraq	N
3. Export-Import Bank	N	7. Sanctuary Cities	Y	11. Homeland Security $$	N
4. Debt Ceiling Increase	N	8. Armor-piercing Bullets	Y	12. Trade Adjustment aid	N

Election Results

Election	Name (Party)	Vote (%)	Cand. Spent	Ind. Exp. Support	Ind. Exp. Oppose
2016 General	Steve Chabot (R)	210,014 (59%)	$671,326	$122	
	Michele Young (D)	144,644 (41%)	$216,871		
2016 Primary	Steve Chabot (R)	(100%)			

Prior winning percentages: 2014 (63%), 2012 (58%), 2010 (52%), 2006 (52%), 2004 (60%), 2002 (65%), 2000 (53%), 1998 (53%), 1996 (54%), 1994 (56%)

Republican Steve Chabot first came to the House in the historic GOP Class of 1994. After losing reelection in 2008, he returned two years later as the most senior member of another huge freshman class. He reclaimed his status as one of the chamber's most conservative members. As Small Business Committee chairman, he has claimed credit for removing obstacles to American entrepreneurism. With the resignation in 2015 of Speaker John Boehner in the adjacent 8th District, he had less need to worry about the dictates of party leaders.

Chabot grew up in the Cincinnati area and graduated from La Salle High School. He earned a degree in history and physical education from the College of William & Mary. He took night classes at Northern Kentucky University to get his law degree while teaching at an elementary school during the day. Chabot won a seat on the Cincinnati City Council, where he served for four years. He followed that with a four-year stint on the Hamilton County Commission. During that time, Chabot tried to find innovative ways to reduce the cost of government, such as using jail inmates for some public services.

In 1994, Chabot was among the successful conservative Republicans who ended 40 years of Democratic control of the House. For 14 years, he sometimes took politically risky stands opposing federal spending on projects in his district and was a leader on social issues, particularly opposition to abortion rights. In 2003, he helped enact a ban on "partial-birth" abortions, and he pushed a bill to prevent minors from crossing state lines to get abortions. Chabot was a House manager during the 1998 impeachment of President Bill Clinton.

Chabot lost his seat in 2008 when Democrat Steve Driehaus defeated him by five percentage points. Spoiling for a rematch, Chabot in 2010 criticized the incumbent for voting with the Democratic majority on the Affordable Care Act and the $787 billion economic-stimulus package. Driehaus defended the actions of the Democrats, including the health care overhaul, which he called "the right thing" to do. On the stump, he asked voters to give Obama and the Democrats more time to implement change. Driehaus had trouble generating voter excitement. In October the Democratic Congressional Campaign Committee pulled the plug on further spending for television ads on his behalf. Each candidate raised about $2 million. Chabot won, 52%-46%.

When he returned to the House, Chabot used his seniority to claim the chairmanship of the Foreign Affairs Subcommittee on the Middle East and South Asia. He criticized the Obama administration's policies in the region and called its explanation of events before and after the deadly 2012 attack at the U.S. consulate in Benghazi, Libya, "ham-handed at best and a cover-up at worst." During the next two years, he chaired the Asia and the Pacific Subcommittee. With Democratic Rep. Joe Crowley of New York, he filed the Burma Human Rights and Democracy Act, which restricted military aid to that country and signaled the Obama administration to move more cautiously to normalize relations. In 2015, he enacted bills to assist in the recovery of works of art taken in violation of international law, and to assist programs overseas that seek to prevent discrimination against young women.

On domestic issues, he filed a bill to revamp the Section 8 housing initiative for low-income residents, calling it "a broken program that rewards dependency on government with our tax dollars." He crusaded against federal funding of Cincinnati's streetcar project on economic grounds. In 2014, Chabot enacted a bipartisan bill to strengthen the law school clinic certification program of the Patent and Trademark Office, which he said would encourage entrepreneurial innovation. In 2015, his *Almanac* voting record was nearly perfect conservative.

With an opening for Small Business chairman after 2014, Chabot played up his conservative bona fides to take over the gavel. "If there's one thing government can do for small business, it's to get the heck off their backs," Chabot told the Associated Press. In addition to scrutinizing the Internal Revenue Service and Environmental Protection Agency, he took steps to streamline the Small Business Administration's lending process. "It's cumbersome, it takes too long, there's far too much paperwork. It just intimidates a lot of people," he said. For 2015, he helped to enact several bills, including: a waiver of the upfront fees for Small Business Administration express loans for veterans and their spouses; assistance for the victims of natural disasters; and provisions in the annual defense spending bill to help small firms compete for Pentagon contracts.

After redistricting made the 1st District substantially more Republican by adding solidly GOP Warren County, Chabot has won reelection easily. "Unless Steve Chabot commits a felony, he will be there for as long as he wants to be," Hamilton County Democratic Party Chairman Tim Burke lamented to *The Cincinnati Enquirer*. During and after the 2016 presidential campaign, Chabot sent "open letters" to Donald Trump that, among other things, advised him to "stop saying thuggish things" and "show some class" at his campaign rallies, and stop referring to the news media as "the enemy."

Western/Northern Cincinnati Metro

Population		**Race and Ethnicity**		**Income**	
Total	727,194	White	70.1%	Median Income	$52,272 (219 out of 435)
Land area	687	Black	21.7%		
Pop/ sq mi	1058.6	Latino	2.8%		
Born in state	72.4%	Asian	2.9%	Under $50,000	48.1%
		Two races	2.1%	$50,000-$99,999	28.7%
Age Groups		Other	0.3%	$100,000-$199,999	18.2%
Under 18	24.6%			$200,000 or more	5.2%
18-34	23.2%	**Education**		Poverty Rate	16.9%
35-64	39.2%	H.S grad or less	39.8%		
Over 64	13.0%	Some college	27.8%	**Health Insurance**	
		College Degree, 4 yr	20.3%	With health insurance coverage	90.9%
Work		Post grad	12.1%		
White Collar	39.2%				
Sales and Service	42.7%	**Military**		**Public Assistance**	
Blue Collar	18.1%	Veteran	8.1%	Cash public assistance income	3.5%
Government	4.7%	Active Duty	0.0%		
				Food stamp/SNAP benefits	14.9%

Voter Turnout			
2015 Total Citizens 18+	529,004	2016 House Turnout as % CVAP	67%
2016 House turnout	354,788	2014 House Turnout as % CVAP	38%

2012 Presidential Vote		
Mitt Romney	190,501	(52%)
Barack Obama	168,195	(46%)

2016 Presidential Vote		
Donald Trump	185,025	(51%)
Hillary Clinton	160,988	(44%)
Gary Johnson	11,250	(3%)

Cook Partisan Voting Index: R+5

Cincinnati, with its long-settled good looks, was Ohio's first major metropolis, a heavily German beehive of riverboats and sausage factories, nicknamed in the 1850s "Porkopolis." In the 19th century, it was the nation's fourth-largest city, and at the outbreak of the Civil War, it was a chief destination for slaves on the Underground Railroad. The National Underground Railroad Freedom Center is now located downtown. In the middle of the city is Mill Creek, lined with factories named by the advocacy group American Rivers the most endangered urban river in North America in 1997. Two decades later, the executive director of Groundwork Cincinnati reported that fish and wildlife had returned to the Mill Creek, with a reduction of sewage, the clean-up of nearby contaminated sites, and improved local planning. On the hills to the west, above the restored Union Terminal housing several museums, are the modest streetcar suburbs of the 19th century.

The Cincinnati area was the site of great innovations: the first municipal fire department; the first professional baseball team, the Red Stockings, who began playing in 1869; and the nation's first concrete skyscraper, the 15-story Ingalls building built in 1902. Not all of the innovations have been salutary; the first train robbery in America occurred in North Bend, just to the west. Cincinnati spawned not flashy but solid industries, including America's biggest concentration of machine tool makers, an industry that's now a fraction of its once-robust size, and the Procter & Gamble soap business, with its twin-towered headquarters at the edge of downtown. In November 2016, General Electric opened downtown its new Global Operations Center with more than 1,000 employees. In suburban Evendale, the company maintains a huge jet-engine manufacturing facility. With more than 15,000 employees statewide, GE is the largest manufacturer in Ohio.

Today, downtown Cincinnati's spruced-up Fountain Square shows off well-maintained skyscrapers plus a revival of museums, arts institutions and retail shops. Old ethnic neighborhoods on the west side, crowded with brick row houses on steep hills, maintain their thick local accents and special foods, from German sauerbraten to Cincinnati chili. (Go for the 5-way at Skyline!) With fewer recent immigrants than comparable northern cities, Cincinnati's population declined in every decade since the 1940s. From

2010 until 2015, there was an increase of 1,600 residents. In the metro area, the 6 percent growth during that period was the best in the state.

The 1st Congressional District of Ohio includes almost all of Cincinnati, except for parts of its affluent eastern side. It contains most of Cincinnati's distinctive neighborhoods, like Over-the-Rhine, named for its heavily German-American early population, where the annual Bockfest (named for the malty bock beer) has attracted 25,000. This was a premier entertainment district until the late 1910s, when Prohibition shut down the breweries, With increased African-American population, it was the epicenter of race riots in 2001, though it has been gentrifying since then. The district takes in Avondale, once the center of Cincinnati's Jewish population, but now more than 90 percent African American; Hebrew Union College, the oldest extant Jewish seminary in the Americas, is just to the west of the neighborhood. Hillary Clinton won Hamilton County, 53%-43%, one of only eight counties that she won statewide. The district takes in overwhelmingly Republican Warren County, suburban territory that is prospering and had the second-highest median household income in the state. P&G planned to complete in late 2017 its new Beauty Innovation Center, a $300 million expansion of its campus in Mason.

Historically, Cincinnati was a pro-Union island of Republicanism in a sea of Democratic sentiment. Today, the reverse is true. It has an overwhelmingly Democratic urban core, but beyond that, the rest of the district is mostly Republican. The 1st includes most of the heavily Republican middle-class suburbs and exurbs to the west of the city and some Democratic-leaning inner suburbs to the north. City-dwellers now comprise about one-third of the district, Warren County is a bit less than one-third and the Hamilton suburbs are the remainder. This is a lean-Republican district. Donald Trump got 51 percent of the vote in 2016, while Mitt Romney got 52 percent in 2012. This was one of only two Republican-held districts in Ohio where the GOP presidential vote declined.

SECOND DISTRICT

Brad Wenstrup (R)

Elected 2012, 3rd term; b. Jun 17, 1958, Cincinnati; University of Cincinnati, B.A.; Rosalind Franklin University (IL), B.S.; William M. Scholl College of Podiatric Medicine, Rosalind Franklin University (IL); Roman Catholic; Married (Monica Klein); 1 child.

Military Career: U.S Army Reserves, 1998-2011 (Iraq).

Professional Career: Physician, Wellington Orthopaedic & Sports Medicine, 1999-2013; Private practice, 1986-1999.

DC Office: 2419 RHOB 20515, 202-225-3164, Fax: 202-225-1992, wenstrup.house.gov.

State Offices: Cincinnati, 513-474-7777; Peebles, 513-605-1380.

Committees: *Armed Services*: Emerging Threats & Capabilities, Military Personnel. *Permanent Select on Intelligence*. *Veterans' Affairs*: Economic Opportunity, Health (Chmn).

Group Ratings

	ADA	ACLU	AFL-CIO	LCV	ITI	COC	HAFA	ACU	CFG	FRC
2016	-	5%	-	0%	100%	100%	82%	92%	83%	100%
2015	0%	C	0%	0%	C	70%	C	88%	85%	100%

Almanac Ratings 2015

	Economy	Social	Foreign	Composite
Liberal	11%	4%	0%	5%
Conservative	89%	96%	100%	95%

Key Votes of the 114th Congress

1. Keystone Pipeline	Y	5. Puerto Rico Debt	Y	9. Offenses by Aliens	Y
2. Trade Deals	Y	6. Medical Marijuana	N	10. Troops in Iraq	N
3. Export-Import Bank	N	7. Sanctuary Cities	Y	11. Homeland Security $$	N
4. Debt Ceiling Increase	N	8. Armor-piercing Bullets	Y	12. Trade Adjustment aid	N

Election Results

Election	Name (Party)	Vote (%)		Cand. Spent	Ind. Exp. Support	Ind. Exp. Oppose
2016 General	Brad Wenstrup (R)	221,193	(65%)	$781,122		
	William R. Smith (D)	111,694	(33%)			
2016 Primary	Brad Wenstrup (R)	99,833	(85%)			
	Jim Lewis (R)	17,666	(15%)			

Prior winning percentages: 2014 (66%), 2012 (59%)

Republican Brad Wenstrup, elected in 2012 when he defeated the Republican incumbent in the primary, is a foot surgeon and Iraq War veteran. He has used those experiences to become an influential player on national security issues.

Wenstrup was born and raised in Cincinnati. His father was an optician, and his mother worked at a Stein Mart department store. As a kid, Wenstrup thought about a career in medicine as well as serving in the military. He got his bachelor's degree from the University of Cincinnati and a medical degree from the Scholl College of Podiatric Medicine in Chicago. His medical practice was incorporated into Wellington Orthopaedic & Sports Medicine. He joined the Army Reserve in 1998 and served as a combat surgeon in Iraq in 2005 and 2006. "I tell people, it's the worst thing I ever had to do, but the best thing I ever got to do," he said. Not long after the prisoner-abuse scandal at the Abu Ghraib prison erupted, he was stationed at a combat support hospital within the prison walls. He treated U.S. troops, civilians and some enemy combatants.

Politics grew more intriguing to Wenstrup when he returned from Iraq. "I started to see people in Washington making military decisions that have never served, making health care plans that have never seen a patient or dealt with insurance companies or Medicaid and Medicare," he said. Running for mayor of Cincinnati in 2009 against incumbent Democrat Mark Mallory, Wenstrup lost but took a respectable 46 percent of the vote in the Democratic-leaning city. The strong showing raised his profile and opportunities.

In 2011, he launched a primary challenge to Rep. Jean Schmidt, who had experienced electoral troubles. She had sometimes offended colleagues in Washington and Ohio and was dubbed "Mean Jean" in the blogosphere. Wenstrup was endorsed by the Ohio Liberty Council, a coalition of tea party groups. The anti-incumbent super PAC, Campaign for Primary Accountability, spent money against Schmidt. Wenstrup criticized her for owing money to lawyers at the Turkish Coalition of America while she sat on the House Foreign Affairs Committee. Her campaign said the money was donated before she served on the committee and that she had reimbursed some of the attorneys' fees. Wenstrup ran an ad attacking Schmidt's votes to raise the debt limit and to support the Wall Street bailout, while mentioning that she planted a kiss on President Barack Obama at the State of the Union address. He won the nomination, 49%-43%. He has not faced a serious primary or general-election challenge since then.

In the House, Wenstrup got seats on the Armed Services, Intelligence and Veterans' Affairs committees. When Congress completed action on the defense spending bill in 2014, he cited his work on additional funding for Reserve and National Guard equipment, new funds to combat suicide within the ranks, and the continued prohibition on transfer of any detainees from the Guantanamo prison facility to the United States. In 2016, he represented the Armed Services Committee on a House task force that investigated accusations from intelligence analysts that senior Obama administration officials responsible for operations in the Middle East had watered down their assessments. The report concluded that the military had taken a rosy view. "We still do not fully understand the reasons and motivations behind this practice, and how often the excluded analyses were proven ultimately to be correct," Wenstrup said.

Veterans issues have drawn Wenstrup's attention. In 2015, he praised the Veterans Affairs Department for integrating its record-keeping with Ohio's automatic prescription reporting system and he highlighted his earlier discussions of the problem with VA officials. He passed bills in the House that improved the electronic processing by the Veterans Benefits Administration of claims for educational assistance, and established the Veterans Economic Opportunity and Transition Administration to assist veterans with health, education assistance and vocational rehabilitation. Those measures became part of a broader veterans bill that was enacted in December 2016. In January 2017, Wenstrup became chairman of the Health Subcommittee at Veterans Affairs and said that he would address "an array of medical challenges further complicated by bureaucracy, delays and significant variance in quality of care depending on where former troops seek treatment."

On other issues, Wenstrup advocated replacing the 2010 health care law with market-based solutions that protect the doctor-patient relationship. He took the lead in seeking to have Congress overturn a District of Columbia law that would permit doctors to prescribe life-ending drugs to terminally ill patients who request them. He has filed a bill - unlikely to win approval - that would withhold pay from members of Congress if they failed to vote on the 12 annual spending bills before the Oct. 1 deadline.

Eastern Cincinnati Metro, Southern Ohio

Population		**Race and Ethnicity**		**Income**	
Total	724,744	White	86.2%	Median Income	$51,468 (232 out of 435)
Land area	3,222	Black	8.5%	Under $50,000	48.6%
Pop/ sq mi	225.0	Latino	1.8%	$50,000-$99,999	30.0%
Born in state	74.6%	Asian	1.3%	$100,000-$199,999	16.7%
		Two races	1.9%	$200,000 or more	4.7%
		Other	0.3%	Poverty Rate	15.0%
Age Groups		**Education**		**Health Insurance**	
Under 18	23.4%	H.S grad or less	43.5%	With health insurance coverage	90.2%
18-34	21.2%	Some college	26.7%		
35-64	40.6%	College Degree, 4 yr	18.6%		
Over 64	14.9%	Post grad	11.2%		
Work		**Military**		**Public Assistance**	
White Collar	38.5%	Veteran	8.7%	Cash public assistance income	2.8%
Sales and Service	40.3%	Active Duty	0.0%	Food stamp/SNAP benefits	14.0%
Blue Collar	21.2%				
Government	5.4%				

Voter Turnout			
2015 Total Citizens 18+	546,920	2016 House Turnout as % CVAP	62%
2016 House turnout	340,279	2014 House Turnout as % CVAP	37%

2012 Presidential Vote		
Mitt Romney	194,385	(55%)
Barack Obama	155,036	(44%)

2016 Presidential Vote		
Donald Trump	197,856	(55%)
Hillary Clinton	140,786	(39%)
Gary Johnson	12,111	(3%)

Cook Partisan Voting Index: R+9

Back in the 1850s, Cincinnati, with its large German population, was heavily Republican and anti-slavery. The city's ethnic character and political preference, like its physical appearance, remained pretty well fixed for a long time. Cincinnati attracted fewer southern and eastern European immigrants than did Great Lakes industrial cities like Cleveland, Detroit and Chicago, so the New Deal had less impact on the local political dynamic. The Appalachians who settled here in the 1940s to work in the factories were typically Republicans. Economically, it was never a strong union town, and culturally it is conservative.

The area to the east on the Ohio River includes distinctly different places - "the richest to the poorest, and everything in between," as one area mayor put it. Chillicothe, on the Scioto River, was the first capital of Ohio.

The city of Ripley was a hub for the Underground Railroad, a natural point of egress from the South because the Ohio River narrows near the city. In 1838, escaped slave Eliza Harris leapt from one ice floe to the next, while carrying her 2-year-old son, to cross the river and make it to the city; a young abolitionist and Underground Railroad participant named Harriet Beecher Stowe lived in Cincinnati at the time and likely borrowed from Harris' experiences to create one of the most riveting scenes in *Uncle Tom's Cabin*. Hillsboro briefly made headlines in 1954 when Philip Partridge, a white city engineer, decided that desegregation in the wake of the recent *Brown v. Board of Education* decision by the Supreme Court was not proceeding quickly enough, and forced the city's hand by burning down the school for African-American children. Partridge went to prison for arson, but the schools were integrated two years later.

Chillicothe was profiled by *The Washington Post* in December 2016 as an example of a small city suffering from the opioid epidemic, with a rising death rate, especially among middle-age women. Work on the Energy Department's uranium clean-up project to decontaminate and decommission the Portsmouth Gaseous Diffusion Plant, which has employed about 2,000 workers, has been extended to 2018.

Ohio's 2nd Congressional District includes the eastern edge of Cincinnati, taking in Hyde Park Square, with its farmer's market and many shops and boutiques; most of the largely affluent suburbs of eastern Hamilton County; and the fast-growing suburbs of Clermont County. In once-rural Clermont, Miami Township has become a bedroom community and a center of commercial development along the Interstate 275 loop. The metropolitan parts of the district, with more than 70 percent of the people, are mostly affluent and Republican. The counties farther east are less well off, with most of the old factories gone and with pockets of high unemployment and poverty. The district still leans substantially Republican, and Democrats have rarely competed here. In 2016, Donald Trump took the district, 55%-39%, compared with Mitt Romney's 55%-44% lead in 2012. In rural Pike County, which has a lengthy Democratic tradition, Trump got 67 percent of the vote.

THIRD DISTRICT

Joyce Beatty (D)

Elected 2012, 3rd term; b. Mar 12, 1950, Dayton; Central State University (OH), B.A.; Wright State University (OH), M.S.; University of Cincinnati, Att.; Baptist; Married (Justice Otto Beatty Jr.); 2 stepchildren.

Elected Office: OH House, 1999-2008.

Professional Career: Sr.Vice President., OH St. University, 2008-2013; President, Joyce Beatty & Associates, 1992-2013; Director, Montgomery County Department of Comm. Human Services, 1983-1992; Director, Adult & Elderly services, Montgomery County Mental Health Board, 1983; Professor, Capital University, 1979-1992; Professor, Sinclair Community College, 1975-1983; Caseworker, City of Dayton, 1971-1975.

DC Office: 133 CHOB 20515, 202-225-4324, Fax: 202-225-1984, beatty.house.gov.
State Offices: Columbus, 614-220-0003.

Committees: *Financial Services*: Housing & Insurance, Oversight & Investigations.

Group Ratings

	ADA	ACLU	AFL-CIO	LCV	ITI	COC	HAFA	ACU	CFG	FRC
2016	-	94%	-	100%	67%	71%	12%	0%	0%	0%
2015	90%	C	100%	97%	C	50%	C	0%	0%	0%

Almanac Ratings 2015

	Economy	Social	Foreign	Composite
Liberal	95%	95%	93%	94%
Conservative	5%	5%	7%	6%

Key Votes of the 114th Congress

1. Keystone Pipeline	N	5. Puerto Rico Debt	Y	9. Offenses by Aliens	N
2. Trade Deals	N	6. Medical Marijuana	Y	10. Troops in Iraq	N
3. Export-Import Bank	Y	7. Sanctuary Cities	N	11. Homeland Security $$	Y
4. Debt Ceiling Increase	Y	8. Armor-piercing Bullets	N	12. Trade Adjustment aid	Y

Election Results

Election	Name (Party)	Vote (%)	Cand. Spent	Ind. Exp. Support	Ind. Exp. Oppose
2016 General	Joyce Beatty (D)	199,791 (69%)	$663,527		
	John Adams (R)	90,319 (31%)			
2016 Primary	Joyce Beatty (D)	(100%)			

Prior winning percentages: 2014 (64%), 2012 (68%)

Democrat Joyce Beatty's election to the House in 2012 gave Ohio its first African-American member outside of Cleveland. Consistent with the spirit of Columbus, Beatty often takes a consensus-building approach. She looks after the large academic and financial interests of her constituents

Beatty is the daughter of a brick mason and stay-at-home mom. Her parents moved from the inner city to a predominantly white neighborhood in Dayton with better schools when Beatty was young. She did her undergraduate work in speech and psychology at Central State University and later earned a master's degree in counseling from Wright State University, both in Ohio. Beatty's interest in politics was fueled by hearing Jesse Jackson speak at the 1984 Democratic National Convention. She had several jobs in local government and academia, eventually becoming senior vice president for engagement and outreach at Ohio State University. She owned a management consulting business and a clothing store in downtown Dayton. Beatty served in the Ohio House for nearly a decade, including a stint as minority leader. She was instrumental in passing measures that helped women without health insurance get cancer screenings, reined in home foreclosures and encouraged financial literacy education. Her husband, Otto Beatty Jr., is an attorney and was a member of the state House for nearly two decades until he resigned and was succeeded by his wife.

When she entered the race in the new Columbus-based district, Beatty cited her knowledge of how to "make a payroll" and her ability to work with businesses and labor unions to bring jobs to central Ohio. She drew on her background to make education a central focus of her campaign, calling for making college more affordable and encouraging public-private partnerships to work on job-training initiatives with community colleges and training centers. With the endorsement of Columbus Mayor Michael Coleman and strong financial support from labor unions, Beatty defeated three other candidates in the Democratic primary. Her toughest opponent was former Rep. Mary Jo Kilroy, who had served one term in the 15th District and was defeated in 2010. Beatty won the primary 38%-35%. She easily won in November. During the campaign, Beatty drew the attention of national Democrats. House Minority Leader Nancy Pelosi traveled to her district to join her at a forum on health care policy, and Beatty spoke at the Democratic convention in Charlotte on the role of women in the economy.

On the Financial Services Committee, Beatty has a useful platform for the robust financial sector in Columbus. She has focused on financial oversight, affordable housing and consumer access to credit. In 2015, she filed the Housing Financial Literacy Act to improve first-time homebuyers' financial knowledge. She has been a leading advocate for placing a woman on the $20 bill, and praised Treasury Secretary Jacob Lew when he announced in 2016 that Civil War-era abolitionist Harriett Tubman would replace President Andrew Jackson on the currency. She urged that the Treasury Department act more speedily than its original timetable, which could extend until 2030.

With Republican Rep. Charlie Dent of Pennsylvania, she has filed legislation to create a presidential commission or intercollegiate athletics, and to secure protections for college athletes, including scholarships, health care and procedural rights. She called for more research on neurological disorders and brain injuries. "Talk is not enough," she said, referring to the actions of the NCAA governing of athletics. During her first term, Beatty praised the Big Ten universities when they adopted a plan similar to what she had advocated to guarantee that students who receive athletic scholarships may keep the award until they graduate.

With Republican Rep. Ann Wagner of Missouri, Beatty won House passage of legislation to combat sex trafficking in the United States by making it easier for people to report incidents. The bill was enacted in June 2015 as part of broader legislation on the issue. *The Washington Post*, in a May 2015 fact-check, found that their claim of 300,000 children at risk was "a figure that is so out of date and discredited [that] they do a disservice to a serious issue." Subsequently, Beatty joined other lawmakers in criticizing the Justice Department for slow implementation of the law.

Beatty has been reelected with no primary opposition and nominal Republican challengers in her safe district.

Columbus Metro

Population		**Race and Ethnicity**		**Income**	
Total	745,041	White	53.7%	Median Income	$41,628 (378 out of 435)
Land area	228	Black	32.3%	Under $50,000	57.7%
Pop/ sq mi	3267.7	Latino	6.3%	$50,000-$99,999	28.9%
Born in state	66.4%	Asian	3.3%	$100,000-$199,999	11.3%
Age Groups		Two races	3.9%	$200,000 or more	2.1%
Under 18	24.6%	Other	0.5%	Poverty Rate	23.6%
18-34	29.7%	**Education**		**Health Insurance**	
35-64	36.2%	H.S grad or less	43.8%	With health insurance coverage	85.5%
Over 64	9.5%	Some college	29.4%	**Public Assistance**	
Work		College Degree, 4 yr	17.8%	Cash public assistance income	4.2%
White Collar	33.5%	Post grad	9.0%	Food stamp/SNAP benefits	21.1%
Sales and Service	46.7%	**Military**			
Blue Collar	19.8%	Veteran	7.4%		
Government	3.7%	Active Duty	0.1%		

Voter Turnout			
2015 Total Citizens 18+	518,931	2016 House Turnout as % CVAP	56%
2016 House turnout	291,351	2014 House Turnout as % CVAP	28%

2012 Presidential Vote		
Barack Obama	217,969	(70%)
Mitt Romney	90,434	(29%)

2016 Presidential Vote		
Hillary Clinton	210,489	(66%)
Donald Trump	89,634	(28%)
Gary Johnson	9,210	(3%)

Cook Partisan Voting Index: D+19

In 1972, the first *Almanac of American Politics* noted that Columbus had just surpassed Cincinnati to become Ohio's second-largest city. Today, Columbus is by far the largest city in the state. Franklin County grew by 9 percent during the 2000s and another brisk 9 percent in the five subsequent years, while four of the seven counties abutting it have enjoyed double-digit growth rates. In 2015, the population of the metro area exceeded 2 million, narrowly trailing the two long-dominant metro areas in Ohio, and it is booming while much of the state has stagnated or declined. The reasons are simple: location, location, location ... and government. Not only the geographical center of Ohio, the city lies just a one-day truck drive from more than half of the nation's population, making it the perfect location for a Midwestern hub. It is also the capital of the nation's seventh-most-populous state and home to Ohio State University system's flagship campus.

In a region known for its blue-collar accents, Columbus has retained a distinctly white-collar flavor and attracted the type of upscale, enterprising people who have produced much of America's growth in recent years. It is home to four *Fortune* 500 companies: Nationwide Insurance, American Electric Power, Limited Brands (parent company to Victoria's Secret and Bath & Body Works) and the big-box chain Big Lots. The area is the home of the Battelle Memorial Institute, the think tank that helped invent photocopying, compact discs and the Universal Product Code. Columbus has been rated as one of the best cities for a start-up business. Its leaders point to an inviting civic culture.

The city's rapidly growing foreign-born population - Latinos, Koreans, Ethiopians, Chinese, Russian Jews and Somalis - exceeds 11 percent. In January 2017, Mayor Andrew Ginther signed an executive order supporting the settlement of refugees in Columbus. It isn't only ethnic diversity: Columbus sits just 90 miles north of the Mason-Dixon Line, and one is as likely to hear an Appalachian twang as a Great Lakes accent. This population growth brought political change. Columbus had been Democratic during the Civil War years but became reliably Republican in the late 1800s. As the metropolitan area grew, more people headed for the suburbs and one of the largest Republican cities in the country slowly became Democratic again.

The 3rd Congressional District represents a bow by Republicans to political and demographic realities. Columbus had traditionally been split between the 12th and 15th districts, enabling suburban areas to trump Democratic-leaning portions of the city even in landslide Democratic years. Republicans chose to protect the 12th and 15th, and create a Democratic "vote sink" in Franklin County, the only district in the state entirely contained in a single county. The 3rd takes in the skyscrapers of downtown Columbus; heavily Jewish Bexley, the site of the governor's mansion; the capitol, with the statue of President William McKinley out front; the university neighborhoods; city slums; and the Democratic portions of upscale New Albany and Westerville. The district includes working-class, mixed-race communities west of the city, like Greater Hilltop and Franklinton. These sometimes disparate areas have Democratic voting patterns in common. The 3rd is the second-most Democratic district in Ohio. Hillary Clinton won here, 66%-28%, a bit smaller than Barack Obama's 70%-29% win in 2012.

FOURTH DISTRICT

Jim Jordan (R)

Elected 2006, 6th term; b. Feb 17, 1964, Urbana; Capital University (OH), J.D.; Ohio State University, M.A.; University of Wisconsin, B.S.; Evangelical; Married (Polly Jordan); 4 children; 2 grandchildren.

Elected Office: OH House, 1994-2000; OH Senate, 2000-2006.

Professional Career: Assistant wrestling coach, OH St. University, 1987-1995; Wrestling camp coach, clinician, 1987-2006.

DC Office: 2056 RHOB 20515, 202-225-2676, Fax: 202-226-0577, jordan.house.gov.

State Offices: Bucyrus, 419-663-1426; Lima, 419-999-6455; Norwalk, 419-663-1426.

Committees: *Judiciary*: Courts, Intellectual Property & Internet, Immigration & Border Security. *Oversight & Government Reform*: Government Operations, Health Care, Benefits & Administrative Rules (Chmn).

Group Ratings

	ADA	ACLU	AFL-CIO	LCV	ITI	COC	HAFA	ACU	CFG	FRC
2016	-	17%	-	0%	50%	93%	95%	100%	99%	100%
2015	10%	C	4%	3%	C	53%	C	100%	97%	100%

Almanac Ratings 2015

	Economy	Social	Foreign	Composite
Liberal	12%	0%	8%	7%
Conservative	88%	100%	92%	93%

Key Votes of the 114th Congress

1. Keystone Pipeline	Y	5. Puerto Rico Debt	N	9. Offenses by Aliens	Y
2. Trade Deals	N	6. Medical Marijuana	N	10. Troops in Iraq	N
3. Export-Import Bank	N	7. Sanctuary Cities	Y	11. Homeland Security $$	N
4. Debt Ceiling Increase	N	8. Armor-piercing Bullets	Y	12. Trade Adjustment aid	N

Election Results

Election	Name (Party)	Vote (%)	Cand. Spent	Ind. Exp. Support	Ind. Exp. Oppose
2016 General	Jim Jordan (R)	210,227 (68%)	$351,094	$2,000	
	Janet Garrett (D)	98,981 (32%)	$77,026		
2016 Primary	Jim Jordan (R)	(100%)			

Prior winning percentages: 2014 (68%), 2012 (58%), 2010 (72%), 2008 (65%), 2006 (60%)

Republican Jim Jordan, elected in 2006, has endeared himself to conservatives while annoying his party's leaders with his confrontational approach. His first platform was as chairman of the Republican

Study Committee. Later, he was a founder and the first chairman of the House Freedom Caucus, which conservative members on economic and social policy organized as a forum for their hostility to President Barack Obama's agenda - and often to conciliators in their own party. Jordan has great influence among House Republicans, which he has used chiefly to stifle the plans of others rather than to press his own legislation or other interests.

Jordan grew up in Champaign County and graduated from Graham High School, where he was a champion wrestler. At the University of Wisconsin, he won two NCAA wrestling championships in the 134-pound weight class and was inducted into the Badger Hall of Fame. With his bachelor's in economics, Jordan worked as an assistant wrestling coach at Ohio State University, where he earned a master's degree in education before getting a law degree at Capital University. Soon, he began thinking about elected office. "You get married and have kids, and you get sick of having the government take your money and tell you what to do," he told columnist George Will in 2011. He won a state House seat in 1994, and served six years before he won a tough primary for the state Senate. His solidly conservative record included legislation creating Ohio's "Choose Life" license plates, a ban on same-sex marriage, and government vouchers for private-school tuition.

Jordan ran for the House when Republican Rep. Michael Oxley retired as chairman of the Financial Services Committee. In the six-way Republican primary, he had the most name recognition plus support from Ohio Right to Life, the National Rifle Association, and the national anti-tax group Club for Growth. Findlay real estate developer Frank Guglielmi self-financed $1.6 million and purchased far more ads than the rest of the field. With the benefits of geography and connections, Jordan won 51 percent, carrying eight of 11 counties. Guglielmi carried his home county and one other to get 30 percent. Despite the tough political environment for Republicans in 2006, Democrats barely mounted a competitive campaign.

In the House, Jordan established an unfailingly conservative voting record, with nine perfect scores and a 100 percent lifetime rating from the American Conservative Union through 2015. "With the exception of the military, the federal government doesn't do anything very well," he told the *Mansfield News Journal.* He said he weighs all issues based on whether they benefit families. He is a father of four whose desk calendar is crowded with his children's athletic schedules.

With his right-wing bona fides well established, Jordan succeeded Tom Price of Georgia as head of the 170-member Republican Study Committee in 2011, when the GOP reclaimed control of the House. "He approaches the world of politics like a wrestling match, with the same kind of intensity, preparation, training and focus," Price told *The Plain Dealer* of Cleveland. He beat back a challenge from Louie Gohmert of Texas, who accused him of being a "wing man" for John Boehner, the GOP leader from a neighboring Ohio district. Jordan vowed to be independent of the leadership, saying his group would lobby lawmakers just as vigorously as did the Republicans' formal whip team.

Under Jordan's guidance, the RSC unveiled a congressional budget plan that called for cuts of $2.5 trillion in planned spending over 10 years. When the House approved a measure in March to keep the government running temporarily as Boehner and Obama tried to hammer out an agreement on spending cuts, Jordan was openly scornful. "We must do more than cut spending in bite-sized pieces," he said. That summer. Jordan dug in his heels during the showdown over whether to raise the federal debt limit. He apologized to Republicans at a closed-door meeting after one of his staffers sent an email to conservative groups identifying which lawmakers were undecided about voting for the increase. He denied speculation that he and allies were eager to shut down the government and said he was not out to undercut Boehner. When Republicans and Obama failed to reach a budget deal in early 2013 and triggered across-the-board spending cuts under the sequester, Jordan shrugged that it "won't be the end of the world" and marked an important step toward savings.

As the founding chairman in January 2015 of the House Freedom Caucus, whose chief purpose was to move the Republican agenda to the right, he created another base for friction with Boehner. Those divisions were apparent on several issues in the next few months, notably opposition by Jordan and many in the Freedom Caucus to giving trade promotion authority to Obama, and their demand that new limits on national security data collection go even further. Unlike some of his more junior and outspoken colleagues, he was less interested in casting the conflict in personal terms. Despite his high regard among the rebels and his continued poor-mouthing of GOP leaders, Jordan pointedly was not among the conservatives who voted for alternatives when Boehner was reelected as House Speaker in 2013 and 2015. He urged Rep. Mark Meadows of North Carolina and others not to take steps that might undermine Boehner. This balancing act, *Politico* reported in September 2016, made Jordan "arguably the second-most influential Republican in the House after Speaker Paul Ryan"

With Republicans in control of the White House and Congress after the 2016 election, some Republicans speculated that Jordan would lose his leverage as President Donald Trump and Ryan took command. Jordan disagreed. "I actually think our influence is as strong as ever," he told *The New York*

Times a week after the election. Initially at least, Jordan proved to be correct. In March 2017, he and his Freedom Caucus allies stood firm against party leaders, whom they criticized for failing to keep their promise to repeal the Affordable Care Act. Singling out Jordan and two others, an unhappy Trump tweeted in response, "The Freedom Caucus will hurt the entire Republican agenda if they don't get on the team, & fast. We must fight them, & Dems, in 2018!"

Jordan has focused his own work on the Oversight and Government Reform Committee, where he has chaired the Health Care, Benefits and Administrative Rules Subcommittee. "Uncovering and investigating government abuse has been my passion in Congress," Jordan said when he took the position. In 2015, he fought unsuccessfully to shut down the Export-Import Bank.

During preparation for the 2012 redistricting in Ohio, *The Columbus Dispatch* reported that Boehner's allies were considering retaliation through a plan that would make Jordan's seat substantially more competitive. Boehner denied any such effort, and Jordan's new district became securely Republican, though it moved well beyond his thinly populated base in western Ohio. The changes have been little problem to Jordan. In 2014 and 2016, he won 68 percent of the vote against weak opposition.

Central Ohio: Lima, Sandusky

Population		**Race and Ethnicity**		**Income**	
Total	714,052	White	88.2%	Median Income	$48,397
Land area	4,665	Black	5.2%		(279 out of 435)
Pop/ sq mi	153.1	Latino	3.4%		
Born in state	82.1%	Asian	0.8%	Under $50,000	51.3%
		Two races	2.1%	$50,000-$99,999	32.9%
Age Groups		Other	0.3%	$100,000-$199,999	13.8%
Under 18	23.2%			$200,000 or more	1.9%
18-34	20.7%	**Education**		Poverty Rate	14.5%
35-64	40.5%	H.S grad or less	52.7%		
Over 64	15.5%	Some college	30.8%	**Health Insurance**	
		College Degree, 4 yr	10.4%	With health insurance coverage	91.3%
Work		Post grad	6.1%		
White Collar	28.0%				
Sales and Service	38.7%	**Military**		**Public Assistance**	
Blue Collar	33.4%	Veteran	9.8%	Cash public assistance income	2.8%
Government	5.0%	Active Duty	0.0%		
				Food stamp/SNAP benefits	14.2%

Voter Turnout			
2015 Total Citizens 18+	543,062	2016 House Turnout as % CVAP	57%
2016 House turnout	309,208	2014 House Turnout as % CVAP	34%

2012 Presidential Vote		
Mitt Romney	185,521	(56%)
Barack Obama	139,189	(42%)

2016 Presidential Vote		
Donald Trump	208,736	(64%)
Hillary Clinton	99,626	(30%)
Gary Johnson	11,741	(4%)

Cook Partisan Voting Index: R+14

Central and western Ohio look mostly like farmland to the traveler. Yet this is manufacturing country, indeed one of America's premier manufacturing areas, where the economy is based on factories in small towns and on rural highways. These places seem far from anywhere "important," yet the region has been quietly prosperous most of the years since World War II. While there have been some manufacturing job losses, most of this area emerged from the recession in better shape than other parts of the state. Each population center has its own pet industry: In Lima, the Joint Systems Manufacturing Center has been building versions of the Abrams tank for 30 years, and Ford spent $500 million to develop "EcoBoost" technology for its F-150 pick-up truck at a plant there. Dannon operates in Minster the world's largest yogurt plant, with adaptations for the transition to Greek yogurt. In Jackson Center, Airstream expanded production of its iconic trailers in 2014. Honda has invested more than $6 billion in Marysville and East Liberty since it opened its first plant in Union County, for motorcycles, in 1979. Today, it employs about 14,300 Ohioans (all but 2,000 on the manufacturing side) and is the largest automobile employer in the state. Ethanol production is a growth industry in the area, and a small but growing Hispanic population is limiting the effects of native outmigration. Still, not all is well. Monthly production of the Abrams fell from double digits to one, as of 2015, though foreign sales have increased at the unique JSMC, a government-owned and contractor-operated plant.

These small towns have historical significance. Marion was the home of President Warren G. Harding and socialist Norman Thomas; the latter, as a young boy, delivered the newspaper edited by the former. Fremont, settled by abstemious Yankees, was the home of President Rutherford B. Hayes, whose wife, Lucy, served only lemonade in the White House. Today it is home to an aromatic Heinz ketchup plant; it produces daily the equivalent of 4.1 million 14-ounce bottles, the most in the world. Tiny Milan is the birthplace of the inventor and capitalist Thomas Edison, while Tiffin still has St. Paul's United Methodist Church, the first public building in the United States to be wired for electricity. Wapakoneta, a typically Ohioan-Indian name, is the hometown of Neil Armstrong, the first man to walk on the moon, and the site of the Neil Armstrong Air and Space Museum.

This terrain in central Ohio makes up the 4th Congressional District. The district extends north and east into Seneca, Sandusky, Erie and Lorain counties, and the outer Cleveland suburbs. But it has been carefully wedged into the countryside to avoid metro areas, including Dayton and Toledo. The GOP lean of the small towns mitigates the impact of places like Oberlin College, one of the most liberal colleges in the country and the first to admit African Americans (1835) and women (1841). Donald Trump in 2016 got 64 percent of the vote, an increase from the 56 percent for Mitt Romney four years earlier.

FIFTH DISTRICT

Bob Latta (R)

Elected 2006, 6th term; b. Apr 18, 1956, Bluffton; Bowling Green State University (OH), B.A.; University of Toledo College of Law (OH), J.D.; Ohio Northern University, Att.; Roman Catholic; Married (Marcia Sloan Latta); 2 children.

Elected Office: Wood County commissioner, 1991-1996; OH Senate, 1997- 2001; OH General Assembly, 2001-2007.

Professional Career: Attorney, 1981-1991.

DC Office: 2448 RHOB 20515, 202-225-6405, Fax: 202-225-1985, latta.house.gov.

State Offices: Bowling Green, 419-354-8700; Defiance, 419-782-1996; Findlay, 419-422-7791.

Committees: *Commission Congressional Mailing Standards*. *Energy & Commerce*: Communications & Technology, Digital Commerce & Consumer Protection (Chmn), Energy.

Group Ratings

	ADA	ACLU	AFL-CIO	LCV	ITI	COC	HAFA	ACU	CFG	FRC
2016	-	11%	-	0%	100%	100%	71%	92%	75%	100%
2015	0%	C	8%	3%	C	75%	C	92%	81%	100%

Almanac Ratings 2015

	Economy	Social	Foreign	Composite
Liberal	1%	0%	0%	0%
Conservative	99%	100%	100%	100%

Key Votes of the 114th Congress

1. Keystone Pipeline	Y	5. Puerto Rico Debt	Y	9. Offenses by Aliens	Y
2. Trade Deals	Y	6. Medical Marijuana	N	10. Troops in Iraq	N
3. Export-Import Bank	N	7. Sanctuary Cities	Y	11. Homeland Security $$	N
4. Debt Ceiling Increase	N	8. Armor-piercing Bullets	Y	12. Trade Adjustment aid	N

Election Results

Election	Name (Party)	Vote (%)	Cand. Spent	Ind. Exp. Support	Ind. Exp. Oppose
2016 General	Bob Latta (R)	244,599 (71%)	$525,934	$777	
	James L. Neu Jr. (D)	100,392 (29%)			$600
2016 Primary	Bob Latta (R)	(100%)			

Prior winning percentages: 2014 (67%), 2012 (57%), 2010 (68%), 2008 (64%), 2007 special (57%)

Republican Bob Latta, who was elected in 2007 to the seat that his father Delbert Latta earlier held for 30 years, has a conservative voting record like his father. He has been a practical legislator on the Energy and Commerce Committee, where he has taken an influential assignment.

Bob Latta was born in Ohio but split his early years between his native Bluffton and Washington, D.C. Helping his father's campaigns, Latta says he learned the business of catering to constituents. Young Latta frequently interrupted his homework to answer their phone calls and remembers his father following up with federal agencies to get results from the bureaucracy. Latta spent time driving around the district with his dad, going to meetings and events. While attending Bowling Green State University, he volunteered in his father's office, where he met his wife, Marcia, who worked for his father. When he graduated from law school at the University of Toledo, his father had one bit of career advice for him: Don't get into politics.

He did his best to follow that guidance and practiced law for several years. When his father retired in 1988, the 31-year-old couldn't pass on the opportunity to follow in his footsteps. First, he had to get by Paul Gillmor, a Republican state senator who had been waiting for a congressional seat to open up during Del Latta's long tenure. In their primary contest, Bob Latta argued that, like his father, he would start out young and eventually gain enough seniority to preside over powerful committees. After a spirited race, Gillmor beat Latta by just 27 votes out of 57,361 cast. Latta retreated to local politics, on the Wood County Commission and then to the Ohio Legislature. One of his major efforts was to repeal the estate tax, which he succeeded in doing for most Ohioans. An avid hunter, Latta championed conservation issues, including longer hunting seasons and expanded wildlife reserves.

After Gillmor in September 2007 died at his Washington home, apparently from a fall down stairs, Latta ran for the open seat and had to win two hard-fought contests. His chief primary opponent was state Sen. Steve Buehrer, who was backed by the Club for Growth, which ran several ads attacking Latta as an advocate of higher taxes. Latta attacked Buehrer for accepting donations from Tom Noe, a former Ohio fundraiser for President George W. Bush and a convicted money launderer. It came to light that Latta had also taken money from Noe. Latta defeated Buehrer by 2,542 votes out of 74,191 cast. Democrat Robin Weirauch, a former public administrator who had twice run against Gillmor, had backing in the general from labor unions and the abortion-rights group EMILY's List. She attacked Latta on economic issues and his support for the Iraq war. Despite the anti-Washington sentiment that year, she fell short. Latta won 57%-43%.

Latta has been reliably conservative, often dismissing Democratic proposals as 'socialist." In 2015, his *Almanac* voting record was nearly perfect conservative. He filed bills to permanently repeal the estate tax, and to issue a Ronald Reagan commemorative coin. On the Energy and Commerce Committee, he initially made energy independence his central issue. He successfully amended a House-passed air-quality bill in 2011 to require the Environmental Protection Agency to take industry costs into account in setting standards under the Clean Air Act. The *Los Angeles Times* editorial board listed him among the "10 biggest enemies of the Earth."

Latta has taken an interest in technology. In 2010, he was the first House member to release an iPhone app. He filed in 2011 a resolution declaring that to continue aggressive growth in telecommunications and technology industries, the federal government "should get out of the way and stay out of the way." He co-chaired the Republican New Media Caucus and the Rural Broadband Caucus. In 2017, Latta became chairman of the revamped Digital Commerce and Consumer Protection Subcommittee at Energy and Commerce, whose jurisdiction included the Federal Trade Commission, manufacturing, data security and many Internet-related policies. He filed a bill to increase transparency at the Federal Communications Commission.

As vice chairman of the Congressional Sportsmen's Caucus, Latta castigated an Obama administration proposal to reclassify pocketknives that can be sprung open with one hand as switchblades. Congress enacted a bill that overturned the rule. Latta's Protect Our Great Lakes Act, which was designed to reduce algal blooms by prohibiting discharge of dredged material into the lakes, evolved and was enacted in 2015 as his Drinking Water Protection Act. That measure required the

Environmental Protection Agency to submit a plan to Congress that assessed and managed risks of those toxins from public water systems.

Latta has won reelection by wide margins. His closest race was in 2012. The Toledo *Blade* endorsed his Democratic opponent, Angela Zimmann, a college professor, and said Latta "has not been pragmatic or constructive." Latta outspent her nearly 3-to-1 and won convincingly, 57%-39%. His father was known for his constituent-service work, and his son has sought to replicate that by personally reading and signing each outgoing letter from his office.

Northwest Ohio: Toledo Area, Bowling Green

Population		**Race and Ethnicity**		**Income**	
Total	723,565	White	89.6%	Median Income	$52,806 (212 out of 435)
Land area	5,626	Black	2.8%	Under $50,000	47.3%
Pop/ sq mi	128.6	Latino	4.7%	$50,000-$99,999	33.4%
Born in state	79.1%	Asian	1.2%	$100,000-$199,999	16.2%
		Two races	1.4%	$200,000 or more	3.0%
		Other	0.2%	Poverty Rate	12.3%
Age Groups		**Education**		**Health Insurance**	
Under 18	23.0%	H.S grad or less	44.6%	With health insurance coverage	92.5%
18-34	21.8%	Some college	30.6%		
35-64	39.4%	College Degree, 4 yr	15.0%		
Over 64	15.8%	Post grad	9.7%		
Work		**Military**		**Public Assistance**	
White Collar	32.6%	Veteran	8.8%	Cash public assistance income	2.0%
Sales and Service	38.2%	Active Duty	0.1%	Food stamp/SNAP benefits	10.3%
Blue Collar	29.1%				
Government	5.1%				

Voter Turnout			
2015 Total Citizens 18+	550,242	2016 House Turnout as % CVAP	63%
2016 House turnout	344,991	2014 House Turnout as % CVAP	37%

2012 Presidential Vote		
Mitt Romney	195,060	(54%)
Barack Obama	159,659	(44%)

2016 Presidential Vote		
Donald Trump	214,661	(59%)
Hillary Clinton	124,407	(34%)
Gary Johnson	15,370	(4%)

Cook Partisan Voting Index: R+11

Undergirded by limestone, as flat and fertile as any place in America, northwest Ohio was economically productive from the time it was settled. That settlement came relatively late. Conflicts with Native Americans played a large role in the delay. In 1791, near Fort Recovery in Mercer County, the United States Army was routed by a confederation of Indian tribes: Only 48 of the 1,000 soldiers led into battle escaped unharmed, and a quarter of them died. Three years later, the Battle of Fallen Timbers near present-day Maumee put a temporary end to outright conflict between Indians and Americans, and the ensuing Treaty of Greenville set aside northwestern Ohio for Native American use; the area wasn't made formally available for white settlement until the end of Tecumseh's War some 20 years later. What we know today as fecund farmland was part of a giant swamp in the early 1800s. The Great Black Swamp, left behind by a retreating glacier thousands of years earlier, ran from present-day Sandusky to the outskirts of Fort Wayne, Indiana. It wasn't drained until the mid-1800s.

Today, this is prime industrial country. Its limestone, rail connections, and location between Lake Michigan and Lake Erie have spurred a factory economy that financially is far more important than agriculture. After the first settlements, northwest Ohio grew steadily for many decades, with Germany supplying many of the immigrants. For decades, its small factories supplied the big auto plants in Detroit and northeast Ohio. Growth lagged in the 1980s when the domestic industry collapsed, but rebounded somewhat as small firms sold not only to the Big Three but to foreign customers. Honda has dozens of suppliers in the area. In February 2017, leaders of the Regional Growth Partnership said that current and prospective business projects were the best they had seen, with about 6,000 new jobs - many of them in the auto industry.

The 5th Congressional District of Ohio sweeps across northwest Ohio, including the suburbs of Toledo, the university town of Bowling Green, the Marathon Petroleum home in Findlay, and the towns of Napoleon and Defiance en route to Ohio's borders with Michigan and Indiana. Its factories are numerous and widespread: Bowling Green is the site of the state's first wind turbines, and locals now call it "Blowing Green." Napoleon has the world's largest Campbell soup plant. Upper Sandusky (more than 60 miles inland from Sandusky on Lake Erie) is home to about 30 industrial firms. In December 2016, the city council in Bowling Green rejected a request to build a natural gas pipeline on city-owned land. In Perrysburg, near Toledo, the Belamere Suites have been rated by TripAdvisor as the most romantic hotel in the nation. On a presumably unrelated note, officials in Perrysburg in February 2017 rejected proposed facilities for medical marijuana.

This had been a solidly Republican district. About one-fourth of the district is in suburban Lucas County, though its Toledo neighborhoods are mostly in the solidly Democratic 9th District. The 5th remains comfortably Republican - like each of the 12 GOP-held districts in Ohio. As with several other mostly rural Ohio districts, Donald Trump in 2016 boosted the Republican presidential performance here - to 59 percent, from the 54 percent for Mitt Romney in 2012.

SIXTH DISTRICT

Bill Johnson (R)

Elected 2010, 4th term; b. Nov 10, 1954, Roseboro, NC; Troy University (AL), B.S.; Georgia Institute of Technology, M.A.; Air Command and Staff College (AL); Protestant; Married (LeeAnn Johnson); 4 children; 6 grandchildren.

Military Career: U.S Air Force, 1973-1999.

Professional Career: President, Johnson-Schley Mgmt. Group, 1999-2003; Owner, J2 Business Solutions, 2003-2006; Director, Lockheed Martin, 2005; CIO, Stoneridge Inc., 2006-2010.

DC Office: 1710 LHOB 20515, 202-225-5705, Fax: 202-225-5907, billjohnson.house.gov.

State Offices: Cambridge, 740-432-2366; Ironton, 740-534-9431; Marietta, 740-376-0868; Salem, 330-337-6951.

Committees: *Budget*. *Energy & Commerce*: Communications & Technology, Energy, Environment.

Group Ratings

	ADA	ACLU	AFL-CIO	LCV	ITI	COC	HAFA	ACU	CFG	FRC
2016	-	5%	-	0%	100%	100%	47%	76%	59%	100%
2015	0%	C	33%	3%	C	100%	C	63%	45%	92%

Almanac Ratings 2015

	Economy	Social	Foreign	Composite
Liberal	14%	0%	4%	6%
Conservative	86%	100%	96%	94%

Key Votes of the 114th Congress

1. Keystone Pipeline	Y	5. Puerto Rico Debt	Y	9. Offenses by Aliens	Y
2. Trade Deals	Y	6. Medical Marijuana	N	10. Troops in Iraq	N
3. Export-Import Bank	Y	7. Sanctuary Cities	Y	11. Homeland Security $$	N
4. Debt Ceiling Increase	Y	8. Armor-piercing Bullets	Y	12. Trade Adjustment aid	Y

Election Results

Election	Name (Party)	Vote (%)		Cand. Spent	Ind. Exp. Support	Ind. Exp. Oppose
2016 General	Bill Johnson (R)	213,975	(71%)	$1,210,808		
	Michael Lorentz (D)	88,780	(29%)	$4,480		
2016 Primary	Bill Johnson (R)		(100%)			

Prior winning percentages: 2014 (58%), 2012 (53%), 2010 (50%)

Republican Bill Johnson, elected in 2010 in what was a Democratic bastion not long ago, had been a business consultant and founded an anti-tax group. After learning the ropes, he has become an active member of the Energy and Commerce Committee, where he has been a zealous opponent of environmental regulation and an advocate of more business-friendly government.

Johnson was born in Roseboro, North Carolina, and raised on his family's cotton and tobacco farm. He joined the Air Force when he was 17. While serving, he graduated with a degree in computer science from Alabama's Troy University. Later, he earned his master's degree in computer science from Georgia Tech. In the military, he was stationed at many bases. As a director at U.S. Special Operations Command, he briefed congressional and intelligence officials. He retired from the military in 1999 as a lieutenant colonel, having managed communications and computer systems. He worked for multiple high-technology companies and became an information-technology consultant, especially for the military. He moved to Ohio in 2006, when he began working for Stoneridge, which makes electronic components for automobiles. Upset that shoppers were pouring across the border into Pennsylvania to buy certain goods free of sales taxes, Johnson in 2009 founded an organization called the Ohio Sales Tax Reform Incentive with the goal of creating tax holidays for shoppers.

Initially, Johnson considered running against Democratic Rep. Tim Ryan in the adjacent district. In challenging two-term Democratic Rep. Charlie Wilson, he picked a much less Democratic district. In the GOP primary, he defeated Donald Allen, a veterinarian, 43%-37%; former Belmont County Sheriff Richard Stobbs got 20 percent. Wilson cast fiscally conservative votes and backed gun rights, but he voted for the Democrats' $787 billion economic stimulus bill and the Affordable Care Act. Johnson characterized Wilson as a puppet of liberal House Speaker Nancy Pelosi and out of touch with his constituents. Wilson accused Johnson's company of exporting jobs. Johnson replied that the company created jobs in Ohio and called Wilson's attacks "the desperate act of a career politician who cannot defend his record for his tax-and-spend policies." Johnson benefited from ads by the U.S. Chamber of Commerce that attacked Wilson as "Party-Line Charlie." Johnson won, 50%-45%, while Wilson was outspending him almost 2-to-1, though each benefited from national party spending.

Johnson's voting record moved closer to the center as he adopted more liberal positions on foreign policy. In 2015, his *Almanac* vote ratings ranked him near the middle of Republicans in the House and those from Ohio. He was an adamant critic of the Obama administration. He won House passage in 2012 of his "Stop the War on Coal Act," which barred the Environmental Protection Agency from restricting greenhouse gas emissions, quashed stricter fuel efficiency standards for cars and gave states control over disposal of coal byproducts. The vote coincided with GOP presidential candidate Mitt Romney's attacks on Obama over coal. Johnson filed a bill to prevent the rewriting of a Bush administration regulation that allowed mining companies to dump debris in stream beds that fill up in rainy seasons but go dry at other times.

On the Energy and Commerce Committee, Johnson gained added leverage to advocate the interests of coal and promote energy independence. In 2015, the House passed his bill to expedite exports of liquefied natural gas by setting a deadline for federal approval. After a trip to four European nations, he said that they were "begging" for U.S. energy exports so they could reduce their dependence on Russia. At a July 2016 committee hearing, he called the EPA "un-American" and said that the agency was "draining the lifeblood out of our businesses." Democrats criticized him as "extreme." In February 2017, President Donald Trump used one of his first bill-signings to enact a Johnson measure to overturn a regulation on mining waste that President Barack Obama had approved shortly before he left office. Johnson said that the sole purpose of the rule was "to put a death knell into the coffin of the coal industry."

Wilson sought a comeback in 2012 and loaned his campaign more than $400,000 to keep pace with Johnson, who tried to preserve his outsider status with ads referring to his rival as "Congressman Charlie Wilson." Wilson got about $2 million in help from the DCCC, but the anti-tax lobbying group Americans for Tax Reform spent more than $3 million on Johnson's behalf. Johnson won again, 53%-47%. Wilson died at age 70 in 2013, highlighting the Democrats' need for younger faces. In 2014, Johnson faced Democrat Jennifer Garrison, a lawyer who served six years in the state Assembly and described herself as "pro-life, pro-gun and pro-coal." She called Johnson "the face of Washington dysfunction." Johnson outspent her $1.9 million to $900,000. He won 58%-39% and took 17 of the 18 counties. In 2016, Johnson out-raised his opponent by more than 100-to-1 and won, 71%-29%, evidence that Democrats had turned their attention elsewhere.

Ohio River Valley: Steubenville

Population		**Race and Ethnicity**		**Income**	
Total	711,496	White	94.6%	Median Income	$43,423 (357 out of 435)
Land area	7,215	Black	2.2%	Under $50,000	56.2%
Pop/ sq mi	98.6	Latino	1.0%	$50,000-$99,999	30.4%
Born in state	70.2%	Asian	0.4%	$100,000-$199,999	11.7%
		Two races	1.5%	$200,000 or more	1.7%
		Other	0.1%	Poverty Rate	16.8%
Age Groups		**Education**		**Health Insurance**	
Under 18	21.3%	H.S grad or less	56.7%	With health insurance coverage	89.6%
18-34	19.3%	Some college	28.0%		
35-64	41.5%	College Degree, 4 yr	9.7%		
Over 64	17.9%	Post grad	5.6%		
Work		**Military**		**Public Assistance**	
White Collar	28.0%	Veteran	10.4%	Cash public assistance income	2.8%
Sales and Service	41.4%	Active Duty	0.0%	Food stamp/SNAP benefits	17.1%
Blue Collar	30.6%				
Government	5.5%				

Voter Turnout			
2015 Total Citizens 18+	556,940	2016 House Turnout as % CVAP	54%
2016 House turnout	302,755	2014 House Turnout as % CVAP	34%

2012 Presidential Vote		
Mitt Romney	176,602	(55%)
Barack Obama	136,518	(43%)

2016 Presidential Vote		
Donald Trump	221,872	(69%)
Hillary Clinton	85,501	(27%)
Gary Johnson	8,833	(3%)

Cook Partisan Voting Index: R+16

In the years after the American Revolution, shipping goods downriver by raft was cheaper than sending them over the Appalachian Mountains, and so the Ohio River became a great highway of commerce. From Pittsburgh, where the Allegheny and Monongahela Rivers meet to form the Ohio, the river led south and west toward the Mississippi and the great port of New Orleans. For hundreds of miles, it twisted this way and that through mountains and rolling hills, land that marked the boundary between post-Revolutionary Virginia and the Northwest Territory, between slaveholding territory and free soil as determined by the Confederation Congress of 1787. Across this boundary, settlers made their way in those years to Ohio - Yankees and, in larger numbers, Virginians.

By the late 19th century, the Ohio was an industrial river. Coal was nearby, barge transportation was available, and railroads were built in the narrow valleys between the hills. Steel mills went up on the riverfront. This produced prosperity for a while, but it also produced pollution - Steubenville on the Ohio River once had the nation's dirtiest air - and after the old-line steel industry fell on hard times, the Ohio River was lined with some of the most impoverished parts of America. Even with mandates from the Clean Air Act, the pollution in much of the area from coal-fired power plants remains. Locally, the positive news was that many landowners recently reaped a windfall after rising prices made feasible the extraction of oil and natural gas from the Marcellus and Utica shale beds miles under their land. Shale production opened the door to large-scale manufacturing of plastics in Columbiana County.

The 6th Congressional District of Ohio is a string of counties running 325 miles along the Ohio River, plus part of the Mahoning Valley. It includes Canfield and a few small suburbs of Youngstown in Mahoning County, and it takes in East Liverpool, where bank robber and Public Enemy No. 1 Charles Arthur "Pretty Boy" Floyd was shot by FBI agents in a cornfield. Nearby are Steubenville, once known as "Sin City" and home to Rat Pack crooner Dean Martin, and Hanoverton, the home for nearly two centuries of the Spread Eagle Tavern - a Republican hang-out. The district curves along the lightly populated stretch of the river south from Marietta, past the old industrial town of Ironton, and extends to Wheelersburg, which is not quite in the Cincinnati metro area. For most of its length, the district extends one or two counties from the river.

This mix of communities recently has made a Republican enclave with a cultural conservatism much like that of West Virginia and eastern Kentucky across the river. The population is 95 percent white, the third highest in the nation, but with the lowest median income of any Republican-held district in Ohio. In 2016, Donald Trump won this district, 69%-26%. That margin, the largest in Ohio, was all the more extraordinary, given that Mitt Romney in 2012 won, 55%-43% -- a 31 percentage point increase in the splits during four years. In Columbiana, the Republican chairman called the area, "the very epicentre of the Trump groundswell." The only local patch of blue in the district is a small piece - less than 10 percent - of university-based Athens County.

SEVENTH DISTRICT

Bob Gibbs (R)

Elected 2010, 4th term; b. Jun 14, 1954, Peru, IN; Ohio State University Agricultural Technical Institute; Methodist; Married (Jody Gibbs); 3 children.

Elected Office: OH House, 2003-2008; OH Senate, 2008-2010.

Professional Career: Technician, OH Ag. Research & Devel. Center, 1974-1978; Owner, Hidden Hollow Farms, 1978-2004; Owner, Gibbs Enterprises.

DC Office: 2446 RHOB 20515, 202-225-6265, Fax: 202-225-3394, gibbs.house.gov.

State Offices: Ashland, 419-207-0650; Canton, 330-737-1631.

Committees: *Agriculture*: Biotechnology, Horticulture & Research, General Farm Commodities & Risk Management. *Transportation & Infrastructure*: Aviation, Highways & Transit, Water Resources & Environment.

Group Ratings

	ADA	ACLU	AFL-CIO	LCV	ITI	COC	HAFA	ACU	CFG	FRC
2016	-	11%	-	0%	100%	100%	66%	88%	83%	100%
2015	0%	C	21%	0%	C	85%	C	88%	71%	100%

Almanac Ratings 2015

	Economy	Social	Foreign	Composite
Liberal	0%	0%	4%	1%
Conservative	100%	100%	96%	99%

Key Votes of the 114th Congress

1. Keystone Pipeline	Y	5. Puerto Rico Debt	Y	9. Offenses by Aliens	Y
2. Trade Deals	Y	6. Medical Marijuana	N	10. Troops in Iraq	N
3. Export-Import Bank	N	7. Sanctuary Cities	Y	11. Homeland Security $$	N
4. Debt Ceiling Increase	N	8. Armor-piercing Bullets	Y	12. Trade Adjustment aid	Y

Election Results

Election	Name (Party)	Vote (%)		Cand. Spent	Ind. Exp. Support	Ind. Exp. Oppose
2016 General	Bob Gibbs (R)	198,221	(64%)	$820,745		
	Roy Rich (D)	89,638	(29%)	$7,829		
	Dan Phillip (L)	21,694	(7%)	$16,642		
2016 Primary	Bob Gibbs (R)	79,853	(75%)			
	Terry Robertson (R)	27,035	(25%)			

Prior winning percentages: 2014 (100%), 2012 (56%), 2010 (54%)

Republican Bob Gibbs, elected in 2010, is a hog farmer and ex-state farm bureau president who takes seriously agriculture and public works projects. As a freshman, he became chairman of the Water Resources and Environment Subcommittee of Transportation and Infrastrcture, which made him a prime dispenser of congressional pork - or, as his website described his domain, "cost effective water infrastructure improvements that provide jobs." After term limits forced him to step down from that position in 2017, he continued his pursuit of excessive regulations.

Gibbs grew up on the west side of Cleveland, "as far away from agriculture as you can get," he said. After working in the garden center of his high school, he enrolled in Ohio State University's Agricultural Institute. Gibbs went into business in Holmes County with his Hidden Hollow Farms, where he mostly raised market hogs. His two terms as president of the Ohio Farm Bureau Federation sparked his interest in politics. In 2002, Gibbs won a seat in the Ohio House. He was elected six years later to the Senate, where he chaired the Ways and Means Committee. He focused on agriculture, small business, and private property issues. He co-authored a 21 percent cut in Ohio's personal income tax rates.

Gibbs challenged two-term Democratic Rep. Zack Space, a moderate and a prolific fundraiser. They attacked each other on climate change, health care reform and the "don't ask, don't tell" policy prohibiting gay men and women from serving openly in the military. Republicans blasted Space for his vote for the 2009 House-passed bill to create a cap-and-trade system to reduce greenhouse-gas emissions blamed for global warming. Gibbs said he doesn't believe human activity causes climate change. Space ran ads with footage of Gibbs telling an audience, "I'm a free-trader," and tying him to trade deals that, Space said, sent Ohio jobs overseas. Space outspent Gibbs, $2.9 million to $1.1 million; each had more than $1 million in national party help. In the 2010 Republican tidal wave, Gibbs won easily, 54%-40%.

Gibbs was among the freshmen most likely to vote with Speaker John Boehner of Ohio and the House leadership. One notable exception was the budget and tax compromise to avert the so-called fiscal cliff in January 2013. "It stifles our already fragile economy, keeping the private sector from prospering. ... [It] is absolutely not the answer to our economic crisis," he said. His *Almanac* vote ratings for 2015 were among the most conservative in the House.

With a boost from Boehner, Gibbs got the Water Resources subcommittee chairmanship -- a prime plum for a newcomer. He enacted in 2014 the Water Resources Reform and Development Act, the first such reauthorization since 2007. The law reformed the review process of the Army Corps of Engineers for the nation's ports and flood control projects, "deauthorized" $18 billion in inactive projects and included no specific earmarks. But Gibbs worked to provide clear guidance to the Army Corps for new projects. "Typically, it would take 10 to 15 years to complete the studies necessary prior to beginning construction. WRRDA will reduce that time to three years so that projects are able to begin as they are needed and create jobs," he summarized. He noted, in particular, the need to protect the health of Great Lakes ports. Subsequently, Gibbs said he was "disappointed" with the slow pace and the priorities of the Army Corps in its implementation of the new law.

His work on water resources gave Gibbs a prominent perch to blast the Environmental Protection Agency. The House in 2011 passed his "Reducing Regulatory Burdens Act," which prevented the implementation of a court order requiring pesticide applications in and around U.S. waters to be covered by Clean Water Act permits. In 2015, he introduced a bill to prohibit the EPA from requiring permits to spray pesticides near bodies of water so long as a state had approved the application and the pesticides had been federally approved. That year, the House passed his bill to nullify the EPA's proposed "Waters of the United States" rules, which Gibbs described as "a vast expansion of federal jurisdiction." His measure deadlocked in the Senate.

The election of President Donald Trump became a breakthrough for the policy agenda of Gibbs. In February 2017, he joined a White House ceremony where Trump signed an executive order that overturned Obama's "Waters of the U.S." rules. Trump called those rules one of the worst examples of government "run amok." Gibbs praised Trump for keeping his campaign promise. In an op-ed, Gibbs wrote that the selection of Scott Pruitt as the new EPA administrator gave Ohio a "partner" with whom it could work.

Redistricting gave Gibbs a district in which six of the 10 counties were completely new to him, but the new district leaned more Republican. In 2012, Democrats nominated Joyce Healy-Abrams, who ran a corporate record-keeping business and whose brother, William Healy, was mayor of Canton. She spent $905,000 to $1.3 million for Gibbs. Healy-Abrams won 55 percent of the vote in Stark, but Gibbs rolled up big majorities in the other counties, and won 56%-44%. In a sign that he had settled into his revamped district, Gibbs was re-elected without opposition in 2014 and his Democratic challenger in 2016 attracted little attention.

North-Central Ohio: Canton, Cleveland Suburbs

Population		**Race and Ethnicity**		**Income**	
Total	724,257	White	91.4%	Median Income	$49,615 (260 out of 435)
Land area	3,865	Black	3.8%		
Pop/ sq mi	187.4	Latino	2.1%		
Born in state	82.9%	Asian	0.6%	Under $50,000	50.4%
		Two races	1.9%	$50,000-$99,999	33.0%
Age Groups		Other	0.2%	$100,000-$199,999	14.3%
Under 18	23.6%			$200,000 or more	2.4%
18-34	19.9%	**Education**		Poverty Rate	13.5%
35-64	40.1%	H.S grad or less	53.6%		
Over 64	16.4%	Some college	27.3%	**Health Insurance**	
		College Degree, 4 yr	12.6%	With health insurance coverage	88.0%
Work		Post grad	6.5%		
White Collar	29.2%				
Sales and Service	40.4%	**Military**		**Public Assistance**	
Blue Collar	30.4%	Veteran	9.5%	Cash public assistance income	4.0%
Government	6.0%	Active Duty	0.1%		
				Food stamp/SNAP benefits	13.2%

Voter Turnout			
2015 Total Citizens 18+	547,712	2016 House Turnout as % CVAP	57%
2016 House turnout	309,553	2014 House Turnout as % CVAP	26%

2012 Presidential Vote		
Mitt Romney	179,375	(54%)
Barack Obama	147,567	(44%)

2016 Presidential Vote		
Donald Trump	205,572	(62%)
Hillary Clinton	107,942	(33%)
Gary Johnson	10,856	(3%)

Cook Partisan Voting Index: R+12

A little more than a century ago, Canton was at the center of American politics. It was already an industrial city, though without the huge steel mills of Youngstown or Cleveland. Its high-skill workers were fashioning new kinds of plows and reapers, making watches and, beginning in 1899, roller bearings. It did not attract masses of immigrants, its factories did not run on harsh stopwatch discipline, and the class-warfare politics of other northern Ohio industrial cities did not take root here. Canton's most famous citizen was Republican President William McKinley, who rose to the rank of major at age 22 in the Civil War, and was later elected to Congress. As the Republican nominee for president in 1896, he campaigned from his front porch in Canton, meeting with delegations brought in by train from around the country. This spectacle, displaying both technological virtuosity and personal modesty, sounded a reverberating note in American politics, as did the McKinley platform - the "full dinner pail," the gold standard, and the enforcement of law and order in labor relations - a platform that mostly severed the Democrats' ties to northern blue-collar whites until the 1930s.

Today, Canton remains based on manufacturing and has had some recovery from job losses, including those stemming from the crash of the auto industry in 2009. It has become best known as the home of the Professional Football Hall of Fame, with a roof shaped like a football. The Canton Bulldogs were one of the first teams in the Ohio League, the predecessor to the modern NFL. The NFL has pursued lavish plans for a $600 million, 200-acre Hall of Fame village in Canton, which is scheduled to open in 2019. Planned facilities include a university for coaches, an Institute for the Integrity of Officials, four-star hotel and conference center, performance center, retirement complex and retail space. The area includes Holmes County, which has been on its way to becoming the first Amish-majority county in the nation. With the doubling of the national Amish population to 300,000 from 1995 to 2015, Hudson County has competed with Lancaster County, Pennsylvania, as the largest Amish community in the world. Each has a settlement of about 34,000 residents, which extends beyond its county lines. Ashland is a rural county where Johnny Appleseed lived on what is now Ashland University. The campus includes the Ashbrook Center, which has become a hub for conservative academicians and politicians.

The 7th Congressional District of Ohio is a hodgepodge of counties forming a crescent across northeastern Ohio and avoiding Democratic areas of Cleveland, Akron and Lorain. It includes all of Canton, the old Ohio and Erie Canal town of Massillon, and most of Stark County, which has about a third of the district's population. Much of the area west and southwest of Canton is part of the Appalachian Plateau. The remaining swath of lightly populated counties arches west to Knox County on the outskirts of Columbus and north to North Ridgeville and Avon nearly to Lake Erie in Lorain County. The district extends through Medina County in the outer reaches of the Cleveland metropolitan area. The Stark County portions of the district are Democratic, but the rest of it is mostly Republican and the net result is that the 7th District leans Republican. In 2016 Donald Trump had a 62%-33% lead over Hillary Clinton, a big increase from Mitt Romney's 54%-44% lead in 2012.

EIGHTH DISTRICT

Warren Davidson (R)

Elected 2016, 1st term; b. Mar 01, 1970, Troy; U.S. Military Academy at West Point, Bach. Deg.; University of Notre Dame (IN), M.B.A.; Married (Lisa Davidson); 2 children.

Military Career: U.S Army, 1988-2000.

DC Office: 1004 LHOB 20515, 202-225-6205, Fax: 202-225-0704, davidson.house.gov.

State Offices: Troy, 937-339-1524; West Chester, 513-779-5400.

Committees: *Financial Services*: Capital Markets, Securities & Investment, Monetary Policy & Trade, Terrorism & Illicit Finance.

Group Ratings

	ADA	ACLU	AFL-CIO	LCV	ITI	COC	HAFA	ACU	CFG	FRC
2016	-	5%	-	0%	-	100%	86%	0%	-	83%
2015	0%	C	-	-	C	-	C	-	-	-

Election Results

Election	Name (Party)	Vote	(%)	Cand. Spent	Ind. Exp. Support	Ind. Exp. Oppose
2016 General	Warren Davidson (R)...................	223,833	(69%)	$860,088	$1,131,365	$293,349
	Steven Fought (D).........................	87,794	(27%)	$3,555		
	Derrick James Hendricks (G).........	13,879	(4%)			
2016 Primary	Warren Davidson (R)...................	42,230	(32%)			
	Timothy Derickson (R)..................	31,303	(24%)			
	Bill Beagle (R).............................	25,672	(20%)			
	Jim Spurlino (R)...........................	9,428	(7%)			

Prior winning percentages: 2016 special (77%)

Warren Davidson won a special election in June 2016 to replace Speaker John Boehner, who resigned from the House in October 2015. Inevitably, Davidson's responsibilities became more focused on his district, in contrast to the Speaker's constitutional responsibilities to preside over the House. Davidson brought other changes to his office. He joined the Freedom Caucus in the House and hired his chief of staff from the Heritage Foundation. Each organization had become anathema to Boehner.

Davidson grew up in Sydney, which is between Dayton and Lima. In high school, he was not a motivated student. As Davidson recounted to *The Cincinnati Enquirer*, he told a guidance counselor during his senior year that he wanted to attend West Point. She told him, "Baby, that's not going to happen." Instead, he enlisted in the Army. He gained a series of promotions and became an elite Army Ranger. He witnessed the fall of the Berlin Wall while he was serving in Germany. With this background, he eventually won an appointment to West Point, where he graduated with a degree in American history.

When he left the military, he returned home and planned to join his father's tool-making manufacturing business. But, the *Enquirer* reported, the business was "floundering" and his father was "leery of change." Davidson started his own tool-making business. He was successful and bought out his father. The company grew from 20 employees to more than 200. During that time, he got an MBA from Notre Dame University. He settled in Concord Township, where he served two years as a trustee. He was appointed to the position after having lost an election for the position.

After Boehner resigned, Republican Rep. Jim Jordan of the neighboring district recalled that he had met Davidson the previous year and had been impressed with him. When Davidson voiced interest in running for the seat, Jordan arranged an appointment for him with the Washington-based Club for Growth. The interview went well and Davidson won the endorsement. "It was a pretty easy call for us," said Andrew Roth, the group's vice president of government affairs told the *Enquirer*. "He doesn't mince words. It was clear that what he was telling us was based on principle." That support proved vital when the Club spent $1.1 million on behalf of Davidson during the primary. His two chief opponents, Bill Beagle and Tim Derickson, raised $500,000 and $300,000 respectively. Each was a member of the state Legislature. For the entire campaign, Davidson raised nearly $1 million.

The 15-candidate March primary for the special election was the same day as the primary for the general election in Ohio, including for the presidential campaign. It attracted a turnout of about 130,000. Davidson won with 32 percent of the vote to 24 percent for Derickson and 20 percent for Beagle. Derickson led in Butler and Beagle led in Miami, the two counties with the largest turnouts. Davidson ran second in those counties and led elsewhere. In this district, the outcome of the special election on June 7 was a formality. Davidson defeated Democrat Corey Foister, 77%-12%, with a thin turnout. Foister was described as a 25-year-old whose biggest political achievement was serving in student government at Northern Kentucky University. In the November election for a full term, Davidson won 69 percent of the vote.

After he won the nomination, Davidson voiced appreciation for Boehner's assistance in educating him about some aspects of his new job. But Boehner could not have been pleased that one of Davidson's first decisions was to join the invitation-only Freedom Caucus, the group that spurred his downfall and where Rep. Jordan has been a leader. Davidson got a seat on the Financial Services Committee. In February 2017, he filed with freshman Rep. Ted Budd of North Carolina the "Drain the Swamp" bill, which required that each federal agency relocate its employees across the nation and retain no more than 10 percent of its staff in the Washington, D.C., area.

West-Central Ohio: Cincinnati and Dayton Suburbs, Springfield

Population		**Race and Ethnicity**		**Income**	
Total	723,955	White	86.9%	Median Income	$51,748 (227 out of 435)
Land area	2,450	Black	5.9%		
Pop/ sq mi	295.4	Latino	3.2%		
Born in state	74.6%	Asian	1.8%	Under $50,000	48.2%
		Two races	2.0%	$50,000-$99,999	32.0%
Age Groups		Other	0.3%	$100,000-$199,999	17.0%
Under 18	24.1%			$200,000 or more	2.9%
18-34	21.6%	**Education**		Poverty Rate	14.3%
35-64	39.5%	H.S grad or less	48.4%		
Over 64	14.8%	Some college	28.8%	**Health Insurance**	
		College Degree, 4 yr	14.7%	With health insurance coverage	91.0%
Work		Post grad	8.1%		
White Collar	32.7%				
Sales and Service	40.7%	**Military**		**Public Assistance**	
Blue Collar	26.6%	Veteran	9.6%	Cash public assistance income	3.0%
Government	5.0%	Active Duty	0.1%		
				Food stamp/SNAP benefits	13.1%

Voter Turnout			
2015 Total Citizens 18+	537,655	2016 House Turnout as % CVAP	61%
2016 House turnout	325,506	2014 House Turnout as % CVAP	35%

2012 Presidential Vote		
Mitt Romney	211,446	(62%)
Barack Obama	124,407	(36%)

2016 Presidential Vote		
Donald Trump	223,215	(65%)
Hillary Clinton	104,929	(30%)
Gary Johnson	10,948	(3%)

Cook Partisan Voting Index: R+17

Since the early 20th century, the far west edge of Ohio - where U.S. 40, the old National Road, heads into Indiana - was some of the nation's prime industrial country. The Great and Little Miami rivers drain south into the Ohio, the Miami and Erie Canal system continues its northward march to Toledo, and U.S. 40 jogs southward to go over the Miami and Stillwater river dams. The small cities and towns around and between Dayton and Cincinnati were rising industrial country a century ago. In the years since, they have weathered economic downturns and sought to adapt to changing markets and circumstances. Butler County, in between the two cities, was dominated by the large factory towns of Hamilton and Middletown.

In recent years, some major employers have shut down operations. Other businesses have started up, and Butler's population has grown with the outflow of people from Cincinnati and Dayton, an increase of 13 percent from 2000 to 2016. The center of growth has been West Chester Township, situated on Interstate 75 south of Wright-Patterson Air Force Base. It has attracted an Amylin Pharmaceuticals facility, which produces diabetes medication and is owned by AstraZeneca. CFM manufactures jet engines in a partnership between GE and French-owned Safran. In January 2017, discussions among local officials about designating the township as a "right to work" center brought strong objections from labor unions. Butler County was largely settled by people from south of the Ohio River, who carried Democratic voting habits with them. Since then, it followed most of the new South and become reliably Republican. The county has had an economic boon since the recession, with a big increase in retail vendor licenses.

The 8th Congressional District of Ohio includes all of Butler County. It extends north along the Indiana border to take in Preble and Darke County, the birthplace of Phoebe Ann Moses, later known as sharpshooter Annie Oakley, plus some townships in southern Mercer County, near Fort Recovery. The district includes Clark County, with economically depressed Springfield, where manufacturing has collapsed, the poverty rate is 29 percent and residents are disproportionately aging. Its declining population is at a 90-year low, with a 9 percent drop from 2000 to 2016; it was rated by Gallup in 2011 as the unhappiest city in the United States. Springfield votes Democratic, but its presence does not alter the partisan balance of the district, which has been comfortably Republican. About half the voters are in Butler County and 20 percent are in Clark. Mitt Romney got 62 percent of the vote here in 2012, which was his best showing in Ohio. Donald Trump increased the GOP vote to 65 percent in 2016. He surpassed that in Ohio only with his 69 percent in the 6th District.

NINTH DISTRICT

Marcy Kaptur (D)

Elected 1982, 18th term; b. Jun 17, 1946, Toledo; Massachusetts Institute of Technology, Att.; University of Manchester (England), Att.; University of Michigan, M.A.; University of Wisconsin, B.A.; St. Ursula Academy (OH), Att.; Catholic; Single.

Professional Career: Urban planner, Lucas County Planning Comm., 1969-1975; Urban planning consultant, 1975-1977; White House Assistant Director for Urban Affairs, 1977-1980; Deputy Secretary, National Consumer Coop. Bank, 1980-1981.

DC Office: 2186 RHOB 20515, 202-225-4146, Fax: 202-225-7711, kaptur.house.gov.

State Offices: Cleveland, 440-799-8499; Lorain, 440-288-1500; Toledo, 419-259-7500.

Committees: *Appropriations*: Defense, Energy & Water Development & Related Agencies (RMM), Interior, Environment & Related Agencies. *Joint Congressional-Executive Commission on China.*

Group Ratings

	ADA	ACLU	AFL-CIO	LCV	ITI	COC	HAFA	ACU	CFG	FRC
2016	-	88%	-	100%	60%	62%	12%	0%	4%	8%
2015	80%	C	100%	89%	C	53%	C	0%	3%	8%

Almanac Ratings 2015

	Economy	Social	Foreign	Composite
Liberal	91%	94%	84%	90%
Conservative	10%	6%	16%	10%

Key Votes of the 114th Congress

1. Keystone Pipeline	NV	5. Puerto Rico Debt	Y	9. Offenses by Aliens	N
2. Trade Deals	N	6. Medical Marijuana	Y	10. Troops in Iraq	Y
3. Export-Import Bank	Y	7. Sanctuary Cities	N	11. Homeland Security $$	Y
4. Debt Ceiling Increase	Y	8. Armor-piercing Bullets	N	12. Trade Adjustment aid	Y

Election Results

Election	Name (Party)	Vote (%)	Cand. Spent	Ind. Exp. Support	Ind. Exp. Oppose
2016 General	Marcy Kaptur (D)	193,967 (69%)	$380,023		
	Donald Larson (R)	88,427 (31%)	$34,586		
2016 Primary	Marcy Kaptur (D)	(100%)			

Prior winning percentages: 2014 (68%), 2012 (73%), 2010 (59%), 2008 (74%), 2006 (74%), 2004 (68%), 2002 (74%), 2000(75%), 1998 (81%), 1996 (77%), 1994 (75%), 1992 (74%), 1990 (78%), 1988 (81%), 1986 (78%), 1984 (56%), 1982 (58%)

Democrat Marcy Kaptur, first elected in 1982, is now the most senior Democratic woman in the House - which she keeps in mind in her occasional clashes with Minority Leader Nancy Pelosi. Kaptur is a plainspoken Democrat and a dedicated opponent of free trade who does not always toe the party line, but whose old-fashioned ways have proven popular at home.

Kaptur grew up in a blue-collar neighborhood in Toledo, the daughter of Polish-American parents who worked at local auto plants. The family also operated a small grocery store, but her father sold it to get a job with health benefits. "It broke his heart," she said. She has spent almost her entire career in public service. She graduated from the University of Wisconsin, the first in her family to attend college, got a master's degree from the University of Michigan, then spent eight years as an urban planner in Toledo. She worked on urban revitalization in the Jimmy Carter White House. She interrupted her studies for a doctorate at M.I.T. to return home and run for office. In 1982, she challenged first-term Republican Rep. Ed Weber and won 58%-39%, despite being outspent 3-to-1.

Kaptur has long been convinced that Toledo and places like it have lost jobs and industry because of unfair trade practices and low-wage competition from countries like Mexico and China. She was featured prominently in liberal filmmaker Michael Moore's 2009 movie *Capitalism: A Love Story*. "I have always said there's a great injustice being done here, because the power rests with a handful of megabanks and millions of Americans are being affected," she told the Toledo *Blade* when the film opened.

She criticized President Bill Clinton for ignoring Democrats opposed to the 1993 North American Free Trade Agreement. In 1995, she made a rousing speech on trade before Texas businessman Ross Perot's United We Stand Party. Perot, running as a third-party candidate for president in 1996, offered her the vice presidential nomination, but she turned it down. She was a vocal opponent of normal trade relations with China and the Central American Free Trade Agreement.

Reflecting on those early trade wars years later, Kaptur criticized Pelosi's support of NAFTA. "That's where the real knife was put in the flesh," she said. In 2002, she ran a quixotic, one-day campaign for minority leader against Pelosi but, predictably, got nowhere. When Pelosi announced in 2007 an agreement with Treasury Secretary Hank Paulson on principles for international trade policy, an uninvited Kaptur glared from the back of the room. In 2008, she challenged Xavier Becerra of California for Democratic Caucus vice chairman and lost badly, 175-67. Kaptur backed Pelosi for minority leader in 2011 when her hold on power within the caucus had grown tenuous.

Kaptur strongly opposed trade agreements with Colombia, Panama and South Korea that passed the House in 2011. Kaptur took to the House floor during the debate to point out that the number of cars the U.S. imported from South Korea dwarfed the number of American cars bought by people in the Northeast

Asian nation. "These unfair, unbalanced agreements will not have a demonstrable, positive impact on job creation. We have lost six million manufacturing jobs in the past decade. Enough is enough," she said. When the House narrowly voted in 2015 to give trade promotion authority to President Barack Obama, she slammed proponents who she said sold out "working families and American industries that have been the backbone of the U.S. economy for decades."

When Rep. Norm Dicks of Washington retired in 2012, Kaptur hoped to succeed him as the ranking Democrat on Appropriations. But the post instead went to Nita Lowey of New York, a more predictable liberal and a favorite of Pelosi's. Kaptur became ranking Democrat on the Energy and Water Development Subcommittee, pointing out that her district had abundant water resources. She is a strong advocate of alternative energy such as ethanol and biofuels for Ohio. Kaptur has promoted solar energy, a growing industry in Toledo. In 2015, she criticized Ohio Gov. John Kasich for freezing an intended increase in the state's renewable energy mandate. He "shouldn't lead us backwards," she said.

Kaptur has departed from party orthodoxy on abortion. She opposes federal funding for the procedure, though she has also voted against proposals to deny federal money to Planned Parenthood. She contended that federal funds were not used for abortions, and that Planned Parenthood provided valuable medical care for women.

Kaptur keeps close tabs on her district. A constituent gave her the idea to sponsor the legislation that created the World War II Memorial on the National Mall. Prior to the House ban on earmarks, she ranked 24th among the top earmark recipients in 2010, according to the group Taxpayers for Common Sense. She once challenged Republicans on the committee to limit farm payments, but when they threatened her favorite spending projects, she backed off. "I may be blockheaded sometimes, but I'm not stupid," Kaptur said.

Kaptur, who wrote a book on women in Congress, is exceedingly popular in the Toledo area and rarely has faced a credible challenge. In 2012, Ohio lost two congressional seats. Republicans drawing the new map put her in a district with Cleveland-based Democratic Rep. Dennis Kucinich. Though the ultraliberal Kucinich's bids for president had made him a national hero to hard-core progressives, he had a reputation at home for hobnobbing with celebrities and not accomplishing much for the district. He didn't help himself by briefly toying with the idea of running in Washington state. Kaptur defeated Kucinich in the Democratic primary, 56%-40%, putting an end to his 16-year House career. In Lucas County, she led 94%-4%. Since then, she has had no primary opposition and has breezed to reelection. She appears secure, at least until the next redistricting.

Kaptur can be unpredictable. She was among a handful of House Democrats who supported Bernie Sanders for the 2016 presidential nomination. When fellow Ohio Democratic Rep. Tim Ryan made a post-election leadership challenge, Kaptur backed Pelosi, though she praised Ryan "for moving the Caucus."

Lakefront: Toledo, Cleveland Suburbs

Population		**Race and Ethnicity**		**Income**	
Total	714,244	White	69.8%	Median Income	$40,471 (396 out of 435)
Land area	465	Black	15.3%		
Pop/ sq mi	1537.2	Latino	10.4%		
Born in state	76.1%	Asian	1.3%	Under $50,000	59.4%
Age Groups		Two races	2.9%	$50,000-$99,999	27.8%
Under 18	22.6%	Other	0.3%	$100,000-$199,999	11.0%
18-34	23.5%	**Education**		$200,000 or more	1.9%
35-64	39.7%	H.S grad or less	47.8%	Poverty Rate	21.6%
Over 64	14.3%	Some college	31.1%	**Health Insurance**	
Work		College Degree, 4 yr	13.7%	With health insurance coverage	88.5%
White Collar	29.6%	Post grad	7.4%		
Sales and Service	45.1%	**Military**		**Public Assistance**	
Blue Collar	25.2%	Veteran	8.6%	Cash public assistance income	4.1%
Government	4.3%	Active Duty	0.0%	Food stamp/SNAP benefits	21.7%

Voter Turnout			
2015 Total Citizens 18+	540,137	2016 House Turnout as % CVAP	52%
2016 House turnout	282,398	2014 House Turnout as % CVAP	30%

2012 Presidential Vote		
Barack Obama	217,169	(68%)
Mitt Romney	99,213	(31%)

2016 Presidential Vote		
Hillary Clinton	177,147	(58%)
Donald Trump	110,178	(36%)
Gary Johnson	9,495	(3%)

Cook Partisan Voting Index: D+14

Lake Erie, the southernmost and shallowest of the Great Lakes, played a critical role in the history of America's interior. For decades, its shoreline was the locus of a four-way battle among French, Indian, British and American claimants. Additional conflicts over various claims to the area made by the various American colonies bubbled underneath. Once the federal government finally assumed full control of the Lake Erie shoreline in 1800, development proceeded quickly. Cleveland, at the mouth of the Cuyahoga River, had a population of 1,000 in 1830. Hamlets sprang up on the shoreline, usually at the mouths of rivers: Huron, at the mouth of the Huron River, in 1804; Lorain, at the mouth of the Black River, in 1807; Sandusky, at the mouth of the Sandusky River, in 1818; and Toledo, at the mouth of the Maumee River, in 1833. Toledo and Cleveland became the biggest cities here once the Ohio & Erie and Miami & Erie canals were completed. All of the towns benefited from the trade that flowed from the Atlantic seaboard, up the Erie Canal to Buffalo, across the lake and into the burgeoning American interior.

The canal traffic declined in the late 1800s, but Lake Erie retained an important role in the economy. Erie contains only 2 percent of the water of the Great Lakes, but 50 percent of its fish. It houses one of the largest commercial freshwater fisheries in the world, including a large yellow perch yield. Port Clinton, on Lake Erie, bills itself as the "Walleye Capital of the World" and drops a plastic walleye in place of a glittering ball on New Year's Eve. Local experts boasted that their world's largest walleye fishery was abundant in 2016. In April 2017, Fiat Chrysler shut down its Toledo assembly line for Jeep Cherokees and moved their production to Belvidere Illinois. In its place, the company has upgraded its plant to increase output of its next-generation, "body on frame" Jeep Wranglers. The plant is scheduled to grow its local workforce of about 5,000. Industrial news was more negative in gritty Lorain, which has managed to survive as a steel town. Republic Steel closed its plant in March 2016. U.S. Steel Corp., which in 2011 expanded with great fanfare its plant to make pipes for natural gas companies, downsized at about the same time, with little immediate prospect for a revival. The high-tech economy has made some local inroads, including innovative ways to clean up the environmental degradation left behind by earlier industries. Pollution poses a continued threat to the native fisheries. The canals brought in invasive species - most recently Asian carp - while runoff from farms still promotes algae blooms.

The 9th Congressional District of Ohio sprawls across the Lake Erie shoreline, rarely venturing more than 10 miles inland and sometimes less than a mile or two. From Toledo-based Clark County, with about 30 percent of its voters, it goes east through Port Clinton and Sandusky, home to the giant Cedar Point amusement park, with some of the country's fastest roller coasters. About 40 percent are in Cuyahoga County, where the district takes in western Cleveland, including Hopkins International Airport. This portion includes some inner suburbs, such as revived Lakewood, with its many Victorian-era houses. The two ends of the district, which are 120 miles apart, have shared two things: generally blue-collar economies and Democratic voting patterns. That changed a bit in 2016. With a minority population of about 30 percent and a large white blue-collar cadre, the 58 percent for Hillary Clinton dropped from the more than two-thirds of the vote that Barack Obama got in his two elections.

TENTH DISTRICT

Michael Turner (R)

Elected 2002, 8th term; b. Jan 11, 1960, Dayton; Case Western Reserve University School of Law (OH), J.D.; Ohio Northern University, B.A.; University of Dayton (OH), M.B.A.; Presbyterian; Married (Lori Turner); 2 children (2 from previous marriage).

Elected Office: Dayton Mayor, 1993-2001.

Professional Career: Practicing attorney.

DC Office: 2368 RHOB 20515, 202-225-6465, Fax: 202-225-6754, turner.house.gov.

State Offices: Dayton, 937-225-2843.

Committees: *Armed Services*: Strategic Forces, Tactical Air & Land Forces (Chmn). *Permanent Select on Intelligence*.

Group Ratings

	ADA	ACLU	AFL-CIO	LCV	ITI	COC	HAFA	ACU	CFG	FRC
2016	-	5%	-	11%	100%	100%	35%	57%	48%	100%
2015	0%	C	33%	3%	C	100%	C	38%	36%	92%

Almanac Ratings 2015

	Economy	Social	Foreign	Composite
Liberal	18%	10%	10%	13%
Conservative	82%	90%	90%	87%

Key Votes of the 114th Congress

1. Keystone Pipeline	Y	5. Puerto Rico Debt	Y	9. Offenses by Aliens	Y
2. Trade Deals	Y	6. Medical Marijuana	N	10. Troops in Iraq	N
3. Export-Import Bank	Y	7. Sanctuary Cities	Y	11. Homeland Security $$	Y
4. Debt Ceiling Increase	Y	8. Armor-piercing Bullets	Y	12. Trade Adjustment aid	Y

Election Results

Election	Name (Party)	Vote (%)		Cand. Spent	Ind. Exp. Support	Ind. Exp. Oppose
2016 General	Michael Turner (R)	215,724	(64%)	$1,129,936	$777	
	Robert Klepinger (D)	109,981	(33%)	$5,174		$600
	Tom McMasters (I)	10,890	(3%)	$20,787		
2016 Primary	Michael Turner (R)		(100%)			

Prior winning percentages: 2014 (65%), 2012 (60%), 2010 (68%), 2008 (63%), 2006 (59%), 2004 (62%), 2002 (59%)

Republican Mike Turner, first elected in 2002, is a former Dayton mayor with a stronger interest in urban issues than most House Republicans. He has gained significant influence and a growing voice on national security policy.

Turner grew up in Dayton, where his father spent his career with General Motors. He graduated from Ohio Northern University, Case Western law school and the University of Dayton business school, and became a corporate lawyer. At age 33, he narrowly defeated a scandal-tainted Democratic incumbent to win the first of two terms as Dayton mayor. He created Rehabarama, an acclaimed private-public partnership to rehabilitate neglected housing in Dayton's historic neighborhoods. He narrowly lost reelection in 2001.

Republican leaders recruited him to challenge Democratic Rep. Tony Hall, who had served 12 terms but was vulnerable after redistricting made his turf considerably more Republican. A week after Turner announced he was running for Congress, President George W. Bush nominated Hall as ambassador to the U.N. Food and Agriculture Organization in Rome. In the Republican primary, Turner faced fierce opposition from newspaper publisher Roy Brown, grandson and son of former Reps. Clarence Brown and Clarence Brown Jr., who had represented a neighboring district from 1938 to 1982. Brown spent $1.3 million of his own money, largely on ads attacking Turner's record on taxes and lambasting him for being insufficiently conservative. Brown owned 10 local newspapers, and Turner contended that Brown's campaign guided the newspapers' coverage of the race. The Ohio Election Commission ruled that Brown violated state law with false statements in a televised ad. Turner defeated Brown 80%-14%. The Democratic nominee in the comparatively sedate general was Rick Carne, Hall's chief of staff. With little support from his national party, he raised nearly $600,000, and benefited from a local appearance by Dayton native Martin Sheen, who played President Josiah Bartlet on the popular *West Wing* television series. Turner won 59%-41%.

Turner has supported his party on most major issues. The *Almanac* vote ratings for 2015 ranked him toward the center of the House, especially on economic issues. He has voted against conservative efforts to cut science funding and to eliminate such agencies as the Legal Services Corporation and the National Endowment for the Arts. He has helped to save the Community Development Block Grant program.

Turner has remained focused on urban issues and formed a caucus of former mayors serving in Congress. He worked on House-passed legislation to accelerate the cleanup of polluted brownfields by making it easier for communities to apply for federal grants. He has promoted the kind of public-private partnerships that he used for economic development in Dayton. In 2009, Turner was one of seven House Republicans to support a bill that would give bankruptcy judges the power to restructure the terms of home mortgages.

On the Armed Services Committee, especially as chairman of its Tactical Air and Land Forces Subcommittee. Turner has offered protection from Defense Department cuts for Wright-Patterson Air Force Base, which is the largest single-site employer in Ohio. He said that the base added 10,000 jobs since he was first elected. He has worked to make Dayton into a center for unmanned aerial vehicle research and testing, and he was strongly critical of the Obama administration's funding cuts for missile defense. Turner served a term as president of the inter-parliamentary organization of legislators from the countries of the North Atlantic Alliance. He was a leader of the House Republicans strategy to ignore requirements to "sequester" spending until the deficit was reduced. In February 2016, he opposed President Barack Obama's proposed budget cuts for the military, which Turner said "could break the Army." He challenged Obama's claims that the Islamic State had been "contained." With his seat on the Intelligence Committee, Turner has worked to retain the National Air and Space Intelligence Center headquarters at Wright-Patt.

Turner and Democratic Rep. Niki Tsongas of Massachusetts led the bipartisan Military Sexual Assault Prevention Caucus. As part of their efforts, they filed a bill in 2016 to encourage increased transparency in the military justice system, greater protection for victims and witnesses from retaliation and better victim access to court information. Turner has tried for years to get Congress to pass a law aimed at protecting service members from losing custody of their children because of military deployments; the measure passed the House and stalled in the Senate. In 2014, when there was an opening for chairman of the Armed Services Committee, he deferred but made clear his interest in the next such vacancy, though more senior committee members could assert their interest.

Turner has not been seriously challenged for reelection. In July 2015, he endorsed Ohio Gov. John Kasich at the start of his campaign for the Republican presidential nomination. During a December interview with CNN, he said that Donald Trump was "not qualified to ... hold any elective office." In May 2016, Turner endorsed Trump, without citing his name, "because Hillary Clinton would be an awful president, as she has shown a blatant disregard for our laws."

Dayton Area

Population		Race and Ethnicity		Income	
Total	722,051	White	75.5%	Median Income	$46,703 (312 out of 435)
Land area	1,130	Black	16.8%		
Pop/ sq mi	639.1	Latino	2.5%		
Born in state	68.6%	Asian	2.1%	Under $50,000	52.9%
Age Groups		Two races	2.6%	$50,000-$99,999	28.9%
Under 18	22.2%	Other	0.4%	$100,000-$199,999	15.1%
18-34	23.3%	**Education**		$200,000 or more	3.1%
35-64	38.5%	H.S grad or less	39.0%	Poverty Rate	17.6%
Over 64	15.9%	Some college	33.1%	**Health Insurance**	
Work		College Degree, 4 yr	16.1%	With health insurance coverage	90.3%
White Collar	37.3%	Post grad	11.8%		
Sales and Service	42.6%	**Military**		**Public Assistance**	
Blue Collar	20.0%	Veteran	11.1%	Cash public assistance income	3.4%
Government	5.1%	Active Duty	0.8%		
				Food stamp/SNAP benefits	15.4%

Voter Turnout			
2015 Total Citizens 18+	547,683	2016 House Turnout as % CVAP	61%
2016 House turnout	336,602	2014 House Turnout as % CVAP	36%

2012 Presidential Vote		
Mitt Romney	179,772	(50%)
Barack Obama	172,981	(48%)

2016 Presidential Vote		
Donald Trump	178,674	(51%)
Hillary Clinton	153,346	(44%)
Gary Johnson	11,898	(3%)

Cook Partisan Voting Index: R+4

The underestimated Dayton can hold its own against bigger cities for fostering creative American genius in commerce. It has strong traditions of tinkering and innovation, practical organization and mechanical dreaming, as well as small-town neighborliness. Just south of the old National Road that spans the Midwest was the home of James Ritty, who in 1879 invented the cash register, that indispensable instrument of retail trade that led to the establishment in 1884 of the National Cash Register Co. Tom Watson Sr., an employee of NCR, feuded with owner John Henry Patterson and went off in a huff to found International Business Machines, better known by its initials, IBM. In 1887, George Huffman moved the Davis Sewing Machine Co. to Dayton, and in 1892 began producing Huffy bicycles. Around the same time, Wilbur and Orville Wright experimented with kites and gliders and constructed the first wind tunnel in the world and the first heavier-than-air flying machine, which they took to windy Kitty Hawk, North Carolina, for a test flight in 1903. A few years later, Dayton's Charles Kettering invented the automatic starter for cars and became one of the leaders of the budding automobile industry. Not long ago, Montgomery County was home to the most patents per capita of any county in the United States. Boston took away that title.

After some recent time when Dayton's economy sputtered, it has been bouncing back. During the latest recession, DHL closed an air cargo hub at the Wilmington Air Park in Clinton County, costing the region 10,000 jobs. In a major psychological and economic blow for the city, NCR departed to suburban Atlanta in 2009, taking away Dayton's last *Fortune* 500 company and the 1,300 jobs it provided. The economic picture has brightened since then. General Electric, which has a huge presence in southwest Ohio, employs 1,200 in the Dayton area. It builds jet engines here, and has a center that develops advanced electric power systems for aircraft, ships and hybrid automobiles, including a partnership with Boeing.

Dayton-area universities and Wright-Patterson Air Force Base have made the area a magnet for technology companies. That includes the world's most advanced centrifuge, which is used for aerospace medical research. Wright-Patt has more than 27,000 military and civilian employees. In 2014, *Site*

Selection magazine ranked Dayton as number-two, behind Greensboro, North Carolina, for business expansion projects in cities with fewer than 1 million people. In December 2016, Bloomberg News listed Dayton among the post-industrial cities with bargain real estate and pockets of economic promise. About half of its home-buyers are younger than 35.

The 10th Congressional District of Ohio includes all of Dayton and surrounding Montgomery County, which is about three-fourths of the district. To the east, it includes Greene County, including upscale Beaver Creek and middle-class Fairborn, and most of rural Fayette County. In Washington Court House, the street grid is arrayed in a northwesterly-southeasterly direction (rather than the classic north/east orientation) so that each face of its courthouse gets some sunshine. This has been a Republican-leaning district, although not overwhelmingly so. After Mitt Romney got 50 percent in 2012. Donald Trump inched up the GOP vote to 51 percent, a smaller increase than in other districts in Ohio.

ELEVENTH DISTRICT

Marcia Fudge (D)

Elected 2008, 5th term; b. Oct 29, 1952, Cleveland; Cleveland State University Marshall College of Law (OH), J.D.; Ohio State University, B.S.; Baptist; Single.

Elected Office: Warrensville Heights Mayor, 2000-2008.

Professional Career: Practicing attorney; Aide, U.S. Rep. Stephanie Tubbs Jones, 1991-2000.

DC Office: 2344 RHOB 20515, 202-225-7032, Fax: 202-225-1339, fudge.house.gov.

State Offices: Akron, 330-835-4758; Warrensville Heights, 216-522-4900.

Committees: *Agriculture*: Conservation & Forestry (RMM), Nutrition. *Education & the Workforce*: Early Childhood, Elementary & Secondary Education, Health, Employment, Labor & Pensions.

Group Ratings

	ADA	ACLU	AFL-CIO	LCV	ITI	COC	HAFA	ACU	CFG	FRC
2016	-	94%	-	100%	67%	64%	14%	0%	0%	0%
2015	100%	C	100%	91%	C	45%	C	0%	0%	0%

Almanac Ratings 2015

	Economy	Social	Foreign	Composite
Liberal	98%	100%	93%	97%
Conservative	2%	0%	7%	3%

Key Votes of the 114th Congress

1. Keystone Pipeline	N	5. Puerto Rico Debt	N	9. Offenses by Aliens	N
2. Trade Deals	N	6. Medical Marijuana	Y	10. Troops in Iraq	Y
3. Export-Import Bank	Y	7. Sanctuary Cities	N	11. Homeland Security $$	Y
4. Debt Ceiling Increase	Y	8. Armor-piercing Bullets	N	12. Trade Adjustment aid	Y

Election Results

Election	Name (Party)	Vote (%)	Cand. Spent	Ind. Exp. Support	Ind. Exp. Oppose
2016 General	Marcia Fudge (D)	242,921 (80%)	$549,077		
	Beverly A. Goldstein (R)	59,769 (20%)	$16,290		
2016 Primary	Marcia Fudge (D)	(100%)			

Prior winning percentages: 2014 (80%), 2012 (100%), 2010 (83%), 2008 (85%)

Democrat Marcia Fudge, elected in 2008, has parlayed her organizational and networking skills into leadership of the Congressional Black Caucus and an active role in the Democratic Caucus. Following the 2016 election, she was an outspoken advocate of change among Democrats, including the candidacy of Rep. Tim Ryan for House Minority Leader.

Like many African Americans of her generation, Fudge was greatly influenced by the civil rights movement and got active politically when she was young. During high school, Fudge volunteered with get-out-the-vote efforts for "Young Folks for Stokes," young people helping to elect Carl Stokes as mayor of Cleveland. After getting her bachelor's in business administration from Ohio State University, she received her law degree from Cleveland State University. She practiced mainly criminal defense law in the Cleveland area, along with some probate and corporate work, until she went to work for her mentor and friend Rep. Stephanie Tubbs Jones.

Fudge and Tubbs Jones had met as members of the national Delta Sigma Theta Sorority alumnae association. Fudge later served as national president of the group of predominantly African-American women. When Tubbs Jones became the Cuyahoga County prosecutor, Fudge was her administrative assistant. When Tubbs Jones was elected to Congress in 1998, Fudge followed her to Washington as chief of staff. After a few years, Fudge felt the pull of elected office. When the Warrensville Heights mayor resigned, she won and became the first African-American woman to be elected mayor of the city. She focused on economic development and claimed credit for creating 3,000 jobs and bringing in $500 million for development and infrastructure.

Tubbs Jones died unexpectedly from a cerebral aneurysm, after having won the Democratic primary for another term. Fudge called each member of the district's Democratic Executive Committee, which selected a replacement on the ballot. She explained why she would be the best choice to carry on Tubbs Jones' legacy. The committee nominated Fudge with 175 votes. Former state Sen. C.J. Prentiss was runner-up among the four candidates, with 64 votes. Fudge won the general election with 85 percent of the vote and had no Republican challenger for the special election.

Fudge has been a staunch and passionate liberal. As chair of the CBC in 2013-14, she advocated on behalf of low-income African Americans in assailing the automatic across-the-board spending cuts after the two parties failed to reach a budget agreement. "If we allow this sequester to happen, we're saying that our political agendas are more important than the ability to take care of our families," she said. When lawmakers unveiled a statue of civil rights icon Rosa Parks at the Capitol, she noted the irony of the event occurring on the same day that several conservative Supreme Court justices raised sharp questions about the Voting Rights Act. Fudge earlier drew attention for her proposal to rein in the powers of the independent Office of Congressional Ethics, after it found that Fudge's chief of staff "improperly influenced" information given to the House Ethics Committee about an annual Caribbean trip for Black Caucus members. In 2009, she filed a bill to place limits on the OCE's jurisdiction and to bar "premature publication" of its findings.

Representing an urban area, Fudge has been outspoken on the Agriculture Committee in defending food stamps. When committee Republicans called for cutting the program, she said in 2013 that the lawmakers "literally do not believe there is poverty in this country." In 2017, she became the senior Democrat on the panel's Conservation and Forestry Subcommittee. Although her district had few farms or forests, Fudge said that such resources were plentiful across Ohio and that she would advocate policies that would grow the economy and increase jobs. During the previous two years, she was ranking Democrat on the Education and the Workforce Subcommittee on Early Childhood, Elementary and Secondary Education, where she helped to enact bipartisan changes in the No Child Left Behind Act. In December 2015, she praised the new law as formula-based and said that it "distributes dollars that fill resource and opportunity gaps based on need and population."

Fudge has been active in the national party. At the Democratic convention in Philadelphia in 2016, she presided for many hours after Rep. Debbie Wasserman Schultz unexpectedly stepped down as DNC chairwoman. After the election, she said that Democrats "have to build our party from the ground up and I think that we've not been doing that." She was a vocal supporter of her neighboring Rep. Ryan in his challenge to Nancy Pelosi. Following the leadership vote, Fudge said that the outcome was a win for the rebels and "a great first step" for change. "I think anytime you've been in office as long as Nancy and you lose a full third of your caucus, it's significant," she told *Politico*.

At home, Fudge focused on the continuing urban decay and tensions in Cleveland. In May 2015, she embraced as "a turning point" for police-community relations the consent decree between the city and the Justice Department that promised systemic changes. In her overwhelmingly Democratic district, Fudge has faced token opposition in primary and general elections.

Cleveland, Akron

Population		Race and Ethnicity		Income	
Total	705,697	White	37.8%	Median Income	$34,045 (429 out of 435)
Land area	244	Black	53.2%	Under $50,000	64.2%
Pop/ sq mi	2886.8	Latino	3.9%	$50,000-$99,999	22.6%
Born in state	73.1%	Asian	2.4%	$100,000-$199,999	10.0%
		Two races	2.3%	$200,000 or more	3.2%
		Other	0.4%	Poverty Rate	27.4%

Age Groups		Education		Health Insurance	
Under 18	22.7%	H.S grad or less	44.2%	With health insurance coverage	88.6%
18-34	23.9%	Some college	29.8%		
35-64	38.4%	College Degree, 4 yr	14.4%		
Over 64	15.0%	Post grad	11.7%		

Work		Military		Public Assistance	
White Collar	36.7%	Veteran	7.5%	Cash public assistance income	6.0%
Sales and Service	45.3%	Active Duty	0.0%	Food stamp/SNAP benefits	27.2%
Blue Collar	18.0%				
Government	4.0%				

Voter Turnout			
2015 Total Citizens 18+	529,306	2016 House Turnout as % CVAP	57%
2016 House turnout	302,686	2014 House Turnout as % CVAP	33%

2012 Presidential Vote		
Barack Obama	299,107	(83%)
Mitt Romney	57,787	(16%)

2016 Presidential Vote		
Hillary Clinton	260,311	(80%)
Donald Trump	55,013	(17%)

Cook Partisan Voting Index: D+32

Like most great American cities, Cleveland grew in great bursts of migration, during periods when the economy expanded and attracted low-wage workers from around the country and the world. After the Ohio and Erie Canal connected Lake Erie with the Ohio River in the 1830s, Cleveland became a critical destination for goods traveling from the north to the interior and vice versa. Its greatest surge of growth started in the 1890s and lasted through the 1920s, when the city was transformed from a bustling city of 250,000 to a burgeoning metropolis of over 900,000. Tens of thousands of immigrants from central and southern Europe arrived, looking for jobs in the steel and automobile factories. Bohemians came to the tightly packed neighborhoods along Broadway, Hungarians settled in the northeast, Jews lived north of University Circle along East 105th Street, and Italians ran produce markets along Mayfield Road. As heavy industries geared up for World War II and enjoyed years of prosperous growth afterward, another surge of immigrants came, this time from the South. African Americans settled on the east side and grew from just 2 percent of Cleveland's population in 1910 to 38 percent by 1970.

These bursts of migration led to political changes. A string of ethnic mayors - Frank Lausche, Anthony Celebrezze, Ralph Locher - was followed by the election in 1967 of Carl Stokes, the nation's first black big-city mayor. Cleveland had racially polarized politics for much of the 1970s. Even so, the west side stayed mostly white, and Cleveland did not have a black majority until the 2000 census, when its declining population was 51 percent black; its 2015 population declined to 388,000 and was only 42 percent of what it was in 1950. In a hopeful sign, the loss of 81,000 people from 2000 to 2010 was reduced to only 9,000 in the next five years. Nearly all Clevelanders exalted in the NBA title that their Cavaliers, led by Akron-native LeBron James, won in 2016. This was the first professional championship for the city since 1964, when the football Browns won the NFL. A few months later, the Indians made it to extra innings of the seventh game of the World Series, before losing to the longer-suffering Chicago Cubs.

For decades, Akron was the rubber capital of the world. The four largest tire companies had their headquarters and factories here, with close to 60,000 workers in the rubber industry in the 1930s. By the 1980s, those plants had largely shut down, except for the production of a few specialty tires. Goodrich, Firestone and General left town to manufacture tires with cheaper labor in the South, and then outside the country. Goodyear remained, with an impressive new office building plus its innovation center. One positive result was that the air was cleaner, and the smell of rubber was gone. The population dropped from 290,000 in 1960 to 198,000 in 2015. Like Cleveland, Akron has benefited from immigration. Many refugees have moved into North Hill - from Myanmar and Bhutan, and more recently from Iraq and Syria. The International Institute of Akron operates a resettlement program for refugees, many with skills in science and technology.

The 11th Congressional District of Ohio includes most of the east side of Cleveland, plus the suburbs just to the east. Some of these areas - East Cleveland, Warrensville Heights - are mostly black. Others, like Shaker Heights, are mostly white. Still others, like the old Slavic enclave of Garfield Heights, are populated by the heirs of the ethnic whites who settled Cleveland in the early 20th century. The district includes exurbs of Cleveland, minority segments of downtown, plus Fairlawn and a few other suburbs of Akron. Nearly one-third of Summit County is in the district, which accounts for about 15 percent of its population. The 11th exists for two reasons: To provide a minority-majority district in compliance with the Voting Rights Act, and to satisfy the desire of Republicans in control of redistricting to place as many Democrats as possible in a single district and protect Republicans in nearby districts. The 11th is 53 percent black, and is among the most heavily Democratic districts in the nation. Hillary Clinton took 80% in 2016.

TWELFTH DISTRICT

Pat Tiberi (R)

Elected 2000, 9th term; b. Oct 21, 1962, Columbus; Ohio State University, B.A.; Roman Catholic; Married (Denice Tiberi); 4 children (triplets).

Elected Office: OH House, 1992-2000, Majority Leader, 1999-2000.

Professional Career: Staff Assistant, U.S. Rep. John Kasich, 1984-1992; Realtor, ReMax Achievers, 1995-2000.

DC Office: 1203 LHOB 20515, 202-225-5355, Fax: 202-226-4523, tiberi.house.gov.

State Offices: Worthington, 614-523-2555.

Committees: *Joint Economic (Chmn)*. *Ways & Means*: Health (Chmn), Tax Policy.

Group Ratings

	ADA	ACLU	AFL-CIO	LCV	ITI	COC	HAFA	ACU	CFG	FRC
2016	-	5%	-	0%	100%	100%	52%	76%	64%	100%
2015	0%	C	33%	3%	C	100%	C	63%	47%	92%

Almanac Ratings 2015

	Economy	Social	Foreign	Composite
Liberal	14%	10%	10%	12%
Conservative	86%	90%	90%	88%

Key Votes of the 114th Congress

1. Keystone Pipeline	Y	5. Puerto Rico Debt	N	9. Offenses by Aliens	Y
2. Trade Deals	Y	6. Medical Marijuana	N	10. Troops in Iraq	N
3. Export-Import Bank	Y	7. Sanctuary Cities	Y	11. Homeland Security $$	Y
4. Debt Ceiling Increase	Y	8. Armor-piercing Bullets	Y	12. Trade Adjustment aid	Y

Election Results

Election	Name (Party)	Vote (%)		Cand. Spent	Ind. Exp. Support	Ind. Exp. Oppose
2016 General	Pat Tiberi (R)	251,266	(67%)	$1,539,328		
	Ed Albertson (D)	112,638	(30%)	$19,741		
	Joe Manchik (G)	13,630	(4%)			
2016 Primary	Pat Tiberi (R)		(100%)			

Prior winning percentages: 2014 (68%), 2012 (64%), 2010 (56%), 2008 (55%), 2006 (57%), 2004 (62%), 2002 (64%), 2000 (53%)

Republican Pat Tiberi, elected in 2000, has been an active and influential member of the powerful Ways and Means Committee, where he chairs the Health Subcommittee. Tiberi has been an adviser to Speaker Paul Ryan and earlier was one of Speaker John Boehner's closest allies. He has shown his own ambitions in the House, and beyond.

The son of Italian immigrants, Tiberi grew up in Columbus and graduated from Ohio State University. He worked as a real estate agent and then as an aide to Republican Rep. John Kasich. He recalled to *The Columbus Dispatch* that Kasich won him over by blasting AC/DC's hard rock on the car radio. "I thought, 'Man, this guy listens to the same music, and he's a Republican congressman,'" Tiberi said. "It broke my entire image of what a Republican congressman is." Kasich helped Tiberi win a seat in the state House, where he became majority leader and supported business-friendly legislation and tort law changes. When Kasich announced his retirement from the House, Tiberi won support to replace his mentor from most of the Republican establishment and the U.S. Chamber of Commerce. He faced a noisy but ineffective primary challenge from state Sen. Gene Watts, who sought to rally conservatives. Tiberi won 73%-21%.

The resounding victory gave him a big boost against Maryellen O'Shaughnessy, a Democratic Columbus City Council member. She had a compelling personal story as the single mother of a 10-year-old son. Tiberi played up his Columbus roots and his membership in the Ohio State marching band. He held O'Shaughnessy responsible for negative Democratic Party ads that labeled him a defender of insurance companies on the issue of affordable prescription drugs. This was a closely watched House race during the tight 2000 election. With more campaign help from Kasich, Tiberi won 53%-44%. Tiberi has not faced significant opposition in his district, especially after it became more Republican in the 2012 redistricting.

Tiberi's voting record has been faithfully Republican, though his *Almanac* vote ratings for 2015 leaned to the center of the House in each of the three issue areas. He supported expansion of the Children's Health Insurance Program and a Democratic overhaul of food safety laws in 2009. A year earlier, at Boehner's urging, he backed the final version of the Troubled Asset Relief Program after initially opposing it.

In the majority, Tiberi chaired the Select Revenue Subcommittee at Ways and Means. He pledged to scrap the income tax code and replace it with a simpler version. He blamed indifference from the Obama administration for the lack of progress. In 2015, he switched to chair the Trade Subcommittee. He spent six months in arduous negotiations to gain House support for trade promotion authority for President Barack Obama until he, Ways and Means Chairman Paul Ryan and GOP leaders were confident they had secured a majority. He tried to rally public support for the proposed Trans-Pacific Partnership. "The pie's going to get smaller because the world is a smaller place. Either we engage and move ahead, or we fall behind," he told business officials in New Albany. He played a leading role in the enactment that year of the accompanying Trade Facilitation and Trade Enforcement Act, which addressed customs procedures and other trade issues. The measure, he said, gave Customs officials "the tools they need to enforce our laws in a timely and transparent way."

Tiberi has been a behind-the-scenes operator in GOP internal politics. He was campaign manager for Boehner's successful bid for majority leader in early 2006, and he later helped Boehner fix organizational problems at the National Republican Congressional Committee. He and Oklahoma Republican Tom Cole served as vote-counters for Cathy McMorris Rodgers of Washington in her successful 2012 bid to chair the Republican Conference.

When more than two dozen House Republicans voted for someone other than Boehner in the January 2015 selection of the Speaker, Tiberi was reported to be among his close allies urging penalties for the rebels and making the case that the Speaker had broad party support. As some conservatives continued to undermine Boehner, Tiberi urged disciplinary actions against lawmakers who abandoned the GOP on what were viewed as routine parliamentary votes. In October 2015, after Ryan replaced Boehner as Speaker and gave up his Ways and Means chairmanship, Tiberi ran for the position against Rep. Kevin Brady of Texas. In what reportedly was a close contest, Ryan sided with Brady - at least in part because of Brady's seniority. Tiberi gained impressive consolation prizes: chairman of the Joint Economic Committee, in addition to the Health Subcommittee.

Tiberi has moved beyond the confines of his congressional district. He chaired the steering committee for Kasich's 2016 presidential campaign, in what became an often bitter clash with Donald Trump during and after the contest for the GOP nomination. In October 2016, following the release of the decade-old video with Trump's lewd comments about women, Tiberi said that Trump's "comments and behavior were reprehensible, vulgar and extremely disrespectful." He added that "Americans deserve better choices for the highest office in the land" and "Trump should consider stepping aside."

Months before the 2016 election, Tiberi said publicly that he was thinking seriously about running against Democratic Sen. Sherrod Brown in 2018. Even when Ohio Treasurer Josh Mandel announced soon after the election that he would seek a rematch against Brown, Tiberi kept the door open to the statewide bid. In May 2017, he announced that he will seek reelection in 2018 and dropped his interest in a Senate campaign. He took a couple of shots at Mandel by saying that he would have been the best GOP challenger to Brown and that Mandel suffered from "the baggage" of his earlier unsuccessful Senate bid. Staying in the House increased the prospect that Tiberi someday will chair Ways and Means.

Central Ohio: Northern Columbus Metro

Population		**Race and Ethnicity**		**Income**	
Total	747,035	White	86.9%	Median Income	$65,680 (89 out of 435)
Land area	2,272	Black	4.3%		
Pop/ sq mi	328.8	Latino	2.3%	Under $50,000	38.7%
Born in state	73.3%	Asian	3.5%	$50,000-$99,999	31.0%
		Two races	2.8%	$100,000-$199,999	23.6%
Age Groups		Other	0.3%	$200,000 or more	6.8%
Under 18	24.1%			Poverty Rate	10.5%
18-34	21.4%	**Education**			
35-64	41.2%	H.S grad or less	34.7%	**Health Insurance**	
Over 64	13.3%	Some college	26.4%	With health insurance coverage	92.6%
		College Degree, 4 yr	24.4%		
Work		Post grad	14.5%		
White Collar	44.9%			**Public Assistance**	
Sales and Service	38.3%	**Military**		Cash public assistance income	2.0%
Blue Collar	16.8%	Veteran	8.5%		
Government	5.8%	Active Duty	0.1%	Food stamp/SNAP benefits	10.3%

Voter Turnout			
2015 Total Citizens 18+	551,037	2016 House Turnout as % CVAP	69%
2016 House turnout	377,534	2014 House Turnout as % CVAP	41%

2012 Presidential Vote		
Mitt Romney	207,339	(54%)
Barack Obama	167,507	(44%)

2016 Presidential Vote		
Donald Trump	205,978	(52%)
Hillary Clinton	162,218	(41%)
Gary Johnson	14,308	(4%)

Cook Partisan Voting Index: R+7

Columbus was long the forgotten city in Ohio. Overshadowed by its much larger cousins for most of its existence - Cincinnati to the south and Cleveland to the north - it was best-known to most Americans as the subject of James Thurber's biting satire, *My Life and Hard Times*. It remained a surprisingly small town for the capital of such an important state; its population in 1920 was roughly the same as Akron's. Today, Columbus is a major metropolis and, with 850,000 people in 2015, has breezed past the total of Cleveland and Cincinnati (though those two cities still have slightly more populous metropolitan areas). Columbus' Franklin County passed the 1 million mark in the 1990s and has grown close to 1.3 million.

With this explosive growth has come sprawl in all directions. Most American cities grew up around a coastline or river, which tended to direct their growth. With its location near the geographic center of the state, Columbus was selected as the state capital in 1812 mainly as a way of placating other aspirants for the designation. The plains to the north and west do little to inhibit growth, while the rolling hills that mark the end of the Appalachian Plateau to the south and east provide no meaningful barrier to expansion.

The 12th Congressional District contains a northern slice of the city, with portions of the University District - bordering the football stadium of Ohio State University - filled with pre-World War II Craftsman-style bungalows, as well as the more spacious homes of Clintonville, one of the original "streetcar" communities. It takes in suburbs to the north and east: Worthington, increasingly indistinguishable from the encroaching city; newly fashionable Dublin, with its lush Muirfield Village Golf Club; Gahanna; and upscale New Albany. With its local warehouse and data centers, Amazon offers two-hour shipping service in the Columbus area. To the north is fast-growing Delaware County, home to the highly-rated Columbus Zoo and solidly Republican. It last voted for a Democratic presidential candidate in 1916. Its upscale suburbs help give Delaware the highest median income of any county in Ohio.

Outside of Columbus' orbit, Licking County is home to picturesque Granville and Denison, its small liberal arts college. Industrial parks across the county have attracted new manufacturing companies. Newark is an old manufacturing town in decay, including the departure of Longaberger Basket Co. from its unusual seven-story basket-shaped building. Rural Zanesville, with its famous "Y"-shaped bridge, provides the only real center of Democratic voting strength outside of Franklin County. Franklin is the population center in the district, with about one-third of the vote, but Delaware and Licking are not far behind.

Filling the new 3rd district with Democratic precincts following the 2012 redistricting produced a significant shift in the 12th. A district that Barack Obama won in 2008 with 54 percent was transformed into one that John McCain would have won with 54 percent; Mitt Romney replicated that number. In 2016, Donald Trump took 52 percent of the district vote.

THIRTEENTH DISTRICT

Tim Ryan (D)

Elected 2002, 8th term; b. Jul 16, 1973, Niles; Bowling Green State University (OH), B.A.; Franklin Pierce Law Center (NH), J.D.; Youngstown State University (OH), Att.; Dickinson School of Law's International Law Program (Italy), Att.; Catholic; Married (Andrea Zetts); 1 child; 2 stepchildren.

Elected Office: OH Senate, 2000-2002.

Professional Career: Aide, U.S. Rep. Jim Traficant, 1995-1997.

DC Office: 1126 LHOB 20515, 202-225-5261, Fax: 202-225-3719, timryan.house.gov.

State Offices: Akron, 330-630-7311; Warren, 800-856-4152; Youngstown, 330-740-0193.

Committees: *Appropriations*: Defense, Legislative Branch (RMM), Military Construction, Veterans Affairs & Related Agencies.

Group Ratings

	ADA	ACLU	AFL-CIO	LCV	ITI	COC	HAFA	ACU	CFG	FRC
2016	-	100%	-	100%	100%	57%	20%	0%	0%	0%
2015	80%	C	100%	91%	C	53%	C	8%	6%	0%

Almanac Ratings 2015

	Economy	Social	Foreign	Composite
Liberal	84%	90%	80%	85%
Conservative	17%	10%	20%	15%

Key Votes of the 114th Congress

1. Keystone Pipeline	N	5. Puerto Rico Debt	N	9. Offenses by Aliens	NV
2. Trade Deals	N	6. Medical Marijuana	Y	10. Troops in Iraq	Y
3. Export-Import Bank	Y	7. Sanctuary Cities	N	11. Homeland Security $$	Y
4. Debt Ceiling Increase	Y	8. Armor-piercing Bullets	N	12. Trade Adjustment aid	Y

Election Results

Election	Name (Party)	Vote (%)		Cand. Spent	Ind. Exp. Support	Ind. Exp. Oppose
2016 General	Tim Ryan (D)	208,610	(68%)	$1,040,561		
	Richard Morckel (R)	99,377	(32%)			
2016 Primary	Tim Ryan (D)	86,203	(89%)			
	John Luchansky (D)	10,296	(11%)			

Prior winning percentages: 2014 (69%), 2012 (73%), 2010 (54%), 2008 (78%), 2006 (80%), 2004 (77%), 2002 (51%)

Tim Ryan, a Democrat elected in 2002 at age 29, has been a pro-union centrist who is usually a party regular. His views on guns and abortion have moved to the left. Following the 2016 election, he criticized Minority Leader Nancy Pelosi's handling of that year's campaign and he challenged her bid for another term. He lost the Democratic Caucus vote, 134-63, which many viewed as a demand for change and an indication that Ryan might be part of the post-Pelosi leadership. Several times, he has considered a bid for statewide office in Ohio.

Ryan grew up in Niles, was a star quarterback before a knee injury ended his career, and graduated from Bowling Green State University. His first job was with Rep. James Traficant, a blue-collar and often maverick Democrat. In 2000, after graduating from Franklin Pierce Law Center, Ryan was elected to the state Senate. His opening to run for Congress came when the increasingly flaky Traficant was forced to resign in disgrace after his conviction in 2002 for racketeering and bribery.

Akron-based Rep. Tom Sawyer, a Democrat who had been thrown into the district by redistricting, was the early favorite to succeed Traficant. He outspent Ryan nearly 6-to-1 and he had the perks of incumbency. But Sawyer had voted for the 1993 North American Free Trade Agreement, and he was one of the few Rust Belt Democrats to vote for normalizing trade relations with China. Ryan hammered on these votes in the Mahoning Valley, where it is gospel that free trade drove the region's high-paying jobs abroad. Ryan was endorsed by the National Rifle Association in a district with many hunters. With greater voter intensity in Youngstown than in Akron, Ryan defeated Sawyer 41%-27%. In the general, Ryan slammed state Rep. Ann Womer Benjamin and the GOP Legislature for votes that he said led to higher tuition at state universities. Republicans fired back with ads highlighting several disorderly conduct charges lodged against Ryan while he was in college. The district's Democratic leanings and Ryan's labor support proved decisive. He won 51 percent of the vote to 34 percent for Womer Benjamin and 15 percent for Traficant, who ran from jail as an independent.

Ryan has leaned to the left on economic and foreign policy. His splits with Democrats on abortion rights and gun control have placed him closer to the center on social issues, and he has worked with others to seek common ground. After the deadly school massacre in Newtown, Connecticut, he held meetings with gun enthusiasts and law enforcement officials to try to "thread the needle" on a solution to gun violence. With Democratic abortion-rights advocate Rosa DeLauro of Connecticut, he sponsored the "Reducing the Need for Abortion and Supporting Parents Act," with federal dollars to fight teen pregnancy and increased aid for women who become pregnant; Democratic activists depicted this as a move toward party consensus on a difficult issue. In January 2015, he said that his position had "evolved" further. "I have come to believe that we must trust women and families - not politicians - to make the best decisions for their lives," he wrote in the *Akron Beacon-Journal*.

In 2006, Ryan endeared himself to Pelosi when he was a vocal backer of her close ally John Murtha of Pennsylvania in his unsuccessful bid for majority leader against Steny Hoyer of Maryland. That earned Ryan a seat on the Appropriations Committee. He used that niche to secure earmarked projects for his hard-pressed district. Those practices ended when Speaker John Boehner from politically distinct southwest Ohio ended earmarks after Republicans regained control in 2011. Reflecting his district, Ryan has remained a harsh critic of international trade deals. For several years, he sponsored the Chinese Currency Act, a proposal to counter China's alleged manipulation and undervaluation of its currency. He co-chairs the Congressional Manufacturing Caucus, which seeks to revive the nation's industrial base and to revise its trade policy.

Ryan has drawn attention for his meditation. He attended a five-day retreat after the 2008 election, turning off his two BlackBerrys and gradually reducing how often he talked until he maintained a 36-hour period of silence. "My mind and body were in the same place at the same time, synchronized in a way I had rarely experienced," he told the *Beacon Journal.* He wrote a book in 2012, *A Mindful Nation: How a Simple Practice Can Help Us Reduce Stress, Improve Performance, and Recapture the American Spirit*, and he has spent 45 minutes a day practicing "mindfulness" - something he says stressed-out Washingtonians and corporate executives should try. In 2015, he expanded his spiritual revival to include healthier eating, with a book, *The Real Food Revolution: Healthy Eating, Green Groceries, and the Return of the American Family Farm.*

When House Democrats convened after the traumatic 2016 election, Ryan joined those calling for political introspection. Some Democrats, mostly junior, were looking for an alternative to Pelosi, who had been Democratic Leader for 14 years, all but four of them in the minority. They urged Ryan to run. In a letter to House Democrats, he agreed. "Keeping our leadership team completely unchanged will simply lead to more disappointment in future elections," he wrote.

Although his voting record was more centrist and consensus-driven than that of Pelosi, his two-week campaign was more generational and geographic, especially in the wake of their party's setbacks during the presidential and congressional elections in places like Ohio and elsewhere in the nation's heartland. Following Pelosi's victory, Ryan ironically became the senior Democrat on the Appropriations Subcommittee on the Legislative Branch, a niche that gave him an opportunity to address the working needs of many House members.

Ryan has not faced serious reelection problems. His political dilemma at home has been a repeated refusal to step up the ladder or other offices. Pelosi and her allies mocked his contest against her as a way to get more publicity for a statewide bid. He considered a run for the Senate in 2006 but decided against challenging the more senior Democrat Sherrod Brown. Democratic Gov. Ted Strickland discussed a shared ticket with Ryan in 2010, but Ryan decided to remain in the House, largely because of his new assignment on Appropriations. He took another serious look at running for governor in 2014 after Strickland said that he wouldn't run, but announced that it still wasn't worth the risk to give up his Appropriations seat. He turned down the opportunity to run for the Senate in 2016, with the explanation that he wanted to be close to his "new and growing family." In February 2017, he said that he would not run for governor in 2018 because " I believe the best way to serve my community, my state and my country is to remain in the United States Congress."

In his mid-40s and with Democrats facing demands for change, Ryan likely will have other opportunities - at home and in the Capitol.

Northeast Ohio: Youngstown, Akron Area

Population		**Race and Ethnicity**		**Income**	
Total	713,291	White	81.5%	Median Income	$41,744 (374 out of 435)
Land area	894	Black	11.3%		
Pop/ sq mi	797.6	Latino	3.1%		
Born in state	77.3%	Asian	1.5%	Under $50,000	58.1%
		Two races	2.4%	$50,000-$99,999	29.5%
Age Groups		Other	0.3%	$100,000-$199,999	11.0%
Under 18	20.5%			$200,000 or more	1.6%
18-34	23.1%	**Education**		Poverty Rate	18.9%
35-64	39.6%	H.S grad or less	50.7%		
Over 64	16.8%	Some college	28.3%	**Health Insurance**	
		College Degree, 4 yr	14.1%	With health insurance coverage	89.6%
Work		Post grad	7.0%		
White Collar	29.5%				
Sales and Service	44.8%	**Military**		**Public Assistance**	
Blue Collar	25.6%	Veteran	9.6%	Cash public assistance income	4.3%
Government	4.6%	Active Duty	0.0%		
				Food stamp/SNAP benefits	17.6%

Voter Turnout			
2015 Total Citizens 18+	555,296	2016 House Turnout as % CVAP	55%
2016 House turnout	308,004	2014 House Turnout as % CVAP	31%

2012 Presidential Vote		
Barack Obama	212,082	(63%)
Mitt Romney	120,913	(36%)

2016 Presidential Vote		
Hillary Clinton	163,600	(51%)
Donald Trump	142,738	(44%)
Gary Johnson	8,810	(3%)

Cook Partisan Voting Index: D+7

For nearly a century, the Mahoning Valley - between the Lake Erie docks that unload iron ore from Great Lakes freighters and the coalfields of western Pennsylvania and West Virginia - was a steel capital of the United States. The first blast furnace opened in 1803, and the first coal mine opened in 1826. Canals followed, and in 1892 the first steel mill was built. The valley soon filled up with mills, converters and furnaces. But big-steel management and unions allowed foreign producers to gain a technological edge in the 1950s and 1960s, and worldwide overcapacity in steel grew as almost every developing country decided it needed its own steel mills. After a 119-day strike in 1959, an agreement between the United Steelworkers and management boosted wages and fringe benefits to levels that helped price domestic steel out of the market. Import restrictions kept the furnaces hot for a while, but the oil shock of the 1970s produced sharply higher energy prices and a collapse in the U.S. auto and steel markets. Every plant in the Mahoning Valley closed, with a loss of 40,000 jobs; the public schools were closed for a few months because city revenues fell so precipitously. In the early 1980s, Youngstown had one of the nation's highest unemployment rates.

Steel has since revived, although not at its previous peak and not in Youngstown. The high-wage living standard of the area vanished. Organized crime infiltrated local government, and a federal investigation in the late 1990s led to more than 70 convictions; among those sentenced were a prosecutor, a sheriff and a congressman. In February 2016, Mayor John McNally pleaded guilty to four misdemeanor charges for conspiracy and bribery in a rental-property scheme. He received no jail time, and remained in office. In 2015, Youngstown's population was 65,000, little more than a third its size in the 1950s. The city has struggled to rebound, though it managed to attract a few high-tech firms, including the Turning Technologies software company, whose goal was to make technology more affordable and user-friendly. The region has also become a locus for shale drilling. Still, there is some benefit to the weak economy. In 2016, the Youngstown area had the lowest home prices in the nation. The median price for single-family home sales was $85,400.

The 13th Congressional District of Ohio encompasses most of the Mahoning Valley industrial area: Youngstown (though not its southern Mahoning County suburbs), Warren and most of Trumbull County. It includes nearly all of Portage County and the less-minority parts of Summit County and Akron. Mahoning, Trumbull and Summit have similar shares of the population. It contains two loci of 1970s protest - Kent State University, where four students were killed by National Guardsmen, and Lordstown, site of the General Motors plant where workers purposely built shoddy cars to protest the tedium of the assembly line. Morale at Lordstown has improved, with its 4,000 workers who received GM profit-sharing checks of up to $12,000 in 2016. This Rustbelt patchwork is the least Democratic and least urban of the four Democratic districts in Ohio. Barack Obama twice won a bit more than 60 percent of the vote. Support for Hillary Clinton fell to 51 percent in 2016. The Democratic lead in Mahoning County dropped from 63%-35% in 2012 to 50%-47%. Whether Donald Trump could retain support in this area was viewed as a key test of his presidency.

FOURTEENTH DISTRICT

Dave Joyce (R)

Elected 2012, 3rd term; b. Mar 17, 1957, Cleveland; University of Dayton (OH), B.S.; University of Dayton (OH), J.D.; Roman Catholic; Married (Kelly Joyce); 3 children.

Elected Office: Prosecutor, Geauga County, 1988-2013.

Professional Career: Public defender, Geauga County, 1985-1988; Public defender, Cuyahoga County, 1983-1984.

DC Office: 1124 LHOB 20515, 202-225-5731, Fax: 202-225-3307, joyce.house.gov.

State Offices: Painesville, 440-352-3939; Twinsburg, 330-357-4139.

Committees: *Appropriations*: Energy & Water Development & Related Agencies, Interior, Environment & Related Agencies, Transportation, HUD & Related Agencies.

Group Ratings

	ADA	ACLU	AFL-CIO	LCV	ITI	COC	HAFA	ACU	CFG	FRC
2016	-	5%	-	5%	83%	100%	52%	50%	54%	92%
2015	5%	C	42%	6%	C	95%	C	50%	48%	83%

Almanac Ratings 2015

	Economy	Social	Foreign	Composite
Liberal	24%	20%	5%	16%
Conservative	76%	80%	95%	84%

Key Votes of the 114th Congress

1. Keystone Pipeline	Y	5. Puerto Rico Debt	N	9. Offenses by Aliens	Y
2. Trade Deals	N	6. Medical Marijuana	Y	10. Troops in Iraq	N
3. Export-Import Bank	N	7. Sanctuary Cities	Y	11. Homeland Security $$	N
4. Debt Ceiling Increase	Y	8. Armor-piercing Bullets	Y	12. Trade Adjustment aid	Y

Election Results

Election	Name (Party)	Vote (%)	Cand. Spent	Ind. Exp. Support	Ind. Exp. Oppose
2016 General	Dave Joyce (R)	219,191 (63%)	$1,954,616	$537,621	$68,210
	Michael Wager (D)	130,907 (37%)	$228,277		
2016 Primary	Dave Joyce (R)	78,765 (65%)			
	Matt Lynch (R)	43,279 (36%)			

Prior winning percentages: 2014 (63%), 2012 (54%)

Republican David Joyce, former prosecutor who was elected in 2012 against a weak opponent after the GOP incumbent unexpectedly retired following the primary, quickly showed his political skills when he got a seat on the Appropriations Committee. He has become a reliable member of the GOP establishment and politically secure at home.

Joyce, born in Cleveland, is the son of a coal salesman. He went to the University of Dayton, where he got his bachelor's in accounting and earned a law degree. He said that he expected to get a job at a national accounting firm, but he was told during interviews that he would have little opportunity for trial work. Instead, he took a job as a public defender in Cuyahoga County, eventually moving to nearby Geauga County. Rising through the ranks quickly, Joyce was elected as the youngest prosecutor in Geauga County's history. During 25 years in that position, he gained attention for a locally famous murder case involving a cult leader and for a failed effort to ban from record stores an album by the hip-hop group 2 Live Crew. Joyce worked in political campaigns, starting on phone banks for then-Cleveland Mayor George Voinovich. In 1999, he organized "Prosecutors for Bush," with George W. Bush's presidential campaign.

In July 2012, nine-term GOP Rep. Steven LaTourette made a stunning announcement that he would not seek reelection in November, despite having won the GOP primary. Without giving specifics, he said that the political climate "has increased the toll that it takes on a person." Another suggested explanation was that LaTourette had felt increasingly isolated as a moderate Republican who was friendly with organized labor. He soon suffered serious health problems and died of cancer in 2016.

Needing a new candidate. a group of 14 Republican leaders selected Joyce, a friend of LaTourette with a credible background and no political record to attack. Democratic nominee Dale Blanchard, an obscure accountant and a 10-time candidate for Congress, continued to run despite pressure to step aside for a stronger challenger. Blanchard failed to report any money raised during the campaign. Joyce spent $672,000, despite not entering the race until mid-August. He ran a mostly positive campaign and generally did not engage Blanchard. He won, 54%-39%.

Although Joyce has been more of a party regular than his predecessor, his *Almanac* vote ratings in 2015 ranked him near the center of the House and as the most moderate member of the Ohio delegation. He got a seat on the Appropriations Committee, where he said that his priority was to reduce the size and scope of government. He hasn't taken the hard line of many GOP newcomers, supporting increased spending on infrastructure, for example. Joyce filed a bill that he said would cut $200 billion in government waste and duplicative programs. He has pursued bipartisan efforts to restore the environmental health of the Great Lakes, with $300 million in annual funding. In December 2016, Joyce claimed a victory when enactment of water resources legislation included a provision for the Great Lakes states to create an action plan to determine future funding projects. That bill continued regular dredging of the Cuyahoga River, with removal of dangerous sediments.

After handing Joyce his seat on a silver platter, Democrats promised a more serious effort in 2014. They failed again. In the Republican primary, Joyce won 55%-45% over pro-life state Rep. Matt Lynch, who criticized GOP congressional leaders for "falling apart" in budget negotiations and was helped by tea party groups. Joyce had more than $600,000 in help from the U.S. Chamber of Commerce, American Hospital Association and a Super PAC run by LaTourette, whose daughter won Lynch's seat in the state House. Michael Wager, a Democratic fund-raiser and former chairman of the Cleveland-Cuyahoga County Port Authority, won the Democratic nomination without opposition. Joyce spent $2.6 million compared with $1 million for Wager, who ran ads that called his opponent "greedy" and criticized him for flying first-class. Despite the early party hype, including his plan to raise at least $2 million, Wager was a disappointing challenger in a poor year for Democrats in Ohio. Joyce won, 63%-33%.

In 2016, Joyce faced two rematches and had little problem in either. In the GOP primary, Lynch voiced similar tea party themes. Joyce increased his margin to 64%-36%. Democrats, who regularly won election to the House from this area prior to 1994, have shown no sign of regaining their competitive edge. Wager tried again in 2016, with rhetorical boosts from national Democrats but not much else. He spent $240,000 to $2 million for Joyce and lost 63%-37%. The biggest challenge for Joyce during the campaign appeared to have been his distancing from Donald Trump. He reportedly was among the congressional Republicans who said that they supported their presidential nominee, without naming him.

Northeast Ohio: Cleveland and Akron Suburbs, Ashtabula

Population		**Race and Ethnicity**		**Income**	
Total	719,406	White	89.6%	Median Income	$61,614 (128 out of 435)
Land area	1,953	Black	4.2%		
Pop/ sq mi	368.3	Latino	2.6%		
Born in state	76.0%	Asian	2.0%	Under $50,000	40.7%
Age Groups		Two races	1.5%	$50,000-$99,999	32.1%
Under 18	22.5%	Other	0.2%	$100,000-$199,999	21.4%
18-34	17.9%	**Education**		$200,000 or more	5.7%
35-64	42.2%	H.S grad or less	39.4%	Poverty Rate	8.9%
Over 64	17.4%	Some college	27.6%	**Health Insurance**	
Work		College Degree, 4 yr	20.5%	With health insurance coverage	91.9%
White Collar	39.7%	Post grad	12.6%		
Sales and Service	39.5%	**Military**		**Public Assistance**	
Blue Collar	20.8%	Veteran	9.0%	Cash public assistance income	1.8%
Government	5.1%	Active Duty	0.0%		
				Food stamp/SNAP benefits	8.5%

Voter Turnout			
2015 Total Citizens 18+	545,353	2016 House Turnout as % CVAP	64%
2016 House turnout	350,269	2014 House Turnout as % CVAP	39%

2012 Presidential Vote		
Mitt Romney	192,895	(51%)
Barack Obama	180,026	(48%)

2016 Presidential Vote		
Donald Trump	197,943	(53%)
Hillary Clinton	155,561	(42%)
Gary Johnson	11,325	(3%)

Cook Partisan Voting Index: R+5

The imprint of the westward track of New England Yankee migration is still apparent today on the shores of Lake Erie in northern Ohio. The British crown had granted the Colony of Connecticut all of the land due west of its borders in 1662. Connecticut ceded most of this land in 1786 in exchange for the newly created federal government taking over its Revolutionary War debts, but it retained a 3 million-acre claim in Ohio for its excess population, which became known as the Western Reserve. As European claims to North America subsided and Native Americans were placed on reservations or relocated, these Yankees, cooped up in New England for 200 years, moved west, through Upstate New York, across Ohio and Michigan to Chicago, and on to Kansas, Oregon and California.

During the Civil War, the Western Reserve, ceded by Connecticut to the federal government in 1800, produced some of the nation's strongest opposition to slavery and hardiest support of the Union armies and the Republican Party; Lake Erie ports were prime transit points for the Underground Railroad to Canada. Its thrifty, hardworking, well-educated citizens built communities with fine schools and, with their accumulated savings, invested in what became some of the nation's leading industries. Now, like Connecticut and Massachusetts, northeastern Ohio has moved toward a post-industrial economy. Factory employment has dropped. Small, adaptive business units with highly skilled workers are the growth sectors. In 2015, a private economic development report found that northeast Ohio will need to find 49,000 manufacturing workers to meet the expected demand in the next decade. In February 2017, FirstEnergy announced plans to sell or shut down by 2018 its nuclear power plant in Lake County. It was losing money because of low price of natural gas and other fuels.

The 14th Congressional District of Ohio takes in parts or all of seven counties of northeast Ohio and the old Western Reserve. It includes the suburbs of eastern and southern Cleveland-based Cuyahoga County; northern Summit; some of Portage to the east; and Geauga. The largest are Lake County, which has nearly one-third of the population, and Summit. The more diverse areas are rural Ashtabula, home to 18 covered bridges and several wineries, and the northern part of Trumbull County, which is industrial and close to Youngstown. Historically, the area was Republican. Since the 1930s, it has remained politically competitive, as Cleveland and the industrial centers on Lake Erie became more Democratic. The 14th District has enough Republican territory to give a GOP lean. Donald Trump got 53 percent of the vote in 2016, compared with the 51 percent for Mitt Romney four years earlier.

FIFTEENTH DISTRICT

Steve Stivers (R)

Elected 2010, 4th term; b. Mar 24, 1965, Cincinnati; Ohio State University, B.A.; Ohio State University, M.B.A.; Army Command and General Staff College (KS), Att.; Methodist; Married (Karen Stivers); 2 children.

Military Career: OH Army National Guard, 1988-2008.

Elected Office: OH Senate, 2003-2008.

Professional Career: Legislative aide; Lobbyist.

DC Office: 1022 LHOB 20515, 202-225-2015, Fax: 202-225-3529, stivers.house.gov.

State Offices: Hilliard, 614-771-4968; Lancaster, 740-654-2654; Wilmington, 937-283-7049.

Committees: House National Republican Congressional Committee Chairman. *Financial Services*: Capital Markets, Securities & Investment, Housing & Insurance.

Group Ratings

	ADA	ACLU	AFL-CIO	LCV	ITI	COC	HAFA	ACU	CFG	FRC
2016	-	5%	-	3%	100%	100%	46%	74%	58%	92%
2015	0%	C	35%	3%	C	100%	C	54%	46%	83%

Almanac Ratings 2015

	Economy	Social	Foreign	Composite
Liberal	14%	12%	14%	13%
Conservative	86%	88%	86%	87%

Key Votes of the 114th Congress

1. Keystone Pipeline	Y	5. Puerto Rico Debt	Y	9. Offenses by Aliens	Y
2. Trade Deals	Y	6. Medical Marijuana	N	10. Troops in Iraq	N
3. Export-Import Bank	Y	7. Sanctuary Cities	Y	11. Homeland Security $$	Y
4. Debt Ceiling Increase	Y	8. Armor-piercing Bullets	Y	12. Trade Adjustment aid	Y

Election Results

Election	Name (Party)	Vote (%)	Cand. Spent	Ind. Exp. Support	Ind. Exp. Oppose
2016 General	Steve Stivers (R)	222,847 (66%)	$1,953,334		
	Scott Wharton (D)	113,960 (34%)	$14,180		
2016 Primary	Steve Stivers (R)	(100%)			

Prior winning percentages: 2014 (66%), 2012 (62%), 2010 (54%)

Republican Steve Stivers, elected in 2010, is generally an economic conservative and a social centrist who has become an up-and-comer in the GOP. With his move to the top ranks at the Financial Services Committee and as chairman of the National Republican Congressional Committee, he is positioned to be part of the next generation of Republican leaders in the House.

Stivers grew up in the Cincinnati suburbs, moved to Columbus to attend Ohio State University, and never left, except for deployments with the Ohio Army National Guard. For most of his career, he was associated with the Ohio Legislature. He was a staffer in the state Senate, and in 1995 began working as a lobbyist for BankOne, which was based in Columbus (and later absorbed into Bank of America). He was appointed by the Senate in 2003 to fill the seat of a retiring state senator. Soon afterward, he served tours in Kuwait and Iraq, for which he received a Bronze Star for his leadership throughout the deployment. In the 2006 election, he ran his campaign from Iraq and won. Stivers was vice chairman of the Finance Committee, supporting state budgets that cut property taxes and froze tuition at state universities. He remained active in the Ohio Army National Guard, where he was promoted in February 2017 to brigadier general.

When Republican Rep. Deborah Pryce retired in 2008, Democrats nominated Franklin County Commissioner Mary Jo Kilroy. After initially declining amid speculation that he wanted to be Ohio Senate president, Stivers entered the contest. He campaigned as a moderate, with a blend of support for abortion rights and fiscal discipline plus his military experience. He supported a two-year federal budget process similar to Ohio's and line-item veto power for the president. Kilroy emphasized her background as a former Columbus school board president and slammed Stivers for his stint as a bank lobbyist. Stivers portrayed Kilroy as "way outside the mainstream," too liberal for the district, and a captive of big labor. In a strongly Democratic year, Kilroy defeated Stivers by a narrower than expected 46%-45%, a margin of 2,312 votes.

In her one term, Kilroy was a faithful supporter of the majority Democrats' programs, including the economic stimulus bill, the cap-and-trade bill to reduce carbon emissions, and the Affordable Care Act. Stivers, preparing for a 2010 rematch, called the health law's mandate to buy insurance "very dangerous" and said the legislation would be a heavy burden on small business. Kilroy portrayed him as a flip-flopper, arguing that he had supported an individual mandate and a carbon emissions bill in the past. She charged that he had supported a national sales tax to replace the income tax, and she again ran ads attacking him as a lobbyist. They raised roughly $2.7 million each, but the Democratic Congressional Campaign Committee abandoned the race in October as unwinnable. Stivers prevailed 54%-41%. Kilroy made an unsuccessful comeback bid in 2012, when she narrowly lost in the Democratic primary to Joyce Beatty in the new heavily Democratic 3rd District.

In the House, Stivers was a loyalist to Speaker John Boehner of Ohio and "the type of sensible moderate that most Ohioans want to see," *The Columbus Dispatch* wrote in endorsing him for reelection. He joined the centrist Main Street Partnership as well as the conservative Republican Study Committee. He opposed conservatives' attempts to abolish or reduce funding for the National Endowment for the Arts and the Legal Services Corporation, and to repeal the Davis-Bacon Act's prevailing union wage requirements. On the Financial Services Committee, Stivers has worked with other Republicans to limit the Dodd-Frank banking overhaul law. In his attempt to boost the housing market, the House in 2015 passed his bipartisan Capital Access for Small Community Financial Institutions bill. He has pressed his proposal to permit credit unions to apply for membership with the Federal Home Loan Banks.

Although the issue is under the control of the Ways and Means Committee, Stivers has called for corporate tax reform that sought to promote the interests of middle-market companies. At Boehner's behest, Stivers served on a party task force on cybersecurity and worked with other allies of the Speaker to find ways to boost infrastructure spending. After Stivers introduced a bill to use projected revenue from offshore drilling leases to back the sale of government bonds for highways, Boehner embraced that approach. He served two years on the House Rules Committee, the "arm of the leadership," but gave up that assignment after Boehner stepped down.

Stivers has become deeply involved in party activities. He initially worked with Rep. Steve Scalise of Louisiana to recruit GOP candidates for the NRCC. Later, he became the NRCC's vice chair for finance. When Scalise was elected in 2014 as GOP whip, Stivers became one of his top deputies. Following the 2016 election, he became the NRCC chairman, after easily defeating Rep. Roger Williams of Texas. Although it would take time for the 2018 campaign to take shape, Stivers likely would be challenged by the usual mid-term challenges facing the party controlling the White House, plus the unconventional political style of President Donald Trump, including his 46 percent of the popular vote in 2016. Four special-election contests to replace House Republicans who joined the Trump administration were a test for the NRCC in the spring of 2017. Following the 2016 election results, House GOP strategists viewed numerous first-term Democrats as vulnerable in 2018. For Stivers, that could be a reprise of his own initial election in 2010.

With his Republican-leaning district, Stivers no longer needed to worry about close campaigns. At the end of 2016, his campaign fund had a balance of $1.3 million, allowing Stivers to spread his wings more broadly.

Central Ohio: Southern Columbus Metro, Athens

Population		**Race and Ethnicity**		**Income**	
Total	737,572	White	89.8%	Median Income	$56,404 (168 out of 435)
Land area	4,739	Black	3.6%		
Pop/ sq mi	155.6	Latino	1.9%		
Born in state	77.3%	Asian	2.3%	Under $50,000	44.4%
		Two races	2.1%	$50,000-$99,999	32.8%
Age Groups		Other	0.2%	$100,000-$199,999	19.0%
Under 18	22.5%			$200,000 or more	3.9%
18-34	23.8%	**Education**		Poverty Rate	13.2%
35-64	40.1%	H.S grad or less	42.7%		
Over 64	13.6%	Some college	27.9%	**Health Insurance**	
		College Degree, 4 yr	18.5%	With health insurance coverage	91.6%
Work		Post grad	11.0%		
White Collar	39.2%				
Sales and Service	40.1%	**Military**		**Public Assistance**	
Blue Collar	20.7%	Veteran	8.9%	Cash public assistance income	2.7%
Government	5.1%	Active Duty	0.1%		
				Food stamp/SNAP benefits	13.2%

Voter Turnout			
2015 Total Citizens 18+	558,256	2016 House Turnout as % CVAP	60%
2016 House turnout	336,807	2014 House Turnout as % CVAP	35%

2012 Presidential Vote		
Mitt Romney	180,487	(52%)
Barack Obama	161,187	(46%)

2016 Presidential Vote		
Donald Trump	196,762	(55%)
Hillary Clinton	141,648	(39%)
Gary Johnson	12,381	(3%)

Cook Partisan Voting Index: R+7

John Kennedy, campaigning for president in Columbus in 1960, was met by large, raucous crowds. He later quipped that Columbus was the city where he received the loudest cheers and the fewest votes. Indeed, Kennedy's 19-point loss in Franklin County was his worst showing in a major urban county in Ohio, affirmation of Franklin's deep Republican roots. Back then, it usually voted Democratic only during a Democratic landslide, as in 1936 and 1964. Columbus had attracted few of the Eastern European immigrants and labor unions that made Cleveland and northeastern Ohio so Democratic after the 1930s. But where JFK and others failed, later Democrats succeeded, starting with Bill Clinton and then narrowly for Al Gore. Hillary Clinton got 61 percent of the vote in 2016, the same as President Barack Obama four years earlier - unlike her lagging statewide result.

With that partisan shift, state Republicans in control of redistricting responded in 2011 by making radical changes in the 15th Congressional District of Ohio. Only about 39 percent of the old 15th was preserved: half of the Short North neighborhood just north of downtown, an up-and-coming area with a large gay population and many of the fashionable new clubs and restaurants of Columbus; a few other downtown communities; the old money suburb of Upper Arlington; and the up-and-coming suburbs of Hilliard and Grove City.

A slim majority of the district's residents live in Columbus and its suburbs, mostly in the southern parts of the metro area, in a vast swath of mostly Republican counties stretching from the exurbs of Cincinnati nearly to West Virginia - disparate areas stitched together to help prevent a non-Columbus Republican from amassing a powerbase in a primary election. About 40 percent of the population is in Franklin, with 20 percent in adjacent Fairfield. The only Democratic county is Athens, the poorest county in the state and home of Ohio University, the oldest college west of the Appalachians. Athens was one of only eight counties in Ohio to vote for Clinton in 2016. Nearby Athens is Hocking Hills, the most visited state park in Ohio, with features that include a cave, a gorge, nature preserves, log cabins and access to the 1,444-mile Buckeye Trail that circles most of the state. The district has a distinct Republican lean. Donald Trump took 55 percent of the vote, an improvement over the 52 percent GOP vote in the two previous presidential elections.

SIXTEENTH DISTRICT

Jim Renacci (R)

Elected 2010, 4th term; b. Dec 03, 1958, Monongahela, PA; Indiana University of Pennsylvania, B.A.; Roman Catholic; Married (Tina Renacci); 3 children.

Elected Office: Wadsworth City Council, 1999-2003; City of Wadsworth Mayor, 2004-2008.

Professional Career: CEO, LTC Mgmt. Services, 1985-2003; CEO, LTC Companies Group, 2003-2010.

DC Office: 328 CHOB 20515, 202-225-3876, Fax: 202-225-3059, renacci.house.gov.

State Offices: Parma, 440-882-6779; Wadsworth, 330-334-0040.

Committees: *Budget*. *Ways & Means*: Social Security, Tax Policy.

Group Ratings

	ADA	ACLU	AFL-CIO	LCV	ITI	COC	HAFA	ACU	CFG	FRC
2016	-	11%	-	0%	100%	100%	64%	72%	65%	92%
2015	5%	C	25%	3%	C	85%	C	67%	65%	100%

Almanac Ratings 2015

	Economy	Social	Foreign	Composite
Liberal	5%	5%	4%	5%
Conservative	95%	95%	96%	95%

Key Votes of the 114th Congress

1. Keystone Pipeline	Y	5. Puerto Rico Debt	N	9. Offenses by Aliens	Y
2. Trade Deals	Y	6. Medical Marijuana	N	10. Troops in Iraq	N
3. Export-Import Bank	Y	7. Sanctuary Cities	Y	11. Homeland Security $$	N
4. Debt Ceiling Increase	N	8. Armor-piercing Bullets	Y	12. Trade Adjustment aid	Y

Election Results

Election	Name (Party)	Vote (%)	Cand. Spent	Ind. Exp. Support	Ind. Exp. Oppose
2016 General	Jim Renacci (R)	225,794 (65%)	$1,748,964	$777	
	Keith Mundy (D)	119,830 (35%)	$48,531		$600
2016 Primary	Jim Renacci (R)	(100%)			

Prior winning percentages: 2014 (64%), 2012 (52%), 2010 (52%)

Republican Jim Renacci, first elected in 2010, is a committed conservative who works with Democrats more than many of his Class of 2010 GOP colleagues. He has the unusual mark of having won his each of his first two elections by defeating a Democratic incumbent - following redistricting in the second case. After having settled into a seat on the tax-writing Ways and Means Committee, he decided to run for governor in 2018.

Renacci grew up in a working-class family outside Pittsburgh. His mother was a nurse, and his father was a railroad worker who lost his job when Renacci was eight years old. Renacci graduated from Indiana University of Pennsylvania, the first in his family to finish college, and became very entrepreneurial. According to his congressional website, Renacci during his 30-year business career "owned and operated over 60 entities, created more than 1,500 jobs and employed over 3,000 people."

As a certified public accountant, he worked for an accounting firm in Pittsburgh with nursing home clients. In 1984, he moved to Wadsworth and started a chain of nursing homes. He sold the chain and formed a company specializing in financial consulting for troubled businesses. Along the way, he accumulated a diverse portfolio of investments, including a share in the Columbus Destroyers, an Arena League football team, a concert promotion firm, and several Harley-Davidson dealerships. He also spent five years as a volunteer firefighter in Wadsworth. He was elected to the Wadsworth Council in 1999 and served as mayor from 2004 to 2008.

As the 2010 election approached, Renacci decided to challenge Democrat John Boccieri, who was elected two years earlier after longtime Canton-area Republican Rep. Ralph Regula retired. Boccieri had served in the Ohio Legislature, was a former professional baseball player, and an Air Force reservist who served in Iraq and Afghanistan. He had a respectable victory of 55%-45% in 2008. On the surface, he did not seem an easy target for Renacci.

But Boccieri had voted for President Barack Obama's $787 billion economic stimulus bill and for the Democrats' cap-and-trade bill to curb carbon emissions. He initially opposed the health care overhaul bill when it passed the House in November 2009, but voted for the final version four months later. Renacci campaigned that Obama administration policies were killing job creation. Democrats referred to Renacci as the "millionaire CEO," who made his fortune off the government and taxpayers. They criticized him for a dispute over taxes in 2000 with Ohio authorities in which Renacci accepted a settlement requiring him to pay $1.3 million. Renacci spent $2.4 million on his campaign, but Boccieri remained competitive with $2.1 million. The outcome wasn't close. In a Republican year, Renacci won 52%-41%, carrying every county in the district.

In the House, Renacci has been reliably conservative on most legislation, but occasionally moved toward the middle with innovative approaches. With Democratic Rep. John Carney of Delaware, he formed a bipartisan breakfast club that grew to 14 members and developed several bills aimed at job creation; Carney was elected governor in 2016. "We need to be able to work together," Renacci told *The New York Times.* He later teamed up with Minnesota's Keith Ellison - one of the chamber's most liberal Democrats - on a bill allowing utility and telecommunications companies to report their customers' on-time payments to credit-reporting agencies. But he opposed the New Year's Day 2013 compromise on taxes and spending aimed at avoiding the so-called "fiscal cliff," saying that it "spends too much, taxes too much, and cuts far too little."

In the 2011 redistricting that eliminated two House seats in Ohio, the Republican-held Legislature merged Renacci and Democratic Rep. Betty Sutton into a single district west of Cleveland that dropped south toward the center of the state. They made sure that the fight would play out more on the turf of Renacci than Sutton. Renacci outspent Sutton, $3.3 million to $2.6 million. Outside groups poured in more than $10 million, which was split about evenly between the two parties. Even in a more favorable environment for Democrats, the new district's GOP lean proved too much for Sutton; Renacci won 52%-48%.

On Ways and Means, Renacci was more willing than most Republicans to discuss the possibility of higher taxes, including a hike in the gasoline tax to pay for highway and bridge construction and repair. "It's easy to sit here in Washington and do nothing. I'd rather be somebody who is going to get something accomplished," he told CNN in 2015. He coauthored a column for CNN with Ways and Means Democratic Rep. Earl Blumenauer of Oregon on the "looming transportation funding crisis" in which they called for "a long-term, sustainable solution to give the American people the infrastructure they deserve and the jobs the economy needs." He has called for unspecified reforms in Social Security and Medicare to protect the retirement systems. In a broader spending bill that was enacted in November 2015, Renacci won inclusion of his legislation that revised tax rules for the audits of large for-profit partnerships.

After his first two close contests, Renacci has not been seriously challenged. That changed with his campaign for governor, which was expected to include multiple Republican candidates. With Sutton seeking the Democratic nomination, Renacci could face a rematch, but with a larger electorate.

Northern Ohio: Cleveland/Akron/Canton Suburbs

Population		**Race and Ethnicity**		**Income**	
Total	722,377	White	92.2%	Median Income	$60,887 (136 out of 435)
Land area	1,205	Black	2.0%		
Pop/ sq mi	599.3	Latino	2.1%		
Born in state	78.2%	Asian	2.1%	Under $50,000	40.0%
Age Groups		Two races	1.4%	$50,000-$99,999	34.5%
Under 18	22.1%	Other	0.3%	$100,000-$199,999	21.1%
18-34	18.8%	**Education**		$200,000 or more	4.4%
35-64	41.5%	H.S grad or less	39.3%	Poverty Rate	7.9%
Over 64	17.6%	Some college	28.8%	**Health Insurance**	
Work		College Degree, 4 yr	20.5%	With health insurance coverage	92.4%
White Collar	39.4%	Post grad	11.4%		
Sales and Service	39.9%	**Military**		**Public Assistance**	
Blue Collar	20.6%	Veteran	9.2%	Cash public assistance income	2.1%
Government	5.4%	Active Duty	0.1%	Food stamp/SNAP benefits	7.3%

Voter Turnout			
2015 Total Citizens 18+	551,516	2016 House Turnout as % CVAP	63%
2016 House turnout	345,624	2014 House Turnout as % CVAP	38%

2012 Presidential Vote		
Mitt Romney	199,697	(54%)
Barack Obama	169,106	(45%)

2016 Presidential Vote		
Donald Trump	207,149	(56%)
Hillary Clinton	145,670	(39%)
Gary Johnson	11,451	(3%)

Cook Partisan Voting Index: R+8

The rapidly growing Cleveland of the early-1900s - it went from 93,000 residents in 1870 to more than 900,000 in 1930 - was crammed into a compact area. The eclectic mix of newcomers that populated the city sorted itself into Cleveland's so-called "cosmo wards:" Italians in Big Italy to the southeast of Public Square; Croats, Serbs and Slovenians in the St. Clair area on the northeast side of town; Irish in

Whiskey Island to the west of downtown; Russians, Germans, Poles and Slovaks in the Ohio City and Tremont areas near present-day Newburgh Heights; and Czechs and Poles in Praha and Slavic Village to the north of present-day Garfield Heights. The cosmo wards began to empty out in the 1950s as the original immigrants died off and their children fled to the suburbs. For a half-century, Cleveland's population has been in decline. Only 14 percent of the population of Greater Cleveland now lives in the city itself, the lowest share since before the Civil War.

The now-graying great-grandchildren of those immigrants live in places like those found in the 16th Congressional District of Ohio, a political creation whose precincts are bound more by Republican voting habits than by any coherent geographic locale. About 40 percent of the district's votes are cast in Cuyahoga County, mostly in Cleveland's western outer suburbs: comfortable places like Westlake, a stone's throw from Lake Erie, plus Strongsville and North Royalton, where median incomes exceed the national average. Many residents here tend to be descended from the Hungarians and Bohemians who settled southwest of Public Square, near present-day Brooklyn. In Westlake, its downtown Crocker Park has developed what it describes as the first lifestyle center of its kind in Ohio -- with homes, businesses, restaurants and stores - that draws more than 16 million visitors annually and has continued to grow.

The district also takes in exurban Medina County, Portage and Stark (but not including Canton) counties, and Wayne County, home to the College of Wooster. Wayne is the headquarters of Smuckers, whose familiar consumer brands have included Smucker jellies, Folgers coffee and Pillsbury; in 2016, it added Big Heart pet foods, which was expected to increase its payroll in Oroville above 2,000. Nerdwallet.com ranked Wooster the sixth best small city in the nation. The southern part of Wayne County is Amish country, where people drive horse-drawn tractors, eschew automobiles and electricity (except from their own generators), and quit school after the eighth grade. Tourism has been a growth industry in the Amish region, with a profusion of restaurants, bed-and-breakfasts, and gift shops. The 16th leans Republican just enough to avoid serious Democratic challenges. Donald Trump won 55 percent in 2016.

★ OKLAHOMA ★

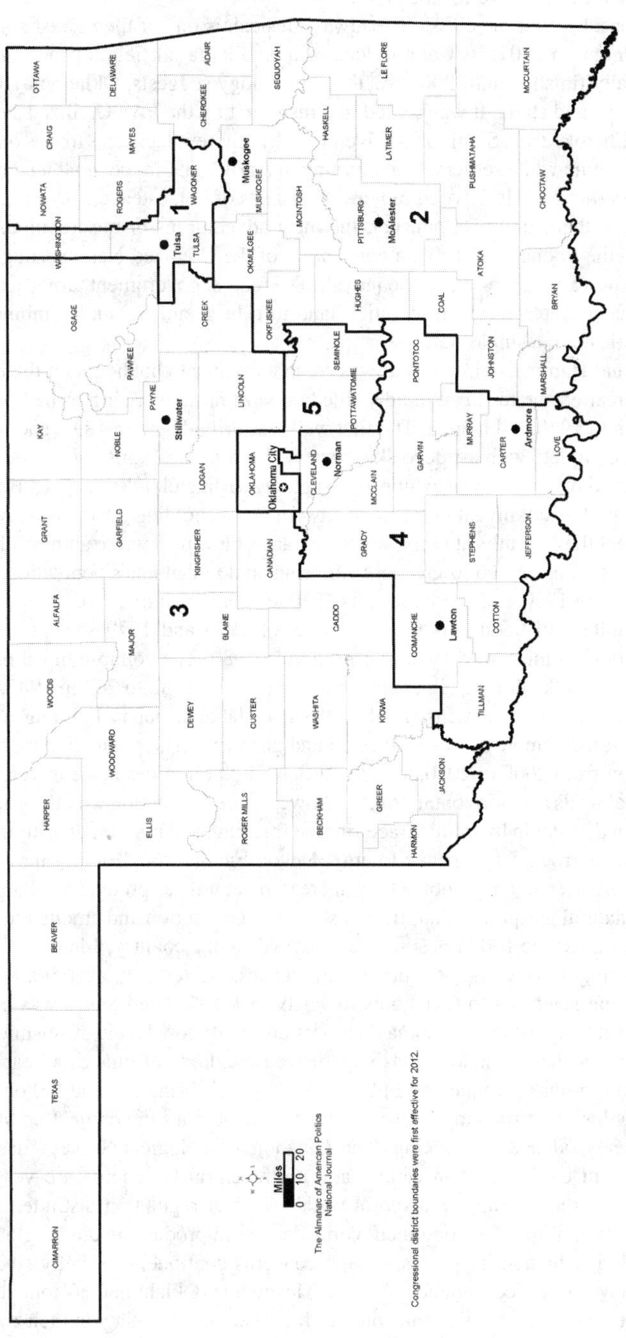
OTTAWA
DELAWARE
ADAIR
SEQUOYAH
LE FLORE
MCCURTAIN
CRAIG
MAYES
CHEROKEE
HASKELL
LATIMER
PUSHMATAHA
NOWATA
ROGERS
WAGONER
Muskogee
MUSKOGEE
MCINTOSH
PITTSBURG
McAlester
CHOCTAW
WASHINGTON
Tulsa
TULSA
OKMULGEE
HUGHES
COAL
ATOKA
BRYAN
OSAGE
PAWNEE
CREEK
OKFUSKEE
SEMINOLE
PONTOTOC
JOHNSTON
MARSHALL
KAY
NOBLE
PAYNE
Stillwater
LINCOLN
POTTAWATOMIE
MURRAY
CARTER
Ardmore
LOVE
LOGAN
OKLAHOMA
Oklahoma City
CLEVELAND
Norman
MCCLAIN
GARVIN
GRANT
GARFIELD
KINGFISHER
CANADIAN
GRADY
STEPHENS
JEFFERSON
ALFALFA
MAJOR
BLAINE
CADDO
COMANCHE
Lawton
COTTON
WOODS
DEWEY
CUSTER
WASHITA
KIOWA
TILLMAN
WOODWARD
JACKSON
HARPER
ELLIS
ROGER MILLS
BECKHAM
GREER
HARMON
BEAVER
TEXAS
CIMARRON
1
2
3
4
5
Miles
0 10 20
The Almanac of American Politics
National Journal
Congressional district boundaries were first effective for 2012.

It wasn't that long ago that Democrats held some sway in Oklahoma. They controlled the state House until 2004, the state Senate until 2008, and the governorship until 2010. Now, though, the GOP has a virtual lock on the state. Not a single county in Oklahoma has voted Democratic in a presidential election since 2000 – a 308 for 308 record for the GOP.

Oklahoma, the subject of the classic Broadway musical, is one of the newest states, the 46th to be admitted to the Union, in 1907. Its Capitol, located atop a large oil field, opened in 1917, though the dome was not finally finished until 2002. As that chronology suggests, Oklahoma's history has been a story of sudden stops and starts. It was settled in a rush, first by the Five Civilized Tribes - Chickasaw, Choctaw, Creek, Cherokee and Seminole - driven west by Andrew Jackson's troops on the Trail of Tears in the 1830s. Then came white settlers. One morning in April 1889, in the great land rush memorialized by novelist Edna Ferber and Hollywood movies, thousands of homesteaders drove their wagons across the territorial line at the sound of a gunshot, the most adventurous or unscrupulous of them literally jumping the gun - the Sooners. In 1905, a convention of the Civilized Nations sought to have eastern Oklahoma admitted as a separate state of Sequoyah. The federal government turned a deaf ear and ended the tribal government, parceled out reservation land to tribe members, and combined the Indian and Oklahoma Territories into a single state.

The Rodgers and Hammerstein musical was set in a mythical Oklahoma on the brink of statehood in 1906. Soon thereafter, the territory rapidly filled up with farmers, rising from 1.5 million people in 1907 to 2.4 million in 1930. Oil helped. The first well was drilled here in 1897, and by 1920 Tulsa was an oil boom town complete with art deco skyscrapers. Then in the 1930s came a decade of bust - and dust - as soil loosened by erosion was whipped into giant swirling clouds: the Dust Bowl. "People sat in Oklahoma City, with the sky invisible for three days in a row, holding dust masks over their faces and wet towels to protect their mouths at night, while the farms blew by," wrote author John Gunther. Okies headed in droves west on U.S. 66 to greener California, and Oklahoma's population steadily declined, falling to 2.2 million in 1950. It did not reach its 1930 level again until 1970.

Then came another oil boom. As the oil shocks of 1973 and 1979 sent prices up, Oklahoma's population rose from 2.5 million in 1970 to 3 million in 1980. The collapse of oil prices in the 1980s produced another bust. Oklahoma's rig count went from 882 in 1982 to 232 in 1983. The 1990 census reported just 3.1 million Oklahomans. In the 1990s, Oklahoma began building a more diversified economy, with high-tech employers as well as oil and gas firms. The population rose 10 percent in the 1990s and 9 percent from 2000 to 2010, to 3.75 million. High oil prices made it worthwhile to squeeze more from marginal wells and horizontal drilling allowed more production with the same number of rigs. Oklahoma has been a leader in hydraulic fracturing, or fracking, and horizontal drilling to extract natural gas embedded in shale rock. Chesapeake Energy, Devon Energy, SandRidge Energy and Continental Resources, all headquartered in Oklahoma City, increased natural gas production sharply. The state now ranks third in dry natural gas production, fifth in shale-gas production and among the top five states for petroleum production. Of the 100 largest natural gas fields in the country, 14 are in Oklahoma.

However, this may have come at a price: earthquakes. As recently as 1990, ScienceLine noted, the Soviet Union sent scientists to Oklahoma to verify that the United States was not testing nuclear weapons underground, choosing Oklahoma due to its unusually low levels of seismic activity. That all changed in 2009; after that, Oklahoma has experienced hundreds of quakes a year and occasionally exceeded California in quake frequency. In 2016, quakes registering 5.8 and 5.0 on the Richter scale hit the state. The culprit isn't fracking per se, scientists believe – it's the reinjection back into "disposal wells" of the water produced in fracking. The Oklahoma Geological Survey "has determined that the majority of recent earthquakes in central and north-central Oklahoma are very likely triggered by the injection of produced water in disposal wells." Tighter regulation instituted by the Oklahoma Corporation Commission in 2015, combined with a decline in production due to global energy trends, has coincided with a reduction in quakes, though concerns continue, especially since building codes in the state were never intended to handle quakes. Meanwhile, Oklahoma has joined Texas in signing legislation to prevent Oklahoma cities and counties from banning fracking on their own.

The influx of energy revenue has juiced the state's capital. The area around its stockyards, the nation's largest, has become a tourist attraction, and civic leaders have channeled the North Canadian River (and renamed it the Oklahoma) to create North America's premier rowing center, even if the arid landscape does not match verdant Henley-on-Thames. Even as Oklahoma harnesses its fossil-fuel legacy, it has also been one of the leading states in developing wind power. Oklahoma now ranks third in wind energy capacity, behind Texas and Iowa, and it generates more than a fifth of its electricity from renewable energy, primarily wind. Wind can also be a serious problem. Between 1890 and 2013, metropolitan Oklahoma City saw at least 156 tornadoes - about one each year, including the 2013 EF5 that killed 24 in and around Moore.

Despite its oil riches, the state has its share of problems. Oklahoma has the third-highest percentage of divorced residents in the nation, its health system is ranked 49th in the nation by the Commonwealth Fund, and its median income is 17 percent below the national average. Oklahoma has above-average rates of teenage pregnancy and crime, a low rate of college graduates, and its cuts in education spending since 2008 were bigger than in any other state, according to the Center on Budget and Policy Priorities. Two studies found that Oklahoma police killed people in 2015 more often than those in any other state, a pattern crystallized that year by the high-profile case of Tulsa reserve deputy Robert Bates, a 73-year-old insurance executive who mistakenly shot an unarmed black man when he meant to use his service taser. Even a positive like the gas boom has not been handled deftly; unlike other states that experienced similar booms, Oklahoma didn't keep excise taxes high, and that added to a fiscal crisis that has lasted half a decade and counting.

On the upside, unemployment in the state has been mild, peaking at 7.1 percent in late 2009 and early 2010, then sinking to 4.1 percent by late 2014 before climbing modestly again by early 2017. In addition to energy, this stemmed from a more stable housing market and some good years for agriculture, conditions that Oklahoma shares with many of its Great Plains neighbors. Oklahoma ranks fourth in the nation in number of farms, in the top five states for cattle, and in the top three states for rye, canola, hay and winter wheat. Statewide, the population has increased by a healthy 4.6 percent since 2010, concentrated in Canadian County (the western suburbs of Oklahoma City, with 15.4 percent growth), Oklahoma County (Oklahoma City, 8.1 percent), Cleveland County (Norman, 7.3 percent) and Tulsa County (5.9 percent). The rest of the state grew by a more modest 1.4 percent. The state got a psychic boost in 2012 when the Oklahoma City Thunder - the first major league pro sports team based in the state - reached the NBA Finals.

Amid all this change, Oklahoma's Indian identity has persisted. With only one small reservation, Oklahomans of Indian ancestry - 9 percent of the population - have made their way forward in the larger society but still cherish their heritage. There has been much intermarriage over the years, and many Oklahomans - and not a few of its politicians - proudly claim Indian blood. (Such murky ancestral ties would eventually cause problems for Massachusetts Sen. Elizabeth Warren, an Oklahoma native whose claims of Native American family history came under scrutiny.) There is an ongoing struggle to keep the Cherokee, Choctaw, Chickasaw and Seminole languages from dying out - you can see street signs in the Cherokee alphabet in Tahlequah, the Cherokees' historical capital. Indians are most numerous in the eastern part of the state. The state has other minorities as well – in fact, white students now account for a minority in the state's public schools. Hispanics, who account for 12 percent of the state's population, are concentrated in the two big cities and in meatpacking counties in the west. Just 7 percent identified as black, and most live in Oklahoma City and Tulsa. The latter was the site of the Tulsa race riot of 1921, "a firestorm of hatred and violence that is perhaps unequaled in the peacetime history of the United States," as historian John Hope Franklin called it. The largely forgotten event destroyed nearly 40 square blocks of African-American homes and businesses and likely killed between 75 and 100 people. More than seven decades later, on April 19, 1995, the state's other major city, Oklahoma City, was the site of mass carnage when a truck bomb placed by domestic terrorists blew apart the Alfred P. Murrah Federal Building, killing 168.

Historically, Oklahoma saw big Democratic margins in eastern counties and in Little Dixie in the southeast, while northwestern Oklahoma, settled by Kansans, has always been Republican. Starting in the 1950s, Tulsa and Oklahoma City leaned Republican too. Then, in the last decade or two, parts of the state outside the metro regions, like Texas outside its big metro areas, moved sharply away from their Democratic heritage and become, in the last two presidential and U.S. Senate races, more Republican than the two big metro areas. This evolution has made Oklahoma one of America's most Republican states. It has not voted Democratic for president since 1964. Since 1966, it has elected only one Democratic senator, David Boren. In 2010, more than 70 percent of voters approved a state constitutional amendment to prevent courts from considering sharia law in judicial decisions. In 2014, the state enacted a law that would have required abortion doctors to have admitting privileges at nearby hospitals, but it was overturned two years later by the state Supreme Court. Meanwhile, the Human Rights Campaign ranked Oklahoma first in the nation for the number of anti-LGBT bills introduced. Dominance has led to factionalization. The state GOP is fractured between tea partiers, Chamber of Commerce types, movement conservatives, evangelicals and others. But Oklahoma Democrats are too decimated to take advantage of the divisions.

In 2016, Donald Trump won the state by a 36-point margin, two points wider than Mitt Romney's edge in 2012. Trump improved on Romney's vote total by 58,000, while Hillary Clinton underperformed Barack Obama's by 23,000. In her best county – Oklahoma County – Clinton managed to win just 41 percent of the vote. Still, echoing national trends, Clinton did marginally better in urban and suburban counties than Obama had. The GOP margin in Tulsa County dropped from 28 points to 22; in Oklahoma County, it fell from 16 to 11; in Canadian County, from 54 to 51; and in Cleveland County, from 26 to 21. With Trump in the White House, Oklahoma may benefit. The president included a 720-mile long transmission line from Oklahoma to Tennessee on a list of 50 priority infrastructure projects, and Trump's pick to head the Environmental Protection Agency was Oklahoma's strongly pro-energy attorney general, Scott Pruitt.

Population		**Race and Ethnicity**		**Income**	
Total	3,849,733	White	67.3%	Median Income	$46,879 (40 out of 50)
Land area	68,595	Black	7.1%	Under $50,000	52.7%
Pop/ sq mi	56.1	Latino	9.6%	$50,000-$99,999	30.3%
Born in state	60.9%	Asian	1.9%	$100,000-$199,999	14.0%
		Two races	6.9%	$200,000 or more	3.1%
Age Groups		Other	7.1%	Poverty Rate	16.7%
Under 18	24.6%	**Education**		**Health Insurance**	
18-34	23.8%	H.S grad or less	44.7%	With health insurance coverage	83.3%
35-64	37.3%	Some college	31.1%		
Over 64	14.2%	College Degree, 4 yr	16.1%	**Public Assistance**	
Work		Post grad	8.0%	Cash public assistance income	3.3%
White Collar	33.3%	**Military**		Food stamp/SNAP benefits	13.9%
Sales and Service	41.9%	Veteran	10.3%		
Blue Collar	24.9%	Active Duty	0.6%		
Government	17.0%				

Voter Turnout			
2015 Total Citizens 18+	2,768,561	2016 Pres Turnout as % CVAP	52%
2016 Pres Votes	1,452,992	2012 Pres Turnout as % CVAP	50%

Legislature	
Senate:	6D, 42R
House:	26D, 74R, 1V

Presidential Politics

2016 Democratic Primary		
Bernie Sanders (D)	174,228	(52%)
Hillary Clinton (D)	139,443	(42%)
2016 Republican Primary		
Ted Cruz (R)	158,078	(34%)
Donald Trump (R)	130,267	(28%)
Marco Rubio (R)	119,633	(26%)
Ben Carson (R)	28,601	(6%)

2016 Presidential Vote		
Donald Trump (R)	949,136	(65%)
Hillary Clinton (D)	420,375	(29%)
Gary Johnson (L)	83,481	(6%)
2012 Presidential Vote		
Mitt Romney (R)	891,325	(67%)
Barack Obama (D)	443,547	(33%)

Since the FDR era, Oklahoma has voted only twice for a Democratic presidential candidate: Harry Truman in 1948 and Lyndon Johnson in 1964. The last Democratic nominee to carry a county in Oklahoma was Al Gore in 2000 (he won nine). Traditionally, Tulsa and Oklahoma City were Republican strongholds, but starting in 2004 the counties outside the two big metro areas have been voting more Republican than the state average in presidential elections. In 1996, Bob Dole defeated Bill Clinton 48%-40%, but Clinton won nearly half the counties, 38. Most of those were in the region's old

Indian Territory, where in-migration from Texas, Arkansas and especially Mississippi brought with it Democratic traditions -- the region became known as "Little Dixie." But in 2016, Donald Trump crushed Hillary Clinton, 65%-29%. Trump won every county in the state. In 66 of 77 counties he won 70 percent or more of the vote. Clinton's best county was Oklahoma (Oklahoma City) where she won 41 percent of the vote, almost the same as the 42 percent Barack Obama garnered in 2008 and 2012.

In 2008, Oklahoma was joined by many other states in voting on Super Tuesday and did not attract much attention. In the Democratic primary, Clinton was the early favorite and beat Obama 55%-31%. Obama carried Oklahoma County (Oklahoma City), and Clinton carried the other 76 counties, with big margins in eastern Oklahoma counties near her longtime home in Arkansas. In 2016, Vermont Sen. Bernie Sanders defeated Clinton 51%-42%. This time around Clinton won only two counties: Oklahoma and Osage, which comprises the Osage Nation Reservation. Oklahoma was one of five states Clinton won in 2008 that she lost in 2016. The others were Indiana, New Hampshire, Rhode Island and West Virginia.

Republican presidential primaries have been closer. John McCain beat Mike Huckabee 37%-33% in 2008 and Rick Santorum beat Mitt Romney 34%-28% in 2012. In 2016, Texas Sen. Ted Cruz spent more than $800,000 on television ads, more than the rest of the GOP candidates combined, and defeated Trump 34%-28%. Marco Rubio was a close third taking 26 percent of the vote. The competitive nature of the race drew a GOP record 459,992 primary voters.

Congressional Districts

115th Congress Lineup	5R	114th Congress Lineup	5R

Oklahoma redistricting following the 2010 census was a breeze. Republicans controlled the process for the first time, and they had little incentive to rock the boat. Democrat Dan Boren, whose family name is revered in state politics, was the sole Democrat in the delegation, but he voted with Republicans more often than any other Democrat in the House.

All five incumbents, including Boren, agreed to minimal changes in their districts, and legislators passed them with a yawn. Then, Boren surprised observers and made the GOP job even easier by announcing his retirement at age 37, from what had long been known as the Little Dixie district - a former Democratic stronghold in the southeast. Fiercely conservative Republican Markwayne Mullin easily picked up the seat the following November. It may be many years before another Democrat is elected from anywhere in Oklahoma. And the redistricting in 2021 should be another breeze.

Governor

Mary Fallin (R)

Elected 2010, term expires 2019, 2nd term; b. Dec. 9, 1954, Warrensburg, MO; OK Baptist U., attended, OK St. U., B.S. 1977; U. of Central OK, attended; Christian; Married (Wade Christiansen); 6 children.

Elected Office: OK House, 1990-1994; OK Lt. Governor, 1994-2006; U.S. House, 2007-2011.

Professional Career: OK Deptartment of Tourism & Recreation; OK Securities Commission; OK Office of Personnel Management, 1977-1982; Hotel Marketing & Management, 1983-1990.

Office: 2300 N. Lincoln Blvd., Room 212, Oklahoma City, 73105; 405-521-2342; Fax: 405-521-3353; Website: ok.gov.

Election Results

Election	Name (Party)	Vote (%)
2014 General	Mary Fallin (R)	460,298 (56%)
	Joe Dorman (D)	338,239 (41%)
	Kimberly Willis (I)	17,169 (2%)
2014 Primary	Mary Fallin (R)	200,035 (76%)
	Chad Moody (R)	40,839 (15%)
	Dax Ewbank (R)	24,020 (9%)

Prior winning percentage: 2010 (60%); House: 2008 (66%), 2006 (60%)

Oklahoma's governor is Mary Fallin, a Republican elected in 2010 as the state's first female chief executive and easily reelected in 2014. A former lieutenant governor and House member, she has delighted conservatives in her deep-red state with an emphasis on trimming government, curbing abortion rights and relaxing handgun restrictions, and she gained a national profile as chair of the National Governors Association in 2013 and 2014. But an oil and gas downturn hit the state hard, and Fallin's popularity flagged during her second term.

Fallin was born in Missouri but raised in Tecumseh, Oklahoma. Her mother and father were Democrats and each served as mayor of the town. After graduating from Oklahoma State University, Fallin managed hotel properties and was a commercial real estate broker. In 1990, she was elected to the state House, where she championed victims' rights and health care reform.

She became lieutenant governor four years later, making her the first Republican and the first woman to hold that office in Oklahoma. During her three terms, she expanded her reach well beyond the office's traditional ribbon-cutting responsibilities. With a focus on economic development, she compiled a pro-business record and played a key role in bringing the right-to-work issue to a successful statewide vote. In 1998, her star dimmed a bit when, in the course of a bitter divorce, she was accused of having a sexual relationship with a state trooper assigned to her security detail; both of them denied the charge.

Fallin decided to run for the seat of GOP Rep. Ernest Istook, who was making a bid for governor in 2006. She joined a wide-open, six-way primary that included state Corporation Commissioner Denise Bode and Oklahoma City Mayor Mick Cornett. In the initial July balloting, Fallin led with 35 percent to Cornett's 24 percent and Bode's 19 percent. In the subsequent runoff, Fallin, with a big fundraising advantage, defeated Cornett, 63%-37%, and she won the general, 60%-37%, becoming the first woman sent to Washington by Oklahoma since 1922.

In June 2007, she saw her first bill pass in the House, a revamping of federal grants for women's business centers. She joined a group of 38 Republicans who staked out negotiating positions in opposition to the Democrats' proposal to expand the Children's Health Insurance Program. Fallin became politically active on the executive committee of the National Republican Congressional Committee, which was chaired by fellow Oklahoman Tom Cole. In the 2008 presidential contest, she was an enthusiastic backer of Alaska Gov. Sarah Palin as the GOP vice presidential nominee, calling her "an excellent model for other women."

With two-term Democratic Gov. Brad Henry ineligible to seek a third term, Fallin announced her candidacy for governor in February 2009. She raised an impressive $2.4 million before the July 2010 primary. Her main opponent was state Sen. Randy Brogdon of Owasso, who sought to generate tea party support by making an issue of her 2008 vote for the bailout of the financial industry. Fallin, however, capitalized on her friendship with Palin and several other big-name Republicans, including Govs. Tim Pawlenty of Minnesota and Jan Brewer of Arizona. She drew 55 percent in the primary, avoiding a runoff. The general election was a two-woman race - Fallin against Democratic Lt. Gov. Jari Askins. To stay competitive in fundraising, Fallin loaned her campaign $1.1 million. She proposed lowering taxes, reducing excessive workers' compensation and legal fees, and cutting the number of state agencies. In October, Fallin suggested she was more qualified than Askins as a result of her experience "being a mother, having children, raising a family." Askins was single and had no children, but Fallin said she didn't intend her remarks as an attack. The controversy didn't end up hurting her; Fallin won 60%-40%, capturing every county except Askins' home of Stephens County and three neighboring counties.

Fallin's first budget had a 3 percent reduction for core state agencies, such as public safety and education, and a 5 percent cut for others. Despite her opposition to President Barack Obama's health care overhaul while in the House, she supported a state bill to set up a framework for the insurance exchanges called for in the federal legislation. At the emphatic urging of the legislature's Republican leaders, though, she eventually rejected setting up an exchange. She also joined numerous other Republican governors in rejecting an expansion of Medicaid. Fallin hit turbulence in February 2013, when she pushed a bill that would have allowed cities and towns to enact stricter smoking bans than exist in state law. She called smoking "a personal issue for me," having lost both of her parents in smoking-related deaths. But a Senate committee rejected the measure.

For the most part, though, Fallin got what she wanted. The number of state employees dropped more than 3 percent in 2011, and she oversaw the consolidation of five state agencies into a single Office of Management and Enterprise Services. Among her other stated goals she met in 2012 were: opening new mental health centers; increasing the number of college graduates; requiring state agencies to reduce energy consumption; and launching a plan to fix structurally deficient state highway bridges. She also got an additional $1 million to reduce infant mortality rates. On social issues, she signed legislation to make it a felony for doctors to perform abortions after a woman reaches 20 weeks of pregnancy and to bar Oklahoma health insurance plans from offering coverage for elective abortions under the federal health care law. In 2012 she signed a bill making Oklahoma the 25th state to adopt an open-carry firearms law.

In May 2013, Fallin found herself in the national spotlight after a deadly tornado struck the Oklahoma City suburbs, killing 24 people. She toured toppled school buildings, consoled victims and quickly became the face of the state's collective determination to rebuild. Her response to the crisis prompted *The Daily Beast* to remark, "Gov. Mary Fallin looks like the star Sarah Palin was supposed to be." But Fallin also drew some scrutiny for her out-of-state travel. *The Oklahoman* newspaper reported in 2012 that her office had spent more than $273,000 on trips, including visits to Arizona for college football bowl games and to Ireland for her daughter's wedding. (She paid her own expenses to Ireland, but her security detail cost taxpayers more than $13,000.)

Overall, though, her efforts proved popular among Oklahomans, and that made her reelection bid against Democratic state Rep. Joe Dorman a breeze. Dorman complained that the state didn't fund schools adequately and attacked Fallin for initially supporting the Common Core academic standards for math and English only to oppose them when they became a national target of conservatives' wrath. She won easily -- 56%-41%, carrying 71 of the state's 77 counties – but it was the lowest-turnout gubernatorial election in the state since 1978, and her margin was actually unimpressive compared with down-ticket Republicans. Still, not a single Democrat won a statewide or congressional office, and the legislature remained overwhelmingly Republican.

With a budget gap fed by a decline in oil and gas tax revenues and a scheduled income tax decrease, fiscal woes dominated the start of Fallin's second term in 2015, and she faced difficulties advancing her agenda through the legislature. By the time Fallin and lawmakers reached a deal, the shortfall had ballooned to more than $600 million, which they agreed to close through cuts to agencies of 5 percent to 7 percent and by drawing from the state's rainy day fund. One of the rare increases in the budget was for corrections, which got an additional $14 million to ease overcrowding. Heavy rains and flooding in May 2015 caused more budgetary worries.

Fallin pleased conservatives when she signed a bill to outlaw an abortion method that critics call "dismemberment," as well as an extension of the mandatory waiting period for an abortion from 24 hours to 72. She also signed a law establishing a backup method of execution - nitrogen gas - amid the state's increasing difficulty in acquiring lethal-injection drugs. A 2014 lethal injection that took 43 minutes made the issue particularly urgent.

In tune with her state's energy industry, Fallin issued an executive order opposing proposed federal regulations on carbon emissions from power plants. She also signed a bill that prevented local governments from banning oil and gas drilling, and another bill to sunset a property-tax exemption for new wind-energy development, saving an estimated $500 million in foregone revenues over 10 years. But she irritated gun-rights supporters by vetoing a bill that would have prevented private businesses from banning the otherwise legal carrying of guns in public places. Critics said the bill could have made it hard for the state to attract major sporting and entertainment events. Meanwhile, Fallin signed a law mandating that school districts develop programs to prevent sexual assault. In 2015, Fallin took a high-profile stance against legal efforts to remove a Ten Commandments statue, but the state Supreme Court decision to remove it was upheld.

Amid continued weakness in the energy industry, budget woes continued into 2016. In March, Fallin once again drew down the rainy day fund to provide education and corrections with emergency funding. In June, she signed the full 2016-2017 budget, which reduced spending by 5 percent but kept education funding level and prevented the closure of hospitals and nursing homes. She signed a bill to help families get outpatient treatment for adult relatives with mental illness, but, somewhat unexpectedly, she vetoed a bill to criminalize abortions, saying it was vague and likely unconstitutional. A spokesman for the socially conservative group Liberty Counsel called the veto "a despicable betrayal of her word and of innocent children whose lives will be cut short because of her cowardly act." One proposal by Fallin went nowhere (though it was presumably in jest) – offering a cabinet position to Oklahoma Thunder superstar Kevin Durant if he would remain with the team. He joined the Golden State Warriors.

Fallin endorsed Donald Trump shortly after he clinched the presidential nomination in May 2016, and her name was periodically floated as a potential running mate. After Trump won the presidency, she was considered for the post of Interior Secretary but was not chosen. Instead, she remained in Oklahoma to grapple with a roughly $870 million budget shortfall. She proposed raising taxes on cigarettes and gasoline while eliminating the sales tax on groceries and the corporate income tax. Oklahoma has a three-fourths supermajority requirement to raise taxes, providing Democrats with some rare leverage in the debate. In the meantime, Fallin announced that an agreement had been reached with Amazon.com to impose sales taxes on customers within the state. However, the years of budget stress took its toll on Fallin's standing; her approval ratings fell to the low 40s. Still, the race to succeed her in 2018 was expected to go easily to a Republican – with the only question being which one. The GOP bench in the state is deep.

Senior Senator

Jim Inhofe (R)

Elected 1994, term expires 2020, 4th full term; b. Nov 17, 1934, Des Moines, IA; University of Tulsa (LK), B.A.; Presbyterian; Married (Kay Kirkpatrick Inhofe); 4 children (1 deceased); 16 grandchildren.

Military Career: U.S Army, 1957-1958.

Elected Office: OK House, 1967-1969; OK Senate, 1969-1977, Republican leader, 1975-1977; Tulsa Mayor, 1978-1984; U.S. House, 1987-1995.

Professional Career: Businessman, land developer, 1962-1986.

DC Office: 205 RSOB 20510, 202-224-4721, Fax: 202-228-0380, inhofe.senate.gov.

State Offices: Enid, 580-234-5105; McAlester, 918-426-0933; Oklahoma City, 405-608-4381; Tulsa, 918-748-5111.

Committees: *Armed Services*: Airland, Readiness & Management Support (Chmn), Strategic Forces. *Commerce, Science & Transportation*: Aviation Operations, Safety & Security, Communications, Technology, Innovation & the Internet, Consumer Protection, Product Safety, Ins & Data Security, Oceans, Atmosphere, Fisheries & Coast Guard, Surface Trans., Merchant Marine Infra., Safety & Security. *Environment & Public Works*: Clean Air & Nuclear Safety, Fisheries, Water, and Wildlife, Transportation & Infrastructure (Chmn). *Small Business & Entrepreneurship*.

Group Ratings

	ADA	ACLU	AFL-CIO	LCV	ITI	COC	HAFA	ACU	CFG	FRC
2016	-	5%	-	12%	100%	100%	66%	88%	82%	100%
2015	0%	C	14%	0%	C	77%	C	92%	78%	100%

Almanac Ratings 2015

	Economy	Social	Foreign	Composite
Liberal	6%	0%	9%	5%
Conservative	94%	100%	91%	95%

Key Votes of the 114th Congress

1. Keystone pipeline	Y	5. National Security Data	Y	9. Gun Sales Checks	N
2. Export-Import Bank	Y	6. Iran Nuclear Deal	Y	10. Sanctuary Cities	Y
3. Debt Ceiling Increase	N	7. Puerto Rico Debt	Y	11. Planned Parenthood	Y
4. Homeland Security $$	N	8. Loretta Lynch A.G	N	12. Trade deals	Y

Election Results

Election	Name (Party)	Vote (%)	Cand. Spent	Ind. Exp. Support	Ind. Exp. Oppose
2014 General	Jim Inhofe (R)............................	558,166 (68%)	$5,152,276	$7,250	
	Matt Silverstein (D)....................	234,307 (29%)	$471,194		
2014 Primary	Jim Inhofe (R)............................	231,131 (88%)			

Prior winning percentages: 2008 (57%), 2002 (57%), 1996 (57%), 1994 special (55%), House: 1992

At the beginning of 2017, Republican James Inhofe, Oklahoma's senior senator, was forced by the rules of the Senate GOP caucus to give up the chairmanship of the Environment and Public Works Committee after three terms. But, if anything, the policy influence of Inhofe -- an outspoken critic of environmental regulation in general and of climate change science in particular -- was poised to increase as the administration of President Donald Trump took power. As former Oklahoma Attorney General Scott Pruitt, to whom Inhofe has long been close, took up new duties as head of the Environmental Protection Agency, at least a half-dozen top Inhofe aides left Capitol Hill to move up Pennsylvania Avenue to work at EPA headquarters or the White House. Inhofe's former chief of staff, after shepherding the controversial nomination of Pruitt through the Senate, became his chief of staff, and other Inhofe alumni subsequently were hired as senior advisers to the new EPA administrator on air, climate and legal issues.

It amounted to something of an outside takeover by loyalists to a veteran senator who in the past has derided the EPA as an "activist organization" that has placed onerous burdens on numerous sectors of the nation's economy. "It gives me a level of comfort to know that we have a bureaucracy that's actually going to be serving instead of ruling," Inhofe said of his former staffers in an interview with the *Washington Post*, adding, "They are going to be very realistic. They're going to do it in a way that will not be punitive. The previous [Obama] administration was almost looking for ways to punish people." During the administration of President Bill Clinton, Inhofe once accused then-administrator EPA Carol Browner of "Gestapo tactics." It's representative of a style that is often blunt and sometimes acerbic. "I'm not afraid of controversy. I'm not afraid to say what's on my mind and what's on a lot of people's minds," Inhofe once said. At the same time, Inhofe has also demonstrated a pragmatic side, working with now-retired California Sen. Barbara Boxer -- who is as liberal as Inhofe is conservative -- on several issues when Inhofe and Boxer were the top Republican and Democrat, respectively, on the Environment and Public Works panel.

Inhofe's political career dates back half a century. He grew up in Tulsa, served in the Army, and worked in real estate and insurance. He was elected to the state House in 1966, and to the state Senate in 1969. (During his time in the Senate, he earned a bachelor's degree from the University of Tulsa.) As a state legislator, he promoted the balanced budget constitutional amendment. His career then hit a couple of bumps at a time when now solidly Republican Oklahoma still tilted Democratic. In 1974, Inhofe ran for governor and lost to Democrat David Boren -- whom he later succeeded in the Senate -- by 64%-36%. Two years later, he ran for the House against Democratic Rep. Jim Jones and lost. Inhofe made a political comeback by winning election as mayor of Tulsa in 1978, and served until 1984.

When Jones left to run unsuccessfully for the Senate in 1986, Inhofe was elected to his House seat. He was re-elected three times, albeit with uninspiring margins: He was held to 53 percent of the vote on two occasions. Negative publicity from a family business lawsuit and charges of campaign finance irregularities impaired his support in what was even then a strongly Republican district. Inhofe's most notable accomplishment while in the House was reforming the arcane rules for discharge petitions, used to force a floor vote on legislation bottled up in committee. For years, House rules kept secret the names of signers of discharge petitions; anonymity allowed lawmakers to claim they had worked to bring legislation to the floor, when they in fact had done the opposite. That was changed in 1993, and one of the first bills to benefit from the new rules was an aviation liability reform bill co-sponsored by Inhofe, an avid flier of small airplanes. The legislation limited the liability of small airplane manufacturers in lawsuits resulting from crashes.

In 1994, when conservative Democrat Boren resigned from the Senate to become president of the University of Oklahoma, Rep. Dave McCurdy, a moderate Democrat, was the initial frontrunner in the special election to fill the last two years of the term. But the Clinton Administration's unpopularity among conservatives was too much for McCurdy, who had voted for 1993 budget increases and tax hikes, and for the 1994 crime bill with its ban on assault weapons. Inhofe won by a solid 55%-40%. In the Senate,

Inhofe was elected president of the large GOP freshman class of 11, as Republicans regained the Senate majority. In 1996, he won a six-year term over James Boren, David Boren's cousin, 57%-40%.

Inhofe's Web site boasts of his placing among the top five most conservative senators in *National Journal*'s 2013 vote ratings. He was fifth that year, and the *Almanac*'s 2015 vote ratings put him almost as high, in seventh place. For the past decade and a half, Inhofe has been an outspoken leader of the GOP faction that disputes the mainstream scientific view of global warming -- which holds that carbon dioxide emissions will cause catastrophic climate change absent action by the United States and other major nations. In 2003, Inhofe termed the contention that man-made emissions have caused global warming "the greatest hoax ever perpetrated on the American people." Nearly a decade later, in 2012, he published a book: *The Greatest Hoax: How the Global Warming Conspiracy Threatens Your Future*. In mid-2016, he again made headlines when, during an appearance on a syndicated radio show, complained that school children were being "brainwashed" on climate change. "...My own granddaughter came home one day and said 'Popi, why is it you don't understand global warming?'," Inhofe related to host Eric Metaxas, adding, "I did some checking and Eric, the stuff that they teach our kids nowadays, you have to un-brainwash them when they get out."

Several years earlier, Inhofe led his grandchildren in building an igloo near the U.S. Capitol after a major snowstorm, which they christened "Al Gore's New Home." But little could top the theatrics of when, on a cold day in February 2015, Inhofe tossed a snowball at the presiding officer while speaking on the Senate floor to challenge climate science. (A Senate page caught it.) "In case we had forgotten, because we keep hearing that 2014 has been the warmest year on record," Inhofe declared, as he reached for a plastic bag next to his lectern. He continued: "I ask the chair, do you know what this is? It's a snowball, just from outside here. It's very, very cold out." A month earlier, Inhofe suggested climate change was due to forces beyond the control of modern civilization. "Climate is changing, and climate has always changed. There's archeological evidence of that. There's biblical evidence of that. There's historic evidence of that," he told the Senate. Advocates of climate change science responded by noting that the record warmth of 2014 was outstripped by new records set in 2015 and then again in 2016.

Notwithstanding his impact on the Trump Administration's policies, Inhofe's first choice for the Republican presidential nomination in 2016 was his Florida colleague, Sen. Marco Rubio. After Rubio dropped out, Inhofe endorsed Ohio Gov. John Kasich. But, when it was clear that Trump would be the nominee, Inhofe reportedly forged ties through his Alabama colleague, Sen. Jeff Sessions -- now Trump's attorney general -- and was named an adviser to the Trump campaign on national security as well as regulatory issues. If President Barack Obama publicly mocked Inhofe's snowball stunt on several occasions, environmental groups weren't laughing in early 2017. "Inhofe was like the original climate-denier in chief. He was one of the first people spouting this gibberish - fact-free but dangerous gibberish," Gene Karpinski, president of the League of Conservation Voters, told *The Washington Post*. "Now he and his cronies have far more reach and are far more dangerous than they've ever been."

Representing a major petroleum-producing state, Inhofe has been an avid proponent of oil drilling in the Arctic National Wildlife Refuge, as well as more oil and gas exploration throughout the nation at large. After the April 2010 BP oil spill in the Gulf of Mexico, he opposed a Democratic initiative to remove the $75 million cap on damages for offshore drilling accidents. Environmental activist Robert F. Kennedy Jr. in 2012 called Inhofe "Big Oil's top call girl."

Inhofe's first stint as chairman of the Environment and Public Works Committee was from 2003 to 2007, when the Democrats regained the majority. He devoted much of his attention to a major non-environmental responsibility of the panel -- reauthorization of the federal surface transportation bill funding highways and transit systems. By early 2004, Inhofe had hammered out an agreement in the Senate for a six-year, $318 billion transportation bill. The House-passed bill was $275 billion. The two versions had significant political differences. Inhofe's goal was to guarantee that every state got 95 percent of its gas tax money back; if total spending was decreased, other states would lose projects. With the conflict deadlocked, the issue was deferred to 2005. By that time, GOP leaders were eager to cut a final deal with Bush, and Inhofe agreed to a scaled-down bill of $286 billion.

It took another decade for Congress to agree on the next long-term surface transportation measure, after a period of short-term extensions of two years or less. In December 2015, Obama signed a five-year, $305 billion extension of the highway bill into law. By that time, the Republicans were back in Senate control, and Inhofe was back for his third and final term as Environment and Public Works chairman. Inhofe, Boxer and Majority Leader Mitch McConnell negotiated a $350 billion bill that authorized funding over six years, but actually paid for only the first three years of that spending. The House, which had approved a $325 billion, six-year measure, balked at the Senate's approach, resulting in the final compromise bill. Left unresolved was a long-term solution to funding the nation's transportation infrastructure: Gas tax revenues continued to decline due to more fuel-efficient vehicles, while lawmakers resisted increasing the per gallon amount of the tax. Earlier, after Democrats had won control of the Senate in the 2006 election, Inhofe withstood a backroom challenge from Virginia Republican John Warner to become the ranking Republican on the committee. Initial prospects for cooperation between Inhofe and Boxer, then the incoming chairman, appeared dim. He spoke out strongly against her bill to impose a mandatory cap on carbon dioxide emissions, which died in the Senate in 2008. But Inhofe insisted their working relations were nonetheless good. Indeed, after they worked together in 2012 to pass a two-year surface transportation bill extension, Boxer told reporters that Inhofe "has been just the best partner for me as chairman...in the best traditions of how the highway bill has been done until now." In 2015, after they collaborated on the longer-term surface transportation measure, Inhofe paid tribute to Boxer in listing the committee's accomplishments in 2015-2016. "While Sen. Boxer and I often did not see eye-to-eye, she and her staff were instrumental to many of the committee's victories in the last two years," Inhofe said.

Besides the surface transportation measure, perhaps the most notable accomplishment of Inhofe's final term as Environment and Public Works chairman was a revision to the federal Toxic Substances Control Act that Obama signed in June 2016. Prior to his death in 2013, New Jersey Democratic Sen. Frank Lautenberg had worked for years to improve the much-criticized law, which had remained largely unchanged since its enactment in 1976. It cleared Inhofe's panel in 2015 on a bipartisan vote, with backing from some environmental groups -- which felt it gave EPA significantly increased powers -- and industry, which liked the fact that, going forward, it provided a single federal regulatory regimen rather than a patchwork of state laws. Inhofe negotiated with New Mexico Democratic Sen. Tom Udall, as Boxer -- joined by several other environmental groups -- initially resisted the bill as not going far enough to regulate industry. She was ultimately assuaged after winning some changes, and the final bill cleared the Senate floor on a voice vote.

In 2013-14, Inhofe served as the top Republican on the Armed Services Committee, after term limits forced Arizona Sen. John McCain to step aside as that panel's ranking minority member. In 2015, with the Republicans back in the majority, McCain was able to claim the Armed Services chairmanship under the GOP term limit rules, and Inhofe returned to Environment and Public Works' top slot. Inhofe began his tenure on Armed Services by crusading against his former Senate colleague, Nebraska Republican Chuck Hagel, to become Obama's secretary of defense after having earlier praised Hagel. While other senators questioned Hagel's support for Israel as a cause for concern, Inhofe went even further: He suggested that Hagel was "cozy" with countries promoting terrorism because Iran had expressed support for his nomination. That led Missouri Democrat Claire McCaskill to respond, "Senator Inhofe, be careful. What if some horrible organization said tomorrow that you were the best guy that they knew?"

In 2014, Inhofe accused Obama of telling an "outrageous lie" during an interview about the 2012 attack on a consulate in Benghazi Libya, and alleged the administration was mounting a Watergate-style cover-up about the incident. Earlier, Inhofe added a provision to the fiscal 2011 defense authorization law barring commanders from collecting information about weapons privately owned by troops. The measure led a group of senior retired generals and admirals in 2012 to ask that the law be changed because it interfered with efforts to prevent military suicides. Inhofe said he disagreed with that view, but he did not block efforts to modify it.

Inhofe has for years regularly flown airplanes and is one of the few certified commercial pilots in Congress. He flew around the world following the historic route of Wiley Post, the first pilot to fly solo around the globe. But he has had several close calls, most recently a July 2016 forced landing in northeastern Oklahoma amid severe weather at the age of 81 (there is no maximum age for pilots of small aircraft). A decade earlier, in October 2006, Inhofe encountered problems when the experimental plane he was flying spun out of control and suffered significant damage on landing in Tulsa, though he and an aide escaped injury. In October 2010, his apparent flouting of air safety rules became a serious issue. Inhofe set his six-seat Cessna down on a runway clearly marked closed at a south Texas airport, and just narrowly missed hitting a group of construction workers during an aborted landing attempt. The Federal Aviation Administration ordered him to take remedial flying lessons, but did not take away his pilot's license.

An unrepentant Inhofe contended he had been cleared to land, and responded by pushing legislation designed to increase the rights of pilots in similar situations. "...They were hiding the voice recording that cleared me to land. That's how bad it was of a system, where you are guilty until proven innocent," he told *Roll Call* in March 2015. He added: "...I didn't know for months on end whether or not I would lose my pilot's license. Now stop and think: I'm a United States senator and I didn't know. What about the guys, these thousands and thousands of airline pilots whose lives, their kids, depend on the job that their daddy or mommy has?" Initially, Inhofe responded with what he called a pilot's bill of rights that gave pilots accused of wrongdoing more authority to review the evidence against them. It was signed into law in 2012. Inhofe didn't stop there: In 2015, he introduced "Pilots Bill of Rights 2", which became law in mid-2016 as part of a Federal Aviation Administration authorization bill.

In November 2013, Inhofe's son Perry died when the small, single-engine plane he was flying crashed in Oklahoma. Discussing how the loss affected him, he told NBC News: "You don't change in terms of your positions, in terms of what you believe in, but you change in terms of your understanding of individuals." The previous month, Sen. Inhofe had quadruple bypass surgery to repair extreme blockages in his arteries. While he will be 86 when his current term ends in 2020, he told Washington-based *E&E News* in September 2016 that he has no plans to retire at that point. Some suspect he would like to close out his career as chairman of the Armed Services Committee, a post which -- assuming the Senate remains in Republican control -- would next come open in early 2021, when the current chairman, McCain, would be forced by step down due to term limits.

Inhofe was re-elected by almost identical margins in 2002 and 2008, both somewhat smaller than recent Republican presidential margins in Oklahoma. In 2002, he beat former Gov. David Walters, who had years earlier pleaded guilty to a misdemeanor count of violating campaign finance laws, 57%-36%. In 2008, he beat state Sen. Andrew Rice, 57%-39%. In 2014, he won a fourth full term with a more convincing 68% of the vote against little-known Democratic challenger Matt Silverstein. If Inhofe does decided to call it quits in 2020, there is already speculation that EPA Administrator Pruitt -- twice elected as state attorney general -- would be interested in succeeding him. Pruitt has "always been talked about as a potential contender" for Senate, Ronald Keith Gaddie, chairman of the political science department at the University of Oklahoma, told *E&E News*. And Inhofe himself, in comments to *The New York Times* in early 2017, said of Pruitt, "I think he'd make a great senator."

Junior Senator

James Lankford (R)

Elected 2014, term expires 2022, 1st full term; b. Mar 04, 1968, Dallas, TX; University of Texas, B.S., 1990; Southwestern Theological Baptist Seminary (TX), M.Div., 1994; Baptist; Married (Cindy Lankford); 2 children.

Professional Career: Youth camp Director, Baptist Gen. Convention of OK, 1995-2009.

DC Office: 316 HSOB 20510, 202-224-5754, Fax: 202-228-1015, lankford.senate.gov.

State Offices: Oklahoma City, 405-231-4941; Tulsa, 918-581-7651.

Committees: *Appropriations*: Commerce, Justice, Science & Related Agencies, Department of Homeland Security, DOL, HHS & Education & Related Agencies, Financial Services & General Government, Legislative Branch (Chmn), State, Foreign Operations & Related Programs. *Homeland Security & Government Affairs*: Federal Spending Oversight & Emergency Management, Investigations, Regulatory Affairs & Federal Management (Chmn). *Indian Affairs*. *Intelligence*. *Joint Congressional-Executive Commission on China*.

Group Ratings

	ADA	ACLU	AFL-CIO	LCV	ITI	COC	HAFA	ACU	CFG	FRC
2016	-	23%	-	6%	100%	88%	74%	92%	100%	100%
2015	0%	C	7%	4%	C	71%	C	96%	84%	100%

Almanac Ratings 2015

	Economy	Social	Foreign	Composite
Liberal	6%	0%	31%	12%
Conservative	94%	100%	69%	88%

Key Votes of the 114th Congress

1. Keystone pipeline	Y	5. National Security Data	Y	9. Gun Sales Checks	N
2. Export-Import Bank	Y	6. Iran Nuclear Deal	Y	10. Sanctuary Cities	Y
3. Debt Ceiling Increase	N	7. Puerto Rico Debt	Y	11. Planned Parenthood	Y
4. Homeland Security $$	N	8. Loretta Lynch A.G	N	12. Trade deals	Y

Election Results

Election	Name (Party)	Vote (%)		Cand. Spent	Ind. Exp. Support	Ind. Exp. Oppose
2016 General	James Lankford (R)	980,892	(68%)	$3,079,878	$2,000	
	Mike Workman (D)	355,911	(25%)			
	Robert Murphy (L)	43,421	(3%)			
	Sean Braddy (I)	40,405	(3%)	$4,518		
2016 Primary	James Lankford (R)	unopposed				

Prior winning percentages: 2014 special (68%), House: 2012 (59%), 2010 (63%)

Less than a decade ago, Republican James Lankford was a little-known church youth camp director without prior political experience. Today, he is Oklahoma's junior senator, first elected in 2014 following four years in the House in which he rose rapidly to occupy a position in the GOP leadership. Since coming to the Senate, Lankford has chaired the subcommittee with jurisdiction over the federal government workforce, while reaching across the political aisle on proposals ranging from personnel policy to governmental effectiveness and transparency. At the same time, reflecting his pre-congressional background, a large part of Lankford's legislative focus has been on maximizing religious freedom both overseas and at home, with the latter efforts sometimes intertwined with a conservative social agenda.

Lankford grew up impoverished in Dallas. His parents divorced when he was four years old, and, with his mother and older brother, he moved into the garage behind his grandparents' house. Lankford says he became a follower of Christ when he was eight, and that his religion has helped him endure tough times. He graduated from the University of Texas with a degree in secondary education, then attended the Southwestern Baptist Theological Seminary and earned a master's degree in divinity. In 1995, Lankford began working for the Baptist General Convention of Oklahoma. A year later, he was made director of the Falls Creek Christian youth summer camp, which touts itself as the largest summer camp in the country. He was in charge of organizing activities for more than 50,000 campers each summer.

In 2009, Lankford resigned to run for the Oklahoma City-based seat of GOP Rep. Mary Fallin after she decided to run for governor. With grassroots support among conservative Christians -- Southern Baptists comprise a significant portion of the Oklahoma population -- Lankford led in the initial round of voting, then won a stunning 65 percent in the primary runoff against state Rep. Kevin Calvey, who had the backing of national Republicans. Lankford also benefited from tea party support during the year in which that insurgent movement first made its mark on the electoral process. In the general election, Lankford easily defeated Democratic attorney Billy Coyle with 63 percent of the vote, even though he was running in the least conservative of Oklahoma's five districts.

In the House, Lankford was given a seat on the Oversight and Government Reform panel and won committee passage of several bills, including a measure setting new standards to promote transparency in the awarding of federal grants. On the Budget Committee, he became a firm supporter of Republican Chairman Paul Ryan's push to cut spending. *Politico* named him, along with California Democrat Karen Bass, as the freshman "most likely to succeed." When Georgia's Tom Price decided to run for GOP Conference chairman after the 2012 election, Lankford quietly lined up support from colleagues to succeed Price as chairman of the Republican Policy Committee. Making the case that he provided fresh blood from the large GOP Class of 2010, he was elected without opposition to the party's fifth-ranking post, a sign of respect from relentlessly ambitious colleagues. In his leadership post, he tried to define agenda items beyond the typical week-ahead congressional perspective, and he described his role as serving as the "eyes and ears" for Speaker John Boehner in the Republican Conference. But, as it turned out, he had little time to make an impact.

GOP Sen. Tom Coburn, a physician first elected to the Senate in 2004, was battling prostate cancer -- and announced in January 2014 that he would resign at the end of that year rather than serve out the final two years of his term. Lankford jumped into the Senate race. Despite his earlier backing from tea party interests, he rankled some in the movement for joining the GOP leadership and for some of his votes.

"We won't support Congressman Lankford's bid for the Senate because of his past votes to increase the debt limit, raise taxes, and fund Obamacare," declared an official of the tea party-aligned Senate Conservatives Fund. Such unhappiness came despite the fact that Lankford had voted with a majority of his House Republican colleagues against the "fiscal cliff" compromise at the end of 2012 that had raised taxes on the wealthiest Americans, as well as against the deal that ended a 16-day federal government shutdown in October 2013. Lankford joined a majority of his GOP colleagues in supporting a budget compromise negotiated at the end of 2013 by Ryan and Democratic Sen. Patty Murray of Washington that was strongly opposed by conservative groups.

Several of the tea party's most visible figures -- including former vice presidential nominee Sarah Palin, Texas Sen. Ted Cruz and Utah Sen. Mike Lee -- coalesced around T.W. Shannon, the former speaker of the Oklahoma House, in the Republican Senate primary. An African American who also is a member of the Chickasaw tribe, Shannon's candidacy was seen by some of his high-profile supporters as an opportunity to rebut criticisms of the Republican Party as lacking in racial diversity. "The Democrats accuse us of not embracing diversity? Oh, my goodness. He is it," Palin declared at an April event also attended by Cruz and Lee. Meanwhile, Coburn, who had emerged as one of the Senate's most outspoken conservatives, said he would remain out of the contest -- but, two weeks before the primary, released a statement calling Lankford "a man of absolute integrity." It was intended as a criticism of outside groups that had been hammering Lankford and not an endorsement, but was widely perceived as the latter. Lankford ran an ad featuring Coburn's words, while also drawing on his long-standing support from the Southern Baptist community, including former Arkansas Governor Mike Huckabee.

Lankford defeated Shannon by an unexpectedly strong 57%-34% in the June 24 primary, with the remaining 9 percent spread among five other candidates. The outcome was a surprise -- particularly for conservative groups, who were planning a big push for Shannon in an August runoff that would have resulted if no candidate got more than 50 percent of the vote. A Mississippi Senate runoff, in which veteran Sen. Thad Cochran faced a serious challenge from a tea party candidate, was taking place the same day as the Oklahoma primary; conservative groups focused their efforts on Mississippi, miscalculating there would be another day to fight in Oklahoma. In the solidly conservative Sooner State, the GOP nomination assured Lankford's election in November to fill the remainder of Coburn's term. He received 68 percent against Democratic state Rep. Connie Johnson, the first woman and the first African-American nominee for Senate from Oklahoma. In 2016, Lankford received a similar percentage of the vote in defeating Democratic political operative Mike Workman to win a full Senate term.

In the Senate, Lankford got a plum assignment to the Appropriations Committee, as well as a seat on the Intelligence panel. The latter slot provided Lankford with increased visibility in early 2017, as he made the rounds of cable news shows while the Intelligence Committee began to grapple with an investigation into allegations of Russian interference in the 2016 president election. Yet another assignment was to the Indian Affairs Committee; Oklahoma's population is 8.5 percent Indian, putting it fourth nationally behind Alaska, New Mexico and South Dakota in terms of its percentage of Native Americans.

Lankford has taken a particular interest in freedom of religion. When the Senate in May 2015 approved expedited trade negotiating authority for President Barack Obama in conjunction with the proposed Trans- Pacific Partnership, Lankford won inclusion of an amendment that U.S. trading partners should encourage religious freedom. He noted that a U.S. commission monitoring international religious freedom had urged the State Department to designate Vietnam as a country of particular concern. Nearly two years later, after President Donald Trump had taken office, Lankford sponsored a resolution with Florida Republican Marco Rubio and Delaware Democrat Chris Coons (who, like Lankford, holds a master's degree in divinity) "reaffirming the commitment of the United States to promoting religious freedom." Pointing to a recent Pew Center finding that nearly 80 percent of the world's population lives in countries where freedom of religion is highly restricted, the resolution encouraged Trump to appoint an ambassador-at-large for international religious freedom within the State Department.

Lankford's interest in religious freedom also has extended to the home front, where his efforts have been more controversial. In early 2015, he introduced resolutions of disapproval aimed at overturning two measures passed by the District of Columbia City Council designed to protect the right to an abortion and the rights of gay student groups. Lankford voiced concern that those policies could restrict the rights of others, including religious groups. In February 2017, Lankford introduced legislation to negate a 1954 provision in the tax code -- included at the behest of then-Sen. Lyndon Johnson -- that prohibits clergy as well as leaders of non-profit groups from advocating for or against candidates for office, at the risk of losing their organizations' tax-exempt status. "The federal government and the IRS should never have the ability to inhibit free speech," declared Lankford. Three months after Lankford introduced his legislation, Trump issued an executive order "promoting free speech and religious liberty" that also took aim at the so-called Johnson amendment. Lankford emphasized that his legislation would maintain the prohibition against monetary contributions to political candidates from churches or non-profit groups that operate under section 501(c)(3) of the tax code.

As chairman of the Homeland Security and Governmental Affairs Subcommittee on Regulatory Affairs and Federal Management, Lankford has worked with Democratic Sen. Heidi Heitkamp of North Dakota, the panel's ranking minority member, on several bills. Citing an increase in embezzlement of government benefits by dishonest representatives of retirees, Lankford and Heitkamp got legislation through the Senate in 2015 to give U.S. attorneys the power to prosecute retiree representatives who misuse funds. In 2017, the two -- along with veteran Republican Sens. Orrin Hatch of Utah and Pat Roberts of Kansas -- sponsored legislation requiring an "advanced notice of proposed rulemaking" at least 90 days before an official notice with the proposed regulation is issued. "An advanced notice of proposed rulemaking for major rules gives everyone an equal opportunity to be able to contribute their ideas before you actually get to the language portion of writing a regulation," Lankford explained.

Lankford has worked with other libertarian-minded Republicans to reduce mandatory questionnaires from the Census Bureau that they viewed as overly intrusive from the standpoint of personal freedom. He also collaborated with two Democratic colleagues, Cory Booker of New Jersey and Mark Warner of Virginia, on one of the last measures that Obama signed before leaving office. The law made permanent what is known as the Presidential Innovation Fellows program, which since 2012 has paired outside technology experts and entrepreneurs with high-ranking civil servants to come up with solutions to challenges facing the public sector.

Since Lankford largely hews to the party line in public pronouncements, it created a bit of a stir when, shortly before Trump took office, there was a leaked transcript of a private conference call in which he expressed nervousness about the incoming president. Alluding to Trump's criticism of trade agreements throughout the campaign, Lankford told a group of Oklahoma business executives, "[Trump] has reassured me that he is a trade person and does want deals-he just wants a good deal, but I have never heard what a good deal is."

Lankford also characterized Trump's campaign trail threats toward other countries belonging to the North Atlantic Treaty Organization (NATO) as "sloppy," adding: "My one nervous moment will be the first state dinner when Trump has a foreign leader over to the White House for dinner, meeting with all those different folks and what is going to be said and done because the president's words do have international effect." Afterward, Lankford's press secretary, in confirming the veracity of the recording, told an Oklahoma City TV station: "This private conference-call meeting was meant to be private and off-the-record, but there isn't anything in this summary that is different than what the senator has said in public venues numerous times. The same James Lankford in private is the same James Lankford in public."

FIRST DISTRICT

Jim Bridenstine (R)

Elected 2012, 3rd term; b. Jun 15, 1975, Ann Arbor, MI; Rice University (TX), B.A.; Cornell University (NY), M.B.A.; Baptist; Married (Michelle D. Ivory); 3 children.

Military Career: U.S Navy, 1998-2007; Navy Reserve, 2010-present.

Professional Career: Defense consultant, Wyle Labs., 2007-2008; Director, Tulsa Air & Space Museum, 2008-2010.

DC Office: 216 CHOB 20515, 202-225-2211, Fax: 202-225-9187, bridenstine.house.gov.

State Offices: Tulsa, 918-935-3222.

Committees: *Armed Services*: Seapower & Projection Forces, Strategic Forces. *Science, Space & Technology*: Energy, Space.

Group Ratings

	ADA	ACLU	AFL-CIO	LCV	ITI	COC	HAFA	ACU	CFG	FRC
2016	5%	11%	17%	0%	67%	92%	92%	100%	96%	100%
2015	5%	C	17%	3%	C	60%	C	96%	92%	100%

Almanac Ratings 2015

	Economy	Social	Foreign	Composite
Liberal	8%	0%	0%	3%
Conservative	93%	100%	100%	98%

Key Votes of the 114th Congress

1. Keystone Pipeline	Y	5. Puerto Rico Debt	N	9. Offenses by Aliens	Y
2. Trade Deals	N	6. Medical Marijuana	N	10. Troops in Iraq	N
3. Export-Import Bank	N	7. Sanctuary Cities	Y	11. Homeland Security $$	N
4. Debt Ceiling Increase	N	8. Armor-piercing Bullets	Y	12. Trade Adjustment aid	N

Election Results

Election	Name (Party)	Vote (%)	Cand. Spent	Ind. Exp. Support	Ind. Exp. Oppose
2016 General	Jim Bridenstine (R)................	(100%)	$1,095,139	$35,818	
2016 Primary	Jim Bridenstine (R)................ 50,595	(81%)			
	Tom Atkinson (R).................. 10,047	(16%)			

Prior winning percentages: 2014 (0%), 2012 (64%)

Republican Jim Bridenstine, first elected in 2012 with tea party-backing against a veteran incumbent in the primary, became a leader of House GOP rebels. His hard-nosed tactics played well at home. He set a six-year term-limit for himself and sought the nomination of President Donald Trump ad administrator of the National Aeronautics and Space Administration.

The son of an accountant and a schoolteacher, Bridenstine was born in Ann Arbor, Michigan. His family moved to Arlington, Texas, and then to Jenks, a suburb of Tulsa, when he was in high school. He attended Rice University in Houston, where he was a triple-major in business administration, economics and psychology.

Bridenstine has shown impressive skills during and after military service. After graduating from Rice, he joined the Navy and became a pilot of the E-2 Hawkeye, an airborne command and control plane. As a naval aviator, he served tours of duty in Iraq and Afghanistan, flying combat missions and logging more than 1,900 hours. He flew the F-18 Hornet with the Naval Strike and Air Warfare Center in Nevada. During that time, he bought a small ranch in Nevada and began to raise alpacas, a small South American mammal that produces fur used for knitted and woven items. After leaving active duty, Bridenstine and his wife, Michelle, worked in Orlando, Florida, at a defense consulting firm, Wyle Laboratories. Simultaneously, he earned his MBA from Cornell University, flying to New York every other weekend for classes. In 2008, they returned to Tulsa, where he became director of the city's Air and Space Museum. He has been a lieutenant commander in the Navy Reserve, flying missions in Central and South America in support of the war on drugs, and later transferred to the air refueling wing of the Oklahoma Air National Guard

In 2011, Bridenstine launched a long-shot primary campaign against veteran Rep. John Sullivan. The incumbent had a conservative voting record and had had no trouble winning reelection. Bridenstine painted Sullivan as an out-of-touch career politician with a proclivity for missing votes. Sullivan had been admitted to a rehabilitation center for alcoholism treatment after the death of his daughter, which he said explained his missed votes. Sullivan accused Bridenstine of operating the Air and Space Museum at a loss and putting it in financial jeopardy. Bridenstine responded that his project to bring a space shuttle to the museum was a secure venture that raised the museum's visibility, though the four shuttles went to museums elsewhere (Florida, Virginia, New York and California). Sullivan outspent Bridenstine $990,000 to $244,000. But Bridenstine won, 54%-46%. He dispatched Democratic businessman John Olson in the general, with 63 percent of the vote. A strong believer in term limits, he vowed to serve no more than three terms in the House.

He made an early start as a House rebel, casting his first vote in 2013 for Majority Leader Eric Cantor of Virginia for Speaker rather than for returning John Boehner. His office issued a statement that his vote "should not have been a surprise to anyone who followed his campaign." In 2015, Bridenstine again voted against Boehner, criticizing him for having "relinquished the power of the purse" to Obama in the bipartisan spending deal during the 2014 lame-duck session. He was among several conservative House Republicans who became targets that year of radio advertisements by the Boehner-affiliated American Action Network urging that they support the spending bill for the Homeland Security Department rather than risk a partial government shutdown over immigration policy.

At the Armed Services Committee, Bridenstine worked on military-space provisions. On the annual defense spending bill in 2015, the House added parts of his initiative to fund the Air Force's Satellite Communications Pathfinder program. The final version of the 2016 defense bill included several provisions from Bridenstine's American Space Renaissance Act, which he described as bold reforms across military, civil, and commercial space sectors.

On the Science, Space and Technology Committee, he chaired the Environment panel for two years. In 2015, the House passed the Weather Research and Forecasting Innovation Act, which he co-authored with fellow Oklahoma Republican Rep. Frank Lucas. The measure was designed to provide additional warnings to states such as Oklahoma that have suffered the devastating effects of severe weather, such as tornadoes and hurricanes. The Senate passed its version in December 2016, but Congress ran out of time to resolve differences. Bridenstine and Lucas renewed their effort in January 2017 and won quick House passage of a measure that was nearly identical to the Senate bill. The legislation extended a pilot program for the National Oceanic and Atmospheric Administration to procure commercial satellite weather data.

Bridenstine has had an easy time winning reelection, with no Democratic opponents. In 2016, he was challenged in the Republican primary by Tom Atkinson, a businessman in the oil industry. Atkinson raised nearly $800,000, including $450,000 in self-financing. Bridenstine raised a similar sum and won 81 percent of the vote, of which four-fifths was cast in Tulsa County. During the presidential campaign, when Speaker Paul Ryan distanced himself from Donald Trump, Bridenstine tweeted, "Given the stakes of this election, if Paul Ryan isn't for Trump, then I'm not for Paul Ryan." In January 2017, with Trump securely elected, he voted for Ryan. Following the election, with the help of friends, Bridenstine promoted himself to head NASA. He talked up the opportunity for space exploration to the moon to obtain billions of tons of water ice believed to exist in lunar craters.

Tulsa Area

Population		**Race and Ethnicity**		**Income**	
Total	773,811	White	65.9%	Median Income	$50,634 (248 out of 435)
Land area	1,632	Black	8.6%		
Pop/ sq mi	474.2	Latino	10.5%		
Born in state	58.0%	Asian	2.4%	Under $50,000	49.3%
		Two races	7.2%	$50,000-$99,999	30.6%
Age Groups		Other	5.5%	$100,000-$199,999	16.0%
Under 18	25.4%			$200,000 or more	4.1%
18-34	23.2%	**Education**		Poverty Rate	15.0%
35-64	38.2%	H.S grad or less	38.6%		
Over 64	13.2%	Some college	32.4%	**Health Insurance**	
		College Degree, 4 yr	20.0%	With health insurance coverage	83.8%
Work		Post grad	9.1%		
White Collar	36.0%				
Sales and Service	42.1%	**Military**		**Public Assistance**	
Blue Collar	21.8%	Veteran	9.3%	Cash public assistance income	2.6%
Government	5.6%	Active Duty	0.1%		
				Food stamp/SNAP benefits	12.5%

Voter Turnout			
2015 Total Citizens 18+	542,574	2016 House Turnout as % CVAP	N/A
2016 House turnout	N/A	2014 House Turnout as % CVAP	N/A

2012 Presidential Vote		
Mitt Romney	188,961	(66%)
Barack Obama	98,321	(34%)

2016 Presidential Vote		
Donald Trump	191,343	(61%)
Hillary Clinton	101,757	(33%)
Gary Johnson	18,406	(6%)

Cook Partisan Voting Index: R+17

The gushers of the 1905 Glenn Pool discovery made Tulsa one of America's oil boomtowns, settled not just by people from the immediate hinterland but also by Midwesterners and New Englanders of Yankee stock. In the 1920s, as its art deco skyscrapers rose on the heights above the Arkansas River, it was still a raw town, but one bent on becoming more cultured. It was optimistic and ready to seek economic change, yet culturally and politically conservative, with a Yankee elite and an American Indian heritage recalled today in one of the nation's best collections of Western art at the Gilcrease Museum - left by oil millionaire Thomas Gilcrease, who was one-eighth Creek Indian. Tulsa, also the home of Oral Roberts University, has remained cosmopolitan but conservative.

In recent decades, Tulsa has boomed and occasionally busted. In 2003, voters approved a $900 million initiative funded by a one-cent sales tax increase, as part of Tulsa's efforts to diversify. That has become the "Vision 2025" tax of six-tenths of a cent. The tax has helped pay for everything from Arkansas River protection work to new university buildings to upgrades at city parks and golf courses. The American Airlines maintenance center in Tulsa, completed in 1992, is the largest such facility in the world. The American hub employs 5,200 people at the primary maintenance base for the world's largest airline. That presence spurred other aerospace-related development in Tulsa, which has become the base of the Oklahoma Aerospace Alliance. More than 500 aerospace firms in the state have an annual output of about $13 billion, including more than 20,000 workers in Tulsa. The next two largest companies are NORDAM, which makes aerospace components, and Spirit AeroSystems, a Boeing supplier.

The 1st Congressional District of Oklahoma includes Tulsa, Wagoner and Washington counties, and small slices of Rogers and Creek counties - just about all of the Tulsa metropolitan area. The political tradition here is heavily Republican, strengthened in recent decades by opposition to national Democrats' cultural liberalism. Donald Trump got 61 percent of the vote here in 2016, but the 1st ranked only fourth among the five Oklahoma districts in its vote for Trump, as well as for Mitt Romney, who got 66 percent in 2012. It's not likely that Republican presidential candidates will need to worry about Oklahoma any time soon.

SECOND DISTRICT

Markwayne Mullin (R)

Elected 2012, 3rd term; b. Jul 26, 1977, Tulsa; Missouri Valley College, 1996; Oklahoma State University Institute of Technology, Assc. Deg., 2010; Pentecostal; Married (Christie Mullin); 5 children (twins).

Professional Career: Owner, Mullin Plumbing, 1996-present.

DC Office: 1113 LHOB 20515, 202-225-2701, Fax: 202-225-3038, mullin.house.gov.

State Offices: McAlester, 918-423-5951; Muskogee, 918-687-2533.

Committees: *Energy & Commerce*: Digital Commerce & Consumer Protection, Energy, Health.

Group Ratings

	ADA	ACLU	AFL-CIO	LCV	ITI	COC	HAFA	ACU	CFG	FRC
2016	-	5%	-	0%	100%	100%	68%	92%	91%	100%
2015	0%	C	21%	3%	C	90%	C	79%	63%	92%

Almanac Ratings 2015

	Economy	Social	Foreign	Composite
Liberal	10%	0%	0%	3%
Conservative	90%	100%	100%	97%

Key Votes of the 114th Congress

1. Keystone Pipeline	Y	5. Puerto Rico Debt	N	9. Offenses by Aliens	Y
2. Trade Deals	Y	6. Medical Marijuana	N	10. Troops in Iraq	N
3. Export-Import Bank	Y	7. Sanctuary Cities	Y	11. Homeland Security $$	N
4. Debt Ceiling Increase	N	8. Armor-piercing Bullets	Y	12. Trade Adjustment aid	N

Election Results

Election	Name (Party)	Vote (%)		Cand. Spent	Ind. Exp. Support	Ind. Exp. Oppose
2016 General	Markwayne Mullin (R)................	189,839	(71%)	$1,453,510	$190	
	Joshua Harris-Till (D)....................	62,387	(23%)			
2016 Primary	Markwayne Mullin (R)..................	20,052	(63%)			
	Jarrin Jackson (R).........................	11,575	(37%)			

Prior winning percentages: 2014 (70%), 2012 (57%)

Republican plumber Markwayne Mullin, elected in 2012, succeeded one of the House's last conservative Southern Democrats. He has been an outspoken conservative, but a more reliable vote for the GOP leadership than some other junior Republicans. A fitness buff, he has spent time in the House gym with Speaker Paul Ryan.

Mullin was born in Tulsa and grew up in Westville, a small town on the Arkansas line, as the youngest of seven children. His father ran a small plumbing business, which Mullin took over at age 19 after briefly attending Missouri Valley College. He expanded the company from six employees to more than 100. He hosted a local talk show advising callers on home repair. Mullin, a Cherokee, operates the Oklahoma Fight Club in Broken Arrow, a training center for jujitsu and mixed martial arts. He earned an associate's degree in business from the Oklahoma State University Institute of Technology in Okmulgee.

Mullin was one of six Republican candidates for the open seat of retiring Democratic Rep. Dan Boren. Arguing against excessive regulation and saying it was "time to fire Barack Obama," he was the first to jump into the race and became the front-runner. His fundraising outpaced that of his GOP rivals, although a good portion was self-financed. In the June primary, he coasted to a first-place finish with 42 percent of the vote to 23 percent for George Faught, a Republican state House member. In the runoff, Faught accused Mullin of carpet-bagging when property records showed that he had claimed homestead tax exemptions in Wagoner County, outside the district. Mullin labeled Faught a career politician and won the runoff handily, 57%-43%.

Democrats nominated Rob Wallace, a former assistant U.S. attorney. In September, news broke that Mullin Plumbing had received about $370,000 in federal economic stimulus money for housing projects with the Cherokee and Muscogee nations. Mullin had campaigned heavily against Obama's stimulus program, and Wallace accused him of acting like an "out-of-touch, typical Washington politician." Mullin claimed not to know that the projects got stimulus money, but documents from the Cherokee Nation obtained by the *Tulsa World* contradicted that assertion. Other business practices of Mullin came under fire, including the storage of firearms and employee background checks for illegal immigrants. Those attacks mostly fell flat. Mullin outspent Wallace, $1.7 million to $1.2 million, and won, 57%-38%.

Mullin has been active on the Energy and Commerce Committee, where he has provided an "Oklahoma business owner perspective" on its broad agenda of regulatory and health care issues. He backed legislation to limit the Obama administration's "Clean Power Plan" to impose big increases in electricity rates. He took on an unusual adversary in 2016, when he filed a bill to require the rapidly growing Ultimate Fighting Championship to disclose more information about its finances, including how it handles its martial-arts competitors. "The only way the sport is sustainable is the fighters being treated on an even playing field," said Mullin, the only member of Congress who has competed in MMA. In December 2016, the Commerce, Manufacturing and Trade Subcommittee, on which he served, held a hearing on the bill. Mullin won the enactment of multiple bills that he filed in 2015-16, including: standards for manufacturers to use internet websites to meet warranty and labeling requirements for consumer products; procedures for low-volume auto manufacturers to meet federal regulations; and three bills related to Indian tribes.

Mullin has taken a personal approach to his work. He used his fitness expertise to bond with members from both parties, including early morning interval training exercises at the House gym and the formation with Democratic Rep. Donald Payne of New Jersey of the Men's Health Caucus. He posts a "Mullin' It Over Column" on his office website most weeks, with informal and home-spun views on his life in Washington and at home.

In 2016, Mullin had a competitive primary against Jarrin Jackson, a West Point graduate who served two tours of duty in Afghanistan. Jackson criticized Mullin for having "only voted to grow government" and for perhaps backing away from his earlier campaign pledge to serve only three terms in the House. Three months before the primary, Mullin had issued a brief statement to *The Oklahoman* that he and his wife "will continue to seek the Lord's guidance and do what is best for our family and the 2nd District of Oklahoma" on his term-limits pledge. Citing Mullin's uncertainty, former Oklahoma Sen. Tom Coburn endorsed Jackson. Current Sens. Jim Inhofe and James Lankford endorsed Mullin. He won the June 2016 primary, 63%-37%, which was the narrowest margin for any of the five House incumbents from Oklahoma, each of whom faced a primary in 2016.

Following the election, Mullin reportedly was under consideration to head the Bureau of Indian Affairs.

East Oklahoma: Tulsa Suburbs, Muskogee

Population		**Race and Ethnicity**		**Income**	
Total	749,607	White	65.2%	Median Income	$39,407 (400 out of 435)
Land area	20,995	Black	3.5%		
Pop/ sq mi	35.7	Latino	4.8%		
Born in state	61.6%	Asian	0.5%	Under $50,000	60.4%
Age Groups		Two races	10.5%	$50,000-$99,999	28.0%
Under 18	23.8%	Other	15.5%	$100,000-$199,999	10.0%
18-34	20.8%	**Education**		$200,000 or more	1.6%
35-64	38.1%	H.S grad or less	52.9%	Poverty Rate	20.6%
Over 64	17.3%	Some college	30.6%	**Health Insurance**	
Work		College Degree, 4 yr	11.2%	With health insurance coverage	79.8%
White Collar	28.6%	Post grad	5.3%		
Sales and Service	41.3%	**Military**		**Public Assistance**	
Blue Collar	30.1%	Veteran	10.7%	Cash public assistance income	4.3%
Government	6.7%	Active Duty	0.0%		
				Food stamp/SNAP benefits	17.9%

Voter Turnout			
2015 Total Citizens 18+	561,906	2016 House Turnout as % CVAP	48%
2016 House turnout	268,870	2014 House Turnout as % CVAP	28%

2012 Presidential Vote		
Mitt Romney	170,983	(68%)
Barack Obama	81,179	(32%)

2016 Presidential Vote		
Donald Trump	198,155	(73%)
Hillary Clinton	62,022	(23%)
Gary Johnson	11,667	(4%)

Cook Partisan Voting Index: R+24

The land that is now northeast Oklahoma used to be Indian territory, the place where in the 1830s the Five Civilized Tribes were driven from Georgia and Alabama over the Trail of Tears. A sizable minority here report their race as American Indian. The Native American identity is highest in the hilly counties west of the Ozarks of Arkansas, where county names - Cherokee, Osage, Sequoyah - recall the Civilized Tribes. The street signs in scenic Tahlequah, the Cherokee capital since 1839, are written in both English and Cherokee. The Creek Nation chose its tribal site in Okmulgee in the belief that tornadoes would not strike the area; history has proven the choice correct so far - tornadoes have done minimal damage here. Bicyclists from the Cherokee Nation have an annual three-week trip for 950 miles across seven states to retrace the Trail of Tears. South of Indian country is Oklahoma's Little Dixie, settled between 1889 and 1907 by white Southerners, most of them poor. Some of the county names - such as Le Flore - are borrowed straight from Mississippi.

This pleasant land of gentle hills and man-made lakes recently has grown at a healthy pace with population spread from Tulsa. Interstate highways and turnpikes connect people to jobs in more-vibrant metropolitan areas, while the lakes have spurred resort and retirement communities. Still, traditional cultural attitudes and folkways remain strong. When Oklahoma voted in 2002 to outlaw cockfighting, voters in many Little Dixie towns turned out in large numbers to oppose the ban. The most populated city here is Muskogee, an old railroad community with a manufacturing economy that had slowed in recent years; there have been signs of local revival, with retail development.

The 2nd Congressional District includes eastern Oklahoma, except for the Tulsa area. It borders on four states and takes in Muskogee; Claremore, Will Rogers' hometown; and McAlester, hometown of former House Speaker Carl Albert. McAlester is the site of a massive Army ammunition plant that manufactures non-nuclear bombs and is the largest local employer. In 2014, the plant began work to upgrade and extend the life of 2,000 Stinger missiles. Tiny Spavinaw in the northeast corner was the birthplace of baseball legend Mickey Mantle. The area was ancestrally Democratic. Since the retirement in 1976 of Albert, a New Deal Democrat, the area has become as solidly Republican as most of Oklahoma. The 2016 election confirmed that the vestiges of Yellow Dog Democrats had mostly disappeared from Little Dixie: Donald Trump won the presidential vote, 73%-23%.

THIRD DISTRICT

Frank Lucas (R)

Elected 1994, 12th term; b. Jan 06, 1960, Cheyenne; Oklahoma State University, B.S., 1982; Baptist; Married (Lynda L. Bradshaw Lucas); 3 children; 2 grandchildren.

Elected Office: OK House, 1988-1994.
Professional Career: Farmer & rancher.

DC Office: 2405 RHOB 20515, 202-225-5565, Fax: 202-225-8698, lucas.house.gov.

State Offices: Yukon, 405-373-1958.

Committees: *Agriculture*: Conservation & Forestry (Chmn), General Farm Commodities & Risk Management. *Financial Services*: Financial Institutions & Consumer Credit, Monetary Policy & Trade. *Science, Space & Technology*: Energy, Research & Technology, Space.

Group Ratings

	ADA	ACLU	AFL-CIO	LCV	ITI	COC	HAFA	ACU	CFG	FRC
2016	-	5%	-	0%	100%	100%	52%	84%	70%	100%
2015	0%	C	22%	3%	C	95%	C	58%	39%	92%

Almanac Ratings 2015

	Economy	Social	Foreign	Composite
Liberal	14%	5%	0%	6%
Conservative	86%	95%	100%	94%

Key Votes of the 114th Congress

1. Keystone Pipeline	Y	5. Puerto Rico Debt	Y	9. Offenses by Aliens	Y
2. Trade Deals	Y	6. Medical Marijuana	N	10. Troops in Iraq	N
3. Export-Import Bank	Y	7. Sanctuary Cities	Y	11. Homeland Security $$	N
4. Debt Ceiling Increase	Y	8. Armor-piercing Bullets	Y	12. Trade Adjustment aid	N

Election Results

Election	Name (Party)	Vote (%)		Cand. Spent	Ind. Exp. Support	Ind. Exp. Oppose
2016 General	Frank Lucas (R)	227,525	(78%)	$635,939		
	Frankie Robbins (D)	63,090	(22%)			
2016 Primary	Frank Lucas (R)	42,006	(78%)			
	Desiree Brown (R)	11,886	(21%)			

Prior winning percentages: 2014 (79%), 2012 (75%), 2010 (78%), 2008 (70%), 2006 (68%), 2004 (82%), 2002 (76%), 2000 (59%), 1998 (65%), 1996 (64%), 1994 (70%)

Republican Frank Lucas, who won a 1994 special election, is a soft-spoken, unflashy farmer and rancher who has become a senior and savvy lawmaker. As chairman of the Agriculture Committee until 2015, he sought to bridge deal-oriented lawmakers from farm states and budget-conscious conservatives. After being term-limited as chairman, he moved to new niches at the Financial Services and Science committees. In 2017, he took the reins at the Agriculture Subcommittee on Conservation and Forestry.

Lucas' family roots in western Oklahoma extend more than 100 years; he owns a 480-acre farm and cattle ranch in Roger Mills County. He studied agricultural economics at Oklahoma State University, where he was active in the College Republicans and student government. He was elected to the Oklahoma House at age 28 after losing two races. He shared an office there with Jim Reese, who became the state's secretary and commissioner of agriculture. "He's not a showboat," Reese told *The New York Times* in 2012. "He just goes about doing his work and tries to work with everybody and is not about getting credit for himself."

He ran for Congress when veteran conservative Democratic Rep. Glenn English resigned to head the National Rural Electric Cooperative Association. In the primary, he trailed state Sen. Brooks Douglass, who campaigned from his Oklahoma City base, 36%-34%. In the runoff, Lucas ridiculed "some Johnny-come-lately dressed up like a drugstore cowboy" and carried the rural areas to win 56%-44%. In the general, he faced Dan Webber, the 27-year-old press secretary for Democratic Sen. David Boren. Lucas ran an ad depicting the Capitol and saying, "This is where Dan Webber has worked his entire adult life." The ad displayed a picture of Oklahoma farmland and said, "This is where Frank Lucas has worked his entire adult life." Lucas won 54%-46%.

Lucas' voting record is mostly conservative. As shown by his *Almanac* vote ratings for 2015, he has broken from conservative orthodoxy on economic matters. He has voted against GOP amendments to abolish or cut funding for federal programs such as rural airport subsidies and the Economic Development Administration. The Club for Growth threatened, but failed, to recruit a primary opponent in 2014 after he scored in the bottom third among Republicans in the anti-tax group's legislative ratings in 2011 and 2012. He said that the criticism didn't bother him. "Any time I have to choose between the influences of D.C. political groups and my fellow Oklahomans, I will always side with my fellow Oklahomans," he told the *Tulsa World.*

His chief base has been the Agriculture Committee. On the 2002 farm bill, Lucas helped to unravel the 1996 Freedom to Farm Act and its rollback of government subsidies, although he had once embraced the law and its conservative philosophical underpinnings. Lucas helped write provisions to control erosion, aid farmers hit by drought, and protect air and water quality. He successfully fought a plan to reduce the number of Farm Service Agency field offices. In the minority during work on the 2008 farm bill, Lucas strongly opposed an overhaul of farm programs as "a threat to the nutrition of the whole, entire world," and he mostly succeeded in preserving subsidies for his district, which ranked 14th in subsidies between 1995 and 2009. With an eye on his district, Lucas helped to write the final provisions in the 2005 energy bill governing rural grants and biodiesel tax credits. He has been a proponent of government support for alternative fuels, particularly switchgrass.

As chairman in 2011, he found himself leading a committee full of freshmen and new members who did not share his bipartisan leanings. "Not everyone on the committee understands the history of farm bills, which have never been partisan by nature," he told *National Journal.* "Getting them to understand the culture is a process." He worked closely with Agriculture's ranking Democrat Collin Peterson of Minnesota to report a five-year farm bill from the committee in 2012.

But the measure never came to a vote that year in the full House. Some conservatives wanted deeper cuts to the food stamp program, which Democrats fiercely resisted. In a closed-door GOP meeting, House Speaker John Boehner reportedly criticized the committee bill's dairy provisions - which contained a new market stabilization plan that major milk processors strongly opposed - as "communism." The delays frustrated Lucas, who labored for months to strike a deal acceptable to House GOP leaders, whom he referred to as "the management."

By that summer, Lucas again thought he had found a political recipe to pass a bill. The legislation he managed to get to the floor looked to be a conservatives' dream: It cut spending $40 billion over 10 years, including $20 billion from the food stamp program, and it had bipartisan support from Peterson and many other farm-state Democrats. Discontented conservatives passed an amendment to give states the option of imposing work requirements on food stamp recipients, a move that shattered the delicate political coalition behind the bill. Lucas made a desperate last-minute plea on the House floor, but the farm bill failed on final passage, 195-234. Sixty-two Republicans voted against it while only 24 Democrats voted for it.

Lucas was the target of radio ads from Washington-based Heritage Action threatening to recruit a "real conservative" to run against him in 2014. "I'm under attack by those people," Lucas said. "They're coming after me. They are all special interest groups that exist to sell subscriptions, to collect seminar fees, and to perpetuate their goals." At one point, he lamented, "it shouldn't be this hard to pass a farm bill."

When he finally passed the bill in 2014, which Lucas called his "single biggest accomplishment" as chairman, he said that its "fundamental guise" was that it became an insurance measure in place of the direct payment program for farm commodities. "When things are beyond our control, or has been the case occasionally in my lifetime, have been manipulated by outside forces, outside governments or even sometimes government actions here at home - then these safety nets are necessary," as he explained the bill. The House passed the bill, 251-166, with bipartisan support in January 2014.

After his term-limited exit from the Agriculture Committee helm in 2015, Lucas found himself, like other term-limited House GOP chairmen, looking for opportunities to remain relevant. Some members urged him to challenge Jeb Hensarling of Texas, the hard-edged chairman at Financial Services. But it's difficult to knock out a sitting chairman, especially one who has the support of the huge Texas delegation and where party leaders had no obvious reason to make a change.

When Hensarling refused to give him a subcommittee chairmanship or other influence, Lucas pursued another Texas chairman - Lamar Smith at Science, Space and Technology - and became vice chairman of that committee. In 2015, Lucas worked to build bridges on the panel to pass legislation. With fellow Oklahoma Republican Jim Bridenstine, Lucas shaped a bipartisan bill to improve weather forecasting, which the House passed that year and again in January 2017. With his Democratic ally Peterson, Lucas in 2015 passed a bill to create a science advisory board to promote fairness and independence at the Environmental Protection Agency.

Lucas has been reelected by wide margins - at least 67 percent since 2000. Despite the unhappiness of national conservative groups, he has not faced serious competition in GOP primaries. The real trouble for the easygoing Lucas seems to be on his ranch. He broke his nose years ago when a cow slammed a gate on him, and he lost a tooth while trying to attach an identification tag to a 250-pound heifer. When drought hit Oklahoma hard in 2011, he found himself forced to sell off some of his herd. "Watching my wife agonize over her mama cows, that's never any fun," he told the *Times*.

Western and Central Oklahoma: Suburbs of Oklahoma City and Tulsa

Population		**Race and Ethnicity**		**Income**	
Total	767,882	White	75.1%	Median Income	$47,952 (286 out of 435)
Land area	34,117	Black	3.6%		
Pop/ sq mi	22.5	Latino	9.2%		
Born in state	64.4%	Asian	1.4%	Under $50,000	51.8%
		Two races	5.0%	$50,000-$99,999	31.3%
Age Groups		Other	5.9%	$100,000-$199,999	14.1%
Under 18	24.4%			$200,000 or more	2.7%
18-34	23.7%	**Education**		Poverty Rate	15.0%
35-64	37.1%	H.S grad or less	48.2%		
Over 64	14.8%	Some college	30.2%	**Health Insurance**	
		College Degree, 4 yr	14.7%	With health insurance coverage	85.3%
Work		Post grad	6.8%		
White Collar	31.0%				
Sales and Service	40.1%	**Military**		**Public Assistance**	
Blue Collar	28.9%	Veteran	9.8%	Cash public assistance income	2.7%
Government	7.1%	Active Duty	0.4%		
				Food stamp/SNAP benefits	11.5%

Voter Turnout			
2015 Total Citizens 18+	559,225	2016 House Turnout as % CVAP	52%
2016 House turnout	290,615	2014 House Turnout as % CVAP	30%

2012 Presidential Vote		
Mitt Romney	199,390	(74%)
Barack Obama	70,346	(26%)

2016 Presidential Vote		
Donald Trump	216,078	(74%)
Hillary Clinton	61,179	(21%)
Gary Johnson	16,160	(6%)

Cook Partisan Voting Index: R+27

Settled at the turn of the 20th century, western Oklahoma is a fertile land forever at the mercy of the elements. The western plains are scorching hot under the summer sun and blown frozen by bitter winter winds. Visitors to the Tallgrass Prairie Preserve, maintained by the Nature Conservancy near Pawhuska, can experience what settlers found when they arrived here: a swaying ocean of 10-foot-high grasses filled with insects emitting a dull, incessant roar. Many rural counties here are not much more populated than they were 100 years ago. Today, local entrepreneurs see the possibility of economic revival in another abundant natural resource: the wind. Kansas company TradeWind has purchased multiple wind farm properties in western Oklahoma. Developers have proposed a transmission line that could transform the prairie into a national wind energy hub.

Solar power has increased in the Panhandle, with a subsidiary of Arkansas Electric Cooperatives owning a 1-megawatt solar project in Hooker. The region is home to the world's largest plot of switchgrass, and there are hopes that it too can become a profitable source of alternative energy. In 2010, the state government set a goal of making Oklahoma 15 percent dependent on renewable energy by 2015. As of November 2016, 30 percent of the state's electricity came from renewables.

The 3rd Congressional District includes Oklahoma's western plains and nearly half of the state's land. It includes the university town of Stillwater, and Osage County, site of the state's lone Indian reservation. A few of the southern counties, settled by farmers crossing the Red River from Texas, are ancestrally Democratic. Farmers coming south from Kansas settled most of these plains, and they were heavily Republican. There are two Air Force bases (Altus and Vance) at opposite corners of the district. Farther west in the Panhandle is Beaver County, which claims to be the cow-chip-throwing capital of the world. Hispanic population has grown to 10 percent, with many moving here to work on hog farms and in meatpacking plants. One of the largest operations is Seaboard Corp.'s plant in Guymon, which has more than 3,000 employees. Texas County, a wheat-growing area in the Panhandle, is 46 percent Hispanic, the highest percentage in the state. This has been the most Republican district in the state, and among the top 10 for the GOP nationwide. Donald Trump got 74 percent of the vote in 2016, virtually the same as the Republican performance in the previous two presidential elections.

FOURTH DISTRICT

Tom Cole (R)

Elected 2002, 8th term; b. Apr 28, 1949, Shreveport, LA; Grinnell College (IA), B.A., 1971; Institute for Historical Research - London (England), 1972; Yale University (CT), M.A., 1974; University of London - Queens College (England), 1978; University of Oklahoma (OK), Ph.D., 1984; Methodist; Married (Ellen Elizabeth Decker Cole); 1 child.

Elected Office: OK Senate, 1988-1991.

Professional Career: Staff, U.S. Rep. Mickey Edwards, 1982-1984; OK GOP Chairman, 1985-1989; Executive Director, NRCC, 1991-1995; OK Secretary of st., 1995-1999; Chief of Staff, RNC, 1999-2000; Political consultant, 2000-2002.

DC Office: 2467 RHOB 20515, 202-225-6165, Fax: 202-225-3512, cole.house.gov.
State Offices: Ada, 580-436-5375; Lawton, 405-310-9736; Norman, 405-329-6500.

Committees: *Appropriations*: Defense, Interior, Environment & Related Agencies, Labor, Health & Human Services, Education & Related Agencies (Chmn). *Budget*. *Rules*.

Group Ratings

	ADA	ACLU	AFL-CIO	LCV	ITI	COC	HAFA	ACU	CFG	FRC
2016	-	5%	-	5%	100%	100%	41%	72%	60%	100%
2015	0%	C	29%	3%	C	100%	C	42%	42%	92%

Almanac Ratings 2015

	Economy	Social	Foreign	Composite
Liberal	14%	10%	10%	12%
Conservative	86%	90%	90%	88%

Key Votes of the 114th Congress

1. Keystone Pipeline	Y	5. Puerto Rico Debt	Y	9. Offenses by Aliens	Y
2. Trade Deals	Y	6. Medical Marijuana	N	10. Troops in Iraq	N
3. Export-Import Bank	Y	7. Sanctuary Cities	Y	11. Homeland Security $$	Y
4. Debt Ceiling Increase	Y	8. Armor-piercing Bullets	Y	12. Trade Adjustment aid	Y

Election Results

Election	Name (Party)	Vote (%)		Cand. Spent	Ind. Exp. Support	Ind. Exp. Oppose
2016 General	Tom Cole (R)	204,143	(70%)	$1,409,421	$57,870	
	Christina Owen (D)	76,472	(26%)			
	Sevier White (L)	12,574	(4%)			
2016 Primary	Tom Cole (R)	28,805	(71%)			
	James Taylor (R)	7,394	(18%)			
	Shawn Roberts (R)	4,151	(10%)			

Prior winning percentages: 2014 (71%), 2012 (68%), 2008 (66%), 2006 (65%), 2004 (78%), 2002 (54%)

Tom Cole, first elected in 2002, is a politically savvy and experienced Republican who has become a key ally of House GOP leaders, including Speaker Paul Ryan. As chairman of the Appropriations subcommittee that handles discretionary spending for health and education programs, he has been an active policy leader for the GOP. Cole has remained a frequent source for reporters seeking to understand the GOP's inner workings.

Cole grew up in Moore, south of Oklahoma City. He is a fifth-generation Oklahoman, and his mother was a state representative and senator. He is a member of the Chickasaw Nation tribe; more than half of the nation's Chickasaw Indians live in his district. Oklahoma GOP colleague Markwayne Mullin and Cole are the only American Indians in Congress. Cole's father served in the Air Force and later worked at Tinker Air Force Base. Cole graduated from Grinnell College, got a master's degree at Yale University, and a Ph.D. in British history at the University of Oklahoma, studying for a year at the University of London. From 1985 to 1989, he was the Oklahoma Republican Party chairman. In 1988, he was elected to the state Senate.

He moved to Washington in 1991 to become executive director of the National Republican Congressional Committee, and over the next decade held jobs as the appointed Oklahoma secretary of state, the president of a polling and political consulting firm in Oklahoma City, and chief of staff for the Republican National Committee during the 2000 election. When Republican Rep. J.C. Watts announced that he would not seek reelection, Cole was the early frontrunner. Despite his party connections and an endorsement from Watts, he faced formidable opposition from attorney Marc Nuttle. The two shared positions on most issues and extensive party connections. Nuttle had been Cole's predecessor at the NRCC and worked on Pat Robertson's 1988 presidential campaign. Nuttle and Cole also had worked together to pass an Oklahoma right-to-work law in a 2001 referendum. In the showdown between the strategists, Cole won 60%-33%.

In the general election, he had tough competition from former state Senate Majority Leader Darryl Roberts, who appealed to the "yellow dog" Democratic tradition that had remained strong in the Red River counties. Cole countered by linking Roberts to past Democratic presidential nominees he had supported, and described him as "pro-tax, pro-abortion, and pro-lawsuit." Cole won 54%-46%, and has been reelected with ease.

Cole has a voting record that usually fits with mainstream conservatives, though the *Almanac* vote ratings for 2015 ranked him as the most-centrist member of the Oklahoma delegation. He differs from many junior conservative colleagues in his willingness to defend some government spending. From his plum seat on the Appropriations Committee, he tends to the needs of his district's military installations and supports federal programs that help his constituents. During the late 2012 negotiations over tax and spending to avoid the so-called "fiscal cliff," he urged his party to accept a tax-cut extension for all but the highest-earning Americans, a position that many Republicans subsequently adopted, leading to the bill's enactment.

In late 2013, Cole took an expanded role in critical budget talks with Senate Democrats, as one of four House Republicans appointed by Speaker John Boehner to a conference committee seeking to end the partisan brinkmanship that had led to a 16-day government shutdown in October. Working with then-Budget Committee Chairman Paul Ryan, Cole was a skillful conciliator trusted by mainstream

Republicans and conservative enough to maintain credibility with the restive tea party faction. A profile on the *Politico* website that October likened him to "the friendly uncle sent out to smoke a cigar and explain to the neighbors what all the noise is about in the basement."

Cole has been an Appropriations "cardinal" as chairman of the Subcommittee on Labor, Health and Human Services, Education and Related Agencies. In recent years, this spending bill has typically made little progress toward agreement with the Senate and instead became part of a status quo "continuing resolution" in the new fiscal year. With Republican Sen. Roy Blunt of Missouri, a Cole ally when he served in the House, serving as chairman of the counterpart Senate panel, the door was opened to possible House-Senate consensus.

The appropriator has warned about the need to control entitlement spending. In a bill filed with Democratic Rep. John Delaney of Maryland, he has called for a bipartisan commission to recommend steps to guarantee the solvency of Social Security for decades to come. "Without immediate changes that modernize the current system, Social Security will not be able to pay the benefits that American workers have earned and have come to rely upon," Cole warned in 2015.

In a sign of his increasing value to Ryan and the GOP, he was named in 2017 as vice-chairman of the leadership-driven Rules Committee. Along with his seat on the Budget Committee, he has become the eyes and ears - and occasionally a gentle enforcer - for Republican strategists. He has used his leadership niches to shape legislation related to American Indians. In the wake of the influence-peddling scandal involving Republican lobbyist Jack Abramoff, who represented several tribes, Cole strongly opposed the proposed limits on the right of tribes to contribute to political campaigns.

Campaign politics have been a longstanding part of Cole's portfolio in the House. Following the dismal 2006 election for Republicans, he defeated Texan Pete Sessions, 102-81, to become chairman of the NRCC, where he had cut his teeth as a political strategist years earlier. He expanded the playing field of competitive seats, but his chairmanship was a difficult time for the GOP. The party suffered a rough transition to the minority with many retirements, and the committee was $19 million in debt. Cole and the Republicans raised $116 million that cycle, compared with $171 million for the Democrats. The biggest obstacle was largely out of Cole's control: President George W. Bush's low public approval ratings, which made reelection an uphill climb for Republicans in competitive seats. The party lost 24 seats during the cycle.

During that period, the relationship between Cole and Minority Leader Boehner was marked by public sniping over who was to blame for the party's electoral failure. When Cole sought another two years as chairman, Sessions had Boehner's active support. Sensing that he could lose a showdown of House Republicans, Cole withdrew. In a spirit of conciliation, Boehner gave Cole the seat on Appropriations. Cole found his way back into Boehner's good graces through aggressive fundraising, plus his savvy combination of legislative skills and political instincts. He called Republicans who voted against Boehner for Speaker in 2015 "pretty unprofessional and very disappointing." Later, he settled into Ryan's good graces. In a 2015 year-end interview with *The Washington Post*, he called Ryan's takeover as Speaker, "the biggest lucky break that the Republican Party got this year." In the event of additional turmoil, Cole could be part of a future leadership team.

South-Central Oklahoma: Parts of Oklahoma City, Norman

Population		**Race and Ethnicity**		**Income**	
Total	773,971	White	71.8%	Median Income	$50,985 (239 out of 435)
Land area	9,777	Black	6.5%		
Pop/ sq mi	79.2	Latino	8.2%		
Born in state	60.8%	Asian	2.2%	Under $50,000	49.1%
		Two races	6.3%	$50,000-$99,999	32.7%
Age Groups		Other	4.9%	$100,000-$199,999	15.5%
Under 18	24.0%			$200,000 or more	2.8%
18-34	26.0%	**Education**		Poverty Rate	14.3%
35-64	36.8%	H.S grad or less	43.7%		
Over 64	13.2%	Some college	32.5%	**Health Insurance**	
		College Degree, 4 yr	15.6%	With health insurance coverage	86.0%
Work		Post grad	8.2%		
White Collar	34.2%				
Sales and Service	42.4%	**Military**		**Public Assistance**	
Blue Collar	23.4%	Veteran	11.9%	Cash public assistance income	3.0%
Government	5.7%	Active Duty	2.2%		
				Food stamp/SNAP benefits	12.1%

Voter Turnout			
2015 Total Citizens 18+	572,157	2016 House Turnout as % CVAP	51%
2016 House turnout	293,189	2014 House Turnout as % CVAP	29%

2012 Presidential Vote		
Mitt Romney	175,956	(67%)
Barack Obama	86,357	(33%)

2016 Presidential Vote		
Donald Trump	194,160	(66%)
Hillary Clinton	83,648	(28%)
Gary Johnson	17,617	(6%)

Cook Partisan Voting Index: R+20

In the years after 1900, the brown hills west of Oklahoma City and north of the Red River suddenly filled up with farmers riding north from Texas, past the quenched green lands of the east toward the bare pasturelands of the west. The first settlers here arrived just as the buffalo were dying out, down from an estimated 60 million animals to no more than 1,000. So in 1901, Republican President William McKinley established the nation's first wildlife preserve in the Wichita Mountains, 25 miles northwest of Lawton. Fifteen bison were donated by the New York Zoological Society and arrived at the preserve via rail in 1907 - a major factor in the survival of the species. Today, this habitat supports grazing for Rocky Mountain elk, white-tailed deer and Texas longhorn cattle.

Government has played a role in the survival of the people, too. Population in southwest Oklahoma clusters around major state and federal institutions: the University of Oklahoma in Norman, which housed the world's first school of petroleum geology and is now home to the National Weather Center; Tinker Air Force Base in southern Oklahoma City; and the Army Field Artillery School at Fort Sill in Lawton. With 120,000 people, Norman is the third-largest city in Oklahoma, with booming commercial and residential development underway. In October 2015, voters approved the Norman Forward initiative, with $148 million of capital improvements financed by bonds and a half-cent increase in the sales tax. The area to the south of Norman is rural. The tiny community of Elmore City, with its prohibition of dancing, became the inspiration for the 1984 movie *Footloose* (dancing was legalized in the town in 1980).

The 4th Congressional District of Oklahoma begins smack dab in the middle of the state not far from the capitol in Oklahoma City, and spreads south and west to cover half of Oklahoma's Red River Valley. Demographically, this district is becoming more suburban, but the cultural tone remains countrified. The area is at the heart of Tornado Alley. Moore, outside Oklahoma City, has been the site of several deadly strikes, including one in 1999 that remains the strongest ever recorded. In May 2013, an EF-5 tornado struck Moore, killing 24 people, damaging at least 12,000 buildings, and leveling entire neighborhoods, including two elementary schools; its estimated $2 billion in damage placed it among the most costly tornados in the nation's history. Ancestrally, this is Democratic country. But Norman, Lawton and the Oklahoma City fringe have voted solidly Republican since the 1990s. This remains a strongly Republican district.

FIFTH DISTRICT

Steve Russell (R)

Elected 2014, 2nd term; b. May 25, 1963, Oklahoma City; Ouachita Baptist University, B.A.; Army Command and General Staff College (KS); Southern Baptist; Married (Cindy Myers); 2 children; 3 adopted children.

Military Career: U.S Army, 1985-2006. (Kosovo, Kuwait, Afghanistan and Iran).

Elected Office: OK Senate, 2008-2012.

Professional Career: Motivational speaker & author, 2007-2014; Founder/owner, Two River Arms gun company, 2010-2014.

DC Office: 128 CHOB 20515, 202-225-2132, Fax: 202-226-1463, russell.house.gov.

State Offices: Del City, 405-602-3074.

Committees: *Armed Services*: Military Personnel, Readiness. *Oversight & Government Reform*: Information Technology, National Security.

Group Ratings

	ADA	ACLU	AFL-CIO	LCV	ITI	COC	HAFA	ACU	CFG	FRC
2016	-	5%	-	0%	83%	100%	67%	88%	79%	100%
2015	5%	C	21%	6%	C	75%	C	78%	53%	100%

Almanac Ratings 2015

	Economy	Social	Foreign	Composite
Liberal	14%	0%	4%	6%
Conservative	86%	100%	96%	94%

Key Votes of the 114th Congress

1. Keystone Pipeline	Y	5. Puerto Rico Debt	Y	9. Offenses by Aliens	Y
2. Trade Deals	N	6. Medical Marijuana	N	10. Troops in Iraq	N
3. Export-Import Bank	Y	7. Sanctuary Cities	Y	11. Homeland Security $$	N
4. Debt Ceiling Increase	N	8. Armor-piercing Bullets	Y	12. Trade Adjustment aid	N

Election Results

Election	Name (Party)	Vote (%)		Cand. Spent	Ind. Exp. Support	Ind. Exp. Oppose
2016 General	Steve Russell (R)	160,184	(57%)	$843,449		
	Al McAffrey (D)	103,273	(37%)	$62,967		
	Zachary Knight (L)	17,113	(6%)			
2016 Primary	Steve Russell (R)	27,426	(80%)			
	Frank Volpe (R)	6,720	(20%)			

Prior winning percentages: 2014 (60%)

Republican Steve Russell, elected in 2014, had a lengthy career as an Army officer and was part of the unit that captured the ousted President Saddam Hussein in Iraq. During his first term, he was an active lawmaker on government management and military issues.

Russell graduated from Ouachita Baptist University on an ROTC scholarship and was commissioned as a second lieutenant in the infantry. He ultimately became a lieutenant colonel during 21 years of service. Russell served in Kosovo, Kuwait, Afghanistan and Iraq, where his unit was part of the effort to find Saddam. Decorated several times for his service, he retired from the military in 2006 and returned to Oklahoma, where he wrote a book, *We Got Him! A Memoir of the Hunt and Capture of Saddam Hussein.*

In 2008, winning a runoff after a highly contested four-way primary, Russell took a seat in the Oklahoma Senate. He authored a law that made military members from the state exempt from taxes and was a vocal opponent of abortion. He declined to run for re-election in 2012 so he could promote his book and start a small rifle-manufacturing business, Two River Arms.

When the House seat opened to succeed James Lankford, who was elected to the Senate, Russell led the six-way Republican primary with 27 percent of the vote. He faced a runoff with Patrice Douglas, commissioner of the Oklahoma Corporation Commission. Douglas was the early frontrunner, as she was better-funded and had more establishment Republican connections. Russell benefited from tea party backing. Both the Russell and Douglas campaigns claimed to have Lankford's support, though Lankford said he hadn't endorsed either of them. Douglas raised $1 million, to about $400,000 for Russell. He won the runoff easily, with 59 percent of the vote. The outcome in November against Democrat Al McAffrey, the first openly gay legislator in Oklahoma, was a foregone conclusion. Russell won 60%-36%.

Russell was the freshman representative on the GOP Steering Committee that made House committee assignments, and supported John Boehner for Speaker based, he said, on the need for "continuity of leadership." Russell retained the practice of retired GOP Sen. Tom Coburn of Oklahoma to issue regular "Waste Watch" reports on government spending. He voted with House Republicans on most major issues, except for his opposition to giving trade promotion authority to President Barack Obama, who he said had "exhibited poor leadership in foreign affairs."

During his first term, Russell enacted two bills from the Oversight and Government Reform Committee. With Democratic Rep. Matt Cartwright of Pennsylvania, he cosponsored the Making Electronic Government Accountable By Yielding Tangible Efficiencies (MEGABYTE) Act, which reformed procurement of software and licenses by giving more authority to agency chief information officers. Russell said the law would save taxpayers more than $4 billion annually. Later in 2016, he worked with other lawmakers from Oklahoma to eliminate the annuity cap for retired air traffic controllers who worked as instructors. The shortage of instructors was acute in the aviation hub of Oklahoma.

On the Armed Services Committee, Russell in 2016 won initial House approval of his religious freedom amendment that protected federal contractors' free exercise of their religious beliefs, including opposition to LGBT rights. His target was an executive order that President Barack Obama had issued, which banned such discrimination. Russell said that the vagueness in Obama's action threatened contracts for Roman Catholic and other religiously affiliated groups. His amendment was dropped by the House-Senate conference committee working on the defense spending bill following the election. Russell pursued the issue again in 2017 and said that he hoped for a more favorable outcome, with the support of President Donald Trump. After Trump took office, Russell voiced differences with some provisions of his executive orders on refugees - specifically, foreigners who had worked with the U.S. armed forces, and children who had been badly injured and needed access to hospitals.

In 2017, Russell said that his objective was to fight waste in government, including in the military. I'm going to focus on duplication in government, stupidity in government," he told *The Oklahoman*. "We've got to be able to beef up agencies with their auditors and inspectors so they can go out and find fraud."

Oklahoma City Area

Population		**Race and Ethnicity**		**Income**	
Total	784,462	White	58.8%	Median Income	$46,251 (320 out of 435)
Land area	2,074	Black	13.2%	Under $50,000	53.1%
Pop/ sq mi	378.3	Latino	15.4%	$50,000-$99,999	28.6%
Born in state	59.8%	Asian	3.0%	$100,000-$199,999	14.2%
Age Groups		Two races	5.4%	$200,000 or more	4.1%
Under 18	25.5%	Other	4.3%	Poverty Rate	18.8%
18-34	25.0%	**Education**		**Health Insurance**	
35-64	36.8%	H.S grad or less	40.5%	With health insurance coverage	81.8%
Over 64	12.7%	Some college	29.9%	**Public Assistance**	
Work		College Degree, 4 yr	19.1%	Cash public assistance income	3.7%
White Collar	35.4%	Post grad	10.5%	Food stamp/SNAP benefits	15.4%
Sales and Service	43.0%	**Military**			
Blue Collar	21.5%	Veteran	9.5%		
Government	6.3%	Active Duty	0.3%		

Voter Turnout			
2015 Total Citizens 18+	532,699	2016 House Turnout as % CVAP	53%
2016 House turnout	280,570	2014 House Turnout as % CVAP	30%

2012 Presidential Vote		
Mitt Romney	156,035	(59%)
Barack Obama	107,344	(41%)

2016 Presidential Vote		
Donald Trump	149,400	(53%)
Hillary Clinton	111,769	(40%)
Gary Johnson	19,631	(7%)

Cook Partisan Voting Index: R+10

Oklahoma City, like many state capitals, was not the spontaneous creation of commerce but the deliberate creation of government, sited in the geographic center of the state on what turned out to be oil land. Rigs were pumping crude on the grounds of the Capitol until 1989. The land here is browner and more eroded by creeks than the rolling Oklahoma farmland to the east. Oklahoma City's population grew briskly from 506,000 in 2000 to 631,000 in 2015, a 25 percent increase, and the city now extends into four counties. Soaring farm commodity prices helped to keep the economy strong while much of the nation was mired in recession. A survey of housing affordability in 2016 ranked Oklahoma City as the sixth most affordable city in the United States; the top five were all in the Rust Belt. In 2016, the local unemployment rate edged up to 4 percent and sales tax receipts dropped by 6 percent, which resulted in part from the fall in oil prices and production.

Oklahoma City was scarred by a profound tragedy: the day in April 1995 when a bomb destroyed the Alfred P. Murrah Federal Building, killing 168 people and injuring more than 680. Five years later, the Oklahoma City National Memorial opened on the site of the blast. Domestic terrorist Timothy McVeigh, a militia movement sympathizer, was put to death in 2001 for his crime. Local pride spiked in 2008 when the Seattle SuperSonics of the National Basketball Association relocated to the city and became the Oklahoma City Thunder, the state's first major sports franchise. The team's successful run to the NBA finals in 2012 energized the city's fan base. Oklahoma City Mayor Mick Cornett told *GQ* that the team helped to promote the city: "Nobody in Paris is waking up thinking about Oklahoma City. But they *might* be watching an international game and see us playing the Lakers." But, alas, the team's star players escaped for more cosmopolitan venues and its title prospects waned. In January 2017, a local developer announced plans to redevelop the historic downtown First National Center into a hotel, with retail stores and apartments.

The 5th Congressional District is centered in Oklahoma City and includes most of Oklahoma County. It takes in Pottawatomie and Seminole counties to the east. Oklahoma County, which is the least-red in the state, casts nearly 90 percent of the vote. In 2016, Donald Trump took the district, 53%-40% -- a drop from the 59 percent that the Republican presidential nominees took in 2008 and 2012 and a notable contrast to the more than 70 percent for Trump in the adjacent 2nd and 3rd districts. Still, the district is comfortably Republican.

★ OREGON ★

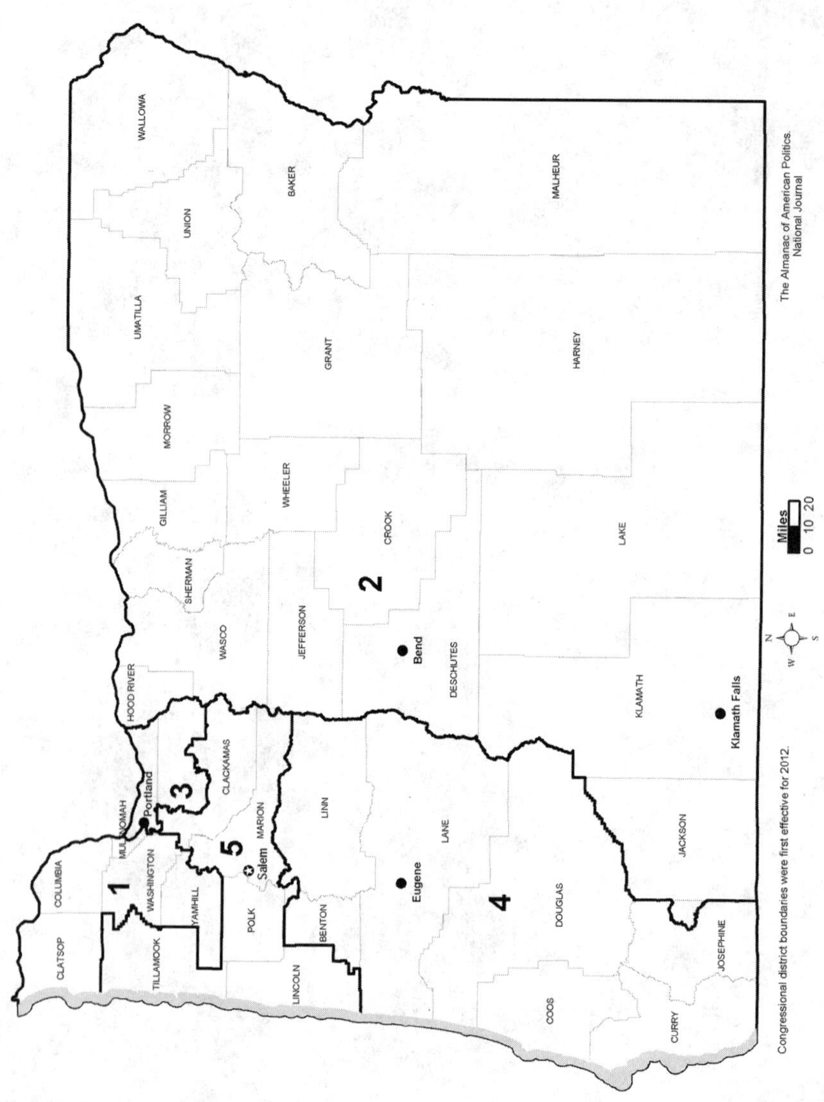
WALLOWA
BAKER
MALHEUR
UNION
UMATILLA
GRANT
HARNEY
MORROW
GILLIAM
WHEELER
CROOK
LAKE
SHERMAN
2
WASCO
JEFFERSON
Bend
DESCHUTES
HOOD RIVER
KLAMATH
Klamath Falls
CLACKAMAS
3
Portland
MULTNOMAH
MARION
LINN
LANE
JACKSON
COLUMBIA
WASHINGTON
5
Salem
1
YAMHILL
Eugene
4
DOUGLAS
CLATSOP
TILLAMOOK
POLK
BENTON
JOSEPHINE
LINCOLN
COOS
CURRY
Miles
0 10 20
N
E
S
W
The Almanac of American Politics,
National Journal
Congressional district boundaries were first effective for 2012.

Almost half of Oregon's population lives in the counties in and around Portland, the city whose hippie-liberal sensitivities are lovingly satirized by Fred Armisen and Carrie Brownstein in the television comedy series *Portlandia*. The Portland area has made Oregon a blue state, but much of the rest of Oregon is as rural and Republican as other portions of the American West.

Oregon is an experimental commonwealth, a laboratory of reform, a maker of national trends — with varying results. Bike trails now exist throughout the country; bike boulevards are catching on, but not as prevalent, yet. You can find light-rail trams in many central cities, but not so many solar energy-powered, plug-in stations for electric cars. Oregon produces (or has manufactured in China) Nike sneakers and Pendleton shirts, but its handcrafted ales don't travel far from the Oregon Brewers Festival. For all its modern advances, however, you can still see much of the same Oregon that Lewis and Clark saw in 1805, when they came down the Columbia River gorge, past the Willamette River to the Pacific Ocean. A few years later, in 1811, John Jacob Astor set up his fur trading post at Astoria. But few Americans came overland until the 1840s, when New England Yankees and Missouri farmers drove wagons along the Oregon Trail and floated down the Columbia to the well-watered Willamette Valley.

In this remote spot, nearly 2,000 miles from the Mississippi River frontier and 700 miles from the small Mexican settlements in California, they built an orderly, productive society — a kind of western New England. It grew steadily, with a few booms — in the early 1900s as timber harvesting surged, during World War II, when Kaiser shipyards in Portland and Vancouver churned out "Liberty" and "Victory" ships, and then again in the 1970s, when home-building skyrocketed and Oregon's natural environment began to be widely appreciated. The settlers brought town-meeting attitudes to Oregon. This was the second state to give people direct decision-making via the initiative and referendum; South Dakota did it first, but Oregon's measure was widely copied, and it has used the procedure more than any other state. It pioneered the election of U.S. senators by popular vote and, with Michigan in 1908, the recall of elected officials. It was the first state to institute Labor Day. In recent decades, it was first to sanction assisted suicide and to adopt mail-in ballot elections.

Oregon grew much faster than the national average in the 1940s, when war industries brought thousands of people to the West Coast, and again in the 1970s, when the pleasant environment attracted so many young people the state's population shot up 26 percent. Containing growth became the hot local issue. "Come and visit us again and again," Republican Gov. Tom McCall told outsiders. "But for heaven's sake don't come here to live." At McCall's prodding, the legislature in 1973 passed a law that in many ways limited development, and in the 1990s, the Portland metropolitan area sharply restricted growth and sprawl. These measures were popular in Portland and the university towns of Eugene and Corvallis and to a lesser extent in the suburbs. The lumber industry, which for decades accounted for most of Oregon's exports, was already sliding when it took another major blow in the 1990s from federal land-use restrictions imposed to protect the threatened spotted owl. While Oregon has remained a leader in producing Christmas trees, mainly in the counties around Salem and mostly for sale in arid California, productivity gains from technology advances and greater automation have contributed to slack employment in the timber sector. "Automation, tougher environmental regulations and a sluggish national housing market, coupled with globalization, led to the collapse of the timber industry," wrote Arlene Stein, a Rutgers University sociologist who has studied the region. Rural areas of Oregon "became laboratories for a right-wing populism that appealed to nostalgia" and demonized elites. In the winter of 2016, a breakaway group of armed protesters occupied the headquarters of the Malheur National Wildlife Refuge in the state's rural, southwestern corner, decrying federal encroachment on private lands and prompting a 41-day standoff that led to one death and more than a dozen guilty pleas for conspiracy and trespassing.

But as rural areas seethed over federal and state land-use policies, those same regulations attracted environment-minded migrants to Portland and the university towns. And some of those newcomers helped build the state's new economy. The growth of high-tech companies around Portland was such that the area became known as Silicon Forest, where Intel, the largest tech employer in the state, shares the stage with homegrown firms like Mentor Graphics, FEI Co. and Rentrack Corp. During the Great Recession, unemployment rose rapidly – from 5.6 percent in May 2008 to 11.9 percent in April 2009, less than a year later. But by February 2017, unemployment was down to 4 percent, about half a percentage point below the national average. The tech industry accounted for a disproportionate number of the state's job gains in the most recent economic rebound, and those jobs were high-paying – the median income is now 7 percent above the national average. In 2013, tech workers accounted for 12 percent of the state's entire payroll, an amount equal to the share of Oregon wages that employees in wood products businesses earned in the 1970s during the peak of the timber industry. Oregon is also a top exporter, with almost $22 billion in 2016. Four of the state's top six export products are in high-tech fields – items related to processors, integrated circuits and semiconductors, with wheat at No. 4 the most traditional export. Befitting Oregon's location on the Pacific Rim, each of the state's top nine trading partners save Canada are in Asia, led by China, Malaysia and Vietnam.

Healthy post-recession growth caused state revenues to soar and trigger the state's "kicker" rebate to Oregon taxpayers. In 1980, voters agreed to a proposal that Oregon's legislators devised to ward off the tax revolt that had swept neighboring California in the late 1970s: when personal income tax receipts grew by more than 2 percent above the state's projections, the excess would be rebated to taxpayers. For 2015, the excess tax receipts amounted to more than $470 million that would be rebated in the form of a credit on the 2016 returns filed by Oregon taxpayers. A comparable kicker was established for corporate income tax revenue, but in 2012, voters approved a ballot measure requiring that any corporate kicker revenue be deposited in the state school fund. For 2015, the corporate kicker was estimated at more than $90 million. Oregon has a $9.75 minimum wage, which is among the half-dozen highest in the nation, and is indexed for inflation.

While Oregon's population growth rate has fallen from its earlier peaks, the state is still expanding at a healthy clip, up 6.8 percent since 2010. Its three biggest counties – Multnomah, Washington and Clackamas, each in the Portland metro area – have each grown by between 8.5 and 10 percent since 2010. The fourth- and fifth-most populous counties, Lane (Eugene) and Marion (Salem) have grown by between 5 percent and 7 percent over that period. Oregon's population is only 2 percent black, 14 percent Hispanic and 4 percent Asian, and metro Portland, with its hugely liberal core neighborhoods, is America's whitest big city -- 72 percent white and 6 percent African American. The highest Hispanic percentages are around the state capital of Salem and farming counties east of the Cascades.

Founded by New England churchmen, Oregon has America's highest percentage of self-described agnostics (8 percent) according to the Pew Research Center's 2014 U.S. Religious Landscape Study; overall, 31 percent of Oregonians are unaffiliated with any faith. This is the core constituency for some of the state's policy innovations over the last two generations, when Oregon legalized most abortions before the Supreme Court's *Roe v. Wade* decision, decriminalized medical marijuana, and legalized assisted suicide in referendums in 1994 and 1997, to the point that doctors can prescribe but not administer lethal drugs, a law upheld by the Supreme Court in 2006. Oregon also passed the nation's first bottle-deposit law and backed limits on land development. In 2007, the Democratic-controlled legislature imposed limits on smoking, banned discrimination on the basis of sexual orientation and mandated recycling of discarded electronics. By 2012, 55,000 Oregonians had a medical marijuana card; penalties for possession of up to one ounce of the substance were the equivalent of a traffic ticket. Then, in 2014, Oregon's voters handily approved a measure legalizing recreational marijuana use among adults 21 and older.

Oregon's voters have repeatedly rejected ballot measures to create a state sales tax and voted to cap property taxes. But in a mail-in ballot in January 2010, Oregonians decided to tax the highest-earners to help fill a budget gap, raising the tax rate on families with incomes of more than $250,000 to 11 percent. In a separate measure, voters also raised taxes on corporations, rejecting the call by Nike founder and Chairman Phil Knight that the new levies amounted to "Oregon's Assisted Suicide Law II." The state eagerly expanded Medicaid under the Affordable Care Act, adding 438,000 mostly able-bodied adults to the rolls. Sometimes, though, Oregon's liberals have moved faster than the state's voters. Oregonians narrowly rejected a 2014 ballot measure requiring labels on genetically engineered foods by 837 votes out of more than 1.5 million cast. And same-sex marriage came relatively late to Oregon, thanks to a 2004 amendment to the state constitution that passed by a 57%-43% margin. The legislature did endorse domestic partnerships in 2007, and in 2014 a federal District Court judge struck down the constitutional prohibition, allowing the legalization of same-sex marriage in the state.

The voting in these elections and on many ballot propositions has followed a similar pattern: Huge margins for liberal candidates and positions in Portland and the university towns of Eugene and Corvallis and huge conservative margins in counties east of the Cascades and in much of southwestern Oregon, where discontent over the policies that decimated the logging industry has lingered. In the last four presidential elections, Democrats won with better than 70 percent in Multnomah County (Portland), while Republicans easily carried the counties east of the Cascades. Voting in all the state's elections is by mail, which voters authorized in a 1998 referendum. There are no polls open on Election Day and voters have until the night of the election to get their ballots to an election clerk. Gradually, other states have followed Oregon's lead: Washington state approved mail-in-only voting in 2011 and Colorado adopted the system starting with the 2014 elections. It hasn't always increased turnout, but it has slowed counting.

In 2016, presidential voting patterns in Oregon didn't change as markedly as they did in some other states, as Hillary Clinton defeated Donald Trump by a 50%-39% margin -- essentially the same gap as in 2012. (In 2016, Libertarian Gary Johnson won 5 percent and Green Party nominee Jill Stein got 2.6 percent.) Both parties saw their raw vote totals increase – by 32,000 for the Democrats and 28,000 for the Republicans. Two counties switched from blue to red – Columbia, northwest of Portland, where the margin shifted by 17 points toward the Republicans, and Tillamook, on the ocean due west of Portland, which shifted 10 points toward the GOP. The heavily Democratic areas around Portland became bluer, but not dramatically so, since they were already solidly blue to begin with. The biggest shift came in Washington County, which is suburban and increasingly diverse ethnically – 10 percent Asian and 16 percent Hispanic, both well above the state as a whole. There, the margin shifted by eight points to the Democrats. All told, in the three core Portland metro counties – Multnomah, Washington and Clackamas-- Clinton improved upon Barack Obama's 2012 showing by 42,000 votes. But outside those counties, her vote totals underperformed Obama by 11,000 votes, even including some slippage in counties that remained Democratic, such as Clatsop (Astoria), where the margin shifted by eight points to the GOP, Lane (Eugene), where the margin shifted by five points to the GOP, and the coastal county of Lincoln, which shifted by 10 points toward the Republicans. Meanwhile, voters defeated the most expensive ballot measure in the state's history – one that would have increased corporate taxes on businesses with annual sales greater than $25 million. Trump's solid loss in the state has led statewide politicians to feel comfortable in opposing his policies. When the newly elected president issued an executive order on immigration, Oregon wasted little time in signing on to neighboring Washington state's lawsuit that challenged the order's legality.

During the spring, political protests in Portland became increasingly raucous from both the left and the right, including the killing of two men by assailants using a knife on a light-rail train.

Population		**Race and Ethnicity**		**Income**	
Total	3,939,233	White	77.2%	Median Income	$51,243 (28 out of 50)
Land area	95,988	Black	1.8%		
Pop/ sq mi	41.0	Latino	12.3%	Under $50,000	48.7%
Born in state	46.0%	Asian	3.9%	$50,000-$99,999	31.1%
		Two races	3.3%	$100,000-$199,999	16.3%
Age Groups		Other	1.4%	$200,000 or more	3.8%
Under 18	21.8%			Poverty Rate	16.5%
18-34	22.9%	**Education**			
35-64	39.8%	H.S grad or less	34.5%	**Health Insurance**	
Over 64	15.4%	Some college	34.7%	With health insurance coverage	87.7%
		College Degree, 4 yr	19.3%		
Work		Post grad	11.5%		
White Collar	37.0%			**Public Assistance**	
Sales and Service	42.1%	**Military**		Cash public assistance income	4.0%
Blue Collar	20.9%	Veteran	10.0%		
Government	14.1%	Active Duty	0.1%	Food stamp/SNAP benefits	19.2%

Voter Turnout			
2015 Total Citizens 18+	2,867,670	2016 Pres Turnout as % CVAP	70%
2016 Pres Votes	2,001,336	2012 Pres Turnout as % CVAP	66%

Legislature	
Senate:	17D, 13R
House:	35D, 25R

Presidential Politics

2016 Democratic Primary		
Bernie Sanders (D)	360,829	(56%)
Hillary Clinton (D)	269,846	(42%)
2016 Republican Primary		
Donald Trump (R)	252,748	(64%)
Ted Cruz (R)	65,513	(17%)
John Kasich (R)	62,248	(16%)

2016 Presidential Vote		
Hillary Clinton (D)	1,002,106	(50%)
Donald Trump (R)	782,403	(39%)
Gary Johnson (L)	94,231	(5%)
Jill Stein (G)	50,002	(3%)
2012 Presidential Vote		
Barack Obama (D)	970,488	(54%)
Mitt Romney (R)	754,175	(42%)

Oregon has the distinction of having hosted the first presidential broadcast debate. During the 1948 GOP primary, Portland radio station KEX hosted Thomas Dewey and Harold Stassen, who debated whether the Communist Party should be outlawed. The debate was carried on national radio networks and some 40 million Americans tuned in to listen for an hour without commercial interruption. Dewey opposed the proposition, won the debate and the primary, and carried the state in the general election. Oregon regularly tilted Republican in close presidential contests, voting for other losing GOP nominees in 1960 and 1976. Another national loser, Democrat Al Gore, won the state by less than 1 point in 2000 (Green Party candidate Ralph Nader won 5 percent of the vote). Still, it has now voted for the Democratic presidential candidate in eight consecutive elections, voting more Democratic than the nation in the last four. In 2016, Hillary Clinton defeated Donald Trump 50%-39%. Clinton won Multnomah County, the state's largest vote producer, by a whopping 73%-17%. She also won Portland suburban counties, Clackamas and Washington, Lane County (Eugene), and four others. Trump won the other 28 of the state's 36 counties.

Oregon once had an important presidential primary held in late May. In 1948, Oregon ended Stassen's presidential prospects, when he lost 52%-48% to Dewey. In 1968, Oregon gave Democrat Robert Kennedy the only defeat in his electoral career when it voted 44%-38% for Eugene McCarthy. In 2008, when the race between Clinton and Barack Obama was still raging, Obama carried Oregon 59%-41%, with especially large margins in Multnomah County and the university towns. Eight years later, Vermont Sen. Bernie Sanders beat Clinton, 56%-42%, winning all but one small rural county, which he lost by one vote. Oregon Democratic Sen. Jeff Merkley was the only one of Sanders's Senate colleagues to endorse him. The May 17 GOP primary was held after all of Trump's Republican rivals had withdrawn from the race and he won 64 percent of the vote.

Congressional Districts

115th Congress Lineup	1R 4D	114th Congress Lineup	1R 4D

Oregon is projected to gain the sixth seat that it narrowly missed following the 2010 census. The good news for Democrats is that they now control the governorship and the Legislature. That is likely to continue through the next redistricting cycle, though it's not a guarantee. The challenge that Democrats would face is whether they can create a safe seat for their party in a delegation that has four Democrats and one Republican. The 4th and 5th districts have been competitive in presidential elections, and each seat might be at risk if the current incumbent retires. The Portland-based 1st and 3rd Districts have plenty of Democrats to sacrifice, though the map-drawers likely would need to divide the city to create a new Democratic-leaning district. Alternatively, Democrats could draw the new district to give their candidate a reasonable opportunity in what could be a competitive district. The Republican-controlled 2nd District east of the Cascade Mountains has few Democratic voters to sacrifice.

In 2011, the legislature accomplished something that it hadn't been able to do in more than 100 years: It passed its own congressional redistricting plan. The prospects had seemed unlikely because the parties were tied at 30 seats apiece in the state House. But there was a compromise to be had: Democrats wanted to shift Corvallis, home of Oregon State University, to the Eugene-based 4th District in case Democrat Peter DeFazio retired. In the deal, Democrats let the 3rd pick up some of Democrat Kurt Schrader's already tiny share of Portland, keeping his 5th District competitive. That kind of deal might be more difficult to pull off with the complexities created by an additional seat. Traditionally progressive Oregon is the last West Coast state without an independent redistricting commission of some kind.

Governor

Kate Brown (D)

Assumed office in 2015, term expires 2019, 1st full term; b. Jun. 21, 1960, Torrejón de Ardoz, Spain; U. of CO Boulder, B.A. 1981; Northwestern Schl. of Law, J.D. 1985; Married (Dan); 2 children.

Elected Office: OR House, 1991-1996; OR Senate, 1997-2008, Majority Leader, 2004; OR Secretary of State, 2008-2015.

Professional Career: Practicing attorney; Instructor, Portland State University.

Office: 900 Court St. NE, Rm. 160, Salem, 97301-4047; 503-378-4582; Fax: 503-378-8970; Website: oregon.gov.

Election Results

Election	Name (Party)	Vote (%)
2016 Primary	Kate Brown (D)	403,730 (84%)
	Julian Bell (D)	33,872 (7%)
2016 Special	Kate Brown (D)	985,027 (51%)
	Bud Pierce (R)	845,609 (44%)
	Cliff Thomason (I)	47,481 (2%)
	James Foster (L)	45,191 (2%)

Democrat Kate Brown was sworn in as Oregon governor in February 2015 following the resignation of John Kitzhaber, who had just been reelected to a fourth term the previous November. Kitzhaber, a Democrat, became enmeshed in a scandal over the awarding of state consulting work to his fiancée that prompted multiple investigations. Brown, the nation's first openly bisexual governor, easily won a special election in 2016 to finish the final two years of Kitzhaber's term. Former aide and longtime friend Kristen Grainger described Brown to the *New Yorker* as "a combination of Snoopy and Katniss Everdeen," the tough heroine of the *Hunger Games* trilogy.

Brown was born in Spain, where her father served in the Air Force, but grew up in Minnesota. She received a bachelor's degree in environmental conservation, with a certificate in women's studies, from the University of Colorado at Boulder, then obtained her law degree from Lewis & Clark College in Portland. She practiced family law in Portland and worked for a non-profit legal services group. Brown got her start in politics in 1991 when, while working as an advocate for the Women's Rights Coalition, she was appointed by the Multnomah County Board of Commissioners to fill a vacancy in the Oregon House. A year later, the state representative that Brown replaced, Judy Bauman, wanted her seat back and challenged Brown in the Democratic primary. Bauman had stronger political connections, but Brown went door-to-door and waged a vigorous grassroots campaign, winning the primary by seven votes. In 1996, Brown won a seat in the Oregon Senate and quickly was named its Democratic caucus leader. Brown married in 1997, and publicly acknowledged her bisexuality after the *Oregonian* reported on it when she was a state lawmaker. She rose to majority leader in 2004, becoming the first woman to occupy that post. In that position, Brown championed government transparency and helped create the state's new online database for campaign transactions. In 2007, she pushed an ethics law limiting the value of lobbyist gifts to lawmakers to $50. She ran for secretary of state in 2008 and won, 51%-46%.

As secretary of state, Brown attracted attention for helping Oregon implement an online voter-registration system - it was the fourth state to do so in 2010 - and for using iPad technology to make voting more accessible to people with disabilities. But in 2012, she came under fire when her office notified two candidates for labor commissioner that their elections would be held in November instead of the following May, a move that critics said appeared to be aimed at helping the Democratic candidate. In her reelection bid, the *Oregonian* endorsed Republican Knute Buehler, saying that while the election switch "isn't, by itself, justification to turn Brown out of office," it has "eroded public confidence in Brown, if not the office itself." Brown won reelection anyway.

Prior to his resignation, Kitzhaber was a giant figure in Oregon politics. During the summer before his fourth and final reelection, he became engaged to Cylvia Hayes, who ran an environmental consulting business. But investigative reporting by the *Willamette Week* in 2014 raised questions about whether Hayes had benefited financially from her relationship with the governor and whether she had properly disclosed the consulting fees she had been paid. Official investigations followed. Although Kitzhaber won his race, the controversy didn't die down. It reached a crescendo in February 2015, and Kitzhaber stepped down. Because Oregon has no lieutenant governor, Brown was next in line as secretary of state.

As governor, Brown emphasized the need to restore trust in government. On the whole, lawmakers welcomed Brown's more collegial approach; Kitzhaber was seen as aloof and arrogant. Within months after taking office, Brown was able to sign an ethics package that included provisions to revitalize the Oregon Government Ethics Commission, to classify the governor's spouse or partner as a public official covered by conflict-of-interest disclosures, to ban speaking fees for the first couple, and to audit how state agencies handle public records. The legislature also set up a campaign finance task force after it had sidelined campaign spending limits the governor had personally lobbied lawmakers to approve. Separately, Brown signed a bill – one she had originally developed as secretary of state -- that would automatically register voters who obtained or renewed their driver's license, becoming the first state to make voter registration automatic. Brown signed a number of other progressive measures approved by the state legislature including: mandatory paid sick leave for most Oregon workers; more permissive rules for acquiring a medical-marijuana card; a bill making it illegal for employers to ask about an applicant's criminal background on job applications; a new system for collecting data about racial profiling by law enforcement officers; an employee-funded workplace-based retirement savings program; a bill to end "conversion therapy" for homosexuality; and protections for transgender students.

The most controversial measure, however, was a bill Brown signed in May 2015 to require a background check for most private sales of guns. The measure highlighted the divide between the liberal Portland area and more conservative rural portions of the state. "There is absolutely no question that there is a rural-urban divide in Oregon," Brown told the *New York Times*. Brown also faced some static on other matters. Efforts to raise the minimum wage fell victim to differences between the two legislative chambers, and the legislature failed to adopt a major transportation bill that she had sought due to squabbling between environmentalists and pro-development forces.

Brown's second year in office began with a crisis, as an armed group protesting federal land policies occupied the headquarters of the Malheur National Wildlife Refuge, deep in rural southeast Oregon. Brown vented frustration with federal officials' take-it-slow approach – local residents, she said during the standoff, "have been overlooked and underserved by federal officials' response." The incident ended after 41 days, with one protester dead; more than a dozen people eventually pled guilty to conspiracy and trespassing charges. The Malheur refuge takeover, combined with lingering anger at Brown's gun control policies, raised concerns about the governor's safety. In July 2016, the *Oregonian* reported that Brown's security procedures had been tightened and coordination with the FBI had increased. Two months later, Brown was burned in effigy on the front steps of the state capitol by gun-rights demonstrators. (Republican state Rep. Bill Post, a gun-rights supporter, was among those who publicly condemned the protesters' actions.)

Despite such tensions, Brown found some legislative success in 2016. She signed a phased-in minimum wage increase scaled to three different territories – Portland, rural areas and everywhere else. She signed new protections for tenants, and she allowed jurisdictions to require builders to include housing priced below market rates. Lawmakers also approved new renewable energy mandates; a lodging-tax increase; a boost for the backlogged testing of rape kits; the lifting of the statute of limitations on rape; and permission for banks to take on marijuana businesses as clients. One problem, however, remained unsolved -- how to tackle the state's $22 billion in unfunded pension liabilities.

Brown was required to run in a 2016 special election for the final two years of Kitzhaber's term. She faced William "Bud" Pierce, a moderate former president of the Oregon Medical Association. During a debate, Pierce said well-educated and accomplished women are less susceptible to sexual harassment; after an outcry, he apologized. Pierce was always going to be an underdog; Republicans hadn't won an Oregon gubernatorial race since 1986, and polls showed Brown with double-digit leads. She even courted opposition among pro-gun Republicans by accepting a $250,000 campaign donation from former New York City mayor and gun-control advocate Michael Bloomberg. In the end, she won by less than the polls had indicated -- only 7 points – but that was still a bigger margin than the weakened

Kitzhaber had managed in 2014. Brown's map of winning counties was similar to Hillary Clinton's, with the only difference being Clackamas County near Portland, which Clinton won by seven points but Pierce took by two points.

As one of a relatively few Democratic governors in office nationally, Brown became a beacon for liberals across the country. "Under my leadership in Oregon, we will continue to be a progressive leader for the country," she told the *Washington Post's* Amber Phillips after her election victory. The day after Donald Trump was inaugurated, Brown promised to do what she could to resist Trump's efforts to force jurisdictions to end their status as "sanctuary cities" for undocumented immigrants, and she called for a "social action team" of volunteers who would use social media to organize for progressive values. Still, despite Brown's growing national profile, she continued to face challenges back home. She again poked pro-gun supporters in the eye by issuing an order to prevent most state employees from carrying guns at work, even if they hold a concealed-carry license. And oddly for a state in such robust economic health, Oregon faced a $1.6 billion budget gap over two years, stemming from a mix of higher Medicaid costs, unfunded pensions and voter-approved tax limitations. In her budget proposal for 2017-18, Brown sought $897 million in new revenue from taxes on tobacco, alcohol, hospitals, insurers and the income of some residents who own corporations. K-12 education would be shielded from cuts, but social service organizations and universities could take a hit. Despite having a Democratic-controlled legislature, intra-party differences and Republican opposition made it unlikely that her fiscal plan would be enacted.

Senior Senator

Ron Wyden (D)

Elected 1996, term expires 2022, 4th full term; b. May 03, 1949; Wichita, KS, University of California, Santa Barbara, 1969; Stanford University (CA), B.A., 1971; University of Oregon Law School, J.D., 1974; Jewish; Married (Nancy Bass Wyden); 5 children (2 from previous marriage).

Elected Office: U.S. House, 1981-1996.

Professional Career: Co-Director & co-founder, OR Gray Panthers, 1974-1980; Director, OR Legal Svcs. for the Elderly, 1977-1979; Instructor, University of OR, 1976, Portland St. University, 1979, University of Portland, 1980.

DC Office: 221 DSOB 20510, 202-224-5244, Fax: 202-228-2717, wyden.senate.gov.

State Offices: Bend, 541-330-9142; Eugene, 541-431-0229; La Grande, 541-962-7691; Medford, 541-858-5122; Portland, 503-326-7525; Salem, 503-589-4555.

Committees: *Budget*. *Energy & Natural Resources*: Energy, Public Lands, Forests & Mining (RMM), Water & Power. *Finance (RMM)*: Energy, Natural Resources & Infrastructure, Fiscal Responsibility & Economic Growth (RMM), Health Care, International Trade, Customs & Global Competitiveness, Social Security, Pensions & Family Policy, Taxation & IRS Oversight. *Intelligence*.

Group Ratings

	ADA	ACLU	AFL-CIO	LCV	ITI	COC	HAFA	ACU	CFG	FRC
2016	-	94%	-	100%	60%	38%	12%	4%	5%	0%
2015	90%	C	50%	92%	C	50%	C	8%	14%	0%

Almanac Ratings 2015

	Economy	Social	Foreign	Composite
Liberal	79%	100%	100%	93%
Conservative	21%	0%	0%	7%

Key Votes of the 114th Congress

1. Keystone pipeline	N	5. National Security Data	Y	9. Gun Sales Checks	Y
2. Export-Import Bank	N	6. Iran Nuclear Deal	N	10. Sanctuary Cities	N
3. Debt Ceiling Increase	Y	7. Puerto Rico Debt	Y	11. Planned Parenthood	N
4. Homeland Security $$	Y	8. Loretta Lynch A.G	Y	12. Trade deals	Y

Election Results

Election	Name (Party)	Vote (%)		Cand. Spent	Ind. Exp. Support	Ind. Exp. Oppose
2016 General	Ron Wyden (D)	1,105,119	(57%)	$6,565,807		
	Mark Callahan (R)	651,106	(33%)	$37,221		
	Eric Navickas (G)	48,823	(3%)			
2016 Primary	Ron Wyden (D)	501,903	(84%)			
	Kevin Stine (D)	78,287	(13%)			

Prior winning percentages: 2010 (57%), 2004 (63%), 1998 (61%), 1996 special (48%), House: 1994 (73%), 1992 (77%), 1990 (81%), 1988 (99%), 1986 (86%), 1984 (59%), 1982 (78%), 1980 (72%)

Now in his late 60s, Democrat Ron Wyden, Oregon's senior senator, has served in Congress for most of his adult life. He arrived in the Senate via a special election in January 1996, after a decade and a half in the House. While he generally has been a reliable vote for his party's leadership, Wyden also has been relentless in his efforts to bridge the partisan divide on such high-wattage issues as health care -- sometimes to the consternation of his Democratic colleagues. At the same time, as a member of the Intelligence Committee, Wyden has emerged as perhaps the Senate's most implacable critic of government efforts to expand electronic surveillance of rank-and-file citizens for the sake of national security.

Wyden's increasing seniority has placed him in several influential positions in recent years. In 2013, he became chairman of the Senate Energy and Natural Resources Committee. Just over a year later, when Montana Sen. Max Baucus resigned in mid-term to become ambassador to China, Wyden took over the gavel of the even higher-profile Finance Committee -- bringing along his reputation for trying to craft bipartisan deals on highly polarizing issues; he is currently the panel's ranking Democrat with the Republicans now in the majority. "Sometimes folks tease him, [saying] if Ron Wyden hasn't used the word bipartisan in a sentence today, it's not our Ron," Alaska Sen. Lisa Murkowski, the ranking Republican on the Energy and Natural Resources panel when Wyden was chairman, told *The Oregonian* in 2013. "But then he's genuine about it, and it's important to him."

Wyden was born in Wichita, Kansas, while his father, Peter, a journalist, was working for the *Wichita Eagle*. Peter shortened the family surname from Weidenreich three years before his son was born; both Wyden's father and his mother, Edith, were Jews who had fled Nazi Germany. Presaging Wyden's involvement in overseeing U.S. intelligence policy years later, Peter Wyden was trained as a U.S. spy during World War II, and returned to Europe to help run an Allied propaganda campaign aimed at Nazi-held territory. Ron Wyden grew up in California, graduated from Stanford University, and moved to Oregon to attend the University of Oregon law school. After graduating in 1974, he founded the Oregon chapter of the Gray Panthers, an advocacy group for the elderly. Under Wyden, the group ventured into electoral politics by sponsoring a successful referendum reducing the price of dentures.

Wyden's first major foray into the political arena had come nearly a decade earlier. As a 19-year old undergraduate, he worked as a campaign driver for Sen. Wayne Morse, who would become Wyden's mentor -- and whose Senate seat Wyden now occupies. In 1968, the famously independent-minded Morse, an early opponent of the Vietnam War, got a challenge in the Democratic primary from former Rep. Robert Duncan, a supporter of the war. Morse won the primary, but lost the general election to a young Republican state legislator, Bob Packwood. Twelve years later, at age 31, Wyden launched a primary challenge to Duncan -- who had returned for a second stint in the House representing the Portland-based 3rd Congressional District. Wyden won the primary, 60%-40%, and easily captured the heavily Democratic seat in the 1980 general election. He breezed to reelection seven times. In the House, Wyden spent most of his tenure on the Energy and Commerce Committee, whose broad jurisdiction ranges from health care to telecommunications.

Wyden's path to the Senate was opened by the Senate Ethics Committee's decision in September 1995 to expel Packwood for sexual harassment of former aides and lobbyists. Wyden, who had long eyed the seat, ran in the special election to replace Packwood. With his home base in Portland, where local television broadcasts reach most of the state, Wyden had greater name identification than his rivals. But he had spirited opposition in the primary from Eugene-based Rep. Peter DeFazio, who carried his own district overwhelmingly, holding Wyden to a 50%-44% win. The Republican nomination went to state Senate President Gordon Smith, a party moderate. Smith, a frozen-vegetable tycoon from eastern

Oregon, spent $2 million of his own money. Most polls suggested a dead heat, and negative ads flooded the airwaves. Wyden picked up strength the week before the Jan. 30 mail-in deadline and won, 48%-47%.

Ten months later, Smith won the state's other Senate seat upon the retirement of Republican Mark Hatfield, marking the instance of two senators being elected who had run against each other in the same year. With the departure of Hatfield and Packwood, Oregon in short order lost 56 years of Senate seniority and gained two senators who everyone expected would be bitter enemies. Instead Wyden and Smith (a cousin of the Democratic Udall family dynasty) became friends and collaborators, holding dozens of joint town meetings across Oregon and having lunch every Thursday with their chiefs of staff. Facing a tough reelection campaign in 2008 against Democrat Jeff Merkley, Smith boasted of bipartisanship in ads that included images of Wyden. Merkley narrowly won, ending the Smith-Wyden working alliance.

As evidenced by Smith, Wyden has often displayed a proclivity for counterintuitive political alliances, along with a knack for coming up with sensible-sounding ideas no one else had thought of. For instance, in early 2009, Wyden and Maine moderate Republican Sen. Olympia Snowe astutely predicted that high-dollar bonuses and "golden parachutes" for executives of financial companies being bailed out by U.S. taxpayers would be unpopular with the public, and they won passage of a provision in that year's economic stimulus bill to prevent such payments. But the stipulation was left out of the final bill at the insistence of the administration of President Barack Obama, which argued that employees might sue to keep their bonuses. Sure enough, in March 2009 came an outpouring of public anger over bonuses paid to employees of troubled insurance giant AIG, which would have been prevented by the Snowe-Wyden provision. Wyden later became one of 13 Democrats who joined Republicans in trying to end the Troubled Asset Relief Program in January 2010, a little more than a year after he voted against creating the $700 billion bailout of the financial industry.

One of the more memorable moments of Wyden's long tenure on Capitol Hill came during a March 2013 Intelligence Committee meeting, when Wyden asked then-Director of National Intelligence James Clapper, "Does the [National Security Agency] collect any type of data at all on millions, or hundreds of millions of Americans?" Replied Clapper, "No, sir." Wyden pressed. "It does not?" Wyden asked. "Not wittingly," Clapper replied. Three months later, whistleblower Edward Snowden created a national firestorm by leaking thousands of NSA documents that proved Clapper had not been straight with Wyden. Snowden, in a column in 2014, said that Clapper's answer to Wyden had been a "major motivating factor" in his decision to leak information illustrating the extent to which intelligence agencies were electronically collecting information on U.S. citizens. (Clapper later acknowledged he had answered Wyden in the "least most untruthful manner.")

For years prior to Snowden's leak, Wyden pushed to reveal the degree to which rank-and-file Americans were being monitored by electronic surveillance. In 2011, Wyden joined Democratic Sen. Mark Udall of Colorado in seeking to force the Justice Department's inspector general to estimate how many Americans were having email and phone calls monitored as part of anti-terrorism efforts, but the Intelligence Committee shot down the proposal. Wyden joined the Intelligence panel in 2001, nine months before the 9/11 attacks. The Patriot Act, which significantly expanded the government's surveillance powers, passed just weeks after 9/11. "Like everyone else, I voted for the Patriot Act," he told *Willamette Week* a decade and a half later. "We had 3,000 people murdered in cold blood." But he was one of only 10 no votes when the law came up for reauthorization in 2015. "Instead of coming back to review it, the Bush Administration put their feet on the pedal and kept expanding and expanding it," he complained.

Following Snowden's revelations, Wyden achieved a large measure of success in 2015, when the USA Freedom Act -- a reauthorization of the Patriot Act -- reined in the government's ability to collect phone data. It put Wyden in yet another bipartisan alliance, this time with libertarian-minded Kentucky Sen. Rand Paul. Two years earlier, Wyden was the only Democrat to stand on the floor with Paul while the Kentucky senator filibustered the nomination of John Brennan as director of the Central Intelligence Agency -- a protest of the Obama White House's use of controversial drone strikes. Wyden did vote to confirm Brennan, but he called on the administration to produce more documents about its drone policy.

In January 2017, Wyden battled President Donald Trump's nominee for CIA director, then-Rep. Mike Pompeo, forcing a six-hour debate on the Senate floor before Pompeo was confirmed. Wyden took aim at an op-ed piece that Pompeo had published in the *Wall Street Journal* a year earlier that called for re-establishing collecting the "metadata" restricted by the 2015 version of the Patriot Act. Pompeo advocated that such metadata should be combined with a publicly available financial and lifestyle information into a "comprehensive searchable database." Declared Wyden on the Senate floor: "I have never heard an idea so extreme, so overarching and so intrusive of Americans' privacy. We are headed into dangerous times."

Wyden's interest in the internet goes back to the mid-1990s, as he was moving from the House to the Senate and the World Wide Web was growing exponentially. He was an early champion of internet freedom, often siding with the high tech sector against Hollywood and other content producers who sought stricter anti-piracy laws. In 2010, he worked to block action on a bill allowing the government to bar credit card companies and information networks from dealing with websites that engaged in copyright infringement. Wyden told *Wired* that the approach was "like using a bunker-busting cluster bomb when what you really need is a precision-guided missile. The collateral damage of this statute could be American innovation, American jobs, and a secure internet."

Earlier, he and then-California Republican Rep. Christopher Cox sponsored a three-year ban on taxation of access to the internet that passed in 1998. The ban on internet access taxation was extended until 2004, and there were another half-dozen extensions of the moratorium until Congress finally voted to make the prohibition permanent in early 2016.

Wyden's efforts to cross the aisle on health care date back to the administration of President George W. Bush. He was one of 11 Senate Democrats to vote for the Republican-authored Medicare prescription drug law in 2003 in the face of criticism from fellow Democrats. "It wasn't a bill I would have written. But I thought it was the right thing to do to get started," he said. He won amendments creating a national commission on health care and extending a managed care option for rural Oregon. Later, with Snowe, he sponsored a bill to allow the federal government to negotiate drug prices with pharmaceutical companies.

As Obama's health care overhaul was debated in 2009, Wyden joined Republican Robert Bennett of Utah on a bill to replace the tax exclusion for employer-provided health insurance with a tax deduction for individuals to buy insurance from private insurers. They lined up six Democratic and four Republican co-sponsors, contending their approach would produce a bipartisan health care bill that included universal coverage. Wyden presciently predicted that the more government-heavy approach Obama favored would be a hard sell. But the Obama Administration and key Senate committee chairmen disagreed that changes in tax incentives alone would achieve the goal of insuring millions of Americans without health insurance. "Ron Wyden's brand is as a guy who wants to get things done," Bennett, defeated for reelection in 2010, later said. "Anything he does with a Republican who is reasonable builds that brand, even if it doesn't come to fruition...He's built this brand and he loves it."

But Wyden did not get a lot of love from his own party when, in December 2011, he joined forces with Rep. Paul Ryan of Wisconsin -- then chairman of the House Budget Committee and now House speaker -- to offer a plan to partially privatize and radically transform Medicare. The Democratic Party had already campaigned against-and strongly condemned-Ryan's budget blueprint to change Medicare, and Wyden's move undermined the party's message. The Obama White House said the plan would "end Medicare as we know it." Wyden and Ryan's plan would have allowed insurers to compete with traditional Medicare, and give patients subsidies they could use for either fee-for-service Medicare or private insurance.

Ryan was later chosen as Republican Mitt Romney's running mate in the 2012 presidential race. In arguing that the Ryan Medicare plan had bipartisan support, the Romney campaign frequently cited Wyden. But by then, Wyden had mostly disavowed his previous support; he denounced Romney's claims, and sought to downplay his role by noting he had not drafted actual legislation with Ryan. Wyden later voted against the Ryan budget blueprint when it came before the Senate. But critics on the left complained that Wyden "gave cover to Ryan" while the Republicans were on the political defensive. For his part, Ryan told *The Oregonian* that Wyden "doesn't have the hostility to free-market ideas, private-sector solutions that many on the left do. And that's what makes Ron a guy Republicans can feel comfortable talking with."

Wyden's ascension to the chairmanship of Finance became possible with Baucus' departure to China and the decision by their ambitious colleague, New York's Charles Schumer, not to challenge Wyden. Wyden signaled he would run the committee with a lighter touch than the sometimes independent Baucus, including letting subcommittee chairs know they would have more freedom to hold their own hearings. He worked with Utah's Orrin Hatch, the panel's ranking Republican, on a proposal to rescue the Highway Trust Fund in part by instituting measures aimed at achieving better compliance with existing tax laws.

During his short-lived Finance chairmanship, Wyden didn't get much of what he wanted, in part because the leaders of his own party were leery of his independent ways. As *The Washington Post* put it, Wyden was "shoved aside by his majority leader, snubbed by his House counterpart and handcuffed by his president." The newspaper even quoted a former aide to Reid, Jim Manley, being dismissive of Wyden's leadership style. "He's prone to quixotic causes and never really got into the nitty-gritty of the legislative process," Manley said.

The debate over the Trans-Pacific Partnership trade deal in 2015, after Wyden had shifted to the ranking member's slot on Finance, put him in alliance with the Obama White House -- albeit on the opposite side from a large majority of his Senate Democratic colleagues. Representing a Pacific Rim state heavily dependent on exports, Wyden already was one of his party's most notable free-trade voices; that role only heightened during the TPP debate. Oregon is "the face of the opportunity to grow more good-paying jobs" from trade, he told the *Post*. Wyden played a prominent role as he and 11 Democrats joined most Republicans in voting to give Obama expedited negotiating authority for the 12-nation trade deal. Those to his left expressed their dismay, from activists back home chasing him with a blimp and an RV to AFL-CIO President Richard Trumka, who made a special visit to Portland to scold Wyden and other free-trade backers in the delegation. (Wyden's home-state colleague, Merkley, joined others in the party's progressive wing in opposing the deal, from which Trump withdrew after taking office.)

In 2011, Wyden finally succeeded in a years-long effort to reform Senate rules -- when, by a vote of 92-4, the Senate voted to require public disclosure of so-called "holds" after two days. It ended the ability of a single senator to secretly stop legislation from advancing. Wyden and Iowa Republican Charles Grassley had first called for public disclosure of the names of senators who placed such holds back in 1997.

Wyden's attention to state issues, and his visibility at home-he holds forums in all 36 counties every year, even in heavily Republican eastern Oregon-has arguably made him the state's most popular politician. Wyden has been a staunch defender of Oregon's landmark assisted-suicide law, fighting various attempts to nullify the law over the years. He irritated allies in the environmental movement by backing a proposed liquefied natural gas terminal at Coos Bay in southern Oregon; he touted its potential for jobs, but opponents said it would encourage significant greenhouse-gas emissions. At the same time, when a company seeking to construct an LNG terminal at the mouth of the Columbia River in northwest Oregon withdrew its application in 2016 amid strong local opposition, Wyden said he was "relieved," adding, "I shared the concerns that the...project would have had negative environmental and economic impacts."

After his narrow win against Smith in the January 1996 special election, Wyden easily won his first full term in November 1998 by 61%-34%. In 2004, he won reelection just as easily, 63%-32%. A year later, Wyden married for the second time; his wife, Nancy Bass, is co-owner of New York City's venerated Strand Bookstore. (Thanks to her holdings, Wyden now ranks among the top 50 in *Roll Call*'s annual list of the wealthiest members of Congress.)

In 2010, he was opposed by Lewis and Clark College law school professor James Huffman. In a heavily Republican year, Wyden won by 57%-39%. A month after the 2010 election, Wyden underwent prostate surgery and made a quick recovery, voting on the Senate floor two days later. In 2016, Wyden won a full fourth term, 57%-33%, defeating Republican Mark Callahan, a perennial candidate who surprised even himself by winning a four-way primary for the GOP nomination.

Wyden returned to Capitol Hill as the Finance panel's ranking Democrat as tax reform, another issue in which he has long been involved, was high on the agenda. Wyden has long promoted a restructuring of the tax code akin to the reform enacted in 1986, including reductions in tax rates and an expansion of the tax base by eliminating tax preferences and deductions. In 2010, he and Republican Judd Gregg of New Hampshire sponsored a measure with three income tax brackets (15%, 25%, 35%), a lower corporate tax rate, and immediate expensing of inventory and equipment for businesses with receipts under $1 million. Wyden reintroduced the bill in 2011, undaunted by the challenge that Congress is too politically polarized to accomplish major tax reform.

Junior Senator

Jeff Merkley (D)

Elected 2008, term expires 2020, 2nd term; b. Oct 24, 1956, Myrtle Creek; Princeton University Woodrow Wilson School of Public and International Affairs (NJ), M.PP; Stanford University (CA), B.A.; Lutheran; Married (Mary Sorteberg); 2 children.

Elected Office: OR House, 1999-2008, Speaker, 2007-2008.

Professional Career: President fellow, Office of the Secretary of Defense, 1982-1985; National security analyst, CBO, 1985-1989; Executive Director, Portland Habitat for Humanity, 1991-1994; Director of housing development, Human Solutions, 1995-1996; President, World Affairs Council of OR, 1996-2003.

DC Office: 313 HSOB 20510, 202-224-3753, Fax: 202-228-3997, merkley.senate.gov.

State Offices: Bend, 541-318-1298; Eugene, 541-465-6750; Medford, 541-608-9102; Pendleton, 541-278-1129; Portland, 503-326-3386; Salem, 503-362-8102.

Committees: *Appropriations*: Agriculture, Rural Development, FDA & Related Agencies (RMM), Department of the Interior, Environment & Related Agencies, DOL, HHS & Education & Related Agencies, Energy & Water Development, State, Foreign Operations & Related Programs. *Budget. Environment & Public Works*: Clean Air & Nuclear Safety, Fisheries, Water, and Wildlife, Transportation & Infrastructure. *Foreign Relations*: Africa & Global Health Policy, East Asia, the Pacific & International Cybersecurity Policy, Internat'l Dev Instit & Internat'l Econ, Energy & Environ Policy (RMM).

Group Ratings

	ADA	ACLU	AFL-CIO	LCV	ITI	COC	HAFA	ACU	CFG	FRC
2016	-	94%	-	100%	40%	38%	17%	0%	9%	0%
2015	100%	C	100%	100%	C	36%	C	4%	8%	0%

Almanac Ratings 2015

	Economy	Social	Foreign	Composite
Liberal	93%	100%	100%	98%
Conservative	7%	0%	0%	2%

Key Votes of the 114th Congress

1. Keystone pipeline	N	5. National Security Data	Y	9. Gun Sales Checks	Y
2. Export-Import Bank	NV	6. Iran Nuclear Deal	N	10. Sanctuary Cities	N
3. Debt Ceiling Increase	Y	7. Puerto Rico Debt	N	11. Planned Parenthood	N
4. Homeland Security $$	Y	8. Loretta Lynch A.G	Y	12. Trade deals	N

Election Results

Election	Name (Party)	Vote (%)		Cand. Spent	Ind. Exp. Support	Ind. Exp. Oppose
2014 General	Jeff Merkley (D)	814,537	(56%)	$11,147,553	$198,099	$1,320,547
	Monica Wehby (R)	538,847	(37%)	$3,896,848	$747,941	$322,424
2014 Primary	Jeff Merkley (D)	256,365	(93%)			

Prior winning percentages: 2008 (49%)

Democrat Jeff Merkley, Oregon's junior senator, arrived on Capitol Hill with neither the celebrity of Minnesota's Al Franken nor the grassroots following of Massachusetts' Elizabeth Warren, *The Oregonian* -- his home state newspaper -- noted as Merkley prepared to seek a second term in 2014. But if Merkley remains lesser known than some colleagues in the Senate's progressive wing, he has attracted a following among activists beyond Oregon for a willingness to aggressively pursue his agenda. "I'm absolutely a risk-taker," Merkley acknowledged, "and it kind of catches people off guard." In the spring of 2016, Merkley became the first and only senator to endorse his colleague, Bernie Sanders of Vermont, for the Democratic presidential nomination -- at a time when at least 40 other Senate Democrats had lined up behind Hillary Clinton. And while Merkley is now a member of his party's Senate leadership -- named chief deputy minority whip in late 2016 -- his hard-charging tactics have caused him at times to run afoul of the current Democratic leader, Charles Schumer of New York, as well as Schumer's predecessor, Harry Reid of Nevada.

Merkley was born in Myrtle Creek in Oregon's Douglas County, where his parents worked at a local sawmill. The sawmill closed when Merkley was two years old, and his father went to work as a logger and a homebuilder in the neighboring town of Roseburg. When those jobs disappeared, the family moved to Portland, about 180 miles to the north, where his father took a job as a mechanic. He still resides in the east Portland neighborhood in which he grew up. "My parents lived with an ethic of making sure they saved and spent very little money on frills," he recalled.

In high school, Merkley spent a summer in Ghana as part of the American Field Service Exchange Program. The first in his family to attend college, he earned admission to a couple of elite universities. As an undergraduate at Stanford, he spent a trimester in Florence, Italy, and a summer hitchhiking around Israel before earning a degree in international affairs. He then took an internship with the Carnegie Endowment for International Peace. In the summer of 1980, Merkley and a fellow intern traveled through war-torn Central America by bus. He earned a master's degree in public policy from Princeton University, landed a presidential fellowship at the Pentagon in 1982, and then worked as an analyst in the Congressional Budget Office.

Merkley moved back to Portland in the early 1990s and accepted a job as director of the city's Habitat for Humanity chapter, where he concentrated on affordable housing and skills training for at-risk youth and low-income families. He later worked for the World Affairs Council of Oregon. In 1998, Merkley was elected to the state House, campaigning on a platform to improve the state's school system. In 2003, he was chosen as minority leader, as fellow House Democrats cited his consensus-building ability. But the state House was plagued by bitter partisanship, making it difficult to get anything done. Merkley exhibited his no-holds-barred side as he campaigned on behalf of Democratic House candidates in 2006, including running a controversial television ad that accused the Republican House speaker of covering up suspected sexual misconduct by her brother-in-law. State Republicans condemned the ad as over the line, but the Democrats won control of the Oregon House for the first time in 16 years, and Merkley was elected speaker.

During his tenure as speaker, the legislature passed such measures as an expanded indoor smoking ban and greater rights for same-sex couples. Merkley also pushed through an ethics bill aimed at curbing gifts by lobbyists to lawmakers. He took on Oregon's payday loan industry with a bill that imposed an interest rate cap of 36 percent annually on consumer loans of less than $50,000, and negotiated establishment of a rainy-day fund to protect schools and other state services from recessions; an increase in the state's corporate minimum tax paid for the fund. *The Oregonian* called the session "one of the most successful...of recent years."

In 2008, after two of the state's House Democrats, Earl Blumenauer and Peter DeFazio, passed on the opportunity to challenge GOP Sen. Gordon Smith, Schumer -- then chairman of the Democratic Senatorial Campaign Committee -- recruited Merkley. "The fact that I ended up in that campaign was a real shock to me," Merkley reminisced years later. National Democrats thought he would appeal to the same voters who had elected the moderate and pragmatic Smith to two terms. But despite the endorsements and financial backing of his national party, Merkley faced stiff primary competition from liberal activist and political consultant Steve Novick, who had opposed Merkley's elevation to House minority leader five years earlier. Merkley initially ignored Novick and focused his campaign on Smith. But Novick labeled Merkley as pro-war for a vote cast in favor of a 2003 resolution that praised both President George W. Bush and U.S. troops for courage in the war against Iraq. Merkley narrowly won the primary, 45%-42%. Novick won liberal Multnomah County, which includes Portland, by 12 points, but Merkley's large victories in rural areas gave him the nomination.

The general election was among the most expensive and closely watched contests of 2008. Smith had broken with his party by voting for higher automobile mileage standards and against oil drilling in the Arctic National Wildlife Refuge. To combat Smith's centrist appeal, Merkley allied himself with Democratic presidential nominee Barack Obama and his campaign theme of change. The message resonated in a state where Bush's approval ratings were particularly weak. In late October, Merkley aired a television ad that featured Obama urging voters to bring about "real change" by casting their ballots for Merkley.

Smith touted his reputation for bipartisanship, particularly his good relationship with fellow Oregon Sen. Ron Wyden, a Democrat. He attempted to distance himself from Bush, running ads that featured shots of Wyden, Democratic icon Sen. Edward Kennedy of Massachusetts, and even Obama. In one of the campaign season's oddest attack ads, the NRSC aired an unflattering clip of Merkley gobbling a hot dog and fielding questions about Russia's invasion of Georgia with his mouth full. In addition to capturing an inelegant moment, the ad also caught Merkley uninformed on the issue. Smith later condemned the ad. Ultimately, Merkley won, 49%-46%, boosted by the 57%-40% percent margin by which Obama defeated GOP presidential nominee John McCain in Oregon. Smith outraised Merkley $13 million to $7 million, but the DSCC and other outside groups poured in $11 million. The election gave Oregon two Democrats in the Senate for the first time in 40 years.

"When he was running, people didn't expect him to be quite as progressive as he turned out to be," Tim Carpenter of the Progressive Democrats of America noted. In 2015, the year after winning a second term, he had the 12th most liberal voting record, according to *Almanac* ratings. Arriving on Capitol Hill just months after the financial crisis of 2008, Merkley was named to the Banking Committee and began hammering Wall Street. During the 2010 Dodd-Frank financial regulatory overhaul, he joined forces with Democrat Carl Levin of Michigan to craft a tough version of the "Volcker Rule" banning banks from engaging in risky investment practices that may have contributed to the crisis. Their provision remained in the final bill, albeit in watered-down form in an effort to attract Republican support.

Earlier in 2010, Merkley was one of just 11 Democrats to oppose Obama's nomination of Ben Bernanke for a second term as Federal Reserve chairman; he contended Bernanke was partly at fault for the recession and was the wrong person to trust with an economic recovery. Four years later, Merkley was among the progressives whose opposition stymied Obama's plan to nominate former Treasury Secretary Larry Summers to succeed Bernanke; the party's left wing saw Summers as too accommodating to Wall Street. Merkley also allied himself with party progressives in the 2010 debate over the Affordable Care Act, as they unsuccessfully pushed for a Senate vote on a government-run "public option" to compete with private insurers.

Merkley has actively courted progressive activists outside the Beltway. "He gets the value of an inside-outside partnership -- of really using pressure from around the country to get Washington, D.C., to pay attention," said Adam Green, co-founder of the Progressive Change Campaign Committee. Merkley has used the Web site of Moveon.org to propose petition campaigns to the group's 8 million members. In turn, some progressive activists floated his name as a running mate for Clinton prior to the Democratic National Convention in July 2016. Notwithstanding his limited name ID outside of his home state and a reputation as a less-than-fiery stump speaker, they argued Merkley would bring progressive enthusiasm to the ticket without the downsides of some other potential running mates. Three months earlier, Merkley had stood alone among his Senate colleagues in endorsing Sanders. "It doesn't feel lonely, it just feels right," Merkley told the *Atlantic*, adding, "I think we need to fundamentally change the system that has been so deeply moving towards consolidation of power by the very few."

Earlier, when Senate Democrats were in the majority, Merkley lobbied outside groups to support efforts to restrict the ability of the GOP minority to block progressive-backed legislation through use of the filibuster. "The clear and undeniable fact is that the Senate is broken," Merkley declared. "Thoughtful deliberation does not occur and far too much gets lost in a tangle of obstruction and delay." Merkley joined Democratic Sen. Tom Udall on a proposal to ban filibustering of motions to proceed to legislation. Their measure required senators opposing a bill to stay on the Senate floor. Initially, Senate leaders resisted their efforts. But in 2013, Reid pushed through a no-filibuster rule for most judicial and executive-branch appointments -- expanded in 2017 by Majority Leader Mitch McConnell, in the face of a filibuster of President Donald Trump's Supreme Court nominee.

By that time, with the Democrats in the minority, Merkley's perspective with regard to filibustering had shifted dramatically. In January 2017, even before Trump's nominations of appeals court judge Neil Gorsuch was announced, Merkley vowed to filibuster = any Trump nominee for the high court -- while utilizing Senate procedures to exact revenge for McConnell's refusal to allow hearings or a vote on Obama's nomination of appeals court judge Merrick Garland to the vacant seat a year earlier. According to *Politico*, an irritated Schumer warned Merkley about making the battle about retribution for Garland, as opposed to the merits of the Trump Administration's nominee. Schumer reportedly told Merkley, as chief deputy minority whip, to make clear he was speaking for himself and not the party. Shortly before McConnell's move to change the filibuster rules on nomination, Merkley delivered the eighth longest floor speech in Senate history, at nearly 15 hours and 30 minutes. He charged the Republicans had "stolen" a Supreme Court seat, while detailing Democratic concerns about Gorsuch. Technically, the speech was not a filibuster: Because McConnell already had set the vote on the Senate rules change, Merkley's move did not delay Senate business.

Merkley was aligned with Sanders, Warren and other leading progressives -- and against most of his fellow Oregon legislators, as well as Obama -- in opposing the Trans-Pacific Partnership trade deal in 2015. While trade receives notable support in export-friendly Oregon, even from Democrats, and while Obama pledged that the deal would be more pro-worker and pro-environment than past agreements, Merkley didn't buy that argument. "Here we are repeating the same basic structure of the other agreements with no changes for America and therefore no improvement for the workers," he said in a floor speech. Only a handful of Senate Democrats joined Republicans in granting Obama expedited negotiating authority for the agreement -- from which Trump withdrew the United States during the first days of his presidency.

As a follow-on to his advocacy of greater rights for same-sex couples while speaker of the Oregon House, Merkley played a leading role in drafting and moving the Employment Non-Discrimination Act, to protect members of the LGBT community from job discrimination. The legislation went nowhere in the Republican-controlled House, but it notched an impressive victory in the Senate -- passing in November 2013 with bipartisan backing, 64-32. Prominent on Merkley's office wall is a letter from Kennedy -- for years the Senate's leading liberal voice -- turning over leadership on the issue to Merkley. It was written not long before Kennedy died of cancer in 2009.

Republicans hoped to unseat Merkley in 2014 by seeking to portray him as out of touch with most Oregon voters. Monica Wehby, a pediatric neurosurgeon with moderate positions, took 50 percent of the vote in a five-way primary. Subsequent media reports alleged that Wehby had "stalked" her ex-husband and a former boyfriend. No charges were ever filed, and Wehby blamed Democrats for trying to "shred" her family. But she never recovered politically from the allegations. Freedom Partners, a group connected to the tea party-aligned billionaire Koch brothers, poured money into the race. However, it proved to be a double-edged sword, as it gave Merkley an angle of attack: He charged that Wehby was beholden to the controversial brothers. Merkley campaigned hard, visiting as many as eight cities in a single day of campaigning, and Freedom Partners pulled out of the state more than a month before the election. In a year that the Democrats suffered a net loss of nine Senate seats, Merkley won easily, 56%-37%.

On the same day he was reelected, Oregon voters -- by a margin of less than 850 votes out of 1.5 million cast -- defeated a ballot initiative that would have required the labeling of food with genetically modified organisms. But Vermont's passage of a similar law several months earlier put the issue in Congress' lap, as major food companies resisted having to comply with a patchwork of state regulations. Merkley and three Democratic colleagues, including Patrick Leahy of Vermont, introduced a bill to require that food labeling either identify each GMO ingredient or include a blanket statement that some ingredients were genetically engineered. Merkley called the proposal a compromise between consumer groups that wanted clear labeling and industry groups fearful that GMO labels would scare away customers. But consumer groups were unhappy when the final version of the bill to come before the Senate allowed the labeling be done through scannable smartphone codes rather than text or symbols. It passed by a 65-30 margin on its way to becoming law. Merkley voted against it, saying it would make it virtually impossible for consumers to access information about GMOs.

Representing a state where the sale of both medical and recreational marijuana is legal, Merkley pushed beginning in 2015 to allow Veterans Administration physicians to discuss medical marijuana as a treatment option for pain and symptoms related to post-traumatic stress disorder. It was in response to VA physicians being barred from doing so in the nearly two dozen states with medical marijuana laws, forcing veterans to turn elsewhere for guidance as well as the paperwork often necessary to acquire the drug. Joining with Republican Sen. Steve Daines of Montana -- another state where medical marijuana is legal -- Merkley sponsored a bill to ease medicinal cannabis access for veterans, and in May 2015 it passed the Senate Appropriations Committee. A year later, similar language was contained in amendments that passed both the House and Senate by wide margins in the annual funding bill for the VA . But the marijuana language was quietly stripped in House-Senate conference committee. Merkley blasted the removal as "outrageous," but failed to get the provision reinserted.

FIRST DISTRICT

Suzanne Bonamici (D)

Elected 2012, 3rd full term; b. Oct 14, 1954, Detroit, MI; Lane Community College (OR), A.A.; University of Oregon Law School, J.D.; University of Oregon (OR), B.A., 1980; Episcopalian; Married (Michael H. Simon); 2 children.

Elected Office: OR House, 2007-2008; OR Senate, 2008-2011.

Professional Career: Attorney, Federal Trade Commission, 1983-1986; Practicing attorney, 1986-1989; Legislative aide, 2001-2006.

DC Office: 439 CHOB 20515, 202-225-0855, Fax: 202-225-9497, bonamici.house.gov.

State Offices: Beaverton, 503-469-6010.

Committees: *Education & the Workforce*: Early Childhood, Elementary & Secondary Education, Health, Employment, Labor & Pensions. *Science, Space & Technology*: Environment (RMM), Research & Technology.

Group Ratings

	ADA	ACLU	AFL-CIO	LCV	ITI	COC	HAFA	ACU	CFG	FRC
2016	-	100%	-	100%	83%	50%	10%	4%	11%	0%
2015	85%	C	92%	97%	C	55%	C	4%	0%	0%

Almanac Ratings 2015

	Economy	Social	Foreign	Composite
Liberal	84%	100%	99%	94%
Conservative	16%	0%	1%	6%

Key Votes of the 114th Congress

1. Keystone Pipeline	N	5. Puerto Rico Debt	Y	9. Offenses by Aliens	N
2. Trade Deals	Y	6. Medical Marijuana	Y	10. Troops in Iraq	Y
3. Export-Import Bank	Y	7. Sanctuary Cities	N	11. Homeland Security $$	Y
4. Debt Ceiling Increase	Y	8. Armor-piercing Bullets	N	12. Trade Adjustment aid	Y

Election Results

Election	Name (Party)	Vote (%)		Cand. Spent	Ind. Exp. Support	Ind. Exp. Oppose
2016 General	Suzanne Bonamici (D)	225,391	(60%)	$589,542		
	Brian Heinrich (R)	139,756	(37%)			
	Kyle Sheahan (L)	12,257	(3%)			
2016 Primary	Suzanne Bonamici (D)	93,884	(90%)			
	Shabba Woodley (D)	10,152	(10%)			

Prior winning percentages: 2014 (57%), 2012 (60%), 2012 special (54%)

Democrat Suzanne Bonamici, who won a special election in 2012, usually has been a reliable liberal. The chief exception has been that she is responsive to the needs and overseas interests of local businesses, often to the dismay of unions on international trade issue.

Bonamici was born in Detroit and grew up in the small town of Northville, Michigan. Her father worked at a local bank, and her mother was a piano teacher. After high school, Bonamici traveled with friends in a van to Oregon, fell in love with the state and moved to Eugene. "It was a very '70s thing to do," Bonamici told *The Oregonian*. She attended Lane Community College and worked at a legal-aid center in Eugene. Bonamici got her bachelor's and law degrees from the University of Oregon. She moved to Washington, D.C., to take a job as a consumer protection lawyer at the Federal Trade Commission. There, she met her husband and they relocated to Oregon, where Bonamici worked as a lawyer in private practice. After working as a legislative assistant in the Oregon House of Representatives, she won her own state House seat and focused on consumer protection. She was appointed to fill a vacancy in the state Senate and then was elected.

When Democratic Rep. David Wu resigned amid charges of improper sexual advances, Bonamici jumped into the Democratic primary in the special election. She faced off against state Labor Commissioner Brad Avakian and state Rep. Brad Witt; both opposed U.S. trade pacts with Colombia, Panama and South Korea that were being debated in Congress. Bonamici initially declined to take a position and drew criticism for indecisiveness. She then came out in favor of the South Korea pact. She raised the most money of the three candidates and won with 66 percent of the vote.

In the general, Bonamici faced Rob Cornilles, a sports business consultant. Cornilles played up his business experience and kept his distance from the national GOP. He touted his endorsements from Democratic mayors, and refused to take the customary no-new-taxes pledge made by most Republicans in Congress. Bonamici ran an ad attacking Cornilles for an old federal tax lien against his business over failure to pay payroll taxes. She advocated the end to some corporate tax breaks to fund education and infrastructure projects. The Democratic Congressional Campaign Committee moved early to paint Cornilles as a tea party extremist. The DCCC, EMILY's List, and other liberal interest groups poured millions into the race, while national Republican groups mostly stayed away. Bonamici won, 54%-40%.

In the House, Bonamici has been a consistent Democratic vote. On the Education and the Workforce Committee, she focused on making college more affordable and reforming the No Child Left Behind Act. On the renewal of student-loan legislation in 2014, she worked with others to add increased financial counseling for recipients. She was a founder of the bipartisan Congressional STEAM Caucus, which encourages innovation in science, technology, engineering, art and design and math education. In January 2017, she became the vice ranking member on the Education and the Workforce Committee, where she said that her interest was to fight for working families and public education. As the ranking Democrat on the Science, Space and Technology Subcommittee on Environment, she has focused on global climate change. In December 2016, the House passed her bill to improve warnings and education in coastal communities about the threat of tsunamis.

In 2015, Bonamici was one of 28 House Democrats who voted to give trade promotion authority to President Barack Obama, whose prospective Trans-Pacific Partnership was touted as an economic boon for West Coast companies and ports. "Our economy is increasingly global, and trade done right creates jobs, helps businesses grow and puts our country on stronger economic footing," she said. She cited the benefits for local wheat and potato farmers. She accompanied Obama on a visit to Nike headquarters, where he said that the deal would benefit Oregon companies and "help level the playing field." In an appearance in Portland a few days later, AFL-CIO President Richard Trumka warned that he was "blowing the whistle, quite frankly" on Bonamici and other Portland-area Democrats in Congress for being on "the wrong side" of TPP, which he said most Oregonians opposed.

Bonamici has been reelected easily. Despite the threat of a challenge backed by organized labor or a loss of enthusiasm among her base, she suffered neither. In the Democratic primary, her opponent was Shabba Woodley, a 25-year-old videographer who had no money or political experience and read poetry to a reporter. Bonamici won the primary with 90 percent of the vote. Likewise, her Republican opponent, Brian Heinrich, was a sales representative who was running his first campaign. He did not file a campaign-finance report. Bonamici won, 60%-37%, and continued to have support from a broad array of interest groups.

Northwest Oregon: Western Portland Area

Population		**Race and Ethnicity**		**Income**	
Total	797,650	White	72.7%	Median Income	$63,770 (103 out of 435)
Land area	3,007	Black	1.5%		
Pop/ sq mi	265.3	Latino	14.2%		
Born in state	44.0%	Asian	7.0%	Under $50,000	39.5%
		Two races	3.6%	$50,000-$99,999	32.1%
Age Groups		Other	0.9%	$100,000-$199,999	22.3%
Under 18	23.5%			$200,000 or more	6.1%
18-34	23.1%	**Education**		Poverty Rate	12.6%
35-64	40.7%	H.S grad or less	29.9%		
Over 64	12.7%	Some college	31.7%	**Health Insurance**	
Work		College Degree, 4 yr	24.1%	With health insurance coverage	88.9%
White Collar	42.7%	Post grad	14.4%		
Sales and Service	39.2%	**Military**		**Public Assistance**	
Blue Collar	18.2%	Veteran	8.4%	Cash public assistance income	3.1%
Government	6.6%	Active Duty	0.1%		
				Food stamp/SNAP benefits	14.2%

Voter Turnout			
2015 Total Citizens 18+	550,623	2016 House Turnout as % CVAP	69%
2016 House turnout	378,095	2014 House Turnout as % CVAP	51%

2012 Presidential Vote		
Barack Obama	200,993	(57%)
Mitt Romney	140,462	(40%)

2016 Presidential Vote		
Hillary Clinton	219,369	(55%)
Donald Trump	132,195	(33%)
Gary Johnson	22,061	(6%)
Jill Stein	9,036	(2%)

Cook Partisan Voting Index: D+9

Just over the hills from downtown Portland are the valleys and interstices between green mountains of suburban Washington County. This was once farm country, with 39,000 people in 1940; now it has almost 575,000 and is an integral part of metro Portland. Its population zoomed up 70 percent between 1990 and 2010, with an increase of another 45,000 in the next five years. Its towns enjoy a high-tech, healthy-lifestyle affluence, cushioned by protected forests and anchored by major employers that include Tektronix, Intel, IBM and Columbia Sportswear, most of which are based out-of-state. Near Beaverton is the world headquarters of Nike, housed in 22 buildings spread over 200 acres. Like Silicon Valley, the Silicon Forest has an environment that appeals to a highly skilled workforce. Nestled at the foot of mountains, it is woodsy and even rustic, but is outfitted with all the comforts of modern life. The Asian population of the county is 10 percent.

The companies went through a rough patch during the recession, cutting jobs and sending unemployment in the Portland area well above 10 percent through 2010. The Portland area has since been on the rebound. Nike continues to expand, and employs more than 10,000 people in Beaverton. Intel is the largest employer in the state with 19,500, many of them at a 530-acre campus in Hillsboro. The company controls more than 90 percent of the chip market; the tech industry's move away from chips has led Intel to new markets, such as data and memory. Biotech firm Genentech has a presence in Hillsboro.

The 1st Congressional District of Oregon includes the western slice of Portland and all of suburban Washington County, which includes more than two-thirds of the voters. It extends nearly 100 miles northwest from Portland along the Columbia River to the rain-swept port of Astoria on the Pacific Coast, where Lewis and Clark spent the winter of 1805-06. (The event is memorialized at the Lewis and Clark National Historical Park.) Yamhill County and Beaverton are known for wineries. Astoria, which retains many century-old buildings, has been a popular site to shoot movies, including *Goonies,* a 1980s small-town cult classic.

Like Oregon overall, the 1st District was historically New England Republican, electing only Republicans to Congress from 1892 to 1972. Also like New England, it trended left on cultural issues, and since 1974 it has elected only Democrats. Hillary Clinton won 55 percent of the presidential vote in 2016; President Barack Obama got 57 percent in 2012.

SECOND DISTRICT

Greg Walden (R)

Elected 1998, 10th term; b. Jan 10, 1957, The Dalles; University of Oregon (OR), B.S.; University of Alaska, Att.; Episcopalian; Married (Mylene Ann Simons Walden); 1 child.

Elected Office: OR House, 1989-1995, Majority Leader, 1991-1993; OR Senate, 1995-1997.

Professional Career: Press Secretary, U.S. Rep. Denny Smith, 1981-1984, chief of Staff, 1984-1986; Owner, Columbia Gorge Broadcasters Inc., 1986-2008.

DC Office: 2185 RHOB 20515, 202-225-6730, Fax: 202-225-5774, walden.house.gov.

State Offices: Bend, 541-389-4408; La Grande, 541-624-2400; Medford, 541-776-4646.

Committees: *Energy & Commerce (Chmn)*: Communications & Technology, Digital Commerce & Consumer Protection, Energy, Environment, Health, Oversight & Investigations.

Group Ratings

	ADA	ACLU	AFL-CIO	LCV	ITI	COC	HAFA	ACU	CFG	FRC
2016	-	5%	-	5%	100%	100%	46%	72%	68%	83%
2015	0%	C	29%	3%	C	100%	C	50%	40%	83%

Almanac Ratings 2015

	Economy	Social	Foreign	Composite
Liberal	10%	20%	10%	13%
Conservative	90%	80%	90%	87%

Key Votes of the 114th Congress

1. Keystone Pipeline	Y	5. Puerto Rico Debt	Y	9. Offenses by Aliens	Y
2. Trade Deals	Y	6. Medical Marijuana	Y	10. Troops in Iraq	N
3. Export-Import Bank	N	7. Sanctuary Cities	Y	11. Homeland Security $$	Y
4. Debt Ceiling Increase	Y	8. Armor-piercing Bullets	Y	12. Trade Adjustment aid	Y

Election Results

Election	Name (Party)	Vote (%)	Cand. Spent	Ind. Exp. Support	Ind. Exp. Oppose
2016 General	Greg Walden (R)	272,952 (72%)	$2,221,030		
	Jim Crary (D)	106,640 (28%)			
2016 Primary	Greg Walden (R)	82,903 (80%)			
	Paul Romero (R)	20,446 (20%)			

Prior winning percentages: 2014 (70%), 2012 (69%), 2010 (74%), 2008 (70%), 2006 (67%), 2004 (72%), 2002 (72%), 2000 (74%), 1998 (62%)

Greg Walden, elected in 1998, has emerged as one of the Republican Party's most highly regarded inside strategists. After two successful terms as chairman of the National Republican Congressional Committee in which the GOP had a net gain in its House majority, he took control in 2017 of the influential Energy and Commerce Committee. That placed him at the center of the debate on the future of the Affordable Care Act. Given his recent campaign management, he understood the political dynamics facing House Republicans.

Walden grew up on an 80-acre cherry orchard near The Dalles in the Columbia River Gorge. His father ran radio stations that had been in the family since the 1930s and also served in the state House.

Walden followed both pursuits. As a young man, he was a disc jockey and talk show host. Then, he got involved in politics as the press secretary and chief of staff for local Republican Rep. Denny Smith from 1981 to 1987. Walden returned to Hood River to run the family's five-station broadcast business, Columbia Gorge Broadcasters. In 1988, he was elected to the state House, eventually becoming majority leader.

When the 2nd District seat opened in 1998, Walden ran and faced substantial primary opposition from Perry Atkinson, a Christian broadcaster who was backed financially by Gary Bauer's Campaign for Working Americans. Walden stayed competitive by raising $500,000 and prevailed over Atkinson with 55 percent of the vote. In the anticlimactic general election against a conservative Democrat, Walden won 61%-35%. He has not faced a serious reelection challenge in his comfortably Republican district.

In the House, as shown by the *Almanac* vote ratings for 2015, Walden has been a mainstream Republican who leans to the center on cultural issues. He caught the eye of Republican leaders with his political knowledge, knack for forming friendships and devotion to the party agenda. In 2011, *The Oregonian* newspaper wrote that Walden is known for being "reliable, self-deprecating, and largely without ego." He has been close to Republican Rep. Pete Sessions of Texas, and when Sessions took over as NRCC chairman, he made Walden his deputy. In early 2010, still in the minority, Republican Leader John Boehner picked Walden to be chairman of the Republican leadership. When Republicans reclaimed the majority that fall, Walden helped steer the GOP's transition to power, handling issues ranging from rules changes governing debate to steps to economize on House operations.

After the 2012 election, Boehner tapped Sessions as Rules Committee chairman and Walden was unanimously elected chairman of the NRCC. His term hit some initial bumps: The NRCC came under criticism for what members of both parties said was an unseemly 2014 fundraising email about the select committee investigating the deadly 2012 terrorist attacks at U.S. facilities in Benghazi, Libya. "There are times when I'm taken aback because that's not the person I knew growing up and I don't think they are always things he believes," Democratic Oregon Rep. Earl Blumenauer, who served with Walden's father in the state Legislature, told *The Oregonian.*

Although the midterm environment was considered highly favorable for his party, Walden's confidence in a wave election startled even fellow Republicans. Walden touted a "Drive for 245," which would require a double-digit increase in Republican seats. Some Republicans dismissed it as an unrealistic fundraising ploy, and lamented the Democrats' ability to out-raise them even as they acknowledged lacking a figure who brought in funds as proficiently as President Barack Obama. Two junior Republicans floated the idea of challenging Walden for another term. Some anonymous Republicans wondered in print whether he was too nice. That talk disappeared after Republicans reaped 247 seats, their largest House majority since 1928. Walden was unopposed for another term as NRCC chairman.

Walden has kept busy on the policy side. In 2011, he took over as chairman of the Energy and Commerce Telecommunications Subcommittee, a prime niche for an ex-broadcaster. As a critic of Federal Communications Commission and its Obama-era policies, his appointment signaled that Republicans would wage a fierce battle against the regulators. Walden filed legislation that would require the FCC to justify any rule change by identifying market implications or potential harm to consumers. His bill passed the House in 2012, but the Democratic-controlled Senate did not take it up.

Walden clashed with the FCC and vowed to upend its proposed internet rules, known as "net neutrality," which prohibit tiered pricing by phone and cable companies that many Republicans regard as excessive interference in the market. His bill passed the House in 2011 but also died in the Senate. Walden co-authored a letter to Obama asking him to halt net neutrality rules expected to take effect. The administration ignored his letter. In February 2015, the FCC under Chairman Tom Wheeler issued its final net neutrality rules. Republicans strongly objected. The FCC's actions did not end the debate, Walden said. "Resorting to Great Depression-era rules will trigger a stampede to the courts, unleashing years of lawsuits and uncertainty at a time when U.S. leadership and the internet economy are more important than ever." Although he pursued legislative alternatives, the Obama administration's embrace of Wheeler left his critics with few options. That quickly changed after the 2016 election when President Donald Trump named new leaders at the FCC. One of their first priorities was repeal of the net neutrality rules.

Another telecommunications priority for Walden was to stifle efforts to restore the Fairness Doctrine, which required broadcasters to offer multiple viewpoints on controversial issues of the day. He worked closely on this issue with then-Rep. Mike Pence of Indiana, before he left the House for larger ambitions; based on his earlier experience as a radio talk-show host, Pence strongly opposed the revival of the Fairness Doctrine. Recalling his own days in broadcasting, Walden told *The Oregonian* that it was difficult to figure out who qualified to offer opposing viewpoints when his father read editorials on the air, so the family stopped airing editorials altogether. Political chatter over the broadcast network tends to be conservative, he said, but that should not matter. "Is it more conservative than liberal? Yeah," Walden told the newspaper. "Are there a lot more country-western stations than polka stations? Yeah. Listeners make these determinations. The marketplace decides." Walden won this battle, as the FCC removed the Fairness Doctrine from the agency's rules.

Walden has had a hand in national issues that affect his rural district. He played a central role in 2003 in assembling bipartisan support for the Healthy Forests Restoration Act, which was a legislative response to wildfires raging across the West worsened by unlogged dry timber. Walden has worked to curb regulations under the Endangered Species Act by encouraging a greater role for outside scientists to review government proposals. In an effort to restore timber payments to rural counties, he joined forces with home-state Democrats. In March 2015, Walden found an unexpected vehicle for action when he added a provision to a time-urgent Medicare bill his plan, cosponsored by Oregon Democratic Rep. Peter DeFazio, to give hundreds of millions of dollars of aid to rural counties that suffered from reduced timber sales. Responding to protests the previous year by ranchers in his district who objected to what they viewed as heavy-handed federal rules, Walden in February 2017 filed legislation to relax restrictions on landowners who set limited fires to protect the value of their property.

Going into the 2016 campaign cycle at the Republicans' high water-mark of House seats, Walden and the NRCC were widely expected to be on the defensive. Most of the competitive seats were Republican-held. Although the GOP majority seemed secure, a double-digit loss of seats was considered likely. His task became all the more challenging when GOP presidential nominee Donald Trump had a limited, or chilly, relationship with many House Republicans, who worried that Trump had become a drag on their own election prospects. In the end, some benefited from Trump's relative strength in exurban and rural districts; Democrats failed to take advantage of opportunities in suburban districts where Trump ran relatively poorly. With the NRCC's useful strategic advice and spending for candidates in battleground districts, the GOP's loss of only six House seats was viewed as an impressive accomplishment for Walden.

During that campaign, his eyes were on a bigger prize: With Fred Upton of Michigan term-limited as Energy and Commerce Committee chairman after 2016, Walden quietly made known his interest in taking the reins. His chief opponent was John Shimkus of Illinois, who had impressive accomplishments on energy and environmental issues. Walden had the big advantage of having protected the Republican majority for four years. He gained the support of many Republicans who owed their seat - or their chairmanship - to him. Speaker Paul Ryan reportedly backed Walden, despite the seniority advantage for Shimkus. Following his selection, Walden worked to avoid recriminations by expanding the jurisdiction of Shimkus's subcommittee.

As committee chairman, Walden quickly turned his attention to House Republican efforts to revise the Affordable Care Act. Prior to the 217-213 passage of the bill in the House on May 4, 2017, Walden and others on his committee worked with Ways and Means Republicans plus GOP leaders in the painstaking deliberations to build majority support. Their objective, he said, was "how to best achieve the goals of protecting America's sickest patients and maintaining market stability….without Obamacare's unpopular individual mandate." Other items on Walden's agenda at Energy and Commerce included revisions in the Children's Health Insurance Program and changes at the Food and Drug Administration. Given his experience at the NRCC, Walden was mindful that the legislative outcomes would affect reelection prospects for some House Republicans.

Eastern Oregon: Medford, Bend

Population		**Race and Ethnicity**		**Income**	
Total	781,254	White	80.7%	Median Income	$44,314 (347 out of 435)
Land area	69,443	Black	0.6%		
Pop/ sq mi	11.3	Latino	13.1%		
Born in state	44.2%	Asian	1.0%	Under $50,000	55.2%
		Two races	2.7%	$50,000-$99,999	30.3%
Age Groups		Other	1.9%	$100,000-$199,999	12.2%
Under 18	22.2%			$200,000 or more	2.3%
18-34	19.9%	**Education**		Poverty Rate	17.8%
35-64	39.3%	H.S grad or less	39.8%		
Over 64	18.5%	Some college	36.8%	**Health Insurance**	
		College Degree, 4 yr	14.9%	With health insurance coverage	85.9%
Work		Post grad	8.6%		
White Collar	31.9%				
Sales and Service	43.8%	**Military**		**Public Assistance**	
Blue Collar	24.3%	Veteran	12.2%	Cash public assistance income	3.9%
Government	9.6%	Active Duty	0.1%		
				Food stamp/SNAP benefits	21.3%

Voter Turnout			
2015 Total Citizens 18+	578,896	2016 House Turnout as % CVAP	66%
2016 House turnout	380,739	2014 House Turnout as % CVAP	50%

2012 Presidential Vote		
Mitt Romney	196,568	(56%)
Barack Obama	139,940	(40%)

2016 Presidential Vote		
Donald Trump	215,711	(55%)
Hillary Clinton	139,059	(35%)
Gary Johnson	18,600	(5%)
Jill Stein	8,191	(2%)

Cook Partisan Voting Index: R+11

The Cascade Mountains that wall off eastern Oregon from the rest of the state are a magnificent chain of once active volcanic mountains that drain almost every drop of moisture out of the air blowing in from the Pacific Ocean. They separate green, wet western Oregon from brown, parched eastern Oregon. The eastern part has 70 percent of the state's land, but only around half a million of its 4 million people, many of whom still make their living off the land: beef and dairy cattle, timber and lumber, fish from the Columbia River, and wheat and sugar beets from the irrigated plains. The effect of the Cascades can be felt in the one place they are breached - at the Columbia River Gorge. Here, funneled winds pound in steadily from the west, making the confluence of the Columbia and Hood rivers the best windsurfing site in the United States. One of the world's largest wind farms, Shepherds Flat, became operational here in 2012. In early 2017, Republicans in Congress were considering options to sell perhaps 3 million acres of public lands in Oregon.

The 2nd Congressional District of Oregon covers nearly three-fourths of the state: everything east of the Cascades and the southernmost valley between the Cascades and the Coast Range. Much of this land is forested and unpopulated. Harney County, with a land area larger than that of nine states, had just 7,292 residents in 2016, a 2 percent drop since 2010. In Bend and the surrounding area, sawmills have closed, but the wilderness and high desert plateau have attracted software developers, outdoor activity, upscale tourists and telecommuters. In the town of The Dalles, Google operates a 200-employee data center on 30 acres of land on the Columbia River. In 2015 and 2016, the company purchased another 97 acres, where it plans to expand its campus for a total investment of close to $2 billion, with generous local tax breaks. The land had been the site of an aluminum smelter until 2000. Facebook has its data center in Prineville, to the south. After getting a property tax exemption from Gov. Kate Brown, Apple announced plans in 2016 for a third data center in Prineville. In January 2017, *The Oregonian* reported that the area was running short of electricity to power the giant facilities. In Klamath County, developers made plans in early 2017 for a 500-acre business park, supported by a projected $1 billion in new infrastructure spending by 2021.

The 2nd District is heavily Republican. This is part of the leave-us-alone Rocky Mountain Basin, not the hipster West Coast. Court decisions protecting the spotted owl hurt the logging industry here. International competition has hurt the timber industry, with Oregon lawmakers blaming Chinese manufacturers for setting artificially low prices for timber-related products. In 2009, rural Jackson County saw its last remaining large sawmill dismantled; it had 91 in its heyday. An unusual coalition of timber industry leaders, environmentalists and government officials joined forces to save the last remaining lumber mill in Grant County in 2012. In 2014, according to *The Oregonian,* "the pendulum had swung so far that Oregon's high-tech industry accounted for the same number of workers and share of wages as the forest sector did in the 1970s."

THIRD DISTRICT

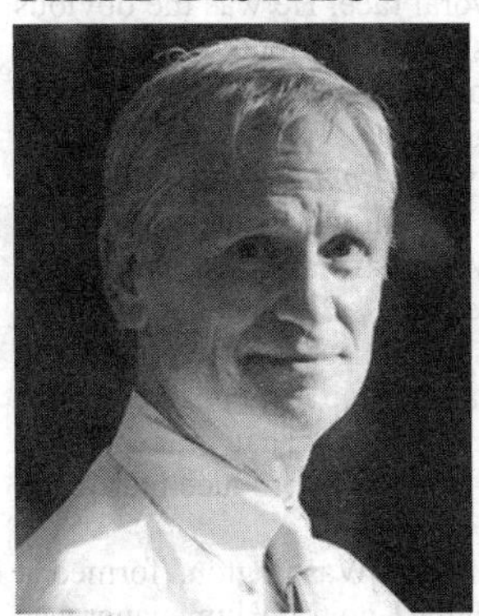

Earl Blumenauer (D)

Elected 1996, 11th term; b. Aug 16, 1948, Portland; Lewis & Clark College (OR), B.A., 1970; Northwestern Law School, Lewis and Clark College (OR), J.D., 1976; Jewish; Married (Margaret Kirkpatrick Blumenauer); 2 children.

Elected Office: OR House, 1973-1978; Multnomah County Commissioner, 1978- 86; Portland City Council, 1986-1996.

Professional Career: Assistant to President, Portland St. University, 1970-1977; Portland Community College Board of Director, 1975-1981.

DC Office: 1111 LHOB 20515, 202-225-4811, Fax: 202-225-8941, blumenauer.house.gov.

State Offices: Portland, 503-231-2300.

Committees: *Ways & Means*: Health, Oversight, Tax Policy.

Group Ratings

	ADA	ACLU	AFL-CIO	LCV	ITI	COC	HAFA	ACU	CFG	FRC
2016	-	100%	-	97%	50%	50%	14%	0%	18%	0%
2015	85%	C	88%	97%	C	55%	C	4%	1%	0%

Almanac Ratings 2015

	Economy	Social	Foreign	Composite
Liberal	89%	100%	100%	96%
Conservative	11%	0%	0%	4%

Key Votes of the 114th Congress

1. Keystone Pipeline	N	5. Puerto Rico Debt	Y	9. Offenses by Aliens	N
2. Trade Deals	Y	6. Medical Marijuana	Y	10. Troops in Iraq	Y
3. Export-Import Bank	Y	7. Sanctuary Cities	N	11. Homeland Security $$	Y
4. Debt Ceiling Increase	Y	8. Armor-piercing Bullets	N	12. Trade Adjustment aid	Y

Election Results

Election	Name (Party)	Vote (%)		Cand. Spent	Ind. Exp. Support	Ind. Exp. Oppose
2016 General	Earl Blumenauer (D)	274,687	(72%)	$878,331		
	David Walker (I)	78,154	(20%)			
	David Delk (P)	29,514	(8%)			
2016 Primary	Earl Blumenauer (D)		(100%)			

Prior winning percentages: 2014 (72%), 2012 (75%), 2010 (70%), 2008 (75%), 2006 (74%), 2004 (71%), 2002 (67%), 2000 (67%), 1998 (84%), 1996 (67%)

Democrat Earl Blumenauer, who won a special election in 1996, has built on his role as Congress' point person on "smart growth" planning strategies that combat urban sprawl and promote alternatives to driving. On the Ways and Means Committee, he has become a leader in promoting international trade - a contentious issue among Democrats. He is known for his distinctive bow ties and bike rides.

Blumenauer grew up in Portland and graduated from Lewis and Clark College and its Northwestern Law School. In his teens, he was inspired by the civil rights and anti-war movements of the 1960s. In college, he headed a statewide campaign to lower Oregon's voting age. He has held public office almost all of his adult life. In 1972, at age 23, he was elected to the Oregon House. He subsequently was elected as a Multnomah County commissioner and as a Portland city councilor; in the latter job, he also served as commissioner of public works.

He championed many of the policies that have made Portland distinctive - regional light-rail transit, curbside recycling and aggressive land-use planning. He encouraged bicycle riding and "regional rail summits," which bring neighborhood residents into the planning for higher densities at transit nodes. Blumenauer has had some setbacks, notably when he lost the 1992 mayoral race. He was the obvious successor when Ron Wyden was elected to the Senate, and he won the special election 68%-25%. His campaign slogan was "Vote Earl, Vote Often." In his Democratic bastion, he has never drawn less than 67 percent of the vote since and has not faced a serious primary challenge.

Blumenauer has had a consistently liberal voting record, as shown by his *Almanac* vote ratings for 2015. He and Rep. Jared Polis of Colorado have been lead sponsors of a bill allowing states to legalize medical marijuana and to regulate it in a manner similar to alcohol. "We're still arresting two-thirds of a million people for use of a substance that a majority feel should be legal," Blumenauer told The Associated Press. In 2015, the House narrowly defeated a proposal that he co-sponsored to give states the authority to legalize marijuana. In April 2016, *Rolling Stone* profiled him as the "top legal pot advocate," and quoted him saying there has been a "sea change" in support within Congress. That year, he filed a bill with Republican Rep. Morgan Griffith of Virginia to permit more growers to produce marijuana for research.

Blumenauer, who has ridden his bicycle everywhere he travels around Washington, formed a Congressional Bike Caucus and argued for showers for bike commuters at the Capitol. Blumenauer was astonished to find that the House subsidized parking for employees, but not mass transit; now, employees can get subsidized transit fares. He is interested in what seem like quixotic projects now but may seem less so in time: an interstate highway system for bicycle paths and reduced dependence on driving as a tool to improve public health. "The rise of bicycles is a metaphor for change in this country," Blumenauer says. He has been active in promoting healthier school lunches. To rescue the depleted highway trust fund, he has called for a 15-cent hike per gallon in the gas tax over a three-year period, plus eventual movement toward a mileage-based tax. "There is a looming transportation funding crisis before us," he wrote with Republican Rep. Jim Renacci of Ohio in a 2015 opinion column for CNN. GOP leaders did not permit a vote during the debate that year on the highway bill.

The sometimes nerdy policy wonk has developed an audience for his gospel of livability and civic values. With his seat on the tax-writing Ways and Means Committee, he has given the panel a new focus on the environment and urban planning - for Democrats, at least. His call for tax subsidies for bicycle commuting was included in the Troubled Asset Relief Program law of 2008. As committee chairman, Rep. Paul Ryan of Wisconsin dismissed his ideas as "central planning."

On economic issues, he has actively promoted trade across the Pacific, a key element of Portland's economy. He was an outspoken supporter of approving Trade Promotion Authority for President Barack Obama, noting in 2015 that "Oregon will not only be able to export more of its products, but also its values," including human rights, worker rights and environmental protections. He was caustic in criticizing other House Democrats, including party leaders, for their votes against extending trade adjustment assistance for workers adversely affected by overseas trade deals. "Political gamesmanship within our party won out over substance," he said. He complained that tariffs imposed on U.S.-designed footwear imported from Asia discriminate against companies like Oregon's Nike.

Blumenauer has been a leader of the Congressional Public Broadcasting Caucus and has been an outspoken critic of Republican proposals to strike funding for National Public Radio, citing polls that it has strong public support. During the 2009 health care debate, he promoted legislation to allow doctors to charge Medicare for end-of-life consultations, a proposal that former Alaska Gov. Sarah Palin famously charged would lead to "death panels." In February 2017, Blumenauer launched a working group to consider how the 25th Amendment to the Constitution might create an opportunity to remove President Donald Trump from office. One option, he said, would be the creation of a bipartisan panel of former presidents and vice presidents to make the determination.

Greater Portland

Population		Race and Ethnicity		Income	
Total	799,338	White	72.2%	Median Income	$54,254 (194 out of 435)
Land area	1,074	Black	5.0%		
Pop/ sq mi	743.9	Latino	10.9%		
Born in state	44.6%	Asian	6.6%	Under $50,000	46.5%
		Two races	3.9%	$50,000-$99,999	30.9%
Age Groups		Other	1.4%	$100,000-$199,999	18.2%
Under 18	20.4%			$200,000 or more	4.5%
18-34	26.5%	**Education**		Poverty Rate	17.6%
35-64	41.3%	H.S grad or less	30.4%		
Over 64	11.8%	Some college	32.3%	**Health Insurance**	
		College Degree, 4 yr	23.1%	With health insurance coverage	87.5%
Work		Post grad	14.2%		
White Collar	40.6%				
Sales and Service	41.2%	**Military**		**Public Assistance**	
Blue Collar	18.1%	Veteran	7.3%	Cash public assistance income	4.5%
Government	7.8%	Active Duty	0.0%		
				Food stamp/SNAP benefits	20.3%

Voter Turnout			
2015 Total Citizens 18+	581,820	2016 House Turnout as % CVAP	66%
2016 House turnout	382,355	2014 House Turnout as % CVAP	51%

2012 Presidential Vote		
Barack Obama	268,004	(72%)
Mitt Romney	91,733	(25%)

2016 Presidential Vote		
Hillary Clinton	282,402	(68%)
Donald Trump	89,631	(22%)
Gary Johnson	14,294	(4%)
Jill Stein	12,886	(3%)

Cook Partisan Voting Index: D+24

Postmodern skyscrapers rising above the riverfront and below a range of hills: This is downtown Portland. The city - which would have been named Boston if a coin toss had gone the other way - started here, along the Willamette River just before it flows into the Columbia. Downtown Portland was once a dowdy place, proper in a New England kind of way, with a few formal buildings above the warehouses and factories. But the past four decades here have witnessed an explosion of affluence and creativity, symbolized by handsome high-rises, restored Victorian storefronts, a downtown transit trolley, and a light-rail line known as MAX (for Metropolitan Area Express).

On the Pacific Rim, Portland makes much of its living on trade with Asia. It has become a home to high-tech industries, particularly in the Silicon Forest suburbs. Local government also has produced change. Metro, the regional agency established just as growth was accelerating, is a counterweight against the endless population sprawl outward. The city encouraged development of high-density commercial space and housing around transit stops, and bicycle paths wind throughout the metropolitan area. In a 2016 survey based on Bike Score ratings, Portland ranked fifth as the nation's most bicycle-friendly large city, though it remained first in the share of commuters who bicycle to work. Local leaders have sought to make Portland the nation's leader for biodiesel and other renewable fuels. In 2018, the local transit authority expects to start using new electric buses. In becoming a city focused on renewable energy, Portland has attracted political and cultural liberals. In 2015, Portland ranked third in the nation in the Clean Tech Leadership Index. The city's hipster sensibility has been satirized on the IFC television show *Portlandia,* which features Carrie Brownstein and Fred Armisen and began its seventh season in January 2017. In 2015, a Gallup survey ranked the Portland metro area second behind San Francisco in the share of its population that is gay, lesbian, bisexual or transgender. In other ways, the city is less diverse: its population is 6 percent African-American and 9 percent Hispanic. In 2016, *The Atlantic* headlined a story about the city, "The Racist History of Portland, the Whitest City in America."

The 3rd Congressional District of Oregon includes most of Portland, including downtown. It also takes in Multnomah County east of the city and a small part of suburban Clackamas County to the south, which includes a bit more than 10 percent of its voters. Politically, the 3rd remains dominated by liberals. In 2016, Hillary Clinton got 76 percent of the vote in Multnomah County and 68 percent in the district.

FOURTH DISTRICT

Peter DeFazio (D)

Elected 1986, 16th term; b. May 27, 1947, Needham, MA; Tufts University (MA), B.A., 1969; University of Oregon (OR), Att., 1971; University of Oregon (OR), M.S., 1977; Roman Catholic; Married (Myrnie Daut).

Military Career: U.S. Air Force Reserve, 1967-1971.

Elected Office: Lane County Board of Commissioners, 1983-1986, chmn, 1985-1986.

Professional Career: District Director, U.S. Rep. James Weaver, 1977-1982.

DC Office: 2134 RHOB 20515, 202-225-6416, Fax: 202-226-3493, defazio.house.gov.

State Offices: Coos Bay, 541-269-2609; Eugene, 541-465-6732; Roseburg, 541-440-3523.

Committees: *Transportation & Infrastructure (RMM)*: Aviation, Coast Guard & Maritime Transportation, Economic Dev't, Public Buildings & Emergency Management, Highways & Transit, Railroads, Pipelines & Hazardous Materials, Water Resources & Environment.

Group Ratings

	ADA	ACLU	AFL-CIO	LCV	ITI	COC	HAFA	ACU	CFG	FRC
2016	-	100%	-	95%	50%	50%	13%	4%	8%	0%
2015	80%	C	95%	91%	C	47%	C	4%	7%	0%

Almanac Ratings 2015

	Economy	Social	Foreign	Composite
Liberal	85%	87%	97%	90%
Conservative	15%	13%	4%	11%

Key Votes of the 114th Congress

1. Keystone Pipeline	N	5. Puerto Rico Debt	Y	9. Offenses by Aliens	Y
2. Trade Deals	N	6. Medical Marijuana	Y	10. Troops in Iraq	Y
3. Export-Import Bank	Y	7. Sanctuary Cities	N	11. Homeland Security $$	Y
4. Debt Ceiling Increase	Y	8. Armor-piercing Bullets	Y	12. Trade Adjustment aid	Y

Election Results

Election	Name (Party)	Vote (%)		Cand. Spent	Ind. Exp. Support	Ind. Exp. Oppose
2016 General	Peter DeFazio (D)	220,628	(56%)	$648,775		
	Art Robinson (R)	157,743	(40%)	$43,344		
	Michael Beilstein (G)	12,670	(3%)			
2016 Primary	Peter DeFazio (D)	109,053	(92%)			
	Joseph McKinney (D)	9,397	(8%)			

Prior winning percentages: 2014 (59%), 2012 (59%), 2010 (55%), 2008 (82%), 2006 (62%), 2004 (61%), 2002 (64%), 2000 (68%), 1998 (70%), 1996 (66%), 1994 (67%), 1992 (71%), 1990 (86%), 1988 (72%), 1986 (54%)

Peter DeFazio, a Democrat first elected in 1986, is a persistent - and sometimes outspoken - populist who doesn't mind showing his independence from his party or loudly criticizing the conservative ideas he disdains. Oregon's longest-serving House member, he has shown legislative skills as the top Democrat on the Natural Resources Committee and, since 2015, on the Transportation and Infrastructure Committee.

DeFazio grew up in Massachusetts, moved to Oregon for graduate school, was a bike mechanic, and went to work for Democratic Rep. Jim Weaver. In 1982, DeFazio moved to Springfield and won a seat on the county commission. When Weaver retired in 1986, DeFazio won his House seat in close contests. He beat Bill Bradbury 34%-33% in the primary and took the general election 54%-46%.

DeFazio has compiled a record that seems to satisfy both Eugene and the rest of the district: The *Almanac* vote ratings for 2015 show that he's liberal on most issues, and moderate on social issues. An original founder of the loose-knit Progressive Caucus, he channeled the anger that millions of working Americans suffered during the boom years before the economic collapse in 2008 and the recession. DeFazio is known for sarcasm and his tendency to yell during debates. Referring to Republicans' fiscal policy, he told MSNBC in 2009: "Tax cuts solve all problems. I mean, we are pretty soon going to fill potholes with tax cuts."

DeFazio often takes idiosyncratic or maverick views. With Democratic Rep. Louise Slaughter of New York, he has long sought to remove the antitrust exemption from the health insurance industry. He introduced a bill in 2011 allowing people to opt out of the health care law's individual mandate reviled by Republicans-but only if they waived the right to any government-backed medical help for at least three years. He voted against climate legislation in 2009 putting caps on carbon emissions, he said, because there were better ways to reduce greenhouse gas emissions, such as a carbon tax. Sometimes, his views are enacted: He took the lead in 2007 in the House effort to permit airline pilots to carry guns in the cockpit. Although the Bush administration initially opposed it, DeFazio won by an astonishing 250-175. The Senate followed suit.

In 2007, DeFazio became chairman of Transportation and Infrastructure's Highways and Transit Subcommittee. He was the only member of Congress to oppose the final 2009 economic stimulus bill after backing the original House version, saying it did not sufficiently boost transportation spending. He got $1.1 billion for Oregon projects in the 2012 two-year surface transportation bill. He made sure the measure contained a temporary extension of federal payments for Oregon counties. DeFazio has called for replacing the federal gasoline tax with a per-barrel tax. "What if we got rid of the tax that people don't like and move it upstream to something that most people don't like - the oil industry?" he asked *The Oregonian.*

In 2013, DeFazio took over as ranking Democrat on the Natural Resources Committee. He promised to "push for a 21st century energy policy that promotes conservation and the development of renewable resources on federal lands and waters," but the next 18 months were an unusually quiet legislative period. In 2014, the committee passed his bipartisan bill to save West Coast fishermen millions of dollars by refinancing high-interest federal loans for fishing vessels in a program that had been created in 2003 to address over-capacity; the House failed to act. DeFazio strongly opposed Republican efforts to revise the Endangered Species Act.

When the top Democratic post on Transportation and Infrastructure opened after the 2014 election, DeFazio urged Congress to get serious about fixing what he called the nation's decaying transportation facilities and stop "relying on short-term patches for long-standing problems." He called for financing the highway trust fund with a one-time 14 percent transition tax on foreign earnings by U.S. companies, followed by a 19 percent minimum tax on their global profits. He pledged bipartisan cooperation and said that his goals were "job creation, increased efficiency and strategic growth."

Long before it became the consensus position for congressional Democrats, he had been a critic of international trade deals. He opposed the Clinton-era North American Free Trade Agreement and was a leader in the fight against normal trade relations with China. In 2015, he was an outspoken foe of granting authority to President Barack Obama to expedite his prospective Trans-Pacific Partnership. The agreement, he said, was "informed and manipulated by corporate interests" and would have "relegated Congress to be used as a doormat… [for an agreement that] has been negotiated in secret and will export jobs, drive down U.S. wages, and undermine U.S. sovereignty." When Obama made a last-ditch plea to House Democrats prior to the initial failed vote on the plan, DeFazio told reporters, "The president tried to both guilt people and impugn their integrity. I was insulted." The House agreed the following week, with support from the other three Democrats from Oregon.

After Republican Sen. Bob Packwood resigned in 1995, DeFazio ran in the special election. His opposition to gun control and NAFTA provided clear contrasts to Portland liberal Democratic Rep. Ron Wyden. The better-funded Wyden won the primary 50%-44% and prevailed in the general. Until 2010, DeFazio routinely won reelection by more than 60 percent in his marginal district. That year, Republican Art Robinson held him to 54 percent of the vote after getting a boost from outside groups' ads tying DeFazio to liberal House Speaker Nancy Pelosi. Robinson, a biochemist who owns a sheep ranch, received hundreds of thousands of dollars of support from Robert Mercer, a hedge-fund manager who became a prominent supporter of Donald Trump in the 2016 campaign. DeFazio faced Robinson three more times. He got 59 percent in 2012 and 2014, and 56 percent in 2016. Robinson continued to receive sizable Super PAC support, though he was largely ignored by Republican groups. Oddly, Robinson raised only $66,000 in the 2016 campaign.

After Trump was elected and called for extensive new building of infrastructure, DeFazio said that he would be willing to work with him. But he added, " I will not hesitate to fight short-sighted proposals that seek to privatize our transportation systems, jeopardize American jobs and manufacturing, or gut critical regulations that protect our workers and communities." He applauded Trump's decision to withdraw from the Trans-Pacific Partnership. At his committee, which also has jurisdiction over the General Services Administration, he demanded information about GSA's lease agreement with the Trump International Hotel on Pennsylvania Avenue.

Southwest Oregon: Eugene, Albany

Population		**Race and Ethnicity**		**Income**	
Total	773,605	White	84.9%	Median Income	$43,138 (360 out of 435)
Land area	17,274	Black	0.7%		
Pop/ sq mi	44.8	Latino	7.3%		
Born in state	46.4%	Asian	2.2%	Under $50,000	56.2%
		Two races	3.4%	$50,000-$99,999	29.8%
Age Groups		Other	1.5%	$100,000-$199,999	11.9%
Under 18	19.4%			$200,000 or more	2.1%
18-34	23.7%	**Education**		Poverty Rate	20.0%
35-64	38.4%	H.S grad or less	36.7%		
Over 64	18.5%	Some college	37.9%	**Health Insurance**	
		College Degree, 4 yr	15.4%	With health insurance coverage	88.0%
Work		Post grad	9.9%		
White Collar	33.7%				
Sales and Service	43.6%	**Military**		**Public Assistance**	
Blue Collar	22.6%	Veteran	11.7%	Cash public assistance income	4.1%
Government	8.1%	Active Duty	0.1%		
				Food stamp/SNAP benefits	21.6%

Voter Turnout			
2015 Total Citizens 18+	600,010	2016 House Turnout as % CVAP	66%
2016 House turnout	397,568	2014 House Turnout as % CVAP	52%

2012 Presidential Vote		
Barack Obama	188,563	(51%)
Mitt Romney	163,931	(45%)

2016 Presidential Vote		
Hillary Clinton	180,872	(45%)
Donald Trump	180,318	(44%)
Gary Johnson	19,141	(5%)
Jill Stein	11,675	(3%)

Cook Partisan Voting Index: EVEN

Eugene is nestled in the southernmost bit of lowland in Oregon's Willamette Valley, and is surrounded by mountains on three sides. It is a farming center, a lumber provider and, most notably, a university town. In 1876, the University of Oregon was established, a symbol of the state's strong Yankee cultural ethic. Eugene and next-door Springfield, which has become a center for the manufacture of computer chips, have grown into comfortable midsized towns. Eugene has bicycle paths along the riverbanks and its main streets. It likes to bill itself as the "Running Capital of the Universe" - Phil Knight and his former University of Oregon track coach, Bill Bowerman, started Nike here, the first soles formed on a waffle iron. Now the third-largest city in Oregon, Eugene has small-town ambience and urban sensibilities, and its liberal voters have been vital to Democrats statewide. The 1978 comedy *National Lampoon's Animal House* was filmed at the University of Oregon after many other schools declined to provide a location for the movie over its raunchy content. The student online news site *Daily Emerald* wrote in 2012 that Knight had donated $300 million for University of Oregon facilities. In 2015, downtown Eugene had high-speed fiber optic internet technology, even before such service was available in downtown Portland.

Beyond Eugene and Springfield are southwest Oregon's green-clad mountains. For years, the region cut more timber than anywhere else in the country. But Timber Country, including forest-product businesses, has struggled. Recent economic development has been diverse, with gains in health care, tourism and retiree migration from California. Springfield is the putative home of the popular television show "The Simpsons," according to its creator, Oregon native Matt Groening. The largest employer in the real Springfield is Peace Health, a Catholic health care and hospital system, whose prominence has spurred residential development in the area. Renewable energy company Ocean Power Technologies has worked on a project to generate electricity for 1,000 homes through ocean wave motion. In December 2016, following local protests, federal regulators rejected a proposal for a liquefied natural gas terminal and pipeline in coastal Coos County.

The 4th Congressional District of Oregon includes Eugene, Springfield and surrounding Lane County. It includes the state's other main college town, Corvallis, home to Oregon State University. South along Interstate 5 it takes in Roseburg in Douglas County. Also in the 4th is the southern half of Oregon's stunning Pacific coastline, a roughly 200-mile drive to the California border. About half of the voters are in Eugene-based Lane County. Eugene is heavily Democratic, while Douglas County and Roseburg vote Republican; the travails of the logging industry hurt the Democrats here. The 4th has leaned Democratic, including for President Barack Obama in his two campaigns, but is far more blue-collar and less liberal than the Portland area's districts. Hillary Clinton led Donald Trump by a few hundred votes in this district in 2016 .

FIFTH DISTRICT

Kurt Schrader (D)

Elected 2008, 5th term; b. Oct 19, 1951, Bridgeport, CT; Cornell University (NY), B.A., 1973; University of Illinois, B.A., 1975; University of Illinois College of Veterinary Medicine (IL), D.V.M., 1977; Episcopalian; Married (Susan Mora); 5 children.

Elected Office: OR House, 1997-2003; OR Senate, 2003-2008.

Professional Career: Former aide, AK gov.; Veterinarian, 1978-2008.

DC Office: 2431 RHOB 20515, 202-225-5711, Fax: 202-225-5699, schrader.house.gov.

State Offices: Oregon City, 503-557-1324; Salem, 503-588-9100.

Committees: *Energy & Commerce*: Energy, Health.

Group Ratings

	ADA	ACLU	AFL-CIO	LCV	ITI	COC	HAFA	ACU	CFG	FRC
2016	-	94%	-	76%	83%	64%	14%	8%	13%	0%
2015	60%	C	78%	57%	C	68%	C	8%	7%	0%

Almanac Ratings 2015

	Economy	Social	Foreign	Composite
Liberal	50%	87%	79%	72%
Conservative	50%	13%	21%	28%

Key Votes of the 114th Congress

1. Keystone Pipeline	Y	5. Puerto Rico Debt	Y	9. Offenses by Aliens	Y
2. Trade Deals	Y	6. Medical Marijuana	Y	10. Troops in Iraq	Y
3. Export-Import Bank	Y	7. Sanctuary Cities	N	11. Homeland Security $$	Y
4. Debt Ceiling Increase	Y	8. Armor-piercing Bullets	Y	12. Trade Adjustment aid	Y

Election Results

Election	Name (Party)	Vote (%)	Cand. Spent	Ind. Exp. Support	Ind. Exp. Oppose
2016 General	Kurt Schrader (D)	199,505 (54%)	$1,237,393	$292,207	$240,457
	Colm Willis (R)	160,443 (43%)	$273,789	$158,234	
2016 Primary	Kurt Schrader (D)	67,124 (73%)			
	Dave McTeague (D)	25,289 (27%)			

Prior winning percentages: 2014 (54%), 2012 (54%), 2010 (51%), 2008 (54%)

Kurt Schrader, elected in 2008, has been a business-oriented Democrat in a district that is divided between urban and rural. A veterinarian and organic farmer, he has dealt with health care and energy issues on the Energy and Commerce Committee.

Schrader was born in Bridgeport, Connecticut, where his father was a chemical engineer. He studied government and got a degree at Cornell University, then received his doctorate in veterinary medicine at the University of Illinois. Schrader ran two veterinary clinics in Canby. From his farm, he sold organic fruits and vegetables. Schrader entered politics on the Canby planning commission, assisting in development of the city's land-use plan. He was elected to the state House, where he served six years, followed by another six in the state Senate. He was co-chairman of the Joint Ways and Means Committee, where he pushed legislation to tax new construction to pay for schools. He developed a reputation as a conservative Democrat and opposed his party on increasing the minimum wage. His wife Martha was his chief of staff in his early years in the Legislature, and later served on the Clackamas County Commission. They divorced in 2011 and he remarried in 2016 to a Washington D.C.-based utility company executive.

When the House seat opened, Schrader lent his campaign $130,000 during the primary and won more than 54 percent of the vote against three opponents. In the general, he faced Republican shipping entrepreneur Mike Erickson, who was the GOP nominee two years earlier. The general election was initially considered wide open. This was George W. Bush territory in 2000 and 2004, but a surge in new voters gave Democrats their first voter-registration advantage in 12 years. Erickson was unable to shake the allegations about his earlier relationship with a woman for whose abortion he had paid. Schrader received endorsements from the Oregon Farm Bureau and several newspapers, and got financial help from the Democratic Congressional Campaign Committee. Erickson outspent Schrader by more than $1 million, but Schrader prevailed 54%-38%. That became the high-water mark for Schrader's vote.

Schrader has been willing to go his own way from his party. He has been co-chair of the fiscally conservative Blue Dog Coalition and was one of 22 House Democrats in 2012 to support fellow Blue Dog Jim Cooper's unsuccessful budget proposal based on the bipartisan Simpson-Bowles commission's recommendations. He has voted for Republican alternatives to weaken the 2010 health care law by allowing consumers to purchase insurance plans that don't meet the terms of that law. He originally cosponsored the DREAM Act for children of illegal immigrants but later voted against it, saying he wanted a more comprehensive immigration reform. In 2015, he voted for the Keystone XL pipeline from Canada, the only Democrat from Oregon to support the project. Also that year, he was among only 28 House Democrats voting for trade promotion authority, though three of them were from Oregon.

Schrader has been an outspoken critic of the Supreme Court's *Citizens United* decision in 2010 that eased campaign finance restrictions, and has proposed a constitutional amendment to allow congressional regulation of campaign contributions and spending. He joined the non-partisan No Labels group, which has urged a bipartisan congressional agenda. He attracted local support by joining a bipartisan plan to place 1.6 million acres of federal lands in Western Oregon into a state trust focused on timber production.

On the influential Energy and Commerce Committee, Schrader advocated more spending on renewable energy and access to health coverage without increased government regulations. He praised the panel's bipartisan handling of several bills, and claimed some credit. The January 2017 takeover as committee chairman by Oregon Rep. Greg Walden opened new opportunity for cooperation.

National Republicans went after Schrader in 2010 and recruited state Rep. Scott Bruun, who accused him of not being the fiscal hawk he portrayed himself as and of going "on a world-class spending spree with your money." Schrader parried that Bruun wanted to privatize Social Security. Schrader won 51%-46%, benefiting from the huge Democratic vote in Multnomah. The 2012 redistricting made Schrader's district slightly more favorable to Republicans by leaving only a sliver of Multnomah and adding more of Clackamas. In 2014, Republicans nominated Clackamas Commissioner Tootie Smith, a conservative who once raffled off a Glock pistol to raise campaign funds. She raised only $64,000 while

Schrader raised $1.6 million. He won 54%-39% and led in all seven counties. Two years later, he again got 54 percent, this time against Colm Willis, the top lobbyist for Oregon Right to Life. Willis criticized Schrader's support for the Obama administration's health care and trade policies. In the 2016 primary, Schrader was challenged by a former state representative who decided to run after Schrader said that he supported the Trans-Pacific trade deal. Schrader won with 72 percent of the vote.

Following the election, he was an outspoken supporter of Rep. Tim Ryan of Ohio to replace Nancy Pelosi as Democratic Leader. When Ryan lost, Schrader told reporters, "I'm very worried we just signed the Democratic Party's death certificate for the next decade and a half."

West-Central Oregon: Salem, Clackamas County

Population		**Race and Ethnicity**		**Income**	
Total	787,386	White	76.0%	Median Income	$54,112 (196 out of 435)
Land area	5,190	Black	0.9%		
Pop/ sq mi	151.7	Latino	16.0%		
Born in state	50.9%	Asian	2.7%	Under $50,000	46.1%
		Two races	3.0%	$50,000-$99,999	32.5%
Age Groups		Other	1.5%	$100,000-$199,999	17.4%
Under 18	23.6%			$200,000 or more	4.0%
18-34	21.4%	**Education**		Poverty Rate	14.6%
35-64	39.3%	H.S grad or less	36.0%		
Over 64	15.7%	Some college	35.3%	**Health Insurance**	
		College Degree, 4 yr	18.4%	With health insurance coverage	88.1%
Work		Post grad	10.3%		
White Collar	34.4%				
Sales and Service	43.2%	**Military**		**Public Assistance**	
Blue Collar	22.4%	Veteran	10.4%	Cash public assistance income	4.5%
Government	7.0%	Active Duty	0.1%		
				Food stamp/SNAP benefits	18.3%

Voter Turnout			
2015 Total Citizens 18+	556,321	2016 House Turnout as % CVAP	67%
2016 House turnout	373,108	2014 House Turnout as % CVAP	51%

2012 Presidential Vote		
Barack Obama	172,986	(50%)
Mitt Romney	161,482	(47%)

2016 Presidential Vote		
Hillary Clinton	180,404	(46%)
Donald Trump	164,548	(42%)
Gary Johnson	20,135	(5%)
Jill Stein	8,214	(2%)

Cook Partisan Voting Index: EVEN

The Willamette Valley was the great Promised Land at the end of the Oregon Trail, shielded from the cold storms of the Pacific by mountains but squeezing most of the moisture out of the clouds in the form of rain, fog and persistent mist. New England Yankees planted small towns they called Salem and Oregon City, founded schools and colleges, built tall-spired churches and eventually Salem's distinctive Art Deco state capitol. This was one of the few valleys in the West that settlers found readily suitable for agriculture. The Willamette Valley's soil is fertile, and the plain created by the waters of the Willamette sweeping down from the mountains is broad. Ironically in this environmentally friendly state, industrial runoff has made the river among the most polluted in the nation. The Willamette Valley is home to a burgeoning wine industry with more than 500 wineries, many of which are known for their pinot noir.

Salem and Eugene have battled for the distinction of Oregon's second-largest city, after Portland. Salem, the state capital, has pulled slightly ahead; its 20 percent Hispanic population is more than twice the share in Eugene. In March 2016, Microsoft began sales of a giant new touch screen that it built in Wilsonville. The product came in 55-inch and 84-inch versions, with a retail price from $9,000 to $22,000, depending on size. The company had gained a local presence when it purchased a Pixel facility. Also based in Wilsonville was Mentor Graphics, a sophisticated electronics company with 1,000 employees. German-based Siemens bought Mentor in November 2016.

The 5th Congressional District of Oregon includes much of the northern Willamette Valley. The district has about 40 percent of its voters in Clackamas County in the outskirts of Portland and spreads south to Salem-based Marion County, also home of Willamette University, the oldest university in the West. It crosses the Coast Range to take in Lincoln and Tillamook counties, which are fishing, logging and cheese-making communities. In the thinly populated coastal areas, Newport has a busy port and a state beach. The Coast Guard announced in 2014 that it was removing its local helicopter because of budget pressures, but Congress the next year responded to local pressure and agreed to retain the base. Historically, the valley was Republican, but it has trended Democratic. Overall, the 5th has been competitive. In 2016. Hillary Clinton took the district, 46%-42%.

★ PENNSYLVANIA ★

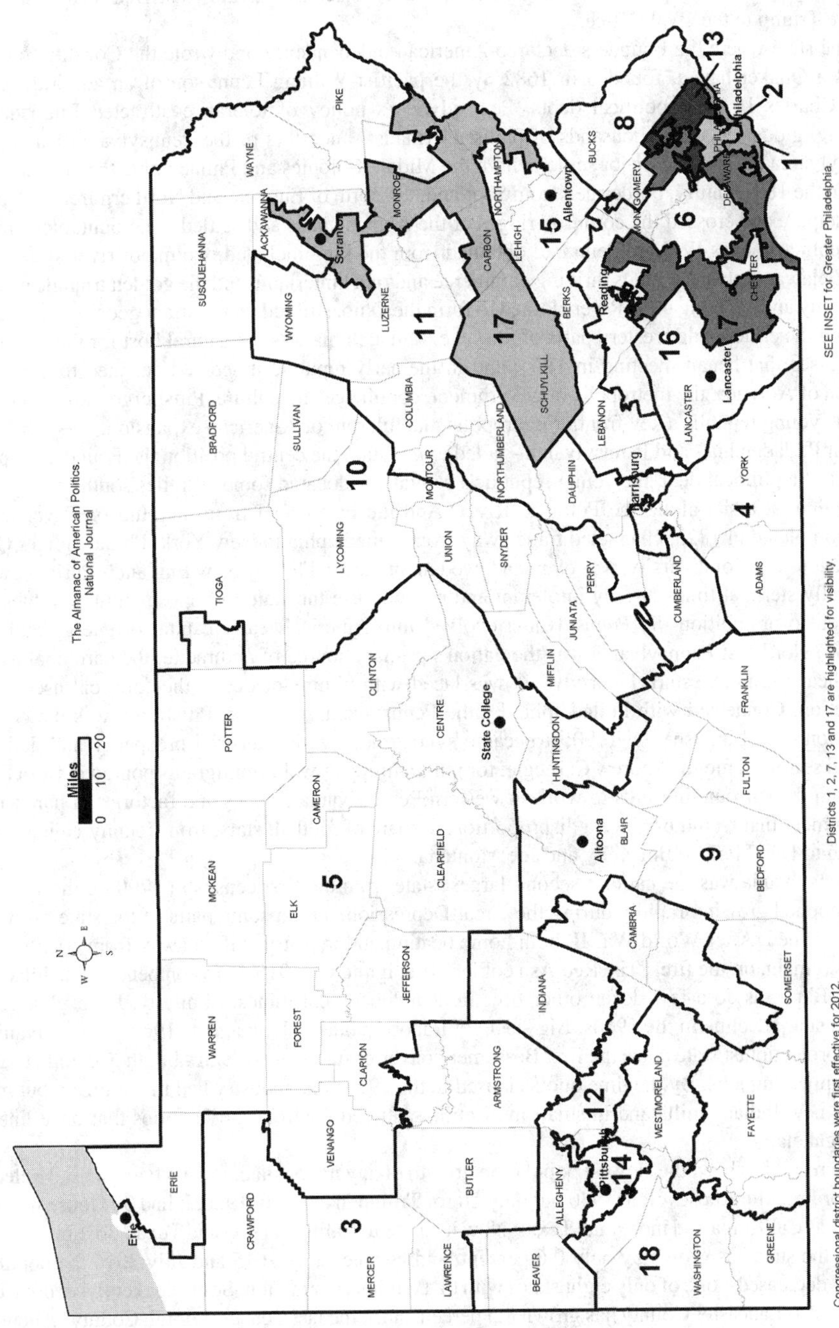

Pennsylvania has long been a state targeted by Democrats and Republicans alike, with competitive contests at almost every level of government. But the Keystone State hadn't voted Republican for president since 1988 – until 2016, when it stunned the nation by backing Donald Trump over Hillary Clinton by about 44,000 votes, joining Michigan and Wisconsin as the Rust Belt states that helped elevate Trump to the Oval Office.

The state where the Founders declared American independence and wrote the Constitution started out as a Quaker haven, founded in 1682 by the pacifist William Penn, son of an admiral to whom King Charles II owed political debts. Pennsylvania's policy of tolerance attracted Englishmen of many religious sects and thousands of pietist Germans - ancestors of the Pennsylvania Dutch. Soon, Pennsylvania became the major settlement in the Middle Colonies and Philadelphia the largest colonial port. In the 18th century, bordermen from Scotland, the north of England and Northern Ireland landed in Philadelphia and crossed the corduroy ridges of the Appalachians and settled the mountainous interior. The geometric lines William Penn had obtained from the king included two major river systems - the wide Delaware estuary with its thriving commerce and rich hinterland, and the golden triangle where the Allegheny and Monongahela Rivers joined to form the Ohio, still today important geographical features defining the eastern and western parts of the state. Philadelphia was the natural host for the Continental Congresses that began meeting in 1774, and in the early republic it seemed destined to become the London of America, the metropolis of government, commerce and culture. Pittsburgh, founded in 1758, was the young republic's key frontier metropolis, the fulcrum of American expansion.

But Philadelphia - and Pennsylvania - failed to maintain the central position the Founders expected. As part of a political deal, the young republic's capital was located some 80 miles south of the Mason-Dixon line, at a site along the Potomac River. And the Erie Canal from the Hudson River to Lake Erie, completed in 1825, channeled trade away from Philadelphia to New York. Philadelphia's Quaker tradition, tolerant of diversity, was overshadowed in intellectual life by New England's Puritan tradition -- morally stern, at times angrily intolerant and ready to use the state to impose cultural values, from abolition to prohibition. So Pennsylvania evolved into America's early capital of energy and heavy industry. Northeast Pennsylvania was the nation's primary source of anthracite, the hard coal used for home heating, and western Pennsylvania was laced with bituminous coal, the soft coal used in steel production. Connected with Philadelphia by the Pennsylvania Railroad, Pittsburgh was the center of the nation's steel industry by 1890; it became synonymous with industrial prosperity and, led by its adopted son, steel mogul Andrew Carnegie, for philanthropy as well. Immigrants poured in from Europe and from the surrounding hills to work in western Pennsylvania's mines and factories, a hardscrabble environment that would produce a disproportionate share of football stars, from Johnny Unitas and Joe Namath to Dan Marino, Jim Kelly and Joe Montana.

Pennsylvania was the nation's second-largest state from the first census in 1790 up through 1940, but it stopped growing rapidly during the Great Depression, and in some parts of the state growth has never returned. After World War II, both home heating and industry shifted away from coal. Only the embers remain, or, the fires: The Red Ash colliery fire, ignited in 1915, burns on beneath the hills above Wilkes-Barre, as do a few dozen other fires in abandoned coal mines. Similarly, Pennsylvania steel began a sharp decline in the 1960s. Big steel got import quotas as long ago as 1969 - Pennsylvania has been a protectionist state since the first Bessemer converter furnaces were lit - but they couldn't save all the disappearing jobs. By the time quotas lapsed in the 1990s, the industry had modernized, but mostly in huge new Indiana mills and in small mini-mills scattered far from the factories that once lined the Monongahela.

The result has been the slowest population growth of any major state. Pennsylvania cast 36 electoral votes for Franklin Roosevelt in 1940 but only 20 for Trump in 2016. In 1960, it had 30 House members, as many as California and more than Texas. Now it has 18 to California's 53 and Texas' 36. Since the 2010 census, the state has grown by only 0.6 percent, and between July 2015 and July 2016 the population actually decreased – one of only eight states with that dubious distinction. Some pockets have done better than others – Lancaster County has grown 8.5 percent since the last Census, Lehigh County (Allentown-Bethlehem) has grown by nearly 4 percent, and Philadelphia, along with two of its collar counties, Montgomery and Chester, grew in the 2 percent to 3 percent range over the same period. But other corners of the state have shrunk by a percentage point or two, including Lackawanna County (Scranton) and Luzerne County (Wilkes-Barre) in the northeast, and Erie County in the northwest. Some smaller counties have shrunk by more than that. For the most part, people growing up in Pennsylvania have been as likely to leave as to stay; relatively few outsiders moved in. This has made the state increasingly old -- only three others (Florida, West Virginia and Maine) have a higher percentage of residents age 65 and over. Pennsylvania also remains one of the whitest big states--10 percent black, 8 percent Hispanic, and 4 percent Asian. Pockets of the state, however, have seen rapid Hispanic increases, notably Hazleton in Luzerne County, a shift that has prompted bitter battles over illegal immigration.

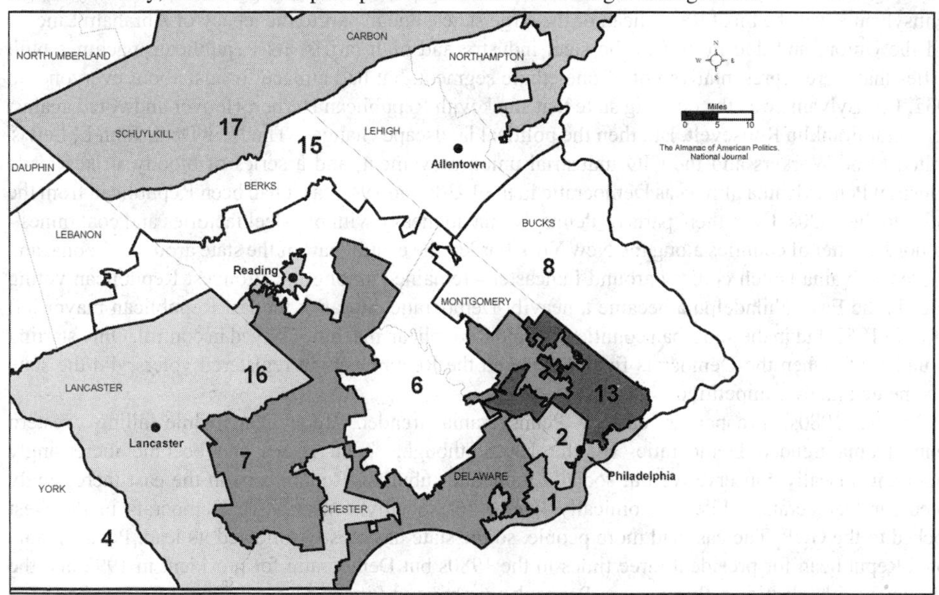

Congressional district boundaries were first effective for 2012. Districts 1, 2, 7, 13, 16 and 17 are highlighted for visibility.

Economically, Pennsylvania has begun to perk up a bit over the past two decades. Big hospitals have replaced big steel mills as employers in metro Pittsburgh, and metro Philadelphia and the surrounding countryside have experienced diversified economic growth, though manufacturing remains important outside the big cities – almost 15 percent of the state's non-urban jobs are in manufacturing, with nearly 175,000 workers in 4,300 companies. Some municipalities have become insolvent, in part because of unwise investment in unprofitable facilities - an incinerator in Harrisburg, parking structures in Scranton. Pennsylvania has held taxes down more than many of its Northeastern neighbors. New Yorkers are moving a couple of miles farther out on Interstate 80 to retire near the Delaware Water Gap and the Poconos, and Hispanics from New York and North Jersey are moving out Interstate 78 to work in Reading, Allentown and Bethlehem, where a big Sands casino opened in 2009 on what was once Bethlehem Steel property. As for the City of Brotherly Love, "while its public school system remains a mess, its crime rate elastic and its poverty rate high, Philadelphia has been revitalized over the last decade and a half, with celebrity chefs, a vibrant technology sector and thriving art scene, all boxes to check for cities on the move these days," the *New York Times* wrote on the city's selection as the site of the 2016 Democratic convention. Agriculture remains a significant industry – Pennsylvania ranks among the top five states for production of eggs, milk, pumpkins, apples, grapes, and peaches, and ranks first nationally in mushroom production, centered on Kennett Square in Chester County, "The Mushroom Capital of the World." Statewide, the unemployment rate peaked a bit lower than the national average during the Great Recession – 8.7 percent in early 2010 – and fell to 4.8 percent in March 2017, roughly in line with the nation as a whole. The median income is 7 percent above the national average.

James Carville once famously described the state as Pittsburgh and Philadelphia with Alabama in between. It's those parts in between in rural Pennsylvania, once the site of the world's first oil well and first commercial nuclear power plant, that are getting a renewed taste of being a major economic engine. The Marcellus Shale beneath 60 percent of Pennsylvania and much of upstate New York contains the nation's largest reserves of natural gas embedded in hard rock. It can be brought to the surface by hydraulic fracturing - better known as "fracking" - in which water and chemicals under high pressure is injected into the shale, fracturing it and releasing gas previously locked inside. With the development of horizontal drilling, fracking became commercially feasible in 2004, and there are now wells through much of the western and northern parts of the state, making Pennsylvania the second biggest producer of natural gas after Texas. Environmental groups have charged that fracking can pollute drinking water sources, but the EPA has cast doubt on those claims and development is still going forward -- although a recent slump in energy prices has put a crimp in the industry's fortunes.

For generations after the Civil War - whose turning point is often pegged to quiet Gettysburg - Pennsylvania was the most Republican of the large states, due in part to the legacy of Abraham Lincoln and the Union, and due in part to the steel industry and high tariffs. Its Republican machines built parties that were representative not of one ethnic segment, but had a place for just about everyone. In 1932, Pennsylvania was the only big state that stuck with Republican Herbert Hoover and voted against Democrat Franklin Roosevelt. But then the political landscape changed. The New Deal, John L. Lewis' United Mine Workers and the CIO industrial union movement, and a series of bloody strikes made industrial Pennsylvania almost as Democratic in the 1930s and 1940s as it had been Republican from the 1860s to the 1920s. Even then, parts of Pennsylvania not heavy with big steel factories and coal mines - the northern tier of counties along the New York border, the central part of the state around Altoona, and the Pennsylvania Dutch country around Lancaster - remained among the strongest Republican voting blocs in the East. Philadelphia became a heavily Democratic city after the last Republican mayor left office in 1952, but in the suburban counties, the old Republican machines stayed in control. Only starting around 1960, when the Democrats finally matched the Republicans in registered voters, did the state become genuinely competitive.

In the 1980s, prosperous eastern Pennsylvania trended Republican while ailing western Pennsylvania trended Democratic. By the 1990s, though, social issues had become increasingly important. Fiscally conservative but socially moderate suburban Republicans in the east increasingly voted for Democrats, while economically liberal but socially conservative Democrats in the west flocked to the GOP. The east had more people, so the state has mostly followed its lead. Pennsylvania voted Republican for president three times in the 1980s but Democratic for president in 1992 and the subsequent five elections. But western Pennsylvania beyond Pittsburgh's Allegheny County has been moving in the other direction. In four heavily working-class counties surrounding Allegheny -- Beaver, Fayette, Greene, and Washington -- Al Gore won better than 53 percent of the two-party vote in 2000, PoliticsPA noted, but by 2016, those four counties gave Hillary Clinton only 29 percent to 40 percent of the two-party vote.

Such shifts underpinned Trump's victory in the state in 2016. He won a state that had gone for Obama by five points in 2012; he won 290,000 more votes than Mitt Romney had four years earlier, while Clinton was underperforming Obama by 64,000 votes. To a greater degree than in some other states, both candidates gained ground in certain regions. Trump flipped three counties Obama had won: Luzerne (by shifting the margin 24 points in the GOP's direction), Erie (by shifting it by 18 points), and Northampton (Easton, by shifting it by nine points). Trump also moved the needle in several blue-collar counties, but not quite enough to win; notably, these included Clinton's (and Joe Biden's) ancestral county of Lackawanna, where the margin shifted from a 27-point Democratic win in 2012 to a four-point victory in 2016. The silver lining for Clinton was her ability to improve on Obama's performance in more affluent and educated cities and suburbs. She flipped Philadelphia-area Chester County from red to blue, and expanded Democratic margins in Centre County, the home of Penn State University. She pulled 5,000 more votes from Philadelphia itself, and extended Obama's margins in the Philadelphia collar counties of Delaware and Montgomery by one and six points, respectively.

But in more modest amounts, Trump managed to wring more votes from less-populated areas, and they added up. The cumulative Republican improvement over 2012 in just five western Pennsylvania counties – Beaver, Fayette, Greene, Washington and Westmoreland – was almost enough by itself to supply Trump's statewide winning margin. The same could be said for Trump's improvement in Luzerne and Lackawanna. In these regions, a combination of social conservatism, support for gun rights and energy development, and a frayed union legacy delivered votes to Trump, although downballot Democrats fared between two and 17 points better than Clinton in both regions, suggesting that the two candidates' personal characteristics – for good and ill -- weighed heavily on the results. "Trump won because he solved a problem that bedeviled Republicans for almost three decades: He solidified white working-class voters in the North. He carried every conceivable one of them he could find, not just in the counties that blinked red on the map, but in the blue ones, too," political analysts Brandon Finnigan and Jeffrey Blehar of DecisionDeskHQ wrote.

Population		**Race and Ethnicity**		**Income**	
Total	12,779,559	White	78.1%	Median Income	$53,599 (21 out of 50)
Land area	44,743	Black	10.5%		
Pop/ sq mi	285.6	Latino	6.4%	Under $50,000	46.7%
Born in state	73.4%	Asian	3.0%	$50,000-$99,999	30.9%
		Two races	1.7%	$100,000-$199,999	17.8%
Age Groups		Other	0.3%	$200,000 or more	4.6%
Under 18	21.3%			Poverty Rate	13.5%
18-34	22.3%	**Education**			
35-64	40.0%	H.S grad or less	47.2%	**Health Insurance**	
Over 64	16.2%	Some college	24.2%	With health insurance coverage	91.2%
		College Degree, 4 yr	17.4%		
Work		Post grad	11.2%		
White Collar	36.7%			**Public Assistance**	
Sales and Service	41.6%	**Military**		Cash public assistance income	3.5%
Blue Collar	21.8%	Veteran	8.7%		
Government	10.8%	Active Duty	0.0%	Food stamp/SNAP benefits	12.9%

Voter Turnout			
2015 Total Citizens 18+	9,710,416	2016 Pres Turnout as % CVAP	63%
2016 Pres Votes	6,165,478	2012 Pres Turnout as % CVAP	60%

Legislature	
Senate:	19D, 31R
House:	83D, 120R

Presidential Politics

2016 Democratic Primary		
Hillary Clinton (D)	935,107	(56%)
Bernie Sanders (D)	731,881	(44%)
2016 Republican Primary		
Donald Trump (R)	902,593	(57%)
Ted Cruz (R)	345,506	(22%)
John Kasich (R)	310,003	(19%)

2016 Presidential Vote		
Donald Trump (R)	2,970,733	(48%)
Hillary Clinton (D)	2,926,441	(47%)
Gary Johnson (L)	146,715	(2%)
2012 Presidential Vote		
Barack Obama (D)	2,990,274	(52%)
Mitt Romney (R)	2,680,434	(47%)

Pennsylvania is one of the best states to look at when assessing what happened in the 2016 presidential election. Unlike its Rustbelt neighbors Michigan and Wisconsin, both Donald Trump and Hillary Clinton campaigned vigorously in the Keystone State, saturating it with television ads. Democrats held their national convention in Philadelphia. And while it doesn't have the demographic diversity of other presidential battlegrounds like Florida and Virginia, it is a state where the shifting political dynamics of the suburbs have been apparent for several elections.

Pennsylvania has been seriously contested in just about every presidential election since 1976, but only once in that time, in 2008, has any candidate received more than 52 percent of the vote. For Democrats, their winning coalition in Pennsylvania came to rely less on working class and union voters in the coal mines and steel mills of Western Pennsylvania and the Lehigh Valley than on suburbanites in the four vote-rich counties-Bucks, Chester, Delaware and Montgomery - surrounding Philadelphia. Many of these blue-collar voters are Catholics and ethnic voters who were drawn to the GOP because of its conservative stance on abortion and other social issues. The reverse was happening in the Philadelphia suburbs where college-educated voters were alienated by the Republicans' courtship of evangelicals and rightward drift on social issues. These suburbanites were happy to vote for Democratic candidates so long as they didn't lurch too far to the left on economic issues. In 2008, Barack Obama defeated John McCain 54%-44%. He carried the Philadelphia suburbs 57%-42%. With Joe Biden as his running mate, Obama carried the Northeast, a 15-county region (from Bradford in the north, to Berks in the south, to Northampton in the east), 54%-45%, which includes Lackawanna County and Scranton, Biden's hometown. Obama's margins throughout the state dipped in 2012, but he still managed to win the Philadelphia suburbs 54%-45% and carry the state 52%-47%.

In 2016, Hillary Clinton won the Philadelphia suburban counties by an even greater margin, 55%-42%. In the largely rural and solidly Republican central part of the state, Clinton's vote dropped about five percentage points from Obama's totals, but it collapsed in the northeast: In 2012, Obama won the area, 51%-48%; in 2016, Trump prevailed there 55%-42%, a 16-point swing to the GOP. Pittsburgh (Allegheny County) has transformed itself from a steel town to a technology hub and contributes 2-out-5 votes cast in the west and votes Democratic. But it was the only county in the 20-county region (from Warren in the north to Cambria and Somerset in the south) that backed Clinton in 2016. Even Eire County, a former Democratic blue-collar bastion, backed Trump, 49%-47%. Trump carried western Pennsylvania 54%-42%, compared with Mitt Romney's margin of 51%-47% in 2012, an eight-point swing. With all these shifts, Trump eked out a 49%-48% victory and became the first Republican since George H.W. Bush in 1988 to carry the state.

Since 1924, Pennsylvania has held its presidential primary in April, usually toward the end of the month. It usually isn't a battleground like it was in the 2008 Democratic primary, when a record 2.3 million Pennsylvanians voted and gave Clinton a 55%-45% victory over Obama, who had his own "basket of deplorables" moment when he spoke at a fundraiser about Pennsylvanians in small towns who were "bitter" about their economic straits and who "cling to guns or religion." In 2016, Pennsylvania was good to Clinton again: she defeated Vermont Sen. Bernie Sanders by a similar 56%-44% in the April 26 primary. Clinton carried Philadelphia and its suburban counties by relatively large margins and won the Lehigh Valley, Pittsburgh and most of western Pennsylvania. Sanders tended to run better in rural counties. On the Republican side, Donald Trump defeated Texas Sen. Ted Cruz 57%-22%. Ohio Gov. John Kasich, a Pittsburgh-area native, was once seen as a potential contender in Pennsylvania, but won only 19 percent of the vote. Trump won all 18 of the state's congressional districts and that was important because the state's Republicans elect their district level delegates directly, making them free agents of sorts. But before the primary several said that they would support the winner of their district. That helped Trump, whose campaign never mastered the art of slating delegate candidates in states.

Congressional Districts

115th Congress Lineup	13R 5D	**114th Congress Lineup**	13R 5D

Pennsylvania is projected to be down another House seat following the next census, having lost two after the 2000 census and one after 2010. At 18 seats, the Keystone State now has half the House members it had at its peak in 1930. With their 13-5 control of the delegation, Republicans likely would be at risk with the status quo, regardless of the politics in Harrisburg. Perhaps the more realistic scenario is that Republicans will lose a seat or two (or more) before then, especially among the five artfully drawn districts they hold in the Philadelphia suburbs and exurbs.

History offers useful insights into the complexities of Pennsylvania redistricting. Republicans held the governorship and legislative majorities in both 2001 and 2011, and were in firm control of redistricting. In 2001, under heavy pressure from White House strategist Karl Rove, they overreached. Republicans could have eliminated two of the Democrats' 10 seats and called it a day; instead they attempted to claim 13 of 19 seats by pairing three sets of Democratic incumbents, drawing Democrat Tim Holden into a Republican Harrisburg-based seat, and creating two new Republican seats in the Pittsburgh and Philadelphia suburbs. But in 2002, Holden upset the septuagenarian incumbent, who proved politically rusty. Then, four years later, Democrats defeated four Republican incumbents in a strong Democratic year, proving Republicans had spread themselves too thin; two GOP incumbents who lost that year were damaged by scandals. In 2008, Democrats defeated a fifth Republican, Phil English, in the Erie area. Still, Republicans showed the utility of that old map in 2010, when they picked up five seats and turned Democrats' 12-7 edge upside-down.

By 2011, Republicans had learned their lesson. Needing to cut a seat while protecting 12 of their own, including five in districts Obama had carried in 2008, Republicans set about to axe only one Democrat. By process of elimination, the choice was easy. Merging any two of the three Philadelphia Democrats would have displaced too many Democratic voters into suburban Republican seats. Democrat Mike Doyle's Pittsburgh seat was too Democratic to break apart. Holden, in the Harrisburg area, had already proven he could run ahead of party lines in 2002 and no neighboring Republican wanted to face him.

That left junior Democrats Jason Altmire in the 4th District and Mark Critz in the 12th District, who could easily be merged in the slow-growing, Republican-trending counties north and east of Pittsburgh.

After months of closed-door negotiations among finicky incumbents, Republicans unveiled their proposal and GOP Gov. Tom Corbett signed it less than 10 days later. The plan ruthlessly sewed the state, particular the Philadelphia suburbs, into a crazy quilt. Montgomery County, about the population of one district, was split five ways to boost three suburban Republicans, who were happy to feed their trickiest inner suburbs to Philadelphia's Democrats. In the northeast, Republicans stuffed Blue Dog Holden's 17th District with the liberal labor bastions of Scranton, Wilkes-Barre and Easton to relieve pressure on freshman Republican Lou Barletta in the 11th District and Charlie Dent in the Lehigh Valley's 15th. In the west, Republicans carefully merged Altmire and Critz in such a way that neither Democrat could plausibly run elsewhere but either would still be vulnerable in a general election. Sure enough, Critz defeated Altmire in a bitter primary and Republican Keith Rothfus defeated Critz in November. Back east, Holden lost his primary to a more liberal Democrat, and in November, Republicans held onto their other 12 seats without much of a fight.

Democrats promise they will do better in 2018. They have suffered since 2012 from a weak bench of candidates in Pennsylvania. Even with Republican retirements in 2016 in the Bucks County-based 8th District and the Lancaster-based 16th, and with the relative unpopularity of Donald Trump in the region, GOP contenders had an easier time than expected in the open seats. The state's projected loss of a seat in the next reapportionment could pose more challenges for Republicans. Of the five Democratic-held seats, the 17th has become less secure and could be at risk, depending on other redistricting dynamics.

Governor

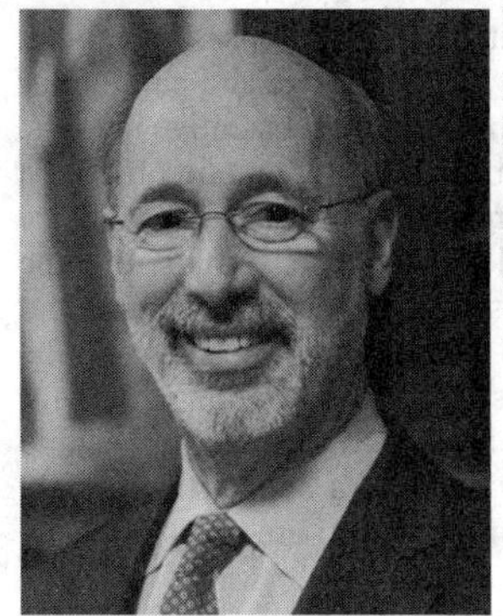

Thomas W. Wolf (D)

Elected 2014, term expires 2019, 1st term; b. Nov. 17, 1948, York, PA; Dartmouth Col., B.A. 1972; U. of London, M.A. 1978; MA Inst. of Technology, PhD 1981; Episcopalian; Married (Frances); 2 children.

Professional Career: Peace Corps, India; CEO & President, Wolf Organization, 1986-2006, Chairman & CEO, 2009-present; Secretary of Revenue, Governor Ed Rendell, 2007-2009.

Office: Main Capitol Building, Rm. 225, Harrisburg, 17120; 717-787-2500; Fax: 717-772-8284; Website: governor.pa.gov.

Election Results

Election	Name (Party)	Vote (%)
2014 General	Tom Wolf (D)	1,920,355 (55%)
	Tom Corbett (R)	1,575,511 (45%)
2014 Primary	Tom Wolf (D)	488,917 (58%)
	Allyson Schwartz (D)	149,027 (18%)
	Rob McCord (D)	142,311 (17%)
	Kate McGinty (D)	64,754 (8%)

Pennsylvanians elected Democrat Tom Wolf, a wealthy latecomer to politics, as their governor in 2014, shattering Pennsylvania's rigid, post-World War II pattern of the two parties trading off the governorship every eight years. Wolf's tenure was marked by a record-long budget battle in 2015 and 2016 that sapped his popularity. While his approval has since stabilized, Wolf now faces a challenging reelection battle in 2018.

Born in York and raised in Mount Wolf - named for his great-great-grandfather - Wolf acquired degrees from Dartmouth College, the University of London, and the Massachusetts Institute of Technology. During that time, he interrupted his studies to join the Peace Corps, serving two years in a village in India. After graduation, Wolf went to work for the family business, initially employed as a forklift operator at the Wolf Organization, a cabinet and building-materials company. In 1985, Wolf and two cousins bought the company and more than doubled its size. After selling the company to a private-equity firm in 2006, Wolf was tapped by Democratic Gov. Ed Rendell to be state revenue secretary in 2007 and 2008. Wolf intended to mount a campaign for governor to succeed Rendell, who was term-limited, but when the family business was on the brink of bankruptcy and collapse, Wolf abandoned the campaign, repurchased the company and restored it to solvency. He stepped down as CEO in 2013 to focus on his 2014 bid for governor, targeting first-term Republican Gov. Tom Corbett, who was saddled with low approval ratings.

Democratic Rep. Allyson Schwartz was anointed the early front-runner in the primary, and state Treasurer Rob McCord and former state Environmental Protection Secretary Kathleen McGinty ran as well. But Wolf poured $10 million of his own money into the race, allowing him to blanket the airwaves from January 2014 until the May primary, which Wolf won easily with 58 percent of the vote. (Wolf later tapped McGinty as his chief of staff. In August 2015, she launched an ultimately unsuccessful campaign for the seat of Republican Sen. Pat Toomey.) In the general, Wolf had the air and campaign strategy of an incumbent, bolstered by double-digit leads in the polls. Corbett touted his tax cuts and his efforts to reduce the size of government, rein in spending and bring businesses back to Pennsylvania. But Wolf hammered away at weak job growth under Corbett and accused him of slashing school funding. Wolf said that, unlike Corbett, he would raise taxes on the fast-growing natural gas industry. Scrutiny of Corbett's role as attorney general in the investigation of former Penn State assistant football coach Jerry Sandusky on accusations of child molestation became another albatross for the incumbent. Ultimately, Wolf won the high-spending race with 55 percent of the vote.

Wolf came into office stressing transparency; he introduced a website to track expenses by cabinet secretaries and signed a gift ban, and he refused the gubernatorial salary and residence and paid out of pocket for office space for the state police officers assigned to protect him. On more substantive matters, he moved to broaden the state's Medicaid expansion under the Affordable Care Act, and he ordered a moratorium on the death penalty. But budget issues proved the most intractable. Wolf came into office facing a $2 billion budget gap – as well as two Republican-controlled legislative chambers. In June 2015, Wolf vetoed the first GOP budget. That instigated a battle that lasted until March 2016 and that included skirmishes not only over revenues and spending but also vetoes of GOP-backed changes to the state pension system and to tightly regulated liquor sales. The standoff also led to a credit downgrade for the state and fears of layoffs and closed public schools. Ultimately, Wolf allowed a budget to become law without signing it, saying, "I cannot in good conscience attach my name to a budget that simply does not add up. But to allow us to move on to face budget challenges of 2016-17, I am going to allow (it) to become law."

During the rest of 2016, the relationship between Wolf and lawmakers was lower-key, and generally more productive. In April 2016, he signed a medical-marijuana law, and he issued an executive order protecting persons from discrimination based on sexual orientation and gender identity. In June 2016, Wolf signed bipartisan legislation to overhaul the state liquor system, including permission for grocery stores to sell wine and for wine to be shipped directly to customers, as well as an extension of hours at state liquor stores. That month, Wolf also signed new regulations governing horizontal oil and gas drilling. In November 2016, he signed a bill to finalize a regulatory system for network transportation companies such as Uber and Lyft, which had been operating under temporary licenses. And that same month Wolf signed several measures aimed at curbing opioid addiction, including restrictions on prescriptions for minors and requirements that medical professionals check a database before issuing prescriptions. Wolf vetoed a bill that would have slowed the release of names of law-enforcement officers involved in incidents that result in deaths or serious incidents.

The 2016 election was a downer for Pennsylvania Democrats, as presidential nominee Hillary Clinton lost the state and Republicans expanded their majorities by three seats in the state Senate and two seats in the state House. That gave Senate Republicans their widest edge in the Senate in seven decades. It was also enough votes to override vetoes if they stuck together, opening the possibility that the GOP might be able to pass agenda items that had previously remained out of reach, including measures on abortion and gun rights. Meanwhile, Wolf and the legislature faced the biggest budgetary shortfall since the recession; in January 2017, the independent legislative fiscal office projected a deficit of about $3 billion for the two-year fiscal period ending in June 2018. By early 2017, Wolf's approval ratings had recovered somewhat from their lows during the extended budget struggle of 2015 and 2016, but they were still only in the 40s, putting his seat at risk in 2018. State Sen. Scott Wagner and businessman Paul Mango entered the Republican race early, with several other possible challengers waiting in the wings, including House Speaker Mike Turzai and former Lt. Gov. Jim Cawley.

Senior Senator

Robert Casey (D)

Elected 2006, term expires 2018, 2nd term; b. Apr 13, 1960, Scranton; College of the Holy Cross (MA), B.A.; Catholic University of America (DC), J.D.; Roman Catholic; Married (Terese Foppiano Casey); 4 children.

Elected Office: PA auditor General, 1997-2005; PA State Treasurer, 2005-2007.

Professional Career: Practicing attorney, 1988-1996.

DC Office: 393 RSOB 20510, 202-224-6324, Fax: 202-228-0604, casey.senate.gov.

State Offices: Allentown, 610-782-9470; Bellefonte, 814-357-0314; Erie, 814-874-5080; Harrisburg, 717-231-7540; Philadelphia, 215-405-9660; Pittsburgh, 412-803-7370; Scranton, 570-941-0930.

Committees: *Aging (RMM)*. *Agriculture, Nutrition & Forestry*: Conservation, Forestry & Natural Resources, Livestock, Marketing & Agriculture Security, Nutrition, Agricultural Research & Specialty Crops (RMM). *Finance*: International Trade, Customs & Global Competitiveness (RMM), Social Security, Pensions & Family Policy, Taxation & IRS Oversight. *Health, Education, Labor & Pensions*: Children & Families (RMM), Employment & Workplace Safety.

Group Ratings

	ADA	ACLU	AFL-CIO	LCV	ITI	COC	HAFA	ACU	CFG	FRC
2016	-	70%	-	100%	80%	50%	9%	4%	5%	0%
2015	85%	C	100%	88%	C	50%	C	4%	4%	9%

Almanac Ratings 2015

	Economy	Social	Foreign	Composite
Liberal	87%	80%	80%	82%
Conservative	13%	20%	20%	18%

Key Votes of the 114th Congress

1. Keystone pipeline	Y	5. National Security Data	Y	9. Gun Sales Checks	Y
2. Export-Import Bank	N	6. Iran Nuclear Deal	N	10. Sanctuary Cities	N
3. Debt Ceiling Increase	Y	7. Puerto Rico Debt	Y	11. Planned Parenthood	N
4. Homeland Security $$	Y	8. Loretta Lynch A.G	Y	12. Trade deals	N

Election Results

Election	Name (Party)	Vote (%)		Cand. Spent	Ind. Exp. Support	Ind. Exp. Oppose
2012 General	Robert Casey (D)	3,021,364	(54%)	$14,342,086	$1,214,669	$1,832,382
	Tom Smith (R)	2,509,132	(45%)	$21,206,326	$1,756,341	$803,659
2012 Primary	Robert Casey (D)	565,488	(81%)			
	Joseph Vodvarka (D)	133,683	(19%)			

Prior winning percentages: 2006 (59%)

Robert Casey Jr., Pennsylvania's senior senator, has never been associated with the Democratic "red hots." So, he attracted attention in early 2017, when he spoke out against several of President Donald Trump's Cabinet nominees and went to the Philadelphia airport to join a protest of Trump's executive order limiting entry by refugees. As he prepared for a potentially competitive campaign in 2018, he had incentive to reach out to the Democratic base. In reality, he had been moving in recent years to the left on social issues, on which he had once defined himself as a different kind of Democrat. Still, the cautious Casey surely was mindful of the 2016 results in Pennsylvania, when Democrats narrowly lost high-stakes presidential and Senate contests. That begged the question of what kind of GOP challenger Casey would face in his prospective bid for a third term. In 2012, he faced a tougher than expected challenge from a largely unknown-but personally wealthy-Republican after the GOP failed to recruit a better-known candidate.

Casey is the son and namesake of a former governor, who served from 1987-1995, and was an anti-abortion Democrat who clashed with national party leaders over that issue. The junior Casey voiced similar views in 2002 when he sought unsuccessfully to follow his late father's footsteps into the governor's mansion in what became a bitter Democratic primary. He appeared to be waiting to make another run at that job when, in 2005, New York Sen. Charles Schumer-then head of the Democratic Senatorial Campaign Committee-convinced him instead to take a run at ousting two-term Republican Sen. Rick Santorum. Schumer's push to recruit the younger Casey rankled a number of the state's socially liberal Democratic activists. In his voting record since assuming the Senate seat, Casey has made moves to assuage the latter group-softening his anti-abortion stance around the edges, even as he told the Philadelphia-based *Inquirer* in 2014, "I'm a pro-life Democrat, always have been, always will be." But a Pennsylvania official of Planned Parenthood offered a more nuanced view when she told the Pittsburgh *Post-Gazette* in early 2017 that Casey had "become more comfortable in distinguishing the women's health work we do" from abortion

Born in the former coal town of Scranton in northeast Pennsylvania, the oldest son in a large Irish-Catholic family, Casey grew up in the Green Ridge neighborhood-also the boyhood home of Vice President Joe Biden. (Biden moved away two years before Casey's birth.) Robert Casey Sr. served as a state senator and Pennsylvania's auditor general, while losing three Democratic primaries for governor before finally winning that office. He was a feisty, tradition-minded practitioner of New Deal-style politics, but was best known nationally for his steadfast opposition to abortion rights. In 1992, he was prevented from speaking at the Democratic National Convention, a decision related to his abortion stance but also brought on by his skepticism about Bill Clinton as the right candidate. (The younger Casey, after backing Barack Obama over Hillary Clinton in the Pennsylvania Democratic primary in 2008, firmly backed Clinton in 2016.)

Like his father, Casey Jr. graduated from the College of the Holy Cross in Massachusetts. He taught in an inner-city Philadelphia school for the Jesuit Volunteer Corps and got his law degree from Catholic University in Washington, D.C. He practiced law in Scranton, and then began his political career by winning election in 1996 as state auditor general, the same post his father had held a couple of decades earlier. He was reelected in 2000, and, two years later, running as a cultural conservative with strong labor support, he lost a nasty and expensive primary for governor to former Philadelphia Mayor Ed Rendell. Casey's tightly scripted campaign and negative ads tarnished his image, but he showed resilience by returning in 2004 to win the state treasurer's office after his second term as auditor general had come to a close.

A year later, national Democrats were looking for a strong challenger to Santorum, a high-profile social conservative with a red-state following and a blue-state constituency. First in the House and then in the Senate, Santorum showed a knack for winning elections against tough odds-but the state's political landscape had shifted considerably since his first election to the Senate in 1994. Schumer wanted Casey to run and quickly cleared the field to avoid a cash-draining primary. While Casey's opposition to abortion rights made him anathema to many cultural liberals in the Philadelphia area, Schumer believed Casey could make inroads into Santorum's culturally conservative and "pro-life" base-particularly in the western part of the state, where Santorum resided. Meanwhile, as the Democratic alternative to Santorum, Casey would be acceptable to "pro-choice" voters in suburban Philadelphia, Schumer reasoned. The national party's heavy-handed involvement in recruiting Casey rankled many Democrats in the state. But resistance to Casey's candidacy faded in the run-up to the election, as he maintained a steady and sizable lead over Santorum in the polls.

Though Santorum was being mentioned as a potential presidential candidate, his standing at home was tenuous. As early as April 2005, he trailed Casey by double digits in the polls. That summer, he released a book titled, *It Takes a Family: Conservatism and the Common Good.* Coming a year before he stood for reelection, it was perhaps not the best timing for a frank discourse on some of the most divisive cultural issues of the day. And Santorum's support of the unpopular Bush administration was not politically helpful to him in 2006, as Casey hammered him for voting "98 percent of the time" with President George W. Bush. In addition, Democrats sought mileage from the issue of Santorum's residence and questioned whether his Virginia home disqualified him from casting a vote in Penn Hills, the Pittsburgh suburb where Santorum owned a home and was registered to vote. As Casey and Santorum clashed on issues ranging from the war in Iraq to immigration to Social Security, Casey's socially conservative positions-at the time, he opposed gun control and same-sex marriage-helped cut into Santorum's advantage outside the state's metropolitan areas. Together the two candidates raised $43 million. Santorum outspent Casey by more than $8 million, but it wasn't enough. Casey won 59%-41%, to become the first Pennsylvania Democrat elected to a full Senate term since 1962.

In the Senate, Casey has been a reliable supporter of his party's agenda, while moving leftward on several social issues since his first election. He angered some anti-abortion groups in 2011 when he voted against denying federal funds to Planned Parenthood, saying the group provides many family planning services beyond abortion. He used a similar line of argument in 2014 when he supported a bill to overturn the Supreme Court's so-called "Hobby Lobby" decision, a move that also irked some abortion foes. The legislation was an effort to put congressional Democrats on record in favor of forcing most businesses to offer employees a full range of contraceptive coverage, even if the businesses' owners raised religious objections. "The health-care service that's at issue here is contraception, which means prior to conception," Casey told the *Inquirer*. Christopher Borick, a political scientist at Muhlenberg College, told the newspaper, "He has remained a pro-life Democrat, but one who has stretched the bounds of that definition."

Casey held to his traditional anti-abortion stand in the spring of 2015, as he joined just three other Democrats in voting with most Republicans to advance a bill relating to human trafficking. Most Democrats were supporting a filibuster of the measure over a provision they believed would expand the scope of the so-called Hyde amendment, which bars federal dollars from being spent on abortions. He signed on again to the pro-life view in September 2015, when he joined only two other Democratic Senators in voting to start debate on a bill to prohibit abortions after 20 weeks of pregnancy.

Two years earlier, Casey had reversed himself on two other social issues of perennial controversy: gun control and same-sex marriage. In April 2013, he supported a measure-co-authored by his Pennsylvania Republican colleague, Pat Toomey-to expand background checks for gun owners. The bill, proposed following the December 2012 school shooting in Newtown, Connecticut in which more than two dozen were killed, failed to overcome a filibuster. The same month, Casey dropped his opposition to same-sex marriage. While he was among the last group of Senate Democrats to do so, his statement came more than two years before the 2015 Supreme Court ruling legalizing same-sex marriage across the country. In June 2016, following the massacre at a gay club in Orlando. he reinforced his shift on guns with a proposal to restrict sales or ownership for individuals convicted of a hate crime.

Casey, who acquired a sought-after seat on the Senate Finance Committee following his 2012 reelection, has usually been a party regular on economic issues. He has shared the skepticism of other Democrats from Rust Belt states toward international trade deals. "Our workers are losing over and over again when you have these trade agreements," Casey told the Allentown-based *Morning Call*. He voted against South Korea, Panama, and Colombia trade agreements that became law in October 2011, and, in the spring of 2015, was among the large majority of Democrats to oppose giving Obama "fast track" negotiating authority to expedite a 12-nation Asian trade agreement.

As part of his move to the Finance Committee, Casey gave up his slot on the Foreign Relations Committee. While on that panel, he visited Pakistan in 2011 and urged government officials to limit exports of chemicals used to make improvised explosive devices, which have been responsible for the deaths of numerous U.S. soldiers in Afghanistan. Another cause during his time on the Foreign Relations panel was the plight of Afghan women. In 2014, the "Scranton Restaurant" opened in western Afghanistan's Herat Province as the country's first female-only restaurant, with assistance from two famous Scranton natives, Casey and Biden, and donations from dozens of Scranton residents.

Closer to home, Casey serves on the Health, Education, Labor and Pensions Committee, where he has taken an interest in issues affecting children and families. He has consistently promoted legislation to award grants to states that provide high-quality, full-day pre-kindergarten programs. He reintroduced the legislation in 2015, while complaining Congress has ignored the business community's support for investment in early childhood education. "It's been terribly frustrating," he told the Easton *Express-Times*. He has sought an expansion of the federal child-care tax credit, saying the current credit-which begins to phase out after the first $15,000 in income-does not sufficiently benefit middle-class families. He has been an avid booster of funding for the State Children's Health Insurance Program, similar to a program his father instituted in Pennsylvania.

Like other coal-state senators, Casey had his differences with the Obama administration on environment and energy policy. Responding in late 2014 to the administration's proposed climate change rules, Casey, emphasizing his commitment to environmental protection, said that a plan by the Environmental Protection Agency was necessary. But, in a 22-page letter to EPA officials, Casey asked for revisions in the plan, saying it set the carbon emissions target for Pennsylvania too high. "Our Commonwealth powers the electricity needs of states across the mid-Atlantic. We should be treated sensibly and fairly," he wrote. In 2015, he was one of only eight Democrats to support an unsuccessful effort to override Obama's veto of the Keystone XL pipeline, a project opposed by environmentalists. In his search for middle ground, Casey sponsored a bill to authorize the federal government to regulate the controversial natural gas drilling technique known as hydraulic fracturing or "fracking," which environmentalists blame for contaminating groundwater in Pennsylvania and elsewhere.

Republicans hoped to unseat Casey in the 2012 campaign, but they had a hard time recruiting a top-tier candidate to take on the well-funded incumbent. None of their four primary candidates had significant name recognition. Former coal company executive Tom Smith, who spent almost $5 million of his own money, won the nomination with almost 40 percent of the vote. Initially, Smith was given little chance to beat Casey. A June 2012 Quinnipiac poll showed Casey with a comfortable lead of almost 20 points. Smith went on the attack, calling Casey "Senator Zero" and claiming he had accomplished little in the Senate. As a precaution, Casey kept his distance from Obama, whose popularity in the state had waned. Casey's supporters worried he was underestimating Smith. "They've run a non-campaign up until now," Rendell told the Scranton *Times-Tribune* just weeks before the general election. Around that time, Smith personally invested another $10 million into his campaign, flooding the airwaves with attack ads. Despite his tea party support, Smith characterized himself as a former "union coal miner with big dreams," and in the campaign's only debate, he portrayed Casey as tight with the Obama Administration. An October Quinnipiac poll found Casey's lead had narrowed to just 3 points. Casey won endorsements from most of the state's major newspapers, including the conservative *Pittsburgh Tribune-Review*. Smith outspent him, $21 million to $14 million, but Casey hung on to win, 54%-45%. He ran slightly ahead of Obama, who garnered 52 percent in winning the state.

Heading into the 2018 campaign, public approval of Casey was unimpressive. In a May 2017 poll by Franklin and Marshall College, 38 percent rated his job performance as "excellent" or "good," while 50 percent responded that it was "fair" or "poor." For a politician who typically has not evoked strong reactions, his 10% excellent and 17% poor were higher than in years past. That may help to explain his uptick in opposition to Trump as he sought to rally Democratic loyalists. In early May, Republican Rep. Lou Barletta said that he was thinking about a challenge to Casey and that he had received encouragement in a phone call from Trump. Barletta, an early and outspoken supporter of Trump in the 2016 campaign, shares Casey's home ground in northeast Pennsylvania. A larger question might be whether Barletta-or another GOP challenger to Casey--would pursue Trump's small-town strategy from the 2016 Pennsylvania campaign or the more-suburban emphasis of Republican Sen. Pat Toomey in his close reelection that year.

Junior Senator

Pat Toomey (R)

Elected 2010, term expires 2022, 2nd term; b. Nov 17, 1961, Providence, RI; Harvard University, B.A.; La Salle Academy (RI); Roman Catholic; Married (Kris Toomey); 3 children.

Elected Office: Allentown Government Study Commissioner, 1994-1996; U.S. House, 1999-2005.

Professional Career: Investment banker, Chemical Bank, 1984-1986; Investment banker, Morgan Grenfell, 1986-1990; Financial consultant, Springfield Ltd., 1990-1991; Restaurateur, 1990-2001; President, Club for Growth, 2005-2009.

DC Office: 248 RSOB 20510, 202-224-4254, Fax: 202-228-0284, toomey.senate.gov.

State Offices: Allentown, 610-434-1444; Erie, 814-453-3010; Harrisburg, 717-782-3951; Johnstown, 814-266-5970; Philadelphia, 215-241-1090; Pittsburgh, 412-803-3501; Wilkes-Barre, 570-820-4088.

Committees: *Banking, Housing & Urban Affairs*: Economic Policy, Financial Institutions & Consumer Protection (Chmn), Securities, Insurance & Investment. *Budget*. *Finance*: Health Care (Chmn), Social Security, Pensions & Family Policy, Taxation & IRS Oversight.

Group Ratings

	ADA	ACLU	AFL-CIO	LCV	ITI	COC	HAFA	ACU	CFG	FRC
2016	-	11%	-	0%	50%	75%	59%	96%	91%	0%
2015	5%	C	17%	0%	C	71%	C	83%	86%	91%

Almanac Ratings 2015

	Economy	Social	Foreign	Composite
Liberal	23%	10%	19%	17%
Conservative	77%	90%	82%	83%

Key Votes of the 114th Congress

1. Keystone pipeline	Y	5. National Security Data	N	9. Gun Sales Checks	Y
2. Export-Import Bank	NV	6. Iran Nuclear Deal	Y	10. Sanctuary Cities	Y
3. Debt Ceiling Increase	N	7. Puerto Rico Debt	Y	11. Planned Parenthood	Y
4. Homeland Security $$	Y	8. Loretta Lynch A.G	N	12. Trade deals	Y

Election Results

Election	Name (Party)	Vote (%)	Cand. Spent	Ind. Exp. Support	Ind. Exp. Oppose
2016 General	Pat Toomey (R)	2,951,702 (49%)	$27,373,876	$15,146,525	$59,455,201
	Kathleen McGinty (D)	2,865,012 (47%)	$14,968,292	$14,558,232	$47,543,382
	Edward Clifford (L)	235,142 (4%)			
2016 Primary	Pat Toomey (R)	unopposed			

Prior winning percentages: 2010 (51%), House: 2002 (57%), 2000 (53%), 1998 (55%)

In his improbable reelection in 2016, Republican Pat Toomey, Pennsylvania's junior senator, showed his political evolution in his state's complex politics. Not incidentally, he took a different approach to victory than did Donald Trump, who won even more narrowly in the Pennsylvania presidential contest that day. With an emphasis on the suburban battlegrounds outside of Philadelphia, Toomey succeeded with more of a coalition-building appeal. Toomey is one of only two surviving Republican senators from the 12 states in the New England and Mid-Atlantic regions. The political complexion of the vast majority of those states-blue or purple-had placed him near the top of national Democrats' takeover prospects in 2016.

His success was all the more notable because of the contrast to the political approach that he took prior to 2010, when he won a similarly narrow election to the Senate. In those earlier days, Toomey had spent several years as the president of the Club for Growth, a national organization that has spent generously to support conservative candidates who share its views. It has frequently backed candidates opposed by the local party establishment in Republican primary contests, sometimes taking on incumbent Republicans in the process. As head of the group, Toomey's view was that the GOP was courting political disaster because it had abandoned conservative principles. During his first term in the Senate, Toomey remained steadfast in his devotion to the Club for Growth's core principles of lower taxes and less spending. But, facing reelection in a state that had become reliably blue in presidential elections, he moved perceptibly to the center on some social issues. The most noteworthy example came in 2013, when Toomey-a gun-rights supporter with an "A" rating from the National Rifle Association-broke with his party to sponsor expanded background checks for gun owners.

A New Englander by birth, Toomey grew up in Providence, Rhode Island, the third of six children of a union worker and a part-time church secretary. He graduated from Harvard University, thanks to scholarship money and earnings from part-time jobs. After college, he worked in investment banking-founding a successful international financial services consulting firm in 1990 and amassing considerable wealth. After six years on Wall Street, Toomey moved to Allentown, where he joined his brothers to start Rookies Restaurant and Sports Bar, which grew into a chain with outlets across the state. In 1994, he was elected to the Allentown Government Study Commission, where he pushed to lower taxes and to require a supermajority vote by the city council to raise taxes.

In 1998, Toomey ran for the seat of a retiring Democrat. One of six candidates in the Republican primary, he advocated individual Social Security investment accounts, a flat tax to replace the current income tax system, and term limits for members of Congress; he promised to serve only six years. He won the close primary with 27 percent, just ahead of the 1996 nominee, Bob Kilbanks, with 25 percent. In the general election, he won, 55%-45%. He was twice reelected with a similar margin in a district that had voted Democratic for president since 1992.

In the House, Toomey focused primarily on economic issues, pushing to limit spending and to force Congress to set aside money for debt reduction. Toomey kept his term limit pledge in 2004 and ran for the Senate seat held by then-Republican Arlen Specter. Specter was supported by President George W. Bush as well as his conservative Pennsylvania colleague, Sen. Rick Santorum. Specter raised far more money than Toomey while spotlighting the projects he had obtained for the state over his 24 years in the Senate. Toomey criticized Specter's voting record as too liberal and emphasized the latter's support from trial lawyers. The result was exceedingly close. Specter won 51%-49%, 17,000 votes out of over 1 million cast. Specter carried metro Philadelphia, his home, with 57 percent, but Toomey carried metro Pittsburgh with 58 percent.

In 2005, Toomey signed on as the head of the Club for Growth, a post he held until 2009, and which enabled him to make contacts around the country with conservative activists and major fundraisers. He defended the Club's strategy in 2008 after Oklahoma Rep. Tom Cole, then chair of the National Republican Congressional Committee, excoriated the Club for Growth's involvement in a contentious Ohio congressional primary. "The problem I have with the Club is I think they're stupid," Cole told *The New York Times*. "They spend more money beating Republicans than Democrats." In a *Wall Street Journal* op-ed piece entitled "In Defense of RINO Hunting," - an acronym for Republican In Name Only-Toomey shot back: "Republicans would be better off, the argument goes, if the Club PAC spent its money targeting Democrats instead of liberal Republicans. This is the argument of politicians who care more about maintaining power than using that power to implement conservative policies." In recent years, the Club has stopped targeting Republican Senate incumbents.

Toomey challenged Specter again in 2010 after the incumbent cast one of three Republican votes for the Democrats' $787 billion economic stimulus bill in 2009. In April 2009, Specter announced he was switching parties to become a Democrat, saying he did not want to put his service at the mercy of Republican primary voters. Unfortunately for Specter, his path to the Democratic nomination was rocky, despite his backing from party heavyweights. Two-term Democratic Rep. Joe Sestak, a retired Navy admiral, subsequently entered the race, despite pressure from the Obama White House and the Senate Democratic leadership to clear the field for Specter. Sestak won the primary, 54%-46%, carrying all but three counties: Philadelphia and those containing Harrisburg and Scranton (Sestak's refusal to yield to the wishes of Democratic leaders left intraparty scars that affected his candidacy in 2016, when Sestak was seeking a rematch against Toomey.)

Toomey had no problem winning the Republican primary, capturing 81 percent. The general election presented a clear contrast on issues: Sestak had voted not only for the stimulus bill, but for the Democrats' health care overhaul and their cap-and-trade bill to limit carbon emission. Toomey called for extending the Bush-era tax cuts for everyone, including the wealthiest bracket, and for lower corporate and capital gains tax rates. He spent $17 million, while Sestak spent $12 million, much of it in the primary. In a year in which Republicans rode a political wave, Toomey beat Sestak, 51%-49%. Toomey lost metro Philadelphia, 62%-38%, but carried metro Pittsburgh, 53%-47%, and the rest of the state, 59%-41%.

In the Senate, Toomey has shown a preference for serious policy over sound bites. Notwithstanding his Club for Growth background, he has won praise for articulating conservative ideals in a manner that has not offended those who may disagree. Keeping up an effort he had begun in the House, Toomey joined with a Democratic centrist, Missouri Sen. Claire McCaskill, in a letter urging colleagues to abandon earmarks in appropriations bills to fund pet projects. He later introduced legislation making an earmark ban permanent; it did not pass, but a combination of opposition to earmarks from the White House and House Republican leaders has placed a *de facto* ban on the practice.

Toomey gained attention while floating a couple of far-reaching plans to reduce the deficit. When a standoff developed in 2011 between President Barack Obama and Republican congressional leaders over raising the federal debt ceiling, Toomey disputed warnings from the Treasury Department and business leaders that a failure to raise the debt ceiling risked a financial default; he argued the United States could prioritize its payments in the event of a debt ceiling breach to avoid a true default. Although he voted against the bill that ended the crisis by raising the federal debt ceiling, he was one of three Republican senators appointed to the Joint Committee on Deficit Reduction-the so-called "Supercommittee"-that was created by the legislation raising the debt limit. The committee, evenly divided between Democrats and Republicans and House and Senate, was charged with coming up with at least $1.2 trillion in budget savings over a 10-year period.

The committee's efforts ended in partisan stalemate prior to a November deadline set by the legislation. Toomey, with the support of several other Republicans, floated a proposal to raise $400 billion in revenue-the majority of it coming from a reduction in tax breaks-coupled with $800 million in spending cuts. But the Democrats reportedly rejected Toomey's plan because it did not phase out the Bush era tax cuts for the wealthiest Americans, which budget analysts said would cost $800 billion over the next decade. Toomey's proposal aimed to balance the budget in nine years with defense cuts already proposed by then-Defense Secretary Robert Gates, along with an overhaul of Medicaid into a block grant program. His plan did not touch two popular entitlement programs, Medicare and Social Security.

In 2013, Toomey won a coveted seat on the Finance Committee. At the same time, he supported the January 2013 compromise on taxes and spending to avoid the so-called "fiscal cliff." But he blunted criticism from conservatives who didn't like the deal by declaring that Republicans needed to be ready to shut down the government in future debates over raising the deficit. "We absolutely have to have this fight over the debt limit," he said. In October of that year, Toomey was one of just 18 senators to vote against the spending deal to end a 16-day federal government shutdown, saying he opposed the new borrowing it allowed.

It is on social issues that Toomey's first-term record was often unpredictable. He surprised some of his supporters in late 2010 by favoring repeal of the ban on openly gay service personnel in the military. "My highest priority is to have the policy that best enables our armed services to do their job," he told the Allentown *Morning Call*. Although he reiterated shortly before the Supreme Court's 2015 ruling on same-sex marriage that he believes marriage should be between a man and a woman, he voted for several measures that acknowledged gay rights. They included domestic violence protections to gay, lesbian and transgender victims; a ban on workplace discrimination; and a requirement that groups receiving some federal money do not discriminate based on sexual orientation.

Toomey's teaming with West Virginia Democrat Joe Manchin in April 2013 on a compromise on gun control rippled across Capitol Hill. Their proposal called for expanding background checks to gun shows and online sales while maintaining record-keeping provisions that law enforcement officials said were essential in tracking criminal gun use. Toomey said that, while the volatile issue was "not something I sought," he considered it important to take action. It followed the December 2012 school shooting in Newtown, Connecticut, in which a deranged gunman killed 26, most of them children. The Manchin-Toomey proposal fell five votes short of the 60-vote supermajority needed to overcome a filibuster, as only three other Republicans joined Toomey in supporting the measure, which was strongly opposed by the NRA. At a subsequent event where he was honored by the families of the Newtown victims, Toomey said that, despite the fallout from his conservative base, he would "do it again in a heartbeat," according to *The Washington Post*. Later, Toomey said he regretted his bill hadn't passed and "that it took me so long before I raised my voice on this very important issue."

In 2015, national Democratic leaders spent months searching for an alternative candidate to Sestak to take on Toomey. Finally, in August, Katie McGinty entered the contest hoping to rally the support of feminists, organized labor and her environmental base as a former top aide to Vice President Al Gore. Republicans pointed out that she ran a distant fourth in the 2014 primary for governor. In a view that became more prevalent in post-election second-guessing, some Democrats argued that Sestak, given his outsider appeal and narrow loss to Toomey in a year not kind to Democrats, would have been a formidable challenger in November, notwithstanding his scratchy relations with the Democratic establishment and history of running weak campaigns. McGinty won the primary, 43%-33%.

Toomey sought to present himself as more well-rounded than a politician who cared only about cutting taxes and regulations, his campaign strategist Jon Lerner told *Roll Call* following the election. Emphasizing that Toomey had not backed away from his conservatism, Lerner said, "It was an attempt to put something else on top of it, it was a tonal aspect. It was a guy who's thoughtful, a guy who's serious." He sought to demonstrate this approach on several issues, including opposition to the Iranian nuclear agreement and the response to sanctuary cities, in addition to his actions on the debt and gay rights.

The approach was designed to appeal, in particular, to voters votes in the moderate Philadelphia suburbs. The results there showed his success. He won narrowly in Bucks and Chester counties, and lost narrowly in Montgomery and Delaware counties. In the four counties combined, Toomey got about 48 percent of the vote, compared to only 43 percent for Trump. Both ran strongly elsewhere, though Trump out-performed Toomey, notably in blue-collar strongholds outside of Pittsburgh, which responded to more socially conservative appeals. Like Trump, Toomey lost Allegheny County by about 100,000. He won every other county west of the Philadelphia suburbs, including Center and Dauphin, which Trump narrowly lost. During the campaign, Toomey would not endorse Trump, though he said on Election Day that he voted for Trump.

The Senate contest was also notable as, by far, the most expensive in congressional history. In addition to about $50 million in spending by the candidates, outside groups spent more than $120 million, which was split nearly evenly between the two parties. [[Confirm these numbers with Duncan]]

Following the election, Toomey was positioned to work on significant Republican policies. As chairman of the Banking, Housing and Urban Affairs Subcommittee on Financial Institutions and Consumer Protection, he took early steps to prepare the Senate response to overhaul of the 2010 Dodd-Frank banking regulation law. In a February 2017 letter to Federal Reserve chairwoman Janet Yellen, Toomey urged the Fed to delay issuing new banking rules until the Trump administration and the Senate had an opportunity to consider the statute and fill vacancies on the Federal Reserve Board.

FIRST DISTRICT

Robert Brady (D)

Elected 1998, 11th term; b. Apr 07, 1945, Philadelphia; Martin Technical School (PA); Roman Catholic; Married (Debra Brady); 2 children.

Elected Office: 34th Ward Executive Committee Member, 1967-present, Ward Leader, 1980.

Professional Career: Carpenter; Sgt-at-arms, Philadelphia City Council, 1975-1983; Philadelphia deputy mayor for labor, 1984-1987; Chairman, Philadelphia Demorcratic Party, 1986-present; Legislative rep., Metro. Regional Council of Carpenters & Joiners, 1987-1998; Lecturer, University of PA, 1997-present.

DC Office: 2004 RHOB 20515, 202-225-4731, Fax: 202-225-0088, brady.house.gov.

State Offices: Chester, 610-874-7094; Philadelphia, 215-389-4627; Philadelphia, 215-426-4616; Philadelphia, 267-519-2252.

Committees: *Armed Services*: Military Personnel. *House Administration (RMM)*.

Group Ratings

	ADA	ACLU	AFL-CIO	LCV	ITI	COC	HAFA	ACU	CFG	FRC
2016	-	94%	-	97%	40%	62%	16%	4%	0%	0%
2015	90%	C	100%	89%	C	45%	C	5%	0%	0%

Almanac Ratings 2015

	Economy	Social	Foreign	Composite
Liberal	88%	93%	93%	92%
Conservative	12%	7%	7%	8%

Key Votes of the 114th Congress

1. Keystone Pipeline	Y	5. Puerto Rico Debt	N	9. Offenses by Aliens	N
2. Trade Deals	N	6. Medical Marijuana	Y	10. Troops in Iraq	Y
3. Export-Import Bank	Y	7. Sanctuary Cities	N	11. Homeland Security $$	Y
4. Debt Ceiling Increase	Y	8. Armor-piercing Bullets	N	12. Trade Adjustment aid	Y

Election Results

Election	Name (Party)	Vote (%)	Cand. Spent	Ind. Exp. Support	Ind. Exp. Oppose
2016 General	Robert Brady (D)	245,791 (82%)	$341,097		
	Deborah Williams (R)	53,219 (18%)			
2016 Primary	Robert Brady (D)	(100%)			

Prior winning percentages: 2014 (83%), 2012 (85%), 2010 (100%), 2008 (91%), 2006 (100%), 2004 (86%), 2002 (86%), 2000 (88%), 1998 (81%)

Democrat Robert Brady, elected in 1998, is the personification of Philadelphia's old-fashioned urban politics, and is one of the few remaining white ethnic party bosses in big-city America. He worked behind the scenes to help his city land and stage-manage the 2016 Democratic National Convention.

Brady grew up in Overbrook Park in West Philadelphia, with an Italian mother and an Irish father who was a policeman. After high school, he went to work as a carpenter, quickly rose through the ranks of the carpenters' union, and remains a dues-paying member. He entered politics at age 22, when the local ward leader wouldn't replace a burned-out streetlight. Brady was elected to the 34th Ward Democratic

Executive Committee, and in 1980 he was elected ward leader. In 1986, he became chairman of the Philadelphia Democratic Party.

He depicts himself as a roll-up-your-sleeves guy who represents working-class voters, and says he's proud to be the boss of what he calls the nation's largest big-city machine - or, as he calls it, an "organization." Brady is known for making "arrangements" with others - "they're always arrangements, never deals," he insists. "Governors come and go, mayors come and go, but he's the party chair," Ed Rendell, a former Philly mayor and Pennsylvania governor, told *Politico.*

In 1997, Brady ran for an open seat. The district's ward leaders determined the nomination for the special election. Not surprisingly, they favored Brady. With the endorsement of many black leaders and a strong Election Day organization, he won the special election with 74 percent of the vote. The same year he married his wife, Debra, a former Eagles cheerleader who later took a position on the city's housing authority board.

After his election to the House, Brady's focus remained back home. "Ninety-five percent of my day is not Congress," he once said. On the eve of the 2016 election, he worked with both sides to negotiate an agreement to prevent a transit strike, which would have jeopardized voter turnout across the city. He has played a similar role in labor negotiations with numerous other public employees. His ties to City Hall and to local unions gave him credibility with both sides. Brady also has worked to resolve countless local intra-party conflicts. After the fatal crash just north of the Philly train station in 2015, an angry Brady criticized Amtrak for failing to have a safety system in place.

Brady keeps a low profile in Washington. On most days that the House is in session, he commutes from home. For "the most powerful man in Philadelphia," *Philadelphia* magazine once wrote, "Washington gas-bagging is not his thing." His initiatives reflect his local orientation. He boasts of once refusing to take a phone call from President Bill Clinton because he was busy dealing with a woman asking if he could send someone to fix her toilet. He says he decided that he was in favor of abortion rights after asking his mother. His loyalty to unions led him to buck environmentalists and most Democrats to vote for drilling in the Arctic National Wildlife Refuge. His *Almanac* vote ratings in 2015 positioned him near the center of House Democrats.

When she was House Speaker, Nancy Pelosi may have found the perfect job for him. Brady became chairman of the House Administration Committee, the so-called "Mayor of Capitol Hill" who oversees operations of the House and doles out favors such as choice office space. He helped get a bill through the House in 2009 to honor African Americans who had been slave laborers during the original construction of the Capitol building. He pays less attention to his assignment with the Armed Services Committee, though he has moved up to the panel's second-ranking Democrat.

In 2013, he began making calls to other leading local Democrats about hosting the 2016 convention. In February 2015, the Democratic National Committee picked the City of Brotherly Love over Brooklyn and Columbus, Ohio. "Did Bob Brady raise a lot of money? No, I raised the most money," Rendell added. "Did he do any work to put the bid together? No. But without Bob Brady bringing us all together and saying, 'Come on guys, let's roll,' we never would have been here."

The limitations of Brady as an inspiring leader were evident when he ran for mayor in 2007. He joined the field late and had significant opposition in the primary, including from three veteran local black officials who had operated largely outside Brady's organization. Brady's platform was standard fare, including a call for more open government, safer streets, improved schools and lower taxes. Democratic ward leaders endorsed him in overwhelming numbers but with varying enthusiasm. He finished a distant third in the primary, with 15 percent of the vote. He even lost his home ward in Overbrook. With chatter about his weak performance, there was talk of a 2008 primary challenge to his House seat by an African-American candidate, but it never materialized. His share of the vote has not dropped below 82 percent since then.

An anecdote from when Pope Francis spoke to a joint session of Congress in September 2015 illustrated his sentimentality. After the Pope concluded his speech and left the podium, Brady retrieved the simple glass that the Pope had used to drink water while he spoke. As reported by the *Philadelphia Daily News*, Brady returned with the glass to his office and carefully shared the water with his family members, staffers and friends. He later emptied the water into a bottle that he would use to bless his grandchildren. Brady also secured the glass that President Barack Obama used during his Inaugural address at the Capitol in 2009. Brady decided that he could not improve on that collection and he has limited his glasses to two, according to the *Daily News*.

Parts of Philadelphia and Delaware County

Population		**Race and Ethnicity**		**Income**	
Total	707,654	White	40.0%	Median Income	$41,321 (384 out of 435)
Land area	78	Black	34.1%	Under $50,000	57.8%
Pop/ sq mi	9083.0	Latino	16.5%	$50,000-$99,999	26.3%
Born in state	67.1%	Asian	7.1%	$100,000-$199,999	12.8%
Age Groups		Two races	1.9%	$200,000 or more	3.2%
Under 18	23.4%	Other	0.4%	Poverty Rate	24.9%
18-34	28.4%	**Education**		**Health Insurance**	
35-64	37.0%	H.S grad or less	53.2%	With health insurance coverage	86.1%
Over 64	11.2%	Some college	21.8%	**Public Assistance**	
Work		College Degree, 4 yr	14.9%	Cash public assistance income	8.0%
White Collar	35.3%	Post grad	10.0%	Food stamp/SNAP benefits	24.6%
Sales and Service	47.2%	**Military**			
Blue Collar	17.6%	Veteran	5.4%		
Government	4.3%	Active Duty	0.0%		

Voter Turnout			
2015 Total Citizens 18+	498,235	2016 House Turnout as % CVAP	60%
2016 House turnout	299,010	2014 House Turnout as % CVAP	32%

2012 Presidential Vote		
Barack Obama	244,505	(82%)
Mitt Romney	50,211	(17%)

2016 Presidential Vote		
Hillary Clinton	250,924	(79%)
Donald Trump	57,521	(18%)

Cook Partisan Voting Index: D+31

Everywhere in Center City Philadelphia, American history is close at hand. Independence Hall is where Americans in the 1780s drew up the Constitution, and not far away are the restored townhouses of Society Hill. Nearby sits the Liberty Bell and its signature crack. City founder William Penn was a Quaker, a member of one of the 17th century sects that prized reason, and he imposed order on his new environment: no cow-path street patterns here, but a grid of numbered and named streets. Penn's "City of Brotherly Love" grew to be a commercial and industrial metropolis that spread out over the countryside until it was the young nation's largest city. From 2005 to 2015, the metro area dropped from the fourth-largest in the nation to seventh.

For all its historical grandeur, Philadelphia seldom has had a city government to be proud of. It has a very expensive government. Its employees' retirement fund was only 47 percent funded in 2015, and the number of individuals receiving benefits was larger than the total of employees making contributions . It has had crime-ravaged neighborhoods, with homicides topping 330 in 2012. Following a decline, that number rose again in 2016, as was the case in other large cities. Also that year, the adult poverty rate of 25 percent was the highest in the nation for big cities. There are signs of renewal. Center City remains attractive to young professionals - a growing number with families. The $575 million Gallery Mall with retail shopping was scheduled to open in late 2018 as part of wider-scale development between City Hall and Independence Mall. Plans were underway to more than double the container cargo facilities at the port and to build an 11-acre park over Interstate 95 at the riverfront.

The 1st Congressional District of Pennsylvania contains parts of Center City and eastern sections of Philadelphia along the Delaware River. Much of 18th century Philadelphia is here: Independence Hall; the U.S. Mint; and historic Christ Church, where George Washington and Benjamin Franklin worshipped. It also takes in Chinatown, Society Hill, the Northern Liberties village, Penn's Landing and Old City, with its flourishing night life. The National Constitution Center is on Independence Mall. The 1st includes once heavily Italian South Philadelphia. Nearby the district takes in the city's stadium and arena complex, as well as Pat's and Geno's, well-established haunts for late-night cheesesteaks. At the Wells Fargo Arena, Democrats nominated Hillary Clinton for president at their 2016 convention. Along the Delaware River into Delaware County, it covers impoverished Chester, where the school system went bankrupt in 2012. Following the order of a federal judge, the state bailed out the city. Three years later, teachers started the school year working for free because Chester was near insolvency.

To keep the neighboring 2nd District an African-American majority, the 2012 redistricting has decreased the black population of the 1st to 35 percent. But this is a two-thirds majority-minority and strongly Democratic district.

SECOND DISTRICT

Dwight Evans (D)

Elected 2016, 1st term; b. May 16, 1954, Philadelphia; Community College of Philadelphia, A.A., 1973; La Salle College (PA), B.A., 1975; Baptist; Single.

Elected Office: PA House, 1980-2016.

Professional Career: Teacher, Philadelphia Public Schools.

DC Office: 1105 LHOB 20515, 202-225-4001, Fax: 202-225-5392, evans.house.gov.

State Offices: Philadelphia, 215-276-0340.

Committees: *Agriculture*: Livestock & Foreign Agriculture, Nutrition. *Small Business*: Contracting & Workforce, Economic Growth, Tax & Capital Access (RMM).

Group Ratings

	ADA	ACLU	AFL-CIO	LCV	ITI	COC	HAFA	ACU	CFG	FRC
2016	-	0%	-	100%	-	50%	-	-	-	-
2015	-	C	-	-	C	NULL	C	C	C	-

Election Results

Election	Name (Party)	Vote (%)		Cand. Spent	Ind. Exp. Support	Ind. Exp. Oppose
2016 General	Dwight Evans (D)	322,514	(90%)	$1,474,407	$19,865	
2016 Primary	Dwight Evans (D)	73,496	(42%)			
	Chaka Fattah (D)	60,061	(35%)			
	Brian Gordon (D)	23,234	(13%)			
	Dan Muroff (D)	17,499	(10%)			

Democrat Dwight Evans won the Democratic primary in April 2016 against 11-term Rep. Chaka Fattah, who was convicted on corruption charges two months later. Evans, who had been influential and well-known locally during his 36 years in the state House, had the support of Democratic state and city leaders. His victory was narrow.

Evans was born in Philadelphia and got his bachelor's degree from La Salle University. He went to work as a teacher in Philly and for the Urban League as a community activist. In 1980, he was elected as a state representative, where he began a busy legislative career. He led the effort to win approval in 1986 of a new downtown convention center in his home town. He helped to create the Public Transportation Assistance Fund, which was a dedicated funding source for mass transit. He was an author of the state's charter school program, which increased the school choices for parents and their children.

For 20 years, Evans was the chairman or senior Democrat on the House Appropriations Committee, where he directed funds to communities across the state. In 2010, he was stripped of the position following an internal squabble among Democrats. As chairman of the Budget Committee of the Southeast Pennsylvania Transportation Authority, Evans participated actively in labor negotiations, including the week-long transit strike in 2016 that was settled on the eve of Election Day. Evans had several unsuccessful runs for higher office, including governor and lieutenant governor and two bids for mayor; in the 2007 campaign, Fattah also was a candidate.

Evans got his big opening when Fattah was indicted in July 2015 on federal corruption charges - including bribery, money laundering and mail fraud - for his mixing of personal and campaign finances during his run for mayor. Fattah remained in the House, but he was required to step down as senior Democrat on the Commerce, Justice, Science Appropriations Subcommittee. Evans was endorsed by, among others, Pennsylvania Gov. Tom Wolf and Philadelphia Mayor Jim Kenney, each of whom Evans had endorsed when they sought their current office. Many of the ward leaders in the Democratic organization stayed with Fattah. Despite his decades serving in Harrisburg, Evans styled himself as a reformer. "We must fix our politics," he said.

Fattah, who was beleaguered by legal bills, raised only $220,000 to $1.5 million for Evans. In the four-candidate April primary, Evans won 42%-34%. Fattah resigned from the House three days after his conviction, though he initially sought to retain his seat until October. He was sentenced in December to 10 years in prison, one of the longest-ever criminal sentences for a current or former member of Congress. In the general election, Evans got 90 percent of the vote against Republican James Jones, who did not report campaign finances. He won a special election for the remainder of Fattah's term, and took office a week after the election.

Evans joined the Agriculture Committee, where he would have the opportunity to work on hunger and nutrition programs during the expected debate on the farm bill. He had spent time on related issues during his years in Harrisburg. A week after President Donald Trump took office, Evans joined local Democrats in criticizing the new administration's decision to deny admission to Syrian refugees who reportedly were seeking to enter the nation legally at the Philadelphia airport. He called the prohibition "cruel and unusual ... [and] a very sad day in the city of Brotherly Love."

North and West Philadelphia, Center City

Population		**Race and Ethnicity**		**Income**	
Total	719,392	White	29.1%	Median Income	$37,038 (415 out of 435)
Land area	74	Black	57.2%		
Pop/ sq mi	9703.2	Latino	5.9%		
Born in state	67.4%	Asian	4.8%	Under $50,000	60.3%
		Two races	2.2%	$50,000-$99,999	22.5%
Age Groups		Other	0.7%	$100,000-$199,999	11.9%
Under 18	20.5%			$200,000 or more	5.4%
18-34	31.6%	**Education**		Poverty Rate	28.2%
35-64	34.6%	H.S grad or less	44.0%		
Over 64	13.3%	Some college	22.6%	**Health Insurance**	
		College Degree, 4 yr	17.2%	With health insurance coverage	89.0%
Work		Post grad	16.2%		
White Collar	44.3%				
Sales and Service	44.4%	**Military**		**Public Assistance**	
Blue Collar	11.3%	Veteran	5.7%	Cash public assistance income	7.8%
Government	4.3%	Active Duty	0.0%		
				Food stamp/SNAP benefits	24.9%

Voter Turnout			
2015 Total Citizens 18+	542,257	2016 House Turnout as % CVAP	66%
2016 House turnout	357,645	2014 House Turnout as % CVAP	38%

2012 Presidential Vote		
Barack Obama	338,343	(90%)
Mitt Romney	33,530	(9%)

2016 Presidential Vote		
Hillary Clinton	334,322	(90%)
Donald Trump	28,067	(8%)

Cook Partisan Voting Index: D+40

Looking out over the Schuylkill River north of Center City Philadelphia, you can still see the landscape painted 100 years ago by Philadelphia artist Thomas Eakins: the tightly packed but formidable rowhouses, the old fieldstone houses of Germantown, and the boat houses below the small Greek temples of the Water Works. Here are some of Philadelphia's long-established black neighborhoods: West Philadelphia, across the Schuylkill on either side of Market Street; and North Philadelphia, on either side of Broad Street. Pennsylvania was the first state to abolish slavery, thanks to William Penn and his Quaker legacy, and Philadelphia has been home to a large African-American community since before the Civil War. That heritage is reflected in places like the John Coltrane House, a national historic landmark in celebration of the jazz innovator's early years here.

Northwest Philadelphia includes distinguished old neighborhoods such as Chestnut Hill, with its cobblestone streets and classic architecture. East Falls was the childhood home of Grace Kelly, who grew up to be a Hollywood starlet and princess of Monaco. Kelly Drive, which runs along the Schuylkill River, was named after Grace's brother, former City Councilman John Kelly Jr. Some neighborhoods here continue to suffer from poverty and blight. But in recent years, city officials have made a concerted effort to bring young, affluent people back to the city. In 2015, local officials said Center City ranked second only to midtown Manhattan for the number of residents living in the heart of a city.

The 2nd Congressional District of Pennsylvania takes in the African-American neighborhoods in North and West Philadelphia, and most of Center City west of 16th Street. It encircles City Hall, an ornate building where a statue of city founder William Penn stands 37 feet high, and includes well-heeled Rittenhouse Square, the Philadelphia Zoo (America's first), and the University of Pennsylvania and Drexel University across the Schuylkill. It includes most of Fairmount Park, the largest landscaped urban park in the world, which climaxes at the Philadelphia Museum of Art, where a *Rocky-like* run up the steps has become *de rigueu*r for tourists.

For many, including visitors, the 30th Street train station is the heart of the district. A $6.5 billion master plan envisioned a new concourse, connections to local rail and bus lines, and long-term development of the area over the tracks. Also ambitious are federal rail plans to straighten the Frankford Curve just north of the station, which was the site of a deadly derailment in 2015. The 2nd, which is 58 percent black but only 6 percent Hispanic, covers wealthier suburbs on the Main Line, including Ardmore, Bala Cynwyd and up the river to Conshohocken Station. These Montgomery County voters are about 10 percent of the district and they significantly increase the otherwise low median income of the district. This has been among the five most Democratic districts in the nation. Hillary Clinton got a 90 percent vote here in 2016, as did Barack Obama in 2012.

THIRD DISTRICT

Mike Kelly (R)

Elected 2010, 4th term; b. May 10, 1948, Pittsburgh; University of Notre Dame (IN), B.A.; Roman Catholic; Married (Victoria Kelly); 4 children; 10 grandchildren.

Elected Office: Butler City Council, 2006-2009.

Professional Career: Butler Area School Board, 1992-1996; Owner, Manager, Kelly Chevrolet-Cadillac Inc.

DC Office: 1707 LHOB 20515, 202-225-5406, Fax: 202-225-3103, kelly.house.gov.

State Offices: Butler, 724-282-2557; Erie, 814-454-8190; Sharon, 724-342-7170.

Committees: *Ways & Means*: Social Security, Tax Policy, Trade.

Group Ratings

	ADA	ACLU	AFL-CIO	LCV	ITI	COC	HAFA	ACU	CFG	FRC
2016	-	5%	-	0%	100%	100%	67%	72%	71%	100%
2015	0%	C	29%	3%	C	85%	C	63%	50%	100%

Almanac Ratings 2015

	Economy	Social	Foreign	Composite
Liberal	10%	0%	4%	5%
Conservative	90%	100%	96%	95%

Key Votes of the 114th Congress

1. Keystone Pipeline	Y	5. Puerto Rico Debt	N	9. Offenses by Aliens	Y
2. Trade Deals	Y	6. Medical Marijuana	N	10. Troops in Iraq	N
3. Export-Import Bank	Y	7. Sanctuary Cities	Y	11. Homeland Security $$	N
4. Debt Ceiling Increase	N	8. Armor-piercing Bullets	Y	12. Trade Adjustment aid	Y

Election Results

Election	Name (Party)	Vote (%)	Cand. Spent	Ind. Exp. Support	Ind. Exp. Oppose
2016 General	Mike Kelly (R)	244,893 (100%)	$960,231		
2016 Primary	Mike Kelly (R)	(100%)			

Prior winning percentages: 2014 (61%), 2012 (55%), 2010 (56%)

Republican Mike Kelly, who defeated a Democratic incumbent in 2010, is an ex-college football player who has been known for his fiery pep talks to colleagues behind closed doors. He has been mostly loyal to his party and its leaders. On the Ways and Means Committee, he has advocated core issues for House Republicans.

Kelly was born in Pittsburgh and four years later his family moved to Butler, where his father started a small automobile business, working seven days a week. "He took the cars off the trains himself, and he serviced them himself. And he built a business, based around a strong work ethic, which was similar to his parents. It's pretty much the story of western Pennsylvania," Kelly said. In high school, Kelly was an all-state football player and was recruited to play for the University of Notre Dame. But he tore up a knee during his freshman year and dislocated it again in his sophomore season, ending his football career. After college, he worked as a salesman in the family business, Kelly Chevrolet-Cadillac, eventually becoming general manager. He bought the dealership from his father, and expanded it to include Hyundai and Kia autos. In 2005, Kelly was elected to the Butler City Council.

Running for Congress in 2010, Kelly's toughest opponent in the primary was Paul Huber, former chief executive of Seco/Warwick, a maker of industrial furnaces. He eked out a victory by 954 votes out of 54,000 cast. His general election foe was Rep. Kathy Dahlkemper, a Democrat who in 2008 had narrowly knocked off seven-term GOP Rep. Phil English, 51%-49%. Dahlkemper opposed abortion rights, but she took heat from conservatives for voting for the Affordable Care Act, which many anti-abortion activists believed opened the door to taxpayer-funded abortions. Dahlkemper outspent Kelly by about 3-to-2. He stressed his football background, which was an asset in the football mecca of western Pennsylvania, and he promised to cut government spending and curtail interference with small business. Dahlkemper ran an ad playing on populist themes, calling Kelly a multimillionaire who has "millions invested in Wall Street and big gas-and-oil companies." With the strong Republican wave at his back, Kelly won 56%-44%.

During the 2011 fight over raising the debt limit, he gave what Rep. Peter King of New York called a well-delivered "Knute Rockne-type speech" to rally conservatives. "Mike Kelly's the one that steps up to the microphone and says, 'Hey, we're all in this together. … Nobody in this room is going to get everything they want. Let's go do this,'" Republican Rep. Austin Scott of Georgia told the *Pittsburgh Tribune-Review*. He got national attention in 2014 when he delivered the Republican weekly address and offered Obama a lump of coal for Christmas to bolster the nation's economic revival. In the *Almanac* vote ratings for 2015, Kelly was conservative on social and foreign policy and more centrist on economic matters.

On Ways and Means, Kelly won approval in 2015 of his bill to remove protections for Internal Revenue Service employees who improperly review or reveal taxpayer information. The committee approved his bill to improve the transparency of Medicare Advantage programs for the individuals who have enrolled. He co-founded the bipartisan Retirement Security Caucus to encourage more savings. Kelly has been a vocal advocate of expanded international trade, which he said is a boost for workers and assures that the nation "is leading, shaping, and dominating the global economy." He was an outspoken supporter of granting trade protection authority to President Barack Obama, a step that he said would be "a crucial victory to the principles of American dominance, domestic prosperity, and government accountability that we hold so dear."

During the 2016 presidential campaign, Kelly was an enthusiastic supporter of Donald Trump. "Only a Trump presidency can undo the current damage caused by explosive government growth and chart a new direction," he wrote for CNN in October 2016. After the election, Kelly told the *Washington Examiner*, "I just thought his approach was so unique … he was a change agent." At home, Kelly has restored the Republican tilt of his district. He easily won reelection in 2012 and 2014 against active Democratic challengers. In 2016, he had no major-party opposition. In May 2017, he ruled out running for governor in 2018, but he kept the door open for a possible Senate bid.

Northwest Pennsylvania: Erie, Pittsburgh Exurbs

Population		**Race and Ethnicity**		**Income**	
Total	700,703	White	90.6%	Median Income	$47,669
Land area	3,851	Black	4.5%		(289 out of 435)
Pop/ sq mi	182.0	Latino	2.1%		
Born in state	82.1%	Asian	0.9%	Under $50,000	52.0%
		Two races	1.7%	$50,000-$99,999	31.0%
Age Groups		Other	0.2%	$100,000-$199,999	14.2%
Under 18	21.3%			$200,000 or more	2.9%
18-34	20.5%	**Education**		Poverty Rate	14.1%
35-64	40.8%	H.S grad or less	51.8%		
Over 64	17.4%	Some college	24.2%	**Health Insurance**	
		College Degree, 4 yr	15.7%	With health insurance coverage	91.6%
Work		Post grad	8.4%		
White Collar	32.2%				
Sales and Service	42.4%	**Military**		**Public Assistance**	
Blue Collar	25.4%	Veteran	10.1%	Cash public assistance income	3.8%
Government	5.6%	Active Duty	0.0%		
				Food stamp/SNAP benefits	15.4%

Voter Turnout			
2015 Total Citizens 18+	545,085	2016 House Turnout as % CVAP	45%
2016 House turnout	244,893	2014 House Turnout as % CVAP	34%

2012 Presidential Vote		
Mitt Romney	171,114	(56%)
Barack Obama	132,486	(43%)

2016 Presidential Vote		
Donald Trump	197,957	(61%)
Hillary Clinton	113,562	(35%)
Gary Johnson	8,979	(3%)

Cook Partisan Voting Index: R+11

The best natural harbor on Lake Erie is in Erie, Pennsylvania, protected by the Presque Isle ("almost an island") peninsula - a cowlick-shaped, seven-mile-long sand spit blanketed by mature forest, with a lighthouse dating to 1872. Erie is in Pennsylvania's far northwest corner, closer to Cleveland (about 100 miles) than to Pittsburgh (125 miles). There are farmlands here, and even some woods, but the land between the Great Lakes and the basin of the Ohio River has been prime heavy industry territory for more than a century. The jeep, which Gen. George Marshall called America's greatest contribution to World War II, was invented in Butler County. In the 1990s, under Republican Gov. Tom Ridge, who grew up in Erie, the state invested $100 million in the city's waterfront to develop a cruise ship terminal, hotel and convention center, a ballpark for the double-A Erie SeaWolves baseball team, and a renovated Warner Theatre.

The effort spruced up a dying downtown, but it didn't buffer Erie from a new downturn during which International Paper, American Meter, Gunite/EMI and American Sterilizer laid off employees and closed plants. General Electric Transportation, one of the area's largest employers, has suffered more cutbacks and its global headquarters moved from Lawrence Park to Chicago. Its workforce suffered from the decline in freight rail traffic. One hopeful sign for the GE plant has been an increase in overseas purchase of locomotives. Erie officials have created a downtown innovation district that they envision as a hub for cybersecurity and data science. James Fallows wrote for *The Atlantic* in January 2017 that young people have been "very prominent in the startup, advanced-manufacturing, and civic-engagement scene in Erie."

The 3rd Congressional District of Pennsylvania occupies the northwest corner of the state. It takes in most of the city of Erie, though a majority of Erie County is in the rural 5th District. It covers Meadville, where the company Talon invented the zipper, and Grove City and Grove City College, a Christian liberal arts school. It includes New Castle and the old glass industry borough, Ford City. The district dips south to politically conservative Butler and Armstrong counties, which include the northern exurbs of Pittsburgh. About one-third of the population is in Butler, and one-sixth is in Erie. The population of the city of Erie declined 9 percent from 1990 to its 2015 total of 99,500. A growing number of refugees are about 18 percent of the city - an increase of 3,400 from 2012 to 2016.

As has been the case throughout western Pennsylvania, the presidential vote in the district has moved steadily to Republicans. The 61 percent for Donald Trump in 2016 was a hefty increase from the 52 percent that John McCain got in these boundaries in 2008.

FOURTH DISTRICT

Scott Perry (R)

Elected 2012, 3rd term; b. May 27, 1962, San Diego, CA; Pennsylvania State University, B.S.; U.S. Army War College (PA), M.S.; Church of the United Brethren in Christ; Married (Christy Perry); 2 children.

Military Career: PA Army National Guard, 1980-present.

Elected Office: PA House, 2007-2012.

Professional Career: Dock worker, Dauphin Distribution, 1981-1982; Insurance sales agent, 1984-1985; Co-owner, Hydrotech Mechanical Services, 1993-present.

DC Office: 1207 LHOB 20515, 202-225-5836, Fax: 202-226-1000, perry.house.gov.

State Offices: Gettysburg, 717-338-1919; Wormleysburg, 717-635-9504; York, 717-600-1919.

Committees: *Foreign Affairs*: Asia & the Pacific, Terrorism, Nonproliferation & Trade. *Homeland Security*: Counterterrorism & Intelligence, Oversight & Management Efficiency (Chmn). *Transportation & Infrastructure*: Aviation, Highways & Transit, Railroads, Pipelines & Hazardous Materials.

Group Ratings

	ADA	ACLU	AFL-CIO	LCV	ITI	COC	HAFA	ACU	CFG	FRC
2016	-	17%	-	0%	67%	100%	85%	96%	91%	92%
2015	10%	C	13%	3%	C	58%	C	100%	81%	82%

Almanac Ratings 2015

	Economy	Social	Foreign	Composite
Liberal	8%	15%	8%	10%
Conservative	93%	85%	92%	90%

Key Votes of the 114th Congress

1. Keystone Pipeline	Y	5. Puerto Rico Debt	N	9. Offenses by Aliens	Y
2. Trade Deals	N	6. Medical Marijuana	Y	10. Troops in Iraq	N
3. Export-Import Bank	N	7. Sanctuary Cities	Y	11. Homeland Security $$	N
4. Debt Ceiling Increase	N	8. Armor-piercing Bullets	Y	12. Trade Adjustment aid	N

Election Results

Election	Name (Party)	Vote (%)	Cand. Spent	Ind. Exp. Support	Ind. Exp. Oppose
2016 General	Scott Perry (R)	220,628 (66%)	$433,608		
	Joshua Burkholder (D)	113,372 (34%)			
2016 Primary	Scott Perry (R)	(100%)			

Prior winning percentages: 2014 (75%), 2012 (60%)

Republican Scott Perry was elected in 2012 after easily prevailing in a crowded primary in which he started as an underdog. With an agenda that emphasized a leaner federal government, gun rights, traditional marriage and his lengthy military career, Perry remained committed to those values, though he has not stirred much attention.

Perry was born in San Diego but moved at age 7 to central Pennsylvania, where he lived in a home without electricity or plumbing. He grew up in what he described to *National Journal* as a "little dysfunctional and a little disjointed family." Perry was the child of a single mother and has met his biological father just once. The family fell on hard times when both his mother, a flight attendant, and stepfather, a pilot, lost their airline jobs. After graduating from high school, Perry worked as an auto mechanic before enlisting in the Pennsylvania Army National Guard. After being commissioned in the field artillery, he transferred to Army aviation. He flew numerous aircraft and became an instructor pilot. He distinguished himself as a helicopter pilot and rose to the rank of brigadier general. While a state representative, he served for a year in Iraq, flying 44 missions. He has commanded the Fort Indiantown Gap National Training Site and remains active as an assistant adjutant general at headquarters.

As a young man, Perry held a series of jobs, including as a dockhand, an insurance sales agent, and a designer and drafter at an engineering firm. He got his bachelor's in business administration from Penn State University. He and a partner founded Hydrotech Mechanical Services and built it into a contracting firm specializing in meter calibration and line work for municipalities. The venture hit a snag in 2002 when the Pennsylvania attorney general's office accused Perry of falsifying reports to the state Environmental Protection Department. Instead of fighting the charge, he entered the Accelerated Rehabilitative Disposition Program, a pretrial avenue similar to probation. The matter ended with a $5,000 fine and his record being expunged. Perry maintained his innocence, asserting that an overzealous "bureaucrat" was the culprit.

His legal ordeal inspired Perry to get more involved in politics. As a past president of the Pennsylvania Young Republicans, he was elected to the state House in 2006. There, Perry expanded the law allowing residents to use deadly force in self-defense. He bucked Republican Gov. Tom Corbett by proposing legislation that would have declined federal money to fund insurance exchanges under the Affordable Care Act.

When he ran for the House, Perry's past legal troubles were raised in the seven-person Republican primary field but they never got traction. He garnered endorsements from Corbett and GOP Sen. Pat Toomey. Retiring Rep. Todd Platts offered kind words about him in a mailer to voters, but not an endorsement. He benefited from his military background. Perry was outspent 2-to-1, but won 54 percent of the primary vote, far ahead of York County Commissioner Christopher Reilly, the runner-up with 19 percent. In November, he had no trouble in this heavily Republican district. The contest attracted scant national attention.

In the House, Perry serves on three committees: Foreign Affairs, Homeland Security, and Transportation and Infrastructure. He is a co-founder of the post-9/11 veterans' caucus. In 2014, when the Iraqi military lost control of major parts of their country, he voiced bitterness as he recalled his own service. "Right now I wonder what that was all about. What was the point of all of that?" In 2015, he criticized President Barack Obama's "lack of leadership" in dealing with terror threats overseas and worried publicly about the potential threat to the homeland from domestic jihadists. But he backed away from an earlier charge that Obama was "working collaboratively with what I would say is the enemy of freedom." In April 2016, Perry chaired a hearing in which he strongly opposed the call by the Obama administration to close the detention camp at Guantanamo Bay.

He voted against trade promotion authority; he said the proposal failed to provide sufficient accountability and transparency in trade negotiations. He has filed legislation to legalize a marijuana-based oil that has been shown to reduce seizures in children with debilitating epilepsy. In February 2017, the House passed his bill to improve management of the vehicle fleet at the Department of Homeland Security.

At home, Perry faced Harrisburg Democratic Mayor Linda Thompson in the 2014 election. She campaigned against the "dysfunction" in Congress, but raised less than $9,000 and was not well known outside of her Democratic base. Perry won 75%-25%. In 2016, Perry got 66 percent of the vote against Joshua Burkholder, a multimedia digital artist who got the Democratic nomination as a write-in candidate.

South-Central Pennsylvania: York, Harrisburg

Population		**Race and Ethnicity**		**Income**	
Total	714,595	White	81.8%	Median Income	$57,680
Land area	1,518	Black	7.2%		(159 out of
Pop/ sq mi	470.8	Latino	6.7%		435)
Born in state	66.2%	Asian	2.1%	Under $50,000	43.1%
		Two races	1.9%	$50,000-$99,999	34.3%
Age Groups		Other	0.2%	$100,000-$199,999	19.3%
Under 18	22.2%			$200,000 or more	3.3%
18-34	20.8%	**Education**		Poverty Rate	11.1%
35-64	41.3%	H.S grad or less	50.3%		
Over 64	15.7%	Some college	24.4%	**Health Insurance**	
		College Degree, 4 yr	16.1%	With health insurance coverage	91.6%
Work		Post grad	9.1%		
White Collar	34.0%				
Sales and Service	40.9%	**Military**		**Public Assistance**	
Blue Collar	25.1%	Veteran	9.6%	Cash public assistance income	2.6%
Government	4.7%	Active Duty	0.1%		
				Food stamp/SNAP benefits	10.8%

Voter Turnout			
2015 Total Citizens 18+	539,767	2016 House Turnout as % CVAP	62%
2016 House turnout	334,000	2014 House Turnout as % CVAP	37%

2012 Presidential Vote		
Mitt Romney	177,707	(57%)
Barack Obama	129,243	(42%)

2016 Presidential Vote		
Donald Trump	198,571	(58%)
Hillary Clinton	125,762	(37%)
Gary Johnson	10,267	(3%)

Cook Partisan Voting Index: R+11

The Mason-Dixon Line, the historic boundary between Maryland and Pennsylvania, runs through pleasant rolling farmlands, west of the Susquehanna River, and through the Appalachian Mountains. The area was home to the westernmost capital of the United States during the Revolutionary War: the city of York, where the Continental Congress passed the Articles of Confederation and received word from Benjamin Franklin in Paris that the French would help the colonies with money and ships. Nearly a century later, Robert E. Lee's Confederate troops crossed this invisible line and were repelled at the Battle of Gettysburg in July 1863. Not much today suggests that these hills were a frontier or the object of bloody struggle. President Dwight Eisenhower, of Pennsylvania Dutch stock, quietly spent his retirement years in Gettysburg. The Pennsylvania Gaming Control Board in 2011 rejected a proposal to build a casino within a half-mile of Gettysburg National Military Park.

York is the site of a large Harley-Davidson manufacturing plant, though automation and fewer sales downsized its payroll from 2,000 workers in 2009 to 1,000 in 2016. Hanover, in York County, is a snack headquarters, home to Snyder's of Hanover and potato chip giant Utz. The city has a growing Hispanic population, many of whom work the abundant orchards near Gettysburg. Harrisburg, the capital of Pennsylvania, features a string of mansions-turned-lobbying headquarters lining the banks of the Susquehanna and boasts Pennsylvania's marvelously restored Capitol building. Despite the presence of state government, the city has run up heavy debts. Harrisburg filed for bankruptcy in October 2011 but it was rejected by the state. In 2012, its $1.5 billion debt was the largest per capita in the nation. In 2014, the state enacted a bill to assist cities to restructure their finances with additional taxing powers. Legislation in 2016 tightened municipal debt procedures in an attempt to prevent a repeat of apparent abuses in Harrisburg. Also that year, the state approved a recovery program for the school system in York, which was having financial problems. During an August 2016 presidential campaign visit, Donald Trump said that Harrisburg "looked like a war zone" because of its closed factories. Local business leaders and journalists disagreed.

The 4th Congressional District is in the south-central part of the state and includes all of Adams and York counties and portions of Cumberland and Dauphin counties. Nearly two-thirds of the voters in the 4th are in York. It takes in most of downtown Harrisburg along the Susquehanna, including the state Capitol. That section of Harrisburg is Democratic, but it is only 5 percent of the district. In an election post mortem, the Cook Political Report noted that Trump would not have won the 2016 election if York-along with Macomb County in Michigan and Waukesha in Wisconsin-had not voted.

FIFTH DISTRICT

Glenn Thompson (R)

Elected 2008, 5th term; b. Jul 27, 1959, Bellefonte; Marywood College (PA); Pennsylvania State University, B.S.; Temple University (PA), M.Ed.; Protestant; Married (Penny Thompson); 3 children.

Elected Office: Bald Eagle Area School Board, 1990-1995.

Professional Career: Therapist, Williamsport Hosp., 1982-1995; Adjunct faculty, Cambria County Comm. College, 1997-1999; Manager, Susquehanna Health Rehabilitation Services, 1995-2008; Centre County GOP Chairman, 2002-2008; Firefighter & EMT.

DC Office: 124 CHOB 20515, 202-225-5121, Fax: 202-225-5796, thompson.house.gov.

State Offices: Bellefonte, 814-353-0215; Titusville, 814-827-3985.

Committees: *Agriculture*: Conservation & Forestry, Nutrition (Chmn). *Education & the Workforce*: Early Childhood, Elementary & Secondary Education, Higher Education & Workforce Development. *Natural Resources*: Energy & Mineral Resources, Federal Lands.

Group Ratings

	ADA	ACLU	AFL-CIO	LCV	ITI	COC	HAFA	ACU	CFG	FRC
2016	-	11%	-	3%	100%	93%	49%	84%	62%	100%
2015	0%	C	21%	3%	C	100%	C	50%	38%	92%

Almanac Ratings 2015

	Economy	Social	Foreign	Composite
Liberal	14%	10%	10%	12%
Conservative	86%	90%	90%	88%

Key Votes of the 114th Congress

1. Keystone Pipeline	Y	5. Puerto Rico Debt	Y	9. Offenses by Aliens	Y
2. Trade Deals	Y	6. Medical Marijuana	N	10. Troops in Iraq	N
3. Export-Import Bank	Y	7. Sanctuary Cities	Y	11. Homeland Security $$	Y
4. Debt Ceiling Increase	Y	8. Armor-piercing Bullets	Y	12. Trade Adjustment aid	Y

Election Results

Election	Name (Party)	Vote (%)		Cand. Spent	Ind. Exp. Support	Ind. Exp. Oppose
2016 General	Glenn Thompson (R)	206,761	(67%)	$1,162,667		
	Kerith Strano Taylor (D)	101,082	(33%)	$103,671		
2016 Primary	Glenn Thompson (R)		(100%)			

Prior winning percentages: 2014 (64%), 2012 (63%), 2010 (69%), 2008 (57%)

Republican Glenn Thompson, who won the seat in 2008, is an amiable centrist and the only Pennsylvanian to serve on the House Agriculture Committee, where he is an influential member. He tries to protect farmers, as well as energy interests, from what he sees as excessive regulation.

A lifelong resident of Centre County, Thompson graduated from nearby Penn State. He launched his career in health care at Williamsport Hospital, where he worked as a rehabilitation services manager. He later worked as a licensed nursing home administrator. As his congressional website states about his career, "GT has touched the lives of thousands of individuals facing life altering conditions. As a result, he … has become a strong advocate for increased access, affordability, quality of care, and patient choice." Thompson served as a member of the board of the Bald Eagle Area School District. He ran twice for state representative, both times unsuccessfully, but was elected to three terms as chairman of the Centre County Republican Party.

When the House seat opened, Thompson jumped into the nine-candidate primary. His hopes appeared dim against big-spending rivals. Businessmen Matt Shaner and Derek Walker self-financed their campaigns, and took to the airwaves to reach voters across the expansive district. Thompson instead hit the pavement, crisscrossing the district in a low-key and low-cost campaign that emphasized his Republican positions and focused on rural issues. He opposed tolls on Interstate 80 and called for expanding rural Medicare initiatives. He spoke of the Iraq war in personal terms; his son, Logan, was injured by a landmine in 2007 while serving.

Two developments helped him to break out of the pack. Less than two weeks before the primary, retiring GOP Rep. John Peterson endorsed Thompson as the candidate who would follow in his footsteps and who best understood rural issues. A week later, the Clearfield County district attorney filed charges against Walker for allegedly breaking into his ex-girlfriend's apartment. Thompson eked out a small victory. Vastly outspent, he won 19 percent of the vote to beat Walker by 835 votes. The general election was a breeze by comparison. Clearfield County Commissioner Mark McCracken, raised only $94,000 and received little help from national or state Democrats. Thompson won 57%-41%. He has not been seriously challenged for reelection.

Thompson has shown some independence. His *Almanac* vote ratings for 2015 ranked him among the one-fourth of Republicans in the center of the House. He dissed tea party advocates by voting to raise the federal debt limit in 2011, to preserve rural air subsidies in 2012, and to support the tax and spending legislation that averted the so-called "fiscal cliff" in 2013. He called the latter "not perfect, but a pretty good deal." In 2014, he included in the year-end spending bill $155 million for the Essential Air Service program, which promotes rural airports and is opposed by many conservatives. In 2015-16, C-SPAN reported that Thompson spoke on the House floor 209 times -- more often than any other member.

Rural causes have been a priority for Thompson. On the Agriculture panel, he chaired the Subcommittee on Conservation and Forestry for six years. He worked to strengthen voluntary conservation programs as part of the farm bill enacted in 2014. With many dairy farmers in his district, he filed a bill in 2015 with Democratic Rep. Joe Courtney of Connecticut to reaffirm the requirement that milk is offered with each school meal. In 2017, he took over as vice chairman of the full committee and chairman of the Nutrition Subcommittee, which encounters frequent controversy with its handling of food stamps.

On the Natural Resources Committee, Thompson has pushed for more natural gas drilling in the Marcellus Shale formation. He dismissed concerns of environmentalists that the gas-drilling technique called hydraulic fracturing was contaminating groundwater. He was highly critical of the Environmental Protection Agency's efforts during the Obama administration to protect Chesapeake Bay from agricultural-related pollution, accusing the EPA of a "quixotic quest to impose unreasonable regulatory mandates." In 2015, he attacked EPA for its proposed Waters of the U.S. rules, which he said would have severe implications for farmers. Thompson retains his interest in education issues as a member of the Education and the Workforce Committee. He has co-chaired both the Career and Technical Education Caucus and the Natural Gas Caucus.

In 2015-16, he won House passage of several bills that he filed and shepherded through his three committees. They included reauthorization of the National Forest Foundation, extension of career education programs and loosening of restrictions on oil and gas development in the Allegheny National Forest.

North-Central Pennsylvania: State College, Erie Suburbs

Population		**Race and Ethnicity**		**Income**	
Total	706,400	White	92.7%	Median Income	$46,621 (314 out of 435)
Land area	10,711	Black	2.3%		
Pop/ sq mi	65.9	Latino	1.9%		
Born in state	79.8%	Asian	1.7%	Under $50,000	53.1%
		Two races	1.2%	$50,000-$99,999	31.8%
Age Groups		Other	0.3%	$100,000-$199,999	12.9%
Under 18	19.0%			$200,000 or more	2.2%
18-34	25.2%	**Education**		Poverty Rate	15.4%
35-64	38.9%	H.S grad or less	53.9%		
Over 64	16.9%	Some college	23.4%	**Health Insurance**	
		College Degree, 4 yr	13.8%	With health insurance coverage	91.9%
Work		Post grad	8.9%		
White Collar	33.0%				
Sales and Service	39.9%	**Military**		**Public Assistance**	
Blue Collar	27.1%	Veteran	9.8%	Cash public assistance income	3.1%
Government	5.9%	Active Duty	0.0%		
				Food stamp/SNAP benefits	12.7%

Voter Turnout			
2015 Total Citizens 18+	559,240	2016 House Turnout as % CVAP	55%
2016 House turnout	307,833	2014 House Turnout as % CVAP	32%

2012 Presidential Vote		
Mitt Romney	165,469	(57%)
Barack Obama	120,026	(41%)

2016 Presidential Vote		
Donald Trump	195,739	(62%)
Hillary Clinton	105,139	(33%)
Gary Johnson	9,256	(3%)

Cook Partisan Voting Index: R+13

North-central Pennsylvania, isolated from the rest of the country by mountains and off the main east-west rail and highway lines until the 1970s, is one of those empty spaces that make even the Northeastern states seem lightly populated compared to the densely packed terrain of Western Europe or East Asia. This is a prime area for hunting, fishing and snowmobiling. The Allegheny National Forest sprawls across four counties and is a popular recreational area. Neatly preserved Ridgway holds the largest chainsaw carving event in the world.

For several years recently, production of natural gas deep underground in the Marcellus Shale formation generated extensive local spending and considerable optimism. But with the worldwide decline in oil and gas prices, production here decreased substantially in 2016, with only 19 rigs in operation. In the previous year, more than 2,200 oil and gas jobs were lost in Pennsylvania. Punxsutawney in Jefferson County is home of the legendary groundhog Phil, who predicts the arrival of spring every Feb. 2 by looking for his shadow on Gobbler's Knob. The 1993 movie *Groundhog Day* sparked a tourism boomlet in the small town, even though the movie was filmed in Woodstock, Illinois.

The economy of Centre County in the Nittany Valley has been more resilient thanks to Pennsylvania State University. Penn State's cutting-edge facilities have spawned a high-skills job market. In 2016, State College was rated the 10th best place in the nation to start a business. The university was long known for its powerful football teams coached by Joe Paterno. Scandal rocked the university in 2011 when former defensive coordinator Jerry Sandusky was charged with 40 counts of child molestation and related crimes. He was found guilty and sentenced to up to 60 years in prison. Once an iconic figure in these parts, Paterno was fired for "failure of leadership;" he died two and a half months later. Criminal charges were brought against three top university officials, including president Graham Spanier. In March 2017, a jury found Spanier guilty on one count of child endangerment. The two others pleaded guilty to child endangerment. All were misdemeanors. In 2015, the university reached a settlement with the National Collegiate Athletic Association in which sanctions were rescinded and a new "integrity agreement" took effect. Even through the scandal and the sanctions, football Saturdays remained a local religion with a huge economic impact in Happy Valley.

The 5th Congressional District of Pennsylvania, rural and sprawling, is the largest district in the state. At its opposite ends and more than 200 miles apart, Erie and Centre counties are the most populous and the least Republican. The district has rarely been politically competitive. The 62 percent of the vote for Donald Trump in 2016 exceeded the 52 percent for John McCain in the 2008 election.

SIXTH DISTRICT

Ryan Costello (R)

Elected 2014, 2nd term; b. Sep 07, 1976, Phoenixville; Ursinus College, Bach. Deg.; Villanova University School of Law (PA), J.D.; Presbyterian; Married (Christine Costello); 1 child.

Elected Office: E. Vincent Township Board of Supervisors, 2002-2007; Chester County recorder of deeds, 2008-2011; Chester County Board of Commissioner, 2011-2013.

Professional Career: Practicing attorney, 1980-2002.

DC Office: 326 CHOB 20515, 202-225-4315, Fax: 202-225-8440, costello.house.gov.

State Offices: West Chester, 610-696-2982; Wyomissing, 610-376-7630.

Committees: *Energy & Commerce*: Communications & Technology, Digital Commerce & Consumer Protection, Oversight & Investigations.

Group Ratings

	ADA	ACLU	AFL-CIO	LCV	ITI	COC	HAFA	ACU	CFG	FRC
2016	-	23%	-	39%	100%	100%	33%	20%	35%	67%
2015	10%	C	42%	14%	C	100%	C	38%	32%	67%

Almanac Ratings 2015

	Economy	Social	Foreign	Composite
Liberal	14%	32%	10%	19%
Conservative	86%	68%	90%	81%

Key Votes of the 114th Congress

1. Keystone Pipeline	Y	5. Puerto Rico Debt	Y	9. Offenses by Aliens	Y
2. Trade Deals	Y	6. Medical Marijuana	Y	10. Troops in Iraq	N
3. Export-Import Bank	Y	7. Sanctuary Cities	Y	11. Homeland Security $$	Y
4. Debt Ceiling Increase	Y	8. Armor-piercing Bullets	Y	12. Trade Adjustment aid	Y

Election Results

Election	Name (Party)	Vote (%)	Cand. Spent	Ind. Exp. Support	Ind. Exp. Oppose
2016 General	Ryan Costello (R)	207,469 (57%)	$1,987,833	$206,300	
	Mike Parrish (D)	155,000 (43%)	$368,561		
2016 Primary	Ryan Costello (R)	(100%)			

Prior winning percentages: 2014 (56%)

Republican Ryan Costello, elected in 2014, sealed the suburban Philadelphia battleground for the GOP in 2014 by keeping GOP control of the 6th District. Democrats have not held any of the five seats since the 2012 redistricting. The self-styled moderate has had two relatively comfortable wins against under-financed opponents. In 2017, he gained a prized seat on the Energy and Commerce Committee, which placed him at the center of the health care debate.

Costello, the son of two public school teachers, grew up in Chester County. He got his bachelor's from Ursinus College and his law degree from Villanova. He served on the East Vincent Township Board of Supervisors, where he was elected chairman, and then as recorder of deeds in Chester. He was elected to Chester's Board of Commissioners, the three-member governing body of the county, and was chosen internally as chairman. He touted a record of balancing budgets of more than $500 million, cutting spending, and improving the county's 911 emergency call system. After six-term GOP Rep. Jim Gerlach retired, Costello ran unopposed for the GOP nomination.

Democrats, who had eagerly eyed the seat, placed their challenger, Manan Trivedi, in the party's "Red to Blue" program in hopes of a pickup. A physician who served with the Marines in the Iraq War and was a campaign adviser for President Barack Obama, Trivedi had lost to Gerlach in 2010 and 2012. But they faced several obstacles, including that redistricting had made the district more conservative. Costello benefited from about $1 million in combined outside spending by the National Association of Realtors, the National Rifle Association and the U.S. Chamber of Commerce. Trivedi, by contrast, benefitted little from spending by groups on the left. He questioned Costello's ethics, accusing him of steering a lucrative health care contract for the county to the company of a campaign donor; the Costello camp denied the charge.

Costello cast Trivedi as a creature of Washington and its liberal Democrats. A National Republican Congressional Committee ad linked Trivedi to House Minority Leader Nancy Pelosi, saying he shared her support of "Obamacare on steroids." Costello won comfortably, 56%-44%. His victory was evenly split: 55 percent each in Chester and Montgomery, 57 percent in Berks, and 69 percent in smaller Lebanon.

In his first term, Costello placed a high priority on oversight of the VA. He followed up on continuing problems at the Philadelphia regional office and worked with Veteran' Affairs Committee Chairman Jeff Miller of Florida on legislation to require that any bad performance or misconduct by a VA employee remain in the employee's permanent file. The House passed the bill in May 2015 and again in January 2017, on the opening day of the new Congress. On the Transportation and Infrastructure Committee, he cited his work on the bipartisan passage of the Passenger Rail Reform and Investment Act, including its plan to upgrade three rail stations in southeast Pennsylvania. Also in 2015, he broke with most House Republicans by voting against the proposal to deport grown children of illegal immigrants who had lost protected status.

As a new member of Energy and Commerce in March 2017, he voted in favor of the House GOP measure to replace the Affordable Care Act as "the appropriate framework." When the bill was modified as the House prepared to vote later that month, he said that he would have voted against the legislation and that he sought additional changes.

The Democratic Congressional Campaign Committee placed Costello on its "one-term wonders" list of 15 GOP freshmen whom it targeted for the 2016 campaign. But the party's challenge again fell far short. Businessman Mike Parrish, the Democratic nominee, had served in the military and was a graduate of the Wharton School of Economics. He demanded that Costello disavow Republican presidential nominee Donald Trump. Costello distanced himself from Trump and criticized his lewd comments about groping women as "incredibly inappropriate for someone who wants to lead our country." He also questioned the business practices and personal finances of Parrish. Costello raised $2.5 million to $400,000 for Parrish, who received minimal party assistance. He won 57%-43%, including 54 percent of the vote in Chester County.

In 2017, the Democratic Congressional Campaign Committee placed Costello on its early target list for reelection and ran Twitter ads against him for his failure to attend town-hall meetings. For his part, Costello was named a vice-chairman of the Patriot Program of the National Republican Congressional Committee, which is designed to aid vulnerable incumbents.

Southeast Pennsylvania: Philadelphia Suburbs, Reading Area

Population		Race and Ethnicity		Income	
Total	719,763	White	84.1%	Median Income	$75,159 (52 out of 435)
Land area	860	Black	4.0%		
Pop/ sq mi	836.5	Latino	5.8%	Under $50,000	32.0%
Born in state	72.0%	Asian	4.4%	$50,000-$99,999	31.8%
Age Groups		Two races	1.6%	$100,000-$199,999	26.4%
Under 18	22.8%	Other	0.2%	$200,000 or more	9.9%
18-34	20.3%	**Education**		Poverty Rate	7.4%
35-64	41.6%	H.S grad or less	36.5%	**Health Insurance**	
Over 64	15.2%	Some college	21.7%	With health insurance coverage	93.9%
Work		College Degree, 4 yr	25.4%		
		Post grad	16.4%		
White Collar	44.8%			**Public Assistance**	
Sales and Service	38.4%	**Military**		Cash public assistance income	2.0%
Blue Collar	16.9%	Veteran	8.0%		
Government	5.2%	Active Duty	0.0%	Food stamp/SNAP benefits	6.0%

Voter Turnout			
2015 Total Citizens 18+	534,548	2016 House Turnout as % CVAP	67%
2016 House turnout	360,046	2014 House Turnout as % CVAP	40%

2012 Presidential Vote		
Mitt Romney	174,415	(51%)
Barack Obama	166,030	(48%)

2016 Presidential Vote		
Hillary Clinton	177,639	(48%)
Donald Trump	175,340	(47%)
Gary Johnson	11,003	(3%)

Cook Partisan Voting Index: R+2

The gentle hills of southeastern Pennsylvania, settled in the 18th century by Quaker townsmen, Welsh farmers, German peasants and members of pietistic sects who became known as the Pennsylvania Dutch, were America's first polyglot interior. Before and after independence, a diverse lot looking for tolerance in the area above Philadelphia and the Delaware River found a land that yielded riches, first in crops, then in ironworking. In Revolutionary times, the area was countryside, a long day's ride from the markets and docks of Philadelphia. Then, rail lines were built from Philadelphia: The Main Line of the Pennsylvania Railroad headed west to industrial Pittsburgh and the Midwest, and the Reading Railroad headed northwest through Berks County and the anthracite coalfields beyond. Factories were built in some of the towns, and many farms continued to thrive, but by the late 19th century, some of the land had become commuter territory. The area along the Main Line was affluent suburbia for the masses, or a large part of them.

Much of this area has a kinship with Philadelphia, but it also offers idyllic, rustic living. Chester is the wealthiest county in the state and has a disproportionate share of well-educated voters. Its median sales price for houses is the highest in the Philadelphia area, and its $86,000 median household income was among the highest in the nation.

The 6th Congressional District of Pennsylvania is an oddly shaped configuration that snakes through nearly two-thirds of Chester County, clips the northwest corner of Montgomery County, stretches through the center of Berks County but does not include the Democratic city of Reading, and takes the southeast corner of heavily Republican Lebanon County. Berwyn, Devon, Malvern and Paoli, sometimes referred to as the Upper Main Line, are all in the district. Chester is the population center, with nearly half the population, followed by Berks and Montgomery. The district had been the site of close House races, but the 2012 shifts made the 6th about five points more Republican. Like the other four artfully drawn Republican-held seats in the suburbs and exurbs of Philadelphia, redistricting changes left the district GOP-friendly but competitive under the right circumstances. Hillary Clinton won the district by less than one point in 2016, after Mitt Romney took it by three points in 2012. Chester was a major battleground in 2016. Clinton won the county, 53%-43%, a margin of more than 25,000 votes, after Mitt Romney took it by about 1,000 votes in 2012.

SEVENTH DISTRICT

Patrick Meehan (R)

Elected 2010, 4th term; b. Oct 20, 1955, Cheltenham Township; Bowdoin College (ME), B.A.; Temple University (PA), J.D.; Roman Catholic; Married (Carolyn Meehan); 3 children.

Elected Office: Delaware County District Attorney, 1996-2001.

Professional Career: Practicing attorney, 1986-1991, 2008-2010; Counsel, Sen. Arlen Specter, 1991-1994; Campaign aide, Sen. Rick Santorum, 1994; U.S. Attorney, 2001-2008.

DC Office: 2305 RHOB 20515, 202-225-2011, Fax: 202-226-0280, meehan.house.gov.

State Offices: Springfield, 610-690-7323.

Committees: *Ethics*. *Ways & Means*: Oversight, Tax Policy, Trade.

Group Ratings

	ADA	ACLU	AFL-CIO	LCV	ITI	COC	HAFA	ACU	CFG	FRC
2016	-	17%	-	29%	100%	100%	36%	32%	38%	67%
2015	0%	C	42%	14%	C	90%	C	46%	37%	83%

Almanac Ratings 2015

	Economy	Social	Foreign	Composite
Liberal	17%	17%	10%	15%
Conservative	83%	83%	90%	85%

Key Votes of the 114th Congress

1. Keystone Pipeline	Y	5. Puerto Rico Debt	N	9. Offenses by Aliens	Y
2. Trade Deals	Y	6. Medical Marijuana	N	10. Troops in Iraq	N
3. Export-Import Bank	Y	7. Sanctuary Cities	Y	11. Homeland Security $$	Y
4. Debt Ceiling Increase	Y	8. Armor-piercing Bullets	Y	12. Trade Adjustment aid	Y

Election Results

Election	Name (Party)	Vote (%)		Cand. Spent	Ind. Exp. Support	Ind. Exp. Oppose
2016 General	Patrick Meehan (R)	225,678	(60%)	$1,783,751	$447,637	
	Mary Ellen Balchunis (D)	153,824	(41%)	$189,693		
2016 Primary	Patrick Meehan (R)	84,638	(76%)			
	Stan Casacio (R)	26,384	(24%)			

Prior winning percentages: 2014 (62%), 2012 (59%), 2010 (55%)

Pat Meehan, elected in 2010, is a moderate Republican in the mold of the late Sen. Arlen Specter, his former boss. He has been an influential legislator, including at the Ways and Means Committee, where he has been a pragmatic problem-solver. In 2016, he refused to endorse Donald Trump for president. In February 2017, he decided not to challenge Democratic Sen. Robert Casey in 2018. The two facts may be related.

Meehan grew up in Cheltenham Township, in Montgomery County. His father was a construction worker, his mother a secretary. Meehan helped pay his tuition at Bowdoin College in Maine by working at a rubber factory, where he shoveled rubber pellets into an incinerator. He played hockey in college and for two years worked as a referee in the National Hockey League, a job that he says was good training for politics. He learned to stand behind controversial calls, to be fair in the public spotlight, and to know when to break up a fight and when to let the players slug it out, Meehan said. He has participated in the annual congressional hockey game between lawmakers and lobbyists.

Meehan graduated from Temple University law school, then went to work at the large law firm founded by Philadelphia Mayor Richardson Dilworth. He left the firm to become counsel to Specter, long before the independent senator switched parties to become a Democrat. In 1994, Meehan was the campaign manager for Republican Rick Santorum when he defeated Democratic Sen. Harris Wofford.

With his solid Republican credentials, Meehan was elected district attorney in Delaware County in 1995. That job gave him wide publicity for the successful prosecution of millionaire John DuPont in the murder of Olympic wrestler Dave Schultz. He created a special victims unit that allowed domestic violence cases to be prosecuted without victims having to testify in open court. In 2001, on Specter's recommendation, Meehan was appointed U.S. attorney in Philadelphia. He won corruption convictions against several high-profile local politicians, Republicans as well as Democrats, some resulting from wiretaps in the office of Philadelphia Mayor John Street.

When Democratic Rep. Joe Sestak challenged Specter for his Senate seat in 2010, Meehan ran for Sestak's House seat. Although the district was trending Democratic, Meehan had an edge as a familiar prosecutor with moderate positions on cultural issues. With his Philadelphia-area contacts, he raised $3 million, almost twice that raised by his Democratic opponent, Bryan Lentz, an Iraq war veteran and two-term state representative from Swarthmore. Both national parties spent lavishly on the contest. Meehan won 55%-44%, carrying all three counties that were then in the district.

Meehan has worked with Republican leadership, while also showing plenty of independence, especially on legal issues. He was one of 17 Republicans to oppose a House-passed amendment in 2012 barring the use of federal funds to defend legal challenges to a provision of the health care law. On the Homeland Security Committee, he chaired the panel on cybersecurity, a timely topic. He won House passage in 2012 of his bill to set guidelines for the Homeland Security Department's sharing of information with state and local law enforcement about threats involving chemical, biological and nuclear weapons. The House passed his bill to boost penalties for people trafficking in counterfeit drugs. In 2014, he worked on a bipartisan legislative package that was enacted to modernize and strengthen the nation's cyber defense.

Meehan has shown a wide range of interests at Ways and Means. He won committee approval of two bills that were subsequently enacted in 2015 and 2016 as part of comprehensive legislation: procedures for the Homeland Security Department to work with the Customs Bureau on overseas terrorism threats, and protection against prescription drug abuse for Medicare beneficiaries. He was among the first Republicans to support the campaign to place a woman on the nation's currency and break what Meehan called the "green ceiling." He organized activities to repeal the medical devices tax in the Affordable Care Act. He also got a seat on the Ethics Committee, which is a useful slot for a former prosecutor.

After redistricting, his Democratic opponent in 2012, Radnor Township Democratic Chair George Badey, highlighted Meehan's conservative votes, such as support of House Budget Committee Chairman Paul Ryan's budget. But Meehan was endorsed by the influential Philadelphia building and construction trades council and he coasted to a 59%-41% victory. In his next two campaigns, he was reelected with 62 percent and 59 percent against Mary Ellen Balchunis, a political science professor at LaSalle University who has taught courses about U.S. government. In this swing district, he showed little vulnerability. In 2016, he took 58 percent in Delaware County, 55 percent in Montgomery and 62 percent in Chester. Balchunis fell short on fundraising each time, failing to raise more than $200,000 while Meehan exceeded $2 million. National Democrats gave little support. In a 2016 primary with businessman Stanley Casacio, who campaigned on his "conservative values," Meehan won, 76%-24%.

Early in the presidential election, Meehan had a top fundraising position with New Jersey Gov. Chris Christie. The two had served together for several years as U.S. attorneys in neighboring offices. Even after Donald Trump became the GOP nominee, Meehan refused to endorse him. "I'm worried about Donald Trump's credibility," he told Chadds Ford Republicans in early October 2016. Later, he said that he planned to write-in Mike Pence on Election Day. Following the election, Meehan showed his independence of the new administration. President Trump's budget, he said in March 2017, "reflects a different set of priorities than the ones I've set." He was among the first congressional Republicans to urge Attorney General Jeff Sessions to recuse himself from the Justice Department investigation of connections between Russia and the Trump campaign. That independence likely would have been problematic for Meehan among Republicans if he had challenged Casey. The Democratic Congressional Campaign Committee listed Meehan with several other Republicans from Pennsylvania on its early list of 2018 targets.

Southern and Western Philadelphia Suburbs: Delaware County

Population		**Race and Ethnicity**		**Income**	
Total	716,023	White	85.4%	Median Income	$80,607 (33 out of 435)
Land area	863	Black	5.2%		
Pop/ sq mi	830.1	Latino	3.2%	Under $50,000	30.7%
Born in state	73.8%	Asian	4.5%	$50,000-$99,999	29.5%
		Two races	1.5%	$100,000-$199,999	28.6%
Age Groups		Other	0.2%	$200,000 or more	11.3%
Under 18	22.5%			Poverty Rate	5.8%
18-34	19.8%	**Education**			
35-64	41.3%	H.S grad or less	36.0%	**Health Insurance**	
Over 64	16.4%	Some college	22.5%	With health insurance coverage	92.9%
		College Degree, 4 yr	24.1%		
Work		Post grad	17.4%		
White Collar	45.5%			**Public Assistance**	
Sales and Service	38.1%	**Military**		Cash public assistance income	1.7%
Blue Collar	16.5%	Veteran	7.7%		
Government	5.7%	Active Duty	0.0%	Food stamp/SNAP benefits	4.8%

Voter Turnout			
2015 Total Citizens 18+	535,934	2016 House Turnout as % CVAP	71%
2016 House turnout	379,502	2014 House Turnout as % CVAP	44%

2012 Presidential Vote		
Mitt Romney	183,343	(50%)
Barack Obama	176,658	(49%)

2016 Presidential Vote		
Hillary Clinton	190,599	(49%)
Donald Trump	181,455	(47%)
Gary Johnson	9,771	(3%)

Cook Partisan Voting Index: R+1

A century ago, Delaware Country, southwest of Philadelphia, was already filling up, with industrial towns strung out along the rail lines paralleling the Delaware River and residential suburbs along the inland commuter rail lines. Politics in Delaware County in those days was run by a Republican machine headed by state Sen. John McClure. Such was his power that, in 1960, presidential candidate Richard Nixon stopped by the ailing McClure's home to pay homage. McClure exercised his influence through the War Board, a 15-member panel that decided on all nominations for public office. The board technically went out of business in 1975, but one of its products, Tom Judge, remained county Republican chairman till 2010.

The area is filled with colonial history. At the Brandywine Battlefield, George Washington and Gen. Henry Knox unsuccessfully tried to prevent British forces from taking Philadelphia during the Revolutionary War. Valley Forge is where Washington and his men spent the terrible winter and spring of 1777-78. Villanova University, the home of the NCAA basketball champions in 2016, is in Radnor. A driving economic force here is Boeing's plant in Ridley Park, with 4,800 employees, where the V-22 Osprey and H-47 helicopters have been assembled for decades. In recent decades, the area has undergone significant demographic and political change: Blacks have moved out of Philadelphia into adjacent Delaware County suburbs in large numbers, and cultural liberalism has led many affluent suburbs to vote Democratic. In the 1988 presidential race, Delaware County voted 60%-39% for Republican George H.W. Bush. But Hillary Clinton got 60 percent in the county in 2016, as did President Barack Obama in 2012.

The 7th Congressional District of Pennsylvania covers most of Delaware County, which is a bit more than half of the population of the district, though Democratic Swarthmore and the black neighborhoods are mostly in the 1st District. It takes in parts of Chester County, such as the refined farm country of Chadds Ford, home to generations of Wyeth artists. The district includes parts of Berks and Montgomery counties and extends to a few conservative precincts in Lancaster County. The unconventional shape of the 7th made it one of the most highlighted gerrymanders in post-2010 redistricting. *The Patriot-News* of Harrisburg called it "some sort of amorphous modern art drawing." *The Washington Post* described it as "Goofy Kicking Donald Duck." The *Philadelphia Daily News* complained that it was "a new poster child for why we must find a better way to do redistricting." The district has remained marginal territory. Hillary Clinton took the 2016 presidential vote, 49%-47%, after Mitt Romney won in 2012, 50%-49%.

EIGHTH DISTRICT

Brian Fitzpatrick (R)

Elected 2016, 1st term; b. Dec 17, 1973, Levittown; Pennsylvania State University, M.B.A.; LaSalle University, Bach. Deg., 1996; Penn State University Dickinson School of Law (PA), J.D., 2001; Roman Catholic; Single.

Professional Career: Judicial Clerk, Eastern District of PA, 2001-2002; Special Agent, FBI.

DC Office: 514 CHOB 20515, 202-225-4276, Fax: 202-225-9511, brianfitzpatrick.house.gov.

State Offices: Langhorne, 215-579-8102.

Committees: *Foreign Affairs*: Europe, Eurasia & Emerging Threats, Middle East & North Africa. *Homeland Security*: Cybersecurity & Infrastructure Protection, Transportation & Protective Security. *Small Business*: Economic Growth, Tax & Capital Access, Health & Technology.

Group Ratings

	ADA	ACLU	AFL-CIO	LCV	ITI	COC	HAFA	ACU	CFG	FRC
2016	-	17%	-	47%	0%	100%	67%	92%	84%	100%
2015	-	C	42%	23%	C	95%	C	C	C	-

Almanac Ratings 2015

	Economy	Social	Foreign	Composite
Liberal	16%	10%	11%	12%
Conservative	85%	90%	89%	88%

Key Votes of the 114th Congress

1. Keystone Pipeline	NV	5. Puerto Rico Debt	Y	9. Offenses by Aliens	Y
2. Trade Deals	Y	6. Medical Marijuana	N	10. Troops in Iraq	N
3. Export-Import Bank	N	7. Sanctuary Cities	Y	11. Homeland Security $$	Y
4. Debt Ceiling Increase	Y	8. Armor-piercing Bullets	Y	12. Trade Adjustment aid	Y

Election Results

Election	Name (Party)	Vote (%)		Cand. Spent	Ind. Exp. Support	Ind. Exp. Oppose
2016 General	Brian Fitzpatrick (R)	207,263	(54%)	$2,012,172	$529,847	$6,097,769
	Steve Santarsiero (D)	173,555	(46%)	$2,781,440	$2,366,081	$7,682,583
2016 Primary	Brian Fitzpatrick (R)	74,087	(78%)			
	Andy Warren (R)	11,817	(13%)			
	Marc Duome (R)	8,621	(9%)			

Republican Brian Fitzpatrick, elected in 2016, succeeded his brother, GOP Rep. Mike Fitzpatrick, who retired to keep his term-limits pledge. The latest Fitzpatrick is a political newcomer, but he has deep experience with law enforcement, where he pursued political corruption and global terrorism. His expertise in campaign-finance and election laws is unusual for a member of Congress.

Brian Fitzpatrick, who is 10 years younger than his brother Mike, was raised in Bucks County. He got his bachelor's degree from LaSalle University and his MBA and law degrees from Penn State University. He has been a licensed certified public accountant and an attorney. Fitzpatrick served as a special assistant U.S. attorney focused on drug crimes. He graduated first in his class at Quantico, the FBI academy, and served for 15 years as an FBI supervisory special agent. During the war in Iraq, Fitzpatrick was embedded with U.S. Special Forces. In his portfolio with the FBI, he was the national director for its Campaign Finance and Election Crimes Enforcement Program and was a national supervisor for its political corruption unit. In 2015, he was an inaugural recipient of the FBI Director's Leadership Award.

Mike Fitzpatrick retired after having served eight years between 2005 and 2017 (He lost reelection to Democrat Patrick Murphy in 2006 and then defeated Rep. Murphy four years later.) Although Brian Fitzpatrick was a newcomer as a political candidate and had not resided in the 8th District for many years, his last name and bio were obvious assets. When he entered the contest, the early front-runner state Rep. Scott Petri dropped out. The Republican primary became a low-key contest in which the candidates had few major differences and Fitzpatrick's two opponents raised less than $50,000 between them. Fitzpatrick, who raised $2.2 million for the cycle, had $450,000 for the primary. He won that contest with 78 percent of the vote. His eclectic platform included a balanced budget constitutional amendment, limits on carbon emissions, building a wall along the border with Mexico and opposition to international trade agreements.

His Democratic challenger, state Rep. Steven Santarsiero, survived a far more competitive primary against Shaughnessy Naughton, a businessman who narrowly lost the Democratic nomination in this district in 2014 and was backed by EMILY's List, which supports Democratic women who favor abortion rights. In the 2016 primary, each Democrat raised more than $1 million; Santarsiero won, 54%-46%.

In the general election, the two candidates signed a pledge to conduct a positive campaign. Santarsiero told *Politico* that Fitzpatrick had spent little time in the district for many years prior to their campaign and that, "It's clear that if his last name were not Fitzpatrick, he wouldn't be running." Local reporters said that Fitzpatrick was rarely available for interviews. His ads described him as "Levittown's own," and he emphasized his professional credentials and national security expertise. He did not endorse Donald Trump during the campaign and said that he could not vote for him. Following the early October 2016 release of the video in which Trump made lewd comments about women, Fitzpatrick said, "Donald Trump's comments and actions are offensive and disgusting and they cannot be rationalized or ignored, regardless of context." Santarsiero raised $2.8 million for the cycle. Each candidate benefited from more than $7 million in national party support. In a district where the presidential election was virtually even, Fitzpatrick had a comfortable 54%-46% win.

With seats on the Foreign Affairs and Homeland Security committees, in addition to Small Business, Fitzpatrick was positioned to pursue issues on which he had worked at the FBI. He quickly showed his independence. In January 2017, he was one of nine Republicans who voted against the plan to permit expedited House votes on health care reform. He said that Trump's initial executive order to limit entry by refugees to the United States "entirely misses the mark." He added, "While serious actions are needed to protect our country, these must not be done in a way that singles out any specific nations or ethnicities." In March, the House unanimously passed his bill to streamline the acquisition process of the Homeland Security Department. House Democrats listed Fitzpatrick as an early target for 2018.

Northern Philadelphia Suburbs: Bucks County

Population		**Race and Ethnicity**		**Income**	
Total	708,560	White	85.4%	Median Income	$77,839 (44 out of 435)
Land area	707	Black	3.7%		
Pop/ sq mi	1002.3	Latino	4.6%	Under $50,000	31.2%
Born in state	68.3%	Asian	4.6%	$50,000-$99,999	30.8%
		Two races	1.4%	$100,000-$199,999	28.4%
Age Groups		Other	0.3%	$200,000 or more	9.7%
Under 18	21.8%			Poverty Rate	5.8%
18-34	18.7%	**Education**			
35-64	43.4%	H.S grad or less	37.4%	**Health Insurance**	
Over 64	16.0%	Some college	25.3%	With health insurance coverage	94.1%
		College Degree, 4 yr	22.8%		
Work		Post grad	14.6%		
White Collar	42.1%			**Public Assistance**	
Sales and Service	39.6%	**Military**		Cash public assistance income	2.0%
Blue Collar	18.4%	Veteran	7.8%		
Government	5.3%	Active Duty	0.1%	Food stamp/SNAP benefits	5.3%

Voter Turnout			
2015 Total Citizens 18+	534,009	2016 House Turnout as % CVAP	71%
2016 House turnout	381,024	2014 House Turnout as % CVAP	42%

2012 Presidential Vote		
Mitt Romney	178,195	(49%)
Barack Obama	177,940	(49%)

2016 Presidential Vote		
Hillary Clinton	185,685	(48%)
Donald Trump	186,607	(48%)
Gary Johnson	9,895	(3%)

Cook Partisan Voting Index: R+2

Bucks County was one of Pennsylvania founding father William Penn's three original settlements and the launching point for George Washington's crossing of the frigid Delaware River to surprise English and Hessian forces on Christmas Day 1776. But it has had a split personality from the start. Upper Bucks County was at once a bucolic paradise of rolling hills and creeks and, after Penn's secretary, James Logan, built the Durham Furnace iron works in 1727, it became one of the nation's major industrial sites. In the 1920s, Bucks County's well-settled farmland, old fieldstone houses and covered bridges captured the imagination of writers and artists, attracting the New York theatrical crowd - Oscar Hammerstein, Moss Hart, Dorothy Parker and S. J. Perelman. Doylestown, the county seat, has beautiful old homes and several impressive museums. New Hope remains a popular weekend spot, with its hip boutiques and restaurants.

After World War II, its location between Philadelphia and Trenton, New Jersey, brought industrial Lower Bucks County to the forefront. The ocean-navigable Delaware River and several rail lines resulted in huge new developments: U.S. Steel's Fairless Works, one of the few big postwar steel plants, and the Levitt organization's second Levittown in what had been a swamp between U.S. 13 and U.S. 1. The steel mill closed in 1991. A wind turbine plant moved onto part of the site. This development came later than in other suburban Philadelphia counties, where most blue-collar immigration settled decades earlier. Fairless Works and Levittown, with their tightly packed homes filled with blue-collar workers, became Democratic. Upper Bucks, attracting trendy New Yorkers, has increasingly favored Democratic policies such as green space programs to keep developers away. Tourism and conventions are big business in Bucks. Once heavily Republican, Bucks County has become politically marginal.

The 8th Congressional District of Pennsylvania includes all of Bucks County. Its small part of northeast Montgomery County is slightly more than 10 percent of the district. Bucks has a notably small minority population of 4 percent black and 5 percent Hispanic and the third-highest income of any county in the state. Compared with surrounding districts, the 8th is relatively compact. The district has hosted some of the most hotly contested House races in the country, and it remains competitive. In both the 2012 and 2016 presidential elections, the district was a battleground and the outcome was virtually even. Mitt Romney and Donald Trump each won by less than 1,000 votes.

NINTH DISTRICT

Bill Shuster (R)

Elected 2001, 9th term; b. Jan 10, 1961, McKeesport; American University (DC), M.A.; Dickinson College (PA), B.A.; Lutheran; Divorced; 2 children.

Professional Career: Manager, Goodyear Tire & Rubber Co., 1983-1987; District Manager, Bandag Inc., 1987-1990; Owner & General Manager, Shuster Chrysler, 1990-2001.

DC Office: 2079 RHOB 20515, 202-225-2431, Fax: 202-225-2486, shuster.house.gov.

State Offices: Chambersburg, 717-264-8308; Hollidaysburg, 814-696-6318; Indiana, 724-463-0516.

Committees: *Armed Services*: Emerging Threats & Capabilities. *Transportation & Infrastructure (Chmn)*: Aviation, Coast Guard & Maritime Transportation, Economic Dev't, Public Buildings & Emergency Management, Highways & Transit, Railroads, Pipelines & Hazardous Materials, Water Resources & Environment.

Group Ratings

	ADA	ACLU	AFL-CIO	LCV	ITI	COC	HAFA	ACU	CFG	FRC
2016	-	5%	-	3%	100%	100%	53%	72%	58%	100%
2015	0%	C	33%	3%	C	90%	C	58%	48%	100%

Almanac Ratings 2015

	Economy	Social	Foreign	Composite
Liberal	5%	0%	4%	3%
Conservative	95%	100%	96%	97%

Key Votes of the 114th Congress

1. Keystone Pipeline	Y	5. Puerto Rico Debt	N	9. Offenses by Aliens	Y
2. Trade Deals	Y	6. Medical Marijuana	N	10. Troops in Iraq	N
3. Export-Import Bank	N	7. Sanctuary Cities	Y	11. Homeland Security $$	N
4. Debt Ceiling Increase	Y	8. Armor-piercing Bullets	Y	12. Trade Adjustment aid	Y

Election Results

Election	Name (Party)	Vote (%)		Cand. Spent	Ind. Exp. Support	Ind. Exp. Oppose
2016 General	Bill Shuster (R)	186,580	(63%)	$3,728,348	$326,883	
	Art Halvorson (D)	107,985	(37%)	$239,651		$226,268
2016 Primary	Bill Shuster (R)	49,393	(51%)			
	Art Halvorson (R)	48,166	(49%)			

Prior winning percentages: 2014 (64%), 2012 (62%), 2010 (73%), 2008 (64%), 2006 (60%), 2004 (69%), 2002 (71%), 2001 special (52%)

Republican Bill Shuster won a May 2001 special election to succeed his father, Bud Shuster, the powerful chairman of the Transportation and Infrastructure Committee in the 1990s. With the support of GOP leaders, the younger Shuster has chaired the same panel, becoming an important figure on transportation issues in his own right. In 2016, he survived an unusual reelection challenge. Critics said that he was too close to lobbyists.

Bill Shuster grew up in the Pittsburgh area, where his father started a successful business. After getting a bachelor's degree from Dickinson College and a master's in business administration from American University, he took over the family's car dealership, Shuster Chrysler in East Freedom, near Altoona. He sold the business in 2002.

Bud Shuster resigned from the House in January 2001, unhappy that Republican leaders refused him an exemption from term limits on committee chairmen. The contest for the House seat was decided for all practical purposes at a district-wide Republican convention. Facing nine other contenders, Bill Shuster, with back-room help from his father, ran an insider campaign that took advantage of his father's name and years of service. Despite local grumbling about a Shuster dynasty, opponents failed to coalesce behind a candidate. Shuster won 69 of the 133 votes, two more than the required majority. Although national Democrats ignored the race in the heavily Republican district, their nominee H. Scott Conklin campaigned vigorously as an opponent of abortion rights and gun control. Shuster won by a closer than expected 52%-44%.

Shuster has a solidly conservative voting record. His *Almanac* voting record in 2015 was the most conservative in the Pennsylvania delegation. In his father's tradition, Shuster was an avid practitioner of earmarked spending for his district, a practice that budget conservatives have attacked as wasteful. He reluctantly went along when Republican Leader John Boehner pushed to ban the practice. Democrats lampooned Shuster in 2009 for taking credit for $9 million sent to his district from President Barack Obama's economic stimulus bill, even though he had voted against the legislation.

As chairman of the Railroads, Pipelines, and Hazardous Materials Subcommittee in 2011, Shuster favored high-speed rail, but only in the busy Northeast corridor, and said that it should be privatized - an idea many Democrats consider unworkable. He sponsored a measure that became law cracking down on unauthorized intercity bus operators. He added an amendment to an aviation bill in 2011 requiring the Federal Aviation Administration to give more weight to economic factors before adopting safety rules. Safety groups sharply criticized the proposal, but it narrowly passed.

Taking the helm of Transportation and Infrastructure in 2013, he vowed to cut through the polarization on the committee. Shuster told the *Pittsburgh Tribune-Review* that he would consider abandoning the Republican no-new-taxes pledge to fund transportation projects. Though he initially said he was open to a vehicle-miles-traveled fee, he abandoned that idea in late 2014 along with an increase in the federal gasoline tax, citing public and political opposition, not least among House Republicans. Shuster has been more approachable and pragmatic than his father, who ran the committee with an iron fist. Part of that is by necessity: Unlike his father, he can no longer use earmarks on transportation authorization bills to help smooth deal-making. He also has an altered budget environment in which to work, partly due to a slowing in the growth of revenues from the gasoline tax.

Shuster has been a busy chairman. After three years of effort, he enacted in December 2015 a five-year extension of the highway program. The Fixing America's Surface Transportation (FAST) Act, which cleared Congress with broad bipartisan support, was the first long-term transportation bill that Congress has passed in a decade. Shuster highlighted the increased focus on freight transportation, bridge repair and the doubling of highway spending for Pennsylvania: $8.7 billion in five years. Earlier, Shuster had resorted to passage of a series of short-term extensions. Conservative groups voiced opposition to their budget gimmicks and even supporters said they were little more than Band-Aids. Shuster hit it off with Obama's Transportation secretary, Anthony Foxx, and they worked to get a longer-term bill into law before the start of the 2016 presidential campaign. The two even held a joint "Twitter Town Hall" discussion in February 2015 to try to drum up support. Even with their collaboration, the continuing deadlock over money had forced Congress to pass two additional short-term extensions in 2015.

In December 2016, Shuster helped to complete bipartisan enactment of new water resources projects, which he described as job-creating measures that also addressed the needs of America's harbors, locks, dams, flood protection and other water resources infrastructure. "Ensuring America's water infrastructure is brought into the 21st century will grow the economy, strengthen our competitiveness, and create jobs," he said. In 2017, the support by President Donald Trump for as much as $1 trillion in additional infrastructure projects opened the door for Shuster to play a leading role on a chief administration initiative. Shuster emphasized that some of the projects would be privately financed.

At home, Shuster has faced strong primary challenges. In 2004, Michael DelGrosso, a management consultant whose family owns a Blair County tomato sauce company, said that the district needed a new economic approach. DelGrosso carried Blair County and three nearby counties in the northern part of the district. Shuster ran strongly elsewhere and squeezed by with a 51%-49% win. A decade later, Art Halvorson, a retired Coast Guard official with tea party ties, attacked Shuster as a loyal lieutenant of Speaker Boehner and said the district needed to be represented by someone not named Shuster for a change. Shuster spent more than $700,000 on TV ads and took 11 of the 12 counties as he won the primary, 53%-35%.

In 2016, Halvorson ran again - twice, actually. Shuster had been damaged by a news story in 2015 when *Politico* reported that he was dating an influential lobbyist who works for Airlines for America, a large trade association with extensive interest in legislation before his committee. Shuster, who was divorced in 2014, acknowledged that he had a private and personal relationship with the lobbyist, Shelley Rubino, but that she "doesn't lobby my office, including myself and my staff." Halvorson said that the relationship showed "collusion" with special interests and said that the relationship could be "criminal." Shuster had a big financial advantage. During the cycle, he raised $4.1 million to $300,000 for Halvorson, and had more than $400,000 in support from outside groups. Shuster barely won, with 50.6% in the GOP primary, a margin of 1,227 votes. Halvorson won five of the 12 counties, chiefly in the eastern part of the district, including Shuster's home territory in Altoona-based Blair County. When no Democrat filed in the primary, Halvorson became the nominee with write-in votes. But he failed to attract much organizational support and his campaign effort was relatively modest. In November, Shuster had an easier time. He won, 63%-37%, and took 11 counties - all except for Westmoreland, which cast less than 2 percent of the vote.

Southwest Pennsylvania: Pittsburgh Exurbs, Altoona

Population		**Race and Ethnicity**		**Income**	
Total	701,011	White	93.1%	Median Income	$45,632 (332 out of 435)
Land area	5,730	Black	2.7%		
Pop/ sq mi	122.3	Latino	2.0%		
Born in state	80.7%	Asian	0.6%	Under $50,000	54.0%
Age Groups		Two races	1.4%	$50,000-$99,999	31.7%
Under 18	20.6%	Other	0.1%	$100,000-$199,999	12.5%
18-34	20.6%	**Education**		$200,000 or more	1.7%
35-64	40.3%	H.S grad or less	59.6%	Poverty Rate	15.3%
Over 64	18.5%	Some college	22.9%	**Health Insurance**	
Work		College Degree, 4 yr	11.3%	With health insurance coverage	90.1%
White Collar	28.8%	Post grad	6.2%		
Sales and Service	41.9%	**Military**		**Public Assistance**	
Blue Collar	29.3%	Veteran	10.5%	Cash public assistance income	3.4%
Government	5.6%	Active Duty	0.0%		
				Food stamp/SNAP benefits	14.8%

Voter Turnout			
2015 Total Citizens 18+	551,480	2016 House Turnout as % CVAP	53%
2016 House turnout	294,565	2014 House Turnout as % CVAP	31%

2012 Presidential Vote		
Mitt Romney	176,451	(63%)
Barack Obama	100,765	(36%)

2016 Presidential Vote		
Donald Trump	213,382	(69%)
Hillary Clinton	83,263	(27%)
Gary Johnson	6,282	(2%)

Cook Partisan Voting Index: R+19

The old towns of the southern tier of Pennsylvania look much as they did a century ago: farmhouses and red barns set amidst rolling hills in the shadow of mountain ridges, seemingly isolated from the pulsing rhythms of modern America. During the 18th century, the Appalachian Mountains provided Quaker Pennsylvania with a rampart against Indian attacks, and allowed the commonwealth to become the richest and most populous of the colonies. But the mountains also became a barrier to commerce for later pioneers, and it took the aggressive capitalists who built the Pennsylvania Railroad to get trains over the ridges. Though Pennsylvania's rail links remained important, a war-bound nation in 1940 opened the road of the future here: the Pennsylvania Turnpike, the first highway in America that was able to move vehicles dependably at high speeds over long distances.

The region made history again much later, although without the happy ending: On Sept. 11, 2001, United Airlines Flight 93 crashed into an empty former coalfield near Shanksville in Somerset County, killing all 40 passengers and crew on board. To Americans, the crash site became a symbol of both sadness and pride at the passengers' effort to wrest back control of the plane and possibly thwart a greater disaster, initiated by the now-famous cry of "Let's roll!" The National Park Service opened a memorial to Flight 93.

The 9th Congressional District takes in a wide swath of southern Pennsylvania, extending almost to the northern panhandle of West Virginia, including six full counties and parts of six others. Most of the 9th is not coal country and was thus spared the boom-bust cycles of northeastern Pennsylvania. But this is still a slow-growth, low-income area today. Blair County includes the city of Altoona, which continues to wither, from 82,000 people in 1930 to 45,300 in 2015. The largest and fastest-growing full county in the district is Franklin, where several international manufacturers have built local plants; its population jumped 19 percent from 2000 to 2015. Pennsylvania Turnpike managers have been reviewing options to build new tunnels to replace two existing 6,070-foot tunnels through the mountains in Somerset County, with an estimated cost as high as $694 million. The original tunnels, opened in the late 1930s and in 1965, were described as deteriorating and lacking adequate capacity. The turnpike was built for an initial cost of $61 million. Also under review have been plans for a bypass that would reduce the traffic nightmare at the Breezewood exit on the turnpike, an idea vehemently opposed by Breezewood business owners.

Politically, this part of Pennsylvania has been solidly Republican since 1860, and has not come close to electing a Democrat to Congress for decades. This is still the strongest GOP district in the state. Donald Trump in 2016 increased the Republican presidential vote to an impressive 69 percent, from the 63 percent that Mitt Romney took in 2012.

TENTH DISTRICT

Tom Marino (R)

Elected 2010, 4th term; b. Aug 15, 1952, Williamsport; Lycoming College (PA), B.A.; Dickinson School of Law (PA), J.D.; Williamsport Area Community College (PA), A.A.; Roman Catholic; Married (Edie Marino); 2 adopted children.

Elected Office: Lycoming County District Attorney, 1992-2002.

Professional Career: U.S. Attorney, 2002-2007; Practicing attorney, 2007-2010.

DC Office: 2242 RHOB 20515, 202-225-3731, Fax: 202-225-9594, marino.house.gov.

State Offices: Lake Ariel, 570-689-6024; Selinsgrove, 570-374-9469; Williamsport, 570-322-3961.

Committees: *Foreign Affairs*: Asia & the Pacific, Europe, Eurasia & Emerging Threats. *Homeland Security*: Emergency Preparedness, Response & Communications, Oversight & Management Efficiency. *Judiciary*: Courts, Intellectual Property & Internet, Regulatory Reform, Commercial & Antitrust Law (Chmn).

Group Ratings

	ADA	ACLU	AFL-CIO	LCV	ITI	COC	HAFA	ACU	CFG	FRC
2016	-	5%	-	5%	100%	92%	61%	86%	73%	100%
2015	0%	C	25%	3%	C	85%	C	63%	56%	100%

Almanac Ratings 2015

	Economy	Social	Foreign	Composite
Liberal	7%	0%	4%	4%
Conservative	93%	100%	96%	96%

Key Votes of the 114th Congress

1. Keystone Pipeline	Y	5. Puerto Rico Debt	N	9. Offenses by Aliens	Y
2. Trade Deals	Y	6. Medical Marijuana	N	10. Troops in Iraq	N
3. Export-Import Bank	Y	7. Sanctuary Cities	Y	11. Homeland Security $$	N
4. Debt Ceiling Increase	N	8. Armor-piercing Bullets	Y	12. Trade Adjustment aid	Y

Election Results

Election	Name (Party)	Vote (%)		Cand. Spent	Ind. Exp. Support	Ind. Exp. Oppose
2016 General	Tom Marino (R)...........................	211,282	(70%)	$819,065		
	Mike Molesevich (D)...............	89,823	(30%)	$65,120		
2016 Primary	Tom Marino (R)...........................		(100%)			

Prior winning percentages: 2014 (63%), 2012 (66%), 2010 (55%)

Republican Tom Marino, elected in 2010, is a former prosecutor who cultivates an image at home as an aggressive guardian of taxpayer interests. "There are few as tough as Tom Marino," a 2012 campaign ad boasted. He has kept a low profile as he dealt with law enforcement and regulatory issues and largely avoided intramural scuffles. In 2016, he gained prominence as an early and outspoken supporter of Donald Trump.

Marino was born and raised in Williamsport. His father was a janitor and a firefighter, and his mother was a homemaker. After high school, Marino worked in manufacturing and managed a bakery for several years before enrolling at Williamsport Area Community College at age 30 and then graduating from Lycoming College. He earned a law degree at Penn State University. In 1992 he was elected district attorney for Lycoming County. After holding that post for a decade, he was selected as U.S. attorney for Pennsylvania's Middle District, which includes Scranton and Harrisburg.

As a federal prosecutor, he was involved in a case that became an issue in his 2010 campaign. Marino had served as a reference for Louis DeNaples on an application for a gambling license for the Mount Airy Casino Resort while his office was investigating DeNaples on another matter. After Marino resigned as U.S. attorney in 2007, he became an in-house counsel for DeNaples on some of his non-casino businesses. When his role in the application surfaced during the campaign, Marino said that he had received authorization from the Justice Department. Two-term Democratic Rep. Chris Carney raised questions about Marino's character and trustworthiness in what became a bitterly negative campaign. Two factors bolstered Marino: Carney's support for the 2010 health care overhaul was unpopular in this conservative stronghold, and $1.7 million in late spending by national Republican and business groups had an impact in the low-cost advertising market. In a big Republican year, Marino won, 55%-45%.

Marino has been mostly conservative, although he has voted against like-minded Republicans on their efforts to cut some federal programs that support his district, including subsidies to rural airports. As chairman of the Judiciary Subcommittee on Regulatory Reform, Commercial and Antitrust Law, he has sought to reduce the adverse economic impact of federal regulations. His signature legislation has been his Responsibly and Professionally Invigorating Development (RAPID) Act, which requires federal agencies to act promptly on proposals for infrastructure or energy construction. In September 2015, the House passed the bill, 233-170. In May 2016, the House passed his bill to expand the scope of activities that can be subject to prosecution for drug trafficking. The measure was enacted as part of broader legislation.

Marino has pushed proposals that would change congressional operations. With Democratic Rep. Scott Peters of California, he called for changes in House rules to require that any House bill may be considered after 60 days. He has filed a constitutional amendment to limit lawmakers to 12 years in the House and 12 years in the Senate, and has seen grounds for optimism with voters' hostility to incumbency.

In his solidly Republican district, against weak opposition, Marino has increased his victory margin with each reelection and he has become entrenched. In 2016, Democrat Mike Molesevich, a former mayor of Lewisburg, became the nominee as a write-in candidate after he learned that Marino was supporting Trump for president. He promised "moderation and cooperation." Marino won 70%-30% and took each county except for Monroe, which Molesevich won by less than one percentage point.

In February 2016, Marino became the fourth House Republican to endorse Trump. That made him part of a small group of members, led by Rep. Chris Collins of New York, who sought to expand their ranks and educate other colleagues about Trump. He also became an informal campaign adviser to Trump and his top aides and served as a surrogate at the Republican convention and elsewhere. According to the Allentown *Morning Call*, Marino and Lou Barletta from the neighboring 11th District were referred to by the Trump campaign team as "Thunder" and "Lightning." Marino was rewarded with membership on the executive committee for Trump's presidential transition, which advised on selection of officials for the new administration.

In April 2017, there were multiple press reports that Trump had decided to nominate Marino as head of the White House Office of National Drug Control Policy. A month later, several news organizations reported that Marino was no longer be considered. There was very little explanation, pro or con.

Northeast Pennsylvania

Population		**Race and Ethnicity**		**Income**	
Total	704,169	White	90.5%	Median Income	$50,354 (252 out of 435)
Land area	8,378	Black	3.3%		
Pop/ sq mi	84.0	Latino	3.9%		
Born in state	69.3%	Asian	0.8%	Under $50,000	49.7%
		Two races	1.1%	$50,000-$99,999	33.3%
Age Groups		Other	0.3%	$100,000-$199,999	14.5%
Under 18	20.6%			$200,000 or more	2.6%
18-34	20.1%	**Education**		Poverty Rate	12.9%
35-64	41.3%	H.S grad or less	54.8%		
Over 64	18.0%	Some college	24.9%	**Health Insurance**	
Work		College Degree, 4 yr	12.8%	With health insurance coverage	89.6%
		Post grad	7.6%		
White Collar	30.3%				
Sales and Service	40.9%	**Military**		**Public Assistance**	
Blue Collar	28.8%	Veteran	10.3%	Cash public assistance income	2.6%
Government	7.0%	Active Duty	0.0%		
				Food stamp/SNAP benefits	11.2%

Voter Turnout			
2015 Total Citizens 18+	550,475	2016 House Turnout as % CVAP	55%
2016 House turnout	301,105	2014 House Turnout as % CVAP	33%

2012 Presidential Vote		
Mitt Romney	170,273	(60%)
Barack Obama	109,011	(39%)

2016 Presidential Vote		
Donald Trump	204,204	(66%)
Hillary Clinton	93,279	(30%)
Gary Johnson	7,794	(3%)

Cook Partisan Voting Index: R+16

The northeast corner of Pennsylvania is a land of crevassed valleys and rugged mountains, crisscrossed by giant viaducts built for the railroads linking the East Coast with the Great Lakes and the mines that produced the region's anthracite coal. Except for a row of anthracite coal cities from Scranton to Wilkes-Barre, this part of Pennsylvania still has a throwback look to it. The region has numerous long-established small towns, with solidly built courthouses and banks and elderly citizens. It's a part of the Northeast that seems worlds away from the region's huge central cities and growing suburbs. Notable towns include Williamsport, home of the Little League World Series, and Lewisburg, home of Bucknell University. Only at the eastern edge has there been significant growth. Pike County on the Delaware River was the state's second-fastest growing county from 2000 to 2010, increasing in population by 24 percent, with many of its new residents fleeing higher taxes in New Jersey and New York. In Pike, Milford is the home of Gifford Pinchot, who served two terms as governor and became a founder of the conservation movement and the first chief of the Forest Service under President Theodore Roosevelt. The Pocono Mountains are a destination for weekend skiers and, for a few days each November, for bear hunters.

The rural area recently has benefited from some major projects. In May 2016, work began on the Central Susquehanna Valley Thruway project, including a $156 million bridge across the Susquehanna River between rural Snyder and Northumberland Counties. The project was scheduled for completion in 2024. In December, work was completed near Williamsport on the $1 billion Marcellus Shale-gas power plant, which was designed to power up to 1 million homes. Between November 2016 and March 2017, 50 permits were issued for drilling of natural-gas wells in Lycoming, Sullivan and Tioga counties.

The 10th Congressional District of Pennsylvania includes the less-populated areas of northeast Pennsylvania. (Democratic-leaning Scranton in the neighboring 17th District is surrounded by the 10th.) The area's most consequential member of Congress was probably David Wilmot, a founding member of the Republican Party who in the 1840s introduced the Wilmot Proviso barring slavery from the New Mexico and California territories acquired in the Mexican War, raising the issue that led proximately to the Civil War. Most people in this part of Pennsylvania have been Republicans ever since. It dips deep into central Pennsylvania west of Harrisburg in the conservative rural counties of Juniata and Mifflin. Williamsport-based Lycoming County is the population center of the 15 counties. Overall, this is the second-most Republican district in the state, with 66 percent of the vote for Donald Trump in 2016.

ELEVENTH DISTRICT

Lou Barletta (R)

Elected 2010, 4th term; b. Jan 28, 1956, Hazelton; Luzerne County Community College (PA); Bloomsburg State College (PA); Catholic; Married (Mary Grace Malloy Barletta); 4 children; 3 grandchildren.

Elected Office: Hazleton City Council, 1998-2000; Hazleton Mayor, 2000-2010.

Professional Career: Co-owner, Interstate Road Marketing, 1984-2000.

DC Office: 2049 RHOB 20515, 202-225-6511, Fax: 202-226-6250, barletta.house.gov.

State Offices: Carlisle, 717-249-0190; Harrisburg, 717-525-7002; Hazleton, 570-751-0050; Sunbury, 570-988-7801.

Committees: *Education & the Workforce*: Health, Employment, Labor & Pensions, Higher Education & Workforce Development. *Homeland Security*: Border & Maritime Security, Counterterrorism & Intelligence. *Transportation & Infrastructure*: Economic Dev't, Public Buildings & Emergency Management (Chmn), Highways & Transit, Railroads, Pipelines & Hazardous Materials.

Group Ratings

	ADA	ACLU	AFL-CIO	LCV	ITI	COC	HAFA	ACU	CFG	FRC
2016	-	5%	-	3%	100%	100%	50%	72%	59%	83%
2015	0%	C	33%	3%	C	90%	C	57%	51%	91%

Almanac Ratings 2015

	Economy	Social	Foreign	Composite
Liberal	13%	4%	9%	8%
Conservative	87%	97%	92%	92%

Key Votes of the 114th Congress

1. Keystone Pipeline	Y	5. Puerto Rico Debt	NV	9. Offenses by Aliens	Y
2. Trade Deals	Y	6. Medical Marijuana	N	10. Troops in Iraq	N
3. Export-Import Bank	Y	7. Sanctuary Cities	Y	11. Homeland Security $$	N
4. Debt Ceiling Increase	N	8. Armor-piercing Bullets	Y	12. Trade Adjustment aid	Y

Election Results

Election	Name (Party)	Vote (%)		Cand. Spent	Ind. Exp. Support	Ind. Exp. Oppose
2016 General	Lou Barletta (R)	199,421	(64%)	$859,398		
	Michael Marsicano (D)	113,800	(36%)	$122,207		
2016 Primary	Lou Barletta (R)		(100%)			

Prior winning percentages: 2014 (66%), 2012 (59%), 2010 (55%)

Republican Lou Barletta was elected in 2010 in his third challenge to 13-term Democrat Paul Kanjorski. Although he has remained a vociferous critic of illegal immigration, he has worked on bipartisan measures on other issues and much of his overall voting record has been in the center of House Republicans. Barletta has been a key congressional ally of Donald Trump.

Barletta hails from Hazleton, where he was mayor for a decade. As a youth, he worked with his parents and three brothers in his family's businesses: A. Barletta and Sons Road Construction and Barletta Heating Oil. He attended Bloomsburg University, but he left early to follow a dream of becoming a professional baseball player. After an unsuccessful tryout with the Cincinnati Reds - "I couldn't hit a curve ball," he told *The Patriot-News* of Harrisburg - he returned to Hazleton, where he opened a pavement-marking business. In 1998, Barletta was elected to the Hazleton City Council, and two years later became mayor. He inherited a budget shortfall and helped return the city to financial health. In 2006, he signed a law allowing the city to deny business permits to employers who hired illegal immigrants and to fine landlords who rented to them. A federal judge struck down the law.

Barletta first challenged Kanjorski in 2002. He lost, 56%-42%, but he maintained ties to national Republicans. In 2004, President George W. Bush appointed him to the United Nations Advisory Committee on Local Authorities. Two years later, the Republican National Committee tapped Barletta for outreach to Catholics. He lost to Kanjorski again in 2008 but narrowed the outcome to 52%-48%. In 2010, he campaigned with ads that characterized Kanjorski as a "couch potato" and asserted, "Paul Kanjorski has just been around too long." The Kanjorski campaign appealed to the district's many senior citizens with ads accusing Barletta of supporting the privatization of Social Security, even though he opposed private Social Security accounts. Kanjorski's ads warned that Barletta's message to seniors was: "Get out of the way because your time may have passed." Kanjorski outspent Barletta, $2.1 million to $1.3 million. Both national parties and their allies spent heavily on the contest. The Republican tide of 2010 gave Barletta enough lift to win, 55%-45%.

Barletta has been a consensus-builder who backs his party on big votes, as do most Pennsylvania Republicans. On immigration, however, he retained a hard line. When others in the GOP saw the 2012 presidential election results as a sign that they needed to reach out to Latino voters, Barletta was having none of it. After a bipartisan Senate group came out in 2013 with a comprehensive immigration plan, he scoffed that it was "amnesty that America can't afford." He told *The Morning Call* of Allentown that courting Hispanics is a waste of time for his party. "The Republican Party is not going to compete over who can give more social programs out," he said. "They will become Democrats because of the social programs they'll depend on." Barletta was equally dismissive of Democratic gun control efforts following the Newtown, Connecticut, elementary school massacre in 2012. "Would banning spoons stop obesity?" he asked on ABC News' *This Week*.

On the Transportation and Infrastructure Committee, Barletta chairs the Economic Development, Public Buildings and Emergency Managements Subcommittee, which oversees all federal buildings and the Federal Emergency Management Agency. Based on the experience of his district with hurricanes and other natural disasters, he has sought to improve disaster relief. In February 2016, the House passed his bipartisan bill to modernize FEMA operations. His proposal was enacted in broader legislation that year. He also won enactment of integrated public alert and warning systems to respond to national disasters. In May 2016, he won House passage of legislation to reduce rental costs and reform management of federal office space, which he said would save billions of dollars annually.

Barletta has worked on issues outside of his committee jurisdiction. He voted to give President Barack Obama trade promotion authority to expedite international trade deals, but only after he won provisions to protect Americans from foreign guest workers and prevent illegal dumping of cheaper foreign products, including steel. He was a leading opponent of Obama's nuclear-fuels agreement with Iran, and enacted his measure to require congressional votes on the deal. He continued strong objections to illegal immigration, including his legislation that would protect legal workers from the competition of such immigrants and stop funding local governments that support sanctuary cities.

These views made Barletta a natural ally of the presidential campaign of Donald Trump. They first met in 2015 when Barletta's subcommittee favorably reviewed Trump's attempt to open a hotel in the former post office building on Washington's Pennsylvania Avenue. With a handful of other House Republicans, he advised Trump and his campaign staff about nitty-gritty political issues and players. Following the election, Barletta served on the executive committee for the presidential transition. He spoke with reporters at Trump Tower in New York City after he met with Trump to discuss his possible nomination as Secretary of Transportation or another Cabinet position.

With the benefit of favorable redistricting changes, Barletta has been easily reelected against lightly funded opponents. In the spring of 2017, Barletta said that Trump had encouraged him to challenge Democratic Sen. Robert Casey in 2018 and that he was giving it thought.

East-Central Pennsylvania: Harrisburg Area, Wilkes-Barre Suburbs

Population		Race and Ethnicity		Income	
Total	707,670	White	86.4%	Median Income	$51,784 (225 out of 435)
Land area	3,356	Black	4.9%		
Pop/ sq mi	210.8	Latino	5.5%		
Born in state	77.7%	Asian	1.5%	Under $50,000	48.1%
		Two races	1.4%	$50,000-$99,999	33.3%
Age Groups		Other	0.2%	$100,000-$199,999	15.9%
Under 18	20.3%			$200,000 or more	2.8%
18-34	21.4%	**Education**		Poverty Rate	12.4%
35-64	40.9%	H.S grad or less	51.7%		
Over 64	17.4%	Some college	25.5%	**Health Insurance**	
Work		College Degree, 4 yr	14.3%	With health insurance coverage	91.8%
White Collar	32.2%	Post grad	8.5%		
Sales and Service	42.6%	**Military**		**Public Assistance**	
Blue Collar	25.1%	Veteran	10.1%	Cash public assistance income	2.8%
Government	4.9%	Active Duty	0.1%	Food stamp/SNAP benefits	11.5%

Voter Turnout			
2015 Total Citizens 18+	549,051	2016 House Turnout as % CVAP	57%
2016 House turnout	313,221	2014 House Turnout as % CVAP	34%

2012 Presidential Vote		
Mitt Romney	157,842	(54%)
Barack Obama	130,429	(45%)

2016 Presidential Vote		
Donald Trump	191,678	(60%)
Hillary Clinton	115,614	(36%)
Gary Johnson	8,007	(3%)

Cook Partisan Voting Index: R+10

The small town of Carlisle has a unique history as one of the unsung stories of rural Pennsylvania. In 1912, the most dominant college football team in the nation belonged to the Carlisle Indian Industrial School. The team of Native Americans starred Olympian Jim Thorpe and was coached by Glenn Scobey "Pop" Warner. "They didn't just change football. They changed prevailing ideas about Indians," wrote author Sally Jenkins in her book, *The Real All Americans*. The epic 1912 game between the Carlisle Indians and the U.S. Military Academy at West Point - which featured Dwight Eisenhower at linebacker - became an extension of fighting between white expansionists and Native Americans. This time, the Carlisle underdogs won, 27-6.

The 11th Congressional District of Pennsylvania stretches from Wyoming County in the northeast to Cumberland in the south, taking in Carlisle, and most of Dauphin with Harrisburg's suburbs and a slice of the capital city. Today, Carlisle is home to Dickinson College, the U.S. Army War College and an Amazon warehouse that is so large that it has moving vehicles and roads inside plus automated vertical shelves. From 2010 to 2016, Cumberland was the fastest-growing county in the state, with a 6 percent increase. Luzerne is the largest county, with 30 percent of the population. The district surrounds on three sides Democratic Wilkes-Barre, which is in the 17th District. Hazleton is a small city that gained national notoriety for its crackdowns on illegal immigrants, which were repeatedly contested in the courts and not implemented. Those problems have subsided with a combination of new warehouse jobs, "white flight" to nearby towns and a population that has become almost 50 percent Hispanic, the *Philadelphia Inquirer* reported in April 2016. Hazleton is the site for much of the nation's supply of anthracite coal. Another hot issue in the region is whether natural gas extraction in the underground Marcellus Shale formation will irrevocably contaminate the Susquehanna River.

The 11th leaned Democratic for decades. Republican redistricting in 2011 removed Wilkes Barre, Scranton and other Democratic urban centers. The district has gained a distinct Republican lean, which increased from 52 percent for John McCain in the 2008 presidential election to 60 percent for Donald Trump in 2016. Luzerne County takes pride that it has voted in every election since 1932 for the presidential candidate who has won Pennsylvania. Its shift in 2016 was extraordinary: The 52%-47% advantage in Luzerne for President Barack Obama in 2012 switched to 58%-39% for Donald Trump.

TWELFTH DISTRICT

Keith Rothfus (R)

Elected 2012, 3rd term; b. Apr 25, 1962, Endicott, NY; State University of New York, Buffalo, B.S.; University of Notre Dame Law School (IN), J.D.; Roman Catholic; Married (Elsie Rothfus); 6 children.

Professional Career: Systems programmer, IBM, 1985-1988; Practicing attorney, 1991-2010; Association dean, Regent University School of Law, 1993-1997; Bush administration faith-based initiatives official, 2004-2007; Staff, U.S. Department of Homeland Security, 2006-2007.

DC Office: 1205 LHOB 20515, 202-225-2065, Fax: 202-225-5709, rothfus.house.gov.

State Offices: Beaver, 724-359-1626; Johnstown, 814-619-3659; Pittsburgh, 412-837-1361.

Committees: *Financial Services*: Financial Institutions & Consumer Credit, Housing & Insurance, Terrorism & Illicit Finance.

Group Ratings

	ADA	ACLU	AFL-CIO	LCV	ITI	COC	HAFA	ACU	CFG	FRC
2016	-	11%	-	0%	83%	100%	79%	92%	81%	100%
2015	5%	C	13%	3%	C	70%	C	88%	80%	100%

Almanac Ratings 2015

	Economy	Social	Foreign	Composite
Liberal	13%	0%	4%	6%
Conservative	87%	100%	96%	94%

Key Votes of the 114th Congress

1. Keystone Pipeline	Y	5. Puerto Rico Debt	Y	9. Offenses by Aliens	Y
2. Trade Deals	N	6. Medical Marijuana	N	10. Troops in Iraq	N
3. Export-Import Bank	N	7. Sanctuary Cities	Y	11. Homeland Security $$	N
4. Debt Ceiling Increase	N	8. Armor-piercing Bullets	Y	12. Trade Adjustment aid	Y

Election Results

Election	Name (Party)	Vote (%)		Cand. Spent	Ind. Exp. Support	Ind. Exp. Oppose
2016 General	Keith Rothfus (R)	221,851	(62%)	$1,346,842		
	Erin McClelland (D)	137,353	(38%)	$238,413		
2016 Primary	Keith Rothfus (R)		(100%)			

Prior winning percentages: 2014 (59%), 2012 (52%)

Republican Keith Rothfus won the seat in 2012, succeeding two House Democrats who had represented local districts before redistricting revamped the area surrounding Pittsburgh and forced them to run in a district where many voters were new to them. The fiscally conservative Rothfus brought a new style less focused on aid from Washington.

Growing up near Binghamton in Endicott, New York, he was a teen-age acolyte in 1980 of Republican presidential candidate Ronald Reagan, especially his plan to cut taxes. He got a bachelor's degree in information systems from Buffalo State College, part of the State University of New York. He worked for IBM for three years, then got a law degree from Notre Dame. He was a litigator in Pittsburgh and became an associate dean at the Regent University School of Law. He later negotiated commercial contracts and established a private practice in Pittsburgh. He became involved in politics, working on faith-based initiatives at the Homeland Security Department in the George W. Bush administration.

Rothfus had never thought that he would run for office. That changed in 2009, when he looked for six months for a congressional candidate to support before putting his own name forward. Passage in

Congress of the $787 billion economic stimulus in 2009 - and the debt it added - heightened his interest. The challenge was daunting: He ran in a district that leaned Democratic and he was an underdog in the Republican primary against former U.S. Attorney Mary Beth Buchanan. With tea party support, Rothfus pulled an upset in the 2010 primary. Then, he nearly won a shocker on Election Day, falling to well-funded Democratic Rep. Jason Altmire 51%-49%.

That close contest encouraged him to run again in 2012, especially when the newly drawn 12th District became more favorable to the GOP. This time, he faced Rep. Mark Critz, a long-time staffer to former Defense Appropriations Subcommittee Chairman John Murtha and the heir to his seat when Murtha died in 2010. In the 2012 Democratic primary between two incumbents, Critz defeated Altmire 51%-49%, by rolling up a large margin in Cambria and Somerset while Altmire won the Pittsburgh-area counties. In the general election, Critz stressed his support for gun owners' rights and opposition to abortion rights, and he sought to tie Rothfus to House Budget Committee Chairman Paul Ryan's plan to overhaul Medicare. Rothfus linked Critz to President Barack Obama and listed as his top priorities the "Three Rs:" repealing "Obamacare," reforming tax and spending policies, and rolling back regulation. He called for transforming southwest Pennsylvania into an energy capital. His strength in Allegheny and Westmoreland counties overcame Critz's big lead in the eastern part of the district. Rothfus won 52%-48%. Two House Democrats in southwest Pennsylvania disappeared.

Rothfus has been a mainstream Republican. His *Almanac* voting record in 2015 was toward the center of the House GOP on economic issues and conservative on social issues. He centered his work at the Financial Services Committee. He said that he wanted to be a conciliator and deal-maker at a time of polarization in Congress. "I have a reputation in my professional work, negotiating contracts, where I've gone into deals where other people haven't closed the deal, and I've been able to get it done," he said. "We need to work with people of goodwill in both parties and start to tackle problems we have." The National Association of Manufacturing praised his support for manufacturing and innovation.

In 2015, Rothfus filed proposals to overhaul the 2010 Dodd-Frank law and permit mutual banks and savings associations to engage in a broader range of financial services. He became vice chairman in 2017 of the Financial Institutions and Consumer Credit Subcommittee and said that his goal was to reduce "the weight of misguided Dodd-Frank regulations." In March 2016, the House passed on a nearly party-line vote his Satisfying Energy Needs and Saving the Environment (SENSE) bill to reduce environmental regulations in the "waste coal" industry. Rothfus won an amendment to the defense spending bill to reverse the Defense Department's decision in 2014 to transfer to the Army control of Apache helicopters at the National Guard complex in Johnstown and in three other states. But President Barack Obama vetoed that bill in October 2015.

Rothfus has twice breezed to reelection against Democratic health care expert Erin McClelland. The party and union spending on her behalf was reduced in 2016, and her vote share dropped from 41 percent in 2014 to 38 percent. Democrats appear unlikely to win back this seat, at least until likely redistricting changes in 2022.

Northern Pittsburgh Suburbs, Johnstown Area

Population		**Race and Ethnicity**		**Income**	
Total	704,203	White	92.4%	Median Income	$56,446 (167 out of 435)
Land area	2,163	Black	3.1%		
Pop/ sq mi	325.6	Latino	1.3%		
Born in state	83.4%	Asian	1.6%	Under $50,000	44.7%
		Two races	1.4%	$50,000-$99,999	31.3%
Age Groups		Other	0.2%	$100,000-$199,999	19.0%
Under 18	20.2%			$200,000 or more	4.9%
18-34	18.2%	**Education**		Poverty Rate	9.6%
35-64	42.2%	H.S grad or less	43.3%		
Over 64	19.4%	Some college	25.5%	**Health Insurance**	
		College Degree, 4 yr	18.9%	With health insurance coverage	94.3%
Work		Post grad	12.2%		
White Collar	39.7%				
Sales and Service	39.8%	**Military**		**Public Assistance**	
Blue Collar	20.4%	Veteran	10.0%	Cash public assistance income	2.4%
Government	5.1%	Active Duty	0.0%		
				Food stamp/SNAP benefits	10.4%

Voter Turnout			
2015 Total Citizens 18+	554,745	2016 House Turnout as % CVAP	65%
2016 House turnout	359,204	2014 House Turnout as % CVAP	39%

2012 Presidential Vote		
Mitt Romney	200,093	(58%)
Barack Obama	141,753	(41%)

2016 Presidential Vote		
Donald Trump	213,109	(58%)
Hillary Clinton	137,603	(38%)
Gary Johnson	9,226	(3%)

Cook Partisan Voting Index: R+11

The mountains and valleys within a 100-mile radius of Pittsburgh comprise one of America's most beautiful - and economically troubled - regions. This has been tough, hard-working country ever since Scots-Irish farmers settled here in the 1790s. Their first big product was whiskey - this was the site of the Whiskey Rebellion of 1794 - but historically the most important product was bituminous coal. Discovered in the 19th century, it was the basic energy source for the production of iron and steel. Johnstown was once known as the "Cradle of the American Steel Industry." It has been on a long downhill slide since the 1979 oil shock. Its population fell from 67,000 in 1920 to below 20,000 in 2015, a decline similar to that of many communities in the region. Johnstown has been ranked as the poorest city in Pennsylvania.

Johnstown was the site of the flood of May 1889, when water from the ruptured South Fork Dam cascaded down steep valley walls, gaining speed and debris during an 18-mile trip, and poured into the little industrial city with a force equal to Niagara Falls. "Everyone heard shouting and screaming, the ear-splitting crash of buildings going down, glass shattering, and the sides of houses ripping apart," historian David McCullough wrote of the flood that killed more than 2,200 people in a disaster that lasted just 10 minutes. In February 2017, a fundraising campaign to improve the flood museum had raised two-thirds of the needed money. Even after the death in 2010 of its long-time Democratic Rep. John Murtha, Johnstown continued to receive a disproportionate share of Defense Department contracts. With government aid, companies in the area have developed improved batteries and energy storage. Southwestern Pennsylvania is also football country: Joe Namath is a grandchild of a Hungarian immigrant steelworker from Beaver Falls, and Hall of Fame quarterbacks Joe Montana and Dan Marino hailed from the region.

The 12th Congressional District stretches from the Ohio border to the Pennsylvania heartland. It covers the shrinking rust belt cities of Aliquippa and Beaver Falls, more upscale northern Pittsburgh suburbs in Allegheny County, Johnstown in Cambria County, and part of nearby Somerset County. About 40 percent of the population is in Allegheny County and 20 percent in Beaver. With the shifting political climate in western Pennsylvania, the district has become safely Republican in presidential elections. Donald Trump got 58 percent of the vote in 2016.

THIRTEENTH DISTRICT

Brendan Boyle (D)

Elected 2014, 2nd term; b. Feb 06, 1977, Philadelphia; University of Notre Dame (IN), Bach. Deg.; Harvard University John F. Kennedy School of Government (MA), M.PP; Roman Catholic; Married (Jennifer Morgan); 1 child.

Elected Office: PA House, 2009-2014.

Professional Career: Radio broadcaster; Management Consultant; Adjunct Professional, Drexel University.

DC Office: 1133 LHOB 20515, 202-225-6111, Fax: 202-226-0611, boyle.house.gov.

State Offices: Glenside, 215-517-6572; Norristown, 610-270-8081; Philadelphia, 215-335-3355; Philadelphia, 267-335-5643.

Committees: *Budget*. *Foreign Affairs*: Middle East & North Africa, Terrorism, Nonproliferation & Trade.

Group Ratings

	ADA	ACLU	AFL-CIO	LCV	ITI	COC	HAFA	ACU	CFG	FRC
2016	-	88%	-	100%	50%	64%	14%	8%	0%	0%
2015	65%	C	100%	100%	C	53%	C	10%	0%	0%

Almanac Ratings 2015

	Economy	Social	Foreign	Composite
Liberal	82%	85%	65%	77%
Conservative	18%	15%	35%	23%

Key Votes of the 114th Congress

1. Keystone Pipeline	N	5. Puerto Rico Debt	N	9. Offenses by Aliens	N
2. Trade Deals	N	6. Medical Marijuana	NV	10. Troops in Iraq	N
3. Export-Import Bank	Y	7. Sanctuary Cities	N	11. Homeland Security $$	Y
4. Debt Ceiling Increase	Y	8. Armor-piercing Bullets	N	12. Trade Adjustment aid	N

Election Results

Election	Name (Party)	Vote (%)	Cand. Spent	Ind. Exp. Support	Ind. Exp. Oppose
2016 General	Brendan Boyle (D)	239,316 (100%)	$466,826		
2016 Primary	Brendan Boyle (D)	(100%)			

Prior winning percentages: 2014 (67%)

Democrat Brendan Boyle in 2014 took an unconventional route to victory in the 13th District by sweeping the north Philadelphia wards while his higher-spending rivals in the Democratic primary focused on upscale Montgomery County. He became one of the youngest members of Congress at age 37 and looked even younger. He and his brother, State Rep. Kevin Boyle, are politically ambitious and have sought to expand their reach.

Raised by working-class parents in northeast Philadelphia, Boyle was the first in his family to go to college. After his bachelor's in government at Notre Dame, he got a master's degree in public policy at Harvard's John F. Kennedy School of Government. In 2008, he was elected to the state House. Kevin was elected two years later, making them the first pair of siblings to serve together in the state House. When Democratic Rep. Allyson Schwartz ran unsuccessfully in the Democratic primary for governor, Boyle was one of four Democrats seeking to replace her. They included former Rep. Marjorie Margolies, who is Chelsea Clinton's mother-in-law. The contest was one of the most expensive in the nation, with Bill Clinton offering fundraising help for Margolies. Boyle was financially outgunned by the three other Democratic contenders, especially Valerie Arkoosh, a well-funded doctor. Each spent at least $1.5 million in the primary, while Boyle spent only $900,000 for his entire campaign.

Boyle hit the pavement with old-school populism and held 225 voter events that played up his grass-roots candidacy, noting that his father was a public-transit maintenance worker and his mother a school crossing guard. He got a boost from union support, with a labor-backed PAC spending $350,000 on Boyle's behalf, despite the opposition of Rep. Robert Brady, the boss of the Philadelphia Democratic organization. His rivals targeted his legislative record on women's health, namely his support for a bill that called for the renovation of health centers but reportedly led to the closing of several abortion clinics. NARAL, a leading abortion-rights group, accused him of "tap dancing around votes he took that would throw roadblocks in front of women seeking reproductive health care."

Boyle's targeted route to victory went decidedly through Philadelphia County, where he got 70 percent of the vote. He called himself "a Northeast guy." He finished a distant fourth with only 16 percent in Montgomery, which cast 54 percent of the primary vote. But that was enough to give him the victory with 41 percent, to 27 percent for runner-up Margolies, whose Clinton ties were not enough to overcome a disorganized campaign. In the general election, Dee Adcock spent $500,000 and a group of anesthesiologists spent another $300,000 on her behalf. But the contest was never in doubt. Boyle won 67%-33%, and won 75 percent of the vote in Philadelphia.

On the Foreign Affairs Committee, Boyle joined a delegation to Dubai for a briefing on the Islamic State and the situation in the Persian Gulf. At the St. Patrick's Day reception at the White House in March 2015, President Barack Obama gave a shout-out to Boyle, plus his brother and father. He told the immigrant story of their father, who was born in Donegal. His *Almanac* vote ratings for 2015 ranked Boyle toward the center of the House, especially on foreign policy. In 2017, he got a seat on the Budget

Committee, where he joined other Democrats in attacking Republican plans to repeal and replace the Affordable Care Act. He said that the GOP alternative broke the promises made by Donald Trump during his presidential campaign. With Democratic Rep. Marc Veasey of Texas, he organized the Blue Collar Caucus for Democrats to reach out to Trump voters.

Boyle was reelected without opposition from either party. In February 2017, *Philadelphia* magazine ran a lengthy profile of the Boyle brothers that described their skill in reaching out to working-class voters, a constituency with which national Democrats had been falling short, they said. "Now that I've been inside the room of the Democratic Congressional Campaign Committee, one of the first questions that's asked when we're looking to recruit a Democratic candidate for Congress is: Can that person self-fund?" Brendan Boyle said critically. He added that Democrats need to "widen the tent" to include voters with different views on abortion and guns, for example.

Montgomery County, Northeast Philadelphia

Population		**Race and Ethnicity**		**Income**	
Total	721,966	White	59.4%	Median Income	$56,794 (165 out of 435)
Land area	155	Black	18.1%		
Pop/ sq mi	4652.4	Latino	11.3%		
Born in state	68.6%	Asian	8.8%	Under $50,000	44.5%
		Two races	2.0%	$50,000-$99,999	29.7%
Age Groups		Other	0.4%	$100,000-$199,999	20.2%
Under 18	23.0%			$200,000 or more	5.4%
18-34	23.3%	**Education**		Poverty Rate	13.7%
35-64	38.9%	H.S grad or less	43.5%		
Over 64	14.8%	Some college	23.7%	**Health Insurance**	
		College Degree, 4 yr	19.9%	With health insurance coverage	89.2%
Work		Post grad	12.9%		
White Collar	38.6%				
Sales and Service	43.5%	**Military**		**Public Assistance**	
Blue Collar	17.9%	Veteran	6.4%	Cash public assistance income	4.2%
Government	4.8%	Active Duty	0.0%		
				Food stamp/SNAP benefits	13.6%

Voter Turnout			
2015 Total Citizens 18+	506,594	2016 House Turnout as % CVAP	47%
2016 House turnout	239,316	2014 House Turnout as % CVAP	37%

2012 Presidential Vote		
Barack Obama	210,902	(66%)
Mitt Romney	105,024	(33%)

2016 Presidential Vote		
Hillary Clinton	217,268	(65%)
Donald Trump	105,558	(32%)

Cook Partisan Voting Index: D+15

Montgomery County is the proximate hinterland of Philadelphia: rolling hills cut on one side by the Schuylkill River and at intervals by the Pennsylvania and Reading Railroad lines radiating outward from Center City. Older suburbs, both rich and modest, grew up around rail stations, with comfortable houses within walking distance for commuters. Farther out are 18th and 19th century villages, once surrounded by farm fields, now encroached upon by subdivisions where people depend on cars, not rail lines, to get to work. Historically, the moderate Republican style of politics in Montgomery was set by Ivy League graduates. In the 1990s, the county swung toward Democrats in national politics, with abortion rights and other cultural issues usually trumping economic concerns. Montgomery County has been the second most affluent county, behind Chester, in the state. It is a distant third as the most populous county, behind Philadelphia and Allegheny.

In Horsham, downsizing of the Willow Grove Naval Air Station resulted in plans for a large housing development following an environmental clean-up of the area. Instead, local officials in February 2017 decided to turn the land into open-space preservation. In 2016, parts of Willow Grove had been revived as a home to pilots of unmanned military drone aircraft flying missions over conflict zones across the world.

Nearby, Northeast Philadelphia is quite a different place. This is relatively new urban territory, with more than half of its houses built after 1950. Many of Philadelphia's Hispanics live in the industrial river wards along the Delaware River, but other wards in the Northeast have remained mostly white and blue-collar. Some industries have settled here, such as Teva Pharmaceuticals USA, which is the largest generic drug manufacturer in North America.

The 13th Congressional District of Pennsylvania includes southeastern and central Montgomery County and parts of Northeast Philadelphia. About 55 percent of the voters are in Montgomery. It extends north in two arms, one to Norristown and King of Prussia and the other to Lansdale. King of Prussia mall was enlarged in August 2016 and became the largest on the East Coast, second in the nation to the Mall of America in Minnesota. ABC aired a comedy series, "The Goldbergs," which was based in the small borough of Jenkintown. About 30 percent of Montgomery is in the 13th. Northern parts of the county have been parceled out to the Republican-held 6th, 7th and 8th Districts, each of which has its population base elsewhere. The 13th is one of three solidly Democratic districts in the Philadelphia area. Hillary Clinton got 65 percent of the vote in 2016, virtually the same as the vote for President Barack Obama in his two campaigns.

FOURTEENTH DISTRICT

Mike Doyle (D)

Elected 1994, 12th term; b. Aug 05, 1953, Swissvale; Pennsylvania State University, B.S.; Roman Catholic; Married (Susan Erlandson Doyle); 4 children.

Elected Office: Swissvale Borough Council, 1977-1981.

Professional Career: Ins. agent, 1975-1977; Executive Director, Turtle Creek Valley Citizens Union, 1977-1979; Chief of Staff, PA Sen. Frank Pecora, 1979-1994; Co-founder/owner, Eastgate Ins. Agency, 1983-present.

DC Office: 239 CHOB 20515, 202-225-2135, Fax: 202-225-3084, doyle.house.gov.

State Offices: Coraopolis, 412-264-3460; McKeesport, 412-664-4049; Penn Hills, 412-241-6055; Pittsburgh, 412-390-1499.

Committees: *Energy & Commerce*: Communications & Technology (RMM), Energy.

Group Ratings

	ADA	ACLU	AFL-CIO	LCV	ITI	COC	HAFA	ACU	CFG	FRC
2016	-	82%	-	100%	50%	64%	14%	0%	0%	8%
2015	90%	C	100%	83%	C	45%	C	4%	0%	0%

Almanac Ratings 2015

	Economy	Social	Foreign	Composite
Liberal	90%	100%	95%	95%
Conservative	10%	0%	5%	5%

Key Votes of the 114th Congress

1. Keystone Pipeline	Y	5. Puerto Rico Debt	Y	9. Offenses by Aliens	N
2. Trade Deals	N	6. Medical Marijuana	Y	10. Troops in Iraq	Y
3. Export-Import Bank	Y	7. Sanctuary Cities	N	11. Homeland Security $$	Y
4. Debt Ceiling Increase	Y	8. Armor-piercing Bullets	N	12. Trade Adjustment aid	Y

Election Results

Election	Name (Party)	Vote	(%)	Cand. Spent	Ind. Exp. Support	Ind. Exp. Oppose
2016 General	Mike Doyle (D)	255,293	(74%)	$493,428		
	Lenny McAllister (R)	87,999	(26%)	$13,270		
2016 Primary	Michael F. Doyle (D)	99,875	(77%)			
	Janis Brooks (D)	30,563	(23%)			

Prior winning percentages: 2014 (100%), 2012 (76.9%), 2010 (69%), 2008 (91%), 2006 (90%), 2004 (100%), 2002 (100%), 2000 (69%), 1998 (68%), 1996 (56%), 1994 (55%)

Mike Doyle, an ardently pro-labor Democrat first elected in 1994, has become a senior member of the Energy and Commerce Committee, where he has shown deal-making skills. In 2017, he took over as the ranking Democrat dealing with communications and technology issues.

Of Irish and Italian descent, Doyle grew up in the Monongahela Valley town of Swissvale and worked in steel mills during summers off from Penn State. He became an insurance agent and was elected to the Swissvale Borough Council at age 24. In 1978, he became chief of staff to state Sen. Frank Pecora, a Republican. In 1994, Doyle, who followed his boss in switching to the Democratic Party, ran for the House seat vacated by Republican Rep. Rick Santorum, who was elected to the Senate. With endorsements from labor unions and community leaders, he won the seven-candidate primary. In November, he faced John McCarty, an aide to the late Republican Sen. John Heinz. McCarty was pro-abortion rights and Doyle opposed abortion rights. Doyle also campaigned for sweeping health care changes. In a Republican year, he won 55%-45%.

Doyle initially had a mixed voting record, often on the right on cultural issues. Over the years, he became more of a progressive populist. As a pro-life Catholic, he helped broker the deal on abortion during the final days of the 2010 health care debate that brought on board other anti-abortion members of his party. When Republicans regained control, he complained that GOP budgets would "eviscerate" social services. Doyle rarely has sought attention or caused much of a ruckus. One notable exception was the 2011 debate over raising the federal debt limit, when in a private meeting he reportedly compared Republicans' negotiating tactics to those of terrorists. Conservative bloggers and commentators heaped criticism on him, and he said, "I wasn't out to defame anybody."

On Energy and Commerce, his focus has been on high-tech initiatives, including increased availability of broadband services in underserved areas. As ranking Democrat on the Communications and Technology Subcommittee, he supported policies such as net neutrality, unlicensed spectrum, modernized 911 services, greater competition for devices and services, and protection of the open internet. He kept the door open for bipartisan cooperation on expanded broadband and a robust public safety communications system.

Doyle has worked to reduce foreign imports, and he pushed a bill to create a national historic site at the former U.S. Steel facilities along the Monongahela River. During the 2009 debate over cap-and-trade legislation, which would have capped carbon emissions while allowing companies to trade emissions credits, he vigorously advocated the interests of steel and other job-creating Rust Belt industries, even as he worked out a compromise with environmentalists. The House-passed bill died in the Senate, largely because of opposition from Rust Belt Democrats. When Republicans in 2011 voted to restrict the Environmental Protection Agency's power to regulate emissions, Doyle accused the GOP of "scaring American people" into wrongly believing that failure to curb EPA's authority would cause gas prices to rise.

During debate over the Keystone XL pipeline, Doyle unsuccessfully offered an amendment that would have required at least three-quarters of the iron and steel in the pipeline to be made in North America. In December 2016, Republicans defeated his effort to add a "buy America" provision to a water infrastructure bill. Doyle founded and co-chaired the House Distributed Generation Caucus, which promotes decentralized power generation technology that is fuel efficient and environmentally friendly. He also has co-chaired the Robotics Caucus.

Before the practice was banned, Doyle was an avid earmarker of spending projects for his district. One of his favorite beneficiaries was the eponymous Doyle Center for Manufacturing Technology in South Oakland, which was started in 2003 by a $1.5 million federal grant he helped secure. In response to criticism from House Republicans, Doyle removed his name from the center, though he continued to seek federal support for its operations. He is active on autism research and cracking down on illegal dog-breeding "puppy mills." His colleagues praise his managing of the Democrats' team in the annual congressional charity baseball game.

On the Democrats' Policy and Communications Committee, Doyle has worked to develop a unified caucus message. He has been politically untouchable at home, though the downsides for his party are that he has become the only House Democrat from southwest Pennsylvania. In 2016, he got 74 percent of the vote against Lenny McAllister, who has hosted local radio and television talk shows. When Doyle was elected in 1994, he was one of five Democrats (with no Republicans) from roughly the same region. That shift helps to illustrate why they are in the minority.

Pittsburgh Metro

Population		**Race and Ethnicity**		**Income**	
Total	704,815	White	70.5%	Median Income	$42,044 (369 out of 435)
Land area	209	Black	21.2%		
Pop/ sq mi	3367.6	Latino	2.1%		
Born in state	78.9%	Asian	3.0%	Under $50,000	56.8%
		Two races	2.9%	$50,000-$99,999	28.2%
Age Groups		Other	0.3%	$100,000-$199,999	12.2%
Under 18	17.8%			$200,000 or more	2.7%
18-34	28.4%	**Education**		Poverty Rate	18.9%
35-64	37.5%	H.S grad or less	41.6%		
Over 64	16.3%	Some college	27.6%	**Health Insurance**	
		College Degree, 4 yr	17.8%	With health insurance coverage	91.1%
Work		Post grad	13.1%		
White Collar	39.2%				
Sales and Service	45.1%	**Military**		**Public Assistance**	
Blue Collar	15.7%	Veteran	8.5%	Cash public assistance income	4.3%
Government	4.2%	Active Duty	0.0%		
				Food stamp/SNAP benefits	18.0%

Voter Turnout			
2015 Total Citizens 18+	559,474	2016 House Turnout as % CVAP	61%
2016 House turnout	343,292	2014 House Turnout as % CVAP	26%

2012 Presidential Vote		
Barack Obama	230,768	(68%)
Mitt Romney	103,964	(31%)

2016 Presidential Vote		
Hillary Clinton	231,983	(65%)
Donald Trump	107,252	(30%)
Gary Johnson	7,818	(2%)

Cook Partisan Voting Index: D+17

The Golden Triangle is the inevitable focus of Pittsburgh, the tip of land where the Allegheny and Monongahela rivers come together to form the Ohio. It has been a strategic site for more than 200 years. During the French and Indian War, British Gen. Edward Braddock's army was heading to Fort Duquesne, with George Washington helping lead the way, when it was ambushed and famously defeated in 1754. A few years later, the first American city west of the Appalachian chain was carved out of the wilderness and named after the English statesman William Pitt. Pittsburgh did nicely when railroads became ascendant, since rail lines tend to run along the riverside. Then Andrew Carnegie, a Scottish immigrant, foresaw that steel would replace iron for railroad bridges. He built a steel factory in Pittsburgh, one blessed with ready deposits of coal and access to iron ore from the Great Lakes. Carnegie built his capacity to the point that when he sold out in 1901, the resulting U.S. Steel Corp. held a near-monopoly.

As the steel industry and other blue-collar industries contracted over the years, so did Pittsburgh. In 1940, it was the nation's 10th largest city, with 672,000 people. In 2015, it was the 63rd largest, with 304,000 people. The population loss has been easing, with an increase in young people. Local universities and hospitals now have far more workers than downsized U.S. Steel. Economic diversity helped Pittsburgh survive the recession better than other Rust Belt cities. The University of Pittsburgh Medical Center is the largest employer in the region, with the UPMC acronym on the old U.S. Steel skyscraper. In 2015, local icon H.J. Heinz purchased Chicago-based Kraft Foods and the company described itself as "global," but "co-headquartered" in the two cities. The city has a rich cultural heritage. Pop artist Andy Warhol grew up in Pittsburgh and the Warhol Museum is located in the downtown area. The predominantly black Hill District inspired playwright August Wilson's chronicles, and along the Monongahela River is the town of Clairton, where *The Deer Hunter* was filmed. The Brookings Institution in February 2017 ranked Pittsburgh third among 100 metro areas in a combination of productivity, wage increases and standard of living. In March 2016, a writer for the *Pittsburgh*

Post-Gazette whimsically suggested that the city should call itself: "Pittsburgh: The Greatest Place that Doesn't Grow."

The 14th Congressional District of Pennsylvania includes Pittsburgh and the mostly working class suburbs to the east, south and west. All of it is in Allegheny County, except for 2 percent who live in the northwest corner of Westmoreland. It is heavily Democratic, with the two districts to the north and south having become more Republican. The 14th is a Democratic island in increasingly Republican southwest Pennsylvania.

FIFTEENTH DISTRICT

Charlie Dent (R)

Elected 2004, 7th term; b. May 24, 1960, Allentown; Lehigh University (PA), M.P.A.; Pennsylvania State University, B.A.; Presbyterian; Married (Pamela Jane Serfass Dent); 3 children.

Elected Office: PA House, 1991-1999; PA Senate, 1999-2005.

Professional Career: Development officer, Lehigh University, 1986-1990.

DC Office: 2082 RHOB 20515, 202-225-6411, Fax: 202-226-0778, dent.house.gov.

State Offices: Allentown, 610-770-3490; Annville, 717-867-1026; Hamburg, 610-562-4281; Hershey, 717-533-3959.

Committees: *Appropriations*: Military Construction, Veterans Affairs & Related Agencies (Chmn), State, Foreign Operations & Related Programs, Transportation, HUD & Related Agencies.

Group Ratings

	ADA	ACLU	AFL-CIO	LCV	ITI	COC	HAFA	ACU	CFG	FRC
2016	-	35%	-	18%	67%	100%	29%	40%	59%	58%
2015	5%	C	25%	6%	C	100%	C	33%	38%	67%

Almanac Ratings 2015

	Economy	Social	Foreign	Composite
Liberal	14%	37%	11%	20%
Conservative	86%	63%	90%	80%

Key Votes of the 114th Congress

1. Keystone Pipeline	Y	5. Puerto Rico Debt	Y	9. Offenses by Aliens	Y
2. Trade Deals	Y	6. Medical Marijuana	N	10. Troops in Iraq	N
3. Export-Import Bank	Y	7. Sanctuary Cities	Y	11. Homeland Security $$	Y
4. Debt Ceiling Increase	Y	8. Armor-piercing Bullets	Y	12. Trade Adjustment aid	Y

Election Results

Election	Name (Party)	Vote (%)	Cand. Spent	Ind. Exp. Support	Ind. Exp. Oppose
2016 General	Charlie Dent (R)	190,618 (58%)	$1,283,465	$12,000	
	Rick Daugherty (D)	124,129 (38%)	$20,559		
	Paul Rizzo (L)	11,727 (4%)			
2016 Primary	Charlie Dent (R)	(100%)			

Prior winning percentages: 2014 (100%), 2012 (57%), 2010 (54%), 2008 (59%), 2006 (54%), 2004 (59%)

Charlie Dent, elected in 2004, is prominent in the dwindling ranks of moderate House Republicans who have shown their survival skills. He has wielded clout as a subcommittee chairman on the Appropriations Committee, and he gained respect for service as chairman of the House Ethics Committee.

Dent grew up in Allentown, graduated from Penn State and got a graduate degree in public administration at Lehigh University, where he later worked as a development officer. In 1990, he was elected to the state House and later to the state Senate. When Republican Rep. Pat Toomey decided to run against Sen. Arlen Specter in the 2004 Republican primary, Dent was the front-runner to succeed him.

Dent's lifelong residence in the Lehigh Valley was a sharp contrast to the background of the Democratic nominee, businessman Joe Driscoll. Driscoll grew up in Massachusetts, where he went sailing with the Kennedys and made enough money to spend $2 million on his campaign. He lived for years in posh Lower Merion in Montgomery County, just outside Philadelphia. Dent framed the campaign as a contest between a native son and a carpetbagging outsider who thought of the Lehigh Valley as "a speed bump on his way to Congress." Driscoll sought to deflect the residency issue with aggressive criticism of the Bush administration, asserting that a vote for Dent was an endorsement of President George W. Bush's policies. Dent's moderate record, which included support for abortion rights, made it difficult to tie him to Bush, and he insisted that he would be an independent voice in Washington. Dent won 59%-39%.

In the House, Dent has one of the least conservative voting records among Republicans. In 2015, his *Almanac* vote ratings ranked him among the 15 most centrist House Republicans, especially on social issues. (He prefers the term "center-right" to "moderate.") When Democrats set the House agenda, he broke from most Republicans to vote for expanding the Children's Health Insurance Program, allowing the Food and Drug Administration to regulate tobacco and overhauling food safety laws. He has been a co-chairman of the Tuesday Group, a caucus of moderates in a GOP Conference dominated by conservatives, where he advocates "responsible, common-sense solutions."

In the majority, Republican leaders regard him as a useful swing vote. He was among 85 Republicans who joined with 172 Democrats on New Year's Day 2013 to pass the compromise bill on spending and taxes to avert the so-called fiscal cliff, and he was among the 49 Republicans who joined with 192 Democrats to pass a relief bill for states hit by Hurricane Sandy. He and Rep. Peter King of New York were the only Republicans who voted for a Democratic proposal that would have avoided the October 2013 government shutdown. "When you're in this business of governing, sometimes you must step up and govern," he told the *New York Times*.

On the influential Appropriations Committee, he became in 2015 a "cardinal" in charge of the bill funding Military Construction and Veterans' Affairs, which is the third largest of the 12 spending bills. His objectives have included enhanced transparency and accountability at the Department of Veterans Affairs through further oversight, increased funding for the inspector general's independent audits and investigations, and modernization of the VA's electronic health records with restrictions on its funding until progress was shown on the system's functionality. Because he won House passage of his subcommittee bill in both 2015 and 2016, unlike most other Appropriations subcommittees, his measure in each case became the vehicle to pass omnibus spending legislation. In 2016, Dent cited the measure's "steps to enhance oversight within the VA to address the mismanagement that has plagued VA facilities for far too long," plus additional overseas funding for NATO operations in Europe.

As chairman of the Ethics Committee for two years, he handled 78 investigations of ethical behavior, he wrote in its January 2017 summary of activities. He also cited the panel's more routine review of thousands of training sessions, responses for ethical guidance and financial disclosure statements for lawmakers and their aides.

Dent has continued to emphasize his independence on hot-button social issues. In 2014, he reversed his earlier opposition to same-sex marriage. "Life is too short to have the force of government stand in the way of two adults whose pursuit of happiness includes marriage," he said. He has worked with a bipartisan group that has sought to update the Voting Rights Act after the Supreme Court overturned a key section on enforcement. In 2015, he was one of four House Republicans who voted against the bill prohibiting most abortions after 20 weeks. In February 2017, Dent joined first-term Rep. John Faso of New York as the only Republicans to vote against House passage of the measure to defund abortion-related services by Planned Parenthood.

Later in the spring, Dent clashed with Tuesday Group co-chair Rep. Tom MacArthur of New Jersey over MacArthur's efforts to find common ground with conservatives on the House GOP's revision of the Affordable Care Act. MacArthur resigned as co-chair but not before voicing criticism about some in the Tuesday Group who were reluctant to make deals, which he appeared to target at Dent.

In 2010, Dent faced his toughest reelection opponent in Bethlehem Mayor John Callahan. The race was a statistical dead heat in polls a month before the election; former President Bill Clinton and Vice President Joe Biden made campaign stops for Callahan. Dent painted Callahan as fiscally irresponsible while portraying himself as a restraint on government spending. Dent won a surprisingly easy 54%-39% victory. Since then, he has reaped the benefits of a redrawn district plus his continued moderation. In 2016, against Rick Daugherty, a former Lehigh County Democratic Party chairman and congressional aide who worked with foster children, Dent out-raised him by 70-to-1 and won 58%-38%. Dent refused to support the election of Donald Trump, calling his tone and behavior "a bridge too far." In October, he urged other Republicans to "abandon" their presidential nominee.

East-Central Pennsylvania: Allentown

Population		**Race and Ethnicity**		**Income**	
Total	716,514	White	76.9%	Median Income	$58,384 (156 out of 435)
Land area	1,285	Black	3.9%		
Pop/ sq mi	557.6	Latino	14.6%		
Born in state	67.4%	Asian	2.6%	Under $50,000	42.4%
		Two races	1.7%	$50,000-$99,999	34.0%
Age Groups		Other	0.3%	$100,000-$199,999	19.0%
Under 18	21.7%			$200,000 or more	4.5%
18-34	21.9%	**Education**		Poverty Rate	11.3%
35-64	40.3%	H.S grad or less	47.3%		
Over 64	16.1%	Some college	24.9%	**Health Insurance**	
		College Degree, 4 yr	16.7%	With health insurance coverage	91.0%
Work		Post grad	11.1%		
White Collar	34.8%				
Sales and Service	41.9%	**Military**		**Public Assistance**	
Blue Collar	23.2%	Veteran	8.5%	Cash public assistance income	2.8%
Government	4.9%	Active Duty	0.1%		
				Food stamp/SNAP benefits	10.5%

Voter Turnout			
2015 Total Citizens 18+	540,005	2016 House Turnout as % CVAP	60%
2016 House turnout	326,474	2014 House Turnout as % CVAP	24%

2012 Presidential Vote		
Mitt Romney	156,165	(51%)
Barack Obama	147,240	(48%)

2016 Presidential Vote		
Donald Trump	173,596	(51%)
Hillary Clinton	148,078	(44%)
Gary Johnson	8,946	(3%)

Cook Partisan Voting Index: R+4

Billy Joel's song "Allentown" was a source of both controversy and praise upon its release in 1982. Its grim picture of closed factories, joblessness and human despair resonated with some area residents, while others found the song derisive and inaccurate. Joel was actually singing about the neighboring town of Bethlehem and the struggles of Bethlehem Steel, which was dissolved in 2003. Fences were mended when a petition drive helped bring Joel to play a concert at Lehigh University's Stabler Arena. The empathy Joel showed toward the region's economic plight has generated mostly pleasant memories.

Today's Lehigh Valley has a much more diverse economy, with a mix of regional health care networks, telephone call centers for insurance companies and banks, and long-surviving industries. The valley's population increased almost 12 percent from 2000 to 2010. Growth slowed to 2 percent in the next five years, though that was still better than most of Pennsylvania. Commuters seeking to avoid big-city housing costs are connected by Interstate 78 to New York City and by the Northeast Extension to Philadelphia. The region has a cluster of colleges - Lehigh, Muhlenberg, and Moravian - and a strong newspaper in *The Morning Call.* It has Dorney Park, one of the nation's oldest amusement parks. A 2013 joint report by two Lehigh Valley community groups found that the area was shedding manufacturing jobs, and that even the health care sector was struggling. In November 2016, Kraft Heinz shut down its large plant in Upper Macungie Township that produced Miracle Whip and Grey Poupon mustard. In Allentown, the 2014 opening of a new $200 million hockey arena was described as "the biggest happening in 30 years." Development of a $325 million, nine-building commercial and residential complex along the Lehigh River broke ground in 2015.

The 15th Congressional District includes most of the Lehigh Valley, covering all of Allentown and most of Bethlehem. The two eastern counties include about 70 percent of the population. The district extends west almost to Harrisburg and takes in parts of Berks, Lebanon and Dauphin counties. It includes Hershey, the town erected by chocolate magnate Milton S. Hershey as a planned, utopian village for his factory workers and their families. The surrounding area is fed by a steady flow of tourists to the Hersheypark amusement site. In 2012, a $300 million expansion of its West Hershey plant reduced the workforce by about 600 jobs. With automation and the smell of chocolate still in the air, the facility produced more than 70 million Kisses each day. Middletown has leafy, gridded streets and handsome homes that give no hint that it is the location of the Three Mile Island nuclear plant, which in 1979 was the site of the worst nuclear accident in U.S. history. Like other GOP-held districts in the Philadelphia area, the 15th can be competitive. Donald Trump won 51 percent of the vote in 2016. President Barack Obama won and then lost similarly narrow contests.

SIXTEENTH DISTRICT

Lloyd Smucker (R)

Elected 2016, 1st term; b. Jan 23, 1964, Lancaster; Franklin & Marshall College; Lebanon Valley College (PA); Lutheran; Married (Cynthia (Cindy) Smucker); 3 children.

Elected Office: Western Lampeter Board of Supervisors, 2001-2005.

Professional Career: Business Owner; West Lampeter Planning Commission.

DC Office: 516 CHOB 20515, 202-225-2411, Fax: 202-225-2013, smucker.house.gov.

State Offices: Lancaster, 717-393-0667.

Committees: *Budget*. *Education & the Workforce*: Health, Employment, Labor & Pensions, Higher Education & Workforce Development. *Transportation & Infrastructure*: Economic Dev't, Public Buildings & Emergency Management, Highways & Transit, Railroads, Pipelines & Hazardous Materials.

Election Results

Election	Name (Party)	Vote (%)	Cand. Spent	Ind. Exp. Support	Ind. Exp. Oppose
2016 General	Lloyd Smucker (R)	168,669 (54%)	$1,445,384	$242,884	
	Christina Hartman (D)	134,586 (43%)	$1,084,740	$359,559	$715,954
	Shawn House (L)	10,518 (3%)			
2016 Primary	Lloyd Smucker (R)	49,549 (54%)			
	Chet Beiler (R)	42,092 (46%)			

Lloyd Smucker, elected to an open seat in 2016, seemed to fit comfortably with the mostly Establishment Republicans in the Pennsylvania delegation. He won competitive contests in both the primary and general election and styled himself as a problem-solver.

Smucker grew up locally and attended but did not graduate from local colleges. He founded Smucker Co., a commercial construction firm that specialized in dry wall, and ran the business for a quarter-century. He served on the West Lampeter Township Planning Commission for four years, and was elected to the state Senate for eight years. In Harrisburg, Smucker chaired the Senate Education Committee and mostly advocated local control over educational standards. He supported steps to encourage legalization of immigrants but was unable to enact such a measure.

When Republican Rep. Joseph Pitts retired after serving 20 years, just as his predecessor Rep. Robert Walker had served 20 years, Smucker became the frontrunner. In the primary, he faced businessman Chet Beiler, whose family-owned Amish Country Gazebos was the nation's leading retailer of custom-built gazebos. The two candidates were second cousins who graduated in the same class at Lancaster Mennonite High School. In the primary, each spent more than $600,000, with a large share self-financed. Smucker was endorsed the Chamber of Commerce and the National Rifle Association. He won, 54%-46%, with 56 percent in Lancaster County, which cast more than 80 percent of the total vote.

The general election was competitive against Democrat Christina Hartman, a local native who was a consultant to non-profit groups after having spent 15 years in international development. She described herself as "moderate to progressive" and said that the district was moving to the left. Her campaign ran negative ads that sought to link Smucker to GOP presidential nominee Donald Trump. In the closing weeks of the campaign, Smucker grew more enthusiastic about Trump and spoke at his rally in Lancaster. David Wasserman of the Cook Political Report wrote that Hartman ran a "surprisingly energetic campaign," and was competitive financially, even though national Democrats did not become active until late in the campaign. Smucker out-raised Hartman, $1.5 million to $1.2 million, and received more than $800,000 in additional support. He won, 54%-43%. Hartman led in Berks and Chester counties. Lancaster cast about three-fourths of the total vote, of which Smucker took 59 percent.

Smucker positioned himself in the House with seats on three committees: Budget, Education and the Workforce, and Transportation and Infrastructure. In March, he filed his first bill, which sought to give senior citizens more flexibility on when they can sign up for Medicare. He advocated other steps to reduce health care costs. That month, he said that he was "very disappointed" by the initial failure of House Republicans to reform the Affordable Care Act. The Democratic Congressional Campaign Committee listed Smucker among four Pennsylvania Republicans - all from the Philadelphia metro area - on its initial list of targets for 2018.

Philadelphia Exurbs: Lancaster, Reading

Population		**Race and Ethnicity**		**Income**	
Total	717,967	White	73.0%	Median Income	$54,296 (192 out of 435)
Land area	998	Black	5.8%		
Pop/ sq mi	719.6	Latino	17.5%		
Born in state	70.3%	Asian	1.8%	Under $50,000	46.1%
Age Groups		Two races	1.6%	$50,000-$99,999	33.2%
Under 18	25.0%	Other	0.2%	$100,000-$199,999	17.2%
18-34	22.3%	**Education**		$200,000 or more	3.4%
35-64	37.9%	H.S grad or less	53.4%	Poverty Rate	14.4%
Over 64	14.8%	Some college	21.8%	**Health Insurance**	
Work		College Degree, 4 yr	16.1%	With health insurance coverage	88.1%
White Collar	32.1%	Post grad	8.8%		
Sales and Service	40.1%	**Military**		**Public Assistance**	
Blue Collar	27.8%	Veteran	8.0%	Cash public assistance income	3.7%
Government	5.7%	Active Duty	0.1%		
				Food stamp/SNAP benefits	13.6%

Voter Turnout			
2015 Total Citizens 18+	512,269	2016 House Turnout as % CVAP	61%
2016 House turnout	313,773	2014 House Turnout as % CVAP	35%

2012 Presidential Vote		
Mitt Romney	153,452	(52%)
Barack Obama	135,469	(46%)

2016 Presidential Vote		
Donald Trump	161,763	(50%)
Hillary Clinton	140,186	(44%)
Gary Johnson	10,447	(3%)

Cook Partisan Voting Index: R+5

The Pennsylvania Dutch Country, settled by Germans in the 18th century when it was Pennsylvania's frontier, remains a distinctive part of America. These Germans were Amish and Mennonite, pietistic sects seeking religious liberty and determined to farm rich lands in the same intensive way they had in Germany. Today, many of their descendants - the Eisenhower family is the most famous example - have blended into mainstream America. But in the Dutch area around Lancaster, many "Plain People" still live in the old way, though today they are willing to use some modern devices, such as battery-powered electricity. Tourists can still see families of Plain People clad in black, clattering over the back roads in horse-drawn carriages, with scrupulously tended farms set amid rolling hills and barns decorated with hex signs. Beneath the surface, Amish communities are facing the strains of modernity and economic dislocation. In October 2006, five Amish girls were killed and five others seriously wounded by a gunman at their one-room schoolhouse in Nickel Mines.

With the rich soil, fruits and vegetables are a pillar of the local economy. In Chester County, Kennett Square is the Mushroom Capital of the World. It grows 65 percent of domestic consumption. The industry employs about 6,000 workers; most of them are permanent residents because many of the mushroom farmers have six crops each year, most of them indoors. In September, the annual mushroom festival attracts about 100,000 persons. With an easy drive from Philadelphia, Baltimore and Washington, the area is home to many outlet malls; the first Woolworth's store opened in Lancaster in 1879. Pennsylvania Dutch Country draws more than 8 million tourists annually.

The 16th Congressional District of Pennsylvania includes most of Lancaster County, parts of southwestern Chester County, and a small slice of mostly Democratic Reading in Berks County. An old industrial town that inspired John Updike's *Rabbit* novels and ranked recently among the poorest cities in the nation, Reading is now 58 percent Hispanic, compared with 18 percent for the district. Until the 1980s, Lancaster County was one of the most Republican counties in the state. Suburbanization and demographic change have reduced that share. But it remains firmly Republican with 57 percent for Donald Trump in 2016, and is the second-fastest growing county in the state. It includes nearly 75 percent of the population in the 16th District. (Amish rarely vote, but their social views seem consistent with the overall local attitudes.) Like the other Republican-held districts in southeast Pennsylvania, the 16th was carefully drawn to share the heavily Republican precincts among those five districts. The 50 percent of the vote for Donald Trump in 2016 fell between the 49 percent for John McCain and the 52 percent for Mitt Romney.

SEVENTEENTH DISTRICT

Matt Cartwright (D)

Elected 2012, 3rd term; b. May 01, 1961, Erie; Hamilton College (NY), A.B., 1983; Temple University School of Law (PA), Att., 1984; University of Pennsylvania, J.D., 1986; Roman Catholic; Married (Marion Munley); 2 children.

Professional Career: Practicing attorney, Munley, Munley & Cartwright, 1986-2012.

DC Office: 1034 LHOB 20515, 202-225-5546, Fax: 202-226-0996, cartwright.house.gov.

State Offices: Easton, 484-546-0776; Pottsville, 570-624-0140; Scranton, 570-341-1050; Wilkes-Barre, 570-371-0317.

Committees: *Appropriations*: Commerce, Justice, Science & Related Agencies, Financial Services & General Government. *Oversight & Government Reform*.

Group Ratings

	ADA	ACLU	AFL-CIO	LCV	ITI	COC	HAFA	ACU	CFG	FRC
2016	-	76%	-	100%	50%	57%	12%	4%	0%	8%
2015	85%	C	100%	94%	C	37%	C	4%	0%	8%

Almanac Ratings 2015

	Economy	Social	Foreign	Composite
Liberal	94%	85%	81%	87%
Conservative	6%	15%	19%	13%

Key Votes of the 114th Congress

1. Keystone Pipeline	NV	5. Puerto Rico Debt	Y	9. Offenses by Aliens	Y
2. Trade Deals	N	6. Medical Marijuana	Y	10. Troops in Iraq	N
3. Export-Import Bank	Y	7. Sanctuary Cities	N	11. Homeland Security $$	Y
4. Debt Ceiling Increase	Y	8. Armor-piercing Bullets	N	12. Trade Adjustment aid	N

Election Results

Election	Name (Party)	Vote (%)		Cand. Spent	Ind. Exp. Support	Ind. Exp. Oppose
2016 General	Matt Cartwright (D)	157,734	(54%)	$630,584		
	Matt Connolly (R)	135,430	(46%)	$29,132		
2016 Primary	Matt Cartwright (D)		(100%)			

Prior winning percentages: 2014 (57%), 2012 (60%)

Scranton lawyer and political newcomer Matt Cartwright was elected in 2012 after he toppled 10-term Rep. Tim Holden in the 2012 Democratic primary by running to the left in a redrawn district. With a seat on the Appropriations Committee, he took on the Pennsylvania tradition of servicing local constituents.

Cartwright was born in Erie. His mother earned a law degree but didn't practice law. After he served in the Army during World War II, his father's wartime experience with radar technology led to a job with General Electric. His father's GE work eventually led the family to relocate to Toronto, where Cartwright got his bachelor's degree from Hamilton College. He studied at the London School of Economics and Political Science. He earned his law degree from the University of Pennsylvania and practiced law in Philadelphia for several years while his wife worked as a judicial clerk. The couple later moved to Scranton to join the law firm of his father-in-law, Robert Munley. Cartwright represented consumers tangling with large corporations on a variety of civil claims. He served on the board of governors of the American Association for Justice, a trial lawyers' group.

Cartwright decided to take on Holden, who had been severely damaged by the Republican-orchestrated redistricting, Holden's hometown areas of St. Clair and Pottsville were joined with unfamiliar territory in Scranton. Cartwright's campaign estimated that 86 percent of the district's likely Democratic voters were new to Holden. "I had always thought about running for high political office, and I was kind of waiting for the stars to line up," Cartwright said. "And, you know, they don't hold the door open for you. You kind of have to muscle your way in."

For the Democratic primary, Cartwright raised around $600,000, much of it from fellow trial lawyers. He got help from the anti-incumbent super PAC Campaign for Primary Accountability. Cartwright ran as a progressive, pushing for environmental protections and criticizing corporate tax breaks. The two candidates differed on health care. Cartwright supported the 2010 Affordable Care Act. Holden had voted against it while serving his more conservative district. Holden ran a hard-hitting ad insinuating that Cartwright's law firm contributed money to jailed Luzerne County Judge Michael Toole in exchange for a favorable verdict in a malpractice case. *The Citizens' Voice* newspaper of Wilkes-Barre pointed out that the political contribution was four years before the malpractice verdict.

The new Democratic district was better suited to Cartwright's liberal views than to Holden's centrism. The challenger won the primary, 57%-43%, with more than 70 percent of the vote in both Lackawanna and Luzerne. Holden took 85 percent in his home base of Schuylkill, but it wasn't enough. In the general election, Cartwright faced Scranton Tea Party founder Laureen Cummings. In Democratic territory, Cartwright won, 60%-40%.

With Rep. Joaquin Castro of Texas, Cartwright was elected one of two presidents of the Democratic freshman class. During his first two years, he took credit for having developed and introduced 60-plus bills, more than any other House Democrat. He joined Democratic Rep. Rick Nolan of Minnesota on a proposed constitutional amendment to reverse the Supreme Court's ruling in the *Citizens United* case that overturned restrictions on federal campaign financing. That bill had faint prospects in the Republican-controlled House. True to his campaign promise, Cartwright mostly voted the party line.

In the *Almanac* vote ratings for 2015, he was more liberal on economic issues and conservative on foreign policy. He was part of a bipartisan group that enacted in July 2016 the Megabyte Act, which reduced government costs for software licenses. In December, the House passed his bill to disseminate information to assist local schools in promoting energy efficiency. He made a big personal move that year when he filled the vacancy on the Appropriations Committee, which resulted when Democrat Chaka Fattah of Pennsylvania resigned after his criminal conviction. Explaining his selection to the *Wilkes Barres Times Leader*, Cartwright said, "As soon as I got to Washington, I set about the business of making friends. And the best way to make friends is to be a friend." Following the election, on the recommendation of Minority Leader Nancy Pelosi, he became one of three co-chairs of the Democratic Policy and Communications Committee.

In the 2016 election, Cartwright showed that he needed to work to secure his seat. Little-known Republican challenger Matt Connolly, a real estate investor who campaigned against excessive federal regulations and unfunded mandates on local governments, said that Cartwright's views were "not aligned with this district." Connolly raised a mere $31,000 to nearly $1 million for Cartwright. The outcome was an unexpectedly close, 54%-46%. House Republicans listed him as an early target for reelection in 2018. Given his carefully drawn district and the shrinking Pennsylvania delegation, perhaps the biggest risk for Cartwright is redistricting in 2021.

East-Central Pennsylvania: Scranton/Wilkes-Barre, Easton

Population		**Race and Ethnicity**		**Income**	
Total	700,379	White	83.0%	Median Income	$48,600 (275 out of 435)
Land area	1,733	Black	5.4%		
Pop/ sq mi	404.1	Latino	8.0%		
Born in state	68.3%	Asian	1.8%	Under $50,000	51.1%
		Two races	1.5%	$50,000-$99,999	31.5%
Age Groups		Other	0.3%	$100,000-$199,999	15.1%
Under 18	20.6%			$200,000 or more	2.4%
18-34	21.0%	**Education**		Poverty Rate	13.7%
35-64	40.8%	H.S grad or less	52.2%		
Over 64	17.7%	Some college	27.2%	**Health Insurance**	
		College Degree, 4 yr	13.3%	With health insurance coverage	90.8%
Work		Post grad	7.3%		
White Collar	30.6%				
Sales and Service	43.6%	**Military**		**Public Assistance**	
Blue Collar	25.8%	Veteran	9.7%	Cash public assistance income	3.3%
Government	4.5%	Active Duty	0.1%		
				Food stamp/SNAP benefits	14.3%

Voter Turnout			
2015 Total Citizens 18+	540,402	2016 House Turnout as % CVAP	54%
2016 House turnout	293,164	2014 House Turnout as % CVAP	31%

2012 Presidential Vote		
Barack Obama	156,015	(55%)
Mitt Romney	121,867	(43%)

2016 Presidential Vote		
Donald Trump	163,734	(53%)
Hillary Clinton	132,699	(43%)
Gary Johnson	6,515	(2%)

Cook Partisan Voting Index: R+1

"Coal is the theme song of this city in the hills," the *WPA Guide* said of Scranton in 1940, but even as those words were written, the anthracite kingdom around Scranton and Wilkes-Barre was crumbling. In the 19th century, anthracite had become America's main home heating fuel, and the valley along the East Branch of the Susquehanna River was the No. 1 source of anthracite. Thousands of immigrants flocked to the valley, settling in a chain of little cities north and south of Wilkes-Barre and Scranton. They took jobs with long hours, modest pay, poor working conditions and high death rates - facts of life that made the violently pro-union Molly Maguires popular here and that spawned periodic clashes between workers and the Pinkerton security forces hired by the industrial moguls. Author John O'Hara grew up in Pottsville and wrote about tough-talking miners in the 1930s and 1940s.

While the supply of coal was endless, demand proved fleeting. Anthracite production peaked in 1917, with long strikes in 1922 and 1925 quickening the conversion to oil and gas. Demand for anthracite began to fall in the 1920s and plummeted in the 1940s. The counties containing Wilkes-Barre and Scranton, Luzerne and Lackawanna, had 755,000 people in 1930 and 528,000 in 2015. The Hispanic population in Luzerne was 10 percent in 2015, a nearly 50 percent increase in the previous five years and one of the fastest-growing Hispanic areas in the nation. Scranton was known from 2005 until 2013 as the location of the fictitious Dunder Mifflin Paper Company on *The Office*, the hit NBC comedy series. It is the birthplace of former Vice President Joe Biden, and Hillary Clinton's paternal grandparents were natives. Pottsville is the home of Yuengling lager (known locally as "Vitamin Y"). In Easton, old industrial buildings have become a magnet for artists seeking inexpensive loft and warehouse space. In March 2017, the world's largest waterpark opened in Pocono Summit.

Scranton's $16 million budget shortfall in 2012 threatened to push the city into bankruptcy. Officials kept the city afloat by issuing $26 million in bonds and getting financial aid from the state. In 2015, the city tripled to $3 a week its local services tax for all workers in the city. The police and firefighter pension funds were near insolvency. In October 2016, State Auditor General Edward DePasquale said that Scranton had made progress, but he warned of the spike in pension payments that remained due.

The 17th Congressional District takes in the Democratic strongholds Scranton and Wilkes-Barre, drops south to Easton and Bethlehem in Northampton, then shifts west to Pottsville and Republican-leaning Schuylkill County. It covers parts of marginal Carbon County and Democratic-leaning Monroe County. The irregularly shaped district was drawn by Republican redistricters to include Democratic bastions and protect nearby GOP districts. But the 2016 election took a sharp and unexpected turn. In a district that President Barack Obama - with Biden -- had won with 57 percent and 55 percent in his two campaigns, Donald Trump won, 53%-43%.

EIGHTEENTH DISTRICT

Tim Murphy (R)

Elected 2002, 8th term; b. Sep 11, 1952, Cleveland, OH; Wheeling Jesuit University (WV), B.S., 1974; Cleveland State University (OH), M.A., 1976; University of Pittsburgh (PA), Ph.D., 1979; Roman Catholic; Married (Nanette Missig); 1 child; 2 grandchildren.

Military Career: U.S. Navy Reserve Medical Service Corps, 2009-present.

Elected Office: PA Senate, 1997-2003.

Professional Career: Practicing psychologist, 1976-2002.

DC Office: 2332 RHOB 20515, 202-225-2301, Fax: 202-225-1844, murphy.house.gov.

State Offices: Greensburg, 724-850-7312; Pittsburgh, 412-344-5583.

Committees: *Energy & Commerce*: Energy, Environment, Health, Oversight & Investigations (Chmn).

Group Ratings

	ADA	ACLU	AFL-CIO	LCV	ITI	COC	HAFA	ACU	CFG	FRC
2016	-	5%	-	3%	100%	100%	46%	76%	58%	100%
2015	0%	C	42%	3%	C	90%	C	54%	50%	100%

Almanac Ratings 2015

	Economy	Social	Foreign	Composite
Liberal	3%	14%	10%	9%
Conservative	97%	86%	90%	91%

Key Votes of the 114th Congress

1. Keystone Pipeline	Y	5. Puerto Rico Debt	Y	9. Offenses by Aliens	Y
2. Trade Deals	Y	6. Medical Marijuana	N	10. Troops in Iraq	N
3. Export-Import Bank	N	7. Sanctuary Cities	Y	11. Homeland Security $$	Y
4. Debt Ceiling Increase	N	8. Armor-piercing Bullets	Y	12. Trade Adjustment aid	Y

Election Results

Election	Name (Party)	Vote (%)	Cand. Spent	Ind. Exp. Support	Ind. Exp. Oppose
2016 General	Tim Murphy (R)	293,684 (100%)	$985,029		
2016 Primary	Tim Murphy (R)	(100%)			

Prior winning percentages: 2014 (100%), 2012 (64%), 2010 (67%), 2008 (64%), 2006 (58%), 2004 (63%), 2002 (60%)

Republican Tim Murphy, elected in 2002, has used his background as a psychologist and his seat on the influential Energy and Commerce Committee to play a role in debates over health care, including the

21st Century Cures Act of 2016. He is a fairly reliable Republican, but occasionally shows independence and has drawn enough backing from labor unions to avoid serious Democratic challenges.

Murphy grew up in Cleveland in a family of 11 children. He took up the guitar as a teenager, and was accomplished enough to play in bands that opened for folk legend John Hartford and banjo master Earl Scruggs. He graduated from Wheeling Jesuit University, got a Ph.D. from the University of Pittsburgh and became a child psychologist. He worked in several Pittsburgh-area hospitals and was an adjunct faculty member in public health and pediatrics at the University of Pittsburgh. He became well-known locally as "Dr. Tim," offering advice in television appearances and on radio talk shows. He co-authored the book, *The Angry Child: Regaining Control When Your Child is Out of Control.* After his election to Congress, he co-authored another book (which was not about Congress) titled, *Overcoming Passive-Aggression.* Murphy served six years in the state Senate, where he sponsored a Patients' Bill of Rights and increased funding for medical research.

Running for the House in a vacant district after redistricting, he presented himself as an experienced and accomplished legislator who opposed abortion rights and supported gun ownership. With extensive support from state and national Republicans, he ran unopposed in the Republican primary. In the general election, he outspent Democratic nominee Jack Machek, a school district administrator, by nearly 8-to-1. Murphy won 60%-40%, an impressive showing in an area that had mostly sent Democrats to Congress.

Murphy has been an active legislator but he has kept a fairly low profile. "He's measured. He doesn't provoke controversy," Franklin & Marshall University politics professor G. Terry Madonna told the *Pittsburgh Post-Gazette.* In 2007 and 2009, he backed the Democrats' plan to expand the Children's Health Insurance Program, and he has supported several priorities of labor unions, including a bill to make unionizing easier by eliminating the secret ballot in worksite elections. But he reversed his position and mollified business groups on that issue in 2012, prompting the conservative *Pittsburgh Tribune-Review*'s editorial page to call him "a weasel."

On Energy and Commerce, his work as chairman of the Oversight and Investigations Subcommittee initially focused on programs for military veterans with mental illness and on improving security for their medical records. After the Newtown, Connecticut, school massacre in 2012 focused attention on mental illness and violence, his oversight panel conducted a thorough overview of federal programs to determine what role mental illness plays in outbreaks of violence. He introduced his landmark mental health reform bill, the Helping Families in Mental Health Crisis Act. He has worked with Democratic Rep. Gene Green of Texas to win House passage of a bill to address the shortage of doctors in underserved communities.

Working on the 21st Century Cures Act, Murphy won several major debates to assure federal enforcement of equal insurance coverage for mental-health illness. Referring to the inclusion of his Helping Families in Mental Health Crisis Act in that broader bill, he said that the new law "fixes the nation's broken mental health system by refocusing programs, reforming grants, and removing federal barriers to care." Murphy co-chairs the Mental Health Caucus and is a founding member of the GOP Doctors Caucus. Serving in the Navy Reserve Medical Service Corps at Walter Reed National Military Medical Center, he has treated service members with traumatic brain injury.

On energy issues, Murphy has sought to reduce regulatory burdens on companies using hydraulic fracturing, better known as "fracking," to extract natural gas. He promoted small "modular" nuclear reactors that could power individual neighborhoods. He formed a bipartisan energy working group that created a plan to free the United States from dependence on foreign oil. The proposal would expedite exploration of oil and gas resources, and invest new revenues from leasing and royalties into rebuilding roads, bridges, locks and dams. He co-chairs the Congressional Steel Caucus, where he took some credit for enactment in 2015 of trade-enforcement legislation "to protect American steel against foreign trade cheats."

He has been successful in helping to keep open his district's 911th Airlift Wing in Moon Township, which the Pentagon had threatened to shut down. In September 2016, when President Barack Obama signed the bill to continue federal spending until after the election, it included funds to construct a facility at the Pittsburgh Air Reserve Station that is scheduled to house a squadron of the huge C-17 cargo transport aircraft.

Murphy has not been seriously challenged for reelection. In 2012, he drew a GOP primary opponent - Evan Feinberg, a 28-year-old tea party favorite who brandished endorsements from his former bosses, Kentucky Sen. Rand Paul and Oklahoma Sen. Tom Coburn. Feinberg failed to gain much traction, and Murphy won 63%-37%. He coasted in November with 64 percent over underfunded Democrat Larry Maggi. In 2014 and 2016, Murphy was reelected without opposition.

Southwestern Pittsburgh Suburbs

Population		**Race and Ethnicity**		**Income**	
Total	707,775	White	92.7%	Median Income	$60,615 (140 out of 435)
Land area	2,073	Black	2.3%		
Pop/ sq mi	341.5	Latino	1.4%		
Born in state	81.1%	Asian	1.9%	Under $50,000	40.8%
		Two races	1.4%	$50,000-$99,999	32.4%
Age Groups		Other	0.2%	$100,000-$199,999	21.3%
Under 18	19.9%			$200,000 or more	5.4%
18-34	18.8%	**Education**		Poverty Rate	8.3%
35-64	42.7%	H.S grad or less	40.1%		
Over 64	18.6%	Some college	25.5%	**Health Insurance**	
		College Degree, 4 yr	21.8%	With health insurance coverage	94.4%
Work		Post grad	12.7%		
White Collar	40.3%				
Sales and Service	40.1%	**Military**		**Public Assistance**	
Blue Collar	19.5%	Veteran	9.6%	Cash public assistance income	2.3%
Government	4.8%	Active Duty	0.0%		
				Food stamp/SNAP benefits	8.5%

Voter Turnout			
2015 Total Citizens 18+	556,846	2016 House Turnout as % CVAP	53%
2016 House turnout	293,684	2014 House Turnout as % CVAP	30%

2012 Presidential Vote		
Mitt Romney	201,320	(58%)
Barack Obama	142,394	(41%)

2016 Presidential Vote		
Donald Trump	215,200	(58%)
Hillary Clinton	142,836	(38%)
Gary Johnson	9,424	(3%)

Cook Partisan Voting Index: R+11

Pittsburgh was built on the unlikeliest terrain of any major U.S. city. Just about the only level places in the city or its suburbs are the bottomlands along the rivers. Everything else is built on hills that approach the magnitude of mountains. Only a propitious location, where the Allegheny and Monongahela rivers join to form the Ohio, and the confluence of economically valuable natural resources - coal from the mountains and iron ore from the Great Lakes - can explain why a large metropolitan area sprang up there. The cities and towns of greater Pittsburgh are separated from each other not just by miles but by altitude. So, the region's high-income suburbs and its gritty factory towns are not concentrated in one quarter, but are scattered all around. This is long-settled country, with many more old towns than sparkling new suburbs. Unlike the economically diverse Pittsburgh-based Allegheny County, Washington and Westmoreland counties here are more dependent on manufacturing and more susceptible to industry-wide cuts. Several small towns in Allegheny County had above-average growth from 2010 to 2015, apparently because of their proximity to the Pittsburgh airport.

The 18th Congressional District of Pennsylvania covers the southern part of the Pittsburgh metropolitan area. It includes substantial portions of southern Allegheny and Westmoreland counties, which are the population centers, plus smaller and more rural Washington and Greene counties in the southwest corner of the state along both sides of the West Virginia border. Westmoreland votes most heavily Republican of the four counties. The district leans strongly Republican. Donald Trump won 58 percent of the vote in 2016, the same as Mitt Romney got in 2012.

★ RHODE ISLAND ★

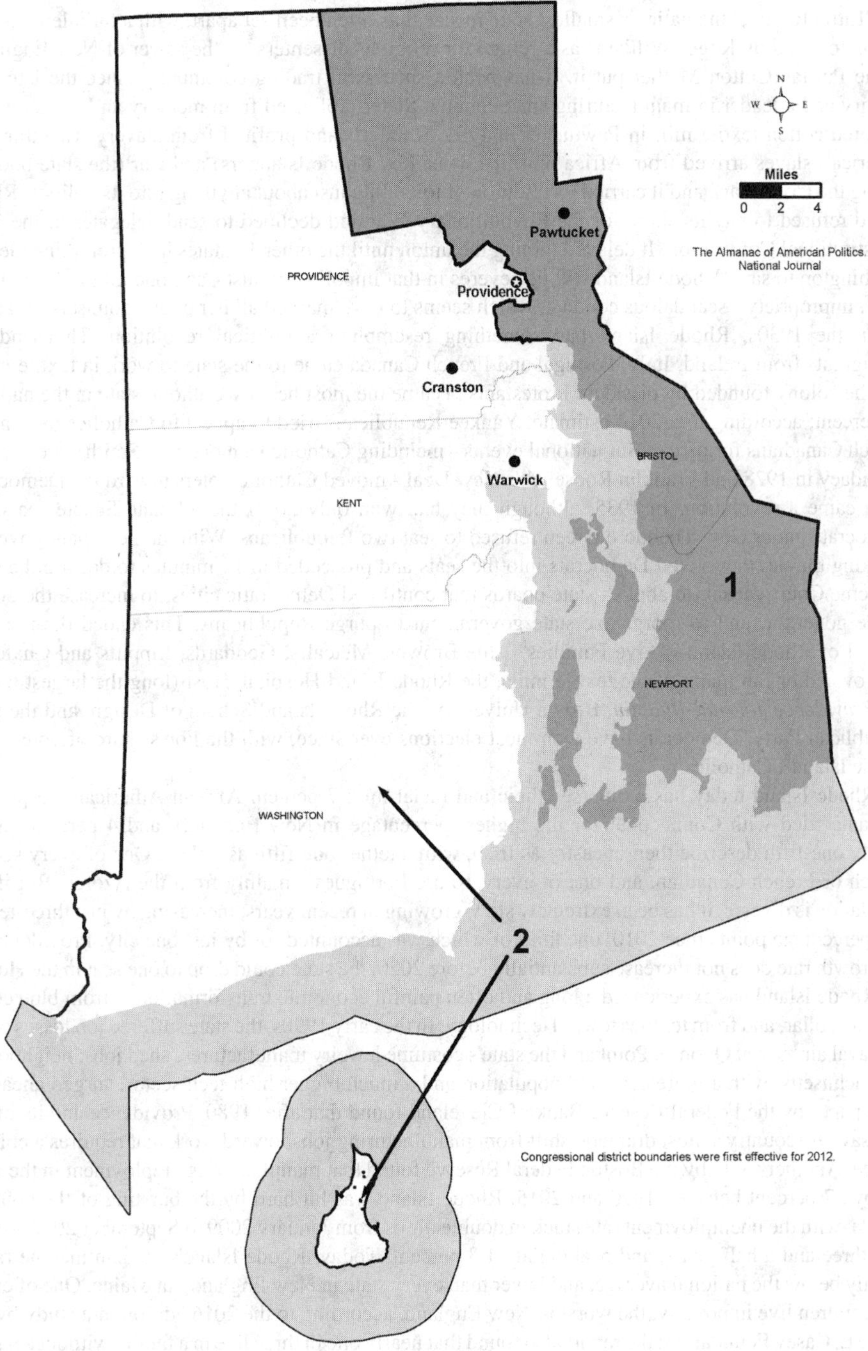

Congressional district boundaries were first effective for 2012.

Rhode Island has a lopsidedly Democratic legislature and a Democratic governor, and it supported Hillary Clinton for president. But like other blue states, it saw Donald Trump make inroads with white working-class voters in 2016, cutting the Democrats' margin of victory in the presidential race by close to half.

"Little Rhody," the nation's smallest state in size, has often been set apart, with a turbulent history. It was founded by Roger Williams as a refuge for religious dissenters -- "the sewer of New England," as the Puritan Cotton Mather put it. It has been a successful trading community since the late 17th century and a leader in manufacturing since Samuel Slater replicated from memory an English water-powered cotton textile mill in Pawtucket in 1791. Rhode Island profited from slavery (two-thirds of America's slaves arrived from Africa on ships owned by Rhode Islanders) and war (the state boomed during the Civil War), and it carried its tradition of tolerating just about anything into its politics. Rhode Island refused to pay its share for the Revolutionary War and declined to send delegates to the 1787 Constitutional Convention. It delayed joining the union until the other 12 states had, prompting George Washington to say, "Rhode Island still perseveres in that impolitic, unjust - and one might add without much impropriety - scandalous conduct, which seems to have marked all her public counsels of late."

In the 1930s, Rhode Island had something resembling a political revolution. Thousands of immigrants from Ireland, Italy, Portugal and French Canada came to the state to work in textile mills, and the colony founded by dissident Protestants became the most heavily Catholic state in the nation – 44 percent, according to a 2014 estimate. Yankee Republicans tried to appeal to Catholics by running French Canadians for office. But national events - including Catholic Democrat Al Smith's presidential candidacy in 1928 and Franklin Roosevelt's New Deal - moved Catholic voters toward the Democrats. Then came a revolution. In 1935, although they had won only 20 of the 42 state Senate seats, the Democrats under Gov. Theodore Green refused to seat two Republicans. With the lieutenant governor breaking the tie, they voted Democrats into the seats and proceeded in 14 minutes to declare the state Supreme Court vacant, to abolish state boards that controlled Democratic cities, to increase the power of the governor, and to reorganize state government to purge Republicans. This ended the political control of Rhode Island's "Five Families" - the Browns, Metcalfs, Goddards, Lippitts and Chafees - who owned or ran many of the textile mills, the Rhode Island Hospital Trust (long the largest bank), the *Providence Journal-Bulletin*, Brown University, the Rhode Island School of Design, and the state Republican Party. Democrats have won most elections ever since, with the lion's share of votes from Rhode Island's Catholics.

Rhode Island today has a diverse ethnic and racial mix: 7 percent African American, 15 percent Hispanic (tied with Connecticut for the highest percentage in New England), and 4 percent Asian. Nearly one-fifth describe their ancestry as Irish, with another one-fifth as Italian. One of every six are French or French Canadian, and one of every 10 are Portuguese, mainly from the Azores. But if the population is diverse, it has been extremely slow-growing in recent years, increasing by just three-tenths of a percentage point since 2010, one third of which was accounted for by just one city, Providence. If the growth rate does not increase substantially before 2020, the state could drop to one seat in the House.

Rhode Island has experienced a long and often painful economic transformation -- from blue collar to white collar, and from textiles toward technology. In the early 1990s, the state suffered job losses when the naval air base at Quonset Point and the state's costume jewelry manufacturers shed jobs; neighboring Massachusetts, with a more educated population and a much bigger high-tech sector, surged ahead. A 2016 paper by the Federal Reserve Bank of Cleveland found that after 1980, Providence and its metro area saw the country's most dramatic shift from manufacturing jobs toward work that requires a college degree. Another study by the Boston Federal Reserve found that manufacturing employment in the state fell by 57 percent between 1990 and 2015. Rhode Island was hit hard by the bursting of the housing bubble, with the unemployment rate stuck in double digits from January 2009 to September 2012 – more than three and a half years, and peaking at 11.3 percent. Today, Rhode Island's median income ranks slightly below the national average, and lower than every state in New England but Maine. One of every five children live in poverty, the worst in New England, according to the 2016 edition of a study by the Annie E. Casey Foundation; the report also found that nearly one in three live in a family without a parent working full-time. One bright spot was the tech sector; in 2016, the Brookings Institution's Metropolitan Policy Program ranked Rhode Island 17th in job growth for advanced industries, beating out both the nation as a whole and its New England rivals. Another bright spot: Latino businesses, which grew by 280 percent between 1997 and 2012, according to the Latino Policy Institute at Roger Williams University. By early 2017, the state had finally returned to the national average for unemployment. Meanwhile, Rhode Island became home to the nation's first operational offshore windfarm, a 30-megawatt project off Block Island.

In 2009, realizing that education was lagging, the state board of regents hired Deborah Gist as state schools superintendent. By the time she left in 2015, Gist had overseen notable improvements, including higher four-year graduation rates and a decrease in dropout rates among minorities. But she also took flak from teachers' unions, and in 2014 the legislature voted to halt the use of standardized test scores for high school graduation. She left to become school superintendent in Tulsa, Oklahoma.

From 1940 to 1980, Democrats won every election in Rhode Island for House seats, and the state has backed the Democrat in every presidential election since Ronald Reagan's 49-state landslide in 1984. Democrats currently hold all of Rhode Island's four seats in Congress, with Sens. Jack Reed, first elected in 1996, and Sheldon Whitehouse, elected in 2006, well-positioned to hold on as long as their Democratic predecessors John Pastore and Claiborne Pell (24 and 36 years, respectively). But Republicans have done well with the governor's office. Starting in 1994, Republicans Lincoln Almond and Donald Carcieri were elected governor twice each; in 2010, Lincoln Chafee, former Republican Sen. John Chafee's son, was elected as an independent. It wasn't until 2014 that Democrats returned to the governor's chair as Gina Raimondo, the state's first female governor, won office. Third parties have been a factor, most recently with the left-leaning, labor-friendly Working Families Party beginning to flex its muscle in legislative races.

Rhode Island is sometimes called "Rogues Island" for its history of public corruption. The rogues gallery includes former Gov. Edward DiPrete, who served time after pleading guilty to bribery and extortion charges in 1998; Joseph Bevilacqua and Thomas Fay, two chief justices of the state Supreme Court who resigned while they were under investigation in 1986 and 1992; longtime House Speaker John Harwood, who resigned in 2002 after reports that he had sexually harassed a researcher in the legislature; and Senate President William Irons, who resigned in 2004 after an investigation by the state Ethics Commission of lawmakers who voted on legislation while they were working for companies that benefited from those bills. The grim parade continued in 2014, when the FBI raided the home and office of then- House Speaker Gordon D. Fox, who quickly resigned his post; in 2015, Fox pleaded guilty to taking bribes, wire fraud and filing a false tax return. Then, in 2016, House Finance Chairman Raymond E. Gallison Jr. resigned from the legislature; he was later charged with stealing from the estate of a deceased client and a youth education charity. But no political figure embodied Rhode Island's spotty ethical history better than Buddy Cianci, the Providence mayor who spent time in a "federally funded gated community" for assaulting with a fire log a man whom he accused of having an affair with his wife. Later, after becoming a radio talk show host, Cianci was reelected as mayor in 1990, before resigning again amid federal racketeering charges that ultimately led to another conviction. Cianci died in 2016; perhaps fittingly, Rhode Island voters later that year approved a constitutional amendment overturning a 2009 state Supreme Court decision that had curbed the powers of the state ethics commission.

In the 2016 presidential election, Clinton won Rhode Island by 15 points, a substantial victory but a narrower one than Barack Obama had managed in 2012, when he won the state by 28 points. (Chafee, Rhode Island's own 2016 presidential contender running as a Democrat, exited the race in October 2015after attracting negligible support.) Clinton underperformed Obama's 2012 showing by 27,000 votes, while Trump overperformed Mitt Romney by 23,000. Of the state's five counties, one switched from blue to red-- Kent (Warwick), which went from an 18-point Obama victory to a narrow win by Trump. The other four counties remained Democratic, although Providence County saw its margin shift by 14 points toward the GOP, Washington County (Narragansett) saw its margin shift by seven points, and Bristol County saw its shift by two points. Newport County gravitated slightly in Trump's direction. Analyzing the returns town-by-town, the *Providence Journal* found that Clinton "drew her support from the wealthiest and poorest places, while Trump drew his from the middle." The newspaper further noted that "all of the communities that touch saltwater voted for Clinton, and all but four of the state's inland communities went for Trump." June S. Speakman, a political science professor at Roger Williams University told the paper, "That looks a lot like the country, doesn't it? The two coasts are blue, and the heartland is red."

Population		Race and Ethnicity		Income	
Total	1,053,661	White	74.5%	Median Income	$56,852 (19 out of 50)
Land area	1,034	Black	5.3%		
Pop/ sq mi	1019.2	Latino	13.6%	Under $50,000	44.6%
Born in state	57.9%	Asian	3.2%	$50,000-$99,999	29.7%
		Two races	2.2%	$100,000-$199,999	20.5%
Age Groups		Other	1.1%	$200,000 or more	5.2%
Under 18	20.4%			Poverty Rate	14.2%
18-34	24.1%	**Education**			
35-64	40.2%	H.S grad or less	41.1%	**Health Insurance**	
Over 64	15.4%	Some college	27.0%	With health insurance coverage	90.7%
Work		College Degree, 4 yr	19.1%		
		Post grad	12.8%		
White Collar	36.9%			**Public Assistance**	
Sales and Service	44.6%	**Military**		Cash public assistance income	3.0%
Blue Collar	18.5%	Veteran	7.9%		
Government	12.7%	Active Duty	0.4%	Food stamp/SNAP benefits	15.9%

Voter Turnout			
2015 Total Citizens 18+	776,565	2016 Pres Turnout as % CVAP	60%
2016 Pres Votes	464,144	2012 Pres Turnout as % CVAP	58%

Legislature	
Senate:	33D, 5R
House:	64D, 11R

Presidential Politics

2016 Democratic Primary		
Bernie Sanders (D)	66,993	(55%)
Hillary Clinton (D)	52,749	(43%)
2016 Republican Primary		
Donald Trump (R)	39,221	(64%)
John Kasich (R)	14,963	(24%)
Ted Cruz (R)	6,416	(10%)

2016 Presidential Vote		
Hillary Clinton (D)	252,525	(54%)
Donald Trump (R)	180,543	(39%)
Gary Johnson (L)	14,746	(3%)
2012 Presidential Vote		
Barack Obama (D)	279,677	(63%)
Mitt Romney (R)	157,204	(35%)

Rhode Island has been one of the most Democratic states in presidential elections. It voted 61%-32% for Al Gore in 2000 - his best state in the country. Hillary Clinton easily beat Donald Trump 54%-39%, but that was a significant drop from Barack Obama's 63%-35% victories in both 2008 and 2012. Registered Democrats outnumber Republicans in Rhode Island by more than three-to-one, but unaffiliated voters make up a plurality of the electorate. Rhode Island is also the most Catholic state in the country, but many Catholics vote with their party rather than with their bishop. White ethnic voters dominate the political culture of the state and places like Johnston, North Providence, West Warwick and Woonsocket can tilt more Republican for a candidate who is conservative on social issues and crime, but is not hostile to bigger government. All of these locales saw their vote for Clinton fall by 13 to 17 percentage points from Obama's levels in 2012.

From 1984 to 2008, Rhode Island held a presidential primary in early-to-mid March, but in 2011 the state legislature moved the date in hopes of increasing its relevance in a regional Eastern states primary. The state succeeded somewhat: In the final days before the April 26 primary, all four of the top contenders campaigned in Rhode Island. Donald Trump defeated Ohio Gov. John Kasich 64%-24%. Trump captured all 39 of the state's cities and towns except for Barrington, a comfortable suburban town that is the hometown of Trump's White House Press Secretary, Sean Spicer. Vermont Sen. Bernie Sanders defeated Clinton 55%-43%, winning all but Barrington, East Greenwich and Pawtucket. In 2008, she won the state 58%-40%

Congressional Districts

115th Congress Lineup	2D	114th Congress Lineup	2D

Rhode Island held onto its two districts in the 2010 census, though not by much, and now houses the least populous districts in the country. Census Bureau projections are that the state won't be so lucky next time.

Redistricting hasn't been much of a problem since the state lost its third seat in 1932: Providence is split and both districts are overwhelmingly Democratic -though a Republican occasionally has been elected against a flawed Democrat. In 2011, the legislature approved a new 18-member Special Commission on Reapportionment, an advisory panel comprising eight legislators and six citizens appointed by the majority leaders (Democrats), and four legislators appointed by the minority.

The commission needed to shift only about 7,000 residents from the 1st District to the 2nd, and could have easily done so by tweaking a few lines in Providence. But freshman Democrat David Cicilline was polling abysmally in the 1st. His ally, state House Speaker Gordon Fox, prevailed on the commission to draft a map shifting three northern towns Cicilline had lost in 2010 - Smithfield, North Smithfield and Burrillville - into Democrat Jim Langevin's 2nd District in exchange for more of liberal Providence, moving nearly 100,000 residents. Langevin, though popular, would have none of it. The commission proposed exchanging only Burrillville for a smaller share of Providence, giving Cicilline one extra percentage point of insurance. The legislature and governor approved. Since then, Cicilline and Langevin have won easily. The state is preparing for a political nightmare when the 2020 census likely will strip its second House seat, and the two Democrats - or their successors - will be forced to run against each other, unless one steps aside. Langevin took a possible move in that direction in February 2017 when he told a reporter for the *Providence Journal* that he was thinking of running for governor-in 2022, but not in 2018. Cicilline might find that an appealing option.

Governor

Gina Raimondo (D)

Elected 2014, term expires 2019, 1st term; b. May. 17, 1971, Smithfield, RI; Harvard U., B.A. 1993; Rhodes Scholar, Oxford U., PhD; Yale Law Schl., J.D. 1998; Catholic; Married (Andy Moffitt); 2 children.

Elected Office: RI Treasurer, 2010-2014.

Professional Career: Clerk, Judge Kimba Wood; Founder & Senior Vice President, Village Ventures; Co-founder, Point Judith Capital.

Office: 82 Smith St., Providence, 02903; 401-222-2371; Fax: 401-222-2012; Website: ri.gov.

Election Results

Election	Name (Party)	Vote (%)
2014 General	Gina Raimondo (D)	131,899 (41%)
	Allan Fung (R)	117,428 (36%)
	Robert Healey (Mod)	69,278 (21%)
2014 Primary	Gina Raimondo (D)	53,990 (42%)
	Angel Taveras (D)	37,326 (29%)
	Clay Pell (D)	34,515 (27%)

Democrat Gina Raimondo - a Harvard graduate, Rhodes scholar, Yale-trained lawyer and venture capitalist - was elected Rhode Island's first female governor in 2014. Though she's under 5-foot-3, Raimondo played rugby in college, which may have helped her prepare for her state's rough-and-tumble politics.

Raimondo's personal history reads like the script for a made-in-Rhode Island public service ad. Her grandfather arrived from Italy at age 14, and learned English by studying at the Providence Public

Library. Her father is a World War II Navy veteran from a family of butchers and used the GI Bill to become the first in his family to attend college. Raimondo grew up in a tight-knit family in Smithfield and graduated with honors from Harvard, where she was named top economics student in her class. She received a doctorate from Oxford University on a Rhodes scholarship and earned a law degree from Yale Law School. She clerked for a federal judge and then entered the venture-capital business.

While Raimondo is a Democrat in one of the nation's bluest states, she has typically positioned herself as a pro-business, reformist politician rather than a creature of the party establishment and its key interest groups, such as organized labor. She was elected Rhode Island treasurer in 2010 and set about overhauling the state's public-employee pension system. Central Falls, a city of about 19,000 people, filed for bankruptcy in 2011 under the weight of underfunded pensions - its retiree health benefit liability was five times the city's annual revenues. Meanwhile, Providence was grappling with the 1991 decision by then-mayor Buddy Cianci to award 6 percent annual increases in pension benefits to hundreds of city employees. Raimondo warned that Rhode Island had the largest unfunded pension debt per capita of any state, spending 10 cents of every dollar of tax revenue on the pensions of 21,000 public employees, with that amount poised to double within five years. So in 2011, Raimondo crafted a pension law that froze automatic cost-of-living increases and raised retirement ages. Additional legislation forced some state workers and teachers to move a portion of their retirement savings into 401(k)-style accounts. It passed with bipartisan support and was signed into law in 2012, but public-employee unions were livid.

The governorship came open in 2014 after independent Lincoln Chafee's decision not to seek another term. At first, it appeared the Democratic primary was headed toward a battle between Raimondo, a fiscal reformer, and Providence Mayor Angel Taveras, running as a progressive who would win support from labor unions. But then former U.S. Education Department official Clay Pell, grandson of the late Democratic Sen. Claiborne Pell and scion of one of Rhode Island's most prominent families, got into the race, and union support was divided, with firefighters, police, supermarket clerks and city employees backing Taveras, and the teachers union - unhappy with Taveras' support of charter schools - siding with Pell. Raimondo benefited from the split and won the primary with 42 percent of the vote.

Raimondo sought to mend fences with organized labor in the general election. She stumped to raise the state minimum wage to $10.10 an hour, and benefited when her Republican opponent, Cranston Mayor Allan Fung, came out against raising the minimum wage and in favor of right-to-work legislation that would ban union shops from requiring workers to pay union dues. In a state where more than one of every seven workers carries a union card -- the highest rate in New England -- that idea was a non-starter with many voters. Fung pledged to cut taxes and spending, while Raimondo called it "wrong-headed economic theory." Raimondo ended up winning, 41%-36%. In a surprise, perennial candidate Robert J. Healey Jr., running on the Moderate Party line, won 21 percent, possibly due to the name recognition he earned from his many campaigns since the mid-1980s as well as dissatisfaction with both of the major-party nominees.

Raimondo got off to an inauspicious start with legislators when she attended a Washington, D.C., conference and criticized the state's budget process. The Rhode Island governor has relatively weak powers, including a requirement that many appointments be approved the state Senate and the absence of line-item veto powers enjoyed by 44 other governors. Her criticism prompted a rebuke from House Speaker Nicholas Mattielo, after which Raimondo called Mattielo to apologize and went to his office to smooth things over. After that flap, Raimondo recovered, quietly working with lawmakers on a budget that ended up winning unanimous approval in the House and near-unanimous approval in the Senate. The budget created new economic-development programs, exempted most Social Security benefits from state taxes, removed the sales tax on energy for businesses, cut Medicaid spending, increased funding for K-12 education, raised the tax on cigarettes by 25 cents to $3.75 a pack, lowered the state's corporate minimum tax, and established a state infrastructure bank. Businesses were unhappy that the legislature and governor agreed to raise the state minimum wage to $9.60 an hour, although that was 50 cents less than what Raimondo had proposed in her campaign.

The budget also authorized the state to settle the lawsuit brought by unions challenging its pension reforms. Earlier, the state and the unions had averted a trial and agreed to soften the pension reforms by modifying retirement ages, increasing defined benefits for longtime public employees and permitting more chances for inflation adjustments. While Raimondo said the state "had a very strong case," the settlement allowed her to remove the uncertainty hanging over the overhaul, which she said remained intact after the settlement. In 2016, *Fortune* magazine named Raimondo to its list of the World's 50 Greatest Leaders on the basis of her work on pensions. However, Raimondo took some heat for the pension investment fund's annual loss in 2015, the first since the financial crisis in 2008. She had long advocated the use of hedge funds to maximize income, but critics were irked by their high fees and secrecy – and now by their weak performance. In September 2016, the State Investment Commission unanimously backed a move to relinquish half of the state's $1.1 billion hedge funds investments.

In February 2016, Raimondo signed a bill to fund bridge repairs through a mix of borrowing, refinancing and new tolls on trucks, and in July she signed a renewable energy package. However, Raimondo suffered an embarrassment over the launch of a tourism campaign in early 2016. Residents were puzzled by the slogan "Rhode Island – Cooler and Warmer," and matters only worsened when a video affiliated with the campaign was discovered to have included footage of Iceland. (Wags called it "Rhode Iceland.") Within days, the marketing director was out, and so was the slogan. Separately, her administration presided over the troubled construction of a $364 million statewide electronic benefits system known as the Unified Health Infrastructure Project. And some criticized the governor for being too fond of incentives to boost business projects, partly a legacy of the disastrous tax breaks the state had previously given 38 Studios, a video-game business founded by former baseball player Curt Schilling.

In early 2017, the state got some good news, as the unemployment rate fell below the national average for the first time since 2005. Raimondo proposed offering residents two years of free tuition at public colleges, requiring employers to offer sick days, and again sought to increase the minimum wage, this time to $10.50 an hour. But with middling approval ratings, Raimondo faced what was likely to be a competitive reelection campaign in 2018. Even if she doesn't face a primary challenge, several credible Republicans are considered potential challengers, including Fung, business executive and former state Sen. Giovanni Feroce, former state Supreme Court Justice Robert Flanders, House Minority Leader Patricia Morgan, and state Reps. Bobby Nardolillo, Joe Trillo and Anthony Giarrusso. Moderate Party founder Ken Block could be in the mix either on the Moderate line or as a Republican, as could former state police superintendent Brendan Doherty, in a party to be determined.

Senior Senator

Jack Reed (D)

Elected 1996, term expires 2020, 4th term; b. Nov 12, 1949, Cranston; Harvard University John F. Kennedy School of Government (MA), M.PP; Harvard University Law School (MA), J.D.; U.S. Military Academy (NY), B.S.; La Salle Academy (RI); Roman Catholic; Married (Julia Hart Reed); 1 child.

Military Career: U.S. Army, 1967-1979; U.S. Army Reserve, 1979-1991.

Elected Office: RI Senate, 1985-1991; U.S. House, 1991-1997.

Professional Career: Association Professor, U.S Military Acad. at West Point, 1977-1979; Practicing attorney, Southerland, Asbill & Brennan, Edwards & Angell, 1982-1990.

DC Office: 728 HSOB 20510, 202-224-4642, Fax: 202-224-4680, reed.senate.gov.
State Offices: Cranston, 401-943-3100; Providence, 401-528-5200.

Committees: *Appropriations*: Commerce, Justice, Science & Related Agencies, Department of Defense, Department of the Interior, Environment & Related Agencies, DOL, HHS & Education & Related Agencies, Military Construction & Veteran Affairs & Related Agencies, Transportation, HUD & Related Agencies (RMM). *Armed Services (RMM)*: Airland, Cybersecurity, Emerging Threats & Capabilities, Personnel, Readiness & Management Support, Seapower, Strategic Forces. *Banking, Housing & Urban Affairs*: Financial Institutions & Consumer Protection, Housing, Transportation & Community Development, Securities, Insurance & Investment. *Intelligence*.

Group Ratings

	ADA	ACLU	AFL-CIO	LCV	ITI	COC	HAFA	ACU	CFG	FRC
2016	-	82%	-	100%	80%	25%	9%	8%	5%	0%
2015	100%	C	100%	100%	C	43%	C	0%	6%	0%

Almanac Ratings 2015

	Economy	Social	Foreign	Composite
Liberal	100%	100%	96%	99%
Conservative	0%	0%	4%	1%

Key Votes of the 114th Congress

1. Keystone pipeline	N	5. National Security Data	Y	9. Gun Sales Checks	Y
2. Export-Import Bank	N	6. Iran Nuclear Deal	N	10. Sanctuary Cities	N
3. Debt Ceiling Increase	Y	7. Puerto Rico Debt	Y	11. Planned Parenthood	N
4. Homeland Security $$	Y	8. Loretta Lynch A.G	Y	12. Trade deals	N

Election Results

Election	Name (Party)	Vote (%)		Cand. Spent	Ind. Exp. Support	Ind. Exp. Oppose
2014 General	Jack Reed (D)	223,675	(71%)	$4,649,761	$5,576	$4,115
	Mark Zaccaria (R)	92,684	(29%)	$54,031		
2014 Primary	Jack Reed (D)	unopposed				

Prior winning percentages: 2008 (73%), 2002 (78%), 1996 (63%), House: 1994 (68%), 1992 (71%), 1990 (59%)

Since first elected in 1996, Democrat Jack Reed, Rhode Island's senior senator, has operated mostly behind the scenes. He hasn't sought much attention, -but he has been numbered among its most respected policy wonks, making his influence felt on banking issues as well as national security matters. As he has moved into the ranks of the most senior Democrats, he has taken on a greater role as a party spokesman. Reed is a graduate of the United States Military Academy, and, as such, is among the few senators of his generation with military experience. Reed has waved off overtures to become defense secretary-in the hope of one day chairing the Senate Armed Services Committee.

As the top Democrat on Armed Services since 2015, Reed has collaborated with Republican Sen. John McCain, the panel chairman. The two have had an unusually respectful relationship, based partly on their common experience as military academy graduates, with lengthy service. They typically share broad objectives, though they often disagree on specifics. During a February 2016 interview with WPRI in Reed's home state, McCain described their partnership. "We work together, never surprise each other.... We also happen to be good friends, which is very helpful. That's not always the case with a Republican and Democrat." In a separate interview, Reed lavished praise on McCain as "an American hero," and emphasized that he-unlike McCain-never saw combat.

Rhode Island has had a tendency over the past century to send scions of the state's blue-blooded families to the Senate; Theodore Green, Reed's predecessor once removed, traced his ancestry to the colonists who arrived with Roger Williams, Rhode Island's founder, in 1636. Reed is an exception to this political pattern: He grew up in working-class Cranston, immediately west of Providence, as the second of three children of a school custodian and a housewife. Disappointed that she never got to go to college, Mary Reed prepared her children for success in school. She insisted on music and art classes for Jack beginning at age 5. Her son, fascinated by history and World War II as a child, eventually decided he wanted to attend the U.S. Military Academy in West Point New York. At LaSalle Academy, a Catholic prep school in Providence, he played football, although he was small for the sport (he today stands at 5 feet, 7 inches). He also ran track, while working for the school newspaper and winning election to the student council.

After graduating from West Point in 1971, Reed served in the 82nd Airborne Division as a paratrooper, and received a master's degree from Harvard's Kennedy School of Government while in the Army. After eight years of active duty (he spent an additional 12 years in the Army Reserve, retiring with the rank of major), Reed enrolled in Harvard Law School. Throughout his life, he has maintained connections to West Point, teaching there briefly in the late 1970s, serving on the academy's governing board, and choosing its chapel as the site of his wedding in April 2005.

Following graduation from law school, Reed was an associate at a Washington, D.C. law firm before returning to Rhode Island in 1983 to work for Providence-based Edwards & Angell, then one of the state's oldest and most prominent law firms. A year later, at 35, Reed won public office for the first time, beating an incumbent in the primary for the state Senate, where he served six years. During his tenure, Reed headed a commission that investigated a corruption scandal involving the Rhode Island Housing and Mortgage Finance Corporation, a state agency created to make affordable loans to low-income Rhode Islanders. When Republican Claudine Schneider gave up her House seat in 1990 to run against Sen. Claiborne Pell, Reed made a run for Congress. He captured 49 percent of the vote in a four-way field. Former Rep. Edward Beard, a colorful figure who had served three terms in the House prior to being ousted by Schneider in 1980, ran a distant second with 27 percent. In the general election,

Reed won the district, covering the western section of the state, by 59%-41%. He was reelected twice by margins exceeding 2-1.

In 1995, when Pell announced his retirement after six terms, Reed ran to succeed him. Reed had no serious competition for the Democratic nomination and faced state Treasurer Nancy Mayer in the general election. National Republicans spent nearly $1 million on ads attacking Reed as a liberal for opposing bills requiring welfare recipients to work and for supporting labor unions-not especially harmful charges in largely liberal, heavily unionized Rhode Island. Reed spent $2.7 million to Mayer's $773,000. His biography was his message: Reed launched his campaign in a public school conference room named for his late father, he stressed his bootstraps rise from a working-class background, and he called for education spending to help others achieve the same success. He won 63%-35%. He has not had serious competition in three reelection bids since.

Reed has served on the Armed Services Committee since 1999. When he was given a sought-after seat on the Appropriations Committee in 2007, he received a waiver from the Democratic leadership to remain on the Armed Services panel. His influence and clout on defense issues is such that former Defense Secretary Robert Gates said Reed was instrumental in persuading him to stay on the job in the early years of the Obama Administration. "In terms of reaching out to me, and whether I would stay on, Obama couldn't have picked a person I was more willing to listen to or respected more than Jack," Gates told *Rhode Island Monthly* in November 2012. In fact, Gates said he had proposed Reed to Obama as a candidate for defense secretary. But the president "shook his head-he clearly has the highest respect for Jack-and he said, 'I can't lose him in the Senate,' " Gates recalled.

Obama's sentiments at the time were likely driven as much by concerns over the partisan makeup of the Senate as by respect for Reed. At the end of 2008, the governorship of Rhode Island was in GOP control: If the governor had appointed a Republican to replace Reed, it could have upset the new administration's aim to have a 60-vote, filibuster-proof Democratic Senate majority in place. Rhode Island law has since been changed to provide for a special election in the case of a Senate vacancy, but Reed-on at least two occasions when Obama was president-reportedly rejected opportunities to become defense secretary. The most recent occurred just after the 2014 election, when Defense Secretary Chuck Hagel was eased out. A Reed spokesman told the *Providence Journal* at that time that Reed "has made it very clear that he does not wish to be considered for secretary of defense or any other Cabinet position."

When Obama was a Democratic presidential candidate, Reed accompanied him on a 2008 trip to Iraq and Afghanistan, and Obama later considered him as a potential running mate until Reed ruled himself out. (Reed's working-class upbringing as well as his military service and expertise were seen as his upsides as a candidate for national office. Among the downsides: His low-key rhetorical style hardly fit the attack-dog role that vice presidential candidates often must play. Nor did he bring many Electoral College votes to the table.) During Obama's first year, as the new president was mulling strategy in Afghanistan, Reed expressed doubts about sending more troops and said the burden of proof was on commanders to justify a troop increase; Obama was sympathetic with that viewpoint, as Reed knew. Reed has traveled to Iraq and Afghanistan frequently, often straying from the safe zones-thanks to his military background and his close relationships with many military commanders.

In October 2016, Reed made his 17th visit to Afghanistan and his 19th visit to Iraq. When he returned, he said that Obama's decision to maintain U.S. troops in Afghanistan and to provide support to the Afghan National Defense "have laid the foundation for a sustainable U.S. and international security presence in Afghanistan," and he urged the incoming Trump Administration to continue a "conditions-based approach" in Afghanistan. He voiced concern that "Iran's unsafe and unprofessional actions in the maritime arena continue," and said, "It is critical that we not cede space or territory to Iranian influence."

Earlier, during the administration of President George W. Bush, Reed in October 2002 opposed the Iraq war resolution. When American forces entered Iraq months later, he argued that Defense Secretary Donald Rumsfeld grossly underestimated the strength of anti-American insurgents in Iraq and failed to send in adequate troops and equipment. In 2005, after a trip to Iraq, he said: "I think my criticism has been accurate, certainly in the operations in this region, in that we didn't organize ourselves for the appropriate occupation and stabilization" following the overthrow of Iraqi leader Saddam Hussein. Reed was at the forefront of Democratic efforts in 2006 to convince Bush to redeploy the forces in Iraq. With Democratic Sen. Carl Levin of Michigan, he sponsored a bill calling for a "phased redeployment" in six months, with no deadline for complete withdrawal and with some U.S. forces remaining to train Iraqi security forces. The Levin-Reed amendment lost 60-39.

Reed has long backed efforts to permanently increase the size of the Army. In 2004, he and Hagel, then a Nebraska Republican senator, called for an increase of 30,000 troops, and the Senate agreed to 20,000. In 2006, Reed worked with Republican leaders to add $3.7 billion for more soldiers and Marines, and he sponsored an amendment to add $10 billion to replace damaged or destroyed equipment. While

Reed defended in 2012 Obama's plans to shrink the size of the Army and Marines, he later expressed concern about the impact on the armed forces of the 2011 Budget Control Act-passed to end a standoff between Obama and Republican congressional leaders over raising the federal debt ceiling. The 2011 BCA created automatic spending cuts-so-called sequestration-while putting both defense and domestic spending limits in place.

When the two of them took the top positions of the Armed Services Committee in 2015, Reed and McCain told leaders of the Senate Budget Committee that those limits "which require nearly $1 trillion of defense spending cuts over 10 years… have become a national security crisis of the first order." They acknowledged some legislators "insist that our nation cannot afford to spend more on defense at this time," but added: "At a time when real worldwide threats are growing, we are compounding those dangers with a national security crisis of our own making." During initial debate in 2016 on the annual defense spending bill, they found themselves on opposite sides as each party made broad fiscal arguments. But they collaborated following the election on a bipartisan agreement with the House.

On most issues, Reed has had a solidly liberal voting record. In 2009, a *National Journal* examination of roll call votes dating to the 1980s found him to be the most liberal senator, slightly ahead of Barbara Boxer of California and Edward Kennedy of Massachusetts. Since then, he has remained among the 20 most-liberal senators. He has supported extensions of unemployment benefits and work-share programs, like those in Rhode Island, in which employers reduce the hours of full-time employees to avoid layoffs during financial hard times. In the *Almanac* vote ratings for 2015, Reed had perfect liberal scores on economic and foreign issues and was nearly perfect on social issues.

Sometimes overlooked in Reed's high-profile status as a defense expert is his grounding in financial issues. In his Banking Committee portfolio, he played a key role in the crafting of the Dodd-Frank financial regulation law in 2010. The committee chairman, Connecticut Democrat Christopher Dodd, asked Reed to work with New Hampshire Republican Judd Gregg on the derivatives issue. According to *Act of Congress*, a book by *Washington Post* editor Robert Kaiser on the making of Dodd-Frank, Reed spent months working with Gregg to craft a regulatory framework in the complex area of derivatives-financial contracts based on the value of other assets, from interest rates to corn and soybeans. "Reed was an atypical senator," Kaiser wrote. "A small, compact man with a formidable intellect, he did mountains of homework. He mastered complicated issues."

The interests of Rhode Island always remain on Reed's mind. In 2008, as his home state was buffeted by the Great Recession-Rhode Island had one of the highest unemployment rates in the nation, and was among the top 10 states in terms of subprime mortgage foreclosures-he played a quiet, but major role in securing an agreement on a foreclosure rescue bill. Accompanied by Dodd, Reed brokered with Alabama Sen. Richard Shelby, the Banking Committee's top Republican, the final terms of the 2008 foreclosure rescue plan. It widened access to federally insured mortgages without tapping taxpayer money-a condition on which Shelby insisted-while, at the same time, allowing Reed to include an affordable housing fund that he had been seeking since 2002. New York Democrat Charles Schumer, a fellow Banking Committee member, told *The New York Times*, "Once again, Jack does it in his quiet, steadfast way, and it is extremely effective." In 2015, Reed used his position on the Appropriations Committee to remove a provision from the transportation funding bill that would have eliminated more than $8.5 million from the Rhode Island Public Transportation Authority.

When Donald Trump became President, Reed voiced mixed sentiments. He welcomed the prospect of increased Pentagon spending, which likely would mean more local jobs in submarine building at General Dynamics Electric Boat. He warned that Trump and other Republicans should not dismiss facts about possible Russian interference in the 2016 election "because they are, for some reason, inconvenient." When Michael Flynn-a Rhode Island native--in February 2017 resigned under pressure as Trump's national security adviser, the unusually outspoken Reed warned, "That disorganization and disarray has to stop."

In 2005, Reed, whom friends long joked was married to his work, married for the first time in his mid-50s. His wife, Julia Hart, was working in the Senate's Interparliamentary Services Office when she and Reed met in 2002-on a congressional delegation trip to Afghanistan. He is only the third Senator-all Democrats-to hold his Senate seat since 1937, and his predecessors became senior Senators. Green served 24 years and retired at the age of 93; Pell served for 36, retiring at 77. Based on those precedents-and Rhode Island's blue voting patterns-Reed is well-positioned to remain an influential force in the Senate for years to come.

Junior Senator

Sheldon Whitehouse (D)

Elected 2006, term expires 2018, 2nd term; b. Oct 20, 1955, New York City, NY; University of Virginia Law School, J.D.; Yale University (CT), B.Arch.; Episcopalian; Married (Dr. Sandra Thornton Whitehouse); 2 children.

Elected Office: RI Attorney General, 1999-2003.

Professional Career: RI special Assistant Attorney General, 1984-1990; Legal counsel, Governor Bruce Sundlun, 1991; Policy Director, Governor Bruce Sundlun, 1992; Director, RI Department of Business Regulation, 1992-1994; U.S Attorney for RI, 1994-1998; Practicing attorney, 2003-2006.

DC Office: 530 HSOB 20510, 202-224-2921, Fax: 202-228-6362, whitehouse.senate.gov.

State Offices: Providence, 401-453-5294.

Committees: *Aging*. *Budget*. *Environment & Public Works*: Clean Air & Nuclear Safety (RMM), Fisheries, Water, and Wildlife, Transportation & Infrastructure. *Health, Education, Labor & Pensions*: Employment & Workplace Safety, Primary Health & Retirement Security. *Joint Security & Cooperation in Europe*. *Judiciary*: Crime & Terrorism (RMM), Oversight, Agency Action, Federal Rights & Federal Courts, Privacy, Technology & the Law.

Group Ratings

	ADA	ACLU	AFL-CIO	LCV	ITI	COC	HAFA	ACU	CFG	FRC
2016	-	64%	-	100%	80%	25%	7%	4%	5%	0%
2015	95%	C	100%	100%	C	43%	C	0%	0%	0%

Almanac Ratings 2015

	Economy	Social	Foreign	Composite
Liberal	100%	100%	96%	99%
Conservative	0%	0%	4%	1%

Key Votes of the 114th Congress

1. Keystone pipeline	N	5. National Security Data	Y	9. Gun Sales Checks	Y
2. Export-Import Bank	N	6. Iran Nuclear Deal	N	10. Sanctuary Cities	N
3. Debt Ceiling Increase	Y	7. Puerto Rico Debt	Y	11. Planned Parenthood	N
4. Homeland Security $$	Y	8. Loretta Lynch A.G	Y	12. Trade deals	Y

Election Results

Election	Name (Party)	Vote (%)	Cand. Spent	Ind. Exp. Support	Ind. Exp. Oppose
2012 General	Sheldon Whitehouse (D)	271,034 (65%)	$4,933,336	$4,103	$183,165
	Barry Hinckley (R)	146,222 (35%)	$1,667,195	$9,084	
2012 Primary	Sheldon Whitehouse (D)	60,754 (100%)			

Prior winning percentages: 2006 (54%)

In November 2016, Democrat Sheldon Whitehouse, Rhode Island's junior senator, delivered the 150th in a series of weekly Senate floor speeches on the dangers he believes are posed by climate change-a green poster with a satellite photo of Earth and the slogan "Time To Wake Up" perched on an easel behind him. The ritual served to underscore that Whitehouse, since first being elected in 2006 from one of the country's bluest states, has emerged as one of the Senate's most vocal liberals-particularly on climate change, but also on other hot-button topics ranging from gun control to campaign finance reform to income equality. On the Judiciary Committee, he has been outspoken about nominations to the Supreme Court and the investigation of Russian interference in U.S. politics.

Whitehouse is only the latest in a series of outspoken congressional liberals in recent decades to come from a background of wealth and privilege. He is a descendant of Charles Crocker, one of California's "Big Four" men who built the Central Pacific Railroad; the latter connected with the Union Pacific line at Promontory Summit, Utah, in 1869 to form the nation's first transcontinental railroad. Whitehouse's grandfather was a diplomat, as was his father, Charles Whitehouse, a World War II Marine Corps pilot who was U.S. ambassador to Laos and Thailand in the 1970s.

Sheldon Whitehouse was born in New York City and spent his formative years overseas, including in Cambodia, South Africa, the Philippines, and Guinea; as a teenager, he taught English to Vietnamese children in Saigon. He graduated from St. Paul's preparatory school, Yale University, and the University of Virginia Law School. After clerking for an appeals court judge, Whitehouse moved to Rhode Island in 1984 to take a job as an assistant state attorney general. He was appointed a top staffer to Democratic Gov. Bruce Sundlun in 1991, and subsequently served two years as the head of the state's department of business regulation under Sundlun. In 1994, on the recommendation of Democratic Sen. Claiborne Pell, a family friend, Whitehouse was appointed U.S. Attorney for Rhode Island. Whitehouse launched an undercover investigation that resulted in the conviction of Providence Mayor Buddy Cianci on corruption charges. He also focused on environmental cleanup, leading an investigation that resulted in the largest fine in state history for an oil spill in Narragansett Bay.

In 1998, Whitehouse ran for state attorney general. In the three-way Democratic primary, his opponents portrayed him as an inexperienced, fox-hunting patrician trying to buy his way into public office. Whitehouse was better known in the state than his two opponents, and he got the nomination, capturing about half of the total vote. In the general election, the Republican nominee, state Treasurer Nancy Mayer forced Whitehouse to concede he had tried drugs as a student, and questioned whether he was tough enough for the job. Whitehouse later told *The Providence Journal*: "The book on me was, 'Smart kid, works hard, but, you know, has no common touch, can't relate to people, will be a disaster.' In fact, I got advice from some political types to run sort of a Rose Garden strategy. You know, 'Don't go out, don't let people see you, 'cause if they see you, they're not going to like you. Just mail your resume around, you know, and spend a lot of money on television.'" But the tide began to turn after Mayer ran highly negative ads on the drug issue that backfired in the absence of evidence that the incident was more than a short chapter from Whitehouse's distant past. He overwhelmingly won the election, 67%-33%.

By 2002, Whitehouse was viewed as a strong contender for governor. He ran but lost the Democratic primary by 926 votes to former state Sen. Myrth York, who outspent Whitehouse by 2-1. The primary battle left scars: When Whitehouse challenged Republican Sen. Lincoln Chafee in 2006, York broke with her party and endorsed Chafee.

Whitehouse had considered running for the Senate in 1999, when four-term incumbent John Chafee announced he would not seek a fifth term. But then, Chafee-who had been a roommate of Whitehouse's father while they were undergraduates at Yale-died in November 1999. Republican Gov. Lincoln Almond appointed the senator's son, Lincoln Chafee, then mayor of Warwick, to fill the vacancy, and Chafee the following year was elected to a full term. In the Senate, Chafee sided with Democrats often enough that there was frequent speculation that he would switch parties. In 2006, Chafee-still a Republican-was opposed in the primary by Cranston Mayor Steve Laffey, a conservative and a sharp-elbowed campaigner backed by a national anti-tax group, the Club for Growth. Though Chafee won the September primary, 54%-46%, he had little cash left after that fight.

After deciding to take on Chafee in 2006, Whitehouse had a relatively easy time in the Democratic primary. The general election pitted two candidates of fairly similar views who shared an upper-crust background: Chafee was an heir of one of Rhode Island's most prominent families, whose members had held high office in the state going back to the 1870s. In 2006, there was little daylight between Chafee and Whitehouse on the issues-both backed federal funding of embryonic stem cell research, abortion rights, and gun control. So Whitehouse campaigned against the then-unpopular Bush Administration, running ads with the tagline, "Finally, a Whitehouse in Washington you can trust." Whitehouse won, 54%-46%. He overwhelmingly won Providence and the fading industrial cities-Central Falls, Pawtucket, and Woonsocket-in the northeastern section of the state. Chafee won in Warwick, where he had been mayor, and some jurisdictions in the western part of the state.

Whitehouse was one of eight new Democratic senators whose election gave the party a majority in the Senate. He quickly gained recognition as a fierce critic of the Bush Administration. Whitehouse blasted Attorney General Alberto Gonzalez for firing U.S. Attorneys for what Democrats alleged were political motivations. After Gonzalez resigned, Whitehouse opposed the nomination of Michael Mukasey as attorney general for refusing to say whether water boarding was an illegal tactic against terrorism detainees.

With President Barack Obama in office, Whitehouse became a stalwart administration defender. His voting record put him on the Senate's liberal end. In the *Almanac* vote ratings for 2015, he tied with home-state colleague Jack Reed among the most liberal Senators. During the first year of the Obama Administration, he supported the $787 billion economic stimulus bill, and even said he would like to see a second stimulus bill focused entirely on the nation's infrastructure. Later, Whitehouse clamored for a Senate vote on the administration's so-called "Buffett Rule" imposing higher taxes on the wealthiest Americans. Republicans in 2012 blocked it from clearing the necessary 60-vote hurdle.

Whitehouse's tendency toward hyperbole has occasionally sparked controversy. He irked conservatives when he said on the Senate floor that opposition to Obama's health care reform measure was driven in part by "right-wing militias and Aryan support groups." Later, in October 2012, he charged that House Budget Committee Chairman Paul Ryan's budget blueprint "gets rid of Medicare in 10 years and turns it into a voucher program," which the fact-checking site *PolitiFact* rated as false.

PolitiFact has been kinder to his regular floor speeches on climate change, rating as "mostly true" claims he has made on issues ranging from rising sea levels to warmer oceans to eroding coastlines. "We're not a very big state, so we don't have a lot of land to give away to the sea," Whitehouse told the *Associated Press*, noting that Rhode Island finds itself "on the receiving end" of the climate change problem because it doesn't have coal mines or oil drilling. He began to give his speeches on climate change in April 2012, accusing Congress of "sleepwalking through history." Speaking weekly when the Senate was in session, he claimed he had never had to give the same speech twice because of the breadth of the topic. Whitehouse credits his wife, a marine scientist, with helping him to recognize the importance of oceans in everyone's lives. In the process, he has become perhaps Congress' most persistent voice on the hazards of climate change. His November 2016 presentation was typically blunt. "It is long past time to wake up to the industry-controlled campaign of calculated misinformation on the dangers of carbon pollution. Opponents of climate action relish operating in the dark," he told the Senate. "If anything is really going to change, we need to shine a light on the sophisticated scheme of denial being foisted on the American people."

In 2013, Whitehouse and now-retired California Democratic Rep. Henry Waxman, long a key congressional player on environmental issues, formed a climate change task force. He has pushed for more funding of ocean protection and rising sea levels, including creation of a National Endowment for the Oceans, Coasts and Great Lakes. Whitehouse's passion on this topic is such that he suggested, in a May 2015 op-ed piece in *The Washington Post*, that the fossil fuel industry's efforts to discredit climate science might constitute deliberate deception similar to what the tobacco industry perpetrated in previous decades. In 2006, a federal judge found the tobacco industry guilty of fraud in a civil lawsuit, and Whitehouse contended fossil fuel companies might ay be a ripe target for a comparable civil lawsuit.

Some of Whitehouse's proposals have faced steep political hurdles even in a Democratic-controlled Congress. With his proposal to impose a carbon fee on industries that emit carbon pollution, he has tried to make it more politically acceptable by crafting it as revenue neutral, with corporate tax cuts and rebates for taxpayers. He has pursued more conciliatory approaches to advance his cause. In 2014, Whitehouse formed an alliance with West Virginia Sen. Joe Manchin, a centrist Democrat from a major coal-producing state. Manchin visited Rhode Island to see the effect of climate change firsthand and Whitehouse toured coal and energy resources in West Virginia. Whitehouse has shown an ability to reach across the aisle on other issues. With Republican Rep. Mike McCaul of Texas, who chaired the House Homeland Security Committee, Whitehouse co-chaired the Cyber Policy Task Force at the Center for Strategic and International Studies.

On the Senate Judiciary Subcommittee on Crime and Terrorism, Whitehouse has worked with South Carolina Republican Lindsey Graham, now the chairman, on several topics. In early 2017, they collaborated on the inquiry into Russian influence in the 2016 presidential election. That included a highly publicized May 2017 hearing in which Sally Yates, the deputy attorney general in the Obama Administration, described the circumstances when Trump fired her as acting attorney general after she warned about the personal conflicts of national security adviser Michael Flynn. The subcommittee's inquiry served broader purposes than the Intelligence Committee's review, Whitehouse said: "to give a thorough public accounting of the known facts, to pose the questions that still need answers, and to help us determine how best to protect the integrity and proper functioning of our government."

Much of Whitehouse's energy has been devoted to keeping the flame alive on a host of liberal causes unlikely to be enacted into law anytime soon. He has become the ideological heir to former Wisconsin Democratic Sen. Russ Feingold in seeking to control the influence of money in elections. He has taken on gun rights advocates, including the National Rifle Association.

Conservative groups have pushed back on occasion. In June 2014, a tea party group filed a complaint with the Senate Ethics Committee, accusing Whitehouse of breaking ethics rules by pressuring the Obama Administration to target conservative groups, according to *The Hill*. The Tea Party Patriots pointed to an April 2013 hearing at which it charged Whitehouse had "publicly berated" the Internal Revenue Service and Justice Department for not prosecuting conservative groups, classified under tax law as social welfare organizations, for engaging in electioneering activity. The complaint was filed about a year after controversy broke out over the IRS targeting tea party groups for audits. Whitehouse defended his actions as proper, with a spokesman saying the senator "noticed that certain legal declarations appear to have violated [federal statutes] making false statements a crime."

In the 2012 campaign, his Republican opponent was software executive Barry Hinckley, who campaigned as a moderate on social issues, while calling for the repeal of the health care reform law and supporting offshore oil drilling. He faced an uphill battle in heavily Democratic Rhode Island, and was defeated 65%-35%. Whitehouse had no cause for concern about reelection in 2018.

FIRST DISTRICT

David Cicilline (D)

Elected 2010, 4th term; b. Jul 15, 1961, Providence; Brown University (RI), B.A., 1983; Georgetown University Law Center (DC), J.D., 1986; Jewish; Single.

Elected Office: RI House, 1995-2003; Providence Mayor, 2003-2011.

Professional Career: Public defender, 1986-1987; Practicing attorney; Faculty, Roger Williams Law School.

DC Office: 2244 RHOB 20515, 202-225-4911, Fax: 202-225-3290, cicilline.house.gov.

State Offices: Pawtucket, 401-729-5600.

Committees: *Foreign Affairs*: Europe, Eurasia & Emerging Threats, Middle East & North Africa. *Judiciary*: Immigration & Border Security, Regulatory Reform, Commercial & Antitrust Law (RMM).

Group Ratings

	ADA	ACLU	AFL-CIO	LCV	ITI	COC	HAFA	ACU	CFG	FRC
2016	-	94%	-	100%	50%	46%	14%	4%	400%	0%
2015	100%	C	100%	97%	C	45%	C	4%	0%	0%

Almanac Ratings 2015

	Economy	Social	Foreign	Composite
Liberal	95%	94%	99%	96%
Conservative	5%	6%	1%	4%

Key Votes of the 114th Congress

1. Keystone Pipeline	N	5. Puerto Rico Debt	Y	9. Offenses by Aliens	Y
2. Trade Deals	N	6. Medical Marijuana	Y	10. Troops in Iraq	Y
3. Export-Import Bank	Y	7. Sanctuary Cities	N	11. Homeland Security $$	Y
4. Debt Ceiling Increase	Y	8. Armor-piercing Bullets	N	12. Trade Adjustment aid	Y

Election Results

Election	Name (Party)	Vote (%)		Cand. Spent	Ind. Exp. Support	Ind. Exp. Oppose
2016 General	David Cicilline (D)	130,534	(65%)	$702,103		
	H. Russell Taub (R)	71,023	(35%)	$66,310		
2016 Primary	David Cicilline (D)	23,995	(68%)			
	Christopher Young (D)	11,559	(33%)			

Prior winning percentages: 2014 (60%), 2012 (53%), 2010 (51%)

Democrat David Cicilline, elected in 2010, has established a socially liberal niche as a gay and often outspoken lawmaker. The former mayor of Providence, Cicilline had a rocky start when his popularity plummeted with news of his messy stewardship of the city's finances. But he has recovered politically at home.

Cicilline was born in Providence, the middle of five children. His parents eloped when his Jewish mother was 16 and his Catholic father 17. He grew up celebrating the traditions of both religions, and now identifies as Jewish. His father was a criminal-defense attorney. Cicilline attended Brown University, where he majored in political science and founded, along with classmate John F. Kennedy Jr., a chapter of the College Democrats. He was active in student government and worked two jobs waiting tables. Cicilline came out as gay in college and says he was fortunate to have a supportive family. After getting a law degree from Georgetown University, he worked in Washington as a public defender for juveniles. In addition to defending the youths in court, Cicilline sometimes enrolled them in school, substance-abuse treatment and other support services.

He returned to Rhode Island to campaign for the state Senate. He lost that bid, but ran for the state House two years later and won. In the legislature, he pushed to raise the legal age to buy a gun from 13 to 18, introduced a bill creating a needle exchange program for drug users, and fought attempts to restrict abortion rights. In 2002, he was elected to the first of two terms as mayor of Providence, becoming the first openly gay mayor of a state capital city. He campaigned as a reformer, promising to clean up the city after the two-decade reign of Buddy Cianci, who was convicted of corruption. In office, Cicilline sought to end cronyism in the police department and expanded after-school programs. As the city's revenue shriveled in the recession, he laid off nearly 500 employees and raised property taxes. Cicilline was president of the National Conference of Democratic Mayors.

When Democratic Rep. Patrick Kennedy decided not to seek reelection, Cicilline won the primary with 37 percent of the vote against three opponents. In the general election, Cicilline campaigned as a pragmatist focused on creating jobs. Republican state Rep. John Loughlin focused on the state's poor economy and said that he would balance the federal budget. Cicilline spent $2 million to $800,000 for Loughlin, and won 51%-45%. The unexpectedly close outcome in a heavily Democratic district highlighted Republican strength in 2010 and residual problems for Cicilline.

Cicilline spent his first term under a cloud. *The Providence Journal* reported in early 2011 that the city had a $180 million deficit for the next two fiscal years and that its reserve fund was almost depleted. A nonpartisan bond rating agency, Fitch Ratings, criticized Cicilline's administration for "imprudent budgeting decisions." Cicilline said he had to use reserve money to prevent sharp cuts to city programs. He went on an apology tour to acknowledge he should have been more forthcoming about Providence's fiscal problems.

Cicilline established a solidly liberal voting record but also co-founded the Common Ground Caucus, a bipartisan group of House members who meet regularly to foster greater cooperation. He spoke out forcefully against proposed GOP budget cuts to programs for low-income citizens, and he tried without success to amend spending bills to take money from Afghanistan reconstruction and apply it to deficit reduction. His *Almanac* vote ratings for 2015 ranked him as a solid liberal in each of the three issue areas.

His agenda likely has no prospects in a Republican-controlled Congress, but it gives Democrats and progressives talking points in the political debate. In 2015, following the shooting deaths of nine people in a Charleston, South Carolina, church, he filed legislation to prohibit gun purchases by children, people with a criminal record and those with a mental illness. "While I understand that some in Congress would prefer not to have this debate right now, it is critical that we find the political will to finally address these urgent concerns," Cicilline said. He has pushed another bill to reinstate a ban on certain classes of semi-automatic weapons. He has sponsored legislation for automatic voter registration in the 50 states, which shifts the burden for registering from the individual to the state. The proposal gives citizens a 21-day period to opt out of registration. In 2016, he enacted his Bathrooms Accessible for Babies in Every Situation (Babies) Act, which requires a diaper-changing station in both male and female bathrooms in all federal buildings.

In 2012, he turned back a Democratic challenge from businessman Anthony Gemma, who was the runner-up in the 2010 primary. Gemma accused Cicilline of voter fraud. The incumbent called the allegation "absolutely absurd" and won 62%-38%. His general election rival was Republican Brendan Doherty, a former state police superintendent. Cicilline outspent Doherty, $2.4 million to $1.5 million, and each received generous party support. Cicilline sought to link Doherty to GOP presidential nominee Mitt Romney, which resonated in the Democratic-dominated district. He again won modestly, 53%-41%, while President Barack Obama took the district with 66 percent of the vote. Since then, Cicilline has won more comfortably against lightly funded opponents.

Eastern Rhode Island: Parts of Providence, Newport

Population		Race and Ethnicity		Income	
Total	528,427	White	69.7%	Median Income	$52,517 (215 out of 435)
Land area	268	Black	7.1%	Under $50,000	47.8%
Pop/ sq mi	1968.1	Latino	15.9%	$50,000-$99,999	28.7%
Born in state	51.9%	Asian	3.3%	$100,000-$199,999	18.4%
		Two races	2.6%	$200,000 or more	5.2%
		Other	1.5%	Poverty Rate	16.1%
Age Groups		**Education**		**Health Insurance**	
Under 18	20.9%	H.S grad or less	42.4%	With health insurance coverage	89.8%
18-34	24.8%	Some college	25.9%	**Public Assistance**	
35-64	38.9%	College Degree, 4 yr	18.5%	Cash public assistance income	3.2%
Over 64	15.4%	Post grad	13.2%	Food stamp/SNAP benefits	18.1%
Work		**Military**			
White Collar	36.8%	Veteran	7.5%		
Sales and Service	44.5%	Active Duty	0.6%		
Blue Collar	18.7%				
Government	11.5%				

Voter Turnout			
2015 Total Citizens 18+	378,899	2016 House Turnout as % CVAP	53%
2016 House turnout	202,371	2014 House Turnout as % CVAP	38%

2012 Presidential Vote		
Barack Obama	141,306	(66%)
Mitt Romney	68,723	(32%)

2016 Presidential Vote		
Hillary Clinton	130,682	(59%)
Donald Trump	75,510	(34%)
Gary Johnson	6,767	(3%)

Cook Partisan Voting Index: D+14

The 1st Congressional District is the eastern half of Rhode Island, divided from the state's other congressional district by a boundary line that circles around the state capital on three nearby streets and extends about 40 miles from Woonsocket along the Massachusetts border to Newport and Little Compton along the Atlantic Ocean. The district takes in much of Providence, including the elite East Side and College Hill around Brown University. Lower-income South Providence is the only sizable part of the district west of the Providence River. In recent years, the once down-on-its-luck city has revived physically, with an accessible waterfront adjacent to downtown, active night life and restoration of neighborhoods around the state capitol. The district captures all of next-door Pawtucket, whose Slater Mill is known as the birthplace of the American Industrial Revolution. Pawtucket created an arts district downtown and it has rehabbed many of its abandoned mills into lofts for artists and commercial space for entrepreneurs.

The onetime textile mill towns of the Blackstone Valley, Woonsocket and Central Falls are in the 1st, along with high-income Barrington and Bristol along the eastern coast of Narragansett Bay. To the south, on the ocean, is the old city of Newport, with its restored 18th-century houses and summer "cottages" that are more like mansions, plus the smaller island of Jamestown. Newport has been home to the America's Cup races and has hosted a popular jazz festival every summer since 1954, with productions occasionally elsewhere. It is also the site of the oldest synagogue in North America, where George Washington once told a congregation that the United States gives "to bigotry no sanction, to persecution no assistance."

Budget woes hit hard in some Rhode Island cities, and have not been easy to shake. Central Falls declared bankruptcy in 2011, becoming the second city in the nation to exhaust its pension fund; it significantly cut benefits for retirees under court direction. In 2012, Providence, on the brink of bankruptcy, averted fiscal disaster by cutting back pensions and education spending, and raising property taxes. By 2016, each city was again struggling with its finances. Following the 2016 election, Providence Mayor Jorge Elorza launched a "One Providence" initiative, based on the state's founding principles of religious freedom and tolerance - and in pointed contrast to President Donald Trump. Ethnically, the 1st District is the more French-Canadian and the less Italian of Rhode Island's two congressional districts. Politically, it is the more strongly Democratic district, though the Democratic vote in each district dropped several points in the 2016 presidential election.

SECOND DISTRICT

Jim Langevin (D)

Elected 2000, 9th term; b. Apr 22, 1964, Providence; Harvard University John F. Kennedy School of Government (MA), M.P.A.; Rhode Island College, B.A.; Roman Catholic; Single.

Elected Office: RI House, 1989-1995; RI Secretary of St., 1995-2001.

DC Office: 2077 RHOB 20515, 202-225-2735, Fax: 202-225-5976, langevin.house.gov.

State Offices: Warwick, 401-732-9400.

Committees: *Armed Services*: Emerging Threats & Capabilities (RMM), Seapower & Projection Forces, Tactical Air & Land Forces. *Homeland Security*: Cybersecurity & Infrastructure Protection, Emergency Preparedness, Response & Communications.

Group Ratings

	ADA	ACLU	AFL-CIO	LCV	ITI	COC	HAFA	ACU	CFG	FRC
2016	-	64%	-	100%	67%	57%	15%	4%	4%	8%
2015	85%	C	100%	100%	C	50%	C	8%	2%	8%

Almanac Ratings 2015

	Economy	Social	Foreign	Composite
Liberal	91%	80%	63%	78%
Conservative	9%	20%	37%	22%

Key Votes of the 114th Congress

1. Keystone Pipeline	N	5. Puerto Rico Debt	Y	9. Offenses by Aliens	Y
2. Trade Deals	N	6. Medical Marijuana	Y	10. Troops in Iraq	N
3. Export-Import Bank	Y	7. Sanctuary Cities	N	11. Homeland Security $$	Y
4. Debt Ceiling Increase	Y	8. Armor-piercing Bullets	N	12. Trade Adjustment aid	Y

Election Results

Election	Name (Party)	Vote (%)		Cand. Spent	Ind. Exp. Support	Ind. Exp. Oppose
2016 General	Jim Langevin (D)	133,108	(58%)	$954,632		
	Rhue Reis (R)	70,301	(31%)	$2,783		
	Jeffrey Johnson (I)	16,253	(7%)			
	Salvatore Caiozzo (I)	9,486	(4%)			
2016 Primary	Jim Langevin (D)	16,264	(64%)			
	Steven Archer (D)	4,748	(19%)			
	John Hamilton (D)	4,244	(17%)			

Prior winning percentages: 2014 (62%), 2012 (56%), 2010 (60%), 2008 (70%), 2006 (73%), 2004 (75%), 2002 (76%), 2000 (62%)

Democrat Jim Langevin, elected in 2000, is the first quadriplegic to serve in Congress and has worked on behalf of others with similar physical challenges. He has been an active and respected participant on cybersecurity and other national security issues on the Armed Services and Homeland Security committees, where he has gained senior slots.

Langevin grew up in Warwick and as a boy hoped to become an FBI agent. in 1980, at age 16, when he was a police cadet in the Boy Scout Explorer program, he was shot by a police officer when a gun accidentally discharged. The bullet went through his upper back and throat and damaged the upper part of his spinal column, making him a quadriplegic. He received a $2.2 million settlement from the city of Warwick. Although he disliked the attention it brought him, he says he became determined to do something meaningful with his life. He worked as an intern at the state House and for Sen. Claiborne Pell. While a student at Rhode Island College, where he got his bachelor's, he was elected to the state House, where he styled himself as a reformer. He got a master's degree in public administration from the John F. Kennedy School of Government at Harvard. In 1994, Langevin was elected Rhode Island's secretary of state.

When the House seat opened, Langevin's strongest opponent was Kate Coyne-McCoy, executive director of the Rhode Island Association of Social Workers, who criticized his opposition to abortion rights. Langevin had support from many Democratic leaders and some unions, and won the party's endorsement at the April convention. Coyne-McCoy waged an aggressive campaign financed by unions, health care workers and EMILY's List. Langevin called her positions "unrealistic and extreme." She said, "There's no such thing as being too liberal." He favored less stringent forms of gun control and said, "No one has to tell me how dangerous weapons can be." He spoke often about the accident that paralyzed him. "Certainly, being disabled is part of who I am, but it doesn't define me," he said. Langevin defeated Coyne-McCoy, 47%-29%. In the general, Rodney Driver, nominee of the Conscience for Congress Party and a retired mathematics professor, spent $300,000 of his retirement savings. Langevin won easily, 62%-21%.

The House chamber in the Capitol was made wheelchair-accessible for Langevin, with two of the fixed seats in the front removed to give him space to maneuver and to talk to colleagues. At his urging, then-Democratic Speaker Nancy Pelosi agreed to far-reaching structural changes to make all parts of the chamber, including the speaker's rostrum, accessible. In July 2010, on the 20th anniversary of the Americans with Disabilities Act, he became the first person in a wheelchair to preside over the House.

Langevin has been a member of Rep. Steny Hoyer's senior whip team. In 2005, he was one of only three House Democrats from New England to side with conservatives in the case of Terri Schiavo, a severely brain-damaged Florida woman at the center of a court battle over removing her life-sustaining feeding tube. He returned to the liberal fold on embryonic stem cell research, which anti-abortion groups opposed. Langevin took the view that the research might alleviate suffering from certain diseases and injuries, which drew heat from the Roman Catholic bishop of Providence.

Langevin has sponsored several gun control bills, including increased inspections of firearms dealers' sales records and stiffened penalties for dealers who have been untruthful. He has called universal health care coverage his top priority. In 2006, Langevin won passage of a bipartisan bill that established a respite program for caregivers of individuals with special needs. He was a staunch supporter of the Democrats' health are initiative in 2009 and 2010. His *Almanac* voting record for 2015 showed that he has been liberal on economic issues and more centrist on cultural and foreign policy issues, an apt reflection of his district's ethnic communities

On the Armed Services Committee, Langevin led efforts to boost spending for missile defense systems above the level requested by the Obama administration. He worked successfully in 2012 with Connecticut independent Sen. Joe Lieberman to thwart the administration's proposed cut in production of Virginia-class submarines in Connecticut and Rhode Island. He has been the ranking Democrat on the Emerging Threats and Capabilities Subcommittee.

Langevin has been the chief House sponsor of a bill to establish cybersecurity offices in the White House and Homeland Security Department and give the president emergency powers to act during a cybersecurity crisis. The House passed the bill in 2010, but it died in the Senate. He later sought to amend the fiscal 2012 defense authorization bill to add the new office, but he failed on a largely party-line vote. After being term-limited on the House Intelligence Committee, he returned in 2015 to the Homeland Security Committee, where he has dealt with some similar issues. That year, he called for the resignation of Katherine Archuleta, director of the Office of Personnel Management, after she failed to take responsibility or suggest steps to respond to the massive cyberattack on OPM records for millions of federal employees. Her failure to create a risk-based cyber strategy was "simply unacceptable," Langevin said. In February 2017, the House passed his bill to create a grant program to enhance cooperation between the United States and Israel on cybersecurity. He urged President Donald Trump to have "an advocate for cybersecurity in the room when budget and policy decisions are made" and to support legislation to develop the workforce needed to address cybersecurity issues.

State and national Democrats urged Langevin to challenge Republican Sen. Lincoln Chafee in 2006, but abortion rights groups objected to his candidacy. Democrat Sheldon Whitehouse challenged Chafee and won. In 2016, he was held to 58 percent of the vote in a four-candidate contest. Republican Russ

Taub, who raised $103,000 to $1.5 million for Langevin, got 31 percent. In 2015, his collegiate alma mater named its state-of-the-art design center in Langevin's honor.

Western Rhode Island: Parts of Providence, Warwick, Cranston

Population		**Race and Ethnicity**		**Income**	
Total	525,234	White	79.4%	Median Income	$61,793 (124 out of 435)
Land area	269	Black	3.6%		
Pop/ sq mi	1949.0	Latino	11.4%		
Born in state	63.9%	Asian	3.1%	Under $50,000	41.6%
		Two races	1.8%	$50,000-$99,999	30.7%
Age Groups		Other	0.7%	$100,000-$199,999	22.7%
Under 18	19.9%			$200,000 or more	5.2%
18-34	23.4%	**Education**		Poverty Rate	12.4%
35-64	41.3%	H.S grad or less	40.0%		
Over 64	15.4%	Some college	28.0%	**Health Insurance**	
		College Degree, 4 yr	19.6%	With health insurance coverage	91.7%
Work		Post grad	12.4%		
White Collar	37.0%				
Sales and Service	44.7%	**Military**		**Public Assistance**	
Blue Collar	18.3%	Veteran	8.3%	Cash public assistance income	2.7%
Government	13.8%	Active Duty	0.1%		
				Food stamp/SNAP benefits	13.6%

Voter Turnout			
2015 Total Citizens 18+	397,666	2016 House Turnout as % CVAP	58%
2016 House turnout	229,148	2014 House Turnout as % CVAP	43%

2012 Presidential Vote		
Barack Obama	138,371	(60%)
Mitt Romney	88,481	(38%)

2016 Presidential Vote		
Hillary Clinton	121,843	(50%)
Donald Trump	105,033	(43%)
Gary Johnson	7,979	(3%)

Cook Partisan Voting Index: D+6

The 2nd Congressional District is the western half of Rhode Island. Most of its population is concentrated in towns like working-class Cranston and more upscale Warwick, which, despite their British names, are inhabited mostly by people with Irish, Italian, French and Portuguese surnames. Cranston was reportedly the inspiration for FOX's animated comedy *Family Guy*; the show ran for several seasons and was set in the fictitious town of Quahog, which happens to be a Rhode Island species of clam. The 2nd includes the fastest-growing part of the state, South County, which is not an official place but the common name for Rhode Island south of East Greenwich. This area takes in the affluent suburbs and beachfront communities along Narragansett Bay, the Kingston home of the University of Rhode Island, and the area around Westerly, where many residents work at the General Dynamics Electric Boat shipyards in Groton, Connecticut. Electric Boat also employs about 3,300 people several miles up the coast in Quonset. The workforce is roughly split between the two states. In January 2017, the company announced a hiring increase as it made plans to manufacture a new class of ballistic missile submarines, which were scheduled for production starting in 2020. The shipyard already has been producing a class of attack submarines.

Another important segment of the economy is sailing and tourism. In addition to its rolling farmland (although there is not much acreage), the district includes communities along the bay and the ocean, where many people still make their living building boats and catching fish. After years of discussion, regulatory hurdles and local opposition, the Block Island Wind Farm in December 2016 began to produce energy with the nation's first off-shore wind farm. The state hoped that the farm near Block Island would position it as a leader in renewable energy. The five-turbine, 30-megawatt facility used a submarine cable to connect to the mainland and it expected to power 17,000 homes. Developers have followed up with a larger and less costly farm off of Long Island. Wind farms on land are cheaper to build, but those in the ocean have stronger winds.

This has been a comfortably Democratic district. President Barack Obama twice won with 60 percent of the vote. In 2016, Hillary Clinton won by only 50%-43%. Donald Trump ran strongly in the small towns.

★ SOUTH CAROLINA ★

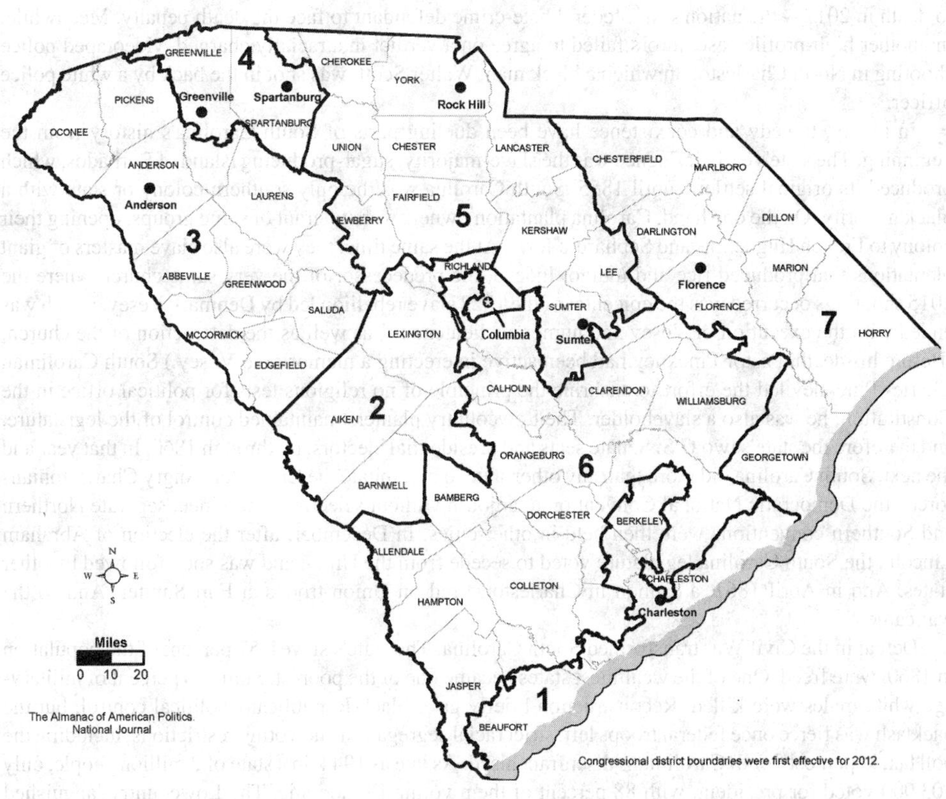

History is inescapable anywhere, but especially so in the South - as Americans have been reminded in recent years, when South Carolina has repeatedly been vaulted into the headlines for tragic incidents, and for efforts at reconciliation.

In 2015, a gunman with a history of white supremacist beliefs entered a historic African-American church in Charleston, sat down for Bible study, and then systematically gunned down nine black worshippers - including the pastor, state Sen. Clementa Pinckney – as he squeezed the trigger more than 75 times. Amid the mourning, a debate about an old subject - race and Confederate heritage - reemerged. Critics said the state should finally do what it had previously balked at - remove the Confederate battle flag from the state capitol grounds in Columbia, where it had flown, in one way or another, since the depths of the civil rights conflict in 1962. Republican Gov. Nikki Haley, who prior to the killings had shown little interest in following her predecessors' (failed) efforts to pull down the flag, offered her support for removal, and the tide began to turn. The Legislature gave its approval, and on July 10, 2015, the flag was lowered from the statehouse grounds for good. The shooter, Dylann Roof, was sentenced to death in 2017 -- the nation's first federal hate-crime defendant to face the death penalty. Meanwhile, in another high-profile case, jurors failed to agree on a verdict in a racially charged, videotaped police shooting in North Charleston in which a black man, Walter Scott, was shot in the back by a white police officer.

In reality, tragedy and coexistence have been dueling parts of South Carolina's history from the beginning. The state's early influence was the slave-majority, sugar-producing island of Barbados, which produced its original settlers; until 1855, South Carolina was the only southern colony or state with a black majority. On the one hand, Carolina plantation owners were tolerant of some groups, opening their colony to French Huguenots and Sephardic Jews. At the same time, they were also slave masters of giant plantations that produced rice and indigo. Indeed, the predecessor of the very same church where the 2015 shootings occurred was the epicenter of the 1822 slave rebellion led by Denmark Vesey, which was ended with the execution of Vesey and numerous lieutenants, as well as the destruction of the church. (Before his death, Pastor Pinckney had been active in erecting a memorial to Vesey.) South Carolinian Charles Pinckney led the effort to enshrine the principle of no religious tests for political office in the Constitution; he was also a slaveholder. The Lowcountry planters maintained control of the legislature, and therefore the state's two U.S. Senate seats and presidential electors, up through 1860. In that year and the next, South Carolina did more than any other state to precipitate the Civil War. Angry Charlestonians forced the Democratic National Convention to adjourn without selecting a nominee; separate Northern and Southern conventions were then held in other cities. In December, after the election of Abraham Lincoln, the South Carolina legislature voted to secede from the Union and was soon followed by other states. And in April 1861, a cannon in Charleston fired on Union troops at Fort Sumter. And so the war came.

Defeat in the Civil War transformed South Carolina. The state's slaves, 57 percent of the population in 1860, were freed. One of the wealthiest states became one of the poorest. Some 30 percent of military-age white males were killed. Reconstruction briefly gave black Republicans political control, but the backlash was fierce once federal troops left; strict racial segregation and voting restrictions, including the poll tax, kept most South Carolinians disenfranchised. As late as 1944, in a state of 2 million people, only 103,000 voted for president, with 88 percent of them voting Democratic. The Lowcountry languished in poverty, with malnutrition on coastal islands. A silver lining was architectural - the old mansions of Charleston were not replaced by commercial buildings, and instead were saved by the nation's first local historic preservation movement (and rebuilt after Hurricane Hugo in 1989), cementing the city's culture and civic pride. Mostly white Upstate South Carolina, with a growing textile industry, took the political lead, led by such politicians as Pitchfork Ben Tillman (governor 1890-94, senator 1895-1918) and a close friend's son, Strom Thurmond (governor 1947-51, senator 1954-2003).

In the last few decades, this once underdeveloped state has taken steps forward. In the 1950s, South Carolina repealed its poll tax, and turnout surged as South Carolina became competitive in the presidential elections of 1952 and 1960. Clemson University was peacefully desegregated thanks to the efforts of Democratic Gov. Ernest Hollings (1959-63). Most South Carolina whites opposed integration, but unlike in Alabama and Mississippi the effort was mostly not punctuated by violence. The Civil Rights Act of 1964 and the Voting Rights Act of 1965 ended legal segregation of public accommodations and workplaces and brought blacks into the electorate. Democratic (and later Republican) Sen. Thurmond, who staged a record-setting filibuster of the 1957 Civil Rights Act, started appointing black staffers and signed off on a black federal judge in the late 1960s and early 1970s. By the 21st century, the state elected Haley, a daughter of immigrants from India, and then Tim Scott, an African-American, to the House and later to the Senate, respectively; in this strongly conservative state, their conservative views were what mattered.

In many ways, the biggest change has been economic. Forty years ago, much of South Carolina's economy depended on military bases and big textile mills in the Interstate 85 corridor around Greenville and Spartanburg. Then South Carolina became the most aggressive state in the South in seeking new industry. It advertised its business climate, with one of the nation's lowest rates of unionization and taxation and a willingness to splurge on tax incentives. Crucially, Hollings as governor spearheaded the creation of the state's technical colleges, which today educate and train hundreds of thousands of residents a year. Michelin opened the first of several South Carolina plants in 1975, and the first BMW vehicles rolled off the Spartanburg assembly line in 1992. As recently as May 2015, Volvo chose a South Carolina site 30 miles northwest of Charleston as the location of its first North American assembly plant, lured by business-friendly laws and $200 million in incentives. Smaller companies built factories throughout much of central and Upstate South Carolina. Navy bases were the mainstay of Charleston's economy in the 1970s, but the bases were closed in the early 1990s. Charleston has not only survived but thrived, thanks in large part to the creative energy of longtime Mayor Joseph P. Riley Jr., who was first elected in 1975 and who served until January 2016. With a keen aesthetic eye, he has made the city's historic center a magnet for tourists, and he has helped Charleston become a major port, which is especially helpful for Michelin and BMW. Meanwhile, shuttered military bases became a center of aircraft production, particularly when Boeing in 2009 chose North Charleston to build a plant to assemble its 787 Dreamliner. The aircraft giant now employs 7,600 people in the Charleston area, though the company has expressed strong opposition to a budding unionization push.

Such industrial expansion has improved South Carolina's fundamentals, and tourism has become a significant source of income: In 2016, the state announced its third straight record-setting year for tourism, reaching $19 billion. But South Carolina counts only one locally headquartered company on the Fortune 500 list – Fort Mill-based paper manufacturer Domtar Corp. at No. 489 – and poverty in many areas of the state has proven intractable. In 2016, five whole counties and parts of several others reported more than 95 percent of their schoolchildren qualifying for free or reduced-cost lunches or Medicaid. Statewide median income is 18 percent below the national average, and the poverty rate is 16.6 percent, compared with 14.7 percent nationally. South Carolina is tied for ninth in the nation in residents without health insurance, and it ranked in the bottom quarter of states for the percentage of residents with a college degree.

By February 2017, the unemployment rate had fallen to 4.4 percent, slightly below the national average. The cumulative changes to the economic base had transformed South Carolina from an inward-looking state to a more outward-looking one. Through the 1960s, few people except military personnel moved in. That has changed in a big way. In 2016, United Van Lines determined that South Carolina was the second-most popular destination for interstate moves, behind Oregon. Most of the newcomers are white, largely with conservative attitudes - the state had the sixth largest percentage of "very religious" residents, according to Gallup - but with less attachment to the state's ancient traditions. South Carolina's population is 28 percent black (tied for the fifth highest in the nation, although far below African-Americans' near-majority of the 1940s) and 5 percent Hispanic. Since 2010, the state has grown by 7.3 percent, with growth fastest on and near the coast – 19.7 percent in Horry County (Myrtle Beach), 18.6 percent in Berkeley County (the northern suburbs of Charleston), 13.2 percent in Charleston County (Charleston), 12.9 percent in Beaufort County (Hilton Head), and 12.6 percent in Dorchester County (the northwestern suburbs of Charleston). These booming areas attract tourists and affluent retirees eager to spend days with pleasant weather on the golf course and in time-shares. Another growth area has been the York County suburbs of booming Charlotte, North Carolina; it grew by 14.4 percent over the same period. The state has only begun to face one of the looming challenges stemming from the influx of newcomers: The fastest-growing portion of South Carolina's population now consists of those 85 and older, and by 2030, the state is expected to have more residents 65 and older than children in school.

The demographic changes have moved South Carolina politically toward the Republicans. Politics cleaves the electorate along racial lines, and the hard math of the population figures - whites have an easy majority - makes it difficult for Democrats to win statewide in South Carolina any more. South Carolina has voted for Republicans for president in every election but one since 1960 – in 1976, when son of the South Jimmy Carter was running. With some bare-knuckled help from wunderkind strategist Lee Atwater, former Gov. Carroll Campbell built a Republican Party capable of electing statewide officials and legislative majorities. In 1988, Campbell and Atwater, who was by then George H.W. Bush's campaign manager, set up the early Republican presidential primary on the Saturday before Super Tuesday, which enabled Bush to clinch the nomination that year. It did the same for Bob Dole in 1996, for George W. Bush in 2000, and for John McCain in 2008. The only hiccup came in 2012, when Newt Gingrich won the state; in 2016, Donald Trump won all but two counties.

Early in the 2016 general election season, polling showed a surprisingly tight race between Trump and Hillary Clinton in South Carolina, but on Election Day, the state gave Trump a 14-point victory, up from Mitt Romney's 11-point margin in 2012. The widened gap had more to do with a surge of support for Trump than a massive decline for Clinton. Trump outperformed Romney by 84,000 votes, but Clinton dropped below Barack Obama's 2012 totals by a modest 11,000 votes. Where Obama had won 21 counties, Clinton held on in 15. The six counties that switched to Trump (Barnwell, Calhoun, Chester, Colleton, Darlington and McCormick) were largely in the interior and jurisdictions where African Americans accounted for a substantial minority, but not a majority, of the population. The margins in each of these six blue-to-red counties moved by between six and 16 percentage points in the GOP's direction. Meanwhile, Clinton, despite losing ground in the state overall, improved on Obama's performance in Richland County (Columbia), where she gained about 4,000 votes, and Charleston County (Charleston), which gained an additional 8,000 and increased the Democratic winning margin from two percentage points to eight. Clinton did better in several solidly red counties even as she lost them overall. In Greenville County (Greenville), she gained 6,000 additional votes, in York she gained more than 2,000 additional votes, and in Horry, she gained slightly. But such gains came on the margins. As the state's dominant party, the South Carolina GOP will need to grapple with fractiousness and the burdens of any voter dissatisfaction with their policies. But it's the Democrats who face a steeper climb in the state.

Population		**Race and Ethnicity**		**Income**	
Total	4,777,576	White	63.9%	Median Income	$45,483 (42 out of 50)
Land area	30,061	Black	27.3%		
Pop/ sq mi	158.9	Latino	5.3%	Under $50,000	53.9%
Born in state	58.0%	Asian	1.4%	$50,000-$99,999	29.3%
		Two races	1.7%	$100,000-$199,999	13.8%
Age Groups		Other	0.5%	$200,000 or more	2.9%
Under 18	22.6%			Poverty Rate	17.9%
18-34	23.0%	**Education**			
35-64	39.1%	H.S grad or less	44.2%	**Health Insurance**	
Over 64	15.2%	Some college	29.9%	With health insurance coverage	85.5%
		College Degree, 4 yr	16.5%		
Work		Post grad	9.3%		
White Collar	33.1%			**Public Assistance**	
Sales and Service	43.1%	**Military**		Cash public assistance income	1.5%
Blue Collar	23.9%	Veteran	10.3%		
Government	15.8%	Active Duty	0.8%	Food stamp/SNAP benefits	15.1%

Voter Turnout			
2015 Total Citizens 18+	3,566,508	2016 Pres Turnout as % CVAP	59%
2016 Pres Votes	2,103,027	2012 Pres Turnout as % CVAP	58%

Legislature	
Senate:	18D, 27R, 1V
House:	44D, 79R, 1V

Presidential Politics

2016 Democratic Primary		
Hillary Clinton (D)	272,379	(73%)
Bernie Sanders (D)	96,498	(26%)
2016 Republican Primary		
Donald Trump (R)	240,882	(32%)
Ted Cruz (R)	165,417	(22%)
Marco Rubio (R)	166,565	(22%)
Jeb Bush (R)	58,056	(8%)
John Kasich (R)	56,410	(8%)
Ben Carson (R)	53,551	(7%)

2016 Presidential Vote		
Donald Trump (R)	1,155,389	(55%)
Hillary Clinton (D)	855,373	(41%)
Gary Johnson (L)	49,204	(2%)
2012 Presidential Vote		
Mitt Romney (R)	1,071,645	(55%)
Barack Obama (D)	865,941	(44%)

In presidential general elections, South Carolina has been reliably Republican for a long time. It was the only Deep South state to vote for Richard Nixon over George Wallace in 1968. Since then, it has voted Democratic only once, for Jimmy Carter in 1976. The primaries are less predictable, but more important. Since 1980, when Republicans began using a primary to allocate their national convention delegates, that contest played a pivotal role in determining the GOP nomination nearly every four years. And with an early spot on the calendar, it also played a major role in the 2008 Democratic race, and is positioned to render important judgments in subsequent party contests.

The primary's significance for Republicans began at the outset, when Ronald Reagan defeated John Connolly in 1980. Connolly had the backing of the state's legendary Sen. Strom Thurmond. Reagan's 55%-30% victory confirmed his widespread popularity among Southern Republicans and helped propel him to the GOP nomination. In 1987, Republican operative Lee Atwater craftily scheduled the GOP primary for the Saturday before Super Tuesday, a collection of mostly Southern primaries that many of the region's Democrats had organized, hoping to push their party toward choosing a moderate Southern standard bearer. Instead, South Carolina moved Republicans toward choosing a moderate Southern Republican, George H.W. Bush of Texas, who won a 49%-21%-19% victory over GOP Senate leader Bob Dole and evangelical champion Pat Robertson. That victory was a precursor of Bush's sweep of the Southern primaries that clinched nomination for him four days later. In 1992, Bush beat Pat Buchanan 67%-26%, squashing Buchanan's claims to conservative Southern support. Four years later, Dole, after his disappointing showings elsewhere, won an impressive 45%-29% victory over Buchanan. In 2000, former GOP governors Carroll Campbell and David Beasley supported George W. Bush, as he beat John McCain 53%-42%, in what was a particularly bruising and bitter contest that left relations between McCain and Bush strained throughout the latter's presidency. In 2008, McCain defeated former Arkansas Gov. Mike Huckabee 33%-30%. The Arizonan's victory established him as the front-runner for the nomination and gave him momentum that he carried into the Florida primary 10 days later and then the subsequent Super Tuesday contests. The 2012 Republican primary was held just 10 days after New Hampshire. Rick Perry and Newt Gingrich saw South Carolina as a must-win state for their campaigns, particularly after their weak finishes in Iowa and New Hampshire. Mitt Romney led in some pre-primary polls, but the hot candidate turned out to be Gingrich, who defeated Romney 40%-28%.

The 2016 edition of the South Carolina GOP primary was another Republican slugfest. Donald Trump questioned Texas Sen. Ted Cruz's citizenship and threatened to sue him over a negative television ad, which featured Trump describing himself in 1999 as "very pro-choice." In a debate, Trump accused former President George W. Bush of lying about the presence of weapons of mass destruction in Iraq in the run-up to the 2003 U.S.-led invasion of that country. After that debate the former president made his only appearance at a campaign rally for his brother, Jeb. Florida Sen. Marco Rubio won endorsements from the state's popular junior senator, Tim Scott, and more importantly, Gov. Nikki Haley. Sen. Lindsey Graham, who had been a candidate for the nomination but withdrew from the race a couple of months before the primary, endorsed Bush. But like Gingrich's victory four years earlier, it was Trump's fiery rhetoric and disdain for the GOP establishment and the media that excited South Carolina Republicans and enabled him to defeat Rubio, 33%-23%. Cruz finished a third with 22 percent and Bush's 8 percent prompted him to withdraw from the race.

The state's two political parties - not the state government - conduct presidential primaries in South Carolina, and they can choose to hold them on different days. In 2008, South Carolina Republicans responded by moving their primary to Jan. 19 to protect the state's coveted first-in-the-South status among GOP contests. The Democratic National Committee chose South Carolina as the only state other than New Hampshire to hold an early primary, and South Carolina Democrats picked Jan. 26. On the Democratic side, the most coveted endorsement was that of Rep. James Clyburn, the assistant Democratic leader in the House and an African American who can be a force in a presidential primary whose electorate is more than 50 percent black. Candidates and surrogates flock to his annual spring fish fry in Columbia, where the crowd consumes more than 1,000 pounds of whiting. Clyburn didn't endorse in the 2008 Democratic race between North Carolina Sen. John Edwards, Barack Obama and Hillary Clinton. Turnout in the Democratic primary was a record 532,000 voters, and Obama won a crushing victory, defeating Clinton 55%-26%. Years later in his memoir, Clyburn, who had voted for Obama, wrote that he received a 2 a.m. phone call the day after the primary from Bill Clinton blaming him for his wife's defeat and vowing, "If you bastards want a fight, you damn well will get one." The 2016 Democratic primary was much less contentious and saw a reversal of fortune for Clinton, who had consolidated African-American support, particularly in the South. She was endorsed by Clyburn one week before the primary, while her rival, Vermont Sen. Bernie Sanders, dispatched rap singer Killer Mike (his given name is Michael Render) to the state in hopes or rallying younger blacks to his candidacy. It didn't work. Clinton won more than four-out-of-five black voters, and they accounted for three-out-of-five of all voters in the primary.

In the 2016 general election the state held to its GOP tendencies and Trump defeated Clinton 55%-41%. Trump won 31 of the state's 46 counties. Clinton carried Charleston and Richland and did well in the counties with a higher African-American population in Clyburn's 6th District.

Congressional Districts

115th Congress Lineup	6R 1D	**114th Congress Lineup**	6R 1D

South Carolina gained a seventh House seat in the reapportionment of 2010, giving the state its largest delegation since the 1910 census. Republicans held the governorship and solid majorities in both houses of the legislature. They held five of six House seats after shoring up their incumbents. So in June 2011, the state House passed a proposal adding a new 7th District in the Pee Dee region anchored by Myrtle Beach and surrounding Horry County, a rapidly growing Republican bastion. But something unexpected happened on the road to full passage. The state Senate, including ambitious Republicans from the Lowcountry region, surprised the House with its own scheme, placing the new 7th District in the Charleston suburbs and Beaufort to the south. The map's plotters had brought on board several Democrats who believed the Senate version would give them a better shot in the 7th District, and they passed it 22-20. The impasse created by Republican infighting threatened to send the entire matter to federal court, where it was possible judges would insist on creating a second black majority seat in addition to Democrat Jim Clyburn's 6th District. After all, African-Americans were 28% of the state's population in 2010.

Republicans in the two chambers reached a compromise, greased by support from Upstate legislators, to place the 7th District in the Pee Dee, which would have the most blacks of any district in the state other than Clyburn's. The Charleston-based 1st District would pick up Beaufort, and 2nd District Republican Joe Wilson, who had taken only 53 percent in 2010, would shed some African-American counties to Clyburn. Gov. Nikki Haley signed the map, and the Obama Justice Department tersely granted preclearance. A group of six Democratic voters sued to block the map on the grounds it failed to create a new African-American seat, but a three-judge panel upheld the map in March 2012. Even though it is the least partisan of the six Republican districts, Tom Rice has easily held the new 7th District for the GOP.

Democrats' best option for 2022 likely will be to seek assistance from the Justice Department or the courts in the creation of a district that leans African American. That likely would require reduction of black voters in the 6th, and carving up the 5th or the 7th.

Governor

Henry McMaster (R)

Assumed office in 2017, term expires 2019, 1st term; b. May. 27, 1947, Columbia, SC; Univ. of South Carolina, BA 1969; Univ. of South Carolina, J.D 1973; Presbyterian; Married (Peggy); 2 children.

Military Career: U.S Army JAG, 1969-1975.

Elected Office: Chairman, SC Republican Party, 1993-2002; SC Attorney General 2003-2011; SC Lt. Governor, 2015-2017.

Professional Career: Legislative Assistant to U.S Sen. Strom Thurmond, 1973-1974; SC Law Enforcement Coordinating Committee head, 1981-1985;

Office: 1205 Pendleton St., Columbia, 29201; 803-734-2100; Fax: 803-734-5167; Website: sc.gov.

Henry McMaster, a longtime Republican officeholder in South Carolina who had lost a gubernatorial primary to Nikki Haley in 2010, was elevated from lieutenant governor in 2017 after Haley, by then in the middle of her second term as governor, was confirmed as President Donald Trump's pick to be U.S. ambassador to the United Nations.

McMaster, a native of Columbia, received his bachelor's degree from the University of South Carolina in 1969 and his law degree from the same university four years later. He then headed to Washington, D.C., for a year to serve as a legislative assistant to Sen. Strom Thurmond, after which he built a private practice in South Carolina. In 1981, on Thurmond's recommendation, President Ronald Reagan appointed McMaster to serve as U.S. attorney. During his four years in the post, his office helped convict more than 100 people for importing nearly $1 billion in illegal drugs. In 1986, McMaster ran for Senate against longtime incumbent Democrat Ernest Hollings but lost. Four years later, he ran for lieutenant governor and lost again. In 1991, then-Gov. Carroll Campbell appointed McMaster to the state Commission on Higher Education, and for most of the 1990s he headed the state Republican Party.

McMaster finally won an elected statewide office – attorney general -- in 2002. After securing the GOP nomination in a contested primary, McMaster defeated Democrat Steve Benjamin, 56%-44%, and he easily won a second term four years later. As attorney general, McMaster took a leading role in opposing the Affordable Care Act. He threw his hat into the ring for the open-seat gubernatorial race in 2010. The large Republican primary field also included Lt. Gov. André Bauer, Rep. Gresham Barrett, state Sen. Larry Grooms, and state Rep. Nikki Haley; Haley won the primary and went on to win the governorship in November. In 2014, McMaster ran for lieutenant governor, placing first in the Republican primary and defeating Democrat Bakari Sellers in the general election, 59%-41%.

During her six years as governor, Haley had attracted national attention as the first woman and the first racial minority to lead the Palmetto State. Born into an Indian Sikh family, Haley had become a symbol of the national Republican Party's efforts to tout an image of inclusiveness. After a lackluster first term, she won reelection in 2014 by a wider margin, then attracted widespread praise for leading the effort to remove the Confederate battle flag from the state capitol complex after years of failed attempts. In the 2016 presidential race, Haley had initially supported Florida Sen. Marco Rubio, and then Texas Sen. Ted Cruz. Itt was only in October that she confirmed she would vote for Trump. Despite this, Haley became one of the president-elect's first major appointments, and she won Senate confirmation by a 96-4 vote.

With Haley's confirmation in January 2017, McMaster at last became governor, at age 69. Coming into office, state legislators said they were hoping he'd be a dealmaker and easier to get along with than either Haley or her predecessor, Mark Sanford, both of whom were perceived to have sharp elbows. Former state Democratic chair Dick Harpootlian told *The State* newspaper that McMaster was "a good guy" who can "disagree without being disagreeable." In his first major act as governor, McMaster wrote to Trump seeking nearly $5.2 billion for infrastructure projects across the state, including $2 billion for repaving interstate and other primary roads, $2 billion for highway congestion relief, $500 million for rural highway safety improvements, $500 million for bridge repair, and $180 million to deepen Charleston's harbor by 52 feet. He also said he would veto a gas tax increase to fund infrastructure repairs. In the meantime, McMaster began preparing for the 2018 election, where he was expected to run for a full term, but in which he was likely to face GOP primary challengers, including former Lt. Gov.

Yancey McGill and former state agency head Catherine Templeton. McMaster, meanwhile, rebuffed Democratic calls for him to leave the all-white Forest Lake Club in Columbia, even though former state Republican Chairman Katon Dawson had resigned his membership in 2008 and called for the club to admit black members.

Senior Senator

Lindsey Graham (R)

Elected 2002, term expires 2020, 3rd term; b. Jul 09, 1955, Central; University of South Carolina, B.S.; University of South Carolina School of Law, J.D.; University of South Carolina, M.P.A.; Baptist; Single.

Military Career: U.S Air Force, 1982-88; SC Air National Guard, 1989-94; U.S Air Force Reserve, 1995-2015.

Elected Office: SC House, 1992-1994; U.S. House, 1995-2003.

Professional Career: U.S Air Forces Europe Circuit Trial Counsel, 1984-1988; Assistant Oconee County Attorney, 1988-1992; Practicing attorney, 1988-1994; Judge advocate, McEntire Air National Guard Base, 1989-1994; Central, SC, city Attorney, 1990-1994.

DC Office: 290 RSOB 20510, 202-224-5972, Fax: 202-224-3808, lgraham.senate.gov.

State Offices: Columbia, 803-933-0112; Florence, 843-669-1505; Greenville, 864-250-1417; Mt. Pleasant, 843-849-3887; Pendleton, 864-646-4090; Rock Hill, 803-366-2828.

Committees: *Appropriations*: Commerce, Justice, Science & Related Agencies, Department of Defense, DOL, HHS & Education & Related Agencies, Energy & Water Development, State, Foreign Operations & Related Programs (Chmn), Transportation, HUD & Related Agencies. *Armed Services*: Cybersecurity, Personnel, Strategic Forces. *Budget*. *Judiciary*: Antitrust, Competition Policy & Consumer Rights, Constitution, Crime & Terrorism (Chmn).

Group Ratings

	ADA	ACLU	AFL-CIO	LCV	ITI	COC	HAFA	ACU	CFG	FRC
2016	-	5%	-	29%	100%	100%	30%	50%	5700%	100%
2015	0%	C	31%	12%	C	100%	C	57%	53%	100%

Almanac Ratings 2015

	Economy	Social	Foreign	Composite
Liberal	38%	25%	37%	33%
Conservative	62%	76%	63%	67%

Key Votes of the 114th Congress

1. Keystone pipeline	Y	5. National Security Data	NV	9. Gun Sales Checks	N
2. Export-Import Bank	N	6. Iran Nuclear Deal	Y	10. Sanctuary Cities	NV
3. Debt Ceiling Increase	Y	7. Puerto Rico Debt	Y	11. Planned Parenthood	Y
4. Homeland Security $$	Y	8. Loretta Lynch A.G	Y	12. Trade deals	Y

Election Results

Election	Name (Party)	Vote (%)		Cand. Spent	Ind. Exp. Support	Ind. Exp. Oppose
2014 General	Lindsey Graham (R)	672,941	(55%)			
	Brad Hutto (D)	456,726	(38%)			
	Thomas Ravenel (I)	47,588	(4%)			
	Victor Kocher (L)	33,839	(3%)			
2014 Primary	Lindsey Graham (R)	178,093	(56%)			
	Lee Bright (R)	48,704	(15%)			
	Richard Cash (R)	26,246	(8%)			
	Det Bowers (R)	23,071	(7%)			
	Nancy Mace (R)	19,560	(6%)			
	Bill Connor (R)	16,847	(5%)			

Prior winning percentages: 2008 (58%), 2002 (54%), House: 2000 (69%), 1998 (100%), 1996 (60%), 1994 (60%)

Republican Lindsey Graham, South Carolina's senior senator, in many ways has made himself an indispensable and unique player on multiple fronts in the Senate and beyond. He and his close friend, Arizona Republican John McCain, are the Senate's two high-profile defense hawks; on domestic issues, Graham sometimes confounds conservatives by collaborating with Democrats, but he also can be a lacerating critic of the other party. First elected to the House in 1994 and to the Senate in 2002, Graham is well-positioned for more influence as a committee chairman, perhaps at Senate Judiciary. As his 2016 presidential candidacy showed, his ideas and comments can have an impact, even if he has limits as a national voice. He frequently irritated Donald Trump during the campaign and made a point of voting in November for independent Evan McMullin, a former CIA agent and national-security hard-liner.

Graham grew up in Pickens County, where his parents owned a tavern in the textile mill town of Central. Both his parents died young, while Graham was still attending the University of South Carolina, and he became his younger sister's legal guardian so that she could receive his military benefits. He was the first in his family to graduate from college, and then received a law degree from the University of South Carolina. He was an Air Force prosecutor who worked on assignments overseas, including one case that led to major changes in the service's drug testing program for soldiers. In 1988, he returned home and practiced law in Seneca. In 1992, he was elected to the state House. Graham was called up to active duty and served stateside during the Gulf War. He joined the Air Force Reserve in 1995 where he served as a senior instructor in the Air Force's JAG school and also as a reserve judge on the Air Force Court of Criminal Appeals. He was awarded the Bronze Star in 2014 for meritorious service for his role as a senior legal adviser to the Air Force during combat operations in Afghanistan. Graham retired from the reserves in June 2015 just as he was launching his presidential campaign.

In 1994, with the retirement of 20-year Democratic Rep. Butler Derrick, Graham ran for the House. Both parties had contested primaries, and Graham won the Republican primary with 52 percent of the vote. In the general election, he faced state Sen. Jim Bryan. Graham called for term limits, supported more defense spending, and opposed gays in the military. His attitude toward the Clinton administration and the Democratic leadership was unequivocal. He said, "I'm one less vote for an agenda that makes you want to throw up." Graham won 60%-40%, a smashing victory in a district represented only by Democrats since Reconstruction.

In the House, Graham had a solidly conservative voting record but did not always support the Republican leadership. In the summer of 1997, he was among a small group of junior House members who plotted with some senior lawmakers to try to oust Speaker Newt Gingrich, who by then had lost the confidence of his Republican troops. The attempt failed. In a Republican Conference meeting, when Majority Leader Dick Armey of Texas, one of the plotters, asserted that no member of the leadership was involved, Graham challenged that assertion as false.

As a member of the House Judiciary Committee, Graham played a major role in the 1998 impeachment of President Bill Clinton. In the Senate trial, Graham's folksy manner and clear description of Clinton's offenses-"Where I come from, a man who calls someone up at 2:30 in the morning is up to no good"-made him one of the most effective GOP impeachment managers. In 2000, Graham was one of McCain's staunchest supporters in his first bid for the presidency.

In 2002, Graham ran for the Senate seat of Republican Sen. Strom Thurmond, who was 99 and did not seek a ninth term. There had not been an open South Carolina Senate seat since 1941. In this now heavily

Republican state, Graham had no opposition in the Republican primary. His work on impeachment and in the McCain campaign made him well-known and popular statewide, and he had the endorsements of three former governors and Thurmond. Democrats portrayed him as lacking in substance and recruited Alex Sanders, president of the College of Charleston who in 1985 was appointed to the state Court of Appeals.

Sanders was a gifted raconteur, charming and well-connected around the state. He was a solid fundraiser as well, eventually raising $4.2 million, less than Graham's $6.2 million, but a considerable achievement for a candidate consistently behind in the polls. Sanders supported the Bush tax cuts and military action in Iraq, but he opposed the death penalty, on religious grounds, as well as a constitutional amendment to allow criminalization of flag burning. Graham hammered him on the death penalty and the flag amendment but most of all tried to label him as a liberal, saying Sanders would advance the agenda of Sens. Hillary Clinton of New York and Edward Kennedy of Massachusetts. Graham won 54%-44% and took the place of a senator first elected in the year before he was born. Graham and Clinton have long had a love-hate relationship - she's cited him as one of the Republicans she worked best with while in the Senate and called him after the Charleston murders, but he was a vocal critic of her tenure as secretary of state. During the closing weeks of the 2016 presidential race, he called for a special prosecutor to investigate the emails that she kept on her private server when she was secretary of state.

Graham has long combined a foreign policy hawkishness with sometimes surprising breaks with his party on domestic issues. Graham was the only Judiciary Committee Republican to support President Barack Obama's choice of Sonia Sotomayor for the Supreme Court in 2009, saying the president deserved the prerogative to nominate a qualified person of his choice even if the GOP disagreed with her ideology. He took the same position a year later when Obama nominated Solicitor General Elena Kagan for the court. In addition to praising her intellect, he said, "She's funny, and that goes a long way in my book." After the Supreme Court legalized gay marriage nationwide he said the party should accept the ruling and drop language calling for a constitutional amendment barring gay marriage nationwide from its platform.

In February 2009, Graham said he supported a limited nationalization of some banks and Obama's proposal to "stress-test" banks. "I'm not going to be the Herbert Hoover of 2009, saying 'Just let the free market work it out,'" he told the *Charlotte Observer*. And he incensed tea party activists by declaring to *The New York Times* in 2010 that the movement would "die out" because it "can never come up with a coherent vision for governing the country." When Kentucky GOP Sen. Rand Paul staged a 13-hour talking filibuster in March 2013 in partial protest of the administration's use of unmanned drones to kill U.S. citizens, Graham dismissed Paul's concerns to the Associated Press as "paranoia between libertarians and the hard left that is unjustified."

Graham has shored up his standing among conservatives by turning aggressively confrontational on several high-profile issues, many of them involving national security. He and McCain led a successful push to derail U.N. Ambassador Susan Rice's chances to become secretary of state after they sharply questioned her role in responding to the deadly September 2012 terrorist consulate attack in Benghazi Libya. Graham told Fox News that Secretary Clinton "got away with murder" for not foreseeing the threat in Benghazi. The two senators also were at the forefront of opposing the nomination of their former colleague, Republican Chuck Hagel of Nebraska, to become secretary of defense because of what they considered his insufficient support for Israel and hawkishness on Iran, although Hagel eventually was confirmed. And he warned in June 2014 that the "seeds of 9/11 are being planted all over Iraq and Syria" in calling for a more aggressive U.S. response in both nations.

Graham occasionally has taken a sharp turn to the right on fiscal and social policy. During the 2012 showdown over spending and taxes, he faulted Obama for not "manning up" and told Fox News his party needed to take a tough approach on the next vote to raise the federal debt limit. "We're not going to let Obama borrow any more money, or any American Congress borrow any more money, until we fix this country from becoming Greece," he said. Meanwhile, Graham took a hard line against new gun control measures including a ban on assault weapons, instead introducing a bill to strengthen mental health provisions in gun background checks. Graham stuck by his view that tighter gun control wasn't necessary in the wake of the murders of nine African-American churchgoers by a white man in Charleston in June 2015, though he suggested he supported more enforcement of background check laws already on the books. Breaking with some other Republican candidates he said there's "no doubt" the murders were racially motivated, but initially demurred when asked if he thought the Confederate Flag should be removed from official use in the state, calling it "part of who we are." Later, he backed South Carolina Gov. Nikki Haley when she called for the removal of the Confederate flag from statehouse grounds after the Charleston murders. In the *Almanac* vote ratings for 2015, he was the fourth least conservative Senator; that placed him literally at the center of the Senate.

Graham has worked in a bipartisan fashion on immigration, an issue with which he has long grappled. In 2006 and 2007, Graham supported the McCain-Kennedy and Kennedy-Kyl immigration bills, positions that got him in considerable trouble with conservatives who opposed giving illegal immigrants a process to achieve citizenship. Radio talk show host Rush Limbaugh belittled him as "Lindsey Grahamnesty," and the Greenville County Republican Party voted to censure him. Graham's public comments suggesting that immigration bill opponents were "bigots" did not help his cause.

Undeterred, Graham joined a group of senators, four Democrats and four Republicans, that hammered out a plan in early 2013 to tighten border security, visa tracking, and workplace verification in exchange for providing a path toward citizenship for the country's estimated 11 million undocumented workers. "I am confident, very confident, that if I help solve this problem in a way that we won't have 20 million illegal immigrants 20 years from now, not only will I get reelected, I can look back and say I was involved in something that was important," he told McClatchy Newspapers. The bill passed by a wide margin in the Senate but House GOP leaders refused to take it up in the face of withering criticism from conservative talk radio. Graham later joined conservatives in calling for an end to birthright citizenship, a position that incensed his usual immigration allies. Following the 2016 election, he again turned more conciliatory when he said that legal protections should be given to undocumented immigrants who arrived in the United States as children. During the campaign, he criticized Trump for his hostility to immigrants. "My party is in a hole with Hispanics. The first rule of politics when you're in a hole is stop digging. And somebody needs to take a shovel out of Donald Trump's hand."

Graham has supported action to combat climate change, though he's been less active on the issue in recent years. He had worked with Massachusetts Democratic Sen. John Kerry and Connecticut independent Sen. Joe Lieberman on a method of pricing carbon that would be an alternative to the House's 2009 bill creating a cap-and-trade system for companies emitting the greenhouse gases. As a presidential candidate in 2015, he told CNN that "Climate change is real" and promised "If I'm president of the United States, we're going to address climate change, CO2 emissions in a business-friendly way."

He has had varied experiences in national politics. Comparing his political style to McCain's, Graham told *The New York Times*: "I've never been a Luke Skywalker; I'm a much more calculating guy than that. I understand that you just don't charge into these things based on some moral belief that you're right and the other guy's wrong." Without much of a threat to his own reelection bid, Graham in 2008 traveled the country with McCain, the Republican presidential nominee. McCain, Graham, and Lieberman formed a bipartisan triumvirate on the campaign trail, dubbed the "Three Amigos." Graham's support was helpful to McCain in the pivotal January 2008 South Carolina primary, in which McCain redeemed his 2000 loss by winning with 33 percent of the vote. "There's nobody I trust more than Lindsey Graham," McCain told the Myrtle Beach *Sun News*. Graham was said to be the member of McCain's inner circle who was the most enthusiastic about him tapping Lieberman as his running mate, according to the 2010 book about the campaign, *Game Change*. But McCain settled on Alaska Gov. Sarah Palin after Graham began privately floating the idea of Lieberman with social conservatives, enraging Limbaugh and others when word leaked out.

Graham's departures from party orthodoxy fueled talk in 2014 of a primary challenger for his reelection to the Senate, and some D.C.-based conservative groups had him high on their target list. But Graham worked assiduously behind the scenes to befriend or scare off serious potential challengers, and managed to ward off any big-name opponents. He raised more than $12 million and put together an impressive on-the-ground operation featuring more than 5,000 precinct captains and six field offices around South Carolina. He kept his most prominent potential opponents out of the race - he helped Rep. Mick Mulvaney land a seat on the House Financial Services Committee, for instance. "When the members of the congressional delegation needed something for their district, their first call was to Lindsey Graham and it was to his cell phone. Lindsey Graham has been accessible to that federal delegation from day one," said former South Carolina Republican Party Chairman Katon Dawson, who ran a super PAC backing Graham.

On the campaign trail, Graham emphasized the areas where he agreed with the conservative base, introducing a bill banning abortions after 20 weeks of pregnancy in the Senate and trumpeting his battles with the Obama administration on national security, ripping the president on his handling of Benghazi, Russia, Syria, Iraq and Israel. Running against six minor challengers, Graham walked away in the June primary with 56 percent. From there, he had little trouble in the general election.

Graham had long mused about running for president in 2016. Many remained doubtful he would run, but he proved his skeptics wrong when he launched his campaign in June 2015, with a heavy focus on national security. "I want to be president to protect our nation that we all love so much from all threats foreign and domestic," he said in his announcement speech. Graham began the campaign as a long-shot candidate, and he failed to rise above that status or to gain much positive attention for himself.

With Donald Trump taking an "America First" approach, Graham emphasized the need for the nation to play a more assertive national-security role. Early in the campaign, he got under Trump's skin so much that the billionaire businessman called him a "light-weight" and he urged supporters at his rallies to call Graham's personal cell phone number. When Trump said that Graham's friend McCain was not a war hero because he had been captured and held prisoner in North Vietnam, Graham called Trump "a jackass." Graham ended his campaign in December 2015 when his failure to break out of the second tier of presidential candidates meant that he failed to become part of the chief field of contenders for GOP debates. "I don't want to be the undercard voice," he said, with frustration. He added that his campaign "has made a real difference" by getting other candidates to focus on security issues.

Following Trump's victory, Graham joined Sen. Ben Cardin of Maryland, the senior Democrat on the Foreign Relations Committee, in voicing concern about Russian attempts to influence the election. They took the lead in the Senate in demanding that Trump retain economic sanctions on Russia. When Graham and McCain said that Trump's efforts to restrict refugee from entering the United States-one of his early actions as president-would "become a self-inflicted wound in the fight against terrorism," the new president Tweeted that they were "sadly weak on immigration" and "always looking to start World War III." As chairman of the Appropriations Subcommittee with control of the State Department and foreign aid, Graham would have a significant voice in the outcome of Trump's budget that proposed major cutbacks for that spending.

Junior Senator

Tim Scott (R)

Appointed Jan. 2013, term expires 2022, 1st full term; b. Sep 19, 1965, North Charleston; Charleston Southern University (SC), B.S.; Presbyterian College (SC), Att., Evangelical; Single.

Elected Office: Charleston County Council, 1995-2008, Chairman, 2007-2008; SC House, 2009-2010; U.S. House, 2011-2013.

Professional Career: Partner, real estate firm; Owner, Tim Scott Allstate.

DC Office: 717 HSOB 20510, 202-224-6121, Fax: 202-228-5143, scott.senate.gov.

State Offices: Columbia, 803-771-6112; Greenville, 864-233-5366; North Charleston, 843-727-4525.

Committees: *Aging*. *Banking, Housing & Urban Affairs*: Financial Institutions & Consumer Protection, Housing, Transportation & Community Development (Chmn), Securities, Insurance & Investment. *Finance*: Energy, Natural Resources & Infrastructure, Fiscal Responsibility & Economic Growth (Chmn), Taxation & IRS Oversight. *Health, Education, Labor & Pensions*: Employment & Workplace Safety, Primary Health & Retirement Security. *Small Business & Entrepreneurship*.

Group Ratings

	ADA	ACLU	AFL-CIO	LCV	ITI	COC	HAFA	ACU	CFG	FRC
2016	-	11%	-	0%	80%	75%	78%	92%	89%	100%
2015	0%	C	8%	0%	C	71%	C	92%	89%	100%

Almanac Ratings 2015

	Economy	Social	Foreign	Composite
Liberal	5%	0%	35%	13%
Conservative	95%	100%	65%	87%

Key Votes of the 114th Congress

1. Keystone pipeline	Y	5. National Security Data	Y	9. Gun Sales Checks	N
2. Export-Import Bank	N	6. Iran Nuclear Deal	Y	10. Sanctuary Cities	Y
3. Debt Ceiling Increase	N	7. Puerto Rico Debt	N	11. Planned Parenthood	Y
4. Homeland Security $$	N	8. Loretta Lynch A.G	N	12. Trade deals	Y

Election Results

Election	Name (Party)	Vote (%)		Cand. Spent	Ind. Exp. Support	Ind. Exp. Oppose
2016 General	Tim Scott (R)	1,241,609	(61%)	$4,751,790	$161,399	
	Thomas Dixon (D)	757,022	(37%)	$35,176		
2016 Primary	Tim Scott (R)	unopposed				

Prior winning percentages: 2014 special (61%); House: 2012 (62%), 2010 (66%)

Republican Tim Scott, South Carolina's junior senator, has had a remarkable ascent in local and state politics and has become a prominent national spokesman on topics from conservatism to police practices. He was appointed to the Senate by Gov. Nikki Haley in January 2013 after GOP Sen. Jim DeMint resigned to head the conservative Heritage Foundation think tank. Since then, as the first black GOP lawmaker to be elected statewide in the South since Reconstruction and the Senate's first black Republican since 1979, Scott has easily won two elections. He previously served one term in the House. Scott has remained ambitious, seeking to influence the selection of the GOP presidential nominee in 2016 and voicing interest in running for governor, though each of those efforts ran into obstacles. In the cauldron of South Carolina Republican politics, Scott has shown that he should be taken seriously.

Scott and his siblings were raised by a single mother who worked 16-hour days as a nurse's assistant. Scott got his first job at age 13. He was on the verge of flunking out of high school when he met the man who he says changed his life-John Moniz, the owner of the fast-food Chick-fil-A restaurant next to the movie theater where Scott worked and where he would regularly buy French fries, the only food he could afford. Moniz, who considered himself a born-again Christian, became a father figure for Scott, teaching him the value of personal discipline and hard work. In a speech at the 2012 Republican National Convention, Scott said Moniz taught him that "having a job is a good thing, but creating jobs was even better." Scott finished high school and went on to earn a partial football scholarship to Presbyterian College. He eventually transferred to Charleston Southern University, where he earned a bachelor's degree in political science.

Scott ran an insurance company and owned part of a real estate agency. His first elected office was a seat on the Charleston County Council in 1995. Just after his election, he received a handwritten note of congratulations from Republican Sen. Strom Thurmond of South Carolina, who had run for president on a pro-segregation platform in 1948. Thurmond's past didn't stop Scott from accepting the job as statewide co-chairman of Thurmond's final senatorial campaign in 1996. Asked how an African American could help Thurmond, Scott told *The New York Times*, "The Strom Thurmond I knew had nothing to do with that" and noted that Thurmond's views on race had evolved. Scott also said that Thurmond taught him the value of constituent service. He later served as chairman of the council and was elected to one term in the state House.

In 2010, Scott ran for an open House seat in the Charleston-based 1st District. In the GOP primary, he faced opposition from candidates with better name recognition, including Carroll Campbell III, son of former South Carolina Gov. Carroll Campbell, Jr.; and Paul Thurmond, the former senator's son. Scott got help from national Republican organizations. He was the frontrunner in the primary, with 31 percent of the vote, which was short of the 50 percent necessary to avoid a runoff; Thurmond took second. There were few policy differences between the two, although Thurmond did not share Scott's willingness to abide by term limits and to swear off earmarked spending. Scott claimed that in his 15 years in elected office, he never voted for a tax increase. His conservative credentials won him praise from prominent Republicans such as former Alaska Gov. Sarah Palin and former House Speaker Newt Gingrich of Georgia. In the runoff election, Scott defeated Thurmond, 68% to 32%. In the general election, he easily beat Democrat Ben Frasier, a retired federal worker, 65% to 29%. His race appeared to be a non-issue for the district's voters, about 70 percent of whom were white.

As a House member, Scott's voting record was marginally more moderate than the rest of South Carolina's deeply conservative delegation. He was less outspoken than the delegation's other members or Florida Republican Rep. Allen West, the chamber's other black Republican during his first term. He joined conservatives in refusing to support a 2011 bill to raise the federal debt limit, a 2012 tax and spending compromise to avert a so-called "fiscal cliff," and several leadership-backed spending bills to keep the government running. Republican leaders professed not to mind; they realized his obvious value to their party and heaped praise on him. "He is leadership personified. He has a lot of magnetism and a lot of charisma," Majority Leader Eric Cantor of Virginia said. Scott served as a deputy whip and a freshman-class liaison to the leadership, and he was given a seat on the influential Rules Committee.

The decision by DeMint to quit the Senate after he suffered setbacks in the 2012 election with the defeat of some Tea Party candidates whom he had supported, which contributed to Republicans' failure to win Senate control, turned attention to whom Haley would appoint. Early speculation revolved around Scott, especially in light of the party's dismal electoral showing among African-American voters. Haley, who is Indian-American, chose Scott over four other finalists, a decision she said was based on his devotion to the state and his ability to advocate for it. "It is very important to me, as a minority female, that Congressman Scott earned this seat," she said. His selection proved extremely popular with Republicans.

Scott mostly shunned the public spotlight, turning down a number of opportunities to raise his national profile, and didn't seek to highlight his race. He concentrated on getting to know the state, holding numerous local town halls and meeting constituents in creative circumstances, such as volunteering incognito at a local Goodwill store to talk about their problems without tipping them off that he was a politician. In 2014, he flew under the national radar without serious primary or general election opposition; he won the general election with 61 percent of the vote.

When major race-related events shook South Carolina in 2015, Scott took advantage of his unique position. After a white policeman killed Walter Scott [no relation], an unarmed black man in Scott's hometown of North Charleston in April 2015, the senator was one of the first to support body cameras for policemen and introduced a bill to provide millions of dollars for local police departments to acquire them. Similar legislation became law in South Carolina in early June. Weeks later, when nine African-American churchgoers were murdered by a white supremacist in Charleston, Scott joined Gov. Haley and other South Carolina leaders to back a move to remove the Confederate flag from statehouse grounds. His emotional speech on the Senate floor generated widespread coverage, as he choked up when repeating comments from a relative of a victim that "this evil attack would lead to reconciliation, restoration, and unity in the nation." He later said on the Senate floor that he had been subject to racial discrimination at the Capitol.

Scott joined with New Jersey Democratic Sen. Cory Booker, who was then the Senate's only other African American, to introduce a bill for tax credits for businesses to create more apprenticeship programs. The idea received bipartisan praise-Hillary Clinton talked up the idea during her presidential campaign. He's been part of a bipartisan working group focused on criminal justice and sentencing reform. He also has been a loud advocate for school choice, a more controversial issue. Scott believes it can help improve education for poor and minority children. "There is a trend that can be broken at its foundation if we focus first on education and second on work skills," he said on ABC's "This Week" in mid-2015.

In July 2016, Scott told the Senate that there was no single solution to law enforcement problems affecting the racial minorities, though he emphasized, "Believe it or not, the government is not the answer to what ails us." He called for improved police training, increased personal inter-action between law-enforcement officers and community groups, and federal legislation to provide broader assistance-including expanded use of police body cameras. His critics pointed out that he received "F" ratings from the NAACP on its annual scorecards, supported voter ID laws many civil rights groups view as discriminatory against minorities, and refused to endorse a congressional fix to the Voting Rights Act after the Supreme Court struck down a key enforcement provision of the law.

In the 2016 campaign, Scott expanded the town halls that he had initiated with presidential candidates four years earlier in his battleground home state; this time, he partnered with his close friend and ally, Rep. Trey Gowdy. Unlike in 2012, Scott didn't rule out endorsing a candidate. Most of the GOP candidates were eager to appear alongside the potential kingmakers. The chief exception was Donald Trump, who preferred to control the format and sponsorship of his campaign events. Two weeks before the South Carolina primary, Scott endorsed Florida Sen. Marco Rubio, who shared Scott's youth and minority status plus a commitment to address poverty with conservative principles. Dimming some of Scott's strength, Trump won the primary with 33 percent of the vote; Rubio ran second with 22 percent, slightly ahead of Texas Sen. Ted Cruz.

Scott had another easy election of his own that year. Perhaps the most notable aspect was that his 61 percent of the vote was six percentage points ahead of Trump's performance on Election Day. The chief difference in their performances was that Scott took 56 percent of the vote in his home county of Charleston, where Trump ran second to Hillary Clinton with 43 percent.

With Gowdy's encouragement, local Republicans enthusiastically discussed the possibility that Scott and Gowdy would run as a ticket in the campaign for governor in 2018, when Haley was term-limited. But that possibility dimmed when Trump appointed Haley as Ambassador to the United Nations and Lieutenant Governor Henry McMaster moved up to governor, with the intention of seeking his own full term.

FIRST DISTRICT

Mark Sanford (R)

Elected 2013, 3rd term; b. May 28, 1960, Fort Lauderdale, FL; University of Virginia Darden School of Business, M.B.A.; Furman University (SC), B.A.; Episcopalian; Engaged (Maria Belen Chapur); 4 children (from previous marriage).

Military Career: U.S Air Force Reserves, 2002-2011.

Elected Office: U.S. House, 1995-2001; SC Governor, 2003-2011.

Professional Career: Real estate investor, 1988-1992; Owner, Norton & Sanford real estate investment firm, 1992-2002; Commentator, FOX News, 2011-2013; real estate investor, 2011-2013.

DC Office: 2211 RHOB 20515, 202-225-3176, sanford.house.gov.

State Offices: Beaufort, 843-521-2530; Mount Pleasant, 843-352-7572.

Committees: *Budget. Oversight & Government Reform*: Government Operations, Health Care, Benefits & Administrative Rules. *Transportation & Infrastructure*: Aviation, Railroads, Pipelines & Hazardous Materials, Water Resources & Environment.

Group Ratings

	ADA	ACLU	AFL-CIO	LCV	ITI	COC	HAFA	ACU	CFG	FRC
2016	-	35%	-	21%	67%	86%	85%	96%	100%	83%
2015	5%	C	13%	6%	C	67%	C	92%	95%	83%

Almanac Ratings 2015

	Economy	Social	Foreign	Composite
Liberal	7%	15%	48%	23%
Conservative	93%	85%	52%	77%

Key Votes of the 114th Congress

1. Keystone Pipeline	Y	5. Puerto Rico Debt	N	9. Offenses by Aliens	Y
2. Trade Deals	Y	6. Medical Marijuana	Y	10. Troops in Iraq	Y
3. Export-Import Bank	N	7. Sanctuary Cities	Y	11. Homeland Security $$	N
4. Debt Ceiling Increase	N	8. Armor-piercing Bullets	Y	12. Trade Adjustment aid	NV

Election Results

Election	Name (Party)	Vote (%)		Cand. Spent	Ind. Exp. Support	Ind. Exp. Oppose
2016 General	Mark Sanford (R)	190,410	(59%)	$161,825		
	Dimitri Cherny (D)	119,799	(37%)	$13,024		
	Michael Crier Jr. (L)	11,614	(4%)			
2016 Primary	Mark Sanford (R)	21,266	(56%)			
	Jenny Horne (R)	16,974	(44%)			

Prior winning percentages: 2014 (93%), 2013 special (54%), Governor: 2006 (55%), 2002 (53%); House: 1998 (91%), 1996 (96%), 1994 (66%)

Republican Mark Sanford won a 2013 special election, completing an extraordinary political comeback. A disgraced former governor whose personal life became a national punch line, Sanford has returned to the House as one of the GOP's most stringent fiscal conservatives. He has been mostly a back bencher and has kept his distance from the House's bomb-throwing activists and from Donald Trump. His candor and perhaps his ambition remain active.

Sanford grew up in Fort Lauderdale, Florida, the son of a heart surgeon. The family spent summers and vacations on a 3,000-acre farm in Beaufort County, once known as Coosaw Plantation, and moved there permanently when Mark was 18. He graduated from Furman University and the University of Virginia business school. He worked in real estate investment in New York and later started his own firm in Charleston.

When the seat was open in 1994, Sanford, with no political experience, ran for the House. He campaigned as an outsider and pledged to serve only three terms, to take no political action committee money, to vote for no tax increases, and to refuse any salary increase until the federal budget was balanced. He won a primary runoff 52%-48% and then easily prevailed in the general election with 66 percent of the vote. In the House, Sanford became a voice for reduced federal spending, and he declined to seek pork barrel projects for his district.

After honoring his term-limit pledge, Sanford in 2002 launched a campaign for governor. He beat two better-known Republicans in the primary, then faced Democratic Gov. Jim Hodges, who played up his modest background and called Sanford a wealthy Charleston plantation owner from South Florida. One of his ads attacked Sanford for having voted "against programs for disabled kids." But then it was revealed that Hodges had transferred $300,000 from a fund for emotionally disturbed children to the operating account for the governor's office. Campaigning in khakis and a plaid shirt, Sanford promised to end politics as usual and won 53%-47%.

As governor, Sanford had an extremely strained relationship with the Republican-controlled legislature. In 2004, he issued 106 budget vetoes to cut spending and the House overrode 105 of them. He angered legislators by sneaking two piglets into the State House - which he dubbed "Pork" and "Barrel" - to symbolize the legislature's wasteful spending; the pigs defecated on the carpet, but the public loved the stunt. Seeking a second term in 2006, Sanford easily won the GOP primary and faced Democratic challenger Tommy Moore, a state senator and veteran legislative dealmaker. Sanford framed the race as a choice between his outsider's approach and the state's business-as-usual political culture. He raised more than $8 million, compared with Moore's $3 million, and won 55%-45%.

Sanford's tightfisted budgeting, popular with some national conservatives, stirred talk of a possible place for him on the Republican national ticket in 2008. During an interview on CNN, host Wolf Blitzer asked Sanford to specify distinctions between Republican presidential candidate John McCain and President George W. Bush on the economy. Sanford drew a blank for several seconds, before citing the North American Free Trade Agreement. Blitzer pointed out Bush and McCain agreed on free trade. The clip probably sank Sanford's chances of joining the ticket. His political future soon worsened.

In June 2009, reports surfaced that Sanford had not been at work for several days. As legislators wondered where he was, Sanford's spokesman reported that the governor was in the mountains hiking the Appalachian Trail. But a reporter for *The State,* acting on a tip, staked out Atlanta's Hartsfield-Jackson airport and confronted Sanford, who admitted that he had not been hiking. Back in Columbia that afternoon, Sanford said in a rambling, unscripted news conference that he had been carrying on an extramarital affair with a woman from Argentina. He made clear he intended to remain as governor, although he resigned as chairman of the Republican Governors Association.

A few days later, Sanford gave an interview to the Associated Press in which the married governor and father of four called his mistress, Maria Belen Chapur, his "soul mate." More than half of the Republicans in the state Senate called for Sanford's resignation. Several members of the state's congressional delegation either publicly or privately urged him to step down. But he refused and finished out his term. The phrase "hiking the Appalachian Trail" entered the vernacular as slang for infidelity, and Sanford seemed to be washed up in politics. He took the well-traveled road of failed political conservatives to a commentator's job at Fox News, and he became engaged to Chapur.

When GOP Rep. Tim Scott was appointed to fill a vacancy in the Senate, Sanford ran for his House seat. Despite his obvious negatives, Sanford had reason to be optimistic: A Democrat had not represented the district since the early 1970s. Sanford had plenty of competition in the primary. He led the 15 GOP candidates in the first round of voting and took the runoff from Curtis Bostic, a former Charleston County Council member, 57%-43%. That set up a contest with Democratic businesswoman Elizabeth Colbert Busch, the sister of political satirist Stephen Colbert. Her brother's fame lent her considerable name recognition, and she stressed her moderate credentials. Sanford, meanwhile, could not escape his scandal. Revelations that his ex-wife, Jenny Sanford, had accused him of trespassing at her home prompted the National Republican Congressional Committee to withdraw its support. He claimed he had just dropped by the house while his ex-wife was away to keep his son company during the Super Bowl.

Still, Colbert Busch would have had to run a perfect race to win, and she didn't. The political novice failed to connect with voters, her campaign themes seemed uninspired, and she made relatively few public appearances compared to the ubiquitous and people-friendly Sanford. He won 54%-45% and said of his unlikely comeback victory, "I am an imperfect man saved by God's grace."

Back in Congress, Sanford learned that many subcommittee chairmen were reluctant to have him on their panels, fearing he could cause an unwanted distraction. House Speaker John Boehner helped smooth things over. Sanford avoided wading into splashy sound-bite fights and dutifully attended hearings; his perseverance was rewarded in 2014 when the House passed his bill to end the

Transportation Security Agency's practice of paying higher wages to workers for skills they don't use at their jobs.

His *Almanac* vote ratings for 2015 showed that Sanford remained a fiscal conservative, but he ranked in the center of the House. He was one of just 10 Republicans to oppose a Homeland Security funding bill that tightened restrictions on illegal immigrants. In June 2015, he issued a statement supporting the decision by Gov. Nikki Haley to remove the Confederate flag from the State House grounds. Also that month, he showed his libertarian instincts when he joined Democratic Rep. Barbara Lee of California on an amendment to eliminate proposed travel restrictions to Cuba. The amendment was defeated, 176-247, on a mostly party-line vote. In early 2017, he worked on a conservative replacement for the Affordable Care Act.

Sanford's return to political life has had some bumps. In 2014, he was reelected without major-party opposition. Two years later, he was challenged in the Republican primary by state Rep. Jenny Horne, who ran a robust campaign and criticized Sanford's vote to close the U.S. detention camp at Guantanamo Bay, Cuba. Sanford spent little money on the contest and was held to a 56%-44% win, a sign of his lingering tension with GOP voters. His Democratic challenger, Dimitri Cherney, crossed the district on a canoe and bicycle. He was "at the mercy of the tides and the winds," which he said was a useful metaphor for millions of Americans. Cherney raised only $28,000 and got little attention. Sanford won, 59%-37%.

In 2015, a former speechwriter wrote a book about working for Sanford, which a review in *The New York Times* described as "a thankless job for an unreasonable person in a dysfunctional office during a period of unusual turmoil." A lengthy profile in *Politico* in February 2017 described Sanford's chilly view of President Donald Trump, whom he criticized for having "fanned the flames of intolerance." Sanford, who castigated Trump during the campaign for refusing to release his tax returns, added that Trump "represents the antithesis, or the undoing, of everything I thought I knew about politics, preparation and life." The story speculated generally about Sanford's ambition for another statewide campaign.

Sanford's personal life has drawn continued headlines. In 2014, he announced in a rambling 2,346-word post on Facebook that he and Chapur were breaking up. He said the "agony of divorce" and a custody fight with his ex-wife had proven too much of a strain. The publicity startled Chapur, who later said that she had asked that he not make public the details of their split. But that didn't end the saga. In 2015, *Politico* reported that the couple "were spotted together again numerous times."

Lowcountry: Charleston, Hilton Head

Population		**Race and Ethnicity**		**Income**	
Total	712,074	White	70.4%	Median Income	$59,613 (146 out of 435)
Land area	1,548	Black	18.9%		
Pop/ sq mi	460.0	Latino	6.5%		
Born in state	43.1%	Asian	1.8%	Under $50,000	41.8%
Age Groups		Two races	2.1%	$50,000-$99,999	33.5%
Under 18	22.2%	Other	0.5%	$100,000-$199,999	19.3%
18-34	23.7%	**Education**		$200,000 or more	5.5%
35-64	38.4%	H.S grad or less	31.1%	Poverty Rate	12.2%
Over 64	15.6%	Some college	31.4%	**Health Insurance**	
Work		College Degree, 4 yr	23.6%	With health insurance coverage	86.9%
White Collar	38.5%	Post grad	13.9%		
Sales and Service	43.1%	**Military**		**Public Assistance**	
Blue Collar	18.5%	Veteran	12.9%	Cash public assistance income	0.9%
Government	17.3%	Active Duty	1.6%		
				Food stamp/SNAP benefits	8.7%

Voter Turnout			
2015 Total Citizens 18+	530,974	2016 House Turnout as % CVAP	61%
2016 House turnout	325,170	2014 House Turnout as % CVAP	24%

2012 Presidential Vote		
Mitt Romney	174,391	(58%)
Barack Obama	119,833	(40%)

2016 Presidential Vote		
Donald Trump	178,181	(54%)
Hillary Clinton	134,541	(40%)
Gary Johnson	12,450	(4%)

Cook Partisan Voting Index: R+10

Looking out across the harbor to Fort Sumter are the glorious mansions of the Battery, gazing on the same view that the hot-blooded young swells of Charleston did in April 1861, when they fired the shots that began the Civil War. Today, there are few more beautiful urban scenes in America than the pastel "single houses" of Charleston, built flush with the sidewalk, turning their shoulders to the streets, with open piazzas inside their iron gateways facing south to catch the breeze. Founded in 1670, Charleston was blessed with one of the finest harbors on the Atlantic, at the point where, Charlestonians like to say, the Ashley and Cooper rivers meet to form the Atlantic Ocean. It was one of the South's two leading cities during the Civil War. Cargoes of rice, indigo, cotton and slaves crossed its docks, enriching the white planters and merchants who dominated the state's economic and political life. After the war, Charleston became an economic backwater, enabling the old buildings to survive. The loving restorations of recent years have made the center city look better than ever and have attracted a considerable tourist trade.

Charleston's old society - descended from planters from Barbados, French Huguenots, Sephardic Jews and the second sons of English gentry - was once a leading force in American political life. The hotheads in the gallery disrupted the 1860 Democratic National Convention here so boisterously that it adjourned and reconvened in Baltimore, while Southern Democrats split off and nominated their own candidate, enabling Abraham Lincoln to win with 38 percent of the popular vote. The history of black South Carolinians, memorialized in George Gershwin's *Porgy and Bess*, is noteworthy, but the tale of slavery, once hidden under a blanket of politeness, was slow to emerge. Many plantations near Charleston have added programs on the history of slavery to tours once dominated by romantic tales of the old South. The decision by Gov. Nikki Haley to remove the Confederate flag from the state capital grounds following the June 2015 shootings at a black church in downtown Charleston accelerated that local rethinking.

The 1st Congressional District of South Carolina stretches along the coast from Charleston down to Hilton Head. It includes the coastal parts of Beaufort County taking in the old county seat of Beaufort and the carefully manicured developments of Hilton Head Island, plus parts of burgeoning inland suburbs in Berkeley and Dorchester counties. It includes the heavily white Battery and the area west of the Ashley River, but not the African-American areas to the north in downtown Charleston. The adjacent 6th District scoops up much of the black population in Charleston and Beaufort counties, leaving the 1st at 20 percent black. About 40 percent of the population of the 1st is in Charleston, another 40 percent in the inland counties, and 20 percent in Beaufort. Beaufort's old mansions provided the backdrop for novelist Pat Conroy, while the posh condominium developments and golfing resorts around Hilton Head help drive up Beaufort County's population, which increased 13 percent between 2010 and 2016, one of the fastest growing areas in the nation. In October 2016, Hurricane Matthew caused extensive flooding and storm damage. On nearby St. Helena Island, slave owners escaping the heat and the mosquitoes ran largely absentee operations, thus allowing Gullah culture - a fusion of English and African elements - to thrive. The district takes in the Marine Corps' Parris Island training base and an air station at Beaufort, which is scheduled to be the base for four squadrons of the F-35 Joint Strike Fighter.

This is comfortable Republican country, but the conservatism of the Lowcountry - the term for South Carolina's coastal counties, including Charleston - is more economic and less cultural than the conservatism of the Upstate region. Many voters here favor environmental restrictions and efforts to curb sprawl. Donald Trump in 2016 won the 1st, 54%-40%, his lowest performance in the state's six Republican districts.

SECOND DISTRICT

Joe Wilson (R)

Elected 2001, 9th term; b. Jul 31, 1947, Charleston; University of South Carolina, J.D.; Washington and Lee University (VA), B.A.; Presbyterian; Married (Roxanne Dusenbury McCrory Wilson); 4 children; 7 grandchildren.

Military Career: U.S Army Reserve, 1972-1975; SC National Guard, 1975-2003.

Elected Office: SC Senate, 1985-2001.

Professional Career: Practicing attorney, 1972-2001.

DC Office: 1436 LHOB 20515, 202-225-2452, Fax: 202-225-2455, joewilson.house.gov.

State Offices: Aiken, 803-642-6416; West Columbia, 803-939-0041.

Committees: *Armed Services*: Emerging Threats & Capabilities, Readiness (Chmn). *Education & the Workforce*: Health, Employment, Labor & Pensions, Workforce Protections. *Foreign Affairs*: Europe, Eurasia & Emerging Threats, Terrorism, Nonproliferation & Trade.

Group Ratings

	ADA	ACLU	AFL-CIO	LCV	ITI	COC	HAFA	ACU	CFG	FRC
2016	-	5%	-	0%	100%	100%	66%	92%	72%	100%
2015	0%	C	9%	0%	C	45%	C	75%	68%	100%

Almanac Ratings 2015

	Economy	Social	Foreign	Composite
Liberal	13%	0%	4%	6%
Conservative	87%	100%	96%	94%

Key Votes of the 114th Congress

1. Keystone Pipeline	Y	5. Puerto Rico Debt	Y	9. Offenses by Aliens	Y
2. Trade Deals	Y	6. Medical Marijuana	N	10. Troops in Iraq	N
3. Export-Import Bank	Y	7. Sanctuary Cities	Y	11. Homeland Security $$	N
4. Debt Ceiling Increase	Y	8. Armor-piercing Bullets	Y	12. Trade Adjustment aid	Y

Election Results

Election	Name (Party)	Vote (%)		Cand. Spent	Ind. Exp. Support	Ind. Exp. Oppose
2016 General	Joe Wilson (R)	183,746	(60%)	$720,133		
	Arik Bjorn (D)	109,452	(36%)	$68,145		
	Eddie McCain (A)	11,798	(4%)			
2016 Primary	Joe Wilson (R)		(100%)			

Prior winning percentages: 2014 (62%), 2012 (96%), 2010 (54%), 2008 (54%), 2006 (63%), 2004 (65%), 2002 (91%)

Republican Joe Wilson, elected in 2001, has a reputation in his committee roles as a hard-working fiscal and defense hawk. With his seniority, he has been a mentor to many junior Republicans. He remains known as the lawmaker who breached congressional decorum in 2009 by shouting, "You lie!" during President Barack Obama's health care address to Congress.

Wilson grew up in Charleston and graduated from Washington & Lee University and the University of South Carolina law school. He got his Republican stripes as an aide to Rep. Floyd Spence and then for Sen. Strom Thurmond. Wilson was deputy general counsel at the Energy Department during the Reagan administration. He practiced law in West Columbia for 25 years while working on several political campaigns. In 1984, he was elected to the state Senate, where he chaired the Transportation Committee. Throughout this period, he served 31 years as a staff judge advocate in the South Carolina Army National Guard. All four of Wilson's sons have been Eagle Scouts and served in the military, two of them in Iraq. His son, Alan, was reelected state attorney general in 2014.

In 2001, when Spence died after more than 30 years in the House, Wilson became the front-runner to replace his longtime friend and mentor. In his campaign, he pledged to continue Spence's focus on defense. He won the Republican primary with 76 percent of the vote and defeated his Democratic opponent easily, 73%-25%.

With a seat on the Armed Services Committee, he has concentrated on military issues. In 2011, he became chairman of the Military Personnel Subcommittee. In the fiscal 2013 defense authorization bill, he kept alive some of the Air Force's Global Hawk unmanned surveillance planes after the Pentagon had sought to retire them. At a 2013 hearing, Wilson rebuked outgoing Secretary of State Hillary Clinton for not going on Sunday talk shows to discuss the terrorist attack in Benghazi, Libya, saying one of her priorities should have been "telling correct information" to the public. Wilson criticized Obama for "holding our military hostage" with the across-the-board defense cut "sequester" that took effect that year after the president and Congress failed to reach a comprehensive spending deal.

Wilson has advocated a closer military relationship with India, and he traveled frequently to Iraq and Afghanistan to review those conflicts when U.S. forces were engaged. He urged President Donald Trump to loosen the restrictions on the U.S. military fighting the Taliban rebels in Afghanistan. In 2017, Wilson took over as chairman of the Readiness Subcommittee at Armed Services, to provide the resources and support for the military to respond to what he described as an "unprecedented readiness crisis."

Wilson was unknown outside of his district, and barely known in Washington, before his outburst during Obama's September 2009 speech at the Capitol. As Obama was answering what he called critics' "bogus claims" of his health care legislation, Wilson called out, "You lie!" His behavior provoked stinging criticism on editorial pages and talk shows around the country. He apologized to Obama in a phone call but rebuffed Democratic demands for a more public apology from the well of the House. His South Carolina colleague, then-Democratic Majority Whip James Clyburn, alleged there was a taint of racism in Wilson's reaction, noting that no other president in memory had been the target of a similar breach in protocol during a joint session. Democrats pushed for a floor vote to sanction Wilson, and the House passed a "resolution of disapproval" on a mostly party-line vote. Seven years later, in an interview with ESPN, former Attorney General (and Obama friend) Eric Holder said of the Wilson incident, "Somebody should have smacked his ass."

Wilson typically has joined most other South Carolina Republicans in opposing trade promotion authority for presidents. In 2011, he refused to support a trade deal with South Korea, which competes against his state's textile industry. Ironically, despite their antipathy for Obama, Wilson and three other House Republicans from South Carolina voted in 2015 to give him trade promotion authority for the prospective Trans-Pacific Partnership. In 2010, he criticized the Obama administration's decision to withhold funding for the Yucca Mountain nuclear waste depository in Nevada, saying that the Savannah River Site would be stuck indefinitely holding 7,200 containers of spent nuclear waste. His legislation to reverse the decision failed to advance.

On the Education and the Workforce Committee, Wilson in 2003 won House passage of a bill to expand college loan forgiveness for math, science, and special education teachers who work in impoverished areas. He worked with Democrats to make permanent the child adoption tax credit. He failed to get the top Republican slot on the committee when it came open in 2009. Although he had more seniority, he lost out to John Kline of Minnesota. After Kline stepped down in 2016, Wilson supported Rep. Virginia Foxx of North Carolina as the next chair. "They are tough issues that I don't have a passion for. My passion is for a strong national defense," he said. Foxx named Wilson as vice chairman.

Over the years, Wilson has been reelected by wide margins. His district includes some of the strongest tea party bastions in the state. Wilson's willingness to counsel South Carolina's four Republicans elected in 2010 led them to dub him "the Scoutmaster."

West-Central South Carolina: Parts of Columbia Metro, Aiken

Population		**Race and Ethnicity**		**Income**	
Total	681,406	White	67.2%	Median Income	$53,547 (205 out of 435)
Land area	3,022	Black	23.3%		
Pop/ sq mi	225.5	Latino	5.2%		
Born in state	53.8%	Asian	1.8%	Under $50,000	46.6%
		Two races	2.0%	$50,000-$99,999	32.0%
Age Groups		Other	0.4%	$100,000-$199,999	17.8%
Under 18	23.5%			$200,000 or more	3.6%
18-34	22.8%	**Education**		Poverty Rate	14.3%
35-64	39.9%	H.S grad or less	37.5%		
Over 64	13.8%	Some college	30.5%	**Health Insurance**	
		College Degree, 4 yr	20.1%	With health insurance coverage	88.0%
Work		Post grad	12.0%		
White Collar	38.2%				
Sales and Service	41.3%	**Military**		**Public Assistance**	
Blue Collar	20.5%	Veteran	11.2%	Cash public assistance income	1.5%
Government	19.7%	Active Duty	2.1%		
				Food stamp/SNAP benefits	12.6%

Voter Turnout			
2015 Total Citizens 18+	503,582	2016 House Turnout as % CVAP	61%
2016 House turnout	304,996	2014 House Turnout as % CVAP	39%

2012 Presidential Vote		
Mitt Romney	171,829	(62%)
Barack Obama	101,354	(37%)

2016 Presidential Vote		
Donald Trump	176,615	(57%)
Hillary Clinton	119,812	(38%)
Gary Johnson	8,289	(3%)

Cook Partisan Voting Index: R+12

In 1786, soon after the Revolutionary War, the South Carolina Legislature decided to move the state capital away from the Charleston aristocracy and into the interior, away from a city named after a king to a new city named after a discoverer of America. So began Columbia. The State House was built on high ground above the Congaree River in a town of one-and-a-half story houses with first-floor porticos, dormers and raised brick basements - "Columbia cottages." In 1865, Gen. William Tecumseh Sherman's army burned almost everything here but the State House - something remembered by a local Presbyterian minister's eight-year-old son, whose name was Thomas Woodrow Wilson. Columbia recovered but grew slowly, with the state government, the state university, the Army's Fort Jackson and local insurance companies providing steady employment.

Columbia's politics were personified by Jimmy Byrnes, the Democrat who was elected to Congress in 1910 and returned from top posts in President Franklin D. Roosevelt's Washington to serve as governor. Byrnes adamantly opposed the *Brown v. Board of Education* decision in 1954. Since then, upwardly mobile white South Carolinians have turned Republican, first in national elections and then at the state and local levels. Metro Columbia is competitive: Richland County, which is 47 percent African American, votes Democratic and gave 64 percent of the vote to Hillary Clinton in 2016. Across the river, Lexington County is 15 percent black and heavily Republican and gave 66 percent to Donald Trump.

The 2nd Congressional District of South Carolina includes parts of metro Columbia, excluding black neighborhoods in central and north Columbia that are in the black-majority 6th District. It contains the city's affluent white neighborhoods and the spread-out towns and countryside beyond. It includes all of Lexington and Aiken counties. Aiken, with its horsey trappings for polo and steeplechase, has long attracted affluent transplants. About 40 percent of the vote is in Lexington, and 30 percent is in Richland. The district takes in Barnwell County and the Savannah River Site, which from 1954 to 1991 was one of the nation's nuclear weapons manufacturing complexes. Since then, the 310 square miles have been undergoing a multibillion-dollar cleanup, an important economic driver regionally. Employment at Savannah River remained at more than 6,000 workers in 2016. The state of South Carolina has pursued extensive litigation with the federal government over the project. In February 2017, a federal judge dismissed part of the lawsuit seeking compensation for the delay, but continued to review the pace of the cleanup. At a plant in Lexington, Michelin manufactures radial and earthmover tires, with a payroll of 1,400.

The district is comfortably Republican, though the Republican voted dropped from 62 percent for Mitt Romney in 2012 to 57 percent for Trump in 2016.

THIRD DISTRICT

Jeff Duncan (R)

Elected 2010, 4th term; b. Jan 07, 1966, Greenville; Clemson University (SC), B.A.; Baptist; Married (Melody Duncan); 3 children.

Elected Office: SC House, 2002-2010.

Professional Career: Assistant Vice President., M.S. Bailey & Son, 1989-1993; Assistant Vice President., Palmetto Bank, 1993-1995; President, J. Duncan & Assocs., 1995-2010.

DC Office: 2229 RHOB 20515, 202-225-5301, Fax: 202-225-3216, jeffduncan.house.gov.

State Offices: Anderson, 864-224-7401; Laurens, 864-681-1028.

Committees: *Foreign Affairs*: Europe, Eurasia & Emerging Threats, Western Hemisphere (Chmn). *Homeland Security*: Border & Maritime Security, Oversight & Management Efficiency.

Group Ratings

	ADA	ACLU	AFL-CIO	LCV	ITI	COC	HAFA	ACU	CFG	FRC
2016	-	17%	-	0%	67%	100%	85%	96%	91%	100%
2015	10%	C	4%	3%	C	53%	C	96%	88%	91%

Almanac Ratings 2015

	Economy	Social	Foreign	Composite
Liberal	9%	15%	8%	11%
Conservative	91%	85%	92%	89%

Key Votes of the 114th Congress

1. Keystone Pipeline	Y	5. Puerto Rico Debt	N	9. Offenses by Aliens	Y
2. Trade Deals	N	6. Medical Marijuana	Y	10. Troops in Iraq	N
3. Export-Import Bank	N	7. Sanctuary Cities	Y	11. Homeland Security $$	N
4. Debt Ceiling Increase	N	8. Armor-piercing Bullets	Y	12. Trade Adjustment aid	N

Election Results

Election	Name (Party)	Vote (%)		Cand. Spent	Ind. Exp. Support	Ind. Exp. Oppose
2016 General	Jeff Duncan (R)	196,325	(73%)	$447,245		
	Hosea Cleveland (D)	72,933	(27%)			
2016 Primary	Jeff Duncan (R)		(100%)			

Prior winning percentages: 2014 (71%), 2012 (67%), 2010 (66%)

Republican Jeff Duncan, elected in 2010 to an open seat, has often gone his own way from GOP leaders. His deeply held conservative beliefs can prompt fierce rhetoric, which angers Democrats but plays well among his like-minded colleagues and at home.

Duncan was born in Greenville. His family moved frequently, mostly in the Carolinas, as they followed his father's job as a textile industry manager tasked with turning around underperforming plants. He got his bachelor's at Clemson University, where he was a wide receiver on the football team and majored in political science. After college, he worked as a community banker and then for a real estate auction company, which inspired him to start his own real-estate marketing firm that specialized in auctions. In the state House, he worked on updating the funding formula for education and on lowering taxes. In 2009, Duncan sponsored a bill creating an alternative state budget that did not use federal stimulus money, as a way of protesting President Barack Obama's $787 billion measure. Then-Gov. Mark Sanford recognized him as a "Taxpayer's Hero."

In the six-candidate GOP primary for the House seat, Duncan was endorsed by the anti-tax group Club for Growth, built a 2-to-1 fundraising advantage and prevailed in a runoff with 51 percent of the vote against businessman Richard Cash. In the general, he faced token Democratic opposition from Air Force veteran Jane Dyer, a FedEx pilot, who had little chance in the solidly Republican district. He won, 62%-36%, and has widened his victory margin in each of his three reelections.

Duncan believes in the "Jeffersonian principles of limited governments, free markets, and individual liberties" and thinks that the federal government has gone beyond its constitutional authority. He would shift some of its powers to the states. In 2011, he became the first member of Congress to receive a perfect score from the conservative activist group Heritage Action. A member of the Tea Party Caucus, Duncan has been part of the cadre of conservatives who have voted against GOP leadership priorities. In January 2015, he was the only South Carolina Republican who voted against giving John Boehner another term as Speaker. "I believe a new Speaker of the House would send the signal to the American people that we're hearing their concerns while also letting the president know that Congress is committed to upholding the rule of law," he said in a statement a few hours before the vote. Soon after that, he quit as a member of the Republican Whip team and was among the GOP rebels who helped to create the Freedom Caucus.

Duncan has been an active member of the Foreign Affairs Committee. In 2012, he enacted a bill that called for a strategy to address the Iranian threat in the Western Hemisphere. At a hearing in 2013 on the terrorist attack in Benghazi, Libya, he rebuked outgoing Secretary of State Hillary Clinton for "gross negligence" in allowing the consulate there to "become a death trap." As chairman of the Foreign Affairs Subcommittee on the Western Hemisphere, Duncan was outspoken in his opposition to President Barack Obama's opening of diplomacy to Cuba. He has demanded tighter enforcement of the border with Mexico. He has filed a bill calling for immediate and mandatory deportation of any non-citizen or permanent resident who has been entered into the terrorist screening database.

During the presidential campaign, Duncan criticized as "horrendous and indefensible" comments about women by Donald Trump. Then, he added, "I continue to be more concerned with Hillary Clinton's actions than I am with Donald Trump's words." Duncan had been interested in running for governor in 2018, when there was the prospect of an open seat. That option faded in January 2017 when Henry McMaster succeeded Nikki Haley, the new U.N. Ambassador.

Northwestern South Carolina: Anderson, Greenville Suburbs

Population		**Race and Ethnicity**		**Income**	
Total	668,814	White	74.4%	Median Income	$41,362 (381 out of 435)
Land area	5,268	Black	18.5%		
Pop/ sq mi	127.0	Latino	4.5%		
Born in state	67.0%	Asian	0.8%	Under $50,000	58.2%
		Two races	1.5%	$50,000-$99,999	28.4%
Age Groups		Other	0.3%	$100,000-$199,999	11.5%
Under 18	22.1%			$200,000 or more	1.9%
18-34	22.2%	**Education**		Poverty Rate	19.0%
35-64	39.2%	H.S grad or less	50.3%		
Over 64	16.6%	Some college	29.9%	**Health Insurance**	
		College Degree, 4 yr	12.7%	With health insurance coverage	85.7%
Work		Post grad	7.1%		
White Collar	30.0%				
Sales and Service	40.3%	**Military**		**Public Assistance**	
Blue Collar	29.6%	Veteran	9.4%	Cash public assistance income	1.5%
Government	14.7%	Active Duty	0.1%		
				Food stamp/SNAP benefits	15.5%

Voter Turnout			
2015 Total Citizens 18+	506,707	2016 House Turnout as % CVAP	53%
2016 House turnout	269,540	2014 House Turnout as % CVAP	32%

2012 Presidential Vote		
Mitt Romney	170,084	(65%)
Barack Obama	89,439	(34%)

2016 Presidential Vote		
Donald Trump	190,605	(67%)
Hillary Clinton	82,618	(29%)
Gary Johnson	5,616	(2%)

Cook Partisan Voting Index: R+19

The Upstate in South Carolina was many days' travel by wagon from the Lowcountry plantations along the coast. It was first settled by Scots-Irish farmers, including the family of future Vice President John C. Calhoun, around the time of the Revolutionary War. The pioneers wanted to make big plantations of these forests, but the land was too hilly for the labor-intensive rice crops grown in the Lowcountry and sometimes too cold for cotton. So relatively few slaves were brought here and the land became mostly small farms. Today, the racial and cultural tone of the Upstate shows traces of these roots. Clemson University was founded here by Calhoun's son-in-law and is one of the state's two land-grant institutions. (South Carolina State, a historically black university, is the other, located in Orangeburg.) This is a mostly white part of the South, with a hell-of-a-fella tone to daily life and a tradition-minded slice of Middle America.

Yet it is not untouched by change. The textile factories and mills have been shutting down, and a way of life in many of these rural areas has vanished with them. During the recession, Greenwood County (not to be confused with more prosperous Greenville County) suffered the largest increase in the poverty rate for any county in the nation. On the positive side, high-tech and automobile manufacturers have expanded, with growth throughout the Upstate. Interstate 85 - once the Main Street of America's textile belt - travels through a booming corridor that runs from Raleigh-Durham to Atlanta, including the northwest corner of South Carolina. In 2016, Clemson became part of a $300 million program, including support from the Defense Department, to expand textile manufacturing and technology. The football team's national championship victory in 2017 was a feel-good moment for the university and the state, with a boost in fundraising and applications for admission.

The 3rd Congressional District of South Carolina follows the Georgia border from Augusta through the tree-harvesting country around McCormick County to mountains along the North Carolina border. The 18 percent black population is the smallest of any district in the state. The southern part of the 3rd has a few heavily African-American areas, like Edgefield County, where the late Sen. Strom Thurmond first won public office in the 1930s. The former segregationist served until he was 100 years old, retiring in 2002 as the oldest member of Congress. Anderson is the largest county in the district, with nearly 30 percent of the voters.

This part of South Carolina, ancestrally Democratic, began trending Republican in the 1950s as cultural issues became more important in this fervently religious region; Thurmond switched to the GOP to support Barry Goldwater for president in 1964. Donald Trump won an impressive 67 percent of the vote here in 2016, his best showing in a South Carolina district.

FOURTH DISTRICT

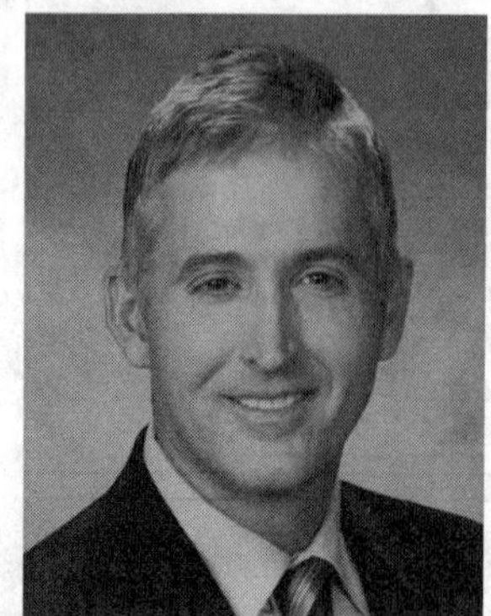

Trey Gowdy (R)

Elected 2010, 4th term; b. Aug 22, 1964, Greenville; Baylor University (TX), B.A.; University of South Carolina School of Law, J.D.; Baptist; Married (Terri Dillard Gowdy); 2 children.

Elected Office: Solicitor, SC 7th Circuit, 2001-2010.

Professional Career: Prosecutor, U.S. Attorney Office SC, 1994-2000.

DC Office: 2418 RHOB 20515, 202-225-6030, Fax: 202-226-1177, gowdy.house.gov.

State Offices: Greenville, 864-241-0175; Spartanburg, 864-583-3264.

Committees: *Ethics*. *Judiciary*: Constitution & Civil Justice, Crime, Terrorism, Homeland Security & Investigations (Chmn). *Oversight & Government Reform (Chmn)*: Government Operations, Health

Care, Benefits & Administrative Rules, Information Technology, Intergovernmental Affairs, Interior, Energy & Environment, National Security. *Permanent Select on Intelligence.*

Group Ratings

	ADA	ACLU	AFL-CIO	LCV	ITI	COC	HAFA	ACU	CFG	FRC
2016	-	5%	-	0%	100%	100%	82%	96%	85%	100%
2015	0%	C	0%	0%	C	63%	C	100%	94%	100%

Almanac Ratings 2015

	Economy	Social	Foreign	Composite
Liberal	1%	4%	11%	5%
Conservative	99%	96%	89%	95%

Key Votes of the 114th Congress

1. Keystone Pipeline	Y	5. Puerto Rico Debt	N	9. Offenses by Aliens	Y
2. Trade Deals	Y	6. Medical Marijuana	N	10. Troops in Iraq	N
3. Export-Import Bank	N	7. Sanctuary Cities	Y	11. Homeland Security $$	N
4. Debt Ceiling Increase	N	8. Armor-piercing Bullets	Y	12. Trade Adjustment aid	N

Election Results

Election	Name (Party)	Vote (%)	Cand. Spent	Ind. Exp. Support	Ind. Exp. Oppose
2016 General	Trey Gowdy (R)	198,648 (67%)	$1,183,682	$22,146	
	Chris Fedalei (D)	91,676 (31%)	$86,168		
2016 Primary	Trey Gowdy (R)	(100%)			

Prior winning percentages: 2014 (85%), 2012 (65%), 2010 (65%)

Republican Trey Gowdy, elected in 2010, likes to call himself "a prosecutor, not a politician." He doggedly pressed investigations of the Obama administration, but he has a politician's gregarious personality. He received widespread attention, receiving both praise and criticism, as head of a select committee investigating the Obama administration's handling of the 2012 terrorist attacks in Benghazi, Libya. He has been on the front-lines of the GOP's handling of immigration issues. He has frequently voiced interest in becoming a federal judge, though he remains well-regarded among House Republicans. In June 2017, he gained additional stature when he was named chairman of the House's chief investigative panel.

Gowdy grew up in Spartanburg. His father grew up poor but put himself through medical school and became a pediatrician. As a teenager, he was inspired by Ronald Reagan's 1980 campaign for president and by a stint as a Senate page, sponsored by home-state Sen. Strom Thurmond. Gowdy graduated from Baylor and earned a law degree from the University of South Carolina.

In 1994, Gowdy became a prosecutor for the U.S. attorney's office in Greenville, where he worked on cases ranging from drug trafficking to murder. In 2000, he was elected as county solicitor and was reelected twice. In that role, he sought the death penalty in seven cases and won them all. Much of the job was managerial, but Gowdy says he tried about half of the cases that came through his office himself, with a focus on violence against women and drunken driving. Gowdy, who named his dogs Judge, Jury and Bailiff, says that being a prosecutor was "the best job I will ever have in my life."

He challenged six-term GOP Rep. Bob Inglis in the 2010 Republican primary after the incumbent had tacked to the left on several issues. Gowdy portrayed his opponent as a Washington insider whose positions were out of step with the district's conservative voters. He criticized Inglis for earmarking funds in appropriations bills, for his opposition to President George W. Bush's 2007 troop surge in Iraq, and for his stand against oil exploration in Alaska's Arctic National Wildlife Refuge. Gowdy declared that he was running against the "sins of Congress," rather than an individual. Gowdy led the initial five-candidate balloting, and soundly defeated Inglis in a runoff, 71%-29%. In November, Gowdy breezed past Democrat Paul Corden, a retired businessman and Vietnam veteran, 63%-29%. He has been reelected with comparable margins.

In the House, Gowdy has been a committed conservative. He has a firm belief in "a limited government that inspires trust and demands accountability." He usually is willing to offer opinions to reporters and to lavishly compliment his colleagues, and he despairs of the lack of civility in Congress. "We, Republicans and Democrats, are as kind and polite to each other as you could possibly be," he told a local audience in 2012. "That changes the moment the cameras come on."

At the same time, Gowdy was as ferocious as any of his Class of 2010 colleagues in taking on the Obama administration. He called for Attorney General Eric Holder to resign or be impeached for his failure to rein in the "Operation Fast and Furious" gun-tracking program. He dismissed as "mind-numbingly stupid" the assertion by Minority Leader Nancy Pelosi that the House panel's investigation of the program was linked to voter suppression. At a 2011 hearing on Nuclear Regulatory Commission Chairman Gregory Jaczko's alleged mistreatment of colleagues, he upbraided Jaczko: "When you have four eyewitnesses that testify to someone under oath, you know what they call a defendant after that? An inmate."

In 2013, Gowdy won a plum assignment as chairman of the Judiciary Subcommittee on Immigration and Border Control. He told *GreenvilleOnline.com* that he wanted to develop an immigration reform bill that reflects "the humanity that I think defines us as a people and the respect for the rule of law that defines us as a republic." But even though the Senate passed a bipartisan bill in 2013, House Republicans could not agree among themselves about what should be included in the measure, and the effort eventually fell apart. As subcommittee chairman, Gowdy has handled scant legislation.

Gowdy has not confined his attacks to his committee work. He has been one of the most outspoken critics of the 2010 health care overhaul, blasting the president for falsely claiming that people would be able to keep their doctors under the law. He sponsored a bill that would authorize Congress to sue the president for failing to "faithfully execute" federal laws, including those with which the chief executive disagrees. It passed the House on a largely party-line vote in 2014 but died in the Democratic-controlled Senate. "To me, it's not a political issue," Gowdy said. "Do you think the chief executive should have to actually enforce the law? I would think every member of the House and Senate would support that."

The Benghazi investigation thrust Gowdy into the spotlight. After the Oversight and Government Reform Committee spent months pursuing allegations that the administration bungled the response to the attack and lied to Congress about it, House GOP leaders created a select committee headed by Gowdy. After House Democrats initially denounced the select committee as a partisan stunt, they agreed to participate. The panel became riven by partisan strife. Ranking Democrat Elijah Cummings of Maryland accused Gowdy of holding secret meetings with witnesses and then withholding or downplaying information from those interviews that undermined the GOP's investigation. Cummings and other Democrats objected to Gowdy's plan to subpoena 22 witnesses without a debate or vote. Gowdy responded that he had tried to work out a deal with Democrats over subpoenas, only to be rebuffed.

As the months passed, the investigation focused increasingly on Democratic presidential candidate Hillary Clinton, the former Secretary of State. In what Democrats alleged was an attempt to influence the 2016 campaign, Gowdy and his GOP colleagues relentlessly pursued Clinton's involvement with Benghazi wherever it led, including the emails that she had sent while in office via a private server, her decision to wipe her computer clean of those files, the emails that were retained by confidants, and the broader circumstances that left Ambassador to Libya Christopher Stevens and three other officials dead. Cummings accused Gowdy of using the investigation as a "fundraising tool." Gowdy denied that the probe had anything to do with presidential politics. "It's my job to report facts," he said. He blamed the length of the investigation on the Obama administration's failure to cooperate.

Gowdy was approached about potentially challenging South Carolina Republican Sen. Lindsey Graham in a 2014 primary, but demurred. Graham returned the favor in February 2015 by saying that if he were president, he would nominate Gowdy to serve on the Supreme Court. Following the 2016 election, Gowdy and Republican Sen. Tim Scott speculated that they might run as a ticket for the expected open seat for governor in 2018. That prospect became less likely when Henry McMaster became governor after Nikki Haley resigned to serve as U.N. Ambassador.

In the 2016 presidential campaign, Gowdy described as “indefensible” Donald Trump’s lewd video comments about women. Still, he reportedly was considered for attorney general in the new administration, though the job went to Sen. Jeff Sessions of Alabama. Gowdy won a new opportunity when House Republicans in June 2017 selected him as the successor to Oversight Committee chairman Jason Chaffetz, who resigned from the House.

Greenville/Spartanburg Area

Population		Race and Ethnicity		Income	
Total	689,104	White	69.1%	Median Income	$47,843 (287 out of 435)
Land area	1,299	Black	18.9%		
Pop/ sq mi	530.4	Latino	7.9%		
Born in state	56.6%	Asian	2.3%	Under $50,000	51.7%
		Two races	1.5%	$50,000-$99,999	29.6%
Age Groups		Other	0.3%	$100,000-$199,999	15.3%
Under 18	23.7%			$200,000 or more	3.4%
18-34	22.8%	**Education**		Poverty Rate	16.3%
35-64	39.3%	H.S grad or less	41.5%		
Over 64	14.2%	Some college	28.9%	**Health Insurance**	
		College Degree, 4 yr	18.9%	With health insurance coverage	85.4%
Work		Post grad	10.7%		
White Collar	35.3%				
Sales and Service	40.9%	**Military**		**Public Assistance**	
Blue Collar	23.8%	Veteran	8.6%	Cash public assistance income	1.5%
Government	10.6%	Active Duty	0.1%		
				Food stamp/SNAP benefits	12.3%

Voter Turnout			
2015 Total Citizens 18+	496,546	2016 House Turnout as % CVAP	60%
2016 House turnout	295,670	2014 House Turnout as % CVAP	30%

2012 Presidential Vote		
Mitt Romney	170,623	(62%)
Barack Obama	99,359	(36%)

2016 Presidential Vote		
Donald Trump	181,637	(60%)
Hillary Clinton	103,848	(34%)
Gary Johnson	8,171	(3%)

Cook Partisan Voting Index: R+15

A century ago, Northern investors seeking sites for textile mills looked at the Upstate of South Carolina and found what was described then as "mild climate, abundant water power, proximity to the cotton fields, and plenty of native labor already accustomed to a low standard of living." As mills fled New England, textile factories settled along the Southern Railway and Seaboard Coast Line tracks between Charlotte and Atlanta, especially in the Piedmont of South Carolina. The textile country might look bucolic, but Greenville, Spartanburg and the dozens of mill towns thick in the surrounding countryside became as industrial as Lancashire or the Ruhr. In the days before child labor laws, factory work sometimes began at age 6, condemning workers to a life of illiteracy. Escapes to a brighter future, such as the brilliant but brief baseball career of West Greenville's "Shoeless" Joe Jackson, were rare.

Today, along Interstate 85, which parallels the Southern Railway, little remains of what was once the largest textile-producing area in the United States. In the four decades after 1973, increasing imports and the productivity gains from technological changes reduced the state's textile and apparel jobs by about 90 percent. Many of those textile jobs went to China, and more recently to Vietnam. In April 2016, *Greenville Online* reported that the 18 textile mills that were operating a century earlier within three miles of downtown had been reduced to three. Some had been converted to condominiums or office buildings. Others had been torn down.

Many former textile workers have taken jobs with the new companies discovering the region's virtues. Michelin has been the largest industrial employer in the Greenville area, with more than 4,000 workers at several plants. In April 2016, GE Power opened in Greenville its first advanced manufacturing center, which employed 3,200. Greenville's revitalized downtown boasts fancy hotels and restaurants, which cater to the new corporate manager class. Financial sweeteners, tax incentives, the absence of unions and solid infrastructure - airports, highways, and the busy Port of Charleston - attracted an enormous BMW plant in Spartanburg. In 2016, the company produced 411,000 vehicles, its biggest plant worldwide, with a payroll of 8,800 people. Most of those cars were sold domestically. A few days before his inauguration, Donald Trump complained about BMW's plans to build a new factory in Mexico that would produce 150,000 sedans annually by 2019, and warned that those imports would be subject to a 35 percent tax. The company defended its commitment to the U.S. market.

The 4th Congressional District of South Carolina includes about 90 percent of Greenville and Spartanburg counties, with nearly two-thirds living in Greenville. Along with Anderson (in the 3rd district), Greenville and Spartanburg comprise the largest population area in South Carolina, with more than 1 million residents. Culturally, the 4th ranges from conservative to very conservative, with strong influence from Greenville's many evangelical and fundamentalist churches. Bob Jones University is here as well; it dropped its ban on interracial dating in 2000, but students are still prohibited from smoking, drinking, dancing and wearing jeans or shorts to class. Here, the real political divide is between religious and economic conservatives. Large new subdivisions have sprouted between Greenville and Spartanburg, and newcomers have brought religious diversity. Greenville has growing numbers not only of Catholics and Jews, but also of Muslims, Buddhists, Hindus, Baha'is and even has a gay-oriented church. Hispanics grew from 4 percent of Greenville County's population in 2000 to 9 percent in 2015, one of the largest countywide totals in the state. Still, the 4th is comfortably Republican. Donald Trump got 60 percent of the vote in 2016, compared with 62 percent for Mitt Romney in 2012.

FIFTH DISTRICT

Ralph Norman (R)

Elected 2017, 1st term; b. Jun 20 1953, York County; Presbyterian College, B.S; married (Elaine Norman); 4 children, 15 grandchildren.

Elected Office: SC House 2009-2017

Professional Career: Real estate developer, Warren Norman Company

State Offices: Gaffney, 864-206-6004; Rock Hill, 803-327-1114; Sumter, 803-774-0186.

Committees: *Science, Space & Technology; Small Business.*

Election Results

Election	Name (Party)	Vote (%)	Cand. Spent	Ind. Exp. Support	Ind. Exp. Oppose
2017 Special	Ralph Norman (R)	44,889 (51%)	$1,155,362	$3,933	
	Archie Parnell (D)	42,053 (48%)	$509,700		
2017 Primary Runoff	Ralph Norman (R)	17,755 (50%)			
	Tommy Pope (R)	17,552 (50%)			
2017 Primary	Tommy Pope (R)	11,943 (30%)			
	Ralph Norman (R)	11,808 (30%)			
	Tom Milikin (R)	7,759 (20%)			
	Chad Connelly (R)	5,546 (14%)			

Republican Ralph Norman won the June 2017 special election to fill the seat of GOP Rep. Mick Mulvaney, who resigned to join the Trump administration as director of the Office of Management and Budget. Although the contest was over-shadowed by another special election the same day about 200 miles west in a suburban Atlanta district, the lower-profile and less expensive South Carolina contest turned out to be closer. Norman defeated Democrat Archie Parnell, 51%-48%, in a district that had Democratic roots.

The Republican primary was a hard-fought contest that featured two experienced state representatives, with neighboring districts in York County. Norman received more than $700,000 of support during the primary from the Club for Growth. Tommy Pope, who had been planning to run for governor in 2018, was backed by the Chamber of Commerce.

In the first round of voting, each got 30 percent of the vote in the seven-candidate primary; Pope led by 135 votes. The run-off was just as close. Norman prevailed by 203 votes of the more than 35,000 that were cast. Pope took 54 percent of the vote in York County, which cast slightly more than half of the vote; Norman won nine of the other 10 counties. A real estate developer, Norman in 2006 had run against the district's long-time Democratic Rep. John Spratt and was defeated, 57%-43%.

Parnell, the Democratic nominee, was new to local politics. But he had extensive experience in Washington and with Congress, as a tax attorney at the Justice Department and with the House Ways and Means Committee. He was an international tax and trade adviser to large companies. Parnell won the three-way primary with 71 percent of the vote.

Mulvaney was elected to the House in 2010 and was a leader of conservative factions. He initially won his seat by defeating Spratt, who was chairman of the House Armed Services Committee. Following the 2014 election, he was defeated in a bid to chair the Republican Study Committee. With other conservatives, he then organized the more renegade Freedom Caucus. Mulvaney's tight-fisted spending views while he was in Congress led Senate Armed Services Committee chairman John McCain of Arizona to oppose his nomination because, he said, "It would be irresponsible to place the future of the defense budget in the hands of a person with such a record and judgment on national security." Mulvaney was confirmed by the Senate, 51-49, with all Democrats, in addition to McCain, voting against him. He quickly became a key domestic-policy adviser to Trump.

North-Central South Carolina: Charlotte Suburbs, Sumter County

Population		**Race and Ethnicity**		**Income**	
Total	678,910	White	65.5%	Median Income	$44,685 (345 out of 435)
Land area	5,506	Black	27.1%	Under $50,000	54.9%
Pop/ sq mi	123.3	Latino	4.2%	$50,000-$99,999	29.1%
Born in state	58.7%	Asian	1.1%	$100,000-$199,999	13.6%
		Two races	1.8%	$200,000 or more	2.4%
		Other	0.5%	Poverty Rate	17.5%
Age Groups		**Education**		**Health Insurance**	
Under 18	23.8%	H.S grad or less	48.3%	With health insurance coverage	86.6%
18-34	21.0%	Some college	29.9%		
35-64	40.4%	College Degree, 4 yr	14.5%		
Over 64	14.8%	Post grad	7.4%		
Work		**Military**		**Public Assistance**	
White Collar	31.1%	Veteran	10.4%	Cash public assistance income	1.6%
Sales and Service	41.7%	Active Duty	0.5%	Food stamp/SNAP benefits	15.9%
Blue Collar	27.2%				
Government	14.8%				

Voter Turnout			
2015 Total Citizens 18+	505,233	2016 House Turnout as % CVAP	54%
2016 House turnout	273,006	2014 House Turnout as % CVAP	35%

2012 Presidential Vote		
Mitt Romney	158,537	(55%)
Barack Obama	124,561	(43%)

2016 Presidential Vote		
Donald Trump	175,488	(57%)
Hillary Clinton	118,656	(39%)
Gary Johnson	6,525	(2%)

Cook Partisan Voting Index: R+9

Some of the fiercest battles of the Revolutionary War were fought in South Carolina's Upstate, on hilly lands just being settled by Scots-Irish farmers moving up from the Lowcountry or down the Virginia Piedmont valley. This was a country of violent passions and unclear lines. Carolinians argued for years over which side of the North and South Carolina boundary Andrew Jackson was born on in 1767. Ever since, the fighting spirit and Calvinist faith of Upstate Carolinians have not wavered. This "Olde English District" remains intensely religious and pro-military, but it is no longer impoverished. The area has been moving on from the Civil War in other ways. In January 2017, the Confederate flag and photos of local war generals were removed from a room in the court house in York. The clerk of courts for the county discovered a long-ago law that required the protection of Civil War relics.

For many years, the dominant industry here was textiles, traditionally the first factory enterprise of industrializing countries, with low pay and poor working conditions. With unemployment exceeding 20 percent in some small counties during the 2007-09 recession, the number of textile jobs has declined markedly, though more sophisticated manufacturing has boomed. The growth of suburbia south of Charlotte in York and Lancaster counties has been rapid: a 57 percent increase in population in the larger York from 2000 to 2016.

Located 30 miles from downtown Charlotte and with an average home price of about $139,000 in 2015, Rock Hill has become an attractive destination for city workers looking for affordable housing. Just to the west in Cherokee County, Gaffney is the heart of South Carolina peach country. It is home to the famed Peachoid, a four-story water tower tank off Interstate 85 that is shaped like a peach. In 2015, when the tower was refurbished and painted, some tourists were alarmed that it was being dismantled. South Carolina has shipped more peaches than neighboring Georgia since the 1950s, despite the latter's Peach State nickname.

The 5th Congressional District consists of all or part of 11 counties, mostly in the Upstate and some in the Midlands. Over half the population is in Lancaster and York counties and in Cherokee County, along I-85 and in the Charlotte exurbs. Politically, this homeland of Andrew Jackson is ancestrally Democratic but has become increasingly Republican. Much of the population growth in York and Lancaster comes from Charlotte suburban commuters with no ancestral ties here but with strong conservative views. In the outskirts of Columbia, the rural counties of Fairfield and Lee are majority-black. Sumter, which is 47% black, has grown only three percent since 2000. The district is 28% black. Overall, this has been a Republican district in presidential elections, although the demographics have placed a lid on the partisan balance. Donald Trump got 57 percent of the vote in 2016.

SIXTH DISTRICT

James Clyburn (D)

Elected 1992, 13th term; b. Jul 21, 1940, Sumter; South Carolina Executive Institute; South Carolina State University, B.S.; University of South Carolina School of Law; Mather Academy, Camden (SC); African Methodist Episcopal; Married (Emily England Clyburn); 3 children.

Professional Career: Teacher, 1962-1966; Director, Charleston Neighborhood Youth Corps, 1966-1968; Executive Director, SC Comm. for Farm Workers, 1968-1971; Assistant, Gov. West, 1971-1974; SC Human Affairs Comm., 1974-1992.

DC Office: 242 CHOB 20515, 202-225-3315, Fax: 202-225-2313, clyburn.house.gov.

State Offices: Columbia, 803-799-1100; Kingstree, 843-355-1211; Santee, 803-854-4700.

Group Ratings

	ADA	ACLU	AFL-CIO	LCV	ITI	COC	HAFA	ACU	CFG	FRC
2016	-	94%	-	92%	80%	62%	12%	0%	0%	0%
2015	80%	C	95%	83%	C	63%	C	0%	0%	0%

Almanac Ratings 2015

	Economy	Social	Foreign	Composite
Liberal	88%	100%	91%	93%
Conservative	13%	0%	9%	7%

Key Votes of the 114th Congress

1. Keystone Pipeline	Y	5. Puerto Rico Debt	Y	9. Offenses by Aliens	N
2. Trade Deals	N	6. Medical Marijuana	Y	10. Troops in Iraq	Y
3. Export-Import Bank	Y	7. Sanctuary Cities	N	11. Homeland Security $$	Y
4. Debt Ceiling Increase	Y	8. Armor-piercing Bullets	N	12. Trade Adjustment aid	NV

Election Results

Election	Name (Party)	Vote (%)		Cand. Spent	Ind. Exp. Support	Ind. Exp. Oppose
2016 General	James Clyburn (D)	177,947	(70%)	$946,558		
	Laura Sterling (R)	70,099	(28%)			
2016 Primary	James Clyburn (D)		(100%)			

Prior winning percentages: 2014 (73%), 2012 (94%), 2010 (63%), 2008 (68%), 2006 (64%), 2004 (68%), 2002 (67%), 2000 (72%), 1998 (73%), 1996 (69%), 1994 (64%), 1992 (65%)

James Clyburn, a Democrat elected in 1992, is the highest ranking African American in Congress and the dean of his state's otherwise all-Republican delegation. He is the assistant minority leader, the third-ranking position in the House Democratic leadership - a job created for him after his party lost its House majority in 2011. Like other House Democratic leaders, he has chafed in the minority and has voiced frustration that national Democrats have not placed a higher priority on regaining the House majority.

Clyburn grew up in Sumter, the son of a minister, and was educated at a private, all-black boarding school. As a young man, he joined the Student Nonviolent Coordinating Committee, which took its cues from the Rev. Martin Luther King Jr.'s Southern Christian Leadership Conference. In 1960, he was one of seven people who organized the state's first sit-ins, at a five-and-dime store in the Orangeburg town square. He met his wife while in jail for three days. Clyburn worked as a teacher, as an employment counselor, and in government antipoverty programs. In 1970, he ran for the South Carolina House and lost narrowly. Democratic Gov. John West appointed Clyburn as state Human Affairs commissioner, and he served 18 years, under two Democratic and two Republican governors. He ran twice for secretary of state, in 1978 and 1986, losing narrowly.

Then, the new black-majority 6th District was created. Clyburn ran for the seat and in the Democratic primary won 56 percent of the vote against four African-American opponents, all with serious claims to the nomination. Clyburn was better known, ran first or second in every part of the district, and piled up 88 percent of the vote in his home county of Sumter. Clyburn became the first African American to represent South Carolina in Congress since George Washington Murray (a distant relative of his) left in 1897. He has not faced serious opposition for reelection.

In the House, Clyburn established a moderate-to-liberal voting record. He joined the moderate New Democrat Coalition at its inception in 1997, the only African-American House member to do so. Like other South Carolina lawmakers, he is a proponent of expanding the use of nuclear power, which provides more than half of the state's electricity. On the Appropriations Committee from 1998 to 2006, Clyburn focused on securing federal funds to develop the Interstate 95 corridor, which passes through rural counties in the district that historically were dependent on tobacco and cotton. The House enacted in 2006 his bill to create a Gullah/Geechee Cultural Heritage Corridor from south of Jacksonville, Florida, to north of Wilmington, North Carolina.

As chairman of the Congressional Black Caucus in 1999, he urged the Democratic National Committee to become more responsive to African Americans. After the 2002 election, he ran for vice chairman of the Democratic Caucus, arguing that the leadership needed to better reflect the party's diversity. He prevailed with 95 votes to 56 for New York Rep. Gregory Meeks and 53 for California Rep. Zoe Lofgren. In 2006, he was elected Democratic Caucus chairman, and later that year, after Democrats won control of the House, he was chosen majority whip, the No. 3 post. Then-Rep. Rahm Emanuel of Illinois also wanted to be whip but had less seniority than Clyburn, and he backed down at the urging of House Speaker Nancy Pelosi, who favored Clyburn. Emanuel took Clyburn's spot as Democratic Caucus chairman in recognition of his success in the 2006 election, when he chaired the Democratic Congressional Campaign Committee.

Clyburn sought enhanced influence for his whip organization in crafting policy, a way of getting more points of view into the drafting of major legislation. In 2007, he held a series of "listening sessions" with Democrats to explore options for an immigration bill. He led the Hurricane Katrina Task Force, which met regularly with local officials to coordinate the House's response to the devastation caused by Hurricane Katrina in 2005. "I truly believe that if the demographics of the affected areas had been different, the response of the federal government would have been different," he said in a 2007 speech in Baton Rouge. Clyburn also finessed a solution to a longstanding complaint by the CBC that they were prevented from advancing in the Democratic caucus because they couldn't pay their "dues" by raising large amounts of political donations in their disproportionately low-income districts. Clyburn persuaded Pelosi to adopt a modified system that rewarded Democrats for non-financial contributions, such as making appearances for candidates and doing press interviews.

As the most prominent black politician in the state, Clyburn has been a player in South Carolina's often pivotal Democratic presidential primary. In 2004, after his initial candidate, Rep. Dick Gephardt of Missouri, withdrew following the Iowa caucuses, Clyburn endorsed front-runner John Kerry rather than South Carolina native John Edwards. Although he did not take sides in the 2008 primary, he clashed with Hillary Clinton when she seemed to suggest that President Lyndon Johnson, in signing the Civil Rights Act of 1964, had a more important role than King and other key civil rights figures at the time. He later wrote in his 2014 memoir *Blessed Experiences: Genuinely Southern, Proudly Black* that an angry Bill Clinton called to blame him for his wife's defeat in the primary.

After the 2008 election, Clyburn got into a conflict with Republican Gov. Mark Sanford, who said that he would not use all of the money available to South Carolina from the economic stimulus bill enacted in 2009. Clyburn called the action a "slap in the face" to the predominately black constituents who would benefit. He wrote a clause into the $787 billion stimulus bill that enabled state legislatures to bypass governors who rejected the money. Clyburn took on another South Carolina conservative, House colleague Joe Wilson, after Wilson infamously called out "You lie!" during Obama's health care address to Congress in 2009. Clyburn pressed a resolution formally reproaching Wilson for a breach of House rules, which passed on a largely party-line vote.

When Democrats lost the House majority in 2010, they no longer controlled the speakership and so lost one spot in their leadership lineup. A battle shaped up for the No. 2 position of minority whip between Clyburn and former Majority Leader Steny Hoyer of Maryland. An intense, behind-the-scenes rivalry unfolded, with each camp touting its greater level of support in the caucus. To avoid a divisive outcome, Pelosi created the new job of assistant leader and made it the No. 3 post in the minority hierarchy. Clyburn was named assistant leader, and Hoyer became minority whip.

Clyburn's new job wasn't well-defined, but he used it to become one of his party's main messengers. After the Newtown, Connecticut, elementary school massacre, he compared the push for gun control to the civil rights movement. When Obama's health care law was a hot topic on the 2012 campaign trail, he told a gathering of South Carolina Democrats, "Do not be afraid to use the term 'Obamacare.' You should be proud of Obamacare." He spoke out forcefully against state voter-identification laws that he and other critics said disenfranchised minority voters.

Black Caucus members in 2013 suggested that Clyburn replace Ray LaHood as Secretary of Transportation, but his spokesman shot down the idea. Several months later, he joined other Black Caucus members in blasting a Supreme Court decision that struck down a key portion of the 1965 Voting Rights Act. "Even before I came to Congress, there has been a drift away from the Voting Rights Act," he said. "And I think it is just the Supreme Court using an excuse to do what they didn't have good excuse to do before."

In February 2016, Clyburn enthusiastically endorsed Hillary Clinton a week before the South Carolina primary. In August, *Politico* reported on Clyburn's efforts to find common ground with Clinton and House Speaker Paul Ryan on a bipartisan proposal for additional federal aid to low-income areas, for both blacks and whites. During the closing weeks of the general election, Clyburn publicly urged the Clinton campaign to step up its activity in minority neighborhoods to assist in down-ballot contests. He turned out to be correct about the lack of grass-roots enthusiasm, but he - like many other Democrats - over-estimated the nominee's strength. In January 2017, after President Donald Trump voiced repeated accusations of voter fraud in 2016, Clyburn joined Democratic Rep. Elijah Cummings of Maryland in requesting details from state election officials and attorneys general.

In 2014, he gained attention from publishing *Blessed Experiences.* He told *The Post & Courier* of Charleston that writing the book made him realize he was "much more faith-based than I thought I was. ... I just found out those teachings in that parsonage [during childhood] shaped me more than I ever thought, and I don't know if I would have come to grips with that if I had not written this book."

Central South Carolina: Parts of Charleston and Columbia

Population		**Race and Ethnicity**		**Income**	
Total	667,105	White	36.0%	Median Income	$34,143 (427 out of 435)
Land area	8,063	Black	56.4%		
Pop/ sq mi	82.7	Latino	4.8%		
Born in state	70.0%	Asian	1.0%	Under $50,000	66.2%
Age Groups		Two races	1.5%	$50,000-$99,999	24.3%
Under 18	21.7%	Other	0.5%	$100,000-$199,999	8.2%
18-34	28.2%	**Education**		$200,000 or more	1.3%
35-64	36.4%	H.S grad or less	52.3%	Poverty Rate	25.8%
Over 64	13.8%	Some college	29.1%	**Health Insurance**	
Work		College Degree, 4 yr	11.8%	With health insurance coverage	82.5%
White Collar	27.1%	Post grad	6.9%		
Sales and Service	46.9%	**Military**		**Public Assistance**	
Blue Collar	26.0%	Veteran	9.5%	Cash public assistance income	2.1%
Government	19.6%	Active Duty	1.1%		
				Food stamp/SNAP benefits	23.1%

Voter Turnout			
2015 Total Citizens 18+	506,394	2016 House Turnout as % CVAP	50%
2016 House turnout	253,901	2014 House Turnout as % CVAP	34%

2012 Presidential Vote		
Barack Obama	206,857	(73%)
Mitt Romney	73,588	(26%)

2016 Presidential Vote		
Hillary Clinton	179,272	(67%)
Donald Trump	79,798	(30%)

Cook Partisan Voting Index: D+19

South Carolina's coastal lowlands and islands are laced with sluggish rivers and swamps. Its early settlers, planters from Barbados, brought thousands of slaves from Africa, and colonial South Carolina quickly became one of the richest parts of North America, with dazzling Georgian architecture in Charleston and classic plantation gardens. The planters built great irrigation systems and grew rice, cotton and the dye-plant indigo, all heavily in demand in Britain and elsewhere. All this wealth, of course, was built on the slave labor of countless African Americans. In colonial times, a majority of South Carolinians were slaves, as were a majority of lowland residents. South Carolina's black heritage has left a lasting imprint on American culture. Gullah, a mixture of English, French and African dialects, is still spoken on the Sea Islands, and Gullah customs survive - oyster roasts and sweet potato feasts at Christmas, handmade dolls and sweetgrass baskets. The poverty that was the almost universal lot of lowland blacks after the Civil War has eased only in the last generation, as development came to the coast and cultural isolation dissipated. But many African Americans decided not to wait for progress. They long ago abandoned South Carolina for opportunities in the North.

At the Emanuel African Methodist Episcopal Church in downtown Charleston in June 2015, a 21-year-old white gunman opened fire on a Bible study group and killed nine people before he escaped and was captured a few hours later driving in North Carolina. The victims included the church pastor, Clementa Pinckney, who also was a state senator. The church was one of the oldest and most respected black churches in the South. "Emanuel A.M.E. Church is the rock upon which the A.M.E. Church throughout the South is built," local Rep. James Clyburn said at a prayer vigil the next day. Dylann Roof, who had earlier produced amateur videos that featured white-supremacist objects and themes, was convicted in December 2016 of the nine murders; a month later, he became the first federal hate-crime defendant to be sentenced to death.

The 6th Congressional District of South Carolina, created in 1992 as a black-majority district, takes in the black central city neighborhoods of Charleston, North Charleston and Columbia, but leaves out their affluent white areas, both urban and suburban, which are in the adjacent 1st and 2nd Districts. Columbia-based Richland has about 30 percent of the population; Charleston and Orangeburg are close to 15 percent each. The remainder of the district is mostly rural. The 6th includes most of Orangeburg County, home of the historically black South Carolina State University. Orangeburg was the scene of a massacre in February 1968, when three black students were killed and 27 were wounded by police while protesting a segregated bowling alley. In its North Charleston assembly plant, adjacent to the airport, Boeing in December 2016 delivered its 500th Dreamliner, its 787 long-distance aircraft.

Republicans packed the 6th District with African-American Democrats, ensuring that the remaining six of the state's seven congressional seats would solidly favor Republicans. Hillary Clinton in 2016 won the district, 67%-30%, compared with President Barack Obama's 73%-26% reelection in 2012.

SEVENTH DISTRICT

Tom Rice (R)

Elected 2012, 3rd term; b. Aug 04, 1957, Charleston; University of South Carolina, Mast. Deg.; University of South Carolina School of Law, J.D.; University of South Carolina, B.S.; Episcopalian; Married (Wrenzie Rice); 3 children.

Elected Office: Horry County Council, 2010-2012.

Professional Career: Staff accountant, Deloitte Haskins & Sells, 1982-1984; Practicing lawyer, 1984-present.

DC Office: 223 CHOB 20515, 202-225-9895, Fax: 202-225-9690, rice.house.gov.

State Offices: Florence, 843-679-9781; Myrtle Beach, 843-445-6459.

Committees: *Ways & Means*: Social Security, Trade.

Group Ratings

	ADA	ACLU	AFL-CIO	LCV	ITI	COC	HAFA	ACU	CFG	FRC
2016	-	17%	-	0%	100%	100%	76%	92%	96%	92%
2015	0%	C	13%	3%	C	80%	C	83%	77%	83%

Almanac Ratings 2015

	Economy	Social	Foreign	Composite
Liberal	6%	15%	14%	12%
Conservative	94%	85%	86%	88%

Key Votes of the 114th Congress

1. Keystone Pipeline	Y	5. Puerto Rico Debt	Y	9. Offenses by Aliens	Y
2. Trade Deals	Y	6. Medical Marijuana	Y	10. Troops in Iraq	Y
3. Export-Import Bank	N	7. Sanctuary Cities	Y	11. Homeland Security $$	N
4. Debt Ceiling Increase	N	8. Armor-piercing Bullets	Y	12. Trade Adjustment aid	N

Election Results

Election	Name (Party)	Vote (%)	Cand. Spent	Ind. Exp. Support	Ind. Exp. Oppose
2016 General	Tom Rice (R)	176,468 (61%)	$621,240		
	Mal Hyman (D)	112,744 (39%)	$87,972		
2016 Primary	Tom Rice (R)	(100%)			

Prior winning percentages: 2014 (60%), 2012 (56%)

Republican Tom Rice was elected in 2012 with a focus on his business background and conservative politics in the growing region. Compared to the often raucous members of the state's congressional delegation, Rice has been more low-profile and focused on his legislative work. That background proved useful when he got a seat on the Ways and Means Committee.

Growing up amid the sand dunes of Myrtle Beach, Rice spent every day playing on the beach. His mother was a schoolteacher; his father, a repairman, died when he was young. Rice worked every summer after he turned 12, busing tables at the local tourist restaurants. At the University of South

Carolina, he volunteered with Big Brothers Big Sisters. He stayed at the university to earn his master's in accounting and a law degree.

Rice moved to Charlotte, North Carolina, to work for the accounting giant Deloitte. After gaining experience on larger cases, he returned home to practice tax law and eventually open his own practice. Rice served on the board of the Myrtle Beach Haven homeless shelter and, during his 10-year term as president, helped it build an expanded facility. He ran successfully for Horry County Council chairman in 2010. In that role, he focused on rebuilding the Myrtle Beach Regional Economic Development Corporation and bringing jobs to the county.

In 2012, Rice came in second in the crowded GOP primary field to former Lt. Gov. André Bauer. His opponent, the conservative favorite, came under attack for comparing public school children who receive free lunches to stray animals who should not be fed. Bauer raised almost double the amount of campaign cash as Rice and labeled him a "moderate" in a wave of attack ads. In the runoff, Rice crushed Bauer, 56%-44%, thanks in part to a powerful endorsement from popular GOP Gov. Nikki Haley. In the general, Rice faced Gloria Bromell Tinubu, who had been the underdog in the Democratic primary running on a platform of union advocacy. A South Carolina native and former economics professor at the mostly African-American Spelman College in Atlanta, she had served in the Georgia state House. Rice got support from the state tea party and National Right to Life Committee. He outspent Bromell Tinubu a bit more than 2-to-1 and won 56%-44%. His entire margin of victory came from his base in Horry County, where he led 65%-35%.

When Rice served on the Transportation and Infrastructure Committee, he was outspoken in his call to raise the gasoline tax by as much as 13 cents per gallon to pay for improvements to highways and bridges. "Infrastructure is the foundation of which competitiveness is based," he said. In a vital caveat, he said that the increase should be offset by cuts in income taxes. He disagreed with GOP conservatives who sought to shut down the Export-Import Bank. "In a perfect world, I wish it wasn't there. And I wish that banks would step up to fill the void. But the problem is it's not a perfect world," Rice said. In October 2015, when he voted to extend the bank, he said that during the previous five years it "has facilitated $4 billion in exports from South Carolina, and has helped over 60 companies in the state."

In November 2015, he was named to fill the vacancy on Ways and Means created when Rep. Paul Ryan of Wisconsin departed the committee to become House Speaker. Rice's background as an accountant and tax lawyer positioned him to deal with the issues facing the panel. He said that he would focus on jobs and American competitiveness.

In a 2014 rematch for reelection, Bromell Tinubu spent $229,000, which was one-third her total in 2012. Rice won 60 percent of the vote. In 2016, he won, 61%-39%, against Mal Hyman, a sociology professor at Coker College, who raised $91,000. Perhaps the biggest challenge facing Rice is redistricting in 2022. His base in booming Horry County likely will serve him well.

Pee Dee/Waccamaw Region: Myrtle Beach, Florence, Georgetown

Population		**Race and Ethnicity**		**Income**	
Total	680,163	White	63.7%	Median Income	$40,063 (398 out of 435)
Land area	5,355	Black	29.0%		
Pop/ sq mi	127.0	Latino	4.1%		
Born in state	58.2%	Asian	0.9%	Under $50,000	59.6%
		Two races	1.5%	$50,000-$99,999	28.1%
Age Groups		Other	0.7%	$100,000-$199,999	10.4%
Under 18	21.6%			$200,000 or more	1.9%
18-34	20.7%	**Education**		Poverty Rate	21.2%
35-64	40.0%	H.S grad or less	49.9%		
Over 64	17.7%	Some college	29.9%	**Health Insurance**	
		College Degree, 4 yr	13.3%	With health insurance coverage	82.9%
Work		Post grad	6.9%		
White Collar	29.1%				
Sales and Service	48.1%	**Military**		**Public Assistance**	
Blue Collar	22.9%	Veteran	10.3%	Cash public assistance income	1.4%
Government	13.8%	Active Duty	0.1%		
				Food stamp/SNAP benefits	18.2%

Voter Turnout

2015 Total Citizens 18+	517,072	2016 House Turnout as % CVAP	56%
2016 House turnout	289,463	2014 House Turnout as % CVAP	33%

2012 Presidential Vote

Mitt Romney	152,577	(55%)
Barack Obama	124,601	(45%)

2016 Presidential Vote

Donald Trump	173,065	(58%)
Hillary Clinton	116,626	(39%)

Cook Partisan Voting Index: R+9

The Pee Dee region of South Carolina, named for the river that lazily winds its way through the northern lowlands of the Palmetto State. It was here that Francis Marion's penchant for conducting lightning fast raids on larger British forces and then vanishing into the swamps earned him the name "Swamp Fox" during the Revolutionary War. In September 2016, researchers raised from the muddy Pee Dee River three cannons, which Confederate forces apparently had pushed overboard from a ship in their futile battle against the oncoming forces of General William Sherman. Discovery of the cannons near Florence provided scholarly insights into military history.

The 7th Congressional District takes in almost the entire Pee Dee region. State Republicans in control of redistricting in 2011 were happy to create the new district that is solidly Republican. The 7th consists of two distinct areas of roughly equal population. The inland counties remain reminiscent of the Old South. Crossroads communities and farms dot the landscape, and on Labor Day weekend the Bojangles' Southern 500 fills the air around Darlington with the roar of stock car engines. Florence, historically the hub of the Pee Dee, is the only city in this portion of the district with a population in excess of 30,000. Unlike the rest of the area, Florence has experienced real economic development over the past decade.

The second half of the district is coastal. A century ago, this was largely uninhabited forestland, and Myrtle Beach wasn't incorporated until 1938. Today, the two coastal counties of the Pee Dee - Horry and Georgetown - are home to the 60-mile Grand Strand, comprising miles of beachfront and golf courses and drawing 17 million visitors annually to the year-round vacation spot. The combined vote of the two counties, which are entirely in the 7th, has increased to a bit more than half of the total for the district. From 2000 to 2016, Horry grew 64 percent, to 322,000 people. After a steel mill in Georgetown was shut down in 2015, causing the loss of more than 200 jobs, local planners explored ways to redevelop the site. The coastal areas of the district are overwhelmingly Republican. The inland portions of Florence and Darlington are more competitive. Rural Marion and Marlboro counties are majority-black, and they vote Democratic.

The district is 28 percent black, virtually the same as the 5th District and the largest in the state other than the black-majority 6th District. With shifts of black communities from the adjacent 5th, this could have been more of a minority-influence district, but a black-majority district likely would have required creative mapmaking. Despite legal challenges, the Obama administration concluded that the state was not required by the Voting Rights Act to draw an additional minority-majority district. Overall, the 7th is Republican, but not overwhelmingly so. Donald Trump won 58 percent of the vote here in 2016, an increase from the 55 percent for Mitt Romney in 2012 and no longer the lowest vote of the state's six GOP-held districts.

★ SOUTH DAKOTA ★

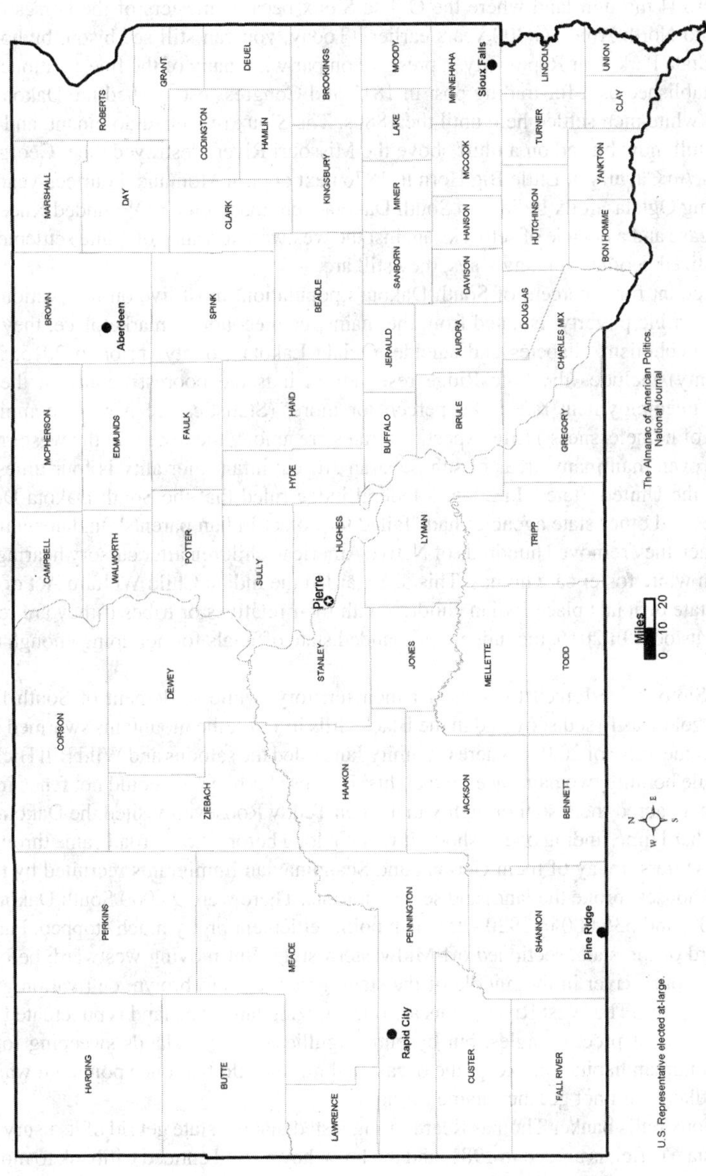

South Dakota is one of the most Republican states in the nation. It last supported a Democratic nominee for president in 1964, and it last elected a Democratic governor in 1974, a Democratic senator in 2006, and a Democratic House member in 2008. Judging by the statewide results of the 2016 presidential election – a 30-point romp by Donald Trump – South Dakota's Republican leaning is, if anything, increasing.

The Lewis and Clark exploration encountered herds of buffalo as they paddled up the Missouri River in the fall of 1804 through land where the Oglala Sioux became masters of the horses the Spaniards had imported to North America 300 years earlier. (Today, you can still see bison, bighorn sheep and elk at Custer State Park near Rapid City, a preserve on par with many of the finest national parks.) Fort Pierre was established as a fur-trading post in 1817 and Congress established the Dakota Territory in 1861, but few white men settled here until the 1880s. The Sioux remained dominant, and their warrior chief Sitting Bull, now buried on a bluff above the Missouri River, destroyed Gen. George Armstrong Custer and his 7th Cavalry at Little Big Horn in 1876 next door in Montana. Fourteen years later, many of the remaining Oglala Sioux Indians in South Dakota were massacred at Wounded Knee. After half a century of disease and a decade of setbacks against the westward advance of white settlement, the Sioux were a traumatized people. In many ways, they still are.

Indians account for 9 percent of South Dakota's population; most live on reservations with proud traditions but terrible poverty. Isolated from the mainstream economic marketplace, they are beset by high rates of alcoholism, diabetes and suicide. Oglala Lakota County (prior to 2015, it was called Shannon County) includes the Pine Ridge reservation; it is the poorest county in the nation, and the estimated unemployment rate is 80 percent or more. (Statistics are hard to compile given the pervasiveness of homelessness.) Life expectancy rates are among the lowest in the western hemisphere and are lower even than many areas of sub-Saharan Africa; infant mortality is four times higher than other areas of the United States. In 2015, a federal judge ruled that the South Dakota Department of Social Services and other state agencies had "failed to protect Indian parents' fundamental rights" over many years when they removed hundreds of Native American children after cursory hearings and placed them mostly in white foster care homes. This disregarded the Indian Child Welfare Act of 1978, which requires that state officials place Indian children with their relatives or tribes if they are removed from their parents' custody. In 2016, the judge reprimanded state officials for not doing enough to rectify the situation.

Once the Sioux were forced to surrender their territory, white settlement of South Dakota came quickly. After gold was first discovered in the Black Hills in 1874, the mountains swarmed with settlers. Deadwood became a city of 20,000 where Calamity Jane ruled the saloons and Wild Bill Hickok was shot in the back while holding two pair - aces and eights. Because barbed wire could not fence in the buffalo, hired hunters massacred them so thoroughly that when Teddy Roosevelt visited the Dakota Territory in 1884, he had a hard time finding one to shoot. It was not long before the railroad came through, followed by permanent settlers, many of them German and Scandinavian immigrants recruited by the railroads. They built sod houses, broke the land, and set down roots. There were 98,000 South Dakotans in 1880; 401,000 in 1900; and 636,000 in 1920 - at which point settlement pretty much stopped. Farmers settled the eastern third of the state, sectioned off Midwestern-style. But moving westward, before a traveler reaches the Missouri River in the middle of the state, green turns to brown, cultivation grows sparse, and then simply stops. The West River plains are open grazing land. The land is punctuated not by roads meeting every mile at precise angles, but by buttes, gullies, and grasslands sweeping to the horizon with no sign of human habitation except the occasional missile silo that once pointed toward the Soviet Union. The badlands did not get their name for nothing.

In 1979, Sioux Falls banker Thomas Reardon suggested that the state get rid of its usury law limiting interest rates; state officials agreed in 1981, and the laws they passed enticed Citibank to move its credit-card operations to Sioux Falls, where it could charge market interest rates, all in a state with no corporate or personal income taxes, and a community with a literate but lower-wage work force. The Citibank operation has grown from 500 employees to nearly 3,000. It didn't take long for other companies such as Wells Fargo and Capital One to move their credit-card operations to the Sioux Falls metro area. Today, South Dakota has $3 trillion in bank assets, more than any other state, according to the Federal Deposit Insurance Corporation data. The arrival of the financial sector enabled residents of an aging agricultural state to gain exposure to and experience in the 21st Century economy of finance. Unlike other largely rural areas of the country, "Sioux Falls has an entire managerial class that trained locally-and stayed local," wrote Amy Sullivan in *National Journal's Next Economy*. The finance sector also bequeathed Sioux Falls a secondary industry -- mail-order pharmaceuticals, which piggybacked on the logistics network built to enable credit-card companies to deliver replacement cards quickly and securely to their customers. And a separate financial specialty has quietly emerged in recent years – trusts for wealthy families, aided by favorable laws. In just one "modest, two-story white-brick building" at 201 South Phillips Ave. in Sioux Falls, $80 billion worth of trust assets are administered, the *Financial Times* reported in 2016. Statewide, the amount has zoomed past $226 billion. "America is the new Switzerland," Swiss-based lawyer David Wilson told the newspaper.

The agriculture sector, meanwhile, had a good run during the Great Recession, but it began a downturn around 2014, as prices for livestock, corn, soybeans and wheat all fell by double-digit percentages. Farm income fell by 76 percent between 2011 and 2016. On balance, though, the new, white-collar industries have helped stabilize South Dakota's economy. The unemployment rate peaked at a modest 5.2 percent in January 2010, and by February 2017 it had fallen to 2.8 percent, tied for second lowest of any state. By the fall of 2016, the city of Sioux Falls registered the nation's lowest unemployment rate for any city – 1.9 percent. South Dakota ranks high in credit ratings, low in foreclosures, and high in repayment of college loans. Median incomes have improved to slightly under the national average. South Dakotans (along with North Dakotans) spend less time commuting to work than Americans elsewhere. Meanwhile, the healthy economy, particularly when bolstered by the tourism sector, has boosted the state's population. South Dakota is coming to resemble the Rocky Mountain States, with most people concentrated around a few prosperous and growing cities and towns, with vast acreage remaining vacant, punctuated by the occasional farm or ranch house. Statewide, the population has grown by 6.3 percent since 2010, with particularly high growth rates in the Sioux Falls area – 10.5 percent in Minnehaha County and 21.5 percent in suburban Lincoln County. African Americans account for only 2 percent of the state's population, ranking in the bottom 10 states nationally, while Hispanics account for just 4 percent, half of the percentage in neighboring Iowa and one-third of the percentage in adjoining Nebraska.

South Dakota's political patterns were largely set by the early 1900s. Its early settlers were mostly Midwesterners who brought their Republicanism with them, of New England Yankee and German stock primarily, and also some Norwegians. South Dakota, unlike North Dakota, never had much use for the Non-Partisan League, and unlike in Minnesota, there was never anything comparable to the Farmer-Labor Party. But the nature of the farm economy - its dependence on the great railroads and milling companies and on the vagaries of international markets - meant that South Dakota was subject to periodic farm revolts. It voted for populists and William Jennings Bryan in the 1890s, then switched to Republicans. In the summer of 1927, when the sculpting of Mount Rushmore began, it welcomed President Calvin Coolidge for a vacation in Custer State Park, where he announced he would not seek another term in 1928. South Dakota briefly supported the New Deal, and it revolted against the Eisenhower administration in the late 1950s by electing to Congress a young Dakota Wesleyan University professor named George McGovern. South Dakota shared the isolationist impulse of much of the Great Plains; McGovern's opposition to the Vietnam War in the late 1960s was not a liability back home.

As in other small states, South Dakotans expect to meet and chat with their elected officials repeatedly. Pierre (pronounced "peer") is the nation's second smallest state capital city, outranking only Montpelier, Vermont, and personal campaigning has enabled Democrats to be competitive at times in congressional elections. Back in 1978, the 29-year-old Tom Daschle's personal campaigning enabled him to beat Congressional Medal of Honor recipient Leo Thorsness by 139 votes in a House race. That led to Daschle's election to the Senate in 1986 and his elevation to Senate Democratic leader in 1995. South Dakota's other Senate seat was won by Democrat Tim Johnson in 1996 by 8,579 votes and, helped by a major turnout drive on the Pine Ridge Indian Reservation, won a narrow reelection in 2002. Briefly, from June 2004 to January 2005, South Dakota had an all-Democratic congressional delegation - with Rep. Stephanie Herseth Sandlin joining Daschle and Johnson -- for only the second time in its history. Johnson suffered a disabling brain hemorrhage in December 2006 and his determined recovery generated wide sympathy; he was reelected 62%-38% in 2008.

In general, though, South Dakota has leaned strongly Republican, beginning with the gubernatorial administration of Bill Janklow, elected in 1978 and 1982 and then again in 1994 and 1998. Since 2008, no Democrat has been elected to statewide office in South Dakota. In the 2016 presidential election, the state became even more heavily red than previously. Donald Trump's winning margin was 30 points, well above Mitt Romney's 18-point edge in 2012. Trump over-performed Romney by 17,000 votes, while Clinton underperformed Obama's 2012 vote total by 28,000. Obama won 10 counties in the state, Clinton just five – and the counties that remained blue in 2016 were either extraordinarily small or heavily Native American. In contrast to other states (but similar to North Dakota), each of South Dakota's five mostpopulous counties not only voted Republican in both 2012 and 2016 but also shifted even more strongly toward the GOP. In Minnehaha County (Sioux Falls), and Pennington County (Rapid City), it shifted by four points toward the GOP; in Lincoln County(the southern suburbs of Sioux Falls) it shifted by three points; in Brown County (Aberdeen) it shifted by 19 points; and in Brookings County (Brookings) it shifted by 12 points. If such patterns persist, the Republicans can expect smooth sailing up and down the South Dakota ballot for the foreseeable future.

Population		**Race and Ethnicity**		**Income**	
Total	843,190	White	83.2%	Median Income	$50,957 (29 out of 50)
Land area	75,811	Black	1.5%		
Pop/ sq mi	11.1	Latino	3.3%	Under $50,000	49.1%
Born in state	64.5%	Asian	1.2%	$50,000-$99,999	33.4%
Age Groups		Two races	2.3%	$100,000-$199,999	14.3%
Under 18	24.6%	Other	8.4%	$200,000 or more	3.2%
18-34	23.1%	**Education**		Poverty Rate	14.1%
35-64	37.4%	H.S grad or less	40.4%	**Health Insurance**	
Over 64	14.9%	Some college	32.6%	With health insurance coverage	89.0%
Work		College Degree, 4 yr	19.0%		
White Collar	34.8%	Post grad	8.0%	**Public Assistance**	
Sales and Service	41.3%	**Military**		Cash public assistance income	2.7%
Blue Collar	23.9%	Veteran	10.1%		
Government	15.5%	Active Duty	0.4%	Food stamp/SNAP benefits	11.1%

Voter Turnout			
2015 Total Citizens 18+	621,770	2016 Pres Turnout as % CVAP	60%
2016 Pres Votes	370,093	2012 Pres Turnout as % CVAP	61%

Legislature	
Senate:	8D, 27R
House:	12D, 57R

Presidential Politics

2016 Democratic Primary		
Hillary Clinton (D)	27,047	(51%)
Bernie Sanders (D)	25,959	(49%)
2016 Republican Primary		
Donald Trump (R)	44,867	(67%)
Ted Cruz (R)	11,352	(17%)
John Kasich (R)	10,660	(16%)

2016 Presidential Vote		
Donald Trump (R)	227,721	(62%)
Hillary Clinton (D)	117,458	(32%)
Gary Johnson (L)	20,850	(6%)
2012 Presidential Vote		
Mitt Romney (R)	210,610	(58%)
Barack Obama (D)	145,039	(40%)

Cook Partisan Voting Index: R+14

South Dakota has voted Democratic for president just four times since statehood - in 1896, 1932, 1936, and 1964. But it was fairly close in five of the seven elections between 1972, when South Dakota's George McGovern was the Democratic nominee, and 1996, when Democrat Bill Clinton came within 3 points of winning. In 2000, Al Gore's environmental policies were unpopular here and Republican George W. Bush carried the state, 60%-38%. In 2004, Bush carried the state by the same margin, winning every county except those with Indian reservations and the University of South Dakota. In 2008, Republican John McCain carried the state 53%-45%. Barack Obama won the Indian reservations, several counties in the northeast and southeast, and won Minnehaha County (Sioux Falls) by 587 votes out of 80,000 cast. For Democrats to have any chance at victory, they need to win Minnehaha. In 2012, South Dakota gave Republican Mitt Romney a 58%-40% victory over Obama, and Romney carried Minnehaha County 53%-45%. The 2016 general election was a smashing Republican victory; Donald Trump defeated Hillary Clinton, 62%-32%, winning 61 of the state's 65 counties. He handily won Minnehaha, 54%-39%.

In 1988, South Dakota switched its presidential primary from the traditional June date to February, but switched back in 1996.There was a robust race for the 2008 Democratic nomination up through June 3, when South Dakota voted. Obama had a long list of endorsements from leading South Dakota Democrats but Hillary Clinton, Bill Clinton, and daughter Chelsea Clinton crisscrossed the state in the two weeks before the primary, and Clinton won 55%-45%. It was only her second victory north of the 42nd parallel and west of Indiana and Michigan. In the 2016 primary South Dakotans stuck with Clinton, giving her a narrow 51%-49% victory over Sen. Bernie Sanders, just over 1,000 votes out of 53,006 cast. Too late to matter in recent GOP contests, Mitt Romney won the 2012 primary with 66 percent, and Donald Trump prevailed in 2016 with 67 percent.

Congressional Districts

115th Congress Lineup	1R	**114th Congress Lineup**	1R

Governor

Dennis M. Daugaard (R)

Elected 2010, term expires 2019, 2nd term; b. Jun. 11, 1953, Garretson, SD; U. of SD, B.S. 1975; Northwestern U., J.D. 1978; Lutheran; Married (Linda); 3 children.

Elected Office: SD Senate, 1996-2002; SD Lt. Governor, 2002-2010.

Professional Career: Business Development & Vice President, U.S. Bank, Sioux Falls, 1981-1990; Development Director, Children's Home Foundation, 1990-2002; Executive Director, Children's Home Society, 2002-2009.

Office: 500 E. Capitol Ave., Pierre, 57501-5070; 605-773-3212; Fax: 605-773-4711; Website: sd.gov/governor.

Election Results

Election	Name (Party)	Vote (%)
2014 General	Dennis Daugaard (R)	195,477 (71%)
	Susan Wismer (D)	70,549 (25%)
	Mike Myers (I)	11,377 (4%)
2014 Primary	Dennis Daugaard (R)	60,017 (81%)
	Lora Hubbel (R)	14,196 (19%)

Prior winning percentage: 2010 (62%)

First elected in 2010, Dennis Daugaard is a Republican who has leavened conservative stances on abortion and guns with more moderate ones on juvenile justice and transgender rights.

Daugaard grew up on his family's dairy farm near Garretson in eastern South Dakota. His grandparents, who emigrated from Denmark, started the farm in 1911. Both of his parents were born deaf, so he principally communicated with them through sign language. He graduated from the University of South Dakota in 1975 and earned his law degree from Northwestern University in 1978. He spent a year at a small law firm in Chicago, then left to concentrate on real estate and settlement negotiations. He returned to South Dakota in 1981, marrying his high school girlfriend, Linda, and working as a trust officer for nine years at U.S. Bank in Sioux Falls. In 1990, he became director of development at the Children's Home Foundation, the fundraising arm of the Children's Home Society, which provides help to victims of abuse and neglect. He became the society's executive director in 2002.

Daugaard made his initial bid for public office in 1996, when he won a seat in the state Senate. He was reelected easily in 1998 and 2000. As a lawmaker, he focused on issues affecting people with disabilities and children. In 2002, Mike Rounds, a former state Senate president, asked him to join his gubernatorial ticket as lieutenant governor. Though they came into the GOP primary as underdogs, Rounds and Daugaard benefited from a nasty battle between their rivals and ended up relatively unscathed. They won the general election with 57 percent of the vote and were reelected four years later with 62 percent. As lieutenant governor, Daugaard chaired the Worker's Compensation Advisory Board and a task force on health care, as well as serving on a commission to revise the state constitution.

With Rounds term-limited in 2010, Daugaard ran for governor, vowing not to raise taxes except to cope with the aftermath of a flood or other emergency. He also called for increasing the value of the state's economic development fund, which provides low-interest loans to startups expanding or relocating to the state, while also continuing to expand wind, ethanol and other alternative energy sources. At the same time, he pushed for a strong increase in science and math education for students. He easily won the June GOP primary with just over 50 percent of the vote, having far outspent his four opponents. In the general election, he faced Scott Heidepriem, the state Senate minority leader. Heidepriem campaigned as an independent Democrat skilled at building consensus, and in recognition of the uphill challenge facing his party he chose a Republican businessman as his running mate. Heidepriem was able to remain competitive on fundraising but was unable to overcome the state's Republican bent, and Daugaard won in a landslide, 62%-38%.

With a more hands-on management style than Rounds, Daugaard focused on fiscal matters during his early months in office, proposing a budget that would cut about 10 percent from almost every aspect of state government. The proposal went deeper than one Rounds had proposed in December that relied on reserve money to limit cuts to 5 percent for such programs as elementary education and Medicaid. Lawmakers approved a budget with his 10 percent cuts. Daugaard also signed a measure that made South Dakota the first state to authorize school employees to carry guns on the job, though it left it up to individual school districts whether to arm teachers. The issue that brought Daugaard the most national attention, however, was a bill he signed into law in March 2011 that instituted the nation's longest waiting period at the time - three days - for women seeking an abortion after meeting with a doctor. The measure also required women to visit an anti-abortion counseling center. Two years later, Daugaard signed another bill that said weekends and holidays did not count as part of the three-day waiting period.

In 2013, Daugaard won bipartisan approval from the state legislature for a bill to reduce the growth of the state's prison population, primarily by not locking up offenders with minor drug-possession charges. The measure also redirected funds to programs to reduce recidivism. He touted this measure, and his budget-cutting ways, when campaigning for reelection in 2014. That year, he faced Democratic state Rep. Susan Wismer, the first woman to win a major party's nomination for South Dakota governor. She criticized Daugaard for refusing to support Medicaid expansion under the Affordable Care Act and attacked his budget cuts to K-12 education as excessive. But voters gave Daugaard a historically large victory, 70%-25%. In the same election, 55 percent of voters approved a ballot measure Daugaard had opposed that increased the state's minimum wage to $8.50 an hour.

At the start of his second term, Daugaard broke his no-new-taxes pledge by signing a six-cent increase in the gasoline tax to fund road and bridge repairs. Daugaard had favored a larger increase spread over several years, but when Republican lawmakers in the GOP-controlled state legislature balked, he agreed to a compromise. The measure also increased the state's motor vehicle excise tax from 3 percent to 4 percent, boosted license plate fees by 20 percent and raised the state speed limit from 75 to 80 mph. Following up on his efforts to reduce the state's prison population, Daugaard enacted juvenile justice reform in early 2015. The measure was designed to cut the number of occupants in state juvenile facilities in half by 2020 by diverting more youths without a criminal record from the juvenile system and expanding access to community-based substance-abuse programs. Daugaard kept to his conservative moorings on budget matters, approving a 2 percent increase in funding for education and signing a bill authorizing a lower minimum wage, $7.50 an hour, for youth under 18.

In 2016, Daugaard surprised observers by once again advocating a tax increase – a half-cent sales tax hike to fund higher pay for teachers – and by junking his previous opposition to expanding Medicaid under the Affordable Care Act. The legislature agreed with the tax increase but balked at the Medicaid expansion, and Daugaard stepped back from the proposal after Donald Trump won the 2016 presidential election with a promise to repeal the law. In March 2016, Daugaard signed another abortion restriction – a ban on the procedure beyond 20 weeks of pregnancy, the point at which many doctors say the unborn child can feel pain. But Daugaard took a more moderate approach on transgender rights the same month, vetoing a bill that would have made the state the first to pass a bill requiring transgender students to use the bathroom of their birth gender. He said the bill did "not address any pressing issue" and added that "if and when these rare situations arise, I believe local school officials are best positioned to address them." The veto spared South Dakota the economic boycott and acrimony that would later hit North Carolina after it passed a similar measure. Daugaard reiterated his opposition in January 2017 when faced with a new bill on the use of bathrooms and locker rooms; he said he would veto that bill as well.

Daugaard took heat in early 2017 after voters approved a ballot measure to tighten ethics rules. One 2015 study had ranked South Dakota 47th for "state integrity," including transparency, and on Election Day 2016, voters approved Measure 22 by a 52%-48% margin. The measure capped contribution limits, increased reporting requirements, banned lobbying and limited gifts to former state officials for two years, established an ethics commission, and created a limited system of public campaign financing. During the campaign, Daugaard had opposed the measure, saying that voters were being "hoodwinked by scam artists" from out of state. Within months after its passage, the legislature approved, and Daugaard signed, a bill to repeal the ballot measure, although some legislators offered measures to replace portions of it.

Meanwhile, facing a slump in the agriculture and tourism sectors, Daugaard proposed a budget that increased spending on education and health care by 1 percent. He also broke with his pro-gun record in March, vetoing a pair of bills that would have expanded gun rights. One would have allowed certain individuals to carry a gun in the state capitol, while the other would have allowed concealed weapons without a permit more generally. Daugaard is term-limited, and a tight GOP primary was widely expected in 2018 between Rep. Kristi Noem and Attorney General Marty Jackley. In the present political climate in the state, it's hard to imagine Democrats making a serious run at the office, even if they could find a credible candidate.

Senior Senator

John Thune (R)

Elected 2004, term expires 2022, 3rd term; b. Jan 07, 1961, Pierre; Biola University, b.B.A., 1983; University of South Dakota, M.B.A., 1984; Evangelical; Married (Kimberley Joe Weems Thune); 2 children; 1 grandchild.

Elected Office: U.S. House, 1997-2003.

Professional Career: Legislative Assistant, U.S Sen. James Abdnor, 1985-1986; Special Assistant, U.S Small Business Admin., 1987-1989; Executive Director, SD Republican Party, 1989-1991; SD railroad Director, 1991-1993; Executive Director, SD Municipal League 1993-1996.

DC Office: 511 DSOB 20510, 202-224-2321, Fax: 202-228-5429, thune.senate.gov.

State Offices: Aberdeen, 605-225-8823; Rapid City, 605-348-7551; Sioux Falls, 605-334-9596.

Committees: Senate Republican Conference Chairman. *Agriculture, Nutrition & Forestry*: Commodities, Risk Management & Trade, Livestock, Marketing & Agriculture Security, Rural Development & Energy. *Commerce, Science & Transportation (Chmn)*: Aviation Operations, Safety & Security, Communications, Technology, Innovation & the Internet, Consumer Protection, Product Safety, Ins & Data Security, Oceans, Atmosphere, Fisheries & Coast Guard, Space, Science & Competitiveness, Surface Trans., Merchant Marine Infra., Safety & Security. *Finance*: Health Care, International Trade, Customs & Global Competitiveness, Taxation & IRS Oversight.

Group Ratings

	ADA	ACLU	AFL-CIO	LCV	ITI	COC	HAFA	ACU	CFG	FRC
2016	-	11%	-	0%	60%	100%	50%	81%	70%	100%
2015	0%	C	14%	4%	C	86%	C	75%	68%	100%

Almanac Ratings 2015

	Economy	Social	Foreign	Composite
Liberal	31%	0%	9%	13%
Conservative	69%	100%	91%	87%

Key Votes of the 114th Congress

1. Keystone pipeline	Y	5. National Security Data	N	9. Gun Sales Checks	N
2. Export-Import Bank	Y	6. Iran Nuclear Deal	Y	10. Sanctuary Cities	Y
3. Debt Ceiling Increase	Y	7. Puerto Rico Debt	Y	11. Planned Parenthood	Y
4. Homeland Security $$	Y	8. Loretta Lynch A.G	N	12. Trade deals	Y

Election Results

Election	Name (Party)	Vote (%)	Cand. Spent	Ind. Exp. Support	Ind. Exp. Oppose
2016 General	John Thune (R)	265,516 (72%)	$2,424,179		
	Jay Williams (D)	104,140 (28%)	$59,126		
2016 Primary	John Thune (R)	unopposed			

Prior winning percentages: 2010 (100%), 2004 (51%), House: 2000 (73%), 1998 (75%), 1996 (58%)

Republican John Thune, the senior senator from South Dakota, wields considerable influence as chairman of the Commerce, Science and Transportation Committee and as chairman of the Republican Conference, the third-ranking GOP leadership slot. He is the only Senate Republican younger than 60 to hold either a top committee post or a party leadership position, let alone both. That leaves him well-positioned to gain additional influence in the years ahead-perhaps more so than any other of the relatively junior GOP Senators. The seniority tables could leave him as the top Republican on the powerful Senate Finance Committee within the next decade. His Senate prospects are all the more intriguing because he gave early consideration to running for president in 2012 and he subsequently drew continued attention for a possible presidential candidacy. "I am not actively pursuing [the presidency] at the moment; I've got my work cut out for me in the Senate," Thune told *The Hill* in December 2014.

He first gained national notice in 2004, when he defeated the Senate Democratic leader, Tom Daschle, in a hard-fought and costly contest. With his relative youth, his extensive Capitol Hill experience and his impressive fundraising, Thune has numerous opportunities, both inside and outside the Senate. Among other possibilities, the Senate Republicans' term-limit rules may leave him as the frontrunner for moving up to party Whip before the next Congress convenes in 2019. In effect, he might become the Republican version of either the senator whom he defeated or perhaps another South Dakota Democratic senator, George McGovern, who was his party's presidential nominee in 1972. In the meantime, his broad portfolio as Commerce Committee chairman gives him jurisdiction over a wide variety of key issues, ranging from telecommunications to insurance and product safety, in addition to aviation and railroads.

Thune grew up in Murdo, on the dusty plains west of the Missouri River, a small town with a cluster of restaurants and motels at the interchange of Interstate 94 and U.S. 83. His father, the son of a Norwegian immigrant and a Navy veteran of World War II, was a teacher and the family was Democratic. Thune graduated from Biola University in La Mirada, California and then earned an M.B.A. from the University of South Dakota. The genesis of Thune's political career dates back to when, as a high school freshman, he was spotted at a grocery store checkout counter by Republican Rep. Jim Abdnor, who recalled the tall young man had missed only one of six free throws in his high school basketball game the previous night. They kept in touch, and years later, when Abdnor was in the Senate (Abdnor won the seat in 1980 by McGovern), he hired Thune on his Washington staff. In the close-knit family of South Dakota politics, Thune joined Abdnor's staff in 1985, a year after finishing business school, and worked there until Abdnor in 1986 lost a bid for reelection to Democrat Tom Daschle. Thune then spent a couple of years working for the Small Business Administration.

Thune returned to South Dakota in 1989 and became executive director of the state Republican Party. In 1991, he was appointed state railroad director by Gov. George Mickelson and in 1993 he became director of the South Dakota Municipal League, which represents incorporated municipalities around the state. In 1996, at the age of 35, Thune entered a race for the state's at-large House seat, which was open due to Democratic Rep. Tim Johnson's decision to run for Senate. The favorite in the Republican primary was Lt. Gov. Carole Hillard. But Thune attracted the support of religious conservatives and won the primary 59%-41%. In the general election, he faced Democrat Rick Weiland, a former state director for Daschle. Thune opposed all tax increases and promised to serve only three terms. He won 58%-37%. In the House, Thune was chosen as freshman class representative to the Republican leadership. He was reelected, 75%-25%, in 1998, the largest percentage margin ever for a statewide candidate in South Dakota. He did almost as well-73 percent-winning a third term in 2000.

As he bumped up against his self-imposed three-term limit in the House, Thune considered running for the open governor's seat in 2002, and was seen as a heavy favorite to win. But, at a White House dinner in April 2001, President George W. Bush urged Thune instead to challenge Johnson, who had won in 1996 by ousting Republican Sen. Larry Pressler. Daschle, who had become Senate Democratic leader in 1995, had vowed to do everything he could to protect Johnson, and got him a seat on the influential Appropriations Committee. Thune decided to challenge Johnson in 2002, clearing the way for Republican Mike Rounds-now Thune's junior colleague in the Senate -to make a successful bid for governor. In taking on Johnson, Thune argued South Dakota would be better off with a bipartisan Senate delegation. Johnson countered that he and Daschle made a uniquely powerful team, and emphasized votes he had cast for Bush Administration policies in a state that had not voted for a Democratic presidential nominee since 1964. Johnson and Thune spent about $6 million each, a record amount for South Dakota, and the national parties and independent groups spent much more.

The election was the closest Senate race in the nation that year. During most of Election Night and into the morning, Thune led. Then the last two precincts came in, from Shannon County, which includes most of the Pine Ridge Indian Reservation. It voted for Johnson by a better than 9-1 margin, putting him over the top by a margin of 524 votes-in percentage terms, 50.1%-49.9%. Many Republicans urged Thune to contest the election results. In a decision that won him respect and appreciation from both parties in South Dakota, he declined and went to work as a lobbyist and consultant in Washington. He was encouraged by Republican leaders and family members to run in 2004 against Daschle, who had beaten lightly funded opponents in 1992 and 1998. Daschle had been majority leader for 18 months in 2001-2002, and he had otherwise been minority leader since 1995. In South Dakota, Thune's favorable ratings remained high after his narrow 2002 defeat; early GOP polls showed him running slightly ahead of Daschle, and it was clear Thune would enjoy the full support of the Bush White House. Bush, who had carried South Dakota 60%-38% in 2000, was at the top of the ballot that year. In January 2004, Thune announced he would take on Daschle.

Thune sought to portray Daschle as the chief obstructionist to the Bush agenda in the Senate. To underscore the Republicans' determination to oust the incumbent, Majority Leader Bill Frist of Tennessee traveled to South Dakota to stump for Thune, breaking with Senate tradition of party leaders refraining from campaigning against each other. Daschle ran ads in the summer of 2003, arguing that a freshman senator could not hope to match his influence in Washington, and emphasizing the federal largesse he had brought to South Dakota. He also cited his support of some Bush initiatives. But Daschle was hobbled politically by the same balancing act as several other Democratic congressional leaders before and since-serving as a spokesman for national Democratic policies without putting off voters in a Republican-leaning or battleground state. "Sen. Daschle at the time was using his leadership position in a way that was contrary to where a majority of South Dakotans were," Thune observed during a CSPAN interview nearly a decade after that campaign. "Eventually, that caught up with him."

During the 2004 contest, Thune portrayed Daschle as a political insider who lived in a $2 million house in Washington and had lost touch with the folks back home. The state Republican Party sent a mailer attacking the work of Daschle's wife, an aviation industry lobbyist. It was the most expensive congressional election of the year, as both national parties and numerous third-party interest groups poured millions of dollars into South Dakota. By the end, they had spent $35 million. The closely fought race brought a huge turnout, up 23 percent from 2000. Thune won 51%-49%, the first defeat for a Senate party leader since Democrat Ernest McFarland of Arizona lost to Republican Barry Goldwater in 1952. The contours of the vote were similar to 2002, although Thune increased his share of the vote significantly in the Pine Ridge and Rosebud Indian reservations-where his decision not to challenge the election outcome two years earlier may have earned him goodwill.

Nationally, Thune was celebrated by Republicans as a giant-killer. He became a talk show favorite, a fundraising star, and a celebrity among Republican freshmen-and quickly rose in the ranks. Named chief deputy whip at the end of 2006, he served as vice-chairman of the Senate Republican Conference before moving up to Republican Policy Committee chairman in 2009, following the resignation of scandal-plagued John Ensign of Nevada. In early 2012, Thune became chairman of the Republican Conference after Tennessee Sen. Lamar Alexander chose to relinquish that post. It made Thune the third-ranking member of the Senate Republican leadership, behind Majority Leader Mitch McConnell of Kentucky and Majority Whip John Cornyn of Texas. With the six-year term limit for all Senate Republican committee chairmen and leadership members (except for McConnell's slot), Thune has the opportunity to move up the leadership ladder following the 2018 election and replace Cornyn in the number-two post, though he could face competition.

In the Senate, Thune has established a mostly conservative voting record, especially on cultural issues. The *Almanac* vote ratings for 2015 ranked him near the center of Senate Republicans; his scores on foreign policy issues were relatively moderate. "He is conservative, but his message usually is not bombastic, and he doesn't say things that scare off moderates and independents," the largest newspaper in Thune's home state, the Sioux Falls-based *Argus Leader*, observed in 2013.

Taking over as Commerce Committee chairman, Thune gave attention to railroads, which were a specialty of his lobbying days and remain a prime interest of many farmers and businesses in South Dakota. He has been especially concerned about the availability of sufficient rail transportation for agriculture. In December 2015, he enacted his bill to reform operations of the Surface Transportation Board, which regulates rail freight. Thune said that the changes were designed to make the Board "more accountable and effective in addressing rail rate and service disputes," including severe rail backlogs and service delays that had recently hindered agricultural shipments. On another transportation issue that is vital to South Dakota, Thune has split with fellow conservatives who have sought to kill the Essential Air Service program, which ensures small airports continue to get commercial flights.

Another prime issue for Thune as Commerce chairman has been the so-called network neutrality rules, which the Democratic majority of the Federal Communications Commission approved on a 3-2 vote in 2015. The rules have been designed to assure that all Internet content is treated equally; they classify Internet providers as public utilities, as telephone companies have long been. Thune called the FCC action the "most radical, polarizing and partisan path possible," and told the FCC majority at a hearing of his committee, "Instead of working with me and my colleagues in the House and Senate on a bipartisan basis to find a consensus, the three of you chose an option that I believe will only increase political, regulatory, and legal uncertainty, which will ultimately hurt average Internet users." In February 2017, Thune said that he was preparing legislation that would define net neutrality principles and codify them into law, including a prohibition on Internet service providers from selectively slowing down traffic or creating special "fast lanes" for sites that pay more. With new leaders appointed by President Donald Trump, the FCC had moved to rescind the earlier rules. On an issue that is vital for rural areas, Thune won committee approval in March 2016 of his bill to increase wireless broadband development by making more spectrum available.

On the Agriculture Committee, Thune prepared a proposal for a new category of land conservation, which he has called the Soil Health and Income Protection Program. The voluntary program, which he plans to advocate during expected debate of a new farm bill in 2018, would compensate farmers during times of excessive crops. Thune called his plan "an income protection program for farmers." Earlier, he helped to author a section of the 2008 farm bill establishing a permanent disaster-relief program to provide financial aid to farmers whose crops are harmed by natural disasters. He pushed successfully for these provisions to be reauthorized in the 2014 farm bill, and made retroactive to 2012 to cover losses from that year's drought in the Upper Midwest.

Thune has used his seat on the Finance Committee to push his legislation to repeal the estate tax. He has blasted the tax as a "nightmare" that "violates the basic premise of the American dream." Such a measure could become part of Republican plans for sweeping tax reform in the new Congress, Thune said following the 2016 election. On other fiscal matters, Thune has supported proposals for a biennial budget and a presidential line-item veto as steps to encourage fiscal discipline.

After close Senate races in 2002 and 2004, Thune has breezed to reelection. In 2010, South Dakota Democrats did not field a candidate. He became only the third Republican senator to run unopposed since direct election of senators began in 1913. Thune faced token opposition in 2016 from Jay Williams, a small businessman who spent $67,000, which was one percent of what Thune spent during the two-year cycle. He won, 72%-28%. With the lack of serious competition, Thune in 2016 gave $2 million to the NRSC to assist other Senate GOP candidates. Following the election, he retained more than $10 million cash on hand in his campaign account..

Thune is young by the standards of the Senate-he turned 56 in January 2017-and he could be an influential presence on Capitol Hill for years to come. With the election of Donald Trump as president, options for other Republicans have become more uncertain. "That might have been the window. You never know," Thune said of his decision not to run in 2012. "Timing's everything." For Thune, another potential wrinkle is that he publicly urged Trump to step aside as the GOP nominee in October 2016 following the release of the decade-old video in which he made lewd comments about women. Thune later suggested that he planned to vote for Trump.

Junior Senator

Mike Rounds (R)

Elected 2014, term expires 2020, 1st term; b. Oct 24, 1954, Huron; South Dakota State University, B.S.; Roman Catholic; Married (Jean Vedvei Rounds); 4 children; 6 grandchildren.

Elected Office: SD Senate, 1991-2000, Majority Leader, 1995-2000; SD governor, 2003-2010.

Professional Career: Insurance & real estate Executive.

DC Office: 502 HSOB 20510, 202-224-5842, Fax: 202-224-7482, rounds.senate.gov.

State Offices: Aberdeen, 605-225-0366; Pierre, 605-224-1450; Rapid City, 605-343-5035; Sioux Falls, 605-336-0486.

Committees: *Armed Services*: Cybersecurity (Chmn), Readiness & Management Support, Seapower. *Banking, Housing & Urban Affairs*: Housing, Transportation & Community Development, National Security & International Trade & Finance, Securities, Insurance & Investment. *Environment & Public Works*: Fisheries, Water, and Wildlife, Superfund, Waste Management, & Regulatory Oversight (Chmn). *Small Business & Entrepreneurship*. *Veterans' Affairs*.

Group Ratings

	ADA	ACLU	AFL-CIO	LCV	ITI	COC	HAFA	ACU	CFG	FRC
2016	-	11%	-	6%	100%	83%	45%	72%	64%	100%
2015	0%	C	14%	0%	C	100%	C	71%	58%	100%

Almanac Ratings 2015

	Economy	Social	Foreign	Composite
Liberal	33%	0%	28%	20%
Conservative	67%	100%	72%	80%

Key Votes of the 114th Congress

1. Keystone pipeline	Y	5. National Security Data	Y	9. Gun Sales Checks	N
2. Export-Import Bank	N	6. Iran Nuclear Deal	Y	10. Sanctuary Cities	Y
3. Debt Ceiling Increase	Y	7. Puerto Rico Debt	Y	11. Planned Parenthood	Y
4. Homeland Security $$	Y	8. Loretta Lynch A.G	N	12. Trade deals	Y

Election Results

Election	Name (Party)	Vote (%)		Cand. Spent	Ind. Exp. Support	Ind. Exp. Oppose
2014 General	Mike Rounds (R)	140,741	(50%	8 9 6 , 1 2 3 $)		
	Rick Weiland (D)	82,456	(30%)	$20,755		
	Larry Pressler (I)	47,741	(17%)			
	Gordon Howie (I)	8,474	(3%)			
2014 Primary	Mike Rounds (R)	41,372	(56%)			
	Stace Nelson (R)	13,591	(18%)			
	Larry Rhodes (R)	13,178	(18%)			
	Annette Bosworth (R)	4,283	(3%)			

Like other former governors in the Senate, Republican Mike Rounds has discovered the contrasts to the more action-oriented and less partisan responsibilities of a chief executive. Arriving in the Senate in 2015, he gravitated to a range of interests, from customary local representation and national line-drawing between the parties to emerging national-security issues where he could pursue more of a consensus-building approach.

Rounds, South Dakota's junior senator, is a former two-term governor who in 2014 was initially expected to walk away with the seat of retiring Democratic Sen. Tim Johnson. He won comfortably, but only after his contest had become one of the most unpredictable of the election cycle. His swearing-in gave South Dakota-a state that has voted reliably Republican in presidential races, but which has had a history of sending Democrats to the Senate and the House-its first all-GOP congressional delegation in more than a half century and left the once-vaunted South Dakota Democrats in disarray.

Rounds, named for an uncle who was killed in World War II, was born in Huron, but has lived in Pierre, the state capital, since he was 3. The eldest of 11 siblings, Rounds earned a degree in political science from South Dakota State University. In 1990, he was elected to the South Dakota Senate, rising to become majority leader during his last six years in that body, which he left in 2000 due to term limits. In 2002, he ran for governor, and won the Republican gubernatorial primary in one of the biggest political upsets in state history. Rounds faced former Lt. Gov. Steve Kirby and state Attorney General Mark Barnett, who waged a highly negative campaign against each other. Those attack ads were so negative that they backfired, benefiting Rounds-who won with 44 percent, to 30 percent for Barnett and 26 percent for Kirby. That fall, Rounds won 57 percent of the vote against Democrat Jim Abbott, who had been president of the University of South Dakota.

As governor, Rounds mostly enjoyed high approval ratings. They slumped in the spring of 2006 after he signed a controversial law banning all abortions except those necessary to save the mother's life. The law was challenged in court and never took effect, and Rounds' approval ratings recovered. The statute-criticized because it did not include exceptions for rape, incest, or the health of the mother-was repealed by voters in a state referendum, 55%-45%, on the same day that Rounds won his second term with 62 percent of the vote. Term-limited in 2010, Rounds was urged by some Republicans to challenge Democratic Sen. Tim Johnson in 2008, but declined to do so. Johnson suffered a cerebral hemorrhage at the end of 2006 that required brain surgery, but had partially recovered and sought a third term. At the end of 2010, Rounds returned to his insurance and real estate firm, Fischer Rounds & Associates, where he had put his ownership interest in a blind trust after being elected governor.

When Johnson did not seek reelection in 2014, Rounds made plans to run. The Democrats hoped that former three-term Rep. Stephanie Herseth Sandlin would run, but she declined. Although she had been defeated for reelection in the Republican wave year of 2010, she was the offshoot of a prominent South Dakota political family and remained popular in the state. She continued with her legal practice. In February 2017, she was named president of Augustana University. "I am done seeking political office," she said. U.S. attorney Brendan Johnson, son of the retiring senator, also declined to run. National Democrats all but threw in the towel on the seat. Rick Weiland, a former congressional aide and a two-time unsuccessful candidate for the state's at-large House seat, became the Democratic nominee. Rounds won a five-way Republican primary with 56 percent. In July, one poll showed Rounds leading in the general election by a 2-1 margin.

Weiland began hammering Rounds on his handling, while governor, of the so-called EB-5 program-which allows foreigners to obtain U.S. green cards by investing $500,000 in U.S. business projects that create jobs. The highest profile EB-5 project in the state was a beef processing plant, Northern Beef Packers that received almost $100 million from EB-5 funding, but nonetheless went bankrupt in 2013, a year after it opened. The problem for Rounds was that, a month before leaving office as governor, his economic development secretary, Richard Benda, had signed a contract with a private firm, SDRC, to take over the state's EB-5 program. Benda subsequently went to work for that firm. It was later revealed that Benda failed to disclose his plans to work for SDRC, while signing contracts on behalf of the state that benefitted that firm. Benda committed suicide in 2013 after the South Dakota attorney general, in a draft indictment, accused him of diverting a $550,000 state grant to his own enrichment. Rounds dropped in the polls amid voter anger over the EB-5 scandal, as he acknowledged he had been aware of Benda's conflict of interest.

Rounds campaigned on a solidly conservative pro-gun rights, anti-abortion and anti-same sex marriage platform; he advocated repeal of the Affordable Care Act and suggested during the campaign that the Department of Education should be abolished. Some Republicans fretted that he was not doing enough to defend himself in a public dispute with national GOP strategists over whether to run negative ads in the state-a move that Rounds opposed, largely because he had never used them in his past races.

Public polling revealed another problem; an independent candidate-former Republican Sen. Larry Pressler-was showing strength and was making the race a three-way contest. Pressler had held the seat for 18 years until losing it to Johnson in 1996. A Rhodes Scholar and Vietnam War veteran who was regarded as something of an oddball by colleagues during his years on Capitol Hill, Pressler had moved back to South Dakota after living in Washington. He ran as a maverick committed to reforming the way things are done in Washington. With Pressler not saying with which party he would join if he won, the Democratic Senatorial Campaign Committee began running ads attacking Rounds. Weiland charged that the DSCC was seeking to undercut him and boost Pressler. Rounds went along with national GOP strategists and began running ads contrasting his views on the Affordable Care Act and the Keystone XL pipeline with those of Pressler and Weiland. Rounds pulled away in the polls, and, on Election Day, won comfortably, taking 50 percent to 30 percent for Weiland and 17 percent for Pressler.

Rounds arrived in the Senate as the one former governor elected in 2014. By 2017, the total of ex-governors in the chamber had grown to 11. Rounds struck a bipartisan tone as a co-chair of the Former Governors Caucus, with Democrat Jeanne Shaheen of New Hampshire and independent Angus King of Maine. "Former governors are accustomed to making decisions and working across party lines to get things done," he said in early 2015. "Our shared background helps us find common ground without checking our credentials at the door." In an appearance on NBC's "Meet the Press," he said other former governors in the Senate had warned him that he should be prepared to be frustrated. Referring to Capitol Hill, he added: "There's no time frame there. There's nobody there that seems to understand that the people outside of Washington expect results."

He directed his problem-solving approach to cybersecurity, especially in national security. That topic had attracted growing bipartisan interest, especially following claims that Russian computer hacks had sought to influence the 2016 presidential election. In January 2017, Rounds became chairman of the newly-created Armed Services Cybersecurity Subcommittee. He was especially interested, he said, in "the Defense Department's role in responding to an attack on our nation's civilian critical infrastructure and in deterring bad actors from conducting such an attack in the first place." It was vital, he said, to deter a potential attack on the nation's infrastructure. In March, he met with Israeli officials to discuss areas where the two nations could expand their cooperation on cyber issues.

Rounds used other committee assignments to pursue constituent-based concerns. As chairman of the Environment and Public Works Subcommittee on Superfund, Waste Management and Regulator Oversight, he advocated repeal of Obama-era environmental regulations, notably new rules that gave the Environmental Protection Agency new authority over water sources. "EPA continuously ignored the concerns of farmers, ranchers, agriculture groups, state governors, attorneys general and the Small Business Administration before moving ahead," he claimed.

As a member of the Banking, Housing and Urban Affairs Committee, Rounds looked after the interests of the large banking and credit-card interests in South Dakota. In February 2017, he reintroduced his bill to require federal banking regulators to consider bank risk profiles and business models. Rounds said that his proposal had been strongly advocated by the American Bankers Association and the alliance of state bankers associations.

REPRESENTATIVE-AT-LARGE

Kristi Noem (R)

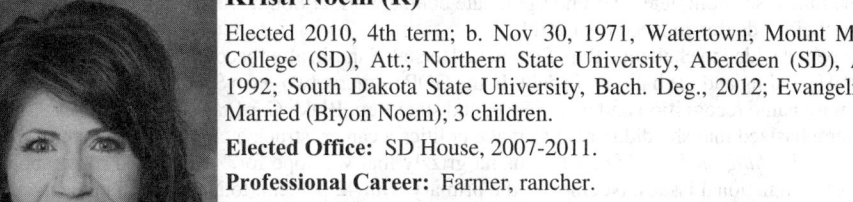

Elected 2010, 4th term; b. Nov 30, 1971, Watertown; Mount Marty College (SD), Att.; Northern State University, Aberdeen (SD), Att., 1992; South Dakota State University, Bach. Deg., 2012; Evangelical; Married (Bryon Noem); 3 children.

Elected Office: SD House, 2007-2011.

Professional Career: Farmer, rancher.

DC Office: 2457 RHOB 20515, 202-225-2801, Fax: 202-225-5823, noem.house.gov.

State Offices: Rapid City, 605-791-4673; Sioux Falls, 605-275-2868; Watertown, 605-878-2868.

Committees: *Ways & Means*: Tax Policy, Trade.

Group Ratings

	ADA	ACLU	AFL-CIO	LCV	ITI	COC	HAFA	ACU	CFG	FRC
2016	-	5%	-	0%	100%	100%	56%	79%	67%	92%
2015	0%	C	8%	3%	C	90%	C	67%	69%	92%

Almanac Ratings 2015

	Economy	Social	Foreign	Composite
Liberal	6%	10%	16%	11%
Conservative	94%	90%	84%	89%

Key Votes of the 114th Congress

1. Keystone Pipeline	Y	5. Puerto Rico Debt	Y	9. Offenses by Aliens	Y
2. Trade Deals	Y	6. Medical Marijuana	N	10. Troops in Iraq	N
3. Export-Import Bank	N	7. Sanctuary Cities	Y	11. Homeland Security $$	Y
4. Debt Ceiling Increase	N	8. Armor-piercing Bullets	Y	12. Trade Adjustment aid	Y

Election Results

Election	Name (Party)	Vote (%)	Cand. Spent	Ind. Exp. Support	Ind. Exp. Oppose
2016 General	Kristi Noem (R)	237,163 (64%)	$1,395,681		
	Paula Hawks (D)	132,810 (36%)	$394,627		
2016 Primary	Kristi Noem (R)	(100%)			

Prior winning percentages: 2014 (67%), 2012 (57%), 2010 (48%)

Republican Kristi Noem, elected in 2010, is a conservative outdoorswoman. Her frontier touches have evoked comparisons to former Alaska Gov. Sarah Palin. But she has been more of a team player and serious student of policy, especially its rural impact. She has become a player on the Ways and Means Committee. That tenure was set to end in 2018, with her run for governor.

Noem was born in Hamlin County, South Dakota. She attended college but returned home to help run the family farm after her father died in a fall into a grain bin while trying to unclog a feeder line, an accident that she discussed in her first campaign ad. She raised Angus cattle and quarter horses on a ranch with her husband, Bryon. An avid hunter of elk, pheasant and other game, Noem owned a hunting lodge and worked a variety of jobs, including a stint as a restaurant manager.

After developing an interest in conservative causes, including unhappiness with the estate tax bill that her family received after her father died, Noem ran for the South Dakota House and narrowly won in 2006. She earned her GOP colleagues' respect when she questioned a Democratic state senator's sponsorship of a bill to expand casino-style gambling in the state while the senator's law firm was representing an American Indian tribe. She became assistant majority leader. Noem knows how to balance a busy schedule. While serving in the Legislature and in the House and raising three children on the ranch, she completed her undergraduate course work at South Dakota State University. She got her bachelor's degree in December 2011.

Noem decided to challenge Rep. Stephanie Herseth Sandlin after becoming disenchanted with rising federal spending and the ballooning debt. In the GOP primary, two-term Secretary of State Chris Nelson had more name recognition and experience, and state Rep. Blake Curd raised more money. But Noem, who emphasized that she didn't plan to make politics a career, struck a chord with voters. One of them told *The Washington Post*, "She's the mama grizzly that we hope for." She talked more about South Dakota than national issues. Noem won the primary with 42 percent, to Nelson's 35 percent and Curd's 23 percent.

With substantial campaign contributions from out-of-state Republicans, Noem out-raised Herseth Sandlin. She was aided by local operatives of popular Republican Sen. John Thune. Outside conservative groups poured about $2 million into the race, more than three times what liberal groups spent. Noem sought to tie her opponent to House Speaker Nancy Pelosi and promised to cut spending and help small businesses create jobs.

Herseth Sandlin, a leader of the Blue Dog Coalition of fiscally conservative House Democrats, touted her credentials as a moderate who opposed Pelosi on several high-profile measures, including the Affordable Care Act. She played down her party affiliation, leaving it out of her campaign literature. The incumbent received help from the state's Democratic Party, which sought to make an issue of Noem's 20 speeding tickets and other traffic violations over two decades; she received six notices for failing to appear in court. She responded to the criticism by saying that she was not proud of her driving record and was working to be a better example to young drivers. Noem won 48%-46%.

In Washington, Noem was named one of two freshman class representatives to the GOP leadership. In 2011, she opposed the Environmental Protection Agency's proposal to regulate dust as part of air quality standards, arguing it would hurt farmers and ranchers. She joined her party in backing a budget that eliminated an Agriculture Department flood control program, but later requested federal disaster aid to cope with South Dakota's spring flooding - a move that led state Democrats to accuse her of hypocrisy. She worked on other issues of local interest, including House passage of a measure to transfer ownership of nine cemeteries in the Black Hills from the federal government to the communities that have managed them.

Noem became a favorite with activists on the right, drawing a cheer at the Conservative Political Action Conference in 2011 when she declared, "A lot of us freshmen don't have a whole lot of knowledge, necessarily, about the way that Washington, D.C., is operated. And, frankly, we don't really care." Though her voting mostly followed the Republican leaders' wishes, she distanced herself from them at times. At a 2012 town hall meeting, she told voters that she understood their anger toward House Speaker John Boehner for striking a deal with the Obama White House on taxes and spending to avoid a "fiscal cliff." She said, "What bothers me is that we don't get out there and tell the American people that the House has already passed these bills that extended all the tax rates."

Noem kept open bridges to GOP leaders. On the House-Senate conference committee that hammered out the final terms of the farm bill enacted in 2014, she won approval of a livestock disaster program that was retroactive. Noem authored a provision that gave the Forest Service additional tools to fight the pine beetle, which had caused considerable damage in the Black Hills.

In 2015, she scored a coup by gaining a seat on Ways and Means. That became the first time since 1978 that South Dakota did not have a member on the Agriculture Committee - a topic of some partisan grumbling at home, though Noem defended the broad spurview of her new panel. She said that the "abysmal" customer service by the Internal Revenue Service was "inexcusable." In April 2016, the House passed her bill to prevent the IRS from rehiring employees who had previously been fired for misconduct. In early 2017, she said that she would seek to improve crop insurance coverage in the farm bill scheduled for 2018.

As a co-chair of the Congressional Caucus on Women's Issues, she worked for bipartisan policies that affect low-income children. "There's so many times I've been in on a discussion on a bill or policy where if the women weren't in the room, it wouldn't have been an adequate solution; it wouldn't have been something that worked for our country," she told the Christian Broadcasting Network.

In 2012, Noem was challenged by Democrat Matt Varilek, a former aide to Democratic Sen. Tim Johnson. Varilek impressed local observers by raising close to $1 million and hitting Noem on missing Agriculture Committee hearings. Noem raised $2.8 million and won by a comfortable 57%-43%. She has won easily since then.

Noem gave serious thought to running for the Senate in 2014, even after former Republican Gov. Mike Rounds said that he was seeking the seat of retiring Sen. Johnson. Less than a week after the 2016 election, she announced her plan to run for governor. Republicans were likely to retain her House seat. She turned down inquiries that she consider serving as Agriculture Secretary for President Donald Trump. Although she criticized as "horrific" his campaign comments about groping women, Noem kept on mostly positive terms with Trump and his policies.

★ TENNESSEE ★

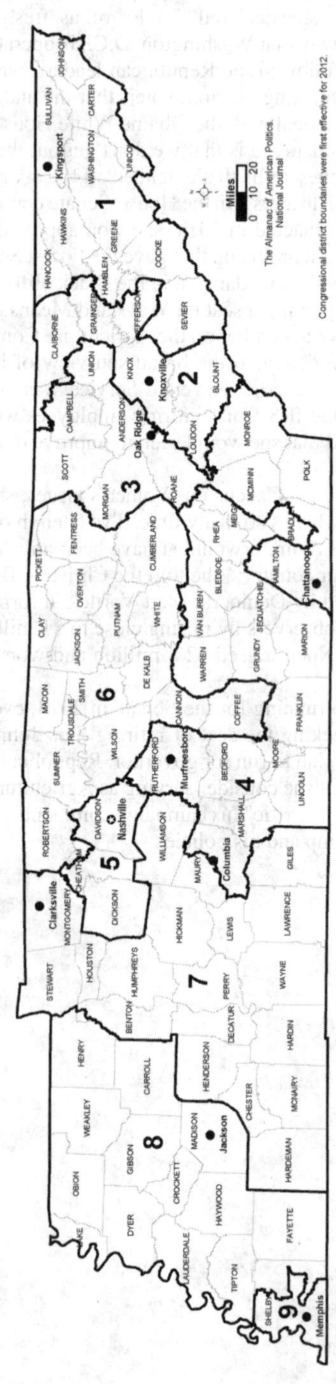
The Almanac of American Politics.
National Journal
Congressional district boundaries were first effective for 2012.
Miles
0 10 20
1
2
3
4
5
6
7
8
9
Kingsport
Knoxville
Oak Ridge
Chattanooga
Murfreesboro
Nashville
Columbia
Clarksville
Jackson
Memphis
SULLIVAN
JOHNSON
CARTER
WASHINGTON
UNICOI
HAWKINS
GREENE
HANCOCK
HAMBLEN
COCKE
CLAIBORNE
GRAINGER
JEFFERSON
SEVIER
UNION
KNOX
BLOUNT
CAMPBELL
ANDERSON
LOUDON
MONROE
SCOTT
ROANE
MCMINN
POLK
MORGAN
FENTRESS
CUMBERLAND
RHEA
BRADLEY
PICKETT
OVERTON
BLEDSOE
HAMILTON
CLAY
PUTNAM
WHITE
VAN BUREN
SEQUATCHIE
JACKSON
WARREN
GRUNDY
MARION
MACON
SMITH
DE KALB
CANNON
COFFEE
FRANKLIN
TROUSDALE
SUMNER
WILSON
RUTHERFORD
BEDFORD
MOORE
LINCOLN
MARSHALL
ROBERTSON
DAVIDSON
WILLIAMSON
GILES
MAURY
CHEATHAM
MONTGOMERY
DICKSON
HICKMAN
LEWIS
LAWRENCE
STEWART
HOUSTON
HUMPHREYS
PERRY
WAYNE
BENTON
DECATUR
HARDIN
HENRY
CARROLL
HENDERSON
CHESTER
MCNAIRY
WEAKLEY
GIBSON
MADISON
HARDEMAN
OBION
CROCKETT
HAYWOOD
FAYETTE
LAKE
DYER
LAUDERDALE
TIPTON
SHELBY

Tennessee, once a political battleground, is no longer. It has become one of the most solidly Republican states in the country, with just a few pockets of blue in its biggest cities. That said, Tennessee still has an active strain of moderate Republicanism, embodied by its senators, Lamar Alexander and Bob Corker, and its governor, Bill Haslam.

Tennessee is almost 500 miles across, closer in the east to Dover, Delaware, than to Memphis, and closer in the west to Dallas, Texas, than to Johnson City. It has had a fighting temperament since the days before the Revolutionary War, when the first settlers crossed the Appalachian ridges and headed for the rolling country in the watersheds of the Cumberland and Tennessee rivers. Tennessee became a state in 1796, the third state after the original 13. Its first congressman was a 29-year-old lawyer who was the son of Scots-Irish immigrants: Andrew Jackson. Jackson, who killed two men in duels, was a general who led Tennessee volunteers - it's still called the Volunteer State - to battle against the Creek Indians at Horseshoe Bend in 1814 and against the British at New Orleans in 1815. He was the first president from an interior state, elected in 1828 and 1832, and was a founder of the Democratic Party, now the oldest political party in the world. Jackson was a strong advocate of the union, but 16 years to the day after his death, Tennessee voted to join the Confederacy. (Today, Jackson's own party largely disowns him, while President Donald Trump made a pilgrimage to his gravesite just weeks after being sworn in.) But Tennessee is a state with a certain civility: Both Confederate and Union generals paid respectful calls on the widow of President James K. Polk, who stayed carefully neutral, in her Nashville mansion.

Tennessee also was a cultural battleground for much of the 20th century. On one side were the Fugitives, writers like John Crowe Ransom and Allen Tate, who contributed to "I'll Take My Stand," a manifesto calling for retaining the South's rural economy and heritage. (Today, the state remains second in the country in most types of tobacco production, third in tomatoes, and fifth in hay and snap beans.) The state is also known for the momentous 1925 trial in which high school biology teacher John T. Scopes in Dayton defied a state ban on teaching evolution in public schools. The legal confrontation in the Rhea County Courthouse featured William Jennings Bryan for the prosecution and Clarence Darrow, a member of the American Civil Liberties Union, for the defense. Bryan won the trial, but Darrow is said to have won the argument by effectively presenting before a national audience the case for evolution. In 1960, John Lewis, a student at Nashville's Fisk University organized sit-in protests at segregated lunch counters at Kress, Woolworth and McClellan stores. The protests sparked confrontations, arrests and ultimately a bombing that destroyed the home of the defense attorney for the protestors. That prompted Nashville Mayor Ben West to make a public appeal calling for an end to discrimination in the city. Within a few weeks, stores began to integrate their lunch counters and Nashville later became the first major city in the South to desegregate public facilities. The campaign became a template for student-run civil rights efforts throughout the South that Lewis, who eventually became a Georgia congressman, would heroically lead. Against this backdrop were business leaders who created the first supermarket (Piggly Wiggly), Holiday Inn, and Moon Pies, and who made FedEx a global leader. The New Deal-era creation of the federal Tennessee Valley Authority also provided the state with bountiful energy, from a mix of coal, nuclear and hydropower plants.

Music is another strong Tennessee tradition. East Tennessee is one of the original homes of bluegrass music and mountain fiddling. Gospel music has long been centered in Nashville, which is also home to the Southern Baptist Convention and a center for religious publishing; justifiably, Nashville is known as the "buckle of the Bible Belt." Country music got its commercial start in Nashville, with broadcasts of the Grand Ole Opry from Ryman Auditorium in 1925, and it remains the capital of country music today. The Mississippi lowlands around Memphis, which is economically and culturally the metropolis of the Mississippi Delta, gave birth to the blues in the years from 1890 to 1920, and the blues were in turn the inspiration for Elvis Presley and countless other rock 'n' roll musicians beginning in the 1950s and 1960s. Presley's Graceland mansion is now one of the state's major tourist destinations, and the tourism bureau celebrated when Tennessee drew more than 100 million visitors for the first time in 2014. The state's musical roots have also generated television success, led by the ABC and Country Music Television hit *Nashville*; Tennessee now ranks seventh in the country for film-industry employment.

While Tennessee's economy trailed the nation's through much of the 20th century, its open climate for entrepreneurism enabled it to grow mightily in the 1980s and 1990s. The absence of strong unions made Tennessee attractive, as did the relative lack of bitter racial discord, with the obvious exception being the assassination of Martin Luther King Jr. in Memphis in 1968. Republican Gov. Lamar

Alexander (now a senator) was a deft salesman in his efforts to bring foreign auto plants to Middle Tennessee and in 1983, Nissan opened a plant in Smyrna, south of Nashville. It has since built another and relocated its U.S. headquarters to Tennessee. Volkswagen built a $1 billion "green" plant for the Passat in Chattanooga that, after a $900 million investment, is now being used to build the Atlas, a new midsize crossover SUV. Today, the state's automotive industry employs 118,000 people in 88 of the state's 95 counties

During the Great Recession, Tennessee had unemployment rates in double digits for more than a year, peaking at 11.1 percent; by mid-to-late 2016, it was in the vicinity of the national average. The state's population has grown by 4.8 percent since 2010, with especially rapid expansion in the Nashville area; Davidson County grew by 9.2 percent while suburban Rutherford and Williamson counties increased by 17.4 percent and 19.6 percent, respectively. Growth in Knox County (Knoxville) and Hamilton County (Chattanooga) grew in the mid-single digits over the same span, but Shelby County (Memphis) lagged with growth of less than 1 percent. Tennessee's population is 17 percent black and 6 percent Hispanic; it has more than 322,000 immigrants, about 5 percent of the state population. In the long-term, however, the state faces challenges to compete in the global economy because its workforce is neither highly skilled nor particularly healthy. Tennessee ranks among the bottom 10 states in the attainment of bachelor's degrees, and the 2016 edition of *America's Health Rankings* placed Tennessee 44th in overall health status, due in part to high rates of obesity, diabetes and smoking. The state's median income is 16 percent below the national average. Meanwhile, a 2015 Federal Reserve Board study found the state's tax system to be the country's most regressive. While Tennessee has some of the nation's lowest overall tax rates, its heavy reliance on the sales tax, which supplies more than half of annual state revenue, means that a disproportionate share of taxes flow from low- and middle-income households. And unlike most states that exempt food and clothing from sales taxes, Tennessee does not. Tennessee is one of seven states that do not have a payroll or state income tax. In 2014, voters by an almost a 2-1 margin ratified a constitutional amendment banning the adoption of any state or local personal income or payroll tax.

For more than a century, Tennessee's political divisions were rooted in Civil War loyalties. In two referenda on secession (first rejecting it in February 1861 and then embracing it in June after the attack on Fort Sumter) most East Tennessee counties voted heavily for the Union and have remained heavily Republican ever since. But pro-secession counties in Middle and West Tennessee long voted heavily Democratic, some even for liberal presidential candidates like George McGovern and Michael Dukakis. Reform-minded liberal Democrats Estes Kefauver and Albert Gore Sr. became national figures, with reliable enough backing from Tennessee's yellow-dog Democratic majority to vote for civil rights bills. Gore was defeated in 1970, but he lived to see his son twice elected vice president before his death in 1998.

As the Democrats' cultural liberalism strained the ancestral loyalties of rural voters in West and Middle Tennessee, and as the surging growth in the ring of counties around Nashville created a new voting bloc that was conservative both economically and culturally, Republicans gained the upper hand. In 2004, as George W. Bush was handily carrying the state, Tennessee voters elected a Republican majority in the state Senate. By 2008, the Republicans won a 50-to-49 majority in the state House, and by 2012, with President Barack Obama at the top of the Democratic ticket, Republicans won supermajorities in both chambers. In the space of a decade, Democrats went from controlling all three branches of state government to being barely relevant in the capital. Today, only five other states (Idaho, Kansas, South Dakota, Utah and Wyoming) have wider GOP legislative supermajorities than Tennessee, leaving Republican lawmakers with few restraints – even a governor from their own party – to push strongly conservative legislation. The rump Democratic Party has become largely urban and more progressive as old-style conservative Democrats have fallen by the wayside. The only significant base of power for Democrats at the moment is in the mayor offices, which they now hold in Memphis, Nashville, Chattanooga and Knoxville; at least one former Democratic mayor, Karl Dean of Nashville, is a serious candidate for governor in 2018.

This political lineup was reinforced in the 2016 presidential election, which Trump won by 26 points,a margin six points wider than Mitt Romney's in 2012. Trump won 61,000 more votes than Romney had,while Hillary Clinton underperformed Barack Obama's 2012 total by 90,000 votes. Just three counties voted Democratic in both elections. Two were the state's largest -- Shelby (Memphis) and Davidson (Nashville) – and both provided Clinton with a modestly wider margin than Obama had seen four years earlier. The third county to remain blue was Haywood, which has a slight black majority. One county– 42 percent black Hardeman -- switched from Obama to Trump. All other counties voted Republican in both elections, although two of the bigger ones – Knox County (Knoxville) and Williamson County(the southwest suburbs of Nashville) – gave Trump narrower margins than they had given Romney.

Population		**Race and Ethnicity**		**Income**	
Total	6,499,615	White	74.7%	Median Income	$45,219 (43 out of 50)
Land area	41,235	Black	16.7%		
Pop/ sq mi	157.6	Latino	4.9%	Under $50,000	54.2%
Born in state	60.8%	Asian	1.6%	$50,000-$99,999	29.2%
		Two races	1.7%	$100,000-$199,999	13.5%
Age Groups		Other	0.3%	$200,000 or more	3.2%
Under 18	23.0%			Poverty Rate	17.6%
18-34	22.8%	**Education**			
35-64	39.8%	H.S grad or less	47.5%	**Health Insurance**	
Over 64	14.6%	Some college	27.6%	With health insurance coverage	87.2%
		College Degree, 4 yr	15.9%		
Work		Post grad	9.0%		
White Collar	33.8%			**Public Assistance**	
Sales and Service	41.9%	**Military**		Cash public assistance income	3.1%
Blue Collar	24.4%	Veteran	9.3%		
Government	14.0%	Active Duty	0.3%	Food stamp/SNAP benefits	17.1%

Voter Turnout			
2015 Total Citizens 18+	4,828,366	2016 Pres Turnout as % CVAP	52%
2016 Pres Votes	2,508,027	2012 Pres Turnout as % CVAP	53%

Legislature	
Senate:	5D, 28R
House:	26D, 73R

Presidential Politics

2016 Democratic Primary		
Hillary Clinton (D)	245,930	(66%)
Bernie Sanders (D)	120,800	(32%)
2016 Republican Primary		
Donald Trump (R)	333,180	(39%)
Ted Cruz (R)	211,471	(25%)
Marco Rubio (R)	181,274	(21%)
Ben Carson (R)	64,951	(8%)
John Kasich (R)	45,301	(5%)

2016 Presidential Vote		
Donald Trump (R)	1,522,925	(61%)
Hillary Clinton (D)	870,695	(35%)
Gary Johnson (L)	70,397	(3%)
2012 Presidential Vote		
Mitt Romney (R)	1,462,330	(59%)
Barack Obama (D)	960,709	(39%)

Most of Tennessee is part of the Jacksonian belt of America running along the Appalachians, territory that has turned more and more Republican since 2000. In 2008, Barack Obama carried Memphis' Shelby County, which is about half African-American, and Nashville's Davidson County, but he won only four of the state's other 93 counties. In 2016, Hillary Clinton also won Shelby and Davidson and one other, Haywood, in western Tennessee. Donald Trump won the other 92 counties on his was to a 61%-35% victory.

For 2008, Tennessee set its primary on Super Tuesday, but did not see much campaigning. Clinton defeated Barack Obama 54%-40%. In 2016, Clinton defeated Vermont Sen. Bernie Sanders 66%-33%. Sanders won only three rural counties in western Tennessee. Recent GOP primaries have offered more mixed results. In 2008, Mike Huckabee carried most of rural Tennessee and Shelby County, abutting his native Arkansas, and won with 34 percent of the vote. John McCain carried Knoxville and its suburbs and won 32 percent. Mitt Romney carried most of metro Nashville and got 24 percent. In 2012, Rick Santorum won with 37 percent, well ahead of Romney's 28 percent. In 2016, Trump defeated Texas Sen. Ted Cruz 39%-25% and carried 94 of the state's 95 counties. But his five worst performing counties were the five largest GOP primary vote producers on Super Tuesday in the Volunteer State: Hamilton,

Knox (Knoxville), Davidson, Shelby, and Williamson, which Trump lost to Florida Sen. Marco Rubio. Rubio, who was endorsed by Republicans Gov. Bill Haslam and former Senate Majority Leader Bill Frist, finished third with 21 percent.

Congressional Districts

115th Congress Lineup	7R 2D	114th Congress Lineup	7R 2D

Republicans swept the governorship and both houses of the Tennessee legislature in 2010, earning unbridled authority to reverse the jig-sawed map Democrats had drawn in 2002. Back then, Democrats had created a fragile arrangement that gave them a 5-4 edge for eight years. Tennessee's cultural shift away from Democrats rendered the map a ticking time bomb even before the next redistricting. In 2010, Republicans defeated one incumbent and had double-digit wins in two open seats where the incumbents may have seen the handwriting on the wall. That gave them 7-2 control of the delegation, which has not been seriously threatened since.

In early 2011, there was chatter that Republicans would seek more revenge by splitting Nashville Democrat Jim Cooper's 5th District four ways. But Republicans determined the move too risky and, in January 2012, passed a map strengthening Cooper and straightening most district lines across the state. They had enough maneuvering room to tweak two of the districts to remove potential primary foes for two of their GOP incumbents. Democrats comfortably control the Memphis-based 9th plus the 5th. Even in the unlikely event that Republicans lose control of the process, that scenario seems likely to prevail for another decade following the redistricting in 2022.

Governor

Bill Haslam (R)

Elected 2010, term expires 2019, 2nd term; b. Aug. 23, 1958, Knoxville, TN; Emory U., B.A. 1980; Presbyterian; Married (Crissy); 3 children.

Elected Office: Knoxville Mayor, 2003-2011.

Professional Career: Manager, Director and President, Pilot Corp., 1980-2003; President of e-strategies, Consultant, Saks Inc., 1999-2001.

Office: Tennessee State Capitol, 1st Floor, Nashville, 37243; 615-741-2001; Fax: 615-532-9711; Website: tn.gov/governor.

Election Results

Election	Name (Party)	Vote (%)
2014 General	Bill Haslam (R)	951,796 (70%)
	Charles V. "Charlie" Brown (D)	309,237 (23%)
	John Jay Hooker (I)	30,579 (2%)
	Shaun Crowell (C)	26,580 (2%)
2014 Primary	Bill Haslam (R)	570,997 (88%)
	Mark "Coonrippy" Brown (R)	44,165 (7%)

Prior winning percentage: 2010 (65%)

As mayor of Knoxville and then governor of Tennessee, Republican Bill Haslam has won plaudits for his practical approach to governing and his low-key personal manner. But he has often sparred with the more conservative members of his own party in the GOP-controlled state legislature, and he declared that he would not vote for Donald Trump in 2016, even though Trump was poised to win the state by 26 points. During his two terms, he has notched significant achievements in education and transportation policy.

Haslam is a product of Knoxville's most influential and powerful family. His father, James, made a fortune by building a single gas station into a chain of Pilot stations, which expanded into an empire of more than 650 travel centers and truck stops in 43 states and Canada. Pilot Flying J is among the largest private companies in the nation, with sales in excess of $38 billion. *Forbes* estimated that the governor, who has a 15 percent stake in the family business, has a net worth of $2 billion. The family has financed numerous projects around the state, many of them at the University of Tennessee. Republican Sen. Lamar Alexander once served on the company's board, and GOP Sen. Bob Corker was a college roommate of James Haslam III, Bill's older brother, who in 2012 became owner of the Cleveland Browns football team. In 2014, the company paid $92 million to avoid criminal prosecution and settle a federal investigation into allegations that it schemed to defraud customers of rebates.

Bill Haslam was a teenager attending the prestigious Webb School in Knoxville when his mother died at the age of 42. Her death prompted Haslam to examine his faith more deeply and he became active in Young Life, a Christian outreach ministry for high school students. Haslam went to Emory University, where he met his future wife, Crissy Garrett, a Memphis native, whose father trained with famed heart surgeon Michael DeBakey. Before graduating in 1980 with a history degree, Haslam thought he might teach high school history for a couple of years and then go to seminary. But one day when he was jogging with his father he asked about a possible role in the family business. His father encouraged the idea. Haslam worked in different aspects of the company and became its president in 1995, but he was always unsure about making his entire career at Pilot, and in 1999 he became the chief executive officer of Saks Direct, the online retail arm of Saks Fifth Avenue. In 2001, Haslam left that post and became a consultant for Saks. According to a lengthy profile of the Haslam family in the *Knoxville News Sentinel*, Haslam was taking a break in Florida in 2001 when he happened to go on a bike ride with Corker, a longtime family friend and the newly elected mayor of Chattanooga. During the ride, Corker described the impact a mayor can have, which piqued Haslam's interest. Haslam floated the idea of running for mayor of Knoxville to a group of friends at Cedar Springs Presbyterian Church. The feedback was encouraging, and he decided to run in 2003.

His Democratic opponent, Madeline Rogero, a nonprofit executive and former Knox County commissioner, depicted him as an inexperienced elitist. He won by 2,000 votes out of nearly 30,000 cast, even though he raised nearly four times as much money as his opponent. He reached out to Rogero and her supporters and embraced some of the issues she championed, such as environmental sustainability. He brought together interested groups to work out a plan for South Knoxville's waterfront and to end homelessness, and he reduced property taxes to their lowest levels in 50 years. He even hired Rogero to serve as the city's director of community development. He gained a reputation as a moderate and was reelected in 2007 with 87 percent of the vote.

Haslam was one of several prominent Republicans who ran to succeed term-limited Democrat Phil Bredesen as governor in 2010, including Chattanooga-area Rep. Zach Wamp and Lt. Gov. Ron Ramsey, both of whom ran to Haslam's right. Haslam's family company became a frequent punching bag. In April 2009, state Attorney General Robert Cooper announced that Pilot was among 16 companies and individuals that settled claims of gasoline price gouging. "When you have that many employees, there are bound to be occasional issues," Haslam responded. He spent more than $9 million -- more than Wamp and Ramsey combined -- and maintained a double-digit lead in polls while collecting endorsements from the state's largest newspapers, which praised his pragmatism. He easily won the August primary with 47 percent of the vote, to 29 percent for Wamp and 22 percent for Ramsey. Haslam was considered the favorite in the general election over Democrat Mike McWherter, a businessman and the son of former Gov. Ned McWherter. Haslam again had the financial advantage, outspending McWherter by a 6-to-1 margin, and he won, 65%-33%, the largest margin of victory for an open-seat gubernatorial race in Tennessee since the 1970s. He lost only the counties containing Memphis and Nashville and three rural counties.

Haslam came into office determined to replicate the inclusive style he used as mayor. He met with teachers over lunch around the state to seek their input. He promised to increase funding for elementary education programs but asked state departments to provide cuts of up to 3 percent. At the same time, he showed his conservative bona fides by proposing a ban on class-action lawsuits and a broad-based illegal immigration bill that would include enhanced powers for law enforcement modeled Arizona's tough law. His budget, which cut $1 billion in spending, passed with overwhelming support. His administration worked out a deal in October with online retailer Amazon to add $350 million in new distribution locations in the state, with the potential to create 3,500 jobs, in exchange for tax breaks.

With Tennessee's economic climate improving, Haslam in 2012 called for relatively small but politically popular reductions in both the state sales tax on food and the state inheritance tax. He also called for more spending in other areas, including cash grants to businesses to expand or locate in the state and a 2.5 percent pay hike for state employees. After saying he would "probably" sign a bill to protect the teaching of "weaknesses" in evolution and other scientific theories, he let it become law without his signature. But he disappointed social conservatives by using his first veto on a measure that would have allowed campus organizations at Vanderbilt University to bar members who disagree with the philosophy of the organization. He also angered conservatives by retaining Democratic as well as gay employees and hiring a Muslim woman as a state economic development official. He brushed aside the criticism, telling the *Knoxville News Sentinel*: "In the end I think it is about, how do we get the very best people to work for the state of Tennessee."

To the delight of Republicans in the legislature, in December 2012 Haslam decided against creating a state-based health insurance exchange as part of President Barack Obama's new health care law. He also announced plans to push a limited school voucher program, though he pulled the plug after Senate Republicans sought a more expansive bill. His relationship with at least some tea party-aligned legislators increasingly became strained. Rep. Rick Womick called Haslam "a traitor to the party" for his past efforts to defeat some of his legislative opponents in party primaries. Lt. Gov. Ron Ramsey and some conservative GOP supporters, including Americans for Prosperity, an advocacy group funded by billionaires Charles G. and David H. Koch, sought to oust three state Supreme Court justices who were facing judicial retention elections in August 2014. The justices, critics argued, bore responsibility for appointing Cooper to be attorney general; Cooper, a Democrat, had not joined other state attorneys general in a lawsuit challenging the Affordable Care Act. Haslam refused to aid Ramsey's effort against the justices, which was ultimately unsuccessful. Haslam's own reelection bid in 2014 was a breeze. He faced unknown political novice Charlie Brown, whose biggest public notice came from saying he'd like to strap Haslam into the electric chair and "give him about half the jolt." Haslam won, 70%-23%. After his victory, Haslam was elected chairman of the Republican Governors Association.

Searching for a way to extend health coverage without backing Medicaid expansion, Haslam crafted Insure Tennessee, a proposal that would set up two programs for those with incomes up to 138 percent of the poverty rate -- vouchers for people whose employers offered insurance that they could not afford, and savings accounts that could be tapped to pay health costs. Haslam called a special session of the legislature in early 2015 to consider his proposal, but the Tennessee chapter of Americans for Prosperity mobilized 200 activists to lobby lawmakers to reject the plan, and when it met in February, a state Senate committee rejected the measure, effectively killing it. During the regular session of the legislature, Haslam won approval for his budget, which included $166 million in incentives for Volkswagen to expand its Chattanooga plant, but another Senate committee overwhelmingly rejected a resolution that would have enabled him to implement his version of Medicaid expansion. Democrats urged Haslam to call another special session to push through his proposal, but the governor demurred, saying supporters first needed to show that they had changed some minds. He also signed a measure to review and replace Common Core educational standards.

In 2015, Haslam signed a bill requiring a 48-hour waiting period before an abortion could be performed, and he signed another requiring medical facilities or physician's offices to be licensed as ambulatory surgical treatment centers if they perform more than 50 abortions in a year. Those measures came after voters in 2014 endorsed an amendment to the state constitution giving state lawmakers more power to regulate abortions. Haslam also signed a measure preventing local governments from barring people with handgun-carry permits from bringing weapons to playgrounds, parks and sports fields, even though as mayor of Knoxville he had backed a ban on guns in city parks. The following year, the legislature sent him a bill to let public-university employees with handgun-carry permits take their weapons onto campus; Haslam allowed it to become law without his signature, saying he would have preferred allowing university administrators to make the decision on such policies.

In May 2016, Haslam allowed another bill to become law without his signature; it allowed Attorney General Herbert Slatery to sue the federal government over refugee resettlement. Haslam continued to grapple with socially conservative measures sent to him by the legislature. He signed one, a measure that allows therapists and counselors to turn down LGBT clients. But he vetoed another bill – only his fourth veto -- that would have made Tennessee the first state to make the Bible the official state book. Haslam said it "trivializes the Bible, which I believe is a sacred text." An override effort in the House failed. In September, Haslam called a special session to get the state's DUI law into compliance with federal standards, hoping to avoid the loss of $60 million in federal highway funds. Lawmakers enacted the fix. Then, in December, Haslam led the state's response to a massive fire in Gatlinburg, a Smoky Mountain town that attracts 11 million tourists annually. Nearly 18,000 acres burned, killing 13 people and destroying more than 2,400 structures.

To kick off his final two years in office in 2017, Haslam proposed tuition-free community college for all adults in the state, $100 million in pay raises for schoolteachers, and – in a significant move backed by the legislature -- increases in the gasoline and diesel fuel taxes to fund infrastructure, partially offset by cuts in business and grocery sales taxes. Meanwhile, attention had already turned to the race to succeed Haslam in 2018. Possible GOP candidates included Rep. Diane Black, state Senate Majority Leader Mark Norris, state House Speaker Beth Harwell, state Sen. Mark Green and outgoing economic development commissioner Randy Boyd. The leading potential Democratic candidate was former Nashville Mayor Karl Dean.

In May 2017, Haslam signed a bill to make it easier for rural areas to get access to the internet.

Senior Senator

Lamar Alexander (R)

Elected 2002, term expires 2020, 3rd term; b. Jul 03, 1940, Maryville; New York University Law School, J.D.; Vanderbilt University (TN), B.A.; Presbyterian; Married (Leslee Buhler Buhler); 4 children; 6 grandchildren.

Elected Office: TN Governor, 1979-1987.

Professional Career: President, University of TN, 1988-1991; U.S Education Secretary, 1991-1993; Co-Director, Empower America, 1994-1995; Professor, Harvard University JFK School Of Government, 2001-2002.

DC Office: 455 DSOB 20510, 202-224-4944, Fax: 202-228-3398; Website: alexander.senate.gov.

State Offices: Blountville, 423-325-6240; Chattanooga, 423-752-5337; Jackson, 731-664-0289; Knoxville, 865-545-4253; Memphis, 901-544-4224; Nashville, 615-736-5129.

Committees: *Appropriations*: Commerce, Justice, Science & Related Agencies, Department of Defense, Department of the Interior, Environment & Related Agencies, DOL, HHS & Education & Related Agencies, Energy & Water Development (Chmn), Transportation, HUD & Related Agencies. *Energy & Natural Resources*: Energy, National Parks, Public Lands, Forests & Mining. *Health, Education, Labor & Pensions (Chmn)*: Children & Families, Employment & Workplace Safety, Primary Health & Retirement Security. *Rules & Administration.*

Group Ratings

	ADA	ACLU	AFL-CIO	LCV	ITI	COC	HAFA	ACU	CFG	FRC
2016	-	17%	-	41%	100%	88%	26%	44%	52%	0%
2015	10%	C	15%	24%	C	100%	C	50%	59%	100%

Almanac Ratings 2015

	Economy	Social	Foreign	Composite
Liberal	48%	5%	41%	31%
Conservative	52%	95%	59%	69%

Key Votes of the 114th Congress

1. Keystone pipeline	Y	5. National Security Data	Y	9. Gun Sales Checks	N
2. Export-Import Bank	N	6. Iran Nuclear Deal	Y	10. Sanctuary Cities	Y
3. Debt Ceiling Increase	Y	7. Puerto Rico Debt	Y	11. Planned Parenthood	Y
4. Homeland Security $$	Y	8. Loretta Lynch A.G	N	12. Trade deals	Y

Election Results

Election	Name (Party)	Vote (%)		Cand. Spent	Ind. Exp. Support	Ind. Exp. Oppose
2014 General	Lamar Alexander (R)	849,629	(62%)	$9,378,379	$973,069	$294,406
	Gordon Ball (D)	437,251	(32%)	$971,372		
	Joe Wilmoth (C)	36,063	(3%)			
2014 Primary	Lamar Alexander (R)	330,088	(50%)			
	Joe Carr (R)	269,169	(41%)			
	George Flinn (R)	34,207	(5%)			

Prior winning percentages: 2008 (65%), 2002 (54%)

Lamar Alexander, elected to the Senate in 2002, has been at the center of Tennessee and Republican politics for a half-century. With a start as an aide in the Senate and the Nixon White House, his career includes: governor of Tennessee, state university president, Education secretary and Republican presidential aspirant. His Senate years have brought added distinction, including as a GOP leader and chairman of the Health, Education, Labor and Pensions (HELP) Committee. Having brought a high-level consistency to his work, he faces the question of whether to retire in 2020, at age 80, at the peak of his influence.

Alexander grew up Maryville, in East Tennessee between Knoxville and the Smoky Mountains, the son of a principal and a teacher. He started piano lessons at age 4 and still plays. He went to Vanderbilt University, where in the early 1960s he wrote editorials for the school newspaper urging integration. He got a law degree from New York University and then clerked for Judge John Minor Wisdom of the 5th Circuit Court of Appeals. In 1966, he wrote to Republican Howard Baker, volunteering to work in Baker's Senate campaign against Democrat Frank Clement. Instead, Baker gave him a job on his Washington staff. In 1969, on Baker's recommendation, Alexander got a job with President Richard Nixon's congressional liaison, Bryce Harlow. On a trip back to Tennessee in 1970, he met Memphis dentist Winfield Dunn, who was running for governor, and Alexander agreed to manage his campaign. Dunn became the first Republican elected governor in 50 years.

Back then, Tennessee governors were limited to one four-year term. Alexander decided that next time, he would be the candidate. So in 1974, at age 34, he ran a conventional campaign for governor. In that Watergate year, he lost to Democratic Rep. Ray Blanton, 55%-44%. He ran again in 1978-by then, Tennessee changed its law to allow two consecutive terms-and undertook a more colorful campaign strategy. Wearing a red plaid shirt that would become his signature, Alexander walked 1,000 miles across Tennessee. He defeated Blanton, 56%-44%.

After the election, Blanton issued many pardons of criminals, who, it turned out, were paying him bribes. The U.S. attorney urged that Alexander be sworn in three days early, and Democratic legislative leaders and the state's chief justice agreed. In a hurried ceremony, Alexander took the oath and named Fred Thompson, famous for his work as Baker's chief counsel in the Senate Watergate hearings, as special prosecutor. In office, Alexander attended a White House meeting where President Jimmy Carter urged governors to get Japanese auto manufacturers to build cars in the United States; he flew to Japan and persuaded Nissan to build its first American plant in Rutherford County. He also persuaded General Motors to build its innovative Saturn plant in Williamson County. The plants became the spark plugs of rapid growth in the counties around Nashville. Alexander was reelected in 1982, 60%-40%. After leaving office, he spent six months living in Australia, writing a book appropriately called *Six Months Off*. In 1988, he became president of the University of Tennessee, and in 1991, President George H.W. Bush tapped him as Secretary of Education.

In 1996, Alexander sought a bigger prize: the White House. He campaigned as a plaid-shirt-wearing outsider. Of members of Congress, he said, "Cut their pay and bring them home!" He called for decentralizing government, and he had a superb fundraising organization that made Nashville a leading Republican money source in the nation. He hired top-notch political consultants and organizers in Iowa and New Hampshire. Alexander finished third in the Iowa caucuses, behind Bob Dole and Pat Buchanan and ahead of Steve Forbes. New Hampshire was his best chance for a breakthrough. Five days before the primary, Dole shrewdly ran ads attacking Alexander. Buchanan was likely to do well in New Hampshire, but probably could not be nominated. If Buchanan finished second in New Hampshire, he would likely become Dole's chief rival, smoothing Dole's path to the nomination. Dole's strategy worked: Buchanan won 27 percent of the vote, edging Dole with 26 percent. Alexander, in third place with 23 percent, dropped by the wayside and Dole cruised to the nomination.

Alexander started to run for president again in 1999, but the shirt grew old and the outsider themes failed to resonate. George W. Bush dominated the race, and left little room for Alexander. His fundraising faltered, and after his disappointing sixth-place finish in the August 1999 straw poll, he dropped out and endorsed Bush. He was later interviewed by Dick Cheney as a possible vice presidential nominee, but Cheney kept the job for himself. Critical of the frontloaded presidential primary calendar, Alexander in 2007 was a chief co-sponsor of legislation to implement a system of rotating regional primaries.

In March 2002, less than a month before the filing deadline, Thompson, by then a senator, announced that he would not seek reelection. He gave Alexander a heads-up on his decision, allowing him to get his campaign underway shortly after the announcement. Republican Rep. Ed Bryant of suburban Memphis also got into the race. On talk radio shows, Alexander ran a series of "plain talk" ads taking conservative stands on taxes, charter schools, and oil drilling in the Arctic National Wildlife Refuge. Bryant's ads urged, "Don't be plaid. Be solid for Bryant," and he attacked Alexander for increasing sales and gasoline taxes as governor. Alexander won, 54%-44%.

In the general election, his opponent was Democratic Rep. Bob Clement of Nashville, the state's largest media market. Clement, with a relatively moderate voting record that supported the Bush tax cuts and the 2002 Iraq war resolution, depicted Alexander as a political insider who became wealthy through political connections. Alexander countered that Clement, while public service commissioner in the 1970s, served on the board of one of the banks of Jake Butcher, whose banks imploded in scandal in the 1980s. Clement maintained that it was an advisory board and his work on it occurred a decade before the scandal. Alexander prevailed, 54%-44%, winning handily in his native (and ancestrally Republican) East Tennessee. Clement carried his base in Davidson County and rural counties in Middle Tennessee, but Alexander carried the fast-growing ring of suburban counties around Nashville. In West Tennessee, Alexander made inroads among Memphis blacks and carried the rural counties. Six years later, prominent Democrats passed on Alexander's reelection and he easily defeated former state Democratic Chairman Robert Tuke, 65%-32%, carrying 94 of 95 counties, including Memphis's black-majority Shelby County. It was the highest percentage ever for a Tennessee Republican senator.

In his early years in the Senate, Alexander sought to become part of his party's leadership. When his home-state colleague Bill Frist retired in 2006, GOP Whip Mitch McConnell of Kentucky was poised to replace Frist as GOP leader. Alexander courted votes to take McConnell's spot as whip. After the election, former majority leader Trent Lott of Mississippi got into the contest. Although Alexander claimed he had sufficient votes to win, Lott prevailed, 25-24. When Lott resigned from the Senate in December 2007, GOP Conference Chairman Jon Kyl was elected whip and Alexander ran for conference chairman. North Carolina's Richard Burr also ran and pulled support from younger conservatives. Alexander won, 31-16, although he showed deference to those on his right by striving to be inclusive.

Alexander holds the unusual mark of attaining a high-ranking Senate GOP leadership post only to resign from it, because he said the job interfered with his attempts at bipartisanship. In September 2011, he baffled much of Washington by announcing that he was resigning as Conference chairman-a rare move in a town where people seldom relinquish power voluntarily. "Stepping down from the Republican leadership will liberate me to spend more time working for results on issues that I care most about," he said. He insisted that he was still a "very Republican Republican."

For the most part, Alexander has stuck to consensus party positions. He opposed the Democrats' health care overhaul, telling the *Tennessee Tribune* that it was "arrogant in its dumping of 15 million low-income Americans into a medical ghetto called Medicaid that none of us or any of our families would ever want to be a part of for our health care." After the Newtown, Connecticut school massacre in 2012 sparked debates over gun control, he told MSNBC: "I think video games are a bigger problem than guns, because video games affect people."

Alexander also sought out bipartisan alliances, and has often found them-with an interest in home-state energy and environment issues. He joined Delaware Democrat Tom Carper on a bill to limit emissions of carbon dioxide and other pollutants, and to create a system of emissions trading. Air pollution had been high in Knoxville and threatened the tourism industry in the Great Smoky Mountains area. To counter the effects of a federal court ruling, he also pushed to restrict emissions from coal-fired power plants. In 2009, he actively opposed the Democrats' cap-and-trade bill to create a system of emissions trading, even though it was similar to the one he had supported with Carper. In 2011, he was one of six Republicans to cross party lines and oppose a move by Sen. Rand Paul of Kentucky to oppose an EPA regulation that limited smog. "There's a lot I admire about our neighbors in Kentucky, including their two distinguished United States senators, but I don't want their dirty air blowing into Tennessee," Alexander told the Senate.

On immigration reform, Alexander joined another Delaware Democrat, Sen. Chris Coons, to introduce a measure in 2012 to create a new temporary visa for immigrants working in high-tech fields.

He was one of 14 Republicans to support the Gang of Eight's comprehensive reform bill that passed the Senate in 2013. Alexander voted for President Barack Obama's Supreme Court nominee, Sonia Sotomayor in 2009, although he voted against his other nominee to the high court, Elena Kagan, a year later. He cited Kagan's action as Harvard Law School dean barring military recruiters from the school.

In 2011, Alexander helped craft bipartisan legislation to enable states to compel online retailers to collect sales taxes from consumers after previous attempts to implement Internet sales taxes failed to get traction. The issue had been especially divisive in Tennessee, where Amazon.com began building distribution centers but dragged its feet on collecting sales taxes. He was a co-sponsor of the controversial Stop Online Piracy Act, which was opposed by much of Silicon Valley but had the support of Nashville's country music artists and songwriters, who were worried about Internet piracy. When public opposition to the bill grew, with an Internet "black out" day sponsored by Wikipedia and Google, he conceded that it had little chance of passage.

On the HELP committee, Alexander worked on successful bills to help states ensure special education teachers meet federal standards, to give parents more choice in special education services, and to create summer academies for teachers and students to study American history. As a former secretary of Education, Alexander opposed greater involvement by the federal government in federal student loans, comparing it to the "European-Soviet higher education model." On a key labor issue for their state, Alexander and fellow Tennessee Republican Bob Corker held up the Federal Aviation Administration authorization in spring 2010 over their opposition to a House provision increasing the power of labor unions to organize Memphis-based FedEx.

In 2014, hoping to avoid the fate of Indiana Sen. Richard Lugar, a moderate who had lost a 2012 primary to a tea-party challenger, Alexander kicked off his reelection bid early, announcing a team that included popular Republican Gov. Bill Haslam and the entire GOP Tennessee delegation except for scandal-ridden Rep. Scott DesJarlais. Some worried that a tea party-aligned rival, state Rep. Joe Carr, could catch fire in the increasingly conservative state. Alexander took no chances, spending a combined $8 million in the primary and the general. He won the August primary, 50%-41%, then defeated Knoxville Democratic attorney Gordon Ball by more than 30 points in the fall.

As chairman of the Appropriations Subcommittee on Energy and Water Development when Republicans took Senate control in 2015, Alexander gained an opportunity to promote his long-time goals of nuclear and alternative energy. He has advocated for 100 new nuclear power plants over the next 20 years and conversion of half the country's automobiles to electric power. When the Senate overwhelmingly passed his subcommittee bill in May 2016, it included funds for new nuclear-energy technologies, including next-generation small modular reactors, plus research and other incentives for wind, solar and hydroelectric power.

Taking over as HELP committee chairman, Alexander was determined to revise the No Child Left Behind education law. He had inveighed against the 2001 law's theory that the federal government should hold states accountable for students' progress. In early 2015, he joined with Sen. Patty Murray of Washington, the senior Democrat on the panel, to propose an overhaul that restored local authority while providing new protections for low-income families. As a former university president and former pre-school teacher, they were a formidable bipartisan duo. In a significant legislative action, the Senate in December 2015 sent the bill to Obama on an 85-12 vote. Alexander was enthusiastic about the final bill. "It will unleash a flood of excitement and innovation and student achievement that we haven't seen in a long time," he said.

Bipartisanship on education didn't last long. When President Donald Trump nominated Betsy DeVos as Education Secretary, Alexander defended her strong advocacy of charter schools against unified Democratic opposition. Overriding objections from Democratic Senators who wanted additional time for hearings during which DeVos sometimes struggled to respond, he said that he was using the same committee procedures that Democrats followed when they were in the majority and handled the nominees of a Democratic president. "I'm trying to be fair," he said in January 2017. Outside of Alexander's office in Nashville, Tennessee teacher unions and other liberal advocacy groups protested the inexperience of DeVos with public schools. Alexander said that she was "on our children's side." In an unprecedented action, Vice President Mike Pence broke the 50-50 Senate tie to confirm DeVos.

The conflict over Trump's nominees paled compared to the challenge facing Alexander and Senate Republicans on their pledge to replace the Affordable Care Act. As chairman, he was eager to find a bipartisan solution, which initially seemed a steep challenge. After having spent six years "shooting at each other" following enactment of the law, he cautioned, "Building consensus in an environment like that is hard to do. But if we keep in mind that we're trying to help people who are hurting and trying to keep people from being hurt, then that will encourage consensus." Given that his committee had held numerous hearings, Alexander said that he accepted McConnell's plan to draft an alternative in a

Republican working group. "There's nothing new in the bill, really. We've debated it and heard it for six years," he said, as Republicans struggled to find consensus.

Speculation began early over Alexander's intentions when his term expires in 2020. In January 2017, the *Knoxville Times Free Press* wrote that Alexander advisers dismissed a report that "GOP insiders" expected that he will retire and that former professional football quarterback Peyton Manning, who first gained fame playing at the University of Tennessee, was a potential successor. Term-limited Gov. Bill Haslam has been cited as perhaps a more realistic option.

Junior Senator

Bob Corker (R)

Elected 2006, term expires 2018, 2nd term; b. Aug 24, 1952, Orangeburg, SC; University of Tennessee, B.S.; Presbyterian; Married (Elizabeth Corker); 2 children.

Elected Office: Chattanooga Mayor, 2001-2005.

Professional Career: Owner, Bencor Corporation, 1978-1990; Commissioner, TN Department of Fin. & Admin., 1995-1996; Owner, Corker Group, 1982-2006.

DC Office: 425 DSOB 20510, 202-224-3344, Fax: 202-228-0566, corker.senate.gov.

State Offices: Chattanooga, 423-756-2757; Jackson, 731-664-2294; Jonesborough, 423-753-2263; Knoxville, 865-637-4180; Memphis, 901-683-1910; Nashville, 615-279-8125.

Committees: *Aging*. *Banking, Housing & Urban Affairs*: Financial Institutions & Consumer Protection, National Security & International Trade & Finance, Securities, Insurance & Investment. *Budget*. *Foreign Relations (Chmn)*: Africa & Global Health Policy, East Asia, the Pacific & International Cybersecurity Policy, Europe & Regional Security Cooperation, Internat'l Dev Instit & Internat'l Econ, Energy & Environ Policy, Near East, South Asia, Central Asia & Counterterrorism, State Dept & USAID Mngmnt, Internat'l Ops & Internat'l Dev, West Hem Crime Civ Sec Dem Rights & Women's Issues.

Group Ratings

	ADA	ACLU	AFL-CIO	LCV	ITI	COC	HAFA	ACU	CFG	FRC
2016	-	17%	-	0%	80%	100%	50%	81%	74%	100%
2015	15%	C	0%	4%	C	92%	C	63%	83%	91%

Almanac Ratings 2015

	Economy	Social	Foreign	Composite
Liberal	46%	0%	31%	26%
Conservative	54%	100%	69%	74%

Key Votes of the 114th Congress

1. Keystone pipeline	Y	5. National Security Data	N	9. Gun Sales Checks	N
2. Export-Import Bank	Y	6. Iran Nuclear Deal	Y	10. Sanctuary Cities	Y
3. Debt Ceiling Increase	N	7. Puerto Rico Debt	Y	11. Planned Parenthood	Y
4. Homeland Security $$	Y	8. Loretta Lynch A.G	N	12. Trade deals	Y

Election Results

Election	Name (Party)	Vote (%)	Cand. Spent	Ind. Exp. Support	Ind. Exp. Oppose
2012 General	Bob Corker (R)	1,506,443 (65%)	$8,472,064	$6,789	
	Mark E. Clayton (D)	705,882 (30%)			
2012 Primary	Bob Corker (R)	389,613 (85%)			
	Zach Poskevich (R)	28,311 (6%)			

Prior winning percentages: 2006 (51%)

Republican Bob Corker, elected in 2006, is a pragmatist who has shown skill in making bipartisan deals. As chairman of the Foreign Relations Committee, the junior senator from Tennessee tried to shape his party's often-fractious approach on international affairs. He sought to tamp down the partisan edge of Senate Republicans in dealing with President Barack Obama, including on the nuclear deal with Iran and on economic sanctions against Russia. With his independence and his success in business, Corker found common ground with Donald Trump during the 2016 presidential campaign and reportedly was considered for both vice president and secretary of state. Corker remains ambitious, including possible opportunities outside of the Senate.

Corker was born in South Carolina, grew up in Chattanooga, and graduated from the University of Tennessee in 1974 with a degree in industrial management. (He roomed with Jimmy Haslam, the older brother of Tennessee Gov. Bill Haslam.) Just a few years out of college, he started a construction company, which he sold before he turned 40 (he was the Senate's sixth-wealthiest member in 2014, with estimated assets of $44.5 million, according to the Center for Responsive Politics). Before he sold his company, Corker helped to create Chattanooga Neighborhood Enterprise, a non-profit organization designed to get low-income families into affordable housing.

In 1994, he ran for the Senate, finishing second in the Republican primary to Bill Frist, who went on to defeat Democratic incumbent Jim Sasser that year and eventually became majority leader. After his defeat, Corker was named state finance commissioner by Republican Gov. Don Sundquist. After 18 months, he returned to private business, purchasing two real estate and development companies in Chattanooga. In 2001, he won election as Chattanooga mayor and got credit for reducing violent crime and revitalizing the city's waterfront.

While still in his first term as mayor, Corker announced in 2004 that he would run to succeed Frist, who stuck to his initial campaign promise to serve just two terms. By the end of the year, Corker had raised $2 million. Two former Republican congressmen also ran, Ed Bryant, who had lost to Lamar Alexander in the 2002 Senate primary, and Van Hilleary, who had lost that year to Democrat Phil Bredesen for governor. Corker drew on his personal wealth to introduce himself to voters and defend against attacks that he was insufficiently conservative. Bryant and Hilleary claimed Corker raised property taxes in Chattanooga and criticized his support for abortion rights during his 1994 Senate campaign. Corker called his opponents "ineffective career politicians" and talked about his background as a successful businessman and mayor. He said he was "wrong" on abortion in 1994 and that he opposed the right to abortion except in cases of rape and incest. Corker won by a comfortable margin, 48 percent to 34 percent for Bryant and 17 percent for Hilleary, carrying nearly every county east of Nashville and a half-dozen west of it.

The Democratic nominee was Rep. Harold Ford, Jr., of Memphis. Youthful, ambitious, and telegenic, Ford was an attractive candidate. The son of former Rep. Harold Ford, Sr., he was elected to the House in 1996, months after graduating from law school, and his record was sufficiently moderate to make him a competitive statewide candidate. For much of the general election campaign, Corker failed to gain traction and it appeared that he might defy Tennessee's recent Republican trend in national elections. His efforts to frame Ford as too liberal for Tennessee fell flat in the face of Ford's centrist, even conservative, positions on illegal immigration, the Iraq war, border security, and same-sex marriage. Ford put Corker on the defensive about his business dealings.

Nevertheless, as the scion of a Memphis African-American political dynasty, Ford had to weather distractions caused by several family members, including his uncle, former state Sen. John Ford, who was indicted on federal corruption charges. Heading into the final weeks of the campaign, the election appeared to be a dead heat. But Corker gained momentum after Republicans launched a series of attack ads and zeroed in on Ford's personal story, characterizing it as a life of privilege. Corker's ads described his own rise from a laborer who poured concrete. In late October, a controversial ad with purported on-the-street interviews with regular people, included an attractive young, blonde, and white woman, claiming that she had "met Harold at the *Playboy* party," a reference to news stories that Ford had attended a Super Bowl party hosted by *Playboy* magazine. The commercial ended with the woman saying, "Harold, call me." Critics called the ad racial politicking, while Republicans insisted it was about values. Ultimately, Corker won, 51%-48%, with whites voting 59%-40% for Corker, and blacks voting 95%-4% for Ford.

In his early years, Corker was a reliable vote for Republicans on issues such as opposing embryonic stem cell research and troop withdrawal timetables in Iraq, but he broke with the party on some high-profile issues. He backed an energy bill to raise gas mileage standards for cars and trucks. He joined a bipartisan effort to promote a 2008 energy bill allowing offshore drilling while also emphasizing renewable energy sources. In 2007, he voted for a Democratic bill to expand the State Children's Health Insurance Program and played a crucial role in negotiations to renew federal funding for the state's TennCare Medicaid program. In 2015, his *Almanac* vote ratings ranked him 45th most conservative of 54 Republican Senators, placing him near the center of the Senate and his home-state GOP colleague Lamar Alexander, especially on economic issues. "I can be a conservative Republican, but I can sit down and find common ground with a liberal Democrat on some issues," he told McClatchy newspapers. "For people to look at that as somehow compromising principles is ridiculous."

Corker got a seat on the Banking Committee, where he was unusually active for a junior member on financial issues. When committee ranking Republican Richard Shelby of Alabama refused to participate in bipartisan talks about a bailout for the collapsing financial industry, Corker engaged in meetings with Democratic Chairman Christopher Dodd of Connecticut that produced the $700 billion Troubled Asset Relief Program. In late 2008, when the big three domestic automakers sought a multi-billion-dollar bailout, Corker criticized auto executives who appeared before the committee, chiding their plans for securing government loans and waiting for mergers. He told the head of Chrysler: "While this is happening, you're going to be going to spas and getting facials and hopefully finding someone to marry you." In December, Corker offered an alternative proposal that required retiring autoworkers to accept most of their benefits in stock rather than in cash, forced bondholders to accept a steep cut in the value of their bonds, and required wages and benefits comparable to American employees of foreign automakers. Corker's conditions angered big auto's supporters in Detroit, but they were in large part followed by President Barack Obama's task force on the auto companies.

On banking regulation, which was the big issue before the Banking Committee in 2009 and 2010, Dodd encouraged Corker to engage in informal meetings with Virginia Democrat Mark Warner. "I think he's somebody who's willing to work with anybody who he thinks has a good idea," Warner later told the Associated Press. When Dodd concluded that negotiations with Shelby on the bill were going nowhere, Corker again agreed to try to work with the chairman. Corker continued to be troubled by what he regarded as the too-big-to-fail treatment of major banks and other financial institutions. When Dodd unveiled what became the Dodd-Frank bill without any Republicans, Corker complained that the unilateral action was ordered by the Obama White House. But he was also critical of fellow Republicans for a major strategic error in not reaching a compromise and said that they had overstated assertions that the bill would increase the likelihood of bailouts.

Corker jumped into the debate over cutting federal spending in 2011, and again, did so in a bipartisan way. He and Missouri Democrat Claire McCaskill sponsored a bill to require reductions of federal spending from 24.7 percent of gross domestic product to the 40-year historic average of 20.6 percent, with the White House budget office charged with making simultaneous cuts in entitlement and discretionary spending if Congress did not meet the targets. When Republican leaders and Obama brokered a deal to raise the debt ceiling in August 2011, some hardline conservatives carped that the legislation failed to achieve substantial deficit reduction, as Corker had proposed. He voted for the deal.

His reelection bid in 2012 was far easier than his first. After beating four Republicans in a primary with 85 percent of the vote, he faced Democrat Mark Clayton, a self-described author and anti-gay rights activist. Within days of the primary, the state Democratic Party disavowed Clayton and made it known that it didn't consider him to be a legitimate nominee. Corker won, 65%-30%.

Following his reelection, Corker drew attention for several bipartisan moves. He complained in September 2013 that his more junior GOP colleagues Ted Cruz of Texas and Mike Lee of Utah sought a government shutdown for what amounted to publicity purposes. He was the only Senate Republican to vote that year with Democrats in favor of considering a minimum-wage increase. He and Warner teamed again in 2014 to tackle housing finance reform, crafting a framework that became incorporated in a draft of Banking committee leaders. He worked with Connecticut Democrat Chris Murphy on a proposal to boost the federal gasoline tax to save the depleted Highway Trust Fund.

While all of these activities made Corker an unusually busy senator, he recently has made his biggest mark at the Senate Foreign Relations Committee. He became the ranking Republican after Indiana's Richard Lugar, one of the Senate's most respected voices on foreign policy, was defeated in the 2012 GOP primary. Corker has acknowledged that he had initially possessed little practical experience in international relations, but he has made up for lost time: By his count, he had visited more than 70 countries.

At times, Corker was more tolerant of the Obama administration than were other Republicans. He was among the Senators voting to ratify the New START arms-reduction treaty with Russia in 2010 after getting assurances from appropriators of funding for the modernization of nuclear weapons. In 2013, rather than joining other GOP panel members in pummeling outgoing Secretary of State Hillary Clinton for her handling of the terrorist attacks in Benghazi Libya, Corker suggested that the incident be used as an opportunity to craft a policy "that reflects the dynamics of the region as they really are today."

As time went on, though, Corker became more critical of the Obama administration's foreign policy. He complained that its officials did not sufficiently consult Congress on military engagement in Libya. He was an early backer of arming Syrian rebels opposed to Bashar Assad and of sending lethal aid to Ukraine, in both cases getting out in front of Obama. By August 2014, Corker's exasperation reached the point where he wrote a blunt op-ed for *The Washington Post* blasting the president as unreliable on foreign affairs. Citing the White House's handling of the situations in Syria, Libya and Eastern Europe, Corker concluded, "More often than not, the president doesn't hit singles and doubles; he just balks. It is hard to watch."

As the panel's new chairman when Republicans took control in 2015, Corker faced an immediate dilemma prompted by Obama's nuclear talks with Iran. Just-elected Republican Sen. Tom Cotton of Arkansas circulated a letter written directly to Iran's leaders, warning them that the Senate could undo any deal Obama struck. In all, 47 GOP senators signed on, including Majority Leader Mitch McConnell. But the move, and the letter's seemingly condescending tone, drew fire from many corners, and not just from Democrats. The seven Republicans who declined to sign it included Corker, who had been engaged in less confrontational, bipartisan negotiations to ensure that any final deal be approved by Congress. Corker's ability to craft broadly agreeable terms won over Democrats; his bill ended up passing the Senate 98-1 (with Cotton as the only dissenting vote) and was signed by Obama in May. In an op-ed, Corker wrote that congressional approval was so important because "a nuclear Iran is a threat to every nation and would lead to a less safe and secure world. It also could create a dangerous arms race with the possibility of a nuclear weapon falling into the hands of terrorists." When the Senate and House reviewed the deal later that year, a majority in each chamber-including all Republicans plus some influential Democrats--voted against it. Corker's deal allowed Obama to prevail with the support of only one-third of the members in either chamber.

Corker showed comparable dexterity in his early dealings with Trump. During the final weeks before the Republican convention in July 2016, Corker had multiple meetings with Trump and his top advisers, to discuss his possible selection as running-mate. Corker said that he concluded that the position failed to play to his policy strengths. "It's a highly political job, and that's not who I am," he told *The Washington Post*. "I know the things I'm good at doing. And knowing what a candidate for vice president has to do, it's just not the right thing for me, and I don't think it's the right thing for them." During the summer, he told *The Tennessean* that he might be selected as Secretary of State or Treasury in a Trump administration. Those post-election discussions apparently were limited. After Trump selected Rex Tillerson for the State Department, Corker aided the nominee as Foreign Relations chairman and rejected Democratic demands for disclosure of additional financial information.

Corker has been widely expected to seek reelection in 2018, although he has mentioned his interest in seeking the open seat for governor. Although it is unlikely that Corker will switch to the gubernatorial contest, GOP Gov. Bill Haslam, who is term limited in 2018, has expressed an interest in running for the seat if it is open. Regardless of who is the Republican nominee, no Democrat has been elected to the Senate from Tennessee since 1990 and that is not likely to change anytime soon.

FIRST DISTRICT

Phil Roe (R)

Elected 2008, 5th term; b. Jul 21, 1945, Clarksville; Austin Peay State University (TN), B.S.; University of Tennessee, Memphis, M.D.; Methodist; Married (Pam Roe); 3 children (3 from previous marriage); 2 grandchildren.

Military Career: U.S Army Medical Corps, 1973-1974.

Elected Office: Johnson City Commission, 2003-2009, vice Mayor, 2005-2007, Mayor, 2007-2009.

Professional Career: Obstetrician/gynecologist, 1970-2008.

DC Office: 336 CHOB 20515, 202-225-6356, Fax: 202-225-5714, roe.house.gov.

State Offices: Kingsport, 423-247-8161; Morristown, 423-254-1400.

Committees: *Education & the Workforce*: Early Childhood, Elementary & Secondary Education, Health, Employment, Labor & Pensions. *Veterans' Affairs (Chmn)*.

Group Ratings

	ADA	ACLU	AFL-CIO	LCV	ITI	COC	HAFA	ACU	CFG	FRC
2016	-	11%	-	0%	83%	100%	75%	96%	83%	100%
2015	0%	C	10%	0%	C	74%	C	100%	79%	100%

Almanac Ratings 2015

	Economy	Social	Foreign	Composite
Liberal	12%	19%	12%	14%
Conservative	88%	81%	88%	86%

Key Votes of the 114th Congress

1. Keystone Pipeline	NV	5. Puerto Rico Debt	Y	9. Offenses by Aliens	Y
2. Trade Deals	Y	6. Medical Marijuana	NV	10. Troops in Iraq	N
3. Export-Import Bank	N	7. Sanctuary Cities	NV	11. Homeland Security $$	NV
4. Debt Ceiling Increase	N	8. Armor-piercing Bullets	NV	12. Trade Adjustment aid	N

Election Results

Election	Name (Party)	Vote (%)	Cand. Spent	Ind. Exp. Support	Ind. Exp. Oppose
2016 General	Phil Roe (R)	198,293 (78%)	$256,284		
	Alam Bohms (D)	39,024 (15%)			
2016 Primary	Phil Roe (R)	34,272 (82%)			
	Clint Tribble (R)	7,310 (18%)			

Prior winning percentages: 2014 (83%), 2012 (76%), 2010 (81%), 2008 (72%)

Republican Phil Roe, elected in 2008, is one of the House's physicians and he has been closely associated with his former profession. He serves on two committees dealing with health issues, regularly espoused his party's opposition to the Affordable Care Act, and issues his news releases with "M.D." after his name. As a reliable partisan but no bomb-thrower, he was selected by House Republicans to take over in 2017 as chairman of the Veterans' Affairs Committee.

Roe grew up in Clarksville and attended a one-room schoolhouse with no running water. He graduated from Austin Peay State University and received a medical degree from the University of Tennessee. He was a captain in the Army Medical Corps, where he was stationed in South Korea near the Demilitarized Zone. He returned to Johnson City, setting up practice as an obstetrician/gynecologist for 30 years. He delivered nearly 5,000 babies, a useful way to connect with voters. In 2003, the political bug bit Roe, and he was elected to the Johnson City Commission. Roe was chosen by commission members to be vice mayor in 2005 and mayor 2007. When the House seat opened in 2006, Roe competed in a crowded GOP primary. He finished fourth with 17 percent of the vote, behind health care business owner David Davis, who went on to win the general election.

Davis quickly gained a reputation as a combative partisan. Roe challenged him for reelection and embarked on a grass-roots campaign, talking to voters, stumping in restaurants and waving signs at busy intersections. In ads featuring an elderly grandmother trying to fill up her car with gas, Roe criticized Davis for accepting money from oil companies, attacks that resonated as gas prices spiked. Davis outspent the challenger 3-to-1. Roe rebounded to upset Davis, becoming the first challenger in more than 40 years to defeat a House member in Tennessee. His margin of victory was 482 votes. He won the district's two largest counties, Washington and Sullivan, while Davis was strong along the western edge of the district, winning Sevier and Hawkins counties. Roe defeated Democrat Robert Russell with 72 percent of the vote and has been reelected with ease.

Roe's positions mirror the conservative bent of the district. He has an upbeat, folksy demeanor and was among the first House Republicans to join the Tea Party Caucus in 2010. With the GOP takeover of the House, he became chairman of the Education and Workforce Committee's health panel and helped to craft his party's free-market alternatives to the new law. He filed a bill in 2011 seeking to repeal an advisory board that was created to rein in Medicare spending increases. The House passed the measure in 2012, but GOP leaders drew criticism from Democrats - including those who supported the bill - for attaching a provision setting caps on medical damage lawsuit awards, and the bill died in the Senate.

With GOP Rep. Austin Scott of Georgia and the backing of the Republican Study Committee, Roe filed in 2015 a bill to repeal the Affordable Care Act and replace it with what the authors called patient-centered reforms and free-market solutions. He worked on the bipartisan bill that was enacted in 2015 to repeal the "doc fix" reducing payments to doctors with Medicare patients and take other steps to strengthen Medicare. With Democratic Rep. Ami Bera of California, another doctor, Roe sought to limit drug abuse by disposing of prescription drugs that the user no longer needs.

After hearings by the Veterans' Affairs Committee revealed problems with the VA Department's contracting procedures, Roe won approval in 2012 of a provision barring its employees who break the law from receiving bonuses. In December 2016, he won enactment of his bill to require clinicians practicing at the VA to report directly to state licensing boards whenever they witness unacceptable behavior from other VA clinicians. After the election, Roe ran to replace Rep. Jeff Miller of Florida, who was term-limited as committee chairman. He won the contest against two Colorado Republicans - moderate Mike Coffman and conservative Doug Lamborn. "There's no federal agency more in need of reform than the VA," Roe said about his plans as chairman. "I am excited by the opportunity to advance Republican solutions aimed at improving veterans' care."

On an issue with a local connection, Roe voted in 2015 to give trade promotion authority to President Barack Obama which, Roe said, could help the 800,000 Tennesseans with jobs that benefit from trade. He harshly criticized restrictions on coal-fired utility plants in the Obama administration's "clean power plan" as an attempt to "take one industry and try to put them out of business." He has supported the fair tax, which would replace the federal income tax with a 23 percent national retail sales tax. His *Almanac* vote ratings in 2015 were near the center of the House and the second-least conservative of the Republicans from Tennessee.

After the release in October 2016 of Donald Trump's crude comments about women, Roe called them "disgusting, inappropriate and reprehensible," and said that he planned to write-in another Republican for president. Following the election, he said that no Republican would want to reduce the number of Americans with health insurance coverage. When the House GOP deadlocked on an alternative health care plan, Roe insisted that they would find an agreement.

Northeast Tennessee: Kingsport, Bristol, Johnson City

Population		**Race and Ethnicity**		**Income**	
Total	709,547	White	91.9%	Median Income	$38,263 (407 out of 435)
Land area	4,142	Black	2.1%		
Pop/ sq mi	171.3	Latino	3.4%		
Born in state	62.2%	Asian	0.7%	Under $50,000	61.3%
		Two races	1.6%	$50,000-$99,999	27.3%
Age Groups		Other	0.2%	$100,000-$199,999	9.5%
Under 18	20.5%			$200,000 or more	1.9%
18-34	19.7%	**Education**		Poverty Rate	19.3%
35-64	41.4%	H.S grad or less	55.2%		
Over 64	18.3%	Some college	26.1%	**Health Insurance**	
		College Degree, 4 yr	11.7%	With health insurance coverage	86.0%
Work		Post grad	7.0%		
White Collar	29.4%				
Sales and Service	44.2%	**Military**		**Public Assistance**	
Blue Collar	26.4%	Veteran	10.5%	Cash public assistance income	2.3%
Government	7.4%	Active Duty	0.1%		
				Food stamp/SNAP benefits	18.9%

Voter Turnout			
2015 Total Citizens 18+	551,605	2016 House Turnout as % CVAP	46%
2016 House turnout	253,025	2014 House Turnout as % CVAP	25%

2012 Presidential Vote		
Mitt Romney	186,318	(73%)
Barack Obama	65,782	(26%)

2016 Presidential Vote		
Donald Trump	203,651	(77%)
Hillary Clinton	52,237	(20%)
Gary Johnson	6,488	(2%)

Cook Partisan Voting Index: R+28

Between the corduroy-like ridges of the Appalachian chains, as they bend west and then south, the Great Valley of Virginia extends far into northeastern Tennessee. These ridges guide travel today (even the interstates follow the valleys here) just as they guided settlement more than 200 years ago. The land rush immediately after the Revolutionary War populated the area, mostly with Scots-Irish immigrants. These settlers and their descendants were often hot-tempered, fierce folk. In tiny Jonesborough, the early settlers attempted to establish the free state of Franklin in 1784. The original town had an ordinance requiring settlers "to within three years build a brick, stone, or well framed house, 20 feet long and 16 feet wide, and at least 10 feet in the pitche, with a brick or stone chimney" - a sort of early restrictive covenant - and many pioneer cabins, Federal-style mansions, and Greek Revival churches are lovingly preserved today. A young Andrew Jackson made his way from North Carolina to the area, set up a legal practice and became a (typically irascible) judge before moving westward.

The building of the railroads in the 1850s determined the winners and losers for the modern era. The small industrial cities that developed - Johnson City, Kingsport and Bristol, now collectively known as the Tri-Cities - were on the main lines of national commerce before the Civil War. The war had a different political impact here than in most of the South: Mountainous Northeast Tennessee had few slaves and, with its connection to Northern industry, was Union and Republican territory. East Tennesseans twice voted against secession. It remains heavily Republican to this day.

The area developed the sort of industrial economy that produced unions and Democrats in the North. Its skilled labor force, low electric power rates because of the Tennessee Valley Authority and good transportation routes (rail lines and Interstates 26 and 81) spurred growth. Its small cities once boasted major paper and printing plants, although most of them are gone. With companies such as Kingsport-based Eastman Chemical Co. and Bell Helicopters taking the lead, the area has been a strong market for exports. In Sevier County near Knoxville, Gatlinburg and Pigeon Forge (home of Dolly Parton's Dollywood theme park) have more than 10,000 hotel rooms near the entry to the Great Smoky Mountains National Park, the nation's busiest. In 2016, the park had more than 11 million visitors, twice as many as runner-up Grand Canyon. In November 2016, a massive wildfire in Gatlinburg caused 14 deaths and devastating property damage. Two months earlier, Tennessee defeated Virginia Tech in a college football game at the Bristol Speedway, with attendance of 156,990, the most ever for a football game in the United States.

The 1st Congressional District takes in the far northeastern end of Tennessee. Sullivan and Washington counties, which include the Tri-Cities, include 40 percent of the population. Mountain City is where fugitive murderer Tom Dula was captured before being returned to North Carolina for hanging (generations of folk musicians would eventually alter his name to the more familiar "Tom Dooley"). Greeneville was the birthplace of Congressman Davy Crockett and the longtime home of President Andrew Johnson. Over the years, this district's politics haven't budged an inch. It hasn't elected a Democrat to the House since 1878. True to its roots, it gave Donald Trump 77 per cent of the vote: his highest in Tennessee and in the top 2 percent of GOP districts nationwide.

SECOND DISTRICT

John Duncan (R)

Elected 1988, 15th term; b. Jul 21, 1947, Lebanon; George Washington University School of Law (DC), J.D.; University of Tennessee, B.S.; Presbyterian; Married (Lynn Hawkins Duncan); 4 children; 9 grandchildren.

Military Career: TN Army National Guard & U.S Army Reserve, 1970-1987.

Professional Career: Practicing attorney, 1973-1981; Knox County judge, 1981-1988.

DC Office: 2207 RHOB 20515, 202-225-5435, Fax: 202-225-6444, duncan.house.gov.

State Offices: Knoxville, 865-523-3772; Maryville, 865-984-5464.

Committees: *Oversight & Government Reform*: Intergovernmental Affairs, National Security. *Transportation & Infrastructure*: Aviation, Highways & Transit, Railroads, Pipelines & Hazardous Materials.

Group Ratings

	ADA	ACLU	AFL-CIO	LCV	ITI	COC	HAFA	ACU	CFG	FRC
2016	-	29%	-	0%	67%	86%	77%	88%	91%	92%
2015	10%	C	17%	6%	C	68%	C	96%	72%	92%

Almanac Ratings 2015

	Economy	Social	Foreign	Composite
Liberal	9%	14%	52%	25%
Conservative	91%	86%	48%	75%

Key Votes of the 114th Congress

1. Keystone Pipeline	Y	5. Puerto Rico Debt	Y	9. Offenses by Aliens	Y
2. Trade Deals	N	6. Medical Marijuana	Y	10. Troops in Iraq	Y
3. Export-Import Bank	N	7. Sanctuary Cities	Y	11. Homeland Security $$	N
4. Debt Ceiling Increase	N	8. Armor-piercing Bullets	Y	12. Trade Adjustment aid	N

Election Results

Election	Name (Party)	Vote (%)	Cand. Spent	Ind. Exp. Support	Ind. Exp. Oppose
2016 General	John Duncan (R)	212,455 (76%)	$468,376		
	Stuart Starr (D)	68,401 (24%)			
2016 Primary	John Duncan (R)	(100%)			

Prior winning percentages: 2014 (73%), 2012 (74%), 2010 (85%), 2008 (78%), 2006 (78%), 2004 (79%), 2002 (79%), 2000 (89%), 1998 (89%), 1996 (71%), 1994 (91%), 1992 (72%), 1990 (81%), 1988 (56%)

Republican John (Jimmy) Duncan, first elected in 1988, has been a maverick on economic and foreign policy issues, something that has hindered his ascension in the House GOP ranks. He has played a modest legislative role, though he remains well-liked by colleagues and constituents.

His similarly low-profile father, John Duncan, a former mayor of Knoxville who became the senior Republican on the House Ways and Means Committee, had held the seat from 1964 until his death in May 1988. Jimmy Duncan got a bachelor's degree in journalism at the University of Tennessee and a law degree from George Washington University. He practiced law and was a trial judge in the 1980s. When his father died, he won the seat despite a spirited challenge from Democrat Dudley Taylor, a scion of another prominent East Tennessee political family. Taylor attacked Duncan for his ties to scandal-tarred banker and Democratic politician Jake Butcher. Duncan won with 57 percent of the vote. He has been reelected every two years since with at least 71 percent.

Duncan is known for his independence, and *Reason* magazine has listed him as one of the consistent libertarians in the House, both at home and abroad. In the *Almanac* vote ratings, which measure ideological consistency with other lawmakers, Duncan ranked in 2015 among the most centrist - or, in his case, independent - members of the House in the three issue categories.

Duncan lacks the appetite for self-promotion but he often speaks his views on the House floor. Duncan has repeatedly called for an end to U.S. involvement in the war in Afghanistan, which he complained in 2011 was "seemingly endless." In 2002, he was one of six Republicans who voted against the use of force in Iraq. Duncan argued that there was not sufficient proof that Iraqi Leader Saddam Hussein had weapons of mass destruction. In 2011, he voted against the budget compromise that Republicans struck with President Barack Obama to avert a government shutdown. Duncan has consistently opposed international trade deals, regardless of who controls the White House, on the grounds that they give too much power to the president and they are a boon chiefly to giant multinational companies. He objects that the trade agreements have led to excessive deficits in the U.S. balance of payments with other large nations.

On domestic issues, the National Taxpayers Union has named Duncan the most fiscally conservative member of the House. He also has been consistently conservative on social issues. Though he voted for the Violence Against Women Act's reauthorization in 2005, he opposed it in 2013 on economic grounds. He raised eyebrows when he told the *Chattanooga Times Free-Press*: "Like most men, I'm more opposed to violence against women than even violence against men. Because most men can handle it a little better than a lot of women can."

In 2011, Duncan became chairman of Transportation and Infrastructure's Subcommittee on Highways and Transit, where he sought to play a major role in getting a multi-year surface transportation bill into law. He slipped a provision into the bill in 2012 barring the use of federal money to buy red-light traffic cameras, though the cameras are funded by violators' fines and safety advocates said it would have little impact. He has disdained "radical environmentalists" whom he accused in 2010 of being insensitive to rural Americans: "Most of them are city people, anyway. They probably think it would be good if everyone was forced to live in 25 or 30 urban areas, with the country left totally empty."

His contrariness has had its price. Duncan was a candidate for the chairmanship of the Natural Resources Committee in 2003, but Speaker Dennis Hastert skipped over him. When Republicans recaptured the House in 2010, Speaker John Boehner gave the chairmanship to a more loyal ally. In 2006, Duncan made a big push for the top Republican position on the Transportation and Infrastructure Committee. He lost to John Mica of Florida, who had less seniority but was more of a party regular. In 2013, the less-senior Bill Shuster of Pennsylvania got the gavel. Instead, Duncan has been the panel's vice chairman.

Duncan hasn't been shy about seeking funding for local projects, from resurfacing the Foothills Parkway near the Great Smoky Mountains National Park to a rail and trolley system for downtown Knoxville. Another of his legislative interests has been a bill to require the disclosure of contributions to presidential libraries, which the House passed three times. The bill died each time in the Senate. Duncan worked on a bill with Democratic Reps. Louise Slaughter of New York and Tim Walz of Minnesota to require disclosure of those who are compensated for providing political intelligence in Washington.

In Knoxville, Duncan's annual barbecue dinner at the downtown coliseum draws as many as 6,000 people and reinforces his local popularity. His father began the event in 1968. In January 2017, *Knoxville News-Sentinel* columnist Jack McElroy speculated that Duncan could be serving his final term and that the seat might soon be held by somebody other than a Duncan for the first time in more than a half-century. McElroy noted that Duncan's son, John Duncan III, had been interested in the seat. But he left office as elected Knox County trustee after pleading guilty in 2013 to a felony charge of official misconduct for having approved more than $50,000 in official bonuses to himself and several employees. After he completed a year of unsupervised probation, a local judge agreed to dismiss the case. Several other Republicans have been mentioned as potential contenders, including term-limited Knox County Mayor Tim Burchett.

In February 2017, about 300 protesters picketed outside of Duncan's office in Knoxville because of his refusal to hold a town hall meeting. Duncan said that he would not give "shouting opportunities for extremists, kooks and radicals." The history of the district makes it highly unlikely for a Democratic takeover. As McElroy cautioned, "the safest bet" may be that Duncan will win another term.

East Tennessee: Knoxville

Population		**Race and Ethnicity**		**Income**	
Total	721,436	White	86.5%	Median Income	$46,952 (307 out of 435)
Land area	2,321	Black	6.4%		
Pop/ sq mi	310.9	Latino	3.7%		
Born in state	60.4%	Asian	1.5%	Under $50,000	52.6%
		Two races	1.6%	$50,000-$99,999	29.7%
Age Groups		Other	0.3%	$100,000-$199,999	14.2%
Under 18	21.3%			$200,000 or more	3.5%
18-34	23.1%	**Education**		Poverty Rate	16.1%
35-64	39.6%	H.S grad or less	42.8%		
Over 64	16.0%	Some college	28.3%	**Health Insurance**	
		College Degree, 4 yr	17.8%	With health insurance coverage	89.1%
Work		Post grad	11.1%		
White Collar	36.3%				
Sales and Service	42.4%	**Military**		**Public Assistance**	
Blue Collar	21.2%	Veteran	9.3%	Cash public assistance income	2.8%
Government	6.4%	Active Duty	0.1%		
				Food stamp/SNAP benefits	14.6%

Voter Turnout			
2015 Total Citizens 18+	551,735	2016 House Turnout as % CVAP	51%
2016 House turnout	280,856	2014 House Turnout as % CVAP	30%

2012 Presidential Vote		
Mitt Romney	186,362	(67%)
Barack Obama	85,510	(31%)

2016 Presidential Vote		
Donald Trump	188,973	(65%)
Hillary Clinton	86,217	(30%)
Gary Johnson	10,457	(4%)

Cook Partisan Voting Index: R+20

Knoxville, the largest city in East Tennessee, was the state's first capital. It is nestled between mountain ridges where the Holston and French Broad rivers join to form the Tennessee River. It was established not long after the first wave of pioneers came through the gaps and down the mountains of the Appalachian chain. During the Civil War, it was Union territory, and it has remained Republican in allegiance and progressive on civil rights ever since. Its Republican heritage has been affected by another tradition, that of the Tennessee Valley Authority. A bold program when created in the 1930s, it is now part of the fabric of life in East Tennessee, sometimes criticized as it has reached capacity to produce hydroelectric power and begun to rely more on expensive and sometimes poorly functioning nuclear power plants. In a competitive electricity market, TVA has labored under billions of dollars in debt mostly incurred in building its nuclear plants. Heavy ozone pollution in Knoxville led the Environmental Protection Agency to impose growth limits, so TVA spent several billion dollars to reduce pollution at its coal-fired power plants. The result has improved local air quality and the EPA has ruled that the Knoxville area met its ozone standard. With its more rigorous standards, the American Lung Association in April 2016 gave Knoxville an "F" for air quality.

Knoxville has overcome other setbacks and grown, at times robustly. Its 4.7 percent job growth in 2016 ranked 16th among U.S. cities. The University of Tennessee's football complex, Neyland Stadium, on fall Saturdays contains one of the nation's largest crowds, cheering on the Vols. Women's basketball is nearly as popular as football here, and in 2009 Lady Vols' Coach Pat Summitt became the first Division I basketball coach, men's or women's, to win 1,000 career games. She retired in 2012 with a diagnosis of early-onset Alzheimer's disease, after having won 1,098 games and eight national championships, and died in 2016. In spring 2016, a new bridge for walkers and bikers opened across the Tennessee River from the campus to South Knoxville.

The 2nd Congressional District of Tennessee includes Knoxville and Knox County, plus all or part of six mountainous counties to the north and south. More than 60 percent live in Knox County, where the landmark Sunsphere tower from the 1982 World's Fair remains visible from Interstate 40. The heavily Republican district has not elected a Democratic congressman since the early 1850s. With its 65 percent vote for Donald Trump in 2016, the 2nd was at the low end of the seven Republican-held districts in Tennessee.

THIRD DISTRICT

Chuck Fleischmann (R)

Elected 2010, 4th term; b. Oct 11, 1962, New York, NY; University of Illinois, B.A.; University of Tennessee College of Law, Knoxville, J.D.; Roman Catholic; Married (Brenda Fleischmann); 3 children.

Professional Career: Practicing attorney, 1987-2010.

DC Office: 2410 RHOB 20515, 202-225-3271, Fax: 202-225-3494, fleischmann.house.gov.

State Offices: Athens, 423-745-4671; Chattanooga, 423-756-2342; Oak Ridge, 865-576-1976.

Committees: *Appropriations*: Energy & Water Development & Related Agencies, Homeland Security, Labor, Health & Human Services, Education & Related Agencies.

Group Ratings

	ADA	ACLU	AFL-CIO	LCV	ITI	COC	HAFA	ACU	CFG	FRC
2016	-	5%	-	3%	100%	100%	72%	80%	65%	100%
2015	0%	C	8%	3%	C	80%	C	88%	75%	100%

Almanac Ratings 2015

	Economy	Social	Foreign	Composite
Liberal	5%	9%	0%	5%
Conservative	95%	91%	100%	95%

Key Votes of the 114th Congress

1. Keystone Pipeline	Y	5. Puerto Rico Debt	N	9. Offenses by Aliens	Y
2. Trade Deals	Y	6. Medical Marijuana	N	10. Troops in Iraq	N
3. Export-Import Bank	NV	7. Sanctuary Cities	Y	11. Homeland Security $$	N
4. Debt Ceiling Increase	N	8. Armor-piercing Bullets	Y	12. Trade Adjustment aid	N

Election Results

Election	Name (Party)	Vote	(%)	Cand. Spent	Ind. Exp. Support	Ind. Exp. Oppose
2016 General	Chuck Fleischmann (R)	176,613	(66%)	$914,926		
	Melody Shekari (D)	76,727	(29%)	$95,655		
2016 Primary	Charles Fleischmann (R)	31,940	(84%)			
	Geoffery Suhmer Smith (R)	3,069	(8%)			
	Allan Levene (R)	3,056	(8%)			

Prior winning percentages: 2014 (62%), 2012 (62%), 2010 (60%)

Republican Charles (Chuck) Fleischmann was elected in 2010 to succeed GOP Rep. Zach Wamp, who ran unsuccessfully for governor. Fleischmann is more of a team player than the independent-minded Wamp. With his seat on the Appropriations Committee, he pursues funding for the Oak Ridge lab. But he has contended with two primary challenges from Zach's son Weston, in which Fleischmann narrowly prevailed.

When he was a boy, Fleischmann's father, Max, worked in the food services business. Fleischmann lived in Philadelphia and New Jersey before finishing high school in Chicago. He graduated from the University of Illinois in three years with a bachelor's degree in political science. He got his law degree at the University of Tennessee, and started his own firm in Knoxville with his wife, Brenda.

When Zach Wamp opened the seat, Fleischmann ran, saying he was "very, very upset with the way things were going in Washington, D.C." In the primary, health care consultant Robin Smith, a former Republican state party chairwoman, was a formidable opponent. Fleischmann put $544,000 of his own money into the campaign and accused Smith of mismanaging funds when she chaired the GOP. Smith attacked Fleischmann's record as a personal injury lawyer, saying that he had sued gun clubs, Wal-Mart stores and churches, all popular institutions in the state. Fleischmann defended himself by saying, "I make a living standing up for the little guy, people who have traditionally not had a voice and who have been dealt injustices and harm." Fleischmann edged out Smith, 30%-28%. In November, he defeated radio talk-show host John Wolfe, 57%-28%.

Fleischmann has been a conservative mainstay. He is capable of serving up red-meat rhetoric. Asked at a debate for his views on climate change, he responded: "I think we ought to take Al Gore, put him on an iceberg, and put him way out there." Although he opposed the debt ceiling hike in 2011 and the deal to avoid the fiscal cliff in 2013, he has been loyal to GOP leaders on other votes. The *Chattanooga Free Press'* editorial page, in endorsing him for reelection, complained that "his unwillingness to vote against his party … is exasperating."

His position on Appropriations, especially its Energy and Water Development Subcommittee, has given Fleischmann a critical voice on those needs. In February 2017, he hosted House Appropriations Committee chairman Rodney Frelinghuysen on a visit to Oak Ridge to make the case for its "vital work" in science, nuclear clean-up and national security. Fleischmann has repeatedly stressed the need to replace Chickamauga's deteriorating 75-year-old river lock by overhauling the project's funding mechanism, the Inland Waterway Trust Fund, for the estimated $680 million project. When the lock shut down in July 2016 because of cracked concrete, he said that its replacement was "very high on the priority list." With Democratic Rep. Ben Ray Lujan of New Mexico, he co-chaired the Nuclear Cleanup Caucus.

Fleischmann survived two grueling primary fights. In 2012, he drew spirited challenges from the 25-year-old Weston Wamp and dairy magnate Scottie Mayfield. Neither Wamp nor Mayfield was as experienced as Fleischmann, who raised much more money. He won the primary with 39 percent, as Mayfield took 31 percent and Wamp 29 percent. His Democratic general election opponent, acute care physician Mary Headrick, accused him of being in the pocket of special interests and blasted his proposal to cut capital gains tax rates. But she raised just $119,000 to his $1.4 million, and he coasted to a 61 percent win.

Wamp returned for another try in 2014 in what became an even tighter primary. He called himself an "independent-minded conservative," and he courted votes from Democrats, who were eligible to vote in the primary. Fleischmann rebuked him at one debate, saying, "If he wants to run as a Democrat, let him run as a Democrat." Wamp responded that the congressman apparently believed "that Democrats have cooties and you can't talk to them." Fleischmann retorted, "They have got a lot worse than that, Weston." Fleischmann accused Wamp of being a "show horse" and supporting "amnesty" for illegal immigrants. He eked out the primary, 51%-49%. The outcome in many of the counties was exceedingly close, and neither candidate had an obvious base.

In 2016, the scare for Fleischmann was a contest that did not happen. Bo Watson, the veteran speaker pro tem in the Tennessee Senate, said publicly that he was giving serious thought to a primary challenge. Instead, Watson decided to stick with his influential state post. That left Fleischmann with his first easy campaign, but no guarantee for the future.

East Tennessee: Chattanooga, Oak Ridge

Population		**Race and Ethnicity**		**Income**	
Total	717,815	White	82.6%	Median Income	$42,612 (365 out of 435)
Land area	4,570	Black	10.8%		
Pop/ sq mi	157.1	Latino	3.6%		
Born in state	64.1%	Asian	1.2%	Under $50,000	56.4%
		Two races	1.6%	$50,000-$99,999	27.8%
Age Groups		Other	0.3%	$100,000-$199,999	13.1%
Under 18	21.3%			$200,000 or more	2.5%
18-34	21.0%	**Education**		Poverty Rate	18.0%
35-64	40.8%	H.S grad or less	50.2%		
Over 64	16.9%	Some college	28.2%	**Health Insurance**	
		College Degree, 4 yr	13.5%	With health insurance coverage	88.1%
Work		Post grad	8.1%		
White Collar	33.0%				
Sales and Service	41.8%	**Military**		**Public Assistance**	
Blue Collar	25.2%	Veteran	9.7%	Cash public assistance income	3.2%
Government	6.2%	Active Duty	0.1%		
				Food stamp/SNAP benefits	18.0%

Voter Turnout			
2015 Total Citizens 18+	551,525	2016 House Turnout as % CVAP	48%
2016 House turnout	266,006	2014 House Turnout as % CVAP	28%

2012 Presidential Vote		
Mitt Romney	172,227	(63%)
Barack Obama	95,014	(35%)

2016 Presidential Vote		
Donald Trump	181,189	(65%)
Hillary Clinton	83,297	(30%)
Gary Johnson	8,665	(3%)

Cook Partisan Voting Index: R+18

Etching its way through the serrated ridges of East Tennessee, with some of the most vivid scenery in the Appalachian Mountain chain, is the river that gave the state its name. From Knoxville, the Tennessee River cuts through a ridge and then plunges down a long valley to the city of Chattanooga at the Georgia line. There it switches course again, winding around the tabletop Lookout Mountain and then moving into northern Alabama before eventually swinging back north to empty into the Ohio River. Chattanooga was just a village when it became a Civil War battlefield. It then grew to be the industrial "Dynamo of Dixie," rising to prominence as a part of the "New South." Four decades ago, it was labeled America's most polluted city. But regional political leaders, prodded by influential and civic-minded scions of its Industrial Age aristocracy, used creative measures, such as locally built electric shuttle buses, to reduce pollution and to spruce up the city's scenic river banks. With big job cuts at the Tennessee Valley Authority, the region has pinned its hopes for economic growth more on the private sector, including tourism and a large food-service industry that includes the MoonPie and Little Debbie confectioners.

Chattanooga is the state's fourth-largest city and in recent years has been challenging Knoxville for third place. After declining in the 1980s and stagnating in the 1990s, the city has had a double-digit increase since 2000. As old businesses have shut down, new ones have arrived. In 2015, Volkswagen announced a $700 million expansion of its plant for production of its new Atlas, a midsize SUV, that was expected to add 2,000 jobs with VW and nearly 8,000 jobs with suppliers. The announcement came a few months after VW workers turned down an organizing campaign by the United Auto Workers at the plant, though 150 maintenance workers affiliated with the UAW a few months later. Amazon.com has expanded its sprawling distribution center in the area, which is the size of 28 football fields and employs more than 3,000 people. The high-tech industry is transforming more than the local economy; the city features a state-of-the-art, publicly owned, citywide fiber network. Its 10 gigabyte service reportedly makes Chattanooga the largest city with such service. The city features the popular Tennessee Aquarium. Chattanooga has moved closer to the growing orbit of metropolitan Atlanta, which is 110 miles away, and it has been discussed as a site for the latter city's second airport.

The 3rd Congressional District of Tennessee includes Chattanooga, stretches from Georgia to Kentucky, and stops a few miles short of both Alabama and Virginia. A bit more than half of its population is in Chattanooga-based Hamilton County. The district includes the Oak Ridge National Laboratory, which was secretly constructed during World War II in virgin Appalachian forest to house the facility that made uranium isotopes for the Hiroshima bomb. For years, it did not appear on maps. The district contains the Museum of Appalachia in Clinton, which maintains dozens of frontier structures, including a cabin owned by Mark Twain's father. Historically, the area was split politically, with Chattanooga voting Democratic and the mountain counties Republican. Today, it is solidly Republican. Donald Trump won 65 percent of the vote; the 63 percent that Mitt Romney got here in 2012 was his smallest vote in the state's seven Republican-controlled districts.

FOURTH DISTRICT

Scott DesJarlais (R)

Elected 2010, 4th term; b. Feb 21, 1964, Des Moines, IA, IN; University of South Dakota, B.S.; University of South Dakota School of Medicine, M.D.; Episcopalian; Married (Amy DesJarlais); 4 children (1 from previous marriage).

Professional Career: Practicing physician, 1993-2010.

DC Office: 2301 RHOB 20515, 202-225-6831, Fax: 202-226-5172, desjarlais.house.gov.

State Offices: Cleveland, 423-472-7500; Columbia, 931-381-9920; Murfreesboro, 615-896-1986; Winchester, 931-962-3180.

Committees: *Agriculture*: General Farm Commodities & Risk Management, Livestock & Foreign Agriculture, Nutrition. *Armed Services*: Readiness, Seapower & Projection Forces. *Oversight & Government Reform*: Health Care, Benefits & Administrative Rules.

Group Ratings

	ADA	ACLU	AFL-CIO	LCV	ITI	COC	HAFA	ACU	CFG	FRC
2016	-	17%	-	0%	67%	100%	93%	96%	96%	100%
2015	5%	C	0%	0%	C	60%	C	100%	100%	100%

Almanac Ratings 2015

	Economy	Social	Foreign	Composite
Liberal	7%	4%	8%	6%
Conservative	93%	96%	92%	94%

Key Votes of the 114th Congress

1. Keystone Pipeline	Y	5. Puerto Rico Debt	N	9. Offenses by Aliens	Y
2. Trade Deals	Y	6. Medical Marijuana	N	10. Troops in Iraq	N
3. Export-Import Bank	NV	7. Sanctuary Cities	Y	11. Homeland Security $$	N
4. Debt Ceiling Increase	N	8. Armor-piercing Bullets	Y	12. Trade Adjustment aid	N

Election Results

Election	Name (Party)	Vote (%)	Cand. Spent	Ind. Exp. Support	Ind. Exp. Oppose
2016 General	Scott DesJarlais (R)	165,796 (65%)	$531,507		
	Steven Reynolds (D)	89,141 (35%)	$36,471		
2016 Primary	Scott DesJarlais (R)	24,207 (52%)			
	Grant Starrett (R)	20,131 (43%)			

Prior winning percentages: 2014 (58%), 2012 (56%), 2010 (60%)

Republican Scott DesJarlais, elected in 2010, has overcome explosive accusations about his personal life and unexpectedly has survived primary challenges. He has continued to show skills as a campaigner, though he's been less active as a legislator.

DesJarlais grew up in Sturgis, South Dakota. He earned a bachelor's degree in chemistry and psychology from the University of South Dakota in 1987. After receiving his medical degree from the school in 1991, DesJarlais moved to Jasper, Tennessee, where he practiced medicine.

The 2010 House race was DesJarlais' first bid for elected office, and he said it was motivated by his patients' concerns about the foundering economy and their fears about losing their jobs. He challenged Rep. Lincoln Davis, who had been the most conservative Democrat in the Tennessee delegation and had earned the endorsements of the U.S. Chamber of Commerce, the National Rifle Association, and National Right to Life. DesJarlais billed himself as a "doctor, not a politician." Davis made headlines with accusations made by DesJarlais' first wife, Susan, who claimed that he physically intimidated her during their 2000 divorce and threatened to commit suicide.

DesJarlais called the charges "completely false," and the ad exposed Davis to accusations of mudslinging. Davis pointed out his votes against the Democrats' health care overhaul and their cap-and-trade bill to limit greenhouse gas emissions, both unpopular in the district. But his limited cooperation with President Barack Obama in voting for the $787 billion economic stimulus bill cost him votes. DesJarlais won 57%-39%.

DesJarlais has been a mainstream conservative. In the *Almanac* vote ratings for 2015, he ranked near the center of House Republicans. He joined fellow Tennessee Republican Charles Fleischmann in opposing an Energy Department plan to consolidate management of Oak Ridge's Y-12 weapons plant with the Pantex facility in Texas. In 2015, DesJarlais voted against giving John Boehner another term as Speaker, on the basis that "we need a new direction and a fresh approach." Instead, he voted for conservative Rep. Jim Jordan of Ohio. He defended as essential outreach his unusually high spending on constituent mailings. On the flip side, C-SPAN found that he spoke on the House floor only once in 2015-16, the fewest of any House Member who served the full term. "When you speak on the floor, it's usually to an empty House, so I don't think it's the best forum to reach out," he told *USA Today*. In 2017, he joined the Armed Services Committee, where he could tend to the needs of the local Arnold Air Force Base, an advanced testing facility.

Scandal so overshadowed DesJarlais' legislative work that survival has seemed his most significant accomplishment. According to the transcript of a phone recording made prior to his divorce made public a few weeks before the 2012 election, DesJarlais reportedly urged his pregnant mistress - who was one of his medical patients - to get an abortion. He issued a statement accusing opponents of "the same gutter politics" as his earlier race, but he later said in a letter to supporters that he encouraged the abortion because he was trying to get her to admit she wasn't pregnant. Conservatives abandoned him in droves, and national Democrats raced to assist challenger Eric Stewart, who had been seen as a long shot. The district's conservative voters gave DesJarlais the benefit of the doubt, as he defeated Stewart 56%-44%.

He won Rutherford County - the district's largest - by 53%-47%, and he easily won the rest of the district except for three small counties in the Cumberland mountains.

After the election, the state Democratic Party released court transcripts showing that DesJarlais and his ex-wife mutually agreed that she would have two abortions, and that he admitted having sex with at least two patients, three coworkers, and a drug company representative. DesJarlais later acknowledged having used "very poor judgment" but dismissed suggestions that he resign or not run again. In 2013, the Tennessee Board of Medical Examiners fined him $500 and reprimanded him for having sex with multiple patients.

In January 2013, state Sen. Jim Tracy announced a primary challenge for 2014 and began to peel off DesJarlais' donors. Tracy told supporters, "I'm a conservative in word and deed. I'm 100 percent pro-life." Tracy outraised DesJarlais and won endorsements from many in the state's GOP establishment; he had run for an open seat in 2010, and finished third in the primary by only 566 votes behind winner Diane Black. He campaigned on bringing "integrity" to the office, but he was slow to attack DesJarlais directly. The incumbent countered that his personal life was old news, noting that he had been married for 12 years to his second wife. He emphasized his conservative values and efforts in Washington. That message resonated with some voters.

DesJarlais won the high-turnout primary by 38 votes. Five other GOP candidates split 10 percent of the vote. Tracy had a big lead in the population center of Rutherford County, but Desjarlais rolled up the vote in the rural areas. After 18 days of recounts, Tracy continued to fault the handling of the election but said that further challenges "would not be the right thing for the Republican Party and the conservative cause in Tennessee." In November, DesJarlais faced a competitive challenge from Democrat Lenda Sherrell, an accountant, who spent more than $1 million. But Republicans rallied around DesJarlais and he won, 58%-35%.

In 2016, his chief Republican challenger was Grant Starrett, a lawyer and real estate investor who worked for Mitt Romney in the 2012 presidential campaign. Starrett moved to the district in 2015 and self-financed nearly $900,000 of the $1.6 million he raised for his campaign. DesJarlais won the four-candidate contest, 52%-43%, again winning all of the counties except for the three in the eastern mountains. In the presidential campaign, Desjarlais was an early supporter of Donald Trump and served as his liaison to the conservative House Republicans in the Freedom Caucus. In October, he criticized what he called the "tepid support" by Speaker Paul Ryan for Trump. That led the liberal *Huffington Post* to headline that the "Congressman who had sex with patients stands by Trump."

Middle Tennessee: Murfreesboro Area

Population		**Race and Ethnicity**		**Income**	
Total	733,717	White	81.4%	Median Income	$46,823 (311 out of 435)
Land area	5,985	Black	8.2%		
Pop/ sq mi	122.6	Latino	5.8%		
Born in state	61.2%	Asian	1.5%	Under $50,000	53.1%
		Two races	2.8%	$50,000-$99,999	31.3%
Age Groups		Other	0.3%	$100,000-$199,999	13.4%
Under 18	23.8%			$200,000 or more	2.3%
18-34	23.3%	**Education**		Poverty Rate	16.2%
35-64	39.2%	H.S grad or less	50.7%		
Over 64	13.7%	Some college	28.1%	**Health Insurance**	
		College Degree, 4 yr	14.4%	With health insurance coverage	87.3%
Work		Post grad	6.8%		
White Collar	30.6%				
Sales and Service	40.6%	**Military**		**Public Assistance**	
Blue Collar	28.8%	Veteran	9.0%	Cash public assistance income	3.0%
Government	6.9%	Active Duty	0.1%		
				Food stamp/SNAP benefits	16.3%

Voter Turnout			
2015 Total Citizens 18+	537,032	2016 House Turnout as % CVAP	47%
2016 House turnout	254,937	2014 House Turnout as % CVAP	27%

2012 Presidential Vote		
Mitt Romney	169,508	(65%)
Barack Obama	86,394	(33%)

2016 Presidential Vote		
Donald Trump	189,318	(68%)
Hillary Clinton	76,133	(27%)
Gary Johnson	7,806	(3%)

Cook Partisan Voting Index: R+20

The invisible line between Republican and Democratic territory during the Civil War in Tennessee ran along Walden Ridge, the westernmost swelling of the Appalachians. This invisible line also separates the Tennessee Valley, which had few slaves and whose economic ties were to the North, from the rolling farmlands of Middle Tennessee, first settled by Andrew Jackson in the 1790s and resolutely Democratic from 1829, when Jackson became the first president to call himself a Democrat. This is an America of small towns, where every hamlet seems to have its own annual festival, like the RC MoonPie Festival in Bell Buckle. Lynchburg is where Jasper Newton Daniel, better known by the nickname "Jack," began brewing his "Old No. 7" whiskey, an operation that continues to this day. In 2016, the company completed a $140 million expansion at its plant, which has 500 workers. Oddly, Moore County, where the distillery is located, is a dry county.

There is an industrial base here as well, particularly in the automobile industry. General Motors launched its Saturn brand in Spring Hill in 1990, igniting growth in the region. When the erstwhile auto giant went bankrupt in 2009, it shut down the factory and furloughed most of its 2,700 employees. Since then, it has had an impressive comeback. Assembly-line production resumed in 2012 on the Chevrolet Equinox, and the plant produces engines and other components for GM assembly plants elsewhere. In January 2017, it added a third shift and raised total employment to 3,300 workers. Nissan has a large engine assembly plant in Decherd in Franklin County and operates a large vehicle production assembly plant in Smyrna, where it also manufactures batteries for its Leaf electric cars. General Mills announced in 2015 a $250 million expansion of its local plant, where 900 workers already produced Yoplait yogurt and Toaster Strudel.

The 4th Congressional District of Tennessee takes in all of these places. About 40 percent of its population is in Rutherford County, which has become part of suburban Nashville. Murfreesboro has more than doubled since 1990, and is the sixth-largest city in the state, with a population exceeding 100,000. This is the most blue-collar of Nashville's major suburban counties and the least-heavily Republican. The rest of the district is a scattering of small towns and rural areas. Dayton is where the famous Scopes Monkey Trial was held in 1925; Scopes was convicted of teaching evolution. This was once reliably Democratic territory. Democrats have become scarce in most of Tennessee outside of Nashville and Memphis. Donald Trump in 2016 won the 4th with 68 percent.

FIFTH DISTRICT

Jim Cooper (D)

Elected 2002, 14th term; b. Jun 19, 1954, Nashville; University of North Carolina, Chapel Hill, B.A., 1975; Oxford University (England), M.A., 1977; Harvard University Law School (MA), J.D., 1980; Episcopalian; Married (Martha Hays Cooper); 3 children.

Elected Office: U.S. House, 1983-1995.

Professional Career: Practicing attorney, 1980-1982; Investment banker, 1995-1999; Founder & partner, investment bank, 1999-2002.

DC Office: 1536 LHOB 20515, 202-225-4311, Fax: 202-226-1035, cooper.house.gov.

State Offices: Nashville, 615-736-5295.

Committees: *Armed Services*: Emerging Threats & Capabilities, Strategic Forces (RMM), Tactical Air & Land Forces. *Oversight & Government Reform*: Health Care, Benefits & Administrative Rules.

Group Ratings

	ADA	ACLU	AFL-CIO	LCV	ITI	COC	HAFA	ACU	CFG	FRC
2016	-	76%	-	82%	83%	79%	17%	8%	10%	0%
2015	55%	C	79%	80%	C	65%	C	21%	10%	0%

Almanac Ratings 2015

	Economy	Social	Foreign	Composite
Liberal	69%	81%	58%	69%
Conservative	31%	19%	42%	31%

Key Votes of the 114th Congress

1. Keystone Pipeline	Y	5. Puerto Rico Debt	Y	9. Offenses by Aliens	N
2. Trade Deals	Y	6. Medical Marijuana	Y	10. Troops in Iraq	N
3. Export-Import Bank	Y	7. Sanctuary Cities	N	11. Homeland Security $$	Y
4. Debt Ceiling Increase	Y	8. Armor-piercing Bullets	Y	12. Trade Adjustment aid	Y

Election Results

Election	Name (Party)	Vote (%)	Cand. Spent	Ind. Exp. Support	Ind. Exp. Oppose
2016 General	Jim Cooper (D)	171,111 (63%)	$439,048		
	Stacy Ries Snyder (R)	102,433 (37%)	$84,834		
2016 Primary	Jim Cooper (D)	(100%)			

Prior winning percentages: 2014 (62%), 2012 (65%), 2010 (57%), 2008 (66%), 2006 (69%), 2004 (69%), 2002 (64%), 1992 (66%), 1990 (69%), 1988 (100%), 1986 (100%), 1984 (75%), 1982 (66%)

Jim Cooper, a Democrat elected in 2002 who also served from 1982 to 1994, is a brainy moderate with a tart tongue - especially when it comes to his own party's leadership. Despite the polarized political climate, he persistently seeks bipartisanship on fiscal matters. He has shifted his legislative focus chiefly to defense issues.

His father, Prentice Cooper, was governor for six years. Jim Cooper, educated at the University of North Carolina, Oxford and Harvard Law School, was first elected in 1982 by defeating Republican Cissy Baker, the daughter of then-Senate Majority Leader Howard Baker. During his first stint in Congress, when his district was mostly rural in contrast to his current district, he spoke out against tobacco use and opposed the National Rifle Association in a state where both were popular. He participated actively in the "Group of Nine" Democrats on the Energy and Commerce Committee that produced a compromise between Michigan Democrat John Dingell, an ally of the auto industry, and California's Henry Waxman, who was pro-environmental regulation, on the Clean Air Act of 1990. In 1994, Cooper ran against Republican Fred Thompson for the Senate seat that Democrat Al Gore had vacated when he was elected vice president; in a bad year for Democrats, Thompson won, 60%-39%.

Cooper went to work as an investment banker in Nashville and as a teacher at Vanderbilt University's business school. In 2002, when the city-based district opened, Cooper joined a flurry of Democratic candidates. His toughest opponent was Davidson County Sheriff Gayle Ray, the first female sheriff in Tennessee, who had support from the Democratic women's fundraising group EMILY's List. Ray attacked Cooper's voting record on abortion. An abortion rights supporter, Cooper said that Ray's charges were inaccurate. He ran positive ads showing his children describing what he does well - banjo playing, helping with homework, getting health care for senior citizens - and what he doesn't do well - cooking, playing basketball. The AFL-CIO and *The Tennessean* endorsed Ray. Cooper had support from the Sierra Club and several smaller newspapers and raised twice as much money as Ray, including $700,000 in self-financing. He won the primary, 47%-23%, in a seven-candidate field. Cooper won the general election easily and has faced no serious reelection challenges.

In his return to Congress, he has served on the Armed Services Committee. He is ranking Democrat on the Strategic Forces Subcommittee, which oversees the nation's nuclear arsenal and usually acts on a bipartisan basis. With Republican Rep. Frank Wolf of Virginia, he called for a panel to examine entitlement spending - an idea that led to President Barack Obama's creation in 2010 of the Simpson-Bowles commission on the national debt. When the House in 2012 debated Cooper's amendment to have a budget resolution based on the commission's recommendations, it drew just 38 votes. *New York Times* columnist Joe Nocera, in a 2011 piece titled "The Last Moderate," praised Cooper as "the House's conscience, a lonely voice for civility in this ugly era." He has introduced numerous measures with GOP support. He said that finding Republicans to support him "is really not hard" but gets overlooked. "The press is only focused on the leaders," he said. "They barely know the names of the backbenchers, and those are the people who can make things happen if they choose to."

One way Cooper builds cooperation is by giving out his cell phone number to everyone. "Phone numbers are kind of a trust issue," he said at a 2013 town hall meeting. "If you trust people, then they will trust you back." It also helps that Cooper eschews name-calling. When others in his party were savaging Republican Paul Ryan of Wisconsin for his budget-cutting proposals in 2011, Cooper said he didn't agree with all of Ryan's proposals but defended him as "genuinely smart and nice and humble and caring." When Speaker John Boehner resigned under pressure in September 2015, Cooper issued a statement that Boehner was "a very honorable man who always tries to do the right thing. ... Unfortunately, he had a nearly impossible job leading an increasingly unreasonable and right-wing party that refuses to work with Democrats for the good of the nation."

Cooper has sought to reform Congress, which he has accused of being "too lazy to prioritize." In 2012, he became the first lawmaker to sign a pledge by the activist group Rootstrikers not to lobby after leaving office. He was an early advocate of limits on spending earmarks - before the earmark moratorium, he had refused for years to seek such special-interest funding - and enforcement of pay-as-you-go rules that require tax cuts or spending increases to be offset elsewhere in the budget. A longtime proponent of increased government oversight, his bill to strengthen the independence of federal inspectors general passed Congress and, despite a veto threat from President George W. Bush, became law in 2008. He has taken the lead in calling for redistricting reform by requiring that each state establish a bipartisan commission to draw House boundaries. His proposed Redistricting Transparency Act would require that such information be made public.

Cooper has been a leader of the fiscally conservative Blue Dog Coalition -- where he has described himself as "the nerd" of the group -- and an advocate of consensus-building among Democrats. He once said of his fellow Democrats under California's Nancy Pelosi, "We're just told how to vote. We are treated like mushrooms most of the time." One reason that the ranks of the Blue Dogs have shrunk, he said, is the fear of retribution. "Lots of things are withheld from members who are not perfectly loyal," he told *Roll Call* in May 2015. In the January 2017 vote for House Speaker, he voted for Democratic Rep. Tim Ryan of Ohio, who earlier had challenged Pelosi within the Democratic Caucus. Cooper was one of four Democrats who voted for somebody other than Pelosi. Rep. Ron Kind of Wisconsin voted for Cooper.

Nashville Metro

Population		**Race and Ethnicity**		**Income**	
Total	737,704	White	60.6%	Median Income	$48,155 (283 out of 435)
Land area	1,249	Black	24.8%		
Pop/ sq mi	590.8	Latino	9.1%		
Born in state	53.3%	Asian	2.9%	Under $50,000	51.8%
		Two races	2.0%	$50,000-$99,999	30.0%
Age Groups		Other	0.6%	$100,000-$199,999	14.1%
Under 18	21.9%			$200,000 or more	4.2%
18-34	28.4%	**Education**		Poverty Rate	17.9%
35-64	38.5%	H.S grad or less	39.0%		
Over 64	11.2%	Some college	26.1%	**Health Insurance**	
		College Degree, 4 yr	22.1%	With health insurance coverage	85.1%
Work		Post grad	12.8%		
White Collar	38.8%				
Sales and Service	42.4%	**Military**		**Public Assistance**	
Blue Collar	18.8%	Veteran	7.2%	Cash public assistance income	4.6%
Government	6.9%	Active Duty	0.1%		
				Food stamp/SNAP benefits	15.3%

Voter Turnout			
2015 Total Citizens 18+	528,937	2016 House Turnout as % CVAP	52%
2016 House turnout	273,544	2014 House Turnout as % CVAP	29%

2012 Presidential Vote		
Barack Obama	152,960	(56%)
Mitt Romney	116,289	(43%)

2016 Presidential Vote		
Hillary Clinton	156,730	(56%)
Donald Trump	105,720	(38%)
Gary Johnson	10,431	(4%)

Cook Partisan Voting Index: D+7

Country music, an art form that emerged from the settlers of the hardscrabble, mountainous counties of East Tennessee, is now a more than $2 billion-a-year business. The heart of country music is located in the city that is increasingly the cultural, political and economic heart of Tennessee: Nashville. Run out of a series of deceptively modest homes-turned-offices on Music Row, the industry congregated in Nashville because local radio station WSM had a clear channel in the 1920s from which to beam its weekly "barn dances" throughout the South. The broadcasts later became known as the Grand Ole Opry, the nation's longest continuously running radio show. Music Row has become a corporate juggernaut that views itself as more influential than the entertainment meccas on the East or West Coast. The city has about 200 recording studios, and Nashville music has more than $1 billion in sales each year. The Country Music Hall of Fame and Museum recently had a $100 million expansion as part of the downtown revitalization. The music industry is increasingly intertwined with the television industry here.

For years, the city's elite and its religious leaders resented the growing local influence of country music. But all three made their peace in the 1970s, and since then Nashville has become one of the South's boom cities - one of the fastest-growing metropolitan areas behind the much larger Atlanta and Dallas-Fort Worth Metroplex. An agreeable quality of life, plenty of highly skilled labor, a central location and absence of urban strife have all enhanced Nashville as the largest metropolitan area in the state, with suburban growth in all directions. After a steady closing of the gap, Nashville in 2015 surpassed Memphis as the largest city. The music industry has supported 57,000 jobs here. It is also a center of the for-profit health industry, the area's largest and fastest-growing employer.

The dominant cultural tone in the metropolitan area is conservative - Nashville has more than 700 churches, and is the headquarters for the publishing arms of the Southern Baptist Convention, United Methodist Church and National Baptist Convention - but Nashville and Davidson County remain Democratic bulwarks and islands in an otherwise Republican environment. Bolstered by the defeat in 2009 of an English-only referendum in Nashville, the metro area has a large immigrant population, which business leaders have sought to welcome.

The 5th Congressional District of Tennessee includes all of consolidated Nashville-Davidson County. Neighboring Cheatham and Dickson counties include about 10 percent of the district's population. The 5th is reliably Democratic, one of only two districts in Tennessee where a Democrat has a chance, but it is much more centrist than the Memphis-based 9th District. Hillary Clinton got 56 percent of the vote, the same that President Barack Obama took in 2012.

SIXTH DISTRICT

Diane Black (R)

Elected 2010, 4th term; b. Jan 16, 1951, Baltimore, MD; Anne Arundel Community College (MD), A.D., 1971; Belmont University (TN), B.S.N., 1992; Lutheran; Married (David Black); 3 children; 6 grandchildren.

Elected Office: TN House, 1998-2004; TN Senate, 2004-2010.

Professional Career: Registered nurse, 1969-2010; Director, Sumner Regional Health Systems, 1993-1998; Owner, Ebon-Falcon.

DC Office: 1131 LHOB 20515, 202-225-4231, Fax: 202-225-6887, black.house.gov.

State Offices: Cookeville, 931-854-0069; Gallatin, 615-206-8204.

Committees: *Budget (Chmn)*. *Ways & Means*: Health.

Group Ratings

	ADA	ACLU	AFL-CIO	LCV	ITI	COC	HAFA	ACU	CFG	FRC
2016	-	11%	-	0%	67%	100%	85%	96%	92%	100%
2015	0%	C	4%	0%	C	75%	C	96%	88%	100%

Almanac Ratings 2015

	Economy	Social	Foreign	Composite
Liberal	0%	0%	4%	1%
Conservative	100%	100%	96%	99%

Key Votes of the 114th Congress

1. Keystone Pipeline	Y	5. Puerto Rico Debt	N	9. Offenses by Aliens	Y
2. Trade Deals	Y	6. Medical Marijuana	N	10. Troops in Iraq	N
3. Export-Import Bank	N	7. Sanctuary Cities	Y	11. Homeland Security $$	N
4. Debt Ceiling Increase	N	8. Armor-piercing Bullets	Y	12. Trade Adjustment aid	N

Election Results

Election	Name (Party)	Vote (%)		Cand. Spent	Ind. Exp. Support	Ind. Exp. Oppose
2016 General	Diane Black (R)	202,234	(71%)	$2,584,120		
	David Kent (D)	61,995	(22%)	$5,025		
	David Ross (I)	20,261	(7%)			
2016 Primary	Diane Black (R)	33,210	(64%)			
	Joe Carr (R)	16,662	(32%)			

Prior winning percentages: 2014 (71%), 2012 (76%), 2010 (70%)

Republican Diane Black, elected in 2010, is an active social conservative and has a background in health care, which has been instrumental in her extensive work on the Ways and Means Committee. She is an avid supporter of tax reform and an outspoken opponent of abortion. In 2017, Speaker Paul Ryan selected her to chair the House Budget Committee, which showed her policy and political skills and her rapid rise in influence.

Black was born in Baltimore and lived in the area for most of her early life. She obtained an associate's degree in nursing from a local community college. In 1985, she and her business executive husband, David Black, moved to Tennessee. Black returned to school to get her bachelor's degree in nursing from Belmont University. She entered politics in 1998, when she was elected to the first of three terms in the Tennessee House. During that time, she joined an anti-tax protest that foreshadowed her later involvement in the tea party. In the state Senate, Black became the first woman to chair the Republican Caucus. She earned her stripes as a small-government conservative, repeatedly voting against a state income tax and increases to the sales tax. She pushed for a traditional definition of marriage, a zero-tolerance policy for illegal immigrants, and a balanced budget constitutional amendment. Her husband became president of a sports anti-doping laboratory at Vanderbilt University, which the two of them co-founded.

When Democratic Rep. Bart Gordon retired after 13 terms rather than face a tea party challenge, Black ran for the seat. She survived a bruising three-way GOP primary with 31 percent of the vote, edging out second-place finisher Lou Ann Zelenik by 283 votes. Zelenik, the Rutherford County GOP chair, made her opposition to a local Muslim community center a top issue and accused Black of not taking a strong enough stand against it. In the general election, Black's conservative views made her a tea party favorite, and she racked up endorsements from Republican luminaries, including former Alaska Gov. Sarah Palin. In calling for repeal of the health care law, Black invoked her experience as a nurse in emergency rooms. She raised $2.4 million, with more than half coming from her own wallet, more than 10 times the amount mustered by her opponent, Iraq war veteran Brett Carter. She won 67%-29%, taking every county in what until then had been a Democratic district.

Black quickly displayed her cachet as a freshman with seats on the Ways and Means and Budget committees. She staunchly defended Budget Chairman Paul Ryan's plan to rein in spending. She was one of four regional directors of the National Republican Congressional Committee, in recognition of her fundraising acumen. In 2015, *Roll Call* listed her as 10th among the wealthiest members of Congress, with a net worth at $46 million, including extensive real estate holdings in the Nashville area. In the *Almanac* vote ratings for 2015, Black ranked among the House's most-conservative members.

She has remained a firm opponent of abortion. Her first legislation sought to deny federal funding to Planned Parenthood. She introduced a half dozen other abortion-related bills. In 2013, she sponsored a measure to give any individual or group that opposes contraception an automatic exemption from the requirement in the Affordable Care Act that employee health insurance plans provide birth control. In 2015, she filed a bill to block Title X federal funding to organizations that perform abortions. She was a strong proponent of the House-passed bill barring most abortions after 20 weeks, and she cited growing evidence that such fetuses feel pain. She joined her Nashville-area colleague Rep. Marsha Blackburn on the House's Select Panel on Infant Lives, where Republicans called for withholding federal funds from family planning providers that performed abortions. In February 2017, the House passed a bill that overturned the regulation issued by President Barack Obama days before he left office that required state and local governments to provide family-planning funds.

Black has engaged on an array of fiscal issues. She has advocated a flatter, fairer and simpler tax code to help create the conditions for economic growth. On Ways and Means, she was tapped to chair the Education and Family Benefits Tax Reform Working Group. When President-elect Donald Trump nominated Rep. Tom Price of Georgia as Secretary of Health and Human Services, Ryan selected Black to replace Price as Budget Committee chair. Not only was she - as Price and Ryan had been - a member of Ways and Means, but she scored points as the first woman to chair the Budget Committee.

Her initial challenge as chairwoman was to work with House GOP leaders and other committee chairmen to replace the Affordable Care Act, an objective that Black fully shared. In March 2017, when the Congressional Budget Office reported that the GOP alternative would eventually remove health insurance coverage for 24 million persons, Black said that the legislation would lower premiums, increase consumer choices and reduce the federal deficit. "If you want to repeal Obamacare, this bill does it," she said. When that proposal failed to attract support from sufficient House Republicans to gain passage, House leaders and committee chairmen spent several more weeks to make additional tweaks in their bill, which the House passed in early May.

At home, Black has easily prevailed against credible Republican challengers. In 2012, Zelenik returned for another primary challenge, once again making her opposition to the Islamic Center of Murfreesboro a focal point. Zelenik found a wealthy ally in Tennessee multimillionaire Andy Miller, who paid for ads attacking Black for supporting a hike in the federal debt limit. But with Zelenik's base of Rutherford County having been removed from the 6th District by redistricting, Black won a suspense-free 69%-31% primary. Democrats didn't bother to field a candidate that year. In 2014, Democrats ran Amos Powers, who worked for a local radio station and held Black accountable for dysfunction in Washington. It didn't seem to make much difference. Black won, 71%-23%.

In 2016, Black faced a tea party candidate, former state Rep. Joe Carr, who had held Sen. Lamar Alexander to a 50%-41% GOP primary win in 2014, a contest for which Alexander raised more than $6 million prior to the primary. Black - a former favorite of the tea party -- took the challenge seriously, as she raised and spent more than $1.3 million prior to the primary. Judson Phillips, the founder of Tea Party Nation who had organized the tea party in Nashville in 2009, wrote in *The Washington Times* a week before the August primary that Carr would defeat Black and become "the Dave Brat of 2016," a reference to the successful primary challenger to Majority Leader Eric Cantor of Virginia in 2014. "Carr, again without outside help, is running an amazing campaign," he wrote. "Polls have him at worst tied with Black." Phillips was wrong. Black won in a blow-out, 65%-33%, taking all 17 counties. She took the general, 71%-22%. Following the election, Black was included among possible candidates to seek the open seat for governor in 2018. Her Budget Committee gavel became an added factor in her decision on whether to run statewide.

Middle Tennessee: Eastern Nashville Suburbs, Cookesville

Population		Race and Ethnicity		Income	
Total	728,457	White	89.2%	Median Income	$46,221 (322 out of 435)
Land area	6,474	Black	4.2%		
Pop/ sq mi	112.5	Latino	3.9%		
Born in state	62.5%	Asian	0.9%	Under $50,000	53.4%
		Two races	1.4%	$50,000-$99,999	30.6%
Age Groups		Other	0.5%	$100,000-$199,999	13.4%
Under 18	23.1%			$200,000 or more	2.6%
18-34	20.0%	**Education**		Poverty Rate	15.2%
35-64	40.5%	H.S grad or less	52.7%		
Over 64	16.4%	Some college	26.9%	**Health Insurance**	
		College Degree, 4 yr	13.5%	With health insurance coverage	88.0%
Work		Post grad	6.8%		
White Collar	31.5%				
Sales and Service	41.4%	**Military**		**Public Assistance**	
Blue Collar	27.1%	Veteran	9.5%	Cash public assistance income	3.5%
Government	8.3%	Active Duty	0.1%		
				Food stamp/SNAP benefits	15.5%

Voter Turnout			
2015 Total Citizens 18+	545,479	2016 House Turnout as % CVAP	52%
2016 House turnout	284,490	2014 House Turnout as % CVAP	30%

2012 Presidential Vote		
Mitt Romney	192,602	(69%)
Barack Obama	82,276	(30%)

2016 Presidential Vote		
Donald Trump	216,516	(72%)
Hillary Clinton	70,428	(24%)
Gary Johnson	7,578	(3%)

Cook Partisan Voting Index: R+24

Middle Tennessee is hilly and fertile, cut by deep, curvy rivers. The terrain was never much suited for plantation crops, and there were few big landholdings. This has long been a land of small farmers and small county-seat towns, nestled amid some of the loveliest scenery in the country. As one of the heartlands of the Democratic Party, it was the political base of President Andrew Jackson and supported him nearly unanimously in his 1832 reelection. For 140 years after Jackson, it voted solidly Democratic and elected as its representatives in Congress some of the luminaries of the national party: Cordell Hull (1907-21, 1923-31), later senator and Secretary of State; Albert Gore Sr. (1939-53), later senator; and Albert Gore Jr. (1977-85), later senator and vice president.

The 6th Congressional District includes 17 Middle Tennessee counties, plus small parts of two others. These counties have a rural heritage. Dan Evans, founder of the Cracker Barrel Old Country Store chain, grew up in Smithville. The populated areas evoke the small-town charm for which those stores are famous. The National Rolley Hole Marble Tournament is held annually at Standing Stone State Park; Jamestown is the headquarters for the World's Longest Yard Sale. Just over half of the district's population lives in the three counties that adjoin Music City, USA. These are generally upscale places with median incomes that are among the highest in the state. Sumner and Wilson, the two largest counties in the district, grew 12 and 16 percent respectively from 2010 to 2016.

Because this part of Tennessee had few African Americans, the racial politics of the 1960s largely bypassed the region, and Democratic loyalties outlasted those in other parts of the South. With Gore, Bill Clinton swept the area in 1992. As the Democratic Party became an increasingly urban coalition in the 2000s, the party's local fortunes plummeted. Its 72 percent for Donald Trump in 2016 placed it among his top 5 percent of districts nationwide. It likely will be a long time before Democrats return to competitiveness in Al Gore's former district.

SEVENTH DISTRICT

Marsha Blackburn (R)

Elected 2002, 8th term; b. Jun 06, 1952, Laurel, MS; Mississippi State University, B.S., 1973; Presbyterian; Married (Chuck Blackburn); 2 children; 2 grandchildren.

Elected Office: TN Senate, 1998-2002.

Professional Career: Retail marketing consultant, 1973-1998.

DC Office: 2266 RHOB 20515, 202-225-2811, Fax: 202-225-3004, blackburn.house.gov.

State Offices: Clarksville, 931-503-0391; Franklin, 615-591-5161.

Committees: *Energy & Commerce*: Communications & Technology (Chmn), Environment, Health.

Group Ratings

	ADA	ACLU	AFL-CIO	LCV	ITI	COC	HAFA	ACU	CFG	FRC
2016	-	11%	-	0%	100%	93%	88%	96%	96%	100%
2015	0%	C	0%	0%	C	63%	C	96%	91%	100%

Almanac Ratings 2015

	Economy	Social	Foreign	Composite
Liberal	1%	0%	0%	0%
Conservative	99%	100%	100%	100%

Key Votes of the 114th Congress

1. Keystone Pipeline	Y	5. Puerto Rico Debt	N	9. Offenses by Aliens	Y
2. Trade Deals	Y	6. Medical Marijuana	N	10. Troops in Iraq	N
3. Export-Import Bank	N	7. Sanctuary Cities	Y	11. Homeland Security $$	N
4. Debt Ceiling Increase	N	8. Armor-piercing Bullets	Y	12. Trade Adjustment aid	N

Election Results

Election	Name (Party)	Vote	(%)	Cand. Spent	Ind. Exp. Support	Ind. Exp. Oppose
2016 General	Marsha Blackburn (R)	200,407	(72%)	$1,485,728		
	Tharon Chandler (D)	65,226	(24%)			
	Leonard Ladner (I)	11,880	(4%)			
2016 Primary	Marsha Blackburn (R)		(100%)			

Prior winning percentages: 2014 (70%), 2012 (71%), 2010 (72%), 2008 (69%), 2006 (66%), 2004 (100%), 2002 (71%)

Republican Marsha Blackburn, elected in 2002, is a conservative firebrand who has become a legislative activist. She has been an influential lawmaker at the Energy and Commerce Committee, where she took over in January 2017 as chairwoman of its Communications and Technology Subcommittee.

Blackburn grew up in Laurel, Mississippi, where her father sold oil-field production equipment. Her interest in gardening and canning won her a 4-H college scholarship at Mississippi State University, where she majored in merchandising and clothing. She helped pay her way through college by selling books door-to-door. She became a sales manager for Southwestern Co., which sold educational materials, and moved to Williamson County. Her hilltop home is known as "Up Yonder," named by its former owner, Grand Ole Opry star Minnie Pearl. Blackburn became director of retail fashion for a Nashville department store and was appointed by Republican Gov. Don Sundquist as executive director of the Tennessee Film, Entertainment, and Music Commission. In 1992, she was the Republican nominee against Democrat Rep. Bart Gordon and lost 57%-41%. Elected in 1998 to the state Senate, she built a grass-roots campaign to defeat Sundquist's proposed income tax. In 2014, Tennessee voters approved a constitutional amendment that expressly prohibited a state income tax.

When the House seat opened, Blackburn was the only well-known candidate from the Nashville area. Of the six other candidates, three were familiar figures in the Memphis area. She benefited from financial support of the national anti-tax Club for Growth and from attacks by the Shelby County candidates on one another. She ran as an anti-abortion, pro-gun and pro-military conservative and won with 40 percent of the vote. She easily won the general election.

Blackburn has often sought a leadership role. In 2006, she lost a bid to chair the Republican Conference. She has been active on the Republican Study Committee, and in 2012 she co-chaired the GOP convention's Platform Committee. She cosponsored the controversial "birther" bill in 2009 requiring future presidential candidates to prove they were born in the United States, a measure that played off attacks on President Barack Obama's qualifications to hold office, although the measure would not have applied to him.

When Republicans regained control of the House in 2011, Blackburn assumed a prominent role on technology policy at Energy and Commerce. A fervent advocate of the Nashville-based music industry and founder of the Congressional Songwriters Caucus, she has fought to protect intellectual property rights of artists against illegal music downloads. In 2015, she cosponsored the bipartisan Fair Play, Fair Pay bill to assure that musicians are compensated for their work. The recording industry has given her a congressional Grammy. Blackburn has often challenged the Federal Communications Commission. In 2014, the House passed on a largely party-line vote her amendment to prevent the FCC from preempting state laws that block the ability of cities to create local government-run broadband networks; she cited state sovereignty on behalf of her proposal, which was supported by large cable companies. In 2015, she sought to deny funding for the FCC to implement its net-neutrality rules that were designed to bar tiered pricing for internet services; she contends that such authority is solely the responsibility of Congress. In taking over in 2017 the revamped Communication and Technology Subcommittee, she encouraged Ajit Pai, President Donald Trump's choice to chair the FCC, to cut back its regulations.

In 2016, she chaired the House's Select Panel on Infant Lives, which was a special committee created to review allegations by anti-abortion activists of an illicit trade in fetal tissue. The panel held hearings and issued recommendations for changes in what Blackburn described as "the abortion and fetal tissue procurement industries." Democrats opposed creation of the panel and its activities. On other issues, Blackburn has regularly sought to repeal the Affordable Care Act. She engaged in presidential politics with a 2015 letter to the Internal Revenue Service challenging the tax-exempt status of the Clinton Foundation. A champion of gun owners' rights, Blackburn boasted about her perfect marksmanship score with her Smith & Wesson .38. After the Newtown, Connecticut, elementary school massacre, she said the debate should focus on mental health because disturbed people disposed toward violence could use "a hammer, a hatchet, a car" instead of a gun.

At home, Blackburn faced a primary challenge in 2008 from Shelby County Register of Deeds Tom Leatherwood, whose campaign revealed that Blackburn had misreported more than $440,000 on campaign finance disclosure forms dating to her first House campaign. Blackburn filed amended returns. The underdog Leatherwood charged that Blackburn had used her campaign funds to help her family's businesses and that she hadn't been effective in Washington. She easily won the primary, 62%-38%, carrying every county except Shelby. Redistricting in 2011 shifted the outlying Shelby area to the 8th District.

During the 2016 campaign, Blackburn was an early supporter of Donald Trump. She served as a vice-chair of his presidential transition team. That sparked speculation that she might be named to a Cabinet position. She has received continued mentions as a possible contender for a House leadership position.

Middle Tennessee: Western Nashville Suburbs, Clarksville

Population		**Race and Ethnicity**		**Income**	
Total	732,702	White	81.2%	Median Income	$50,736 (244 out of 435)
Land area	9,160	Black	9.8%		
Pop/ sq mi	80.0	Latino	4.8%		
Born in state	53.7%	Asian	1.7%	Under $50,000	49.3%
		Two races	2.0%	$50,000-$99,999	29.9%
Age Groups		Other	0.5%	$100,000-$199,999	15.6%
Under 18	25.2%			$200,000 or more	5.3%
18-34	21.6%	**Education**		Poverty Rate	15.2%
35-64	39.6%	H.S grad or less	45.8%		
Over 64	13.5%	Some college	27.2%	**Health Insurance**	
		College Degree, 4 yr	17.4%	With health insurance coverage	88.9%
Work		Post grad	9.4%		
White Collar	36.8%				
Sales and Service	39.5%	**Military**		**Public Assistance**	
Blue Collar	23.7%	Veteran	11.3%	Cash public assistance income	3.0%
Government	8.3%	Active Duty	2.2%		
				Food stamp/SNAP benefits	14.9%

Voter Turnout			
2015 Total Citizens 18+	534,887	2016 House Turnout as % CVAP	52%
2016 House turnout	277,513	2014 House Turnout as % CVAP	30%

2012 Presidential Vote		
Mitt Romney	183,840	(66%)
Barack Obama	91,987	(33%)

2016 Presidential Vote		
Donald Trump	196,893	(67%)
Hillary Clinton	82,236	(28%)
Gary Johnson	9,071	(3%)

Cook Partisan Voting Index: R+20

Rural Tennessee north of Mississippi is mostly a sparsely settled area. Along each side of the Tennessee River, as it flows north and widens out into Kentucky Lake, are small rural communities. Many date to pre-Civil War days and have not grown much since. One of these is Waynesboro, where Davy Crockett delivered campaign speeches from the base of a huge natural stone double bridge overlooking the Buffalo River. Farther west is McNairy County, where Sheriff Buford Pusser of *Walking Tall* fame carried his big stick and fought organized crime until his death in a 1974 car crash. Even some of the roads have changed little; the Natchez Trace Parkway follows the same basic path as the trail carved out by prehistoric bison from Mississippi grazing lands to the salt licks of central Tennessee. Meriwether Lewis met a violent and mysterious death - most likely a suicide - while traveling on the Trace in 1807.

This land is complemented by two urban areas: Greater Nashville to the east and Clarksville to the north. South of Nashville is Williamson County, where the bedroom communities of Franklin and Brentwood are affluent, highly educated and fast-growing. Each grew by more than 13 percent from 2010 to 2015. Nissan North America took advantage of the low cost of doing business in Tennessee by moving its headquarters from California to the Cool Springs area of Franklin. Along the Cumberland River is Clarksville, the fifth-largest city in the state, with many restored 19th-century homes and a large industrial park. In 2016, Google projected a $600 million cost for its vast new data center near Clarksville. Straddling the Kentucky border north of Clarksville is the Army's sprawling Fort Campbell, home of the 101st Airborne Division, which has become a rapid deployment unit and is the Army's only air assault division; Campbell is the Army's fifth largest base and a military boomtown, though it suffered a setback in 2014 when the 2,400-soldier Combat Aviation Brigade was deactivated.

The 7th Congressional District covers this territory, which is the largest district in Tennessee. Close to 40 percent live in Tennessee's Central Basin, in Williamson County. Another fifth of its population live in Clarksville-based Montgomery County. This is the wealthiest county in the state, measured by median income, and is heavily Republican. The remainder live in the lightly populated, rural counties traversing the state from northern border to southern. The area around Clarksville retains some of its historic attachment to the Democratic Party dating to the Civil War. In 2016, Donald Trump got 65 percent in Williamson and 56 percent in Montgomery. The district overall has remained solidly Republican. Trump took the district with 67 percent after Mitt Romney got 66 percent in 2012.

EIGHTH DISTRICT

David Kustoff (R)

Elected 2016, 1st term; b. Oct 08, 1966, Memphis; University of Memphis; b.B.A., 1989; University of Memphis, Cecil C. Humphreys School of Law (TN), J.D., 1992; Jewish; Married (Roberta Kustoff); 2 children.

Professional Career: Practicing attorney; Chairman, Shelby County GOP, 1995-1999; U.S. Attorney, Western District of Tennessee, 2006-2008.

DC Office: 508 CHOB 20515, 202-225-4714, Fax: 202-225-1765; Website: kustoff.house.gov.

State Offices: Dyersburg, 731-412-1037; Jackson, 731-423-4848; Martin, 731-412-1043; Memphis, 901-682-4422.

Committees: *Financial Services*: Financial Institutions & Consumer Credit, Oversight & Investigations, Terrorism & Illicit Finance.

Election Results

Election	Name (Party)	Vote (%)	Cand. Spent	Ind. Exp. Support	Ind. Exp. Oppose
2016 General	David Kustoff (R)	194,386 (69%)	$1,201,938		
	Rickey Hobson (D)	70,925 (25%)			
	Shelia Godwin (I)	6,442 (2%)			
2016 Primary	David Kustoff (R)	16,886 (27%)			
	George Flinn Jr. (R)	14,197 (23%)			
	Mark Luttrell (R)	10,878 (18%)			
	Brian Kelsey (R)	7,941 (13%)			

Republican David Kustoff was elected to an open seat in 2016, after winning a hard-fought primary. With his experience as a U.S. attorney in Western Tennessee and his political connections to leading Republicans in the state, Kustoff was the establishment favorite in the contest.

Born and raised in Shelby County, Kustoff got his bachelor's and law degrees from the University of Memphis. He opened a law firm with Jim Strickland, a Democrat who was elected mayor of Memphis in 2016. Kustoff served in various positions for the Republican Party, including Shelby County chairman, and state chairman of the George W. Bush presidential campaigns in 2000 and 2004. In 2002, he ran for the Congress in the 7th District in 2002, but finished second with 20 percent, to 40 percent for Marsha Blackburn in the Republican primary, when he split the vote from Shelby County with two other local Republicans. Kustoff was nominated as U.S. attorney in 2006 and served until 2009. He gained attention for winning the conviction of state Sen. John Ford and others in the "Tennessee Waltz" political corruption trial. Later, Kustoff served on the board of BankTennessee, a community bank, and was appointed by Gov. Bill Haslam as vice-chairman of the Tennessee Higher Education Commission, where he oversaw the implementation of state assistance programs.

When three-term GOP Rep. Steven Fincher retired, there was a wide-open field of 13 Republican candidates, two Democrats and five independents. He emphasized his law-enforcement background by criticizing President Barack Obama for having "unfairly and severely impugned the reputation of law enforcement" officers in high-profile cases of alleged police misconduct. Other leading Republican candidates were former Shelby County Commissioner George Flinn, a physician who had two previous unsuccessful runs for Congress, Shelby County Mayor Mark Luttrell and state Sen. Brian Kelsey.

Flinn raised by far the most money with $3 million, of which $2.7 million was self-financed. Kustoff raised about $700,000 for the primary, including $100,000 from a personal loan. Kustoff won the primary with 28 percent of the vote to 23 percent for Flinn, 18 percent for Luttrell and 13 percent for Kelsey. Kustoff took nearly half the vote in Shelby County, which was a larger margin than in the overall district. Democratic nominee Rickey Hobson did not file a financial report with the Federal Election Commission, and Kustoff won the general, 69%-25%.

Kustoff got a seat on the Financial Services Committee, where he sought to reduce the restrictions imposed by the 2010 Dodd-Frank banking law. He urged quick action on a replacement for the Affordable Care Act.

West Tennessee: Memphis Suburbs, Jackson

Population		**Race and Ethnicity**		**Income**	
Total	707,982	White	73.6%	Median Income	$52,752 (213 out of 435)
Land area	6,851	Black	19.7%	Under $50,000	47.6%
Pop/ sq mi	103.3	Latino	3.1%	$50,000-$99,999	29.3%
Born in state	66.0%	Asian	1.9%	$100,000-$199,999	17.9%
		Two races	1.3%	$200,000 or more	5.3%
Age Groups		Other	0.4%	Poverty Rate	14.2%
Under 18	24.0%	**Education**		**Health Insurance**	
18-34	19.8%	H.S grad or less	44.6%	With health insurance coverage	89.8%
35-64	40.8%	Some college	26.8%	**Public Assistance**	
Over 64	15.4%	College Degree, 4 yr	17.8%	Cash public assistance income	2.5%
Work		Post grad	10.8%	Food stamp/SNAP benefits	15.0%
White Collar	37.2%	**Military**			
Sales and Service	39.4%	Veteran	9.7%		
Blue Collar	23.4%	Active Duty	0.2%		
Government	6.6%				

Voter Turnout			
2015 Total Citizens 18+	526,721	2016 House Turnout as % CVAP	54%
2016 House turnout	282,733	2014 House Turnout as % CVAP	33%

2012 Presidential Vote		
Mitt Romney	202,041	(66%)
Barack Obama	99,608	(33%)

2016 Presidential Vote		
Donald Trump	197,432	(66%)
Hillary Clinton	90,006	(30%)
Gary Johnson	6,370	(2%)

Cook Partisan Voting Index: R+19

West of Nashville and north of Memphis, the rivers roll lazily through flat or gently rolling land that has similarities to the northern end of Mississippi. Cotton and soybeans are the main crops - the annual Tennessee Soybean Festival is held in Martin, near the Kentucky border - and they often are abundant. African Americans remain in rural areas here, a reminder of the old plantation economy. Henning is the hometown of Alex Haley, who used to sit on his porch and listen to his aunts tell him stories about slave ships and the Civil War; these became his book *Roots.* The plantation economy also bequeathed a fierce loyalty to the Democratic Party; before 2011, much of this district hadn't been represented by a Republican since Reconstruction. The small towns in this area are sustained by manufacturers such as the NSK automotive plant and light industry such as Dot Foods, the nation's largest food redistributor, both in Dyersburg. Kentucky Lake draws big crowds for its annual BASSfest in Henry County.

Crockett County, with a county seat named Alamo, is named after Davy Crockett, who represented the area for three terms in the House before he moved to Texas. The area carries the highest earthquake risk in the United States outside of the West Coast. In the early 1800s, four earthquakes rocked the region, permanently altering the topography. Perhaps the most extreme example is Reelfoot Lake, the only large natural lake in Tennessee, which was a dry area before the quakes occurred; the land dropped almost 20 feet in places before the Mississippi River filled in the newly formed depression.

The 8th Congressional District of Tennessee includes much of this West Tennessee farmland. Its largest city is Jackson, founded shortly after the area was opened for white settlement in 1818, and the site of one of Crockett's final speeches before heading west to his doom at the Alamo. Jackson has become 49 percent black. Nearby Haywood is a black-majority county. Overall, the population is 21 percent black. Suburban Shelby County east of Memphis includes 40 percent of the district population. Redistricting changes in 2011 dropped President Barack Obama's 2008 vote share by eight percentage points, and this is now a strongly Republican seat, like the six other GOP-held districts in Tennessee. Donald Trump got 66 percent of the vote in 2016, the same share that went for Mitt Romney in 2012.

NINTH DISTRICT

Steve Cohen (D)

Elected 2006, 6th term; b. May 24, 1949, Memphis; Vanderbilt University (TN), B.A., 1971; Memphis State University - Cecil C. Humphreys School of Law (TN), J.D., 1973; Jewish; Single1 child.

Elected Office: Shelby County Commissioner, 1977-1978; TN Senate, 1982-2006.

Professional Career: Practicing attorney, 1974-2006.

DC Office: 2404 RHOB 20515, 202-225-3265, Fax: 202-225-5663, cohen.house.gov.

State Offices: Memphis, 901-544-4131.

Committees: *Ethics. Joint Security & Cooperation in Europe. Judiciary*: Constitution & Civil Justice (RMM), Courts, Intellectual Property & Internet. *Transportation & Infrastructure*: Aviation, Highways & Transit, Railroads, Pipelines & Hazardous Materials.

Group Ratings

	ADA	ACLU	AFL-CIO	LCV	ITI	COC	HAFA	ACU	CFG	FRC
2016	-	94%	-	100%	67%	50%	14%	4%	4%	0%
2015	100%	C	100%	100%	C	45%	C	8%	3%	0%

Almanac Ratings 2015

	Economy	Social	Foreign	Composite
Liberal	92%	94%	99%	95%
Conservative	8%	6%	1%	5%

Key Votes of the 114th Congress

1. Keystone Pipeline	N	5. Puerto Rico Debt	Y	9. Offenses by Aliens	Y
2. Trade Deals	N	6. Medical Marijuana	Y	10. Troops in Iraq	Y
3. Export-Import Bank	Y	7. Sanctuary Cities	N	11. Homeland Security $$	Y
4. Debt Ceiling Increase	Y	8. Armor-piercing Bullets	N	12. Trade Adjustment aid	Y

Election Results

Election	Name (Party)	Vote (%)		Cand. Spent	Ind. Exp. Support	Ind. Exp. Oppose
2016 General	Steve Cohen (D)	171,631	(79%)	$272,443		
	Wayne Albertson (R)	41,123	(19%)			
	Paul Cook (I)	5,203	(2%)			
2016 Primary	Steve Cohen (D)	35,628	(86%)			
	Justin Ford (D)	4,164	(10%)			

Prior winning percentages: 2014 (75%), 2012 (75%), 2010 (74%), 2008 (88%), 2006 (60%)

Democrat Steve Cohen, elected in 2006, is a rare white member of Congress representing a majority-minority district. He has easily fended off primary challenges from the district's African-American majority by maintaining one of the House's most liberal voting records and concentrating on issues of strong interest to his constituents.

Cohen is a fourth-generation Memphian and the son of a psychiatrist. At age 5, Cohen was diagnosed with polio. Cohen got his bachelor's at Vanderbilt University and his law degree from the University of Memphis. He worked as a legal adviser for the Memphis Police Department and then started a law practice. He was elected to the Shelby County Commission and, in 1982, to the state Senate, where he served for 24 years. He became known as the father of the Tennessee State Lottery for his efforts in 2002 to pass a referendum creating a lottery, with revenue to fund college scholarships.

Cohen wanted to run for Congress in 1996 when 22-year African-American Rep. Harold Ford Sr., announced his retirement, but he found his path blocked by the incumbent's 26-year-old son, who secured the seat. He got his chance in 2006 when Harold Ford Jr. ran unsuccessfully for the Senate. As the only serious white contender among the 15 candidates who filed to run, Cohen faced criticism from local black leaders, who said that an African American should represent the district. Cohen's supporters charged that another primary foe paid for a push poll that asked, "Are you more likely to vote for a born-again Christian or a Jew?" Cohen quipped that his staunchly liberal record would make people mistake him for a black woman.

The district's black leaders did not sufficiently narrow the field, and the primary results splintered. Cohen won with 31 percent. Nikki Tinker, the former campaign manager for Ford Jr., finished second with 25 percent. The incumbent's cousin, Joe Ford Jr., finished third with 12 percent. Cohen faced a challenge in November from yet another Ford - Jake, the incumbent's younger brother, who ran as an independent. Jake Ford was a high school dropout who had had a few scrapes with the law, but he had support from his father and other African-American leaders who opposed Cohen. He argued that he was in better sync with the community, noting that more than two-thirds of the primary vote went against Cohen. Cohen's critics made an issue of the fact that he supported same-sex marriage. He won the general election with 60 percent of the vote, ending the Ford family's 32-year hold on the district. Cohen wanted to join the Congressional Black Caucus, but backed off when CBC leaders made it clear that they objected.

Cohen worked to quickly secure his hold on the seat. Among his first moves was a resolution apologizing for slavery. While it seemed like a relatively harmless motion that easily passed the House on a voice vote, Cohen's office was slammed with constituent calls charging the measure was a political ploy. It was approved just days before the August 2008 primary. Cohen also got a Memphis federal building and post offices named after prominent African Americans.

In that primary, African-American leaders in the district coalesced around Tinker, who staged a rematch. "He's not black, and he can't represent me," one minister told the Memphis *Commercial Appeal.* Tinker got financial help from the CBC and EMILY's List, the abortion-rights fundraising group that supports women candidates. But prominent black leaders from outside the district, including Judiciary Chairman John Conyers of Michigan and Rep. Jesse Jackson Jr. of Illinois, made radio ads for Cohen and donated to his campaign. He outraised Tinker by more than 2-to-1 and crushed her, 79%-19%.

Winning a plum seat on the Judiciary Committee, Cohen worked on bills to force radio broadcasters to pay money to performers whose music is played and on studying racial disparities in the criminal justice system. He enacted a measure in 2010 protecting authors and journalists from having foreign libel judgments honored in U.S. courts and another to help members of the National Guard and Reserve obtain bankruptcy relief. As the ranking Democrat on the Constitution and Civil Justice Subcommittee, whose jurisdiction includes civil rights issues, Cohen has a bipartisan bill that would make marijuana legal for some medical purposes. His *Almanac* vote ratings for 2015 ranked him among the House's liberals. A week before the 2016 election, he said that FBI director James Comey should resign because of his handling of the emails of Hillary Clinton. In 2017, Cohen joined the House Ethics Committee.

In the face of repeated primary challenges, Cohen seems to have become entrenched. In 2010, his opponent was Willie Herenton, Memphis' first elected black mayor. Cohen was ready, with an endorsement from President Barack Obama, a popular figure in the district, as well as support from a dozen CBC members. He trounced Herenton, 79%-21%, in the primary and sailed to reelection. Two years later, his challenger was Memphis Urban League CEO and school board member Tomeka Hart. *The Cook Political Report* observed that her campaign "seems to be focusing more on promoting her brand than giving voters a reason to replace Cohen," and the incumbent won the primary, 89%-11%.

Against the less well-known Ricky Wilkins in 2014, Cohen had his closest primary since he was first elected. Wilkins campaigned publicly on how Cohen's race and ethnicity differed from that of most of his constituents. Cohen won, 66%-33%. His chief Democratic challenger in 2016 was Justin Ford, a Shelby County commissioner and another member of the clan. But Ford filed late and did not run much of a campaign. Cohen took 86 percent of the vote in the four-candidate contest.

Memphis Metro

Population		**Race and Ethnicity**		**Income**	
Total	710,255	White	25.1%	Median Income	$37,233 (414 out of 435)
Land area	483	Black	64.7%		
Pop/ sq mi	1469.3	Latino	6.8%		
Born in state	64.4%	Asian	1.8%	Under $50,000	62.0%
		Two races	1.4%	$50,000-$99,999	26.2%
Age Groups		Other	0.3%	$100,000-$199,999	10.0%
Under 18	25.6%			$200,000 or more	1.8%
18-34	27.1%	**Education**		Poverty Rate	26.7%
35-64	37.1%	H.S grad or less	46.5%		
Over 64	10.3%	Some college	30.3%	**Health Insurance**	
Work		College Degree, 4 yr	14.8%	With health insurance coverage	82.4%
White Collar	29.4%	Post grad	8.5%		
Sales and Service	45.1%	**Military**		**Public Assistance**	
Blue Collar	25.4%	Veteran	7.2%	Cash public assistance income	3.2%
Government	4.7%	Active Duty	0.1%		
				Food stamp/SNAP benefits	25.7%

Voter Turnout			
2015 Total Citizens 18+	500,445	2016 House Turnout as % CVAP	44%
2016 House turnout	217,957	2014 House Turnout as % CVAP	23%

2012 Presidential Vote		
Barack Obama	201,171	(79%)
Mitt Romney	53,147	(21%)

2016 Presidential Vote		
Hillary Clinton	173,411	(78%)
Donald Trump	43,233	(19%)

Cook Partisan Voting Index: D+28

Memphis had long been the largest city in Tennessee, though it lost that title in 2015 to fast-growing Nashville, which also has a much larger metropolitan area. In the state's southwestern corner, 20 miles from Mississippi's cotton fields and riverboat casinos, Memphis's share of African Americans is among the largest in the country, evidence of the city's economic heritage as a capital of the Cotton Kingdom. Big Mississippi planters used to come north to sell their crops in the courtyard of the Peabody Hotel, then make financial arrangements for the next growing season. According to tradition, ducks still famously march daily to the hotel's fountain for a dip.

The city's most celebrated tradition is blues music. Unlike Nashville's country music, which emerged from mountainous East Tennessee, the Memphis sound originated from the self-taught musical stylings of poor, rural blacks in the Mississippi Delta. Throughout the first half of the 20th century, talented black musicians migrated north to Memphis and congregated downtown on Beale Street. The blues sound was adapted by Elvis Presley, a poor white from rural Mississippi, in July 1954 at Sam Phillips' Sun Studio in Memphis - the birth of rock 'n' roll. In the early 1960s, Memphis again became the crucible of a new sound, soul music, which emerged as a counterpoint to rock, its increasingly white-dominated cousin. Otis Redding, Isaac Hayes, the Staple Singers, and Sam & Dave made their records at the Stax studio. For some years, Memphis tried to downplay its musical heritage. Much of Beale Street was razed and set on a misguided path toward urban renewal. But the city came to recognize its history as an asset. Graceland, Presley's garishly decorated mansion, which attracts hordes of musical pilgrims from all over the world, in March 2017 marked its latest expansion with a 450-room resort hotel. The Museum of American Soul Music, at the downtown site of the Stax studio, is the world's only soul music museum and attracts about 500,000 visitors annually

Memphis is the home of the first supermarket chain: Piggly Wiggly, founded in 1916 (its symbol, Mr. Pig, has slimmed down since then). It also hosted the first Holiday Inn. The biggest employer by far is FedEx, where nearly 10,000 employees scan, sort, weigh and route 1.4 million packages on 42 miles of conveyor belts to and from 150 aircraft that arrive and depart within a six-hour period almost every night at the world's busiest cargo airport. For some years, racial discord scarred the political life of Memphis. Rev. Martin Luther King Jr., was assassinated there in 1968, and the site, the Lorraine Motel, has been converted into a civil rights museum. Even today, resurgent Beale Street is one of the few racially integrated spaces in the city, a division that holds equally true in voting. Blacks vote almost unanimously Democratic, and whites vote Republican by margins almost as great. The city has been ranked as the fourth most-segregated city in the nation. Many African Americans in Memphis have moved into the middle class. In 2016, it relinquished to Tucson, Arizona, its listing as the metro area with the highest poverty rate.

The 9th Congressional District of Tennessee remains the strongest Democratic district in the state and is essential to any chance of success for Democrats running statewide. African Americans are 65 percent of the population. In 2016, Hillary Clinton won 78 percent in the district.

★ TEXAS ★

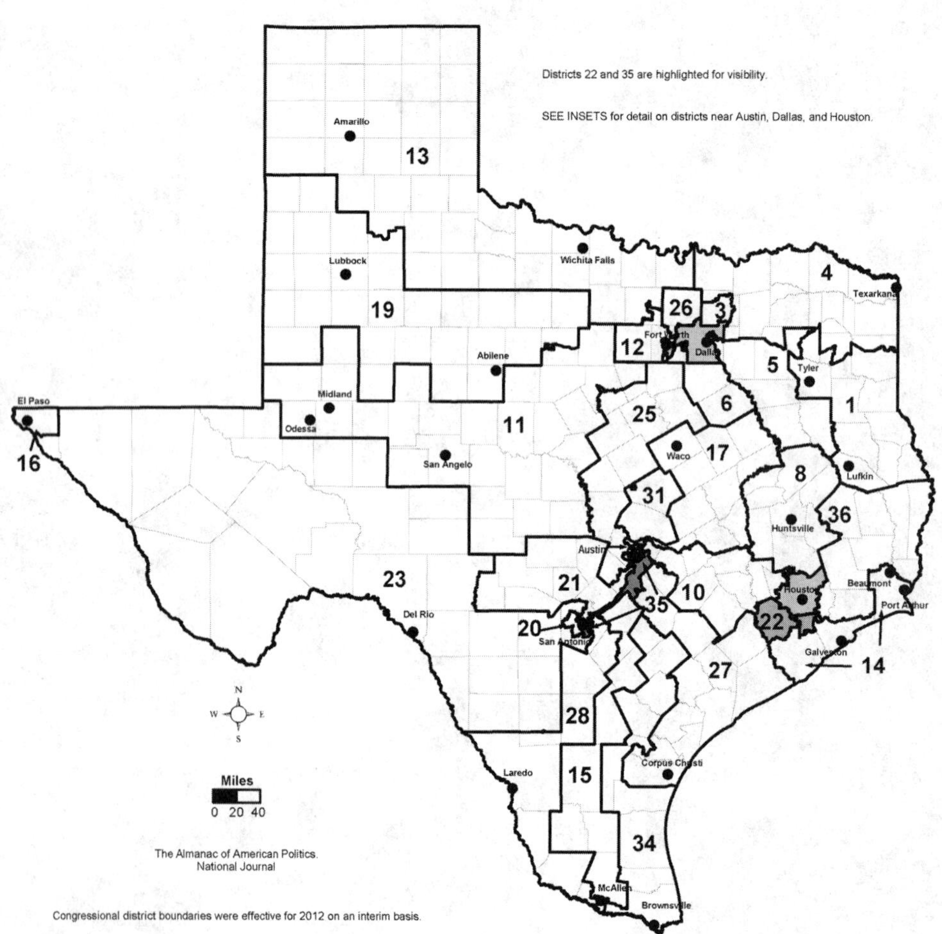

Districts 22 and 35 are highlighted for visibility.
SEE INSETS for detail on districts near Austin, Dallas, and Houston.
Amarillo
13
Lubbock
19
Wichita Falls
4
Texarkana
26
3
12
Fort Worth
Dallas
5
Tyler
1
Abilene
El Paso
Midland
Odessa
16
11
San Angelo
25
6
Waco
17
31
8
Lufkin
36
Huntsville
Austin
21
35
10
23
Houston
Beaumont
Port Arthur
22
Del Rio
20
San Antonio
Galveston
14
27
N
W
E
S
28
Laredo
15
Corpus Christi
Miles
0 20 40
34
The Almanac of American Politics.
National Journal
McAllen
Brownsville
Congressional district boundaries were effective for 2012 on an interim basis.

Texas hasn't elected a Democrat to statewide office in about a quarter century, and it hasn't voted for a Democratic presidential candidate since Jimmy Carter. But while Texas remains in the Republican camp in most ways, its demographics are – ever so slowly – beginning to reshape its politics. The state, which is now majority-minority, displayed one of the nation's sharpest shifts against Donald Trump in 2016. Trump won, but the GOP's margin of victory was about half what it was in 2012.

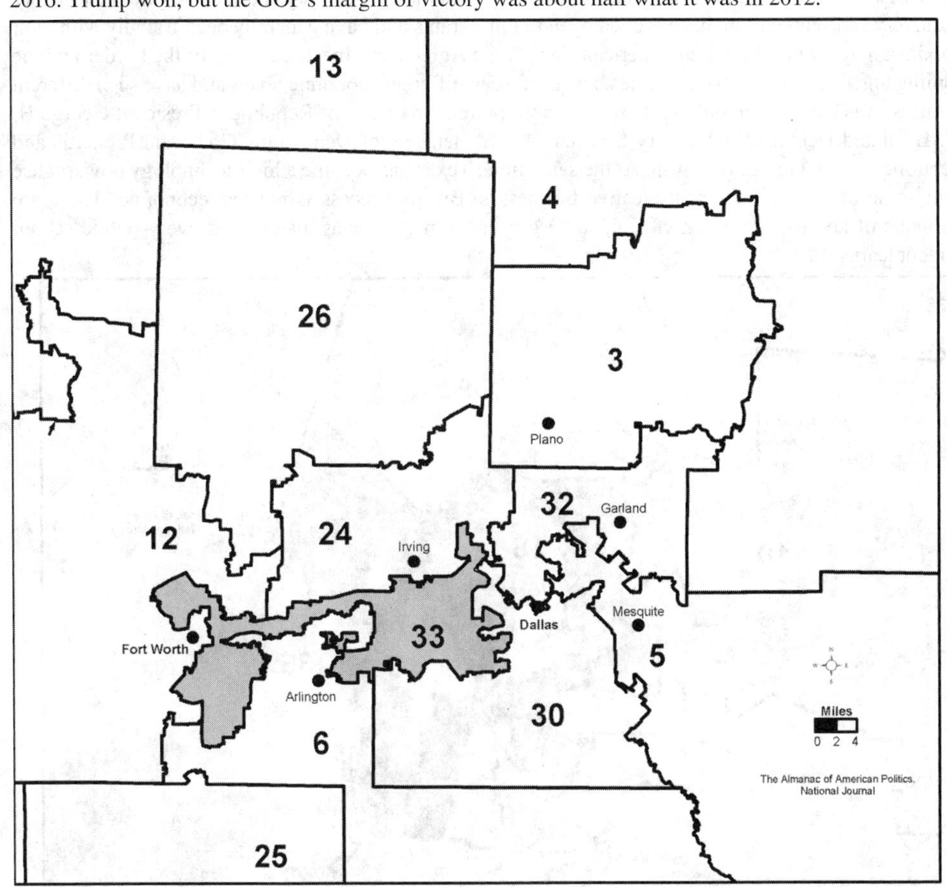

Congressional district boundaries were effective for 2012 on an interim basis. District 33 is highlighted for visibility.

At its origin, Texas was an independent republic, freed from Mexico before it agreed to annexation by the United States in 1845. Today it is a nation-state, almost 28 million strong, larger in area than any of the 28 nations of the European Union and more populous than all but six. The two largest states – California and Texas -- have put their stamp on national politics in our time. In the 14 presidential elections since 1960, Americans have elected Texans four times and Californians four times, just as New York did from 1900 to 1960, when it produced five of the winners and eight of the losers in 15 presidential elections. Texas has been the second-largest state in area since Alaska was admitted to the Union in 1959, and it became the second largest in population in 1994, when it surpassed New York. A formative strain in the state's history is that it is a society without an aristocratic past, a state not formed by plantation owners or plutocrats, but by dirt farmers and citizen-soldiers like Sam Houston. Texas was founded by Southerners, particularly Tennesseans, who were invited to establish their own enclave within the borders of Mexico, then dreamed of a republic with Anglo-Saxon freedoms and African-American slavery. They defended their dream to the death at the Alamo and to a bloody victory at San Jacinto. They entered the Union willingly in 1845 and left it enthusiastically in 1861. The Texas that emerged from the Civil War was still young and poor. Not until 1901 was oil discovered at Spindletop, setting Texas wildcatters on the road to riches.

Without the underpinnings and burdens of tradition, 20th century Texas produced fabulous wealth, generously rewarding success while being unforgiving of failure. It has respect for learning and style - think of its great universities and Neiman Marcus - and it revels in rough manners and Western wear. Texans are prone to wild swings in fortune - think of Sam Houston and Lyndon B. Johnson, the Yankee wildcatter George H. W. Bush and his son George W. In the 21st century. Texans, despite their history of slavery and segregation, have proved open to immigrants and have generally been friendly with their Mexican neighbors. The North American Free Trade Agreement, the opening up of the border and the coming together of these two countries that are at such different economic levels and have such different cultures, was a project mainly of Texans of both political parties - of Republican President George H. W. Bush and Democratic Treasury Secretary Lloyd Bentsen, of Democratic Gov. Ann Richards and Republican Gov. George W. Bush. At the same time, Texas has become a high-technology powerhouse with some of the nation's most creative businesses. But its success is not just economic. There are elements of heroism - some mythical, some genuine - in the Texas history that every public school student learns.

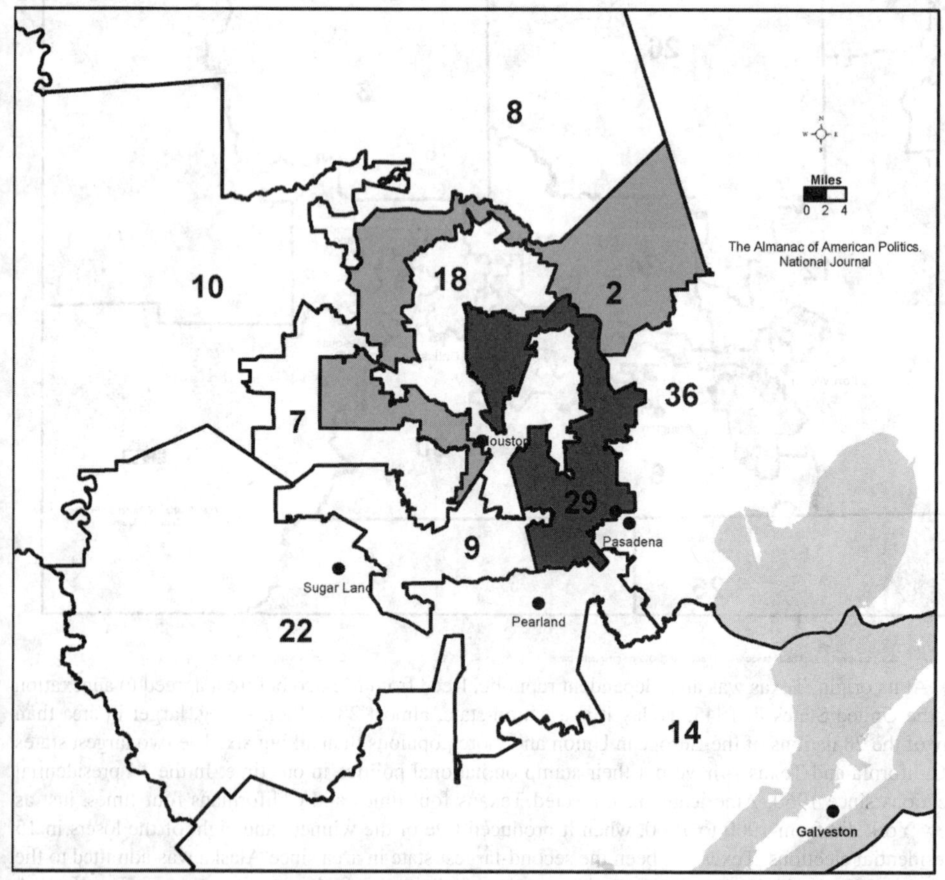

Congressional district boundaries were effective for 2012 on an interim basis. Districts 2 and 29 are highlighted for visibility.

Texas started off as a marshland on the border of the Third World, with an economy based on commodities, mainly cotton, when cotton prices were in long-term decline. Its farmers felt as if they were part of a colonial economy controlled by bankers and Wall Street financiers. After Spindletop, Texas became the nation's - and for a time the world's - leading producer of oil. But oil prices, too, fell in free markets and producers were propped up by politicians. There was the 1935 "hot oil" act that Democrat Sam Rayburn, as chairman of the House Commerce Committee, pushed through. Then came the oil depletion allowance, maintained for years by Rayburn when he was Speaker of the House and by Johnson when he was Senate majority leader and later by Bentsen as Senate Finance Committee chairman. These politicians also secured subsidies for cotton growers and contracts for defense plants and space facilities during World War II and through the Cold War years. Most Texas voters stayed Democratic up to 1970 because of Confederate memories, New Deal affections, and the clout and competence of Texas Democratic officeholders.

By the 1970s, Texas was no longer dependent on raw commodities. The "awl bidness" here became less a matter of extracting oil than it was playing host to the greatest concentration of highly skilled specialists in extracting oil and natural gas in any part of the world. Also beginning in the 1960s, Texas became a center for technology with the critical mass of knowledge and finances needed to produce firms like Texas Instruments and Dell Computer and a university infrastructure in the University of Texas and Texas A&M. (A&M educated three of the 2015 *Fortune* 100 CEOs, the only public university to tie the Ivy League universities Cornell, Harvard, Princeton and Yale.) Today, oil extraction remains important in the state, and revered. Texas accounts for 45 percent of the nation's crude oil production, bolstered by horizontal drilling and fracking, which were protected by a 2015 law that keeps localities from banning it. In November 2016, the U.S. Geological Survey announced that one basin under Midland and Lubbock in west Texas appears to have three times as much oil as North Dakota's massive Bakken formation. At the same time, Texas already leads the nation in wind-powered electricity capacity. That's useful because Texas ranks sixth per capita among the states in energy consumption, due in part to high demand for air conditioning during the hot summer months. In typically Texas fashion, it is the only state that has a stand-alone electric grid entirely within its borders.

The energy sector helped Texas ride out the Great Recession; the unemployment rate topped out at 8.4 percent in 2009, which was below the peak for the nation as a whole. Impressively, the unemployment rate was at 5 percent or below from July 2014 to March 2017, though it has been rising modestly since January 2015, due in part to the global oil price collapse. Still, the recent oil slump has not hurt Texas' economy as severely as the 1980s oil bust, which helped tank the real estate and banking sectors. During the post-recession recovery, professional services generated nearly three times as many jobs in Texas as the natural resources sector. Foreclosure rates were well below the national average and far below those in other Sunbelt states including California, Nevada, Arizona and Florida. Meanwhile, lower energy costs bolster the state's thriving petrochemical industry.

The Dallas-Fort Worth Metroplex is rich with defense contractors and with small firms that grew large with exports to Mexico, and it is in the midst of building a U.S. headquarters complex for Toyota that is projected to cost $1 billion for relocation and construction. Houston is home to firms like Schlumberger, the global oil services company, as well as many of the high-tech spinoffs from the space program and the enormous Texas Medical Center. (Houston used to be home to oil service giants Halliburton and Weatherford, but those two companies moved their headquarters to Dubai and Ireland, respectively.) San Antonio, with the Air Force's prime hospital, has significant medical technology and biotech industries. Austin became a technology center vying for second place after California's Silicon Valley, as well as a mecca for the arts and culture. In 2015, Texas ranked second to California in *Fortune* 500 companies headquartered there. Those corporations helped make the Dallas-Fort Worth and Houston metro areas the fourth and fifth largest in the country, ahead of Philadelphia and Washington.

By some indicators, though, the state is underperforming. As its public colleges prosper, the rest of the public school system complains of being cash-starved. In May 2016, the state Supreme Court ruled that the state's funding formula for public schools was constitutional but urged lawmakers to reform it. Texas also faces health care challenges. Its 17 percent uninsured rate is the highest in the nation. But Texas has developed a civic culture of adaptability and resilience, as it demonstrated by taking in thousands of Hurricane Katrina evacuees in 2005. Three years later, Houston weathered Hurricane Ike with orderly and timely evacuations.

Newcomers - think of the Bushes - have done much to put the stamp of Texas on the whole of the United States. Its population grew from 21 million in 2000 to 25 million in 2010, a 21 percent increase. The reapportionment of House seats among the states reflects relative population growth; after the 2010 census, six states gained one seat, Florida gained two, California for the first time in its history gained none - and Texas gained four. Texas' growth came from a combination of immigration and domestic migration. Since 2010, the state has grown by an additional 10.8 percent, trailing only North Dakota in its percentage increase during that period. Texas' fastest-growing counties since 2010 have been suburban areas around the big cities -- Fort Bend County near Houston grew by 26.8 percent, while Denton and Collin counties near Dallas grew by 21.7 percent and 20.1 percent, respectively. Close behind were the core urban counties, led by Travis County (Austin), which has grown by 17.1 percent since 2010. Bexar (San Antonio), Harris (Houston) and Tarrant (Fort Worth) counties all grew by between 11 percent and 13 percent during that period. Even the big counties with below-average growth rates expanded at a pace that many areas in other states would envy – 9.7 percent in Hidalgo County (McAllen), 8.8 percent in Dallas County, and 4.7 percent in El Paso County.

Today, Texas is 44 percent white – down from 66 percent in 1980 and lower than any state save California, New Mexico and Hawaii. Hispanics account for 37 percent, blacks 12 percent and Asians 5 percent. Illegal immigration along the state's border with Mexico reached crisis proportions in 2014, when there was a surge of children from El Salvador, Guatemala and Honduras seeking to flee to the United States. Of those who were apprehended trying to enter the U.S., more than three quarters were caught crossing along the Rio Grande Valley. The Texas governor at the time, Rick Perry, complained that the federal government had failed to secure the border and dispatched hundreds of Texas National Guard troops and Department of Public Safety officers to provide additional surveillance, deter crossings and interdict the flow of illegal drugs. Over the decades, though, Texas has surged in part because it has nurtured and profited from its relationship with its southern neighbor. The border is long, some 1,200 miles, and porous. Nearly half of merchandise exports to Mexico are from Texas; the busiest truck crossing between the countries is the new World Trade Bridge near Laredo and Nuevo Laredo.

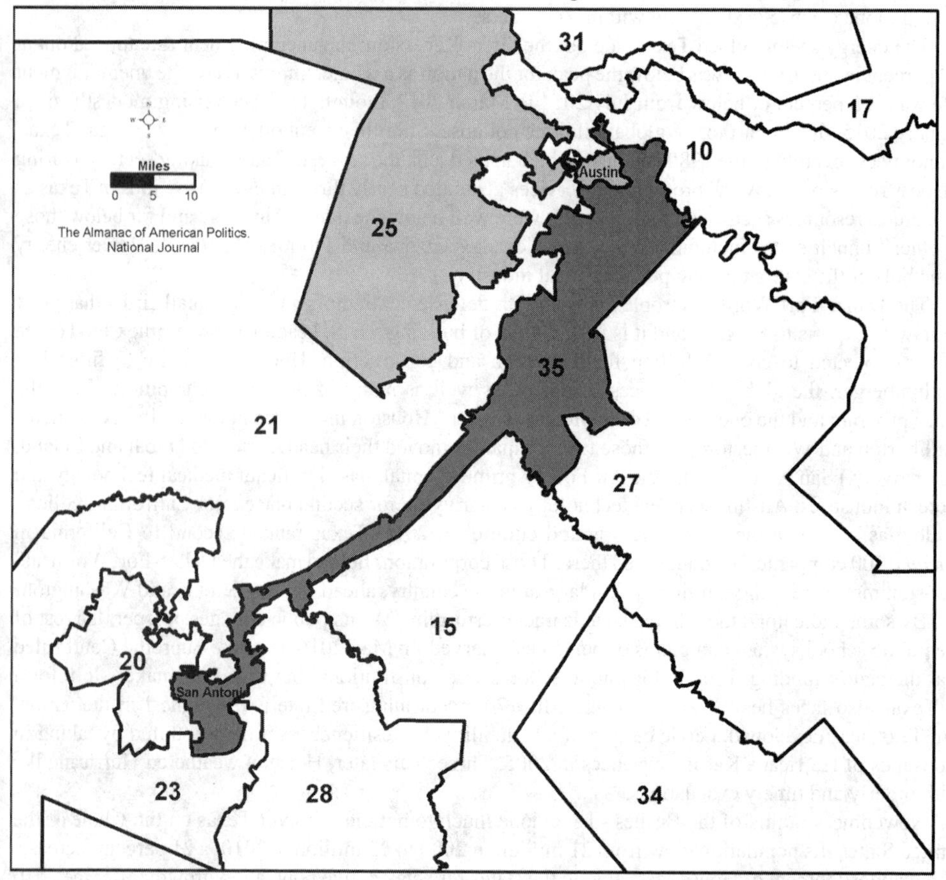

Congressional district boundaries were effective for 2012 on an interim basis. Districts 25 and 35 are highlighted for visibility.

Politically, Texas is now predominantly Republican. Republicans hold both Senate seats, more than two-thirds of the congressional seats, all nine statewide elective offices in the executive branch, all nine elected seats on the state Supreme Court, and all nine statewide elected judges on the Court of Criminal Appeals. Republicans have large margins in both houses of the state legislature, although moderate Republicans in the House often team with Democrats to stifle conservative initiatives, such as school choice. Demographic factors seem to threaten Republican dominance in the state sooner or later, but there are few signs of it yet. Most parts of rural, small-town Texas - the kinds of places portrayed in *Friday Night Lights* - are GOP strongholds, but they are being outpaced in population growth by the rest of the state. The political impact of these changes has been delayed somewhat due to a gap between the make-up of the state's population and the electorate that shows up at the polls. A big challenge for Texas Democrats is that they are largely an urban party, other than the stretch of rural counties from El Paso to Brownsville in the Rio Grande Valley that have heavy Hispanic populations. An even bigger challenge is that it has seen its bench of candidates decimated during the past quarter-century of Republican dominance.

Despite the clear victory by Trump, the 2016 presidential election showed the first indications in a long time that Democrats may have a path forward in the state. Whereas Mitt Romney won the state by 16 points in 2012, Trump won it by only nine points in 2016. Part of that stemmed from gains by third-party candidates and write-in votes, but Clinton's tally increased by about 570,000 votes, far more than Trump's increase of 115,000. Most historically Republican counties didn't pull the lever for Clinton, but in many of the bigger ones, the GOP's margins narrowed considerably. In Collin, Denton and Tarrant counties in the Dallas-Fort Worth area, Trump's margins of victory were between two and 15 points smaller than Romney's. Meanwhile, Texas' islands of blue became even bluer in 2016. In Travis, Harris, Dallas, El Paso and Bexar counties, the Democratic winning margin grew by between eight and 15 points. Perhaps the most notable shifts came in Fort Bend County near Houston, the state's most racially and ethnically diverse, and where about 45 percent of residents have bachelor's degrees, compared with28.4% statewide. Fort Bend backed Romney by a seven-point margin, but flipped to support Clinton by six. Such electoral results give Democrats hope that they can make inroads in 2018 in some of the more affluent suburban congressional districts long held by the GOP, while Sen. Ted Cruz is getting a challenge from Rep. Beto O'Rourke, one of the Democratic Party's relatively few rising stars in the state. Still, the Texas Tribune noted that even as Fort Bend flipped to Clinton, Republicans continued to win most county-level races in 2016. The demographic shift in Texas may finally be making itself felt, but it still has a long way to go.

Population		**Race and Ethnicity**		**Income**	
Total	26,538,614	White	43.8%	Median Income	$53,207 (23 out of 50)
Land area	261,232	Black	11.6%		
Pop/ sq mi	101.6	Latino	38.4%	Under $50,000	46.9%
Born in state	60.2%	Asian	4.2%	$50,000-$99,999	29.6%
		Two races	1.5%	$100,000-$199,999	18.2%
Age Groups		Other	0.4%	$200,000 or more	5.3%
Under 18	26.6%			Poverty Rate	17.3%
18-34	24.8%	**Education**			
35-64	37.6%	H.S grad or less	43.3%	**Health Insurance**	
Over 64	11.2%	Some college	29.2%	With health insurance coverage	79.4%
		College Degree, 4 yr	18.2%		
Work		Post grad	9.4%		
White Collar	35.1%			**Public Assistance**	
Sales and Service	42.1%	**Military**		Cash public assistance income	1.7%
Blue Collar	22.8%	Veteran	7.9%		
Government	13.8%	Active Duty	0.5%	Food stamp/SNAP benefits	13.4%

Voter Turnout			
2015 Total Citizens 18+	16,864,962	2016 Pres Turnout as % CVAP	53%
2016 Pres Votes	8,969,226	2012 Pres Turnout as % CVAP	51%

Legislature	
Senate:	11D, 20R
House:	55D, 95R

Presidential Politics

2016 Democratic Primary		
Hillary Clinton (D)	936,004	(65%)
Bernie Sanders (D)	476,547	(33%)
2016 Republican Primary		
Ted Cruz (R)	1,241,118	(44%)
Donald Trump (R)	758,762	(27%)
Marco Rubio (R)	503,055	(18%)

2016 Presidential Vote		
Donald Trump (R)	4,685,047	(52%)
Hillary Clinton (D)	3,877,868	(43%)
Gary Johnson (L)	283,492	(3%)
2012 Presidential Vote		
Mitt Romney (R)	4,569,843	(57%)
Barack Obama (D)	3,308,124	(41%)

In presidential elections, Texas has gone Republican in the last 10 contests. Jimmy Carter in 1976 was the last Democrat to win its then-26 electoral votes. Since the Georgian's narrow victory, the closest a Democratic nominee has come to carrying Texas was in 1996, when Texan Ross Perot split the opposition to Bill Clinton, and Bob Dole carried the state 49%-44%. George W. Bush carried the state with 59 percent and 61 percent of the vote in 2000 and 2004, respectively. In 2008, Barack Obama increased the Democratic percentage, but only to 44 percent , against John McCain's 55 percent. In 2012, Mitt Romney carried the state 57%-41%. Romney lost 58%-41% in the heavily Hispanic South Texas that includes the Rio Grande Valley, San Antonio and Corpus Christi. Obama also won 52%-45% in metro Austin. But Romney won a solid 54 percent in the Dallas-Fort Worth Metroplex (Collin, Dallas, Denton and Tarrant Counties), 52 percent in metro Houston (Brazoria, Chambers, Fort Bend, Galveston and Harris Counties). He won rural East and West Texas by 73 percent and 78 percent, respectively.

In 2016, Hillary Clinton restored the Democratic performance in the Lone Star State to close to its recent high. Donald Trump won 52%-43%, a margin of victory comparable to his victory in the battleground state of Ohio. Clinton won South Texas by roughly 59%-37%, improving a bit on Obama's 2012 showing. Clinton's breakthrough of sorts came when she won the Dallas-Fort Worth area by less than a percentage point, and captured the Houston Metro by roughly 51%-45%. Trump won East and West Texas with roughly 73 percent and 77 percent of the vote, respectively. And while he didn't carry Austin, he did handily carry the rest of south central Texas. The comparisons to 2012 are not exact because of the greater vote for third-party candidates in 2016. But the jump in the Democratic presidential vote in urban Texas, coupled with a growing Hispanic population could make the state more competitive in coming elections. Almost one-quarter of the Texas electorate was Hispanic and according to the television network exit poll they voted for Clinton by 61%-34%, a far cry from 2004, when Bush lost that group by only one percentage point. Democrats need to improve their appeal among white voters who made up more than half the state's electorate in 2016: Trump won white Texans by a whopping 69%-26%. Almost 1 million more Texans voted in 2016 than in 2012. That represented a 12.2% increase, the largest percentage gain in total votes of any state in the country. That is in part a reflection of the state's seemingly non-stop growth, which has given Texas 38 Electoral College votes, second only to California's 55. And if population trends continue, that number could climb to 41 or even 42, after the next decennial reapportionment occurs.

For the first time in 20 years, Texas was an important state in the presidential nomination process in 2008. Texas voted on March 4, after Obama had won a string of primaries and caucuses in February. Clinton won 51%-47%. But Obama won more delegates overall because one-third of them were selected in caucuses held on primary night and more Obama voters showed up. The caucus counting continued for days after the primary and was never completed, casting doubt on the actual results. In the 2016 Democratic presidential primary, Clinton swamped Vermont Sen. Bernie Sanders, 65%-33%. Sanders narrowly carried Travis County (Austin and University of Texas), next-door Hays, Brazos (Texas A&M University) as well as a handful of rural counties. Clinton won 239 of the state's 254 counties (two were tied).

On the Republican side in 2016, the primary was conducted early as the GOP nominating contest was entering a critical phase to sort out which candidates would survive. Texas Sen. Ted Cruz campaigned hard in the state, knowing that if he lost it, he was out. Another Texan, former Gov. Rick Perry also sought the Republican nomination, but his candidacy failed to catch on and he bowed out of the race in September 2015 and endorsed Cruz. A CNN debate in Houston days before the March primary was a raucous affair with candidates hurling insults at each other. Cruz ended up defeating Trump 44%-27% and claimed 248 of the state's counties; Trump won six.

Congressional Districts

115th Congress Lineup	25R 11D	**114th Congress Lineup**	25R 11D

Texas redistricting, once the plain prerogative of Anglo Democrats, now involves one of the most complex sets of partisan, racial and legal considerations in the country. In the 2000 census, Texas gained two seats, and in 2010, another four. The early projection is for a three or four-seat gain in 2020. In 2001, after a split legislature failed to agree on a map, a federal court drew a plan protecting 17 Democratic incumbents and adding two new Republican seats, for a 17-15 breakdown. Since then, as the Republicans' strengthening grip on state politics has coincided with a Hispanic population boom, Texas has endured what seems like a never-ending legislative and legal rollercoaster ride. Between 2000 and 2012, the state held its elections under five separate sets of boundaries, and a sixth is possible in 2018.

Republicans took over the legislature in 2002, and House Majority Leader Tom DeLay (whose 2011 conviction for charges related to his role was overturned by an appeals court) pressured his party to replace the court plan with a design to maximize Republican seats. Famously, 51 Texas House Democrats, who became known as the "Killer D's," fled to Oklahoma to thwart a two-thirds quorum. But Republicans eventually rammed through their map, converting a 15-17 deficit that wildly underrepresented GOP strength into a 21-11 edge in 2004 by defeating five "WD-40s" - white Democrats over age 40 - whom DeLay had targeted for extinction. In 2006, the U.S. Supreme Court insisted on minor changes in South Texas to protect Hispanics. In 2010, Republicans captured 23 of 32 seats, and it was Democrats rather than Republicans who were severely underrepresented.

In early 2011, holding a gluttony of seats, Republicans faced a dilemma. The most rapid growth in the state had taken place in exurban counties, almost all of them Republican. But Hispanics had accounted for 65 percent of all growth between 2000 and 2010, and the state's plans were subject to review by the Obama administration's Justice Department. The prevailing interpretation of the Voting Rights Act seemed to require maximizing black- and Hispanic-majority seats. So, mindful of federal scrutiny, a group of pragmatic House Republicans led by Rep. Lamar Smith lobbied legislators in Austin to simply shore up incumbents and split the four new seats evenly: two new Democratic-leaning, Hispanic-majority seats, and two new Republican seats in fast-growing exurban areas, for a 25-11 delegation.

Republican legislators, and Perry, were horror-struck by the idea of "giving" Democrats *any* seats. In June, they disregarded their own delegation's advice and passed their own plan to split the Metroplex's Hispanic population six ways, stuff Austin Democrat Lloyd Doggett into a heavily Hispanic seat stretching to San Antonio, and create three new safely Republican enclaves: one in Fort Worth's western suburbs, another in Houston's eastern suburbs, and a third running along the I-35 corridor from the fringes of the Metroplex to the outskirts of Austin. The plan created one new Democratic seat in the Rio Grande Valley. But it did so by dropping the neighboring 27th District of Republican Blake Farenthold, a surprise 2010 winner, from 73 percent to 49 percent Hispanic.

Doggett and the Democrats immediately blasted the "Perry-mander" as a gross overreach. Hispanic advocacy groups denounced it as discriminatory and sued in a San Antonio federal court. The groups argued that while Republicans had created a "new" Hispanic majority 35th District stretching from Austin to San Antonio, they had weakened the sprawling 23rd District between El Paso and San Antonio by underhandedly swapping out high-turnout Hispanic precincts for low-turnout precincts to boost freshman Republican Quico Canseco's Anglo share.

The Justice Department declared the map had been drawn with discriminatory intent and assumed the opposition as Attorney General Greg Abbott, in an end-around attempt, sought preclearance from a three-judge panel at the U.S. Court of Appeals in Washington. Back in San Antonio, Republicans weren't faring much better before a separate three-judge panel. The state's own expert witness, Rice University professor John Alford, admitted on the stand the Republican map didn't create an effective new Hispanic seat. The San Antonio panel halted the map's implementation and announced its intent to draw its own interim plan if the state map did not obtain federal preclearance before the December 2011 opening of the candidate filing period.

Sure enough, the D.C. court denied Abbott's request for quick summary judgment, setting up a protracted preclearance trial that couldn't possibly be resolved by a December deadline. So the San Antonio judges delighted Democrats with their own plan: Not only did it preserve Doggett's existing

Austin-based 25th District, it essentially drew three of four new seats for Democrats - one minority "coalition" seat in Fort Worth, and one Hispanic majority seat each in the Rio Grande Valley and San Antonio areas. In yet another surprise twist, the high court granted Abbott's request for a stay, in turn forcing Texas to delay its primary until May.

In January 2012, the Supreme Court ruled that the San Antonio court had "exceeded its mission" to fix only the districts that had violated the Voting Rights Act and faulted the court for failing to use an elected legislature's original plan as a baseline for its own. So in February, the San Antonio court issued a second interim map. This time, it resembled Republicans' plan, except it created a new 66 percent Hispanic seat linking Dallas and Fort Worth and restored Hispanic voting strength in the 23rd District. The end result was nearly identical to what Republican incumbents had lobbied for in the first place: a 2-2 division of new seats. Democrats scored another pickup in November by ousting Canseco in the 23rd, for 12 of 36 seats overall.

Following further legal maneuvering, the San Antonio panel ruled in March 2017 that Doggett's 35th District, plus the districts of Republican Reps. Will Hurd and Blake Farenthold were drawn in ways that discriminated against Hispanics. But the judges failed to offer an immediate alternative, leaving uncertainty about the timing and details of a potential replacement - and the possibility of a Supreme Court review before any new map was implemented. Even if no immediate changes are made in the current map, the court ruling raises the prospect that the additional seats for Texas following the 2020 reapportionment will be chiefly Democratic-held.

Of note, although the 2012 interim map increased the number of Hispanic majority districts from seven to nine, the number of Hispanics representing them remained at five. Anglo Democrats Doggett and Gene Green won reelection in overwhelmingly Hispanic districts, black Democrat Marc Veasey narrowly captured the new Dallas-area 33rd District, and although Democrat Filemon Vela won the new 34th District in the Rio Grande Valley, Democrat Silvestre Reyes lost a primary challenge to an Anglo, Beto O'Rourke, in the El Paso 16th District. (In a sign of how times have changed, no white Democrat represents an Anglo-majority district in Texas.) In 2014, African-American Republican Will Hurd ousted Hispanic Democrat Pete Gallego in the heavily Hispanic 23rd District. Also noteworthy is that the Texas Republican delegation includes seven committee chairman and three Appropriations subcommittee chairmen, the kind of clout that Texas Democrats wielded in the heyday of Democratic control. Some of those current chairmen would be at risk if there are major redistricting changes. It may take more decades of naturalization, mobilization, and litigation before Texas' share of Hispanic officeholders catches up to the fast-maturing Hispanic share of the state's total residents - 39 percent in 2015.

Governor

Greg Abbott (R)

Elected 2014, term expires 2019, 1st term; b. Nov. 13, 1957, Wichita Falls, TX; U. of TX, B.B.A. 1981; Vanderbilt U., J.D. 1984; Catholic; Married (Cecilia); 1 child.

Elected Office: TX State Trial Judge 129th District Court, 1992-1995; TX Supreme Court, 1995-2001; TX Attorney General, 2002-2014.

Professional Career: Practicing attorney, Butler & Binion, 1984-1992.

Office: PO Box 12428, Austin, 78711-2428; 512-463-2000; Fax: 512-463-5571; Website: gov.texas.gov.

Election Results

Election	Name (Party)	Vote (%)
2014 General	Greg Abbott (R)	2,796,547 (59%)
	Wendy Davis (D)	1,835,596 (39%)
2014 Primary	Greg Abbott (R)	1,224,014 (92%)

Republican Greg Abbott once described his job as the state's attorney general this way: "I go into the office in the morning, I sue Barack Obama, and then I go home." It was that reputation that helped Abbott win the governorship in 2014, entrenching Republican domination in a state that has not elected a Democrat to statewide office since 1994. With Obama's exit from the White House, Abbott has generally supported President Donald Trump, particularly on immigration and border security.

Abbott was born in Wichita Falls and raised in Duncanville in Dallas County. He earned a bachelor's degree in finance from the University of Texas at Austin and got his law degree from Vanderbilt University in Nashville. The year he finished law school, in 1984, a falling tree injured Abbott while he was out for a run. The incident left him a paraplegic, and he has used a wheelchair ever since. After a stint in private practice, Abbott became an associate justice on the Texas Supreme Court in 1995, appointed to fill a vacancy by then-Gov. George W. Bush. Abbott won election twice more to the state's highest civil court, and in 2001 he resigned to run for attorney general in 2002. Abbott won reelection twice and became the longest-serving state attorney general in Texas history. As the state's highest law enforcement officer, Abbott was a pure Texas conservative. He sued the federal government more than two dozen times, on issues ranging from the Affordable Care Act to abortion, voter ID, and environmental regulations. In 2005, Abbott appeared before the U.S. Supreme Court to argue in favor of the constitutionality of the Ten Commandments monument on the Texas State Capitol grounds. (He won, with the high court ruling 5-4 that the display did not violate the Constitution's Establishment Clause.)

Less than a week after Gov. Rick Perry announced he would not seek another term, Abbott declared his candidacy for the job. He faced only token opposition in the GOP primary; in the general, he squared off against state Sen. Wendy Davis, whom supporters hoped would benefit from the national attention she got from her unsuccessful filibuster of a bill to ban most abortions after the 20th week of pregnancy. Democrats saw Texas, with its growing Hispanic population, as a state gradually swinging in their direction, and Davis tapped Hispanic state Sen. Leticia Van de Putte as her running mate. Abbott was joined at the top of the GOP ticket by state Sen. Dan Patrick, the nominee for lieutenant governor, and state Sen. Ken Paxton, the nominee for attorney general; both were tea party favorites who had prevailed over establishment favorites in contentious primaries and runoffs. Davis sought to portray Abbott as an Austin "insider" siding with the interests of his rich and powerful friends at the expense of "hard-working Texans." Abbott saturated the airwaves with spots that reminded voters how, despite using a wheelchair, he had persevered and succeeded in life. His ads portrayed Davis as closely aligned with Obama, who was not popular in the Lone Star State, and he featured his Hispanic mother-in-law in TV ads and on billboards to appeal to Hispanic voters. In October, the Davis campaign released the "wheelchair ad." The spot opened with a picture of a wheelchair, noted Abbott's crippling accident and said, "He sued and got millions. Since then he spent his career working against other victims." The ad then cited cases as evidence that Abbott had thwarted or ruled against other victims trying to get compensation. The ad got a lot of attention, including criticism that it was in bad taste. But there was probably nothing that was going to save Davis' campaign; Abbott ended up trouncing her, 59%-39%. Exit polls showed he won roughly 44 percent of the Hispanic vote. Abbott carried 235 of the state's 254 counties, limiting Davis to the Democratic strongholds of Dallas, El Paso and Travis County (Austin) and 16 others in the heavily Hispanic Rio Grande Valley.

Abbott made progress on some of his key agenda items in 2015. He signed legislation in May to provide $130 million in funding to school districts whose pre-kindergarten programs met certain standards, including having certified teachers and using a state-approved curriculum. The measure won bipartisan approval in the legislature, though it was briefly stalled in the Senate when Lt. Gov. Patrick's "Grassroots Advisory Board," a council of mostly tea party activists, distributed a letter to lawmakers calling the proposal "socialistic" and a "threat to parental rights." Patrick distanced himself from that opposition, and the measure passed the 31-member chamber with only six Republican tea party allies defecting to vote no. Then, in June, Abbott steamrolled critics who said border-crossing from Mexico was at a years-long low, signing legislation that expedited hiring of law-enforcement officers on the border, increased penalties for human trafficking, and established a center to analyze border-crime data. Abbott got a further boost when a federal judge in Brownsville blocked Obama's executive order on immigration, which he had personally fought in court in his waning days as attorney general. Abbott's push for broad ethics reform sputtered, however, as he vetoed legislation with a last-minute amendment that weakened standards. (In 2017, he signed an ethics bill .) Meanwhile, Abbott pleased social conservatives by removing a mock Nativity display at the state Capitol that had been mounted by an atheist group; he then made sure that the state fought a lawsuit filed by the organization that had placed the display.

In the 2016 presidential race, Abbott initially supported home-state Sen. Ted Cruz, but later threw his support to Trump. Abbott, like the GOP presidential candidates, continued to articulate a tough stance on immigration. In November 2015, he said the state would refuse to accept Syrian refugees. Just over a year later, he threatened to cut funding to any public university that considered itself a "sanctuary" campus. Two months later, he kept a promise to cut state grants to Travis County Sheriff Sally Hernandez, who had moved to limit cooperation with federal immigration officials over arrestees accused of minor crimes. After Trump took office, Abbott praised the new president's efforts to build a border wall and to expand federal spending on border security.

In his 2017 state of the state address, Abbott urged changes to the state Child Protective Services agency, which had been accused of neglect, and spoke in favor of expanded school choice, including taxpayer-funded vouchers for private schools. He declared a state hiring freeze through August, and called on lawmakers to pass a law requiring burial or cremation for fetal remains. He signed a measure to cut state funding for sanctuary cities. Abbott reiterated a prior call for a constitutional convention that would refocus powers away from the federal government and toward the states. One issue Abbott touched only gingerly was a "bathroom bill" that would require transgender individuals to use the bathroom of their birth sex; a similar law in North Carolina had become a target of boycotts and contributed to the defeat of the incumbent Republican governor before being repealed in 2017. As the bill worked its way through the legislature, Abbott ranged from neutral to supportive of a more moderate version. By early 2017, Abbott's approval rating hovered in the mid-60s, and he had a sizable war chest. When he officially announced that he was running again, a significant potential primary challenger – Patrick -- decided against running. While a challenge from the right was still possible, and while Democrats were heartened by a relatively strong showing in the 2016 presidential race in Texas, Abbott remained the frontrunner to win a second term as governor.

Senior Senator

John Cornyn (R)

Elected 2002, term expires 2020, 3rd term; b. Feb 02, 1952, Houston; St. Mary's School of Law (TX), J.D.; Trinity University (TX), B.A.; University of Virginia, LL.M.; Church of Christ; Married (Sandra Hansen Cornyn); 2 children.

Elected Office: Bexar County District court judge, 1985-1991; TX Supreme Court, 1991-1997; TX Attorney General, 1999-2002.

Professional Career: Practicing attorney, 1977-1984.

DC Office: 517 HSOB 20510, 202-224-2934, Fax: 202-228-2856, cornyn.senate.gov.

State Offices: Austin, 512-469-6034; Dallas, 972-239-1310; Harlingen, 956-423-0162; Houston, 713-572-3337; Lubbock, 806-472-7533; San Antonio, 210-224-7485; Tyler, 903-593-0902.

Committees: Senate Majority Whip & Assistant Majority Leader. *Finance*: Energy, Natural Resources & Infrastructure, International Trade, Customs & Global Competitiveness (Chmn), Taxation & IRS Oversight. *Intelligence*. *Judiciary*: Border Security & Immigration (Chmn), Constitution, Crime & Terrorism.

Group Ratings

	ADA	ACLU	AFL-CIO	LCV	ITI	COC	HAFA	ACU	CFG	FRC
2016	-	5%	-	6%	100%	100%	47%	79%	72%	0%
2015	0%	C	14%	0%	C	93%	C	71%	65%	100%

Almanac Ratings 2015

	Economy	Social	Foreign	Composite
Liberal	28%	0%	28%	19%
Conservative	72%	100%	72%	81%

Key Votes of the 114th Congress

1. Keystone pipeline	Y	5. National Security Data	Y	9. Gun Sales Checks	N
2. Export-Import Bank	Y	6. Iran Nuclear Deal	Y	10. Sanctuary Cities	Y
3. Debt Ceiling Increase	Y	7. Puerto Rico Debt	Y	11. Planned Parenthood	Y
4. Homeland Security $$	Y	8. Loretta Lynch A.G	N	12. Trade deals	Y

Election Results

Election	Name (Party)	Vote (%)	Cand. Spent	Ind. Exp. Support	Ind. Exp. Oppose
2014 General	John Cornyn (R)........................	2,860,678 (62%)	$14,672,004	$635,391	$27,244
	David Alameel (D).....................	1,597,272 (34%)	$5,715,984		
	Rebecca Paddock (L)..................	133,738 (3%)			
2014 Primary	John Cornyn (R)...........................	781,259 (59%)			
	Steve Stockman (R)....................	251,577 (19%)			
	Dwayne Stovall (R).....................	140,794 (11%)			

Prior winning percentages: 2008 (55%), 2002 (55%)

Republican John Cornyn, Texas' senior senator, has risen quickly through his party's leadership ranks since his initial election in 2002. After two terms as chairman of the National Republican Senatorial Committee, he was chosen minority whip -- the second-ranking slot in the Senate GOP hierarchy -- in 2013. Two years later, after the Republicans retook control of the Senate, Cornyn became majority whip. No Texas senator has risen as high in that chamber since the 1950s, when Democrat Lyndon Johnson was majority leader.

Nevertheless, the workload has been bumpy for Cornyn at times. Since 2013, he has shared representation of the Lone Star State with tea party firebrand -- and erstwhile presidential contender -- Ted Cruz: Cornyn and Cruz have perhaps the chilliest relationship of any two current Senators representing the same state . In 2015, Cornyn, a former state Supreme Court justice and state Attorney General, put together a bipartisan and ideologically diverse coalition behind a criminal justice reform bill, which seemed poised to become one of the few significant legislative accomplishments in that Congress. But it ultimately failed to reach the Senate floor amid hardline opposition from several of the most conservative Republicans , including Cruz. In 2017, Cornyn was interviewed to be director of the Federal Bureau of Investigation -- only to withdraw his name when it became clear that the appointment of a partisan Republican would have created a firestorm, in light of the politically charged circumstances in which President Donald Trump had dismissed the previous FBI head, James Comey.

Cornyn's willingness to be considered for the FBI post appeared to stem, in part, from his uncertain future in the Senate leadership: Under the Republican Conference's internal rules, he will have to step down as whip at the end of 2018, after serving three terms. Cornyn, who turned 65 in early 2017, has made little secret of his desire to eventually succeed Majority Leader Mitch McConnell, telling *Politico* that it is "something I would be interested in doing." But McConnell, who holds the one Republican leadership post not subject to term limits, is not up for reelection from Kentucky until 2020, and there is no guarantee that he will step down -- even though he will be 78 at that point. "And so I think a lot depends on what his decision is going to be," acknowledged Cornyn, who also faces reelection in 2020.

Cornyn was born in Houston and spent much of his childhood in San Antonio. His father was an oral pathologist in the Air Force stationed in Japan, where Cornyn went to high school. After his father retired from the service, the family settled in San Antonio. Cornyn graduated from Trinity University and St. Mary's University School of Law, both in San Antonio. He practiced law for five years with a firm that defended physicians and insurance companies in medical malpractice cases. In 1984, he ran for district court judge in Bexar County and, at 32, upset a strong favorite in the race. In 1990, Cornyn was elected to the state Supreme Court. Five years later, he wrote the 5-4 decision upholding the state's "Robin Hood" school finance system, in which property-wealthy school districts had to send money to property-poor districts.

In 1997, Cornyn resigned from the court to run for attorney general. Against two better known opponents, he placed second in the initial round of the primary, but went on to win the runoff. In the general election, he faced a grizzled political veteran -- former Attorney General Jim Mattox, a populist Democrat who had been a House member from Dallas. Cornyn won 54%-44%, becoming the first Republican attorney general in Texas since Reconstruction. He argued two cases before the U.S. Supreme Court, including the Santa Fe Independent School District's defense of reading the Lord's Prayer at football games. (The high court nixed it.)

When GOP Sen. Phil Gramm announced he would not seek reelection in 2002, Cornyn got into the contest to succeed him, and had no serious opposition in the Republican primary. Democrats nominated two-term Dallas Mayor Ron Kirk, who was vying to become Texas' first African-American senator. Cornyn ran as a strong supporter of President -- and former Texas Governor -- George W. Bush; he called for making Bush's 2001 tax cuts permanent. He supported government vouchers for private school tuition, individual investment accounts as part of Social Security, and color-blind standards for college and university admissions. Kirk took opposite stands on most issues, but portrayed himself as a moderate Democrat who would support Bush in many instances. Republicans ran ads linking Kirk to then-New York Senator Hillary Clinton, and to liberal out-of-state contributors.

Kirk (who later served as U.S. trade representative under President Barack Obama) campaigned with a sense of humor, making fun of his bald pate, but he made some mistakes. He refused to disclose his income tax returns, except for allowing reporters a peek at his 2001 return. Cornyn came out in favor of a bill in the Texas legislature requiring district attorneys to seek the death penalty for killers of law enforcement officials, after the Austin-based district attorney had not done so for the killer of a Travis County sheriff's deputy. Kirk said Cornyn was acting like he was running for district attorney, and then apologized to a convention of law enforcement officials a few days later -- as Cornyn met with the deputy's widow. Democrats operated on the assumption that Kirk had to win 85% of African Americans, 65% of Hispanics, and 35% of whites to win. He clearly achieved the first and probably achieved the second of those goals, but failed by a solid margin to achieve the third. Cornyn won 55%-43%-almost the same percentages as in his race for attorney general in 1998, and a fair reflection of basic party identification in Texas in recent years. Kirk carried historically Republican Dallas County by a narrow margin -- but Cornyn won the entire Dallas-Fort Worth Metroplex, and also carried metropolitan Houston and the combined San Antonio and Austin metro areas.

Cornyn often is described as "genial," and generally favors reasoned language over angry rhetoric. "He's quiet by nature and isn't excitable," his friend Jim Lunz, a retired San Antonio businessman, told *The New Republic*. "So when he does speak, you are more inclined to listen to what he has to say." Because of his reputation, South Carolina Republican Sen. Lindsey Graham told NPR in December 2014 that Cornyn was "the best guy in the [GOP] conference to bring us together" as Republicans prepared to assume the majority. "Nobody doubts his conservatism," said Graham, who arrived in the Senate at the same time as Cornyn. "But he's a very practical, let's-move-the-ball-forward kind of guy."

In contrast, Cornyn's in-state colleague, Cruz, has a reputation for slash-and-burn legislative tactics that have alienated senators on both sides of the aisle. Ironically, Cornyn's dealings with Cruz mirrored the sometimes uneasy relationship between McConnell and his junior Kentucky colleague, tea party-aligned Rand Paul. But, after Paul was nominated in 2010 over McConnell's opposition, the two reached a rapprochement of sorts: Paul endorsed McConnell over a tea party challenger in the 2014 primary, and McConnell backed Paul's bid for the party's presidential nomination two years later. Such an accommodation proved to be a bridge too far for Cornyn and Cruz. In the 2012 primary, in which Cruz scored a come-from-behind win over Lieutenant Governor David Dewhurst, Cruz was criticized for refusing to back Cornyn's bid for GOP Senate whip. Cruz subsequently declined to endorse Cornyn when the latter faced a challenge from the right in the 2014 primary. Cornyn, in turn, stayed out of the 2016 race for the GOP presidential nomination in which Cruz emerged as the leading challenger to Trump; the presence of several candidates with Texas ties gave Cornyn political cover. Cornyn has served notice that he plans to remain neutral in Texas' 2018 Republican Senate primary -- when Cruz may face a serious challenge.

"Obviously I would have loved for Ted and I to be exactly two peas in a pod on everything," Cornyn mused to the *Austin American-Statesman* editorial board in February 2014. Days earlier, in what he described as "an uncomfortable moment," Cornyn had moved to shut down a Cruz filibuster of an increase in the federal debt ceiling. Upon Cruz's arrival on Capitol Hill, Cornyn sought to work with him -- helping Cruz to land a seat on the Judiciary Committee, where Cornyn also serves, and initially signing on to Cruz's effort in late 2013 to shut down the government in an effort to de-fund the Affordable Care Act. Cornyn subsequently withdrew his support and criticized the highly controversial tactic, which resulted in a 16-day shutdown. *The Dallas Morning News*' editorial page in January 2015 suggested Cornyn was often guilty of "straying from his signature sound judgment and allowing the party's extremists, including Cruz, to set an agenda that feeds gridlock." Six months later, Cornyn did call out his colleague when Cruz, in a startling departure from Senate norms, accused McConnell of a "flat-out lie" on an Export-Import Bank bill. Cornyn, in a remark considered blunt by the chamber's genteel standards, responded, "I have listened to the comments of my colleague, the junior senator from Texas, both last week and this week, and I would have to say that he is mistaken."

Cornyn's move to end Cruz's 2014 filibuster of the debt ceiling increase came after he helped to strike a compromise on the matter, joining McConnell and breaking with most members of the Republican conference to vote for a clean increase after they failed to convince other Republicans to take those votes instead. The episode ended years of repeated brinksmanship over government spending that often hurt Republicans in the polls.

With the Republicans back in the majority in 2015, Cornyn took over as chairman of Judiciary's Constitution, Civil Rights and Human Rights Subcommittee. He changed its name to the Constitution Subcommittee, angering civil rights groups. In October of that year, Cornyn led a diverse group of eight senators -- including two members of the Senate Democratic leadership as well as the Republican chairman of the Judiciary panel -- in introducing a major criminal justice reform measure. "This is the way the system is supposed to work--people with different views come together, find common ground. You won't get everything you want, and if your attitude is 'I get everything I want or nothing,' you'll always get nothing," declared Cornyn, in what some saw as a dig at Cruz. The bill proposed to reduce sentences for some non-violent drug offenses and give judges more leeway with lower-level drug crimes, while also increasing rehabilitation and job training programs for inmates to cut down on recidivism. Cornyn said it drew on reforms that had worked in Texas.

The bill cleared the Judiciary Committee on a bipartisan vote, with leading liberals such the panel's ranking Democrat, Patrick Leahy of Vermont, joining tea party-aligned Republican Mike Lee of Utah in embracing it. But it then ran into objections from Cruz and several other conservative hardliners, and, despite revisions designed to assuage the dissenters, McConnell opted not to bring it to the floor. McConnell "understandably did not want to tee up an issue that split our caucus right before the 2016 election," Cornyn told *The New York Times*, while expressing consternation about the demise of the legislation. "It is one of the things that makes this a frustrating place to work," he observed.

Another bipartisan bill Cornyn introduced in 2015 ended up leading to major partisan conflict. His bill targeting sexual abuse and human trafficking passed the Judiciary panel unanimously before Democrats realized it had language that would limit the ability of victims to receive abortions. An incensed Cornyn pointed out the bill had been public for weeks before Democrats noticed the provision just before the bill was up for passage by the full Senate. "The idea that there's been some sort of ambush is just preposterous, it's just not credible," he declared. But Democrats refused to accept the language, despite quietly acknowledging they had failed to notice it earlier. Republicans retaliated by holding up the nomination of Loretta Lynch for attorney general, putting them in the position of blocking the first African-American woman to hold the job over an unrelated issue. Cornyn and Washington state Democrat Patty Murray eventually worked out a compromise that led to unanimous passage of the bill and paved the way for Lynch's confirmation.

A year later, Cornyn worked with another senior Democrat on the Judiciary panel, Dianne Feinstein of California, to attempt to find common ground on the gun control issue following the deadliest mass shooting in U.S. history: the June 2016 Orlando, Florida nightclub massacre in which 49 were killed. Ultimately, Cornyn and Feinstein produced competing proposals, neither of which was able to get enough votes to advance -- as has repeatedly been the case in recent years when gun control measures have been considered on the Senate floor. "We all agree that terrorists should not be able to purchase a weapon; that is not up for debate," Cornyn was quoted as saying by the *Texas Tribune*. "The question before us is whether we're going to do so in a way that's constitutional."

Under Cornyn's amendment, which had the backing of the National Rifle Association, the attorney general would be given 72 hours to prove there was a probable cause for denying a suspected terrorist the ability to purchase a gun. Feinstein's amendment permitted the attorney general to ban gun sales to those on the Federal Bureau of Investigation's database of known or suspected terrorists if there was "reasonable belief" the weapons might be used to carry out an attack. Feinstein questioned the feasibility of providing evidence in 72 hours as called for by Cornyn's plan, and contended that the FBI database was "clearly vetted." Cornyn argued that Feinstein's proposal would deny due process, while saying his amendment "would stop terrorists from buying guns while ensuring law-abiding citizens placed on a watch list by mistake don't have their rights taken away because of some secret list created by the Obama Administration…" At the outset of the Trump administration, Cornyn introduced legislation to allow gun owners to carry firearms across state lines by requiring a given state to recognize gun permits issued elsewhere.

Earlier, Cornyn emerged as a leading critic of the Obama administration's "Operation Fast and Furious" initiative, an ill-fated plan that allegedly allowed guns to cross the border into Mexico as a way to track drug cartels, but that were later linked to fatal shootings. In 2011, Cornyn's bill blocking the Justice Department from undertaking future Fast and Furious-type programs passed the Senate unanimously. He later called on Lynch's predecessor, Attorney General Eric Holder, to resign over the matter.

Cornyn worked on immigration reform legislation in 2007 before abandoning his efforts. Arizona Republican John McCain angrily accused Cornyn at the time of raising arcane legal issues to scuttle the bill. Cornyn said of the talks, "I didn't so much walk away as got chased away." His amendment to bar illegal immigrants convicted of identity theft from legalization processes was defeated 51-46. From then on, he opposed the larger immigration bill. As reform heated up in 2013 with the bipartisan "Gang of Eight" of which McCain was part, Cornyn remained a skeptic about a comprehensive approach. He said giving illegal immigrants a path to citizenship remained premature and insisted on focusing on border enforcement. Frank Sharry, founder of the pro-immigration group America's Voice, complained in the *Huffington Post* that Cornyn "is famous for posing as a reformer even as he works to derail reform."

Cornyn voted against the bipartisan comprehensive reform bill that passed the Senate in 2013 after the chamber rejected his amendment that would have required 100 percent surveillance of the southern border and 90 percent apprehension of border-crossers before undocumented immigrants could begin a pathway to citizenship. When a crisis involving Central American refugees along the border became a major controversy in 2014, Cornyn joined with Texas Democratic Rep. Henry Cuellar on a bill expediting the deportation of undocumented children from countries other than Mexico and Canada. Democrats and immigration advocates criticized the bill, saying an easier deportation process would return the children to potentially dangerous situations back home. Cornyn was among a number of border state Republicans who in early 2017 took issue with Trump's call for a contiguous wall along the 1,900 mile U.S.-Mexico border, advocating instead for 700 miles of border fence as called for in a 2006 statute.

Cornyn began his campaign for a second term in 2008 with polls showing he was less popular than his then-Republican colleague, Kay Bailey Hutchison. But Democratic attempts to attract a well-known challenger failed. Their nominee was Houston state Rep. Rick Noriega, a veteran of the war in Afghanistan. Cornyn outraised Noriega by better than 4-1, and won 55%-43%, the same margin as in 2002. He captured 36 percent of the Hispanic vote, an improvement over 2002.

Following his reelection victory, Cornyn became chairman of the NRSC, the political arm of the Senate GOP. Democrats had gained 14 Senate seats in the 2006 and 2008 campaign cycles, when their Senate campaign committee was headed by New York Sen. Charles Schumer; Cornyn wanted to reverse those results. Cornyn adopted Schumer's strategy of recruiting candidates who could win in states not naturally inclined to his party. It didn't always work out. Cornyn urged Gov. Charlie Crist to run in Florida and Rep. Mike Castle to run in Delaware. In Florida, former state House Speaker Marco Rubio gained steam against Crist, eventually forcing him from the party and then crushing his independent bid. And Castle lost in a stunning primary upset to a tea party challenger, Christine O'Donnell, with the Democrats retaining the seat in the fall.

Despite these setbacks, Cornyn succeeded in the chairman's major duty: raising large sums. He brought in $115 million for the cycle and came close to matching the $130 million raised by rival Democrats for the 2010 election . The Republicans ended up gaining six seats, many more than seemed likely in January 2009, when insiders were predicting further Democratic gains, but less than seemed possible over the summer and fall. In addition to O'Donnell's defeat in Delaware, where Castle would almost certainly have won, tea party candidates Sharron Angle in Nevada and Ken Buck in Colorado both lost their races.

After the election, Cornyn got another term as NRSC chairman for the 2012 elections without serious opposition. Irritated by then-South Carolina Republican Sen. Jim DeMint's endorsements of candidates whose chances Cornyn had thought to be dim in 2010, notably Angle and O'Donnell, he urged colleagues to bring concerns they had about candidates to him. DeMint pledged not to oppose any incumbent Republican senators. Cornyn, in turn, made it plain that he would be more wary of taking sides in primaries. The upshot was that a pair of far-right Republicans became nominees: Richard Mourdock in Indiana and Todd Akin in Missouri. Both blew what were seen as nearly sure-thing opportunities after they made politically disastrous comments about rape and abortion. Democrats ended up netting two Senate seats in a year they were expected to lose a handful.

When Republican Whip Jon Kyl of Arizona announced that he would retire at the end of 2012, Cornyn announced he would run for the position. Lamar Alexander of Tennessee initially said he would run for whip, but later dropped out. Richard Burr of North Carolina also briefly considered running, but decided against it, giving Cornyn a clear path to the post.

In 2014, Cornyn's biggest reelection threat appeared to be from the right following Cruz's surprise primary win over Dewhurst, an establishment Republican like Cornyn. But Cornyn assiduously courted conservatives in the state, careful not to split with Cruz's hardline postures on most high-profile votes. And he brought in some of the conservative strategists who had helped Cruz win. His efforts, and huge early fundraising, helped scare off serious primary challengers. Even though Cruz declined to endorse him, Cornyn drew no serious tea-party primary opposition-just an impulsive last-minute challenge from quirky far-right Rep. Steve Stockman. Cornyn finished way ahead of Stockman, 59%-19%. In heavily Republican Texas, Cornyn's race against Democratic businessman David Alameel was little more than a formality, as he won 62%-34%.

In the Senate, Cornyn was close to Alabama Republican Jeff Sessions, who -- as Trump's attorney general -- asked Cornyn to consider the FBI job after Trump fired Comey in May 2017. Cornyn was quickly interviewed, but a week after Comey's ouster, he took himself out of the running. "Now more than ever the country needs a well-credentialed, independent FBI director," Cornyn said. "I've informed the administration that I'm committed to helping them find such an individual, and that the best way I can serve is continuing to fight for a conservative agenda in the U.S. Senate." His statement hinted at what even many of his Republican colleagues were suggesting: Given allegations that Trump had fired Comey to slow down an investigation of possible collusion by the Trump campaign with Russia in the 2016 election, appointment of a partisan as FBI director -- even a well-liked one such as Cornyn -- would have yielded a bruising confirmation battle. "I told him I thought he'd be a good FBI director under normal circumstances," his Senate colleague, Graham, told *The Washington Post*. "But I just, quite frankly, think that last week made it tough."

Junior Senator

Ted Cruz (R)

Elected 2012, term expires 2018, 1st term; b. Dec 22, 1970, Calgary, Alberta, Canada, AB; Princeton University (NJ), A.B.; Harvard University, J.D.; Southern Baptist; Married (Heidi Nelson); 2 children.

Professional Career: Clerk, U.S Appeals Court, 1995; Clerk, Supreme Court Justice William Rehnquist, 1996; Attorney, Cooper, Carvin & Rosenthal, 1997-1999; Domestic policy adviser, Bush-Cheney campaign, 1999- 2000; Association deputy U.S Attorney General, 2001; Policy-planning office Director, Fed. Trade Commission, 2001-2002; Texas solicitor General, 2003-2008; Adjunct Professor, University of TX, 2004-2009; Attorney, Morgan, Lewis & Bockius, 2008-2012.

DC Office: 404 RSOB 20510, 202-224-5922, Fax: 202-228-0755, cruz.senate.gov.

State Offices: Austin, 512-916-5834; Dallas, 214-599-8749; Houston, 713-718-3057; McAllen, 956-686-7339; San Antonio, 210-340-2885; Tyler, 903-593-5130.

Committees: *Armed Services*: Airland, Emerging Threats & Capabilities, Strategic Forces. *Commerce, Science & Transportation*: Aviation Operations, Safety & Security, Communications, Technology, Innovation & the Internet, Consumer Protection, Product Safety, Ins & Data Security, Space, Science & Competitiveness (Chmn). *Judiciary*: Border Security & Immigration, Constitution (Chmn), Crime & Terrorism. *Rules & Administration*.

Group Ratings

	ADA	ACLU	AFL-CIO	LCV	ITI	COC	HAFA	ACU	CFG	FRC
2016	-	35%	-	0%	33%	100%	94%	0%	-	0%
2015	0%	C	23%	0%	C	54%	C	100%	95%	100%

Almanac Ratings 2015

	Economy	Social	Foreign	Composite
Liberal	19%	10%	40%	23%
Conservative	81%	90%	60%	77%

Key Votes of the 114th Congress

1. Keystone pipeline	Y	5. National Security Data	Y	9. Gun Sales Checks	N
2. Export-Import Bank	Y	6. Iran Nuclear Deal	Y	10. Sanctuary Cities	Y
3. Debt Ceiling Increase	N	7. Puerto Rico Debt	N	11. Planned Parenthood	Y
4. Homeland Security $$	N	8. Loretta Lynch A.G	NV	12. Trade deals	Y

Election Results

Election	Name (Party)	Vote (%)	Cand. Spent	Ind. Exp. Support	Ind. Exp. Oppose
2012 General	Ted Cruz (R)	4,440,137 (56%)	$14,031,864	$3,160,012	$5,872,431
	Paul Sadler (D)	3,194,927 (41%)	$510,439	$30,867	
	John Jay Myers (L)	162,354 (2%)	$15,341		
2012 Primary Run Off	Ted Cruz (R)	631,812 (57%)			
	David Dewhurst (R)	480,126 (43%)			
2012 Primary	David Dewhurst (R)	627,731 (45%)			
	Ted Cruz (R)	480,558 (34%)			
	Tom Leppert (R)	187,900 (13%)			

In the modern political era, there rarely has been a U.S. senator as controversial -- or who has attracted as much animosity in the still-clubby chamber -- as Ted Cruz. Within a year of his 2012 election as Texas' junior senator, Cruz dominated national politics with headstrong, take-no-prisoners legislative tactics that helped to bring about a 16-day shutdown of the federal government -- thrilling tea party activists, but infuriating not just Democrats, but many of his Republican colleagues. "If you killed Ted Cruz on the floor of the Senate, and the trial was in the Senate, nobody would convict you," South Carolina Republican Lindsey Graham wisecracked in early 2016, a couple of months after dropping out of the crowded race for the GOP presidential nomination in which Cruz had emerged as a leading contender.

In March 2015, a little more than two years after being sworn in to the Senate, Cruz announced his candidacy for his party's presidential nomination combining a hard-right ideology with an outsider's appeal. He won nearly a dozen state primaries and caucuses and raised a record amount of money in finishing as the runner-up to another outsider, Donald Trump, in the nastiest presidential campaign in modern times. Cruz was slow to rebound from the bitterness of that campaign: He was virtually booed off the stage at the Republican National Convention in July 2016 when he delivered a speech in which he refused to endorse Trump. The backlash from that episode spurred some intraparty fence-mending on his part. And Trump's unexpected victory in November prompted Cruz -- his path to the White House blocked for at least eight years -- to further pull in his political fangs, as he prepared for what could be a competitive 2018 reelection contest.

Cruz was born in Calgary Alberta, where his parents worked in the oil business. (Thanks to an American-born mother, he is considered a natural-born citizen under the Constitution, notwithstanding Trump's suggestion during the 2016 race that Cruz's place of birth made him ineligible for the White House.) His father's life story figures prominently into Cruz's political narrative. Rafael Cruz fought to overthrow the Fulgencio Batista regime in Cuba in the 1950s before fleeing to Texas at the age of 18, with nothing more than $100 sewn into his underwear. He worked as a dishwasher for 50 cents an hour to put himself through the University of Texas and ultimately started a business in Houston. There, he met Cruz's mother, an Irish-American who studied math at Rice University.

As a high school student, Ted Cruz earned scholarship money by entering speech contests organized by the Free Enterprise Institute, in which participants studied the "Ten Pillars of Economic Wisdom," a libertarian manifesto, and delivered 20-minute speeches about it. As part of the program, Cruz memorized the Constitution and traveled around Texas discussing conservative ideas. He was educated at a couple of elite Eastern universities not usually associated with political outsiders: After earning his undergraduate degree from Princeton, where he was a champion debater, Cruz graduated from Harvard Law School, followed by a clerkship for Supreme Court Chief Justice William Rehnquist.

After a few years with a Washington law firm, Cruz joined George W. Bush's campaign in 2000 as a domestic policy adviser. It was there that he met his wife, Heidi Nelson Cruz, another member of the Bush policy team. Both were dispatched to Florida in the chaos of the recount between Bush and Democratic nominee Al Gore, which led to jobs in the Bush administration. In his autobiography, Cruz admits he was "far too cocky for my own good" in those years and "burned a fair number of bridges" that hurt his chances at landing a higher-level administration job. He served as associate deputy attorney general at the Justice Department and then as director of the Office of Policy Planning for the Federal Trade Commission.

Cruz returned to Texas in 2003 when he was appointed state solicitor general, making him the first Hispanic American to hold the position. During his five-year tenure, Cruz argued before the U.S. Supreme Court nine times and participated in a number of high-profile cases, including one in which Texas fought to execute a Mexican citizen who raped and murdered two teenage girls and another in which he defended the display of the Ten Commandments on the state Capitol grounds. Cruz in July 2012 told the *Texas Tribune:* "We ended up, year after year, arguing some of the biggest cases in the country. There was a degree of serendipity in that, but there was also a concerted effort to seek out and lead conservative fights." His successor, James Ho, told *The New Yorker:* "He was and is the best appellate litigator in the state of Texas."

Cruz was in private practice when he decided to run in 2012 for the seat opened by the retirement of Republican Sen. Kay Bailey Hutchison. He began the race as an underdog against Lt. Gov. David Dewhurst, an influential figure in the Texas GOP establishment who had the backing of almost every prominent Republican officeholder, including Gov. Rick Perry. Dewhurst also was much better known than Cruz and had millions of dollars to throw into the race. But Cruz got the backing of such national conservative heavyweights as former Alaska Gov. Sarah Palin, South Carolina Sen. Jim DeMint, former Rep. Ron Paul of Texas and his son, Kentucky Sen. Rand Paul -- as well as outside groups such as the Club for Growth and Freedom Works. Cruz sank $1 million of his own money into the primary in an effort to keep Dewhurst under 50 percent and force a runoff. In the nine-candidate first round, Dewhurst finished in front -- but with only 45 percent, followed by Cruz with 34 percent.

Dewhurst sought to cast Cruz as a creature of Washington, given his government experience, and suggested Cruz did not have the state's best interests in mind. Cruz portrayed Dewhurst as just another moderate Republican. It wasn't so much that Dewhurst was a moderate, but that, as lieutenant governor -- a position more powerful in Texas than many other states -- he served as president of the state Senate; it was a position that required a large amount of deal-cutting and horse trading. Cruz trounced Dewhurst, 57%-43%, capturing every major county. In the general election, he had little trouble beating his Democratic opponent, former Texas state Rep. Paul Sadler, 56%-41%.

In the Senate, Cruz quickly established himself as a strong intellectual voice for the far right, following in the iconoclastic mold of DeMint -- who resigned to head the conservative Heritage Foundation just as Cruz was taking office. Summarizing what he would do to enact a conservative agenda, Cruz told *National Review*, "What it takes is backbone, the willingness to stand and fight for those principles in the face of opposition and derision. Of those who have firm principles, even fewer have the backbones to stand for those principles when the heat is on." Underpinning such convictions was a political calculation: At least prior to Trump's surprise 2016 victory, the Republican Party was divided in recent years over whether success lay in seeking to energize the political right or following a more centrist approach in an effort to broaden the party's base. Cruz was firmly in the former camp. "The way you win [the White House] … is you draw a line in the sand," he told the Club for Growth's annual meeting in 2015.

He won ecstatic reviews from conservative activists for his aggressiveness on issues, but his hyper-confident style won him few friends of either party among his new Senate colleagues. When he reviewed the origins of the Bill of Rights to California Democrat Dianne Feinstein at a Judiciary Committee hearing two months after being sworn in, she snapped, "It's fine you want to lecture me on the Constitution. I appreciate it. Just know that I've been here a long time." When Cruz lent assistance to the libertarian-leading Paul during the latter's 2013 filibuster of the Obama administration's nomination of John Brennan to head the Central Intelligence Agency over the government's drone policy, Arizona Republican John McCain called Cruz and Paul "wacko birds." Cruz didn't seem to care. At a conservative awards dinner, he joked, "It is wonderful to be among friends or, as some might say, fellow wacko birds."

As 2013 progressed, Cruz eclipsed another junior Republican senator, Marco Rubio of Florida, who also came to power on the tea party wave -- and whom *Time* had anointed on its cover as the party's "savior." Cruz opposed Rubio's efforts to enact a comprehensive immigration reform bill being pushed by a bipartisan group of senators. But Cruz had an even bigger goal in mind. He sought to block a vote on a measure to fund the federal government past the Sept. 30 budget deadline unless Congress barred any funding to implement the Affordable Care Act. "I believe we can win this fight," he told reporters and conservative activists.

But other Republicans weren't buying it; North Carolina Sen. Richard Burr called it "the dumbest idea I've ever heard." In September, Cruz staged a 21-hour talk marathon on the Senate floor in which he memorably read portions of Dr. Seuss's "Green Eggs and Ham" as a bedtime story to his two young daughters supposedly watching via C-SPAN. (While there is some dispute as to whether Cruz's speech qualified as a filibuster, it ranked as the fourth longest speech in Senate history.) The resulting 16-day shutdown damaged the GOP brand, and Cruz took a significant share of the blame. "It wasn't about the shutdown. It wasn't about the Affordable Care Act. It was about launching Ted Cruz," Oklahoma GOP Sen. Tom Coburn told *The Washington Post*.

Indeed, the episode caused Cruz's star to shine even brighter in right-wing circles-he won a number of straw polls at conservative events during and after the shutdown. He traveled across the country giving speeches, accompanied by his father Rafael, who introduced him with the assertion, "He will not compromise!" (Rafael Cruz also was in the spotlight later during the presidential campaign after Trump, citing a *National Enquirer* story, made the unfounded claim that the elder Cruz had been with Lee Harvey Oswald prior to the assassination of President John F. Kennedy.) Ted Cruz's numbers as a potential 2016 presidential contender crept upward, reaching double digits in some mid-2014 surveys.

By February 2014, Cruz was emboldened to the point where he objected to a deal crafted by Republican Leader Mitch McConnell of Kentucky that would require 51 votes instead of 60 to raise the debt ceiling. The lower threshold would give senators like McConnell in tough reelection races the political cover to vote against the increase, while ensuring the chances that it would pass and government could continue to function. Cruz later acknowledged that his effort to scuttle the deal enraged his colleagues more than any of his actions, but was unrepentant. "It's part of the reason why I've said many times that I think the biggest divide we've got in this country is not between Republicans and Democrats," he told *The New Yorker*. "It's between entrenched politicians in Washington in both parties and the American people."

In what he later allowed was an "uncomfortable moment," it was left to Cruz's senior Texas colleague, Republican Whip John Cornyn, to move shut off Cruz's efforts to filibuster the debt ceiling. Cruz's tactics created a continuing series of headaches for Cornyn, leading to a frosty relationship between the two Texans. The year after the debt ceiling confrontation, Cruz defied Senate floor protocol by accusing McConnell of telling a "flat-out lie" regarding a bill on the Export-Import Bank -- prompting Cornyn, a former judge, to publicly chide his junior colleague.

Cruz became the first major Republican in the presidential race when he launched his long-expected bid in March 2015 at Liberty University, a hotbed of social conservatism founded by the late Jerry Falwell. But his star had faded somewhat with the base since his first years in office-he began the race in the low single digits in national polling, stuck in the second tier of a crowded GOP field. Undeterred, Cruz kept up his bomb-throwing rhetorical approach on the campaign trail, seeking to put together a coalition of religious and economic ultra-conservatives. His calls to "abolish the IRS" and Common Core national education standards earned regular cheers on the campaign trail. Cruz leaned hard into religious liberty arguments as well, introducing legislation for a constitutional amendment that would reinstate states' rights to bar gay marriage just days before the Supreme Court legalized it nationwide.

At first, Cruz went out of his way to maintain a "bromance" with Trump -- to the point of defending the New York businessman when Trump described most Mexican undocumented immigrants as "rapists" and "criminals" in launching his candidacy. Cruz even invited Trump to appear at a Capitol Hill rally against the Obama administration's Iranian nuclear deal in September 2015. Behind this strategy was a belief by Cruz's advisers that Trump had shifted the campaign narrative to their advantage by highlighting voter distrust of Washington. "The Establishment's only hope: Trump & me in a cage match. Sorry to disappoint - @realDonaldTrump is terrific. #DealWithIt," Cruz tweeted at the end of 2015. In contrast to the insult-laden blasts aimed at other rivals, Trump was noticeably milder with Cruz, repeatedly calling him a "nice guy." This era of good feeling would resurface after Trump's election -- but only after a year-long conflict filled with toxic rhetoric and allegations. Before it was over, Trump would post an unflattering picture of Heidi Cruz-- on whom he threatened to "spill the beans" -- while Ted Cruz would blast Trump as a "serial philanderer" and "utterly amoral."

Cruz pulled off a surprise win in the first delegate selection contest, the Iowa caucuses -- where Trump was thought to be in the lead heading into the contest. But in their eagerness to capitalize on their momentum, Cruz campaign officials made an error that would haunt them. Retired neurosurgeon Ben Carson, who finished fourth in the caucuses, signaled that he was speaking early Monday and heading home to Florida -- prompting the Cruz campaign to suggest incorrectly via email and social media that Carson was pulling out of the race as the voting was taking place. Cruz apologized the next day after Carson accused him of "dirty tricks," but Trump also chimed in -- accusing Cruz of "fraud" and suggesting a new election be held. The episode gave rise to a damning Trump nickname: "Lyin' Ted." It stuck with Cruz in part because of the widespread perception on Capitol Hill and throughout the party establishment that the Texas senator would stop at nothing to advance his own interests.

The Cruz campaign raised $93.2 million on its own, a record for a Republican presidential primary candidate. (According to a compilation by *The Washington Post*, this does not include another $89.6 million raised by "super PACs" and other independent groups in support of Cruz.) In addition to Iowa and his home state of Texas, Cruz won primaries and caucuses in nine other states and outlasted two fellow freshman senators seeking the nomination: Paul, who dropped out after Iowa, and Rubio, who called it quits in early March after losing his home state of Florida to Trump. But, for most of the rest of the campaign after the Iowa win, Cruz had a bumpy ride. Trump recovered to win the first-in-the-nation New Hampshire primary, and followed with a victory in South Carolina -- where exit polls showed him winning evangelical voters that the Cruz campaign saw as a key part of their base. On "Super Tuesday" March 1, Trump captured seven states to Cruz's three.

Cruz did score a significant victory over Trump, 48%-35% in the Wisconsin primary, but, by that time, there was no mathematical possibility of Cruz winning the nomination outright. In an informal alliance with the other remaining contender besides Trump, Ohio Gov. John Kasich, Cruz pursued a strategy of seeking to deny Trump a first-ballot victory -- and thereby force a contested convention. As Trump continued to win primaries during March and April, Cruz's campaign worked to recruit hardcore party activists, as opposed to newly minted Trump supporters, to serve as delegates who would vote for Trump on the first ballot -- and then abandon the frontrunner. And Cruz designated another former contender for the GOP nomination, businesswoman Carly Fiorina, as his running mate, as he sought to present himself as the true conservative in the race -- in contrast to Trump, whose ideological credentials remained the subject of suspicion among many in the GOP.

In the end, the animosity toward Cruz precluded him from emerging at the standard-bearer of the so-called "Never Trump" movement. Former House Speaker John Boehner of Ohio called Cruz "Lucifer in the flesh" and a "miserable son of a bitch." Josh Holmes, McConnell's chief of staff when Cruz arrived in the Senate, told *Politico*, "The idea that there's ever been a spokesperson less equipped to make an argument for party unity - I don't think there is anybody." In early May, Cruz lost the Indiana primary to Trump, 53%-36%, and withdrew from the race.

Cruz quickly announced he would seek reelection in Texas in 2018, but the blowback from his primetime speech at the Republican National Convention in Cleveland -- including criticism of his refusal to endorse Trump from fellow Texas Republicans -- prompted speculation that his Senate seat could be at risk. Rep. Michael McCaul, one of the wealthiest men in Congress, was reported to be considering taking on Cruz in a primary. "You don't come to the convention after you have lost the nomination and not support the nominee," Cornyn told Fox News Radio. "I think the right thing to do would be to stay home. I think it was a mistake and I don't know what it means in terms of his future, but I think he miscalculated."

Cruz took steps to repair the damage: He and Cornyn co-sponsored a couple of October events in Texas to raise money for endangered Senate Republicans, even as one of those incumbents, New Hampshire's Kelly Ayotte, was running an ad critical of Cruz's role in the 2013 government shutdown. A month earlier, Cruz endorsed Trump in a Facebook post, declaring: "After many months of careful consideration, of prayer and searching my own conscience, I have decided that on Election Day, I will vote for the Republican nominee, Donald Trump...If you don't want to see a Hillary Clinton presidency, I encourage you to vote for him."

At that time, Trump was considered the clear underdog in November, and Cruz appeared to be contemplating a bid for the 2020 GOP nomination against a President Hillary Clinton. After the results on Nov. 8, he pivoted again. According to *Politico*, Cruz visited Trump Tower in New York in mid-November, told the Trump transition team that the incoming president would need a "champion" -- and volunteered for the task. "I think everyone recognizes we are in a markedly different environment today than we were four years ago, or three years ago, or two years ago, or a year ago, or even three months ago," Cruz told the newspaper in January 2017. "And that environment is going to change how everyone approaches getting our job done."

Two months later, less than a year after Trump and Cruz had slung insults at each other over their wives and respective moral standards, the two dined at the White House at Trump's invitation -- accompanied by their spouses. On Capitol Hill, an apparently kinder, gentler Cruz invited colleagues to weekly basketball games, while toning down his rhetoric. While critical of the House Republicans' initial version of the repeal of the Affordable Care Act, he skipped a press conference at which his fellow tea party conservatives, Lee and Paul, blasted it. He told reporters that, while he had concerns, "the proper way to address those concerns is working with colleagues in the House, the Senate and the administration."

If some were skeptical about the authenticity of Cruz's changed modus operandi, McConnell -- at a weekly luncheon of Republican senators -- labeled his erstwhile tormentor "the new Ted Cruz," and

Graham apologized for his much-quoted wisecrack of a year earlier. "Love is everywhere," Graham quipped as he and Cruz made a joint appearance on MSNBC. "I want to apologize to Ted for saying he should be killed on the Senate floor." Observed Cruz, "At least we're not on the Senate floor now."

At home, Cruz could still face a battle in 2018. Even if McCaul or another high-profile Republican does not take him on in a primary, the state's demographics have begun trending back to the Democrats, and Rep. Beto O'Rourke announced plans to take on Cruz in a general election. (A second Democrat, Rep. Julian Castro, considered the contest, but appeared to take himself out of the running in the spring of 2017.)

FIRST DISTRICT

Louie Gohmert (R)

Elected 2004, 7th term; b. Aug 18, 1953, Pittsburg; Baylor University School of Law (TX), J.D.; Texas Agricultural and Mechanical University, B.A.; Baptist; Married (Kathy Gohmert); 3 children.

Military Career: U.S Army, 1978-1982.

Elected Office: Smith County District Court judge, 1993-2002.

Professional Career: Practicing attorney, 1982-1992; Chief justice, TX 12th Court of Appeals, 2002-2003.

DC Office: 2243 RHOB 20515, 202-225-3035, Fax: 202-226-1230, gohmert.house.gov.

State Offices: Longview, 903-236-8597; Lufkin, 936-632-3180; Marshall, 903-938-8386; Nacogdoches, 936-715-9514; Tyler, 903-561-6349.

Committees: *Judiciary*: Constitution & Civil Justice, Crime, Terrorism, Homeland Security & Investigations. *Natural Resources*: Energy & Mineral Resources, Oversight & Investigations.

Group Ratings

	ADA	ACLU	AFL-CIO	LCV	ITI	COC	HAFA	ACU	CFG	FRC
2016	-	5%	-	0%	25%	100%	92%	100%	94%	100%
2015	10%	C	4%	3%	C	55%	C	96%	96%	100%

Almanac Ratings 2015

	Economy	Social	Foreign	Composite
Liberal	13%	5%	8%	9%
Conservative	87%	95%	92%	91%

Key Votes of the 114th Congress

1. Keystone Pipeline	Y	5. Puerto Rico Debt	N	9. Offenses by Aliens	Y
2. Trade Deals	N	6. Medical Marijuana	N	10. Troops in Iraq	N
3. Export-Import Bank	N	7. Sanctuary Cities	Y	11. Homeland Security $$	N
4. Debt Ceiling Increase	N	8. Armor-piercing Bullets	Y	12. Trade Adjustment aid	N

Election Results

Election	Name (Party)	Vote (%)		Cand. Spent	Ind. Exp. Support	Ind. Exp. Oppose
2016 General	Louie Gohmert (R)	192,434	(74%)	$840,220	$3,387	
	Shirley McKellar (D)	62,847	(24%)	$11,202		
2016 Primary	Louie Gohmert (R)	95,710	(82%)			
	Simon Winston (R)	16,212	(14%)			

Prior winning percentages: 2014 (78%), 2012 (71%), 2010 (90%), 2008 (88%), 2006 (68%), 2004 (62%)

Louie Gohmert, a Republican first elected in 2004, is a devout tea party conservative with a knack for provoking Democrats, fellow Republicans, and even the U.S. Park Police. He had his "15 minutes of fame" when he challenged John Boehner in the House vote for Speaker in 2015 and got three votes. He turned down a similar challenge to Paul Ryan after the 2016 election.

Gohmert grew up in Mount Pleasant and graduated on an Army scholarship at Texas A&M University, where he was class president. He got a law degree from Baylor University, then served as a captain in the Army. He practiced law in Tyler and spent a decade as a district court judge. Republican Gov. Rick Perry named him chief justice of the Texas Appellate Court in 2002. He earned a reputation as a tough law-and-order judge with a knack for attracting attention. In 1996, he ordered an HIV-positive convicted car thief, as a condition of probation, to notify future sexual partners of his HIV status and to obtain written consent from them before engaging in sexual activity.

After the 2003 redistricting in Texas, Gohmert was one of six Republicans to challenge four-term Democratic Rep. Max Sandlin, who had a moderate voting record but was a close ally of Minority Leader Nancy Pelosi. Gohmert led in the primary with 42 percent of the vote to 30 percent for lawyer John Graves. In the runoff campaign, few differences separated the two conservatives, and Gohmert prevailed 57%-43%. Gohmert won 77 percent of the vote in his home base of Smith County, where half the votes were cast. In the general election, Gohmert linked Sandlin to the national Democratic Party and its 2004 presidential nominee, John Kerry. The result wasn't close. Gohmert beat Sandlin, 61%-38%, winning 79 percent in Smith County.

When the bailout for the financial industry came to the House floor in 2008, Gohmert made a motion to adjourn the chamber "so we don't do this terrible thing to our nation." It was defeated 394-8. When the House voted in 2012 to remove the archaic word "lunatic" from laws referring to the mentally ill, there was one dissenting vote - Gohmert's. "Not only should we not eliminate the word 'lunatic' from federal law when the most pressing issue of the day is saving our country from bankruptcy, we should use the word to describe the people who want to continue with business as usual in Washington," he said.

Gohmert had little regard for President Barack Obama or Hillary Clinton. In 2012, he drew criticism from Sen. John McCain of Arizona after Gohmert joined several Republicans in accusing a top State Department official of having ties to the Muslim Brotherhood. During a September 2016 speech to the Values Voters Summit of social conservatives, he said that Clinton was "mentally impaired." "We need to be praying for Hillary Clinton," he added. "There's special needs there."

Gohmert's work on the Judiciary Committee has drawn television talk-show invitations and scorn from liberal blogs for his provocative views. During a September 2013 press conference in Cairo after he and two other House conservatives met with new Egyptian leader Abdel Fatah el-Sissi, the Army general who had ousted the Muslim Brotherhood government in a coup two months earlier, Gohmert compared him to George Washington. In May 2016, he said on the House floor that gay people should not be sent into space.

Gohmert, who often speaks to tea party groups, often has tangled with House Republican leaders. After the 2014 election, Gohmert launched his own candidacy as conservative unhappiness with Speaker John Boehner deepened. He received three votes, including his own, while GOP Rep. Daniel Webster of Florida got 12 votes, though he stepped into the race the morning of the vote. Allies referred to Gohmert as "a stalking horse" who encouraged others to enter the contest. After Boehner resigned in October 2015, Gohmert was one of nine who voted against Paul Ryan for Speaker. "I simply cannot vote for a candidate who demands more power before he agrees to be Speaker," Gohmert said. That opposition didn't hurt him on the Natural Resources Committee, where he became vice chairman in 2017.

Gohmert has never been reelected with less than 68 percent of the vote. After the 2016 election, he cut back on town-hall meetings with constituents. I don't need a town hall to prevent me from trying to accomplish the agenda" from the election, he said. "I know where a majority of East Texans stand."

East Texas: Tyler, Longview

Population		**Race and Ethnicity**		**Income**	
Total	709,646	White	63.1%	Median Income	$45,131 (339 out of 435)
Land area	7,859	Black	17.7%		
Pop/ sq mi	90.3	Latino	16.7%		
Born in state	71.0%	Asian	1.1%	Under $50,000	54.6%
		Two races	1.0%	$50,000-$99,999	28.9%
Age Groups		Other	0.4%	$100,000-$199,999	13.6%
Under 18	24.8%			$200,000 or more	2.9%
18-34	23.3%	**Education**		Poverty Rate	18.6%
35-64	36.7%	H.S grad or less	47.1%		
Over 64	15.2%	Some college	32.9%	**Health Insurance**	
Work		College Degree, 4 yr	13.6%	With health insurance coverage	79.8%
White Collar	30.1%	Post grad	6.4%		
Sales and Service	41.0%	**Military**		**Public Assistance**	
Blue Collar	28.9%	Veteran	9.1%	Cash public assistance income	1.7%
Government	6.4%	Active Duty	0.1%	Food stamp/SNAP benefits	14.0%

Voter Turnout			
2015 Total Citizens 18+	497,152	2016 House Turnout as % CVAP	52%
2016 House turnout	260,409	2014 House Turnout as % CVAP	30%

2012 Presidential Vote		
Mitt Romney	181,835	(72%)
Barack Obama	69,858	(28%)

2016 Presidential Vote		
Donald Trump	189,604	(72%)
Hillary Clinton	66,389	(25%)
Gary Johnson	5,501	(2%)

Cook Partisan Voting Index: R+25

The gently rolling land of East Texas was settled by Tennessee farmers in the years before the Civil War. It sits at the western edge of Scots-Irish America, a swath of territory that starts in the Appalachian ridge and is inhabited by a combative, honor-bound, and highly religious populace. A hundred years ago, this was one of the poorest parts of America, where farmers scratched a living off the land and hoped for good weather and decent prices in the marketplace. When a peach blight in the early 20th century wiped out much of the local fruit industry, many farmers turned to growing roses, which proved ideally suited to the climate and soil of East Texas. By the 1940s, more than half the nation's rose bushes were grown within 10 miles of Tyler, which has become known for its annual Texas Rose Festival, which draws 120,000 visitors. About 75 percent of the garden roses in the country have found their way through Tyler and are distributed throughout the country. The municipal gardens feature 38,000 rose bushes and more than 600 varieties. Longview, which in the 1870s was the western terminus of the Southern Pacific Railroad, became a trading center for wagon trains and local cotton growers and timber cutters. In 1943, the Big Inch pipeline began sending millions of barrels of crude oil from the "Black Giant" oil field near Longview - at the time, the largest ever in the state - to the East for refining. Since then, the Longview area has become an industrial center for earth-moving equipment and chemicals. Eastman Chemical Co., which once produced chemicals for film company Eastman Kodak, has had a booming business because of lower natural gas prices; its Longview site has employed about 1,500.

The fields and woodlands around Nacogdoches - the oldest city in Texas - are the site where debris from the Space Shuttle *Columbia* fell in February 2003. An organized search by 25,000 people recovered more than 84,000 pieces - 38 percent of the shuttle. The Keystone XL pipeline runs through the district in eastern Wood and Smith counties and western Nacogdoches County. Unlike the pipeline's northern end, mired in regulatory holdups, oil began flowing through the Gulf Coast portion in January 2014.

The 1st Congressional District of Texas, covering the heart of East Texas, is made up of 12 counties, the most populous being Tyler's Smith County and Longview's Gregg County, which total nearly half the population. East Texas is ancestrally Democratic, a region that responded to the populist rhetoric of presidential candidate William Jennings Bryan in the 1890s and President Franklin D. Roosevelt in the 1930s and 1940s. But Republicans began making inroads in Tyler and Longview in the 1950s. By the time George W. Bush ran for reelection as Texas governor in 1998, it was solidly Republican.

Democrats held onto the district until the 2003 redistricting, masterminded by former House Majority Leader Tom DeLay of Texas to give the GOP a strong advantage. GOP-friendly Smith and Gregg counties were added to the district, and overall the district today is solidly Republican. In the Cook Political Report's PVI listings, this is the 18th most Republican district in the nation. But it is only the 7th most Republican district in Texas.

SECOND DISTRICT

Ted Poe (R)

Elected 2004, 7th term; b. Sep 10, 1948, Temple; Abilene Christian University (TX), B.A.; University of Houston Bates College of Law (TX), J.D.; Church of Christ; Married (Carol Poe); 4 children.

Military Career: U.S. Air Force Reserve, 1970-1976.

Elected Office: Harris County judge, 1981-2003.

Professional Career: Teacher; Practicing attorney; Assistant District Attorney, 1973-1981.

DC Office: 2132 RHOB 20515, 202-225-6565, Fax: 202-225-5547, poe.house.gov.

State Offices: Kingwood, 281-446-0242.

Committees: *Foreign Affairs*: Europe, Eurasia & Emerging Threats, Terrorism, Nonproliferation & Trade (Chmn). *Judiciary*: Courts, Intellectual Property & Internet, Crime, Terrorism, Homeland Security & Investigations.

Group Ratings

	ADA	ACLU	AFL-CIO	LCV	ITI	COC	HAFA	ACU	CFG	FRC
2016	-	17%	-	0%	83%	100%	79%	0%	81%	100%
2015	0%	C	21%	0%	C	68%	C	92%	76%	100%

Almanac Ratings 2015

	Economy	Social	Foreign	Composite
Liberal	8%	9%	1%	6%
Conservative	93%	91%	99%	94%

Key Votes of the 114th Congress

1. Keystone Pipeline	Y	5. Puerto Rico Debt	N	9. Offenses by Aliens	Y
2. Trade Deals	Y	6. Medical Marijuana	N	10. Troops in Iraq	N
3. Export-Import Bank	Y	7. Sanctuary Cities	Y	11. Homeland Security $$	N
4. Debt Ceiling Increase	N	8. Armor-piercing Bullets	Y	12. Trade Adjustment aid	N

Election Results

Election	Name (Party)	Vote (%)		Cand. Spent	Ind. Exp. Support	Ind. Exp. Oppose
2016 General	Ted Poe (R)	168,692	(61%)	$369,923		
	Pat Bryan (D)	100,231	(36%)	$7,066		
	James B. Veasaw (L)	6,429	(2%)			
2016 Primary	Ted Poe (R)		(100%)			

Prior winning percentages: 2014 (68%), 2012 (65%), 2010 (89%), 2008 (89%), 2006 (68%), 2004 (56%)

Ted Poe, a Republican first elected in 2004, is best known for his loquaciousness on the House floor. He has used his chairmanship of a Foreign Affairs subcommittee to engage on terrorism issues. As chairman of the all-GOP House Immigration Reform Caucus, he has been a well-informed hardline lawmaker to watch as conservatives wrestle with the issue.

A sixth-generation Texan, Poe got a bachelor's degree from Abilene Christian University and enlisted in the Air Force Reserve. He received his law degree from the University of Houston and became a prosecutor in Harris County where, he boasts, he never lost a jury trial. Poe then became a criminal court judge in the county, becoming a judicial celebrity during his 22 years on the bench for meting out humiliating "Poe-tic justice" punishments to criminals. He required murderers to hang pictures of their victims in their prison cells and ordered drunken drivers and shoplifters to stand at the entrances to taverns and stores carrying signs publicizing their offenses. He gained national recognition as a legal commentator on national television.

In 2003, Poe stepped down as a judge to run for Congress. In a six-candidate Republican primary, his high name recognition and bench experience earned him 61 percent of the vote and the right to challenge Democratic Rep. Nick Lampson. The incumbent was running in largely unfamiliar territory because of the 2003 Republican-engineered redistricting of congressional boundaries. Lampson had a moderate voting record, a low-key style, and was a big booster of NASA. At first, national Republicans fretted about Poe's fundraising and his seemingly complacent campaign. Lampson outspent Poe nearly 2-to-1. On Election Day, the new district's shift of residents and its solid Republican bent were decisive. Lampson led 68%-31% in Jefferson County, the area that was his base and where 36 percent of votes were cast. But Poe won 70%-28% in Harris County, which cast 58 percent of the votes. Overall, Poe won 56%-43%. He has not been seriously challenged for reelection. His district has had major changes, including the loss of Jefferson County to the 14th District.

In the House, Poe evolved from what started as a relatively moderate voting record for a Republican from Texas. Saying that they did not go far enough in reducing spending, he opposed compromises that Republicans struck with President Barack Obama on the 2011 budget and the January 2013 tax and spending deal to avert the so-called "fiscal cliff." One of Poe's causes has been the Keystone XL pipeline, designed to bring oil from Canada to Texas refineries; he pushed for legislation to put the decision in the hands of Congress instead of the White House. In March 2017, he went his own way again when he resigned from the Freedom Caucus because of the conservative group's objections to revisions in the Affordable Care Act. "Saying no is easy, leading is hard, but that is what we were elected to do," he said. "Leaving this caucus will allow me to be a more effective member of Congress and advocate for the people of Texas. It is time to lead."

In the Immigration Reform Caucus, Poe has sought tighter enforcement at the border with Mexico. He travels regularly to the border to meet directly with local law enforcement officials. In 2014, he took the lead in advocating legislation to prohibit funding to implement Obama's executive action on immigration. Federal judges in Texas later delayed its implementation. Poe has successfully amended spending bills to add money for fencing and border infrastructure, but failed to add $100 million for more detention beds for immigrants facing deportation. With Sen. Ted Cruz of Texas, he filed a proposal in January 2017 to empower governors to reject the relocation of refugees into their states.

As chairman of the Foreign Affairs Subcommittee on Terrorism, Nonproliferation and Trade, he has used his megaphone to complain that Pakistan has done too little to help the U.S. in the war on terror. In June 2016, he objected to giving additional money to that nation. "Pakistan cannot be trusted," he wrote. "It has actually supported those very terrorists who kill our service men and women in Afghanistan. It is time to call it like it is." Poe has urged Twitter to remove accounts associated with terrorist groups. "Terrorists should not have access to an American-controlled social media platform so they can kill, rape, pillage and burn," he told the House. He worked in 2015 with Democrat Zoe Lofgren of California to influence the legislation to ban the National Security Agency from searching for data without a search warrant. Following the deadly terrorist attack in Brussels in March 2016, he called the Obama administration's strategy against ISIS "a complete failure."

Poe takes a keen interest in victim's rights, something he said stems partly from his maternal grandfather's death at the hands of a drunk driver. In February 2013, he and Blake Farenthold were the only two Texas Republicans to join Democrats in supporting the reauthorization of the Violence Against Women Act. The Victims of Human Trafficking Act, which Poe cosponsored with Democratic Rep. Carolyn Maloney of New York, was enacted in May 2015. The bill supports victims with a fund collected from trafficking fines. In December 2016, he enacted another bill to assure funding of a human trafficking hotline.

For years, Poe was best known to C-SPAN junkies for his loquaciousness. In 2009-10, according to C-SPAN, Poe spoke on 234 of the 317 days that the chamber was in session. "The people of Southeast Texas can't come up here and do it, so I speak for them," he told *the Houston Chronicle*. Poe typically ends speeches on the House floor with his trademark, "And that's just the way it is." He has remained as outspoken as ever. But in 2015, Republican Rep. Glenn Thompson took the title as the most frequent talker in the House. In January 2017, following six months of treatment, Poe announced that he was in remission from leukemia but not cancer-free.

West Houston and Northern Suburbs

Population		**Race and Ethnicity**		**Income**	
Total	745,283	White	49.0%	Median Income	$72,729 (61 out of 435)
Land area	309	Black	10.5%		
Pop/ sq mi	2413.9	Latino	30.8%	Under $50,000	33.6%
Born in state	50.4%	Asian	7.3%	$50,000-$99,999	30.7%
Age Groups		Two races	1.7%	$100,000-$199,999	25.3%
Under 18	24.5%	Other	0.6%	$200,000 or more	10.5%
18-34	25.7%	**Education**		Poverty Rate	11.3%
35-64	40.1%	H.S grad or less	31.9%	**Health Insurance**	
Over 64	9.7%	Some college	28.5%	With health insurance coverage	82.7%
Work		College Degree, 4 yr	25.1%		
White Collar	44.2%	Post grad	14.4%	**Public Assistance**	
Sales and Service	37.3%	**Military**		Cash public assistance income	1.0%
Blue Collar	18.6%	Veteran	6.3%		
Government	5.9%	Active Duty	0.0%	Food stamp/SNAP benefits	6.7%

Voter Turnout			
2015 Total Citizens 18+	477,527	2016 House Turnout as % CVAP	58%
2016 House turnout	278,236	2014 House Turnout as % CVAP	33%

2012 Presidential Vote		
Mitt Romney	157,094	(63%)
Barack Obama	88,751	(36%)

2016 Presidential Vote		
Donald Trump	145,530	(52%)
Hillary Clinton	119,659	(43%)
Gary Johnson	10,323	(4%)

Cook Partisan Voting Index: R+11

Houston, which remains one of the fastest growing metropolitan areas in the country, has become an internationally renowned energy hub that provides the largest share of the nation's jobs in oil and gas extraction. The city's Energy Corridor, a sprawling 4,000-acre business district on both sides of the Katy Freeway west of the city, is a state-established district whose vision is to become the world's premier location for energy-related businesses. It houses more than 300 companies and 94,000 employees, including U.S. headquarters for BP, ConocoPhillips and Shell. Northeast of downtown near Lake Houston along the Sam Houston Tollway, the first phase of construction was completed in early 2016 when 1,500 workers moved into Generation Park, a 4,000-acre master-planned enterprise park for corporate and residential development. Developers have described this area, which could eventually host 150,000 employees, as a "sleeping giant."

Growth in the Houston area has been phenomenal. Unlike past booms in Texas, this one has survived a drop in oil prices. The oil and gas rush in South Texas' Eagle Ford Shale region alone supported 155,000 jobs in Texas, according to a 2013 University of Texas-San Antonio study. Many of those field operation and management jobs have been centered in Harris County. Its growth to 4.6 million from 2000 to 2016 was a 35 percent increase; the metropolitan area's 12 percent growth since 2010 was the fastest in the nation, though many of the area's most affluent residents are moving to Montgomery County. New office space and condominiums have been concentrated on the west side of Houston, where expanding energy corporate headquarters are found.

The 2nd Congressional District of Texas is a swirl-shaped district located entirely within Harris County. It comes close to the downtown, covering Rice University, the museum district, and Memorial Park, which at 1,466 acres is larger than New York City's Central Park. It also takes in the heavily Democratic neighborhood of Montrose, which has been the center of Houston's gay and lesbian community and claims President Lyndon Baines Johnson (who lived there after he graduated from Southwest Texas State) and Howard Hughes as former residents. In March 2017, the *Houston Chronicle* reported "there's a sense among some Houstonians" that increasingly upscale Montrose was no longer "the center for gay culture in Houston."

The district includes some of the most Republican precincts in Harris County. With the shift in the 7th District, this was the only district of the five that are mostly in Houston that voted for Donald Trump in 2016. His 52% of the vote in the 2nd was a big drop from the 63 percent for Mitt Romney in 2012.

THIRD DISTRICT

Sam Johnson (R)

Elected 1991, 14th term; b. Oct 11, 1930, San Antonio; George Washington University (DC), M.A.; Southern Methodist University, Dallas (TX); b.B.A.; Armed Forces Staff College (VA); Naval War College (DC); Methodist; Widower (Shirley); 3 children; 10 grandchildren.

Military Career: U.S. Air Force, 1950-1979 (Korea & Vietnam, POW), 1966-1973.

Elected Office: TX House, 1985-1991.

Professional Career: Homebuilder.

DC Office: 2304 RHOB 20515, 202-225-4201, Fax: 202-225-1485, samjohnson.house.gov.

State Offices: Plano, 469-304-0382.

Committees: *Ways & Means*: Health, Social Security (Chmn).

Group Ratings

	ADA	ACLU	AFL-CIO	LCV	ITI	COC	HAFA	ACU	CFG	FRC
2016	-	5%	-	0%	100%	100%	89%	95%	90%	100%
2015	0%	C	0%	0%	C	67%	C	100%	99%	100%

Almanac Ratings 2015

	Economy	Social	Foreign	Composite
Liberal	5%	4%	0%	3%
Conservative	95%	97%	100%	97%

Key Votes of the 114th Congress

1. Keystone Pipeline	Y	5. Puerto Rico Debt	N	9. Offenses by Aliens	Y
2. Trade Deals	Y	6. Medical Marijuana	N	10. Troops in Iraq	N
3. Export-Import Bank	N	7. Sanctuary Cities	Y	11. Homeland Security $$	N
4. Debt Ceiling Increase	N	8. Armor-piercing Bullets	Y	12. Trade Adjustment aid	N

Election Results

Election	Name (Party)	Vote (%)		Cand. Spent	Ind. Exp. Support	Ind. Exp. Oppose
2016 General	Sam Johnson (R)	193,684	(61%)	$1,151,324		
	Adam Bell (D)	109,420	(35%)			
	Scott Jameson (L)	10,448	(3%)			
2016 Primary	Sam Johnson (R)	65,288	(75%)			
	John Slavens (R)	10,022	(12%)			
	Keith Thurgood (R)	7,157	(8%)			
	Dave Cornette (R)	5,032	(6%)			

Prior winning percentages: 2014 (82%), 2012 (100%), 2010 (66%), 2008 (60%), 2006 (63%), 2004 (63%), 2002 (74%), 2000 (72%), 1998 (91%), 1996 (73%), 1994 (91%), 1992 (86%)

Sam Johnson, an ardent conservative first elected in 1991, will retire in 2018 from what has been a safe Republican seat. He has been honored by Congress for his service in Vietnam, including seven years as a prisoner of war, and was a founder of the Republican Study Committee - the influential caucus of House conservatives. As chairman of the Ways and Means Subcommittee on Social Security, he has a prominent perch from which to oversee the program. During his final term, he is the oldest Republican in Congress and a year younger than Democratic Reps. John Conyers of Michigan and Louise Slaughter of New York.

Johnson grew up in Dallas, graduated from Southern Methodist University and got a master's degree from George Washington University. He was a director of the Air Force Fighter Weapons (Top Gun) School, and as a fighter pilot, flew 87 combat missions during the wars in Korea and Vietnam. After his F-4 was shot down over North Vietnam during his 25th mission, he was imprisoned from 1966 to 1973 in the "Hanoi Hilton," where he spent 42 months in solitary confinement and was forced into leg stocks for more than two years. He weighed 120 pounds upon his release, having subsisted on river weeds and pig fat, and was left with a slight stoop in his walk and a disfigured hand. "His scars bear witness to his tenacity and toughness," House Speaker John Boehner said in a 2013 speech honoring the 40th anniversary of his release. In 2009, the Congressional Medal of Honor Society gave Johnson its highest civilian honor, the National Patriots Award.

After his military service, Johnson started a homebuilding company and was elected to the Texas House in 1984. He won a 1991 special election, after Republican Steve Bartlett resigned to become mayor of Dallas. Johnson ran second in the primary, behind former Peace Corps director Tom Pauken. In the runoff, he emphasized his war record and won 53%-47%. Although his district has shifted substantially into the former countryside from its north Dallas roots, he has not faced a serious challenger since then.

Johnson is among the House's most conservative members, though he is a comparative moderate within the Texas Republican delegation, as shown by the *Almanac* vote ratings for 2015. He was a founder of the Conservative Action Team, the precursor to the Republican Study Committee, which has pressed Republican leaders to support goals ranging from a balanced budget amendment to shutting down the National Endowment for the Arts. Mostly junior House conservatives in 2015 created the Freedom Caucus after they complained that the RSC had become too large and less aggressive.

Johnson has pushed for lower taxes. Every two years, he offers a constitutional amendment to repeal the 16th Amendment, which authorized the federal income tax. He has supported GOP leaders on most tax and spending measures, but drew the line at the late 2012 compromise to avert a so-called "fiscal cliff," calling it "a bad bill that raises taxes on families and small businesses." On Ways and Means, he is the senior Republican behind fellow Texan Kevin Brady, who leapfrogged him to become chairman after Paul Ryan stepped up to Speaker. Johnson has raised the specter of the U.S. "corporate structure" incrementally relocating overseas to avoid high rates if the tax code is not reformed. Earlier, he sponsored the successful repeal in 2000 of the earnings limit for Social Security recipients, and he was a leading proponent of pension reform that was enacted in 2006. In December 2016, he filed a bill that he said would "permanently save Social Security," with steps such as means testing and a gradual increase in the retirement age to 69.

Johnson has focused on military issues. He staunchly opposed setting arbitrary troop withdrawal deadlines in Afghanistan. When Obama announced an economic aid plan for Egypt in 2011, Johnson blasted the idea: "America has no business sending large sums of money to volatile nations in the Middle East that may end up with radical Islamists at the helm." He helped to enact the Military Family Tax Relief Act of 2003, which doubled the death benefit for families of active service members who pass away and also reduced taxes for those families. He spent four years on a bipartisan working group on comprehensive immigration reform legislation. But, with fellow Texas GOP Rep. John Carter, he withdrew in September 2013 with a statement blasting President Barack Obama for his disregard of the Constitution "to advance his political agenda."

Johnson gained national attention in 2007 when he spoke emotionally on the House floor against a plan by Democratic Speaker Nancy Pelosi to set a timetable to withdraw from Iraq. Invoking his memories of Vietnam, he said, "I know what it's like to be far from home and hear that your country and your Congress don't care about you." Even though he and Sen. John McCain of Arizona, also a well-known Vietnam prisoner of war, shared a cell for 18 months and each publicly has spoken warmly about their shared experience, they have had a chilly political relationship. Johnson strongly backed George W. Bush for the 2000 GOP presidential nomination, stating that McCain "cannot hold a candle to George Bush."

In recent elections, Johnson regularly has drawn GOP primary challengers who have sought public attention for the day when he decided to retire. In 2016, Johnson got 75 percent of the vote against three GOP challengers. "I love Sam Johnson," said John Slavens, a retired CPA who finished second with 11 percent, but "we never see him on television shows or fighting for the cause we believe in." Slavens and others likely will have a battle royale in the 2018 primary to determine Johnson's successor.

Northern Dallas Suburbs: Plano, McKinney

Population		**Race and Ethnicity**		**Income**	
Total	770,105	White	59.9%	Median Income	$85,752 (25 out of 435)
Land area	481	Black	8.7%	Under $50,000	28.4%
Pop/ sq mi	1601.4	Latino	14.8%	$50,000-$99,999	28.9%
Born in state	44.3%	Asian	13.6%	$100,000-$199,999	31.2%
		Two races	2.3%	$200,000 or more	11.7%
Age Groups		Other	0.7%	Poverty Rate	7.4%
Under 18	27.3%				
18-34	21.2%	**Education**		**Health Insurance**	
35-64	42.2%	H.S grad or less	20.5%	With health insurance coverage	87.2%
Over 64	9.3%	Some college	27.5%		
		College Degree, 4 yr	33.3%		
Work		Post grad	18.6%	**Public Assistance**	
White Collar	53.0%			Cash public assistance income	0.8%
Sales and Service	36.8%	**Military**			
Blue Collar	10.2%	Veteran	6.6%	Food stamp/SNAP benefits	3.6%
Government	5.8%	Active Duty	0.1%		

Voter Turnout			
2015 Total Citizens 18+	487,711	2016 House Turnout as % CVAP	65%
2016 House turnout	316,467	2014 House Turnout as % CVAP	28%

2012 Presidential Vote		
Mitt Romney	175,383	(64%)
Barack Obama	93,290	(34%)

2016 Presidential Vote		
Donald Trump	174,561	(54%)
Hillary Clinton	129,384	(40%)
Gary Johnson	12,304	(4%)

Cook Partisan Voting Index: R+13

The Dallas and Fort Worth metropolitan area, once a railroad junction and cotton-shipping center, now has 7 million people, the fourth largest in the nation and more than all of Texas had during World War II. More than two-thirds of them live beyond the city limits of Dallas and Fort Worth. In Dallas, the city's old elite occupies the mansions of Highland Park north of downtown, but its business and professional classes have moved farther up into Collin County's scrub-covered hills. Collin's population exploded from 67,000 in 1970 to 940,000 in 2016, with an impressive 20 percent growth since 2010. Demographers projected in 2016 that the population of Collin will increase to 2.1 million by 2054. It is now the sixth-largest and second-wealthiest county in Texas. County officials agreed that the local highways had become "totally inadequate." The median income in the county is the highest in the Dallas Metroplex. Its biggest city is Plano, with 284,000 people. The former farming community is the corporate headquarters of Dr. Pepper, J.C. Penney and HP Enterprise Services. In mid-2017, Toyota planned to move about 4,000 employees into its seven-building headquarters at a state-of-the-art campus on 100 acres near the Dallas North Tollway in Plano. Construction and relocation costs were expected to be at least $1 billion. Toyota officials reviewed more than 100 other potential sites before they decided to shift from Torrance, California. JPMorgan Chase expects 6,000 employees at its new campus in Plano by 2019. Not surprisingly, WalletHub in 2016 ranked Plano as the top city in the nation to find a job.

Plano and nearby Richardson have growing Asian-American populations that were 17 percent and 15 percent in 2010. Sixty Chinese cultural organizations are based in North Texas, mostly in Collin County, serving more than 30,000 Chinese-American residents. Recruited by then-Gov. Rick Perry, the Chinese telecommunications company Huawei established its North American headquarters in Plano in 2001. More than 20,000 Indian-American residents moved into Collin County from 2000 to 2010, with many working at high-tech firms and medical centers in the region. Restaurants, grocery stores and boutiques cater to the Indian community.

Even with the growing diversity, one traditional Texas pastime continues strong in these parts: high school football. Collin County boasts some of the top high school football programs in the country, and the well-heeled suburb of Allen opened a $60 million high school football stadium in 2012 that seats

18,000 fans, with amenities comparable to many college football facilities. Eagle Stadium reopened in 2015 after more than $10 million of concrete and other repairs, which took more than a year.

The 3rd Congressional District of Texas, based entirely within Collin County, includes all but two small corners of the county and centers on Plano. Collin is heavily Republican. As in other relatively upscale suburban GOP districts in Texas, its 54 percent vote for Donald Trump in 2016 was a big drop from the 64 percent for Mitt Romney in 2012.

FOURTH DISTRICT

John Ratcliffe (R)

Elected 2014, 2nd term; b. Oct 20, 1965, Chicago, IL; University of Notre Dame Law School (IN), Bach. Deg.; Southern Methodist University Law School (TX), J.D.; Roman Catholic; Married (Michele Ratcliffe); 2 children.

Elected Office: Heath City Council, 2001-2004; Heath Mayor, 2004-2012.

Professional Career: Practicing attorney; Heath Board of Adjustment, 1997-1998; Heath Planning & Zoning Commission, 1998-2001; E. TX District Chief, Anti-Terrorism & National Security, 2004-2007; U.S. Attorney, TX East District, 2007-2008.

DC Office: 325 CHOB 20515, 202-225-6673, Fax: 202-225-3332, ratcliffe.house.gov.

State Offices: Rockwall, 972-771-0100; Sherman, 903-813-5270; Texarkana, 903-823-3173.

Committees: *Homeland Security*: Cybersecurity & Infrastructure Protection (Chmn), Oversight & Management Efficiency. *Judiciary*: Crime, Terrorism, Homeland Security & Investigations, Regulatory Reform, Commercial & Antitrust Law.

Group Ratings

	ADA	ACLU	AFL-CIO	LCV	ITI	COC	HAFA	ACU	CFG	FRC
2016	-	11%	-	0%	100%	100%	95%	100%	96%	100%
2015	0%	C	0%	0%	C	65%	C	100%	100%	100%

Almanac Ratings 2015

	Economy	Social	Foreign	Composite
Liberal	0%	0%	0%	0%
Conservative	100%	100%	100%	100%

Key Votes of the 114th Congress

1. Keystone Pipeline	Y	5. Puerto Rico Debt	N	9. Offenses by Aliens	Y
2. Trade Deals	Y	6. Medical Marijuana	N	10. Troops in Iraq	N
3. Export-Import Bank	N	7. Sanctuary Cities	Y	11. Homeland Security $$	N
4. Debt Ceiling Increase	N	8. Armor-piercing Bullets	Y	12. Trade Adjustment aid	N

Election Results

Election	Name (Party)	Vote (%)		Cand. Spent	Ind. Exp. Support	Ind. Exp. Oppose
2016 General	John Ratcliffe (R)	216,643	(88%)	$759,377		
	Cody Wommack (L)	29,577	(12%)			
2016 Primary	John Ratcliffe (R)	76,973	(68%)			
	Lou Gigliotti (R)	23,877	(21%)			
	Ray Hall (R)	12,303	(11%)			

Prior winning percentages: 2014 (100%)

Republican John Ratcliffe, elected in 2014, won the GOP primary runoff against 91-year-old Rep. Ralph Hall, the oldest member of Congress, who was seeking his 18th term. With his background as a federal prosecutor, Ratcliffe has worked on law-enforcement and homeland-security issues and has gained expertise and influence on cybersecurity laws.

Ratcliffe, the youngest of six children, earned a scholarship to Notre Dame, where he graduated in three years, and got his law degree from Southern Methodist University. He served eight years as mayor in the town of Heath. He took credit for the town being the only municipality in Rockwall County not to have a tax increase during those years.

He served under President George W. Bush as U.S. attorney for northern and eastern Texas, where his caseload included terrorism, illegal immigration, drug trafficking, public corruption and internet child predators. During that time, he led a national operation, which resulted in the single-day arrest of more than 300 illegal immigrants and the subsequent successful prosecution of hundreds who committed identity theft and Social Security fraud, plus a $4.5 million criminal penalty for the company that hired them. Later, he became a partner in a law firm run by former Attorney General John Ashcroft.

In the primary, Ratcliffe sought to refer to the issue of Hall's age without offending seniors, who make up more than 15 percent of the district's electorate. He told voters he admired Hall as a man and as a politician while portraying the congressman's Washington experience as a liability. After so much time in the nation's capital, "the problems are getting worse, not better," Ratcliffe said in one ad.

In terms of substance, little distinguished the two. Hall, a former Democrat who switched parties following the redistricting in 2003, had one of the most conservative voting records in the House. Ratcliffe was endorsed by the Club for Growth and the Senate Conservatives Fund. He opposed raising the debt ceiling. When asked about continuing with John Boehner as Speaker, he said that the House should have "better leadership at the top." A bigger campaign difference was tactical: Ratcliffe pursued a data-driven approach, while Hall favored old-style stumping. The challenger cited his background in law enforcement - particularly, immigration and homeland security - as a chief reason to seek higher office.

In the six-candidate primary in March, Hall led 45%-29%. That triggered a runoff in May. With turnout one-third lower this time, committed conservatives flocked to Ratcliffe. He edged out Hall, 52.8%-47.2%, a margin of 2,372 votes, and was unopposed in November.

Ratcliffe joined the Judiciary and Homeland Security committees. As a freshman, he became chairman of the latter's Cybersecurity, Infrastructure Protection and Security Technologies Subcommittee, which has a timely portfolio. He worked with Homeland Security Chairman Michael McCaul, a fellow Texan, on bipartisan passage in 2015 of the National Cybersecurity Protection Advancement Act, which Ratcliffe said "will help safeguard personal privacy and prevent cyber intrusions from occurring." The legislation was enacted later that year as part of the Cybersecurity Information Sharing Act. He urged the resignation of Katherine Archuleta as director of the Office of Personnel Management before she finally stepped down in July 2015 following revelations of massive data breaches of federal records. Even with her departure, he said, there were "serious vulnerabilities that must be fully addressed."

Following Ratcliffe's trip to Israel in July 2016 with Democratic Rep. James Langevin of Rhode Island, the two of them collaborated to enact in December the United States-Israel Advanced Research Partnership Act, which includes Israel in an international cooperation program with the Homeland Security Department for research on terrorism. "My work as a cybersecurity subcommittee chairman over the past two years has focused on ensuring American citizens are protected from the growing national security threats posed by malicious cyber actors who intend to do our nation harm," Ratcliffe said. In January 2017, the House passed his bill to encourage cooperation between the Homeland Security Department and emerging technology developers to help improve the federal government's cybersecurity defense and response capabilities.

Contrary to his campaign comments, Ratcliffe voted for Boehner for Speaker once he took office. "I certainly don't see myself as an establishment guy or a leadership guy, but I also don't see myself as a bomb-thrower who's anti-establishment or [an] anti-leadership guy," he said in an interview with *The Texas Tribune* a month after he took office. "Republicans need a big tent," he added. Ratcliffe stayed busy with his work and kept his distance from junior House Republicans - including some from Texas - who have demanded change.

In his reelection campaign, Ratcliffe had a primary challenge from Lou Gigliotti, who got 16 percent and finished third in the first round of Ratcliffe's 2014 challenge to Hall. Gigliotti was a businessman who claimed tea party support. Ratcliffe won their rematch, 68%-21%, and again had no Democratic opposition.

Northeast Texas: Eastern Dallas Area, Denison

Population		**Race and Ethnicity**		**Income**	
Total	714,953	White	72.8%	Median Income	$48,391 (280 out of 435)
Land area	10,123	Black	10.5%		
Pop/ sq mi	70.6	Latino	13.0%		
Born in state	67.5%	Asian	1.0%	Under $50,000	51.2%
		Two races	2.0%	$50,000-$99,999	29.8%
Age Groups		Other	0.8%	$100,000-$199,999	15.6%
Under 18	24.6%			$200,000 or more	3.3%
18-34	20.4%	**Education**		Poverty Rate	16.3%
35-64	39.2%	H.S grad or less	47.9%		
Over 64	15.8%	Some college	32.4%	**Health Insurance**	
Work		College Degree, 4 yr	13.1%	With health insurance coverage	81.9%
White Collar	31.7%	Post grad	6.7%		
Sales and Service	41.2%	**Military**		**Public Assistance**	
Blue Collar	27.2%	Veteran	10.4%	Cash public assistance income	1.8%
Government	7.3%	Active Duty	0.1%		
				Food stamp/SNAP benefits	14.2%

Voter Turnout			
2015 Total Citizens 18+	511,502	2016 House Turnout as % CVAP	48%
2016 House turnout	246,220	2014 House Turnout as % CVAP	23%

2012 Presidential Vote		
Mitt Romney	189,554	(74%)
Barack Obama	63,559	(25%)

2016 Presidential Vote		
Donald Trump	210,587	(75%)
Hillary Clinton	60,841	(22%)
Gary Johnson	6,530	(2%)

Cook Partisan Voting Index: R+28

The Red River Valley is hardscrabble farm country along an unnavigable river. First settled in the 1830s, in the days of the Texas Republic, many counties here reached their population peak around 1900, when a large extended farm family worked every 160 acres. It includes towns like Denison, due north of Dallas, best-known as the birthplace of Dwight Eisenhower, and Sherman, which was the site of a major race riot in 1930 when a black farm worker accused of rape was attacked by a white mob. To the east is Texarkana, noteworthy because its neat grid streets cross the Texas-Arkansas state line, which is straddled by the city's downtown post office. The contrast between the laws of the two states has created competition for which side of the border is more attractive. Arkansas accepted the Medicaid expansion of the 2010 health care law, for example, but Texas did not. This small city and its hinterland have produced three recent presidential candidates: Ross Perot grew up in Texarkana, while Bill Clinton and Mike Huckabee hail from Hope, Arkansas, just 30 miles east.

Northeast Texas in 1912 sent Democrat Sam Rayburn to Congress, where he became the powerful House Speaker from 1940 until his death in 1961 (except for two terms when Republicans had the majority). The region was once a Democratic bastion, with a sentimental regard for Confederate veterans and a seething hatred of Wall Street bankers. That was Rayburn's politics, and he arguably was the most skillful lawmaker of the 20th century. Today, Rayburn's style of politics has almost completely vanished from the area. Rafael de la Garza, a Republican-turned-Democrat who unsuccessfully ran for Collin County district attorney in 2010, told *The Dallas Morning News* that his backers feared that neighbors would assume they supported the deeply unpopular President Barack Obama.

The 4th Congressional District of Texas is the lineal descendant of the seat that Rayburn held, and still includes his hometown of Bonham in Fannin County, which houses a Rayburn museum. But it is quite a different district today. In Rayburn's time, it was farm country, separate and distinct from citified Dallas. Today, it retains its farm counties, but they are only a short hop on the interstate from the Dallas-Fort Worth Metroplex, and about one-third of the district's residents live in the DFW metropolitan area. Rockwall County, at the edge of the Metroplex, has been the third-fastest growing county in the nation;

its population increased 118 percent between 2000 and 2016. In 2016, its median household income of $86,600 made it the wealthiest county in Texas, the Census Bureau reported. In addition to Rockwall, other population centers are Denton-based Grayson County and Texarkana-based Bowie. Less than 10 percent of the district is in suburban Collin County.

In 1940, the year Rayburn became Speaker, his district voted 90 percent for Franklin D. Roosevelt. In 2016, the 4th District voted 75% for Donald Trump, which placed it among his top 2 percent of districts in the nation.

FIFTH DISTRICT

Jeb Hensarling (R)

Elected 2002, 8th term; b. May 29, 1957, Stephenville; Texas Agricultural and Mechanical University, B.A.; University of Texas Law School, J.D.; Episcopalian; Married (Melissa Fore Hensarling); 2 children.

Professional Career: Practicing attorney, 1982-1984; TX Director, U.S. Sen. Phil Gramm, 1985-1989; Executive Director, NRSC, 1991-1993; Communications Executive, 1993-2002.

DC Office: 2228 RHOB 20515, 202-225-3484, Fax: 202-226-4888, hensarling.house.gov.

State Offices: Athens, 903-675-8288; Dallas, 214-349-9996.

Committees: *Financial Services (Chmn)*: Capital Markets, Securities & Investment, Financial Institutions & Consumer Credit, Housing & Insurance, Monetary Policy & Trade, Oversight & Investigations, Terrorism & Illicit Finance.

Group Ratings

	ADA	ACLU	AFL-CIO	LCV	ITI	COC	HAFA	ACU	CFG	FRC
2016	-	11%	-	0%	100%	93%	83%	96%	95%	100%
2015	0%	C	4%	0%	C	75%	C	96%	92%	100%

Almanac Ratings 2015

	Economy	Social	Foreign	Composite
Liberal	2%	0%	0%	1%
Conservative	99%	100%	100%	100%

Key Votes of the 114th Congress

1. Keystone Pipeline	Y	5. Puerto Rico Debt	Y	9. Offenses by Aliens	Y
2. Trade Deals	Y	6. Medical Marijuana	N	10. Troops in Iraq	N
3. Export-Import Bank	N	7. Sanctuary Cities	Y	11. Homeland Security $$	N
4. Debt Ceiling Increase	N	8. Armor-piercing Bullets	Y	12. Trade Adjustment aid	N

Election Results

Election	Name (Party)	Vote (%)	Cand. Spent	Ind. Exp. Support	Ind. Exp. Oppose
2016 General	Jeb Hensarling (R)	155,469 (81%)	$1,116,916		
	Ken Ashby (L)	37,406 (19%)			
2016 Primary	Jeb Hensarling (R)	(100%)			

Prior winning percentages: 2014 (85%), 2012 (64%), 2010 (71%), 2008 (84%), 2006 (62%), 2004 (65%), 2002 (58%)

Jeb Hensarling, a Republican first elected in 2002, is an influential and politically savvy conservative who is often in the thick of debates on economic policy. As chairman of the Financial Services Committee, he has led the GOP attacks on the Dodd-Frank financial reform law. His hardline stances have limited his achievements and occasionally put him at odds with the corporate world, including his failed efforts to shut down the Export-Import Bank. He previously served as Republican Conference chairman and retains leadership interest.

Hensarling grew up in Morris County in East Texas. He worked on his father's poultry farm near College Station as a teenager and decided that he did not want to be a farmer. In high school, he started a Republican club and began organizing political events. He graduated from Texas A&M University and got a law degree from the University of Texas. After briefly practicing law, he got a job on the staff of Sen. Phil Gramm. Hensarling rose quickly through the ranks and became Gramm's campaign manager in 1990. When GOP senators chose Gramm to chair the National Republican Senatorial Committee, he named Hensarling as his executive director. Hensarling later returned to Texas to become vice president of communications for Green Mountain Energy, a local utility, and was co-founder of Family Support Assurance, a firm that aided child support collections.

After the redistricting in 2001, Republican Rep. Pete Sessions, who had represented the 5th District, decided to run in the new and more affluent 32nd District on the north side of Dallas. Hensarling became the front-runner for the Republican nomination in the 5th. Like his mentor, Gramm, he listed cutting taxes as his top priority. Against four opponents, he won the nomination with 54 percent of the vote. Democrats nominated Ron Chapman, a former Dallas County appellate judge. Hensarling referred to his opponent as "Judge Softie" for his record on capital murder cases. The folksy Chapman tried to paint Hensarling as too extreme for the district, but his message failed to take hold. Hensarling won 58%-40% and has been reelected easily since. Democrats did not run a challenger in 2014 and 2016.

In 2007, he became chairman of the Republican Study Committee, which typically advocated conservative views. In that role, Hensarling crafted a seven-point strategy for House Republicans that included a constitutional amendment to limit spending and a flat tax on goods and services to replace the federal income tax. The party embraced his platform, except for his call for a moratorium on spending earmarks in appropriations bills. He helped lead the conservative revolt in 2008 against the call by President George W. Bush for the Troubled Asset Relief Program. His votes are usually market-oriented, which means not always business friendly. He told *Fortune* in 2014: "I do not subscribe to the theory that what is good for GM is necessarily good for America." Hensarling ranked nearly perfect conservative in the *Almanac* ratings for 2015.

As other Republicans have moved on, Hensarling has remained active and well-connected in leadership politics. In 2006, he managed Indiana Republican Mike Pence's unsuccessful challenge to John Boehner for minority leader. After Pence became governor and then running mate to Donald Trump, Hensarling remained close and joined him at the 2016 vice presidential debate. He was a key ally of another GOP leader, Eric Cantor of Virginia. With Cantor's backing, he easily succeeded Pence as conference chairman after the 2010 election. When Hensarling stepped down from that post to become Financial Services chairman, he endorsed Georgia Rep. Tom Price over Washington's Cathy McMorris Rodgers - a Boehner favorite - as his successor. McMorris Rodgers won. Hensarling, who was fundraising head of the National Republican Congressional Committee in 2010, has remained a prodigious fundraiser.

As Financial Services chairman, Hensarling has been generally supportive of Wall Street and hostile to banking regulations. He has firmly stood his ground, whether it's on a cable TV show or in committee business. He has often clashed with California's Maxine Waters, the panel's ranking Democrat who is as liberal as he is conservative. One area of disagreement was the Federal Housing Administration, which Hensarling accused of overextending credit to risky borrowers. He has called for the abolition of the government-sponsored mortgage giants Fannie Mae and Freddie Mac, which he said abused their power. Making these changes would take several years, he said. "Nobody can wave a magic wand and get this done overnight," he told *The Dallas Morning News* in November 2012.

His legislative limitations became apparent at the start of his chairmanship. In 2013, Hensarling pushed through his committee the Protecting American Taxpayers and Homeowners (PATH) Act on a largely party-line vote. The bill called for winding down Fannie Mae and Freddie Mac and almost completely privatizing the housing finance industry. It drew criticism from the real estate and home-builder lobbies, whose members benefit greatly from the current system, and did not muster enough support to make it to the House floor. His bill to kill the Emergency Homeowners' Relief Program, which was set up to provide loans to recently unemployed homeowners who have missed mortgage payments, prompted a veto threat from President Barack Obama and made little progress. Hensarling ran into another problem in 2013 when he objected to a flood-insurance bill; his erstwhile ally Cantor took it away from him. The bill eventually passed the House, 306-91.

Hensarling faced two major challenges in 2015. Early that year, soon after the GOP took Senate control, he enacted a six-year renewal of the Terrorism Risk Insurance Act (TRIA), which backstops financial losses from a terrorist attack. He was less successful with his attempt to shut down the Export-Import Bank, a government-sponsored agency that helps sell American-made products overseas. Hensarling and other conservatives disparaged the bank as a shining example of crony capitalism. "On a macro-economic level, the bank is of little consequence," Hensarling told *The Texas Tribune* in June 2015. "But what is important is what direction we take as a nation." Business interests that benefit from the bank mounted a sustained lobbying campaign to extend its charter. With other Republicans, including some on Financial Services, remaining supportive of Ex-Im and joining with House Democrats to force House action by a rare discharge petition, Hensarling fought a losing battle. In December 2015, Obama signed legislation extending the bank. "Even though I'm a chairman, I don't always get my way," Hensarling said.

Hensarling has waved off criticism of his productivity, saying he should be judged by his entire six-year stint as chairman. "I play a long game," he told *National Journal* in 2014. As 2017 began, it was clear that his legacy as chairman would be determined by his plan to reshape banking regulation, including major changes to Dodd-Frank. He has likened that law to "a legislative drive-by shooting" and harshly criticized the work of the Consumer Financial Protection Bureau, which was created to enforce parts of Dodd-Frank. He contended that the law's burdensome rules had become a drag on economic growth. After the election of Donald Trump in 2016, Hensarling took the lead in dismantling large parts of the Obama-era centerpiece. "Supporters of Dodd-Frank promised it would lift the economy, end bailouts and protect consumers," he said in April 2017, as his committee began work on a major rewrite of banking regulations. "Yet Americans have suffered through the worst recovery in 70 years, Dodd-Frank guarantees future bailouts for Wall Street, and consumers are paying more and have fewer choices." In June 2017, the House passed on a nearly party-line vote Hensarling's Financial Choice Act, which would repeal many key provisions of Dodd-Frank, including its capital requirements for big banks and a weakening of the authority of the Consumer Financial Protection Bureau.

Outside of his committee work, Hensarling has maintained his focus on fiscal issues. He served on the Simpson-Bowles deficit commission in 2010, where he preferred that it concentrate on domestic spending. He opposed the commission's findings as insufficient in containing health care costs. He disdained the 2011 budget-cutting deal that Obama struck with Republicans, saying it did not cut spending enough and that "we probably all deserve to be tarred and feathered."

Following that protracted standoff over raising the federal debt limit, Boehner selected Hensarling to work with Washington Democratic Sen. Patty Murray as co-chairs of the Joint Select Committee on Deficit Reduction, the so-called "super committee," which was given three months to forge a bipartisan deal or face the alternative of more automatic spending "sequesters." The effort proved fruitless and failed to produce proposals for public consumption; Hensarling called the outcome "a huge blown opportunity." He blamed Democrats' unwillingness to negotiate and said that Republicans were willing to increase taxes if Democrats agreed to pro-growth tax reform. He blamed Obama for trying to fit $450 billion in stimulus spending into the super committee's mandate and vowing to veto any plan that altered Medicare without raising taxes on the highest earners.

Hensarling hasn't hid his continuing ambition for a top leadership post, though he turned down opportunities to step to the plate. In a May 2014 radio interview, he did not rule out a challenge to Boehner for Speaker after the November election. "I'm not going to say 'no,' just in case the invitation comes," he told conservative host Hugh Hewitt. When Cantor unexpectedly lost his primary in June 2014, Hensarling declined to run for majority leader, despite intensive discussions and encouragement from conservatives who wanted a credible challenger to Majority Whip Kevin McCarthy of California, who did not hesitate in his own bid. "After prayerful reflection, I have come to the conclusion that this is not the right office at the right time for me and my family," Hensarling said. He faced new opportunities when Boehner resigned in October 2015. Instead, he stepped aside when McCarthy initially sought to become the new Speaker. Hensarling said that he would have supported Price to replace McCarthy as majority leader, though that option never ensued. Ryan had extensive private discussions with Hensarling before agreeing to step into the breach, at his urging.

Following the 2016 election, Hensarling was on Donald Trump's early list to be Secretary of Treasury and they met in Manhattan. But, as the *Dallas News* wrote, financier Steven Mnuchin "beat him out" for the job. His future appeared to remain in the House. Whether he eventually makes a leadership bid likely will depend on his ability to gain support. The period following the 2018 election, when he will be term-limited as committee chairman and House Republicans might be facing new internal dynamics, could be his moment of truth.

Eastern Dallas Suburbs, Mesquite

Population		**Race and Ethnicity**		**Income**	
Total	724,157	White	54.3%	Median Income	$45,811 (328 out of 435)
Land area	5,044	Black	14.5%		
Pop/ sq mi	143.6	Latino	27.2%		
Born in state	65.6%	Asian	1.9%	Under $50,000	53.6%
		Two races	1.5%	$50,000-$99,999	28.8%
Age Groups		Other	0.5%	$100,000-$199,999	14.7%
Under 18	26.8%			$200,000 or more	3.0%
18-34	22.6%	**Education**		Poverty Rate	18.6%
35-64	37.9%	H.S grad or less	51.1%		
Over 64	12.6%	Some college	29.8%	**Health Insurance**	
		College Degree, 4 yr	12.8%	With health insurance coverage	76.6%
Work		Post grad	6.4%		
White Collar	28.9%				
Sales and Service	44.1%	**Military**		**Public Assistance**	
Blue Collar	27.0%	Veteran	8.0%	Cash public assistance income	1.7%
Government	7.5%	Active Duty	0.0%		
				Food stamp/SNAP benefits	14.9%

Voter Turnout			
2015 Total Citizens 18+	462,739	2016 House Turnout as % CVAP	42%
2016 House turnout	192,875	2014 House Turnout as % CVAP	22%

2012 Presidential Vote		
Mitt Romney	137,239	(65%)
Barack Obama	73,085	(34%)

2016 Presidential Vote		
Donald Trump	145,841	(62%)
Hillary Clinton	79,759	(34%)
Gary Johnson	5,776	(3%)

Cook Partisan Voting Index: R+16

Not all of Dallas is glitz and postmodern marble. East of downtown is an older Dallas with neighborhoods of old mansions, modest bungalows and shotgun houses. Some of these areas have been renovated and rebuilt, with chic cafes and trendy stores. Other once middle-class neighborhoods are filling up with immigrants from Mexico and are again noisy with children as they were in the 1950s when people moved here not from Mexico or Central America, but from the almost all-Anglo counties of North and Central Texas.

The 5th Congressional District includes much of east and southeast Dallas County, including neighborhoods in east Dallas and suburban Mesquite, which has become a destination for immigrants moving up the economic ladder. The population is 32 percent Hispanic and 22 percent black. In April 2015, the Breitbart.com website ran a story headlined, "Mesquite Texas - The Gun Show Capital of America," which described its several hundred shows annually as a mix of "trade shows, swap meets and raw capitalism," with crowds that are usually male, white and over 40. The district also covers a more upscale slice of Dallas inside the LBJ freeway, including parts of Lakewood and White Rock Lake.

The minority population in the district has been steadily increasing, from 26 percent Hispanic and 14 percent black in 2010 to 28 percent and 16 percent in 2015. About one-third of the district's voters are in Dallas County. The 5th also takes in six other counties in East Texas, the largest of which are Henderson and Kaufman. One of the booming small towns is Forney, which has become a destination for young families. Anderson County was the site in 1910 of the little-noted Slocum Massacre in which a white mob attacked and killed as many as 25 black residents and forced the remainder to flee, according to a 2015 report on Texas Public Radio. Each of the outlying counties is more heavily Republican than the Dallas portion of the district. As rural areas have swung away from the Democrats, the district switched from being a battleground in the early 1990s to safely Republican. In 2016, Donald Trump won 62 percent of the presidential vote in the 5th. The rural vote gave him a larger share of the vote here than in other Dallas-area districts.

SIXTH DISTRICT

Joe Barton (R)

Elected 1984, 17th term; b. Sep 15, 1949, Waco; Purdue University (IN), M.S.; Texas Agricultural and Mechanical University, B.S.; Methodist; Married (Terri Barton); 4 children (3 from previous marriage); 2 stepchildren; 5 grandchildren.

Professional Career: Assistant to Vice President., Ennis Business Forms, 1973-1981; White House Fellow, U.S. Department of Energy, 1981-1982; Consultant, Atlantic Richfield Oil & Gas Co., 1982-1984.

DC Office: 2107 RHOB 20515, 202-225-2002, Fax: 202-225-3052, joebarton.house.gov.

State Offices: Arlington, 817-543-1000; Ennis, 972-875-8488.

Committees: *Energy & Commerce*: Energy, Environment, Health, Oversight & Investigations.

Group Ratings

	ADA	ACLU	AFL-CIO	LCV	ITI	COC	HAFA	ACU	CFG	FRC
2016	-	11%	-	0%	100%	100%	63%	92%	70%	100%
2015	0%	C	18%	3%	C	84%	C	74%	69%	100%

Almanac Ratings 2015

	Economy	Social	Foreign	Composite
Liberal	3%	5%	4%	4%
Conservative	97%	95%	96%	96%

Key Votes of the 114th Congress

1. Keystone Pipeline	Y	5. Puerto Rico Debt	Y	9.* Offenses by Aliens	Y
2. Trade Deals	Y	6. Medical Marijuana	N	10. Troops in Iraq	N
3. Export-Import Bank	N	7. Sanctuary Cities	Y	11. Homeland Security $$	N
4. Debt Ceiling Increase	N	8. Armor-piercing Bullets	Y	12. Trade Adjustment aid	Y

Election Results

Election	Name (Party)	Vote (%)	Cand. Spent	Ind. Exp. Support	Ind. Exp. Oppose
2016 General	Joe Barton (R)	159,444 (58%)	$1,329,822		
	Ruby Fay Woolridge (D)	106,667 (39%)	$13,052		
	Darrel Smith Jr. (G)	7,185 (3%)			
2016 Primary	Joe Barton (R)	55,197 (69%)			
	Steven Fowler (R)	17,927 (22%)			
	Collin Baker (R)	7,279 (9%)			

Prior winning percentages: 2014 (61%), 2012 (58%), 2010 (66%), 2008 (62%), 2006 (61%), 2004 (66%), 2002 (70%), 2000 (88%), 1998 (73%), 1996 (77%), 1994 (76%), 1992 (72%), 1990 (67%), 1988 (68%), 1986 (56%), 1984 (57%)

Republican Joe Barton, first elected in 1984, has been an outspoken champion for the oil industry and a leading skeptic of man-made global warming. Barton's influence waned after he was term-limited and lost his bid in 2010 to remain as chairman of the Energy and Commerce Committee. In 2017, he became vice chairman of the committee, a sort of elder statesman without legislative portfolio.

Barton grew up in Ennis, in then-rural Ellis County. He graduated from Texas A&M and got a master's degree in industrial administration from Purdue, worked as an oil company engineer, then was a White House fellow at the Energy Department in 1981. When Republican Rep. Phil Gramm ran successfully for the Senate in 1984, Barton ran for his House seat. Barton won the Republican runoff by only 10 votes, then won the general election with 57 percent of the vote.

Barton has enjoyed a degree of success on the busy Energy and Commerce Committee. In 1995, he became chairman of the panel's Oversight and Investigations Subcommittee and used the platform to conduct extensive hearings of the nation's food and drug laws. The result was enactment, with bipartisan support, of significant modernization of the Food and Drug Administration, which encouraged the agency to more quickly review innovative drugs and medical devices. In 1999, he became chairman of the Energy and Power Subcommittee with jurisdiction over energy legislation. He managed to reach agreement in 2001 with ranking committee Democrat John Dingell of Michigan on higher fuel economy standards. Barton pressed for action on electricity regulation, but he retreated from requiring utilities to join regional transmission organizations and sought to encourage them to do so. His bill passed the House but died in the Senate.

In 2004, after committee Chairman Billy Tauzin of Louisiana stepped down because of health problems, Barton was his successor. He aroused some partisan ire that September when he blocked committee Democrats' demand for information about Vice President Dick Cheney's 2001 energy task force. But he worked successfully to win Democratic votes on some issues and to defend and expand the committee's jurisdiction. Telecommunications issues are a major responsibility of Energy and Commerce, and in 2006 the House passed Barton's bill to make it easier for telephone companies to enter the broadband market. Influential Democrats opposed the measure, and it died in the Senate. Barton became a leading opponent of a Federal Communications Commission plan to increase regulation of broadband service companies.

Barton fought the Democrats' health care proposals tooth-and-nail in 2009, but was usually outgunned by California's Henry Waxman, who had taken over as chairman of Energy and Commerce. On some issues, Barton led Republicans in seeking common ground with Waxman, as he had with Dingell. He worked with committee Democrats on a proposal to approve generic versions of biologic drugs following a 12-year period of exclusivity for the inventor.

Barton's contrariness has sometimes landed him in controversy. Discussing global warming with former Democratic Vice President Al Gore at a hearing in 2007, Barton told Gore, who'd written a book on the topic, "You're not just off a little. You're totally wrong." In a 2009 C-SPAN interview, Barton said, "There's ample evidence that warming generically, however it is caused, is a net benefit to mankind." He was the party's lead spokesman against the sweeping climate change bill passed by the House in 2009. He offered his own bill that would have set emission standards for new coal and natural gas plants, but would not have penalized existing plants. Barton's plan failed on a party-line vote. The climate-change bill proved to be politically damaging for many House Democrats in 2010, when they lost 63 seats. In 2011, with Republicans back in the majority, the House passed his bill to prevent the Environmental Protection Agency from regulating greenhouse gases, but it did not move in the Democratic-controlled Senate. When some scientists pronounced 2012 the hottest year on record in the continental United States, Barton scoffed to *The Dallas Morning News:* "What are they going to say in the next three or four years when [the temperature] goes down a little bit?"

Barton hoped to retain the committee chairmanship when Republicans regained House control in 2010, despite GOP-imposed term limits. He organized an aggressive campaign to boost his chances against Michigan's Fred Upton, the Republican next in line on the panel. A 22-page critique of the moderate Upton's record was circulated that accused him of being a "part-time Republican." Though Barton said he wasn't behind the effort, many Republicans were skeptical. The leadership-controlled GOP Steering Committee picked Upton, and Barton chose not to challenge its decision.

The chairmanship defeat capped what had been a tough year for Barton. During a June committee hearing at which BP executives were grilled on the catastrophic spill in the Gulf, Barton apologized to the executives for the Obama administration's decision to force it to establish a $20 billion fund - which he called "a shakedown" - to compensate people who lost their livelihoods in the aftermath. In light of the public's anger over the spill, his remarks sparked a political uproar. GOP leaders threatened to strip him of his ranking spot on the committee and Barton issued a retraction.

In the past, Barton sometimes strayed to the center on economic and social issues. But since George W. Bush left the White House, he has been a rock-solid conservative. In 2012, most House Republicans sought to end the administration's energy loan guarantee program following the collapse of California solar company Solyndra Corp. Barton, who helped write the 2005 law setting up the program, initially called for reforming it instead. He ended up voting for the "No More Solyndras" legislation after *The Wall Street Journal's* editorial page and other conservatives ratcheted up pressure on him. In 2015, he took the lead in the successful effort to lift the ban on crude-oil exports from the United States. Following the 2016 election, he made another bid to regain the chairmanship at Energy and Commerce. But the other contenders this time were mainstream Republicans who had pulled their weight for the House GOP. Barton reportedly got little support. But he handled himself well enough that he was named vice chairman of the panel, which gave him a leadership seat.

Barton has had some political disappointments. He ran for the Senate in 1993 after Democrat Lloyd Bentsen resigned to become President Bill Clinton's Treasury secretary. He finished third with 14 percent of the vote in the all-party primary. In 2001, when Gramm announced his retirement from the Senate, Barton considered running for his seat. But the Bush White House favored Texas Attorney General John Cornyn and Barton stepped aside. After the 2006 election, he made a bid for minority leader, but discovered that John Boehner of Ohio had wrapped up sufficient votes to win. Barton withdrew after six days.

He has been reelected easily in the 6th District. He suffered a heart attack in December 2005 but made a full recovery. He reportedly got into a spat with fellow Texas Republican Lamar Smith in early 2011 over the state's redistricted congressional boundaries. Smith sought to evenly split four new districts between Republicans and Democrats, giving Texas' booming Hispanic population minority-majority seats in the Dallas and Houston areas. But Barton wanted to keep Republican voters dominant in three of the new districts. His plan passed the state legislature, but ultimately was tossed out in federal court, leading to a court-drawn map that made his 6th District seat more Democratic. In 2016, he was challenged by Ruby Woolridge, a community activist and retired educator. The *Dallas Morning News,* rarely an ally of Barton, editorialized for his reelection because of his influence in Congress, but cautioned, "this district could use a shot of new blood."

He seems secure for now but, with other Republicans, faces demographic challenges in the Metroplex.

Southwest Metroplex: Arlington, Fort Worth Area

Population		**Race and Ethnicity**		**Income**	
Total	732,310	White	51.9%	Median Income	$61,110 (133 out of 435)
Land area	2,148	Black	19.1%		
Pop/ sq mi	340.9	Latino	21.7%		
Born in state	59.5%	Asian	4.8%	Under $50,000	40.3%
Age Groups		Two races	1.9%	$50,000-$99,999	33.4%
Under 18	26.8%	Other	0.5%	$100,000-$199,999	22.0%
18-34	23.7%	**Education**		$200,000 or more	4.3%
35-64	39.3%	H.S grad or less	37.0%	Poverty Rate	13.2%
Over 64	10.2%	Some college	33.8%	**Health Insurance**	
Work		College Degree, 4 yr	20.2%	With health insurance coverage	82.4%
White Collar	36.9%	Post grad	9.0%		
Sales and Service	41.7%	**Military**		**Public Assistance**	
Blue Collar	21.5%	Veteran	8.3%	Cash public assistance income	1.5%
Government	5.6%	Active Duty	0.1%	Food stamp/SNAP benefits	10.8%

Voter Turnout			
2015 Total Citizens 18+	488,824	2016 House Turnout as % CVAP	56%
2016 House turnout	273,296	2014 House Turnout as % CVAP	31%

2012 Presidential Vote		
Mitt Romney	146,985	(58%)
Barack Obama	103,444	(41%)

2016 Presidential Vote		
Donald Trump	148,945	(54%)
Hillary Clinton	115,272	(42%)
Gary Johnson	8,552	(3%)

Cook Partisan Voting Index: R+9

The Dallas-Fort Worth Metroplex - a name even the locals use - has spread outward from its historic nodes in downtown Dallas and downtown Fort Worth. Although Dallas is the larger population center, much of the development has moved west, across the plains and the barely perceptible Balcones Escarpment, the geologist's boundary between green and grassy East Texas and brown, barren and hilly West Texas. The plains have been filled in with subdivisions and shopping centers under the enormous Texas sky. Among the larger suburbs is Arlington, right between Dallas and Fort Worth and an easy highway commute to both cities. Named in 1877 after Robert E. Lee's hometown in Virginia (another suburb, but not quite so booming as the Texas locale), its location has been ideal as a site for regional attractions like Six Flags over Texas and the Ballpark in Arlington, commissioned by the former part-owner of the Texas Rangers, George W. Bush. In 2009, the Dallas Cowboys opened the $1.1 billion domed AT&T Stadium in Arlington, which hosted the 2011 Super Bowl and the 2014 NCAA "Final Four" basketball tournament. (Redistricting in 2011 put both complexes just outside the 6th District.)

The city's population of 388,000 in 2015 was 27 percent Hispanic, 19 percent African American, and 7 percent Asian. Enrollment at the University of Texas campus in Arlington reached a new high of 40,000 students in 2016, making it the second-largest in the UT system behind Austin. GM's Arlington assembly plant produces the company's popular and highly profitable SUVs and employs about 4,000 workers. GM plans to fuel the factory entirely by wind power in 2018 and to complete by 2019 a $1.4 billion expansion. As Arlington has filled up, the big growth is to the south in Mansfield, where the population more than doubled to 64,000 between 2000 and 2015. Klein Tools, a major tool manufacturer, relocated from the Chicago suburbs to Mansfield.

The 6th Congressional District of Texas includes most of Arlington and the southern and northeastern fringes of Fort Worth to the west. Nearly three-fourths of the people live in Arlington and Tarrant County, which is the 16th largest in the nation. To the south is Ellis County, which grew 50 percent between 2000 and 2016. Beyond Ellis is small-town Navarro County, home to the Collin Street Bakery, which ships its famed fruitcakes around the world during Christmas season each year. Ellis and Navarro lean heavily Republican and provide the partisan ballast for the 6th. Politically, this territory was ancestrally Democratic for many years, then became solidly Republican, but its minority population in Arlington -- non-Hispanic whites are barely a majority of the district - has reduced GOP margins at the presidential level.

SEVENTH DISTRICT

John Culberson (R)

Elected 2000, 9th term; b. Aug 24, 1956, Houston; South Texas College of Law, J.D.; Southern Methodist University (TX), B.A.; Methodist; Married (Belinda Burney Culberson); 1 child.

Elected Office: TX House, 1987-2001, Majority whip, 1999-2001.

Professional Career: Jim Culberson Advertising, 1981-1985; Practicing attorney, 1988-2000.

DC Office: 2161 RHOB 20515, 202-225-2571, Fax: 202-225-4381, culberson.house.gov.

State Offices: Houston, 713-682-8828.

Committees: *Appropriations*: Commerce, Justice, Science & Related Agencies (Chmn), Homeland Security, Transportation, HUD & Related Agencies.

Group Ratings

	ADA	ACLU	AFL-CIO	LCV	ITI	COC	HAFA	ACU	CFG	FRC
2016	-	5%	-	3%	100%	93%	79%	92%	86%	100%
2015	0%	C	4%	0%	C	79%	C	76%	78%	100%

Key Votes of the 114th Congress

1. Keystone Pipeline	Y	5. Puerto Rico Debt	Y	9. Offenses by Aliens	Y
2. Trade Deals	Y	6. Medical Marijuana	N	10. Troops in Iraq	N
3. Export-Import Bank	N	7. Sanctuary Cities	Y	11. Homeland Security $$	N
4. Debt Ceiling Increase	Y	8. Armor-piercing Bullets	Y	12. Trade Adjustment aid	N

Election Results

Election	Name (Party)	Vote (%)		Cand. Spent	Ind. Exp. Support	Ind. Exp. Oppose
2016 General	John Culberson (R)	143,542	(56%)	$1,104,602		
	James Cargas (D)	111,991	(44%)	$57,517		
2016 Primary	John Culberson (R)	44,202	(57%)			
	James Lloyd (R)	19,182	(25%)			
	Maria Espinoza (R)	13,772	(18%)			

Prior winning percentages: 2014(63%), 2012 (61%), 2010 (81%), 2008 (56%), 2006 (59%), 2004 (64%), 2002 (89%), 2000 (74%)

John Culberson, a conservative first elected in 2000, calls himself a "Jeffersonian Republican" and is passionate about transferring power to local governments. That viewpoint has faced tension in serving as a senior appropriator who controls funding for several large federal agencies, including NASA, which has a major presence in his district. With occasional softening of his hard-edged fiscal views plus the demographic shifts in his district, Culberson found himself squeezed from both the right and left in the 2016 election.

Culberson grew up in Houston, the son of the owner of an advertising agency. He graduated from Southern Methodist University, South Texas College of Law, and then worked as a defense lawyer. In 1986, while still in law school at age 29, Culberson won a seat in the Texas House, where he served for 14 years. In 2000, Republican Rep. Bill Archer, who succeeded George H. W. Bush in the House, retired after being term-limited as chairman of the Ways and Means Committee. The front-runners in the GOP primary were Culberson and Peter Wareing, a Houston merchant banker and son-in-law of Texas oilman Jack Blanton. Wareing spent nearly $4 million to Culberson's $650,000. Culberson had an extensive grassroots campaign; he led the first round 38%-27% and won the runoff four weeks later 60%-40%. The general election was no contest.

Consistent with his frequent advice to "let Texans run Texas," Culberson has shown his disdain for how Congress does its work. During the final days of the health care debate in November 2009, he attended a Capitol Hill rally of the bill's opponents and tossed loose pages of the 2,000-page document to the crowd. Like his predecessor, Archer, he has dreamed of junking the current tax code and replacing it with a national sales tax. Culberson sometimes has gone his own way. He ruffled feathers as one of only two Texas Republicans to oppose passage of the $400 billion Medicare expansion and prescription-drug coverage in 2003. The *Almanac* vote ratings for 2015 showed that he had shifted toward the center of House Republicans.

Culberson has a coveted spot on Appropriations, as chairman of the subcommittee that handles spending for the Commerce and Justice departments and science agencies. He has used his post to finance projects in his district and elsewhere in the Houston area, including medical research, flood control projects and improvements to the Houston Ship Channel. He fought with Houston officials who wanted money for light rail projects, filing a formal objection in 2009 with the Federal Transit Administration to stop a light-rail line because he said the local transit agency was in precarious financial shape - a charge agency officials said was based on outdated information. When he sought to block funds for an expansion of two rail lines, the *Houston* Chr*onicle's* editorial page rebuked him for "trying to impose his own rules rather than work with local leaders." In 2015, the *Chronicle* reported that he had called a truce in his war with the Metro agency. Culberson takes some credit for the Katy Freeway expansion, which combined the interstate with several locally owned toll lanes.

An amateur astronomer and self-proclaimed science buff since he was a kid, Culberson is an enthusiast for NASA and has an interest in nanotechnology research, which is a specialty at Rice University. "I want to get the politicians and knuckleheads out of their way," he told the *Chronicle.* Since 2012, he has filed legislation to give the space agency's administrator a 10-year term similar to that given to the FBI director, which he said would promote better planning and a return to what he believes should be its core mission of space travel. In 2013, he called for restructuring NASA, saying it lacked vision. Democrats on his subcommittee have welcomed Culberson's support for more NASA funding. In January 2017, he said that he would continue his work to "restore NASA to the glory days of Apollo by ensuring that American scientists are the first to discover life on another world and an American spacecraft is the first to achieve interstellar travel."

He has advocated changes in House procedures to improve internal operations. He was an early proponent of requiring the House to post all non-emergency legislation online at least 72 hours before debate, a rules change that Republicans approved in 2011. Following the 2016 election, he joined two other GOP appropriators to push the Republican Conference to change House rules and restore spending earmarks in legislation "as long as the sponsoring member is identified, the earmarks initiate in committee, and they don't increase spending." After the proposal gained significant internal support, Speaker Paul Ryan unilaterally nixed it, at least temporarily.

In 2008, Culberson faced his first well-financed Democratic challenger. Wind energy executive Michael Skelly spent nearly $3.1 million, including $1 million of his own money. Culberson spent a relatively modest $1.8 million. Skelly criticized Culberson's lack of support for alternative energy and said he was not sufficiently helpful to the space program. Culberson ran as a strong social and fiscal conservative and won, 56%-42%.

In 2016, Culberson had two competitive contests. In the Republican primary, Houston lawyer James Lloyd said that Culberson was disconnected from his district. Anti-immigration activist Maria Espinoza focused on illegal immigration and border security. Culberson cited his "impeccable conservative credentials." Lloyd spent $168,000 and Espinoza spent $89,000, but they fell short of their goal of denying him a majority and forcing a runoff. Culberson took 57 percent of the vote to 25 percent for Lloyd and 18 percent for Espinoza. In the general election, he faced Democrat James Cargas, an energy lawyer who worked in the Clinton White House and in the Houston mayor's office. In their third contest since 2012, Cargas spent $62,000 to Culberson's $1.2 million for the cycle. The Chronicle editorial section, which did not endorse either candidate, summarized the contest: "Cargas' passion has grown listless, especially when placed next to Culberson's machine-gun staccato during their editorial board meeting." After Culberson won 56%-44%, his closest contest to date, he told the *Dallas Morning News* that the 2016 election was "highly unusual" and that he would be working hard to increase his support in 2018. "We don't want Harris County to go the way of Dallas County," he said.

West Houston and Suburbs

Population		**Race and Ethnicity**		**Income**	
Total	742,386	White	44.7%	Median Income	$70,257 (72 out of 435)
Land area	162	Black	12.3%		
Pop/ sq mi	4584.3	Latino	30.6%	Under $50,000	36.4%
Born in state	46.0%	Asian	10.2%	$50,000-$99,999	27.4%
		Two races	1.8%	$100,000-$199,999	22.5%
Age Groups		Other	0.4%	$200,000 or more	13.7%
Under 18	25.7%			Poverty Rate	12.8%
18-34	24.8%	**Education**			
35-64	39.6%	H.S grad or less	27.1%	**Health Insurance**	
Over 64	9.9%	Some college	24.8%	With health insurance coverage	82.3%
		College Degree, 4 yr	28.8%		
Work		Post grad	19.3%		
White Collar	48.1%			**Public Assistance**	
Sales and Service	36.9%	**Military**		Cash public assistance income	1.0%
Blue Collar	15.1%	Veteran	5.2%		
Government	6.9%	Active Duty	0.0%	Food stamp/SNAP benefits	7.0%

Voter Turnout			
2015 Total Citizens 18+	434,491	2016 House Turnout as % CVAP	59%
2016 House turnout	255,533	2014 House Turnout as % CVAP	33%

2012 Presidential Vote		
Mitt Romney	143,631	(60%)
Barack Obama	92,499	(39%)

2016 Presidential Vote		
Hillary Clinton	124,722	(48%)
Donald Trump	121,204	(47%)
Gary Johnson	9,126	(4%)

Cook Partisan Voting Index: R+7

When George H.W. Bush moved from Midland in West Texas to Houston in 1960, he bought a house in Briarwood in what were then the western outskirts of the fast-growing city. He returned to Houston in 1993 after losing his reelection bid for the presidency and built a new house one mile from his old one, near lush Memorial Park. The lavish Galleria, one of the largest malls in the United States with an ice rink and tennis club, draws more than 30 million visitors a year under its impressive glass atriums. Downtown Houston is sprouting apartment buildings. Oil companies have prospered, and many businesses moved here from the New Orleans area following the devastation of Hurricane Katrina in 2005. Despite the drop in oil prices, construction of luxury hotels, residences, offices and shopping areas has continued, the *Houston Chronicle* reported in April 2016.

The 7th Congressional District of Texas is the lineal descendant of the district that in 1966 elected Bush as the first Republican to represent Houston in the House. It occupied far more territory then, half of Harris County. It now includes only 17 percent of the county. In successive redistricting rounds, its boundaries have been pared back, as the population of the west side of Houston has skyrocketed. Today, more than 2 million people live in an area where 350,000 lived when Bush was first elected. The district, based entirely in Harris County, includes most of the territory between the Katy Freeway (Interstate 10) and Westheimer Road from downtown. In Texas style, Katy's 26 lanes when it crosses Beltway 8 may be the widest highway in the world. The district takes in the affluent neighborhoods southwest of downtown Houston, Bellaire and a swath of Houston west of the 610 highway loop. Outside the loop is Gulfton, a rural area in the 1950s that became a haven for young oil workers in the 1970s and is now a predominantly Hispanic town that the *Houston Chronicle* called an "ersatz Ellis Island for economic refugees from Mexico and Central America." Continued surges of immigration from Mexico have strained the public schools in Gulfton, whose sprawling apartment complexes have become the most densely populated neighborhood in Houston. In 2016, its 9 percent growth in real estate values was the biggest in Houston.

Most of Houston's business and professional elite live within the district's boundaries: the partners of the big law firms, cutting-edge medical researchers and society mavens. The district is also home to Rev. Joel Osteen's Lakewood evangelical megachurch, which describes itself as the largest congregation in the nation and draws more than 52,000 worshipers a week, with many more viewing the service on an internationally televised Sunday program. The church is housed in the former home of the Houston Rockets basketball team.

The 7th District has been a solidly Republican district, but its demographics are changing. After redistricting in 2011, this became a majority-minority district: Whites are about 45 percent of the population, Hispanics 31 percent, blacks 12 percent and Asian Americans 10 percent. Among the voting-age population, Hispanics had skewed younger and turned out to vote at a lower rate. But that pattern has changed dramatically. In a district that Mitt Romney won with 60 percent in 2012, down from George W. Bush's 66 percent in 2004, Donald Trump lost to Hillary Clinton, 48%-47%.

EIGHTH DISTRICT

Kevin Brady (R)

Elected 1996, 11th term; b. Apr 11, 1955, Vermillion, SD; University of South Dakota, B.S.; Roman Catholic; Married (Cathy Brady); 2 children.

Elected Office: TX House, 1991-1996.

Professional Career: Executive, The Woodlands Chamber of Commerce, 1978-1996.

DC Office: 1011 LHOB 20515, 202-225-4901, Fax: 202-225-5524, kevinbrady.house.gov.

State Offices: Conroe, 936-441-5700; Huntsville, 936-439-9532.

Committees: *Ways & Means (Chmn)*: Health, Human Resources, Oversight, Social Security, Tax Policy, Trade.

Group Ratings

	ADA	ACLU	AFL-CIO	LCV	ITI	COC	HAFA	ACU	CFG	FRC
2016	-	5%	-	0%	100%	100%	62%	96%	84%	100%
2015	0%	C	13%	0%	C	100%	C	83%	64%	100%

Almanac Ratings 2015

	Economy	Social	Foreign	Composite
Liberal	8%	0%	4%	4%
Conservative	92%	100%	96%	96%

Key Votes of the 114th Congress

1. Keystone Pipeline	Y	5. Puerto Rico Debt	Y	9. Offenses by Aliens	Y
2. Trade Deals	Y	6. Medical Marijuana	N	10. Troops in Iraq	N
3. Export-Import Bank	N	7. Sanctuary Cities	Y	11. Homeland Security $$	N
4. Debt Ceiling Increase	Y	8. Armor-piercing Bullets	Y	12. Trade Adjustment aid	Y

Election Results

Election	Name (Party)	Vote (%)	Cand. Spent	Ind. Exp. Support	Ind. Exp. Oppose
2016 General	Kevin Brady (R)	236,379 (100%)	$3,709,675	$200,030	$61,502
2016 Primary	Kevin Brady (R)	64,983 (53%)			
	Steve Toth (R)	45,413 (37%)			
	Craig McMichael (R)	6,042 (5%)			

Prior winning percentages: 2014 (89%), 2012 (77%), 2010 (80%), 2008 (73%), 2006 (67%), 2004 (69%), 2002 (93%), 2000 (92%), 1998 (93%), 1996 (59%)

Republican Kevin Brady, first elected in 1996, has settled in as chairman of the House Ways and Means Committee. One of the most powerful players in Congress, he sits at the starting point for much of President Donald Trump's legislative program. Brady, a Texan who has been largely a team player on economic issues, was positioned to reach deals on health care, taxes, and possibly international trade. He took the job after Paul Ryan moved up to House Speaker in October 2015. Brady had unsuccessfully vied with Ryan for the committee gavel less than a year earlier. He has largely avoided the public spotlight and partisan in-fighting. Coincidentally, he faced a close primary contest four months after he became chairman.

Brady comes easily to his pro-business viewpoint. He grew up and went to college in South Dakota, moved in 1978 to what was then rural Texas in Montgomery County and headed The Woodlands Chamber of Commerce for 18 years. In 1990, he was elected to the Texas House. When Brady ran for the open seat in Congress, his chief opponent in the decisive Republican primary was Eugene Fontenot, a physician who said he wanted "to restore America to its Christian heritage." Brady was the choice of party regulars; Fontenot was backed by religious conservatives.

Fontenot attacked Brady for being one of two Republicans to vote against the state's concealed weapons law. Brady had opposed most gun control bills but not the concealed weapons bill. When he was 12 years old, his father, an attorney, was shot and killed while trying a case in a South Dakota courtroom. "I couldn't look Mom in the eye and vote for this," he told the *Houston Chronicle* after the vote. (In 2013, he said he regretted the vote. "I've been remarkably impressed with how well concealed-carry has worked in Texas," he told *National Journal.*) The campaign was grueling and convoluted. After Fontenot led Brady in the March primary, Brady won the April runoff 53%-47%. After the U.S. Supreme Court in June ordered a redrawing of 13 districts, Brady led Fontenot 41%-39% in an all-party primary in November. Finally, in the December runoff, turnout was sharply down and Brady won their third face-off, 59%-41%.

Brady has compiled a conservative voting record, though he has often been more of a pragmatist than other Texas conservatives. Brady has been a deputy whip for the House Republican leadership and in 2011 joined with Oklahoma Republican Tom Cole on a National Republican Congressional Committee effort to raise money from colleagues, which led them to be dubbed "the Dues Brothers." He is known for being easygoing and soft-spoken, but that doesn't mean he never gets mad. His November 2009 showdown with Treasury Secretary Timothy Geithner made national news when Brady savaged Geithner's handling of the Wall Street crisis, saying, "The public has lost all confidence in your ability to do the job." A year earlier, Brady was the only Houston-area member of the House in either party to vote for the financial industry rescue. "As much as I detest this bill, doing nothing is worse," he said.

Brady has focused on economic issues. As chairman of the Trade Subcommittee at Ways and Means, he persistently fought for more free-trade agreements, which he contends are essential to the U.S. economic recovery. Taking over the Health Subcommittee in 2013, his agenda included repealing unpopular parts of the Affordable Care Act, such as a tax on medical devices and an advisory panel that critics say usurps Congress' responsibilities. He got those bills through the House, but they stalled in the Democratic-controlled Senate. For many weeks in early 2015, he worked closely with Ways and Means and House GOP leaders to win the House's narrow approval of trade promotion authority for President Barack Obama to submit his Trans-Pacific Partnership.

Much of his work has been on the tax code. Brady in 2014 got a bipartisan bill through the House to make permanent and expand the research and development tax credit. The Obama administration, however, opposed the measure because it would expand the credit without offsetting the cost. Three months later, Brady released the draft text of a bill to find those savings by curtailing Medicare and Medicaid fraud and abuse with bipartisan suggestions that he collected from committee members. In 2015, he again won passage of a measure to make permanent the R&D tax credit and provide more certainty to businesses. Again, White House officials said Obama would veto the bill. On an important local matter, Brady was a central figure in the successful effort in 2004 to make state and local sales taxes deductible in the seven states, including Texas, that have no personal income tax.

Even before term-limited Ways and Means Chairman Dave Camp of Michigan announced that he wouldn't seek reelection in 2014, Brady publicly made his case for the job in media interviews. He said that he was ready to challenge Ryan, the 2012 vice presidential nominee and a policy maven, who had chaired the House Budget Committee. "I'm qualified and prepared to lead this committee. At the right time, I'm going to make that case to my colleagues," Brady told Bloomberg TV. "This is all about the ideas and how we can move tax reform, trade, entitlement reform forward, so it's good to have a healthy competition."

Ryan took Ways and Means after a November 2014 meeting of the House GOP Steering Committee. He had less seniority than Brady, but he had the support of Speaker John Boehner and made at least an implicit disavowal of plans for another national campaign. Brady remained the senior committee Republican behind aging Rep. Sam Johnson of Texas and he retained his Health Subcommittee post. He seemed to benefit from running a respectful campaign. Given that Ryan's career options remained abundant, it was possible that Brady would have another opportunity to take the top committee post before Ryan's six-year term limit expired. Brady was active on other committee issues in 2015, in addition to the international-trade debate. In April, the House passed his bill to repeal the estate tax, which also died in the Senate.

Brady also continued as the senior House Republican of the Joint Economic Committee, which studies fiscal policy but has no power to pass legislation, Brady used that post to preach the gospel of getting Washington out of the way to let the private sector create jobs. "The 'government spending is the answer' crowd had their chance to jump-start the economy. They failed," he wrote in a *National Review Online* op-ed in February 2013. "It's time for a proven, pro-growth approach." Concerned about the Federal Reserve's repeated lowering of interest rates, he called for reforming the agency and appointing a bipartisan commission to study its operations, though Federal Reserve leaders have taken a dim view of his efforts. The JEC chairmanship rotates every two years between the House and Senate majority parties; in 2015, Brady served as vice-chairman of the panel.

His next opportunity at Ways and Means came sooner than expected amid the internal House Republican chaos. When Boehner in late September 2015 unexpectedly announced his resignation as Speaker under pressure, House Republicans struggled to find a successor. After other contenders fell short, it became clear that Ryan was the consensus choice of virtually all Republicans; he continued his deliberations with the various party factions, while Boehner "cleaned out the stable" of major legislation - chiefly, a two-year extension of federal budget caps. That created an additional two weeks of uncertainty and awkwardness at Ways and Means, especially for Brady. Although Brady seemed to be the heir apparent, Rep. Pat Tiberi of Ohio - a Boehner ally - said that he would seek the Ways and Means chairmanship if it was available. Brady had seniority and support from the large and influential Texas GOP delegation, but that had not been enough to secure the chairmanship months earlier.

Five days after Ryan won the gavel as Speaker, one of his first official duties was to chair the leadership committee meeting as it selected his Ways and Means successor. Shortly before the secret-ballot vote, Ryan said that he was supporting Brady. This time, Brady won. As the new chairman, he said that he supported "a pro-growth agenda," with the objectives of "real steps toward fixing this broken tax code, reforming welfare, saving Social Security and Medicare for the long term and enlarging America's economic freedom to trade."

With the following year consumed by the presidential election, Brady's start as chairman was relatively quiet. That respite unexpectedly ended with Republicans in control of Congress and the White House. Brady and GOP leaders knew their general policy goals, but it took time for them to establish a working relationship with Trump on the handling of major legislation. That resulted in missed deadlines on budget actions and an extended scramble before the House passed in early May its first major legislation during the Trump presidency: the bill to repeal and revise the Affordable Care Act. Scheduled next was tax reform.

Amid his new prominence in Washington, Brady ran into a major problem at home: his first significant Republican primary contest during the 20 years since he was elected. He faced three challengers, who spent a total of less than $200,000, compared with the $4 million that Brady spent during the campaign cycle. Steven Toth, an ordained minister and a former state representative, was his chief challenger. He raised concerns such as Syrian refugees, funding for Planned Parenthood and "back-door" illegal immigration. We've got to speak the truth to the American people so that we can engage them, and they can become a part of the solution," Toth told a reporter for the *Woodlands Monocle.*

In a pre-primary story, *The Texas Tribune* reported, "Brady is in enough trouble that outside groups -- including the leadership-aligned Congressional Leadership Fund super PAC -- are spending big to protect him." The Fund reported spending nearly $180,000 on Brady's behalf during the closing days of the campaign. Brady barely avoided the embarrassment and potential peril of a run-off, with 53 percent of the vote to 37 percent for Toth. Brady had no opposition in November. But the scare in the high-turnout March primary surely got his attention and that of other would-be giant killers.

Northern Houston Suburbs: East-Central Texas

Population		**Race and Ethnicity**		**Income**	
Total	759,942	White	66.3%	Median Income	$61,863 (121 out of 435)
Land area	6,054	Black	7.5%		
Pop/ sq mi	125.5	Latino	21.3%		
Born in state	59.8%	Asian	2.5%	Under $50,000	40.7%
		Two races	2.0%	$50,000-$99,999	30.0%
Age Groups		Other	0.4%	$100,000-$199,999	21.3%
Under 18	25.6%			$200,000 or more	7.9%
18-34	22.0%	**Education**		Poverty Rate	13.6%
35-64	40.0%	H.S grad or less	42.2%		
Over 64	12.3%	Some college	29.7%	**Health Insurance**	
		College Degree, 4 yr	19.0%	With health insurance coverage	83.1%
Work		Post grad	9.1%		
White Collar	36.5%				
Sales and Service	41.4%	**Military**		**Public Assistance**	
Blue Collar	22.1%	Veteran	8.9%	Cash public assistance income	1.2%
Government	7.5%	Active Duty	0.1%		
				Food stamp/SNAP benefits	8.6%

Voter Turnout			
2015 Total Citizens 18+	511,507	2016 House Turnout as % CVAP	46%
2016 House turnout	236,379	2014 House Turnout as % CVAP	28%

2012 Presidential Vote		
Mitt Romney	195,742	(77%)
Barack Obama	55,273	(22%)

2016 Presidential Vote		
Donald Trump	214,605	(72%)
Hillary Clinton	70,532	(24%)
Gary Johnson	8,418	(3%)

Cook Partisan Voting Index: R+28

Montgomery County, to the north of Houston, was once fenceless cattle country, dotted with roadside stands and barbecues. In 1931, wildcatter George Strake struck oil near Conroe. Thousands of other wildcatters and roughnecks quickly joined in the boom, and this became one of the richest oil-producing areas in the nation. Active production continues today.

The oil boom centered on Conroe was followed by a population and economic boom. In 1974, a planned community called The Woodlands opened 30 miles north of Houston and 15 miles south of Conroe. Development of this new city has barreled along since then, with corporate parks, glistening condo towers, pristine golf courses and a man-made waterway. Its real estate, which is among the most expensive in the Houston area, is home to more than 110,000 residents and 1,900 businesses with 63,000 employees. Anadarko Petroleum, with two office towers, had been the chief corporate presence, with 4,000 employees before layoffs in 2016. The Cynthia Woods Mitchell Pavilion in the Woodlands, which opened in 1990, described itself as the busiest outdoor concert venue in the world in 2016. ExxonMobil built a 385-acre campus with 20 office buildings close to the Woodlands, which consolidated other Houston-area sites and is projected to house 10,000 jobs. The campus is a research center of resources, technologies and products, including the company's chemical work. Entergy planned to start construction in 2019 on a $1 billion natural gas-fired power plant north of Conroe.

The 8th Congressional District includes all of Montgomery County, which is the sixth fastest-growing county in Texas and contains about two-thirds of the district's people. About 10 percent of the district is a small slice of Harris County, a few miles from George Bush International Airport. The district extends north through parts of the thinly populated Brazos Valley and covers Sam Houston National Forest and Davy Crockett National Forest. It spans through all of seven counties and parts of two. The district takes in Huntsville, with one of Texas' oldest prisons and "Big Sam," a 67-foot-tall statue of Sam Houston outside the town along Interstate 45. This is one of the most Republican districts in the country, and Donald Trump got 72 percent of the vote in 2016.

NINTH DISTRICT

Al Green (D)

Elected 2004, 7th term; b. Sep 01, 1947, New Orleans, LA; Florida Agricultural and Mechanical University, Att.; Texas Southern University, Thurgood Marshall School of Law, J.D.; Tuskegee University (AL), Bach. Deg.; Baptist; Not Stated.

Elected Office: Harris County justice of the peace, 1977-2004.

Professional Career: Practicing attorney, 1973-1977; President, Houston NAACP, 1986-1995.

DC Office: 2347 RHOB 20515, 202-225-7508, Fax: 202-225-2947, algreen.house.gov.

State Offices: Houston, 713-383-9234.

Committees: *Financial Services*: Financial Institutions & Consumer Credit, Monetary Policy & Trade, Oversight & Investigations (RMM).

Group Ratings

	ADA	ACLU	AFL-CIO	LCV	ITI	COC	HAFA	ACU	CFG	FRC
2016	-	88%	-	95%	50%	64%	16%	4%	0%	0%
2015	100%	C	100%	86%	C	50%	C	4%	2%	0%

Almanac Ratings 2015

	Economy	Social	Foreign	Composite
Liberal	86%	100%	94%	93%
Conservative	14%	0%	6%	7%

Key Votes of the 114th Congress

1. Keystone Pipeline	Y	5. Puerto Rico Debt	Y	9. Offenses by Aliens	N
2. Trade Deals	N	6. Medical Marijuana	Y	10. Troops in Iraq	N
3. Export-Import Bank	Y	7. Sanctuary Cities	N	11. Homeland Security $$	Y
4. Debt Ceiling Increase	Y	8. Armor-piercing Bullets	N	12. Trade Adjustment aid	Y

Election Results

Election	Name (Party)	Vote (%)		Cand. Spent	Ind. Exp. Support	Ind. Exp. Oppose
2016 General	Al Green (D)	152,032	(81%)	$185,970		
	Jeff Martin (R)	36,491	(19%)			
2016 Primary	Al Green (D)		(100%)			

Prior winning percentages: 2014 (91%), 2012 (78%), 2010 (76%), 2008 (94%), 2006 (100%), 2004 (72%)

Democrat Al Green, first elected in 2004, champions the concerns of the homeless and poor. Like his namesake soul-singer-turned-preacher, Green is deeply religious, usually sporting a "God Is Good" lapel pin. His legislative work has focused on the Financial Services Committee, where he represents the interests of low-income groups. With his engaging demeanor, he has had some success in building bipartisanship.

Green grew up in New Orleans. He attended college at Florida A&M University and graduated from Texas Southern University's law school, where he later taught. He was elected justice of the peace for Harris County in 1977 and served 26 years. For a decade, he also was president of the Houston chapter of the NAACP. After the congressional redistricting in 2003 that largely benefited Republicans, Green saw an opening to run for Congress. The representative from the old district that covered much of this area was Chris Bell, a white Democrat elected in 2002, when he ran with liberal support and beat a more conservative black candidate. The primary against Green was a different matter. Green said that he wanted to fight racial profiling and discrimination in law enforcement, and used subtle racial references on the campaign trail, including his promise to bring "a mountain of soul" to the new district. He amassed an impressive roster of endorsements from prominent local and national black leaders.

Bell responded by asking voters "not to focus on the color of my skin, but on the size of my heart." He was endorsed by the AFL-CIO, Texas teachers unions, abortion rights groups, and Democratic Minority Leader Nancy Pelosi. But he struggled as a white candidate running in a heavily minority district. As the primary neared, the racially charged atmosphere intensified. When state Democratic Chairman Charles Soechting endorsed Bell, Green said it reminded him of "the double standards when African Americans had to ride on the back of the bus and drink from colored-only water fountains." Green won the primary in a landslide, 66%-31%, and faced no real opposition in the general election.

Green began with a relatively moderate voting record but has become a more liberal Democrat. The *Almanac* ratings for 2015 ranked him as the most liberal House member from Texas and near the center of all Democrats. On the Financial Services Committee, where he is the ranking Democrat on the Oversight and Investigations Subcommittee, he has worked to eliminate housing practices that discriminate against minorities, at times successfully enlisting Republicans in his efforts. In 2015, the House passed his "Homes for Heroes" bill to increase housing assistance to low-income and homeless veterans, and give the topic a higher priority at the Department of Housing and Urban Development. An estimated 50,000 veterans are homeless.

Green has focused on a diverse set of social issues. After Democrats were criticized before their 2012 convention for initially leaving the word "God" out of the party platform, Green was added as a speaker to reinforce the party's commitment to religion. "Our faith tells us we have a moral obligation to better our communities, to accept responsibility and care for each other," he said in his remarks. At a controversial Homeland Security Committee hearing on Muslim extremism in 2011, he passionately told panel members that other groups using religion as the basis for their views, such as the Ku Klux Klan, also should be examined. In March 2016, he was part of the congressional delegation that accompanied President Barack Obama to Cuba. He voiced concern about the racism that he said is experienced by Afro-Cubans, who are more than one-fourth of the population on the island.

Like most Texas lawmakers, Green is protective of the oil and gas industry, joining a group of Democrats in 2009 warning that Obama's proposal to raise taxes and impose new fees on the industry would hamper domestic production. Green broke with House Democrats by voting in 2012 for a bill to double the number of offshore oil and gas drilling leases, probably the smart vote in a Houston-based district that relies on oil profits. In 2015, he was one of 28 House Democrats who voted for the Keystone XL oil pipeline.

South Houston, Eastern Fort Bend County

Population		**Race and Ethnicity**		**Income**	
Total	741,226	White	11.8%	Median Income	$42,967 (363 out of 435)
Land area	166	Black	37.6%		
Pop/ sq mi	4474.9	Latino	37.6%		
Born in state	49.9%	Asian	11.2%	Under $50,000	56.8%
		Two races	1.3%	$50,000-$99,999	28.3%
Age Groups		Other	0.4%	$100,000-$199,999	12.6%
Under 18	26.7%			$200,000 or more	2.4%
18-34	27.7%	**Education**		Poverty Rate	22.1%
35-64	37.0%	H.S grad or less	48.2%		
Over 64	8.6%	Some college	26.8%	**Health Insurance**	
		College Degree, 4 yr	16.7%	With health insurance coverage	71.2%
Work		Post grad	8.2%		
White Collar	28.2%				
Sales and Service	47.4%	**Military**		**Public Assistance**	
Blue Collar	24.5%	Veteran	4.6%	Cash public assistance income	1.9%
Government	6.7%	Active Duty	0.0%		
				Food stamp/SNAP benefits	18.7%

Voter Turnout			
2015 Total Citizens 18+	399,503	2016 House Turnout as % CVAP	47%
2016 House turnout	188,523	2014 House Turnout as % CVAP	21%

2012 Presidential Vote		
Barack Obama	145,332	(78%)
Mitt Romney	39,392	(21%)

2016 Presidential Vote		
Hillary Clinton	151,559	(79%)
Donald Trump	34,447	(18%)

Cook Partisan Voting Index: D+29

A half-century ago, the steaming flatlands south of Houston running down to the Gulf of Mexico did not seem a likely site for one of the world's most advanced civilizations. But spreading out in all directions from its historic center at Allen's Landing on Buffalo Bayou, Houston has become one of the great metropolises of North America. Most of the scientific work in NASA's early years was done in Houston, and the first word spoken when man landed on the moon was "Houston." It is the undisputed center of expertise in the oil business and has been at the center of innovations in hydraulic fracking, leading to a resurgence in drilling throughout South Texas. Houston has also become a medical mecca, with the giant Texas Medical Center and its 14 hospitals leaving their mark on the health care statewide. The Memorial Hermann Health System is scheduled to complete in 2019 a $650 million expansion of its 13 hospitals across Houston, which will include renovation of its renowned Texas Medical Center, its original facility. The famed Astrodome, which was once the "Eighth Wonder of the World," has been closed since 2009 and had a yard sale in 2013. After voters in 2013 rejected a referendum to turn it into a giant convention center, the Harris County Commission in September 2016 decided to create a parking lot on its lower levels, with the hope that developers would use the remainder of the edifice for conferences or other commercial purposes.

Twenty-four *Fortune* 500 companies are headquartered in Houston, second only to New York City; all but three of them are chiefly in the energy business. This success is in part a triumph of air conditioning, which made Houston's five-month summer tolerable. Today, it is the fourth-largest city in the nation, with a population that grew 18 percent from 2000 to 2015. It is now the most ethnically diverse major metropolitan area, according to a Rice University report, citing its status as an "immigration gateway."

The 9th Congressional District of Texas slices across the southern part of metropolitan Houston in Harris County. It takes in two wedges of Fort Bend County, which form a crescent around the 22nd District and include about 30 percent of the district's voters. The 9th includes many African-American neighborhoods, low-income and middle-income, in both counties. Its population is 38 percent black and 38 percent Hispanic, although many of the latter are not citizens or do not vote. Another 12 percent are

Asians, many clustered along Bellaire Boulevard in the Chinese-American community. Entrepreneurial Vietnamese boat people settled in Alieve and have created quality schools, an Asian-oriented shopping mall and businesses that serve one of the largest Vietnamese communities in the nation. Overall, this is a heavily Democratic district, which gave Hillary Clinton 79 percent of the vote in 2016, her second best in Texas and barely behind the Dallas-based 30th District.

TENTH DISTRICT

Michael McCaul (R)

Elected 2004, 7th term; b. Jan 14, 1962, Dallas; Harvard University John F. Kennedy School of Government (MA), Att.; St. Mary's School of Law (TX), J.D.; Trinity University (TX), B.A.; Catholic; Married (Linda McCaul); 5 children (triplets).

Professional Career: Federal prosecutor, 1990-1999; Deputy Attorney General, 1999-2003; Chief, Western Div. of TX. U.S. Attorney's Office, 2003-2004.

DC Office: 2001 RHOB 20515, 202-225-2401, Fax: 202-225-5955, mccaul.house.gov.

State Offices: Austin, 512-473-2357; Brenham, 979-830-8497; Katy, 281-398-1247; Tomball, 281-255-8372.

Committees: *Foreign Affairs*: Western Hemisphere. *Homeland Security (Chmn)*: Border & Maritime Security, Counterterrorism & Intelligence, Cybersecurity & Infrastructure Protection, Emergency Preparedness, Response & Communications, Oversight & Management Efficiency, Transportation & Protective Security.

Group Ratings

	ADA	ACLU	AFL-CIO	LCV	ITI	COC	HAFA	ACU	CFG	FRC
2016	-	0%	-	3%	100%	100%	68%	83%	66%	100%
2015	0%	C	8%	3%	C	80%	C	88%	80%	100%

Almanac Ratings 2015

	Economy	Social	Foreign	Composite
Liberal	3%	5%	6%	5%
Conservative	97%	95%	94%	95%

Key Votes of the 114th Congress

1. Keystone Pipeline	Y	5. Puerto Rico Debt	Y	9. Offenses by Aliens	Y
2. Trade Deals	Y	6. Medical Marijuana	N	10. Troops in Iraq	N
3. Export-Import Bank	N	7. Sanctuary Cities	Y	11. Homeland Security $$	Y
4. Debt Ceiling Increase	N	8. Armor-piercing Bullets	Y	12. Trade Adjustment aid	N

Election Results

Election	Name (Party)	Vote (%)		Cand. Spent	Ind. Exp. Support	Ind. Exp. Oppose
2016 General	Michael McCaul (R)	179,221	(57%)	$1,582,845		
	Tawana Cadien (D)	120,170	(38%)	$6,101		
	Bill Kelsey (L)	13,209	(4%)			
2016 Primary	Michael McCaul (R)		(100%)			

Prior winning percentages: 2014 (62%), 2012 (61%), 2010 (65%), 2008 (54%), 2006 (55%), 2004 (79%)

Michael McCaul, a Republican first elected in 2004 as a protégé of Texas GOP Sen. John Cornyn, chairs the Homeland Security Committee. He has pursued an activist agenda of timely issues, often on a bipartisan basis, and has warned of threats facing the nation. In 2016, he roiled the political water with talk of challenging Republican Sen. Ted Cruz in 2018, but appeared to back down after Cruz plunged back into Texas politics. Following the election, McCaul discussed with Donald Trump a possible Cabinet appointment.

McCaul grew up in Dallas, studied business and history at Trinity University, and got his law degree at St. Mary's University, both in San Antonio. He worked as a federal prosecutor and then moved to Austin in 1999 to be a deputy to state Attorney General Cornyn. In 2002, he joined the U.S. attorney's office and was chief of the Terrorism and National Security Section for West Texas.

McCaul was one of eight candidates in the 2004 Republican primary for the newly created congressional district. The other top Republican contenders were mortgage company owner Ben Streusand and former Judge John Devine. McCaul focused on his anti-terrorism work, calling himself the only candidate who "won't have a learning curve." Streusand, based in Harris County, called for less government regulation and opposed the Bush administration's immigration proposals. Devine, who had refused to remove a Ten Commandments display from his Harris County courtroom, had the support of Christian conservatives and called for a crackdown on illegal immigration. In the primary, Streusand carried seven of the eight counties to finish with 28 percent of the vote, to 24 percent for McCaul, who ran strongly in his Travis County base, and 21 percent for Devine.

In the runoff campaign, McCaul and Streusand agreed on most issues. McCaul criticized Streusand's past donations to Democratic candidates, while Streusand questioned McCaul's service in the Clinton administration Justice Department. McCaul used his connections - his father-in-law is Clear Channel Communications founder and Chairman Lowry Mays - to collect major Republican endorsements. McCaul won 63%-37%, carrying both Travis and Harris counties. He faced no major party opposition in the general election. *Roll Call* lists him as the second wealthiest member of the House with a net worth of at least $108 million.

In the House, McCaul has a mostly conservative voting record. Early in his career, he cast moderate votes that included requiring insurers to treat mental illness the same as other health conditions in 2008, and allowing the Food and Drug Administration to regulate tobacco products in 2009. He worked with Democratic Rep. G.K. Butterfield of North Carolina in 2012 to enact a bill encouraging companies to develop drugs for rare childhood cancers and other diseases. After Republicans took control of the House in 2011, his voting record grew more conservative, particularly on fiscal matters.

McCaul earned the gratitude of House GOP leaders for leading the protracted 2010 ethics investigation of Democratic Rep. Charles Rangel of New York that culminated in Rangel's censure by the full House. A former chief counsel and staff director on Ethics accused McCaul and then-chairman GOP Rep. Jo Bonner of Alabama of having had secret conversations with two ex-staffers on the committee about the Rangel investigation and a separate probe involving Democratic Rep. Maxine Waters of California. Such interactions are not permitted under Ethics Committee rules, in certain circumstances. Both Bonner and McCaul recused themselves in the Waters case.

In 2011, as chairman of Homeland Security's Oversight, Investigations and Management Subcommittee, McCaul filed legislation to have six Mexican drug cartels designated as foreign terrorist organizations, a move that could have led to much stiffer penalties for drug traffickers. Later, he pressed Obama administration officials at a hearing over their failure to define "spill-over violence" from the drug wars in Mexico. McCaul co-sponsored a cybersecurity bill with Democratic Rep. Daniel Lipinski of Illinois that would develop standards for dealing with cyberthreats; it passed the House in 2012 but fell victim to partisan squabbling in the Senate. With Democratic Rep. Jim Langevin of Rhode Island, he founded and co-chaired the Cybersecurity Caucus.

Taking over as committee chairman in 2013, McCaul blasted a Homeland Security Department decision to release hundreds of immigrants from around the country for budgetary reasons as "indicative of the department's weak stance on national security." After former National Security Agency contractor Edward Snowden fled to China and then Russia with a laptop full of secret documents, McCaul speculated that he had been "cultivated by a foreign power" to leak sensitive intelligence information. In December 2015, he cited parts of a classified U.S. intelligence document to allege that terrorists were seeking to enter the nation as refugees. Following the 2016 election, McCaul said that he was eager to consolidate jurisdiction over homeland security so his committee could pass the first authorization bill for those programs since 2002.

McCaul has moved legislation on several fronts. In 2014, he worked with a bipartisan group to enact the National Cybersecurity Protection Act, which provided private and government digital networks additional protection against attacks. He joined the bipartisan coalition that enacted in 2015 the USA Freedom Act to reduce the bulk collection of phone data and other records by the National Security Agency. He helped to preserve and update other key provisions, including surveillance of suspected "lone wolf" terrorists who are not affiliated with a government or organized group, plus the "roving wiretap" provision that allowed government agents to target suspected individuals. Also that year, he worked with Republican Rep. John Ratcliffe of Texas to enact a measure to give the Homeland Security Department authority to pursue cyberthreat data sharing. McCaul was stymied in early 2015 when he tried to move a border-security bill, which became part of the debate on an appropriations bill; House Republicans ultimately failed to restrict President Barack Obama's executive actions on immigration (which were eventually halted by a federal judge).

McCaul spoke out during the 2016 presidential campaign. During the final week, he cited Hillary Clinton's use of her private email server while she was Secretary of State as possible grounds for the House to impeach her, if she was elected president. In another interview, he said that her conduct was "treason." After the election, he was on Donald Trump's initial short list to lead the Homeland Security Department and he publicly voiced interest in the job. This was one of several positions that Trump filled with a former military leader, Gen. John Kelly. Although McCaul had advised the Trump campaign and transition team on immigration enforcement, he said in January 2017 that the new president's executive order on immigration "went too far" in restricting lawful entry.

Talk of a possible McCaul challenge to Cruz in 2018 mounted at the 2016 Republican national convention when many of the party faithful were unhappy with Cruz's failure to endorse Trump. McCaul left the door open to a candidacy with a "never say never" response. With his deep pockets and law-enforcement persona, he could be a credible statewide contender. Cruz eventually endorsed Trump and rebuilt his bridges with the Texas GOP. As veteran Texan Republican leader David Dewhurst discovered in the 2012 primary, an intra-party contest with Cruz would be a heavy lift.

Austin/Houston Corridor

Population		**Race and Ethnicity**		**Income**	
Total	760,755	White	55.4%	Median Income	$66,188 (86 out of 435)
Land area	5,071	Black	10.0%		
Pop/ sq mi	150.0	Latino	27.5%	Under $50,000	38.2%
Born in state	58.0%	Asian	5.1%	$50,000-$99,999	30.4%
		Two races	1.6%	$100,000-$199,999	23.4%
Age Groups		Other	0.3%	$200,000 or more	8.1%
Under 18	26.1%			Poverty Rate	11.9%
18-34	23.4%	**Education**			
35-64	39.7%	H.S grad or less	35.1%	**Health Insurance**	
Over 64	10.8%	Some college	27.9%	With health insurance coverage	84.1%
		College Degree, 4 yr	24.5%		
Work		Post grad	12.4%		
White Collar	42.3%			**Public Assistance**	
Sales and Service	38.6%	**Military**		Cash public assistance income	1.1%
Blue Collar	19.1%	Veteran	7.4%		
Government	6.7%	Active Duty	0.1%	Food stamp/SNAP benefits	8.5%

Voter Turnout			
2015 Total Citizens 18+	493,635	2016 House Turnout as % CVAP	63%
2016 House turnout	312,600	2014 House Turnout as % CVAP	36%

2012 Presidential Vote		
Mitt Romney	159,714	(59%)
Barack Obama	104,839	(39%)

2016 Presidential Vote		
Donald Trump	164,912	(52%)
Hillary Clinton	135,984	(43%)
Gary Johnson	11,251	(4%)

Cook Partisan Voting Index: R+9

Two of Texas' major cities are named for leaders of the old Texas Republic, Sam Houston and Stephen Austin. They were not entirely attractive characters: Houston had episodes of alcoholic depression, and Austin was a slaveholder who argued that Mexico infringed on Texas' liberty when it freed its slaves. But they were also men of courage and determination who built a distinctively American culture in what was then the northeast of Mexico. Today, the two metropolises named for them are quite different in character. Houston is about commerce, the capital of the oil business, an entrepreneurial hub spread out over the swampy, humid plains north of the Gulf of Mexico. Austin is the creature of the state government headquartered in the grand Capitol building and of the University of Texas, with a huge endowment of land in West Texas that turned out to be full of oil. Still, Austin has as much oil in its DNA as does Houston. Former Gov. Rick Perry, who was the state's chief executive for 14 years, told late-night TV host Jimmy Kimmel in March 2014 that Austin was "kind of the blueberry in the tomato soup of the state. It's a little different than the rest of the place."

Politically, these two urban centers have moved in very different directions. The historic Austin is a liberal enclave in the heart of a conservative state. North of the Capitol and the university, an entrepreneurial Austin has taken shape, one that embraces technology and the free market, and is a major center for technology start-ups and the manufacturing of computer and electronic products. It is host to the annual South by Southwest conference, which had 260,000 participants in 2016, including President Barack Obama and first lady Michelle Obama. Started in 1986 by journalists chiefly as a music festival, it has become a 10-day phenomenon of policy, culture, food, entertainment and networking. The area around north Austin and its suburbs has taken on some of Houston's character in recent years, despite the continuing popularity of "Keep Austin Weird" bumper stickers. Apple has built a new campus in northwest Austin, which handles hardware technologies, customer service and human resources; its payroll of 5,100 at the end of 2015 was scheduled to grow to 6,700 by 2022, with an average salary of $73,500. IBM has a major research lab that has employed about 6,000.

Curiously, there is no superhighway connecting the 160 miles between Austin and Houston, though there has been improved motor-coach service and discussion of a rail line. To get from one to the other, the drive goes through thinly populated counties dotted with plaques recalling the days of the Texas Republic. This area includes seven lightly populated rural counties, including Austin County and its small town of Sealy, where the same-named mattress company was founded. The town of Brenham is home to renowned ice cream manufacturer Blue Bell Creamery. The company suffered a setback with Listeria contamination that caused three deaths and closed the facility for most of 2015; it reopened with a smaller workforce. With its trendy shops, red-brick inns and fancy restaurants, Brenham is a popular rest stop for travelers between the two cities.

The 10th Congressional District of Texas is like a bar-bell (politically, if not visually) that connects the western suburbs of Houston with the northern precincts of Austin through a corridor of rural counties. It is split into three parts. About 38 percent live in the western edge of Houston's Harris County, a fast-growing and overwhelmingly Republican area, with lots of young families, new subdivisions, and mega churches. Another 36 percent of the voters are in Austin and Travis County, where the Democratic arm of the district includes the northern third of Austin, with one tentacle reaching northwest beyond the city limits and another dropping south to Austin State Hospital. In 2016, the congressional vote in the 10th was 68 percent Republican in Harris and 60 percent Democratic in Travis. The small towns between the two ends are heavily Republican, which make the district comfortably Republican. With minority growth on each end, the Hispanic population is 29 percent and blacks account for 11 percent. In 2016, Donald Trump took 52 percent of the district vote. Four years earlier, Mitt Romney got 59 percent.

ELEVENTH DISTRICT

Mike Conaway (R)

Elected 2004, 7th term; b. Jun 11, 1948, Borger; Texas A & M University, Commerce; b.B.A.; Abilene Christian University (TX); Baptist; Married (Suzanne Conaway); 4 children; 7 grandchildren.

Military Career: U.S. Army, 1970-1972.

Elected Office: Midland School Board, 1985-1988.

Professional Career: Tax Manager, Price Waterhouse & Co., 1972-1980; CFO, Keith G. Graham, 1980-1981; CFO, Lantern Petroleum Co., 1981; CFO, Arbusto Energy Inc./Bush Exploration Co., 1982-1984; CFO, Spectrum 7 Energy Corporation, 1984-1986; CFO, United Bank, 1987-1990; Sr. Vice President., TX Community Bank, 1990-1992; Owner, K. Michael Conaway, CPA, 1993- 2004; TX St. Board of Public Accountancy, 1995-2002.

DC Office: 2430 RHOB 20515, 202-225-3605, Fax: 202-225-1783, conaway.house.gov.
State Offices: Brownwood, 325-646-1950; Granbury, 682-936-2577; Llano, 325-247-2826; Midland, 432-687-2390; Odessa, 432-331-9667; San Angelo, 325-659-4010.

Committees: *Agriculture (Chmn)*: Biotechnology, Horticulture & Research, Commodity Exchanges, Energy & Credit, Conservation & Forestry, General Farm Commodities & Risk Management, Livestock

& Foreign Agriculture, Nutrition. *Armed Services*: Oversight & Investigations, Seapower & Projection Forces. *Permanent Select on Intelligence*.

Group Ratings

	ADA	ACLU	AFL-CIO	LCV	ITI	COC	HAFA	ACU	CFG	FRC
2016	-	11%	-	0%	100%	100%	72%	96%	70%	100%
2015	0%	C	4%	0%	C	85%	C	92%	77%	100%

Almanac Ratings 2015

	Economy	Social	Foreign	Composite
Liberal	5%	0%	0%	2%
Conservative	95%	100%	100%	98%

Key Votes of the 114th Congress

1. Keystone Pipeline	Y	5. Puerto Rico Debt	Y	9. Offenses by Aliens	Y
2. Trade Deals	Y	6. Medical Marijuana	N	10. Troops in Iraq	N
3. Export-Import Bank	N	7. Sanctuary Cities	Y	11. Homeland Security $$	N
4. Debt Ceiling Increase	Y	8. Armor-piercing Bullets	Y	12. Trade Adjustment aid	N

Election Results

Election	Name (Party)	Vote (%)		Cand. Spent	Ind. Exp. Support	Ind. Exp. Oppose
2016 General	Mike Conaway (R)	201,871	(90%)	$1,315,570		
	Nicholas Landholt (L)	23,677	(11%)			
2016 Primary	Mike Conaway (R)		(100%)			

Prior winning percentages: 2014 (90%), 2012 (79%), 2010 (81%), 2008 (88%), 2006 (100%), 2004 (77%)

Mike Conaway, a Republican first elected in 2004, is a low-profile, well-regarded conservative. He has become an all-purpose handyman who has taken on numerous assignments for his party, including generously fundraising for GOP colleagues, serving as chairman of the House Ethics Committee and taking over the Intelligence Committee investigation of Russian influence in the 2016 election. He was rewarded in 2015 with the gavel of the Agriculture Committee. With the current farm program set to expire in 2018, he held hearings and private discussions on what would come next.

Conaway grew up in Odessa, playing offensive and defensive line on the Odessa Permian High School team that won the 1965 state championship and became the inspiration for the TV show *Friday Night Lights*. He graduated from East Texas State University, before it became known as Texas A&M-Commerce. He worked as a certified public accountant with Price Waterhouse for, among others, George W. Bush, and was chief financial officer in Arbusto/Bush Exploration during the 1980s. After Bush became governor, he named Conaway to the state Board of Public Accountancy, and Conaway later chaired the National Association of State Boards of Accountancy. In May 2003, he finished second in the all-party primary for a special election in the 19th District. In June, he lost by fewer than 600 votes in a hard-fought runoff with Republican Randy Neugebauer of Lubbock, who later won the seat.

After state Republicans pushed through a new redistricting plan that October, Conaway was the obvious front-runner in the redrawn 11th District, which is immediately south of the 19th. Veteran Democratic Rep. Charles Stenholm, who represented much of the area, decided to run against Neugebauer. Conaway's GOP primary opponent was Bill Lester, a little-known political science professor who campaigned against Bush's proposed guest worker program. Conaway supported increased documentation of people crossing the border. He won 75%- 25%, carrying 33 of the 36 counties. In the general election, he won 77%-22% and has been reelected with ease ever since.

Through 2016, Conaway had a lifetime rating of nearly 93 percent from the American Conservative Union. His *Almanac* vote ratings for 2015 ranked him among the most conservative House members. He is known for requiring his staff to read and understand the Constitution. "It's only 4,500 words - it's not like reading *War and Peace*," he told the *Houston Chronicle*. He favors state-based regulatory actions over federal ones, arguing that they are far more nimble and responsive. He was critical of Obama administration efforts to promote renewable energy and sponsored legislation to limit the purchase of biofuels, which compete against his state's oil and natural gas. He voted against the original $700 billion bailout of the financial services industry in 2008, but voted for the final version after his long-time friend President Bush called to urge his support.

As an accountant, Conaway served on the executive committee of the National Republican Congressional Committee. In 2007, he uncovered an internal fraud scheme by the committee's longtime treasurer, who had embezzled almost $1 million. Speaker John Boehner personally asked Conaway to become chairman in 2013 of the Ethics Committee, an undesirable posting but one that often brings later leadership rewards with other opportunities. Conaway said he sought to enhance Congress' low public standing by conducting investigations thoroughly and fairly. "I have a long history of accepting the responsibilities I have been offered and doing the best I can," he told *The San Angelo Standard-Times*. He and California's Linda Sanchez, the panel's top Democrat, declined to act on a recommendation from the Office of Congressional Ethics that the panel set up a special committee to look into allegations that Washington's Cathy McMorris Rodgers, a member of the GOP leadership, improperly used funds in a leadership race and to cover other campaign activities.

When Oklahoma's Frank Lucas was term-limited as Agriculture's chairman, Conaway solidified his hold on the job by raising more than $800,000 for other Republicans during 2014, including fundraising events with Boehner in Conaway's district. As the new chairman, he noted that there are "fewer and fewer voices" in Congress that represent rural America, and he was honored to be one of them. In an ongoing international trade dispute, Conaway supported repeal of "country of origin labeling" on exports of beef, pork and chicken. In 2015, the House passed on a 300-131 vote his bill to repeal the labeling requirement. He urged the Trump administration to craft new trade agreements to boost exports.

In preparing to meet his priority of a timely renewal of the farm bill in 2018, Conaway led a comprehensive committee review of the Supplemental Nutrition Assistance Program, also known as food stamps, a target for numerous fiscal conservatives' ire. He explored options for when recipients should start - and stop - receiving benefits. An overriding question on that program, he said, is the impact on the price of food. "There is sincere, bipartisan interest in ensuring that SNAP is meeting the needs of those it is intended to serve," he said in a December 2016 committee report. Having previously chaired the Agriculture Subcommittee on General Farm Commodities and Risk Management, Conaway has been willing to challenge fellow conservatives who have criticized subsidies for mohair, a fabric yielded from Angora goats. Numerous Angora farmers live in his district. Another interest of constituents was gaining better coverage for cotton in the commodity program.

Conaway has kept busy on other issues as a member of the Armed Services and Intelligence committees. When Intelligence Committee Chairman Devin Nunes of California in April 2017 stepped aside under pressure from control of that panel's investigation of Russian interference in the election following questions about his release of classified information, committee and party leaders designated Conaway to lead the high-pressure inquiry. Earlier, he did not deny that Russian computer hacks were intended to influence the election results, but he added that the documents from the Clinton campaign were valid. "I am confident that he will oversee a professional investigation into Russia's actions and follow the facts wherever they may lead," said Speaker Paul Ryan. Conaway had been among a few House members mentioned to succeed Boehner as Speaker in October 2015 if Ryan did not take the position.

During the 2016 campaign, Conaway was a consistent supporter of Trump. "It is what it is, awful, but by the same token, no candidate is perfect," he said, following the release in October 2016 of a controversial video with lewd comments by Trump. "I refuse to do anything that would help Hillary [Clinton] become president."

West-Central Texas: Midland, Odessa

Population		**Race and Ethnicity**		**Income**	
Total	733,162	White	57.8%	Median Income	$51,050 (237 out of 435)
Land area	27,832	Black	3.6%		
Pop/ sq mi	26.3	Latino	36.2%		
Born in state	70.7%	Asian	0.9%	Under $50,000	49.0%
		Two races	1.1%	$50,000-$99,999	29.7%
Age Groups		Other	0.4%	$100,000-$199,999	16.6%
Under 18	25.2%			$200,000 or more	4.7%
18-34	24.0%	**Education**		Poverty Rate	14.2%
35-64	35.8%	H.S grad or less	49.0%		
Over 64	15.0%	Some college	31.1%	**Health Insurance**	
		College Degree, 4 yr	13.9%	With health insurance coverage	79.1%
Work		Post grad	5.9%		
White Collar	29.1%				
Sales and Service	40.8%	**Military**		**Public Assistance**	
Blue Collar	30.2%	Veteran	9.4%	Cash public assistance income	1.7%
Government	8.2%	Active Duty	0.7%		
				Food stamp/SNAP benefits	11.1%

Voter Turnout			
2015 Total Citizens 18+	509,645	2016 House Turnout as % CVAP	44%
2016 House turnout	225,548	2014 House Turnout as % CVAP	24%

2012 Presidential Vote		
Mitt Romney	182,438	(79%)
Barack Obama	45,083	(20%)

2016 Presidential Vote		
Donald Trump	193,620	(78%)
Hillary Clinton	47,468	(19%)
Gary Johnson	6,659	(3%)

Cook Partisan Voting Index: R+32

In the 1540s, the conquistador Francisco Coronado and his men rode their horses over the plains of the land they called the Llano Estacado, or "palisaded plains," which is now West Texas. They found a vast emptiness, gradually and imperceptibly rising in elevation to the west, with only scrub vegetation and small bands of Comanche Indians. What they did not see, lying far beneath the surface, was oil, discovered in the 1940s in large amounts in the Permian Basin. When oil was found, two tiny county seats 25 miles apart suddenly became small cities - Odessa, home of the roughneck oil well workers, and Midland, the more upscale town where oil entrepreneurs lived and started their own Petroleum Club. The Permian Basin boomed in the years just after World War II. In 1940, Ector and Midland counties had a population of 26,000. By 1960, they had grown to 159,000. Midland in the 1950s was an affluent town by West Texas standards, but hardly luxurious. Air conditioning had not yet become standard in homes or schools, and there were no mansions at the edge of town, just barren desert and oil derricks. George and Barbara Bush moved to the Permian Basin in 1948 in search of success in the oil industry and room for a growing family. They rented houses in Odessa before upgrading to a series of larger, but by no means grand, ranch houses in Midland. President George W. Bush's wife, Laura, also is from Midland. Odessa is now perhaps best known as the high school football-crazed town depicted in the 1990 book *Friday Night Lights*, later turned into a movie and hit TV series.

In an area that still yields much of the state's oil, production and land sales have increasingly been driven by new hydraulic fracturing techniques. As recently as early 2014, 536 of the 1,540 on-shore oil rigs operating in the United States were in the Permian Basin. The plunge in the price of oil later in 2014 caused a drop in shale-oil production and the closing of some small businesses, a boom-and-bust pattern that is common to the area. In January 2017, ExxonMobil announced a $6.6 billion purchase of 275,000 acres, chiefly for shale production. The total of $27 billion in land sales in West Texas during the previous year signaled confidence that oil prices had returned to levels that were sufficiently high to warrant production and make a profit. Midland's population grew by 18 percent from 2000 to 2010 and an even more impressive 20 percent in the next five years. Optimistic city leaders have projected that, if the boom holds, population could double over the next three decades.

The 11th Congressional District of Texas covers much of West Texas. It sweeps through 29 counties and across 300 miles of often barren land from the New Mexico border to the outskirts of both Fort Worth and Austin. more than half the population is in Midland, Ector and Tom Green (San Angelo) counties. The district's Hispanic population has steadily increased to 38 percent. West Texas in the 1940s was, like nearly every other part of Texas, almost totally Democratic. That began to change in the 1950s as Midland moved toward Republicans. Newcomers like the Bushes were an important part of this trend. The 11th today is overwhelmingly Republican, giving Donald Trump 78 percent of the vote in 2016. Slightly behind the adjacent 13th District, it is the second-most Republican district in the nation, the same top-two results as in 2012.

TWELFTH DISTRICT

Kay Granger (R)

Elected 1996, 11th term; b. Jan 18, 1943, Greenville; Texas Wesleyan University, B.S.; University of Texas - Arlington, 1976; Methodist; Divorced; 3 children; 5 grandchildren.

Elected Office: Ft. Worth City Council, 1989-1991; Ft. Worth Mayor, 1991-1996.

Professional Career: Teacher, 1965-1978; Life ins. agent, 1978-1985; Chairman, Ft. Worth Zoning Comm., 1981-1989; Founder & President, Kay Granger Ins. Co. Inc.

DC Office: 1026 LHOB 20515, 202-225-5071, Fax: 202-225-5683, kaygranger.house.gov.

State Offices: Fort Worth, 817-338-0909.

Committees: *Appropriations*: Defense (Chmn), Energy & Water Development & Related Agencies, State, Foreign Operations & Related Programs.

Group Ratings

	ADA	ACLU	AFL-CIO	LCV	ITI	COC	HAFA	ACU	CFG	FRC
2016	-	5%	-	3%	100%	100%	58%	85%	85%	100%
2015	0%	C	23%	0%	C	95%	C	67%	67%	100%

Almanac Ratings 2015

	Economy	Social	Foreign	Composite
Liberal	7%	5%	11%	8%
Conservative	93%	95%	90%	93%

Key Votes of the 114th Congress

1. Keystone Pipeline	Y	5. Puerto Rico Debt	Y	9. Offenses by Aliens	Y
2. Trade Deals	Y	6. Medical Marijuana	N	10. Troops in Iraq	N
3. Export-Import Bank	N	7. Sanctuary Cities	Y	11. Homeland Security $$	Y
4. Debt Ceiling Increase	Y	8. Armor-piercing Bullets	Y	12. Trade Adjustment aid	Y

Election Results

Election	Name (Party)	Vote (%)	Cand. Spent	Ind. Exp. Support	Ind. Exp. Oppose
2016 General	Kay Granger (R)	196,482 (69%)	$717,753		
	Bill Bradshaw (D)	76,029 (27%)			
	Ed Colliver (L)	10,604 (4%)			
2016 Primary	Kay Granger (R)	(100%)			

Prior winning percentages: 2014 (71%), 2012 (71%), 2010 (72%), 2008 (68%), 2006 (67%), 2004 (72%), 2002 (92%), 2000 (63%), 1998 (62%), 1996 (58%)

Kay Granger, first elected in 1996, is the only Republican woman to represent the Lone Star State in Congress. Less conservative than most other Texans, she has climbed the ladder of the Appropriations Committee. After six years chairing the subcommittee that controls spending for the State Department and foreign aid, she took over in January 2017 as chairwoman of the Defense Subcommittee. Her expertise on national security issues and local funding will be instrumental for the major defense plants in her district. Coincidentally, House Armed Services Committee chairman Mac Thornberry represents the adjacent 13th District.

Granger grew up in Fort Worth, graduated from Texas Wesleyan College and worked as a high school journalism and English teacher in North Richland Hills. She raised three children and started her own insurance agency, which she operated for more than 20 years. In 1989, she was elected to the Fort Worth Council, and two years later was elected as the non-partisan mayor. When the House seat became open, leaders of both parties tried to recruit Granger.

She decided to run in the Republican primary. In a three-candidate race, she was attacked as a liberal, partly for her support of abortion rights. She won with 69 percent of the vote. Her Democratic opponent was Hugh Parmer, a former Fort Worth mayor and the challenger to GOP Sen. Phil Gramm in 1990. Parmer attacked Republican cuts in Medicare and the stewardship of House Speaker Newt Gingrich. Granger called for a balanced budget and tax cuts for business and ran on her record as mayor. She won 58%-41%, a stunning Republican victory in the district held for 18 terms by Democratic Speaker Jim Wright until 1989.

Granger's voting record has been in the center of House Republicans, as shown by the *Almanac* vote ratings for 2015. In 2007-08, she was vice chair of the Republican Conference, but her leadership ambitions were limited. One of Granger's legislative achievements was enactment of tax-free savings accounts for higher education expenses. She and Democratic Rep. Emanuel Cleaver of Missouri, another former big-city mayor, launched in 2013 an effort to build bipartisanship in the deeply polarized House. In 2014, Speaker John Boehner named her to chair a working group on the border crisis, chiefly in the Rio Grande valley. Her proposal was far less costly than the plan submitted by President Barack Obama. She takes her work seriously and she rarely seeks news-media attention. "Kay Granger chooses work over recognition," the *Fort Worth Star-Telegram* headlined a March 2015 news story.

On the Appropriations Committee, Granger became an expert on foreign assistance. In 2005, she traveled to Iraq with Democratic Rep. Ellen Tauscher of California, where they conducted an election training session for women candidates. In 2009, she visited U.S. troops in Afghanistan, and was among the Republicans who urged the Obama administration to step up pressure on Afghan President Hamid Karzai to establish a "functional, transparent government that does not condone corruption." She served on a private commission that reviewed global health policy.

In 2011, she became chairwoman of the State and Foreign Operations Subcommittee, where her experience with military spending and her interest in human rights were useful to her goals of global security and stability. She warned freshman Republicans against cutting foreign aid too deeply. "I think that there is more pressure [to cut foreign aid] because there's this misunderstanding of how much that part of the budget is," she said on the PBS *NewsHour*. But she did not embrace major increases in foreign aid. Despite personal lobbying from U2 singer and human rights activist Bono, she said that the Agency for International Development's request for a 22 percent increase for fiscal 2012 was "unrealistic in today's budget environment." She backed off slightly to permit Secretary of State John Kerry to announce $250 million in aid to Egypt during his 2013 trip to Cairo. In the spending bill enacted in December 2015, she secured nearly $1 billion in aid for Mexico and Central America. Also that year, she worked to freeze $370 million to the Palestinian Authority because of its incitement of violence in Israel. In January 2017, she called for a cut in funding of the United Nations until the Security Council repealed its latest anti-Israel resolution. On her subcommittee, Granger formed a close and productive working relationship with Rep. Nita Lowey of New York, the committee's top Democrat.

Granger pursued an active campaign to chair the Defense Subcommittee, a goal that she had set when she was first elected 20 years earlier. Over the years, she has kept a close eye on local Pentagon spending and worked to maintain production in her district of Lockheed Martin planes, especially the F-35 fighter jet. In an unusual and mostly closed-door process, she was selected by Rep. Rodney Frelinghuysen, the new chairman of the committee. Rep. Hal Rogers of Kentucky, who was term-limited as committee chairman, had sought the Defense Subcommittee but instead took the State and Foreign Operations panel that Granger had chaired. In addition to her long experience and local interests, she had the support of the influential Texas GOP delegation. Her selection was all the more timely because President-elect Donald Trump had tweeted, "F-35 program and cost is out of control." Following the October 2016 release of Trump's crude comments about women, Granger had said that he "should remove himself from consideration as commander in chief." Following the election, she said that Trump had a "mandate for change" and "I will work with whoever is the president."

Granger has been reelected by wide margins. Her moderate tendencies inspired challenges in the 2010 and 2012 Republican primaries by underfunded challengers from her right, whom she dispatched with ease. She wrote a book, *What's Right About America: Celebrating Our Nation's Values*, published in 2006.

Fort Worth and Western Suburbs

Population		Race and Ethnicity		Income	
Total	742,964	White	63.8%	Median Income	$60,933 (134 out of 435)
Land area	1,441	Black	8.2%		
Pop/ sq mi	515.5	Latino	22.2%		
Born in state	60.5%	Asian	3.3%	Under $50,000	40.5%
		Two races	1.9%	$50,000-$99,999	33.6%
Age Groups		Other	0.6%	$100,000-$199,999	20.5%
Under 18	25.4%			$200,000 or more	5.3%
18-34	24.3%	**Education**		Poverty Rate	12.3%
35-64	38.5%	H.S grad or less	37.7%		
Over 64	11.8%	Some college	32.7%	**Health Insurance**	
		College Degree, 4 yr	19.9%	With health insurance coverage	83.0%
Work		Post grad	9.8%		
White Collar	37.0%				
Sales and Service	41.3%	**Military**		**Public Assistance**	
Blue Collar	21.7%	Veteran	9.8%	Cash public assistance income	1.6%
Government	5.9%	Active Duty	0.3%		
				Food stamp/SNAP benefits	9.5%

Voter Turnout			
2015 Total Citizens 18+	512,749	2016 House Turnout as % CVAP	55%
2016 House turnout	283,115	2014 House Turnout as % CVAP	31%

2012 Presidential Vote		
Mitt Romney	166,992	(67%)
Barack Obama	79,147	(32%)

2016 Presidential Vote		
Donald Trump	177,939	(62%)
Hillary Clinton	92,549	(33%)
Gary Johnson	10,173	(4%)

Cook Partisan Voting Index: R+18

Fort Worth has a fair claim to being the quintessential mid-American city. It sits halfway across the continent, just west of the Balcones Escarpment that divides the dry, treeless grazing lands of West Texas from the humid green croplands of East Texas, "where the West begins," as its 19th century boosters proclaimed, coining the slogan that's still used by the city. This was the last stop for cattle drives before they returned to Kansas. It is Southern in heritage and Northern in its advanced post-industrial economy. It has the nation's longest row of Western wear shops and one of the nation's richest families, the Basses, whose steel skyscrapers dominate the skyline. The family developed Sundance Square, a 35-block entertainment, office and retail district that has helped revive the downtown district. The area was named for the running mate of famed outlaw Butch Cassidy, who regularly frequented Fort Worth for its saloons and gambling establishments at the turn of the 20th century.

"Cowtown," as the city is sometimes called, is the 16th most populous city in the nation, larger than Boston, Memphis and Baltimore. It has a high-tech economy and has been an aviation center since the 1940s, though one that was hard hit by defense cuts. The huge Lockheed Martin plant, which employs about 14,000 people, produces numerous bombers and fighter planes for the armed forces, including the F-35 fighter jet. In January 2017, the company announced plans to hire an additional 1,800 workers to increase production of the F-35. Next door is the Naval Air Station Fort Worth Joint Reserve Base, formerly Carswell Air Force Base, the home of B-52 bombers for years. In January 2017, the Air Force announced that the base will be the home to a squadron of F-35s. *The New York Times* has called the city "an irresistible combination of cowboys and culture," in part because it has some of the nation's premier small museums, including the Amon Carter Museum, the Kimbell Art Museum, the Modern Art Museum of Fort Worth, and the Sid Richardson Museum. The Aviation Hall of Fame, moving from Dayton, Ohio, was scheduled to open in October 2017. Under construction and scheduled to open in 2019 in Fort Worth is a $450 million arena, where the sports events will include rodeos.

The 12th Congressional District includes about half of Fort Worth and western suburban Tarrant County, as well as all of Parker County to the west and part of Wise County to the north. About 76 percent of the population is in Tarrant, which has grown an impressive 39 percent since 2000. It has narrowed its population gap with Dallas County to less than 600,000 residents. Parts of Tarrant are in six districts, of which the 12th has the largest share. The district includes northern and western Fort Worth neighborhoods and the affluent southwest quarter beyond Texas Christian University, downtown and the Stockyards. Parker County was once windswept open land around the courthouse town of Weatherford, where former House Speaker Jim Wright, a Democrat, grew up and was first elected to the House in 1954. (Facing ethics sanctions, he quit the House in 1989 after two-plus years as Speaker, and he returned to Texas to write and teach; he died in 2015.) Today, Parker is sprouting subdivisions and grew 46 percent from 2000 to 2016, to a population of 129,000. Fort Worth and Tarrant County stayed Democratic in the 1950s when Dallas went Republican. With Dallas recently swinging back to Democrats, Fort Worth and Tarrant County have swung Republican. The 12th District has become solidly Republican, giving Donald Trump 62 percent of the vote in 2016. Democratic parts of Fort Worth are in the 33rd District, which extends to Dallas.

THIRTEENTH DISTRICT

Mac Thornberry (R)

Elected 1994, 12th term; b. Jul 15, 1958, Clarendon; Texas Technical University Law School, B.A.; University of Texas Law School, J.D.; Presbyterian; Married (Sally Adams Thornberry); 2 children.

Professional Career: Legislative counsel, Rep. Tom Loeffler, 1983-1985; Chief of Staff, Rep. Larry Combest, 1985-1988; Deputy Assistant Secretary of st. for Legislative affairs, 1988-1989; Practicing attorney, 1989-1994; Rancher, 1989-1994.

DC Office: 2208 RHOB 20515, 202-225-3706, Fax: 202-225-3486, thornberry.house.gov.

State Offices: Amarillo, 806-371-8844; Wichita Falls, 940-692-1700.

Committees: *Armed Services (Chmn)*: Emerging Threats & Capabilities, Military Personnel, Oversight & Investigations, Readiness, Seapower & Projection Forces, Strategic Forces, Tactical Air & Land Forces.

Group Ratings

	ADA	ACLU	AFL-CIO	LCV	ITI	COC	HAFA	ACU	CFG	FRC
2016	-	5%	-	0%	100%	100%	55%	80%	62%	100%
2015	0%	C	17%	0%	C	100%	C	83%	66%	92%

Almanac Ratings 2015

	Economy	Social	Foreign	Composite
Liberal	10%	0%	4%	5%
Conservative	90%	100%	96%	95%

Key Votes of the 114th Congress

1. Keystone Pipeline	Y	5. Puerto Rico Debt	Y	9. Offenses by Aliens	Y
2. Trade Deals	Y	6. Medical Marijuana	N	10. Troops in Iraq	N
3. Export-Import Bank	N	7. Sanctuary Cities	Y	11. Homeland Security $$	N
4. Debt Ceiling Increase	Y	8. Armor-piercing Bullets	Y	12. Trade Adjustment aid	Y

Election Results

Election	Name (Party)	Vote (%)		Cand. Spent	Ind. Exp. Support	Ind. Exp. Oppose
2016 General	Mac Thornberry (R)	199,050	(90%)	$908,271		
	Calvin DeWeese (L)	14,725	(7%)			
	Rusty Tomlinson (G)	7,467	(3%)			
2016 Primary	Mac Thornberry (R)		(100%)			

Prior winning percentages: 2014 (84%), 2012 (91%), 2010 (87%), 2008 (78%), 2006 (74%), 2004 (92%), 2002 (79%), 2000 (68%), 1998 (68%), 1996 (67%), 1994 (55%)

Republican Mac Thornberry, first elected in 1994, has been one of Congress' brainiest and most thoughtful members on national and domestic security issues. As chairman of the House Armed Services Committee, the first Texan of either party to hold that post, he has been outspoken about the need for more defense spending and has challenged anybody who has delayed that objective.

His great-great-grandfather, Amos Thornberry, a Union Army veteran and staunch Republican, moved to Clay County, just east of Wichita Falls, in the 1880s. A year after Amos died in 1925, his son bought the cattle ranch in sparsely populated Donley County, closer to Amarillo, which Mac Thornberry and his family now run. After college at Texas Tech and law school at the University of Texas, Thornberry worked for influential West Texas GOP Reps. Tom Loeffler and Larry Combest. He returned to practice law in West Texas, and in 1994 challenged Democratic Rep. Bill Sarpalius, whom he attacked for voting for President Bill Clinton's budget and tax legislation. He profited from news stories that Sarpalius failed to pay a company that moved him to Washington, and then accepted a fee for speaking at the company's convention in Las Vegas. Thornberry won 55%-45%, and has rolled up large reelection margins since.

Thornberry has a solidly conservative voting record, though he is hardly the most ideological Republican in the Texas delegation. In keeping with his scholarly nature, his official website includes a section on "Mac's reading list." The *Dallas Morning News*, in a January 2015 profile with a headline saying he brought "expertise, not notoriety" to his work, wrote that his office bookshelves are "filled with tomes on spy craft, military history and strategy."

On domestic issues, Thornberry has pressed for repeal of the estate tax and adoption of a national sales tax. In 2010, he enacted a bill expanding access to state veterans' homes for parents whose children died while serving in the military. He filed a bill in 2011 to help states set up special health care courts staffed by judges with health policy expertise. The judges would serve as an alternative to juries that Republicans say are inclined to award unnecessarily large damage amounts in malpractice cases. He has supported a two-year budget cycle, an idea that reform groups have said would make the budget process run far more smoothly. On a vital local issue, Thornberry won House passage in February 2017 of his bill to require a that the Bureau of Land Management survey the lands along the Texas side of the Red River as a step toward resolving long-time disagreements between landowners and the federal government.

Thornberry has long been at the forefront of national security issues. In 2002, after the Sept. 11 terrorist attacks, he played a key role in establishment of the new Homeland Security Department. In 2011, he took over as chairman of the Armed Services' terrorism panel and Speaker John Boehner asked him to lead an effort to develop a cybersecurity strategy for the country. The House in 2012 passed a series of bills based on his task force's recommendations that were in keeping with his desire to take up issues in "bite-sized chunks" rather than in a single sweeping measure. But partisan disagreements stalled action in the Senate. He has championed missile defense and called for better coordination of military space programs. In 2014, he told reporters that the leaks of confidential information by Edward Snowden were acts of espionage that worked to "compromise the military capability and defense of the country" and would cost billions of dollars to repair.

In 2013, Thornberry led a long-term effort to reform the Pentagon's acquisition programs. Thornberry told *Federal Computer Week* that he wanted to change the underlying principles of acquisition instead of merely trying to eliminate wasteful programs. "I think the key is looking … to the incentives that exist in the system, both on the side of government and on the side of industry," he said.

Taking over as committee chairman, Thornberry sought to be a firm check on the Obama administration. "Congress is sometimes criticized for exercising its proper role in defense," he said in a forceful January 2015 speech that made clear he would be an activist. He cited Capitol Hill's decision to block the Pentagon's decision to shut down the country's lone tank-production line and its insistence on using Predator drones as a weapon against terrorists. At the same time, though, he acknowledged that Congress can be "parochial" and get things wrong. He said that he was open to "any solution" that would stave off the steep spending cuts under automatic sequestration procedures.

Thornberry won House approval in May 2015 of the military authorization bill, which reflected the view of his committee's defense hawks that the Pentagon needed an infusion of funds for new and expanded programs. Many liberals and a few Republican budget hawks complained that he used budget tricks to break spending ceilings. Defense Secretary Ash Carter called the bill "a road to nowhere" that would be vetoed unless Congress revised both domestic and military spending ceilings. An analysis by business consultants that was published by *Defense One* said the bill's overhaul of Pentagon acquisition procedures "makes considerable strides toward disrupting a procurement process that is widely considered broken, but the bill is far from a fix-all." After a House-Senate agreement on the defense spending bill was vetoed by Obama in October 2015, the two sides came together at the end of the year when congressional leaders reached a budget agreement to raise spending caps.

Thornberry has continued his interest in improving the efficiency of the Pentagon. In 2016, he set acquisition reform as a key feature of the annual defense spending bill, including steps such as more experimentation with technology, encouragement of competition and clarification of intellectual property rights of Pentagon contractors. Several of these changes gained bipartisan support and were included in the final version of what otherwise was mostly a stand-pat measure, which was enacted in in the lame-duck session following the election.

Although the election of President Donald Trump gave him opportunities to set Pentagon policy with a more sympathetic administration, Thornberry had early problems with Trump's free-wheeling style as the GOP nominee. "I'm troubled by some of the things Mr. Trump has said and done," he said when the presidential nominee had an extended rhetorical showdown during the summer with a Muslim family whose son had died in Iraq while serving in the Army. "There is a responsibility for all of us … to reaffirm that we honor and appreciate their service and nothing that is said or done in politics changes that." During a broadcast interview in September 2016 when he had not yet formally endorsed Trump, he refused to respond directly to a question of whether he had confidence in Trump. "Sure. I've got concerns about what both candidates have said," he told MSNBC.

When Trump in March 2017 submitted initial budget plans for the entire government, Thornberry responded that they fell short of what he had expected for rebuilding the military. "Do people at the White House understand how much damage has been done over the past several years? I don't know," Thornberry told reporters. "But, you know, that is part of our job as an independent branch of government, to understand that and to try to convey that. That is why this is a continuing conversation."

North Texas/Panhandle: Amarillo, Wichita Falls

Population		**Race and Ethnicity**		**Income**	
Total	705,632	White	64.8%	Median Income	$48,160 (282 out of 435)
Land area	38,349	Black	5.2%		
Pop/ sq mi	18.4	Latino	25.7%		
Born in state	67.0%	Asian	1.9%	Under $50,000	51.4%
		Two races	1.8%	$50,000-$99,999	30.8%
Age Groups		Other	0.7%	$100,000-$199,999	15.2%
Under 18	25.2%			$200,000 or more	2.6%
18-34	23.7%	**Education**		Poverty Rate	15.9%
35-64	36.9%	H.S grad or less	47.0%		
Over 64	14.2%	Some college	33.3%	**Health Insurance**	
		College Degree, 4 yr	13.8%	With health insurance coverage	81.6%
Work		Post grad	6.0%		
White Collar	30.0%				
Sales and Service	41.9%	**Military**		**Public Assistance**	
Blue Collar	28.1%	Veteran	9.5%	Cash public assistance income	1.4%
Government	7.4%	Active Duty	1.2%		
				Food stamp/SNAP benefits	12.3%

Voter Turnout			
2015 Total Citizens 18+	488,404	2016 House Turnout as % CVAP	45%
2016 House turnout	221,242	2014 House Turnout as % CVAP	27%

2012 Presidential Vote		
Mitt Romney	184,104	(80%)
Barack Obama	42,521	(19%)

2016 Presidential Vote		
Donald Trump	190,838	(80%)
Hillary Clinton	40,253	(17%)
Gary Johnson	6,709	(3%)

Cook Partisan Voting Index: R+33

North TexaThe farther west one travels in Texas, the browner the land gets and the smaller the towns get, until you arrive at counties containing only a few hundred people each - plus quite a few more head of cattle. At that point, the land rises nearly 1,000 feet in elevation, up steep hillsides from the gullies along the rivers that for most of the year are just trickles, to the tilted tableland that makes up the High Plains of West Texas. The winds here sweep down from the Rockies, the land is barren except where irrigated, often with the now dangerously depleted waters of the Ogallala Aquifer. The land alternates between grazing areas and cotton fields. But here and there in this demanding environment - sticky hot in the summer, swept by north winds from Canada in winter, always threatened by tornadoes - comfortable cities have been built to house the people and businesses that bring forth some of the nation's most abundant oil, natural gas, helium and other elements from the earth. The area produces cotton and milo, a variety of sorghum, and is home to one of the nation's oldest cattle auctions. Researchers have discovered dangerous levels of uranium at some sites in the Ogallala Aquifer. Support has grown for greater use of renewable energy in the Panhandle. In 2015, a utility report showed that wind accounted for 19 percent of energy production.

Still, the population in the region has been either in decline or stagnant for nearly three decades. Around Wichita Falls is the agricultural land of the Red River Valley. Cadillac Ranch, located just off I-40 west of Amarillo, is a famous roadside sculpture featuring "10 tail-finned, brightly painted Cadillacs planted nose down in a pasture," as *Texas Monthly* describes it. Built in 1974, the attraction inspired the 1980 Bruce Springsteen song "Cadillac Ranch." Archer City, home of novelist Larry McMurtry, was chronicled in *The Last Picture Show* and *Texasville*.

The 13th Congressional District of Texas spans 39 counties and parts of two others, from the New Mexico border to just north of Denton in the Dallas exurbs. That is a Texas-sized drive of more than 450 miles. The area was long dominated by Texas Anglos, but Latinos lately have been moving here in large numbers to work in the fields or in crop processing. Today, the district is 26 percent Hispanic. Amarillo is the largest city in the heart of cowboy country. It is famously windy - windier than Chicago, in fact. Just outside town is the Pantex plant that secretly assembled and then dismantled thousands of nuclear warheads and was the epicenter of American defense in the Cold War. Much of the facility has decayed, including leaky roofs, the *Lubbock Avalanche Journal* reported in 2014. A Pentagon study in 2016 showed $3.7 billion in deferred maintenance for nuclear-weapons facilities. Pantex has become the site of a renewable energy project that removes carbon dioxide emissions from the air. At its other end, close to the Red River Valley, the district reaches but does not include Denton County at the northwest corner of the Metroplex.

Settled by Confederate veterans, the valley was heavily Democratic through the 1970s. The High Plains were for years more Republican. Both are now solidly Republican, and so is the 13th District. In 2016, Donald Trump got 80 percent of the vote here, which was his strongest performance in the nation.

FOURTEENTH DISTRICT

Randy Weber (R)

Elected 2012, 3rd term; b. Jul 02, 1953, Pearland; University of Houston, Clear Lake (TX), B.S.; Baptist; Married (Brenda Weber); 3 children; 7 grandchildren.

Elected Office: Pearland City Council, 1990-1996; TX House, 2008-2013.

Professional Career: Owner, Weber's Air & Heat, 1981-present.

DC Office: 1708 LHOB 20515, 202-225-2831, Fax: 202-225-0271, weber.house.gov.

State Offices: Beaumont, 409-835-0108; Lake Jackson, 979-285-0231; League City, 281-316-0231.

Committees: *Science, Space & Technology*: Energy (Chmn), Environment. *Transportation & Infrastructure*: Coast Guard & Maritime Transportation, Railroads, Pipelines & Hazardous Materials, Water Resources & Environment.

Group Ratings

	ADA	ACLU	AFL-CIO	LCV	ITI	COC	HAFA	ACU	CFG	FRC
2016	-	11%	-	0%	83%	100%	85%	96%	86%	100%
2015	0%	C	8%	3%	C	75%	C	88%	88%	100%

Almanac Ratings 2015

	Economy	Social	Foreign	Composite
Liberal	5%	0%	1%	2%
Conservative	95%	100%	99%	98%

Key Votes of the 114th Congress

1. Keystone Pipeline	Y	5. Puerto Rico Debt	N	9. Offenses by Aliens	Y
2. Trade Deals	Y	6. Medical Marijuana	N	10. Troops in Iraq	N
3. Export-Import Bank	Y	7. Sanctuary Cities	Y	11. Homeland Security $$	N
4. Debt Ceiling Increase	N	8. Armor-piercing Bullets	Y	12. Trade Adjustment aid	N

Election Results

Election	Name (Party)	Vote (%)		Cand. Spent	Ind. Exp. Support	Ind. Exp. Oppose
2016 General	Randy Weber (R)	160,631	(62%)	$425,093		
	Michael Cole (D)	99,054	(38%)	$22,433		
2016 Primary	Randy Weber (R)	57,769	(84%)			
	Keith Casey (R)	10,971	(16%)			

Prior winning percentages: 2014 (62%), 2012 (54%)

Republican Randy Weber in 2012 prevailed in a crowded primary and claimed the seat of retiring libertarian icon Rep. Ron Paul. Although he lacked the fame of his predecessor, Weber often spoke his mind and posed challenges to House GOP leaders. In October 2015, he was one of nine Republicans who voted for an alternative to Paul Ryan as Speaker.

Before he was elected to Congress, Weber had always resided within a five-mile radius of his hometown of Pearland. His father owned a gas station and later ran an RV business. After getting his bachelor's from the University of Houston, he started Weber's Air and Heat, making all the service calls as an air conditioning contractor and putting flyers on every doorstep in town to drum up business. "Did we struggle? Man, did we," Weber said, recalling the number of times the electric company threatened to turn off his power. "Nobody came to bail out Randy Weber. My company, I made it the old-fashioned way." The business had 10 employees when he entered Congress. In the 1980s, President Ronald Reagan's message of limited government inspired Weber to get politically involved. From 1990 to 1996, he served on the Pearland City Council. Twelve years later, he was elected to the Texas House, where he worked on issues ranging from veterans affairs to domestic human trafficking - usually with a strongly conservative view.

Running for the House, Weber emerged from a field of nine GOP contenders. He was endorsed by Paul and Texas Gov. Rick Perry. Weber styled himself as a devoted family man and Christian and he ran "to everyone else's right," wrote David Wasserman of the Cook Political Report. He bought a new home in nearby Alvin in 2012 after his residence just outside the district became a frequent target of attacks against him in the campaign. After leading the first round with 28 percent to 19 percent for Felicia Harris, an attorney and councilwoman from Pearland, he easily won the runoff with 63 percent of the vote.

Weber faced off in the general election against former Democratic Rep. Nick Lampson, who distanced himself from the national party and retained some of his local popularity from two earlier stints in the House when he served five terms and represented Jefferson County. The unique makeup of the district - rife with working-class voters - coupled with the political chops of both candidates led the *Texas Tribune* to dub it the only "real, true, honest-to-goodness competition" in the deeply red state in 2012. Republicans needed to work harder than expected, especially when Weber ran short of cash in the final weeks of the campaign. Each candidate spent a bit more than a million dollars. Lampson benefited from his name ID and the local Democratic lean to take 58 percent of the vote in Jefferson. Weber ran stronger in his base, with 68 percent in Brazoria. In the swing county of Galveston, which cast 45 percent of the total vote, Weber got 57 percent. Overall, he won, 53%-45%. He has been twice reelected with 62 percent of the vote against opponents whom he vastly outspent.

In the House, Weber unabashedly said that nobody would "out-conservative" him - unlike Paul, whose libertarian views on some social and foreign policy issues sometimes fit more comfortably with Democrats. In 2014, he filed a resolution condemning President Barack Obama for having routinely refused to enforce the law and said that the president was provoking a constitutional crisis. "In my view, the president has not faithfully executed the law," Weber said.

He got an opportunity to deal with local issues as chairman of the Science, Space and Technology Subcommittee on Energy. When the House passed in January 2017 an authorization bill for the Energy Department, it included Weber's provisions to encourage spending on advance nuclear reactor technologies.

Weber clashed frequently with Republican leaders. In January 2015, he voted for Rep. Louie Gohmert of Texas - and against John Boehner - for House Speaker, and explained, "I voted according to my constituents' wishes." He said that he hoped that his vote sent a signal to GOP leaders that "we need to be more forceful in fighting this president and his liberal agenda." He later told reporters that he paid a political price when his plan to sponsor a routine bill on Energy Department research was given to another GOP member. After Weber voted for Rep. Daniel Webster of Florida in the October 2015 selection of a successor to Boehner, he congratulated Paul Ryan and expressed hope that he "will take this opportunity to forward our conservative cause, restore order in the House, and have the strength to make tough decisions."

Weber was outspoken on topics outside of Congress. When Supreme Court Justice Ruth Bader Ginsburg voiced critical comments about Donald Trump in July 2016, Weber said that she should resign. During the presidential transition in January 2017, he tweeted that CNN should fire its White House reporter who confronted Trump at a press conference.

Gulf Coast: Galveston, Beaumont-Port Arthur

Population		**Race and Ethnicity**		**Income**	
Total	717,656	White	51.8%	Median Income	$53,716 (203 out of 435)
Land area	2,441	Black	19.8%	Under $50,000	46.7%
Pop/ sq mi	294.0	Latino	23.7%	$50,000-$99,999	28.9%
Born in state	66.4%	Asian	2.9%	$100,000-$199,999	19.6%
		Two races	1.4%	$200,000 or more	4.9%
		Other	0.3%	Poverty Rate	16.0%
Age Groups		**Education**		**Health Insurance**	
Under 18	24.6%	H.S grad or less	44.2%	With health insurance coverage	81.0%
18-34	23.1%	Some college	33.0%		
35-64	39.8%	College Degree, 4 yr	15.5%		
Over 64	12.5%	Post grad	7.4%		
Work		**Military**		**Public Assistance**	
White Collar	34.1%	Veteran	8.7%	Cash public assistance income	1.5%
Sales and Service	40.6%	Active Duty	0.1%	Food stamp/SNAP benefits	13.7%
Blue Collar	25.3%				
Government	5.4%				

Voter Turnout			
2015 Total Citizens 18+	498,579	2016 House Turnout as % CVAP	52%
2016 House turnout	259,685	2014 House Turnout as % CVAP	29%

2012 Presidential Vote		
Mitt Romney	147,213	(59%)
Barack Obama	97,958	(40%)

2016 Presidential Vote		
Donald Trump	153,191	(58%)
Hillary Clinton	101,228	(38%)
Gary Johnson	7,352	(3%)

Cook Partisan Voting Index: R+12

The spongy land of the Texas Gulf Coast remained mostly unsettled until well into the 19th century. When oil was found at the Spindletop field near Beaumont in 1901, the area all around it boomed, first with oil exploration, then petroleum refining, then petrochemical production. The rig workers and mechanical engineers they attracted have given a kind of permanent roughneck air to the region, and it's one of the few places in Texas where unions have any strength. The Humble oil field was once the largest in Texas, and the local Humble Oil and Refining Company is now known as ExxonMobil. Galveston, on a barrier island in the Gulf, was an immigrant port until a 1900 hurricane killed thousands. It is now guarded by a 17-foot seawall and connected to the mainland by a hurricane-resistant bridge. Its cruise port in 2015 ranked fourth in total passengers and serves several of the largest cruise lines; all of the top three ports are in Florida. The nearby refinery town of Texas City was home to one of the state's worst disasters: In April 1947, more than 500 people died after two freighters containing ammonium nitrate fertilizer exploded, demolishing the port. More recently, Hurricanes Gustav and Ike in 2008 shut down oil pipelines for months and toppled some platforms. Galveston was scheduled to complete by the summer of 2017 a four-mile beach expansion, with sand removed from the Galveston Ship Channel.

The 14th Congressional District of Texas stretches along the southeast Gulf Coast, from Port Arthur and Beaumont to Freeport at its southernmost point. Nearly half of the district is in the solidly Republican confines of Galveston. One-third of the population lives in Jefferson County, around the highly polluted "Golden Triangle" oil refining area of Beaumont and Port Arthur. Of the two, Port Arthur is smaller and suffered greatly during the recession. While refineries are Port Arthur's economic lifeline, the city's downtown has been virtually abandoned, and over a quarter of residents live below the poverty level. The BP oil spill disaster and subsequent offshore drilling moratorium hurt that industry and the local shrimping economy, as well. The local economy received a boost from the 2014 opening of the southern leg of the Keystone XL pipeline from Cushing, Oklahoma, to the Port Arthur refineries. Construction of additional terminals and infrastructure likely will benefit the area, regardless of the price of oil and its destination. In November 2016, ExxonMobil announced a $1.2 billion expansion of the polyethylene unit in its local refinery complex, with 1,400 additional workers expected. These developments helped to place Beaumont-Port Arthur on a website that listed the top 10 places with booming incomes in 2016. The population in Jefferson County is 34 percent African American and 20 percent Hispanic; the county leans Democratic. The remainder of the district is inland Brazoria County, home to the first capital of the Republic of Texas; about half of Brazoria is in the 14th.

The 14th is a working-class, ancestrally Democratic district that since the 1980s has become safely Republican, with help from redistricting changes. Overall, the 24 percent Latino and 20 percent black population have not affected the comfortably Republican tilt. In this area, where local Rep. Ron Paul was once the favorite son in presidential campaigns, Donald Trump took 58 percent of the vote; Mitt Romney had 59 percent in 2012.

FIFTEENTH DISTRICT

Vicente Gonzalez (D)

Elected 2016, 1st term; b. Sep 04, 1967, Corpus Christi; Harvard University School of Law (MA); Embry Riddle Aeronautical University, B.S., 1992; Texas A & M University School of Law (formerly Texas Wesleyan School of Law), J.D., 1996; Catholic; Married (Lorena Saenz).

Professional Career: Attorney and Owner, V. Gonzalez & Associates..

DC Office: 113 CHOB 20515, 202-225-2531, Fax: 202-225-5688, gonzalez.house.gov.

State Offices: Edinburg, 956-682-5545.

Committees: *Financial Services*: Capital Markets, Securities & Investment, Housing & Insurance, Oversight & Investigations.

Election Results

Election	Name (Party)	Vote (%)		Cand. Spent	Ind. Exp. Support	Ind. Exp. Oppose
2016 General	Vicente Gonzalez (D)	101,712	(57%)	$2,288,715		
	Tom Westley (R)	66,877	(38%)	$286,697		
	Vanessa Tijerina (G)	5,448	(3%)			
2016 Primary Run Off	Vicente Gonzalez (D)	16,071	(66%)			
	Juan Palacios Jr. (D)	8,379	(34%)			
2016 Primary	Vicente Gonzalez (D)	22,122	(42%)			
	Juan Palacios Jr. (D)	9,907	(19%)			
	Dolly Elizondo (D)	8,881	(17%)			
	Joel Quintanilla (D)	6,144	(12%)			

Democrat Vicente Gonzalez of Texas was elected in 2016 to an open seat along the border with Mexico. His years growing up had a boot-strap quality. But the fact that he mostly self-financed his campaign showed that he had succeeded professionally, as a trial lawyer. With his ample funds, the political newcomer significantly outspent his opposition.

Gonzalez was born to a military family in Corpus Christi. His mother stressed the importance of education, which motivated Gonzalez to go back to high school and get his GED certificate. He attended community college classes at Del Mar College and earned his bachelor's in business aviation at Embry Riddle Aeronautical University at Corpus Christi Naval Air Station. Continuing to heed his mother's advice, he got a law degree at Texas A&M. While in law school, he interned for Democratic Rep. Solomon Ortiz of Texas to learn more about government. He founded his own law firm, which focused on business litigation, catastrophic accidents and property damage. In that work, he successfully handled several major lawsuits against South Texas school districts, which recovered millions of dollars from contractors who misspent bond money.

When Rep. Rubén Hinojosa announced his retirement, Gonzalez faced five other candidates in the Democratic primary. Gonzalez said that he self-financed his campaign so he would not have to accept corporate contributions. The $2.3 million that he spent more than doubled the total for all of his opponents combined in both parties. With the benefit of some Washington connections, Gonzalez won the endorsement of the Congressional Progressive Caucus and campaign contributions from several House Democrats, including Minority Whip Steny Hoyer of Maryland. In the first round of voting, Gonzalez got 42 percent; the runner-up with 19 percent was Juan "Sonny" Palacios Jr., an attorney who was a member of the Edinburg school board. Gonzalez won the runoff with 66 percent of the vote.

In the general election, Republican nominee Tim Westley was an Army veteran whose campaign slogan was "Putting God Back into Politics." He spent $16,000, which was less than 1 percent of the total for his opponent. Gonzalez won, 57%-38%. That might seem close, but it was roughly the share of the vote that Hinojosa typically received during his 10 terms as Gonzalez's predecessor.

Gonzalez showed insider skills by gaining a seat on the Financial Services Committee. He joined the bipartisan Problem Solvers Caucus. "For too long we have fallen victim to partisan bickering and witnessed congressional inaction," he said. "Legislators must find practical, common sense solutions to the nation's most pressing issues." A week after President Donald Trump took office, Gonzalez invited him to the Rio Grande Valley to discuss international trade policy. "I would appreciate having the opportunity to visit with you in a bipartisan way to discuss how commerce between the two nations affects border communities and the overall economy," he wrote to Trump.

McAllen/San Antonio Corridor

Population		Race and Ethnicity		Income	
Total	740,657	White	15.9%	Median Income	$40,685 (393 out of 435)
Land area	7,804	Black	1.7%		
Pop/ sq mi	94.9	Latino	80.7%		
Born in state	64.0%	Asian	1.1%	Under $50,000	58.3%
		Two races	0.4%	$50,000-$99,999	26.8%
Age Groups		Other	0.1%	$100,000-$199,999	12.6%
Under 18	31.8%			$200,000 or more	2.2%
18-34	24.6%	**Education**		Poverty Rate	29.2%
35-64	33.2%	H.S grad or less	56.5%		
Over 64	10.4%	Some college	24.7%	**Health Insurance**	
		College Degree, 4 yr	13.4%	With health insurance coverage	69.4%
Work		Post grad	5.4%		
White Collar	28.1%			**Public Assistance**	
Sales and Service	48.1%	**Military**			
Blue Collar	23.8%	Veteran	6.0%	Cash public assistance income	2.4%
Government	10.1%	Active Duty	0.2%		
				Food stamp/SNAP benefits	26.9%

Voter Turnout			
2015 Total Citizens 18+	392,516	2016 House Turnout as % CVAP	45%
2016 House turnout	177,479	2014 House Turnout as % CVAP	23%

2012 Presidential Vote		
Barack Obama	86,941	(57%)
Mitt Romney	62,885	(42%)

2016 Presidential Vote		
Hillary Clinton	104,454	(57%)
Donald Trump	73,689	(40%)
Gary Johnson	4,501	(2%)

Cook Partisan Voting Index: D+7

A century ago, there was little but desert wilderness in the Lower Rio Grande Valley in South Texas. Only a handful of people lived anywhere near the shallow, sluggish Rio Grande. There was no U.S. Border Patrol because very few people wanted to venture across desert. Then came pioneers like Lloyd Bentsen Sr., father of the former senator and Treasury secretary, who arrived after World War I with $5 in his pocket and became one of the Valley's biggest landowners. Bentsen and others cleared the land and dug canals, hired Mexican and Mexican-American workers, and with irrigated water from the Rio Grande planted citrus groves, cornfields and palm windbreaks, ran cattle and drilled for oil and gas. Along U.S. 83, north of the Rio Grande, these pioneers built a string of towns with Anglo names and storefronts. But most of the people were Latino in culture and language. Wage levels higher than in Mexico, though low by U.S. standards, brought more Mexicans over the border.

The 15th Congressional District of Texas is one of three districts in the Lower Rio Grande Valley that run from the heavily populated areas along the border to just north of San Antonio. The days are past when ranchers and oilmen wielded absolute political power here. There is instead a robust, mostly Hispanic politics. The Hispanic population in the district is 81 percent, the second-highest in the state. Although the district reaches as far north as the rural area between Corpus Christi and San Antonio, three-quarters of its residents live just north of the river in McAllen-based Hidalgo County. Reasonably priced real estate contributed to fast-paced growth in the region and Hidalgo's population increased 49 percent from 2000 to 2016, when it reached 850,000. Hidalgo has surpassed El Paso as the largest Texas metro area along the border.

The local infrastructure has barely kept up as subdivisions have replaced citrus groves. In the McAllen area, new suburbanites work just across the border as corporate managers in the low-wage "maquiladoras," or factories. Poverty is pervasive. As of 2012, 34 percent of residents lived below the poverty line, the second highest rate for a metro area in the nation. The abortion clinic in McAllen became a flashpoint in federal litigation over state-imposed restrictions. The region is struggling to handle crime from the trade in illegal immigration and drugs. A Gallup survey in 2014 found that McAllen had the highest rate of fear of walking alone at night.

The district is heavily Democratic in the border areas but more conservative elsewhere. Hillary Clinton carried the district with 57 percent in 2016, a couple of points less than she got in each of the two adjacent heavily Hispanic districts. The 15th shares Hidalgo with the 28th and 34th Districts, but includes about 70 percent of the total population.

SIXTEENTH DISTRICT

Beto O'Rourke (D)

Elected 2012, 3rd term; b. Sep 26, 1972, El Paso; Columbia University (NY), B.A.; Roman Catholic; Married (Amy Sanders); 3 children.

Elected Office: El Paso City Council, 2005-2011.

Professional Career: Owner, Stanton St. Tech. Group, 1999-present.

DC Office: 1330 LHOB 20515, 202-225-4831, Fax: 202-225-2016, orourke.house.gov.

State Offices: El Paso, 915-541-1400.

Committees: *Armed Services*: Emerging Threats & Capabilities, Strategic Forces. *Veterans' Affairs*: Economic Opportunity (RMM), Health.

Group Ratings

	ADA	ACLU	AFL-CIO	LCV	ITI	COC	HAFA	ACU	CFG	FRC
2016	-	88%	-	89%	83%	62%	11%	5%	0%	0%
2015	80%	C	91%	94%	C	50%	C	4%	3%	8%

Almanac Ratings 2015

	Economy	Social	Foreign	Composite
Liberal	81%	100%	86%	89%
Conservative	19%	0%	15%	11%

Key Votes of the 114th Congress

1. Keystone Pipeline	N	5. Puerto Rico Debt	Y	9. Offenses by Aliens	N
2. Trade Deals	Y	6. Medical Marijuana	Y	10. Troops in Iraq	Y
3. Export-Import Bank	Y	7. Sanctuary Cities	N	11. Homeland Security $$	Y
4. Debt Ceiling Increase	Y	8. Armor-piercing Bullets	N	12. Trade Adjustment aid	Y

Election Results

Election	Name (Party)	Vote (%)		Cand. Spent	Ind. Exp. Support	Ind. Exp. Oppose
2016 General	Beto O'Rourke (D)	150,228	(86%)	$204,914		
	Jaime O. Perez (L)	17,491	(10%)			
	Mary Gourdoux (G)	7,510	(4%)			
2016 Primary	Beto O'Rourke (D)	39,958	(86%)			
	Ben Mendoza (D)	6,732	(14%)			

Prior winning percentages: 2014 (68%), 2012 (65%)

Democrat Beto O'Rourke, a sort of preppy Anglo and former El Paso city councilman, won this heavily Latino district in 2012. He worked on military and immigration issues that are vital locally and he was successful in gaining bipartisan opportunities in the Republican-controlled House. O'Rourke settled comfortably into an outsider niche within both the House and his party. He took on an uphill challenge when he launched his challenge to Republican Sen. Ted Cruz in the 2018 election.

Born to a family that has lived in El Paso for four generations, O'Rourke's roots in the district run deep. His first name is short for Roberto. His grandmother opened a furniture store there in 1950 that his mother owned, and his father, also a Democrat, served on the El Paso County Commissioners Court and as a county judge in the 1980s. At Columbia University, O'Rourke majored in English and played guitar in a rock band called Foss, which toured and was part of the do-it-yourself punk movement. O'Rourke and his bandmates often were dependent on the goodwill of club owners and nearby residents for meals and places to sleep. He described it as an "absolutely magical" time in his life. "We met wonderful people involved in that culture of rock 'n' roll and in their community," he said. After college, O'Rourke landed a job in the then-developing web technology field. He spent three years working in Manhattan, then returned to El Paso to start his own company, Stanton Street Technology Group, which continued to provide tech services throughout El Paso and nationally.

O'Rourke became involved in civic work, seeking to reverse a trend of young people leaving El Paso. With an economy dependent on low-wage, low-skill jobs, the city was "not a place you wanted to be," he said. Many jobs had been outsourced to Mexico, and bridges from Ciudad Juárez into El Paso had some of the longest waiting times along the border. He served two terms on the City Council, where he worked to save Sun Metro, public transportation in El Paso, from a fiscal meltdown.

In his primary challenge, O'Rourke argued that eight-term Rep. Silvestre Reyes, who had been chairman of the Intelligence Committee and of the Hispanic Caucus, had accomplished little on the Veterans' Affairs Committee and failed to seek a solution to reduce bridge traffic. Reyes attacked O'Rourke for his support of legalizing marijuana and painted him as unfit for office based on his arrest for drunken driving 16 years earlier. The charge had been dismissed. O'Rourke unexpectedly defeated Reyes 50%-44%, assuring his victory in the heavily Democratic district.

Serving on the Armed Services and Veterans' Affairs committees, O'Rourke was not reluctant to criticize the Obama administration. He criticized the more than two months that were required for El Paso veterans to meet with a mental health counselor at the local VA facility, which he said was a factor in the suicides among local veterans. Eager to move immigration legislation, he told *The Washington Post* in 2014 that President Barack Obama's proposed executive order was "noble" in its intention, but "terrible" by adding to "the precedent of presidents bypassing Congress to achieve something they think is important to the national interest." With Republican Rep. Steve Pearce of New Mexico, he filed a bill that sought to increase transparency and accountability at the Customs and Border Protection agency. He said that he was responding to growing reports of abuses by officers along the border. In January 2017, he filed a bill that would keep confidential the personal information of undocumented minors who he claimed were at greater risk with President Donald Trump taking office. He added that Trump's proposed border wall was "racist."

O'Rourke remained a rebel in Congress. In a 2013 interview with the elpasoinc.com web site, he said that the biggest surprise to him about serving in Congress was, "They set your expectations so low when you come in the door." The advice of senior Democrats, he explained, was "You will not pass any legislation or be able to get anything done. You should focus on raising money, winning re-election and returning us to a majority so that you can do those things you ran for in Congress." In 2014, he was among 22 House Democrats who condemned the Obama administration's handling of the swap of Army deserter Bowe Bergdahl for five Taliban prisoners at Guantanamo.

He joined Republican Rep. Jim Bridenstine of Oklahoma in sponsoring a bill imposing 10-year term limits for members of Congress. "The longer you're there, the more these interests and access agreements you've implicitly developed," he explained. Following the 2016 election, he backed the challenge of Rep. Tim Ryan of Ohio to Minority Leader Nancy Pelosi. "For any organization to succeed, there must be change in leadership to ensure that it continues to meet new and evolving opportunities and challenges," O'Rourke said. In March 2017, he had an unusual experience when he and Republican Rep. Will Hurd of Texas took a "road trip" return to Washington because bad weather had disrupted air travel. Their rental-car adventure attracted a cult-ish following on social media, where the travelers had diverse exchanges with each other and with callers. The new friends agreed to sponsor each other's legislation.

O'Rourke term-limited his House career when he announced in March 2017 his candidacy against Cruz. Initially, he talked up his own appeal and spent little time attacking the well-known senator.

El Paso

Population		**Race and Ethnicity**		**Income**	
Total	728,187	White	14.8%	Median Income	$43,234 (359 out of 435)
Land area	710	Black	3.5%		
Pop/ sq mi	1025.1	Latino	79.2%		
Born in state	55.2%	Asian	1.2%	Under $50,000	56.7%
Age Groups		Two races	0.9%	$50,000-$99,999	28.1%
Under 18	28.0%	Other	0.4%	$100,000-$199,999	12.9%
18-34	25.9%	**Education**		$200,000 or more	2.3%
35-64	34.8%	H.S grad or less	46.1%	Poverty Rate	20.9%
Over 64	11.3%	Some college	30.7%	**Health Insurance**	
Work		College Degree, 4 yr	15.9%	With health insurance coverage	75.9%
White Collar	31.6%	Post grad	7.2%		
Sales and Service	48.0%	**Military**		**Public Assistance**	
Blue Collar	20.4%	Veteran	9.4%	Cash public assistance income	3.5%
Government	6.0%	Active Duty	3.5%	Food stamp/SNAP benefits	21.9%

Voter Turnout			
2015 Total Citizens 18+	430,941	2016 House Turnout as % CVAP	41%
2016 House turnout	175,229	2014 House Turnout as % CVAP	17%

2012 Presidential Vote		
Barack Obama	100,993	(64%)
Mitt Romney	54,315	(35%)

2016 Presidential Vote		
Hillary Clinton	130,784	(68%)
Donald Trump	52,334	(27%)
Gary Johnson	6,900	(4%)

Cook Partisan Voting Index: D+17

El Paso, Texas, and Ciudad Juaréz, Mexico, face each other across the narrow Rio Grande, their tree-shaded streets spread out below the rough brown face of Comanche Peak. Downtown El Paso is only a few blocks from the bridge to Ciudad Juaréz. The two border cities are surrounded by hundreds of miles of some of North America's most rugged and desolate landscape. El Paso is closer to San Diego than to Houston, and it's in a different time zone from the rest of the state. Still, the region has grown significantly. In the 1950s, El Paso and Ciudad Juaréz each had a population around 130,000. In 2016, there were 838,000 people in El Paso County (including 681,000 in the city of El Paso), 81 percent of them Hispanic; the Mexican census counted 1.4 million in metro Juaréz. This is a bilingual, bicultural pair of cities, where most people have a Mexican heritage. El Paso is one of the lowest-wage and lowest-education locales in the United States, though statistically it is also one of the safest, with the lowest crime rate of any large U.S. city. Ciudad Juaréz, though struggling with drug cartel violence and crime, is one of the highest-wage cities in Mexico.

In the wake of the North American Free Trade Agreement, *maquiladora* factories created a cross-border economy. Much of the local economy is built on cheap, low-skill labor. South of the border, there is a large General Motors technical center. Many factories on both sides of the border were shuttered during the 2007-09 recession, but trade with Mexico helped shield El Paso from the worst of the economic downturn. The other important factor sustaining the economy was Fort Bliss, a big winner in the 2005 base closing review, with a $5 billion expansion and a total of nearly 41,000 employees. The base is home to the First Armored Division and covers 1,700 square miles, which is nearly four times the size of Delaware. One in three jobs in El Paso depends directly or indirectly on Fort Bliss. There has been deep concern about the potentially devastating impact of another base-closing review. Most of the local job growth has been in leisure and hospitality, jobs that carry lower wages than new jobs in the rest of the state. Only 76 percent of El Paso County residents are high school graduates.

The 16th Congressional District of Texas is based entirely in El Paso County - the city itself, the suburban fringe, giant Fort Bliss to the north, and rural housing settlements known as *colonias*, most without electricity and running water, spreading out to the east and south. The district is solidly Democratic. The remaining 9 percent of El Paso voters are in the sprawling 23rd District. In 2016, Hillary Clinton won the 16th with 68 percent of the vote.

SEVENTEENTH DISTRICT

Bill Flores (R)

Elected 2010, 4th term; b. Feb 25, 1954, Warren Air Force Base, Cheyenne, WY; Texas Agricultural and Mechanical University; b.B.A.; Houston Baptist University (TX), M.B.A.; Baptist; Married (Gina Flores); 2 children; 2 grandchildren.

Professional Career: Keyes Offshore, 1980-1990; Marine Drilling, 1990-1997; Western Atlas, 1997-1998; Gryphon Exploration, 2001-2005; Accountant, financial Manager, Phoenix Exploration, 2006-2009.

DC Office: 2440 RHOB 20515, 202-225-6105, Fax: 202-225-0350, flores.house.gov.

State Offices: Austin, 512-373-3378; Bryan, 979-703-4037; Waco, 254-732-0748.

Committees: *Energy & Commerce*: Communications & Technology, Energy, Environment.

Group Ratings

	ADA	ACLU	AFL-CIO	LCV	ITI	COC	HAFA	ACU	CFG	FRC
2016	-	5%	-	0%	100%	100%	83%	88%	88%	100%
2015	0%	C	4%	0%	C	75%	C	92%	89%	100%

Almanac Ratings 2015

	Economy	Social	Foreign	Composite
Liberal	3%	0%	0%	1%
Conservative	97%	100%	100%	99%

Key Votes of the 114th Congress

1. Keystone Pipeline	Y	5. Puerto Rico Debt	N	9. Offenses by Aliens	Y
2. Trade Deals	Y	6. Medical Marijuana	N	10. Troops in Iraq	N
3. Export-Import Bank	N	7. Sanctuary Cities	Y	11. Homeland Security $$	N
4. Debt Ceiling Increase	N	8. Armor-piercing Bullets	Y	12. Trade Adjustment aid	N

Election Results

Election	Name (Party)	Vote (%)	Cand. Spent	Ind. Exp. Support	Ind. Exp. Oppose
2016 General	Bill Flores (R)	149,417 (61%)	$1,377,578		
	William Matta (D)	86,603 (35%)	$42,828		
	Clark Patterson (L)	9,708 (4%)			
2016 Primary	Bill Flores (R)	60,434 (73%)			
	Ralph Patterson (R)	15,387 (18%)			
	Kaleb Sims (R)	7,591 (9%)			

Prior winning percentages: 2014 (65%), 2012 (80%), 2010 (62%)

Republican Bill Flores, a retired oil and gas executive, won his seat in 2010 by defeating a long-time Democratic incumbent and GOP nemesis. In addition to zealously guarding home-state interests with a seat on the Energy and Commerce Committee, Flores served as chairman of the conservative Republican Study Committee in 2015-16. He defeated a more activist contender, which led some to depict Flores as the establishment candidate. He rejected that characterization, though dissidents then created the outspoken Freedom Caucus.

Flores was born at Warren Air Force Base in Cheyenne, Wyoming. After his father's military tour of duty, the family moved back to Stratford, in the northern tip of the Texas Panhandle. From age 9, Flores helped work cattle on the family's ranch. Flores helped pay his way through Texas A&M, where he was a member of the Corps of Cadets, the student body government, and the honor guard. He has remained active as an alumnus, donating millions of dollars to his alma mater to fund scholarships. After graduation, he went to work for the KPMG accounting firm and built a career as a financial manager for several large corporations, eventually settling in the oil and gas industry in Houston. He was president and chief executive officer of Phoenix Exploration until he ran for Congress.

In 2010, he had four opponents in the Republican primary. After leading 2008 GOP nominee Rob Curnock in the first round, 33%-29%, Flores won the runoff, 65%-35%. He ran against Rep. Chet Edwards, the final remaining "yellow dog" Texas Democrat, a 20-year incumbent with considerable political skills. But Edwards' standing with conservatives was damaged when liberal House Speaker Nancy Pelosi in July 2008 mentioned him as a possible Democratic vice presidential candidate. That year, Curnock held the Democratic incumbent to a 53%-46% victory, even though Edwards outspent him $2 million to $96,000. Flores targeted Edwards' vote for the 2009 economic stimulus bill. And he emphasized his own business credentials, saying that he would bring to Congress the discipline of a successful accountant. Flores touted his role in the early 1990s helping to turn around a financially struggling oil and gas company called Marine Drilling. However, *The Dallas Morning News* reported that a Marine subsidiary filed for bankruptcy in 1992, leaving the government with $7.5 million in unpaid debt.

It was a high-dollar race, with Edwards spending $3.8 million and Flores $3.3 million ($1.5 million of it his own money). Outside groups spent another $720,000 against Edwards and $1 million against Flores. By summer, Edwards was trailing badly in polls, and the Democratic Congressional Campaign Committee mostly pulled out of the race to focus resources on more winnable contests. Flores won by an impressive 62%-37%, carrying all but one small county. He won with 52 percent in Waco's McLennan County, but got 64 percent in College Station's Brazos County and 71 percent in Johnson County, south of Fort Worth.

As part of the new House majority, Flores' first bills were measures to set more stringent deadlines for government approval of offshore oil and gas drilling and to extend for 12 months all leases in the Gulf of Mexico affected by Interior Department's drilling moratoriums after the massive BP spill. He successfully amended several House-passed bills to block a provision in the 2007 energy law promoting the use of alternative fuels in federal vehicles. In one instance, he said, "The Defense Department should not be wasting its time studying fuel emissions and should not have to be stifled by the arguments over how to interpret a small section of an energy law." He took heat from constituents at home for voting in 2011 to raise the federal debt limit, but opposed the subsequent tax and spending compromise in 2013 to avoid the so-called "fiscal cliff."

With his seat on Energy and Commerce, a valuable niche for a former oil executive from Texas, Flores pursued energy issues. In November 2015, he filed a bill to cut back what he called "over-reaching" by the Environmental Protection Agency in setting ozone limitations as part of the national ambient-air standards. In May 2015, he joined a bipartisan coalition that sought to reduce the mandate for ethanol use by vehicles.

Flores became active in the Republican Study Committee, which had been the caucus of the House's most conservative members. He ran for chairman after the 2014 election, after years in which the confrontational RSC often spent more time attacking other Republicans than Democrats. He sought a more constructive relationship that would push the party agenda to the right. He also wanted to lower the press profile of the RSC. In the contest for the chairmanship, his chief foe was South Carolina Rep. Mick Mulvaney, a far more outspoken member of the GOP class first elected in 2010. After the easy victory by Flores, which was encouraged by allies of Speaker John Boehner, Mulvaney and other mavericks created the Freedom Caucus to give them a separate forum to challenge Boehner and other party leaders. Later, Mulvaney joined the Trump administration as director of the Office of Management and Budget.

As RSC chairman, Flores launched the America Without Faith project, which sought to explore the value that faith-based institutions contribute to America's communities, especially for the poor. He laid out a policy agenda for the RSC that was based on five principles: expand economic opportunity, fix Washington's fiscal mess, rebuild national security, protect American values and "restrict the federal government to its constitutionally limited role." After the 2016 election, he sought a leadership position as vice chairman of the Republican Conference, but was defeated by Doug Collins of Georgia.

At home, he had a GOP primary challenge in 2016 from Ralph Patterson, an ordained Baptist deacon who had chaired the McLennan County Republican Party. Patterson spent $403,000 to $1.5 million for Flores, who won, 72%-18%. In November, he was opposed by William Matta, who was an English professor at McLennan Community College and a retired Air Force colonel; Flores won, 61%-35%. In the presidential campaign that year, he cited the "inappropriate attacks" by Donald Trump on a federal judge as a reason why he did not endorse Trump after he had wrapped up the nomination. Later, Flores endorsed Trump at the GOP convention.

Central Texas: Waco, College Station

Population		**Race and Ethnicity**		**Income**	
Total	727,840	White	56.4%	Median Income	$47,333 (297 out of 435)
Land area	7,651	Black	12.9%		
Pop/ sq mi	95.1	Latino	24.3%		
Born in state	67.2%	Asian	4.5%	Under $50,000	52.2%
		Two races	1.7%	$50,000-$99,999	29.1%
Age Groups		Other	0.3%	$100,000-$199,999	15.4%
Under 18	23.2%			$200,000 or more	3.2%
18-34	30.9%	**Education**		Poverty Rate	20.1%
35-64	34.6%	H.S grad or less	40.5%		
Over 64	11.3%	Some college	30.4%	**Health Insurance**	
		College Degree, 4 yr	18.6%	With health insurance coverage	83.2%
Work		Post grad	10.6%		
White Collar	37.1%				
Sales and Service	42.0%	**Military**		**Public Assistance**	
Blue Collar	20.9%	Veteran	7.8%	Cash public assistance income	1.8%
Government	6.2%	Active Duty	0.1%		
				Food stamp/SNAP benefits	11.5%

Voter Turnout			
2015 Total Citizens 18+	504,972	2016 House Turnout as % CVAP	49%
2016 House turnout	245,728	2014 House Turnout as % CVAP	26%

2012 Presidential Vote		
Mitt Romney	135,309	(60%)
Barack Obama	84,531	(38%)

2016 Presidential Vote		
Donald Trump	139,415	(56%)
Hillary Clinton	96,156	(38%)
Gary Johnson	10,055	(4%)

Cook Partisan Voting Index: R+12

Waco, about midway between Dallas and Austin, is deep in the heart of Texas. In the late 19th century, it was one of the largest cotton markets in the world, a rip-roaring town with legalized prostitution. In 1870, Waco opened across the Brazos River what was then the largest single-span suspension bridge in the United States. It became the main depot along the Chisholm Trail, which cattlemen used to drive their longhorns north to Kansas stockyards. In 1885, a Waco pharmacist concocted the first Dr. Pepper. Waco is the home of Baylor University, the oldest college in Texas and the largest Baptist university in the world. Kenneth Starr, the former independent counsel who investigated President Bill Clinton, was demoted from university president and then resigned in 2016 following revelations of sexual assaults by football players; the coach was fired. The city has embarked on an "Imagine Waco" program to restore a walkable downtown; development along the riverfront also is underway. In Waco's McLennan County is the tiny town of Crawford, where the White House press corps huddled when President George W. Bush stayed at his 1,583-acre Prairie Chapel Ranch.

The 17th Congressional District of Texas includes all of eight counties and parts of four more, but centers on Waco and all of McLennan County, which has a third of the district's population. The southwestern tip of the district covers a small slice of northern Austin and most of socially diverse suburban Pflugerville, whose population jumped from 4,400 in 1990 to more than 50,000 residents in 2010. The other population center is Brazos County, whose largest city, College Station, is home to Texas A&M University; Brazos is entirely in the 17th and is one-fourth of the population. The school's agricultural and military traditions have given it a much more conservative ambience than the similarly selective University of Texas at Austin. Fast-growing College Station is the site of the George H.W. Bush Presidential Library. The university is one of three federally funded centers to prepare the country for a biological attack.

The political tradition in Central Texas for more than a century after the Civil War was heavily Democratic. This area voted for Hubert Humphrey in 1968, while most of the rural South went for George Wallace and Richard Nixon. As recently as 1990, it voted Democratic for governor, supporting Waco native Ann Richards. Since then, the district has followed most of non-urban Texas to the Republican Party. The arm of the district that extends into Austin and Travis County is its Democratic enclave. Donald Trump won 56 percent of the district-wide vote in 2016, a dip from the 60 percent for Mitt Romney four years earlier.

EIGHTEENTH DISTRICT

Sheila Jackson Lee (D)

Elected 1994, 12th term; b. Jan 12, 1950, Jamaica, NY; University of Virginia Law School, J.D.; Yale University (CT), B.A.; New York University; Seventh-Day Adventist; Married (Elwyn C. Lee); 2 children.

Elected Office: Houston City Council, 1990-1994.

Professional Career: Practicing attorney, 1975-1977, 1978-1987; Staff counsel, U.S. House Select Assassinations Committee, 1977-1978; Houston Association municipal judge, 1987-1990.

DC Office: 2187 RHOB 20515, 202-225-3816, Fax: 202-225-3317, jacksonlee.house.gov.

State Offices: Houston, 713-691-4882; Houston, 713-861-4070; Houston, 713-655-0050; Houston, 713-227-7740.

Committees: *Budget*. *Homeland Security*: Counterterrorism & Intelligence, Cybersecurity & Infrastructure Protection. *Joint Security & Cooperation in Europe*. *Judiciary*: Crime, Terrorism, Homeland Security & Investigations (RMM), Immigration & Border Security.

Group Ratings

	ADA	ACLU	AFL-CIO	LCV	ITI	COC	HAFA	ACU	CFG	FRC
2016	-	94%	-	92%	60%	67%	16%	0%	0%	8%
2015	100%	C	100%	86%	C	55%	C	5%	2%	0%

Almanac Ratings 2015

	Economy	Social	Foreign	Composite
Liberal	89%	83%	85%	86%
Conservative	11%	17%	15%	14%

Key Votes of the 114th Congress

1. Keystone Pipeline	Y	5. Puerto Rico Debt	Y	9. Offenses by Aliens	N
2. Trade Deals	N	6. Medical Marijuana	NV	10. Troops in Iraq	Y
3. Export-Import Bank	Y	7. Sanctuary Cities	NV	11. Homeland Security $$	Y
4. Debt Ceiling Increase	Y	8. Armor-piercing Bullets	NV	12. Trade Adjustment aid	Y

Election Results

Election	Name (Party)	Vote (%)	Cand. Spent	Ind. Exp. Support	Ind. Exp. Oppose
2016 General	Sheila Jackson Lee (D)	150,157 (74%)	$461,136		
	Lori Bartley (R)	48,306 (24%)	$32,997		
	Thomas Kleven (G)	5,845 (3%)			
2016 Primary	Sheila Jackson Lee (D)	(100%)			

Prior winning percentages: 2014 (72%), 2012 (75%), 2010 (70%), 2008 (77%), 2006 (77%), 2004 (89%), 2002 (77%), 2000 (77%), 1998 (90%), 1996 (77%), 1994 (74%)

Sheila Jackson Lee, a Democrat first elected in 1994, has been known as one of Congress' most difficult members - she has had more staff turnover than any other lawmaker and fares poorly in *Washingtonian's* annual survey of Hill aides. As she has gained seniority on her committees, she has become more preoccupied with her work. She is hugely popular at home, always winning at least 70 percent of the vote in elections and rarely facing a primary challenge.

A native of Queens, New York, Jackson Lee graduated from Yale University and the University of Virginia law school. She practiced law in Houston, where she was a local judge and won two terms as an at-large member of the Houston City Council. After a local term-limits law took effect in 1994, she ran against Democratic Rep. Craig Washington, a talented but iconoclastic legislator. He had voted against funding for the space station, a source of many local jobs, and against the 1993 North American Free Trade Agreement, which was a boon to Houston's port traffic. Jackson Lee supported NAFTA and raised a lot of money from business interests that favored it. She won the primary, 63%-37%, and swept the general election.

The *Almanac* vote ratings for 2015 showed that Jackson Lee has shifted toward the center of the House in each of the three issue areas. She has been prolific in proposing bills and offering amendments on the floor. In 2015-16, she filed 76 bills, the second most in the House. Typically, her measures call for studies on one topic or another, add small amounts to spending bills, or are noncontroversial, such as one that called on Afghanistan to prohibit the use of children as soldiers. In December 2016, one of her bills was enacted. It required the Transportation Security Administration to make a comprehensive risk analysis of security threat assessment procedures for vessels and maritime facilities. In June 2015 and again in January 2017, the House passed her bill to require the Homeland Security Department to prepare a report on the effectiveness and availability of First Responders in the case of a terrorist threat or attack.

According to C-SPAN records, Jackson Lee in 2015-16 spoke to the House on 164 days, which was the most of any Democrat. She trailed only Republican Rep. Glenn Thompson of Pennsylvania, who spoke on 209 days during those two years. She told the *Houston Chronicle* that while she can ruffle feathers, she is unflagging in her desire to serve constituents. "I just want to be called an Energizer bunny that keeps on working for the people of this great district," she said.

She has been active on the Homeland Security Committee, especially the Border and Maritime Security Subcommittee, an assignment that suits a port city. On the Judiciary Committee, she has faced conflicting tensions from Latino constituents, who favor more generous treatment of immigrants, and African-American constituents, who see immigrants as competition for jobs. She frequently takes the pro-immigrant side. She favors an increase in visas and access to permanent resident status. As the ranking Democrat on the Subcommittee on Crime, Terrorism, Homeland Security, and Investigations, Jackson Lee has introduced the "Build Trust Act," which was intended to decrease the excessive reliance by some local governments on traffic fines and court costs to generate revenue to fund government operations. She has generated controversy at home with gun-rights groups for her support of universal background checks for firearms purchasers.

Jackson Lee has been outspoken in her opposition to Donald Trump. At the Democratic national convention in July 2016, she delivered a speech in which she called him "a man of fear" and "willfully ignorant to the outcry of young people who want real criminal justice reform." In January 2017, during the usually routine joint session of Congress that certifies the Electoral College count, she led several House members who protested the vote count in some states. When she failed to get the required support of at least one senator, Vice President Joe Biden overruled her objections. Jackson Lee is known for grabbing a prominent aisle seat for State of the Union addresses, ensuring her a moment of national television time with the president as he enters. She abandoned that practice when Trump made his initial appearance in February 2017, though she did attend the event.

In 2010, Jackson Lee faced a primary challenge from Houston City Councilman Jarvis Johnson, who cited her reputation as difficult to work with, and local lawyer Sean Roberts. Neither came remotely close to her in fundraising. In February, she unveiled her trump card - an endorsement from President Barack Obama calling her "a tireless champion for Houston's working families." She drew 67 percent of the vote to Johnson's 28 percent and Roberts' 5 percent. She faced no primary challenge in the next three elections.

Central and Northern Houston

Population		**Race and Ethnicity**		**Income**	
Total	736,283	White	16.3%	Median Income	$41,435 (380 out of 435)
Land area	235	Black	37.8%		
Pop/ sq mi	3130.5	Latino	41.0%		
Born in state	60.2%	Asian	3.6%	Under $50,000	57.8%
		Two races	0.9%	$50,000-$99,999	26.3%
Age Groups		Other	0.4%	$100,000-$199,999	12.2%
Under 18	27.2%			$200,000 or more	3.7%
18-34	28.3%	**Education**		Poverty Rate	24.6%
35-64	36.0%	H.S grad or less	53.2%		
Over 64	8.6%	Some college	26.4%	**Health Insurance**	
		College Degree, 4 yr	13.1%	With health insurance coverage	74.1%
Work		Post grad	7.3%		
White Collar	28.0%				
Sales and Service	44.2%	**Military**		**Public Assistance**	
Blue Collar	27.9%	Veteran	5.0%	Cash public assistance income	2.6%
Government	6.3%	Active Duty	0.0%		
				Food stamp/SNAP benefits	19.7%

Voter Turnout			
2015 Total Citizens 18+	431,588	2016 House Turnout as % CVAP	47%
2016 House turnout	204,308	2014 House Turnout as % CVAP	24%

2012 Presidential Vote		
Barack Obama	150,129	(76%)
Mitt Romney	44,991	(23%)

2016 Presidential Vote		
Hillary Clinton	157,117	(76%)
Donald Trump	41,011	(20%)
Gary Johnson	5,346	(3%)

Cook Partisan Voting Index: D+27

Within its sprawling boundaries, Houston contains income and wealth disparities as striking as any city in America, the product of an expanding city with dynamic economic growth, a high rate of immigration, and the absence of centralized planning. The contrast is most obvious at the edge of Houston's gleaming downtown. Just blocks from the Heritage Plaza, Pennzoil and Bank of America buildings, and the sports complexes for baseball's Astros and basketball's Rockets are slums where many people live in unpainted frame houses with cracks wide enough to let in Houston's humid, smoggy air.

Until the 1960s, Houston had a Third World economy. It was a low-skill producer of basic commodities, where a few got rich and many lived near subsistence level. Since then, Houston has built a high-tech economy offering myriad opportunities and a wider range of economic outcomes. It has also greatly expanded its international trade. Many of Houston's African Americans and Hispanics have moved to comfortable middle-class neighborhoods. In 2007, Hispanics for the first time outnumbered Anglos in Harris County, which grew 20 percent from 2000 to 2010 and another 12 percent from 2010 to 2016. The Houston metropolitan area was ranked the most ethnically diverse in the country in a Rice University study in 2012, though many neighborhoods remain largely segregated. With its rapid growth, Houston was expected to surpass Chicago as the third-largest city in the nation by about 2025. By 2050, state demographers project, Houston will be 60 percent Hispanic and 15 percent black.

While the city has diversified economically, oil has remained king. With economic growth getting a lift from the demand for fuel by China and other emerging nations, Houston was largely shielded from the 2007-09 recession. In 2015, *Forbes* ranked Houston as the fastest-growing city in the nation, though the collapse in the price of oil has accelerated economic diversification. The contrasts between rich and poor remain. In a 2014 report, the Brookings Institution ranked Houston 11th among cities with the highest income inequality. In 2015, a study by New World Wealth reported that Houston has the fastest growing community of multi-millionaires in the country. The diversity also has applied to local elections. With the retirement of three-term Mayor Annise Parker, one of the first mayors in the nation who was openly gay, voters in December 2015 selected veteran African-American state Sen. Sylvester Turner over Republican Bill King, a longtime local businessman, 50.2%-49.8%. A month earlier, a proposed equal rights ordinance for Houston lost in a referendum, with 61 percent opposed.

The 18th Congressional District of Texas contains Houston's downtown area and the African-American and Latino neighborhoods immediately south of it. The district has two arms running beyond Loop 610 - one is northeast, between the Eastex Freeway and Beaumont Highway, and the larger one is northwest, between the Northwest Freeway and Interstate 45, extending east to take in George Bush Intercontinental Airport. African Americans make up a declining 36 percent of the district's population and Hispanics a rising 43 percent. This is the third most Democratic district in Texas. Hillary Clinton got 76 percent of the vote here in 2016, the same as Barack Obama won in 2012.

NINETEENTH DISTRICT

Jodey Arrington (R)

Elected 2016, 1st term; b. Mar 09, 1972, Kansas City, MO; Texas Tech University, B.A., 1994; Texas Tech University, M.P.A., 1997; Georgetown University-McDonough School of Business, 2004; Presbyterian; Married (Anne Arrington); 3 children.

Professional Career: Special Assistant, President George W. Bush, 2001; Chief of Staff, FDIC Chairman Don Powell, 2001-2005; Deputy Federal Coordinator, COO, Office of the Federal Coordinator for Gulf Cost Rebuilding, 2005-2006; Administrator, Texas Tech University, 2007-2014.

DC Office: 1029 LHOB 20515, 202-225-4005, Fax: 202-225-9615, arrington.house.gov.

State Offices: Abilene, 325-675-9779; Lubbock, 806-763-1611.

Committees: *Agriculture*: Biotechnology, Horticulture & Research, General Farm Commodities & Risk Management, Nutrition. *Budget*. *Veterans' Affairs*: Economic Opportunity (Chmn), Oversight & Investigations.

Election Results

Election	Name (Party)	Vote (%)		Cand. Spent	Ind. Exp. Support	Ind. Exp. Oppose
2016 General	Jodey Arrington (R)	176,314	(87%)	$1,249,237	$73,000	
	Troy Bonar (L)	17,376	(9%)			
	Mark Lawson (G)	9,785	(5%)			
2016 Primary Run Off	Jodey Arrington (R)	25,322	(54%)			
	Glen Robertson (R)	21,832	(46%)			
2016 Primary	Glen Robertson (R)	27,791	(27%)			
	Jodey Arrington (R)	26,980	(26%)			
	Michael Bob Starr (R)	22,256	(21%)			
	Donald May (R)	9,592	(9%)			

Republican Jodey Arrington was elected in 2016 to an open seat. His narrow win in the primary run-off was tantamount to victory in this Republican stronghold. Arrington benefited from strong political connections, which resulted from his extended experience as an aide to President George W. Bush. Taking office at age 46, he said that his objective in the House is to chair the Agriculture Committee.

Arrington was born in Plainview, where his father was a farm equipment salesman. He got a bachelor's and a master's degree in public administration from Texas Tech University. Soon after that, he joined the staff of then-Gov. Bush as a manager of appointments in state government. After Bush was elected president, Arrington become a White House staff special assistant to the president and associate director of presidential personnel. He specialized in appointments relating to energy, the environment and natural resources. In late 2001, he became chief of staff to the chairman of the Federal Deposit

Insurance Corporation, who was a native of Amarillo. A year later, Arrington returned to Texas to become chief of staff for the Texas Tech University System, which now has more than 40,000 students, nearly 20,000 employees and a budget of about $1.3 billion. Initially, he worked for Chancellor Kent Hance, who had defeated Bush a quarter-century earlier in a campaign for Congress. Later, he was appointed vice chancellor of research and commercialization, where he helped to spur the university's growth. In 2014, he ran for the state Senate and lost the Republican primary, 53%-30%. In the private sector, he became president of Scott Laboratories, which commercializes health care innovations.

When Rep. Randy Neugebauer retired, nine Republican candidates ran for the open seat. The chief contenders, in addition to Arrington, were Glen Robertson, who was completing four years as mayor of Lubbock, and Michael Bob Starr, who had been commander of Dyess Air Force Base near Abilene. In the first round of the primary, Starr got 48 percent of the vote in Abilene-based Taylor County. Arrington and Robertson each got 30 percent in Lubbock County, which was the base for both. The district-wide vote in the primary gave 27 percent to Arrington, 26 percent to Robertson and 21 percent to Starr, with the top two advancing to the runoff.

Arrington touted his support from Bush and many of this advisers, plus former Gov. Rick Perry, and said that he was the candidate who best represented "conservative values." Robertson said he had more political experience as mayor and as a local businessman for 38 years. Robertson had an edge in campaign spending with $1.8 million, of which 90 percent was self-financed. Arrington spent $1.3 million during the cycle. He won, 54%-46%, and led in both Lubbock and Taylor counties. In November, no Democrat had filed and Arrington took 87 percent of the vote.

In the House, Arrington was assigned to the Agriculture Committee, his first choice. He said that a priority on the farm bill would be to resume commodity coverage for cotton. That objective will be bolstered by the fact that committee Chairman Mike Conaway represents the neighboring 11th District, which also is heavily rural. "I want to carry his water, help him any way I can," Arrington said. He also joined Budget and Veterans' Affairs, where he chaired the Economic Opportunity Subcommittee. As one of the few freshmen to get a chairmanship, he said that his chief priority was to encourage job opportunities for veterans.

West Texas: Lubbock, Abilene

Population		**Race and Ethnicity**		**Income**	
Total	713,951	White	55.4%	Median Income	$45,606 (334 out of 435)
Land area	25,836	Black	5.8%	Under $50,000	54.2%
Pop/ sq mi	27.6	Latino	35.6%	$50,000-$99,999	29.5%
Born in state	73.1%	Asian	1.3%	$100,000-$199,999	13.3%
		Two races	1.5%	$200,000 or more	3.0%
		Other	0.5%	Poverty Rate	18.1%
Age Groups		**Education**		**Health Insurance**	
Under 18	24.9%	H.S grad or less	48.4%	With health insurance coverage	80.7%
18-34	27.7%	Some college	30.3%		
35-64	34.3%	College Degree, 4 yr	14.0%		
Over 64	13.1%	Post grad	7.2%		
Work		**Military**		**Public Assistance**	
White Collar	30.7%	Veteran	8.0%	Cash public assistance income	1.7%
Sales and Service	43.6%	Active Duty	0.6%	Food stamp/SNAP benefits	13.4%
Blue Collar	25.6%				
Government	7.1%				

Voter Turnout			
2015 Total Citizens 18+	502,016	2016 House Turnout as % CVAP	41%
2016 House turnout	203,475	2014 House Turnout as % CVAP	23%

2012 Presidential Vote		
Mitt Romney	160,058	(74%)
Barack Obama	54,448	(25%)

2016 Presidential Vote		
Donald Trump	165,384	(72%)
Hillary Clinton	53,519	(23%)
Gary Johnson	7,849	(3%)

Cook Partisan Voting Index: R+27

Until water was discovered in the giant Ogallala Aquifer that lies under Lubbock and its environs, this was Indian country, a land of Army forts and cattle ranches. When the water was tapped, well into the 20th century, what had been grazing land suddenly became cotton-growing territory, with green crops grown in circles where the sprinklers reached and parched ground beyond. Lubbock became a regional center, the home of Texas Tech University, and grew rapidly at mid-century. Lubbock County's population increased from 101,000 in 1950 to 156,000 in 1960. Since then, the regional economy has grown more slowly, though it had a 9 percent gain from 2010 to 2016, when the county's population reached 303,000. Nearby Gaines County led the nation in cotton production in 2015. Cotton growers have struggled with international competitors and adverse trade rulings, as well as pressure to reduce agricultural subsidies. Wind power has become a new industry here, with hundreds of towers between Abilene and Sweetwater. In early 2017, developers began construction of a wind farm near Plainview that they earlier described as the largest in the nation, with 340 landowners over 190 square miles. The local utility company projected that nearly 40 percent of its energy will be wind-generated by 2021. Lubbock and nearby counties have made an outsized contribution to American popular culture with a disproportionate share of renowned musicians: Buddy Holly, Tanya Tucker, Jimmy Dean, Waylon Jennings, Mac Davis, Joe Ely, Roy Orbison, Don Williams and the Dixie Chicks' Natalie Maines.

Nearly 200 miles southeast of Lubbock, over gully-ridden territory, are Abilene and the surrounding Big Country, with ranches specializing in Angora goats and sheep and exotic animals like ostriches, emus and aoudad sheep. Sweetwater, near Abilene, features an annual "rattlesnake roundup," with a noise from thousands of snakes that apparently can be fearsome. There also are cotton fields, pecan trees, mesquite and many oil wells. Some of the nation's B-1 bombers are stationed at Dyess Air Force Base. Like other parts of Texas, Abilene has become a haven for resettlement of refugees, mostly from Africa. In January 2017, about 1,200 resided in Abilene, a city of 120,000.

The 19th Congressional District of Texas takes in the Lubbock and Abilene areas. The two counties combined account for about 62 percent of the district's population. In 1978, this part of West Texas was Democratic enough that in an open-seat election, voters rejected the candidacy of a young Midland oilman named George W. Bush in favor of Lubbock Democrat Kent Hance. Those two careers would take some interesting turns. Today, the area is heavily Republican. Bush received 77 percent of the vote in his 2004 reelection, and Republican candidate Mitt Romney won the district with 74 percent in 2012 - among their highest scores in the nation, but only third-best among districts in West Texas. In 2016, the vote for Donald Trump dipped to 72 percent; that was eight percentage points less than his vote in the 13th District to the north, which can be explained partly by the larger Hispanic population in the 19th.

TWENTIETH DISTRICT

Joaquin Castro (D)

Elected 2012, 3rd term; b. Sep 16, 1974, San Antonio; Stanford University (CA), A.B.; Harvard University Law School (MA), J.D.; Roman Catholic; Married (Anna Flores); 2 children.

Elected Office: TX House, 2003-2013.

Professional Career: Practicing attorney, 2000-2013.

DC Office: 1221 LHOB 20515, 202-225-3236, Fax: 202-225-1915, castro.house.gov.

State Offices: San Antonio, 210-348-8216.

Committees: *Foreign Affairs*: Africa, Global Health, Global Human Rights & Internat'l Orgs, Western Hemisphere. *Permanent Select on Intelligence.*

Group Ratings

	ADA	ACLU	AFL-CIO	LCV	ITI	COC	HAFA	ACU	CFG	FRC
2016	-	94%	-	92%	60%	62%	11%	0%	0%	0%
2015	95%	C	100%	97%	C	45%	C	0%	0%	0%

Almanac Ratings 2015

	Economy	Social	Foreign	Composite
Liberal	90%	100%	87%	92%
Conservative	10%	0%	13%	8%

Key Votes of the 114th Congress

1. Keystone Pipeline	N	5. Puerto Rico Debt	Y	9. Offenses by Aliens	N
2. Trade Deals	N	6. Medical Marijuana	Y	10. Troops in Iraq	N
3. Export-Import Bank	Y	7. Sanctuary Cities	N	11. Homeland Security $$	Y
4. Debt Ceiling Increase	Y	8. Armor-piercing Bullets	N	12. Trade Adjustment aid	Y

Election Results

Election	Name (Party)	Vote (%)	Cand. Spent	Ind. Exp. Support	Ind. Exp. Oppose
2016 General	Joaquin Castro (D)........................	149,640 (80%)	$765,598		
	Jeffrey C. Blunt (L).....................	29,055 (16%)			
	Paul Pipkin (G)................................	8,974 (5%)			
2016 Primary	Joaquin Castro (D)....................................	(100%)			

Prior winning percentages: 2014 (76%), 2012 (64%)

Democrat Joaquin Castro was elected to his San Antonio-based seat in 2012. As a young, telegenic Hispanic, he gained prominence along with his twin brother, Julián, a former San Antonio mayor who was the secretary of Housing and Urban Development for the final two-plus years of the Obama administration. Texas Democrats have been eagerly waiting for one or both of them to run statewide. But their reluctance to seize the opportunity has highlighted the continuing woes of the state party.

Politics is in Castro's blood. His mother, Rosie Castro, was a noted Latina activist in the 1960s and 1970s, and she instilled a belief in civil rights and equality of opportunity in her sons. Both he and his brother earned their bachelor's in political science at Stanford University. Both continued to Harvard Law School, where they graduated and then returned to San Antonio to join the politically well-connected Akin, Gump, Strauss, Hauer & Feld law firm and launch their local political careers. Joaquin Castro successfully challenged a Democratic incumbent in the Texas House in 2002, running a change-themed campaign. In the legislature, he focused on education and eventually became the Democratic floor leader. "I've always been in deep minorities" in the legislature, Castro said. "The silver lining is that you learn, almost in a Darwinian way, how to be effective without using sheer force of numbers." That included restoring education funding amid budget-cutting after the 2010 elections.

Castro has had an unusually charmed electoral history. He initially announced he would run in 2012 for Texas' new 35th Congressional District, a thin ribbon of a district from San Antonio's east side to Austin. That pitted him against veteran Democratic Rep. Lloyd Doggett and foretold an expensive primary battle dividing two cities and two ethnic groups of Democrats. Long-time Democratic Rep. Charles Gonzalez of San Antonio later called Castro and said he had decided to retire. "At that point," Castro said, "it became clear I should run for my home district." No other Democrat filed to run against him and he has faced perfunctory Republican opposition, which has freed Castro to help other Democratic candidates with their campaigns.

Castro has been a reliable party man, with *Almanac* vote ratings in 2015 that ranked him near the center of House Democrats. He has focused on education, introducing multiple measures to expand a pre-kindergarten program that his brother started as mayor of San Antonio. His objective has been to give cities a direct line to federal funds, bypassing state legislatures. "Local entities must have the ability to step up to the plate and pick up the slack where their state governments are failing," he wrote in a *Dallas Morning News* op-ed column. In February 2017, he filed a bill to give individuals involved in early childhood education programs the tax breaks that are available to elementary and secondary school teachers.

He pushed on various fronts to urge legislative action on immigration, including a pathway to citizenship for those in the country illegally. A measure of his uphill battle came in June 2016, when he unsuccessfully pleaded to the House Rules Committee to abandon Republican efforts to force the Library of Congress to continue using the term "alien" to refer to immigrants, which he described as "a prejudicial term that's particularly offensive to Hispanics." He added, "These folks may not be U.S. citizens, but they're not from outer space."

As a member of the Armed Services Committee, Castro voiced disappointment in 2015 that the panel rejected his efforts to include in the annual spending bill a provision to take military sexual assault prosecutions out of the chain of command to ensure that victims are comfortable in bringing charges. He was successful in gaining House passage in September 2016 of a bill that he filed with Republican Rep. Mike McCaul of Texas to create a Global Development Lab in the U.S. Agency for International Development. Their goal, he said, was "applying science and building partnerships to solve urgent, complex development challenges." As a new member of the House Intelligence Committee in 2017, Castro spoke out on the "need to determine not only the extent of Russia's attempts to undermine our election and democracy, but also whether any Americans participated in those efforts.

Castro has been an in-demand figure on the political circuit. During the final days of the 2016 presidential campaign, he and his brother barnstormed battleground states, plus Texas, to get out the vote for Hillary Clinton. In 2017, he became chairman of the non-profit Congressional Hispanic Caucus Institute. Castro is a chief deputy whip for Minority Whip Steny Hoyer, which could be his initial step up the Democrats' leadership ladder.

Castro leaves no doubt that his political ambition is not confined to the House. A statewide bid remains a daunting challenge for any Texas Democrat, though some Democrats were encouraged that Clinton's loss to Donald Trump in Texas was in the single digits. Journalists have written about Castro's frequent travels to meet with grass-roots Democrats across the state. In April 2017, an aide told reporters that Castro was not planning to challenge Republican Sen. Ted Cruz in 2018, though he added that Castro did not rule out entering the contest closer to the election. A recent statewide poll had given Castro a slight lead over Cruz. Democratic Rep. Beto O'Rourke had already declared his candidacy against Cruz.

San Antonio

Population		**Race and Ethnicity**		**Income**	
Total	749,530	White	22.5%	Median Income	$47,361 (296 out of 435)
Land area	200	Black	5.0%		
Pop/ sq mi	3753.7	Latino	68.0%		
Born in state	65.0%	Asian	2.9%	Under $50,000	52.4%
Age Groups		Two races	1.4%	$50,000-$99,999	31.0%
Under 18	26.3%	Other	0.2%	$100,000-$199,999	14.7%
18-34	28.1%	**Education**		$200,000 or more	2.0%
35-64	35.4%	H.S grad or less	45.2%	Poverty Rate	19.4%
Over 64	10.2%	Some college	31.5%	**Health Insurance**	
Work		College Degree, 4 yr	15.3%	With health insurance coverage	80.3%
White Collar	32.3%	Post grad	8.0%		
Sales and Service	47.7%	**Military**		**Public Assistance**	
Blue Collar	20.0%	Veteran	10.4%	Cash public assistance income	2.1%
Government	4.8%	Active Duty	1.5%	Food stamp/SNAP benefits	16.1%

Voter Turnout			
2015 Total Citizens 18+	488,832	2016 House Turnout as % CVAP	38%
2016 House turnout	187,669	2014 House Turnout as % CVAP	18%

2012 Presidential Vote		
Barack Obama	110,663	(59%)
Mitt Romney	74,540	(40%)

2016 Presidential Vote		
Hillary Clinton	132,363	(61%)
Donald Trump	74,386	(34%)
Gary Johnson	7,373	(3%)

Cook Partisan Voting Index: D+10

With its antique past and Hispanic heritage, San Antonio is unlike any other city in the United States. It is the home of the Alamo, preserved by the Daughters of the Republic of Texas, where Davy Crockett, Jim Bowie and 184 others were killed in 1836. (Crockett was a Tennessee congressman for three terms; if he had not lost his reelection in 1834, he presumably would not have left Tennessee for Texas.) Its Spanish architecture recalls San Antonio's days as the most important town in Texas, when the state was part of Mexico; it contrasts with the 30-story Tower Life Building and with the armadillo-like Alamodome. Its Paseo del Rio, the Riverwalk along the tiny San Antonio River that was redeveloped in the 1970s, recalls an earlier era.

For most of the 20th century, San Antonio's economy was built on the military. What the locals call "Military City, U.S.A." remains the home of Lackland Air Force Base, Fort Sam Houston and a giant military hospital. San Antonio has many military retirees and is the largest tourist center in Texas. The city's recent strength has resulted from a diversifying economy that has attracted good-paying jobs in its booming medical research industry. Health care and biosciences in 2015 had grown to a $37 billion business, led by the military units and the University of Texas Health Science Center. More than one of every six San Antonio employees works in these fields, according to the city's Chamber of Commerce. San Antonio's manufacturing center contributes more than $22 billion to the local economy, more than triple the revenue it generated in 1991. It is home to the world headquarters of Valero Energy, Clear Channel Communications and USAA Insurance.

The growth has shown continued social diversity. From 2000 to 2015, San Antonio's population increased 28 percent, and it has surpassed Dallas as Texas' second-largest city, after Houston. Its metropolitan area population of 2.4 million is about one-third the size of metro Houston or of the Dallas-Fort Worth Metroplex; 56 percent are Hispanic and that share is growing. The low education and income levels locally have been partially due to the large numbers of new immigrants in the city. In the metro area, the Anglo growth between 2010 and 2012 was 2.1 percent; the non-Anglo growth was 5.5 percent. Overall, its "gross metropolitan product" expanded by 22 percent from 2010 to 2015, the seventh strongest metro area in the nation.

Just under half of San Antonio's population - or one-third of Bexar County -- is located in the 20th Congressional District of Texas, which is centered in its lower-income west side; the downtown area where most of the city's attractions are located is mostly in the 35th District. Parts of five districts are in Bexar, but only the 20th is wholly contained in the county. With a Hispanic population share of 68 percent, it is one of the state's nine Hispanic-majority districts. It leans Democratic. Hillary Clinton took 61 percent of the district vote - two percentage points higher than President Barack Obama got in 2012.

TWENTY-FIRST DISTRICT

Lamar Smith (R)

Elected 1986, 16th term; b. Nov 19, 1947, San Antonio; Southern Methodist University Law School (TX), J.D.; Texas Military Institute; Yale University (CT), B.A.; Christian Scientist; Married (Elizabeth Schaefer); 2 children.

Elected Office: TX House, 1981-1982; Bexar County comm., 1983-1985.

Professional Career: U.S. Small Business Admin., 1969-1970; Business writer, Christian Science Monitor, 1970-1972; Practicing attorney, 1975-1978.

DC Office: 2409 RHOB 20515, 202-225-4236, Fax: 202-225-8628, lamarsmith.house.gov.

State Offices: Austin, 512-912-7508; Kerrville, 830-896-0154; San Antonio, 210-821-5024.

Committees: *Homeland Security*: Border & Maritime Security. *Judiciary*: Courts, Intellectual Property & Internet, Immigration & Border Security. *Science, Space & Technology (Chmn)*: Energy, Environment, Oversight, Research & Technology, Space.

Group Ratings

	ADA	ACLU	AFL-CIO	LCV	ITI	COC	HAFA	ACU	CFG	FRC
2016	-	5%	-	0%	100%	100%	80%	92%	67%	100%
2015	0%	C	0%	3%	C	70%	C	100%	91%	100%

Almanac Ratings 2015

	Economy	Social	Foreign	Composite
Liberal	0%	0%	0%	0%
Conservative	100%	100%	100%	100%

Key Votes of the 114th Congress

1. Keystone Pipeline	Y	5. Puerto Rico Debt	N	9. Offenses by Aliens	Y
2. Trade Deals	Y	6. Medical Marijuana	N	10. Troops in Iraq	N
3. Export-Import Bank	N	7. Sanctuary Cities	Y	11. Homeland Security $$	N
4. Debt Ceiling Increase	N	8. Armor-piercing Bullets	Y	12. Trade Adjustment aid	N

Election Results

Election	Name (Party)	Vote	(%)	Cand. Spent	Ind. Exp. Support	Ind. Exp. Oppose
2016 General	Lamar Smith (R)	202,967	(57%)	$1,640,734		$3,000
	Tom Wakely (D)	129,765	(36%)	$63,057	$14,950	
	Mark Loewe (L)	14,735	(4%)			
	Antonio Diaz (G)	8,564	(2%)			
2016 Primary	Lamar Smith (R)	69,872	(60%)			
	Matt McCall (R)	33,597	(29%)			
	Todd Phelps (R)	6,591	(6%)			
	John Murphy (R)	6,189	(5%)			

Prior winning percentages: 2014 (60%), 2012 (61%), 2010 (69%), 2008 (80%), 2006 (60%), 2004 (62%), 2002 (73%), 2000 (76%), 1998 (91%), 1996 (76%), 1994 (90%), 1992 (72%), 1990 (75%), 1988 (93%), 1986 (61%)

Republican Lamar Smith, first elected in 1986, has long been among his party's most influential conservatives on issues ranging from climate change to immigration. After being term-limited as chairman at Judiciary, he has chaired the Science, Space and Technology Committee. He has used that position to advance both national and state interests, and he has voiced hope for collaboration with President Donald Trump.

Smith is from an old San Antonio and South Texas ranching family. Their Jim Wells County ranch has been in the family for four generations. Smith graduated from Texas Military Institute (now TMI, the Episcopal School of Texas), Yale University and Southern Methodist University's law school. He worked as a reporter for the *Christian Science Monitor* and as a lawyer in San Antonio.

He was elected to the Texas House in 1980 and the Bexar County Commissioners Court in 1982. In 1986, Smith ran for the open House seat. He defeated two other San Antonio-based candidates in the primary and won the runoff 54%-46% against a religious conservative. His campaign was run by then little-known Texas political consultant Karl Rove, who became President George W. Bush's top political advisor. Until 2016, Smith had been consistently reelected with at least 60 percent of the vote.

Smith was one of three House Republican with a perfect conservative score on the 2015 *Almanac* vote ratings. Like other veteran Republicans, his rhetoric was noticeably sharper while Barack Obama was president. Smith said on the Family Research Council's radio program in 2015 that Obama wasn't taking the threat of the Islamic State "seriously" and was doing "nothing" to stop the terrorist group because, he contended, the president thinks "America's not exceptional."

Smith was an activist as the top Republican on the Judiciary Committee for six years before he was term-limited in 2012. He pressed for tougher enforcement of immigration laws as an alternative to comprehensive reform, which he and many Republicans insist cannot include provisions giving illegal immigrants a path to citizenship. He is a firm believer in stronger action to stop illegal immigration. Smith irked Democrats in 2010 when he called the DREAM Act - which would have made legal status available to some children of illegal immigrants - an "American nightmare." Smith was a leading House Republican voice in support of an Arizona law that allowed police to demand proof of citizenship from people stopped or questioned by police for other reasons.

In early 2013, Smith blasted a reform initiative offered by a bipartisan group of senators: "By granting amnesty, the Senate proposal actually compounds the problem by encouraging more illegal immigration." As an alternative, he proposed in 2011 a program to bring 500,000 foreign migrant farm workers to the United States each year to placate farmers who complain about shortages of legally authorized labor. At the behest of technology firms, he proposed another bill to provide permanent resident visas for foreigners who graduate from U.S. universities with advanced degrees in science and technology. That measure passed the House in 2012 on a mostly party-line vote. Smith was sharply critical of Obama's executive order protecting some of the nation's illegal immigrants and joined a group of lawmakers supporting a successful lawsuit to stop it. "Putting a stop to these overreaching executive actions isn't about Republicans or Democrats; it's about respecting and restoring the rule of law," he said.

Perhaps his most significant achievement in this area was passage of the Illegal Immigration Reform and Immigrant Responsibility Act of 1996. Smith was the chief House architect of several of its provisions, including a dramatic increase in the number of Border Patrol agents, more wiretap authority for law enforcement authorities, and funds for state-of-the-art equipment such as helicopters, four-wheel-drive vehicles and night goggles. Smith found common ground with Democrats at Judiciary on other bills, such as strengthened cybersecurity and intellectual property enforcement. He worked closely with ranking Judiciary Democrat John Conyers of Michigan on patent reform issues, including structural changes at the Patent and Trademark Office aimed at improving review quality, which were enacted in 2011. Smith parted with Conyers and opposed a committee proposal that eliminated mandatory minimum prison sentences for crack cocaine use.

In taking over as chairman of the Science Committee, his priorities have included cybersecurity and investigating the Obama administration's science-related work. Smith placed a priority on the future of NASA, an important agency in Texas that he wants to focus more on space exploration and less on scientific research, where he contends the agency wastes money studying climate change.

In March 2017, Smith won quick enactment of an authorization bill for NASA, which featured a detailed plan for manned exploration programs, with the long-term goal of sending humans to Mars. His other priorities with the Trump administration included "sound science" at the Environmental Protection Agency, increased energy research and more spending on advanced technology.

On the dangers posed by man-made climate change, Smith is a bit less of a skeptic than other conservatives on the Science committee, conceding that it "has the potential to impact agriculture, ecosystems, sea levels, weather patterns, and human health." But when the Intergovernmental Panel on Climate Change issued a report in 2014 warning the problem was becoming worse and assigning even more blame to humans, Smith told Bloomberg TV that the report was "clearly biased" and added: "There's still no explanation and no one can tell me yet what percentage of so-called climate change is due to human activity [and] what percentage is due to natural trends, natural cycles."

In a September 2016 profile that was critical of Smith, the *New Yorker* wrote, "With a focus that is unprecedented, [Smith is] now using his position to attack scientists and activists who work on climate change." He introduced a bill with Wyoming GOP Sen. John Barrasso in 2015 that banned the Environmental Protection Agency from writing any regulations unless they were based on the "best available science" that is made publicly available. The lawmakers said too much of the agency's rulemaking was secret. In 2014, the House passed his bill restricting research by the NSF. In January 2015, he co-authored with Republican Sen. Rand Paul of Kentucky a column for *Politico* in which they refuted Democratic accusations that Republicans were "at war with science." They demanded that money be spent for "not just any science but the *best* science."

Smith displayed his broad command when he chaired the House Ethics Committee in 1999-2000, an unusual case of a House member having chaired three separate panels. If he plays his cards right, he is in line to chair the Homeland Security Committee after his six years at the Science panel.

Smith quarterbacked the 2011 redistricting for Texas Republicans and got into a spat with GOP colleague Joe Barton over the racial makeup of the state's new map. Smith sought to evenly split four new districts between Republicans and Democrats, giving Texas' booming Hispanic population minority-majority seats in the Dallas and south Texas areas. Barton wanted to keep Republican voters dominant in three of the new districts. Barton's plan passed the state legislature, but Smith ultimately prevailed on a court-drawn map that created what have become 24 secure Republican seats of 36.

Although Smith remains safe at home, he received unusual warnings in 2016. In the primary, he was held to 60 percent of the vote by three challengers. Businessman Matt McCall ran with tea party support and got 29 percent, though that fell short of McCall's 60%-34% outcome with Smith in 2014. In the general election, Smith faced Tom Wakely, who spent $70,000, compared with the $1.7 million that Smith spent during the campaign cycle. Wakely, a former farm-worker organizer, warned about the local ramifications of climate change. Smith's 57%-36% victory was the narrowest of his career, though it did not make him a prime Democratic target for 2018, as was the case with other senior Texas Republicans. In Travis County, Wakely led Smith, 62%-29%. But Smith took 78 percent in New Braunfels-based Comal County.

San Antonio/South Austin Corridor

Population		**Race and Ethnicity**		**Income**	
Total	746,822	White	63.3%	Median Income	$61,733 (125 out of 435)
Land area	5,921	Black	3.3%		
Pop/ sq mi	126.1	Latino	28.0%		
Born in state	58.1%	Asian	3.2%	Under $50,000	40.9%
Age Groups		Two races	1.9%	$50,000-$99,999	30.2%
Under 18	20.6%	Other	0.4%	$100,000-$199,999	21.5%
18-34	26.6%	**Education**		$200,000 or more	7.3%
35-64	38.3%	H.S grad or less	25.9%	Poverty Rate	12.1%
Over 64	14.5%	Some college	29.4%	**Health Insurance**	
Work		College Degree, 4 yr	28.5%	With health insurance coverage	86.0%
White Collar	47.0%	Post grad	16.2%		
Sales and Service	40.5%	**Military**		**Public Assistance**	
Blue Collar	12.6%	Veteran	11.1%	Cash public assistance income	1.0%
Government	8.2%	Active Duty	0.8%	Food stamp/SNAP benefits	6.4%

Voter Turnout			
2015 Total Citizens 18+	557,097	2016 House Turnout as % CVAP	64%
2016 House turnout	356,031	2014 House Turnout as % CVAP	34%

2012 Presidential Vote		
Mitt Romney	188,241	(60%)
Barack Obama	119,220	(38%)

2016 Presidential Vote		
Donald Trump	188,336	(52%)
Hillary Clinton	152,528	(42%)
Gary Johnson	14,130	(4%)

Cook Partisan Voting Index: R+10

The Balcones Escarpment is a bulwark of cracked and weathered rock that crosses Texas diagonally from the Dallas-Fort Worth Metroplex southwest to Austin and San Antonio and all the way to the Rio Grande. It separates the flatlands of central Texas from the stony hills to the north and west. It is a boundary between cropland and grazing land, between acres rich with greenery and acres whose rolling brown hills blaze out in color when the wildflowers bloom in early spring. But the Balcones Escarpment is less familiar to Texans today than the highway that runs pretty much along the same line: Interstate 35. This is one of the most heavily traveled and congested interstates in America, thick with truck traffic in the populated stretches between the Metroplex and the Mexican border even as it passes through the lightly populated near-desert between San Antonio and Laredo. I-35 connects Austin and San Antonio, two booming Texan cities with very different beginnings and different characters now.

In the counties between these two cities and in the Hill Country to the west is the Texas German country, originally settled by Germans in the mid-1800s. It consists of economically prosperous communities that were anti-slavery and politically Republican in a state whose enthusiasm for the Democratic Party had roots in Confederate loyalties and populist rebellions. Texas Germans introduced the long-barbecued beef brisket that has become synonymous with Lone Star State cuisine and has become increasingly available in other states; an antique German dialect is sometimes heard on the streets of New Braunfels, Boerne and Fredericksburg. These communities, with their neat houses, low cost of living and Hill Country ambience are attracting residents to new subdivisions. Parts of this area, chiefly small cities, are among the most rapidly growing in the nation. Nearby Georgetown and New Braunfels ranked first and second in the nation in 2015; San Marcos, which is about halfway between the two anchors on I-35, was the fastest-growing city in 2014.

The 21st Congressional District of Texas includes much of this territory. One-third of its people are in San Antonio and Bexar County. It includes the northeast corner of the city and county, taking in Fort Sam Houston, and the affluent northside neighborhoods of Terrell Hills, Olmos Park and Alamo Heights just outside San Antonio. Fort Sam's renowned Brooke Army Medical Center was transformed into a regional military medical center for a net gain of more than 4,000 jobs. In the expansive Hill Country, the district takes in Gillespie County; along the Pedernales River is the LBJ Ranch, where the 36th president was born, vacationed during his presidency and is buried. He grew up in neighboring Blanco County's Johnson City, where he ran his first race for the House. When he was a New Deal congressman, Johnson famously brought electricity and other services to this hinterland, which remains countrified today.

Another one-fourth of the district is in Travis County, with parts of downtown Austin's central business district that border the University of Texas and the state capital. Amid the booming corporate development, downtown Austin has cherished its fame of more bars per capita than any other ZIP code in the nation. The political heritage of the district is mixed. While Travis County was always Democratic and the Texas German country was Republican, San Antonio was mixed. Overall, the district has been solidly Republican. As was the case in other suburban parts of Texas, Donald Trump underperformed the GOP presidential vote here; he got 52 percent, compared with 60 percent for Mitt Romney in 2012.

TWENTY-SECOND DISTRICT

Pete Olson (R)

Elected 2008, 5th term; b. Dec 09, 1962, Fort Lewis, WA; Rice University (TX), B.A.; University of Texas Law School, J.D.; Methodist; Married (Nancy Olson); 2 children.

Military Career: U.S Navy 1988-98, Naval Reserves, 1998-Present.

Professional Career: Naval officer, 1995; Staffer, U.S. Sen. Phil Gramm, 1998-2002; Staffer, U.S. Sen. John Cornyn, 2002-2007.

DC Office: 2133 RHOB 20515, 202-225-5951, Fax: 202-225-5241, olson.house.gov.

State Offices: Katy, 281-889-7134; Pearland, 281-485-4855; Sugar Land, 281-494-2690.

Committees: *Energy & Commerce*: Communications & Technology, Energy, Environment.

Group Ratings

	ADA	ACLU	AFL-CIO	LCV	ITI	COC	HAFA	ACU	CFG	FRC
2016	-	5%	-	0%	100%	100%	73%	96%	78%	100%
2015	0%	C	8%	0%	C	79%	C	92%	81%	100%

Almanac Ratings 2015

	Economy	Social	Foreign	Composite
Liberal	3%	0%	0%	1%
Conservative	97%	100%	100%	99%

Key Votes of the 114th Congress

1. Keystone Pipeline	Y	5. Puerto Rico Debt	N	9. Offenses by Aliens	Y
2. Trade Deals	Y	6. Medical Marijuana	N	10. Troops in Iraq	N
3. Export-Import Bank	N	7. Sanctuary Cities	Y	11. Homeland Security $$	N
4. Debt Ceiling Increase	N	8. Armor-piercing Bullets	Y	12. Trade Adjustment aid	N

Election Results

Election	Name (Party)	Vote (%)	Cand. Spent	Ind. Exp. Support	Ind. Exp. Oppose
2016 General	Pete Olson (R)	181,864 (60%)	$1,254,091		
	Mark Gibson (D)	123,679 (41%)	$24,048		
2016 Primary	Pete Olson (R)	(100%)			

Prior winning percentages: 2014 (67%), 2012 (64%), 2010 (68%), 2008 (52%)

Pete Olson, a Republican elected in 2008, represents the district once overseen by Tom DeLay, the powerful former House majority leader. On the Energy and Commerce Committee, he advocates on behalf of oil and gas interests and Houston's diverse business community. Olson is every bit as conservative and just as vigilant as DeLay, though few House members could match his clout.

A graduate of Rice University and the University of Texas Law School, Olson entered the Navy on the same day he took the Texas bar exam. He served as a naval aviator and flew anti-submarine missions, including in the Persian Gulf following the war against Iraq in 1991. He finished his military career in Washington, D.C., as a liaison to the Senate (the same job that Arizona Republican Sen. John McCain had before he entered politics). His next job was as a staff member for Republican Sen. Phil Gramm of Texas. After Gramm retired in 2002, Olson was chief of staff for his successor, Republican Sen. John Cornyn.

In 2006, DeLay resigned his seat after his September 2005 indictment in Texas required him to give up his leadership post. He was convicted in 2011 and sentenced to a three-year prison term for money laundering and conspiracy stemming from his role funneling corporate contributions to Texas state races. The state criminal appeals court in 2014 overturned the conviction on the basis that prosecutors failed to prove that the contributions were illegal. Former Democratic Rep. Nick Lampson took advantage of disarray among local Republicans and won the seat.

Two years later, Republicans targeted Lampson for defeat. In a crowded primary field, Shelley Sekula-Gibbs - who held the seat for a few weeks when she won a special election after DeLay resigned -- finished first in the primary but with only 30 percent of the vote. Republicans at the state and national levels regarded her as a weak candidate and coalesced around Olson, who won the runoff with 69 percent. In the general election, Olson touted a conservative message, while Lampson tried to tar him with DeLay's image, charging that Olson employed consultants who had previously worked for DeLay. Democratic leaders came to Lampson's aid, saying that if reelected he would chair the House subcommittee with jurisdiction over NASA, an important local employer. But all of this could not stop the district from returning to its GOP roots after a two-year interlude. In a Democratic year, Olson won 52%-45%.

Olson has been a rock-solid conservative, with nearly perfect conservative *Almanac* vote ratings in 2015. With a plum seat on the Energy and Commerce Committee, he has been a staunch defender of the Texas oil and gas industry. The House passed his bill in 2012 letting power companies off the hook if they violate environmental laws while attempting to comply with federal mandates to maintain the reliability of their electricity grids during power emergencies. Olson has been an outspoken advocate of the Keystone XL pipeline, which will carry Canadian oil to Texas refineries. He sought to permit more oil and gas drilling on public lands. With Democratic Rep. Cedric Richmond of Louisiana, he co-founded the Congressional Refinery Caucus, which was designed to educate lawmakers about the industry's interests. In 2016, the House passed Olson's bill to extend the time for implementation by the Environmental Protection Agency of its ozone-reduction standards under the Clean Air Act.

In January 2017, the House passed Olson's bill to create a national clinical care commission to consider a better federal response to a disease resulting from insulin deficiency or resistance. He has been a champion of NASA's Johnson Space Center and criticized President Barack Obama's budget requests for ignoring Congress' interest in human space flight. He called for a return to the moon to set the stage for an eventual manned mission to Mars.

Olson has pursued conservative initiatives. In 2013, he called for the Government Accountability Office to release a study on the use of federal funding by Planned Parenthood and other organizations that perform abortions. He took the lead in filing articles of impeachment against Attorney General Eric Holder for his mismanagement of the "Fast and Furious" gun-running program in Mexico. Republican leaders did not pursue the charges and Holder stepped down in 2015.

Olson has not been seriously challenged for reelection, despite Democrats managing to win the ethnically diverse Republican-leaning seat in the past decade. In February 2017, Fort Bend County Sheriff Troy Nehls, a Republican, opened the door to a challenge. "I am seriously considering running for Congress in 2018," he said. Nehls has been an outspoken critic of federal handling of illegal immigration. An internal GOP clash could give a boost to Democrats.

Southern Houston Suburbs: Sugar Land

Population		**Race and Ethnicity**		**Income**	
Total	786,002	White	42.9%	Median Income	$88,466 (21 out of 435)
Land area	1,033	Black	13.0%		
Pop/ sq mi	761.0	Latino	24.8%	Under $50,000	26.9%
Born in state	51.7%	Asian	17.2%	$50,000-$99,999	29.1%
		Two races	1.8%	$100,000-$199,999	31.3%
Age Groups		Other	0.3%	$200,000 or more	12.7%
Under 18	28.2%			Poverty Rate	7.9%
18-34	21.5%	**Education**			
35-64	41.0%	H.S grad or less	28.4%	**Health Insurance**	
Over 64	9.3%	Some college	28.6%	With health insurance coverage	86.0%
Work		College Degree, 4 yr	27.2%		
		Post grad	15.8%		
White Collar	49.6%			**Public Assistance**	
Sales and Service	35.1%	**Military**		Cash public assistance income	0.9%
Blue Collar	15.3%	Veteran	6.3%		
Government	5.2%	Active Duty	0.1%	Food stamp/SNAP benefits	6.6%

Voter Turnout			
2015 Total Citizens 18+	489,745	2016 House Turnout as % CVAP	62%
2016 House turnout	305,543	2014 House Turnout as % CVAP	31%

2012 Presidential Vote		
Mitt Romney	158,452	(62%)
Barack Obama	93,582	(37%)

2016 Presidential Vote		
Donald Trump	159,717	(52%)
Hillary Clinton	135,525	(44%)
Gary Johnson	9,322	(3%)

Cook Partisan Voting Index: R+10

The story of the Houston area's booming growth is well captured in a drive out the Southwest Freeway to Sugar Land. Much has changed from the days before the Civil War, when sugar plantations flourished here. Sugar Land is a privately planned city of more than 88,000 people, with privatized water and other services. (In 1990, its population was 45,000.) The surrounding Fort Bend County was fifth in the nation in job growth between 2000 and 2009. In 2014, *Money* magazine ranked Sugar Land number one in the nation on its list of "Best Places to Find a New Job." The local baseball team is the Sugar Land Skeeters, a reference to the area's uncomfortable proliferation of the biting insects.

When former House Majority Leader Tom DeLay represented the 22nd Congressional District, whites were a majority. Although much of Fort Bend's black population resides in the adjacent 9th District, the 22nd is a minority-majority district. Suburban Sugar Land and Fort Bend County are among the most-diverse areas in the country. Almost a quarter of the county's population is Hispanic, 21 percent is African American, and 20 percent is Asian. Sugar Land has elected a Chinese American to the city council, and a native of India has served on the board of the Chamber of Commerce. In 2016, Hillary Clinton took the county, 52%-45%, a 13-point swing from 2012 and an encouraging omen for Democrats. The district includes 80 percent of the voters in Fort Bend County, including Sugar Land, and a bit more than half of Brazoria County, centering on Pearland, just south of Houston. Pearland, a suburb whose population exploded from 46,000 in 2000 to 109,000 in 2015, when it was the seventh fastest-growing city in the nation, is positioning itself as a health care hub for the region. The district, which takes in a small slice of southwestern Houston, has been solidly Republican, with Mitt Romney getting 62 percent of the vote in 2012. Four years later, Donald Trump was not so good a fit and took only 52 percent.

TWENTY-THIRD DISTRICT

Will Hurd (R)

Elected 2014, 2nd term; b. Aug 19, 1977, San Antonio; Texas A&M University System, B.S.; Christian - Non-Denominational; Single.

Elected Office: TX House, 1990-2013.

Professional Career: Operations officer, CIA, 2000-2009; Partner, Crumpton Group, 2010-2013; Senior advisor, FusionX, 2010-present.

DC Office: 317 CHOB 20515, 202-225-4511, Fax: 202-225-2237, hurd.house.gov.

State Offices: Del Rio, 830-422-2040; Eagle Pass, 210-784-5023; Fort Stockton, 210-245-1548; San Antonio, 210-921-3130; San Antonio, 210-784-5023; Socorro, 915-235-6421.

Committees: *Homeland Security*: Border & Maritime Security, Counterterrorism & Intelligence. *Oversight & Government Reform*: Information Technology (Chmn). *Permanent Select on Intelligence*.

Group Ratings

	ADA	ACLU	AFL-CIO	LCV	ITI	COC	HAFA	ACU	CFG	FRC
2016	-	5%	-	3%	100%	100%	54%	80%	64%	83%
2015	0%	C	17%	0%	C	90%	C	83%	74%	92%

Almanac Ratings 2015

	Economy	Social	Foreign	Composite
Liberal	6%	5%	6%	6%
Conservative	94%	95%	94%	94%

Key Votes of the 114th Congress

1. Keystone Pipeline	Y	5. Puerto Rico Debt	Y	9. Offenses by Aliens	Y
2. Trade Deals	Y	6. Medical Marijuana	N	10. Troops in Iraq	N
3. Export-Import Bank	N	7. Sanctuary Cities	Y	11. Homeland Security $$	Y
4. Debt Ceiling Increase	N	8. Armor-piercing Bullets	Y	12. Trade Adjustment aid	N

Election Results

Election	Name (Party)	Vote (%)	Cand. Spent	Ind. Exp. Support	Ind. Exp. Oppose
2016 General	Will Hurd (R)	110,577 (48%)	$4,113,847	$187,197	$4,968,488
	Pete Gallego (D)	107,526 (47%)	$2,151,758	$1,717,426	$5,776,754
	Ruben S. Corvalan (L)	10,862 (5%)			
2016 Primary	Will Hurd (R)	39,762 (82%)			
	William Peterson (R)	8,590 (18%)			

Prior winning percentages: 2014 (50%)

In a district known for its frequent change of party control, Republican Will Hurd, a former CIA officer, in 2016 became the first incumbent to win reelection since 2008. Through extensive constituent outreach and an active legislative record, he defied the odds, with the additional handicap that Democrats sought to link him to Donald Trump in this 70 percent Hispanic district, though Hurd did not endorse in the presidential campaign. In a lengthy profile, *Politico* described him as "a phenom," with "a rare combination of competence as a policymaker, responsiveness as a representative and ferocity as a campaigner."

Hurd, a native of San Antonio, is the youngest of three children of a mixed-race couple. He graduated from Texas A&M University with a degree in computer science. As student body president, he helped a grieving campus recover from the 1999 collapse of the traditional football bonfire, which killed 12 students and injured 27 others. On the day after the September 11 attacks, he joined a new counter-terrorism unit in Afghanistan. When he left the agency after nine years and returned to Texas, he became a partner in the strategic advisory firm Crumpton Group, founded by former CIA officer and counterterrorism director Henry "Hank" Crumpton. Hurd also was a senior adviser with the cybersecurity firm FusionX. The *Houston Chronicle* headlined him as the spy "who came in from the shadows."

Hurd ran for the House seat in 2010, and he led the first round of primary voting with 34 percent. But he lost the GOP runoff to Francisco "Quico" Canseco, 53%-47%, a margin of 722 votes. Canseco then defeated Democratic Rep. Ciro Rodriguez. In 2012, Pete Gallego, a former prosecutor and former state representative, took the seat back for Democrats, 50%-46%. In 2014, Hurd easily defeated Canseco, 59%-41%, in the runoff. Tea party supporters backed Hurd's campaign, which emphasized his intelligence service "in this time of heartbreak and troubles throughout the world." Gallego portrayed himself as a moderate Blue Dog Democrat, but Hurd criticized him as too aligned with President Barack Obama and "radical environmentalists." Painting Gallego as a job killer, Hurd attacked his votes against the Keystone XL pipeline and drilling on public lands.

The race remained tight to the end. Gallego outspent Hurd, $2.7 million to $1.4 million. Each candidate was helped by more than $2.5 million in spending by national party committees and other outside groups that made huge ad purchases. The *San Antonio Express-News* endorsed Hurd as a young, charismatic conservative "with equal appeal to grizzled West Texas ranchers and upwardly mobile urban twentysomethings." Hurd won by about 2,400 votes, 49.8%-47.7%. In Bexar, which cast nearly half the votes, Hurd led, 57%-40%. In a district with only a 3% black population, Hurd explained to *The Washington Post* how "the black dude" was successful: "We did it by engaging people on the issues that they care about," notably, a good income, housing and health. "So we have to translate our agenda in a way that hits at those issues."

Hurd quickly settled in and made his mark in the House, including an impressive record of legislative accomplishments. He got a plum assignment for a freshman as chairman of the Oversight and Government Reform Subcommittee on Information Technology. In a February 2015 interview with *Baseline* magazine, Hurd said that the nation needs to do more to prepare against a cyberattack. "We do not have clear rules of engagement for a pure digital-on-digital attack. Knowing the rules of engagement deters some of this undesirable behavior." Seven months after taking office, he enacted his bill to cut the number of information technology systems at the Homeland Security Department to reduce duplication.

He took a broad perspective on cyber issues. "It's no secret that federal agencies need to improve their cybersecurity posture," Hurd said, as he chaired a June 2015 hearing on the data breach at the Office of Personnel Management that affected millions of federal employees and their family members. "Until agency leadership takes control of these basic cybersecurity measures … we will always be playing catch-up against our highly sophisticated and well-resourced adversaries." Hurd joined Democratic Rep. Ted Lieu of California in urging caution about new rules that required business to give law-enforcement officials access to their encrypted data. "Any vulnerability to encryption or security technology that can be accessed by law enforcement is one that can be exploited by bad actors such as criminals, spies and those engaged in economic espionage," they wrote to FBI Director James Comey.

Demonstrating his familiarity with national security and intelligence issues, Hurd encountered Comey in another forum in July 2016, which the *Express-News* described as "a star-making moment." As the Oversight Committee grilled Comey about the FBI's investigation of Hillary Clinton's handling of her personal email server when she was Secretary of State, Hurd said that Clinton had "a server in her basement that had information that was collected from our most sensitive assets and it was not protected by anyone. … And that's not a crime? That's outrageous."

Hurd was not shy in taking on the leadership of his own party. Following the October 2016 release of the 2005 video in which Donald Trump made lewd comments about women, Hurd called them "repulsive for women and all Americans" and said that Trump should "step aside for a true conservative to beat Hillary Clinton." After Trump was elected, Hurd said that he would be able to work with him. But he found plenty of opportunities to distance himself. Five days after Trump took office and repeated that he wanted to build a wall along the border with Mexico, Hurd - whose district includes more than 800 miles of that border - said that the proposed wall was "the most expensive and least effective way to secure the border." Also in January 2017, Hurd got a plum assignment, given his background: a seat on the Intelligence Committee. That didn't keep him from being one of 20 Republicans in May who voted against House passage of the GOP's American Health Care Act.

Given his initial tight victory, it was no surprise that the Democratic Congressional Campaign Committee made him a prime target in 2016. In a rematch, Gallego relentlessly sought to link Hurd with Trump. Hurd ran a well-organized campaign, which featured three district visits by House Speaker Paul Ryan, and he was well-financed. He turned the tables on Gallego from their previous campaign by outspending him, $4.1 million to $2.2 million. The two candidates roughly split more than $9 million in outside support from their respective parties and outside groups. Hurd won, 48.3%-47.0%, a margin of 3,000 votes. Hurd led in Bexar County by 13,600 votes and trailed with the much smaller electorate in El Paso by 14,000 votes. The margin of difference was in the district's vast rural areas.

Hurd's political future has been a topic of growing speculation. Assuming that he continues to win reelection in his swing district, the profile in *Politico* reported, he might eventually run for the Senate. "Hurd is too young, too talented, too ambitious not to push the limits and enter the arena with bigger and better competition."

San Antonio Exurbs, West Texas

Population		**Race and Ethnicity**		**Income**	
Total	730,817	White	25.0%	Median Income	$50,003 (256 out of 435)
Land area	58,059	Black	2.8%		
Pop/ sq mi	12.6	Latino	69.6%		
Born in state	64.9%	Asian	1.2%	Under $50,000	50.0%
Age Groups		Two races	0.9%	$50,000-$99,999	28.7%
Under 18	29.0%	Other	0.5%	$100,000-$199,999	16.3%
18-34	23.5%	**Education**		$200,000 or more	5.0%
35-64	35.7%	H.S grad or less	51.8%	Poverty Rate	19.4%
Over 64	11.8%	Some college	27.2%	**Health Insurance**	
Work		College Degree, 4 yr	13.7%	With health insurance coverage	78.8%
White Collar	29.8%	Post grad	7.4%		
Sales and Service	43.7%	**Military**		**Public Assistance**	
Blue Collar	26.5%	Veteran	9.0%	Cash public assistance income	1.5%
Government	6.7%	Active Duty	0.7%		
				Food stamp/SNAP benefits	18.6%

Voter Turnout			
2015 Total Citizens 18+	445,968	2016 House Turnout as % CVAP	51%
2016 House turnout	228,965	2014 House Turnout as % CVAP	26%

2012 Presidential Vote		
Mitt Romney	99,666	(51%)
Barack Obama	94,419	(48%)

2016 Presidential Vote		
Hillary Clinton	115,157	(50%)
Donald Trump	107,273	(46%)
Gary Johnson	7,077	(3%)

Cook Partisan Voting Index: R+1

Fifty or so miles west of San Antonio, the hills flatten out and become the parched uplands of West Texas. This is a borderland, just north of Mexico, where people are concentrated in tiny hamlets amid the empty ranchlands. Most are Hispanic. Once, Indians were the threat on this frontier. Now the challenge is a lack of water. The aquifers of West Texas are being drained, and state law still permits landowners to pump out as much water as they want. The Rio Grande, dried out by a dam in New Mexico, gets most of its water from the Rio Conchos in the Mexican state of Chihuahua. The mountains of Big Bend National Park rise above the Rio Grande, where in the clean air you can see for 180 miles. Texas' frontier in many ways is thriving; its remote location makes it one of the least-visited national parks. Eccentrics established an art colony in Marfa and stage a chili cook-off in Terlingua. In 2013, the CBS "60 Minutes" program reported on Marfa as "the capital of quirkiness," chiefly because of the gentrification that the new arrivals have brought. Near the Mexican border is Dimmit County, where more than a dozen companies have drilled thousands of wells in an oil and gas field known as the Eagle Ford shale formation. Huge wind farms have flowered along the interstate in Crockett County. Near the New Mexico border is oil-producing Loving County. From 2010 to 2016, the population grew from 82 to 113 residents, which made it the fastest-growing - as well as least populous -- county in the nation; Mentone, its only town, remained unincorporated. The increase may have resulted from the local interest in serving as a dump site for radioactive waste. Discovery of shale oil and improved fracking techniques have opened additional parts of the Permian Basin to production. That has resulted in huge local projects in these vast lands, including drilling rigs, a refinery and pipeline. Since 2010, land prices in some of these areas have soared.

The 23rd Congressional District of Texas is geographically the largest in the state, stretching from the outskirts of San Antonio to the edge of El Paso, from Eagle Pass and Maverick County to the New Mexico border. It takes in 23 percent of the state's land area, spanning more than 800 miles of the Texas-Mexico border and covering 29 counties. About 9 percent of the district's residents are military veterans, with many working as active duty personnel at Fort Sam Houston, Lackland Air Force Base, and Randolph Air Force Base, all just outside the district in or near San Antonio. Many local communities along the border have strong views - often hostile - about national politicians who want to build a large wall here. Local residents also understand the logistical complications, especially in Big Bend.

About 48 percent of the district's population is in Bexar County, chiefly in a C-shaped ring in the county's western suburbs that surround downtown San Antonio and is the more heavily Republican part of the district. The Mexican-American tradition in the part of South Texas radiating from San Antonio is anchored in two culturally conservative institutions: The Catholic Church and the U.S. military. San Antonio's Mexican-American community has produced many politicians who are liberal on economic issues and civil rights but also are pro-military and at home with traditional religious and cultural values. Only 6 percent of the 23rd is in El Paso County, which is disproportionately Democratic, as are most of the rural counties that lie between the urban anchors. The district is 70 percent Hispanic, but this is still a battleground district. This was among the few seats won by Hillary Clinton that Mitt Romney carried four years earlier - narrowly, in each case.

TWENTY-FOURTH DISTRICT

Kenny Marchant (R)

Elected 2004, 7th term; b. Feb 23, 1951, Bonham; Nazarene Theological Seminary (MO), Att.; Southern Nazarene University (OK), B.A.; Nazarene; Married (Donna Walker Marchant); 4 children; 2 grandchildren.

Elected Office: Carrollton City Council, 1980-1984; Carrolton Mayor, 1984-1986; TX House, 1987-2005.

Professional Career: Founder & owner, construction & home building business, 1975-2004.

DC Office: 2369 RHOB 20515, 202-225-6605, Fax: 202-225-0074, marchant.house.gov.

State Offices: Irving, 972-556-0162.

Committees: *Ethics*. *Ways & Means*: Health, Tax Policy.

Group Ratings

	ADA	ACLU	AFL-CIO	LCV	ITI	COC	HAFA	ACU	CFG	FRC
2016	-	5%	-	0%	100%	92%	88%	91%	77%	100%
2015	0%	C	4%	0%	C	75%	C	96%	95%	100%

Almanac Ratings 2015

	Economy	Social	Foreign	Composite
Liberal	3%	7%	4%	5%
Conservative	97%	93%	96%	95%

Key Votes of the 114th Congress

1. Keystone Pipeline	Y	5. Puerto Rico Debt	Y	9. Offenses by Aliens	Y
2. Trade Deals	Y	6. Medical Marijuana	N	10. Troops in Iraq	N
3. Export-Import Bank	N	7. Sanctuary Cities	Y	11. Homeland Security $$	N
4. Debt Ceiling Increase	N	8. Armor-piercing Bullets	Y	12. Trade Adjustment aid	Y

Election Results

Election	Name (Party)	Vote (%)		Cand. Spent	Ind. Exp. Support	Ind. Exp. Oppose
2016 General	Kenny Marchant (R)	154,845	(56%)	$324,586		
	Jan McDowell (D)	108,389	(39%)	$16,590		
	Mike Kolls (L)	8,625	(3%)			
2016 Primary	Kenny Marchant (R)		(100%)			

Prior winning percentages: 2014 (65%), 2012 (61%), 2010 (82%), 2008 (56%), 2006 (60%), 2004 (64%)

Republican Kenny Marchant, elected in 2004, is moving up in seniority on the Ways and Means Committee and is close to a subcommittee chairmanship. On the committee, he has been a player on taxes and international trade issues. He typically is loyal to GOP leadership and the party agenda. Mild-mannered and deeply religious, he does not have the sharp rhetorical edge of many Texas conservatives.

Marchant graduated from Southern Nazarene University and became a homebuilder and successful developer. He said that he got involved in politics when the head of the local homebuilders association told him that officials planned to change the construction codes and make it more expensive to build. Marchant served a quarter-century in local elected offices, including stints on the Carrollton City Council, as Carrollton mayor, and then in the state House. (His son, Matthew, stepped down as Carrollton's mayor in 2017, when he was term-limited.) He has been active in humanitarian projects around the world; the Ken Marchant Foundation funds church loans, mission projects and scholarships. He has a ranch about an hour from Dallas, where he maintains 400 cows and likes to fish and hunt. He had a net worth of at least $13.9 million in 2015, according to *Roll Call.*

In the state House, he enjoyed a reputation on both sides of the aisle as a levelheaded peacemaker. Despite serving in some of the legislature's most partisan leadership posts, Marchant refrained from engaging in the acrimonious battles all around him. Marchant had been chairman of the Banking and Investments Committee, and spent four years as floor leader of the Texas House Republican caucus. He served on the House Redistricting Committee during the bitter 2003 mapping battle.

Unsurprisingly, the redistricting plan couldn't have been more favorable to him. The new 24th District was heavily Republican and inhospitable to Democratic Rep. Martin Frost, an effective partisan who was targeted by then-Majority Leader Tom DeLay of Texas, the mastermind behind the effort. Frost opted to run in the new 32nd District and lost. Marchant has thrived in the redrawn 24th, which incorporated nearly his entire state legislative district. In the primary, he defeated three other candidates with 73 percent of the vote, and in the general election he won 64%-34%.

Marchant has a solidly conservative voting record that ranked him in the top one-third of Republicans in the *Almanac* vote ratings for 2015. He was among the original members of the Tea Party Caucus. "My vision for America is one where government is limited, taxes are low, success is celebrated, and the public sector flourishes," he told the *Fort Worth Star-Telegram* in 2012. He developed a fruitful relationship with Speaker John Boehner; he joined the Education and the Workforce Committee that Boehner chaired in 2005 and was one of the few Texans to back Boehner when he ran for majority leader in 2006. Marchant serves on the House Ethics Committee.

On Ways and Means in 2013, Marchant chaired the tax reform working group on debt, equity and capital. In response to the political-targeting controversy at the IRS, which he said jeopardized the security of confidential taxpayer information, he prepared a bill to prohibit IRS employees from using personal email accounts for official business. The House passed the measure on a voice vote in 2015. He has proposed a phase-out of the $6 billion production tax credit for wind energy. As a member of the Trade Subcommittee, he was an enthusiastic supporter of the prospective Trans-Pacific Partnership agreement. In an op-ed piece in June 2015, he urged prospective opponents not to take the bait. "Every objection is based on misinformation or economic fallacy," he said.

Marchant drew a spirited GOP primary challenger in 2012 in Grant Stinchfield, a former TV news investigative reporter. He accused Marchant of failing to adequately represent conservatives and chastised him for requesting in an email to a GOP operative that his "grandbabies'" schools be included in his district as part of the recent redistricting. Stinchfield won the endorsement of the *Star-Telegram*, which called Marchant "a good argument for term limits" and cited his lack of legislative productivity. Marchant's campaign noted that Stinchfield lived outside the district and that most of his support came from there. Stinchfield spent a relatively modest $239,000. The incumbent won 68%-32%. Marchant has not had a primary challenge since.

In 2016, Democratic nominee Jan McDowell, a certified public accountant, called for Congress to take a new approach based not on the interests of campaign donors but on "what benefits the greatest number of people." She spent only $21,000. Marchant won, 56%-39%, which tied for his lowest share of the vote since he was first elected.

North-Central Metroplex: Fort Worth Suburbs

Population		**Race and Ethnicity**		**Income**	
Total	747,381	White	50.6%	Median Income	$65,004 (94 out of 435)
Land area	263	Black	10.5%	Under $50,000	38.4%
Pop/ sq mi	2844.3	Latino	23.7%	$50,000-$99,999	30.5%
Born in state	45.3%	Asian	12.2%	$100,000-$199,999	22.1%
		Two races	2.2%	$200,000 or more	9.2%
Age Groups		Other	0.7%	Poverty Rate	10.1%
Under 18	23.8%				
18-34	25.5%	**Education**			
35-64	41.0%	H.S grad or less	28.0%	**Health Insurance**	
Over 64	9.7%	Some college	28.3%	With health insurance coverage	82.2%
		College Degree, 4 yr	28.6%		
Work		Post grad	15.1%		
White Collar	43.7%			**Public Assistance**	
Sales and Service	40.8%	**Military**		Cash public assistance income	1.3%
Blue Collar	15.6%	Veteran	6.8%		
Government	5.9%	Active Duty	0.0%	Food stamp/SNAP benefits	6.4%

Voter Turnout			
2015 Total Citizens 18+	471,590	2016 House Turnout as % CVAP	58%
2016 House turnout	275,635	2014 House Turnout as % CVAP	31%

2012 Presidential Vote		
Mitt Romney	150,547	(60%)
Barack Obama	94,634	(38%)

2016 Presidential Vote		
Donald Trump	140,128	(50%)
Hillary Clinton	122,872	(44%)
Gary Johnson	10,753	(4%)

Cook Partisan Voting Index: R+9

The gigantic (larger than Manhattan Island) Dallas-Fort Worth International Airport bisects the Metroplex and its two adjacent counties with its large terminals and the Texas-sized highway network that feeds them. Its total of flight operations makes it the third largest airport in the world, with seven runways, five terminals, 165 gates and 60,000 employees in an area of 27 square miles. DFW, as the locals call it, has been a focal point for development in both Dallas and Tarrant counties. Airport improvements for future growth, at a cost of $2.7 billion, began in 2011 and are scheduled to be completed in 2020. "DFW is no longer solely an airport. DFW is our home," the *Fort Worth Star-Telegram* wrote. New cities, with as many people as Dallas and Fort Worth had in the 1950s - Grand Prairie and Irving - grew up around the airport during the next two decades in an area that had been an open prairie. The merger of American Airlines and US Airways made the combined company the largest airline in the nation, with its headquarters remaining in Fort Worth. It remains the dominant carrier at DFW, though its share of passengers dropped below 85 percent earlier this decade.

North and west of DFW are newer and more upscale suburbs in northeast Tarrant County: Southlake, with huge shopping malls and resort centers, and Grapevine, home to the largest consumer-judged wine competition in the country. The Texas 114 corridor (also known as the Northwest Freeway) has become a booming business zone from Southlake to Roanoke. Across the International Parkway in northwest Dallas County are Coppell, Farmers Branch, and Carrollton. To the north are the fast-growing suburbs and exurbs of Denton County. The Dallas-Fort Worth-Arlington Metropolitan Statistical Area has passed Philadelphia as the nation's fourth-largest MSA. In 2015, it was the second fastest-growing metro area, trailing only Houston.

The 24th Congressional District of Texas is based in the suburban territory around DFW Airport. The line between its two principal counties, which goes through the eastern part of the terminal, is roughly the central axis of the district. Dallas and Tarrant each provide slightly more than 40 percent of the population, with the remainder beyond Dallas in Denton County. The area in Dallas takes in Irving, including ExxonMobil's corporate headquarters, part of Carrolton and all of Farmers Branch and Coppell. The slice in Tarrant, which includes Grapevine, Bedford, Colleyville and Southlake, is the strongest Republican part of the district. This has been solidly Republican territory, though the 50 percent vote for Donald Trump in 2016 was a sharp drop from the 60 percent that Mitt Romney got four years earlier.

TWENTY-FIFTH DISTRICT

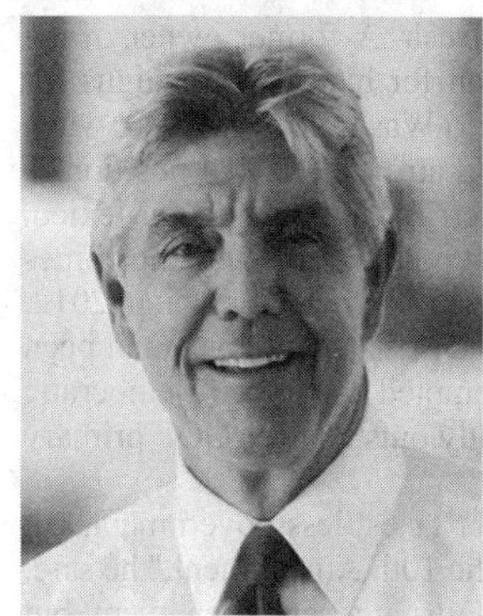

Roger Williams (R)

Elected 2012, 3rd term; b. Sep 13, 1949, Evanston, IL; Texas Christian University, B.S.; Disciples of Christ; Married (Patty Williams); 2 children.

Professional Career: Owner, Roger Williams Chrysler Dodge Jeep Ram, 1971-present; Atlanta Braves farm team, 1971-1974; Baseball coach, TX Christian University, 1974-1976; TX Secretary of st., 2005-2007.

DC Office: 1323 LHOB 20515, 202-225-9896, Fax: 202-225-9692, williams.house.gov.

State Offices: Austin, 512-473-8910; Cleburne, 817-774-2575.

Committees: *Financial Services*: Financial Institutions & Consumer Credit, Monetary Policy & Trade, Terrorism & Illicit Finance.

Group Ratings

	ADA	ACLU	AFL-CIO	LCV	ITI	COC	HAFA	ACU	CFG	FRC
2016	-	5%	-	0%	100%	100%	84%	92%	75%	100%
2015	0%	C	0%	0%	C	72%	C	96%	90%	100%

Almanac Ratings 2015

	Economy	Social	Foreign	Composite
Liberal	3%	4%	4%	3%
Conservative	98%	96%	97%	97%

Key Votes of the 114th Congress

1. Keystone Pipeline	Y	5. Puerto Rico Debt	Y	9. Offenses by Aliens	Y
2. Trade Deals	Y	6. Medical Marijuana	N	10. Troops in Iraq	N
3. Export-Import Bank	N	7. Sanctuary Cities	Y	11. Homeland Security $$	N
4. Debt Ceiling Increase	N	8. Armor-piercing Bullets	Y	12. Trade Adjustment aid	N

Election Results

Election	Name (Party)	Vote (%)		Cand. Spent	Ind. Exp. Support	Ind. Exp. Oppose
2016 General	Roger Williams (R)	180,988	(58%)	$1,164,817		
	Kathi Thomas (D)	117,073	(38%)	$44,739		
	Loren Marc Schneiderman (L)	12,135	(4%)			
2016 Primary	Roger Williams (R)		(100%)			

Prior winning percentages: 2014 (60%), 2012 (58%)

Republican Roger Williams, a former Texas secretary of state and prolific fundraiser, easily won a wide-open GOP primary in 2012 to take the district that had become reliably Republican in redistricting. He has quietly gone about his work, which includes a seat on the Financial Services Committee. He has suffered setbacks on two non-legislative matters in the House. In November 2016, he lost a bid to chair the National Republican Congressional Committee. Plus, an ethics complaint dealing with his business ownership was unresolved for many months.

Williams grew up in Fort Worth, where his father was a Chevrolet dealer and his mother ran a needlepoint business. He distinctly remembers that, as a 14-year-old, he was the last person to shake President John Kennedy's hand as he left the Texas Hotel in Fort Worth on the morning of Nov. 22, 1963. He attended Texas Christian University on a baseball scholarship. After graduating, he played in the Atlanta Braves minor league system for four years until he injured a shoulder while sliding into first base. He returned home to run the family car dealership and to coach baseball at TCU for three years. "I always thought I'd be a major league baseball player," he said. "When you're young, you never think you're going to get hurt or get old." Baseball is still important to Williams; he checks box scores every morning in season and considers pitching legend Nolan Ryan a good friend. He continues to own the dealership, which later led to the ethics inquiry.

Their shared love for baseball connected Williams and George W. Bush. A former owner of the Texas Rangers, Bush invited Williams to be a regional finance chairman for his two campaigns for governor, which was Williams' first foray into politics. He made his way to Washington in 2000, when Bush appointed him to the Republican National Committee's Eagles program. He left that position to accept Gov. Rick Perry's appointment as secretary of state. He was also Perry's chief liaison to Mexico.

Williams, who was Sen. John Cornyn's finance chair in 2002, said that political fund-raising comes easily to him. Having voiced interest in running for the open Senate seat that Ted Cruz later won in 2012, Williams announced in June 2011 that he would instead run for the 25th District seat, which had been altered to become securely Republican. The GOP-engineered changes prompted its veteran Democratic Rep. Lloyd Doggett to move to the 35th District. Williams overwhelmingly outspent the GOP primary field and defeated tea party activist Wes Riddle in a runoff, 58%-42%.

Williams ran on what he called a "pretty simple" platform. "It's lower taxes, less government, cut the spending, defend the borders, listen to your generals, and understand the 10th Amendment," he said. He generated controversy when he called President Barack Obama a socialist at a campaign event, but said he saw no reason to apologize. "Here's a man that wants to own the banks, the car manufacturers, the student loan programs," he said. "It's basically socialism versus entrepreneurialism and capitalism. That's what we're fighting." In November, Williams defeated Democrat Elaine Henderson, 58%-37%.

On the Financial Services Committee, Williams joined the terrorism financing task force; its work was conducted largely behind closed doors. He generated controversy in seeking to give the Medal of Honor to former Navy SEAL Chris Kyle, who inspired the movie "American Sniper" for having killed more than 160 people during combat in Iraq, and then was the victim of a shooting at a Texas rifle range. Critics from some veterans' groups contended that Kyle did not meet the required standard of a single extraordinary act of valor. Williams disagreed, and filed his bill in February 2015. The House took no action on his proposal. Questions dealing with his legislation related to car dealerships led the Office of Congressional Ethics to recommend that the House Ethics Committee conduct an investigation, given his continued ownership of a large auto dealership in the Fort Worth area. Williams denied any conflict. In June 2016, the committee said that it was investigating Williams, but gave no details. *Roll Call* in 2015 listed his wealth as $27.5 million.

Williams became finance chairman of the National Republican Congressional Committee in 2013. From that base, he voiced interest in taking over as chairman of the full committee after the 2014 election, regardless of the intentions of then-chairman Greg Walden of Oregon. When House Republicans made a double-digit gain in the 2014 election and Walden made clear that he was not giving up the post, Williams quietly abandoned his bid. Following the 2016 election, Williams and Rep. Steve Stivers of Ohio competed to replace Walden. Stivers, who had more experience within the NRCC, won on a 143-96 vote among House Republicans.

In 2016, Democrat Kathi Thomas, a special events planner, challenged Williams for reelection. She talked about the need for bipartisanship and getting big money out of politics. Like other Democratic challengers in Texas, she had little money to make her case. Williams won, 58%-38%, though he trailed in Travis County, 55%-40%.

Austin; the Hill Country

Population		**Race and Ethnicity**		**Income**	
Total	738,761	White	68.7%	Median Income	$61,730 (126 out of 435)
Land area	7,621	Black	6.9%		
Pop/ sq mi	96.9	Latino	18.6%		
Born in state	57.9%	Asian	2.6%	Under $50,000	40.7%
Age Groups		Two races	2.3%	$50,000-$99,999	30.3%
Under 18	25.0%	Other	0.8%	$100,000-$199,999	20.9%
18-34	23.7%	**Education**		$200,000 or more	8.0%
35-64	38.8%	H.S grad or less	33.7%	Poverty Rate	12.9%
Over 64	12.4%	Some college	30.8%	**Health Insurance**	
Work		College Degree, 4 yr	22.7%	With health insurance coverage	85.7%
White Collar	42.7%	Post grad	12.8%		
Sales and Service	38.2%	**Military**		**Public Assistance**	
Blue Collar	19.1%	Veteran	10.7%	Cash public assistance income	1.6%
Government	7.7%	Active Duty	2.4%	Food stamp/SNAP benefits	9.3%

Voter Turnout			
2015 Total Citizens 18+	521,459	2016 House Turnout as % CVAP	59%
2016 House turnout	310,196	2014 House Turnout as % CVAP	34%

2012 Presidential Vote		
Mitt Romney	162,279	(60%)
Barack Obama	102,433	(38%)

2016 Presidential Vote		
Donald Trump	172,476	(55%)
Hillary Clinton	125,949	(40%)
Gary Johnson	11,772	(4%)

Cook Partisan Voting Index: R+11

Austin, the capital of the second-largest state in the country and the site of the largest capitol building, was laid-back and countrified until fairly recently. After World War II, in Sen. Lyndon Johnson's time, Austin had a metropolitan population of just over 130,000. There had never been much commerce. State government provided much of the local employment. Its skies were untainted by industrial smoke. Its biggest industry was the University of Texas, with 50,000 students and an endowment of thousands of West Texas acres that turned out to sit on top of oil. The university has long had a distinguished faculty and some of the world's great scholarly collections, including the LBJ Presidential Library and its 45 million pages of documents. The Austin of old was also the central focus of Texas' hardy but almost always outnumbered liberals, based in the university, state government and *Texas Observer* magazine. They mocked the business lobbyists who called the shots when the "Leg" (pronounced *lej*) was in session.

Today's Austin is quite a different place. The metropolitan area has doubled every 20 years, and today Greater Austin's population stands at 2 million, the fourth-largest in the state. In the 12 months ending in June 2015, for the fifth consecutive year, it was the fastest-growing metro area in the nation with at least 1 million people. The city, with a 15 percent increase from 2010 to 2015, has a population of 930,000. Hillary Clinton won 66 percent of the vote in Travis County in 2016, an increase from the 60 percent for President Barack Obama in 2012. Some businesses cater to the old liberal bastions: The upscale organic-food chain Whole Foods Market is based in Austin. The tone of the area overall has grown more corporate, especially as its private sector began to make up a larger share of the local economy. The techies who settled in the Silicon Hills extending from Austin's Travis County to once-rural Williamson County tended to vote Republican. When Austin's local government in 2014 shifted from at-large to district representation, Republicans picked up seats. Housing prices across much of the city have soared, though they still seem cheap compared with San Francisco and Boston. In a sign that the local liberal ethos has not become totally outdated, Travis in March 2017 declared itself a "sanctuary" for immigrants, which led Gov. Greg Abbott to deny it some state funds.

The 25th Congressional District of Texas, which includes the capitol and the nearby UT campus, has about 30 percent of the residents of Travis County. To dilute the liberal votes cast in Austin, they have been split among five districts, of which the 25th has the largest share. That part of the district leans Democratic, though not nearly as much as the lower-income neighborhoods of southeast Austin, which are in the 35th District; studies have shown that poor neighborhoods in Austin are more "economically segregated" than in comparable large metro areas. To the west of downtown, Mopac Boulevard operates as a dividing line between overwhelmingly Democratic Austin and the more suburban, Republican-leaning areas of the county near Lake Travis. The remaining 60 percent of the district's population resides in a string of Republican-leaning counties that include the Hill Country. This stretch, which extends 180 miles north to Burleson in the Fort Worth exurbs, politically overwhelms the liberal enclaves in Austin. Rural Coryell County include much of Fort Hood, which covers more than 25 percent of the county's land area, though its official home in Killeen is in the 31st District. In Lampasas, the first chapter of the Farmers' Alliance, a precursor to the Populists, was founded in 1877. The 25th has been a solidly Republican district, though many of its new business class did not respond well to Donald Trump. His 55 percent of the vote in 2016 was less robust than the 60 percent for Mitt Romney in 2012.

TWENTY-SIXTH DISTRICT

Michael Burgess (R)

Elected 2002, 8th term; b. Dec 23, 1950, Rochester, MN; North Texas State University, M.S.; North Texas State University, Dallas, B.S.; University of Texas-Houston, M.D.; The Selwyn School (TX); University of Texas - Dallas, M.S.; Anglican; Married (Laura Burgess); 3 children; 2 grandchildren.

Professional Career: Practicing obstetrician, 1981-2003.

DC Office: 2336 RHOB 20515, 202-225-7772, Fax: 202-225-2919, burgess.house.gov.

State Offices: Lake Dallas, 940-497-5031.

Committees: *Energy & Commerce*: Digital Commerce & Consumer Protection, Health (Chmn), Oversight & Investigations. *Joint Security & Cooperation in Europe*. *Rules*: Legislative & Budget Process.

Group Ratings

	ADA	ACLU	AFL-CIO	LCV	ITI	COC	HAFA	ACU	CFG	FRC
2016	-	11%	-	0%	67%	93%	88%	92%	96%	100%
2015	10%	C	4%	3%	C	70%	C	92%	85%	100%

Almanac Ratings 2015

	Economy	Social	Foreign	Composite
Liberal	10%	0%	7%	6%
Conservative	90%	100%	93%	94%

Key Votes of the 114th Congress

1. Keystone Pipeline	Y	5. Puerto Rico Debt	N	9. Offenses by Aliens	Y
2. Trade Deals	N	6. Medical Marijuana	N	10. Troops in Iraq	Y
3. Export-Import Bank	N	7. Sanctuary Cities	Y	11. Homeland Security $$	N
4. Debt Ceiling Increase	N	8. Armor-piercing Bullets	Y	12. Trade Adjustment aid	N

Election Results

Election	Name (Party)	Vote (%)		Cand. Spent	Ind. Exp. Support	Ind. Exp. Oppose
2016 General	Michael Burgess (R)	211,730	(66%)	$874,077		
	Eric Mauck (D)	94,507	(30%)			
	Mark Boler (L)	12,843	(4%)			
2016 Primary	Michael Burgess (R)	73,515	(79%)			
	Joel Krause (R)	13,183	(14%)			
	Micah Beebe (R)	5,938	(6%)			

Prior winning percentages: 2014 (83%), 2012 (68%), 2010 (67%), 2008 (60%), 2006 (60%), 2004 (66%), 2002 (75%)

Michael Burgess, a conservative Republican physician first elected in 2002, has become an activist House leader and GOP spokesman on health care. An outspoken member of the Energy and Commerce Committee, he became chairman of its Health Subcommittee in January 2017, a pivotal time for the panel.

Burgess grew up in Denton County, the son of a physician, and graduated from the University of North Texas and the University of Texas Medical School in Houston. He trained at Parkland Hospital in Dallas and set up an obstetrics-gynecology practice in Lewisville. After 21 years in practice, Burgess made an unlikely run for Congress, his first bid for elective office. When Majority Leader Dick Armey announced in 2001 that he would not run again, there was no doubt that a Republican would succeed him in his overwhelmingly Republican district. Almost no one expected that the winner would be Burgess. The widespread expectation was that the winner would be the majority leader's son, Scott Armey, a former Denton County judge.

In the primary, Armey outspent Burgess by more than 6-to-1. Turnout was light - only 25,000 of 456,000 voting-age residents took part. With no statewide Republican contests on the ballot, there seemed to be no suspense about the outcome. Armey took 45 percent of the vote, failing to gain the required majority. Burgess won 23 percent. In the four-week runoff campaign, Burgess benefited from a series of hard-hitting articles in the *Dallas Morning News* about Armey's record as a county judge, which suggested he had used his position to steer county jobs and contracts to close friends. Burgess focused on health care and taxes. He had helped to draft the Texas Patients' Bill of Rights and vowed to do the same on a national level. In another low-turnout affair of 19,259 voters, Burgess won the runoff 55%-45%. Armey tellingly lost 60%-40% in Denton County, where he was known best. After the runoff, his father bitterly attacked the newspaper's "vicious unprofessionalism" and accused it of a vendetta against the Armey family. Burgess breezed to victory in November, 75%-23%. He has been reelected comfortably since.

Burgess has a reliably conservative voting record, especially on social issues, according to the *Almanac* vote ratings. He joined the Tea Party Caucus when it was formed in 2010. He drew headlines the next year when, while attending a tea party meeting, he responded to a question about whether impeaching President Barack Obama would tie up Obama's agenda by saying there was "no question" that it would. He said later that he didn't advocate impeachment. He has pushed legislation to replace the federal income tax with a 23 percent sales tax on goods and services.

Burgess has focused his work chiefly on health care. On Energy and Commerce, he has been an effective inquisitor on the 2010 health reform law, and was a persistent opponent of Obama administration policies. He was vocal about seeking to fully defund the law in the fiscal 2011 budget, an idea that House Republican leaders sought to defuse. His nine-part plan for health care included many ideas that GOP candidates have espoused and that have become mainstream within the party, including allowing patients to shop for insurance across state lines and limiting damages in malpractice lawsuits.

He has made a steady rise to influence, with work on a cross-section of health care issues. On pharmaceutical issues, he has shown that he is not a reflexive partisan. In 2009, he joined a bipartisan agreement to permit the Food and Drug Administration to approve generic versions of biologic drugs. He was part of a bipartisan group in 2011 that proposed legislation ensuring that seniors who show signs of Alzheimer's receive a formal diagnosis from their doctor. In 2015, he filed with then-Rep. Chris Van Hollen of Maryland the Advancing Research for Neurological Diseases Act of 2015, which would create a national data collection system at the Centers for Disease Control and Prevention for disorders such as Parkinson's disease and multiple sclerosis.

In 2015, he was the chief sponsor of a landmark law when Congress finally resolved the "doc fix" issue that limited reimbursements for patients with Medicare coverage. "May we never speak of it again," he concluded. The bipartisan deal, which he called the most significant entitlement reform in years, included other changes in Medicare, such as performance incentives and new payment procedures for health care providers. Several provisions from Burgess were part of the enactment in 2016 of the Twenty First Century Cures Act, including neurological research and interoperability standards for electronic health records. In 2015-16, he chaired the Commerce, Manufacturing and Trade subcommittee, which has jurisdiction over consumer and tourism issues.

When Burgess became chairman of the Health Subcommittee in 2017, he said the position is "what I asked for" when first elected to Congress. "That's going to be my life for the next two years," he told the *Texas Tribune* in February. He promised many fresh ideas for replacement of the Affordable Care Act. Although he hasn't been shy about expressing his views, he doesn't demand attention. Asked by the *Tribune* whether he will be the quarterback of the initiative, he responded, "Nooooo. ... Water boy?" More seriously, he described his role as "educator," of other members of Congress as well as the public. Conveniently, he and the subcommittee's ranking Democrat - fellow Texas Rep. Gene Green - have worked closely over the years, though they often disagree. In a profile, McClatchy News headlined that Burgess was "the GOP's policy wonk behind Obamacare repeal." One of the first bills that the House passed in 2017 was the bipartisan Improving Access to Maternity Care Act, of which he has been the lead sponsor. The proposal sought to improve the availability of maternity services, a topic with which he has deep familiarity.At home, Burgess has kept his distance from the Texas GOP establishment. He was an early supporter of Ted Cruz, including his successful Senate primary bid against Lt. Gov. David Dewhurst in 2012. While other Lone Star State lawmakers were backing Gov. Rick Perry for president that year, Burgess was an early backer of Newt Gingrich. Early in the 2016 campaign, he said that it would be "inappropriate" for vaccination against measles to become an issue. His position took issue with Donald Trump, who occasionally raised questions about vaccines when he was a candidate.

Northern Metroplex: Denton

Population		**Race and Ethnicity**		**Income**	
Total	771,286	White	66.4%	Median Income	$79,792 (36 out of 435)
Land area	907	Black	7.2%		
Pop/ sq mi	850.2	Latino	17.7%	Under $50,000	29.5%
Born in state	51.1%	Asian	5.5%	$50,000-$99,999	31.9%
		Two races	2.7%	$100,000-$199,999	30.1%
Age Groups		Other	0.5%	$200,000 or more	8.6%
Under 18	28.0%			Poverty Rate	8.0%
18-34	23.2%	**Education**			
35-64	40.5%	H.S grad or less	27.3%	**Health Insurance**	
Over 64	8.3%	Some college	32.1%	With health insurance coverage	87.2%
		College Degree, 4 yr	27.9%		
Work		Post grad	12.7%		
White Collar	44.2%			**Public Assistance**	
Sales and Service	40.4%	**Military**		Cash public assistance income	1.1%
Blue Collar	15.3%	Veteran	8.1%		
Government	5.4%	Active Duty	0.1%	Food stamp/SNAP benefits	5.9%

Voter Turnout			
2015 Total Citizens 18+	506,857	2016 House Turnout as % CVAP	63%
2016 House turnout	319,080	2014 House Turnout as % CVAP	28%

2012 Presidential Vote		
Mitt Romney	177,941	(68%)
Barack Obama	80,828	(31%)

2016 Presidential Vote		
Donald Trump	194,033	(60%)
Hillary Clinton	109,536	(34%)
Gary Johnson	12,577	(4%)

Cook Partisan Voting Index: R+18

Until the Texas Land and Immigration Company settled this portion of northeast Texas with a land grant from the Texas Congress in 1841, settlers were scarce and Indian raids were common. The area now known as Denton County takes its name from John Bunyan Denton, a Methodist pioneer preacher and lawyer killed in a skirmish with Indians. Today, this area on the northern edge of the Dallas-Fort

Worth Metroplex is teeming with new arrivals and filling up with young, well-educated, middle-class families. In 1940, there were 34,000 people in Denton County, and they voted 88 percent Democratic for president. Population for the county grew from 432,000 in 2000 in 806,000 in 2016, an 86 percent increase. The fast-growing county voted 65 percent for Mitt Romney in 2012, though it fell to 58% for Donald Trump in 2016. The University of North Texas, with more than 38,000 students, is the fifth-largest in the state, while Texas Woman's University is the largest state-supported university for women in the United States (although it does accept men).

The county's chief cities are Denton, Flower Mound and Lewisville, and there is plenty of room for more growth along Interstates 35E and 35W. Truck manufacturer Peterbilt Motors, the largest employer in Denton with 2,000 employees, completed in March 2017 a large expansion to improve its efficiency. In Frisco, near the North Dallas Tollway, four mega-developments recently opened along what became known as Five Billion Dollar Mile. Near Justin, in the southwest corner of Denton County, a pipeline allows for production of up to 1 billion cubic feet of natural gas daily. With sophisticated imaging and drilling technology, other natural gas wells operate within 10 miles of downtown Fort Worth. On the downside, GE Transportation, which manufactures rail locomotives in Fort Worth, has suffered layoffs because of a lack of sales. Sufficient open space remains so that Denton has more horse ranches than any other county in the United States. The county inflicted an unusual setback on the oil and gas industry, but it didn't last long. Denton voters in November 2014 approved a referendum to ban hydraulic fracturing within city limits; six months later, Gov. Greg Abbott signed a law prohibiting such local bans.

The 26th Congressional District of Texas is at the heart of the northern expansion of the Metroplex. It includes more than 80 percent of suburban and exurban Denton County, and a small fragment of urban Tarrant County, including the old railroad town of Keller, now a bustling upscale suburb with a median family income in excess of $100,000. There are some Democratic areas here, especially around Denton's universities. Overall, this was the second-strongest Republican district in the Metroplex for Trump; he got 60 percent here, short of the 62 percent in the 5th District.

TWENTY-SEVENTH DISTRICT

Blake Farenthold (R)

Elected 2010, 4th term; b. Dec 12, 1961, Corpus Christi; Saint Mary's University School of Law, San Antonio (TX), J.D.; University of Texas, B.S.; Incarnate Word Academy (TX); Episcopalian; Married (Debbie Farenthold); 2 children.

Professional Career: Practicing attorney, 1989-1995; Owner, Farenthold LLC, 1995-2010; Radio host, 1999-2010.

DC Office: 2331 RHOB 20515, 202-225-7742, Fax: 202-226-1134, farenthold.house.gov.

State Offices: Corpus Christi, 361-884-2222; Victoria, 361-894-6446.

Committees: *Judiciary*: Courts, Intellectual Property & Internet, Regulatory Reform, Commercial & Antitrust Law. *Oversight & Government Reform*: Information Technology, Interior, Energy & Environment (Chmn). *Transportation & Infrastructure*: Aviation, Highways & Transit, Railroads, Pipelines & Hazardous Materials.

Group Ratings

	ADA	ACLU	AFL-CIO	LCV	ITI	COC	HAFA	ACU	CFG	FRC
2016	-	17%	-	0%	83%	100%	88%	-	92%	92%
2015	5%	C	13%	3%	C	65%	C	-	83%	100%

Almanac Ratings 2015

	Economy	Social	Foreign	Composite
Liberal	8%	5%	0%	4%
Conservative	93%	95%	100%	96%

Key Votes of the 114th Congress

1. Keystone Pipeline	Y	5. Puerto Rico Debt	N	9. Offenses by Aliens	Y
2. Trade Deals	N	6. Medical Marijuana	N	10. Troops in Iraq	N
3. Export-Import Bank	N	7. Sanctuary Cities	Y	11. Homeland Security $$	N
4. Debt Ceiling Increase	N	8. Armor-piercing Bullets	Y	12. Trade Adjustment aid	N

Election Results

Election	Name (Party)	Vote (%)		Cand. Spent	Ind. Exp. Support	Ind. Exp. Oppose
2016 General	Blake Farenthold (R)	142,251	(62%)	$1,096,491		
	Roy Barrera (D)	88,329	(38%)	$14,806		
2016 Primary	Blake Farenthold (R)	42,872	(56%)			
	Gregg Deeb (R)	33,699	(44%)			

Prior winning percentages: 2014 (64%), 2012 (57%), 2010 (48%)

Republican Blake Farenthold was elected in 2010 with one of the most surprising GOP wins of that cycle, then emerged as a big winner in Texas redistricting with a more solidly Republican district. His major legislative achievement has been House passage of a bill that would weaken the authority of the Federal Trade Commission. In 2015, he privately settled a lawsuit filed against him by a former congressional aide, which led him to become a leading critic of congressional ethics rules. He had an unexpectedly close Republican primary in 2016.

Farenthold was born and raised in Corpus Christi, where his family has farmed for three generations. His grandfather's second wife was Sissy Farenthold, a Democratic state legislator and a pioneer of the women's rights movement who was a serious contender to be Democrat George McGovern's running mate in 1972. Blake Farenthold studied radio, film and television at the University of Texas. After earning his law degree at St. Mary's University, he joined his step-grandfather's law practice, focusing on agricultural law. He became dissatisfied with the legal profession, and launched a computer consulting and website design firm. He began dabbling in radio, appearing as an occasional guest to talk about computer-related issues. Eventually, he became a sidekick on the morning program of Corpus Christi's news radio station KKTX, airing his conservative views and gaining name recognition.

Motivated by his opposition to the Affordable Care Act, Farenthold ran against 14-term Democratic Rep. Solomon Ortiz. In a tough fight for the Republican nomination against Corpus Christi real estate agent James Duerr, Farenthold drew on his personal wealth to outspend Duerr and prevailed in the April runoff, 51%-49%. He started as a decided underdog against Ortiz, who had built a moderate voting record in a Hispanic-majority district and had shepherded money to local projects as a senior member of the Armed Services Committee.

Farenthold's campaign suffered a credibility deficit after images surfaced of him wearing pajamas featuring yellow ducks while out for a night on the town with a young woman wearing what appeared to be a sheer nightie. (It turned out to be a photo at a costume party, and the woman was a waitress.) Ortiz touted the photograph as evidence that his opponent could not be taken seriously. Farenthold's campaign got a boost from the support of local tea party activists, but he was outspent 2-to-1. After a recount showed that he trailed by 799 votes, Ortiz conceded.

Farenthold got early attention in the House when he sponsored amendments to the fiscal 2011 spending bill, including one to ban funding for Planned Parenthood. He grew disillusioned with House Republicans' inability to cut spending enough to suit him. "Imagine going real fast in a *Flintstones* car, and my heel is out there," he said in Robert Draper's 2012 book *Do Not Ask What Good We Do*. "I went to Washington to change the world, and all I can do is put my heel out." He lamented his party's inability to get its message across: "What the Democrats can say in two emotion-packed sentences takes us 10 PowerPoint slides."

Perhaps his most significant legislative achievement was House passage in March 2016 of his bill to require that the Federal Trade Commission use the same enforcement standards in antitrust cases as the Justice Department. His proposal, which would overrule 100 years of FTC practice, would have the effect of significantly weakening the commission's authority. "Currently, the two agencies use different procedures to challenge a merger and cause unequal burdens on merging parties," Farenthold said. The bill passed, 235-171, on a nearly party-line vote. On the Oversight and Government Reform Committee, Farenthold spent two years as chairman of the federal workforce subcommittee. He expressed concerns about agencies' spending on outside conferences. In 2017, he became chairman of its Interior, Energy and Environment Subcommittee,

In December 2014, a 27-year-old former aide on his House staff filed a lawsuit against Farenthold in which she accused him of excessive drinking, flirting and firing her after she complained of a hostile work environment. He told the *Houston Chronicle* that he was shocked by the allegations that were "far out in left field" and that he had "good reason" for the dismissal. His lawyers wrote in a court filing that the aide had failed to report for work. In late 2015, the lawsuit was settled in a private agreement between Farenthold and his aide; details were not made public.

After its own inquiry, the Office of Congressional Ethics found that there was not substantial reason for the House Ethics Committee to investigate. Farenthold's unhappiness with the handling of his case reportedly led him to join other critics who sought to weaken the authority of the ethics office under House rules. Meanwhile, Farenthold drew unwanted attention in October 2016 when he downplayed Donald Trump's controversial comment about groping women. He told an interviewer for MSNBC that he "would have to consider" whether a hypothetical rape charge against Trump would be acceptable. Farenthold later Tweeted his apology.

After redistricting shifts in 2012 made his district more safely Republican, Farenthold's first two reelection campaigns were uneventful. Following the revelation of his former aide's complaint, the *Texas Tribune* reported that the Democratic Congressional Campaign Committee saw the lawsuit as an opportunity in 2016 to seek a credible challenger to Farenthold who would publicize his ethics problems.

His greater challenge came in the GOP primary. Gregg Deeb, a businessman in Corpus Christi and a military veteran, said that he sought "real solutions" to problems facing the nation. The two candidates agreed not to run negative campaigns, and there was no public indication that Deeb raised the ethics issues. Following his unexpectedly close 56%-44% victory, Farenthold attributed the outcome to "the fact that folks are angry with Washington." Although his November reelection was more routine with 62 percent of the vote, Deeb's challenge might prompt a more serious contest in 2018.

Central Gulf Coast: Corpus Christi, Victoria

Population		**Race and Ethnicity**		**Income**	
Total	719,002	White	41.1%	Median Income	$49,960 (257 out of 435)
Land area	9,128	Black	5.1%		
Pop/ sq mi	78.8	Latino	51.0%		
Born in state	75.7%	Asian	1.4%	Under $50,000	50.1%
Age Groups		Two races	1.1%	$50,000-$99,999	30.0%
Under 18	25.3%	Other	0.4%	$100,000-$199,999	16.9%
18-34	22.8%	**Education**		$200,000 or more	3.0%
35-64	37.6%	H.S grad or less	50.1%	Poverty Rate	17.0%
Over 64	14.3%	Some college	31.5%	**Health Insurance**	
Work		College Degree, 4 yr	12.3%	With health insurance coverage	80.7%
White Collar	28.0%	Post grad	6.1%		
Sales and Service	43.7%	**Military**		**Public Assistance**	
Blue Collar	28.4%	Veteran	10.0%	Cash public assistance income	1.7%
Government	7.4%	Active Duty	0.4%	Food stamp/SNAP benefits	15.1%

Voter Turnout			
2015 Total Citizens 18+	501,495	2016 House Turnout as % CVAP	46%
2016 House turnout	230,580	2014 House Turnout as % CVAP	26%

2012 Presidential Vote		
Mitt Romney	131,803	(61%)
Barack Obama	83,152	(38%)

2016 Presidential Vote		
Donald Trump	140,787	(60%)
Hillary Clinton	85,589	(36%)
Gary Johnson	6,491	(3%)

Cook Partisan Voting Index: R+13

The Nueces River rises on the Edwards Plateau in Central Texas, almost a half mile above sea level. From there it cascades across the Texas Hill Country and passes through the coastal plain before emptying into the Gulf of Corpus Christi. Early attempts at establishing settlements near the river's terminus were half-hearted and unsuccessful, and the area was uninhabited until Henry Lawrence Kinney and William Aubrey established a trading post on the west shore of the bay in 1839. Growth came slowly here at first; a population of 2,100 in 1870 was barely 11,000 in 1920. Hurricanes, the occasional outbreak of yellow fever and, more importantly, the lack of a deep-water port, frustrated attempts to expand the city.

Then, in 1926, the federal government completed the dredging of a shipping channel and the modern Port of Corpus Christi was born. The city's population almost tripled in the 1920s, then doubled in the 1930s. By 2015, it topped 324,000. The port is the fifth largest in the United States in total tonnage shipped, a center for exporting cotton, sorghum and grains, and importing steel and construction equipment; the port includes numerous factories and industrial plants. Barge traffic of oil has increased greatly along the Gulf Intracoastal Waterway. In August 2016, Corpus Christ had groundbreaking for the $900 million Harbor Bridge, which will give larger ships entry to the port. The Naval Air Station at Corpus Christi is another major contributor to the local economy, while sport fishing is a burgeoning industry. Starting in 2010, the Eagle Ford Shale yielded more than 1.5 million barrels of daily oil production, though the oil-price slump shut down some rigs; production in 2016 fell below 1 million barrels daily before prices rebounded. In March 2017, San Patricio County approved a $10 billion petrochemical complex, which expected to hire 11,000 workers for the construction. Corpus Christi's population is 60 percent Hispanic. According to a Pew Research Center report in 2013, only 8 percent of them were foreign-born. That was the smallest share for any of the 60 metro areas with sizable Hispanic populations.

The 27th Congressional District of Texas is centered on Corpus Christi, and almost half of its residents live in the city and surrounding Nueces County. Corpus Christi is the county seat and 90 percent of Nueces; the city extends into three adjacent smaller counties. The district takes in most of the Gulf Coast north of Corpus Christi, up to Bay City and the outskirts of Houston's suburbs. The only other city of any size in the district is Victoria, an industrial town of 68,000. Formosa Plastics is undergoing a $1.7 billion expansion of its plastics and petrochemicals site in nearby Point Comfort. An arm of the 27th reaches to Bastrop and Caldwell counties, in the Austin area, and takes in Gonzales, where the first shots of the Texas Revolution were fired. The redrawn district, unlike its predecessor, is safe Republican territory, even with its 52 percent Hispanic population. In 2016, Donald Trump got 60 percent of the district vote.

TWENTY-EIGHTH DISTRICT

Henry Cuellar (D)

Elected 2004, 7th term; b. Sep 19, 1955, Laredo; Georgetown University (DC), B.S.; Laredo Community College (TX), A.A.; Texas A and M International University, M.B.A.; University of Texas, Ph.D.; University of Texas Law School, J.D.; Roman Catholic; Married (Imelda Rios Cuellar); 2 children.

Elected Office: TX House,1987-2001; TX Secretary of st., 2001.

Professional Career: Practicing attorney, 1981-2004; Adjunct Professional, TX A&M University, 1984-1986.

DC Office: 2209 RHOB 20515, 202-225-1640, Fax: 202-225-1641, cuellar.house.gov.

State Offices: Laredo, 956-725-0639; Mission City, 956-424-3942; Rio Grande City, 956-487-5603; San Antonio, 210-271-2851.

Committees: *Appropriations*: Defense, Homeland Security.

Group Ratings

	ADA	ACLU	AFL-CIO	LCV	ITI	COC	HAFA	ACU	CFG	FRC
2016	-	29%	-	32%	100%	93%	28%	12%	17%	42%
2015	35%	C	55%	20%	C	94%	C	27%	26%	58%

Almanac Ratings 2015

	Economy	Social	Foreign	Composite
Liberal	41%	49%	34%	41%
Conservative	59%	51%	66%	59%

Key Votes of the 114th Congress

1. Keystone Pipeline	Y	5. Puerto Rico Debt	Y	9. Offenses by Aliens	Y
2. Trade Deals	Y	6. Medical Marijuana	N	10. Troops in Iraq	N
3. Export-Import Bank	Y	7. Sanctuary Cities	N	11. Homeland Security $$	Y
4. Debt Ceiling Increase	Y	8. Armor-piercing Bullets	Y	12. Trade Adjustment aid	Y

Election Results

Election	Name (Party)	Vote (%)		Cand. Spent	Ind. Exp. Support	Ind. Exp. Oppose
2016 General	Henry Cuellar (D)	122,086	(66%)	$715,450		
	Zeffen Hardin (R)	57,740	(31%)			
	Michael Cary (G)	4,616	(3%)			
2016 Primary	Henry Cuellar (D)	49,962	(90%)			
	William Hayward (D)	5,682	(10%)			

Prior winning percentages: 2014 (82%), 2012 (68%), 2010 (56%), 2008 (69%), 2006 (68%), 2004 (59%)

Henry Cuellar, elected in 2004, is one of the most conservative Hispanic Democrats, with a voting record putting him near the center of the House as a whole. Despite his maverick tendencies, he has shown enough loyalty to his party to earn a coveted seat on the Appropriations Committee. He has delivered funds to his district for its many needs, including homeland security and agriculture.

Cuellar was the oldest of eight children of migrant workers who had only elementary school educations. He graduated from Georgetown University and the University of Texas law school, and later got a Ph.D. in government from UT. With his five degrees, he claims to be the "most degreed" member of the House. From his base in Laredo, he served in the Texas House from 1986 to 2000, where he helped to author the Texas Grant college aid program. In 2001, Republican Gov. Rick Perry appointed him secretary of state even though he is a Democrat.

Cuellar resigned in 2002 to run against veteran Republican Rep. Henry Bonilla in the sprawling 23rd District. Bonilla claimed he didn't need Laredo to win. In response, the Webb County GOP chairman endorsed Cuellar. The challenger attacked Bonilla for his votes against funding for the Children's Health Insurance Program, the Family and Medical Leave Act, and Pell grants. Bonilla had the money advantage. Cuellar carried Webb County 84%-15%. When the Bexar County votes were counted a few days later, Bonilla's confidence turned out to be warranted. He won 52%-47%.

Redistricting in 2003 gave Cuellar an opportunity to run in the 28th against Democratic Rep. Ciro Rodriguez of San Antonio, who had the most liberal voting record of Texas' Hispanic Democrats in Congress and was chairman of the Hispanic Caucus. Rodriguez expressed disbelief that a friend and former legislative colleague for whom he had raised money in 2002 would run against him. The ambitious Cuellar sealed the end of the friendship when he told a local reporter, "Nobody died and made him king."

Cuellar criticized Rodriguez for voting against the GOP's 2003 Medicare prescription drug bill, while Rodriguez pointed out Cuellar's collusion with Republicans as secretary of state. Cuellar was declared the Democratic nominee by 58 votes out of 49,000 cast. He won in November, 59%-39%. In 2007, the Federal Election Commission fined Cuellar $28,500 for failing to disclose a $200,000 bank loan in his 2004 campaign.

Cuellar's voting has placed him among the most conservative Democrats. The *Almanac* ratings for 2015 gave him the second-highest conservative score for a Democrat behind Collin Peterson of Minnesota, though he was still more liberal than all House Republicans. The Heritage Action scorecard for 2016 ranked him as the third-most conservative House Democrat in 2016. In response to criticism of his independence, Cuellar told a San Antonio audience in September 2014, "I will die as a Democrat."

Many Democrats were slow to embrace him, given his endorsement of George W. Bush in the 2000 presidential election. He is a member of the shrinking Blue Dog Coalition of his party's fiscal conservatives and was one of just 22 Democrats to support a failed amendment for a fiscal 2013 budget based on the recommendations of the Simpson-Bowles deficit reduction commission. In 2015, he was one of 28 House Democrats to vote for the Keystone XL pipeline. He joined most of the Texas delegation in voting against lifting the financial liability cap on oil spills.

His middle ground positions on immigration have irritated many Democrats, the *Houston Chronicle* reported in September 2014. He was the only House Democrat who voted for a bill that would have made it easier to deport unaccompanied minors from Central America. He criticized President Barack Obama, including for his handling of immigration. On MSNBC, he said that Obama looked "aloof and detached" by not going to the Mexican border when he was in Texas for political fundraisers in 2014. When Donald Trump became president, Cuellar attacked his proposal for a border wall as "a 14th century solution," and said that illegal immigration ought to be addressed as a 21st century problem, with steps such as military surveillance and a "virtual border."

With his bipartisan approach, Cuellar has had success passing legislation that has benefited his district. In December 2016, he enacted his bill for alternative financing arrangements to construct and maintain facilities at ports of entry along the border. The water-resources bill that became law the same month included a provision for the Army Corps of Engineers to study a flood-control project along Chacon Creek in Laredo. In the spending bill that was approved in May 2017 for the remainder of the fiscal year, he claimed credit for $947 million for his 10-20-30 agriculture program: at least 10 percent of funds goes to counties where 20 percent or more of the population has lived in poverty for the past 30 years

In Cuellar's first reelection bid in 2006, Rodriguez challenged him in the primary but struggled to match his fundraising. Cuellar won the primary comfortably this time, 53%-40%. He has won reelection easily since. Cuellar told the *Chronicle* that he would like to seek a statewide office, and mentioned the possibility of running for governor or the Senate in 2018. As of May 2017, he had not taken steps for such a campaign.

Laredo/San Antonio Corridor

Population		**Race and Ethnicity**		**Income**	
Total	730,332	White	16.8%	Median Income	$44,230
Land area	9,379	Black	4.0%		(349 out of 435)
Pop/ sq mi	77.9	Latino	77.2%		
Born in state	63.4%	Asian	0.8%	Under $50,000	55.2%
		Two races	0.9%	$50,000-$99,999	29.0%
Age Groups		Other	0.2%	$100,000-$199,999	13.7%
Under 18	31.6%			$200,000 or more	2.2%
18-34	23.4%	**Education**		Poverty Rate	26.7%
35-64	34.5%	H.S grad or less	56.2%		
Over 64	10.5%	Some college	26.5%	**Health Insurance**	
		College Degree, 4 yr	11.7%	With health insurance coverage	72.0%
Work		Post grad	5.6%		
White Collar	26.9%				
Sales and Service	47.7%	**Military**		**Public Assistance**	
Blue Collar	25.4%	Veteran	7.9%	Cash public assistance income	1.9%
Government	7.5%	Active Duty	0.4%		
				Food stamp/SNAP benefits	25.4%

Voter Turnout			
2015 Total Citizens 18+	396,815	2016 House Turnout as % CVAP	46%
2016 House turnout	184,442	2014 House Turnout as % CVAP	19%

2012 Presidential Vote		
Barack Obama	101,843	(60%)
Mitt Romney	65,372	(39%)

2016 Presidential Vote		
Hillary Clinton	110,020	(58%)
Donald Trump	72,520	(38%)
Gary Johnson	4,401	(2%)

Cook Partisan Voting Index: D+9

The border country along the Rio Grande is in some ways a region all its own, a mixture of the United States and Mexico. As former Laredo Mayor Betty Flores has said, "The river for us is more like some street that we cross. It's really not a border." This is where, in "Streets of Laredo," singer

Marty Robbins (and many others over the years, including Johnny Cash) summoned up images of lonely cowboys on dusty streets outside of saloons in a tiny town. But that is not the Laredo of today. It is the busiest border crossing for U.S.-Mexico trade. About 14,000 trucks and railcars cross its four bridges daily; with about $283 billion in two-way trade crossing the Rio Grande in 2016, the Laredo customs district was the third busiest in the nation behind Los Angeles and New York. Local enthusiasts refer to the Laredo area as "NAFTA on Wheels." Laredo grew at a 34 percent pace in the first decade of the 21st century and another 8 percent from 2010 to 2015. Its old downtown streets are filled with Mexicans who cross the border on foot.

Laredo's Webb County had a population of 271,000 in 2016, of which 95 percent was Hispanic. Local fast-food restaurants feature enchiladas more often than hamburgers. Nearly three-fourths of all businesses are minority owned, which is the largest share in the nation. The region has its problems, including crime from the trade in illegal immigration and drugs; its positioning at the end of Interstate 35 makes it an important point of entry for both. The county retained a 32 percent poverty rate in 2016, even with a revival in oil drilling in the Eagle Ford Shale.

The 28th Congressional District of Texas is centered in Laredo and Webb County, which has the largest population in the district. South along the Rio Grande, it crosses Starr County, one of the poorest counties in Texas and home of many blatant and wealthy drug smugglers. It also takes in Mission in a narrow strip of Hidalgo County. These border counties make up about two-thirds of the district. To the north, it extends through thinly settled ranch and oil well country, plus about 160,000 residents on the eastern side of Bexar County, including a small portion of San Antonio. It includes the Joint Base San Antonio, formed from the joining of Randolph and Lackland Air Force bases and Fort Sam Houston in 2010. About 78 percent of the residents of the 28th are Hispanic. The district leans Democratic locally, but Republicans sometimes do well. President George W. Bush in 2004 and some state GOP officials have carried the district as currently configured. In 2016, Hillary Clinton got 58 percent, the same share of the vote that Barack Obama received in 2008.

TWENTY-NINTH DISTRICT

Gene Green (D)

Elected 1992, 13th term; b. Oct 17, 1947, Houston; University of Houston (TX), B.A.; University of Houston Bates College of Law (TX), J.D.; Methodist; Married (Helen Alders Green); 2 children; 4 grandchildren.

Elected Office: TX House, 1973-1985; TX Senate, 1985-1993.

Professional Career: Practicing attorney, 1977-1992.

DC Office: 2470 RHOB 20515, 202-225-1688, Fax: 202-225-9903, green.house.gov.

State Offices: Houston, 281-999-5879; Houston, 713-330-0761.

Committees: *Energy & Commerce*: Digital Commerce & Consumer Protection, Energy, Environment, Health (RMM).

Group Ratings

	ADA	ACLU	AFL-CIO	LCV	ITI	COC	HAFA	ACU	CFG	FRC
2016	-	76%	-	82%	67%	69%	16%	8%	6%	0%
2015	70%	C	100%	63%	C	63%	C	13%	0%	0%

Almanac Ratings 2015

	Economy	Social	Foreign	Composite
Liberal	77%	84%	39%	67%
Conservative	23%	16%	61%	33%

Key Votes of the 114th Congress

1. Keystone Pipeline	Y	5. Puerto Rico Debt	Y	9. Offenses by Aliens	N
2. Trade Deals	N	6. Medical Marijuana	Y	10. Troops in Iraq	N
3. Export-Import Bank	Y	7. Sanctuary Cities	N	11. Homeland Security $$	Y
4. Debt Ceiling Increase	Y	8. Armor-piercing Bullets	Y	12. Trade Adjustment aid	Y

Election Results

Election	Name (Party)	Vote (%)		Cand. Spent	Ind. Exp. Support	Ind. Exp. Oppose
2016 General	Gene Green (D)	95,649	(73%)	$1,515,239	$67,653	$40,251
	Julio Garza (R)	31,646	(24%)			
	N. Ruben Perez (L)	3,234	(3%)			
2016 Primary	Gene Green (D)	17,750	(57%)			
	Adrian Garcia (D)	11,935	(39%)			

Prior winning percentages: 2014 (90%), 2012 (90%), 2010 (65%), 2008 (75%), 2006 (74%), 2004 (94%), 2002 (95%), 2000 (73%), 1998 (93%), 1996 (68%), 1994 (73%), 1992 (65%)

Democrat Gene Green, first elected in 1992, is a gregarious centrist with a bipartisan streak. As an Anglo, he has shown political skill and paid close attention to constituents in remaining popular in a district that is more than three-fourths Hispanic. In 2016, he faced a serious primary challenge for the first time in two decades from a former local Latino official. In a low-turnout contest, Green won 57%-39%, a warning that his lock on the district might be weakening. In the House, his senior position on the Energy and Commerce Committee has made him an active player on health care issues.

Green grew up in the largely Hispanic Lindale section of north Houston, the son of a home-improvement business owner who enlisted his sons to provide him with free labor. He worked as a printer's apprentice and got business and law degrees from the University of Houston. He was elected to the state House in 1972, at age 25, and to the state Senate in a special election in 1985. As a friend to organized labor and trial lawyers in Austin and Washington, and an opponent of gun control, his political base has been Texas' small, blue-collar unions.

In the 1992 primary for the House seat, he faced Ben Reyes, a tempestuous Houston councilman who once protested official inaction on crime by demolishing a crack house. Green went door-to-door and carried lawn signs and a hammer in his trunk while appearing as a frequent guest on Spanish-language radio shows. In the primary, Reyes led 34%-28%. In the runoff, Green came out ahead by 180 votes out of 31,508 cast. Reyes went to court and charged that Republican voters had illegally crossed over to vote in the runoff. That got him a re-runoff, but to no avail. This time, Green won with 52 percent. He went on to win the general election with 65 percent.

In the House, Green has a moderate voting record, especially for a lawmaker in a heavily minority urban district. His *Almanac* vote ratings in 2015 ranked him as the 12th most conservative Democrat, with a notably conservative score on foreign policy issues. He has been a loyal partisan in assailing Republican budgets for their supposed impact on senior citizens and low-income residents. But he occasionally has gone his own way. In 2012, he joined most Republicans in defeating a Democratic amendment to cut $400 million from the missile defense budget and he backed a GOP proposal to try suspected terrorists at Cuba's Guantanamo Bay rather than in U.S. civilian courts.

On the influential Energy and Commerce Committee, Green has focused on issues important to the oil industry. In 2008, he became chairman of the Environment and Hazardous Materials Subcommittee. But Democrat Henry Waxman of California eliminated the panel - and Green's chairmanship - after taking over as Energy and Commerce chairman. Green had been an ally of Michigan Democrat John Dingell in the pitched battle with Waxman for the committee chairmanship after the 2008 election.

During debate on the climate change bill in 2009, Green got significant concessions from Waxman for oil refineries. That measure forced Green to strike a balance between the industry's desires and quality-of-life issues in the district. He fought Republican proposals to encourage new oil refineries, claiming the environmental exemptions could have jeopardized the clean air program in Houston. Green sided with other Texas delegation members after the 2010 BP oil spill in the Gulf of Mexico and opposed lifting the liability cap on spills. In 2011, he sponsored a bipartisan resolution to support continued deep-water drilling in the Gulf of Mexico. He led Democrats who advocated approval of the Keystone XL pipeline, which will bring Canadian oil to Texas refineries. Following the Republican takeover of the House in 2011, Green became ranking Democrat on the Environment and Economy Subcommittee.

With Dingell and Waxman retired in 2015, Green became the ranking Democrat on the Health Subcommittee. More of a liberal on health care, this became a more comfortable assignment for him. He was part of the bipartisan group that enacted the 21st Century Cures Act, which encouraged more rapid introduction of new pharmaceuticals. Green has joined on several initiatives with Republican Rep. Mike Burgess of Texas, who has become the Health Subcommittee chairman. In June 2016, they filed a bill to promote greater transparency for the costs of health care services for patients. But there have been clear limits on cooperation for Green who, during debate on the Affordable Care Act in 2009, backed the government-run "public option" to compete with private insurers. In February 2016, he filed a bill that was based on the budget submitted by President Barack Obama, which would have given states three years of full funding if they expanded Medicaid coverage under the health care law. Green criticized Republicans in Texas who turned down that option

Despite the fact that the 29th has been an inviting opportunity for an ambitious Hispanic politician, Green has been reelected easily and without significant primary challenges. With a population of 2.3 million, of whom 44 percent are Hispanic, Houston is the only city or metro area with a large Hispanic presence that does not have a Hispanic representative in Congress. Green has consistently defended his representation and the voters. "We're not South Africa under apartheid. They've had the opportunity, and they made that decision," he told the *Houston Chronicle* in September 2014.

That changed in 2016, when former Harris County Sheriff Adrian Garcia challenged Green and pointed to the continuing poverty and low education performance in the district. "It's about not accepting the status quo anymore, and it's about giving the community a loud and active and engaged voice," Garcia told *The Atlantic.* In a measure of incumbency, Green was endorsed by BOLD PAC, the campaign arm of the Congressional Hispanic Caucus. Garcia spent $387,000, compared with the $1.9 million that Green spent during the cycle. In the March 1 primary, which was the day of the presidential contests in Texas, Green's 57 percent of the vote came from a turnout of 31,000, nearly one-third less than minority districts in the Houston area that did not have competitive congressional primaries. In the general, Green got 72 percent against Julio Garza, who had a scant campaign presence. The potential for higher voter registration and Democratic primary turnout among Hispanics may be the biggest threat facing Green.

East Houston and Pasadena

Population		**Race and Ethnicity**		**Income**	
Total	730,411	White	10.6%	Median Income	$38,833 (404 out of 435)
Land area	187	Black	10.3%	Under $50,000	61.6%
Pop/ sq mi	3904.5	Latino	76.8%	$50,000-$99,999	27.7%
Born in state	57.1%	Asian	1.6%	$100,000-$199,999	9.8%
Age Groups		Two races	0.5%	$200,000 or more	1.0%
Under 18	31.4%	Other	0.3%	Poverty Rate	26.5%
18-34	27.1%	**Education**		**Health Insurance**	
35-64	34.1%	H.S grad or less	69.9%	With health insurance coverage	65.7%
Over 64	7.3%	Some college	20.9%	**Public Assistance**	
Work		College Degree, 4 yr	6.7%	Cash public assistance income	1.8%
White Collar	15.8%	Post grad	2.5%	Food stamp/SNAP benefits	21.3%
Sales and Service	42.2%	**Military**			
Blue Collar	41.9%	Veteran	3.8%		
Government	7.1%	Active Duty	0.0%		

Voter Turnout			
2015 Total Citizens 18+	335,284	2016 House Turnout as % CVAP	39%
2016 House turnout	131,982	2014 House Turnout as % CVAP	14%

2012 Presidential Vote		
Barack Obama	75,720	(66%)
Mitt Romney	37,909	(33%)

2016 Presidential Vote		
Hillary Clinton	95,027	(71%)
Donald Trump	34,011	(25%)
Gary Johnson	3,136	(2%)

Cook Partisan Voting Index: D+19

Many areas of Texas have large Mexican-American communities that can be traced back to statehood. But not Houston. The swampy area in what was originally called Harrisburg County had few inhabitants of any ethnicity until the 20th century. Houston and its Mexican-American community had to be built from the ground up. The city's economy was also built from the ground up, based on a combination of cotton, oil and trade via the 52-mile Houston Ship Channel. Cotton and oil were gifts of nature, though they required much human effort and ingenuity to produce in commercial quantities. The ship channel has been almost totally man's creation and a massive public works project. Along with the unsettled conditions created by the Mexican Revolution of 1910, it provided the impetus for Mexican immigration to the city.

After the sand-spit port of Galveston was destroyed by a hurricane in 1900, Houston's elders decided to dredge out Buffalo Bayou and make their inland city a seaport. When the channel officially opened in November 1914, a sluggish, 6-foot-deep creek had become a 40-foot-deep waterway that would turn Houston into one of the nation's biggest ports. Today, the channel is 45 feet deep and 530 feet wide. To accommodate the giant container ships that began to arrive in 2016 from the expanded Panama Canal, the channel has made $1 billion in upgrades. In the port, which is the second-largest in the nation in tonnage, more than half the cargo is energy-related. In a dramatic shift, Houston in 2016 had a $14 billion surplus in its net exports of energy, including a growing amount of liquid natural gas that is shipped to petrochemical manufacturers in Asia and Latin America. The port is the site of the largest petrochemical complex in the nation. On its west side, Houston seems entirely a white-collar, office-bound city. But on the east and north, around the port and through the maze of refinery towers and pipelines, it remains blue-collar and a job magnet for Mexican Americans and workers from the rural South. To the south is Hobby Airport, whose art-deco terminal served the city until what is now called the George Bush International Airport opened in 1969 on much larger land just north of the Sam Houston Tollway. Hobby, where Southwest Airlines is the dominant carrier, opened a new international terminal in October 2015 and serves about 20 percent of the area's airline passengers.

The 29th Congressional District of Texas, which is entirely in Harris County, covers much of the ship channel area and working-class Houston. Its unusual shape - some say it resembles a seated dragon - connects heavily Hispanic sections north of Houston with the Hispanic community around the ship channel and Pasadena. The district wraps around the Sam Houston Tollway, taking in blue-collar neighborhoods in northeast Houston as well. In the southeast, Pasadena, once part of the giant Allen Ranch, is now a working-class city of 154,000 centered on the oil and aerospace industries. In July 2016, plans were announced for a $335 million high-capacity marine terminal along the ship channel in Pasadena. It will chiefly handle refined petroleum products and will be able to dock Panamax-size ships when it is scheduled to open in 2019. The district is 77 percent Hispanic and firmly Democratic. The 71 percent for Hillary Clinton in the 2016 election was five percentage points higher than the vote for President Barack Obama in 2012.

THIRTIETH DISTRICT

Eddie Bernice Johnson (D)

Elected 1992, 13th term; b. Dec 03, 1935, Waco; Texas Christian University, B.S.; St. Mary's College at the University of Notre Dame (IN); Southern Methodist University (TX), M.P.A.; Baptist; Divorced; 1 child; 3 grandchildren.

Elected Office: TX House, 1973-1977; TX Senate, 1987-1993.

Professional Career: Registered nurse, 1955-1972; Regional Director, U.S. Department of HEW, 1977-1981; Mgmt. consultant, Sammons Corporation, 1979-1981; Owner, Eddie Bernice Johnson & Association.

DC Office: 2468 RHOB 20515, 202-225-8885, Fax: 202-226-1477, ebjohnson.house.gov.

State Offices: Dallas, 214-922-8885.

Committees: *Science, Space & Technology (RMM)*: Energy, Environment, Oversight, Research & Technology, Space. *Transportation & Infrastructure*: Aviation, Highways & Transit, Water Resources & Environment.

Group Ratings

	ADA	ACLU	AFL-CIO	LCV	ITI	COC	HAFA	ACU	CFG	FRC
2016	-	94%	-	95%	67%	64%	11%	0%	0%	0%
2015	90%	C	78%	89%	C	53%	C	0%	0%	0%

Almanac Ratings 2015

	Economy	Social	Foreign	Composite
Liberal	87%	100%	93%	93%
Conservative	13%	0%	7%	7%

Key Votes of the 114th Congress

1. Keystone Pipeline	N	5. Puerto Rico Debt	Y	9. Offenses by Aliens	N
2. Trade Deals	Y	6. Medical Marijuana	Y	10. Troops in Iraq	Y
3. Export-Import Bank	Y	7. Sanctuary Cities	N	11. Homeland Security $$	Y
4. Debt Ceiling Increase	Y	8. Armor-piercing Bullets	N	12. Trade Adjustment aid	Y

Election Results

Election	Name (Party)	Vote (%)	Cand. Spent	Ind. Exp. Support	Ind. Exp. Oppose
2016 General	Eddie Bernice Johnson (D)	170,502 (78%)	$324,735		
	Charles Lingerfelt (R)	41,518 (19%)			
	Jarrett R. Woods (L)	4,753 (2%)			
2016 Primary	Eddie Bernice Johnson (D)	44,505 (69%)			
	Barbara Mallory Caraway (D)	15,266 (24%)			
	Brandon Vance (D)	4,336 (7%)			

Prior winning percentages: 2014 (88%), 2012 (79%), 2010 (76%), 2008 (82%), 2006 (80%), 2004 (93%), 2002 (74%), 2000 (92%), 1998 (72%), 1996 (55%), 1994 (73%), 1992 (72%)

Eddie Bernice Johnson, a Democrat first elected in 1992, is a revered figure in Dallas politics, having spent four decades as an advocate for the city. Some of her younger rivals and *The Dallas Morning News*' editorial page have said that it's time for her to step aside, but she remained a potent political force even as she passed age 80. Her chief legislative work has been on the Science, Space and Technology Committee, where she has had an often-fractious relationship with the Republican chairman, a fellow Texan.

Johnson grew up in Texas, graduated from Texas Christian University with a nursing degree, and later got a master's degree in public administration at Southern Methodist University. She worked at St. Paul Hospital and was the chief psychiatric nurse at the Veterans Administration Hospital in Dallas. She told *The Morning News* in 1987 that she first got interested in politics in the early 1960s, when she went to buy a new hat and was shocked to learn that blacks in the city weren't allowed to try on such headgear. She organized a boycott of the store. In 1972, she was elected to the Texas House, the first black woman elected to the legislature from Dallas. She became a regional director of the old Health, Education and Welfare Department under President Jimmy Carter. She was elected to the Texas Senate in 1986. As the Senate's Redistricting Committee chair in 1991, she was instrumental in creating the new 30th District, and she went on to win the Democratic primary with 92 percent of the vote. She remains the only person to have held the seat.

In the House, Johnson - known by her initials "EBJ" - has a mostly liberal voting record. A former chairwoman of the Congressional Black Caucus, she was more supportive of President Barack Obama than other caucus members critical of his limited efforts for low-income and unemployed blacks. She has been attentive to business interests in Dallas, which helps to explain why her *Almanac* vote ratings for 2015 placed her at the center of House Democrats on economic issues. Johnson once pledged to labor unions to oppose the North American Free Trade Agreement, but she changed her mind and voted for it in 1993. Dallas is a large exporter to Mexico, and many jobs depend on that trade. Johnson also sided with business on normalizing trade relations with China, and was one of 28 House Democrats who backed trade promotion authority for Obama in June 2015. National unions were unhappy, though she suffered no immediate political damage.

Johnson became ranking Democrat on the Science, Space, and Technology Committee in 2011. What had long been a bipartisan committee has become increasingly polarized. At an August 2013 hearing, she accused Chairman Lamar Smith, a fellow Texan, of representing the interests of "industry hacks." At a hearing in December 2015, Johnson clashed with Smith over his criticism of scientists at the National Oceanic and Atmospheric Administration who had studied global warming. Smith's claims that the researchers altered historical climate data were "the most outrageous statements ever made by a chair of the Committee on Science," she said. While lambasting Republican cuts in science funding, she sought to encourage more students to enter science- and technology-related fields. She shared credit for passing the Networking and Information Research and Development Act to double funding for information research. As a health care professional, she takes an interest in minority health issues. In 2017, she reintroduced her bipartisan bill to have a federal National Nurse for Public Health work alongside the surgeon general.

As a senior member of the Transportation and Infrastructure Committee, Johnson has worked to secure funds for the Interstate 30 suspension bridge over the Trinity River, and she continues to support Trinity River projects. The Trinity River Corridor toll-road project, in the works for decades and including three new suspension bridges, remains controversial and unresolved. She has supported the Dallas-Fort Worth area's mass transit projects to alleviate traffic congestion.

Johnson generally has sailed to reelection. In the months before the 2010 election, the *Morning News* reported that she had awarded college scholarships to four relatives and the two children of a top aide who otherwise would have been ineligible under the Congressional Black Caucus Foundation's guidelines. Johnson said she had not been familiar with the rules and agreed to repay the foundation. The scandal provided an opening for her Republican challenger, minister Stephen Broden. The *Morning News* endorsed Broden and rebuked Johnson for being among the South Dallas leaders "who treat their districts as if they were their fiefdoms." Johnson chalked up another landslide, 76%-22%.

Two years later, Johnson faced two young Democratic challengers: attorney Taj Clayton and state Rep. Barbara Mallory Caraway, who avoided criticizing Johnson directly but made clear their view that the district needed fresh representation. The *Morning News* endorsed Clayton this time, saying Johnson "once had what it takes, but now it's time for new leadership." The normally even-keeled Johnson ripped into both of her opponents, calling Clayton a stooge for Republicans. She won the primary with ease, reaping 70 percent to Caraway's 18 percent and Clayton's 12 percent, and coasted to another reelection. In subsequent rematches with Caraway, whose husband Dwaine Caraway was interim mayor of Dallas in 2011, Johnson won the primary with 70 percent in 2014 and 69 percent in 2016. Following the 2016 election, Johnson broadly hinted that she would not seek reelection. "I want to wind it down and move on to what's out there for me," she told a local television station. By April 2017, the *News* reported that she had changed her tune and was planning to seek one more term. If nothing else, her uncertainty and the recent futile challenges have opened the door for Johnson's potential successors to make plans.

Central and Southern Dallas Metro

Population		**Race and Ethnicity**		**Income**	
Total	733,277	White	15.8%	Median Income	$42,146 (367 out of 435)
Land area	356	Black	43.8%		
Pop/ sq mi	2058.2	Latino	37.0%		
Born in state	64.2%	Asian	1.8%	Under $50,000	57.2%
Age Groups		Two races	1.3%	$50,000-$99,999	28.3%
Under 18	28.1%	Other	0.2%	$100,000-$199,999	12.4%
18-34	25.1%	**Education**		$200,000 or more	2.2%
35-64	37.6%	H.S grad or less	51.8%	Poverty Rate	24.2%
Over 64	9.2%	Some college	28.6%	**Health Insurance**	
Work		College Degree, 4 yr	13.3%	With health insurance coverage	74.9%
White Collar	28.1%	Post grad	6.4%		
Sales and Service	45.1%	**Military**		**Public Assistance**	
Blue Collar	26.8%	Veteran	6.2%	Cash public assistance income	2.3%
Government	5.3%	Active Duty	0.1%	Food stamp/SNAP benefits	20.6%

Voter Turnout			
2015 Total Citizens 18+	443,709	2016 House Turnout as % CVAP	47%
2016 House turnout	208,826	2014 House Turnout as % CVAP	24%

2012 Presidential Vote		
Barack Obama	175,637	(80%)
Mitt Romney	43,333	(20%)

2016 Presidential Vote		
Hillary Clinton	174,528	(79%)
Donald Trump	40,333	(18%)
Gary Johnson	4,276	(2%)

Cook Partisan Voting Index: D+29

In 1923, Texas adopted the "white primary," which barred blacks from participating in statewide Democratic primary elections, although blacks who could pay a poll tax were permitted to vote in general elections, municipal elections, school board elections, special elections and on ballot propositions. By 1947, Dallas County had a majority-black electorate, and yet despite this, there was no congressional district in North Texas that was considered likely to elect a black representative until the creation of the 30th Congressional District in 1991. Its creation was insisted on by the then-chairwoman of the Texas Senate's redistricting committee, and the result was a grotesquely shaped district. Its center was south and east Dallas, but it had tentacles as complex as a Portuguese Man O' War. Since then, lawsuits and four more rounds of redistricting have smoothed out the lines and left the 30th as one of two heavily minority Democratic districts in the Dallas-Fort Worth Metroplex.

The Dallas-Fort Worth metro area in 2015 was the second-fastest growing area in the nation, behind only Houston; Dallas can continue to claim bragging rights as the largest metro area in Texas, though Houston was only 7 percent smaller. Dallas-area officials have been responding to the growth. In October 2016, the board of Dallas Area Rapid Transit approved plans for a new downtown subway line. Two months later, the city approved a 10,000-acre nature district along the Trinity River.

Today, the 30th District consists of most of the south side of Dallas, with one tentacle running northwest, out Stemmons Freeway to Love Field. In between is the "mixmaster," where three busy highways - Interstates 30, 35E and 45 - come together within a square mile, surrounding many of the prominent sites in Dallas. Further south, it embraces African-American majority towns such as Cedar Hill, Glenn Heights and upscale DeSoto, as well as minority-majority locales like Duncanville and Hutchins. The court-drawn map in the latest redistricting removed much of the district's previous Hispanic population and placed it in the newly created 33rd District. But Hispanics have continued to surge in South Dallas. The 30th District's population is now 44 percent African American and 39 percent Hispanic; the latter are mostly young and foreign-born and less likely to vote, and 90 percent of them are from Mexico. The growing influence of racial minorities in the city has been a major factor in Democrats' gaining control of many Dallas County offices and seats in the Texas Legislature. This district is overwhelmingly Democratic, and the party's strongest in Texas.

THIRTY-FIRST DISTRICT

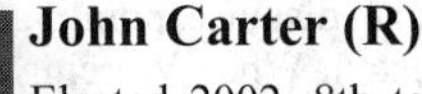

John Carter (R)

Elected 2002, 8th term; b. Nov 06, 1941, Houston; Texas Technical University, B.A.; University of Texas Law School, J.D.; Lutheran; Married (Erika Carter); 4 children; 6 grandchildren.

Elected Office: Williamson County TX District Court judge, 1981-2001.

Professional Career: Practicing attorney, 1969-1981.

DC Office: 2110 RHOB 20515, 202-225-3864, Fax: 202-225-5886, carter.house.gov.

State Offices: Round Rock, 512-246-1600; Temple, 254-933-1392.

Committees: *Appropriations*: Commerce, Justice, Science & Related Agencies, Defense, Homeland Security (Chmn).

Group Ratings

	ADA	ACLU	AFL-CIO	LCV	ITI	COC	HAFA	ACU	CFG	FRC
2016	-	5%	-	0%	100%	100%	65%	80%	70%	100%
2015	0%	C	10%	0%	C	89%	C	74%	76%	100%

Almanac Ratings 2015

	Economy	Social	Foreign	Composite
Liberal	9%	12%	11%	10%
Conservative	92%	88%	90%	90%

Key Votes of the 114th Congress

1. Keystone Pipeline	Y	5. Puerto Rico Debt	N	9. Offenses by Aliens	Y
2. Trade Deals	Y	6. Medical Marijuana	N	10. Troops in Iraq	N
3. Export-Import Bank	N	7. Sanctuary Cities	Y	11. Homeland Security $$	Y
4. Debt Ceiling Increase	Y	8. Armor-piercing Bullets	Y	12. Trade Adjustment aid	Y

Election Results

Election	Name (Party)	Vote (%)		Cand. Spent	Ind. Exp. Support	Ind. Exp. Oppose
2016 General	John Carter (R)	166,060	(58%)	$1,172,397		
	Mike Clark (D)	103,852	(37%)	$24,361		
	Scott Ballard (L)	14,676	(5%)			
2016 Primary	John Carter (R)	62,718	(71%)			
	Mike Sweeney (R)	25,270	(29%)			

Prior winning percentages: 2014 (64%), 2012 (61%), 2010 (83%), 2008 (60%), 2006 (59%), 2004 (65%), 2002 (69%)

John Carter, a conservative Republican first elected in 2002, brings an ex-judge's no-nonsense, law-and-order perspective to homeland security and immigration as chairman of the Appropriations subcommittee with jurisdiction over those issues. He is respected as an informal leader among House Republicans, though he has not been afraid to show his independence of party leadership.

Carter grew up in Houston and graduated from Texas Tech University and the University of Texas law school. He practiced law in Williamson County and served as a municipal judge in Round Rock. He was appointed a district judge in 1981 by Republican Gov. Bill Clements and in 1982 stood for election. Judicial elections are partisan in Texas, and Carter was the first GOP judge elected in Williamson County. He became known as the father of the county Republican Party.

In 2001, after a three-judge district court created a new Republican district stretching from Williamson County to Houston, Carter retired from the bench and ran for the seat. The real contest was among the eight candidates for the Republican nomination. Carter's main rivals were Peter Wareing, the son-in-law of Texas oilman Jack Blanton, and Brad Barton, son of Rep. Joe Barton of the 6th District. In the primary, Wareing led with 37 percent to 26 percent for Carter and 16 percent for Barton.

In the runoff, Carter attacked Wareing as a liberal in disguise, pointing to his campaign contributions to Democrats like Rep. Sheila Jackson Lee of Houston. When Wareing proposed that each candidate sign a "clean campaign pledge," Carter offered what he called a "homestead pledge" - a ploy to highlight his charge that Wareing was a Houston carpetbagger who had rented an apartment in the district to run for the seat. Rep. Barton endorsed Carter as "the only true conservative in this race." Wareing outspent Carter more than 2-to-1, but Carter won 57%-43%. He got 78 percent of the vote in Williamson County, which cast 33 percent of the vote. Carter won the general election easily and has had little trouble winning reelection.

Carter has been a reliable conservative, but not a hard-liner. His *Almanac* ratings for 2015 placed him in the center of House Republicans, the least conservative GOP member from Texas. As an Appropriations Committee member, he opposed some of the bolder GOP proposals to cut spending in 2012, such as an across-the-board cut in energy and water spending. He fought off a Republican attempt in 2011 to sharply cut spending for military bands, arguing that they "are an integral part to the patriotism that keeps our soldiers' hearts beating fast." In 2010, he accused the Pentagon of watering down a report on the 2009 Fort Hood shootings to avoid discussing Islamic terrorism. After years of efforts, he was successful in enacting a bill in 2015 that awarded Purple Heart medals to the shooting victims so their families could receive benefits. In 2016, he enacted his POLICE (Protecting Our Lives through Initiating COPS Expansion) Act, which was designed to increase active shooter training for law-enforcement officers - partly in response to the Fort Hood incident.

As chairman of the Homeland Security Appropriations Subcommittee, Carter fought for spending more to secure the U.S.-Mexico border, but also acknowledged the need to "show compassion" to immigrants who are already in the United States. In February 2015, he cooperated with Speaker John Boehner on the House GOP leadership strategy to use the Homeland Security spending bill to try to force President Barack Obama to back down on his executive actions to loosen restrictions on immigrants from Mexico. Senate Democrats held firm against any compromise, and Republicans eventually agreed to approve full-year funding of Carter's bill rather than force a shutdown. His work on Appropriations brought benefits to Fort Hood, including funding of a new hospital, $61 million to upgrade the barracks and $50 million to renovate the cavalry headquarters. He has served four terms as co-chairman of the bipartisan House Army Caucus.

Carter took part in bipartisan discussions to seek a legislative compromise on a broader immigration measure. With fellow GOP Rep. Sam Johnson of Texas, he quit the group in September 2013 because, they said, Obama was using the immigration issue to "advance his political agenda." With President Donald Trump supporting a wall along the border with Mexico, Carter was supportive in general terms. In February 2017, he joined Speaker Paul Ryan for a horseback tour of part of the border.

Before he joined Appropriations, Carter served on the Judiciary Committee, where he passed his Terrorist Penalties Enhancement Act and a bill to establish penalties for identity theft. In January 2017, he joined Republican Rep. Jeff Duncan of South Carolina in filing a bill to relax restrictions on gun silencers, which is a priority of the National Rifle Association. Carter has been a leader of the Texas Republican delegation and still likes to be called "Judge." He served three terms in the leadership as House Republican Conference secretary, and was in 2009 the chief antagonist on ethics charges against Democratic Rep. Charles Rangel, who was chairman of the Ways and Means Committee.

In 2016, Carter had a GOP primary challenge from political newcomer Mike Sweeney, who called for elimination of several federal agencies and criticized Carter for his "votes to fund the Obama agenda." Sweeney, who had a successful software business, spent $10,000, of which half was self-financed. Carter spent $1.2 million in the campaign cycle and got 71 percent of the vote, a signal of some conservative unrest.

Central Texas: Williamson and Bell Counties

Population		**Race and Ethnicity**		**Income**	
Total	759,528	White	58.0%	Median Income	$63,625 (104 out of 435)
Land area	2,154	Black	10.8%		
Pop/ sq mi	352.5	Latino	23.5%		
Born in state	51.9%	Asian	4.4%	Under $50,000	38.6%
		Two races	2.7%	$50,000-$99,999	34.1%
Age Groups		Other	0.6%	$100,000-$199,999	22.6%
Under 18	27.3%			$200,000 or more	4.7%
18-34	24.5%	**Education**		Poverty Rate	10.7%
35-64	37.7%	H.S grad or less	32.4%		
Over 64	10.5%	Some college	34.1%	**Health Insurance**	
		College Degree, 4 yr	22.4%	With health insurance coverage	86.7%
Work		Post grad	11.1%		
White Collar	41.2%				
Sales and Service	41.5%	**Military**		**Public Assistance**	
Blue Collar	17.3%	Veteran	13.7%	Cash public assistance income	1.7%
Government	5.7%	Active Duty	2.9%	Food stamp/SNAP benefits	8.7%

Voter Turnout			
2015 Total Citizens 18+	514,420	2016 House Turnout as % CVAP	55%
2016 House turnout	284,588	2014 House Turnout as % CVAP	27%

2012 Presidential Vote		
Mitt Romney	144,634	(60%)
Barack Obama	92,842	(38%)

2016 Presidential Vote		
Donald Trump	153,823	(53%)
Hillary Clinton	117,181	(40%)
Gary Johnson	13,735	(5%)

Cook Partisan Voting Index: R+10

In 1932, Williamson County was a rural backwater that cast a little more than 7,000 votes for president; Franklin Roosevelt won all but 431 of them. Today it has become a major population and business center deep in the heart of Texas, casting 200,000 votes in 2016. Its population has virtually doubled in every recent decade. It had 40,000 people in 1970, 80,000 in 1980, 140,000 in 1990, 250,000 in 2000, 427,000 in 2010 and 529,000 in 2016. Williamson County is just north of Austin, and much of this growth has been generated by the area's high-technology boom - Austin's city limits actually now spill over into Williamson. The county long ago moved beyond a bedroom suburb. Hugely successful computer producer Dell is headquartered in Round Rock (the rock, which served as an important wagon crossing, is in the middle of Brushy Creek, with wheel ruts still visible). Dell had more than 14,000 local employees, though it suffered layoffs following its merger in 2016 with EMC Corp. Texas 130, a 49-mile, 10-lane toll road with a speed limit of 85 miles per hour in parts, has generated more growth. Georgetown, which has become a popular retirement destination, was the fastest-growing city in the nation in 2015, with a population increase from 28,000 in 2000 to 64,000 in 2015. In March 2017, the city became one of the first in the country that is powered entirely on renewable energy, both wind and solar.

Bell County, just north of Williamson County, is home to part of Fort Hood, the largest U.S. military base in the world in terms of acreage. The base is the only U.S. post capable of supporting two full armored divisions. Its mission - maintaining combat readiness, including training Army reservists in urban combat - explains its size; it covers 218,000 acres, or, 340 square miles, an area larger than New York's five boroughs. Killeen, home of the base, has been growing rapidly and had the most affordable housing of a mid-sized Texas city in 2014. Ford Hood is where Maj. Nidal Malik Hasan in 2009 killed 13 people and wounded 38 others. East of Fort Hood is Temple, a rail center and the birthplace of Miriam "Ma" Ferguson, wife of Gov. James "Pa" Ferguson, who was elected governor in 1925 after her husband was impeached and convicted.

The 31st Congressional District is an unusually compact district by modern Texas standards. It is entirely contained within Bell and Williamson counties, and takes in almost all of each. Williamson has 70 percent of the population. Historically this was solidly Democratic country, devoted to the party of the Confederacy and then the New Deal. It was populated by cotton farmers who distrusted Wall Street and railroads and who trusted politicians like Sam Rayburn and Lyndon Johnson and, later, Gov. Ann Richards and Sen. Lloyd Bentsen. These people took a shine to Ronald Reagan's and George W. Bush's brand of Republicanism. It became a safely Republican area, Mitt Romney got 60 percent of the vote in 2012. With the large tech workforce, the GOP presidential vote dropped to 53 percent for Donald Trump in 2016.

THIRTY-SECOND DISTRICT

Pete Sessions (R)

Elected 1996, 11th term; b. Mar 22, 1955, Waco; Southwestern University (TX), B.S.; Southwest Texas State University, Att.; Methodist; Married (Karen Sessions); 2 children; 3 stepchildren.

Professional Career: District Manager, SW Bell Telephone Co., 1978-1993; Vice President, Public Policy, National Center for Policy Analysis, 1994-1995.

DC Office: 2233 RHOB 20515, 202-225-2231, Fax: 202-225-5878, sessions.house.gov.

State Offices: Dallas, 972-392-0505.

Committees: *Rules (Chmn)*: Rules & Organization of the House.

Group Ratings

	ADA	ACLU	AFL-CIO	LCV	ITI	COC	HAFA	ACU	CFG	FRC
2016	-	5%	-	0%	100%	100%	70%	92%	85%	100%
2015	0%	C	13%	0%	C	84%	C	88%	79%	100%

Almanac Ratings 2015

	Economy	Social	Foreign	Composite
Liberal	3%	0%	0%	1%
Conservative	97%	100%	100%	99%

Key Votes of the 114th Congress

1. Keystone Pipeline	Y	5. Puerto Rico Debt	Y	9. Offenses by Aliens	Y
2. Trade Deals	Y	6. Medical Marijuana	N	10. Troops in Iraq	N
3. Export-Import Bank	N	7. Sanctuary Cities	Y	11. Homeland Security $$	N
4. Debt Ceiling Increase	N	8. Armor-piercing Bullets	Y	12. Trade Adjustment aid	N

Election Results

Election	Name (Party)	Vote	(%)	Cand. Spent	Ind. Exp. Support	Ind. Exp. Oppose
2016 General	Pete Sessions (R)	162,868	(71%)	$2,269,937	$31,230	
	Ed Rankin (L)	43,490	(19%)			
	Gary Stuard (G)	22,813	(10%)	$1,710		
2016 Primary	Pete Sessions (R)	49,632	(61%)			
	Russ Ramsland (R)	19,105	(24%)			
	Paul Brown (R)	9,462	(12%)			

Prior winning percentages: 2014 (62%), 2012 (58%), 2010 (63%), 2008 (57%), 2006 (56%), 2004 (54%), 2002 (68%), 2000 (54%), 1998 (56%), 1996 (53%)

Pete Sessions, a Republican first elected in 1996, chairs the Rules Committee, a job that allows him to indulge his fondness for ritual sparring with Democrats while upholding the leadership's priorities. He previously chaired the National Republican Congressional Committee, where he guided his party to a 63-seat gain and control of the House in 2010. He has been stymied in his hopes to move up in GOP leadership. Election Day 2016 unexpectedly revealed that he likely will face a well-supported Democratic challenger in 2018 - and perhaps beyond.

Sessions grew up in Waco, graduated from Southwestern University, then worked at Southwestern Bell in Dallas for 16 years. His father is William Sessions, a federal judge who served as director of the Federal Bureau of Investigation from 1987 to 1993. The vagaries of redistricting in Texas have led Sessions to run for Congress in several different House districts. In 1991, he ran and finished sixth in the special election in the 3rd District, which then included much of North Dallas.

In 1993, he resigned from the phone company to run against Democratic Rep. John Bryant in the 5th District, which included much of the east side of Dallas and several rural counties to the south. Sessions ran a vigorous campaign, making a two-day, 12-city tour of the district's rural portions with a livestock trailer full of horse manure and a sign saying, "The Clinton health care plan stinks worse than this trailer." Although he outspent Sessions 2-to-1 in 1994, Bryant won by just 50%-47%. Two years later, Bryant ran, unsuccessfully, for the Senate. Sessions faced Democrat John Pouland, a former regional General Services Administration director. Sessions charged that Pouland was a big-government liberal and would abandon U.S. military bases overseas. Pouland criticized Republican cuts in Medicare. Sessions won 53%-47%.

Sessions' voting record placed him in the top 10 percent of conservative Republicans in the 2015 *Almanac* vote ratings. Still, some conservative blogs and websites have questioned whether he is too much a part of the Washington establishment that they loathe. He has had a litany of actions that reveal his leanings. Sessions sponsored the constitutional amendment to require a two-thirds vote to raise taxes, was a leading advocate of the Republican proposal to stop the government from spending Social Security and Medicare surpluses, and called for scrapping the income tax code. When President Barack Obama laid out a liberal agenda in his 2013 State of the Union address, Sessions told *The New York Times*: "We're now managing America's demise, not America's great future." He is generally tightfisted but is apt to support government spending to help families with disabled children. Sessions has a son with Down syndrome.

Sessions sought to get on the House leadership track by running in 2006 for chairman of the NRCC, which raises money for Republicans and recruits challengers in House races. He lost to Republican Tom Cole of Oklahoma. After the 2008 election, Sessions won a second try to head the NRCC. He had the strong support of Republican Leader John Boehner: Sessions was among the few Texas Republicans who had backed Boehner for party leader against Roy Blunt of Missouri in 2006. Cole wanted a second term as NRCC chairman, but he carried the burden of the party's 21-seat loss in the November 2008 election.

Sessions had a rocky start as chairman. Republicans lost a seat in a special election in upstate New York. He drew criticism for holding fundraisers at risqué venues that were at odds with the party's family-values image. He was lampooned by Democrats for what they considered odd comments, including his statement that Obama was trying "to inflict damage and hardship on the free enterprise system, if not to kill it." Sessions set a challenging goal of gaining the 40 seats the party needed to recapture the majority in 2010, and reorganized the committee to improve fundraising, communications and candidate recruitment. He was not in complete command of the job, as Boehner reportedly sat in on major strategy meetings. Sessions joined the Tea Party Caucus and channeled its members' anger at big spending, while helping to mesh the GOP message to that theme. The Republicans' huge gain in November was the largest party switch since 1948.

Sessions considered using his political capital to run for majority whip in November 2010, but decided against challenging California's politically savvy Kevin McCarthy. Boehner gave Sessions added responsibilities as NRCC chairman to advise new members taking office on how to coordinate their House work schedule with their reelection campaigns.

In the 2012 election season, Sessions predicted that Republicans would pick up as many as seven new seats "because we are playing offense, not trying to protect what we have." Democrats netted eight seats and outgained the GOP in the total popular vote. But the nationwide redistricting gave Republicans the edge, and they retained control that year-and until at least the 2022 redistricting, many House experts have believed.

With his seat on the Rules Committee, Sessions has promoted the Republican message. Boehner chose him in November 2012 to succeed retiring chairman David Dreier of California. Rules meetings can often set off partisan sparks, as was the case in February 2015. Outspoken Democrat Alcee Hastings of Florida declared that Texas is "a crazy state" and that he would never want to live there. Though Sessions wasn't present at the hearing, he took the House floor to defend his state. "Texans are a proud people, and we've been a proud people since the days of the Alamo," Sessions said. "While some people may think that limited government and empowering families is 'crazy,' I disagree."

When Majority Leader Eric Cantor unexpectedly lost his primary in June 2014, Sessions flirted again with seeking a leadership post. He told reporters that he was running and cited the big boost that he expected to receive from the Texas delegation. Less than 48 hours after Cantor's defeat, he changed his mind and decided for a second time not to challenge McCarthy, saying that running a successful campaign "would have created unnecessary and painful division within our party." Other Republicans said that McCarthy already had locked up the needed support. Some conservatives reportedly approached Sessions about running for McCarthy's old whip job, but he declined after brief consideration. A failed leadership bid would have jeopardized his continuation as chairman of Rules, where Sessions remained influential in the business of the House. Likewise, when Boehner stepped down in October 2015, Sessions briefly voiced interest in replacing him - after McCarthy fell short and before Republicans rallied behind Ryan.

In 2016, Sessions became part of two internal House conflicts. After Democrats held their overnight sit-in on the House floor to protest Republicans' refusal to consider gun-control legislation, he threatened an investigation of House rules violations. Republicans later changes House rules to penalize lawmakers who use their phones to broadcast videos in the House. He supported a change in House ethics rules to reduce the independence of the Office of Congressional Ethics. Following widespread public objections, including from President-elect Donald Trump, GOP leaders dropped the proposal.

Sessions has had his own roller-coaster electoral history. In 2001, he unexpectedly left the safe 5th to run in the newly created and more upscale 32nd, which had no incumbent but included only 16 percent of his old district. He said he wanted to spend less time traveling around his district - the 32nd was considerably more compact - and he thought it more compatible with his pro-business philosophy. Sessions had only token primary opposition and won the seat, 68%-30%. Ironically, his successor in the 5th was Jeb Hensarling, who has become the influential chairman of the Financial Services Committee and has continuing leadership ambitions.

In 2003, Tom DeLay of Texas, the powerful House majority leader, persuaded the Republican-controlled Texas Legislature to draw the lines yet again. Although most GOP members were well-served by the new lines, Sessions wound up in a somewhat less Republican district and with a reelection challenge from 13-term Democratic incumbent Martin Frost, whose 24th District had been shorn of its most Democratic precincts. The contest became the most expensive House campaign of 2004. Sessions spent $4.5 million and Frost $4.8 million, and much more was spent by party committees and independent groups. Sessions won 54%-44%, capturing more than 80 percent of the vote in some Park Cities precincts; Frost failed to get the higher turnout he needed in increasingly Hispanic Oak Cliff.

Sessions has been reelected without difficulty since then. In 2014, he fended off a primary challenge from Katrina Pierson, a tea party activist who was a top volunteer on Republican Ted Cruz's 2012 Senate campaign and later became a prominent spokesman for Trump in his presidential campaign. But she failed to raise serious money - $144,000 to Sessions' $1.5 million - and Sessions won 64%-36%. In 2016, he easily disposed of credible challengers in the GOP primary. Businessman Russ Ramsland spent $332,000 and had tea party support, but trailed, 61%-24%; the well-financed Sessions spent $2.6 million during the campaign cycle. In the general election, when no Democrat ran, Sessions got 71 percent of the vote against Libertarian and Green Party challengers.

Following the 2016 election, Democrats sought to make up for their missed opportunity by listing Sessions as a top target in 2018 and contended that Trump's brand of conservatism would cause complications for the incumbent. Sessions and GOP campaign strategists dismissed the Democrats' claims, though he likely will be prepared. "If the Democrats want to think they can take their party, that is dead, and resurrect something in Texas 32, bring it on," he told the *Dallas Morning News* in December. A potential complication remained the possibility of a credible GOP primary challenger to Sessions.

Northern Dallas Metro

Population		**Race and Ethnicity**		**Income**	
Total	732,953	White	50.4%	Median Income	$63,573 (105 out of 435)
Land area	186	Black	12.0%		
Pop/ sq mi	3947.8	Latino	26.8%		
Born in state	51.4%	Asian	7.8%	Under $50,000	39.3%
		Two races	2.7%	$50,000-$99,999	29.9%
Age Groups		Other	0.4%	$100,000-$199,999	21.1%
Under 18	24.3%			$200,000 or more	9.8%
18-34	25.1%	**Education**		Poverty Rate	13.9%
35-64	39.6%	H.S grad or less	31.8%		
Over 64	11.0%	Some college	26.1%	**Health Insurance**	
Work		College Degree, 4 yr	26.7%	With health insurance coverage	80.7%
White Collar	43.1%	Post grad	15.4%		
Sales and Service	40.4%	**Military**		**Public Assistance**	
Blue Collar	16.5%	Veteran	6.2%	Cash public assistance income	1.2%
Government	7.3%	Active Duty	0.0%		
				Food stamp/SNAP benefits	9.3%

Voter Turnout			
2015 Total Citizens 18+	468,242	2016 House Turnout as % CVAP	49%
2016 House turnout	229,171	2014 House Turnout as % CVAP	34%

2012 Presidential Vote		
Mitt Romney	146,420	(57%)
Barack Obama	106,563	(42%)

2016 Presidential Vote		
Hillary Clinton	134,895	(48%)
Donald Trump	129,701	(46%)
Gary Johnson	11,358	(4%)

Cook Partisan Voting Index: R+5

North Dallas has long been the home of the city's elite and, indeed, a slice of the nation's elite. Early in the 20th century, the richest citizens started moving away from old neighborhoods adjacent to downtown and out past Turtle Creek to the area around the suburbs of Highland Park and University Park - the Park Cities. Dallas grew lustily from mid-century. Beyond the Park Cities, miles of affluent neighborhoods were built, especially between the Central Expressway and the Dallas North Tollway. Gallerias and office complexes followed. An entertainment and singles apartment corridor runs along Greenville Avenue, plus working-class neighborhoods here and there, and pockets of Latino neighborhoods near the freeways. Overall, the tone has been set by Dallas' upper crust.

Highland Park and University Park are well-heeled and over 90 percent white in increasingly diverse Dallas. University Park is the larger of the two, which have a combined population of 34,000 and median household income of about $180,000. In the 1990s, George W. Bush and Dick Cheney lived in or near the Park Cities. After eight years in the White House, the Bushes returned to their Preston Hollow neighborhood, to an 8,500-square-foot home on an acre of land a few miles from his presidential library at Southern Methodist University. In November 2015, local voters approved, 55%-45%, a $361 million school bond, with some opponents reportedly raising fears that the result would increase the minority population. The much larger and still-growing urban center is Garland, with a population of 240,000, majority-minority residents and household income of $52,000. Its largest private-sector employers are the Baylor Medical Center and Kraft Foods. Just to the east in Rowlett, developers began work in March 2017 on a $1 billion mixed-use development project on 260 acres along the shores of Lake Ray Hubbard, including an eight-acre constructed lagoon.

In 1954, voters here elected strict conservative Rep. Bruce Alger, who was only the third Republican to represent any portion of the state in the 20th century. But North Dallas and the 32nd Congressional District of Texas now reflect the political trends driving 21st century politics: As upper-income suburbanites drifted toward the Democrats and the minority population of north Dallas County increased, the district has moved leftward. Mitt Romney won here with 57 percent of the vote in 2012, and its Republican congressman has struggled to exceed 60 percent in recent elections. Still, few were prepared for the stunning outcome in 2016, when Hillary Clinton led Donald Trump, 48%-46%. Local Democrats who failed to run a congressional challenger were among the most surprised.

The Republican-engineered redistricting in 2011 dropped the Hispanic share of the population from 43 percent to 28 percent, and improved Republican performance by a few points. The district includes a thin slice of Collin County that takes in some of fast-growing, upscale Wylie; more than 90 percent of the 32nd is in Dallas County. The district still has Democratic pockets around racially diverse Richardson and the downtown area.

THIRTY-THIRD DISTRICT

Marc Veasey (D)

Elected 2012, 3rd term; b. Jan 03, 1971, Tarrant County; Texas Wesleyan University, B.S.; Christian Church; Married (Tonya Veasey); 1 child.

Elected Office: TX House, 2005-2013.

Professional Career: Staffer, Rep. Martin Frost, 1998-2004; Commercial real-estate broker.

DC Office: 1519 LHOB 20515, 202-225-9897, Fax: 202-225-9702, veasey.house.gov.

State Offices: Dallas, 214-741-1387; Fort Worth, 817-920-9086.

Committees: *Armed Services*: Emerging Threats & Capabilities, Tactical Air & Land Forces. *Science, Space & Technology*: Energy (RMM), Space.

Group Ratings

	ADA	ACLU	AFL-CIO	LCV	ITI	COC	HAFA	ACU	CFG	FRC
2016	-	76%	-	84%	67%	71%	17%	0%	16%	0%
2015	80%	C	100%	86%	C	60%	C	0%	2%	0%

Almanac Ratings 2015

	Economy	Social	Foreign	Composite
Liberal	82%	95%	58%	78%
Conservative	18%	5%	42%	22%

Key Votes of the 114th Congress

1. Keystone Pipeline	Y	5. Puerto Rico Debt	Y	9. Offenses by Aliens	N
2. Trade Deals	N	6. Medical Marijuana	Y	10. Troops in Iraq	N
3. Export-Import Bank	Y	7. Sanctuary Cities	N	11. Homeland Security $$	Y
4. Debt Ceiling Increase	Y	8. Armor-piercing Bullets	N	12. Trade Adjustment aid	Y

Election Results

Election	Name (Party)	Vote (%)		Cand. Spent	Ind. Exp. Support	Ind. Exp. Oppose
2016 General	Marc Veasey (D)	93,147	(74%)	$1,186,155		
	Mark Mitchell (R)	33,222	(26%)	$24,302		
2016 Primary	Marc Veasey (D)	20,494	(63%)			
	Carlos Quintanilla (D)	11,837	(37%)			

Prior winning percentages: 2014 (87%), 2012 (73%)

Democrat Marc Veasey won a hard-fought primary in 2012 to claim the seat in the 33rd District, which was created by the 2011 redistricting. As an African American in this heavily Hispanic district, he has faced continuing challenges. His deep political background has educated him on those dynamics. That experience gave him a head start in the House, where he uses his seat on the Armed Services Committee to look after the needs of local defense contractors.

Veasey, a commercial real estate broker, was born and still lives in Fort Worth. He credits his involvement in politics to his uncle, who worked for Fort Worth's Jim Wright, the Democratic Speaker of the House from 1987 to 1989. After watching a White House press briefing on television in his mid-teens, Veasey remembers asking his uncle what it would take to get such a job, and his uncle advised he get a college degree.

After graduating from Texas Wesleyan University, Veasey held a string of jobs, including substitute teaching, writing phone-book ads and working for local Democratic Rep. Martin Frost. As a Frost staffer, he worked to attract a grocery store to a poor section of Fort Worth to create jobs and enable residents to buy fresh produce. He secured transportation funding for the district's roads. Veasey ran for the state House in 2004 out of frustration with an incumbent who refused to join other Texas Democrats in leaving the state to protest GOP-led redistricting. He chaired the Democratic Caucus, served on an environmental regulations committee and dealt with banking and pension issues - all while suffering the limitations of the minority party.

His main competition in the decisive primary for the House seat was Dallas attorney Domingo Garcia. The contest polarized black voters who supported Veasey and Hispanics who largely supported Garcia; it also developed into a regional spat between Veasey from Fort Worth and Garcia from crosstown rival Dallas. In the initial balloting, Veasey bested Garcia, 37%-25%, not enough to avoid a runoff. In the runoff campaign, Veasey targeted the Democratic base and black voters on his home turf. Garcia accused him of "playing the race card" by spending a lot of time in Fort Worth's black neighborhoods. But it turned out to be a good strategy. Voters in Tarrant County turned out in higher proportions than those in Dallas County.

Garcia failed to galvanize Hispanics the way that Veasey excited African Americans as the first black to represent Tarrant County in Congress, despite Hispanics outnumbering blacks four-to-one, though more narrowly among registered voters. He made costly mistakes in the campaign, such as his call to scrap the F-35 plane even though it was responsible for more than 40,000 local jobs. And he labeled Veasey an "errand boy for the establishment" - and then refused to apologize for use of the racially charged term "boy" because, he said, he didn't mean it as a slur. Veasey won the runoff 53%-47%. He got 68 percent of the vote in Tarrant County, which cast 59 percent of the total, and was careful to sound a conciliatory note in his acceptance speech. "Despite what the pundits said, this election was never about Dallas versus Fort Worth. It was never about African Americans versus Hispanics," he said to cheering supporters in Fort Worth, according to *The Dallas Morning News*. "This election was about making sure North Texans were represented fairly and honestly. In November, Veasey had no trouble defeating Republican Chuck Bradley, 73%-26%.

Veasey got a seat on the Armed Services Committee, where he tended to the interests of the many military contractors in or near his district. When the annual defense spending bill passed the House in May 2015, he claimed credit for additional weapons procurement that will benefit his district plus a bipartisan agreement that required the Pentagon to review how illegal immigrants were serving in the military, including their eligibility for service. Veasey supported the merger of Fort Worth-based

American Airlines and U.S. Airways as a plus for local jobs, and he broke with the Obama administration in its 2013 objections to the deal on anti-competitive grounds. He was one of five Texas Democrats who split with Obama and their party to support the Keystone XL pipeline.

In 2016, Veasey organized two party caucuses to promote Democratic interests. The Congressional Voting Rights Caucus was designed to update the Voting Rights Act, following the 2013 ruling by the Supreme Court that struck down a key enforcement provision. Following the election, he and Rep. Brendan Boyle of Pennsylvania launched the Blue Collar Caucus to understand and address the economic anxiety of workers in various industries and to respond to what Veasey called the "scam" of President Donald Trump's outreach to workers.

He has faced primary challenges from Latino opponents, with varied results. In 2014, Tom Sanchez, a telecommunications lawyer, self-financed nearly all of his $1.5 million campaign. Although outspent, Veasey won easily, 73%-27%, and showed increased strength in Dallas County where he took 62 percent of the vote. The turnout in his home base of Tarrant County nearly doubled that in Dallas. The 2016 primary sent a warning to Veasey. Democratic challenger Carlos Quintanilla, a self-described "activist," did not report spending any money. But his grass-roots campaign gave him 52 percent of the vote in Dallas County, which cast 43 percent of the total vote in the higher presidential-year turnout. Veasey prevailed by taking 75 percent in Tarrant, which gave him 63 percent overall.

Local Democrats have talked up the possibility that another round of redistricting could create separate minority seats for blacks and Hispanics in the Metroplex, in addition to the longstanding 30th District.

Central Metroplex: Parts of Fort Worth and Dallas

Population		**Race and Ethnicity**		**Income**	
Total	720,668	White	16.1%	Median Income	$35,858 (421 out of 435)
Land area	212	Black	15.5%		
Pop/ sq mi	3400.3	Latino	65.1%		
Born in state	54.9%	Asian	2.2%	Under $50,000	65.9%
		Two races	0.8%	$50,000-$99,999	26.3%
Age Groups		Other	0.3%	$100,000-$199,999	6.9%
Under 18	31.6%			$200,000 or more	0.8%
18-34	26.4%	**Education**		Poverty Rate	28.3%
35-64	34.2%	H.S grad or less	70.4%		
Over 64	7.8%	Some college	20.1%	**Health Insurance**	
		College Degree, 4 yr	6.7%	With health insurance coverage	64.7%
Work		Post grad	2.6%		
White Collar	15.3%				
Sales and Service	44.0%	**Military**		**Public Assistance**	
Blue Collar	40.8%	Veteran	4.0%	Cash public assistance income	3.3%
Government	5.9%	Active Duty	0.0%		
				Food stamp/SNAP benefits	25.2%

Voter Turnout			
2015 Total Citizens 18+	321,492	2016 House Turnout as % CVAP	39%
2016 House turnout	126,369	2014 House Turnout as % CVAP	16%

2012 Presidential Vote		
Barack Obama	86,686	(72%)
Mitt Romney	32,641	(27%)

2016 Presidential Vote		
Hillary Clinton	94,513	(73%)
Donald Trump	30,787	(24%)
Gary Johnson	3,157	(2%)

Cook Partisan Voting Index: D+23

In the 1950s, the Dallas-Fort Worth Turnpike was built on empty land to link the two cities' downtowns. Over the next three decades, the land filled up, with as many people as the central cities had. Irving, Grand Prairie and Arlington grew up along the highway in the once impoverished region and became central to one of America's richest and most productive metropolitan areas. Major civic landmarks followed: Rangers Ballpark in Arlington, built by one-time managing partner George W. Bush, and the domed AT&T Stadium, home of the Dallas Cowboys.

Arlington and Grand Prairie are in their second generation, taking on the patina of age, but above them you still see the big Texas sky and, in the distance, the small bluffs that mark the Balcones Escarpment, the geological divide between flat and lush East Texas and rolling and dry West Texas. The turnover brought newcomers to these fast-growing areas: Arlington is now only 45 percent non-Hispanic white; Irving is 31 percent; Grand Prairie 29 percent.

The 33rd Congressional District of Texas, which covers this suburban zone, is a judicial creation. After the 2010 census, state Republicans in control of redistricting drew a 33rd District that combined Arlington with heavily Republican Parker and Wise counties. The court found that the arrangement violated the Voting Rights Act and created the minority-majority district, which is 67 percent Hispanic and 16 percent African American. Its jagged boundaries mesh with those of the African-American-controlled 30th District in Dallas.

The 33rd doesn't take in many of the industrial plants in the area, but its blue-collar workforce provides much of the manpower for Northrop Grumman, General Motors, Hughes Training, Bell Textron Helicopter and Lockheed Martin, all of which have facilities in or near the district. It has neighborhoods in western Dallas, including Oak Cliff, a collection of Victorian era mansions near the Trinity River that became heavily African American in the 1970s and 1980s as a result of white flight; it is now heavily Hispanic. Lee Harvey Oswald, who lived in a rooming house in Oak Cliff, took a cab the short distance from near Dealey Plaza to his home after killing President John Kennedy in November 1963 and then was arrested in the nearby Texas Theater.

The district also includes much of Grand Prairie and Irving, as well as tiny, almost-entirely Hispanic Cockrell Hill. Across a narrow tentacle of lightly populated precincts, the district has about a third of Fort Worth, including the old stockyards, where cattle drives are still conducted twice a day by real cattle drovers. The Tarrant County part of the district includes Forest Hill and parts of Arlington, including the sports stadiums. Several major commercial and retail projects are underway in the district: the $175 million Stockyards development in Fort Worth; the $180 million Music Factory entertainment and retail venue in Irving; and the voter-approved $1 billion baseball stadium in an entertainment complex adjacent to the site where the Rangers now play. Tarrant and Dallas counties each have about 50 percent of the voters of the 33rd. Overall, its 73 percent for Hillary Clinton in 2016 fell short of her 79 percent in the 30th, which is the other strongly Democratic district in the Metroplex.

THIRTY-FOURTH DISTRICT

Filemon Vela (D)

Elected 2012, 3rd term; b. Feb 13, 1963, Harlingen; Georgetown University (DC), B.A.; University of Texas, J.D.; Loyola University, New Orleans (LA), Att.; Roman Catholic; Married (Rose Vela).

Professional Career: Practicing attorney, 1988-2012.

DC Office: 437 CHOB 20515, 202-225-9901, Fax: 202-225-9770, vela.house.gov.

State Offices: Alice, 361-230-9776; Brownsville, 956-544-8352; San Benito, 956-276-4497; Weslaco, 956-520-8273.

Committees: *Agriculture*: Conservation & Forestry, Livestock & Foreign Agriculture. *Homeland Security*: Border & Maritime Security (RMM).

Group Ratings

	ADA	ACLU	AFL-CIO	LCV	ITI	COC	HAFA	ACU	CFG	FRC
2016	-	76%	-	82%	67%	77%	19%	4%	16%	0%
2015	70%	C	96%	80%	C	55%	C	8%	2%	0%

Almanac Ratings 2015

	Economy	Social	Foreign	Composite
Liberal	73%	91%	40%	68%
Conservative	28%	9%	60%	32%

Key Votes of the 114th Congress

1. Keystone Pipeline	Y	5. Puerto Rico Debt	N	9. Offenses by Aliens	N
2. Trade Deals	N	6. Medical Marijuana	Y	10. Troops in Iraq	N
3. Export-Import Bank	Y	7. Sanctuary Cities	NV	11. Homeland Security $$	Y
4. Debt Ceiling Increase	Y	8. Armor-piercing Bullets	N	12. Trade Adjustment aid	Y

Election Results

Election	Name (Party)	Vote (%)	Cand. Spent	Ind. Exp. Support	Ind. Exp. Oppose
2016 General	Filemon Vela (D).........................	104,638 (63%)	$451,528		
	Rey Gonzalez (R).........................	62,323 (37%)			
2016 Primary	Filemon Vela (D).....................	(100%)			

Prior winning percentages: 2014 (59.5%), 2012 (61.9%)

Democrat Filemon Vela won the 34th District House seat in part on the strength of his illustrious political family. Brownsville's federal courthouse bears the name of his late father, a federal district judge who was nominated by President Jimmy Carter and served more than two decades, and his mother was the city's first elected woman mayor. In his first elected office, Vela focused on local concerns: the border and agriculture.

Vela was born in Harlingen, at the southern tip of Texas, and raised in nearby Brownsville. After receiving a bachelor's degree from Georgetown University and a law degree from the University of Texas, he returned to Brownsville to practice law. As a civil attorney for 25 years, Vela represented school districts seeking restitution for shoddy construction by independent contractors. In one case, he recovered money spent by the district on a poorly built facility; in another, he won recompense for a malfunctioning air-quality control system.

When Vela launched his campaign, some political observers were surprised by the "D" next to his name. His wife was a Republican justice on the Texas Court of Appeals, and Vela acknowledged that he sometimes backed GOP office-seekers. He aligned himself with the Democratic agenda, calling for "a realistic and fair way" to deal with illegal immigration, protection of Medicare and Social Security benefits, and tax cuts for small businesses as an incentive to hire workers. Undoubtedly, he was mindful of the district's Democratic tilt.

His main rival for the Democratic nomination, Cameron County District Attorney Armando Villalobos, led the field in fundraising but was indicted on federal fraud charges two weeks before the May primary. Vela had a 40%-13% lead in the opening round and got 67 percent of the vote in the July runoff against Denise Saenz Blanchard, who was chief of staff to former Democratic Rep. Solomon Ortiz, who had represented the area for 28 years before he was defeated in 2010. Following the runoff, she told the Associated Press, "We now have a Republican who has converted to being a Democrat who I believe is taking a seat from the Democrats." In the general election, Vela gained the imprimatur of Nancy Pelosi, the House Democratic leader who headlined a fundraiser for Vela in August. He won, 62%-36%, and has retained that margin since.

Vela showed a strong interest in immigration issues and he has served as the ranking Democrat on the Homeland Security Subcommittee on Border and Maritime Security. He resigned from the Hispanic Caucus because he felt that the caucus was not objecting strongly enough to a provision in the Senate-passed immigration reform bill in 2013, which he believed was spending too much money on new barriers and border officials. The caucus agreed to his return. That year, he filed with Democratic Rep. Raul Grijalva of Arizona a comprehensive immigration bill in an effort to jump-start the House debate. In September 2015, the House passed Vela's bill to protect the United States from high-risk rail shipments involving radiation that cross the border. During the 2016 campaign, he was outspoken in his opposition to Donald Trump, especially his views on immigration. Vela sent him an open letter in June 2016 after Trump said that he would not get a fair trail from a judge who was Hispanic in a case dealing with Trump University. "Your ignorant anti-immigrant opinions, your border wall rhetoric, and your recent bigoted attack on an American jurist are just plain despicable," he wrote. "Mr. Trump, you're a racist and you can take your border wall and shove it up your ass." When Trump took initial steps to build a wall during his first few days as president in January 2017, Vela called it "a ridiculous proposition."

On the Agriculture Committee, Vela was a member of the House-Senate conference committee that approved the 2014 farm bill. He focused on assuring sufficient water from the Rio Grande for South Texas farmers and opposed cuts in food stamps. In 2017, House Democrats tapped him as their vice ranking member of the panel. His *Almanac* vote ratings in 2015 ranked him among the 10 percent most conservative House Democrats.

In 2014, Vela was reelected 59%-39% over Republican Larry Smith, who spent $120,000 and had a small lead among the one-third of district voters who did not reside in Cameron or Hidalgo counties. The same pattern applied in 2016 against his opponent, Rey Gonzalez Jr., who did not file a spending report for his campaign. Vela has become entrenched along the border. The growth of Hispanic political power in Texas could give him opportunities for increased influence.

Southern Gulf Coast: Brownsville, McAllen

Population		**Race and Ethnicity**		**Income**	
Total	717,149	White	14.4%	Median Income	$35,196 (424 out of 435)
Land area	8,190	Black	1.3%		
Pop/ sq mi	87.6	Latino	83.4%		
Born in state	69.1%	Asian	0.6%	Under $50,000	63.1%
		Two races	0.2%	$50,000-$99,999	24.5%
Age Groups		Other	0.1%	$100,000-$199,999	10.4%
Under 18	30.3%			$200,000 or more	2.0%
18-34	23.5%	**Education**		Poverty Rate	31.5%
35-64	33.5%	H.S grad or less	61.0%		
Over 64	12.7%	Some college	24.2%	**Health Insurance**	
		College Degree, 4 yr	10.4%	With health insurance coverage	70.1%
Work		Post grad	4.4%		
White Collar	26.7%				
Sales and Service	48.2%	**Military**		**Public Assistance**	
Blue Collar	25.2%	Veteran	6.2%	Cash public assistance income	2.3%
Government	8.7%	Active Duty	0.1%		
				Food stamp/SNAP benefits	26.3%

Voter Turnout			
2015 Total Citizens 18+	406,218	2016 House Turnout as % CVAP	41%
2016 House turnout	166,961	2014 House Turnout as % CVAP	20%

2012 Presidential Vote		
Barack Obama	90,885	(61%)
Mitt Romney	57,303	(38%)

2016 Presidential Vote		
Hillary Clinton	101,796	(59%)
Donald Trump	64,767	(38%)
Gary Johnson	4,042	(2%)

Cook Partisan Voting Index: D+10

At the far southern tip of Texas, just before the waters of the Rio Grande end their 1,900-mile journey from southern Colorado by washing out into the Gulf of Mexico, stands the fast-growing city of Brownsville. Situated across the river from Matamoros, Mexico, it is one of the country's major border crossings, and its history has been intertwined with U.S.-Mexican relations for much of its existence. Fort Texas, later renamed Fort Brown, was established in the run-up to the Mexican-American War. After the war ended, land speculators bought up property nearby, and the town of Brownsville was born. The First and Second Cortina wars took place here, as a private army under Juan Cortina did battle with Texas Rangers over perceived mistreatment of Mexican-American laborers. The last land engagement of the Civil War, the Battle of Palmito Ranch, was fought nearby, more than a month after Robert E. Lee surrendered at Appomattox. Later, Teddy Roosevelt notoriously gave dishonorable discharges to an entire regiment of African-American soldiers stationed in Brownsville for a purported cover-up of a murder. An investigation held more than 60 years later concluded the soldiers were innocent, and President Richard Nixon granted them pardons, all but two of which were issued posthumously.

Fort Brown was decommissioned in 1946, but Brownsville still stands at the crossroads of Mexican-American relations. A makeshift 18-foot steel fence has been constructed a mile north of the border, avoiding the complications of poor building conditions and private land ownership. The 1993 North American Free Trade Agreement has lifted the economy in parts of the area, and there has been a boom in commercial construction. Increased trade was expected to boost the local economy with completion of parts of Interstate 69 through the redesignation of former state highways; it eventually will link Brownsville with Port Huron, Michigan. But the slow-moving I-69 project has run into obstacles from state and local officials, including small-town business interests that fear a loss of retail transactions. In 2015, Brownsville had the highest poverty rate in the nation. The next two on the grim list are up the Rio Grande, Laredo and McAllen. Not far from the border is the *colonia* of Cameron Park, where people live in trailers or makeshift structures without water or sewer service. It is rated by the Census Bureau as one of the poorest places in the nation, with an annual per capita income of $8,100. One sign of hope has come from a new niche for Brownsville as the "ship-breaking" capital of the nation. In 2014, it dismantled a former aircraft carrier, the *Constellation*. The next year, three local companies were dismantling other Navy hulks. More than 90 percent of the cargo in the Brownsville port is to or from Mexico.

The 34th Congressional District of Texas stretches nearly 300 miles while reaching across 11 counties. More than half of its population is at the far southern end in Brownsville-based Cameron County and another 15 percent is in Hidalgo County. The rest of the district is mostly ranching country, with a handful of small towns that lean heavily Republican. Kleberg County is home to the vast grazing and oil lands of the 825,000-acre - that's 1,289 square miles, part-nuh! - King Ranch, which is bigger than Rhode Island. South Padre Island, part of the lengthy national seashore, is a popular spring-break beach destination. In the latest redistricting, this new district replaced much of the old 27th District, which has become Republican and is based north of Corpus Christi. With its 83 percent Hispanic population and solidly Democratic locales along the border, the 34th is a Democratic district. Hillary Clinton got 59 percent of the vote, compared with 61 percent for President Barack Obama in 2012; the turnout in 2016 was 10 percent lower.

THIRTY-FIFTH DISTRICT

Lloyd Doggett (D)

Elected 1994, 12th term; b. Oct 06, 1946, Austin; University of Texas; b.B.A.; University of Texas Law School, J.D.; Methodist; Married (Libby Belk Doggett); 2 children; 3 grandchildren.

Elected Office: TX Senate, 1973-1985; TX Supreme Court justice, 1989-1994.

Professional Career: Practicing attorney, 1970-1989; Adjunct Professional, University of TX Law School, 1989-1994.

DC Office: 2307 RHOB 20515, 202-225-4865, Fax: 202-225-3073, doggett.house.gov.

State Offices: Austin, 512-916-5921; San Antonio, 210-704-1080.

Committees: *Ways & Means*: Human Resources, Tax Policy (RMM), Trade.

Group Ratings

	ADA	ACLU	AFL-CIO	LCV	ITI	COC	HAFA	ACU	CFG	FRC
2016	-	94%	-	100%	50%	64%	14%	4%	0%	0%
2015	90%	C	100%	97%	C	39%	C	8%	3%	0%

Almanac Ratings 2015

	Economy	Social	Foreign	Composite
Liberal	95%	100%	81%	92%
Conservative	6%	0%	19%	8%

Key Votes of the 114th Congress

1. Keystone Pipeline	NV	5. Puerto Rico Debt	Y	9. Offenses by Aliens	N
2. Trade Deals	N	6. Medical Marijuana	Y	10. Troops in Iraq	N
3. Export-Import Bank	Y	7. Sanctuary Cities	N	11. Homeland Security $$	Y
4. Debt Ceiling Increase	Y	8. Armor-piercing Bullets	N	12. Trade Adjustment aid	Y

Election Results

Election	Name (Party)	Vote (%)		Cand. Spent	Ind. Exp. Support	Ind. Exp. Oppose
2016 General	Lloyd Doggett (D)	124,612	(63%)	$183,422		
	Susan Narvaiz (R)	62,384	(32%)	$127,131		
	Rhett Rosenquest Smith (L)	6,504	(3%)			
	Scott Trimble (G)	4,076	(2%)			
2016 Primary	Lloyd Doggett (D)		(100%)			

Prior winning percentages: 2014 (63%), 2012 (64%), 2010 (53%), 2008 (66%), 2006 (67%), 2004 (68%), 2002 (84%), 2000 (85%), 1998 (85%), 1996 (56%), 1994 (56%)

Lloyd Doggett, first elected in 1994, is a liberal Democrat and a respected voice in his party ontax and social-welfare issues, among others. His political views and pugnacity have made him a target of Texas' GOP-led redistricting, but he has eluded repeated efforts to draw him out of a seat. With a boost in seniority at the House Ways and Means Committee, he took over in 2017 as the ranking Democrat on the Tax Policy Subcommittee.

Doggett grew up in Austin, finished first in his class at the University of Texas, and was student body president. At age 26, he began his lengthy and relentless career with election to the state Senate, which had been under the control of conservative Democrats. In the 1970s, as part of a large liberal bloc, he pushed for laws against job discrimination and cop-killer bullets, and for generic drugs. He has long been a close ally of trial lawyers, a strong force supporting liberal Democrats in Texas. In the legislature, he was one of the "Killer Bees" who hid out to prevent a quorum on changing the rules in the Democratic primary and filibustered what he called anti-consumer bills.

In 1984, he ran for the Senate, narrowly edging out two House members to win the Democratic nomination. He lost the general election 59%-41% to Rep. Phil Gramm, a former who had switched parties. Doggett was elected to the Texas Supreme Court in 1988. When Democratic Rep. Jake Pickle retired after 31 years, Doggett ran for his Austin-based seat. He won the Democratic primary with token opposition and took the general 56%-40%.

Doggett's *Almanac* vote ratings in 2015 ranked him among the most liberal Democrats in Texas and near the center of his party nationally. He has worked closely with Democratic Leader Nancy Pelosi and was a leader in opposing the resolution authorizing the use of force in Iraq. At times highly partisan, he was a frequent critic of Republican Speaker Newt Gingrich and an ally of Minority Whip David Bonior of Michigan in seeking to diminish Gingrich's power by raising continual questions about his ethics.

When Democrats controlled the House between 2007 and 2010, Doggett was active and often influential on Ways and Means. His priorities included eliminating tax shelters and loopholes and giving the federal government power to negotiate prescription drug prices for Medicare. He sought tax incentives for purchasers of plug-in hybrid electric cars. In 2009, when President Barack Obama announced his plan to reform international tax policy, he cited Doggett's input on proposals to crack down on overseas tax evasion. Doggett pressed the president's Simpson-Bowles fiscal commission to scrutinize the more than $1 trillion a year that the tax code provides in the form of reduced taxes or refunds to companies and individuals.

Since returning to the minority in the House, Doggett has found ways to be effective. As the senior Democrat on the Human Resources Subcommittee at Ways and Means, he got a bill into law in 2013 setting up a national commission to examine ways to reduce the number of children who die from abuse and neglect. Texas has had the highest rate of child abuse and neglect fatalities. He worked at Ways and Means with Texas Republican Sam Johnson to get a bill through the House in 2012 to authorize the phased removal of Social Security numbers from Medicare cards to crack down on identity theft. In 2015, Doggett helped found the House Prescription Drug Task Force to tackle the skyrocketing cost of prescription drugs. Although an outspoken foe of Obama's international trade deals, he scored a modest triumph that year when he convinced White House officials to increase the transparency of the agreements. Later in 2015, he enacted his proposal to give Medicare beneficiaries notification of the details of out-patient services. In 2017, he lost party-line votes in committee on his proposals to force President Donald Trump to release his tax returns for closed-door congressional review.

Republicans have sought and failed with numerous redistricting schemes to end Doggett's congressional career. In 2004, the GOP stretched his district 300 miles south to the Mexican border. But he took up the challenge. As other dislocated Texas Democrats took their fight to the courts, Doggett took his case to the voters of his new district. If he lost, Doggett told voters, "Tom DeLay will have won," a reference to the powerful GOP majority leader from Texas who had orchestrated the remap. Doggett won the primary 64%-36%. He led 88%-12% in Travis County and held Leticia Hinojosa, a former district court judge from McAllen, to a standoff in Hidalgo County. He won handily in November. In 2010, he drew a tough challenge from Republican Donna Campbell, a doctor and hospital emergency department director who raised $765,000. But Doggett spent $1.2 million and won 53%-45%, carrying Travis by 2-to-1.

In 2011, Texas Republicans again sought to carve up Doggett's stronghold. The eventual map added his liberal Austin base to a predominantly San Antonio district that included some conservative rural counties. Doggett easily won a three-way Democratic primary with 73 percent of the vote and then crushed Republican San Marcos Mayor Susan Narvaiz in November with 64 percent. In two rematches with Narvaiz, he has won with similar margins. In March 2017, after federal judges ruled that his district had been unconstitutionally gerrymandered, Doggett agreed and said that the GOP map "reduces the amount of accessibility and accountability of elected officials, regardless of their party."

He has remained active in the politics of both his home and adopted cities. In 2013, he sent a letter urging the San Antonio City Council to approve a measure barring workplace discrimination against gays; the plan was approved a few days later. In February 2017, he condemned the "vindictiveness" and "anti-immigrant hysteria" of Texas Governor Greg Abbott in seeking to punish Austin with a loss of state funding because of its "sanctuary" policies to protect illegal immigrants.

San Antonio/East Austin Corridor

Population		**Race and Ethnicity**		**Income**	
Total	758,070	White	25.3%	Median Income	$41,317 (385 out of 435)
Land area	594	Black	9.0%		
Pop/ sq mi	1276.7	Latino	62.6%		
Born in state	64.5%	Asian	1.4%	Under $50,000	58.5%
Age Groups		Two races	1.4%	$50,000-$99,999	29.1%
Under 18	26.7%	Other	0.3%	$100,000-$199,999	11.1%
18-34	29.9%	**Education**		$200,000 or more	1.3%
35-64	34.7%	H.S grad or less	53.4%	Poverty Rate	24.0%
Over 64	8.7%	Some college	28.6%	**Health Insurance**	
Work		College Degree, 4 yr	12.9%	With health insurance coverage	76.0%
White Collar	26.0%	Post grad	5.1%		
Sales and Service	48.8%	**Military**		**Public Assistance**	
Blue Collar	25.1%	Veteran	7.7%	Cash public assistance income	2.5%
Government	6.1%	Active Duty	0.3%	Food stamp/SNAP benefits	20.1%

Voter Turnout			
2015 Total Citizens 18+	466,860	2016 House Turnout as % CVAP	42%
2016 House turnout	197,576	2014 House Turnout as % CVAP	21%

2012 Presidential Vote		
Barack Obama	105,550	(63%)
Mitt Romney	58,007	(35%)

2016 Presidential Vote		
Hillary Clinton	128,535	(64%)
Donald Trump	61,136	(30%)
Gary Johnson	7,664	(4%)

Cook Partisan Voting Index: D+15

"There are only four unique cities in America: Boston, New Orleans, San Francisco and San Antonio." This quote may well be apocryphal - it has been attributed to both Mark Twain and Will

Rogers - and today one would have to add a few other cities to the list. But San Antonio still stands as a one-of-a-kind American locale. It started out as a collection of five Spanish missions, including the Mission San Antonio de Valero, better known today as the Alamo. From there it grew into a colonial capital, a hub for cattle drives, a railroad base, and eventually the heart of South Texas' increasingly transnational economy. Southerners and Mexicans played a large role in the city's growth, but Germans also settled here in large numbers in the mid-19th century. Frederick Law Olmsted referred to antebellum San Antonio as a "jumble of races, costumes, languages, and buildings," and as late as 1877, German speakers outnumbered Anglos and Mexican Americans.

Even the city's politics ran against the grain. In 1920, a district that included Bexar County elected Republican Harry Wurzbach to Congress, the only member of his party the Lone Star State sent to Congress in the first half of the 20th century. He lost in 1928, but, even as the country was engaged in a historic shift toward Democrats, won a special election after he contested that outcome and served again until he died in November 1931.

The 35th Congressional District of Texas covers many of the downtown features that helped make San Antonio unique. After 110 years in which it had been maintained by the private Daughters of the Republic of Texas, state lands commissioner George P. Bush in March 2015 switched management of the Alamo to the state's general land office. The district takes in the 2.5-mile-long River Walk, lined with restaurants, museums, and hotels; the 30-story, octagonal Tower Life Building; and the Alamodome, a 65,000 seat basketball/football stadium and the new Henry B. Gonzalez Convention Center. About 40 percent of the district's voters live in Bexar County. There has been rapid growth in the often-thin strip of neighborhoods running along Interstate 35 through the outskirts of Texas Hill Country, in the German settlement of New Braunfels, the old mill town of San Marcos, and Kyle, a booming suburb of Austin. New Braunfels, with 7 percent growth in 2015, was the second-fastest growing city in the nation, behind Georgetown, Texas.

The remaining 30 percent of the district's population lives in southeastern Travis County, in the mostly minority neighborhoods of east Austin. The Austin airport, once a former military base, which had been about even with San Antonio in its passenger load, has had a spurt in traffic and is expanding its facilities with nine new gates scheduled to open in 2018. A new highway to the airport, including toll lanes, is scheduled for completion in 2020. Along Lady Bird Lake in southeast Austin, Oracle has been building a new campus that will focus on cloud computing technologies, which will be its fifth office building in the Austin area.

The district owes its unique shape to two goals of Republicans during the 2011 redistricting. They wanted to pack as many Democrats as possible into a single district, and they wanted to make a majority-Hispanic district that would endanger longtime Austin-based Democratic Rep. Lloyd Doggett in a primary. They attained their objective of a district, which has become 83 percent Hispanic. But Doggett has shown remarkable resilience, and has not faced serious competition from either party. In March 2017, a three-judge federal court ruled that the gerrymandered shape of the district is unconstitutional, though the panel did not offer a solution.

THIRTY-SIXTH DISTRICT

Brian Babin (R)

Elected 2014, 2nd term; b. Mar 23, 1948, Port Arthur; Lamur University (TX), B.S.; University of Texas-Houston, Att.; University of Texas-Houston, D.D.S.; Southern Baptist; Married (Roxanne Babin); 5 children; 12 grandchildren.

Military Career: TX Army National Guard, 1969-1971; U.S. Army Reserve, 1971-1975; U.S. Air Force, 1976-1979.

Elected Office: Woodville City Council, 1981-1982, 1984-1989; Woodville Mayor, 1982-1984; Woodville School Board, 1992-1995.

Professional Career: Dentist, 1979-2014; TX St. Board of Dental Examiners, 1981-1987; TX Historical Comm., 1989-1995; Lower Neches Valley Authority, 1999-2014.

DC Office: 316 CHOB 20515, 202-225-1555, Fax: 202-226-0396, babin.house.gov.
State Offices: Deer Park, 832-780-0966; Orange, 409-883-8075; Woodville, 844-303-8934.

Committees: *Science, Space & Technology*: Environment, Space (Chmn). *Transportation & Infrastructure*: Highways & Transit, Railroads, Pipelines & Hazardous Materials, Water Resources & Environment.

Group Ratings

	ADA	ACLU	AFL-CIO	LCV	ITI	COC	HAFA	ACU	CFG	FRC
2016	-	11%	-	0%	100%	100%	83%	100%	90%	100%
2015	0%	C	9%	0%	C	70%	C	100%	85%	100%

Almanac Ratings 2015

	Economy	Social	Foreign	Composite
Liberal	0%	0%	0%	0%
Conservative	100%	100%	100%	100%

Key Votes of the 114th Congress

1. Keystone Pipeline	Y	5. Puerto Rico Debt	N	9. Offenses by Aliens	Y
2. Trade Deals	Y	6. Medical Marijuana	N	10. Troops in Iraq	N
3. Export-Import Bank	N	7. Sanctuary Cities	Y	11. Homeland Security $$	N
4. Debt Ceiling Increase	N	8. Armor-piercing Bullets	Y	12. Trade Adjustment aid	N

Election Results

Election	Name (Party)	Vote (%)	Cand. Spent	Ind. Exp. Support	Ind. Exp. Oppose
2016 General	Brian Babin (R)	193,675 (89%)	$592,024		
	Hal Ridley Jr. (G)	24,890 (11%)			
2016 Primary	Brian Babin (R)	(100%)			

Prior winning percentages: 2014 (76%)

Brian Babin, a dentist and local Republican leader who made his third run for Congress in 2014, sealed this victory in a primary runoff. He moved quickly to bolster NASA and make his own mark as chairman of the Space Subcommittee, an apt assignment for his district.

Babin grew up in Beaumont, attended Lamar University and got his degree in dentistry at the University of Texas at Houston; friends refer to him as "Doc Babin." After dental school, he served overseas in the Air Force, and later was an airborne artilleryman in the Army Reserve. He settled in Woodville in rural Tyler County, where he has maintained his dental practice. Babin entered local politics by serving as an alderman and mayor of Woodville. He was a regional chairman for Ronald Reagan's 1980 presidential campaign and claims some credit for the shift in local politics to the Republican Party. He has served on various local and state authorities, including a 1999 appointment by Gov. George W. Bush to the Lower Neches Valley Authority.

Not long ago, these parts of east Texas were "yellow dog" conservative Democratic territory and home to the colorful late Democratic Rep. Charlie Wilson, the subject of the book and movie *Charlie Wilson's War*. When Wilson retired in 1996, Babin ran for the seat, only to lose to Democrat Jim Turner 52%-46%. He tried again two years later and lost by a wider margin. The area covered by the 36th has skewed toward the GOP over the past decade. When the outspokenly conservative Steve Stockman gave up his House seat in a quixotic challenge to Republican Sen. John Cornyn, Babin sought to convert his decades of political activism into a congressional run.

In a 12-candidate field in the March primary, Babin ran first with 33 percent of the vote, followed by tea-party favorite Ben Streusand at 23 percent. The May runoff was contentious. Streusand brought up Babin's role in a Texas campaign finance scandal, noting that he received $37,000 in illegal corporate money from his friend, businessman Peter Cloeren, when he ran for the House in 1996. Cloeren pleaded guilty to campaign violations and paid a fine of $200,000. The FEC gave Babin a relative pass, ordering him to pay $30,000 in civil fines. His years of local political work gave him the edge. Streusand, a Houston banker who lived outside the district, won his base in Harris County with 65 percent of the vote, but he underperformed on turnout as Harris cast only one-third of the total vote. Babin rolled up huge majorities in the rural areas, including 85 percent in his native Tyler County. He won the runoff, 58%-42%. The general election was largely a formality.

In the House, Babin won seats on two committees well-suited to his district: Transportation and Infrastructure; and Science, Space and Technology. He was given the chairmanship of the Space

Subcommittee when it opened in June 2015, due to a shuffle of other committee assignments. His goal, he said, was to "strengthen NASA's core exploration mission, create an environment for commercial space ventures to thrive, and build a clear vision for America's space program." More specifically, he wanted to resume manned space flight as NASA's top priority, and to end NASA's reliance on other nations to send astronauts to the International Space Station. He supported expansion of commercial space flight.

When he took over as chairman, Babin criticized the agency's lack of focus. "NASA's primary missions are aeronautics and human spaceflight," he told the *Houston Chronicle.* "We seem to have gotten off of that in many respects." With other Texans, he sought to revitalize the Johnson Space Center, whose share of the NASA budget dropped from about half to less than one-fourth during the Obama administration. The NASA authorization bill, which he helped to enact in March 2017, included Babin's provision to care for former astronauts and enhance public understanding of the effects of spaceflight on the human body.

In his other committee, Babin won approval of two provisions in the water resources bill, which the Transportation Committee helped to enact in 2016. They improved the navigation and maintenance of the Houston Ship Channel. He introduced in 2015, and refiled in January 2017 a bill to halt the plan of President Barack Obama to bring in tens of thousands of refugees from Syria and other Muslim nations. This proposal presaged a comparable executive order that President Donald Trump issued. In March 2017, Babin voiced disappointment that the Freedom Caucus - of which he was a member - delayed House approval of the revision of the Affordable Care Act. "I worked very hard to get President Trump elected," Babin said. "So we need to support that agenda." In the 2015 *Almanac* vote ratings, Babin was among three House Republicans - each from Texas - with perfect conservative scores.

With his subcommittee niche, Babin is positioned to bring stability to his House district.

Eastern Houston Suburbs, Southeast Texas

Population		**Race and Ethnicity**		**Income**	
Total	719,530	White	63.1%	Median Income	$55,067 (183 out of 435)
Land area	7,126	Black	9.4%	Under $50,000	45.5%
Pop/ sq mi	101.0	Latino	23.2%	$50,000-$99,999	31.1%
Born in state	68.2%	Asian	2.2%	$100,000-$199,999	19.4%
		Two races	1.5%	$200,000 or more	3.9%
		Other	0.6%	Poverty Rate	14.4%
Age Groups		**Education**		**Health Insurance**	
Under 18	25.4%	H.S grad or less	48.9%	With health insurance coverage	80.2%
18-34	22.1%	Some college	32.7%		
35-64	39.6%	College Degree, 4 yr	12.5%		
Over 64	12.9%	Post grad	5.9%		
Work		**Military**		**Public Assistance**	
White Collar	31.2%	Veteran	8.9%	Cash public assistance income	1.7%
Sales and Service	38.6%	Active Duty	0.1%	Food stamp/SNAP benefits	12.8%
Blue Collar	30.1%				
Government	5.8%				

Voter Turnout			
2015 Total Citizens 18+	492,878	2016 House Turnout as % CVAP	44%
2016 House turnout	218,565	2014 House Turnout as % CVAP	27%

2012 Presidential Vote		
Mitt Romney	175,883	(73%)
Barack Obama	61,786	(26%)

2016 Presidential Vote		
Donald Trump	183,176	(72%)
Hillary Clinton	64,225	(25%)
Gary Johnson	5,704	(2%)

Cook Partisan Voting Index: R+26

East Texas is thick with landmarks of Lone Star history. There's still an Indian reservation in Polk County, and the swampland Big Thicket National Preserve reminds you of what the area looked like before humans first settled the region some 2,500 years ago. (It is called "America's Ark" because of its vast array of animals and plants.) These were some of the first parts of Texas to be settled by Anglos; Anahuac in Chambers County was a port of entry for early colonists. Later, the area became a destination for other colonists during the famed "Runaway Scrape," as they fled eastward, leaving beds unmade and breakfasts sitting on the table, in the face of Santa Anna's approaching army. Today, much of East Texas looks frozen in time - farm towns that the railroads passed by and the interstates overlooked. One can still get a sense of what the wildcatters saw when they crisscrossed the land buying up mineral rights in Mont Belvieu, hoping to cash in on the oil boom taking place in nearby Spindletop. Of course, some things have changed. Racial segregation has been abolished - this area is home to a large portion of the state's rural black population - and the isolation of the small town has been reduced by television, the regional shopping mall and the internet.

Urban development, sprinting outward from Houston's loop freeways, is spreading in between the pine forests and reservoirs. The industrial age is on steroids in Baytown, where Exxon is building its second refinery, with about 10,000 construction workers; production was scheduled to start in 2017, with a major expansion of chemical manufacturing and promises of a reduction in carbon emissions. Also scheduled for completion is Chevron's $6.5 billion expansion of its petrochemical plant. "Low oil prices dragging down the rest of Houston are feeding a $50 billion to $60 billion construction burst at east-side refineries and chemical plants now flush with cheap natural gas and oil -- feedstock for plastics and other products they make," the *Houston Chronicle* reported in March 2016. The growth of Houston's port has added to local industrial expansion.

The southeastern corner of Harris County tends to be more upscale, populated by highly educated employees of the Lyndon B. Johnson Space Center and the space and aeronautics industry that grew around it. The location of that iconic center, which opened in 1961, was influenced by its namesake, the Texas senator who was the majority leader when the site was selected and later became the 36th president and a continuing advocate of NASA. After discouraging recent years, during which the *Houston Press* in 2014 reported that the JSC "lost its identity and purpose" with the demise of NASA's manned space flights and roughly half of its buildings were torn down or consolidated, several factors have contributed to an apparent brightening of prospects. They include three Texas Republicans taking key House and Senate subcommittee chairmanships that handle NASA finances, plus the apparent support of President Donald Trump for space exploration. Backers were enthusiastic about the Orion human spaceflight capsule, which got a big boost from NASA legislation that Trump signed in March 2017.

The 36th Congressional District of Texas is a compromise: Both suburban Houston Republicans and East Texas Republicans wanted a new congressional district, and the result is one evenly divided between the two groups. About half of the district's population lives in a collection of eight lightly populated counties, where lumbering, farming, ranching, and oil and gas dominate. The other half of the district's population lives in the suburbs on the eastern edge of Harris County. They include blue-collar Baytown, Deer Park, La Porte and part of Pasadena, near the Houston Ship Channel. Further south are Clear Lake, Taylor Lake Village and part of Webster. The district is among the top 5 percent of the most Republican nationwide. Donald Trump got 72 percent in 2016.

★ UTAH ★

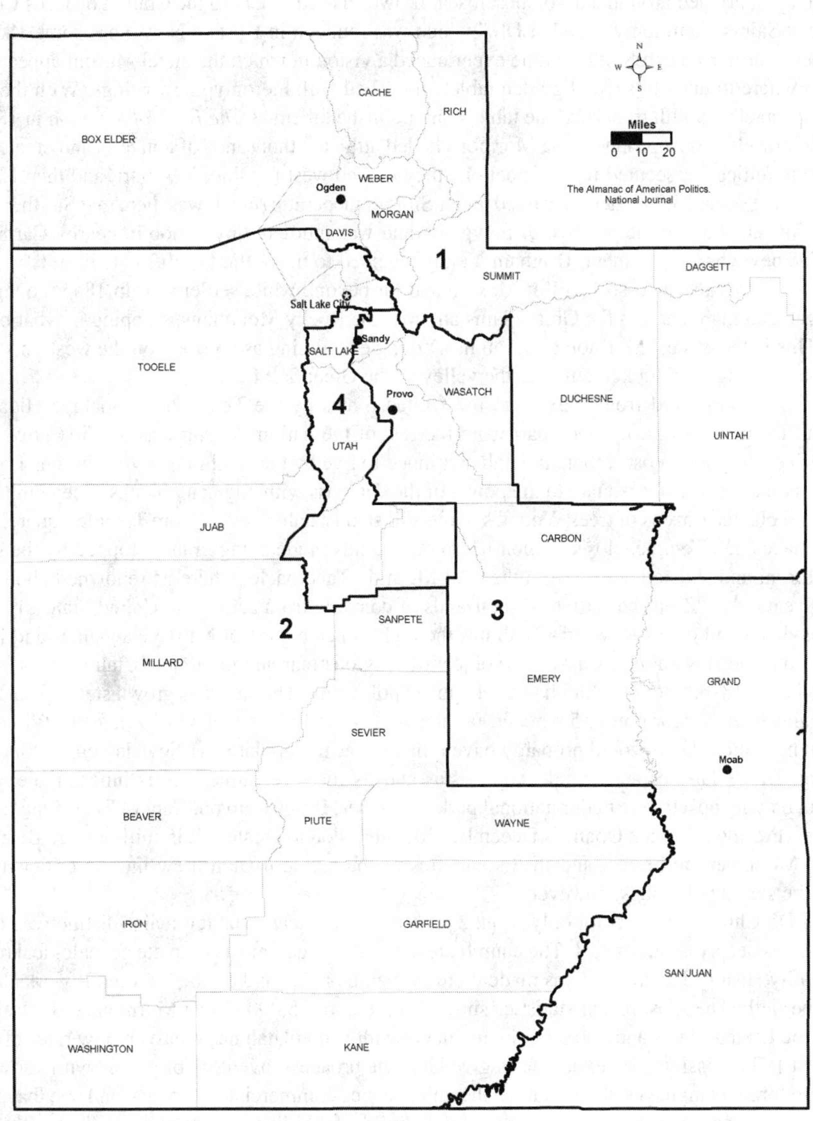

Congressional district boundaries were first effective for 2012.

Utah has long been one of the most Republican states in the union, but the 2016 presidential election – featuring a Republican candidate whose behavior repulsed many in the highly religious state – scrambled the electoral map, though for how long is unclear.

Other American states were founded by leaders of religious sects - Massachusetts, Connecticut, Pennsylvania - but only in colonial times and along waters navigable by ocean ships. Utah, a triumph of man over nature, was the creation of a productive and orderly civilization in a remote expanse of desert and mountain, arrayed around a desolate salt sea. It owes its settlement to the Church of Jesus Christ of Latter-day Saints, commonly called "LDS," which was founded in Upstate New York some 185 years ago. There, farmer Joseph Smith said he experienced a vision in which the angel Moroni appeared and told him where to unearth several golden tablets inscribed with hieroglyphic writings. With the aid of special spectacles, Smith translated the tablets and published them as *The Book of Mormon* in 1830; he declared himself to be a prophet. The Mormons he led attracted thousands of converts and created their own communities. Persecuted for their beliefs, they moved west to Ohio, Missouri, and then Nauvoo, Illinois, where some 15,000 members lived under Smith's theocratic rule. It was there that Smith received a revelation sanctioning the practice of polygamy and was murdered by a mob in nearby Carthage in 1844. The new church president, Brigham Young, decided to move the faithful - "the saints" - farther west into territory that was still part of Mexico and far beyond white settlement. In 1847 Young led a well-organized march across the Great Plains and into the Rocky Mountains, stopping in what became Utah. "This is the place," Mormon tradition has Young exclaiming as he stood on the western slope of the Wasatch Range and looked out over the valley of the Great Salt Lake.

Utah was transferred from Mexico to the United States by the Treaty of Guadalupe Hidalgo of 1848, but for many years, it lived apart from the rest of the nation. Young was the first governor of the Utah Territory and most settlers in Utah continued to live by the teachings of the church. The early pioneers laid out towns foursquare to the points of the compass with huge city blocks. They built sturdy houses and planted dozens of trees. Young's home still stands a block away from Temple Square, where the Salt Lake LDS Temple, closed to non-Mormons, stands in gleaming granite, topped by the golden angel Moroni and situated across from the oval Mormon Tabernacle, where its renowned choir sings. For 160 years, this "Zion" has attracted thousands of converts from across the United States, England, Scandinavia and all over the world - Utah has the highest percentage of Native Hawaiians and Pacific Islanders outside Hawaii and Alaska. The object of religious fear and prejudice, Utah was not granted statehood until 1896, after the church had renounced polygamy. The state has grown steadily since then and remains heavily Mormon - 55 percent, far ahead of second-place Idaho at 19 percent. Without the Mormon migration, Utah would probably have remained as unpopulated as Nevada before it legalized gambling; Utah's landscape of sand-swept vistas and its massive saline lake is inhospitable, if also beautiful, playing host to five major national parks -- Arches, Bryce Canyon, Capitol Reef, Canyonlands and Zion. (President Barack Obama's December 2016 decision to create a 1.35 million-acre Bears Ears National Monument to protect ancient Indian sites in southeastern Utah drew intense criticism from most of the state's politicians, however.)

The LDS Church accounts for only about 2 percent of Americans, but it remains distinctive in many ways. It cares deeply about its past. The church preserves America's most complete genealogical records in its Family History Library and has made them available on site and on the Internet. It works hard to spread the faith: The most recent statistics show that a record 75,000 young Mormons did missionary work in the United States and abroad. (An ancillary result is that Utah has relatively low rates of Army enlistment.) The missionaries' experiences give Utah the broadest inventory of people with knowledge of obscure foreign languages of any state in the union, a nice commercial advantage, and one that played a role in the National Security Agency's decision to build a $2 billion cloud-based facility in Bluffdale, south of Salt Lake City. By law, the state now prioritizes teaching languages in public schools as early as first grade.

Utah, according to Gallup, is the third most religious state in the nation, trailing only Mississippi and Alabama. Mormon teaching prohibits the consumption of tobacco, alcohol, coffee and tea. (A possible side effect: Utahns buy candy at the highest rate in the United States, about 50 percent higher than the national average.) The church encourages hard work and large families; 30 percent of Utah residents in 2015 were under 18, compared with the national average of 23 percent. On average, Mormons are better educated, work longer hours, and earn more money. The LDS Church has no paid clergy, but members serve in positions for which they are chosen, conducting religious services but also keeping in touch with members and counseling them when they need help. The church also maintains its own social-service organizations. While American mainline denominations have been losing members, the LDS Church is growing. Starting with just 30 members, the church took a century to reach 1 million. There were 2.9 million Mormons in 1970, 5 million in 1982 and almost 15.9 million today - a bit more than the estimated number of Jews worldwide. More than half of LDS members today live outside the United States.

In some ways, Utah resembles the America of the 1950s. It has the highest percentage of households headed by married couples and households with children, the highest fertility rate for non-Hispanic whites, the youngest median age of first marriages, and the lowest birth rate for unmarried women. It has many more children per capita than any other state, which can make its economic statistics misleading: Utah has a per capita income 15 percent below the national average - because all those kids aren't earning salaries - yet its median household income is 17 percent above the national average and its poverty rate is well below the nation's as a whole. It also has the highest rate of volunteerism, and its residents have the nation's highest rate of charitable giving, according to the *Chronicle of Philanthropy*. Utahns' trusting nature has even prompted the state to launch the nation's first white-collar-crime database. Utah is "sadly known for its high level of financial vulnerability to affinity fraud" - scams that take advantage of personal relationships, state Attorney General Sean Reyes said. Utah was the first state where women voted (Wyoming gave the right first, but Utah's elections were held before Wyoming's that year) and it elected the first female state senator. But in recent years, the percentage of women in elected office has been below the national average.

Historically, the state has been a bastion of social conservatism. The LDS Church's opposition to abortion rights is widely shared by its membership, and the church has always discouraged gambling. It is one of only two states (Hawaii is the other) with no form of legal gambling, although many Mormons are employed in the gaming industry in neighboring Nevada. The church has made notable overtures to the LGBT community in recent years -- in 2015, Mormon leaders worked with lawmakers to pass a measure that banned employment and housing discrimination based on sexual orientation while carving out protections for religious institutions that oppose homosexuality - but a new church policy leaked later that year sent mixed signals, saying that Mormons in same-sex unions would be considered apostates and that their children would face obstacles to receiving blessings and baptism rituals. Reflecting church attitudes, Utah has been ahead of the rest of the nation in discouraging the use of tobacco, and it has had restrictive liquor laws. Only in July 2009, amid concerns about the impact on tourism, could you finally get a drink served at a bar without joining a private club, and even then it had to be poured out of sight, behind what became known as a "Zion curtain." After years of trying, legislative efforts to get rid of the curtain are gaining momentum.

Still, the state isn't frozen in time. While its black population – 1 percent – is among the nation's lowest, Utah's Hispanic population is now 13 percent. While that's far lower than Arizona or Nevada, it still represents a sharp contrast with Utah's past, and the Utah Hispanic population is even younger than the state's population as a whole, making it a growing demographic force. This shift has evoked quite a different response in Utah than in Arizona. Utah businesses have been interested in maintaining an immigrant work force, and LDS leaders, many with experience as overseas missionaries, have expressed compassion. Gov. Jon Huntsman, before his resignation to become ambassador to China in 2009, and his successor, Republican Gary Herbert, worked to create a "Utah Compact," which was enacted in March 2011. Law-enforcement personnel were authorized to check the immigration status only of those arrested for felonies or serious misdemeanors, and illegal immigrants who paid a fine of $2,500 (or $1,000 if they had overstayed a legal visa) and passed criminal background checks could get work permits.

Overall, Utah has been on a growth spurt. From 2000 to 2010, the state's population rose by 24 percent, to nearly 2.8 million - the third-highest growth rate in the nation after Nevada and Arizona. Since 2010, the state has grown by another 10.4 percent, with several areas exceeding that, including Washington County (St. George), Utah County (Provo), Summit County (Park City), Davis County (the northern suburbs of Salt Lake City), and, biggest of all, Wasatch County (Heber City) with a nearly 30 percent increase since 2010. Utah's economy has done well, too: It had a much smaller housing bubble than other states, and unemployment peaked at only 8 percent in early 2010, well below the national average. By February 2017, it was at 3.1 percent, the seventh-lowest in the nation.

In the 19th century, Republicans led the fight to keep Utah out of the union, and Democratic President Grover Cleveland signed the statehood act. Before World War II, Utah saw itself as a colonial victim of East Coast bankers and financiers, and Mormons saw themselves as suffering religious discrimination and bigotry - with considerable cause. Utah's income levels were well below the national average, and its cost of living was higher. In political terms, this perspective translated into a Democratic allegiance. In 1940, Utah was represented by staunch New Dealers in Congress and voted 62%-38% for Franklin Roosevelt. Since then, Utah has come to see itself as a busy generator of wealth, with a raft of successful businesses, a knack for high-tech innovation, and longer workweeks than the rest of the nation. But in recent years – and in ordinary circumstances -- Mormons and Utahns have become heavily Republican, indeed the most Republican state in the nation, according to Gallup. Utah has not voted Democratic for president since 1964, hasn't elected a Democratic governor since Scott Matheson in 1980, and hasn't sent a Democratic senator to Washington since 1970. Utah's last Democratic congressman, Scott Matheson's son Jim, retired in 2014 and was succeeded by Mia Love, a Brooklyn native of Haitian ancestry who had converted to the LDS church.

Salt Lake City has been the state's primary pocket of liberalism, with the resort area of Park City a close second. The neighborhoods close to the church headquarters, with their gracious old houses and a smaller street grid, have attracted academic and professional newcomers and so have become the most heavily "gentile" (the Mormon term for non-Mormons) part of the state. In 2008, Democrats won control of the Salt Lake County government and elected most of its state legislators. But Democrats have won few legislative seats in the rest of the state. The Republican dominance has grown so great that tea party factions have flexed their muscle, worrying establishment figures in the party. Prompted by an activist-dominated convention in 2010 in which insurgent Mike Lee won enough votes to keep incumbent Sen. Robert Bennett off the primary ballot, establishment Republicans pushed successfully to allow candidates alternate paths to the primary, a system that took effect in 2016.

The 2016 presidential race in Utah was the most topsy-turvy in memory. The eventual Republican nominee, Donald Trump, got a measly 14 percent of the GOP primary vote, and he was so unpopular that even Democratic nominee Hillary Clinton made the rare move of spending money in the state, sending a mailer to Utah voters in late August. In late October, a *Salt Lake Tribune* poll found Trump only two points ahead of Utah native and independent candidate Evan McMullin; Clinton's disapproval numbers among Utah voters were even worse than Trump's, but she was still in the hunt at another six points back. About two weeks before the election, the Trump campaign dispatched vice presidential nominee Mike Pence to Salt Lake City, a move unheard of for a Republican nominee. In the end, though, many Republican voters heeded Pence's call to "come home" – on Election Day, Trump exceeded his standing in most late polls and the McMullin bubble shrank.

While Trump won the state's electoral votes, his showing was atrocious for a Republican in Utah. Mitt Romney had won the state with 73 percent in 2012; Trump won it with 45 percent four years later– the lowest percentage he reached in any state he won – and garnered a stunning 225,000 fewer votes statewide than Romney had. Most of the "missing" Republican vote went to McMullin, who took 21.3 percent. (Libertarian Gary Johnson, who initially had high hopes in the state, ended up with 3.5 percent.)While Clinton didn't end up much above Obama's percentage of the vote in 2012, she exceeded his raw-vote total by 59,000 and actually won two counties outright – Salt Lake County, where the margin had shifted 29 points in the Democratic direction, and Summit County, where the margin shifted by 19 points. Clinton's 30,000-vote gain in Salt Lake County accounted for much of her improvement, but she also improved on Obama's showing in such solidly red jurisdictions as Utah County (11,000 more votes than Obama), Davis County (7,000 more), and both Washington County and Cache County(Logan), with about 2,000 additional votes each. It was hardly the stuff of a major partisan realignment, but if anti-Trump sentiment remains high in Utah, the state could become one of the nation's more interesting electoral laboratories.

Population		Race and Ethnicity		Income	
Total	2,903,379	White	79.5%	Median Income	$60,727 (12 out of 50)
Land area	82,170	Black	1.0%		
Pop/ sq mi	35.3	Latino	13.4%	Under $50,000	40.3%
Born in state	62.1%	Asian	2.2%	$50,000-$99,999	36.1%
Age Groups		Two races	1.9%	$100,000-$199,999	19.4%
Under 18	30.9%	Other	2.0%	$200,000 or more	4.2%
18-34	26.6%	**Education**		Poverty Rate	12.3%
35-64	32.8%	H.S grad or less	32.0%	**Health Insurance**	
Over 64	9.7%	Some college	37.0%	With health insurance coverage	86.8%
Work		College Degree, 4 yr	20.8%		
White Collar	36.8%	Post grad	10.4%	**Public Assistance**	
Sales and Service	41.8%	**Military**		Cash public assistance income	2.0%
Blue Collar	21.4%	Veteran	6.7%		
Government	15.3%	Active Duty	0.2%	Food stamp/SNAP benefits	8.9%

Voter Turnout			
2015 Total Citizens 18+	1,868,008	2016 Pres Turnout as % CVAP	61%
2016 Pres Votes	1,131,430	2012 Pres Turnout as % CVAP	59%

Legislature	
Senate:	5D, 29R
House:	13D, 62R

Presidential Politics

2016 Democratic Caucus		
Bernie Sanders (D)	62,991	(79%)
Hillary Clinton (D)	16,162	(20%)
2016 Republican Caucus		
Ted Cruz (R)	132,904	(69%)
John Kasich (R)	31,992	(17%)
Donald Trump (R)	26,434	(14%)

2016 Presidential Vote		
Donald Trump (R)	515,231	(45%)
Hillary Clinton (D)	310,676	(27%)
Evan McMullin (I)	243,690	(21%)
Gary Johnson (L)	39,608	(3%)
2012 Presidential Vote		
Mitt Romney (R)	740,600	(73%)
Barack Obama (D)	251,813	(25%)

Utah has been the most Republican state in seven of the last 10 presidential elections. In 1992, this was also the least Democratic state: Third-party candidate Ross Perot finished ahead of Bill Clinton, 27%-25%. Barack Obama's 34.4 percent showing in 2008 was the best Democratic performance since Hubert Humphrey won 37 percent of the vote in 1968. He even carried Salt Lake County, if only by 296 votes. The trend was, unsurprisingly, reversed in 2012, when Republicans nominated Mitt Romney, a Mormon who was widely known for his work in rescuing the 2002 Salt Lake City Winter Olympics. Utah saw the biggest swing toward Romney in the nation, as he carried the state 73%-25% and Salt Lake County 58%-38%. The 2016 presidential race was further scrambled when shortly after Republicans formally nominated Donald Trump, Utah native Evan McMullin, a Mormon and former senior GOP congressional aide and ex-CIA operative, launched an independent presidential bid. His name wound up on the ballot in 11 states, including Utah. Trump won the state over Hillary Clinton, 46%-28%, with McMullin taking 21 percent, his best showing by far. Clinton carried two counties, Salt Lake and Summit (Park City). McMullin didn't win a single one of the state's 29 counties, but finished ahead of Clinton in 15.

Utah's attempts to become a force in presidential primaries have not been successful. Republican Gov. Mike Leavitt spent much time and effort promoting a Western regional primary, but only Colorado and Wyoming (with a caucus, not a primary) joined together in March 2000, but candidates paid less attention to Western issues than Leavitt had hoped. In 2016, Democrats opted to hold a March caucus that gave Vermont Sen. Bernie Sanders a 79%-20% landslide over Clinton. Republicans also held a caucus. Romney, who stumped for Ohio Gov. John Kasich in that state's primary a week earlier, cut radio ads for Sen. Ted Cruz in Utah, and the Texan captured 70 percent of the vote, to Kasich's 17 percent and Trump's 14 percent.

Congressional Districts

115th Congress Lineup	4R	**114th Congress Lineup**	4R

Fast-growing Utah waited longer than expected for a fourth seat in the House. After 2012, Republicans had to wait another two years. For now, they appear to have a lock on all four seats.

Utahns had expected that the 2000 census would boost their delegation from three to four. But under the reapportionment formula, Utah fell 857 residents short of getting a new seat. After growing 24 percent between 2000 and 2010, Utah was a slam dunk to finally get its fourth seat. Republicans' safe play would have been to create one solid Democratic district in Salt Lake City - a "doughnut hole" - for Jim Matheson, a savvy centrist Blue Dog, and simply draw a safe new Republican seat somewhere else. But for decades, many Utah Republicans argued, in their party's interest, that all the state's districts should contain both urban and rural areas, splitting Salt Lake City like a "pizza pie." After lengthy debate and some Republican internal bickering, the state House and Senate passed a map: The new 4th District would be a "doughnut hole," but it would stretch south to the heavily Republican suburbs south of Salt Lake City and the northern reaches of prohibitively Republican northern Utah County. Each of the remaining three districts included parts of the metropolitan area plus vast open spaces.

Matheson ran in the 4th. Like Houdini, he cheated the Republicans' plan, prevailing by 768 votes. The feat was all the more impressive in light of his opponent, Mia Love, a black Mormon small-town mayor who gained a national following. To boot, Mitt Romney atop the ballot won 68 percent in the 4th. Had Republicans carved just one more Utah County precinct into the 4th, Matheson would almost certainly have lost. Still, Matheson decided that he had struggled enough, including with Democratic leaders in the House. He retired in 2014. Love has prevailed twice - though by unexpectedly narrow margins, partly due to the local peculiarities of the 2016 presidential contest.

Governor

Gary Herbert (R)

Assumed office in 2009, term expires 2021, 2nd term; b. May. 7, 1947, American Fork, UT; Brigham Young U., attended 1968-70, Mormon; Married (Jeanette); 6 children.

Military Career: UT Army National Guard, 1970-76.

Elected Office: UT County Commissioner, 1990-2004; UT Lt. Governor, 2005-2009.

Professional Career: Realtor, Herbert & Assocs. Realtors; Co-owner, The Kids Connection, 1985-2008.

Office: 350 North State St., Suite 200, Salt Lake City, 84114-2220; 801-538-1000; Fax: 801-538-1133; Website: utah.gov/governor.

Election Results

Election	Name (Party)	Vote (%)
2016 General	Gary Herbert (R)	750,828 (67%)
	Mike Weinholtz (D)	322,462 (29%)
	Brian Kamerath (L)	34,687 (3%)
2016 Primary	Gary Herbert (R)	165,678 (72%)
	Jonathan Johnson (R)	63,978 (28%)

Prior winning percentage: 2012 (68%), 2010 (64%)

Republican Gov. Gary Herbert assumed office in August 2009 following the resignation of Republican Gov. Jon Huntsman Jr., who was tapped by President Barack Obama to become U.S.

ambassador to China. Herbert was easily elected in 2010 to serve out the remainder of Huntsman's term, then won reelection comfortably on his own in 2012. He then survived a credible primary challenge to win another term in 2016. Herbert has steered a relatively moderate course despite his state's overwhelmingly Republican leanings, and his approval ratings have been consistently high.

Herbert was born in American Fork, where his father owned a construction company. He studied engineering and accounting at Brigham Young University but left school before graduating and established Herbert and Associates Realtors. He ran for the Orem City Council in 1989, losing by 32 votes. The next year, he was elected to the Utah County Commission and served as its chairman for 13 years. During his tenure, Utah County had one of the state's lowest tax rates. He entered the 1994 race to unseat Democratic Rep. Bill Orton but dropped out after struggling to raise money. Orton went on to win reelection.

In 2003, Herbert left the Utah County Commission to run for governor. The field for the 2004 Republican primary was crowded with better known politicians, including former Rep. Jim Hansen, former Utah House Speaker Nolan Karras, and Huntsman, the son of industrialist Jon Huntsman Sr., the wealthiest man in Utah, Herbert cast himself as a "David" in a field of "Goliaths" and stressed his rural roots and ties to local government. Unable to generate enough support for his candidacy, Herbert accepted Huntsman's invitation to join his ticket as the nominee for lieutenant governor. At the time, Huntsman was perceived as lacking credibility in state politics and rural issues, two areas where Herbert was strong. The ticket won with 58 percent of the vote.

Under Utah's constitution, the lieutenant governor's sole official duty is overseeing the state Elections Office, but Huntsman expanded Herbert's responsibilities to include managing the state's public lands policies, transportation plans and homeland security operations. He pushed for the creation of a Public Lands Policy Coordination Office to help manage the state's role in land-management issues. In 2008, Huntsman won a second term as governor but soon handed the office over to Herbert after accepting the ambassadorship. Herbert is considered unflashy and unpretentious. "He's plainspoken," the *Salt Lake Tribune* said in endorsing him for reelection in 2012. "With Gary, what you see is what you get." Legislatively, Herbert made few changes to Huntsman's cabinet and continued a policy of opposing most tax increases. He agreed not to veto a bill that raised the state's cigarette tax by $1 a pack to reduce an education budget shortfall from $300 million to around $10 million. He also retained a four-day workweek - since repealed - that his predecessor had initiated as a way to cut costs.

Herbert was strongly favored for election in 2010 and won the GOP nomination at the state party's convention in May with 71 percent of the vote. He ran on his state's fiscal stability during the 2007-09 recession. His Democratic opponent was Salt Lake County Mayor Peter Corroon, a conservative who tapped Republican state Rep. Sheryl Allen as his running mate and who ran ads vowing to put "ideas ahead of ideology." The state's GOP leanings and the strong election cycle for the party enabled Herbert to easily beat Corroon, 64%-32%, carrying every county except Summit (Park City).

Early in his new term in 2011, Herbert enraged open-government advocates and the news media by signing a bill to restrict disclosure of some state information, such as text messages and instant messages. Three days later, activists filed a petition to start a referendum drive, and newspaper editorials condemned the measure. Herbert agreed to seek repeal, saying the public's response "demands us to push the reset button." The law was overwhelmingly repealed.

On immigration, Herbert signed a package of bills that authorized a guest-worker program that allowed undocumented immigrants to remain in the state if they paid fines. At the same time, it required police to check the legal status of people arrested on felony or serious misdemeanor charges; established a partnership with the Mexican state of Nuevo León to allow workers to come to Utah; and allowed Utah citizens to sponsor immigrants.

Herbert addressed another controversial issue in March 2012, when he vetoed a bill that would have allowed school districts to drop sex education and required abstinence-only instruction in those that kept it. The measure had sparked emotional protests and petition drives, and Herbert argued that it "simply goes too far by constricting parental options." His action displeased conservatives, but they were mollified when he signed another measure asking the federal government to give back more than 20 million acres of land to the state.

In running for a full four-year term of his own in 2012, Herbert drew five Republican challengers but won 58 percent on the first ballot at the state's GOP convention, then proceeded to trounce runner-up Morgan Philpot, a former state representative, 63%-37%, in the primary. With Mitt Romney, a Mormon, on the presidential ballot, any Democrat running in 2012 faced overwhelming odds in Utah. Herbert's Democratic opponent, Peter Cooke, was a retired Army Reserve general; Herbert couldn't match Romney's 73 percent, but he still won, 68%-28%, carrying every county, including Summit this time by a 50%-47% margin.

After that election, Herbert - and the overwhelmingly Republican Legislature - displayed a moderate streak. He signed a bill urging treatment rather than prison for drug offenders, and signed another to permit the use of cannabis oil as a medical treatment. He also said he was open to broader medical-marijuana legislation. He created a Clean Air Action Team to craft ideas for improving air quality along the Wasatch Front. He hiked property taxes to spend on education and raised the gasoline tax to boost transportation initiatives. He also worked with the Obama administration to propose a middle ground on the expansion of Medicaid under the Affordable Care Act.

Most strikingly, Herbert worked with leaders of the LDS church and gay-rights groups to enact a measure that simultaneously outlawed discrimination against members of the LGBT community while protecting religious freedoms. The landmark measure was seen as a compromise that might be replicated elsewhere. "I have no doubt the eyes of the nation are upon us," Herbert said at the signing ceremony. "We can do difficult things because we are determined to work together, one with another, as opposed to working against one another." At the same time, Herbert took some stands that pleased conservatives. He supported a resolution opposing federal protections for two areas, Cedar Mesa and San Rafael Swell, and signed into a law a measure that allowed firing squads for executions if no drugs were available for lethal injections.

As Herbert prepared to run for his second full term in 2016, he continued to balance conservative and moderate positions. Conservatives were pleased to see him sign the nation's first law requiring women seeking an abortion after 20 weeks to be given anesthesia. He also signed a package of measures addressing pornography. The most far-reaching provision would require computer technicians to report child pornography they find, and would deem the failure to do so a misdemeanor. Herbert also made moves to reverse his past support for the Common Core curriculum and related education reforms. He cheered moderates by approving one bill to spend $27 million over three years on homeless services, and another to spend $15 million on an expansion of Medicaid to a projected 16,000 residents. Herbert also withdrew his support for Republican presidential nominee Donald Trump in October after the emergence of a 2005 recording showing the future Republican candidate making remarks offensive to women. "While I cannot vote for Hillary Clinton," he tweeted, "I will not vote for Trump."

In his reelection bid, Herbert first faced a primary challenge from his right by Overstock.com chairman Jonathan Johnson, who received the backing of the conservative group FreedomWorks. At the diehard-dominated state GOP convention, Johnson beat Herbert, 55%-45% -- not enough to push Herbert out of the race, but enough for the challenger to secure a spot on the primary ballot. After it came out that Herbert had referred to himself at a meeting with lobbyists as "Available Jones" – someone open to doing business in exchange for campaign contributions – Johnson attacked his comment and Herbert apologized. But critics also raised questions about Johnson's fundraising efforts; he received some $900,000 from one donor, Overstock.com founder Patrick Byrne. In the June primary, with a broader electorate, Herbert defeated Johnson, garnering more than 70 percent of the vote. In the general election, Herbert was the heavy favorite against Democrat Mike Weinholtz, a largely self-funding candidate who was chairman of a health care company. Weinholtz sent mailers pairing Herbert with Trump and Russian President Vladimir Putin, but they weren't enough to overcome the state's strong partisan leanings. Herbert won, 67%-29%, carrying every county except for Summit, which Weinholtz won by fewer than 600 votes.

In 2017, Herbert proposed "Talent Ready Utah," a program to promote apprenticeships for high school graduates, as well as a measure to tax online sales. And he expressed support for a bill to end the state's "Zion curtains," which shield customers from the pouring of alcoholic beverages. Some lawmakers had been trying to end the practice for years without success. Meanwhile, when Trump issued an executive order curbing refugee admissions, Herbert reiterated his and the state's support for refugees. "We have a lot of people from Syria that are probably running from terrorism that aren't terrorists," he said. "More important to me is who they are, what they are - as opposed to where they come from." But the governor suffered a disappointment in February 2017 when the Outdoor Retailer show, a major event held twice annually in Salt Lake City, said it was abandoning the state because of Herbert's stance on public lands policy. The show's organizers said he had refused to end support for congressional efforts to transfer federal land to states; for overturning the Antiquities Act, which allows the president to unilaterally designate federally protected lands; and for overturning President Barack Obama's designation of the Bears Ears National Monument in the southeastern part of the state.

Regardless, all indications were that Herbert remained popular, and if he serves out his entire term, he will have been in office for more than 11 years, making him the state's second-longest-serving governor. A possible successor for 2020 emerged in April 2017, when GOP Rep. Jason Chaffetz announced that he would not be running for reelection in 2018 and he then decided to resign from the House in June 2017.

Senior Senator

Orrin Hatch (R)

Elected 1976, term expires 2018, 7th term; b. Mar 22, 1934, Homestead Park (Pittsburgh), PA; Brigham Young University (UT), B.S.; University of Pittsburgh School of Law (PA), J.D.; Mormon; Married (Elaine Hansen Hatch); 6 children; 23 grandchildren; 10 great-grandchildren.

Professional Career: Practicing attorney, 1962-1976.

DC Office: 104 HSOB 20510, 202-224-5251, Fax: 202-224-6331, hatch.senate.gov.

State Offices: Cedar City, 435-586-8435; Ogden, 801-625-5672; Provo, 801-375-7881; Salt Lake City, 801-524-4380; St George, 435-634-1795.

Committees: Senate President Pro Tempore. *Aging*. *Finance (Chmn)*: Energy, Natural Resources & Infrastructure, Fiscal Responsibility & Economic Growth, Health Care, International Trade, Customs & Global Competitiveness, Social Security, Pensions & Family Policy, Taxation & IRS Oversight. *Health, Education, Labor & Pensions*: Children & Families, Primary Health & Retirement Security. *Judiciary*: Antitrust, Competition Policy & Consumer Rights, Oversight, Agency Action, Federal Rights & Federal Courts, Privacy, Technology & the Law.

Group Ratings

	ADA	ACLU	AFL-CIO	LCV	ITI	COC	HAFA	ACU	CFG	FRC
2016	-	11%	-	12%	80%	100%	33%	62%	73%	0%
2015	0%	C	14%	0%	C	92%	C	65%	61%	100%

Almanac Ratings 2015

	Economy	Social	Foreign	Composite
Liberal	44%	9%	19%	24%
Conservative	56%	91%	82%	76%

Key Votes of the 114th Congress

1. Keystone pipeline	Y	5. National Security Data	N	9. Gun Sales Checks	N
2. Export-Import Bank	N	6. Iran Nuclear Deal	Y	10. Sanctuary Cities	Y
3. Debt Ceiling Increase	Y	7. Puerto Rico Debt	Y	11. Planned Parenthood	Y
4. Homeland Security $$	Y	8. Loretta Lynch A.G	Y	12. Trade deals	Y

Election Results

Election	Name (Party)	Vote (%)		Cand. Spent	Ind. Exp. Support	Ind. Exp. Oppose
2012 General	Orrin Hatch (R)	657,608	(65%)	$13,140,209	$475,982	$947,793
	Scott Howell (D)	301,873	(30%)	$420,779	$46,209	
	Shaun Lynn McCausland (C)	31,905	(3%)			
2012 Primary	Orrin Hatch (R)	160,359	(66%)			
	Dan Liljenquist (R)	80,915	(34%)			

Prior winning percentages: 2006 (62%), 2000 (66%), 1994 (69%), 1988 (67%), 1982 (58%), 1976 (56%)

Republican Orrin Hatch, Utah's senior senator who was first elected to the Senate in 1976, is president pro tem, his party's longest-serving member in the chamber. Like few others in Congress, he has been consistent in his inconsistency-he veers between collaborating enthusiastically with Democrats and attacking them with vigor. He tacked rightward in the face of a 2012 tea party challenge, but displayed greater bipartisanship after winning a primary to ensure reelection to what he said at the time would be his final term. As the chairman of the Finance Committee, his eagerness to cooperate with President Donald Trump could provide a big boost to prospects for health care, tax and trade legislation. His eagerness to support Trump was ironic, given that Utah voters-Mormons, especially-had been unusually hostile to Trump.

Hatch grew up in Pittsburgh, where his father was a metal lather. The family lost their home during the Depression, and lived for a time in a shelter made of salvaged wood and metal and without plumbing. He worked his way through Brigham Young University as a janitor and a metal lather, like his father. He went on to get a law degree from the University of Pittsburgh, and practiced law in the Steel City. He and his wife and their young family later moved to Salt Lake City, and the newly-minted lawyer got interested in politics. In 1976, he ran for the Senate. An endorsement from Republican presidential candidate Ronald Reagan helped him get attention, and he won the GOP nomination. In the general election, he upset three-term Democrat Frank Moss, defeating him, 54%-45%. His toughest reelection fight came in 1982, when he was opposed by Democratic Salt Lake City Mayor Ted Wilson. Hatch won 58% to 41%.

His Senate career has been shaped by two impulses that are sometimes at odds with each other: a strong conservative philosophy and a sense of responsibility to pass meaningful legislation. As the Finance chairman, Hatch has been a tough critic of the Affordable Care Act. The courtly senator has taken a leadership role on trade, another area in which he has reached across the aisle. He stressed the importance of trade to Utah, which has become a large exporting state. When the Senate, in 2015, passed legislation to renew Trade Promotion Authority, Hatch called it "perhaps the most important bill we'll pass in the Senate this year." Months later, he voiced serious reservations about Obama's proposed Trans-Pacific Partnership on the grounds that the deal gave insufficient protection to biologics, a new class of pharmaceuticals.

As one of only nine Senators who has served at least 40 years, he has both witnessed and created a great deal of Senate history. Democrat Carl Hayden of Arizona, who retired in 1969, was the only Senator among those nine with whom Hatch has not served. As the Trump presidency began, Hatch was second in Senate seniority to Vermont Democrat Patrick Leahy. His ascension to the pro-tem position (technically third in line in presidential succession) earned him a $19,400 raise as well as a security detail. At age 82, Hatch was less than one year younger than the two oldest Senators: Democrat Dianne Feinstein of California and Republican Charles Grassley of Iowa.

At least as remarkable as the length of his tenure has been its variety and impact. After entering the Senate as the conservative firebrand who brought down key elements of the liberal agenda under President Jimmy Carter, Hatch served as a leading and productive supporter of Ronald Reagan. He later crafted several pieces of significant social legislation (especially, health care) with liberal lions, notably Ted Kennedy of Massachusetts in the Senate and Henry Waxman in the House. He clashed with Barack Obama because Hatch felt that the young President was too partisan and unwilling to seek common ground, plus he felt a home-state imperative to defend conservative principles. Then, he attempted to steer Donald Trump through his rocky agenda.

Consider his multiple committee chairmanships. After only four years in the Senate, Hatch took the helm in 1981 at what was then the Labor and Human Resources Committee. At Judiciary, he was chairman intermittently during the presidencies of Bill Clinton and George W. Bush, depending on which party held the Senate majority. Forced out at Judiciary by term limits on chairmen, Hatch bided his time at the Finance Committee until Grassley ran up against his own term limits.

Less than half-way through his Senate career, the 1994 *Almanac* highlighted what already had become Hatch's sweeping range, noting that he had been an important legislator almost from the start. "In the late 1970s, he filibustered the AFL-CIO's labor law reform bill and killed it; when Republicans unexpectedly won control of the Senate in 1980, he was suddenly chairman of the Labor and Human Resources Committee. He became a legislative workhorse, taking seriously his responsibilities of superintending welfare and labor programs and working hard on the details. He moved many programs into block grants and to the states early on, but also became a "big booster" of the Job Corps. He eventually won a sub-minimum wage for teenagers, but only after market wages rose well above the minimum. He backed the Americans with Disabilities Act, and his child care bill include many provisions from the Children's Defense Fund ABC bill. He is staunchly against abortion and, on the Judiciary Committee, opposed civil rights bills he considered quota legislation and staunchly supported the Supreme Court nominations of Robert Bork and Clarence Thomas. But he worked to build compromises on civil rights and family and medical leave. He has pushed for more funding for vaccinations, the WIC program and AIDS babies…." And on, and on….

Hatch has aggressively defended traditional Republican positions, sponsoring bills to restrict class action lawsuits and to set limits on medical malpractice cases. In 1995, when he became chairman of the Judiciary Committee, he worked on limiting tort liability and regulatory law. He managed the balanced budget amendment proposal to one-vote defeats in 1995 and 1997. He helped draft the 2001 USA Patriot

Act, the Bush administration's centerpiece anti-terrorism law, and in 2004 defended it against attempts to eliminate some of its main provisions. During negotiations to reauthorize the Foreign Intelligence Surveillance Act, Hatch supported a provision to grant retroactive immunity to phone companies that had participated in the administration's warrantless wiretapping program. Hatch described the phone companies as "patriotic" in a speech on the Senate floor. The FISA reauthorization passed the Senate in 2008 with retroactive immunity for the companies.

Another of Hatch's preoccupations has been protecting intellectual property in the face of technological advance. He supported the Digital Millennium Copyright Act of 1998 banning unlawful downloading of copyrighted music and movies, and he backed the record industry against the threat raised by Napster. In 2004, the Senate passed his bill, co-sponsored with Leahy, to authorize the Justice Department to bring civil lawsuits as well as criminal actions for illegal downloading.

Hatch's interest in these issues has not been merely theoretical. He has long written poetry and hundreds of songs, some of which have been recorded by a Utah firm, including a 13-song album of Christmas music. Some of his songs were recorded by singer Gladys Knight, a convert to the Mormon Church. His music earned praise from Bono, the lead singer of the popular and politically-oriented rock band U2. In 2003, the two men met to discuss the AIDS crisis in Africa, and the singer suggested for Hatch the stage name "Johnny Trapdoor." One of his songs, "Souls Along the Way," was written for his friend Kennedy and was used in the movie *Ocean's 12.* In 2009, he even wrote a Jewish holiday tune called "Eight Days of Hanukkah."

Every senator, it sometimes seems, feels compelled to run for president, and that time came for Hatch with the 2000 election. He argued that he had more experience in federal office than the other candidates and that he was not "beholden to the Republican establishment." In the Iowa caucuses in January 2000, he won only 1 percent of the vote, even fewer than Republican John McCain, who did not campaign in the state. Two days later, he withdrew from the race and endorsed George W. Bush. In the 2008 presidential primaries, Hatch endorsed fellow Mormon Mitt Romney of Massachusetts. But after Romney dropped out, Hatch endorsed his colleague McCain and wrote a patriotic campaign song for him called "Together Forever."

When Obama took office in 2009, Hatch expressed a willingness to work with his longtime friend, the seriously-ailing liberal Massachusetts Democrat Edward Kennedy, on comprehensive health care legislation. But even before Kennedy's death in August of that year, Hatch was assailing the measure as big-government overreach. In March 2011, he was one of only nine senators to oppose a fiscal 2011 budget deal that staved off a government shutdown, arguing that it did not cut spending enough. He called on the Treasury Department to delay implementation of the Dodd-Frank financial services overhaul law. Even though he had voted to confirm Elena Kagan as solicitor general, Hatch opposed her nomination to the Supreme Court in 2010 because, he contended, she "embraces an essentially activist view of judicial power."

Hatch's strong endorsement of conservative positions was an acknowledgment that he had received the message Utah Republicans delivered in 2010, when they dumped three-term Sen. Robert Bennett at the state party nominating convention after he backed the controversial bank bailout legislation as well as the $787 billion stimulus bill favored by Obama. Bennett's perceived apostasy paved the way for conservative Republican Mike Lee to defeat him. With rhetorical over-reach plus an eye toward the 2012 state party convention, Hatch told a conference of conservatives in Washington in 2011 that he was so much a deficit hawk that, "I'm prepared to be the most hated man in this Godforsaken city in order to save this country."

Hatch had some vulnerabilities, as the hard-charging conservative activists who dominate the state's nominating convention knew. Like Bennett, he backed the Wall Street bailout measure and he had a long history of working across the aisle. So Hatch went into overdrive to emphasize his strong conservative credentials. He may not have been the most hated, but for those two years Hatch was among the most conservative. He cosponsored legislation forcing government-sponsored mortgage giants Fannie Mae and Freddie Mac, both tea party targets, into gradual privatization.

Hatch scoffed at the idea that he was operating any differently. "The fact of the matter is, I've been a tea party person, I think, since before the tea party came into existence," he told Fox News. Given his past work with Democrats, especially Kennedy, that notion was a hard sell. Even Lee, his Utah colleague, declined to endorse him, putting even more strain on their relationship. Hatch's rhetoric took a noticeably sharper bite. He told Fox News that Obama was a "scaredy cat hiding in some closet in the White House" for not moving faster on the Keystone XL pipeline, designed to bring Canadian oil to U.S. refineries.

Hatch energetically courted support. By early 2012, FreedomWorks, one of the largest of the tea party movement's groups and one that has a close relationship with Lee, had raised more than $615,000 to try to oust him. Hatch responded by calling FreedomWorks "the sleaziest bunch I've ever seen in my life." The group's favored challenger, Rep. Jason Chaffetz, declined to take on Hatch. At the April 2012 convention, Hatch fell just short-with 59.19 percent of the vote during the second round of balloting-of attaining the 60 percent threshold to avoid a primary in June. His primary opponent, Dan Liljenquist, a former state senator, accused Hatch of "fiscal child abuse" for repeatedly voting to raise the nation's debt limit. Hatch was much more popular with rank-and-file Republican primary voters than with the tea party activists that dominate party conventions, and easily sailed to a 66% to 34% victory, winning every county. That lopsided victory sealed his easy win in the general election.

In October 2013, Hatch was secure enough politically to warn, on MSNBC, that the conservative Heritage Foundation think tank was "in danger of losing its clout and its power" because it had lurched so far rightward. He also had some unsolicited advice for Lee in a radio station interview with KSL in Salt Lake City in 2014, after some Republicans criticized the junior Utah senator, one of the architects of the government shutdown in 2013: "You can't be devoted to just one strain of the Republican Party without making sure you represent everybody, and I think that's where some of this resentment comes." He declined to endorse Lee's reelection in 2016, taking a page from Lee's failure to endorse him as the tea party made him a target in 2012.

In an earlier interview with that radio station in 2014, Hatch sounded a more pragmatic note than Lee about same-sex marriage despite the fact that he personally opposed such unions. He predicted that rainbow marriages inevitably would become legal at some point, in a ruling of the Supreme Court. Lee, by contrast, on the same radio show, did not think such a ruling was inevitable and said that it's wrong for judges to make that call because the decision should rest with the people of the states. The following year, Hatch proved to be prescient and the Court legalized same-sex marriage.

To counter Democrats' criticism that the GOP had no alternative to the Affordable Care Act, Hatch unveiled a proposal in 2014 with Republican Sens. Richard Burr of North Carolina and Tom Coburn of Oklahoma. The bill retained many of the most popular elements of the law but repealed the mandate that Americans obtain insurance or pay a penalty. It would only guarantee coverage for people with pre-existing medical conditions if they maintained "continuous coverage." The idea drew widespread attention but failed to gain much political traction.

Following the Republican convention, Hatch and Trump talked regularly by phone, perhaps a dozen calls before the end of the year. *The Wall Street Journal* reported in early December 2016, "Since the election, the two have spoken regularly about potential nominations for the Supreme Court and the Trump administration, as well as about Mr. Trump's legislative agenda, according to people familiar with the conversations." In the face of unyielding opposition by Finance Committee Democrats to the new president's cabinet members, Hatch circumvented long-time Senate traditions to win their confirmation. As the debate began on the future of the Affordable Care Act, Hatch voiced his flexibility. "I'm open to anything," he told The Washington Post. "Anything that will improve the system, I'm for."

In 2000, Hatch easily defeated former state senator Scott Howell, 66% to 31%, and he became the first Utahn popularly elected five times to the Senate. Howell would challenge him again 12 years later. The only other five-term senator in Utah history, Reed Smoot, who served from 1903 to 1933, was elected to his first term by the legislature. Hatch broke the record with a sixth, and then a seventh term. During his 2012 campaign, Hatch told voters that he would not seek another term. By 2016, he was having second thoughts and was urged by some Republicans and business groups to run in 2018 for an eighth term, which only five Senators-including Kennedy and Leahy-have achieved. In January 2017, a poll by the *Salt Lake Tribune* found that 78 percent said that he should retire and that he could be vulnerable in a GOP primary. Former 2012 GOP presidential nominee Mitt Romney, an ex-governor of Massachusetts, said he would consider running if Hatch retired. Romney, a Mormon leader, has a home in Utah. That fueled speculation that Hatch was delaying his retirement announcement to limit his time as a Senate lame duck.

During a private June 2017 meeting that he hosted with many of his contributors, Romney reportedly did not dismiss a suggestion during a discussion with former Vice President Joe Biden that Romney should consider running for the Senate.

Junior Senator

Mike Lee (R)

Elected 2010, term expires 2022, 2nd term; b. Jun 04, 1971, Mesa, AZ; Brigham Young University (UT), B.A.; Brigham Young University (UT), J.D.; Mormon; Married (Sharon Lee); 3 children.

Professional Career: Law clerk, Judge Samuel Alito, U.S Court of Appeals, 3rd Circuit, 1998-1999; Practicing attorney, 1999-2002; Assistant U.S Attorney, 2002-2005; Gen. counsel, Gov. Jon Huntsman, 2005-2006; Law clerk, Supreme Court Justice Samuel Alito, 2006-2007; Practicing attorney, 2007-2010.

DC Office: 361-A RSOB 20510, 202-224-5444, Fax: 202-228-1168, lee.senate.gov.

State Offices: Ogden, 801-392-9633; Salt Lake City, 801-524-5933; St. George, 435-628-5514.

Committees: *Commerce, Science & Transportation*: Aviation Operations, Safety & Security, Communications, Technology, Innovation & the Internet, Consumer Protection, Product Safety, Ins & Data Security, Oceans, Atmosphere, Fisheries & Coast Guard, Space, Science & Competitiveness. *Energy & Natural Resources*: National Parks, Public Lands, Forests & Mining (Chmn), Water & Power. *Judiciary*: Antitrust, Competition Policy & Consumer Rights (Chmn), Border Security & Immigration, Oversight, Agency Action, Federal Rights & Federal Courts, Privacy, Technology & the Law.

Group Ratings

	ADA	ACLU	AFL-CIO	LCV	ITI	COC	HAFA	ACU	CFG	FRC
2016	-	58%	-	6%	33%	71%	100%	100%	100%	100%
2015	5%	C	23%	4%	C	58%	C	100%	100%	100%

Almanac Ratings 2015

	Economy	Social	Foreign	Composite
Liberal	14%	0%	38%	17%
Conservative	86%	100%	62%	83%

Key Votes of the 114th Congress

1. Keystone pipeline	Y	5. National Security Data	Y	9. Gun Sales Checks	N
2. Export-Import Bank	Y	6. Iran Nuclear Deal	Y	10. Sanctuary Cities	Y
3. Debt Ceiling Increase	N	7. Puerto Rico Debt	N	11. Planned Parenthood	Y
4. Homeland Security $$	N	8. Loretta Lynch A.G	N	12. Trade deals	N

Election Results

Election	Name (Party)	Vote (%)		Cand. Spent	Ind. Exp. Support	Ind. Exp. Oppose
2016 General	Mike Lee (R)	760,241	(68%)	$4,420,800	$316,173	
	Misty Snow (D)	301,860	(27%)	$95,199		
	Stoney Fonua (I)	26,167	(2%)			
2016 Primary	Mike Lee (R)	unopposed				

Prior winning percentages: 2010 (62%)

Utah's junior senator is Republican Mike Lee, who toppled 18-year Senate veteran Robert Bennett at the state GOP convention in 2010. Though low-key and outwardly unassuming, Lee has strong convictions, especially an abiding interest in spreading his tea party-influenced views. Aside from his easy reelection, the 2016 campaign was marked by his enthusiastic support for Sen. Ted Cruz of Texas for the GOP presidential nomination and his own refusal to endorse Donald Trump in the general election.

Lee grew up in Provo, where his father, Rex Lee, was the founding dean of Brigham Young University law school. He also lived part of the time in McLean, Virginia, when Rex Lee was an assistant attorney general from 1975 to 1976 and solicitor general from 1981 to 1985. Senate Democratic Leader Harry Reid of Nevada, then a House member, was his Mormon (Church of Jesus Christ of Latter-day

Saints) "home teacher," and he was schoolmates with children of Republican Sen. Strom Thurmond of South Carolina and Democratic Rep. Dick Gephardt of Missouri. As a teenager, Lee remembers watching his father argue cases before the Supreme Court. "It took me a while before I realized it wasn't entirely an ordinary experience to get to do that frequently," he recalled.

Lee returned to Provo at age 14, and later entered Brigham Young University, where he ran for student body president on a platform that the university should end the practice of vetting candidates for student government. "There were a number of people who called me a radical because of that. It's hardly radical to say students ought to be able to conduct their own elections," he said. He graduated from college and law school at Brigham Young, and then served as a law clerk to District Judge Dee Benson in Utah and Third Circuit Court of Appeals Judge Samuel Alito in New Jersey. He went on to practice law in Washington D.C. and Utah. In 2005, he served as legal counsel to Republican Gov. Jon Huntsman, and in 2006, after Alito was confirmed to the Supreme Court, Lee returned to Washington to clerk for him once again.

Lee had joined a Utah law firm by the time the 2010 election rolled around. He said he decided to challenge Bennett after Congress passed the $700 billion bailout of the financial industry and the $787 billion stimulus bill that President Barack Obama sought. "The Republican Party had in so many ways deviated from what it professes," Lee said. Bennett was in his third term and regarded as a solid conservative. But he had voted for the Troubled Asset Relief Program for the financial industry, and he also had been a chief supporter of a bipartisan approach to health care legislation with Oregon Democrat Ron Wyden.

Bennett was endorsed by soon-to-be presidential nominee Mitt Romney and fellow Utah GOP Senator Orrin Hatch. But to get on the primary ballot, he had to get 60 percent of the delegate vote, or finish first or second at the Utah Republican convention in May 2010. In the meantime, Lee had caught the fancy of tea party activists, who were beginning to make inroads with their attacks on government spending and the expanded reach of government into the health care system. He was endorsed by DeMint, who was trying to influence the selection of a more conservative crop of GOP candidates in 2010.

At the convention, involving roughly 3,500 delegates from around the state, Bennett survived a first round of balloting despite being pilloried for backing the TARP, which was decried as a bank bailout, and for working on bipartisan health care legislation. He was hammered for being a member of the Appropriations Committee when the government debt kept growing. Bennett was swept out in the second round. Business consultant Tim Bridgewater came in first with 37 percent, and Lee was second, with 35 percent of the delegates; Bennett finished third with 27 percent.

When neither Lee nor Bridgewater reached the 60-percent threshold to win outright, the contest went to a primary election. Lee prevailed, 51%-49%. Of the state's two most populous counties, Bridgewater carried Salt Lake County, where relatively less-conservative voters live, but Lee won in Utah County. The general election was anticlimactic in this heavily Republican state. Lee easily defeated Democrat Sam Granato, 62%-33%.

At age 38, Lee was the youngest senator when he took office in 2011. One of his first moves was to introduce a bill for a balanced budget amendment that would require a two-thirds vote of both houses of Congress to override the limitation on spending. It did not go far in the Democratic-controlled Senate. Lee got some notice when he was one of the few Republicans to vote against extending the USA Patriot Act after expressing concern that it did not sufficiently protect civil liberties and privacy.

In 2011, Lee penned a book titled *The Freedom Agenda: Why a Balanced Budget Amendment is Necessary to Restore Constitutional Government*. During the standoff over raising the debt limit in the summer of 2011, he tried to push the balanced budget amendment as part of any deal. But the Senate eventually approved a plan with more modest deficit reduction. Lee voted against it. In December 2011, he and fellow Utahn Orrin Hatch offered a balanced budget amendment that was rejected, 47-53. In May 2012, Lee offered a proposal to balance the budget in five years, implement a flat tax, and reform health care coverage. The Senate rejected it, 17-82. After Hurricane Sandy, Lee offered another amendment in 2013 to cut federal programs across the board by a half of a percentage point through 2021 as a way to prevent disaster aid from raising the debt; it failed 35-62.

Lee jumped into the fray on judicial nominations. Outraged over President Obama's recess appointments, he voted, from his seat on the Judiciary Committee, against Utah lawyer Robert Shelby for a federal judgeship in April 2012. He made it clear that he supported Shelby, but voted "no" as a protest against the recess appointments. That underscored his willingness to press a fight for a principle, which, in this case, was what he saw as an unconstitutional power grab by the Executive Branch. His persistence was rewarded when the Supreme Court ruled unanimously in 2014 that such recess appointments were unconstitutional if made when the Senate says that it is in session.

Lee's tenacity became evident in his battle to dismantle the Affordable Care Act. During the initial legal challenge to the law, Lee was active as the lawsuit wended its way to the Supreme Court. He put out three *YouTube* videos related to health care. But the Court, in 2012, upheld the law's requirement that individuals must carry health insurance or face a penalty as part of the government's tax authority.

That setback did not stop Lee from continuing his efforts to target the law. He emerged as a leader, along with his friend and ally, Republican Sen. Ted Cruz of Texas, in formulating the strategy to defund what came to be derided as Obamacare. That approach led to a government shutdown, much to the consternation of party leaders. When the 16-day shutdown ended without having made a dent in Obamacare, Lee faced widespread unhappiness in the Senate from fellow Republicans, as Democrats looked to make political hay from the unpopular maneuver. Lee suffered back home, where the federal government is the largest employer. Between shutting down national parks and furloughing federal workers, Utah took a hit and Lee's poll numbers sagged.

That downturn proved to be temporary as Lee rebounded by reaching out to reassure the business community and explain his relentless push for smaller and less meddlesome government. He had the strong backing of aggressive, well-funded conservative groups that were poised to spend lavishly to help him fend off would-be GOP primary challengers. As it turned out, their help was not needed in his 2016 reelection.

Lee roiled the clubby Senate when he declined to endorse his colleague, Hatch, in 2012 when the long-time incumbent was facing the fight of his political life from tea party-backed challengers. Hatch survived to win a seventh term. Lee's stance further strained the relationship between the two Republican senators.

Lee does not shy from shaking up his party's establishment and has continued to press some controversial stances. With other conservative Republicans, he co-sponsored a bill declaring that the 14th Amendment's birthright citizenship is limited to children of citizens, legal residents, and members of the military, and does not extend to illegal immigrants. He also pushed for loosening some immigration restrictions. He crossed party lines in an unusual alliance with New York Democratic Sen. Charles Schumer to advance a visa reform bill that included helping foreigners who have invested at least $500,000 in a house in the United States. At Schumer's behest, Lee took part in bipartisan talks on a comprehensive immigration reform bill in late 2012 and early 2013, but backed out and refused to sign the group's draft giving immigrants a path to legal citizenship. "Reforms to our complex and dysfunctional immigration system should not in any way favor those who came here illegally over the millions of applicants who seek to come here lawfully," he said.

On foreign policy, Lee has been less hawkish than some other conservatives. In a Senate Foreign Relations Committee vote in 2011, Lee opposed a congressional resolution authorizing U.S. military involvement in Libya. He was the first GOP senator to join his Kentucky colleague Rand Paul during Paul's 13-hour filibuster in 2013 that protested the Obama administration's potential use of unmanned drones to attack U.S. citizens.

His ideological kinship with Paul and Cruz came to the fore when they said they would filibuster any attempt to bring gun-control legislation to the Senate floor. Lee continued to cause some upset with Republican Senate leaders. During the high-stakes fight for the Trans-Pacific Partnership trade legislation, Lee was the subject of a *Politico* story that reported that he had blindsided his party leaders by failing to show up on a critical vote. Though he had stated he backed the effort, he stayed in Utah when the vote was called, because, his office said, he had a family commitment to be with his sons who had just completed their Mormon missions. Though the measure narrowly passed, Lee's absence did not endear him to the GOP leaders, who had counted on his vote. In 2016, he pursued a quixotic bid for a GOP leadership seat, even though there appeared to be no opening. He abandoned his quest months before the election, for the time being at least.

Lee has worked hard to elect other tea party-backed candidates. In 2012, he formed a political action committee to support like-minded conservative candidates and also produced a policy blueprint for them to use on the trail. Lee has traveled across the country to campaign with such candidates who are involved in tough party primaries. In 2016, he coasted to reelection, 68%-27%, against Misty Snow, the first known transgender person to win a major-party nomination for a congressional seat. After his enthusiastic support for Cruz during the presidential primaries, Lee was outspokenly "NeverTrump" at the Republican convention and during the fall campaign. He complained that Republican officials violated party rules by denying the anti-Trump forces their right to participate in convention activities.

FIRST DISTRICT

Rob Bishop (R)

Elected 2002, 8th term; b. Jul 13, 1951, Kaysville; University of Utah, B.A., 1974; Mormon; Married (Jeralynn Hansen Bishop); 5 children; 7 grandchildren.

Elected Office: UT House, 1978-1994, speaker 1993-1994.

Professional Career: H.S. teacher, 1974-2002; Chair, UT Republican Party, 1997-2001.

DC Office: 123 CHOB 20515, 202-225-0453, Fax: 202-225-5857, robbishop.house.gov.

State Offices: Brigham City, 435-734-2270; Ogden, 801-625-0107.

Committees: *Armed Services*: Readiness, Tactical Air & Land Forces. *Natural Resources (Chmn)*: Energy & Mineral Resources, Federal Lands, Indian, Insular & Alaska Native Affairs, Oversight & Investigations, Water, Power & Oceans.

Group Ratings

	ADA	ACLU	AFL-CIO	LCV	ITI	COC	HAFA	ACU	CFG	FRC
2016	-	5%	-	0%	100%	100%	71%	92%	74%	100%
2015	0%	C	9%	0%	C	75%	C	78%	81%	92%

Almanac Ratings 2015

	Economy	Social	Foreign	Composite
Liberal	2%	18%	0%	7%
Conservative	98%	82%	100%	93%

Key Votes of the 114th Congress

1. Keystone Pipeline	Y	5. Puerto Rico Debt	Y	9. Offenses by Aliens	Y
2. Trade Deals	Y	6. Medical Marijuana	Y	10. Troops in Iraq	N
3. Export-Import Bank	N	7. Sanctuary Cities	Y	11. Homeland Security $$	N
4. Debt Ceiling Increase	N	8. Armor-piercing Bullets	Y	12. Trade Adjustment aid	N

Election Results

Election	Name (Party)	Vote (%)	Cand. Spent	Ind. Exp. Support	Ind. Exp. Oppose
2016 General	Rob Bishop (R)	182,928 (66%)	$372,342		
	Peter Clemens (D)	73,381 (26%)	$121,790		
	Craig Bowden (L)	16,296 (6%)			
2016 Primary	Rob Bishop (R)	(100%)			

Prior winning percentages: 2014 (64%), 2012 (72%), 2010 (69%), 2008 (65%), 2006 (63%), 2004 (68%), 2002 (61%)

Republican Rob Bishop, first elected in 2002, is a leading advocate of states' rights and a sharp critic of federal management of public lands, both hot-button issues in the rural West. As chairman of the Natural Resources Committee, he has sought to reshape the debate and to challenge an activist president willing to go his own way. Bishop pressed President Donald Trump to rescind many of the executive actions affecting the West that were taken by President Barack Obama, especially during his final days in office.

Bishop grew up in Davis County and graduated from the University of Utah. He became a high school history and government teacher in Box Elder County. (He remains fond of giving guided historical tours of the Capitol. In one, videotaped for *The Salt Lake Tribune*'s website, he pointed out religious-themed paintings displayed in the Rotunda and quipped, "So much for the separation of church and state.") In 1978, he was elected to the state House and served two years as House speaker. He continued working as a teacher after leaving the legislature, and also worked as a lobbyist for state Republicans and for the National Rifle Association.

When the House seat became open, both Bishop and former House Majority Leader Kevin Garn ran. As a former state party chair for four years, Bishop won 58 percent of the vote at the Republican nominating convention. With mostly similar conservative views, their chief difference was a contentious issue in Utah: the ongoing battle between banks and credit unions. The credit union lobby endorsed Bishop who, as a lobbyist in 1999, helped defeat legislation to curtail the credit unions' tax-exempt status. Bishop won the primary 60%-40%. Democrat Dave Thomas, a wealthy advertising executive and an anti-abortion rights Mormon bishop, presented himself as a fiscal conservative and "a regular guy" not tied to special interests. Bishop won, 61%-37%.

Bishop has been an active conservative voice, often on behalf of Western land interests. He started a "10th Amendment Task Force" to advocate allowing states to assume control of federal programs, and proposed a constitutional amendment to allow any federal law or regulation to be overturned if two-thirds of states opposed it. In the Utah Legislature, "I learned to hate the federal government," he told *The Salt Lake Tribune* in 2010. "I could point to [highway] overpasses that were made because there was a 10-to-1 [funding] match, or programs we ran simply because the government bribed us with money."

On Natural Resources, Bishop has demonstrated skill at deal-making during his long legislative career. The *Standard-Examiner* of Ogden, in endorsing him for reelection in 2014, said: "Rep. Bishop has matured. He's less of the tea party wannabe and more of a statesman willing to both listen and work hard for his constituents. ... In fact, he expressed concern to us about some of the extreme right-wing conspiracy theories that he sometimes hears at town hall meetings, particularly on immigration." He accommodated Democrats by agreeing to their request to include climate change on the committee's agenda for 2015-16. Still, Bishop sometimes has been averse to bipartisanship. Soon after taking over as chairman in 2015, he included in a border-security bill a provision to exempt from some environmental laws immigration enforcement activities within 100 miles of U.S. borders, a move that critics condemned as a ruse to bar any regulation of those lands.

Bishop has signaled that he wants to think broadly and that he sees his chairmanship "as a chance to shake up the way the United States manages federal and Indian lands, from protecting treasured areas to permitting drilling in others," the *Houston Chronicle* reported. As Bishop told the *Chronicle* in 2015, "We haven't had a change in the way people look at the stewardship of the federal government and land in 50 or 60 years. … We are timed for a paradigm shift, and I want to be part of that." He and fellow Utah Republican Rep. Chris Stewart created an informal Federal Land Action Group, with a goal of finding ways to transfer federal land to local control. In 2016, Bishop filed a sweeping bill, the Public Lands Initiative, that would give states more authority to approve permits or energy development on federal lands. When an Obama administration official testified before his committee in defense of federal control, Bishop responded, "The state can do it in a reasonable process, you can't."

Bishop has been highly critical of unilateral presidential attempts, especially by Obama, to designate new national monuments in the West. In 2015, he objected when Obama proposed to set aside more than 12 million acres of the Arctic National Wildlife Refuge as wilderness, with tight restrictions on oil and gas leasing. "By tightening his grasp on these resources, the president has revealed another lack of leadership on the global stage," he wrote in a *Washington Times* op-ed. "This time, it's America's future leverage in world affairs and our nation's path to energy security that's at stake." Bishop, noting the opposition to the action by local Native American tribes, was furious when Obama in his final month in office unilaterally declared the 1.3 million-acre Bears Ears National Monument in Utah. "It has to be a gotcha moment where the president unveils something unilaterally," he told NPR. Bishop urged Trump to rescind or substantially cut back the Bears Ears site. Interior Secretary Ryan Zinke, a former House colleague from Montana, told Congress that a president lacks the authority to rescind a monument.

Bishop remains an active member of the Armed Services Committee; the military has numerous facilities in Utah. On the annual defense spending bill in 2015, he cited his efforts to "protect the Utah Test and Training Range, Dugway Proving Ground, the Tooele Army Depot, and other lands used for military training, from intrusion by the Obama administration."

Bishop has been comfortably reelected every two years. In 2012, his Democratic rival was Donna McAleer, an Army veteran and technology executive who blamed him for contributing to Congress' gridlock. The *Tribune* called her the best-qualified candidate her party had fielded in years, but it endorsed Bishop, who trounced her, 71%-25%. In a 2014 rematch, in which McAleer spent $268,000 to his $526,000, Bishop's victory was a bit tighter at 64%-29%. In 2016, Democratic challenger Peter Clemens, a family doctor and hyperbaric specialist at an Ogden hospital, challenged Bishop's views on lands issues. Bishop largely ignored him and won, 66%-26%. Short of serious wrongdoing, he seems secure in this district.

Northern Utah: Ogden, Logan

Population		**Race and Ethnicity**		**Income**	
Total	720,434	White	82.0%	Median Income	$61,224 (132 out of 435)
Land area	19,561	Black	0.9%		
Pop/ sq mi	36.8	Latino	12.3%		
Born in state	65.1%	Asian	1.5%	Under $50,000	39.6%
		Two races	1.9%	$50,000-$99,999	36.9%
Age Groups		Other	1.3%	$100,000-$199,999	19.7%
Under 18	31.8%			$200,000 or more	3.8%
18-34	25.8%	**Education**		Poverty Rate	11.0%
35-64	33.1%	H.S grad or less	34.4%		
Over 64	9.3%	Some college	37.2%	**Health Insurance**	
		College Degree, 4 yr	19.5%	With health insurance coverage	88.9%
Work		Post grad	8.9%		
White Collar	35.3%				
Sales and Service	39.6%	**Military**		**Public Assistance**	
Blue Collar	25.1%	Veteran	8.4%	Cash public assistance income	2.2%
Government	4.2%	Active Duty	0.5%		
				Food stamp/SNAP benefits	9.1%

Voter Turnout			
2015 Total Citizens 18+	467,360	2016 House Turnout as % CVAP	59%
2016 House turnout	277,455	2014 House Turnout as % CVAP	28%

2012 Presidential Vote		
Mitt Romney	193,672	(78%)
Barack Obama	51,098	(20%)

2016 Presidential Vote		
Donald Trump	139,503	(49%)
Evan McMullin	62,547	(22%)
Hillary Clinton	62,733	(22%)
Gary Johnson	10,231	(4%)

Cook Partisan Voting Index: R+26

In May 1869, a motley crowd of Irish and Chinese laborers, teamsters, engineers, train crews, officials and guests from Salt Lake City gathered at Promontory Summit, Utah, to watch the opening of the transcontinental railroad. Leland Stanford's blow with a silver sledge, intended to drive the ceremonial "Last Spike" into the railroad ties, missed its mark, but telegraphs nevertheless conveyed the word "done" across the nation. It wasn't just the railroad that was complete. As long as America had been America, there had been a frontier, but as the civilized East and the mostly untamed West were finally united, that frontier began to shrink and then vanish.

Ogden, Utah, is in many ways a microcosm of the impact the railway could have. At the time the railroad was completed, Ogden was a small farming community of 1,500 inhabitants. Had it not won the right to become the junction of the Union Pacific and Central Pacific railroads - which meant that all of the passengers and shipping crossing the nation changed trains in Ogden - it might have suffered the same fate as Corinne, the nearby and forgotten town that lost out to Ogden in the competition for the railroad. The city adopted the motto, "You can't get anywhere without coming to Ogden!" Today, with a population of 85,000, Ogden has developed as a hub for outdoor sports equipment makers. Amer Sports, founded in Finland and with operations in 34 nations, has consolidated its North American operations in Ogden; it owns Wilson, Atomic and other brands. As a manufacturing center for bicycles, it has become known as "biketown." Like other cities in Utah, Ogden has become a center for technology jobs.

The 1st Congressional District of Utah takes in Ogden and areas to the north of Salt Lake City. While it sprawls from the Colorado border to Idaho, about two thirds of its residents live in the stretch north of Salt Lake City from Kaysville to Brigham City. Hill Air Force Base, which houses F-35 fighter jets, is in the district, as is Utah State University, farther north in Logan. The Great Salt Lake, which is the largest water mass west of the Mississippi River and much of which is in this district, was at record low levels in the summer of 2016, posing a threat to the eco-system of the area. The record rains in the West during the following winter brought some improvement, but the water level remained well below its historic average. Much of the district is farm country and heavily Mormon. An exception is Park City, in the mountains east of Salt Lake City, which is a fashionable ski resort and home of actor Robert Redford's annual Sundance Film Festival, the largest independent film festival in the nation and in 2016 attracted 46,000, including more than 1,000 journalists.

The 1st has been among the top 10 most heavily Republican districts in the nation. Mitt Romney got 78 percent in 2012. The antipathy of Mormons for Donald Trump changed that. But the 49 percent for Trump in the District was his highest in the state and the 22 percent for Hillary Clinton was her lowest.

SECOND DISTRICT

Chris Stewart (R)

Elected 2012, 3rd term; b. Jul 15, 1960, Logan; Utah State University, B.S.; Mormon; Married (Evie Stewart); 6 children.

Military Career: U.S. Air Force, 1984-1998.

Professional Career: Owner, Shipley Group, 2000-present.

DC Office: 323 CHOB 20515, 202-225-9730, Fax: 202-225-5629, stewart.house.gov.

State Offices: Salt Lake City, 801-364-5550; St. George, 801-364-5550.

Committees: *Appropriations*: Financial Services & General Government, Interior, Environment & Related Agencies, State, Foreign Operations & Related Programs. *Permanent Select on Intelligence.*

Group Ratings

	ADA	ACLU	AFL-CIO	LCV	ITI	COC	HAFA	ACU	CFG	FRC
2016	-	5%	-	0%	100%	100%	78%	92%	84%	100%
2015	0%	C	0%	3%	C	70%	C	86%	88%	92%

Almanac Ratings 2015

	Economy	Social	Foreign	Composite
Liberal	2%	18%	0%	6%
Conservative	99%	83%	100%	94%

Key Votes of the 114th Congress

1. Keystone Pipeline	Y	5. Puerto Rico Debt	Y	9. Offenses by Aliens	Y
2. Trade Deals	Y	6. Medical Marijuana	Y	10. Troops in Iraq	N
3. Export-Import Bank	N	7. Sanctuary Cities	NV	11. Homeland Security $$	N
4. Debt Ceiling Increase	N	8. Armor-piercing Bullets	NV	12. Trade Adjustment aid	N

Election Results

Election	Name (Party)	Vote (%)		Cand. Spent	Ind. Exp. Support	Ind. Exp. Oppose
2016 General	Chris Stewart (R)	170,542	(62%)	$894,774		
	Charlene Albarran (D)	93,780	(34%)	$585,781		
	Paul J. McCollaum (C)	12,519	(5%)			
2016 Primary	Chris Stewart (R)		(100%)			

Prior winning percentages: 2014 (60%), 2012 (62%)

Republican Chris Stewart, a former Air Force pilot and author, won an open seat in 2012. Following impressive careers in the military and private sector, he established his credentials as a member of the Appropriations and Intelligence committees. In the 2016 presidential campaign, Stewart gained public notoriety with occasional shifts in his support for Donald Trump.

Stewart and his nine siblings grew up on a dairy farm in southern Idaho. His parents, both Mormon, had moved there from nearby Utah. Stewart enrolled in Utah State University, serving as a Mormon missionary in Texas before completing a degree in economics. After graduating from college, he entered the Air Force. He was first in his class in both officer training school and undergraduate pilot training. In 14 years in uniform, he attained the rank of major and in 1995 set the world record for the fastest, nonstop flight around the world in a B-1 Lancer. (His crew flew nearly 23,000 miles in just over 36 hours, for an average speed of about 630 mph.) He also flew rescue helicopters. Five of Stewart's six sons have served in the military.

Stewart began writing in the military, and took it up full time after his discharge to spend more time with his children. After two years, he bought the Shipley Group, an energy and environment consulting firm that did government and corporate security work. While he ran the business, Stewart's writing career flourished. He has written 18 books, including three *New York Times* best sellers, *Seven Miracles That Saved America* in 2009, *The Miracle of Freedom* in 2011 and a collaboration in 2013 with Utah native Elizabeth Smart on the story of her kidnapping. He says that he found more meaning in writing a six-part fiction series, *The Great and Terrible*, a religious epic about the struggle between good and evil. In his writing, he favored a balanced-budget amendment, a 25 percent top marginal income-tax rate and a dramatically reduced federal budget.

When Democratic Rep. Jim Matheson decided to run in 2012 in the newly created 4th District, Stewart got into the open-seat contest, emerging on top in an acrimonious GOP primary. One of the candidates, Eureka Mayor Milt Hanks, alleged just before delegates began casting ballots at the April party convention that four other contenders tried to pull him into a plan to hit Stewart with negative attacks. The other candidates angrily denied the charges and accused Stewart of starting a rumor of a conspiracy against him to attract voter sympathy. A subsequent Utah Republican Party investigation found no evidence of plots among candidates. Stewart prevailed with more than 60 percent of the vote in the only contest that really mattered in the heavily Republican district. He had no trouble dispatching Democrat Jay Seegmiller in the general election, 62%-33%.

After the October 2013 government shutdown, which cost local Utah governments and businesses millions of dollars, Stewart filed a bill that would allow states to fund the operations of national parks, monuments and other facilities related to tourism and other commercial activity in the event of a future lapse of federal spending. In 2014, the House passed on a largely party-line vote his bill to revamp the selection of members to the Environmental Protection Agency's Science Advisory Board to require more representatives of state and local governments. With Democratic Rep. Gregory Meeks of New York, he created a congressional caucus on Peru, chiefly because that nation had become the source for the second-largest number of immigrants to Utah. The Mormon Church has 13 missions in Peru.

His seats on the Appropriations Committee, including its State and Foreign Operations Subcommittee, and the Intelligence Committee positioned him to use his Air Force experience to oversee national security activities, notably the Obama administration's nuclear-arms talks with Iran. In March 2015, Stewart wrote in *The Wall Street Journal* that, as a B-1 pilot, he was a military representative in arms-reduction talks with the former Soviet Union. Based on that experience, he wrote, negotiating parties must be reliable partners who want an agreement to succeed. On that basis, he contended, "the record is bare" of Iran partnering with the United States or an ally "in a productive way." When the international agreement with Iran was reached in July, he said that President Barack Obama was "naïve." The deal, he added, was "an incredibly dangerous agreement and Congress must do everything in its power to stop it." The House and Senate failed to secure the two-thirds to prevent that.

In December 2016, Stewart voiced concern that the "Cold War-esque" relationship with Russia had become difficult and dangerous, especially its cyber-attacks against American interests. "What Russia is doing is aggressive. It's illegal and harmful," he told a Utah reporter. Stewart became chairman in 2017 of the Defense Intelligence and Overhead Architecture Subcommittee of the Intelligence panel, which had jurisdiction over the National Reconnaissance Program and some Pentagon programs.

During the Republican presidential primaries, Stewart supported Sen. Marco Rubio of Florida. While speaking to University of Utah students in March 2016, he called Donald Trump "our Mussolini," referring negatively to the fascist dictator of Italy. Following the release of Trump's lewd comments about groping women, Stewart said that he should withdraw his candidacy. A few days before the election, he said that he would vote for Trump as "a better choice than Hillary Clinton." Following the election, Stewart was considered for Secretary of the Air Force, the *Deseret News* reported.

Salt Lake City and Western Utah

Population		**Race and Ethnicity**		**Income**	
Total	718,869	White	77.3%	Median Income	$54,299 (191 out of 435)
Land area	39,988	Black	1.2%		
Pop/ sq mi	18.0	Latino	14.9%		
Born in state	58.8%	Asian	2.5%	Under $50,000	45.9%
		Two races	1.7%	$50,000-$99,999	34.3%
Age Groups		Other	2.4%	$100,000-$199,999	15.8%
Under 18	28.5%			$200,000 or more	4.0%
18-34	26.5%	**Education**		Poverty Rate	14.6%
35-64	33.0%	H.S grad or less	34.2%		
Over 64	12.0%	Some college	35.1%	**Health Insurance**	
		College Degree, 4 yr	19.3%	With health insurance coverage	84.1%
Work		Post grad	11.4%		
White Collar	35.7%				
Sales and Service	42.7%	**Military**		**Public Assistance**	
Blue Collar	21.7%	Veteran	7.3%	Cash public assistance income	2.1%
Government	4.8%	Active Duty	0.1%		
				Food stamp/SNAP benefits	9.9%

Voter Turnout			
2015 Total Citizens 18+	471,918	2016 House Turnout as % CVAP	59%
2016 House turnout	276,841	2014 House Turnout as % CVAP	31%

2012 Presidential Vote		
Mitt Romney	173,513	(68%)
Barack Obama	74,556	(29%)

2016 Presidential Vote		
Donald Trump	130,525	(46%)
Hillary Clinton	90,686	(32%)
Evan McMullin	47,862	(17%)
Gary Johnson	8,914	(3%)

Cook Partisan Voting Index: R+16

In Salt Lake City, at the center of the Mormon Church is Temple Square, illuminated by 300,000 lights during Christmas week and nestled beneath the towering mountains that flank Salt Lake City. The Mormon Tabernacle is here, home to the famous choir, as is the Salt Lake LDS Temple itself, crowned with the golden angel Moroni. The area has been the focal point of Utah since Mormon leader Brigham Young, looking down at the valley, said (according to church tradition), "This is the place." Ironically, this part of Salt Lake City is the least Mormon and most cosmopolitan part of Utah, with the state university and businesses bringing in outsiders who, flouting Mormon strictures, keep purveyors of alcohol and caffeine in business. The state has ended its private club system at bars, though prohibitions remained on bartenders pouring drinks in plain sight. In 2015, Salt Lake City elected Jackie Biskupski as mayor. She was a Democrat (which was nothing new for the city) and lesbian.

The 2nd Congressional District of Utah consists of most of Salt Lake City, its northern and southwestern suburbs, and the vast and mostly empty southwestern portion of the state. In Salt Lake, which includes about one-third of the district's population, it takes in the historic downtown, its distinctive Avenues District, and the airport. The county has had one Mormon chapel every 1.3 square miles, many of which are relatively small. The Milken Institute, in its annual report on best-performing cities, ranked Salt Lake City 11th in 2016, with its "well-educated workforce and relatively lower wages and business costs." The already huge reconstruction of the terminal at the airport has been expanded to add a second concourse. The $2.9 billion project is scheduled to be completed in 2020.

To the west are the desolate Bonneville Salt Flats, where land speeds records have been set. After having been closed for three years to preserve the salts, the area reopened in August 2016 with races at up to 400 miles per hour. This land of stark beauty, much of it federally owned, has been used roughly by man, as a repository for hazardous wastes at civilian and military dumps in Tooele County and as a place for military experimentations at the Dugway Proving Grounds, where scientists test defenses against chemical and biological agents. In 2015, the facility opened a center for biological warfare readiness.

The Skull Valley Band of Goshute Indians has pressed for a temporary nuclear waste storage site near Dugway, but it has remained on hold for years because of Utah's reluctance to take waste from other states.

About 20 percent of the district's residents live in the stretch of the Wasatch Front, between the mountains and Great Salt Lake, just north of Salt Lake City, in suburban and fairly affluent Davis County. Another 25 percent live in the stretch of lightly populated counties in the southwest corner of the state, chiefly Washington County, which is the home of Zion National Park. The park has been struggling to cope with a surge of visitors, which exceeded 4 million in 2016.

Politically, this is a mostly Republican area, with pockets of Democratic strength. Hillary Clinton carried Salt Lake County by nearly 38,000 votes over Donald Trump in 2016. That year, many of the usual Republican voters supported third-party candidates instead of Donald Trump. The 68%-29% win in 2012 for Mitt Romney, a Mormon, dropped to a 46%-32% lead for Trump four years later.

THIRD DISTRICT

Jason Chaffetz (R)

Elected 2008, 5th term; b. Mar 26, 1967, Los Gatos, CA; Brigham Young University (UT), B.A., 1989; Mormon; Married (Julie Marie Johnson Chaffetz); 3 children.

Professional Career: Spokesman & Public Relations, Nu Skin Intl.; President Maxtera Utah; Chief of Staff, Gov. Jon Huntsman, 2005-2008.

DC Office: 2236 RHOB 20515, 202-225-7751, Fax: 202-225-5629, chaffetz.house.gov.

State Offices: Provo, 801-851-2500.

Committees: *Judiciary*: Courts, Intellectual Property & Internet, Crime, Terrorism, Homeland Security & Investigations. *Oversight & Government Reform.*

Group Ratings

	ADA	ACLU	AFL-CIO	LCV	ITI	COC	HAFA	ACU	CFG	FRC
2016	-	11%	-	0%	100%	100%	74%	92%	93%	92%
2015	0%	C	4%	0%	C	70%	C	96%	88%	83%

Almanac Ratings 2015

	Economy	Social	Foreign	Composite
Liberal	3%	9%	0%	4%
Conservative	97%	91%	100%	96%

Key Votes of the 114th Congress

1. Keystone Pipeline	Y	5. Puerto Rico Debt	Y	9. Offenses by Aliens	Y
2. Trade Deals	Y	6. Medical Marijuana	Y	10. Troops in Iraq	N
3. Export-Import Bank	N	7. Sanctuary Cities	Y	11. Homeland Security $$	N
4. Debt Ceiling Increase	N	8. Armor-piercing Bullets	Y	12. Trade Adjustment aid	N

Election Results

Election	Name (Party)	Vote (%)		Cand. Spent	Ind. Exp. Support	Ind. Exp. Oppose
2016 General	Jason Chaffetz (R)	209,589	(74%)	$1,242,187		
	Stephen Tryon (D)	75,716	(27%)	$10,000		
2016 Primary	Jason Chaffetz (R)	44,655	(79%)			
	Chia-Chi Teng (R)	12,043	(21%)			

Prior winning percentages: 2014 (72%), 2012 (77%), 2010 (72%), 2012 (77%), 2010 (72%), 2008 (66%)

Republican Jason Chaffetz, a media-savvy conservative, was elected in 2008 and had close kinship with the tea party-backed Republicans who arrived two years later. As chairman of the Oversight and Government Reform Committee during the final two years of the Obama administration, he relentlessly pressed investigations - occasionally on a bipartisan basis. Like many Republicans, he was preparing to confront Hillary Clinton as president with endless inquiries. But he was flummoxed by Donald Trump's presidential campaign and the start of his administration. In April 2017, he announced that he would not seek reelection to the House, though he kept the door open to other election campaigns. Soon after that, he said that he would resign in June. Utah officials said that they plan a special election for his seat later in the year. House Republicans selected Rep. Trey Gowdy of South Carolina to replace him as Oversight chairman.

Born in Los Gatos, California, Chaffetz grew up in Arizona. His family's politics were Democratic, and they boasted one notable link: His father's first wife, Katharine Dickson, would later enter the national consciousness as "Kitty," whose second husband was Michael Dukakis, the 1988 Democratic presidential nominee. During college, Chaffetz was named an honorary co-chairman of the Dukakis campaign for Utah in 1988.

He won an athletic scholarship to Brigham Young University, where he was the place-kicker for the football team. More significantly, he converted to Mormonism and began what he views in hindsight as a natural movement toward the political right. After college, Chaffetz worked in public relations, first as an executive for Nu Skin Enterprises, a company that sells skin care products. In 2003, he volunteered for Republican Jon Huntsman Jr.'s gubernatorial campaign. When his campaign manager abruptly resigned, Huntsman asked Chaffetz to replace him. After the election, Chaffetz served a year as the new governor's chief of staff.

Chaffetz sensed an opportunity as perennial discontent with Republican Rep. Chris Cannon simmered among Utah conservatives. Chaffetz entered the race in early 2007, at a steep disadvantage in both cash and name recognition. He criticized Cannon's support of President George W. Bush's proposal for a guest worker program and a path to citizenship for illegal immigrants, both deeply unpopular in the conservative district. He called for immediate deportation of all illegal immigrants and the construction of tent cities, ringed by barbed-wire fences, to detain those who had committed crimes while in the United States. Bush and most of the state's Republican establishment endorsed Cannon, although Huntsman stayed neutral. Cannon attacked Chaffetz as an opportunist and raised more than $840,000. Chaffetz spent less than $200,000. In the low-turnout June contest, he won by a whopping 20 points. The outcome of the general election was never in doubt. He has gone unchallenged in his heavily Republican district.

Chaffetz typically votes the conservative line in accordance with his district's wishes, and often has been out front in in trying to shape the debate. During the battle over raising the debt limit in 2011, he became a chief sponsor of the "cut, cap and balance" proposal favored by deficit hawks, which passed the House. The plan, which included a spending cap and a proposed balanced budget amendment to the Constitution, was tabled by the Senate. But he can be unpredictable. He was one of 36 House Republicans who refused to back the 2010 deal extending the Bush-era tax cuts, contending the move would only contribute to the national debt.

In his early work on Oversight and Government Reform, Chaffetz got a bill through the House in 2009 to bar primary scanning at airports using whole body imaging machines, which he considered unnecessarily intrusive. He had a confrontation at Salt Lake's airport after trying to avoid an image scanner. He also was an outspoken opponent of the District of Columbia's legalization of same-sex marriage. He filed bills to allow for the firing of federal workers who are delinquent paying taxes and bar them from receiving government contracts or grants. In February 2017, he said that he would seek to overturn a D.C. law permitting assisted suicide.

Chaffetz, who views accountability as a hallmark of his work, became a leading critic of President Barack Obama's response to the deadly September 2012 terrorist attack at the U.S. consulate in Benghazi, Libya. He was among the first congressional investigators to Libya in the weeks following the attack and his concerns became the impetus for a broader investigation and the appointment of a select committee. When his subcommittee publicly released unclassified but sensitive documents a month later that included the names of Libyan human rights activists who had worked with the U.S. government, prompting criticism from the State Department, Chaffetz was unapologetic. "That's right out of the Democrat playbook: Attack the messenger," he told *The Huffington Post.*

Chaffetz is known for his media accessibility and quotability, appearing in a CNN video project highlighting his freshman year and giving numerous interviews to publications, TV stations and websites. He regularly posted videos on *YouTube* and collected more than 250,000 followers on Twitter. "He's impossible not to like on a personal level," said South Carolina GOP Rep. Trey Gowdy, another favorite of Hill journalists. Coincidentally, Gowdy gained broad support among House Republicans to succeed Chaffetz as committee chairman.

His media savvy was a boost in helping Chaffetz to defeat three more senior Republicans - John Mica of Florida and Jim Jordan and Mike Turner, both of Ohio - who challenged him for the Oversight and Government Reform chairmanship in 2014. "We as a party often make the mistake of just talking to the same people that agree with us," he said. "We talk a lot about being a big tent, but we tend not to talk to other audiences." Chaffetz brought in dozens of new staffers and created a new panel devoted to information technology. He gave Jordan, a well-regarded figure among conservatives, an enhanced role in scrutinizing the Obama administration's regulations.

Chaffetz was serious about promoting bipartisanship at the committee. He started by reaching out to ranking Democrat Elijah Cummings of Maryland, and they spent time with each other in visits to each other's district during the summer of 2014. "We're going to disagree on most issues," Chaffetz told *Time*. "I just don't want to be disagreeable." That proved to be no easy matter. At the first committee meeting in January, Chaffetz pushed through a rules package that Cummings complained was "worse than the rules we had" under the previous chairman, Darrell Issa of California.

Chaffetz launched an ambitious schedule of investigations and nearly daily committee hearings, much of which he sought to peg to pending controversies. When the Secret Service was plagued by continuing misbehavior within its ranks, including among senior officers, Chaffetz called a hearing to review compliance with the agency's protocols. With Cummings, he issued a joint statement in May 2015 that "a major cultural overhaul is essential to restoring the Secret Service to its former stature." Later that year, *The Washington Post* reported that Secret Service agents had been improperly compiling embarrassing information about Chaffetz. He called the report "a little bit scary." Chaffetz held hearings on criminal justice reform at the request of Cummings, who said that he appreciated the cooperation. Following reports of a data breach at the Office of Personnel Management involving the records of millions of federal employees, Chaffetz quickly launched hearings and moved with other committee Republicans to demand the removal of OPM Director Katherine Archuleta from her job. With similar statements from congressional Democrats, she stepped down two weeks later in July 2015. In an unusual move for a Republican, he investigated the problems that journalists have faced in gaining compliance with the Freedom of Information Act. He blamed "the yahoos at the White House having to review each and every document."

Chaffetz became enmeshed in intramural Republican politics when he decided in June 2015 to remove Rep. Mark Meadows of North Carolina as chairman of the Government Operations Subcommittee for various acts of party disloyalty, including voting against procedural steps on giving trade promotion authority to Obama. The move, which Speaker John Boehner appeared to have encouraged, sparked a furor among conservatives and lengthy closed-door talks. A few days later, they issued a joint statement restoring Meadows to the post. "I think we both better understand each other" following several discussions, Chaffetz said. "I respect Mark and his approach." Meadows responded prior to the August recess by filing a resolution that would force Boehner to step down as Speaker. When it became apparent that he was losing support among Republicans, the Speaker announced his resignation at the end of September.

During the skirmishing for a new GOP leadership team, Chaffetz voiced interest. He told Fox News that he had been "recruited" by members unhappy with Majority Leader Kevin McCarthy and that he would "bridge the divide" in the House GOP. "We don't seem to win the argument, and that's a problem." It turned out that neither of them had sufficient support to become Speaker. Chaffetz urged Paul Ryan to take the position.

During the 2016 campaign, Chaffetz was preparing to investigate a Clinton presidency. "It's a target-rich environment," he told *The Washington Post* two weeks before the election. He showed ambivalence about Trump, who was unpopular among Mormons. When a video was released in October with Trump's lewd comments about women, Chaffetz responded, "I'm out," and said he could not "in good conscience" support Trump. "I've been in a lot of locker rooms. This is not just locker room talk." After the election, Chaffetz offered indirect support by criticizing the head of the Office of Government Ethics, who had questioned Trump's financial conflicts. Chaffetz briefly threatened an investigation of the ethics official. Less than a month after the election, he was challenged by protesters in his district for not investigating Trump. Chaffetz responded that he would investigate if warranted, but that he would not pursue "a fishing investigation."

Those new circumstances that left Chaffetz in an awkward position of figuring out how to investigate a controversial president of his own party may have been a factor in his unexpected decision to step down from the House. Following his resignation, Chaffetz said, he left the door open to remaining in public life. He joined Fox News as a contributor. He made clear that he retained his long-standing interest in running statewide in Utah. That could become a bid for governor in 2020. Or, given that he tested the waters in 2011 for a primary challenge to Sen. Orrin Hatch, which Chaffetz said would be a "multimillion dollar bloodbath," a Senate campaign remained a possibility-though less likely if Hatch decided to seek another term in 2018. He retained plenty of career options.

Central and East Utah: Provo Area, Salt Lake City Suburbs

Population		**Race and Ethnicity**		**Income**	
Total	720,828	White	83.2%	Median Income	$64,445 (101 out of 435)
Land area	20,071	Black	0.5%		
Pop/ sq mi	35.9	Latino	10.2%		
Born in state	60.6%	Asian	1.9%	Under $50,000	38.0%
		Two races	2.0%	$50,000-$99,999	34.2%
Age Groups		Other	2.1%	$100,000-$199,999	22.1%
Under 18	31.4%			$200,000 or more	5.6%
18-34	28.6%	**Education**		Poverty Rate	12.5%
35-64	30.8%	H.S grad or less	24.3%		
Over 64	9.2%	Some college	37.4%	**Health Insurance**	
		College Degree, 4 yr	25.4%	With health insurance coverage	88.2%
Work		Post grad	12.8%		
White Collar	41.1%				
Sales and Service	42.0%	**Military**		**Public Assistance**	
Blue Collar	17.0%	Veteran	5.2%	Cash public assistance income	1.8%
Government	5.0%	Active Duty	0.1%		
				Food stamp/SNAP benefits	7.6%

Voter Turnout			
2015 Total Citizens 18+	466,894	2016 House Turnout as % CVAP	61%
2016 House turnout	285,305	2014 House Turnout as % CVAP	31%

2012 Presidential Vote		
Mitt Romney	208,121	(79%)
Barack Obama	51,791	(20%)

2016 Presidential Vote		
Donald Trump	136,782	(47%)
Evan McMullin	70,933	(24%)
Hillary Clinton	67,461	(23%)
Gary Johnson	9,580	(3%)

Cook Partisan Voting Index: R+25

Provo is in a geographically isolated valley between 11,000-foot peaks of the Wasatch Range and the shores of Utah Lake. It is the third-largest city in the state and home of Brigham Young University, the heart of Mormonism and an institution long known for old-fashioned moral standards and the conservative views of its faculty. Its student population in 2015 was 98.5 percent Mormon, and 36 percent of seniors were married. It is annually ranked as the most-sober university in the nation. BYU is known for its welcoming of technological innovation. The Mormon commonwealth, after all, started off with a huge shortage of both labor and water, and its inhabitants were motivated to use technology to prosper in the fearsome terrain. Provo is where the vast majority of Mormon missionaries are trained; 36,000 annually have gone through Provo's Missionary Training Center, which has had the effect of producing a disproportionately high number of foreign language speakers in the area. In 2015, the 5 percent job growth in Provo was the strongest in the nation; Provo was rated in a 2014 Gallup poll as the best city to live in the United States.

Today, the city is a technology center, the home of Novell and hundreds of other computer-related firms. Provo produced Philo Farnsworth, the inventor of television, and Harvey Fletcher, inventor of the hearing aid. Nearby Lehi is home to a large office site for the software maker Adobe and to Micron's master planned community for technology leadership, which envisions more than 20,000 employees and 3,000 residents. Micron and Intel jointly operate the IM Flash plant, where 1,700 employees have been developing new computer chips for use in manufacturing, in an effort to reverse the big drop in the U.S. share of the chip market.

The 3rd Congressional District of Utah includes all or part of seven counties in central and eastern Utah. Close to 60 percent of the district's residents live in Utah County and 30 percent in Salt Lake. The 3rd takes in affluent suburbs southeast of Salt Lake City, including Holladay, Cottonwood Heights and Draper. In Utah County, which grew by 15 percent from 2010 to 2016, the district takes in Provo and the string of towns between the mountains and Utah Lake. The area around Moab is a destination for outdoor-loving tourists. The land is mostly owned by one federal agency or another, and there have been bitter fights between locals dependent on mining and environmentalists who want to preserve the scenery, including recently discovered dinosaur tracks. In San Juan County, lame-duck President Barack Obama sparked huge controversy when he declared the 1.3 million acre Bears Ears National Monument. Sen. Orrin Hatch of Utah called the executive action "an attack on an entire way of life." President Donald Trump fared poorly throughout Utah. He won the 3rd with 47 percent of the vote in 2016, where Mitt Romney got 79 percent four years earlier.

FOURTH DISTRICT

Mia Love (R)

Elected 2014, 2nd term; b. Dec 06, 1975, Brooklyn, NY; University of Hartford; b.F.A.; Mormon; Married (Jason Love); 3 children.

Elected Office: Saratoga Springs, UT City Council, 2003-2009; Saratoga Springs, UT Mayor, 2010-2014.

Professional Career: Flight attendant, 1997-1998; Call center employee, 1998-2000; Software company marketing director, 2000.

DC Office: 217 CHOB 20515, 202-225-3011, Fax: 202-225-5638, love.house.gov.

State Offices: West Jordan, 801-996-8729.

Committees: *Financial Services*: Financial Institutions & Consumer Credit, Monetary Policy & Trade, Terrorism & Illicit Finance.

Group Ratings

	ADA	ACLU	AFL-CIO	LCV	ITI	COC	HAFA	ACU	CFG	FRC
2016	-	5%	-	3%	100%	100%	76%	92%	84%	92%
2015	0%	C	4%	0%	C	75%	C	96%	85%	83%

Almanac Ratings 2015

	Economy	Social	Foreign	Composite
Liberal	2%	9%	0%	4%
Conservative	99%	91%	100%	96%

Key Votes of the 114th Congress

1. Keystone Pipeline	Y	5. Puerto Rico Debt	Y	9. Offenses by Aliens	Y
2. Trade Deals	Y	6. Medical Marijuana	Y	10. Troops in Iraq	N
3. Export-Import Bank	N	7. Sanctuary Cities	Y	11. Homeland Security $$	N
4. Debt Ceiling Increase	N	8. Armor-piercing Bullets	Y	12. Trade Adjustment aid	N

Election Results

Election	Name (Party)	Vote (%)		Cand. Spent	Ind. Exp. Support	Ind. Exp. Oppose
2016 General	Mia Love (R)	147,597	(54%)	$5,494,953	$331,069	$850,985
	Doug Owens (D)	113,413	(41%)	$2,067,952		$358,661
	Collin R. Simonsen (C)	13,559	(5%)			
2016 Primary	Mia Love (R)		(100%)			

Prior winning percentages: 2014 (50%)

The first black Republican woman in Congress when she was elected in 2014, Mia Love had been proclaimed a rising star two years earlier when she fell barely short against a Democratic incumbent. His subsequent retirement paved the way for easier - but hardly routine - contests for Love.

Love told her life story at the 2012 Republican National Convention. Her parents immigrated to Brooklyn from Haiti with $10 and became legal citizens shortly after she was born. The family then moved to Connecticut, where she stayed until she graduated from the University of Hartford with a degree in fine arts. Love worked as a flight attendant for Continental Airlines. The job allowed her to live almost anywhere, so she decided to move to Utah. She met Jason Love on a Mormon mission, married him and converted to Mormonism. She remembers being upset when hearing news stories about groups trying to remove "under God" from the Pledge of Allegiance and decided to enter politics. In 2003, she won a seat on the Saratoga Springs City Council, where she served for six years before voters elected her mayor.

The first black mayor of a Utah city, Love took a firmly conservative line on limited government, immigration and social issues. When she challenged veteran Democratic Rep. Jim Matheson in 2012, she became a national sensation within the GOP. She won praise for her Republican convention speech in which she said, "Mr. President, I am here to tell you we are not buying what you are selling in 2012." In the new district lines, Love had been widely expected to win. But Matheson was one of the House's most conservative Democrats, and Republicans found it difficult to tie him closely to President Barack Obama. Love lost by 768 votes.

When Love announced that she would run again, Matheson retired in the face of a tough path to victory in the midterm election with a smaller voter turnout. Love won the nomination at the state Republican convention with 78 percent of the vote. Democratic nominee Doug Owens campaigned against her in much the way Matheson had, seeking to appeal to moderate Republicans and independents. He blasted Love for statements in 2012 that she would do away with the Department of Education, eliminate federally subsidized student loans and cut other federal programs. Love said those positions weren't etched in stone and accused Owens of resorting to personal attacks. Love spent $5.2 million, compared with only $867,000 for Owens, and she notched a 50%-46% victory. Owens had a 2,100 vote lead in Salt Lake County, but Love had a 3-to-1 lead in Utah County.

After being sworn into office, Love joined a ceremonial swearing-in for the Congressional Black Caucus, a Democratic-dominated group, despite having previously accused it of "demagoguery," and told the *Deseret News* in 2012 that she would "take that thing apart from the inside out." She prominently defended Majority Whip Steve Scalise after it was revealed in December 2014 that he had spoken to a white nationalist group while he was serving in the Louisiana Legislature. She told ABC News: "He's apologized, and I think that we need to move on and get the work of the American people done."

In the House, Love kept a low profile during her first term. Her first bill was "The Student Right to Know Before You Go Act," which was designed to assure that college students and their families understand the consequences of their financial decisions, especially student loans. Florida GOP Sen. Marco Rubio earlier introduced a similar measure in the Senate. Serving on the Financial Services Committee, she won House passage in April 2016 of a bill raising limits on the assets and loans of community banks.

Her *Almanac* vote ratings for 2015 were mostly conservative, except that she ranked toward the center of House Republicans on social issues. She was the most conservative member of the Utah delegation. During a speech to the Utah Legislature in February 2017, she talked up her legislation to permit over-the-counter sale of contraceptives without a prescription. "This is my way of empowering American women and making sure they are in charge of their decision-making," she said.

In her first reelection campaign, Love had a rematch with Owens, whose $2.1 million in campaign funds were more than twice what he raised in 2014. Her $5.5 million included a $1,000 contribution from a House member of the opposition party: Democrat David Scott of Georgia. "Mia has proven herself. She is very smart, very talented," Scott told the *Salt Lake Tribune*. "It is very important for us as African Americans to look at the big picture and realize that we are in a big game here and we have to have alliances."

During their only campaign debate, Owens criticized Love for excessive spending on her constituent mail, which he called "self-promoting campaign pieces that were paid for by taxpayers." Love responded that such criticism was "absolutely dishonest" and showed that "he's got nothing else." Love won, 54%-41%. Of her 34,000-vote margin, more than 19,000 came from Utah County, which cast less than 15 percent of the vote. She won by about 10,000 votes in Salt Lake, which cast more than 80 percent of the vote. Love did not endorse a presidential candidate. There was no evidence that Donald Trump's poor performance in Utah had an adverse impact on the reelection vote for the state's three other House Republicans.

Central Utah: Suburbs of Salt Lake City and Provo

Population		**Race and Ethnicity**		**Income**	
Total	743,248	White	75.6%	Median Income	$62,860 (113 out of 435)
Land area	2,550	Black	1.4%		
Pop/ sq mi	291.4	Latino	16.2%		
Born in state	63.8%	Asian	2.8%	Under $50,000	37.4%
		Two races	1.9%	$50,000-$99,999	38.7%
Age Groups		Other	2.1%	$100,000-$199,999	20.6%
Under 18	31.9%			$200,000 or more	3.4%
18-34	25.9%	**Education**		Poverty Rate	11.1%
35-64	33.7%	H.S grad or less	34.2%		
Over 64	8.5%	Some college	37.9%	**Health Insurance**	
		College Degree, 4 yr	19.3%	With health insurance coverage	85.9%
Work		Post grad	8.6%		
White Collar	35.4%				
Sales and Service	42.9%	**Military**		**Public Assistance**	
Blue Collar	21.7%	Veteran	5.9%	Cash public assistance income	1.8%
Government	4.3%	Active Duty	0.1%		
				Food stamp/SNAP benefits	8.6%

Voter Turnout			
2015 Total Citizens 18+	461,836	2016 House Turnout as % CVAP	59%
2016 House turnout	274,569	2014 House Turnout as % CVAP	32%

2012 Presidential Vote		
Mitt Romney	165,294	(68%)
Barack Obama	74,368	(30%)

2016 Presidential Vote		
Donald Trump	108,421	(39%)
Hillary Clinton	89,796	(32%)
Evan McMullin	62,348	(22%)
Gary Johnson	10,883	(4%)

Cook Partisan Voting Index: R+13

Driving along the Wasatch Front on the 90-mile stretch of Interstate 15 from North Ogden to Provo, one passes within about five miles of two-thirds of the state's population. In Utah, 65 percent of the people occupy about 2 percent of the land area. Salt Lake City accounts for a surprisingly small portion of this: Its population of 193,000 is only slightly larger than the 180,000 it had in 1950. Like many Western cities, Salt Lake City mostly grew up with automobiles and suburbs and houses with yards for children in mind, and the settlement patterns reflect that. Suburbs and small cities stretch out to the north, south, and west of the city, and even into the foothills of the Wasatch. Salt Lake County, consequently, quadrupled its population from 275,000 in 1950 to 1.1 million in 2015.

The 4th Congressional District of Utah, the smallest district in the state, takes in much of the suburban area to the south of Salt Lake City. Although the city sections of Salt Lake County lean Democratic, about 40 percent of the district's population is in that county south of the Interstate 215 Belt Route - West Jordan, South Jordan, Sandy and Riverton - all of which are Republican. Sandy was an old mining town and West Jordan was a farming community, but their populations shot up as suburban growth took off in the 1960s. Today, West Jordan has more than 110,000 people. South Jordan and Lehi are the new growth centers. Each has been among the fastest-growing cities in the nation between 2010 and 2015: 32 percent and 24 percent, respectively. Technology-related employment has expanded strongly in this area since 2010. Bluffdale is the site of the Intelligence Community Comprehensive National Cybersecurity Initiative Data Center. These are all upscale places, with median incomes well above the national average. About 80percent% of the 4th is in Sale Lake County. The district also takes in western Utah County, including Eagle Mountain and Saratoga Springs, which were created in the early 1990s and have grown rapidly.

This has been a solidly Republican district, which Mitt Romney won in 2012 with 68 percent of the vote, though it is the least Republican district in deep-red Utah. The antipathy toward Donald Trump throughout Utah was especially pronounced here. He won the 4th, 39%-32%, with much of the remaining vote going to Evan McMullin.

★ VERMONT ★

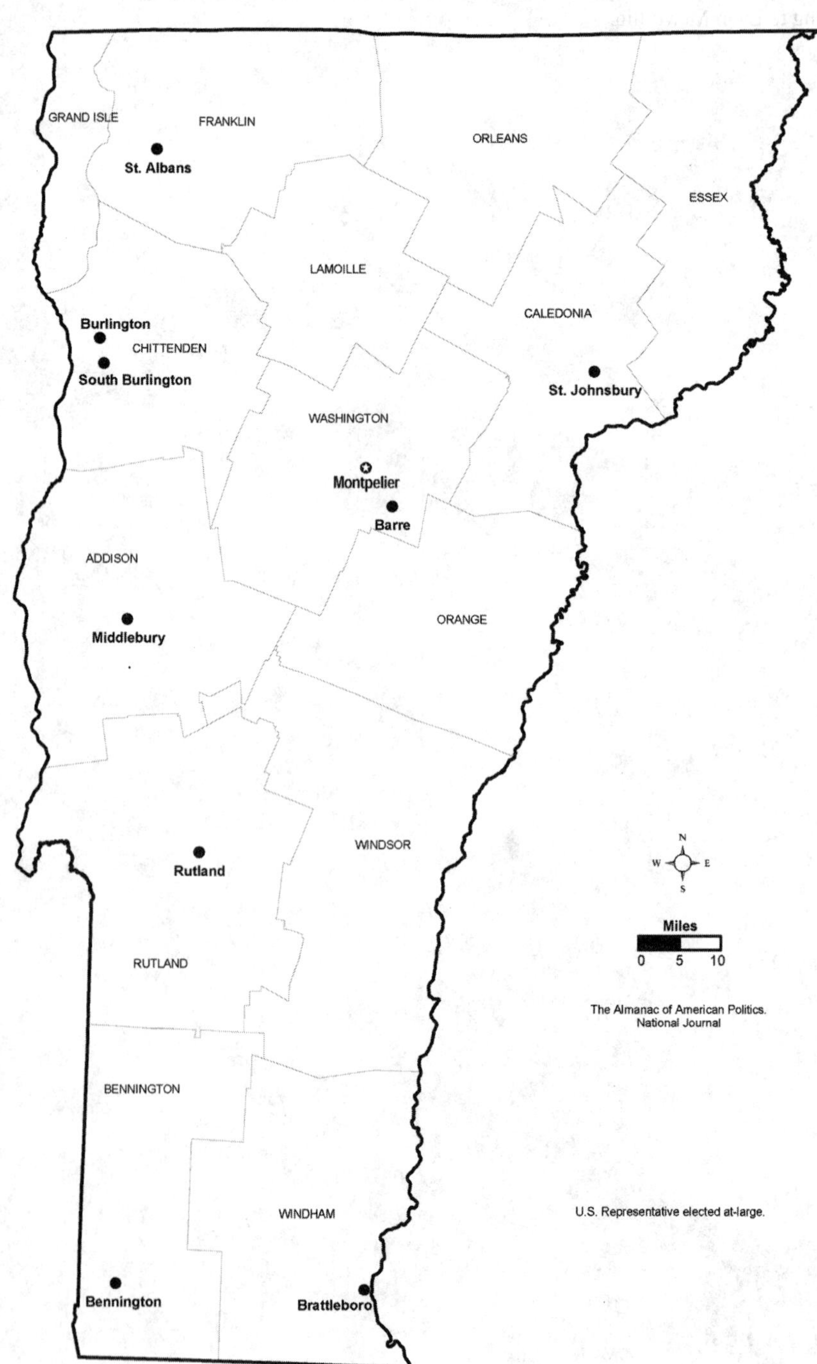
GRAND ISLE
FRANKLIN
St. Albans
ORLEANS
ESSEX
LAMOILLE
CALEDONIA
Burlington
CHITTENDEN
South Burlington
St. Johnsbury
WASHINGTON
Montpelier
Barre
ADDISON
Middlebury
ORANGE
WINDSOR
Rutland
RUTLAND
BENNINGTON
WINDHAM
Bennington
Brattleboro
N
W
E
S
Miles
0 5 10
The Almanac of American Politics.
National Journal
U.S. Representative elected at-large.

Vermont is one of the bluest states in America. But while the state has repeatedly elected socialist Bernie Sanders to Congress, and while Hillary Clinton won the state easily in the 2016 presidential race, that's not the whole story. A Republican won the open-seat governorship in 2016, and Clinton fared worse than Barack Obama did four years earlier, especially in more rural counties.

Early America and contemporary America come together in Vermont. The state is a mixture of the 19th and 21st centuries-maple syrup and Ben & Jerry's ice cream, tiny clapboard villages and carefully zoned towns with unobtrusively signed outlet malls, covered bridges and same-sex marriages. It was the first state where the legislature rather than a court legalized same-sex marriage. Not so long ago, Vermont seemed an antique state, almost as carefully preserved as its Shelburne Museum, with its barn and jail, railroad station and blacksmith shop, and its 37 buildings of folk art; its new Center for Art and Education, by contrast, is sleekly contemporary. In just two decades, Vermont was transformed by newcomers, who were attracted to its throwback look but who have since transformed Vermont's culture in their own image. Now, in-migration is down – Vermont is one of just four states where the population has fallen since 2010, especially beyond Chittenden County (Burlington), where it rose by about 3 percent during that time -- and the population is aging. Vermont also remains the whitest state in the nation, with blacks, Hispanics and Asian-Americans each accounting for just 1 percent of the population.

Vermont was first settled by flinty Yankees from Connecticut, and it showed an independent streak from the beginning. After Ethan Allen's Green Mountain Boys repulsed the British in 1777, Vermont called itself an independent republic for 14 years, claimed(to no avail) by New York and New Hampshire. Allen tried to persuade George Washington to make it a new state, but several histories argue that Vermont never voluntarily joined the United States. In any case, Vermont was admitted as the 14th state in 1791. Its economy then was almost entirely agricultural, as second sons and daughters from small New England farms struggled to scratch out livings from the rocky soil. Eventually many gave up and moved west, while those who remained raised dairy cows, producing milk for the masses in New York City, and harvested maple syrup in the spring.

With their legendary thriftiness, Vermonters accumulated capital that, invested wisely, was used to build the solid stone office buildings and courthouses, the thick-timbered houses, and gold-topped state Capitol in Montpelier, the nation's smallest state capital. Vermont also made an economic asset of its maple trees and its quaintness. Beginning in the 1890s, the state government promoted Vermont as a tourist destination and passed a law requiring Vermont maple syrup to be made only from local trees. (As recently as February 2016, Vermont led an effort to oppose syrup brands with additives through a letter to the Food and Drug Administration.) But the state never developed labor-intensive industry, so over the years it exported people and its population aged. Two presidents were born in Vermont, but both made their careers elsewhere-Chester Arthur in New York City and Calvin Coolidge in Massachusetts. Two great foreign writers lived there for years-Rudyard Kipling and Aleksandr Solzhenitsyn-but neither wrote much about Vermont.

Starting in the 1960s-perhaps the key date was 1963, when people first outnumbered cows-Vermont changed rapidly. Its economy boomed, led by leisure-time industries-ski resorts and summer homes-and technology companies, starting with IBM in 1957, in and around the Burlington area on the mostly undeveloped shores of glorious Lake Champlain. You can find big-box retailers in Williston, but also ethnic diversity-Vietnamese, Bosnians, and Koreans-in Winooski. Homegrown firms started by baby boomers-Ben & Jerry's, founded in 1978, is the archetype-have flourished. There were 45 separate communes in Vermont during the late 1960s and early 1970s, according to the Vermont Historical Society, though they represented just the furthest edge of a much wider movement within the state. Next-door New Hampshire may have trumpeted its low taxes and aversion to government regulation, attracting right-leaning migrants from Massachusetts and elsewhere to settle spanking-new developments, but Vermont, proclaiming its desire to preserve the environment and the past, attracted left-leaning migrants from New York and elsewhere who were willing to pay higher taxes and higher prices and submit to tough environmental restrictions for the privilege of living in a pristine setting. Gallup rates Vermont as the second-most liberal state, slightly behind Massachusetts, as well as the most non-religious state and the state where residents are most likely to eat produce frequently. (Organic produce, in all likelihood, and without genetically modified ingredients – although a landmark state law requiring the labeling of GMO foods was preempted by a federal law in July 2016.)

Indeed, public policy has shaped the state's arc. In 1970, Republican Gov. Deane Davis (the last Vermont native to hold the job until Democrat Peter Shumlin was elected in 2010) pushed through Act 250, a sweeping land use law that helped give Vermont its environmental reputation. Housing developments and new ski resorts were required to meet 10 environmental criteria and get the approval of five different commissions, with opponents granted a right to appeal. Later, Vermont passed its own Clean Air Act, levying a tax on new cars that get less than 20 miles per gallon. It bans billboards and rooftop air conditioning units. Residents also passed Act 60, which attempted to equalize property taxes throughout the state. Vermont maintains a land trust that buys development rights of farmland to stop the disappearance of family farms. Distressed by the demise of dairy farming-the number of dairy farms declined from 3,300 in 1983 to 992 in 2011-the state government loans money to help farmers buy water buffalo to produce mozzarella cheese. In 2014, two landmark events occurred in the state's energy sector: The Vermont Yankee nuclear power plant on the Connecticut River shut down after more than four decades of operation, and the city of Burlington announced that 100 percent of its electricity came from renewable sources. Today, about half the city's electricity comes from renewably farmed wood chips, with the remainder coming from a combination of hydroelectric power, wind turbines, and solar panels. "The net energy costs are cheap enough that the city has not had to raise electric rates for its customers in eight years," *Politico* reported. Liberal policies have proven to be compatible with economic success: Vermont's median income is 5.2 percent above the national average, and the unemployment rate, which peaked at just 7 percent in May 2009, was at 3 percent in February 2017, the sixth-best rate of any state in the nation.

The quintessential Vermont commercial strip is the Church Street Marketplace in downtown Burlington, a four-block pedestrian mall known for its tasteful shopping venues and street fairs-the polar opposite of the big-box stores sprouting elsewhere. There were four Walmarts in the state in 2011, but two of them are in pre-existing buildings and the developer trying to expand one in Bennington had to pay $225,000 to refurbish downtown buildings and support watershed development. (It finally opened in August 2016.) Dollar General was required to face its Chester store with clapboard wood rather than vinyl siding and keep its shopping carts off the street. Some dairy farmers are processing their animals' solid waste, mixed with bacteria from their digestive systems, into methane fuel. Other farmers are making biodiesel fuel from canola beans, sunflower seeds, and flax. But Vermont does not try to regulate everything. The state has some of the laxest gun-control laws in the country, (coincidentally accompanied by the lowest violent crime rate) tolerated even by leading Vermont Democrats, to the consternation of others in their party who represent more urbanized areas. (In the 2016 Democratic primary, Clinton used gun policy as a wedge issue against Sanders – outside Vermont, at least.)

Vermonters love their natural environment, but nature can sometimes be cruel. In August 2011, Hurricane Irene roared inland and devastated major sections of Vermont. Water crashed down the Green Mountains and the White River crested at 28 feet above normal. Hundreds of miles of roads that followed mountainside streambeds were washed away along with hundreds of dairy cows. Farmers were stranded on hilltops, and 73,000 homes lost electric power. Vermonters responded with Yankee alacrity. Neighbors hiked in with shovels to clear new paths; local fire and rescue squads improvised new roadways; electric power was restored to all but 5,900 homes within three days. State government reopened 500 miles of road, replaced a dozen bridges, and repaired 200 more by December, working with Google to keep maps updated to show passable roads. The new Vermont responded in a way that would make the old Yankee Vermont proud. But the state has also suffered from a scourge that stems from humans rather than nature-drug addiction. In a high-profile speech in 2014, Shumlin said that $2 million worth of heroin enters the state every week, and that heroin addiction had risen a stunning 770 percent since 2000. In 2016, preliminary figures pegged the number of overdoses at a record level. The following year, officials considered establishing a facility in Burlington where addicts could shoot heroin in a protective environment. At the same time, Vermont has been weighing the legalization of marijuana for years; while the drug is already consumed widely, full legalization hasn't gained sufficient momentum to pass.

As Vermont has changed culturally, it has also changed politically. In the 19th century, Yankee Vermont was the most Republican state in the nation, voting Republican in every presidential election from 1856 to 1960. In 1936, Vermont and Maine were the only states to resist Franklin D. Roosevelt's landslide, inspiring Roosevelt's campaign manager, James Farley, to joke, "As Maine goes, so goes

Vermont." For three decades thereafter, Vermont's Yankee Protestant Republicans outnumbered its French Canadian and Irish Catholic Democrats. As newcomers kept arriving, Vermont was divided politically along different lines: between liberal, highly educated newcomers and conservative, less educated, old Vermonters. A key figure was Howard Dean, who grew up on Park Avenue in New York City, was educated at Yale and moved to Vermont, where he and his wife practiced medicine. He was elected lieutenant governor in 1986 and became governor when incumbent Republican Richard Snelling died in August 1991, learning of his elevation while treating a patient. He was elected to five terms in his own right (Vermont and New Hampshire are the last states with two-year gubernatorial terms) and set out to run for president in January 2003. His campaign took off briefly because of his full-throated opposition to the Iraq war. This was the point at which Vermont had moved way to the left on America's political spectrum.

Republicans didn't become extinct in Vermont, but the ones who survived tended to be much more moderate than their peers within the national GOP, such as Sen. James Jeffords, whose switch from Republican to independent in 2001 enabled the Democrats to take over the chamber mid-session, and Jim Douglas, who was elected governor in 2002, 2004, 2006 and 2008. But Democrats have done increasingly well in Vermont. Obama recorded his third-highest margin of victory there in both 2008 and 2012, trailing only the District of Columbia and Hawaii. Sen. Patrick Leahy-through a combination of the state's Republican roots, the recent service of two Senate independents and Leahy's own long tenure in the chamber-oddly remains the only Democratic senator ever elected from Vermont. He has been elected to his eighth term, and in December 2012 became the most senior member of the Senate. His Senate colleague, Sanders, is a self-styled socialist who has managed to hold office almost continuously in Vermont since 1981, first as Burlington mayor, then as the at-large House member and, since the 2006 election, as a senator. Sanders is an example of the liberal inflow to the state, having graduated from Brooklyn's James Madison High School (the same one as Sen. Charles Schumer of New York, former Sen. Norm Coleman of Minnesota, and Supreme Court Justice Ruth Bader Ginsburg). Sanders would later muster an unexpectedly potent presidential bid in the 2016 Democratic primaries, consolidating a large share of the national party's most liberal voters with his anti-Wall Street rhetoric.

The governor's office has been a dicier proposition for Democrats. Shumlin won in 2010, 2012 and 2014 and pursued a progressive agenda, increasing the minimum wage to $10.50 an hour by 2018 and shielding doctors and others from liability for helping terminal patients ingest lethal drugs. But he also faced the limits of liberalism even in a liberal state: He pulled back from his proposal for a single-payer health insurance system in 2014, citing the pitfalls of financing it. When Shumlin opted not to seek another term in 2016, Phil Scott, the Republican lieutenant governor, won the open seat while highlighting the kind of moderate profile that allowed Jeffords and Douglas to win in previous years.

In Vermont's 2016 GOP presidential primary, Trump narrowly defeated Ohio Gov. John Kasich, on the heels of an almost surreal Trump rally in Burlington that was held without the backing of the state GOP and, as *Politico* put it,at a venue "just yards from Sanders' campaign headquarters on one side, the birthplace of Howard Dean's presidential campaign on another, and the bar where (the Vermont-based jam band) Phish played its first gig on a third." In November, Vermont was far from competitive – Clinton's percentage in Vermont was her sixth highest of any state –but in many parts of the state, Clinton lost ground compared to Obama. Trump even managed to flip one county from blue to red -- Essex, in the state's rural "Northeast Kingdom." Statewide, Clinton won 57 percent, well below Obama's 67 percent four years earlier. Most of the vote share that Clinton bled, however, didn't go to Trump -- he actually won a slightly smaller percentage statewide than Mitt Romney did in 2012. Some went to third- party candidates – 3 percent for Libertarian Gary Johnson and 2 percent for Green Party nominee Jill Stein – but a stunning 7 percent of the statewide tally went to write-in votes, including nearly 6 percent for favorite son Sanders. That was way up from 2012, when write-in votes accounted for less than half a percent of presidential ballots cast. Another 1.4 percent of presidential ballots in 2016 were left blank. It was one of the oddest electoral patterns of any state in 2016.

Population		Race and Ethnicity		Income	
Total	626,604	White	93.6%	Median Income	$55,176 (20 out of 50)
Land area	9,217	Black	1.1%	Under $50,000	45.3%
Pop/ sq mi	68.0	Latino	1.7%	$50,000-$99,999	33.3%
Born in state	51.0%	Asian	1.4%	$100,000-$199,999	17.6%
Age Groups		Two races	1.8%	$200,000 or more	3.7%
Under 18	19.7%	Other	0.4%	Poverty Rate	11.5%
18-34	22.0%	**Education**			
35-64	42.1%	H.S grad or less	38.3%	**Health Insurance**	
Over 64	16.3%	Some college	25.8%	With health insurance coverage	94.2%
Work		College Degree, 4 yr	21.7%		
White Collar	40.4%	Post grad	14.3%	**Public Assistance**	
Sales and Service	38.8%	**Military**		Cash public assistance income	4.2%
Blue Collar	20.8%	Veteran	8.9%		
Government	14.6%	Active Duty	0.1%	Food stamp/SNAP benefits	13.7%

Voter Turnout			
2015 Total Citizens 18+	493,124	2016 Pres Turnout as % CVAP	64%
2016 Pres Votes	315,067	2012 Pres Turnout as % CVAP	62%

Legislature	
Senate:	21D, 4P, 7R
House:	83D, 7P, 53R, 7I

Presidential Politics

2016 Democratic Primary		
Bernie Sanders (D)	115,900	(86%)
Hillary Clinton (D)	18,338	(14%)
2016 Republican Primary		
Donald Trump (R)	19,974	(33%)
John Kasich (R)	18,534	(30%)
Marco Rubio (R)	11,781	(19%)
Ted Cruz (R)	5,932	(10%)

2016 Presidential Vote		
Hillary Clinton (D)	178,573	(57%)
Donald Trump (R)	95,369	(30%)
Gary Johnson (L)	10,078	(3%)
Jill Stein (G)	6,758	(2%)
2012 Presidential Vote		
Barack Obama (D)	199,239	(67%)
Mitt Romney (R)	92,698	(31%)

Cook Partisan Voting Index: D+15

While Vermont is the home of Sen. Bernie Sanders, the liberal champion of the 2016 election, no state has voted more often for Republican presidential candidates. Since the birth of the GOP in 1856 until the 1992 election, Vermont voted once for the Democratic presidential nominee, Lyndon Johnson in 1964. Times changed. Starting in 1992, Vermonters have voted Democratic in every presidential election. In 2008 and 2012, it was the second-most Democratic state, trailing only D.C. and Barack Obama's birthplace of Hawaii. Republican Mitt Romney journeyed to Vermont for debate preparation in 2012, but he carried only two of the state's 246 cities and towns. Vermont has become solidly liberal on foreign policy and cultural issues (except gun control) and it is not very conservative on economics, either.In 2016 Hillary Clinton defeated Donald Trump, 57%-30%, dropping the state to the sixth most Democratic (seventh if you include D.C.). What dropped Democratic Party performance is that some 18,183 Vermonters wrote in Sanders' name on the general election ballot, almost 6 percent of the vote. Sanders' tally exceeded the totals garnered by Libertarian Gary Johnson and Green Party candidate Jill Stein combined. Trump won a majority of the votes cast in 18 of Vermont's towns and won another 43 with a plurality.

The Vermont presidential primary, abolished for 1992, reappeared in 1996, but got little notice that year or in 2000. Former Gov. Howard Dean's 2004 presidential campaign was headquartered in Burlington, and although Dean was effectively eliminated by the time Vermont voted on March 2, Vermonters still came out in droves to give Dean his only Democratic primary victory. In 2008, Vermont voted on March 4, when Obama and Hillary Clinton were locked in a struggle for the nomination. Obama beat Clinton 59%-39%. In 2012, Vermont voted on March 6, when the Republican race was still raging. Romney led with 40 percent, to 26 percent for Ron Paul and 24 percent for Rick Santorum. In 2016,

Sanders crushed Clinton, 86%-14%. Clinton didn't even break the 15 percent threshold required to earn any pledged delegates. In the Republican race, Ohio Gov. John Kasich held several town hall events in the Burlington area, a hallmark of his New Hampshire campaign, hoping that his moderate profile would appeal to the state's voters, butTrump beat him, 33%-30%.

Congressional Districts

115th Congress Lineup	1D	114th Congress Lineup	1D

Governor

Phil Scott (R)

Elected 2016, term expires 2019, 1st term; b. Aug. 4, 1958, Barre, VT; Univ. of Vermont, BS 1980; Married (Diana); 2 children.

Elected Office: VT Senate 2001-2010; VT Lt. Governor 2011-2017

Professional Career: Stock Car Racer 1996-2005; Co-owner, DuBois Construction, 1986-2016.

Office: 109 State Street Pavilion, Montpelier, 05609-0101; 802-828-3333; Fax: 802-828-3339; Website: vermont.gov.

Election Results

Election	Name (Party)	Vote (%)
2016 General	Phil Scott (R)	166,817 (53%)
	Sue Minter (D)	139,253 (44%)
2016 Primary	Phil Scott (R)	27,728 (60%)
	Bruce Lisman (R)	18,113 (39%)

Vermont may be one of the most liberal states in the union, but in 2016, voters elected Phil Scott -- a Republican -- as governor by an almost nine-point margin. His victory continued the tradition since the 1960s of Vermont voters filling an open-seat governorship with a replacement from the out-of-power party.

Scott was born in Barre, earned a bachelor's degree from the University of Vermont, and co-owned a company, DuBois Construction, that he sold, as he had promised, prior to his inauguration as governor. A stock-car enthusiast, Scott also founded a program called Wheels for Warmth, which enabled Vermont residents to donate tires they no longer need, with some of them being resold to benefit heating-fuel assistance programs and others recycled. Scott won a race for the state Senate in 2000 and served a decade. In 2010, he ran for lieutenant governor, which in Vermont is elected separately from the governor. In the general election, he defeated Democrat Steven Howard, 49%-42%, as Democrat Peter Shumlin was winning an open-seat gubernatorial race. As lieutenant governor, Scott started the "Vermont Everyday Jobs" initiative, in which he worked a few hours several times a month in different jobs, aiming to promote state businesses and highlight local workers. Scott was fiscally conservative but steered a moderate course overall; by the time he ran for reelection in 2012, he was endorsed by the state affiliate of the National Education Association. Scott won a second term over Democrat Cassandra Gekas, 57%-40% -- an even wider margin than in his initial run. Two years later, he won a third term without even facing a Democratic candidate; instead, Scott's main opponent was Dean Corren from the left-wing Progressive Party. Corren was endorsed by the senior Democratic politicians in the state, but Scott prevailed by his largest margin yet, 62%-36%.

When Shumlin decided against running for a fourth two-year term as governor in 2016, Scott jumped into the race. Shumlin had sweated through a tough 2014 race in which neither he nor his opponent, Republican Scott Milne, won a majority of votes cast, which, according to Vermont law, required the Democratic-dominated legislature to cast ballots to resolve the election, which they did in his favor. Shumlin's close call in 2014 amounted to a death blow for his pursuit of a single-payer health-insurance system, which by then was already on life-support. Early in his tenure, Shumlin had succeeded in getting the legislature to pass a bill establishing Green Mountain Care, a single-payer system, with a planned launch in 2017. The proposal was designed to blend universal coverage with cost controls. But despite some seeming advantages—Vermont's small size, its already high coverage rates and its liberal electorate—the complex implementation lagged, and worries grew as it became clear that expanding coverage would require sizable new state payroll and income taxes. In December 2014, Shumlin acknowledged that the revenue increases would be too heavy a lift for the state. Liberals were disappointed, and Shumlin called the scuttling of the plan "the biggest disappointment of my political life." The slow disillusionment with single-payer health care, combined with general fatigue over Shumlin's tenure, gave Republicans – particularly one as moderate as Scott -- an opening in the 2016 gubernatorial race.

First, though, Scott had to win the August GOP primary against former Wall Street executive Bruce Lisman. On the big issues – such as their stances toward business, taxation and the state's health care system – Scott and Lisman were generally on the same page. Instead, the race boiled down to a faceoff between a Montpelier insider (Scott) and a political outsider (Lisman). In one direct mail piece, Lisman linked Scott to Shumlin by showing a photograph of the two together with the headline, "Peter Shumlin and Phil Scott have taken Vermont in the wrong direction."Lisman also criticized Scott's proposal for a car mileage tax, and he accused Scott of leveraging his political position to win government contracts for his company. But Scott won the support of Republican lawmakers and much of the party establishment and won the primary, 60%-39%. Afterward, Lisman endorsed Scott. Meanwhile, in a competitive Democratic primary, state transportation secretary Sue Minter prevailed decisively over former state Sens. Matt Dunne and Peter Galbraith.

In the general election – the state's most expensive in history -- Scott and his allies at the Republican Governors Association sought to tie Minter to Shumlin. "Everything that I've heard from Sue is about spending more money, finding other ways of taxing, whether it's a tax on services or a carbon tax or this cap and trade type of scheme," Scott told Vermont Public Radio. Minter, meanwhile, declared her independence from Shumlin and touted her support from Sanders, the state's most popular politician, and President Barack Obama, who cut an ad for her.The support didn't transfer, however. Scott was able to maintain his image as a moderate pragmatist in the mold of the state's two most recent Republican governors, Richard Snelling and Jim Douglas.On Election Day, even as the state was voting for Hillary Clinton over Donald Trump by a 61%-33% margin, voters backed Scott over Minter, 53%-44%. (Scott had withheld his support from Trump.) Bill Lee, an eccentric former pitcher for the Boston Red Sox known as "Spaceman," took almost 3 percent of the vote running on the Liberty Union Party ballot line.Scott won all but three counties – Chittenden, Windsor and Windham.

Scott's victory made him the only Republican to hold statewide office in Vermont. After he was sworn in, he warned lawmakers that Vermont faced a budget gap of $70 million. His headline proposal was to keep funding level for K-12 education and to increase from 15 percent to 20 percent the portion that teachers must pay for their health insurance. Scott touted the plan as "bold," but legislators were unimpressed. The Republican governor and the Democratic legislature were poised to tangle further on how to address the budget gap.

Senior Senator

Patrick Leahy (D)

Elected 1974, term expires 2022, 8th term; b. Mar 31, 1940, Montpelier; St. Michael's College (VT), B.A., 1961; Georgetown University Law Center (DC), J.D., 1964; Roman Catholic; Married (Marcelle Pomerleau Leahy); 3 children; 5 grandchildren.

Elected Office: VT State Attorney, Chittenden County, 1966-1974.

Professional Career: Practicing attorney, 1964-1974.

DC Office: 437 RSOB 20510, 202-224-4242, Fax: 202-224-3479, leahy.senate.gov.

State Offices: Burlington, 802-863-2525; Montpelier, 802-229-0569.

Committees: *Agriculture, Nutrition & Forestry*: Conservation, Forestry & Natural Resources, Livestock, Marketing & Agriculture Security, Nutrition, Agricultural Research & Specialty Crops. *Appropriations (RMM)*: Agriculture, Rural Development, FDA & Related Agencies, Commerce, Justice, Science & Related Agencies, Department of Defense, Department of Homeland Security, Department of the Interior, Environment & Related Agencies, DOL, HHS & Education & Related Agencies, Energy & Water Development, Financial Services & General Government, Legislative Branch, Military Construction & Veteran Affairs & Related Agencies, State, Foreign Operations & Related Programs (RMM), Transportation, HUD & Related Agencies. *Judiciary*: Antitrust, Competition Policy & Consumer Rights, Border Security & Immigration, Oversight, Agency Action, Federal Rights & Federal Courts, Privacy, Technology & the Law. *Rules & Administration.*

Group Ratings

	ADA	ACLU	AFL-CIO	LCV	ITI	COC	HAFA	ACU	CFG	FRC
2016	-	94%	-	100%	50%	50%	7%	0%	0%	0%
2015	100%	C	100%	100%	C	46%	C	0%	0%	0%

Almanac Ratings 2015

	Economy	Social	Foreign	Composite
Liberal	100%	100%	100%	100%
Conservative	0%	0%	0%	0%

Key Votes of the 114th Congress

1. Keystone pipeline	N	5. National Security Data	Y	9. Gun Sales Checks	Y
2. Export-Import Bank	N	6. Iran Nuclear Deal	N	10. Sanctuary Cities	N
3. Debt Ceiling Increase	Y	7. Puerto Rico Debt	Y	11. Planned Parenthood	N
4. Homeland Security $$	Y	8. Loretta Lynch A.G	Y	12. Trade deals	N

Election Results

Election	Name (Party)	Vote (%)		Cand. Spent	Ind. Exp. Support	Ind. Exp. Oppose
2016 General	Patrick Leahy (D)	192,243	(61%)	$2,558,664		
	Scott Miline (R)	103,637	(33%)	$57,826		
	Cris Ericson (M)	9,156	(3%)			
2016 Primary	Patrick Leahy (D)	62,249	(89%)			
	Cris Ericson (D)	7,596	(11%)			

Prior winning percentages: 2010 (64%), 2004 (71%), 1998 (72%), 1992 (54%), 1986 (63%), 1980 (50%), 1974 (47%)

Democrat Patrick Leahy, Vermont's senior senator, was first elected in 1974, and, in late 2012, became the chamber's current senior member. Reelected to an eighth term in 2016, he is now the fifth longest serving senator in U.S. history. Leahy has wielded influence in his more than four decades on Capitol Hill over a wide variety of issues-ranging from civil liberties, intellectual property rights and agriculture policy at home to human rights abroad. Leahy has chaired two Senate committees: the Agriculture Committee, from 1987-1995, and the Judiciary panel, from 2001-2003 and again from 2007-2015. He could have ascended to chairman of a third committee, the Appropriations panel, when a vacancy occurred in late 2012. But, as a former prosecuting attorney, Leahy stayed as Judiciary chairman and continued to focus on a host of legal issues that have been his legislative passion. The Republican takeover of the Senate in the 2014 election cost him the gavel, but he continued to play a key role as the Judiciary panel's ranking Democrat-notably in the 2015 debate over renewal of the controversial surveillance provisions in the USA Patriot Act, first enacted in the wake of the 9/11 attacks.

In early 2017, he exercised his seniority and become the top Democrat on Appropriations, replacing Sen. Barbara Mikulski of Maryland, who had retired. Leahy cited the results of the 2016 election, with President Donald Trump coming to power and the Democrat's failure to recapture a Senate majority, as the major factor in his decision. "Right now, at this unusual time, with these results, the best way for me to amplify Vermonter's voices is as the ranking member of the Appropriations Committee," he declared.

Leahy is a stalwart liberal. In 2015, he was in a three-way tie for first place as the most liberal member of the Senate, according to *Almanac* rankings. He was as much of an influential ally of President Barack Obama as he was a stubborn antagonist of President George W. Bush. Bush's vice president, Dick Cheney, infamously told Leahy to "Go f-yourself" following a 2004 picture-taking session at the Capitol; Cheney was apparently angered by Leahy's criticism of the activities of Halliburton, a company once headed by Cheney, during the Iraq war.

While Leahy, too, is known for periodic flashes of temper, he has been credited by Republicans for efforts to reach across the aisle. He has found common ground on civil liberties and criminal justice issues with some of the Senate's most outspoken GOP conservatives, including Kentucky Sen. Rand Paul, and has enjoyed a good working relationship with the current Judiciary Committee chairman, Iowa Republican Charles Grassley. In 2016, Leahy and Republican Whip John Cornyn of Texas-- a fellow member of the Judiciary panel -- combined on legislation, signed by Obama, to expand public access to government records through a strengthening of the federal Freedom of Information Act. "He's a good listener who will take into account the views of others," Maine Sen. Susan Collins, a GOP moderate, told *The Boston Globe.* The more conservative Mississippi Sen. Thad Cochran, chairman of the Appropriations panel and a colleague of Leahy for more than a third of a century, told the *Associated Press*: "I'm fond of him. I shouldn't be, but I am."

Leahy grew up in Vermont at a time when the Green Mountain State-now one of the nation's bluest-was rock-ribbed Republican. He graduated from St. Michael's College in Winooski, just north of where he grew up in Burlington. He earned a law degree at Georgetown University before returning home to practice law. Leahy joined the law firm of Philip Hoff, who, in 1962, had become the first Democrat since before the Civil War to win election as Vermont's governor. In 1966, Hoff appointed Leahy, then just 26, to fill a vacancy as state's attorney for Chittenden County, which includes Burlington. Leahy was elected to full terms in 1966 and 1970, and still often invokes recollections of his years in that post.

In 1974, after eight years as state's attorney, he ran for the Senate at age 34. The seat was being vacated by George Aiken, a liberal Republican who was first elected the year that Leahy was born. Leahy had made a name for himself in the pocket-sized state as a prosecutor who tried all major felony cases personally, and who criticized the big oil companies during the 1970s energy crisis. He had a solid base in predominantly Democratic Burlington, the state's largest city, along with the kind of thoughtful temperament Vermonters like in their public officials. In a year when the political fallout from the Watergate scandal benefited Democrats nationwide, Leahy outpolled GOP Rep. Richard Mallary by 50%-46%. Leahy became the first Democrat in history to win a Senate seat from Vermont, and remains the only Democratic senator ever elected from the state. (His in-state colleague, Sen. Bernie Sanders, although now a force in the national Democratic Party, has been elected twice as an independent who caucuses with the Democrats.)

A key reason that Leahy opted to stay at the helm of the Judiciary Committee at the end of 2012-rather than move over to chair the Appropriations panel upon the death of Hawaii Sen. Daniel Inouye -- was that the Judiciary Committee was confronting two issues that could shape his legislative legacy. One was the first attempt at comprehensive immigration reform in six years; the other was the first major gun control legislation in nearly two decades. He was an unlikely figure on the latter issue: An avid gun enthusiast, he was a member of his college shooting team and still enjoys the sport. But he has a mixed legislative record that earned him a "C" rating from the National Rifle Association. In 1993, Leahy voted against passage of the so-called Brady Bill, which requires background checks for individuals purchasing firearms. Notwithstanding its recent reputation as a bastion of liberalism, Vermont continues to have one of the highest rates of gun ownership in the country, along with some of the least restrictive gun laws of any state.

Nevertheless, with Democrats demanding action in the wake of the December 2012 elementary school massacre in Newtown Connecticut, in which 26 were killed, most of them children, Leahy took up the challenge. He moved a series of bills through his committee to bar the straw purchase and trafficking of guns, and to strengthen other law enforcement tools to assist investigations of those crimes. His legislation included reinstatement of a ban on assault weapons, which then-Senate Majority Leader Harry Reid refused to go along with on the grounds that it lacked the votes for passage. Even so, efforts to pass modest gun control legislation fell apart during floor debate in April 2013: A compromise proposal by West Virginia Democratic Sen. Joe Manchin and Pennsylvania GOP Sen. Pat Toomey to expand the background check process for would-be gun buyers fell five votes short of the 60 votes necessary to end a GOP filibuster.

On immigration, Leahy held hearings to try to build support for reform, while leaving much of the legislative work to a bipartisan group of eight senators. His combative side was on display in April 2013, when he accused Republicans of politicizing the issue by tying their objections to the Boston Marathon bombings-which involved two suspects from Chechnya. No one, Leahy declared at a hearing, should "be so cruel as to try to use the heinous acts of two young men… to derail the dreams and futures of millions." Leahy guided a major overhaul of immigration laws, providing a path to citizenship for undocumented residents, through the Judiciary Committee in May 2013-where it garnered the support of all Democrats and three Republicans. The legislation cleared the Senate a month later on a bipartisan 68-32 vote, after provisions were added to beef up security along the U.S.-Mexico border. The GOP-controlled House never took up the measure, as the immigration issue became increasingly politicized.

Leahy's first stint as Judiciary chairman coincided with the Sept. 11, 2001 attacks, as he and his staff worked with the Bush administration to hammer out the USA Patriot Act-the sweeping law that sparked a national debate over whether government investigators should be given broader powers at the expense of individual liberties. It is a debate in which Leahy continued to play a major role nearly a decade and a half later. After onetime National Security Agency contractor Edward Snowden revealed in 2013 that the agency was collecting Americans' phone records, sentiment grew in Congress for restricting such authority, contained in Section 215 of the law. As Section 215 was due to expire at the end of May 2015, Leahy and Utah Republican Sen. Mike Lee, a tea party conservative, introduced legislation to require targeted warrants to obtain phone metadata from telecommunications companies. The bill attracted 18 co-sponsors, running the gamut from the most liberal to the most conservative members of the Senate.

As a bill similar to the one proposed by Leahy and Lee moved through the House, Leahy hoped to get Grassley to sign on to the legislation. Grassley ultimately declined, but his failure to move a bill through the Judiciary Committee strengthened the hand of Leahy, as the ranking Democrat on the committee. It left the Leahy-Lee measure and a rival proposal by Senate Majority Leader Mitch McConnell and Senate Intelligence Committee Richard Burr-to continue the law in its current form-as the two major options. A filibuster by McConnell's Kentucky junior colleague, Rand Paul, caused provisions of the USA Patriot Act to lapse for a couple of days. It gave McConnell, who had argued that extending Section 215 was essential to national security, little choice but to concede to the approach passed by the House and contained in the Leahy-Lee bill. "It's historical. It's the first major overhaul of government surveillance in decades," Leahy declared after Congress stripped the NSA of its authority to collect phone records.

The original USA Patriot Act, enacted a month after the 9/11 attacks, was essentially the Senate version of the legislation crafted in Leahy's committee, as opposed to the House version of the bill. Leahy fought the Bush administration when it sought to expand police powers in the wake of the attacks. He opposed a proposal to allow the government to detain and deport immigrants suspected of terrorism without presenting evidence in court. In 2002, he contended the Justice Department should be required to disclose the number of U.S. citizens being spied on, the number of secret foreign intelligence wiretaps that had become part of criminal proceedings, and the total number of persons targeted by foreign intelligence surveillance warrants. During Bush's second term, Leahy objected to government surveillance of communications between suspected al-Qaida terrorists abroad and individuals in the United States. Back for a second stint as Judiciary chairman when the Democrats recaptured the Senate majority in 2006, Leahy placed Bush Attorney General Michael Mukasey on the spot with demands that he denounce use of waterboarding, an interrogation tactic for terrorism suspects that simulates drowning.

Leahy was an early supporter of Obama in the 2008 presidential primaries. He guided Obama's two Supreme Court nominees, Sonia Sotomayor and Elena Kagan, to swift confirmation, even while working with a new ranking Republican, Alabama's Jeff Sessions, who was considerably more partisan than his predecessor in that role, Pennsylvania's Arlen Specter-who had switched to the Democratic Party in early 2009. Leahy accused Republicans of seeking to play the race card against Sotomayor, the court's first Latina justice, and of gender bias toward Kagan. As the GOP blocked numerous Obama nominees to federal district and appeals courts, Leahy lamented in 2013, "I have repeatedly asked Senate Republicans to abandon their destructive tactics."

Leahy was in the forefront of the criticism in 2016 when Republicans, spearheaded by McConnell, refused to vote on or even hold hearings into Obama's nomination of federal appeals court judge Merrick Garland to succeed the late Supreme Court Justice Antonin Scalia. "It's sleazy," Leahy railed at the Republican majority in an interview with *USAToday*. "Have the courage to do your job and actually ask the questions. Why would you want to be a senator if you don't have the courage to stand up and do the right thing?" It put Leahy at odds with his old friend Grassley -- whom Leahy sought to needle into breaking with McConnell to convene Judiciary Committee hearings on the nomination. "The only option is for the chairman of the committee to say, 'We're going to have a hearing,' " Leahy said with a mischievous smile. "I showed a lot of independence when I was chairman of that committee. I held hearings on even controversial things, whether the leadership liked it or not." His prodding didn't work: Grassley had breakfast with Garland, but went no further, and the seat remained vacant until Trump took office and nominated appeals court judge Neil Gorsuch in early 2017.

Earlier, when Leahy became chairman during the Democrats' year and a half in the majority starting in mid-2001, he, in turn, often held up Bush's judicial nominations. Later, as ranking Democrat on the panel from 2003-2007, he led filibusters against 10 Bush appeals court nominees, tactics that the Republicans bitterly attacked. Leahy countered that the committee had approved the vast majority of appellate nominees and almost every trial court nominee, and argued he had been fairer to Bush's appointees than Republicans had been to those put forth by Bush's predecessor, President Bill Clinton.

In 2005, Leahy led the Democratic minority's questioning of Bush's Supreme Court nominees, John Roberts and Samuel Alito, both of whom were confirmed. Leahy surprised many when he voted to approve the conservative Roberts. "I came here to do what I thought was right, and as a Vermonter I can do nothing different," he said. He also asked tough questions of Alito, but voted no in that instance. "This president is in the midst of a radical realignment of the powers of government and its intrusiveness into the private lives of Americans. This nomination is part of that plan," Leahy charged. In 2017, he joined all but a handful of his Democratic colleagues in voting against the conservative Gorsuch's nomination, taking aim at not only several of Gorsuch's rulings but at what Leahy termed his "nonresponsive testimony" before the Judiciary panel. "Compared to Chief Justice Roberts, there is a yawning crevasse between the words Judge Gorsuch spoke to us, and his actual record," Leahy asserted.

Intellectual property rights also have been a major focus for Leahy at the Judiciary Committee, particularly as the dawn of the digital age posed new challenges in this area. (In 2003, Leahy became the first member of Congress with a blog.) He enacted an overhaul of the nation's patent system in September 2011, ending a seven-year stalemate. But in mid-2014, Leahy was forced to throw in the towel on legislation to rein in so-called patent trolls-firms which accumulate patents not to produce tangible goods, but rather to use the legal system to extract fees and legal judgments from other companies. Leahy reportedly withdrew the measure under pressure from Reid, as the legislation faced opposition from such powerful lobbies as the pharmaceutical industry and the nation's trial lawyers. Leahy tried again in 2015 with the new Congress, but a patent trolling measure co-authored by him and Grassley -- and cosponsored by five other members of the Judiciary panel -- failed to advance. It was yet another collaboration between Leahy and Grassley, who, in the past, have worked together on such matters as satellite television access and cellphone unlocking technology.

Leahy is ranking member of the Appropriations subcommittee with jurisdiction over the State Department and foreign aid programs, and has chaired that subcommittee in the past-giving him a platform to advance several foreign policy-related causes. He has been a major force behind the Trafficking Victims Protection Act, first passed in 2000 and reauthorized several times since; the law is designed to pressure foreign countries engaged in human trafficking, while providing legal recourse to victims of the practice in the United States. Another Leahy cause is the elimination of land mines. Since 1989, he has been crusading against the export and use of such devices, which are easy and cheap to implant yet difficult and expensive to remove. In 1994, he persuaded the United Nations to unanimously call for the eventual elimination of land mines. He pushed Obama in 2010 to join an international treaty banning the mines.

As an opponent of the U.S. embargo against Cuba, Leahy was actively involved in the successful effort to free government contractor Alan Gross from a Cuban prison at the end of 2014-a move that paved the way for Obama's decision to restore diplomatic relations. Leahy was among several lawmakers who flew to Cuba to bring Gross home, and then accompanied Obama to Cuba during a visit in the spring of 2016. He took aim at critics of Obama's initiative to normalize relations, accusing them of applying a "flagrant double standard." In an op-ed in his hometown newspaper, the *Burlington*

Free Press , Leahy noted the critics had not raised objections to U.S. engagement with allies, such as Egypt and Saudi Arabia, despite their poor human rights records. "The critics apparently believe that engagement through diplomatic relations and trade everywhere except Cuba is in our national interest, despite the repressive and corrupt policies of other governments." Leahy gibed.

Earlier in his career, Leahy became one of the few senators to chair the Agriculture Committee who did not represent a state with crops such as wheat, corn or cotton. As the panel's ranking Democrat, he worked with Indiana Republican Richard Lugar in the 1990s to phase out the subsidy system. But after their success in enacting the Freedom to Farm Act of 1996, crop prices fell, and lawmakers' resolve dissipated. Congress took to supporting large annual subsidies in the form of emergency relief to farmers, and in 2002, largely rolled back the 1996 act. Closer to home, Leahy has used his perch on the Agriculture panel to deliver for the roughly 1,000 dairy farms in Vermont. He got an extension of a safety net program for dairy farmers into the January 2013 tax and spending bill that averted the so-called "fiscal cliff."

Around the Capitol, Leahy is known for his hobbies. He is a gadgeteer and an accomplished amateur photographer, despite being legally blind in his left eye since birth; his work has been published in *The New York Times, USAToday* and several news magazines. He is a huge fan of the *Batman* movies, appearing briefly in four of them, most recently *Batman v. Superman: Dawn of Justice* in 2016. He had a speaking part in 2008's *The Dark Knight,* as Leahy tells the Joker, "We're not intimidated by thugs." (Since 2015, Leahy's daughter, Alicia, has been a lobbyist for the Motion Picture Association of America.) Leahy also has been a high-profile fan of the Grateful Dead, and can recite lyrics from their songs-along with verses from Shakespeare.

Leahy had a close call in his first reelection bid, surviving a 1980 challenge from Republican Stewart Ledbetter, then the state's banking and insurance commissioner, by 50%-49% amid a national Republican landslide. Six years later, in a year more favorable for Democrats, he had little trouble defeating popular Gov. Richard Snelling, 63%-35%. In 1992, Leahy was held to 54 percent by Jim Douglas, who was later elected governor-and among the few Republicans to achieve electoral success in Vermont in recent years. Leahy easily won reelection in 1998, 2004, and 2010, garnering more than 70 percent of the vote on a couple of occasions.

Running in 2016 at age 76, Leahy faced businessman Scott Milne, who had come close to upsetting Gov. Peter Shumlin two years earlier. Milne made campaign finance an issue: He reported taking in just$128,000 in unsolicited contributions and donations from himself. "I'm running against a gentleman who charges special-interest lobbyists $5,000 a piece to sit around a table with him and have lunch," Milne declared of Leahy, who raised more than $3.9 million. Milne also sought to tie Leahy's past advocacy of the EB-5 program -- which provides foreigners with path to permanent residency in exchange for investments in U.S. projects -- to a scandal in Vermont. Milne's charges followed a Securities and Exchange Commission lawsuit alleging that two developers in the state's northeast region had operated what the agency called a "Ponzi-like scheme" to defraud foreign investors of $200 million.

"Taken together, these facts raise legitimate questions about Pat Leahy's interest in EB-5," Milne told *Vermont Public Radio*, while demanding that Leahy's office release all communications regarding the program. "If he is accusing me of doing something wrong, he should call the U.S. attorney's office," Leahy shot back -- while pointing out that Milne had traveled to China in 2009 to explore tapping into the EB-5 program for a development project. However, weeks before Election Day, as Congress passed a continuing resolution to fund the government that included an extension of the EB-5 program, Leahy voted against the measure because it did not include proposed EB-5 reforms. He called fraud in the program "rampant," according to the *Vermont Digger*, an online news site, saying he would feel betrayed if allegations against one of the involved developers -- Bill Stenger, to whom Leahy has had close ties -- were proven to be true.

Leahy easily defeated Milne, 61%-33%. When another continuing resolution to keep the government operating came up in the post-election lame-duck session of Congress without changes to EB-5, Leahy again voted no, saying, "It is time we fix it. If EB-5 cannot be reformed due to a paralysis of leadership, the time has come for it to end."

Junior Senator

Bernie Sanders (I)

Elected 2006, term expires 2018, 2nd term; b. Sep 08, 1941, Brooklyn, NY; University of Chicago (IL), B.A.; Brooklyn College (NY), Att.; Jewish; Married (Jane O'Meara Driscoll); 1 child; 3 stepchildren.

Elected Office: Burlington Mayor, 1981-1989; U.S. House, 1991-2007.

Professional Career: Writer; Director, American People's Historical Soc., 1977-1981; Lecturer, Harvard University, 1989; Lecturer, Hamilton College, 1990.

DC Office: 332 DSOB 20510, 202-224-5141, Fax: 202-228-0776, sanders.senate.gov.

State Offices: Burlington, 802-862-0697; St. Johnsbury, 802-748-9269.

Committees: Senate Democratic Outreach Committee Chairman. *Budget (RMM)*. *Energy & Natural Resources*: Energy, National Parks, Water & Power. *Environment & Public Works*: Clean Air & Nuclear Safety, Superfund, Waste Management, & Regulatory Oversight, Transportation & Infrastructure. *Health, Education, Labor & Pensions*: Children & Families, Primary Health & Retirement Security (RMM). *Veterans' Affairs*.

Group Ratings

	ADA	ACLU	AFL-CIO	LCV	ITI	COC	HAFA	ACU	CFG	FRC
2016	-	94%	-	6%	0%	25%	23%	0%	N/A	0%
2015	100%	C	100%	100%	C	15%	C	9%	11%	0%

Almanac Ratings 2015

	Economy	Social	Foreign	Composite
Liberal	91%	95%	91%	92%
Conservative	9%	5%	9%	8%

Key Votes of the 114th Congress

1. Keystone pipeline	N	5. National Security Data	N	9. Gun Sales Checks	Y
2. Export-Import Bank	Y	6. Iran Nuclear Deal	N	10. Sanctuary Cities	N
3. Debt Ceiling Increase	Y	7. Puerto Rico Debt	N	11. Planned Parenthood	NV
4. Homeland Security $$	Y	8. Loretta Lynch A.G	Y	12. Trade deals	N

Election Results

Election	Name (Party)	Vote (%)		Cand. Spent	Ind. Exp. Support	Ind. Exp. Oppose
2012 General	Bernie Sanders (I)	207,848	(71%)	$3,247,555		
	John MacGovern (R)	72,898	(25%)	$131,927		
	Cris Ericson (UMJ)	5,924	(2%)			
2012 Primary	Bernie Sanders (I)	36,902	(99%)			

Prior winning percentages: 2006 (65%)

At first, few took Bernie Sanders seriously as a contender for the Democratic presidential nomination -- a rumpled, self-styled socialist in his mid-70s, who, despite a quarter of a century on Capitol Hill, was regarded by many of his colleagues as a preachy out lier with a limited record of legislative accomplishment. "We didn't have a strategy to win this when we started," Tad Devine, a leading Sanders' strategist, told Clinton herself to the left. As he returned to Capitol Hill in early 2017, Senate Democratic colleagues USA Today. "We were just trying to be competitive." Nearly 50 points down in some polls when he started, Vermont's junior senator battled the front-running candidate, Hillary Clinton, to the end of the primary election season. By the time he arrived at the Democratic National Convention in July 2016, Sanders could claim victories in 22 states, along with the backing of 45 percent of the pledged delegates, while energizing and attracting millennial voters. "That gives me a lot of leverage, leverage that I intend to use," Sanders vowed to The Washington Post shortly before the general election.

In the wake of Clinton's surprise loss to Donald Trump, post-mortem debates continue within party circles about just how close Sanders came to actually derailing Clinton's nomination, and which of them might have fared better in November. What is not in dispute is that Sanders emerged from the 2016 campaign as a major player in the national Democratic Party, after pushing both the party platform and Clinton herself to the left. As he returned to Capitol Hill in early 2017, Senate Democratic colleagues reached out to Sanders to help deal with the widening gulf between the party's establishment and progressive wings -- as the two sides battled over tactics in responding to the new Trump administration.

Such newly minted attention and clout was particularly notable for a legislator who had made eight successful runs for the House and two for the Senate without appearing on the Democratic ballot line. "No, I'm an independent," Sanders said on MSNBC in April 2017 when asked whether he now identifies as a Democrat. But his goal is nothing less than a transformation of the Democratic Party -- a point he has voiced repeatedly since his presidential bid. "If the Democratic Party is going to succeed - and I want to see it succeed - it's gonna have to open its door to independents…It's got to open its doors to working people and to young people, create a grassroots party," he said during the MSNBC appearance.

Shortly after announcing his candidacy in April 2015, Sanders appeared on CBS' "Face The Nation",during which he criticized President Barack Obama's efforts to compromise early in his White House tenure. Sanders made clear he felt Obama had wasted time trying to engage Republican congressional leaders, asserting: "The truth is Republicans never wanted to negotiate. All they wanted to do was obstruct." Such comments-while hardly in keeping with the more compromising tones historically adopted by presidential contenders-are nonetheless consistent with Sanders' long-time public persona. His unapologetic stance also presaged the fiery rhetoric throughout his presidential bid -- which was viewed with increasing seriousness as Sanders drew frequently massive crowds early on, while railing against the "billionaire class" and urging a "political revolution."

Behind the fomenter of this political revolution is a savvy strategist who, on occasion, has demonstrated a willingness to -- yes, compromise, both during his congressional career and earlier. "The thing about Bernie which is different than most socialists is Bernie wants to win," Garrison Nelson, a University of Vermont professor who has known Sanders for four decades, told *Politico*. Taking over the chairmanship of the Senate Veterans' Affairs Committee in 2013, Sanders steered an overhaul of the VA into law a year later, making it one of the few major bipartisan accomplishments of a politically gridlocked Congress. Shortly after closing that legislative deal in 2014, Sanders adopted a more conciliatory tone as he harkened back to his days as the first socialist mayor of Burlington, in the 1980s. "When I took office, [in terms of] people who supported me on the city council, we had two out of 13, and I had to make things happen while being in the minority," Sanders told *Roll Call*. "So I do know how to negotiate fairly. Negotiation is part of the political process. I certainly have been prepared to do that since day one."

As his still-thick Brooklyn accent indicates, Sanders grew up in the Flat bush section of New York City's largest borough, the son of a paint salesman who had emigrated from Poland. He graduated from James Madison High School (also the *alma mater* of Minority Leader Charles Schumer, who named Sanders to a post in the Senate Democratic leadership in late 2016) before attending Brooklyn College. He graduated from the University of Chicago, where he became involved in radical leftist politics. Sanders moved to Vermont as part of the hippie migration of 1968; a continuing influx of urbanites in the 1960s and 1970s transformed the once solidly Republican state into the deep blue bastion it is today. Sanders worked as a carpenter upon arriving in Vermont. In 1971, he ran in a special election to replace Republican Senator Winston Prouty, who had died in office. Sanders won just 2 percent of the vote as the candidate of the Liberty Union Party. He went on to lose four more statewide races (including a 1974 Senate bid when, running against Democrat Patrick Leahy, now his senior colleague from the Green Mountain State, Sanders raised his share of the vote on the Liberty Union line to 4 percent.)

Sanders' earnest persona finally won over the people of Burlington, who elected him mayor in 1981 by just 10 votes. "There was anger in the air, plenty of it," the *Burlington Free Press* recalled more than three decades later. "Bernie Sanders, a self-proclaimed socialist of all people, had somehow stolen City Hall from [the Democrats]." He served as mayor until 1989, winning re-election three times. "I am a socialist, of course I am a socialist," Sanders declared during a 1983 mayoral debate, according to an *Associated Press* account. He added, "To hold a vision that society can be fundamentally different, to believe that all people can be equal, that is not a new idea." He called a change he had made to give city employees input into policies such as sick leave and grievance procedures "a socialist idea." More than three decades later, as many Sanders supporters argued that he would have been a stronger general election candidate than Clinton, other Democrats contended that Trump and the Republicans would have highlighted the socialist label to the detriment of his candidacy.

In 1988, when Republican Rep. James Jeffords ran for the Senate, Sanders made a bid for the House as an independent, but lost to Republican Peter Smith in a close, three-way race by 41%-38%. Two years later, Sanders ran again, and defeated Smith, 56%-40%, becoming only the third socialist ever elected to the House, after Victor Berger of Milwaukee (1911-13, 1923-29) and Meyer London of Manhattan's Lower East Side (1915-23).Sanders benefited politically in 1990 from his opposition to gun control: Smith had voted to ban semi-automatic weapons, and the National Rifle Association came out against him.Three years later, in 1993, Sanders voted against the so-called Brady Bill requiring background checks for individuals purchasing firearms. And in 2005, Sanders supported a NRA-backed bill to shield gun manufacturers and dealers from most lawsuits.

Sanders' early gun control stance has haunted him; Clinton raised it in candidate forums in 2016, and it was used in ads by a "super PAC" supporting her candidacy. More recently, Sanders has sided with gun control advocates -- voting in 2013 in favor of legislation to expand background checks in the wake of the Newtown Connecticut school shootings, and in 2016 to bar firearm sales to those on the government's terrorist watch list. But he represents a state where gun ownership is widespread with few restrictions in place, and Sanders appeared to be playing the role of pragmatic politician during his successful 1990 campaign. "Bernie's response is that he doesn't just represent liberals and progressives. He was sent to Washington to represent all of Vermont," Sanders' chief of staff was quoted as saying shortly after he won. "It's not inappropriate for a congressman to support a majority position, particularly on something Vermonters have been very clear about."

During his 16 years in the House, Sanders was Vermont's single, at-large member. Democrats initially balked at accepting a socialist in their caucus, but granted him seniority as a Democrat after he arrived on Capitol Hill in 1991. (To gain appointment to committees, a member of Congress must caucus with one of the two major parties.) Sanders formed a Progressive Caucus with a quixotic agenda: progressive tax reform, a Canada-style single-payer health care system, a 50-percent cut in military spending, a national energy policy, and-a Vermont touch-support for family farms. A number of these ideas later formed the heart of his presidential bid. After announcing in 2015, Sanders called for significantly raising tax rates on the highest earners and instituting a government-run single-payer system for health care; a similar public option was considered as part of the debate over the Affordable Care Act in 2009-10, but dropped for lack of support. Notwithstanding that much of what he has advocated is unlikely to be enacted anytime soon, Sanders has sought to play the long game throughout his career, hoping to influence opinion by speaking out early and often."Everybody [now] talks about income inequality," he told *The New YorkTimes* in 2015. "Well, check it out. Find out who was talking about it 20 years ago."

One of Sanders' House proposalsexhibited appeal across the political aisle. In 2001, he proposed a $300-per-person income tax rebate. It quickly became Democratic Party policy, and Republicans, in assembling majorities for the Bush Administration tax cuts, included it in diluted form-a $300 rebate for income-tax-paying adults. Sanders and the Democrats noted ruefully that President George W. Bush took credit for a tax-cutting proposal that was initially theirs. As much as any member of Congress, Sanders made the cost of prescription drugs a national issue. Since the 1980s, he had called for government programs to pay for prescription drugs, and was the first member of Congress to lead bus trips to Canada to buy lower cost pharmaceuticals there.

All of this played well at home, and by the late 1990s, Sanders was regularly winning re-election with more than 60 percent of the vote. In April 2005, Jeffords announced he would not run for another Senate term in 2006. Sanders became the early frontrunner and quickly amassed endorsements from top Vermont Democrats, including state Senate President Pro Tempore Peter Welch (who succeeded Sanders in the state's at-large House seat). With Sanders' consent, Democrats ran his name on their primary ballot, and he won 94 percent of the vote, although he formally declined the nomination and petitioned the state to list him on the general election ballot as an independent.On the GOP side, Gov. Jim Douglas was considered the one Republican with a real shot at defeating Sanders, but Douglas declined to run. Richard Tarrant, a multi-millionaire businessman, became the nominee. His ads sought to portray Sanders as an ineffective radical who was soft on sexual predators and drug dealers. The strategy might have worked elsewhere, but not in Vermont, where voters were well-acquainted with Sanders and his iconoclastic ways. Although outspent, Sanders won handily, 65%-32%. Sanders had even less trouble winning a second term in 2012, easily dispatching underfunded Republican John MacGovern, 71%-25%.

Sanders settled with surprising ease into the Senate's more structured ways, and grew more sensitive to his reputation as a troublemaker. Leahy told a Vermont reporter that other senators-presumably expecting a political bomb-thrower in their midst-had confided "what a pleasant surprise [Sanders] has turned out to be" with his willingness to craft legislative deals. Sanders found himself in a position of influence as Veterans' Affairs chairman in 2013-14, shortly after winning a second term.

Revelations about the poor treatment that veterans faced forced out VA Secretary Eric Shinseki and led to considerable pressure to pass a reform bill. Over several months, Sanders engaged in a regular and often bitter war of words with his conservative House counterpart, Jeff Miller of Florida, but the two men struck a compromise at the conclusion of what Sanders called "a very, very difficult process." The $17 billion package sailed through the House unanimously and drew just three dissenting votes in the Senate. It represented one of the largest expansions of the federal government since the Republicans had taken over the House majority at the beginning of 2011.

But the uncompromising side of Sanders that would later be on prominent display in the presidential contest remained very much in evidence-as he at one point likened skeptics of human-caused global warming to non-Germans who had denied the spread of Nazism before World War II. When Obama nominated Ben Bernanke in 2009 for a second term asFederal Reserve chairman, Sanders bristled, "When the people voted for change in 2008, they did not vote to have one of the key architects of the Bush economy be reappointed." In June 2012, Sanders released the names of 18 Federal Reserve regional bank directors (current and former) whose businesses had received close to zero interest loans from the Fed. A couple of years earlier, as Congress debated the so-called Dodd-Frank bill overhauling regulation of the financial industry, Sanders got a provision into the Senate version ordering an audit of the Fed.

When in 2011 the "Occupy Wall Street" protest movement energized the American left, Sanders endorsed the goals of the upstart movement. But his breakout moment on the national political stage came with an eight-hour, often apoplectic floor speech at the end of 2010: He excoriated the extension of tax cuts for the highest-income Americans--enacted early in the Bush administration -- as "Robin Hood in reverse." At one point, Sanders sarcastically asked: "How can I get by on one house? I need five houses, 10 houses! I need three jet planes to take me all over the world! Sorry, American people. We've got the money, we've got the power, we've got the lobbyists here and on Wall Street. Tough luck." The speech proved so popular that it temporarily shut down the Senate video server and put Sanders' name atop Twitter's list of trending topics. In early 2011, it was sold as a book, *The Speech: A Historic Filibuster on Corporate Greed and the Decline of Our Middle Class,* with the proceeds going to Vermont charities. In the monthsfollowing the speech, Sanders made the rounds of television shows ranging from MSNBC to *The Daily Show with Jon Stewart,* as he released a list of 10 large corporations that he said had paid disproportionately low taxes, including GE, Exxon Mobil, and Bank of America.

Sanders drew attention in fall 2013 when he toured several Southern states and declared he would consider running for president in 2016. "Anyone who really, really wants to be president is slightly crazy because this is an unbelievably difficult job given the crises that this country faces today," he said during one appearance. Nevertheless, he said that if no one else with his views ended up in the race, he would contemplate it to ensure someone raised the issues important to him-reining in Wall Street, addressing the "collapse" of the middle class and fighting the spread of poverty. He took the plunge after the first choice of the party's left wing, Massachusetts Sen. Elizabeth Warren, spent a year insisting she had no plans to mount a White House bid.

Like Trump, Sanders exhibited a populist appeal, albeit from the opposite end of the spectrum -- and, also like Trump, was seen as a political outsider taking aim at the *status quo*. The latter appeared to be a key element of his allure to 18-to-29 year-olds, some more than half a century his junior, as he captured them by a 5-2 margin over Clinton. "To some young people, his candidacy is irresistibly attractive, not necessarily because his policies make a lot of sense, but because they are drawn to one thing: his unmistakable sense of outrage at how things are," Cass Sunstein -- a former Obama administration official who was once a colleague of Obama's on the University of Chicago Law School faculty -- opined for *Bloomberg View.*Sanders' fundraising efforts were, in and of themselves, something of a phenomenon: He relied heavily on small individual donors, thereby helping to lend credibility to his attacks on moneyed interests and their influence on the political system. Sanders' campaign committee collected nearly $234 million from 8 million donations that it said averaged $27 each, setting it apart from many of the 2016 presidential candidates that were fueled by super PACs and other outside groups. (Despite discouraging the support of super PACs, the Sanders campaign did benefit from $6.3 million inspending byindependent expenditure groups.)

Sanders' fundraising success allowed his campaign to keep going through the primary season, even as the mathematical odds against his capturing nomination mounted. But if he had the enthusiastic support of young voters, Sanders -- who represents a state that is 96 percent white -- struggled to attract non-white voters, who cast an estimated 40 percent of the ballots during the Democratic primaries and caucuses. According to exit polling data compiled by the *Wall Street Journal*, African-American voters favored Clinton by better than 3-1. With the notable exception of Sanders' surprise victory in the Michigan primary on March 8 -- which infused him with hope that he still had a shot at the nomination -- the vast majority of his primary season wins were in more sparsely populated states with limited minority populations.

Also working against Sanders was the Democratic establishment, many of whom were among more than 700 "super-delegates" who automatically have a vote at the nominating convention as elected officeholders or high-ranking party officials. A large majority of super-delegates backed Clinton early on. This extended to Sanders' own state, where four of five super-delegates lined up behind Clinton, despite Vermont giving more than 85 percent of its primary vote to its favorite son. (One of the pro-Clinton super-delegates, Sanders' senior colleague Leahy, said he had committed to supporting Clinton as far back as 2012.) Sanders' supporters complained repeatedly about the influence of the super-delegates,but his sharpest criticisms of the nominating process were reserved for the Democratic National Committee and what he considered its rigging of the system to bolster Clinton. The DNC's chairman, Rep. Debbie Wasserman Schultz,resigned just prior to the Democratic National Convention after a series of leaked e-mails confirmed Sanders' suspicions.

Some of Sanders' problems, however, were self-inflicted -- not unusual for a first-time candidate for national office. Early on, he gave Clinton a pass on her use of private email server while secretary of state, a controversy that would later help sink her candidacy in the general election. "Let me say something that may not be great politics," Sanders acknowledged during a televised debate in the fall of 2015, and then proceeded to tell Clinton, "The American people are sick and tired about hearing about your damn emails."By the same token, Sanders did himself no favors six months later, when he said Clinton wasn't qualified to be president during another debate. He later backed away from that statement, but -- coming off a string of primary and caucus wins at the time -- it may have cost him a shot at an upset victory in Clinton's home state of New York.

In early June, as Clinton gained enough delegates to clinch the nomination, and Sanders, after initially vowing to take his campaign all the way to the convention, backed off and endorsed Clinton two weeks prior to the Philadelphia gathering. Seeking to ensure a harmonious convention, the Clinton campaign agreed to put almost as many Sanders supporters on the platform committee as Clinton backers. And Clinton later embraced variations of a couple of Sanders's major campaign proposals -- free tuition at public universities and an expanded role for the federal government providing health care coverage --into her general election campaign.

Notwithstanding some significant inroads for what started as a longshot candidacy,it was apparent that Sanders felt the nomination had been within his grasp, and his disappointment was palpable. "I understand that many people here in this convention hall and around the country are disappointed about the final results of the nominating process," he said while addressing the delegates in Philadelphia. "I think it's fair to say that no one is more disappointed than I am." Appearing on CNN in early 2017, Sanders pointedly declined to rule out another bid in 2020. "It's much too early to be talking about that," he said. If he runs, Sanders would be 79, two years older than the oldest president to date -- Ronald Reagan, who left the White House at 77. First, he must win re-election in 2018, for which he is a prohibitive favorite:

As Congress convened in January 2017, Sanders continued in his role as ranking member of the Senate Budget Committee -- a post he first assumed two years earlier -- while seeking to exercise his new-found clout. As the Senate debated a congressional budget resolution for the coming year, Sanders called out 13 Democratic senators who voted against an amendment that pushed one of his long-time causes: allowing reimportation of prescription drugs from Canada."The Democratic Party has got to make it very clear that they are prepared to stand up to powerful special interests like the pharmaceutical industry and like Wall Street -- and they're not going to win elections and they're not going to be doing the right thing for the American people unless they have the guts to do that," he declared. A month later, one of the 13, New Jersey Sen. Cory Booker joined Sanders at a press conference introducing a bill to allow allowing importation of pharmaceuticals from Canada. Booker -- who represents a state that is headquarters to several large pharmaceutical firms -- shifted after taking heat from the party's progressive activist wing. It was an early sample of what may lay in store for Booker, a potential aspirant for the 2020 Democratic presidential nomination, as well as other contenders -- with or without Sanders in the race.

REPRESENTATIVE-AT-LARGE

Peter Welch (D)

Elected 2006, 6th term; b. May 02, 1947, Springfield, MA; College of The Holy Cross (MA), B.A., 1969; University of California, Berkeley, J.D., 1973; Roman Catholic; Married (Margaret Cheney); 5 children; 3 stepchildren.

Elected Office: Elected Office: VT Senate, 1981-1989, 2002-2007, Minority Leader, 1983-1985, President pro tem, 1985-1989, 2003-2007.

Professional Career: Robert F. Kennedy fellow, 1969-1970; Practicing attorney, 1974-2006.

DC Office: 2303 RHOB 20515, 202-225-4115, Fax: 202-225-6790, welch.house.gov.

State Offices: Burlington, 888-605-7270.

Committees: *Energy & Commerce*: Communications & Technology, Digital Commerce & Consumer Protection, Energy. *Oversight & Government Reform*: National Security.

Group Ratings

	ADA	ACLU	AFL-CIO	LCV	ITI	COC	HAFA	ACU	CFG	FRC
2016	-	100%	-	97%	50%	57%	14%	4%	4%	0%
2015	90%	C	100%	94%	C	37%	C	9%	6%	0%

Almanac Ratings 2015

	Economy	Social	Foreign	Composite
Liberal	97%	100%	93%	96%
Conservative	3%	0%	7%	4%

Key Votes of the 114th Congress

1. Keystone Pipeline	N	5. Puerto Rico Debt	Y	9. Offenses by Aliens	N
2. Trade Deals	N	6. Medical Marijuana	Y	10. Troops in Iraq	N
3. Export-Import Bank	Y	7. Sanctuary Cities	N	11. Homeland Security $$	Y
4. Debt Ceiling Increase	Y	8. Armor-piercing Bullets	N	12. Trade Adjustment aid	Y

Election Results

Election	Name (Party)	Vote (%)	Cand. Spent	Ind. Exp. Support	Ind. Exp. Oppose
2016 General	Peter Welch (D)	264,414 (90%)	$381,437		
	Erica Clawson (L)	30,943 (10%)			
2016 Primary	Peter Welch (D)	(100%)			

Prior winning percentages: 2014 (64%), 2012 (72%), 2010 (65%), 2008 (83%), 2006 (53%)

Vermont's only House member is Peter Welch, a Democrat first elected in 2006. He is highly regarded within his party as a strategist and spokesman. He serves as a chief deputy whip and has been active on energy and health care issues-occasionally on a bipartisan basis. One of his proposals to lower Medicare costs drew the direct interest of President Donald Trump, who invited Welch and a colleague to meet with him. Welch has been viewed as the heir apparent to a Senate seat if either of Vermont's more elderly senators creates a vacancy.

Welch grew up in Springfield, Massachusetts, the son of a dentist, and graduated from the College of the Holy Cross. The summer before his junior year, he worked for a Jesuit group that did community outreach in poor black neighborhoods in Chicago, where he was inspired by a speech by the Rev. Martin Luther King Jr. After graduating from law school at the University of California, Berkeley, Welch backpacked down the Pan-American Highway to Santiago, Chile, went overland to Brazil, then worked on a freighter that sailed to Portugal. After that, he was ready to practice law and chose White River Junction, Vermont, as his home. He worked as a public defender before founding his small firm.

In 1980, Welch became the first Democrat to represent Windsor County in the state Senate since the Civil War. Two years later, he became Senate minority leader. After Democrats won a majority in the

Senate for the first time ever, he was elected president pro tem. He focused on environment, education, and tax issues and helped establish the Housing and Land Conservation Trust, which worked to create affordable housing and to conserve farmland and forests. In 1988, when Republican Rep. James Jeffords ran for the Senate, Welch aimed for the House but lost the Democratic primary by 266 votes. In 1990, he ran for governor, but lost 52%-46% to Republican Richard Snelling. For some years after that, Welch was out of political life. His wife, Joan, who had been his closest adviser and campaign manager, fought cancer for nine years, and Welch at times was her full-time caregiver. She died in 2004.

In 2001, Democratic Gov. Howard Dean appointed Welch to the state Senate to fill a vacancy. In 2003, he became president pro tem once again and focused on health care issues. Jeffords did not seek reelection in 2006. Rep. Bernie Sanders, after 15 years in the House, ran for the Senate and attracted little opposition. Welch ran again for the House and won the Democratic primary unopposed. Martha Rainville, commander of the Vermont National Guard, won the Republican primary 71%-28%. In the general election, Welch ran as an opponent-from the start-of military action in Iraq, and he condemned the "corrupt" Republicans in Washington. He supported universal health care. Rainville said she would have voted for military action in Iraq in 2002 given what was known then, but she criticized some decisions of the Bush administration. Both candidates favored abortion rights.

Following an agreement by the candidates, this was probably the only seriously contested House race in 2006 without a single negative ad. But there was some dispute. Welch called Rainville the "hand-picked" candidate of the unpopular national Republicans. Rainville countered that Vermont Republicans are "something very different," and insisted that "the party has a lot of room for diversity." Welch spent $1.7 million to Rainville's $1.1 million. The House Republican campaign committee outspent its Democratic counterpart, $750,000 to $300,000. Welch won, 53%-45%.

Welch has been known for legislative skill, which features an understated and collegial style. On the Energy and Commerce Committee, he helped to shape energy and climate-change legislation. He got a provision in a House-passed bill to spend billions of dollars on energy efficiency. He won committee approval of a measure to provide tax rebates to consumers for installing upgraded insulation, storm windows and other energy-efficiency aids. Practicing what he preached, he made his office the first in the House to install new lights and water fixtures to reduce energy use.

After the GOP takeover of the House, he became a chief deputy for Minority Whip Steny Hoyer. He helped liberals articulate their opposition on various issues and maintained a liberal voting record. Welch is not a strict partisan. He worked with Republicans on a measure in 2013 to allow states to ensure online merchants collect sales taxes in return for simplified tax procedures. He joined Republican Rep. David McKinley of West Virginia on a broad proposal that included efficiency standards for utility companies and a requirement that federally backed home mortgages must include efficiency ratings for the property. The House passed the bill in 2015 and it was enacted with Senate revisions. In November 2016, he joined a bipartisan group that enacted a bill that directed the Commerce Department to quantify the financial impact of outdoor recreation. Welch has been a member of the bipartisan citizen activist effort No Labels.

Overseas, he broke with Obama in 2014 on the call to train and equip rebels opposing the Islamic State and the regime in Syria. "I do not believe that that plan has any reasonable prospect of success," Welch said. In December 2015, he was among the leaders of a bipartisan, bicameral group that filed the first resolution to authorize the use of military force against ISIS.

In March 2017, Welch and Democratic Rep. Elijah Cummings of Maryland met with Trump to discuss their proposal for the federal government to negotiate lower prices for prescription-drug coverage under Medicare. Following the nearly hour-long meeting, the two Democrats said that Trump agreed to support their plan.

At home, Welch has faced no serious reelection threats. In 2009, he married state Rep. Margaret Cheney, who later became a member of the Vermont Public Service Board. After a question arose about a possible conflict, he said that he would not accept campaign contributions from political action committees of companies with cases before the board. Welch turned down an opportunity to run for governor in 2016.At age 70, he remained a distinct possibility to run for the Senate if an opening occurs.

★ VIRGINIA ★

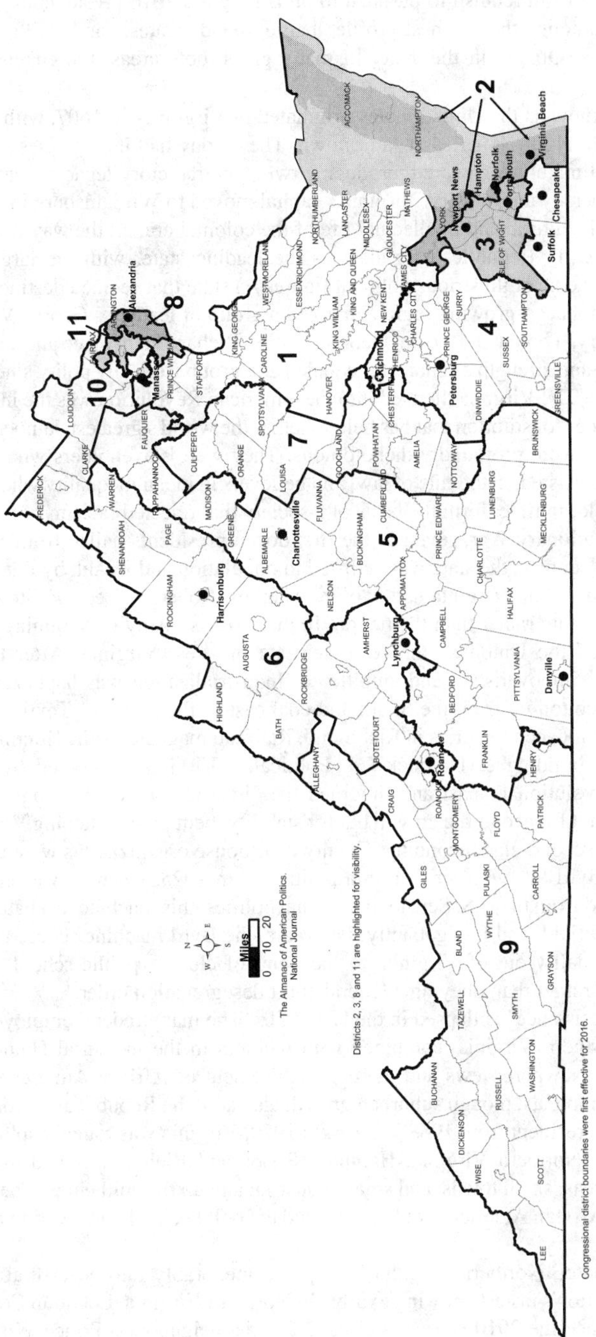
Alexandria
Manassas
Charlottesville
Harrisonburg
Lynchburg
Roanoke
Danville
Richmond
Petersburg
Newport News
Hampton
Norfolk
Portsmouth
Virginia Beach
Chesapeake
Suffolk
1
2
3
4
5
6
7
8
9
10
11
Miles
0 10 20
The Almanac of American Politics.
National Journal
Districts 2, 3, 8 and 11 are highlighted for visibility.
Congressional district boundaries were first effective for 2016.

Virginia may have been the home to the capital of the Confederacy a century and a half ago, but in recent years, the state – and its political evolution – has been driven to a large degree by the increasingly diverse suburbs of Washington, D.C. Election by election, at the statewide level, Virginia has gradually shifted from reddish to purplish to bluish; by the 2016 presidential race, Virginia wasn't even considered among the highest-profile battleground states, and Hillary Clinton slightly outperformed Barack Obama in the state. In many grass-roots areas, the change has been slow or continues to evolve.

What we now know as the United States originated in Virginia - in 1607, with the first permanent English settlement in North America at Jamestown. The colony had its struggles - with food, weather and Indians - but ultimately persevered, producing twin, contradictory legacies that shaped the nation: representative democracy and slavery. Virginia's capital moved to Williamsburg in 1699, becoming the locus of commercial, cultural and intellectual life of the colonial era, all the way through the American Revolution. In the early Republic, Virginia was the leading state, with the largest population, the greatest wealth and the most illustrious political figures - a state that seemed destined to lead and shape a nation. From this tobacco-growing region emerged a group of leaders - George Washington, George Mason, Patrick Henry, Thomas Jefferson, George Wythe, Richard Henry Lee and James Madison - that in learning, wisdom and strength of character equaled any group from any polity since Periclean Athens or Republican Rome. The Virginia they led into the American Revolution was the indispensable creator of the republic and the Constitution that has held together the world's greatest democracy. But these men embodied ideals that were profoundly dichotomous. They were slaveholders who insisted on liberty, revolutionaries who insisted on the rule of law, and believers in racial inequality who set forth principles of equality that would, in time, form the basis of a society that rejected racism.

After the Revolutionary War, seven of the first dozen presidents hailed from Virginia. But in the first half of the 19th century, the state was eclipsed in population and wealth by Pennsylvania and New York. During the Civil War, Virginia had two great heroes, Robert E. Lee and Stonewall Jackson, but they fought for their state rather than the nation. In the process, many of Virginia's mountain counties broke off and joined the Union as the separate state of West Virginia. After the war, Virginia's leadership class was impoverished and embittered. Industrialization was haphazard. Railroads were constructed to ship cotton up from the South and coal east to the seaports. Textile mills were built in Southside towns and tobacco factories in Richmond. Railroad magnate Collis Huntington built the giant Newport News Shipbuilding & Drydock Co. Politically, Virginia was ruled by local gentry who worshipped their revolutionary past and mourned the "Lost Cause" of the Confederacy. They were pessimists, looking not for economic growth but for stability, bent on maintaining Virginia's segregation and content with its second-class economy. County courthouse organizations were united in a political machine by Harry Byrd Sr., who ran Virginia politics from 1925, when he was elected governor, to 1965, when he retired from the U.S. Senate. In national politics, this machine lost battles more often than Lee lost on the battlefield, and less gallantly. For years, the Byrd machine succeeded in keeping most vestiges of racial equality out of Virginia, to the point of closing public schools in Prince Edward County in the 1950s rather than obeying a federal court desegregation order.

This "massive resistance" collapsed in the late 1950s. The many federal employees in the bedroom communities of Northern Virginia, combined with workers in the industrial Hampton Roads region around Norfolk and Newport News and the enfranchisement of African Americans, provided a new political base for Democrats, though suburban growth also kept the Republicans strong; the state would vote Republican for president from 1968 to 2004. In 1970, Virginia was roughly split between its major metropolitan areas - Northern Virginia, Hampton Roads and Richmond - and the rest of Virginia, consisting of rural areas, small towns, and small industrial and textile-mill cities. The latter were solidly conservative. Most African Americans didn't vote, and the poll tax held down voting among poor whites until it was banned.

A half-century later, Northern Virginia had spread inexorably into once-rural counties, some of which became the nation's fastest-growing exurbs. In Northern Virginia, Loudoun County has grown by nearly 24 percent since the 2010 census, and its D.C.-area neighbors – Prince William, Stafford and Arlington counties and the cities of Manassas Park and Alexandria – had each grown by double digits over the same period. Further to the south, Hampton Roads grew out into swampy lands on either side of the James River and swelled due to a large military presence, while metropolitan Richmond, undeterred by the increasing marginalization of tobacco, expanded outward, with places like New Kent

County growing by almost 15 percent since 2010. Some jurisdictions elsewhere in the state exceeded Virginia's overall growth rate of 5.1 percent, including Fredericksburg, Harrisonburg and the university area of Charlottesville. But traditional Virginia -- places like the Northern Neck, the two Eastern Shore counties, South side Virginia, and the Shenandoah Valley – saw its population, and in many cases the economies, stagnate. The mountains of Southwest Virginia suffered the most: Since 2010, the Appalachian counties of Buchanan, Dickenson and Wise saw their populations decline by between 5 percent and 8 percent.

Virginia's population growth was accompanied by significant demographic change, especially in Northern Virginia. Statewide, the population was 19 percent black, 10 percent Hispanic and 6 percent Asian; both the black and Asian percentages ranked Virginia among the top 10 states in the nation. But the state's northern suburbs near Washington, D.C., saw the heaviest diversification. Prince William County is 22 percent Hispanic and 9 percent Asian; the city of Alexandria is 17 percent Hispanic and 7 percent Asian; Fairfax County is 17 percent Hispanic and 17 percent Asian; Arlington County is 16 percent Hispanic and 11 percent Asian; and Loudoun County is 14 percent Hispanic and 18 percent Asian. Each of these jurisdictions was not just diverse but also affluent – Loudoun County, the city of Falls Church and Fairfax County ranked first, second and third in the nation in median household income, each of them easily exceeding six figures, beneficiaries of the growth of the federal government and the relatively high wages and good benefits enjoyed by federal employees. Virginia ranks high in median income and educational attainment; it has the sixth-highest percentage of any state for residents with bachelor's degrees. Virginia's unemployment peaked at 7.4 percent during the Great Recession, well below the national high, and it was below the national average in March 2017, at 3.8 percent. Virginia ranked first among states as a recipient for Defense Department spending, accounting for almost 12 percent of state gross domestic product. Virginia's aerospace and aviation industry employs more than 44,000 people. Other tech-minded enterprises, riding the defense industry's coattails, dot the Dulles Airport corridor.

Growth and change produced unstable politics. In the 1970s, conservatives who left the Democratic Party and ran as independents or Republicans held Democrats at bay. In the 1980s, three moderate Democrats were elected governor - Charles Robb in 1981, Gerald Baliles in 1985 and Douglas Wilder in 1989. (Virginia is the last state that bars its governors from running for reelection, though they can run again after at least one term out of office.) The three Democratic governors did not attempt to impose a liberal agenda on an unwilling Virginia, instead arguing that government could be used effectively to improve education and build the state's economy. In the 1990s, Virginia split increasingly along ideological lines. George Allen, elected governor by a wide margin in 1993, was a Republican who believed in lower taxes and traditional cultural values. He leavened confrontational issue positions with a sunny temperament. Four years later, Republican James Gilmore made his centerpiece issue the phasing-out of the property tax on automobiles and won a 56%-43% victory. Republicans for the first time swept the top three statewide offices, and in the 1999 legislative elections Gilmore led Republicans to majorities in both chambers for the first time ever.

The 21st century has tilted Virginia more toward the Democrats. Mark Warner won the governorship in 2001 after an intensive, 18-month campaign in rural Virginia in which he paid attention to the parts of the state not blessed by 1990s growth. Warner carried Northern Virginia and the Hampton Roads area only narrowly, but he also carried non-urban Virginia. Warner left office with high ratings and is now a senator (though he experienced a scare in his 2014 reelection bid, thanks to the national GOP wave and an erosion of support in the state's increasingly Republican rural areas). Warner's success represented the first of several Democratic breakthroughs, fueled in large part by the diversification of Northern Virginia.

While George W. Bush carried Northern Virginia in 2000, he lost it four years later, 51%-48%. The trend accelerated as Democrat Tim Kaine was elected governor in 2005 over Republican Jerry Kilgore, whose conservative stands were a tough sell in Northern Virginia as well as suburban Richmond and Hampton Roads. Three years later, Barack Obama became the first Democratic presidential candidate to carry Virginia since 1964, and he did so by his national average of 53%-46%. A grateful Obama installed Kaine as Democratic National Committee chairman. Virginia politics zig-zagged back, at least temporarily, in 2009, amid dissatisfaction with Obama's agenda; Attorney General Bob McDonnell deemphasized cultural issues and ran instead as a job-creating candidate ready to tackle the recession. He won a smashing 59%-41% victory, the biggest margin for any Virginia governor since the last big victory of the Byrd machine in 1961. Virginia's relative prosperity-plus a never-ending organization, with 60 offices, 20,000 volunteers, and 580,000 door knocks-enabled Obama to carry the commonwealth again in 2012, though by the reduced margin of 51%-47%. After a money-and-influence scandal hobbled McDonnell, voters returned the governor's mansion to the Democrats, as national party fixer Terry McAuliffe defeated socially conservative attorney general Ken Cuccinelli. But wary about trusting one party with all levers of power, voters continued to give Republicans a large margin in the state House and a narrow one in the state Senate.

In the 2016 presidential election, Clinton, with Kaine as her running mate, won Virginia by a slightly wider margin than Obama had in 2012. She exceeded Obama's vote total by about 10,000, while Donald Trump fell short of Mitt Romney's total by about 53,000. In Northern Virginia, already a Democratic stronghold, such jurisdictions as Arlington, Fairfax, Loudoun and Prince William counties and the city of Alexandria saw their winning margins shift by between five and 20 points in the Democrats' direction. The Richmond suburbs also moved toward the Democrats. In Henrico County, which went for Clinton, the winning margin shifted by 8 points toward the Democrats. And in two Richmond-area counties that went red in both 2012 and 2016 – Hanover and Chesterfield – Trump fell several percentage points short of matching Romney's margins. Trump did notch a modest improvement over Romney in Hampton Roads and made substantial gains in more rural areas. As the state looked ahead to a closely watched and highly competitive gubernatorial race in 2017, there were signs of heightened energy in the progressive wing of the Democratic Party. Opportunities and potential pitfalls lay ahead.

Population		**Race and Ethnicity**		**Income**	
Total	8,256,630	White	63.4%	Median Income	$65,015 (8 out of 50)
Land area	39,490	Black	18.9%		
Pop/ sq mi	209.1	Latino	8.6%	Under $50,000	38.9%
Born in state	49.6%	Asian	5.9%	$50,000-$99,999	30.1%
		Two races	2.7%	$100,000-$199,999	23.0%
Age Groups		Other	0.5%	$200,000 or more	8.1%
Under 18	22.6%			Poverty Rate	11.5%
18-34	24.0%	**Education**			
35-64	40.1%	H.S grad or less	36.5%	**Health Insurance**	
Over 64	13.3%	Some college	27.2%	With health insurance coverage	88.6%
		College Degree, 4 yr	21.0%		
Work		Post grad	15.4%		
White Collar	42.7%			**Public Assistance**	
Sales and Service	39.4%	**Military**		Cash public assistance income	2.1%
Blue Collar	17.9%	Veteran	11.2%		
Government	20.5%	Active Duty	1.7%	Food stamp/SNAP benefits	9.7%

Voter Turnout			
2015 Total Citizens 18+	5,948,625	2016 Pres Turnout as % CVAP	67%
2016 Pres Votes	3,984,631	2012 Pres Turnout as % CVAP	68%

Legislature	
Senate:	19D, 21R
House:	34D, 66R

Presidential Politics

2016 Democratic Primary		
Hillary Clinton (D)	504,791	(64%)
Bernie Sanders (D)	276,387	(35%)
2016 Republican Primary		
Donald Trump (R)	356,896	(35%)
Marco Rubio (R)	327,936	(32%)
Ted Cruz (R)	171,162	(17%)
John Kasich (R)	97,791	(10%)
Ben Carson (R)	60,237	(6%)

2016 Presidential Vote		
Hillary Clinton (D)	1,981,473	(50%)
Donald Trump (R)	1,769,443	(44%)
Gary Johnson (L)	118,274	(3%)
2012 Presidential Vote		
Barack Obama (D)	1,971,820	(51%)
Mitt Romney (R)	1,822,522	(47%)

Long ignored in presidential politics, Virginia suddenly became a national bellwether in 2008 and 2012, when its 53%-46% and 51%-47% margins for Barack Obama were the same as those in the nation as a whole. With its diverse electorate, steady growth and urban-rural mix, Virginia is battleground state reflective of the country. In the first half of the 20th century, it was part of the solid Democratic South. But from 1952 to 1960 it voted Republican, following the "golden silence" of Democratic Sen. Harry Byrd Sr., who declined to endorse presidential candidates, but quietly signaled his preference for the more fiscally conservative GOP standard bearers. It voted for Democrat Lyndon Johnson for president in 1964 and then backed Republicans in the next 10 elections. But over time, the GOP margins narrowed. Democrat Bill Clinton lost here by 47%-45% in 1996. In 2000, George W. Bush won 53%-44%. In 2004, Bush won statewide 54%-46%, while losing the increasingly Democratic close-in D.C. suburbs in Northern Virginia 57%-42%. In 2008, Barack Obama targeted Virginia from start to finish. His organizing efforts for the February primary gave him a head start when he defeated Hillary Clinton 64%-35%. Republicans didn't believe polls showing Obama leading throughout most of the summer and fall, but the polls proved accurate. Obama ran seven percentage points ahead of John Kerry's showing in 2004. In 2012, intensive campaigning - national candidates made some 90 appearances in Virginia - didn't change the result appreciably. Obama's margin over Republican Mitt Romney was reduced to 51%-47%. The patterns of support were similar. Close-in Northern Virginia D.C. suburbs voted heavily for Obama, and he narrowly carried the Northern Virginia exurbs. The vote was almost identical to 2008 in the Tidewater and metro Richmond, while Romney increased the Republican margins in the rural parts of the state. Without Northern Virginia, Obama would have barely won the state in 2008, by 50%-49%, and barely lost it in 2012, by 50%-48%.

The growth and diversity of the Northern Virginia suburbs and exurbs will continue to make the region's voters a critical component of the Democratic coalition in the state. And while the area includes a Donald Trump golf club up the Potomac River in Loudon County, the Republican nominee was not a local favorite in 2016. Hillary Clinton defeated Trump 50%-44%, a margin that some believe shows the state has moved from a battleground to one that will increasingly tilt Democratic in presidential races. That may be premature, but the Democrat tide in the suburbs is unmistakable. The immigrants, highly educated, and young singles of the D.C. suburbs gave Clinton a 70%-27% advantage over Trump, better than either of Obama's margins. Clinton also narrowly captured the Northern Virginia exurbs that stretch from the wealthy Loudon County to Frederick County on the border with West Virginia and south to Spotsylvania County, 49%-47%. She also carried the central and eastern portions of the state that include Richmond and more rural counties with relatively high numbers of African-American voters. Sen. Tim Kaine, her running mate, was once the mayor of Richmond and the suburban county that surrounds the city, Henrico, saw a jump in Democratic voting in 2016. Clinton also carried the Tidewater (Hampton Roads) region of the state, albeit by a smaller margin than Obama did in 2012. The blue-collar towns of Norfolk and Portsmouth, the massive Navy base at Newport News, the more white-collar and tourism oriented Virginia Beach which is also home to Pat Robertson's Christian Broadcast Network, makes this a complex Democratic-leaning battleground. Clinton won the Tidewater, 53%-43%, a bit under Obama's 57%-42% margin in 2012. The western and central region of the state that stretches down the Blue Ridge and Appalachian Mountains from Shenandoah County in the north to the cities of Danville and Bristol on the borders of North Carolina and Tennessee, respectively, was Trump country in 2016. He carried this mostly rural region 65%-32%, better than Romney's 61%-37% margin in 2012. Indeed, the 15 Virginia counties that saw the greatest falloff from Obama's percentage of the vote in 2012 to Clinton's percentage in 2016 were all in this region.

Virginia held primaries on the original Super Tuesday in March 1988, when it voted for George H.W. Bush and Jesse Jackson, then switched back to choosing delegates at state conventions for the next two cycles. Republicans held a primary in 2000 in which George W. Bush beat McCain 53%-44%. In 2004, John Kerry carried every part of the state and won 52%-27% over John Edwards. In 2008, Obama captured the state the same day he won in neighboring Maryland and the District of Columbia. The Republican contest attracted less attention and, significantly in a state with no party registration, only 489,000 votes. In 2012, the Republican primary was held on March 6. But only two candidates amassed the number of signatures required to get on the ballot; Romney beat Ron Paul 60%-40%. This was Paul's highest percentage in any primary.

The 2016 primary was held on March 1, when both parties' nominations were up for grabs. The Republican contest saw Trump narrowly defeat Florida Sen. Marco Rubio, 33%-30%. Texas Sen. Ted Cruz finished third with 17 percent. Rubio thrashed Trump in the close-in D.C. suburbs of Northern

Virginia, 42%-23% and also defeated him in Loudon and Prince William Counties, the two largest Northern Virginia exurban tracts outside of Washington, foreshadowing a weakness that would become even more apparent in November. The Democratic primary was a one-sided affair where Clinton reversed her 2008 fate and defeated Vermont Sen. Bernie Sanders, 64%-35%.

Congressional Districts

115th Congress Lineup	7R 4D	**114th Congress Lineup**	8R 3D

Despite above national average population growth, Virginia has failed to gain a seat in reapportionment since 1991 and the size of its delegation appeared unlikely to change in 2021. The big recent change resulted in 2016 following the relentless push by state Democrats, led by Governor Terry McAuliffe, to seek court revision of the plan that had been enacted in 2011 by the Republican-controlled Legislature and Governor Bob McDonnell. That map had shored up incumbents in both parties, especially Republicans, and left the 8-3 GOP delegation - in a state whose statewide officials are all Democrats and Republican haven't won a presidential campaign since 2004. At the time, Democrats offered a competing plan converting Republican Rep. Randy Forbes' 4th District into a second minority-majority seat.

The Senate Democrats' plan took on new life in October 2014, when a three-judge federal court panel ruled that the state's map was an unconstitutional violation of the 14th Amendment's civil rights protections. The court found that the Legislature had improperly packed minorities into the 3rd District of Democratic Rep. Bobby Scott and ordered the Republican-controlled legislature to draw a new map by September 2015. Not surprisingly, Republicans were unwilling to make the sacrifice and Democrats persisted on court resolution. Democrats got their way. The judges agreed to a version of the Democrats' map, in which Petersburg and large parts of Richmond were moved to the 4th, and much of Forbes' base of Chesapeake was shifted to the 3rd District. Forbes concluded that he could not win his revised district. With little time to prepare, he ran in the revamped Virginia Beach-based 2nd District, which had none of his previous constituents. Even though its incumbent Republican Rep. Scott Rigell had retired, Forbes ran as an outsider against Delegate Scott Taylor and fared poorly. The court's map made changes in the 1st and 7th Districts, but their Republican incumbents were unscathed. The remaining six districts in Virginia were untouched, which left the Republican-held 11th as competitive and the object of further campaign contests and likely redistricting attention. The challenge facing the District's GOP Rep. Barbara Comstock has been that the Northern Virginia suburbs had become so overwhelmingly Democratic that few sufficiently Republican precincts remained, forcing her district farther into the changing exurbs plus rural Virginia.

Governor

Terry McAuliffe (D)

Elected 2013, term expires 2018, 1st term; b. Feb. 9, 1957, Syracuse, NY; Catholic U., B.A. 1979; Georgetown U., J.D. 1984; Catholic; Married (Dorothy); 5 children.

Elected Office: Chairman, Democratic Natl. Committee, 2001-2005.

Professional Career: Founder, McAuliffe Driveway Maintenance, 1971; Board member & Chairman, Federal City National Bank, 1987-1991; Campaign finance Director, U.S. Rep. Richard Gephardt, 1988; Co-founder & Partner, McAuliffe, Kelly, Raffaelli, 1990-1994; Co-director, President Bill Clinton re-election campaign, 1996; Director, Hilary Clinton presidential campaign, 2008; Chairman, GreenTech Automotive, 2009.

Office: P.O. Box 1475, Richmond, 23218; 804-786-2211; Fax: 804-371-6351; Website: governor.virginia.gov.

Election Results

Election	Name (Party)	Vote (%)
2013 General	Terry McAuliffe (D)	1,069,789 (48%)
	Ken Cuccinelli (R)	1,013,354 (45%)
	Robert Sarvis (L)	146,084 (7%)

Democrat Terry McAuliffe was elected Virginia governor in 2013. A longtime fundraiser and all-around Democratic impresario known for his wheeler-dealer style, McAuliffe won in an epic contest against Ken Cuccinelli, a state attorney general known for his fiery conservatism. It was widely believed during the campaign that, because of their polarizing natures, each man may have been the only one the other could have defeated.

McAuliffe was born in Syracuse, New York, son of the treasurer of the Onondaga County Democratic Committee. At age 8, he began helping the party raise money. At 14, McAuliffe built a driveway-tarring company - the first of many businesses he has been involved with during his career, from banking to real estate to investing to manufacturing. Whatever the business, McAuliffe has always kept a foot -or more - in politics. He gravitated to Washington early on, attending Catholic University as an undergraduate and then Georgetown for law school. He served as finance director of the Jimmy Carter-Walter Mondale reelection committee, as national finance chairman of Rep. Richard Gephardt's presidential committee, as national co-chairman of the Bill Clinton-Al Gore reelection committee and as chairman of Hillary Clinton's 2008 presidential campaign. McAuliffe has chaired party conventions and inaugurations, and from 2001 to 2005 he chaired the Democratic National Committee.

But such resume entries don't fully capture what sets McAuliffe apart - his eccentrically effective skills at separating political donors from their money. By the time he was elected governor, McAuliffe's aggressive salesmanship had been the stuff of legend for more than a quarter-century. In 1984, a Seattle newspaper said McAuliffe "could sell an icebox to an Eskimo or soda water to W. C. Fields." In 1987, the *New York Times'* Maureen Dowd noted that McAuliffe alternately cajoled and sweet-talked donors and their gatekeepers using the peppy language of a 1930s screwball-comedy character. He was known, she wrote, to lurk "in the dim light of dawn in driveways and on airport taxiways, interrupting dinners and vacations" just to bag an elusive donation, once even wrestling an alligator in Florida to secure a $15,000 contribution. His infectious enthusiasm and optimism got people to open their checkbooks; in his autobiography, he dubbed himself a "huckster." McAuliffe grew particularly close to Bill and Hillary Clinton; in addition to golfing and vacationing with them, he put up $1.35 million in cash to backstop the couple's mortgage when they purchased their post-presidential home in Chappaqua, New York.

In 2009, McAuliffe moved beyond being a surrogate and a strategist by seeking the Democratic nomination for governor. McAuliffe's connections were golden, and he was extraordinarily well prepared for the nitty-gritty of running for office. But his stature within the national party wasn't enough to scare off challengers in Virginia, where he was seen as a carpetbagger. In the primary, he faced former state Del. Brian Moran from northern Virginia - the brother of then-Rep. James Moran - and state Sen. Creigh Deeds from the Shenandoah Valley, who four years earlier had lost an excruciatingly close race for attorney general to Republican Bob McDonnell. With the campaign under way during the Great Recession, McAuliffe touted his business background, but this proved to be a double-edged sword. To some, McAuliffe's wheeler-dealer style was off-putting, and his opponents reinforced that part of his background.

It became clear during the campaign that with McAuliffe, the lines between politicians, political donors and business partners had often become blurred. The *Washington Post* in 2013 detailed a "pattern of investments in which McAuliffe has used government programs, political connections and access to wealthy investors of both parties in pursuit of big profits for himself. ... A review of McAuliffe's business history shows him often coming out ahead personally, even if some investments fail or become embroiled in controversy." One such deal was a $100,000 investment in Global Crossing Holdings that earned him a reported $8 million, even though the company eventually flamed out. His opponents questioned whether the deals he put together actually created significant numbers of new jobs, as opposed to helping his own bottom line. Ultimately, primary voters gave the low-key, little-known Deeds the nod with a surprisingly large 50 percent of the vote. McAuliffe drew 26 percent and Moran took 24 percent. In the general election, Deeds faced McDonnell. The Republican came into the race known for his strong socially conservative views, but he ran a campaign that downplayed social issues in favor of economic ones, and that proved attractive to swing voters. Just as he had against Deeds four years earlier, McDonnell prevailed in the gubernatorial race, but this time his margin was much larger -

59%-41%. The Republican won such northern Virginia swing counties as Loudoun and Prince William easily, and Fairfax more narrowly.

With Deeds' second consecutive statewide loss, McAuliffe became the presumed front-runner for the Democratic gubernatorial nomination in 2013, and he devoted significant effort to retail politicking over the next four years, aiming to build up his credibility with Virginia voters. It eventually became clear that his general-election opponent would be Cuccinelli, producing a clash of titans, each with strikingly high negatives. Virginia gubernatorial elections usually attract special attention nationally because they occur in off-years, with only New Jersey voting on the same schedule. But this national focus was heightened in 2013 because of the ideological gap between McAuliffe and Cuccinelli, the pivotal role Virginia was expected to play in the looming presidential election, and the intense competitiveness displayed by both men.

As attorney general, Cuccinelli had taken an aggressively conservative approach, often in tune with the tea party. He focused on such social issues as abortion and gay rights, and he hammered away at President Barack Obama's health care law and sought to probe a University of Virginia climate-change scientist. Cuccinelli won the nomination at a convention - one that he himself had pushed the state party to hold, rather than holding a nominating primary. The convention was dominated by conservative activists to a greater degree than a primary would have been, giving Cuccinelli such an edge over his leading rival, the more moderate Lt. Gov. Bill Bolling, that Bolling exited the race before it was even held. The convention also nominated other statewide Republicans who tilted heavily to the right. McAuliffe, for his part, ran further to the left on social issues than previous statewide Democratic nominees had-openly backing gun control, same-sex marriage and abortion rights-while taking a more moderate approach to economic issues. He promoted investments in such areas as alternative energy, cybersecurity and biotechnology. He also backed a roads bill popular in suburban areas that McDonnell had pushed and that Cuccinelli had opposed.

McAuliffe took some hits, several self-inflicted. Critics noted that in his 2007 memoir, he had bragged about leaving his wife Dorothy in the middle of childbirth in order to attend a party for a *Washington Post* reporter, and he added that he'd stopped on the way home from the hospital with another newborn in order to attend a fundraiser. ("I felt bad for Dorothy," McAuliffe wrote, "but it was a million bucks for the Democratic Party and by the time we got home and the kids had their new little brother in their arms, Dorothy was all smiles and we were one big happy family again.") He also attracted negative attention over GreenTech, an electric car company he had founded. McAuliffe took heat for planning to build a facility in Mississippi instead of Virginia. The company also caused problems for McAuliffe after news reports of federal investigations into possible irregularities in special visas the firm had sought for some of its foreign investors. In April 2013, McAuliffe stepped away from the company.

Despite such challenges for McAuliffe, Cuccinelli was unable to take full advantage because he had his own problem - a metastasizing scandal surrounding McDonnell, the outgoing governor. McDonnell and his wife, Maureen, had been wooed by Jonnie R. Williams Sr., the CEO of a dietary supplement company who hoped that McDonnell could provide credibility for his business. Williams gave the first family $177,000 in loans and gifts, ranging from catering to fancy vacations to a Rolex watch. Ten days after the election, McDonnell and his wife were indicted; eventually, they were both convicted of public corruption, and the former governor was sentenced to two years in prison. (In June 2016, the U.S. Supreme Court unanimously overturned McDonnell's conviction, saying the prosecutors' definition of "official act" was too broad.) Cuccinelli was never charged with anything related to the case, but he had to disclose during the campaign that he'd received more than $18,000 from Williams. The spiraling allegations about McDonnell also became a more generalized problem for the Republican slate. Not surprisingly given his background, McAuliffe amassed a fundraising advantage - $34.4 million to $19.7 million. He successfully drew a contrast with Cuccinelli's tea party views, which worried elements of the business establishment. Even so, Cuccinelli appeared to gain ground in the final days. McAuliffe won, 48%-45%, with Libertarian Robert Sarvis taking 7%. The most striking finding by political analysts was that McAuliffe had managed to draw an off-year electorate that looked more like a presidential-year electorate - one much more favorable to Democrats. It was the first time in three and a half decades that Virginia voters chose a governor from the same party as the one controlling the White House.

After being sworn in, McAuliffe quickly signed executive orders establishing a gift ban and protecting state employees from discrimination based on sexual orientation or gender identity. He proposed bringing back a one-gun-per-month purchase limit and an end to the so-called gun show loophole, and he added abortion-rights supporters to a state health board in a bid to undo anti-abortion policies instituted under Cuccinelli. He also sought to allow same-sex marriage in the state. But with Republicans holding key levers of power in the legislature, McAuliffe's most-liberal efforts were largely stymied. This was seen most clearly in his bid to expand Medicaid under the Affordable Care Act.

Despite an aggressive effort to sell the policy, McAuliffe drew fierce opposition in the GOP-held House of Delegates. He then faced an endgame when Democratic state Sen. Phillip Puckett resigned amid controversy surrounding a job offer and a judgeship for his daughter; Puckett's departure tipped the chamber to the GOP, putting the kibosh on any hopes for Medicaid expansion. Meanwhile, taking executive-branch actions that would once have been considered heretical in the state, McAuliffe and Attorney General Mark Herring banned firearms from state buildings and ended a policy of honoring concealed handgun permits from two dozen states that did not meet Virginia's standards.

McAuliffe tried to change the calculus by taking an active role in the 2015 legislative elections, campaigning aggressively for legislative candidates who would be open to passing his agenda. The Democrats, with the tie-breaking lieutenant governor's office already in hand, could have seized control of the Senate by netting just one seat. But on Election Day, the GOP held on to all their vulnerable Senate seats. Undaunted, McAuliffe used his 2016 state of the commonwealth address to reiterate his call for expanding Medicaid. But he also touted ideas with greater cross-party appeal, including a trade mission to Cuba he had recently completed (he presented Republican House Speaker William Howell with a Cuban cigar) and new limits on standardized testing in schools. But McAuliffe's most controversial move came in April 2016, when he unilaterally restored voting rights to some 200,000 convicted felons. The qualifying felons were disproportionately black, and many Republicans saw McAuliffe's action as a naked ploy to enlarge the state's Democratic voter rolls. Legal scholars questioned whether the state's gubernatorial powers allowed such a mass restoration of voting rights. In a closely divided decision, the state Supreme Court overturned his action. But McAuliffe pledged to pursue restorations on an individual – rather than a blanket -- basis, an approach the court's ruling seemed to allow.

McAuliffe's longstanding connections to the Clinton family meant that questions involving Hillary Clinton's presidential campaign were never far away. In 2015, the *Post* determined that more than 175 donors to the Clinton Foundation and Clinton's campaign had also given to McAuliffe, despite frequently lacking ties to Virginia. Then, in May 2016, it was reported that donations to McAuliffe's gubernatorial campaign were under investigation by the FBI and the Justice Department's public integrity unit. (Nothing appears to have emerged from the inquiry.) Clinton's campaign manager, Robby Mook, had run McAuliffe's gubernatorial campaign, just one of many aides and advisers with ties to both camps; Clinton ended up choosing Virginia Sen. Tim Kaine as her running mate, a move that, had they won, would have enabled McAuliffe to appoint his successor. But McAuliffe also caused Clinton some heartache: In an interview at the Democratic National Convention in July, he said he expected that the nominee would shift back to supporting the Trans-Pacific Partnership trade deal – a stance sure to rile many in the Democratic base. (A spokesman later walked the comment back.)

Despite McAuliffe's deep ties in Clinton world, he had also established some surprising connections to her opponent, Donald Trump. "I have known Donald Trump for 20 years, had dinner with him, golfed with him," McAuliffe told Washington's WTOP radio shortly after Trump won. "When I ran in '09, he actually wrote me a $25,000 check. So I look forward to a productive relationship." But as time went on, McAuliffe put increasing distance between himself and the new president. McAuliffe declined to attend Trump's inauguration but took part in the women's protest march the following day. Then, after Trump issued an executive order curbing immigration from certain Muslim-majority countries, he and Herring signed the state on to an existing legal challenge. Meanwhile, McAuliffe signed an executive order preventing the state from doing business with organizations that discriminate based on sexual orientation or gender identity. All told, Virginia voters gave McAuliffe favorable approval ratings, but at somewhat less exalted levels than some of his predecessors, and with wider partisan divergence.

With McAuliffe barred from reelection by state law, candidates from both parties lined up to succeed him. The June 13 primaries appeared to boost Democrats. Lt. Gov. Ralph Northam won the Democratic nomination, 56% to 44%, following an unexpectedly robust challenge by former Rep. Tom Perriello, who was backed by 2016 Democratic presidential candidate Bernie Sanders. On the Republican side, Ed Gillespie – a Washington insider and lobbyist who made a surprisingly strong run at Democratic Sen. Mark Warner in 2014 – narrowly prevailed over Prince William County board chairman Corey Stewart, who ran as a champion of the Confederate legacy. Gillespie led Stewart by little more than one percentage point in the unofficial count; state Sen. Frank Wagner took 14 percent of the vote. Democratic turnout was nearly 50 percent higher than the GOP vote, which suggested an enthusiasm gap heading into the November election.

Senior Senator

Mark Warner (D)

Elected 2008, term expires 2020, 2nd term; b. Dec 15, 1954, Indianapolis, IN; George Washington University (DC), B.A.; Harvard University Law School (MA), J.D.; Presbyterian; Married (Lisa Collis); 3 children.

Elected Office: VA Governor, 2002-2006.

Professional Career: Fundraiser, Democratic National Committee, 1980-1982; Venture capitalist, 1982-1989; Mng. Director, Columbia Capital Corporation, 1989-2001; Commonwealth Transportation Board, 1990-1994; Chairman, VA Democratic Party, 1993-1995; Chmn, Nat'l Governors Association, 2004-2005.

DC Office: 703 HSOB 20510, 202-224-2023, Fax: 202-224-6920, warner.senate.gov.

State Offices: Abingdon, 276-628-8158; Norfolk, 757-441-3079; Richmond, 804-775-2314; Roanoke, 540-857-2676; Vienna, 703-442-0670.

Committees: Senate Democratic Conference Vice Chairman. *Banking, Housing & Urban Affairs*: Financial Institutions & Consumer Protection, National Security & International Trade & Finance, Securities, Insurance & Investment (RMM). *Budget*. *Finance*: Energy, Natural Resources & Infrastructure, Health Care, Taxation & IRS Oversight (RMM). *Intelligence (RMM). Rules & Administration.*

Group Ratings

	ADA	ACLU	AFL-CIO	LCV	ITI	COC	HAFA	ACU	CFG	FRC
2016	-	52%	-	88%	100%	63%	7%	5%	6%	0%
2015	65%	C	57%	80%	C	69%	C	0%	15%	0%

Almanac Ratings 2015

	Economy	Social	Foreign	Composite
Liberal	76%	85%	80%	80%
Conservative	24%	15%	20%	20%

Key Votes of the 114th Congress

1. Keystone pipeline	Y	5. National Security Data	Y	9. Gun Sales Checks	NV
2. Export-Import Bank	N	6. Iran Nuclear Deal	N	10. Sanctuary Cities	N
3. Debt Ceiling Increase	Y	7. Puerto Rico Debt	NV	11. Planned Parenthood	N
4. Homeland Security $$	Y	8. Loretta Lynch A.G	Y	12. Trade deals	Y

Election Results

Election	Name (Party)	Vote (%)		Cand. Spent	Ind. Exp. Support	Ind. Exp. Oppose
2014 General	Mark Warner (D)	1,073,667	(49%)	$18,114,108	$345,891	$321,800
	Ed Gillespie (R)	1,055,940	(48%)	$7,875,545	$486,890	$1,827,242
	Robert Sarvis (L)	53,102	(2%)	$84,949		
2014 Primary	Mark Warner (D)	unopposed				

Prior winning percentages: 2008 (72%)

Democrat Mark Warner, Virginia's senior senator, is a former governor whose tenure in Richmond was widely seen as a template for fellow Democrats seeking ways to win and effectively govern in the states of the Old Confederacy. Warner's success in his 2001-2005 gubernatorial tenure was such that many viewed him as a leading presidential contender in 2008, an option he seriously considered. Warner instead ran for an open Senate seat that year, and won by a 2-1 margin. In 2014, he narrowly survived what was supposed to be an easy reelection bid. In a big career move, he took over in 2017 as the ranking Democrat on the Senate Intelligence Committee as it was launching its investigation of Russian efforts to influence the 2016 presidential election-in which, incidentally, his Senate colleague from Virginia was the Democratic vice-presidential nominee.

Warner was born in Indianapolis, where his father was a safety evaluator for Aetna Life & Casualty Inc. The family moved to Vernon, Connecticut, when Warner was in the eighth grade. He graduated from George Washington University, the first college graduate in his family, and from Harvard Law School. Although he has emphasized his business experience in his campaigns, his first love appears to have been politics: Soon after graduating from law school in 1980, he took a job fundraising for the Democratic National Committee. In 1989, he managed Democrat Douglas Wilder's successful campaign to become the first African-American governor elected anywhere in the nation since Reconstruction.

Warner spent most of the 1980s and 1990s as a highly successful venture capitalist, with the origins of that success the result of his political contacts. While working for the DNC, Warner met Rep. Tom McMillen, a Maryland Democrat, who told him about the potential of cell phone markets just as the Reagan administration was about to award 1,500 free licenses for metropolitan markets. Warner cobbled together investor groups and packaged their applications in exchange for a fee and a 5-percent ownership stake if they received the licenses. The best known of these ventures was Nextel, and Warner soon became a wealthy man. His average net worth in 2014 was estimated at $243 million, making him the second wealthiest member of Congress, according to an analysis of financial disclosure reports by the nonpartisan Center for Responsive Politics.

A political career remained very much on Warner's mind. From 1993-1995, he was Virginia Democratic chairman. In 1996, he ran against Republican Sen. John Warner (no relation) in what seemed a quixotic race: The senior Warner, elected narrowly in 1978, had won reelection in a landslide in 1984 and had no Democratic opponent in 1990. Mark Warner pitched his campaign not to his home turf in northern Virginia, but to the Shenandoah Valley and southwest Virginia. He carried southwest Virginia, and lost the part of the state outside the three big metropolitan areas by only 51%-49%, a considerable achievement for a Democrat. But John Warner's strength among moderates enabled him to carry northern Virginia 55%-45% and to win the Tidewater region and metropolitan Richmond with smaller majorities. The result was a 52%-47% statewide win for John Warner, but certainly not an end to upstart Mark Warner's electoral ambitions.

In the late 1990s, Mark Warner put millions of dollars into philanthropic efforts and set up four regional business investment funds in Tidewater, Richmond, and Southside-the area south of Richmond-as well as southwest Virginia. By 1999, he had an eye on running for governor in 2001 as an entrepreneur who could bring savvy business methods to government. He picked a good year. Republican Gov. Jim Gilmore had helped to elect Republican majorities in both houses of the legislature, but then battled with them over the budget. Republicans had an intraparty fight over the gubernatorial nomination in 2001 between Lt. Gov. John Hager and Attorney General Mark Earley. Earley resigned as attorney general immediately after winning the nomination to focus on the campaign, but had little money and no clear strategy. Warner poured $5 million of his own money into his candidacy.

Warner lived in a mansion in Old Town Alexandria but avoided being typecast as an urban liberal. He characterized himself as a fiscal conservative and pledged not to raise income or sales taxes. Responding to complaints from traffic-choked northern Virginia and Tidewater, he called for regional referenda on local sales tax increases for transportation. He opposed any new gun control laws and wooed the National Rifle Association, which remained neutral in the contest. Warner ran ads featuring old pickup trucks and bluegrass music, and he sponsored a NASCAR race truck. He traveled to all parts of rural Virginia, much as Wilder had in 1989, to show he was in touch with everyday folks and to remind them of his investment funds and philanthropic initiatives.

Warner defeated Easley, but not resoundingly, by 52%-47%, a reversal of the numbers in the 1996 Senate race. He carried all major regions of the state, albeit by narrow margins. And he attracted notice from national Democrats for winning a Southern state through business-friendly, fiscally responsible policies combined with cultural conservatism-a combination Warner dubbed "radical centrism."

Once in office, Warner convinced the legislature to approve transportation tax referenda in northern Virginia and Tidewater, but the House of Delegates rejected his education initiative in 2002. As a budget shortfall grew, Warner cut more than $850 million in spending and laid off 1,800 state employees. In November 2003, after the legislative elections and when Virginia seemed to be in danger of losing its AAA bond rating, Warner presented his new fiscal plan: a $1 billion tax increase, with increases in the income, sales, and cigarette taxes, and tax reductions for those with low incomes and in car and food taxes. In early 2004, his plan was rejected by the heavily Republican House of Delegates, which increased taxes by just $520 million and provided few spending increases. But House Speaker William Howell was unable to hold his Republicans in line, and 17 of them abandoned their anti-tax positions. The Senate agreed to a $1.3 billion tax increase, more than Warner had requested, and the House went along, a major victory for the governor. By December 2004, the fiscal picture had changed: State government was facing a $1.2 billion surplus, and Warner called for more spending.

When John Warner in August 2007 announced his retirement from the Senate after five terms, Mark Warner's next career move seemed obvious. He had no serious opposition for the Democratic nomination. On the Republican side, Gilmore, Warner's predecessor as governor, decided to run. At the 2008 state GOP nominating convention, he barely prevailed after being challenged from the right because of his support for abortion rights in some cases. It turned out not to be a seriously contested campaign. Warner argued Gilmore had left the state in poor fiscal shape, and that he had been able to turn things around as Gilmore's successor. Warner won 65%-34%, losing only two counties in the Shenandoah Valley, two exurban Richmond counties, and two small independent cities. He ran far ahead of Democratic presidential nominee Barack Obama, even as Obama was carrying the state by 6 points. For the first time since 1970, when Harry Byrd, Jr. declared himself an independent, Virginia had two Democratic senators.

In the Senate, Warner lamented the adjustment ex-governors face in becoming one of 100 legislators. (In 2013, he toyed with running again for governor, which he called "the best job I ever had," but ultimately opted against it.) His driven and frenetic personality became a source of humor among his colleagues. In recounting his close working relationship with the laid-back Republican Saxby Chambliss of Georgia, Warner told reporters in January 2013, "The way he starts each day is, 'Well, Mark, did you take your Ritalin today?'"

Warner's voting habits have put him in the political center. He was the 5th most conservative Democratic senator in the Almanac vote ratings for 2015. He supported President Barack Obama on some major legislation, notably the health care overhaul in 2009; during that debate, he led 11 freshman Democrats in proposing a series of amendments intended to control costs and boost accountability of the new program. He also backed the Budget Control Act of 2011 and other Obama administration efforts to raise the federal debt ceiling, but he joined Republicans in backing caps on discretionary spending.

Despite his "A" rating from the NRA, Warner declared after the December 2012 Newtown, Connecticut school massacre in which 26 were killed that "the status quo isn't acceptable" on guns. "There needs to be appropriate restrictions on these tools of mass-killing," he said. In April 2013, Warner joined most Democrats in backing a compromise measure-opposed by the NRA-to expand background checks on gun buyers. But he was among 15 Democrats to vote against an assault weapons ban, and one of 10 Democrats to oppose a ban on high-capacity magazines. Warner took blowback from the party's liberal wing, as the president of MoveOn.org called Warner's votes on the latter issues "shameful.

As he frequently reached across the political aisle, Warner became best known for joining forces with Chambliss-Warner's closest Republican friend until he retired at the end of 2014-in leading the "Gang of Six." The group, consisting of three Republicans and three Democrats, came together in 2011 in the hope of putting the recommendations of the bipartisan Simpson-Bowles deficit reduction commission into legislation. To keep the group's closed-door meetings from becoming too partisan, Warner reportedly would occasionally push a comic buzzer that sounded the message: "Bull-detected. Take precautions."

By 2011, as the House and Senate faced a controversial increase in the federal debt limit, the Warner-Chambliss group had developed a $3.7 trillion deficit-reduction plan. Of that total, $2.7 trillion in cuts came from adjustments to Medicaid and Social Security. Meanwhile, federal revenues would be increased $1.1 trillion over 10 years through changes to tax deductions for home mortgage interest, charitable giving, and health care insurance. Republicans remained resolutely opposed to any revenue increases, and the deficit-reduction "supercommittee"-formed by the Budget Control Act that provided for a 2011 increase in the federal debt ceiling-failed to make headway in addressing the partisan deadlock. The Gang of Six proposal never became formal legislation, and the leadership of both parties paid the group scant attention. Warner repeatedly expressed frustration over his inability to get a deal. "In Washington there is no support group, or institutional structure, to support people doing the right thing," he complained at a 2012 gathering in Richmond.

Tennessee Republican Bob Corker has been a frequent Warner collaborator. As fellow members of the Banking Committee, they worked together on ways to prevent financial institutions from becoming "too big to fail" as part of the crafting of the 2010 Dodd-Frank bill overhauling the federal financial regulatory structure. Later, Warner and Corker coauthored legislation to wind down mortgage giants Fannie Mae and Freddie Mac and make changes to the mortgage finance system. A similar measure cleared the Banking Committee in 2014, but stalled due to the opposition of liberal Democrats including Charles Schumer of New York and Elizabeth Warren of Massachusetts, amid concerns it might limit access to mortgages by middle-income Americans. Meanwhile, Warner won a seat on the Finance Committee in 2014, a plum assignment he had pursued for years. It provided him with an influential platform to pursue long-time interests in reforming the tax code and curbing entitlement spending.

After the 2010 election, Warner was offered the chairmanship of the Democratic Senatorial Campaign Committee. His business connections made him a highly desirable candidate. but he turned down the post-which would have required him to become much more of a partisan. He gained a place at the leadership table as a "policy development advisor" to the Democratic Policy and Communications Center. The appointment came despite the fact Warner was one of a handful of moderate Democrats to vote against the reelection of Senate Democratic Leader Harry Reid, with whom Warner has had a bumpy relationship. When Schumer replaced Reid, he named Warner and Warren as vice-chairs of the Democratic Conference.

His vote against Reid came shortly after Warner came within a percentage point of losing reelection in 2014. He started the campaign as a prohibitive favorite, and polls as late as September showed him up by 20 points over his challenger, former Republican National Committee Chairman Ed Gillespie. By the end of the campaign, Warner had outspent Gillespie by almost 2-1, $15.7 million to $7.9 million. Warner's ad campaign attacked Gillespie, founder of a prominent Washington lobbying firm, for lobbying on behalf of Enron-the Texas-based energy firm that collapsed amid scandal in 2001. Gillespie, meanwhile, in 2010 had helped to found American Crossroads, an outside group that pumped millions into Republican campaigns around the country. But he was unable to attract the group's interest to his seemingly long-shot bid, and his own campaign couldn't afford to go on the air until October.

Two major factors conspired to almost do in Warner. First, Democratic turnout was off in 2014 around the country-but especially so in Virginia, and particularly in Democratic leaning areas such as the northern Virginia suburbs. Warner was later criticized in Democratic circles for not getting his campaign up and running earlier in the cycle and for not doing more to turn out the vote in such areas. Plus, Gillespie relentlessly tied Warner to Obama, pointing to a *CQ/Roll Call* analysis that found Warner had voted with Obama 97 percent of the time. *PolitiFact* noted the 97 percent figure was based on just 419 of the 1,473 votes Warner had cast in the Senate, and that more than half of the 419 votes came on presidential nominations. This line of attack proved potent. Obama's approval ratings had sunk to 40 percent after he carried the state in 2008 and 2012. Warner eked out a win, 49%-48%, a statewide margin of less than 17,000 votes.

Warner, who focused heavily during the campaign on the centrist, fiscally responsible persona he had developed during his time as governor, afterward brushed aside suggestions that the election results were an indication his moderate stance no longer plays well in an increasingly polarized state. "I'm going to continue to be bipartisan," he said. But he also vowed to be more of a "disrupter" in his second term, as he attributed his close call to voters "grumpy" over congressional inaction and saying that "they want results." The voters, he added, were telling him: "'Warner, show us some more of being that change agent.' I'm taking that message to heart."

His big opportunity arrived in January 2017 when changes at the Intelligence Committee left Warner as the ranking Democrat as the panel became the Senate vehicle to investigate the claims of Russian interference in the 2016 presidential election. As Warner told *The New York Times*, the investigation would be "probably the most important thing I've done in public life." After committee chairman Republican Richard Burr of North Carolina-backed by Majority Leader Mitch McConnell-initially rejected demands for an inquiry, Warner organized the committee Democrats to reverse his decision. With a combination of public and private pressures, Warner succeeded. As the investigation began, Warner seemed to have succeeded with his practice of bonding with a relatively pragmatic Republican Senator. In this case, Warner and Burr were both mid-South white men of similar age and-once aroused-serious purpose. By contrast, the House Intelligence Committee seemed to be less well-organized to deal with the increasingly complex circumstances, including President Donald Trump's firing of James Comey, the FBI director.

In what may have been a timely coincidence, Warner and Republican Sen, Cory Gardner of Colorado created in June 2016 a Senate Cybersecurity Caucus to explore the impact of cyber policy on national security, the economy and digital security. Earlier, Warner-the former tech executive-joined Republican Rep. Mike McFaul of Texas in calling for a commission to study the challenges encryption poses to law enforcement. With a series of seemingly separate developments, Warner seemed to have placed himself at the center of a complex and increasingly vital-but unpredictable-international web of 21st century statecraft and competition.

Junior Senator

Tim Kaine (D)

Elected 2012, term expires 2018, 1st term; b. Feb 26, 1958, St. Paul. MN, MN; University of Missouri, A.B.; Harvard University Law School (MA), J.D.; Roman Catholic; Married (Anne Bright Holton); 3 children.

Elected Office: Richmond City Council, 1994-1998; Richmond Mayor, 1998-2001; VA Lt.Governor, 2002-2006; VA Governor, 2006-2010; Chairman, Democratic National Committee, 2009-2011.

Professional Career: Practicing attorney, 1983-2000; Lecturer, University of Richmond, 1987-1993, 2010-2012;

DC Office: 231 RSOB 20510, 202-224-4024, Fax: 202-228-6363, kaine.senate.gov.

State Offices: Abingdon, 276-525-4790; Danville, 434-792-0976; Manassas, 703-361-3192; Richmond, 804-771-2221; Roanoke, 540-682-5693; Virginia Beach, 757-518-1674.

Committees: *Armed Services*: Readiness & Management Support (RMM), Seapower. *Budget. Foreign Relations*: East Asia, the Pacific & International Cybersecurity Policy, Near East, South Asia, Central Asia & Counterterrorism (RMM), West Hem Crime Civ Sec Dem Rights & Women's Issues. *Health, Education, Labor & Pensions*: Children & Families, Primary Health & Retirement Security.

Group Ratings

	ADA	ACLU	AFL-CIO	LCV	ITI	COC	HAFA	ACU	CFG	FRC
2016	-	76%	-	100%	100%	75%	2%	4%	5%	0%
2015	80%	C	57%	88%	C	57%	C	0%	6%	0%

Almanac Ratings 2015

	Economy	Social	Foreign	Composite
Liberal	83%	100%	80%	88%
Conservative	17%	0%	20%	13%

Key Votes of the 114th Congress

1. Keystone pipeline	N	5. National Security Data	Y	9. Gun Sales Checks	Y
2. Export-Import Bank	N	6. Iran Nuclear Deal	N	10. Sanctuary Cities	N
3. Debt Ceiling Increase	Y	7. Puerto Rico Debt	Y	11. Planned Parenthood	N
4. Homeland Security $$	Y	8. Loretta Lynch A.G	Y	12. Trade deals	Y

Election Results

Election	Name (Party)	Vote	(%)	Cand. Spent	Ind. Exp. Support	Ind. Exp. Oppose
2012 General	Tim Kaine (D)	2,010,067	(53%)	$17,918,247	$3,220,901	$28,008,366
	George F. Allen (R)	1,785,542	(47%)	$14,392,354	$2,782,563	$18,399,356
2012 Primary	Tim Kaine (D)	Unopposed				

Democrat Tim Kaine, a former Virginia governor who was elected in 2012 as the state's junior senator, took a star turn in 2016 as the vice-presidential nominee in a campaign that had seemed likely to cap his diverse career in local and national government and politics. Hillary Clinton's loss of that presidential campaign initially marked a retreat for Kaine, too. Kaine had been close to President Barack Obama and chaired the Democratic National Committee. His career in the Senate has been marked by efforts to question the White House's authority to conduct military operations without authorization from Congress, including clashes with terrorist groups.

Born in St. Paul, Minnesota, Kaine grew up in Overland Park, Kansas, a suburb of Kansas City. His father ran his own ironworking and welding shop, with Kaine and his younger brothers frequently helping out. Kaine attended the University of Missouri, where he graduated in three years, before going on to Harvard Law School. Midway through law school, Kaine left to spend nine months teaching at a Jesuit mission in Honduras. In a *Washington Post* interview three decades later, Kaine said of his time in

Honduras: "It made a public servant out of me…And the Jesuits themselves kind of became my heroes." It also gave him fluency in Spanish. As the Senate debated a major immigration overhaul bill in 2013, Kaine became the first senator ever to deliver a floor speech entirely in Spanish. "I think people were probably surprised," Kaine told *The New York Times* afterward. "One of my people got a call by a Latino staffer in the House [who] said, 'I have waited 20 years to see this happen.' "

Kaine returned to Harvard from Honduras to complete his law degree in 1983. It was there that he met his wife, Anne Holton, a daughter of A. Linwood Holton, Virginia's first Republican governor since Reconstruction. Anne Holton made national headlines as a child when her father, as governor from 1969-1973, declared an end to the state's policy of resistance to desegregation-and enrolled his children in Richmond's public schools, whose student population was largely African American. For a time, Kaine worked for a federal judge in Macon, Georgia, while Holton was working for a federal judge in Richmond. They decided to get married and settle in Richmond. Kaine subsequently worked as a civil rights lawyer, specializing in representing those who had been denied housing due to race or disability. In 1994, he won a seat on the Richmond City Council and four years later was elected mayor. In 2001, he was elected lieutenant governor. (Holton worked as a legal aid attorney before serving as a juvenile court judge; she stepped down as Virginia's secretary of education after Kaine became the vice-presidential nominee.)

Kaine ran for governor in 2005 against former state Attorney General Jerry Kilgore. Kaine, a former big city mayor who held positions well to the left of Kilgore, pitched a quality-of-life agenda designed to appeal to urban and suburban voters. He emphasized tax relief for homeowners, a statewide pre-kindergarten initiative, a balanced approach to growth, and new transportation solutions. Kilgore relied on hot-button issues such as the death penalty and illegal immigration, while dismissing Kaine as "too liberal for Virginia." In one Kilgore ad, a man whose son and daughter-in-law were murdered criticized Kaine for opposing the death penalty for "the worst mass murderer in modern times." Kaine said his opposition to capital punishment was based on religious convictions, and the issue gave him an opportunity to talk about his Catholic faith. Kaine emphasized that, despite his personal beliefs, he would allow executions as governor.

Kaine won 52%-46%, a victory powered by large margins in suburban northern Virginia. Kaine's focus on managing growth enabled him to carry six of the state's 10 fastest-growing counties, including two in the Washington D.C. suburbs, Loudoun and Prince William, that were among the fastest growing in the nation. In his first year, Kaine had some successes dealing with the Republican-controlled legislature, including passage of a bill requiring rigorous teacher evaluations. But he was unable to deliver on his primary objective of finding a reliable source of transportation financing to relieve traffic congestion. Kaine did not stand in the way of four executions of death row inmates, although he delayed the execution of a fifth after questions were raised about the inmate's mental capacity.

A year later, Kaine reached agreement with the Republican-controlled House and Senate in 2007 on a $1 billion transportation bill, representing the state's biggest funding increase in two decades. Since Republicans would not agree to a significant statewide tax increase, the scheme called for borrowing up to $3 billion over 10 years and giving taxing powers to regional authorities in the two traffic-choked big metro areas, northern Virginia and Tidewater. But the plan was frustrated when the state Supreme Court ruled that the regional authorities couldn't raise taxes. In 2008, Kaine proposed $1.1 billion for transportation, with a penny sales tax increase in northern Virginia and Tidewater. But House Republicans steadfastly resisted it.

While Kaine was in Japan on an overseas trade mission in April 2007, a deranged Virginia Tech student opened fire on fellow students during classes, killing 32 before taking his own life. He immediately flew back home and won praise for his handling of the tragedy. Kaine in his last year in office reached agreement with House Speaker William Howell, a Republican, to ban smoking in bars and restaurants, but he failed to get the legislature to agree to proposals for background checks on sales at gun shows and universal pre-kindergarten.

In February 2007, Kaine endorsed Obama for the Democratic presidential nomination, the first governor to do so outside of Obama's home state. He campaigned heavily for Obama in Virginia and helped him win one of his biggest primary victories there. He made Obama's list of potential vice presidential nominees. Named chairman of the Democratic National Committee in 2009, Kaine held the post until 2011. Kaine says that he is among roughly 20 individuals in U.S. history to have served as mayor, governor and senator.

When Democratic Sen. Jim Webb decided not to seek reelection in 2012 after serving just one term, Kaine got into the Senate race at the urging of Obama and other leading Democrats eager to find a high-profile challenger to George Allen. The son and namesake of a legendary football coach, Allen was first elected to the Senate in 2000, and his name was frequently mentioned as a potential presidential candidate in 2008. But he narrowly lost reelection in 2006 to Webb in a major upset, after Allen sparked widespread controversy when he referred to an Indian-American aide to Webb-who had been assigned to tape Allen's public campaign appearances-with the racially derogatory term "macaca."

Kaine and Allen flooded the airwaves with ads. Kaine spent nearly $18 million, as compared to about $14.4 million for Allen. The outside group Crossroads GPS spent millions attacking Kaine. Allen ridiculed Kaine for accepting a position to head the DNC while still governor; Kaine criticized Allen for increased spending while in the statehouse. Kaine hit Allen for past support of partial privatization of Social Security. Allen said he did not support changes for current retirees, but was open to a voluntary retirement investment plan as a supplement. During one debate, the normally disciplined Kaine made a rare gaffe. After Republican presidential candidate Mitt Romney was caught on tape complaining about 47 percent of Americans not paying taxes, Kaine said he was "open to a proposal that would have some minimum tax level for everyone." Republicans jumped on the comment, and Allen ran ads highlighting it. Kaine scored a big victory for Democrats, 53%-47%.

Kaine was assigned to seats on the Foreign Relations and Armed Services committees. The latter panel is of key importance to his home state, given the large Navy presence in the Tidewater area. He focused on national security-and, specifically, the process for authorizing the United States to engage in military action. Kaine and Arizona Republican John McCain, now the chairman of the Armed Services Committee, in January 2014 introduced legislation to clarify the 40-year old War Powers Act-and the underlying question of the degree to which the president and Congress possess, or share, the power to initiate military action abroad. In April 2016, he said that it was hypocritical for the Obama administration to criticize Russia's invasion of Ukraine when it has put troops into Syria without authority. "We are carrying out escalating military operations in Syria without the permission and really even against the will of the sovereign nation," he told a Senate hearing.

In addition, Kaine has pushed repeatedly for congressional debate and a vote on a new authorization for U.S. military action against the Islamic State, or ISIS. This stance put him at odds with Obama, who had asserted that an Authorization for Use of Military Force (AUMF) passed in 2001, a week after the 9/11 attacks, was sufficient for current U.S. military activities in and around Syria and Iraq. Kaine has contended that current military action against ISIS "goes well beyond the intent" of the 2001 AUMF. In June 2014, after writing an op-ed piece arguing for constraints on the president's unilateral power to conduct war, Kaine engaged Obama at the White House in what the senator later referred to as a "spirited discussion." Kaine is reported to have firmly told Obama that, if he intended to go to war, he would need Congress' permission, while the president-politely, but just as firmly-disagreed. With Republican Jeff Flake of Arizona at the Foreign Relations Committee in 2015, Kaine advocated authorization for action against ISIS, but they did not succeed.

Kaine, in an interview with the *New York Times* in late 2014, said that his adamant position on this issue grew not only out of the large military presence in his home state, but also Virginia's unique place in the nation's founding. "They know I feel strongly about this because I'm a Virginian," Kaine said of the Obama White House. "Until we have a vote, and we live by that vote, I am going to keep pushing them hard."

In the wake of the Democrats' loss of the Senate majority in the 2014 election, Kaine and his colleague, Mark Warner, were among a half-dozen Democrats to vote against the election of Sen. Harry Reid of Nevada as minority leader. An aide said Kaine "voted no because he believes the caucus should have had a more thorough discussion on strategy before taking a leadership vote."

Clinton's selection of Kaine as her running mate, which she announced the weekend before the Democratic convention, generally was well-received. His limitations included that he did not excite liberal activists, and that his support for international-trade deals did little to generate enthusiasm among blue-collar union members.. Clinton based the selection, in part, on their compatibility and his preparation to do the job. In an interview with PBS, she said that her decision showed that she was "afflicted with the responsibility gene."

During the most-watched performance for any vice-presidential candidate, the debate of the two nominees, Kaine's persistent attack mode was described by commentators as "over-caffeinated." He played the attack dog, especially against Republican presidential nominee Donald Trump. "A dark and twisted journey through the mind of Donald Trump [is] a very scary place to be," was an occasional attack line. But, like the Clinton campaign generally, he failed to convince battleground-state voters that Trump was an unacceptable choice. Kaine's Spanish-speaking and his experience in Latin American nations did not have a noticeable impact with Hispanic voters.

In the aftermath of the unexpected defeat, he may have become even more settled into the Senate. "I have a job to do here that in some ways may have gotten more important," Kaine told reporters when he returned to the Capitol a week after the election. When the Secret Service agents departed after he returned home to Richmond the day after the election, he said that he felt a sense of relief.

Kaine likely will face a competitive reelection race in 2018, particularly in light of his senior colleague, Democrat Mark Warner, barely eking out a win in the 2014 election. The identity of his challenger and the start of that campaign were largely delayed during the 2017 campaign for governor of Virginia. Among the Republicans expressing an early interest in the contest were former presidential candidate Carly Fiorina and conservative activist Laura Ingraham.

Kaine has said that he does not expect to run for president and that he wants a lengthy career in the Senate, like Virginia Republican John Warner, who served for 30 years. He retains an introspective view of his work. When asked by the *Washington Post* in 2015 about one of his hobbies, playing the harmonica in bluegrass bands, he chuckled, "...The way I look at it is, in politics you've got to have a fallback in our line of work because your career can be over in an instant." Asked about the quality of his harmonica playing, Kaine replied, "My wife is the most honest. She says, 'Hey, you ought to play anytime they ask you because as soon as you're not in elected office, they're not going to ask you anymore'."

FIRST DISTRICT

Rob Wittman (R)

Elected 2007, 6th term; b. Feb 03, 1959, Washington, DC; University of North Carolina, Chapel Hill, M.PH; Virginia Commonwealth University, Ph.D.; Virginia Polytechnic Institute, B.S.; Episcopalian; Married (Kathryn Jane Sisson Wittman); 2 children; 3 grandchildren.

Elected Office: Montross Town Council, 1986-1996; Montross Mayor, 1992-1996; Westmoreland County Board of Supervisors, 1996-2005, chmn, 2004-2005; VA House, 2006-2007.

Professional Career: Environmental health specialist, VA health Department; Field Director, VA Health Department Div. of Shellfish Sanitation.

DC Office: 2055 RHOB 20515, 202-225-4261, Fax: 202-225-4382, wittman.house.gov.

State Offices: Mechanicsville, 804-730-6595; Stafford, 540-659-2734; Tappahannock, 804-443-0668.

Committees: *Armed Services*: Seapower & Projection Forces (Chmn), Tactical Air & Land Forces. *Natural Resources*: Energy & Mineral Resources, Water, Power & Oceans.

Group Ratings

	ADA	ACLU	AFL-CIO	LCV	ITI	COC	HAFA	ACU	CFG	FRC
2016	-	5%	-	0%	83%	92%	82%	96%	85%	100%
2015	5%	C	17%	3%	C	70%	C	96%	73%	100%

Almanac Ratings 2015

	Economy	Social	Foreign	Composite
Liberal	8%	0%	0%	3%
Conservative	92%	100%	100%	97%

Key Votes of the 114th Congress

1. Keystone Pipeline	Y	5. Puerto Rico Debt	N	9. Offenses by Aliens	Y
2. Trade Deals	N	6. Medical Marijuana	N	10. Troops in Iraq	N
3. Export-Import Bank	N	7. Sanctuary Cities	Y	11. Homeland Security $$	N
4. Debt Ceiling Increase	N	8. Armor-piercing Bullets	Y	12. Trade Adjustment aid	N

Election Results

Election	Name (Party)	Vote (%)	Cand. Spent	Ind. Exp. Support	Ind. Exp. Oppose
2016 General	Rob Wittman (R)	230,213 (60%)	$960,915		
	Matt Rowe (D)	140,785 (37%)	$44,480		
	Glenda Parker (I)	12,866 (3%)			

Prior winning percentages: 2014 (63%), 2012 (56%), 2010 (64%), 2008 (57%), 2007 special (61%)

Republican Rob Wittman, who won the seat in a 2007 special election, has engaged on national security, with a focus that goes beyond the parochial concerns of his district. He combines military expertise with a professional interest in environmental protection, a pairing not often found among either conservative Republicans like Wittman or liberal Democrats. He had been seeking grass-roots support to run for governor in 2017, or potentially to succeed Sen. Tim Kaine if he had been elected vice president. Wittman abandoned his statewide ambitions after the 2016 election, and pursued increased influence in the House.

Wittman was born in Washington, D.C., and became a marine scientist. He has a Ph.D. in public policy and administration from Virginia Commonwealth University. Wittman served for many years as an environmental health specialist in the Northern Neck and Peninsula regions, including as field director for the state's shellfish sanitation division. His first public office was a seat on the Montross Town Council, where he served for 10 years, including four as mayor. In 1995, he began a decade on the Westmoreland County Board of Supervisors. In 2005, he was elected to the Virginia House of Delegates.

In 2007, after GOP Rep. Jo Ann Davis died of breast cancer, Republicans held a convention to choose their nominee. Wittman's chief opponent was Paul Jost, a businessman and anti-tax activist. Wittman cited his experience in public office and "the basics of good government." With help from several busloads of supporters, Jost led in early balloting, which began with 11 candidates. The key moment came after five ballots, when Davis' widower, Chuck Davis, threw his support to Wittman. Democratic nominee Philip Forgit, a school teacher and Navy reservist who won a Bronze Star in Iraq, described himself as a centrist and called for improved training to bring strategic change in Iraq. Wittman emphasized his conservative credentials, including his support for gun rights and his opposition to abortion. He touted the fact that House Minority Leader John Boehner pledged to give him a seat on the Armed Services Committee. The Democratic Congressional Campaign Committee paid little attention to the Republican district, and Wittman won 61%-37%.

Wittman got a seat on Armed Services as promised, and also a seat on the Natural Resources Committee, another good fit for his district. He usually sticks with Republicans on major issues but is not an automatic vote. Coming from a district with a large government presence, he is less enamored of eliminating federal programs and dramatically reducing spending than other conservatives. The House in 2009 passed his bill to improve management of efforts to clean up Chesapeake Bay. He won Natural Resources approval in 2011 of his bill to streamline the process to develop offshore wind energy. His *Almanac* vote ratings for 2015 ranked him with consistently conservative scores.

As chairman of the Armed Services' Oversight and Investigations Subcommittee in 2011, he delved into the management scandal at Arlington National Cemetery, where an Army report found mismarked graves and numerous other problems. In 2013, he became chairman of the Readiness Subcommittee. Like others from his state and the committee, he aggressively advocates expanding the Navy's fleet. As co-chair of the Congressional Shipbuilding Caucus, he has maintained that it is more critical than ever for the military to project power around the world. During a 2014 visit by a delegation of House members with King Abdullah of Jordan, Wittman said the United States can assist in the fight against the Islamic State but added, "this effort needs an Arab face."

Republican Rep. Randy Forbes of Virginia lost re-election following the redistricting changes in 2016, conveniently opening for Wittman the chairmanship of the Seapower and Projection Forces Subcommittee. Wittman grabbed that opportunity, a vital position for the extensive ship-building interests of Virginia. "As chairman, I will have the opportunity to serve both our nation and the commonwealth of Virginia, and I am committed to ensuring that our military remains the greatest fighting force the world has ever known," Wittman said.

That subcommittee chairmanship was all the more attractive because of the call by President Donald Trump to expand the Navy to 350 ships from its roughly 275 ships, a long-term objective that Wittman enthusiastically embraced, not least because Hampton Roads is home to the world's largest naval base and the headquarters for Huntington Ingalls Industries, the largest U.S. military shipbuilder. In turn, that gave Wittman a graceful exit from the contest for governor, where he was facing a competitive Republican primary and uncertain prospects in November.

Wittman has not been seriously threatened for re-election . In 2016, Democratic challenger Matt Rowe, a council member in Bowling Green and data analyst for Stafford County, criticized the dysfunction in Congress and Wittman's support for Trump. Wittman won, 60%-37%, taking all of the counties and the cities except for Fredericksburg. He is young enough and respected enough that he eventually could be positioned to chair one of his two committees, especially now that his statewide plans have been curtailed.

Eastern Virginia: DC and Richmond Exurbs,

Demographics data for new House districts were not prepared by the Census Bureau prior to our editorial deadline.

Voter Turnout			
2016 House Turnout as % CVAP	N/A	2016 House turnout	384,601

2012 Presidential Vote information unavailable due to recent redistricting.

2016 Presidential Vote		
Donald Trump	210,618	(53%)
Hillary Clinton	161,476	(41%)
Gary Johnson	12,298	(3%)

Cook Partisan Voting Index: R+8

When the English first sailed up the estuaries that flow into the Chesapeake Bay, they were searching for gold. But they couldn't help noticing that the spot where the James River fed into the bay, now Hampton Roads, was a fine natural harbor with calm, deep water and good anchorages. So some of them stayed and established communities farther up the river that achieved not only the high craftsmanship of Williamsburg, but endured the pitiless hardship of Jamestown and other early settlements. Tidewater Virginia brought slavery to America and tobacco to the world, and slave-raised tobacco was the center of its economy in the colonial era and in the years afterward. Today, more than 1.7 million people live in the area. Because of the heavy military presence, it's a population collected from all over the country. So, like most of Northern Virginia, it has less of a Southern atmosphere than other regions of the Old Dominion.

About half the population of the 1st Congressional District of Virginia lives south and east of Fredericksburg, the unofficial southern terminus of Northern Virginia. The court-ordered redistricting in 2016 shifted this part of the district by adding exurban and largely Republican Hanover and New Kent Counties, which were shifted from the old 7th District. In exchange, the 1st lost Williamsburg, Yorktown and surrounding areas, which moved to the 2nd District. The effect of these changes was to extend the new 1st west of Interstate 95 in the area north of Richmond, with offsetting losses east of Richmond. Most of the major Hampton Roads military installations are in surrounding congressional districts. But the 1st remains steeped in military culture, and the Department of Defense and NASA are significant employers. In Caroline County, Fort A.P. Hill serves as a training site for active and reserve-component units. Not far from there is the Naval Surface Warfare Center in Dahlgren, located on the Potomac River, originally established as the Navy's main proving ground for large-caliber guns.

The other half of the district's population lives in the southern reaches of exurban Washington, D.C., effectively making its representative the fourth member of Congress from Northern Virginia. This part leans Republican with Fredericksburg, Stafford County and portions of Prince William and Fauquier counties. Prince William and Stafford remain the two largest counties in the district. They comprise nearly 40 percent of the population and were not affected by redistricting. Stafford County, which is 42 miles from Washington, is rapidly growing, with a 54 percent increase from 2000 to 2015; projections are that it will more than double between 2015 and 2040. The district has a large military presence here as well, including the Quantico Marine Corps base. With drivers in this area suffering some of the worst commutes in the nation, Virginia transportation officials have prepared plans to upgrade the rail line between Richmond and Washington to reduce the time along that route by about an hour; the changes could be completed by 2025. With its military population and growing retirement communities, the 1st has been reliably Republican in most elections. The redistricting changes in 2016 increased the GOP vote by about three percentage points. Donald Trump won 53 percent of the vote. With the new lines, Mitt Romney would have had 56 percent, instead of the 53 percent that he got with the old lines in 2012.

SECOND DISTRICT

Scott Taylor (R)

Elected 2016, 1st term; b. Jun 27, 1979, Baltimore, MD; Old Dominion University (VA); Harvard University Extension School (MA); Christian - Non-Denominational; Single1 child.

Military Career: U.S Navy SEAL (Iraq), 1997-2005.

Professional Career: Real estate broker; Entrepeneur; Author.

DC Office: 412 CHOB 20515, 202-225-4215, Fax: 202-225-4218, taylor.house.gov.

State Offices: Virginia Beach, 757-364-7650.

Committees: *Appropriations*: Homeland Security, Legislative Branch, Military Construction, Veterans Affairs & Related Agencies.

Election Results

Election	Name (Party)	Vote (%)	Cand. Spent	Ind. Exp. Support	Ind. Exp. Oppose
2016 General	Scott Taylor (R)	190,475 (61%)	$690,693	$32,645	
	Shaun D. Brown (D)	119,440 (39%)	$22,364		
2016 Primary	Scott Taylor (R)	21,403 (53%)			
	Randy Forbes (R)	16,553 (41%)			
	Pat Cardwell (R)	2,773 (7%)			

Republican Scott Taylor was elected in 2016 when he defeated a veteran incumbent in a primary, with a boost from redistricting. His extensive experience as a Navy SEAL provided useful background to his candidacy and to his early service in Congress, including his unusual achievement of securing a seat on the Appropriations Committee as a House freshman. He was a state legislator and has worked in business.

Taylor grew up on a farm in the small town of Hebron on the Eastern Shore of Maryland. Raised by a single mother, he was introduced to the Big Brothers/Big Sisters Program of America. He said that his Big Brother changed his life and helped to set him on a path to success. After graduating from high school, where he was an accomplished wrestler, he enlisted in the U.S. Navy and served as a Navy SEAL sniper in South and Central America. He reenlisted after the 9/11 attacks and was sent to Iraq in 2005. While on a combat mission in Iraq, Taylor was severely injured while on a combat mission in Ramadi and eventually returned to the United States. According to the Associated Press, he fell 20 feet through the floor of a dark, vacant building while searching for insurgents and suffered broken ribs, a concussion and a collapsed lung. After his recuperation, he completed his SEAL service as a marksmanship and reconnaissance instructor.

Taylor became a security and asset protection adviser for multinational companies and traveled extensively to Yemen as a security consultant for a multinational energy company. He was also a real estate broker in Virginia Beach. He used the education benefits of the GI Bill to earn a bachelor's degree in International Relations from Harvard University and has completed the coursework for his master's degree at Harvard. He holds a Master's Certificate in Government Contracting from Old Dominion University. He ran for Congress in the 2nd District in 2010 and finished fourth in the six-candidate Republican primary, with 8 percent of the vote. Scott Rigell won the primary and served three terms. In 2013, he was elected from Virginia Beach to the state House of Delegates, where he focused on energy, workforce and veterans' issues. In 2015, he wrote a book, *Trust Betrayed: Barack Obama, Hillary Clinton, and the Selling Out of America's National Security*, which accused Obama of taking too much credit for the SEALs' successful raid on Osama bin Laden's compound in Pakistan. "I got involved in that specifically because I felt like our leaders were releasing national security secrets ... to gain credit politically and get re-elected," he told AP.

When Rigell retired, Taylor found himself in a primary against 16-year House veteran Randy Forbes, whose 4th District seat had been revamped by redistricting and had become largely unwinnable for a Republican. A senior member of the Armed Service Committee, Forbes decided to run in a new constituency that was east and north of his base in Chesapeake. In what became a nasty campaign,

Forbes focused on Taylor's past driving violations, financial mismanagement of his real-estate business and other legal problems, plus his failures to comply with federal campaign laws during 2010. Taylor criticized Forbes for aspects of his congressional record and for not living in the 2nd District; he said that Forbes should have run in the revamped 4th District. Forbes reported raising $1.4 million for the primary, to $170,000 for Taylor. With the four-month campaign, Forbes was unable to get traction in the new district and took only four lightly voting jurisdictions. Taylor won, 53%-41%. He took 57 percent of the vote in Virginia Beach, which cast 69 percent of the vote.

Taylor had an easy time in the general election against Democratic nominee Shaun Brown, a business consultant who had lost several previous local campaigns in the area and was a Bernie Sanders delegate at the 2016 Democratic convention. Brown raised $28,000 and was largely ignored by her national party and its allies, despite the recent competitive history of the district. Taylor won 61%-38% and swept all of the jurisdictions except for Williamsburg.

With his seat on the Appropriations Committee, Taylor said that he would "protect and enhance [the]federal assets" of his district. "We have the duty to thread the needle between fiscal responsibility and providing the funds for a strong national defense," he added. He gained seats on three subcommittees: Homeland Security, Military Construction/Veterans Affairs and Legislative Branch. But his first bill sought to prohibit discrimination in housing based on sexual orientation or gender identity. Amid the early controversies that President Donald Trump had with the intelligence community, Taylor said, "they need to get on the same page very quickly."

Hampton Roads: Virginia Beach, Colonial Virginia

Demographics data for new House districts were not prepared by the Census Bureau prior to our editorial deadline.

Voter Turnout			
2016 House Turnout as % CVAP	N/A	2016 House turnout	310,568

2012 Presidential Vote information unavailable due to recent redistricting.

2016 Presidential Vote		
Donald Trump	158,067	(48%)
Hillary Clinton	147,217	(45%)
Gary Johnson	12,379	(4%)

Cook Partisan Voting Index: R+3

Virginia Beach, once a sleepy beach resort, is now the state's largest city, with 453,000 people. It began attracting tourists when rail service to Norfolk began in 1883. Later, it became the anchor to a metropolitan area of 1.7 million people that is centered on the local Navy community -- active duty and civilian personnel, dependents, retirees and workers at the Newport News Shipyard. Virginia Beach also is home to the headquarters of the Christian Broadcasting Network, which produces "The 700 Club" and features evangelist Pat Robertson, the son of former Democratic Sen. A. Willis Robertson of Virginia. In 1974, the city converted a local landfill into a grass-covered park, and Mount Trashmore Park was born, with its basketball courts, walking trails and fishing in the adjoining Lake Trashmore. The city has a growing industrial base, including a large power tool plant of the German-based Stihl company. Like Norfolk, Virginia Beach is infused with military culture. The city is the base of East Coast Navy SEAL teams; these elite commandos endure punishing training, and they took on some of the military's most secretive and daring missions in Iraq and Afghanistan, including participating in the Pakistan compound raid that killed Osama bin Laden in 2011. A monument in tribute to the SEALs was scheduled to be built along the boardwalk in the spring of 2017.

Military history of a different sort is commemorated in Yorktown, the site of the decisive battle of the Revolutionary War in 1781, which is adjacent to a naval weapons station on the banks of the York River. Not far away is Williamsburg, where major parts have been restored to look as they did in colonial times; actors play the roles of colonists, which is a major tourist draw. Also in Williamsburg is the College of William & Mary. America's second-oldest college claims as alumni presidents Thomas Jefferson, James Monroe and John Tyler, as well as Chief Justice John Marshall. Another historic site, on a spit of land in the Chesapeake Bay, is Fort Monroe, where Jefferson Davis was confined after the Civil War.

The 2nd Congressional District of Virginia includes all of Virginia Beach, plus several small cities on thin stretches of land that Virginians refer to as necks (peninsulas to outsiders). Across the Chesapeake Bay Bridge-Tunnel, the district transforms into a more placid area, including the two Virginia counties of the Delmarva Peninsula, the site of the annual roundup of wild Chincoteague ponies in the national wildlife refuge. In October 2016, Dominion Resources began operating in Accomack County what was promoted as the largest solar power facility on the East Coast. The solar farm is providing power to Amazon for its data centers in the area. Redistricting in 2016 shifted Norfolk and Newport News to the 3rd District. In exchange, the 2nd picked up some of the colonial sites of the Tidewater area. More than 60 percent of the district's population is in Virginia Beach, and it leans Republican. Under the old lines, Barack Obama narrowly carried the district twice, each time by a few thousand votes. With the shifts, Mitt Romney would have gained about two percentage points and taken the district. In 2016, Donald Trump had a similar narrow lead, 48%-45%..

THIRD DISTRICT

Bobby Scott (D)

Elected 1992, 13th term; b. Apr 30, 1947, Washington, DC; Boston College Law School (MA), J.D.; Harvard University, B.A.; Episcopalian; Divorced.

Military Career: U.S. Army Reserve, 1970-1974; MA Army National Guard, 1974-1976.

Elected Office: VA House, 1978-1983; VA Senate, 1983-1993.

Professional Career: Practicing attorney, 1973-1991.

DC Office: 1201 LHOB 20515, 202-225-8351, Fax: 202-225-8354, bobbyscott.house.gov.

State Offices: Newport News, 757-380-1000.

Committees: *Education & the Workforce (RMM)*: Early Childhood, Elementary & Secondary Education, Higher Education & Workforce Development, Workforce Protections.

Group Ratings

	ADA	ACLU	AFL-CIO	LCV	ITI	COC	HAFA	ACU	CFG	FRC
2016	-	100%	-	100%	67%	57%	12%	0%	0%	0%
2015	100%	C	100%	100%	C	37%	C	0%	0%	0%

Almanac Ratings 2015

	Economy	Social	Foreign	Composite
Liberal	98%	100%	97%	98%
Conservative	2%	0%	4%	2%

Key Votes of the 114th Congress

1. Keystone Pipeline	N	5. Puerto Rico Debt	Y	9. Offenses by Aliens	N
2. Trade Deals	N	6. Medical Marijuana	Y	10. Troops in Iraq	Y
3. Export-Import Bank	Y	7. Sanctuary Cities	N	11. Homeland Security $$	Y
4. Debt Ceiling Increase	Y	8. Armor-piercing Bullets	N	12. Trade Adjustment aid	NV

Election Results

Election	Name (Party)	Vote (%)		Cand. Spent	Ind. Exp. Support	Ind. Exp. Oppose
2016 General	Bobby Scott (D)	208,337	(67%)	$53,748		
	Marty Williams (R)	103,289	(33%)	$69,271		

Prior winning percentages: 2014 (94%), 2012 (81%), 2010 (70%), 2008 (97%), 2006 (96%), 2004 (69%), 2002 (96%), 2000 (98%), 1998 (76%), 1996 (82%), 1994 (79%), 1992 (79%)

Democrat Bobby Scott, first elected in 1992, has been an influential civil libertarian, an intellectual force in the Congressional Black Caucus, and an important figure in Virginia politics. In 2015, he gained new authority as the Education and Workforce Committee's top Democrat. The prospect that Sen. Tim Kaine would be elected vice president in 2016 fueled widespread speculation that Scott would gain new prominence as the Senate successor to Kaine. That was one of many Democratic dreams that were quashed by the November election.

Scott grew up in Newport News, the son of a doctor. His maternal grandfather was Filipino, which led him to join the Congressional Asian Pacific American Caucus. He got his bachelor's at Harvard University, where he was a classmate of Al Gore, and got his law degree at Boston College. He served in the National Guard and Army Reserves and returned home to practice law. In 1977, he was elected to the House of Delegates, and later to the state Senate, representing a multi-racial district in a community where, because of the military tradition of integration, such diverse politics came more naturally than in other places.

In 1986, he ran a credible race for Congress and lost to Republican Rep. Herb Bateman, 56%-44%. In 1992, with his base in a district that had been redrawn to become African-American majority, Scott won the Democratic primary with 67 percent of the vote against two Richmond-based candidates. He easily won the general election to become the first African-American elected from Virginia since 1891. He has been reelected by overwhelming margins, with occasional changes in his district lines.

Scott has a solidly liberal voting record, as shown by his *Almanac* vote ratings in 2015 that placed him among the 5 percent of House members who were the most liberal. As one of the most outspoken civil libertarians on the Judiciary Committee, he joined like-minded Reps. Jerrold Nadler of New York and John Conyers of Michigan in 2012 in seeking more scrutiny of the Obama administration's use of unmanned drones to kill suspected terrorists. When bipartisan coalitions passed legislation to permit states to display the Ten Commandments in schools or government buildings, he raised First Amendment objections. After the September 11 attacks, he opposed the USA Patriot Act, the nation's tough new anti-terrorism law, arguing that it might promote racial profiling. Scott was one of three lawmakers to oppose condemnation of a federal court decision declaring unconstitutional the words "one nation under God" in the Pledge of Allegiance. "We ought to be standing up for unpopular decisions" and not voting for a resolution that "everyone knows is stupid, but it sounds popular," he said.

After the Newtown, Connecticut, elementary school massacre in 2012, Minority Leader Nancy Pelosi named Scott vice chair of the Democrats' gun-violence prevention task force. One of his legislative successes was the bipartisan Death in Custody Reporting Act, which requires states to report deaths of arrestees and prisoners. Also in 2010, he enacted the Fair Sentencing Act to narrow the discrepancies between sentences for powder and crack cocaine, an issue he had long contended led to blacks receiving disproportionately longer sentences.

As the Education and the Workforce's ranking member, Scott has built on his longtime interest in K-12 education, with a special focus on equity. He introduced a bill in 2014 to authorize the Obama administration's "Promise Neighborhood" program, augmenting K-12 classes with health and arts programs. In 2015, he was among the four lawmakers chiefly responsible for rewriting the No Child Left Behind education law, which Scott had contended was outdated. Despite his initial objections to Republican alternatives, Scott praised the final version of the Every Student Succeeds Act, as "the embodiment of what we can do when we work together in Washington--a workable compromise that does not force either side to desert its core beliefs." Also that year, he filed the administration's proposal for two years of tuition-free community college for millions of students.

Scott is a fervent advocate of boosting funding to reduce juvenile crime. He joined Republican Rep. Carlos Curbelo of Florida in gaining House passage in September 2016 of a bill to upgrade juvenile justice programs and end what Scott called the "school-to-prison pipeline." With GOP Rep. Raul Labrador of Idaho in 2015, he filed a bill to reduce certain mandatory drug sentences, restore judicial discretion in sentencing for some offenses, and promote alternatives to incarceration. He worked with members of both parties to reduce national security collection of telephone metadata records, as part of a revision of the Patriot Act that was enacted in June 2015.

He has taken a leadership role on issues that go beyond his committee work. In 2007, Scott joined with then-Sens. Barack Obama of Illinois and Joe Biden of Delaware in pushing legislation to compensate black farmers who had been victims of government discrimination; the bill was enacted in 2010. Scott opposed the bipartisan fiscal cliff budget deal in 2012 that extended most of the Bush-era tax cuts, and he has been the prime sponsor of the CBC's alternative budget plan to phase out those tax cuts for upper-income taxpayers and finance more spending on domestic programs. The House has routinely defeated his annual proposal.

Scott hosts an annual Labor Day picnic that has become a required stop for Democratic candidates for state and federal office. He used the 2011 picnic to announce that he wouldn't run for retiring Democrat Jim Webb's Senate seat, clearing the way for former Gov. Kaine to get the nomination. Earlier that year, he said he was considering a Senate bid because he had become disenchanted with the "fiscal insanity" in the House and the scant opportunity for debate and compromise. At the 2016 picnic, guests enthusiastically speculated that Scott would be the front-runner for Gov. Terry McAuliffe's appointment to succeed Kaine. He did not object. Privately, some Democrats worried that Scott would have been too liberal and unknown outside his district to win statewide. For now, that has become a moot point.

As Scott and his district became the focal point of redistricting litigation over the Republican congressional map, he kept a behind-the-scenes role. He consistently encouraged a second district in the Tidewater area with a substantial minority presence, which ultimately removed from his district many African-American locales.

Bobby Scott (D)

Democrat Bobby Scott, first elected in 1992, has been an influential civil libertarian, an intellectual force in the Congressional Black Caucus, and an important figure in Virginia politics. In 2015, he gained new authority as the Education and Workforce Committee's top Democrat. The prospect that Sen. Tim Kaine would be elected vice president in 2016 fueled widespread speculation that Scott would gain new prominence as the Senate successor to Kaine. That was one of many Democratic dreams that were quashed by the November election.

Scott grew up in Newport News, the son of a doctor. His maternal grandfather was Filipino, which led him to join the Congressional Asian Pacific American Caucus. He got his bachelor's at Harvard University, where he was a classmate of Al Gore, and got his law degree at Boston College. He served in the National Guard and Army Reserves and returned home to practice law. In 1977, he was elected to the House of Delegates, and later to the state Senate, representing a multi-racial district in a community where, because of the military tradition of integration, such diverse politics came more naturally than in other places.

In 1986, he ran a credible race for Congress and lost to Republican Rep. Herb Bateman, 56%-44%. In 1992, with his base in a district that had been redrawn to become African-American majority, Scott won the Democratic primary with 67 percent of the vote against two Richmond-based candidates. He easily won the general election to become the first African-American elected from Virginia since 1891. He has been reelected by overwhelming margins, with occasional changes in his district lines.

Scott has a solidly liberal voting record, as shown by his Almanac vote ratings in 2015 that placed him among the 5 percent of House members who were the most liberal. As one of the most outspoken civil libertarians on the Judiciary Committee, he joined like-minded Reps. Jerrold Nadler of New York and John Conyers of Michigan in 2012 in seeking more scrutiny of the Obama administration's use of unmanned drones to kill suspected terrorists. When bipartisan coalitions passed legislation to permit states to display the Ten Commandments in schools or government buildings, he raised First Amendment objections. After the September 11 attacks, he opposed the USA Patriot Act, the nation's tough new anti-terrorism law, arguing that it might promote racial profiling. Scott was one of three lawmakers to oppose condemnation of a federal court decision declaring unconstitutional the words "one nation under God" in the Pledge of Allegiance. "We ought to be standing up for unpopular decisions" and not voting for a resolution that "everyone knows is stupid, but it sounds popular," he said.

After the Newtown, Connecticut, elementary school massacre in 2012, Minority Leader Nancy Pelosi named Scott vice chair of the Democrats' gun-violence prevention task force. One of his legislative successes was the bipartisan Death in Custody Reporting Act, which requires states to report deaths of arrestees and prisoners. Also in 2010, he enacted the Fair Sentencing Act to narrow the discrepancies between sentences for powder and crack cocaine, an issue he had long contended led to blacks receiving disproportionately longer sentences.

As the Education and the Workforce's ranking member, Scott has built on his longtime interest in K-12 education, with a special focus on equity. He introduced a bill in 2014 to authorize the Obama administration's "Promise Neighborhood" program, augmenting K-12 classes with health and arts programs. In 2015, he was among the four lawmakers chiefly responsible for rewriting the No Child Left Behind education law, which Scott had contended was outdated. Despite his initial objections to Republican alternatives, Scott praised the final version of the Every Student Succeeds Act, as "the embodiment of what we can do when we work together in Washington--a workable compromise that does not force either side to desert its core beliefs." Also that year, he filed the administration's proposal for two years of tuition-free community college for millions of students.

Scott is a fervent advocate of boosting funding to reduce juvenile crime. He joined Republican Rep. Carlos Curbelo of Florida in gaining House passage in September 2016 of a bill to upgrade juvenile justice programs and end what Scott called the "school-to-prison pipeline." With GOP Rep. Raul Labrador of Idaho in 2015, he filed a bill to reduce certain mandatory drug sentences, restore judicial discretion in sentencing for some offenses, and promote alternatives to incarceration. He worked with members of both parties to reduce national security collection of telephone metadata records, as part of a revision of the Patriot Act that was enacted in June 2015.

He has taken a leadership role on issues that go beyond his committee work. In 2007, Scott joined with then-Sens. Barack Obama of Illinois and Joe Biden of Delaware in pushing legislation to compensate black farmers who had been victims of government discrimination; the bill was enacted in 2010. Scott opposed the bipartisan fiscal cliff budget deal in 2012 that extended most of the Bush-era tax cuts, and he has been the prime sponsor of the CBC's alternative budget plan to phase out those tax cuts for upper-income taxpayers and finance more spending on domestic programs. The House has routinely defeated his annual proposal.

Scott hosts an annual Labor Day picnic that has become a required stop for Democratic candidates for state and federal office. He used the 2011 picnic to announce that he wouldn't run for retiring Democrat Jim Webb's Senate seat, clearing the way for former Gov. Kaine to get the nomination. Earlier that year, he said he was considering a Senate bid because he had become disenchanted with the "fiscal insanity" in the House and the scant opportunity for debate and compromise. At the 2016 picnic, guests enthusiastically speculated that Scott would be the front-runner for Gov. Terry McAuliffe's appointment to succeed Kaine. He did not object. Privately, some Democrats worried that Scott would have been too liberal and unknown outside his district to win statewide. For now, that has become a moot point.

As Scott and his district became the focal point of redistricting litigation over the Republican congressional map, he kept a behind-the-scenes role. He consistently encouraged a second district in the Tidewater area with a substantial minority presence, which ultimately removed from his district many African-American locales.

Newport News, Norfolk

Demographics data for new House districts were not prepared by the Census Bureau prior to our editorial deadline.

Voter Turnout			
2016 House Turnout as % CVAP	N/A	2016 House turnout	312,340

2012 Presidential Vote information unavailable due to recent redistricting.

2016 Presidential Vote		
Hillary Clinton	205,746	(63%)
Donald Trump	103,064	(32%)
Gary Johnson	9,072	(3%)

Cook Partisan Voting Index: D+16

The U.S. Navy Atlantic fleet berthed in its home port of Norfolk is one of the most awe-inspiring sights in America, or anywhere. Norfolk has been a Navy port since 1801 and has long been recognized as having one of the best natural harbors on the East Coast, one that never freezes, has a channel 50 feet deep, and is within 750 miles of three-quarters of U.S. manufacturing capacity. The Norfolk Naval Station is the world's largest naval base, situated on 4,300 acres on Sewell's Point. Almost a quarter of the nation's uniformed military personnel are stationed in the Hampton Roads area, and the aggregation of destructive power in the line of towering gray ships is probably greater than in any other single port. Once a small city, Norfolk is now part of a metropolitan area of 1.7 million people, anchored by Virginia Beach. The local Navy community - active duty and civilian personnel, dependents, retirees, and workers at the Newport News Shipyard - is estimated at more than 300,000, and military spending pours some $11 billion annually into the local economy. The shipyard, a division of Huntington Ingalls Industries, and Virginia's largest industrial employer, in 2015 lost 1,200 workers from its workforce of more than 22,000, chiefly the result of military spending cutbacks in Washington. It expected to add at least 3,000 workers in 2017, with further growth likely in coming years, given the Pentagon's budget for new ships, including replacement of the Navy's *Ohio*-class nuclear submarines.

The 3rd Congressional District of Virginia includes all of the majority-black city of Portsmouth, a Navy port and industrial town with a charming old section. It travels up the James River to the communities of Norfolk and Newport News, which form its population center. The economy here depends heavily on the Newport News Shipyard. The district takes in areas with high concentrations of white liberals, such as Ghent in Norfolk. As the result of the redistricting changes in 2016, the district no longer includes parts of Richmond. Those areas, especially the African-American neighborhoods, have shifted to the new 4th District, which gained a sizable increase in its black population. In exchange for losing Richmond plus areas on both sides of the James River, including Jamestown, the new 3rd has picked up large parts of Chesapeake, Suffolk and Franklin, which is close to the North Carolina border. The District has dropped to 46 percent black from the 56 percent black population of the old 3rd District, which had been drawn to place the largest possible number of Democrats in a single district.

In 2012, President Barack Obama carried the 3rd District, 79%-20%, one of his best showings in the South and by far his strongest in Virginia. The ruling of a three-judge federal court in June 2015 that the district had been an unconstitutional racial gerrymander and must be redrawn for the 2016 election, which the Supreme Court affirmed, would have given Obama 68 percent in the new 3rd. In 2016, Hillary Clinton won the 3rd, 63%-32%. As a result, the partisan ranking of the district dropped below the two more strongly Democratic districts in northern Virginia. In exchange, a black plurality - and Democrats -- gained control of a second district in Tidewater.

FOURTH DISTRICT

Donald McEachin (D)

Elected 2016, 1st term; b. Oct 10, 1961, Nuremberg, Germany; Virginia Union University Samuel DeWitt Proctor School of Theology; American University (DC), B.S., 1982; University of Virginia Law School, J.D., 1986; Baptist; Married (Colette Wallace McEachin); 3 children.

Elected Office: VA Assembly, 1996-2002, 2006-2008; VA Senate, 2008-2016.

DC Office: 314 CHOB 20515, 202-225-6365, Fax: 202-226-1170, mceachin.house.gov.

State Offices: Richmond, 804-486-1840.

Committees: *Armed Services*: Readiness, Seapower & Projection Forces. *Commission Congressional Mailing Standards*. *Natural Resources*: Federal Lands, Oversight & Investigations (RMM).

Election Results

Election	Name (Party)	Vote	(%)	Cand. Spent	Ind. Exp. Support	Ind. Exp. Oppose
2016 General	Donald McEachin (D)	200,136	(58%)	$412,002		
	Mike Wade (R)	145,731	(42%)	$142,690		
2016 Primary	Donald McEachin (D)	11,837	(75%)			
	Ella Ward (D)	3,982	(25%)			

Democrat Donald McEachin was elected in 2016 to represent a district that changed significantly in a court-ordered redistricting plan, which led its incumbent Republican Rep. Randy Forbes to conclude that he could not win in the new district. McEachin had a relatively easy route to election and brought extensive experience as a legislator. He is the second member of the Virginia delegation to join the Congressional Black Caucus.

McEachin was born in Nuremberg, Germany, to an Army veteran and a public school teacher. He grew up in Richmond, got his bachelor's degree from American University and law degree from the University of Virginia. He served six years in the state House of Delegates and then ran unsuccessfully in 2001 for state attorney general. "The defeat stung, and he found himself struggling to find a purpose," *The Washington Post* reported. McEachin enrolled in the Samuel Proctor Theological Seminary at Virginia Union University, received his masters of divinity degree and became an ordained Baptist minister. Meanwhile, he returned to the state House and later was elected to the state Senate, where he chaired the Democratic Caucus. He co-founded and practiced with his law firm in Richmond.

When a federal court reviewed redistricting in Virginia, it agreed to a version of the map proposed by Democratic Gov. Terry McAuliffe, which revamped the Republican-held 4th District. It appeared to be tailor-made politically and geographically for McEachin. He ran and got 75 percent of the vote in the low-turnout Democratic primary against Ella Ward, a member of the Chesapeake City Council. After Forbes decided to run in the Virginia Beach-based 2nd District, Henrico County Sheriff Mike Wade, who spent his career in law enforcement, won the Republican nomination. Wade originally challenged

Rep. Dave Brat in the Republican primary in the adjacent 7th District, but switched to the 4th after it became an open seat.

With McEachin running a mostly quiet campaign, the lightly funded Ward had little opportunity to engage. He referred to his opponent as "Dodging Don." During a debate in October, they disagreed on offshore drilling and alternative energy, the Affordable Care Act and Syrian refugees, the *Richmond Times-Dispatch* reported. Although they agreed on the need for law enforcement officers to wear body cameras, Wade took offense at McEachin's claim of excessive police profiling of racial minorities. The greater problem, he said, was with individuals who have mental-health or substance-abuse problems. "When I got pulled over … I didn't have a mental health problem and I wasn't on my way to jail," McEachin responded. He won, 57%-43%, rolling up huge majorities in Richmond, Petersburg and Henrico, which cast nearly half of the vote. Ward took 64 percent of the vote in Chesapeake and won four outlying counties - areas that had been Forbes' base in the old 4th.

McEachin got a seat on the Armed Services Committee, where he promoted "quality of life" issues for the military and veterans. He joined the Natural Resources Committee and became ranking minority member on the Oversight and Investigations Subcommittee, where he said that he would "spotlight the consequences of shortsighted policies that promote climate change, threaten public health, or reduce Americans' access to public lands."

Southeast Virginia: Richmond and its Exurbs, parts of Chesapeake

Demographics data for new House districts were not prepared by the Census Bureau prior to our editorial deadline.

Voter Turnout			
2016 House Turnout as % CVAP	N/A	2016 House turnout	346,656

2012 Presidential Vote information unavailable due to recent redistricting.

2016 Presidential Vote		
Hillary Clinton	212,677	(58%)
Donald Trump	134,676	(37%)
Gary Johnson	9,595	(3%)

Cook Partisan Voting Index: D+10

The history of American slavery literally began along the tidal expanse of the James River. Only a dozen years after the founding of Jamestown in 1607, the first slave ship sailed up the James and offloaded its human cargo, giving birth to the slave-based economy of the American South. In the 21st century, some of the big plantation houses of the Tidewater still dot the banks of the James. Charles City County - the site of William Byrd II's Westover, Benjamin Harrison III's Berkeley, and John Carter's Shirley - also was the birthplace of two successive presidents, William Henry Harrison and John Tyler. Virginia famously produced a total of eight U.S. presidents - almost 20 percent of the individuals to serve - but none for almost a century.

The 4th Congressional District of Virginia travels back and forth across the James River north of Jamestown to string together black precincts and communities. Upriver on the south bank of the James, it takes in 77 percent African-American Petersburg, where much of the movie *Lincoln* was filmed, as well as eastern Henrico County. All of Richmond is in the district, including the state's Capitol, designed by Thomas Jefferson; the historic Jefferson Hotel; and the African-American neighborhoods around Church Hill, where Patrick Henry famously proclaimed "give me liberty or give me death." Monument Avenue has statues of Confederate luminaries and tennis player Arthur Ashe. Old tobacco warehouses on the banks of the James have been converted into loft apartments. Hollywood Cemetery is where Presidents James Monroe and John Tyler share a final resting place with 25 Confederate generals, Jefferson Davis, and Davis' son, Joseph, who died at age 5 in 1864 after falling from the Confederate White House balcony.

The district also takes in the flat lands of Southside Virginia. These were tobacco fields after the English first settled here in the 17th century. The tiny town of Wakefield is home to the Shad Planking, the fish-eating event where Virginia politicians still make pilgrimages every spring to meet and greet each other and voters; these days, most of them are Republicans. In January 2017, plans were unveiled to construct in Southampton County the largest solar facility in the state; the power will be used by

Amazon. Parts of the district are in suburban Henrico and fast-growing Chesterfield County, where the population increased by 30 percent from 2000 to 2015 and surpassed Henrico. The district includes all of the city of Hopewell, with its Honeywell plant and 18th century plantations. By picking up Richmond and Petersburg from the old 3rd and giving in exchange Suffolk and large parts of Chesapeake to the new 3rd, the redistricting changes in 2016 increased the African American population in the district from 31 percent to 43 percent. That, in turn, increased the vote in 2012 for President Barack Obama from 49 percent to 61 percent, making this a Democratic district. In 2016, Hillary Clinton took 58 percent of the vote.

FIFTH DISTRICT

Thomas Garrett (R)

Elected 2016, 1st term; b. Mar 27, 1972, Atlanta, GA; University of Richmond (VA), B.S., 1995; University of Richmond School of Law, J.D., 2003; Disciples of Christ; Married (Flanna Garrett); 2 children (2 from previous marriage).

Military Career: U.S Army, 1995-2000.

Elected Office: VA Senate, 2012-2016.

Professional Career: Louisa County Commonwealth Attorney, 2008-2012; VA Assistant Attorney General, 2002-2007.

DC Office: 415 CHOB 20515, 202-225-4711, Fax: 202-225-5681, tomgarrett.house.gov.

State Offices: Charlottesville, 434-973-9631; Danville, 434-791-2596.

Committees: *Education & the Workforce*: Early Childhood, Elementary & Secondary Education, Higher Education & Workforce Development. *Foreign Affairs*: Africa, Global Health, Global Human Rights & Internat'l Orgs, Terrorism, Nonproliferation & Trade. *Homeland Security*: Cybersecurity & Infrastructure Protection, Emergency Preparedness, Response & Communications.

Key Votes of the 114th Congress

1. Keystone Pipeline	Y	5. Puerto Rico Debt	Y	9. Offenses by Aliens	Y
2. Trade Deals	N	6. Medical Marijuana	Y	10. Troops in Iraq	Y
3. Export-Import Bank	N	7. Sanctuary Cities	Y	11. Homeland Security $$	N
4. Debt Ceiling Increase	N	8. Armor-piercing Bullets	Y	12. Trade Adjustment aid	N

Election Results

Election	Name (Party)	Vote (%)	Cand. Spent	Ind. Exp. Support	Ind. Exp. Oppose
2016 General	Tom Garrett (R)	207,758 (58%)	$602,667	$15,903	
	Jane Dittmar (D)	148,339 (42%)	$1,344,423		$1,331,313

Republican Tom Garrett won an open seat in 2016 in a mostly rural area that has become safely Republican. A former state senator and prosecutor, he brought strong conservative credentials. His Democratic opponent failed to grow beyond her Charlottesville base.

Garrett was born in Atlanta and got his bachelor's and law degrees from the University of Richmond. He served in the Army for six years and reached the rank of captain as a combat arms officer in Bosnia. He was a prosecutor with the state attorney general's office before he was elected as commonwealth attorney for Louisa County. Garrett was twice elected to the state Senate from a district that includes parts of three congressional districts. He supported Sen. Ted Cruz in the 2016 presidential primary.

When Republican Rep. Robert Hurt decided to retire after three terms, citing the Virginia tradition of citizen service, Garrett announced his candidacy the same day. He was endorsed by the National Rifle Association and 15 of the 21 members of the Republican Senate Caucus. The Republican nomination was settled in May at a convention with four candidates; Garrett was the only one with experience in elected office. He benefited when he got the support of Bedford-area developer Jim McKelvey, who was eliminated after the first ballot. Garrett won on the third ballot against Charlottesville-area technology executive Michael Del Rosso.

In the general, he faced Jane Dittmar, a professional mediator who had served as an Albemarle County supervisor and was unopposed for the Democratic nomination. She was endorsed by several prominent national liberal organizations, including EMILY's List, the Sierra Club and Priorities USA. Their financial support assisted Dittmar in raising $1.4 million, which was twice the total for Garrett, though he had nearly $1 million in additional support from national Republican groups. At an October press conference in Charlottesville that Dittmar had called to criticize harsh attacks on her that had been made on Facebook and Twitter, Garrett attended and joined her call for civility. Dittmar took 64 percent of the vote in Charlottesville and surrounding Albemarle, plus she won Brunswick County and Danville. That wasn't nearly enough. Garrett won, 58%-42%.

Garrett got seats on the Education and the Workforce, Foreign Affairs and Homeland Security committees. In February, he filed a bill to remove marijuana from the federal controlled substances list, which would end federal criminal prosecution for its use. "Statistics indicate that minor narcotics crimes disproportionately hurt areas of lower socio-economic status, and what I find most troubling is that we continue to keep laws on the books that we do not enforce," he said. Democratic Rep. Tulsi Gabbard of Hawaii was the chief cosponsor of the bill.

Southside: Charlottesville, Danville

Population		**Race and Ethnicity**		**Income**	
Total	731,594	White	72.7%	Median Income	$48,713 (273 out of 435)
Land area	10,030	Black	20.1%		
Pop/ sq mi	72.9	Latino	3.4%		
Born in state	65.2%	Asian	1.5%	Under $50,000	50.9%
		Two races	2.0%	$50,000-$99,999	29.6%
Age Groups		Other	0.3%	$100,000-$199,999	15.6%
Under 18	20.5%			$200,000 or more	3.8%
18-34	21.5%	**Education**		Poverty Rate	15.3%
35-64	40.2%	H.S grad or less	46.5%		
Over 64	17.8%	Some college	27.6%	**Health Insurance**	
		College Degree, 4 yr	14.9%	With health insurance coverage	88.2%
Work		Post grad	11.1%		
White Collar	36.2%				
Sales and Service	40.1%	**Military**		**Public Assistance**	
Blue Collar	23.6%	Veteran	9.9%	Cash public assistance income	2.2%
Government	6.9%	Active Duty	0.1%		
				Food stamp/SNAP benefits	12.6%

Voter Turnout			
2015 Total Citizens 18+	564,423	2016 House Turnout as % CVAP	63%
2016 House turnout	356,756	2014 House Turnout as % CVAP	36%

2012 Presidential Vote		
Mitt Romney	188,485	(53%)
Barack Obama	164,555	(46%)

2016 Presidential Vote		
Donald Trump	195,190	(53%)
Hillary Clinton	154,665	(42%)
Gary Johnson	9,230	(3%)

Cook Partisan Voting Index: R+6

Southside Virginia is technically defined as the parts of the commonwealth east of the Blue Ridge, west of the Fall Line and south of the James River. But it really is a cultural designation: an outcropping of Deep South culture in the Old Dominion. The eastern counties are flat and humid - frontier in the late-colonial period, plantation country by 1800, and now peanut fields and pine forests. Along U.S. 58, which snakes across southern Virginia from Virginia Beach almost to the Cumberland Gap, are the vestiges of the state's Tobacco Road, including the Tobacco Farm Life Museum of Virginia in South Hill. Further west, into the Piedmont, the land gradually gets hillier. The largest metropolitan area in Southside is Danville, where the tobacco auction originated in 1858. Tobacco magnates later built "Millionaire's Row," one of the finest extant collections of Edwardian and Victorian architecture. Two of the most important battles for African-

American equality were won northeast of Danville. The first was at Appomattox Court House, the serene little hamlet where Robert E. Lee surrendered to his onetime subordinate Ulysses S. Grant. The second was in Prince Edward County, where one of the five cases consolidated into the landmark *Brown v. Board of Education* case arose.

Southside blends the old and the new. In 2015, Duke Energy agreed to pay $2.5 million to clean up a coal ash spill that coated with a gray sludge 70 miles of the Dan River, including parts of Danville. The residue was dumped in a nearby landfill. In November 2016, Microsoft announced the fifth expansion of its data center in Mecklenburg County, at a total cost of $2 billion. There is a D-Day memorial in Bedford, which lost more men per capita (23 of its 35 soldiers) in the Normandy invasion than any other town in the country.

The 5th District of Virginia covers most of Southside Virginia west of metro Richmond, spreading out to the Blue Ridge Mountains. This is the heart of the district; about two-thirds of its population lives south of the James River. The district includes overwhelmingly liberal Charlottesville, with Thomas Jefferson's University of Virginia, and surrounding Albemarle County, but their 20 percent of the vote has little impact in this district. An arm extends north to the western part of Fauquier County in the Washington, D.C., exurbs. Southside Virginia was long conservative and Democratic; it was the last part of Virginia to elect a Republican to Congress. In recent decades, the district has voted predominantly Republican. Democrats running statewide have energized the Charlottesville area and the African-American precincts, especially in Danville, which is 50 percent black. Donald Trump in 2016 won 53 percent of the vote, the same as Mitt Romney got four years earlier.

SIXTH DISTRICT

Bob Goodlatte (R)

Elected 1992, 13th term; b. Sep 22, 1952, Holyoke, MA; Bates College (ME), B.A.; Washington and Lee University School of Law (VA), J.D.; Christian Scientist; Married (Maryellen Flaherty Goodlatte); 2 children.

Professional Career: District Director, U.S. Rep. Caldwell Butler, 1977-1979; Practicing attorney, 1979-1992; Partner, Bird, Kinder & Huffman, 1981-1992.

DC Office: 2309 RHOB 20515, 202-225-5431, Fax: 202-225-9681, goodlatte.house.gov.

State Offices: Harrisonburg, 540-432-2391; Lynchburg, 434-845-8306; Roanoke, 540-857-2672; Staunton, 540-885-3861.

Committees: *Agriculture*: Commodity Exchanges, Energy & Credit, Livestock & Foreign Agriculture. *Judiciary (Chmn)*: Constitution & Civil Justice, Courts, Intellectual Property & Internet, Crime, Terrorism, Homeland Security & Investigations, Immigration & Border Security, Regulatory Reform, Commercial & Antitrust Law.

Group Ratings

	ADA	ACLU	AFL-CIO	LCV	ITI	COC	HAFA	ACU	CFG	FRC
2016	-	5%	-	0%	83%	93%	79%	96%	77%	100%
2015	0%	C	8%	0%	C	75%	C	100%	84%	100%

Almanac Ratings 2015

	Economy	Social	Foreign	Composite
Liberal	0%	4%	0%	1%
Conservative	100%	96%	100%	99%

Key Votes of the 114th Congress

1. Keystone Pipeline	Y	5. Puerto Rico Debt	N	9. Offenses by Aliens	Y
2. Trade Deals	Y	6. Medical Marijuana	N	10. Troops in Iraq	N
3. Export-Import Bank	N	7. Sanctuary Cities	Y	11. Homeland Security $$	N
4. Debt Ceiling Increase	N	8. Armor-piercing Bullets	Y	12. Trade Adjustment aid	N

Election Results

Election	Name (Party)	Vote (%)		Cand. Spent	Ind. Exp. Support	Ind. Exp. Oppose
2016 General	Bob Goodlatte (R)	225,471	(67%)	$1,788,477	$1,463	
	Kai Degner (D)	112,170	(33%)	$134,269		$702
2016 Primary	Bob Goodlatte (R)	19,810	(77%)			
	Harry Griego (R)	5,816	(23%)			

Prior winning percentages: 2014 (75%), 2012 (65%), 2010 (76%), 2008 (62%), 2006 (75%), 2004 (97%), 2002 (97%), 2000 (99%), 1998 (69%), 1996 (67%), 1994 (100%), 1992 (60%)

Bob Goodlatte, a Republican first elected in 1992, serves as chairman of the Judiciary Committee. He has found common ground with Democrats on technology and patent matters and some budget issues, though not on gun control, immigration and other hot-button social issues. Although he has not called attention to himself, he has not been shy to assert his views, including early collaboration with President Donald Trump on immigration.

Goodlatte grew up in Holyoke, Massachusetts, the son of a Friendly's ice cream store manager and a part-time retail clerk. He attended Bates College in Maine, where he was president of the College Republicans, and got his law degree at Washington and Lee University. He was an aide to Republican Rep. Caldwell Butler of Roanoke. Goodlatte practiced law in Roanoke and stayed active in politics. In 1992, when Democratic Rep. Jim Olin retired, Goodlatte was nominated by the Republican convention; he won his first elected office, 60%-40%.

Goodlatte has been conservative on most fiscal and social issues. His *Almanac* vote ratings for 2015 were nearly perfect conservative. He tiptoed into the "birther" controversy in 2009 by co-sponsoring a bill to require presidential candidates to make their birth certificates public - a reaction to a discredited theory that President Barack Obama is foreign-born, although the bill would not have applied to Obama. Goodlatte regularly introduced bills to abolish the tax code. He has sponsored measures to implement a constitutional balanced-budget amendment, which fell short of the two-thirds majority required for passage in 2011, and to stop the Environmental Protection Agency from setting the parameters for cleaning up Chesapeake Bay by regulating stormwater runoff. In recent years, Goodlatte's zeal for deficit reduction has made him more willing to break with his party to reduce defense spending.

Goodlatte got the Judiciary gavel in 2013, just as comprehensive immigration reform won bipartisan approval in the Senate. Goodlatte threw cold water on a central sticking point, whether to grant illegal immigrants a potential path to citizenship. "I don't think [it's] going to happen," he told National Public Radio. He said that so-called "dreamers" who were brought in illegally by their parents should get an "earned pathway to citizenship." When waves of migrants from Central America sparked a crisis at the U.S.-Mexico border in 2014, Goodlatte blasted Obama's request for $3.7 billion as a "slap in the face" and a "blank check" without any limits. He was incensed when Obama issued an executive order protecting some categories of illegal immigrants, saying that overturning it would be his top priority. "We cannot allow one man to nullify the law of the land with either a stroke of his pen or a phone call," he said after a federal judge prevented the order from taking effect in February 2015. When Trump was preparing his initial executive order to limit entry by immigrants, Goodlatte stirred controversy when he permitted his aides to assist in the technical drafting. He defended the executive order and said that the cooperation was common for congressional staffers.

He has been outspoken on other issues at Judiciary. On gun control, Goodlatte said in 2013 that a Democratic push for universal background checks is "not a very practical thing to do." In February 2017, he won House passage of a bill to reverse an Obama administration regulation that limited gun rights of individuals who were classified by the Social Security Administration as having a mental disorder. Goodlatte called the regulation a denial of constitutional rights and "a slap in the face for those in the disabled community," a position endorsed by the American Civil Liberties Union. Trump signed the repeal that month.

In 2015, Goodlatte won House passage of a bill that would ban most abortions after 20 weeks. The bill, which passed on a nearly party-line vote, had been slightly modified to respond to the concerns of some women in the Republican Conference who objected that the original version was too far-reaching. The Pain-Capable Unborn Child Protection Act died in the Senate. Goodlatte said that his position was in line with a growing consensus in public opinion, as well as a political talking point for conservatives. "Current medical research tells us that late-term abortions are cruel to unborn children and do not exist in the gray areas of morality," he said.

Goodlatte has a less partisan side. He co-chairs the bipartisan Congressional Internet Caucus and often has worked with its Democratic members. He also chaired the House Republican Technology Working Group. He was a vocal proponent of the bipartisan Stop Online Piracy Act (SOPA) aimed at cracking down on foreign-based websites offering pirated movies, music and other content. The bill received strong backing from movie studios and unions, both traditional Democratic allies, but ran into fierce opposition in 2012 from Internet giants such as Google and did not advance. He and Democratic Rep. Anna Eshoo of California pushed for a permanent ban on internet-access taxes. When he failed to achieve that goal, he helped to broker in 2007 an agreement for a four-year prohibition. "I don't think there is a single issue related to tech that isn't bipartisan," Goodlatte has said.

The House in 2013 approved his Innovation Act to fight abusive patent litigation. To combat so-called "patent trolls" seeking to hide behind shell companies, the bill required plaintiffs to disclose who is the owner of a patent before filing litigation. Goodlatte's Democratic counterpart in the Senate, Patrick Leahy of Vermont, refused to move it. Goodlatte won committee approval of his proposal in 2015, but House action was postponed after small inventors voiced opposition.

In 2015, Goodlatte was part of a wide-ranging bipartisan group that worked to revise and extend the Patriot Act, but with limits on the government's collection of phone metadata from telecommunications companies. He worked closely with Republican Jim Sensenbrenner of Wisconsin and Democrat John Conyers of Michigan, both former chairmen of the committee who had earlier helped to enact the measure, and with former Senate Judiciary Chairman Leahy. Their new USA Freedom Act contained the most sweeping reforms of government surveillance practices since the 1970s.

"The ceaseless effort to restrain the reach of government is in our DNA as Americans. And for 225 years, we have refused to accept the idea that in order to have national security, we must sacrifice our personal freedoms," Goodlatte and Sensenbrenner wrote in an op-ed for *The Hill* newspaper. "The USA Freedom Act lives up to these ideals, proving once again that we can protect both Americans' civil liberties and our national security without compromising either one." The libertarian approach by these two GOP old bulls was well-received by House Republicans, including party leaders, who had voiced growing concerns about Big Government.

On the Agriculture Committee, which he chaired from 2003 to 2007, Goodlatte worked closely with Democratic Chairman Collin Peterson of Minnesota to enact the 2008 farm bill, serving as the committee's informal liaison with the Bush White House. He helped to broker a compromise on country-of-origin labeling of meat in the bill. In 2008, he joined 50 other House Republicans in urging the Environmental Protection Agency to reduce ethanol production requirements.

Following the 2016 election, Goodlatte was a leading proponent of a proposed change in House rules that would have limited the autonomy of the Office of Congressional Ethics to review ethics complaints and make recommendations to the House Ethics Committee. He said that his proposal protected the due process rights for lawmakers under investigation, but did not jeopardize the authority of the OCE. Strong objections by Democrats, good-government groups and two negative tweets by Trump led Speaker Paul Ryan to remove the proposal from the customary opening-day rules package when the House convened in January 2017. Goodlatte criticized the "gross misrepresentation by opponents" of his proposal.

Goodlatte has been reelected without difficulty. He encountered no problem in 2002 when he abandoned his pledge to serve no more than 12 years. His support of SOPA prompted a primary challenge in 2012 from libertarian Karen Kwiatkowski, who lost 65%-35%. In 2016, he received an unusual primary challenge from Harry Griego, a retired Air Force pilot who had tea party support and said that voters "want a change." Goodlatte won, 78%-22%. In the general election, Democratic nominee Kai Degner accused Goodlatte of benefiting from an investment that his wife had made in a local company that was seeking to build a natural gas pipeline in the area. Degner added that Goodlatte, as Judiciary Committee chairman, had "a unique role in our dysfunctional, partisan, and out-of-touch Congress." Goodlatte was routinely reelected with 67 percent of the vote.

During the closing days of the 2016 presidential campaign, he publicly encouraged FBI Director James Comey to assure that voters were fully informed about the Bureau's investigation of Hillary Clinton's emails that were stored on a private server when she was Secretary of State. Comey's subsequent disclosure on election eve led to furious criticism by many Democrats.

Shenandoah Valley: Roanoke, Harrisonburg

Population		**Race and Ethnicity**		**Income**	
Total	740,643	White	80.6%	Median Income	$48,924 (270 out of 435)
Land area	5,930	Black	10.6%	Under $50,000	51.0%
Pop/ sq mi	124.9	Latino	4.7%	$50,000-$99,999	31.9%
Born in state	64.7%	Asian	1.8%	$100,000-$199,999	14.5%
		Two races	1.9%	$200,000 or more	2.6%
		Other	0.2%	Poverty Rate	15.4%
Age Groups		**Education**		**Health Insurance**	
Under 18	20.6%	H.S grad or less	46.9%	With health insurance coverage	88.1%
18-34	24.3%	Some college	26.9%	**Public Assistance**	
35-64	38.5%	College Degree, 4 yr	16.5%	Cash public assistance income	2.2%
Over 64	16.6%	Post grad	9.7%	Food stamp/SNAP benefits	11.2%
Work		**Military**			
White Collar	34.2%	Veteran	9.2%		
Sales and Service	42.7%	Active Duty	0.1%		
Blue Collar	23.2%				
Government	5.4%				

Voter Turnout			
2015 Total Citizens 18+	566,740	2016 House Turnout as % CVAP	60%
2016 House turnout	338,409	2014 House Turnout as % CVAP	32%

2012 Presidential Vote		
Mitt Romney	197,045	(59%)
Barack Obama	132,153	(39%)

2016 Presidential Vote		
Donald Trump	206,303	(59%)
Hillary Clinton	120,596	(35%)
Gary Johnson	10,801	(3%)

Cook Partisan Voting Index: R+13

The sturdy men and women who settled the Shenandoah Valley of Virginia west of the Blue Ridge were quite different from the "second sons" of the European aristocracy who cleared the marshy forests of the Tidewater and built grand plantations. Even before the Revolutionary War, Scots and Scots-Irish, German Protestants, and Mennonites and Moravians - members of religious communities and fiercely independent farmers - poured down the Great Wagon Road from Pennsylvania to the valley, planting farms and founding towns with names like Strasburg, Edinburg, Mount Jackson, and Glasgow. They were looking not for the flat, mahogany colored land that Eastern tobacco growers sought, but for land that could support wheat, corn and hay - crops that could be rotated and that an individual farmer and his family could handle. A young George Washington surveyed portions of the land; what are believed to be his carved initials are still visible on Natural Bridge in Rockbridge County.

The same independent spirit nurtured the growth of higher education here. In Lexington are Washington and Lee University, which Robert E. Lee headed, and the Virginia Military Institute, where Stonewall Jackson taught philosophy and artillery tactics and which did not admit women until required by the U.S. Supreme Court in 1996. Harrisonburg is the home of James Madison University. A trio of distinguished women's colleges is nearby: Mary Baldwin College in Staunton, Hollins University in Roanoke and Sweet Briar College in Sweet Briar, which has been revived after nearly shutting down in June 2015 because of financial woes. President Woodrow Wilson's birthplace is in Staunton.

Industry flourished here more than in most of Virginia east of the Blue Ridge. In the 19th century, the Norfolk and Western Railway established its chief junction at Roanoke, and as the years passed, the city became the headquarters of the railroad and many other companies. In 2015, the company, now Norfolk Southern, moved its corporate headquarters to Norfolk. The population of Roanoke has remained flat since the 1970s.

The 6th Congressional District of Virginia covers the heart of the Valley of Virginia, from Strasburg to Roanoke. It crosses over the Blue Ridge to take in Lynchburg, the home of Liberty University, the largest university in Virginia and a fundamentalist Baptist college where Sen. Ted Cruz in March 2015 launched his presidential campaign. In January 2016, university president Jerry Falwell Jr. announced his enthusiastic support for Donald Trump. In recent decades, the ancestral conservatism of the region and the feisty politics of the mountain rebels have melded into a single conservative Republicanism, more populist than elitist in tone, as concerned with moral values as with economic freedom, and prickly about interference from Washington and Richmond. Those roots here go deep: Many of these counties have shown Republican tendencies dating back more than 100 years. In 1952, the district's voters did something extremely rare at the time: They voted out an incumbent Southern Democrat in favor of a Republican. The GOP has held the seat ever since, save for an interlude in the 1980s. Donald Trump in 2016 won 59 percent of the vote, though Hillary Clinton took the cities of Roanoke, Harrisonburg and Lexington.

SEVENTH DISTRICT

Dave Brat (R)

Elected 2014, 2nd full term; b. Jul 27, 1964, Detroit, MI; Princeton Theological Seminary (NJ), M.Div.; American University (DC), Ph.D.; Hope College (MI), B.A.; Catholic; Married (Laura Sonderman); 2 children.

Professional Career: Consultant, Arthur Anderson, 1986-1988; Economic consultant, World Bank, 1993-1995; Faculty, Randolph-Macon College, 1996-present; VA Governor Board of Economic Advisors, 2006-2013.

DC Office: 1628 LHOB 20515, 202-225-2815, Fax: 202-225-0011, brat.house.gov.

State Offices: Glen Allen, 804-747-4073; Spotsylvania, 540-507-7216.

Committees: *Budget*. *Education & the Workforce*: Early Childhood, Elementary & Secondary Education, Workforce Protections. *Small Business*: Economic Growth, Tax & Capital Access (Chmn), Health & Technology.

Group Ratings

	ADA	ACLU	AFL-CIO	LCV	ITI	COC	HAFA	ACU	CFG	FRC
2016	-	11%	-	0%	50%	93%	94%	100%	96%	100%
2015	5%	C	8%	3%	C	55%	C	100%	97%	100%

Almanac Ratings 2015

	Economy	Social	Foreign	Composite
Liberal	10%	4%	1%	5%
Conservative	90%	96%	99%	95%

Key Votes of the 114th Congress

1. Keystone Pipeline	Y	5. Puerto Rico Debt	N	9. Offenses by Aliens	Y
2. Trade Deals	N	6. Medical Marijuana	N	10. Troops in Iraq	N
3. Export-Import Bank	N	7. Sanctuary Cities	Y	11. Homeland Security $$	N
4. Debt Ceiling Increase	N	8. Armor-piercing Bullets	Y	12. Trade Adjustment aid	N

Election Results

Election	Name (Party)	Vote (%)	Cand. Spent	Ind. Exp. Support	Ind. Exp. Oppose
2016 General	Dave Brat (R)	218,057 (58%)	$1,128,778	$58,532	
	Eileen Bedell (D)	160,159 (42%)	$243,516		

Prior winning percentages: 2014 (61%), 2014 special (62%)

Republican Dave Brat was elected in 2014 in one of the biggest political shocks in that cycle - and arguably in years - with his primary defeat of House Majority Leader Eric Cantor. An obscure college professor, Brat tapped into voters' anti-Washington mood to topple the House's No. 2 Republican. Brat became a leader of the Freedom Caucus, a group of conservative Republicans who made themselves a nuisance to GOP leaders.

Brat was an unlikely tea party hero. Born and raised in Dearborn, Michigan, he studied business and religion before completing a Ph.D. in economics at American University. He taught economics at Randolph-Macon College, focusing on the ethics of capitalism. Apart from a failed run in 2011 for the state House of Delegates, he stayed out of politics and led the quiet life of an academic.

But Brat's political timing was impeccable. After the 2011 redistricting, the 7th became more conservative and rural, dropping parts of Richmond and taking in more of New Kent County. Cantor had thought that would shore up his reelection, but in fact it brought in more blue-collar voters amenable to the tea party message rather than white-collar professionals who had made up his base. Also changing the dynamics, Cantor's leadership duties and fundraising increasingly kept him away from the retail politics that his constituents expected. The race ultimately turned on the issue of immigration. Although the House GOP refused to take up a bipartisan bill that the Senate passed in 2013, Cantor staked out a position to the left of many in his party when he proposed limited legal immigration status for children of undocumented workers who were brought into the United States as minors. Conservatives saw that as a bridge too far, and Brat picked up on their anger.

As the primary campaign progressed, Cantor committed several unforced errors. He used much of his huge cash advantage to launch a negative ad campaign that increased Brat's name recognition rather than hurting him. Cantor also took comfort from the only two polls issued, both of which happened to be favorable. Although Brat got little formal support from the tea party movement, which largely saw his campaign as hopeless, he benefited from a powerful local grass-roots conservative movement, abetted by a rallying cry from conservative media personalities such as Laura Ingraham and Mark Levin. Cantor spent $6 million through the primary, some of which went for leadership activities not related to his district; Brat spent $392,000 on the primary.

In June, Brat defeated Cantor by a stunning 56%-44%. The first House party leader to lose a primary, Cantor soon resigned his seat to join an investment bank. Former Rep. Tom Davis, a Republican from Virginia, wrote in a book, *The Partisan Divide*, "Cantor was defeated because he was viewed as too soft on Obama, too willing to compromise, and too eager to abandon conservative principles by a constituency (particularly the primary voting universe) that wanted the opposite."

In the January 2015 vote for House Speaker, Brat voted for Republican Rep. Jeff Duncan of South Carolina, one of 24 Republicans who voted against another term for John Boehner. He continued his anti-leadership actions later that year when he initially opposed Majority Leader Kevin McCarthy to replace Boehner, who had resigned, then was one of nine Republicans who voted for Republican Rep. Daniel Webster of Florida rather than Paul Ryan, who had been selected by the House Republican Conference. Brat often went his own way on legislation. In March 2017, he was one of three Republicans on the House Budget Committee who voted against the GOP leadership's plan to revise the Affordable Care Act.

At home, he faced a competitive challenge for reelection from political newcomer Eileen Bedell, an attorney in Richmond. She attacked Brat for having "embraced Trump" and accomplished little in Congress, and she discussed the need to address the "financial problem" of Social Security and Medicare. Brat raised $1.3 million and continued to receive tea party support. Bedell had $228,000, though she got little attention from national Democrats. Brat won 58%-42%, but took only 50.6 percent in Henrico and 54 percent in Chesterfield. Following the election, Brat became the target of anti-Trump protesters, and he wasn't happy about it. In January, a video from his district showed him complaining, "the women are in my grill, no matter where I go."

During the campaign, Brat said that he might run to replace Sen. Tim Kaine if he was elected vice president. But he later showed no interest in challenging Kaine directly.

Central Virginia: Richmond Suburbs

Demographics data for new House districts were not prepared by the Census Bureau prior to our editorial deadline.

Voter Turnout			
2016 House Turnout as % CVAP	N/A	2016 House turnout	379,163

2012 Presidential Vote information unavailable due to recent redistricting.

2016 Presidential Vote		
Donald Trump	198,032	(50%)
Hillary Clinton	172,544	(44%)
Gary Johnson	14,206	(4%)

Cook Partisan Voting Index: R+6

Richmond, the centrally located capital of Virginia, still sets the tone for the Commonwealth. It is home to many of the state's great institutions - Dominion Resources, Main Street banks, big law firms and the *Richmond Times-Dispatch*. Its metro area, now the third-largest in the commonwealth, has grown far past its city borders, covering most of suburban Henrico and Chesterfield counties and spreading into what was, until recently, countryside. As the area has grown, its tone has shifted.

The 7th Congressional District of Virginia sprawls across 120 miles from southwest of Richmond to the outer reaches of the Washington, D.C., exurbs, though it is centered in Henrico and Chesterfield Counties. Each county is about 30 percent of the population. Surrounding much of Richmond, Henrico was once a linchpin of the state Republican coalition - it gave GOP nominee Barry Goldwater 70 percent of the vote in 1964. But demographic change, especially in the eastern portion of the county, and the movement of suburbanites toward the Democrats in the past two decades have changed its makeup. In 2008, Barack Obama became the first Democrat to carry Henrico since Franklin Roosevelt. In 2016, Hillary Clinton increased the Democratic vote in Henrico to 58 percent. Henrico's Republican-leaning areas - the upscale Tuckahoe and Glen Allen and the fast-growing Short Pump area - are in the 7th District. To the south of Richmond, Chesterfield County has been exurban and largely Republican. With rapid population growth, Chesterfield has become more competitive. Donald Trump won the county, 48%-46%, a marked tightening from Bob Dole's 60%-32% lead over Bill Clinton in 1996.

The outlying parts of the district are rural and heavily Republican. For Washingtonians willing to endure a long commute or simply wanting to get away from the metro area, Spotsylvania and Culpeper counties have become popular destinations in the Washington exurbs; each grew by nearly 50 percent from 2000 to 2016. The redistricting in 2016 added areas west of Richmond that had been in the old 4th District, and in exchange removed New Hanover and Kent counties north and east of Richmond to the 1st District. That switch resulted in a slight increase in the Democratic vote. The demographic and redistricting shifts have made this a more competitive area. George W. Bush twice took the District with 61 percent of the vote. Donald Trump won, 50%-44%.

EIGHTH DISTRICT

Don Beyer (D)

Elected 2014, 2nd term; b. Jun 20, 1950, Trieste, Italy; Williams College, B.A.; Episcopalian; Married (Megan Carroll); 4 children; 2 grandchildren.

Elected Office: VA Lt. Governor, 1990-1998.

Professional Career: Automobile dealer; Chairman, Jobs for VA Graduates, 1999-2013; U.S. Ambassador to Switzerland and Liechtenstein, 2009-2013.

DC Office: 1119 LHOB 20515, 202-225-4376, Fax: 202-225-0017, beyer.house.gov.

State Offices: Alexandria, 703-658-5403.

Committees: *Joint Economic*. *Natural Resources*: Energy & Mineral Resources, Water, Power & Oceans. *Science, Space & Technology*: Oversight (RMM), Research & Technology, Space.

Group Ratings

	ADA	ACLU	AFL-CIO	LCV	ITI	COC	HAFA	ACU	CFG	FRC
2016	-	100%	-	100%	83%	57%	12%	0%	11%	0%
2015	80%	C	83%	97%	C	55%	C	4%	0%	0%

Almanac Ratings 2015

	Economy	Social	Foreign	Composite
Liberal	88%	100%	99%	96%
Conservative	12%	0%	1%	4%

Key Votes of the 114th Congress

1. Keystone Pipeline	N	5. Puerto Rico Debt	Y	9. Offenses by Aliens	N
2. Trade Deals	Y	6. Medical Marijuana	Y	10. Troops in Iraq	Y
3. Export-Import Bank	Y	7. Sanctuary Cities	N	11. Homeland Security $$	Y
4. Debt Ceiling Increase	Y	8. Armor-piercing Bullets	N	12. Trade Adjustment aid	Y

Election Results

Election	Name (Party)	Vote (%)	Cand. Spent	Ind. Exp. Support	Ind. Exp. Oppose
2016 General	Don Beyer (D)	246,653 (68%)	$960,241	$1,069	
	Charles Hernick (R)	98,387 (27%)	$73,228		
	Julio Gracia (I)	14,664 (4%)			

Prior winning percentages: 2014 (63%)

Democrat Don Beyer easily won election in 2014 in this district, which covers the wealthy and heavily Democratic Northern Virginia suburbs, giving him the shortest commute to his district and home of any member - around "18 minutes," he says. Although he has a long record as a successful businessman and public official, he faced an adjustment to service in the minority party. He sought opportunities for bipartisanship, though he made few headlines.

Beyer was born in Trieste, Italy, where his father was serving as an Army officer, grew up in Washington, went to Gonzaga High School in the shadow of the Capitol, and got his bachelor's degree from Williams College. American politics is rich in examples of second and third chances, and Beyer is no exception. He built a reputation as an affable deal-maker who could work with both sides of the aisle when he served two terms as Virginia's lieutenant governor, starting in 1990. But in 1997, when he sought the prize of the governorship, he floundered in his campaign against Republican James Gilmore III, stumbling in particular over the issue of the state's contested car tax. When he lost by 10 percentage points, many Virginians thought it would mark the end of Beyer's political career.

Beyer turned toward building his family's car-dealership business, which features Volvos, but he found he couldn't stay away from politics for good. In 2004, he served as campaign treasurer for Howard Dean's presidential campaign, and in 2008 he helped raise substantial sums for the Obama campaign. He led the new administration's transition planning at the Commerce Department and was rewarded with a plum ambassadorship to Switzerland and Liechtenstein, which he held for four years.

When 12-term Democratic Rep. Jim Moran announced his retirement, Beyer promptly launched his bid and tapped his extensive network of high-level Democratic contacts. His name recognition and his connections proved to be an advantage in a crowded primary race that drew six other Democrats. Of the $2.7 million that he spent, $415,000 was self-financed. He stood out in candidate forums by demonstrating a strong grasp of both foreign and domestic policy. In the June primary, he topped the field with 46 percent of the vote, followed by state Del. Patrick Hope at 18 percent.

On the Science, Space and Technology Committee, Beyer has been the ranking Democrat on the Oversight Subcommittee. He worked with Republicans on cybersecurity issues, including at the Office of Personnel Management and in the banking industry. The House passed his Science Prize Competition Act, which encourages federal agencies to use prize competitions as incentives for innovative scientific research and development. Beyer said he identified with the more than 70,000 federal employees in his district: Three of his four grandparents were federal employees. To the dismay of labor unions that had supported him, he was an enthusiastic backer in 2015 of President Barack Obama's request for trade promotion authority and the prospective trans-Pacific trade deal. Union threats to challenge his reelection proved empty in this upscale district. With the election of President Donald Trump, Beyer said that his job was "to play careful defense" on behalf of federal employees. In November 2016, he won enactment of his bill for the outdoor recreation economy to be counted as part of the nation's gross domestic product.

Beyer brought his international experience to the job. He praised Obama's nuclear-arms agreement with Iran, and took a bit of credit. As ambassador to Switzerland, he recounted, he hosted the initial discussions with Iran that launched the broader negotiations. Following the election, he sought unsuccessfully to delay the vote of the Electoral College until the electors had an intelligence briefing on Russian influence during the election. In March 2017, as co-chairman of the Safe Climate Caucus, he urged the Trump administration to comply with international climate-control agreements.

Northern Virginia: Fairfax, Arlington, Alexandria

Population		**Race and Ethnicity**		**Income**	
Total	772,740	White	52.5%	Median Income	$98,851 (8 out of 435)
Land area	149	Black	13.4%		
Pop/ sq mi	5177.8	Latino	19.1%	Under $50,000	22.6%
Born in state	23.6%	Asian	11.4%	$50,000-$99,999	27.9%
		Two races	3.0%	$100,000-$199,999	32.7%
Age Groups		Other	0.6%	$200,000 or more	16.8%
Under 18	20.8%			Poverty Rate	8.0%
18-34	28.5%	**Education**			
35-64	40.8%	H.S grad or less	22.3%	**Health Insurance**	
Over 64	9.9%	Some college	17.1%	With health insurance coverage	87.1%
		College Degree, 4 yr	29.9%		
Work		Post grad	30.7%	**Public Assistance**	
White Collar	57.1%				
Sales and Service	32.7%	**Military**		Cash public assistance income	1.0%
Blue Collar	10.2%	Veteran	8.4%		
Government	4.9%	Active Duty	1.8%	Food stamp/SNAP benefits	4.7%

Voter Turnout			
2015 Total Citizens 18+	500,843	2016 House Turnout as % CVAP	72%
2016 House turnout	360,676	2014 House Turnout as % CVAP	40%

2012 Presidential Vote		
Barack Obama	243,746	(68%)
Mitt Romney	111,518	(31%)

2016 Presidential Vote		
Hillary Clinton	270,415	(72%)
Donald Trump	76,854	(21%)
Gary Johnson	10,396	(3%)
Evan McMullin	7,334	(2%)

Cook Partisan Voting Index: D+21

When George Washington strolled the brick sidewalks of Alexandria on his way to market or church or Gadsby's Tavern (where he celebrated his final two birthdays), it was the largest city in Northern Virginia, and larger than Georgetown just up the Potomac River. The areas that are now Capitol Hill and downtown Washington, D.C., were hills above the river's mud flats. But Washington became the national capital, and as it grew, Northern Virginia seemed left behind. In 1846, the District of Columbia retroceded its land south of the Potomac - now Alexandria and Arlington - to Virginia because it seemed then that the federal government would never need it. It would be another 97 years before the first federal building was constructed on the Virginia side - the Pentagon. When that occurred, Alexandria and the rural countryside of Northern Virginia were represented in Congress by Judge Howard W. Smith, for many years the influential chairman of the House Rules Committee, a Democrat who saw as his mission the maintenance of the standards of George Washington, Thomas Jefferson and Robert E. Lee, including on racial segregation. Yet by the 1950s, the area was changing around him.

New subdivision dwellers with white-collar jobs wanted schools with good academic programs, not the segregated schoolhouses Judge Smith's friends were willing to finance. The new generation wanted freeways, parks and recreation facilities. Today, the onetime suburbs of Arlington and Alexandria are "edge cities," with far more liberal policies. In 2014, Arlington County led the nation with the greatest share of its people who have college degrees (72 percent) and graduate degrees (37 percent). Cranes dot its cityscape, as giant office and housing developments have sprung up from rail yards in Crystal City and from used car lots upriver in Rosslyn. Commuters find roads jammed: Washington suffers from some of the worst traffic congestion in the country, plus nagging slowdowns with its Metrorail system. In 2016, the Army negotiated with Arlington County on expansion of Arlington National Cemetery.

The 8th Congressional District of Virginia consists of Arlington County and the cities of Alexandria and Falls Church, where slightly more than half its population resides. The district covers all of Virginia that is inside the Capital Beltway except for small pockets in Annandale and McLean. The balance lives in Fairfax County, either in precincts near the perimeter of Arlington/Falls Church/Alexandria or in areas south of the Beltway. The district also takes in George Washington's Mount Vernon estate and the more rural areas around Fort Belvoir. Plans by Alexandria to remove a Confederate monument in the center of town have been rejected by state legislators. The district is solidly Democratic. The 72 percent of the vote in 2016 for Hillary Clinton was an increase over the 68 percent that Barack Obama twice received. This is the most Democratic district in Virginia.

NINTH DISTRICT

Morgan Griffith (R)

Elected 2010, 4th term; b. Mar 15, 1958, Philadelphia, PA; Emory and Henry College (VA), B.A., 1980; Washington and Lee University School of Law (VA), J.D., 1983; Episcopalian; Married (Hilary Davis); 3 children.

Elected Office: VA House, 1994-2010, MajorityLeader, 2000-2010.

Professional Career: Practicing attorney, 2008-2010.

DC Office: 2202 RHOB 20515, 202-225-3861, Fax: 202-225-0076, morgangriffith.house.gov.

State Offices: Abingdon, 276-525-1405; Christiansburg, 540-381-5671.

Committees: *Energy & Commerce*: Energy, Health, Oversight & Investigations.

Group Ratings

	ADA	ACLU	AFL-CIO	LCV	ITI	COC	HAFA	ACU	CFG	FRC
2016	-	29%	-	0%	67%	86%	70%	92%	78%	100%
2015	15%	C	29%	9%	C	70%	C	75%	55%	100%

Almanac Ratings 2015

	Economy	Social	Foreign	Composite
Liberal	18%	9%	26%	18%
Conservative	82%	91%	74%	82%

Key Votes of the 114th Congress

1. Keystone Pipeline	Y	5. Puerto Rico Debt	Y	9. Offenses by Aliens	Y
2. Trade Deals	N	6. Medical Marijuana	N	10. Troops in Iraq	Y
3. Export-Import Bank	N	7. Sanctuary Cities	Y	11. Homeland Security $$	N
4. Debt Ceiling Increase	N	8. Armor-piercing Bullets	Y	12. Trade Adjustment aid	Y

Election Results

Election	Name (Party)	Vote (%)	Cand. Spent	Ind. Exp. Support	Ind. Exp. Oppose
2016 General	Morgan Griffith (R)	212,838 (69%)	$567,260	$702	
	Derek Kitts (D)	87,877 (28%)	$96,337		$702
	Janice Boyd (I)	9,050 (3%)			

Prior winning percentages: 2014 (72%), 2012 (61%), 2010 (51%)

Republican Morgan Griffith, a former Virginia House majority leader, uses his Energy and Commerce Committee seat to protect his region's coal industry, inveigh against the Environmental Protection Agency and cut back federal regulation. Following his election in 2010, he has quickly become entrenched in a district that his predecessor, Democrat Rick Boucher, had held for 28 years. He has shown his insider skills and occasional independence.

Griffith was born in Philadelphia and moved to Salem as a child. He was president of his high school student body and an avid swimmer. He attended Emory & Henry College, in part because it had just completed a new pool. He graduated in 1980 and received a law degree three years later from Washington and Lee University. Griffith opened a private practice in Salem and joined a statewide firm in 2008. After winning a seat in the state House of Delegates in 1994, Griffith pursued conservative efforts to repeal restrictions on gun ownership, limit abortion rights, and block a $1.4 billion tax increase. In 2000, he became the first Republican in Virginia to serve as the House majority leader and earned a reputation as a skilled parliamentarian. Griffith sometimes bucked his party, as when he helped draft a bill in 2010 to legalize marijuana for medicinal use.

In the House race, Griffith easily won the Republican nomination, but he was at a significant financial disadvantage in the general election, outspent by Boucher 3-to-1. Boucher, though he sought a middle ground, had been a leader at the Energy and Commerce Committee on the party's cap-and-trade bill aimed at limiting greenhouse gas emissions, which passed the House in 2009. The bill was unpopular in Appalachia's coal country, and Griffith made Boucher's work on the bill a centerpiece of his campaign. He argued that the measure would have killed jobs and raised electricity costs. Boucher framed his support for the bill as a way to ensure that Congress - and not conservatives' nemesis, the EPA - had power over carbon emissions. Griffith ran an ad with a video clip of President Barack Obama saying, "I love Rick Boucher." Boucher attacked Griffith as a carpetbagger who lived outside the district, running a television ad that said, "Morgan Griffith: He's not from here ... and it shows." Griffith was bolstered by nearly $2 million in spending by national party and conservative groups. As Republicans swept across the country, especially in rural areas, Griffith won 51%-46%.

In the House, Griffith has mostly been a loyal Republican, though less of an ideologue than many of his GOP classmates. The *Almanac* vote ratings for 2015 placed him precisely at the center of the House. On foreign policy issues, he was among the most liberal Republicans.

He followed Boucher with a plum seat on Energy and Commerce and steered a bill through the House in 2011 that sought to limit the EPA's power to regulate boilers. He and West Virginia Republican David McKinley complained in a 2013 op-ed about "the destructive consequences of this administration's regulatory assault" on the coal industry. He also contended that EPA regulations treated dairy milk spills the same as oil spills, an assertion that the fact-checking site *PolitiFact* labeled false. When Appalachian Power in June 2015 shut down two coal-fired power plants in Virginia and three in West Virginia in response to an EPA mandate of stricter emissions standards, Griffith said the agency was threatening the stability of the electrical grid. He added that Virginia Gov. Terry McAuliffe had joined the "war on coal," which was jeopardizing the economy of Southwest Virginia. Griffith took the lead in seeking to reverse "stream protection" regulations imposed by the Obama administration, which were designed to prevent coal debris from being dumped into nearby waters. In February 2017, he praised President Donald Trump for signing a bill to overturn the new rules and "bring relief" to coal miners.

On other issues at Energy and Commerce, Griffith filed with Democratic Rep. Joyce Beatty of Ohio the Furthering Access to Stroke Telemedicine (FAST) Act, to expand Medicare coverage of health technology in rural areas. During debate on proposals to repeal the Affordable Care Act, he sought to protect benefits for coal miners suffering from black lung disease. He urged that expansion of broadband services be included in any legislation to pay for additional infrastructure.

Democrats have not seriously challenged Griffith for reelection. In 2016, Democratic nominee Derek Kitts had served with the Army in Iraq and Afghanistan. He called for changes in the Affordable Care Act and for protection of Second Amendment rights, and said that the incumbent "doesn't represent who we are." Griffith won, 69%-28%, reinforcing the political transformation of rural America.

In supporting the reelection of Speaker John Boehner in 2015, Griffith issued a lengthy statement that no viable candidate had circulated plans or sought his support prior to the vote and that he would have given serious consideration to such a contender "due to my frustrations with the leadership style of John Boehner." He seemed comfortable with Boehner's successor, Paul Ryan.

Southwest Virginia: Blacksburg, Bristol

Population		**Race and Ethnicity**		**Income**	
Total	721,066	White	89.7%	Median Income	$39,759 (399 out of 435)
Land area	9,114	Black	5.4%	Under $50,000	59.8%
Pop/ sq mi	79.1	Latino	2.2%	$50,000-$99,999	27.7%
Born in state	65.8%	Asian	1.3%	$100,000-$199,999	10.3%
		Two races	1.2%	$200,000 or more	2.1%
		Other	0.3%	Poverty Rate	19.0%
Age Groups		**Education**		**Health Insurance**	
Under 18	19.0%	H.S grad or less	51.9%	With health insurance coverage	88.1%
18-34	23.0%	Some college	28.8%		
35-64	39.9%	College Degree, 4 yr	11.8%		
Over 64	18.1%	Post grad	7.6%		
Work		**Military**		**Public Assistance**	
White Collar	32.1%	Veteran	8.4%	Cash public assistance income	3.0%
Sales and Service	41.3%	Active Duty	0.1%	Food stamp/SNAP benefits	15.5%
Blue Collar	26.6%				
Government	5.2%				

Voter Turnout			
2015 Total Citizens 18+	572,209	2016 House Turnout as % CVAP	54%
2016 House turnout	310,314	2014 House Turnout as % CVAP	28%

2012 Presidential Vote		
Mitt Romney	196,354	(63%)
Barack Obama	108,641	(35%)

2016 Presidential Vote		
Donald Trump	217,837	(68%)
Hillary Clinton	86,463	(27%)
Gary Johnson	7,481	(2%)

Cook Partisan Voting Index: R+19

As early as 1765, settlements were carved out of the great Valley of Virginia, bending westward and south toward Tennessee and the Cumberland Gap. Most of these founders were of Scots-Irish lineage, and they moved to a mountainous area that developed almost apart from the rest of Virginia. The fiercely independent settlers eventually spilled over the ridges that bound the valley to the west and into the heart of the Appalachian Mountains. Here, they followed the same political and economic development patterns as those in West Virginia, which wasn't a separate state until 1863. They were first farmers and later coal miners. Politically, this virtually all-white area opposed slavery and was skeptical, if not hostile, to the Confederacy. It is a long way from here to plantation country - the state's extreme southwest corner is closer to nine other state capitals than to Richmond. Out of the crucible of struggle between secessionists and unionists, Southwest Virginia developed a robust two-party politics after the Civil War, sooner than in the rest of the state.

In recent decades, as development has moved down Interstate 81, the region has become more like the rest of Virginia. With encouragement from state officials, businesses have created jobs at high-tech companies and telephone call centers. Agriculture has been thriving, especially produce and dairy, while the role of coal mining has diminished. Coal has not entirely disappeared, either economically or socially. *Big Stone Gap*, a movie that was shot in the coal-mining town with the same name in the southwest corner of the state and stars Ashley Judd seeking love and herself, opened in October 2015, with local festivities and a celebration of its 1970s culture. During the 2016 campaign, both presidential candidates promised - in separate ways - to revive Coal Country. Even with Sen. Tim Kaine of Virginia as her running mate, Hillary Clinton fell short. In September 2016, Donald Trump had a huge campaign rally in Roanoke.

The 9th Congressional District covers all of Southwest Virginia west of Roanoke; the city and most of Roanoke County are in the 6th District. Over the years, it became known as the "Fighting Ninth" because of its taste for raucous politics, which by and large were culturally conservative and economically populist. This is NASCAR country; Martinsville's speedway is here, and Bristol's is just across the Tennessee line. Blacksburg, with a population of 44,000 plus the 31,000 students at Virginia Tech University, is the largest city in the area. The university features a 300 acre "automation park" for testing drones and self-driving cars. Buchanan County, in the far western part of the district, shows how the political winds have shifted. It gave Bill Clinton 63 percent of the vote in both 1992 and 1996, but the Democrats' vote share dropped precipitously in each succeeding election. In 2016, Donald Trump took Buchanan by a stunning 79%-19%. As Democratic support collapsed, this has become the most Republican district in the state. Trump won 68%-27% in 2016.

TENTH DISTRICT

Barbara Comstock (R)

Elected 2014, 2nd term; b. Jun 30, 1959, Springfield, MA; Middlebury College (VT), B.A., 1981; Georgetown University Law Center (DC), J.D., 1986; Roman Catholic; Married (Elwyn (Chip) Charles Comstock); 3 children; 2 grandchildren.

Elected Office: VA House, 2010-2015.

Professional Career: Practicing attorney; Staffer, U.S. Rep. Frank Wolf, 1991-1995; Staff, U.S. House Oversight & Gov't Reform Committee, 1995-1999; Director, U.S. Department of Justice Office of Public Affairs, 2002-2003; Sr. partner & principal, Blank Rome LLP & Blank Rome Gov't Relations LLC, 2003-2006; Founding partner, Corallo Comstock; Founding partner, Comstock Strategies, present.

DC Office: 229 CHOB 20515, 202-225-5136, Fax: 202-225-0437, comstock.house.gov.
State Offices: Sterling, 703-404-6903; Winchester, 540-773-3600.

Committees: *Commission Congressional Mailing Standards. House Administration. Joint Economic. Science, Space & Technology*: Research & Technology (Chmn), Space. *Transportation & Infrastructure*: Aviation, Economic Dev't, Public Buildings & Emergency Management, Highways & Transit.

Group Ratings

	ADA	ACLU	AFL-CIO	LCV	ITI	COC	HAFA	ACU	CFG	FRC
2016	-	5%	-	3%	100%	100%	47%	76%	66%	92%
2015	0%	C	25%	3%	C	100%	C	50%	47%	91%

Almanac Ratings 2015

	Economy	Social	Foreign	Composite
Liberal	15%	13%	10%	13%
Conservative	85%	87%	90%	87%

Key Votes of the 114th Congress

1. Keystone Pipeline	Y	5. Puerto Rico Debt	Y	9. Offenses by Aliens	Y
2. Trade Deals	Y	6. Medical Marijuana	N	10. Troops in Iraq	N
3. Export-Import Bank	N	7. Sanctuary Cities	Y	11. Homeland Security $$	Y
4. Debt Ceiling Increase	Y	8. Armor-piercing Bullets	Y	12. Trade Adjustment aid	Y

Election Results

Election	Name (Party)	Vote (%)		Cand. Spent	Ind. Exp. Support	Ind. Exp. Oppose
2016 General	Barbara Comstock (R)	210,791	(53%)	$5,238,246	$299,863	$5,509,279
	LuAnn Bennett (D)	187,712	(47%)	$2,675,924	$2,977,098	$8,804,447

Prior winning percentages: 2014 (57%)

Republican Barbara Comstock, elected in 2014, took her seat with lengthy political experience. Initially, she had an easier time than expected in a contest that both parties had viewed as a toss-up in this wealthy Northern Virginia district. Then, the local unpopularity of Donald Trump proved a formidable test for Comstock and resulted in a costly reelection campaign. Her survival may have been aided by her disavowal of Trump in the closing weeks of her campaign. She has drawn continued attention as a possible statewide candidate.

Comstock was born in Springfield, Massachusetts, and was an intern for the late Democratic Sen. Edward Kennedy. After getting her bachelor's from Middlebury College and her law degree from Georgetown University, Comstock went into private practice as an attorney. She spent four years on the staff of GOP Rep. Frank Wolf, whom she would later succeed, and then spent another four years as chief investigative counsel and senior counsel for the House Oversight and Government Reform Committee.

Comstock became a valuable strategic and legal operative for Republicans, including opposition research on Vice President Al Gore for George W. Bush's 2000 presidential campaign. She was director of public affairs at the Justice Department, and returned to the private sector to help the legal defense of former House Majority Leader Tom DeLay and Scooter Libby, the former aide to Vice President Dick Cheney. Comstock worked as a lobbyist for the Motion Picture Association of America, was a consultant for the Mitt Romney campaign in 2012 and for the Workplace Fairness Institute, which opposes the Democratic-supported effort by organized labor to ban private ballots for union elections.

Comstock was elected to Virginia's House of Delegates in 2009, ousting a Democratic incumbent. When Wolf announced he would retire after 34 years, Comstock ran, as many had long expected. In a January "firehouse primary" - which gave the nominee a head start on general-election campaigning - Comstock won in a crowded field with 54 percent of the vote. Democrats believed that they could use Comstock's votes in Richmond against transportation funding and for anti-abortion legislation against her. Democrat John Foust attacked her as a creature of Washington and for failing to disclose the Workplace Fairness Institute as a client. The Comstock campaign called it an oversight, which it corrected. Foust made a critical error when he put down his opponent to a campaign audience, "I don't think that she has even had a real job." The comment was obviously inaccurate. Comstock called it "offensive and demeaning." It seemed to deflate Foust's campaign and the Democrats' "war on women" rhetoric. Later, Foust told an interviewer that he had misspoke, and that he had intended to say that the jobs were hyper-partisan. In October, the Democratic Congressional Campaign Committee pulled its ads from the contest. Comstock outspent Foust, $3.4 million to $3 million, and had another $4 million spent on her behalf. She won easily 57%-40%, and she took all five counties by comfortable margins.

On the Science, Space and Technology Committee, Comstock chaired the Research and Technology Subcommittee. With the many technology firms and entrepreneurs in her district, she viewed the assignment as an opportunity to address "innovation issues that can revolutionize our education, economy, health care, and national security." She enacted a bill that directed NASA to encourage women to pursue careers in science, mathematics and engineering. Much as her predecessor Wolf had done, Comstock calibrated some of her House votes to appeal to moderates and government workers. In 2015, she voted against the House Republican budget because she said that its employee benefit changes were unfair to federal employees. With her local focus, she filed a bill to rewrite the complex charter of the struggling Metro transit agency. She criticized GOP appropriators for their $75 million cut in transit funds for Metro.

Comstock faced a more competitive challenger in 2016 than she and other Republicans had expected. LuAnn Bennett, the Democratic nominee, was a local real estate agent with no campaign experience. She was known among local Democrats as the ex-wife of former Rep. Jim Moran in the 8th District. Bennett emphasized that Comstock's views were similar to those of Trump, and tried to force the incumbent to take sides on her party's nominee. Some Republicans charged that Bennett's chief residence was in the District of Columbia. Comstock raised $5.3 million to $2.8 million for Bennett. The two candidates roughly split more than $16 million in support from the national parties and their allies.

For much of her campaign, Comstock maintained an awkward silence on Donald Trump - limiting her contacts with the news media and refusing to offer her views. Early in 2016, she donated to charity a $3,000 contribution that Trump had made to her campaign in 2014, noting that he was not a good role model and "doesn't represent" the Republican Party. In early October, following the release of the Access Hollywood video in which Trump made lewd comments about groping women, Comstock said that Trump's remarks were "disgusting, vile and disqualifying," and said that he "should step aside and allow our party to replace him with Mike Pence or another appropriate nominee." Two weeks before the election, David Wasserman of the Cook Political Report wrote that Comstock's opponent "may be less … Bennett and more Donald Trump." A crucial development may have been the first-time endorsement of Comstock by *The Washington Post*, which praised her for "steps to temper her hard-right conservatism" and for her "withering assessment" of Trump - a bipartisanship that, the *Post* wrote, would be "invaluable" after the election.

Comstock won, 52%-46%. The vote in Loudoun was virtually a tie and Comstock won Fairfax narrowly. More than two-thirds of her 23,000-vote victory margin came in Frederick County, which cast 10 percent of the vote. Although Comstock made no moves for a statewide office, such a campaign might be no more difficult than biennial contests in her district, where she seemed certain to remain a Democratic target.

Northern Virginia: Loudoun and Fairfax Counties

Population		**Race and Ethnicity**		**Income**	
Total	782,678	White	63.7%	Median Income	$1,14,566 (1 out of 435)
Land area	1,372	Black	6.7%		
Pop/ sq mi	570.4	Latino	12.7%	Under $50,000	19.3%
Born in state	36.1%	Asian	13.1%	$50,000-$99,999	23.4%
		Two races	3.3%	$100,000-$199,999	35.4%
Age Groups		Other	0.6%	$200,000 or more	21.9%
Under 18	27.4%			Poverty Rate	5.2%
18-34	19.3%	**Education**			
35-64	43.0%	H.S grad or less	24.1%	**Health Insurance**	
Over 64	10.4%	Some college	22.1%	With health insurance coverage	90.9%
		College Degree, 4 yr	30.2%		
Work		Post grad	23.6%		
White Collar	53.9%			**Public Assistance**	
Sales and Service	34.1%	**Military**		Cash public assistance income	1.2%
Blue Collar	11.9%	Veteran	9.6%		
Government	5.1%	Active Duty	0.4%	Food stamp/SNAP benefits	3.9%

Voter Turnout			
2015 Total Citizens 18+	503,968	2016 House Turnout as % CVAP	79%
2016 House turnout	400,083	2014 House Turnout as % CVAP	44%

2012 Presidential Vote		
Mitt Romney	186,650	(50%)
Barack Obama	182,432	(49%)

2016 Presidential Vote		
Hillary Clinton	210,692	(52%)
Donald Trump	170,580	(42%)
Gary Johnson	12,563	(3%)

Cook Partisan Voting Index: D+1

What we think of today as the outer suburbs and exurbs of Washington, D.C., was still open country as late as World War II. Gen. George Marshall, driving from his office in the Pentagon to the old house he bought in Leesburg 40 miles away, would pass a few gas stations, crossroads villages and countless acres of farm fields. If Marshall made the trip today, his drive would take much more time and he would see something very different. As the federal government grew, Fairfax County's population doubled in the 1940s and very nearly tripled in the 1950s. It has continued to grow, though at a much slower rate, passing 1 million in 2002 and 1.1 million in 2011. Loudoun County, where Dulles International Airport opened in the 1960s as the outer limit to the region, lately has experienced that type of explosive growth. Its population fell just short of doubling in each of the past two decades, with an increase from 174,000 in 2000 to 386,000 in 2016. This has become the richest area of the country: Loudoun and Fairfax counties ranked first and third, respectively, in the nation in median household income in 2011. Nearby Falls Church, which the Census Bureau classifies as a county for these purposes, was second. The Asian and Latino populations have increased rapidly in both Fairfax and Loudoun: a combined 36 percent and 32 percent, respectively. Growth continues apace, and the Washington metro area now extends past those two counties and over the Blue Ridge into the Shenandoah Valley.

No longer simply a collection of bedroom communities, Northern Virginia has become an employment center and focus of innovation in its own right. The Dulles Access Road is lined with high-tech firms and entrepreneurial startups, defense contractors and "Beltway bandit" lobbying firms. Traffic is mightily congested and Loudoun has taken steps to curb sprawl. This is family country: 46 percent of households have children under 18, in contrast to 15 percent in gentrified Arlington County.

The 10th Congressional District covers much of Northern Virginia's western suburbs. It includes most of well-heeled McLean, home of many of Washington's political and lawyer-lobbyist elites, but it skirts the increasingly liberal residential enclaves in the booming Tysons commercial area. It includes the conservative Clifton area of southwest Fairfax, northern Prince William County, and the cities of Manassas and Manassas Park. Beyond the Beltway, it takes in woodsy Great Falls and the Dulles Airport corridor. It includes all of Loudoun County, which is heavily built-up in the east with some still-rural areas west of Leesburg. Middleburg, with both old and new money, is horse country with many gated mansions. Beyond the Blue Ridge, it takes in the fast-growing, Republican Winchester-based Frederick County, which not long ago was best known for its apple orchards. About 45 percent of the population is in Loudoun, and 25 percent in Fairfax.

The district was once reliably Republican; it gave George W. Bush 56 percent of the vote in 2000 and 55 percent in 2004. With an influx of immigrants and federal workers, Northern Virginia is becoming notably friendlier to Democrats. Hillary Clinton in 2016 won the district, 52%-42%, after Barack Obama narrowly lost in 2012.

ELEVENTH DISTRICT

Gerald Connolly (D)

Elected 2008, 5th term; b. Mar 30, 1950, Boston, MA; Maryknoll College (IL), B.A., 1971; Harvard University, M.P.A., 1979; Roman Catholic; Married (Cathy Connolly); 1 child.

Elected Office: Fairfax County Board of Supervisors, 1995-2009, Chairman, 2004-2009.

Professional Career: Non-profit Executive; U.S. Senate aide; Defense contractor.

DC Office: 2238 RHOB 20515, 202-225-1492, Fax: 202-225-3071, connolly.house.gov.

State Offices: Annandale, 703-256-3071; Woodbridge, 571-408-4407.

Committees: *Foreign Affairs*: Asia & the Pacific, Middle East & North Africa. *Oversight & Government Reform*: Government Operations (RMM), Information Technology.

Group Ratings

	ADA	ACLU	AFL-CIO	LCV	ITI	COC	HAFA	ACU	CFG	FRC
2016	-	100%	-	100%	67%	64%	10%	0%	4%	0%
2015	70%	C	92%	94%	C	60%	C	4%	0%	0%

Almanac Ratings 2015

	Economy	Social	Foreign	Composite
Liberal	75%	94%	78%	82%
Conservative	25%	6%	22%	18%

Key Votes of the 114th Congress

1. Keystone Pipeline	N	5. Puerto Rico Debt	Y	9. Offenses by Aliens	Y
2. Trade Deals	Y	6. Medical Marijuana	Y	10. Troops in Iraq	N
3. Export-Import Bank	Y	7. Sanctuary Cities	N	11. Homeland Security $$	Y
4. Debt Ceiling Increase	Y	8. Armor-piercing Bullets	N	12. Trade Adjustment aid	Y

Election Results

Election	Name (Party)	Vote (%)	Cand. Spent	Ind. Exp. Support	Ind. Exp. Oppose
2016 General	Gerald Connolly (D)....................	247,818 (88%)	$981,115	$534	

Prior winning percentages: 2014 (57%), 2012 (61%), 2010 (49%), 2008 (55%)

Democrat Gerald (Gerry) Connolly, elected in 2008, is a former Capitol Hill staffer and county executive who remains an ardent champion of the federal workers and government contractors who populate his Northern Virginia district, which is almost entirely outside the Capital Beltway.

Connolly grew up in the Boston area and graduated from Maryknoll College. He considered joining the priesthood and studied for six years at a Catholic seminary. His interest in public policy led him to Washington, where he managed the American Freedom from Hunger Foundation and the U.S. Committee for Refugees. He got a master's degree from Harvard and worked for a decade on the staff of the Senate Foreign Relations Committee, where he specialized in Middle Eastern affairs and foreign aid. He left Capitol Hill to run the Washington office of Stanford Research Institute International and then became vice president of the San Diego-based defense contractor SAIC. In 1995, Connolly won a seat on the Fairfax County Board of Supervisors, and later was elected board chairman, taking responsibility for a large government at a time of rapid growth. His biggest project was the Metrorail extension to Tysons and Dulles.

In these battles, Connolly often worked with Republican Rep. Tom Davis, who continued to pay close attention to local issues. Davis, an expert on political demographics, could see that Northern Virginia was moving away from the GOP; he also was term-limited as the top Republican on the Oversight and Government Reform Committee. In 2008, he decided not to seek reelection. In the primary, Connolly faced former Rep. Leslie Byrne, whom Davis defeated in 1994. She had the backing of the national abortion rights fundraising group EMILY's List, but Connolly outpaced her finances, with support from defense contractors. In a low-turnout June primary, Connolly won by a solid 58%-33%. Republican nominee Keith Fimian, a businessman and newcomer to Northern Virginia politics, self-financed much of his campaign. Democrats attacked Fimian as a conservative on cultural issues, in contrast to Davis' moderate record, and Fimian got little help from national Republicans. Connolly won 55%-43%.

Connolly has been a leader of the dwindling centrist New Democrat Coalition and established a moderate voting record. His *Almanac* vote ratings in 2015 placed him toward the center of the House, though he was relatively liberal on social issues. Connolly was among the Democrats who joined a majority of Republicans in backing free-trade deals with Colombia, Panama and South Korea in 2011. In 2015, he was an enthusiastic supporter among an even smaller number of House Democrats who supported trade promotion authority for President Barack Obama and his prospective Trans-Pacific Partnership deal. In turn, he was strongly criticized by labor and liberal groups that opposed the measure. Connolly's close alliance with federal employees' unions gave him some political cover.

On the Oversight and Government Reform Committee, Connolly has generally worked well with Republicans. He set aside occasional differences with Chairman Darrell Issa of California in 2014 to enact the landmark Federal Information Technology Acquisition Reform Act, which was the first major overhaul of federal IT management since 1996. He enacted a bill in 2010 to encourage teleworking.

As the ranking Democrat on the Oversight Subcommittee on Government Operations, as well as the vice-ranking Democrat of the full committee, Connolly has blasted Republican budget-cutting efforts that he said unfairly target government workers. "Federal employees are now fair game, because [Republicans] see some short-term political advantage in making them a scapegoat," he said in 2012. With President Donald Trump, he warned of an onslaught of attacks against federal workers.

Following up on his work as a Senate staffer, Connolly has been an active member of the House Foreign Affairs Committee, where he tends to voice an internationalist view. In March 2017, he said that Trump's proposed budget cuts for the State Department would harm American security and diminish its leadership on the global stage. "You don't make America great again by unilaterally withdrawing from the world," he said.

At home, Fimian returned for a rematch in 2010, a perilous year for Democrats. This time, Fimian did not have to rely on self-financing and raised $2.9 million to Connolly's $2.4 million. Fimian stuck to the national Republican message of "outrageous spending" and rising deficits and attacked Connolly as a "career politician." Five days after the election, Fimian conceded, having won 48.8 percent to his opponent's 49.2 percent - a margin of 981 votes out of 227,000 cast. Connolly has had it easier since, with assistance from new district lines and the Democrats' domination of Northern Virginia. In 2016, he was reelected without major-party opposition.

Northern Virginia: Fairfax and Prince William Counties

Population		**Race and Ethnicity**		**Income**	
Total	771,956	White	47.5%	Median Income	$1,04,292 (3 out of 435)
Land area	185	Black	12.5%		
Pop/ sq mi	4170.7	Latino	18.0%	Under $50,000	18.9%
Born in state	28.5%	Asian	17.8%	$50,000-$99,999	28.4%
		Two races	3.8%	$100,000-$199,999	36.3%
Age Groups		Other	0.4%	$200,000 or more	16.6%
Under 18	24.2%			Poverty Rate	6.5%
18-34	24.3%	**Education**			
35-64	41.3%	H.S grad or less	23.9%	**Health Insurance**	
Over 64	10.2%	Some college	21.8%	With health insurance coverage	88.0%
Work		College Degree, 4 yr	29.3%		
White Collar	52.7%	Post grad	24.9%	**Public Assistance**	
Sales and Service	36.2%	**Military**		Cash public assistance income	1.3%
Blue Collar	11.1%	Veteran	10.1%		
Government	4.9%	Active Duty	0.9%	Food stamp/SNAP benefits	5.1%

Voter Turnout			
2015 Total Citizens 18+	484,699	2016 House Turnout as % CVAP	58%
2016 House turnout	282,003	2014 House Turnout as % CVAP	39%

2012 Presidential Vote		
Barack Obama	212,181	(62%)
Mitt Romney	123,317	(36%)

2016 Presidential Vote		
Hillary Clinton	238,982	(66%)
Donald Trump	98,222	(27%)
Gary Johnson	10,253	(3%)

Cook Partisan Voting Index: D+15

Rising on a hill west of Washington D.C., Tysons Corner was a back-country intersection 50 years ago. By the late 1980s, it was an edge city, with the largest concentration of office space to be found anywhere between Washington and Atlanta, and with a modern skyline and busy multi-lane avenues that served as arteries to the Capital Beltway. Fairfax County, which includes Tysons Corner, had been a typical postwar suburb. It had only 99,000 people in 1950, far fewer than Washington's 802,000. But in the years that followed, the trickle moving into Fairfax became a gusher. In 2016, it had 1.1 million people, nearly twice as many as Washington. Today, it is packed with mostly affluent communities, with dazzlingly high percentages of residents with college degrees and two or more cars.

In the last decade, the once-sedate "Mother Fairfax" has once again changed. Just as Tysons Corner (now referred to as simply Tysons) made it a major corporate and shopping center, plans are underway to transform that complex to approximate a walkable, downtown urban area. By 2050, planners envision 100,000 residents and 200,000 jobs in Tysons, which will become a 24-hour urban center. Population growth has slowed since the 1980s; the 12 percent growth rate of the 2000s was the slowest since the 1910s. Meanwhile, Prince William County has been growing at a fast clip, 62 percent between 2000 and 2016, attracting the young families that Fairfax once did. Immigrants - Koreans and Vietnamese, Ethiopians and Afghans, Salvadorans and Mexicans - have put their stamp in Fairfax on what once were mostly white, heavily Protestant neighborhoods.

The 11.7 mile extension of the Washington-area Metrorail system to Tysons and Reston, which opened in 2014, has reduced traffic congestion in the area and increased the number of shoppers who use public transit. The next Silver Line extension from Reston to Dulles Airport, which is scheduled for completion in 2020, is expected to boost the number of passengers who fly from Dulles, where flight loads recently have dipped.

The 11th Congressional District of Virginia consists of much of Fairfax County and southeastern Prince William County. Republicans in control of redistricting packed as many Democratic voters into the district as possible in order to shore up neighboring Republican districts. Fairfax County has had a dramatic political shift. Bill Clinton won 46 percent of the county vote in his 1996 reelection; Hillary

Clinton took 64 percent in 2016. The 11th takes in sprawling Tysons, parts of Annandale that are the only area of the district inside the Capital Beltway, and also Oakton, Vienna, Fairfax City, Lorton, Burke and part of Centreville. An arm extends west to the heavily Democratic planned community of Reston and neighboring Herndon. In Prince William County, it includes Woodbridge and Dale City, areas with large Latino immigrant populations. The district is majority-minority: 18 percent Asian, 18 percent Hispanic, and 14 percent African American. It is solidly Democratic, as intended. In 2016, Hillary Clinton got 66 percent of the vote.

★ WASHINGTON ★

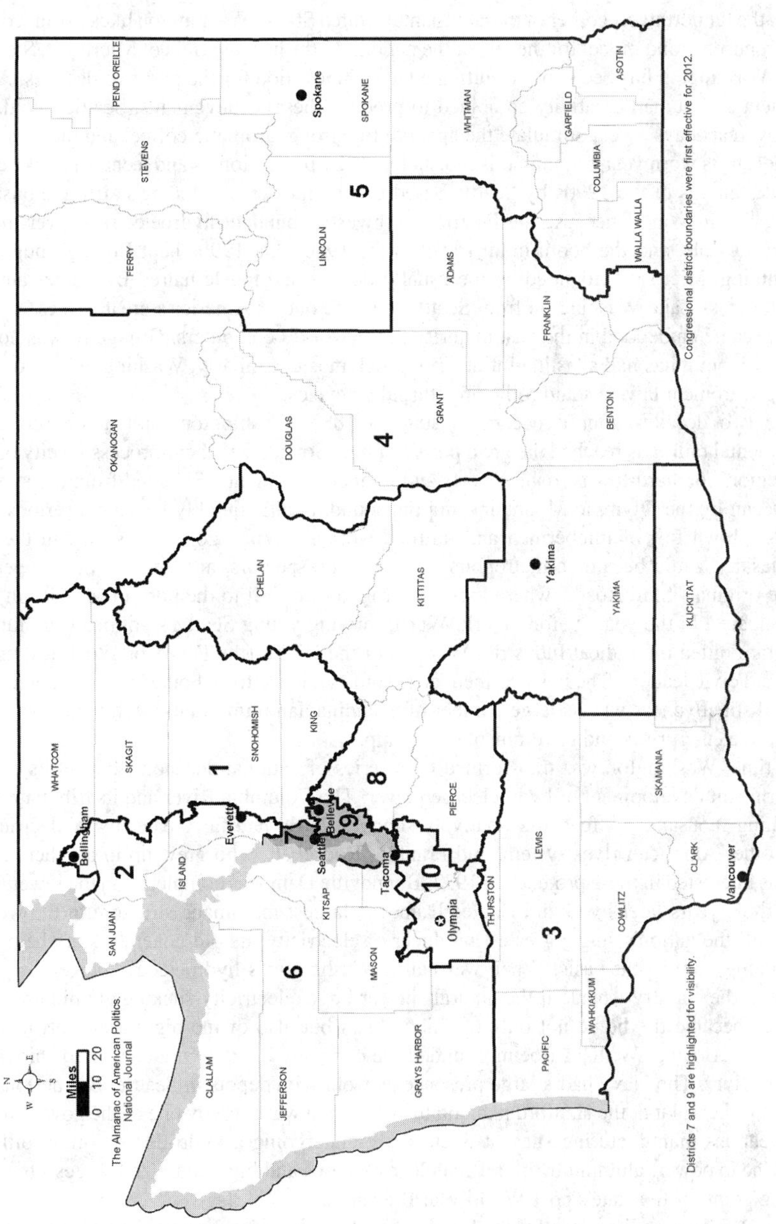
Congressional district boundaries were first effective for 2012.
Districts 7 and 9 are highlighted for visibility.
The Almanac of American Politics, National Journal
Miles
0 10 20
N
E
S
W
PEND OREILLE
STEVENS
FERRY
OKANOGAN
SPOKANE
Spokane
LINCOLN
WHITMAN
GARFIELD
ASOTIN
COLUMBIA
WALLA WALLA
ADAMS
FRANKLIN
GRANT
DOUGLAS
CHELAN
BENTON
KITTITAS
YAKIMA
Yakima
KLICKITAT
WHATCOM
Bellingham
SKAGIT
SNOHOMISH
Everett
ISLAND
SAN JUAN
KING
Seattle
Bellevue
KITSAP
Tacoma
PIERCE
Olympia
THURSTON
MASON
LEWIS
SKAMANIA
CLARK
Vancouver
COWLITZ
WAHKIAKUM
PACIFIC
GRAYS HARBOR
JEFFERSON
CLALLAM
1
2
3
4
5
6
7
8
9
10

Washington state is a hotbed for high-tech and export industries, disproportionately populated by affluent, well-educated, and culturally liberal residents, at least in the Seattle metropolitan area, which accounts for more than half the state's population. As such, it embodies a key wing of the modern Democratic Party, and in 2016, Washington was the rare state in which Hillary Clinton expanded on Barack Obama's 2012 margin of victory, though only modestly.

Off in the far northwest corner of the continental United States, Washington likes to think of itself as a national trendsetter and model for the rest of the nation. As the headquarters of Microsoft, Starbucks and Amazon, Washington has been on the cutting edge of innovation for the past two decades. An unusual environment and human creativity combined to produce these achievements. Seattle's cold, misty air and 225 overcast days a year stimulate the appetite for strong, aromatic coffee, and the torn blue jeans and flannel shirts worn year-round in this moist climate by professionals and teenagers alike created the trend made famous in the 1990s by Seattle-based grunge musicians. Boeing's airframe business took off during World War II because the Pacific Northwest's abundant hydroelectric power made cheap aluminum possible, and the boom in air travel in the 1980s and 1990s kept Boeing's huge assembly lines humming. Microsoft, founded by the usually tie-less and tousle-haired Bill Gates and based in Redmond, across Lake Washington from Seattle, became one of America's great success stories as its software became embedded in the vast majority of the world's computers. Grunge rock is no longer in the vanguard, but it has had a lasting influence on rock music; similarly, Washington's innovators have survived government lawsuits and rollicking, turbulent cycles.

In the two decades after it became a state in 1889, Washington built a new civilization as transcontinental railroads reached the great ports of Puget Sound, the wheat-processing city of Spokane, and the region's orchard towns, fishing ports and lumber settlements. Shielded from the storms of the Pacific Ocean by the Olympic Mountains and the sound, Seattle quickly became a serious American city, a lusty town full of lumbermen and railroad workers. When gold was struck in the Klondike and in Alaska, Seattle became a metropolis of miners, prospectors, and get-rich-quick operators, the site of the original "Skid Road," where logs were rolled downhill to the port. (Today it's in gentrified Pioneer Square.) In the years before World War I, thriving young Seattle's politics were turbulent, as class warfare pitted the radical Industrial Workers of the World (the IWW, or Wobblies) against city business and civic leaders. The businessmen, after some violence from both sides, prevailed. Adding to the area's distinctiveness was its large number of Scandinavian immigrants, with their favorable views of cooperative enterprises and government ownership.

Over time, Washington was transformed by a series of national decisions that set its course. One was government development of hydroelectric power. The Columbia River and its tributary, the Snake River, falling thousands of feet in a relatively short distance, had far greater hydroelectric potential than any other American river system, and Franklin Roosevelt, who grew up in another scenic river valley, was interested in these projects. In 1937, Bonneville Dam was completed on the lower Columbia, followed three years later by Grand Coulee Dam, the largest man-made structure in the world at the time and still the nation's single greatest producer of electricity; its old generators are being replaced on an ongoing, multi-year basis. When war came, Washington's hydroelectric power - the cheapest electricity in the country - made it the natural site for huge, electricity-sucking aluminum plants. The Seattle area became the home not only of shipbuilders but also of the biggest aircraft manufacturer in the country, Boeing. William Boeing founded the company in 1916 in a converted shipyard on the Duwamish River. The Navy had a large presence as well, with depots in Seattle, Bremerton and other locations. Further inland, the Hanford plant on the Columbia was secretly one of the government's main nuclear weapons manufacturing sites; it is currently undergoing a multi-decade, multi-billion-dollar cleanup. Cheap power, aluminum, aircraft, nuclear weapons and high unionized wages - these became the starting point for the state's post-World War II economy.

Today, Washington lives less off the brawn of hydroelectric power and rail and ship tonnage, and more off the brains that made Boeing the world leader in aircraft and Microsoft the world leader in software. Yet it hit a rough patch at the turn of the 21st century. Violent demonstrators trashed the streets of Seattle during the World Trade Organization meeting in December 1999, keeping Bill Clinton and other world leaders indoors, while the city's police chief and mayor, showing an abundance of tolerance, did little to stop the violence. In March 2000, the tech bubble, inflated as businesses retooled to avoid Y2K problems, suddenly burst. Microsoft was fending off an antitrust suit initiated in 1998 by the Clinton administration, and over the next decade, the company failed to achieve the dominance in computer games and search engines that it has enjoyed in PC software. In March 2001, Boeing announced it was moving its headquarters (though not its factories) to Chicago; then it saw its order book go blank after the September 11 attacks. In the recession of the early 2000s Washington's unemployment was the second highest in the nation, after Oregon's.

Washington has bounced back pretty well. Boeing's 787 Dreamliner was introduced, although the plane was grounded temporarily in 2013 while a problem with recurring battery fires was remedied. The company also got a controversial contract for the Air Force's KC-46 refueling tanker. However, the company shed thousands of jobs in 2016, including many in Washington state, and it planned to reduce payrolls further in 2017, citing slack sales. Microsoft survived the federal antitrust case, a huge fine from European Union antitrust authorities, Gates' retirement, and vigorous competition from California-based Apple and Google. It now has about 120,000 full-time employees, more than one-third of them in metro Seattle. Starbucks cut back during the recession but started expanding again, abroad and at home. Amazon was transformed from an internet bookseller that wreaked havoc on the big bookstores to an all-purpose retailer challenging almost every brick-and-mortar retailer. The company expanded into streaming video and even toyed with the idea of delivery by drones; its founder, Jeff Bezos, purchased the *Washington Post* (in the other Washington) and proceeded to bolster its fortunes. Washington's exports to China tripled in a decade, and it is estimated that exports drive 40 percent of the state's economy. Unemployment during the Great Recession peaked at 10.4 percent and was at 4.7 percent by early 2017, largely tracking the nationwide pattern. The state has the nation's ninth-highest median income, 19 percent above the national average; attainment of bachelor's degrees ranks 11th among the states.

Amid such economic success, Washington's population increased by 14 percent between 2000 and 2010 -- faster than Oregon's or California's – and it has risen by another 8.4 percent since 2010. The state's biggest counties have expanded at healthy rates: King County by 11.3 percent since 2010, and neighboring Snohomish County (Everett) and Pierce County (Tacoma) by 10.4 percent and 8.3 percent respectively. Outside of metro Seattle, Clark County (Vancouver, across from Portland, Oregon) has grown by 9.8 percent. Even Spokane County, in the slower-growing eastern half of the state, has grown by 5.9 percent since 2010. Washington remains predominantly white – 69 percent -- but the white percentage has fallen in each of the state's 39 counties since 2010. Overall, the state is 13 percent Hispanic and 8 percent Asian. King County has a fast-growing Asian population, rising from 14.6 percent in 2010 to 16.9 percent in 2015. But some of the highest minority proportions are in agricultural areas, such as apple-growing Yakima County, a minority-majority jurisdiction that is 48 percent Hispanic and 6 percent Native American. People are continuing to flock to Washington despite the growing evidence of catastrophic risk - either a major volcanic event at Mount Rainier, just 60 miles from Seattle and Tacoma, or an earthquake and tsunami stemming from the little-known Cascadia subduction zone. A regional director of the Federal Emergency Management Agency told the *New Yorker* in 2015 that, in the worst-case scenario, "our operating assumption is that everything west of Interstate 5 will be toast," meaning 140,000 square miles and 7 million people living in and around Seattle, Tacoma and Olympia in Washington and Portland, Eugene and Salem in Oregon.

Situated in a region with abundant natural beauty, Washington has taken environmental concerns seriously, but this often has pitted green priorities against industries that created the state's original wealth. A key flashpoint has been coal – not extracted from mines in the state, but rather shipped by rail from places like Wyoming, destined for terminals that would send shiploads to growing Asian economies. Activists have fought the construction of a half-dozen new cargo terminals, and they have been successful; by early 2017, only one proposed terminal, in the southwestern port of Longview, remained a live possibility, though even that project was in limbo after failing to obtain a required state permit. But the state's environmental leanings had limits: In 2016, voters rejected a ballot measure that would have taxed carbon dioxide emissions at $25 per ton, in exchange for sales tax rollbacks. The measure failed by a surprisingly large 18-point margin. Some environmentalists opposed the tax as too weak.

Politically, Washington was one of the most Democratic northern states in the 1930s. Roosevelt's campaign manager, James Farley, used to refer to "the 47 states and the Soviet of Washington." Its mainstream Democrats - notably Warren Magnuson and Henry "Scoop" Jackson, who represented the state in Congress for a cumulative 87 years - believed in an active and compassionate federal government that built dams, bought military aircraft and pursued an internationalist, anti-Communist foreign policy abroad. Their political strength came out of a blue-collar base, augmented by the respect big business had for their political clout. Today, the state remains one of the most unionized in the nation, but the fulcrum of the electorate has moved from blue collar to white collar, and from economic class warfare to culture wars, with the Democrats benefiting, on balance; according to Gallup, Washington ranks sixth nationally in the percentage of nonreligious residents. In presidential races, Washington has voted exclusively Democratic since 1988 and has elected only Democratic governors since 1984. For eight years from 2004 to 2012, Washington's governor and both of its senators were Democratic women. However, a number of the state's recent gubernatorial and senatorial contests have been competitive, and the GOP currently holds the offices of state treasurer and secretary of state. In the legislature, the state Senate is GOP-controlled thanks to a partnership with a renegade Democrat, and the Democrats control the state House only narrowly.

Politically, Washington is divided along geographic lines. The biggest share of votes comes from the three counties closest to Seattle – King, Snohomish and Pierce counties; together, they accounted for 53 percent of the statewide votes cast for president in 2016. In the 1980s, King County was closely divided, with higher-income suburbs voting Republican and working-class neighborhoods in Seattle voting Democratic. But Seattle has become a relatively childless city with a small black population. Hispanics have been moving to southern King County suburbs, and a rising number of Asians have been relocating to suburbs like Bellevue and Redmond east of Lake Washington. All these groups tend to vote heavily Democratic. Seattle in particular has pursued a solidly liberal course, raising its minimum wage to $15 and even electing Kshama Sawant, an Indian-born Trotskyist socialist, to the city council. Pierce County has long been a blue-collar Democratic bastion, as has, to a lesser extent, Snohomish County. But both have seen suburban overflow from Seattle; all three Seattle-area counties are reliably Democratic.

Two other regions account for the remainder of the statewide vote. One is eastern Washington beyond the Cascade Range; this region votes consistently Republican. (Many of the Hispanics in eastern Washington are not eligible to vote and thus haven't had a large impact on political outcomes.) Cultural issues have produced results in this part of the state that are sharply at odds with the state as a whole. In 2012, for instance, when Washington joined Maine and Maryland in endorsing same-sex marriage, it passed with 67 percent in King County but failed by 60 percent in eastern Washington. The third area that casts the remainder of the state's votes is west of the Cascades but outside King, Snohomish and Pierce. A notable portion of this region is Clark County, a fast-growing area adjoining Portland. (Washington has no income tax and Oregon no sales tax, so you can avoid lots of taxes by living in Clark County and shopping across the line in Oregon.) Efforts to split the state in two along the Cascades have popped up periodically -- and as recently as 2017 -- though the idea remains the longest of longshots.

In the 2016 presidential race, Clinton won by 16 points, a slightly wider margin than Barack Obama had achieved in 2012. Clinton actually fell short of Obama's vote total by about 13,000 statewide, but Donald Trump fared even worse, underperforming Mitt Romney's 2012 total by 69,000. Many of the missing votes for both candidates likely went to third-party candidates – Libertarian Gary Johnson got 5 percent statewide and Green Party nominee Jill Stein got nearly 2 percent. Clinton won 12 counties, four fewer than Obama. She saw five Obama counties slip away – Clallam, Cowlitz, Gray's Harbor, Mason and Pacific, all modestly populated western counties well beyond the Seattle metro area. The winning margin in these five counties shifted by between two and 21 points in the GOP's direction in 2016. At the same time, Clinton was able to flip one Romney county – Whitman, which includes Pullman, the home of Washington State University. The three big counties near Seattle remained blue, but they took somewhat different paths. In aggressively liberal King County, Clinton improved on Obama's winning margin by eightpoints. In Pierce County, with more white working-class voters who were receptive to Trump's message, Clinton held on but saw her margin slip to seven points from Obama's 11. In more mixed Snohomish, the Democratic winning margin stayed roughly the same between 2012 and 2016.All told, Clinton's weak performance in less-populated areas of the state meant that she had to rely more heavily on the Seattle area to win. The share of the Democratic presidential vote coming from King, Snohomish and Pierce counties rose from 59 percent in 2012 to 62 percent in 2016

Meanwhile, Democrats cheered other victories in 2016. Cyrus Habib, a blind Rhodes Scholar and Iranian-American lawyer-legislator with a passion for karate and jazz piano, was elected lieutenant governor. Voters passed ballot measures to raise the statewide minimum wage and to allow courts to remove individuals' access to firearms if they are deemed to be at risk to themselves or others. But one-third of the state's 12 Democratic electors defected from Clinton, one as a Native American protest against the Dakota Access Pipeline. After Trump took office, Washington state officials assumed a leading role in trying to block his agenda. State Attorney General Bob Ferguson filed a successful lawsuit against Trump's first attempt at a temporary ban on immigrants from Muslim-majority countries posing a terrorism threat (the first judge to rule against the policy was based in Seattle); his challenge to Trump's policy drew rhetorical support from such locally based companies as Amazon.com and Expedia. Ferguson also pledged to defend the state's recreational marijuana law from any threat posed by the U.S. Justice Department.

Population		**Race and Ethnicity**		**Income**	
Total	6,985,464	White	70.8%	Median Income	$61,062 (11 out of 50)
Land area	66,456	Black	3.5%		
Pop/ sq mi	105.1	Latino	12.0%	Under $50,000	41.0%
Born in state	47.5%	Asian	7.6%	$50,000-$99,999	32.0%
		Two races	4.3%	$100,000-$199,999	21.2%
Age Groups		Other	1.9%	$200,000 or more	5.7%
Under 18	22.9%			Poverty Rate	13.3%
18-34	23.7%	**Education**			
35-64	39.7%	H.S grad or less	32.8%	**Health Insurance**	
Over 64	13.7%	Some college	34.4%	With health insurance coverage	88.6%
		College Degree, 4 yr	20.9%		
Work		Post grad	12.0%		
White Collar	39.0%			**Public Assistance**	
Sales and Service	40.1%	**Military**		Cash public assistance income	3.9%
Blue Collar	20.9%	Veteran	10.6%		
Government	16.2%	Active Duty	0.9%	Food stamp/SNAP benefits	14.3%

Voter Turnout			
2015 Total Citizens 18+	4,937,212	2016 Pres Turnout as % CVAP	67%
2016 Pres Votes	3,317,019	2012 Pres Turnout as % CVAP	67%

Legislature	
Senate:	24D, 25R
House:	50D, 48R

Presidential Politics

2016 Democratic Caucus		
Hillary Clinton (D)	420,461	(52%)
Bernie Sanders (D)	382,293	(48%)
2016 Republican Primary		
Donald Trump (R)	455,023	(75%)
Ted Cruz (R)	65,172	(11%)
John Kasich (R)	58,954	(10%)

2016 Presidential Vote		
Hillary Clinton (D)	1,742,718	(53%)
Donald Trump (R)	1,221,747	(37%)
Gary Johnson (L)	160,879	(5%)
2012 Presidential Vote		
Barack Obama (D)	1,755,396	(56%)
Mitt Romney (R)	1,290,670	(41%)

For three decades, Washington was one of the most contrarian states in presidential politics, voting for Republican losers Richard Nixon in 1960 and Gerald Ford in 1976 and Democratic losers Hubert Humphrey in 1968 and Michael Dukakis in 1988. In the 1990s, it tilted Democratic, with the nation, voting for Bill Clinton twice. Since then, it has moved significantly toward the Democrats, voting 53%-46% for John Kerry in 2004, and 58%-40% and 56%-41% for Barack Obama in 2008 and 2012, respectively. Hillary Clinton's margin over Donald Trump comfortably fit with Obama's: she won the state 53%-37%. The traditional partisan dividing line is the Cascades mountain range. West to the Pacific is Democratic territory. East to the Idaho border is Republican turf. Anchoring the Democratic terrain is King County, which accounts for almost one-third of the state's vote. King once had plenty of Seattle suburbs that were content to back moderate Republicans. But as the GOP adopted more conservative stands on social issues and Seattle became a high-tech haven that attracted younger voters, the county became a Democratic bastion. It voted for Clinton over Trump, 70%-21%, better than Obama's 69%-29% margin over Mitt Romney. According to *The Seattle Times*, only two towns in the county, Black Diamond and Enumclaw, voted for Trump. The paper reported that Trump received 8 percent of the vote in Seattle, less than the 10 percent he garnered in the liberal temple of San Francisco. Adjoining Pierce and Snohomish Counties, the next two largest vote-producers that include Seattle suburbs and exurbs, also backed Clinton. But the Obama administration's hostility toward the timber industry shifted some of the old allegiances in eastern Washington. The five counties in the state that saw the biggest percentage drop-off in the Democratic vote from 2012 were in the west: Cowlitz, Gray's Harbor, Mason, Pacific and Wahkiakum. All five have lumber and logging concerns. All five backed Trump. The first four were carried by Obama in 2012. All the counties east of the Cascades backed Trump except for Whitman, home to Washington State University. But even with blue-collar support, a Republican needs to be competitive in the Seattle suburbs to prevail statewide.

When it came to the two parties' presidential nominating contests, there was no divide in the state. Democrats held a caucus on March 26 and Vermont Sen. Bernie Sanders walloped Clinton 73%-27% and carried every county in the state. The caucuses gave him a larger delegate boost than any other caucus or primary. For Clinton it must have felt like deja vu all over again: In the 2008 caucuses, Obama beat Clinton 68%-31%, winning every county. Republicans held a May primary, after all of Trump's GOP rivals had withdrawn from the race. The New Yorker garnered 76 percent of the vote.

Congressional Districts

115th Congress Lineup	4R 6D	**114th Congress Lineup**	4R 6D

Washington gained a House seat in the reapportionment following the 2010 census. In 1983, voters had approved a constitutional amendment that created a bipartisan redistricting commission, made up of two Democrats and two Republicans appointed by legislative leaders. If the commission deadlocks, the issue goes to the Supreme Court; lines also can be changed by a two-thirds vote in both houses of the legislature. The Washington plan originally was lauded for encouraging cooperation and creating more districts that both parties can win. But unlike Iowa or California, where commissions are not supposed to take political considerations into account, the result in Washington has become incumbent protection.

In 2011, Democrats held just a 5-4 lead in House seats, and 56 percent of the state's growth between 2000 and 2010 had taken place in the four Republican-held districts. The two Republican commissioners, including former Sen. Slade Gorton, proposed placing a new "fair fight" 10th District in the state's highly competitive northwest and North Puget Sound. The two Democrats countered with proposals putting the new 10th District in the more reliably Democratic South Puget Sound area around Olympia. Three days before their New Year's Eve deadline, the commissioners forged a compromise in a display of bipartisanship rare for the 2012 cycle. The new 10th District went to the South Sound and was a perfect fit for Democrat Denny Heck, who had lost to Republican Rep. Jaime Herrera Beutler in 2010. In exchange, Democrats strengthened two incumbent Republicans, and stretched the suburban Seattle 1st District all the way north to the Canadian border to make it marginally more competitive. In November 2012, Heck won the 10th, Democrat Suzan DelBene comfortably won the open 1st, and every other incumbent won reelection, for a 6-4 Democratic lead.

In Washington, the six districts that border on vast Puget Sound are comfortably Democratic. The three that are in the hinterlands have become safely Republican. Parts of the 8th District of Republican Dave Reichert moved east of the Cascades following the 2011 redistricting, though most of it has remained in the Seattle metropolitan area, leaving it the one truly competitive district. This self-styled good-government state, with its bipartisan commission, largely accepted political reality and reduced the prospect of competitive general elections, though Washington has had feisty primaries. Though unlikely, the next redistricting will provide opportunities to draw new battlegrounds. The focus probably will be on the 8th, depending partly on what happens before then.

Governor

Jay Inslee (D)

Elected 2012, term expires 2021, 2nd term; b. Feb. 9, 1951, Seattle, WA; Stanford U., 1969-70, U. of WA, B.A. 1973; Willamette U., J.D. 1976; Protestant; Married (Trudi); 3 children.

Elected Office: WA House, 1988-1992; U.S. House, 1993-1995, 1999-2012.

Professional Career: City prosecutor, Selah, WA, 1976-1984; Practicing attorney, 1976-1992, 1995-1996; Regional Director, U.S. Department of Health and Human Services, 1997-1998.

Office: PO Box 40002, Olympia, 98404-0002; 360-902-4111; Fax: 360-753-4110; Website: governor.wa.gov.

Election Results

Election	Name (Party)	Vote (%)
2016 General	Jay Inslee (D)	1,760,520 (54%)
	Bill Bryant (R)	1,476,346 (45%)
2016 Primary	Jay Inslee (D)	687,412 (49%)
	Patrick O Rourke (R)	40,572 (3%)

Prior winning percentage: 2012 (52%); House: 2010 (58%), 2008 (68%), 2006 (68%), 2004 (62%), 2002 (60%), 2000 (55%), 1998 (50%), 1992 (51%)

Democrat Jay Inslee was narrowly elected Washington's governor in 2012, after serving 15 years in the House. He won a second term in 2016 by a nine-point margin, only about half the winning statewide margin for Hillary Clinton in the same election.

Inslee grew up in north Seattle, the son of a high school biology teacher and football coach. He graduated from the University of Washington and Willamette University College of Law. He moved to Selah, in Yakima County east of the Cascades, to practice law and served on the State Trial Lawyers Association board of directors. In 1988, at age 37, he was elected to the state House over a former Yakima mayor.

In 1992, when 4th District Rep. Sid Morrison ran for governor, Inslee won the general election to succeed him, 51%-49%, over Doc Hastings, a conservative supported by the Christian Coalition. In the House, Inslee voted for the Clinton budget and tax increase and for a crime bill with a ban on certain types of semi-automatic weapons that gun-rights opponents call "assault weapons." In the 1994 Republican wave election, Hastings challenged Inslee and beat him, 53%-47%. After his defeat, Inslee moved to Bainbridge Island and practiced law in Seattle. In 1996, he ran for governor and finished fifth, with 10 percent of the vote, in the all-party primary. He briefly served as regional director of the U.S. Health and Human Services Department.

In 1998, Inslee decided to run for Congress again, this time in the 1st District against Republican incumbent Rick White, an economic conservative with liberal votes on some cultural issues. In the September all-party primary, White led 50%-44%. But by November, with the two pitted head to head exclusively, two issues changed the balance. Inslee ran ads claiming that White intended to spend 10 years in the House and then become a lobbyist, a charge his ex-wife had made in divorce papers. He also ran ads highlighting White's vote to impeach President Bill Clinton. In the acrimony, the primary numbers were reversed in November, and Inslee won 50%-44%.

In Congress, Inslee was a moderate-to-liberal Democrat. He joined in protecting the privacy of consumer financial records - an issue important to Microsoft, his largest single source of campaign funds as a congressman. He and Democratic Sen. Maria Cantwell of Washington pressed the Federal Communications Commission in December 2010 for stricter rules on the FCC's proposed net-neutrality order that some Republicans said was already too heavy a hand in the market. When security experts reported in 2011 that Apple's iPhone could secretly track its users' movements, Inslee called for greater government oversight of data collection. In February 2011, Inslee seconded the GOP's alarm about growing budget deficits and called for closing tax loopholes. On the Energy and Commerce Committee, Inslee focused on conservation and increasing renewable energy sources. As early as 2005, he introduced bills to address global warming and reduce U.S. dependence on foreign oil. When Republicans skeptical of alarmist warnings about climate change took control of the House, Inslee criticized what he called the GOP's "allergy to science," and toted a stack of more than 20 books to a March 2011 hearing, claiming they contained irrefutable evidence of the problem.

By the time two-term Democratic Gov. Christine Gregoire decided to retire in 2012, Inslee already had laid the groundwork for a bid, alerting his campaign donors of the possibility. Nine months after launching his candidacy, he decided in March 2012 to resign his House seat to campaign full-time, saying, "I am not one for half measures or half-hearted efforts." The situation created a dilemma for state officials, who had not budgeted the $1 million needed to hold a special election. They decided to leave the seat vacant until November, with the winner serving the remaining two months of his unexpired term.

Inslee's stature cleared the field of top-tier contenders, and he won the state's top-two primary in August with 47 percent of the vote. That set up a general-election matchup against Republican Rob McKenna, the state's attorney general, who took 43 percent in the all-party primary. Republicans accused Inslee of notching no significant legislative accomplishments or attaining a leadership position. But with the state tilting Democratic, especially in presidential politics, Inslee was regarded as having a slight edge.

Even though a Republican hadn't won a gubernatorial race in the state since 1980, the GOP liked McKenna's chances. As attorney general, he focused on consumer protection issues and, as president of the National Association of Attorneys General, played a key role in a $25-billion, multi-state settlement with banks over their mortgage practices. Democrats sought to tie him to the tea party movement, citing his decision to join other states in challenging the federal health care law. But McKenna campaigned as a business-friendly moderate who promised to reprioritize government spending and devote more money to education without raising taxes. He played up his pro-environment beliefs and said that, in contrast to several GOP governors elected in 2010, he did not oppose collective bargaining and would work with unions if elected. He said he personally opposed abortion, but that ultimately it was up to the woman to decide. He got help from state Republicans who played up the failure of some of the clean-energy companies that Inslee had highlighted in a book he'd written.

Polls showed the race to be close. But Barack Obama's strong reelection showing in the state - he won with 56 percent of the vote - helped put Inslee over the top with a 52%-48% victory. McKenna eked out a 52%-48% win in Tacoma's Pierce County and dominated the rural eastern half of the state. But Inslee decisively won Seattle's King County, 62%-38%, and took Everett's Snohomish County 51%-49%. He also joined Obama in winning the Asian and Hispanic vote by large margins.

As governor in 2013, Inslee floated the idea of extending tax breaks for Boeing to 2040, as long as the company agreed to build its next-generation plane, the 777X, in Washington rather than elsewhere, such as South Carolina, where the company had recently been expanding. In February 2014, Inslee established a moratorium on the death penalty, covering the nine men on death row in the state. In 2015, Senate Republicans blocked his bid for a $12 statewide minimum wage. On taxes, Inslee in December 2014 proposed a roughly $1.5 billion package that would include a capital gains tax, a carbon tax, a hike in the cigarette tax and a tax on e-cigarettes, along with several narrower provisions. None were voted on in the Democratic-controlled state House, and six months later, following an unexpectedly strong revenue forecast, he said a tax package that extensive was no longer necessary, although individual elements might remain on the table. The final budget was closer to the one passed in April by the Republican majority in the state Senate.

For much of his term, Inslee grappled with the issue of carbon emission cuts - a signature accomplishment if he could achieve it. In April 2014, Inslee proposed a cap-and-trade program aimed at reducing greenhouse gases in stages by 2020, 2035 and 2050, in order to reach target levels that had been enacted in 2008. He also urged phasing out coal-derived electricity, reducing vehicular emissions, increasing investment in alternative energy and curbing emissions by state government. But the centerpiece of his agenda - the cap-and-trade plan - faced resistance, including from some Democrats. By June 2015, even modified versions of the proposal fell by the wayside. On a different environmental front, Inslee in May 2015 signed a statewide emergency declaration in the wake of a historically low snowpack. This freed up aid for fighting wildfires and helping the agricultural and fishery sectors. Meanwhile, Inslee supported the "Connecting Washington" program, which allocated billions of dollars for expanding and replacing state highways, paid for by gasoline and car taxes. He also worked with the legislature to raise salaries for school employees and cut college tuition.

But spending on K-12 education proved to be particularly thorny. A 2012 state Supreme Court ruling upended the state's education funding system, requiring the state to pay more for teacher salaries and other basic education costs. After the ruling, lawmakers and the governor reallocated some state money to schools but never fully satisfied the court's dictates; the justices responded by levying contempt fines on the state. But with an election under way in 2016, the state's politicians largely kicked the can to 2017.

The 2016 election pitted Inslee against Republican Bill Bryant, a former Port of Seattle commissioner. In the August all-party primary, Inslee took first place with 49 percent and Bryant took second with 38 percent. In the general election, Bryant attacked Inslee's oversight of the state's biggest psychiatric facility as well as the corrections system, which had been shown to have released thousands of inmates too early as a result of incorrect computerized calculations – a systemic problem that was not rectified immediately after discovery. Inslee countered by touting the state's economic health and reductions in tuition at state colleges and universities; he was also a leading supporter of a ballot measure that would raise the minimum wage in steps to $13.50 an hour. In the general election, Inslee beat Bryant by a nine-point margin, on the strength of a 68%-32% edge in King County and victories in neighboring Pierce and Snohomish counties. Democrats won several other statewide offices and kept their House majority, but the GOP held their majority in the state Senate and won races for state treasurer and secretary of state. Voters approved the minimum-wage ballot measure, but – abetted by dissatisfied environmentalists who said it didn't go far enough -- rejected one that would have imposed the nation's first carbon tax.

In early 2017, Inslee prepared for battle with the legislature over plans to fulfill the mandates of the school funding decision. He proposed $2.75 billion to satisfy the court, as well as $732 million in raises for state employees, $300 million for the state's mental health system, $56 million for tuition freezes, and $324 million for K-12 counselors, psychologists and social workers. Overall, his plan totaled a whopping 20 percent increase over the previous two-year budget. The increases would be funded by hikes in the capital gains tax and some business taxes, as well as a rewritten carbon tax and the elimination of some exemptions.

Meanwhile, Inslee's national profile grew as he became a leading Democratic voice against the policies of President Donald Trump. As early as his election-night victory party, Inslee had set a tone by saying that "Washington was, is and will always be a beacon for progressive values across the United States of America." This was not a new role for Inslee. As early as 2015, he had taken a stand in favor of continuing to accept Syrian refugees, even as other governors, mostly Republican, sought to bar their settlement. But as the state, led by Attorney General Bob Ferguson, became an important – and, at least initially, successful -- litigant against Trump's travel ban, Inslee became a frequent guest on cable news shows. He also signed an executive order limiting state cooperation on federal immigration enforcement. Some pundits even began wondering whether Inslee had higher office in mind; the *Wall Street Journal* ran a story headlined, "With Challenge to Trump Travel Ban, Is Washington's Jay Inslee Setting Up 2020 Run?" Inslee dismissed the idea, but he was scheduled to chair the Democratic Governors Association in 2018, meaning that he would have a pipeline to national politics, whatever his plans turned out to be.

In May 2017, Inslee signed a bill to require gun dealers to notify the Washington Association of Sheriffs and Police Chiefs if a prospective purchaser failed a background check after trying to buy a gun.

Senior Senator

Patty Murray (D)

Elected 1992, term expires 2022, 5th term; b. Oct 11, 1950, Bothell; Washington State University, B.A.; Roman Catholic; Married (Robert Randall Murray); 2 children.

Elected Office: Shoreline School Board, 1985-1989, President, 1985-1986; WA Senate, 1988-1992.

DC Office: 154 RSOB 20510, 202-224-2621, Fax: 202-224-0238, murray.senate.gov.

State Offices: Everett, 425-259-6515; Seattle, 206-553-5545; Spokane, 509-624-9515; Tacoma, 253-572-3636; Vancouver, 360-696-7797; Yakima, 509-453-7462.

Committees: Senate Assistant Minority Leader. *Appropriations*: Department of Defense, Department of Homeland Security, DOL, HHS & Education & Related Agencies (RMM), Energy & Water Development, Military Construction & Veteran Affairs & Related Agencies, Transportation, HUD

& Related Agencies. *Budget. Health, Education, Labor & Pensions (RMM)*: Children & Families, Employment & Workplace Safety, Primary Health & Retirement Security. *Veterans' Affairs.*

Group Ratings

	ADA	ACLU	AFL-CIO	LCV	ITI	COC	HAFA	ACU	CFG	FRC
2016	-	82%	-	100%	100%	38%	7%	4%	5%	0%
2015	95%	C	62%	96%	C	57%	C	0%	6%	0%

Almanac Ratings 2015

	Economy	Social	Foreign	Composite
Liberal	83%	95%	80%	86%
Conservative	17%	5%	20%	14%

Key Votes of the 114th Congress

1. Keystone pipeline	N	5. National Security Data	Y	9. Gun Sales Checks	Y
2. Export-Import Bank	N	6. Iran Nuclear Deal	N	10. Sanctuary Cities	N
3. Debt Ceiling Increase	Y	7. Puerto Rico Debt	N	11. Planned Parenthood	N
4. Homeland Security $$	Y	8. Loretta Lynch A.G	Y	12. Trade deals	Y

Election Results

Election	Name (Party)	Vote (%)	Cand. Spent	Ind. Exp. Support	Ind. Exp. Oppose
2016 General	Patty Murray (D)	1,913,979 (59%)	$5,676,043	$33,423	
	Chris Vance (R)	1,329,338 (41%)	$441,718		
2016 Primary	Patty Murray (D)	745,421 (54%)			
	Chris Vance (R)	381,004 (28%)			

Prior winning percentages: 2010 (52%), 2004 (55%), 1998 (58%), 1992 (54%)

Patty Murray is the senior senator from Washington, first elected in 1992. She has come a long way from her entry into politics as a parent-activist. Even as Murray maintains a low-key, plainspoken style, she has become a powerful and senior backroom player, with a seat at her party's leadership table. She plays a key role in advancing the Democrats' positions-a lofty status she ascribes partly to her training as an educator of young children. "You don't walk into a class with 4-year-olds without a direction of where you're going to go," she told *The Huffington Post*. In 2015, the ex-teacher helped to enact a new education bill. The next year, she won a fifth term with her biggest election vote.

Murray grew up in the Seattle suburb of Bothell, one of seven children of a disabled World War II veteran. She graduated from Washington State University in 1972, married, and stayed home to raise her children. In 1980, she was in Olympia trying to save a parent education class she was teaching at Shoreline Community College, which was the target of budget cuts. A state legislator told her gruffly, "You're just a mom in tennis shoes. You can't make a difference." As she said later, "Almost every woman I've ever met in politics got into it because she was mad about something." She won her fight over the parents' class and then ran for the Shoreline School District board. She eventually was chosen board president. In 1988, she challenged a Republican state senator, knocked on 17,000 doors and won the seat. While there, she worked on issues that resonated with voters, from school bus safety to extending a family leave bill for a parent whose child is ill or dying. In late 1991, Murray decided to run against Sen. Brock Adams, a Democrat who was under a cloud following charges of sexual molestation. He decided not to seek reelection.

Amid a crowd of better-known, conventional male politicians, Murray, with her flat, Midwestern-style accent and "mom in tennis shoes" line, attracted most of the campaign attention. In the 1992 all-party primary, her main Democratic opponent was former Rep. Don Bonker, who had narrowly lost a Senate nomination in 1988. Murray won 28 percent of the total vote to Bonker's 19 percent. She sprinted to a big lead in polls against Republican Rep. Rod Chandler, who had served his district for a decade. She won, 54% to 46% in November in what came to be called "the year of the woman."

Murray has had a largely liberal voting record. She is known for being attuned to the needs of Senate conservatives, for being adept at ingratiating herself with her veteran colleagues, and for recognizing and exploiting the possibility of a deal for legislation even in a very partisan environment. That helps to explain why her *Almanac* vote ratings in 2015 placed her among the more conservative Democrats. "She's a pretty good arbiter and proxy for the caucus as a whole," Rich Tarplin, a lobbyist close to

Senate Democrats, told *National Journal*. Murray generally leaves the spotlight to others, but does not shy from asserting senatorial prerogatives. In what she calls her "angry mom" voice, she has rebuked Republican and Democratic secretaries of the Department of Veterans Affairs for proposals that would make veterans pay more for health care. "Ask my kids about it," she said of such confrontations to *The Olympian* newspaper in 2010. "There is a line they knew they shouldn't cross."

Murray assumed the chairmanship of the Budget Committee in 2013. To counter the controversial budget proposal offered by her House counterpart, Wisconsin Republican Paul Ryan, she unveiled a proposed budget that was the first from her party since 2009. It included about $1 trillion in new revenues over 10 years, from the closing of tax loopholes and incentives, to match about $1 trillion in spending cuts. Unlike Ryan's budget, which some House GOP moderates found draconian, her plan was geared toward getting broad Democratic support. It included $100 billion for a new "economic recovery protection plan" that would fund infrastructure projects and education programs. But in something of a surprise, it contained more than double the cuts to the biggest health entitlement, Medicare, than Ryan's. Though Republicans vilified her proposal as unworkable, they said Murray was easy to work with. "You've allowed us to have free ability to speak out; you've been respectful," Budget ranking Republican Jeff Sessions of Alabama told her at a hearing.

Murray forged a working relationship with Ryan through her combination of affability and a can-do, pragmatic style. Her development of a partnership with Ryan enabled them in December 2013 to strike a two-year budget deal that called for raising new revenue through fee increases without tax increases or controversial reforms to Social Security or Medicare. It replaced steep across-the-board spending cuts under the looming "sequester" in January with targeted spending cuts. Democrats groused about the deal, which didn't add much money for party priorities such as infrastructure spending, and it failed to close any of the tax loopholes they had targeted. But it easily passed both chambers and became law. Each chairman scored a personal achievement.

The Budget chairmanship represented Murray's second turn as a leader on the issue. After the protracted standoff over raising the federal debt limit in 2011, she and Texas Republican Rep. Jeb Hensarling were named as co-chairs of the Joint Select Committee on Deficit Reduction, the "super committee" charged with finding a bipartisan consensus on future spending in just a few months. To almost no one's surprise, the effort was fruitless. In this case, she had less maneuverability. "The one thing the Republicans wouldn't put on the table was revenue," Murray told *The Seattle Times* about her experience. "I knew what a bad deal would mean for the middle class in this country. Many of us are where we are in our lives because we had a country that was there for us."

On the Appropriations Committee, Murray made a point as a junior member to get along with senior senators. After Alaska's Ted Stevens, the former GOP chairman, lost his bid for reelection in 2008, he gave Murray the desk that once belonged to legendary Washington Democrat Warren Magnuson (1944-81). When West Virginia Democrat Robert Byrd was too ill in 2007 and 2008 to manage spending bills on the floor as chairman, he gave Murray the task ahead of more senior members. Now, only Patrick Leahy of Vermont has served more years than Murray (plus Dianne Feinstein, whose tenure also began after the 1992 election) among Democrats, both on Appropriations and in the entire Senate . She has delivered for her state and then some: $219 million in home-state projects in 2010, which was the ninth highest amount among senators that year. The Washington watchdog group Taxpayers for Common Sense dubbed her the "Queen of Pork." Despite a subsequent ban on earmarking, Murray still worked to include funding for a variety of Washington projects in spending bills, including money for a Seattle light-rail system and a bridge over the Columbia River.

In 2015, Murray took the top Democratic seat on the Appropriations panel overseeing the departments of Labor, Health and Human Services and Education. With the retirement of Iowa Sen. Tom Harkin, she also claimed the ranking-member post on the Health, Education, Labor and Pensions Committee, giving her a powerful platform on domestic policy.

At the HELP Committee, she worked closely with Tennessee Republican Sen. Lamar Alexander, the chairman of the committee, on a measure to overhaul No Child Left Behind. She dissuaded him from writing his own bill and then seeking some moderate Democrats' support and, instead, he agreed to develop a bipartisan proposal from the start. No Child Left Behind had become very unpopular because of its heavy reliance on standardized testing. "I've heard from parent after parent and teacher after teacher in Washington state who has told me that not only are students taking too many tests, oftentimes the tests are of low quality or redundant," Murray said.

Though previous efforts to reform the law had failed for several years, Alexander and Murray crafted a proposal that cut back the heavy reliance on testing and gave states and local school districts more control of academic standards and teacher and school performance. Remarkably, the HELP Committee, whose members' views span the ideological spectrum, voted unanimously for the bill in April 2015. The

Senate passed it, 81-17. Murray successfully insisted that the bill assured that all schools would be able to offer opportunities to students. That collaboration at the HELP Committee ended with the election of President Donald Trump. The confirmation of Betsy DeVos as Education Secretary was a contentious affair. Murray complained that DeVos had not sufficiently disclosed her complex personal finances or responded to questions from Democrats, who were unhappy with Alexander's rush to confirm DeVos.

In 2015, Murray worked with Senate Republican Whip John Cornyn of Texas to end a stalemate over a noncontroversial measure to combat human trafficking that became ensnared in the always-combustible abortion debate. Democrats objected to what they saw as an anti-abortion provision in the legislation that would prevent money from the victims' fund from being used for abortions in keeping with the Hyde Amendment's prevention of taxpayer funds from being used for abortion services. Murray and Cornyn led the way to a creative compromise. They clarified that money from the fines would go to non-health care concerns, which would not be subject to the Hyde prohibition, and that federal funds, which are subject to the prohibition, would cover heath care.

Earlier, Murray had earned chits with her Democratic colleagues for her work in the 2012 election cycle as head of the Democratic Senatorial Campaign Committee, the party's campaign recruiting and fundraising arm. Not only were Murray and fellow Democrats able to hold the Senate, they picked up two seats. They got some fortunate breaks from flawed Republicans. Murray also recruited successful female candidates, such as Massachusetts' Elizabeth Warren, Wisconsin's Tammy Baldwin, and North Dakota's Heidi Heitkamp. "Oftentimes, when you're looking at people to run, they rule the women out, saying they can't win," Murray told *The Oregonian*. "I ruled them in." In 2006, her colleagues had elected her Democratic Conference Secretary, the fourth-ranking position in the leadership.

In her first years on Capitol Hill, Murray was criticized as too staff reliant, but she grew into the role of senator. She immersed herself in Washington state issues, becoming one of the Senate's staunchest proponents of normal trade relations with China, a position strongly backed by Boeing, a major Washington-based employer. Murray also has worked to remove restrictions on abortion rights and has prevailed in the Senate on legislation allowing abortions in military hospitals. With then-Democratic Sen. Hillary Clinton of New York, she waged a fight with the Bush administration regarding the approval of over-the-counter sales of the Plan B contraceptive.

Murray's 2016 reelection was her easiest, a 59%-41% victory over Chris Vance, a former chairman of the Washington Republican Party, which failed to recruit a more formidable challenger. Vance was out-spent, 19-to-1. In earlier campaigns, she had won reelection three times by steadily diminishing margins. In 1998, she was challenged by Rep. Linda Smith, a Republican and a strong opponent of abortion and free trade deals. Murray raised far more money than Smith and won 58% to 42%. In 2004, she faced Republican George Nethercutt, another House member, who in 1994 earned a reputation as a giant killer by defeating Democratic House Speaker Tom Foley. The former mom in tennis shoes had become a hardball fundraiser. An aide put out the word to lobbyists that the senator would regard contributions to Nethercutt as hostile, even if contributors gave to her too. Murray raised $11.5 million, compared with Nethercutt's $7.7 million. Murray won 55% to 43%. Republicans initially considered Murray vulnerable in 2010. They landed a top-tier recruit in former state Sen. Dino Rossi, a fiscal conservative who had twice run impressive but losing campaigns against Democratic Gov. Christine Gregoire. He criticized her involvement in shaping the Democratic agenda. But Murray did not back down from her record and said Rossi would bankrupt the nation by giving tax breaks to the wealthy. She won 52% to 48%.

When Harry Reid announced in March 2015 that he would not seek reelection, Murray did not rule out a move to climb up the Democratic leadership ladder. Though she endorsed New York Sen. Chuck Schumer to succeed Reid in the top post in 2017, she declined to back Sen. Richard Durbin of Illinois to retain his position as Democratic whip. When pressed by reporters about whether she planned to seek the whip post, Murray sidestepped the question, saying that her first priority and focus was her own reelection. After the election and the Democratic setbacks, she decided not to challenge Durbin, who said that he had a majority of the votes. Schumer gave her enhanced responsibilities and the title of assistant Democratic leader. As the relentless Murray has shown in playing the long game, it's a good bet that she will have additional opportunities.

Junior Senator

Maria Cantwell (D)

Elected 2000, term expires 2018, 3rd term; b. Oct 13, 1958, Indianapolis, IN; Miami University of Ohio, B.A.; Roman Catholic; Single.

Elected Office: WA House, 1987-1993; U.S. House, 1993-1995.

Professional Career: Owner, Cantwell & Association PR firm, 1985-1991; RealNetworks, 1995-2000.

DC Office: 511 HSOB 20510, 202-224-3441, Fax: 202-228-0514, cantwell.senate.gov.

State Offices: Everett, 425-303-0114; Richland, 509-946-8106; Seattle, 206-220-6400; Spokane, 509-353-2507; Tacoma, 253-572-2281; Vancouver, 360-696-7838.

Committees: *Commerce, Science & Transportation*: Aviation Operations, Safety & Security (RMM), Communications, Technology, Innovation & the Internet, Oceans, Atmosphere, Fisheries & Coast Guard, Surface Trans., Merchant Marine Infra., Safety & Security. *Energy & Natural Resources (RMM)*: Energy, National Parks, Public Lands, Forests & Mining, Water & Power. *Finance*: Energy, Natural Resources & Infrastructure, Health Care, Taxation & IRS Oversight. *Indian Affairs*. *Small Business & Entrepreneurship*.

Group Ratings

	ADA	ACLU	AFL-CIO	LCV	ITI	COC	HAFA	ACU	CFG	FRC
2016	-	88%	-	100%	100%	38%	7%	4%	5%	0%
2015	95%	C	64%	96%	C	50%	C	0%	6%	0%

Almanac Ratings 2015

	Economy	Social	Foreign	Composite
Liberal	83%	100%	80%	88%
Conservative	17%	0%	20%	13%

Key Votes of the 114th Congress

1. Keystone pipeline	N	5. National Security Data	Y	9. Gun Sales Checks	Y
2. Export-Import Bank	N	6. Iran Nuclear Deal	N	10. Sanctuary Cities	N
3. Debt Ceiling Increase	Y	7. Puerto Rico Debt	N	11. Planned Parenthood	N
4. Homeland Security $$	Y	8. Loretta Lynch A.G	Y	12. Trade deals	Y

Election Results

Election	Name (Party)	Vote (%)		Cand. Spent	Ind. Exp. Support	Ind. Exp. Oppose
2012 General	Maria Cantwell (D)	1,855,493	(60%)	$11,198,862	$183,709	
	Michael Baumgartner (R)	1,213,924	(40%)	$998,360		
2012 Primary	Maria Cantwell (D)	772,058	(56%)			
	Michael Baumgartner (R)	417,141	(30%)			
	Art Coday (R)	79,727	(6%)			

Prior winning percentages: 2006 (57%), 2000 (49%)

Democrat Maria Cantwell, Washington's junior senator, was elected in 2000. She is active on energy, technology, and tax matters, often working with Republicans, and is known for her tenacity. As the ranking member on the Energy and Natural Resources Committee, she has developed a close partnership with Republican chairwoman Lisa Murkowski of Alaska, with their shared Northwest perspective and similar views on many issues.

Cantwell grew up in Indianapolis, where her father, Paul Cantwell, a construction worker, served as county commissioner, a city councilman, and a state legislator. As a child, Cantwell observed politics firsthand as her father dispensed advice to union members, laborers, and politicians who stopped by to talk politics. During her father's stint as an aide to Democratic Rep. Andy Jacobs of Indiana, she awoke one morning to the distinctive Boston accent of Sen. Edward Kennedy of Massachusetts downstairs.

Cantwell graduated from Miami University of Ohio, the first in her family to graduate from college. She worked in Ohio for former Cincinnati Mayor turned television personality Jerry Springer's 1982 campaign for governor. Then she worked for California Democratic Sen. Alan Cranston's presidential campaign in 1984, going to Seattle to set up a regional campaign office. The Cranston campaign went nowhere, but Cantwell loved the Pacific Northwest and decided to stay. She moved to Mountlake Terrace, a suburb in Snohomish County, where she organized a coalition to build a new library. In 1986, she was elected to the Washington state House.

In 1992, Cantwell ran for an open House seat and won a solid 55% to 42% victory-the first Democrat to prevail in the district in 40 years. In the House, she showed her independence by not supporting President Bill Clinton's health care plan, but she did back the family and medical leave bill, the Clinton economic plan and NAFTA. Cantwell was a strong supporter of abortion rights and an unwavering champion of stands backed by environmental advocacy groups. She sounded early alarms about encroachments on privacy, and persuaded the Clinton administration to drop its support for the "clipper chip," which would have enabled the government to monitor personal electronic communications. Still, she lost her 1994 bid for reelection to Republican Rick White, 52% to 48%, in a huge wave year for the GOP, when Democrats lost six seats in the nine-seat Washington delegation.

Back in the Seattle area, Cantwell joined a start-up firm called Progressive Networks in 1995. Five years later, it had become RealNetworks, a leader in Internet-based audio and visual software. In late 1999, her stock was worth about $40 million, and Cantwell was ready to resume her political career. She challenged Republican Sen. Slade Gorton. Gorton had an increasingly conservative record on environmental and economic issues. Insurance Commissioner Deborah Senn, who also was running, was widely considered too liberal to win. Cantwell called herself a New Democrat in the Clinton mode and backed permanent normal trade relations with China-a move that Senn opposed. But the real difference was money. Cantwell, who liquidated more than $5 million in stock, spent freely, while Senn was on television only during the last two weeks before the September all-party primary. In the first round of balloting, Gorton got the most votes, 44 percent of the total. Cantwell got 37 percent, and Senn received only 13 percent.

Cantwell said she would spend "whatever it takes" to win. At the same time, she made her support of McCain-Feingold-type campaign finance regulation a major issue and refused to take contributions from political action committees or large donations known as "soft money" from the Democratic Party (though it put $640,000 into the state before Cantwell won the primary). She charged that Gorton was beholden to special-interest contributors, singling out his late-night Senate amendment that paved the way for a cyanide-leach gold mine in rural Okanogan County, which environmentalists were fighting. She spoke of her work in high-tech and contrasted her experience with his, saying: "I've just spent the last five years in the private sector learning how to do things on the outside. Senator Gorton's been in office for 41 years. He seems to like government a lot." Gorton described Cantwell as an old-style liberal Democrat who would have government meddling in health care, education, and the local environment. Overall, she spent $11.5 million, $10.3 million of it her own money, to Gorton's $6.4 million. Gorton was hurt when Indian tribes, some flush with casino cash, weighed in against him as they felt that he did not respect their sovereignty when he sought to have them bound by the same laws that bind other people.

Gorton led on Election Night, but not by much. The absentee ballots from heavily Democratic King County put Cantwell over the top by 1,953 votes. A mandated recount left the margin at 2,229 for Cantwell, out of 2.4 million cast, the closest Senate contest of 2000. Cantwell carried only five counties: King, Snohomish, Thurston, which includes the state capital of Olympia, and two small counties in the west. Gorton carried eastern Washington with 61 percent. Cantwell's victory created a tie in the Senate, until Vermont's James Jeffords became an independent in May 2001 and gave Democrats a razor-thin majority.

Cantwell's voting record is consistently liberal on social issues, but more moderate on economic and foreign policy matters. With scores close to those of her home-state colleague Patty Murray, her *Almanac* vote ratings in 2015 ranked her with centrist Democrats. She was one of just nine Senate Democrats to oppose the 2008 law creating the Troubled Asset Relief Fund for ailing financial institutions, saying the government had no business getting so deeply involved with the private sector. Three years later, she was one of six Democrats to support a failed GOP amendment to halt tax breaks and incentives for corn-based ethanol products popular with farm-state lawmakers.

During the 2010 debate on overhauling the banking and financial services regulatory system, Cantwell pushed for more radical reforms. She co-sponsored a bill with GOP Sen. John McCain of Arizona that would have reinstated the Glass-Steagall Banking Act of 1933, which created a wall between commercial and investment banking. She wanted to close loopholes on unregulated derivatives trading. Cantwell was one of only two Democrats to vote against initial passage of the White House-backed banking reform bill. She joined her party in voting for the final conference report on the bill, reasoning that the updated bill offered at least tougher regulation and greater transparency of the derivatives market.

To help her state's hydropower industry, which produces almost three-fourths of Washington's electricity, Cantwell has been active in efforts to remove barriers to licensing new facilities. In 2010, when the Obama administration and Democrats in Congress pushed for ultimately unsuccessful legislation aimed at curbing greenhouse gases, she jumped into the debate. The Obama White House bill, which allowed energy efficient companies to trade credits to larger greenhouse gas emitters as a way to reduce overall levels of carbon dioxide emissions, proved a hard sell. Cantwell and GOP Sen. Susan Collins of Maine stepped up efforts to push their "cap-and-dividend" bill that skirted the idea of a carbon trading market. Instead, their bill would cap emissions from sources such as coal mines and oil refineries, and those emitters would be required to purchase carbon permits. The Senate failed to take action on the bill. Cantwell opposed legislation to authorize the Keystone XL pipeline.

When Montana Sen. Max Baucus quit the Senate in early 2014 to become Ambassador to China, that led Oregon's Ron Wyden to take over the Finance Committee and Louisiana's Mary Landrieu to move into Wyden's chair on Energy and Natural Resources, Cantwell assumed the gavel at the Small Business Committee. She worked with Jim Risch of Idaho, the panel's ranking Republican, on a measure to renew the State Trade and Export Promotion program, which awards grants to states to help small businesses begin or expand exports of their products. She held separate hearings on helping veteran and women entrepreneurs. Cantwell spent less than a year in the Small Business top post. After Landrieu lost reelection, Cantwell took the top Democratic seat at Energy, now in the minority.

Working with Murkowski as chairwoman, Cantwell put together a bill on multiple energy topics that won bipartisan approval in committee and overwhelmingly passed the Senate in April 2016. "Most provisos are very modest, but that doesn't mean they're not useful," former Democratic Rep. Philip Sharp of Indiana, who has worked on energy issues for decades, told *The Washington Post*. "It's a positive test for the Congress being able to legislate across the bitter partisan divide, and frankly Chairman Murkowski and Sen. Cantwell deserve considerable credit." The Senate bill addressed such issues as enhancement of the electric grid, energy efficiency in buildings and exports of natural gas. Negotiators failed to resolve differences with the House, which had passed a measure that focused more on resource production. "It is really irresponsible for our House colleagues to drop the ball," Cantwell said. She and Murkowski also collaborated on a proposal to increase the fleet of polar icebreaking ships for the Coast Guard, which has an active presence in their home states.

In 2017, President Donald Trump's nomination of former Texas Gov. Rick Perry as Energy Secretary initially halted bipartisanship on the Energy committee. Perry was "not the direction that the Energy Department needs to go," including energy efficiency, Cantwell said.

Cantwell has a coveted seat on the Finance Committee. She secured passage of a 2008 measure to temporarily extend the deductibility of state sales taxes, a popular tax break in Washington as it doesn't have a personal income tax. On the Commerce, Science and Transportation Committee, she has been the senior Democrat on the aviation panel, where she keeps a close eye for Boeing and the rest of her state's aerospace businesses. In 2012, Cantwell was the point person on the ambitious NextGen air traffic control modernization effort, which was part of the Federal Aviation Administration reauthorization bill that became law.

In 2015, Cantwell sought to extend the life of the U.S. Export-Import Bank, which expired as Congress started its July 4th recess. The bank, which finances U.S. exports abroad, became the center of a fierce political debate. Tea party conservatives argued that it is a prime example of corporate cronyism and welfare to companies that don't need it against. Defenders, like Cantwell, saw it as vital to U.S. competitiveness. With her Washington colleague Patty Murray, Cantwell led the charge for renewal of the Bank as a way to promote jobs. They played tough with Senate Majority Leader Mitch McConnell and won a promise for a floor vote later in the year on renewal of the bank, in return for which they supported the bill to give President Barack Obama fast-track authority to negotiate new trade deals. That led to a sequence of votes in which Congress agreed to revive the Bank, which has provided assistance to Washington-based Boeing's jet sales. *The Seattle Times* editorialized in December 2015 that Cantwell deserved "credit for helping bring back the Ex-Im Bank."

Although a strong supporter of campaign finance regulation, Cantwell has had campaign finance problems of her own. To fund her 2000 campaign, she had sold $5.6 million of her RealNetworks stock and had borrowed $3.8 million from a bank using the company's stock as collateral. That enabled her to run the last-minute ads that were essential to her victory. The Federal Election Commission ruled in

January 2004 that she had violated the law by failing to disclose the terms of the loans, but it took no punitive action. With her earlier net worth of $40 million, paying off the loans should have been easy. But RealNetworks, like other high-tech firms, saw its stock price plummet, from $80 per share in spring 2000 to $6 in spring 2001. Suddenly Cantwell owed far more than the collateral was worth. Over the course of the next several years, she paid off the debt.

Cantwell's narrow victory in 2000 placed her high on the Republicans target list for 2006. National Republicans recruited Mike McGavick, chairman and chief executive officer at Safeco insurance. McGavick, a successful businessman, with moderate positions and political smarts developed while he managed Gorton's 1988 campaign and served as his chief of staff, appeared formidable. McGavick acknowledged that he had been charged with drunken driving in 1993. Cantwell faced lingering discontent from liberals in the party for her 2002 vote in favor of the Iraq war resolution. In a Democratic year in a Democratic-leaning state, she won 57 percent to 40 percent. In 2012, another good year for Democrats, Cantwell had an easy race against Republican state Sen. Michael Baumgartner. He was from eastern Washington, which hasn't produced a senator since 1934, and was unable to raise the kind of money necessary to compete with Cantwell. She won 60%-40%. National Republicans have shifted their campaign attention elsewhere.

FIRST DISTRICT

Suzan DelBene (D)

Elected 2012, 3rd term; b. Feb 17, 1962, Selma, AL; Reed College (OR), B.A., 1983; University of Washington, M.B.A., 1990; Episcopalian; Married (Kurt Delbene); 2 children.

Professional Career: Director of Marketing, Microsoft, 1989-1998; Vice President., Drugstore.com, 1998-2000; President, CEO, Nimble Tech., 2000-2003; Vice President., Microsoft, 2004-2007; Consultant, Global Partnerships, 2008-2009; Director, WA Department of Revenue, 2010-2012.

DC Office: 2442 RHOB 20515, 202-225-6311, Fax: 202-225-1606, delbene.house.gov.

State Offices: Bothell, 425-485-0085; Mount Vernon, 360-416-7879.

Committees: *Budget*. *Ways & Means*: Oversight, Tax Policy.

Group Ratings

	ADA	ACLU	AFL-CIO	LCV	ITI	COC	HAFA	ACU	CFG	FRC
2016	-	100%	-	97%	100%	54%	9%	0%	0%	0%
2015	75%	C	92%	94%	C	55%	C	4%	0%	0%

Almanac Ratings 2015

	Economy	Social	Foreign	Composite
Liberal	67%	100%	93%	86%
Conservative	33%	0%	7%	14%

Key Votes of the 114th Congress

1. Keystone Pipeline	N	5. Puerto Rico Debt	Y	9. Offenses by Aliens	N
2. Trade Deals	Y	6. Medical Marijuana	Y	10. Troops in Iraq	Y
3. Export-Import Bank	Y	7. Sanctuary Cities	N	11. Homeland Security $$	Y
4. Debt Ceiling Increase	Y	8. Armor-piercing Bullets	N	12. Trade Adjustment aid	Y

Election Results

Election	Name (Party)	Vote (%)	Cand. Spent	Ind. Exp. Support	Ind. Exp. Oppose
2016 General	Suzan DelBene (D)	193,619 (55%)	$1,114,584	$1,322	
	Robert Sutherland (R)	155,779 (45%)	$26,415		
2016 Primary	Suzan DelBene (D)	47,058 (54%)			
	Robert Sutherland (R)	27,200 (31%)			
	John Orlinski (R)	8,357 (10%)			

Prior winning percentages: 2014 (55%), 2012 (54%)

Democrat Suzan DelBene, a former Microsoft executive, was elected to an open seat in 2012. With her corporate experience, she settled in with the dwindling ranks of business-oriented Democrats in the House and backed President Barack Obama's international trade agenda. In 2017, she got a coveted seat on the Ways and Means Committee.

DelBene was born in Selma, Alabama. When she was a toddler, her parents divorced and DelBene lived with her mother, who married an airline pilot. The family moved often. When she was in high school, DelBene's stepfather got a job with Iran Air and her parents relocated overseas. She majored in biology at Reed College, originally hoping to become a veterinarian. Undergraduate research changed her career interests and her first job after college was with a biotechnology firm in Seattle. She got her master's degree in business administration and interned at Microsoft. She landed a full-time job there and met and married her husband, Kurt, president of Microsoft's Office division. She spent 12 years at Microsoft, rising to the position of corporate vice president of the company's mobile communications business. DelBene left Microsoft in 1998 and joined two high-tech startups. She later worked on microfinance with an international nonprofit, a job that she said taught her the ways in which policy could create opportunities for families. In her spare time, DelBene has been a marathon runner.

Inspired to run for Congress, she spent more than $2 million of her own money in a 2010 challenge to Republican Rep. Dave Reichert in the east Seattle suburbs. Her narrow 52%-48% loss in the GOP-leaning district was impressive during a disastrous year for national Democrats. Shortly after that setback, Democratic Gov. Christine Gregoire appointed DelBene director of the state Department of Revenue, where she helped to enact a tax amnesty program that generated $345 million to help close the state's budget gap. That job didn't last long. In 2012, DelBene was one of five Democrats in the newly drawn 1st District. With a reported net worth of more than $50 million, her personal wealth was a prime topic in the race. Her Democratic opponents cast her as just another millionaire running for Congress. Her background was appealing to the Democratic establishment for her ability to self-fund, and she was endorsed by Gregoire and Rep. Rick Larsen. DelBene's campaign aired a series of biographical ads that focused on the financial struggles of her youth.

DelBene's chief Democratic opponent was liberal Darcy Burner, also a Microsoft executive. The only Republican in the all-party primary was state legislator John Koster, who had lost two earlier contests a decade apart in the adjacent 2nd District. Koster finished first with 45 percent of vote. DelBene won the battle to enter the runoff with 22 percent to 14 percent for Burner. DelBene consolidated support among Democrats and won, 54%-46%. She got 60 percent in King County, and 52 percent in Snohomish; Koster took 55 percent in Whatcom. On the same day, DelBene won a special election to complete the term of Democratic Rep. Jay Inslee, who had resigned to run for governor. In that contest, she defeated Koster by the wider margin of 60%-40%. The special election was waged in the more Democratic boundaries prior to redistricting and consequently had a different electorate.

DelBene spent much of her time during her first year tending to two unexpected local disasters and their follow-up: the collapse of a bridge on Interstate 5 in Skagit Valley and a destructive mudslide in rural Oso. She served on the Judiciary Committee, where she spoke out on technology and privacy. She advocated greater transparency and oversight of the National Security Agency. In June 2015, DelBene voted to give trade promotion authority to Obama, noting that "Washington is the most trade-dependent state in the nation and 40 percent of our jobs depend on trade."

In 2016, DelBene served on the temporary Panel on Infant Lives that House Republicans created to investigate Planned Parenthood and the procuring of fetal tissue. Calling the panel "a brazenly partisan and ideological witch-hunt and it should never have been created in the first place," she added when Republicans issued their final report, "this so-called investigation has repeatedly shown contempt for the facts and disdain for the truth." On another social issue, she filed a bill with California Democratic Rep. Ted Lieu to create a federal ban on conversion therapy for gays and lesbians. In the *Almanac* vote ratings for 2015, she joined three other Democrats from Washington who were ranked near the center of the House. Her scores were centrist on the economy and liberal on social issues.

In January 2017, as DelBene took her seat on Ways and Means, she said that Congress should reject "dangerous proposals" from Republicans on health care, and instead should work on "incentivizing high-quality patient care, reducing costs for small business, and expanding access for our most vulnerable citizens." At the same time, she became the finance co-chair of the Democratic Congressional Campaign Committee. After President Donald Trump issued executive orders on immigrants and refugees a week after he took office, DelBene went to the Seattle-Tacoma airport to seek information about people who had been detained and denied entry. She immediately wrote to the Customs Bureau seeking explanations.

DelBene has had relatively easy reelection campaigns. In each of her two contests, she raised more than $2 million and got 55 percent of the vote. Her husband Kurt spent about a year in Washington with the challenging assignment of managing the government website for citizen enrollment in the Affordable Care Act. Soon after that, he returned home to Microsoft as executive vice-president of corporate strategy and planning.

Interior Northwest Washington: Seattle and Everett Suburbs

Population		**Race and Ethnicity**		**Income**	
Total	706,079	White	75.9%	Median Income	$82,358 (29 out of 435)
Land area	6,186	Black	1.1%		
Pop/ sq mi	114.1	Latino	8.7%	Under $50,000	29.1%
Born in state	49.0%	Asian	9.6%	$50,000-$99,999	30.7%
		Two races	3.4%	$100,000-$199,999	30.0%
Age Groups		Other	1.3%	$200,000 or more	10.2%
Under 18	24.0%			Poverty Rate	8.5%
18-34	20.9%	**Education**			
35-64	43.0%	H.S grad or less	26.8%	**Health Insurance**	
Over 64	12.1%	Some college	32.4%	With health insurance coverage	91.2%
Work		College Degree, 4 yr	26.2%		
		Post grad	14.6%	**Public Assistance**	
White Collar	45.8%				
Sales and Service	36.1%	**Military**		Cash public assistance income	2.8%
Blue Collar	18.2%	Veteran	8.3%		
Government	6.0%	Active Duty	0.2%	Food stamp/SNAP benefits	9.0%

Voter Turnout			
2015 Total Citizens 18+	482,839	2016 House Turnout as % CVAP	72%
2016 House turnout	349,398	2014 House Turnout as % CVAP	47%

2012 Presidential Vote		
Barack Obama	183,802	(54%)
Mitt Romney	147,074	(43%)

2016 Presidential Vote		
Hillary Clinton	188,952	(52%)
Donald Trump	132,109	(37%)
Gary Johnson	19,396	(5%)

Cook Partisan Voting Index: D+6

With the high-tech growth since the 1980s, metropolitan Seattle grew to the north and to the east, as a wave of newcomers arrived seeking the area's distinctive blend of natural beauty, robust and creative economic expansion, and freewheeling culture. The heart of the new Seattle is east of Lake Washington, in the edge city of Redmond. That is where you find the turquoise, pine-shaded, low-rise buildings of the Microsoft campus - a tranquil environment for a booming and boisterously aggressive company. With 45,400 employees in the Puget Sound area in December 2016, the company has expanded its campus in Redmond and leased major chunks of office space in Seattle and Bellevue. Microsoft has fueled Redmond's transformation from a sleepy hamlet of 1,426 people in 1960 to a hip center of commerce with a population of more than 61,000, of whom 25 percent are Asian. Immediately after President Donald Trump in January 2017 issued his executive order restricting immigrants and refugees, Microsoft offered assistance to Muslims and others in its workforce who might have been affected.

The 1st Congressional District of Washington includes most of Redmond and many of the other King County suburbs east of Seattle. Technology is a huge factor in the local economy. Redmond is also home of Nintendo of North America. In neighboring Kirkland, Google in February 2016 doubled the office space on its campus, where the research and development center developed Google Maps. On the eastern shore of Lake Washington are the homes and estates of the "Microsoft millionaires," many of whom exercised company stock options before the economic bust. The affluent suburbs include Medina, Clyde Hill, Yarrow Point and Hunts Point, as well as Bill Gates' $60 million, 66,000-square-foot home.

The 1st goes through the Cascades to take in the eastern extremities of King County. It also takes in the interior portions away from coastline of Snohomish, Skagit and Whatcom counties, all the way to the Canadian border. Along the way, the economy gradually shifts from software code to raspberries and dairy farming. At the far north end of the district is the fishing and lumber town of Blaine, with America's most attractively landscaped border crossing and the International Peace Arch, just south of British Columbia. About 40 percent of the population is in King, and nearly as many in Snohomish.

The King County areas of the district are strongly Democratic, while the inland portions are swing territory. The resulting district leans Democratic, but can be competitive. Hillary Clinton, like Barack Obama four years earlier, won 52 percent of the vote in 2016. For Obama, that was his smallest win in the state's six Democratic-held districts. Clinton's performance was a bit lower in the two districts west of Puget Sound.

SECOND DISTRICT

Rick Larsen (D)

Elected 2000, 9th term; b. Jun 15, 1965, Arlington; Pacific Lutheran University (WA), B.A., 1987; University of Minnesota, M.P.A., 1990; Methodist; Married (Tiia Karlen Larsen); 2 children.

Elected Office: Snohomish City Council, 1998-2000, President, 1999-2000.

Professional Career: Econ. dev. official, Port of Everett, 1990-1991; Director pub. affairs, WA St. Dental Assn., 1991-1998.

DC Office: 2113 RHOB 20515, 202-225-2605, Fax: 202-225-4420, larsen.house.gov.

State Offices: Bellingham, 360-733-4500; Everett, 425-252-3188.

Committees: *Armed Services*: Emerging Threats & Capabilities, Strategic Forces. *Transportation & Infrastructure*: Aviation (RMM), Coast Guard & Maritime Transportation.

Group Ratings

	ADA	ACLU	AFL-CIO	LCV	ITI	COC	HAFA	ACU	CFG	FRC
2016	-	94%	-	100%	83%	57%	10%	0%	0%	0%
2015	75%	C	88%	94%	C	55%	C	0%	0%	0%

Almanac Ratings 2015

	Economy	Social	Foreign	Composite
Liberal	78%	100%	86%	88%
Conservative	22%	0%	15%	12%

Key Votes of the 114th Congress

1. Keystone Pipeline	N	5. Puerto Rico Debt	Y	9. Offenses by Aliens	N
2. Trade Deals	Y	6. Medical Marijuana	Y	10. Troops in Iraq	Y
3. Export-Import Bank	Y	7. Sanctuary Cities	N	11. Homeland Security $$	Y
4. Debt Ceiling Increase	Y	8. Armor-piercing Bullets	N	12. Trade Adjustment aid	Y

Election Results

Election	Name (Party)	Vote (%)	Cand. Spent	Ind. Exp. Support	Ind. Exp. Oppose
2016 General	Rick Larsen (D)	208,314 (64%)	$813,669	$1,280	
	Marc Hennemann (R)	117,094 (36%)			
2016 Primary	Rick Larsen (D)	46,642 (53%)			
	Marc Hennemann (R)	27,931 (32%)			
	Mike Lapointe (D)	8,963 (10%)			

Prior winning percentages: 2014 (61%), 2012 (61%), 2010 (51%), 2008 (62%), 2006 (64%), 2004 (64%), 2002 (50%), 2000 (50%)

Rick Larsen, a moderate Democrat first elected in 2000, takes an avid interest in issues related to China, a country that does substantial business with his state. He is well-positioned in the House on aviation matters to assist Boeing Co., the largest employer in his district. In the state's tradition, he remains an outspoken proponent of international trade.

Larsen grew up in Arlington, in Snohomish County, graduated from Pacific Lutheran University, and got a master's degree at the University of Minnesota. He spent a year doing research on economic development for the Port of Everett. For six years, he was director of public affairs for the Washington State Dental Association. In 1998, he won a seat on the Snohomish County Council and later became its president.

In 2000, Republican Jack Metcalf kept his promise to retire after three terms in Congress. The Democratic field was cleared for Larsen. Republicans nominated state Rep. John Koster. The general election became a battleground for political action committees and one of the premier contests in the nation. Anti-abortion rights groups and the National Rifle Association backed Koster, and unions and abortion-rights groups fought for Larsen. Larsen criticized Koster for referring to "our American holocaust," a familiar term among anti-abortion activists. Larsen won 50%-46%.

Larsen has been a leader of the New Democrat Coalition and leans toward the center in his voting record, although he became more reliably Democratic after President Barack Obama took office. He backed the 2009 economic stimulus and 2010 health care legislation. Earlier, he voted for the Bush-era tax cuts in 2001, but later opposed extending the cuts for upper-income taxpayers. He was one of 22 Democrats in 2012 to support a failed plan for a budget along the lines of the Simpson-Bowles deficit reduction commission. Though he opposed the 2005 Central America Free Trade Agreement, he joined with most Republicans six years later to back free-trade pacts with Korea, Panama and Colombia. In June 2015, he was one of 28 House Democrats who voted to give trade promotion authority to Obama, especially for the prospective Trans-Pacific Partnership.

Larsen has co-chaired the U.S.-China Working Group, a bipartisan group of House members that seeks to build lasting diplomatic ties with China. Washington state exports to China nearly quadrupled from 2000 to 2009. In 2011, Larsen got a bill into law creating a new type of business card aimed at expediting travel in the Asia-Pacific region for qualified American travelers. The working group has called for greater U.S. engagement with China on military issues, despite reports of widespread computer-security breaches that were blamed on that nation's army. In April 2016, he applauded an agreement by China to reduce its export subsidies. He has made similar demands on the European Union to reduce its subsidies for the European-made Airbus.

As the "Congressman from Boeing," Larsen has a plum assignment as the top Democrat on the Transportation and Infrastructure Aviation Subcommittee. In a sign of the importance of aviation to Washington, his home-state Sen. Maria Cantwell holds a comparable position in the Senate. Boeing and its employees are among Larsen's major campaign contributors. He supported the Federal Aviation Administration's decision in 2013 to ground the company's new 787 Dreamliner fleet over concerns about the plane's fire-plagued batteries, saying that safety should be paramount. He said that Congress must assure that the FAA is "positioned to understand and challenge assumptions put forward by manufacturers regarding new technologies."

On other issues, Larsen has pushed to secure funds for upgraded border security at Bellingham and helped get a pipeline safety bill into law in 2002 after a lethal explosion in his district. He co-founded the Congressional Arctic Working Group, with the chief focus of protecting U.S. environmental, economic and strategic interests in the region.

Larsen won reelection easily until 2010, when he was challenged by Koster, his opponent of a decade earlier. Koster won endorsements from leading national conservatives, which inspired tea party activists to pump hundreds of thousands of dollars into the Republican's campaign. Larsen outspent the challenger $2.1 million to $1.1. million. Their second battle was a microcosm of the two major parties' talking points that year: Koster blasted the Democrats' "socialist" health care bill and the rising federal debt, while Larsen stressed job creation and expanding credit for small business. He declared victory a week after the election with a 51%-49% edge, a margin of 6,500 votes.

After the 2011 redistricting boosted the Democratic base in the district by five percentage points, Larsen has won more than 60 percent of the vote in each general election. But he often faces a difficult political balance. In 2016, the State Labor Council withheld its endorsement and environmentalists objected to refineries in Puget Sound. Democrat Mike LaPointe, a coffee shop owner in Everett, challenged Larsen in the primary from the left, with objections to his international trade votes. In the all-party primary, Larsen got 52 percent and LaPointe had 11 percent, with the remainder going to Republicans.

Following the 2016 election, Larsen was vocal in warning against Donald Trump's calls to restrict international trade. "Trade is a two-way street. If the president-elect believes that we are the country of the 1950s, where we can merely punish countries on trade without them taking reciprocal action, he's wrong," he said.

Upper Puget Sound: Everett Metro

Population		**Race and Ethnicity**		**Income**	
Total	696,458	White	72.8%	Median Income	$59,665 (144 out of 435)
Land area	1,015	Black	2.6%		
Pop/ sq mi	686.2	Latino	10.3%		
Born in state	48.1%	Asian	8.0%	Under $50,000	41.8%
Age Groups		Two races	4.5%	$50,000-$99,999	33.8%
Under 18	21.4%	Other	1.8%	$100,000-$199,999	20.8%
18-34	25.3%	**Education**		$200,000 or more	3.5%
35-64	39.2%	H.S grad or less	32.4%	Poverty Rate	13.1%
Over 64	14.2%	Some college	38.0%	**Health Insurance**	
Work		College Degree, 4 yr	20.0%	With health insurance coverage	88.3%
White Collar	34.7%	Post grad	9.5%		
Sales and Service	43.0%	**Military**		**Public Assistance**	
Blue Collar	22.3%	Veteran	10.8%	Cash public assistance income	3.9%
Government	6.3%	Active Duty	1.5%	Food stamp/SNAP benefits	14.1%

Voter Turnout			
2015 Total Citizens 18+	505,499	2016 House Turnout as % CVAP	64%
2016 House turnout	325,408	2014 House Turnout as % CVAP	40%

2012 Presidential Vote		
Barack Obama	185,771	(59%)
Mitt Romney	119,266	(38%)

2016 Presidential Vote		
Hillary Clinton	185,821	(55%)
Donald Trump	113,670	(34%)
Gary Johnson	16,880	(5%)
Jill Stein	7,477	(2%)

Cook Partisan Voting Index: D+10

The Seattle metropolitan area has marched north along the shore of Puget Sound, beyond the old lumber port and railroad terminus of Everett, where the huge Boeing plant produces 747s, 767s, 777s, and the new long-range 787s. Sales of the 787 Dreamliner, which made its maiden flight in 2009, have been especially strong, following some delay when the Dreamliner was grounded because of battery failures. In December 2016, the company said that it planned to cut production of the 777, the company's biggest money-maker, which is being replaced by the 777X. In a May 2015 interview with the *Seattle Times*, a Boeing executive said that the company will be hiring as many as 30,000 workers in the next few years because of expected retirements. Some of the assembly-line jobs have been replaced by robots. Further north is Bellingham, which grew up as a supply station for gold miners in the 1850s and was the source of much of the lumber used to rebuild San Francisco after the 1906 earthquake and fire. It still plays an important role in the local fishing industry. Officials at the region's deep-water ports, two days closer to Asia than Southern California's ports, have been nervous that the widening of the competing Panama Canal will divert traffic to East Coast ports that are closer to markets.

In the waters of Puget Sound are the 176 San Juan Islands, which were the last part of the continental United States to be turned over to this country. The waters were great whaling grounds, and not until 1860 did the British relinquish them. Today, ferryboats ply the waters of the sound, connecting the islands to mainland Washington and to British Columbia, directly to the west. The publicly operated Washington State Ferries system in 2016 had more than 24 million passengers and 10 million vehicles on 22 auto-passenger ferries to 20 ports, the largest ferry operator in the United States. Whale-watching is popular not only with tourists but among scientists on both sides of the border. This is some of the most beautiful coastline in North America: the steely blue sound with forested hills rising behind it, shielded from the full force of Pacific rains by the Olympic Mountains, though still seldom dry. The little towns, on bits of level land between the water and the mountains, have the look of pristine New England villages, and the stores are stocked with fresh produce and local seafood.

The 2nd Congressional District of Washington encompasses the San Juan Islands, including 45-mile-long Whidbey Island, and most of the mainland along the east side of the sound. The district has several military installations, including a Navy base at Everett and a naval air station on Whidbey. The political tradition in most of the lumbering and fishing areas here is Democratic, as is the political culture in Everett. In addition to Everett, the district takes in most of the major ports on Puget Sound. Nearly 60 percent of the population resides in Snohomish County, which is closest to Seattle. The remainder are spread among four other counties. Following a *Los Angeles Times* investigation of opioid addiction in Everett, the city in January 2017 filed a lawsuit against the manufacturer of OxyContin. North of Bellingham, the district line is a few miles short of the Canadian border. The 2nd leans strongly Democratic. Hillary Clinton took 55 percent of the vote in 2016.

THIRD DISTRICT

Jaime Herrera Beutler (R)

Elected 2010, 4th term; b. Nov 03, 1978, Glendale, CA; Seattle Pacific University (WA), Att., 1998; Bellevue Community College (WA), A.A., 2003; University of Washington, B.A., 2004; Christian Church; Married (Daniel Beutler); 1 child.

Elected Office: WA House, 2007-2011.

Professional Career: Legislative aide, Rep. Cathy McMorris Rodgers, 2005-2007.

DC Office: 1107 LHOB 20515, 202-225-3536, Fax: 202-225-3478, jaimehb.house.gov.

State Offices: Chehalis, 360-695-6292; Vancouver, 360-695-6292.

Committees: *Appropriations*: Energy & Water Development & Related Agencies, Financial Services & General Government, Labor, Health & Human Services, Education & Related Agencies.

Group Ratings

	ADA	ACLU	AFL-CIO	LCV	ITI	COC	HAFA	ACU	CFG	FRC
2016	-	5%	-	8%	83%	100%	52%	0%	84%	100%
2015	0%	C	14%	6%	C	95%	C	58%	60%	90%

Almanac Ratings 2015

	Economy	Social	Foreign	Composite
Liberal	10%	9%	5%	8%
Conservative	90%	91%	95%	92%

Key Votes of the 114th Congress

1. Keystone Pipeline	Y	5. Puerto Rico Debt	NV	9. Offenses by Aliens	Y
2. Trade Deals	Y	6. Medical Marijuana	N	10. Troops in Iraq	N
3. Export-Import Bank	Y	7. Sanctuary Cities	Y	11. Homeland Security $$	N
4. Debt Ceiling Increase	N	8. Armor-piercing Bullets	Y	12. Trade Adjustment aid	Y

Election Results

Election	Name (Party)	Vote (%)	Cand. Spent	Ind. Exp. Support	Ind. Exp. Oppose
2016 General	Jaime Herrera Beutler (R)	193,457 (62%)	$1,668,020		
	Jim Moeller (D)	119,820 (38%)	$110,107		
2016 Primary	Jaime Herrera Beutler (R)	54,114 (55%)			
	Jim Moeller (D)	25,042 (25%)			
	David McDevitt (D)	9,984 (10%)			

Prior winning percentages: 2014 (62%), 2012 (60%), 2010 (53%)

Republican Jaime Herrera Beutler, elected in 2010, is a young Latina - exactly the kind of politician that many in her party wantin their ranks. She assists the GOP in its outreach while compiling a business-friendly centrist voting record. On the Appropriations Committee, she tends to local resource funding. In the 2016 presidential campaign, she said that she was open to supporting Donald Trump. Following the early October release of a 2005 tape in which Trump made lewd comments about women, she said, "That door has now slammed shut."

Herrera Beutler grew up in the region. Her father was a printer, her parents raised six children, and finances were tight. It was a blended family: Her parents took in an uncle's children to shelter them from gangs and violence in Southern California. She took a job as a nanny to help pay for college. After concluding that nursing studies weren't the right field for her, Herrera Beutler got a degree in communications from the University of Washington. She was involved in politics as a teenager, knocking on doors for Republicans in 1994. During college, she had a White House internship. After graduating, she was a legislative aide to Rep. Cathy McMorris Rodgers of eastern Washington, who became her mentor. When a seat opened in the state legislature in 2007, she was appointed. She won election in her own right the next year with 60 percent of the vote. She became the assistant floor leader, the only woman and minority on the Republican leadership team.

When six-term Democratic Rep. Brian Baird announced that he would retire in 2010, Herrera Beutler, then 31 and a newlywed, discussed getting into the race with her husband, Daniel Beutler, who was about to start law school. They decided to delay his plans so she could run. "We didn't want to look back in 10 or 20 years and say to our children we were too comfortable to do what was right," she said. In the all-party primary, Herrera Beutler led a crowded Republican field that included two tea party-backed candidates, with 28 percent of the vote, doubling the total for runner-up David Hendrick. She got help in the primary from the National Republican Congressional Committee, which put her on its "Young Guns" list of candidates worthy of funding and advertising.

In the general, Herrera Beutler was outspent. Media and technology entrepreneur Denny Heck spent $2 million, including $350,000 of his own money, to her $1.5 million. National party and interest-group money helped her close the gap. Heck ran as a moderate Democrat and emphasized his experience creating jobs. She criticized Heck for his support of the health care overhaul championed by Democrats and of President Barack Obama's economic stimulus bill. Her television ads concluded, "For fiscal sanity, Jaime Herrera for Congress." Riding that year's GOP tidal wave, she won 53%-47%. In 2012, Heck was elected in a nearby district that was created by redistricting.

Herrera Beutler has been among the moderate members of the Class of 2010. She has been loyal to the GOP leadership on most major votes, partly with a boost from McMorris Rodgers. In her first year, she opposed conservative attempts to eliminate or drastically reduce funding for agencies such as the Legal Services Corporation and Foreign Agricultural Service. Oregon GOP Rep. Greg Walden appointed her vice chair of the minority outreach effort at the National Republican Congressional Committee. "I think we can do a better job of tone," she told *The Columbian* of Vancouver about her party's relationship with Hispanics. She expressed reservations about legislative proposals to restrict gun rights, citing her own experience in her early 20s when a man repeatedly tried to break into her home. She said owning a gun gave her peace of mind. On immigration, she favored comprehensive reform, but opposed Obama's unilateral efforts to impose changes. She joined Democrat Rep. Kurt Schrader of Oregon in leading objections to a federal court's 2011 decision that water runoff from forest roads must be regulated the same as runoff from factories and sewage treatment plants. The Supreme Court in 2013 reversed the decision.

She switched in 2013 to her plum seat on Appropriations. She has worked to secure funds for the nuclear waste clean-up at the Hanford plant in her home state. In 2017, she joined the Subcommittee on Labor, Health and Human Services and Education, where she said that she would focus on cures for diseases, opioid abuse and workforce training.

In 2013, her daughter Abigail was born premature and without kidneys. Herrera Beutler took six months away from the Capitol to be with her daughter, who unexpectedly survived with unprecedented surgical intervention and kidney dialysis. In March 2016, her husband Daniel gave a kidney transplant to their daughter, whose health seemed miraculously robust. As a result of that experience, Herrera Beutler has pushed for a bill to help create a nationwide network of providers to assist medically complex children.

Herrera Beutler has coasted to reelection with at least 60 percent of the vote and has entrenched herself in the previously Democratic district. In 2015, some conservative Republicans unhappy with her House votes for additional spending and regulations discussed calls for a censure by the Clark County GOP. Instead, they reconsidered and agreed to a mechanism to monitor the votes of all elected officials. As a woman with Mexican ancestry, she struggled during the 2016 campaign with her views on Trump. For now, her political future remains bright. House Democrats listed her among their early targets in the 2018 campaign. In early 2017, she objected to Republican proposals to cut back Medicaid funding.

Southwest Washington: Vancouver

Population		**Race and Ethnicity**		**Income**	
Total	692,893	White	81.6%	Median Income	$54,685 (187 out of 435)
Land area	9,114	Black	1.4%		
Pop/ sq mi	76.0	Latino	8.8%		
Born in state	41.3%	Asian	3.1%	Under $50,000	45.2%
		Two races	3.7%	$50,000-$99,999	33.4%
Age Groups		Other	1.4%	$100,000-$199,999	18.0%
Under 18	24.4%			$200,000 or more	3.2%
18-34	23.2%	**Education**		Poverty Rate	13.2%
35-64	40.1%	H.S grad or less	37.3%		
Over 64	12.4%	Some college	39.4%	**Health Insurance**	
Work		College Degree, 4 yr	15.1%	With health insurance coverage	88.7%
White Collar	32.5%	Post grad	8.2%		
Sales and Service	42.0%	**Military**		**Public Assistance**	
Blue Collar	25.4%	Veteran	11.6%	Cash public assistance income	5.1%
Government	6.5%	Active Duty	0.1%	Food stamp/SNAP benefits	17.8%

Voter Turnout			
2015 Total Citizens 18+	497,860	2016 House Turnout as % CVAP	63%
2016 House turnout	313,277	2014 House Turnout as % CVAP	41%

2012 Presidential Vote		
Mitt Romney	150,409	(50%)
Barack Obama	145,442	(48%)

2016 Presidential Vote		
Donald Trump	157,359	(48%)
Hillary Clinton	134,009	(41%)
Gary Johnson	15,707	(5%)

Cook Partisan Voting Index: R+4

From the Pacific Ocean to the majestic row of active and inactive volcanoes of the Cascades, southwest Washington was long one of America's most productive lumber areas. The moist air and almost constant rain blown in from the Pacific have kept the trees on the coast growing rapidly. Precipitation is heavy in the valleys just past the Coast Range, and the forests there are also fast growing. Then come the high mountains. The Cascades are a genuine divide, wringing almost all of the moisture out of the atmosphere and making an arid climate eastward for a thousand miles. Americans had long been taught that the lower 48 states had no active volcanoes, but Mount St. Helens in Skamania County proved that wrong in 1980 when it erupted after laying dormant for 123 years, killing 57 people, destroying its own peak, and paving the land around it with lava. Tiny quakes were detected there in November 2016.

For many years, this part of Washington was sparsely settled, with lumber-mill and fishing-boat towns scattered between mountains and water. It was flannel shirt country, Democratic since New Deal days. In the early 1990s, its resource-based economy was threatened by the environmental movement, which restricted fishing practices and produced a court decision shutting down logging in old-growth forests to save spotted owl habitat. This roiled local politics and gave Republicans an opening. The GOP's efforts in the region have been assisted by the growth of Clark County, across the Columbia River from Portland, Oregon, which has filled with new residents eager to avoid Oregon's income tax, one of the highest in the country, but who want to make big purchases in Oregon free of sales tax. Clark County, where one-third of the residents commute to work in Portland, grew by 35 percent from 2000 to 2016; 9 percent of the county population is Hispanic.

The 3rd Congressional District of Washington covers the southwestern corner of the state, between the ocean and the Cascades. Economic growth and diversification and the arrival of many new residents with no roots in the old industries have made the area politically marginal. Nearly two-thirds of the district's residents live in Clark County. To the north, the district includes a small slice of Thurston

County, but not the state's capital, Olympia. The 3rd now leans Republican by a few percentage points. Donald Trump won in 2016, 48%-41%, after Mitt Romney led here 50%-48%.

FOURTH DISTRICT

Dan Newhouse (R)

Elected 2014, 2nd term; b. Jul 10, 1955, Sunnyside; Washington State University, B.S., 1977; Presbyterian; Widower; 2 children.

Elected Office: WA House, 2003-2009.

Professional Career: Farmer; WA Director of Agriculture, 2009-2013.

DC Office: 1318 LHOB 20515, 202-225-5816, Fax: 202-225-3251, newhouse.house.gov.

State Offices: Richland, 509-713-7374; Twisp, 509-433-7760; Yakima, 509-452-3243.

Committees: *Appropriations*: Energy & Water Development & Related Agencies, Homeland Security, Legislative Branch. *Rules*: Legislative & Budget Process, Rules & Organization of the House.

Group Ratings

	ADA	ACLU	AFL-CIO	LCV	ITI	COC	HAFA	ACU	CFG	FRC
2016	-	5%	-	0%	100%	100%	62%	83%	71%	92%
2015	0%	C	17%	3%	C	90%	C	75%	58%	75%

Almanac Ratings 2015

	Economy	Social	Foreign	Composite
Liberal	10%	15%	0%	8%
Conservative	90%	85%	100%	92%

Key Votes of the 114th Congress

1. Keystone Pipeline	Y	5. Puerto Rico Debt	N	9. Offenses by Aliens	Y
2. Trade Deals	Y	6. Medical Marijuana	Y	10. Troops in Iraq	N
3. Export-Import Bank	Y	7. Sanctuary Cities	Y	11. Homeland Security $$	N
4. Debt Ceiling Increase	N	8. Armor-piercing Bullets	Y	12. Trade Adjustment aid	N

Election Results

Election	Name (Party)	Vote (%)		Cand. Spent	Ind. Exp. Support	Ind. Exp. Oppose
2016 General	Dan Newhouse (R)	132,517	(58%)	$1,234,530		
	Clint Didier (R)	97,402	(42%)	$74,390		
2016 Primary	Dan Newhouse (R)	32,875	(46%)			
	Clint Didier (R)	19,383	(27%)			
	Doug McKinley (D)	15,547	(22%)			

Prior winning percentages: 2014 (51%)

Dan Newhouse won the seat in 2014 over fellow Republican Clint Didier after they were the top two in the August primary. Newhouse's promise of greater bipartisanship has been difficult to fulfill in the polarized Congress. He has been willing to buck conservative Republican renegades on issues that are vital to business. His assignments to two prime House committees have shown that he is well-regarded by GOP leaders.

Newhouse grew up in a Yakima Valley family that was active in local politics. His father, Irv, was a state legislator for 34 years. The younger Newhouse and his wife operate a 600-acre farm where they grow hops, grapes and alfalfa. He got his bachelor's degree in agricultural economics from Washington State University and is a former president of the Hop Growers of America. Newhouse won election to the state House in 2002. Democratic Gov. Christine Gregoire named him state agriculture director, calling him "the best person for the job." He served four years in the position. When Gregoire's successor,

Democrat Jay Inslee, declined to keep Newhouse in the position, he became a frequent television spokesman for opponents of a failed 2013 state ballot initiative that would have required labeling of genetically modified food products.

When Republican Rep. Doc Hastings, chairman of the Natural Resources Committee, announced his retirement, Republicans were confident they would keep the seat. In the all-party primary, Didier and Newhouse led the field with 32 percent and 26 percent, respectively. It marked the first time in state history that two Republicans faced off in the general election. That left voters a choice between two starkly different Republicans. Didier, a former tight end in the National Football League who ran for the Senate in 2010 and finished third in that all-party primary with 13 percent of the vote, was a major figure in the state's tea party movement. He was endorsed by former Alaska Gov. Sarah Palin and former Rep. Ron Paul of Texas, and emphasized gun rights, patriotism and religion.

Newhouse won endorsements from Hastings as well as the National Rifle Association. His campaign criticized Didier for reporting $291,000 in federal farm subsidies between 1995 and 2010, alleging the payments were at odds with his limited-government message. In its endorsement of Newhouse, the *Yakima Herald-Republic* noted the importance of the federal government in the district, which includes multiple federal dams. "Newhouse by far shows a better grasp of the federal government's influence and the need to work with others for the interests of Central Washington, all while representing the region's conservative slant," the newspaper said. Newhouse outspent Didier, $982,000 to $579,000, and won the general election, 51%-49%, a margin of 2,465 votes. Didier led in six of the eight counties. But Newhouse took Benton and Yakima counties, which cast 64 percent of the total votes. He won 60 percent in his Yakima base, which was the deciding factor.

Newhouse initially won assignments on the district-connected Agriculture and Natural Resources committees. When an opening occurred in early 2015 on the Rules Committee, which operates as an arm of the leadership, Speaker John Boehner tapped him as the only freshman on the panel. Newhouse supported renewal of the Export-Import Bank, a split with many junior Republicans but a popular move in his home state, where Boeing-manufactured aircraft are major beneficiaries of the loans, as are many farmers. "It's something I've seen as a very effective tool to help increase the exports coming out of the state of Washington," Newhouse said. In January 2017, he gained a seat on the Appropriations Committee; with Republican Jaime Herrera Beutler and Democrat Derek Kilmer, he became the third member from the Washington delegation to join that powerful panel. His subcommittee assignments, Newhouse added, "ensure that federal responsibilities to support Hanford cleanup and the groundbreaking scientific research and development at the Pacific Northwest National Laboratory are fulfilled." He remained on the Rules panel.

In the 2016 campaign, Newhouse unexpectedly found himself in a rematch with Didier in the general election. This time, Didier - who had a radio show on a Christian network - was an enthusiastic supporter of Donald Trump, but he declared his candidacy shortly before the filing deadline and was less-prepared. Newhouse, who had a fundraising advantage of 15-to-1, led handily in both the primary and general elections. Following the election, Newhouse voiced concerns about the impact of Trump's crackdown on immigration. "It is darned hard to get people to work on farms," Newhouse responded. He said that he hoped to work with the new president on trade issues, despite their disagreements. He was more supportive of the administration's plans to cut back environmental regulations.

Central Washington: Richland, Yakima

Population		**Race and Ethnicity**		**Income**	
Total	699,457	White	55.4%	Median Income	$50,313 (253 out of 435)
Land area	19,250	Black	1.0%		
Pop/ sq mi	36.3	Latino	37.6%		
Born in state	55.4%	Asian	1.5%	Under $50,000	49.7%
		Two races	2.1%	$50,000-$99,999	32.4%
Age Groups		Other	2.4%	$100,000-$199,999	15.1%
Under 18	29.3%			$200,000 or more	2.8%
18-34	22.8%	**Education**		Poverty Rate	18.3%
35-64	35.5%	H.S grad or less	48.5%		
Over 64	12.4%	Some college	31.7%	**Health Insurance**	
		College Degree, 4 yr	12.6%	With health insurance coverage	82.3%
Work		Post grad	7.2%		
White Collar	29.0%				
Sales and Service	36.9%	**Military**		**Public Assistance**	
Blue Collar	34.1%	Veteran	8.6%	Cash public assistance income	4.3%
Government	5.3%	Active Duty	0.1%		
				Food stamp/SNAP benefits	20.0%

Voter Turnout			
2015 Total Citizens 18+	417,073	2016 House Turnout as % CVAP	55%
2016 House turnout	229,919	2014 House Turnout as % CVAP	37%

2012 Presidential Vote		
Mitt Romney	142,741	(60%)
Barack Obama	90,612	(38%)

2016 Presidential Vote		
Donald Trump	140,560	(56%)
Hillary Clinton	85,083	(34%)
Gary Johnson	12,039	(5%)

Cook Partisan Voting Index: R+13

The rugged peaks of the Cascade Mountains divide the State of Washington into two starkly different climate zones and two almost as starkly different political cultures. West of the Cascades, Washington is moist, green and crammed with watery inlets. To the east, it is barren and brown, except where irrigation ditches channel the water of the Columbia River into thirsty valleys and where the mountaintop waters fall east, as they do above the apple orchards in the Yakima Valley.

As Washington has become mostly Democratic west of the Cascades, it has become mostly Republican on the eastern side. This shift in political inclinations has followed the development of national politics and the local economy. The federal government has been a presence east of the Cascades since the 1930s, when it began to build dams to provide cheap power and boost economic development in this forbidding landscape. A giant bust of Franklin D. Roosevelt gazes out from a bluff on the Columbia over 550-foot-high Grand Coulee Dam, one of Roosevelt's favorite projects. Other dams are strung along the Columbia to Bonneville Dam near Portland, where the river breaks through the Cascades. This was Democratic territory then; Grant County, which includes the dam, gave Franklin Roosevelt 86 percent of the vote in 1936. As the region became wealthier - in part because of the federal projects - and as the nation's politics took on a cultural cast, the area shifted to the Republicans. Lumber towns in the Cascades responded angrily when the logging business was harmed by efforts to preserve the spotted owl. Farmers in the Yakima Valley, which produces most of the nation's apples and many other crops, were enraged when environmentalists proposed breaching the Snake River dams upriver to save salmon.

The 4th Congressional District of Washington covers much of the center of the state east of the Cascades, running from the vast wilderness of Okanogan County, which has long been gold country, past the Grand Coulee and the Columbia River. The biggest population center here is the Tri-Cities of Richland, Kennewick and Pasco in Benton County. Like Benton, Yakima County has about one-third of the voters in the district. Yakima has a larger population, of which 48 percent is Hispanic. In June 2016, ConAgra Foods announced that it was spending $200 million on a second french fry processing line at its manufacturing campus in Richland. The city also is the site of a 455,000-square-foot freezer, the largest in North America, which is a processing center for millions of pounds of cherries, tater tots and frozen dinners. Benton is the location of the Hanford Nuclear Reservation; in 2015, its research facility proved the existence of gravitational waves. A note on Donald Trump's Cabinet: After Trump announced James Mattis as his Defense Secretary, and before he took office, the retired general served on a Benton County jury for a misdemeanor case; the jury found the defendant not guilty.

The district's population is 38 percent Hispanic. Many are farm workers or the children of farm workers who have picked fruit for generations. The area was narrowly split between the parties as recently as the 1990s, but the 4th has become the most Republican district in the state; the cultural liberalism of Seattle seems very far away from here. Donald Trump got 56 percent in 2016, short of the 60 percent who voted for Mitt Romney in 2012.

FIFTH DISTRICT

Cathy McMorris Rodgers (R)

Elected 2004, 7th term; b. May 22, 1969, Salem, OR; Pensacola Christian College (FL), B.A.; University of Washington, M.B.A.; Evangelical; Married (Brian Rodgers); 3 children.

Elected Office: WA House, 1994-2004, Minority Leader, 2002-2004.

Professional Career: Owner-operator, Peachcrest Fruit Basket orchard, 1984-1998; St. Legislative aide, 1990-1994.

DC Office: 1314 LHOB 20515, 202-225-2006, Fax: 202-225-3392, mcmorris.house.gov.

State Offices: Colville, 509-684-3481; Spokane, 509-353-2374; Walla Walla, 509-529-9358.

Committees: House Republican Conference Chairman. *Energy & Commerce*: Health.

Group Ratings

	ADA	ACLU	AFL-CIO	LCV	ITI	COC	HAFA	ACU	CFG	FRC
2016	-	5%	-	0%	100%	100%	58%	96%	72%	100%
2015	0%	C	13%	0%	C	100%	C	75%	58%	92%

Almanac Ratings 2015

	Economy	Social	Foreign	Composite
Liberal	10%	10%	10%	10%
Conservative	90%	90%	90%	90%

Key Votes of the 114th Congress

1. Keystone Pipeline	Y	5. Puerto Rico Debt	N	9. Offenses by Aliens	Y
2. Trade Deals	Y	6. Medical Marijuana	N	10. Troops in Iraq	N
3. Export-Import Bank	N	7. Sanctuary Cities	Y	11. Homeland Security $$	Y
4. Debt Ceiling Increase	Y	8. Armor-piercing Bullets	Y	12. Trade Adjustment aid	Y

Election Results

Election	Name (Party)	Vote (%)		Cand. Spent	Ind. Exp. Support	Ind. Exp. Oppose
2016 General	Cathy McMorris Rodgers (R).........	192,959	(60%)	$3,268,996		
	Joe Pakootas (D).........................	130,575	(40%)	$342,676		
2016 Primary	Cathy McMorris Rodgers (R).........	43,089	(41%)			
	Joe Pakootas (D).........................	33,432	(32%)			
	Dave Wilson (I)..........................	14,241	(14%)			
	Tom Horne (R)............................	11,280	(11%)			

Prior winning percentages: 2014 (61%), 2012 (62%), 2010 (68%), 2008 (65%), 2006 (56%), 2004 (60%)

Cathy McMorris Rodgers, elected in 2004, heads the House Republican Conference, the fourth-ranking post in the party leadership. She is the top woman among House GOP leaders and a trusted on-message lieutenant. Despite her interest in moving up, other Republicans subsequently have leap-frogged her in the leadership ranks.

McMorris Rodgers spent much of her childhood in northern British Columbia but moved with her family to Kettle Falls, where her parents bought a fruit orchard and operated a stand selling apples, peaches, cherries and strawberries. Her father was a county Republican chairman. She graduated from Pensacola Christian College in Florida and got an MBA from the University of Washington. After college, she became a legislative assistant to a state House member. McMorris Rodgers was appointed to her state House seat at age 24, and later was elected in her own right. She served for 10 years and chaired the Commerce and Labor Committee. She rose to minority leader, the first woman to hold such a post in state history.

In 2004, George Nethercutt, who defeated Democratic House Speaker Tom Foley in 1994, ran for the Senate. McMorris Rodgers and two other Republicans competed in the primary. They agreed on most major issues, including opposing abortion and favoring a constitutional amendment banning same-sex marriage. McMorris Rodgers won 50 percent of the vote in the primary to 27 percent for state Sen. Larry Sheahan. The Democratic nominee, businessman Don Barbieri, was from Spokane, while she was from rural northeastern Washington. Barbieri also had a heavy financial advantage and no primary opposition. The National Republican Congressional Committee spent heavily for McMorris Rodgers, highlighting her pro-business credentials and agricultural background. That was enough to give her a comfortable victory, 60%-40%, a sign of the change in Foley's old district. She has not faced a serious reelection challenge.

She leaned toward the center of the House on some issues. In 2007, she voted to expand the Children's Health Insurance Plan, a move favored by Democrats but opposed by President George W. Bush. (She opposed the final version that became law in 2009.) She backed Bush's Iraq war policies, but also criticized the administration on veterans' health care and on a delay in rules for country-of-origin meat labeling. With her seat on the Energy and Commerce Committee, she has worked across the aisle on several issues. With Democratic Rep. Diana DeGette, she enacted in 2013 the Hydropower Regulatory Efficiency Act, which streamlined the permitting process for small hydropower projects as a tool to expand clean energy.

McMorris Rodgers became an ally of Republican Leader John Boehner, with whom she served on the Education and the Workforce Committee. She became the GOP Conference vice chair with his backing and took on several tasks. He selected her in 2009 to head a GOP task force that sought to develop a policy on earmarks. She has helped to recruit women to run and has served as a liaison to newly elected Republican women, including with fund-raising. McMorris Rodgers has broadened her party's use of social media tools. During the 2012 presidential campaign, Mitt Romney tapped McMorris Rodgers to serve as his House liaison, partly as a reward for her early endorsement.

She pitched to move up to Republican Conference chair after the 2012 election, stressing her communications skills and her recruiting of successful candidates. She touted raising more than $1 million for the National Republican Congressional Committee and contributing more than $300,000 to candidates. She defeated Tom Price of Georgia, a favorite of the tea party who had the backing of Paul Ryan of Wisconsin.

The Office of Congressional Ethics recommended that the Ethics Committee investigate whether McMorris Rodgers improperly used official funds in that leadership contest as well as to cover campaign-related activities. The allegations came from a former aide, who told OCE investigators that he wrote campaign speeches and did other political work on official time. Her attorney denied the allegations, and in 2014 the committee said it would not appoint a special investigative panel on the matter.

Along with senior GOP leaders, she considered the party's perceived weaknesses to be less about its policies than about how it conveys its message. "I don't think it's about the Republican Party needing to become more moderate," she told CNN. "I really believe it's the Republican Party becoming more modern." She hired a Hispanic staffer to provide the party's message to Spanish-language television networks and set up a Twitter feed in Spanish. She created video products for other members to use on social media and in their districts.

McMorris Rodgers hosted meetings between groups of young Republican voters and younger members of Congress. Much of her work remained behind the scenes. "I'm trying to promote a Republican cause," she said. "And part of that is [about] message as well as messengers. It's not about me, it's not about my profile, it is about doing that which I think is going to help our overall effort to advance the conservative cause." In 2015, McMorris Rodgers was instrumental in crafting a compromise between GOP women and pro-life conservatives on a House-passed abortion bill that would have barred most abortions after 20 weeks.

In April 2007, McMorris Rodgers and her husband had their first child, a boy, Cole McMorris Rodgers, who was born four weeks premature and was diagnosed with Down syndrome. She subsequently gave birth to two daughters, making her the first member of Congress to deliver multiple babies while in office. She formed the Congressional Down Syndrome Caucus in 2008 to raise awareness about institutional barriers that face individuals with Down syndrome, and she became a leader in the disabilities community. In 2013, she enacted her National Pediatric Research Network Act. In 2014, she helped to enact the Achieving a Better Life Experience (ABLE) Act, which was designed to empower individuals with disabilities.

Her voting record has become more conservative. *The Spokesman-Review* of Spokane editorialized in 2012, "Too often she appears the ideologue in her solidarity with House leadership." She was chosen to give the GOP response to Obama's 2014 State of the Union address and played up her party's attempt to "trust people" to make their own economic decisions. Republican colleagues praised McMorris Rodgers for her hard work. When Majority Leader Eric Cantor's unexpected primary defeat in June 2014 opened two GOP leadership seats, she quickly said she would not run for either of them. Her staffers said that the timing wasn't right and that she remained open to pursuing a higher post. She showed a similar reticence in the October 2015 leadership shuffle after Boehner's resignation as Speaker.

McMorris Rodgers seems positioned to wield continued influence in the House, regardless of her leadership prospects. On Energy and Commerce, her seniority has moved her close to a subcommittee chair. Following the 2016 election, she reportedly was the front-runner for Interior Secretary before Donald Trump gave the position to the junior Rep. Ryan Zinke. *The Spokesman-Review* earlier reported that she had a "tepid alliance" with Trump during the presidential campaign, though she maintained support for him while other congressional Republicans were withdrawing or qualifying their endorsement.

Eastern Washington: Spokane

Population		Race and Ethnicity		Income	
Total	685,344	White	84.7%	Median Income	$47,491
Land area	15,473	Black	1.5%		(294 out of 435)
Pop/ sq mi	44.3	Latino	6.1%		
Born in state	52.8%	Asian	2.3%	Under $50,000	52.1%
Age Groups		Two races	3.4%	$50,000-$99,999	31.2%
Under 18	21.8%	Other	2.0%	$100,000-$199,999	14.1%
18-34	25.4%	**Education**		$200,000 or more	2.6%
35-64	37.7%	H.S grad or less	33.9%	Poverty Rate	17.3%
Over 64	15.1%	Some college	38.3%	**Health Insurance**	
Work		College Degree, 4 yr	17.4%	With health insurance coverage	89.1%
White Collar	36.0%	Post grad	10.4%		
Sales and Service	44.1%	**Military**		**Public Assistance**	
Blue Collar	19.8%	Veteran	12.0%	Cash public assistance income	4.8%
Government	6.2%	Active Duty	0.5%		
				Food stamp/SNAP benefits	17.9%

Voter Turnout			
2015 Total Citizens 18+	515,660	2016 House Turnout as % CVAP	63%
2016 House turnout	323,534	2014 House Turnout as % CVAP	44%

2012 Presidential Vote		
Mitt Romney	168,671	(54%)
Barack Obama	137,771	(44%)

2016 Presidential Vote		
Donald Trump	166,765	(50%)
Hillary Clinton	125,112	(38%)
Gary Johnson	18,499	(6%)

Cook Partisan Voting Index: R+8

Eastern Washington is a land of great rivers and bare parched land, where the Columbia, Spokane and Snake rivers wind among vast plateaus, bringing water from the Rockies to the desert. Spokane grew up at the falls of the Spokane River when the railroads first came through. It was initially a gold rush town, and later became a major wheat, mining and railroad center. Nearby are some of the most fascinating landscapes in the United States: undulating yellow wheat fields on the rolling ridges of the Palouse, where the wheat-growing topsoil is 200 feet deep; acres of protected forestland in Colville National Forest, home to the last surviving herd of caribou in the lower 48 states; and bare-rock coulees rising above dammed-up lakes and barren desert. Much of this area is remote and inhospitable. The summers can be blazingly hot and the winters bitterly cold. But the water from the Grand Coulee and other dams irrigates some of the richest farmland in the country. In 2015, the Forest Service expanded Colville by 2,391 acres to increase user access to the Pacific Northwest Scenic National Trail, a 1,200-mile system that snakes its way from Montana's Glacier National Park to the Pacific Ocean

The 5th Congressional District of Washington covers the easternmost part of the state. Nearly three-fourths of the people live in Spokane County, where the voting habits have grown apart from the Washington west of the Cascades, especially on natural resource issues. Several Spokane-area politicians have called for creating a 51st state of Eastern Washington, which would cover 60 percent of the state. A prospective new round of base closures has residents concerned about the fate of Fairchild Air Force Base, the area's largest employer. In 2016, Fairchild was on the short list of bases under consideration as a home for the new KC-46A aerial tankers. With recent wage and job growth, there recently have been positive signs that Spokane, with four local universities, has become a "second-tier" city where companies locate for quality of life and lower housing costs. Caterpillar opened a $37 million distribution center. In 2014, JP Morgan Chase & Co. took majority control of the Palouse wind farm that has powered 30,000 homes. Near the Oregon border is Walla Walla, long dependent on wheat and sweet onions but now attracting tourists with its budding wine industry. The city's name is an American Indian term for "many waters."

The district's political inclinations lean Republican. Spokane County voted for Democrat Bill Clinton in 1992 and 1996, but Republicans have won it since. In 2016, Donald Trump took 50 percent of the vote, his second-best district in the state. Democrat Tom Foley was the local congressman for 30 years and served as Speaker of the House from 1989 until 1994, when he lost his seat and Democrats lost their majority. Democrats have not been competitive for the seat since then.

SIXTH DISTRICT

Derek Kilmer (D)

Elected 2012, 3rd term; b. Jan 01, 1974, Port Angeles; Princeton University (NJ), A.B., 1996; Oxford University (England), Ph.D., 2003; Methodist; Married (Jennifer Kilmer); 2 children.

Elected Office: WA House, 2005-2007; WA Senate, 2007-2013.

Professional Career: Mgmt. consultant, McKinsey & Co., 1999-2002; Vice President., Economic Development Board, Tacoma-Pierce County, 2002-2012.

DC Office: 1520 LHOB 20515, 202-225-5916, Fax: 202-226-3575, kilmer.house.gov.

State Offices: Bremerton, 360-373-9725; Port Angeles, 360-797-3623; Tacoma, 253-272-3515.

Committees: *Appropriations*: Commerce, Justice, Science & Related Agencies, Interior, Environment & Related Agencies.

Group Ratings

	ADA	ACLU	AFL-CIO	LCV	ITI	COC	HAFA	ACU	CFG	FRC
2016	-	88%	-	97%	100%	46%	10%	0%	0%	0%
2015	75%	C	92%	94%	C	60%	C	0%	0%	0%

Almanac Ratings 2015

	Economy	Social	Foreign	Composite
Liberal	67%	100%	72%	80%
Conservative	33%	0%	28%	20%

Key Votes of the 114th Congress

1. Keystone Pipeline	N	5. Puerto Rico Debt	Y	9. Offenses by Aliens	N
2. Trade Deals	Y	6. Medical Marijuana	Y	10. Troops in Iraq	N
3. Export-Import Bank	Y	7. Sanctuary Cities	N	11. Homeland Security $$	Y
4. Debt Ceiling Increase	Y	8. Armor-piercing Bullets	N	12. Trade Adjustment aid	Y

Election Results

Election	Name (Party)	Vote (%)		Cand. Spent	Ind. Exp. Support	Ind. Exp. Oppose
2016 General	Derek Kilmer (D)	201,718	(62%)	$652,317	$1,280	
	Todd Bloom (R)	126,116	(39%)	$5,172		
2016 Primary	Derek Kilmer (D)	65,954	(59%)			
	Todd Bloom (R)	27,211	(24%)			
	Stephan Andrew Brodhead (R)	9,143	(8%)			

Prior winning percentages: 2014 (63%), 2012 (59%)

Democrat Derek Kilmer, elected in 2012, succeeded his political mentor, Rep. Norm Dicks, in the 6th District and with a seat on the Appropriations Committee, where Dicks had been the senior Democrat. Like his mentor, Kilmer has been a centrist and has shown interest in defense and resource issues.

Kilmer grew up as the son of two public school teachers in Port Angeles. Watching the town's economic struggles in the wake of the timber industry's decline led Kilmer to pursue a career linking public policy and economic development. He got a bachelor's from Princeton University and a doctorate in social policy from the University of Oxford in England, with a focus on economic development. After working as a business consultant for McKinsey and Co., he went to work for the nonprofit Economic Development Board for Tacoma-Pierce County. As a vice president, he talked with 200 businesses a year in an effort to broaden the economies of communities like Port Angeles, long dependent on timber. Kilmer was elected to the state House in 2004 and two years later moved to the state Senate, where he was the chief author of the state's capital budget and promoted legislation to create jobs by borrowing money for public construction.

Dicks gave his protégé early word in 2012 that he would not seek a 19th term. "He told me, 'In about an hour I'm going to announce my retirement, and you should figure out what you're going to do,'" Kilmer recalled. He moved quickly and was the only Democratic contender. In the all-party primary, Kilmer got 53 percent of the total vote and Republican businessman Bill Driscoll led the six Republican candidates with 18 percent. Driscoll had served with the Marines in Iraq and Afghanistan and also worked in the timber and real estate industries. He called the federal deficit the biggest threat to national security and departed from Republican orthodoxy in calling for tax increases tied to specific spending cuts. Driscoll also supported abortion rights and same-sex marriage. Kilmer made sure to let voters know that he was running with Dicks' backing. *The Seattle Times* endorsed him as "a problem solver who can be bipartisan." Each candidate spent close to $2 million. Kilmer won 59%-41%, including 58 percent in Kitsap and 64 percent in Pierce.

Kilmer made an early effort at consensus-building with the Bipartisan Working Group and the Problem Solvers Caucus, which have tried to forge greater consensus on a variety of issues. With Republican Rep. Doug Collins of Georgia, he filed the "Keeping American Jobs Act," which seeks to assure that employers can't require American workers to train cheaper staff who are working with U.S. visas. He helped to organize the Puget Sound Recovery Caucus to bring increased focus and attention to cleanup work that needs to be done. Kilmer has filed legislation to reorganize the selection of members to the Federal Election Commission in a bid to break its typical deadlock. He also sought to limit contributions and increase transparency in campaigns. As vice-chairman of policy for the New Democrat Coalition, he created task forces in 2017 to prepare alternatives to Republican proposals. His *Almanac* vote ratings in 2015 were the most centrist of the Democrats in the Washington delegation.

On the Appropriations Committee, he has added district-oriented provisions to subcommittee bills. He seemed ready to follow in Dicks' footsteps with a long run on the panel, much as Dicks earlier was mentored as an aide to Sen. Warren Magnuson of Washington, who chaired the Senate

Appropriations Committee. On the committee-approved bill in 2016 for the Commerce, Justice and Science appropriations, he got funds to encourage innovation and advancement in ocean acidification research, boost efforts to recover endangered salmon populations in Washington state, and increase trade enforcement. With Rep. Joe Kennedy of Massachusetts following the 2016 election, Kilmer won Democratic Caucus approval of a requirement that Democrats add a "vice ranking member" to each House committee - with the goal of giving more leadership opportunities to junior Democrats. Fortuitously, Kilmer took that new position at Appropriations.

On local interests, Kilmer enacted a bill in 2014 that renamed a memorial on Bainbridge Island in honor of Japanese Americans who were forced from their local homes during World War II. With his encouragement, the Navy and National Park Service coordinated efforts to monitor military jet noise over Olympic National Park during training missions. He has been reelected easily and appears to have settled in for a lengthy and productive career.

Central Tacoma, Olympic Peninsula

Population		**Race and Ethnicity**		**Income**	
Total	680,773	White	77.7%	Median Income	$55,608 (176 out of 435)
Land area	6,903	Black	3.5%	Under $50,000	44.8%
Pop/ sq mi	98.6	Latino	7.2%	$50,000-$99,999	33.1%
Born in state	48.5%	Asian	4.0%	$100,000-$199,999	18.3%
		Two races	5.1%	$200,000 or more	3.9%
		Other	2.4%	Poverty Rate	13.2%
Age Groups		**Education**		**Health Insurance**	
Under 18	20.2%	H.S grad or less	33.7%	With health insurance coverage	88.6%
18-34	22.0%	Some college	38.2%		
35-64	40.2%	College Degree, 4 yr	17.6%		
Over 64	17.6%	Post grad	10.4%		
Work		**Military**		**Public Assistance**	
White Collar	35.2%	Veteran	15.6%	Cash public assistance income	4.5%
Sales and Service	43.7%	Active Duty	2.5%	Food stamp/SNAP benefits	15.3%
Blue Collar	21.1%				
Government	7.3%				

Voter Turnout			
2015 Total Citizens 18+	525,322	2016 House Turnout as % CVAP	62%
2016 House turnout	327,834	2014 House Turnout as % CVAP	42%

2012 Presidential Vote		
Barack Obama	184,820	(56%)
Mitt Romney	135,573	(41%)

2016 Presidential Vote		
Hillary Clinton	172,596	(50%)
Donald Trump	131,449	(38%)
Gary Johnson	19,038	(6%)
Jill Stein	6,950	(2%)

Cook Partisan Voting Index: D+6

The rainiest part of the continental United States is its far northwest corner, where the Olympic Mountains of Washington jut into the Pacific Ocean. The waters of the Pacific evaporate, condense, and then mist or rain on the hills and mountains along Puget Sound. The mountains here are always green, the trees that line the inlets towering, and during heavy rainfalls the rivers can rise six feet in a day. This has long been lumbering and fishing country, where people start work at 6 a.m. and where the vagaries of nature and environmental laws - like the ban on old-growth logging to protect the habitat of the spotted owl - have strengthened a traditional surly independence and suspicion of authority. Still, respect for the beauty of nature endures, including at the 3,310-square-mile Olympic Coast National Marine Sanctuary, a vast underwater reserve. The small city of Forks is where the "Twilight" teen vampire novels were set, and some of the locals complain about the influx of outsiders who visit the scenery firsthand. But the local Chamber of Commerce operates a welcoming station for the tourism boomlet to give out maps of the can't-miss locales in the novels.

The many inlets of Puget Sound, winding sinuously through mountains, are among America's most picturesque waterways and strategically among its most important. During World War II, shipyards were built to shelter much of the Navy's Pacific fleet. During the Cold War, some of the nuclear submarine fleet was anchored at the giant Kitsap Navy base. The shipyard now has five installations, including a shipyard. It employed 12,800 in 2015, with plans to add a few hundred more workers. The Tacoma Narrows Bridge replaced the original bridge which, in a scene preserved on newsreel and still viewed by civil engineering students, started vibrating on the wrong harmonic in high winds and collapsed in 1940. On the other side is Tacoma, long the second city on Puget Sound, with its massive docks, former pulp mills, pleasant hilly residential neighborhoods and recently revived waterfront. On the northern coast, across from British Columbia, Port Angeles been ranked among the nation's best small towns. In March 2017, a local paper mill was sold to a Mexican firm and was shut down for retooling. The Olympic Peninsula extends from the Pacific Ocean to Puget Sound, and from the Canadian border to Oregon. The national park in Olympic Mountains covers 1,442 square miles.

The 6th Congressional District of Washington includes the Olympic Peninsula, Bremerton and about 30 percent of Tacoma. Kitsap is the largest population center, including Bainbridge Island, where residents commute by ferry to downtown Seattle. About two-thirds of the 6th's residents live in Kitsap or in Tacoma's Pierce County. Politically, the Olympic Peninsula and Tacoma are working-class Democrat, as is the district overall, though not overwhelmingly. Hillary Clinton in 2016 got 50 percent of the vote, compared with the 56 percent for President Barack Obama in 2012. Coastal and blue-collar Grays Harbor County voted Republican in the 2016 presidential election for the first time since 1928.

SEVENTH DISTRICT

Pramila Jayapal (D)

Elected 2016, 1st term; b. Sep 21, 1965, Chennai, India; Georgetown University (DC), B.A., 1986; Northwestern University Kellogg School Management (IL), M.B.A., 1990; Hinduism; Married (Steve Williamson); 1 child; 1 stepchild.

Elected Office: WA Senate, 2015-2016.

Professional Career: Financial Analyst; Non Profit Executive.

DC Office: 319 CHOB 20515, 202-225-3106, Fax: 202-226-1169; Website: jayapal.house.gov.

State Offices: Seattle, 206-674-0040.

Committees: *Budget*. *Judiciary*: Immigration & Border Security, Regulatory Reform, Commercial & Antitrust Law.

Election Results

Election	Name (Party)	Vote (%)		Cand. Spent	Ind. Exp. Support	Ind. Exp. Oppose
2016 General	Pramila Jayapal (D)	212,010	(56%)	$2,959,177	$538,828	
	Brady Walkinshaw (D)	166,744	(44%)	$1,911,395	$353,000	
2016 Primary	Pramila Jayapal (D)	44,540	(39%)			
	Brady Walkinshaw (D)	24,285	(21%)			
	Joe McDermott (D)	23,798	(21%)			
	Craig Keller (R)	10,083	(9%)			
	Scott Sutherland (R)	5,781	(5%)			

Pramila Jayapal of Washington won an open seat in 2016 in a nonpartisan runoff, in which she campaigned as the more ardently liberal candidate against another Democratic state legislator. Her early actions in the House showed her progressive activism. She is the first Indian-American woman elected to Congress.

Jayapal was born in Chennai, India, where her parents have continued to reside. Her father was in the oil business, and the family traveled in Asia when she was a child. At 16, she moved to the United States to attend Georgetown University. She worked on Wall Street for PaineWebber as a financial analyst in leveraged buy-outs and got an MBA from Northwestern University. After briefly working on the sales of cardiac defibrillators in the medical equipment industry, she pursued a career in the nonprofit world, starting with a Seattle-based group working on international public health. During that time, she spent two years living in small towns in India. She wrote a book about that experience: *Pilgrimage to India: A Woman Revisits Her Homeland.*

Following the 9/11 terrorist attacks, Jayapal started and was executive director of Hate Free Zone, an advocacy group for South Asians, Arabs and Muslims. The organization, which changed its name to OneAmerica, worked on local and state issues. She led a national coalition, We Belong Together, which addressed gender-related issues in the Senate-passed immigration reform bill in 2013. She was recognized by President Barack Obama as a White House "Champion of Change." In 2014, Jayapal was elected as the first woman of color to the state Senate, where she worked on tuition-free community college, a state voting rights act, automatic voter registration and measures to help survivors of sexual assault. Her husband, Steve Williamson, has held senior positions with labor unions.

When Democratic Rep. Jim McDermott announced his retirement after 14 terms, five Democrats entered the contest to succeed him. Under state law, the top two advanced to the general election, regardless of party affiliation. In the first round of voting in August, in which Democrats received 85 percent of the total vote, Jayapal was the front-runner with 42 percent. The runner-up with 21 percent was Brady Walkinshaw, an openly gay state representative who was a native of Whatcom County and styled himself as a bipartisan bridge-builder. In the general election, Jayapal was endorsed by EMILY's List, several labor unions and Sen. Bernie Sanders of Vermont. She raised $3 million to $1.9 million for Walkinshaw, who won endorsements from many local Democrats and had $353,000 in support from a Latino advocacy group; he is Cuban-American. Jayapal won the runoff, 56%-44%.

Jayapal got seats on the Budget and Judiciary committees, and was selected by Democrats as vice ranking member at Budget. She didn't wait long to get attention. Three days after taking office, during the typically ceremonial count of the Electoral College vote, she raised objections to the November presidential vote count in Georgia. Vice President Joe Biden, who was presiding over the joint session of Congress, gaveled her to silence and advised her, to some laughter, "It's over." Jayapal later told *The Seattle Times* that she had hoped to state her full objections, though the rules required that at least one senator join her. In April, she filed in coordination with Sanders a bill to make public colleges and universities tuition-free for some families and to significantly reduce student debt.

Seattle

Population		**Race and Ethnicity**		**Income**	
Total	713,395	White	71.3%	Median Income	$71,615 (67 out of 435)
Land area	144	Black	4.3%		
Pop/ sq mi	4949.7	Latino	7.5%	Under $50,000	35.9%
Born in state	41.1%	Asian	10.6%	$50,000-$99,999	28.3%
Age Groups		Two races	5.0%	$100,000-$199,999	25.6%
Under 18	16.0%	Other	1.3%	$200,000 or more	10.2%
18-34	30.6%	**Education**		Poverty Rate	11.8%
35-64	40.7%	H.S grad or less	17.5%	**Health Insurance**	
Over 64	12.7%	Some college	25.6%	With health insurance coverage	91.5%
Work		College Degree, 4 yr	34.0%		
White Collar	55.5%	Post grad	22.9%	**Public Assistance**	
Sales and Service	34.4%	**Military**		Cash public assistance income	2.5%
Blue Collar	10.1%	Veteran	6.7%		
Government	6.4%	Active Duty	0.2%	Food stamp/SNAP benefits	8.9%

Voter Turnout			
2015 Total Citizens 18+	546,611	2016 House Turnout as % CVAP	69%
2016 House turnout	378,754	2014 House Turnout as % CVAP	46%

2012 Presidential Vote		
Barack Obama	310,828	(79%)
Mitt Romney	70,973	(18%)

2016 Presidential Vote		
Hillary Clinton	341,412	(80%)
Donald Trump	50,615	(12%)
Gary Johnson	13,495	(3%)
Jill Stein	8,374	(2%)

Cook Partisan Voting Index: D+33

Seattle rises from the Puget Sound harbor of Elliott Bay on steep hills once covered with 300-foot-high Douglas firs. Behind the hills and buildings, on a clear day you can see the nimbus of Mount Rainier. On the picturesque waterfront, below gleaming high-rises, is Pike Place Market, where you can get fresh salmon and Dungeness crabs. Nearby, where the ferries from Bainbridge and Vashon Islands and Bremerton dock in the nation's busiest ferry system, is Pioneer Square, where stores and warehouses from the turn of the 20th century have been restored. Yesler Way was America's original Skid Road - literally a path for skidding newly cut logs to transportation terminals. It remains a haven for the homeless and a frequent locale for open-air drug dealing.

Seattle has some old ethnic neighborhoods, like the once heavily Scandinavian Ballard, which now features boutiques and nightspots, and the countercultural Capitol Hill, where shoppers jam busy stores, galleries, and clubs. Highly educated, affluent single professionals have made the Victorian houses overlooking the harbor and the 1940s houses in Capitol Hill among the nation's highest-priced residential real estate. The city has a new ethnic mix, with thousands of recent Asian immigrants boosting the total to 14 percent. The activism of local immigrant-rights groups led to the successful lawsuit by the state attorney general that delayed enforcement of the travel ban imposed by the Trump administration during its first week in office.

The city's economic foundation is sound, and parts are bustling. Rejecting Microsoft's local model of a suburban campus, the robust Amazon has expanded into a huge new campus with three new office towers in the South Lake Union area. In 2016, the company had more than 25,000 local workers and more than 5,000 newly created openings. Amazon founder and CEO Jeff Bezos checks in occasionally with the other Washington on his part-time investment property, *The Washington Post*. Microsoft founder Bill Gates' decision to turn his attention to global health philanthropy has made Seattle the Davos of health care, drawing experts in malaria, tuberculosis, AIDS and other global scourges. Seattle is the headquarters, in an old industrial district, of Starbucks. From 2012 to 2016, the company had a growth spurt from 18,000 to 25,000 stores worldwide; about half are in the United States. For 2017, Starbucks projected adding 2,100 new shops, of which 1,000 would be in China and elsewhere in Asia and the Pacific. In 2014, the city council spurred a nationwide movement when it increased Seattle's minimum wage to $15 per hour, on a phased timetable from 2017 to 2021, depending on the size of a business. Although the city has continued to boom, some conservative economists contend that there has been a subsequent dip in minimum-wage jobs.

Seattle ranks as one of the nation's most desirable cities, but it has its flaws and limitations. The Justice Department investigated the city's police after several episodes in which officers were accused of using unnecessary force and discriminating against minorities, and concluded that the department had engaged in a pattern of excessive force that violated the Constitution and federal law. The *Seattle Post-Intelligencer* now publishes exclusively online, leaving *The Seattle Times* as the city's only daily newspaper. The city is a growing haven for young singles, as married couples with children make up only 13 percent of Seattle households. As many as 40 percent of Seattle households have a single occupant.

The 7th Congressional District of Washington includes nearly all of the city of Seattle, some industrial suburban fringe to the south, a white-collar suburban fringe to the north, and artsy, bucolic Vashon Island in Puget Sound. It is a Democratic enclave. Less than 10 percent of the population is in the southwest corner of Snohomish County, in Lynnwood. Hillary Clinton's 80 percent of the district vote in 2016 exceeded President Barack Obama's 79 percent four years earlier.

EIGHTH DISTRICT

Dave Reichert (R)

Elected 2004, 7th term; b. Aug 29, 1950, Detroit Lakes, MN; Concordia Lutheran College (OR), A.A., 1970; Lutheran; Married (Julie Reichert); 3 children; 6 grandchildren.

Military Career: U.S Air Force Reserve, 1971-1976.

Elected Office: King County sheriff, 1997-2004.

Professional Career: King County police officer, 1972-1997.

DC Office: 1127 LHOB 20515, 202-225-7761, Fax: 202-225-4282, reichert.house.gov.

State Offices: Issaquah, 425-677-7414; Wenatchee, 509-885-6615.

Committees: *Ways & Means*: Human Resources, Tax Policy, Trade (Chmn).

Group Ratings

	ADA	ACLU	AFL-CIO	LCV	ITI	COC	HAFA	ACU	CFG	FRC
2016	-	11%	-	34%	100%	92%	33%	32%	39%	83%
2015	10%	C	42%	6%	C	100%	C	26%	34%	100%

Almanac Ratings 2015

	Economy	Social	Foreign	Composite
Liberal	12%	34%	14%	20%
Conservative	88%	66%	86%	80%

Key Votes of the 114th Congress

1. Keystone Pipeline	Y	5. Puerto Rico Debt	Y	9. Offenses by Aliens	Y
2. Trade Deals	Y	6. Medical Marijuana	N	10. Troops in Iraq	N
3. Export-Import Bank	Y	7. Sanctuary Cities	N	11. Homeland Security $$	Y
4. Debt Ceiling Increase	Y	8. Armor-piercing Bullets	Y	12. Trade Adjustment aid	Y

Election Results

Election	Name (Party)	Vote (%)		Cand. Spent	Ind. Exp. Support	Ind. Exp. Oppose
2016 General	Dave Reichert (R)	193,145	(60%)	$1,711,500	$1,000	
	Tony Ventrella (D)	127,720	(40%)	$19,163		
2016 Primary	Dave Reichert (R)	49,291	(57%)			
	Tony Ventrella (D)	15,032	(18%)			
	Santiago Ramos (D)	10,954	(13%)			
	Alida Skold (D)	7,138	(8%)			

Prior winning percentages: 2014 (63%), 2012 (60%), 2010 (52%), 2008 (53%), 2006 (52%), 2004 (52%)

Dave Reichert, a Republican elected in 2004, is a party loyalist on most economic matters but he regularly joins Democrats on environmental issues. That approach, along with a seat on the powerful Ways and Means Committee that opened fundraising doors, have enabled him to thwart Democratic attempts to unseat him in close contests. He has shown interest in statewide office, though he has not made the plunge. That probably has been wise on his part. Washington has not elected a Republican senator or governor since 1994. And his seniority has increased his clout on Ways and Means.

Reichert was born in Detroit Lakes, Minnesota, and his family moved to the Seattle area when he was an infant. To escape his father's alcoholism and his family's disorder, he ran away from home as a high school senior. He graduated from Concordia Lutheran College in Portland and joined the Air Force Reserve. He worked for 32 years in the King County sheriff's office and was elected sheriff in 1997. He became a national leader on firearms reduction and methamphetamine prevention. During the riots that hampered the 1999 international trade meeting in Seattle, he criticized city leaders and the police force for inadequate preparation. He gained national attention for capturing Gary Ridgway, the "Green

River Killer" who had terrorized the Seattle area with a two-decade murder spree that left 48 women dead. After Ridgway's capture in 2001, Reichert was featured on television shows and in documentaries. He published a book about the experience, *Chasing the Devil: My Twenty-Year Quest to Capture the Green River Killer.*

When the long-time GOP seat opened, Republicans recruited Reichert. He defeated three opponents in the September primary with 43 percent of the vote. The Democratic nominee was Dave Ross, a veteran Seattle radio talk show host. In the general election, the national parties spent heavily and organized visits by party leaders. Each candidate tried to portray the other as lacking policy experience and holding views too extreme for the district. Both Seattle newspapers, with strong liberal traditions, endorsed Ross for his greater familiarity with issues and suggested that Reichert was too conservative for the district. Reichert won 52%-47%.

When Reichert arrived in the House, he was rewarded with the chairmanship of the Homeland Security Subcommittee on Emergency Preparedness, making him the only freshman in his class to chair a panel. With his law-enforcement background, he won enactment of a bill that established standards for interoperable communications. He later sponsored a successful bill to fund programs that foster intelligence-sharing with state and local governments. In 2015, following a series of controversial police incidents in cities run by Democrats, he urged Republicans to conduct more oversight of local police departments. As a co-chairman of the Law Enforcement Caucus, he said that trust had broken down between local police and many communities.

With a prized seat on Ways and Means, he has chaired three subcommittees since 2011: Human Resources, which deals with job creation; Select Revenue Measures Subcommittee, which handles tax legislation; and the Trade Subcommittee, following a committee shuffle in November 2015 when Paul Ryan became House Speaker. In 2012, Reichert advocated an extension of the wind-energy tax credit, which became part of the budget deal to avoid the "fiscal cliff" of automatic spending cuts and tax hikes. With his district's heavy reliance on trade, he was an enthusiastic Ways and Means supporter of the Trans-Pacific Partnership, which was a potential boon for his home state; President Barack Obama unsuccessfully sought congressional approval of the deal. In a February 2016 interview with McClatchy News, Reichert criticized presidential candidate Donald Trump's hostility to trade. "It's a cop-out. The easiest message to deliver is to just bash whatever. He bashes everything, so he's going to bash trade."

Reichert has been one of the House Republicans friendliest to restrictive environmental regulation. According to the League of Conservation Voters' scorecard for 2016, his lifetime score of 37 percent was the fourth best of all incumbent House Republicans. He was among eight Republicans who voted for the 2009 House-passed bill to cap carbon dioxide emissions blamed for global warming. In 2011, he was the lone Republican to support a Democratic amendment putting the House on record as accepting the scientific view that human beings are a major cause of climate change. He opposed oil drilling in Alaska's Arctic National Wildlife Refuge. On occasion, he has split with environmentalists. He voted with his party to block enforcement by the Obama administration's Environmental Protection Agency of air pollution requirements for many older coal-fired power plants and to oppose its oceans management policy. In a 2015 interview with the *Seattle Times*, Reichert said that Republicans need to "fill the room" with more conservationists in their ranks. In the *Almanac* vote ratings for 2015, Reichert was among the most centrist House Republicans, especially on social issues.

National Democrats consistently targeted Reichert for reelection, but he has defeated well-financed challengers who had been top managers at Microsoft. In 2006, former Microsoft executive Darcy Burner, the Democratic nominee, dubbed him "Rubber Stamp Reichert" for his support of President George W. Bush. The candidates each spent $3 million, and together, the national parties poured in more than $4 million. In a tough year for Republicans, Reichert won 51%-49%. Two years later, he was the 53%-47% winner of a rematch in which Burner outspent him by more than $1 million. In 2010, his Democratic opponent was Suzan DelBene, another former Microsoft executive. She ran a strong campaign in which she outspent him and got substantial national party help, but Reichert won in a big GOP year, 52%-48%. (DelBene won election in 2012 in the open 1st District.) Since then, he has benefited from redistricting shifts that added conservative areas across the Cascades, and has won with at least 60 percent against weak challengers.

Reichert fanned local speculation by saying that he was "keeping my option open" to run statewide in 2016. In October 2015, he announced that he was not running for governor. "I am in a unique position to work with both Democrats and Republicans on some of the most important issues facing this nation and Washington state," he said, referring to tax reform and international trade. He kept his distance from Trump during the 2016 campaign. "Unfortunately, with these comments, Donald Trump has lost my vote," he said in early October, following the release of the video with Trump's lewd comments about women.

Outer Seattle-Tacoma Suburbs

Population		**Race and Ethnicity**		**Income**	
Total	705,178	White	73.6%	Median Income	$73,749 (56 out of 435)
Land area	7,360	Black	2.6%		
Pop/ sq mi	95.8	Latino	10.4%	Under $50,000	32.5%
Born in state	52.2%	Asian	7.7%	$50,000-$99,999	32.8%
Age Groups		Two races	4.1%	$100,000-$199,999	27.3%
Under 18	25.3%	Other	1.6%	$200,000 or more	7.6%
18-34	21.0%	**Education**		Poverty Rate	10.3%
35-64	42.2%	H.S grad or less	34.2%	**Health Insurance**	
Over 64	11.5%	Some college	33.5%	With health insurance coverage	89.8%
Work		College Degree, 4 yr	21.4%		
White Collar	38.3%	Post grad	10.9%	**Public Assistance**	
Sales and Service	39.0%	**Military**		Cash public assistance income	3.1%
Blue Collar	22.7%	Veteran	10.0%		
Government	5.6%	Active Duty	0.2%	Food stamp/SNAP benefits	10.8%

Voter Turnout			
2015 Total Citizens 18+	487,104	2016 House Turnout as % CVAP	66%
2016 House turnout	320,865	2014 House Turnout as % CVAP	41%

2012 Presidential Vote		
Barack Obama	155,982	(50%)
Mitt Romney	151,069	(48%)

2016 Presidential Vote		
Hillary Clinton	153,167	(46%)
Donald Trump	143,403	(43%)
Gary Johnson	17,644	(5%)

Cook Partisan Voting Index: EVEN

In the shadow of the majestic 14,410-foot Mount Rainier, Seattle in the last 50 years has spread out to all four points of the compass. In 1960, surrounding King County had 935,000 residents, 557,000 of whom lived in Seattle. Since then, the city has added about 127,000 people, but the county has more than doubled to 2.1 million. At first these newcomers moved into places like Bellevue, Redmond and Renton, on the flat lands to the north and west of Cougar Mountain. But as those places have filled in, the metropolitan area expanded out past Lake Sammamish and into the foothills of the Cascades, the valleys between the peaks of the Issaquah Alps, and the southern flatlands of the Puget Trough. Auburn, an old center for hop farming that became a factory town for Boeing in the 1960s, nearly doubled its population from 2000 to 2015, as a new super mall attracted businesses, jobs, and new residents.

The 8th Congressional District of Washington takes in much of this new frontier in greater Seattle's development, as well as some of its last remaining areas of undeveloped land. It encompasses all of Mount Rainier, as well as one of the nation's last inland old-growth rain forests. Other areas include the southern edge of King County, including Auburn and smaller towns like Algona, Milton and Lakeland North. The district extends into Pierce County, where it includes some of the suburbs around Tacoma. The risk of mud slides and volcanic debris at Rainier have led Pierce County officials to prepare improved detections and warnings. The district also takes in three agricultural counties that extend east of the Cascades. Kittitas County is a major producer of hay, most of which is shipped overseas. In Chelan County, growers in 2015 replaced a camp area with a state-required $6 million facility to house seasonal workers who pick cherries, apples and pears. In Chelan, marijuana producers protested in March 2017 when the county proposed the elimination of outdoor growing plus restrictions on indoor growing. About 60 percent of the district is in King, nearly 25 percent in Pierce, and the remainder is in or beyond the Cascades.

Of the three districts that are based chiefly in King County, the 8th has the preponderance of Republican precincts. Even with redistricting changes in 2012 that increased the GOP vote by several percentage points, the District has remained competitive in presidential elections. In 2016, Hillary

Clinton led, 46%-43%, the only one of the four Republican-held districts in Washington in which she took a plurality of the vote.

NINTH DISTRICT

Adam Smith (D)

Elected 1996, 11th term; b. Jun 15, 1965, Washington, DC; Western Washington University, Att.; Fordham University (NY), B.A., 1987; University of Washington, J.D., 1990; Christian Church; Married (Sara Bickle-Eldridge Smith); 2 children.

Elected Office: WA Senate, 1990-1996.

Professional Career: Practicing attorney, 1991-1992; City prosecutor, 1993-1995.

DC Office: 2264 RHOB 20515, 202-225-8901, Fax: 202-225-5893, adamsmith.house.gov.

State Offices: Renton, 425-793-5180.

Committees: *Armed Services (RMM)*: Emerging Threats & Capabilities, Military Personnel, Oversight & Investigations, Readiness, Seapower & Projection Forces, Strategic Forces, Tactical Air & Land Forces.

Group Ratings

	ADA	ACLU	AFL-CIO	LCV	ITI	COC	HAFA	ACU	CFG	FRC
2016	-	82%	-	82%	60%	54%	15%	0%	4%	0%
2015	80%	C	100%	89%	C	50%	C	0%	0%	0%

Almanac Ratings 2015

	Economy	Social	Foreign	Composite
Liberal	94%	93%	93%	93%
Conservative	6%	7%	7%	7%

Key Votes of the 114th Congress

1. Keystone Pipeline	N	5. Puerto Rico Debt	Y	9. Offenses by Aliens	N
2. Trade Deals	N	6. Medical Marijuana	Y	10. Troops in Iraq	N
3. Export-Import Bank	Y	7. Sanctuary Cities	N	11. Homeland Security $$	Y
4. Debt Ceiling Increase	Y	8. Armor-piercing Bullets	N	12. Trade Adjustment aid	Y

Election Results

Election	Name (Party)	Vote (%)		Cand. Spent	Ind. Exp. Support	Ind. Exp. Oppose
2016 General	Adam Smith (D)	205,165	(73%)	$866,912	$1,771	
	Doug Basler (R)	76,317	(27%)	$29,536		
2016 Primary	Adam Smith (D)	41,744	(57%)			
	Doug Basler (R)	18,090	(25%)			
	Jesse Wineberry (D)	9,561	(13%)			

Prior winning percentages: 2014 (71%), 2012 (72%), 2010 (55%), 2008 (65%), 2006 (66%), 2004 (63%), 2002 (59%), 2000 (62%), 1998 (65%), 1996 (50%)

Adam Smith, a Democrat first elected in 1996, has been a pro-business moderate who isn't shy about expressing his irritations with both political parties. Since 2011, he has been the Armed Services Committee's ranking Democrat, giving his state added clout on defense matters. For the most part, he has joined the panel's tradition of bipartisanship. The polarization of Congress occasionally has affected that panel, leading Smith to go his own way.

Smith grew up in the Sea-Tac area. His father, a baggage handler for United Airlines who was active in the Machinists Union, died when Smith was 17. The family went on welfare. Smith worked his way through Fordham University driving trucks for UPS, and got his law degree at the University of Washington. He worked as a Seattle prosecutor, handling drunk-driving and domestic-abuse cases.

In 1990, at age 25, he was elected to the state Senate, beating an incumbent Republican by canvassing the district door-to-door.

In 1996, he ran against first-term Republican Rep. Randy Tate. The two had similar backgrounds. They had been born in the same year to families of modest means, were elected to office at a young age, and were firm believers in grass-roots campaigning. Tate was a religious conservative and a strong supporter of House Speaker Newt Gingrich, while Smith campaigned as a moderate Democrat, supporting the death penalty and tougher penalties for criminals. He attacked Tate for his support of Gingrich and for backing cuts in Medicare. Tate attacked Smith for his opposition to assigning youthful offenders to adult courts and prisons and for voting for a tax increase in 1993. This was one of the closest races in the country. In the September all-party primary, Smith led 49%-48%. In November, he won 50%-47%.

Smith joined the New Democrat Coalition, established a moderate voting record, and showed a willingness to take on established views and interests in his party. He voted to authorize military action in Iraq and sought to improve compensation and other quality-of-life benefits for military personnel. He supported the House-passed health care overhaul in 2009, but refused to commit publicly on the final version until the very end in March 2010, finally agreeing to back it after pleas from President Barack Obama and others. He joined Republicans in 2011 in voting to extend key expiring provisions of the Patriot Act anti-terrorism law. In 2012, he lamented "the hyper-partisanship that is making Congress so dysfunctional." In opposing the New Year's Day 2013 tax and spending deal to avoid the so-called fiscal cliff, he accused Obama of "bad math" and of being unrealistic. "His insistence that we only tax the rich has put us in a box," he told *The Seattle Times.* In 2015, in a switch of his customary free-trade view, Smith cited problems for workers and the environment when he voted against giving trade promotion authority to Obama. His *Almanac* vote ratings for 2015 placed him in the more liberal half of House Democrats-a reversal of his customary ranking among moderate Democrats, especially on foreign policy.

On the Armed Services Committee, Smith rose quickly and earned praise for his work as chairman of two of its subcommittees. He served on the Intelligence Committee, further bolstering his credentials on military and foreign affairs issues. When Armed Services Chairman Ike Skelton lost his reelection bid in 2010, Smith jumped into the race to succeed the Missourian as the senior Democrat on the panel. Intelligence Committee Chairman Silvestre Reyes of Texas was the early favorite for the job, and California Rep. Loretta Sanchez also got into the race. When the House Democratic Caucus voted, Sanchez and Smith tied at 64 votes apiece, while Reyes got 53. In the two-person runoff, Smith won by 11 votes. (Reyes subsequently was defeated for reelection. Sanchez lost a bid for the Senate.)

He joined efforts to help the military adapt to automatic spending cuts that took effect in 2013 after Obama and Congress failed to reach a budget accord. He introduced a bill calling for spending reductions to be split about evenly between defense and domestic spending programs. Republican Rep. Mac Thornberry of Texas, who took over in 2015 as Armed Services chairman, said that Smith has helped make the committee less partisan. Ironically, Smith for the first time voted in May 2015 against passage of the defense spending bill, and called it "extremely damaging" to national security because it did not remove the budgetary spending caps and shifted some funding off-budget. In November, after a bipartisan budget deal had been made, he rejoined the bipartisan majority on the defense bill. In May 2016, he changed course and voted against the defense bill after Republicans added religious-liberty provisions for defense contractors, which opponents said were hostile to gay rights. On the House-Senate conference report in December, he again switched after hot-button issues were removed and the bill made "positive improvements" to defense policy.

Smith generally supported the Obama administration's defense and foreign policies. In 2014, he was appointed to the select committee investigating the terrorist attacks at U.S. facilities in Benghazi, Libya. "This is a committee that should not have been formed," he said when it was unveiled. "But since the Republicans chose to form it, I think we have to participate to do our best to bring out the correct arguments." Earlier, he said Obama "could have done a better job" in working with Congress before taking military action against Libya in 2011 as part of a NATO coalition, but he backed the president's strategy. When Chuck Hagel stepped down as Defense secretary in November 2014, Smith was mentioned as a possible successor. "I'm open to it, but I don't anticipate being asked," he told a broadcast interviewer in Seattle. "It would be a difficult decision."

In the debate over the Islamic State, he dismissed hawks' calls for swift military action and emphasized the need to build coalitions. "We need reliable partners to work with in the region," Smith told CBS News. "We can't simply bomb first and ask questions later." He said that a formal request to involve the military - known as an authorization for use of military force (AUMF) - should be sharply limited in how much power it gave to the president. "I don't think we should give the executive a blank check," he said. After Donald Trump was elected, Smith voiced serious doubts about his national security views. "I don't think it's intellectually possible to digest what he's talking about, and I'm not just being a wise-ass here," he told McClatchy News in November 2016.

Smith's independence has worked well for him at home, and he usually has won reelection easily. His closest contest was a 55%-45% win over Pierce County Council member Dick Muri during the Republican wave in 2010. Redistricting changes in 2012 removed much of his base in Pierce County and gave him a King County-based district that was ethnically diverse and largely new to him, but more safely Democratic.

In 2016, he ran into the potential downside of his realigned district when Democrat Jesse Wineberry, an African American and former state representative, challenged Smith for not being a strong advocate. "Diversity is under attack in this country," Wineberry said. "Let me utilize the power of the office to benefit the community." Smith responded that 160 languages were spoken in the district and said, "I consistently reach out to these communities." In the all-party primary, Smith got 56 percent to 23 percent for Republican Doug Basler and 15 percent for Wineberry. He had no trouble defeating Basler in the general election, 73%-27%. Basler raised $33,000 and Wineberry did not file a campaign-finance report, while Smith raised nearly $1 million. Smith eagerly supported Pramila Jayapal, who prevailed against another Democrat in the open-seat contest for the neighboring 7th District. She was a resident of the 9th and might have been a serious threat if she had instead challenged Smith. His relationship with the more outspoken minority community bears watching.

Southern and Eastern Seattle Metro

Population		**Race and Ethnicity**		**Income**	
Total	705,071	White	47.5%	Median Income	$66,344 (85 out of 435)
Land area	183	Black	10.8%		
Pop/ sq mi	3843.8	Latino	12.0%	Under $50,000	38.5%
Born in state	38.8%	Asian	22.3%	$50,000-$99,999	30.0%
		Two races	5.5%	$100,000-$199,999	23.1%
Age Groups		Other	2.0%	$200,000 or more	8.4%
Under 18	22.1%			Poverty Rate	13.7%
18-34	25.3%	**Education**			
35-64	40.2%	H.S grad or less	31.7%	**Health Insurance**	
Over 64	12.4%	Some college	28.8%	With health insurance coverage	87.3%
		College Degree, 4 yr	24.8%		
Work		Post grad	14.5%		
White Collar	41.1%			**Public Assistance**	
Sales and Service	40.8%	**Military**		Cash public assistance income	3.7%
Blue Collar	18.1%	Veteran	7.3%		
Government	5.2%	Active Duty	0.2%	Food stamp/SNAP benefits	14.9%

Voter Turnout			
2015 Total Citizens 18+	457,814	2016 House Turnout as % CVAP	61%
2016 House turnout	281,482	2014 House Turnout as % CVAP	37%

2012 Presidential Vote		
Barack Obama	195,863	(68%)
Mitt Romney	84,828	(30%)

2016 Presidential Vote		
Hillary Clinton	205,193	(69%)
Donald Trump	67,956	(23%)
Gary Johnson	11,178	(4%)

Cook Partisan Voting Index: D+21

The misty shores of Puget Sound have seen some of America's most vibrant economic growth over the past two decades. It has spread south and west from Seattle, over suburban territory to the outskirts of the once-industrial city of Tacoma. The subdivisions along the sound, which have some of the loveliest views in the U.S., tend to be high-income. But much of greater Seattle's prime industrial territory lies between the ridges that run north and south inland. Weyerhaeuser, the world's largest private owner of softwood timber, is headquartered in Federal Way. Boeing is a major presence in Renton, on the south end of Lake Washington. Boeing's aircraft and electronic components plants have made it the nation's No. 1 exporter for many years. Renton manufactures 737s, the best-selling commercial jet in history. In March 2017, Boeing unveiled the MAX version of its 737, with a capacity of 220 passengers. Three months earlier, the company reported a backlog of nearly 4,500 orders for the 737, including the MAX. Production at Renton was scheduled to increase in 2019 to 57 planes per month. A host of smaller factories cluster near the rail lines that are the terminus from Minneapolis-St. Paul across the Great Plains to Puget Sound.

The 9th Congressional District of Washington covers much of this area. It includes Sea-Tac Airport and Renton, just south of Seattle, as well as Des Moines, and most of Kent and Federal Way. It includes the container port of Tacoma, though most of the rest of that city is in the 6th and 10th Districts. The 9th extends northward from the south Seattle suburbs, where it takes in the southeastern neighborhoods of Seattle proper. It also pushes into the eastern suburbs. As the city grew over the years, newcomers crossed the pontoon bridge across Mercer Island to Bellevue and made that area one of the most vibrant parts of metropolitan Seattle; Bellevue's population almost quintupled in the 1960s and then doubled again over the next 40 years. Online auction house eBay has its operations there. With its vibrant downtown, including new office towers and residential high-rises, Bellevue today is an "edge city." The long-time rival Seattle and Tacoma ports unified their management in August 2015 in an alliance for their cargo facilities to compete more effectively. Their container cargo made the combined ports the fourth-largest in the United States, supporting 48,000 jobs. Passenger traffic at Sea-Tac in 2016 grew to the ninth-busiest airport in the nation. A week after he took office, Sea-Tac was the site of one of the largest protests of President Donald Trump's initial travel ban for immigrants and refugees.

More than 95 percent of the district is in King County. The 9th takes in much of Seattle's minority population and is the city's first majority-minority district. It is 24 percent Asian, 13 percent Hispanic, 12 percent African American. In 2016, Hillary Clinton led, 69%-23%, after President Barack Obama twice won here, 68%-30%.

TENTH DISTRICT

Denny Heck (D)

Elected 2012, 3rd term; b. Jul 29, 1952, Vancouver; Evergreen State College (WA), B.A., 1973; Portland State University (OR), Att., 1975; Lutheran; Married (Paula Heck); 2 children.

Elected Office: WA House, 1976-1986.

Professional Career: Chief of Staff, Gov. Booth Gardner, 1989-1993; Co-founder & CEO, TVW, 1993-2003; Co-founder, bd. member, Intrepid Learning Solutions, 1999-2012.

DC Office: 425 CHOB 20515, 202-225-9740, dennyheck.house.gov.

State Offices: Lacey, 360-459-8514; Lakewood, 253-533-8332.

Committees: *Financial Services*: Financial Institutions & Consumer Credit, Monetary Policy & Trade. *Permanent Select on Intelligence*.

Group Ratings

	ADA	ACLU	AFL-CIO	LCV	ITI	COC	HAFA	ACU	CFG	FRC
2016	-	88%	-	97%	83%	57%	12%	0%	0%	0%
2015	85%	C	96%	97%	C	50%	C	0%	0%	0%

Almanac Ratings 2015

	Economy	Social	Foreign	Composite
Liberal	80%	100%	69%	83%
Conservative	20%	0%	31%	17%

Key Votes of the 114th Congress

1. Keystone Pipeline	N	5. Puerto Rico Debt	Y	9. Offenses by Aliens	N
2. Trade Deals	N	6. Medical Marijuana	Y	10. Troops in Iraq	Y
3. Export-Import Bank	Y	7. Sanctuary Cities	N	11. Homeland Security $$	Y
4. Debt Ceiling Increase	Y	8. Armor-piercing Bullets	N	12. Trade Adjustment aid	Y

Election Results

Election	Name (Party)	Vote (%)		Cand. Spent	Ind. Exp. Support	Ind. Exp. Oppose
2016 General	Denny Heck (D)	170,460	(59%)	$653,179	$1,553	
	Jim Postma (R)	120,104	(41%)			
2016 Primary	Denny Heck (D)	47,612	(47%)			
	Jim Postma (R)	37,406	(37%)			
	Jennifer Ferguson (D)	12,959	(13%)			

Prior winning percentages: 2014 (55%), 2012 (59%)

Democrat Denny Heck was elected in 2012 in the new Democratic-friendly and Olympia-based 10th District. He had lost a tough race in 2010 in a nearby marginal district to Jaime Herrera Beutler, a rising Republican star. With his long and diverse career in politics and business, he found ways to make an impact in the House.

Heck had a working-class upbringing in Vancouver. His father was a truck driver and Heck began working at a nearby strawberry farm at age 9. After graduating from Evergreen State College, he applied for a position as an assistant to a school district superintendent. At the school board meeting where Heck was officially hired, he met his wife, Paula, who was monitoring the meeting as a local union representative. In 1976, he was elected to the state House, where he was an author of the state's Basic Education Act and its funding formula. He became House majority leader before retiring at age 34. Two years later, he became chief of staff to Democratic Gov. Booth Gardner.

In the 1990s, Heck cofounded TVW, a statewide public affairs network modeled after C-SPAN. He hosted a public affairs program and won an Emmy for a documentary he produced. Soon afterward, one of TVW's board members, Rob Glaser, created RealNetworks, an early audio and video internet service. Glaser convinced Heck to invest in RealNetworks, which pioneered streaming video. "He said, 'Do you want to get in on this idea I've got for a software that pushes audio and video over the internet?' And my question was, 'What's the internet?' I mean, this was really early," Heck recalled. Later, he cofounded an education and worker training company called Intrepid Learning Solutions.

By 2010, Heck hadn't worked in politics in years. He entered the race for the open 3rd District, which had been Democratic-held. He raised almost $2 million to $1.5 million for Herrera Beutler. Heck ran as a moderate Democrat and emphasized his business experience in creating jobs. Herrera Beutler criticized his support of the congressional Democrats' agenda and ran on a campaign of "fiscal sanity," a message that resonated that year, and won, 53%-47%. Not discouraged, Heck had another opportunity in 2012 when Washington gained a new district in more favorable territory. In the all-party primary with six candidates, he led Republican Dick Muri 40%-28%. As a veteran of the 1991 Gulf War and a retired Air Force lieutenant colonel, Muri's military experience was a strong selling point in a district that includes Joint Base Lewis-McChord. Heck called for phasing out tax breaks for households earning more than $250,000 a year, but he pushed for a lower estate-tax rate. He outspent Muri nearly 8-to-1 in the campaign, and national funding groups showed little interest. Heck won, 59%-41%.

He gained a seat on the Financial Services Committee and found some areas of bipartisan cooperation. With Republican Rep. Robert Pittenger of North Carolina, Heck moved legislation that gave small businesses a formal advisory role at the Consumer Financial Protection Bureau. He was an outspoken advocate for extending the authority of the Export-Import Bank of the United States, which is a popular agency in the trade-friendly state of Washington. He worked with Republican Rep. Bradley Byrne of Alabama to re-launch the Congressional Singapore Caucus to encourage bilateral relations.

Heck opposed legislation to provide trade promotion authority to Obama because, he said, prospective trade deals would not do enough to protect workers or the environment. A few days before the 2016 election, when labor unions had been threatening to withhold support from him, he posted a lengthy essay stating that he could not support the Trans-Pacific Partnership unless there were tougher enforcement procedures against unfair trade practices by other nations and more training for workers who lose their jobs. His *Almanac* vote rating for 2015 was close to the center of the House; he was more conservative on foreign policy and liberal on social issues.

In 2017, Heck got a seat on the House Intelligence Committee, which led the *Seattle Post-Intelligencer* to describe him as "an adult in the fractious House chamber." He took on party-related assignments. With the centrist New Democrat Coalition, he co-chaired the housing task force. At the Democratic Congressional Campaign Committee, he took on the vital role of recruitment chairman. Although he voiced optimism about prospects for 2018, he cautioned as "a starting point" that most of the seats that Democrats needed to win had been held by Republicans "for quite some time."

At home, he under-performed in the 2014 election against Joyce McDonald, a former member of the Pierce County Council. McDonald, a native of Scotland who became a naturalized citizen and served in the state House, called for tighter limits on federal spending. She raised only $88,000, while Heck raised $1.9 million. McDonald held him to a 55%-45% win. The two candidates were less than 400 votes apart in Pierce; Heck took 60 percent of the vote in his base of Thurston. In 2016, he breezed to re-election with 59 percent against Jim Postma, a perennial candidate who did not file a federal campaign report.

Tacoma Metro, Olympia

Population		**Race and Ethnicity**		**Income**	
Total	700,816	White	67.8%	Median Income	$57,542 (161 out of 435)
Land area	827	Black	5.9%		
Pop/ sq mi	847.8	Latino	10.9%		
Born in state	47.4%	Asian	6.4%	Under $50,000	42.3%
		Two races	6.0%	$50,000-$99,999	35.7%
Age Groups		Other	3.0%	$100,000-$199,999	19.0%
Under 18	24.1%			$200,000 or more	3.0%
18-34	25.1%	**Education**		Poverty Rate	13.5%
35-64	38.0%	H.S grad or less	35.5%		
Over 64	12.8%	Some college	38.4%	**Health Insurance**	
		College Degree, 4 yr	16.9%	With health insurance coverage	88.7%
Work		Post grad	9.3%		
White Collar	34.4%				
Sales and Service	43.6%	**Military**		**Public Assistance**	
Blue Collar	22.0%	Veteran	15.4%	Cash public assistance income	4.3%
Government	5.3%	Active Duty	3.3%		
				Food stamp/SNAP benefits	15.6%

Voter Turnout			
2015 Total Citizens 18+	501,430	2016 House Turnout as % CVAP	58%
2016 House turnout	290,564	2014 House Turnout as % CVAP	37%

2012 Presidential Vote		
Barack Obama	164,505	(56%)
Mitt Romney	120,066	(41%)

2016 Presidential Vote		
Hillary Clinton	151,373	(50%)
Donald Trump	117,861	(39%)
Gary Johnson	17,003	(6%)
Jill Stein	6,481	(2%)

Cook Partisan Voting Index: D+5

Beginning at Deception Pass, near present-day Mount Vernon and Anacortes, Puget Sound winds its way southward from the Strait of Juan de Fuca for more than 100 miles, through an intricate latticework of bays, straits and islands. At the far southern end of the sound, off of Budd Inlet, is Olympia, the capital of Washington. In 1846, two New England natives, Lathrop Smith and Edmund Sylvester, hoping to take advantage of the location near the end of the Cowlitz Trail, platted a town in the New England style: a town square, carefully planned streets and land reserved for schools. They initially opted to name the town Smithster - a portmanteau of their surnames - but eventually opted for Olympia, after the mountains that are visible to the north on a clear day. It soon thereafter became the capital of Washington territory. As late as 1880, Olympia's population rivaled that of other major Washington cities. But the railroads passed it by, and other ports were developed in more advantageous positions closer to the mouth of Puget Sound. Olympia grew at a relatively slow but steady pace, sustained mostly by the lumber industry and state government.

Today, the lumber industry is in decline in Olympia; the Georgia Pacific and St. Regis mills are all long closed. Olympia is a relatively small city, with an economy that revolves mostly around government. The city has tried to diversify into tourism and as a hub for hydraulic fracturing, known as "fracking," a technique for extracting oil and natural gas. In November 2016, environmentalists protested shipments through the Olympia port of materials for fracking in North Dakota and Wyoming. Percival Landing, one of three waterfront parks in Olympia, features a mile-long boardwalk, restaurants, and piers for boats.

Since 2000, Thurston County has grown by 33 percent; nearby Lacey has grown almost as large as Olympia and has larger households. In December 2016, Olympia declared itself a "sanctuary city," joining Seattle in refusing to cooperate with federal immigration officials. Pierce County, which has grown by 23 percent since 2000, has become a destination for homeowners who cannot afford high real-estate prices in Seattle and King County. In 2015, Pierce was first in the nation in the number of persons migrating from within the nation; Snohomish County, which is north of Seattle, ranked second. In Tacoma, where 41 percent of the population is minority, the city decided in March 2017 not to expand its immigrant detention center, out of fear that it might facilitate round-ups and deportations by the Trump administration.

The 10th Congressional District centers around Olympia-based Thurston County and Tacoma-based Pierce County. A small fraction lives in Mason County, to the northwest. That county takes in the town of Shelton, where a local lumber mill with 275 employees shut down in 2015. Sierra Pacific shut down two other nearby mills and opened a state-of-the-art facility along the waterfront in Shelton. A bit more than half the population is in Pierce and 40 percent in Thurston. Politically, the district leans comfortably toward Democrats. Hillary Clinton won with 50 percent in 2016, a dip from the 56 percent for President Barack Obama in 2012.

★ WEST VIRGINIA ★

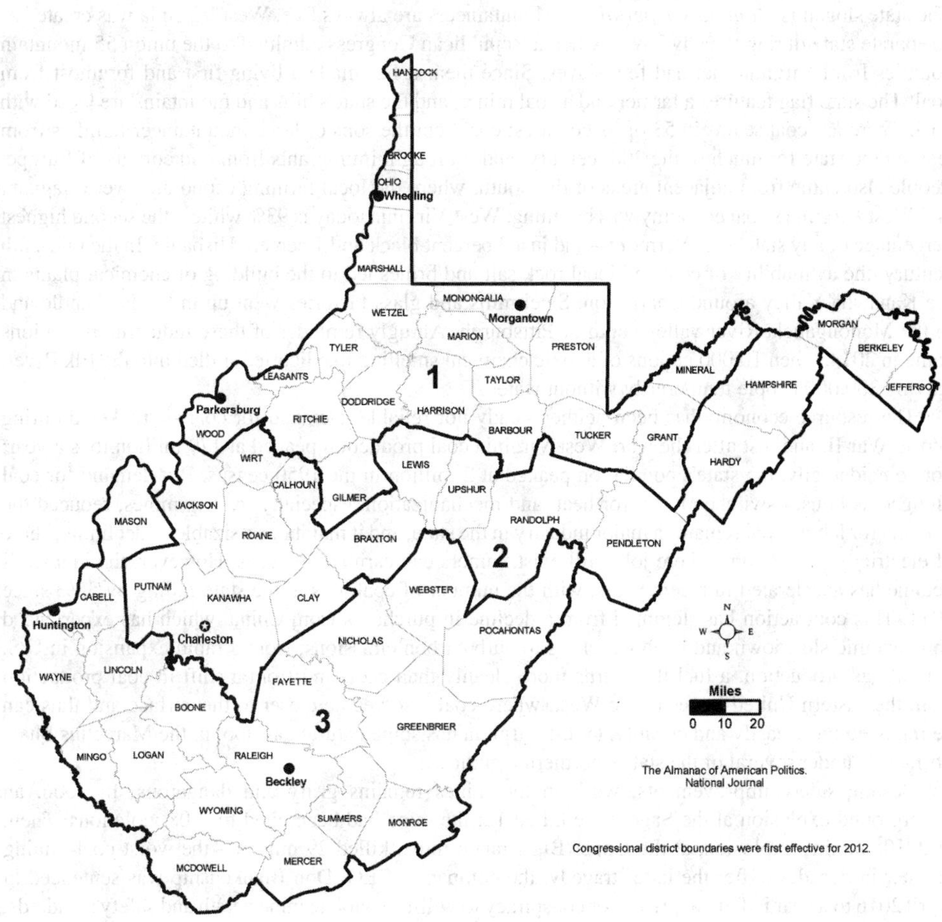

Few states have shifted more quickly, and more completely, from Democratic to Republican than West Virginia. Democratic presidential candidates haven't won the state since 1996, and 2016, Hillary Clinton – hobbled by an awkward comment about putting coal miners out of work – lost the state by a whopping 42-point margin, the second-widest margin for Donald Trump anywhere in the United States except for Wyoming. All this has happened while the state has grappled with severe industrial decline and the resulting economic and social woes.

"Almost heaven" is what the song says about West Virginia, and there's something to it, at least in the minds of West Virginians who have never lost their affection for the state's hills and mountains. Yet the state has had more than its share of tragedy and heartbreak. It was first settled by Scots-Irish immigrants, fresh from internecine fighting in the British Isles and determined to stake out comfortable homesteads. The state slogan is *Montani semper liberi*: Mountaineers are always free. West Virginia was created as a separate state during the Civil War, when a Republican Congress admitted to the union 55 mountain counties from Virginia that had few slaves. Since then, it has made a living first and foremost from coal. The state flag features a farmer and a coal miner, and the state's hills and mountains are laced with coal. There are coal seams in 53 of its counties; coal kept the sons of large mountaineer families from leaving the state for much of the 20th century, and it brought immigrants from odd corners of Europe. People also came from adjacent areas of the South, where the local farming economies were stagnant and West Virginia's coal economy was booming. West Virginia today is 93% white – the second highest percentage of any state after Vermont – and just 3 percent black and 1 percent Hispanic. In the mid-20th century, the availability of coal and local rock salt and brines led to the building of chemical plants in the Kanawha Valley around Charleston. Steel mills and glass factories went up in the Panhandle and in the Monongahela River valley south of Pittsburgh. An ugly reminder of these industrial operations came in 2014, when 10,000 gallons of a toxic chemical smelling like licorice spilled into the Elk River, leaving 300,000 people temporarily without water.

The resource economy has been neither steady nor reliable. Demand for coal skyrocketed during World War II, and just after the war, West Virginia coal production peaked at 179 million tons a year; not coincidentally, the state's population peaked at 2 million in the 1950 census. But demand for coal plunged as houses switched to oil for heat, and mechanization, especially in strip mines, reduced the demand for labor. Coal remains a major industry in the state, and it maintains a sizable, if declining, share of electricity generation. Where jobs still exist, miners can earn solid wages. However, the industry's decline has accelerated in recent years, with the number of coal jobs in the state falling by 35% since 2011. This contraction has stemmed from a decline in purchases from China, which has experienced an economic slowdown and is now seeking to curb carbon emissions; from a rapid expansion in U.S. natural gas production, a fuel that burns more cleanly than coal; and from a shift in coal production from the eastern United States to the West, where coal reserves lie closer to the surface and thus can be removed more easily and cheaply. (West Virginia has some natural gas, too, in the Marcellus Shale Formation under several of the state's northern counties.)

Despite safety improvements, work in the mines remains gritty and dangerous. In 2006, an underground explosion at the Sago mine killed 12; the mine had been cited for 208 violations. Then, in 2010, another explosion, at the Upper Big Branch mine, killed 29 miners – the worst coal-mining disaster in decades. After the latter tragedy, the company's CEO, Don Blankenship was sentenced in April 2016 to a year in federal prison for conspiracy to willfully violate mine health and safety standards. But the ability of workers to protect themselves has declined along with membership in the United Mine Workers. The union's rolls included 90% of the state's miners when it staged a black lung strike in 1969, but that share has since crumbled by two-thirds. By 2016, the Republican-controlled legislature went so far as to pass a right-to-work law detested by labor unions, though it has been temporarily blocked in court.

West Virginia's median income is almost one-fourth below the national average, exceeding only those of Arkansas, Kentucky and Mississippi. The poverty rate is seventh-highest in the nation at 17.9%, with rates even higher in depressed coal-mining areas in the state's southern tier, such as McDowell County at 34.5% and Mingo County at 29%. Statewide, 20% of residents receive food stamps, compared to 14% nationally. In 2015, the state achieved the grim dual landmarks of finishing first in the nation in its opioid overdose death rate, at 41.5 per 100,000 people, and last in the labor-force participation rate, at 52.8%. Health care companies dominate the list of biggest employers, with WVU Medicine dethroning WalMart in 2016 as the state's biggest employer. Government has inevitably played a role. During his 50 years on the Senate Appropriations Committee, Democratic Sen. Robert Byrd exceeded his goal of steering $1 billion of federal projects into the state, including the FBI's biggest division, with a growing workforce of 3,000 workers plus contractors in Clarksburg. The quest to attract high-tech jobs has been hobbled by the state's weak levels of educational attainment. West Virginia ranks dead last in the percentage of residents with a bachelor's degree, and eighth from the bottom in the percentage who have a high-school degree.

In this difficult economic environment, West Virginia's population has contracted. Since the 2010 Census, the state has lost 1.2 percent of its population. The state's biggest county, Kanawha (Charleston) shrank by 3.5 percent over that period, and other populous counties – Cabell (Huntington), Wood (Parkersburg), Ohio (Wheeling) and Raleigh (Beckley) -- have each declined by percentages in the low single digits during that time. The decline in impoverished coal counties has been even bigger; Mingo's population fell by 8.2% and McDowell's fell by 13.4%. The few growing areas of the state include the Eastern Panhandle, now a long-distance suburb of Washington, D.C., and Morgantown, the home of WVU, both of which have expanded by high single-digit percentages since the last Census. Generations of out-migration by children raised in the state has left West Virginia with the second-highest percentage of residents 65 and older of any state, trailing only Florida.

West Virginia's political heritage from the Civil War days was Republican, though some counties tilted toward the Confederacy and the Democrats. The United Mine Workers organized most of the West Virginia mines by 1902, and there were bloody strikes in 1912-13 and 1920-21. Under the UMW's John L. Lewis, coal country shifted toward the New Deal Democrats, and for more than half a century, West Virginia was one of the most Democratic states, deserting the national ticket only in Republican landslide years (1956, 1972, and 1984).]In the 21st century, it has swung to the Republicans -- hard. A big reason has been the national party leaders' attitudes toward coal. In the 2000 presidential race, George W. Bush's strategist Karl Rove ignored precedent and targeted West Virginia, smartly calculating that Bush's support for mountaintop mining and his opposition to gun control could make the state winnable for a Republican. In office, Bush continued to push Congress to spend billions of dollars on clean coal technology and backed import quotas to help the steel industry, a major coal user. That helped Bush and John McCain carry the state by almost identical margins in 2004 and 2008.

After Barack Obama took office, the Environmental Protection Agency revoked a 2007 permit issued to Arch Coal for mountaintop mining in Logan County-the first time such a permit had been denied under clean water rules. Democratic Gov. Joe Manchin sued to overturn federal rules on mountaintop mining in October 2010, when he was running in the special election to fill Byrd's Senate seat. An ad that helped him clinch the election showed Manchin taking aim with a rifle and shooting a hole in a copy of the cap-and-trade energy bill that Democrats had passed in the House in June 2009. It helped Manchin win, 53%-43%. In 2012, West Virginians' anger at Obama administration policies was apparent in the May presidential primary, in which 41% of registered Democrats voted for a convict instead of the president; in the general election, Mitt Romney won the state, 62%-36%, and carried all 55 counties. Then, in 2014, the dominoes really started falling, in dramatic fashion. That year, the legislature – which had been Democratic since the 1930s – fell to the GOP, first the state House on Election Night and then the state Senate after a post-election party switch. That same year, Republicans won all of the state's House seats for the first time since 1921, and they flipped the seat held by five-term Democratic Sen. John (Jay) Rockefeller. Today, aside from newly elected Gov. Jim Justice (who conspicuously distanced himself from Hillary Clinton, who was above him on the ticket) and state Treasurer John Perdue, all the statewide elected officials on the state's board of public works are Republicans. That was a far cry from just a few election cycles earlier, when Republicans had trouble even fielding credible candidates for many legislative and statewide seats.

The swing toward the GOP continued in 2016. West Virginians positively recoiled from Clinton, who had blundered in a March televised town hall when she said, "We're going to put a lot of coal miners and coal companies out of business." While Clinton had said this in the context of urging new opportunities for ex-miners in growing fields such as renewable energy, the words stung in coal country, and they were easily turned into a cudgel by her critics. When Clinton made a pre-primary visit to the state in May, she was met by chants of "Go home!" Vermont Sen. Bernie Sanders ended up winning the primary, 51%-36%. However, relatively few of those Sanders supporters backed Clinton in November.

Many supported Donald Trump, who trounced Clinton in the general election and widened the GOP's margin of victory from 27 points in 2012 to 42 points in 2016. In raw votes, Trump exceeded Romney's total by 72,000, while Clinton under-performed even the unpopular Obama by 49,000 votes. For the second time in a row, the Democratic nominee failed to win a single West Virginia county. (Obama had taken seven in 2008.) Most of West Virginia's biggest counties shifted their winning margins by eight to 15 points in the GOP's direction; in coal counties like Mingo and McDowell, the shifts in the winning margin exceeded 20 points in the GOP's direction. By all indications, West Virginians held out high hopes for the new president, awaiting new investments in infrastructure and for progress on his promise to bring back coal-mining jobs. But reviving the coal industry is expected to be an exceedingly uphill task.

Population		**Race and Ethnicity**		**Income**	
Total	1,851,420	White	92.5%	Median Income	$41,751 (48 out of 50)
Land area	24,038	Black	3.3%		
Pop/ sq mi	77.0	Latino	1.4%	Under $50,000	57.7%
Born in state	70.0%	Asian	0.7%	$50,000-$99,999	28.3%
		Two races	1.9%	$100,000-$199,999	11.8%
Age Groups		Other	0.2%	$200,000 or more	2.1%
Under 18	20.7%			Poverty Rate	18.0%
18-34	21.0%	**Education**			
35-64	41.1%	H.S grad or less	55.7%	**Health Insurance**	
Over 64	17.3%	Some college	25.1%	With health insurance coverage	88.5%
		College Degree, 4 yr	11.7%		
Work		Post grad	7.4%		
White Collar	32.2%			**Public Assistance**	
Sales and Service	43.0%	**Military**		Cash public assistance income	2.3%
Blue Collar	24.8%	Veteran	10.2%		
Government	19.0%	Active Duty	0.1%	Food stamp/SNAP benefits	16.1%

Voter Turnout			
2015 Total Citizens 18+	1,455,848	2016 Pres Turnout as % CVAP	49%
2016 Pres Votes	714,423	2012 Pres Turnout as % CVAP	46%

Legislature	
Senate:	12D, 22R
House:	36D, 63R, 1I

Presidential Politics

2016 Democratic Primary		
Bernie Sanders (D)	124,700	(51%)
Hillary Clinton (D)	86,914	(36%)
2016 Republican Primary		
Donald Trump (R)	157,238	(77%)
Ted Cruz (R)	18,301	(9%)
John Kasich (R)	13,721	(7%)

2016 Presidential Vote		
Donald Trump (R)	489,371	(69%)
Hillary Clinton (D)	188,794	(26%)
Gary Johnson (L)	23,004	(3%)
2012 Presidential Vote		
Mitt Romney (R)	417,655	(62%)
Barack Obama (D)	238,269	(36%)

From 1932 to 1996, the only Republican nominees who carried West Virginia were incumbents headed for landslide reelection victories - Dwight Eisenhower in 1956, Richard Nixon in 1972, and Ronald Reagan in 1984. But West Virginia has voted Republican in the last five presidential elections. That change in the new millennium can be explained by two factors: culture and coal. West Virginians tend to be more religious and tradition-minded than Americans generally. At a time when national Democrats are bent on reducing carbon emissions to address climate change, West Virginia's once dominant coal economy is staggering under market and regulatory forces. According to the Bureau of Economic Affairs, government now accounts for a bigger share of the state's GDP than mining. Still, the state's voters can back Democrats and split their tickets. West Virginians elect their governor in the same year they cast their ballots for president. And in each of those past five elections, they have sent a Democrat to their statehouse in Charleston. But those Democrats were ones in tune with the West Virginia electorate.

he party's decline began when GOP nominee George W. Bush targeted West Virginia in his 2000 campaign. Bush's support of mountaintop mining and his promotion of clean coal technology enabled him to beat Al Gore 52%-46% in 2000 and John Kerry 56%-43% in 2004. In 2008, John McCain beat Obama 56%-43%, carrying 48 of 55 counties. Four years later, Mitt Romney carried the state 62%-36%, winning all 55 counties - the first nominee of either party to do so since the Civil War. Donald Trump became the second, defeating Hillary Clinton 69%-27%. That was probably a forgone outcome when Clinton, campaigning in next-door Ohio, told a CNN town hall, "We're going to put a lot of coal miners and coal companies out of business," in explaining her proposals to move the country toward other sources of energy. These comments were not welcomed in West Virginia, which reached a record 158 million short tons of coal production in 2008, the year before Obama came to office. The Bureau of Business and Economic Research at West Virginia University estimated that for 2016, Obama's last year in office, production fell to 68 million short tons.

West Virginia's presidential primary, held in May, has not attracted much attention since 1960, when John Kennedy took on Hubert Humphrey and beat him with 61 percent of the vote, proving that a Catholic could succeed in a virtually all-Protestant state. The 2008 Democratic contest was not an epic battle like 1960, but it was hard fought nonetheless. Turnout was a robust 356,000, well above the levels in recent primaries. Clinton won 67%-26%, her biggest victory except for Arkansas, carrying every county. In the 2016 primary, Vermont Sen. Bernie Sanders defeated Clinton, 51%-36%. Not only did Sanders win every county, a majority of his supporters in the *Democratic* primary told the television network exit poll that they would vote for Trump in the general election. Coming right after Trump's remaining GOP rivals abandoned their nomination bids, his 77%-9% victory over Texas Sen. Ted Cruz was anticlimactic.

Congressional Districts

115th Congress Lineup	3R	**114th Congress Lineup**	3R

West Virginia elected six members of the House in 1960 but only three in 1992. Current population projections show that it will lose another district in the 2020 reapportionment. As recently as 1998, the state elected three Democrats. With voter hostility to the national party, Republicans have taken all three. Assuming no changes in the partisan control of those seats, one of those incumbents likely will draw the short straw or lose at musical chairs. (Pick your metaphor!). With only two districts, the map-drawers would have few options, regardless of which party is in control. They could split the state with a line that goes roughly east-west, or one that goes north-south. In either case, the geographic realities appear to dictate one district that is Charleston-based and the other that hugs the Pennsylvania and Maryland state lines, with the remainder of the state split accordingly.

In 2011, Beltway Democratic strategists pressured West Virginia's legislators to be aggressive. Democratic state Sen. John Unger unveiled a proposal to keep untouched the district of Democrat Rep. Nick Rahall, who had held the southern 3rd District since 1976, and run the 1st and 2nd districts north-south rather than east-west, in effect pairing Republican Reps. Shelley Moore Capito and David McKinley and creating an open Eastern Panhandle seat. Furious Republicans pointed out that moving Mason County (population, 27,324) from the 2nd District to the 3rd District was all that was needed to equalize seats. The Unger plan earned tepid reception from Democrats, too. Some were fearful that rocking the boat would prompt Capito to run statewide; others didn't see the need to satisfy their party's Washington, D.C., leaders. So, a few days later, the legislature passed and Democratic Gov. Earl Ray Tomblin signed the "Mason County flip" into law. Redistricting notwithstanding, in 2014, Rahall lost reelection and Republicans retained Capito's seat when she was elected to the Senate. Nothing could avert the unpopularity of the Democratic brand.

Governor

Jim Justice (D)

Elected 2016, term expires 2021, 1st term; b. Apr. 27, 1951, Raleigh County, WV; Marshall University, BA & MBA; Married (Cathy); 2 children.

Professional Career: Entrepeneur

Office: 1900 Kanawha Blvd., East, Charleston, 25305; 304-558-2000; Fax: 304-342-7025; Website: governor.wv.gov.

Election Results

Election	Name (Party)	Vote (%)
2016 General	Jim Justice (D)	350,408 (49%)
	Bill Cole (R)	301,987 (42%)
	Charlotte Jean Pritt (MT)	42,068 (6%)
	David Moran (L)	15,354 (2%)
2016 Primary	Jim Justice (D)	132,704 (51%)
	Booth Goodwin (D)	65,416 (25%)
	Jeff Kessler (D)	60,230 (23%)

Jim Justice, a billionaire often described as West Virginia's richest man, was elected governor in 2016. He won despite running as a Democrat in a state that, on the same Election Day, overwhelmingly backed Republican presidential nominee Donald Trump. However, many observers noted that Justice and Trump shared key attributes, including their wealth, a range of controversies over their businesses, support for the coal industry, and an outspoken style. "I am not a career politician; I am a career businessman," Justice wrote in an op-ed in the Charleston *Gazette-Mail*.

Justice was born in West Virginia and continued and diversified his family's businesses. After earning a bachelor's and M.B.A. at Marshall University, Justice started Bluestone Farms in 1977 and expanded it to cover 50,000 acres of corn, wheat, and soybeans in West Virginia, Virginia, North Carolina, and South Carolina. Following his father's death in 1993, Justice assumed control of Bluestone Industries Inc. and Bluestone Coal Corp. He proceeded to expand the company's operations in coal, Christmas tree farms, cotton gins, turfgrass, timber, and golf courses. By the time he was elected governor, Justice ran approximately 100 different companies. In 2009, he sold his coal company to the Russian firm Mechel OAO. But the new owner failed, and Justice purchased back his controlling interest in 2015 for a reported $5 million -- less than 1 percent of what he'd sold it for. In the meantime, Justice had purchased the Greenbrier – the debt-plagued resort in in White Sulphur Springs, West Virginia, that was one of the nation's finest and most storied getaways -- for $20.5 million in 2009. He added a casino and brought in such high-profile events as the PGA Tour and NFL and NBA training camps. He also acquired other resorts and country clubs around the state. While running for governor, Justice had his daughter Jill run the Greenbrier while his son Jay oversaw the coal and agriculture businesses.

Despite his wealth, Justice cultivated a down-home image. He has been involved with Little League baseball in Beckley for a quarter-century, and he has coached girls and boys basketball teams for more than 35 years, most recently for Greenbrier East High School in Lewisburg, West Virginia. Shortly after winning the governorship, he notched his 1,000th career win as a basketball coach. At times, Justice has showed little patience for political niceties. He rejected his Republican opponent's claim that he supported President Barack Obama as "complete dog snot" and, after winning the governorship, punctuated his veto of a budget passed by the Republican-controlled legislature by unveiling a copy of the budget topped by a pile of real-life bull feces. "We don't have a nothingburger today, and we don't have a mayonnaise sandwich today," he said. "We all should take ownership for this, but what we have is nothing more than a bunch of political bull-you-know-what."

Justice's business activities have been dogged by controversy. In 2014, NPR reported that his companies owed almost $2 million in unpaid fines. In 2015, Justice agreed to pay a $220,000 fine for failing to obtain Clean Water Act permits before building 20 dams at a hunting and fishing preserve. In September 2016, the Environmental Protection Agency announced a nearly $6 million agreement to settle thousands of pollution violations at coal facilities owned by Justice in West Virginia and other states. The violations included excess pollution, insufficient sampling, failure to file reports and inattention to federal requests, dating back to 2011. He and his companies have also faced problems with delinquent taxes in state and local jurisdictions in Kentucky, Virginia, and West Virginia. A follow-up to the NPR investigation in October 2016 concluded that Justice had become "the nation's top mine-safety delinquent," owing $15 million from operations in six states, ranging from property and minerals taxes to unemployment taxes to mine-safety penalties. The NPR investigation found injury rates at Justice's mines to be twice the national average, with violations rates more than four times the national rate during the period of delinquency. When issues such as these surfaced in the gubernatorial campaign, Justice said at a news conference, "I'm a safety fanatic. So I'm the last person in the world that's wanting something to where you would put an employee in a situation that would be unsafe."

Justice got into politics by running to succeed Gov. Earl Ray Tomblin, a culturally conservative Democrat who assumed office on Nov. 15, 2010. The former president of the state Senate, Tomblin had succeeded Democrat Joe Manchin, who stepped down as governor to run successfully for the late Sen. Robert Byrd's seat in the Senate. Tomblin won an October 2011 special election to serve the remaining year of Manchin's unexpired term and 13 months later won a four-year term of his own. Like many other West Virginia Democrats, Tomblin opposed abortion rights and disdained many of the national Democratic Party's other priorities. Justice did not have a clear path to the Democratic nomination, however. He faced a competitive three-way primary against former United States Attorney Booth Goodwin and state Senate Majority Leader Jeff Kessler. Goodwin touted his prosecution of cases stemming from one of the worst mine explosions in United States history, at West Virginia's Upper Big Branch mine that killed 29 men in 2010. Kessler, the candidate in the primary with the most extensive political experience, ran somewhat to the left of his rivals. But Justice, bolstered by his deep pockets and his statewide familiarity, won the primary with an outright majority of 51%; Goodwin got 25% and Kessler pulled 23%.

In the general election, Justice positioned himself as a conservative Democrat, almost an Independent – a necessity for any successful West Virginia Democrat in recent years, including Tomblin and Manchin. "I cannot be a supporter of Hillary Clinton," he said in a radio interview. "The reason I can't be is her position on coal is diametrically, completely wrong in many, many different ways." He also exhibited a higher tolerance for government spending and investment than many politicians today. Justice faced Republican state Senate president Bill Cole. Cole had attracted notice as a key player in state budget negotiations, but he preferred to emphasize his business background – he owned a car dealership and a share of a metal manufacturing plant in Tennessee. Cole offered a traditional conservative agenda that included tax and spending cuts, curbs on abortion, and charter schools. He also tied himself to Trump. In one ad, the narrator said, "Together, the Bill Cole-Donald Trump team will fight for working families, helping make West Virginia, and America, great again." On the campaign trail, Cole attacked Justice's business record, which offered plenty of material. But Justice's ace in the hole was that he seemed to fit the national and state mood for an outsider willing to break up politics-as-usual, negating any drag from his Democratic party affiliation. Justice also got a public-relations boost after severe floods hit portions of the state in July 2016, killing 23 people. He closed the Greenbrier and allowed hundreds of local residents displaced by the storm to stay there. On Election Day, Justice won 49%-42%. Ardent environmentalist Charlotte Pritt – no fan of Justice's mountaintop-removal mining -- took almost 6% running on the Mountain Party line, while Libertarian David Moran took 2%. Cole won only 19 counties, many of them in the historically Republican Eastern Panhandle region; in almost every other region, Justice won the lion's share of counties.

After his victory, Justice aligned himself with Trump, who had won the state overwhelmingly and with whom he had spoken during the transition. At his inauguration, Justice said, "Whether you like it or don't like it, Donald Trump is our president. And let me just tell you this: I'm friends with the Trump family. I know 'em; I know them well. And I truly believe that he will provide us with opportunities in West Virginia." Inheriting a budget of roughly $500 million, Justice didn't shy away from proposing revenue increases, saying in his inauguration speech, "We have got to find a way to raise revenue. We cannot continue to just kick the can down the road" and drain the state's rainy-day fund. Justice proposed a $4.5 billion budget, then reduced it to just under $4.3 billion. The proposal included a toll hike on the

West Virginia Turnpike for out-of-state motorists, a gasoline tax increase, a tax on sugary drinks, and an increase for motor-vehicle fees. In April, the legislature approved a $4.1 billion budget, which prompted a veto and Justice's bull-feces display. Over the longer term, he proposed adjusting the severance tax on energy resources so that it rose during good times for the industry and retreated during bad times. In something of a surprise, the legislature passed and Justice signed a law legalizing medical marijuana, making West Virginia the 29th state to do so. Meanwhile, the governor pledged to keep coaching kids' basketball. "I love kids," Justice said. "It's my release. I don't go on vacation. I work all the bloomin' time. This is my vacation."

Senior Senator

Joe Manchin (D)

Elected 2010, term expires 2018, 2nd term; b. Aug 24, 1947, Farmington, West Virginia University, B.S.; Catholic; Married (Gayle Conelly); 3 children; 8 grandchildren.

Elected Office: WV House, 1982-1986; WV Senate, 1986-1996; WV Secretary Of State, 2000-2004; WV Governor, 2004-2010.

Professional Career: Co-owner, Manchin's Carpet & Tile, 1968-1982; Owner, Enersystems, 1989-2000.

DC Office: 306 HSOB 20510, 202-224-3954, Fax: 202-228-0002, manchin.senate.gov.

State Offices: Charleston, 304-342-5855; Fairmont, 304-368-0567; Martinsburg, 304-264-4626.

Committees: Senate Democratic Policy and Communications Center Vice Chairman. *Appropriations*: Commerce, Justice, Science & Related Agencies, Department of Homeland Security, DOL, HHS & Education & Related Agencies, Financial Services & General Government, Transportation, HUD & Related Agencies. *Energy & Natural Resources*: Energy (RMM), Public Lands, Forests & Mining, Water & Power. *Intelligence*. *Veterans' Affairs*.

Group Ratings

	ADA	ACLU	AFL-CIO	LCV	ITI	COC	HAFA	ACU	CFG	FRC
2016	-	41%	-	47%	60%	100%	21%	27%	26%	0%
2015	60%	C	93%	40%	C	64%	C	33%	23%	45%

Almanac Ratings 2015

	Economy	Social	Foreign	Composite
Liberal	75%	50%	83%	69%
Conservative	25%	51%	17%	31%

Key Votes of the 114th Congress

1. Keystone pipeline	Y	5. National Security Data	Y	9. Gun Sales Checks	Y
2. Export-Import Bank	N	6. Iran Nuclear Deal	Y	10. Sanctuary Cities	Y
3. Debt Ceiling Increase	Y	7. Puerto Rico Debt	NV	11. Planned Parenthood	N
4. Homeland Security $$	Y	8. Loretta Lynch A.G	Y	12. Trade deals	N

Election Results

Election	Name (Party)	Vote (%)		Cand. Spent	Ind. Exp. Support	Ind. Exp. Oppose
2012 General	Joe Manchin (D)	399,898	(61%)	$7,678,708	$204,219	$97,225
	John R. Raese (R)	240,787	(36%)	$1,610,493	$40,392	$89,252
	Bob Henry Baber (MT)	19,517	(3%)			
2012 Primary	Joe Manchin (D)	163,891	(80%)			
	Sheirl Fletcher (D)	41,118	(20%)			

Prior winning percentages: 2010 special (53%); Governor: 2008 (70%), 2004 (64%)

Democrat Joe Manchin, who won a special election in 2010 to succeed the late, legendary Robert Byrd, is West Virginia's senior senator. A popular former governor, he has used his political capital to try to break through the Senate's gridlock, most notably on gun control and student loan rates. With his home state's tilt away from Democrats, he faced a potentially challenging reelection campaign in 2018. He turned down Republican invites to switch parties or join President Donald Trump's cabinet.

Manchin hails from a prominent political family. He grew up in Farmington, a few miles up Buffalo Creek from the industrial city of Fairmont. Manchin took a semester off from college to help his father rebuild his carpet and furniture store after a fire. His grandfather and father both served as mayor of Farmington. His uncle, A. James Manchin, was elected to the West Virginia House of Delegates and was secretary of state and state treasurer.

After graduating from West Virginia University, Joe Manchin went to work in the carpet and furniture business, helping to send his four siblings to college. Then he started a coal brokerage company and moved to Fairmont. Manchin was elected to the House of Delegates in 1982 and the state Senate in 1986. He ran for governor in 1996, only to lose in the Democratic primary to legislator Charlotte Pritt. When Secretary of State Ken Hechler ran for the House in 2000, Manchin ran to succeed him, as did Pritt. This time, Manchin beat her in the primary, 51% to 29%. He won the general election.

In 2003, Manchin announced that he would challenge Democratic Gov. Bob Wise in the 2004 primary. Later that month, Wise admitted that he'd had an extramarital affair and would not seek reelection. Manchin got support from both unions and business. His stands on cultural issues were impeccably conservative and in line with state preferences: He was opposed to abortion rights, gun control, and same sex marriage. Manchin won the Democratic primary with 53 percent, and he defeated Republican Monty Warner in the general election, 64% to 34%, carrying 52 of 55 counties.

Manchin had been in office for just one year when he gained renown as the public face of desperate attempts to rescue 13 trapped coal miners after the January 2006 explosion at the Sago Mine in central West Virginia. Manchin, whose uncle was killed in a 1968 mine accident that claimed 78 lives, gave numerous televised interviews from the mine site. He mistakenly announced "the miracle of all miracles"-that 12 of the miners had survived-when in fact they had died. The blunder could have been career-ending, but Manchin's standing skyrocketed in the polls, partly because West Virginia Republicans decided that invoking the accident politically was a line that they would not cross. After two other deadly mining accidents, Manchin ordered safety inspections at all mines in the state. In 2007, he signed new laws mandating certain ventilation practices and giving the state authority to temporarily shut down mines with violations.

Manchin had success on other issues. In 2006, he signed into law eight bills designed to improve health care in the state, including giving low-income families basic care at clinics and creating a catastrophic health care insurance program and a new mental health commission. His tenure was marred by a controversy involving his daughter and politically potent institutions in the state. The *Pittsburgh Post-Gazette* reported that the governor's daughter, Heather Bresch, falsely claimed to have earned a master's degree in business in 1998 at West Virginia University. The school then awarded her the degree in 2007 even though she had completed only about half the required 48 credit hours. Under pressure, several top university officials, including the school's president, resigned. Bresch-by then, a high-level executive at Mylan, a generic drug maker that had donated heavily to the university and, through its top executives, to Manchin's campaigns-never admitted wrongdoing. Manchin expressed support for Bresch. Although the scandal made headlines in 2008, he was reelected that year without serious competition, 70% to 26%. (In 2016, Bresch created new awkwardness for Manchin, following bipartisan criticism from senators that Mylan was charging exorbitant sums for its EpiPen, a self-injected dose of epinephrine used in the event of life-threatening allergic reactions.)

His popularity prompted speculation about his political future. When Byrd died in June 2010-after a record 51 years in the Senate and six more in the House-Manchin was seen as the Democrats' best hope for keeping the seat. Although he could have appointed himself to the Senate pending a special election, Manchin declined to do so. Instead, he appointed his former chief counsel, Carte Goodwin, as a placeholder pending a 2010 special election. Republicans initially hadn't planned to invest in the race. In September, a Rasmussen survey showed Manchin with a soaring job approval rating of 69 percent. His GOP opponent was John Raese, a wealthy businessman whom Byrd had defeated four years earlier by a nearly 2-to-1 margin. But Raese, who poured his own money into the contest, had the wind at his back in a strong election cycle for the GOP. He ran ads seeking to tie Manchin to President Barack Obama, and the NRSC launched its own ads portraying Manchin as a rubber stamp for Obama's agenda. Before long, the race was a toss-up.

Manchin distanced himself from the president, even to the extent of flip-flopping. Early in 2010, he supported Obama's health care overhaul. By October, Manchin was saying he would have voted against it had he been serving as a senator at the time. The Democrats' cap-and-trade bill to curb carbon emissions was highly unpopular in West Virginia coal country. Manchin famously ran an ad in which he shot a mock copy of the carbon emissions bill with a rifle. Manchin raised questions about Raese's commitment to the state, pointing out repeatedly on the stump and in television ads that the steel and limestone magnate owned a home in Palm Beach, Florida (complete with a pink marble driveway) and that his wife was registered to vote there. Manchin hammered Raese for his support for eliminating the minimum wage and abolishing the Education Department. Although he was outspent $6.3 million to $4.4 million, Manchin won, 53% to 43%.

Taking office immediately after the election to begin serving the final two years of Byrd's term, he voted to extend the Bush-era tax cuts except for taxpayers earning over $1 million. He had said during his campaign he favored the Republican position of extending them for all taxpayers. He was the only Democrat to vote "no" on a proposal to repeal the ban on openly gay members in the military. Still, Manchin was roundly criticized back home for missing a final vote on repeal of "don't ask, don't tell," and also for missing a major vote on a bill to give legal status to the children of some illegal immigrants. *The Charleston Gazette* called him "absolutely gutless." Manchin apologized publicly, saying he missed the December votes to be with his grandchildren over the holidays. He further angered the newspaper in 2012 when he declined to say whether he would vote for Obama's reelection. It refused to endorse him in that April's Democratic primary, questioning whether he was "on course to follow Connecticut's Joe Lieberman and register as independent." It hardly mattered; Manchin beat former Monongalia County legislator Sheirl Fletcher with 80 percent of the vote. His win set up a general-election rematch with Raese for a full six-year term. Raese resurrected his main campaign theme that Manchin was an Obama rubber stamp. The senator now had a voting record that demonstrated otherwise. Manchin easily improved upon his earlier victory, winning 61%-36% in a state in which GOP presidential nominee Mitt Romney took 62 percent of the vote.

Even before his reelection, Manchin showed signs of wanting to change the Senate's stalemated course. In September, he blasted the chamber for adjourning six weeks before the election. He later teamed up with former Utah Republican Gov. Jon Huntsman to form a "Problem Solvers" initiative enlisting lawmakers from both parties through the group NoLabels.org. "We will either work across the aisle to fix problems or we will achieve nothing," Manchin and Huntsman wrote in a January 2013 op-ed column.

In April 2013, after several months of taking colleagues out on his boat *Black Tie* for evenings of beer and pizza, Manchin announced a compromise on gun control with Republicans Mark Kirk of Illinois-his best friend in the chamber-and Pat Toomey of Pennsylvania. Its most significant feature was a proposal to expand background checks for gun buyers to cover transactions at gun shows and Internet sales. It did not go as far as Obama wanted-it exempted sales between private citizens in some instances-but was seen as the best chance to advance gun control legislation in years. "This is common sense," said Manchin, who previously had boasted of his "A" rating from the National Rifle Association. "This is gun sense." But the measure couldn't attract enough votes to overcome a GOP filibuster, and some gun control proponents said Manchin didn't handle the issue with enough finesse. They noted that his spokesman had said the NRA was "neutral" on the measure when it was unveiled; the powerful group denied that was the case. The NRA ended up taking its attacks on the proposal to Manchin's home state, spending six figures on ads.

Manchin had more success attacking political gridlock during the student loan debate in the summer of 2013. The two parties had spent months bickering about how to prevent an automatic doubling of student-loan rates from 3.4% to 6.8% by a statutory deadline of July 1. Manchin was a key negotiator in a deal that brought the rates back down and tied them to the market. He got involved after Senate Democratic leaders presented a doomed plan to temporarily extend lower rates. "You want me to vote for the extension. You know it's going to fail, but you just want to make a political point with the extension like we're trying to keep the rates down. And I said ... I know that we can do so much better, we can reduce everybody's rates," Manchin said. The deal that passed, and was ultimately signed into law, brought rates down for undergraduates to 3.9 percent. It was crafted by a bipartisan group of senators, including Manchin, and aides to Obama.

On the Energy and Natural Resources Committee, where he is the ranking member òn the energy subcommittee, Manchin backed the Keystone XL pipeline. He became the only Democrat to co-sponsor the Affordable Reliable Energy Now Act of 2015, a bill shepherded by his fellow West Virginia senator, Republican Shelley Moore Capito. The bill-which Obama would have vetoed-pushed back against efforts by the administration's Environmental Protection Agency to curb carbon emissions. Manchin cosponsored a measure to lift the ban on exporting domestic crude oil, joining several Republicans and Democrat Heidi Heitkamp, who represents oil and gas behemoth North Dakota. Manchin formed an unlikely partnership with Senate liberal icon Elizabeth Warren to offer legislation that would publicize the details of trade deals before lawmakers were asked to approve presidential fast-track trade authority. In 2017, he joined the Appropriations Committee, where Capito already had a seat and where Byrd earlier had reigned as chairman for many years.

After the Democrats lost the Senate in the 2014 election-a development Manchin called "a real ass-whuppin'"-he expressed deep frustration to the *Washington Post* about Obama and Senate Democratic Leader Harry Reid of Nevada, and said he might not back Reid for party leader. But he recommitted to remaining with his party rather than switching to the GOP. "I'm a moderate Democrat, proud West Virginian. If you don't have moderates on both sides, you don't get anything done," he said. As for Obama, Manchin told *Time* magazine that "people just don't believe he cares." Expressing continued frustration with the Senate, Manchin toyed with leaving the chamber two years early in 2016 to run instead for governor, a job that would provide him with executive powers he had enjoyed before. But in the spring of 2015, Manchin announced that he would remain in the Senate-a big boost for Democrats, who had few other options for winning his seat in increasingly Republican West Virginia.

The Republican-controlled Senate gave Manchin opportunities to work on legislation and to display his differences with Democrats. On the popular legislation to attack opioid abuse, which was enacted in July 2016, he contributed a section promoting public education of the crisis. Going his own way, he and Joe Donnelly of Indiana were the only Democrats who voted in August 2015 to force a vote to prohibit federal funding of Planned Parenthood. In February 2017, he was the only Democrat to vote to confirm Jeff Sessions for Attorney General. "Jeff's extensive career in public service and legal expertise make him qualified to be our country's next Attorney General," Manchin said, prompting harsh criticism of him from liberal advocates. In April, Manchin joined Donnelly and Heitkamp as the only Democratic Senators voting to confirm Neil Gorsuch to the Supreme Court.

In a November 2016 interview, Manchin said that he gets asked "every day" to switch parties, to which he responds that he has not considered it. "I would be dishonest to myself and the people who voted for me if I changed parties," he told the *Washington Examiner*. Instead, he took a seat on the leadership team of Democratic Leader Charles Schumer. During the presidential transition, Manchin met in New York City with Donald Trump to discuss a Cabinet position, perhaps Secretary of Energy. He decided that he wasn't interested, though he said that he would be working with the new president. "I've had more personal time with Trump in two months than I had with [Barack] Obama in eight years," he told *Politico* in March 2017.

Having a presidential pal apparently will offer no protection to Manchin for what Republicans promise will be a competitive reelection challenge in 2018. Rep. Evan Jenkins , who became a Republican giant-killer in 2014 when he defeated veteran Democratic Rep. Nick Rahall, announced in May that he will challenge Manchin. In a video, he criticized Manchin for "violating our values and pushing gun control."

Junior Senator

Shelley Moore Capito (R)

Elected 2014, term expires 2020, 1st term; b. Nov 26, 1953; Glen Dale; Duke University (NC), B.S.; University of Virginia, M.Ed.; Presbyterian; Married (Dr. Charles Lewis Capito); 3 children; 4 grandchildren.

Elected Office: WV House, 1997-2001; US House, 2001-2015.

Professional Career: Career counselor, WV St. College, 1976-1978; Director, Education Information Center, WV Board of Regents, 1978-1981.

DC Office: 172 RSOB 20510, 202-224-6472, Fax: 202-224-7665, capito.senate.gov.

State Offices: Beckley, 304-347-5372; Charleston, 304-347-5372; Martinsburg, 304-262-9285; Morgantown, 304-292-2310.

Committees: *Appropriations*: Commerce, Justice, Science & Related Agencies, Department of the Interior, Environment & Related Agencies, DOL, HHS & Education & Related Agencies, Financial Services & General Government (Chmn), Military Construction & Veteran Affairs & Related Agencies,

Transportation, HUD & Related Agencies. *Commerce, Science & Transportation*: Aviation Operations, Safety & Security, Communications, Technology, Innovation & the Internet, Consumer Protection, Product Safety, Ins & Data Security, Space, Science & Competitiveness, Surface Trans., Merchant Marine Infra., Safety & Security. *Environment & Public Works*: Clean Air & Nuclear Safety (Chmn), Fisheries, Water, and Wildlife, Transportation & Infrastructure. *Rules & Administration.*

Group Ratings

	ADA	ACLU	AFL-CIO	LCV	ITI	COC	HAFA	ACU	CFG	FRC
2016	-	11%	-	24%	100%	100%	32%	62%	56%	100%
2015	5%	C	29%	4%	C	92%	C	63%	54%	73%

Almanac Ratings 2015

	Economy	Social	Foreign	Composite
Liberal	45%	0%	28%	24%
Conservative	55%	100%	72%	76%

Key Votes of the 114th Congress

1. Keystone pipeline	Y	5. National Security Data	Y	9. Gun Sales Checks	N
2. Export-Import Bank	Y	6. Iran Nuclear Deal	Y	10. Sanctuary Cities	Y
3. Debt Ceiling Increase	Y	7. Puerto Rico Debt	N	11. Planned Parenthood	Y
4. Homeland Security $$	Y	8. Loretta Lynch A.G	N	12. Trade deals	Y

Election Results

Election	Name (Party)	Vote (%)		Cand. Spent	Ind. Exp. Support	Ind. Exp. Oppose
2014 General	Shelley Moore Capito (R)............	280,400	(62%)	$8,779,918	$640,871	$227,388
	Natalie Tennant (D)......................	155,730	(35%)	$3,499,419	$34,000	$290,776
2014 Primary	Shelley Moore Capito (R)............	74,655	(88%)			
	Matthew Dodrill (R).......................	7,072	(8%)			

Prior winning percentages: House: 2012 (70%), 2010 (69%), 2008 (57%), 2006 (57%), 2004 (58%), 2002 (60%), 2000 (49%)

Republican Shelley Moore Capito was elected West Virginia's junior senator in 2014 after serving seven terms in the House. As the state's first Republican in the Senate since the 1950s, she is a well-liked moderate who is unwavering in her advocacy of West Virginia's coal industry. She got along well with Majority Leader Mitch McConnell, another Senator from coal country, and joined his leadership team. Her policy focus has been largely tied to home-state interests and needs.

Capito grew up in northern West Virginia and in the Washington, D.C. area, where her father, Arch Moore, served in the House from 1957 to 1969. He was elected governor of West Virginia in 1968 and 1972, and then again in 1984. Capito graduated from Duke University and received a master's degree in education from the University of Virginia. She worked for two years as a career counselor at West Virginia State University and then as director of the state's Educational Information Center from 1978 to 1981. She served two terms in the West Virginia House of Delegates.

Capito's opportunity to follow in her father's footsteps in the House came when Democratic Rep. Bob Wise ran for governor in 2000. She benefited from a divisive Democratic primary won by Jim Humphreys, a former state senator and a lawyer. Capito, who supported abortion rights, started off as the underdog, but Humphreys proved to be a poor candidate despite spending $6 million of his own money in the general election. Capito won, 48% to 46%, becoming the first Cherry Blossom Princess elected to Congress.

In the House, Capito had a relatively moderate voting record; she was a member of the centrist Republican Main Street Caucus. She broke from conservatives to support programs important to her state, such as continued funding of rural air service and opposing drastic cutbacks in food stamps. In a rare encounter with controversy in 2006, she dealt with the fallout from revelations of inappropriate sexual advances by GOP Rep. Mark Foley of Florida, which included contact with House pages. Capito, a member of the three-lawmaker board that oversaw the teenage page program, said she was not informed of the allegations until after the scandal became public.

Capito became more inclined to side with her party after the election of President Barack Obama, who was highly unpopular in West Virginia. In 2011, she took over as chairwoman of the Financial Services Subcommittee on Financial Institutions and Consumer Credit. She focused on the regulatory burdens facing community banks and credit unions. Her husband, Charles, is a longtime banking executive, which has raised eyebrows among watchdog groups. Capito said she makes her own decisions, telling *Esquire* magazine in 2010 that "no matter what your decisions are, no matter what your votes are, if you're not playing by the rules you're taking a big risk."

After winning a seventh term in 2012, Capito announced she would challenge Democratic Sen. Jay Rockefeller for his seat when it came up in 2014. Rockefeller, in his late-70s and with health problems, clearly wanted no part of a tough race against Capito. During his 42 years as a statewide elected official, his only defeat came against her father in the 1972 contest for governor. Rockefeller announced his retirement after a poll showed her with a slight lead in a head-to-head matchup. Capito caught a break when Pat McGeehan, a former state House member to her ideological right, exited the race early on.

In the general, Capito's opponent was Natalie Tennant, West Virginia's secretary of state and a former television reporter. (Tennant's husband, Erik Wells, had lost to Capito in a 2004 challenge for her House seat.) Tennant sought to make an issue of Capito and her spouse's close ties to banking interests, saying her own "West Virginia first" approach contrasted with Capito's record "working for Wall Street banks where her husband works." Capito ran a quietly effective campaign, largely overshadowed nationally by more intensely watched races elsewhere, and was aided by Obama's deep unpopularity among West Virginians. Indeed, her ascension from the House to the Senate was seen as such a certainty that by July, friends and colleagues reportedly began addressing her as "Senator." In November, she defeated Tennant by an even larger margin than expected, 62%-35%.

Capito settled into the Senate with a seat on the influential Appropriations Committee, becoming the only new senator tapped as a "cardinal," or subcommittee chair. She took charge of the panel that funds congressional operations, a good way to make connections with Senate insiders. In 2017, she became chairwoman of the Financial Services and General Government Subcommittee at Appropriations. She has been one of four Senators who serve as counsel to McConnell, providing him advice on various topics. Capito had an interest in assuring that repeal or revisions of the Affordable Care Act did not jeopardize Medicaid services. In March 2017, she joined three other GOP senators who wrote to McConnell about the need for "stability and certainty for individuals and families in Medicaid expansion programs or the necessary flexibility for states," including West Virginia.

She was assigned to join two panels of great importance to coal-producing West Virginia-the Energy and Natural Resources Committee and the Environment and Public Works Committee. On the latter, she served as chairwoman of the Clean Air and Nuclear Safety Subcommittee. She was lead sponsor of the Affordable Reliable Energy Now Act, which sought to preempt the Obama administration's proposal to tackle climate change. "We're asking for a common-sense agreement that assures reliable and affordable energy, protects our economy and jobs and allows states to make their own decisions," she told reporters. The measure won co-sponsorship of nearly three dozen senators, including one Democrat, Joe Manchin, Capito's West Virginia colleague. In May 2015, she filed a bill to roll back Obama's Clean Power Plan, which was designed to cut back the use of coal by utility companies. The election of Donald Trump became a vital opportunity for Capito and her allies to reverse regulations and enforcement by the Environmental Protection Agency. On a related topic, she advocated health-care coverage for retired miners. McConnell spearheaded a related plan that was enacted as part of the government funding bill in May 2017.

Although Capito has mostly supported Trump during his campaign and presidency, she reacted to the October 2016 release of the lewd "Access Hollywood" video from 2005 by saying that Trump should "reexamine his candidacy." She added, "As a woman, a mother, and a grandmother to three young girls, I am deeply offended by Mr. Trump's remarks, and there is no excuse for the disgusting and demeaning language."

FIRST DISTRICT

David McKinley (R)

Elected 2010, 4th term; b. Mar 28, 1947, Wheeling; Purdue University (IN), B.S.; Episcopalian; Married (Mary McKinley); 4 children; 6 grandchildren.

Elected Office: WV House, 1980-1994.

Professional Career: Principal, McKinley & Association, 1981-2010; Chair, WV GOP, 1990-1994.

DC Office: 2239 RHOB 20515, 202-225-4172, Fax: 202-225-7564, mckinley.house.gov.

State Offices: Morgantown, 304-284-8506; Parkersburg, 304-422-5972; Wheeling, 304-232-3801.

Committees: *Energy & Commerce*: Digital Commerce & Consumer Protection, Energy, Environment.

Group Ratings

	ADA	ACLU	AFL-CIO	LCV	ITI	COC	HAFA	ACU	CFG	FRC
2016	-	5%	-	0%	83%	100%	54%	68%	53%	100%
2015	5%	C	42%	6%	C	80%	C	58%	53%	92%

Almanac Ratings 2015

	Economy	Social	Foreign	Composite
Liberal	17%	5%	4%	9%
Conservative	83%	95%	96%	91%

Key Votes of the 114th Congress

1. Keystone Pipeline	Y	5. Puerto Rico Debt	Y	9. Offenses by Aliens	Y
2. Trade Deals	N	6. Medical Marijuana	N	10. Troops in Iraq	N
3. Export-Import Bank	N	7. Sanctuary Cities	Y	11. Homeland Security $$	N
4. Debt Ceiling Increase	N	8. Armor-piercing Bullets	Y	12. Trade Adjustment aid	Y

Election Results

Election	Name (Party)	Vote (%)	Cand. Spent	Ind. Exp. Support	Ind. Exp. Oppose
2016 General	David McKinley (R)	163,469 (69%)	$751,674		
	Mike Panypenny (D)	73,534 (31%)	$26,752		
2016 Primary	David McKinley (R)	(100%)			

Prior winning percentages: 2014 (64%), 2012 (62%), 2010 (50%)

Republican David McKinley, elected in 2010 in a district that Democrats had held for 40 years, is a coal-championing centrist. He has been an active legislator and has shown some independence from the party on big issues.

McKinley is a seventh-generation native of Wheeling. McKinley's great-grandfather ran for West Virginia governor as a Democrat in 1908. His father was a civil engineer who taught him to read blueprints when he was in third grade. He majored in civil engineering at Purdue University. After college, McKinley worked for several engineering and construction companies until he founded his own firm, McKinley & Associates, which restores historic properties and does other construction work. In West Virginia's House of Delegates, McKinley pushed for a bill to allow school and prison cafeterias to donate unused food to homeless shelters. He authored a law that prohibited insurance companies from canceling policies of people diagnosed with HIV. He ran for governor in 1996 but lost the primary to Cecil Underwood, who won the general election.

In his House bid, McKinley had the backing of national Republicans and won the primary with 35 percent of the vote. In the general election, he faced state Sen. Mike Oliverio, who had toppled 14-term Democratic Rep. Alan Mollohan in the primary after several newspaper accounts raised questions about whether Mollohan profited personally from business deals with people and nonprofit groups that got federal funds he earmarked in appropriations bills.

McKinley's ads labeled Oliverio as a "career politician" who supported "job-killing liberal Nancy Pelosi," a reference to the then-House Speaker. McKinley emphasized his opposition to the Democrats' energy bill that would limit carbon emissions, arguing that it would hurt West Virginia's coal industry. Oliverio also opposed the bill. He charged that McKinley got rich from government contracts even as he criticized government spending, citing federal economic stimulus money that McKinley's architectural and engineering firm received to design a Marshall County school. Despite his call for repeal of the Affordable Care Act, McKinley supported the provision that prohibited insurance companies from denying coverage to people with preexisting conditions. McKinley eked out a victory of 1,440 votes, a split of 50.4%-49.6%.

McKinley was one of a handful of Republicans in 2011 and 2012 to vote against Budget Committee Chairman Paul Ryan's budget blueprint, complaining that it did not adequately protect Medicare. Among Class of 2010 GOP members, he had the second-lowest score on the anti-tax Club for Growth's legislative scorecard in those two years. He got a plum seat on the Energy and Commerce Committee and co-founded a Marcellus Shale Caucus to oppose regulation of drilling in the oil-and-gas-rich area stretching along the East Coast. In 2015, he took the lead for House Republicans in the enactment of tougher standards for energy efficiency. With Democratic Rep. Matt Cartwright of Pennsylvania, McKinley passed a bill in 2015 that authorized the Bureau of Prisons to permit its officers to carry pepper spray for self-defense. He authored the bill after a federal correctional officer was murdered by an inmate. It was enacted in a separate measure in March 2016.

McKinley has aggressively fought so-called coal ash rules that affect industries such as concrete production and manufacturing of wallboard. He introduced a bill to create an enforceable minimum standard for the regulation of coal ash by the states, allowing its use in a manner that he said would protect jobs. It passed the House but stalled in the Senate. When House Republicans sought in 2012 to add the measure to the surface transportation bill, West Virginia Democratic Sen. Jay Rockefeller - who earlier co-sponsored similar legislation - blocked the move, saying it would jeopardize the bill's passage. McKinley told *The Charleston Gazette* he was "frankly shocked" at Rockefeller's decision, but Rockefeller prevailed. In February 2017, the House rescinded on a nearly party-line vote the coal-ash rule that the Interior Department had written during the Obama administration; President Donald Trump signed the repeal measure.

McKinley applauded Trump's selection of Scott Pruitt as administrator of the Environmental Protection Agency was "a breath of fresh air for West Virginia." He cautioned that the coal industry would not be hiring nearly as many West Virginians as had worked in the mines a half-century ago, but he voiced hope that the coal industry would find new markets for overseas exports.

McKinley has strengthened himself politically. With a boost from serving on Energy and Commerce, he has stockpiled large contributions from coal interests. He has been reelected each time with at least 62 percent of the vote. In June 2015, after extensive review, he ruled out a run in 2016 for the open seat for governor. After recent layoffs of more than 1,400 mine workers in the state, McKinley said he decided, "I can do much more for West Virginia right here in Congress." Voters granted his preference. Democrats appear to have given up on this district, like others in Appalachia. In September 2016, the House Ethics Committee issued a letter of reproval - its mildest sanction - to McKinley because of his failure to remove his name from his engineering business, even after he had sold the company.

Northern West Virginia: Morgantown, Parkersburg

Population		Race and Ethnicity		Income	
Total	617,868	White	93.8%	Median Income	$42,057 (368 out of 435)
Land area	6,276	Black	2.4%	Under $50,000	57.3%
Pop/ sq mi	98.5	Latino	1.3%	$50,000-$99,999	28.4%
Born in state	69.0%	Asian	0.9%	$100,000-$199,999	12.1%
		Two races	1.5%	$200,000 or more	2.1%
		Other	0.1%	Poverty Rate	17.5%
Age Groups		**Education**		**Health Insurance**	
Under 18	19.6%	H.S grad or less	52.8%	With health insurance coverage	89.0%
18-34	23.4%	Some college	25.9%		
35-64	39.9%	College Degree, 4 yr	13.0%		
Over 64	17.2%	Post grad	8.2%		
Work		**Military**		**Public Assistance**	
White Collar	32.2%	Veteran	9.8%	Cash public assistance income	2.2%
Sales and Service	42.9%	Active Duty	0.0%	Food stamp/SNAP benefits	13.6%
Blue Collar	24.9%				
Government	4.4%				

Voter Turnout			
2015 Total Citizens 18+	491,707	2016 House Turnout as % CVAP	48%
2016 House turnout	237,003	2014 House Turnout as % CVAP	29%

2012 Presidential Vote		
Mitt Romney	141,736	(62%)
Barack Obama	81,017	(36%)

2016 Presidential Vote		
Donald Trump	165,934	(68%)
Hillary Clinton	64,384	(26%)
Gary Johnson	8,862	(4%)

Cook Partisan Voting Index: R+19

The northern part of West Virginia is in many ways an extension of the Pittsburgh metropolitan area. People here are Steelers and Pirates fans, they drink Iron City and Rolling Rock beer, they watch Pittsburgh television, and they live in the crevasses between hills cut by the Monongahela and Ohio rivers. The terrain here would seem to forbid manufacturing and urban development, yet this has been one of America's prime industrial areas. Northern West Virginia is part of the same coal-and-steel economy that made Pittsburgh one of the nation's largest cities and filled the narrow bottomlands along the rivers with steel and glass factories, foundries and coal yards.

As in Pennsylvania, these industries have been declining and they have become far less labor-intensive. Local jobs and population have declined. Since 1980, the 12,000 mining jobs in this part of West Virginia have dropped by more than two-thirds, with comparable fall-offs in manufacturing. The Weirton tin and steel mill (now called Arcelor Mittal and owned by an integrated steel and mining company headquartered in Luxembourg) employed 14,000 workers in the mid-1970s and was down to fewer than 900 in 2015. Service jobs have replaced some of these losses. Walmart has been West Virginia's largest employer since 1998, and the government has brought in thousands more jobs, compliments of the late Sen. Robert Byrd, the West Virginia Democrat and powerful Senate appropriator, whose legacy endured years after his death. One of the largest employers in Harrison County has been the U.S. Department of Justice. The county has become the state's leader in the Marcellus Shale natural gas boom, with an influx of jobs and money that have resulted from more than 3,000 wells drilled in the state.

The 1st Congressional District of West Virginia includes 20 counties in the northern third of the state. On the Panhandle along the Ohio River is Victorian Wheeling, once one of the richest cities in the country with its steel and glass companies. There is Weirton, named for Ernest T. Weir, the anti-union Pittsburgh industrialist who transformed it from a farming community to a steel town in the early 1900s. South of Pittsburgh on the Monongahela River is Morgantown, with human capital from West Virginia University, the largest employer in the state; in February 2017, the university announced a project to explore new manufacturing technologies to utilize natural gas. In 2014, the Milken Institute ranked Morgantown seventh best-performing among 179 small metro areas. On the Ohio River is the former oil-refining and shipping center of Parkersburg, which has become a plastics and manufacturing hub. Parts of the district are stagnant while others are on a growth path. Morgantown's population grew 15 percent from 2000 to 2015, while Wheeling's fell by 12 percent - part of a consistent decline since the 1930s - and Parkersburg's decreased by 6 percent.

To the west, the district includes three lonely mountain counties - Doddridge, Ritchie and Tyler - that were never heavily industrialized and have remained firmly Republican since the Civil War. Doddridge was the only one of West Virginia's 55 counties to vote against Byrd in 2006. For most of the 20th century, much of the territory in the 1st District was solidly Democratic. But dissatisfaction with the Clinton-Gore policies on coal mining and the environment helped Republican George W. Bush carry the district twice, and the local hostility accelerated with Obama policies. Donald Trump in 2016 took at least 66 percent of the vote in each of West Virginia's three districts, with 68 percent in the 1st.

SECOND DISTRICT

Alex Mooney (R)

Elected 2014, 2nd term; b. Jun 07, 1971, Washington, DC; Dartmouth College, B.A.; Roman Catholic; Married (Grace Gonzalez); 3 children.

Elected Office: MD Senate, 1999-2010.

Professional Career: Aide, Rep. Roscoe Bartlett, 1993-1995; Executive, Council for National Policy Action, Inc, 1995-1998; Director, The National Journalism Center, 2005-2012; Chair, MD GOP, 2010-2013; Owner, consulting firm, 2011-2014.

DC Office: 1232 LHOB 20515, 202-225-2711, Fax: 202-225-7856, mooney.house.gov.

State Offices: Charleston, 304-925-5964; Martinsburg, 304-264-8810.

Committees: *Financial Services*: Capital Markets, Securities & Investment, Monetary Policy & Trade.

Group Ratings

	ADA	ACLU	AFL-CIO	LCV	ITI	COC	HAFA	ACU	CFG	FRC
2016	-	17%	-	0%	67%	93%	83%	88%	75%	91%
2015	5%	C	13%	3%	C	60%	C	88%	79%	83%

Almanac Ratings 2015

	Economy	Social	Foreign	Composite
Liberal	8%	9%	13%	10%
Conservative	93%	91%	87%	90%

Key Votes of the 114th Congress

1. Keystone Pipeline	Y	5. Puerto Rico Debt	N	9. Offenses by Aliens	Y
2. Trade Deals	N	6. Medical Marijuana	Y	10. Troops in Iraq	N
3. Export-Import Bank	N	7. Sanctuary Cities	Y	11. Homeland Security $$	N
4. Debt Ceiling Increase	N	8. Armor-piercing Bullets	Y	12. Trade Adjustment aid	N

Election Results

Election	Name (Party)	Vote (%)		Cand. Spent	Ind. Exp. Support	Ind. Exp. Oppose
2016 General	Alex Mooney (R).........................	140,807	(58%)	$806	$9,910	
	Mark Hunt (D).............................	101,207	(42%)	$423,447		
2016 Primary	Alexander Mooney (R)..................	45,262	(73%)			
	Marc Savitt (R)............................	16,803	(27%)			

Prior winning percentages: 2014 (47%)

Republican Alex Mooney, a onetime Marylander, found a receptive home in West Virginia in 2014 when he won an open seat. Mooney, who has run for office in three states, won a costly and contentious contest in the sprawling 2nd District. He was reelected more easily.

Mooney was born in Washington, D.C., to a Cuban refugee mother and a father from an Irish immigrant family who served in Vietnam. He graduated from Dartmouth College, where he was president of the Coalition for Life; during his time there, he ran for the New Hampshire House of Representatives but got just 8 percent of the vote and finished last of the seven candidates in the general election. After college, he was an aide to GOP Rep. Roscoe Bartlett of Maryland. Mooney won a Maryland state Senate seat in 1998 at age 27, and became Maryland GOP chairman after he lost reelection to the Senate in 2010. (His official bio deleted reference to his service in Annapolis.) He set his sights on Bartlett's House seat and started raising money for a potential run in 2012. But he abandoned the effort after Bartlett announced he would run in what turned out to be a losing effort. Mooney kept the campaign cash, saying he would run in 2014, and went back to work for Bartlett part-time in 2012. But he had a change of plan and moved to West Virginia, where he entered a seven-way GOP primary after Rep. Shelley Moore Capito ran successfully for the Senate. He won with 36 percent of the vote to 22 percent for Ken Reed, a pharmacist.

In the general election, Mooney campaigned on an anti-Obama platform, vowing to repeal the Affordable Care Act and pledging to fight any government overreach. Nick Casey, a former Democratic state chairman, said that he wanted to scrap some parts of the health care law, such as the mandate for employers to provide coverage, and argued that Washington needed more moderate voices. Both candidates pledged strong support for coal, a key litmus test in West Virginia. The central fight was over whether geography or ideology mattered more. Casey, calling himself a "true West Virginian," branded Mooney a carpetbagger and opportunist. Mooney countered that he was a "West Virginian by choice," and therefore more committed to his adopted district's conservative values. He said that his Maryland state Senate seat bordered West Virginia and that the two areas are similar.

The district agreed with Mooney, though some voters undoubtedly were turned off by his river-crossing. Neil Berch, a West Virginia University political science professor told *The New York Times* that a segment of voters would believe that "the best preacher's a convert" who "wrapped himself in West Virginia values." Each candidate spent about $2 million. Mooney benefited from more than $2.3 million in additional spending from Republican and conservative groups, compared with less than $900,000 that national Democrats delivered to Casey. Mooney won, 47%-44%.

In the House, Mooney joined the Budget Committee, where he supported the Republicans' spending plan and took credit for provisions that opposed funding of ozone standards by the Environmental Protection Agency and blocked regulations that would prohibit surface mining in West Virginia. On the Natural Resources Committee, he maintained attacks against Obama administration initiatives that were designed to limit the mining and use of coal. "West Virginia is blessed to be abundant in natural resources," Mooney said in 2015. "Unfortunately, the president is intent on destroying coal as a domestic energy source." He joined the Freedom Caucus of activist conservatives. And he bucked party leaders in June 2015 during votes on trade promotion authority for the president, but he later received campaign support from Speaker Paul Ryan. Mooney's *Almanac* vote ratings in 2015 ranked near the ideological center of House Republicans and not far from the other two House Republicans from West Virginia. In 2017, he got a seat on the Financial Services Committee, where he pursued his interest in community banking and housing issues.

After Casey decided not to seek a rematch, the Democratic Congressional Campaign Committee expressed interest in Cory Simpson - who had been an active-duty attorney in the Army, while residing in Silver Spring Maryland -- as its preferred choice in the primary in 2016. But Simpson finished second in the five-candidate primary to Mark Hunt, who self-financed $280,000 of the $480,000 that he raised, and won the primary, 29%-26%. Hunt, a Charleston-area attorney, had served 14 years in the state House of Delegates before he lost the primary for reelection in 2014. He described Mooney as "missing in action" but received little support from national Democrats or their allies in the general election. Mooney won, 58%-42%.

Central West Virginia: Charleston, Martinsburg

Population		**Race and Ethnicity**		**Income**	
Total	624,926	White	90.7%	Median Income	$46,254 (319 out of 435)
Land area	8,017	Black	3.7%		
Pop/ sq mi	77.9	Latino	1.9%		
Born in state	63.8%	Asian	0.7%	Under $50,000	53.4%
		Two races	2.7%	$50,000-$99,999	30.1%
Age Groups		Other	0.2%	$100,000-$199,999	13.8%
Under 18	21.7%			$200,000 or more	2.7%
18-34	19.7%	**Education**		Poverty Rate	15.5%
35-64	41.9%	H.S grad or less	54.1%		
Over 64	16.8%	Some college	24.9%	**Health Insurance**	
		College Degree, 4 yr	12.8%	With health insurance coverage	88.8%
Work		Post grad	8.2%		
White Collar	33.8%				
Sales and Service	42.6%	**Military**		**Public Assistance**	
Blue Collar	23.7%	Veteran	10.9%	Cash public assistance income	2.3%
Government	4.6%	Active Duty	0.1%		
				Food stamp/SNAP benefits	14.3%

Voter Turnout			
2015 Total Citizens 18+	484,765	2016 House Turnout as % CVAP	50%
2016 House turnout	242,014	2014 House Turnout as % CVAP	31%

2012 Presidential Vote		
Mitt Romney	140,783	(60%)
Barack Obama	89,079	(38%)

2016 Presidential Vote		
Donald Trump	164,674	(66%)
Hillary Clinton	73,487	(29%)
Gary Johnson	8,232	(3%)

Cook Partisan Voting Index: R+17

Not all of West Virginia has been coal country, and not all of its hills have been scarred by strip mining. Large parts of this naturally beautiful state look as verdant and unchanged as they must have when George Washington was speculating in land here. For miles, there are gentle hills and rugged mountains. Yet over another hill you may find, amid scenery primeval and rural, sudden evidence of industrialization: a pulp mill or charcoal factory in a clearing scraped out of the forest; a small factory town, built close to a river in a cleft bordered with hills; the entrance to an underground coal mine or a mountaintop blasted open to allow surface mining.

The 2nd Congressional District of West Virginia is a central slice of the state, from Berkeley Springs and Harpers Ferry in the Washington, D.C., exurbs, more than 300 miles to beyond Charleston and the Ohio River town of Ravenswood. The district includes fast-growing parts of the state: the Eastern Panhandle counties, which are part of the Washington metropolitan area, and chemical-producing Putnam County, which is increasingly home to suburbanites commuting to Charleston. The local Toyota engine and transmission plant, which employs 1,600 people, celebrated its 20th anniversary in 2016 with plans for a $400 million expansion. In Charleston, the state Capitol sits on the banks of the Kanawha River, designed by Cass Gilbert with a dome higher than that of the U.S. Capitol. When the city's two newspapers - *The Charleston Gazette*, which leans Democratic, and the Republican-tilting *Charleston Daily Mail* - combined into the *Charleston Gazette-Mail* in 2015, it created one news staff and two separate editorial pages.

In the 1940s, the area produced all of the nation's Lucite, polyethylenes and nylon, as well as much of its artificial rubber and antifreeze. Today, the state boasts that it is home to more polymer producers than any other place on the planet; the chemical industry makes products used in the manufacturing of cosmetics, detergents, shampoo and other products. Those chemical plants employ 22,500 workers in Kanawha and Putnam counties, but they can be hazardous. In 2014, a spill from a chemical tank farm on the Elk River just north of Charleston caused more than 300,000 people in the metropolitan area to lose fresh drinking water for days or weeks in some cases. Charleston is West Virginia's professional center, with a few downtown office towers and some affluent residential districts. Politically, this ancestrally Democratic district is now trending Republican. Berkeley County, which has commuter rail to Washington, has grown 50 percent since 2000 to become the second-largest county in the state. During that period, Charleston-based Kanawha County has dropped 7 percent. Donald Trump in 2016 won here with 66 percent of the vote, his weakest performance in the state, but six points higher than what Mitt Romney got in this district in 2012.

THIRD DISTRICT

Evan Jenkins (R)

Elected 2014, 2nd term; b. Sep 12, 1960, Huntington; University of Florida, B.S.; Marshall University Cumberland School of Law (WV), J.D.; Presbyterian; Married (Elizabeth Weiler); 3 children.

Elected Office: WV House 1994-2000; WV Senate 2002-2014.

Professional Career: Practicing attorney, Business law instructor, Marshall University, Executive Director, West Virginia State Medical Association.

DC Office: 1609 LHOB 20515, 202-225-3452, Fax: 202-225-9061, evanjenkins.house.gov.

State Offices: Beckley, 304-250-6177; Bluefield, 304-325-6800; Huntington, 304-522-2201.

Committees: *Appropriations*: Commerce, Justice, Science & Related Agencies, Interior, Environment & Related Agencies, Military Construction, Veterans Affairs & Related Agencies.

Group Ratings

	ADA	ACLU	AFL-CIO	LCV	ITI	COC	HAFA	ACU	CFG	FRC
2016	-	11%	-	3%	83%	100%	56%	68%	52%	100%
2015	5%	C	38%	6%	C	90%	C	54%	53%	92%

Almanac Ratings 2015

	Economy	Social	Foreign	Composite
Liberal	14%	9%	5%	9%
Conservative	86%	91%	95%	91%

Key Votes of the 114th Congress

1. Keystone Pipeline	Y	5. Puerto Rico Debt	N	9. Offenses by Aliens	Y
2. Trade Deals	N	6. Medical Marijuana	N	10. Troops in Iraq	N
3. Export-Import Bank	N	7. Sanctuary Cities	Y	11. Homeland Security $$	N
4. Debt Ceiling Increase	N	8. Armor-piercing Bullets	Y	12. Trade Adjustment aid	Y

Election Results

Election	Name (Party)	Vote (%)	Cand. Spent	Ind. Exp. Support	Ind. Exp. Oppose
2016 General	Evan Jenkins (R)	140,741 (68%)	$364,158		
	Matt Detch (D)	49,708 (24%)	$50,991		
	Zane Lawhorn (L)	16,883 (8%)	$88,298		
2016 Primary	Evan Jenkins (R)	(100%)			

Prior winning percentages: 2014 (55%)

Republican Evan Jenkins, elected in 2014, defeated 19-term Democratic Rep. Nick Rahall by convincing voters that he would be a better protector of the 3rd District's most defining resource: coal. He got a seat on the Appropriations Committee, which was unusual for a freshman, and tended to local needs, chiefly efforts to undo Obama-era regulations of coal.

Jenkins, born in Huntington, earned his bachelor's degree from the University of Florida and a law degree from the Cumberland School of Law at Samford University. He was the CEO of the West Virginia Medical Foundation and taught business law at Marshall University.

He was elected in 1994 as a Democrat to three terms in the state House of Delegates. In 2002, he won a state Senate seat after defeating the Democratic incumbent in the primary. Jenkins later won two more terms in the Senate. Jenkins said he was most proud of his work to create the Hatfield-McCoy Trail System, 700-plus miles of off-road trails designed to bring an economic boost to nine counties. He cited his actions on newborn-infant hearing tests, drug-abuse prevention and a sex-offender registry database. In 2013, he changed his party registration to Republican and challenged Rahall, a senior member of the House. He was nominated without opposition.

Jenkins and Rahall had similar views on issues such as gun control and gay marriage (both of which each opposed). It was Jenkins's repeated mentions of two highly charged issues in West Virginia - President Barack Obama and coal - that drove this contest and gave the GOP a pickup of the final House Democratic seat in a state delegation that had been solidly Democratic in 2010 but had turned sharply conservative. Jenkins pledged to lead the effort to repeal the Affordable Care Act, a law Rahall supported. When Rahall emphasized the value his seniority brought to the state, Jenkins dismissed the longtime incumbent as just another vote for a president who did not win a single county in West Virginia in 2012 (and who lost 41 percent of the Democratic primary vote to a prisoner). "West Virginia," Jenkins said as he announced his candidacy, "is under attack from President Obama and a Democratic Party that our parents and grandparents would not recognize." Rahall shot back that Jenkins was "spineless" and "two-faced."

Both candidates and their parties spent lavishly in this low-cost media market. Rahall outspent Jenkins \$2.6 million to \$1.6 million, while each national party and its allies spent a bit more than \$5 million for their candidate. The fight came down to which man voters believed was more committed to reversing the decline of the state's coal industry. Jenkins accused Rahall of backing a carbon tax (which Rahall denied), while the incumbent retorted that Jenkins would vote to cut black-lung benefits (which Jenkins denied). Obama's unpopularity put the Republican on top 55%-45%.

Jenkins got a seat on Appropriations, including its Interior Subcommittee, which oversees a host of federal regulations that many West Virginians view as burdensome. During his first two years, he said that he used the power of the purse to fight "the anti-coal agenda of Barack Obama through the EPA's budget." In June 2015, he took credit for \$1.2 billion that the committee cut from EPA. He cited legislative restrictions that the Interior Subcommittee crafted, including prohibitions on implementation of new greenhouse gas regulations and on expanded regulatory authority under the Clean Water Act. Jenkins also set a priority of financing new highway projects in southern West Virginia. That objective seemed ironic given that Rahall had lavishly delivered such benefits as the senior Democrat on the House Transportation and Infrastructure Committee.

In 2017, Jenkins touted his assignment to two other Appropriations subcommittees: Commerce, Justice, Science, where he could focus on the opioid epidemic in his district; and Veterans, Military Construction, where he could tend to the needs of the nearly 10 percent of West Virginians who served in the military, including the reopening of a veterans' clinic in Greenbrier County. With President Donald Trump, Jenkins applauded the February 2017 congressional repeal of the Interior Department's Stream Buffer Zone Rule, which severely restricted mountain-top mining and had taken effect on Obama's final full day in office.

He was reelected in 2016 with 68 percent of the vote and ended the year with \$717,000 in his campaign account. Jenkins announced in May 2017 his challenge to Democratic Sen. Joe Manchin in the 2018 campaign. He praised President Donald Trump, called Manchin a Washington insider and criticized his support in 2016 for Hillary Clinton. Jenkins might face a Republican primary.

Southern West Virginia: Huntington, Beckley

Population		**Race and Ethnicity**		**Income**	
Total	608,626	White	93.2%	Median Income	$36,902 (418 out of 435)
Land area	9,745	Black	3.7%	Under $50,000	62.8%
Pop/ sq mi	62.5	Latino	1.0%	$50,000-$99,999	26.3%
Born in state	77.3%	Asian	0.5%	$100,000-$199,999	9.4%
		Two races	1.4%	$200,000 or more	1.6%
		Other	0.3%	Poverty Rate	21.1%
Age Groups		**Education**		**Health Insurance**	
Under 18	20.7%	H.S grad or less	60.3%	With health insurance coverage	87.8%
18-34	20.1%	Some college	24.3%		
35-64	41.4%	College Degree, 4 yr	9.4%		
Over 64	17.8%	Post grad	5.9%		
Work		**Military**		**Public Assistance**	
White Collar	30.1%	Veteran	9.9%	Cash public assistance income	2.4%
Sales and Service	43.7%	Active Duty	0.0%	Food stamp/SNAP benefits	20.4%
Blue Collar	26.2%				
Government	4.3%				

Voter Turnout			
2015 Total Citizens 18+	479,376	2016 House Turnout as % CVAP	43%
2016 House turnout	207,332	2014 House Turnout as % CVAP	29%

2012 Presidential Vote		
Mitt Romney	135,136	(65%)
Barack Obama	68,173	(33%)

2016 Presidential Vote		
Donald Trump	158,763	(73%)
Hillary Clinton	50,923	(23%)
Gary Johnson	5,910	(3%)

Cook Partisan Voting Index: R+23

Early in the 20th century, the coal fields of southern West Virginia were one of America's boom areas. Into rural farmland and hollows, inhabited by the same families that settled the mountains 100 years before, came coal company lawyers with mineral rights' leases to sign, coal company engineers to design and sink mineshafts, and men from other mountain counties to work the mines. Company houses were built, company stores were stocked with goods as the company dictated and company paymasters kept close tabs on the finances of every employee. These conditions bred discontent, which ignited into the fire of industrial unionism. The Battle of Blair Mountain in Logan County, where 10,000 armed unionists faced off against 3,000 law enforcement officers and strikebreakers, presaged later efforts at organization by John L. Lewis, president of the United Mine Workers. Lewis was not only a militant unionist, but also an isolationist. During and after World War II, he called out his coal miners on strikes, to the fury of Democratic Presidents Franklin Roosevelt and Harry Truman. The national war effort and postwar economic recovery were threatened by these labor stoppages involving some 300,000 workers, centered in back corners of the country like southern West Virginia.

Coal no longer is the dominant U.S. source of electricity. In 2016, it supplied 30 percent of the fuel to power utility plants, compared with 34 percent -- and growing -- for natural gas. That share from coal has dropped markedly in recent years. Most of the coal mining in this region is done in Boone, Logan, Raleigh and Mingo counties, each of which produced more than 10 million tons of coal in 2009. In 2012, Boone had been overtaken by Marshall County in the northern part of the state as the county that produced the most coal. Production in the southern part of the state dropped from 116 million tons in 2008 to 79 million tons in 2012, while the northern counties had a slight increase. Raleigh is the site of Massey Energy's Upper Big Branch Mine, where a 2010 disaster killed 29 miners in the worst industry accident in four decades. Former Massey CEO Don Blankenship was convicted in December 2015 on conspiracy charges, but he was cleared of other felony charges]. After he served his time and was released in May 2017, he sent a letter to President Donald Trump that urged him to be lenient with coal-company executives who have been guilty of safety violations. A tragedy of a different kind was the loss of 6,700 jobs in the West Virginia mines between 2011 and 2015, with a 15 percent drop in coal that was mined during that timeframe. Mingo and nearby counties have suffered among the highest rates in the nation for opioid drug addiction and deaths.

The 3rd Congressional District of West Virginia includes most of the mountainous coal country in the southern part of the state, which for years was heavily Democratic. But the coal mining counties make up less than half of the district. About a quarter of the population is in and around the industrial city of Huntington on the Ohio River, which includes Marshall University. Another quarter is to the east, in Beckley and the farming uplands. Also located there is the Greenbrier Resort, where the government built a massive secret fallout shelter, code-named "Project Greek Island," to house the entire Congress in the event of nuclear war. The district has shifted to Republicans in the past two decades. In 2016, Donald Trump won here, 72%-23%, among his strongest districts in the nation. This remarkable historical turnaround resulted largely from discontent with the energy and environmental policies of national Democrats.

★ WISCONSIN ★

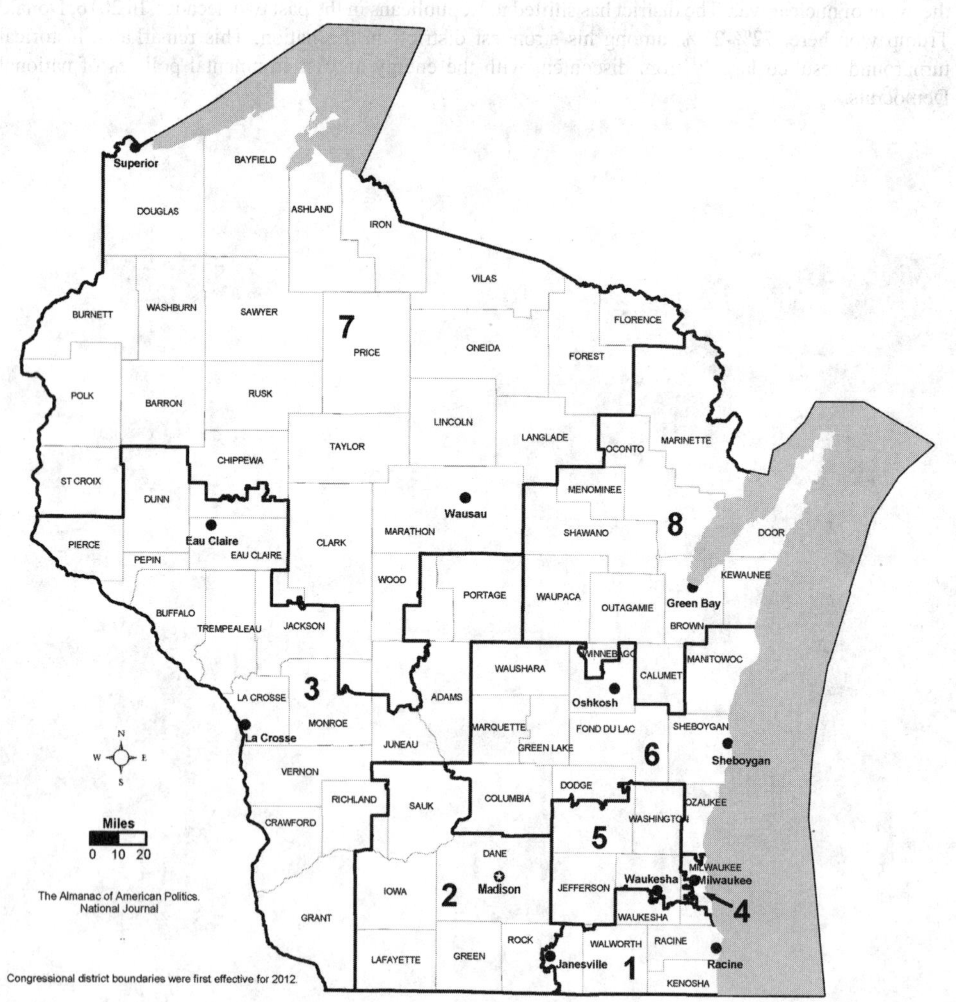
Superior
BAYFIELD
DOUGLAS
ASHLAND
IRON
VILAS
BURNETT
WASHBURN
SAWYER
7
PRICE
ONEIDA
FLORENCE
FOREST
POLK
BARRON
RUSK
LINCOLN
LANGLADE
TAYLOR
OCONTO
MARINETTE
CHIPPEWA
ST CROIX
DUNN
MENOMINEE
Wausau
Eau Claire
MARATHON
SHAWANO
8
DOOR
PIERCE
CLARK
EAU CLAIRE
PEPIN
KEWAUNEE
WOOD
PORTAGE
WAUPACA
OUTAGAMIE
Green Bay
BUFFALO
TREMPEALEAU
JACKSON
BROWN
WINNEBAGO
MANITOWOC
WAUSHARA
CALUMET
3
LA CROSSE
ADAMS
Oshkosh
MONROE
MARQUETTE
FOND DU LAC
SHEBOYGAN
La Crosse
JUNEAU
GREEN LAKE
6
Sheboygan
N
W
E
S
VERNON
DODGE
RICHLAND
SAUK
COLUMBIA
OZAUKEE
WASHINGTON
CRAWFORD
Miles
0 10 20
5
DANE
MILWAUKEE
IOWA
2
Madison
JEFFERSON
Waukesha
Milwaukee
The Almanac of American Politics.
National Journal
4
WAUKESHA
GRANT
ROCK
WALWORTH
RACINE
LAFAYETTE
GREEN
Janesville
1
Racine
KENOSHA
Congressional district boundaries were first effective for 2012.

Heading into the 2016 presidential election, Wisconsin was considered one of the Democrats' "blue wall" states – a supposed bulwark against Republicans in the Electoral College. But that ignored that the state had turned somewhat to the right after the 2010 gubernatorial election of Scott Walker. As it turned out, Hillary Clinton had an unhappy surprise in store, as Donald Trump won the state, albeit by less than 23,000 votes, or about eight-tenths of a percentage point.

Wisconsin has long been one of America's premier "laboratories of reform," in Justice Louis Brandeis' phrase -- a state developing new public policies, debating them vigorously and even tumultuously, observing whether they worked, and serving as an example for other states. North of the dominant westward paths of migration, the state was sparsely settled first by New England Yankees and then by waves of immigrants from Germany and Scandinavia. The German language is seldom heard now, but German place names and surnames are common and, like the once plainly German beer and brat brands, now seem quintessentially American. But from the 1840s into the 20th century, Germans were the most distinctive immigrants. On the rolling dairy land of Wisconsin and the orderly streets of Milwaukee, they built their own churches, kept their own language, and maintained old customs, from country weddings to Christmas trees to beer gardens - a source of friction in temperance-minded America. Wisconsin still has an orderliness and steadiness that owes something to its Germanic heritage, evident in its excellence in precision manufacturing, respect for higher learning, and its hold on its people. About half of Wisconsin residents, more than in any other state, reported in the 2010 census that they are of German descent.

Wisconsin's economy has been an outgrowth of its immigrant and manufacturing heritage. Its high-skill, precision instrument production at companies like Johnson Controls and Rockwell Automation jumped into gear in the late 1980s, and helped lead the nation's export boom of the 1990s. Wisconsin ranks either first or second in the nation in most categories of milk and cheese. But due to improved productivity and competition from foreign countries -- and from California's giant agribusiness enterprises -- the number of dairy farms has declined by close to 90 percent since 1960. Wisconsin, of course, is also a prime source of beer and sausage. Pabst, which began in Milwaukee in 1844, closed its operations there in 1996 but was set to open a new brewery, taproom and restaurant in the city in 2017. Over time, Wisconsin's economy has ranked right around where the country is. The state's median income ranks just slightly below the national average. The unemployment rate peaked at 9.2 percent in early 2010, which was slightly better than country as a whole; by early 2017, it was 3.4 percent, about a full point better than national average.

Wisconsin's reputation for innovative public policy was established during the Progressive Era that began around 1900 and owes its development to an extraordinary governor, Robert La Follette Sr., and the state's German heritage. This is one of the two states that gave birth to the Republican Party in 1854 (the other is Michigan), and Germans, then arriving in America in vast numbers, heavily favored the GOP. They opposed slavery and welcomed the free lands Republicans delivered in the Homestead Act, the free education provided by land grant colleges, and the transportation routes constructed by subsidized railroad builders. This was the seedbed from which sprouted the Progressive movement founded and symbolized by La Follette. At a time when Germany was the world's leader in graduate education and the application of science to government, La Follette had professors at the University of Wisconsin help develop the state workmen's compensation system and income tax. The Progressive movement favored the use of government to improve the lot of ordinary citizens, an idea borrowed partly from German liberals and adopted by the New Dealers a generation later. La Follette became a national figure, and after he died in 1925, his sons, and then liberal Democrats such as Sens. William Proxmire and Gaylord Nelson and Gov. Patrick Lucey, carried on his tradition -- progressive at home and isolationist abroad.

Wisconsin also has a long history of labor activism. Before the violence of the 1892 Homestead steel strike in Pittsburgh and Colorado's Ludlow Massacre in 1914, Milwaukee saw bloodshed on May 5, 1886, when 1,500 tradesmen and Polish immigrants demanding an eight-hour work day marched on the Rolling Mills iron plant in the city's Bay View neighborhood. Gov. Jeremiah Rusk, who had served as a U.S. Army general in the Civil War, was in Milwaukee commanding 700 Wisconsin National Guard troops and gave the order to fire on the workers if they approached the iron works. Seven people, including a young boy, were killed. After the incident, Rusk famously said, "I seen my duty, and I done it." South of downtown Milwaukee, a memorial stands in the Bay View area not far from where the blood was spilled, and local union activists gather there to commemorate the anniversary of the tragedy. Wisconsin was the first state to grant collective-bargaining rights to public employees, in 1959. The state also had its conservative elements – it was the place where Sen. Joe McCarthy rose to prominence.

Starting in the 1990s, Wisconsin became a laboratory for reforms driven by Republican Gov. Tommy Thompson, who beat a liberal Democrat in 1986 and was reelected three times. He cut taxes, sponsored a school choice program, and passed a series of welfare reforms - the nation's most sweeping - that cut caseloads by equipping recipients to work. Governors elsewhere, and Republicans in Congress, watched Wisconsin's experiments with interest. The 1996 overhaul of federal welfare policy may not have passed without Wisconsin's example to give its backers confidence. When Thompson left to become George W. Bush's Health and Human Services secretary in 2001, Wisconsin moved back toward the Democrats, though it remained a presidential battleground. From 1992 to 2006, it elected only Democratic senators, although sometimes by narrow margins, and Democrat Jim Doyle was elected governor in 2002 and 2006. The 2010 election produced another experiment in conservative reform when Republican Scott Walker, a former Milwaukee County executive, took office and proceeded to set off a firestorm with a proposal to limit the power of unions. The effort was successful, and Walker turned back an energetic, labor-driven effort to recall him in 2012 before winning reelection in 2014. By 2017, union membership in the state had fallen substantially. Walker joined two other national Republican figures from Wisconsin – Rep. Paul Ryan, the party's 2012 vice presidential nominee and later House Speaker, and Reince Priebus, the former Wisconsin GOP state chair who became chairman of the Republican National Committee and then White House chief of staff under Trump.

Wisconsin's population has grown, but at a slow rate – up by only 1.5 percent since the 2010 Census. Milwaukee itself grew by less than 1%, and its suburban counties – unlike many suburbs in other states – grew by only about 2 percent. The state's fastest growth has occurred in Dane County (Madison), which has expanded by nearly 9 percent since 2010. The state remains primarily white, with a small, if rising, foreign-born population. Overall, Wisconsin is 6 percent black, 10 percent Hispanic and 3 percent Asian.

Politically, the three large "WOW" counties in the Milwaukee suburbs - Washington, Ozaukee and Waukesha - have traditionally been Republican, sometimes enough to cancel out Milwaukee County and its lopsided Democratic margins. Eastern Wisconsin - the counties along Lake Michigan and two or three counties inland, with small industrial cities in the Fox River Valley like Kenosha, Sheboygan, Appleton, and Green Bay - is historically Republican turf. Western and northern Wisconsin -areas along the Mississippi River, the small inland cities such as Wausau and Eau Claire and the counties along Lake Superior - have tended to be more Democratic. The *Milwaukee Journal Sentinel's* Craig Gilbert, in his fine-grained analysis of Wisconsin election results, has suggested that these patterns stem from ethnic differences: Eastern Wisconsin is more German, and western and northern Wisconsin more Scandinavian. The most Democratic region by far is around Madison, the state capital and home of the University of Wisconsin, whose college-town atmosphere and unionized state employees have spread to rural counties to the south and northeast. La Crosse and Eau Claire host University of Wisconsin system campuses, as does Rock County (Janesville), which is also home to Beloit College. The arc from Janesville to Eau Claire creates a university belt that has helped this territory lean Democratic. With statewide races in Wisconsin often won by 10 percent of the vote or less, a significant number of Wisconsinites are swing voters. In 2010, Wisconsin elected conservative Republican businessman Ron Johnson to the Senate, then two years later promoted liberal Democratic Rep. Tammy Baldwin to the Senate, making her the first openly gay person to serve in that chamber.

The 2016 presidential election in Wisconsin was dramatic from start to finish. The state had not voted Republican for president since Ronald Reagan's 1984 landslide, and for much of the contest, Trump seemed to test Republican voters' patience. Ted Cruz easily beat him in the primary, even though his Texas stylings were not an obvious fit for Wisconsin. After it became clear that Trump was going to be the GOP nominee, he and Ryan, by then the House Speaker, engaged in an on-again, off-again, awkward dance. Even a few days out from Election Day, the polls – and expert opinion – had Trump trailing. The full extent of Clinton's struggles in the state were hard to spot and were largely ignored by her campaign team. As was the case in other states, Trump's key strength -- and Clinton's key weakness -- was in rural areas and small towns where Democrats had often been competitive, locales that are common in Wisconsin. Meanwhile, the distaste for Trump among suburban Republicans, personified by the transformation of longtime conservative radio host Charlie Sykes into an anti-Trumper, was strong enough to even out the numbers.

On Election Day, a state Barack Obama had won by seven points in 2012 ended up voting for Trump by less than a point.The shortfall in Democratic votes in Milwaukee was more than enough to have cost Clinton the win, but Milwaukee was not her only underperforming area – her vote shortfalls in Milwaukee accounted for only about one-sixth of Clinton's vote decline compared with 2012. Trump actually underperformed 2012 nominee Mitt Romney, too, but by the much smaller margin of about 2,700 votes, largely due to diminished Republican margins in the affluent, educated Milwaukee suburbs. Trump's margins underperformed Romney's by 12 points in Ozaukee and by eight points in Waukesha. But in most areas of the state, Trump soundly defeated soundly defeated Clinton. She won only about a third of the counties Obama had won four years earlier, and many of those that switched from blue to red saw their winning margins shift in the GOP's direction by double digits, as high as a 31-point shift in Forest County, located between Green Bay and Lake Superior. The *Journal-Sentinel* calculated that in Wisconsin communities of less than 2,000 people, Trump won by 24 points, six times bigger than Romney's margin. And while Trump lost the metro areas by five points, the newspaper calculated, he won non-metro areas by 19 points. The one potential silver lining for Democrats, the Journal-Sentinel's Gilbert has written, is the historical swinginess of many areas where Trump did well; these areas have often voted against the party controlling the White House. The question is whether the chasm between white- and blue-collar voters, and between rural and suburban voters, has grown so wide that these areas will become much less swingy going forward. Either way, Wisconsin promises to be a hotly contested political battleground even more than in the recent past.

Population		**Race and Ethnicity**		**Income**	
Total	5,742,117	White	82.4%	Median Income	$53,357 (22 out of 50)
Land area	54,158	Black	6.2%	Under $50,000	46.8%
Pop/ sq mi	106.0	Latino	6.3%	$50,000-$99,999	33.2%
Born in state	71.5%	Asian	2.5%	$100,000-$199,999	16.9%
		Two races	1.7%	$200,000 or more	3.3%
Age Groups		Other	0.9%	Poverty Rate	13.0%
Under 18	22.8%				
18-34	22.5%	**Education**			
35-64	39.9%	H.S grad or less	40.9%	**Health Insurance**	
Over 64	14.8%	Some college	31.2%	With health insurance coverage	92.1%
		College Degree, 4 yr	18.4%		
Work		Post grad	9.4%		
White Collar	34.5%			**Public Assistance**	
Sales and Service	40.1%	**Military**		Cash public assistance income	2.2%
Blue Collar	25.4%	Veteran	8.6%		
Government	12.4%	Active Duty	0.1%	Food stamp/SNAP benefits	12.9%

Voter Turnout			
2015 Total Citizens 18+	4,294,321	2016 Pres Turnout as % CVAP	69%
2016 Pres Votes	2,976,150	2012 Pres Turnout as % CVAP	73%

Legislature	
Senate:	13D, 20R
House:	34D, 64R

Presidential Politics

2016 Democratic Primary		
Bernie Sanders (D)	570,192	(57%)
Hillary Clinton (D)	433,739	(43%)
2016 Republican Primary		
Ted Cruz (R)	533,079	(48%)
Donald Trump (R)	387,295	(35%)
John Kasich (R)	155,902	(14%)

2016 Presidential Vote		
Donald Trump (R)	1,405,284	(47%)
Hillary Clinton (D)	1,382,536	(46%)
Gary Johnson (L)	106,674	(4%)
2012 Presidential Vote		
Barack Obama (D)	1,620,985	(53%)
Mitt Romney (R)	1,407,966	(46%)

Wisconsin has seen some very close presidential elections: Al Gore carried the state 47.8%-47.6%, a margin of only 5,708 votes in 2000, and John Kerry won it 49.7%-49.3%, a margin of only 11,384 votes in 2004. But in 2016, the Badger State tipped the other way and Donald Trump defeated Hillary Clinton, 47.2%-46.5%, a relatively generous margin of 22,748 votes. Much of the blame for Clinton's loss of a state that had voted Democratic in the previous seven presidential elections was laid on her middling effort there. The day before the election in 2012, Barack Obama's team staged a huge rally with the president and Bruce Springsteen in Madison. Clinton never returned to the state after her primary loss to Sanders in April. Veteran Democratic pollster Paul Maslin, who is based in Wisconsin, called that lack of attention "political malpractice." According to University of Wisconsin political scientist Barry Burden, the last time a major party nominee didn't visit the state during the general election campaign was President Richard Nixon in 1972, who was headed for a 49-state landslide. As Election Day neared, the Clinton campaign realized the state was a toss-up and pumped some $3 million in ads onto Wisconsin television and radio in the final week. But it was not enough to stem the erosion in the Democratic vote in this vital swing state.

Perhaps the biggest factor in Trump's victory was the shift in the vote in Wisconsin's rural (and largely white) territory. Among the 34 counties that saw a 10-percentage point decline in the Democratic share of the two-party (Democratic and Republican) presidential vote, nearly every one of those counties was in the western half of the state and north of the more industrial Fox River Valley. All total, Clinton received roughly 109,000 fewer votes than Obama did in 2012 - nearly five times her total statewide margin of defeat. Total turnout was down by just 4,569 in those counties. President Barack Obama carried 15 of these counties in 2012, and in another six he came within 2.5 percentage points of Mitt Romney. The western portion of the state is populated by many voters of Scandinavian ancestry who are traditionally more liberal than the German descendants who are more prevalent in and around Milwaukee and its suburbs.

In Milwaukee County, Clinton garnered roughly 43,600 fewer votes than Obama did in 2012. Turnout in the county - which has a relatively high share of African-American voters for Wisconsin - was down by more than 51,000. Clinton won roughly 70 percent of the vote in the county and had the turnout from 2016 matched the level of 2012, she would have picked up more than 15,000 votes on Trump, making up about two-thirds of her statewide deficit. In the three suburban counties that make up the rest of the Milwaukee metropolitan area -- Washington, Ozaukee and Waukesha -- Trump saw the GOP margin drop from some 132,500 votes scored by Romney in 2012 to roughly 104,500 votes in 2016. Clinton came out of the entire Milwaukee metro nearly 13,000 votes ahead of Obama's performance.

Clinton's other pockets of strength came in the University Belt stretching from Rock County - home to the University of Wisconsin-Rock County and liberal arts Beloit College - to La Cross, Eu Claire, and Portage Counties, which also have University of Wisconsin systems. But otherwise, Clinton carried only Menominee County, whose borders encompass the Menominee Indian Reservation and three counties at the northern tip of the state: Ashland, Bayfield, and Douglas, along the Gogebic iron range. In addition to the rural territory, Trump carried the Fox River Valley, which includes smaller industrial cities like Appleton, Fon du Lac, Green Bay and Oshkosh. He also won Kenosha and Racine Counties with their blue-collar communities. Obama won both of those counties in 2012. The election in Wisconsin did not end on Nov. 8. In late November, Wisconsin elections officials were the first in the country to grant Green Party nominee Jill Stein's request for a recount. After their review concluded and the results were certified on Dec. 12, Trump had gained 131 votes on his Election Night numbers.

Wisconsin once had one of the nation's most influential presidential primaries. It knocked Wendell Willkie out of the race in 1944, helped John Kennedy establish his lead over Hubert Humphrey in 1960, prompted Lyndon Johnson to withdraw as Eugene McCarthy was about to beat him here in 1968, gave George McGovern his first victory in 1972, gave Jimmy Carter a key victory in 1976 - after ABC and NBC mistakenly called the primary for Mo Udall - and chose "New Democrat" Gary Hart over Minnesota neighbor Walter Mondale in 1984.

In 2016, the "never Trump" movement coalesced around Texas Sen. Ted Cruz before the April 5 GOP primary. Conservative radio talk show host Charlie Sykes lead the charge against Trump Monday-through-Friday mornings. Republican Gov. Scott Walker, who briefly sought his party's nomination, endorsed Cruz and appeared in television spots boosting the Texan's candidacy. It was enough to give Cruz a 48%-35% victory. But Wisconsin would be the last primary or caucus that Trump would lose on his way to the GOP nomination. On the Democratic side, Vermont Sen. Bernie Sanders held multiple rallies across the state and outspent Clinton on television advertising. She stumped primarily in the

Milwaukee area. But on the Sunday before the primary she was speaking in black churches in New York City, basically conceding the state. Sanders won 56%-44% and carried 71 of the state's 72 counties. Clinton's lone win was Milwaukee County.

Congressional Districts

115th Congress Lineup	5R 3D	**114th Congress Lineup**	5R 3D

Wisconsin lost a congressional district in the 2000 census. After Democratic Rep. Tom Barrett retired to run for governor, his north Milwaukee district was easy to eliminate. The resulting consensus plan enabled all four Democrats and four Republicans running for reelection to win in 2002. The Green Bay-based 8th District has shifted twice since then and has returned to GOP control. Republican Sean Duffy picked up retiring Democrat David Obey's northwestern 7th District.

In 2011, Republicans had total control over redistricting. With the state Senate under siege over a petition to oust six members in recall elections, Gov. Scott Walker quietly signed a pro-Republican map into law. The map shored up Duffy, giving him friendly St. Croix County in the Twin Cities exurbs and trading the liberal cities of Stevens Point and Wisconsin Rapids to 3rd District Democrat Ron Kind. It also boosted Republicans Paul Ryan in the 1st District and Tom Petri in the 6th District with an eye toward possible future open seats. In November 2012, Republicans won 49 percent of all votes cast for the House but kept their 5-3 edge. Following his retirement in 2014, Petri was replaced by the more conservative Glenn Grothman. In June 2017, the U.S. Supreme Court agreed to review the ruling of a three-judge federal court that had found the GOP plan an unconstitutional "partisan gerrymander." The earlier ruling was stayed pending the Court's review.

Governor

Scott Walker (R)

Elected 2010, term expires 2019, 2nd term; b. Nov. 2, 1967, Colorado Springs, CO; Marquette U., attended 1986-90; Christian; Married (Tonette); 2 children.

Elected Office: WI Assembly, 1993-2002; Milwaukee County Executive, 2002-2010.

Professional Career: Salesman, IBM Corp., 1988-1990; Financial developer, American Red Cross, 1990-1994.

Office: 115 E. Capitol, Madison, 53702; 608-266-1212; Fax: 608-267-8983; Website: wisconsin.gov.

Election Results

Election	Name (Party)	Vote (%)
2014 General	Scott Walker (R)	1,259,706 (52%)
	Mary Burke (D)	1,122,913 (47%)

Prior winning percentage: 2010 (52%)

Scott Walker won the governorship of Wisconsin and proceeded to implement a muscular conservative agenda. He survived a 2012 recall election and won a second term in 2014, and while he flopped as a presidential candidate two years later, he starts as a modest favorite to win a third term as governor in 2018.

Walker was born in Colorado Springs, Colorado, and moved with his family at age 10 to Delavan, a small town 60 miles southeast of Madison. His mother kept the books for a local department store and his father was a Baptist preacher who Walker stood next to on Sundays to help greet worshippers. Walker was an Eagle Scout and represented Wisconsin at the Boys Nation student government program in Washington, D.C., in 1985, an achievement that he says spurred his interest in politics. Republican Ronald Reagan was president at the time and served as an inspiration to him. He attended Marquette University but left before graduating to take a job in his senior year with the American Red Cross in marketing and development.

Walker ran for the state Assembly in 1990 in a Democratic district but lost to incumbent Gwen Moore, who went on to serve in the U.S. House. Three years later, Walker tried in a more GOP-friendly district and won. He reportedly considered running for governor, but a pension scandal that led to Tom Ament's resignation as Milwaukee County executive changed Walker's plans. Promising to run a clean government, Walker was elected to that job in 2002. Liberal Democrats had previously held the nonpartisan county executive's post and Walker put a fiscally conservative stamp on the job. He cut the workforce by 20 percent, clashed with unions, and used his veto more than 100 times to force $44 million in spending cuts. Each of his budgets held property taxes in check, and he returned a portion of his salary to the county's coffers. Some Democrats accused him of being overly stingy in financing basic services. But others hailed his low-key personality and political skills.

Walker entered the race for governor in 2006 but backed out after 14 months, citing fundraising difficulties. In hindsight that was a wise call, as 2006 turned out to be a banner year for Democrats. In April 2009, though, he announced another bid, criticizing Democratic Gov. Jim Doyle for increased spending and taxes and emphasizing what he called a common-sense, "brown bag" approach to cutbacks. Four months after Walker entered the race, Doyle, by then trailing Walker in some polls, announced he would not seek a third term. Walker faced a GOP primary challenger in Mark Neumann, a homebuilder and developer who served two terms in the House in the 1990s; Walker prevailed in the September 2010 primary, 59%-39%. In the general election, Walker's Democratic opponent was another former House member-Tom Barrett, a representative from 1993 to 2003 before losing the 2002 gubernatorial primary to Doyle, and then winning election as Milwaukee's mayor in 2004. Wisconsin Republicans were clearly more energized than Democrats in the election, partly due to their efforts to oust veteran Democratic Sen. Russ Feingold, who was up for reelection. Walker ended up winning, 52%-47%. Barrett carried Milwaukee County 62%-38%, Dane County (Madison) 68%-31%, as well as Eau Clair, La Crosse and Rock Counties, but Walker won the Milwaukee suburbs, the Fox River Valley and most of the rest of the state.

On his first official day in office, Walker called the legislature into session to address the state's economy and swiftly won two victories. Republicans passed bills to allow concealed carry for handguns, to tighten personal injury laws and to provide tax breaks for people with health savings accounts. He also shuttered the state's Department of Commerce and replaced it with a public-private agency, the Wisconsin Economic Development Corporation. And in a state with same-day voter registration and a large transitory college student population, Walker and the GOP legislature tightened state voter ID laws. But the true uproar came after he called for curtailing collective bargaining rights for many of the state's public employees, describing those rights as an obstacle to reducing state and local budget deficits. Fourteen Senate Democrats fled the state to block a vote. Union workers showed up at the Capitol by the tens of thousands, carrying angry signs and inspiring similar protests against GOP governors' tactics in other states. Activists gathered petitions to recall GOP Wisconsin state senators. Walker became an instant political celebrity. Prospective Republican presidential candidates stampeded to support him, he appeared on national television shows, and he even was mentioned as a possible vice presidential candidate for 2012.

In the face of the noisy protests, Walker refused to back down, and in March the state Senate passed a bill with the collective bargaining provisions without Democratic senators present. A *Milwaukee Journal Sentinel* poll that month showed just how polarized public opinion about the governor had become: 90 percent of Republicans approved of his job performance, while 91 percent of Democrats disapproved. In April, an election for state Supreme Court judges turned into a proxy for the battling sides. Justice David Prosser, a self-described judicial conservative, defeated challenger JoAnne Kloppenburg after a concerted effort by liberal interest groups to topple Prosser in retaliation for Walker's crackdown on unions. Conservatives maintained their 4-3 majority on the court.

Walker's collective bargaining changes survived court challenges and became law. But the anger that flared up over the changes did not subside. With the help of labor groups, Democrats tried to gain control of the state Senate by attempting to recall six Republican incumbents, all Walker allies, in August 2011. But enough of the Republicans survived to allow the GOP to keep a 17-16 majority. Also percolating was an investigation into whether Milwaukee County staffers in Walker's former office did political work with taxpayer money. In early 2012, two of Walker's appointees were charged with embezzling money and spending the money on trips and personal items after one of his staffers noticed missing funds; eventually, they and four other aides and associates of the governor were convicted as part of the state probe. Walker supporters said the outcome showed that the governor was never a target of the investigation, while critics said it demonstrated he was at least guilty of bad judgment.

An official movement to recall Walker began in late 2011. United Wisconsin, the group managing the recall and working with the state Democratic Party, collected almost 1 million signatures to put the issue on the ballot, far above the 540,208 required. Subsequent polls showed that the public narrowly opposed the recall, with even some of Walker's opponents saying they preferred to settle differences through the regular election process. But the effort forged ahead and the June recall became the most expensive election in Wisconsin history. Candidates and outside groups poured in more than $63 million, according to the Center for Public Integrity, compared with the $37.4 million spent in the 2010 race. Barrett won a five-way primary to take on Walker again, but suffered a substantial fundraising disadvantage. Walker notched a 53%-46% triumph, becoming the first governor in history to survive a recall. The vast campaign spending on Walker's behalf by conservative groups prompted a so-called "John Doe" investigation - which involved strict secrecy and barred the conservative targets of the probe from discussing it - to see if campaign contribution limits or laws barring coordination between candidates and independent groups had been breached. John Chisholm, the Democratic Milwaukee County district attorney who had investigated Walker county executive staffers earlier, drove the new probe, assisted by the state's Government Accountability Board. After a long investigation that involved pre-dawn armed raids on the homes of political activists, the state Supreme Court shut down the investigation and rebuked investigators for overzealousness and flimsy legal reasoning, and the legislature disbanded the GAB.

Walker's political success over the unions earned him a spot on *Time* magazine's list of the 100 most influential people of 2014, and he began that year – a reelection year for him – by signing a $541 million tax cut for families and businesses as state officials were forecasting a $1 billion surplus for the coming year. Unable to entice a marquee candidate to take on Walker, Democrats nominated Mary Burke, a former state Commerce secretary and a former executive at her family's business, Trek Bicycle Co. President Barack Obama, former President Bill Clinton and first lady Michelle Obama campaigned for Burke. Outside groups and unions joined the fray on Burke's behalf, helping to highlight Walker's failure to meet his 2010 pledge to create 250,000 new jobs in Wisconsin, and pushing other attacks. Democrats painted Walker as a social extremist who had signed a law requiring women to get an ultrasound before having an abortion. Walker responded by portraying Burke as a liberal, and his campaign ran negative ads mocking Burke's wealth while her family business outsourced jobs by building bikes overseas. In the end, he defeated Burke, 52%-47%, carrying almost the exact same counties he had in 2010. While not especially large, his victory was comprehensive -- he carried college and non-college voters, every age group except for those between 25 and 39, and independents. He lost self-described moderates to Burke 52%-46%, an uncommonly good showing for a Republican and three percentage points better than in his 2010 race.

A presidential run beckoned, even though the 2014 state exit poll found that 55 percent of voters didn't think he would make a good president. Walker got some good news in July when the Wisconsin Supreme Court brought a halt to the "John Doe" investigation that had been dogging Walker and his allies. On fiscal matters, Walker was less fortunate. The $1 billion projected surplus from the previous year never materialized and he had to cope with a shortfall of about $280 billion. His proposals to cut funding for the University of Wisconsin system and state aid to education were met with resistance, including from the GOP-controlled legislature. Republican lawmakers pruned his cuts to the university system, which still took a $250 million hit, and blocked his proposed reduction in K-12 education funding. But Walker signed a new budget without raising taxes, and used his line-item veto on more than 100 items in the measure. The two-year, $73-billion budget removed tenure protections for state university professors, partially repealed the state's prevailing wage law, and made Wisconsin a right-to-work state, a proposal Walker had forsworn as a candidate but was quick to embrace once it gained momentum among the GOP legislators.

Walker also signed a bill that banned abortion after the 20th week of pregnancy and that heightened requirements for abortion doctors' admitting privileges. (The latter provision was struck down by the Supreme Court in June 2016.) Meanwhile, an ongoing series of audits of the Wisconsin Economic Development Corporation, which Walker established in his first year in office, described a sloppily run agency that handed out grants and loans to unqualified businesses, some with ties to the governor's financial supporters. Walker called on the legislature to reform the beleaguered agency and remove all elected officials from its board.

Leading up to his presidential run, Walker articulated some conservative positions likely to play well with national GOP primary voters, but his words and actions did not always come off smoothly. During a February 2015 trip to London, he was asked about evolution and replied, "I'm going to punt on that one." He said his record fighting organized labor was good preparation for defeating ISIS, and he not only urged tough policies at the U.S. border with Mexico, but at one point said it was "legitimate" to consider building a wall along the U.S.-Canada border. (Sen. Patrick Leahy, a Democrat from Canada-neighboring Vermont, called it "one of the craziest" ideas he'd heard during the election season.) Walker also flirted with supporting an end to birthright citizenship before backing off. Floating the extension of his anti-union policies to the federal level, Walker proposed a national right-to-work law and elimination of the National Labor Relations Board. But despite some support within the GOP establishment and from some key donors, Walker failed to gain traction with voters. By the time he dropped out in September 2015, he was polling around 1 percent nationally and was mired in 10th place in Iowa, where he had initially excited conservative activists.

Walker gained a new platform to influence national politics shortly after the 2016 election, when he became chairman of the Republican Governors Association. He was almost certain to run for a third term as governor, and while Democrats saw Wisconsin as winnable, they were hampered early on by their inability to entice a top-tier challenger into the race.

Senior Senator

Ron Johnson (R)

Elected 2010, term expires 2022, 2nd term; b. Apr 08, 1955, Mankato, MN; University of Minnesota; University of Minnesota, B.S.; Lutheran; Married (Jane Johnson); 3 children; 2 grandchildren.

Professional Career: Owner, PACUR; Accountant, Josten's.

DC Office: 328 HSOB 20510, 202-224-5323, Fax: 202-228-6965, ronjohnson.senate.gov.

State Offices: Milwaukee, 414-276-7282; Oshkosh, 920-230-7250.

Committees: *Budget. Commerce, Science & Transportation*: Communications, Technology, Innovation & the Internet, Oceans, Atmosphere, Fisheries & Coast Guard, Space, Science & Competitiveness, Surface Trans., Merchant Marine Infra., Safety & Security. *Foreign Relations*: Europe & Regional Security Cooperation (Chmn), Near East, South Asia, Central Asia & Counterterrorism, West Hem Crime Civ Sec Dem Rights & Women's Issues. *Homeland Security & Government Affairs (Chmn)*: Federal Spending Oversight & Emergency Management, Investigations, Regulatory Affairs & Federal Management.

Group Ratings

	ADA	ACLU	AFL-CIO	LCV	ITI	COC	HAFA	ACU	CFG	FRC
2016	-	23%	-	6%	100%	100%	45%	84%	78%	100%
2015	10%	C	14%	0%	C	100%	C	75%	72%	73%

Almanac Ratings 2015

	Economy	Social	Foreign	Composite
Liberal	28%	24%	31%	27%
Conservative	73%	76%	69%	73%

Key Votes of the 114th Congress

1. Keystone pipeline	Y	5. National Security Data	Y	9. Gun Sales Checks	NV
2. Export-Import Bank	N	6. Iran Nuclear Deal	Y	10. Sanctuary Cities	Y
3. Debt Ceiling Increase	N	7. Puerto Rico Debt	Y	11. Planned Parenthood	Y
4. Homeland Security $$	Y	8. Loretta Lynch A.G	Y	12. Trade deals	Y

Election Results

Election	Name (Party)	Vote (%)		Cand. Spent	Ind. Exp. Support	Ind. Exp. Oppose
2016 General	Ron Johnson (R)	1,479,471	(50%)	$27,590,817	$2,187,944	$8,418,011
	Russ Feingold (D)	1,380,335	(47%)	$25,190,356	$1,565,370	$16,527,845
	Phil Anderson (L)	87,531	(3%)			
2016 Primary	Ron Johnson (R)	unopposed				

Prior winning percentages: 2010 (52%)

Republican Ron Johnson, Wisconsin's senior senator, won his seat in one of 2010's biggest upsets, dispatching 18-year Democratic Sen. Russ Feingold. Six years later, he defended it in a rematch against Feingold, once again beating the odds. His victory in 2016 enabled Johnson to become the first Republican in Wisconsin since 1980 to win a Senate contest in a presidential year.

Johnson grew up in Mankato Minnesota. He says he developed a strong work ethic at an early age, delivering newspapers, caddying at a golf course, and baling hay on his uncle's dairy farm. He was a restaurant dishwasher at 15 and within a year won a promotion to night manager. Although Johnson didn't finish high school, he attended college, working full-time and graduating with $7,000 in the bank. While working as an accountant, Johnson went to night school to earn an MBA. Just short of a degree in 1979, he decided to move to Oshkosh to start a plastics company, PACUR, with his brother-in-law. Their first customer was a company co-founded by his father-in-law. Since then, the business has become a major producer of specialty packaging for medical devices, employing about 120 workers. Johnson has said his political views have been influenced by Ayn Rand's 1957 novel *Atlas Shrugged*, which argues that civilization cannot exist where men are slaves to society and government.

Johnson said that his motivation to run against Feingold was the senator's support of the Democrats' 2010 health care overhaul, which he called "the single greatest assault to our freedom in my lifetime." He entered the race in May, just days before the state Republican nominating convention. Three GOP candidates were already competing, including beer mogul and former state Commerce Secretary Dick Leinenkugel and Madison developer Terrence Wall. Johnson's ability to self-finance made an immediate impact. At the convention, Leinenkugel surprised everyone, including Johnson, by taking his turn at the lectern to drop out and endorse Johnson, saying, "It's not my time ... it's Ron Johnson's time." Wall then reluctantly followed suit. Spending more than $4 million of his own money, Johnson went on to crush businessman Dave Westlake in the September primary.

The campaign between Johnson and Feingold-a liberal with a quirky, maverick streak-was nasty, especially by Wisconsin's normally civil standards. Without a legislative record of his opponent to mine, Feingold sought to concentrate on Johnson's record in business, attempting to depict him as someone more concerned about profits than people-someone "with a country club view of reality." Feingold also called Johnson a hypocrite for opposing federal economic stimulus funds and then allegedly seeking those funds for renovation of an opera house. Johnson fought back, noting in an ad that the Senate had 57 lawyers, including Feingold, but just one accountant and no manufacturers like himself. His GOP allies also did a textbook job of depicting the incumbent-who had contemplated running for president in 2008-as an entrenched Washington insider supportive of deficit spending. Feingold had $21 million to Johnson's $15 million, but it was not enough in a Republican wave year. Johnson won, 52% to 47%.

Johnson initially got seats on the Appropriations and Budget committees, but he left Appropriations for Foreign Relations in 2013 after saying he was tired of being the only committee member opposed to more spending. In 2011, he notably did not support fellow Wisconsin Republican Rep. Paul Ryan's controversial budget plan to dramatically reduce the deficit and transform Medicare, arguing that Ryan's proposal did not cut spending enough. Also that year, Johnson blocked a resolution to support military action in Libya as a way of calling attention to debt reduction, saying on the floor that the debt is "the single most important issue facing this nation." Hoping for more radical spending cuts, he joined 18 other Senate Republicans in opposing the August 2011 deal that raised the debt limit. In December 2011, Johnson launched a bid for a Senate Republican leadership post as conference vice chairman. The race was a classic outsider-vs.-insider battle, with Johnson the maverick running against the establishment candidate, Roy Blunt of Missouri. The conference selected Blunt over Johnson, 25-22.

In Washington, Johnson has been blunt; one of his strategists, Brad Todd, has described him as "straight as a shot of uncut whiskey." He drew particular attention for grilling outgoing Secretary of State Hillary Clinton at a Foreign Relations Committee hearing in January 2013 on the deadly terrorist attack at the U.S. consulate in Benghazi Libya. Johnson complained that lawmakers had been "misled" about the incident, and when Clinton said it would have been inappropriate to contact diplomatic staff for details immediately afterward because of an FBI investigation, he replied, "I realize that's a good excuse." An exasperated Clinton retorted: "No, it's a fact ... What difference, at this point, does it make?" After *The Washington Post* awarded Johnson its "Worst Week in Washington" accolade for his aggressiveness, the senator said, "In Washington, demanding the truth is apparently a sin." In the long run, however, Johnson may have fought to at least a draw: The footage of her incensed answer was unspooled repeatedly by conservatives to remind voters of Clinton's biggest foreign policy blemish.

As a senator, Johnson has compiled a conservative voting record. But when tea party-backed candidates failed to topple incumbent GOP senators in several primary elections in 2014, Johnson drew attention for emphasizing pragmatism over political purity, and that continued in advance of his 2016 reelection bid. Johnson won Senate passage of the Integrated Public Alert and Warning System Modernization Act of 2015 by unanimous consent, and rhetorically, he put some distance between himself and the tea party. "I sprang out of the tea-party movement, no question," he told *National Journal*, but he emphasized that "I've never joined any kind of tea-party caucus or tea-party group."

The rematch with Feingold became a marquee Senate race of 2016. According to political analyst Nathan Gonzales, it is rare for a fallen incumbent to avenge his loss against the candidate who defeated him. The last time it happened was in 1934. In 1928, two-term Sen. Peter Gerry, a Democrat from Rhode Island, lost reelection to Republican Felix Hebert. Six years later, Gerry came back to handily defeat Heber. For much of Johnson's reelection campaign, Feingold was considered the frontrunner, with polls vacillating between a mid-single-digit lead and a low double-digit lead for the Democrat. The widespread assumption was that Feingold would do better in a presidential election year than a low-turnout midterm year; by late summer, Republican groups and their allies showed indications of writing off Johnson and moving on to Senate contests in other states. But Johnson regrouped in September with the help of his older brother, Dean, a veteran television executive producer and host, and a new team of consultants. They took the gloves off against Feingold, relentlessly attacking him as a creature of Washington, while painting Johnson in softer hues, including efforts to highlight the Joseph Project, a faith-oriented jobs program Johnson was involved in. Johnson also targeted small, rural towns and worked to boost turnout in traditionally Republican areas that were lagging, using detailed data from the state party that had previously helped Scott Walker's gubernatorial campaigns.

On Election Day, Johnson won 74,000 more votes than Trump did, and he defeated Feingold by 3 percentage points, which was higher than Trump's fraction-of-a-point margin over Clinton in Wisconsin. To a large degree, Johnson's wider margin than Trump in the state can be traced to the "WOW" counties in the Milwaukee suburbs-Washington, Ozaukee and Waukesha. These counties are historically Republican, but their relatively high education and income levels made them less fertile ground for Trump's message. By contrast, Johnson, a more conventional Republican, was able to hold on to a larger fraction of the GOP vote. In Ozaukee, Johnson won 65% of the vote, compared to 56% for Trump. In Waukesha, Johnson won 68% to Trump's 60%. And in Washington County, Johnson won72% to Trump's 67%.

Once he had won a new term, Johnson urged leveraging the newly all-Republican federal government to eliminate federal regulations through the Congressional Review Act, a tool rarely used previously. But Johnson also floated the idea of bipartisan cooperation to "fix" Obamacare. Either way, his second term likely would be Johnson's last in the Senate. During the campaign, he announced that he would not run again in 2022.

Junior Senator

Tammy Baldwin (D)

Elected 2012, term expires 2018, 1st term; b. Feb 11, 1962, Madison; Smith College (MA), A.B.; University of Wisconsin Law School, J.D.; Single.

Elected Office: Dane County Board of Supervisors, 1986-1994; WI Assembly, 1992-1998; U.S. House, 1998-2012.

Professional Career: Practicing attorney, 1989-1992.

DC Office: 709 HSOB 20510, 202-224-5653, Fax: 202-224-9787, baldwin.senate.gov.

State Offices: Eau Claire, 715-832-8424; La Crosse, 608-796-0045; Madison, 608-264-5338; Milwaukee, 414-297-4451.

Committees: Senate Democratic Conference Secretary. *Appropriations*: Agriculture, Rural Development, FDA & Related Agencies, Department of Defense, Department of Homeland Security, DOL, HHS & Education & Related Agencies, Military Construction & Veteran Affairs & Related Agencies. *Commerce, Science & Transportation*: Aviation Operations, Safety & Security, Communications, Technology, Innovation & the Internet, Oceans, Atmosphere, Fisheries & Coast Guard, Space, Science & Competitiveness, Surface Trans., Merchant Marine Infra., Safety & Security. *Health, Education, Labor & Pensions*: Employment & Workplace Safety, Primary Health & Retirement Security.

Group Ratings

	ADA	ACLU	AFL-CIO	LCV	ITI	COC	HAFA	ACU	CFG	FRC
2016	-	94%	-	100%	40%	63%	7%	4%	5%	0%
2015	100%	C	100%	100%	C	43%	C	0%	0%	0%

Almanac Ratings 2015

	Economy	Social	Foreign	Composite
Liberal	100%	100%	91%	97%
Conservative	0%	0%	9%	3%

Key Votes of the 114th Congress

1. Keystone pipeline	N	5. National Security Data	Y	9. Gun Sales Checks	Y
2. Export-Import Bank	N	6. Iran Nuclear Deal	N	10. Sanctuary Cities	N
3. Debt Ceiling Increase	Y	7. Puerto Rico Debt	N	11. Planned Parenthood	N
4. Homeland Security $$	Y	8. Loretta Lynch A.G	Y	12. Trade deals	N

Election Results

Election	Name (Party)	Vote (%)	Cand. Spent	Ind. Exp. Support	Ind. Exp. Oppose
2012 General	Tammy Baldwin (D)	1,547,104 (51%)	$15,204,940	$3,269,678	$15,461,680
	Tommy Thompson (R)	1,380,126 (46%)	$9,582,888	$4,030,898	$19,024,651
	Joseph Kexel (L)	62,240 (2%)			
2012 Primary	Tammy Baldwin (D)	185,265 (100%)			

Prior winning percentages: House: 2010 (62%), 2008 (69%), 2006 (63%), 2004 (63%), 2002 (66%), 2000 (51%), 1998 (53%)

Democrat Tammy Baldwin of Wisconsin is the first openly gay member of the Senate, as well as the first woman elected to the chamber from Wisconsin. She won her seat in 2012, when Baldwin, a House member, defeated former Gov. Tommy Thompson to succeed retiring Democratic Sen. Herb Kohl.

Baldwin grew up in Madison, where she was raised mostly by her maternal grandparents, a University of Wisconsin biochemist and the theater department's head costume designer. Her mother, who was 19 and a UW student when she was born, was "in the middle of a divorce and overwhelmed,"

Baldwin told the *New York Times*, adding that her mother had long battles with pain and addiction. "My grandparents were there, and I'm very, very grateful." Baldwin graduated first in her class at Madison West High School and went on to Smith College and UW law school. It was in college that it became "very clear" that she was gay. Her grandfather was deceased by the time she came out, but her grandmother was supportive.

In 1986, at age 24 and still in law school, Baldwin was elected to the Board of Supervisors of Dane County (Madison). In 1992, she was elected to the Wisconsin Assembly. Six years later, when moderate Republican Scott Klug honored his promise to serve only four terms in the House, Baldwin got into the race, along with three other Democrats and six Republicans. As a woman who favored abortion rights, she was supported by EMILY's List, which helped her raise about one-quarter of her $1.5 million campaign chest. Baldwin won with 37 percent of the vote; then, in the general election, she beat former state Insurance Commissioner Jo Musser. This made her the first openly gay non-incumbent to win a seat in the House.

Baldwin's voting record was consistently one of the most liberal in the House. She secured a coveted seat on the Energy and Commerce Committee, but with the chamber in Republican hands for 10 of her 14 years in the House, her ability to accomplish many of her progressive goals was limited. She was sharply critical of many GOP proposals, including the controversial budget of Wisconsin Rep. Paul Ryan and of Gov. Scott Walker's equally controversial but successful effort to limit collective bargaining rights for state workers, the issue that touched off a recall campaign against Walker. (Baldwin told the *Times* that Walker had been "a nice guy" when they served together in the Assembly and that she felt "deceived" by his agenda as governor.)

Baldwin's driving issue has been guaranteed health care for all Americans. The issue was personal: A serious illness as a child kept her in the hospital for three months, making her a patient with a pre-existing condition. Baldwin supported the Democrats' 2010 overhaul of the health insurance system even though it did not include a government-run "public option" to compete with private insurers, a provision she had favored. She was also a leading advocate for the right to same-sex marriage. In 2008, she and Massachusetts Democrat Barney Frank, another gay lawmaker, established the House LGBT Equality Caucus. In an interview with the *New York Times*, Baldwin recalled that in the House, "I did a lot of sitting down with Republicans to talk about these bills. Often there was a real sort of intimacy in those conversations. People talked about gay brothers, or a child who was gay, lesbian or transgender. I can't tell you how many of those stories I accumulated. I think I moved a number of my colleagues, and I think it at least caused a lot of internal conflict for those I didn't move." Baldwin is also one of just a handful of lawmakers who hasn't specified a religious affiliation. "They didn't let me put the phrase, 'It's complicated,' as Facebook might have," she told the *Times*.

After Baldwin decided to run for Kohl's seat, she was unchallenged in the Democratic primary, giving her ample time to organize her campaign and raise money. Tommy Thompson, a popular former governor known as a pragmatic conservative, won the GOP primary against three more conservative candidates and started with a lead over Baldwin in the general election campaign. But Baldwin and her allies outspent Thompson and his backers by 3-to-1 in the weeks after the primary, and the race turned unrelentingly negative. Baldwin ran a disciplined campaign, seeking to convince voters that she would be more attuned to the needs of Wisconsin than the 70-year-old Thompson, a former Health and Human Services secretary under George W. Bush who hadn't been a candidate for office in 14 years. Realizing it made little sense to attack Thompson's gubernatorial record, which many Wisconsinites of both parties still remembered fondly, Baldwin instead blasted Thompson with negative television ads about his post-gubernatorial career, highlighting his work for a Washington D.C. lobbying firm. Meanwhile, Thompson and Republicans accused Baldwin of being a radical, but she downplayed her liberal views and highlighted her populist stands against China's trade policies and her efforts at bipartisanship. One outside analysis of both campaigns' ads found that over a 30-day period, 99 percent were negative. As the race neared its conclusion, Thompson veered to the right-he told a tea party group that he wanted to "do away with the Medicare and Medicaid," a stark departure from his previous positions-but the maneuver rang hollow with voters. The former governor failed to attract a significant number of Democratic crossover voters, and Baldwin won, 51% to 46%.

In the Senate, Baldwin holds seats on the Appropriations; Commerce, Science, and Transportation; and Health, Education, Labor, and Pensions committees. She has voted a consistently liberal line, almost always taking the opposite stance from the state's senior senator, conservative Republican Ron Johnson. As Craig Gilbert noted in the Milwaukee *Journal Sentinel*, the two Wisconsin senators split over the Affordable Care Act, fast-track trade authority, the Keystone XL pipeline, gun control, immigration, the minimum wage and a host of other issues. A rare point of unison, Gilbert found, was a shared vote in favor of ensuring that same-sex spouses have access to Social Security and veterans' benefits.

Baldwin joined her fellow midwestern Democratic senators Sherrod Brown of Ohio and Bob Casey of Pennsylvania in an effort to insert a "Buy America" provision in a major water resources bill, and she introduced a measure to end the carried-interest tax loophole that benefits hedge fund managers. After the Pulse nightclub shootings in Orlando in June 2016, Baldwin worked to make sure that LGBT concerns were not overlooked in the rush to discuss gun violence and terrorism. "They needed someone on the floor to come and say, 'This is all of these things. Do not just sweep away the hate crime aspect of it -- give these people's lives, give them, a voice," she told *Glamour* magazine. Baldwin was also among the leaders in an effort to lift a longstanding Food and Drug Administration ban against blood donation by gay and bisexual individuals. Language authored by Baldwin made it into the Comprehensive Addiction and Recovery Act signed by President Barack Obama in 2016. However, Baldwin – along with Johnson and former Sen. Russ Feingold – took heat for failing to heed whistleblower complaints about a mushrooming opioid over-prescription scandal at the Veterans Affairs Medical Center in Tomah, Wisconsin. A strong supporter of Hillary Clinton in the 2016 Democratic presidential primary, Baldwin was reportedly among three dozen people considered for the vice presidential slot that eventually went to Virginia Sen. Tim Kaine.

In 2017, Baldwin received an assignment in the Senate Democratic leadership -- conference secretary. With a reelection campaign looming in 2018, Baldwin faced a balancing act between her party's drift to the left and her state's status as a linchpin of Donald Trump's presidential victory in 2016. She opposed more Trump nominees than most of the other Trump-state Democrats who are up for reelection in 2018. But back home, she began emphasizing more populist themes such as improving trade deals and lowering the cost of prescription drugs. In March 2016, Baldwin had an approval rating of 40% in the Marquette University Law School poll – up three points from the previous October and five points higher than her disapproval rating. She got a break when two of the highest-profile Republicans who could have run against her – Rep. Sean Duffy and Milwaukee Sheriff David Clarke – opted against entering the race, but Baldwin still faced a potentially long list of GOP challengers, including several state legislators.

FIRST DISTRICT

Paul Ryan (R)

Elected 1998, 10th term; b. Jan 29, 1970, Janesville; Miami University of Ohio, B.A., 1991; Roman Catholic; Married (Janna Little Ryan); 3 children.

Professional Career: Aide, U.S. Sen. Bob Kasten, 1992; Advisor & speechwriter, Empower America, 1993-1995; Legislative Director, U.S. Sen. Sam Brownback, 1995-1997; Marketing consultant, Ryan Inc., 1997-1998.

DC Office: 1233 LHOB 20515, 202-225-3031, Fax: 202-225-3393, paulryan.house.gov.

State Offices: Janesville, 608-752-4050; Kenosha, 262-654-1901; Racine, 262-637-0510.

Group Ratings

	ADA	ACLU	AFL-CIO	LCV	ITI	COC	HAFA	ACU	CFG	FRC
2016	-	0%	-	N/A	100%	-	-	0%	N/A	100%
2015	0%	C	11%	0%	C	94%	C	78%	73%	92%

Almanac Ratings 2015

	Economy	Social	Foreign	Composite
Liberal	11%	9%	10%	10%
Conservative	89%	91%	90%	90%

Key Votes of the 114th Congress

1. Keystone Pipeline	Y	5. Puerto Rico Debt	Y	9. Offenses by Aliens	Y
2. Trade Deals	Y	6. Medical Marijuana	N	10. Troops in Iraq	N
3. Export-Import Bank	N	7. Sanctuary Cities	Y	11. Homeland Security $$	Y
4. Debt Ceiling Increase	Y	8. Armor-piercing Bullets	Y	12. Trade Adjustment aid	Y

Election Results

Election	Name (Party)	Vote (%)		Cand. Spent	Ind. Exp. Support	Ind. Exp. Oppose
2016 General	Paul Ryan (R)	230,072	(65%)	$7,687,473	$50,001	$42,441
	Ryan Solen (D)	107,003	(30%)	$15,448		
	Jason LeBeck (L)	7,486	(2%)	$291		
2016 Primary	Paul Ryan (R)	57,391	(84%)			
	Paul Nehlen (R)	10,852	(16%)			

Prior winning percentages: 2014 (63%), 2012 (55%), 2010 (68%), 2008 (64%), 2006 (63%), 2004 (65%), 2002 (67%), 2000 (67%), 1998 (57%)

Paul Ryan, a Republican elected in 1998, became the reluctant Speaker in October 2015 after other Republicans tried and failed to win support after John Boehner announced his resignation, under pressure. During his career, Ryan has emphasized his policy chops. In the prior 10 months, he had chaired the powerful Ways and Means Committee, where his priorities were tax and international trade proposals. He already had served four years as chairman of the Budget Committee, where he was regarded as an intellectual leader in the GOP with unrivaled influence on fiscal matters. In 2012, he demonstrated the requisite political skills in his quick run as the GOP's vice presidential nominee. When he took over Ways and Means, he said that he would not run for president in 2016. "Our party has a responsibility to offer a real alternative," he said. "So I'm going to do what I can to lay out conservative solutions and to help our nominee lead us to victory." Both during and after the campaign, his relationship with Donald Trump had its ups and downs, as Ryan struggled to keep him focused on policy.

Ryan grew up in Janesville, where in 1884 his great-grandfather started a family construction firm, now run by his cousins. His father, a Republican lawyer, and former Democratic Sen. Russ Feingold's father had law offices in the same building, and the two sons were friends in Congress before Feingold's 2010 defeat. Ryan got started in politics early, as a staffer for Republican Sen. Bob Kasten while attending college at Miami University in Ohio. During summers, he was a salesman for Oscar Mayer and can boast that he once drove the company's incomparable Wienermobile. He planned to apply to the University of Chicago and eventually become an economist, but says he "just kept getting really interesting jobs" in politics.

Ryan was hired as a speechwriter for Republican Rep. Jack Kemp of New York and then worked for the think tank Empower America founded by Kemp and conservative writer William Bennett. He later was legislative director for GOP Sen. Sam Brownback of Kansas. In his days as a poorly paid congressional staffer, Ryan moonlighted as a waiter and fitness trainer. His father and grandfather both died of heart attacks in their 50s, making Ryan, the father of three young children, particularly mindful of a healthy diet and an exercise regimen.

In 1998, Ryan returned to the 1st District to run for the House when GOP Rep. Mark Neumann ran for the Senate (Neumann lost to Feingold). Ryan won the Republican primary with 81 percent of the vote. Democrats nominated Kenosha County official Lydia Spottswood, who had lost to Neumann in 1996. Ryan campaigned against tax increases and in favor of gun rights. In a district that liberal Democrat Les Aspin held for a quarter-century before he became Bill Clinton's first Defense secretary, this was a fiercely contested election, one of the Democrats' top 10 priorities in the nation that year. Spottswood spent $1.33 million, and Ryan spent $1.24 million. But the outcome was not close. Ryan won 57%-43%. He hasn't had a competitive challenge since.

Ryan has been a loyal conservative, especially when Barack Obama was president. Previously he had a reputation as someone who occasionally bucked his party and took centrist positions on foreign policy and some social issues. In 2007, he voted for a bill to prohibit employment discrimination on the basis of sexual orientation and later said he supported the bill because he had friends "who didn't choose to be gay … they were just created that way." He said he "took a lot of crap" for the vote from social conservatives. He also voted for the 2008 government bailout of the domestic auto industry, citing mounting hardships in his district because of factory layoffs.

Ryan was the top Republican on Budget for eight years. In 2007, he vaulted over 12 more senior Republicans on the committee. Like his political mentor, the late supply-sider Kemp, Ryan advocated tax cuts to spur economic growth but said his views have evolved to put equal weight on keeping deficits low and government growth in check. His beliefs drew widespread attention in 2009, when he began warning of future fiscal problems in dire terms. The debt, he told *The Washington Post*, was "completely unsustainable" and would "crash our economy." Democrats said such rhetoric came to typify Ryan's approach. Though they praised his affability, they accused him of overstating budgetary hazards and then refusing to accept any solutions other than his own. "It's very important not to mistake congeniality with compromise," then-Rep. Chris Van Hollen of Maryland, the ranking Democrat on Budget, told the *Los Angeles Times* in 2012.

In 2009, Ryan helped write the Republicans' alternative to Obama's first budget. He worked closely with Republican Conference Chairman Mike Pence of Indiana and Minority Whip Eric Cantor of Virginia, each of whom gained considerably more influence. They pushed Minority Leader John Boehner to include details about how the party would control spending and trim the deficit, but Boehner steered them away from specifics that could be picked apart by Democratic critics. The plan ultimately was panned in the press for lacking detail, and the effort was scrapped.

Undeterred, Ryan in 2010 produced a detailed "roadmap" to economic recovery as an alternative to the majority Democrats' budget, which he said was chock full of "reckless borrowing." His document called for a dramatically simpler tax code of two rates, 10 percent on annual income up to $100,000 for joint filers and 25 percent on income above that. Ryan's plan also called for breaking the link between employment and health insurance by switching from tax incentives for employer-provided insurance plans to tax credits for individual purchases of insurance. It would transform Medicare for Americans younger than 55 into a voucher or "premium support" system providing an average $11,000 for the purchase of government-approved policies. Most of the Republicans who won House seats in 2010, when the GOP scored a historic 63-seat gain, campaigned on Ryan's message of immediate and bold action on the deficit.

As Budget Committee chairman, Ryan pronounced himself highly disappointed with Obama's fiscal 2012 budget proposal, contending it did little to rein in spending over 10 years. Answering Democratic taunts that Republicans had no detailed response of their own, Ryan rolled out an alternative to much conservative fanfare. Titled "The Path to Prosperity," it called for freezing most domestic spending for five years and repealing the economic stimulus law in the course of cutting spending more than $6 trillion over 10 years, shrinking federal spending as a percentage of the economy to its lowest level since 1949.

The most immediately controversial feature of Ryan's budget was its plan for Medicare. As with his earlier "roadmap," individuals who turned 65 before 2022 would continue under the current program, while new seniors would get a government subsidy to buy private insurance. Many Democrats and some economic commentators sharply questioned the impact such cuts would have on the poor and middle class. In an April speech, Obama – in a bit of historic hyperbole -- said Ryan's approach would lead to a country that is "fundamentally different than what we've known throughout our history." Medicare was created in 1965. The House passed the budget in April, with 235 of the chamber's 239 Republicans backing it and every single Democrat opposing it.

Polls showed strong majorities of Americans opposed to the Medicare aspects of his budget. Democrats quickly began incorporating such sentiments into their effort to retake control of the House in 2012. Even some Republicans grew uneasy. Former Speaker Newt Gingrich, fresh from announcing his intention to run for president, called the budget "radical" in May and added, "I don't think right-wing social engineering is any more desirable than left-wing social engineering." Ryan responded to a conservative talk-radio host, "Hardly is that social engineering and radical. What's radical is kicking the can down the road."

In 2012, Ryan offered another budget plan that cut discretionary spending below the levels agreed upon by Congress in 2011. It would have overhauled Medicare and Medicaid and repealed the 2010 health care law signed by Obama. His budget squeaked out of committee and passed the full House, 228-191; it later failed in the Democratic-controlled Senate, 41-58, with five Republicans opposing the measure.

In what had been a swing district, Ryan has remained secure at home, without serious challenge. As his political stock rose, he was mentioned as a possible 2012 presidential candidate, but Ryan told numerous interviewers that he wasn't interested: "My head's not that big, and my kids are too small." Still, he emerged as a potential vice presidential pick during the summer of 2012. Prospective nominee Mitt Romney was also considering Ohio Sen. Rob Portman and Minnesota Gov. Tim Pawlenty. He selected Ryan, viewed by some political observers as the riskier choice given his views on the budget and his willingness to enact sweeping entitlement reforms. Romney and Ryan had a strong working rapport. Aides to Ryan said later that before he accepted the offer, he received assurances that he would play a central role on economic matters, as Vice President Dick Cheney did on national security during George W. Bush's presidency.

The selection of Ryan kicked off a debate about Medicare that hindered Republicans' desire to make the election a referendum on Obama's handling of the economy. The Romney-Ryan plan called for a new premium support plan beginning with new Medicare beneficiaries in 2023. Seniors would pick from private plans or could choose traditional Medicare, all of which would be offered on a new Medicare exchange. Democrats portrayed those efforts as intended to dismantle the social safety net, leading Ryan to respond that Obama "robbed Medicare" to pay for his health care law. Fact-checking sites such as *PolitFact.com* noted that, although Obama's health care law was slated to reduce the amount of future spending growth in Medicare, it did not actually cut Medicare (although Democrats deride the same kind of restraint as cuts when it serves their own purposes). The Obama campaign also pointed out that Ryan's own past budget plan had relied on the same $700 billion savings in Medicare.

Democrats portrayed Ryan as someone who couldn't be trusted to tell the truth. His address to the Republican National Convention fed that narrative. Ryan mentioned the shuttered General Motors auto plant in his hometown that he said Obama had promised to keep open; the plant had closed in December 2008, a month after the president was elected.

Despite the carping from Democrats, Ryan drew mostly positive marks for his spirited performance on the stump. Still, his presence on the ticket didn't enable Romney to win Wisconsin. Obama, who lived his adult life in neighboring Chicago, prevailed in Wisconsin by seven percentage points, which was half of his 56%-42% win there in 2008. Four years later, Donald Trump won Wisconsin by less than one point, a margin of 22,700 votes. Because he was already on the ballot for reelection to the House when Romney chose him, Ryan stayed in that race and defeated Democrat Rob Zerban, 55%-43%, which was his closest margin for the House.

Back in Washington in 2013, Ryan received a waiver from GOP term limits to continue as Budget chairman - a request that Boehner had denied to less prominent Republicans, though the Speaker has more authority to select the Budget chairman. In response to criticism that his earlier budgets took too long to get into balance, his fiscal 2014 proposal called for reaching that level within a decade, again through steep spending restraints. It passed the House on a 221-207 vote with no Democratic support.

Ryan later that year showed that he was willing and able to work with Democrats. He and Senate Democratic Budget Committee Chairman Patty Murray of Washington struck a two-year budget deal that called for raising new revenue through fee hikes, without tax increases or reforms to Social Security or Medicare. It deferred for two years across=the=board spending cuts under the looming "sequester" and replaced them with targeted cuts. Despite criticism from conservative groups such as the Club For Growth and Heritage Action, Ryan's clout helped it pass the House on a 332-94 vote, with 169 Republicans voting in favor.

Ryan's work on the budget deal, and his informal discussions in search of a deal to get an immigration overhaul through the chamber, sparked speculation that he might one day seek to become Speaker of the House. But Ryan told a San Antonio luncheon audience that he wasn't interested. "I could've decided to go on the elected leadership route years ago," he said. "I'm more of a policy person." He already had made clear his goal to take over Ways and Means after term limits forced Chairman Dave Camp of Michigan to step down in 2015.

In 2014, Ryan's visits to the crucial presidential states of Iowa and New Hampshire sparked renewed talk about his future. He said he hadn't made any decisions about 2016, though he reportedly told a group of donors at a private meeting in New York to "keep their powder dry" as he considered his options. As he prepared to take over the Ways and Means chairmanship, he decided that it wasn't worth entering a crowded GOP field. In any case, he would have other opportunities. And he kept the door open to seeking to influence the selection of the nominee, and perhaps working with another prospective Republican president. Ryan affirmed his considerable fundraising prowess by taking in $9.4 million during the 2013-14 cycle.

During that time, he touched off renewed partisan criticism when he said he was looking at overhauling poverty programs to address the "real culture problem ... of men not working." He said safety-net programs such as unemployment insurance were a "hammock that ends up lulling people in their lives into dependency and complacency." His anti-poverty plan, which called for giving states more autonomy to administer their own programs. "We don't want to have a poverty management system that simply perpetuates poverty," he said on NBC's *Meet the Press* in July 2014 "We want to get at the root causes of poverty." To receive so-called "opportunity grants" offering federal assistance, poor families would be required to work with government agencies, nonprofit or for-profit groups to develop "life plans" that would include time limits for receiving money and sanctions for not meeting goals. Democratic critics said while the plan offered some positive ideas, such as reforming mandatory sentences to reduce prison overcrowding and expanding the earned income tax credit, it amounted to a fresh repackaging of old conservative ideas.

As he took over Ways and Means in January 2015, Ryan signaled his strong desire to find agreement with Obama on a few potential areas, including tax reform, trade and infrastructure. He provoked Democrats when the committee approved routine extensions of tax breaks. "I think it goes counter to tax reform," Michigan's Sander Levin, the top Democrat on Ways and Means, told *The Hill*. "You're sending the wrong signal, that somehow you're going to do this piecemeal instead of sending the signal that, let's do something comprehensively." The few Democratic proponents of tax reform had been advocating a tax overhaul that would raise taxes on the highest earners.

It was Ryan, not Levin, with whom Obama worked on his administration's top legislative priority in 2015: Congressional approval in June of trade promotion authority, which was designed to open the door for "fast-track" congressional consideration of international trade deals that Obama and most Republicans saw as a spur to economic growth. Ryan worked for months, with little public attention, to craft the details of the trade legislation that would satisfy Obama and his aides, and to round up the mostly Republican votes needed to reach 218. Congress took no action on the Trans-Pacific Partnership that Obama had reached with Asian nations. Soon after he took office, Trump shelved the deal.

With action expected later in the year by Congress and Obama on a new budget framework, possibly including tax changes and a sweeping highway bill, Ryan found himself unexpectedly positioned as the "gate-keeper" for Obama's agenda, potentially "to burnish the president's legacy," as *The New York Times* described in February 2015. Then, in September, the unexpected resignation of Boehner forced Ryan to consider stepping away from his chairmanship to become Speaker. When Majority Leader Kevin McCarthy was unable to win support from 218 of the 247 Republicans at that time, the pressure on Ryan increased. He faced a politically risky move that would reshape his future: Whether to take the more powerful position of Speaker, though with independent GOP factions and the uncertainty of a presidential election a year later, or retain the more hands-on opportunity to shape legislation as a committee chairman.

At a moment that might come to be viewed in retrospect as the zenith of influence for the 45-year-old Ryan, he went for the brass ring. Conservative writer Matthew Continetti saw this as a seminal moment for Republicans and the takeover by a younger generation. "Ryan's election as Speaker would be the culmination of a long journey not only for him but also for his party. This journey began when he embraced the so-called third rail of American politics - reform of Social Security and Medicare - and refashioned it into the GOP platform," he wrote. "Liberals are terrified of what these young conservatives might accomplish. Liberals should be. We're approaching the end of phase one of the Ryan Revolution. Phase two? That's where it gets interesting."

Republican politics certainly grew more interesting, though not always in ways that Ryan, Continetti and their cadres had hoped. With the wide-open field for the party's presidential nomination in 2016, Ryan remained neutral and sought to encourage the broader debate and to shape the views of the eventual nominee. "We should not hide our disagreements - we should embrace them. We have nothing to fear from honest differences, honestly stated," he told the House when he accepted the gavel in October 2015. As would become clear a few months later, the younger proponents of fresh conservative thinking within the GOP fell short in the Republican primaries.

Instead, an older newcomer - Donald Trump -- prevailed, in many ways as the antithesis to Ryan. Trump's views were "a dagger aimed directly at Ryan's vision for the party," wrote *New York Times* columnist Ross Douthat. "On issue after issue, from trade to immigration to entitlement reform, a Trumpized party would simply bury [Ryan and his allies] under white identity politics." Even after Trump had effectively won the GOP nomination following the Indiana primary in early May 2016 and his opponents had ended their candidacy, Ryan was not ready to endorse the party standard-bearer. Instead, Ryan gently tried to re-shape Trump's "America first" views.

Over time, Ryan voiced qualified support for Trump, amid intermittent nasty Tweets from the presidential nominee about Ryan's hesitation and lack of enthusiasm. The Speaker shifted his focus to crafting and publicizing the House Republicans' agenda of "A Better Way." With ample fundraising and relentless campaigning for House GOP candidates in battleground districts, he placed his overriding attention on preserving their House majority - often, while seeking to ignore Trump.

The awkwardness played out in various ways. Ryan was a distant presence at the Republican convention in July, at which he nominally presided. At home, he faced a Republican primary challenge in August from little-known newcomer Paul Nehlen, who embraced Trump's views on policies such as immigration and trade and harshly attacked Ryan who, he said, "will thwart President Trump at every opportunity." Trump endorsed Ryan in the primary, after having Tweeted favorable comments about Nehlen. Ryan won, 84%-16%, which reinforced his independence. In early October, following the release of the decade-old Access Hollywood video that publicized Trump's lewd comments about groping women, Ryan told House Republicans in a conference call that he would no longer defend Trump or campaign with him, though he stood by his endorsement. Like many other Republicans, Ryan was expecting that Hillary Clinton would be elected president.

Trump's victory was accompanied by a loss of only six Republican seats in the House. Ryan moved quickly to planning for the presidential transition, including hosting Trump at the Capitol two days after the election. In the following months, the two sought to collaborate on identifying and gaining congressional support for key Republican initiatives, starting with replacement of the Affordable Care Act and an overhaul of the tax code. So long as things were going well, they spoke positively about each other even as each preserved some independence.

After Ryan postponed a House vote on health care in late March because of divisions among Republicans on what had been scheduled as the first major legislative test, that deadlock gradually turned to legislative compromises. When the House passed the revised bill by a bare majority in early May, Trump that afternoon hosted a celebration at the White House. By late spring, the legislative and electoral outcomes were more unclear than ever. If anything, the future of Ryan's Speakership seemed at least as much in doubt as the future of Trump's presidency.

Southeast Wisconsin: Janesville, Kenosha

Population		**Race and Ethnicity**		**Income**	
Total	714,836	White	81.3%	Median Income	$59,528 (148 out of 435)
Land area	1,728	Black	5.3%		
Pop/ sq mi	413.7	Latino	9.3%		
Born in state	67.4%	Asian	1.9%	Under $50,000	41.5%
		Two races	1.7%	$50,000-$99,999	33.8%
Age Groups		Other	0.4%	$100,000-$199,999	20.9%
Under 18	23.6%			$200,000 or more	3.7%
18-34	20.2%	**Education**		Poverty Rate	11.2%
35-64	42.0%	H.S grad or less	40.6%		
Over 64	14.1%	Some college	32.6%	**Health Insurance**	
		College Degree, 4 yr	17.8%	With health insurance coverage	92.2%
Work		Post grad	8.9%		
White Collar	34.4%				
Sales and Service	39.9%	**Military**		**Public Assistance**	
Blue Collar	25.6%	Veteran	8.8%	Cash public assistance income	2.8%
Government	4.3%	Active Duty	0.1%		
				Food stamp/SNAP benefits	12.6%

Voter Turnout			
2015 Total Citizens 18+	528,090	2016 House Turnout as % CVAP	67%
2016 House turnout	354,245	2014 House Turnout as % CVAP	55%

2012 Presidential Vote		
Mitt Romney	195,835	(52%)
Barack Obama	179,872	(47%)

2016 Presidential Vote		
Donald Trump	187,372	(52%)
Hillary Clinton	150,436	(42%)
Gary Johnson	12,926	(4%)

Cook Partisan Voting Index: R+5

The southern tier of Wisconsin, from Lake Michigan to the Rock River Valley, is some of America's prime industrial country. Settled by Yankee and German farmers 170 years ago, it was once primarily dairy land. By the early 20th century, the steady habits and high skills of the local dairy farmers had made them a good labor pool for factories. There are still major plants here, including the headquarters of S. C. Johnson in Racine, with its Frank Lloyd Wright–designed tower. But the collapse of the domestic auto industry had a powerful impact on the local economy. In December 2008, General Motors closed its Janesville plant, laying off more than 5,000 workers, and in 2010 Chrysler shuttered its Kenosha plant, which once employed 14,000. (The GM layoffs became a line of attack for 2012 GOP vice presidential nominee Paul Ryan, of Janesville, who slammed President Barack Obama for saying in 2008 that the plant would "be here for another hundred years.")

Local innovation remains alive. Kenosha, once primarily a factory town, has undergone a transformation, with some of the old smokestacks and shipyards along its lakefront replaced with museums, a marina, restaurants and boutiques that attract Chicagoans on weekends. Kenosha has competed with other towns in the region in trying to lure Chicago businesses north with lower tax rates. Most of the region is becoming metropolitan, part of the almost continuously suburban zone where metro Milwaukee melds into metro Chicago. In February 2017, REjournals.com, a website that covers commercial real estate in the Midwest, reported that much of the business growth in southeast Wisconsin has been in-state, rather than the "border-hopping" of the past. A month later, German candymaker Haribo announced plans for a $242 million plant in Pleasant Prairie to produce gummy bears, with 400 workers. Some old lake resorts continue to thrive, most notably on Lake Geneva, long a favorite weekend getaway for residents of Chicagoland. In nearby Williams Bay is the University of Chicago's historic Yerkes Observatory, one of the nation's largest astronomy research centers.

The 1st Congressional District of Wisconsin runs from Lake Michigan west to Janesville in Rock County and encompasses all of Racine and Kenosha counties on Lake Michigan as well as parts of Walworth County, including Lake Geneva. It also takes in the southern Milwaukee County suburbs of Oak Creek and Greenfield and the southern tier of townships in suburban Waukesha County, including New Berlin.

The district has been a competitive battleground. In 2008, Obama led, 51%-48%. Boosted a bit by Ryan's presence on the ticket, Mitt Romney in 2012 took the District, 52%-47%. Donald Trump doubled that margin, with his 52%-42% win in the 1st. Kenosha and Racine counties are the swing areas. They voted for Obama in 2012 by 13 and 3 percentage points, respectively, and then for Trump by 0.3 and 4 points, respectively. Waukesha County is heavily Republican. Rock County, where Janesville is located, gave Obama 61 percent of the vote in 2012. Four years later, Hillary Clinton won Rock with 52 percent. Though the overall change in four years was significant in the 1st, each of the four districts in the northern part of Wisconsin had a larger shift toward the GOP in 2016.

SECOND DISTRICT

Mark Pocan (D)

Elected 2012, 3rd term; b. Aug 14, 1964, Kenosha; University of Wisconsin - Madison, B.A., 1986; Married (Philip Frank).

Elected Office: Dane County Board of Supervisors, 1991-1996; WI Assembly, 1998-2012.

Professional Career: Owner, Budget Signs & Specialties, 1988-present; Public-relations specialist, WI Realtors Association, 1986-1988.

DC Office: 1421 LHOB 20515, 202-225-2906, Fax: 202-225-6942, pocan.house.gov.

State Offices: Beloit, 608-365-8001; Madison, 608-258-9800.

Committees: *Appropriations*: Agriculture, Rural Development, FDA & Related Agencies, Labor, Health & Human Services, Education & Related Agencies.

Group Ratings

	ADA	ACLU	AFL-CIO	LCV	ITI	COC	HAFA	ACU	CFG	FRC
2016	-	100%	-	100%	33%	50%	14%	0%	4%	0%
2015	100%	C	100%	97%	C	35%	C	8%	2%	0%

Almanac Ratings 2015

	Economy	Social	Foreign	Composite
Liberal	99%	100%	100%	99%
Conservative	2%	0%	0%	1%

Key Votes of the 114th Congress

1. Keystone Pipeline	N	5. Puerto Rico Debt	Y	9. Offenses by Aliens	N
2. Trade Deals	N	6. Medical Marijuana	Y	10. Troops in Iraq	Y
3. Export-Import Bank	Y	7. Sanctuary Cities	N	11. Homeland Security $$	Y
4. Debt Ceiling Increase	Y	8. Armor-piercing Bullets	N	12. Trade Adjustment aid	Y

Election Results

Election	Name (Party)	Vote (%)	Cand. Spent	Ind. Exp. Support	Ind. Exp. Oppose
2016 General	Mark Pocan (D)...........................	273,537 (69%)	$515,857	$2,119	
	Peter Theron (R)...........................	124,044 (31%)	$36,625		
2016 Primary	Mark Pocan (D)..	(100%)			

Prior winning percentages: 2014 (68%), 2012 (68%)

Democrat Mark Pocan, elected in 2012, is cut from the same political cloth as his predecessor, Tammy Baldwin, whom he also succeeded in the Wisconsin State Assembly. Like Baldwin, who was elected to the Senate, Pocan is openly gay, progressive and a Democrat. In the House, he took up many of Baldwin's issues, plus her outspoken advocacy.

Pocan was born and raised in Kenosha, the child of two small-business owners. His father ran a specialty print shop, and his mother owned a beauty-supply store. Pocan's father served on the Kenosha City Council, and as a kid Pocan campaigned with him and attended council meetings. At the University of Wisconsin, Pocan said, "I started out as a poli-sci major until I took my first poli-sci class that talked about the Ottoman Empire and not political campaigns. So I decided to switch" to journalism. He helped pay for college by working as a magician and tending bar.

After graduating, Pocan worked in public relations. Then, he followed in his father's footsteps and opened his own Madison-based print shop. Around that time, Pocan dealt with personal trauma. After leaving a gay bar one night, he was physically assaulted by two men and needed stitches. "I was not out to everyone, to friends, mostly. ... But that was kind of a turning point because after that happened, that's when I got very active with a number of LGBT nonprofits," he said. Since gay marriage was not legal in Wisconsin in 2006, Pocan married in Canada. He still dabbles as a magician for a hobby.

In 1991, Pocan won a seat on the Dane County Board of Supervisors. He later spent 14 years in the state Assembly. He landed a seat on the influential Joint Finance Committee and co-chaired the panel for two years. Pocan helped expand health care coverage for children and extend domestic-partner benefits for gay couples. In 2008, he coauthored the Compassionate Care for Rape Victims Act to ensure that hospitals provide information on emergency contraception to victims of sexual assault. *Milwaukee Magazine* named him "best legislator" in 2009.

In the acrimonious contest for Baldwin's House seat, Pocan's chief rival was Kelda Helen Roys, also a Madison-area state representative. Pocan had support from unions and much of the party establishment, plus a roughly 2-to-1 fundraising advantage. Roys attacked him for compromising with Republicans and for taking money from political action committees. She criticized his votes for two business tax-credit bills, describing them as Republican Gov. Scott Walker's "corporate tax giveaways." Pocan did not back away from his image as a strong progressive willing to work across the aisle. "There are those who scream and holler and put out a press release," he told the *Wisconsin State Journal*. "I decided I wanted to be the kind that gets things done." He tried to stay above the fray and emphasized his roots as a small businessman. Pocan won with 72 percent of the vote to Roys' 22 percent. In the general election, he got 68 percent against Chad Lee, a 29-year-old businessman.

Pocan has emphasized the need for bipartisanship, which is the only way that he can get much done in a Republican-controlled House. On the Education and the Workforce Committee, he introduced with Republican Rep. Luke Messer of Indiana a resolution to support continuation of the Perkins student loan program. He and conservative Republican Rep. Glenn Grothman of Wisconsin pursued steps to reduce student loan debt, including their bill to permit loan-holders to refinance at any time. His *Almanac* vote ratings for 2015 listed him among the top 3 percent of the most liberal House members. In January 2017, Pocan joined other gay House members in opposing the nomination of Betsy DeVos as Secretary of Education, accusing her of supporting anti-gay causes. Also that month, he joined the Appropriations Committee, where he pledged to "fight for middle-class families and those aspiring to be in the middle class."

Pocan pursued his liberal agenda as first vice chair of the Progressive Caucus. In 2015, he joined New York City Mayor Bill de Blasio and others to launch The Progressive Agenda to Combat Income Inequality, which Pocan said would "put meat on the bone of our progressive values." As a chair of the LGBT Equality Caucus, he drew attention to the problem of LGBT youth homelessness. He co-chaired the House Democrats' Labor Council.

Pocan has twice been reelected uneventfully against a perennial Republican challenger, and with no primary opposition.

South-Central Wisconsin: Madison

Population		**Race and Ethnicity**		**Income**	
Total	734,213	White	83.1%	Median Income	$59,229 (150 out of 435)
Land area	4,537	Black	4.2%		
Pop/ sq mi	161.8	Latino	6.2%		
Born in state	65.5%	Asian	3.9%	Under $50,000	42.5%
Age Groups		Two races	2.2%	$50,000-$99,999	33.0%
Under 18	22.1%	Other	0.3%	$100,000-$199,999	20.1%
18-34	26.2%	**Education**		$200,000 or more	4.4%
35-64	39.0%	H.S grad or less	31.5%	Poverty Rate	12.9%
Over 64	12.8%	Some college	29.2%	**Health Insurance**	
Work		College Degree, 4 yr	23.8%	With health insurance coverage	93.2%
White Collar	43.5%	Post grad	15.6%		
Sales and Service	38.1%	**Military**		**Public Assistance**	
Blue Collar	18.4%	Veteran	7.3%	Cash public assistance income	1.7%
Government	5.2%	Active Duty	0.0%	Food stamp/SNAP benefits	10.9%

Voter Turnout			
2015 Total Citizens 18+	544,781	2016 House Turnout as % CVAP	73%
2016 House turnout	398,060	2014 House Turnout as % CVAP	61%

2012 Presidential Vote		
Barack Obama	284,084	(68%)
Mitt Romney	126,688	(30%)

2016 Presidential Vote		
Hillary Clinton	271,507	(65%)
Donald Trump	119,608	(29%)
Gary Johnson	14,385	(3%)

Cook Partisan Voting Index: D+18

On a narrow isthmus between Lakes Mendota and Monona is the center of Madison, and in many ways, the center of Wisconsin. The state Capitol rises at one end of State Street, and at the other end is the main campus of the University of Wisconsin, in a beautiful, park-like setting above Lake Mendota. For most of the 20th century, Wisconsin politics was dominated by the Madison-based LaFollettes and their liberal Democratic successors. University faculty were devoted to Robert LaFollette's "Wisconsin idea" of a supposedly apolitical bureaucracy and to his Wisconsin Tax Commission and workmen's compensation law - both firsts in the nation and conceived of by the former governor and senator. Madison spawned an activist and sometimes violent student movement during the Vietnam War. A graduate student was killed in a laboratory by a bomb set off by a protester. Since then, the liberal campus opposed the welfare reform and school choice laws enacted while Republican Tommy Thompson was governor. The Madison community was the center of vocal opposition to Gov. Scott Walker's plan to end collective bargaining for most state workers and then led the unsuccessful recall effort to oust him in June 2012. The labor and student protests continued, with a renewed focus in early 2015 on right-to-work legislation. Walker took revenge of sorts with the July 2015 enactment of a plan for the state to wield more control over the university, including faculty hiring, through its Board of Regents. With that new structure in place and the end of Walker's presidential ambitions, a calm ensued after the 2016 election. The University president said that Walker's 2017 budget proposal for the campus was "the best … we've had in over a decade, and we need to be appreciative."

Madison is the center of Wisconsin's 2nd Congressional District, nearly half of which is urban and the remainder split between suburban and rural. It includes surrounding Dane County and dairy and alfalfa country to the north and south, as well as several rural dairy counties that have traditionally been Republican. It takes in the birthplace of the Ringling Brothers Circus in Baraboo, and the Swiss-settled town of New Glarus, known for the brewing company that makes Fat Squirrel and Spotted Cow beers. A local landmark disappeared in 2015 when the merger of Kraft and Heinz led to the shutdown of the Oscar Mayer meat headquarters and plant in Madison, after 96 years. Dodgeville, in Iowa County (not on the Iowa border), is the headquarters of Lands' End, the catalog retailer. Dane is about three-fourths of the district.

Madison remains economically vibrant. A sympathetic study in 2015 found that the university has an impact of $15 billion on the state's economy. The effect of reduced state funding on the campus was expected to take a few years to determine. The metropolitan area boasts one of the best-educated workforces in the country - 51 percent of residents hold a college degree and 17 percent have a graduate degree. The growth industries include health care (Madison is home to American Family Insurance) and biotechnology start-ups tied to the university.

In the 1990s, rural Dane County was open to Republicans like Thompson and Rep. Scott Klug. The rural areas have become bluer as Madison-area liberals move to the countryside, even as other parts of the state have become more crimson. The 2nd is a heavily Democratic district, though not quite as strong as the Milwaukee-based 4th District. In 2016, Hillary Clinton won 65%-29%, a slight dip from the 68%-30% win for President Barack Obama in 2012.

THIRD DISTRICT

Ron Kind (D)

Elected 1996, 11th term; b. Mar 16, 1963, La Crosse; Harvard University, Bach. Deg., 1985; London School of Economics (England), M.A., 1987; University of Minnesota, J.D., 1990; Lutheran; Married (Tawni Zappa Kind); 2 children.

Professional Career: Practicing attorney, 1990-1992; Assistant State Prosecutor, La Crosse County, 1992-1996.

DC Office: 1502 LHOB 20515, 202-225-5506, Fax: 202-225-5739, kind.house.gov.

State Offices: Eau Claire, 715-831-9214; La Crosse, 608-782-2558.

Committees: *Ways & Means*: Health, Trade.

Group Ratings

	ADA	ACLU	AFL-CIO	LCV	ITI	COC	HAFA	ACU	CFG	FRC
2016	-	94%	-	87%	83%	64%	10%	4%	7%	0%
2015	70%	C	78%	86%	C	58%	C	4%	1%	0%

Almanac Ratings 2015

	Economy	Social	Foreign	Composite
Liberal	75%	84%	80%	80%
Conservative	25%	16%	20%	20%

Key Votes of the 114th Congress

1. Keystone Pipeline	N	5. Puerto Rico Debt	Y	9. Offenses by Aliens	Y
2. Trade Deals	Y	6. Medical Marijuana	Y	10. Troops in Iraq	N
3. Export-Import Bank	Y	7. Sanctuary Cities	N	11. Homeland Security $$	Y
4. Debt Ceiling Increase	Y	8. Armor-piercing Bullets	Y	12. Trade Adjustment aid	Y

Election Results

Election	Name (Party)	Vote (%)	Cand. Spent	Ind. Exp. Support	Ind. Exp. Oppose
2016 General	Ron Kind (D)	257,401 (99%)	$1,110,052		
2016 Primary	Ron Kind (D)	33,283 (81%)			
	Myron Buchholz (D)	7,680 (19%)			

Prior winning percentages: 2014 (57%), 2012 (64%) 2010 (50%), 2008 (63%), 2006 (65%), 2004 (56%), 2002 (63%), 2000 (64%), 1998 (72%), 1996 (52%)

Ron Kind, a Democrat elected in 1996, is a moderate who focuses on health and agriculture issues and seeks bipartisanship on the Ways and Means Committee. In contrast to the dominant liberal core of Wisconsin Democrats, he has been chairman of the New Democrat Coalition, a business-oriented group that attempts to break through partisan gridlock. In 2015, he was the leading Democratic proponent in the bitter intra-party battle to give trade promotion authority to President Barack Obama. Though badly outnumbered, he appeared to survive that clash, both at home and in Washington.

Kind grew up in a large family in La Crosse, the son of a telephone repairman and a secretary in the local schools. He went to Harvard University on a scholarship and played quarterback. He was a summer intern for Democratic Sen. William Proxmire, doing research for Proxmire's Golden Fleece awards pointing out wasteful government spending. Kind attended the London School of Economics and the University of Minnesota's law school, practiced law in a large firm in Milwaukee, then returned home to La Crosse to work as an assistant prosecutor on rape and sexual abuse cases.

Kind ran for an open seat that had been Republican-held. Former state Sen. Jim Harsdorf won the Republican primary and made a case for a balanced budget and for Republican Gov. Tommy Thompson's "Wisconsin Works" welfare reform program. Kind presented his own balanced budget proposal and urged reform of campaign finance. Kind won, 52%-48%.

Early in his House career, Kind took an interest in improving the health of the upper Mississippi River, which is vital to the well-being of his district. He has worked to restore the river, combat invasive species and ensure that it remains a resource for recreation and transportation.

In the health care debate in 2009, he co-sponsored a bill to put greater emphasis on quality and coordination of care in reimbursing providers. He was dissatisfied with the version that Ways and Means approved and was one of three Democrats who joined committee Republicans in opposing it. After lengthy meetings that he and others held with Speaker Nancy Pelosi on containing the spiraling costs of Medicare, he agreed to support the legislation.

With dairy farming prominent in his district, Kind has been vitally interested in agriculture issues. In 2007, he joined with conservative deficit hawks and suburban and urban Democrats in an attempt to add provisions to the farm bill that would have limited subsidies and provided more funds for land conservation and school nutrition. "For too long, we've had large taxpayer subsidies going to a few very large farming entities to the disadvantage of family farmers," Kind said. He won 200 votes for similar provisions in the 2002 farm bill. This time around, Democratic leaders were worried about angering farmers' groups in rural swing districts and refused to allow a House vote. The plan died in committee. Kind voted against the final version of the farm bill, calling it a "nightmare." In 2012, he complained in a letter to colleagues that the GOP-written farm bill that passed the Agriculture Committee "takes us backward in terms of budget-busting crop subsidies, unlimited insurance subsidies, and trade-distorting programs." Despite the farm subsidies that flow to his district, he said that most producers he represents don't get huge agriculture subsidies because they're not large agribusinesses.

In 2013, Kind took over as head of the New Democrat Coalition. "We want to work hard to find that sensible center on policy and move the ball," he told *The Hill* newspaper. Following the Democrats' disastrous 2010 election performance, he refused to support Pelosi in her bid for minority leader in January 2011, casting his vote for Tennessee Democrat Jim Cooper, another moderate. He subsequently has backed Pelosi. He irked his party again as one of the 17 House Democrats to vote in favor of criminal contempt charges in 2012 against Attorney General Eric Holder in connection with the "Fast and Furious" gun-tracing operation.

On Obama's request in 2015 for trade promotion authority, which is essential in approving international trade deals, Kind quietly and methodically assembled Democratic support. He faced fierce opposition from labor unions and many of his Democratic colleagues in his advocacy of Obama's top legislative priority of the year. Working closely with home-state Ways and Means Chairman Paul Ryan and other GOP leaders, he preserved cohesion among the 28 depleted but still vital Democratic supporters of international trade engagement. *Roll Call* described Kind's role as "integral" - starting with guest speakers to discuss the framework months in advance at lunch meetings of the New Democrat Coalition and continuing with his whip check and one-on-one discussions with dozens of Democratic members who were potential supporters. He compared notes daily with White House officials. "Sometimes the phone rang and it was Obama himself," *Roll Call* reported. When President Donald Trump in January 2017 withdrew the United States from the proposed Trans-Pacific Partnership, Kind voiced concern that the move "will cost us jobs in Wisconsin."

At home, Kind in 2004 had his first credible challenger, Republican state Sen. Dale Schultz, a moderate in the Wisconsin legislature. Schultz ran with an unlikely Republican theme, criticizing Kind as a free trader who had sent jobs overseas. Kind affirmed his support for trade agreements, but he criticized the Bush administration for failing to enforce their labor and environmental protection terms. Kind won, 56%-43%. In 2010, another serious challenger emerged, Dan Kapanke, a Republican state senator who lambasted Kind for his support of the health care bill and Obama's economic agenda. Kind survived with a 50%-46% win. He has won comfortably since 2012 with redrawn district lines that are more favorable for him. In 2016, he was unopposed.

Kind has considered runs for statewide office, and could be a strong contender in a general election. He likely would face problems in a primary with a liberal from Milwaukee or Madison. In March 2017, he decided, "after much consideration," not to run for governor in 2018. In his Republican-trending district, he was among the early House GOP targets for the 2018 election.

West-Central Wisconsin: Eau Claire, La Crosse

Population		**Race and Ethnicity**		**Income**	
Total	716,980	White	92.5%	Median Income	$49,851 (258 out of 435)
Land area	11,112	Black	1.0%		
Pop/ sq mi	64.5	Latino	2.3%		
Born in state	71.8%	Asian	2.1%	Under $50,000	50.1%
Age Groups		Two races	1.4%	$50,000-$99,999	33.5%
Under 18	21.4%	Other	0.6%	$100,000-$199,999	14.2%
18-34	24.9%	**Education**		$200,000 or more	2.2%
35-64	38.0%	H.S grad or less	43.3%	Poverty Rate	14.2%
Over 64	15.7%	Some college	33.0%	**Health Insurance**	
Work		College Degree, 4 yr	15.6%	With health insurance coverage	91.6%
White Collar	31.2%	Post grad	8.1%		
Sales and Service	40.9%	**Military**		**Public Assistance**	
Blue Collar	27.9%	Veteran	9.5%	Cash public assistance income	2.0%
Government	6.4%	Active Duty	0.1%	Food stamp/SNAP benefits	12.0%

Voter Turnout			
2015 Total Citizens 18+	556,036	2016 House Turnout as % CVAP	47%
2016 House turnout	260,370	2014 House Turnout as % CVAP	50%

2012 Presidential Vote		
Barack Obama	199,188	(55%)
Mitt Romney	159,205	(44%)

2016 Presidential Vote		
Donald Trump	177,172	(49%)
Hillary Clinton	160,999	(44%)
Gary Johnson	14,511	(4%)

Cook Partisan Voting Index: EVEN

On the rolling land of western Wisconsin, in the knobby hills just east of the Mississippi River, is some of the most beautiful river landscape in the country. This is where author Laura Ingalls Wilder's family built their little house in the big woods in the 1870s, before the first railroad came steaming up the narrow floodplain alongside the Mississippi River. Today, it is hard to imagine the big woods. The trees have long since been cut down, and the hillsides are covered with grass grazed by placid dairy cattle. Where the pioneers tried to scratch out diversified crops, later generations of farmers created America's premier dairy region, producing milk, butter and cheese. Some Amish communities from Pennsylvania have relocated here in recent years because land is cheaper than in the East. But since 1980, the dairy economy here has been in flux. Numerous dairy farmers have gone out of business. Wisconsin also has had trouble competing against the European Union's subsidized cheese and butter, and more recently, with products from California's large-scale agribusiness. Cows have become more productive, and demand for milk has decreased. In the 1980s, many communities here lost population, but there has been some growth since then. Eau Claire County's population surpassed 100,000 in 2012.

The 3rd Congressional District of Wisconsin follows the Mississippi from the border with Illinois north to Dunn County, covering the southern half of the western edge of the state. The district's two largest cities are La Crosse and Eau Claire, home to home-improvement giant Menards. Both cities have won recognition for their livability. The district now stretches east to Democratic-leaning Portage County and Stevens Point, where the lakes, streams and trails make the area a recreational hotspot.

Settled largely by German and Scandinavian immigrants, the region once consistently voted for Wisconsin's LaFollette Progressives and its voters cannot be taken for granted. In recent years, the district leaned Democratic at the presidential level. Western Wisconsin was one of the few segments of rural America where President Barack Obama in 2012 ran even with historic Democratic percentages, which was vital to his statewide victory. Still, Obama carried the district with 55 percent of the vote, compared to his 2008 performance of 59 percent. This area was a bulwark for Republican Gov. Scott Walker in his 2010 election and June 2012 recall, when he won every county in the district except La Crosse. That shift continued in 2016. Donald Trump won the district, 49%-44% -- a 15 percentage point drop for the Democrats in eight years. Eau Claire, LaCrosse and Portage Counties all voted for Hillary Clinton, but narrowly. The rural counties went heavily for Trump.

FOURTH DISTRICT

Gwen Moore (D)

Elected 2004, 7th term; b. Apr 18, 1951, Racine; Marquette University (WI), B.A., 1978; Milwaukee Area Technical College (WI), Att., 1983; Harvard University, Att., 2000; Baptist; Single3 children; 3 grandchildren.

Elected Office: WI Assembly, 1989-1992; WI Senate, 1992-2004, President pro tem, 1997-1998.

Professional Career: Housing & urban dev. specialist, 1985-1989.

DC Office: 2252 RHOB 20515, 202-225-4572, Fax: 202-225-8135, gwenmoore.house.gov.

State Offices: Milwaukee, 414-297-1140.

Committees: *Financial Services*: Financial Institutions & Consumer Credit, Monetary Policy & Trade (RMM), Oversight & Investigations. *Joint Security & Cooperation in Europe.*

Group Ratings

	ADA	ACLU	AFL-CIO	LCV	ITI	COC	HAFA	ACU	CFG	FRC
2016	-	100%	-	97%	60%	54%	14%	4%	5%	0%
2015	100%	C	96%	91%	C	45%	C	0%	0%	0%

Almanac Ratings 2015

	Economy	Social	Foreign	Composite
Liberal	98%	100%	99%	99%
Conservative	2%	0%	1%	1%

Key Votes of the 114th Congress

1. Keystone Pipeline	N	5. Puerto Rico Debt	Y	9. Offenses by Aliens	N
2. Trade Deals	N	6. Medical Marijuana	Y	10. Troops in Iraq	Y
3. Export-Import Bank	Y	7. Sanctuary Cities	N	11. Homeland Security $$	Y
4. Debt Ceiling Increase	Y	8. Armor-piercing Bullets	N	12. Trade Adjustment aid	Y

Election Results

Election	Name (Party)	Vote (%)		Cand. Spent	Ind. Exp. Support	Ind. Exp. Oppose
2016 General	Gwen Moore (D)	220,181	(77%)	$837,599	$36,266	
	Robert Raymond (I)	33,494	(12%)			
	Andy Craig (L)	32,183	(11%)	$2,427		
2016 Primary	Gwen Moore (D)	55,093	(85%)			
	Gary George (D)	10,000	(15%)			

Prior winning percentages: 2014 (70%), 2012 (72%), 2010 (69%), 2008 (88%), 2006 (71%), 2004 (70%)

Gwen Moore, a Democrat elected in 2004, is Wisconsin's first African-American member of Congress. A former welfare recipient, she often recounts her struggles -- in spirited and candid detail -- of standing up for the poor, homeless and victims of domestic violence. On a larger stage, she has expanded her horizons to raise questions about the management of the World Bank.

Moore was born in Racine, the eighth of nine children, and raised on the North Side of Milwaukee. As an 18-year-old college freshman, she became a single mother who relied on welfare to help support her daughter. She graduated from Marquette University and worked as a housing and urban development specialist. Moore said she got active in politics when a rent-to-own center repossessed her washer and dryer even though she had paid three times their value in interest. She led an effort to establish a community credit union. Elected to the state Assembly in 1989 and the Senate in 1992, she was the state's first black woman senator. In 1990, she defeated Republican Scott Walker, the only election defeat for the future governor of Wisconsin.

In 2003, when blue-collar Democratic Rep. Gerald Kleczka announced that he was retiring, Moore was the front-runner. She was challenged in the primary by two political veterans, state Sen. Tim Carpenter and former state Democratic Chairman Matt Flynn, both white. The candidates agreed on most issues: All three supported abortion rights, focused on jobs and economic concerns, and called for eliminating the Bush administration's tax cuts for people with incomes exceeding $200,000 a year. Moore took advantage of the energized black voter base, and she leveraged financial support from liberal women's organizations, teachers' unions, and other progressive groups. Flynn was endorsed by Kleczka. But he was damaged politically by his work as general counsel for the local Roman Catholic archdiocese in a priest sex abuse scandal. Carpenter was the only openly gay member of the Senate and had the support of national gay rights groups. Moore won 64 percent of the vote to 25 percent for Flynn and 10 percent for Carpenter. In the general election, Moore won easily, 70%-28%.

Moore has a staunchly liberal voting record, with *Almanac* vote ratings in 2015 that listed her in the top 5 percent of House liberals. She often is hyperbolic in her criticism of Republican policies. She said in 2012 that a Wisconsin voter ID law "does nothing but attempt to return us to an era of Jim Crow politics." When House Republicans sought to defund Planned Parenthood during the 2011 budget debate, Moore drew on her own unwelcome experience of an unplanned pregnancy at age 18. "I just want to tell you a little bit about what it's like to not have Planned Parenthood," she said on the House floor. "You have to add water to the formula to make it stretch. You have to give your kids Ramen noodles at the end of the month to fill up their little bellies so they won't cry. You have to give them mayonnaise sandwiches." In 2017, she became whip for the Congressional Black Caucus.

She has introduced legislation to increase spending on school lunch programs, crackdown on foreclosure fraud, and boost grants to crime-ravaged communities. In 2005, the House incorporated provisions of her Shield Act into the reauthorization of the Violence Against Women Act, to protect the identity of domestic-violence victims who receive homeless assistance. When the law came up in 2012, Moore stunned House colleagues by taking to the floor to graphically recount how a group of young men once discussed having sex with her. "The appointed boy, when he saw that I wasn't going to be so willing, completed a date rape and then took my underwear to display it to the rest of the boys. I mean, this is what American women are facing," she said.

As ranking member of the Financial Services Subcommittee on Monetary Policy and Trade, Moore has taken an interest in the World Bank and International Monetary Fund. In April 2016, she wrote to the Bank that she was "increasingly uneasy" with its funding and promotion of water privatization through public-private partnerships. She cited the catastrophic consequences of the water supply crisis in Flint, Michigan, and raised concerns about discussions of water privatization in Wisconsin.

Since Walker's emergence as one of the nation's most polarizing governors and then a presidential candidate, Moore has been among his most vocal critics. She accused him of eliminating a women's cancer screening program in 2012 "for political gain," an assertion that the website *PolitiFact* called "false and ridiculous." On the *Colbert Report* in 2013, she criticized Walker for having thrown many groups "under the bus." But at a 2011 Oversight and Government Reform hearing at which he appeared, Moore said that she considers Walker a friend. "I'm crazy about his kids and his wife," she said. "But I'm not going to spend my five minutes pretending we agree on anything."

Moore harshly criticized Donald Trump's views of women when she spoke to the Democratic convention in Philadelphia. She was more temperate when the CBC met with President Trump at the White House in March 2017. "It was important to sort of just clear the air," she said. "I don't think that our communities would be served well by our not engaging."

Moore remains firmly entrenched in her district. In 2014 and 2016, former state Sen. Gary George challenged her in the Democratic primary and criticized her failure to use the "bully pulpit" to address crime and economic issues. George failed to raise the $5,000 required to file a campaign-finance report. Moore won with 71 percent and 84 percent of the vote, respectively.

Milwaukee

Population		**Race and Ethnicity**		**Income**	
Total	716,353	White	43.3%	Median Income	$39,329 (401 out of 435)
Land area	128	Black	33.6%		
Pop/ sq mi	5581.2	Latino	16.4%		
Born in state	65.8%	Asian	3.5%	Under $50,000	59.8%
		Two races	2.6%	$50,000-$99,999	27.1%
Age Groups		Other	0.6%	$100,000-$199,999	10.9%
Under 18	25.8%			$200,000 or more	2.2%
18-34	27.9%	**Education**		Poverty Rate	25.7%
35-64	35.7%	H.S grad or less	44.3%		
Over 64	10.6%	Some college	28.9%	**Health Insurance**	
		College Degree, 4 yr	17.2%	With health insurance coverage	87.7%
Work		Post grad	9.6%		
White Collar	33.1%				
Sales and Service	45.1%	**Military**		**Public Assistance**	
Blue Collar	21.8%	Veteran	6.2%	Cash public assistance income	4.0%
Government	3.4%	Active Duty	0.0%		
				Food stamp/SNAP benefits	27.2%

Voter Turnout			
2015 Total Citizens 18+	493,162	2016 House Turnout as % CVAP	58%
2016 House turnout	286,909	2014 House Turnout as % CVAP	51%

2012 Presidential Vote		
Barack Obama	268,440	(75%)
Mitt Romney	84,751	(24%)

2016 Presidential Vote		
Hillary Clinton	228,226	(73%)
Donald Trump	67,287	(22%)
Gary Johnson	8,501	(3%)

Cook Partisan Voting Index: D+25

Milwaukee is America's most German city, with an ethnic heritage noticeable not just in the names of its beers and its old German restaurants, but in the sturdiness of its houses and the orderliness of its streets. Until World War I inflamed sensitivities to all things German, the language was spoken on the streets and read in city newspapers; German beer was produced in dozens of breweries. A huge four-sided clock, nearly twice the size of London's Big Ben, rises above the Allen-Bradley factory, looking out over the industrial city. It is an apt symbol, a piece of precision engineering in this high-skill manufacturing town, with its skyline of smokestacks and church steeples - the closest thing in America to the German factory cities that inspired Milwaukee's early citizens. The city has led the nation in beer brewing, industrial control equipment, mining gear, cranes and independent foundries.

Like other Rust Belt cities, downtown Milwaukee has seen major changes in the past few decades - with recent signs of an uptick. During the past three decades, many of the plants in Milwaukee shut down. It hemorrhaged population, with a drop from 740,000 in 1960 to 595,000 in 2010. The city has stopped shrinking, thanks to its rapidly expanding Hispanic population. For the most part, the city has embraced Latinos. Many Hispanics have settled in the old immigrant neighborhoods of the city's South Side. The West Side and North Side are home to many of the city's African-American neighborhoods, such as Sherman Park and Bronzeville. From 2010 to 2015, the city grew by 1 percent.

That population growth has been followed by a downtown "building boom," the Milwaukee *Journal-Sentinel* reported in March 2017. The newspaper listed a $524 million arena for the NBA Milwaukee Bucks that is scheduled to open in 2018, Northwestern Mutual's office tower and apartment high-rise, the BMO Harris Financial Center office tower, the conversion of the Warner Grand Theater into the Milwaukee Symphony Orchestra's performance hall and a $50 million Westin Hotel. Led by MillerCoors, the brewing industry continues to employ more than 7,000 in Milwaukee. The city is focusing on becoming a global hub for water technology and research, with the University of Wisconsin-Milwaukee opening the first graduate school in the nation dedicated solely to the study of freshwater.

The 4th District of Wisconsin covers the entire city of Milwaukee and a few of its working-class suburbs - St. Francis, Cudahy and South Milwaukee on Lake Michigan, and West Milwaukee and part of West Allis. It includes to the north tonier suburbs along the lake, many with sizable Jewish populations - Shorewood, Whitefish Bay and Fox Point. These communities are politically competitive and closely attuned to state politics. Before he was elected governor, Republican Scott Walker served two terms as Milwaukee County Executive. But he drew only 36 percent of the county vote when he was reelected in 2014. About 30 percent of Milwaukee County voters reside in parts of three Republican-held districts in Wisconsin. In the 4th, blacks make up 33 percent of the population, while Hispanics comprise another 17 percent. It is easily Wisconsin's most Democratic district, with Hillary Clinton getting 73 percent of the vote here in 2016, close to the 75 percent for President Barack Obama in 2012. As the *Journal-Sentinel* reported following the election, the big difference was that turnout in Milwaukee County dropped by 50,000 voters in four years. That reduced Clinton's lead in the county by 27,000 votes. She lost statewide by fewer than 23,000 votes.

FIFTH DISTRICT

Jim Sensenbrenner (R)

Elected 1978, 20th term; b. Jun 14, 1943, Chicago, IL; Milwaukee County Day School (WI), 1961; Stanford University (CA), B.A., 1965; University of Wisconsin Law School, J.D., 1968; Roman Catholic; Married (Cheryl Warren Sensenbrenner); 2 children.

Elected Office: WI Assembly, 1968-1974; WI Senate, 1974-1978.
Professional Career: Staff Assistant, U.S. Rep. Arthur Younger, 1965; Practicing attorney, 1968-1969.

DC Office: 2449 RHOB 20515, 202-225-5101, Fax: 202-225-3190, sensenbrenner.house.gov.

State Offices: Brookfield, 262-784-1111.

Committees: *Foreign Affairs*: Africa, Global Health, Global Human Rights & Internat'l Orgs, Europe, Eurasia & Emerging Threats. *Judiciary*: Crime, Terrorism, Homeland Security & Investigations, Immigration & Border Security (Chmn).

Group Ratings

	ADA	ACLU	AFL-CIO	LCV	ITI	COC	HAFA	ACU	CFG	FRC
2016	-	17%	-	0%	100%	86%	83%	100%	90%	100%
2015	5%	C	8%	6%	C	75%	C	96%	90%	92%

Almanac Ratings 2015

	Economy	Social	Foreign	Composite
Liberal	11%	9%	13%	11%
Conservative	89%	91%	87%	89%

Key Votes of the 114th Congress

1. Keystone Pipeline	Y	5. Puerto Rico Debt	Y	9. Offenses by Aliens	Y
2. Trade Deals	Y	6. Medical Marijuana	Y	10. Troops in Iraq	Y
3. Export-Import Bank	N	7. Sanctuary Cities	Y	11. Homeland Security $$	N
4. Debt Ceiling Increase	N	8. Armor-piercing Bullets	Y	12. Trade Adjustment aid	N

Election Results

Election	Name (Party)	Vote (%)	Cand. Spent	Ind. Exp. Support	Ind. Exp. Oppose
2016 General	Jim Sensenbrenner (R)................	260,706 (67%)	$290,071		
	Khary Penebaker (D)....................	114,477 (29%)	$73,296		
	John Arndt (L)...............................	15,324 (4%)			
2016 Primary	Jim Sensenbrenner (R).............	(100%)			

Prior winning percentages: 2014 (70%), 2012 (68%), 2010 (69%), 2008 (80%), 2006 (62%), 2004 (67%), 2002 (86%), 2000 (74%), 1998 (91%), 1996 (74%), 1994 (100%), 1992 (70%), 1990 (100%), 1988 (75%), 1986 (78%), 1984 (73%), 1982 (100%), 1980 (78%), 1978 (61%)

Republican Jim Sensenbrenner, first elected in 1978, is a forceful conservative whose prickly personality has rankled liberals even as he has racked up many impressive legislative accomplishments. He is the second most-senior Republican, and one of only three House members who served before the election of Ronald Reagan. As something of an elder statesman in the House, he offers useful historical memory plus savvy in how to get things done. That has made him a useful adviser to Speaker Paul Ryan; their districts share Waukesha County.

Sensenbrenner was born in Chicago and grew up in the Milwaukee area, with strong Wisconsin roots. His great-grandfather was a founder of Kimberly-Clark, which invented the sanitary napkin, and Sensenbrenner is an heir to the paper and cellulose fortune. He graduated from Stanford University and the University of Wisconsin Law School, and has spent most of his adult life in politics. He served briefly as a staffer in the House, then was elected to the Wisconsin Assembly in 1968 and to the Senate in 1974. (His son, Bob, has been general counsel of the House Administration Committee.) When Republican Rep. Bob Kasten ran for governor, Sensenbrenner won the Republican primary by 589 votes. He was elected in November with 61 percent of the vote, which was the lowest vote of his career. His net worth exceeds $20 million, according to the Center for Responsive Politics. As an example of how the rich get richer, he won $250,000 in the District of Columbia lottery after buying two tickets at a Capitol Hill liquor store.

Sensenbrenner's pugnaciousness has endeared him to conservatives. *Human Events* named him as its man of the year in 2006. His legislative skills have earned him respect on Capitol Hill. He was one of the first to urge that Congress apply to itself the same laws it imposes on the rest of the country. Despite his conservatism, he occasionally opposes his party on principle. In 2003, he said he saw no need to amend the Constitution to ban same-sex marriages. He was one of 17 House Republicans to vote against a 2012 amendment to bar the Obama administration from using taxpayer funds to defend its health care law in court. That independence helps to explain why his 2015 *Almanac* vote ratings were toward the center of the House and the least conservative of the five Republicans from Wisconsin.

He chaired the Judiciary Committee starting in 2001, where he is best known for his work after the September 11 attacks. He pressed for a thorough congressional review of Attorney General John Ashcroft's proposal for beefed-up investigative powers for law enforcement. Concerned about possible violations of civil liberties, he insisted on a sunset provision for the USA Patriot Act, the anti-terrorism law passed after the attacks on New York and Washington, ensuring it would expire in four years and giving Congress a chance to study its impact.

By 2005, he decided that his concerns about civil liberties had been addressed and he pushed to make most of the law permanent. After a difficult conference committee with the Senate, he won an extension of the law for the Bush administration. Sensenbrenner had differences with Attorney General Alberto Gonzales over the scope of the domestic surveillance program and demanded steps to protect "the freedoms we cherish." Sensenbrenner presciently pushed for a permanent extension of the law's so-called "lone wolf" provision allowing the government to monitor terrorists even if they are not suspected of ties to a specific group.

In 2015, he was instrumental in reducing the sweep of the Patriot Act, which had become unpopular with both tea party conservatives suspicious of government and civil libertarians. Following revelations of the National Security Agency's bulk collection of data, Sensenbrenner authored what became known as the USA Freedom Act, a bipartisan, bicameral and comprehensive measure that put an end to collection of meta-data, increased the transparency of the Foreign Intelligence Surveillance Court and found a new balance between national security and privacy. "Sensenbrenner could savor the kind of victory that doesn't come along too often in a polarized, party-line political world," the Milwaukee *Journal Sentinel* wrote after the bill was enacted. "[President Obama and I] both realized there was a problem that had to be fixed. And we worked together to fix it," he recounted. When Republican

Sen. Marco Rubio of Florida later said that it was a mistake to end meta-data collection, Sensenbrenner responded that he was "wrong" and that the data did not prevent a single terrorist attack.

Sensenbrenner worked steadily for years on some bills. Bankruptcy reform was enacted in 2005 after being held up for years by a Democratic provision preventing abortion protesters from filing for bankruptcy to avoid fines and damages in attacks on abortion clinics. He has backed limitations in tort law on class action, medical malpractice and asbestos liability, and has sought to increase penalties for frivolous lawsuits. He was instrumental in passing a congressional authorization of the Department of Justice, citing the vital role that it gave the Judiciary Committee in improving oversight of the department. He was instrumental in enacting in 2003 the Child Abduction Prevention Act, which enhanced the AMBER Alert system. One of his final actions as chairman was the bipartisan extension of the Voting Rights Act. With liberal Democratic Rep. John Conyers of Michigan, he has begun to explore ways to reform the criminal justice system - including, as he has said, "changing the way evidence is collected and analyzed, defending innocent Americans against a bloated criminal code, and protecting citizens' property rights."

With immigration, he successfully added to the 2004 intelligence reorganization bill provisions setting national standards for driver's licenses that denied licenses to illegal immigrants, prohibited the use of Mexican *matricula consular* cards for identification, tightened standards for asylum, and overrode state laws and regulations blocking border barriers. He was skeptical of bipartisan Senate passage in 2013 of a comprehensive immigration reform bill, saying, "extending amnesty to those who came here illegally or overstayed their visas is dangerous waters." He now chairs the Judiciary Subcommittee on Crime, Terrorism, Homeland Security and Investigations. He wants to use money forfeited by drug traffickers for increased security on the border, perhaps for a wall.

After the House Republicans' six-year term limit for senior committee members forced Sensenbrenner to give up the top slot on Judiciary in 2007, Minority Leader John Boehner named him the ranking Republican on the Select Committee on Energy Independence and Global Warming, which Speaker Nancy Pelosi had created to accommodate environmentalists. A skeptic of alarmist predictions about global warming, Sensenbrenner had voted against creation of the panel, saying it was nothing more than a publicity stunt, but he promised to participate in the debate. As chairman of the Science, Space, and Technology Committee in the late 1990s, he attacked the conclusions of some climate scientists. He sought to regain that chairmanship in 2013, but lost out to Lamar Smith of Texas.

Sensenbrenner has been reelected easily every two years. In 2009, he announced his plans for reelection at the same time he revealed that he had prostate cancer. He prided himself on not missing votes, scheduling his cancer treatments around the House schedule and keeping his customary schedule of town meetings in his district. In early 2017, he was among the few House Republicans who vigorously continued to hold frequent constituent meetings in the face of liberal protests of President Donald Trump.

Sensenbrenner has had reservations about Trump. "I'm not confident Trump will do the right thing, but I am confident Hillary Clinton will always do the wrong thing," he told the *Journal-Sentinel* before the Wisconsin primary. That news story added, "Sensenbrenner says he doesn't view Trump as a conservative, disapproves of his language and tone, and fears a GOP disaster in November." He was wrong on at least one point.

Western Milwaukee Suburbs, Waukesha

Population		**Race and Ethnicity**		**Income**	
Total	717,385	White	88.5%	Median Income	$64,701 (98 out of 435)
Land area	1,891	Black	1.9%		
Pop/ sq mi	379.4	Latino	5.5%	Under $50,000	38.4%
Born in state	76.6%	Asian	2.5%	$50,000-$99,999	34.1%
		Two races	1.4%	$100,000-$199,999	22.3%
Age Groups		Other	0.3%	$200,000 or more	5.3%
Under 18	22.1%			Poverty Rate	7.8%
18-34	20.7%	**Education**			
35-64	41.5%	H.S grad or less	34.0%	**Health Insurance**	
Over 64	15.7%	Some college	30.9%	With health insurance coverage	94.6%
		College Degree, 4 yr	23.8%		
Work		Post grad	11.3%		
White Collar	39.2%			**Public Assistance**	
Sales and Service	39.3%	**Military**		Cash public assistance income	1.5%
Blue Collar	21.5%	Veteran	8.1%		
Government	4.2%	Active Duty	0.0%	Food stamp/SNAP benefits	8.0%

Voter Turnout			
2015 Total Citizens 18+	543,287	2016 House Turnout as % CVAP	72%
2016 House turnout	390,844	2014 House Turnout as % CVAP	61%

2012 Presidential Vote		
Mitt Romney	257,017	(61%)
Barack Obama	158,226	(38%)

2016 Presidential Vote		
Donald Trump	229,325	(57%)
Hillary Clinton	148,900	(37%)
Gary Johnson	15,756	(4%)

Cook Partisan Voting Index: R+13

For decades, the orderly, heavily German-American factory city of Milwaukee has been spreading slowly, mostly west and north, into Wisconsin dairy country. There are high-income enclaves here, such as close-in Elm Grove and exurban Oconomowoc, halfway to Madison and tucked in around numerous lakes. There is office development in Brookfield, and subdivisions have spread to Menomonee Falls and farther, reaching small towns with roots in the 19th century. This is comfortable but not fancy territory, and the economy is still based heavily on skilled manufacturing. Not far from Milwaukee are West Bend, with West Bend kitchen appliances; and Pewaukee, with Harken sailboat hardware. Harley-Davidson began manufacturing on the city's West Side a century ago and has a payroll of about 1,000 employees who manufacture engines at the plant, now in Menomonee Falls. In September 2015, GE announced plans to shut down its engine plant and shift its 350 employees to Canada in 2018. The company blamed congressional uncertainty over the future of the Export-Import Bank. House Speaker Paul Ryan, who represents the southern part of Waukesha and opposed the Ex-Im as "corporate welfare," criticized the move and said that GE officials were not telling the whole story about their decision.

The 5th Congressional District of Wisconsin includes most of the western and northwestern suburbs of Milwaukee, spanning the Milwaukee County suburbs of Wauwatosa, Greenfield and West Allis; the northern half of Waukesha County, including New Berlin; and Jefferson County farther west. To the north, it includes all of Washington County and part of Dodge County. Nearly half the population is in Waukesha. This has been the most Republican district in the state, and voters here tend to be better-off than Republicans elsewhere in Wisconsin. The median household income is nearly $67,000, the highest of any district in the state, even the well-educated, Madison-based 2nd District.

Waukesha County, more than three-fourths of which is in the district, is the conservative core of the state, providing the grassroots energy that fueled Gov. Scott Walker's victory during the June 2012 recall campaign. Waukesha gave Walker 72 percent of the vote in the recall and reported the second highest countywide turnout in the state. Donald Trump, for his part, under-performed in Waukesha. His victory margin in the county was 63,000 votes with 61 percent of the vote, compared with Mitt Romney's 84,000-vote lead and 67 percent in 2012 - even though Trump won and Romney lost statewide. In the

April primary, Ted Cruz led Trump in Waukesha, 61%-22%. Overall, the District voted 57 percent for Trump in November, which was virtually the same as his share in the 6th, 7th and 8th Districts. Romney, by contrast, took 61 percent in the 5th, which was roughly 10 percentage points higher than his performance in those three other GOP-leaning districts. Turnout in November 2016 was a few thousand votes less than in 2012.

SIXTH DISTRICT

Glenn Grothman (R)

Elected 2014, 2nd term; b. Jul 03, 1955, Milwaukee; University of Wisconsin - Madison; b.B.A., 1977; University of Wisconsin Law School, J.D., 1983; Lutheran; Single (Growth Muhn).

Elected Office: WI Assembly, 1994-2004; Assistant Minority Leader, WI Senate, 2012-2013; Assistant Majority Leader, WI Senate 2013; WI Senate, 2004-2014.

Professional Career: Attorney.

DC Office: 1217 LHOB 20515, 202-225-2476, Fax: 202-225-2356, grothman.house.gov.

State Offices: Fond du Lac, 920-907-0624.

Committees: *Budget. Education & the Workforce*: Higher Education & Workforce Development, Workforce Protections. *Oversight & Government Reform*: Health Care, Benefits & Administrative Rules, Intergovernmental Affairs.

Group Ratings

	ADA	ACLU	AFL-CIO	LCV	ITI	COC	HAFA	ACU	CFG	FRC
2016	-	11%	-	0%	100%	100%	74%	100%	93%	91%
2015	0%	C	8%	0%	C	80%	C	88%	90%	92%

Almanac Ratings 2015

	Economy	Social	Foreign	Composite
Liberal	2%	9%	8%	6%
Conservative	99%	91%	92%	94%

Key Votes of the 114th Congress

1. Keystone Pipeline	Y	5. Puerto Rico Debt	Y	9. Offenses by Aliens	Y
2. Trade Deals	Y	6. Medical Marijuana	Y	10. Troops in Iraq	N
3. Export-Import Bank	N	7. Sanctuary Cities	Y	11. Homeland Security $$	N
4. Debt Ceiling Increase	N	8. Armor-piercing Bullets	Y	12. Trade Adjustment aid	Y

Election Results

Election	Name (Party)	Vote (%)		Cand. Spent	Ind. Exp. Support	Ind. Exp. Oppose
2016 General	Glenn Grothman (R)	204,147	(57%)	$1,027,145		
	Sarah Lloyd (D)	133,072	(37%)	$182,501		
	Jeff Dahlke (I)	19,716	(6%)	$38,010		
2016 Primary	Glenn Grothman (R)		(100%)			

Prior winning percentages: 2014 (57%)

Republican Glenn Grothman, elected in 2014, is a staunch conservative who had a lengthy record of provocative comments that raised national GOP concerns during the campaign. After taking office, he was relatively mainstream and seemed to settle in with Wisconsin's influential Republicans.

Born in Milwaukee, Grothman earned his bachelor's and law degrees from the University of Wisconsin. He won a special election to the Wisconsin Assembly in 1993, then easily took the GOP nomination for a Senate seat in 2004, arguing that the incumbent was insufficiently conservative. He became assistant Republican leader in 2009, and was a vocal supporter of GOP Gov. Scott Walker's budget and policy changes.

In 2014, Grothman said that he would challenge the moderate, low-profile Rep. Tom Petri. After 35 years in the House, Petri decided to retire in the face of what likely would have been a competitive contest. In the closest congressional race in Wisconsin since 1970, Grothman won the primary over state Sen. Joe Leibham by 219 votes, with 36 percent each. State Rep. Duey Stroebel finished third with 25 percent. Leibham declined to ask for a recount. The primary results showed unusual disparities. Grothman led Liebham nearly 4-to-1 in Ozaukee County and 3-to-2 in Fond du Lac. Liebham led 2-to-1 in Sheboygan and 5-to-1 in Manitowoc. Strobel won two small counties in the western part of the district.

Grothman was a dream candidate for opposition researchers. In the legislature, he supported Walker's decision to repeal the state's Equal Pay Enforcement Act, saying that "you could argue that money is more important for men." He introduced a bill that would have required a state board to list single parenthood as a contributor to child abuse. Grothman proposed an unsuccessful amendment to delete language prohibiting sex-education teachers from displaying "bias" against gay and lesbian students. He told *The Capital Times* that when he was in high school, "Homosexuality was not on anybody's radar. And that's a good thing." Grothman opposed Martin Luther King Day as a public holiday and called the promotion of Kwanzaa "deplorable," urging people to "treat Kwanzaa with the contempt it deserves before it becomes a permanent part of our culture." He described welfare programs as "a bribe not to work that hard or a bribe not to marry someone with a full-time job."

Both Grothman and Winnebago County Executive Mark Harris, the Democratic nominee, argued that the other was too extreme for the district. Harris said Grothman was weak on "women's issues," while Grothman in a fundraising email labeled Harris a "far-left politician." Harris cast himself as being more like Petri - a "thoughtful, quiet moderate." Grothman had demographics and money on his side. Grothman spent $1.2 million, more than four times as much as Harris. Neither national party showed much interest in this contest. Grothman won 57%-41% - four percentage points better than Mitt Romney in 2012. He took nine of the 11 counties; Harris narrowly won Columbia and Winnebago.

Grothman attracted little attention in the House and kept busy with work on his committees: Budget, Education and the Workforce, and Oversight and Government Reform. After his first two months, the Milwaukee *Journal Sentinel* reported, "we've hardly heard a word from him." He occasionally made provocative statements, but nothing sufficient to get him in trouble. During a TV interview in Milwaukee days before the Wisconsin presidential primary in April 2016, Grothman suggested that the state's new voter ID laws might reduce turnout by Democrats and increase the prospect that Republicans might win the presidential election in November. "Photo ID is going to make a little bit of a difference," he said. Martha Laning, the head of Wisconsin's Democratic Party responded that Grothman was accidentally telling the truth. "He might as well have said Republicans are working to rig elections to win," Laning said. The unexpected defeat of Hillary Clinton in November showed that Democrats had larger problems in Wisconsin.

Grothman's candor extended to his dismissive comments about Donald Trump during the Wisconsin presidential primary. "You look at the way he behaves. If your 8-year-old child behaved that way, you'd wonder if there was something wrong with them," said Grothman, who had endorsed Ted Cruz. "So, he is not a human being who I think we want to emulate."

Grothman had an uneventful reelection. Despite his tight primary when he was first elected, no Republican challenged him in 2016. Democratic nominee Sarah Lloyd was a dairy farmer who was on leave from a job at the Wisconsin Farmers Union. She had served on the Columbia County Board for four years and was a member of the state's Milk Marketing Board for six years. That rural background apparently did not strike a chord in this working-class district. Grothman, who spent $1 million on the campaign to $184,000 for Lloyd, won 57%-41%, nearly the same as his victory in 2014.

East-Central Wisconsin: Oshkosh, Sheboygan

Population		**Race and Ethnicity**		**Income**	
Total	711,964	White	90.2%	Median Income	$54,218 (195 out of 435)
Land area	4,918	Black	1.5%		
Pop/ sq mi	144.8	Latino	4.2%		
Born in state	79.1%	Asian	2.3%	Under $50,000	45.7%
		Two races	1.3%	$50,000-$99,999	35.0%
Age Groups		Other	0.4%	$100,000-$199,999	16.2%
Under 18	21.8%			$200,000 or more	3.2%
18-34	20.7%	**Education**		Poverty Rate	9.8%
35-64	41.2%	H.S grad or less	44.3%		
Over 64	16.3%	Some college	30.9%	**Health Insurance**	
		College Degree, 4 yr	17.1%	With health insurance coverage	93.5%
Work		Post grad	7.7%		
White Collar	31.0%				
Sales and Service	39.1%	**Military**		**Public Assistance**	
Blue Collar	30.0%	Veteran	9.2%	Cash public assistance income	1.9%
Government	4.9%	Active Duty	0.1%		
				Food stamp/SNAP benefits	10.5%

Voter Turnout			
2015 Total Citizens 18+	545,825	2016 House Turnout as % CVAP	65%
2016 House turnout	357,183	2014 House Turnout as % CVAP	55%

2012 Presidential Vote		
Mitt Romney	202,979	(53%)
Barack Obama	174,988	(46%)

2016 Presidential Vote		
Donald Trump	203,433	(55%)
Hillary Clinton	141,917	(38%)
Gary Johnson	14,291	(4%)

Cook Partisan Voting Index: R+8

Central Wisconsin is a producer of basic commodities - milk, butter, cheese, Kleenex, Mercury Marine outboard motors and military trucks. This is where the rolling hills and prairies of southern Wisconsin begin to give way to the pine and hardwood forests and glacial lakes of the Northwoods. First settled by Yankee Protestants, the 1850s brought the first large surge of German migration into the United States, and central Wisconsin was a favorite destination. They built the dairy farms and factory towns that seemed steadfastly prosperous, and they developed a manufacturing economy. Central Wisconsin was one of the birthplaces of the Republican Party, when a group of Whigs, Free Soilers and anti-slavery Democrats met in February 1854 in a small white schoolhouse in Ripon and proclaimed themselves Republicans. (A similar gathering took place in Jackson, Michigan, which also claims to be the birthplace of the party.) The party grew rapidly, winning a near majority in the House in that year's elections.

The German influence is still felt. Sheboygan is the Bratwurst Capital of the World. Johnsonville Foods, which began as a small family-owned company in 1945, employs more than 1,600 workers, sells more sausage than any of its national competitors and remains privately owned. New immigrant groups recently have moved into Sheboygan. The city and surrounding county are home to more than 6,300 Hispanics and 6,000 Asians, mostly Hmong. Sheboygan, which hosts an annual Hmong summer festival, is the site of the Lao, Hmong and American Veterans Memorial, which was dedicated in 2010 "to recognize and to honor the people who served and who died for the U.S. secret war." In March 2017, more than 500 protesters successfully lobbied against a proposal to toughen Sheboygan's immigration enforcement. Oshkosh is no longer the place where children's clothing maker Oshkosh B'Gosh manufactures its products. It is home to the Oshkosh Corp., which produces everything from dump trucks to military vehicles, including a $6.7 billion contract to build a new Joint Light Tactical Vehicle for the Army.

The 6th Congressional District is a slice of central Wisconsin from Lake Michigan to the Wisconsin River. It takes in the conservative, northern Milwaukee suburbs in Ozaukee County, including Port

Washington, and less than 1 percent of Milwaukee County. It includes Oshkosh-based Winnebago, the largest city and county in the district; Sheboygan and Manitowoc on Lake Michigan; and Fond du Lac on the south shore of Lake Winnebago. The district includes four rural counties plus the Wisconsin Dells and its giant water park, a longtime vacation destination for city dwellers in Milwaukee and Chicago. Overall, the district has been Republican territory since that first meeting in Ripon. As with the 7th and 8th Districts to the north, Donald Trump's victory margin in the 6th was at least 10 percentage points greater than Mitt Romney's victory in 2012. That pattern is all the more noteworthy, given that Barack Obama won each of the three districts in 2008.

SEVENTH DISTRICT

Sean Duffy (R)

Elected 2010, 4th term; b. Oct 03, 1971, Hayward; St. Mary's University (MN), Bach. Deg., 1994; William Mitchell College of Law (MN), J.D., 1999; Roman Catholic; Married (Rachel Campos-Duffy); 8 children.

Elected Office: District Attorney, Ashland County, 2002-2010.

Professional Career: Practicing attorney, 1999-2000; Special prosecutor, Ashland County, 2000-2002.

DC Office: 2330 RHOB 20515, 202-225-3365, duffy.house.gov.

State Offices: Hudson, 715-808-8160; Wausau, 715-298-9344.

Committees: *Financial Services*: Capital Markets, Securities & Investment, Housing & Insurance (Chmn).

Group Ratings

	ADA	ACLU	AFL-CIO	LCV	ITI	COC	HAFA	ACU	CFG	FRC
2016	-	11%	-	3%	100%	100%	67%	73%	53%	100%
2015	0%	C	8%	0%	C	75%	C	79%	86%	100%

Almanac Ratings 2015

	Economy	Social	Foreign	Composite
Liberal	2%	4%	0%	2%
Conservative	99%	96%	100%	98%

Key Votes of the 114th Congress

1. Keystone Pipeline	Y	5. Puerto Rico Debt	Y	9. Offenses by Aliens	Y
2. Trade Deals	Y	6. Medical Marijuana	N	10. Troops in Iraq	N
3. Export-Import Bank	N	7. Sanctuary Cities	Y	11. Homeland Security $$	N
4. Debt Ceiling Increase	N	8. Armor-piercing Bullets	Y	12. Trade Adjustment aid	N

Election Results

Election	Name (Party)	Vote (%)	Cand. Spent	Ind. Exp. Support	Ind. Exp. Oppose
2016 General	Sean Duffy (R)	223,418 (62%)	$1,930,755		$128,528
	Mary Hoeft (D)	138,643 (38%)	$113,774		
2016 Primary	Sean Duffy (R)	29,421 (90%)			
	Donald Raihala (R)	3,465 (11%)			

Prior winning percentages: 2014 (59%), 2012 (56%), 2010 (52%)

When Republican Sean Duffy in 2010 succeeded retiring Democratic stalwart David Obey, the House Appropriations Committee chairman, it was a stunning turnaround for the district. The telegenic Duffy, a former prosecutor, has largely avoided intra-party conflicts and tended to his work on the Financial Services Committee. With his friend Paul Ryan as Speaker, Duffy gained influence in a House that looked more like him.

Duffy hails from the thickly forested northern area of the state, the 10th of 11 children. He became adept at the local craft of lumberjacking, eventually earning multiple world-champion titles in the 60-foot and 90-foot pole speed climb. At St. Mary's College in Minnesota, he got his degree in business marketing. On a lark after graduation, Duffy joined the cast of MTV's *The Real World: Boston.* The program brought young people with diverse backgrounds together to live as roommates. Duffy was cast as the conservative in the show. He met his future wife, Rachel Campos-Duffy, a Latina who had been cast as the conservative foil in the *Real World* season taped in San Francisco. She later made many appearances on "The View," the syndicated talk show and wrote a book in 2009, *Stay Home, Stay Happy: 10 Secrets to Loving At-Home Motherhood,* which she calls "a love letter to at-home moms." The couple has eight children.

Duffy got a law degree from William Mitchell College of Law in St. Paul. He returned to Wisconsin to work briefly for his family's law firm. Appointed as Ashland County district attorney, he boasted a 90 percent success rate in jury trials and prosecuting child sex offenders. He resigned to challenge Obey in 2010. Obey unexpectedly announced that he would not seek reelection after more than four decades as a powerful Washington insider, removing a target for Duffy and his conservative message in the anti-incumbent climate. Instead, Duffy faced a young Washington outsider like himself, Democratic state Sen. Julie Lassa.

In his campaign, Duffy made an issue of the $787 billion economic stimulus bill that Obey had initially crafted. He was adept at raising money, and he ran as an unabashedly family-values and small-government conservative. Lassa accused Duffy of supporting deep cuts in entitlement spending after he embraced Paul Ryan's budget plan. She campaigned as a champion of the middle class but had difficulty connecting with voters, giving stump speeches that relied heavily on notes. Duffy was at ease and even charming in a crowd. He won, 52%-44%.

Duffy has backed his party on big votes, especially on fiscal issues, but has been independent on constituent matters. He refused to join most other tea party-backed freshmen in voting to end subsidies to rural airports and to defund National Public Radio, which maintains a strong audience in some rural areas. He talked up conservative themes. In January 2016, Duffy clashed on the House floor with Democratic Rep. Gwen Moore of Wisconsin, when he criticized the large number of abortions by black women. "Black lives matter," he said. "All those lives matter. We should fight for all life, including the life of the unborn." Moore responded, "It's painfully obvious that Rep. Duffy's concern for life ends as soon as the umbilical cord is cut."

On the Financial Services Committee, he chaired the Oversight and Investigations Subcommittee for two years. With committee Chairman Jeb Hensarling of Texas, he investigated a leak of market-sensitive information from the Federal Open Market Committee of the Federal Reserve. At a July 2015 hearing, he accused Fed Chairwoman Janet Yellen of hiding documents that the committee had subpoenaed. She replied that she could not jeopardize a criminal investigation. Duffy held hearings on allegations of discrimination and retaliation by managers of the Consumer Financial Protection Bureau against the agency's employees. At a September 2016 hearing with a State Department witness, Duffy demanded details of the Obama administration's cash payments to Iran during the nuclear deal a year earlier. In April 2017, as chairman of the Housing and Insurance Subcommittee, he released a draft of a bipartisan proposal for greater oversight and transparency on international insurance standards.

At home, Duffy gained attention when he tried to show empathy with an economically struggling constituent at a 2011 town hall meeting. When the man pointed out that Duffy's salary was "three times what I make," Duffy responded, "If you think I'm living high off the hog, I've got one paycheck. ... I struggle to meet my bills right now." Democrats pounced on the comment, contending that it illustrated how out of touch Duffy was, and launched aggressive attempts to unseat him.

Pat Kreitlow, a former Democratic state senator, spent $1.3 million in his 2012 challenge. Duffy drew on the financial industry's largesse and spent twice that amount. Each national party spent more than $2 million for its candidate. Duffy won, 56%-44%. In 2014, Duffy faced Kelly Westlund, a 30-year-old liberal activist who served on the city council in Ashland and spent $527,000. Duffy increased his win to 59%-39%, carrying every county except Douglas. Democrats' opposition faded and they turned their attention elsewhere. In 2016, Democratic challenger Mary Hoeft, a retired professor of communications arts at the University of Wisconsin, attacked Duffy's alliance with Donald Trump. A union-backed Super PAC spent $129,000 against Duffy, which was a bit more than Hoeft spent on her campaign. Duffy won, 62%-38%.

Duffy opened the door to additional political options. He was an early and consistent supporter of Trump, joined his wife as a featured speaker at the Republican National Convention and served on the executive committee for Trump's presidential transition. In February 2017, he turned down the opportunity to challenge Democratic Sen. Tammy Baldwin in 2018. "This is not the right time for me to run for Senate," Duffy said, leaving the door open to a possible run in 2022 when GOP Sen. Ron Johnson has said he will not seek reelection.

North-Central Wisconsin: Wausau

Population		**Race and Ethnicity**		**Income**	
Total	709,686	White	92.2%	Median Income	$49,512 (262 out of 435)
Land area	23,037	Black	0.7%		
Pop/ sq mi	30.8	Latino	2.1%		
Born in state	67.6%	Asian	1.5%	Under $50,000	50.4%
		Two races	1.5%	$50,000-$99,999	33.6%
Age Groups		Other	1.9%	$100,000-$199,999	13.7%
Under 18	22.3%			$200,000 or more	2.3%
18-34	18.1%	**Education**		Poverty Rate	11.7%
35-64	41.6%	H.S grad or less	45.8%		
Over 64	18.0%	Some college	32.6%	**Health Insurance**	
		College Degree, 4 yr	14.5%	With health insurance coverage	91.1%
Work		Post grad	7.0%		
White Collar	30.9%				
Sales and Service	39.3%	**Military**		**Public Assistance**	
Blue Collar	29.8%	Veteran	10.6%	Cash public assistance income	2.0%
Government	7.5%	Active Duty	0.1%		
				Food stamp/SNAP benefits	12.0%

Voter Turnout			
2015 Total Citizens 18+	545,149	2016 House Turnout as % CVAP	66%
2016 House turnout	362,271	2014 House Turnout as % CVAP	52%

2012 Presidential Vote		
Mitt Romney	190,364	(51%)
Barack Obama	178,841	(48%)

2016 Presidential Vote		
Donald Trump	213,467	(57%)
Hillary Clinton	137,874	(37%)
Gary Johnson	12,613	(3%)

Cook Partisan Voting Index: R+8

In the late 19th century, thousands of migrants traveled the rail lines radiating northwest from Chicago and Milwaukee to settle the northern reaches of Wisconsin, the most thickly settled land this far north in the United States and east of the Mississippi. What attracted them was not cropland - there are no large wheat farms as in the Red River Valley of North Dakota - but trees, iron and cows. This was one of America's largest virgin timberlands, and the river towns are still dotted with paper mills. Farther north, iron brought Finns and Italians to the port of Superior, across the St. Louis Bay from Duluth, Minnesota, and to smaller towns on the chilly lake. Nearby Apostle Islands National Lakeshore has eight lighthouses and breeding grounds for 240 species of birds that migrate through the archipelago. The cleared forest lands became dairy farms. Dairy cattle, properly cared for, thrived in these northern uplands, and the sons of Wisconsin dairymen, many of them immigrants from Germany and Norway, moved their herds even farther north toward Canada. Small cities grew, and some became home to big enterprises.

Those long-standing industries have encountered tough times. In Wausau, the city's eponymous paper industry has shrunk, as has household income in surrounding Marathon County. In 2011, Wausau Paper Corp. closed its mill in Brokaw, shedding 450 jobs. The company was purchased in 2015 by Sweden-based SCA, which had other paper mills in the United States but no plans to resume operations in Wausau. The number of dairy farmers in the region is in sharp decline as the economics of their business have become less attractive. Prices have been low, as national consumption of milk has decreased for more than a decade. Cheese and butter consumption remained high, but those products are more costly to produce. Dairy farmers complained that the threats by President Donald Trump against undocumented immigrant workers jeopardized their workforce. Some farmers have turned to potatoes, vegetables, cranberries and even ginseng. Wausau, which the 1980 census found to be the most ethnically homogeneous city in the nation, now has a sizeable immigrant community. Many Hmong refugees moved there in the 1980s; as of 2010, 11percent of the city's population was Asian.

This region makes up Wisconsin's 7th Congressional District. Its 21 counties stretch more than 200 miles from Lake Superior in the north to part of Monroe County, next to La Crosse. Commuter-oriented St. Croix County, part of the Minneapolis-St. Paul metro area, was the fastest-growing county in Wisconsin from 2000 to 2010, with its population now 88,000. In northern Iron County, a resource firm abandoned in 2015 a downsized proposal for an open-pit mine in an area rich with iron ore. Environmentalists and Native American tribes had fought the plan. Other developers reportedly were exploring opportunities.

The politics of the 7th District have a rough-hewn quality, a lumberjack-populist flavor. Ancestrally Republican, the area favored the progressivism of Wisconsin's LaFollettes. Superior-based Douglas County has been the chief Democratic outpost, while Marathon, St. Croix and many of the smaller counties have leaned Republican. Barack Obama carried the new boundaries, 53%-45%, 2008. There has been a remarkable transformation since then. Mitt Romney won the District with 51 percent of the vote. In 2016, Donald Trump's 57%-37% put the 7th in a tie with the 5th for his best district in the state. Douglas and two small neighboring counties, Bayfield and Ashland, were the only ones that supported Hillary Clinton.

EIGHTH DISTRICT

Mike Gallagher (R)

Elected 2016, 1st term; b. Mar 03, 1984, Green Bay; Princeton University Woodrow Wilson School of Public and International Affairs (NJ), B.A., 2006; National Intelligence University (DC), M.S., 2010; Georgetown University (DC), M.A., 2012; Georgetown University (DC), M.A., 2013; Georgetown University (DC), Ph.D., 2015; Catholic; Single.

Military Career: U.S Marine Corps (Iraq), 2006-2013.

Professional Career: Staff, United States Senate Foreign Relations Committee, 2013-2016; Foreign Policy Advisor.

DC Office: 1007 LHOB 20515, 202-225-5665, Fax: 202-225-5729, gallagher.house.gov.

State Offices: Appleton, 920-903-9806; Green Bay, 920-301-4500.

Committees: *Armed Services*: Readiness, Seapower & Projection Forces. *Homeland Security*: Counterterrorism & Intelligence, Cybersecurity & Infrastructure Protection.

Election Results

Election	Name (Party)	Vote (%)		Cand. Spent	Ind. Exp. Support	Ind. Exp. Oppose
2016 General	Mike Gallagher (R)	227,892	(63%)	$2,708,699	$76,556	$565,383
	Tom Nelson (D)	135,682	(37%)	$1,818,156	$59,877	$1,681,139
2016 Primary	Mike Gallagher (R)	40,150	(74%)			
	Frank Lasee (R)	10,683	(20%)			
	Terry McNulty (R)	3,103	(6%)			

Republican Mike Gallagher was elected in 2016 to an open seat in a district that has switched party control seven times since 1975. A former Marine captain who worked in top-level intelligence circles, he is the first newly elected local representative in that time who succeeded a member of his own party. Gallagher, who won impressively in what was expected to be a close contest, might have been bolstered by Donald Trump's coattails.

Gallagher was born in Green Bay. He moved with his mother to Costa Mesa, California, after his parents divorced when he was a toddler, though he spent summers with his father in Green Bay. He got his bachelor's from Princeton's Woodrow Wilson School of Public and International Affairs and joined the Marine Corps the day he graduated. He served seven years on active duty as a human intelligence and counterintelligence officer, and as a regional affairs officer for the Middle East and North Africa. During that time, he learned to speak Arabic, served on General David Petraeus's Central Command Assessment Team in the Middle East and spent three years working in the intelligence community. During two tours in Iraq, he was deployed to Anbar Province and attempted to work with local Iraqis to identify both opportunities for action and threats to the safety of his Marine battalion. He later questioned the U.S.

decisions both to invade Iraq and to remove troops from the region after it was pacified. "I do think it was an analytical failure and an intelligence failure," he told the Milwaukee *Journal-Sentinel*. "The fact that we won the war and lost the peace I think is shameful."

Gallagher got a master's degree in strategic intelligence from the National Intelligence University, and another master's followed by a Ph.D in government from Georgetown University. After he left the Marines, Gallagher was the Republican aide for the Middle East, North Africa and counterterrorism on the Senate Foreign Relations Committee and later was the national security adviser for the presidential campaign of Wisconsin Gov. Scott Walker. He spent time in the private sector as the senior global market strategist at Breakthrough Fuel, a Green Bay-based energy and supply chain management company.

In the contest for the open seat after three-term GOP Rep. Reid Ribble retired, Gallagher won the Republican primary with 75 percent of the vote against Frank Lasee, a two-term state senator, who got 20 percent. Democratic nominee Tom Nelson, the Outagamie county executive and a former state legislator, was a prime recruit for his party. Nelson said that the limited time Gallagher had lived in Wisconsin combined with his support for international trade agreements showed that he was out of touch with local voters. Each candidate ran attack ads about his opponent's positions on taxes and Social Security. Fact-checking organizations pointed out that each side was not always truthful.

The contest was a high-dollar affair. Gallagher out-spent Nelson, $2.7 million to $1.8 million. Gallagher also had an advantage in support from party organizations, $1.8 million to $600,000. During the summer, the Democratic Congressional Campaign Committee said that it would spend $750,000 on behalf of Nelson. As Nelson slipped in the polls, the DCCC trimmed that support to $268,000. Gallagher's unexpectedly wide 63%-37% win was part of a strong Republican performance in rural and small-town Wisconsin. He took 61 percent in Brown County, 59 percent in Nelson's base of Outagamie and more than two-thirds of the vote in most of the smaller counties.

Gallagher got seats on the Armed Services and Homeland Security committees. A month after he took office, he hosted Republican Rep. Rob Wittman of Virginia at a tour of the Marinette Marine Shipyard, a Pentagon contractor and a vital employer in his district; Wittman chaired the Seapower and Projection Forces Subcommittee, to which Gallagher was assigned.

Northeast Wisconsin: Green Bay, Appleton

Population		**Race and Ethnicity**		**Income**	
Total	720,700	White	87.8%	Median Income	$54,446 (190 out of 435)
Land area	6,807	Black	1.2%		
Pop/ sq mi	105.9	Latino	4.8%		
Born in state	78.3%	Asian	2.2%	Under $50,000	45.6%
		Two races	1.6%	$50,000-$99,999	35.3%
Age Groups		Other	2.3%	$100,000-$199,999	16.4%
Under 18	23.4%			$200,000 or more	2.8%
18-34	20.6%	**Education**		Poverty Rate	10.4%
35-64	41.0%	H.S grad or less	44.2%		
Over 64	15.0%	Some college	31.3%	**Health Insurance**	
		College Degree, 4 yr	17.4%	With health insurance coverage	92.9%
Work		Post grad	7.1%		
White Collar	31.5%				
Sales and Service	39.6%	**Military**		**Public Assistance**	
Blue Collar	28.9%	Veteran	9.3%	Cash public assistance income	1.9%
Government	5.2%	Active Duty	0.0%		
				Food stamp/SNAP benefits	10.4%

Voter Turnout			
2015 Total Citizens 18+	537,991	2016 House Turnout as % CVAP	68%
2016 House turnout	363,780	2014 House Turnout as % CVAP	54%

2012 Presidential Vote		
Mitt Romney	191,127	(51%)
Barack Obama	177,346	(48%)

2016 Presidential Vote		
Donald Trump	207,620	(56%)
Hillary Clinton	142,677	(38%)
Gary Johnson	13,691	(4%)

Cook Partisan Voting Index: R+7

In 1673, the French Catholic missionary and explorer Jacques Marquette sailed from the open waters of Lake Michigan into what is now the expansive Green Bay. He had hoped to find the Northwest Passage to the Pacific. Instead, he found the Fox River, which leads to Lake Winnebago and, after a not-too-difficult portage, the Wisconsin River, which flows into the Mississippi. Green Bay and the Fox River Valley remained mostly wilderness and Indian country for more than 150 years. But once settled by Europeans, they became, as Father Marquette would have liked, one of the most heavily Catholic parts of the United States. The area thrived economically, with paper mills, a busy port, and high-skill manufacturing in Green Bay and Appleton. The port economy rebounded from the recession with double-digit annual percentage increases in domestic cargo. In Marinette County, located on the bay, the Marinette Marine shipyard has spurred an economic boomlet with a multibillion dollar Navy contract to build new littoral combat ships by 2030, with a workforce of about 2,000; the contract for the 11th LCS was awarded in 2016.

No reference to Green Bay is complete without a mention of professional football's Packers, the locally beloved franchise owned by 361,000 shareholders and unlikely ever to move. Under the team's charter, if the Packers are sold, the proceeds would go to the local Sullivan-Wallen American Legion Post 11 "for the purposes of erecting a proper soldier's memorial." (The proceeds might be enough to rebuild the city!) Individual shares cannot be traded and they pay no dividend. The city, by far the smallest with an NFL franchise, has earned the nickname "Titletown" for the Packers' numerous championships, including the 2011 Super Bowl. Thirty miles south is Appleton, which has produced famous, and infamous, Americans: novelist Edna Ferber, escape artist Harry Houdini, and demagogue Sen. Joseph McCarthy, the central figure in the "red scare" of the 1950s. Both Green Bay and Appleton are growing, thanks in part to surging Hispanic populations. Green Bay's Latino community has increased from approximately 1,000 people in 1990 to nearly 14,000; the city is more than 13 percent Hispanic. Following the 2016 election, Appleton officials said that the city will operate as a "sanctuary city" in terms of national immigration policy, though it did not officially adapt the designation.

The 8th Congressional District of Wisconsin includes Green Bay and the Fox River Valley south to Appleton. It also includes the inland dairy counties and the Northwoods, which has hundreds of pine-ringed lakes where city dwellers keep summer homes. The Door County peninsula, which extends from Green Bay into Lake Michigan, is a more upscale summer destination, with art galleries, boutiques and restaurants. Green Bay-based Brown County is one-third of the population; Appleton-based Outagamie is about one-fourth.

Politically, this has often been malleable territory and a must-win region in this traditional swing state. With other non-urban parts of Wisconsin, the 8th has shifted dramatically. Barack Obama carried the district with 54 percent of the vote in 2008. Eight years later, Donald Trump took 56 percent. Tiny Menominee County, the site of an Indian reservation, was the only county Trump lost.

★ WYOMING ★

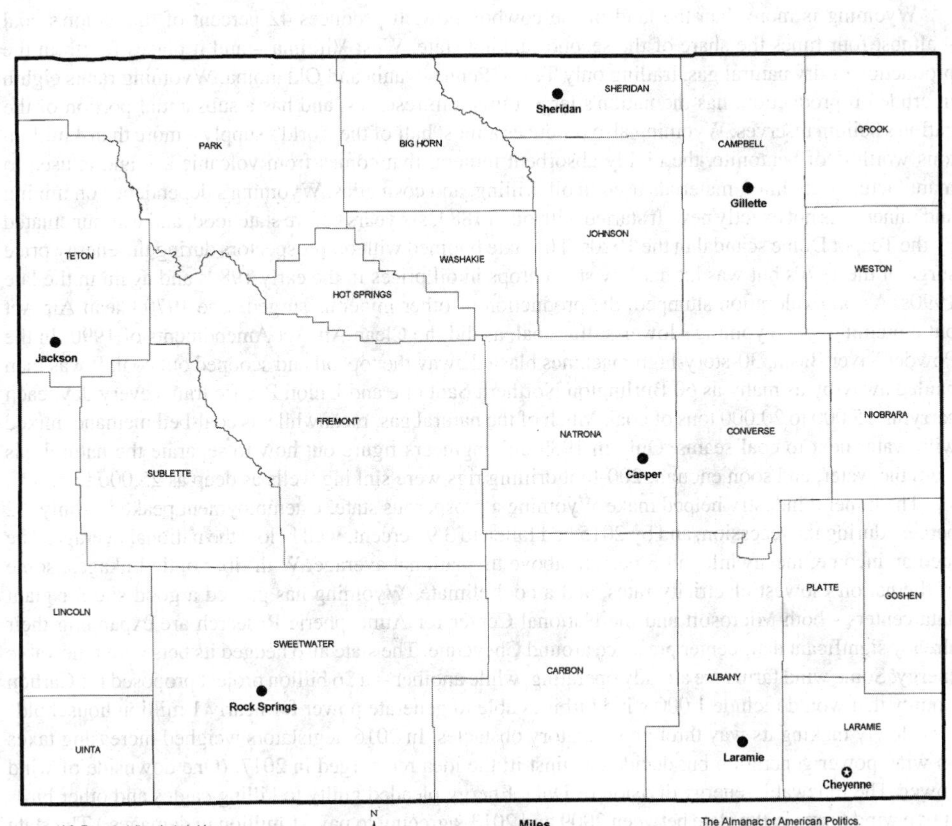
PARK
BIG HORN
SHERIDAN
Sheridan
CAMPBELL
CROOK
Gillette
JOHNSON
TETON
WASHAKIE
HOT SPRINGS
WESTON
Jackson
FREMONT
NATRONA
CONVERSE
NIOBRARA
SUBLETTE
Casper
LINCOLN
SWEETWATER
CARBON
PLATTE
GOSHEN
ALBANY
Rock Springs
LARAMIE
UINTA
Laramie
Cheyenne
U.S. Representative elected at-large.
N
W
E
S
Miles
0 10 20
The Almanac of American Politics.
National Journal

As one might expect of a state that's the nation's leading producer of coal, Wyoming has the biggest Republican advantage in party affiliation of any state, and Hillary Clinton won a smaller percentage of Wyoming's vote than she did in any other state. Meanwhile, the state has suffered from a downturn in the energy sector that has hit the economy and the budget hard.

America's frontier disappeared in 1890, according to the Census Bureau and historian Frederick Jackson Turner, but some people in Wyoming still believe they are living on the frontier. The state – symbolized by the cowboy astride a bucking bronco that graces its license plates -- remains the most western of states in spirit. Largely unsettled even by western standards, its thin veneer of civilization stretches thinly across a forbidding and beautiful land. After the open range era, cattle ranches were made possible by the barbed wire that could fence in roaming herds and the steam locomotives that could carry cattle to markets in the East.

Wyoming is more than the land of the cowboy now. It produces 42 percent of the nation's coal – almost four times the share of the second-ranking state, West Virginia – and it places fourth in the production of dry natural gas, trailing only Texas, Pennsylvania and Oklahoma. Wyoming ranks eighth in crude oil production, has the nation's largest uranium reserves, and has a substantial portion of the nation's helium reserves. Wyoming also produces almost half of the world's supply – more than 4 million tons worth -- of bentonite, the highly absorbent mineral that comes from volcanic ash and is used to manufacture kitty litter, materials used in oil drilling, and cosmetics. Wyoming's dependence on mining and minerals is not exactly new. It started with oil in 1884, six years before statehood, and was punctuated by the Teapot Dome scandal in the 1920s. The state boomed with oil prospectors during the energy price surge of the 1970s but was hit hard by steep drops in oil prices in the early 1980s and again in the late 1990s. As oil exploration slumped, the production of other minerals surged. The 1970 Clean Air Act put a premium on Wyoming's lower-sulfur coal, as did the Clean Air Act Amendments of 1990. In the Powder River Basin, 30-story-high machines blasted away the topsoil and scooped out coal. It was then hauled away by as many as 60 Burlington Northern Santa Fe and Union Pacific trains every day, each carrying 15,000 to 20,000 tons of coal. Much of the natural gas, meanwhile, is coal-bed methane, mixed with water next to coal seams. Only in 1989 did engineers figure out how to separate the natural gas from the water, and soon enough, 200-foot drilling rigs were sinking wells as deep as 25,000 feet.

The mineral industry helped make Wyoming a prosperous state. Unemployment peaked at only 7.2 percent during the recession, and by 2015 had fallen to 3.9 percent, well below the national average. The median income, meanwhile, hit 8 percent above the national average. With fiber optic linkages, some of the nation's lowest electricity rates, and a cool climate, Wyoming has proved a good site for giant data centers - both Microsoft and the National Center for Atmospheric Research are expanding their already significant data-center presence around Cheyenne. The state also hedged its bets with renewable energy. Some wind farms are already operating, while another -- a $6 billion project proposed for Carbon County that would include 1,000 wind turbines able to generate power for nearly 1 million households -- is slowly making its way through regulatory obstacles. In 2016, legislators weighed increasing taxes on wind power generation but decided against it; the idea reemerged in 2017. (One downside of wind power: The renewable-energy division of Duke Energy pleaded guilty to killing eagles and other birds at two wind farms in the state between 2009 and 2013, agreeing to pay $1 million in damages.) The state is dabbling in solar power as well, with a project proposed partially on federal land.

The energy sector buttressed the state during the Great Recession, but as the sector subsequently experienced a downturn, Wyoming has suffered. The unemployment rate has begun edging above the national average, and between September 2014 and February 2017, the number of people employed in Wyoming's mining and logging sector declined by 9,000, or about one-third. The decline has hit the state budget particularly hard – the energy and mining sector typically provides the treasury with about two-thirds of its revenue, and gains in such fields as tourism and high-tech centers haven't been enough to fill in the gaps. The state's population has taken a hit as well. Wyoming is still the least populous state - Washington, D.C., is 16 percent bigger in population despite being 1,400 times smaller in area - though its population grew by 14 percent the decade ending in 2010, and then by an additional 4 percent through 2015. But as energy and mining payrolls were downsized and workers sought jobs elsewhere, the state population began falling. Four of the five most populous counties in the state have shrunk since the downturn began. Two had expanded rapidly during the energy boom (Casper-based Natrona and

Gillette-based Campbell) while two had barely been increasing even before the decline started (Green River-based Sweetwater and Lander-based Fremont).

The few counties that have both grown rapidly and kept expanding are supported by other industries -- government (Laramie County, which includes the state capital of Cheyenne), higher education (Albany County, which includes Laramie, home of the University of Wyoming), and tourism (Teton County, which includes the resort area around Jackson Hole). Teton in particular has benefited from Wyoming's remarkable landscape. Yellowstone, established in 1872, was the nation's first national park; it has averaged about 3 million visitors annually in recent years, and Grand Teton National Park draws even more. Jackson Hole, just south of the parks, has become one of America's elite year-round resort areas since the early 1980s, thanks in part to a policy of promoting air service to the regional airport through tax expenditures. Teton County now has a median income 28 percent higher than the state as a whole.

The juxtaposition of civilization and wilderness has created some thorny policy issues. For years, the state has run feeding grounds for elk near Jackson Hole, and the herd has grown to tens of thousands. Environmental groups, worried about the spread of chronic wasting disease, want the feeding stopped, though thousands of elk induced over generations to depend on the feeding grounds likely will die. Local ranchers want it continued, to keep the elk away from their cattle, especially in winter. Grizzly bears, once endangered and protected in Yellowstone, have now increased in number and have been removed from the endangered list. The Interior Department agreed that the wolves previously reintroduced into the state and protected could be shot on sight, as long as the state committed to preserve 10 breeding pairs and 100 wolves outside Yellowstone; a court battle continues over whether to de-list the state's wolves from the endangered species list. Meanwhile, after protests from locals, the National Park Service agreed to allow snowmobiles and snow coaches into Yellowstone, and the National Forest Service permitted ice climbs on the Shoshone River to the east. On petition from the Northern Arapaho, the Fish and Wildlife Service granted the tribe permits to kill bald eagles. Then there's the sage grouse, which has a habitat that covers about a quarter of the state's land area. The federal government and private landowners have worked on conservation efforts, but the future of such activities under the Trump administration remains in question.

The settled part of Wyoming consists of medium-sized towns, which are the state's largest cities. It is a small state, a single community really, where people remember who played what position, when and how well, and for what high school football team. The locals set the tone of life. Wyoming remains 85 percent white, tied for sixth-highest nationally. It is only 1 percent black -- one of six states registering at just 1 percent – but it is 9 percent Hispanic, a higher percentage than in such larger and more diverse states as Michigan, Missouri, Ohio and Pennsylvania. When it was still a territory in 1869, Wyoming was the first to give women the vote. (The exception: New Jersey allowed women with property to vote between 1776 and 1807, but there weren't many women with property.) Wyoming also had the nation's first woman governor, Nellie Tayloe Ross, in the 1920s, although it hasn't had one since.

There was once a sharp economic and regional split reflected in its partisan politics. The big economic interests - cattle ranchers, organized in the Wyoming Stock Growers Association, and the Union Pacific Railroad management - favored the Republicans, as did the wildcatters, independent producers and oil company geologists. The main Democratic constituency was made up of Union Pacific Railroad workers who built the first transcontinental line across southern Wyoming in the 1860s. (Cheyenne was established because it was the midpoint between the UP's operations in Omaha and Ogden, Utah.) The southern tier of counties, from Cheyenne through Laramie to Evanston, once voted Democratic. But now the Democrats are strongest in Teton County, the home of Jackson Hole, the state's only county to vote for Barack Obama in both 2008 and 2012, and in Albany County, home of Laramie and the University of Wyoming, which Obama carried in 2008.

Wyoming hasn't elected a Democrat to the Senate since 1970, or to the House since 1976, though it has had Democratic governors over that time, thanks to the importance of personal campaigning in such a tight-knit state. Democrats Ed Herschler, Mike Sullivan, and Dave Freudenthal have occupied the governor's chair for 28 of the past 42 years. But it may be a while before the Democrats win the governorship-or any statewide office-again. In 2014, the party couldn't even field a candidate for secretary of state, state treasurer and state auditor, and their candidate for education secretary, a credible business executive, won less than 40 percent of the vote. Both chambers of the legislature have Democratic caucuses numbering in the single digits. Still, compared with other solidly Republican states where religious conservatives are dominant, Wyoming has a libertarian, live-and-let-live ethos. In 1994, on the same Election Day when the GOP was winning a competitive gubernatorial race by a 3-2 margin (and rolling to big gains nationally), Wyoming voters rejected a tough anti-abortion ballot measure by an equivalent 3- 2 margin. Wyoming attracted negative attention with the gruesome 1998 murder of Matthew Shepard, a gay college student, in Laramie. Since then, Laramie, home of the University of Wyoming, approved an ordinance that banned discrimination on the basis of sexual orientation or gender identity, the first such ban in the state.

In the 2016 presidential election, Donald Trump expanded the GOP's already expansive winning margin by seven points over what it was in 2012, winning more than 3,000 more votes than Mitt Romney's total while Hillary Clinton dropped by 13,000 compared with Obama that year. The winning margins in the state's biggest counties all expanded in the GOP's direction, typically by seven to 14 points more per county than in 2012. The one that broke the pattern was Teton, which not only remained in the Democratic camp but actually gave Clinton a winning margin 15 points bigger than Obama's in2012. But in Wyoming, Teton County is the exception that proves the rule.

Population		**Race and Ethnicity**		**Income**	
Total	5,742,117	White	84.5%	Median Income	$58,840 (16 out of 50)
Land area	97,093	Black	1.0%		
Pop/ sq mi	59.1	Latino	9.6%	Under $50,000	42.7%
Born in state	40.9%	Asian	0.9%	$50,000-$99,999	33.3%
		Two races	2.0%	$100,000-$199,999	20.7%
Age Groups		Other	2.0%	$200,000 or more	3.2%
Under 18	23.8%			Poverty Rate	11.5%
18-34	24.0%	**Education**			
35-64	38.8%	H.S grad or less	37.1%	**Health Insurance**	
Over 64	13.5%	Some college	37.2%	With health insurance coverage	86.6%
		College Degree, 4 yr	17.1%		
Work		Post grad	8.6%		
White Collar	32.5%			**Public Assistance**	
Sales and Service	39.0%	**Military**		Cash public assistance income	1.6%
Blue Collar	28.4%	Veteran	11.0%		
Government	21.1%	Active Duty	0.5%	Food stamp/SNAP benefits	5.9%

Voter Turnout			
2015 Total Citizens 18+	430,026	2016 Pres Turnout as % CVAP	59%
2016 Pres Votes	255,849	2012 Pres Turnout as % CVAP	60%

Legislature	
Senate:	4D, 26R
House:	9D, 51R

Presidential Politics

2016 Democratic Caucus		
Bernie Sanders (D)	4,122	(57%)
Hillary Clinton (D)	3,131	(43%)
2016 Republican Convention		
Ted Cruz (R)	1,128	(69%)
Marco Rubio (R)	231	(14%)
Donald Trump (R)	112	(7%)

2016 Presidential Vote		
Donald Trump (R)	174,419	(68%)
Hillary Clinton (D)	55,973	(22%)
Gary Johnson (L)	13,287	(5%)
2012 Presidential Vote		
Mitt Romney (R)	170,962	(69%)
Barack Obama (D)	69,286	(28%)
Gary Johnson (L)	5,326	(2%)

Cook Partisan Voting Index: R+25

Wyoming was Republican Donald Trump's best state in 2016. His 46-percentage point margin of victory over Hillary Clinton was his biggest of all 50. Clinton's 22 percent showing was her worst. This was also George W. Bush's best state in 2000, when he carried it 68%-28%, and his second best state in 2004, when he carried it 69%-29%. It was Mitt Romney's No. 2 state in 2012, when he carried it 69%-28%. Clinton did carry one of the state's 23 counties: Teton, 60%-32%, home to Jackson Hole, the outdoors playground of the super-rich. According to the Economic Policy Institute, the top 1 percent of earners in the Jackson metro had average incomes of $19,995,835 in 2013, 213 times the bottom 99 percent, which marked the greatest disparity in the country, yet another sign of the changing bifurcated demographics of the Democratic Party's electorate.

Clinton fared a little better when Wyoming Democrats held their caucuses on April 9. Sanders stumped in the state - he held a rally there on the night of his victory in the Wisconsin primary - and garnered 56 percent of the state convention delegates. Clinton captured Laramie (Cheyenne) and Natrona (Casper) counties. Sanders won Teton, Sweetwater, an old Democratic base of Union Pacific Railroad workers, and Albany, home of the University of Wyoming. Republicans held county conventions on March 11 and Texas Sen. Ted Cruz defeated Florida Sen. Marco Rubio 66%-20%. Trump finished third with 7 percent.

Congressional Districts

115th Congress Lineup	1R	114th Congress Lineup	1R

Governor

Matt Mead (R)

Elected 2010, term expires 2019, 2nd term; b. Mar. 11, 1962, Jackson, WY; Trinity U. TX, B.A. 1984; U. of WY, J.D. 1987; Episcopalian; Married (Carol); 2 children.

Professional Career: Campbell County prosecutor, 1987-1990; Fed. prosecutor, U.S. Attorney, Cheyenne, 1991-1994; Special Assistant U.S. Attorney, 1994-1995; Special Assistant Attorney General., WY, 1998-2001; Practicing attorney, 1995-2001; U.S. Attorney, WY, 2001-2007; Farm/ranch operator, 2007-present.

Office: 200 W. 24th St., Cheyenne, 82002-0010; 307-777-7434; Fax: 307-632-3909; Website: governor.wyo.gov.

Election Results

Election	Name (Party)	Vote (%)
2014 General	Matt Mead (R)	99,700 (59%)
	Pete Gosar (D)	45,752 (27%)
	Don Wills (I)	9,895 (6%)
	Dee Cozzens (L)	4,040 (2%)
2014 Primary	Matt Mead (R)	53,673 (55%)
	Taylor Haynes (R)	31,532 (32%)
	Cindy Hill (R)	12,464 (13%)

Prior winning percentage: 2010 (66%)

Wyoming's governor is Matt Mead, a Republican elected in 2010 to succeed two-term Democrat Dave Freudenthal. Mead drew positive reviews and easily won a second term in 2014, though he grappled with declining revenues as the state's large energy sector experienced a slump.

Mead was born in Jackson and raised on his family's Teton County ranch. He is the grandson of Clifford Hansen, a former Republican governor of Wyoming (1963-67) and a senator (1967-78). Mead's mother, Mary, ran unsuccessfully for governor in 1990, six years before her death in a horseback riding accident. After receiving a bachelor's degree from Trinity University in San Antonio, Mead returned home to attend the University of Wyoming's law school. He worked as a prosecutor in Campbell County and in the U.S. attorney's office in Cheyenne, and he practiced law for six years at a Cheyenne firm.

He was chosen to serve as U.S. attorney for Wyoming in 2001 and spent nearly six years in the job. When Republican Sen. Craig Thomas died in 2007, Mead resigned his position in the hopes of getting an appointment to the vacant seat. But the Republican State Central Committee instead picked three other candidates, including state Sen. John Barrasso, whom Democratic Gov. Dave Freudenthal subsequently appointed. Barrasso won a 2008 special election to serve the remaining four years of Thomas' term.

After the Senate setback, Mead returned to working in his family's ranching business. Meanwhile, Freudenthal - who had won reelection in 2006 with an impressive 70 percent of the vote - decided against running again. Mead got into a crowded Republican field for governor, emphasizing his family's record of service. His opponents included state Auditor Rita Meyer, who served as GOP Gov. Jim Geringer's chief of staff; former state Rep. Ron Micheli; and state House Speaker Colin Simpson, son of former Sen. Alan Simpson. The candidates shared similar conservative views. Meyer got the endorsement of former Alaska Gov. Sarah Palin, while Simpson used his family connections to win the backing of former President George H.W. Bush. But Mead put nearly $900,000 of his own money into the contest to give him a 2-1 cash advantage, and that helped him build name recognition against his better-known competitors. He won 29 percent of the vote in the September primary, to Meyer's 28 percent. Micheli took 26 percent, and Simpson won 16 percent. In the general election, Mead benefited from running as a Republican at a time when Wyoming was increasingly negative about the Democratic Party. Mead easily defeated Leslie Petersen, Wyoming's former state Democratic Party chairman, by a 66%-23% margin, carrying every county.

Taking office, Mead noted that Wyoming's relatively sound fiscal health made it the envy of other states coping with severe budget shortfalls. He displayed his fiscal conservatism by trimming the payroll in the governor's office by about $100,000 a year. And he signed into law $15 million in incentives to entice large computer data centers to the state. He also proposed spending more state money on highways by using a portion of the proceeds from Wyoming's statutory severance tax on minerals. The state legislature rejected the idea but committed to an interim study to look at new non-tax and non-toll-based revenue sources to fund roads.

On other issues, Mead signed into law a bill that would eliminate the right of suspected drunk drivers to refuse testing, and a measure allowing residents to carry concealed guns without a permit. He called this "an appropriate law for Wyoming." He won praise for his dealings with the federal government, particularly on the U.S. Fish and Wildlife Service's agreement to remove some wolves from the endangered species list. By January 2012, his approval rating in a Colorado College poll stood at an astronomical 77 percent, the highest of any Rocky Mountain governor.

In 2012, Mead urged lawmakers to adopt a budget plan that financed one-time expenses in construction projects, highway maintenance and aid to local governments for infrastructure needs. He later called on agency heads to cut 8 percent of their budgets for fiscal year 2014, as a hedge against fluctuating coal and natural gas prices, and froze $4.4 million planned for a new state office building. At year's end, he proposed raising the state fuels tax by 10 cents, quickly expanding its rainy-day fund and slightly shrinking the size of its operating budget. Lawmakers gave him most of what he wanted. In 2013, a Wyoming House-passed bill that drew national publicity sought to exempt the state from new federal laws. But after Mead raised concerns about potentially pitting police against federal agents charged with enforcing those laws, the measure died in the state Senate.

Mead, after some prodding by the legislature, fought with Cindy Hill, the state superintendent of schools whose stormy tenure included accusations that she had exercised poor management skills; Hill was ousted following passage of a bill signed by Mead, then reinstated after the courts deemed it unconstitutional. Hill sought revenge against Mead by running in the 2014 gubernatorial primary. She had a base in the tea party, and in the state GOP convention her supporters nearly succeeded in tagging Mead with a censure resolution. But Mead consolidated establishment support and won the primary. In the general, Mead was the overwhelming favorite over Democrat Pete Gosar, Libertarian Dee Cozzens and independents Don Wills and Taylor Haynes, ultimately winning with nearly 60 percent of the vote.

Mead's view on the Affordable Care Act evolved. He had said in November 2012 that Wyoming would decline to set up a state insurance exchange under the federal health care law, defaulting to a federally operated exchange. He also recommended that the state not participate in an expansion of Medicaid. But in his State of the State Address in 2015, Mead made the case for negotiations to expand Medicaid that were already under way with the federal government. "The fact is many of us don't like the ACA, including me," Mead said. "But here's another fact: Our federal tax dollars help pay for the ACA, and Wyoming tax dollars pay for the ACA. Do we choose to have that Wyoming money be returned to Colorado, California or Wyoming? I say Wyoming." However, the legislature put the kibosh on the idea -- and continued to do so, despite Mead's efforts.

On other issues, Mead has also taken a more pragmatic approach than some fellow Republican governors, particularly those seeking a national profile with presidential bids. Mead worked with the legislature and Hill's successor as schools superintendent to navigate the controversies over Common Core. He signed a repeal of a ban on adopting science-education standards that say global warming is caused by humans. And he quietly prepared for the possibility that President Barack Obama's Clean Power Plan – which would have dealt a severe blow to the state's crucial coal sector – would be enacted, even though he opposed the plan. Eventually, though, Wyoming lucked out: With the plan already in legal limbo stemming from legal challenges by states including Wyoming, newly elected President Donald Trump began the process of reversing the plan's implementation. The election of Trump – who Mead consistently supported during the 2016 campaign – promised to help the state's resource industry in other ways by overturning Obama-era environmental policies. (Mead was reportedly in the mix for a senior job in the administration, but he withdrew his name.)

By 2016, Mead's biggest challenge was figuring out how to address revenue shortfalls stemming from the downturn in the energy sector. In June 2016, he offered a plan to cut agencies by an average of 8 percent, with the University of Wyoming and the corrections, family services and health departments taking big hits. When revenue projections once again fell short later that year, Mead avoided an additional round of cuts by drawing from the state's rainy day fund, as well as issuing bonds and finding miscellaneous sources of revenue. Especially worrisome was a cumulative projected shortfall in K-12 education of $1.8 billion by 2022. In 2017, Mead offered a cautious budget, proposing only a historically modest $8.6 million in new programs, including one to aid diversification of the state's economy. With Mead not running again in 2018, potential Republican candidates included former Rep. Cynthia Lummis, Secretary of State Ed Murray, Treasurer Mark Gordon, former House speaker Ed Buchanan, attorney and former congressional candidate Darin Smith and former gubernatorial candidate Taylor Haynes. Possible Democrats included former state Rep. Mary Throne, state Sen. Chris Rothfuss, former congressional candidate Ryan Greene and state Nature Conservancy director Milward Simpson.

Senior Senator

Mike Enzi (R)

Elected 1996, term expires 2020, 4th term; b. Feb 01, 1944, Bremerton, WA; George Washington University (DC), b.B.A.; University of Denver (CO), M.B.A.; Presbyterian; Married (Diana Buckley Enzi); 3 children; 4 grandchildren.

Military Career: U.S Air Force & WY Air National Guard, 1967-1973.

Elected Office: Gillette Mayor, 1975-1982; WY House, 1986-1990; WY Senate, 1990-1996.

Professional Career: Owner, NZ Shoes, 1969-1995; Director & Chairman, First WY Bank of Gillette, 1978-1988; Accounting Manager & computer programmer, Dunbar Well Service, 1985-1997; Ed. Comm. of States, 1989-1993; Director, Black Hills Corporation, 1992-1996; Western Interstate Comm. for Higher Ed., 1995-1996.

DC Office: 379-A RSOB 20510, 202-224-3424, Fax: 202-228-0359, enzi.senate.gov.
State Offices: Casper, 307-261-6572; Cheyenne, 307-772-2477; Cody, 307-527-9444; Gillette, 307-682-6268; Jackson, 307-739-9507.

Committees: *Budget (Chmn)*. *Finance*: Energy, Natural Resources & Infrastructure, Health Care, Taxation & IRS Oversight. *Health, Education, Labor & Pensions*: Primary Health & Retirement Security (Chmn). *Homeland Security & Government Affairs*: Federal Spending Oversight & Emergency Management, Regulatory Affairs & Federal Management. *Small Business & Entrepreneurship*.

Group Ratings

	ADA	ACLU	AFL-CIO	LCV	ITI	COC	HAFA	ACU	CFG	FRC
2016	-	35%	-	12%	60%	88%	57%	88%	8400%	100%
2015	0%	C	20%	0%	C	85%	C	91%	72%	100%

Almanac Ratings 2015

	Economy	Social	Foreign	Composite
Liberal	13%	0%	16%	9%
Conservative	87%	100%	84%	91%

Key Votes of the 114th Congress

1. Keystone pipeline	Y	5. National Security Data	N	9. Gun Sales Checks	N
2. Export-Import Bank	Y	6. Iran Nuclear Deal	Y	10. Sanctuary Cities	Y
3. Debt Ceiling Increase	N	7. Puerto Rico Debt	Y	11. Planned Parenthood	Y
4. Homeland Security $$	Y	8. Loretta Lynch A.G	N	12. Trade deals	Y

Election Results

Election	Name (Party)	Vote (%)		Cand. Spent	Ind. Exp. Support	Ind. Exp. Oppose
2014 General	Mike Enzi (R)	121,554	(72%)	$3,486,953		
	Charlie Hardy (D)	29,377	(17%)	$88,284		
	Curt Gottshall (I)	13,311	(8%)	$76,431		
	Joe Porambo (L)	3,677	(2%)			
2014 Primary	Mike Enzi (R)	77,965	(82%)			
	Bryan Miller (R)	9,330	(10%)			

Prior winning percentages: 2008 (76%), 2002 (73%), 1996 (54%)

Michael Enzi, the senior senator from Wyoming, was elected in 1996. He is a mild-mannered conservative who's skillful in working both sides of the aisle and in winning back-room legislative battles. As the current chairman of the Budget Committee, he has the opportunity to assist in crafting a Republican game plan on fiscal issues. Enzi's widespread support among Republicans helped to thwart a 2014 primary challenge from ex-Vice President Dick Cheney's daughter Liz, who now serves in the House.

Enzi grew up in Thermopolis and Sheridan, the son of a shoe salesman. He earned degrees in accounting and retail marketing, moved to Gillette, and became an accountant for an oil well servicing company. He and his wife, Diana, started a small business, NZ Shoes. In the 1970s, at a meeting of his local Jaycee business group, Enzi met Republican Sen. Alan Simpson, who was impressed by his volunteerism and suggested he run for public office. In 1975, Enzi was elected mayor of Gillette, the center of Wyoming's coal belt and its fastest-growing town. He was mayor for eight years. In 1986, he was elected to the Wyoming state House and in 1990 to the state Senate.

After Simpson announced his retirement in December 1995, Enzi was one of nine Republicans and two Democrats who ran for the seat. With support from a grassroots network of conservatives, Enzi finished first in a straw poll at the Republican state convention. His key difference with second-place finisher John Barrasso was on abortion rights-Enzi opposed abortion rights, and Barrasso favored them. Barrasso had more money, but Enzi won 32%-30%. (Barrasso and Enzi have become friendly colleague in the Senate.) In the general, the Democratic nominee, former Secretary of State Kathy Karpan, opposed gun control and abortion rights. Her support for President Bill Clinton and his Interior Secretary, former Arizona Gov. Bruce Babbitt, doomed her candidacy in solidly Republican Wyoming. Enzi led from the outset and won, 54%-42%.

Enzi offers several indices for his conservative credentials. He has been a conservative stalwart-his lifetime rating from the anti-tax American Conservative Union through 2016 was 91 percent, one of the highest among senators. The Almanac vote ratings for 2015 placed Enzi in the top one-third of most conservative Republicans-two notches to the left of Barrasso. Enzi has regularly introduced his "Repeal Amendment," a constitutional amendment enabling two-thirds of the states to overturn a federal law; tea party activists have applauded the proposal.

Enzi left his biggest mark at the Health, Education, Labor, and Pensions Committee. Despite his ideological differences with the late Sen. Edward M. Kennedy of Massachusetts, with whom he alternated the chairmanship for years as party control switched in the Senate, Enzi forged a productive relationship with the liberal lion. They operated on the "80-20 principle"-reach broad agreement on 80 percent of an issue and leave out the 20 percent where no agreement can be found. The legislation that the two successfully pushed through the committee included a bill requiring insurance companies to treat mental illness the same as other ailments in coverage decisions, reauthorization of Head Start early education and renewal of college-aid programs.

As chairman of the HELP panel in 2005, Enzi sided with Kennedy in opposing a proposal by the Bush administration to encourage more use of government vouchers for private school tuition in Gulf states recovering from Hurricane Katrina. On an issue of special interest with constituents, he helped to enact a bill to expedite the cleanup of abandoned coal mines. He was instrumental in resolving conflicts over the funding formula to renew domestic AIDS programs.

Enzi participated in bipartisan negotiations in 2009 on the health care proposal submitted by President Barack Obama. His alternative called for tax credits for buying health insurance, assistance to help small businesses provide coverage for their employees, and requirements for the states to reduce the cost of medical malpractice insurance. The "Gang of Six" senators that met during the summer that year failed to hammer out a solution acceptable to both parties. Since then, Enzi has been a critic of the Affordable Care Act.

In 2011, Democrat Tom Harkin of Iowa, then chairman of the HELP Committee, worked with Enzi in an attempt to rewrite the No Child Left Behind education law. Some Republicans on the panel derailed a drafting session, complaining that they had been left out of the process. The bill passed the committee with Enzi and two other Republicans joining all committee Democrats in support, but it never came to a vote on the Senate floor. In sharp disagreement when Harkin planned a hearing to examine for-profit colleges, Enzi sent him two letters urging that he broaden the hearing to include all higher education institutions. When Harkin went ahead with the hearing, Enzi led other Republicans in a boycott of the meeting.

On other legislation, Enzi has regularly sought common ground. As the only accountant in the Senate, Enzi played a key role in the enactment in 2002 of a corporate accountability bill. With Banking, Housing, and Urban Affairs Committee Chairman Paul Sarbanes of Maryland, he reached a compromise to establish an accounting board independent of the Securities and Exchange Commission with the power to oversee accounting firms. He opposed a move by the SEC to bar accounting firms from doing auditing and consulting work for the same corporation. The compromise was part of what became known as the Sarbanes-Oxley corporate accounting law.

His bipartisan collaboration has helped Enzi to win the "nicest senator" award in *Washingtonian's* occasional anonymous survey of congressional staffers. With California Democrat Dianne Feinstein, Enzi worked in 2010 to limit the use of the controversial chemical bisphenol A as part of food safety legislation, though the chemical industry successfully blocked the move. Enzi and Democrat Bob Casey of Pennsylvania co-sponsored a bill that aimed to help small businesses pool together as regional associations to secure federal government contracts.

For years, Enzi sought a seat on the Finance Committee. Twice in 2007, he was bypassed when GOP Senate leaders gave a committee vacancy to less senior Senators: John Ensign of Nevada, as a reward for his work as chairman of the National Republican Senatorial Committee, and John Sununu of New Hampshire, who was facing a difficult reelection in 2008. An unhappy Enzi briefly considered retiring in 2008. Instead, he was reelected that year, and finally filled a vacant seat on the powerful Finance panel after the election.

After Republicans took back the majority in the 2014 election, Enzi was part of an unexpected battle for the chairmanship of the Budget Committee with Jeff Sessions of Alabama. Sessions, a staunch conservative and outspoken partisan, had been the top Republican on the panel and was widely expected to take over as chairman. Instead, the lower-key Enzi startled fellow senators when he decided to use his edge in seniority over Sessions to claim the slot. (His seniority edge had been determined by a coin flip, since the two men entered the Senate at the same time.) Ultimately, Sessions deferred to Enzi, avoiding what could have been a nasty battle. (Two years later, during Donald Trump's presidential transition, Sessions accepted the offer to become his Attorney General.)

In taking over as Budget chairman, Enzi promised to offer a blueprint bringing the budget into balance within 10 years "without gimmicks and bad accounting." At the end of 2016, he unveiled a plan to move to a two-year appropriations process and to eliminate the possibility of a shutdown by automatically funding the government if appropriations measures have not been enacted on time. He called the reforms "one of my top priorities."

On the handling of the annual budget resolution, Enzi worked in 2015-16 with House Budget Committee chairman Tom Price of Georgia to win approval by congressional Republicans of a budget with big increases in defense spending and steep cuts in domestic programs. Following the expected rejection by congressional Democrats and President Barack Obama, the bipartisan congressional leaders in late 2015 agreed on a deal with a two-year budget framework. In February 2016, Enzi took the unusual step of refusing to invite officials from the Obama administration to present their annual budget to the

Budget Committee. "It's not a significant budget, and holding a hearing on it doesn't do anything," he said.

On the opening day of Congress in 2017, Enzi filed a resolution in which he triggered the start of the annual budget process with a provision calling for repeal of the Affordable Care Act. The Republican-controlled Congress quickly agreed to his resolution, but the House and Senate did not come to close to meeting their schedule to repeal the actual law.

Enzi's success in avoiding serious opposition to reelection appeared to be at risk in 2013 when Liz Cheney took steps toward a Republican primary challenge. Cheney, a State Department official and prominent conservative activist in her own right, declared that "the Washington establishment is the problem." But she was tagged as a carpetbagger who had lived extensively in the Washington area. Her candidacy led to a nasty intra-family split over same-sex marriage with her sister, Mary, who is a lesbian.

Enzi won unwavering public backing from colleagues of all stripes. Republican Sen. Orrin Hatch of Utah told *Politico* that Enzi is "honest and decent, hard-working; he's got very important positions in the Senate. He's highly respected. And these are all things that would cause anybody to say: 'Why would anybody run against him?'" Facing a poll that showed Enzi ahead by 55 percentage points, Cheney ended her bid in January 2014, citing "serious health issues" in her family. Enzi subsequently had another easy reelection. Cheney's election to the House two years later suggested that she was prepared to take a longer route to the Senate, though it's far from clear that Enzi will accommodate her with his retirement in 2020, at age 76.

Junior Senator

John Barrasso (R)

Appointed Jun. 2007, term expires 2018, 1st full term; b. Jul 21, 1952, Reading, PA; Georgetown University (DC), B.S.; Georgetown University School of Medicine (DC), M.D.,; Presbyterian; Married (Bobbi Brown); 3 children (2 from previous marriage).

Elected Office: WY Senate, 2002-2007.

Professional Career: Orthopedic surgeon, 1983-2007; RNC Chairman, 1992-1996; Chief of staff, WY Med. Center, 2003-2005.

DC Office: 307 DSOB 20510, 202-224-6441, Fax: 202-224-1724, barrasso.senate.gov.

State Offices: Casper, 307-261-6413; Cheyenne, 307-772-2451; Riverton, 307-856-6642; Rock Springs, 307-362-5012; Sheridan, 307-672-6456.

Committees: Senate Republican Policy Committee Chairman. *Energy & Natural Resources*: National Parks, Public Lands, Forests & Mining, Water & Power. *Environment & Public Works (Chmn)*: Clean Air & Nuclear Safety, Fisheries, Water, and Wildlife, Superfund, Waste Management, & Regulatory Oversight, Transportation & Infrastructure. *Foreign Relations*: Africa & Global Health Policy, East Asia, the Pacific & International Cybersecurity Policy, Europe & Regional Security Cooperation, Internat'l Dev Instit & Internat'l Econ, Energy & Environ Policy. *Indian Affairs*.

Group Ratings

	ADA	ACLU	AFL-CIO	LCV	ITI	COC	HAFA	ACU	CFG	FRC
2016	-	11%	-	12%	80%	100%	54%	85%	79%	100%
2015	0%	C	14%	0%	C	86%	C	79%	67%	100%

Almanac Ratings 2015

	Economy	Social	Foreign	Composite
Liberal	17%	0%	9%	9%
Conservative	83%	100%	91%	91%

Key Votes of the 114th Congress

1. Keystone pipeline	Y	5. National Security Data	N	9. Gun Sales Checks	N
2. Export-Import Bank	Y	6. Iran Nuclear Deal	Y	10. Sanctuary Cities	Y
3. Debt Ceiling Increase	Y	7. Puerto Rico Debt	Y	11. Planned Parenthood	Y
4. Homeland Security $$	N	8. Loretta Lynch A.G	N	12. Trade deals	Y

Election Results

Election	Name (Party)	Vote (%)	Cand. Spent	Ind. Exp. Support	Ind. Exp. Oppose
2012 General	John Barrasso (R)	185,250 (76%)	$4,511,679	$14,534	
	Tim Chesnut (D)	53,019 (22%)			
	Joel Otto (C)	6,176 (3%)			
2012 Primary	John Barrasso (R)	73,516 (90%)			
	Thomas Bleming (R)	5,080 (6%)			

Prior winning percentages: 2008 special (73%)

Republican John Barrasso, Wyoming's junior senator, was appointed in June 2007 after Republican Sen. Craig Thomas died in office of leukemia. He has moved into a Senate leadership role as chairman of both the Environment and Public Works Committee and the Republican Policy Committee, which he has used as platforms to identify policy priorities and move legislation, especially those serving Western interests. He has been an outspoken foe of President Barack Obama's nuclear deal with Iran.

Barrasso grew up in Reading, Pennsylvania, the son of a World War II veteran who made a living as a cement finisher and who took his family to Washington every four years for the president's inauguration. John Barrasso got his undergraduate and medical degrees from Georgetown University, moved to Wyoming in the 1980s, and set up practice as an orthopedic surgeon in Casper. Barrasso quickly made his name in local Republican politics, serving as a Republican national committeeman and as state party treasurer. He was a local radio and television personality, dispensing practical medical advice on news programs and in public service announcements, including as host of the annual Jerry Lewis telethon for muscular dystrophy.

In 1996, a decade before his appointment to the Senate, Barrasso ran for the open seat created when Republican Sen. Alan Simpson retired. He faced then-state Sen. Michael Enzi in a crowded GOP primary where abortion played a key role. Running as a moderate, Barrasso favored abortion rights and had opposed a 1994 constitutional amendment to ban most abortions. Enzi, who had support from social conservatives, opposed abortion rights and narrowly edged out Barrasso 32% to 30%. The two joined forces for the general election, with Barrasso serving as Enzi's finance chairman in the fall.

In 2002, Barrasso won election to the state Senate, where he worked on health care issues and chaired the Transportation, Highways, and Military Affairs Committee. He sponsored a bill to increase the criminal penalty for killing a pregnant woman, but then-Democratic Gov. Dave Freudenthal vetoed it. He occasionally crossed the political aisle to join with Democrats, backing a bill to exempt food from the state sales tax and supporting a ban on smoking in public buildings. He sponsored a law enabling physicians to talk freely with patients about medical complications, without the risk that the conversations could be used against them in a lawsuit.

After Thomas died on June 4, 2007, Wyoming's Republican State Central Committee had 15 days to select three candidates to fill the vacancy, from which the governor was required to pick the successor. That triggered a scramble by 31 candidates who applied for consideration. They conducted a week-long beauty pageant among the 71 members of the party committee. The roster of applicants included state Rep. Colin Simpson, the son of former Sen. Simpson, and numerous state legislators, lawyers, ranchers and other professionals. Unlike in his Senate bid 11 years earlier, Barrasso emphasized his conservative credentials. "I believe in limited government, lower taxes, less spending, traditional family values, local control, and a strong national defense," he told the committee. He noted that he had an "A" rating from the National Rifle Association, voted for prayer in public schools, sponsored legislation "to protect the sanctity of life," and opposed gay marriage.

The Republican committee named three finalists: Barrasso; Cynthia Lummis, who had served 14 years in the legislature and two terms as state treasurer; and Tom Sansonetti, who had been Thomas' chief of staff and an assistant attorney general in the Bush administration. Lummis was not on good terms with the governor, and Sansonetti had been a lobbyist for mining and ranching interests, a profession that is not popular with voters of any stripe. Barrasso, by contrast, had worked with Freudenthal on health care issues. On June 22, the governor tapped him for the seat. He quickly prepared to run in November of 2008 to fill out Thomas' term. Barrasso was unopposed in the Republican primary. In the general he defeated Democratic lawyer Nick Carter, an underfunded political newcomer, 73%-27%. Barrasso won a full six-year term in 2012 with 76% of the vote. Wyoming has not elected a Democrat to the Senate since 1970.

Barrasso opposed the Democratic proposal to extend the State Children's Health Insurance Program in 2009. But he showed his early interest in health-care and regional issues when he successfully included a provision in the bill to benefit rural doctors and hospitals. He broke with many conservatives in calling for lifting the U.S. ban on travel to Cuba, saying U.S. citizens should be free to visit relatives in the communist country. He proposed legislation to protect undeveloped areas of the Wyoming range from oil and gas development and to preserve 387 miles around the Snake River. It became law as part of a larger land management bill in 2009. Barrasso introduced a bipartisan bill in 2011 that became law a year later, paving the way for Indian tribes to pursue homeownership and other economic development opportunities on tribal lands. As Indian Affairs chairman in 2015, he and Montana Democrat Jon Tester, the committee's vice chairman, reintroduced a bill they had sponsored to streamline federal reviews of Indian energy projects. Meanwhile, he worked on a bipartisan compromise aimed at tamping down Republicans' widespread use of filibusters, telling the *New York Times*: "I hope we're more functional. I want (the Senate) to function."

Other stances have had a distinct conservative lean, often with a regional tilt. As a member of the Energy and Natural Resources Committee and the Environment and Public Works Committee, Barrasso has reflected the views of constituents and industries back home by expressing skepticism about federal regulation, and in this area, he's found some success legislatively. Barrasso supported removing gray wolves from the Endangered Species List, telling the Associated Press, "This is a Wyoming concern that requires a Wyoming solution. It does not require interference from Washington." In 2013, he angered Indian tribes when he opposed a reauthorization of the Violence Against Women Act that would have allowed tribal courts to have jurisdiction over non-Indians who commit crimes against Indians on reservations. The U.S. Fish and Wildlife Service eventually removed gray wolves from the list. Barrasso objected loudly to a CIA center on climate change, an area that experts increasingly regard as a national security challenge. The agency closed the center in 2012.

With Oklahoma Sen. James Inhofe term-limited as committee chairman of the Environment Committee, Barrasso took control in January 2017, at the same time that President Donald Trump brought radical change in resource policies and enforcement. Barrasso offered support during the confirmation hearing for Scott Pruitt, the new head of the Environmental Protection Agency. Pruitt, the former attorney general of Oklahoma, "will be the strong leader the EPA needs," Barrasso said. In response to the Democrats' boycott of the committee meeting to send Pruitt's nomination to the Senate, Barrasso got the approval of the Parliamentarian to change the rules so that the committee could act without Democrats in attendance. At a February hearing on proposals to "modernize" the Endangered Species Act, he said that the law "is not working today," and he cited the many public officials and rural groups that have sought change.

Barrasso has deep experience with the issues before his committee. In 2009, he said that the Democrats' cap-and-trade bill regulating carbon emissions would have unfairly punished his state's farmers and ranchers. In 2013, he lashed out at Obama's nominee to head the EPA, Gina McCarthy, asserting that the agency was "making it impossible for our coal miners to feed their families." He has filed legislation to bar the EPA from regulating greenhouse gases blamed for global warming. "This is not your parents' EPA," Barrasso said in a 2011 speech. "Your parents' EPA focused on rebuilding the environment. This EPA is focused on remaking society."

Barrasso gained his broader partisan platform, becoming a firm ally of Republican Leader Mitch McConnell, when he became Republican Conference vice chairman in 2010. A year later, he took control of the Republican Policy Committee, making him the fourth-ranking leader among Senate Republicans. With the prospect that he will be term-limited in that position in 2018, Barrasso could seek another leadership slot. A member of the Foreign Relations Committee, Barrasso was an early and outspoken opponent of the nuclear deal that the Obama administration reached with Iran in 2015. "The White House seemed fixated on getting a deal, even a bad deal," he said.

In 2016, he chaired the Platform Committee of the Republican convention, where he worked with officials of the Trump campaign to find acceptable provisions. While reaching agreement on that document, Barrasso has occasionally offered mild critiques or warnings to Trump-during the campaign and after he took office. Asked in an interview on CNN whether Trump should release his tax returns, Barrasso said, "I think it would be a good idea....I'm somebody's who's in favor of transparency and openness." In response to Trump's travel ban on immigrants from several Muslim nations, which he issued a week after he took office, Barrasso said, "a religious test or ban is against everything our country stands for." His plain-spoken comments often get attention.

REPRESENTATIVE-AT-LARGE

Liz Cheney (R)

Elected 2016, 1st term; b. Jul 28, 1966, Madison, WI; Colorado College, B.A., 1988; University of Chicago Law School, J.D., 1996; Methodist; Married (Philip Perry); 5 children.

Professional Career: Staff, United States Agency for International Development, 1989-1992; Staff, United States Department of State, 1992; Attorney, International Finance Coporation, 199-2002; Deputy Assistant Secretary of State for Near Eastern Affairs, United States Department of State, 2002-2004; Presidential Campaign Staff, George W. Bush, 2004; Principal Deputy Assistant Secretary of State for Near Eastern Affairs, United States Department of State, 2005-2009; Non profit executive; Television commentator.

DC Office: 416 CHOB 20515, 202-225-2311, Fax: 202-225-3057, cheney.house.gov.
State Offices: Casper, 307-261-6595; Cheyenne, 307-772-2595; Gillette, 307-414-1677; Sheridan, 307-673-4608.

Committees: *Armed Services*: Emerging Threats & Capabilities, Oversight & Investigations. *Natural Resources*: Energy & Mineral Resources, Federal Lands. *Rules*: Rules & Organization of the House.

Election Results

Election	Name (Party)	Vote	(%)	Cand. Spent	Ind. Exp. Support	Ind. Exp. Oppose
2016 General	Liz Cheney (R)	156,176	(62%)	$2,080,393	$6,916	
	Ryan Greene (D)	75,466	(30%)	$173,440		
	Daniel Clyde Cummings (C)	11,101	(4%)	$443		
	Lawrence Struempf (L)	9,033	(4%)			
2016 Primary	Liz Cheney (R)	35,668	(40%)			
	Leland Christensen (R)	19,594	(22%)			
	Tim Stubson (R)	15,635	(18%)			
	Darin Smith (R)	13,680	(15%)			

Liz Cheney was elected in 2016 to the seat that her father, Dick Cheney, held for a decade before he became Secretary of Defense and, later, Vice President. She has worked closely with her father and shared many of his views, especially on national security issues.

Growing up with the Cheney family, she resided chiefly in the Washington, D.C., area and said that she split her time in Casper, Wyoming. She got her bachelor's from Colorado College and her law degree from the University of Chicago. Before law school, she worked with the State Department and the U.S. Agency for International Development, and joined the consulting firm of Richard Armitage. Cheney practiced international law in the private sector. In 2002, she was appointed deputy assistant secretary of state for Near Eastern affairs and remained at the State Department until the end of the Bush presidency, except for a break to work on the Bush-Cheney re-election campaign. With the change in administration, she served as chair of Keep America Safe, a non-profit organization, and assisted her father with his writing.

In 2013, Cheney mounted a controversial challenge to Republican Sen. Mike Enzi of Wyoming. She was criticized as an outsider who had spent little time living in the state; she was distracted by an unexpected intra-family split over same-sex marriage with her sister Mary, who is a lesbian. Trailing by more than 50 points in a poll, Cheney withdrew from the race in January 2014, citing health issues in her family.

When Republican Rep. Barbara Lummis announced that she would retire in 2016, Cheney ran for the open seat. She was endorsed by a wide range of national Republican sand conservative leaders. In the eight-candidate GOP primary, her chief challenger was state Sen. Leland Christensen, a leader of the "constitutionalist" movement; he was endorsed by Sen. Rand Paul, who frequently clashed with the Cheneys on national security issues. Christensen accused Cheney of repeatedly lying or misleading voters about her campaign and experience in Wyoming. Cheney spent $2.1 million for the campaign cycle, more than three times as much as her top three GOP opponents combined. Cheney took 40 percent of the vote to 22 percent for Christensen.

In the general election, Democratic nominee Ryan Greene was a political newcomer who worked for an oil-field services company. He called himself a "persuader" and said that Cheney was "a bomb-thrower" and "long on political ambition but short on Wyoming experience." He spent $184,000, but that was not enough to get traction in this Republican bastion. Greene was largely ignored by national Democrats and liberal groups. Cheney supported Donald Trump for president, though she described as "appalling" his comments about groping women, which were publicized in October. Cheney won, 62%-30%.

In the House, Cheney got committee assignments that catered to her local and national interests, on Natural Resources and Armed Services. In February 2017, the House passed her bill to repeal the Bureau of Land Management's land planning and management strategies, which were approved during the final days of the Obama administration. Trump signed the bill in March. Revisiting an approach that her father had pursued years earlier, she urged Trump to restore enhanced interrogation techniques in the war on terror.

★ THE INSULAR TERRITORIES ★

AMERICAN SAMOA

American Samoa, the only American territory south of the equator, remains almost as Polynesian today as it was when the United States took possession of it in 1900 at the request of tribal chiefs. These seven hot, rainy islands are 2,500 miles southwest of Hawaii, 1,700 miles northeast of New Zealand, and have a land area slightly larger than the District of Columbia.

American Samoa has 57,000 people, the vast majority of them on the island of Tutuila. The islands' population doubled in the past quarter century. Fear that outsiders will change the culture has prompted demands for stricter immigration standards. A federal law in1940 classified American Samoans as U.S. nationals but not as U.S. citizens; they can serve in the military, but not as officers. In 2012, a group of American Samoans challenged the law by arguing that it violated the 14th Amendment. The territorial government refused to back them over fears that automatic citizenship could dilute what Samoans call fa'asamoa, the "Samoan way of life." An appellate court in June 2015 ruled against the plaintiffs. The Supreme Court declined to take up the case the following year. The territory has had a non-voting delegate in Congress since 1981.

The Interior Department has overseen administration of American Samoa since 1956 and operates a National Park based in northern Tutuila, which attracts close to 14,000 visitors per year. Due to local customs that prohibit selling the land on which the park sits, the U.S. government has leased it from local villages, contributing $600,000 per year to the local economy. American Samoa adopted its own constitution in 1967. Residents elect a governor and a two-house legislature known as the Fono. The secretary of the Interior appoints the chief justice and associate justice of the High Court. About 16 percent of American Samoans are Mormon. Many are bilingual. Close to 90 percent of the population speaks Samoan at home. Government is mostly conducted in English. Fono proceedings are in Samoan, and court sessions are conducted in English but translated into Samoan. Within this governmental framework, older Samoan traditions and politicsremain. Local chiefs, or matai, oversee communal lands and kinship systems called aigas.

Pago Pago, the largest town in American Samoa, has one of the finest natural harbors in the Pacific. But the market economy has not made much progress here. American Samoa leans heavily on the federal government, which contributes more than half of its revenues. The territorial government employs almost 45 percent of the workforce. For years, the private sector economy consisted of two big StarKist and Chicken of the Sea tuna canneries, which provided one-third of U.S. canned tuna and employed more than 5,000 workers. But demand for tuna has been stagnant in recent years. Chicken of the Sea in 2009 announced the closing of its Samoa packing plant, with 2,100 jobs lost. StarKist, owned by the Korean firm Dongwon, reduced its workforce from 3,000 to 1,200 in 2010. Another cannery, Washington-based Tri Marine, which opened its operation in American Samoa in 2015 with a $70 million investment, suspended production in October 2016. On a brighter note, a Filipino company broke ground in January 2016 on a multimillion dollar food-processing plant that the company said will create 700 jobs. Wages have been a perpetual problem in the territory. Average household incomes in American Samoa hover around $22,000, less than half the national average. In 2007, Congress passed a law raising the minimum wage in American Samoa to $7.25 an hour by 2014, but federally mandated delays had frozen wages for cannery workers . In late 2015, Congress approved an immediate 40 cent hourly wage increase and scheduled additional increases .

Health is a major issue in American Samoa. The territory has one of the highest obesity rates in the world.With obesity have come diabetes and heart disease. One in five babies born in American Samoa is overweight, and usually within a year most infants are obese, according to a Brown University study. One in three American Samoans suffer from diabetes. Still, American Samoans have developed a reputation for athleticism, most notably in regards to their success in American football. American Samoa has sent 30 players to the NFL and more than 200 to colleges in the NCAA. Top coaches make the long flight to Pago Pago to scout high school players.

American Samoa does not cast electoral votes for president, but it does send delegates to the major parties' national conventions. In 2016, its nine Republican delegateswere unpledged, but they lined up behind Donald Trump after his victory in Indiana. Hillary Clinton won the territory's Democratic caucuses in 2008 and 2016.

Governor Democrat Lolo Letalu Matalasi Moliga was elected in 2012 to succeed term-limited Gov. TogiolaTulafono. He was a High Talking Chief (Lolo) in the village of Sili in the Manu'a islands and High Chief (Letalu) from Ta'u, the largest island in the Manu'a group. He received an education degree from Chadron State College in Nebraska and an M.P.A. in 2012 from San Diego State University. He worked as a teacher and principal at Manu'a High School. He later became a school administrator, head of the American Samoa budget office, and chief procurement officer for the territory. He was elected to four terms in the territorial House of Representatives and to the Senate. In the November 2012 election for governor, Moliga, running as an independent, defeated former lieutenant governor Faoa Aitofele Sunia (D) 53%-47% in a runoff election. He faced Sunia again in 2016, this time defeating him in the general election 60.2%-35.8%. In the territory's 2016 Democratic caucuses, he endorsed Hillary Clinton for president.

As governor, Moliga has sought increased autonomy for the territorial government in American Samoan affairs. He supported the decision of federal courts in 2015 and 2016 not to grant automatic citizenship rights to American Samoans, saying that the territory should "determine for itself the political relationship it wishes to establish with the United States." He opposed the Obama administration's expansion of protected marine reserves in the Pacific Ocean and has been critical of federal aviation laws and minimum wage hikes, which he once called "well intentioned" but "inappropriate for our small economy." In June 2015, he requested that the U.S. government subsidize wage increases mandated by Congress. His administration has viewed immigration reform as a way to bolster the territory's stagnant population growth. Under Moliga, American Samoa has granted amnesty to more than 4,000 foreigners living illegally on the islands, and he supported legislation in 2016 increasing the number of foreigners who may receive permanent residency status in the territory.

DELEGATE

Aumua Amata Coleman Radewagen (R)

Elected 2014, term expires 2018, 2nd term, b. Dec 29, 1947; Pago Pago, American Samoa; Sacred Hearts Academy (HI); Loyola Marymount University; University of Guam, B.S.; George Mason University (VA); Roman Catholic; Married (Fred Radewagen); 3 children; 1 grandchild.

Professional Career: Journalist; Trainer; Staff, U.S. Rep. Philip Crane (IL), 1997-1999; Staff, U.S. Rep. J.C. Watts Jr. (OK), 1999-2003; White House Commissioner for Asian Americans & Pacific Islanders, 2001.

DC Office: 1339 LHOB 20515, 202-225-8577, Fax: 202-225-8757, radewagen.house.gov.

Committees: *Natural Resources*: Indian, Insular & Alaska Native Affairs, Oversight & Investigations. *Small Business*: Agriculture, Energy & Trade, Health & Technology (Chmn). *Veterans' Affairs*: Disability Assistance & Memorial Affairs, Health.

Aumua Amata Coleman Radewagen, a Republican, became the first woman to represent American Samoa in Congress after defeating 13-term Democrat Eni F. H. Faleomavaega in 2014. A cancer survivor, Radewagen grew up with 12 siblings and earned a degree from the University of Guam.

Her family has deep roots in Samoan politics. Peter Tali Coleman, her father, was the first Samoan appointed to serve as governor of the territory and its first popularly elected governor. Collectively, his tenure spanned five decades, from 1956 to 1993, and he founded the territory's Republican Party. Radewagen is the most senior member of the Republican National Committee. She has served on the Executive Council and the Standing Committee on Rules, and in 2013 she received the organization's Trailblazer Award. She supported Donald Trump at the 2016 Republican National Convention, both as a delegate and as a member of the convention rules committee. She has voiced approval of Trump's proposal to withdraw the U.S. from the Trans-Pacific Partnership and has lobbied the administration to reverse President Obama's expansion of marine reserves in the Pacific Ocean. In December 2016, she was appointed to serve on the executive council of Trump's White House transition team.

In the House, Radewagen chairs a Small Business subcommittee on health and technology and is a member of a Natural Resources subcommittee responsible for insular affairs. Despite being a non-voting member of Congress, she has had some legislative successes. In October 2016, President Obama signed into law her bill raising the minimum wage in American Samoa 40 cents every three years until it aligns with the federal minimum. Obama signed into law another bill from Radewagen related to international fishery management agreements in December 2016. In 2015 and 2016, she supported decisions by federal courts not to grant birthright citizenship status to American Samoans, saying in a press release that the courts had reaffirmed "the bedrock principle that the American Samoan people, and not outside interest groups or federal courts, should have the final say in matters concerning their political status."

Radewagen challenged long-term delegate Eni Faleomavaega on eight different occasions before finally winning the seat in 2014. Her first run was in 1994. In her 2008, 2010, and 2012 attempts, she came up short by 16 points or more in each contest. But in 2013, Faleomavaega began experiencing complications from exposure to Agent Orange in the Vietnam War and his health became a major issue. In 2014, he faced a field of eight challengers, and Radewagen was able to pull in 42% of the vote to Faleomavaega's 30%. Radewagen easily won reelection in 2016, defeating four challengers and winning 75% of the vote.

GUAM

Some 6,300 miles west of Los Angeles and 3,800 miles west of Hawaii, 17 hours of flying time from Washington, D.C., is Guam, an American possession since 1898. Geographically, this island is in the center of the Marianas Islands, though Guam is legally separate. It was acquired from Spain after the Spanish-American War, while the U.S. let Germany purchase the rest of the Mariana chain. It was ruled by Navy captains from 1898 to 1949, except for 31 months of Japanese occupation during World War II. In 1950, the Guam Organic Act made Guamanians U.S. citizens. Carlton Skinner, who as a captain integrated the crew of his Navy ship in 1943, became the first civilian governor in 1949 and helped write the territorial constitution. The local government is known as GovGuam, but Congress retains final power over the territory. It gave Guam a non-voting delegate to the House in 1972.

Guam is 36 miles long by four to nine miles wide, with an estimated 162,750 people. Some 37 percent of the population is Chamorro (descendants of the original islanders) or from elsewhere in Micronesia; 26 percentis Filipino; 12 percent other Pacific Islander; 6 percent other Asian; and 7 percent white. The population is politically mixed and overwhelmingly Catholic, yet in 2015 Guam became the first U.S. territory to recognize same-sex marriage. More than 100 marriage licenses had been issued to same-sex couples in Guam by October 2016. The island's tropical environment can be dangerous. In August 1993, Guam experienced an earthquake measuring 8.2 on the Richter scale, comparable to San Francisco's in 1906. Guam suffers from almost 300 invasive species, the most problematic of which is the brown tree snake. It has killed off nearly all of the island's bird population and has caused an estimated $4.5 million in damage. In addition to using traps and repellants to eradicate the species, the Agriculture Department has dropped mice packed with acetaminophen from helicopters.

Guam depends heavily on tourism—especially from Japan—and service businesses, but most of all on the U.S. military. Guam's visitor spending in 2015 was $1.6 billion, a 6.8 percent increase over the previous year. Guam is America's forward position in Asia. In August 2016, North Korean dictator Kim Jong Un threatened U.S. bases after the U.S. deployed bombers at Guam's Andersen Air Force Base. Bases occupy one-third of the land, and an estimated 60 percent of the island's income is derived from the federal government. In 2013, the Pentagon announced plans to relocate 5,000 marines and 1,300 dependents from Okinawa to Guam, a move that defense officials predicted would add upwards of $37 million per year to Guam's economy. About 2,500 marines are expected to move to Guam by 2021, while the remaining half will arrive by 2026. In 2017, the federal government announced that it will begin paying reparations to Guam residents who experienced wartime atrocities under Japan's occupation of the island during World War II. Since a 2012 surplus, the island's finances have had several years of deficits. By the end of the 2015 fiscal year, Guam's government had a $120 million deficit. Republican Gov. Eddie Calvo has blamed Guam's debt problems on federal mandates and the $1 billion spent over the past 13 years on providing services to immigrants. Meanwhile, Guam's first new luxury resort in 15 years opened in 2015.

Guam does not cast any electoral votes for president, but elects delegates to national party conventions. In the 2016 Democratic caucuses, Hillary Clinton defeated Bernie Sanders 60%-40%. Guam Republicans held a convention in 2016, and all nine delegates pledged to back Donald Trump. In lieu of a general election, Guam began holding non-binding straw polls every four years in 1984. For the first time in its history, the straw poll in 2016 did not accurately predict the next president. About 72 percent of Guam voters chose Clinton over Trump.

Governor Eddie Calvo, a Republican, was elected governor of Guam in 2010 and won a second term in 2014. Calvo grew up in Guam before moving to California where he graduated from a Catholic high school in Mountain View and Notre Dame de Namur University in Belmont. His father, Paul Calvo, was elected governor of Guam in 1978. After school, Eddie Calvo returned to Guam and worked for the Pacific Construction Co. and the Pepsi Bottling Co. of Guam. In 1998, he was elected to the Guam legislature. In 2002, he ran for lieutenant governor with running mate Tony Unpingco, who lost to Felix Camacho, also a Republican. In 2010, Calvo ran for governor and defeated independent Carl Gutierrez by just 487 votes, 20,066 to 19,579. Calvo faced Gutierrez again in 2014 and won 63%-35%. Calvo is term-limited in 2018. Three Democrats, former Gov. Carl Gutierrez, Sen. Frank Aguon Jr., and former Sen. Lou Leon Guerrero have all declared their candidacy to succeed him.

Since Calvo assumed office, Guam's finances have fluctuated between surpluses and deficits. The island's finances stabilized in 2012 and 2013, but the general fund carried a deficit in 2014 and 2015. In 2017, Calvo announced that the 2016 fiscal year ended with a $10 million surplus, which reduced the total deficit to $110 million. After the 2012 surplus, Calvo proposed to sell $343 million of bonds to pay overdue tax refunds. The legislature pushed back, but enough bonds were sold to satisfy a court requirement that refunds be paid within a year of when they were owed. Since then, issuing tax refunds on time has become a focal point of his administration.

Calvo has been a frequent critic of federal policy in Guam. In 2015, after a U.S. District judge ruled in favor of a gay couple to whom Calvo's administration had refused to issue a marriage license, he stated that the territory's laws were "being challenged by federal judges that were nominated by a U.S. president and confirmed by a U.S Senate, none of whom were elected through a process that included the people of Guam." Calvo met with Donald Trump's transition team after the 2016 general election with the goal to "make as many people as possible aware of the problems we face with federal overreach," Calvo said. He has argued that the federal government has ignored the impact that some national decisions have had on Guam. Calvo served as co-chair of Trump's Asian Pacific American advisory committee during the 2016 campaign.

DELEGATE

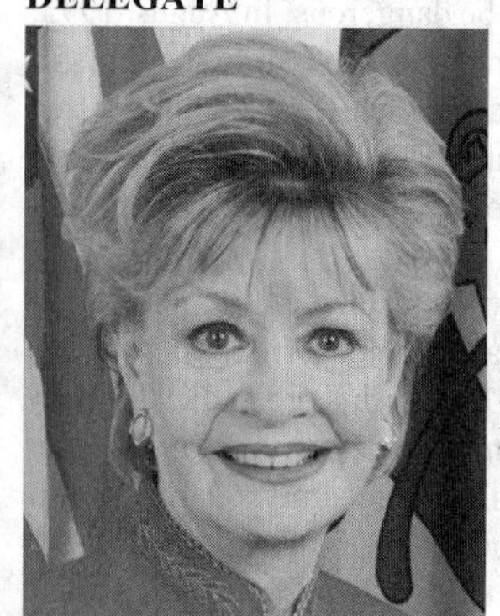

Madeleine Bordallo (D)

Elected 2002, term expires 2018, 7th term, b. May 31, 1933; Graceville, MN; St. Katherine's College (MN), Att.; St. Mary's College (IN), Att.; Roman Catholic; Widow1 child; 1 grandchild.

Elected Office: GU Senate, 1981-1982, 1987-1994; GU Lt. Governor, 1995-2002.

Professional Career: Radio & TV broadcaster KUAM, 1954.

DC Office: 2441 RHOB 20515, 202-225-1188, Fax: 202-226-0341, bordallo.house.gov.

Committees: *Armed Services*: Readiness (RMM), Seapower & Projection Forces. *Natural Resources*: Indian, Insular & Alaska Native Affairs, Water, Power & Oceans.

Madeleine Bordallo, a Democrat, was first elected delegate from Guam in 2002. She grew up in Minnesota and, after age 14, in Guam. She studied vocal music at St. Catherine's College in St. Paul and worked for Guam radio stations. She was elected to the Guam legislature in 1980. Her late husband, Ricardo Bordallo, was elected governor in 1974, was defeated for reelection in 1978 by Paul Calvo, the father of current Gov. Eddie Calvo, and was elected governor again in 1982. Then, in a tragic turn of events, Ricardo Bordallo, facing a prison term for bribery in 1990, chained himself to the statue of Chief Quipuha and shot himself in the head, dying later that day. Madeleine Bordallo was a candidate for governor that year, and lost 57%-43% to incumbent Republican Joseph Ada. In 1994, she was elected lieutenant governor and was reelected in 1998.

In 2002, when Del. Robert Underwood decided to run for governor, Bordallo ran for delegate. In the Democratic primary, she faced Judith Won Pat, daughter of Guam's first delegate, Antonio Borja Won Pat, after whom Guam's international airport is named. Bordallo defeated Won Pat 59%-41%. In the general election, she defeated Ada 65%-35%.

Bordallo did not face major party opposition from 2004 to 2010. In 2012, she was opposed for the Democratic nomination by KarloDizon, a Philippine-born Guamanian and graduate of Yale and the London School of Economics. She won 73%-26%. In the general election, she easily defeated Republican Frank Blas Jr., 58%-38%. In 2014, she won by a similar margin against Republican Margaret Metcalfe. In 2016, Bordallo won re-election against Republican Felix P. Camacho by a narrower 54%-46% margin.

Bordallo became the ranking Democrat on the Readiness Subcommittee of the House Armed Services Committee in 2011 with reappointments in 2013, 2015, and 2017. She has strongly supported the military buildup on Guam and has sought aid for infrastructure. In 2014, she angered both environmentalists and land-rights advocates by proposing a wildlife refuge and Chamorro archaeological site in Guam as a potential site for a Marines' live-fire training range. She sparred with Republican Sen. John McCain of Arizona in 2013, accusing him of lacking a "sense of history" when he opposed $120 million for Guam wastewater treatment, water infrastructure and a public health laboratory. Bordallo has received the Distinguished Public Service Awards from the U.S. Air Force and the U.S. Navy for her advocacy of military resources for Guam.

Bordallo has sought reparations for human rights abuses suffered during Japan's occupation during World War II, even though the 1951 treaty between the United States and Japan absolved Japan of any claims. The House approved her bill for reparations in 2009, but the Senate limited it to living survivors and relatives of those killed—terms that Bordallo rejected. She succeeded, however, in 2016, when Congress approved the National Defense Authorization Act of 2017, which included her proposal for reparations. This legislation also added $170 million for military construction projects in Guam including a Marine base.

MARIANA ISLANDS

The Commonwealth of the Northern Mariana Islands, in American hands since 1944, is a chain of 14 islands, only three permanently inhabited, running north from Guam in the Western Pacific. The northern islands are volcanic and the southern islands are limestone and fringed with coral reefs. They are closer to mainland Asia than to the mainland United States, sitting roughly 2,100 miles southeast of Hong Kong and some 7,800 miles southwest of Los Angeles.

The Northern Marianas have a storied history. They were first peopled by Micronesians three millennia ago and were visited by Magellan in 1521. Spanish Jesuits arrived in 1668, and the islands were a possession of Spain until the Spanish-American War in 1898. Over the centuries, they became depopulated, and then in the middle 19th century, began to be settled by Chamorros from Guam. In 1898, the United States acquired Guam as a coaling station but was content to see the Northern Marianas sold to Germany in 1899. They were seized by Japan in 1914 soon after it entered World War I, and the League of Nations gave Japan legal claim to them in 1920. They were occupied by U.S. forces in 1944, in the midst of World War II. In August 1945, the *Enola Gay* took off from Tinian on its mission to drop the atomic bomb on Hiroshima. That same year, the Northern Marianas were put in the custody of the new United Nations Security Council, and in 1947 they were declared part of the U.S. Trust Territory of the Pacific Islands. While the other islands in time opted for independence, the Northern Marianas voted in 1975 to approve a covenant with the United States creating the Commonwealth of the Northern Mariana Islands, which went into effect in 1976. Under its terms, the CNMI was not subject to federal immigration or labor laws and not obliged to pay U.S. taxes, but it deferred entirely to the United States in foreign and military affairs. Foreign investors were limited to a 49 percent share of businesses or property, and land could be owned only by "persons of Northern Marianas descent." The CNMI government started operating after the 1977 elections.

In the early 1970s, the Northern Marianas had only 12,000 people. There were no modern runways and only one rickety flight a day from Guam. Then, in the mid-1980s, the CNMI government opened up the economy to foreign investment and rewrote its immigration laws to permit an influx of guest workers. This resulted in heavy investment in garment factories that imported workers, mostly female, from low-wage countries such as the Philippines, China and Vietnam. Products made here could be labeled "Made in U.S.A." and imported into the United States without being subject to textile import quotas. By the mid-1990s, there were some 34 garment factories, employing 17,000 guest workers. Japanese investors began building tourist destinations, with low-wage jobs for guest workers. The result was a population boom. The 2000 census counted 69,000 people in the Northern Marianas, with more than 90 percent on Saipan.

Two outside developments transformed this situation. In January 2005, a treaty that set quotas on textile imports into the U.S. expired. Suddenly the CNMI's exemption from those quotas became irrelevant, and Saipan was subject to lower-wage competition from Vietnam, Cambodia and China. By January 2009, all of the islands' garment factories were shuttered. The second major blow occurred in October 2005 when Japan Airlines canceled its daily flights to Saipan. Japanese investors sold three hotels, a golf course and a shopping center. Tourism, which had employed half the workforce, nosedived. Gross domestic product dropped about 20 percent in 2009, and the CNMI's population decreased to less than 54,000 as of 2016.

In response to concerns about labor abuses and national security issues, Congress brought the CNMI under federal immigration law in 2008. The transition established a guest worker system to ensure an adequate labor supply to support the tourism and garment industries. Most CNMI politicians opposed the bill but had little power to stop it. It also gave the CNMI its first-ever delegate in Congress, replacing the territory's Resident Representative, a position funded by the CNMI that had been in place since 1978. In 2014, the guest worker program and all other elements of the transition program were extended for five years to help CNMI businesses meet their labor needs. CNMI government officials have asked Congress to extend the guest worker program past 2019 to meet labor demands. In 2007, legislation required the CNMI to increase the minimum wage. twas scheduled to increase to $7.05 in September 2017.

In 2012 the CNMI's pension fund became the first public pension fund in the U.S. to file for bankruptcy. Signs of a recovery began appearing in 2013 when the GDP reversed course and grew by 4.4 percent. The gaming industry has had a significant impact on the economy. Imperial Pacific, a Hong Kong-based company, committed to invest $3.1 billion in building a casino resort on Saipan, the first-of-its-kind on the island, with more than 4,000 hotel rooms. The Imperial Pacific Resort Hotel was scheduled to open in June 2017 Licensing fees of $30 million have helped the CNMI to address its pension crisis.

After the CIA closed its covert training base on Saipan in 1962, the U.S. military presence in the Northern Marianas became more limited than in nearby Guam. But the realignment of U.S. military operations in the Pacific could change that. The Marine Corps announced its intention to use the islands of Pagan and Tinian for live-fire amphibious training. Locals have hotly protested the plan, citing historical and environmental concerns. In response, the Navy has conducted additional studies and has been preparing alternative plans. A final decision about the training ranges was expected to be released in 2020.

Governor Republican Ralph Torres became governor of the CNMI on December 29, 2015, following the death of Gov. Eloy Inos. Torres is the territory's third governor in the past four years. In February 2013, Inos succeeded Republican BeningoFitial who left office that same month amid impeachment proceedings and multiple allegations of corruption and misconduct. Torres, who previously served as lieutenant governor, ran as Inos' running mate in 2014. Inos won that election 57%-43%, defeating former CNMI House Speaker Heinz Sablan Hofschneider, an independent.

Torres was born in Saipan but attended high school and college in Idaho, earning a degree in political science from Boise State in 2001. After returning to the CNMI, he won election to the territory's legislature in 2008 and served as senate president from 2013 to 2015. As governor, Torres has sought to boost tourism and grow the territory's workforce, and he has supported raising the cap on permits for foreign workers in the CNMI. In April 2016, he drew national attention for his support of a law restricting ownership of assault-style weapons and imposing a $1,000 excise tax on pistols. In the 2016 presidential race, Torres initially supported retired neurosurgeon Ben Carson. Ahead of the CNMI's March caucuses, however, he threw his support behind Donald Trump. Torres went on to serve alongside Gov. Eddie Calvo of Guam as co-chair of the Trump campaign's Asian-Pacific Advisory Committee.

DELEGATE

Gregorio Kilili Camacho Sablan (D)

Elected 2008, term expires 2018, 4th term, b. Jan 19, 1955; Saipan; University of Hawaii, Manoa, Att.; University of Guam, Att.; Roman Catholic; Married (Andrea C. Sablan); 6 children.

Elected Office: N. Marianas Islands Legislature, 1982-1986.

Professional Career: Gov.'s deputy chief admin. officer, CNMI Government, 1980-1981; Special Assistant for Management & budget, CNMI Government, 1994-1995; Executive Director, Commonwealth Election Commission, 1999-2008.

DC Office: 2411 RHOB 20515, 202-225-2646, Fax: 202-226-4249, sablan.house.gov.

Committees: *Education & the Workforce*: Health, Employment, Labor & Pensions (RMM), Higher Education & Workforce Development. *Natural Resources*: Indian, Insular & Alaska Native Affairs, Water, Power & Oceans. *Veterans' Affairs*: Disability Assistance & Memorial Affairs, Oversight & Investigations.

The first delegate to the House from the Commonwealth of the Northern Mariana Islands, Gregorio Kilili Camacho Sablan was elected in November 2008.

He grew up in Saipan in an extended family much involved in politics. His grandfather was the first elected mayor of Saipan, and his uncle was the city's longest-serving mayor. At age 11, Sablan moved to the Federated States of Micronesia and attended boarding school, the only ethnic Chamorro there. He attended the University of Guam and the University of California, Berkeley, but did not get a degree.

He worked for Democratic Gov. Carlos Camacho, the CNMI's first elected governor, then served in the legislature from 1982 to 1986. Sablan also worked for 18 months on the Washington staff of former Hawaii Democratic Sen. Daniel Inouye, who long had an interest in the Pacific territories. When he returned to Saipan, Sablan worked as special assistant for management and budget for Democratic Gov. FroilanTenorio. Later, he was appointed executive director of the Commonwealth Election Commission and won praise for his conduct of CNMI's closely contested election in 2006.

After Congress voted in April 2008 to give the CNMI a non-voting delegate in Congress, Sablan joined a field of nine candidates seeking the seat. Sablan ran as an independent rather than as a Democrat because, he said, the local Democratic Party was poorly organized. Of 10,161 votes cast, Sablan received 2,474, edging his nearest competition, Republican Pete A. Tenorio, by 357 votes. Sablan, who has been reelected by increasingly wide margins, ran unopposed in 2016. Although he runs as an independent in elections, he caucuses with the Democratic Party. He endorsed Hillary Clinton for president in 2016.

Sablan has had some legislative successes, including enactment of a measure in 2013 giving the CNMI ownership of submerged lands three miles out to sea and a December 2012 amendment to the defense authorization bill requiring that the flags of the CNMI and other territories be displayed whenever military units display all of the states' flags. In 2014, he helped prolong a visa program that allows long-term foreign investors to reside on the islands. In 2016 and 2017, the House passed his bills increasing caps on foreign workers in the CNMI. After years of trying to create a national park on the island of Rota, Sablan came one step closer in 2017 when the National Park Service announced that it will study Rota to determine whether it is suitable to designate it as a unit of the national park system. Sablan has called for extending U.S. voting rights protections to the territories and has supported increases to the minimum wage. He has been an opponent of militarizing the island of Pagan, saying in April 2015, "I have made my personal position on Pagan clear for over two years: I oppose the bombing of Pagan." Sablan serves on the Education and Workforce, Veterans' Affairs, and Natural Resources committees.

PUERTO RICO

Puerto Rico has a unique history. From Columbus' landing in 1493 until the Spanish-American War of 1898, it was a Spanish colony—and an important one in the three centuries when the port of San Juan was the gathering place for its annual convoy of gold and silver from the Americas to Spain. From the time it became an American territory in 1898 to the 1950s, it was considered "the poorhouse of the Caribbean," a sugar-producing island with a tiny elite. In the second half of the 20th century, it developed a recognizably first world economy and a solidly democratic—though sometimes turbulent—political system.

In the 21st century, Puerto Rico's forward momentum has ground to a halt. A combination of overspending and overborrowing by the territorial government and Congress' removal of tax breaks that had traditionally brought corporations and big businesses to the island led to an economic crisis. Growth became virtually non-existent. The territory's economy has shrunk by 15percent since 2006. Unemployment hit 12.4 percent in December 2016, more than twice the national average. In the meantime, the government borrowed to make ends meet. By May 2015, its debt had reached $72 billion, four times the amount that brought Detroit to its knees in 2013, prompting some to refer to Puerto Rico as the "Greece of the Caribbean." U.S. bankruptcy law prohibits Puerto Rico from restructuring its debt under Chapter 9. The Supreme Court reaffirmed that policy in June 2016, when it struck down a 2014 law passed by the Puerto Rican government aimed at allowing the territory's public utilities to restructure $20 billion in debt. Lacking bankruptcy as an option, government officials in San Juan have looked to spending cuts and tax hikes to slow the bleeding, causing anti-austerity protests to erupt in the capital, as worried residents left in droves. Between 2000 and 2015, Puerto Rico's population shrank by 9 percent, from roughly 3.8 million to 3.4 million. In 2014, an estimated 230 people left per day—most of them relocating to Florida. The situation has shown signs of deteriorating into a humanitarian crisis. The poverty rate on the island has been estimated to be about 45 percent. In 2014 and 2015, Puerto Rico lost more than one doctor per day. In August 2016, the Department of Health and Human Services declared a public health emergency due to an outbreak of the Zika virus on the island.

In June 2015, former Gov. Alejandro García Padilla concluded that Puerto Rico could not meet its financial obligations. A year later, the territory defaulted on a $422 million payment. In June 2016, Congress intervened. The Puerto Rico Oversight, Management, and Economic Stability Act, or PROMESA, halted all litigation between Puerto Rico and its creditors and established a seven-member federal oversight board responsible for managing the territory's finances, negotiating and settling with creditors, and restructuring debts. Members of the board were to be chosen by the president from a list provided by congressional leaders. The broad powers granted to the board attracted criticism among residents of Puerto Rico, with some characterizing it as colonialism and calling the board a "junta." In March 2017, newly elected Gov. Ricardo Rosselló released a blueprint for fiscal reforms and debt management. The plan requires approval from the federal oversight board.

The financial crisis revived the fundamental question of whether Puerto Rico should seek statehood, continue its current commonwealth status, or, in what has traditionally been a minority view, declare independence. A transition to statehood would require congressional approval. Puerto Rico didn't elect its own governor until 1948. From the 1940s until the early 1960s, it was transformed by Gov. Luis MuÑoz Marín and his Popular Democratic Party. MuÑoz initiated "Operation Bootstrap" to lure businesses to Puerto Rico with promises of low-wage labor, government-built factories and tax exemptions.Hedeveloped Puerto Rico's commonwealth form of government—in Spanish, Estado LibreAsociado, or, ELA, meaning Free Associated State—that was approved by referendum in 1952. Puerto Rico is part of the United States for purposes of international trade, foreign policy and war, but it has its own laws, taxes and representative government. It is not subject to federal income taxes and is not eligible for all federal benefits. The island has developed its own political parties: MuÑoz's Popular Democrats (the Spanish acronym is PPD), the New Progressive Party (PNP) which favors statehood, and two small pro-independence parties. PPD politicians have long been affiliated with the mainland Democratic Party, while PNP politicians have been split, with some favoring mainland Democrats and some favoring mainland Republicans. The New Progressives' Ricardo Rosselló, who was elected governor in November 2016, ran on a pro-statehood platform, arguing that statehood could boost the territory's lagging economy.

Residents of Puerto Rico have voted on the issue of statehood four times since 1967. In the 1967 referendum, Puerto Ricans voted to continue commonwealth status over statehood 60%-39%. In 1993, the vote was 48%-46% for continuing the commonwealth. In a 1998 referendum, the vote was 47 percent for statehood and 50 percent for "none of the above," the option favored by the PPD. In 2012, voters faced a two-part referendum. The first question was whether to continue the present status. The second was a choice between statehood, independence, or a "sovereign commonwealth." On the first question, 52 percent of those who turned out voted against the current status and 44 percent voted for it. On the second question, statehood won a plurality. But, taking into account all those who turned out, it got only 44 percent of the vote—roughly comparable to statehood's showing in past referenda. In June 2017, Puerto Rico voters were scheduled to choose between statehood and free association/independence.

The Obama administration largely avoided taking a firm stance on statehood. When Obama visited Puerto Rico in June 2011, the first president to do so since Gerald Ford in 1976, he said, "When the people of Puerto Rico make a clear decision, I will stand by you," without being specific about what would constitute "a clear decision." The Trump administration initially took a similar approach. On his campaign website, Donald Trump stated that Puerto Ricans "should be entitled to determine for themselves their political status. I am firmly committed to the process where Puerto Ricans might resolve their status according to Constitutional and Congressional protocols." House Republicans were unlikely to raise the issue for fear that Puerto Rico as a state would elect five Democratic House members and cast seven Democratic electoral votes. Rosseló\sought to alleviate this concern by arguing that the island could become a swing-state.

Puerto Rico does not vote for president, but it elects delegations to the Democratic and Republican national conventions. Hillary Clinton, who as a former senator from New York had many constituents with roots in Puerto Rico, won a majority of the territory's delegates in her two campaigns for president. In 2016 , Florida Sen. Marco Rubio received 75 percent of the Republican vote, earning him all 23 Puerto Rican delegates. He was the only Republican candidate to campaign on the island.

Governor Ricardo Rosselló, a member of the New Progressive Party (PNP), was elected Puerto Rico's 12th governor in 2016. Like his predecessor, Alejandro García Padilla—who chose not to run for a second term in 2016—Rosselló comes from a political family. His father, Pedro Rosselló was governor from 1993 to 2001. But prior to his election in November, much of Rosselló's life was spent in academia and in the scientific community. He studied at M.I.T., making him the second M.I.T.-educated governor of Puerto Rico. The first was Luis Ferre (1969-1973). Rossello earned a doctorate in biomedical engineering from the University of Michigan in 2007 and spent time as a neurobiology researcher at Duke. In 2010, he co-founded Beijing Prosperous Biopharm Co., a pharmaceutical research and development company.

In the territory's contest for the PNP nomination, Rosselló faced former Puerto Rico resident commissioner Pedro Pierluisi. The race turned bitter as the candidates sparred over PROMESA, a bill passed by Congress in 2016 aimed at addressing Puerto Rico's economic crisis. Rosselló opposed the legislation, while Pierluisi tepidly supported it. In the June 2016 primaries, Rosselló won a narrow 51%-49% victory. The general election also proved competitive, but Rosselló managed to defeat former Puerto Rico Secretary of State David Bernier, whose Popular Democratic Party, at the time, was navigating its way through a corruption scandal. Rosselló won 42%-39%. An independent candidate took more than 10% of the vote.

Statehood has so far been the bedrock of Rosselló's political agenda. In his campaign, he advocated for drafting a state constitution and electing senators and representatives to lobby Congress to recognize Puerto Rico as a U.S. state. Tennessee successfully utilized a similar strategy in the late 18th century. He has been a vocal supporter of the referendum vote that will take place in June 2017. After taking office, he signed executive orders promoting bilingualism and requiring territorial agencies to reduce budgets. He has supported the privatization of certain public services and the creation of financial incentives to attract more doctors to the island.

RESIDENT COMMISSIONER

Jenniffer Gonzalez Colon (R)

Elected 2016, term expires 2018, 1st term, b. Aug 05, 1976; San Juan; University of Puerto Rico, Bach. Deg.; Inter-American University of Puerto Rico; Inter-American University of Puerto Rico, LL.M.; Single.

Elected Office: President, Puerto Rico Republian Party, 2004-2016; Vice President, New Progressive Party, 2008-2016; PR House, 2002-2016, Speaker, 2009-2012, Minority Leader, 2012-2016.

DC Office: 1529 LHOB 20515, 202-225-2615, Fax: 202-225-2154, gonzalez-colon.house.gov.

Committees: *Natural Resources*: Indian, Insular & Alaska Native Affairs, Oversight & Investigations. *Small Business*: Economic Growth, Tax & Capital Access, Health & Technology. *Veterans' Affairs*: Health, Oversight & Investigations.

Jenniffer González, a member of Puerto Rico's pro-statehood New Progressive Party (PNP), was elected in 2016. At 40 years old, González is the youngest person ever to serve as resident commissioner for the territory and the first woman to hold the position. She became a legislator in Puerto Rico in 2002 at the age of 25 and became the island's youngest speaker of the house seven years later. She earned a J.D. from Puerto Rico's Interamerican University and has worked in San Juan as an attorney. While PNP politicians affiliate with both the Democratic and Republican parties on the mainland, González is the chair of the territory's Republican Party. This did not keep her from speaking critically of Donald Trump throughout the 2016 primary season, however. In May, she pledged not to vote for Trump at the Republican National Convention, saying, "I cannot validate the attack on the Latino community. I won't vote for him." González endorsed Marco Rubio ahead of the territory's March primary, which Rubio won with more than 70 percent of the vote.

González succeeded two-term commissioner Pedro Pierluisi, who decided against seeking a third term in order to run for governor. She won the PNP's primary with roughly 70 percent of the vote. In the general election, she defeated Popular Democratic Party candidate Hector Ferrer, 48.77%-47.25%.

In the House, González serves on the committees on Natural Resources, Small Business and Veterans' Affairs. She is the vice-chair of the subcommittee with jurisdiction on territorial affairs. As with Puerto Rico's newly-elected Gov. Ricardo Rossello, statehood has been a key issue for her. In January 2017, she filed a bill that would make Puerto Rico a state by 2025. She has also submitted legislation aimed at expanding healthcare access and preserving Medicaid in the territory.

VIRGIN ISLANDS

The U.S. Virgin Islands, acquired from Denmark in 1917, are near the northern end of the Antilles chain between the Caribbean Sea and the Atlantic Ocean. They were settled by the Dutch and Danish and had a polyglot colonial society, with one of the oldest Jewish communities in the Western Hemisphere. Their most famous son is Alexander Hamilton, who grew up on St. Croix but moved to New York and never came back. Almost all of the territory's 103,000 people live on the three main islands of St. Thomas, St. John and St. Croix. Its population is the fifth-oldest in the world with a median age of 45.6 years.

The Virgin Islands have lived primarily off tourism and, until 2013, an oil refinery. St. Thomas has long been one of the top cruise ship destinations in the world and the islands together receive nearly 3 million visitors each year. Tourism accounts for approximately 60 percent of the territory's GDP and the government continues to incentivize travel to the islands, offering spending credit vouchers to celebrate in 2017 its centennial as a U.S. territory and increasing the number of airplane flights from Atlanta and Houston.

Even with its reliable tourism industry, the Virgin Islands' economy was weakened after Hovensa, an oil refinery built on St. Croix by Hess Oil in 1966, was closed. Once one of the largest refineries in the world, it closed in 2012, with a loss of 2,200 jobs and $100 million revenue to the territorial government. After nearly four years of inactivity, the Hovensa oil refinery was given a second chance in December

2015 when the legislature approved a purchase agreement with Limetree Bay Holdings, a subsidiary of ArcLight Capital Partners. The refinery will act as an oil storage facility; Sinopec, Asia's largest oil refiner, will lease 75 percent of its capacity over the next decade. Limetree Bay expressed interest in reviving Hovensa's refining operations.

Rum sales in the Virgin Islands are a staple of the economy. Rum-producing U.S. territories have received $13.25 of the $13.50 per-gallon federal tax on rum since 1999. These payments have been used to incentivize rum producers to relocate to the Virgin Islands. In 2008, the Virgin Islands government made a deal with the British-based liquor company Diageo to move its Captain Morgan rum operations from Puerto Rico to a new $165 million distillery in the Virgin Islands. The islands' government estimated it would get $119 million in annual revenue, of which $36 million would go to Diageo as an incentive to move. Puerto Rican politicians were unhappy with the plan and argued that it was illegitimate to use rum tax funds to lure a distillery operation from one territory to another. In 2009, former Puerto Rico Resident Commissioner Pedro Pierluisi sponsored a bill to limit payment to liquor companies to 10 percent of rum tax funds. The rum tax rebate has been renewed every two years, though criticism of the practice from fiscal hawks in Congress has been growing louder.

Unemployment in the Virgin Islands has remained above 11 percent since 2012. More than one quarter of workers on the islands are employed by the government. In addition to a budget deficit, the islandshave a crushing burden of $2.4 billion in bond debt. The Virgin Islands have $3,000 more debt per person than their neighbor, Puerto Rico, which defaulted on $779 million of debt in July 2016, an event adding to anxiety over the islands' fiscal future. In February 2017, the territory's legislature passed the Revenue Enhancement and Economic Recovery Act, taxing alcohol, tobacco and carbonated beverages to generate new revenue.

The Virgin Islands usually play a small role in the presidential selection process. The territory gained attention in 2016 when two factions within the local GOP disputed which slate of at-large delegates would attend the Republican National Convention in Cleveland—the elected delegates, who were disqualified for failing to properly file paperwork, or the alternate delegates put forward by the Virgin Islands' party chair. Ultimately, the Republican National Committee's Committee on Contests reinstated the original delegates prior to the convention. Eight delegates backed Donald Trump and one abstained. In the Democratic caucus, Hillary Clinton defeated Bernie Sanders, 84-12%, securing all seven pledged delegates. Eight years earlier, Barack Obama had bested Clinton by a similarly large margin, 90%-8%.

Governor Kenneth Mapp, an independent, was elected to replace term-limited Democrat John de Jongh in 2014, in an upset over Donna Christensen, the territory's long-time delegate to Congress. Christensen entered the race as the favorite, but trailed Mapp by almost nine points in the first round of voting and suffered a crushing defeat in the runoff. Mapp, running on an economic platform that included a plan to create 1,000 jobs during his first year in office, won 62%-37%. He is the Virgin Islands' first non-Democratic governor since 1999.

A former police officer in New York City, Mapp served three terms as a Republican in the Virgin Islands Legislature and one term as lieutenant governor from 1995 to 1999 under Roy Lester Schneider. He ran as an independent for governor in 2006 and 2010, losing both times to de Jongh. Mapp earned a masters in public administration from Harvard University and worked in the administration of Gov. Charles Turnbull as director of finance and administration for the Virgin Islands Public Finance Authority from 2002 to 2006.

In office, Mapp has tangled with Hovensa over the fate of its shuttered oil refinery on St. Croix. He pushed to remove the company from the property, and in March 2015, proposed repurposing the refinery as a military installation, similar to—or as a potential replacement for—Guantanamo Bay. The St. Croix refinery was eventually purchased by Limetree Bay Holdings, a subsidiary of ArcLight Capital Partners, to serve as an oil storage facility. Mapp applauded the agreement in December 2015, highlighting the $220 million payment Limetree would make to the government as part of the deal.

To address the islands' ailing economy, Mapp has advocated improved sports tourism infrastructure, including refurbishing two horse racing tracks in a $27 million agreement ratified in December 2016. He also supported the passage of the Revenue Enhancement and Economic Recovery Act in February 2017, which taxes alcohol, tobacco, and carbonated beverages, to generate new revenue. In March 2017, Mapp expressed concerns over plans in Washington to repeal and replace Obamacare, saying that the territorial government would be unable to cover costs if Congress and the White House cut Medicaid funding. The USVI opted into the Affordable Care Act's expansion of Medicaid in 2014 and has received more than $300 million in federal funding.

DELEGATE

Stacey Plaskett (D)

Elected 2014, term expires 2018, 2nd term, b. May 13, 1964; New York, NY; Georgetown University Foreign Service School (DC), B.S.; American University, Washington College of Law, J.D.; Lutheran; Married (Jeremy Buckney Small); 5 children.

Professional Career: Assistant District Attorney, Bronx; Consultant & legal counsel, Mitchel Madison Group; Practicing attorney; Staff, U.S. Department of Justice, 2002-2004; General counsel, Virgin Isl. econ. dev't. auth. 2007-2014.

DC Office: 331 CHOB 20515, 202-225-1790, Fax: 202-225-5517, plaskett.house.gov.

Committees: *Agriculture*: Commodity Exchanges, Energy & Credit, General Farm Commodities & Risk Management, Livestock & Foreign Agriculture. *Oversight & Government Reform*: Health Care, Benefits & Administrative Rules, Interior, Energy & Environment (RMM).

Stacey Plaskett, a Democrat, was elected delegate from the Virgin Islands in 2014. Plaskett grew up in Brooklyn, raised by parents who migrated to New York from the Virgin Islands in the 1950s. She attended Choate Rosemary Hall, where a young John F. Kennedy was voted "most likely to succeed" by his graduating class in 1935 (the school became co-educational in the 1970s). She earned a degree in history and diplomacy from Georgetown University and a law degree from American University. Afterwards, she worked as an assistant district attorney in the Bronx and later as counsel to the House Ethics Committee. Before relocating to the Virgin Islands, Plaskett was a political appointee in the Department of Justice from 2002 to 2004 and served on the staff of Deputy Attorney General Larry Thompson.

Plaskett first ran for the delegate seat in 2012 when she lost to incumbent Donna Christensen in the primary 57%-42%. In 2014, Plaskett ran again and won the general election with more than 90% of the vote. Plaskett kept her seat in 2016 by defeating former State Senator Ronald Russell in the primary 85%-14%. Facing write-in candidate Gordon Ackley in the general election, Plaskett came away with 98% of the vote.

In the House, Plaskett serves on the Oversight and Government Reform Committee and is the first delegate from the Virgin Islands to hold a seat on the Agriculture Committee. In December 2016, she ran for a newly-created position on the House Democrats' leadership team but lost to California Rep. Tony Cardenas. She has been active on territorial issues, including advocating for voting rights for the insular territories. In 2015, Plaskett introduced legislation to increase the rebate the Virgin Islands receives from federal taxes on rum sales. The bill failed, but she took up the issue again in February 2017, arguing that the territory may be owed $100 million in cover-over revenues dues. Her bill calling attention to the centennial anniversary of the U.S. acquisition of the Virgin Islands in 1917 was signed into law in September 2016.

★ LEADERSHIP ★

The 115th Congress
2017-2018

U.S. Senate

46D, 52R, 2I

Republicans

Majority Leader...Mitch McConnell (KY)
President Pro Tempore..Orrin Hatch (UT)
Majority Whip & Assistant Majority Leader...John Cornyn (TX)
Republican Conference Chairman..John Thune (SD)
Republican Conference Vice Chairman...Roy Blunt (MO)
Republican Policy Committee Chairman...John Barrasso (WY)
National Republican Senatorial Committee Chairman.................. .....Cory Gardner (CO)

Democrats

Minority Leader...Charles Schumer (NY)
Minority Whip..Dick Durbin (IL)
Assistant Minority Leader..Patty Murray (WA)
Democratic Policy and Communications Center Chairman.................Debbie Stabenow (MI)
Democratic Conference Vice Chairman...Elizabeth Warren (MA)
Democratic Conference Vice Chairman...................................... .....Mark Warner (VA)
Democratic Steering Committee Chairman................................. .....Amy Klobuchar (MN)
Democratic Outreach Committee Chairman..Bernie Sanders (VT)
Democratic Policy and Communications Center Vice Chairman.... .....Joe Manchin (WV)
Democratic Conference Secretary...Tammy Baldwin (WI)
Democratic Senatorial Campaign Committee Chairman................ .....Chris Van Hollen (MD)

U.S. House of Representatives

194D, 241R

Republicans

Speaker of the House.. .....Paul Ryan (WI-1)
Majority Leader...Kevin McCarthy (CA-23)
Majority Whip... .....Steve Scalise (LA-1)
Republican Conference Chairman..Cathy McMorris Rodgers (WA-5)
Republican Policy Committee Chairman...Luke Messer (IN-6)
Chief Deputy Whip..Patrick McHenry (NC-10)
National Republican Congressional Committee Chairman...................Steve Stivers (OH-15)
Republican Conference Vice Chairman...Doug Collins (GA-9)
Republican Conference Secretary...Jason Smith (MO-8)

Democrats

Minority Leader...Nancy Pelosi (CA-12)
Minority Whip..Steny Hoyer (MD-5)
Assistant Democratic Leader.. .....James Clyburn (SC-6)
Democratic Caucus Chairman...Joseph Crowley (NY-14)
Democratic Congressional Campaign Committee Chairman.................Ben Lujan (NM-3)
Democratic Caucus Vice Chairman..Linda Sanchez (CA-38)
Democratic Steering and Policy Committee Co-Chair.................. .....Rosa DeLauro (CT-3)
Democratic Steering and Policy Committee Co-Chair.................. .....Eric Swalwell (CA-15)

★ SENATE SENIORITY ★

Senators are ranked by length of consecutive service in the Senate. If necessary, ties are broken based on previous public service and state population. The Senate seniority list was compiled from Senate Historical Office records. It is current as of Jun 30, 2017.

Senator (Party and State)	Start of Service
Patrick Leahy (D-VT)	Jan 03, 1975
Orrin Hatch (R-UT)	Jan 03, 1977
Thad Cochran (R-MS)	Dec 27, 1978
Chuck Grassley (R-IA)	Jan 03, 1981
Mitch McConnell (R-KY)	Jan 03, 1985
John McCain (R-AZ)	Jan 03, 1987
Richard Shelby (R-AL)	Jan 03, 1987
Dianne Feinstein (D-CA)	Nov 10, 1992
Patty Murray (D-WA)	Jan 03, 1993
Jim Inhofe (R-OK)	Nov 17, 1994
Ron Wyden (D-OR)	Feb 06, 1996
Pat Roberts (R-KS)	Jan 03, 1997
Jack Reed (D-RI)	Jan 03, 1997
Dick Durbin (D-IL)	Jan 03, 1997
Mike Enzi (R-WY)	Jan 03, 1997
Susan Collins (R-ME)	Jan 03, 1997
Mike Crapo (R-ID)	Jan 03, 1999
Chuck Schumer (D-NY)	Jan 03, 1999
Debbie Stabenow (D-MI)	Jan 03, 2001
Tom Carper (D-DE)	Jan 03, 2001
Maria Cantwell (D-WA)	Jan 03, 2001
Bill Nelson (D-FL)	Jan 03, 2001
John Cornyn (R-TX)	Dec 01, 2002
Lisa Murkowski (R-AK)	Dec 20, 2002
Lindsey Graham (R-SC)	Jan 03, 2003
Lamar Alexander (R-TN)	Jan 03, 2003
Richard Burr (R-NC)	Jan 03, 2005
Johnny Isakson (R-GA)	Jan 03, 2005
John Thune (R-SD)	Jan 03, 2005
Robert Menendez (D-NJ)	Jan 18, 2006
Claire McCaskill (D-MO)	Jan 03, 2007
Amy Klobuchar (D-MN)	Jan 03, 2007
Ben Cardin (D-MD)	Jan 03, 2007
Robert Casey (D-PA)	Jan 03, 2007
Sherrod Brown (D-OH)	Jan 03, 2007
Bob Corker (R-TN)	Jan 03, 2007
Jon Tester (D-MT)	Jan 03, 2007
Bernie Sanders (I-VT)	Jan 03, 2007
Sheldon Whitehouse (D-RI)	Jan 03, 2007
John Barrasso (R-WY)	Jun 25, 2007
Roger Wicker (R-MS)	Dec 31, 2007
Tom Udall (D-NM)	Jan 03, 2009
Mark Warner (D-VA)	Jan 03, 2009
Jeanne Shaheen (D-NH)	Jan 03, 2009
Jeff Merkley (D-OR)	Jan 03, 2009
Jim Risch (R-ID)	Jan 03, 2009
Michael Bennet (D-CO)	Jan 21, 2009
Kirsten Gillibrand (D-NY)	Jan 26, 2009
Al Franken (D-MN)	Jul 07, 2009
Chris Coons (D-DE)	Nov 15, 2010
Joe Manchin (D-WV)	Nov 15, 2010
Jerry Moran (R-KS)	Jan 03, 2011
Rand Paul (R-KY)	Jan 03, 2011
Mike Lee (R-UT)	Jan 03, 2011
John Hoeven (R-ND)	Jan 03, 2011
Ron Johnson (R-WI)	Jan 03, 2011
Richard Blumenthal (D-CT)	Jan 03, 2011
Roy Blunt (R-MO)	Jan 03, 2011
John Boozman (R-AR)	Jan 03, 2011
Rob Portman (R-OH)	Jan 03, 2011
Marco Rubio (R-FL)	Jan 03, 2011
Pat Toomey (R-PA)	Jan 03, 2011
Dean Heller (R-NV)	May 09, 2011
Brian Schatz (D-HI)	Dec 27, 2012
Tim Scott (R-SC)	Jan 02, 2013
Elizabeth Warren (D-MA)	Jan 03, 2013
Mazie Hirono (D-HI)	Jan 03, 2013
Angus King (I-ME)	Jan 03, 2013
Tim Kaine (D-VA)	Jan 03, 2013
Martin Heinrich (D-NM)	Jan 03, 2013
Heidi Heitkamp (D-NPL-ND)	Jan 03, 2013
Chris Murphy (D-CT)	Jan 03, 2013
Tammy Baldwin (D-WI)	Jan 03, 2013
Deb Fischer (R-NE)	Jan 03, 2013
Jeff Flake (R-AZ)	Jan 03, 2013
Ted Cruz (R-TX)	Jan 03, 2013
Joe Donnelly (D-IN)	Jan 03, 2013
Ed Markey (D-MA)	Jul 16, 2013
Cory Booker (D-NJ)	Oct 31, 2013
Bill Cassidy (R-LA)	Jan 03, 2015
Shelley Moore Capito (R-WV)	Jan 03, 2015
Steve Daines (R-MT)	Jan 03, 2015
Tom Cotton (R-AR)	Jan 03, 2015
Joni Ernst (R-IA)	Jan 03, 2015
Cory Gardner (R-CO)	Jan 03, 2015
David Perdue (R-GA)	Jan 03, 2015
Gary Peters (D-MI)	Jan 03, 2015
James Lankford (R-OK)	Jan 03, 2015
Ben Sasse (R-NE)	Jan 03, 2015
Mike Rounds (R-SD)	Jan 03, 2015
Dan Sullivan (R-AK)	Jan 03, 2015
Thom Tillis (R-NC)	Jan 03, 2015
Chris Van Hollen (D-MD)	Jan 03, 2017
Todd Young (R-IN)	Jan 03, 2017
Kamala Harris (D-CA)	Jan 03, 2017
Maggie Hassan (D-NH)	Jan 03, 2017
John Kennedy (R-LA)	Jan 03, 2017
Catherine Cortez Masto (D-NV)	Jan 03, 2017
Tammy Duckworth (D-IL)	Jan 03, 2017
Luther Strange (R-AL)	Feb 09, 2017

★ HOUSE SENIORITY ★

Representatives are ranked by the total length of time served in the House. Members are given credit for prior service, and ties are broken alphabetically. The House seniority list was provided was compiled from information records and rules provided by the office of the Clerk of the House. It is current as of Jun 30, 2017.

Member (Party and State)	Start of Service
John Conyers (D-MI)	Jan 03, 1965
Don Young (R-AK)	Mar 06, 1973
Jim Sensenbrenner (R-WI)	Jan 03, 1979
Lamar Smith (R-TX)	Jan 03, 1981
Hal Rogers (R-KY)	Jan 03, 1981
Chris Smith (R-NJ)	Jan 03, 1981
Jason Smith (R-MO)	Jan 03, 1981
Mike Rogers (R-AL)	Jan 03, 1981
Steny Hoyer (D-MD)	May 19, 1981
Sander Levin (D-MI)	Jan 03, 1983
Marcy Kaptur (D-OH)	Jan 03, 1983
Joe Barton (R-TX)	Jan 03, 1985
Pete Visclosky (D-IN)	Jan 03, 1985
Louise Slaughter (D-NY)	Jan 03, 1987
John Lewis (D-GA)	Jan 03, 1987
Fred Upton (R-MI)	Jan 03, 1987
Peter DeFazio (D-OR)	Jan 03, 1987
Nancy Pelosi (D-CA)	Jun 02, 1987
John Duncan (R-TN)	Nov 08, 1988
Frank Pallone (D-NJ)	Nov 08, 1988
Dana Rohrabacher (R-CA)	Jan 03, 1989
Nita Lowey (D-NY)	Jan 03, 1989
Richard Neal (D-MA)	Jan 03, 1989
Eliot Engel (D-NY)	Jan 03, 1989
Ileana Ros-Lehtinen (R-FL)	Aug 29, 1989
Jose Serrano (D-NY)	Mar 20, 1990
Collin Peterson (D-MN)	Jan 03, 1991
Rosa DeLauro (D-CT)	Jan 03, 1991
Maxine Waters (D-CA)	Jan 03, 1991
Eleanor Holmes Norton (D-DC)	Jan 03, 1991
Eddie Bernice Johnson (D-TX)	May 08, 1991
Sam Johnson (R-TX)	May 08, 1991
Jerrold Nadler (D-NY)	Nov 03, 1992
Lucille Roybal-Allard (D-CA)	Jan 03, 1993
Bob Goodlatte (R-VA)	Jan 03, 1993
Anna Eshoo (D-CA)	Jan 03, 1993
Luis Gutierrez (D-IL)	Jan 03, 1993
James Clyburn (D-SC)	Jan 03, 1993
Nydia Velazquez (D-NY)	Jan 03, 1993
Peter King (R-NY)	Jan 03, 1993
Alcee Hastings (D-FL)	Jan 03, 1993
Ed Royce (R-CA)	Jan 03, 1993
Carolyn Maloney (D-NY)	Jan 03, 1993
Gene Green (D-TX)	Jan 03, 1993
Ken Calvert (R-CA)	Jan 03, 1993
Sanford Bishop (D-GA)	Jan 03, 1993
Bobby Scott (D-VA)	Jan 03, 1993
Bobby Rush (D-IL)	Jan 03, 1993
Sean Maloney (D-NY)	Jan 03, 1993

Member (Party and State)	Start of Service
Michael Bishop (R-MI)	Jan 03, 1993
Bennie Thompson (D-MS)	Apr 13, 1993
Frank Lucas (R-OK)	May 10, 1994
Zoe Lofgren (D-CA)	Jan 03, 1995
Walter Jones (R-NC)	Jan 03, 1995
Rodney Frelinghuysen (R-NJ)	Jan 03, 1995
Sheila Jackson Lee (D-TX)	Jan 03, 1995
Frank LoBiondo (R-NJ)	Jan 03, 1995
Mac Thornberry (R-TX)	Jan 03, 1995
Mike Doyle (D-PA)	Jan 03, 1995
Lloyd Doggett (D-TX)	Jan 03, 1995
Elijah Cummings (D-MD)	Apr 16, 1996
Earl Blumenauer (D-OR)	May 21, 1996
Robert Aderholt (R-AL)	Jan 03, 1997
Diana DeGette (D-CO)	Jan 03, 1997
Ron Kind (D-WI)	Jan 03, 1997
Bill Pascrell (D-NJ)	Jan 03, 1997
Pete Sessions (R-TX)	Jan 03, 1997
Rodney Davis (R-IL)	Jan 03, 1997
John Shimkus (R-IL)	Jan 03, 1997
Kay Granger (R-TX)	Jan 03, 1997
Adam Smith (D-WA)	Jan 03, 1997
Kevin Brady (R-TX)	Jan 03, 1997
Jim McGovern (D-MA)	Jan 03, 1997
David Price (D-NC)	Jan 03, 1997
Brad Sherman (D-CA)	Jan 03, 1997
Danny Davis (D-IL)	Jan 03, 1997
Robert Brady (D-PA)	Jan 03, 1997
Gregory Meeks (D-NY)	Feb 03, 1998
Barbara Lee (D-CA)	Apr 07, 1998
Michael Capuano (D-MA)	Jan 03, 1999
John Larson (D-CT)	Jan 03, 1999
Grace Napolitano (D-CA)	Jan 03, 1999
Mike Thompson (D-CA)	Jan 03, 1999
Jan Schakowsky (D-IL)	Jan 03, 1999
Paul Ryan (R-WI)	Jan 03, 1999
Greg Walden (R-OR)	Jan 03, 1999
Joseph Crowley (D-NY)	Jan 03, 1999
Mike Simpson (R-ID)	Jan 03, 1999
Darrell Issa (R-CA)	Jan 03, 2001
John Culberson (R-TX)	Jan 03, 2001
Sam Graves (R-MO)	Jan 03, 2001
Betty McCollum (D-MN)	Jan 03, 2001
Jim Langevin (D-RI)	Jan 03, 2001
Susan Davis (D-CA)	Jan 03, 2001
Adam Schiff (D-CA)	Jan 03, 2001
Rick Larsen (D-WA)	Jan 03, 2001
Pat Tiberi (R-OH)	Jan 03, 2001
Lacy Clay (D-MO)	Jan 03, 2001

Member (Party and State)	Start of Service
Bill Shuster (R-PA)	May 15, 2001
Stephen Lynch (D-MA)	Oct 16, 2001
Joe Wilson (R-SC)	Dec 18, 2001
Madeleine Bordallo (D-GU)	Nov 05, 2002
Raul Grijalva (D-AZ)	Jan 03, 2003
Michael Burgess (R-TX)	Jan 03, 2003
Dutch Ruppersberger (D-MD)	Jan 03, 2003
Jeb Hensarling (R-TX)	Jan 03, 2003
David Scott (D-GA)	Jan 03, 2003
Trent Franks (R-AZ)	Jan 03, 2003
Steve King (R-IA)	Jan 03, 2003
Michael Turner (R-OH)	Jan 03, 2003
Marsha Blackburn (R-TN)	Jan 03, 2003
Mario Diaz-Balart (R-FL)	Jan 03, 2003
Rob Bishop (R-UT)	Jan 03, 2003
Devin Nunes (R-CA)	Jan 03, 2003
Tom Cole (R-OK)	Jan 03, 2003
John Carter (R-TX)	Jan 03, 2003
Tim Murphy (R-PA)	Jan 03, 2003
Tim Ryan (D-OH)	Jan 03, 2003
Linda Sanchez (D-CA)	Jan 03, 2003
Jim Cooper (D-TN)	Jan 03, 2003
G.K. Butterfield (D-NC)	Jul 20, 2004
Jim Costa (D-CA)	Jan 03, 2005
Emanuel Cleaver (D-MO)	Jan 03, 2005
Al Green (D-TX)	Jan 03, 2005
Brian Higgins (D-NY)	Jan 03, 2005
Ted Poe (R-TX)	Jan 03, 2005
Patrick McHenry (R-NC)	Jan 03, 2005
Virginia Foxx (R-NC)	Jan 03, 2005
Daniel Lipinski (D-IL)	Jan 03, 2005
Mike Conaway (R-TX)	Jan 03, 2005
Dave Reichert (R-WA)	Jan 03, 2005
Henry Cuellar (D-TX)	Jan 03, 2005
Cathy McMorris Rodgers (R-WA)	Jan 03, 2005
Louie Gohmert (R-TX)	Jan 03, 2005
Kenny Marchant (R-TX)	Jan 03, 2005
Gwen Moore (D-WI)	Jan 03, 2005
Debbie Wasserman Schultz (D-FL)	Jan 03, 2005
Michael McCaul (R-TX)	Jan 03, 2005
Charlie Dent (R-PA)	Jan 03, 2005
Jeff Fortenberry (R-NE)	Jan 03, 2005
Doris Matsui (D-CA)	Mar 08, 2005
Albio Sires (D-NJ)	Nov 07, 2006
Ed Perlmutter (D-CO)	Jan 03, 2007
John Yarmuth (D-KY)	Jan 03, 2007
John Sarbanes (D-MD)	Jan 03, 2007
Joe Courtney (D-CT)	Jan 03, 2007
Gus Bilirakis (R-FL)	Jan 03, 2007
Peter Roskam (R-IL)	Jan 03, 2007
Steve Cohen (D-TN)	Jan 03, 2007
Doug Lamborn (R-CO)	Jan 03, 2007
Adrian Smith (R-NE)	Jan 03, 2007
Kathy Castor (D-FL)	Jan 03, 2007
Kevin McCarthy (R-CA)	Jan 03, 2007
Tim Walz (D-MN)	Jan 03, 2007
Hank Johnson (D-GA)	Jan 03, 2007
Vern Buchanan (R-FL)	Jan 03, 2007
Jim Jordan (R-OH)	Jan 03, 2007

Member (Party and State)	Start of Service
Peter Welch (D-VT)	Jan 03, 2007
Yvette Clarke (D-NY)	Jan 03, 2007
Keith Ellison (D-MN)	Jan 03, 2007
Dave Loebsack (D-IA)	Jan 03, 2007
Jerry McNerney (D-CA)	Jan 03, 2007
Niki Tsongas (D-MA)	Oct 16, 2007
Rob Wittman (R-VA)	Dec 11, 2007
Bob Latta (R-OH)	Dec 11, 2007
Andre Carson (D-IN)	Mar 11, 2008
Jackie Speier (D-CA)	Apr 08, 2008
Steve Scalise (R-LA)	May 03, 2008
Gregorio Sablan (D-MP)	Nov 04, 2008
Marcia Fudge (D-OH)	Nov 18, 2008
Kurt Schrader (D-OR)	Jan 03, 2009
Tom Rooney (R-FL)	Jan 03, 2009
Bill Posey (R-FL)	Jan 03, 2009
Blaine Luetkemeyer (R-MO)	Jan 03, 2009
Gerald Connolly (D-VA)	Jan 03, 2009
Paul Tonko (D-NY)	Jan 03, 2009
Gregg Harper (R-MS)	Jan 03, 2009
Lynn Jenkins (R-KS)	Jan 03, 2009
Mike Coffman (R-CO)	Jan 03, 2009
Glenn Thompson (R-PA)	Jan 03, 2009
Jason Chaffetz (R-UT)	Jan 03, 2009
Erik Paulsen (R-MN)	Jan 03, 2009
Brett Guthrie (R-KY)	Jan 03, 2009
Duncan Hunter (R-CA)	Jan 03, 2009
Leonard Lance (R-NJ)	Jan 03, 2009
Jared Polis (D-CO)	Jan 03, 2009
Phil Roe (R-TN)	Jan 03, 2009
Pete Olson (R-TX)	Jan 03, 2009
Jim Himes (D-CT)	Jan 03, 2009
Chellie Pingree (D-ME)	Jan 03, 2009
Tom McClintock (R-CA)	Jan 03, 2009
Ben Lujan (D-NM)	Jan 03, 2009
Mike Quigley (D-IL)	Apr 07, 2009
Judy Chu (D-CA)	Jul 14, 2009
John Garamendi (D-CA)	Nov 03, 2009
Ted Deutch (D-FL)	Apr 13, 2010
Tom Graves (R-GA)	Jun 08, 2010
Tom Reed (R-NY)	Nov 02, 2010
Adam Kinzinger (R-IL)	Jan 03, 2011
Andy Harris (R-MD)	Jan 03, 2011
Austin Scott (R-GA)	Jan 03, 2011
Billy Long (R-MO)	Jan 03, 2011
Blake Farenthold (R-TX)	Jan 03, 2011
Bob Gibbs (R-OH)	Jan 03, 2011
Cedric Richmond (D-LA)	Jan 03, 2011
Chuck Fleischmann (R-TN)	Jan 03, 2011
Daniel Webster (R-FL)	Jan 03, 2011
David McKinley (R-WV)	Jan 03, 2011
David Cicilline (D-RI)	Jan 03, 2011
David Schweikert (R-AZ)	Jan 03, 2011
Dennis Ross (R-FL)	Jan 03, 2011
Diane Black (R-TN)	Jan 03, 2011
Rick Crawford (R-AR)	Jan 03, 2011
Frederica Wilson (D-FL)	Jan 03, 2011
Morgan Griffith (R-VA)	Jan 03, 2011
Jaime Herrera Beutler (R-WA)	Jan 03, 2011

Member (Party and State)	Start of Service
Jim Renacci (R-OH)	Jan 03, 2011
Jeff Duncan (R-SC)	Jan 03, 2011
Jeff Denham (R-CA)	Jan 03, 2011
Justin Amash (R-MI)	Jan 03, 2011
Karen Bass (D-CA)	Jan 03, 2011
Kevin Yoder (R-KS)	Jan 03, 2011
Kristi Noem (R-SD)	Jan 03, 2011
Larry Bucshon (R-IN)	Jan 03, 2011
Lou Barletta (R-PA)	Jan 03, 2011
Martha Roby (R-AL)	Jan 03, 2011
Mike Kelly (R-PA)	Jan 03, 2011
Mo Brooks (R-AL)	Jan 03, 2011
Patrick Meehan (R-PA)	Jan 03, 2011
Paul Gosar (R-AZ)	Jan 03, 2011
Randy Hultgren (R-IL)	Jan 03, 2011
Raul Labrador (R-ID)	Jan 03, 2011
Rob Woodall (R-GA)	Jan 03, 2011
Scott DesJarlais (R-TN)	Jan 03, 2011
Scott Tipton (R-CO)	Jan 03, 2011
Sean Duffy (R-WI)	Jan 03, 2011
Steve Pearce (R-NM)	Jan 03, 2011
Steve Womack (R-AR)	Jan 03, 2011
Steve Chabot (R-OH)	Jan 03, 2011
Steve Stivers (R-OH)	Jan 03, 2011
Steven Palazzo (R-MS)	Jan 03, 2011
Terri Sewell (D-AL)	Jan 03, 2011
Tom Marino (R-PA)	Jan 03, 2011
Tim Walberg (R-MI)	Jan 03, 2011
Todd Rokita (R-IN)	Jan 03, 2011
Trey Gowdy (R-SC)	Jan 03, 2011
Vicky Hartzler (R-MO)	Jan 03, 2011
Bill Flores (R-TX)	Jan 03, 2011
Bill Johnson (R-OH)	Jan 03, 2011
William Keating (D-MA)	Jan 03, 2011
Bill Huizenga (R-MI)	Jan 03, 2011
Mark Amodei (R-NV)	Sep 13, 2011
Suzanne Bonamici (D-OR)	Jan 31, 2012
Thomas Massie (R-KY)	Nov 06, 2012
Donald Payne (D-NJ)	Nov 06, 2012
Suzan DelBene (D-WA)	Nov 06, 2012
Alan Lowenthal (D-CA)	Jan 03, 2013
Andy Barr (R-KY)	Jan 03, 2013
Brad Wenstrup (R-OH)	Jan 03, 2013
Bill Foster (D-IL)	Jan 03, 2013
Ann Wagner (R-MO)	Jan 03, 2013
Tom Rice (R-SC)	Jan 03, 2013
Grace Meng (D-NY)	Jan 03, 2013
Scott Perry (R-PA)	Jan 03, 2013
Filemon Vela (D-TX)	Jan 03, 2013
Ann Kuster (D-NH)	Jan 03, 2013
Marc Veasey (D-TX)	Jan 03, 2013
Michelle Lujan Grisham (D-NM)	Jan 03, 2013
Richard Nolan (D-MN)	Jan 03, 2013
Kyrsten Sinema (D-AZ)	Jan 03, 2013
Dan Kildee (D-MI)	Jan 03, 2013
Chris Stewart (R-UT)	Jan 03, 2013
Denny Heck (D-WA)	Jan 03, 2013
Elizabeth Esty (D-CT)	Jan 03, 2013
Susan Brooks (R-IN)	Jan 03, 2013

Member (Party and State)	Start of Service
Cheri Bustos (D-IL)	Jan 03, 2013
Doug Collins (R-GA)	Jan 03, 2013
George Holding (R-NC)	Jan 03, 2013
Jim Bridenstine (R-OK)	Jan 03, 2013
Jackie Walorski (R-IN)	Jan 03, 2013
Joe Kennedy (D-MA)	Jan 03, 2013
Joyce Beatty (D-OH)	Jan 03, 2013
Lois Frankel (D-FL)	Jan 03, 2013
Juan Vargas (D-CA)	Jan 03, 2013
Markwayne Mullin (R-OK)	Jan 03, 2013
Mark Meadows (R-NC)	Jan 03, 2013
Luke Messer (R-IN)	Jan 03, 2013
Ron DeSantis (R-FL)	Jan 03, 2013
Scott Peters (D-CA)	Jan 03, 2013
Robert Pittenger (R-NC)	Jan 03, 2013
Tulsi Gabbard (D-HI)	Jan 03, 2013
Ted Yoho (R-FL)	Jan 03, 2013
Derek Kilmer (D-WA)	Jan 03, 2013
Keith Rothfus (R-PA)	Jan 03, 2013
Matt Cartwright (D-PA)	Jan 03, 2013
Mark Pocan (D-WI)	Jan 03, 2013
Ami Bera (D-CA)	Jan 03, 2013
Beto O'Rourke (D-TX)	Jan 03, 2013
David Valadao (R-CA)	Jan 03, 2013
Eric Swalwell (D-CA)	Jan 03, 2013
Dave Joyce (R-OH)	Jan 03, 2013
Chris Collins (R-NY)	Jan 03, 2013
Joaquin Castro (D-TX)	Jan 03, 2013
Julia Brownley (D-CA)	Jan 03, 2013
Kevin Cramer (R-ND)	Jan 03, 2013
Mark Takano (D-CA)	Jan 03, 2013
Paul Cook (R-CA)	Jan 03, 2013
Randy Weber (R-TX)	Jan 03, 2013
Raul Ruiz (D-CA)	Jan 03, 2013
Roger Williams (R-TX)	Jan 03, 2013
Tony Cardenas (D-CA)	Jan 03, 2013
Doug LaMalfa (R-CA)	Jan 03, 2013
John Delaney (D-MD)	Jan 03, 2013
Jared Huffman (D-CA)	Jan 03, 2013
Hakeem Jeffries (D-NY)	Jan 03, 2013
Richard Hudson (R-NC)	Jan 03, 2013
Dina Titus (D-NV)	Jan 03, 2013
Robin Kelly (D-IL)	Apr 09, 2013
Mark Sanford (R-SC)	May 07, 2013
Katherine Clark (D-MA)	Dec 10, 2013
Bradley Byrne (R-AL)	Dec 17, 2013
Alma Adams (D-NC)	Nov 04, 2014
Donald Norcross (D-NJ)	Nov 04, 2014
Dave Brat (R-VA)	Nov 04, 2014
Stacey Plaskett (D-VI)	Nov 04, 2014
Aumua Radewagen (R-AS)	Nov 04, 2014
French Hill (R-AR)	Jan 03, 2015
Gary Palmer (R-AL)	Jan 03, 2015
Buddy Carter (R-GA)	Jan 03, 2015
Jody Hice (R-GA)	Jan 03, 2015
Rod Blum (R-IA)	Jan 03, 2015
David Young (R-IA)	Jan 03, 2015
Mike Bost (R-IL)	Jan 03, 2015
Debbie Dingell (D-MI)	Jan 03, 2015

Member (Party and State)	Start of Service
Brenda Lawrence (D-MI)	Jan 03, 2015
John Moolenaar (R-MI)	Jan 03, 2015
Mark Walker (R-NC)	Jan 03, 2015
David Rouzer (R-NC)	Jan 03, 2015
Tom MacArthur (R-NJ)	Jan 03, 2015
Bonnie Watson Coleman (D-NJ)	Jan 03, 2015
Kathleen Rice (D-NY)	Jan 03, 2015
Elise Stefanik (R-NY)	Jan 03, 2015
Seth Moulton (D-MA)	Jan 03, 2015
Garret Graves (R-LA)	Jan 03, 2015
John Katko (R-NY)	Jan 03, 2015
Steve Russell (R-OK)	Jan 03, 2015
Brendan Boyle (D-PA)	Jan 03, 2015
John Ratcliffe (R-TX)	Jan 03, 2015
Will Hurd (R-TX)	Jan 03, 2015
Don Beyer (D-VA)	Jan 03, 2015
Barbara Comstock (R-VA)	Jan 03, 2015
Dan Newhouse (R-WA)	Jan 03, 2015
Glenn Grothman (R-WI)	Jan 03, 2015
Evan Jenkins (R-WV)	Jan 03, 2015
Bruce Westerman (R-AR)	Jan 03, 2015
Tom Emmer (R-MN)	Jan 03, 2015
Steve Knight (R-CA)	Jan 03, 2015
Pete Aguilar (D-CA)	Jan 03, 2015
Norma Torres (D-CA)	Jan 03, 2015
Mimi Walters (R-CA)	Jan 03, 2015
Mark DeSaulnier (D-CA)	Jan 03, 2015
Alex Mooney (R-WV)	Jan 03, 2015
Ted Lieu (D-CA)	Jan 03, 2015
Ken Buck (R-CO)	Jan 03, 2015
Ryan Costello (R-PA)	Jan 03, 2015
Barry Loudermilk (R-GA)	Jan 03, 2015
Bruce Poliquin (R-ME)	Jan 03, 2015
David Trott (R-MI)	Jan 03, 2015
Lee Zeldin (R-NY)	Jan 03, 2015
Ruben Gallego (D-AZ)	Jan 03, 2015
Rick Allen (R-GA)	Jan 03, 2015
Ralph Abraham (R-LA)	Jan 03, 2015
Martha McSally (R-AZ)	Jan 03, 2015
Brian Babin (R-TX)	Jan 03, 2015
Mia Love (R-UT)	Jan 03, 2015
Carlos Curbelo (R-FL)	Jan 03, 2015
Daniel Donovan (R-NY)	May 05, 2015
Trent Kelly (R-MS)	Jun 02, 2015
Darin LaHood (R-IL)	Sep 10, 2015
Warren Davidson (R-OH)	Jun 07, 2016
Jenniffer Gonzalez Colon (R-PR)	Nov 01, 2016
James Comer (R-KY)	Nov 08, 2016
Dwight Evans (D-PA)	Nov 08, 2016
Colleen Hanabusa (D-HI)	Nov 08, 2016
Brad Schneider (D-IL)	Jan 03, 2017
Carol Shea-Porter (D-NH)	Jan 03, 2017
Anthony Brown (D-MD)	Jan 03, 2017
Adriano Espaillat (D-NY)	Jan 03, 2017
Donald McEachin (D-VA)	Jan 03, 2017

Member (Party and State)	Start of Service
Al Lawson (D-FL)	Jan 03, 2017
Andy Biggs (R-AZ)	Jan 03, 2017
Brian Mast (R-FL)	Jan 03, 2017
Clay Higgins (R-LA)	Jan 03, 2017
Claudia Tenney (R-NY)	Jan 03, 2017
Brian Fitzpatrick (R-PA)	Jan 03, 2017
Darren Soto (D-FL)	Jan 03, 2017
Francis Rooney (R-FL)	Jan 03, 2017
Drew Ferguson (R-GA)	Jan 03, 2017
Don Bacon (R-NE)	Jan 03, 2017
David Kustoff (R-TN)	Jan 03, 2017
Salud Carbajal (D-CA)	Jan 03, 2017
Stephanie Murphy (D-FL)	Jan 03, 2017
Val Demings (D-FL)	Jan 03, 2017
Raja Krishnamoorthi (D-IL)	Jan 03, 2017
Trey Hollingsworth (R-IN)	Jan 03, 2017
Roger Marshall (R-KS)	Jan 03, 2017
Tom Suozzi (D-NY)	Jan 03, 2017
Vicente Gonzalez (D-TX)	Jan 03, 2017
Thomas Garrett (R-VA)	Jan 03, 2017
Scott Taylor (R-VA)	Jan 03, 2017
Tom O'Halleran (D-AZ)	Jan 03, 2017
Ted Budd (R-NC)	Jan 03, 2017
Ruben Kihuen (D-NV)	Jan 03, 2017
Ro Khanna (D-CA)	Jan 03, 2017
Jodey Arrington (R-TX)	Jan 03, 2017
Jacky Rosen (D-NV)	Jan 03, 2017
Paul Mitchell (R-MI)	Jan 03, 2017
Jamie Raskin (D-MD)	Jan 03, 2017
Josh Gottheimer (D-NJ)	Jan 03, 2017
Jason Lewis (R-MN)	Jan 03, 2017
Matt Gaetz (R-FL)	Jan 03, 2017
John Rutherford (R-FL)	Jan 03, 2017
Liz Cheney (R-WY)	Jan 03, 2017
Mike Gallagher (R-WI)	Jan 03, 2017
Pramila Jayapal (D-WA)	Jan 03, 2017
Lloyd Smucker (R-PA)	Jan 03, 2017
John Faso (R-NY)	Jan 03, 2017
Jack Bergman (R-MI)	Jan 03, 2017
Mike Johnson (R-LA)	Jan 03, 2017
Jim Banks (R-IN)	Jan 03, 2017
Neal Dunn (R-FL)	Jan 03, 2017
Lisa Rochester (D-DE)	Jan 03, 2017
Lou Correa (D-CA)	Jan 03, 2017
Nanette Barragan (D-CA)	Jan 03, 2017
Jimmy Panetta (D-CA)	Jan 03, 2017
Charlie Crist (D-FL)	Jan 03, 2017
Ron Estes (R-KS)	Apr 11, 2017
Greg Gianforte (R-MT)	Jun 14, 2017
Ralph Norman (R-SC)	Jun 26, 2017
Karen Handel (R-GA)	Jun 26, 2017
Jimmy Gomez (D-CA)	TBD

★ SENATE COMMITTEES ★

Agriculture, Nutrition & Forestry | **328A RSOB**
agriculture.senate.gov | **202-224-2035**

Majority (R 11): Roberts (KS), Chmn; Cochran (MS), McConnell (KY), Boozman (AR), Hoeven (ND), Ernst (IA), Grassley (IA), Thune (SD), Daines (MT), Perdue (GA), Strange (AL)
Minority (D 10): Stabenow (MI), RMM; Leahy (VT), Brown (OH), Klobuchar (MN), Bennet (CO), Gillibrand (NY), Donnelly (IN), Heitkamp (ND), Casey (PA), Van Hollen (MD)

SUBCOMMITTEES

Commodities, Risk Management & Trade
Majority (R 8): Boozman (AR), Chmn; Cochran (MS), Hoeven (ND), Grassley (IA), Thune (SD), Daines (MT), Perdue (GA), Roberts (KS)
Minority (D 7): Heitkamp (ND), RMM; Brown (OH), Bennet (CO), Gillibrand (NY), Donnelly (IN), Van Hollen (MD), Stabenow (MI)

Conservation, Forestry & Natural Resources
Majority (R 7): Daines (MT), Chmn; Cochran (MS), McConnell (KY), Boozman (AR), Grassley (IA), Strange (AL), Roberts (KS)
Minority (D 6): Bennet (CO), RMM; Leahy (VT), Klobuchar (MN), Donnelly (IN), Casey (PA), Stabenow (MI)

Livestock, Marketing & Agriculture Security
Majority (R 7): Perdue (GA), Chmn; McConnell (KY), Ernst (IA), Grassley (IA), Thune (SD), Daines (MT), Roberts (KS)
Minority (D 6): Gillibrand (NY), RMM; Leahy (VT), Klobuchar (MN), Heitkamp (ND), Casey (PA), Stabenow (MI)

Nutrition, Agricultural Research & Specialty Crops
Majority (R 7): Strange (AL), Chmn; McConnell (KY), Boozman (AR), Hoeven (ND), Ernst (IA), Perdue (GA), Roberts (KS)
Minority (D 6): Casey (PA), RMM; Leahy (VT), Brown (OH), Gillibrand (NY), Van Hollen (MD), Stabenow (MI)

Rural Development & Energy
Majority (R 8): Ernst (IA), Chmn; Cochran (MS), Boozman (AR), Hoeven (ND), Thune (SD), Daines (MT), Strange (AL), Roberts (KS)
Minority (D 7): Van Hollen (MD), RMM; Brown (OH), Klobuchar (MN), Bennet (CO), Donnelly (IN), Heitkamp (ND), Stabenow (MI)

Appropriations | **S-128 The Capitol**
appropriations.senate.gov | **202-224-7257**

Majority (R 16): Cochran (MS), Chmn; McConnell (KY), Shelby (AL), Alexander (TN), Collins (ME), Murkowski (AK), Graham (SC), Blunt (MO), Moran (KS), Hoeven (ND), Boozman (AR), Capito (WV), Lankford (OK), Daines (MT), Kennedy (LA), Rubio (FL)
Minority (D 15): Leahy (VT), RMM; Murray (WA), Feinstein (CA), Durbin (IL), Reed (RI), Tester (MT), Udall (NM), Shaheen (NH), Merkley (OR), Coons (DE), Schatz (HI), Baldwin (WI), Murphy (CT), Manchin (WV), Van Hollen (MD)

SUBCOMMITTEES

Agriculture, Rural Development, FDA & Related Agencies
Majority (R 7): Hoeven (ND), Chmn; Cochran (MS), McConnell (KY), Collins (ME), Blunt (MO), Moran (KS), Rubio (FL)
Minority (D 6): Merkley (OR), RMM; Feinstein (CA), Tester (MT), Udall (NM), Leahy (VT), Baldwin (WI)

Commerce, Justice, Science & Related Agencies
Majority (R 10): Shelby (AL), Chmn; Alexander (TN), Murkowski (AK), Collins (ME), Graham (SC), Boozman (AR), Capito (WV), Lankford (OK), Kennedy (LA), Cochran (MS)
Minority (D 8): Shaheen (NH), RMM; Leahy (VT), Feinstein (CA), Reed (RI), Coons (DE), Schatz (HI), Manchin (WV), Van Hollen (MD)

Department of Defense
Majority (R 10): Cochran (MS), Chmn; McConnell (KY), Shelby (AL), Alexander (TN), Collins (ME), Murkowski (AK), Graham (SC), Blunt (MO), Daines (MT), Moran (KS)
Minority (D 9): Durbin (IL), RMM; Leahy (VT), Feinstein (CA), Murray (WA), Reed (RI), Tester (MT), Udall (NM), Schatz (HI), Baldwin (WI)

Department of Homeland Security
Majority (R 7): Boozman (AR), Chmn; Cochran (MS), Shelby (AL), Murkowski (AK), Hoeven (ND), Lankford (OK), Kennedy (LA)
Minority (D 6): Tester (MT), RMM; Shaheen (NH), Leahy (VT), Murray (WA), Baldwin (WI), Manchin (WV)

Department of the Interior, Environment & Related Agencies
Majority (R 8): Murkowski (AK), Chmn; Cochran (MS), Alexander (TN), Blunt (MO), Hoeven (ND), McConnell (KY), Daines (MT), Capito (WV)
Minority (D 7): Udall (NM), RMM; Feinstein (CA), Leahy (VT), Reed (RI), Tester (MT), Merkley (OR), Van Hollen (MD)

DOL, HHS & Education & Related Agencies
Majority (R 10): Blunt (MO), Chmn; Cochran (MS), Shelby (AL), Alexander (TN), Graham (SC), Moran (KS), Capito (WV), Lankford (OK), Kennedy (LA), Rubio (FL)
Minority (D 10): Murray (WA), RMM; Durbin (IL), Reed (RI), Shaheen (NH), Merkley (OR), Schatz (HI), Baldwin (WI), Murphy (CT), Manchin (WV), Leahy (VT)

Energy & Water Development
Majority (R 9): Alexander (TN), Chmn; Cochran (MS), McConnell (KY), Shelby (AL), Collins (ME), Murkowski (AK), Graham (SC), Hoeven (ND), Kennedy (LA)
Minority (D 9): Feinstein (CA), RMM; Murray (WA), Tester (MT), Durbin (IL), Udall (NM), Shaheen (NH), Merkley (OR), Coons (DE), Leahy (VT)

Financial Services & General Government
Majority (R 6): Capito (WV), Chmn; Moran (KS), Boozman (AR), Lankford (OK), Daines (MT), Cochran (MS)
Minority (D 5): Coons (DE), RMM; Durbin (IL), Manchin (WV), Van Hollen (MD), Leahy (VT)

Legislative Branch
Majority (R 4): Lankford (OK), Chmn; Kennedy (LA), Rubio (FL), Cochran (MS)
Minority (D 3): Murphy (CT), RMM; Van Hollen (MD), Leahy (VT)

Military Construction & Veteran Affairs & Related Agencies
Majority (R 9): Moran (KS), Chmn; McConnell (KY), Murkowski (AK), Hoeven (ND), Collins (ME), Boozman (AR), Capito (WV), Rubio (FL), Cochran (MS)
Minority (D 8): Schatz (HI), RMM; Tester (MT), Murray (WA), Reed (RI), Udall (NM), Baldwin (WI), Murphy (CT), Leahy (VT)

State, Foreign Operations & Related Programs
Majority (R 9): Graham (SC), Chmn; McConnell (KY), Blunt (MO), Boozman (AR), Moran (KS), Lankford (OK), Daines (MT), Rubio (FL), Cochran (MS)
Minority (D 7): Leahy (VT), RMM; Durbin (IL), Shaheen (NH), Coons (DE), Merkley (OR), Murphy (CT), Van Hollen (MD)

Transportation, HUD & Related Agencies
Majority (R 10): Collins (ME), Chmn; Shelby (AL), Alexander (TN), Blunt (MO), Boozman (AR), Capito (WV), Daines (MT), Graham (SC), Hoeven (ND), Cochran (MS)
Minority (D 9): Reed (RI), RMM; Murray (WA), Durbin (IL), Feinstein (CA), Coons (DE), Schatz (HI), Murphy (CT), Manchin (WV), Leahy (VT)

Armed Services — **228 RSOB**
armed-services.senate.gov — **202-224-3871**

Majority (R 14): McCain (AZ), Chmn; Inhofe (OK), Wicker (MS), Fischer (NE), Cotton (AR), Rounds (SD), Ernst (IA), Tillis (NC), Sullivan (AK), Perdue (GA), Cruz (TX), Graham (SC), Sasse (NE), Strange (AL)
Minority (D 13): Reed (RI), RMM; Nelson (FL), McCaskill (MO), Shaheen (NH), Gillibrand (NY), Blumenthal (CT), Donnelly (IN), Hirono (HI), Kaine (VA), King (ME), Heinrich (NM), Warren (MA), Peters (MI)

SUBCOMMITTEES

Airland
Majority (R 8): Cotton (AR), Chmn; Inhofe (OK), Wicker (MS), Tillis (NC), Sullivan (AK), Cruz (TX), Sasse (NE), McCain (AZ)
Minority (D 7): King (ME), RMM; McCaskill (MO), Blumenthal (CT), Donnelly (IN), Warren (MA), Peters (MI), Reed (RI)

Cybersecurity
Majority (R 6): Rounds (SD), Chmn; Fischer (NE), Perdue (GA), Graham (SC), Sasse (NE), McCain (AZ)
Minority (D 5): Nelson (FL), RMM; McCaskill (MO), Gillibrand (NY), Blumenthal (CT), Reed (RI)

Emerging Threats & Capabilities
Majority (R 6): Ernst (IA), Chmn; Wicker (MS), Fischer (NE), Perdue (GA), Cruz (TX), McCain (AZ)
Minority (D 5): Heinrich (NM), RMM; Nelson (FL), Shaheen (NH), Peters (MI), Reed (RI)

Personnel
Majority (R 5): Tillis (NC), Chmn; Ernst (IA), Graham (SC), Sasse (NE), McCain (AZ)
Minority (D 4): Gillibrand (NY), RMM; McCaskill (MO), Warren (MA), Reed (RI)

Readiness & Management Support
Majority (R 6): Inhofe (OK), Chmn; Rounds (SD), Ernst (IA), Perdue (GA), Strange (AL), McCain (AZ)
Minority (D 4): Kaine (VA), RMM; Shaheen (NH), Hirono (HI), Reed (RI)

Seapower
Majority (R 7): Wicker (MS), Chmn; Cotton (AR), Rounds (SD), Tillis (NC), Sullivan (AK), Strange (AL), McCain (AZ)
Minority (D 6): Hirono (HI), RMM; Shaheen (NH), Blumenthal (CT), Kaine (VA), King (ME), Reed (RI)

Strategic Forces
Majority (R 7): Fischer (NE), Chmn; Inhofe (OK), Cotton (AR), Sullivan (AK), Cruz (TX), Graham (SC), McCain (AZ)
Minority (D 5): Donnelly (IN), RMM; Heinrich (NM), Warren (MA), Peters (MI), Reed (RI)

Banking, Housing & Urban Affairs
banking.senate.gov
534 DSOB
202-224-7391

Majority (R 12): Crapo (ID), Chmn; Shelby (AL), Corker (TN), Toomey (PA), Heller (NV), Scott (SC), Sasse (NE), Cotton (AR), Rounds (SD), Perdue (GA), Tillis (NC), Kennedy (LA)
Minority (D 11): Brown (OH), RMM; Reed (RI), Menendez (NJ), Tester (MT), Warner (VA), Warren (MA), Heitkamp (ND), Donnelly (IN), Schatz (HI), Van Hollen (MD), Cortez Masto (NV)

SUBCOMMITTEES

Economic Policy
Majority (R 6): Cotton (AR), Chmn; Toomey (PA), Perdue (GA), Tillis (NC), Kennedy (LA), Crapo (ID)
Minority (D 5): Heitkamp (ND), RMM; Menendez (NJ), Warren (MA), Donnelly (IN), Brown (OH)

Financial Institutions & Consumer Protection
Majority (R 10): Toomey (PA), Chmn; Shelby (AL), Corker (TN), Heller (NV), Scott (SC), Sasse (NE), Cotton (AR), Perdue (GA), Kennedy (LA), Crapo (ID)
Minority (D 9): Warren (MA), RMM; Reed (RI), Tester (MT), Warner (VA), Donnelly (IN), Schatz (HI), Van Hollen (MD), Cortez Masto (NV), Brown (OH)

Housing, Transportation & Community Development
Majority (R 7): Scott (SC), Chmn; Shelby (AL), Heller (NV), Rounds (SD), Tillis (NC), Kennedy (LA), Crapo (ID)
Minority (D 6): Menendez (NJ), RMM; Reed (RI), Heitkamp (ND), Schatz (HI), Van Hollen (MD), Brown (OH)

National Security & International Trade & Finance
Majority (R 6): Sasse (NE), Chmn; Corker (TN), Cotton (AR), Rounds (SD), Perdue (GA), Crapo (ID)
Minority (D 5): Donnelly (IN), RMM; Warner (VA), Heitkamp (ND), Schatz (HI), Brown (OH)

Securities, Insurance & Investment
Majority (R 9): Heller (NV), Chmn; Shelby (AL), Corker (TN), Toomey (PA), Scott (SC), Sasse (NE), Rounds (SD), Tillis (NC), Crapo (ID)
Minority (D 8): Warner (VA), RMM; Reed (RI), Menendez (NJ), Tester (MT), Warren (MA), Van Hollen (MD), Cortez Masto (NV), Brown (OH)

Budget — 624 DSOB
budget.senate.gov — 202-224-0642

Majority (R 12): Enzi (WY), Chmn; Grassley (IA), Crapo (ID), Graham (SC), Toomey (PA), Johnson (WI), Corker (TN), Perdue (GA), Gardner (CO), Kennedy (LA), Boozman (AR), Strange (AL)
Minority (D 11): Sanders (VT), RMM; Murray (WA), Wyden (OR), Stabenow (MI), Whitehouse (RI), Warner (VA), Merkley (OR), Kaine (VA), King (ME), Van Hollen (MD), Harris (CA)

Commerce, Science & Transportation — 512 DSOB
commerce.senate.gov — 202-224-1251

Majority (R 14): Thune (SD), Chmn; Wicker (MS), Blunt (MO), Cruz (TX), Fischer (NE), Moran (KS), Sullivan (AK), Heller (NV), Inhofe (OK), Lee (UT), Johnson (WI), Capito (WV), Gardner (CO), Young (IN)
Minority (D 13): Nelson (FL), RMM; Cantwell (WA), Klobuchar (MN), Blumenthal (CT), Schatz (HI), Markey (MA), Booker (NJ), Udall (NM), Peters (MI), Baldwin (WI), Duckworth (IL), Hassan (NH), Cortez Masto (NV)

SUBCOMMITTEES

Aviation Operations, Safety & Security
Majority (R 13): Blunt (MO), Chmn; Wicker (MS), Cruz (TX), Fischer (NE), Moran (KS), Sullivan (AK), Heller (NV), Inhofe (OK), Lee (UT), Capito (WV), Gardner (CO), Young (IN), Thune (SD)
Minority (D 12): Cantwell (WA), RMM; Klobuchar (MN), Blumenthal (CT), Schatz (HI), Markey (MA), Booker (NJ), Udall (NM), Peters (MI), Baldwin (WI), Duckworth (IL), Hassan (NH), Nelson (FL)

Communications, Technology, Innovation & the Internet
Majority (R 14): Wicker (MS), Chmn; Blunt (MO), Cruz (TX), Fischer (NE), Moran (KS), Sullivan (AK), Heller (NV), Inhofe (OK), Lee (UT), Johnson (WI), Capito (WV), Gardner (CO), Young (IN), Thune (SD)
Minority (D 13): Schatz (HI), RMM; Cantwell (WA), Klobuchar (MN), Blumenthal (CT), Markey (MA), Booker (NJ), Udall (NM), Peters (MI), Baldwin (WI), Duckworth (IL), Hassan (NH), Cortez Masto (NV), Nelson (FL)

Consumer Protection, Product Safety, Ins & Data Security
Majority (R 10): Moran (KS), Chmn; Blunt (MO), Cruz (TX), Fischer (NE), Heller (NV), Inhofe (OK), Lee (UT), Capito (WV), Young (IN), Thune (SD)
Minority (D 9): Blumenthal (CT), RMM; Klobuchar (MN), Markey (MA), Booker (NJ), Udall (NM), Duckworth (IL), Hassan (NH), Cortez Masto (NV), Nelson (FL)

Oceans, Atmosphere, Fisheries & Coast Guard
Majority (R 9): Sullivan (AK), Chmn; Wicker (MS), Fischer (NE), Inhofe (OK), Lee (UT), Johnson (WI), Gardner (CO), Young (IN), Thune (SD)
Minority (D 8): Peters (MI), RMM; Cantwell (WA), Blumenthal (CT), Schatz (HI), Markey (MA), Booker (NJ), Baldwin (WI), Nelson (FL)

Space, Science & Competitiveness
Majority (R 8): Cruz (TX), Chmn; Moran (KS), Sullivan (AK), Lee (UT), Johnson (WI), Capito (WV), Gardner (CO), Thune (SD)
Minority (D 7): Markey (MA), RMM; Schatz (HI), Udall (NM), Peters (MI), Baldwin (WI), Hassan (NH), Nelson (FL)

Surface Trans., Merchant Marine Infra., Safety & Security
Majority (R 10): Fischer (NE), Chmn; Wicker (MS), Blunt (MO), Heller (NV), Inhofe (OK), Johnson (WI), Capito (WV), Gardner (CO), Young (IN), Thune (SD)
Minority (D 9): Booker (NJ), RMM; Cantwell (WA), Klobuchar (MN), Blumenthal (CT), Udall (NM), Baldwin (WI), Duckworth (IL), Hassan (NH), Nelson (FL)

Energy & Natural Resources — 304 DSOB
energy.senate.gov — 202-224-4971

Majority (R 12): Murkowski (AK), Chmn; Barrasso (WY), Risch (ID), Lee (UT), Flake (AZ), Daines (MT), Gardner (CO), Alexander (TN), Hoeven (ND), Cassidy (LA), Portman (OH), Strange (AL)
Minority (D 11): Cantwell (WA), RMM; Wyden (OR), Sanders (VT), Stabenow (MI), Franken (MN), Manchin (WV), Heinrich (NM), Hirono (HI), King (ME), Duckworth (IL), Cortez Masto (NV)

SUBCOMMITTEES

Energy
Majority (R 10): Gardner (CO), Chmn; Risch (ID), Flake (AZ), Daines (MT), Alexander (TN), Hoeven (ND), Cassidy (LA), Portman (OH), Strange (AL), Murkowski (AK)
Minority (D 9): Manchin (WV), RMM; Wyden (OR), Sanders (VT), Franken (MN), Heinrich (NM), King (ME), Duckworth (IL), Cortez Masto (NV), Cantwell (WA)

National Parks
Majority (R 8): Daines (MT), Chmn; Barrasso (WY), Lee (UT), Gardner (CO), Alexander (TN), Hoeven (ND), Portman (OH), Murkowski (AK)
Minority (D 7): Hirono (HI), RMM; Sanders (VT), Stabenow (MI), Heinrich (NM), King (ME), Duckworth (IL), Cantwell (WA)

Public Lands, Forests & Mining
Majority (R 11): Lee (UT), Chmn; Barrasso (WY), Risch (ID), Flake (AZ), Daines (MT), Gardner (CO), Alexander (TN), Hoeven (ND), Cassidy (LA), Strange (AL), Murkowski (AK)
Minority (D 8): Wyden (OR), RMM; Stabenow (MI), Franken (MN), Manchin (WV), Heinrich (NM), Hirono (HI), Cortez Masto (NV), Cantwell (WA)

Water & Power
Majority (R 8): Flake (AZ), Chmn; Barrasso (WY), Risch (ID), Lee (UT), Cassidy (LA), Portman (OH), Strange (AL), Murkowski (AK)
Minority (D 7): King (ME), RMM; Wyden (OR), Sanders (VT), Franken (MN), Manchin (WV), Duckworth (IL), Cantwell (WA)

Environment & Public Works

epw.senate.gov — **410 DSOB**, **202-224-6176**

Majority (R 11): Barrasso (WY), Chmn; Inhofe (OK), Capito (WV), Boozman (AR), Wicker (MS), Fischer (NE), Moran (KS), Rounds (SD), Ernst (IA), Sullivan (AK), Shelby (AL)
Minority (D 10): Carper (DE), RMM; Cardin (MD), Sanders (VT), Whitehouse (RI), Merkley (OR), Gillibrand (NY), Booker (NJ), Markey (MA), Duckworth (IL), Harris (CA)

SUBCOMMITTEES

Clean Air & Nuclear Safety
Majority (R 9): Capito (WV), Chmn; Inhofe (OK), Boozman (AR), Wicker (MS), Fischer (NE), Moran (KS), Ernst (IA), Shelby (AL), Barrasso (WY)
Minority (D 8): Whitehouse (RI), RMM; Cardin (MD), Sanders (VT), Merkley (OR), Gillibrand (NY), Markey (MA), Duckworth (IL), Carper (DE)

Fisheries, Water, and Wildlife
Majority (R 9): Boozman (AR), Chmn; Inhofe (OK), Capito (WV), Wicker (MS), Fischer (NE), Rounds (SD), Sullivan (AK), Shelby (AL), Barrasso (WY)
Minority (D 8): Duckworth (IL), RMM; Cardin (MD), Whitehouse (RI), Merkley (OR), Gillibrand (NY), Booker (NJ), Markey (MA), Carper (DE)

Superfund, Waste Management, & Regulatory Oversight
Majority (R 5): Rounds (SD), Chmn; Moran (KS), Ernst (IA), Sullivan (AK), Barrasso (WY)
Minority (D 4): Harris (CA), RMM; Sanders (VT), Booker (NJ), Carper (DE)

Transportation & Infrastructure
Majority (R 10): Inhofe (OK), Chmn; Capito (WV), Boozman (AR), Wicker (MS), Fischer (NE), Moran (KS), Ernst (IA), Sullivan (AK), Shelby (AL), Barrasso (WY)
Minority (D 9): Cardin (MD), RMM; Sanders (VT), Whitehouse (RI), Merkley (OR), Gillibrand (NY), Markey (MA), Duckworth (IL), Harris (CA), Carper (DE)

Finance

finance.senate.gov — **219 DSOB**, **202-224-4515**

Majority (R 14): Hatch (UT), Chmn; Grassley (IA), Crapo (ID), Roberts (KS), Enzi (WY), Cornyn (TX), Thune (SD), Burr (NC), Isakson (GA), Portman (OH), Toomey (PA), Heller (NV), Scott (SC), Cassidy (LA)
Minority (D 12): Wyden (OR), RMM; Stabenow (MI), Cantwell (WA), Nelson (FL), Menendez (NJ), Carper (DE), Cardin (MD), Brown (OH), Bennet (CO), Casey (PA), Warner (VA), McCaskill (MO)

SUBCOMMITTEES

Energy, Natural Resources & Infrastructure
Majority (R 9): Heller (NV), Chmn; Grassley (IA), Crapo (ID), Enzi (WY), Cornyn (TX), Burr (NC), Scott (SC), Cassidy (LA), Hatch (UT)
Minority (D 7): Bennet (CO), RMM; Cantwell (WA), Nelson (FL), Menendez (NJ), Carper (DE), Warner (VA), Wyden (OR)

Fiscal Responsibility & Economic Growth
Majority (R 2): Scott (SC), Chmn; Hatch (UT)
Minority (D 1): Wyden (OR), RMM

Health Care
Majority (R 11): Toomey (PA), Chmn; Grassley (IA), Roberts (KS), Enzi (WY), Thune (SD), Burr (NC), Isakson (GA), Portman (OH), Heller (NV), Cassidy (LA), Hatch (UT)
Minority (D 8): Stabenow (MI), RMM; Menendez (NJ), Cantwell (WA), Carper (DE), Cardin (MD), Brown (OH), Warner (VA), Wyden (OR)

International Trade, Customs & Global Competitiveness
Majority (R 7): Cornyn (TX), Chmn; Grassley (IA), Roberts (KS), Isakson (GA), Thune (SD), Heller (NV), Hatch (UT)
Minority (D 5): Casey (PA), RMM; Stabenow (MI), Nelson (FL), McCaskill (MO), Wyden (OR)

Social Security, Pensions & Family Policy
Majority (R 5): Cassidy (LA), Chmn; Portman (OH), Crapo (ID), Toomey (PA), Hatch (UT)
Minority (D 3): Brown (OH), RMM; Casey (PA), Wyden (OR)

Taxation & IRS Oversight
Majority (R 11): Portman (OH), Chmn; Crapo (ID), Roberts (KS), Enzi (WY), Cornyn (TX), Thune (SD), Burr (NC), Isakson (GA), Toomey (PA), Scott (SC), Hatch (UT)
Minority (D 9): Warner (VA), RMM; Carper (DE), Cardin (MD), McCaskill (MO), Menendez (NJ), Bennet (CO), Casey (PA), Cantwell (WA), Wyden (OR)

Foreign Relations **423 DSOB**
foreign.senate.gov **202-224-4651**

Majority (R 11): Corker (TN), Chmn; Risch (ID), Rubio (FL), Johnson (WI), Flake (AZ), Gardner (CO), Young (IN), Barrasso (WY), Isakson (GA), Portman (OH), Paul (KY)
Minority (D 10): Cardin (MD), RMM; Menendez (NJ), Shaheen (NH), Coons (DE), Udall (NM), Murphy (CT), Kaine (VA), Markey (MA), Merkley (OR), Booker (NJ)

SUBCOMMITTEES

Africa & Global Health Policy
Majority (R 6): Flake (AZ), Chmn; Young (IN), Barrasso (WY), Isakson (GA), Paul (KY), Corker (TN)
Minority (D 5): Booker (NJ), RMM; Coons (DE), Udall (NM), Merkley (OR), Cardin (MD)

East Asia, the Pacific & International Cybersecurity Policy
Majority (R 6): Gardner (CO), Chmn; Risch (ID), Rubio (FL), Barrasso (WY), Isakson (GA), Corker (TN)
Minority (D 5): Markey (MA), RMM; Merkley (OR), Murphy (CT), Kaine (VA), Cardin (MD)

Europe & Regional Security Cooperation
Majority (R 6): Johnson (WI), Chmn; Risch (ID), Barrasso (WY), Portman (OH), Paul (KY), Corker (TN)
Minority (D 5): Murphy (CT), RMM; Markey (MA), Menendez (NJ), Shaheen (NH), Cardin (MD)

Internat'l Dev Instit & Internat'l Econ, Energy & Environ Policy
Majority (R 6): Young (IN), Chmn; Flake (AZ), Gardner (CO), Barrasso (WY), Portman (OH), Corker (TN)
Minority (D 5): Merkley (OR), RMM; Udall (NM), Coons (DE), Markey (MA), Cardin (MD)

Near East, South Asia, Central Asia & Counterterrorism
Majority (R 6): Risch (ID), Chmn; Rubio (FL), Johnson (WI), Young (IN), Portman (OH), Corker (TN)
Minority (D 5): Kaine (VA), RMM; Menendez (NJ), Murphy (CT), Booker (NJ), Cardin (MD)

State Dept & USAID Mngmnt, Internat'l Ops & Internat'l Dev
Majority (R 6): Isakson (GA), Chmn; Risch (ID), Rubio (FL), Portman (OH), Paul (KY), Corker (TN)
Minority (D 5): Shaheen (NH), RMM; Coons (DE), Booker (NJ), Udall (NM), Cardin (MD)

West Hem Crime Civ Sec Dem Rights & Women's Issues
Majority (R 6): Rubio (FL), Chmn; Johnson (WI), Flake (AZ), Gardner (CO), Isakson (GA), Corker (TN)
Minority (D 5): Menendez (NJ), RMM; Udall (NM), Shaheen (NH), Kaine (VA), Cardin (MD)

Health, Education, Labor & Pensions 428 DSOB
help.senate.gov 202-224-5375

Majority (R 12): Alexander (TN), Chmn; Enzi (WY), Burr (NC), Isakson (GA), Paul (KY), Collins (ME), Cassidy (LA), Young (IN), Hatch (UT), Roberts (KS), Murkowski (AK), Scott (SC)
Minority (D 11): Murray (WA), RMM; Sanders (VT), Casey (PA), Franken (MN), Bennet (CO), Whitehouse (RI), Baldwin (WI), Murphy (CT), Warren (MA), Kaine (VA), Hassan (NH)

SUBCOMMITTEES

Children & Families
Majority (R 8): Paul (KY), Chmn; Murkowski (AK), Burr (NC), Cassidy (LA), Young (IN), Hatch (UT), Roberts (KS), Alexander (TN)
Minority (D 7): Casey (PA), RMM; Sanders (VT), Franken (MN), Bennet (CO), Kaine (VA), Hassan (NH), Murray (WA)

Employment & Workplace Safety
Majority (R 8): Isakson (GA), Chmn; Roberts (KS), Scott (SC), Burr (NC), Paul (KY), Cassidy (LA), Young (IN), Alexander (TN)
Minority (D 7): Franken (MN), RMM; Casey (PA), Whitehouse (RI), Baldwin (WI), Murphy (CT), Warren (MA), Murray (WA)

Primary Health & Retirement Security
Majority (R 10): Enzi (WY), Chmn; Burr (NC), Collins (ME), Cassidy (LA), Young (IN), Hatch (UT), Roberts (KS), Scott (SC), Murkowski (AK), Alexander (TN)
Minority (D 9): Sanders (VT), RMM; Bennet (CO), Whitehouse (RI), Baldwin (WI), Murphy (CT), Warren (MA), Kaine (VA), Hassan (NH), Murray (WA)

Homeland Security & Government Affairs 340 DSOB
hsgac.senate.gov 202-224-4751

Majority (R 8): Johnson (WI), Chmn; McCain (AZ), Portman (OH), Paul (KY), Lankford (OK), Enzi (WY), Hoeven (ND), Daines (MT)
Minority (D 7): McCaskill (MO), RMM; Carper (DE), Tester (MT), Heitkamp (ND), Peters (MI), Hassan (NH), Harris (CA)

SUBCOMMITTEES

Federal Spending Oversight & Emergency Management
Majority (R 5): Paul (KY), Chmn; Lankford (OK), Enzi (WY), Hoeven (ND), Johnson (WI)
Minority (D 4): Peters (MI), RMM; Hassan (NH), Harris (CA), McCaskill (MO)

Investigations
Majority (R 6): Portman (OH), Chmn; McCain (AZ), Paul (KY), Lankford (OK), Daines (MT), Johnson (WI)
Minority (D 5): Carper (DE), RMM; Tester (MT), Heitkamp (ND), Peters (MI), McCaskill (MO)

Regulatory Affairs & Federal Management
Majority (R 6): Lankford (OK), Chmn; McCain (AZ), Portman (OH), Enzi (WY), Daines (MT), Johnson (WI)
Minority (D 5): Heitkamp (ND), RMM; Carper (DE), Hassan (NH), Harris (CA), McCaskill (MO)

Judiciary 224 DSOB
judiciary.senate.gov 202-224-5225

Majority (R 11): Grassley (IA), Chmn; Hatch (UT), Graham (SC), Cornyn (TX), Lee (UT), Cruz (TX), Sasse (NE), Flake (AZ), Crapo (ID), Tillis (NC), Kennedy (LA)
Minority (D 9): Feinstein (CA), RMM; Leahy (VT), Durbin (IL), Whitehouse (RI), Klobuchar (MN), Franken (MN), Coons (DE), Blumenthal (CT), Hirono (HI)

SUBCOMMITTEES

Antitrust, Competition Policy & Consumer Rights
Majority (R 5): Lee (UT), Chmn; Grassley (IA), Hatch (UT), Graham (SC), Tillis (NC)
Minority (D 4): Klobuchar (MN), RMM; Leahy (VT), Franken (MN), Blumenthal (CT)

Border Security & Immigration
Majority (R 8): Cornyn (TX), Chmn; Tillis (NC), Kennedy (LA), Grassley (IA), Cruz (TX), Flake (AZ), Crapo (ID), Lee (UT)
Minority (D 7): Durbin (IL), RMM; Feinstein (CA), Leahy (VT), Klobuchar (MN), Franken (MN), Blumenthal (CT), Hirono (HI)

Constitution
Majority (R 5): Cruz (TX), Chmn; Cornyn (TX), Crapo (ID), Sasse (NE), Graham (SC)
Minority (D 4): Blumenthal (CT), RMM; Durbin (IL), Franken (MN), Coons (DE)

Crime & Terrorism
Majority (R 5): Graham (SC), Chmn; Cornyn (TX), Cruz (TX), Sasse (NE), Kennedy (LA)
Minority (D 4): Whitehouse (RI), RMM; Durbin (IL), Klobuchar (MN), Coons (DE)

Oversight, Agency Action, Federal Rights & Federal Courts
Majority (R 8): Sasse (NE), Chmn; Grassley (IA), Crapo (ID), Kennedy (LA), Hatch (UT), Lee (UT), Flake (AZ), Tillis (NC)
Minority (D 7): Coons (DE), RMM; Leahy (VT), Whitehouse (RI), Klobuchar (MN), Franken (MN), Blumenthal (CT), Hirono (HI)

Privacy, Technology & the Law
Majority (R 6): Flake (AZ), Chmn; Hatch (UT), Lee (UT), Tillis (NC), Crapo (ID), Kennedy (LA)
Minority (D 5): Franken (MN), RMM; Leahy (VT), Whitehouse (RI), Coons (DE), Hirono (HI)

Rules & Administration — **305 RSOB**
rules.senate.gov — **202-224-6352**

Majority (R 10): Shelby (AL), Chmn; McConnell (KY), Cochran (MS), Alexander (TN), Roberts (KS), Blunt (MO), Cruz (TX), Capito (WV), Wicker (MS), Fischer (NE)
Minority (D 9): Klobuchar (MN), RMM; Feinstein (CA), Schumer (NY), Durbin (IL), Udall (NM), Warner (VA), Leahy (VT), King (ME), Cortez Masto (NV)

Small Business & Entrepreneurship — **428A RSOB**
sbc.senate.gov — **202-224-5175**

Majority (R 10): Risch (ID), Chmn; Rubio (FL), Paul (KY), Scott (SC), Ernst (IA), Inhofe (OK), Young (IN), Enzi (WY), Rounds (SD), Kennedy (LA)
Minority (D 9): Shaheen (NH), RMM; Cantwell (WA), Cardin (MD), Heitkamp (ND), Markey (MA), Booker (NJ), Coons (DE), Hirono (HI), Duckworth (IL)

Veterans' Affairs — **412 RSOB**
veterans.senate.gov — **202-224-9126**

Majority (R 8): Isakson (GA), Chmn; Moran (KS), Boozman (AR), Heller (NV), Cassidy (LA), Rounds (SD), Tillis (NC), Sullivan (AK)
Minority (D 7): Tester (MT), RMM; Murray (WA), Sanders (VT), Brown (OH), Blumenthal (CT), Hirono (HI), Manchin (WV)

SPECIAL AND SELECT

Aging — **G-31 DSOB**
aging.senate.gov — **202-224-5364**

Majority (R 9): Collins (ME), Chmn; Hatch (UT), Flake (AZ), Scott (SC), Tillis (NC), Corker (TN), Burr (NC), Rubio (FL), Fischer (NE)
Minority (D 8): Casey (PA), RMM; Nelson (FL), Whitehouse (RI), Gillibrand (NY), Blumenthal (CT), Donnelly (IN), Warren (MA), Cortez Masto (NV)

Ethics — **220 HSOB**
ethics.senate.gov — **202-224-2981**

Majority (R 3): Isakson (GA), Chmn; Roberts (KS), Risch (ID)
Minority (D 3): Coons (DE), Schatz (HI), Shaheen (NH)

Indian Affairs — **838 HSOB**
indian.senate.gov — **202-224-2251**

Majority (R 8): Hoeven (ND), Chmn; Barrasso (WY), McCain (AZ), Murkowski (AK), Lankford (OK), Daines (MT), Crapo (ID), Moran (KS)
Minority (D 7): Udall (NM), Tester (MT), Cantwell (WA), Franken (MN), Schatz (HI), Heitkamp (ND), Cortez Masto (NV)

Intelligence **211 HSOB**
intelligence.senate.gov **202-224-1700**

Majority (R 10): Burr (NC), Chmn; Risch (ID), Rubio (FL), Collins (ME), Blunt (MO), Lankford (OK), Cotton (AR), Cornyn (TX), McConnell (KY), McCain (AZ)
Minority (D 9): Warner (VA), Feinstein (CA), Wyden (OR), Heinrich (NM), King (ME), Manchin (WV), Harris (CA), Schumer (NY), Reed (RI)

★ HOUSE COMMITTEES ★

Agriculture
agriculture.house.gov

1301 LHOB
202-225-2171

Majority (R 26): Conaway (TX), Chmn; Thompson (PA), Goodlatte (VA), Lucas (OK), King (IA), Rogers (AL), Gibbs (OH), Scott (GA), Crawford (AR), DesJarlais (TN), Hartzler (MO), Denham (CA), LaMalfa (CA), Davis (IL), Yoho (FL), Allen (GA), Bost (IL), Rouzer (NC), Abraham (LA), Kelly (MS), Comer (KY), Marshall (KS), Bacon (NE), Faso (NY), Dunn (FL), Arrington (TX)
Minority (D 20): Peterson (MN), RMM; Scott (GA), Costa (CA), Walz (MN), Fudge (OH), McGovern (MA), Vela (TX), Lujan Grisham (NM), Kuster (NH), Nolan (MN), Bustos (IL), Maloney (NY), Plaskett (VI), Adams (NC), Evans (PA), Lawson (FL), Panetta (CA), O'Halleran (AZ), Soto (FL), Rochester (DE)

SUBCOMMITTEES

Biotechnology, Horticulture & Research
Majority (R 8): Davis (IL), Chmn; Gibbs (OH), Denham (CA), Yoho (FL), Rouzer (NC), Bacon (NE), Dunn (FL), Arrington (TX)
Minority (D 6): Lujan Grisham (NM), RMM; Lawson (FL), Panetta (CA), Costa (CA), McGovern (MA), Rochester (DE)

Commodity Exchanges, Energy & Credit
Majority (R 8): Scott (GA), Chmn; Goodlatte (VA), Rogers (AL), LaMalfa (CA), Davis (IL), Comer (KY), Marshall (KS), Faso (NY)
Minority (D 6): Scott (GA), RMM; Maloney (NY), Kuster (NH), Plaskett (VI), O'Halleran (AZ), Soto (FL)

Conservation & Forestry
Majority (R 9): Lucas (OK), Chmn; Thompson (PA), Denham (CA), LaMalfa (CA), Allen (GA), Bost (IL), Abraham (LA), Kelly (MS), Conaway (TX)
Minority (D 7): Fudge (OH), RMM; Walz (MN), Kuster (NH), Nolan (MN), O'Halleran (AZ), Vela (TX), Peterson (MN)

General Farm Commodities & Risk Management
Majority (R 13): Crawford (AR), Chmn; Lucas (OK), Rogers (AL), Gibbs (OH), Scott (GA), DesJarlais (TN), Allen (GA), Bost (IL), Abraham (LA), Bacon (NE), Dunn (FL), Arrington (TX),
Minority (D 9): Nolan (MN), RMM; Walz (MN), Bustos (IL), Rochester (DE), Scott (GA), Maloney (NY), Plaskett (VI), Lawson (FL), O'Halleran (AZ)

Livestock & Foreign Agriculture
Majority (R 8): Rouzer (NC), Chmn; Goodlatte (VA), King (IA), DesJarlais (TN), Hartzler (MO), Yoho (FL), Kelly (MS), Marshall (KS)
Minority (D 5): Costa (CA), RMM; Vela (TX), Bustos (IL), Plaskett (VI), Evans (PA)

Nutrition
Majority (R 12): Thompson (PA), Chmn; King (IA), Crawford (AR), DesJarlais (TN), Hartzler (MO), Davis (IL), Yoho (FL), Rouzer (NC), Comer (KY), Marshall (KS), Faso (NY), Arrington (TX)
Minority (D 9): McGovern (MA), RMM; Adams (NC), Evans (PA), Fudge (OH), Lujan Grisham (NM), Lawson (FL), Panetta (CA), Soto (FL), Maloney (NY)

Appropriations
appropriations.house.gov

H-305 The Capitol
202-225-2771

Majority (R 30): Frelinghuysen (NJ), Chmn; Rogers (KY), Aderholt (AL), Granger (TX), Simpson (ID), Culberson (TX), Carter (TX), Calvert (CA), Cole (OK), Diaz-Balart (FL), Dent (PA), Graves (GA), Yoder (KS), Womack (AR), Fortenberry (NE), Rooney (FL), Fleischmann (TN), Herrera Beutler (WA), Joyce (OH), Valadao (CA), Harris (MD), Roby (AL), Amodei (NV), Stewart (UT), Young (IA), Jenkins (WV), Palazzo (MS), Newhouse (WA), Moolenaar (MI), Taylor (VA)
Minority (D 22): Lowey (NY), RMM; Kaptur (OH), Visclosky (IN), Serrano (NY), DeLauro (CT), Price (NC), Roybal-Allard (CA), Bishop (GA), Lee (CA), McCollum (MN), Ryan (OH), Ruppersberger (MD), Wasserman Schultz (FL), Cuellar (TX), Pingree (ME), Quigley (IL), Kilmer (WA), Cartwright (PA), Meng (NY), Pocan (WI), Clark (MA), Aguilar (CA)

SUBCOMMITTEES

Agriculture, Rural Development, FDA & Related Agencies
Majority (R 7): Aderholt (AL), Chmn; Yoder (KS), Rooney (FL), Valadao (CA), Harris (MD), Young (IA), Palazzo (MS)
Minority (D 4): Bishop (GA), RMM; DeLauro (CT), Pingree (ME), Pocan (WI)

Commerce, Justice, Science & Related Agencies
Majority (R 7): Culberson (TX), Chmn; Rogers (KY), Aderholt (AL), Carter (TX), Roby (AL), Palazzo (MS), Jenkins (WV)
Minority (D 5): Serrano (NY), RMM; Kilmer (WA), Cartwright (PA), Meng (NY), Lowey (NY)

Defense
Majority (R 10): Granger (TX), Chmn; Rogers (KY), Calvert (CA), Cole (OK), Womack (AR), Aderholt (AL), Carter (TX), Diaz-Balart (FL), Graves (GA), Roby (AL)
Minority (D 6): Visclosky (IN), RMM; McCollum (MN), Ryan (OH), Ruppersberger (MD), Kaptur (OH), Cuellar (TX)

Energy & Water Development & Related Agencies
Majority (R 8): Simpson (ID), Chmn; Calvert (CA), Fleischmann (TN), Fortenberry (NE), Granger (TX), Herrera Beutler (WA), Joyce (OH), Newhouse (WA)
Minority (D 5): Kaptur (OH), RMM; Visclosky (IN), Wasserman Schultz (FL), Aguilar (CA), Serrano (NY)

Financial Services & General Government
Majority (R 7): Graves (GA), Chmn; Yoder (KS), Herrera Beutler (WA), Amodei (NV), Stewart (UT), Young (IA), Moolenaar (MI)
Minority (D 4): Quigley (IL), RMM; Serrano (NY), Cartwright (PA), Bishop (GA)

Homeland Security
Majority (R 7): Carter (TX), Chmn; Culberson (TX), Fleischmann (TN), Harris (MD), Palazzo (MS), Newhouse (WA), Taylor (VA)
Minority (D 4): Roybal-Allard (CA), RMM; Cuellar (TX), Price (NC), Ruppersberger (MD)

Interior, Environment & Related Agencies
Majority (R 7): Calvert (CA), Chmn; Simpson (ID), Cole (OK), Joyce (OH), Stewart (UT), Amodei (NV), Jenkins (WV)
Minority (D 4): McCollum (MN), RMM; Pingree (ME), Kilmer (WA), Kaptur (OH)

Labor, Health & Human Services, Education & Related Agencies
Majority (R 9): Cole (OK), Chmn; Simpson (ID), Womack (AR), Fleischmann (TN), Harris (MD), Roby (AL), Herrera Beutler (WA), Moolenaar (MI),
Minority (D 5): DeLauro (CT), RMM; Roybal-Allard (CA), Lee (CA), Pocan (WI), Clark (MA)

Legislative Branch
Majority (R 5): Yoder (KS), Chmn; Amodei (NV), Newhouse (WA), Moolenaar (MI), Taylor (VA)
Minority (D 3): Ryan (OH), RMM; McCollum (MN), Wasserman Schultz (FL)

Military Construction, Veterans Affairs & Related Agencies
Majority (R 7): Dent (PA), Chmn; Fortenberry (NE), Rooney (FL), Valadao (CA), Womack (AR), Jenkins (WV), Taylor (VA)
Minority (D 4): Wasserman Schultz (FL), RMM; Bishop (GA), Lee (CA), Ryan (OH)

State, Foreign Operations & Related Programs
Majority (R 6): Rogers (KY), Chmn; Balart (FL), Dent (PA), Rooney (FL), Fortenberry (NE), Stewart (UT)
Minority (D 5): Lowey (NY), RMM; Lee (CA), Ruppersberger (MD), Meng (NY), Price (NC)

Transportation, HUD & Related Agencies
Majority (R 7): Diaz-Balart (FL), Chmn; Dent (PA), Joyce (OH), Culberson (TX), Young (IA), Valadao (CA), Graves (GA)
Minority (D 4): Price (NC), RMM; Quigley (IL), Clark (MA), Aguilar (CA)

Armed Services
armedservices.house.gov — **2216 RHOB** — **202-225-4151**

Majority (R 34): Thornberry (TX), Chmn; Jones (NC), Wilson (SC), LoBiondo (NJ), Bishop (UT), Turner (OH), Rogers (AL), Franks (AZ), Shuster (PA), Conaway (TX), Lamborn (CO), Wittman (VA), Hunter (CA), Coffman (CO), Hartzler (MO), Scott (GA), Brooks (AL), Cook (CA), Bridenstine (OK), Wenstrup (OH), Byrne (AL), Graves (MO), Stefanik (NY), McSally (AZ), Knight (CA), Russell (OK), DesJarlais (TN), Abraham (LA), Kelly (MS), Gallagher (WI), Gaetz (FL), Bacon (NE), Banks (IN), Cheney (WY)

Minority (D 27): Smith (WA), RMM; Brady (PA), Davis (CA), Langevin (RI), Larsen (WA), Cooper (TN), Bordallo (GU), Courtney (CT), Tsongas (MA), Garamendi (CA), Speier (CA), Veasey (TX), Gabbard (HI), O'Rourke (TX), Norcross (NJ), Gallego (AZ), Moulton (MA), Hanabusa (HI), Shea-Porter (NH), Rosen (NV), McEachin (VA), Carbajal (CA), Brown (MD), Murphy (FL), Khanna (CA), O'Halleran (AZ), Suozzi (NY)

SUBCOMMITTEES

Emerging Threats & Capabilities

Majority (R 10): Stefanik (NY), Chmn; Shuster (PA), Wenstrup (OH), Abraham (LA), Cheney (WY), Wilson (SC), LoBiondo (NJ), Franks (AZ), Lamborn (CO), Scott (GA)
Minority (D 8): Langevin (RI), RMM; Larsen (WA), Cooper (TN), Speier (CA), Veasey (TX), Gabbard (HI), O'Rourke (TX), Murphy (FL)

Military Personnel

Majority (R 8): Coffman (CO), Chmn; Jones (NC), Wenstrup (OH), Russell (OK), Bacon (NE), McSally (AZ), Abraham (LA), Kelly (MS)
Minority (D 6): Speier (CA), RMM; Brady (PA), Tsongas (MA), Gallego (AZ), Shea-Porter (NH), Rosen (NV)

Oversight & Investigations

Majority (R 6): Hartzler (MO), Chmn; Conaway (TX), Gaetz (FL), Banks (IN), Cheney (WY), Scott (GA)
Minority (D 3): Moulton (MA), RMM; O'Halleran (AZ), Suozzi (NY)

Readiness

Majority (R 10): Wilson (SC), Chmn; l (OK), Scott (GA), Rogers (AL), Hartzler (MO), Stefanik (NY), McSally (AZ), DesJarlais (TN), Kelly (MS), Gallagher (WI)
Minority (D 9): Bordallo (GU), RMM; Courtney (CT), Gabbard (HI), Shea-Porter (NH), McEachin (VA), Carbajal (CA), Brown (MD), Murphy (FL), Khanna (CA)

Seapower & Projection Forces

Majority (R 11): Wittman (VA), Chmn; Conaway (TX), Hartzler (MO), Byrne (AL), DesJarlais (TN), Gallagher (WI), Hunter (CA), Cook (CA), Bridenstine (OK), Knight (CA), Abraham (LA)
Minority (D 9): Courtney (CT), RMM; Davis (CA), Langevin (RI), Bordallo (GU), Garamendi (CA), Norcross (NJ), Moulton (MA), Hanabusa (HI), McEachin (VA)

Strategic Forces

Majority (R 10): Rogers (AL), Chmn; Franks (AZ), Lamborn (CO), Hunter (CA), Brooks (AL), Bridenstine (OK), Turner (OH), Coffman (CO), Byrne (AL), Graves (MO)
Minority (D 8): Cooper (TN), RMM; Davis (CA), Larsen (WA), Garamendi (CA), O'Rourke (TX), Norcross (NJ), Hanabusa (HI), Khanna (CA)

Tactical Air & Land Forces

Majority (R 14): Turner (OH), Chmn; LoBiondo (NJ), Cook (CA), Graves (MO), McSally (AZ), Knight (CA), Kelly (MS), Gaetz (FL), Bacon (NE), Banks (IN), Jones (NC), Bishop (UT), Wittman (VA), Brooks (AL)
Minority (D 10): Tsongas (MA), RMM; Langevin (RI), Cooper (TN), Veasey (TX), Gallego (AZ), Rosen (NV), Carbajal (CA), Brown (MD), O'Halleran (AZ), Suozzi (NY)

Budget
budget.house.gov

B-234 LHOB
202-226-7270

Majority (R 22): Black (TN), Chmn; Rokita (IN), Diaz-Balart (FL), Cole (OK), McClintock (CA), Woodall (GA), Sanford (SC), Womack (AR), Brat (VA), Grothman (WI), Palmer (AL), Westerman (AR), Renacci (OH), Johnson (OH), Smith (MO), Lewis (MN), Bergman (MI), Faso (NY), Smucker (PA), Gaetz (FL), Arrington (TX), Ferguson (GA)
Minority (D 14): Yarmuth (KY), RMM; Lee (CA), Lujan Grisham (NM), Moulton (MA), Jeffries (NY), Higgins (NY), DelBene (WA), Wasserman Schultz (FL), Boyle (PA), Khanna (CA), Jayapal (WA), Carbajal (CA), Jackson Lee (TX), Schakowsky (IL)

Education & the Workforce
edworkforce.house.gov

2176 RHOB
202-225-4527

Majority (R 22): Foxx (NC), Chmn; Wilson (SC), Hunter (CA), Roe (TN), Thompson (PA), Walberg (MI), Guthrie (KY), Rokita (IN), Barletta (PA), Messer (IN), Byrne (AL), Brat (VA), Grothman (WI), Stefanik (NY), Allen (GA), Lewis (MN), Rooney (FL), Mitchell (MI), Garrett (VA), Smucker (PA), Ferguson (GA), Estes (KS), Handel (GA)
Minority (D 17): Scott (VA), RMM; Davis (CA), Grijalva (AZ), Courtney (CT), Fudge (OH), Polis (CO), Sablan (MP), Wilson (FL), Bonamici (OR), Takano (CA), Adams (NC), DeSaulnier (CA), Norcross (NJ), Rochester (DE), Krishnamoorthi (IL), Shea-Porter (NH), Espaillat (NY)

SUBCOMMITTEES

Early Childhood, Elementary & Secondary Education
Majority (R 7): Rokita (IN), Chmn; Hunter (CA), Roe (TN), Thompson (PA), Messer (IN), Brat (VA), Garrett (VA)
Minority (D 6): Polis (CO), RMM; Grijalva (AZ), Fudge (OH), Bonamici (OR), Davis (CA), Wilson (FL)

Health, Employment, Labor & Pensions
Majority (R 12): Walberg (MI), Chmn; Wilson (SC), Roe (TN), Rokita (IN), Barletta (PA), Allen (GA), Lewis (MN), Rooney (FL), Mitchell (MI), Smucker (PA), Ferguson (GA), Estes (KS)
Minority (D 9): Sablan (MP), RMM; Wilson (FL), Norcross (NJ), Rochester (DE), Shea-Porter (NH), Espaillat (NY), Courtney (CT), Fudge (OH), Bonamici (OR)

Higher Education & Workforce Development
Majority (R 13): Guthrie (KY), Chmn; Thompson (PA), Barletta (PA), Messer (IN), Byrne (AL), Grothman (WI), Stefanik (NY), Allen (GA), Lewis (MN), Mitchell (MI), Garrett (VA), Smucker (PA), Estes (KS)
Minority (D 10): Davis (CA), RMM; Courtney (CT), Adams (NC), DeSaulnier (CA), Krishnamoorthi (IL), Polis (CO), Sablan (MP), Takano (CA), Rochester (DE), Espaillat (NY)

Workforce Protections
Majority (R 8): Byrne (AL), Chmn; Wilson (SC), Hunter (CA), Brat (VA), Grothman (WI), Stefanik (NY), Rooney (FL), Ferguson (GA)
Minority (D 7): Takano (CA), RMM; Grijalva (AZ), Adams (NC), DeSaulnier (CA), Norcross (NJ), Krishnamoorthi (IL), Shea-Porter (NH)

Energy & Commerce
energycommerce.house.gov

2125 RHOB
202-225-2927

Majority (R 31): Walden (OR), Chmn; Barton (TX), Upton (MI), Shimkus (IL), Murphy (PA), Burgess (TX), Blackburn (TN), Scalise (LA), Latta (OH), McMorris Rodgers (WA), Harper (MS), Lance (NJ), Guthrie (KY), Olson (TX), McKinley (WV), Kinzinger (IL), Griffith (VA), Bilirakis (FL), Johnson (OH), Long (MO), Bucshon (IN), Flores (TX), Brooks (IN), Mullin (OK), Hudson (NC), Collins (NY), Cramer (ND), Walberg (MI), Walters (CA), Costello (PA), Carter (GA)
Minority (D 24): Pallone (NJ), RMM; Rush (IL), Eshoo (CA), Engel (NY), Green (TX), DeGette (CO), Doyle (PA), Schakowsky (IL), Butterfield (NC), Matsui (CA), Castor (FL), Sarbanes (MD), McNerney (CA), Welch (VT), Lujan (NM), Tonko (NY), Clarke (NY), Loebsack (IA), Schrader (OR), Kennedy (MA), Cardenas (CA), Ruiz (CA), Peters (CA), Dingell (MI)

SUBCOMMITTEES

Communications & Technology
Majority (R 18): Blackburn (TN), Chmn; Lance (NJ), Shimkus (IL), Scalise (LA), Latta (OH), Guthrie (KY), Olson (TX), Kinzinger (IL), Bilirakis (FL), Johnson (OH), Long (MO), Flores (TX), Brooks (IN), Collins (NY), Cramer (ND), Walters (CA), Costello (PA), Walden (OR)
Minority (D 13): Doyle (PA), RMM; Welch (VT), Clarke (NY), Loebsack (IA), Ruiz (CA), Dingell (MI), Rush (IL), Eshoo (CA), Engel (NY), Butterfield (NC), Matsui (CA), McNerney (CA), Pallone (NJ)

Digital Commerce & Consumer Protection
Majority (R 14): Latta (OH), Chmn; Harper (MS), Upton (MI), Burgess (TX), Lance (NJ), Guthrie (KY), McKinley (WV), Kinzinger (IL), Bilirakis (FL), Bucshon (IN), Mullin (OK), Walters (CA), Costello (PA), Walden (OR)
Minority (D 10): Schakowsky (IL), RMM; Lujan (NM), Clarke (NY), Cardenas (CA), Dingell (MI), Matsui (CA), Welch (VT), Kennedy (MA), Green (TX), Pallone (NJ)

Energy
Majority (R 19): Upton (MI), Chmn; Olson (TX), Barton (TX), Shimkus (IL), Murphy (PA), Latta (OH), Harper (MS), McKinley (WV), Kinzinger (IL), Griffith (VA), Johnson (OH), Long (MO), Bucshon (IN), Flores (TX), Mullin (OK), Hudson (NC), Cramer (ND), Walberg (MI), Walden (OR)
Minority (D 14): Rush (IL), RMM; McNerney (CA), Peters (CA), Green (TX), Doyle (PA), Castor (FL), Sarbanes (MD), Welch (VT), Tonko (NY), Loebsack (IA), Schrader (OR), Kennedy (MA), Butterfield (NC), Pallone (NJ)

Environment
Majority (R 14): Shimkus (IL), Chmn; McKinley (WV), Barton (TX), Murphy (PA), Blackburn (TN), Harper (MS), Olson (TX), Johnson (OH), Flores (TX), Hudson (NC), Cramer (ND), Walberg (MI), Carter (GA), Walden (OR)
Minority (D 10): Tonko (NY), RMM; Ruiz (CA), Peters (CA), Green (TX), DeGette (CO), McNerney (CA), Cardenas (CA), Dingell (MI), Matsui (CA), Pallone (NJ)

Health
Majority (R 19): Burgess (TX), Chmn; Guthrie (KY), Barton (TX), Upton (MI), Shimkus (IL), Murphy (PA), Blackburn (TN), McMorris Rodgers (WA), Lance (NJ), Griffith (VA), Bilirakis (FL), Long (MO), Bucshon (IN), Brooks (IN), Mullin (OK), Hudson (NC), Collins (NY), Carter (GA), Walden (OR)
Minority (D 14): Green (TX), RMM; Engel (NY), Schakowsky (IL), Butterfield (NC), Matsui (CA), Castor (FL), Sarbanes (MD), Lujan (NM), Schrader (OR), Kennedy (MA), Cardenas (CA), Eshoo (CA), DeGette (CO), Pallone (NJ)

Oversight & Investigations
Majority (R 11): Murphy (PA), Chmn; Griffith (VA), Barton (TX), Burgess (TX), Brooks (IN), Collins (NY), Walberg (MI), Walters (CA), Costello (PA), Carter (GA), Walden (OR)
Minority (D 8): DeGette (CO), RMM; Schakowsky (IL), Castor (FL), Tonko (NY), Clarke (NY), Ruiz (CA), Peters (CA), Pallone (NJ)

Ethics
ethics.house.gov

1015 LHOB
202-225-7103

Majority (R 5): Brooks (IN), Chmn; Meehan (PA), Gowdy (SC), Marchant (TX), Lance (NJ)
Minority (D 6): Deutch (FL), RMM; Clarke (NY), Polis (CO), Brown (MD), Cohen (TN)

SUBCOMMITTEES

Pittenger
Majority (R 2): Dent (PA), Chmn; Katko (NY)
Minority (D 2): Sanchez (CA), RMM; Perlmutter (CO)

Financial Services
financialservices.house.gov

2129 RHOB
202-225-7502

Majority (R 34): Hensarling (TX), Chmn; King (NY), Royce (CA), Lucas (OK), McHenry (NC), Pearce (NM), Posey (FL), Luetkemeyer (MO), Huizenga (MI), Duffy (WI), Stivers (OH), Hultgren (IL), Ross (FL), Pittenger (NC), Wagner (MO), Barr (KY), Rothfus (PA), Messer (IN), Tipton (CO), Williams (TX), Poliquin (ME), Love (UT), Hill (AR), Emmer (MN), Zeldin (NY), Trott (MI), Loudermilk (GA), Mooney (WV), MacArthur (NJ), Davidson (OH), Budd (NC), Kustoff (TN), Tenney (NY), Hollingsworth (IN)
Minority (D 26): Waters (CA), RMM; Maloney (NY), Velazquez (NY), Sherman (CA), Meeks (NY), Capuano (MA), Clay (MO), Lynch (MA), Scott (GA), Green (TX), Cleaver (MO), Moore (WI), Ellison (MN), Perlmutter (CO), Himes (CT), Foster (IL), Kildee (MI), Delaney (MD), Sinema (AZ), Beatty (OH), Heck (WA), Vargas (CA), Gottheimer (NJ), Gonzalez (TX), Crist (FL), Kihuen (NV)

SUBCOMMITTEES

Capital Markets, Securities & Investment
Majority (R 17): Huizenga (MI), Chmn; Hultgren (IL), King (NY), McHenry (NC), Duffy (WI), Stivers (OH), Wagner (MO), Messer (IN), Poliquin (ME), Hill (AR), Emmer (MN), Mooney (WV), MacArthur (NJ), Davidson (OH), Budd (NC), Hollingsworth (IN), Hensarling (TX)
Minority (D 13): Maloney (NY), RMM; Sherman (CA), Lynch (MA), Scott (GA), Himes (CT), Ellison (MN), Foster (IL), Meeks (NY), Sinema (AZ), Vargas (CA), Gottheimer (NJ), Gonzalez (TX), Waters (CA)

Financial Institutions & Consumer Credit
Majority (R 16): Luetkemeyer (MO), Chmn; Rothfus (PA), Royce (CA), Lucas (OK), Posey (FL), Ross (FL), Pittenger (NC), Barr (KY), Tipton (CO), Williams (TX), Love (UT), Trott (MI), Loudermilk (GA), Kustoff (TN), Tenney (NY), Hensarling (TX)
Minority (D 12): Clay (MO), RMM; Maloney (NY), Meeks (NY), Scott (GA), Velazquez (NY), Green (TX), Ellison (MN), Capuano (MA), Heck (WA), Moore (WI), Crist (FL), Waters (CA)

Housing & Insurance
Majority (R 14): Duffy (WI), Chmn; Ross (FL), Royce (CA), Pearce (NM), Posey (FL), Luetkemeyer (MO), Stivers (OH), Hultgren (IL), Rothfus (PA), Zeldin (NY), Trott (MI), MacArthur (NJ), Budd (NC), Hensarling (TX)
Minority (D 11): Cleaver (MO), RMM; Velazquez (NY), Capuano (MA), Clay (MO), Sherman (CA), Beatty (OH), Kildee (MI), Delaney (MD), Kihuen (NV), Gonzalez (TX), Waters (CA)

Monetary Policy & Trade
Majority (R 13): Barr (KY), Chmn; Williams (TX), Lucas (OK), Huizenga (MI), Pittenger (NC), Love (UT), Hill (AR), Emmer (MN), Mooney (WV), Davidson (OH), Tenney (NY), Hollingsworth (IN), Hensarling (TX)
Minority (D 10): Moore (WI), RMM; Meeks (NY), Foster (IL), Sherman (CA), Green (TX), Heck (WA), Kildee (MI), Vargas (CA), Crist (FL), Waters (CA)

Oversight & Investigations
Majority (R 13): Wagner (MO), Chmn; Tipton (CO), King (NY), McHenry (NC), Ross (FL), Messer (IN), Zeldin (NY), Trott (MI), Loudermilk (GA), Kustoff (TN), Tenney (NY), Hollingsworth (IN), Hensarling (TX)
Minority (D 10): Green (TX), RMM; Ellison (MN), Cleaver (MO), Beatty (OH), Capuano (MA), Moore (WI), Gottheimer (NJ), Gonzalez (TX), Crist (FL), Waters (CA)

Terrorism & Illicit Finance
Majority (R 15): Pearce (NM), Chmn; Pittenger (NC), Rothfus (PA), Messer (IN), Tipton (CO), Williams (TX), Poliquin (ME), Love (UT), Hill (AR), Emmer (MN), Zeldin (NY), Davidson (OH), Budd (NC), Kustoff (TN), Hensarling (TX)
Minority (D 12): Perlmutter (CO), RMM; Maloney (NY), Himes (CT), Foster (IL), Kildee (MI), Delaney (MD), Sinema (AZ), Vargas (CA), Gottheimer (NJ), Kihuen (NV), Lynch (MA), Waters (CA)

Foreign Affairs

foreignaffairs.house.gov — **2170 RHOB**, **202-225-5021**

Majority (R 26): Royce (CA), Chmn; Smith (NJ), Ros-Lehtinen (FL), Rohrabacher (CA), Chabot (OH), Wilson (SC), McCaul (TX), Poe (TX), Issa (CA), Marino (PA), Duncan (SC), Brooks (AL), Cook (CA), Perry (PA), DeSantis (FL), Meadows (NC), Yoho (FL), Kinzinger (IL), Zeldin (NY), Donovan (NY), Sensenbrenner (WI), Wagner (MO), Mast (FL), Rooney (FL), Fitzpatrick (PA), Garrett (VA)
Minority (D 21): Engel (NY), RMM; Sherman (CA), Meeks (NY), Sires (NJ), Connolly (VA), Deutch (FL), Bass (CA), Keating (MA), Cicilline (RI), Bera (CA), Frankel (FL), Gabbard (HI), Castro (TX), Kelly (IL), Boyle (PA), Titus (NV), Torres (CA), Schneider (IL), Suozzi (NY), Espaillat (NY), Lieu (CA)

SUBCOMMITTEES

Africa, Global Health, Global Human Rights & Internat'l Orgs
Majority (R 5): Smith (NJ), Chmn; Meadows (NC), Donovan (NY), Sensenbrenner (WI), Garrett (VA)
Minority (D 4): Bass (CA), RMM; Bera (CA), Castro (TX), Suozzi (NY)

Asia & the Pacific
Majority (R 8): Yoho (FL), Chmn; Rohrabacher (CA), Chabot (OH), Marino (PA), Brooks (AL), Perry (PA), Kinzinger (IL), Wagner (MO)
Minority (D 6): Sherman (CA), RMM; Bera (CA), Titus (NV), Connolly (VA), Deutch (FL), Gabbard (HI)

Europe, Eurasia & Emerging Threats
Majority (R 8): Rohrabacher (CA), Chmn; Wilson (SC), Poe (TX), Marino (PA), Duncan (SC), Sensenbrenner (WI), Rooney (FL), Fitzpatrick (PA)
Minority (D 6): Meeks (NY), RMM; Sherman (CA), Sires (NJ), Keating (MA), Cicilline (RI), Kelly (IL)

Middle East & North Africa
Majority (R 12): Ros-Lehtinen (FL), Chmn; Chabot (OH), Issa (CA), DeSantis (FL), Meadows (NC), Cook (CA), Kinzinger (IL), Zeldin (NY), Donovan (NY), Wagner (MO), Mast (FL), Fitzpatrick (PA)
Minority (D 9): Deutch (FL), RMM; Connolly (VA), Cicilline (RI), Frankel (FL), Boyle (PA), Gabbard (HI), Schneider (IL), Suozzi (NY), Lieu (CA)

Terrorism, Nonproliferation & Trade
Majority (R 8): Poe (TX), Chmn; Wilson (SC), Issa (CA), Cook (CA), Perry (PA), Zeldin (NY), Mast (FL), Garrett (VA)
Minority (D 6): Keating (MA), RMM; Frankel (FL), Boyle (PA), Titus (NV), Torres (CA), Schneider (IL)

Western Hemisphere
Majority (R 8): Duncan (SC), Chmn; Smith (NJ), Ros-Lehtinen (FL), McCaul (TX), Brooks (AL), DeSantis (FL), Yoho (FL), Rooney (FL)
Minority (D 6): Sires (NJ), RMM; Castro (TX), Kelly (IL), Torres (CA), Espaillat (NY), Meeks (NY)

Homeland Security
homeland.house.gov — **H2-176 FHOB** — **202-226-8417**

Majority (R 18): McCaul (TX), Chmn; Smith (TX), King (NY), Rogers (AL), Duncan (SC), Marino (PA), Barletta (PA), Perry (PA), Katko (NY), Hurd (TX), McSally (AZ), Ratcliffe (TX), Donovan (NY), Gallagher (WI), Higgins (LA), Rutherford (FL), Garrett (VA), Fitzpatrick (PA)
Minority (D 12): Thompson (MS), RMM; Jackson Lee (TX), Langevin (RI), Richmond (LA), Keating (MA), Payne (NJ), Vela (TX), Watson Coleman (NJ), Rice (NY), Correa (CA), Demings (FL), Barragan (CA)

SUBCOMMITTEES

Border & Maritime Security
Majority (R 7): McSally (AZ), Chmn; Smith (TX), Rogers (AL), Duncan (SC), Barletta (PA), Hurd (TX), Rutherford (FL)
Minority (D 6): Vela (TX), RMM; Richmond (LA), Correa (CA), Demings (FL), Barragan (CA), Thompson (MS)

Counterterrorism & Intelligence
Majority (R 5): King (NY), Chmn; Barletta (PA), Perry (PA), Hurd (TX), Gallagher (WI)
Minority (D 3): Rice (NY), RMM; Jackson Lee (TX), Keating (MA)

Cybersecurity & Infrastructure Protection
Majority (R 6): Ratcliffe (TX), Chmn; Katko (NY), Donovan (NY), Gallagher (WI), Garrett (VA), Fitzpatrick (PA)
Minority (D 4): Richmond (LA), RMM; Jackson Lee (TX), Langevin (RI), Demings (FL)

Emergency Preparedness, Response & Communications
Majority (R 5): Donovan (NY), Chmn; Marino (PA), McSally (AZ), Rutherford (FL), Garrett (VA)
Minority (D 3): Payne (NJ), RMM; Langevin (RI), Watson Coleman (NJ)

Oversight & Management Efficiency
Majority (R 5): Perry (PA), Chmn; Duncan (SC), Marino (PA), Ratcliffe (TX), Higgins (LA)
Minority (D 4): Correa (CA), RMM; Rice (NY), Barragan (CA), Thompson (MS)

Transportation & Protective Security
Majority (R 5): Katko (NY), Chmn; King (NY), Rogers (AL), Higgins (LA), Fitzpatrick (PA)
Minority (D 3): Watson Coleman (NJ), RMM; Keating (MA), Payne (NJ)

House Administration
cha.house.gov — **1309 LHOB** — **202-225-8281**

Majority (R 6): Harper (MS), Chmn; Davis (IL), Comstock (VA), Walker (NC), Smith (NE), Loudermilk (GA)
Minority (D 3): Brady (PA), RMM; Lofgren (CA), Raskin (MD)

Judiciary
judiciary.house.gov — **2138 RHOB** — **202-225-3951**

Majority (R 24): Goodlatte (VA), Chmn; Sensenbrenner (WI), Smith (TX), Chabot (OH), Issa (CA), King (IA), Franks (AZ), Gohmert (TX), Jordan (OH), Poe (TX), Chaffetz (UT), Marino (PA), Gowdy (SC), Labrador (ID), Farenthold (TX), Collins (GA), DeSantis (FL), Buck (CO), Ratcliffe (TX), Roby (AL), Gaetz (FL), Johnson (LA), Biggs (AZ), Rutherford (FL), Handel (GA)
Minority (D 17): Conyers (MI), RMM; Nadler (NY), Lofgren (CA), Jackson Lee (TX), Cohen (TN), Johnson (GA), Deutch (FL), Gutierrez (IL), Bass (CA), Richmond (LA), Jeffries (NY), Cicilline (RI), Swalwell (CA), Lieu (CA), Raskin (MD), Jayapal (WA), Schneider (IL)

SUBCOMMITTEES

Constitution & Civil Justice
Majority (R 5): King (IA), Chmn; DeSantis (FL), Franks (AZ), Gohmert (TX), Gowdy (SC)
Minority (D 3): Cohen (TN), RMM; Raskin (MD), Nadler (NY)

Courts, Intellectual Property & Internet
Majority (R 14): Issa (CA), Chmn; Collins (GA), Smith (TX), Chabot (OH), Franks (AZ), Jordan (OH), Poe (TX), Chaffetz (UT), Marino (PA), Labrador (ID), Farenthold (TX), DeSantis (FL), Gaetz (FL), Biggs (AZ)
Minority (D 12): Nadler (NY), RMM; Johnson (GA), Deutch (FL), Bass (CA), Richmond (LA), Jeffries (NY), Swalwell (CA), Lieu (CA), Schneider (IL), Lofgren (CA), Cohen (TN), Gutierrez (IL)

Crime, Terrorism, Homeland Security & Investigations
Majority (R 9): Gowdy (SC), Chmn; Gohmert (TX), Sensenbrenner (WI), Chabot (OH), Poe (TX), Chaffetz (UT), Ratcliffe (TX), Roby (AL), Johnson (LA)
Minority (D 7): Jackson Lee (TX), RMM; Deutch (FL), Bass (CA), Richmond (LA), Jeffries (NY), Lieu (CA), Raskin (MD)

Immigration & Border Security
Majority (R 8): Sensenbrenner (WI), Chmn; Labrador (ID), Smith (TX), King (IA), Jordan (OH), Buck (CO), Johnson (LA), Biggs (AZ)
Minority (D 5): Lofgren (CA), RMM; Gutierrez (IL), Jayapal (WA), Jackson Lee (TX), Cicilline (RI)

Regulatory Reform, Commercial & Antitrust Law
Majority (R 7): Marino (PA), Chmn; Farenthold (TX), Issa (CA), Collins (GA), Buck (CO), Ratcliffe (TX), Gaetz (FL)
Minority (D 5): Cicilline (RI), RMM; Johnson (GA), Swalwell (CA), Jayapal (WA), Schneider (IL)

Natural Resources — 1324 LHOB
naturalresources.house.gov — 202-225-2761

Majority (R 25): Bishop (UT), Chmn; Young (AK), Gohmert (TX), Lamborn (CO), Wittman (VA), McClintock (CA), Pearce (NM), Thompson (PA), Gosar (AZ), Labrador (ID), Tipton (CO), LaMalfa (CA), Denham (CA), Cook (CA), Westerman (AR), Graves (LA), Hice (GA), Radewagen (AS), LaHood (IL), Webster (FL), Rouzer (NC), Bergman (MI), Cheney (WY), Johnson (LA), Gonzalez Colon (PR), Gianforte (MT)
Minority (D 18): Grijalva (AZ), RMM; Napolitano (CA), Bordallo (GU), Costa (CA), Sablan (MP), Tsongas (MA), Huffman (CA), Lowenthal (CA), Beyer (VA), Torres (CA), Gallego (AZ), Hanabusa (HI), Barragan (CA), Soto (FL), Panetta (CA), McEachin (VA), Brown (MD), Clay (MO)

SUBCOMMITTEES

Energy & Mineral Resources
Majority (R 14): Gosar (AZ), Chmn; Gohmert (TX), Lamborn (CO), Wittman (VA), Pearce (NM), Thompson (PA), Tipton (CO), Cook (CA), Westerman (AR), Graves (LA), Hice (GA), LaHood (IL), Cheney (WY), Bishop (UT)
Minority (D 9): Lowenthal (CA), RMM; Brown (MD), Costa (CA), Tsongas (MA), Huffman (CA), Beyer (VA), Soto (FL), Barragan (CA), Grijalva (AZ)

Federal Lands
Majority (R 13): McClintock (CA), Chmn; Young (AK), Pearce (NM), Thompson (PA), Labrador (ID), Tipton (CO), Westerman (AR), LaHood (IL), Webster (FL), Rouzer (NC), Bergman (MI), Cheney (WY), Bishop (UT)
Minority (D 9): Hanabusa (HI), RMM; Tsongas (MA), Lowenthal (CA), Torres (CA), Gallego (AZ), Panetta (CA), McEachin (VA), Brown (MD), Grijalva (AZ)

Indian, Insular & Alaska Native Affairs
Majority (R 9): LaMalfa (CA), Chmn; Young (AK), Denham (CA), Cook (CA), Radewagen (AS), LaHood (IL), Bergman (MI), Gonzalez Colon (PR), Bishop (UT)
Minority (D 7): Torres (CA), RMM; Bordallo (GU), Sablan (MP), Gallego (AZ), Soto (FL), Hanabusa (HI), Grijalva (AZ)

Oversight & Investigations
Majority (R 7): Labrador (ID), Chmn; Gohmert (TX), Radewagen (AS), Bergman (MI), Johnson (LA), Gonzalez Colon (PR), Bishop (UT)
Minority (D 6): McEachin (VA), RMM; Gallego (AZ), Huffman (CA), Soto (FL), Clay (MO), Grijalva (AZ)

Water, Power & Oceans
Majority (R 12): Lamborn (CO), Chmn; Wittman (VA), McClintock (CA), Gosar (AZ), LaMalfa (CA), Denham (CA), Graves (LA), Hice (GA), Webster (FL), Rouzer (NC), Johnson (LA), Bishop (UT)
Minority (D 9): Huffman (CA), RMM; Napolitano (CA), Costa (CA), Beyer (VA), Barragan (CA), Panetta (CA), Bordallo (GU), Sablan (MP), Grijalva (AZ)

Oversight & Government Reform — 2157 RHOB

oversight.house.gov **202-225-5074**

Majority (R 23): Gowdy (SC), Chmn; Duncan (TN), Issa (CA), Jordan (OH), Chaffetz(UT), Sanford (SC), Gosar (AZ), DesJarlais (TN), Farenthold (TX), Foxx (NC), Massie (KY), Meadows (NC), DeSantis (FL), Ross (FL), Walker (NC), Blum (IA), Hice (GA), Russell (OK), Grothman (WI), Hurd (TX), Palmer (AL), Comer (KY), Mitchell (MI), Amash (MI), Gianforte (MT)
Minority (D 18): Cummings (MD), RMM; Maloney (NY), Norton (DC), Clay (MO), Lynch (MA), Cooper (TN), Connolly (VA), Kelly (IL), Lawrence (MI), Watson Coleman (NJ), Plaskett (VI), Demings (FL), Krishnamoorthi (IL), Raskin (MD), Welch (VT), Cartwright (PA), DeSaulnier (CA), Sarbanes (MD)

SUBCOMMITTEES

Government Operations
Majority (R 8): Meadows (NC), Chmn; Hice (GA), Jordan (OH), Sanford (SC), Massie (KY), DeSantis (FL), Ross (FL), Blum (IA)
Minority (D 6): Connolly (VA), RMM; Maloney (NY), Norton (DC), Clay (MO), Lawrence (MI), Watson Coleman (NJ)

Health Care, Benefits & Administrative Rules
Majority (R 8): Jordan (OH), Chmn; Walker (NC), Issa (CA), Sanford (SC), DesJarlais (TN), Meadows (NC), Grothman (WI), Mitchell (MI)
Minority (D 6): Krishnamoorthi (IL), RMM; Cooper (TN), Norton (DC), Kelly (IL), Watson Coleman (NJ), Plaskett (VI)

Information Technology
Majority (R 7): Hurd (TX), Chmn; Mitchell (MI), Issa (CA), Amash (MI), Farenthold (TX), Russell (OK), Chaffetz (UT), Amash (MI)
Minority (D 6): Kelly (IL), RMM; Raskin (MD), Lynch (MA), Connolly (VA), Krishnamoorthi (IL), Cummings (MD)

Intergovernmental Affairs
Majority (R 6): Palmer (AL), Chmn; Grothman (WI), Duncan (TN), Foxx (NC), Massie (KY), Walker (NC)
Minority (D 2): Demings (FL), RMM; DeSaulnier (CA)

Interior, Energy & Environment
Majority (R 5): Farenthold (TX), Chmn; Gosar (AZ), Ross (FL), Palmer (AL), Comer (KY)
Minority (D 2): Plaskett (VI), RMM; Raskin (MD)

National Security
Majority (R 8): DeSantis (FL), Chmn; Russell (OK), Duncan (TN), Amash (MI), Gosar (AZ), Foxx (NC), Hice (GA), Comer (KY), Amash (MI)
Minority (D 5): Lynch (MA), RMM; Welch (VT), Demings (FL), DeSaulnier (CA), John Sarbanes (MD)

Rules **H-312 The Capitol**
rules.house.gov **202-225-9191**

Majority (R 9): Sessions (TX), Chmn; Cole (OK), Woodall (GA), Burgess (TX), Collins (GA), Byrne (AL), Newhouse (WA), Buck (CO), Cheney (WY)
Minority (D 4): Slaughter (NY), RMM; McGovern (MA), Hastings (FL), Polis (CO)

SUBCOMMITTEES

Legislative & Budget Process
Majority (R 5): Woodall (GA), Chmn; Burgess (TX), Byrne (AL), Newhouse (WA), Buck (CO)
Minority (D 2): Hastings (FL), RMM; Polis (CO)

Rules & Organization of the House
Majority (R 5): Collins (GA), Chmn; Byrne (AL), Newhouse (WA), Cheney (WY), Sessions (TX)
Minority (D 2): Slaughter (NY), RMM; McGovern (MA)

Science, Space & Technology **2321 RHOB**
science.house.gov **202-225-6371**

Majority (R 22): Smith (TX), Chmn; Lucas (OK), Rohrabacher (CA), Brooks (AL), Hultgren (IL), Posey (FL), Massie (KY), Bridenstine (OK), Weber (TX), Knight (CA), Babin (TX), Comstock (VA), Palmer (AL),

Loudermilk (GA), Abraham (LA), LaHood (IL), Webster (FL), Banks (IN), Biggs (AZ), Marshall (KS), Dunn (FL), Higgins (LA), Norman (SC)
Minority (D 16): Johnson (TX), RMM; Lofgren (CA), Lipinski (IL), Bonamici (OR), Bera (CA), Esty (CT), Veasey (TX), Beyer (VA), Rosen (NV), McNerney (CA), Perlmutter (CO), Tonko (NY), Takano (CA), Foster (IL), Hanabusa (HI), Crist (FL)

SUBCOMMITTEES

Energy
Majority (R 11): Weber (TX), Chmn; Knight (CA), Rohrabacher (CA), Lucas (OK), Brooks (AL), Hultgren (IL), Massie (KY), Bridenstine (OK), LaHood (IL), Webster (FL), Dunn (FL)
Minority (D 8): Veasey (TX), RMM; Lofgren (CA), Lipinski (IL), Rosen (NV), McNerney (CA), Tonko (NY), Foster (IL), Takano (CA)

Environment
Majority (R 10): Biggs (AZ), Chmn; Banks (IN), Rohrabacher (CA), Posey (FL), Brooks (AL), Weber (TX), Babin (TX), Palmer (AL), Loudermilk (GA), Higgins (LA)
Minority (D 3): Bonamici (OR), RMM; Hanabusa (HI), Crist (FL)

Oversight
Majority (R 7): LaHood (IL), Chmn; Marshall (KS), Posey (FL), Massie (KY), Palmer (AL), Loudermilk (GA), Higgins (LA)
Minority (D 3): Beyer (VA), RMM; McNerney (CA), Perlmutter (CO)

Research & Technology
Majority (R 9): Comstock (VA), Chmn; Abraham (LA), Lucas (OK), Hultgren (IL), Knight (CA), LaHood (IL), Webster (FL), Banks (IN), Marshall (KS)
Minority (D 7): Lipinski (IL), RMM; Esty (CT), Rosen (NV), Bonamici (OR), Bera (CA), Beyer (VA), Johnson (TX)

Space
Majority (R 14): Babin (TX), Chmn; Brooks (AL), Rohrabacher (CA), Lucas (OK), Posey (FL), Bridenstine (OK), Knight (CA), Comstock (VA), Abraham (LA), Webster (FL), Banks (IN), Biggs (AZ), Dunn (FL), Higgins (LA)
Minority (D 8): Bera (CA), RMM; Lofgren (CA), Beyer (VA), Veasey (TX), Lipinski (IL), Perlmutter (CO), Crist (FL), Foster (IL)

Small Business — **2361 RHOB**
smallbusiness.house.gov — **202-225-5821**

Majority (R 14): Chabot (OH), Chmn; King (IA), Luetkemeyer (MO), Brat (VA), Radewagen (AS), Knight (CA), Kelly (MS), Blum (IA), Comer (KY), Gonzalez Colon (PR), Bacon (NE), Fitzpatrick (PA), Marshall (KS), Estes (KS), Norman (SC)
Minority (D 9): Velazquez (NY), RMM; Evans (PA), Murphy (FL), Lawson (FL), Clarke (NY), Chu (CA), Adams (NC), Espaillat (NY), Schneider (IL)

SUBCOMMITTEES

Agriculture, Energy & Trade
Majority (R 6): Blum (IA), Chmn; King (IA), Luetkemeyer (MO), Radewagen (AS), Comer (KY), Bacon (NE)
Minority (D 2): Schneider (IL), RMM; Lawson (FL)

Contracting & Workforce
Majority (R 4): Knight (CA), Chmn; Comer (KY), King (IA), Estes (KS)
Minority (D 4): Murphy (FL), RMM; Clarke (NY), Evans (PA), Lawson (FL)

Economic Growth, Tax & Capital Access
Majority (R 5): Brat (VA), Chmn; Knight (CA), Kelly (MS), Gonzalez Colon (PR), Fitzpatrick (PA)
Minority (D 4): Evans (PA), RMM; Chu (CA), Murphy (FL), Clarke (NY)

Health & Technology
Majority (R 6): Radewagen (AS), Chmn; Luetkemeyer (MO), Brat (VA), Gonzalez Colon (PR), Fitzpatrick (PA), Marshall (KS)
Minority (D 2): Lawson (FL), RMM; Espaillat (NY)

Investigations, Oversight & Regulations
Majority (R 5): Kelly (MS), Chmn; Blum (IA), Bacon (NE), Marshall (KS), Estes (KS)
Minority (D 2): Adams (NC), RMM;

Transportation & Infrastructure
transportation.house.gov

2251 RHOB
202-225-9446

Majority (R 34): Shuster (PA), Chmn; Young (AK), Duncan (TN), LoBiondo (NJ), Graves (MO), Hunter (CA), Crawford (AR), Barletta (PA), Farenthold (TX), Gibbs (OH), Webster (FL), Denham (CA), Massie (KY), Meadows (NC), Perry (PA), Davis (IL), Sanford (SC), Woodall (GA), Rokita (IN), Katko (NY), Babin (TX), Graves (LA), Comstock (VA), Rouzer (NC), Bost (IL), Weber (TX), LaMalfa (CA), Westerman (AR), Smucker (PA), Mitchell (MI), Faso (NY), Ferguson (GA), Mast (FL), Lewis (MN)
Minority (D 27): DeFazio (OR), RMM; Norton (DC), Nadler (NY), Johnson (TX), Cummings (MD), Larsen (WA), Capuano (MA), Napolitano (CA), Lipinski (IL), Cohen (TN), Sires (NJ), Garamendi (CA), Johnson (GA), Carson (IN), Nolan (MN), Titus (NV), Maloney (NY), Esty (CT), Frankel (FL), Bustos (IL), Huffman (CA), Brownley (CA), Wilson (FL), Payne (NJ), Lowenthal (CA), Lawrence (MI), DeSaulnier (CA)

SUBCOMMITTEES

Aviation
Majority (R 22): LoBiondo (NJ), Chmn; Mitchell (MI), Young (AK), Duncan (TN), Graves (MO), Hunter (CA), Farenthold (TX), Gibbs (OH), Webster (FL), Denham (CA), Massie (KY), Meadows (NC), Perry (PA), Davis (IL), Sanford (SC), Woodall (GA), Rokita (IN), Comstock (VA), LaMalfa (CA), Westerman (AR), Lewis (MN), Shuster (PA)
Minority (D 17): Larsen (WA), RMM; Johnson (TX), Lipinski (IL), Carson (IN), Bustos (IL), Norton (DC), Titus (NV), Maloney (NY), Brownley (CA), Payne (NJ), Lawrence (MI), Capuano (MA), Napolitano (CA), Cohen (TN), Johnson (GA), Nolan (MN), DeFazio (OR)

Coast Guard & Maritime Transportation
Majority (R 9): Hunter (CA), Chmn; Young (AK), LoBiondo (NJ), Graves (LA), Rouzer (NC), Weber (TX), Mast (FL), Lewis (MN), Shuster (PA)
Minority (D 7): Garamendi (CA), RMM; Cummings (MD), Larsen (WA), Huffman (CA), Lowenthal (CA), Norton (DC), DeFazio (OR)

Economic Dev't, Public Buildings & Emergency Management
Majority (R 9): Barletta (PA), Chmn; Crawford (AR), Comstock (VA), Bost (IL), Smucker (PA), Faso (NY), Ferguson (GA), Mast (FL), Shuster (PA)
Minority (D 6): Johnson (GA), RMM; Norton (DC), Sires (NJ), Napolitano (CA), Capuano (MA), DeFazio (OR)

Highways & Transit
Majority (R 28): Graves (MO), Chmn; Young (AK), Duncan (TN), LoBiondo (NJ), Hunter (CA), Crawford (AR), Barletta (PA), Farenthold (TX), Gibbs (OH), Denham (CA), Massie (KY), Meadows (NC), Perry (PA), Davis (IL), Woodall (GA), Katko (NY), Babin (TX), Graves (LA), Comstock (VA), Rouzer (NC), Bost (IL), LaMalfa (CA), Westerman (AR), Smucker (PA), Mitchell (MI), Faso (NY), Ferguson (GA), Shuster (PA)
Minority (D 22): Norton (DC), RMM; Nadler (NY), Cohen (TN), Sires (NJ), Nolan (MN), Titus (NV), Maloney (NY), Esty (CT), Huffman (CA), Brownley (CA), Lowenthal (CA), Lawrence (MI), DeSaulnier (CA), Johnson (TX), Capuano (MA), Napolitano (CA), Lipinski (IL), Johnson (GA), Frankel (FL), Bustos (IL), Wilson (FL), DeFazio (OR)

Railroads, Pipelines & Hazardous Materials
Majority (R 19): Denham (CA), Chmn; Duncan (TN), Graves (MO), Barletta (PA), Farenthold (TX), Webster (FL), Meadows (NC), Perry (PA), Sanford (SC), Rokita (IN), Katko (NY), Babin (TX), Weber (TX), Westerman (AR), Smucker (PA), Mitchell (MI), Faso (NY), Lewis (MN), Shuster (PA)
Minority (D 15): Capuano (MA), RMM; Payne (NJ), Nadler (NY), Cummings (MD), Cohen (TN), Sires (NJ), Garamendi (CA), Carson (IN), Nolan (MN), Esty (CT), Bustos (IL), Wilson (FL), DeSaulnier (CA), Lipinski (IL), DeFazio (OR)

Water Resources & Environment
Majority (R 18): Graves (LA), Chmn; Crawford (AR), Gibbs (OH), Webster (FL), Massie (KY), Davis (IL), Sanford (SC), Woodall (GA), Rokita (IN), Katko (NY), Babin (TX), Rouzer (NC), Bost (IL), Weber (TX), LaMalfa (CA), Ferguson (GA), Mast (FL), Shuster (PA)
Minority (D 14): Napolitano (CA), RMM; Frankel (FL), Wilson (FL), Huffman (CA), Lowenthal (CA), Johnson (TX), Garamendi (CA), Titus (NV), Maloney (NY), Esty (CT), Bustos (IL), Brownley (CA), Lawrence (MI), DeFazio (OR)

Veterans' Affairs
veterans.house.gov

335 CHOB
202-225-3527

Majority (R 14): Roe (TN), Chmn; Bilirakis (FL), Coffman (CO), Wenstrup (OH), Radewagen (AS), Bost (IL), Poliquin (ME), Dunn (FL), Arrington (TX), Rutherford (FL), Higgins (LA), Bergman (MI), Banks (IN), Gonzalez Colon (PR)
Minority (D 10): Walz (MN), RMM; Takano (CA), Brownley (CA), Kuster (NH), O'Rourke (TX), Rice (NY), Correa (CA), Sablan (MP), Esty (CT), Peters (CA)

SUBCOMMITTEES

Disability Assistance & Memorial Affairs
Majority (R 5): Bost (IL), Chmn; Coffman (CO), Radewagen (AS), Bergman (MI), Banks (IN)
Minority (D 3): Esty (CT), RMM; Brownley (CA), Sablan (MP)

Economic Opportunity
Majority (R 5): Arrington (TX), Chmn; Bilirakis (FL), Wenstrup (OH), Rutherford (FL), Banks (IN)
Minority (D 4): O'Rourke (TX), RMM; Takano (CA), Correa (CA), Rice (NY)

Health
Majority (R 7): Wenstrup (OH), Chmn; Bilirakis (FL), Radewagen (AS), Dunn (FL), Rutherford (FL), Higgins (LA), Gonzalez Colon (PR)
Minority (D 5): Brownley (CA), RMM; Takano (CA), Kuster (NH), O'Rourke (TX), Correa (CA)

Oversight & Investigations
Majority (R 6): Bergman (MI), Chmn; Bost (IL), Poliquin (ME), Dunn (FL), Arrington (TX), Gonzalez Colon (PR)
Minority (D 4): Kuster (NH), RMM; Rice (NY), Peters (CA), Sablan (MP)

Ways & Means — 1102 LHOB
waysandmeans.house.gov — **202-225-3625**

Majority (R 24): Brady (TX), Chmn; Johnson (TX), Nunes (CA), Tiberi (OH), Reichert (WA), Roskam (IL), Buchanan (FL), Smith (NE), Jenkins (KS), Paulsen (MN), Marchant (TX), Black (TN), Reed (NY), Kelly (PA), Renacci (OH), Meehan (PA), Noem (SD), Holding (NC), Smith (MO), Rice (SC), Schweikert (AZ), Walorski (IN), Curbelo (FL), Bishop (MI)
Minority (D 16): Neal (MA), RMM; Levin (MI), Lewis (GA), Doggett (TX), Thompson (CA), Larson (CT), Blumenauer (OR), Kind (WI), Pascrell (NJ), Crowley (NY), Davis (IL), Sanchez (CA), Higgins (NY), Sewell (AL), DelBene (WA), Chu (CA)

SUBCOMMITTEES

Health
Majority (R 11): Tiberi (OH), Chmn; Johnson (TX), Nunes (CA), Roskam (IL), Buchanan (FL), Smith (NE), Jenkins (KS), Marchant (TX), Black (TN), Paulsen (MN), Reed (NY)
Minority (D 7): Levin (MI), RMM; Thompson (CA), Kind (WI), Blumenauer (OR), Higgins (NY), Sewell (AL), Chu (CA)

Human Resources
Majority (R 7): Smith (NE), Chmn; Smith (MO), Walorski (IN), Curbelo (FL), Bishop (MI), Reichert (WA), Reed (NY)
Minority (D 4): Davis (IL), RMM; Doggett (TX), Sewell (AL), Chu (CA)

Oversight
Majority (R 7): Buchanan (FL), Chmn; Schweikert (AZ), Walorski (IN), Curbelo (FL), Bishop (MI), Meehan (PA), Holding (NC)
Minority (D 4): Lewis (GA), RMM; Crowley (NY), DelBene (WA), Blumenauer (OR)

Social Security
Majority (R 7): Johnson (TX), Chmn; Rice (SC), Schweikert (AZ), Buchanan (FL), Kelly (PA), Renacci (OH), Smith (MO)
Minority (D 4): Larson (CT), RMM; Pascrell (NJ), Crowley (NY), Sanchez (CA)

Tax Policy
Majority (R 9): Roskam (IL), Chmn; Reichert (WA), Tiberi (OH), Kelly (PA), Renacci (OH), Noem (SD), Holding (NC), Marchant (TX), Meehan (PA)
Minority (D 6): Doggett (TX), RMM; Larson (CT), Sanchez (CA), Thompson (CA), DelBene (WA), Blumenauer (OR)

Trade
Majority (R 10): Reichert (WA), Chmn; Nunes (CA), Jenkins (KS), Paulsen (MN), Kelly (PA), Meehan (PA), Reed (NY), Noem (SD), Holding (NC), Rice (SC)
Minority (D 6): Pascrell (NJ), RMM; Kind (WI), Doggett (TX), Levin (MI), Davis (IL), Higgins (NY)

OTHER COMMITTEES

Commission on Congressional Mailing Standards **1216 LHOB**
cha.house.gov **202-226-0647**

Majority (R 3): Davis (IL), Chmn; Latta (OH), Comstock (VA)
Minority (D 3): Davis (CA), RMM; Sherman (CA), McEachin (VA)

Permanent Select on Intelligence **HVC-304 The Capitol Visitors Center**
intelligence.house.gov **202-225-4121**

Majority (R 13): Nunes (CA), Chmn; Conaway (TX), King (NY), LoBiondo (NJ), Rooney (FL), Ros-Lehtinen (FL), Turner (OH), Wenstrup (OH), Stewart (UT), Crawford (AR), Gowdy (SC), Stefanik (NY), Hurd (TX)
Minority (D 9): Schiff (CA), RMM; Himes (CT), Sewell (AL), Carson (IN), Speier (CA), Quigley (IL), Swalwell (CA), Castro (TX), Heck (WA)

JOINT COMMITTEES

Joint Congressional-Executive Commission on China **243 Ford**
cecc.gov/about/commissioners/115th-congress **202-226-3766**

House (7): Smith (NJ), Pittenger (NC), Franks (AZ), Hultgren (IL), Kaptur (OH), Walz (MN), Lieu (CA)
Senate (9): Rubio (FL), Chmn; Lankford (OK), Cotton (AR), Daines (MT), Young (IN); Feinstein (CA); Merkley (OR); Peters (MI); King (ME)

Joint Economic **G-01 DSOB**
jec.senate.gov/public/index.cfm/about **202-224-5171**

House (10): Tiberi (OH), Chmn; Maloney (NY), Paulsen (MN), Delaney (MD), Adams (NC), Schweikert (AZ), Beyer (VA), Comstock (VA), LaHood (IL), Rooney (FL)
Senate (10): Heinrich (NM), RMM; Klobuchar (MN), Peters (MI), Lee (UT), Cotton (AR), Hassan (NH), Portman (OH), Cruz (TX), Cassidy (LA), Sasse (NE)

Joint Library **1309 LHOB**
cha.house.gov/jointcommittees/joint-committee-library **202-225-8281**

House (5): Harper (MS), Chmn; Yoder (KS), Loudermilk (GA), Brady (PA), Lofgren (CA)
Senate (5): Shelby (AL), VChmn; Roberts (KS), Blunt (MO), Klobuchar (MN), Leahy (VT)

Joint Printing **1309 LHOB**
cha.house.gov/jointcommittees/joint-committee-on-printing **202-225-8281**

House (5): Davis (IL), VChmn; Harper (MS), Walker (NC), Brady (PA), Raskin (MD)
Senate (5): Shelby (AL), Chmn; Roberts (KS), Wicker (MS), Klobuchar (MN), Udall (NM)

Joint Security & Cooperation in Europe **234 Ford**
csce.gov/commissioners **202-225-1901**

House (3): Hastings (FL), Jackson Lee (TX), Moore (WI)
Senate (5): Wicker (MS), Chmn; Boozman (AR), Gardner (CO), Rubio (FL), Tillis (NC)

Joint Taxation **502 Ford**
www.jct.gov **202-225-3621**

House (5): Brady (TX) Chmn, Johnson (TX), Nunes (CA), Neal (MA), Lewis (GA)
Senate (5): Hatch (UT) VChmn, Grassley (IA), Crapo (ID), Wyden (OR), Stabenow (MI)

Vital Statistics on Congress

Vital Statistics on Congress, first published in 1980, long ago became the go-to source of impartial data on the United States Congress. Vital Statistics' purpose is to collect and provide useful data on America's first branch of government, including data on the composition of its membership, its formal procedure (such as the use of the filibuster), informal norms, party structure, and staff. With some chapters of data dating back nearly 100 years, Vital Statistics also documents how Congress has changed over time, illustrating, for example, the increasing polarization of Congress and the diversifying demographics of those who are elected to serve.

Vital Statistics began as a joint effort undertaken by Thomas E. Mann of Brookings and Norman J. Ornstein of the American Enterprise Institute, in collaboration with Michael Malbin of the Campaign Finance Institute. The datasets were published in print until 2013 when the project migrated online for the first time. This year, Brookings' Molly E. Reynolds spearheaded Vital Statistics' most recent update.

The Almanac team obtained permission from the Brookings Institution to provide select tables of data relevant to Almanac readers. The following tables can be found in this section:

- 1-1 Apportionment of Congressional Seats, by Region and State, 1910-2010 (435 seats)
- 1-3 Democratic and Republican Seats in the House, by Region, 101st-115th Congresses, 1989-2017
- 1-5 Democratic and Republican Seats in the Senate, by Region, 101st-115th Congresses, 1989-2018
- 1-16 African Americans in Congress, 41st - 115th Congresses, 1869 - 2017
- 1-17 Asian Americans in Congress, 58th - 115th Congresses, 1903-2017
- 1-18 Hispanic Americans in Congress, 41st - 115th Congresses, 1869 - 2017
- 1-19 Women in Congress, 65th - 115th Congresses, 1917 - 2017
- 1-20 Political Parties of Senators and Representatives, 34th - 115th Congresses, 1855 - 2017
- 2-4 Losses by the President's Party in Midterm Elections, 1862 - 2014
- 2-5 House Seats That Changed Party, 1954 - 2016
- 2-6 Senate Seats That Changed Party, 1954 - 2016
- 2-7 House Incumbents Retired, Defeated, or Reelected, 1946 - 2016
- 2-8 Senate Incumbents Retired, Defeated, or Reelected, 1946 - 2016
- 2-9 House and Senate Retirements by Party, 1930 - 2016
- 2-10 Defeated House Incumbents, 1946 - 2016
- 2-11 Defeated Senate Incumbents, 1946 - 2016

The full Vital Statistics on Congress report contains a great deal more data and information that Almanac readers may find useful. For more information, visit www.brookings.edu/multi-chapter-report/vital-statistics-on-congress.

Table 1-1 Apportionment of Congressional Seats, by Region and State, 1910-2010 (435 seats)

Region and State	1910	1920	1930	1940	1950	1960	1970	1980	1990	2000	2010
South	104		102	105	106	106	108	116	125	131	138
Alabama	10		9	9	9	8	7	7	7	7	7
Arkansas	7		7	7	6	4	4	4	4	4	4
Florida	4		5	6	8	12	15	19	23	25	27
Georgia	12		10	10	10	10	10	10	11	13	14
Louisiana	8		8	8	8	8	8	8	7	7	6
Mississippi	8		7	7	6	5	5	5	5	4	4
North Carolina	10		11	12	12	11	11	11	12	13	13
South Carolina	7		6	6	6	6	6	6	6	6	7
Tennessee	10		9	10	9	9	8	9	9	9	9
Texas	18		21	21	22	23	24	27	30	32	36
Virginia	10		9	9	10	10	10	10	11	11	11
Border	47		43	42	38	36	35	34	32	31	30
Kentucky	11		9	9	8	7	7	7	6	6	6
Maryland	6		6	6	7	8	8	8	8	8	8
Missouri	16		13	13	11	10	10	9	9	9	8
Oklahoma	8		9	8	6	6	6	6	6	5	5
West Virginia	6		6	6	6	5	4	4	3	3	3
New England	32		29	28	28	25	25	24	23	22	21
Connecticut	5		6	6	6	6	6	6	6	5	5
Maine	4		3	3	3	2	2	2	2	2	2
Massachusetts	16		15	14	14	12	12	11	10	10	9
New Hampshire	2		2	2	2	2	2	2	2	2	2
Rhode Island	3		2	2	2	2	2	2	2	2	2
Vermont	2		1	1	1	1	1	1	1	1	1
Mid-Atlantic	92		94	93	88	84	80	72	66	62	58
Delaware	1		1	1	1	1	1	1	1	1	1
New Jersey	12		14	14	14	15	15	14	13	13	12
New York	43		45	45	43	41	39	34	31	29	27
Pennsylvania	36		34	33	30	27	25	23	21	19	18
Midwest	86		90	87	87	88	86	80	74	69	65
Illinois	27		27	26	25	24	24	22	20	19	18
Indiana	13		12	11	11	11	11	10	10	9	9
Michigan	13		17	17	18	19	19	18	16	15	14
Ohio	22		24	23	23	24	23	21	19	18	16
Wisconsin	11		10	10	10	10	9	9	9	8	8
Plains	41		34	31	31	27	25	24	22	22	21
Iowa	11		9	8	8	7	6	6	5	5	4
Kansas	8		7	6	6	5	5	5	4	4	4
Minnesota	10		9	9	9	8	8	8	8	8	8
Nebraska	6		5	4	4	3	3	3	3	3	3
North Dakota	3		2	2	2	2	1	1	1	1	1
South Dakota	3		2	2	2	2	2	1	1	1	1
Rocky Mountains	14		14	16	16	17	19	24	24	28	31
Arizona	1		1	2	2	3	4	5	6	8	9
Colorado	4		4	4	4	4	5	6	6	7	7
Idaho	2		2	2	2	2	2	2	2	2	2
Montana	2		2	2	2	2	2	2	1	1	1

Nevada	1		1	1	1	1	1	2	2	3	4
New Mexico	1[a]		1	2	2	2	2	3	3	3	3
Utah	2		2	2	2	2	2	3	3	3	4
Wyoming	1		1	1	1	1	1	1	1	1	1
Pacific Coast	**19**		**29**	**33**	**43**	**52**	**57**	**61**	**69**	**70**	**71**
Alaska					1[b]	1	1	1	1	1	1
California	11		20	23	30	38	43	45	52	53	53
Hawaii					1[c]	2	2	2	2	2	2
Oregon	3		3	4	4	4	4	5	5	5	5
Washington	5		6	6	7	7	7	8	9	9	10

a. New Mexico became a state in 1912; in 1910 it had a nonvoting delegate in Congress.

b. Alaska became a state on January 3, 1959. In 1950 Alaska had a nonvoting delegate in Congress, making the total for that year 437; subsequent reapportionment reduced the total to 435.

c. Hawaii became a state on August 21, 1959. In 1950 Hawaii had a nonvoting delegate in Congress, making the total for that year 437; subsequent reapportionment reduced the total to 435.

Source: Congressional Quarterly's Guide to U.S. Elections (Washington, D.C.: Congressional Quarterly, various editions); Congressional Quarterly Weekly Report, various issues; U.S. Census data 2000, www.census.gov

Table 1-3** Democratic and Republican Seats in the House, by Region, 101st-115th Congresses, 1989-2017

Congress	101st		102nd		103rd		104th		105th		106th		107th		108th		109th		110th		111th		112th		113th		114th		115th*	
	1989-1990		1991-1992		1993-1994		1995-1996		1997-1998		1999-2000		2001-2002		2003-2004		2005-2006		2007-2008		2009-2010		2011-2012		2013-2014		2015-2016		2017-2018	
Region	D	R	D	R	D	R	D	R	D	R	D	R	D	R	D	R	D	R	D	R	D	R	D	R	D	R	D	R	D	R
South																														
Percent	29.3	22.4	28.8	23.4	29.8	27.3	29.9	27.8	26.1	31.3	25.6	31.5	25.1	32.3	26.8	33.2	24.4	35.3	23.2	38.1	23.5	40.5	19.2	39.0	19.8	42.0	19.7	40.9	20.1	41.1
Seats	76	39	77	39	77	48	61	64	54	71	54	70	53	71	55	76	49	82	54	77	59	72	37	94	40	98	37	101	39	99
Border																														
Percent	8.9	6.3	8.6	6.6	8.1	6.3	7.8	7.0	6.3	8.4	6.2	8.6	5.7	9.1	6.8	7.4	7.0	7.3	6.4	7.9	6.3	8.4	6.7	7.4	5.4	8.2	5.3	8.1	5.2	8.3
Seats	23	11	23	11	21	11	16	16	13	19	13	19	12	20	14	17	14	17	15	16	16	15	13	18	11	19	10	20	10	20
New England																														
Percent	5.4	5.7	6.0	4.2	5.4	4.5	6.9	3.5	8.7	1.8	8.5	1.8	8.1	2.3	7.8	2.2	8.0	2.2	9.0	0.5	8.6	0.0	10.4	0.8	10.4	0.0	10.1	0.8	10.3	0.4
Seats	14	10	16	7	14	8	14	8	18	4	18	4	17	5	16	5	16	5	21	1	22	0	20	2	21	0	19	2	20	1
Mid-Atlantic																														
Percent	16.2	17.2	15.4	18.6	14.0	17.0	16.2	14.3	16.9	13.7	17.1	13.5	17.1	13.6	16.1	12.7	16.9	12.1	17.6	10.4	18.0	9.0	18.7	10.7	17.3	9.9	16.0	11.3	16.0	11.2
Seats	42	30	41	31	36	30	33	33	35	31	36	30	36	30	33	29	34	28	41	21	46	16	36	26	35	23	30	28	31	27
Midwest																														
Percent	18.1	18.4	18.4	18.6	16.7	17.6	15.7	18.3	17.9	16.3	17.5	16.7	17.5	16.8	13.7	17.9	13.9	17.7	14.2	17.8	15.2	9.0	15.2	16.3	12.4	17.2	12.8	16.6	12.9	16.6
Seats	47	32	49	31	43	31	32	42	37	37	37	37	37	37	28	41	28	41	33	36	39	16	39	29	25	40	24	41	25	40
Plains																														
Percent	4.6	6.9	4.9	6.6	4.7	5.7	3.9	6.1	3.9	6.2	4.3	5.9	3.8	6.4	3.4	6.6	4.0	6.0	5.2	5.0	4.3	6.2	3.6	6.2	3.5	6.0	3.7	5.7	3.1	6.2
Seats	12	12	13	11	12	10	8	14	8	14	9	13	8	14	7	15	8	14	12	10	11	11	7	15	7	14	7	14	6	15
Rocky Mountains																														
Percent	3.5	8.6	4.1	7.8	4.3	7.4	2.9	7.8	1.9	8.8	2.4	8.6	2.8	8.2	3.4	9.2	4.0	8.6	4.7	8.4	6.6	6.2	5.2	7.4	6.4	7.7	5.3	8.5	6.2	7.9
Seats	9	15	11	13	11	13	6	18	4	20	5	19	6	18	7	21	8	20	11	17	17	11	10	18	13	18	10	21	12	19
Pacific Coast																														
Percent	13.9	14.4	13.9	14.4	17.1	14.2	16.7	15.2	18.4	13.7	18.5	13.5	19.9	11.4	22.0	10.9	21.9	10.8	19.7	11.9	18.0	13.5	23.3	10.3	24.8	9.0	27.1	8.1	26.3	8.3
Seats	36	25	37	24	44	25	34	35	38	31	39	30	42	25	45	25	44	25	46	24	46	24	45	25	50	21	51	20	51	20
Total Seats	259	174	267	167	258	176	204	230	207	227	211	222	211	220	205	229	201	232	233	202	256	178	193	242	202	233	188	247	194	241

Table 1-5** Democratic and Republican Seats in the Senate, by Region, 101st-115th Congresses, 1989-2018

Congress	101st		102nd		103rd		104th		105th		106th		107th		108th		109th		110th		111th		112th		113th		114th		115th*	
	1989-1990		1991-1992		1993-1994		1995-1996		1997-1998		1999-2000		2001-2002		2003-2004		2005-2006		2007-2008		2009-2010		2011-2012		2013-2014		2015-2016		2017-2018	
Region	D	R	D	R	D	R	D	R	D	R	D	R	D	R	D	R	D	R	D	R	D	R	D	R	D	R	D	R	D	R
South																														
Percent	27.3	15.6	26.8	15.9	22.8	20.9	19.1	24.5	15.6	27.3	17.8	25.5	16.0	28.0	18.8	25.5	9.1	32.7	10.2	34.7	12.7	36.6	11.8	34.0	11.3	35.6	6.8	35.2	6.5	36.5
Seats	15	7	15	7	13	9	9	13[a]	7	15	8	14	8	14	9	13	4	18	5	17	7	15	6	16	6	16	3	19	3	19
Border																														
Percent	10.9	8.9	10.7	9.1	10.5	9.3	10.6	9.4	11.1	9.1	8.9	10.9	10.0	10.0	8.3	11.8	9.1	10.9	10.2	10.2	9.1	12.2	9.8	10.6	9.4	11.1	9.1	11.1	8.7	11.5
Seats	6	4	6	4	6	4	5	5	5	5	4	6	5	5	4	6	4	6	5	5	5	5	5	5	5	5	4	6	4	6
New England																														
Percent	12.7	11.1	12.5	11.4	12.3	11.6	12.8	11.3	13.3	10.9	13.3	10.9	12.0	12.0	12.5	9.8	13.6	9.1	12.2	8.2	12.7	7.3	11.8	8.5	15.1	4.4	18.2	3.7	19.6	1.9
Seats	7	5	7	5	7	5	6	6	6	6	6	6	6	6	6	5	6	5	6	4	7	3	6	4	8	2	8	2	9	1
Mid-Atlantic																														
Percent	7.3	8.9	7.1	9.1	8.8	7.0	8.5	7.5	8.9	7.3	11.1	5.5	12.0	4.0	12.5	3.9	13.6	3.6	14.3	2.0	12.7	2.4	13.7	2.1	13.2	2.2	15.9	1.9	15.2	1.9
Seats	4	4	4	4	5	3	4	4	4	4	5	3	6	2	6	2	6	2	7	1	7	1	7	1	7	1	7	1	7	1
Midwest																														
Percent	12.7	6.7	12.5	6.8	14.0	4.7	12.8	7.5	13.3	7.3	11.1	9.1	12.0	8.0	12.5	7.8	15.9	5.5	16.3	4.1	12.7	4.9	9.8	10.6	11.3	8.9	13.6	7.4	15.2	5.8
Seats	7	3	7	3	8	2	6	4	6	4	5	5	6	4	6	4	7	3	8	2	7	2	5	5	6	4	6	4	7	3
Plains																														
Percent	10.9	13.3	12.5	11.4	12.3	11.6	14.9	9.4	15.6	9.1	15.6	9.1	16.0	8.0	14.6	9.8	13.6	10.9	12.2	12.2	10.9	12.2	11.8	12.8	9.4	15.6	6.8	16.7	6.5	17.3
Seats	6	6	7	5	7	5	7	5	7	5	7	5	8	4	7	5	6	6	6	6	6	5	6	6	5	7	3	9	3	9
Rocky Mountains																														
Percent	10.9	22.2	10.7	22.7	10.5	23.3	10.6	20.8	8.9	21.8	8.9	21.8	8.0	24.0	6.3	25.5	9.1	21.8	10.2	22.4	12.7	22.0	13.7	19.2	13.2	20.0	11.4	20.4	10.9	21.1
Seats	6	10	6	10	6	10	5	11	4	12	4	12	4	12	3	13	4	12	5	11	7	9	7	9	7	9	5	11	5	11
Pacific Coast																														
Percent	7.3	13.3	7.1	13.6	8.8	11.6	10.6	9.4	13.3	7.3	13.3	7.3	14.0	6.0	14.6	5.9	15.9	5.5	14.3	6.1	16.4	2.4	17.7	2.1	17.0	2.2	18.2	3.7	17.4	3.8
Seats	4	6	4	6	5	5	5	5	6	4	6	4	7	3	7	3	7	3	7	3	9	1	9	1	9	1	8	2	8	2
Total Seats	55	45	56	44	57	43	47	53	45	55	45	55	50	50	48	51	44	55	49	49	55	41	51	47	53	45	44	54	46	52

Supplemental Text for Tables 1-3 and 1-5

1-3:

Note: D indicates Democrats; R indicates Republicans. Third parties are omitted. Figures represent the makeup of Congress on the first day of the session.

Source: Congressional Directory, various editions; Congressional Quarterly Weekly Report, various issues; Clerk of the U.S. House of Representatives, http://clerk.house.gov; The Almanac of American Politics (Washington, D.C.: National Journal Group, various editions).

* 115th data compiled by Almanac of American Politics editorial staff
** In source material, Vital Statistics makes available data on regional representation by party going back to 1925 and the 69th Congress. Due to space limitations, data prior to 1989 was truncated.

1-5:

Note: D indicates Democrats; R indicates Republicans. Third parties are omitted. Figures represent the makeup of Congress on the first day of the session.

a. Includes Richard Shelby (AL) who switched from the Democratic to the Republican Party on the day following the election and before the beginning of the 104th Congress.

Source: Congressional Directory, various editions; Congressional Quarterly Weekly Report, various issues; US Senate, http://www.senate.gov; The Almanac of American Politics (Washington, D.C.: National Journal Group, various editions).

* 115th data compiled by Almanac of American Politics editorial staff
** In source material, Vital Statistics makes available data on regional representation by party going back to 1925 and the 69th Congress. Due to space limitations, data prior to 1989 was truncated.

Table 1-16 African Americans in Congress, 41st - 115th Congresses, 1869 - 2017

Congress		House		Senate	
		D	R	D	R
41st	(1869)		2		1
42nd	(1871)		5		
43rd	(1873)		7		
44th	(1875)		7		1
45th	(1877)		3		1
46th	(1879)				1
47th	(1881)		2		
48th	(1883)		2		
49th	(1885)		2		
50th	(1887)				
51st	(1889)		3		
52nd	(1891)		1		
53rd	(1893)		1		
54th	(1895)		1		
55th	(1897)		1		
56th	(1899)[a]				
71st	(1929)		1		
72nd	(1931)		1		
73rd	(1933)		1		
74th	(1935)	1			
75th	(1937)	1			
76th	(1939)	1			
77th	(1941)	1			
78th	(1943)	1			
79th	(1945)	2			
80th	(1947)	2			
81st	(1949)	2			
82nd	(1951)	2			
83rd	(1953)	2			
84th	(1955)	3			
85th	(1957)	3			
86th	(1959)	3			
87th	(1961)	3			
88th	(1963)	4			
89th	(1965)	5			
90th	(1967)	5			1
91st	(1969)	9			1
92nd	(1971)	13			1
93rd	(1973)	16			1
94th	(1975)	16			1
95th	(1977)	15			1
96th	(1979)	15			
97th	(1981)	17			
98th	(1983)	20			
99th	(1985)	20			
100th	(1987)	22			
101th	(1989)	23			
102nd	(1991)	25	1		
103rd	(1993)	38	1	1	
104th	(1995)	37	2	1	
105th	(1997)	36	1	1	
106th	(1999)	36	1		
107th	(2001)	35	1		
108th	(2003)	37			
109th	(2005)	40		1	
110th	(2007)	40		1	
111th[b]	(2009)	39			
112th	(2011)	40	2		
113th[c]	(2013)	41			1
114th	(2015)	42	2	1	1
115th*	(2017)	44	2	2	1

Note: The data do not include nonvoting delegates or commissioners. Figures represent the makeup of Congress on the first day of the session.

a. After the 56th Congress, there were no African American members in either the House or Senate until the 71st Congress.
b. Roland Burris was not seated on the first day of the 111th session.
c. Tim Scott, who was appointed on December 17th to replace outgoing Senator Jim DeMint, is included inthe Senate totals.

Source: Black Americans in Congress, 1870-1977, H. Doc. 95-258, 95th Cong., 1st sess., 1977; Congressional Quarterly Almanac (Washington, D.C.: Congressional Quarterly, various editions); Congressional Quarterly Weekly Report, various issues; Clerk of the U.S. House of Representatives, http://clerk.house.gov; "Membership of the 114th Congress: A Profile," Congressional Research Service

* 115th data compiled by Almanac of American Politics editorial staff

Table 1-17 Asian Americans in Congress, 58th - 115th Congresses, 1903-2017

Congress		House		Senate	
		D	R	D	R
58th	(1903)				
59th	(1905)				
60th	(1907)				
61st	(1909)				
62nd	(1911)				
63rd	(1913)				
64th	(1915)				
65th	(1917)				
66th	(1919)				
67th	(1921)				
68th	(1923)				
69th	(1925)				
70th	(1927)				
71st	(1929)				
72nd	(1931)				
73rd	(1933)				
74th	(1935)				
75th	(1937)				
76th	(1939)				
77th	(1941)				
78th	(1943)				
79th	(1945)				
80th	(1947)				
81st	(1949)				
82nd	(1951)				
83rd	(1953)				
84th	(1955)				
85th	(1957)	1			
86th	(1959)	2			1
87th	(1961)	2			1
88th	(1963)	1		1	1
89th	(1965)	2		1	1
90th	(1967)	2		1	1
91st	(1969)	2		1	1
92nd	(1971)	2		1	1
93rd	(1973)	2		1	1
94th	(1975)	3		1	1
95th	(1977)	2		2	1
96th	(1979)	3		2	1
97th	(1981)	3		2	1
98th	(1983)	3		2	
99th	(1985)	3		2	
100th	(1987)	3	1	2	
101st	(1989)	3	1	3	
102nd	(1991)	3		2	
103rd	(1993)	4	1	2	
104th	(1995)	4	1	2	
105th	(1997)	4	1	2	
106th	(1999)	4		2	
107th	(2001)	5		2	
108th	(2003)	4		2	
109th	(2005)	4	1	2	
110th	(2007)	5	1	2	
111th	(2009)	4	1	2	
112th	(2011)	7	1	2	
113th	(2013)	10	0	1	0
114th	(2015)	11	0	1	0
115th*	(2017)	12	0	3	0

Note: The data do not include nonvoting delegates or commissioners. Figures represent the makeup of Congress on the first day of the session.

Source: "Asian Pacific Americans in the United States Congress;" "Membership of the 114th Congress: A Profile", Congressional Research Service

* 115th data compiled by Almanac of American Politics editorial staff

Table 1-18 Hispanic Americans in Congress, 41st - 115th Congresses, 1869 - 2017

Congress		House		Senate	
		D	R	D	R
41st	(1869)				
42nd	(1871)				
43rd	(1873)				
63rd	(1913)	1			
64th	(1915)	1	1		
65th	(1917)	1			
66th	(1919)	1	1		
67th	(1921)	1	1		
68th	(1923)	1			
69th	(1925)	1			
70th	(1927)	1			1
71st	(1929)				
72nd	(1931)	2			
73rd	(1933)	2			
74th	(1935)	1		1	
75th	(1937)	1		1	
76th	(1939)	1		1	
77th	(1941)			1	
78th	(1943)	1		1	
79th	(1945)	1		1	
80th	(1947)	1		1	
81st	(1949)	1		1	
82nd	(1951)	1		1	
83rd	(1953)	1		1	
84th	(1955)	1		1	
85th	(1957)	1		1	
86th	(1959)	1		1	
87th	(1961)	2		1	
88th	(1963)	3		1	
89th	(1965)	3		1	
90th	(1967)	3		1	
91st	(1969)	3	1	1	
92nd	(1971)	4	1	1	
93rd	(1973)	4	1	1	
94th	(1975)	4	1	1	
95th	(1977)	4	1		
96th	(1979)	5	1		
97th	(1981)	6	1		
98th	(1983)	9	1		
99th	(1985)	10	1		
100th	(1987)	10	1		
101st	(1989)	9	1		
102nd	(1991)	10	1		
103rd	(1993)	14	3		
104th	(1995)	14	3		
105th	(1997)	14	3		
106th	(1999)	16	3		
107th	(2001)	16	3		
108th	(2003)	18	4		
109th	(2005)	19	4	1	1
110th	(2007)	20	3	2	1
111th	(2009)	21	3	1	1
112th	(2011)	19	8	1	1
113th	(2013)	23	5	1	2
114th	(2015)	23	9	1	2
115th*	(2017)	26	8	2	2

Note: The data do not include nonvoting delegates or commissioners. Figures represent the makeup of Congress on the first day of the session.

Source: Biographical Directory of the United States Congress 1774-1989; Congressional Quarterly Almanac (Washington, D.C.: Congressional Quarterly, various editions); Congressional Quarterly Weekly Report, various issues; Clerk of the U.S. House of Representatives, http://clerk.house.gov; http://www.senate.gov/galleries/daily/minority.htm; "Membership of the 114th Congress: A Profile", Congressional Research Service

* 115th data compiled by Almanac of American Politics editorial staff

Table 1-19 Women in Congress, 65th - 115th Congresses, 1917 - 2017

Congress		House		Senate	
		D	R	D	R
65th	(1917)		1		
66th	(1919)				
67th	(1921)		2		1
68th	(1923)		1		
69th	(1925)	1	2		
70th	(1927)	2	3		
71st	(1929)	4	5		
72nd	(1931)	4	3	1	
73rd	(1933)	4	3	1	
74th	(1935)	4	2	2	
75th	(1937)	4	1	2	
76th	(1939)	4	4	1	
77th	(1941)	4	5	1	
78th	(1943)	2	6	1	
79th	(1945)	6	5		
80th	(1947)	3	4		1
81st	(1949)	5	4		1
82nd	(1951)	4	6		1
83rd	(1953)	5	7		1
84th	(1955)	10	7		1
85th	(1957)	9	6		1
86th	(1959)	9	8		1
87th	(1961)	11	7	1	1
88th	(1963)	6	6	1	1
89th	(1965)	7	4	1	1
90th	(1967)	5	5		1
91st	(1969)	6	4		1
92nd	(1971)	10	3		1
93rd	(1973)	14	2	1	
94th	(1975)	14	5		
95th	(1977)	13	5		
96th	(1979)	11	5	1	1
97th	(1981)	10	9		2
98th	(1983)	13	9		2
99th	(1985)	13	9		2
100th	(1987)	12	11	1	1
101st	(1989)	14	11	1	1
102nd	(1991)	19	9	1	1
103rd	(1993)	36	12	5	1
104th	(1995)	31	17	5	3
105th	(1997)	35	16	6	3
106th	(1999)	40	16	6	3
107th	(2001)	41	18	10	3
108th	(2003)	38	21	9	5
109th	(2005)	42	23	9	5
110th	(2007)	50	21	11	5
111th	(2009)	57	17	13	4
112th	(2011)	52	24	12	5
113th	(2013)	56	20	16	4
114th	(2015)	62	22	14	6
115th*	(2017)	62	21	16	5

Note: The data include only women who were sworn in as members and served more than one day. Figures represent the makeup of Congress on the first day of the session.

Source: Women in Congress, H. Rept. 94-1732, 94th Cong., 2nd sess., 1976; Congressional Quarterly Almanac (Washington, D.C.: Congressional Quarterly, various editions); Congressional Quarterly Weekly Report, various issues; Clerk of the U.S. House of Representatives, http://clerk.house.gov; US Senate, http://www.senate.gov.; "Membership of the 114th Congress: A Profile", Congressional Research Service

* 115th data compiled by Almanac of American Politics editorial staff

Table 1-20 Political Parties of Senators and Representatives, 34th - 115th Congresses, 1855 - 2017

Congress		Senate					House of Representatives				
		# Senators	D	R	Other	Vacant	# Reps	D	R	Other	Vacant
34th	(1855 - 1857)	62	42	15	5		234	83	108	43	
35th	(1857 - 1859)	64	39	20	5		237	131	92	14	
36th	(1859 - 1861)	66	38	26	2		237	101	113	23	
37th	(1861 - 1863)	50	11	31	7	1	178	42	106	28	2
38th	(1863 - 1865)	51	12	39			183	80	103		
39th	(1865 - 1867)	52	10	42			191	46	145		
40th	(1867 - 1869)	53	11	42			193	49	143		1
41st	(1869 - 1871)	74	11	61		2	243	73	170		
42nd	(1871 - 1873)	74	17	57			243	104	139		
43rd	(1873 - 1875)	74	19	54		1	293	88	203		2
44th	(1875 - 1877)	76	29	46		1	293	181	107	3	2
45th	(1877 - 1879)	76	36	39	1		293	156	137		
46th	(1879 - 1881)	76	43	33			293	150	128	14	1
47th	(1881 - 1883)	76	37	37	2		293	130	152	11	
48th	(1883 - 1885)	76	36	40			325	200	119	6	
49th	(1885 - 1887)	76	34	41		1	325	182	140	2	1
50th	(1887 - 1889)	76	37	39			325	170	151	4	
51st	(1889 - 1891)	84	37	47			330	156	173	1	
52nd	(1891 - 1893)	88	39	47	2		333	231	88	14	
53rd	(1893 - 1895)	88	44	38	3	3	356	220	126	10	
54th	(1895 - 1897)	88	39	44	5		357	104	246	7	
55th	(1897 - 1899)	90	34	46	10		357	134	206	16	1
56th	(1899 - 1901)	90	26	53	11		357	163	185	9	
57th	(1901 - 1903)	90	29	56	3	2	357	153	198	5	1
58th	(1903 - 1905)	90	32	58			386	178	207		1
59th	(1905 - 1907)	90	32	58			386	136	250		
60th	(1907 - 1909)	92	29	61		2	386	164	222		
61st	(1909 - 1911)	92	32	59		1	391	172	219		
62nd	(1911 - 1913)	92	42	49		1	391	228	162	1	
63rd	(1913 - 1915)	96	51	44	1		435	290	127	18	
64th	(1915 - 1917)	96	56	39	1		435	231	193	8	3
65th	(1917 - 1919)	96	53	42	1		435	210[a]	216	9	
66th	(1919 - 1921)	96	47	48	1		435	191	237	7	
67th	(1921 - 1923)	96	37	59			435	132	300	1	2
68th	(1923 - 1925)	96	43	51	2		435	207	225	3	
69th	(1925 - 1927)	96	40	54	1	1	435	183	247	5	
70th	(1927 - 1929)	96	47	48	1		435	195	237	3	
71st	(1929 - 1931)	96	39	56	1		435	163	267	1	4
72nd	(1931 - 1933)	96	47	48	1		435	216[b]	218	1	
73rd	(1933 - 1935)	96	59	36	1		435	313	117	5	
74th	(1935 - 1937)	96	69	25	2		435	322	103	10	
75th	(1937 - 1939)	96	75	17	4		435	333	89	13	
76th	(1939 - 1941)	96	69	23	4		435	262	169	4	
77th	(1941 - 1943)	96	66	28	2		435	267	162	6	
78th	(1943 - 1945)	96	57	38	1		435	222	209	4	
79th	(1945 - 1947)	96	57	38	1		435	243	190	2	
80th	(1947 - 1949)	96	45	51			435	188	246	1	

Congress		Senate					House of Representatives				
		# Senators	D	R	Other	Vacant	# Reps	D	R	Other	Vacant
81st	(1949 - 1951)	96	54	42			435	263	171	1	
82nd	(1951 - 1953)	96	48	47	1		435	234	199	2	
83rd	(1953 - 1955)	96	46	48	2		435	213	221	1	
84th	(1955 - 1957)	96	48	47	1		435	232	203		
85th	(1957 - 1959)	96	49	47			435	234	201		
86th	(1959 - 1961)	98	64	34			436[c]	283	153		
87th	(1961 - 1963)	100	64	36			437[d]	262	175		
88th	(1963 - 1965)	100	67	33			435	258	176		1
89th	(1965 - 1967)	100	68	32			435	295	140		
90th	(1967 - 1969)	100	64	36			435	246	187		2
91st	(1969 - 1971)	100	58	42			435	243	192		
92nd	(1971 - 1973)	100	54	44	2		435	255	180		
93rd	(1973 - 1975)	100	56	42	2		435	239	192	1	3
94th	(1975 - 1977)	100	61	37	2		435	291	144		
95th	(1977 - 1979)	100	61	38	1		435	292	143		
96th	(1979 - 1981)	100	58	41	1		435	276	157		2
97th	(1981 - 1983)	100	46	53	1		435	243	192		
98th	(1983 - 1985)	100	46	54			435	268	166		1
99th	(1985 - 1987)	100	47	53			435	252	182		1
100th	(1987 - 1989)	100	55	45			435	258	177		
101st	(1989 - 1991)	100	55	45			435	259	174		2
102nd	(1991 - 1993)	100	56	44			435	267	167	1	
103rd	(1993 - 1995)	100	57	43			435	258	176	1	
104th	(1995 - 1997)	100	47	53			435	204	230	1	
105th	(1997 - 1999)	100	45	55			435	207	227	1	
106th	(1999 - 2001)	100	45	55			435	211	223	1	
107th	(2001 - 2003)	100	50	50			435	211	221	2	1
108th	(2003 - 2005)	100	48	51	1		435	205	229	1	
109th	(2005 - 2007)	100	44	55	1		435	201	232	1	1
110th	(2007 - 2009)	100	49	49	2		435	233	202		
111th	(2009 - 2011)	100	55	41	2	1	435	256	178		1
112th	(2011 - 2013)	100	51	47	2		435	193	242		
113th	(2013 - 2015)	100	53	45	2	0	435	200	233	0	2
114th	(2015 - 2017)	100	44	54	2	0	435	188	247	0	0
115th*	(2017 - 2019)	100	46	52	2	0	435	194	241	0	0

Note: Figures represent the makeup of Congress on the first day of the session.

a. Democrats organized House with help of other parties.
b. Democrats organized House because of Republican deaths.
c. Alaska was admitted as a state in 1958. The total figure includes the addition of Alaska's representative.
d. Alaska was admitted as a state in 1958 and Hawaii in 1959. The total figure includes the addition of Alaska's and Hawaii's representatives.

Source: Congressional Directory, various editions; Congressional Quarterly Weekly Report, various issues; Clerk of the U.S. House of Representatives, http://clerk.house.gov; US Senate, http://www.senate.gov; The Almanac of American Politics (Washington, D.C.: National Journal Group, various editions).

* 115th data compiled by Almanac of American Politics editorial staff

Table 2-4 Losses by the President's Party in Midterm Elections, 1862 - 2014

Year	Party holding presidency	President's party gain/loss of seats in House	President's party gain/loss of seats in Senate
1862	R	-3	8
1866	R	-2	0
1870	R	-31	-4
1874	R	-96	-8
1878	R	-9	-6
1882	R	-33	3
1886	D	-15	3
1890	R	-85	0
1894	D	-125	-4
1898	R	-19	9
1902	R	9[a]	2
1906	R	-28	3
1910	R	-57	-8
1914	D	-61	5
1918	D	-22	-6
1922	R	-77	-6
1926	R	-9	-6
1930	R	-52	-8
1934	D	9	10
1938	D	-72	-7
1942	D	-44	-9
1946	D	-55	-12
1950	D	-28	-5
1954	R	-18	-1
1958	R	-48	-12
1962	D	-4	2
1966	D	-48	-4
1970	R	-12	1
1974	R	-48	-4
1978	D	-15	-3
1982	R	-26	1
1986	R	-5	-8
1990	R	-8	-1
1994	D	-54	-8[b]
1998	D	5	0
2002	R	8	1
2006	R	-30	-6
2010	D	-63	-6
2014	D	-13	-9

Note: D indicates Democrats; R indicates Republicans.
Each entry is the difference between the number of seats won by the president's party in that midterm election and the number of seats won by that party in the preceding general election. Because of changes inthe overall number of seats in the Senate and House, in the number of seats won by third parties, and in the number of vacancies, a Republican loss is not always matched precisely by a Democratic gain, or vice versa. Data reflects immediate election results.

a. Although the Republicans gained nine seats in the 1902 elections, they actually lost ground to the Democrats, who gained twenty-five seats after the increase in the overall number of Representativesafter the 1900 census.
b. Sen. Richard Shelby (AL) switched from the Democratic to the Republican Party the day following the election, so that the total loss was nine seats.

Source: Biographical Directory of the United States Congress 1774–1989 (Washington, D.C.: Government Printing Office, 1989); Congressional Quarterly Almanac (Washington, D.C.: Congressional Quarterly, various years); National Journal, various issues; The Almanac of American Politics (Washington, D.C.: National Journal Group, various years), Clerk of the U.S. House of Representatives, http://clerk.house.gov; Clerk of the U.S. Senate, http://clerk.senate.gov.

Table 2-5 House Seats That Changed Party, 1954 - 2016

		Incumbent defeated		Open seat	
Year	Total changes	D->R	R->D	D->R	R->D
1954	26	3	18	2	3
1956	20	7	7	2	4
1958	49	1	34	0	14
1960	37	23	2	6	6
1962	19	9	5	2	3
1964	55	5	39	3	8
1966	47	38	2	5	2
1968	11	5	0	2	4
1970	25	2	9	6	8
1972	21	8	3	6	4
1974	55	4	36	2	13
1976	22	7	5	3	7
1978	32	15	5	7	5
1980	41	28	3	9	1
1982	31	1	23	3	4
1984	22	13	3	5	1
1986	22	2	7	7	6
1988	9	2	4	1	2
1990	20	6	8	0	6
1992	43	19	12	10	2
1994	60	35	0	21	4
1996	31	3	16	9	3
1998	18	1	5	5	7
2000	18	2	4	6	6
2002	15	2	2	6	5
2004	13	6	2	2	3
2006	31	0	22	0	9
2008	31	5	14	0	12
2010	69	52	2	14	1
2012	29	4	15	7	3
2014	19	11	2	5	1
2016*	12	1	6	2	3

Note: This table reflects shifts in party control of seats from immediately before to immediately after the November elections. It does not include party gains resulting from the creation of new districts and does not account for situations in which two districts were reduced to one, thus forcing incumbents to run againsteach other. Party gains that resulted from an incumbent being defeated in either a primary or generalelection are classified as incumbent defeats. In situations where the incumbent declined to run again, ranfor another political office, or died or resigned before the end of the term are classified as open seats.

Source: Biographical Directory of the United States Congress 1774–1989 (Washington, D.C.: Government Printing Office, 1989); Congressional Quarterly Almanac (Washington, D.C.: Congressional Quarterly, various years); National Journal, various issues; The Almanac of American Politics (Washington, D.C.:National Journal Group, various years); Election 2012 Data: The Impact on the House (The Brookings Institution)., The Green Papers, http://thegreenpapers.com

* 2016 data compiled by Almanac of American Politics editorial staff

Table 2-6 Senate Seats That Changed Party, 1954 - 2016

Year	Total changes	Incumbent defeated		Open seat	
		D->R	R->D	D->R	R->D
1954	6	2	3	1	0
1956	8	1	3	3	1
1958	13	0	10	0	3
1960	3	1	1	1	0
1962	8	2	4	0	2
1964	4	1	3	0	0
1966	3	2	0	1	0
1968	9	5	1	2	1
1970	6	3	2	1	0
1972	10	2	4	2	2
1974	6	0	2	1[a]	3
1976	14	5	4	2	3
1978	13	5	3	3	2
1980	12	12	0	0	0
1982	3	1	1	0	1
1984	4	1	2	0	1
1986	10	0	7	1	2
1988	7	1	3	2	1
1990	1	0	1	0	0
1992	4	1	3	0	0
1994	8[b]	2	0	6	0
1996	3	0	1	2	0
1998	6	1	2	2	1
2000	8	1	5	1	1
2002	3	1	1	1[c]	0
2004	8	1	0	5	2
2006	6	0	6	0	0
2008	7	0	4[d]	0	3
2010	6[e]	2[f]	0	4	0
2012	1	0	1	0	0
2014	9	5	0	4[g]	0
2016*	2	0	2	0	0

Note: D indicates Democrat; R indicates Republican.
This table reflects shifts in party control of seats from immediately before to immediately after the November election. Party gains that resulted from an incumbent being defeated in either a primary or general election are classified as incumbent defeats. In situations where the incumbent declined to run again, ran for another political office, or died or resigned before the end of the term are classified as open seats.

a. Includes John Durkin (D-NH). After a contested election in which incumbent Sen. Norris Cotton did not run, the Senate declared the seat vacant as of August 8, 1975. Sen. Durkin was then elected by special election, September 16, 1975, to fill the vacancy.
b. Sen. Richard Shelby (AL) switched from the Democratic to the Republican Party the day after the election and brought the total change to nine.
c. Includes Norm Coleman (R-MN) who beat Walter Mondale (D-MN) after the death of Sen. Paul Wellstone (D-MN).
d. Does not include Al Franken (D-MN), who was declared on 30 June 2009 to have won the US Senate contest defeating Incumbent Senator Norm Coleman (R-MN). This brings the R—>D Incumbent Defeat up to 5, and the Total Changes up to 8.
e. Does not include Incumbent Senator Lisa Murkowski (R-AK), who lost her primary to Joe Miller (R-AK) but won the general election as a Republican write-in candidate.

f. Includes Pat Toomey (R-PA), who defeated Senator Arlen Specter (D-PA). Specter had changed his affiliation from Republican to Democrat in office on April 30, 2009.

g. Includes Montana Senate race, in which incumbent John Walsh withdrew from race after winning Democratic primary and was replaced at party convention.

Source: Congressional Quarterly Almanac (Washington, D.C.: Congressional Quarterly, various years); Congressional Quarterly Weekly Report, various issues; National Journal, various issues, The Green Papers, http://thegreenpapers.com.

* 2016 data compiled by Almanac of American Politics editorial staff

Table 2-7 House Incumbents Retired, Defeated, or Reelected, 1946 - 2016

Year	Retired	Total seeking reelection	Defeated in primaries	Defeated in general election	Total reelected	Percentage of those seeking reelection	Reelected as percentage of House membership
1946	32	398	18	52	328	82.4	75.4
1948	29	400	15	68	317	79.3	72.9
1950	29	400	6	32	362	90.5	83.2
1952	42	389	9	26	354	91.0	81.4
1954	24	407	6	22	379	93.1	87.1
1956	21	411	6	16	389	94.6	89.4
1958	33	396	3	37	356	89.9	81.8
1960	26	405	5	25	375	92.6	86.2
1962	24	402	12	22	368	91.5	84.6
1964	33	397	8	45	344	86.6	79.1
1966	22	411	8	41	362[c]	88.1	83.2
1968	23	409	4	9	396	96.8	91.0
1970	29	401	10	12	379	94.5	87.1
1972	40	393	11	13	365	92.9	83.9
1974	43	391	8	40	343	87.7	78.9
1976	47	384	3	13	368	95.8	84.6
1978	49	382	5	19	358	93.7	82.3
1980	34	398	6	31	361	90.7	83.0
1982	40	393	10	29	354	90.1	81.4
1984	22	411	3	16	392	95.4	90.1
1986	40	394	3	6	385	97.7	88.5
1988	23	409	1	6	402	98.3	92.4
1990	27	406	1	15	390	96.1	89.7
1992	65	368	19	24	325	88.3	74.7
1994	48	387	4	34	349	90.2	80.0
1996	49	384	2	21	361	94.0	83.0
1998	33	402	1	6	395	98.3	90.8
2000	30	403	3	6	394	97.8	90.6
2002	35	398[b]	8	8	383[c]	96.2	88.0
2004	29	404	2	7	395	97.8	90.8
2006	28	403	2	22	379	94.0	87.1
2008	25	400	4[d]	18	377	94.3	86.7
2010	32	397	4	54	339	85.4	77.9
2012	25	391	13	27	351	89.8	80.7
2014	24	392	5	13	374	95.4	86.0
2016*	40	393	5	8	380	96.7	87.4

Note: Some data from previous versions of Vital Statistics have been updated. See errata for more detail.

a. This entry does not include persons who died or resigned before the election.
b. Includes Jim Traficant (D- OH), who ran as an Independent in the election despite being expelled from the House of Representatives in July 2002.
c. Includes Patsy Mink (D-HI) who died shortly before the election yet remained on the ballot.
d. Includes Albert R. Wynn (D-MD) who lost his primary on February 13, 2008, and promptly resigned his seat effective May 31, 2008. Donna Edwards (D-MD) who won the primary and then won the special election to fill Wynn's seat for the remainder of the term is not counted as an incumbent in this table.

Source: Biographical Directory of the United States Congress 1774–1989 (Washington, D.C.: Government Printing Office, 1989); Congressional Quarterly Almanac (Washington, D.C.: Congressional Quarterly, various years); National Journal, various issues; The Almanac of American Politics (Washington, D.C.: National Journal Group, various years), Center for Responsive Politics, http://opensecrets.org.

Most recent update source: Tabulations of data from Federal Election Commission, http://www.fec.gov

* 2016 data compiled by Almanac of American Politics editorial staff

Table 2-8 Senate Incumbents Retired, Defeated, or Reelected, 1946 - 2016

Year	Not seeking reelection	Total seeking reelection	Defeated in primaries	Defeated in general election	Total reelected	Reelected as percentage of those seeking reelection
1946	9	30	6	7	17	56.7
1948	8	25	2	8	15	60.0
1950	4	32	5	5	22	68.8
1952	4	29	1	10	18	62.1
1954	6	32	2	5	25	78.1
1956	5	30	0	4	26	86.7
1958	6	27	0	10	17	63.0
1960	5	29	0	2	27	93.1
1962	4	35	1	5	29	82.9
1964	3	32	0	4	28	87.5
1966	3	32	3	1	28	87.5
1968	7	27	4	4	19	70.4
1970	4	31	1	6	24	77.4
1972	6	27	2	5	20	74.1
1974	7	27	2	2	23	85.2
1976	8	25	0	9	16	64.0
1978	10	25	3	7	15	60.0
1980	5	29	4	9	16	55.2
1982	3	30	0	2	28	93.3
1984	4	29	0	3	26	89.7
1986	6	28	0	7	21	75.0
1988	6	27	0	4	23	85.2
1990	4	32	0	1	31	96.9
1992	9	28	1	4	23	82.1
1994	9	26	0	2	24	92.3
1996	13	21	1[b]	1	19	90.5
1998	5	29	0	3	26	89.7
2000	5	29	0	6	23	79.3
2002	7	27	1	2	24	88.9
2004	8	26	0	1	25	96.2
2006	5	28	1[c]	6	22	78.6
2008	5	30	0	5	25	83.3
2010	12	25	3[d]	2	21	84.0
2012	10	23	1	1	21[e]	91.3
2014	7[f]	29	0	5	23[g]	79.3
2016*	5	29	0	2	27	93.1

Note: Table includes all Senate contests in a given year, whether for full or partial terms.

a. This entry includes Senators who died or resigned before the election and those retiring at the end oftheir terms.

b. Sheila Frahm, appointed to fill Robert Dole's term, is counted as an incumbent in Kansas's "B" seat.

c. Sen. Joe Lieberman (CT) lost in the Democratic primary, but ran in the general election as an independent and won reelection.

d. Sen. Lisa Murkowski (R-AK) lost her primary to Joe Miller (R-AK), but ran in the general election asa Republican write-in candidate and won reelection.

e. Total includes Dean Heller (R-NV), who was appointed on May 9, 2011 and won reelection.

f. Includes the resignation of Tom Coburn (R-OK) and the resulting special election to finish his term.

g. John Walsh (D-MT) withdrew from race after primary and was replaced on the ballot at a party convention.

Source: Congressional Quarterly Almanac (Washington, D.C.: Congressional Quarterly, various years); Congressional Quarterly Weekly Report, various issues; National Journal, various issues, Center for Responsive Politics, http://opensecrets.org.

Most recent update source: Tabulations of data from Federal Election Commission, http://www.fec.gov

* 2016 data compiled by Almanac of American Politics editorial staff

Table 2-9 House and Senate Retirements by Party, 1930 - 2016

Year	House		Senate	
	D	R	D	R
1930	8	15	2	5
1932	16	23	1	1
1934	29	9	3	1
1936	29	3	4	2
1938	21	5	3	1
1940	16	6	1	2
1942	20	12	0	0
1944	17	5	3	2
1946	17	15	4	3
1948	17	12	3	4
1950	12	17	3	1
1952	25	17	2	1
1954	11	13	1	1
1956	7	13	4	1
1958	6	27	0	6
1960	11	15	3	1
1962	10	14	2	2
1964	17	16	1	1
1966	14	8	1	2
1968	13	10	4	3
1970	11	19	3	1
1972	20	20	3	3
1974	23	21	3	4
1976	31	16	4	4
1978	31	18	4	5
1980	21	13	2	3
1982	19	21	1	2
1984	9	13	2	2
1986	20	20	3	3
1988	10	13	3	3
1990	10	17	0	3
1992	41	24	4	3
1994	28	20	6	3
1996	28	21	8	5
1998	17	16	3	2
2000	7	23	4	1
2002	13	22	1	5[a]
2004	12	17	5	3
2006	9	17	2	1
2008	3	24	0	5
2010	17	15	6	6
2012	20	18	7[b]	3
2014	10	14	4	3
2016*	16	24	3	2

Note: D indicates Democrat; R indicates Republican.

These figures include members who did not run again for the office they held and members who sought other offices; the figures do not include members who died or resigned before the end of the particular Congress.

a. Includes Frank Murkowski (R-AK) who ran for governor, won and appointed Lisa Murkoswki to finish the last two years of his term.
b. This total includes Sen. Joe Lieberman (I-CT), who caucused with Democrats.

Source: Mildred L. Amer, "Information on the Number of House Retirees, 1930–1992," (Washington, D.C.:Congressional Research Service, Staff Report, May 19, 1992); Congressional Quarterly Weekly Report, various issues; National Journal, various issues; Roll Call, Casualty List: 112th Congress., Center for Responsive Politics, http://opensecrets.org

* 2016 data compiled by Almanac of American Politics editorial staff

Table 2-10 Defeated House Incumbents, 1946 - 2016

Election	Party	Incumbents lost	Average terms	Consecutive terms served						
				1	2	3	1 - 3	4 - 6	7 - 9	10+
1946	Democrat	62	2.7	35	5	4	44	11	5	2
	Republican	7	3.6	2	0	1	3	3	1	0
	Total	69	2.8	37	5	5	47	14	6	2
1948	Democrat[a]	9	2.7	4	1	1	6	3	0	0
	Republican	73	2.2	41	3	12	56	14	2	1
	Total	82	2.3	45	4	13	62	17	2	1
1958	Democrat[b]	6	5	1	1	0	2	2	1	1
	Republican	34	4.3	9	0	4	13	14	6	1
	Total	40	4.4	10	1	4	15	16	7	2
1966	Democrat	43	3.3	26	6	0	32	4	1	6
	Republican	2	11	1	0	0	1	0	0	1
	Total	45	3.6	27	6	0	33	4	1	7
1974	Democrat	9	4.7	1	1	1	3	3	2	1
	Republican	39	3.8	11	2	6	19	15	2	3
	Total	48	4	12	3	7	22	18	4	4
1978	Democrat	19	4	3	8	2	13	2	1	3
	Republican	5	5.4	2	0	0	2	2	0	1
	Total	24	4.3	5	8	2	15	4	1	4
1980	Democrat	32	5.2	5	2	10	17	5	4	6
	Republican	5	5.3	1	0	1	2	1	1	1
	Total	37	5.2	6	2	11	19	6	5	7
1982	Democrat	4	2.9	1	0	1	2	2	0	0
	Republican[c]	23	3	12	3	2	17	2	2	2
	Total	27	3	13	3	3	19	4	2	2
1984	Democrat	16	4.1	6	1	2	9	4	1	2
	Republican	3	3.7	0	0	2	2	1	0	0
	Total	19	4	6	1	4	11	5	1	2
1986	Democrat	3	1.8	2	0	0	2	1	0	0
	Republican	6	1.5	4	1	1	6	0	0	0
	Total	9	1.6	6	1	1	8	1	0	0
1988	Democrat	2	12	0	0	0	0	0	0	2
	Republican	5	1.6	2	3	0	5	0	0	0
	Total	7	4.6	2	3	0	5	0	0	2
1990	Democrat	6	6.3	0	1	0	1	3	1	1
	Republican[d]	10	3.6	2	3	0	5	4	1	0
	Total	16	4.6	2	4	0	6	7	2	1
1992	Democrat	30	5.6	2	1	4	7	12	10	1
	Republican	13	6.8	2	0	2	4	1	6	2
	Total	43	6	4	1	6	11	13	16	3
1994	Democrat	37	4.2	16	3	5	24	7	2	4
	Republican	0	0	0	0	0	0	0	0	0
	Total	37	4.2	16	3	5	24	7	2	4
1996	Democrat[e]	3	4.7	1	0	1	2	0	0	1
	Republican	18	1.8	12	4	1	17	0	1	0
	Total	21	2.2	13	4	2	19	0	1	1
1998	Democrat	1	1	1	0	0	1	0	0	0
	Republican	6	1.7	3	2	1	6	0	0	0
	Total	7	1.6	4	2	1	7	0	0	0

Election	Party	Incumbents lost	Average terms	Consecutive terms served						
				1	2	3	1 - 3	4 - 6	7 - 9	10+
2000	Democrat	4	6.5	0	0	1	1	1	1	1
	Republican	5	2.4	1	2	1	4	1	0	0
	Total	9	4.2	1	2	2	5	1	1	1
2002	Democrat[f]	12	4.6	0	2	2	4	5	3	0
	Republican	5	4.8	2	0	0	2	1	1	1
	Total	17	4.7	2	2	2	6	6	4	1
2004	Democrat[g]	5	3	1	0	2	3	2	0	0
	Republican	2	9	1	0	0	1	0	0	1
	Total	7	4.7	2	0	2	4	2	0	1
2006	Democrat	0	0	0	0	0	0	0	0	0
	Republican	22	5.9	2	2	2	6	9	3	4
	Total	22	5.9	2	2	2	6	9	3	4
2008	Democrat[h]	6	3.2	4	0	0	4	1	1	0
	Republican	17	4.4	3	2	4	6	4	3	1
	Total	23	4.1	7	2	4	13	5	4	1
2010	Democrat	54	3.8	23	15	3	41	1	4	7
	Republican[i]	4	1.5	3	0	1	4	0	0	0
	Total	58	3.6	26	15	4	45	1	4	7
2012	Democrat	10	6.2	2	2	1	5	2	1	2
	Republican	17	2.5	12	0	1	13	1	2	1
	Total	27	3.9	14	2	2	18	3	3	3
2014	Democrat	12	4.3	7	1	0	8	2	1	1
	Republican	6	6	2	1	0	3	0	2	1
	Total	18[j]	4.8	9	2	0	11	2	3	2
2016*	Democrat	4	8	1	0	0	1	0	1	2
	Republican	9	4.2	3	1	2	6	0	2	1
	Total	13	5.4	4	1	2	7	0	3	3

Note: The 1966 and 1982 numbers do not include races where incumbents ran against incumbents due to redistricting. We counted incumbents who lost in the primary as their party's incumbent but then ran in the general election as a write-in or third-party candidate as an incumbent loss.

a. This includes Leo Isacson (NY), who was a member of the American Labor Party.
b. This includes Vincent Dellay (NJ), who was elected as a Republican but switched to a Democrat. He ran for reelection as an Independent.
c. This includes Eugene Atkinson (PA), who began his House service January 3, 1979, as a Democrat. He became a Republican on October 14, 1981.
d. This includes Donald Lukens (OH) who was defeated in the primary and then resigned on October 24, 1990 and Bill Grant (Fla.) who began his House service January 6, 1987, as a Democrat, but later switched parties. The Republican Conference let his seniority count from 1987.
e. One Democratic incumbent, who served more than ten terms in office, was defeated.
f. Includes Jim Traficant (OH) who ran as an Independent after being expelled from the House.
g. Excludes two 13-term representatives, Charles Stenholm (TX) and Martin Frost (TX), that ran against incumbents as a result of redistricting.
h. Includes Albert R. Wynn (D-MD) who lost his primary on February 13, 2008, and promptly resigned his seat effective May 31, 2008.
i. Includes Parker Griffith (AL) who began his House service January 3, 2009, as a Democrat but switched to a Republican on December 22, 2009.
j. Excludes the defeat of Eni Faleomavaega (D-Samoa) seeking 14th term as a non-voting delegate.

Source: Biographical Directory of the United States Congress 1774-2012, http://bioguide.congress.gov; Congressional Quarterly Almanac (Washington, D.C.: Congressional Quarterly, various years); National Journal, various issues; The Almanac of American Politics (Washington, D.C.: National Journal Group,various years); Roll Call, Casualty List: 112th Congress, Center for Responsive Politics, http://opensecrets.org

* 2016 data compiled by Almanac of American Politics editorial staff

Table 2-11 Defeated Senate Incumbents, 1946 - 2016

Election	Party	Incumbents lost	Average terms	Consecutive terms served					
				1	2	3	4	5	6+
1946	Democrat	11	1.6	7	2	1	1	0	0
	Republican	2	4	0	0	0	2	0	0
	Total	13	2	7	2	1	3	0	0
1948	Democrat	2	1.5	1	1	0	0	0	0
	Republican	8	1	8	0	0	0	0	0
	Total	10	1.1	9	1	0	0	0	0
1958	Republican	10	1.4	6	4	0	0	0	0
	Total	10	1.4	6	4	0	0	0	0
1966	Democrat	4	2	2	0	2	0	0	0
	Total	4	2	2	0	2	0	0	0
1974	Democrat	2	3	1	0	0	0	1	0
	Republican	2	1.5	1	1	0	0	0	0
	Total	4	2.2	2	1	0	0	1	0
1978	Democrat	7	0.9	6	0	1	0	0	0
	Republican	3	2.7	0	2	0	1	0	0
	Total	10	1.4	6	2	1	1	0	0
1980	Democrat	12	2.4	5	1	3	2	0	1
	Republican	1	4	0	0	0	1	0	0
	Total	13	2.6	5	1	3	3	0	1
1982	Democrat	1	4	0	0	0	1	0	0
	Republican	1	1	1	0	0	0	0	0
	Total	2	2.5	1	0	0	1	0	0
1984	Democrat	1	2	0	1	0	0	0	0
	Republican	2	2	1	0	1	0	0	0
	Total	3	2	1	1	1	0	0	0
1986	Republican[a]	7	0.9	7	0	0	0	0	0
	Total	7	0.9	7	0	0	0	0	0
1988	Democrat	1	2	0	1	0	0	0	0
	Republican	3	1.4	2	0	1	0	0	0
	Total	4	1.6	2	1	1	0	0	0
1990	Republican	1	2	0	1	0	0	0	0
	Total	1	2	0	1	0	0	0	0
1992	Democrat	3	1.3	2	1	0	0	0	0
	Republican	2	1.2	1	1	0	0	0	0
	Total	5	1.3	3	2	0	0	0	0
1994	Democrat	2	1.8	1	0	1	0	0	0
	Total	2	1.8	1	0	1	0	0	0
1996	Republican[c]	2	1.5	1	0	1	0	0	0
	Total	2	1.5	1	0	1	0	0	0
1998	Democrat	1	1	1	0	0	0	0	0
	Repbulican	2	2	1	1	0	0	0	0
	Total	3	1.7	2	1	0	0	0	0
2000	Democrat	1	2	0	1	0	0	0	0
	Republican	5	2	3	1	0	0	1	0
	Total	6	2	3	2	0	0	1	0
2002	Democrat[d]	2	0.7	2	0	0	0	0	0
	Republican	2	1.5	1	1	0	0	0	0
	Total	4	1.3	3	1	0	0	0	0

Election	Party	Incumbents lost	Average terms	Consecutive terms served					
				1	2	3	4	5	6+
2004	Democrat	1	3	0	0	1	0	0	0
	Republican	0	0	0	0	0	0	0	0
	Total	1	3	0	0	1	0	0	0
2006	Republican	5	1.8	2	2	1	0	0	0
	Total	5	1.8	2	2	1	0	0	0
2008	Republican	5	2.2	3	1	0	0	0	1
	Total	5	2.2	3	1	0	0	0	1
2010	Democrat	3	3.3	0	1	1	0	1	0
	Republican	1	3	0	0	1	0	0	0
	Total	4	3.3	0	1	2	0	1	0
2012	Republican	1	1	1	0	0	0	0	0
	Total	1	1	1	0	0	0	0	0
2014	Democrat[e]	5	2	3	0	1	1	0	0
	Republican	0	0	0	0	0	0	0	0
	Total	5	2	3	0	1	1	0	0
2016*	Republican	2	1	2	0	0	0	0	0
	Total	2	1	2	0	0	0	0	0

Note: Some data from previous versions of Vital Statistics have been updated. See errata for more detail.

a. This includes James Broyhill (R-NC) who was appointed on July 14, 1986, until November 14, 1986. He lost to Terry Sanford (D-NC) who took over the seat on November 5, 1986.
b. Includes John Seymour (R-CA) who was appointed on January 7, 1991, until November 3, 1992.
c. Includes Sheila Frahm (R-KS) who was appointed on June 11, 1996 until November 7, 1996.
d. Includes Jean Carnahan (D-MO) who was appointed to fill her husband's seat in 2001.
e. Does not include John Walsh (D-MT) who withdrew from the race after the primary and was replaced on the ballot.

Source: Biographical Directory of the United States Congress 1774–1989 (Washington, D.C.: Government Printing Office, 1989); Congressional Quarterly Almanac (Washington, D.C.: Congressional Quarterly, various years); National Journal, various issues; The Almanac of American Politics (Washington, D.C.: National Journal Group, various years).

Most recent update source: Tabulations of data from Federal Election Commission, http://www.fec.gov

* 2016 data compiled by Almanac of American Politics editorial staff

★ PROFILE LIST ★